NEW REVISED

VELÁZQUEZ

Spanish and English

DICTIONARY

NEW REVISED
VELÁZQUEZ
Spanish and English
DICTIONARY

by
Mariano Velazquez de la Cadena,
Late Professor of Spanish, Columbia University
and
Edward Gray, A.B., M.D., F.R.M.S.
and
Juan L. Iribas, A.B., L.L.D.

NEWLY REVISED BY

Ida Navarro Hinojosa,
Manuel Blanco-Gonzalez, M.A.

and

R.J. Nelson, Ph.D.

NEW CENTURY PUBLISHERS, INC.

Printing Code
15 16 17

Library of Congress Cataloging in Publication Data

Velázquez de la Cadena, Mariano, 1778-1860.
Velázquez Spanish and English dictionary.

Spanish-English and Inglés-Espanol.
Published in 1852 under title: A pronouncing dictionary of the Spanish and English languages.
1. Spanish language — Dictionaries — English.
2. English language — Dictionaries — Spanish. I. Gray, Edward, 1849-1920. II. Iribas, Juan L. III. Navarro Hinjosa, Ida. IV. Title.
PC4640.V55 1985 463'.21 84-27199
ISBN 0-8329-0265-9

TABLE OF CONTENTS

Preface

Humanity marches on at a rapidly advancing rhythm, and reference works intended to serve it, such as this dictionary, should keep in step with progress if they are to provide satisfactorily the information sought. That is why the *Velázquez Dictionary*, recognized throughout the world as the highest authority in bilingual Spanish-English dictionaries, needs to keep pace with all the new terms which the prodigious progress of our times is introducing in the fields of science, inventions and discoveries, as well as with those terms which constantly evolving customs and events introduce into both languages.

Thus the NEW REVISED VELÁZQUEZ DICTIONARY, without sacrificing any of the traditional characteristics which have made predecessor editions the pattern for dictionaries of this type, is without doubt the most modern and complete edition of the work ever published. Included in the main alphabetical word lists are thousands of new terms and idiomatic expressions of general use, replacing expressions no longer in common usage which consequently have no place in a book as eminently practical as this one.

This latest revision of the text has been exhaustive. The aim has been to have the *Velázquez Dictionary* respond more efficiently each day to the needs of those consulting it as a practical medium to solve their translation problems in the fields of business, of current events, of technology, of science in general, of literature, etc. At the same time particular attention has been paid to the terms and idioms commonly used in Spanish America and in the United States, since commercial and friendly relations between these two great regions of the modern world are daily becoming more frequent and important.

The equivalents of geographical names and adjectives which are not written identically in Spanish and English have been meticulously revised. The lists making up the present edition include all the changes which such names have undergone through recent historical events.

A similar study has been made of the lists of proper names appearing in the supplements of the book, as well as those of weights and measures. The list of abbreviations has been brought up-to-date so that it may also respond to the fundamentally practical nature of the book.

Through such innovations the usefulness of this dictionary has been tremendously enhanced, and its editors and publishers dare to hope that it may prove even more valuable than earlier editions to its users, whether they be students in process of learning a second tongue, scholars engaged in literary research in either or both languages, or professional and commercial translators—in fact anyone and everyone who has need of authoritative guidance over the difficult road of English-Spanish or Spanish-English translation.

To better serve contemporary needs, the newly revised 1985 edition incorporates a supplement of an additional 700 entries complete with multiple clarifications of the most modern scientific, technical, commercial, cultural and political terms and gives regional variations of local usages, idioms, and colloquialisms for Latin American and Castilian Spanish as well.

A Synopsis of the

Spanish or Castilian Language.

THE PARTS OF SPEECH are: the *Article*, the *Noun* (substantive and adjective), the *Pronoun*, the *Verb*, the *Participle*, the *Adverb*, the *Preposition*, the *Conjunction*, and the *Interjection*.

THE DEFINITE ARTICLE.

Masculine, sing. *The*, El: pl. *The*, Los.
Feminine, " " La: " " Las.

When the article *el* comes after *de* (of or from), or *a* (to), the *e* is suppressed and they are thus written; of the, *del*, to the, *al*, instead of *de el*, *a el*. No apostrophe (') is used in Spanish.

1. *Agua*, water; *águila*, eagle; *alma*, soul; *hacha*, hatchet; *hambre*, hunger, etc., though feminine, take the masculine article; but only in the singular, and when they are immediately preceded by it. This is merely to avoid the concurrence of two a's broadly pronounced and by no means changes the gender.

2. Common nouns taken in a general sense in English require the definite article in Spanish: as, Man is mortal, *El hombre es mortal.* Charity is the first of virtues, *La caridad es la primera de las virtudes.* But when the sense is indeterminate, they do not admit it: as, Give him bread, *Dale pan.*

3. Before nouns of measure, weight, or number, the English *indefinite article* is rendered into Spanish by the *definite*, and frequently omitted: as, He paid six dollars a barrel, *El pagó a cinco pesos el barril*, or *cinco pesos barril.*

4. The English definite and indefinite articles before ordinal numbers preceded by proper names, nouns in apposition, national nouns, as well as those signifying dignity, profession, trade, etc., of persons, and in exclamations, are omitted in Spanish: as, Charles *the* Fifth, *Carlos Quinto;* Madrid *the* capital of Spain, *Madrid capital de España;* He is *an* American, *Él es americano;* She is *a* milliner, *Ella es modista;* What *a* pity! *¡ Qué lástima!*

THE INDEFINITE ARTICLE.

Masculine, sing. *A* or *an*, Un. Feminine, sing. *A* or *an*, Una. The plural *unos* (masculine) and *unas* (feminine) are translated into English by the pronoun *some:* as, a man, *un hombre;* some men, *unos hombres.*

5. The English indefinite article coming between an adjective or a pronoun and a noun, generally is not translated; but when it is emphatical it is placed before the adjective: as, So beautiful *a* woman, *Tan hermosa mujer*, or *Una* mujer tan hermosa. Such *a* man, *Tal hombre*, or *Un* tal hombre.

THE NOUN.

Spanish *Nouns* have *Gender*, *Number*, and *Case.*

GENDER.

It is *masculine* or *feminine.* Every he, or male animal, is of the masculine gender; every she or female is of the feminine.

6. The names of inanimate objects, or of things ending in *a*, *ad*, *ion* (*bre*, when it signifies quality), are for the most part feminine; and those terminating in *e*, *i*, *o*, or *u*, are generally masculine.

7. *Common nouns* ending in *o*, change *o* into *a* to form the feminine; as, son, *hijo*, daughter, *hija.* Those terminating in *an*, *on*, or *or*, add *a* for the feminine; as, a man loiterer, *un holgazán;* a woman loiterer, *una holgazana;* patron, *patrón;* patroness, *patrona;* shepherd, *pastor;* shepherdess, *pastora.*

8. There are some nouns that express the difference of gender by a different word or termination; as, father, *padre;* mother, *madre;* poet, *poeta;* poetess, *poetisa.*

NUMBER.

Singular and *Plural.*

9. Nouns ending in a short, or unaccented vowel, form the plural by adding *s* to the singular; as, boy, *muchacho;* boys, *muchachos.*

10. Nouns terminating in a long, or accented vowel, or in any consonant, or in *y*, add *es* to form the plural; as, ruby, *rubí;* rubies, *rubíes;* captain, *capitán;* captains, *capitanes;* ox, *buey;* oxen, *bueyes.* Nouns terminating in *z*, change it into *c*, and add *es;* as judge, *juez;* judges, *jueces.* *Papá*, *mamá*, *café*, etc., are exceptions.

CASE.

11. The *Nominative* case expresses the subject of the verb; as, The man gives, *El hombre da.*

12. The *Objective* case *direct* points out the immediate object of the action of the verb; as, The man gives alms, *El hombre da limosna.*

13. The *Objective* case *indirect*, or *complement*, indicates the term, or end of the action expressed by the verb; as, The man gives alms to the poor, *El hombre da limosna a los pobres* (=Latin dative).

14. When the *object direct* of an active transitive verb is a *person*, a *proper* or *personified noun*, it must be preceded by the preposition *a;* as, A man must love man, *El hombre debe amar* al *hombre;* Isabella conquered Granada, *Isabel conquistó a Granada;* The miser loves no other God but his money, *El avaro no ama otro Dios que a su dinero.*

AUGMENTATIVE AND DIMINUTIVE NOUNS.

15. *Augmentative* nouns are those that increase the extent of their signification by adding *on*, *ote*, or *azo* to the masculine nouns, and *ona*, *ota*, or *aza* to the feminine, suppressing their final letter, should it be *a*, *e*, or *o;* as (a boy), "un *muchacho*," "un *muchachón*" (a *big* boy); "una *muchacha*" (a girl), "una *muchachona*" (a *big* girl).

16. The termination *azo* frequently signifies the blow or injury caused by the object to which it is added; as, *látigo* (whip), un *latigazo* (a very large whip; a stroke with a whip).

17. *Diminutive* nouns are formed by adding *ito*, *illo*, *ico*, or *uelo* for the masculine, and *ita*, *illa*, *ica*, or *uela* for the feminine, suppressing the final letter if it be *a*, *o*, or *e:* as, "un *muchacho*" (a boy), un *muchachito*, *muchachillo*, or *muchachuelo* (a *little* boy); "una *muchacha*" (a girl), una *muchachita*, *muchachilla*, or *muchachuela* (a *little* girl).

18. The terminations *ito*, *ita*, etc., added to Christian names, or those that express relationship, indicate love, affection, and regard towards the object; thus, "*hermanita*" (dear sister); "*Juanito*" (esteemed John), etc.

THE ADJECTIVE.

19. In Spanish the *Adjective* must agree with its noun, in *Gender* and *Number;* as, "un hombre *rico*" (a

rich man), "una mujer *rica*" (a *rich* woman); "hombres *ricos*" (rich men), "mujeres *ricas*" (*rich* women).

Gender of Adjectives.

20. Adjectives ending in *o* are masculine, and change it into *a* to form the feminine; as, *rico, rica* (rich). Adjectives ending in *on* or *an* add *a* for the feminine; as, *gritón, gritona* (clamorous); *haragán, haragana* (idle). Those ending in any other letter are common to both genders; as, "un hombre *prudente*" (a *prudent* man), "una mujer *prudente*" (a *prudent* woman).

Exception.—Adjectives ending in a consonant, and derived from the names of countries, add *a* to form their feminine; as, *Español, Española* (Spanish); *Inglés, Inglesa* (English); *Andaluz, Andaluza* (Andalusian).

Number.

21. Adjectives form their plural according to the rules set forth for nouns; as, *blanco, blancos* (white); *turquí, turquíes* (deep blue); *natural, naturales* (natural); *feliz, felices* (happy).

Degrees of Signification.

Adjectives have three degrees of signification, the *positive*, the *comparative*, and the *superlative*.

Comparatives.

Comparatives may be considered under the three divisions of the *comparative of equality*, the *comparative of superiority*, and the *comparative of inferiority*.

The *comparative of equality* with adjectives is formed with *tan* . . . *como* (as, so . . . as): as, "El es *tan* rico *como* ella" (He is *as* rich *as* she); "Ella no es *tan* hermosa *como* su hermana" (She is not *so* handsome *as* her sister).

The *comparative of equality* with nouns is formed with *tanto, tanta* . . . *como* (as much, so much . . . as); *tantos, tantas* . . . *como* (as many, so many . . . as): as, "Ella tiene *tanto* dinero *como* él" (She has *as much* money *as* he); "El tiene *tantas* casas *como* su hermano" (He has *as many* houses *as* his brother).

In the *comparative of equality* with verbs, *cuanto* is sometimes substituted for *como:* as, *Tanto* leo *cuanto* escribo" (I read *as much as* I write).

The *comparative of superiority* with adjectives is formed with *más* . . . *que* (*more*, or the termination *er* . . . *than*); as, "El es *más* rico *que* ella" (He is *richer than* she); "El honor es *más* precioso *que* las riquezas" (Honour is *more* precious *than* riches).

Before nouns of number, *more than* is rendered by *más de;* as, "Ellos gastaron *más de* quinientos pesos" (They spent *more than* five hundred dollars). But if the phrase be negative, *más que* is used; as, "No tengo *más que* dos libras" (I have *no more* than two pounds).

The more . . . *the more*, with an intervening verb, is rendered by *cuanto más* . . . *más*, or *cuanto más* . . . *tanto más;* as, "*Cuanto más* estudia, *tanto más* aprende" (*The more* he studies, *the more* he learns).

The *comparative of inferiority* is formed with *menos* . . . *que* (less . . . than); as, "La plata es *menos* útil *que* el hierro" (Silver is *less* useful *than* iron).

Before nouns of number, *less than* is translated by *menos de;* as, "Necesito *menos de* tres reales" (I need *less than* three shillings).

The less . . . *the less*, with an intervening verb, is rendered by *cuanto menos* . . . *tanto menos;* as, "*Cuanto menos* trabaja, *tanto menos* gana" (*The less* he works, *the less* he gains).

Superlatives.

English superlatives ending in *est*, or formed by *most*, are rendered by prefixing the definite article to the Spanish comparative; as, "*El* más sabio" (the wisest); "*la* más ingrata" (the most ungrateful).

Superlatives in English with *very* are formed in Spanish by prefixing *muy* to the adjective, or by affixing to it the termination *ísimo;* as, "*Muy hábil* or *habilísimo*" (*very* skilful); "*muy fácil* or *facilísimo*" (*very* easy).

Irregular Comparatives and Superlatives.

Pos.	Comp.	Super.
Bueno,	mejor,	óptimo.
Malo,	peor,	pésimo.
Grande,	mayor,	máximo.
Pequeño,	menor,	mínimo.
Alto,	superior,	supremo.
Bajo,	inferior,	ínfimo.
Mucho,	más.	
Poco,	menos.	

PRONOUNS.

Personal Pronouns.

I, yo.	*We*, nosotros, nosotras.
Me, me.	*Us*, nos, nos.
Me, mí.	*Us*, nosotros, nosotras.
With me, conmigo.	*With us*, con nosotros, as.
You, tú.	*You*, vosotros, vosotras.
You, te.	*You*, os, os.
You, ti.	*You*, vosotros, vosotras.
With you, contigo.	*With you*, con vosotros, as.

You, in familiar polite style, is translated *usted* for both genders, and the verb agrees with it in the singular or plural, according to the sense. *Usted* and its plural are always written in abbreviation, thus: *V.* or *Vd.* for the first, and *VV.* or *Vds.* for the latter.

You, usted, (V.).	*You*, ustedes, (VV.).
You, a usted, le, la, se.	*You*, a VV. los, las, se.
You, a V. le, se; a él, ella, sí.	*You*, a VV. les, se; a ellos, ellas, sí.
With you, con V. or consigo.	*With you*, con VV. or consigo.
He or *it*, él.	*They*, ellos.
Him or *it*, le, se; él, sí.	*Them*, los, se; ellos, sí.
Him or *it*, le, se; él, sí.	*Them*, les, se; ellos, sí.
With him, it, con él, consigo.	*With them*, con ellos, consigo.
She or *it*, ella.	*They*, ellas.
Her or *it*, la, se; ella, sí.	*Them*, las, se; ellas, sí.
Her or *it*, le, se; ella, sí.	*Them*, les, se; ellas, sí.
With her, it, con ella, consigo.	*With them*, con ellas, consigo.

Mí, ti, sí, are always preceded by prepositions.

Me, te, se, le, los, la, las, les, are governed by verbs and never placed after prepositions.

Possessive Adjectives.

My, mi, mis.	*His*, su, sus.	*Its*, su, sus.
Your, tu, tus.	*Her*, su, sus.	*Their*, su, sus.

Your, with reference to *Usted* or *Ustedes*, su, sus.

These adjectives agree in number with the noun that follows them; as, He sold *his* horses (*él vendió* sus *caballos*); they fulfilled *their* promise (*ellos cumplieron* su *promesa*).

Possessive Pronouns.

Mine, mío, míos. mía, mías.	*His*, suyo, suyos. suya, suyas.	*Its*, suyo, suyos. suya, suyas.
Your, tuyo, tuyos. tuya, tuyas.	*Hers*, suyo, suyos. suya, suyas.	*Theirs*, suyo, suyos. suya, suyas.
Our, nuestro, nuestros. nuestra, nuestras.	*Your*, vuestro, vuestros. vuestra, vuestras.	*Your*, de Usted. de Ustedes.

Your, with reference to *Usted*, is also translated suyo, suyos, suya, suyas, or su, sus . . . de V. or VV.

Relative and Interrogative Pronouns.

Who, which, que, quien, quienes. *What, that*, que.
Which, what, cual, cuales; *also*, el cual, los cuales, la cual, las cuales.
Whose, cuyo, cuyos, cuya, cuyas; *also*, de quien, de cual, etc.

Demonstrative Pronouns

This, este,	*These*, estos.	*That*, aquel.	*Those*, aquellos.
" esta.	" estas.	" aquella.	" aquellas.
That, ese,	*Those*, esos.	*This*, esto.	*That*, aquello.
" esa.	" esas.	*That*, eso.	*It*, ello, lo.

Indefinite Pronouns

One, uno.	*Such*, tal.
Each, cada.	*Something*, algo.
Nobody, nadie, ninguno.	*Nothing*, nada.
Somebody, alguien.	*Each one*, cada cual.
Anybody, Any, some, Someone, Somebody, alguno.	*Each other*, uno y otro.
	One another, uno a otro.
	Either, uno u otro.
	Neither, ni uno ni otro.
	Everyone, cada uno.
Whichever, cualquiera.	*Everyone, Everybody, Everything, All, every*, todo, todos.
Whomsoever, quienquiera.	
Both, ambos, entrambos, ambos a dos.	*It is said*, dicen *or* se dice.

VERBS.

All Spanish verbs are classed into *three conjugations.* Verbs ending in *ar* belong to the *first;* those in *er*, to the *second;* and those in *ir*, to the *third.*

A TABLE

OF THE TERMINATIONS OF ALL THE REGULAR VERBS.

The numbers in the margin refer to the Conjugation, those at the head of the columns, to the Persons.

Infinitive Mode.

1. Present, *ar.*	Gerund, *ando.*	Past or Passive Part. *ado.*
2. " *er.*	" *iendo.*	" " " *ido.*
3. " *ir.*	" *iendo.*	" " " *ido.*

INDICATIVE MODE.

Present.

	Singular.			Plural.		
	1.	2	3.	1.	2.	3.
1.	o,	as,	a:	amos,	áis,	an.
2.	o,	es,	e:	emos,	éis,	en.
3.	o,	es,	e:	imos,	ís,	en.

Imperfect.

1.	aba,	abas,	aba:	ábamos,	abais,	aban.
2.	ía.	ías,	ía:	íamos,	íais,	ían.
3.	ía,	ías,	ía:	íamos,	íais,	ían.

Preterite or Perfect.

1.	é,	aste,	ó:	amos,	asteis,	aron.
2	í,	iste,	ió:	imos,	isteis,	ieron.
3	í,	iste,	ió:	imos,	isteis,	ieron.

Future.

1.	aré,	arás,	ará:	aremos,	aréis,	arán.
2	eré,	erás,	erá:	eremos,	eréis,	erán.
3.	iré,	irás,	irá:	iremos,	iréis,	irán.

IMPERATIVE MODE.

1.		a,	e:	emos,	ad,	en.
2.		e,	a:	amos,	ed,	an.
3.		e,	a:	amos,	id,	an.

SUBJUNCTIVE MODE.

Present.

	Singular.			Plural.		
	1.	2.	3.	1.	2.	3.
1.	e,	es,	e:	emos,	éis,	en.
2.	a,	as,	a:	amos,	áis,	an.
3.	a,	as,	a:	amos,	áis,	an.

Imperfect.—(First Termination.)

1.	ara,	aras,	ara:	áramos,	arais,	aran.
2.	iera,	ieras,	iera:	iéramos,	ierais,	ieran.
3.	iera,	ieras,	iera:	iéramos,	ierais,	ieran.

Imperfect.—(Second Termination.)

1.	aría,	arías,	aría:	aríamos,	aríais,	arían.
2.	ería,	erías,	ería:	eríamos,	eríais,	erían.
3.	iría,	irías,	iría:	iríamos,	iríais,	irían.

Imperfect.—(Third Termination.)

1.	ase,	ases,	ase:	ásemos,	aseis,	asen.
2.	iese,	ieses,	iese:	iésemos,	ieseis,	iesen.
3.	iese,	ieses,	iese:	iésemos,	ieseis,	iesen.

Future.

1.	are,	ares,	are:	áremos,	areis,	aren.
2.	iere,	ieres,	iere:	iéremos,	iereis,	ieren.
3.	iere,	ieres,	iere:	iéremos,	iereis,	ieren.

COMPOUND TENSES.

These tenses are formed by placing after the verb *haber* (to have), the participle past of the verb that is conjugated; as (I *have* armed), "yo *he* armado."

CONJUGATION OF THE AUXILIARY VERBS.

INFINITIVE MODE.

		Present.			
Haber.	Tener.	*To have.*	Ser.	Estar.	*To be.*
		Gerund.			
Habiendo.	Teniendo.	*Having.*	Siendo.	Estando.	*Being.*
		Past Participle.			
Habido.	Tenido.	*Had.*	Sido.	Estado.	*Been.*

INDICATIVE MODE.

Present.

I have.		*I am.*	
1. He.	Tengo.	Soy.	Estoy.
2. Has.	Tienes.	Eres.	Estás.
3. Ha.	Tiene.	Es.	Está.
1. Hemos.	Tenemos.	Somos.	Estamos.
2. Habéis.	Tenéis.	Sois.	Estáis.
3. Han.	Tienen.	Son.	Están.

Imperfect.

I had.		*I was.*	
1. Había.	Tenía.	Era.	Estaba.
2. Habías.	Tenías.	Eras.	Estabas.
3. Había.	Tenía.	Era.	Estaba.
1. Habíamos.	Teníamos.	Éramos.	Estábamos.
2. Habíais.	Teníais.	Erais.	Estabais.
3. Habían.	Tenían.	Eran.	Estaban.

Preterite.

I had.		*I was.*	
1. Hube.	Tuve.	Fui.	Estuve.
2. Hubiste.	Tuviste.	Fuiste.	Estuviste.
3. Hubo.	Tuvo.	Fue.	Estuvo.
1. Hubimos.	Tuvimos.	Fuimos.	Estuvimos.
2. Hubisteis.	Tuvisteis.	Fuisteis.	Estuvisteis.
3. Hubieron.	Tuvieron.	Fueron.	Estuvieron.

Future.

I shall have.		*I shall be.*	
1. Habré.	Tendré.	Seré.	Estaré.
2. Habrás.	Tendrás.	Serás.	Estarás.
3. Habrá.	Tendrá.	Será.	Estará.
1. Habremos.	Tendremos.	Seremos.	Estaremos.
2. Habréis.	Tendréis.	Seréis.	Estaréis.
3. Habrán.	Tendrán.	Serán.	Estarán.

IMPERATIVE MODE.

Let me have.		*Let me be.*	
1. Let me have.	Tenga yo.	Sea.	Esté.
2. Have you.	Ten tú.	Sé.	Está.
2. Have not.	No tengas.	No seas.	No estés.
3 Let him have.	Tenga él.	Sea.	Esté.
2. Have.	Tenga V.	Sea V.	Esté V.
1. Let us have.	Tengamos.	Seamos.	Estemos.
2. Have ye.	Tened.	Sed.	Estad.
2. Have not.	No tengáis.	No seáis.	No estéis.
3. Let them have.	Tengan.	Sean.	Estén.
2. Have you.	Tengan VV.	Sean VV.	Estén VV.

SUBJUNCTIVE MODE.

Present.

I may have.		*I may be.*	
1. Haya.	Tenga.	Sea.	Esté.
2. Hayas.	Tengas.	Seas.	Estés.
3. Haya.	Tenga.	Sea.	Esté.
1. Hayamos.	Tengamos.	Seamos.	Estemos.
2. Hayáis.	Tengáis.	Seáis.	Estéis.
3. Hayan.	Tengan.	Sean.	Estén.

Imperfect.—(First Termination.)

I would have.		*I would be.*	
1. Hubiera	Tuviera.	Fuera.	Estuviera.
2. Hubieras.	Tuvieras.	Fueras.	Estuvieras.
3. Hubiera.	Tuviera.	Fuera.	Estuviera.
1. Hubiéramos.	Tuviéramos.	Fuéramos.	Estuviéramos.
2. Hubierais.	Tuvierais.	Fuerais.	Estuvierais.
3. Hubieran.	Tuvieran.	Fueran.	Estuvieran.

Imperfect. - (Second Termination.)

I would have.		*I would be.*	
1. Habría.	Tendría.	Sería.	Estaría.
2. Habrías.	Tendrías.	Serías.	Estarías.
3. Habría.	Tendría.	Sería.	Estaría.
1. Habríamos.	Tendríamos.	Seríamos.	Estaríamos.
2 Habríais.	Tendríais.	Seríais.	Estaríais.
3. Habrían.	Tendrían.	Serían.	Estarían.

Imperfect.—(Third Termination.)

I should have.		*I should be.*	
1. Hubiese.	Tuviese.	Fuese.	Estuviese.
2. Hubieses.	Tuvieses.	Fueses.	Estuvieses.
3. Hubiese.	Tuviese.	Fuese.	Estuviese.
1. Hubiésemos.	Tuviésemos.	Fuésemos.	Estuviésemos.
2. Hubieseis.	Tuvieseis.	Fueseis.	Estuvieseis.
3. Hubiesen.	Tuviesen.	Fuesen.	Estuviesen.

Future.

When I shall have.		*When I shall be.*	
1. Hubiere.	Tuviere.	Fuere.	Estuviere.
2. Hubieres.	Tuvieres.	Fueres.	Estuvieres.
3 Hubiere.	Tuviere.	Fuere.	Estuviere.
1. Hubiéremos.	Tuviéremos.	Fuéremos.	Estuviéremos.
2. Hubiereis.	Tuviereis.	Fuereis.	Estuviereis.
3. Hubieren.	Tuvieren.	Fueren.	Estuvieren.

PASSIVE VERBS.

Passive verbs are formed from active transitive verbs by adding their *participle past* to the auxiliary verb *ser* (to be), through all its changes, as in English; thus, from the active verb *amar* (to love), is formed the passive verb *ser amado* (to be loved).

The participle must agree in gender and number with the nominative it refers to; thus, He is loved (*él es amado*); she is loved (*ella es amada*); they are loved (*ellos son amados*).

PRONOMINAL OR REFLEXIVE VERBS.

A *pronominal* or *reflexive verb* is conjugated by prefixing the pronouns *me, te, se, V. se; nos, os, se, VV. se* to the verb according to its person and number; as, he arms himself, *él se arma.*

In the infinitive and imperative modes the pronouns are placed after the verb, and in one word with it; the pronoun, therefore, must be suppressed, in order to find out the conjugation: thus, To approach; *acercarse*, (se) acercar, first conjugation.

REMARKS ON THE USE OF THE SUBJUNCTIVE MODE.

Three are the terminations of the imperfect tense subjunctive mode; *ra*, *ría*, *se*.—The termination *ra*, or *se*, is used when the verb is governed by a conditional conjunction, and the verb that completes the sense of the phrase is placed in the termination *ría*; *If* he *had* money, he *would buy* the house, *Si él* tuviera *dinero*, compraría *la casa*:—If the verb begins without a conditional conjunction, the termination *ra* or *ría* may be used, placing the verb that completes the sense in the termination *se*; as, It would be proper that you should write to him, *Fuera* or *sería bueno que V. le escribiese.*

Verbs signifying *command*, *wish*, *supplication*, etc., being in the present indicative, require the governed verb in the present subjunctive; and if they be in any of the past tenses of the indicative, the governed verb must be in the termination *ra* or *se*, of the subjunctive.

THE GERUND.

The *gerund* is that part of the verb that terminates in *ando* in verbs of the first conjugation, and in *iendo* in those of the second and third; as *publicando* (publishing), from *publicar; prometiendo* (promising), from *prometer; asistiendo* (assisting), from *asistir*. It admits no change for gender or number.

It is translated by the English present participle, and conjugated with the verb *estar* (to be); as, Anastasia is reading, and Mary Ann is playing on the piano (*Anastasia está leyendo, y María Ana está tocando el piano*).

PARTICIPLE.

The passive or past participle terminates in *ado* in the first conjugation, and in *ido* in the second and third. It changes its termination according to the number and gender of the person it refers to; except when it follows immediately after the verb *haber*, in which case it does not admit of any change.

All passive participles that do not terminate in *ado* or *ido* are called irregular; such are the following from the verbs:

To open, **abrir, abierto.**	To die, **morir, muerto.**
To cover, **cubrir, cubierto.**	To resolve, **resolver, resuelto.**
To say, **decir, dicho.**	To see, **ver, visto.**
To write, **escribir, escrito.**	To put, **poner, puesto.**
To fry, **freir, frito.**	To turn, **volver, vuelto.**
To do, **hacer, hecho.**	
To print. **imprimir, impreso.**	

Their compounds have the same irregularity.

VERBS THAT HAVE TWO PARTICIPLES.

There are some verbs that have *two passive participles*, the one regular and the other irregular. They are eighty-three in number. Such are: To bless, *bendecir*, bendecido, *bendito*; to compel, *compeler*, compelido, *compulso*; to convert, *convertir*, convertido, *converso*; to awake, *despertar*, despertado, *despierto*; to elect, *elegir*, elegido, *electo*; to express, *expresar*, expresado, *expreso*; to fix, *fijar*, fijado, *fijo*; to satiate, *hartar*, hartado, *harto*; to include, *incluir*, incluido, *incluso*; to join, *juntar*, juntado, *junto*; to arrest, *prender*, prendido, *preso*; to provide, *proveer*, proveído, *provisto*; to break, *romper*, rompido, *roto*; to loosen, *soltar*, soltado, *suelto*; to suspend, *suspender*, suspendido, *suspenso*, etc.

The *regular* participles of these verbs are used to form the compound tenses with *haber*; as, He has awaked early (*él ha despertado temprano*).

The irregular participles are used as verbal adjectives, and with the verbs *ser*, etc., and do not form compound tenses with *haber*; excepting *preso*, *prescrito*, *provisto*, *roto*, *injerto*, *proscrito*, and *supreso*, which have both uses; as, He is early awaked (*el está despierto temprano*); They have provided (*ellos han provisto* or *proveído*).

ADVERBS.

Adverbs are formed from adjectives of one termination by the addition of *mente*; as, *dulce*, dulce*mente*; and from those of two terminations, by adding *mente* to the feminine; as, *gracioso*, graciosa*mente*. They admit the superlative; as, *graciosísimamente*.

When two or more adverbs ending in *ly* occur in the same sentence, the termination *mente* is added to the last only; as, He speaks elegantly and correctly (*él habla correcta y elegantemente*).

PREPOSITIONS.

The most frequent are:

At, to, for,	*A.*	Towards,	*hacia.*
Before,	*antes, ante.*	Until,	*hasta.*
With,	*con.*	For, to,	*para.*
Against,	*contra.*	By, for, through,	*por.*
Of, from,	*de.*	According,	*según.*
From,	*desde.*	Without,	*sin.*
In, on, at,	*en.*	On, upon,	*sobre.*
Between, among,	*entre.*	Behind,	*tras, detrás.*

CONJUNCTIONS.

The principal conjunctions are:

That,	*que.*	Since,	*pues, pues que.*
Also,	*también.*	By, for,	*por.*
Moreover,	*además.*	Therefore,	*por tanto.*
And,	*y, e.*	Whereas,	*por cuanto.*
Neither, nor,	*ni.*	That,	*para que.*
Or, either, / Whether,	*o, u, ya.*	That, / In order that,	*para que. / a fin de.*
Whether,	*sea que.*	If,	*si.*
Neither,	*tampoco.*	But,	*sino.*
But,	*mas, pero.*	Provided,	*con tal que.*
Even,	*aun cuando. / aun, cuando.*	Unless,	*a menos que.*
Although, / Though,	*aunque.*	Since,	*pues, puesto que.*
Because,	*porque, que.*	As,	*como, así como.*
Why?	*¿por qué?*	So,	*así.*

E is used instead of *y* when the following word begins by *i* or *hi*.—*U* is employed instead of *ó*, when the word immediately following begins by *o*, or *ho*.

INTERJECTIONS.

Alas!	*¡Ay!*	Take care!	*¡Tate!*
Ah!	*¡Ah!*	Hurrah!	*¡Viva!*
Woe to me!	*¡Ay de mí!*	Here!	*¡Ce!*
Lo!	*¡He!*	Ugh! Fie!	*¡Puf!*
Well!	*¡Ea!*	God grant!	*¡Ojalá!*
Holla!	*¡Hola!*	Gracious!	*¡Cáspita!*
Phew! ouch!	*¡Huy!*	By jingo!	*¡Caramba!*
No, indeed!	*¡Ca! ¡quiá!*	Whoa!	*¡So! ¡jo! ¡cho!*
Indeed! really!	*¡Toma! ¡Vaya!*	Get up!	*¡Arre! ¡anda!*

GENERAL IRREGULARITIES OF SPANISH VERBS.

EUPHONIC CHANGES.

VERBS THAT REQUIRE A CHANGE IN THEIR RADICAL LETTERS.

1 Verbs ending in CAR change the C into QU when the first letter of the termination is E.

2. Verbs ending in	CER	change the	C	into Z	when the first letter of the termination is O *or* A.
3. " "	CIR	"	C	" Z	
4. " "	GER	"	G	" J	
5. " "	GIR	"	G	" J	
6. " "	QUIR	"	QU	" C	
7. " "	GUIR	drop	U		when the first letter of the termination is E.
8. " "	GAR	add	U		
9. " "	ZAR	change	Z	" C	

THE IRREGULAR VERBS.

Irregular verbs are such as suffer some change either in their radical letters or in the terminations of the conjugations to which they belong, or in both these cases. The total number of such verbs in the Spanish language is about eight hundred and seventy-six. Of these, however, four hundred and sixty-one are compound forms. But this apparently very long list may be reduced to six classes, as follows:

I. To the first class belong certain verbs like **acertar, ascender, sentir,** which have the vowel **e** in the penultimate syllable of the infinitive, and change this **e** when it bears the tonic accent, or is in the singular or the third person plural of the present tense (indicative, subjunctive, imperative), into **ie.** As a general rule, and with very rare exceptions, if in the kindred noun there is the diphthong *ie*, the verb is irregular of this class. Verbs of the third conjugation belonging to this class have the further peculiarity that the vowel *e* of the stem subsides into *i* when unaccented and followed by a strong termination (that is, containing a strong vowel, viz., *a* or *o*), and in the preterite (or aorist) system before a diphthong. To this class belong also the verbs **adquirir, concernir** (defective), **and discernir.**

II. To the second class belong certain verbs like **acordar**, **mover**, and **dormir**, which have the vowel **o** in the penultimate syllable of the infinitive, and change this **o** into **ue** when it bears the tonic accent or is in the singular and the third person plural of the present tense (indicative, subjunctive, and imperative). If the kindred noun has the diphthong *ue*, the verb generally belongs to this class. *Dormir* and *morir* (3d conj.) have *ue* in the same positions where *sentir* (class I) has *i*. The gerund in this class belongs uniformly to the aorist (or preterite) system.

III. To the third class belong verbs of the second and third conjugations ending in **cer** or **cir** preceded by a vowel, the irregularity consisting in their taking a **z** before the **c** when the terminations begin with *a* or *o*. This occurs in the first person singular of the present indicative, in all persons of the present subjunctive, and in those of the imperative which are formed from the subjunctive. About two hundred and eight verbs belong to this class, the forms in **ecer** being very numerous.

IV. This class is composed wholly of verbs of the third conjugation with the stem vowel **e** (like **pedir**), and change this **e** for **i** in the gerund in the third person (singular and plural) of the present indicative, the whole of the present subjunctive, and the imperative formed therefrom; the third persons of the past definite, and all those of the imperfect and future subjunctive.

NOTE.—The verbs which end in **eir** and **ñir**, like **reir**, **ceñir**, lose the **i** of their endings when it is not accented (gerund, third person past definite, and imperfect and future subjunctive), and thus is avoided the double sound of *i* which results; thus:

Ri / Ciñ:
(i)endo.
—, —, (i)ó, —, —, (i)eron.
(i)era, eras, etc.
(i)ese, eses, etc.
(i)ere, eres, etc.

V. To this class belong those verbs ending in **uir** in which both vowels are sounded, like **argüir** (excluding therefore those in *guir*, *quir*). Their irregularity consists in adding **y** to the stem when this is accented or followed by a strong vowel.

The preterite (aorist) stem is regular, but the initial *i* of the diphthongal terminations *ie*, *io*, is changed to *y*, since it comes between two vowels. The gerund in this class belongs always to the aorist system.

VI. To this class are assigned all the remaining irregular verbs, among which there is, however, no common principle of classification. A portion of these have aorist (preterite) systems resembling more or less closely the Latin, while the remainder are irregular in the strictest sense. These verbs are therefore given individually.

EXAMPLES:

1.	*Acrecentar*,	Acreciento, acrecientas, etc.: acreciente, acrecienta, etc.; acreciente, acrecientes, etc.
	Atender,	Atiendo, atiendes, etc.; atienda, atiende, etc.; atienda, atiendas, etc.
	Asentir,	Asiento, asientes, etc.; asienta, asiente, etc.; asienta, asientas, etc.
	"	Asintió, asintieron; asintiera: asintiese; asintiere.
2.	*Acordar*,	Acuerdo, acuerdas, etc.; acuerde, acuerda, etc.; acuerde, acuerdes, etc.
	Mover,	Muevo, mueves, etc.; mueva, mueve, etc.; mueva, muevas, etc.
	Dormir,	Duermo, duermes, etc.; duerma, duerme, etc.; duerma, duermas, etc.
3.	*Conocer*,	Conozco, conozca. *Obedecer*, obedezco, obedezca. *Lucir*, luzco, luzca.
	Conducir,	Conduzco; conduzca, conduzcas, conduzcamos, etc.
	"	Conduje, condujiste, condujo, V. condujo; condujimos, condujisteis, condujeron, VV. condujeron.—*Subj. Imperf. 1st term.* Condujera, etc.—*2d term.* Conduciría, etc.—*3d term.* Condujese, etc.—*Fut.* Condujere, etc.
4.	*Poseer*,	Poseyendo; poseyó, poseyera, etc.; poseyese, etc.; poseyere, etc.
	Pedir,	Pido, pides, etc.; pida, pide, etc.; pida. pidas, etc.
	"	Pidió, pidieron, pidiera, etc.; pidiese, etc.; pidiere, etc.
5.	*Instruir*,	Instruyendo, instruyo, **instruyeron**, instruyera, etc.; instruyese, **etc.**; instruyere, etc.
	"	Instruyo, instruyes, etc.; **instruya, ins**truye, etc.; instruya, **instruyas**, etc.
6.		The auxiliary verbs *Ser*, *Estar*, *Haber*; *Tener*; *Dar*, *Caber*, etc., given individually just below.

VERBS WHOSE IRREGULARITY IS CONFINED TO THEM AND THEIR COMPOUNDS.

N. B. The tenses not conjugated in the following verbs are regular. Thus in *Andar*, for instance, the present of the indicative mood is: 1 *ando*, 2 *andas*, 3 *anda*, etc. The imperfect tense: 1 *andaba*, 2 *andabas*, etc. The tenses or persons printed in *italics* are also regular.

ADQUIRIR, *to acquire.* Cl. I.

Indic. Pres. 1 Adquiero, 2 adquieres, 3 adquiere, V. adquiere: 1 *adquirimos*, 2 *adquirís*, 3 adquieren, VV. adquieren.

Imperative. 1 Adquiera, 2 adquiere, 3 adquiera, adquiera V., 2 no adquieras: 1 *adquiramos*, 2 *adquirid*, 3 adquieran, adquieran VV., 2 *no adquiráis.*

Subj. Pres. 1 Adquiera, 2 adquieras, 3 adquiera, V. adquiera: 1 *adquiramos*, 2 *adquiráis*, 3 adquieran, VV. adquieran.

ANDAR, *to walk.* Cl. VI.

Indic. Preterit. 1 Anduve, 2 anduviste, 3 anduvo, V. anduvo: 1 anduvimos, 2 anduvisteis, 3 anduvieron, VV. anduvieron.

Subj. Imperf. 1st term. 1 Anduviera, 2 anduvieras, 3 anduviera, V. anduviera: 1 anduviéramos, 2 anduvierais, 3 anduvieran, VV. anduvieran.—*2d term.* 1 *Andaría*, etc. *3d term.* 1 Anduviese, 2 anduvieses, etc.—*Fut.* 1 Anduviere, 2 anduvieres, etc.

ASIR, *to seize.* Cl. VI.

Indic. Pres. 1 Asgo, 2 *ases*, 3 *ase*, V. *ase:* 1 *asimos*, 2 *asís*, 3 *asen*, VV. *asen.*—*Subj.* 1 Asga, 2 asgas, 3 asga, V. asga: 1 asgamos, 2 asgáis, 3 asgan, VV. asgan.—*Imperative.* 1 Asga yo, 2 *ase* tú, 3 asga él, asga V., 2 no asgas: 1 asgamos, 2 *asid*, 3 asgan, asgan VV., 2 no asgáis.

BENDECIR, *to bless.* Cl. VI.

Is conjugated like *Decir*, except in the tenses and persons following, which are regular.

Past participle. Bendito. / *Bendecido.*

Indic. Future. 1. Bendeciré, 2 bendecirás, 3 bendecirá: V. bendecirá; 1 bendeciremos, 2 bendeciréis, 3 bendecirán, VV. bendecirán.—*Subj. Imper. 2d term.* 1 Bendeciría, 2 bendecirías, 3 bendeciría, V. bendeciría: 1 bendeciríamos, 2 bendeciríais, 3 bendecirían, VV. bendecirían.—*Imperative.* 2 Bendice tú: 2 Bendecid.

CABER, *to be contained.* Cl. VI.

Indic. Pres. 1 Quepo, 2 *cabes*, 3 *cabe*, V. *cabe:* 1 *cabemos*, 2 *cabéis*, 3 *caben*, VV. *caben.*—*Perf.* 1 Cupe, 2 cupiste, 3 cupo, V. cupo: 1 cupimos, 2 cupisteis, 3 cupieron, VV. cupieron.

Fut. 1 Cabré, 2 cabrás, 3 cabrá, V. cabrá: 1 cabremos, 2 cabréis, 3 cabrán, VV. cabrán.—*Imperative.* 1 Quepa yo, 2 *cabe*, 3 quepa, quepa V., 2 no quepas, 1 quepamos, 2 *cabed*, 3 quepan, quepan VV., 2 no quepáis.

Subj. Pres. 1 Quepa, 2 quepas, 3 quepa, V. quepa: 1 quepamos, 2 quepáis, 3 quepan, VV. quepan.—*Imperf. 1st term.* 1 Cupiera, 2 cupieras, 3 cupiera, V. cupiera: 1 cupiéramos, 2 cupierais, 3 cupieran, VV. cupieran.—*2d term.* 1 Cabría, 2 cabrías, 3 cabría, V. cabría: 1 cabríamos, 2 cabríais, 3 cabrían, VV. cabrían.—*3d term* 1 Cupiese, 2 cupieses, 3 cupiese, V. cupiese: 1 cupiésemos, 2 cupieseis, 3 cupiesen, VV. cupiesen.—*Fut.* 1 Cupiere, 2 cupieres, 3 cupiere, V. cupiere: 1 cupiéremos, 2 cupiereis, 3 cupieren, VV. cupieren.

CAER, *to fall.* Cl. VI.

Gerund. Cayendo. *Past participle. Caído.*

Indic. Pres. 1 Caigo, 2 *caes*, 3 *cae*, V. *cae:* 1 *caemos*, 2 *caéis*, 3 *caen*, VV. *caen.*—*Pret.* 1 *Caí*, 2 *caiste*, 3 cayó, V. cayó: 1 *caimos*, 2 *caisteis*, 3 cayeron, VV. cayeron.

Imper. 1 Caiga yo, 2 *cae*, 3 caiga él, caiga V., 2 no caigas: 1 caigamos, 2 *caed*, 3 caigan, caigan VV., 2 no caigáis.—*Subj. Pres.* 1 Caiga, 2 caigas, 3 caiga, V. caiga: 1 caigamos, 2 caigáis, 3 caigan, VV. caigan.—*Imperf. 1st term.* 1 Cayera, 2 cayeras, 3 cayera, V. cayera: 1

cayéramos, 2 cayerais, 3 cayeran, VV. cayeran.—*2d term.* 1 *Caería*, etc., 1 *caeríamos*, etc.—*3d term.* 1 Cayese, 2 cayeses, 3 cayese, V. cayese : 1. cayésemos, 2 cayeseis, 3 cayesen, VV. cayesen.—*Fut.* 1 Cayere, 2 cayeres, 3 cayere, V. cayere : 1 cayéremos, 2 cayereis, 3 cayeren, VV. cayeren.

COCER, *to boil.* Cl. II.

Indic. Pres. 1 Cuezo, 2 cueces, 3 cuece, V. cuece : 1 *cocemos*, 2 *cocéis*, 3 cuecen, VV. cuecen.—*Subj. Pres.* 1 Cueza, 2 cuezas, 3 cueza, V. cueza : 1 cozamos, 2 cozáis, 3 cuezan, VV. cuezan.—*Imper.* 1 Cueza yo, 2 cuece, 3 cueza él, cueza V., 2 no cuezas : 1 cozamos, 2 *coced*, 3 cuezan, cuezan VV., 2 no cozáis.—*Subj. Pres.* 1. Cueza, 2 cuezas, etc.

DAR, *to give.* Cl. VI.

Indic. Pres. 1 Doy, 2 *das*, 3 *da*, V. *da* : 1 *damos*, 2 *dáis*, 3 *dan*, VV. *dan*.—*Imperf.* 1 *Daba*, etc. 1 *Dábamos*, etc.—*Perf.* 1 Di, 2 diste, 3 dio, V. dio : 1 dimos, 2 disteis, 3 dieron, VV. dieron.

Fut. 1 *Daré*, etc. 1 *Daremos*.—*Imper.* 1 *Dé* yo, etc. 1 *Demos*, etc.—*Subj. Pres.* 1 *Dé*, etc. : 1 *Demos*, etc. —*Imperf. 1st term.* 1 Diera, 2 dieras, 3 diera, V. diera : 1 diéramos, 2 dierais, 3 dieran, VV. dieran.—*2d term.* 1 *Daría*, etc. : 1 *daríamos*, etc.—*3d term.* 1 Diese, 2 dieses, 3 diese, V. diese : 1 diésemos, 2 dieseis, 3 diesen, VV. diesen.

Fut. 1 diere, 2 dieres, 3 diere, V. diere : 1 diéremos, 2 diereis, 3 dieren, VV. dieren.

DECIR, *to say.* Cl. VI.

Gerund, Diciendo. *Past participle.* Dicho.

Indic. Pres. 1 Digo, 2 dices, 3 dice, V. dice : 1 *decimos*, 2 *decís*, 3 dicen, VV. dicen.—*Imperf.* 1 *Decía*, etc. —*Pret.* 1 Dije, 2 dijiste, 3 dijo, V. dijo : 1 dijimos, 2 dijisteis, 3 dijeron, VV. dijeron.

Fut. 1 Diré, 2 dirás, 3 dirá, V. dirá : 1 diremos, 2 diréis, 3 dirán, VV. dirán.—*Imper.* 1 Diga yo, 2 di tú, 3 diga él, diga V., 2 no digas : 1 digamos, 2 *decid*, 3 digan, digan VV., 2 no digáis.—*Subj. Pres.* 1 Diga, 2 digas, 3 diga, V. diga : 1 digamos, 2 digáis, 3 digan, VV. digan.—*Imperf. 1st term.* 1 Dijera, 2 dijeras, 3 dijera, V. dijera : 1 dijéramos, 2 dijerais, 3 dijeran, VV. dijeran.—*2d term.* 1 Diría, 2 dirías, 3 diría, V. diría : 1 diríamos, 2 diríais, 3 dirían, VV. dirían.—*3d term.* 1 Dijese, 2 dijeses, 3 dijese, V. dijese : 1 dijésemos, 2 dijeseis, 3 dijesen, VV. dijesen.—*Fut.* 1 Dijere, 2 dijeres, 3 dijere, V. dijere : 1 dijéremos, 2 dijereis, 3 dijeren, VV. dijeren.

CONTRADECIR, *to contradict* ; DESDECIRSE, *to retract* ; PREDECIR, *to predict.* These three verbs are conjugated like *decir*, except in the second person singular of the imperative, which is *contradice, predice, desdícete.*

DORMIR, *to sleep.* Cl. II.

Gerund. Durmiendo. *Past participle.* Dormido.

Indic. Pres. 1 Duermo, 2 duermes, 3 duerme, V. duerme : 1 *dormimos*, 2 *dormís*, 3 duermen, VV. duermen.

Pret. 1 *Dormí*, 2 *dormiste*, 3 durmió : 1 *dormimos*, 2 *dormisteis*, 3 durmieren, VV. durmieren.—*Imper.* 1 Duerma yo, 2 duerme, 3 duerma él, duerma V., 2 no duermas : 1 durmamos, 2 *dormid*, 3 duerman, duerman VV., 2 no durmáis.—*Subj. Pres.* 1 Duerma, 2 duermas, 3 duerma, V. duerma : 1 durmamos, 2 durmáis, 3 duerman, VV. duerman.—*Imperf. 1st term.* 1 Durmiera, 2 durmieras, 3 durmiera, V. durmiera : 1 durmiéramos, 2 durmierais, 3 durmieran, VV. durmieran.—*2d term.* 1 *Dormiría*, etc.—*3d term.* 1 Durmiese, 2 durmieses, 3 durmiese, V. durmiese : 1 durmiésemos, 2 durmieseis, 3 durmiesen, VV. durmiesen.—*Fut.* 1 Durmiere, 2 durmieres, 3 durmiere, V. durmiere : 1 durmiéremos, 2 durmiereis, 3 durmieren, VV durmieren.

MORIR, *to die.* Cl. II.

Past participle. Muerto.

The rest is conjugated like *Dormir.*

ERGUIR, *to hold up the head.* Cl. I.

Gerund. Irguiendo. *Past participle. Erguido.*

Indic. Pres. 1 Yergo, 2 yergues, 3 yergue, V. yergue : 1 *erguimos*, 2 *erguís*, 3 yerguen, VV. yerguen.—*Pret.* 1 *Erguí*, 2 *erguiste*, 3 irguió, V. irguió : 1 *erguimos*, 2 *erguisteis*, 3 irguieron, VV. irguieron.—*Imper.* 1 Yerga yo, 2 yergue, 3 yerga él, yerga V., 2 no yergas : 1 irgamos, 2 *erguid*, 3 yergan, yergan VV., 2 no irgáis. —*Subj. Pres.* 1 Yerga, 2 yergas, 3 yerga, V. yerga : 1 irgamos, 2 irgáis, 3 yergan, VV. yergan.—*Imperf. 1st term.* 1 Irguiera, 2 irguieras, 3 irguiera, V. irguiera : 1 irguiéramos, 2 irguierais, 3 irguieran, VV. irguieran.—*2d term.* 1 *Erguiría*, etc.—*3d term.* 1 Irguiese, 2 irguieses, 3 irguiese, V. irguiese : 1 irguiésemos, 2 irguieseis, 3 irguiesen, VV. irguiesen.

ERRAR, *to err.* Cl. I.

Indic. Pres. 1 Yerro, 2 yerras, 3 yerra, V. yerra : 1 *erramos*, 2 *erráis*, 3 yerran, VV. yerran.—*Subj. Pres.* 1 Yerre, 2 yerres, 3 yerre, V. yerre : 1 *erremos*, 2 *erréis*, 3 yerren, VV. yerren.—*Imper.* 1. Yerre yo, 2 yerra, 3 yerre él, yerre V., 2 no yerres : 1 *erremos*, 2 *errad*, 3 yerren, yerren VV., 2 no *erréis.*

ESTAR, *to be.* Cl. VI.

See page 9.

HABER, *to have.* Cl. VI.

As an auxiliary verb, see page 9

HABER, when signifying *there to be*, is conjugated only in the third person singular of each tense, whether the nominative be singular or plural ; thus :

There to be, *Haber.* There being, *Habiendo.*

There is There are	*hay*	There had been	*había habido*
There was	*había*	There shall have been	*habrá habido*
There were	*hubo*		
There will be	*habrá*	There may have been	*haya habido*
Let there be	*haya*		
There may be	*haya*	There might, could, would, or should have been	*hubiera habido* *habría habido* *hubiese habido*
There might, could, would, or should be	*hubiera* *habría* *hubiese*		
When there shall be	*cuando hubiere*		
There has been There have been	*ha habido*	When there shall have been	*cuando hubiere habido*

HACER, *to make.* Cl. VI.

Gerund. Haciendo. *Past Participle.* Hecho.

Indic. Pres. 1 Hago, 2 *haces*, etc.—*Imperf.* 1. *Hacía*, etc.—*Pret.* 1 Hice, 2 hiciste, 3 hizo, V. hizo : 1 hicimos, 2 hicisteis, 3 hicieron, VV. hicieron.—*Fut.* 1 Haré, 2 harás, 3 hará : 1 haremos, 2 haréis, 3 harán.—*Imper.* 1 Haga, 2 haz, 3 haga : 1 hagamos, 2 *haced*, 3 hagan.—*Subj. Pres.* 1 Haga, 2 hagas, etc.—*Imperf. 1st term.* 1 Hiciera, 2 hicieras, 3 hiciera : 1 hiciéramos, 2 hicierais, 3 hicieran.—*2d term.* 1 Haría, 2 harías, 3 haría : 1 haríamos, 2 haríais, 3 harían.—*3d term.* 1 Hiciese, 2 hicieses, 3 hiciese : 1 hiciésemos, 2 hicieseis, 3 hiciesen.—*Fut.* 1 Hiciere, 2 hicieres, 3 hiciere : 1 hiciéremos, 2 hiciereis, 3 hicieren.

IR, *to go.* Cl. VI.

Gerund. Yendo. *Past participle.* Ido.

Indic. Pres. 1 Voy, 2 vas, 3 va : 1 vamos, 2 váis, 3 van.—*Imperf.* 1 Iba, 2 ibas, 3 iba : 1 íbamos, 2 ibais, 3 iban.—*Pret.* 1 Fui, 2 fuiste, 3 fue : 1 fuimos, 2 fuisteis, 3 fueron.—*Fut.* 1 Iré, 2 irás, 3 irá : 1 iremos, 2 iréis, 3 irán.—*Imper.* 1 Vaya, 2 ve, 3 vaya : 1 vamos, 2 *id*, 3 vayan.—*Subj. Pres.* 1 Vaya, 2 vayas, 3 vaya : 1 vayamos, 2 vayáis, 3 vayan.—*Imperf. 1st term.* 1 Fuera, 2 fueras, 3 fuera : 1 fuéramos, 2 fuerais, 3 fueran.—*2d term.* 1 Iría, 2 irías, 3 iría : 1 iríamos, 2 iríais, 3 irían.—*3d term.* 1 Fuese, 2 fueses, 3 fuese : 1 fuésemos, 2 fueseis, 3 fuesen.—*Fut.* 1 Fuere, 2 fueres, etc.

JUGAR, *to play.* Cl. II.

Gerund. Jugando. *Past participle.* Jugado.

Indic. Pres. 1 Juego, 2 juegas, 3 juega : 1 *jugamos*, 2 *jugáis*, 3 juegan.—*Imperf.* 1 *Jugaba*, etc.—*Pret.* 1 Jugué, 2 *jugaste*, etc.—*Fut.* 1 *Jugaré*, etc.—*Imperf.* 1 Juegue, 2 juega, 3 juegue : 1 juguemos, 2 *jugad*, 3 jueguen.—*Subj. Pres.* 1 Juegue, 2 juegues, 3 juegue : 1 juguemos, 2 juguéis, 3 jueguen.—*Imperf. 1st term.* 1 *Jugara*, etc.—*2d term.* 1 *Jugaría*, etc.—*3d term.* 1 *Jugase*, etc.—*Fut.* 1 *Jugare*, etc.

OIR, *to hear.* Cl. VI.

Gerund. Oyendo. *Past participle.* Oído.

Indic. Pres. 1 Oigo, 2 oyes, 3 oye : 1 *oímos*, 2 *oís*, 3 oyen.—*Imperf.* 1 *Oía*, etc.—*Pret.* 1 *Oí*, 2 *oíste*, 3 oyó : 1 *oímos*, 2 *oísteis*, 3 oyeron.—*Fut.* 1 *Oiré*, etc.—*Imper.* 1 Oiga, 2 oye, 3 oiga : 1 oigamos, 2 *oíd*, 3 oigan.—*Subj. Pres.* 1 Oiga, 2 oigas, 3 oiga : 1 oigamos, 2 oigáis, 3 oigan.—*Imperf. 1st term.* 1 Oyera, 2 oyeras, oyera : 1 oyéramos, 2 oyerais, 3 oyeran.—*2d term.* 1 *Oiría*, etc. —*3d term.* 1 Oyese, 2 oyeses, 3 oyese : 1 oyésemos, 2 oyeseis, 3 oyesen.—*Fut.* 1 Oyere, 2 oyeres, 3 oyere: 1 oyéremos, 2 oyereis, 3 oyeren.

OLER, *to smell.* Cl. II.

Gerund. Oliendo. *Past participle.* Olido.

Indic. Pres. 1 Huelo, 2 hueles, 3 huele: 1 *olemos*, 2 *oléis*, 3 huelen.—*Imperf.* 1 *Olía*, etc.—*Pret.* 1 *Olí*, etc.—*Fut.* 1 *Oleré*, etc.—*Imper.* 1 Huela, 2 huele, 3 huela: 1 *olamos*, 2 *oled*, 3 huelan.—*Subj. Pres.* 1 Huela, 2 huelas, 3 huela: 1 *olamos*, 2 *oláis*, 3 huelan.—*Imperf. 1st term.* 1 *Oliera*, etc.—*2d term.* 1 *Olería*, etc.—*3d term.* 1 *Oliese*, etc.—*Fut.* 1 Oliere, etc.

PODER, *to be able.* Cl. VI.

Gerund. Pudiendo. *Past participle.* Podido.

Indic. Pres. 1 Puedo, 2 puedes, 3 puede: 1 *podemos*, 2 *podéis*, 3 pueden.—*Imperf.* 1 *Podía*, etc.—*Pret.* 1 Pude, 2 pudiste, 3 pudo: 1 pudimos, 2 pudisteis, 3 pudieron.—*Fut.* 1 Podré, 2 podrás, 3 podrá: 1 podremos, 2 podréis, 3 podrán.—It has no *Imperative*.—*Subj. Pres.* 1 Pueda, 2 puedas, 3 pueda: 1 *podamos*, 2 *podáis*, 3 puedan.—*Imperf. 1st term.* 1 Pudiera, 2 pudieras, 3 pudiera: 1 pudiéramos, 2 pudierais, 3 pudieran.—*2d term.* 1 Podría, 2 podrías, 3 podría: 1 podríamos, 2 podríais, 3 podrían.—*3d term.* 1 Pudiese, 2 pudieses, 3 pudiese: 1 pudiésemos, 2 pudieseis, 3 pudiesen.—*Fut.* 1 Pudiere, 2 pudieres, 3 pudiere: 1 pudiéremos, 2 pudiereis, 3 pudieren.

PODRIR or PUDRIR, *to rot.* Cl. VI.

Gerund. Pudriendo. *Past Participle.* Podrido.

Indic. Pres. 1 Pudro, 2 pudres, 3 pudre: 1 *podrimos*, 2 *podrís*, 3 pudren.—*Imperf.* 1 *Pudría* or *podría*, etc.—*Pret.* 1 *Podrí*, 2 *podriste*, 3 pudrió: 1 *podrimos*, 2 *podristeis*, 3 pudrieron.—*Fut.* 1 *Podriré*, etc.—*Imper.* 1 Pudra, 2 pudre, 3 pudra: 1 pudramos, 2 *podrid*, 3 pudran.—*Subj. Pres.* 1 Pudra, 2 pudras, 3 pudra, etc.—*Imperf. 1st term.* 1 Pudriera, 2 pudrieras, 3 pudriera: 1 pudriéramos, 2 pudrierais, 3 pudrieran.—*2d term.* 1 *Pudriría*, *podriría*, etc.—*3d term.* 1 Pudriese, 2 pudrieses, 3 pudriese: 1 pudriésemos, 2 pudrieseis, 3 pudriesen.—*Fut.* 1 Pudriere, 2 pudrieres, 3 pudriere: 1 pudriéremos, 2 pudriereis, 3 pudrieren.

PONER, *to put.* Cl. VI.

Gerund. Poniendo. *Past participle.* Puesto.

Indic. Pres. 1 Pongo, 2 *pones*, etc.—*Imperf.* 1 *Ponía*, etc.—*Pret.* 1 Puse, 2 pusiste, 3 puso: 1 pusimos, 2 pusisteis, 3 pusieron.—*Fut.* 1 Pondré, 2 pondrás, 3 pondrá: 1 pondremos, 2 pondréis, 3 pondrán.—*Imper.* 1 Ponga, 2 pon, 3 ponga: 1 pongamos, 2 *poned*, 3 pongan.—*Subj. Pres.* 1 Ponga, 2 pongas, 3 ponga: 1 pongamos, 2 pongáis, 3 pongan.—*Imperf. 1st term.* 1 Pusiera, 2 pusieras, 3 pusiera: 1 pusiéramos, 2 pusierais, 3 pusieran.—*2d term.* 1 Pondría, 2 pondrías, 3 pondría: 1 pondríamos, 2 pondríais, 3 pondrían.—*3d term.* 1 Pusiese, 2 pusieses, 3 pusiese: 1 pusiésemos, 2 pusieseis, 3 pusiesen.—*Fut.* 1 Pusiere, 2 pusieres, 3 pusiere: 1 pusiéremos, 2 pusiereis, 3 pusieren.

QUERER, *to will.* Cl. VI.

Gerund. Queriendo. *Past Participle.* Querido.

Indic. Pres. 1 Quiero, 2 quieres, 3 quiere: 1 *queremos*, 2 *queréis*, 3 quieren.—*Imperf.* 1 *Quería*, etc.—*Pret.* 1 Quise, 2 quisiste, 3 quiso: 1 quisimos, 2 quisisteis, 3 quisieron.—*Fut.* 1 Querré, 2 querrás, 3 querrá: 1 querremos, 2 querréis, 3 querrán.—*Subj. Pres.* 1 Quiera, 2 quieras, 3 quiera: 1 *queramos*, 2 *queráis*, 3 quieran.—*Imperf. 1st term.* 1 Quisiera, 2 quisieras, 3 quisiera: 1 quisiéramos, 2 quisierais, 3 quisieran.—*2d term.* 1 Querría, 2 querrías, 3 querría: 1 querríamos, 2 querríais, 3 querrían.—*3d term.* 1 Quisiese, 2 quisieses, 3 quisiese: 1 quisiésemos, 2 quisieseis, 3 quisiesen.—*Fut.* 1 Quisiere, 2 quisieres, 3 quisiere: 1 quisiéremos, 2 quisiereis, 3 quisieren.

REIR, *to laugh.* Cl. IV.

Gerund. Riendo. *Past participle.* Reído.

Indic. Pres. 1 Río, 2 ríes, 3 ríe: 1 *reímos*, 2 *reís*, 3 ríen.—*Imperf.* 1 *Reía*, etc.—*Pret.* 1 *Reí*, 2 *reiste*, 3 rio: 1 *reímos*, 2 *reisteis*, 3 rieron.—*Fut.* 1 *Reiré*, etc.—*Imper.* 1 Ría, 2 ríe, 3 ría: 1 riamos, 2 *reid*, 3 rían.—*Subj Pres.* 1 Ría, 2 rías, 3 ría: 1 riamos, 2 riáis, 3 rían.—*Imperf. 1st term.* 1 Riera, 2 rieras, 3 riera, etc.—*2d term.* 1 *Reiría*, etc.—*3d term.* 1 Riese, 2 rieses, 3 riese: 1 riésemos, 2 rieseis, 3 riesen, etc.—*Fut.* 1 Riere, 2 rieres, 3 riere: 1 riéremos, 2 riereis, 3 rieren, etc.

FREIR, *to fry.* *Past participle.* Frito.

SABER, *to know.* Cl. VI.

Gerund. Sabiendo. *Past participle.* Sabido.

Indic. Pres. 1 Sé, 2 *sabes*, etc.—*Imperf.* 1 *Sabía*, etc.—*Pret.* 1 Supe, 2 supiste, 3 supo: 1 supimos, 2 supisteis, 3 supieron.—*Fut.* 1 Sabré, 2 sabrás, 3 sabrá: 1 sabremos, 2 sabréis, 3 sabrán.—*Imper.* 1 Sepa, 2 *sabe*, 3 sepa: 1 sepamos, 2 *sabed*, 3 sepan.—*Subj. Pres.* 1 Sepa, 2 sepas, 3 sepa: 1 sepamos, 2 sepáis, 3 sepan.—*Imperf. 1st term.* 1 Supiera, 2 supieras, 3 supiera: 1 supiéramos, 2 supierais, 3 supieran.—*2d term.* 1 Sabría, 2 sabrías, 3 sabría: 1 sabríamos, 2 sabríais, 3 sabrían.—*3d term.* 1 Supiese, 2 supieses, 3 supiese, etc.—*Fut.* 1 Supiere, 2 supieres, 3 supiere: 1 supiéremos, 2 supiereis, 3 supieren.

SALIR, *to go out.* Cl. VI.

Gerund. Saliendo. *Past participle.* Salido.

Indic. Pres. 1 Salgo, 2 *sales*, etc.—*Imperf.* *Salía*, etc.—*Pret.* 1 *Salí*, etc.—*Fut.* 1 Saldré, 2 saldrás, 3 saldrá: 1 saldremos, 2 saldréis, 3 saldrán.—*Imper.* 1 Salga, 2 sal, 3 salga: 1 salgamos, 2 *salid*, 3 salgan.—*Subj. Pres.* 1 Salga, 2 salgas, 3 salga: 1 salgamos, 2 salgáis, 3 salgan.—*Imperf. 1st term.* 1 *Saliera*, etc.—*2d term.* 1 Saldría, 2 saldrías, 3 saldría: 1 saldríamos, 2 saldríais, 3 saldrían.—*3d term.* 1 *Saliese*, etc.—*Fut.* 1 *Saliere*, etc.

SATISFACER, *to satisfy.* Cl. VI.

SATISFACER is a verb compounded of *satis* and *hacer*, and is conjugated like *hacer*, changing the *h* into *f*; thus, *satisfago*, *satisfaces*, etc., satisfacía, etc., *satisfice*, *satisficiste*, *satisfizo*, etc. Except the imperative, the second person singular of which is, *satisface*, or *satisfaz*.

TRAER, *to bring.* Cl. VI.

Gerund. Trayendo. *Past participle.* Traído.

Indic. Pres. 1 Traigo, 2 *traes*, etc.—*Imperf.* 1 *Traía*, etc.—*Pret.* 1 Traje, 2 trajiste, 3 trajo: 1 trajimos, 2 trajisteis, 3 trajeron.—*Fut.* 1 *Traeré*, etc.—*Imper.* 1 Traiga, 2 *trae*, 3 traiga, traiga V., 2 no traigas: 1 traigamos, 2 *traed*, 3 traigan, traigan VV., 2 no traigáis.—*Subj. Pres.* 1 Traiga, 2 traigas, 3 traiga, etc.—*Imperf. 1st term.* 1 Trajera, 2 trajeras, 3 trajera: 1 trajéramos, 2 trajerais, 3 trajeran.—*2d term.* 1 *Traería*, etc.—*3d term.* 1 Trajese, 2 trajeses, 3 trajese, etc.—*Fut.* 1 Trajere, 2 trajeres, 3 trajere: 1 trajéremos, 2 trajereis, 3 trajeren.

VALER, *to be worth.* Cl. VI.

Indic. Pres. 1 Valgo, 2 *vales*, etc.: 1 *valemos*, etc.—*Fut.* 1 valdré, 2 valdrás, 3 valdrá, V. valdrá: 1 valdremos, 2 valdréis, 3 valdrán, VV. valdrán.—*Imper.* 1 Valga yo, 2 *vale*, 3 valga, valga V., 2 no valgas, etc., 2 no valgáis.—*Subj. Pres.* 1 Valga, 2 valgas, 3 valga, V. valga: 1 valgamos, 2 valgáis, 3 valgan, VV. valgan.—*Imperf. 1st term.* 1 *Valiera*, etc.—*2d term.* 1 Valdría, 2 valdrías, 3 valdría, V. valdría: 1 valdríamos, 2 valdríais, 3 valdrían, VV. valdrían.—*3d term.* 1 *Valiese*, 2 *valieses*, etc.—*Fut.* 1 *Valiere*, etc.

VENIR, *to come.* Cl. VI.

Gerund. Viniendo. *Past participle.* Venido.

Indic. Pres. 1 Vengo, 2 vienes, 3 viene, V. viene. 1 *venimos*, 2 *venís*, 3 vienen, VV. vienen.—*Pret.* 1 Vine, 2 *viniste*, 3 vino, V. vino: 1 *vinimos*, 2 *vinisteis*, 3 vinieron, VV. vinieron.—*Fut.* 1 Vendré, 2 vendrás, 3 vendrá, V. vendrá: 1 vendremos, 2 vendréis, 3 vendrán, VV. vendrán.—*Imper.* 1 Venga yo, 2 ven tú, 3 venga él, venga V., 2 no vengas: 1 vengamos, 2 *venid*, 3 vengan, vengan VV., 2 no vengáis.—*Subj. Pres.* 1 Venga, 2 vengas, 3 venga, V. venga: 1 vengamos, 2 vengáis, 3 vengan, VV. vengan.—*Imperf. 1st term.* 1 Viniera, 2 vinieras, 3 viniera, V. viniera: 1 viniéramos, 2 vinierais, 3 vinieran, VV. vinieran.—*2d term.* 1 Vendría, 2 vendrías, 3 vendría, V. vendría: 1 vendríamos, 2 vendríais, 3 vendrían, VV. vendrían.—*3d term.* 1 Viniese, 2 vinieses, 3 viniese, V. viniese: 1 viniésemos, 2 vinieseis, 3 viniesen, VV. viniesen.—*Fut.* 1 Viniere, 2 vinieres, 3 viniere, V. viniere: 1 viniéremos, 2 viniereis, 3 vinieren, VV. vinieren.

VER, *to see.* Cl. VI.

Gerund. Viendo. *Past participle.* Visto.

Indic. Pres. 1 Veo, 2 *ves* 3 *ve*, V. *ve*: 1 *vemos*, 2 *veis*, 3 *ven*, VV. *ven*.—*Imperf.* 1 Veía,* 2 veías, 3 veía, V. veía: 1 veíamos, 2 veíais, 3 veían, VV. veían.—*Pret.* 1 *Vi*, 2

* Formerly it was said *vía*, *vías*, *vía*, *víamos*, *víais*, *vían*.

viste, 3 *vio*, V. *vio:* 1 *vimos*, 2 *visteis*, 3 *vieron*, VV. *vieron*.—*Fut.* 1 *Veré*, 2 *verás*, 3 *verá*, V. *verá*, etc.—*Imper.* 1 Vea yo, 2 *ve* tú, 3 vea él, vea V., 2 no veas: 1 veamos, 2 *ved*, 3 vean, vean VV., 2 no veáis.—*Subj. Pres.* 1 Vea, 2 veas, 3 vea, V. vea: 1 veamos, veáis, 3 vean, VV. vean.—*Imperf. 1st term.* 1 *Viera*, 2 *vieras*, etc.—*2d term.* 1 *Vería*, 2 *verías*, etc.—*3d term.* 1 *Viese*, 2 *vieses*, etc.—*Fut.* 1 *Viere*, 2 *vieres*, 3 *viere*, etc.

YACER, *to lie down.* Cl. III.

This verb is rarely used, but in epitaphs; and it is conjugated only in the following tenses and persons:

Gerund. Yaciendo.—*Indic. Pres.* 1 Yazco, yazgo, yago, 2 *yaces*, 3 *yace*, V. *yace:* 1 *yacemos*, 2 *yacéis*, 3 *yacen*, VV. *yacen*.—*Imperf.* 1 *Yacía*, 2 *yacías*, 3 *yacía*, V. *yacía:* 1 *yacíamos*, 2 *yacíais*, 3 *yacían*, VV. *yacían*.—*Subj. Yazga* or *Yazca*.—*Imper. Yace*, yaz.

IMPERSONAL VERBS.

Impersonal verbs are those which are conjugated in the third person singular of each tense only, without expressing the nominative, as:

GRANIZAR, *to hail.*

It hails	*graniza*	It has hailed	*ha granizado*
It hailed	*granizaba* / *granizó*	It had hailed	*había granizado.*
It will hail	*granizará*	It shall have hailed	*habrá granizado*
Let it hail	*granice*	It may have hailed	*haya granizado*
It may hail	*granice*		
It might, could, would, or should hail.	*granizara* / *granizaría* / *granizase*	It might, could, would, or should have hailed	*hubiera granizado* / *habría granizado* / *hubiese granizado*
When it shall hail	*granizare*	When it shall have hailed	*cuando hubiere granizado*

The following are some of the impersonal verbs:

To freeze	*helar*, irr.	To lighten	*relampaguear*
To frost	*escarchar*	To thunder	*tronar*, irr.
		To rain	*llover*, irr.
To thaw	*deshelar*	To happen	*suceder* / *acaecer* / *acontecer*
To drizzle	*lloviznar*		
To snow,	*nevar*, irr.	To dawn	*amanecer*
To be cold	*hacer frío*	To become night	*anochecer*

DEFECTIVE VERBS.

SOLER, *to accustom.* Cl. II.

This verb is used only in the two following tenses:

Indic. Pres. 1 Suelo, 2 sueles, 3 suele, 2 V. suele: 1 *solemos*, 2 *soléis*, 3 suelen, 2 VV. suelen.—*Imperf.* 1 *Solía*, 2 *solías*, 3 *solía*. 2 V. *solía:* 1 *solíamos*, 2 *solíais*, 3 *solían*, 2 VV. *solían*.

PLACER, *to please.* Cl. III.

This verb is used only in the third person singular or plural, in the moods and tenses as follows: it is always accompanied by a personal pronoun in the objective case.

Indic. Pres. 1 *Me* place, 2 *te* place, 3 *le* place, 2 *le* place *a V.:* 1 *nos* place, 2 *os* place, 3 *les* place, 2 *les* place *a VV.; or* 1 *Me* placen, 2 *te* placen, etc.—*Imperf.* 1 *Me* placía, *or* placían, 2 *te* placía, *or* placían, etc.—*Pret.* 1 *Me* plugo, 2 *te* plugo, etc.: 1 *me* pluguieron, 2 *te* pluguieron, etc.—*Subj. Pres.* 1 *Me* plegue, etc.—*Imperf. 1st term. Me* pluguiera, etc.—*3d term. Me* pluguiese, etc. —*Fut. Me* pluguiere.

ROER, *to gnaw.* Cl. VI.

Indic. Pres. 1 Roo, roigo, royo, 2 roes, 3 roe: 1 roemos, 2 roéis, 3 roen.—*Subj. Pres.* 1 Roa, roiga, roya, 2 roas, roigas, royas, 3 roa, roiga, roya: 1 roamos, roigamos, royamos, 2 roáis, roigáis, royáis, 3 roan, roigan, royan.

REMARK.—Corroer, *to corrode*, makes corroe, corroen, in the present indicative, and corroa, corroan, in the subjunctive.

Obs. The verbs *gustar*, to like; *pesar*, to be sorry for; *acomodar*, to suit; *convenir*, to agree, etc., are frequently used only in the third person singular or plural, as in the verb *placer*. Ex.: He likes music, *le gusta la música*, or *él gusta de la música*.

A LIST OF ALL THE IRREGULAR VERBS.

Obs. 1. The compound verbs are not inserted, when they have the same irregularity as the simple ones from which they are derived: as, *componer*, *contraponer*, etc., which are conjugated like *poner*.

For the convenience of the learner the strictness of this principle has been departed from in the two cases following: 1st. When the simple is no longer used by itself. To this list belong these nine: *cluir* (Cl. V), *cordar* (Cl. I), *ducir* (Cl. III), *manecer* (Cl. III), *stituir* (Cl. V), *tribuir* (Cl. V), *vertir* (Cl. I), *blandecer*, *bravecer* (Cl. III). 2d. Some compounds of *ad* (reduced to *a*) have been included, such as *asonar*, *atender*, and *asentir*.

On the other hand, compounds from nominal roots, as *enflaquecer*, *florecer*, have been inserted.

Obs. 2. The most general irregularities of the Spanish verbs consist in their taking *i*, *j*, *y*, or *ue*, or *i*, instead of *o*, or *e*. To find the infinitive mode of such verbs, separate the regular termination, and omit the letter or letters that do not belong to the radicals of such verbs: as in *comienzo*, *muestras*, *sintió*, *condujeron*, *trajeran*, *construyesen*, the terminations are *o*, *as*, *ió*, *eron*, *eran*, *esen*. The remaining letters are, *comienz*, *muestr*, *sint*, *conduj*, *traj*, *construy*. Add to these the regular terminations of the infinitive mode, and they will read *comienzar*, *muestrar*, *sintir*, *condujir*, *trajer*, *construyir*. Take off the *i*, *j*, and *y*, change *ue* into *o*, and the *i* into *e;* add a *c* before the termination to those in *ij or uj;* and they will be *comenzar*, *mostrar*, *sentir*, *conducir*, *traer*, *construir*.

Obs. 3. The irregular participles are set in italics after their verbs.

☞ The verbs of the first column are conjugated like those of the second, which must be consulted in their respective places.

	Cl.
Abastecer,	III
Aborrecer,	III
Abrir, reg. *Abierto.*	
Abstenerse,	VI
(Abs)traer,	VI
Abstracto and Abstraído.	
Abuñolar,	II
Acaecer,	III
Acertar,	I
Aclocar,	II
Acollar,	II
Acontecer,	III
Acordar,	II
Acornar,	II
Acostar,	II
Acrecentar,	I
Acrecer,	III
Adestrar,	I
(Ad)herir,	I
Adolecer,	III
Adormecer,	III
Adquirir,	I
Advertir,	I
Aducir,	III
Aferrar,	I
Afluir,	V
Afollar,	II
Aforar,	II
Agorar,	II
Agradecer,	III
Aguerrir, (defective)	IV
Alborecer,	III
Alebrarse,	I
Alentar,	I
Aliquebrar,	I
Almorzar,	II
Alongar,	II
Altivecerse,	III
Amarillecer,	III
Amoblar,	II
Amolar,	II
Amollecer,	III
Amorecer,	III
Amortecer,	III
Andar,	VI
Anochecer,	III
Apacentar,	I
Aparecer,	III
Apercollar,	II
Apernar,	I
Apetecer,	III
Apostar,	II
Apretar,	I
Aprobar,	II
Argüir,	V

	Cl.
Aridecer,	III
Arrecirse,	IV
Arrendar,	I
Arrepentirse,	I
Ascender,	I
Asentar,	I
Asentir,	I
Aserrar,	I
Asir,	VI
Asolar,	II
Asoldar,	II
Asonar,	II
Asosegar,	I
Atender,	I
Atento and Atendido.	
(A)tentar,	I
Aterirse,	I
Aterrar, (echar por tierra)	I
Atestar, (rellenar)	I
Atontecer,	III
(A)traer,	VI
Atravesar,	I
Atribuir,	V
(A)tronar,	II
Avanecerse,	III
(A)venir,	VI
Aventar(se),	I
Avergonzar,	II
Azolar,	II
Bendecir,	VI
Bendito and Bendecido.	
Bienquerer,	VI
Blanquecer,	III
Caber,	VI
Caer,	VI
Calentar,	I
Canecer,	III
Carecer,	III
Cegar,	I
Ceñir,	IV
Cerner,	I
Cernir,	IV
Cerrar,	I
Cimentar,	I
Circuir,	V
Clarecer,	III
Clocar,	II
Cocer,	II
Colar,	II
Colegir,	IV
Colgar,	II
Comedirse,	IV
Comenzar,	I

	Cl.
Competir,	IV
Complacer,	III
Concebir,	IV
Concernir,	I
Concertar,	I
Concluir,	V
Concluso and Concluído.	
Concordar,	II
Condescender,	I
Condolerse,	II
Conducir,	III
Conferir,	I
Confesar,	I
Confluir,	V
Conocer,	III
Conseguir,	IV
Consentir,	I
Consolar,	II
Constituir,	V
Constreñir,	IV
Construir,	V
Contar,	II
(Con)tener,	VI
Contorcerse.	II
Contribuir,	V
Controvertir,	I
Convalecer,	III
Convertir,	I
Converso and Convertido.	
Corregir,	IV
Correcto and Corregido.	
Costar,	II
Crecer,	III
Cubrir, reg.	
Cubierto.	
Dar,	VI
Decentar,	I
Decir,	VI
Dicho.	
Deducir,	III
Defender,	I
Deferir,	I
Degollar,	II
Demoler,	II
Demostrar,	II
Denegar,	I
Denodarse,	II
Denostar.	II
Dentar,	I
Derrengar,	I
Derretir,	IV
Derrocar,	II
Derruir,	V
Desbastecer,	III
Desbravecer,	III
Descaecer,	III
Descender,	I
Descollar,	II
Descordar,	II
Descornar,	II
Describir, reg.	
Descrito, or *descripto.*	
Desertar,	I
Desflocar,	II
Desherbar,	I
Deshombrecerse,	III
Desleir,	IV
Deslendrar,	I
Desmajolar,	II
Desmembrar	I
Desolar,	II
Desollar,	II
Desosar,	II
Desovar,	II
Despernar,	I
Despertar,	I
Despierto and Despertado.	
Desterrar,	I
Destruir,	V
Desvergonzarse,	II
Dezmar,	I
Diferir,	I
Digerir,	I
Diluir,	V
Discernir,	I
Discordar,	II
Disminuir,	V
Disolver,	II
Dispertar,	I
Dispierto and Dispertado.	
Distribuir,	V
Divertir,	I
Doler,	II
Dormir,	II
Educir,	III
Elegir,	IV
Electo and Elegido.	
Embarbecer,	III
Embebecer(se),	III
Embellecer,	III
Embermejecer,	III
Embestir,	IV
Emblandecer,	III
Embobecer,	III
Embosquecer,	III
Embravecer,	III
Embrutecer,	III
Emparentar,	I
Empecer,	III
Empedernecerse,	III
Empedernir,	IV
Empedrar,	I
Empellar,	I
Empequeñecer,	III
Empezar,	I
Emplastecer,	III
Emplumecer,	III
Empobrecer,	III
Empodrecer,	III
Empoltronecerse,	III
Emporcar,	II
Enaltecer,	III
Enardecer,	III
Encabellecerse,	III
Encalvecer,	III
Encallecer,	III
Encandecer,	III
Encanecer,	III
Encarecer,	III
Encender,	I
Encentar,	I
Encerrar,	I
Encloquecer,	III
Encomendar,	I
Encontrar,	II
Encorar,	II
Encordar,	II
Encorecer,	III
Encornar,	II
Encovar,	II
Encrudecer,	III
Encruelecer(se),	III
Encubertar,	I
Endentecer,	III
Endurecer,	III
Enfierecer(se),	III
Enflaquecer,	III
Enfranquecer,	III
Enfurecer	III
Engorar,	II
Engrandecer,	III
Engreirse,	IV
Engrosar,	II
Engrumecer(se),	III
Enhambrecer,	III
Enhambrentar,	I
Enhestar,	I
Enlenzar,	I
Enloquecer,	III
Enlentecer,	III
Enmagrecer,	III
Enmalecer,	III
Enmarillecer(se),	III
Enmelar,	I
Enmendar,	I
(En)mohecer,	III
Enmollecer,	III
Enmudecer,	III
Ennoblecer,	III
Ennudecer,	III
Enorgullecer(se),	III
Enrarecer.	III
Enriquecer,	III
Enrobustecer,	III
Enrodar,	II
Enrojecer,	III
Enronquecer,	III
Enroñecer,	III
Enrudecer,	III
Enruinecerse,	III
Ensalmorar,	II
Ensandecer,	III
Ensangrentar,	I
Ensarnecer,	III
Ensoberbecer,	III
Ensordecer,	III
Entallecer,	III
Entender,	I
Entenebrecer,	III
Enternecer(se),	III
Enterrar,	I
Entesar,	I
Entigrecerse,	III
Entontecer,	III
Entorpecer,	III
Entortar,	II
Entristecer,	III
Entullecer,	III
Entumecer,	III
Envanecer,	III
Envejecer,	III
(En)verdecer	III
Envestir,	IV
Envilecer,	III
Enzurdecer,	III
Erguir,	I or IV
Errar,	I
Escandecer,	III
Escarmentar,	I
Escarnecer,	III
Esclarecer,	III
Escocer,	II
Escribir, reg.	
Escrito.	
Esforzar,	II
Establecer,	III
Estar (see the auxiliary verbs),	VI
Estatuir,	V
Estregar,	I
Estremecer(se),	III
Estreñir,	IV
Excluir,	V
Excluso and Excluído.	
Expedir,	IV
Extender,	I
Extenso and Extendido.	
Fallecer,	III
Favorecer,	III
Fenecer,	III
Ferrar,	I
Florecer,	III
Fluir,	V
Follar,	II
Fortalecer,	III
Forzar,	II
Fregar,	I
Freir,	IV
Frito and Freído.	
Frutecer,	III
Gemir,	IV
Gobernar,	I
Gruir,	V
Guarecer(se),	III
Guarnecer,	III
Haber (see auxiliary verbs),	VI
Hacendar,	I
Hacer,	VI
Hecho.	
Heder,	I
Helar,	I
Henchir,	IV
Hender,	I
Heñir,	IV
Herbar,	I
Herbecer,	III
Herir,	I
Herrar,	I
Hervir,	I
Holgar,	II
Hollar,	II
Huir,	V
Humedecer,	III
Imbuir,	V
Imprimir, reg.	
Impreso.	
Incensar,	I
Incluir,	V
Incluso and Incluído.	
Inducir,	III
Inferir,	I
Infernar,	I
Ingerir,	I
Ingerto and Ingerido.	
Ingerir(se),	I
Inquirir,	I
Instituir,	V
Instruir,	V
Introducir,	III
Invernar,	I
Invertir,	I
Inverso and Invertido.	
Investir,	IV
Ir, irse,	VI
Jimenzar,	I
Jugar,	II
Languidecer,	III
Leer,	IV
Liquefacer, *V.* SATISFACER,	VI
Lobreguecer,	III
Lucir,	III
Luir,	V
Llover,	II
(Mal)decir,	VI
Maldito and Maldecido.	
Mancornar,	II
Manifestar,	I
Manifiesto and Manifestado.	
(Man)tener,	VI
Mecer,	III
Medir(se),	IV
Melar,	I
Mentar,	I
Mentir,	I
Merecer,	III
Merendar,	I
Moblar,	II
Mohecer,	III
Moler,	II
Morder,	II
Morir,	II
Muerto.	
Mostrar,	II
Mover,	II
Muir,	V
Nacer,	III
Nato and Nacido.	
Negar,	I
Negrecer,	III
Nevar,	I
Obedecer,	III
Obscurecer,	III
Obstruir,	V
Ofrecer,	III
Oir,	VI
Oler,	II
Oponer,	VI
Oscurecer,	III
Pacer,	III
Padecer,	III
Palidecer,	III
Parecer(se),	III
Pedir,	IV
Pensar,	I
Perder,	I
Perecer,	III
Permanecer,	III
Perniquebrar,	I
Pertenecer,	III
Pervertir,	I
Pimpollecer,	III
Placer (def.),	III
Plastecer,	III
Plegar,	I
Poblar,	II
Poder,	VI
Podrecer,	III
Podrir,	VI
Poner,	VI
Puesto.	
Poseer,	IV
Poseso and Poseído.	
Preferir,	I
Prescribir, reg.	
Prescripto.	
Preterir,	I
Prevalecer,	III
Probar,	II
Producir,	III
Proferir,	I
Proscribir, reg.	
Proscripto.	
Prostituir,	V
Proveer,	IV
Provisto and Proveído.	

	Cl.
Quebrar,	I
Querer,	VI
Raer (def.),	VI
Reblandecer,	III
Recordar,	II
Recostar,	II
Recrudecer,	III
Reducir,	III
Referir,	I
Regar,	I
Regimentar,	I
Regir,	IV
Regoldar,	I
Reir,	IV
Rejuvenecer,	III
Relentecer,	III
Remanecer,	III
Remendar,	I
Rendir,	IV
Renovar,	II
Reñir,	IV
Repetir,	IV
Requebrar,	I
Requerir,	I
Resçontrar,	II
Resollar,	II
Resplandecer,	III
Restablecer,	III
Restituir,	V
Restregar,	I
Retentar,	I
Retoñecer,	III
Retribuir,	V
Revejecer,	III
Reventar,	I
Reverdecer,	III
Revolcar,	II
Robustecer,	III
Rodar,	II
Roer (def.),	VI
Rogar,	II
Saber,	VI
Salir,	VI
Salpimentar,	I
Sarmentar,	I
Satisfacer,	VI
Seducir,	V
Segar,	I
Seguir,	IV
Sembrar,	I
Sementar,	I
Sentar(se),	I
Sentir(se),	I
Ser (see auxiliary verbs)	VI
Serrar,	I
Servir(se),	IV
Simenzar,	I

	Cl.
Sofreir, *V.* Reir,	IV
Sofrito and Sofreído.	
Solar,	II
Soldar,	II
Soler (def.),	II
Soltar,	II
Suelto and Soltado.	
Solver,	II
Suelto.	
Sonar,	II
Soñar,	II
Sonreir, *V.* Reir,	IV
Sosegar,	I
Soterrar,	I
Sugerir,	I
Tallecer,	III
Temblar,	I
Tender,	I
Tener,	VI
Tentar,	I
Teñir,	IV
Tinto and Teñido	
Torcer,	II
Tuerto and Torcido.	
Tostar,	II
Traducir,	III
Traer,	VI
Transcender,	I
Transferir,	I
Trascender,	I
Trascordarse,	II
Trasegar,	I
Travesar,	I
Trocar,	II
Tronar,	II
Tropezar,	I
Tumefacerse,	VI
Tumefacto.	
Valer(se),	VI
Venir,	VI
Ventar,	I
Ver,	VI
Visto.	
Verdecer,	III
Vertir,	I
Vestir,	IV
Volar,	II
Volcar,	II
Volver,	II
Vuelto.	
Yacer,	III
Zaherir,	I

WORD-DERIVATION.

Prefixes derived from the Latin are common to Spanish and English and need little elucidation. Some remarks upon the more usual suffixes may, however, prove helpful.

-ada.

(*a*) Expresses the capacity or duration of what is denoted by the primitive noun:

Cuchara, spoon. **Cucharada**, spoonful.
Mano, hand. **Manada**, handful.

(*b*) Signifies a collection of things of the same class:

Caballo, horse. **Cabalgada**, cavalcade.
Perro, dog. **Perrada**, pack of dogs.

(*c*) Denotes a stroke or thrust, usually with a cutting or pointed instrument:

Cuchillo, knife. **Cuchillada**, gash with a knife.

-ada, -ida.

In form the feminine of the past participle makes nouns expressing completed action, usually from verbs of motion:

Entrar, to enter. **Entrada**, entry.
Venir, to come. **Venida**, coming.

-ado.

Forms adjectives denoting resemblance to the primitive:

Corazón, heart. **Acorazonado**, heart-shaped, cordate.
Naranja, orange. **Naranjado**, orange-coloured.

-aje.

(*a*) Derivative nouns in *aje* express a fee or payment connected with the primitive:

Carreta, cart. **Carretaje**, cartage.
Puente, bridge. **Pontage**, bridge toll.

(*b*) Denotes usually collective nouns, sometimes like the English -age:

Ancla, anchor. **Anclaje**, anchorage.
Hierro, iron. **Herraje**, iron-work.

-al, -ar.

Denotes a collection of what is connoted by the primitive noun:

Zarza, bramble. **Zarzal**, bramble thicket.
Naranja, orange. **Naranjal**, orange orchard.
Manzana, apple. **Manzanar**, apple orchard.

-anza.

Forms abstract verbal nouns:

Mudar, to change. **Mudanza**, change.
Esperar, to hope. **Esperanza**, hope.

-azgo.

This suffix denotes the office, functions, or jurisdiction of the person designated by the primitive noun:

Arzobispo, archbishop. **Arzobispazgo**, (obs.) archbishopric (function or jurisdiction)
Primo, cousin. **Primazgo**, cousinship.

-azo.

Denotes a stroke or wound with the object expressed by the primitive noun:

Látigo, whip. **Latigazo**, lash with a whip.
Sable, sabre. **Sablazo**, sabre-cut.

-dera.

Feminine suffix denoting the instrument for accomplishing the action expressed by the primitive verb:

Abrazar, to embrace. **Abrazadera**, ferrule.
Chiflar, to whistle. **Chifladera**, whistle (instrument).
Limpiar, to clean. **Limpiadera**, clothes-brush, plough-scraper.

-dero.

(*a*) Expresses the place where the action of the verb comes to pass.

Beber, to drink. **Bebedero**, drinking-trough or vessel.
Fondear, to cast anchor. **Fondeadero**, anchoring-ground.

(*b*) Forms adjectives expressing fitness to perform or to undergo the action of the verb:

Beber, to drink. **Bebedero**, drinkable, potable.
Casar, to marry. **Casadero**, marriageable.
Durar, to last. **Duradero**, lasting, durable.

-dizo.

Forms adjectives denoting fitness or capability for the action denoted by the primitive verb:

Arrojar, to hurl. **Arrojadizo**, missile.
Regar, to irrigate. **Regadizo**, irrigable.
Serrar, to saw. **Serradizo**, fit to be sawed.

-dumbre.

Forms abstract nouns from adjectives:

Cierto, certain. **Certidumbre**, certainty.
Manso, meek. **Mansedumbre**, meekness.

-dura.

(*a*) Added to verbs forms nouns denoting the action of the verb and the effect resulting:

Cortar, to cut. **Cortadura**, cut, gash.
Aserrar, to saw. **Aserradura**, sawing, saw-cut. **Aserraduras**, sawdust.
Acepillar, to plane. **Acepilladura**, act of planing. **Cepilladuras**, shavings.

(*b*) Added to nouns denotes a set of what is expressed by the primitive:

Diente, tooth. **Dentadura**, set of teeth.
Broche, hook. **Brochadura**, set of hooks and eyes.

-era.

Expresses an article for containing that which the primitive noun connotes:

Sombrero, hat. **Sombrerera**, hat-box.
Carta, letter. **Cartera**, portfolio.
Mostaza, mustard. **Mostacera**, mustard-pot.

-ero.

(*a*) Affixed to nouns denoting the place for containing what is expressed by the primitive:

Grano, grain. **Granero**, granary.
Azúcar, sugar. **Azucarero**, sugar-bowl.
Tinta, ink. **Tintero**, inkstand.

(*b*) Affixed to nouns indicates the person in charge of what is expressed by the primitive:

Cárcel, jail. **Carcelero**, jailer.
Coche, coach. **Cochero**, coachman.
Vaca, cow. **Vaquero**, cowherd, cowboy.

(*c*) Forms derivative adjectives from nouns:

Chanza, joke, jest. **Chancero**, jocose, sportive.
Guerra, war. **Guerrero**, warlike.

(*d*) Denotes the dealer in commercial articles, or the manufacturer of them:

Alfar, pottery. **Alfarero**, potter.
Reloj, watch, clock. **Relojero**, watch-maker, clock-maker.
Cerveza, beer. **Cervecero**, brewer.

-ez and -eza.

Form abstract nouns from adjectives:

Árido, arid. **Aridez**, aridity.
Maduro, ripe. **Madurez**, ripeness, maturity.
Grande, great. **Grandeza**, greatness.
Triste, sad. **Tristeza**, sorrow; sadness.

-ia.

(*a*) Expresses the vocation or business of the person denoted by the primitive, and the place where it is carried on (particularly when affixed to nouns in *ero*):

Abad, abbot. **Abadía**, abbey; office of an abbot.
Alfarero, potter. **Alfarería**, potter's shop; pottery trade.
Librero, bookseller. **Librería**, bookstore; book trade.
Obrero, workman. **Obrería**, task of a workman.

(*b*) Expresses often the name of an art or science (derived from the Greek).

Astronomía, astronomy. **Fotografía**, photography.
Geometría, geometry. **Telegrafía**, telegraphy.

(*c*) Forms sometimes abstract nouns from adjectives:

Cortés, courteous. **Cortesía**, courtesy.
Bizarro, gallant, high-minded. **Bizarría**, gallantry, high-mindedness.
Mentecato, silly **Mentecatería**, silliness, nonsense.
Mejor, better. **Mejoría**, betterment, advantage.

-iento and -ino.

Form adjectives expressing resemblance:

Ceniza, ashes. **Ceniciento**, ash-coloured.
Sed, thirst. **Sediento**, thirsty.
Cuervo, crow. **Corvino**, crow-like.
Púrpura, purple. **Purpurino**, purplish.

-izo.

Forms adjectives which denote a tendency towards the quality or action implied in the primitive word:

Rojo, red. **Rojizo**, reddish.
Enfermo, sick. **Enfermizo**, sickly.
Mover, to move. **Movedizo**, movable, shifting.

-mento, -miento.

Form verbal nouns expressing the act or effect of the primitive verb:

Abastecer, to provide, to supply. **Abastecimiento**, provisioning, supplying; supplies.
Salvar, to save. **Salvamiento**, safety, salvage.

-ón.

(*a*) Added to stems of verbs forms nouns expressing the result of the action of the primitive:

Apretar, to press. **Apretón**, pressure.
Trasquilar, to shear. **Trasquilón**, clipping of wool.

(*b*) Forms adjectives from nouns and verbs, having a frequentative value suggestive of augmentatives in this same termination:

Burlar, to jest. **Burlón**, waggish, roguish.
Preguntar, to inquire. **Preguntón**, inquisitive.
Juguete, plaything. **Juguetón**, playful, frolicsome.

-or, -dor.

Denotes the actor:

Esculpir, to sculpture. **Escultor**, sculptor.
Amar, to love. **Amador**, lover.
Hacer, to make, to create. **Hacedor**, maker, creator.

-oso.

Forms adjectives expressing the quality or characteristic of the primitive noun or verb:

Cariño, affection. **Cariñoso**, affectionate.
Leche, milk. **Lechoso**, milky.
Orgullo, pride. **Orgulloso**, proud.

-udo.

Forms adjectives which express a high degree of the characteristic quality of the primitive noun:

Barriga, belly. **Barrigudo**, big-bellied, corpulent.
Capricho, caprice. **Caprichudo**, stubborn.
Hombro, shoulder. **Hombrudo**, broad-shouldered.
Zanca, shank. **Zancudo**, long-shanked.

-uno.

Forms adjectives denoting species applied commonly to animals:

Buey, ox. **Boyuno**, bovine.
Puerco, pig. **Porcuno**, porcine.

-ura.

Forms abstract nouns from adjectives:

Alto, high. **Altura**, height.
Dulce, sweet. **Dulzura**, sweetness.

-zón.

Forms nouns of allied meaning when affixed to nouns and stems of verbs:

Cargar, to load. **Cargazón**, cargo.
Ligar, to bind. **Ligazón**, bond, ligament.
Pollo, chicken **Pollazón**, brood, hatching.

A Key to the Pronunciation as Represented in This Dictionary.

SPANISH ALPHABET.

Give to the vowel the sound that the syllable that follows it in *italics* has in English; and sound also, as in English, each of the syllables that represent said sound throughout all the dictionary.

VOWELS.

Pronounce a, *ah;* e, *ay;* i, *ee;* o, *oh;* u, *u* (in *bull*); y, *ee*.

The vowels have invariably the same sound, and must be fully and distinctly pronounced. The *u* is silent in the syllables *gue, gui, que, qui,* which are pronounced *gay, gee, kay, kee:* when the *u* is to be sounded, it is marked thus, *ü*, as in *argüir* (ar-goo-eer).

CONSONANTS.

b, *bay,*	**f, *ai'fay,***	**l, *ai'lay,***	**ñ, *ai'nyay,***	**s, *es'say,***	**y griega *or* ye, *jay,***
c, *thay,*	**g, *hay,***	**ll, *ai'lyay,***	**p, *pay,***	**t, *tay,***	**z, *thai tah.***
ch, *tchay,*	**h, *ah'tchay,***	**m, *ai'may,***	**q, *coo,***	**v, *vay,***	
d, *day,*	**j, *hoe'tah,***	**n, *ai'nay,***	**r, *er'ay, er'ray,***	**x, *ay'kiss.***	

N. B. The *z* and the *c* (when the latter precedes *e* and *i*) are marked in this Dictionary to be pronounced as the English *th* in *thought*, which is the Castilian pronunciation. However, throughout Latin America they have the regular sound of *s*.

EXPLANATION OF THE ABBREVIATIONS.

a. . adjective.
Acad. . Dictionary of the Spanish Academy.
adv. . adverb.
Aer. . Aeronautics.
Agr. . Agriculture.
Alg. . Algebra.
Amer. . American.
Anat. . Anatomy.
ant. . antiquated.
Ar. . Arabic.
Arch. . Architecture.
Arg. . Argentina.
Arith. . Arithmetic.
Ast. . Astronomy.
aug. . augmentative.
Biol. . Biology.
Bol. . Bolivia.
Bot. . Botany.
cf. . (Confer) compare.
Chem. . Chemistry.
Ch. . Chile.
Col. . Colombia.
coll. . colloquial.
Com.; com. Commerce; common gender.
comp. . comparative; compound.
conj. . conjunction.
def. . definition.
dim. . diminutive.
Ec. . Ecuador.
Elec. . Electricity
Ent. . Entomology.
f. . feminine (noun).
F. . French.
fig. . figurative(ly).
for. . forensic; law term.
fr. . from.
Fen. . Fencing.
G., Ger. . German.
Geog. . Geography.
Geol. . Geology.
Geom. . Geometry.
Gr. . Greek.
Gram. . Grammar.
Heb. . Hebrew.
Her. . Heraldry.
Hort. . Horticulture.
imp. . imperfect; impersonal; imperative.
int. . interjection.
irr. . irregular.
It. . Italian.
Lat. . Latin.
Lit. . Literature.
m. . masculine (noun).
Mas. . Masonry.
Math. . Mathematics.
Mech. . Mechanics.
Med. . Medicine.
Met. . Metaphorical.
Mex. . Mexican or Mexico.
Mil. . Military.
Min. . Mineralogy; mining.
Mus. . Music.
n. . noun.
Nau., Naut. Nautical.
Neol. . Neologism.
obs. . obsolete.
Opt. . Optics.
Orn. . Ornithology.
Pap. . Paper-making.
pa. . present participle (active).
Per. . Persia(n).
Pg. . Portuguese.
Phil. . Philosophy.
Phot. . Photography.
Phy. . Physics.
pl. . plural.
pp. . past participle.
prep. . preposition.
pro. . pronoun.
Prov.; prov. Provincial; proverb.
r. w. . railway.
sing. . singular.
Sp. Am. Spanish American.
sup. . superlative.
Surg. . Surgery.
Th. . Theatre.
Turk. . Turkish.
typ. . typography.
V. . Vide, see; usted.
v. . verb.
va. . verb active (transitive).
Vd. . (usted) you.
v. def. . verb defective.
vn. . verb neuter (intransitive).
vr. . verb reflexive.
vulg. vulgar, low.
Vet. . Veterinary.
Ven. . Venezuela.
Vds. or *VV.* . ustedes.
Zool. . Zoology.

Nuevo Diccionario Velázquez REVISADO

Español e Inglés — Spanish and English

A

A [ah], first letter of the alphabet in the Spanish language, has but one sound, and is pronounced as the open English *a* in *alarm*.

A, *prep.* which signifies to, in, at, according to, on, by, for, and of; as *Voy á Madrid*, I am going to Madrid. *A la inglesa*, In the English fashion. *Á oriente*, In the east. *Jugar a los naipes*, To play at cards. *A las ocho*, At eight o'clock. *A ley de Castilla*, According to the law of Castile. *Vino a pie*, He came on foot. *Quien a hierro mata, a hierro muere*, He who kills by the sword, dies by the sword. *Dos a dos*, Two by two. *¿A cómo vale la fanega? A treinta reales*, For how much a bushel? for thirty reals. *Este vaso huele a vino*, This glass smells of wine. *Real de a ocho*, Piece of eight. *V.* REAL.—*A* coalesces with the masculine article *el*, and instead of *a el*, as anciently used, *al* is now written, as *Al rey*, To the king. *Al papa*, To the pope. This masculine article is also used before the infinitive mood of verbs taken substantively, as *Al amanecer*, At the break of day. *Al ir yo allá*, When I was going there.—*A* is equivalent to the limit or end of any place or time. *A la cosecha pagaré*, I shall pay at harvest-time. *Desde aquí a San Juan*, From this to St. John's day. *Me llegaba el agua a la garganta*, The water was up to my throat.—*A* sometimes signifies the motive or principle, as *A instancia de la ciudad*, At the request of the city. *¿A qué propósito?* To what purpose?—It also serves to express distributive numbers, as *A perdiz por barba*, A partridge a head.—Before the infinitive mood, and at the beginning of a sentence, it has sometimes a *conditional* sense, as *A decir verdad*, If we must speak the truth.—This preposition governs almost all parts of speech, whether substantives, adjectives, pronouns, or verbs: *A los hombres*, To men. *De bueno a malo*, From good to bad. *A mí, a tí, a vosotros*, To me, to thee, to you. *A jugar*, To play. *Vamos a pasear*, Let us take a walk.—It points out the person in whom the action of the verb terminates, and then is placed before the accusative or objective case, as *Amo a Pedro*, I love Peter.—*A* is still used in some phrases instead of *por, en, sin, para*, and *la*; and in obsolete writings for *con* and *de*.—In composition it serves to convert substantives and adjectives into verbs, as *abocar* from *boca*, *ablandar* from *blando*. Formerly it was prefixed to many words, as *abajar, amatar*, etc.; but being redundant, these words are now written *bajar, matar*, etc.—*A* is frequently used adverbially, as *A deshora*, Unseasonably. *A diferencia de esto*, Contrary to this. *A consecuencia de eso*, In consequence of that. *A la verdad*, Truly. *A lo menos*, At least. *A sabiendas*, Knowingly. *A veces*, Sometimes. *A ojos vistas*, Plainly, publicly; barefacedly. *A cuestas*, On the back, on the shoulders. *A escondidas*, Privately, in a secret manner. *A prueba de bomba*, Bomb-proof.—*A* denotes the number, price, rate, manner of action, instrument, height, depth, etc., as *El gasto sube a cien pesos*, The expense amounts to a hundred dollars. *Se hizo el seguro a tres por ciento*, The insurance was effected at three per cent. *El azúcar se vende a tres pesos quintal*, or *el*, or *por quintal*, Sugar is sold at three dollars a quintal. *Él se viste a la española*, He dresses after the Spanish fashion. *Pasaron el río con el agua a la cintura*, They crossed the river with the water up to the waist. *No le llega el vestido a la rodilla*, His dress does not reach to his knees. *A fe de hombre de bien*, On the faith of an honest man.

Aa [ah-ah], contraction for *Autores*, authors; and *A.* for *Alteza*, Highness, or for approval.

Aarón [ah-ah-ron'], *m.* *V.* BARBA.

Aba [ah'-bah], *m.* 1. A woollen fabric, manufactured in the East. 2. Patriarch of Alexandria in olden times.

Ababa [ah-bah'-bah], *f.* Red poppy. Papaver rhoeas. *V.* AMAPOLA.

Ababol [ah-bah-bole'], *m.* (Prov.) *V.* AMAPOLA MORADA and ABABA.

Abacá [ah-bah-cah'], *m.* Abaca, Manila hemp, inner fibre of a plant (*Musa textilis*) of the banana family, a native of the Philippine Islands.

Abacería [ah-bah-thay-ree'-ah], *f.* A shop where oil, vinegar, etc., are sold. Grocery.

Abacero, ra [ah-bah-thay'-ro, rah], *m.* & *f.* A retailer of provisions, oil, vinegar, etc. Grocer.

Abacial [ah-bah-the-ahl'], *a.* Belonging to an abbot.

Abaco [ah'-bah-co], *m.* 1. (Arch.) Abacus, highest moulding on the capital of a column. 2. Abacus, a calculating frame. 3. (Min.) A washing-trough.

Abad [ah-bahd'], *m.* 1. An abbot. 2. In some provinces the rector of a parish. *Abad bendito*, Abbot having almost episcopal jurisdiction.

Abada [ah-bah'-dah], *f.* The female rhinoceros.

Abadejo [ah-bah-day'-ho], *m.* 1. The codfish, pollack, or other gadoid fish; properly, Poor-john. *V.* BACALAO. 2. Yellow wren. Motacilla trochilus. 3. (Ant.) Cantharides.

Abadengo, ga [ah-bah-den'-go, gah], *a.* Abbatial, belonging to an abbot.

Abadesa [ah-bah-day'-sah], *f.* An abbess.

Abadía [ah-bah-dee'-ah], *f.* 1. An abbey. 2. (Prov.) A parsonage-house.

Abadiado [ah-bah-de-ah'-do], *m.* (Obs.) Abbey-lands.

Abadir [ah-bah-deer'], *m.* A stone of which the ancients made idols, and to which they attributed marvellous virtues.

Abajador [ah-bah-hah-dor'], *m.* 1. Stable-boy in mines. 2. An abater, he that takes down.

Abajamiento [ah-bah-hah-me-en'-to], *m.* (Obs.) 1. Dejection, casting down. 2. Abatement.

Abajarse [ah-bah-har'-say], *vr.* To abase one's self, be humbled.

Abajeño, ña [ah-bah-hay'-nyo, nyah], *a.* (Amer.) A lowlander.

Abajero [ah-bah-hay'-ro], *m.* Cliff, precipice.

Abajo [ah-bah'-ho], *adv.* Under, underneath, below. *Venirse abajo*, To fall, to tumble.

Abalado, da [ah-bah-lah'-do, dah], *a.* (Obs.) Spongy, soft.

Abalanzar [ah-bah-lan-thar'], *va.* 1. To balance. 2. To weigh, to compare. 3. To dart, to impel.—*vr.* 1. To rush on with impetuosity. 2. To venture.

Abalaustrado, da [ah-bah-lah-oos-trah'-do, dah], *a.* Balustered. *V.* BALAUSTRADO.

Abaldonar [ah-bal-do-nar'], *va.* (Obs.)

1. To debase, to revile, to undervalue, to reproach. 2. To abandon.

Abalear [ah-bah-lay-ar'], *va.* To fan or winnow corn.

Abalizar [ah-bah-le-thar'], *va.* (Naut. To lay down buoys.

Abalone [ah-bah-lo'-nay], *m.* A large Californian mollusk: Haliotis; sea-ear (fr. Aulone).

Abalorios [ah-bah-lo'-re-os], *m. pl.* Bugles, glass beads.

Aballar [ah-bal-lyar'], *va.* (Obs.) 1. To strike down. 2. To carry off. 3. To move. 4. (Pict.) *V.* REBAJAR.

Aballestar [ah-bal-lyes-tar'], *va.* (Naut.) To haul a cable.

Abanderado [ah-ban-day-rah'-do], *m.* 1. A standard-bearer.

Abanderizador, ra [ah-ban-day-re-thah-dor', rah], *m.* & *f.* A factious person; a ringleader, agitator.

Abanderizar [ah-ban-day-re-thar'], *va.* To cabal; to stir up disturbances, incite to revolution.

Abandonado, da [ah-ban-do-nah'-do, dah], *a.* 1. Abandoned, helpless, forlorn, despondent. 2. Abandoned, profligate, graceless.—*pp.* of ABANDONAR.

Abandonamiento [ah-ban-do-nah-me en'-to], *m.* 1. The act of abandoning. 2. Lewdness, debauchery. 3. Forlornness.

Abandonar [ah-ban-do-nar'], *va.* 1. To abandon, to leave, to desert, to fling up; to forego, to fall from; to fail. 2. To give away, to relinquish.—*vr.* To despond, to despair; to flinch; to give one's self up to.

Abandono [ah-ban-do'-no], *m.* *V.* ABANDONAMIENTO. Abandon.

Abanicar [ah-bah-ne-car'], *va.* To fan.

Abanicazo [ah-bah-ne-cah'-tho], *m.* 1. Stroke with a fan. 2. A large fan.

Abanico [ah-bah-nee'-co], *m.* 1. A fan. 2. A sprit-sail. *En abanico*, fan-shaped, like a fan. 3. (Mil.) Defensive parapet of wood. 4. (Naut.) Derrick, sheers, a machine used for setting up and taking out masts; crane, outrigger, sprit-sail. 5. (Phot.) Screen. 6. (Arch.) Winding stairs; semicircular window. 7. (Min.) Ventilator.

Abanillo [ah-bah-neel'-lyoh], *m.* 1. (Obs.) Small fan. 2. A ruff, fold; ruffle, frill, puff.

Abanino [ah-bah-nee'-no], *m.* (Obs.) Ruffle, frill.

Abaniquero [ah-bah-ne-kay'-ro], *m.* A fan-maker.

Abanto [ah-bahn'-to], *m.* A bird of the vulture species.

Abaratar [ah-bah-rah-tar'], *va.* To cheapen, to abate.—*vn.* To fall in price.

Abarbetar [ah-bar-bay-tar'], *va.* (Naut.) To rack, to seize; to span, to lash, to jam, to mouse.

Abarca [ah-bar'-cah], *f.* A piece of coarse leather tied on the soles of the feet, worn by Spanish peasants; brogan.

Abarcado, da [ah-bar-cah'-do, dah], *a.* Having the feet supported by pieces of dry skin.—*pp.* of ABARCAR. Embraced, contained.

Abarcador, ra [ah-bar-cah-dor', rah], *m.* & *f.* 1. Embracer, clasper. 2. Monopolist.

Abarcadura [ah-bar-cah-doo'-rah], *f.* ABARCAMIENTO, *m.* An embrace.

Abarcar [ah-bar-car'], *va.* 1. To clasp, to embrace. 2. To contain; to undertake many things at once. 3. To go round and inspect. *Abarcar el viento*, To go round cattle, game, a hill, etc., with the wind in the face. 4. To monopolize goods, etc.

Abarcón [ah-bar-cone'], *m.* 1. A pole-ring in carriages. 2. Large iron clamp.

Abarloar [ah-bar-lo-ar'], *va.* (Naut.) To bring alongside a ship or dock.

(*Yo abarqué, abarquemos*, from *Abarcar. V.* verbs in *car.*)

Abarquillar [ah-bar-keel-lyar'], *va.* To give a thing the form of a boat, also of a tube. To warp.

Abarracarse [ah-bar-rah-car'-say], *vr.* To withdraw into barracks.

Abarrado, da [ah-bar-rah'-do, dah], *a.* (Obs.) Striped, clouded. *V.* BARRADO.

Abarraganamiento [ah-bar-rah-gah-nah-me-en'-to], *m.* *V.* AMANCEBAMIENTO.

Abarraganarse [ah-bar-rah-gah-nar'-say], *vr.* To live in concubinage.

Abarrajado, da [ah-bar-rah-hah'-do, dah], *a.* (Amer.) Libertine.

Abarrancadero [ah-bar-ran-cah-day'-ro], *m.* 1. A deep, heavy road. 2. A precipice, rocky ledge. 3. (Met.) Difficult business.

Abarrancamiento [ah-bar-ran-cah-me-en'-to], *m.* Act of making or falling into holes or pits; embarrassment.

Abarrancar [ah-bar-ran-car'], *va.* To break up a road; to dig holes.—*vr.* To fall into a pit; to become embarrassed.

Abarrar [ah-bar-rar'], *va.* (Obs.) *V.* ACIBARRAR.

Abarraz [ah-bar-rath'], *m.* (Obs.) (Bot.) Lousewort, stavesacre. *V.* ALBARRAZ.

Abarrera [ah-bar-ray'-rah], *f.* (Prov.) *V.* REGATONA.

Abarrisco [ah-bar-rees'-co], *adv.* (Obs.) Indiscriminately, promiscuously.

Abarrotar [ah-bar-ro-tar'], *va.* 1. To tie down, to bind with cords. 2. (Naut.) To stow the cargo. 3. To overstock.

Abarrote [ah-bar-ro'-tay], *m.* (Naut.) Fill-in package.—*pl.* (Amer.) 1. Groceries, provisions. 2. Grocery store.

Abarrotería [ah-bar-ro-tay-ree'-ah], *f.* (Amer.) Grocery store, general store.

Abarrotero, ra [ah-bar-ro-tay'-ro, rah], *m.* & *f.* (Amer.) Grocer.

Abastar [ah-bas-tar']. (Obs.) *V.* ABASTECER and BASTAR.

Abastardarse [ah-bas-tar-dar'-say], *vr.* To degenerate, to vitiate.

Abastecedor, ra [ah-bas-tay-thay-dor', rah], *m.* & *f.* A caterer, provider, purveyor.

Abastecer [ah-bas-tay-therr'], *va.* 1. To provide necessaries, to purvey. 2. To find, to supply.

(*Yo abastezco, abastezca*, from *Abastecer. V.* verbs in *ecer.*)

Abastecimiento [ah-bas-tay-the-me-en'-to], *m.* 1. The act and the effect of providing. 2. Provisions.

Abastionar [ah-bas-te-o-nar'], *va.* To construct bastions.

Abasto [ah-bas'-to], *m.* 1. The supply of a town with provisions, grist. 2. (Met.) Any thing abundant. Small embroideries. 3. *Adv.* Copiously, abundantly.

Abatanar [ah-bah-tah-nar'], *va.* To beat or full cloth.

Abate [ah-bah'-tay], *m.* An abbé wearing a short cloak.

Ábate [ah'-bah-tay], *int.* Take care! Stand out of the way!

Abatidamente [ah-bah-tee-dah-men' tay], *adv.* Dejectedly, heavily; basely.

Abatidísimo [ah-bah-te-dee'-se-mo], *a. sup.* Very low-spirited, very dejected.

Abatido, da [ah-bah-tee'-do, dah], *a.* 1. Dejected, spiritless, flat, low, faint; vapid. 2. Abject, mean, base.—*pp.* of ABATIR.

Abatimiento [ah-bah-te-me-en'-to], *m.* 1. Discouragement, lowness of spirits, heaviness, faintness, flatness. 2. Humbleness, obscure condition. *Abatimiento del rumbo*, (Naut.) The leeway of a ship.

Abatir [ah-bah-teer'], *va.* 1. To throw down, to overthrow, to cut down, to flatten, to fall. 2. To humble, to debase, to overwhelm, to lower, to discourage. 3. (Mech.) To depress, lower.—*vn.* To descend, to stoop.—*vr.* 1. To be disheartened, to be dismayed; to crouch. 2. (Naut.) To have leeway.

Abdicación [ab-de-cah-the-on'], *f.* Abdication.

Abdicar [ab-de-car'], *va.* 1. To abdicate. 2. To revoke, to annul.

Abdomen [ab-doh'-men], *m.* Abdomen, belly.

Abdominal [ab-doh-me-nahl'], *a.* Abdominal.

Abducción [ab-dooc-the-on'], *f.* (Anat.) Abduction.

Abductor [ab-dooc-tor'], *m.* (Anat.) Abductor, the muscles which draw back the several members.

Abecé [ah-bay-thay'], *m.* The alphabet.

Abecedario [ah-bay-thay-dah'-re-o], *m.* 1. The alphabet. 2. A spelling-book. 3. A table of contents.

Abedul [ah-bay-dool'], *m.* The common birch-tree.

Abeja [ah-bay'-hah], *f.* A bee. *Abeja maestra, guía o madre.* The queen or queen-bee. *Abeja machiega*, Breeding-bee. *Abeja albañila*, Mason-bee. *Abeja obrera*, a worker-bee.

Abejar [ah-bay-har'], *m.* A bee-hive. *V.* COLMENAR.

Abejar [ah-bay-har'], *a.* *Uva abejar*, A grape of which bees are very fond.

Abejarrón, Abejorro [ah-bay-har-rone', or ah-bay-hor'-ro], *m.* 1. Death's-head moth. Acherontia atropos. (Acad.) 2. A large fly. *V.* ATROPOS.

Abejaruco, Abejeruco [ah-bay-ha-roo'-co, or ah-bay-hay-roo'-co], *m.* 1. The bee-eater, a bird. Merops apiaster. 2. (Met.) A mean, despicable fellow.

Abejera [ah-bay-hay'-rah], *f.* Balm-mint or bee-wort. Melissa officinalis. *V.* TORONJIL.

Abejero [ah-bay-hay'-ro], *m.* 1. A keeper of bee-hives. 2. *V.* ABEJARUCO.

Abejica, illa, ita, juela [ah-bay-hee'-cah] *f. dim.* A little bee.

Abejón [ah-bay-hone'], *m.* 1. A drone; a hornet; humble-bee. *Jugar al abejón con* uno, (Coll.) To make light of one, mock at him. 2. A rustic play of buzzing in and striking the ear.

Abejonazo [ah-bay-ho-nah'-tho], *m.* A large wild bee.

Abejoncillo [ah-bay-hon-theel'-lyoh], *m. dim.* A small wild bee, a small drone.

Abejorro [ah-bay-hor'-ro], *m.* *V* ABEJARRÓN.

Abejuno, na [ah-bay-hoo'-no, nah], *a.* Belonging to bees; bee.

Abellacado, da [ah-bel-lyah-cah'-do, dah], *a.* Mean-spirited, accustomed to meanness.—*pp.* of ABELLACARSE.

Abellacarse [ah-bel-lyah-car'-say], *vr.* To become mean; to degrade one's self.

Abellar [ah-bel-lyar'], *m.* (Littl. us.) *V.* ABEJAR.

Abellotado [ah-bel-lyo-tah'-do], *a.* Made in the form of acorns.

Aben [ah'-ben], *m.* An oriental word, signifying son, which forms part of some Hebrew and Arab names.

Abenuz [ah-bay-nooth'], *m.* (Obs.) The ebony-tree. *V.* ÉBANO.

Aberengenado, da [ah-bay-ren-hay-nah'-do, dah], *a.* 1. Having the colour or form of the egg-plant, lilac. 2. (In carpentry) Cut slantwise.

Aberración [ah-ber-rah-the-on'], *f.* 1. (Ast.) Aberration. 2. (Med.) Hallucination, aberration. 3. (Opt.) Aberration, divergence of light-rays.

Aberrugado, da [ah-ber-roo-gah'-do, dah], *a.* Full of warts, warty.

Abertal [ah-ber-tahl'], *a.* Flaking or splitting readily; applied to earth or stone.

Abertura [ah-ber-too'-rah], *f.* 1. Aperture. 2. Outset, beginning. 3. An opening, chink, cleft, crevice, fissure, gap, loophole, a hole to give a passage: (Opt.) stop. 4. Openness of mind; plain dealing. 5. A leak. 6. (Mus.) Overture.

Abestiar [ah-bes-te-ar'], *va.* To stupefy.

Abetal [ah-bay-tahl'], *m.* A spot covered with silver firs.

Abete [ah-bay'-tay], *m.* 1. Hook for holding cloth while shearing it. 2. *V.* Abeto.

Abeterno [ab-ay-ter'-no] (or *ab eterno*, Lat.). From all eternity.

Abetinote, or **Abietino** [ah-bay-te-no'-tay, ah-be-ay-te'-no], *m.* Resin which distils from the fir-tree. *V.* Aceite.

Abeto [ah-bay'-to], *m.* The silver-tree; the yew-leaved fir. Pinus picea.

Abetunado, da [ah-bay-too-nah'-do, dah], *a.* Resembling bitumen, bituminous.

Abetunar [ah-bay-too-nar'], *va.* To bituminize; to do over with bitumen.

Abiertamente [ah-be-er-tah-men'-tay], *adv.* Frankly, openly, fairly, plainly.

Abierto, ta [ah-be-er'-to, tah], *a.* 1. Open, free, clear. 2. Sincere, candid, open-hearted, generous. 3. Full-blown.—*pp. irr.* of Abrir.

Abigarrado, da [ah-be-gar-rah'-do, dah], *a.* Variegated, motley.—*pp.* of Abigarrar.

Abigarrar [ah-be-gar-rar'], *va.* To paint with a diversity of colours, without order or union; to fleck.

Abigeato [ah-be-hay-ah'-to], *m.* (Law) Theft of cattle.

Abigeo [ah-be-hay'-oh], *m.* (Law) A thief or stealer of cattle.

Abigotado, da [ah-be-go-tah'-do, dah], *a.* A person wearing long mustaches.

Abihares [ah-be-ah'-res], *m.* 1. Narcissus or daffodil. 2. A precious stone of the colour of the daffodil.

Abiltar [a-beel-tar'], *va.* To depress, humiliate, depreciate.

Abinicio [ab-e-nee'-the-o] (or *ab initio*, Lat.). From the beginning.

Abintestato [ab-in-tes-tah'-to], *a.* (Lat.) Intestate.—*m.* Process of a judge in cases of no will.

Abiosa [ah-be-oh'-sah], *f.* The boa snake. The boa constrictor.

Abiselar [ah-be-say-lar'], *va.* To bevel.

Abisinio, a [ah-be-see'-ne-o, ah], *a.* Abyssinian.

Abismado, da [ah-bis-mah'-do, dah], *a.* 1. Cast down, dejected, depressed. 2. Absorbed in profound meditation.

Abismal [ah-bis-mahl'], *a.* Belonging to an abyss.

Abismal [ah-bis-mahl'], *m.* Clasp nail, shingle nail.

Abismar [ah-bis-mar'], *va.* To depress, to humble, to destroy.

Abismarse [ah-bis-mar'-say], *vr.* (Sp. Am.) To be astonished, to be shocked or astounded.

Abismo [ah-bees'-mo], *m.* 1. Abyss; gulf. 2. That which is immense, or incomprehensible. 3. Hell.

Abitadura [ah-be-ta-doo'-rah], *f.* (Naut.) A turn of the cable around the bitts.

Abitaque [ah-be-tah'-kay], *m.* A rafter or joist, the fourth part of a girder.

Abitar [ah-be-tar'], *va.* *Abitar el cable*, To bite the cable.

Abitas [ah-bee'-tas], *m. pl.* (Naut.) Bitts. *Abitas del molinete*, Carrick-bitts.

Abitones [ah-be-to'-nes], *m. pl.* Top-sail sheet, bitts.

Abizcochado, da [ah-beth-co-chah'-do, dah], *a.* In the form of a biscuit.

Abjuración [ab-hoo-rah-the-on'], *f.* Abjuration, recantation.

Abjurar [ab-hoo-rar'], *va.* To abjure, to recant upon oath.

Ablación [ah-blah-the-on'], *f.* The removal of an organ or portion of the body by surgical means; ablation.

Ablandador, ra [ah-blan-dah-dor', rah], *m.* & *f.* Mollifier.

Ablandamiento [ah-blan-dah-me-en'-to], *m.* Making mellow; relenting.

Ablandar [ah-blan-dar'], *va.* & *n.* 1. To soften, to mellow, to relent. 2. To loosen. 3. To assuage, to mitigate, to melt, to soothe. 4. To grow mild or temperate; to give.

Ablano [ah-blah'-no], *m* (Prov. Ast.) The hazel-tree.

Ablativo [ah-blah-tee'-voh], *m.* The sixth case in the declension of Latin nouns, the ablative.

Ablución [ah-bloo-the-on'], *f.* 1. Ablution, lotion. 2. The water with which Roman Catholic priests purify the chalice at mass.

Abnegación [ab-nay-gah-the-on'], *f.* Abnegation, self-denial.

Abnegadamente [ab-nay-gah-dah-men'-tay], *adv.* With abnegation.

Abnegar [ab-nay-gar'], *va.* To renounce, to deny one's self any thing. (*Yo abniego, abniegue*, from *Abnegar*. *V.* Acrecentar.)

Abobado, da [ah-bo-bah'-do, dah], *a.* Stultified, simple, silly.—*pp.* of Abobar.

Abobamiento [ah-bo-bah-me-en'-to], *m.* Stupefaction, stupidity.

Abobar [ah-bo-bar'], *va.* 1. To stupefy. 2. *V.* Embobar.—*vr.* To grow stupid.

Abocado [ah-bo-cah'-do], *a.* Mild, agreeable: applied to wine.—*pp.* of Abocar.

Abocamiento [ah-bo-cah-me-en'-to], *m.* A meeting, an interview.

Abocar [ah-bo-car'], *va.* To take or catch with the mouth. *Abocar la artillería*, To bring the guns to bear. *Abocar un estrecho*, To enter the mouth of a channel or strait —*vr.* To meet by agreement.

Abocardado, da [ah-bo-car-dah'-do, dah], *a.* Wide-mouthed, like a trumpet.

Abocardar [ah-bo-car-dar'], *va.* To countersink, to widen the mouth.

Abocardo [ah-bo-car'-do], *m.* (Min.) Countersinking drill.

Abocinado [ah-bo-the-nah'-do], *a.* Bent: applied to an elliptic arch, the two faces of which are nearly the same. —*pp.* of Abocinar.

Abocinar [ah-bo-the-nar'], *vn.* (Low) To fall upon the face. *va.* To raise, to broaden an arch upon one side.

Abochornado, da [ah-bo-chor-nah'-do, dah], *a.* Out of countenance, flushed. —*pp.* of Abochornar. *Quedar abochornado*, To feel mortified.

Abochornar [ah-bo-chor-nar'], *va.* 1. To swelter, to overheat. 2. To provoke by abusive language.—*vr.* To blush, to feel mortified.

Abofellar [ah-bo-fel-lyar'], *vn.* To puff, to pant.

Abofeteador, ra [ah-bo-fay-tay-ah-dor' rah], *m.* & *f.* Buffeter, one who insults.

Abofetear [ah-bo-fay-tay-ar'], *va.* 1. To slap one's face. 2. To insult.

Abogacía [ah-bo-gah-thee'-ah], *f.* Profession of a lawyer or advocate.

Abogada [ah-bo-gah'-dah], *f.* 1. A mediatrix. 2. A counsellor's wife.

Abogadear [ah-bo-gah-day-ar'], *vn.* To play the advocate: used in contempt.

Abogadillo [ah-bo-gah-deel'-lyo], *m.* Dim. of Abogado. Ignorant or poor lawyer.

Abogado [ah-bo-gah'-do], *m.* 1. Advocate, counsellor. 2. A mediator.—*pp.* of Abogar.

Abogar [ah-bo-gar'], *vn.* 1. To advocate, to plead the cause of another. 2. To intercede in behalf of another. (*Yo abogué*, from *Abogar*. *V.* verbs in *gar*.)

Abohetado, da [ah-bo-ay-tah'-do, dah] *a.* Inflated, swollen.

Abolengo [ah-bo-len'-go], *m.* 1. Ancestry. 2. Inheritance coming from ancestors.

Abolición [ah-bo-le-the-on'], *f.* Abolition, abrogation, extinction.

Abolicionista [ah-bo-le-the-o-nees'-tah], *m.* Abolitionist.

Abolir [ah-bo-leer'], *va.* To abolish, to annul, to revoke, to repeal.

Abolorio [ah-bo-lo'-re-o], *m.* Ancestry. *V.* Abolengo.

Abolsado, da [ah-bol-sah'-do, dah], *a.* Puckered, folded in the form of a purse.

Abollado [ah-bol-lyah'-do], *a.* & *m.* *V.* Alechugado.—*pp.* of Abollar.

Abolladura [ah-bol-lya-doo'-rah], *f.* 1. Inequality. 2. Embossed work, relievo. 3. Bruise. 4. Dent.

Abollar [ah-bol-lyar'], *va.* 1. To emboss. 2. To annoy with an unpleasant discourse. 3. To stun and confound. 4. To bruise. 5. To dent.

Abollón [ah-bol-lyon'], *m.* (Prov.) A bud, in particular of the vine.

Abollonar [ah-bol-lyo-nar'], *va.* To emboss.—*vn.* (Prov.) To bud, applied in particular to the vine.

Abomaso [ah-bo-mah'-so], *m.* Abomasum, the fourth stomach of ruminating animals.

Abominablemente [ah-bo-me-nah-blay-men'-tay], *adv.* Abominably, detestably, execrably.

Abominable [ah-bo-me-nah'-blay], *a* Detestable, abominable, execrable, odious, heinous, cursed.

Abominación [ah-bo-me-nah-the-on'], *f.* Abomination, detestation, execration, cursedness.

Abominar [ah-bo-me-nar'], *va.* To detest, to abhor, to execrate.

Abonado, da [ah-bo-nah'-do, dah], *m.* & *f.* A subscriber to a work or any other thing. Holder of a season-ticket.

Abonado, da [ah-bo-nah'-do, dah], *a.* 1. Creditable, rich. 2. Fit and disposed for any thing: commonly understood in an ill sense. 3. Manured land. *Testigo abonado*, An irrefragable witness.—*pp.* of Abonar.

Abonador, ra [ah-bo-nah-dor', rah], *m.* & *f.* A bail or surety.

Abonamiento [ah-bo-nah-me-en'-to], *m.* *V.* Abono. Bail, security.

Abonanzar [ah-bo-nan-thar'], *vn.* To grow calm: said of a storm. To clear up: applied to the weather.

Abonar [ah-bo-nar'], *va.* 1. To bail, to insure. 2. To improve or meliorate. 3. To make good an assertion. 4. To manure lands, to compost. 5. To give one credit; to allow. (Com.) To indemnify, to compensate.—*vr.* To subscribe to any work; to buy a season-ticket (for a theatre, etc.); to pay in advance for any thing.—*vn.* *V.* Abonanzar.

Abonaré [ah-bo-na-ray'], *m.* Promissory note: a security for payment of a sum. *V.* Pagaré.

Abono [ah-bo' no], *m.* 1 Season ticket. 2. Part payment. 3. Dung, manure. *Abono verde*, Green manure.

Abordable [ah-bor-dah'-blay], *a.* Accessible, easy of access.
Abordador [ah-bor-dah-dor'], *m.* 1. He that boards a ship. 2. An intruder, who accosts a person with an air of impudence.
Abordaje [ah-bor-dah'-hay], *m.* (Naut.) The act of boarding a ship.
Abordar [ah-bor-dar'], *va.* 1. To board a ship, to fall aboard. 2. To run foul of a ship. 3. To put into a port.
Abordo [ah-bor'-do], *m.* 1. (Met.) Address, attack, shock or force in execution. 2. (Obs.) *V.* ABORDAJE.
Aborigen [ah-bo-ree'-hen], *a.* Aboriginal, indigenous.
Aborígenes [ah-bo-ree'-hay-nes], *m. pl.* Aborigines, the earliest inhabitants of a country.
Aborrachado, da [ah-bor-rah-chah'-do, dah], *a.* 1. High-coloured. 2. Inflamed, fiery, flushed.
Aborrascarse [ah-bor-ras-car'-say], *vr.* To be tempestuous or stormy.
Aborrecedor, ra [ah-bor-ray-thay-dor', rah], *m.* & *f.* A detester, a hater.
Aborrecer [ah-bor-ray-therr'], *va.* 1. To hate, to abhor. 2. To relinquish, to desert: in the last sense it is chiefly applied to birds, which desert their eggs or young ones. 3. To adventure or spend money.
Aborrecible [ah-bor-ray-thee'-blay], *a.* Hateful, detestable, loathsome, cursed, damned, forbidding.
Aborreciblemente [ah-bor-ray-thee-blay-men'-tay], *adv.* With abhorrence, hatefully.
Aborrecimiento [ah-bor-ray-thee-me-en'-to], *m.* Abhorrence, detestation, dislike, hate, grudge.
Aborregarse [ah-bor-ray-gar'-say], *vr.* To be covered with light, fleecy clouds: said of the sky.
Aborrer, Aborrescer [ah-bor-rerr', ah-bor-res-therr'], *va.* (Obs.) *V.* ABORRECER.
(*Aborrezco.* *V.* ABORRECER.)
Abortamiento [ah-bor-tah-me-en'-to], *m.* Abortion.
Abortar [ah-bor-tar'], *va.* 1. To miscarry, abort. 2. To fail.
Abortivamente [ah-bor-te-vah-men'-tay], *adv.* Abortively, untimely.
Abortivo, va [ah-bor-tee'-vo, vah], *a.* Abortive; producing abortion.
Aborto [ah-bor'-to], *m.* 1. A miscarriage, abortion. 2. A monster.
Abortón [ah-bor-tone'], *m.* 1. The abortion of a quadruped. 2. The skin of a lamb born before its time.
Aborujar [ah-bo-roo-har'], *va.* To make parcels.—*vr.* To be muffled or wrapped up.
Abotagarse [ah-bo-tah-gar'-say], *vr.* 1. To be swollen, to be inflated. 2. (Met.) To grow foolish, or stupid.
Abotinado, da [ah-bo-te-nah'-do, dah], *a.* Made in the form of half-gaiters (Bluchers), closing at the instep.
Abotonador [ah-bo-to-nah-dor'], *m.* An instrument used for buttoning gaiters; button-hook.
Abotonar [ah-bo-to-nar'], *va.* 1. To button, to fasten with buttons. 2. (Naut.) To lash, to rack, to seize.—*vn.* 1. To bud, to germinate. 2. To form a button: applied to eggs boiled with the white obtruding.
Abovedado, da [ah-bo-vay-dah'-do, dah], *a.* Arched, vaulted.—*pp.* of ABOVEDAR.
Abovedar [ah-bo-vay-dar'], *va.* To arch, to vault, to shape as a vault.
Aboyado, da [ah-bo-yah'-do, dah], *a.* A farm rented, with the necessary stock of oxen for ploughing the ground.—*pp.* of ABOYAR.
Aboyar [ah-bo-yar'], *va.* (Naut.) To lay down buoys.
Abozalar [ah-bo-tha-lar'], *va.* To muzzle.
Abra [ah'-brah], *f.* 1. A bay, a haven; a cove or creek. 2. A dale or valley. 3. A fissure in mountains; gorge.
Abracijo [ah-brah-thee'-ho], *m.* (Coll.) An embrace, a hug.
Abrahonar [ah-brah-o-nar'], *va.* (Coll.) To hold one fast by the garment.
Abrasadamente [ah-brah-sah-dah-men'-tay], *adv.* Ardently, eagerly.
Abrasador, ra [a-brah-sah-dor', rah], *a.* Very hot, burning, steaming. *Un sol abrasador,* A steaming, burning sun. *Una llama abrasadora,* An ardent flame.
Abrasamiento [ah-brah-sah-me-en'-to], *m.* 1. The act of burning. 2. Inflammation. 3. The excess of passion. 4. Flagrancy.
Abrasar [ah-brah-sar'], *va.* 1. To burn; to fire; to parch the ground. 2. To dissipate, to squander. 3. To provoke. —*vr.* To be agitated by any violent passion, to glow. *Abrasarse vivo,* To be inflamed with passion; to feel extremely hot. *Abrasarse las pajarillas,* To be burning hot.
Abrasilado, da [ah-brah-se-lah'-do, dah], *a.* Of the colour of Brazil-wood.
Abrazadera [ah-brah-thah-day'-rah], *f.* 1. Ferule, clasp. 2. A ring put around a thing as a band. 3. A cleat. 4. A piece of timber which fastens the plough-tail to the plough. 5. (Printing) A brace or bracket {.—*a.* *V.* SIERRA ABRAZADERA.
Abrazador, ra [ah-brah-tha-dor', rah], *m.* & *f.* 1. One that embraces. 2. (Low) A thief-taker. 3. A hook which serves to keep up the pole of a draw-well. 4. (Obs.) One who seduces others into gambling-houses.
Abrazamiento [ah-brah-thah-me-en'-to], *m.* Embracing.
Abrazar [ah-brah-thar'], *va.* 1. To embrace, to hug, to caress; to clasp, to clip, to lock in, to fathom, to comprpress. 2. To surround. 3. To embrace the opinion of another; to go into. 4. To take one's charge. 5. To comprise.
Abrazo [ah-brah'-tho], *m.* A hug, an embrace.
Ábrego [ah'-bray-go], *m.* A south-west wind.
Abrelatas [ah-bray-lah'-tahs], *m.* Can opener.
Abrenuncio [ah-rray-noon'-the-oh], *int.* (Lat.) Far be it from me: used to express detestation.
Abrepuño [ah-bray-poo'-nyo], *m.* (Bot.) Milk-thistle. *V.* CARDO LECHERO.
Abrevadero [ah-bray-vah-day'-ro], *m.* A watering-place for cattle.
Abrevado [ah-bray-vah'-do], *a.* Softened in water: applied to skins.—*pp.* of ABREVAR.
Abrevador [ah-bray-vah-dor'], *m.* 1. He who waters cattle. 2. Waterer. 3. Watering-place.
Abrevar [ah-bray-var'], *va.* To water cattle.
Abreviación [ah-bray-vee-ah-the-on'], *f.* Abbreviation.
Abreviadamente [ah-bray-vee-ah-dah-men'-tay], *adv.* In few words, concisely.
Abreviador, ra [ah-bray-vee-ah-dor', rah], *m.* & *f.* An abridger, one who abridges writings. 2. A breviator, an officer employed in expediting the pope's bulls.
Abreviar [ah-bray-vee-ar'], *va.* To abridge, to cut short.
Abreviatura [ah-bray-vee-ah-too'-rah], *f.* 1. Abbreviation, contraction. 2. Shorthand. *En abreviatura,* In an abbreviated form, briefly; expeditiously.
Abreviaturía [ah-bray-vee-ah-too-ree'-ah], *f.* Office of a breviator.
Abribonarse [ah-bre-bo-nar'-say], *vr.* 1. To grow abject, to degenerate. 2. To act the scoundrel; to stroll about.
Abridero [ah-bre-day'-ro], *m.* A sort of peach, which, when ripe, opens easily and drops the stone; freestone.
Abridero, ra [ah-bre-day'-ro, rah], *a.* Of an aperitive nature; easily opened; freestone.
Abridor [ah-bre-dor'], *m.* 1. (Bot.) Nectarine, a species of the peach-tree. 2. Opener, the person who opens or unlocks. *Abridor de láminas,* An engraver. *Abridor en hueco,* A die or punch sinker. 3. Iron used for opening ruffs or plaits. 4. (Agr.) Grafting-knife. 5. *Abridor de guantes,* Glove-stretcher. 6. *Abridor de heno,* Hay-spreader, tedder. 7. *Abridor de latas,* Can-opener.
Abrigadamente [ah-bre-gah-dah-men'-tay], *adv.* Warmly, well protected.
Abrigadero [ah-bre-gah-day'-ro], *m.* Sheltered place.
Abrigado [ah-bre-gah'-do], *m.* *V* ABRIGADERO.—*pp.* of ABRIGAR.
Abrigaña [ah-bre-gah'-nyah], *f.* (Hort.) Canvas screen, awning.
Abrigaño [ah-bre-gah'-nyoh], *m.* A shelter for cattle.
Abrigar [ah-bre-gar'], *va.* To shelter, to protect, to patronize; to overshadow, to cover; to warm, to lodge. *Abríguese Vd. con ello,* (Coll.) Defend yourself with it.
Abrigo [ah-bree'-go], *m.* 1. Coat, overcoat, topcoat, wrap. 2 Shelter, protection, cover. 3. (Naut.) Harbor, haven.
Abril [ah-breel'], *m.* April, the fourth month of the year. *Estar hecho un abril o parecer un abril,* To be gay, florid, handsome. *Abril, aguas mil,* denotes the copious showers of this month. *Abril y Mayo, llaves de todo el año*: i. e. On the weather of these two months depends the fulness of the crops.
Abrillantador [ah-brel-lyan-tah-dor'], *m.* A diamond-cutter; lapidary.
Abrillantar [ah-brel-lyan-tar'], *va.* 1. To cut a diamond into angles; to make any precious stone sparkle by polishing it. 2. To impart brilliancy; to glaze, to polish.
Abrimiento [ah-bre-me-en'-to], *m.* 1. The act of opening. 2. An opening.
Abrir [ah-breer'], *va.* 1. To open, begin, inaugurate, to unlock. 2. To remove obstacles. 3. To engrave. To expand, as flowers; to distend. *Abrir a chasco,* (Coll.) To jest, to mock. *Abrir el día,* To dawn. *Abrir el ojo,* To be alert. *Abrir la mano,* To accept bribes; to be generous. *Abrir los ojos a uno,* To undeceive; to enlighten.—*vr.* 1. To be open, to tear. 2. To extend itself. 3. To chink, to cleave, to yawn. 4. (Met.) To communicate, to disclose a secret. *Abrirse con alguno,* To disclose one's secret, or to unbosom and reveal it to a friend. *Abrirse o abrir una entrada al agua,* (Naut.) To spring a leak. 5. *Abrir registro* (speaking of a vessel), To begin to take a cargo.
Abrochador [ah-bro-chah-dor'], *m.* An instrument used by tailors to button on clothes; button-hook. *V.* ABOTONADOR.
Abrochadura, *f.* **Abrochamiento,** *m.* [ah-bro-chah-doo'-rah, ah-bro-chah-me-en'-to]. The act of lacing or buttoning on.
Abrochar [ah-bro-char'], *va.* To clasp, to buckle; to button on, to fasten with hooks and eyes.

Abrogable [ah-bro-gah'-blay], *a.* Repealable, abrogable.
Abrogación [ah-bro-gah-the-on'], *f.* Abrogation, repeal, the act of repealing a law.
Abrogar [ah-bro-gar'], *va.* To abrogate, to annul, to repeal.
(*Yo abrogué*, from *Abrogar*. *V.* verbs in *gar*.
Abrojal [ah-bro-hahl'], *m.* A place covered with thistles.
Abrojo [ah-bro'-ho], *m.* 1. (Bot.) Caltrops. Tribulus terrestris. Thistle, thorn, prickle. 2. (Mil.) A thistle; a crowfoot. 3. Thistle fixed on a whip, and used by the flagellants to flog the shoulders. 4. A crab whose carapace has eight spines.—*pl.* Hidden rocks in the sea.
Abromado, da [ah-bro-mah'-do, dah], *a.* (Naut.) 1. Dark, hazy, foggy. 2. Worm-eaten.—*pp.* of ABROMARSE.
Abromarse [ah-bro-mar'-say], *vr.* (Naut.) To be worm-eaten.
Abroncar [ah-bron-car'], *va.* (Coll.) To tease, to vex, to make angry.
Abroquelado, da [ah-bro-kay-lah'-do, dah], *a.* (Bot.) Shield-shaped.
Abroquelar [ah-bro-kay-lar'], *va.* (Naut.) To boxhaul. *vr.* 1. To cover one's self with a shield. 2. To use means of defence in support of one's character or opinion.
Abrótano [ah-bro'-tah-no], *m.* (Bot.) Southernwood, allied to wormwood.
Abrumado, da [ah-broo-mah'-do, dah], *a.* Weary.—*pp.* of ABRUMAR.
Abrumador, ra [ah-broo-mah-dor', rah], *m.* & *f.* A teaser; an oppressor; annoying.
Abrumar [ah-broo-mar'], *va.* 1. To crush, to overwhelm, to oppress. 2. To cause great pains or trouble.
Abrupto, ta [ah-broop'-to, tah], *a.* Craggy, rugged.
Abrutado, da [ah-broo-tah'-do, dah], *a.* Brutish, ungovernable in manners and habits.
Abs, Latin preposition denoting privation.
Absceso [abs-thay'-so], *m.* An abscess; collection of pus.
Abscisa [abs-thee'-sah], *f.* (Geom.) Abscissa.
Abscisión [abs-the-se-on'], *f.* (Med.) 1. An ulcer. 2. Incision.
Absentista [ab-sen-tees'-tah], *a.* Absentee.—*m.* & *f.* Absentee landowner.
Ábside [ab'-se-day], *m.* & *f.* 1. The central arch of a temple. 2. *V.* ÁPSIDE.
Absintio [ab-seen'-te-o], *m.* *V.* AJENJO.
Absit [ab-seet'], *int.* (Lat.) God forbid!
Absolución [ab-so-loo-the-on'], *f.* 1. The act of pardoning. 2. Absolution. 3. Acquittal.
Absoluta [ab-so-loo'-tah], *f.* Dogma, universal proposition.
Absolutamente [ab-so-loo-tah-men'-tay], *adv.* Absolutely, without limits or restrictions.
Absolutismo [ab-so-loo-tees'-mo], *m.* Absolutism, unrestrained despotism.
Absoluto, ta [ab-so-loo'-to, tah], *a.* 1. Absolute; unconditional, without condition or stipulation. 2. Imperious, domineering.
Absolutorio, a [ab-so-loo-to'-re-o, ah], *a.* Absolutory, absolving.
Absolvederas [ab-sol-vay-day'-ras], *f. pl.* The facility of giving absolution.
Absolver [ab-sol-verr'], *va.* 1. To absolve. 2. To acquit.
(*Yo absuelvo, yo absuelva*, from *Absolver*. *V.* MOVER.)
Absorbencia [ab-sor-ben'-the-ah], *f.* The act of absorbing.
Absorbente [ab-sor-ben'-tay], *m.* (Med.) Absorbent.—*pa.* of ABSORBER.
Absorber [ab-sor-berr'], *va.* 1. To absorb, to imbibe. *V.* EMPAPAR. 2. (Met.) To attract, to charm. *Absorber la atención*, To captivate the attention.
Absorbido [ab-sor-bee'-do], *a.* (Med.) Absorbed.—*pp.* of ABSORBER.
Absorción [ab-sor-the-on'], *f.* (Med.) Absorption.
Absortar [ab-sor-tar'], *va.* (Obs.) To strike with amazement.
Absorto, ta [ab-sor'-to, tah], *a.* Amazed, absorbed in thought.—*pp. irr.* of ABSORBER and of ABSORTAR.
Abstemio, mia [abs-tay'-me-o, me-ah], *a.* Abstemious.
Abstención [abs-ten-the-on'], *f.* Forbearance, self-denial.
Abstenerse [abs-tay-ner-say], *vr.* To abstain, to forbear.
Abstergente, Abstersivo, va [abs-ter-hen'-tay, abs-ter-see'-vo, vah], *a.* Detergent, cleansing, abstergent.
Absterger [abs-ter-herr'], *va.* To cleanse; to dispel purulent matter.
Abstersión [abs-ter-se-on'], *f.* Abstersion, purification.
Abstinencia [abs-te-nen'-the-ah], *f.* Forbearance, abstinence. *Día de abstinencia*, A day of abstinence, a fast-day.
Abstinente [abs-te-nen'-tay], *a.* Abstinent, abstemious.
Abstracción [abs-trac-the-on'], *f.* 1 Abstraction, the act of abstracting and state of being abstracted. 2. Retirement from the world. 3. In art, pure abstraction, an abstract composition.
Abstraccionismo [abs-trac-the-o-nees'-mo], *m.* Abstractionism.
Abstractivo, va [abs-trac-tee'-vo, vah], *a.* Abstractive.
Abstracto, ta [abs-trac'-to, tah], *a.* Abstract.—*pp. irr.* of ABSTRAER.
Abstraer [abs-trah-err'], *va.* 1. To abstract, to separate ideas. 2. To pass over in silence. 3. To refrain from. 4. To differ in opinion.—*vr.* To withdraw the intellect from sensible objects, in order to employ it in contemplation.
Abstraído, da [abs-trah-ee'-do, dah], *a.* Retired.—*pp.* of ABSTRAER.
(*Yo abstraigo, yo abstraje, yo abstraiga*, from *Abstraer*. *V.* TRAER.)
Abstruso, sa [abs-troo'-so, sah], *a.* Abstruse, difficult, recondite.
Absuelto, ta [ab-soo-el'-to, tah], *a.* Free.—*pp. irr.* of ABSOLVER.
(*Yo absuelvo, yo absuelva*, from *Absolver*. *V.* MOVER.)
Absurdo [ab-soor'-do], *m.* Absurdity, nonsense.
Absurdo, da [ab-soor'-do, dah], *a.* Nonsensical, absurd.
Abubilla [ah-boo-beel'-lyah], *f.* (Orn.) The hoopoe, or hoopoo, a bird with a beautiful crest. Upupa epops.
Abucate [ah-boo-cah'-tay], *m.* The runner of a velvet loom.
Abuela [ah-boo-ay'-la], *f.* Grandmother.
Abuelo [ah-boo-ay'-lo], *m.* Grandfather, ancestor.
Abulense [ah-boo-len'-say], *a.* Native of Ávila: = Avilés.
Abultado, da [ah-bool-tah'-do, dah], *a.* 1. Increased. 2. Bulky, massive.—*pp.* of ABULTAR.
Abultar [ah-bool-tar'], *va.* To increase, to enlarge.—*vn.* To be bulky or large.
Abundancia [ah-boon-dan'-the-ah], *f.* Abundance, fruitfulness, fertility, opulence, plenty.
Abundante [ah-boon-dahn'-tay], *a.* Abundant, plentiful.
Abundantemente [ah-boon-dan-tay-men'-tay], *adv.* Abundantly, plentifully, luxuriantly.
Abundar [ah-boon-dar'], *vn.* To abound, to have plenty. (Met.) Followed by *en*, to hold identical opinions.
Abuñuelar [ah-boo-nyoo-ay-lar'], *va.* To make something in the shape of a fritter.
Abur [ah-boor'], *int.* *V.* AGUR.
Aburar [ah-boo-rar'], *va.* (Prov.) To burn, scorch.
Aburelado, da [ah-boo-ray-lah'-do, dah], *a.* Of a dark red colour.
Aburguesarse [ah-boor-gay-sar'-say], *vr.* To turn bourgeois, to become middle class.
Aburrición [a-boor-ree-the-on'], *f.* (Coll.) *V.* ABURRIMIENTO.
Aburridamente [ah-boor-re-dah-men'-tay], *adv.* Wearily.
Aburrido, da [ah-boor-ree'-do, dah], *a.* Weary.—*pp.* of ABURRIR.
Aburrimiento [ah-boor-re-me-en'-to], *m.* Uneasiness of mind, despondency, tediousness; weariness, heaviness, tiresomeness, disquiet, sorrow.
Aburrir [ah-boor-reer'], *va.* 1. To vex, to perplex, to weary; to be tedious, tired, dull; to grow impatient; to bore. 2. To venture, to hazard. *Aburriré mil libras esterlinas en esta flota*, I will hazard a thousand pounds in this convoy. 3. To relinquish.
Aburujado, da [ah-boo-roo-hah'-do, dah], *a.* 1. Pressed together. 2. Perplexed, entangled in difficulties.—*pp.* of ABURUJAR.
Aburujar [ah-boo-roo-har'], *va.* To press or heap together.
Aburujonarse [ah-boo-roo-ho-nar'-say] *vr.* To clot, to curdle.
Abusar [ah-boo-sar'], *va.* To abuse or misapply a thing; impose upon.
Abusivamente [ah-boo-se-vah-men'-tay], *adv.* Abusively.
Abusivo, va [ah-boo-see'-vo, vah], *a.* Abusive.
Abuso [ah-boo'-so], *m.* Misusage, the abuse or ill use of a thing.
Abyección [ab-yec-the-on'], *f.* Abjection, abjectness.
Abyecto, ta [ab-yec'-to, tah], *a.* Abject, dejected.
Acá [ah-cah'], *adv.* Here, hither, this way, this side. *¿ De cuando acá?* Since when? *Acá no se estila*, That's not the custom here. *Ven acá*, Come along. *Acá y allá*. Here and there. *Acá*, Hey, used in calling. *Sin más acá, ni más allá*, Without further winks or nods.
Acabable [ah-cah-bah'-blay], *a.* What may be finished, achievable.
Acabadamente [ah-cah-bah-dah-men'-tay], *adv.* 1. Perfectly. 2. (Iron.) Imperfectly, badly.
Acabado, da [ah-cah-bah'-do, dah], *a.* 1. Perfect, complete, faultless. 2. Old, ill-dressed; dejected.—*pp.* of ACABAR.
Acabador, ra [ah-cah-bah-dor', rah], *m.* & *f.* Finisher, completer.
Acabalar [ah-cah-bah-lar'], *va.* To complete, to finish.
Acaballadero [ah-cah-bal-lyah-day'-ro], *m.* The time and place when horses cover mares.
Acaballado, da [ah-cah-bal-lyah'-do dah], *a.* Like a horse.—*pp.* of ACABALLAR, Covered.
Acaballar [ah-cah-bal-lyar'], *va.* To cover a mare.
Acaballerado, da [ah-cah-bal-lyay-rah'-do, dah], *a.* Gentleman-like.—*pp.* of ACABALLERAR.
Acaballerar [ah-cah-bal-lyay-rar'], *va.* 1. To render genteel. 2. To make a person behave as a gentleman.
Acabamiento [ah-cah-bah-me-en'-to], *m.* End, completion, death, consummation.
Acabar [ah-cah-bar'], *va.* & *vn.* 1. To

finish, to conclude, to complete, to make up; to compass; to achieve; to grow toward an end. *Acaba ya*, Determine, resolve. 2. To harass. 3. To obtain. 4. To terminate in any thing, as a sword which ends in a point. 5. To die; to consume; to extinguish; to fail. *Acabar con el negocio*, To make an end of the affair. *Está acabado de salir*, It is just fresh from.—*vr.* To grow feeble. *La vela se está acabando*, The candle is flickering. *Es cosa de nunca acabarse*, It is an endless affair. *Acaba de llegar*, He is just arrived. *Acabar de*, To have just . . . *Acabóse*, (Coll.) No more to be said; that's an end of it.

Acabestrillar [ah-cah-bes-tril-lyar'], *vn.* To stalk, or to fowl with a stalking-horse or ox, that approaches the game and shelters the fowler.

Acabildar [ah-cah-bil-dar'], *va.* To unite many persons by dint of persuasion to do something. 2. To put to vote.

Acacia [ah-cah'-the-ah], *f.* 1. Acacia, a shrub of the thorn kind. 2. Acacia, the inspissated juice of acacia.

Acachetear [ah-cah-chay-tay-ar'], *va.* To tap, to pat, to strike.

Academia [ah-cah-day'-me-ah], *f.* 1. Academy; university; literary society. In particular, the Spanish Academy, officially charged with the pureness of the language. It was founded in Madrid early in the eighteenth century. 2. A naked figure designed from nature.

Académico [ah-cah-day'-me-co], *m.* An academician.

Académico, ca [ah-cah-day'-me-co, cah], *a.* Academical, belonging to a university, etc.

Acaecedero, ra [ah-cah-ay-thay-day'-ro, rah], *a.* Incidental.

Acaecer [ah-cah-ay-therr'], *vn. def.* To happen, to come to pass.

Acaecimiento [ah-cah-ay-the-me-en'-to], *m.* Event, incident, occurrence.

Acal [ah-cahl'], *m.* A canoe used by Mexicans.

Acalambrado, da [ah-cah-lam-brah'-do, dah], *a.* Cramped.

Acalefos [ah-ca-lay'-fos], *m. pl.* Acalephs, a group of radiates, including jelly-fishes and hydroids.

Acalenturarse [ah-cah-len-too-rar'-say], *vr.* To be feverish.

Acalia [ah-cah'-le-ah], *f.* *V.* MALVAVISCO. Marsh-mallow.

Acalicino, na [ah-cah-le-thee'-no, nah], *a.* Wanting a calyx.

Acaloradamente [ah-cah-lo-rah-dah-men'-tay], *adv.* Warmly, with vehemency.

Acaloramiento [ah-cah-lo-rah-me-en'-to], *m.* Ardour, heat; agitation.

Acalorar [ah-cah-lo-rar'], *va.* 1. To warm. 2. To inflame, to overheat. 3. To urge on. 4. To forward, to promote.—*vr.* To grow warm in debate.

Acallar [ah-cal-lyar'], *va.* 1. To quiet, to silence, to hush. 2. To mitigate, to soften, to assuage.

Acamado, da [ah-cah-mah'-do, dah], *a.* Laid flat. *Mieses acamadas*, Crops laid by heavy storms.

Acambrayado, da [ah-cam-brah-yah'-do, dah], *a.* Cambric-like.

Acamellado, da [ah-cah-mel-lyah'-do, dah], *a.* Camel-like.

Acampamento [ah-cam-pah-men'-to], *m.* (Mil.) Encampment, camp.

Acampar [ah-cam-par'], *va.* To encamp.

Acampo [ah-cahm'-po], *m.* Portion of common given to graziers or herds for pasture.

Acamuzado, da [ah-cah-moo-thah'-do, dah], *a.* Chamois-coloured. *V.* AGAMUZADO.

Acana [ah'-cah-nah], *f.* A hard reddish wood, which grows in the island of Cuba, used in ship-building.

Acanalado, da [ah-cah-nah-lah'-do, dah], *a.* 1. What passes through a narrow passage or channel. 2. Striated, fluted.—*pp.* of ACANALAR.

Acanalador [ah-cah-nah-lah-dor'], *m.* An instrument to cut grooves in timber; chamfering-plane, grooving-plane.

Acanalados [ah-cah-nah-lah'-dos], *m. pl.* The ridge of a horse's back.

Acanalar [ah-cah-nah-lar'], *va.* 1. To make a canal or channel. 2. To flute, to groove, to chamfer.

Acandilado, da [ah-can-de-lah'-do, dah], *a.* *Sombrero acandilado*, A hat cocked with sharp points, worn in poor-houses in Spain.

Acanelado, da [ah-cah-nay-lah'-do, dah], *a.* Of a cinnamon colour.

Acangrenarse [ah-can-gray-nar-say], *vr.* To mortify.

Acanillado, da [ah-cah-nil-lyah'-do, dah], *a.* Ribbed. Applied to any sort of cloth which forms furrows from the unevenness of its threads.

Acantalear [ah-can-tah-lay-ar'], *vn.* (Coll.) To hail large hail-stones.

Acantarar [ah-can-tah-rar'], *va.* To measure by *cántaras* or four-gallon vessels.

Acantilado, da [ah-can-te-lah'-do, dah], *a.* Bold, steep. *Costa acantilada*, An accessible coast.

Acantio [ah-cahn'-te-oh], *m.* *V.* TOBA.

Acanto [ah-cahn'-to], *m.* (Bot.) 1. Prickly thistle. 2. (Arch.) Acanthus leaf.

Acantonamiento [ah-can-to-nah-me-en'-to], *m.* Cantonment.

Acantonar [ah-can-to-nar'], *va.* To canton, to quarter troops.

Acañaverear [ah-cah-nyah-vay-ray-ar'], *va.* To wound the flesh with sharp-pointed canes.

Acañonear [ah-cah-nyo-nay-ar'], *va.* To cannonade.

Acap [ah-cahp'], *m.* A Mexican wood suitable for cabinet-work.

Acaparar [ah-cah-pah-rar'], *va.* To monopolize, engross. *V.* ACOPIAR.

Acaparrarse [ah-cah-par-rar'-say], *vr.* 1. To take refuge under another's cloak. 2. To resort to the protection of some one else; to take sides with.

Acaparrosado, da [ah-cah-par-ro-sah'-do, dah], *a.* Of a copperas colour.

Acaponado, da [ah-cah-po-nah'-do, dah], *a.* Capon-like; eunuch.

Acaramelar [a-cah-rah-may-lar'], *va.* To reduce sugar to caramel.

Acarar [ah-cah-rar'], *va.* *V.* CAREAR.

Acardenalar [ah-car-day-nah-lar'], *va.* To make livid, to beat black and blue, to pinch.—*vr.* To be covered with livid spots.

Acareamiento [ah-cah-ray-ah-me-en'-to], *m.* Comparing, confronting.

Acariciador, ra [ah-cah-re-the-ah-dor', rah], *m.* & *f.* One who fondles and caresses.

Acariciar [ah-ca-re-the-ar'], *va.* To fondle, to caress, to hug.

Ácaro [ah'-ca-ro], *m.* Acarus, mite. *Ácaro de queso*, Cheese-mite.

Acarrarse [ah-car-rar'-say], *vr.* To shelter one's self from the heat of the sun: applied to sheep.

Acarreadizo, za [ah-car-ray-ah-dee'-tho, thah], *a.* Portable.

Acarreador, ra [ah-car-ray-ah-dor', rah], *m.* & *f.* A carrier; a porter.

Acarrear [ah-car-ray-ar'], *va.* 1. To carry something in a cart or other carriage; convey, to forward. 2. (Met.) To occasion, to cause. 3. *vr.* To bring upon one's self.

Acarreo [ah-car-ray'-oh], *m.* Carriage, the act of carrying, conveyance, cartage.—*pl.* Supplies. *Cosas de acarreo*, Goods forwarded.

Acartonado [ah-car-to-nah'-do], *a.* Resembling pasteboard.

Acaso [ah-cah'-so], *m.* Chance, casualty.

Acaso [ah-cah'-so], *adv.* By chance, by accident; may be, mayhap, perhaps. *¿ Acaso ?* How ? how now ?

Acastillaje [ah-cas-til-lyah'-hay], *m.* (Obs. Naut.) The upper works of a ship.

Acastorado, da [ah-cas-to-rah'-do, dah], *a.* Beavered; resembling the texture of beaver.

Acatable [ah-cah-tah'-blay], *a.* (Archaic) Venerable.

Acataléctico [ah-cah-tah-lec'-te-co], *a.* Verse which has the complete number of syllables; acatalectic.

Acatamiento [ah-cah-tah-me-en'-to], *m.* 1. Esteem, veneration, respect, reverence, obeisance. 2. Acknowledgment. 3. Presence, view.

Acatar [ah-cah-tar'], *va.* To respect, to revere, to venerate.

Acatarrarse [ah-cah-tar-rar'-say], *vr.* To catch cold.

Acaudalado, da [ah-cah-oo-dah-lah'-do, dah], *a.* Rich, wealthy, opulent.—*pp.* of ACAUDALAR.

Acaudalar [ah-cah-oo-dah-lar'], *va.* 1. To hoard up riches. 2. To acquire a reputation.

Acaudillador [ah-cah-oo-dil-lyah-dor'], *m.* Commander of troops.

Acaudillar [ah-cah-oo-dil-lyar'], *va.* To command troops.

Acaule [ah-cah'-oo-lay], *a.* (Bot.) Acaulous: wanting a stem.

Accedente [ac-thay-den'-tay], *pa.* Acceding; he who accedes in state treaties.

Acceder [ac-thay-derr'], *vn.* To accede, to become accessory to a treaty or agreement concluded by others: to fall in or into an agreement.

Accesible [ac-thay-see'-blay], *a.* 1. Accessible. 2. Attainable. 3. Of easy access, approachable.

Accesión [ac-thay-se-on'], *f.* 1. Accession, the act of acceding. 2. Access or paroxysm of a fever.

Acceso [ac-thay'-so]. 1. Access. 2. Sexual intercourse. 3. Approach. *Acceso dirigido desde tierra*, (Aer.) Ground-control approach.

Accesoria [ac-thay-so'-re-ah], *f.* 1. Outbuilding. 2. (Andal.) A room in the lower story of a house with the door opening to the street.

Accesoriamente [ac-thay-so-re-ah-men'-tay], *adv.* Accessorily.

Accesorio, a [ac-thay-so'-re-o, ah], *a.* Accessory, additional. *Obras accesorias*, (Mil.) The outworks of a fortress.

Accidentado, da [ac-the-den-tah'-do, dah], *a.* Affected with fits.—*pp.* of ACCIDENTARSE.

Accidental [ac-the-den-tahl'], *a.* Accidental, casual, fortuitous, contingent.

Accidentalmente, Accidentariamente [ac-the-den-tal-men'-tay, ac-the-den-tah-re-ah-men'-tay], *adv.* Accidentally, casually, fortuitously.

Accidentarse [ac-the-den-tar'-say], *vr.* To be seized with a fit, or suddenly affected with a disease.

Accidentazo [ac-the-den-tah'-tho], *m. aug.* A severe fit of illness.

Accidente [ac-the-den'-tay], *m.* 1. Accident, an unessential quality of any thing. 2. Casualty, that which happens unforeseen, accident. 3. Privation of sensation. 4. Mode, integral part. 5. Accidental, in music.

Acción [ac-the-on'], *f.* 1. Action; feat. *Acción de gracias*, Act of thanking, thanksgiving. 2. Faculty of doing something. 3. Lawsuit. 4. Gesticulation, gesture. 5. Battle. 6. Action, in the series of events represented in a fable, and the manner of representing them. 7. (Art) Posture. 8. (Com.) Stock, capital in a company; share. 9. (Poet.) The principal subject of a poem. *Acción industrial* (Com. e. g. *de ferrocarril*), Share (e. g. railway share).

Accionamiento [ac-the-o-nah-me-en'-to], *m.* Drive, propulsion, operation.

Accionar [ac-the-o-nar'], *vn.* To gesticulate.—*va.* 1. To sue, to bring suit. 2. To activate, to drive, to propel.

Accionista [ac-the-o-nees'-tah], *m.* A shareholder in a company's stock, actionary.

Acebadamiento [ah-thay-bah-dah-me-en'-to], *m.* A disease contracted by beasts in drinking water after being surfeited with barley.

Acebadar [ah-thay-bah-dar'], *va.* *V.* ENCEBADAR.

Acebedo [ah-thay-bay'-do], *m.* A plantation of holly-trees.

Acebo [ah-thay'-bo], *m.* (Bot.) Holly-tree. Ilex aquifolium.

Acebolladura [ah-thay-bol-lyah-doo'-rah], *f.* Damage to a tree from splitting of the woody layers.

Acebuchal [ah-thay-boo-chahl'], *m.* A plantation of wild olive-trees.

Acebuchal [ah-thay-boo-chahl'], *a.* Belonging to wild olives.

Acebuche [ah-thay-boo'-chay], *m.* (Bot.) The wild olive-tree. Olea.

Acebucheno, na [ah-thay-boo-chay'-no, nah], *a.* Belonging to the wild olive.

Acebuchina [ah-thay-boo-chee'-nah], *f.* Fruit of the wild olive-tree.

Acecinar [ah-thay-the-nar'], *va.* To salt meat and dry it in the air or smoke.—*vr.* To grow old, dry, and withered.

Acechador, ra [ah-thay-chah-dor', rah], *m. & f.* 1. A thief lying in ambush. 2. An intruder who pries into other people's affairs.

Acechar [ah-thay-char'], *va.* 1. To waylay, to lie in ambush, to lurk. 2. To pry into other people's affairs.

Aceche [ah-thay'-chay], *m.* *V.* CAPARROSA.

Acecho [ah-thay'-cho], *m.* The act of waylaying, or laying in ambush. *Al acecho* or *en acecho*, *a.* In wait, in ambush.

Acechón, na [ah-thay-chone', nah], *m. & f.* (Coll.) *V.* ACECHADOR. *Hacer la acechona*, To scrutinize, to inquire with care, to be inquisitive.

Acedar [ah-thay-dar'], *va.* 1. To sour, to make sour. 2. To displease, to vex.

Acedera [ah-thay-day'-rah], *f.* (Bot.) Sorrel. Rumex acetosa. *Acedera de Indias*, (Bot.) Indian sorrel.

Acederilla [ah-thay-day-reel'-lyah], *f.* (Bot.) Wood-sorrel. Rumex acetosella.

Acedía [ah-thay-dee'-ah], *f.* 1. Acidity, sourness. 2. Squeamishness, roughness. 3. Asperity of address. 4. A flounder, or plaice. Pleuronectes flesus.

Acedo, da [ah-thay'-do, dah], *a.* 1. Acid, sour. 2. Harsh, unpleasant.

Acefalia [ah-thay-fah-lee'-ah], *f.* Deprivation of a head; headlessness.

Acéfalo, la [ah-thay'-fah-lo, lah], *a.* Headless, acephalous.

Aceitada [ah-thay-e-tah'-dah], *f.* (Coll.) 1. Oil spilled. 2. Cake kneaded with oil.

Aceitar [ah-thay-e-tar'], *va.* To oil, to rub with oil.

Aceite [ah-thay'-e-tay], *m.* 1. Oil; any unctuous liquor drawn from olives, almonds, nuts, fish, etc. 2. Resin which distils from the fir-tree. *Aceite de comer*, Olive, or sweet oil. *Aceite de bergamota*, Essence of bergamot. *Aceite de espliego*, Oil of spike. *Aceite de trementina*, Oil of turpentine. *Aceite de pescado*, Train oil. *Aceite de merluza*, Cod oil. *Aceite de palo*, Balsam copaiba. *Aceite abetinote*, Oil or juice of spruce fir. *Aceite de linaza*, Linseed oil. *Aceite de ricino*, Castor oil. *Aceite de hígado de bacalao*, Cod-liver oil. *Aceite de carbón, o aceite mineral*, Coal-oil, petroleum. *Aceite lubricante*, (Mech.) Lube.

Aceitera [ah-thay-e-tay'-rah], *f.* An oil jar, oil cruet, oil horn, *Aceiteras*, Vials for oil and vinegar.

Aceitería [ah-thay-e-tay-ree'-ah], *f.* Oil-shop.

Aceitero, ra [ah-thay-e-tay'-ro, rah], *m. & f.* 1. An oil-man, oil-seller. 2. Any vessel for holding oil.

Aceitoso, sa [ah-thay-e-toh'-so, sah], *a.* Oily, containing oil.

Aceituna [ah-thay-e-too'-nah], *f.* Olive, the fruit of the olive-tree. *Aceitunas zapateras*, Olives which stand a long time in pickle.

Aceitunada [ah-thay-e-too-nah'-dah], *f.* The season for gathering olives.

Aceitunado, da [ah-thay-e-too-nah'-do, dah], *a.* Of an olive colour.

Aceitunero [ah-thay-e-too-nay'-ro], *m.* A person who gathers, carries, or sells olives.

Aceituno [ah-thay-e-too'-no], *m.* (Bot.) Olive-tree. Olea Europæa. *V.* OLIVO.

Aceleración [ah-thay-lay-rah-the-on'], *f.* Acceleration, hastening.

Aceleradamente [ah-thay-lay-rah-dah-men'-tay], *adv.* Speedily, swiftly, hastily.

Acelerador [ah-thay-lay-rah-dor'], *m.* Accelerator.

Aceleramiento [ah-thay-lay-rah-me-en'to], *m.* *V.* ACELERACIÓN.

Acelerar [ah-thay-lay-rar'], *va.* To accelerate, to hasten, to hurry, to forward, to expedite.

Aceleratriz [ah-thay-lay-rah-treeth'], *a.* Accelerative.

Acelerómetro [ah-thay-lay-ro'-may-tro], *m.* (Aer.) Accelerometer.

Acelga [ah-thel'-gah], *f.* (Bot.) Beet. Beta vulgaris. *Cara de acelga amarga*, A nick-name given to a pale-faced person.

Acémila [ah-thay'-me-la], *f.* 1. A mule, a beast of burden. 2. (Obs.) Tax paid for mules.

Acemilar [ah-thay-me-lar'], *a.* Belonging to mules and muleteers.

Acemilería [ah-thay-me-lay-ree'-ah], *f.* The stable or place where mules are kept.

Acemilero, ra [ah-thay-me-lay'-ro, rah], *a.* Belonging to mules, in particular to the king's mules.—*m.* A muleteer.

Acemita [ah-thay-mee'-tah], *f.* Bread made of fine bran. Graham bread.

Acemite [ah-thay-mee'-tay], *m.* Fine bran, middlings.

Acendrado, da [ah-then-drah'-do, dah], *a.* 1. Purified. 2. Refined.—*pp.* of ACENDRAR.

Acendrar [ah-then-drar'], *va.* 1. To purify or refine metals. 2. To free from stain or blemish.

Acensuar [ah-then-soo-ar'], *va.* To lease out for a certain rent; impose a tax.

Acento [ah-then'-to], *m.* 1. Accent, a modulation of the voice. 2. Accent, a character placed over a syllable, to mark the modulation of the voice.

Acentuación [ah-then-too-ah-the-on'], *f.* Accent, accentuation.

Acentuar [ah-then-too-ar'], *va.* 1. To accent, to stress. 2. To put a written accent on. 3. (Met.) To accentuate, to stress.

Aceña [ah-thay'-nyah], *f.* Water mill (for grinding flour).

Acepar [ah-thay-par'], *vn.* To take root, to become rooted.

Acepción [ah-thep-the-on'], *f.* Meaning, acceptation. *Acepción de personas*, Partiality, prejudice.

Acepilladora [ah-thay-pil-lyah-do'-rah], *f.* Plane

Acepilladura [ah-thay-pil-lyah-doo'-rah], *f.* 1. The act of planing. 2. The shavings of timber.

Acepillar [ah-thay-pil-lyar'], *va.* 1. To plane. 2. To brush clothes. 3. To polish the manners.

Aceptabilidad [ah-thep-tah-be-le-dad'], *f.* Acceptability.

Aceptable [ah-thep-tah'-blay], *a.* Worthy of acceptance, acceptable.

Aceptablemente [ah-thep-tah-blay-men'-tay], *adv.* Acceptably.

Aceptación [ah-thep-tah-the-on'], *f.* 1. Acceptation. 2. Approbation. 3. Acceptance of a bill of exchange. *Aceptación de herencia*, Acceptance of an inheritance. *Aceptación de personas*, *V.* ACEPCIÓN.

Aceptador, ra [ah-thep-tah-dor', rah], *m. & f.* Acceptor.

Aceptante [ah-thep-tahn'-tay], *pa.* He who accepts.

Aceptar [ah-thep-tar'], *va.* To accept. *Aceptar personas*, To favour particular persons. *Aceptar una letra*, To accept or to honour a bill.—*vr.* To be pleased.

Acepto, ta [ah-thep'-to, tah], *a.* Acceptable, agreeable.

Acequia [ah-thay'-ke-ah], *f.* A canal, trench, or drain. (Arabic.)

Acequiado, da [ah-thay-ke-ah'-do, dah], *a.* Intersected by canals.—*pp.* of ACEQUIAR.

Acequiador [ah-thay-ke-ah-dor'], *m.* Canal-maker.

Acequiar [ah-thay-ke-ar'], *va.* To construct canals or drains.

Acequiero [ah-thay-ke-ay'-ro], *m.* A person appointed to construct canals, a dike-reeve.

Acera [ah-thay'-rah], *f.* 1. Sidewalk. 2. The stones which form the face of a wall.

Acerado, da [ah-thay-rah'-do, dah], *a.* 1. Steeled, made of steel. 2. Strong.—*pp.* of ACERAR.

Acerar [ah-thay-rar'], *va.* 1. To steel, to point or edge with steel. 2. To impregnate liquors with steel. 3. To strengthen.

Acerbamente [ah-ther-bah-men'-tay], *adv.* Harshly, rudely.

Acerbidad [ah-ther-be-dad'], *f.* 1. Acerbity, asperity. 2. Rigour, cruelty.

Acerbo, ba [ah-ther'-bo, bah], *a.* 1. Rough to the taste, as unripe fruit. 2. Severe, cruel.

Acerca [ah-ther'-cah], *prep.* About, relating to. *Acerca de lo que hemos hablado*, In regard to what we have said.

Acercar [ah-ther-car'], *va.* To approach, to place a person or thing close to another.—*vr.* To accost, to come near to, or up to.

Acería [ah-thay-ree'-ah], *f.* Steel mill.

Acerico, Acerillo [ah-thay-ree'-co, ah-thay-reel'-lyo], *m.* 1. A pin-cushion. 2. A small pillow.

Acerino, na [ah-thay-ree'-no, nah], *a.* (Poet.) Made of, or belonging to steel

Acerista [ah-thay-rees'-tah], *m.* Steel manufacturer.

Acernadar [ah-ther-nah-dar'], *va.* To cover with ashes.

Acero [ah-thay'-ro], *m.* 1. Steel. *Acero colado,* Cast steel. *Acero inoxidable,* Stainless steel. 2. Edged or pointed small arms. *Espada de buenos aceros,* Sword of well-tempered steel. *Aceros,* (fig.) Spirit, courage.

Acerola [ah-thay-ro'-lah], *f.* Azarole, the fruit of the parsley-leaved hawthorn.

Acerolo [ah-thay-ro'-lo], *m.* (Bot.) The parsley-leaved hawthorn. Cratægus azarolus.

Acerrar [ah-ther-rar'], *va.* (Low) To seize, to grasp.

Acérrimamente [ah-ther'-re-mah-men-tay], *adv.* Strenuously.

Acérrimo, ma [ah-ther'-re-mo, mah], *a. sup.* Very vigorous and strong.

Acertadamente [ah-ther-tah-dah-men'-tay], *adv.* Opportunely, fitly.

Acertado, da [ah-ther-tah'-do, dah], *a.* Fit, proper. *Su conducta fué acertada,* He conducted himself with propriety.—*pp.* of Acertar.

Acertador, ra [ah-ther-tah-dor', rah], *m* & *f.* One who hits right upon any thing.

Acertajo [ah-ther-tah'-ho], *m.* (Coll.) V. Acertijo.

Acertar [ah-ther-tar'], *va.* 1. To hit the mark. 2. To hit by chance; to meet or find, to succeed. 3. To conjecture right. *vn.* 1. To happen unexpectedly. 2. To take root, as plants.

Acertijo [ah-ther-tee'-ho], *m.* A riddle.

Aceruelo [ah-thay-roo-ay'-lo], *m.* A sort of small pack-saddle used for riding.

Acervo [ah-ther'-vo], *m.* 1. A heap. 2. The totality of tithes, or of an inheritance.

Acescencia [ah-thes-then'-the-ah], *f.* Acidosis.

Acetábulo [ah-thay-tah'-boo-lo], *m.* 1. Acetabulum, cruet; a Roman measure. 2. (Anat.) Acetabulum, the cavity receiving the head of the thigh-bone.

Acetato [ah-thay-tah'-to], *m.* Acetate.

Acético, ca [ah-thay'-te-co, cah], *a.* Acetic; pertaining to vinegar.

Acetificar [ah-thay-te-fe-car'], *va.* To acetify, convert into vinegar.

Acetileno [ah-thay-te-lay'-no], *m.* (Chem.) Acetylene.

Acetimetro [ah-thay-tee'-may-tro], *m.* Acetimeter.

Acetona [ah-thay-to'-nah], *f.* Acetone; pyroacetic spirit.

Acetosa [ah-thay-to'-sah], *f.* (Bot.) Sorrel. *V.* Acedera.

Acetosilla [ah-thay-to-seel'-lyah], *f.* (Bot.) Wood-sorrel. Oxalis acetosella.

Acetoso, sa [ah-thay-to'-so, sah], *a.* 1. Acetous. 2. (Obs.) Acid.

Acetre [ah-thay'-tray], *m.* 1. A small bucket with which water is taken out of jars or wells. 2. The holy-water pot used in Roman Catholic churches.

Aciago, ga [ah-the-ah'-go, gah], *a.* Unfortunate, melancholy, sad.

Acial, Aciar [ah-the-ahl', ah-the-ar'], *m.* Barnacle, twitch, an instrument put upon the nose of a horse to make him stand quiet. *Más vale acial que fuerza de oficial* (prov.), Craft is better than violence.

Aciano [ah-the-ah'-no], *m.* Corn-flower. V. Estrellamar.

Acíbar [ah-thee'-bar], *m.* 1. The juice pressed from the aloes. 2. Aloes-tree. *Acíbar caballuno,* Horse aloes;—*hepático,* Barbadoes aloes;—*socotrino,* Socotrine aloes. (Met.) Harshness, bitterness, displeasure.

Acibarar [ah-the-bah-rar'], *va.* 1. To put the juice of aloes into any thing; to make bitter. 2. (Met.) To imbitter, to cause displeasure.

Acicalador, ra [ah-the-cah-lah-dor', rah], *m.* & *f.* 1. A polisher, burnisher, furbisher. 2. A tool used for burnishing.

Acicaladura, *f.* **Acicalamiento,** *m.* [ah-the-cah-lah-doo'-rah, ah-the-cah-lah-me-en'-to]. The act and effect of burnishing.

Acicalar [ah-the-cah-lar'], *vn.* To polish, to burnish.—*vr.* (Met.) To dress in style, to set one's self off to advantage; to prink.

Acicate [ah-the-cah'-tay], *m.* A long necked Moorish spur with a rowel at the end of it.

Aciche [ah-thee'-chay], *m.* A two-edged tool used by tilers for cutting and adjusting tiles.

Acidez [ah-the-deth'], f. 1. (Med.) Acidosis. 2. Acidity.

Acidia [ah-thee'-de-ah], *f.* (Obs.) *V.* Pereza. Laziness.

Acidificación [ah-the-de-fe-cah-the-on'], *f.* (Chem.) Acidification.

Acidificar [ah-the-de-fe-car'], *va.* To acidify.

Acidímetro [ah-the-dee'-may-tro], *m.* Acidimeter.

Acidismo [ah-the-dees'-mo], *m.* Acidosis.

Acido [ah'-the-do], *m.* (Chem.) Acid. *Acido acético,* Acetic acid. *Acido deoxiribonucleico,* Deoxyribonucleic acid.

Acido, da [ah'-the-do, dah], *a.* Acid, sour.

Acidular [ah-the-doo-lar'], *va.* To acidulate, to make sour.

Acídulo, la [ah-thee'-doo-lo, lah], *a.* (Chem.) Acidulous.

Acierto [ah-the-er'-to], *m.* 1. The act and effect of hitting; a good hit. *Con acierto,* With effect. 2. Prudence, dexterity. 3. Chance, casualty.

(*Yo acierto, yo acierte. V.* Acertar.)

Aciguatado, da [ah-the-goo-ah-tah'-do, dah], *a.* Jaundiced.—*pp.* of Aciguatarse.

Acijado, da [ah-the-hah'-do, dah], *a.* Copperas-coloured; of the colour of *acije.*

Acijoso, sa [ah-the-ho'-so, sah], *a.* Brownish: participating in the nature of *acije.*

Acimboga [ah-thim-bo'-gah], *f.* The citron-tree. Citrus medica.

Ación [ah-the-on'], *f.* Stirrup-leather.

Acionero [ah-thi-o-nay'-ro], *m.* A maker of stirrup-leathers.

Acipado, da [ah-the-pah'-do, dah], *a.* Well-milled; applied to broadcloth and other woollens.

Acirate [ah-the-rah'-tay], *m.* A landmark which shows the limits and boundaries of fields.

Acitara [ah-the-tah'-rah], *f.* A thin wall, a partition wall; the rail of a bridge.

Acitrón [ah-the-tron'], *m.* A citron dried and made into sweetmeat; candied lemon.

Aclamación [ah-clah-mah-the-on'], *f.* Acclamation, the act of shouting with joy. *Elegir por aclamación,* To elect by acclamation.

Aclamador, ra [ah-clah-mah-dor', rah], *m.* & *f.* Applauder.

Aclamar [ah-clah-mar'], *va.* 1. To shout with joy, to applaud. 2. To cry up.

Aclamídeo, a [ah-clah-mee'-day-o, ah], *a.* Achlamydeous; having no floral envelopes; naked.

Aclaración [ah-clah-rah-the-on'], *f.* Illustration, explanation.

Aclarador, ra [ah-clah-rah-dor', rah], *a.* Explanatory, illustrative.—*m.* A kind of comb in looms for making silk fringes.

Aclarar [ah-clah-rar'], *va.* 1. To clear from obscurity, to make bright. 2. To illustrate, to explain. 3. To widen; to clarify.—*vn.* To clear up, to recover brightness.

Aclimatación [ah-cle-mah-tah-the-on'], *f.* Acclimation; acclimatization.

Aclimatar [ah-cle-mah-tar'], *va.* To acclimatize, habituate to a strange climate.

Aclocado, da [ah-cloh-cah'-do, dah], *a.* Stretched at a fire, table, etc.—*pp.* of Aclocarse.

Aclocarse [ah-cloh-car'-say], *vr.* 1. To brood, to hatch eggs. 2. To stretch one's self on the ground, bench, etc.

Acne [ac'-nay], *f.* Acne, a cutaneous disease.

Acobardar [ah-co-bar-dar'], *va.* To daunt, intimidate, terrify.

Acoceador, ra [ah-co-thay-ah-dor', rah], *m.* & *f.* A horse that kicks.

Acoceamiento [ah-co-thay-ah-me-en'-to], *m.* The act and effect of kicking.

Acocear [ah-co-thay-ar'], *va.* To kick, to wince, or flinch.

Acocotar [ah-co-co-tar'], *va.* To kill by a blow upon the neck.

Acocote [ah-co-coh'-tay], *m.* A long gourd pointed at both ends, used in Mexico for extracting the nectar of the maguey.

Acocharse [ah-co-char'-say], *vr.* To squat, to stoop down.

Acochinar [ah-co-che-nar'], *va.* 1. To murder, to assassinate. 2. (Met.) To prevent or obstruct the regular course of a suit at law; to hush up. 3. To humble

Acodadura [ah-co-dah-doo'-rah], *f.* 1. The act of bending the elbow. 2. (Agr.) Layering.

Acodalar [ah-co-dah-lar'], *va.* (Arch.) To put lintels or transoms in a wall to support a window or niche.

Acodar [ah-co-dar'], *va.* 1. (Obs.) To lean the elbow upon. 2. To lay cuttings of vines or other plants in the ground, that they may take root. 3. To square timber.

Acoderarse [ah-co-day-rar'-say], *vr.* 1. To put a spring on a cable. 2. (Naut.) To bring the broadside to bear.

Acodiciar [ah-co-de-the-ar'], *va.* (Obs.) To urge on; to urgently long for, covet, something.—*vr.* To be provoked, to be inflamed with passion.

Acodillar [ah-co-dil-lyar'], *va.* 1. To bend any thing to an elbow or angle. 2. To sink down under a burden. *Acodillarse con la carga,* (Met.) Not to be able to fulfil one's engagements.

Acodo [ah-co'-do], *m.* A shoot or knot of a layer; a scion.

Acogedizo, za [ah-co-hay-dee'-tho, thah], *a.* Collected or gathered promiscuously.

Acogedor, ra [ah-co-hay-dor', rah], *m.* & *f.* Harbourer, protector.

Acoger [ah-co-herr'], *va.* 1. To admit one into our house or company; to receive. 2. (Met.) To protect, to give an asylum.—*vr.* 1. To take refuge, to resort to. 2. (Obs.) To embrace the opinion of another. 3. To make use of a pretext for dissimulation.

Acogida [ah-co-hee'-dah], *f.* 1. Reception. 2. The concurrence of a multitude of things in the same place; confluence; asylum. *Dar acogida a una letra,* (Com.) To honour or protect a bill. *Reservar buena acogida a,* To meet prompt attention.

Acogido [ah-co-hee'-do], *m.* 1. Collection of breeding mares given to the owner of the principal steed, to keep them at a certain price. 2. Temporary admission of flocks into pasture-ground.—*pp.* of Acoger.

Acogimiento [ah-co-he-me-en'-to], *m.* *V.* Acogida.

Acogollar [ah-co-gol-lyar'], *va.* To cover delicate plants with straw or any thing affording shelter.

Acogolladura [ah-co-gol-lyah-doo'-rah], *f.* Earthing up of plants.

Acogombradura [ah-co-gom-brah-doo'-rah], *f.* Digging up of the ground about plants.

Acogombrar [ah-co-gom-brar'], *va.* To dig up the ground about plants; to cover plants with earth.

Acogotar [ah-co-go-tar'], *va.* To kill by a blow on the neck. (Coll.) To overcome a person.

Acolada [ah-co-lah'-dah], *f.* Accolade, a ceremony which consisted of an embrace and a touch with the flat of the sword on each shoulder of one who was receiving knighthood.

Acolar [ah-co-lar'], *va.* (Her.) To arrange or unite two coats of arms under the same crown, shield, etc.

Acolchar [ah-col-char'], *va.* To quilt.

Acólito [ah-co'-le-to], *m.* 1. Acolyte, assistant to a priest at mass. 2. An assistant.

Acolladores [ah-col-lyah-do'-res], *m. pl.* (Naut.) Lanyards. *Acolladores de los obenques*, The lanyards of the shrouds.

Acollarado, da [ah-col-lyah-rah'-do, dah], *a.* *Pájaros acollarados*, Birds having about their necks a ring of feathers of a different colour.

Acollarar [ah-col-lyah-rar'], *va.* 1. To yoke or harness horses, oxen, etc. 2. To couple hounds.

Acombar [ah-com-bar'], *va.* To bend, to crook.

Acomendador [ah-co-men-dah-dor'], *m.* (Obs.) Protector, aider.

Acometedor, ra [ah-co-may-tay-dor', rah], *m.* & *f.* An aggressor.

Acometer [ah-co-may-terr'], *va.* 1. To attack, to assault. 2. To undertake. 3. To tempt. *Acometerse mutuamente*, To jostle.

Acometida, *f.* **Acometimiento**, *m.* [ah-co-may-tee'-dah, ah-co-may-te-me-en'-to]. An attack, an assault. *Acometimiento de calentura*, A fit or access of the fever.

Acomodable [ah-co-mo-dah'-blay], *a.* Accommodable.

Acomodación [ah-co-mo-dah-the-on'], *f.* Accommodation.

Acomodadamente [ah-co-mo-dah-dah-men'-tay], *adv.* Commodiously, suitably.

Acomodado, da [ah-co-mo-dah'-do, dah], *a.* 1. Convenient, fit. 2. Rich, wealthy. 3. Fond of accommodation. 4. Moderate.—*pp.* of Acomodar.

Acomodador, ra [ah-co-mo-dah-dor', rah], *m.* & *f.* The person that accommodates; box-keeper in the theatre.

Acomodamiento [ah-co-mo-dah-me-en'-to], *m.* Accommodation, the act and effect of accommodating.

Acomodar [ah-co-mo-dar'], *va.* 1. To accommodate. 2. To put in a convenient place. 3. To reconcile; to compound. 4. To furnish.—*vn.* To fit, to suit.—*vr.* To condescend, to conform one's self, to comply.

Acomodaticio, cia [ah-co-mo-dah-tee'-the-o, ah], *a.* 1. Accommodating, compliant. 2. (Ant.) Figurative, metaphorical.

Acomodo [ah-co-mo'-do], *m.* Employment, place, situation; lodgings.

Acompañado, da [ah-com-pah-nyah'-do, dah], *a.* 1. Accompanied. 2. *m.* An assistant judge, surgeon, physician, etc.—*pp.* of Acompañar.

Acompañador, ra [ah-com-pah-nyah-dor', rah], *m.* & *f.* 1. A chaperon, an attendant; companion. 2. (Mus.) Accompanist.

Acompañamiento [ah-com-pah-nyah-me-en'-to], *m.* 1. Attendance. 2. Retinue. 3. (Mus.) Accompaniment. 4. Supernumeraries at a theatre. 5. (Her.) The ornament which is constantly placed at the side of the escutcheon.

Acompañar [ah-com-pah-nyar'], *va.* 1. To accompany, to attend, to conduct, to follow, to lead along. 2. To join, or unite. 3. (Mus.) To sing or play in concert with others.—*vr.* To hold a consultation.

Acompasado, da [ah-com-pah-sah'-do, dah], *a.* 1. Measured by the compass. 2. (Coll.) Monotonous and slow in tone. 3. Of fixed, regular habits.

Acomplexionado, da [ah-com-plex-e-o-nah'-do, dah], *a.* Of a good or bad complexion or constitution.

Aconcia [ah-con'-the-ah], *f.* (Ast.) Generic name of comets with a thick nebulosity and delicate tail.

Aconchabarse [ah-con-chah-bar'-say], *vr.* (Coll.) *V.* Acomodarse.

Aconchar [ah-con-char'], *va.* 1. (Naut.) To fit out or repair a ship. 2. To drive ashore.

Acondicionado, da [ah-con-de-the-o-nah'-do, dah], *a.* Of a good or bad condition. *Hombre bien o mal acondicionado*, A man of a good or bad disposition. *Géneros bien o mal acondicionados*, Goods in a good or bad condition.—*pp.* of Acondicionar.

Acondicionamiento del aire [ah-con-de-the-o-nah-me-en'-to dell ah'-e-ray], *m*, or **clima artificial** [clee'-mah ar-te-fe-the-ahl'], *m.* Air conditioning.

Acondicionar [ah-con-de-the-o-nar'], *va.* 1. To prepare, to arrange, to dispose, to fit. 2. To affect. 3. To constitute.—*vr.* To acquire a determined quality or condition. *Acondicionar para uso invernal*, To winterize.

Acongojar [ah-con-go-har'], *va.* To vex, to oppress, to afflict.

Acónito [ah-co'-ne-to], *m.* (Bot.) Aconite, wolf's-bane.

Aconsejable [ah-con-say-hah'-blay], *a.* Advisable.

Aconsejador, ra [ah-con-say-hah-dor', rah], *m.* & *f.* An adviser, counsellor.

Aconsejar [ah-con-say-har'], *va.* To advise, to counsel.—*vr.* To take advice, to be advised.

Aconsonantar [ah-con-so-nan-tar'], *va.* 1. To observe a complete rhyme at the end of each verse. 2. To use in prose rhymes suitable to poetry only.

Acontecedero, ra [ah-con-tay-thay-day'-ro, rah], *a.* That which may happen.

Acontecer [ah-con-tay-therr'], *v. impers.* To happen, to come about, to fare. *Hacer y acontecer*. A common phrase signifying the promises of any good or benefit; also a threat, a menace.

Acontecimiento [ah-con-tay-the-me-en'-to], *m.* Event, incident, casualty, occurrence.

Acopado, da [ah-coh-pah'-do, dah], *a.* Having the form of a cup or vase.—*pp.* of Acopar.

Acopar [ah-co-par'], *vn.* To form a round head in the shape of a cup: applied to trees and plants.

Acopiador [ah-co-pe-ah-dor'], *m.* (Com.) One who buys up goods to keep them from the market.

Acopiamiento [ah-co-pe-ah-me-en'-to], *m.* The act and effect of gathering.

Acopiar [ah-co-pe-ar'], *va.* To gather, to store up, to forestall.

Acopio [ah-co'-pe-o], *m.* Gathering, storing. *Acopio usurario*, Illicit or unfair buying up of goods; "rigging the market."

Acoplado, da [ah-co-plah'-do, dah], *a.* Fitted, adjusted.—*pp.* of Acoplar.

Acopladura [ah-co-plah-doo'-rah], *f.* (Carp.) Coupling, junction.

Acoplar [ah-co-plar'], *va.* 1. To accouple, to join. 2. To frame timber. 3. To settle differences.—*vr.* To make up matters, to be agreed.

Acoquinarse [ah-ko-kee-nar'-say], *vr.* To become terrified.

Acorar [ah-ko-rar'], *va.* To grieve.

Acorazado [ah-ko-rah-thah'-do], *m.* Battleship, battlewagon.

Acorazar [ah-ko-rah-thar'], *va.* To armor, to cover with armor plate.—*vr.* to steel oneself.

Acorazonado, da [ah-co-rah-tho-nah'-do, dah], *a.* Heart-shaped.

Acorcharse [ah-cor-char'-say], *vr.* 1. To shrivel: applied to the fruits (from *corcho*, cork). 2. To become torpid.

Acordación [ah-cor-dah-the-on'], *f.* (Obs.) Remembrance.

Acordada [ah-cor-dah'-dah], *f.* (For.) Resolution, decision.

Acordadamente [ah-cor-dah-dah-men'-tay], *adv.* By common consent, jointly; with mature deliberation.

Acordado, da [ah-cor-dah'-do, dah], *a.* 1. Agreed. 2. Done with mature deliberation. *Lo acordado*, Decree of a tribunal enforcing the observance of prior proceedings.—*pp.* of Acordar.

Acordar [ah-cor-dar'], *va.* 1. To resolve by common consent, to concert. 2. To remind. 3. To tune musical instruments; to dispose figures in a picture.—*vn.* To agree, to level.—*vr.* 1. To remember, to recollect. 2. To come to an agreement. *Tú te acordarás de mí*, You shall remember me. *Acordarse o estar de acuerdo con uno*, To close with one.

(*Yo acuerdo, yo acuerde. V.* Acordar).

Acorde [ah-cor'day], *a.* 1. Conformable, correspondent. 2. Coinciding in opinion.—*m.* 1. Consonance. 2. Harmony of sounds or colours.

Acordelar [ah-cor-day-lar'], *va.* To measure with a cord; to draw a right line by a wall or street, in order to make it straight.

Acordemente [ah-cor-day-men'-tay], *adv.* By common consent.

Acordeón [ah-cor-day-on'], *m.* Accordion, musical instrument.

Acordonado, da [ah-cor-do-nah'-do, dah], *a.* 1. Surrounded. 2. Made in the form of a cord.—*pp.* of Acordonar.

Acordonar [ah-cor-do-nar'], *va.* 1. To make in the form of a cord or rope. 2. To surround.

Acores [ah-co'-res], *m. pl.* (Med.) Achor, a species of the herpes.

Acorneador, ra [ah-cor-nay-ah-dor', rah], *m.* & *f.* A horned beast fighting with its horns.

Acornear [ah-cor-nay-ar'], *va.* To fight or strike with the horns.

Ácoro [ah'-co-ro], *m.* (Bot.) Sweet-smelling flag, sweet cane, sweet grass. Acorus calamus.

Acorralar [ah-cor-rah-lar'], *va.* 1. To shut up cattle or sheep in pens; to corral. 2. To intimidate. 3. To silence.

Acorrer [ah-cor-rerr'], *va.* (Littl. us.) 1. To help. 2. To run to. 3. To shame.

Acortamiento [ah-cor-tah-me-en'-to], *m.* 1. Shortening. 2. (Ast.) Difference in the distance from the centre of the globe to the ecliptic and centre of a planet in its orbit. 3. (Littl. us.) Restraint.

Acortar [ah-cor-tar'], *va.* 1. To shorten, to lessen. 2. To obstruct. *Acortar la vela*, (Naut.) To shorten sail.—*vr.* 1. To shrivel, to be contracted. 2. To be bashful; to fall back.

Acorullar [ah-cor-rool-lyar'], *va.* (Naut.) To bridle or hold up the oars.

Acorvar [ah-cor-var'], *va.* To double, to bend. *V.* ENCORVAR.

Acosador, ra [ah-co-sah-dor', rah], *m.* & *f.* A pursuer, persecutor.

Acosamiento [ah-co-sah-me-en'-to], *m.* Persecution, molestation.

Acosar [ah-co-sar'], *va.* 1. To pursue close. 2. To vex, to molest, to harass.

Acostado, da [ah-cos-tah'-do, dah], *a.* 1. Stretched, laid down. 2. (Obs.) Salaried. 3. (Her.) Accosted.—*pp.* of ACOSTAR.

Acostamiento [ah-cos-tah-me-en'-to], *m.* 1. The act of stretching or laying down. 2. (Obs.) A certain pay, a salary.

Acostar [ah-cos-tar'], *va.* To lay down, to put one in bed.—*vr.* 1. To incline to one side; to lie down. 2. To approach. 3. (Naut.) To stand inshore. 4. (Naut.) To lie along; to have a list. *Acostarse con*, To sleep with.

Acostumbradamente [ah-cos-toom-brah-dah-men'-tay], *adv.* Customarily, according to custom.

Acostumbrar [ah-cos-toom-brar'], *va.* To accustom, to use.—*vn.* To be accustomed, to habituate.

Acotación [ah-co-tah-the-on'], *f.* 1. The act and the effect of setting bounds; limit. 2. Annotation or quotation in the margin.

Acotamiento [ah-co-tah-me-en'-to], *m.* Limitation.

Acotar [ah-co-tar'], *va.* 1. To limit, to set bounds. *Acótome a Dios*, Let God fix my end; used at sports to express confidence in the actual safety of the place. 2. To fix, to mark. 3. To quote, to make annotations in the margin. 4. To accept for a certain price. 5. To witness. *Acoto estorbos*, Including all obstacles: used at juvenile games.

Acotiledóneo, a [ah-co-te-lay-do'-nay-o, ah], *a.* Acotyledonous, not provided with seed-leaves.

Acotillo [ah-co-teel'-lyo], *m.* A large hammer used by smiths — sledge-hammer.

Acoyundar [ah-co-yoon-dar'], *va.* To yoke oxen to a load.

Acre [ah'-cray], *a.* 1. Sour, acrimonious, hot. 2. Mordant, keen. 3. Rough, rude.

Acrebite [ah-cray-bee'-tay], *m.* & *f.* Sulphur. *V.* ALCREBITE. (Arabic.)

Acrecencia, *f.* **Acrecentamiento**, *m.* [ah-cray-then'-the-ah, ah-cray-then-tah-me-en'-to], Increase, augmentation, growth.

Acrecentador, ra [ah-cray-then-tah-dor', rah], *m.* & *f.* One that increases.

Acrecentar, Acrecer ah-cray-then-tar', ah-cray-therr'], *va.* To increase. *Derecho de acrecer*, The right of accretion in cathedral chapters, where a distribution is made according to the present residence of the prebendaries.

(*Yo acreciento, yo acreciente*, from *Acrecentar*. *V.* ACERTAR.)

Acreditado, da [ah-cray-de-tah'-do, dah], *a.* Accredited, distinguished.—*pp.* of ACREDITAR.

Acreditar [ah-cray-de-tar'], *va.* 1. To assure, to affirm a thing for certain. 2. To credit, to procure credit. 3. To prove.

Acreedor [ah-cray-ay-dor'], *m.* 1. A creditor. 2. (Met.) A meritorious person.

Acreedora [ah-cray-ay-do'-rah], *f.* Creditrix, creditress.

Acreencia [ah-cray-en'-the ah], *f.* (Com.) Claim.

Acremente [ah-cray-men'-tay], *adv.* Sourly, with acrimony.

Acribadura [ah-cre-bah-doo'-rah], *f.* Sifting.—*pl.* Siftings, the remains of grain which has been sifted.

Acribar [ah-cre-bar'], *va.* 1. To sift. 2. (Met.) To pierce like a sieve.

Acribillar [ah-cre-bil-lyar'], *va.* 1. To pierce like a sieve. 2. (Met.) To molest, to torment.

Acridia [ah-cree'-de-ah], *f.* Acridia, a genus of locusts.

Acridófago [ah-cre-do'-fah-go], *a.* Living on locusts.

Acrílico, ca [ah-cree'-le-co, cah], *a.* Acrylic.

Acriminación [ah-cre-me-nah-the-on'], *f.* Crimination, the act of accusing or impeaching.

Acriminador, ra [ah-cre-me-nah-dor', rah], *m.* & *f.* Accuser, informer.

Acriminar [ah-cre-me-nar'], *va.* 1. To exaggerate a crime or fault. 2. To accuse, to impeach. 3. (Law) To aggravate.

Acrimonia [ah-cre-mo'-ne-ah], *f.* 1. Acrimony, sharpness, sourness. 2. (Met.) Asperity of expression, keenness, fieriness, sharpness of temper. 3. (Met.) Vehemence in talking.

Acrisolar [ah-cre-so-lar'], *va.* 1. To refine, to purify gold or other metals, to cleanse. 2. (Met.) To clear up a thing by means of witnesses.

Acristianar [ah-cris-te-ah-nar'], *va.* (Coll.) To baptize, christen.

Acritud [ah-cree-tood'], *f.* *V.* ACRIMONIA.

Acrobacia [ah-cro-bah'-the-ah], *f.* Acrobatics; *Acrobacia aérea*, Stunt flying.

Acróbata [ah-cro'-ba-tah], *m.* & *f.* Rope-dancer, acrobat.

Acrobático, ca [ah-cro-bah'-te-co, cah], *a.* Acrobatic.

Acromático, ca [ah-cro-mah'-te-co, cah], *a.* (Opt.) Achromatic.

Acromatismo [ah-cro-mah-tees'-mo], *m.* Achromatism, freedom from spherical aberration.

Acromatizar [ah-cro-mah-tee-thar'], *va.* To render achromatic; to achromatize.

Acrónicamente [ah-cro'-ne-cah-men'-tay], *adv.* (Ast.) Acronycally.

Acrónico, ca [ah-cro'-ne-co, cah], *a.* Acronycal, applied to the rising of a star when the sun sets, or its setting when the sun rises.

Acróstico, ca [ah-cros'-te-co, cah], *a.* *Versos acrósticos*, Acrostics.

Acrotera, Acroteria [ah-cro-tay'-ra, ah-cro-tay'-re-a], *f.* 1. A small pedestal placed at the extremities of pediments, and serving also to support figures, etc. 2. The highest part of columns or buildings.

Acroterio [ah-cro-tay'-re-o], *m.* The superior of the three parts of which the frontispiece of a building is composed.

Acta [ahc'-tah], *f.* Act or record of proceedings.—*pl.* 1. The acts or records of communities, chapters, councils. Papers, file, etc. (Com.) 2. *Actas de los santos*, The lives of the saints.

Actimo [ac-tee'-mo], *m.* The twelfth part of a measure called *punto;* there are 1,728 *actimos* in a geometric foot

Actina [ac-tee'-nah], *m.* Actin.

Actinia [ac-tee'-ne-ah], *f.* Actinia, sea-anemone.

Actitud [ac-te-tood'], *f.* Attitude, position, posture.

Activador [ac-te-vah-dor'], *m.* (Chem.) Activator.

Activamente [ac-te-vah-men'-tay], *adv.* Actively.

Activar [ac-te-var'], *va.* To push, make brisk, hasten.

Activas, *f. pl.* **Activo**, *m.* [ac-tee'-vahs, ac-tee'-vo]. (Com.) Assets, outstanding claims.

Actividad [ac-te-ve-dad'], *f.* 1. Activity. 2. Quickness in performing; liveliness, nimbleness.

Activo, va [ac-tee'-vo, vah], *a.* Active, diligent, forward, fiery. *Voz activa*, Suffrage.

Acto [ahc'-to], *m.* 1. Act or action. 2. Act of a play. 3. Thesis defended in universities. 4. Carnal communication. *Actos*, (Obs.) 1. *V.* AUTOS. 2. Document, papers.

Actor [ac-tor'], *m.* 1. Performer, player. 2. (Obs.) Author. 3. Plaintiff, claimant. 4. Proctor, attorney.

Actora [ac-to'-rah], *f.* Plaintiff, she who seeks justice.

Actriz [ac-treeth'], *f.* Actress.

Actuación [ac-too-ah-the-on'], *f.* Actuation, moving.

Actuado, da [ac-too-ah'-do, dah], *a.* 1. Actuated. 2. Skilled, experienced.—*pp.* of ACTUAR.

Actual [ac-too-ahl'], *a.* Actual, present.

Actualidad [ac-too-ah-le-dad'], *f.* The actual or present state of things.

Actualizar [ac-too-ah-le-thar'], *va.* (Prov.) To realize.

Actualmente [ac-too-al-men'-tay], *adv.* Actually, at present.

Actuante [ac-too-an'-tay], *pa.* Defender of a thesis in colleges.

Actuar [ac-too-ar'], *va.* 1. To digest. 2. (Met.) To consider, to weigh maturely. 3. To perform judicial acts. 4. To instruct; to support a thesis.

Actuario [ac-too-ah'-re-o], *m.* The clerk of a court of justice (who is always a notary public).

Acuadrillar [ah-coo-ah-dril-lyar'], *va.* To collect or head a band of armed men; to conduct a squadron of soldiers; to form or to head parties.

Acuafortista [ah-coo-ah-for-tees'-tah], *m.* Etcher.

Acuanauta [ah-coo-ah-nah'-oo-tah], *m.* Aquanaut.

Acuarela [ah-coo-ah-ray'-lah], *f.* Watercolor.

Acuarelista [ah-coo-ah-ray-lees'-tah], *com.* Watercolorist.

Acuarelístico, ca [ah-coo-ah-ray-lees'-te-co, cah], *a.* Watercolor.

Acuario [ah-coo-ah'-re-o], *m.* 1. Aquarium. 2. Aquarius.

Acuartelado, da [ah-coo-ar-tay-lah'-do, dah], *a.* Divided into quarters.—*pp.* of ACUARTELAR.

Acuartelamiento [ah-coo-ar-tay-lah-me-en'-to], *m.* 1. The act of quartering the troops. 2. Quarters.

Acuartelar [ah-coo-ar-tay-lar'], *va.* To quarter troops. *Acuartelar las velas*, (Naut.) To flat in the sails.

Acuartillar [ah-coo-ar-til-lyar'], *vn.* To bend in the quarters under a heavy load; applied to beasts of burden.

Acuático, ca [ah-coo-ah'-te-co, cah], *a.* *V.* ACUÁTIL.

Acuátil [ah-coo-ah'-teel], *a.* Aquatic, living or growing in water.

Acucia [ah-coo'-the-ah], *f.* Zeal, diligence, haste.

Acuciar [ah-coo-the-ar'], *va.* 1. (Obs.) To stimulate, to hasten. 2. *V.* CODICIAR.

Acucioso, sa [ah-coo-the-o'-so, sah], *a.* Zealous, hasty.

Acuclillado, da [ah-coo-cleel-lyah'-do, dah], *a.* Cowering, squatting (fr. Cuclillas).

Acuclillarse [ah-coo-cleel-lyar'-say], *vr.* To crouch, squat.

Acucharado, da [ah-coo-chah-rah'-do, dah], *a.* Spoon-like

Acuchillado, da [ah-coo-cheel-lyah'-do, dah], *a.* 1. Slashed, stabbed. 2. (Met.) Experienced, skilful by long practice. 3. Slashed or cut in oblong pieces: applied to garments.—*pp.* of ACUCHILLAR.

Acuchillador, ra [ah-coo-cheel-lyah-dor', rah], *m.* & *f.* 1. A quarrelsome person, a bully. 2. Gladiator.

Acuchillar [ah-coo-cheel-lyar'], *va.* 1. To cut or hack, to give cuts with a sabre. 2. (Obs.) To murder.—*vr.* To fight with knives or swords.

Acudimiento [ah-coo-de-me-en'-to], *m.* Aid, assistance.

Acudir [ah-coo-deer'], *vn.* 1. To assist, to succour, to support; to run to, to repair to. 2. To produce; to be docile. 3. To have recourse. *La casa quemada acudir con el agua,* To come with the water when the house is burnt down.

Acueducto [ah-coo-ay-dooc'-to], *m.* 1. Aqueduct. 2. Eustachian tube. It was anciently written *acueducho.*

Acuén, Acuende [ah-coo-en', ah-coo-en'-day], *adv.* (Obs.) Hither.

Acueo, a [ah'-coo-ay-oh, ah], *a.* Watery.

Acuerdado, da [ah-coo-er-dah'-do, dah], *a.* Constructed by line or rule.

Acuerdo [ah-coo-er'-do], *m.* 1. Result of the deliberation of a tribunal, assembly, or meeting. 2. Body of the members of a tribunal assembled in the form of a court. 3. Opinion, advice. 4. Concurrence, accord. 5. Reflection, prudence. 6. Memory. 7. (Art) Harmony of colours. *De acuerdo,* Unanimously, by common consent. *Ponerse* or *estar de acuerdo,* To agree unanimously, to come to an understanding. *Acuerdos del reino,* Remonstrances made by the states of the realm.

(*Yo acuerdo, yo acuerde,* from *Acordar. V.* ACORDAR.)

(*Yo me acuerdo, yo me acuerde,* from *Acordarse. V.* ACORDAR.)

(*Yo acuesto, yo acueste,* from *Acostar. V.* ACORDAR.)

(*Yo me acuesto, yo me acueste,* from *Acostarse. V.* ACORDAR.)

Acuitar [ah-coo-e-tar'], *va.* To afflict, to oppress.—*vr.* To grieve.

Acular [ah-coo-lar'], *va.* (Coll.) To force one into a corner; to oblige one to retreat.

Aculebrinado, da [ah-coo-lay-bree-nah'-do, dah], *a.* Made in the form of a culverin: applied to cannon which from their length resemble culverins.

Acúleo, a [ah-coo'-lay-o, ah], *a.* Aculeate, possessing a string.—*m.* A section of hymenoptera. (Bot.) Aculeate, having prickles.

Acullá [ah-cool-lyah'], *adv.* On the other side, yonder; opposite. *Aquí y acullá,* Here and there.

Acúmetro [ah-coo'-may-tro], *m.* An acoumeter, a device for testing the hearing.

Acumineo, ea [ah-coo-me'-nay-o, ah], *a.* Acuminate, ending in a point.

Acumulación [ah-coo-moo-lah-the-on'], *f.* 1. Accumulation, gathering. 2. Act of filing records.

Acumulador, ra [ah-coo-moo-lah-dor', rah], *a.* Accumulating —*m.* & *f.* Accumulator.—*m.* Storage battery.

Acumular [ah-coo-moo-lar'], *va.* 1. To accumulate, to heap together, to treasure up, to hoard, to lay up. 2. To impute, to upbraid with a fault. 3. To file records.

Acumulativamente [ah-coo-moo-lah-te-vah-men'-tay], *adv.* (Law) 1. By way of prevention; by way of precaution. 2. Jointly, accumulatively.

Acumulativo, va [ah-coo-moo-lah-te'-vo, vah], *a.* 1. Precautionary. 2. Accumulative.

Acuñación [ah-coo-nyah-the-on'], *f.* Coining, milling.

Acuñador, ra [ah-coo-nyah-dor, rah], *m.* & *f.* Coiner.

Acuñar [ah-coo-nyar'], *va.* 1. To coin. 2. To wedge, or fasten with wedges. *Acuñar dinero,* (Met.) To hoard up money. *Hermano ayuda y cuñado acuña,* Brothers and sisters-in-law are always at variance.

Acuosidad [ah-coo-o-se-dad'], *f.* Wateriness.

Acuoso, sa [ah-coo-o'-so, sah], *a.* Watery, aqueous.

Acupuntura [ah-coo-poon-too'-rah], *f.* Acupuncture, a surgical mode of counter-irritation by needle thrusts.

Acurrucarse [ah-coor-roo-car'-say], *vr.* To muffle one's self up.

Acurrullar [ah-coor-rool-lyar'] *va.* (Naut.) To take down the sails of a galley.

Acusable [ah-coo-sah'-blay], *a.* Accusable, indictable.

Acusación [ah-cooh-sah-the-on'], *f.* Accusation, impeachment, charge, expostulation.

Acusador, ra [ah-coo-sah-dor', rah], *m.* & *f.* Accuser, informer.

Acusar [ah-coo-sar'], *va.* 1. To accuse, to criminate, to lay against, to indict. 2. To acknowledge the receipt of. 3. To take charge of.—*vr.* To acknowledge sins to a confessor.

Acusativo [ah-coo-sah-tee'-vo], *m.* Accusative, the fourth case in the declension of the Latin nouns.

Acusatorio, ria [ah-coo-sah-to'-re-o, ah], *a.* Accusatory, belonging to an accusation.

Acuse [ah-coo'-say], *m.* At cards, a certain number estimated to win so much.

Acústica [ah-coos'-te-cah], *f.* Acoustics, the doctrine or theory of sounds.

Acústico, ca [ah-coos'-te-co, cah], *a.* Acoustic.

Acutángulo [ah-coo-tahn'-goo-lo], *a.* (Geom.) Acute-angled.

Achacar [ah-chah-car'], *va.* 1. To impute; to father. 2. To frame an excuse.—*vr.* To ascribe a thing or action to one's self.

Achacosamente [ah-chah-co-sah-men'-tay], *adv.* Sickly.

Achacoso, sa [ah-chah-co'-so, sah], *a.* Sickly, unhealthy.

Achaflanar [ah-chah-flah-nar'], *va.* To lower one end of a table, plank, or board; to chamfer, bevel.

Achancharse [ah-chan-char'-say], *vr.* (Peru.) To become lazy like a hog.

Achantarse [ah-chan-tar'-say], *vr.* (Coll.) To hide during danger.

Achaparrado, da [ah-chah-par-rah'-do, dah], *a.* Of the size of a shrub. *Hombre achaparrado,* A short and lusty man.

Achaparrarse [ah-chah-par-rahr'-say], *vr.* To grow stunted.

Achaque [ah-chah'-kay], *m.* 1. Habitual indisposition. 2. Monthly courses. 3. Excuse, pretext. 4. A failing. 5. Composition with a smuggler. 6. (Law) Mulct, penalty.

Achaquero [ah-chah-kay'-ro], *m.* 1. A magistrate of the board of *mesta* in Spain. 2. He who farms the fines laid on by the magistrate called *achaquero.*

Achaquiento, ta [ah-chah-kee-en'-to, tah], *a. V.* ACHACOSO.

Achaquillo, ito [ah-chah-keel'-lyo, kee'-to], *m. dim.* A slight complaint.

Acharolar [ah-chah-ro-lar'], *va.* To japan, or to paint in imitation of varnish.

Achatar [ah-chah-tar'], *va.* To flatter, (fr. Chato).

Achicado, da [ah-che-cah'-do, dah], *a.* Diminished. *V.* ANIÑADO, childish. —*pp.* of ACHICAR.

Achicador, ra [ah-che-cah-dor', rah], *m.* & *f.* 1. Diminisher, reducer. 2. (Naut.) Scoop for baling boats. 3. He who bales a mine.

Achicadura [ah-che-cah-doo'-rah], *f.* Diminution, reduction.

Achicar [ah-che-car'], *va.* 1. To diminish, to lessen. 2. To bale a boat or drain a mine. *Achicar un cabo,* To shorten a rope. *Achicar el agua del navío,* To free the ship.

Achicharrar [ah-che-char-rar'], *va.* To fry meat too much; to over-heat.

Achichinque [ah-che-cheen'-kay], *m.* A miner whose business is to drain the mines of water.

Achicoria [ah-che-co'-re-ah], *f.* (Bot.) Succory, wild endive, chicory. Cichorium intybus, sive sylvestre.

Achinar [ah-che-nar'], *va.* (Coll.) To intimidate, to terrify.

Achinelado, da [ah-che-nay-lah'-do, dah], *a.* Slipper-shaped.

Achiote, Achote [ah-che-o'-tay, ah-cho'-tay], *m.* (Bot.) The heart-leaved bixa or anotta. Bixa orellana.

Achispado, da [ah-chis-pah'-do, dah], *a.* Tipsy.

Achisparse [ah-chis-par'-say], *vr.* (Coll.) To get tipsy.

Achocar [ah-cho-car'], *va.* 1. To throw one against the wall. 2. To knock asunder. 3. (Coll.) To hoard money.

Achorizado, da [ah-cho-re-thah'-do, dah], *a.* Slashed; made into sausages.

Achubascarse [ah-choo-bas-car'-say], *vr.* (Naut.) To get squally and showery.

Achuchar, Achuchurrar [ah-choo-char', ah-choo-choor-rar'], *va.* (Coll.) To crush with a blow.

Achuchón [ah-choo-chone'], *m.* (Coll.) A push, a squeeze.

Achulado, da [ah-choo-lah'-do, dah], *a.* Waggish, frolicsome.

Ada [ah'-dah], *f.* 1. A small apple of the pippin kind. 2. A very poisonous plant of Numidia. 3. (Zool.) A kind of fly-catcher.

Adad [ah-dahd'], *m.* Name of the Creator among the Syrians; the dragon, a noted idol among the Philistines.

Adafina [ah-dah-fee'-nah], *f.* Sort of stewed meat or fricassee, formerly used by the Jews in Spain.

Adagio [ah-dah'-he-o], *m.* 1. Proverb. 2. (Mus.) Adagio, a term used by musicians to mark a slow time. 3. A piece of music in adagio time.

Adaguar [ah-dah-goo-ar'], *va.* (Obs.) *V.* ABREVAR.

Adala [ah-dah'-lah], *f.* (Naut.) Pump-deal.

Adalid [ah-dah-leed'], *m.* A chief, a commander.

Adamado, da [ah-dah-mah'-do, dah], *a.* Lady-like: applied to vulgar women.

Adamantino, na [ah-dah-man-tee'-no, nah], *a.* (Obs.) Adamantine.

Adamar [ah-dah-mar'], *va.* (Obs.) To love violently.—*vr.* To become as delicate in the face, or in manners, as a lady: to degenerate.

Adamascado, da [ah-dah-mas-cah'-do, dah], *a.* Damask-like.—*pp.* of ADAMASCAR.

Adamascar [ah-dah-mas-car'], *va.* To damask.

Adamita [ah-dah-mee'-tah], *m.* Adamite.

Adán [ah-dahn'], *m.* Adam.

Adaptabilidad [ah-dap-tah-be-le-dahd'], *f* Adaptability adjustment to environmental conditions.

Adaptable [ah-dap-tah'-blay], *a.* Capable of being adapted.

Adaptación [ah-dap-tah-the-on'], *f.* The act of fitting one thing to another accommodation.

Adaptadamente [ah-dap-tah-dah-men'-tay], *adv.* In a fit manner.

Adaptar [ah-dap-tar'], *va.* To adapt, to fit, to apply one thing to another, to fashion.—*vr.* To cohere.

Adaraja [ah-dah-rah'-hah], *f.* (Arch.) Projecting stones left to continue a wall.

Adarce [ah-dar'-thay], *m.* 1. Salt froth of the sea dried on canes. 2. *pl.* Carbonate of lime which certain mineral waters deposit.

Adarga [ah-dar'-gah], *f.* A shield of an oval form made of leather.

Adargar [ah-dar-gar'], *va.* To shield.

Adarguero [ah-dar-gay'-ro], *m.* (Obs.) One who used a shield.

Adarguilla [ah-dar-geel'-lyah], *f.* A small shield.

Adarme [ah-dar'-may], *m.* Half a drachm, the sixteenth part of an ounce. *Por adarmes*, Very sparingly.

Adarvar [ah-dar-var'], *va.* (Obs.) To astonish, astound.

Adarve [ah-dar'-vay], *m.* The flat top of a wall.

Adatar [ah-dah-tar'], *va.* To open an account; to credit. 2. To annotate, to comment.

Adatoda [ah-dah-to'-dah], *f.* (Bot.) The willow-leaved Malabar nut-tree.

Adaza [ah-dah'-thah], *f.* (Bot.) Common panic-grass. *V.* Panizo.

Adecenamiento [ah-day-thay-nah-me-en'-to], *m.* Act of forming by ten and ten.

Adecenar [ah-day-thay-nar'], *va.* To form people by ten and ten.

Adecentar [ah-day-then-tar'], *va.* To render decent.

Adecuación [ah-day-coo-ah-the-on'], *f.* Fitness.

Adecuadamente [ah-day-coo-ah-dah-men'-tay], *adv.* Fitly, properly, to the purpose.

Adecuado, da [ah-day-coo-ah'-do, dah], *a.* Adequate, fit, competent.—*pp.* of Adecuar.

Adecuar [ah-day-coo-ar'], *va.* To fit, to accommodate.

Adefesio [ah-day-fay'-se-o], *m.* (Coll.) Extravagance, folly; any thing not to the purpose. Ridiculous attire.

Adehala [ah-day-ah'-lah], *f.* Gratuity, perquisite.

Adehesado [ah-day-ay-sah'-do], *m.* Place converted into pasture.—*pp.* of Adehesar.

Adehesamiento [ah-day-ay-sah-me-en'-to], *m.* Turning land to pasture, pasturage.

Adehesar [ah-day-ay-sar'], *va.* To convert land into pasture.

Adelantadamente [ah-day-lan-tah-dah-men'-tay], *adv.* Beforehand.

Adelantadillo [ah-day-lan-tah-deel'-lyo], *a.* (Ant.) Red wine made of the first ripe grapes.

Adelantado [ah-day-lan-tah'-do], *m.* An appellation formerly given to the governor of a province.

Adelantado, da [ah-day-lan-tah'-do, dah], *a.* 1. Anticipated, advanced, forehand, onward, bold, forward. 2. Early, when applied to fruit or plants.—*pp.* of Adelantar.

Adelantador, ra [ah-day-lan-tah-dor', rah], *m.* & *f.* One that advances, extends, or amplifies.

Adelantamiento [ah-day-lan-tah-me-en'-to], *m.* 1. Progress, improvement, increase; growth, furtherance; cultivation, good. 2. Anticipation. 3. The dignity of the governor formerly called *adelantado*, and the district of his jurisdiction.

Adelantar [ah-day-lan-tar'], *va.* 1. To advance, to accelerate, to forward; to graduate; to grow, to keep on. 2. To anticipate, to pay beforehand. 3. (Met.) To improve. 4. (Obs.) To push forward. 5. To get ahead.—*vr.* 1. To take the lead, to overrun, to come forward. 2. (Met.) To excel, to outdo.

Adelante [ah-day-lahn'-tay], *adv.* Farther off; higher up; forward, onward. *En adelante*, Henceforth, in future, or for the future. *Quien adelante no mira, atrás se queda*, Look before you leap. *Adelante*, Go on; or, I understand.

Adelanto [ah-day-lahn'-to], *m.* (Com.) Advance, progress. Advance payment.

Adelfa [ah-del'-fah], *f.* (Bot.) Oleander. Rose-bay. Nerium oleander.

Adelfal [ah-del-fahl'], *m.* Plantation of rose-bay trees.

Adelfilla [ah-del-feel'-lyah], *f.* The flowering osier, a shrub.

Adelfo, fa [ah-del'-fo, fah], *a.* (Bot.) Adelphous, having stamens united by their filaments; chiefly used in composition.

Adelgazado, da [ah-del-gah-thah'-do, dah], *a.* Made slender or thin.—*pp.* of Adelgazar.

Adelgazador, ra [ah-del-gah-thah-dor', rah], *m.* & *f.* One that makes thin or slender.

Adelgazamiento [ah-del-gah-thah-me-en'-to], *m.* Act of making slender.

Adelgazar [ah-del-gah-thar'], *va.* 1. To attenuate, to make thin, slender. 2. To lessen. 3. To refine. 4. (Met.) To discuss with subtilty.—*vr.* To become slender.

Adelógeno, na [ah-day-lo'-hay-no, nah], *a.* Adelogenous, a term used of rocks, whose chemical composition is undetermined or obscure.

Adema [ah-day'-mah], *f.* **Ademe** [ah-day'-may], *m.* (Min.) The timber with which the sides of mines are secured. Shore, strut.

Ademador [ah-day-mah-dor'], *m.* (Min.) A workman employed in lining the sides of mines with boards.

Ademán [ah-day-mahn'], *m.* 1. A gesture, by which approbation or dislike is expressed; look, manner. 2. (Art) Attitude. *En ademán*, In the attitude or posture of performing something.

Ademar [ah-day-mar'], *va.* (Min.) To secure the sides of mines with planks or timber; to shore.

Además [ah-day-mahs'], *adv.* 1. Moreover, likewise, further; short of this; besides. 2. (Obs.) Too much.

Adementar [ah-day-men-tar'], *va.* To disturb the reason, to addle.

Adenitis [ah-day-nee'-tis], *f.* Adenitis, inflammation of a gland.

Adenografía [ah-day-no-grah-fee'-ah], *f.* A treatise on the glands.

Adenología [ah-day-no-lo-hee'-ah], *f.* (Anat.) Description of the glands.

Adenoso, sa [ah-day-no'-so, sah], *a.* Glandular.

Adentellar [ah-den-tel-lyar'], *va.* To bite, to catch with the teeth. *Adentellar una pared*, To leave toothing-stones or bricks to continue a wall.

Adentro [ah-den'-tro], *adv.* Within. Come in, calling to persons knocking at a door. *De botones adentro*, In my heart. *Ser muy de adentro*, To be intimate in a house. *¡Ah de adentro!* Within there! *Adentros*, The interior, the recesses of the mind, the secret thought.

Adepto [ah-dep'-to], *m.* Adept; initiated into the mysteries of a science or secret sect.

Aderezar [ah-day-ray-thar'], *va.* 1. To dress, to adorn. 2. (Obs.) To prepare. 3. To clean, to repair. *Aderezar la comida*, To dress victuals.

Aderezo [ah-day-ray'-tho], *m.* 1. Dressing and adorning; finery. 2. Gum, starch, and other ingredients, used to stiffen cloth with. *Aderezo de mesa*, A service for the table; applied to oil, vinegar, and salt. *Aderezo de comida*, Condiment. *Aderezo de diamantes*, A set of diamonds. *Aderezo de caballo*, Trappings or caparisons of a saddle-horse. *Aderezo de casa*, Furniture. *Aderezo de espada*, Hilt, hook, and other appendages of a sword.

Aderra [ah-der'-rah], *f.* A rope, made of rush, used for pressing the husks of grapes.

Adestrado, da [ah-des-trah'-do, dah], *a.* 1. Broken in. 2. (Her.) On the dexter side of the escutcheon; it is also applied to the principal figure in an escutcheon, on the right of which is another.—*pp.* of Adestrar.

Adestrador, ra [ah-des-trah-dor', rah], *m.* & *f.* 1. Teacher. 2. Censor, critic.

Adestrar [ah-des-trar'], *va.* 1. To guide, to lead. 2. To teach. 3. To train.—*vr.* To exercise one's self.

Adeudado, da [ah-day-oo-dah'-do, dah], *a.* 1. Indebted. 2. (Obs.) Obliged.—*pp.* of Adeudar.

Adeudar [ah-day-oo-dar'], *va.* 1. To pay duty. 2. (Com.) To charge, debit.—*vr.* To be indebted, incur debt.

Adherencia [ad-ay-ren'-the-ah], *f.* 1. Alliance, adherence to a sect or party. 2 Relationship, friendship. 3. Adhesion.—*pl.* (Surg.) Adhesions.

Adherente [ad-ay-ren'-tay], *a.* Adherent.—*m.* Follower.—*pl.* Ingredients.

Adherir [ad-ay-reer'], *vn.* To adhere to a sect or party; to espouse an opinion, to cleave to.—*vr.* To hold.

Adhesión [ad-ay-se-on'], *f.* Adhesion; cohesion, attachment.

Adhesivo, va [ad-ay-see'-vo, vah], *a.* Adhesive, capable of adhering.

(*Yo adhiero, yo adhiera; él adhirió, él adhiriera*, from *Adherir. V.* Asentir.)

Adiado [ah-de-ah'-do].—*pp.* Adiar.

Adiamantado, da [ah-de-ah-man-tah'-do, dah], *a.* Adamantine.

Adiar [ah-de-ahr'], *va.* (Obs.) To appoint, to set a day.

Adición [ah-de-the-on'], *f.* 1. Addition. 2. Remark or note put to accounts. *Adición de la herencia*, Acceptance of an inheritance. 3. Addition, the first rule of arithmetic. 4. Advance (of salary).

Adicionador, ra [ah-de-the-o-nah-dor', rah], *m.* & *f.* One that makes additions.

Adicional [ah-de-the-o-nahl'], *a.* Supplementary.

Adicionalmente [ah-de-the-o-nal-men'-tay], *adv.* Additionally.

Adicionar [ah-de-the-o-nar'], *va.* To make additions.

Adicto, ta [ah-deec'-to, tah], *a.* Addicted, attached.

Adicto, *m.* Addict.

Adieso [ah-de-ay'-so], *adv.* (Obs.) At the moment, instantly.

Adiestrar [ah-de-es-trar'], *va.* *V.* Adestrar.

(*Yo adiestro, yo adiestre*, from *Adestrar. V.* Acertar.)

Adietar [ah-de-ay-tar'], *va.* To diet.

Adinamia [ah-de-nah'-me-ah], *f.* Adynamia, debility, great weakness.

Adinámico, ca [ah-de-nah'-me-co, cah], *a.* Adynamic, lacking force.

Adinas [ah-dee'-nas], *f. pl.* *V.* Adivas.

Adinerado, da [ah-de-nay-rah'-do, dah], *a.* Rich, wealthy.

Adintelado, da [ah-din-tay-lah'-do, dah], *a.* Falling from an arch gradually into a straight line.

Adiós [a-de-os'], *int.* Good-bye, adieu.

Adipocira [ah-de-po-thee'-rah], *f.* Adipocere, a soft, unctuous substance sometimes replacing the materials of dead bodies after submersion or burial in moist places.

Adiposo, sa [ah-de-po'-so, sah], *a.* (Med.) Fat, adipose. *V.* SEBOSO.

Adir [ah-deer'], *va.* To accept, to receive an inheritance.

Aditamento [ah-de-tah-men'-to], *m.* Addition.

Adiva [ah-dee'-vah], *f.* **Adive** [ah-dee'-vay], *m.* Jackal. Canis aureus. *Adivas*, Vives, some swellings in the glands under the ears of horses, much resembling the strangles.

Adivina, *f.* = ADIVINANZA.

Adivinable [ah -de-ve-nah'-blay], *a.* Capable of conjecture, or foretelling.

Adivinación [ah-de-ve-nah-the-on'], *f.* Divination.

Adivinador, ra [ah-de-ve-nah-dor', rah], *m. & f.* A diviner, a soothsayer.

Adivinamiento [ah-de-ve-nah-me-en'-to], *m.* *V.* ADIVINACIÓN.

Adivinanza [ah-de-ve-nan'-thah], *f.* (Coll.) 1. Prophecy, prediction. 2. Enigma, riddle, conundrum. 3. Guess. 4. *V.* ADIVINACIÓN.

Adivinar [ah-de-ve-nar'], *va.* 1. To foretell future events, to soothsay. 2. To conjecture, anticipate, or divine, to give a guess. 3. To unriddle an enigma or difficult problem; to find out.

Adivino, na [ah-de-vee'-no, nah], *m. & f.* 1. Soothsayer. 2. Foreboder, fortuneteller.

Adjetivación [ad-hay-te-vah-the-on'], *f.* Act of uniting one thing to another.

Adjetivar [ad-hay-te-var'], *va.* (Coll.) To unite.

Adjetivo [ad-hay-tee'-vo], *m.* (Gram.) Adjective.

Adjudicación [ad-hoo-de-cah-the-on'], *f.* Act of adjudging. *A. a pública subasta*, Auction-sale; "knocking-down" at auction—*al mejor postor*, to the highest bidder.

Adjudicar [ad-hoo-de-car'], *va.* To adjudge, to sell at auction.—*vr.* To appropriate to one's self.

Adjudicativo, va [ad-hoo-de-cah-tee'-vo, vah], *a.* Adjudicating.

Adjudicatario, ria [ad-hoo-de-cah-tah'-re-o, ah], *m. & f.* One to whom something is adjudged; grantee.

Adjunta [ad-hoon'-tah], *f.* Letter inclosed in another.

Adjunto, ta [ad-hoon'-to, tah], *a.* Joined, annexed, inclosed. Adjunct.

Adjunto [ad-hoon'-to], *m.* *V.* ADJETIVO and ADITAMENTO. *Adjuntos*, A body of judges commissioned or appointed jointly to try a cause.

Adjurar [ad-hoo-rar'], *va.* (Obs.) To conjure, exorcise; supplicate.

Adjutor, ra [ad-hoo-tor', rah], *a. & n.* Adjuvant; helper.

Adminicular [ad-me-ne-coo-lar'], *va.* (Law) To increase the power and efficacy of a thing by adding collateral aids.

Adminículo [ad-me-nee'-coo-lo], *m.* Prop, support, aid.

Administración [ad-me-nis-trah-the-on'], *f.* 1. Administration, management. 2. Office of an administrator. *En administración*, In trust: applied to places in which the occupant has no property.

Administrador, ra [ad-me-nis-trah-dor', rah], *m. & f.* Administrator, manager; steward, director, trustee. *Administrador de orden*, A knight who administers a commandery for another, incapable of doing it himself.

Administrar [ad-me-nis-trar'], *va.* 1. To administer, to govern. 2. To serve an office.

Administrativo, va [ad-me-nis-trah-tee'-vo, vah], *a.* Administrative, that does administer.

Administratorio, ria [ad-me-nis-trah-to'-re-o, ah], *a.* (Law) Belonging to an administration or administrator.

Admirable [ad-me-rah'-blay], *a.* Admirable, excellent.

Admirable [ad-me-rah'-blay], *m.* A hymn in Roman Catholic churches in praise of the eucharist, at the time it is reserved in the tabernacle.

Admirablemente [ad-me-rah-blay-men'-tay], *adv.* Admirably, marvellously.

Admiración [ad-me-rah-the-on'], *f.* 1. Wonder; sudden surprise. 2. Point of exclamation, ¡!. 3. Prodigy. *Es una admiración*, It is a thing worthy of admiration.

Admirador, ra [ad-me-rah-dor', rah], *m. & f.* Admirer.

Admirar [ad-me-rar'], *va.* To cause admiration; to marvel, to contemplate.—*vr.* To be seized with admiration; to make a wonder.

Admirativo, va [ad-me-rah-tee'-vo, vah], *a.* Admiring, wondering.

Admisible [ad-me-see'-blay], *a.* Admissible.

Admisión [ad-me-se-on'], *f.* Admission, acceptance.

Admitir [ad-me-teer'], *va.* 1. To receive, to give entrance. 2. To concede; to accept. 3. To admit; to permit; to find. *Bien admitido*, Well received. *El asunto no admite dilación*, The affair admits of no delay.

Admonición [ad-mo-ne-the-on'], *f.* Warning, counsel, advice.

Admonitor [ad-mo-ne-tor'], *m.* Monitor, in some religious communities.

Adnado, da [ad-nah'-do, dah], *m. & f.* Step-son, step-daughter.

Adnata [ad-nah'-tah], *f.* (Anat.) Adnata, the external white membrane of the eye.

Adnato, ta [ad-nah'-to, tah], *a.* (Bot.) Adnate, adherent.

Adnotación [ad-no-tah-the-on'], *f.* The papal seal affixed to certain concessions.

Adobado, da [ah-do-bah'-do, dah], *a.* Pickled; curried, dressed.—*pp.* of ADOBAR.

Adobado [ah-do-bah'-do], *m.* 1. Pickled pork. 2. (Obs.) Any sort of dressed meat.

Adobador, ra [ah-do-bah-dor', rah], *m. & f.* Dresser, preparer.

Adobamiento, *m.* A kind of stew, so-called from the French *á la daube.*

Adobar [ah-do-bar'], *va.* 1. To dress or make any thing up. 2. To pickle pork or other meat. 3. To cook. 4. To tan hides. 5. (Obs.) To contract, to stipulate.

Adobasillas [ah-do-bah-seel'-lyas], *m.* One that makes or repairs straw bottoms for chairs.

Adobe [ah-do'-bay], *m.* A brick not yet burnt, baked in the sun. (Arab. Atob.)

Adobera [ah-do-bay'-rah], *f.* A mould for making bricks.

Adobería [ah-do-bay-ree'-ah], *f.* 1. A brick-yard. 2. *V.* TENERÍA.

Adobo [ah-do'-bo], *m.* 1. Repairing, mending. 2. Pickle-sauce. 3. Ingredients for dressing leather or cloth. 4. Pomade, cosmetic.

Adocenado, da [ah-do-thay-nah'-do, dah], *a.* Common, ordinary, vulgar. —*pp.* ADOCENAR.

Adocenar [ah-do-thay-nar'], *va.* 1. To count or sell by dozens. 2. To despise.

Adoctrinar [ah-doc-tree-nar'], *va.* To instruct. *V.* DOCTRINAR.

Adolecer [ah-do-lay-therr'], *vn.* 1. To be seized with illness. 2. To labour under disease or affliction.—*va.* (Obs.) To produce pain or disease.

Adolescencia [ah-do-les-then'-the-ah], *f.* Adolescence.

Adolescente [ah-do-les-then -tay], *a.* Adolescent, young.—*m. & f.* Adolescent, teen ager.

(*Yo adolezco*, from *Adolecer.* V. ABORRECER.)

Adolorado, Adolorido, *a.* *V.* DOLORIDO.

Adomiciliarse [ah-do-me-the-le-ar'-say], *va.* *V.* DOMICILIARSE.

Adonado, da [ah-do-nah'-do, dah], *a.* (Obs.) 1. Endowed by Nature; gifted. 2. Witty.

Adonde [ah-don'-day], *adv.* Whither? to what place? where. *Adonde quiera*, To whatever place you please.

Adónico, Adonio [ah-do'-ne-co, ah-do'-ne-o], *m.* A Latin verse consisting of a dactyl and a spondee.

Adonis [ah-do'-nis], *m.* Adonis, handsome youth.

Adopción [ah-dop-the-on'], *f.* Adoption taking another man's child for one's own.

Adoptable [ah-dop-tah'-blay], *a.* Adoptable, suitable for adopting.

Adoptador, ra [ah-dop-tah-dor', rah], *m. & f.* Adopter.

Adoptar [ah-dop-tar'], *va.* 1. To adopt, to father. 2. To embrace an opinion. 3. (Obs.) To graft.

Adoptivo, va [ah-dop-tee'-vo, vah], *a.* Adoptive.

Adoquier, Adoquiera [ah-do-ke-err', ah-do-ke-ay'-rah], *adv.* (Obs.) Where you please.

Adoquín [ah-do-keen'], *m.* Paving-stone, binding-stone of a pavement. (Coll.) A dull, sluggish person.

Adoquinar [ah-do-ke-nar'], *va.* To pave.

Ador [ah-dor'], *m.* The time for watering land, where the water is distributed.

Adorable [ah-do-rah'-blay], *a.* Adorable, worshipful.

Adoración [ah-do-rah-the-on'], *f.* Adoration, worship.

Adorador, ra [ah-do-rah-dor', rah], *m. & f.* One that adores, worshipper.

Adorar [ah-do-rar'], *va.* 1. To adore to reverence with religious worship, to idolatrize. 2. To love excessively.

Adoratorio [ah-do-rah-to'-re-o], *m.* A name given by the Spaniards to the temples of idols in America; teocalli.

Adormecedor, ra [ah-dor-may-thay-dor', rah], *a.* Soporiferous, soporific.

Adormecer [ah-dor-may-therr'], *vr.* 1. To cause drowsiness or sleep; to lull asleep. 2. To calm, to lull.—*vr.* 1. To fall asleep. 2. To grow benumbed or torpid. 3. (Met.) To grow or persist in vice.

Adormecido, da [ah-dor-may-thee'-do, dah], *a.* Mopish; sleepy, drowsy.—*pp.* of ADORMECER.

Adormecimiento [ah-dor-may-the-me-en'-to], *m.* Drowsiness, slumber, sleepiness, numbness, mopishness.

(*Yo adormezco*, from *Adormecer.* *V.* ABORRECER.)

Adormidera [ah-dor-me-day'-rah], *f.* (Bot.) Poppy. Papaver somniferum.

Adormir [ah-dor-meer'], *vn.* 1. To fall asleep. 2. (Obs.) To sound softly (said of a musical instrument).

Adormitarse [ah-dor-me-tar'-say], *vr.* *V.* DORMITAR.
Adornador, ra [ah-dor-nah-dor', rah], *m.* & *f.* Adorner.
Adornar [ah-dor-nar'], *va.* 1. To beautify, to embellish, to grace, to ornament. 2. To furnish; to garnish. 3. To accomplish; to adorn with talents.
Adornista [ah-dor-nees'-tah], *m.* Painter of ornaments.
Adorno [ah-dor'-no], *m.* 1. Adorning, accomplishment. 2. Ornament, finery, decoration, habiliment. 3. Garniture, 4. *Adorno de una casa*, Furniture.
Adquiridor, ra [ad-ke-re-dor', rah], *m.* & *f.* Acquirer. *A buen adquiridor buen expendedor*, After a gatherer comes a scatterer.
Adquirir [ad-ke-reer'], *va.* To acquire, to obtain, to get.
(*Yo adquiero, yo adquiera; él adquirió, él adquiriera. V.* ADQUIRIR.)
Adquisición [ad-ke-se-the-on'], *f.* 1. Acquisition; attainment; accomplishment 2. Goods obtained by purchase or gift, not inherited. *Poder de adquisición*, Purchasing power.
Adquisidor, ra [ad-ke-se-dor', rah], *m.* & *f.* Purchaser, acquirer.
Adquisitivo, va [ad-ke-se-tee'-vo, vah], *a.* (*For.*) Acquisitive.
Adquisitorio, ria [ad-ke-se-to'-re-o, reah], *a.* Purchasing, purchase.
Adra [ah'-drah], *f.* 1. Turn. 2. Section of town, neighborhood.
Adragantina [ah-drah-gahn-tee'-nah], *f.* Tragacanthin.
Adraganto [ah-drah-gahn'-to], *m.* Tragacanth.
Adral [ah-drahl'], *m.* Sideboard (of a truck).
Adrede, Adredemente [ah-dray'-day, ah-dray-day-men'-tay], *adv.* Purposely, on purpose, knowingly.
Adrenalina [ah-dray-nah-lee'-nah], *f.* Adrenaline, type of heart stimulant.
Adriático, ca [ah-dree-ah'-te-co, cah], *a.* Adriatic.
Adrizar [ah-dree-thar'], *va.* (Naut.) To right. *Adrizar un navío*, To right a ship.
Adrolla [ah-drol'-lya], *f.* (Obs.) Deceit in trade.
Adscribir [ads-cre-beer'], *va.* To appoint a person to a place or employment.
Adscripción [ads-crip-the-on'], *f.* Nomination, appointment.
Aduana [ah-doo-ah'-nah], *f.* A customhouse. *Pasar por todas las aduanas*, To undergo a close examination. *En la aduana*, (Com.) In bond.
Aduanar [ah-doo-ah-nar'], *va.* 1. To enter goods at the custom-house. 2. To pay duty, to put in bond.
Aduanero [ah-doo-ah-nay'-ro], *m.* Custom-house officer.
Aduar [ah-doo-ar'], *m.* 1. Horde, a migratory crew. 2. Village of Arabs. 3. A horde of gipsies.
Adúcar [ah-doo'-car], *m.* A coarse sort of silk stuff, silk refuse, ferret silk.
Aducir [ah-doo-theer'], *va.* 1. To adduce, to cite. 2. To guide, to bring.
Aductor [ah-dooc-tór'], *m.* (Anat.) Adductor (muscle).
Aduendado, da [ah-doo-en-dah'-do, dah], *a.* Ghost-like, walking about like a ghost.
Adueñarse ah-doo-ay-nyar'-say], *vr.* To take possession of, to seize (fr. Dueño).
Adufa [ah-doo'-fah], *f.* A half-door.
Adufazo [ah-doo-fah'-tho], *m.* Blow with a timbrel or tambourine.
Adufe [ah-doo'-fay], *m.* Timbrel or tambourine. *V.* PANDERO.
Adufero, ra [ah-doo-fay'-ro, rah], *m.* & *f.* Timbrel or tambourine player.
Adujadas, Adujas [ah-doo-hah'-das, ah-doo'-has], *f. pl.* (Naut.) Coil or a coiled cable.
Adujar [ah-doo-har'], *va.* (Naut.) To coil a cable.
Adula [ah-doo'-lah], *f.* 1. (Prov.) A piece of ground for which there is no particular manner of irrigation.
Adulación [ah-doo-lah-the-on], *f.* Flattery, fawning, coaxing, cogging, soothing.
Adulador, ra [ah-doo-lah-dor', rah], *m.* & *f.* Flatterer, fawner, soother.
Adular [ah-doo-lar'], *va.* 1. To flatter, to soothe, to coax, to court, to compliment. 2. To fawn, to creep, to crouch.
Adulatorio, ria [ah-doo-lah-to'-re-o, ah], *a.* Flattering, honey-mouthed; parasitical.
Adulear [ah-doo-lay-ar'], *vn.* To bawl, to cry out.
Adulero [ah-doo-lay'-ro], *m.* Driver of horses or mules.
Adulón, na [ah-doo-lone', nah], *m.* & *f.* (Coll. Amer.) Flatterer.
Adúltera [ah-dool'-tay-rah], *f.* Adulteress.
Adulteración [ah-dool-tay-rah-the-on'], *f.* Adulteration, falsification (of goods, etc.)
Adulterado, da [ah-dool-tay-rah-do, dah], *a.* Sophisticated.—*pp.* of ADULTERAR.
Adulterador, ra [ah-dool-tay-rah-dor', rah], *m.* & *f.* One who adulterates; falsifier.
Adulterar [ah-dool-tay-rar'], *va* To adulterate, to falsify.—*vn.* To commit adultery.
Adulterinamente [ah-dool-tay-re-nah-men'-tay], *adv.* In an adulterous manner.
Adulterino, na [ah-dool-tay-ree'-no, nah], *a.* 1. Adulterous; begotten in adultery. 2. Adulterated, falsified, forged.
Adulterio [ah-dool-tay'-re-o], *m.* Adultery.
Adúltero, ra [ah-dool'-tay-ro, rah], *m.* & *f.* Adulterer.
Adulto, ta [ah-dool'-to, tah], *a.* Adult, grown up.
Adulzar [ah-dool-thar'], *va.* (Obs.) 1. To sweeten. 2. To soften. *Adulzar los metales*, To render metals more ductile.
Adunación [ah-doo-nah-the-on'], *f.* (Obs.) The act of uniting, and the union itself.
Adunar [ah-doo-nar'], *va.* To unite, to join; to unify.
Aduneo, ca [ah-doon'-co, cah], *a.* Aduncous, curved.
Adustez [ah-doos-teth'], *f.* Disdain, aversion, asperity.
Adustamente [ah-doos-tah-men'-tay], *adv.* Austerely, severely.
Adustión [ah-doos-te-on'], *f.* (Med.) Burning up or drying as by fire; cauterization.
Adustivo, va [ah-doos-tee'-vo, vah], *a.* That which has the power of burning up.
Adusto, ta [ah-doos'-to, tah], *a.* Gloomy, austere, untractable, sullen.
Adútero [ah-doo'-tay-ro], *m.* (Anat.) The Fallopian tube.
(*Yo aduzco, yo aduzca; él adujo, él adujera;* from *Aducir. V.* CONDUCIR.)
Advenedizo, za [ad-vay-nay-dee'-tho, thah], *a.* 1. Foreign. 2. Applied to a foreign immigrant.
Advenimiento [ad-vay-ne-me-en'-to], *m.* Arrival; advent.
Adventaja [ad-ven-tah'-hah], *f.* (Law. Prov.) A jewel or piece of furniture, which the surviving husband or wife takes out of the estate of the deceased consort before the division of the inheritance is made.
Adventicio, cia [ad-ven-tee'-the-o, ah], *a.* 1. Adventitious; accidental. 2. (Law) Acquired by industry or inheritance, independent of a paternal fortune.
Adverar [ad-vay-rar'], *va.* (Obs.) To aver, affirm.
Adverbial [ad-ver-be-ahl'], *a.* Belonging to an adverb.
Adverbialmente [ad-ver-be-al-men'-tay], *adv.* Adverbially.
Adverbio [ad-ver'-be-o], *m.* Adverb, one of the parts of speech.
Adversamente [ad-ver-sah-men'-tay], *adv.* Adversely, unfortunately, contrariwise.
Adversario [ad-ver-sah'-re-o], *m.* Opponent; antagonist, foe.—*pl.* Notes in a common-place book; a common-place book.
Adversativo, va [ad-ver-sah-tee'-vo, vah], *a.* (Gram.) A particle which expresses some difference and opposition between that which precedes and follows.
Adversidad [ad-ver-se-dad'], *f.* Calamity, misfortune, affliction.
Adverso, sa [ad-ver'-so, sah], *a.* 1. Adverse, calamitous, afflictive. 2. Opposite, averse. 3. Favourless. 4. Facing, in front of.
Advertencia [ad-ver-ten'-the-ah], *f.* 1. Attention to; regard to. 2. Advice. 3. Advertisement to the reader, remark. 4. Monition, counsel.
Advertidamente [ad-ver-te-dah-men'-tay], *adv.* Advisedly, deliberately.
Advertido, da [ad-ver-tee'-do, dah], *a.* 1. Noticed. 2. Skilful, intelligent; acting with deliberation, sagacious, clever, prudent.—*pp.* of ADVERTIR.
Advertimiento [ad-ver-te-me-en'-to], *m.* *V.* ADVERTENCIA.
Advertir [ad-ver-teer'], *va.* 1. To take notice of, to observe. 2. To instruct, to advise, to give notice or warning. 3. To acquaint. 4. To mark, to note. *Se lo advierto a Vd.*, I warn you. *El Señor N. no dejó de advertir esta observación, este reparo, movimiento, etc.*, This remark (objection, etc.) was not lost upon Mr. N.
Adviento [ad-ve-en'-to], *m.* Advent, the four weeks before Christmas.
(*Yo advierto, yo advierta; él advirtió, él advirtiera;* from *Advertir. V* ASENTIR.)
Advocación [ad-vo-cah-the-on'], *f.* 1. Appellation given to a church, chapel or altar, dedicated to the holy Virgin or a saint. 2. (Obs.) Profession of a lawyer. *V.* ABOGACIÓN. Patronage, protection.
Advocatorio, ria [ad-vo-cah-to'-re-o, ah], *a.* *Carta advocatoria* or *convocatoria*, A letter of convocation calling an assembly.
Adyacente [ad-yah-then'-tay], *a.* Adjacent; contiguous.
Adyuntivo, va [ad-yoon-tee'-vo, vah], *a.* Conjunctive; joining.
Aechadero [ah-ay-chah-day'-ro], *m.* The place where grain is winnowed from the chaff; winnowing-floor.
Aechador, ra [ah-ay-chah-dor', rah], *m.* & *f.* Winnower.
Aechaduras [ah-ay-chah-doo'-ras], *f. pl.* The refuse of grain, chaff.
Aechar [ah-ay-char'], *va.* To winnow, to sift grain from chaff.
Aecho [ah-ay'-cho], *m.* Winnowing, cleansing.
Aeración [ah-ay-rah-the-on'], *f.* 1. Aeration, charging with gas. 2. Ventilation of air. (Acad.)

Aéreo, rea [ah-ay'-ray-o, ah], *a.* 1. Aerial. 2. (Met.) Airy, fantastic.
Aerífero, a [ah-ay-ree'-fay-ro, rah], *a.* Air-conducting.
Aeriforme [ah-ay-re-for'-may], *a* (Chem.) Aeriform, gaseous.
Aerodinámica [ah-ay-ro-de-nah'-me-cah], *f.* Aerodynamics.
Aerodinámico, ca [ah-ay-ro-de-nah'-me-co, cah], *a.* 1. Aerodynamic, 2. Streamlined.
Aeródromo [ah-ay-ro'-dro-mo], *m.* Airdrome.
Aeroembolismo [ah-ay-ro-em-bo-lees'-mo], *m.* (Med.) Aeroembolism.
Aerografía [ah-ay-ro-grah-fee'-ah], *f.* Aerography.
Aerógrafo [ah-ay-ro'-grah-fo], *m.* Air brush.
Aerograma [ah-ay-ro-grah'-mah], *m.* Wireless message.
Aerolínea [ah-ay-ro-lee'-nay-ah], *f.* Airline.
Aerolito [ah-ay-ro-lee'-to], *m.* Aerolite.
Aerología [ah-ay-ro-lo-hee'-ah], *f.* Aerology.
Aeromancia [ah-ay-ro-mahn'-the-ah], *f.* Aeromancy.
Aeromedicina [ah-ay-ro-may-de-thee'-nah], *f.* Aeromedicine.
Aerómetro [ah-ay-ro'-may-tro], *m.* (Chem.) Aerometer.
Aeromoza [ah-ay-ro-mo'-thah], *f.* Airline hostess, stewardess.
Aeronauta [ah-ay-ro-nah'-oo-tah], *m.* Aeronaut.
Aeronáutica [ah-ay-ro-nah'-oo-te-cah], *f.* Aeronautics.
Aeronáutico, ca [ah-ay-ro-nah'-oo-te-co, cah], *a.* Aeronautic.
Aeronave [ah-ay-ro-nah'-vay], *f.* Airship.
Aeroplano [ah-ay-ro-plah'-no], *m.* Airplane; *Aeroplano de combate*, Fighter plane.
Aeropostal [ah-ay-ro-pos-tahl'], *a.* Airmail.
Aeropuerto [ah-ay-ro-poo-err'-to], *m.* Airport. *Aeropuerto para helicópteros*, Heliport.
Aerosol [ah-ay-ro-sol'], *m.* Aerosol.
Aerospacio [ah-ay'ro-spah'-the-o], *m.* Aerospace.
Aerostático, ca [ah-ay-ros-tah'-te-co, cah], *a.* Aerostatic.
Aerotermodinámica [ah-ay-ro-ter-mo-de-nah'-me-cah], *f.* Aerothermodynamics.
Aerotransportado, da [ah-ay-ro-trans-por-tah'-do, dah], *a.* Airlifted, airborne.
Aerovía [ah-ay ro-vee'-ah], *f.* Airway.
Afabilidad [ah-fah-be-le-dad'], *f.* Affability, graciousness, courteousness.
Afable [ah-fah'-blay], *a.* Affable, complacent, kind; agreeable, familiar.
Afablemente [ah-fah-blay-men'-tay], *adv.* Affably, good-naturedly.
Afamado, da [ah-fah-mah'-do, dah], *a.* 1. Celebrated, noted. 2. (Obs.) Hungry.
Afán [ah-fahn'], *m.* 1. Anxiety, solicitude, eagerness, laboriousness in pursuit of worldly affairs. 2. (Obs.) Toil, fatigue.
Afanadamente, Afanosamente [ah-fa-nah-dah-men'-tay, ah-fah-no-sah-men'-tay], *adv.* Anxiously, laboriously.
Afanador, ra [ah-fah-nah-dor', rah], *m.* & *f.* One eager for riches; painstaker.
Afanar [ah-fah-nar'], *vn.* & *vr.* 1. To toil, to labour; to be over-solicitous. 2. (Obs.) To be engaged in corporeal labour. *Afanar, afanar y nunca medrar*, Much toil and little profit.—*vr.* To toil, etc., too much. (Coll.) *Afanarse por nada*, To fidget.
Afaneso [ah-fah-nay'-so], *m.* Arsenite of copper; Scheele's green.
Afanoso, sa [ah-fah-no'-so, sah], *a.* Solicitous; laborious, painstaking.
Afasia [ah-fah'-see-a], *f.* Aphasia.
Afeador, ra [ah-fay-ah-dor', rah], *m.* & *f.* One that deforms or makes ugly.
Afear [ah-fay-ar'], *va.* 1. To deform, to deface, to misshape. 2. (Met.) To decry, to censure, to condemn.
Afeblecerse [ah-fay-blay-ther'-say], *vr.* To grow feeble, or delicate.
Afección [ah-fec-the-on'], *f.* 1. Affection, inclination, fondness. 2. Affection, the state of being affected by any cause or agent. 3. (Phil.) Quality, property. 4. Right of bestowing a benefice.
Afectación [ah-fec-tah-the-on'], *f.* 1. Affectation, artificial appearance; daintiness, finicalness. 2. Presumption, pride.
Afectadamente [ah-fec-tah-dah-men'-tay], *adv.* Affectedly, formally, hypocritically.
Afectado, da [ah-fec-tah'-do, dah], *a.* Affected, formal, conceited, finical, foppish.—*pp.* of Afectar.
Afectar [ah-fec-tar'], *va.* 1. To make a show of something, to feign. 2. To affect, to act upon, to produce effect in any other thing; to affect, assume a manner. 3. To unite benefices or livings. 4. *vr.* To wound, to sadden.
Afectísimo, ma [ah-fec-tee'-se-mo, mah], *a.* Yours devotedly, yours affectionately (ending of a letter).
Afectivo, va [ah-fec-tee'-vo, vah], *a.* Affective, proceeding from affection.
Afecto [ah-fec'-to], *m.* 1. Affection, love, kindness, fancy; concern. 2. Passion, sensation. 3. Pain, disease. 4. (Art) Lively representation. *Afectos desordenados*, Inordinate desires.
Afecto, ta [ah-fec'-to, tah], *a.* 1. Affectionate, loving. 2. Inclined. 3. Reserved: applied to benefices, the collation whereof is reserved to the Pope. 4. Subject to some charge or obligation for lands, rents.
Afectuosidad [ah-fec-too-o-se-dad'], *f.* Tenderness, benevolence, kindness.
Afectuoso, sa [ah-fec-too-o'-so, sah], *a.* Kind, gracious, loving, tender.
Afeitada [ah-fay-tah'-dah], *f.* Shave.
Afeitadora [ah-fay-e-tah-do'-rah], *f.* Razor, shaver.
Afeitar [ah-fay-e-tar'], *va.* 1. To shave. 2. To clip the box, wall-trees, etc., in a garden. 3. To trim the tails and manes of horses.—*vr.* To use paints or rouge.
Afeite [ah-fay'-e-tay], *m.* Paint, rouge, cosmetic.
Afelio [ah-fay'-le-o], *m.* (Ast.) Aphelion, that part of a planet's orbit which is most remote from the sun.
Afelpado, da [ah-fel-pah'-do, dah], *a.* Shaggy, villous, like plush or velvet.
Afelpar [ah-fel-par'], *va.* To make a nap, to shag or velvet.
Afeminación [ah-fay-me-nah-the-on'], *f.* Effemination; emasculation.
Afeminadamente [ah-fay-me-nah-dah-men'-tay], *adv.* Womanly.
Afeminado, da [ah-fay-me-nah'-do, dah], *a.* Effeminate.—*pp.* of Afeminar.
Afeminamiento [ah-fay-me-nah-me-en'-to], *m.* *V.* Afeminación.
Afeminar [ah-fay-me-nar'], *va.* 1. To effeminate, to unman. 2. To debilitate, to enervate, to melt into weakness.—*vr.* To become weak, feeble, lose courage.
Aferente [ah-fay-ren'-tay], *a.* Afferent, conducting inward to a part or organ.
Aféresis [ah-fay'-ray-sis], *f.* Aphæresis, a figure in grammar that takes away a letter or syllable from the beginning of a word, as *Norabuena* for *Enhorabuena*, Well.
Aferrado, da [ah-fer-rah'-do, dah], *a.* Headstrong.—*pp.* of Aferrar.
Aferramiento [ah-fer-rah-me-en'-to], *m.* 1. Grasping, grappling; seizing or binding. *Aferramiento de las velas*, (Naut.) The furling of the sails. 2. Headstrongness.
Aferrar [ah-fer-rar'], *va.* 1. To grapple, to grasp, to seize. 2. (Naut.) To furl. 3. (Naut.) To moor.—*vr.* 1. (Naut.) To grasp one another strongly. 2. (Met.) To persist obstinately in an opinion.
Afgán, na [af-gahn', gah'-nah], *a.* Afgnan, of Afghanistan.
Afianzamiento [ah-fe-an-thah-me-en'-to], *m.* 1. Security, guarantee, bail. 2. Prop, support.
Afianzar [ah-fe-an-thar'], *va.* 1. To become bail or security, to guarantee. 2. To prop, to secure with stays, ropes, etc.; buttress. 3. To obligate, to make fast, to clinch.
Afición [ah-fe-the-on'], *f.* Affection, inclination for a person or thing; mind.
Aficionado, da [ah-fe-the-o-nah'-do, dah], *a.* Fond of, enthusiastic about. —*m.* & *f.* 1. Fan, admirer, enthusiast. 2. Amateur.—*pp.* of Aficionar.
Aficionar [ah-fe-the-o-nar'], *va.* To affect, to cause or inspire affection. *Aficionarse con exceso á*, To fancy, to give one's mind to.
Afidos [ah'-fe-dohs], m. *pl.* (Ent.) Aphids, aphidians.
Afijo, ja [ah-fee'-ho, hah], *a.* (Gram.) Affix, united to the end of a word.
Afiladera [ah-fe-lah-day'-rah], *f.* Whetstone.
Afiladísimo, ma [ah-fe-lah-dee'-se-mo, mah], *a. sup.* Extremely sharp, sharpest.
Afilado [ah-fe-lah'-do], *pp.* of Afilar.—*a.* Sharp, keen.
Afiladura [ah-fe-lah-doo'-rah], *f.* Sharpening, whetting.
Afilamiento [ah-fe-lah-me-en'-to], *m.* 1. The slenderness of the face or nose. 2. *V.* Afiladura.
Afilar [ah-fe-lar'], *va.* 1. To whet, to grind. 2. To render keen. *Afilar las uñas*, To make an extraordinary effort of genius or skill.—*vr.* To grow thin and meagre.
Afiliado [ah-fe-le-ah'-do], *pp.* & *a.* Affiliated, adopted.
Afiliar [ah-fe-le-ar'], *va.* To adopt; to affiliate; to connect with a central body or society.
Afiligranado, da [ah-fe-le-grah-nah'-do, dah], *a.* 1. Resembling filigree. 2. (Met.) Applied to persons who are slender, and small-featured.
Afilo, la [ah-fee'-lo, lah], *a.* (Bot.) Aphyllous, destitute of leaves.
Afilón [ah-fe-lone'], *m.* 1. Whetstone. 2. An instrument made of steel for whetting any edged tool. 3. Leather strap, or strop (for razors, etc.).
Afilosofado, da [ah-fe-lo-so-fah'-do, dah], *a.* 1. Eccentric. 2. Applied to the person who plays the philosopher.
Afín [ah-feen'], *a.* Close by, contiguous, adjacent.—*m.* Relation by affinity.
Afinación [ah-fe-nah-the-on'], *f.* 1. Completion; the act of finishing. 2. Refining. 3. Tuning of instruments.
Afinadamente [ah-fe-nah-dah-men'-tay], *adv.* Completely, perfectly.
Afinado, da [ah-fe-nah'-do, dah], *a.* Well-finished, perfect, complete.—*pp.* of Afinar.
Afinador, ra [ah-fe-nah-dor', rah], *m.* & *f.* 1. Finisher. 2. Key with which stringed instruments are tuned, as harp, piano, etc.

Afinamiento [ah-fe-nah-me-en'-to], *m.* 1. *V.* AFINACIÓN. 2. Refinement. *V.* FINURA.

Afinar [ah-fe-nar'], *va.* 1. To complete, to polish. 2. To tune musical instruments. *Afinar los metales*, To refine metals. *Afinar la voz*, To tune the voice.—*vr.* To become polished, civilized.

Afincamiento [ah-fin-cah-me-en'-to], *m.* (Obs.) 1. Eagerness. 2. Anxiety, affliction.

Afincar [ah-fin-car'], *va.* To buy up real estate; to acquire real property.

Afine [ah-fee'-nay], *a.* Related, affinal, analogous.—*Cf.* AFÍN. (Lat. affinis.)

Afinidad [ah-fe-ne-dad'], *f.* 1. Affinity, relation by marriage. 2. (Met.) Analogy. 3. Relation to, connection with. 4. Friendship.

Afir [ah-feer'], *m.* Horse-medicine made up of juniper-berries.

Afirmación [ah-feer-mah-the-on'], *f.* Affirming, declaring; assertion.

Afirmadamente [ah-feer-mah-dah-men'-tay], *adv.* Firmly.

Afirmador, ra [ah-feer-mah-dor', rah], *m.* & *f.* One who affirms.

Afirmante [ah-feer-man'-tay], *pa.* The person who affirms.

Afirmar [ah-feer-mar'], *va.* 1. To make fast, to secure, to clinch. 2. To affirm, to assure for certain; to contend. *Afirma una carta*, At cards, to give one card a fixed value.—*vn.* To inhabit, to reside.—*vr.* 1. To fix one's self in the saddle or stirrup. 2. To maintain firmly; to advance steadily.

Afirmativa [ah-feer-mah-tee'-vah], *f.* *V.* AFIRMACIÓN.

Afirmativamente [ah-feer-mah-te-vah-men'-tay], *adv.* Affirmatively; positively.

Afirmativo, va [ah-feer-mah-tee'-vo, vah], *a.* Affirmative; opposed to negative.

Afistolar [ah-fis-to-lar'], *va.* To render fistulous; applied to a wound.

Aflechada [ah-flay-chah'-dah], *a.* Arrow-shaped: used of leaves.

Aflicción [ah-flic-the-on'], *f.* 1. Affliction, sorrow, grief, painfulness, mournfulness. 2. Heaviness, anguish of mind.

Aflictivo, va [ah-flic-tee'-vo, vah], *a.* Afflictive, distressing; causing pain and grief. *Pena aflictiva*, Corporeal punishment.

Aflicto, ta [ah-flic'-to, tah], *pp. irr.* of AFLIGIR.

Afligidamente [ah-fle-he-dah-men'-tay], *adv.* Grievously.

Afligimiento [ah-fle-he-me-en'-to], *m.* *V.* AFLICCIÓN.

Afligir [ah-fle-heer'], *va.* To afflict, to put to pain, to grieve, to torment, to curse, to mortify.—*vr.* To make one miserable, to lament, to languish, to repine.

Aflojadura [ah-flo-hah-doo'-rah], *f.* (

Aflojamiento [ah-flo-hah-me-en'-to], *m* 1. Relaxation, loosening or slackening. 2. Looseness. 3. Cooling.

Aflojar [ah-flo-har'], *va.* 1. To loosen, to slacken, to relax, to let loose; to relent; to debilitate. 2. (Pict.) To soften the colour in shading. 3 (Naut.) *Aflojar los obenques*, To ease the shrouds.—*vn.* 1. To grow weak; to abate. 2. To grow cool in fervour or zeal; to lose courage, to languish.

Aflorado [ah-flo-rah'-do], *a.* *V.* FLOREADO.

Afluencia [ah-floo-en'-the-ah], *f.* 1 Plenty, abundance. 2. Fluency, volubility.

Afluente [ah-floo-en'-tay], *a.* 1. Affluent, copious, abundant. 2. Loquacious.—*m.* Affluent, a tributary of a river.

Afluir [ah-floo-eer'], *vn.* 1. To congregate, assemble. 2. To discharge into, or join, another stream.

Afocador, ra [ah-fo-cah-dor', rah], *a.* Focusing; as, *Cremallera afocadora*, Focusing-rack.

Afocar [ah-fo-car'], *va.* To focus (optical instruments).

Afogarar [ah-fo-gah-rar'], *va.* 1. To scorch a sowed field through excessive heat. 2. To scorch a stew, by lack of juices or water. 3. (Met.) To be irritated or distressed.

Afollado, da [ah-fol-lyah'-do, dah], *a.* Wearing large or wide trousers.—*pp.* of AFOLLAR.

Afollar [ah-fol-lyar'], *va.* 1. To blow with bellows. 2. (Obs.) To ill-treat.

Afondar [ah-fon-dar'], *va.* 1. To put under water. 2. (Naut.) To sink.—*vn.* (Naut.) To founder.

Afonía [ah-fo-nee'-ah] *f.* (Med.) Loss of voice, from disease of larynx, as distinguished from aphasia, loss of power to speak, due to brain-disease.

Afónico, ca [ah-fo'-ne-co, cah], *a.* 1. Aphonic, not able to use or control the voice. 2. Silent; used of letters, as *h* in *hacer*.

Áfono = AFÓNICO.

Aforado [ah-fo-rah'-do], *a.* Privileged person.—*pp.* of AFORAR.

Aforador [ah-fo-rah-dor'], *m.* Gauger, appraiser.

Aforamiento [ah-fo-rah-me-en'-to], *m.* 1. Gauging. 2. Duty on foreign goods.

Aforar [ah-fo-rar'], *va.* 1. To gauge, to measure vessels or quantities. 2. To examine goods for determining the duty. 3. To take to a court of justice. To give or take lands or tenements under the tenure of melioration. 4. To give privileges. 5. To appraise.

Aforisma [ah-fo-rees'-mah], *f.* A swelling in the arteries of beasts: aneurism.

Aforismo [ah-fo-rees'-mo], *m.* Aphorism, brief sentence, maxim.

Aforístico, ca [ah-fo-rees'-te-co, cah], *a.* Aphoristical.

Aforo [ah-fo'-ro], *m.* Gauging, examination and appraisal of wine and other commodities for the duties; appraisement.

Aforrador, ra [ah-for-rah-dor', rah], *m.* & *f.* One who lines the inside of clothes.

Aforrar [ah-for-rar'], *va.* 1. To line, to cover the inside of clothes; to face. *Aforrar una casa*, To ceil a house. 2. (Naut.) To sheathe. 4. (Naut.) *Aforrar un cabo*, To serve a cable.

Aforro [ah-for'-ro], *m.* 1. Lining. 2. (Naut.) Sheathing. 3. (Naut.) Waist of a ship.

Afortunadamente [ah-for-too-nah-dah-men'-tay], *adv.* Luckily.

Afortunado, da [ah-for-too-nah'-do, dah], *a.* Fortunate, happy, lucky. *Tiempo afortunado*, (Obs.) Blowing weather.—*pp.* of AFORTUNAR.

Afortunar [ah-for-too-nar'], *va.* To make happy.

Afosarse [ah-fo-sar'-say], *vr.* (Mil.) To defend one's self by making a ditch.

Afrailar [ah-frah-e-lar'], *va.* (Prov.) To trim trees.

Afrancesado, da [ah-fran-thay-sah'-do, dah], *a.* Frenchified, French-like.—*pp.* of AFRANCESAR.

Afrancesar [ah-fran-thay-sar'], *va.* To Gallicize, to give a French termination to words.—*vr.* 1. To imitate the French. 2. To be naturalized in France.

Afrecho [ah-fray'-cho], *m.* (Prov.) Bran, the husks of grain ground.

Afrenillar [ah-fray-nil-lyar'], *vn.* (Naut.) To bridle the oars.

Afrenta [ah-fren'-tah], *f.* 1. Affront, dishonour, or reproach: outrage; an insult offered to the face; abuse. 2. Infamy resulting from the sentence passed upon a criminal. 3. Stigma.

Afrentar [ah-fren-tar'], *va.* To affront; to insult to the face.—*vr.* To be affronted; to blush.

Afrentosamente [ah-fren-to-sah-men'-tay], *adv.* Ignominiously; disgracefully.

Afrentoso, sa [ah-fren-to'-so, sah], *a.* Ignominious; insulting.

Afretar [ah-fray-tar'], *va.* To scrub and clean the bottom of a vessel.

Africanizar [ah-fre-cah-ne-thar'], *va.* To Africanize.

Africano, na, or **Afro** [ah-fre-cah'-no, nah], *a.* African.

Africo [ah'-fre-co], *m.* The south-west wind. *V.* ÁBREGO.

Afrisonado, da [ah-fre-so-nah'-do, dah], *a.* Resembling a Friesland draught-horse.

Afroamericano, na [ah-fro-ah-may-re-cah'-no, nah], *a.* Afro-American.

Afrocubano, na [ah-fro-coo-bah'-no, nah], *a.* Afro-Cuban.

Afrodisíaco [ah-fro-de-see'-ah-co], *a.* Aphrodisiac; exciting venereal appetite.

Afrontar [ah-fron-tar'], *va.* 1. (Obs.) To confront. 2. To reproach one with a crime to his face.—*vn.* To face.

Aftoso, sa [ahf-to'-so, sah], *a.* Aphthous. *Fiebre aftosa*, (Vet.) Hoof-and-mouth disease.

Afuera [ah-foo-ay'-ra], *adv.* 1. Abroad, out of the house, outward. 2. In public. 3. Besides, moreover. *¡ Afuera! ¡ Afuera!* Stand out of the way, clear the way.

Afueras [ah-foo-ay'-ras], *f. pl.* Environs of a place.

Afufa [ah-foo'-fah], *f.* (Coll.) Flight. *Estar sobre las afufas*, (Coll.) Preparing for flight; looking for "a soft place."

Afufar, Afufarse [ah-foo-far', ah-foo-far'-say], *vn.* & *r.* (Coll.) To run away, to escape. *No pudo afufarlas*, He could not escape.

Afusión [ah-foo-se-on'], *f.* Affusion, dashing on water.

Afuste [ah-foos'-tay], *m.* A gun-carriage. *Afuste de mortero*, A mortar-bed.

Agá [ah-gah'], *m.* A Turkish official.

Agabachado, da [ah-gah-bah-chah'-do, dah], *a.* Frenchified.

Agachada [ah-gah-chah'-dah], *f.* (Coll.) Stratagem, artifice.

Agachadiza [ah-gah-chah-dee'-thah], *f.* (Zool.) A snipe. *Hacer la agachadiza*, (Coll.) To stoop down, to conceal one's self.

Agacharse [ah-gah-char'-say], *vr.* 1 To stoop, to squat, to crouch, to cower. *Agachar las orejas*, (Coll.) To be humble; also, to be dejected, dispirited, chopfallen.

Agalbanado, da [ah-gal-bah-nah'-do, dah], *a.* *V.* GALBANERO.

Agalerar [ah-gah-lay-rar'], *va.* (Naut.) To tip an awning so as to shed rain.

Agalla [ah-gal'-lyah], *f.* (Bot.) Gall-nut. *Agalla de ciprés*, Cypress gall. *Quedarse de la agalla*, or *colgado de la agalla*, To be deceived in his hopes.—*pl.* 1. Glands in the inside of the throat. 2. Gills of fishes. 3. Distemper of the glands under the cheeks or in the tonsils. 4. Wind-galls of a horse. 5. Beaks of a shuttle. 6. The side of the head of birds corresponding to the temple. 7. Forced courage.

Agallado, da [ah-gal-lyah'-doh, dah], *a.* Steeped in an infusion of galls.

Agallón [ah-gal-lyone'], *m.* A large gall-nut. *Agallones, pl.* 1. Strings of large silver beads hollowed like gall-nuts. 2. Wooden beads put to rosaries.

Agalluela [ah-gal-lyoo-ay'-lah], *f.dim.* A small gall-nut.

Agamitar [ah-gah-me-tar'], *va.* To imitate the voice of a fawn.

Agamo, ma [ah'-gah-mo, mah], *a.* Agamous, deprived of sexual organs: said of mollusks, and of such plants as fungi and algæ.

Agamuzado, da [ah-gah-moo-thah'-do, dah], *a.* Chamois-coloured.

Agangrenarse [ah-gan-gray-nar'-say], *vr.* To become gangrenous.

Agapas [ah-gah'-pas], *f. pl.* Agapæ. love-feast. (Gr. ἀγάπη.)

Agape [ah'-gah-pay], *m.* Banquet, testimonial dinner.

Agarbado, da [ah-gar-bah'-do, dah], *a.* *V.* GARBOSO.—*pp.* of AGARBARSE.

Agarbanzar [ah-gar-ban-thar']. *vn.* (Prov.) To bud.

Agarbarse [ah-gar-bar'-say], *vr.* To hide away, to hide one's self.

Agarbillar [ah-gar-beel-lyar']. *V.* AGAVILLAR.

Agarbizonarse [ah-gar-be-tho-nar'-say], *vr.* To make up into sheaves.

Agareno, na [ah-gah-ray'-no, nah], *a.* A descendant of Agar; a Mohammedan.

Agárico [ah-gah'-re-co], *m.* (Bot.) Agaric, a fungous excrescence on the trunks of larch-trees.

Agarrada [ah-gar-rah'-dah], *f.* (Coll.) Altercation, wordy quarrel.

Agarradero [ah-gar-rah-day'-ro], *m.* 1. (Naut.) Anchoring-ground. 2. (Coll.) Hold, haft.

Agarrado, da [ah-gar-rah'-do, dah], *a.* Miserable, stingy, close-fisted.—*pp.* of AGARRAR.

Agarrador, ra [ah-gar-rah-dor', rah], *m.* & *f.* 1. One that grasps or seizes. 2. Catch-pole, bailiff. 3. Holder, utensil to grasp plates when hot.

Agarrama [ah-gar-rah'-mah], *f.* *V.* GARRAMA.

Agarrar [ah-gar-rar'], *va.* 1. To grasp, to seize, to lay hold of, to compass. 2. To obtain, to come upon.—*vr.* To clinch, to grapple. *Agarrarse de un pelo*, To grasp at a hair to support an opinion or furnish an excuse.

Agarro [ah-gar'-ro], *m.* Grasp.

Agarrochador [ah-gar-ro-chah-dor'], *m.* Pricker, goader.

Agarrochar, Agarrochear [ah-gar-ro-char', ah-gar-ro-chay-ar'], *va.* To prick with a pike or spear; to goad.

Agarrotar [ah-gar-ro-tar'], *va.* To compress bales with ropes and cords.

Agasajador, ra [ah-gah-sah-hah-dor', rah], *m.* & *f.* Officious, kind, obliging person.

Agasajar [ah-gah-sah-har'], *va.* 1. To receive and treat kindly; to fondle. 2. (Coll.) To regale.

Agasajo [ah-gah-sah'-ho], *m.* 1. Graceful and affectionate reception. 2. Kindness. 3. A friendly present. 4. Refreshment or collation served up in the evening.

Agata [ah'-gah-tah], *f.* Agate, a precious stone.

Agavanzo [ah-gah-vahn'-tho], *m.* or **Agavanza** [ah-gah-vahn'-thah], *f.* (Bot.) Hip-tree, dog-rose. Rosa canina. *V.* ESCARAMUJO. (Per.)

Agave [ah-gah'-vay], *m.* *V.* PITA.

Agavillar [ah-gah-veel-lyar'], *va.* To bind or tie in sheaves.—*vr.* (Met.) To associate with a gang of sharpers.

Agazapar [ah-gah-thah-par'], *va.* (Coll.) To nab a person.—*vr.* To hide one's self.

Agencia [ah-hen'-the-ah], *f.* 1. Agency; ministration, commission. 2. Diligence, activity.

Agenciar [ah-hen-the-ar'], *va.* To solicit.

Agencioso, sa [ah-hen-the-oh'-so, sah], *a.* 1. Diligent, active. 2. Officious.

Agenda [ah-hen'-dah], *f.* Note-book: memorandum. (Lat.)

Agenesia [ah-hay-nay'-se-ah], *f.* (Med.) Impotence.

Agente [ah-hen'-tay], *m.* 1. Agent, actor, minister. 2. Solicitor, attorney. *Agente de cambios*, Bill broker. *Agente publicitario*, Adman.

Agerasia [ah-hay-rah'-se-ah], *f.* Old age free from indispositions.

Agerato [ah-hay-rah'-to], *m.* (Bot.) Sweet milfoil or maudlin. Achillea ageratum.

Agestado, da [ah-hes-tah'-do, dah] (*Bien ó mal*), *a.* Well or ill featured.

Agibilibus [ah-he-bee'-le-boos], *m.* (Coll.) Application and industry to obtain the conveniences of life.

Agible [ah-hee'-blay], *a.* Feasible.

Agigantado, da [ah-he-gan-tah'-do, dah], *a.* Gigantic; extraordinary, out of the general rules.

Ágil [ah'-heel], *a.* Nimble, ready, fast, light.

Agilidad [ah-he-le-dad'], *f.* Agility, nimbleness, activity, lightness, liveliness, sprightliness.

Agilitar [ah-he-le-tar'], *va.* To render nimble, to make active.

Ágilmente [ah'-heel-men-tay], *adv.* Nimbly, actively.

Agio, agiotaje [ah'-he-oh, ah-he-o-tah'-hay], *m.* 1. Usury, high rate of interest on loans. 2. Premium on exchange of drafts, foreign money, etc.

Agiógrafo [ah-he-oh'-grah-fo], *m.* Hagiographer, a holy writer.

Agiógrafos [ah-he-oh'-grah-fos], *m. pl.* Hagiographa, holy writings, a name given to part of the books of Scripture. (Gr.)

Agiotador [ah-he-oh-tah-dor'], *m.* Bill-broker, stock-broker.

Agiotaje [ah-he-o-tah'-hay], *m* Jobbing: "ring" in America.

Agiotista [ah-he-oh-tees'-tah], *m.* Money-changer, bill-broker.

Agitable [ah-he-tah'-blay], *a.* Agitable, capable of agitation.

Agitación [ah-he-tah-the-on'], *f.* 1. Agitation, flurry, flutter, jactitation, fluctuation; fidget. 2. Fretting.

Agitador, ra [ah-he-tah-dor', rah], *m.* & *f.* Fretter, agitator.

Agitanado, da [ah-he-tah-nah'-do, dah], *a.* 1. Gipsy-like. 2. Bewitching.

Agitar [ah-he-tar'], *va.* 1. To agitate, to ruffle, to fret, to irritate. 2. To stir, to discuss.—*vr* To flutter, palpitate.

Aglomeración [ah-glo-may-rah-the-on'], *f.* Agglomeration, heaping up.

Aglomerar [ah-glo-may-rar'], *va.* To heap upon.

Aglutinación [ah-gloo-te-nah-the-on'], *f.* Agglutination.

Aglutinante [ah-gloo-te-nan'-tay], *a.* Agglutinating.—*pa.* of AGLUTINAR.—*f.* (Med.) Sticking-plaster.

Aglutinar [ah-gloo-te-nar'], *va.* To glue together, to agglutinate.

Aglutinativo, va [ah-gloo-te-nah-tee'-vo, vah], *a.* Agglutinative.

Agnación [ag-nah-the-on'], *f.* (Law) Relation by blood on the father's side.

Agnado, da [ag-nah'-do, dah], *a.* (Law) Related to a descendant of the same paternal line.—*Cf.* COGNADO, A relative on the mother's side.

Agnaticio, cia [ag-nah-tee'-the-o, ah], *a.* Belonging to the *agnado*.

Agnición [ag-ne-the-on'], *f.* Recognition of a person on the stage.

Agnocasto [ag-no-cahs'-to], *m.* (Bot.) Agnus castus or chaste-tree. *V.* SAUZGATILLO.

Agnomento [ag-no-men'-to], *m.* (Obs.) *V.* COGNOMENTO and SOBRENOMBRE.

Agnominación [ag-no-me-na-the-on'], *f.* (Rhet.) Paronomasia.

Agnosticismo [ag-nos-te-thees'-mo], *m.* Agnosticism.

Agnóstico, ca [ag-nos'-te-co, cah], *a.* & *m.* & *f.* Agnostic.

Agnus-Dei [ag-noos-day'-ee], *m.* 1. Agnus, a small, thin wax cake, with the figure of a lamb blessed by the Pope. 2. A part of the service of the mass where these words are repeated three times. 3. A coin of the time of John I. of Castile, of smallest value.

Agobiar [ah-go-be-ar'], *va.* 1. To bend the body down. 2. (Met.) To oppress, to grind.—*vr.* To bow, to couch.

Agolar [ah-go-lar'], *va.* (Naut.) To furl the sails. *V.* AMAINAR.

Agolparse [ah-gol-par'-say], *vr.* To crowd, to rush.

Agonales [ah-go-nah'-les], *a. pl.* Games in honour of Janus.

Agone [ah-go'-nay], (In) (Lat.) *o en la agonía de la muerte*, In agony, in the struggle of death.

Agonía [ah-go-nee'-ah], *f.* 1. Agony the pangs of death. 2. Violent pain of body or mind. 3. An anxious or vehement desire.

Agonista [ah-go-nees'-tah], *m.* (Obs.) A dying person.

Agonizante [ah-go-ne-thahn'-tay], *pa.* 1. One that assists a dying person. 2. A monk of the order of St. Camillus. 3. A dying person. 4. In some universities, he who assists students in their examinations.

Agonizar [ah-go-ne-thar'], *va.* 1. To assist dying persons. 2. (Obs.) To desire anxiously. 3. (Met.) To annoy, to importune intolerably. *Estar agonizando*, To be in the agony of death.

Agono [ah-go'-no], *a* Without angles

Agora [ah-go'-rah], *adv.* (Obs.) *V.* AHORA.

Ágora [ah'-go-rah], *f.* Agora, public place in Greek cities.

Agorar [ah-go-rar'], *va.* To divine to prognosticate.

Agorería [ah-go-ray-ree'-ah], *f.* Divination.

Agorero, ra [ah-go-ray'-ro, rah], *m.* & *f* Diviner.

Agorgojarse [ah-gor-go-har'-say], *vr.* To be destroyed by grubs; applied to corn.

Agostadero [ah-gos-tah-day'-ro], *m* Summer pasture.

Agostar [ah-gos-tar'], *va.* 1. To be parched. 2. (Prov.) To plough the land in August.—*vn.* To pasture cattle on stubbles in summer.

Agostero [ah-gos-tay'-ro], *m.* 1. A labourer in the harvest. 2. A religious mendicant who begs corn in August.

Agostizo, za [ah-gos-tee'-tho, thah], *a.* A person born in August; a colt foaled in that month; weak.

Agosto [ah-gos'-to], *m.* 1. August. 2. Harvest-time. 3. Harvest.

Agotable [ah-go-tah'-blay], *a.* Exhaustible.

Agotamiento [ah-go-tah-me-en'-to], *m.* Exhaustion.

Agotar [ah-go-tar'], *va.* 1. To drain off waters. 2. (Met.) To beat out one's brains. 3. To run through a fortune: to misspend it. 4. To exhaust. *Agotar la paciencia*, To tire one's patience.

Agote [ah-go'-tay], *m.* Name of a race of people in the province of Navarre in Spain.

Agracejo [ah-grah-thay'-ho], *m.* 1. A grape remaining small and failing to ripen. 2. (Prov.) An olive which falls before it is ripe. 3. A kind of shrub. *V.* MAROJO.

Agraceño, ña [ah-grah-thay'-nyo, nyah], *a.* Resembling verjuice.

Agracera [ah-grah-thay'-rah], *f.* Vessel to hold verjuice.—*a.* Applied to vines when their fruit never ripen.

Agraciado, da [ah-grah-the-ah'-do, dah], *a.* Graceful, genteel, handsome.—*pp.* of AGRACIAR.—*m.* A grantee.

Agraciar [ah-grah-the-ar'], *va.* 1. To adorn or embellish. 2. To grant a favour. 3. To communicate divine grace. 4. To give employment.

Agracillo [ah-grah-theel'-lyo], *m.* *V.* AGRACEJO, 3d def.

Agradable [ah-grah-dah'-blay], *a.* 1. Agreeable, pleasing. 2. Merry, lovely, glad, gracious. 3. Luscious, grateful. *Ser agradable*, (Com.) To accommodate.

Agradablemente [ah-grah-dah-blay-men'-tay], *adv.* Merrily, graciously.

Agradar [ah-grah-dar'], *va.* To please, to gratify, to render acceptable; to humour, to like.—*vr.* To be pleased.

Agradecer [ah-grah-day-therr'], *va.* 1. To acknowledge a favour, to show gratitude in any way. 2. To reward, to recompense.

Agradecidamente [ah-grah-day-the-dah-men'-tay], *adv.* Gratefully.

Agradecido, da [ah-grah-day-thee'-do, dah], *a.* 1. Acknowledged. 2. Grateful, thankful.—*pp.* of AGRADECER.

Agradecimiento [ah-grah-day-the-me-en'-to], *m.* Gratefulness; act of acknowledging a favour conferred.

(*Yo agradezco*, from *Agradecer. V.* ABORRECER.)

Agrado [ah-grah'-do], *m.* 1. Affability, agreeableness, the quality of pleasing, courteousness, grace; favourableness. 2. Comfortableness, gratefulness. 3. Pleasure, liking. *Esto no es de mi agrado*, That does not please me, I do not like that.

Agramadera [ah-grah-mah-day'-rah], *f.* Brake, an instrument for dressing flax or hemp; scutcher.

Agramar [ah-grah-mar'], *va.* To dress flax or hemp with a brake.

Agramilar [ah-grah-me-lar'], *va.* To point and colour a brick wall; to make even, adjust, the bricks.

Agramiza [ah-grah-mee'-thah], *f.* 1. The stalk of hemp. 2. Refuse of dressed hemp.

Agrandamiento [ah-gran-dah-me-en'-to], *m.* Enlargement.

Agrandar [ah-gran-dar'], *va.* To increase, to greaten, to make larger.

Agranujado, da [ah-grah-noo-hah'-do, dah], *a.* 1. Filled or covered with grain. 2. Grain-shaped.

Agrario, ria [ah-grah'-re-o, ah], *a.* Agrarian, rustic. *Ley agraria*, Agrarian law.

Agravación [ah-grah-vah-the-on'], *f.* Aggravation.

Agravador, ra [ah-grah-vah-dor', rah], *m.* & *f.* Oppressor.

Agravamiento [ah-grah-vah-me-en'-to], *m.* The act of aggravating.

Agravante [ah-grah-vahn'-tay], *a.* Aggravating, irritating, trying. *Circunstancia agravante*, (for.) Aggravating circumstance.

Agravar [ah-grah-var'], *va.* 1. To oppress with taxes and public burdens; to aggrieve. 2. To render more intolerable. 3. To exaggerate, to complicate, aggravate. 4. To ponder.

Agravatorio, ria [ah-grah-vah-to'-re-o, ah], *a.* (Law) Compulsory, aggravating.

Agraviadamente [ah-grah-ve-ah-dah-men'-tay], *adv.* (Obs.) 1. Injuriously, insultingly. 2. Efficaciously, strongly.

Agraviador, ra [ah-grah-ve-ah-dor', rah], *m.* & *f.* One that gives offence or injuries.

Agraviar [ah-grah-ve-ar'], *va.* To wrong, to offend, to grieve, to harm.—*vr.* To be aggrieved; to be piqued.

Agravio [ah-grah'-ve-o], *m.* 1. Offence, harm, grievance, mischief; insult; injury, affront. 2. (Obs.) Appeal.

Agraz [ah-grath'], *m.* 1. Verjuice, the juice expressed from unripe grapes. 2. An unripe grape. 3. Displeasure, disgust. *En agraz, adv.* Unseasonably; unsuitably.

Agrazar [ah-grah-thar'], *vn.* To have a sour taste.—*va.* To disgust, to vex.

Agrazón [ah-grah-thone'], *m.* 1. Wild grape, grapes which do not ripen. 2. (Bot.) Gooseberry-bush. 3. Displeasure, resentment, disgust.

Agredir [ah-gray-deer'], *va.* To assume the aggressive, assault, attack.

Agregación [ah-gray-gah-the-on'], *f.* Aggregation, collecting into one mass.

Agregado [ah-gray-gah'-do], *m.* 1. Aggregate. 2. Congregation. 3. An assistant, a supernumerary.

Agregar [ah-gray-gar'], *va.* 1. To aggregate, to collect and unite, to heap together. 2. To collate, to nominate.

Agremiación [ah-gray-me-ah-the-on'], *f.* 1. Unionization. 2. Labor union.

Agremiar [ah-gray'-me-ar], *va.* & *r.* To form a guild or society.

Agresión [ah-gray-se-on'], *f.* Aggression, attack, assault.

Agresivamente [ah-gray-se-vah-men'-tay], *adv.* Aggressively.

Agresividad [ah-gray-se-ve-dahd'], *f.* Aggressiveness.

Agresivo, va [ah-gray-see'-vo, vah], *a.* Aggressive, provoking.

Agresor, ra [ah-gray-sor', rah], *m.* & *f.* Aggressor, assaulter.

Agreste [ah-gres'-tay], *a.* 1. Rustic, clownish, illiterate, churlish, home-bred. 2. Wild.

Agrete [ah-gray'-tay], *m.* Sourness with a mixture of sweet.

Agriamente [ah-gre-ah-men'-tay], *adv.* Sourly; with asperity or harshness.

Agriar [ah-gre-ar'], *va.* 1. To make sour or tart. 2. (Met.) To make peevish, to irritate, to exasperate.—*vr.* To sour, turn acid.

Agrícola [ah-gree'-co-lah], *a.* & *n.* Agricultural; agriculturist.

Agricultor [ah-gre-cool-tor'], *m.* Husbandman, farmer. 2. A writer upon agriculture.

Agricultora [ah-gre-cool-to'-rah], *f.* The woman who tills the ground.

Agricultura [ah-gre-cool-too'-rah], *f.* Agriculture.

Agridulce [ah-gre-dool'-thay], *a.* Between sweet and sour, sub-sour.

Agrietado, da [ah-gre-ay-tah'-do, dah], *a.* Flawy, defective.

Agrietarse [ah-gre-ay-tar'-say], *vr.* To be filled with cracks.

Agrifolio [ah-gre-fo'-le-o], *m.* (Bot.) Holly-tree. Ibex aquifolium.

Agrillado, da [ah-greel-lyah'-do, dah], *a.* Chained; put in irons.—*pp.* of AGRILLARSE.

Agrillarse [ah-greel-lyar'-say], *vr.* V. GRILLARSE.

Agrillo, lla [ah-greel'-lyo, lyah], *a. dim.* Sourish, tartish.

Agrimensor [ah-gre-men-sor'], *m.* Land surveyor.

Agrimensura [ah-gre-men-soo'-rah], *f.* Art of surveying land.

Agrimonia [ah-gre-mo'-ne-ah], *f.* (Bot.) Agrimony, liverwort. Agrimonia.

Agrio, ria [ah'-gre-o, ah], *a.* 1. Sour, acrid. 2. (Met.) Rough; applied to a road full of stones. 3. (Met.) Sharp, rude, unpleasant. *Una respuesta agria*, A smart reply. 4. Brittle, apt to break, unmalleable; applied to metals. 5. (Art) Of bad taste in colouring or drawing.

Agrio [ah'-gre-o], *m.* The acidity of some fruits; sour. *Agrios*, Sour fruit-trees.

Agrión [ah-gre-on'], *m.* (Vet.) Callosity in the joint of a horse's knee.

Agrisetado, da [ah-gre-say-tah'-do, dah], *a.* 1. Flowered like silks. 2. Gray-coloured.

Agrobiología [ah-gro-be-o-lo-hee'-ah], *f.* Agrobiology.

Agronomía [ah-gro-no-mee'-ah], *f.* Theory of agriculture.

Agronómico, ca [ah-gro-no'-me-co, cah], *a.* Agronomical.

Agrónomo, ma [ah-gro'-no-mo, mah], *a.* Agronomous.—*m.* Agronomist.

Agrumarse [ah-groo-mar'-say], *vr.* To curdle, as in making cheese.

Agrupación [ah-groo-pah-the-on'], *f.* 1. Association, group. 2. Crowding, crowd.

Agrupar [ah-groo-par'], *va.* To group, to cluster.

Agrura [ah-groo'-rah], *f.* 1. Acidity; acerbity. 2. (Obs.) A group of trees which yield fruit of sourish taste.

Agua [ah'-goo-ah], *f.* 1. Water. 2. (Chem.) Liquor distilled from herbs, flowers, or fruit. 3. Lustre of diamonds. 4. (Naut.) Leak. *Agua de azahar*, Orange-flower water. *Agua de olor*, Scented water. *Agua rica*, A name given indifferently to all kinds of scented water in several provinces of Peru. *Agua llovediza*, Rain-water. *Agua fuerte*, Aqua fortis. *Agua regia*, Aqua regia. *Agua bendita*, Holy water. *¡Agua va!* A notice to passers-by that water will be thrown. *Agua viva*, Running water. —*pl.* 1. Mineral waters in general. 2. Clouds in silk and other stuffs. 3. Urine. 4. Tide. *Aguas muertas*, Neap-tides. *Aguas vivas*, Spring tides. *Entre dos aguas*, Between wind and water; in doubt, perplexed. *Agua abajo, adv.* Down the stream. *Agua arriba, adv.* 1. Against the stream. 2. (Met.) With great difficulty. *Agua de Colonia*, Cologne-water. *Agua dulce*, Fresh water. *Agua oxigenada*, Peroxide of hydrogen. *Agua del pantoque*, Bilge-water. *Agua del timón*, Wake of a ship. *Agua de cepas*, (Coll.) Wine.

Aguacate, or **Agualate** [ah-goo-ah-cah'-tay, or ah-goo-ah-lah'-tay], *m.* 1. (In Peru, *Palta.*) A tree of this name and its fruit, resembling a large pear, miscalled alligator-pear. (From Mexican *ahuacatl.*) The fruit of Persea gratissima. 2. Shaped as a pear.

Aguacero [ah-goo-ah-thay'-ro], *m.* A heavy shower of rain.

Aguacibera [ah-goo-ah-the-bay'-rah], *f.* (Prov.) A piece of ground sowed when dry and afterward irrigated.

Aguacil [ah-goo-ah-theel'], *m.* A constable. V. ALGUACIL.

Aguachirle [ah-goo-ah-cheer'-lay], *f.* 1. Inferior wine. 2. Slipslop; any bad liquor.

Aguada [ah-goo-ah'-dah], *f.* 1. (Naut.) Water on board a ship. *Hacer aguada*, To water. 2. (Art) Sketch, outline.

Aguaderas [ah-goo-ah-day'-ras], *f. pl.* Frames in which jars of water are carried by horses.

Aguadero [ah-goo-ah-day'-ro], *m.* 1. Watering-place for cattle. 2. (Naut.) Watering-port for ships.
Aguadija [ah-goo-ah-dee'-hah], *f.* Humour in pimples or sores.
Aguado, da [ah-goo-ah'-do, dah], *a.* 1. Watered. 2. Abstemious, like a teetotaller.—*pp.* of AGUAR.
Aguador, ra [ah-goo-ah-dor', rah], *m.* & *f.* 1. Water-carrier. 2. (Mil.) *Aguador del real*, Sutler. 3. Bucket of a water-wheel.
Aguaducho [ah-goo-ah-doo'-cho], *m.* 1. Water-course. 2. Stall for selling water. 3. (Prov.) Place where earthen vessels with drinking water are kept.
Agua dulce [ah'-goo-ah dool'-thay], *f.* 1. Fresh water. 2. Sweet water.
Aguadura [ah-goo-ah-doo'-rah], *f.* Disease in horses arising from a surfeit of water: contraction of the muscles.
Aguafiestas [ah-goo-ah-fee-ess'-tahs], *m* & *f.* Wet blanket, kill-joy.
Aguafuerte [ah-goo-ah-foo-err'-tay], *m.* or *f.* Etching.
Aguafuertista [ah-goo-ah-foo-err-tees'-tah], *m* & *f.* Etcher
Aguagoma [ah-goo-ah-go'-mah], *f.* Gum-water, used in the preparation of paints.
Aguaitador, ra [ah-goo-ah-e-tah-dor', rah], *m.* & *f.* (Obs.) A spy.
Aguaitar [ah-goo-ah-e-tar'], *va.* (Low) To discover by close examination or artifice.
Aguajaque [ah-goo-ah-hah'-kay], *m.* A sort of ammoniac gum.
Aguajas [ah-goo-ah'-has], *f. pl.* Ulcers above the hoofs of a horse.
Aguaje [ah-goo-ah'-hay], *m.* 1. A running spring. 2. (Naut.) A current in the sea, persistent or periodical; e. g. the Gulf Stream. 3. Place where ships go for water.
Aguamanil [ah-goo-ah-mah-neel'], *m.* 1. Water-jug, laver. 2. A wash-stand.
Aguamanos [ah-goo-ah-mah'-nos], *m.* Water for washing the hands. *Dar aguamanos*, To procure water for washing the hands.
Aguamarina [ah-goo-ah-mah-ree'-nah], *f.* Aqua marina, a precious stone, pale green; a variety of beryl.
Aguamelado, da [ah-goo-ah-may-lah'-do, dah], *a.* Washed or rubbed over with water and honey.
Aguamiel [ah-goo-ah-me-el'], *f.* 1. Hydromel, honey and water, mead, metheglin. 2. The unfermented juice of the Mexican agave or *maguey.*
Aguana [ah-goo-ah'-nah], *f.* A wood used in canoe-making in South America.
Aguanafa [ah-goo-ah-nah'-fah], *f.* (Prov.) Orange-flower water.
Aguanieve [ah-goo-ah-ne-ay'-vay], *f.* 1. Bird of the family of magpies. 2. Sleet, snow; in this sense it is properly two words, *agua nieve.*
Aguanosidad [ah-goo-ah-no-se-dad'], *f.* Serous humours in the body.
Aguanoso, sa [ah-goo-ah-no'-so, sah], *a.* Aqueous; extremely moist.
Aguantar [ah-goo-an-tar'], *va.* 1. To sustain, to suffer, to bear, to endure; to abide. 2. To maintain. 3. (Naut.) To carry a stiff sail.
Aguante [ah-goo-ahn'-tay], *m.* 1. Fortitude, firmness; vigour in bearing labour and fatigue. 2. Patience. 3. (Naut.) *Navío de aguante*, A ship that carries a stiff sail.
Aguañón [ah-goo-ah-nyon'], *m.* Constructor of hydraulic machines.
Aguapa [ah-goo-ah'-pah], *f.* The white water-lily.
Aguapié [ah-goo-ah-pe-ay'], *m.* Small wine. *V.* AGUACHIRLE.
Aguar [ah-goo-ar'], *va.* 1. To mix water with wine, vinegar, or other liquor. 2. (Met.) To disturb or interrupt pleasure. 3. *vr.* To be filled with water.
Aguardar [ah-goo-ar-dar'], *va.* 1. To expect, to wait. 2. To grant time, e. g. to a debtor.
Aguardentería [ah-goo-ar-den-tay-ree'-ah], *f.* Liquor-shop.
Aguardentero, ra [ah-goo-ar-den-tay'-ro, rah], *m.* & *f.* Retailer of liquors.
Aguardiente [ah-goo-ar-de-en'-tay], *m.* 1. Brandy. 2. Whisky.—*Aguardiente de cabeza*, The first and strongest spirits drawn from the still.
Aguardo [ah-goo-ar'-do], *m.* Place where a sportsman waits to fire at the game.
Aguarrás [ah-goo-ar-rahs'], *m.* Oil of turpentine.
Aguarse [ah-goo-ar'-say], *vr.* 1. To be inundated. 2. To get stiff after much fatigue: applied to horses or mules.
Aguatero [ah-goo-ah-tay'-ro], *m.* Water carrier.
Aguatocha [ah-goo-ah-to'-chah], *f.* Pump.
Aguatocho [ah-goo-ah-to'-cho], *m.* (Prov.) Small quagmire.
Aguaturma [ah-goo-ah-toor'-mah], *f.* (Bot.) Jerusalem artichoke. Helianthus tuberosa.
Aguavientos [ah-goo-ah-ve-en'-tos], *m.* (Bot.) Yellow sage-tree.
Aguaza [ah-goo-ah'-thah], *f.* 1. Aqueous humour. 2. Juice extracted from trees by incision.
Aguazal [ah-goo-ah-thahl'], *m.* Marsh, fen. *V.* PANTANO.
Aguazo [ah-goo-ah'-tho] (Pintura de). Painting drawn with gum-water of a dull, cloudy colour.
Aguazoso, sa [ah-goo-ah-tho'-so, sah], *a.* Aqueous.
Aguazur [ah-goo-ah-thoor'], *m.* Kind of dark green large-leaved barilla plant.
Agudamente [ah-goo-dah-men'-tay]. *adv.* 1. Sharply, lively, keenly. 2. Ingeniously, finely; clearly.
Agudeza [ah-goo-day'-thah], *f.* 1. Sharpness of instruments. 2. Acuteness, force of intellect, subtilty, fineness. 3. Witty saying, repartee. 4. Acidity of fruits and plants. 5. Smartness.
Agudo, da [ah-goo'-do, dah], *a.* 1. Sharp-pointed, keen-edged; smart. 2. (Met.) Acute, witty. 3. Dangerous. 4. Brisk, ready, active. 5. (Med.) Acute, of rapid development.
Agüela [ah-goo-ay'-lah], *f.* A cloak, mantle.
Agüelo, la [ah-goo-ay'-lo, lah], *m.* & *f.* (Obs.) Grandfather, grandmother.
Agüera [ah-goo-ay'-rah], *f.* (Prov.) Trench for conveying water to a piece of ground.
Agüero [ah-goo-ay'-ro], *m.* Augury, prognostication, omen.
(*Yo agüero, yo agüere*, from *Agorar. V.* ACORDAR.)
Aguerrido, da [ah-ger-ree'-do, dah], *a.* Inured to war; veteran.—*pp.* of AGUERRIR.
Aguerrir [ah-ger-reer'], *va.* To accustom to war.
Aguijada [ah-ge-hah'-dah], *f.* 1. Spur, goad. 2. Stimulant, pungency.
Aguijador, ra [ah-ge-hah-dor', rah], *m.* & *f.* One that goads or stimulates.
Aguijadura [ah-ge-hah-doo'-rah], *f.* Spurring; the act of exciting.
Aguijar [ah-ge-har'], *va.* 1. To prick, to spur, to goad. 2. To incite, to stimulate.—*vn.* To march fast.
Aguijón [ah-ge-hone'], *m.* 1. Sting of a bee, wasp, etc. 2. Power of exciting motion or sensation. 3. Prick, spur, goad. *Dar o tirar coces contra el aguijón*, To kick against the spur or goad.
Aguijonazo [ah-ge-ho-nah'-tho], *m.* Thrust with a goad.
Aguijoncillo [ah-ge-hon-theel'-lyo], *m. dim.* Petty exciter.
Aguijoneador, ra [ah-ge-ho-nay-ah-dor', rah], *m.* & *f.* One who pricks or goads.
Aguijonear [ah-ge-ho-nay-ar'], *va.* 1. To thrust. *V.* AGUIJAR. 2. To incite.
Águila [ah'-ge-lah], *f.* 1. Eagle. *Ve más que un águila*, He is more sharp-sighted than an eagle. 2. A gold coin with an eagle of the reign of Charles V. 3. Eagle, $10 gold coin of the United States.
Aguileño, ña [ah-ge-lay'-nyo, nyah], *a.* Aquiline; hooked, hawk-nosed.
Aguililla [ah-ge-leel'-lyah], *f. dim.* A little eagle, an eaglet. *V.* CABALLO AGUILILLA.
Aguilón [ah-ge-lone'], *m.* 1. The boom of the instrument called a crane, used for lifting heavy weights. 2. Aug. of ÁGUILA.
Aguilucho [ah-ge-loo'-cho], *m.* 1. A young eagle. 2. Hobby.
Aguinaldo [ah-ge-nahl'-do], *m.* New-year's gift, Christmas box.
Aguisado [ah-gee-sah'-do], *a.* & *n.* (Obs.) Just, reasonable, prudent.
Aguisar [ah-ge-sar'], *va.* (Obs.) 1. To dress, to arrange. 2. To cook or provide provisions.
Agüita [ah-goo-ee'-tah], *f. dim.* A little rain or mist.
Aguja [ah-goo'-hah], *f.* 1. Needle, bodkin. 2. Spire of an obelisk, steeple. 3. Needle-fish, horn-fish. 4. Needle-shell. 5. Hand of a watch, style of a dial. 6. Switch-rail (r. w.). 7. Spindle. 8. Pin (in typography and in artillery); a brad. 9. Graft. *Aguja de marear*, (Naut.) A mariner's compass. *Aguja de cámara*, (Naut.) A hanging compass. *Aguja capotera*, (Naut.) Sailing needle. *Aguja de relinga*, (Naut.) Boltrope-needle. *Aguja de hacer media*, Knitting-needle. *Aguja de pastor*, (Bot.) Shepherd's needle. *Aguja de mechar*, Skewer. —*pl.* 1. Ribs of the fore quarter of an animal. 2. Distemper of horses, affecting the legs, neck, and throat. 3. The southernmost point of Africa. *Vino de agujas*, Wine of a sharp, acrid taste.
Agujazo [ah-goo-hah'-tho], *m.* A prick with a needle.
Agujerar [ah-goo-hay-rar'], *va.* To pierce. *V.* AGUJEREAR.
Agujerazo [ah-goo-hay-rah'-tho], *m.* A wide hole.
Agujerear [ah-goo-hay-ray-ar'], *va.* To pierce, to bore, to make holes.
Agujerico, illo, uelo [ah-goo-hay-ree'-co, reel'-lyo, oo-ay'-lo], *m. dim.* A small hole.
Agujero [ah-goo-hay'-ro], *m.* 1. Hole in clothes, walls, etc. 2. Needle-maker, needle-seller. 3. (Obs.) Pin-case; needle-case. 4. (Naut.) Port, mouth of a river, or any opening in the coast. 5. A dug-out.
Agujeta [ah-goo-hay'-tah], *f.* String or strap of leather.—*pl.* 1. Grog-money given to post-boys or drivers of mail-coaches. 2. Pains felt from fatigue. *Alabar sus agujetas*, To praise one's own merchandise.
Agujetear [ah-goo-hay-tay-ar'], *va.* To sew or join together pieces of leather with strips or thongs.
Agujetería [ah-goo-hay-tay-ree'-ah], *f.* Shop where leather straps, or girths, called *agujetas*, are made or sold.
Agujetero, ra [ah-goo-hay-tay'-ro, rah], *m.* & *f.* Maker or seller of *agujetas* or laces.

Agujón [ah-goo-hone'], *m. aug.* A large needle.
Aguosidad [ah-goo-o-se-dad'], *f.* Lymph, a transparent, colourless liquor in the human body.
Aguoso, sa [ah-goo-o'-so, sah], *a.* Aqueous.
Agur [ah-goor'], *adv.* (Coll.) Adieu, farewell. Good-bye, by-bye. (Lat. augurium, through late form agurium. According to the Sp. Acad. it is from Turkish.)
Agusanarse [ah-goo-sah-nar'-say], *vr.* To be worm eaten, to be rotten.
Agustiniano, na [ah-goos-te-ne-ah'-no, nah], *m.* & *f.* 1. *V.* Agustino. 2. Belonging to the order of St. Augustin.
Agustino, na [ah-goos-tee'-no, nah], *m.* & *f.* Monk or nun of the order of St. Augustin.
Agutí [ah-goo-tee'], *m.* Agouti, a rodent of tropical America.
Aguzadera [ah-goo-thah-day'-rah], *f.* Whetstone.
Aguzadero [ah-goo-thah-day'-ro], *m.* Haunt of wild boars, where they whet their tusks.
Aguzado, da [ah-goo-thah'-do], *a.* Sharp, pointed, keen.
Aguzadura [ah-goo-thah-doo'-rah], *f.* Whetting or sharpening a tool or weapon.
Aguzanieve [ah-goo-thah-ne-ay'-vay], *f.* Wagtail, a small bird.
Aguzar [ah-goo-thar'], *va.* 1. To whet or sharpen. 2. (Met.) To stimulate, to excite. *Aguzar el ingenio,* To sharpen the wit. *Aguzar las orejas,* To cock up the ears, to listen quickly. *Aguzar la vista,* To sharpen the sight.
Aguzonazo [ah-goo-tho-nah'-tho], *m.* *V.* Hurgonazo.
¡Ah! [ah], *interj.* Ah! *V.* ¡Ay!
Ahebrado, da [ah-ay-brah'-do, dah], *a.* Thread-like, fibrous.
Ahelear [ah-ay-lay-ar'], *va.* To give gall to drink, to make bitter.—*vn.* To taste very bitter (fr. Hiel).
Ahembrado, da [ah-em-brah'-do, dah], *a.* (Obs.) Effeminate. *V.* Afeminado.
Aherrojamiento [ah-er-ro-hah-me-en'-to], *m.* Putting in irons.
Aherrojar [ah-er-ro-har'], *va.* To chain, to put in irons.
Aherrumbrarse [ah-er-room-brar'-say], *vr.* 1. To have the taste and colour of iron or copper, to be ferruginous: applied especially to water which has percolated through an iron-bearing stratum. 2. To be full of scoria.
Ahervorarse [ah-er-vo-rar'-say], *vr.* To be heated by fermentation: applied to piled-up grain.
Ahí [ah-ee'], *adv.* There, in that place; in that; yonder. *De por ahí,* About that, indicating a common trifling thing.
Ahidalgado, da [ah-e-dal-gah'-do, dah], *a.* Gentlemanly.
Ahijada [ah-e-hah'-dah], *f.* 1. God-child, goddaughter. 2. *V.* Ahijado.—3. A paddle-staff.—*pp.* of Ahijar.
Ahijado [ah-e-hah'-do], *m.* 1. God-child. 2. Client, one protected or peculiarly favoured.
Ahijador [ah-e-hah-dor'], *m.* One who puts a young animal to suck.
Ahijar [ah-e-har'], *va.* 1. To adopt. 2. (Among shepherds) To put every lamb with its dam. 3. (Met.) To impute.—*vn.* 1. To bring forth young: applied only to cattle. 2. To bud, to shoot out.
Ahilado [ah-e-lah'-do], *a.* Withered (of plants and trees).—*Cf.* Ahilarse, 4.
Ahilarse [ah-e-lar'-say], *vr.* 1. To be faint for want of nourishment. 2. To grow sour, applied to leaven and bread 3. To grow thin. 4. To be weak, applied to plants.—*vn.* To go single file. *Ahilarse el vino,* To turn ropy, applied to wine.
Ahilo [ah-ee'-lo], *m.* Faintness, weakness for want of food.
Ahinco [ah-een'-co], *m.* Earnestness, eagerness, ardour.
Ahitar [ah-e-tar'], *va.* To surfeit; to overload the stomach, to cloy, to satiate.—*vr.* To be surfeited.
Ahitera [ah-e-tay'-rah], *f.* (Coll.) Violent or continued indigestion.
Ahito, ta [ah-ee'-to, tah], *a.* 1. One that labours under an indigestion. 2. (Met.) Disgusted; tired of a person or thing.—*pp. irr.* of Ahitar.
Ahito [ah-ee'-to], *m.* Indigestion; surfeit; repletion.
¡Aho! *int.* (Obs.) Hallo!
Ahobachonado, da [ah-o-bah-cho-nah'-do, dah], *a.* (Coll.) Dull, slovenly, lazy; cowardly.
Ahocicar [ah-o-the-car'], *vn.* (Naut.) To pitch or plunge.
Ahocinarse [ah-o-the-nar'-say], *vr.* To run precipitately: applies to a stream.
Ahogadero [ah-o-gah-day'-ro], *m.* 1. Hangman's rope. 2. Place difficult to breathe in. 3. Throat-band, a part of the head-stall of a bridle or halter.
Ahogadizo, za [ah-o-gah-dee'-tho, thah], *a.* Harsh, unpalatable. *Carne ahogadiza,* Flesh of animals suffocated or drowned.
Ahogado, da [ah-o-gah'-do, dah], *a.* Suffocated; close, unventilated. *Carnero ahogado,* Stewed mutton. *Dar mate ahogado,* To pin up the king at the game of chess. (Met.) To insist upon things being done without delay. *Estar ahogado* or *verse ahogado,* To be overwhelmed with business or trouble.—*pp.* of Ahogar.
Ahogador, ra [ah-o-gah-dor', rah], *m.* & *f.* Suffocater, hangman.
Ahogamiento [ah-o-gah-me-en'-to], *m.* 1. Suffocation. 2. *V.* Ahogo. *Ahogamiento de la madre,* Hysterics, an hysteric fit.
Ahogar [ah-o-gar'], *va.* 1. To choke, to throttle, to kill by stopping the breath, to smother. 2. To drown. 3. (Met.) To oppress. 4. (Met.) To quench, to extinguish. 5. To water plants to excess. 6. (Naut.) To founder.—*vr.* 1. To be suffocated. 2. To drown one's self, be drowned.
Ahogo [ah-o'-go], *m.* Oppression, anguish, pain, severe affliction.
Ahoguido [ah-o-gee'-do], *m.* *V.* Ahoguío.
Ahoguijo [ah-o-gee'-ho], *m.* (Vet.) A quinsy, a swelled throat. *V.* Esquinencia.
Ahoguío [ah-o-gee'-o], *m.* Oppression in the breast which hinders breathing with ease.
Ahojar [ah-o-har'], *vn.* (Prov.) To eat the leaves of trees; applied to cattle.
Ahombrado, da [ah-om-brah'-do, dah], *a.* (Coll.) Masculine: applied to a woman. *V.* Hombruno.
Ahondar [ah-on-dar'], *va.* To sink.—*vn.* 1. To penetrate into a thing; to hollow out; to dip, as of the ground. 2. (Met.) To advance in the knowledge of things; to investigate.
Ahonde [ah-on'-day], *m.* 1. Act and effect of sinking. 2. The depth to which a mine ought to reach in some countries of America to acquire title of ownership (7 varas).
Ahora [ah-o'-rah], *adv.* Now, at present. *Ahora ahora,* Just now. *Ahora mismo ha empezado el sermón,* The sermon began this moment. *Por ahora,* For the present. *Ahora bien,* Well, granted, nevertheless. *Hasta ahora,* Hitherto. (Lat. hac hora.)
Ahora [ah-o'-rah], *conj.* Whether, or.
Ahorcado [ah-or-cah'-do], *m.* Hanged man.—*pp.* of Ahorcar.
Ahorcadura [ah-or-cah-doo'-rah], *f.* The act of hanging.
Ahorcajarse [ah-or-cah-har'-say], *vr.* To sit astride.
Ahorcar [ah-or-car'], *va.* To kill by hanging. *Ahorcar los hábitos,* To abandon the ecclesiastical garb for another profession. *Que me ahorquen si lo hago,* Hang me if I do.—*vr.* To be vexed, to be very angry.
Ahorita [ah-o-ree'-tah], *adv.* (Coll.) Just now; this minute.
Ahormar [ah-or-mar'], *va.* 1. To fit or adjust. 2. To wear clothes or shoes until they fit easy. 3. (Met.) To bring one to a sense of his duty.
Ahornagarse [ah-or-nah-gar'-say], *vr.* To get scorched or burned: said of young leaves or shoots of plants.
Ahornar [ah-or-nar'], *va.* To put in an oven.—*vr.* To be scorched or burnt in the oven without being baked inwardly: applied to bread.
Ahorquillado, da [ah-or-keel-lyah'-do, dah], *a.* Forked.—*pp.* of Ahorquillar.
Ahorquillar [ah-or-keel-lyar'], *va.* To stay, to prop up with forks.—*vr.* To become forked.
Ahorrado, da [ah-or-rah'-do, dah], *a.* Unembarrassed.—*pp.* of Ahorrar.
Ahorrador, ra [ah-or-rah-dor', rah], *m.* & *f.* Emancipator.
Ahorramiento [ah-or-rah-me-en'-to], *m.* Emancipation, enfranchisement.
Ahorrar [ah-or-rar'], *va.* 1. To enfranchise, to emancipate. 2. To economize, to save, to spare. 3. To shun labour, danger, or difficulties. 4. Among graziers, to give the elder shepherds leave to keep a certain number of sheep in the pastures.
Ahorrativa [ah-or-rah-tee'-vah], *f.* (Coll.) *V.* Ahorro.
Ahorrativo, va [ah-or-rah-tee'-vo, vah], *a.* Frugal, thrifty, saving. *Andar* or *ir a la ahorrativa,* To go frugally to work.
Ahorro [ah-or'-ro], *m.* 1. Parsimony, frugality, husbandry. 2. Saving, sparingness. *Banco de ahorros,* Savings-bank.
Ahoyador [ah-o-yah-dor'], *m.* 1. (Prov.) One that makes holes for the purpose of planting. 2. (Met.) Grave-digger.
Ahoyadura [ah-o-yah-doo'-rah], *f.* Making holes in the ground.
Ahoyar [ah-o-yar'], *va.* To dig holes for trees.
Ahuchador, ra [ah-oo-chah-dor', rah], *m.* & *f.* One who hoards; a miser.
Ahuchar [ah-oo-char'], *va.* To hoard up.
Ahuecamiento [ah-oo-ay-cah-me-en'-to], *m.* Excavation.
Ahuecar [ah-oo-ay-car'], *va.* 1. To excavate, to scoop out. 2. To loosen a thing which was close pressed or matted.—*vr.* To grow haughty, proud, or elated.
Ahuehué, or **Ahuehuete** [ah-oo-ay-oo-ay']. (Bot.) Tree of Mexico, like a cypress.
Ahumada [ah-oo-mah'-dah], *f.* 1. Signal given with smoke, from the coast, watch-towers, or high places. 2. A sea-fish.
Ahumar [ah-oo-mar'], *va.* To smoke, to cure in smoke.—*vn.* To fume.
Ahur [ah-oor']. *V.* Agur.
Ahusado, da [ah-oo-sah'-do, dah], *a.* Spindle-shaped.—*pp.* of Ahusar.
Ahusar [ah-oo-sar'], *va.* To make slender as a spindle.—*vr.* To taper.
Ahuyentador, ra [ah-oo-yen-tah-dor', rah], *m.* & *f.* A scarecrow.

Ahuyentar [ah-oo-yen-tar'], *va.* 1. To drive away, to put to flight. *Ahuyentar los pájaros, o las moscas,* To scare away birds or flies. 2. (Met.) To overcome a passion; to banish care.

Aijada [ah-e-hah'-dah], *f.* Goad. *V.* AGUIJADA.

Aiófilo, la [ah-e-o'-fe-lo, lah], *a.* Evergreen, whose leaves last more than a year.

Airadamente [ah-e-rah-dah-men'-tay], *adv.* Angrily; in an angry manner, hastily.

Airado, da [ah-e-rah'-do, dah], *a.* Angry, wrathful. (Met.) Furious, vexed.

Airar [ah-e-rar'], *va.* To anger, to irritate.—*vr.* To grow angry.

Airazo [ah-e-rah'-tho], *m. aug.* A violent gust of wind.

Aire [ah'-e-ray], *m.* 1. Air. 2. Briskness, of the motion of a horse. 3. (Met.) Gracefulness of manners and gait; air, carriage, demeanour, sprightliness. 4. Aspect, countenance, look. 5. Musical composition. 6. Frivolity. 7. The veil which covers the chalice and paten in the Greek rite. *Aires naturales,* The native air. *Beber los aires* or *los vientos,* To desire anxiously. *Creerse del aire,* To be credulous. *Hablar al aire,* To talk idly. *¿ Qué aires le traen a Vd. por acá?* What good wind brings you here? *Tomar el aire,* To take a walk. *En aire,* In a good humour. *De buen o mal aire,* In a pleasing or peevish manner. *En el aire,* In a moment.

Airear [ah-e-ray-ar'], *va.* 1. To give air, to ventilate. 2. To aerate, charge with gas.—*vr.* 1. To take the air. 2. To cool one's self, to obstruct perspiration.

Airecico, llo, to [ah-e-ray-thee'-co, theel'-lyo, thee'-to], *m. dim.* A gentle breeze.

Airón [ah-e-ron'], *m. aug.* 1. Violent gale. 2. Ornament of plumes; crest of hats or caps, or feminine headgear. 3. The crested heron, egret. 4. A deep Moorish well.

Airosamente [ah-e-ro-sah-men'-tay], *adv.* Gracefully, lightly.

Airosidad [ah-e-ro-se-dad'], *f.* Graceful deportment.

Airoso, sa [ah-e-ro'-so, sah], *a.* 1. Airy, windy. 2. Graceful, genteel, lively. 3. Successful.

Aislable [ah-is-lah'-blay], *a.* Insoluble; capable of being obtained pure.

Aislacionismo [ah-is-lah-the-o-nees'-mo], *m.* Isolation, keeping aloof from other countries.

Aislacionista [ah-is-lah-the-o-nees'-tah], *m. & f.* Isolationist, advocate of isolationism in international relations.

Aisladamente [ah-is-lah-dah-men'-tay], *adv.* Isolately; one by one.

Aislado, da [ah-is-lah'-do, dah], *a.* Isolated, embarrassed.—*pp.* of AISLAR.

Aislador, ra [ah-is-lah-dor', rah], *a.* Isolating insulating.

Aislamiento [ah-is-lah-me-en'-to], *m.* Isolation. (Arch.) Isolation, the distance between columns and pilasters.

Aislante [ah-is-lahn'-tay), *a.* Insulating. *Material aislante* or *aislador,* (Elec.) Insulating material.

Aislar [ah-is-lar'], *va.* 1. To surround with water. 2. To insulate.

Ajá! [ah-hah'], *int.* Aha! (from Arabic *hasha,* joy. Acad.). Also *¡ Ajajá !*

Ajada [ah-hah'-dah], *f.* A sauce made of bread steeped in water, garlic, and salt.

Ajado, da [ah-hah'-do, dah], *a.* Garlicky.—*pp.* of AJAR.

Ajamiento [ah-hah-me-en'-to], *m.* Disfiguration; deformity.

Ajar [ah-har'], *m.* Garlic-field.

Ajar [ah-har'], *va* 1. To spoil, to mar, to tarnish, to fade. 2. To abuse. *Ajar la vanidad a alguno,* To pull down one's pride.

Ajarafe [ah-hah-rah'-fay], *m.* 1. A royal seat, or possession of a Mussulman prince or king, during the Arabic dominion in Spain. 2. (Obs.) *V.* AZOTEA and TERRADO.

Ajazo [ah-hah'-tho], *m.* A large head of garlic.

Aje [ah'-hay], *m.* 1. A chronic complaint. 2. (Bot.) A tuber from the Antilles, like a yam, or sweet potato. 3. (Met.) Humiliation, disrespect.

Ajea [ah-hay'-ah], *f.* A sort of brushwood used for firing in the environs of Toledo.

Ajear [ah-hay-ar'], *va.* To cry like a partridge closely pursued.

Ajedrecista [ah-hay-dray-thees'-tah], *m. & f.* Chess player.

Ajedrez [ah-hay-dreth'], *m.* 1. Chess, a game. 2. (Naut.) Netting, grating.

Ajedrezado, da [ah-hay-dray-thah'-do, dah], *a.* Checkered.

Ajenabe [ah-hay-nah'-bay], *m.* (Bot.) Wild mustard.

Ajenable [ah-hay-nah'-blay], *a.* Alienable.

Ajengibre [ah-hen-hee'-bray], *m.* *V.* JENGIBRE.

Ajenjo [ah-hen'-ho], *m.* 1. (Bot.) Wormwood. 2. Sage-brush.

Ajeno, na [ah-hay-no, nah], *a.* 1. Another's. 2. Foreign, strange. 3. Abhorrent, contrary to, remote. 4. Ignorant. 5. (Met.) Improper. *Ajeno de verdad,* Void of truth. *Estar ajeno de sí,* To be unselfish, without self-love. *Estar ajeno de una cosa,* Not to have heard a rumour.

Ajenuz [ah-hay-nooth'], *m.* (Bot.) Field fennel-flower. Nigella arvensis.

Ajeo [ah-hay'-oh], *m.* *Perro de ajeo,* Setter-dog.

Ajete [ah-hay'-tay], *m.* 1. Young or tender garlic. 2. Sauce made with garlic.

Ajetrearse [ah-hay-tray-ar'-say], *vr.* To become bodily fatigued, to fidget.

Ají [ah-hee'], *m.* 1. The red Indian dwarf pepper. *V.* CHILE. Capsicum. 2. A sort of sauce made in America of the ají-pepper.

Ajiaceite [ah-he-ah-thay'-e-tay], *m.* Mixture of garlic and oil.

Ajiaco [ah-he-ah'-co], *m.* 1. A dish made of boiled meat and vegetables. 2. A sort of sauce made with the *ají* for certain dishes in America.

Ajicola [ah-he-co'-lah], *f.* Glue made of cuttings of leather boiled with garlic.

Ajilimoje, or **Ajilimójili** [ah-he-le-mo'-hay, ah-he-le-mo'-he-lee], *m.* Sauce of pepper and garlic.

Ajillo [ah-heel'-lyo], *m.* Tender young garlic.

Ajimez [ah-he-meth'], *m.* An arched window with a pillar in the centre to support it.

Ajipuerro [ah-he-poo-er'-ro], *m.* Leek. *V.* PUERRO.

Ajo [ah'-ho], *m.* 1. (Bot.) Garlic. 2. Garlic-sauce for meat. 3. (Met.) Paint for ladies. 4. (Met.) Affair discussed by many. *Revolver el ajo* or *el ruido,* To stir up new disturbances. *Ajo blanco,* Dish made of bruised garlic, bread, oil, and water. *Echar ajos y cebollas,* To insult one vilely. *Se fué echando ajos y cebollas,* (Coll.) He went off uttering oaths and imprecations.

Ajobar [ah-ho-bar'], *va.* (Coll.) To carry upon one's back heavy loads.

Ajobilla [ah-ho-beel'-lya], *f.* A common sea-shell of the Spanish coast, with small teeth.

Ajobo [ah-ho'-bo], *m.* 1. (Obs.) Carrying heavy loads. 2. A heavy load.

Ajofaina [ah-ho-fah'-e-nah], *f.* *V.* ALJOFAINA.

Ajolio [ah-ho'-le-o], *m.* (Prov.) Sauce made of oil and garlic.

Ajolote [ah-ho-lo'-tay], *m.* An amphibian of the Lake of Mexico; the axolotl.

Ajomate [ah-ho-mah'-tay], *m.* (Bot.) A delicate aquatic plant.

Ajonjera [ah-hon-hay'-rah], *f* **Ajonjero** [ah-hon-hay'-ro], *m.* (Bot.) The low carline thistle, yielding ajonje. Carlina acaulis.

Ajonjolí, Aljonjolí [ah-hon-ho-lee', al-hon-ho-lee'], *m.* (Bot.) Benne, sesame, an oily grain. Sesamum orientale.

Ajoqueso [ah-ho-kay'-so], *m.* Dish made of garlic and cheese.

Ajorca [ah-hor'-cah], *f.* Rings worn by the Moorish women about the wrists or ankles.

Ajordar [ah-hor-dar'], *va.* (Prov.) To bawl, to cry out.

Ajornalar [ah-hor-nah-lar'], *va.* To hire by the day.

Ajuagas [ah-hoo-ah'-gas], *f. pl.* Malanders, a disease in horses; or ulcers over the hoofs. *V.* ESPARAVÁN.

Ajuar [ah-hoo-ar'], *m.* 1. Apparel and furniture which a bride brings to her husband. 2. Household furniture. *Ajuar de novia,* Trousseau.

Ajudiado, da [ah-hoo-de-ah'-do, dah], *a.* Jewish; Jew-like.

Ajuiciado, da [ah-hoo-e-the-ah'-do, dah], *a.* Judicious, prudent.—*pp.* AJUICIAR.

Ajuiciar [ah-hoo-e-the-ar'], *vn.* To acquire judgment; to become prudent.

Ajustadamente [ah-hoos-tah-dah-men'-tay], *adv.* Justly, rightly.

Ajustado, da [ah-hoos-tah'-do, dah], *a.* Exact. right; stingy. *Es un hombre ajustado,* He is a man of strict morals.—*pp.* of AJUSTAR.

Ajustador [ah-hoos-tah-dor'], *m.* 1. Close waistcoat, jacket. 2. Waist, jacket. 3. The person in a printing-office who arranges the form; justifier. 4. (Mech.) Adapter, coupler, adjusting tool.

Ajustamiento [ah-hoos-tah-me-en'-to], *m.* 1. Agreement. 2. Settling of accounts. 3. Receipts.

Ajustar [ah-hoos-tar'], *va.* 1. To regulate, to adjust, to accord, to compose, to guide, to measure, to justify type. 2. To concert, to make an agreement, to bargain. 3. To reconcile, to heal. 4. To examine accounts. 5. To settle a balance. 6. To press close, to oppress. 7. To fit; to fashion; to accommodate.—*vr.* 1. To settle matters. 2. To conform; to combine. 3. To approach. 4. To engage.

Ajuste [ah-hoos'-tay], *m.* 1. Proportion of the constituent parts of a thing. 2. Agreement, contract, covenant, accommodation; engagement; settlement.—*pl.* Couplings.

Ajusticiar [ah-hoos-te-the-ar'], *va.* To execute, to put to death.

Al [al], *art.* 1. An article formed by a syncope of the preposition *a* and the article *el,* and placed before nouns, etc.; e. g. *El juez debe castigar al delincuente,* The judge ought to punish the delinquent. 2. An Arabic article corresponding to the Spanish articles *el* and *la* in compound words; e. g. *Alárabe,* The Arab. 3. Used with the infinitive of divers verbs; e. g. ***Al amanecer,*** **At the dawn of day.**

Al [al], *pron. indef.* (Obs.) Other, contrary, all other things. *V.* DEMÁS and OTRO. *Por al, V.* POR TANTO.

Ala [ah'-lah], *f.* 1. Wing; aisle. 2. Row or file. 3. (Mil.) Flank, wing, of army. 4. Brim of the hat. 5. Auricle, the external fleshy part of the ear. *Alas del corazón* (Anat.), Auricles of the heart. 6. Fin of a fish. 7. Leaf of a hinge; of a door, of a table. *Ala de mesana*, (Naut.) A driver.—*pl.* (Naut.) Upper studding-sails. *Alas de gavia*, Main-top studding-sails. *Alas de velacho*, Fore studding-sails. *Alas de sobremesana*, Mizzen-top studding-sails. *Alas de proa*, Head of the ship.—*Alas*, Protection. Boldness. *Cortar las alas*, To take one down a peg. (Poet.) Velocity.

Alá [ah-lah'], *m.* Allah, an Arabic word for God.

Alabado [ah-lah-bah'-do], *m.* Hymn sung in praise of the sacrament when it is put into the tabernacle.—*pp.* of ALABAR.

Alabador, ra [ah-lah-bah-dor', rah], *m.* & *f.* Applauder, commender.

Alabancioso, sa [ah-lah-ban-the-oh'-so, sah], *a.* (Coll.) Boastful, ostentatious.

Alabandina [ah-lah-ban-dee'-nah], *f.* 1. Manganese sulphide. 2. Alabandine, spinel ruby.

Alabanza [ah-lah-bahn'-thah], *f.* Praise, commendation; glory.

Alabar [ah-lah-bar'], *va.* To praise, to extol, to glorify, to magnify, to commend, to cry up.—*vr.* To praise one's self.

Alabarda [ah-lah-bar'-dah], *f.* 1. Halberd, a kind of battle-axe and pike at the end of a long staff. 2. (Obs.) Sergeant's place, from a halberd having formerly been borne by sergeants.

Alabardazo [ah-lah-bar-dah'-tho], *m.* A blow with a halberd.

Alabardero [ah-lah-bar-day'-ro], *m.* 1. Halberdier, armed with a halberd. 2. Claquer, clapper, hired to applaud in a theatre. (Recent.)

Alabastrado, da [ah-lah-bas-trah'-do, dah], *a.* Resembling alabaster.

Alabastrina [ah-lah-bas-tree'-nah], *f.* A thin sheet of alabaster.

Alabastrino, na [ah-lah-bas-tree'-no, nah], *a.* (Poet.) 1. Made of alabaster. 2. Like alabaster.

Alabastro [ah-lah-bas'-tro], *m.* Alabaster.

Álabe [ah'-lah-bay], *m.* 1. Drooping branch of an olive or other tree. 2. Bucket, flier of a water-wheel, float-board, which serves to set it in motion. 3. Mat used in carts. 4. Cam. 5. Tile of the eaves.

Alabearse [ah-lah-bay-ar'-say], *vr.* To warp, to grow bent or crooked.

Alabega [ah-lah-bay'-gah], *f.* (Bot.) Sweet basil. *V.* ALBAHACA.

Alabeo [ah-lah-bay'-o], *m.* Warping, the state of being warped.

Alabiado, da [ah-lah-be-ah'-do, dah], *a.* Lipped or ragged; applied to uneven coined money.

Alacena [ah-lah-thay'-na], *f.* 1. Sideboard, buffet, a cupboard, small pantry in the wall. 2. (Naut.) Locker, a small box in the cabin and sides of a ship.

Alacha [ah-lah'-chah], *f.* Shad. Clupea alosa parva.

Alaciar [ah-lah-the-ar'], *vn.* *V.* ENLACIAR.

Alacrán [ah-lah-crahn'], *m.* 1. A scorpion, a small poisonous animal. 2. Ring of the bit of a bridle. 3. Stop or hook fixed to the rocker of organ-bellows. 4. Chain or link of a sleeve-button. 5. Swivel.

Alacranado, da [ah-lah-crah-nah'-do, dah], *a.* 1. Bit by a scorpion. 2. (Met.) Infected with some vice.

Alacranera [ah-lah-crah-nay'-rah], *f.* (Bot.) Mouse-ear scorpion-grass. Myosotis scorpioides.

Alacridad [ah-lah-cre-dad'], *f.* Alacrity.

Alada [ah-lah'-dah], *f.* Fluttering of the wings.

Aladares [ah-lah-dah'-res], *m. pl.* Locks of hair over the temples; forelocks.

Aladierna [ah-lah-de-er'-nah]. *V.* ALATERNO.

Alado, da [ah-lah'-do, dah], *a.* Winged, feathered.

Aladrada [ah-lah-drah'-dah], *f.* (Prov.) A furrow.

Aladrar [ah-lah-drar'], *va.* (Prov.) To plough the ground.

Aladro [ah-lah'-dro], *m.* 1. Plough. 2. Ploughed land.

Aladroque [ah-lah-dro'-kay], *m.* (Prov.) An unsalted anchovy.

Alafia [ah-lah'-fe-ah], *f.* (Coll.) *Pedir alafia*, To implore mercy and pardon.

Álaga [ah'-lah-gah], *f.* A species of yellow wheat.

Alagartado, da [ah-lah-gar-tah'-do, dah], *a.* Variegated; motley.

Alaica [ah-lah'-ee-cah], *f.* Winged ant or emmet.

Alajor [ah-lah-hor'], *m.* Ground-rent. (Arab. alhushor.)

Alajú [ah-lah-hoo'], *m.* Paste made of almonds, walnuts, honey, etc.

Alama [ah-lah'-mah], *f.* (Prov.) Gold or silver cloth.

Alamar [ah-lah-mar'], *m.* Loop of silk-en twist, or cord, used for button-holes or trimming.

Alambicado, da [ah-lam-be-cah-do, dah], *a.* 1. Distilled. 2. Euphuistic, pedantic (of diction). 3. (Met.) Given with a sparing hand.—*pp.* of ALAMBICAR.

Alambicamiento [ah-lam-be-cah-me-en'-to], *m.* 1. Distillation. 2. Subtilty, euphuism of language.

Alambicar [ah-lam-be-car'], *va.* 1. To distil. 2. To investigate closely. *Alambicar los sesos*, To cudgel one's wits.

Alambique [ah-lam-bee'-kay], *m.* Alembic, still. *Por alambique*, Sparingly, in a penurious manner.

Alambor [ah-lam-bor'], *m.* (Obs. Mil.) Inside slope of a ditch. *V.* ESCARPA.

Alambre [ah-lam'-bray], *m.* 1. Wire of any metal. 2. In olden times copper, or an alloy of copper; bronze. *Alambre de latón*, Brass wire. 3. Bells belonging to sheep, or to beasts of burden. 4. File for papers.

Alambre de tierra [ah-lam'-bray day te-er'-rah], *m.* (Elec.) Ground wire.

Alambrera [ah-lam-bray'-rah], *f.* 1. Wire netting. 2. (Agr.) Wire trellis. 3. Car basket (r. w.).

Alameda [ah-lah-may'-dah], *f.* 1. A grove of poplar-trees. 2. Public walk, mall.

Alamín [ah-lah-meen'], *m.* 1. (Obs.) Clerk of the market appointed to inspect weights and measures. 2. (Prov.) Architect, surveyor of buildings. 3. (Prov.) Farmer appointed to superintend irrigation or distribution of water.

Alamina [ah-lah-mee'-nah], *f.* A fine paid by the potters of Seville for exceeding the number of vessels to be baked at once in an oven.

Alaminazgo [ah-lah-me-nath'-go], *m.* Office of a clerk, etc.

Alamirré [ah-lah-mir-ray'], *m.* Musical sign (fr. la, mi, re).

Álamo [ah'-lah-mo], *m.* (Bot.) Poplar. *Álamo blanco*, White poplar. *Álamo temblón*, Aspen-tree, trembling poplar-tree. *Álamo negro*, Black poplar-tree.

Alampar, *va.* **Alamparse** [ah-lam-par'-say], *vr.* (Coll.) To long for, to crave.

Alamud [ah-lah-mood'], *m.* A square bolt for a door.

Alanceador [ah-lan-thay-ah-dor'], *m.* One who throws a lance, lancer.

Alancear [ah-lan-thay-ar'], *va.* To dart, to spear.

Alandrearse [ah-lan-dray-ar'-say], *vr.* To become dry, stiff, and blanched: applied to silk-worms.

Alanés [ah-lah-ness'], *m.* A kind of stag in New Mexico (Cervus alces).

Alano [ah-lah'-no], *m.* Mastiff of a large kind.

Alano, na [ah-lah'-no, nah], *a.* Belonging to the *Alans* or Vandals of the fifth century.

Alanquía [ah-lan-kee'-ah], *f.* Cardass, waste-card used in silk-weaving.

Alantoides [ah-lan-to'-e-des], *f.* & *a.* Allantois, the fœtal urinary vesicle.

Alanzada [ah-lan-thah'-dah], *f.* (Obs.) *V.* ARANZADA.

Alanzar [ah-lan-thar'], *va.* To throw lances.

Alaqueca [ah-lah-kay'-cah], *f.* Blood-stone.

Alaqueques [ah-lah-kay'-kes], *m. pl.* *V.* ALAQUECA.

Alar [ah-lar'], *m.* 1. Overhanging roof. *V.* ALERO. 2. Snare of horse-hair.

Alar [ah-lar'], *va.* (Naut.) To haul. *V* HALAR.

Alara [ah-lah'-rah] (Huevo en). (Obs.) An egg without a shell.

Alárabe [ah-lah'-rah-bay], **Alarbe** [ah-lar'-bay], *m.* 1. Arabian. 2. An unmannerly person.

Alarde [ah-lar'-day], *m.* 1. Review of soldiers, muster, parade. 2. Ostentation, boasting, vanity. *Hacer alarde*, (Met.) To boast or brag of something. 3. Manifestation.

Alardear [ah-lar-day-ar'], *vn.* 1. To brag. 2. (Obs.) To review.

Alargadera [ah-lar-gah-day'-rah], *f.* (Chem.) Nozzle, adapter; lengthening tube.

Alargador, ra [ah-lar-gah-dor', rah], *m.* & *f.* One who delays, or lengthens out a thing.

Alargamiento [ah-lar-gah-me-en'-to], *m.* The act of lengthening out.

Alargar [ah-lar-gar'], *va.* 1. To lengthen, to expand, to extend. 2. (Met.) To protract, to dwell upon. 3. To increase a marked number or quantity. 4. To reach or hand a thing to another. 5. To resign: yet in this sense *largar* is more used. 6. To send before; to hold out. *Alargar la conversación*, To spin out a conversation. *Alargar el salario*, To increase or augment the pay. *Alargar el cabo*, (Naut.) To pay out the cable.—*vr.* 1. To be prolonged. *Se alargan los días*, The days grow longer. 2. To launch; to withdraw from a place. 3. To expatiate or enlarge on an argument, to go beyond, to exceed. 4. (Naut.) To sheer off.

Alarguez [ah-lar-geth'], *m.* (Bot.) Dog-rose.

Alaria [ah-lah'-re-ah], *f.* A flat iron instrument used by potters to finish and polish their work; plat chisel.

Alarida [ah-lah-ree'-dah], *f.* Hue and cry.

Alarido [ah-lah-ree'-do], *m.* Outcry, shout, howl.

Alarifazgo [ah-lah-re-fath'-go], *m.* (Obs.) Office of an architect and surveyor.

Alarife [ah-lah-ree'-fay], *m.* (Obs.) Architect, builder. (Arab. al'arisha.)
Alarijes [ah-lah-ree'-hes], *f. pl.* A large sort of grapes. *V.* Arije.
Alarma [ah-lar'-mah], *m.* 1. (Mil.) Alarm. 2. Notice of any sudden danger.
Alarmante [ah-lar-mahn'-tay], *a.* Alarming, dangerous.
Alarmar [ah-lar-mar'], *va.* To alarm, to call to arms.
Alarmista [ah-lar-mees'-tah], *m.* An alarmist.
Alasálet [ah-lah-sah'-let], *m.* Sal ammoniac.
Alastrar [ah-las-trar'], *va.* 1. To throw back the ears. *V.* Amusgar. 2. (Naut.) To ballast. *Alastrar un navío,* To ballast a ship.—*vr.* To squat close: applied to game.
Alaterno [ah-lah-ter'-no), *m.* (Bot.) Mock-privet.
Alatón [ah-lah-tone'], *m.* 1. (Obs.) Latten, brass. *V.* Latón. 2. (Bot. Prov.) The fruit of the lote-tree.
Alatonero [ah-lah-to-nay'-ro], *m.* (Bot. Prov.) Nettle or lote-tree.
Alatrón [ah-lah-trone'], *m.* Froth of saltpetre. Afronitro.
Alavanco [ah-lah-vahn'-co], *m.* *V.* Lavanco.
Alavense, Alavés [ah-lah-ven'-say, ah-la-vess'], *a.* Of Alava, Alavese.
Alazán, na [ah-lah-thahn', nah], *a.* Sorrel-coloured.
Alazo [ah-lah'-tho], *m.* A stroke with the wings.
Alazor [ah-lah-thor'], *m.* (Bot.) Bastard saffron.
Alba [ahl'-bah], *f.* 1. Dawn of day, day-spring. 2. Alb, the white gown worn by priests. *No, sino al alba,* Nothing but the dawn (ironical reply to those who ask what they ought to know already).
Albacea [al-bah-thay'-ah], *m.* Testamentary executor.—*f.* Executrix. *V.* Testamentario.
Albaceazgo [al-bah-thay-ahth'-go], *m.* Executorship.
Albacora [al-bah-co'-rah], *f.* 1. A sea-fish much resembling a tunny. Albicore. 2. An early fig of the largest kind. *V.* Breva.
Albada [al-bah'-dah], *f.* (Prov.) Matinade, music which young men in the country give their sweethearts at the break of day. *V.* Alborada. (Mex.) An attack at daybreak.
Albahaca [al-bah-ah'-cah], *f.* (Bot.) Sweet basil. *Albahaca acuática,* A sort of winter thistle. *Albahaca salvaje* or *silvestre,* Stone or wild thistle.
Albahaquero [al-bah-ah-kay'-ro], *m.* 1. A flower-pot. 2. A vender of sweet basil.
Albahaquilla (de río) [al-bah-ah-keel'-lyah], *f.* *V.* Parietaria.
Albaida [al-bah'-e-dah], *f.* (Bot.) The shrubby gypsophila.
Albalá [al-bah-lah'], *m.* & *f.* 1. (Obs.) Royal letters patent. 2. A quittance given by the custom-house. *Albalá de guía,* A passport.
Albanega [al-bah-nay'-gah], *f.* Net for catching partridges or rabbits.
Albanés, esa [al-bah-ness', sah], *a.* Albanian.
Albañal, Albañar [al-bah-nyahl', al-bah-nyar'], *m.* Common sewer, gully-hole.
Albañil [al-bah-nyeel'], *m.* A mason, bricklayer.
Albañilería [al-bah-nye-lay-ree'-ah], *f.* Masonry.
Albaquía [al-bah-kee'-ah], *f.* 1. (Obs.) Remnant. 2. In collecting tithes, an odd portion which does not admit of division. (Ar.)
Albar [al-bar'], *a.* White. This adjective is confined to a few botanical terms only.
Albara [al-bah'-rah], *f.* Arab name for the common bee.
Albarán [al-bah-rahn'], *m.* 1. Placard of apartments to let. 2. (Prov.) Note of hand or other private instrument.
Albarás [al-bah-rahs'], *m.* *V.* Albarazo.
Albarazada [al-bah-rah-thah'-dah], *f.* A marble-coloured grape, common in Andalucia.
Albarazado, da [al-bah-rah-thah'-do, dah], *a.* 1. Affected with the white leprosy. 2. Pale, pallid.
Albarazo [al-bah-rah'-tho], *m.* White leprosy.
Albarca [al-bar'-cah], *f.* *V.* Abarca.
Albarcoquero [al-bar-co-kay'-ro], *m.* (Prov.) Apricot-tree.
Albarda [al-bar'-dah], *f.* Pack-saddle. *Bestia de albarda,* Beast of burden. *Albarda sobre albarda,* Verbiage, useless repetition.
Albardado, da [al-bar-dah'-do, dah], *a.* Applied to animals having a different-coloured skin at the loins.—*pp.* of Albardar.
Albardán [al-bar-dahn'], *m.* (Obs.) Jester, buffoon.
Albardar [al-bar-dar'], *va.* 1. To put on a pack-saddle. 2. To cover fowls which are to be roasted with large slices of bacon. 3. (Met.) To put upon one, take advantage of another's patience. *No se deja poner la albarda,* Not to allow one's self to be maltreated.
Albardela [al-bar-day'-lah], *f.* Small saddle.
Albardería [al-bar-day-ree'-ah], *f.* 1. A place where pack-saddles are made and sold. 2. The trade of a pack-saddle maker.
Albardero [al-bar-day'-ro], *m.* Pack-saddle maker.
Albardilla [al-bar-deel'-lyah], *f.* 1. Small pack-saddle. 2. Coping of a wall. 3. Border of a garden-bed. 4. Small saddle made use of to tame colts. 5. Wool on the back of sheep or lambs. 6. Earth which sticks to a ploughshare. 7. Batter, with which hogs' tongues and feet are covered.—*pl.* Ridges of earth on the sides of deep foot-paths.
Albardín [al-bar-deen'], *m.* (Bot.) Mat-weed. Lygeum spartum.
Albardón [al-bar-done'], *m.* A pannel, a pack-saddle.
Albardoncillo [al-bar-don-theel'-lyo], *m. dim.* A small pack-saddle.
Albarejo, Albarigo [al-bah-ray'-ho, al-bah-ree'-go], *m.* (Prov.) A species of wheat. *V.* Candeal.
Albarela [al-bah-ray'-lah], *f.* (Bot.) A species of edible fungus which grows upon the chestnut and poplar.
Albaricoque [al-bah-re-co'-kay], *m.* (Bot.) Apricot.
Albaricoquero [al-bah-re-co-kay'-ro], *m.* Apricot-tree.
Albarillo [al-bah-reel'-lyo], *m.* 1. A tune played on the guitar, for country dances. 2. A small kind of apricot.
Albarino [al-bah-ree'-no], *m.* A white paint formerly used by women.
Albarrada [al-bar-rah'-dah], *f.* 1. A dry wall, inclosure. 2. Ditch for defence in war.
Albarradón [al-bar-rah-done'], *m.* A mound to hinder inundation.
Albarrana [al-bar-rah'-nah], *f.* (Bot.) *Cebolla albarrana,* Squill. Scilla maritima. *Torre albarrana,* A sort of watch-tower.
Albarranilla [al-bar-rah-neel'-lya], *f.* A blue-flowered variety of onion.
Albarraz [al-bar-rath'], *m.* (Bot.) 1. *V.* Albarazo. 2. Lousewort. Delphinium staphisagria.
Albatoza [al-bah-to'-thah], *f.* A small covered boat.
Albatros [al-bah'-tros], *m.* The albatross.
Albayaldado, da [al-bah-yal-dah'-do, dah], *a.* Covered with white-lead.
Albayalde [al-bah-yahl'-day], *m.* White-lead, ceruse, lead carbonate.
Albazano, na [al-bah-thah'-no, nah], *a.* Of a dark chestnut colour.
Albazo [al-bah'-tho], *m.* (Obs.) A military term implying an assault at day-break.
Albear [al-bay-ar'], *va.* To whiten. *V.* Blanquear.
Albedrío [al-bay-dree'-o], *m.* 1. Freedom of will. 2. Free-will directed by caprice, and not by reason. *Libre albedrío,* Liberty.
Albéitar [al-bay'-e-tar], *m.* A farrier, veterinary surgeon.
Albeitería [al-bay-e-tay-ree'-ah], *f.* Farriery; veterinary surgery.
Albenda [al-ben'-dah], *f.* Hangings of white linen.
Albendera [al-ben-day'-rah], *f.* 1. Woman who makes hangings. 2. A gadding idle woman.
Albengala [al-ben-gah'-lah], *f.* A sort of gauze worn in the turbans of the Moors in Spain.
Albéntola [al-ben'-to-lah], *f.* A slight net, made of a very fine thread.
Alberca [al-ber'-cah], *f.* 1. A pond or pool. 2. Reservoir, tank, mill-pond. 3. Vat (of tannery).
Albercón [al-ber-cone'], *m. aug.* A large pool or pond.
Albérchiga, or **Albérchigo** [al-ber'-che-gah, or al-ber'-che-go], *m.* & *f.* (Bot.) Peach, strictly a clingstone peach. Amygdalus Persica.
Alberengena [al-bay-ren-hay'-nah], *f.* (Bot.) Egg-plant. Solanum melongena. *V.* Berengena.
Albergador, ra [al-ber-gah-dor', rah], *m.* & *f.* A hotel-keeper.
Albergar [al-ber-gar'], *va.* 1. To lodge, to harbour. 2. To keep a lodging-house.—*vr.* To take a lodging.
Albergue [al-ber'-gay], *m.* 1. Lodging or lodging-house. 2. Den for wild beasts. 3. Hospital for orphans. 4. Place, space, shelter.
Alberguería [al-ber-gay-ree'-ah], *f.* (Obs.) 1. Inn. 2. Hospital for poor travellers. *V.* Posada.
Alberguero [al-ber-gay'-ro], *m.* (Obs.) Innkeeper.
Albericoque [al-bay-re-co'-kay]. *V.* Albaricoque.
Albero [al-bay'-ro], *m.* 1. Whitish earth. 2. A cloth for cleaning plates and dishes.
Alberquero [al-ber-kay'-ro], *m.* One who takes care of the pond where flax is steeped.
Alberquilla [al-ber-keel'-lyah], *f. dim.* A little pool.
Albicante [al-be-can'-tay], *a.* That which whitens or blanches.
Albigense [al-be-hen'-say], *a.* Belonging to the sect of Albigenses, which sprang up in Albis in France.
Albihar [al-be-ar'], *m.* (Bot.) Ox-eye. Buphthalmum.
Albilla [al-beel'-lyah], *f.* **Albillo** [al-beel'-lyo], *m.* An early white grape. Sweet water.
Albillo [al-beel'lyo], *a.* Applied to the wine of a white grape.
Albín [al-been'], *m.* 1. Hæmatites or bloodstone, a sort of iron ore of a brown colour. 2. Dark carmine pigment from this ore, used in alfresco painting.
Albina [al-bee'-nah], *f.* A marshy

piece of ground covered with nitre in the summer season.
Albino, na [al-bee'-no, nah], *a.* 1. Albino. 2. *m.* A person having the skin and hair perfectly white, and the iris of the eye generally pink.
Albión [al-be-on'], *f.* Albion, the ancient name of England.
Albis [ahl'-bis]. (Met.) *Quedarse in albis,* To be frustrated in one's hopes, to be disappointed.
Albitana [al-be-tah'-nah], *f.* 1. Fence used by gardeners to inclose plants. 2. (Naut.) An apron. *Albitana del codaste,* (Naut.) Inner post.
Albo, ba [ahl'-bo, bah], *a.* Very white. (Poetic.)
Alboaire [al-bo-ah'-ee-ray], *m.* Glazed tile work.
Albogalla [al-bo-gahl'-lyah], *f.* A kind of gall-nut.
Albogue [al-bo'-gay], *m.* 1. A pastoral flute much used in Biscay. 2. Martial music, played with two plates of brass resembling the *crotalum* of the ancients; a cymbal.
Alboguero, ra [al-bo-gay'-ro, rah], *m.* & *f.* One who makes *albogues,* or pastoral flutes, or plays on them.
Albohol [al-bo-ole'], *m.* (Bot.) A red poppy. *V.* Amapola.
Albóndiga [al-bon'-de-gah], *f.* A ball made of forced meat chopped fine with eggs and spice.
Albondiguilla [al-bon-de-geel'-lyah], *f. dim.* A small ball of forced meat.
Albor [al-bor'], *m.* (Poet.) 1. Whiteness. 2. Dawn. *Los primeros albores del juicio,* The first dawnings of the mind.
Alborada [al-bo-rah'-dah], *f.* 1. Twilight, the first dawn of day. 2. (Mil.) Action fought at the dawn of day. 3. Reveille, the first military call of the day. 4. Morning watch. *V.* Alba-da.
Alborear [al-bo-ray-ar'], *vn.* To dawn.
Alborga [al-bor'-gah], *f.* A sort of sandal made of mat-weed.
Albornía [al-bor-nee'-ah], *f.* A large glazed jug.
Alborno [al-bor'-no], *m.* (Bot.) Alburnum.
Albornoz [al-bor-noth'], *m.* 1. Coarse woollen stuff. 2. Cloak which forms part of the Moorish dress.
Alboronía [al-bo-ro-nee'-ah], *f.* A dish made with egg-plant, tomatoes, pumpkins, and pimento.
Alboroque [al-bo-ro'-kay], *m.* Regalement given at the conclusion of a bargain: treat.
Alborotadamente [al-bo-ro-tah-dah-men'-tay], *adv.* Noisily, confusedly.
Alborotadizo, za [al-bo-ro-tah-dee-tho', thah], *a.* *V.* Alborotado.
Alborotado, da [al-bo-ro-tah'-do, dah], *a.* Of a restless disposition, turbulent.—*pp.* of Alborotar.
Alborotador, ra [al-bo-ro-tah-dor', rah], *m.* & *f.* A violator of peace, rioter.
Alborotapueblos [al-bo-ro-tah-poo-ay'-blos], *m.* 1. A mover of sedition. 2. (Coll.) A good-natured person who always proposes feasts in companies and parties.
Alborotar [al-bo-ro-tar'], *va.* To disturb, to vex.—*vr.* 1. To come over. 2. To fling out.
Alboroto [al-bo-ro'-to], *m.* 1. Disturbance, tumult, riot, faction; convulsion. 2. Outcry, clatter, noisiness; vulgarly, fuss, hubbub.
Alborozador, ra [al-bo-ro-thah-dor', rah], *m.* & *f.* Promoter of mirth.
Alborozar [al-bo-ro-thar'], *va.* To exhilarate, to promote mirth.
Alborozo [al-bo-ro'-tho], *m.* Merriment, exhilaration, gaiety.
Albortante [al-bor-tahn'-tay], *m.* A branch for a candle, or light in the wall, or in the candelabra.
Albrán [al-brahn'], *m.* A duckling.
Albricias [al-bree'-the-as], *f. pl.* Reward given for some good news. *Ganar las albricias,* To obtain a reward for some good news.—*int.* *¡Albricias, albricias!* Joy! joy!
Albudeca [al-boo-day'-cah], *f.* (Bot.) A watermelon. *V.* Sandía.
Albuérbola [al-boo-er'-bo-lah], *f.* Exhilaration, acclamation.
Albufera [al-boo-fay'-rah], *f.* A large lake formed by the sea.
Albugíneo, nea [al-boo-hee'-nay-o, nay-ah], *a.* Albugineous, entirely white, like the sclerotic. (Anat.) Albuminous.
Albuginoso, sa [al-boo-he-no'-so, sah], *a.* *V.* Albugíneo.
Albugo [al-boo'-go], *m.* Leucoma, a white opacity upon the cornea of the eye.
Albuhera [al-boo-ay'-rah], *f.* A fresh-water lake. *V.* Albufera.
Álbum [ahl'-boom], *m.* Album.
Albumen [al-boo'-men], *m.* (Bot.) Albumen. Nourishing matter, not a part of the embryo, stored up in the seed.
Albúmina [al-boo'-me-nah], *f.* (Chem.) Albumin, as represented in the white of egg; a constituent of some animal fluids, and sparingly found likewise in some plants.
Albuminoso, sa [al-boo-me-no'-so, sah], *a.* Albuminous.
Albur [al-boor'], *m.* 1. Dace, a river fish. Cyprinus leuciscus. 2. A sort of game at cards. 3. Risk, contingency. *Correr un albur,* To venture, to chance.
Albura [al-boo'-rah], *f.* 1. Whiteness. 2. (Bot.) *V.* Alborno. *Albura de huevo,* (Obs.) *V.* Clara de huevo.
Alburero [al-boo-ray'-ro], *m.* A player at the game *albures.*
Albures [al-boo'-res], *m. pl.* A game at cards.
Alburno [al-boor'-no], *m.* 1. (Bot.) *V.* Alborno. 2. The bleak, a fish.
Alca [ahl'-cah], *f.* Razorbill, a bird.
Alcabala [al-cah-bah'-lah], *f.* 1. Excise. *Alcabala del viento,* Duty paid on goods sold by chance. *El caudal de fulano está en alcabala de viento,* He lives upon what he earns. 2. A net. *V.* Jábega.
Alcabalatorio [al-cah-bah-lah-to'-re-o], *m.* Book of rates of the *alcabala.*
Alcabalero [al-cah-bah-lay'-ro], *m.* A tax-gatherer; revenue officer.
Alcabiaz [al-cah-be-ath'], *m.* Aviary, a large cage for birds. *V.* Alcahaz.
Alcabor [al-cah-bor'], *m.* (Prov.) Flue of a chimney.
Alcabuz [al-cah-booth'], *m.* (Obs.) *V.* Arcabuz.
Alcacel, Alcacer [al-cah-thel', al-cah-therr'], *m.* Green barley.
Alcachofa [al-cah-cho'-fah], *f.* 1. (Bot.) Artichoke. 2. Instrument serving to stop a flux of blood. 3. Fluted mallets used by ropemakers.
Alcachofado, da [al-cah-cho-fah'-do, dah], *a.* Resembling an artichoke.
Alcachofado [al-cah-cho-fah'-do], *m.* Dish of artichokes.
Alcachofal [al-cah-cho-fahl'], *m.* Ground where artichokes grow.
Alcachofera [al-cah-cho-fay'-rah], *f.* An artichoke-plant.
Alcahaz [al-cah-ahth'], *m.* A large cage for birds.
Alcahazada [al-cah-ah-thah'-dah], *f.* A number of birds in a cage.
Alcahazar [al-cah-ah-thar'], *va.* To shut up birds in the *alcahaz.*
Alcaheta [al-cah-ay'-tah], *f.* Alcahest, a supposed universal solvent.
Alcahuete, ta [al-cah-oo-ay'-tay, tah], *m.* & *f.* Pimp, procurer, bawd, whoremonger.
Alcahuetear [al-cah-oo-ay-tay-ar'], *va.* To bawd, to pander, to procure women.
Alcahuetería [al-cah-oo-ay-tay-ree'-ah], *f.* 1. Bawdry. 2. Hiding persons who want concealment.
Alcahuetillo, lla [al-cah-oo-ay-teel'-lyo, lyah], *m.* & *f. dim.* A little pimp.
Alcahuetón, na, Alcahuetazo, za [al-cah-oo-ay-tone', nah, al-cah-oo-ay-tah'-tho, thah], *m.* & *f. aug.* A great pander, a great bawd.
Alcaicería [al-cah-e-thay-ree'-ah], *f.* Market-place for raw silk.
Alcaico [al-cah'-e-co], *a.* (Poet.) Alcaic verse in Latin.
Alcaide [al-cah'-e-day], *m.* 1. Governor of a castle or fort. 2. Jailer, warden.
Alcaidesa [al-cah-e-day'-sah], *f.* Wife of a governor or jailer.
Alcaidía [al-cah-e-dee'-ah], *f.* 1. Office of a governor, and district of his jurisdiction; wardenship. 2. Office of a jailer. 3. Ancient duty paid for the passage of cattle.
Alcaldada [al-cal-dah'-dah], *f.* 1. An inconsiderate action of an *alcalde* or petty judge. 2. (Coll.) Any word said, or action performed, with an air of mock authority. 3. A preposterous act or deed that causes a great noise.
Alcalde [al-cahl'-day], *m.* 1. Justice of the peace. 2. Mayor of a city, or chairman of a council (of town government). 3. He who leads off a country dance. *Tener al padre alcalde,* To enjoy the protection of a judge or other man in power. 4. Game at cards. *Alcalde de barrio,* Justice of the peace of a ward. *Alcalde de primera elección,* The senior judge. —— *de segunda elección,* The junior judge. The *alcalde* acts as the *mayor* of the city council.
Alcaldear [al-cal-day-ar'], *vn.* (Coll.) To play the alcalde.
Alcaldesa [al-cal-day'-sah], *f.* The wife of an alcalde.
Alcaldía [al-cal-dee'-ah], *f.* Office and jurisdiction of an alcalde.
Alcalescencia [al-cah-les-then'-the-ah], *f.* (Chem.) *V.* Alcalización.
Alcalescente [al-cah-les-then'-tay], *a.* (Chem.) Partaking of alkaline properties.
Álcali [ahl'-cah-le], *m.* (Chem.) An alkali. *Álcali fijo,* Fixed alkali.
Alcalificable [al-cah-le-fe-cah'-blay], *a.* Changeable into an alkali.
Alcalígeno, na [al-cah-lee'-hay-no, nah], *a.* Alkaligenous, producing alkali.
Alcalímetro [al-cah-lee'-may-tro], *m.* Alkalimeter, an instrument for estimating percentage of fixed alkali.
Alcalinidad [al-cah-le-ne-dad'], *f.* Alkalinity, state of being alkaline.
Alcalino, na, Alcalizado, da [al-cah-lee'-no, nah, al-cah-le-thah'-do, dah], *a.* Alkaline.—*Alcalizado, da, pp.* of Alcalizar.
Alcalización [al-cah-le-thah-the-on'], *f.* (Chem.) Alkalization.
Alcalizar [al-cah-le-thar'], *va.* (Chem.) To render alkaline.
Alcaloide [al-cah-lo'-e-day], *m.* Alkaloid, an organic base.
Alcam [al-cahm'], *m.* (Bot.) Bitter apple. Cucumis colocynthis.
Alcamonías [al-cah-mo-nee'-as], *f. pl.* 1. Various aromatic seeds used in the kitchen, and other stimulants. 2. *m.* *V.* Alcahuete.
Alcaná [al-cah-nah'], *f.* 1. (Obs.) A place where shops are kept. 2. (Bot.)

Alcanna, from which henna is obtained. Alkanet. Lawsonia inermis.

Alcance [al-cahn'-thay], *m.* 1. Following and overtaking a person. 2. Balance of an account. 3. Arm's length. 4. Range of fire-arms. 5. Capacity, ability. 6. Fathom, compass. 7. The supplement of a newspaper; a postscript. 8. Portion of copy which a compositor takes for setting up. 9. Capacity, talent. *Ir á los alcances*, To be at one's heels. *No poderle dar alcance*, To be unable to get sight of one.

Alcancía [al-can-thee'-ah], *f.* 1. Money-box. 2. (Mil.) Inflamed combustible balls.

Alcanciazo [al-can-the-ah'-tho], *m.* A blow with a money-box or ball.

Alcándara [al-cahn'-dah-rah], *f.* Perch of a falcon.

Alcandía [al-can-dee'-ah], *f.* (Bot.) Turkey millet. *V.* ZAHINA.

Alcandial [al-can-de-ahl'], *m.* Ground sown with millet.

Alcanfeno [al-can-fay'-no], *m.* Camphene.

Alcanfor [al-can-fore'], *m.* Camphor.

Alcanforada [al-can-fo-rah'-dah], *f.* Camphor-tree.

Alcanforado, da [al-can-fo-rah'-do, dah], *a.* Impregnated with camphor.

Alcanforero [al-can-fo-ray'-ro], *m.* The camphor-tree. Cinnamonum camphora.

Alcántara [al-cahn'-tah-rah], *f.* Box to hold velvet in the loom.

Alcantarilla [al-can-tah-reel'-lyah], *f.* 1. Small bridge. 2. Sewer. 3. Drain. 4. Culvert.

Alcantarillado [al-can-tah-reel-lyah'-do], *m.* Sewerage system, sewerage.

Alcantarillar [al-can-tah-reel-lyar'], *va.* To put sewers in.

Alcantarillero [al-can-tah-reel-lyay'-ro], *m.* Sewer man.

Alcanzable [al-can-thah'-blay], *a.* Attainable.

Alcanzadizo, za [al-can-thah-dee'-tho, thah], *a.* Within reach, easily reached. *Hacerse alcanzadizo*, (Met.) To affect ignorance.

Alcanzado, da [al-can-thah'-do, dah], *a.* Necessitous.—*pp.* of ALCANZAR.

Alcanzador, ra [al-can-thah-dor', rah], *m.* & *f.* A pursuer.

Alcanzadura [al-can-thah-doo'-rah], *f.* (Vet.) 1. A tumour or wound in the pastern of a horse. 2. Wound or contusion arising from a horse's cutting the fore hoof with the hind shoe.

Alcanzamiento [al-can-thah-me-en'-to], *m.* (Obs.) *V.* ALCANCE.

Alcanzar [al-can-thar'], *va.* 1. To follow or pursue. 2. To overtake, to come up, to reach, to carry far. 3. To reach a thing, to extend the hand to take it. 4. To acquire, to obtain, to possess power of obtaining a thing desired. 5. To comprehend. 6. To be creditor of a balance. 7. To know a long while. *Yo alcancé a Pedro, cuando empecé a estudiar*, I knew Peter when I began my studies.—*vn.* 1. To share. 2. To suffice. 3. To reach: applied to a ball. 4. *Alcanzar en días*, To survive.—*vr.* To wound the pasterns with the feet, as horses do. *Alcanzársele poco a alguno* or *no alcanzársele más*, (Coll.) To be of a weak understanding. *Alcanzar de alguno*, To prevail upon any one. *Alcanzar a ver*, To descry. *No alcanzar con mucho*, To fall short.

Alcaparra, *f.* **Alcaparro**, *m.* [al-cah-pahr'-rah, al-cah-pahr'-roh]. (Bot.) 1. Caper-bush. Capparis. 2. Caper, the bud of the caper-bush.

Alcaparrado, da [al-cah-par-rah'-do, dah], *a.* Dressed with capers.

Alcaparral [al-cah-par-rahl'], *m.* Ground planted with caper-bushes.

Alcaparrón [al-cah-par-rone'], *m. aug.* A large caper.

Alcaparrosa [al-cah-par-ro'-sah], *f.* *V.* CAPARROSA.

Alcarahueya [al-cah-rah-oo-ay'-yah], *f.* (Bot.) Caraway-seed.

Alcaraván [al-cah-rah-vahn'], *m.* (Orn.) Bittern. Ardea stellaris.

Alcaravanero [al-cah-rah-vah-nay'-ro], *m.* A hawk trained to pursue the bittern.

Alcaravea [al-cah-rah-vay'-ah], *f.* (Bot.) *V.* ALCARAHUEYA.

Alcarceñal [al-car-thay-nyahl'], *m.* Plantation of officinal tare.

Alcarón [al-cah-rone'], *m.* Alcaron, a species of scorpion found in Africa.

Alcarracero, ra [al-car-rah-thay'-ro, rah], *m.* & *f.* 1. A potter. 2. Shelf on which earthenware is placed.

Alcarraza [al-car-rah'-thah], *f.* Pitcher or jug unglazed and porous.

Alcartaz [al-car-tath'], *m.* *V.* CUCURUCHO.

Alcatifa [al-cah-tee'-fah], *f.* 1. A sort of fine carpet. 2. Layer of earth put under bricks in paving. 3. Roof of a house.

Alcatife [al-cah-tee'-fay], *m.* Silk. *V.* SEDA.

Alcatraz [al-cah-trath'], *m.* 1. Pelican. *V.* CUCURUCHO.

Alcaucil [al-cah-oo-theel'], *m.* (Prov.) Wild artichoke. *V.* ALCACHOFA.

Alcayata [al-cah-yah'-tah], *f.* 1. A hook. 2. Scarp of a fortification. 3. A kind of knot often used on board ship. *V.* ESCARPIA.

Alcázar [al-cah'-thar], *m.* 1. Castle. 2. Fortress. 3. (Naut.) Quarter-deck.

Alcazuz [al-cah-thooth'], *m.* *V.* REGALIZA and OROZUZ. Licorice.

Alce [ahl'-thay], *m.* 1. (Zool.) Elk or moose. *V.* ANTA. 2. The "cut," at cards.

Alcea [al-thay'-ah], *f.* (Bot.) Marshmallow. Althea officinalis.

Alcedón [al-thay-done'], *m.* A kingfisher. *V.* MARTÍN PESCADOR.

Alcino [al-thee'-no], *m.* (Bot.) Wild basil. Clinopodium vulgare.

Alción [al-the-on'], *m.* 1. *V.* ALCEDÓN. 2. A swallow which makes the edible nests of the Chinese. Collocalia nidifica et al.

Alcista [al-thees'-tah], *f.* (Coll.) Bull, a speculator for a rise in the stock exchange.

Alcoba [al-co'-bah], *f.* 1. Alcove. 2. Bed-room. 3. Case in which the tongue of a balance moves to regulate the weight.

Alcobilla, Alcobita [al-co-beel'-lyah, bee'-tah], *f. dim.* A small alcove.

Alcohol [al-co-ole'], *m.* Alcohol. *Alcohol etílico*, Ethyl alcohol, grain alcohol. *Alcohol de granos*, Grain alcohol. *Alcohol metílico*, Wood alcohol.

Alcoholado, da [al-co-o-lah'-do, dah], *a.* Being of a darker colour around the eyes than the rest of the body; applied to cattle.—*pp.* of ALCOHOLAR.

Alcoholador, ra [al-co-o-lah-dor', rah], *m.* & *f.* One employed in rectifying spirits, or who paints and dyes with antimony.

Alcoholar [al-co-o-lar'], *va.* 1. To paint or dye with antimony. 2. To rectify spirits. 3. To reduce to an impalpable powder.—*vn.* (Obs.) To pass in a tilt the adverse party of combatants.

Alcoholera [al-co-o-lay'-rah], *f.* Vessel for antimony or alcohol.

Alcohólico, ca [al-co-o'-le-co, cah], *a.* Alcoholic, containing alcohol or spirits of wine.

Alcoholímetro [al-co-o-lee'-may-tro], *m.* Alcoholimeter, alcoholometer.

Alcoholismo [al-co-o-lees'-mo], *m.* Alcoholism, a diseased state caused by continued abuse of alcoholic beverages.

Alcoholización [al-co-o-le-thah-the-on'], *f.* (Chem.) Alcoholization.

Alcoholizado, da [al-co-le-thah'-do, dah], *a.* 1. Containing alcohol. 2. Affected by alcoholism.

Alcoholizar [al-co-o-le-thar'], *va.* To alcoholize. *V.* ALCOHOLAR.

Alcor [al-cor'], *m.* *V.* CERRO.

Alcorán [al-co-rahn'], *m.* The Koran, the sacred book of the Mohammedans.

Alcoranista [al-co-rah-nees'-tah], *m.* One who expounds the law of Mohammed.

Alcornocal [al-cor-no-cahl'], *m.* Plantation of cork-trees.

Alcornoque [al-cor-no'-kay], *m.* 1. (Bot.) Cork-tree. 2. (Met.) A person of rude, uncouth manners.

Alcornoqueño, ña [al-cor-no-kay'-nyo, nyah], *a.* Belonging to the cork-tree.

Alcorque [al-cor'-kay], *m.* 1. Cork-wood clogs or soles. 2. *V.* CORCHO. 3. A hollow for holding water about the roots of plants or trees.

Alcorza [al-cor'-thah], *f.* 1. A paste for sweetmeats. 2. A piece of sweetmeat. *Parece hecho de alcorza*, He looks as if he were made of sweetmeat.

Alcorzar [al-cor-thar'], *va.* To cover with iced sugar.

Alcotán [al-co-tahn'], *m.* Lanner, a bird of prey. Falco lanarius.

Alcotana [al-co-tah'-nah], *f.* Pickaxe, gurlet.

Alcotancillo [al-co-tan-theel'-lyo], *m. dim.* A young lanner.

Alcrebite [al-cray-bee'-tay], *m.* Sulphur. *V.* AZUFRE.

Alcribis [al-cree'-bis], *m.* A small tube at the back of a forge through which runs the pipe of the bellows; tewel, tuyere.

Alcubilla [al-coo-beel'-lyah], *f.* (Prov.) Reservoir of an aqueduct; basin, mill-pond.

Alcucero, ra [al-coo-thay'-ro, rah], *m.* & *f.* One who makes oil-bottles, cruets, and vials, which in Spain are commonly made of tin.

Alcucero, ra [al-coo-thay'-ro], *a.* Belonging to an oil-bottle.

Alcucilla [al-coo-theel'-lyah], *f. dim.* A small oil-bottle or can.

Alcuña [al-coo'-nyah], *f.* (Obs.) *V.* ALCURNIA.

Alcurnia [al-coor'-ne-ah], *f.* Family, lineage, race.

Alcuza [al-coo'-thah], *f.* Oil-bottle or cruet; oil-can, oiler. = ACEITERA.

Alcuzada [al-coo-thah'-dah], *f.* The oil contained in a full cruet.

Alcuzazo [al-coo-thah'-tho], *m.* Blow given with an oil-can.

Alcuzcuz [al-cooth-cooth'], *m.* Flour, water, and honey, made into balls, and esteemed by the Moors.

Alcuzón [al-coo-thone'], *m. aug.* A large oil-bottle.

Aldaba [al-dah'-bah], *f.* 1. Knocker, hammer on the door, clapper; door-handle, latch. 2. A cross-bar to secure doors and windows. *Caballo de aldaba*, A steed, a horse for state or war.

Aldabada [al-dah-bah'-dah], *f.* 1. Rap given with the knocker. 2. Sudden fear or apprehension; stings of conscience.

Aldabazo, Aldabonazo [al-dah-bah'-tho, al-dah-bo-nah'-tho], *m.* Knocking.

Aldabear [al-dah-bay-ar'], *vn.* To rap or knock at the door.

Aldabía [al-dah-bee'-ah], *f.* Beam hori-

zontally placed on two walls, to which is a hanging partition.
Aldabilla [al-dah-beel'-yah], *f. dim.* A small knocker.
Aldabón [al-dah-bone'], *m.* 1. (Aug.) A large knocker. 2. An iron handle of trunks.
Aldea [al-day'-ah], *f.* A small village, hamlet, a large farm. (Arab. addeya.)
Aldeana [al-day-ah'-nah], *f.* Villager, countrywoman, lass.
Aldeano [al-day-ah'-no], *m.* Villager, a countryman.
Aldebarán [al-day-bah-rahn'], *m.* (Ast.) Aldebaran or Bull's-Eye, a fixed star of first magnitude in the constellation of Taurus.
Aldehida [al-day-ee'-dah], *f.* Aldehyde, a volatile, colourless fluid obtained by the oxidation of alcohol.
Aldehuela, Aldeilla [al-day-oo-ay'-lah, al-day-eel'-lyah], *f. dim.* A little village.
Aldeorrio [al-day-or'-re-o], *m.* 1. A small, unpleasant village. 2. A town whose inhabitants are rude.
Aldiza [al-dee'-thah], *f.* A sort of small reed without knots.
Aldrán [al-drahn'], *m.* One who sells wine to shepherds.
Aleación [ah-lay-ah-the-on'], *f.* The art of alloying metals; alloy, compound metal.
Aleador [ah-lay-ah-dor'], *m.* Alloyer.
Alear [ah-lay-ar'], *vn.* 1. To flutter. 2. (Met.) To move the arms quickly. 3. (Met.) To recover from sickness, to regain strength after fatigue.—*va.* To alloy.
Alebrado, da [ah-lay-brah'-do, dah], *a.* Hare-hearted.—*pp.* of ALEBRARSE.
Alebrarse, Alebrastrarse, Alebrestarse [ah-lay-brar'-say, ah-lay-bras-trar'-say, ah-lay-brays-tar'-say], *vr.* 1. To squat close to the ground as hares do. 2. To cower.
Alebronarse [ah-lay-bro-nar'-say], *vr.* To be dispirited.
Aleccionar [ah-lec-the-o-nar'], *va.* To teach, to instruct.
Alece [ah-lay'-thay], *m.* A ragout made of the livers of a large fish, called *mújol*, caught on the coast of Valencia.
Alechigar [ah-lay-che-gar'], *va.* To soften.—*vr.* To turn milky.
Alechugado, da [ah-lay-choo-gah'-do, dah], *a.* Curled like the leaf of lettuce. Fluted, plaited.—*pp.* of ALECHUGAR.
Alechugar [ah-lay-choo-gar'], *va.* 1. To curl or contract like the leaf of lettuce. 2. To plait, to flute.
Aleda [ah-lay'-dah], *f.* V. CERA ALEDA. Propolis, or bee-glue, used by bees in stopping cracks and cementing the comb to the hive.
Aledaño [ah-lay-dah'-nyo], *m.* & *a.* Common boundary, border, limit.
Alefanginas [ah-lay-fan-hee'-nas], *f. pl.* Purgative pills made of cinnamon, nutmeg, and the juice of aloes.
Alefris, Alefriz [ah-lay-frees'], *m.* 1. Mortise, a hole cut into wood. 2. Rabbet.
Alefrizar [ah-lay-fre-thar'], *va.* To rabbet.
Alegación [ah-lay-gah-the-on'], *f.* Allegation; argument.
Alegar [ah-lay-gar'], *va.* To allege, to affirm, to quote, to maintain, to adduce.
Alegato [ah-lay-gah'-to], *m.* (Law) Allegation, showing the ground of complaint by the plaintiff. Complaint, petition.
Alegoría [ah-lay-go-ree'-ah], *f.* Allegory.
Alegóricamente [ah-lay-go'-re-cah-men-tay], *adv.* Allegorically.
Alegórico, ca [ah-lay-go'-re-co, cah], *a.* Allegorical, not literal.
Alegorista [ah-lay-go-rees'-tah], *m.* Allegorist.
Alegorizar [ah-lay-go-re-thar'], *va.* To turn into allegory.
Alegrado, da [ah-lay-grah'-do, dah], *a.* Delighted.—*pp.* of ALEGRAR.
Alegrador, ra [ah-lay-grah-dor', rah], *m.* & *f.* 1. (Obs.) One who produces merriment; a jester. 2. (Coll.) Twisted slip of paper to shake the snuff of a candle. 3. (Mech.) Reamer, round broach; riming bit.
Alegrar [ah-lay-grar'], *va.* 1. To make merry, to gladden, to comfort, to exhilarate. 2. (Met.) To enliven, to beautify. 3. (Mech.) To round, make a bore; to ream, widen. *Alegrar las luces*, To snuff the candles.—*vr.* 1. To rejoice, to congratulate, to exult. 2. To grow merry by drinking.
Alegre [ah-lay'-gray], *a.* 1. Merry, joyful, content, light-hearted, full of gaiety, gleeful. 2. Lightsome, comic, ludicrous, facetious. 3. Gay, showy, fine: applied to inanimate things. *Un cielo alegre*, A clear, beautiful sky. 4. Brilliant, pleasing: applied to colours. 5. Lucky, fortunate, genial.
Alegremente [ah-lay-gray-men'-tay] *adv.* 1. Merrily, gladly, gaily. 2. Facetiously, mirthfully, laughingly, good-humouredly.
Alegría [ah-lay-gree'-ah], *f.* 1. Mirth, merriment, exhilaration, gaiety, glee, rejoicing. 2. Festivity. 3. Lightsomeness. 4. Ecstasy, pleasure. 5. (Bot). Sesamum, oily grain. 6. Paste made of sesamum and honey.—*pl.* Rejoicings, public festivals.
Alegrillo [ah-lay-greel'-lyo], *a.* Sprightly, gay.
Alegro [ah-lay'-gro], *m.* 1. (Mus.) Allegro, a word denoting in music a sprightly motion. 2. A movement, or division of a sonata, in this time.
Alegrón [ah-lay-grone'], *m.* (Coll.) 1. Sudden, unexpected joy. 2. A flash.
Alejamiento [ah-lay-hah-me-en'-to], *m.* 1. Elongation, removal to a distance. 2. Distance. 3. Strangeness.
Alejandrino, na [ah-lay-han-dree'-no, nah], *a.* *Verso alejandrino*, Alexandrine.
Alejar [ah-lay-har'], *va.* To remove to a greater distance, to separate.
Alejijas [ah-lay-hee'-has], *f. pl.* Porridge made of barley, cleaned and roasted. *Tiene cara de alejijas*, He looks half-starved.
Alelarse [ah-lay-lar'-say], *vr.* To become stupid.
Alelí [ah-lay-lee'], *m.* (*Bot.*) The winter gilliflower of various colours; also a general name for violets.
Aleluya [ah-lay-loo'-yah], *f.* 1. Allelujah. 2. Joy, merriment. 3. Easter time. *Al aleluya nos veremos*, We shall see each other at Easter. 4. Small pictures with the word *aleluya* printed on them, and thrown among the people on Easter-eve. 5. (Bot.) Wood-sorrel. V. ACEDERILLA. So called because it flowers at Easter. 6. *pl.* (Coll.) Dull, poor verses.
Alema [ah-lay'-mah], *f.* The allotted quantity of water for irrigating a piece of ground.
Alemán, na [ah-lay-mahn', mah'-nah], *a.* & *m.* 1. German. 2. German language.
Alemana, or Alemanda [ah-lay-mah'nah, ah-lay-mahn'-dah], *f.* An ancient Spanish dance of German origin.
Alemanisco, ca [ah-lay-mah-nees'-co, cah], *a.* Germanic: cloth made in Germany; huckaback: damask table-linen.
Alenguamiento [ah-len-goo-ah-me-en'-to], *m.* An agreement relative to pasture.
Alenguar [ah-len-goo-ar'], *va.* To agree respecting sheep-walks or pasturage.
Alentada [ah-len-tah'-dah], *f.* (Obs.) Interval between two respirations, a continued respiration; a full, deep breath.
Alentadamente [ah-len-tah-dah-men'-tay], *adv.* Bravely, gallantly.
Alentado, da [ah-len-tah'-do, dah], *a.* 1. Spirited, courageous, valiant. 2. (Obs.) Bold.—*pp.* of ALENTAR.
Alentador, ra [ah-len-ta-dor', rah], *m.* & *f.* One who inspires courage.—*a.* Encouraging, animating.
Alentar [ah-len-tar'], *vn.* To breathe. —*va.* To animate, to encourage, to comfort.
Alepín [ah-lay-peen'], *m.* A kind of bombasin, or bombazine.
Alerce [ah-ler'-thay], *m.* (Bot.) Larch-tree. Pinus larix.
Alergeno [ah-lehr-hay'-no], *m.* Allergen.
Alergia [ah-lehr'-he-ah], *f.* Allergy.
Alérgico, ca [ah-lehr'-hee-co, cah], *a.* Allergic.
Alero [ah-lay'-ro], *m.* The projecting part of a roof; eaves, gable-end, corona, hood moulding, water-table; splash-board of a carriage.—*pl.* Snares for partridges.
Alerón [ah-lay-rone'], *m.* Aileron (of an airplane).
Alerta [ah-ler'-tah], *f.* (Mil.) Watch-word.
Alerta, Alertamente [ah-ler'-tah, ah-ler-tah-men'-tay], *adv.* Vigilantly, carefully. *Estar alerta*, To be on the watch. *Alerta a la buena guardia a proa*, (Naut.) Lookout well there afore.
Alertar [ah-ler-tar'], *va.* To render vigilant, to put one on his guard.
Alerto, ta [ah-ler'-to, tah], *a.* Vigilant, alert, guarded.
Alesna [ah-lays'-nah], *f.* (Obs.) Awl, a pointed instrument. *V.* LESNA.
Alesnado, da [ah-les-nah'-do, dah], *a.* Awl-shaped, pointed like an awl.
Aleta [ah-lay'-tah], *f.* 1. (Dim.) A small wing. 2. Fin of a fish. *Aletas*, (Naut.) Fashion pieces. 3. (Arch.) Aletta. 4. (Mech.) Leaf of a hinge, leaf of a pinion, teeth of a pinion. 5. (Aer.) Flap. *Aleta de la hélice*, 1. (Aer.) Propeller blade. 2. (Naut.) Screw blade.
Aletada [ah-lay-tah'-dah], *f.* Motion of the wings.
Aletargado, da [ah-lay-tar-gah'-do, dah], *a.* Lethargic.—*pp.* of ALETARGARSE.
Aletargarse [ah-lay-tar-gar'-say], *vr.* To fall into a state of lethargy.
Aletazo [ah-lay-tah'-tho], *m.* Stroke of the wing, flapping.
Aleteado, da [ah-lay-tay-ah'-do, dah], *a.* Finlike, finned.—*pp.* of ALETEAR.
Aletear [ah-lay-tay-ar'], *vn.* To flutter, to take short flights, to flit.
Aleteo [ah-lay-tay'-o], *m.* Clapping of the wings.
Aleto [ah-lay'-to], *m.* (Orn.) The Peruvian falcon. Falco Peruvianus.
Aletón [ah-lay-tone'], *m. aug.* A large wing.
Aletría [ah-lay-tree'-ah], *m.* (Prov.) Vermicelli. *V.* FIDEOS.
Aleudarse [ah-lay-oo-dar'-say], *vr.* (Obs.) To become fermented: applied to dough.
Aleve [ah-lay'-vay], *a.* Treacherous, perfidious, guileful.
Alevilla [ah-le-veel'-lya], *a.* A moth like that of the silkworm, but differ-

ing in having the wings entirely white.
Alevosa [ah-lay-vo'-sah], *f.* (Vet.) A tumour under the tongue of cows and horses. *V.* RÁNULA.
Alevosamente [ah-lay-vo-sah-men'-tay], *adv.* Treacherously, guilefully.
Alevosía [ah-lay-vo-see'-ah], *f.* Perfidy, breach of trust.
Alevoso, sa [ah-lay-vo'-so, sah], *a.* Treacherous.
Alexifármaco, ca [ah-lex-e-far'-mah-co, cah], *a.* (Med.) Antidotal, possessing the power of destroying or expelling poison.
Alfa [ahl'-fah], *f.* Alpha, the first letter of the Greek alphabet. (Met.) The beginning.
Alfábega [al-fah'-bay-gah], *f.* *V.* ALBAHACA.
Alfabéticamente [al-fah-bay'-te-cah-men-tay], *adv.* Alphabetically.
Alfabético, ca [al-fah-bay'-te-co, cah], *a.* Alphabetical.
Alfabetista [al-fah-bay-tees'-tah], *m.* One that studies the alphabet and orthography.
Alfabeto [al-fah-bay'-to], *m.* Alphabet.
Alfadía [al-fah-dee'-ah], *f.* (Obs.) Bribe.
Alfahar, Alfaharero [al-fah-ar', al-fah-ah-ray'-ro]. *V.* ALFAR, ALFARERO.
Alfaharería [al-fah-ah-ray-ree'-ah]. *V.* ALFAR, ALFARERÍA.
Alfajía [al-fah-hee'-ah], *f.* Wood for windows and doors.
Alfajor [al-fah-hor'], *m.* *V.* ALAJÚ.
Alfalfa, *f.* **Alfalfe,** *m.* [al-fahl'-fah, al-fahl'-fay]. (Bot.) Lucerne, alfalfa. Medicago sativa.
Alfalfal, Alfalfar [al-fal-fahl', al-fal-far'], *m.* A piece of ground sown with lucerne.
Alfana [al-fah'-nah], *f.* A strong and spirited horse.
Alfandoque [al-fan-do'-kay], *m.* A hollow cane shaken for a musical instrument. (Ec.)
Alfaneque [al-fah-nay'-kay], *m.* 1. The white eagle. Falco albus. 2. Tent or booth.
Alfanjazo [al-fan-hah'-tho], *m.* A wound with a cutlass.
Alfanje [al-fahn'-hay], *m.* Hanger, cutlass.
Alfanjete [al-fan-hay'-tay], *m. dim.* A small cutlass.
Alfanjón [al-fan-hone'], *m. aug.* A large hanger or cutlass.
Alfanjonazo [al-fan-ho-nah'-tho], *m.* A cut with a large hanger.
Alfaque [al-fah'-kay], *m.* A shoal or bar.
Alfaquí [al-fah-kee'], *m.* A doctor of, or wise in, the law, among Mussulmans.—*Cf.* FAKIR.
Alfar [al-far'], *m.* 1. Pottery. 2. *V.* ARCILLA.—*a.* That raises the head too much: relating to horses.
Alfar [al-far'], *vn.* To raise the forehead too much.
Alfaraz [al-fah-rath'], *a.* Applied formerly to the horses on which the light cavalry of the Moors rode.
Alfarda [al-far'-dah], *f.* 1. (Prov.) Duty paid for the irrigation of lands. 2. Thin beam.
Alfardero [al-far-day'-ro], *m.* (Prov.) A collector of the duty for watering lands.
Alfardilla [al-far-deel'-lyah], *f.* 1. Silk, now called galloon. 2. (Dim. Prov.) A small duty for watering lands.
Alfardón [al-far-done'], *m.* (Prov.) 1. Washer of a wheel. 2. Duty paid for watering lands.
Alfarería [al-fah-ray-ree'-ah], *f.* 1. The art of a potter. 2. Pottery.
Alfarero [al-fah-ray'-ro]. *m.* Potter.
Alfarje [al-far'-hay], *m.* 1. The lower stone of an oil-mill. 2. Ceiling of a room adorned with carved work. Wainscot.
Alfarjía [al-far-hee'-ah], *f.* *V.* ALFAJÍA.
Alfayate [al-fah-yah'-tay], *m.* (Obs.) A tailor.
Alféizar [al-fay'-e-thar], *m.* The aperture in a wall at the inside of a door or window; embrasure.
Alfeñicado, da [al-fay-nye-cah'-do, da], *a.* Weakly, delicate.
Alfeñicar [al-fay-nye-car'], *va.* To ice with sugar.
Alfeñicarse [al-fay-nye-car'-say], *vr.* (Coll.) To affect peculiar delicacy.
Alfeñique [al-fay-nyee'-kay], *m.* 1. A sugar-paste made with oil of sweet almonds. 2. (Met.) A person of a delicate constitution.
Alferecía [al-fay-ray-thee'-ah], *f.* 1. Epilepsy, a nervous affection, in which the patient often falls. 2. (Obs.) An ensign's commission.
Alférez [al-fay'-reth], *m.* 1. Ensign. 2. *Alférez de navío,* Ensign of the navy. 3. *Alférez real,* The chief ensign of the town.
Alfil [al-feel'], *m.* Bishop in the game of chess. (Arab. from Per.)
Alfiler [al-fe-lerr'], *m.* 1. A pin. 2. Jeweller's broach. *Alfileres de gancho o de pelo,* Hair-pins. *Alfileres,* Pin-money. *Con todos sus alfileres* or *de veinte y cinco alfileres,* In full dress, dressed in style. *No estar con todos sus alfileres* (speaking of ladies). Not to be in good humour. *Pedir* or *dar para alfileres,* Money given to servants in public-houses. (Ar.)
Alfilerazo [al-fe-lay-rah'-tho], *m.* 1. Prick of a pin. 2. A large pin.
Alfilerera [al-fe-lay-ray'-rah], *f.* Alfileria, the seed of some of the geranium family; from its shape.
Alfilerero [al-fe-lay-ray-ro], *m.* A maker or seller of pins.
Alfilete, Alfiletete [al-fe-lay'-tay, al-fe-lay-tay'-tay], *m.* Paste made of coarse wheat flour.
Alfiletero [al-fe-lay-tay'-ro], *m.* Pin-case, needle-case, pin-cushion.
Alfolí [al-fo-lee'], *m.* 1. Granary. 2. Magazine of salt.
Alfoliero, Alfolinero [al-fo-le-ay'-ro, al-fo-le-nay'-ro], *m.* Keeper of a granary or magazine.
Alfombra [al-fom'-brah], *f.* 1. Floor-carpet. 2. (Poet.) Field adorned with flowers. 3. (Med.) Measles, an eruptive fever.
Alfombrar [al-fom-brar'], *va.* To spread with carpets.
Alfombraza [al-fom-brah'-tha], *f. aug.* A large carpet.
Alfombrero, ra [al-fom-bray'-ro, rah], *m.* & *f.* Carpet-maker.
Alfombrilla [al-fom-breel'-lyah], *f.* 1. (Dim.) A small carpet. 2. (Med.) Measles. 3. *V.* ALFOMBRA.
Alfóncigo [al-fon'-the-go], *m.* 1. Pistachio, the fruit of the pistachio-tree. 2. Pistachio-tree. Pistacia vera.
Alfonsearse [al-fon-say-ar'-say], *vr.* (Coll.) To joke with each other, to ridicule each other.
Alfonsí [al-fon-see'], *m.* (Obs.) *V.* ALFONSÍN.
Alfonsín, no, na [al-fon-seen', no, nah], *a.* Belonging to the Spanish kings called Alphonso.
Alfonsina [al-fon-see'-nah], *f.* A solemn act held in the church of the Alphonsine college of Alcalá, where several questions, either theological or medical, are publicly discussed.
Alforja [al-for'-hah], *f.* Saddle-bag. knapsack. *Hacerle a alguno la alforja.* To fill one's saddle-bag with provisions.
Alforjero [al-for-hay'-ro], *m.* 1. Maker or seller of saddle-bags. 2. A lay-brother of some religious orders who goes about begging bread. 3. One who carries the bag with provisions. 4. Sportsman's dog taught to guard the bag of game.
Alforjilla, ita, uela [al-for-heel'-lyah, hee'-tah, hoo-ay'-lah], *f. dim.* A small saddle-bag, a small wallet or knapsack.
Alforza [al-for'-thah], *f.* A plait in a skirt, a tuck.
Alfronitro [al-fro-nee'-tro], *m.* *V.* ALATRÓN.
Alga [ahl'-gah], *f.* (Bot.) Sea-weed, alga; sea-wrack. *V.* OVA.
Algadonera [al-gah-do-nay'-rah], *f.* (Bot.) Cudweed, graphalium.
Algaida [al-gah'-e-dah], *f.* A ridge of shifting sand; sand-dune.
Algaido, da [al-gah'-e-do, dah], *a.* (Prov.) Thatched, covered with straw. *Casas algaidas,* Thatched houses.
Algalaba [al-gah-lah'-bah], *f.* (Bot.) White briony, wild hops. Bryonia alba.
Algalia [al-gah'-le-ah], *f.* 1. Civet, a perfume. 2. Catheter, a hollow instrument used in surgery.
Algaliar [al-gah-le-ar'], *va.* (Obs.) To perfume with civet.
Algara [al-gah'-rah], *f.* 1. The thin integument which covers an egg, onion, etc. 2. (Obs.) A foraging party of cavalry.
Algarabía [al-gah-rah-bee'-ah], *f.* 1. The Arabic tongue. 2. (Met.) Gabble, jargon. 3. (Met.) A confused noise of several speaking or shouting at once. 4. (Bot.) Centaury. Centaurea salmantica.
Algarada [al-gah-rah'-dah], *f.* 1. A loud cry. 2. A sudden attack. 3. A sort of battering-ram of the ancients.
Algarero, ra [al-gah-ray'-ro, rah], *a.* Prating, chattering, talkative. *La mujer algarera nunca hace larga tela,* A prating woman works but little.
Algarero [al-gah-ray'-ro], *m.* (Obs.) A horseman of the foraging party called *algara.*
Algarrada [al-gar-rah'-dah], *f.* 1. Driving bulls into the pen for the bull-fight. 2. (Obs.) Battering-ram.
Algarroba [al-gar-ro'-bah], *f.* (Bot.) 1. Carob bean. 2. The honey-mesquit.
Algarrobal [al-gar-ro-bahl'], *m.* Ground planted with carob-trees.
Algarrobera, *f.* **Algarrobo,** *m.* [al-gar-ro-bay'-rah, al-gar-ro'-bo]. (Bot.) Carob-tree, or St. John's bread. Ceratonia siliqua.
Algazara [al-gah-thah'-rah], *f.* 1. Huzza. 2. The shout of a multitude.
Algazul [al-gah-thool'], *m.* A sea-weed, which when burned produces barilla, or impure soda.
Álgebra [ahl'-hay-brah], *f.* 1. Algebra, a branch of the higher mathematics. 2. (Obs.) Art of setting joints.
Algebraico, ca [al-hay-brah'-e-co, cah], *a.* Algebraic.
Algebrista [al-hay-brees'-tah], *m.* 1. Algebraist, a person that understands algebra. 2. (Obs.) One who understands setting dislocated members. Bone-setter.
Algidez [al-he-deth'], *f.* (Med.) Icy coldness.
Algido, da [ahl'-he-do, dah], *a.* Algid, icy.
Algo [ahl'-go], *pro.* Somewhat, some thing, aught.
Algo [ahl'-go], *adv.* Somewhat. *La medida es algo escasa,* The measure is somewhat short. *Algo o nada.* All or

nothing. *Ser algo que*, To be worth something. *Algo*, Property, faculty.
Algodón [al-go-done'], *m.* 1. Cotton. 2. (Bot.) The cotton-plant. Gossypium herbaceum. *Algodón en rama*, Raw cotton. *Algodones*, *V.* Cendales.
Algodonado, da [al-go-do-nah'-do dah], *a.* Filled with cotton.
Algodonal [al-go-do-nahl'], *m.* A cotton-plantation.
Algodonar [al-go-do-nar'], *va.* To cover or fill with cotton.
Algodonería [al-go-do-nay-ree'-ah], *f.* 1. Cotton-factory. 2. Cotton-trade.
Algodonero [al-go-do-nay'-ro], *m.* The cotton-plant. 2. The cottonwood poplar: Populus angulatus.
Algodonero, ra [al-go-do-nay'-ro, rah], *m.* & *f.* A cotton-broker.
Algodonoso, sa [al-go-do-no'-so, sah], *a.* Cottony, covered with thick down; woolly, tasteless (of fruits).
Algol [al-gole'], *m.* Name of a variable star in the constellation Perseus.
Algología [al-go-lo-hee'-ah], *f.* Algology, that branch of botany which treats of algæ, marine or fresh-water.
Algorín [al-go-reen'], *m.* (Prov.) A place in oil-mills for receiving the olives which are to be ground.
Algoritmo [al-go-reet'-mo], *m.* Algorithm, an Arabic word signifying the science of numbers; arithmetic.
Algoso, sa [al-go'-so, sah], *a.* Weedy, full of sea-weeds.
Alguacil [al-goo-ah-theel'], *m.* 1. Constable, a peace officer; a bum-bailiff. 2. The short-legged spider. 3. *Alguacil mayor*, High constable. *Alguacil de campo* or *del campo*, Guard or watchman of corn-fields or vineyards.
Alguacilazgo [al-goo-ah-the-lath'-go], *m.* The place or office of an *alguacil*.
Alguarín [al-goo-ah-reen'], *m.* (Prov.) 1. A small room on the ground-floor in which anything is kept. 2. Bucket in which flour falls from the mill-stones.
Alguaza [al-goo-ah'-thah], *f.* (Prov.) Hinge.
Alguien [ahl'-gee-en], *pro.* Somebody, some one.
Algún [al-goon'], *pro.*. *V.* Alguno. *Algún tiempo*, Sometime. *Algún tanto*, A little, somewhat.
Alguno, na [al-goo'-no, nah], *a.* Some person, some thing, any one. *¿Ha venido alguno?* Has any one come? *Alguna vez*, Sometimes, now and then.
Alhábega [al-ah'-bay-gah], *f.* (Prov.) *V.* Albahaca. Murcia.
Alhadida [al-ah-dee'-dah], *f.* 1. (Chem.) Burnt copper from which the saffron of copper is extracted. 2. *V.* Malaquita.
Alhaja [al-ah'-hah], *f.* 1. Jewel, a thing of great value. 2. Showy furniture, gaudy ornament. *El es una buena alhaja* (ironically), He is a good fellow: he is a good-for-nothing; beware of him. *Quien trabaja tiene alhaja*, He that labours spins gold.
Alhajar [al-ah-har'], *va.* 1. To adorn. 2. To furnish, to fit up.
Alhajuela [al-ah-hoo-ay'-lah], *f. dim.* A little jewel.
Alhamel [al-ah-mel'], *m.* (Prov.) 1. A beast of burden. 2. A porter. 3. Muleteer.
Alhana [al-ah'-nah], *f.* Alhanna, Tripoli earth.
Alhandal [al-an-dahl'], *m.* (Pharm.) Colocynth, bitter apple.
Alharaca [al-ah-rah'-cah], *f.* Clamour, angry vociferation, complaint without sufficient reason.
Alharaquiento, ta [al-ah-rah-ke-en'-to, tah], *a.* Noisy, clamorous, grumbling.
Alhárgama, Alharma [al-ar'-gah-mah, al-ar'-mah], *f.* (Bot.) Wild rue. Peganum harmala.
Alhasa [al-ah'-sah], *f.* Hydroa, a vesicular disease of the skin.
Alhelí [al-ay-lee']. *V.* Alelí.
Alheña [al-ay'-nyah], *f.* 1. (Bot.) Privet. Ligustrum vulgare. 2. Flower of privet; privet ground to powder. 3. *V.* Azúmbar. 4. Laurestinus. 5. The blasting of corn. *V.* Roya.
Alheñar [al-ay-nyar'], *va.* To dye with the powder of privet.—*vr.* To be mildewed: applied to corn. *V.* Arroyarse.
Alhoja [al-o'-hah], *f.* A small bird resembling a lark.
Alholva [al-ol'-vah], *f.* (Bot.) Fenugreek. Trigonella fœnum græcum.
Alhóndiga [al-on'-de-gah], *f.* A public granary. *V.* Pósito.
Alhondiguero [al-on-de-gay'-ro], *m.* The keeper of a public granary.
Alhorma [al-or'-mah], *f.* Moorish camp, or royal tent.
Alhorre [al-or'-ray], *m.* 1. Meconium, the first dark discharge from an infant's bowels. 2. Eruption in the skin of infants.
Alhoz [al-oth'], *m.* Limit or lot of land.
Alhucema [al-oo-thay'-mah], *f.* (Bot.) Lavender. Lavandula spica. (Andal.) *V.* Espliego.
Alhumajo [al-oo-mah'-ho], *m.* Name applied to leaves of the pine-tree.
Aliabierto, ta [ah-le-ah-be-er'-to, tah], *a.* Open-winged: applied to birds that have the wings expanded.
Aliacán [ah-le-ah-cahn'], *m.* Jaundice. *V.* Ictericia.
Aliacanado, da [ah-le-ah-cah-nah'-do, dah], *a.* Jaundiced.
Aliáceo, a [ah-le-ah'-thay-o, ah], *a.* Alliaceous: like onions or garlic.
Aliado, da [ah-le-ah'-do, dah], *a.* & *n.* 1. Ally. 2. Allied, confederate; leagued.—*pp.* of Aliarse.
Aliaga [ah-le-ah'-gah], *f.* (Bot.) Furze, whin. Ulex Europæus.
Aliagar [ah-le-ah-gar'], *m.* Place covered with furze.
Alianza [ah-le-ahn'-thah], *f.* 1. Alliance, league, coalition, confederacy, consociation. 2. Agreement, convention, covenant. 3. An alliance contracted by marriage.
Aliara [ah-le-ah'-rah], *f.* A goblet made of a cow's horn.
Aliaria [ah-le-ah'-re-ah], *f.* (Bot.) Garlic hedge-mustard. Erysimum alliaria.
Aliarse [ah-le-ar'-say], *vr.* To be allied, leagued, or coalesced.
Alias [ah'-le-as], *adv.* (Lat.) 1. Otherwise. 2. By another name.
Alible [ah-lee'-blay], *a.* Nutritive.
Alica [ah-lee'-cah], *f. dim.* A small wing.
Álica [ah'-le-cah], *f.* Pottage made of corn, wheat, and pulse.
Alicaído, da [ah-le-cah-ee'-do, dah], *a.* 1. Drooping. 2. Weak, extenuated. *Sombrero alicaído*, An uncocked hat.
Alicántara [ah-le-cahn'-ta-rah], *f.* A kind of viper whose bite is said to be mortal.
Alicante [ah-le-cahn'-tay], *m.* A poisonous snake. *V.* Alicántara.
Alicantina [ah - le - can - tee'-nah], *f.* (Coll.) Artifice, stratagem, cunning. *Tiene muchas alicantinas*, He is full of stratagems.
Alicantino, na [ah-le-can-tee'-no, nah], *a.* Of Alicante.
Alicatado [ah-le-cah-tah'-do], *m.* Work inlaid with Dutch tiles.
Alicates [ah-le-cah'-tes], *m. pl.* Fine-pointed pincers; nippers.
Aliciente [ah-le-the-en'-tay], *m.* Attraction, incitement, inducement.
Alicón [ah-le-cone'], *m.* The name of the seventh heaven to which the angel Azrael carries the souls of the just (Mohammedan).
Alicuanta [ah-lee-coo-ahn'-tah], *a.* *Parte alicuanta*, Aliquant number, or odd part of a number.
Alicuota [ah-lee'-coo-oh-tah], *a.* *Parte alícuota*, Aliquot number, or even part of a number.
Alidada [ah-le-dah'-dah], *f.* Geometrical ruler, sight vane, transom; alidade.
Alidona [ah-le-do'-nah], *f.* 1. Stone in the intestines of a swallow. 2. Chalk
Alienación [ah-le-ay-nah-the-on'], *f.* Alienation (of mind).
Alienar [ah-le-ay-nar'], *va.* (Obs.) *V* Enajenar.
Alienista [ah-le-ay-nees'-tah], *m.* Alienist, specialist in treating disorders of the mind.
Aliento [ah-le-en'-to], *m.* 1. Breath. 2. Vigour of mind, spirit, manfulness, courageousness. *Yo fuí allá de un aliento*, I went thither in a whiff, without drawing breath.
(*Yo me aliento*, from *Alentarse*. *V.* Acertar.)
Alier [ah-le-err'], *m.* (Naut.) 1. A rower. 2. Marine stationed on board a ship.
Alifafe [ah-le-fah'-fay], *m.* 1. A callous tumour growing on a horse's hock. 2. (Coll.) Chronic complaint.
Alifar [ah-le-far'], *va.* (Prov.) To polish, to burnish.
Alifara [ah-le-fah'-rah], *f.* (Prov.) Collation, luncheon.
Alífero, ra [ah-lee'-fay-ro, rah], *a.* Aliferous, bearing wings.
Aliforme [ah-le-for'-may], *a.* Aliform, wing-shaped.
Aligación [ah-le-gah-the-on'], *f.* Alligation, tying together. *Regla de aligación*, Rule of alligation, in arithmetic.
Aligador [ah-le-gah-dor'], *m.* Alligator.
Aligamiento [ah-le-gah-me-en'-to], *m.* Alligation, the act of binding together.
Aligar [ah-le-gar'], *va.* 1. To tie, to unite. 2. (Met.) To oblige, to lie down.
Aligeramiento [ah-le-hay-rah-me-en'-to], *m.* Alleviation; lightening.
Aligerar [ah-le-hay-rar'], *va.* 1. To lighten. 2. (Met.) To alleviate, to ease. 3. To hasten. 4. To shorten. *Aligerar un caballo*, To make a horse move light and free.
Alígero, ra [ah-lee'-hay-ro, rah], *a.* (Poet.) Winged, quick, fast, fleet.
Alijador, ra [ah-le-hah-dor', rah], *m.* & *f.* 1. Smuggler. 2. (Naut.) One who lightens. *Lanchón alijador*, A lighter, used in unloading ships. 3. He who separates the seed from cotton wool.
Alijar [ah-le-har'], *va.* 1. (Naut.) To lighten. 2. To separate cotton from the seed, with the hand or with a gin. 3. To smuggle.
Alijar [ah-le-har'], *m.* Waste, stony ground.
Alijarar [ah-le-hah-rar'], *va.* To divide waste lands for cultivation.
Alijarero [ah-le-hah-ray'-ro], *m.* One who takes waste lands to cultivate.
Alijares [ah-le-hah'-res], *m. pl.* A royal pleasure resort of Granada.
Alijariego, ga [ah-le-hah-re-ay'-go, gah], *a.* Relating to waste lands.
Alijo [ah-lee'-ho], *m.* 1. (Naut.) Lightening of a ship. *Embarcación de alijo*, (Naut.) Lighter. 2. Alleviation. 3. Smuggled goods.
Alilla [ah-leel'-lyah], *f.* 1. (Dim.) A small wing. 2. Fin of a fish.

Alimaña [ah-le-mah'-nyah], *f.* Animal which destroys game, as the fox, etc.
Alimentación [ah-le-men-tah-the-on'], *f.* Act of nourishing.
Alimentar [ah-le-men-tar'], *va.* 1. To feed, to nourish, to nurse, to fatten. 2. To supply a person with the necessaries of life.—*vr.* To gorge.
Alimentario, Alimentista [ah-le-men-tah'-re-o, ah-le-men-tees'-tah], *m.* & *f.* One who enjoys a maintenance.
Alimenticio, cia [ah-le-men-tee'-the-o, ah], *a.* Nutritious.
Alimento [ah-le-men'-to], *m.* 1. Nourishment, food, nutriment. 2. (Met.) Encouragement, incentive.—*pl.* 1. Allowance given by the heir to his relatives; a pension, alimony, means of living.
Alimentoso, sa [ah-le-men-to'-so, sah], *a.* Alimentary, nutritious.
Alindado, da [ah-lin-dah-do, dah], *a.* Affectedly nice, or elegant.—*pp.* of ALINDAR.
Alindar [ah-lin-dar'], *va.* 1. To mark limits. 2. To embellish, to adorn. *Alindar el ganado*, To drive the cattle to pasture as far as the limits extend. *V.* LINDAR.
Alinde [ah-leen'-day], *m.* (Obs.) Quicksilver prepared for mirrors.
Alineación [ah-le-nay-ah-the-on'], *m.* Laying out a line.
Alinear [ah-le-nay-ar'], *va.* To lay out by line. *Alinearse los soldados*, To fall in.
Aliñador, ra [ah-le-nyah-dor', ah], *m.* & *f.* 1. One who embellishes. 2. (Obs.) Executor, administrator.
Aliñar [ah-le-nyar'], *va.* 1. To arrange, to adorn. 2. To dress or cook victuals. 3. To season.
Aliño [ah-lee'-nyo], *m.* 1. Dress, ornament, decoration, cleanliness. 2. Preparation for the performance of something.
Aliñoso, sa [ah-le-nyo'-so, sah], *a.* Dressed, decked out, decorated.
Alioli [ah-le-o'-le], *m.* (Prov.) *V.* AJIACEITE.
Alionín [ah-le-o-neen'], *m.* The blue-feathered duck.
Alipata [ah-le-pah'-tah], *m.* A tree of the Philippine Islands whose shade is harmful.
Alipede [ah-lee'-pay-day], *a.* (Poet.) One with winged feet, swift, nimble.
Alipedo, da [ah-lee'-pay-do, dah], *a.* Cheiropterous, provided with a wing like membrane between the toes.
Aliquebrado, da [ah-le-kay-brah'-do, dah], *a.* 1. Broken-winged. 2. Dejected.
Alisador, ra [ah-le-sah-dor', rah], *m.* & *f.* 1. Polisher, planisher, smoothing-iron; silk stick. 2. An instrument used to make wax candles round and tapering.
Alisadura [ah-le-sah-doo'-rah], *f.* Planing, smoothing, or polishing.
Alisaduras [ah-le-sah-doo'-ras], *f. pl.* Shavings, cuttings of any thing made smooth.
Alisar [ah-le-sar'], *va.* To plane, to make smooth, to polish, to mangle.
Alisar, *m.* **Aliseda,** *f.* [ah-le-sar', ah-le-say'-dah]. Plantation of alder-trees.
Alisios [ah-lee'-se-os], *m. pl.* East winds, more particular those which blow in the tropics. Trade-winds.
Alisma [ah-lees'-mah], *f.* (Bot.) Water-plantain.
Aliso [ah-lee'-so], *m.* (Bot.) Alder-tree. Betula alnus.
Alistado, da [ah-lees-tah'-do, dah], *a.* 1. Enlisted. 2. Striped.—*pp.* of ALISTAR.
Alistador [ah-lis-tah-dor'], *m.* 1. One who keeps accounts. 2. One who enlists.
Alistamiento [ah-lis-tah-me-en'-to], *m.* Enrolment, conscription, levy.
Alistar [ah-lis-tar'], *va.* 1. To enlist, to enrol, to recruit. 2. To get ready.
Aliteración [ah-le-tay-rah-the-on'], *f.* *V.* PARONOMASIA.
Alitúrgico, ca [ah-le-toor'-he-co, cah], *a.* Said of days when there is no liturgy.
Aliviador, ra [ah-le-ve-ah-dor', rah], *m.* & *f.* 1. An assistant. 2. A spindle that serves to raise or lower the running mill-stone.
Aliviar [ah-le-ve-ar'], *va.* 1. To lighten, to help, to loose. 2. (Met.) To mitigate grief, to relieve, to exonerate. 3. To hasten, to move with swiftness.
Alivio [al-lee'-ve-o], *m.* 1. Alleviation, ease. 2. Mitigation of pain; comfort.
Alizace [ah-le-thah'-thay], *m.* A trench for the foundations of a building.
Alizarina [ah-le-thah-ree'-nah], *f.* Alizarine.
Aljaba [al-hah'-bah], *f.* A quiver.
Aljafana [al-hah-fah'-nah], *f.* *V.* ALJOFAINA.
Aljama [al-hah'-mah], *f.* An assembly of Moors or Jews. A synagogue.
Aljamía [al-hah-mee'-ah], *f.* (Obs.) 1. Corrupted Arabic spoken by the Moors. 2. Moorish name of the Spanish language. 3. (Prov.) Synagogue.
Aljarfa, *f.* **Aljarfe,** *m.* [al-har'-fah, al-har'-fay]. A tarred net with small meshes.
Aljecero, ra [al-hay-thay'-ro, rah], *m.* & *f.* (Prov.) Plasterer.
Aljevena [al-hay-vay'-na], *f.* (Prov.) *V.* ALJOFAINA.
Aljez [al-heth'], *m.* Gypsum in its crude state.
Aljezar [al-hay-thar'], *m.* Pit of gypsum. *V.* YESAR.
Aljezón [al-hay-thone'], *m.* Gypsum, plaster of Paris. *V.* YESÓN.
Aljibe [al-hee'-bay], *m.* 1. A cistern, a reservoir of water. 2. (Mar.) A tank-boat for supplying vessels with water.
Aljibero [al-hee-bay'-ro], *m.* One who takes care of cisterns.
Aljimierado [al-he-me-ay'-rah-do], *a.* Shaved, trimmed.
Aljofaina [al-ho-fah'-e-nah], *f.* 1. An earthen jug. 2. A wash-bowl.
Aljófar [al-ho'-far], *m.* 1. A misshapen pearl. 2. (Met. Poet.) Drops of water or dew.
Aljofarado, da [al-ho-fah-rah'-do, dah], *a.* (Poet.) Full of little drops or pearls.—*pp.* of ALJOFARAR.
Aljofarar [al-ho-fah-rar'], *va.* 1. To adorn with pearls. 2. To imitate pearls.
Aljofifa [al-ho-fee'-fah], *f.* A mop for floors.
Aljofifar [al-ho-fe-far'], *va.* To rub with a cloth, to mop.
Aljonje [al-hon'-hay], *m.* *V.* AJONJE.
Aljonjera [al-hon-hay'-rah], *f.* *V.* AJONJERA.
Aljonjero [al-hon-hay'-ro], *a.* *V.* AJONJERO.
Aljonjolí [al-hon-ho-lee'], *m.* *V.* ALEGRÍA.
Aljor [al-hor'], *m.* Gypsum in its crude state.
Aljorozar [al-ho-ro-thar'], *va.* To level, render smooth; to plaster.
Aljorra [al-hor'-rah], *m.* (Cuba.) A very small insect which, carried by the wind, destroys plantations.
Aljuba [al-hoo'-bah], *f.* A Moorish garment, formerly worn by Christians in Spain.
Alma [ahl'-mah], *f.* 1. Soul, the spirit of man. 2. Human being. *No parece ni se ve un alma en la plaza*, There is not a soul in the market-place. 3. That which imparts spirit or vigour. *Un buen general es el alma de un ejército*, A good general is the soul of an army. 4. The principal part of a thing. (Mech.) Attic ridge, scaffolding pole. (Arm.) Bore. Core (of rope, of a casting). *Vamos al alma del negocio*, Let us come to the main point of the business. 5. (Naut.) Body of a mast. *En mi alma*, Upon my soul. 6. Ghost. 7. The sounding-post in a fiddle, etc. *Alma mía, mi alma*, My dear, my love. *Alma de cántaro*, An ignorant, insignificant fellow. *El alma me da*, My heart tells me. *Dar el alma*, To expire. *Dar el alma al diablo*, To sacrifice everything to a caprice. *Alma de Dios*, He who is good-natured and simple. *Con el alma y la vida*, With all my heart. *Hablar al alma*, To speak plainly and fearlessly. *Irsele a uno el alma por* or *tras alguna cosa*, To be anxious.
Almacaero [al-mah-cah-ay'-ro], *m.* A member of the company of fishermen on the river Guadalquivir.
Almacén [al-mah-then'], *m.* 1. Warehouse. 2. Magazine. 3. Naval arsenal or dock-yard. 4. (Naut.) *Almacén de agua*, A water-cask. 5. (Naut.) *Almacén de una bomba de agua*, The chamber of a pump.
Almacenado, da [al-mah-thay-nah'-do, dah], *a.* Warehoused, stored, bonded.
Almacenador [al-mah-thay-nah-dor'], *m.* Warehouseman.
Almacenaje [al-mah-thay-nah'-hay], *m.* Warehouse rent, housage.
Almacenar [al-mah-thay-nar'], *va.* To lay up, to hoard; to warehouse.
Almacenero [al-mah-thay-nay-ro], *m.* Warehouse-keeper.
Almacenista [al-mah-thay-nees'-tah], *m.* The person who sells goods in a warehouse.
Almáciga [al-mah'-the-gah], *f.* 1. Mastic, a gum of the Pistacia lentiscus. 2. A nursery of trees or plants.
Almacigado, da [al-mah-the-gah'-do, dah], *a.* Composed of or perfumed with mastic.
Almacigar [al-mah-the-gar'], *va.* To perfume any thing with mastic.
Almácigo [al-mah'-the-go], *m.* 1. Collection of plants for transplanting. 2. Mastic-tree. *V.* LENTISCO.
Almaciguero, ra [al-mah-the-gay'-ro, rah], *a.* Relating to mastic.
Almadana, ena, ina [al-mah-dah'-nah, day'-nah, dee'-nah], *f.* A large hammer.
Almadén [al-mah-den'], *m.* (Obs.) Mine or mineral.
Almadia [al-mah-dee'-ah], *f.* 1. Canoe used in India. 2. Raft.
Almadiado, da [al-mah-de-ah'-do, dah], *a.* (Obs.) Fainting.
Almadiero [al-mah-de-ay'-ro], *m.* A raft-pilot.
Almadraba [al-mah-drah'-bah], *f.* 1. Tunny-fishery. 2. Net used in the tunny-fishery. 3. (Obs.) Brickyard.
Almadrabero [al-mah-drah-bay'-ro], *m.* 1. Tunny-fisher. 2. *V.* TEJERO.
Almadraque [al-mah-drah'-kay], *m.* (Obs.) 1. A quilted cushion. 2. A mattress.
Almadreña [al-mah-dray'-nyah], *f.* Wooden shoes or sabots. *V.* ZUECO.
Almagacén [al-ma-gah-then'], *m.* (Obs.) Magazine. *V.* ALMACÉN.
Almaganeta [al-mah-gah-nay'-tah], *f.* *V.* ALMADANA or ALMADENA.
Almagesto [al-mah-hays'-to], *m.* Almagesta, work on astronomy written by Ptolemy.
Almagra [al-mah'-grah], *f.* *V.* ALMAGRE.

Almagral [al-mah-grahl'], *m.* Place abounding in ochre.

Almagrar [al-mah-grar'], *va.* 1. To colour with red ochre. 2. (Low) To draw blood in a quarrel.

Almagre [al-mah'-gray], *m.* Red ochre, red earth, Indian red.

Almaizal, Almaizar [al-mah-e-thahl', al-mah-e-thar'], *m.* 1. A gauze veil worn by Moors. 2. A belt or sash worn by priests and sub-deacons.

Almajara [al-mah-hah'-rah], *f.* (Prov.) *V.* ALMÁCIGA and SEMILLERO. A forcing-bed, hot-bed.

Almajo [al-mah'-ho], *m.* A fucus or other sea-weed yielding barilla.

Almaleque [al-mah-lay'-kay], *f.* (Obs.) A long robe resembling a surtout, worn by Moors.

Alma mater [ahl'-mah mah'-ter], f. Alma mater, one's university or college.

Almanac, Almanaque [al-mah-nak', al-mah-nah'-kay], *m.* Almanac. *Hacer almanaques,* (Met.) To muse, to be pensive. (Ar.)

Almanaquero [al-mah-nah-kay-ro], *m.* A maker and vender of almanacs.

Almancebe [al-man-thay'-bay], *m.* (Obs.) A fishing-boat used on the river Guadalquivir near Seville.

Almandina [al-man-dee'-nah], *f.* (Min.) The common red variety of garnet; almandine. Rubinus alabundicus.

Almanguena [al-man-gay'-nah], *f.* *V.* ALMAGRE.

Almanta [al-mahn'-tah], *f.* 1. Space between the rows of vines and olive-trees. 2. Ridge between two furrows. *Poner a almanta,* To plant vines irregularly.

Almarada [al-mah-rah'-dah], *f.* A triangular poniard. 2. Iron poker with wooden handle. Shoemaker's needle.

Almarcha [al-mar'-chah], *f.* A town situated on marshy ground.

Almario [al-mah'-re-o], *m.* *V.* ARMARIO.

Almarjal [al-mar-hahl'], *m.* 1. Plantation of glass-wort. 2. Marshy ground where cattle graze.

Almarjo [al-mar'-ho], *m.* (Bot.) Glass-wort. Salicornia.

Almaro [al-mah'-ro], *m.* (Bot.) Common clary. Salvia horminum.

Almarraes [al-mar-rah'-ess], *m. pl.* Instrument (cotton-gin) with which cotton is separated from the seed.

Almarraja, Almarraza [al-mar-rah'-hah, al-mar-rah'-thah], *f.* A glass vial with holes formerly used in sprinkling water.

Almártaga, Almártega, Almártiga [al-mar'-tah-gah, al-mar'-tay-gah, al-mar'-tee-gah], *f.* 1. Litharge. 2. A sort of halter. 3. Massicot or lead made up with linseed-oil for painting.

Almástiga [al-mahs'-te-gah], *f.* *V.* ALMÁCIGA. Mastic.

Almastigado, da [al-mas-te-gah'-do, dah], *a.* Containing mastic.

Almatrero [al-mah-tray'-ro], *m.* One fishing with shad-nets.

Almatriche [al-mah-tree'-chay], *m.* A canal for irrigating land. *V.* REGUERA.

Almazara [al-mah-thah'-rah], *f.* (Prov.) Oil-mill.

Almazarero [al-mah-thah-ray'-ro], *m.* Oil-miller.

Almazarrón [al-mah-thar-rone'], *m.* *V.* ALMAGRE.

Almea [al-may'-ah], *f.* 1. A woman who improvises verses among the orientals. 2. The bark of the storax-tree. Styrax officinalis. 3. (Bot.) The star-headed water-plantain. Alisma damasonium.

Almear [al-may-ar'], *m.* A stack of hay, corn, or straw.

Almeja [al-may'-hah], *f.* Mussel, a shell-fish.

Almejia [al-may-hee'-ah], *f.* A small cloak used by poor Moors.

Almelga [al-mel'-gah], *f.* (Agr.) *V.* AMELGA.

Almena [al-may'-nah], *f.* Each of the merlons of a battlement.

Almenado [al-may-nah'-do], *m.* *V.* ALMENAJE.

Almenado, da [al-may-nah'-do, dah], *a.* Embattled.—*pp.* of ALMENAR.

Almenaje [al-may-nah'-hay], *m.* A series of merlons around a rampart; battlement.

Almenar [al-may-nar'], *va.* To crown a rampart or castle with merlons.

Almenara [al-may-nah'-rah], *f.* 1. A beacon-light. 2. (Prov.) A channel which conveys back the overplus water in irrigation.

Almendra [al-men'-drah], *f.* 1. Kernel, the seed of pulpy fruits. 2. An almond. 3. (Among jewellers) A diamond of an almond-shape. 4. (Prov.) A cocoon which contains but one worm. *Almendras de garapiña,* or *garapiñadas,* Sugar almonds.

Almendrada [al-men-drah'-dah], *f.* 1. Almond milk, an emulsion made of almonds and sugar. 2. (Met.) *Dar una almendrada,* To say something pleasing or pretty.

Almendrado, da [al-men-drah'-do, dah], *a.* Almond-like.

Almendrado [al-men-drah'-do], *m.* Macaroon, a kind of sweet biscuit.

Almendral [al-men-drahl'], *m.* 1. A plantation of almond-trees. 2. *V.* ALMENDRO.

Almendrera [al-men-dray'-rah], *f.* **Almendrero** [al-men-dray'-ro], *m.* *V.* ALMENDRO.

Almendrero, ra [al-men-dray'-ro, rah], *a.* *Plato almendrero,* A dish in which almonds are served.

Almendrica, illa, ita [al-men-dree'-cah, eel'-lyah, ee'-tah], *f. dim.* A small almond.

Almendrilla [al-men-dreel'-lyah], *f.* A locksmith's file in the shape of an almond. *Almendrillas,* Almond-shaped diamond ear-rings.

Almendro [al-men'-dro], *m.* Almond-tree.

Almendrón [al-men-drone'], *m.* An American (cherry) tree and its fruit.

Almendruco [al-men-droo'-co], *m.* A green almond.

Almenilla [al-may-neel'-lyah], *f.* 1. (Dim.) A small merlon. 2. Ancient fringe for dresses.

Almete [al-may'-tay], *m.* 1. A helmet. 2. A soldier wearing a helmet.

Almez, Almezo [al-meth', al-may'-tho], *m.* The lote-tree, or Indian nettle-tree. Celtis australis.

Almeza [al-may'-thah], *f.* (Bot.) The fruit of the lote-tree.

Almiar [al-me-ar'], *m.* Haystack.

Almíbar [al-mee'-bar], *m.* Simple sirup. *Almíbares,* Preserved fruit.

Almibarado, da [al-me-bah-rah'-do, dah], *a.* 1. (Met.) Soft, endearing, applied to words. 2. Effeminate.—*pp.* of ALMIBARAR.

Almibarar [al-me-bah-rar'], *va.* 1. To preserve fruit in sugar. 2. (Met.) To conciliate with soft words.

Almicantáradas [al-me-can-tah'-rah-das], *f. pl.* (Ast.) Circles parallel to the horizon imagined to pass through all the degrees of the meridian, and indicating the altitude and depression of the stars.

Almidón [al-me-done'], *m.* Starch; amylum, fecula.

Almidonado, da [al-me-do-nah'-do, dah], *a.* 1. Starched. 2. (Met.) Dressed with affected nicety; spruce.—*pp.* of ALMIDONAR.

Almidonar [al-me-do-nar'], *va.* To starch.

Almijara [al-me-hah'-rah], *f.* Oil-tank (mining and railway term).

Almijarero [al-me-hah-ray'-ro], *m.* Porter in the mines of Almadén.

Almilla [al-meel'-lyah], *f.* 1. An under waistcoat. 2. A short military jacket. 3. Tenon. 4. Pork-chop.

Almimbar [al-meem-bar'], *m.* The pulpit of a mosque.

Alminar [al-me-nar'], *m.* Minaret, turret of a mosque.

Almiranta [al-me-rahn'-tah], *f.* (Naut.) 1. The vice-admiral's ship, the flagship. 2. The admiral's lady.

Almirantazgo [al-me-ran-tath'-go], *m.* (Naut.) 1. Board of admiralty. 2. Admiralty court. 3. Admiral's dues. 4. Duty of an admiral.

Almirante [al-me-rahn'-tay], *m.* 1. Admiral. A commander of a fleet. *Vicealmirante,* Vice-admiral. *Contraalmirante,* Rear-admiral. 2. (Prov.) Swimming-master. 3. A beautiful shell, belonging to the species of rhomb-shells or volutæ.

Almirez [al-me-reth'], *m.* 1. A brass mortar, for kitchen use. 2. A wood-engraver's tool of tempered steel.

Almirón [al-me-rone'], *m.* Wild chicory.

Almizclar [al-mith-clar'], *va.* To perfume with musk.

Almizcle [al-mith'-clay], *m.* Musk. Moschus moschiferus.

Almizcleña [al-mith-clay'-nyah], *f.* (Bot.) Musk, grape-hyacinth. Hyacinthus muscari.

Almizcleño, ña [al-mith-clay'-nyo, ah], *a.* Musky.

Almizclera [al-mith-clay'-rah], *f.* Musk-rat.

Almizclero, ra [al-mith-clay'-ro, rah], *a.* *V.* ALMIZCLEÑO. The musk-deer which yields musk.

Almizteca [al-mith-tay'-cah], *f.* (Obs.) *V.* ALMÁCIGA.

Almo, ma [ahl'-mo, mah], *a.* (Poet.) 1. Any source of support or maintenance; creating, vivifying. 2. (Poet.) Venerable, holy.

Almocadén [al-mo-cah-den'], *m.* The commander of a troop of militia.

Almocafrar [al-mo-ca-frar'], *va.* To make holes with a dibble.

Almocafre [al-mo-cah'-fray], *m.* A gardener's hoe, dibble.

Almoceda [al-mo-thay'-dah], *f.* 1. Impost on water for irrigation. 2. Right of taking water for irrigation upon fixed days.

Almocrate [al-mo-crah'-tay], *m.* Sal ammoniac.

Almocri [al-mo-cree'], *m.* Reader of the Koran in a mosque.

Almodi [al-mo-dee'], *m.* *V.* ALMUDÍ.

Almodrote [al-mo-dro'-tay], *m.* 1. A sauce for the egg-plant, composed of oil, garlic, cheese, etc. 2. Hodge-podge, a confused mixture of various ingredients.

Almofar [al-mo-far'], *m.* A part of ancient armour reclining on the helmet.

Almofía [al-mo-fee'-ah], *f.* *V.* ALJOFAINA.

Almofrej [al-mo-fray'], *m.* A coarse woollen bag; a seaman's canvas bag; a leather case for a mattress.

Almogama [al-mo-gah'-mah], *f.* (Naut.) The stern-post of a ship. *V.* REDEL.

Almogárabe, Almogávar [al-mo-gah'-rah-bay, al-mo-gah'-var], *m.* An expert forager. *Almogávares,* A sort of light troops in the ancient militia of Spain chiefly employed to make frequent incursions into the Moorish dominions.

Almohada [al-mo-ah'-dah], *f.* 1. Pillow or bolster, cushion, pillow-case. 2. (Naut.) A piece of timber on which the bowsprit rests. *Consultar con la almohada,* To take time for weighing any thing maturely. *Almohada para arrodillarse,* A cushion to kneel upon.
Almohadilla [al-mo-ah-deel'-lyah], *f.* 1. (Dim.) A small bolster or pillow. 2. Working-case; sewing cushion; the pads of a harness. 3. Stone projecting out of a wall. 4. A callous excrescence on the backs of mules where the saddle is put. *Cantar a la almohadilla,* To sing alone, without musical instruments.
Almohadillado, da [al-mo-ah-deel-lyah'-do, dah], *a.* In the form of a cushion.
Almohadón [al-mo-ah-done'], *m. aug.* A large cushion.
Almohatre, Almojatre [al-mo-ah'-tray, al-mo-hah'-tray], *m.* Sal ammoniac.
Almohaza [al-mo-ah'-thah], *f.* Curry-comb.
Almohazado, da [al-mo-ah-thah'-do, dah], *a.* Curried.—*pp.* of ALMOHAZAR.
Almohazador [al-mo-ah-thah-dor], *m.* A groom.
Almohazar [al-mo-ah-thar'], *va.* To curry with a curry-comb.
Almojaba [al-mo-hah'-bah], *f.* (Obs.) Smoked tunny-fish.
Almojábana [al-mo-hah'-bah-nah], *f.* 1. Cake made of cheese and flour. 2. Hard sauce.
Almojarifadgo, Almojarifazgo [al-mo-hah-re-fad'-go, al-mo-hah-re-fath'-go], *m.* A duty on imports or exports.
Almojarife [al-mo-ha-ree'-fay], *m.* 1. Tax-gatherer for the king. 2. Custom-house officer.
Almojaya [al-mo-hah'-yah], *f.* Putlog, a cross-piece used in scaffolding.
Almona [al-mo'-nah], *f.* 1. (Prov.) Soap manufactory. 2. (Obs.) A public magazine, store-house. 3. Shad-fishery.
Almóndiga, Almondiguilla [al-mon'-de-gah, al-mon-de-geel'-lyah], *f.* *V.* ALBÓNDIGA and ALBONDINGUILLA.
Almoneda [al-mo-nay'-dah], *f.* An auction.
Almonedear [al-mo-nay-day-ar'], *va.* To sell by auction.
Almoradux [al-mo-rah-dooks'], *m.* 1. (Bot.) Sweet marjoram. Origanum majorana. 2. *V.* SÁNDALO.
Almorí, Almurí [al-mo-ree', al-moo-ree'], *m.* A sweetmeat or cake.
Almoronía [al-mo-ro-nee'-ah], *f.* *V.* ALBORONÍA.
Almorranas [al-mor-rah'-nas], *f. pl.* (Med.) Hemorrhoids or piles.
Almorrefa [al-mor-ray'-fah], *f.* A mosaic floor; tiled floor.
Almorta [al-mor'-tah], *f.* (Bot.) Blue vetch. Lathyrus sativus.
Almorzada [al-mor-thah'-dah], *f.* (Prov.) *V.* ALMUERZA.
Almorzado, da [al-mor-thah'-do, dah], *a.* One who has breakfasted.—*pp.* of ALMORZAR.
Almorzador [al-mor-thah-dor'], *m.* Breakfast-case, which contains things necessary for serving up a breakfast.
Almorzar [al-mor-thar'], *va.* To breakfast.
Almotacén [al-mo-tah-then'], *m.* 1. Inspector of weights and measures. 2. Clerk of the market. 3. A revenue in Toledo, consisting of a third part of the fines imposed by the magistrates.
Almotacenazgo [al-mo-tah-thay-nath'-go], *m.* The office of an inspector, or of a clerk of the market.
Almotacenía [al-mo-tah-thay-nee'-ah], *f.* (Obs.) Custom or duty to the market-clerk.
Almotalafe [al-mo-tah-lah'-fay], *m.* (Obs.) Inspector of silks.
Almotazaf [al-mo-tah-thaf'], *m.* (Obs.) The weigher of wool.
Almotazala [al-mo-tah-thah'-lah], *f.* (Ant.) Counterpane for a bed.
Almozárabe [al-mo-thah'-rah-bay], *m.* A Christian who lived subject to the Moors.
Almud [al-mood'], *m.* A measure of grain and dry fruit, in some places the twelfth part of a *fanega,* and in some others half a *fanega.* *Almud de tierra,* (Prov.) About half an acre of ground.
Almudada [al-moo-dah'-dah], *f.* A piece of ground which takes half a *fanega* of grain for sowing it.
Almudí, Almudín [al-moo-dee', al-moo-deen'], *m.* 1. (Prov.) *V.* ALHÓNDIGA. 2. (Prov.) A measure containing six *cahíces* or bushels.
Almuédano [al-moo-ay'-dah-no], *m.* Muezzin, one who calls to prayer from the minaret.
Almuérdago [al-moo-er'-dah-go], *m.* Bird-lime. *V.* MUÉRDAGO.
Almuerza [al-moo-er'-thah], *f.* A double-handful.
(*Yo almuerzo, yo almuerce,* from *Almorzar.* *V.* ACORDAR.)
Almuerzo [al-moo-er'-tho], *m.* 1. Breakfast. 2. Set of dishes, etc., for breakfast: breakfast cover.
Alnado, da [al-nah'-do, dah], *m.* & *f.* A step-child. *V.* HIJASTRO.
Alobadado, da [ah-lo-bah-dah'-do, dah], *a.* 1. Bit by a wolf. 2. Labouring under morbid swellings.
Alobunadillo, lla [ah-lo-boo-nah-deel'-lyo, lyah], *a.* Resembling a wolf somewhat.
Alobunado, da [ah-lo-boo-nah'-do, dah], *a.* Resembling a wolf in colour.
Alocadamente [ah-lo-cah-dah-men'-tay], *adv.* Rashly, inconsiderately.
Alocado, da [ah-lo-cah'-do, dah], *a.* 1. Half-witted, foolish. 2. Wild.
Alocución [ah-lo-coo-the-on'], *f.* 1. Allocution. 2. Address, speech, harangue. 3. Address of the Pope to the cardinals.
Alodial [ah-lo-de-ahl'], *a.* (Law) Allodial, free, exempt.
Alodio [ah-lo'-de-o], *m.* Allodium, a possession not held by tenure of a superior lord.
Áloe [ah'-lo-ay], *m.* 1. (Bot.) Aloes-tree. 2. Aloes.
Aloético, ca [ah-lo-ay'-te-co, cah], *a.* Aloetic, any drug containing aloes.
Aloina [ah-lo-ee'-nah], *f.* Aloin, active principle of aloes.
Aloja [ah-lo'-hah], *f.* A beverage made of water, honey, and spice; metheglin. In South America, a fermented liquor from carob-beans.
Alojamiento [ah-lo-hah-me-en'-to], *m.* 1. Lodging. 2. (Naut.) Steerage.
Alojar [ah-lo-har'], *va.* 1. To lodge, to let lodgings. 2. To dwell, reside.—*vr.* To station troops.
Alojería [ah-lo-hay-ree'-ah], *f.* A place where metheglin is prepared and sold.
Alojero [ah-lo-hay'-ro], *m.* 1. One who prepares or sells metheglin. 2. A box near the pit in some theatres of Spain, where the justice sits to keep order.
Alomado, da [ah-lo-mah'-do, dah], *a.* Having a curved back: applied to horses.—*pp.* of ALOMAR.
Alomar [ah-lo-mar'], *va.* 1. To distribute equally the load on a horse. 2. To cover with a seed-plough.—*vr.* To grow strong and vigorous.
Alón [ah-lone'], *m.* The plucked wing of any bird.
¡ Alón ! [ah-lone'], *int.* Taken from the French *allons,* Let us go.
Alondra [ah-lon'-drah], *f.* (Orn.) A lark.
Alongadero [ah-lon-gah-day'-ro], *a.* Dilatory. *V.* LARGA.
Alongamiento [ah-lon-gah-me-en'-to], *m.* Delay.
Alongar [ah-lon-gar'], *va.* To enlarge, to extend.
Alónimo [ah-lo'-ne-mo], *m.* Allonymous, published under an assumed name.
Alópata [ah-lo'-pah-tah], *m.* Allopath (ist).
Alopatía [ah-lo-pah-tee'-ah], *f.* Allopathy.
Alopático, ca [ah-lo-pah'-te-co, cah], *a.* Allopathic.
Alopecia [ah-lo-pay'-the-ah], *f.* (Med.) Alopecia, loss of the hair; baldness.
Alopiado, da [ah-lo-pe-ah'-do, dah], *a.* Composed of opium.
Aloque [ah-lo'-kay], *a.* Applied to clear white wine, or a mixture of red and white.
Aloquín [ah-lo-keen'], *m.* A stone wall of the inclosure where wax is bleached.
Alosa [ah-lo'-sah], *f.* Shad. Clupea alosa.
Alosna [ah-los'-nah], *f.* (Bot. Prov.) Wormwood. Artemisia absinthium.
Alotar [ah-lo-tar'], *va.* (Naut.) *V.* ARRIZAR. *Alotar las anclas,* (Naut.) 1. To stow the anchors. 2. To sell fish by auction on the beach.
Alpaca [al-pah'-cah], or **Alpaga** [al-pah'-gah], *f.* 1. Alpaca and *Llama,* a ruminant of South America, esteemed for the fineness of its wool. 2. A fabric made from the wool of this animal. 3. An alloy of copper, zinc, and nickel, called white metal.
Alpañata [al-pah-nyah'-tah], *f.* A piece of chamois-skin which potters use to smooth their work.
Alpargata, *f.* **Alpargate,** *m.* [al-par-gah'-tah, al-par-gah'-tay]. A sort of shoes or sandals made of hemp. *Compañía de la alpargata,* (Prov.) A set of ragamuffins.
Alpargatado, da [al-par-gah-tah'-do, dah], *a.* Wearing hempen sandals.—*pp.* of ALPARGATAR.
Alpargatar [al-par-gah-tar'], *va.* To make hempen sandals.
Alpargatazo [al-par-gah-tah'-tho], *m.* A blow with a hempen sandal.
Alpargatería [al-par-gah-tay-ree'-ah], *f.* A manufactory of hempen sandals.
Alpargatero [al-par-gah-tay'-ro], *m.* A manufacturer of hempen sandals.
Alpargatilla [al-par-gah-teel'-lyah], *f.* 1. (Dim.) A small hempen sandal. 2. (Met.) A crafty, designing fellow.
Alpechín [al-pay-cheen'], *m.* Water which oozes from a heap of olives.
Alpende [al-pen'-day], *m.* Shed to keep mining implements in.
Alpestre, Alpino, na [al-pes'-tray, al-pee'-no, nah], *a.* Alpine.
Alpícola [al-pee'-co-lah], *a.* Growing in the Alps.
Alpicoz [al-pe-coth'], *m.* (Prov.) *V.* ALFICOZ.
Alpinismo [al-pe-nees'-mo], *m.* Alpinism, climbing the Alps.
Alpinista [al-pe-nees'-tah], *m.* & *f.* Alpinist, Alps climber.
Alpiste [al-pees'-tay], *m.* Canary-seed. Phalaris canariensis. *Quedarse alpiste,* To be disappointed.
Alpistela, Alpistera [al-pis-tay'-lah, al-pis-tay'-rah], *f.* A cake made of flour, eggs, sesamum, and honey.
Alpistero [al-pis-tay'-ro], *m.* A sieve for canary-seed.
Alquequenje [al-kay-kane'-hay], *m.* Barbadoes winter-cherry, used as diuretic. Physalis pubescens.

Alquería [al-kay-ree'-ah], *f.* A grange, farm-house, generally a farm with a house at a distance from neighbours.

Alquermes [al-ker'-mes], *m.* 1. A compound cordial, of exciting character, in which the kermes is a principal ingredient. 2. A celebrated confection.

Alquerque [al-ker'-kay], *m.* Place in oil-mills for laying the bruised olives.

Alquez [al-keth'], *m.* A wine measure containing 12 *cántaras.*

Alquibla [al-kee'-blah], *f.* The point toward which Mohammedans direct their eyes when praying.

Alquicel, Alquicer [al-ke-thel', al-ke-therr'], *m.* 1. Moorish garment resembling a cloak. 2. Covers for benches, tables, etc.

Alquifol [al-ke-fol'], *m.* (Min.) Alquifou, or potter's ore: lead ore.

Alquilador, ra [al-ke-lah-dor', rah], *m.* & *f.* One who lets coaches on hire; hirer.

Alquilamiento [al-ke-lah-me-en'-to], *m.* The act of hiring or letting.

Alquilar [al-ke-lar'], *va.* To let, to hire, to rent, to fee.—*vr.* To serve for wages.

Alquiler [al-ke-lerr'], *m.* 1. Wages or hire. 2. The act of hiring or letting. *Alquiler de una casa,* House-rent.

Alquilón, na [al-ke-lone', nah], *a.* That which can be let or hired.

Alquilona [al-ke-lo'-nah], *f.* A woman hired occasionally for odd work.

Alquimia [al-kee'-me-ah], *f.* Alchemy.

Alquímico, ca [al-kee'-me-co, cah], *a.* Relating to alchemy.

Alquimila [al-ke-mee'-lah], *f.* (Bot.) Ladies' mantle. Alchemilla.

Alquimista [al-ke-mees'-tah], *m.* Alchemist.

Alquinal [al-ke-nahl'], *m.* A veil or head-dress for women.

Alquitara [al-ke-tah'-rah], *f.* *V.* ALAMBIQUE.

Alquitarar [al-ke-tah-rar'], *va.* To distil, to let fall in drops.

Alquitira [al-ke-tee'-rah], *f.* Tragacanth, a gum.

Alquitrán [al-ke-trahn'], *m.* 1. Tar or liquid pitch. 2. (Naut.) Stuff for paying a ship's bottom, composed of pitch, grease, resin, and oil: it is also used as a combustible matter. (Met.) ***Es un alquitrán,*** He is a passionate man.

Alquitranado [al-ke-trah-nah'-do], *m.* (Naut.) Tarpaulin, a tarred hempen cloth. ***Cabos alquitranados,*** (Naut.) Black or tarred cordage.—*Alquitranado, da, pp.* of ALQUITRANAR.

Alquitranar [al-ke-trah-nar'], *va.* To tar.

Alrededor [al-ray-day-dor'], *adv.* Around.

Alrededores [al-ray-day-do'-res], *m. pl.* Environs.

Alrota [al-ro'-tah], *f.* A very coarse sort of tow. *V.* ARLOTA.

Alsaciano, na [al-sah-the-ah'-no, nah], *a.* Alsatian: of Alsace or Elsass.

Alta [ahl'-tah], *f.* 1. (Mil.) Orders to active duty. 2. Discharge (from a hospital). 3. New member. *Dar de alta,* To discharge, to release. *Darse de alta,* To join, to become a member. *Ser alta,* (Mil.) To go on active duty.

Altabaque [al-tah-bah'-kay], *m.* Wicker basket.

Altabaquillo [al-tah-bah-keel'-lyo], *m.* (Bot.) Field bindweed.

Alta fidelidad [ahl'-tah fe-day-le-dahd'], *f.* High fidelity.

Altaico, ca [al-tah'-e-co, cah], *a.* Altaic.

Altamente [al-tah-men'-tay] *adv.* Highly, extremely, exceedingly.

Altamía [al-tah-mee'-ah], *f.* (Obs.) A deep plate.

Altamisa [al-tah-mee'-sah], *f.* *V.* ARTEMISA.

Altanería [al-tah-nay-ree'-ah], *f.* 1. (Littl. us.) The towering flight of some birds. 2. Hawking. 3. (Met.) Haughtiness, loftiness, contemptuousness.

Altanero, ra [al-tah-nay'-ro, rah], *a.* 1. Soaring, towering. 2. (Met.) Haughty, arrogant, proud.

Altar [al-tar'], *m.* 1. The table in Christian churches where the mass is celebrated, and where the communion is administered. *Altar de alma* or *de ánima,* A privileged altar. 2. (Ast.) A southern constellation.

Altarero [al-tah-ray'-ro], *m.* One who adorns altars for great festivals.

Altavoz [al-tah-voth'], *m.* Loudspeaker. *Altavoz para sonidos agudos,* Tweeter. *Altavoz para sonidos graves,* Woofer.

Altea [al-tay'-ah], *f.* (Bot.) Common mallow, marsh-mallow. Malva sylvestris.

Altear [al-tay-ar'], *vn.* (Naut.) To rise above; said of a portion of a coast which rises beyond what adjoins it.

Alterabilidad [al-tay-rah-be-le-dahd'], *f.* Changeableness, mutability.

Alterable [al-tay-rah'-blay], *a.* That may be changed, alterable.

Alteración [al-tay-rah-the-on'], *f.* 1. Alteration, mutation. 2. Unevenness of the pulse. 3. Strong emotion of anger or other passion. 4. Disturbance, tumult, commotion.

Alterado, da [al-tay-rah'-do, dah], *a.* Alterative. *Caldo alterado,* Medicated or alterative broth.—*pp.* of ALTERAR.

Alterador, ra [al-tay-rah-dor', rah], *m.* & *f.* Alterer, one who alters.

Alterante [al-tay-rahn'-tay], *pa.* (Med.) Alterative.

Alterar [al-tay-rar'], *va.* 1. To alter, to change. 2. To disturb, to stir up. *Alterar la moneda,* To raise or lower the value of coin.—*vr.* To fling.

Alterativo, va [al-tay-rah-tee'-vo, vah], *a.* Alterative.

Altercación, *f.* **Altercado,** *m.* [al-ter-cah-the-on', al-ter-cah'-do]. A controversy; contest, strife, quarrel.

Altercado [al-ter-cah'-do], *m.* Altercation, wrangle, quarrel.

Altercador, ra [al-ter-cah-dor', rah], *m.* & *f.* One who argues obstinately.

Altercar [al-ter-car'], *va.* To contend, to dispute obstinately, to debate, to quarrel, to bicker, to expostulate.

Alternación [al-ter-nah-the-on'], *f.* Alternation, reciprocal succession.

Alternadamente [al-ter-nah-dah-men'-tay], *adv.* *V.* ALTERNATIVAMENTE.

Alternar [al-ter-nar'], *va.* To alternate, to perform by turns, to change one for another.—*vn.* To succeed reciprocally. *Los gustos y los pesares alternan,* Pleasures and sorrows alternate.

Alternativa [al-ter-nah-tee'-vah], *f.* 1. Alternative, choice of two things. 2. The right of archbishops and bishops to dispose of prebends and benefices alternately with the Pope in their dioceses.

Alternativamente [al-ter-nah-te-vah-men'-tay], *adv.* Alternatively.

Alternativo, va [al-ter-nah-tee'-vo, vah], *a.* Alternate.—*m.* Rotation of crops.

Alterno, na [al-ter'-no, nah], *a.* (Poet.) Alternate. (Bot.) Alternate.

Alteza [al-tay'-thah], *f.* 1. Elevation, sublimity. 2. Highness, a title given to the board of Castile, exchequer, etc. 3. (Obs.) Height.

Altibajo [al-te-bah'-ho], *m.* 1. A downright blow in fencing. 2. (Obs.) A kind of flowered velvet.—*pl.* 1. Uneven ground. 2. (Met.) Vicissitudes, the ups and downs in life.

Altillo, lla [al-teel'-lyo, lyah], *a. dim.* Somewhat high.

Altillo [al-teel'-lyo], *m. dim.* A hillock.

Altilocuencia [al-te-lo-coo-en'-the-ah], *f.* Grandiloquence, high-sounding words.

Altilocuente [al-te-lo-coo-en'-tay], *a.* (Poet.) Pompous in language, grandiloquent.

Altimetría [al-te-may-tree'-ah], *f.* The art of taking or measuring altitudes or heights.

Altímetro [al-tee'-may-tro], *m.* (Naut., Aer.) Altimeter.

Altiplanicie [al-te-plah-nee'-the-ay], *f.* Highland.

Altísimo, ma [al-tee'-se-mo, mah], *a. aug.* Extremely lofty.

Altísimo [al-tee'-se-mo], *m.* The Most High, God.

Altisonante, Altísono, na [al-te-so-nahn'-tay, al-tee'-so-no, nah], *a.* High-sounding.

Altitonante [al-te-to-nahn'-tay], *a.* (Poet.) Thundering.

Altitud [al-te-tood'], *f.* (Geog.) *V.* ALTURA. Elevation, or altitude above the level of the ocean. *Altitud absoluta,* (Aer.) Absolute altitude.

Altivamente [al-te-vah-men'-tay], *adv.* Highly, loftily, lordly.

Altivez [al-te-veth'], *f.* Haughtiness, arrogance, pride, lordliness.

Altivo, va [al-tee'-vo, vah], *a.* 1. Haughty, proud, lofty, lord-like. 2. High, high-minded, consequential. 3. Overbearing.

Alto, ta [ahl'-to, tah], *a.* 1. High, elevated. *Alta mar,* (Naut.) High seas. 2. Tall. 3. (Met.) Arduous, difficult. 4. (Met.) Eminent. 5. Enormous. 6. Deep. 7. Late: applied to movable feasts. ***Altas por abril son las pascuas.*** Easter falls late in April.

Alto [ahl'-to], *m.* 1. Height. 2. Story. *Casa de tres altos,* A house three stories high. 3. (Naut.) Depth or height of a ship. 4. High ground. 5. (Mil.) Halt; command to stop; and a place or time of rest. 6. (Mus.) Notes put over the bass. Contralto (voice). Alto, or tenor violin; viola. 7. *No hacer alto,* Not to mind, not to observe. *Pasar por alto,* To overlook.

Alto [ahl'-to], *int.* 1. *Alto ahí,* Stop there. 2. *Alto de aquí,* Move off.

Alto [ahl'-to], *adv.* 1. Loud. 2. High. *De lo alto,* From above. 3. *Se me pasó por alto,* I forgot. 4. *Por alto,* By stealth; by particular favour. *Metió los géneros por alto,* He smuggled the goods.

Altoparlante [al-to-par-lahn'-tay], *m.* Loudspeaker.

Altozano [al-to-thah'-no], *m.* A height or hill.

Altramuz [al-trah-mooth'], *m.* (Bot.) Lupine. Lupinus. *Altramuces,* Lupines which are mixed with ivory beads, and used as black balls in giving votes in cathedral chapters, especially in Castile.

Altruismo [al-troo-ees'-mo], *m.* Altruism, unselfishness.

Altura [al-too'-rah], *f.* 1. Height, loftiness. 2. One of the three dimensions of a solid body. 3. Summit of mountains. 4. Altitude, the elevation of the pole or of any of the heavenly bodies. (Naut.) The latitude. 5. (Met.) Exaltation of spirits. ***Estar en grande altura,*** To be raised to a high degree of dignity, favour, or fortune. ***Alturas,*** The heavens. ***Dios de las alturas,*** God, the Lord of the heavens.

Aluar, or **Tomar por la lúa**, *vn.* (Naut.) To bring under the lee.

Alubia [ah-loo'-be-ah], *f.* (Bot.) French bean. Phaseolus vulgaris. *V.* JUDÍA.

Aluciar [ah-loo-the-ar'], *va.* To polish an article.

Alucinación, *f.* **Alucinamiento**, *m.* [ah-loo-the-nah-the-on' ah-loo-the-nah-me-en'-to]. Hallucination.

Alucinadamente [ah-loo-the-nah-dah-men'-tay], *adv.* Erroneously.

Alucinar [ah-loo-the-nar'], *va.* To deceive, to lead into error, to fascinate, to delude.

Alucón [ah-loo-cone'], *m.* The barn owl. Strix aluco.

Alud [ah-lood'], *m.* Avalanche.

Aluda [ah-loo'-dah], *f.* (Ent.) Winged ant or emmet. Formica.

Aludel [ah-loo-del'], *m.* (Chem.) Subliming pots used in chemistry.

Aludir [ah-loo-deer'], *vn.* To allude, to refer to.

Aludo, da [ah-loo'-do, dah], *a.* Winged; large-winged.

Aluengar [ah-loo-en-gar'], *va. V.* ALONGAR.

Alueñe [ah-loo-ay'-nyay], *adv.* (Obs.) Far off.

Alumbrado, da [ah-loom-brah'-do, dah], *a.* 1. Aluminous, relating to alum. 2. (Coll.) Flustered with wine.—*pp.* of ALUMBRAR.

Alumbrado [ah-loom-brah'-do], *m.* Illumination. *Alumbrado fluorescente,* Fluorescent lighting. *Luz fluorescente,* Fluorescent light.

Alumbrador, ra [ah-loom-brah-dor', rah], *m.* & *f.* One who gives light, link-boy.

Alumbramiento [ah-loom-brah-me-en'-to], *m.* 1. The act of supplying with light. 2. (Obs.) Illusion, deceit, false appearance. 3. (Met.) Child-birth. *V.* PARTO. *Alumbramiento bueno,* or *feliz,* A happy child-birth.

Alumbrar [ah-loom-brar'], *va.* 1. To light, to supply with light. 2. (Obs.) To restore sight to the blind. 3. To enlighten, to instruct, to adorn with knowledge. 4. Among dyers, to dip cloth into alum-water. 5. To dig about the roots of vines. 6. To bring forth. *Dios alumbre a Vd. con bien,* or *Dios dé a Vd. feliz parto,* God grant you a safe delivery.—*vr.* (Coll.) To be intoxicated.

Alumbre [ah-loom'-bray], *m.* Alum, a mineral salt. *Alumbre catino,* A kind of alkali drawn from the plant glasswort. *Alumbre de rasuras,* Salt of tartar. *Alumbre sacarino* or *zucarino,* Alum and the white of an egg formed into a paste: alum-whey.

Alumbrera [ah-loom-bray'-rah], *f.* Alum-mine. *Alumbrera artificial,* Alum-works.

Alúmina [ah-loo'-me-nah], *f.* (Chem.) Alumina or alumine.

Aluminado, da [ah-loo-me-nah'-do, dah], *a.* (Chem.) Mixed with alum.

Aluminio [ah-loo-mee'-ne-o], *m.* Aluminium or aluminum, one of the metallic elements.

Aluminoso, sa [ah-loo-me-no'-so, sah], *a.* Aluminous, consisting of alum.

Alumno, na [ah-loom'-no, nah], *m.* & *f.* Foster-child; disciple, pupil.

Alunado, da [ah-loo-nah'-do, dah], *a.* 1. Insane, lunatic. 2. Spasmodic. 3. Spoiled, tainted.

Alunita [ah-loo-nee'-tah], *f.* Alunite.

Alunizaje [ah-loo-ne-thah'-hay], *m.* Landing on the moon.

Alunizar [ah-loo-ne-thar'], *vn.* To land on the moon.

Alusión [ah-loo-se-on'], *f.* Allusion, reference.

Alusivamente [ah-loo-se-vah-men'-tay], *adv.* Allusively.

Alusivo, va [ah-loo-see'-vo, vah], *a.* Allusive, hinting at.

Alustrar [ah-loos-trar'], *va.* To give lustre to any thing.

Alutación [ah-loo-tah-the-on'], *f.* (Min.) Stratum of grains of gold, found in some mines.

Aluvial [ah-loo-ve-ahl'], *a.* (Littl. us.) Alluvial.

Aluvión [ah-loo-ve-on'], *f.* Alluvion, wash.

Alveario [al-vay-ah'-re-o], *m.* (Anat.) The inward cavity of the ear.

Álveo [ahl'-vay-o], *m.* 1. Bed of a river. 2. Source of a river.

Alveolar [al-vay-o-lar'], *a.* Alveolar, relating to the alveolus.

Alvéolo [al-vay'-o-lo], *m.* 1. Alveolus or socket of the teeth. 2. (Bot.) Alveolus, the cavity in which the seeds of plants are lodged.

Alverja, Alverjana [al-ver'-hah, al-ver-hah'-nah], *f.* (Bot.) Common vetch or tare. Vicia sativa.

Alverjas [al-ver'-has], *f. pl.* (Bot.) (Sp. Am.) Peas.

Alvidriar [al-ve-dree-ar'], *va.* (Prov.) To glaze earthenware.

Alvino, na [al-vee'-no, nah], *a.* (Med.) Alvine, relating to the bowels.

Alvitana [al-ve-tah'-nah], *f.* A windbreak (hedge or fence).

Alza [ahl'-thah], *f.* 1. A piece of leather put round the last to make the shoe wider. 2. An instrument used in rope-walks to keep up the rope-yarn in the act of spinning it. 3. Advance in the price of any thing. 4. (Typ.) Overlay, frisket sheet. *Alza y baja,* or *caída de los fondos públicos,* The rise and fall of public stocks.

Alzacuello [al-thah-coo-ayl'-lyo], *m.* A black collar bound with linen, which clergymen wear.

Alzada [al-thah'-dah], *f.* 1. Height, stature; of horses. 2. A town, village, etc., situated on an eminence. 3. Appeal. *Juez de alzadas,* A judge in appeal causes.

Alzadamente [al-thah-dah-men'-tay], *adv.* Wholesale.

Alzado [al-thah'-do], *m.* 1. A plan of a building which shows its front and elevation. 2. A fraudulent bankrupt. *Alzados,* Spare stores.—*Alzado, da, pp.* of ALZAR.—*a.* Fraudulent.

Alzadura [al-thah-doo'-rah], *f.* Elevation.

Alzamiento [al-thah-me-en'-to], *m.* 1. The act of lifting or raising up. 2. Bidding a higher price at an auction.

Alzapaño [al-thah-pah'-nyo], *m.* A hook to keep up a curtain.

Alzapié [al-thah-pe-ay'], *m.* A foot-stool.

Alzaprima [al-thah-pree'-mah], *f.* 1. A lever. 2. (Naut.) Heaver. 3. (Mech.) Fulcrum. *Dar alzaprima,* (Met.) To deceive, to ruin by artifice.

Alzaprimar [al-thah-pre-mar'], *va.* 1. To raise by means of a lever. 2. (Naut.) To move with handspikes. 3. To incite, spur on.

Alzapuertas [al-thah-poo-er'-tas], *m.* A player who acts only the part of a dumb servant.

Alzar [al-thar'], *va.* 1. To raise, to lift up, to heave; to erect, to construct. 2. To repeal a decree of excommunication; to recall from banishment. 3. To carry off. 4. To hide, to lock up. 5. To cut the cards; to gather up and arrange in order the printed sheets for the binder. 6. To elevate the host, in mass. 7. (Naut.) To heave. *Alzar cabeza,* To recover from a calamity or disease. *Alzar de codo* or *el codo,* To drink much wine or liquor. *Alzar de obra,* To cease working. *Alzar de eras,* To finish the harvesting of grain in the farm-yards. *Alzar figura,* To assume an air of importance. *Alzar el dedo,* To raise the forefinger in asseveration or affirmation of any thing. *Alzar la casa,* To quit a house, to move out of it. *Alzar velas,* (Naut.) To set the sails. (Met.) To move off.—*vr.* 1. To rise in rebellion. 2. To rise from kneeling. 3. To make a fraudulent bankruptcy. 4. To appeal. *Alzarse con el dinero,* To run away with the money. *Alzarse a mayores,* To be petulant. *Alzarse con algo.* V. APROPIARSE.

Alzatirantes [al-thah-te-rahn'-tes], *m. pl.* Straps attached to the harness of a horse to suspend the traces.

Allá [al-lyah'], *adv.* There, in that place; thither, or to that place; anciently, in other times. *Allá va con Dios,* (Naut.) About ship.

Allanador [al-lyah-nah-dor'], *m.* 1. Leveller. 2. Gold-beater's paper which contains the beaten gold-leaves. 3. Consent, agreement.

Allanamiento [al-lyah-nah-me-en'-to], *m.* 1. Levelling, the act of making even. 2. Consent. 3. (Met.) Affability, suavity.

Allanar [al-lyah-nar'], *va.* 1. To level, to make even, to flatten, to reduce to a flat surface. 2. To remove or overcome difficulties. 3. To pacify, to subdue. *Allanar la casa,* To enter a house by force with a search-warrant. *Allanar el camino,* To pave the way for obtaining something.—*vr.* 1. To abide by a law or agreement, to acquiesce to conform. 2. To fall to ruin.

Allegadizo, za [al-lyay-gah-dee'-tho, thah], *a.* Collected without choice.

Allegado, da [al-lyay-gah'-do, dah], *a.* Near, conjunct.—*m.* Friend, ally.—*pp.* of ALLEGAR.

Allegador, ra [al-lyay-gah-dor', rah], *m.* & *f.* One who gathers or collects. *A padre allegador hijo expendedor,* After a gatherer comes a scatterer.

Allegamiento [al-lyay-gah-me-en'-to], *m.* 1. Collecting, uniting. 2. Close friendship, union.

Allegar [al-lyay-gar'], *va.* 1. To gather, to unite. 2. To draw near. 3. To solicit, to procure.—*vr.* To come near, to approach.

Allende [al-lyen'-day], *adv.* (Obs.) On the other side. *Allende de. V.* ADEMÁS.

Allí [al-lyee'], *adv.* 1. There, in that place. *Allí mismo,* In that very place. *De allí,* Thence, from that place. 2. At that moment.

Allo [ahl'-lyo], *m.* (Amer.) *V.* GUACAMAYO.

Alloza [al-lyo'-thah], *f.* A green almond. *V.* ALMENDRUCO.

Allozo [al-lyo'-tho], *m.* (Bot.) The wild almond-tree. Amygdalus communis.

Alludel [al-lyoo-del'], *m.* Earthen water-pipe. *V.* ALUDEL.

Ama [ah'-mah], *f.* A mistress of the house. *El ama de casa,* The lady or mistress of the house. *Ama de llaves* or *de gobierno,* A house-keeper. *Ama de leche,* A wet-nurse.

Amabilidad [ah-mah-be-le-dahd'], *f.* Amiability, affability, loveliness.

Amable [ah-mah'-blay], *a.* Amiable, pleasing, lovely.

Amablemente [ah-mah-blay-men'-tay], *adv.* Amiably, lovely.

Amacena [ah-mah-thay'-nah], *f.* (Bot.) A damson plum. Prunus damascena.

Amaceno, na [ah-mah-thay'-no, nah], *a.* Damascene.

Amacollarse [ah-mah-col-lyar'-say], *vr.* To throw out shoots.

Amacrático, ca [ah-ma-crah'-te-co, cah], *a.* Amacratic, said of a photographic lens which brings all the chemical rays to one focus.

Amadamado, da [ah-mah-dah-mah'-do, dah], *a.* Effeminate, womanish, frivolous.

Amador, ra [ah-mah-dor', rah], *m.* & *f.* A lover, a sweetheart, suitor.

Amadriada [ah-mah-dree'-ah-dah], *f.* Hamadryad, a wood nymph.

Amadrigar [ah-mah-dre-gar'], *va.* To receive well, especially one not deserving.—*vr.* 1. To burrow. 2. (Met.) To live retired, to decline all inter course with the world.

Amadrinar [ah-mah-dre-nar'], *va.* 1. To couple, to yoke together. 2. (Naut.) To join one thing to another. 3. To act as godmother or bridesmaid.

Amadroñado, da [ah-mah-dro-nyah'-do, dah], *a.* Resembling *madroños*, the fruit of the madroño-tree. *Rosario amadroñado*, A rosary, the beads of which resemble *madroños.*

Amaestrado, da [ah-mah-es-trah'-do, dah], *a.* 1. Taught, tutored. *Caballo amaestrado*, A horse completely broken in. 2. (Obs.) Artfully contrived.—*pp.* of AMAESTRAR.

Amaestradura [ah-mah-es-trah-doo'-rah], *f.* 1. Artifice, cunning. 2. Awning before a window.

Amaestrar [ah-mah-es-trar'], *va.* To instruct, to break in, to lead.

Amagar [ah-mah-gar'], *va.* 1. To be in a threatening attitude. 2. To threaten. 3. To have some symptoms of a disease. 4. (Met.) To manifest a desire.—*vr.* (Prov.) To couch, to stoop.

Amago [ah-mah'-go], *m.* 1. The act of threatening. 2. Doing or saying something not realized. 3. Symptom of disease which does not follow.

Amago [ah'-mah-go], *m.* Bitter stuff found in some bee-cells. (Met.) Nausea, loathing.

Amainar [ah-mah-e-nar'], *va.* 1. (Naut.) To lower the sails. 2. To relax.

Amaitinar [ah-mah-e-te-nar'], *va.* To observe attentively, to watch closely.

Amajadar [ah-mah-hah-dar'], *vn.* 1. To seek shelter in a sheep-fold. 2. To secure sheep.

Amalecita [ah-mah-lay-thee'-tah], *m.* Amalekite.

Amalgama [ah-mal-gah'-mah], *f.* Amalgam.

Amalgamación [ah-mal-gah-mah-the-on'], *f.* Amalgamation.

Amalgamar [ah-mal-gah-mar'], *va.* To amalgamate, to unite metals with quicksilver.

Amalo, la [ah-mah'-lo, lah], *a.* One of the most noted families of the Goths.

Amamantar [ah-mah-man-tar'], *va.* To nurse, to give suck.

Amambluoea [ah-mam-bloo-thay'-ah], *f.* A sort of cotton stuff.

Amancebado, da [ah-man-thay-bah'-do, dah], *a.* Attached, excessively devoted.—*pp.* of AMANCEBARSE.

Amancebamiento [ah-man-thay-bah-me-en'-to], *m.* Concubinage.

Amancebarse [ah-man-thay-bar'-say], *vr.* To live in concubinage.

Amancillar [ah-man-theel-lyar'], *va.* 1. To stain, to pollute. 2. To offend, to injure. 3. (Met.) To tarnish one's reputation.

Amanecer [ah-mah-nay-therr'], *vn.* 1. To dawn. 2. To arrive at break of day. *Al amanecer*, At the break of day. 3. (Met.) To begin to appear, or to show itself.

Amanerado, da [ah-mah-nay-rah'-do, dah], *a.* Applied to painters, mannerists, and to their works.

Amanerarse [ah-mah-nay-rar'-say], *vr.* To adopt a mannerism, or affectation in style. Used of artists or writers.

Amanojar [ah-mah-no-har'], *va.* To gather by handfuls.

Amansador, ra [ah-man-sah-dor', rah] *m.* & *f.* 1. Tamer, subduer. 2. Soother, appeaser.

Amansamiento [ah-man-sah-me-en'-to], *m.* The act of taming.

Amansar [ah-man-sar'], *va.* 1. To tame, to domesticate, to subdue. 2. (Met.) To soften, to pacify.

Amantar [ah-man-tar'], *va.* (Coll.) To cover with any loose garment.

Amante [ah-mahn'-tay], *pa.* & *n.* Loving, lover, sweetheart.—*pl.* (Naut.) Ropes which form part of the running rigging of a ship.

Amantillar [ah-man-teel-lyar'], *va.* (Naut.) To top the lifts, to hoist one end of the yard-arms higher than the other.

Amantillo [ah-man-teel'-lyo], *m.* (Naut.) Lift.

Amanuense [ah-mah-noo-en'-say], *m.* Amanuensis, clerk.

Amañar [ah-mah-nyar'], *va.* To do a thing cleverly.—*vr.* To accustom one's self to do things with skill, to be handy.

Amaño [ah-mah'-nyo], *m.* Way or means of doing a thing.—*pl.* 1. Tools or implements. 2. (Met.) Intrigue or machinations.

Amapola [ah-mah-po'-lah], *f.* (Bot.) Poppy. Papaver. *Amapola morada*, Corn-poppy, corn-rose. Papaver rhœas.

Amar [ah-mar'], *va.* 1. To love, to like, to fancy. 2. (Met.) To have a tendency to; applied to inanimate things.

Amaracino [ah-mah-rah-thee'-no], *a.* *Ungüento amaracino*, A sort of ointment made of marjoram.

Amáraco [ah-mah'-rah-co]. Marjoram. *V.* MEJORANA.

Amaranto [ah-mah-rahn'-to], *m.* (Bot.) Amaranth, flowering bush. Amaranthus.

Amargado, da [ah-mar-gah'-do, dah], *a.* Embittered.—*pp.* of AMARGAR.

Amargaleja [ah-mar-gah-lay'-hah], *f.* The bitter or wild plum. *V.* ENDRINA.

Amargamente [ah-mar-gah-men'-tay], *adv.* Bitterly.

Amargar [ah-mar-gar'], *va.* 1. To make bitter. 2. (Met.) To exasperate, to offend.—*vn.* To be bitter or acrid; to taste bitter.

Amargo, ga [ah-mar'-go, gah], *a.* 1. Bitter, having a hot, acrid taste. 2. Painful.

Amargo [ah-mar'-go], *m.* 1. *V.* AMARGOR. 2. Sweetmeat made up of bitter almonds.—*pl.* Bitters.

Amargón [ah-mar-gone'], *m.* (Bot.) Dandelion. Leontodon taraxacum.

Amargor [ah-mar-gor'], *m.* 1. Bitterness. 2. Sorrow, vexation.

Amargosamente [ah-mar-go-sah-men'tay], *V.* AMARGAMENTE.

Amargoso, sa [ah-mar-go'-so, sah], *a.* Bitter. *V.* AMARGO.

Amarguillo, lla [ah-mar-geel'-lyo, lyah], *a. dim.* Somewhat bitter. It is also used as a substantive.

Amargura [ah-mar-goo'-rah, *f.* Bitterness, acerbity, sorrow.

Amaricado, da [ah-mah-re-cah'-do, dah], *a.* (Coll.) Effeminate.

Amarilis [ah-mah-ree'-lis], *f.* Amaryllis.

Amarilla [ah-mah-reel'-lyah], *f.* 1. Gold coin, especially the ounce. 2. A vat. 3. A liver disease of woolly flocks.

Amarillazo, za [ah-mah-reel-lyah'-tho, thah], *a.* Of a pale yellow colour.

Amarillear [ah-mah-reel-lyay-ar'], *vn.* To incline to yellow.

Amarillejo, ja [ah-mah-reel-lyay'-ho, hah], *a. dim.* Yellowish.

Amarillento, ta [ah-mah-reel-lyen'-to, tah], *a.* Inclining to yellow, golden.

Amarillez [ah-mah-reel-lyeth'], *f.* The yellow colour of the body.

Amarillito, ta [ah-mah-reel-lyee'-to, tah], *a. dim.* *V.* AMARILLEJO.

Amarillo, lla [ah-mah-reel'-lyo, lyah], *a.* Yellow; gold colour.

Amarillo [ah-mah-reel'-lyo], *m.* 1. Jaundice. 2. A disease of silkworms.

Amarinar [ah-mah-re-nar'], *va.* *V.* MARINAR.

Amariposado, da [ah-mah-re-po-sah'-do dah], *a.* 1. (Bot.) Papilionaceous, applied to flowers. 2. Butterfly-like.

Amaro [ah-mah'-ro], *m.* (Bot.) Common clary. Salvia sclarea.

Amarra [ah-mar'-rah], *f.* 1. A cable. 2. A martingale. *Amarra*, (Naut.) A word of command, corresponding to the English belay, lash, or fasten. *Amarras fijas*, Moorings. *Amarras de popa*, Stern-fasts. *Amarras de proa*, Bow-fasts. *Amarras de través*, Fasts amidships. *Tener buenas amarras*, (Met.) To have powerful friends or interest.

Amarradero [ah-mar-rah-day'-ro], *m.* 1. A post to which anything is made fast. 2. (Naut.) A berth, the place where a ship is moored.

Amarrar [ah-mar-rar'], *va.* To tie, to fasten, to lash. *Amarrar un cabo de labor*, To belay a running rope. *Amarrar un bajel entre viento y marea*, To moor a vessel between wind and tide. *Amarrar un bajel con codera sobre el cable*, To moor a ship with a spring on the cable. *Amarrar con reguera*, To moor by the stern.

Amarrazones [ah-mar-rah-tho'-nes], *pl.* (Naut.) Ground-tackle.

Amarrido, da [ah-mar-ree'-do, dah], *a.* Dejected, gloomy, melancholy.

Amartelar [ah-mar-tay-lar'], *va.* 1. To court, to make love to a lady. 2. To love most devotedly.

Amartillar [ah-mar-teel-lyar'], *va.* 1. To hammer, to knock in. 2. To cock a gun or pistol.

Amasadera [ah-mah-sah-day-rah], *f.* A kneading-trough.

Amasador, ra [ah-mah-sah-dor', rah], *m.* & *f.* Kneader.

Amasadura [ah-mah-sah-doo'-rah], *f.* Act of kneading.

Amasamiento [ah-mah-sah-me-en'-to], *m.* 1. The act of uniting or joining. 2. *V.* AMASADURA.

Amasar [ah-mah-sar'], *va.* 1. To knead. 2. To mould. 3. (Met.) To arrange matters well for the attainment of some purpose.

Amasiato [ah-mah-se-ah'-to], *m.* (Sp. Am.) Concubinage.

Amasijo [ah-mah-see'-ho], *m.* 1. Dough. 2. The act of kneading, or the preparation for it. 3. A quantity of mortar or plaster. 4. (Met.) A medley. 5. A task. 6. A plotting agreement. 7. The place where the dough for bread is made.

Amate [ah-mah'-tay], *m.* (Mex.) A fig-tree, the milky juice of which is used as a resolvent.

Amatista [ah-mah-tees'-tah], *f.* (Min.) Amethyst, a precious stone of purplish violet colour.

Amatorio, ria [ah-mah-to'-re-o, ah], *a.* Amatory.

Amauris [ah-mah-oo'-ris], *m.* A kind of Indian linen.

Amaurosis [ah-mah-oo-ro'-sis], *f.* Blindness from disease of the optic nerve.

Amaurótico, ca [ah-mah-oo-ro'-te-co, cah], *a.* Amaurotic, affected by amaurosis.

Amayorazgado, da [ah-mah-yo-rath-gah'-do, dah], *a.* Entailed.
Amazona [ah-mah-tho'-nah], *f.* 1. An amazon; a masculine woman. 2. A large parrot of Brazil. 3. A long riding-skirt or habit.
Amazónico, ca [ah-mah-tho'-ne-co, cah], *a.* Amazonian.
Ambages [am-bah'-hes], *m. pl.* 1. (Obs.) Circuit. 2. (Met.) Circumlocution or multiplicity of words used to describe or explain a thing.
Ambar [ahm'-bar], *m.* Amber. Succinum. *Ambar gris,* Ambergris. *Es un ámbar,* It is excellent, it is very sweet: applied to liquors.
Ambarilla [am-bah-reel'-lyah], *f.* (Bot.) Amber-seed or musk-seed. Hibiscus abelmoschus.
Ambarina [am-bah-ree'-nah], *f.* *V.* ALGALIA.
Ambarino, na [am-bah-ree'-no, nah], *a.* Relating to amber.
Ambición [am-be-the-on'], *f.* 1. Ambition, a desire of preferment or honour. 2. Covetousness.
Ambicionar [am-be-the-o-nar'], *va.* To pursue with anxious desire, to covet.
Ambiciosamente [am-be-the-oh-sah-men'-tay], *adv.* Ambitiously; highly.
Ambicioso, sa [am-be-the-oh'-so, sah], *a.* 1. Ambitious, aspiring. 2. Covetous. 3. High-minded.
Ambidextro, tra [am-be-decs'-tro, trah], *a.* Ambidextrous.
Ambiental [am-be-en-tahl'], *a.* Environmental.
Ambientar [am-be-en-tar'], *va.* To provide with a suitable environment.
Ambiente [am-be-en'-tay], *m.* Environment.
Ambigú [am-be-goo'], *m.* Ambigu, a French word signifying a meal, usually served in the evening at entertainments or receptions, and composed of cold and warm dishes, set all at once on the table.
Ambiguamente [am-be-goo-ah-men'-tay], *adv.* Ambiguously.
Ambigüedad [am-be-goo-ay-dahd'], *f.* Ambiguity, doubt, uncertainty, double meaning.
Ambiguo, gua [am-be'-goo-o, ah], *a.* Ambiguous, doubtful.
Ambito [am'-be-to], *m.* Circuit, circumference, compass.
Ambivertido [am-be-ver-tee'-do], *m.* Ambivert.
Amblar [am-blar'], *va.* (Obs.) To amble; to pace.
Ambleo [am-blay'-o], *m.* A short, thick wax-candle.
Ambligonio [am-ble-go'-ne-o], *m.* Obtuse-angled. *V.* TRIÁNGULO.
Ambliopia [am-ble-o-pee'-ah], *f.* Weakness of sight, without any opacity of the cornea.
Ambo [ahm'-bo], *m.* Combination of two numbers in the lottery.
Ambón [am-bone'], *m.* A pulpit on each side of the high altar.
Ambos, bas [ahm'-bos, bas], *a.* Both. *Ambos* or *Ambas a dos,* Both, or both together.
Ambrosía [am-bro-see'-ah], *f.* 1. Ambrosia. 2. (fig.) Any delicious viand or liquor. 3. (Bot.) Ragweed.
Ambulancia [am-boo-lahn'-the-ah], *f.* Ambulance, a field hospital; also the conveyance.
Ambulante [am-boo-lahn'-tay], *a.* Ambulatory.
Ambulativo, va [am-boo-lah-tee'-vo, vah], *a.* Of a roving turn: applied to persons.
Ambulatorio, a [am-boo-lah-to'-re-o, ah], *a.* Ambulatory, used for walking or progressing. (Zool.)
Amebeo, bea [ah-may-bay'-o, ah], *a.* Amebean, a kind of dialogue in verse.
Amedrentador, ra [ah-may-dren-tah-dor', rah], *m.* & *f.* Threatener, discourager.—*a.* Terrifying, frightening.
Amedrentar [ah-may-dren-tar'], *va.* To frighten, to deter, to discourage, to fear; to intimidate; vulgarly, to cow.
Amelga [ah-mel'-gah], *f.* A ridge between two furrows thrown up by the plough.
Amelgado [ah-mel-gah'-do], *m.* (Prov.) A little hillock to mark the boundaries of a field. *Amelgado, da, pp.* of AMELGAR.
Amelgar [ah-mel-gar'], *va.* 1. To open furrows. 2. (Prov.) To throw up earth to mark boundaries.
Amelo [ah-may'-lo], *m.* (Bot.) Golden star-wort. Aster amellus.
Amelonado, da [ah-may-lo-nah'-do, dah], *a.* Shaped liked a melon.
Amén [ah-men'], *m.* Amen, so be it. *Voto de amén,* A partial vote, given without the least previous discussion or inquiry. *Sacristán de amén,* One who blindly adheres to the opinion of another. *Amén de,* (Coll.) Besides; except; over and above.
Amenaza [ah-may-nah'-thah], *f.* A threat, a menace.
Amenazador, ra [ah-may-nah-thah-dor', rah], *m.* & *f.* One who threatens.—*a.* Threatening.
Amenazante [ah-may-nah-thahn'-tay], *pa.* Minacious, threatening.
Amenazar [ah-may-nah-thar'], *va.* To threaten, to menace.
Amencia [ah-men'-the-ah], *f.* (Ant. and Amer.) Dementia; insanity.
Amenguar [ah-men-goo-ar'], *va.* 1. To diminish. 2. To defame.
Amenidad [ah-may-ne-dahd'], *f.* 1. Amenity, agreeableness. 2. (Met.) A pleasant strain of language.
Amenizar [ah-may-nee-thar'], *va.* 1. To render pleasant or agreeable. 2. (Met.) To adorn a speech with pleasing sentiments.
Ameno, na [ah-may'-no, nah], *a.* 1. Pleasant, delicious. 2. Delightful, elegant: applied to the language of a work.
Amentáceo, cea [ah-men-tah'-thay-o, ah], *a.* (Bot.) Amentaceous, resembling a thong.
Amento [ah-men'-to], *m.* (Bot.) Ament, amentum; catkin.
Ameos. *V.* AMÍ.
Amerar [ah-may-rar'], *va.* To mix wine or liquor with water.—*vr.* To soak or enter gradually, as water.
Amerengado, da [ah-may-ren-gah'-do, dah], *a.* 1. Like, or having, meringue. 2. (Coll.) Nice, prudish.
Americana [ah-may-re-cah'-nah], *f.* Sackcoat, man's suitcoat.
Americanismo [ah-may-re-cah-nees'-mo], *m.* 1. Americanism, feeling for Spanish-American culture. 2. Spanish-American expression.
Americanización [ah-may-re-cah-ne-thah-the-on'], *f.* Americanization.
Americanizar [ah-may-re-cah-ne-thar'], *va.* To Americanize, to make Spanish-American, to make North American.—*vr.* To be Americanized.
Americano, na [ah-may-re-cah'-no, nah], *a.* & *m.* & *f.* American.
Ametalado, da [ah-may-tah-lah'-do, dah], *a.* Having the colour of brass.
Ametista, *f.* **Ametisto,** *m.* [ah-may-tees'-tah, ah-me-tees'-to]. *V.* AMATISTA.
Ametralladora [ah-may-tral-lyah-do'-rah], *f.* Machine gun.
Ametrallar [ah-may-tral-lyar'], *va.* To machine-gun.
Amia [ah'-me-ah], *f.* Lamia, the white shark. Scomber amia.
Amianto, *m.* **Amianta,** *f.* [ah-me-ahn'-to, ah-me-ahn'-tah]. (Min.) Amianthus a filamentous fossil; asbestos.
Amiba [ah-mee'-bah], *f.* Amœba, a rhizopod; a type of the simplest animal life.
Amiento [ah-me-en'-to], *m.* A leather strap, with which a helmet is tied on.
Amiga [ah-mee'-gah], *f.* 1. (Prov.) A school for girls. 2. (Obs.) *V.* BARRAGANA. Mistress.
Amigable [ah-me-gah'-blay], *a.* 1. Friendly. 2. (Met.) Fit, suitable.
Amigablemente [ah-me-gah'-blay-men'tay], *adv.* Amicably.
Amigdala [ah-meeg'-dah-lah], *f.* A tonsil.
Amigdalitis [ah-meeg-dah-lee'-tis], *f.* (Med.) Tonsilitis.
Amigo, ga [ah-mee'-go, gah], *m.* & *f.* 1. A friend; comrade. 2. Lover. *Un amigo íntimo,* A familiar, an intimate. *Es amigo de ganar la vida,* He is fond of gain; he is eager to do any thing to procure a livelihood.
Amigo, ga [ah-mee'-go, gah], *a.* *V.* AMISTOSO and AMIGABLE.
Amigote [ah-me-go'-tay], *m. aug.* (Coll.) A great friend, an intimate.
Amiláceo [ah-me-lah'-thay-o], *a.* Amylaceous, starchy.
Amilanamiento [ah-me-lah-nah-me-en'-to], *m.* Spiritlessness.
Amilanar [ah-me-lah-nar'], *va.* To frighten, to terrify, to crush.—*vr.* To flag.
Amillaramiento [ah-meel-lyah-rah-me-en'-to], *m.* Assessment of a tax.
Amillarar [ah-meel-lyah-rar'], *va.* To assess a tax.
Amillonado, da [ah-meel-lyo-nah'-do, dah], *a.* 1. Liable to pay a tax called *millones,* which is levied on wine, vinegar, etc. 2. Very rich.—*m.* A millionaire.
Aminoácido [ah-mee-no-ah'-thee-do], *m.* Amino acid.
Aminorar [ah-me-no-rar'], *va.* To lessen, to enfeeble.
Amir [ah-meer'], *m.* Ameer, one of the Mohammedan nobility of Afghanistan and Scinde.
Amistad [ah-mis-tahd'], *f.* 1. Amity, friendship; commerce. 2. A connection founded upon a carnal intercourse. 3. Gallantry. 4. Civility, favour. 5. (Obs.) Inclination, desire. *Hacer las amistades,* To make friends.
Amistar [ah-mis-tar'], *va.* & *vr.* To reconcile.
Amistosamente [ah-mis-to-sah-men'-tay], *adv.* In a friendly manner, familiarly.
Amistoso, sa [ah-mis-toh'-so, sah], *a.* Friendly, amicable, cordial.
Amito [ah-mee'-to], *m.* Amice, a square piece of linen with a cross in the middle, which forms the undermost part of a priest's garment when he officiates at the mass.
Amnesia [am-nay'-se-ah], *f.* Amnesia, loss of memory.
Amnios [ahm'-ne-os], *f.* Amnion, a fœtal envelope.
Amnistia [am-nis-tee'-ah], *f.* An amnesty.
Amnistiar [am-nis-te-ar'], *va.* To grant a pardon, to amnesty.—*vr.* To receive amnesty.
Amo [ah'-mo], *m.* 1. Master of a house. 2. Proprietor. 3. Foster-father. 4. Overseer. 5. (Vulg.) Good-man. 6. Lord. *Amo de casa,* A householder. *V.* AMA. *Amo de buque,* A ship-owner.
Amoblar [ah-mo-blar'], *va.* *V.* MOBLAR = AMUEBLAR.
Amodita [ah-mo-dee'-tah], *f.* A sort of horned serpent. *V.* ALICANTE.

Amodorrado, da [ah-mo-dor-rah'-do, dah], *a.* Heavy with sleep.—*pp.* of AMODORRARSE.

Amodorrarse [ah-mo-dor-rar'-say], *vr.* To be drowsy, to grow heavy with sleep.

Amodorrido, da [ah-mo-dor-ree'-do, dah], *a.* *V.* AMODORRADO.

Amogotado, da [ah-mo-go-tah'-do, dah], *a.* Steep with a flat crown: applied to a mountain descried at sea.

Amohecerse [ah-mo-ay-therr'-say], *vr.* To grow mouldy or rusty. *V.* ENMOHECERSE.

Amohinar [ah-mo-e-nar'], *va.* To irritate.

Amojonador [ah-mo-ho-nah-dor'], *m.* One who sets landmarks.

Amojonamiento [ah-mo-ho-nah-me-en'-to], *m.* The act of setting landmarks.

Amojonar [ah-mo-ho-nar'], *va.* To set landmarks, to mark roads.

Amoladera [ah-mo-lah-day'-rah], *f.* Whetstone, grindstone.

Amolador [ah-mo-lah-dor'], *m.* 1. Grinder, whetter. 2. (Coll.) An unskilful coachman. 3. An unskilful artist.

Amoladura [an-mo-lah-doo'-rah], *f.* The act of whetting or grinding. *Amoladuras,* The small sand which falls from the whetstone at the time of whetting.

Amolar [ah-mo-lar'], *va.* To whet, grind, or sharpen an edged tool by attrition.

Amoldador, ra [ah-mol-dah-dor'.rah], *m.* & *f.* A moulder: one who moulds.

Amoldar [ah-mol-dar'], *va.* 1. To cast in a mould, to fashion, to figure. *Amoldar las agujas,* To polish needles. 2. (Met.) To adjust according to reason, to bring one to his duty. 3. (Obs.) To brand or mark cattle.

Amole [ah-mo'-lay], *m.* Soap-root. (Mex.) Chlorogalum.

Amollar [ah-mol-lyar'], *va.* 1. (Naut.) To ease off. 2. To play an inferior card to a winning one.

Amolletado, da [ah-mol-lyay-tah'-do, dah], *a.* Having the shape of a loaf of bread.

Amomo [ah-mo'-mo], *m.* (Bot.) Grain of paradise. Grana paradisi.

Amondongado, da [ah-mon-don-gah'-do, dah], *a.* (Coll.) Sallow, coarse, stout. *Mujer amondongada,* A coarse-featured stout woman.

Amonedar [ah-mo-nay-dar'], *va.* To coin.

Amonestación [ah-mo-nes-tah-the-on'], *f.* 1. Advice, admonition, warning. 2. Publication of marriage banns. *Correr las amonestaciones,* To publish the banns of marriage.

Amonestador, ra [ah-mo-nes-tah-dor', rah], *m.* & *f.* A monitor, an admonisher.

Amonestar [ah-mo-nes-tar'], *va.* 1. To advise, to admonish; to correct. 2. To publish banns of marriage, or of ordination.

Amoniacal [ah-mo-ne-ah-cahl'], *a.* Ammoniacal.

Amoníaco [ah-mo-nee'-ah-co], *m.* 1. Ammonia, NH_3. 2. Ammoniac, a gum-resin.

Amonio [ah-mo'-ne-o], *m.* (Chem.) Ammonium.

Amonita [ah-mo-nee'-tah], *f.* 1. Ammonite, a fossil mollusk. 2. *m.* Ammonite, tribe.

Amontarse [ah-mon-tar'-say], *vr.* To flee or take to the mountains.

Amontonador, ra [ah-mon-to-nah-dor', rah], *m.* & *f.* Heaper, accumulator.

Amontonamiento [ah-mon-to-nah-me-en'-to], *m.* The act of heaping, accumulating, hoarding, gathering; lodgment.

Amontonar [ah-mon-to-nar'], *va.* 1. To heap or throw things together without order or choice; to accumulate, to gather, to hoard, to lay up, to congest. 2. (Pict.) To group a crowd of figures in a painting.—*vr.* (Coll.) To fly into a passion; to grow angry or vexed, and not listen to reason.

Amor [ah-mor'], *m.* 1. Tenderness, affection, love. fancy. 2. The object of love. 3. A word of endearment. *Amor mío* or *mis amores,* My love. *Por amor de Dios,* For God's sake. *Amor de hortelano,* (Bot.) Goose-grass. Galium aparine. *Al amor de la lumbre,* Close to the fire. *Amor propio,* Self-love; conceitedness.—*m.* & *f. pl.* 1. Gallantry. 2. Amours, criminal love. *De mil amores, adv.* With all my heart.

Amoral [ah-mo-ral'], *a.* Amoral, without a sense of moral responsibility.

Amoratado, da [ah-mo-rah-tah'-do, dah], *a.* Livid.

Amorcillo [ah-mor-theel'-lyo], *m. dim.* Slight love, kindness.

Amordazar [ah-mor-dah-thar'], *va.* 1. To gag. (Naut.) To fasten with bitts. 2. (Met.) To deprive of the liberty of speaking or writing.

Amores, or **Amores mil** [ah-mo'-res], *m.* (Bot.) Red valerian. Valeriana rubra.

Amorfo, fa [ah-mor'-fo, fah], *a.* Amorphous, without definite shape.

Amorgado, da [ah-mor-gah'-do, dah], *a.* Stupefied from eating the husks of pressed olives: applied to fish.

Amoricones [ah-mo-re-co'-nes], *m. pl.* (Coll.) Looks, gestures, and actions, expressive of love and fondness.

Amorio [ah-mo-ree'-o], *m.* (Coll.) Friendship. *V.* ENAMORAMIENTO.

Amoriscado, da [ah-mo-ris-cah'-do, dah], *a.* Resembling the Moors.

Amormado, da [ah-mor-mah'-do, dah], *a.* Applied to horses having the glanders.

Amorosamente [ah-mo-ro-sah-men'-tay], *adv.* Lovingly.

Amoroso, sa [ah-mo-ro'-so, sah], *a.* 1. Affectionate, kind, loving. 2. Pleasing. 3. Gentle, mild, serene. *La tarde está amorosa,* It is a charming evening. 4. Tractable, easy.

Amorrar [ah-mor-rar'], *vn.* (Coll.) 1. To hold down the head; to muse. 2. To remain silent with downcast looks.

Amortajar [ah-mor-tah-har'], *va.* To shroud a corpse.

Amortecer [ah-mor-tay-therr'], *va.* *V.* AMORTIGUAR.—*vr.* To faint, to be in a swoon.

Amortecimiento [ah-mor-tay-the-me-en'-to], *m.* Swoon; fainting.

(*Yo me amortezco,* from *Amortecerse.* *V.* ABORRECER.)

Amortiguación, *f.* **Amortiguamiento,** *m.* [ah-mor-te-goo-ah-the-on', ah-mor-te-goo-ah-me-en'-to]. 1. Deadening, absorption. 2. Softening, toning down.

Amortiguador, ra [ah-mor-te-goo-ah-dor', rah], *a.* Cushioning, absorbing. —*m.* Bumper. *Amortiguador de golpes,* Shock absorber. *Amortiguador de luz,* Dimmer. *Amortiguador de sonido,* Muffler, silencer.

Amortiguar [ah-mor-te-goo-ar'], *va.* 1. To cushion, to deaden, to absorb. 2. To tone down, to lessen. 3. To soften.

Amortizable [ah-mor-te-thah'-blay], *a.* Amortizable.

Amortización [ah-mor-te-thah-the-on'], *f.* Amortization, paying off.

Amortizar [ah-mor-te-thar'], *va.* 1. To amortize, to pay back. 2. To write off, to depreciate. 3. To recuperate, to regain.—*vn.* To depreciate, to decrease in value.

Amoscar [ah-mos-car'], *va.* To flap flies.—*vr.* 1. To shake off the flies. 2. To become irritated.

Amosquilado, da [ah-mos-ke-lah'-do, dah], *a.* Applied to cattle when tormented with flies.

Amostachado [ah-mos-tah-chah'-do], *a.* Wearing mustaches.

Amostazar [ah-mos-tah-thar'], *va.* (Coll.) To exasperate, to provoke.—*vr.* To fly into a violent passion; to be vexed.

Amotinadamente [ah-mo-te-nah-dah-men'-tay], *adv.* Mutinously.

Amotinado, da [ah-mo-te-nah'-do, dah], *a.* Mutinous, rebellious.—*pp.* of AMOTINAR.

Amotinador, ra [ah-mo-te-nah-dor', rah], *m.* & *f.* Mutineer.

Amotinamiento [ah-mo-te-nah-me-en'-to], *m.* The act of stirring up a sedition; mutiny.

Amotinar [ah-mo-te-nar'], *va.* 1. To excite rebellion. 2. (Met.) To disorder the mind.—*vr.* To rise against authority.

Amover [ah-mo-verr'], *va.* To remove, to dismiss from employment.

Amovibilidad [ah-mo-ve-be-le-dahd'], *f.* The possibility of being removed, or revoked.

Amovible [ah-mo-vee'-blay], *a.* Removable: a term applied to ecclesiastical livings.

Ampac [am-pahk'], *m.* (Bot.) Champak, a tree of the East Indies, possessing an odour like styrax.

Ampara [am-pah'-rah], *f.* 1. (Law) Seizure of chattels or movable property. 2. (Obs.) *V.* AMPARO.

Amparada [am-pah-rah'-dah]. *V.* MINA.

Amparador, ra [am-pah-rah-dor', rah], *m.* & *f.* Protector; shelter.

Amparar [am-pah-rar'], *va.* 1. To shelter, to protect, to help, to support, to assist. 2. (Law. Prov.) To make a seizure of chattels or movable property; to sequestrate. *Amparar en la posesión,* (Law) To maintain in possession.—*vr.* 1. To claim or enjoy protection. 2. To preserve; to recover. 3. To avail one's self of.

Amparo [am-pah'-ro], *m.* 1. Favour, aid, protection, sanction, support, countenance. 2. Guardship, refuge, asylum. 3. (Obs.) Breastwork, parapet.

Ampelita [am-pay-lee'-tah], *f.* Cannel-coal.

Ampelografía [am-pay-lo-grah-fee'-ah], *f.* (Agr.) Ampelography, a description of the vine.

Amperaje [am-pay-rah'-hay], *m.* (Elec.) Amperage.

Amperímetro [am-pay-ree'-may-tro], *m.* (Elec.) Ammeter.

Amplectivo, va [am-plec-tee'-vo, vah], *a.* Amplective, embracing other organs (of plants).

Ampliación [am-ple-ah-the-on'], *f.* Enlargement; the act of enlarging.

Ampliador, ra [am-ple-ah-dor', rah], *m.* & *f.* Amplifier.

Ampliamente [am-ple-ah-men'-tay], *adv.* Largely, copiously, fully.

Ampliar [am-ple-ar'], *va.* To amplify, to enlarge.

Ampliativo, va [am-ple-ah-tee'-vo, vah], *a.* Amplifying, having the power of enlarging.

Amplificación [am-ple-fe-cah-the-on'], *f.* 1. Enlargement. 2. (Rhet.) Amplification.

Amplificador [am-ple-fe-cah-dor'], *m.* Amplifier, loudspeaker.

Amplificar [am-ple-fe-car'], *va.* 1. To amplify, to enlarge, to extend. 2. To use the figure of speech termed *amplification.*

Amplio, lia [ahm'-ple-o, ah], *a.* Ample, extensive; large; handsome; absolute.

Amplitud [am-ple-tood'], *f.* 1. Extent, greatness, largeness. 2. (Naut.) *Amplitud magnética*, Magnetic amplitude. 3. (Astr.) Amplitude, an arch of the horizon intercepted between the true east and west point thereof, and the centre of the sun or star at their rising or setting. 4. Absoluteness.

Amplo, la [ahm'-plo, plah]. (Obs.) *V.* AMPLIO.

Ampo *de la nieve*, Whiteness. *Blanco como el ampo de la nieve*, White as the driven snow. *V.* LAMPO.

Ampolla [am-pol'-lyah], *f.* 1. A blister on the skin. 2. Avial, a cruet. 3. A small bubble of water.

Ampollar [am-pol-lyar'], *va.* 1. To blister. 2. To make hollow, to excavate. —*vr.* To rise in bubbles by the force of the wind.

Ampollar [am-pol-lyar'], *a.* Resembling a blister.

Ampolleta [am-pol-lyay'-tah], *f. dim.* 1. A small vial: a cruet. 2. An hour-glass. 3. (Naut.) Watch-glass.

Amprar [am-prar'], *vn.* (Prov.) To borrow.

Ampuloso, sa [am-poo-lo'-so, sah], *a.* Pompous, bombastic.

Amputación [am-poo-tah-the-on'], *f.* Amputation.

Amputar [am-poo-tar'], *va.* To amputate, or to cut off a limb.

Amuchachado, da [ah-moo-chah-chah'-do, dah], *a.* Boyish, childish.

Amuchiguar [ah-moo-chee-goo-ar'], *vn.* (Obs.) To augment, to multiply.

Amueblar [ah-moo-ay-blar'], *va.* To furnish.

(*Yo amuelo, amuele*, etc., from *Amolar. V.* ACORDAR.)

Amugamiento [ah-moo-gah-me-en'-to], *m. V.* AMOJONAMIENTO.

Amugronador, ra [ah-moo-gro-nah-dor', rah], *m. & f.* One who trains vine-shoots.

Amugronar [ah-moo-gro-nar'], *va.* To lay the shoot of a vine under the earth in order that it may take root.

Amujerado, da [ah-moo-hay-rah'-do, dah], *a.* Effeminate.

Amujeramiento [ah-moo-hay-rah-me-en'-to], *m. V.* AFEMINACIÓN.

Amularse [ah-moo-lar'-say], *vr.* To become sterile: speaking of mares.

Amulatado, da [ah-moo-lah-tah'-do, dah], *a.* Of a tawny complexion, resembling a mulatto.

Amuleto [ah-moo-lay'-to], *m.* An amulet.

Amunicionar [ah-moo-ne-the-o-nar'], *va.* To supply with ammunition.

Amuñecado, da [ah-moo-nyay-cah'-do, dah], *a.* Puppet-like.

Amura [ah-moo'-rah], *f.* 1. (Naut.) Tack of a sail. *Amura mayor*, Main-tack. *Amura del trinquete*, The fore-tack. 2. (Naut.) A word of command. *Amura a babor*, Aboard larboard-tacks. *Amura a estribor*, Aboard starboard-tacks. *Amura trinquete*, Aboard fore-tacks. *Cambiar la amura*, To stand on the other tack.

Amuradas [ah-moo-rah'-das], *f. pl.* (Naut.) The range of planks between the water-ways and the lower edge of the gun-ports of a ship of war.

Amurallar [ah-moo-ral-lyar'], *va.* To wall. *V.* MURAR.

Amurar [ah-moo-rar'], *va.* (Naut.) To haul the tack aboard.

Amurcar [ah-moor-car'], *va.* To gore with the horns.

Amurco [ah-moor'-co], *m.* Blow or stroke with the horns.

Amurillar [ah-moo-reel-lyar'], *va.* (Agr.) To earth up.

Amusco [ah-moos'-co], *a.* Brown.

Amusgar [ah-moos-gar'], *va.* 1. To throw back the ears as horses and mules, as if to bite, or kick. *Amusgar las orejas*, (Met. Obs.) To listen. 2. To contract the eyes to see better.

Ana [ah'-nah], *f.* 1. An ell. 2. An animal of the fox kind in the Indies. 3. An abbreviation used by medical men to signify equal parts.

Anabaina [ah-nah-bah'-e-nah], *f.* (Bot.) Euphorbiaceous plant of Brazil.

Anabatista, Anabaptista [ah-nah-bah-tees'-tah, ah-nah-bap-tees'-tah], *m.* Anabaptist.

Anabás [ah-nah-bahs'], *m.* The climbing-fish. Anabas.

Anabeno, na [ah-nah-bay'-no, nah], *a.* (Zool.) Tree-climbing.

Anacalifa [ah-nah-cah-lee'-fah], *m.* A poisonous animal of Madagascar.

Anacalo, la [ah-nah-cah'-lo, lah], *m. & f.* (Obs.) A baker's servant.

Anacarado, da [ah-nah-cah-rah'-do, dah], *a.* Of a pearly white colour.

Anacardel [ah-nah-car-del'], *m.* A kind of Madagascar serpent.

Anacardina [ah-nah-car-dee'-nah], *f.* Confection made of anacardium or cashew-nut.

Anacardio [ah-nah-car'-de-o], *m.* (Bot.) Cashew-tree. Anacardium occidentale.

Anacatártico, ca [ah-nah-cah-tar'-te-co, cah], *a. & m.* (Med.) Emetic.

Anaco [ah-nah'-co], *m.* Dress of Indian women in Peru and Bolivia; in Ecuador their hair-dressing.

Anaconda [ah-nah-con'-dah], *f.* (Zool.) Anaconda.

Anacoreta [ah-nah-co-ray'-tah], *m.* An anchorite, a hermit.

Anacorético, ca [ah-nah-co-ray'-te-co, cah], *a.* Anchoretical, belonging to a recluse.

Anacosta [ah-nah-cos'-tah], *f.* A sort of woollen stuff.

Anacreóntico, ca [ah-nah-cray-on'-te-co, cah], *a.* Anacreontic.

Anacronismo [ah-nah-cro-nees'-mo], *m.* Anachronism, an error in computing time.

Ánade [ah'-nah-day], *m. & f.* Duck. Anas boschas.

Anadear [ah-nah-day-ar'], *vn.* To waddle.

Anadeja [ah-nah-day'-hah], *f. dim.* A duckling.

Anadino, na [ah-nah-dee'-no, nah], *m. & f.* A young duck.

Anadón [ah-nah-done'], *m.* Mallard.

Anadoncillo [ah-nah-don-theel'-lyo], *m. dim.* A grown duckling.

Anafalla, or **Anafaya** [ah-nah-fahl'-lyah], *f.* A kind of thick corded silk.

Anafe, or **Anafre** [ah-nah'-fay], *m.* A portable furnace or stove.

Anáfora [ah-nah'-fo-rah], *f.* Anaphora, a figure in rhetoric when several periods of a speech are begun with the same word.

Anafrodisia [ah-nah-fro-dee'-se-ah], *f.* Anaphrodisia, loss of sexual appetite.

Anáglifo [ah-nah'-glee-fo], *m.* Vase, vessel, or other work adorned with sculpture in *basso relievo.*

Anagoge, *m.* **Anagogía**, *f.* [ah-nah-go'-hay, ah-nah-go-hee'-ah]. Anagogics, the mystic sense of the Holy Scriptures.

Anagógicamente [ah-nah-go'-he-cah-men-tay], *adv.* In an anagogical manner.

Anagógico, ca [ah-nah-go'-he-co, cah], *a.* Anagogical.

Anagrama [ah-nah-grah'-mah], *f.* An anagram, a transposition of the letters of a name.

Anal, *a.* Anal, relating to the anus.

Analéptico, ca [ah-nah-lep'-te-co, cah], *a.* (Med.) Analeptic, restorative, comforting.

Analepsia [ah-nah-lep'-se-ah], *f.* (Med.) Analepsis.

Anales [ah-nah'-les], *m. pl.* Annals or historical accounts digested in order.

Analfabeta [ah-nahl-fah-bay'-tah], *m. & f.* Illiterate person.—*a.* Illiterate, ignorant.

Analfabetismo [ah-nahl-fah-bay-tees'-mo], *m.* Illiteracy.

Analgésico, ca [ah-nal-hay'-se-co, cah], *m. & a.* Analgesic.

Análisis [ah-nah'-le-sis], *m. & f.* 1. Analysis. 2. (Gram.) Parsing. 3. (Math.) Algebraic solution. *Análisis de mercados*, Marketing research, market research.

Analista [ah-nah-lees'-tah], *m.* Annalist.

Analíticamente [ah-nah-lee'-te-cah-men-tay], *adv.* Analytically.

Analítico, ca [ah-nah-lee'-te-co, cah], *a.* Analytical, method of resolving any thing into first principles.

Analizable [ah-nah-le-thah'-blay], *a.* Capable of analysis, analyzable.

Analizador [ah-nah-le-thah-dor'], *m.* Analyzer.

Analizar [ah-nah-le-thar'], *va.* To analyze.

Análogamente [ah-nah'-lo-gah-men-tay]. *V.* ANALÓGICAMENTE.

Analogía [ah-nah-lo-hee'-ah], *f.* 1. Analogy, resemblance or relation which things bear to each other. 2. A part of grammar.

Analógicamente [ah-nah-lo'-he-cah-men-tay], *adv.* Analogically.

Analógico, ca, Análogo, ga [ah-nah-lo'-he-co, cah, ah-nah'-lo-go, gah], *a.* Analogous.

Analogismo [ah-nah-lo-hees'-mo], *m.* Analogism, an argument from the cause to the effect.

Analogizar [ah-nah-lo-he-thar'], *va.* (Littl. us.) To explain by way of analogy.

Análogo, ga [ah-nah'-lo-go, gah], *a.* Analogous, similar.

Anama [ah-nah'-mah], *m.* A longicorn beetle of Java.

Anamnesia [ah-nam-nay'-se-ah], *f.* Mnemonics, the art of remembering or acquiring memory.

Anamorfosis [ah-nah-mor-fo'-sis], *f.* A deformed image drawn upon a curved or plane surface in such a way that when viewed from some particular point it appears perfectly regular and well-proportioned.

Anana [ah-nah'-nah], *f.* or **Ananas** (Bot.) Ananas, pineapple. This is the European name; in America it is called Piña. Bromelia ananas.

Anapelo [ah-nah-pay'-lo], *m.* (Bot.) Wolf's bane. Aconitum lychoctonum.

Anapesto [ah-nah-pes'-to], *m.* Anapæst, a Latin verse, ⏑ ⏑ —.

Anaplastia [ah-nah-plas'-te-ah], *f.* Anaplasty, plastic surgery.

Anaquel [ah-nah-kel'], *m.* Shelf or board on which any thing may be placed.

Anaquelería [ah-nah-kay-lay-ree'-ah], *f.* Shelving, case of shelves.

Anaranjado, da [ah-nah-ran-hah'-do, dah], *a.* Orange-coloured.

Anarquía [ah-nar-kee'-ah], *f.* Anarchy.

Anárquico, ca [ah-nar'-ke-co, cah], *a.* Anarchical, confused, without rule.

Anarquista [ah-nar-kees'-tah], *m.* Anarchist: enemy of organized government.

Anasarca [ah-nah-sar'-cah], *f.* (Med.) Anasarca, general dropsy of the connective tissue.
Anascote [ah-nas-co'-tay], *m.* A kind of woollen stuff like serge.
Anastasia [ah-nas-tah'-se-ah], *f.* *V.* ARTEMISA.
Anastomosis [ah-nas-to-mo'-sis], *f.* (Anat.) Anastomosis, the inosculation of blood-vessels. (Bot.) Junction of branches which should be separate.
Anástrofe [ah-nahs'-tro-fay], *m.* (Rhet.) Anastrophe, an inversion of words.
Anata [ah-nah'-tah], *f.* Annats, the first fruits or emoluments which a benefice or employ produces. *Media anata*, The annats of the half year.
Anatema [ah-nah-tay'-mah], *m.* & *f.* 1. Anathema, excommunication. 2. (Obs.) A person anathematized or excommunicated.
Anatematismo [ah-nah-tay-mah-tees'-mo], *m.* *V.* EXCOMUNIÓN.
Anatematizar [ah-nah-tay-mah-te-thar'], *va.* 1. To anathematize, to excommunicate. 2. To curse.
Anatista [ah-nah-tees'-tah], *m.* Officer for the half-year's annats.
Anatomía [ah-nah-to-mee'-ah], *f.* 1. Anatomy. 2. (Pict.) Skeleton by which painters and sculptors study the structure of the human frame.
Anatómicamente [ah-nah-to'-me-cah-men-tay], *adv.* Anatomically.
Anatómico, ca [ah-nah-to'-me-co, cah], *a.* Anatomical.
Anatomista [ah-nah-to-mees'-tah], *m.* Anatomist.
Anatomizar [ah-nah-to-me-thar'], *va.* 1. To anatomize or dissect. 2. (Pict.) To draw, with the utmost exactness, the bones and muscles in statues and figures.
Anca [ahn'-cah], *f.* The croup of a horse, haunch. *A ancas* or *a las ancas*, Behind. *A ancas* or *a las ancas de fulano*, With the assistance of Mr. Such-a-one.
Ancado [an-cah'-do], *m.* (Vet.) A distemper, consisting in a painful contraction of the muscles.
Ancianar [an-the-ah-nar'], *vn.* (Poet.) *V.* ENVEJECER.
Ancianidad [an-the-ah-ne-dahd'], *f.* 1. Old age. 2. Antiquity.
Anciano, na [an-the-ah'-no, nah], *a.* Old, stricken in years.
Ancla [ahn'-clah], *f.* Anchor. *Zafar el ancla para dar fondo*, To clear the anchor for coming to. *El ancla viene al bajel*, The anchor comes home. *El ancla ha soltado el fondo*, The anchor is a-trip. *Pescar un ancla*, To drag for an anchor. *Alotar las anclas*, To stow the anchors. *Arganeo de ancla*, An anchoring. *Caña del ancla*, The shank of the anchor. *Cepo del ancla*, The anchor-stock. *Cruz del ancla*, The crown of the anchor. *Orejas del ancla*, The flukes of the anchor. *Uñas del ancla*, The anchor arms. *Pico del ancla*, The bill of the anchor. *Al ancla* or *anclado*, At anchor. *Ancla de esperanza*, Sheet-anchor. *Ancla del ayuste* or *de uso*, The best bower-anchor. *Ancla sencilla* or *de leva*, The small bower-anchor, *Ancla del creciente*, The flood-anchor. *Ancla del menguante*, The ebb-anchor. *Ancla de la mar hacia fuera*, Sea-anchor. *Ancla de la tierra* or *playa*, Shore-anchor. *Anclas de servidumbre*, Bower-anchors.
Ancladero [an-clah-day'-ro], *m.* (Naut.) Anchorage, anchoring-place.
Anclaje [an-clah'-hay], *m.* 1. The act of casting anchor. 2. Anchoring-ground. *Derecho de anclaje*, Anchorage.
Anclar [an-clar'], *vn.* To anchor.
Anclote [an-clo'-tay], *m.* Stream-anchor, grapnel, kedge.
Anclotillo [an-clo-teel'-lyo], *m.* Kedge anchor.
Ancón, *m.* **Anconada**, *f.* [an-cone', an-co-nah'-dah]. An open road, a bay.
Áncora [ahn'-co-rah]. V. ANCLA. *Echar áncoras*, To cast anchor. *Llevar áncoras*, To weigh anchor. *Estar en áncoras* or *sobre las áncoras*, To lie at anchor.
Ancoraje [an-co-rah'-hay], *m.* *V.* ANCLAJE.
Ancorar [an-co-rar']. *V.* ANCLAR.
Ancorca [an-cor'-cah], *f.* A yellow ochre.
Ancorel [an-co-rel'], *m.* A large stone used by fishermen to secure their nets.
Ancorería [an-co-ray-ree'-ah], *f.* Anchor-forge.
Ancorero [an-co-ray'-ro], *m.* Anchor-smith.
Ancusa [an-coo'-sah], *f.* (Bot.) *V.* ANCHUSA. *Ancusa oficinal*, Common alkanet. Anchusa officinalis. *Lengua de buey.*
Anchaguantes [an-chah-goo-ahn'-tes], *m.* A glove-stretcher.
Anchamente [an-chah-men'-tay], *adv.* Widely, largely.
Ancharia [an-chah'-re-ah], *f.* (Obs.) Among merchants and traders, the width of cloth.
Ancheta [an-chay'-tah], *f.* Venture. Goods which a person, not engaged in trade, exports.
Anchicorto, ta [an-che-cor'-to, tah], *a.* That which is wider than it is long.
Ancho, cha [ahn'-cho, chah], *a.* Broad, large. *Ponerse muy ancho*, (Met.) To look big; to be elated with pride. *Vida ancha*, A loose life.
Ancho, Anchor [ahn'-cho, an-chor'], *m.* *V.* ANCHURA.
Anchoa, Anchova [an-cho'-ah, an-cho'-vah], *f.* Anchovy. Clupea encrasicolas.
Anchoas [an-cho'-ahs], *f. pl.* (Mex.) Pin curls (in hair curling).
Anchuelo, la [an-choo-ay'-lo, lah], *a. dim.* Somewhat wide.
Anchura [an-choo'-rah], *f.* 1. Width, largeness, extensiveness; latitude. 2. Laxity. *A mis anchuras*, or *a sus anchuras*, At large, at full liberty. *Vivo a mis anchuras*, I live just as I choose.
Anchuroso, sa [an-choo-ro'-so, sah], *a.* Large, spacious, extensive, broad.
Anchusa [an-choo'-sah], *f.* (Bot.) Alkanet. Anchusa.
Andada [an-dah'-dah], *f.* 1. Track, trail, pathway. 2. A thin, hard-baked cake. *Andadas*, The traces of game on the ground. *Volver a las andadas*, To relapse back into some vice or bad habit.
Andaderas [an-dah-day'-ras], *f. pl.* Go-carts, in which children learn to walk.
Andadero, ra [an-dah-day'-ro, rah], *a.* Of easy access: applied to the ground.
Andado [an-dah'-do], *m.* Step-child. *V.* ALNADO.
Andado, da [an-dah'-do, dah], *a.* 1. Beaten: applied to a path. 2. Worse for use, threadbare. 3. Customary.—*pp.* of ANDAR.
Andador, ra [an-dah-dor', rah], *m.* & *f.* 1. A good walker. 2. Messenger of a court. 3. (Naut.) A fine sailer. 4. Leading-string. 5. Alley or small walk in a garden.
Andadura [an-dah-doo'-rah], *f.* 1. Gait; pacing. 2. Amble.
Andalia [an-dah'-le-ah], *f.* (Obs.) Sandal. *V.* SANDALIA.
Andaluz, za [an-da-looth', thah], *a.* Andalusian.
Andaluzada [an-dah-loo-thah'-dah], *f.* 1. Bullying, boasting, rhodomontade. 2. Exaggeration.
Andamiada [an-dah-me-ah'-dah], *f.* Scaffolding.
Andamiaje [an-dah-me-ah'-hay], *m.* Scaffolding.
Andamio [an-dah'-me-o], *m.* 1. Scaffold. 2. (Obs.) Platform of a rampart. 3. (Naut.) Gang-board.
Andana [an-dah'-nah], *f.* 1. Row, line. 2. (Naut.) *Andana de los cañones de un costado*, A tier of guns. 3. (Naut.) *Andana de rizos*, The reefs in the sails of ships. 4. *Andana de cuartos*, A suite of apartments. 5. A tier. *Llamarse andana*, Not to fulfil a promise
Andanada [an-dah-nah'-dah], *f.* 1. Barrage. 2. Grandstand. 3. Tirade, severe reprimand.
Andaniño [an-dah-nee'-nyo], *m.* A kind of go-cart in which children learn to walk. *V.* POLLERA.
Andante [an-dahn'-tay], *m.* (Mus.) Andante.
Andantesco, ca [an-dan-tes'-co, cah], *a.* Belonging to knighthood, or knight-errants.
Andantino [an-dan-tee'-no], *m.* (Mus.) Andantino.
Andanza [an-dahn'-thah], *f.* (Obs.) Occurrence, event. *Buena* or *mala andanza*, Good or bad fortune.
Andar [an-dar'], *va.* 1. To go, to walk, to come, or to move along. 2. To act, to behave, to transact. 3. To elapse, 4. To act: applied to machines. 5. To be. *Andar en cuerpo*, To go abroad without a cloak or surtout. *Andar por decir* or *por hacer una cosa*, To be determined to say or do a thing. *Andar a caza de gangas*, To waste one's time in fruitless pursuits. *Andar en carnes* or *en cueros*, To go stark naked. *Andar de Ceca en Meca*, To be roving and wandering about. *Todo se andará*, Every thing will be looked into. *Es preciso andar con el tiempo*, It is necessary to conform to the times. *Andar en dares y tomares* or *en dimes y diretes*, To dispute and quarrel. *Andar a sombra de tejado*, To hide, to skulk. *Andar a trompis*, To come to fisticuffs. *Andar en buena vela*, (Naut.) To keep the sails full. *Andar todo*, (Naut.) To put up the helm. *A mejor andar*, At best, at most. *A peor andar*, At worst. *A más andar*, In full speed. *Andar el mundo al revés*, To reverse the order of nature, to do any thing contrary to the manner it ought to be. *No andar en contemplaciones*, Not to spare a person; to have recourse to hard measures. *El poco andar del barco*, (Naut.) The slow way of the vessel. *Andando el tiempo*, In the lapse of time. *Anden y ténganse*, Fast and loose. *Andar de nones*, To be idle. *Andar con mosca*, To fly into a passion. *Mal me andarán las manos*, If nothing prevents I will do it. *Andar a derechas*, To act honestly. *Andársele a uno la cabeza*, To have vertigo, to became dizzy. *Andarse en flores*, To decline entering into a debate.
¡Andar! [an-dar'], *int.* Well, never mind. *¡Anda!* Stand out of the way. *¡Anda, hijo!* Come along, child.
Andaraje [an-dah-rah'-hay], *m.* The wheel of a well.
Andaribel [an-dah-re-bel'], *m.* (Naut.) A light rope improvised to lower or lift some object; a gant-line.
Andariego, ga [an-dah-re-ay'-go gah], *a.* Restless, of a roving disposition.
Andarín [an-dah-reen'], *m.* (Coll.) A fast walker. *Andarines*, An Italian paste used for soups.

Andarío [an-dah-ree'-o], *m.* (Orn.) The white wagtail. Motacilla alba.

Andas [ahn'-das], *f. pl.* 1. A frame on which a person or most commonly an image is carried; a stretcher. 2. A bier with shafts, to be carried on men's shoulders.

Andén [an-den'], *m.* 1. A shelf. *V.* ANAQUEL. 2. A path for the horse round the draw-well or in a mill. 3. The sidewalk by a road or on a dock. 4. The platform of a railway station.

Andero [an-day'-ro], *m.* One who carries the shafts of a bier on his shoulders.

Andilú [an-de-loo'], *m.* A burnishing stick used by shoemakers.

Andito [ahn'-de-to], *m.* A gallery which surrounds the whole or a part of a building.

Andola [an-do'-lah], *f.* An unmeaning jocular expletive.

Andolina, Andorina, Andarina [an-do-lee'-nah, an-do-ree'-nah, an-dah-ree'-nah], *f.* *V.* GOLONDRINA.

Andorga [an-dor'-gah], *f.* (Coll.) Belly. *Llenar la andorga,* To eat much.

Andorina [an-do-ree'-nah], *f.* (Naut.) A truss.

Andorra [an-dor'-rah], *f.* (Obs.) *V.* ANDORRERA.

Andorrear [an-dor-ray-ar'], *vn.* To gad about.

Andorrera [an-dor-ray'-rah], *f.* Street-walker.

Andorrero [an-dor-ray'-ro], *m.* A person of a roving disposition; tramp.

Andosco, ca [an-dos'-co, cah], *a.* Two years old: applied to sheep.

Andrajo [an-drah'-ho], *m.* 1. Rag, tatter. 2. (Met.) A despicable person. *Hacer andrajos,* To tear to rags.

Andrajosamente [an-drah-ho-sah-men'-tay], *adv.* Raggedly.

Andrajoso, sa [an-drah-ho'-so, sah], *a.* Ragged, dressed in tatters.

Andriana [an-dree-ah'-nah], *f.* A kind of gown formerly worn by women.

Andrina [an-dree'-nah], *f.* A sloe. *V.* ENDRINA.

Andrino [an-dree'-no], *m.* (Bot.) Sloe-tree, blackthorn. Prunus spinosa. *L.*

Andrógeno [an-dro'-hay-no], *m.* Androgen.

Andrógino [an-dro'-he-no], *m.* Hermaphrodite, androgynus, androgyne.

Andrómina [an-dro'-me-nah], *f.* (Coll.) Trick, fraud, artifice.

Androsemo [an-dro-say'-mo], *m.* (Bot.) Parkleaves. Hypericum androsemum. *V.* TODABUENA.

Androtomía [an-dro-to-mee'-ah], *f.* Dissection of human bodies.

Andularios [an-doo-lah'-re-os], *m. pl.* (Coll.) A long and wide gown.

Andullo [an-dool'-lyo], *m.* A long, rolled leaf of tobacco (Cuban).

Andurriales [an-door-re-ah'-les], *m. pl.* By-roads, retired places.

(*Yo anduve, yo anduviera.* etc. *V.* ANDAR.)

Anea [ah-nay'-ah], *f.* (Bot.) Cattail. Typha. *Anea hojiancha,* Great cattail. Typha latifolia. *V.* ESPADAÑA.

Aneaje [ah-nay-ah'-hay], *m.* Alnage, ell measure.

Anear [ah-nay-ar'], *va.* 1. To measure by ells. 2. (Prov. Sant.) To rock in a cradle.

Aneblar [ah-nay-blar'], *va.* To cloud, to darken, to obscure.

Anécdota [ah-nec'-do-tah], *f.* Anecdote.

Anegación [ah-nay-gah-the-on'], *f.* Overflowing, inundation.

Anegadizo, za [ah-nay-gah-dee'-tho, thah], *a.* Liable to be overflowed.

Anegado, da [ah-nay-gah'-do, dah], *a.* Overflowed. *Navío anegado,* (Naut.) A water-logged ship.—*pp.* of ANEGAR.

Anegamiento [ah-nay-gah-me-en'-to], *m.* (Obs.) *V.* ANEGACIÓN.

Anegar [ah-nay-gar'], *va.* To inundate, to submerge.—*vr.* To be inundated.

Anegociado, da [ah-nay-go-the-ah'-do, dah], *a.* (Obs.) Overwhelmed with business.

Anejir [ah-nay-heer'], *m.* A proverb or popular phrase, in verse, which may be sung.

Anejo, ja [ah-nay'-ho, hah], *a.* Annexed, joined. *V.* ANEXO, XA.

Anejo [ah-nay'-ho], *m.* A benefice or church depending on another as its principal or head.

Anélido [ah-nay'-le-do], *m.* (Zool.) Annelid, a many-jointed worm.

Anemia [ah-nay'-me-ah], *f.* (Med.) Anæmia, diminution of red corpuscles in the blood.

Anémico, ca [ah-nay'-me-co, cah], *a.* Anæmic, affected with anæmia.

Anemografía [ah-nay-mo-grah-fee'-ah], *f.* Anemography, the description of the winds.

Anemometría [ah-nay-mo-may-tree'-ah], *f.* Anemometry, measuring the force of the winds.

Anemómetro [ah-nay-mo'-may-tro], *m.* Anemometre, an instrument to measure the force of the wind.

Anémona, or **Anémone** [ah-nay'-mo-nay], *f.* (Bot.) Anemone or wind-flower. Anemone.

Anemoscopio [ah-nay-mos-co'-pe-o], *m.* Anemoscope, a machine to show the changes of the wind.

Anepígrafo, fa [ah-nay-pee'-grah-fo, fah], *a.* Without title or inscription. *V.* MEDALLA.

Anequín (A), or **De Anequín** [ah-nay-keen'], *adv.* So much a head: applied to the shearing of sheep.

Aneroide [ah-nay-ro'-e-day], *a.* & *m.* Aneroid, without fluid; barometer in clock-form.

Anestesia [ah-nes-tay'-se-ah], *f.* Anæsthesia.

Anestesiar [ah-nes-tay-se-ar'], *va.* To anæsthetize.

Anestésico, ca [ah-nes-tay'-se-co, cah], *a.* Anesthetic, producing insensibility.—*m.* Anesthetic.

Aneurisma [ah-nay-oo-rees'-mah], *m.* & *f.* (Med.) Aneurism, a disease of the arteries and of the heart.

Anexar [ah-necs-sar'], *va.* To annex, to join, to unite.

Anexidades [ah-necs-se-dah'-des], *f. pl.* Annexes, belongings.

Anexión [ah-necs-se-on'], *f.* Annexion, union; annexation.

Anexionista [ah-necs-se-o-nees'-tah], *m.* Annexationist.

Anexo, xa [ah-necs'-so, sah], *a.* *V.* ANEJO, JA.

Anfibio, bia [an-fee'-be-o, ah], *a.* Amphibious.

Anfibología [an-fe-bo-lo-hee'-ah], *f.* Amphibology, words or sentences of a double or doubtful meaning.

Anfibológicamente [an-fe-bo-lo'-he-cah-men-tay], *adv.* Amphibologically.

Anfibológico, ca [an-fe-bo-lo'-he-co, cah], *a.* Amphibological, doubtful.

Anfíbraco [an-fee'-brah-co], *m.* Amphibrachys, a foot in Latin verse, ⏑ – ⏑.

Anfímacro [an-fee'-mah-cro], *m.* Amphimacer, a foot in Latin verse, – ⏑ –.

Anfión [an-fe-on'], *m.* A name given to opium in the East Indies.

Anfisbena, Anfisibena [an-fis-bay'-nah, an-fe-se-bay'-nah], *f.* Amphisbæna, an amphibious serpent of America.

Anfiscios [an-fees'-the-os], *m. pl.* Amphiscii, people of the torrid zone, whose shadows at different times fall north and south.

Anfiteatro [an-fe-tay-ah'-tro], *m.* Amphitheatre.

Anfitrión [an-fe-tre-on'], *m.* (Met.) Host, he who does the honours at the table before invited company.

Anfitrite [an-fe-tree'-tay], *f.* Amphitrite. (Poet. and Zool.)

Ánfora [ahn'-fo-rah], *f.* 1. Amphora, ancient vase. 2. (*pl.*) Jars or cruets of silver to preserve consecrated oils. 3. Ancient name of the sign Aquarius. 4. The lower valve of certain fruits which opens on ripening. 5. Ancient Greek and Roman measure for liquids equivalent to about eight gallons.

Anfractuosidad [an-frac-too-o-se-dahd'], *f.* Crookedness.—*f. pl.* (Ant.) Anfractuosities, convolutions of the brain or cerebrum.

Anfractuoso, sa [an-frac-too-oh'-so, sah], *a.* Anfractuous, sinuous, unequal.

Angaria [an-gah'-re-ah], *f.* 1. Ancient servitude. 2. Forced delay in the sailing of a ship, for employ in public service.

Angarillas [an-gah-reel'-lyas], *f. pl.* 1. Hand-barrow. 2. Panniers. 3. Cruet-stands. *V.* AGUADERAS.

Angarillón [an-gah-reel-lyon'], *m.* A large wicker basket; a large hand-barrow.

Angaripola [an-gah-re-po'-lah], *f.* Calico. *Angaripolas,* Gaudy ornaments on clothes.

Angaro [ahn'-gah-ro], *m.* Fire or smoke, used as a signal.

Angel [ahn'-hel], *m.* 1. Angel, a spiritual being. 2. A sort of fish much resembling a ray. *Manga de ángel,* Sleeve of a coat ruffled or plaited. *Angel custodio,* or *de la guarda,* Guardian angel. *Angel de guarda,* Protector. *Angel patudo,* Nickname of a person more malicious than commonly supposed.

Angélica [an-hay'-le-cah], *f.* (Bot.) Garden angelica. Angelica archangelica. *Angélica carlina,* (Bot.) Carline thistles. Carlina acaulis. *Angélica palustre,* Wild angelica. Angelica sylvestris.

Angelical, Angélico, ca [an-hay-le-cahl', an-hay'-le-co, cah], *a.* Angelical or angelic, heavenborn.

Angelicalmente [an-hay-le-cal-men-tay], *adv.* Angelically.

Angelico, ito [an-hay-lee'-co, an-hay-lee'-to], *m. dim.* A little angel.

Angelón, Angelonazo [an-hay-lone', an-hay-lo-nah'-tho], *m. aug.* Great angel. *Angelón de retablo,* Nickname given to a person, commonly a child, disproportionately corpulent.

Angelote [an-hay-lo'-tay], *m. aug.* 1. A large figure of an angel placed on altars. 2. A fat, good-natured child.

Ángelus [ahn'-hay-loos], *m.* The angelus, an evening prayer in the Roman Catholic church.

Angeo [an-hay'-o], *m.* A coarse sort of linen: upholsterer's canvas.

Angina [an-hee'-nah], *f.* Tonsilitis, sore throat. *Angina de pecho,* Angina pectoris.

Angiografía [an-he-o-grah-fee'-ah], *f.* Angiography, a description of vessels in the human body.

Angiología [an-he-o-lo-he'-ah], *f.* Angiology, the doctrine of the vessels of the human body.

Angiosperma [an-he-os-per'-mah], *a.* (Bot.) Angiospermous.

Anglicanismo [an-gle-cah-nees'-mo], *m.* Anglicanism, the church religion in England.

Anglicano, na [an-gle-cah'-no, nah], *a.* Anglican, belonging to England. *La iglesia anglicana*, The established church.
Anglicismo [an-gle-thees'-mo], *m.* Anglicism.
Anglo, gla [ahn'-glo, ah], *a.* Anglian, English-speaking.—*m.* & *f.* Englishman.
Angloamericano, na [an-glo-ah-may-re-cah'-no, nah], *a.* Anglo-American.
Anglomanía [an-glo-mah-nee'-ah], *f.* Anglomania, excessive enthusiasm for the English people and their belongings.
Anglómano [an-glo'-mah-no], *m.* Anglomaniac, servile imitator of the English.
Anglosajón, na [an-glo-sah-hone', nah], *a.* & *n.* Anglo-Saxon.
Angora [an-go'-rah], *a.* The Angora cat or goat: long-haired creatures.
Angostamente [an-gos-tah-men'-tay], *adv.* Narrowly.
Angostar [an-gos-tar'], *va.* To narrow, to contract.
Angosto, ta [an-gos'-to, tah], *a.* Narrow, close. *Venir angosto*, To fall short of one's expectations, ambition, or merit.
Angostura [an-gos-too'-rah], *f.* 1. Narrowness. 2. A narrow pass.
Angra [ahn'-grah], *f.* A small bay, a cove.
Anguarina [an-goo-ah-ree'-nah], *f.* A loose coat hanging down to the knees.
Anguila [an-gee'-lah], *f.* (Zool.) Eel. Muræna anguila. *Anguila de cabo*, (Naut.) A port rope with which the sailors are flogged on board the galleys. *Anguilas*, Ways on which a ship slides when launching.
Anguilazo [an-ge-lah'-tho], *m.* A stroke with a port-rope.
Anguilero, ra [an-ge-lay'-ro, rah], *m.* & *f.* Basket or pannier for eels.
Anguina [an-gee'-nah], *f.* (Vet.) The vein of the groins.
Angula [an-goo'-lah], *f.* The brood of eels.
Angulado, da [an-goo-lah'-do, dah], *a.* Having angles.
Angular [an-goo-lar'], *a.* Angular. *Piedra angular*, The corner-stone.
Angularmente [an-goo-lar-men'-tay], *adv.* With angles; in the form of an angle.
Angulema [an-goo-lay'-mah], *f.* A sort of coarse linen manufactured at Angouleme of hemp or tow.—*pl.* (Coll.) Fulsome flatteries. *V.* Zalamerías.
Ángulo [ahn'-goo-lo], *m.* Angle, corner; nook. *Angulo óptico*, The visual angle. *Ángulos de un picadero*, The corners of a riding-house.
Anguloso, sa [an-goo-lo'-so, sah], *a.* Angular, cornered.
Angustia [an-goos'-te-ah], *f.* Anguish, affliction, pang; heartache, heaviness.
Angustiadamente [an-goos-te-ah-dah-men'-tay], *adv.* Painfully.
Angustiado, da [an-goos-te-ah'-do, dah], *a.* 1. Painful. 2. (Met.) Narrow-minded, miserable.—*pp.* of Angustiar.
Angustiar [an-goos-te-ar'], *va.* To cause anguish, to afflict.
Angustura [an-goos-too'-rah], *f.* (Bot.) Angustura bark.
Anhelación [an-ay-lah-the-on'], *f.* Panting, difficulty of breathing.
Anhelante [an-ay-lahn'-tay], *a.* Eager, avid, keenly desirous.
Anhelar [an-ay-lar'], *vn.* 1. To breathe with difficulty. 2. To desire anxiously, to long, to covet. 3. To gape, to gasp. *Anhelar honores*, To aspire at honours.
Anhélito [an-ay'-le-to], *m.* Difficult respiration.
Anhelo [an-ay'-lo], *m.* A vehement desire; anxiousness, eagerness.
Anheloso, sa [an-ay-lo'-so, sah], *a.* Anxiously desirous.
Anhídrico, ca [an-ee'-dre-co, cah], *a.* *V.* Anhidro.
Anhidrita [an-e-dree'-tah], *f.* Anhydrite, a rock, the base of which is sulphate of lime.
Anhidro, dra [an-ee'-dro, drah], *a.* Anhydrous, destitute of water.
Anhinga [an-een'-gah], *f.* (Orn.) An aquatic bird of prey in Brazil, called the darter. Plotus ahinga.
Ani [ah-nee'], *m.* A pretty creeping bird indigenous to South America.
Aniaga [ah-ne-ah'-gah], *f.* (Mur.) The yearly wages of a labourer.
Anidar [ah-ne-dar'], *vn.* 1. To nestle, to make a nest. 2. (Met.) To dwell, to reside. 3. To cherish, to shelter. *Andar anidando*, To prepare for lying in.
Anieblar [ah-ne-ay-blar'], *va.* To darken, to obscure, to mystify.
Anilina [ah-ne-lee'-nah], *f.* (Chem.) Aniline.
Anillado, da [ah-neel-lyah'-do, dah], *a.* Annulated, ringed.—*pl.* Annelids, worms whose bodies are a series of ringed segments.
Anillar [ah-neel-lyar'], *va.* To form rings or circles in work; used by cutlers.
Anillejo, Anillete [ah-neel-lyay'-ho, ah-neel-lyay'-tay], *m. dim.* A small ring.
Anillo [ah-neel'-lyo], *m.* 1. A finger ring; circlet. 2. (Naut.) Hank or grommet. *Venir como anillo al dedo*, To come in the very nick of time. 3. (Arch.) Astragal.
Ánima [ah'-ne-mah], *f.* 1. Soul. *V.* Alma. 2. (Mech.) The bore of a gun. *Animas*, Ringing of bells at a certain hour, generally at sunsetting, which admonishes the faithful to pray for the souls in purgatory. *A las ánimas me volví a casa*, At sunsetting I returned home.
Animable [ah-ne-mah'-blay], *a.* Susceptible of animation.
Animación [ah-ne-mah-the-on'], *f.* Animation.
Animado, da [ah-ne-mah'-do, dah], *a.* Manful.—*pp.* of Animar.
Animador, ra [ah-ne-mah-dor', rah], *m.* & *f.* One who animates or enlivens.
Animadversión [ah-ne-mad-ver-se-on'], *f.* Animadversion, remark, stricture.
Animal [ah-ne-mahl'], *m.* 1. Animal. 2. Animal: used in contempt, to express that a person is very ignorant or stupid.
Animal [ah-ne-mahl'], *a.* Animal, relating to an animal.
Animalización [ah-ne-mah-le-thah-the-on'], *f.* Animalization: effect of making an animal.
Animalizar [ah-ne-mah-le-thar'], *va.* To animalize.—*vr.* To grow brutish.
Animalazo [ah-ne-mah-lah'-tho], *m. aug.* A large or big animal.
Animalejo, ico, illo [ah-ne-mah-lay'-ho, lee'-co, leel'-lyo], *m. dim.* A small animal, animalcule.
Animalón, Animalote [ah-ne-mah-lone', ah-ne-mah-lo'-tay], *m. aug.* A large or big animal.
Animalucho [ah-ne-mah-loo'-cho], *m.* An ugly, hideous animal.
Animar [ah-ne-mar'], *va.* 1. To animate, to enliven, to comfort, to revive. 2. To incite, to excite. 3. To give power or vigour to inanimate things.
Anime, or **Goma Anime** [ah-nee'-may], *f.* A resin resembling myrrh.
Animero [ah-ne-may'-ro], *m.* One who asks charity for the souls in purgatory.
Ánimo [ah'-ne-mo], *m.* 1. Spirit. 2. Courage, valour, fortitude, manfulness; hardiness. 3. Mind, intention, meaning, will. 4. Thought, attention. *Hacer buen ánimo*, To bear up under adversities.—*int.* Come on!
Animosamente [ah-ne-mo-sah-men'-tay], *adv.* In a spirited manner, courageously.
Animosidad [ah-ne-mo-se-dahd'], *f.* Animosity, valour, courage; boldness.
Animoso, sa [ah-ne-mo'-so, sah], *a.* Brave, spirited, courageous, gallant.
Aniñadamente [ah-nee-nyah-dah-men'-tay], *adv.* In a childish, puerile manner.
Aniñado, da [ah-nee-nyah'-do, dah], *a.* Childish.
Aniñarse [ah-nee-nyar'-say], *vr.* To grow childish.
Aniquilable [ah-ne-ke-lah'-blay], *a.* Annihilable, destructible.
Aniquilación [ah-ne-ke-lah-the-on'], *f.* Annihilation, extinction.
Aniquilador, ra [ah-ne-ke-lah-dor', rah], *m.* & *f.* A destroyer.
Aniquilar [ah-ne-ke-lar'], *va.* To annihilate, to destroy, to overthrow.—*vr.* To decline, to decay; to humble; to consume.
Anís [ah-nees'], *m.* (Bot.) Anise. Pimpinella anisum. *Anises*, Anise-seeds preserved in sugar. *Llegar a los anises*, To come the day after the feast.
Anisado, da [ah-ne-sah'-do, dah], *a.* Applied to spirits tinctured with anise.—*pp.* of Anisar.
Anisar [ah-ne-sar'], *va.* To tincture with anise.
Anisete [ah-ne-say'-tay], *m.* Anisette.
Anisófilo, la [ah-ne-so'-fe-lo, lah], *a.* Anisophyllous, having unequal leaves.
Anisol [ah-ne-sole'], *m.* A liquid substance isomeric with creasote.
Anisómero, ra [ah-ne-so'-may-ro, rah], *a.* An isomeric, composed of unequal parts.
Aniversario, ria [ah-ne-ver-sah'-re-o, ah], *a.* Annual, yearly.
Aniversario [ah-ne-ver-sah'-re-o], *m.* 1. Anniversary; holiday. 2. A mass or service yearly performed for the soul of a person deceased, on the day of his or her death. *Libro de aniversarios*, An obituary of the persons for whom anniversaries are to be performed.
¡Anjá! [an-hah'], *int.* (Cuba) Well! bravo!
Ano [ah'-no], *m.* The anus.
Anoche [ah-no'-chay], *adv.* Last night.
Anochecer [ah-no-chay-therr'], *vn.* To grow dark. *Anochecerle a uno en alguna parte*, To be benighted somewhere. *Al anochecer*, At nightfall.—*vr.* (Poet.) To grow dark. *Yo amanecí en Madrid, y anochecí en Toledo*, I was in Madrid at dawn, and Toledo at dusk.
Anochecida [ah-no-chay-thee'-dah], *f.* Dusk, nightfall.
Anodinar [ah-no-de-nar'], *va.* To administer anodyne medicines.
Anodino, na [ah-no-dee'-no, nah], *a.* (Med.) Anodyne, allaying pain.
Anodizar [ah-no-de-thar'], *va.* To anodize.
Anodo [ah'-no-do], *m.* (Elec.) Anode.
Anomalía [ah-no-mah-lee'-ah], *f.* 1. Anomaly, deviation from rules. 2. (Ast.) Distance of a planet at its aphelion.
Anómalo, la [ah-no'-mah-lo, lah], *a.* (Gram.) Anomalous.
Anón [ah-none'], *m.* (Bot.) The custard apple-tree. Annona.
Anona [ah-no'-nah], *f.* 1. Annona or custard-apple. In some parts it is

called *guanava*. 2. Store of provisions. *V.* Chirimoya.

Anonadación [ah-no-nah-dah-the-on'], *f.* **Anonadamiento,** *m.* 1. Annihilation. 2. Self-contempt.

Anonadar [ah-no-nah-dar'], *va.* 1. To annihilate. 2. (Met.) To diminish or lessen in a considerable degree.—*vr.* To humble one's self to a low degree.

Anónimamente [ah-no'-ne-mah-men-tay], *ad.* Anonymously.

Anónimo, ma [ah-no'-ne-mo, mah], *a.* Anonymous; nameless.

Anorexia [ah-no-rec'-se-ah], *f.* (Med.) Anorexia, loss of appetite.

Anormal [ah-nor-mahl'], *a.* Abnormal.

Anotación [ah-no-tah-the-on'], *f.* Annotation, note, notation.

Anotador, ra [ah-no-tah-dor', rah], *m.* & *f.* Commentator.

Anotar [ah-no-tar'], *va.* To write notes, to comment.

Anoxia [ah-noc'-se-ah], *f.* (Med.) Anoxia.

Anquera [an-kay'-rah], *f.* (Mex.) A round covering for the hind quarter of a horse; semi-lunar tail-piece of a saddle.

Anqueta [an-kay'-tah]. *Estar de media anqueta,* To be incommodiously seated.

Anquiboyuno, na [an-ke-bo-yoo'-no, nah], *a.* Having a croup like an ox; applied to horses and mules.

Anquilosis [an-ke-lo'-sis], *f.* (Anat.) Anchylosis, a stiff joint.

Anquiseco, ca [an-ke-say'-co, cah], *a.* Lean crouped.

Ansa [ahn'-sah], *f.* Commercial bond among the free cities of Germany.

Ánsar [ahn'-sar], *m.* A goose. Anas anser. *Ánsar macho,* Gander.

Ansarería [an-sah-ray-ree'-ah], *f.* The place where geese are reared.

Ansarero [an-sah-ray'-ro], *m.* A goose-herd.

Ansarino, na [an-sah-ree'-no, nah], *a.* (Poet.) Belonging to geese.

Ansarino [an-sah-ree'-no], *m.* A gosling.

Anseático, ca [an-say-ah'-te-co, cah], *a.* Hanseatic, relating to the Hanse-towns in Germany.

Ansí [an-see']. (Obs.) *V.* Así.

Ansia [ahn'-see-ah], *f.* Anxiety, anguish, eagerness, ardent desire; longing, hankering; greediness.

Ansiadamente [an-se-ah-dah-men'-tay], *adv.* Anxiously, earnestly.

Ansiar [an-se-ar'], *va.* To desire anxiously, to long, to hanker.

Ansiedad [an-se-ay-dahd'], *f.* A state of anxiety. *V.* Ansia.

Ansina [an-see'-nah]. (Obs.) *V.* Así.

Ansiosamente [an-se-o-sah-men'-tay], *adv.* Anxiously, earnestly, ardently, eagerly, fervently; heartily.

Ansioso, sa [an-se-oh'-so, sah], *a.* 1. Anxious, eager, greedy; hot. 2. Attended with great uneasiness.

Anta [ahn'-tah], *f.* An elk.—*pl.* (Arch.) Antes, pillars of a building.

Antaceo [an-tah'-thay-o], *m.* (Zool.) A large fish of the family of sturgeons, from which *isinglass* is prepared. Acipenser huso.

Antagallas [an-tah-gahl'-lyas], *f. pl.* (Naut.) Sprit-sail reef-bands.

Antagónico, ca [an-tah-go'-ne-co, cah], *a.* Antagonistic; in opposition.

Antagonismo [an-tah-go-nees'-mo], *m.* Antagonism, antipathy.

Antagonista [an-tah-go-nees'-tah], *m.* 1. Antagonist, an opponent; competitor. 2. Opposer, foe, foeman.

Antana [an-tah'-nah]. *Llamarse antana,* To contradict, to retract.

Antañazo [an-tah-nyah'-tho], *adv.* A long time since.

Antaño [an-tah'-nyo], *adv.* 1. Last year *En los nidos de antaño no hay pájaros hogaño,* Time must be seized by the forelock. (Lit.) There are no bird's in last year's nest. 2. Long ago.

Antártico, ca [an-tar'-te-co, cah], *a.* Antarctic.

Ante [ahn'-tay], *m.* 1. Buckskin, a dressed buck or buffalo skin. 2. An elk. *Piel de ante,* Suede. *Guantes de ante,* Suede gloves.

Ante [ahn'-tay], *prep.* Before. *Ante mí,* Before me, in my presence. *Ante todas cosas* or *ante todo,* Before all things, above all.

Anteado, da [an-tay-ah'-do, dah], *a.* Buff-coloured, of a pale-yellow colour.

Anteanoche [an-tay-ah-no'-chay], *adv.* The night before last.

Anteanteanoche [an-tay-an-tay-ah-no'-chay], *adv.* Three nights ago.

Anteanteayer [an-tay-an-tay-ah-yerr'], *adv.* Three days ago.

Anteantier [an-tay-an-te-err'], *adv.* (Obs.) *V.* Anteanteayer.

Anteayer [an-tay-ah-yerr'], *adv.* The day before yesterday.

Antebrazo [an-tay-brah'-tho], *m.* The fore-arm.

Antecama [an-tay-cah'-mah], *f.* A carpet laid in front of a bed.

Antecámara [an-tay-cah'-mah-rah], *f.* 1. Ante-chamber. 2. Lobby; hall. 3. (Naut.) The steerage.

Antecamarilla [an-tay-cah-mah-reel'-lyah], *f.* A room leading to the king's ante-chamber.

Antecapilla [an-tay-cah-peel'-lyah], *f.* The porch.

Antecedente [an-tay-thay-den'-tay], *m.* Antecedent.

Antecedentemente [an-tay-thay-den-tay-men'-tay], *adv.* Antecedently, previously, beforehand.

Anteceder [an-tay-thay-derr'], *va.* To precede, to forego.

Antecesor, ra [an-tay-thay-sor', rah], *m.* & *f.* Predecessor, forefather. *Antecesores,* Ancestors.

Antechinos [an-tay-chee'-nos], *m. pl.* (Arch.) Fluted mouldings.

Anteco, ca [an-tay'-co, cah], *a.* Applied to the Antoeci, or inhabitants of the same meridian at the same distance on each side the equator. It is sometimes used as a substantive.

Antecoger [an-tay-co-herr'], *va.* 1. To bring any person or thing before one. 2. To gather in fruit before the due time.

Antecolumna [an-tay-co-loom'-nah], *f.* (Arch.) A column of a portico.

Antecoro [an-tay-co'-ro], *m.* The entrance which leads to the choir.

Antecristo [an-tay-crees'-to], *m.* Antichrist.

Antedata [an-tay-dah'-tah], *f.* Antedate.

Antedatar [an-tay-dah-tar'], *va.* To antedate.

Antedecir [an-tay-day-theer'], *va.* To predict, to foretell.

Antedicho, cha [an-tay-dee'-cho, chah], *a.* Foresaid.

Ante diem [an-tay-dee'-em]. (Lat.) The preceding day.

Antediluviano, na [an-tay-de-loo-ve-ah'-no, nah], *a.* Antediluvian.

Antefechar [an-tay-fay-char'], *va.* To anticipate the date of. *V.* Antedatar.

Antefirma [an-tay-feer'-mah], *f.* The style of address which is put before the signature in any communication.

Anteiglesia [an-tay-e-glay'-se-ah], *f.* 1. (Obs.) The porch of a church. 2. The parochial church of some places in Biscay, and the district belonging to any of those parishes.

Antelación [an-tay-lah-the-on'], *f.* Precedence in order of time.

Antemano [an-tay-mah'-no], *adv. De antemano,* Beforehand.

Antemeridiano, na [an-tay-may-re-de ah'-no, nah], *a.* In the forenoon.

Antemural [an-tay-moo-rahl'], *m.* 1. A fort, rock, or mountain, which serves for the defence of a fortress. 2. (Met.) A safeguard.

Antemuralla [an-tay-moo-rahl'-lyah], *f.* or **Antemuro** [an-tay-moo'-ro], *m.* *V* Antemural.

Antena [an-tay'-nah], *f.* 1. (Radio) Aerial. 2. Antenna or feeler of insects.

Antenallas [an-tay-nahl'-lyas], *f. pl.* Pincers.

Antenoche [an-tay-no'-chay], *adv.* 1. The night before last. 2. (Obs.) Before nightfall.

Antenombre [an-tay-nom'-bray], *m.* A title prefixed to a proper name, and equivalent to Sir, Saint, etc., in the English, as *Don Pedro, San Juan,* etc.

Anténula [an-tay'-noo-lah], *f.* Antennule: applied to the smaller pair of antennæ or feelers of crustacea: maxillary palpi.

Antenupcial [an-te-noop-the-ahl'], *a.* Antenuptial, before marriage.

Anteojera [an-tay-o-hay'-rah], *f.* 1. Spectacle-case. 2. Eye-flap.

Anteojero [an-tay-o-hay'-ro], *m.* Spectacle-maker.

Anteojo [an-tay-o'-ho], *m.* A spy-glass; an eye-glass. *Anteojo de larga vista,* A telescope. *Anteojo de puño,* or *de teatro,* Opera-glass.—*pl.* 1. Spectacles. *Anteojos de camino,* or *de enfermos,* Goggles. 2. Pieces of felt or leather put before the eyes of vicious horses.

Ante-ómnia [an-tay-om'-ne-ah]. (Lat.) Before all things; above all.

Antepagar [an-tay-pah-gar'], *va.* To pay beforehand.

Antepasado, da [an-tay-pah-sah'-do, dah], *a.* Passed, elapsed.

Antepasados [an-tay-pah-sah'-dos], *m. pl.* Ancestors, predecessors.

Antepecho [an-tay-pay'-cho], *m.* 1. Balcony, bridge-rail; sill of a window. 2. Breastwork, parapet, battlement. 3. Footstep of a coach. 4. Harness for the breast of a draught-horse; poitrel. 5. Breast roller of a loom. 6. The part of a ribbon frame or loom, which passes from the right to the left, to the point in which the weaver's strap is placed. *Antepechos,* (Naut.) The iron horse of the head.

Antepenúltimo, ma [an-tay-pay-nool'-te-mo, mah], *a.* Antepenult.

Anteponer [an-tay-po-nerr'], *va.* 1. To prefer. 2. (Obs.) To place before.

(*Yo antepongo,* from *Anteponer. V* Poner.)

Anteportada [an-te-por-tah'-dah], *f.* A fly-leaf bearing the title only of a book.

Anteportal, or **Antepórtico** [an-tay-por'-te-co], *m.* Vestibule or porch.

Antepuerta [an-tay-poo-er'-tah], *f.* 1. A curtain placed before a door. 2. Anteport.

Antepuerto, *m.* (Naut.) Anteport.

Antequino [an-tay-kee'-no], *m.* (Arch.) *V.* Esgucio.

Antera [an-tay'-rah], *f.* (Bot.) Anther, the part of the stamen which contains the pollen of flowers.

Antérico-tardío [an-tay'-re-co-tar-dee'-oh], *m.* (Bot.) Mountain spider-wort.

Anterior [an-tay-re-or'], *a.* Anterior, former.

Anterioridad [an-tay-re-o-re-dahd'], *f.* Priority: preference.

Anteriormente [an-tay-re-or-men'-tay], *adv.* Previously.

Anteroversión [an-tay-ro-ver-se-on'], *f.* (Med.) Anteversion of an organ.

Antes [ahn'-tes], *prep.* Before, of place, or time; beforehand. *Antes de* or *antes que*, Before.

Antes [ahn'-tes], *adv.* First, rather, better; heretofore. *Haga Vd. esto antes*, Do this first. *Quisiera antes esto que aquello*, I would rather have this than that. *Antes morir que pecar*, Better to die than to sin.—It also denotes preference of time or place. *Antes bien*, Rather. *Antes del día*, Before day or at daybreak. *Antes con antes*, As soon as possible. *Cuanto antes*, Forthwith, as soon as possible. *De antes*, In ancient times. *Las cosas de antes son muy diferentes de las de ahora*, The affairs of ancient times widely differ from those of the present day.

Antesacristía [an-tay-sah-cris-tee'-ah], *f.* An apartment which leads to the sacristy.

Antesala [an-tay-sah'-lah], *f.* Antechamber. *Hacer antesala*, To dance attendance in an ante-chamber.

Antestatura [an-tes-tah-too'-rah], *f.* (Mil.) A small intrenchment of palisadoes and sandbags.

Antetemplo [an-tay-tem'-plo], *m.* Portico.

Antever [an-tay-verr'], *va.* To foresee. (*Yo anteveo*, from *Antever. V.* VER.)

Antevíspera [an-tay-vees'-pay-rah], *f.* The day before yesterday.

Anti [ahn'-te]. *Inseparable prefix.* 1. Ante-, as in *antiparras*. 2. Anti-, as in *anticristo*.

Antiácido, da [an-te-ah'-the-do, dah], *a.* Antacid.

Antiaéreo, rea [an-te-ah-ay'-ray-o, ray-ah], *a.* Antiaircraft.

Antiafrodisiaco, ca [an-te-ah-fro-de-se-ah'-co, cah], *a.* Anaphrodisiac.

Antialcoholismo [an-te-al-co-o-lees'-mo], *m.* Antialcoholism.

Antiartrítico, ca [an-te-ar-tree'-te-co, cah], *a.* Arthritis-combatting.

Antiasmático, ca [an-te-as-mah'-te-co, cah], *a.* Asthma-combatting.

Antibiótico, ca [an-te-be-o'-te-co, cah], *a.* & *m.* Antibiotic.

Anticanceroso, sa [an-te-can-the-ro'-so, sah], *a.* Cancer-fighting.

Anticarro [an-te-car'-ro], *a.* Antitank.

Anticatarral [an-te-ca-tar-rahl'], *a.* Cold-fighting, cold-curing.

Anticiclón [an-te-the-clon'], *m.* Anticyclone.

Anticipación [an-te-the-pah-the-on'], *f.* 1. Anticipation. 2. Expectation.

Anticipada [an-te-the-pah'-dah], *f.* Catching one's opponent off guard.

Anticipadamente [an-te-the-pah-da-men'-tay], *adv.* In advance, ahead of time.

Anticipar [an-te-the-par'], *va.* 1. To anticipate. 2. To move up (a date), to move up the date of. —*vr.* 1. To get ahead. 2. To come early, to occur early.

Anticipo [an-te-thee'-po], *m.* 1. Anticipation. 2. Advance payment.

Anticlerical [an-te-clay-re-cahl'], *a.* Anticlerical.

Anticoagulante [an-te-co-a-goo-lahn'-tay], *m.* & *a.* Anticoagulant.

Anticolonialismo [an-te-co-lo-ne-a-lees'-mo], *m.* Anticolonialism.

Anticomunismo [an-te-co-moo-nees'-mo], *m.* Anticommunism.

Anticomunista [an-te-co-moo-nees'-tah], *com.* Anticommunist.

Anticoncepcional [an-te-con-thep-the-o-nahl'], *m.* & *a.* Contraceptive.

Anticoncepcionismo [an-te-con-thep-the-o-nees'-mo], *m.* Birth control, use of contraceptives.

Anticonformismo [an-te-con-for-mees'-mo], *m.* Nonconformity.

Anticonformista [an-te-con-for-mees'-tah], *a.* & *m.* & *f.* Nonconformist.

Anticongelante [an-te-con-hay-lahn'-tay], *m.* & *a.* Antifreeze.

Anticonstitucional [an-te-cons-te-too-the-o-nahl'], *a.* Unconstitutional.

Anticresis [an-te-cray'-sis], *f.* A contract between debtor and creditor by which the former yields to the latter the fruits of a farm until the debt is paid.

Anticresista [an-te-cre-sees'-tah], *m.* The creditor in anticresis.

Anticristiano, na [an-te-cris-te-ah'-no, nah], *a.* & *m.* & *f.* Antichristian.

Anticrítico [an-te-cree'-te-co], *m.* Anticritic, an opponent to a critic.

Anticuado, da [an-te-coo-ah'-do, dah], *a.* Antiquated; obsolete, out of use.—*pp.* of ANTICUAR.

Anticuar [an-te-coo-ar'], *va.* To antiquate, to outdate.

Anticuario [an-te-coo-ah'-re-o], *m.* Antiquary, antiquarian.

Anticuerpo [an-te-coo-err'-po], *m.* (Chem.) Antibody.

Antidemocrático, ca [an-te-day-mo-crah'-te-co, cah], *a.* Nondemocratic.

Antideslizante [an-te-des-le-thahn'-tay], *a.* Nonskid.

Antidetonante [an-te-day-to-nahn'-tay], *a.* Antiknock.

Antidiabético, ca [an-te-de-ah-bay'-te-co, cah], *a.* To control diabetes.

Antídoto [an-tee'-do-to], *m.* 1. Antidote, counterpoison. 2. (Met.) A preventive or preservative against vice or error.

Antiemético, ca [an-te-ay-may'-te-co, cah], *a.* (Med.) Antemetic.

Antiepiléptico, ca [an-te-ay-pe-lep'-te-co, cah], *a.* (Med.) Antepileptic.

Antiescorbútico, ca [an-te-es-cor-boo'-te-co, cah], *a.* (Med.) Antiscorbutic.

Antier [an-te-err'], *adv.* (Coll.) The day before yesterday; a contraction of *antes de ayer*.

Antiespasmódico, ca [an-te-es-pas-mo'-de-co, cah], *a.* (Med.) Antispasmodic.

Antifanático, ca [an-te-fah-nah'-te-co, cah], *a.* Antifanatic.

Antifaz [an-te-fath'], *m.* A veil which covers the face. A mask.

Antifebril [an-te-fay-breel'], *a.* (Med.) Antifebrile.

Antiflogístico, ca [an-te-flo-hees'-te-co, cah], *a.* (Med.) Antiphlogistic. It is also used as a substantive.

Antífona [an-tee'-fo-nah], *f.* Antiphony, an anthem.

Antifonal, Antifonario [an-te-fo-nahl', an-te-fo-nah'-re-o], *m.* Antiphonal, a book of anthems.

Antífrasis [an-tee'-frah-sis], *f.* Antiphrasis.

Antifricción [an-te-frec-the-on'], *f.* Antifriction alloy.

Antígeno [an-tee'-hay-no], *m.* Antigen.

Antigravedad [an-te-grah-vay-dahd'], *f.* Weightlessness.

Antigualla [an-te-goo-ahl'-lyah], *f.* 1. A monument of antiquity; antique. 2. Antiquity. 3. Ancient custom out of use.

Antiguamente [an-te-goo-ah-men'-tay], *adv.* Anciently, formerly; heretofore.

Antiguar [an-te-goo-ar'], *vn.* To obtain seniority, as member of a tribunal, college, etc.—*va.* (Obs.) 1. To make obsolete. 2. To abolish the ancient use of a thing.

Antigüedad [an-te-goo-ay-dahd'], *f.* 1. Antiquity, oldness. 2. Ancient times, the days of yore. 3. The ancients. 4. Antique.

Antiguo, gua [an-tee'-goo-o, goo-ah], *a.* Antique, stricken in years, old; having long held an employment or place.

Antiguo [an-tee'-goo-o], *m.* 1. An antique of Greece or Rome. 2. An aged member of a college or community: senior of a college. *Antiguos*, The ancients; the illustrious men of antiquity.

Antihelmíntico, ca [an-te-el-meen'-te-co, cah], *a.* (Med.) Anthelminthic.

Antihigiénico, ca [an-te-he-ay'-ne-co, cah], *a.* Unsanitary, unhygienic.

Antihistamina [an-tees-tah-me'-nah], *f.* Antihistamine.

Antilogaritmo [an-te-lo-gah-reet'-mo], *m.* Antilogarithm.

Antilogía [an-te-lo-hee'-ah], *f.* An apparent contradiction between two sentences or passages of an author.

Antilógico, ca [an-te-lo'-he-co, cah], *a.* Illogical, contrary to logic.

Antílope [an-tee'-lo-pay], *m.* Antelope.

Antillano, na [an-teel-lyah'-no, nah], *a.* Native or relating to the Antilles.

Antimateria [an-te-mah-tay'-re-ah], *f.* Antimatter.

Antimonárquico, ca [an-te-mo-nar'-ke-co, cah], *a.* Antimonarchic, antimonarchical.

Antimonial [an-te-mo-ne-ahl'], *a.* Antimonial, belonging to antimony.

Antimonio [an-te-mo'-ne-o], *m.* Antimony.

Antimonopolio [an-te-mo-no-po'-le-o], *a.* Antitrust, antimonopoly.

Antinacional [an-te-nah-the-o-nahl'], *a.* Against one's national interests.

Antinatural [an-te-nah-too-rahl'], *a.* Unnatural.

Antineutrón [an-te-ne-oo-tron'], *m.* Antineutron.

Antimoral [an-te-mo-rahl'], *a.* Contrary to morality.

Antinomia [an-te-no'-me-ah], *f.* (Law) A conflict between laws or parts of a law.

Antipapa [an-te-pah'-pah], *m.* An antipope, a pope who is not canonically elected.

Antipapado [an-te-pah-pah'-do], *m.* The unlawful dignity of antipope.

Antipapal [an-te-pah-pahl'], *a.* Antipapal.

Antipara [an-te-pah'-rah], *f.* 1. A screen, or anything which serves as a screen.

Antiparásito, Antiparasitario [an-te-pah-rah'-se-to, an-te-pah-rah-se-tah'-re-o], *a.* Preventing or reducing static or interference. — *m.* Static suppressor, interference filter.

Antiparras [an-te-pahr'-ras], *f. pl.* (Coll.) Specs, glasses.

Antipartícula [an-te-par-tee'-coo-lah], *f.* Antiparticle.

Antipatía [an-te-pah-tee'-ah], *f.* Antipathy.

Antipático, ca [an-te-pah'-te-co, cah], *a.* Having a natural aversion for any thing.

Antipatizar [an-te-pah-te-thar'], *vn.* (Amer.) To dislike, to have a feeling against.

Antiperistasis [an-te-pay-rees'-tan-sis], *f.* Antiperistasis, the action of two contrary qualities.

Antiperistáltico, ca [an-te-pay-ris-tahl'-te-co, cah], *a.* Antiperistaltic, a reverse movement of the intestines; also, quieting the natural peristalsis.

Antípodas [an-tee'-po-das], *m. pl.* 1. Antipodes. 2. (Met.) Persons of contrary dispositions, sentiments, or manners.

Antiprotón [an-te-pro-ton'], *m.* Antiproton.
Antipútrido, da [an-te-poo'-tre-do, dah], *a.* Antiseptic.
Antiquísimo, ma [an-te-kee'-se-mo, mah], *a. sup.* Very ancient.
Antirradar [an-teer-rah-dar'], *a.* Antiradar.
Antirreligioso, sa [an-te-ray-le-he-oh'-so, sah], *a.* Antireligious.
Antirrevolucionario, ria [an-teer-ray-vo-loo-the-o-nah'-re-o, ah], *a.* Antirevolutionary.
Antisemita [an-te-say-mee'-tah], *a.* Anti-Semitic.—*m. & f.* Anti-Semite.
Antisemítico, ca [an-te-say-mee'-te-co, cah], *a.* Anti-Semitic.
Antisemitismo [an-te-say-me-tees'-mo], *m.* Anti-Semitism.
Antiséptico, ca [an-te-sep'-te-co, cah], *a.* Antiseptic, counteracting existing sepsis, and thus contrasted with aseptic.
Antisifilítico, ca [an-te-se-fe-lee'-te-co, cah], *a.* Antisyphilitic.
Antisociable [an-te-so-the-ah'-blay], *a.* Antisocial.
Antisocial [an-te-so-the-ahl'], *a.* Antisocial.
Antisubmarino, na [an-te-soob-mah-ree'-no, nah], *a.* Antisubmarine.
Antisuero [an-te-soo-ay'-ro], *m.* Antiserum.
Antitesis [an-tee'-tay-sis], *f.* 1. (Gram.) Antithesis. 2. (Rhet.) A contrast or opposition in the words of a discourse.
Antitético, ca [an-te-tay'-te-co, cah], *a.* Antithetical.
Antitipo [an-te-tee'-po], *m.* Antitype, figure, image, symbol.
Antitoxina [an-te-toc-see'-nah], *f.* Antitoxin.
Antivirus [an-te-vee'-roos], *m.* Antivirus
Antófago, ga [an-to'-fah-go, gah] *a.* Living on flowers.
Antojadizo, za [an-to-ha-dee'-tho, thah], *a.* Capricious, whimsical, fickle.
Antojado, da [an-to-hah'-do, dah], *a.* Anxious, longing.—*pp.* of ANTOJARSE.
Antojarse [an-to-har'-say], *vr.* To long, to desire earnestly. *Antojársele a uno alguna cosa,* To desire or judge without reflection.
Antojera [an-to-hay'-rah], *f.* 1. A spectacle-case. 2. An eye-flap for horses; blinder, blinker.
Antojo [an-to'-ho], *m.* 1. Whim; a vehement desire, a longing, a hankering; fancy. 2. A surmise.
Antología [an-to-lo-hee'-ah], *f.* Anthology.
Antónimo [an-to'-ne-mo], *m.* Antonym.
Antonomasia [an-to-no-mah'-se-ah], *f.* (Rhet.) Antonomasia, a figure by which a title is put for a proper name; as, The Orator, for Cicero.
Antor [an-tor'], *m.* (Law. Prov.) Vender of stolen goods, bought in good faith.
Antorcha [an-tor'-chah], *f.* 1. Torch, flambeau, taper. 2. A cresset.
Antorchero [an-tor-chay'-ro], *m.* (Obs.) A candlestick for tapers, etc.
Antoría [an-to-ree'-ah], *f.* 1. (Law. Prov.) The action of discovering the first seller of stolen goods. 2. Right of reclaiming against the seller of stolen goods.
Antracita [an-trah-thee'-tah], *f.* Anthracite coal; hard coal.
Antrax [ahn'-trahx], *m.* (Med.) Carbuncle; also anthrax or splenic fever
Antro [ahn'-tro], *m.* 1. (Poet.) Cavern, den, grotto. 2. (Med.) Antrum, a cavity in bone.
Antropofagia [an-tro-po-fah-hee'-ah], *f.* Anthropophagy.
Antropófago [an-tro-po'-fah-go], *m.* A cannibal.—*s. pl,* Anthropophagi. In English it has no singular.
Antropografía [an-tro-po-grah-fee'-ah], *f.* Anthropography, descriptive anatomy of man.
Antropoide [an-tro-poy'-day], *m.* & *a.* Anthropoid
Antropoideo [an-tro-poy'-day-oh], *a.* Anthropoid. *Mono antropoideo,* Anthropoid.
Antropología [an-tro-po-lo-hee'-ah], *f.* Anthropology, the science of the human structure.
Antropológico, ca [an-tro-po-lo'-he-co, cah], *a.* Anthropological.
Antropólogo [an-tro-po'-lo-go], *m.* Anthropologist.
Antropomorfismo [an-tro-po-mor-fees'-mo], *m.* The attribution to God of a human body.
Antropomorfo, fa [an-tro-po-mor'-fo, fah], *a.* Anthropomorphous, said of apes.
Antroposofía [an-tro-po-so-fee'-ah], *f.* Anthroposophy, the knowledge of the nature of man.
Antruejar [an-troo-ay-har'], *va.* (Prov.) To wet with water, or play some trick.
Antruejo [an-troo-ay'-ho], *m.* The three days of the carnival.
Antruido [an-troo-ee'-do], *m.* (Obs.) *V.* ANTRUEJO.
Antuvión [an-too-ve-on'], *m.* (Coll.) A sudden, unexpected stroke or attack. *De antuvión,* Unexpectedly. *Fulano vino de antuvión,* Such-a-one came unexpectedly.
Anual [ah-noo-ahl'], *a.* Annual. *Plantas anuales,* (Bot.) Annual plants.
Anualidad [ah-noo-ah-le-dahd'], *f.* 1. State or quality of being annual. 2. Pensions paid by the state. 3. Annuity. (Com.)
Anualmente [ah-noo-al-men'-tay], *adv.* Annually.
Anuario [ah-noo-ah'-re-o], *m.* A year-book of information.
Anúbada [ah-noo'-bah-dah], *f.* 1. (Obs.) An ancient tax paid in Spain. 2. A call to arms.
Anubarrado, da [ah-noo-bar-rah'-do, dah], *a.* Clouded.
Anubarse [ah-noo-bar'-say], *vr.* To vanish.
Anubladamente [ah-noo-blah-dah-men'-tay], *adv.* Mistily.
Anublado, da [ah-noo-blah'-do, dah], *a.* 1. Overcast, clouded, dim, mistful. 2. (Speaking of colours), Somewhat more obscure than the rest.—*pp.* of ANUBLAR.
Anublar [ah-noo-blar'], *va.* 1. To cloud, to darken the light of the sun. 2. To overcast. 3. (Met.) To cloud or obscure merit.—*vr.* 1. To be blasted, withered, or mildewed: applied to corn and plants. 2. (Met.) To miscarry, to be disconcerted: speaking of plans.
Anudar [ah-noo-dar'], *va.* 1. To knot. 2. To join, to unite.—*vn.* To wither, to fade, to pine away. *Anudarse la voz,* (Met.) To throb from passion or grief; not to be able to speak.
Anuencia [ah-noo-en'-the-ah], *f.* Compliance, consent.
Anuente [ah-noo-en'-tay], *a.* Condescending, courteous.
Anulable [ah-noo-lah'-blay], *a.* That which can be annulled.
Anulación [ah-noo-lah-the-on'], *f.* 1. Cessation, abrogation. 2. Abscission.
Anulador, ra [ah-noo-lah-dor', rah], *m.* & *f.* A repealer.
Anular [ah-noo-lar'], *va.* 1. To annul, to make void, to frustrate. 2. To cancel, rescind. (For.) To irritate.
Anular [ah-noo-lar'], *a.* Annular, ring-shaped. *Dedo anular,* The ring-finger, or fourth finger.
Anulativo, va [ah-noo-lah-tee'-vo, vah], *a.* Having the power of making void.
Anuloso, sa [ah-noo-lo'-so, sah]. Annular, composed of many rings.
Anunciación [ah-noon-the-ah-the-on'], *f.* Annunciation; the angel's salutation to the blessed Virgin.
Anunciada [ah-noon-the-ah'-dah], *f.* 1. An order of monks. 2. A religious order for women. 3. An order of knights, instituted by Amadeus VI., Duke of Savoy.
Anunciador, ra [ah-noon-the-ah-dor', rah], *m.* & *f.* Announcer, one who announces.
Anunciar [ah-noon-the-ar'], *va.* 1. To announce, to proclaim, to declare. 2. To advertise, to publicize. 3. To forbode, to portend.
Anuncio [ah-noon'-the-o], *m.* 1. Omen, forerunner. 2. Advertisement. 3. (Com.) Statement, advice.
Anuo, ua [ah'-noo-o, ah], *a.* *V.* ANUAL.
Anúteba [ah-noo'-tay-bah], *f.* 1. *V.* ANÚBADA. 2. Call to war.
Anverso [an-verr'-so], *m.* Obverse: applied to the head side in coins and medals.
Anvir [ahn'-veer], *m.* (South Amer.) A red liquor expressed from the fermented leaves of tobacco.
Anzolero [an-tho-lay'-ro], *m.* (Prov.) One whose trade it is to make fish-hooks.
Anzuelo [an-thoo-ay'-lo], *m.* 1. Fish-hook. 2. (Met.) Allurement, incitement. 3. A kind of fritters made in the shape of a hook. *Caer en el anzuelo,* To be tricked or defrauded. *Roer el anzuelo,* To escape a danger. *Tragar el anzuelo,* To swallow the bait.
Aña [ah'-nyah], *f.* Hyena.
Añada [ah-nyah'-dah], *f.* 1. The good or bad season in a year. 2. Moiety of arable land.
Añadido [ah-nyah-dee'-do], *m.* False hair.
Añadidura [ah-nyah-de-doo'-rah], *f.*
Añadimiento [ah-nyah-de-me-en'-to], *m.* Addition. *Añadidura a los pesos en la venta de cosas,* Over-weight allowed in the sale of goods.
Añadir [ah-nyah-deer'], *va.* 1. To add. 2. To exaggerate.
Añafea [ah-nyah-fay'-ah], *f.* *Papel de añafea,* Brown paper.
Añafil [ah-nyah-feel'], *m.* A musical pipe used by the Moors.
Añafilero [ah-nyah-fe-lay'-ro], *m.* A player on the *añafil.*
Añagaza [ah-nyah-gah'-thah], *f.* 1. A call, lure, or decoy, for catching birds. 2. (Met.) Allurement, enticement to mischief.
Añal [ah-nyahl'], *a.* Annual. *Cordero añal,* A yearling lamb.
Añal [ah-nyahl'], *m.* 1. An annual offering on the tomb of a person deceased. 2. (Obs.) Anniversary.
Añalejo [ah-nyah-lay'-ho], *m.* An ecclesiastical almanac, pointing out the regulations of the divine service.
Añascar [ah-nyas-car'], *va.* 1. (Coll.) To collect by degrees small things of little value. 2. (Obs.) To entangle.
Añejar [ah-nyay-har'], *va.* To make old.—*vr.* To grow old, to become stale.
Añejo, ja [ah-nyay'-ho, hah], *a.* Old, stale, musty.
Añicos [ah-nyee'-cos], *m. pl.* Bits or small pieces of any thing. *Hacer añi*

cos, To break into small bits. *Hacerse añicos*, To take too much exercise, to overheat one's self.

Añil [ah-nyeel'], *m.* 1. (Bot.) The indigo plant. Indigofera tinctoria. 2. Indigo, a mass extracted from the indigo plant: the best quality is called *añil flor*, or *tisate;* the middling sort, *sobresaliente;* and the common kind, *corte.*

Añilar [ah-nye-lar'], *va.* To treat the clothes with bluing, in laundry-work.

Añinero [ah-nye-nay'-ro], *m.* A dealer in lambskins.

Añinos [ah-nyee'-nos], *m.pl,* The fleecy skins of yearling lambs.

Año [ah'-nyo], *m.* 1. A year. 2. A long space of time. 3. The companion or partner who falls to one's lot in family diversions, the first day of the year. *Mal año*, Surely, without doubt. *Mal año para él*, The deuce take him. *Años*, The birthday of a person. *Celebrar los años*, To keep the birthday. *Tener años*, To be old. *Año bisiesto*, Leap-year. *Viva Vd. muchos años* or *mil años*, I am obliged to you.

Añojal [ah-nyo-hahl'], *m.* Fallow land.

Añojo, ja [ah-nyo'-ho, hah], *m. & f.* A yearling calf.

Año luz [ah'-nyo looth], *m.* (Ast.) Light year.

Añoso, sa [ah-nyo'-so, sah], *a.* Old, stricken in years.

Añublado, da [ah-nyoo-blah'-do, dah], *a.* Blindfolded.—*pp.* of AÑUBLAR.

Añublar, Añublarse [ah-nyoo-blar', ah-nyoo-blar'-say]. *V.* ANUBLAR.

Añublo [ah-nyoo'-blo], *m.* Mildew. *V.* TIZÓN.

Añudador, ra [ah-nyoo-dah-dor', rah], *m. & f.* One who knots or ties.

Añudar [ah-nyoo-dar'], *va.* 1. *V.* ANUDAR. 2. To make fast, to unite, to tie close. *Añudar los labios*, To impose silence.

Añusgar [ah-nyoos-gar'], *va.* 1 (Littl. us.) To choke. 2. To vex to annoy. —*vn.* To be displeased.

Aojado, da [ah-o-hah'-do, dah], *a.* Bewitched.—*pp.* of AOJAR.

Aojador, ra [ah-o-hah-dor', rah], *m. & f.* A conjurer.

Aojadura [ah-o-hah-doo'-rah], *f.* **Aojamiento** [ah-o-hah-me-en'-to], *m.* Witchcraft, fascination.

Aojar [ah-o-har'], *va.* To fascinate, to charm, to bewitch.

Aorta [ah-or'-tah], *f.* (Anat.) Aorta, the great artery.

Aorteurismo [ah-or-tay-oo-rees'-mo], *m.* Aneurism of the aorta.

Aórtico, ca [ah-or'-te-co, cah], *a.* Aortic: relating to the aorta.

Aovado, da [ah-o-vah'-do, dah], *a.* Oviform, in the shape of an egg.—*pp.* of AOVAR.

Aovar [ah-o-var'], *va.* To lay eggs.

Aovillarse [ah-o-veel-lyar'-say], *vr.* To grow or be contracted into the shape of a clew.

Apabilar [ah-pah-be-lar'], *va.* To prepare the wick of a wax-candle for being lighted.—*vr.* 1. (Obs.) To die away; applied to the light of a candle. 2. (Met.) To sink under the hand of death.

Apabullar [ah-pah-bool-lyar'], *va.* (Coll.) To flatten, squeeze, crush.

Apacentadero [ah-pah-then-tah-day'-ro], *m.* Pasture; feeding-place for cattle.

Apacentador [ah-pah-then-tah-dor'], *m.* A herdsman.

Apacentamiento [ah-pah-then-tah-me-en'-to], *m.* 1. The act of tending grazing cattle. 2. Pasturage.

Apacentar [ah-pah-then-tar'], *va.* 1. To tend grazing cattle. 2. To graze, to feed cattle. 3. (Met.) To teach, to instruct spiritually. 4. (Met.) To inflame the passions.

Apacibilidad [ah-pah-the-be-le-dahd'], *f.* Affability, mildness of manners, meekness of temper.

Apacible [ah-pah-thee'-blay], *a.* 1. Affable, meek, gentle, inoffensive. 2. Placid, still, quiet. 3. Pleasant, calm, moderate. *Tiempo apacible*, (Naut.) Moderate weather. *Semblante apacible*, A serene countenance. *Sitio apacible*, A pleasant place.

Apaciblemente [ah-pah-the-blay-men'-tay], *adv.* Mildly, gently, agreeably. (*Yo apaciento, yo apaciente*, from *Apacentar. V.* ACERTAR.)

Apaciguador, ra [ah-pah-the-goo-ah-dor', rah], *m. & f.* Pacificator, peace-maker.

Apaciguamiento [ah-pa-the-goo-ah-me-en'-to], *m.* Pacification.

Apaciguar [ah-pah-the-goo-ar'], *va.* To appease, to pacify, to calm, to compose.—*vn.* (Naut.) To grow moderate; applied to the wind and sea.

Apacheta [ah-pah-chay'-tah], *f.* (Amer.) A heap of stones on hills. (Met.) *Hacer la apacheta*, To accomplish the most difficult part of a task. *Hacer su apacheta*, To have made a fortune; to make one's "pile."

Apachurrar [ah-pah-choor-rar'], *va.* (Amer.) To crush, to squeeze, to flatten. *Morir a apachurrones*, To be squeezed to death. *V.* DESPACHURRAR.

Apadrinador, ra [ah-pah-dre-nah-dor', rah], *m. & f.* 1. Patron, defender, protector. 2. Second, in a duel.

Apadrinar [ah-pah-dre-nar'], *va.* 1. To support, to favor, to patronize, to protect. 2. To sponsor. 3. To serve as godfather. 4. To act as second in a duel.

Apagado, da [ah-pah-gah'-do, dah], *a.* Humble-minded, submissive, pusillanimous.—*pp.* of APAGAR.

Apagador [ah-pah-gah-dor'], *m.* 1. One who extinguishes. 2. Damper, extinguisher, a hollow cone. 3. A small bit of cloth to deaden the echo of the strings; damper.

Apagaincendios [ah-pah-gah-in-then'-de-os], *m.* A fire-engine.

Apagamiento [ah-pah-gah-me-en'-to], *m.* The act of quenching.

Apagapenoles [ah-pah-gah-pay-no'-les], *m. pl.* (Naut.) Leech-ropes, leech-lines.

Apagar [ah-pah-gar'], *va.* 1. To quench, to extinguish. 2. (Met.) To efface, to destroy. 3. (Art) To soften colours which are too bright or glaring. 4. To moderate the light of a room. 5. (Mech.) To dead, deaden. *Apagar la cal*, To slake lime. *Apagar la sed*, To quench the thirst. *Apagar la voz*, To put a mute on the bridge of stringed musical instruments for the purpose of softening the sound. *Apagarse la lumbre, la luz* or *el fuego*, To go out.

Apagógico, ca [ah-pah-go'-he-co, cah], *a.* Apagogical, that shows the absurdity which arises from denying a thing.

Apagón [ah-pah-gone'], *s.* (Mex.) Blackout.

Apainelado, da [ah-pah-e-nay-lah'-do, dah], *a.* (Arch.) In imitation of half an ellipsis; applied to an arch.

Apaisado, da [ah-pah-e-sah'-do, dah], *a.* Resembling a landscape; applied to a painting broader than it is high.

Apalabrar [ah-pah-lah-brar'], *va.* 1. To appoint a meeting for consultation. 2. To treat personally. 3. To bespeak, to engage beforehand.

Apalambrar [ah-pah-lam-brar'], *va.* (Obs.) To set on fire. *Apalambrarse de sed*, To be parched with thirst.

Apalancar [ah-pah-lan-car'], *va.* To move with a lever.

Apaleador, ra [ah-pah-lay-ah-dor', rah], *m. & f.* One who uses cudgels, cudgeller.

Apaleamiento [ah-pah-lay-ah-me-en'-to], *m.* Drubbing; beating.

Apalear [ah-pah-lay-ar'], *va.* 1. To cane, to drub, to cudgel, to maul. 2. To beat out the dust, to horsewhip. 3. To move grain to prevent its being spoiled. *Apalear el dinero*, To heap up money with shovels, to be excessively rich.

Apaleo [ah-pah-lay'-o], *m.* Act of moving or shovelling grain.

Apalmada [ah-pal-mah'-dah], *a.* (Her.) Palm of the hand stretched out in a coat of arms.

Apanaje [ah-pah-nah'-hay], *m.* Appanage, yearly income.

Apanalado, da [ah-pah-nah-lah'-do, dah], *a.* Like honeycomb; deeply pitted.

Apancora [ah-pan-co'-rah], *f.* The sea-hedgehog: echinus.

Apandar [ah-pan-dar'], *va.* (Coll.) To pilfer, to steal.

Apandillar [ah-pan-deel-lyar'], *va.* To form a league, a party, or a faction.—*vr.* To be united to form a party or a faction; it is taken generally in a bad sense.

Apandorgarse [ah-pan-dor-gar'-say], *vr.* To grow fat (used of women).

Apanojado, da [ah-pah-no-hah'-do, dah], *a.* (Bot.) Paniculate, bearded like seeds.

Apantanar [ah-pan-tah-nar'], *va.* 1. To fill a piece of ground with water; to make a pool of water.

Apantuflado, da [ah-pan-too-flah'-do, dah], *a.* Wearing slippers.

Apañado, da [ah-pah-nyah'-do, dah], *a.* 1. Resembling woollen cloth in body. (Coll.) 2. Suitable, fit (for), apposite. 3. Dexterous, skilful.—*pp.* of APAÑAR.

Apañador, ra [ah-pah-nyah-dor', rah], *m. & f.* 1. One who grasps or seizes. 2. A pilferer.

Apañadura [ah-pah-nyah-doo'-rah], *f.* The act of seizing, snatching, or grasping away.

Apañamiento [ah-pah-nyah-me-en'-to], *m.* *V.* APAÑO.

Apañar [ah-pah-nyar'], *va.* 1. To grasp or seize. 2. (Met.) To carry away. 3. To pilfer. 4. To dress, to clothe. 5. To patch, to mend.—*vr.* (Coll.) To submit to, to reconcile one's self to a thing.

Apaño [ah-pah'-nyo], *m.* 1. The act of seizing or grasping. 2. Cleverness or ability to do a thing. 3. (Prov.) A patch or other way of mending a thing.

Apañuscador, ra [ah-pah-nyoos-cah-dor', rah], *m. & f.* (Coll.) One who crumples a thing.

Apañuscar [ah-pah-nyoos-car'], *va.* (Coll.) To rumple, to crush.

Apapagayado, da [ah-pah-pah-gah-yah'-do, dah], *a.* Parrot-like; very often applied to the nose.

Aparador [ah-pah-rah-dor'], *m.* 1. Sideboard; dresser. 2. Side-table in churches for the service of the altar. 3. Workshop of an artisan. 4. Plate-rack. *Estar de aparador*, (Coll.) To be decked out or dressed in style.

Aparadura [ah-pah-rah-doo'-rah], *f* (Naut.) Garbel, garboard-plank.

Aparar [ah-pah-rar'], *va.* 1. To stretch out the hands or skirts for catching any thing. 2. To heap the earth round plants. 3. Among shoemakers, to close the quarters of a shoe. 4. To dress with an adze, dub. *Aparar un navío*, (Naut.) To dub a ship.

Aparasolado, da [ah-pah-rah-so-lah'-do, dah], *a.* (Bot.) Umbelliferous.

Aparato [ah-pah-rah'-to], *m.* 1. Apparatus, preparation, disposition. 2. Pomp, ostentation, show. 3. Circumstance or token which precedes or accompanies something. *Hay aparatos de llover*, It looks as if it were going to rain. *El mal viene con aparatos de ser grave* or *con malos aparatos*, The disease is attended with indications of danger. *El aparato de una mesa*, The covering of a table. 4. Appliance, engine, machine. 5. Collection of instruments for a surgical operation.

Aparatoso, sa [ah-pah-rah-to'-so, sah], *a.* (Ant.) Pompous, showy, ushered in with great preparations.

Aparcamiento [ah-par-ca-me-en'-to], *m.* 1. Parking. 2. Parking lot. *Aparcamiento subterráneo*, Underground garage.

Aparcar [ah-par-car'], *va.* To park.

Aparcería [ah-par-thay-ree'-ah], *f.* Partnership.

Aparcero [ah-par-thay'-ro], *m.* 1. Partner in a farm. 2. An associate in general.

Aparear [ah-pah-ray-ar'], *va.* To match, to mate, to suit one thing to another. —*vr.* To be coupled in pairs.

Aparecer [ah-pah-ray-therr'], *vn.* & *vr.* To appear unexpectedly, to go forth, to come up.

Aparecido [ah-pah-ray-thee'-do], *m.* Ghost.—*Aparecido, da, pp.* of APARECER.

Aparecimiento [ah-pah-ray-the-me-en'-to], *m.* An apparition, appearing.

Aparejado, da [ah-pah-ray-hah'-do, dah], *a.* Prepared, fit, ready.—*pp.* of APAREJAR.

Aparejador, ra [ah-pah-ray-hah-dor', rah], *m.* & *f.* 1. One who prepares or gets ready. 2. Overseer of a building. 3. (Naut.) Rigger.

Aparejar [ah-pah-ray-har'], *va.* 1. To get ready. 2. To saddle or harness horses. 3. (Naut.) To rig a ship, to furnish. 4. To prepare the work which is to be painted or gilded. 5. To prepare the timber and stones for a building.—*vr.* To get ready, to equip.

Aparejo [ah-pah-ray'-ho], *m.* 1. Preparation, disposition. 2. Harness, gear. 3. (Pict.) Sizing of a piece of linen or board. 4. (Naut.) Tackle and rigging on a ship, furniture. *Aparejo de amante y estrella*, Runner and tackle. *Aparejo de amura*, Tack-tackle. *Aparejo de bolinear*, Bow-line tackle. *Aparejo de combés*, Luff-tackle. *Aparejo de estrelleras de combés*, Winding-tackle. *Aparejo de estrique*, Garnet, a tackle wherewith goods are hoisted in and out of the hold. *Aparejo de peñol*, Yard-tackle. *Aparejo de pescante*, Fish-tackle. *Aparejo de polea*, Burton, a small tackle used in hoisting things in and out of a ship. *Aparejo real*, Main-tackle. *Aparejo de virador*, Top-tackle. *Aparejo de rolin*, Rolling-tackle. *Aparejo del tercio de las vergas mayores*, Quarter-tackle. 5. Pack-saddle. *V.* ALBARDA.—*pl.* 1. The apparatus, tools, or instruments necessary for a trade. 2. (Art) The materials necessary for priming, burnishing, and gilding.

Aparejuelo [ah-pah-ray-hoo-ay'-lo], *m. dim.* A small apparatus. *Aparejuelos*, (Naut.) Small-tackle. *Aparejuelos de portas*, Port-tackle.

Aparentado, da [ah-pah-ren-tah'-do, dah], *a.* (Obs.) Related, allied.—*pp.* of APARENTAR.

Aparentar [ah-pah-ren-tar'], *va.* To make a false show. *El rico aparenta pobreza y el vicioso virtud*, The rich man affects poverty, and the vicious virtue.

Aparente [ah-pah-ren'-tay], *a.* 1. Apparent, not real, flashy. 2. Convenient, seasonable, fit, suited. 3. Conspicuous, evident.

Aparentemente [ah-pah-ren-tay-men'-tay], *adv.* Apparently, outwardly.

Aparición [ah-pah-re-the-on'], *f.* Apparition, act of appearing.

Apariencia [ah-pah-re-en'-the-ah], *f.* 1. Appearance, outside. 2. Face, likeness, resemblance. 3. Vestige. 4. Pageant. 5. (Obs.) Probability, conjecture. *Caballo de apariencia*, A stately horse.—*pl.* 1. Phenomena discovered by astronomical observations. 2. Decorations of the stage.

Aparrado, da [ah-par-rah'-do, dah], *a.* Crooked, or like vines, shrubby: applied to trees and plants.

Aparroquiado, da [ah-par-ro-ke-ah'-do, dah], *a.* Belonging to a parish, parishioner.—*pp.* of APARROQUIAR.

Aparroquiar [ah-par-ro-ke-ar'], *va.* To bring or attract customers.

Apartación [ah-par-tah-the-on'], *f.* (Chem.) Separation of some one or more of the component parts of a body.

Apartadamente, *adv.* Privately, apart.

Apartadero [ah-par-tah-day'-ro], *m.* 1. Parting-place, cross-roads, cross-way, side-track, siding, railroad switch; shunting. 2. A turn-out; widened space, in canals. 3. A sorting-room for wool or other materials.

Apartadijo [ah-par-tah-dee'-ho], *m.* A small part, share, or portion. *Hacer apartadijos*, To divide a whole into shares.

Apartadizo [ah-par-tah-dee'-tho], *m.* A small room, separated or taken from another apartment.

Apartado, da [ah-par-tah'-do, dah], *a.* 1. Separated. 2. Distant, retired. 3. Distinct, different.—*pp.* of APARTAR.

Apartado [ah-par-tah'-do], *m.* 1. Post-office box. 2. A room separate from the rest of the house. 3. A smelting house.

Apartador, ra [ah-par-tah-dor', rah], *m.* & *f.* 1. One who divides or separates. 2. A sorter in paper-mills. *Apartador de ganado*, One who steals sheep or cattle. *Apartador de metales*, Smelter, one who smelts ores.

Apartamiento [ah-par-tah-me-en'-to], *m.* 1. Apartment. *Apartamiento amueblado*, Furnished apartment. 2. Separation, withdrawal.

Apartar [ah-par-tar'], *va.* 1. To part, to separate, to divide. 2. To dissuade one. 3. To remove a thing. 4. To sort letters.—*vr.* 1. To withdraw from a place; to hold off. 2. To be divorced. 3. To desist from a claim, action, or plea. 4. *va.* & *vr. Apartar*, or *apartarse del derecho*, To cancel any claim or right.

Aparte [ah-par'-tay], *m.* 1. Break in a line, space marking a paragraph. 2. (Theat.) An aside.

Aparte [ah-par'-tay], *adv.* 1. Apart, separately. 2. Aside on the stage.

Aparvar [ah-par-var'], *va.* 1. To arrange the corn for being thrashed. 2. To heap, to throw together.

Apasionadamente [ah-pah-se-o-nah-dah-men'-tay], *adv.* Passionately.

Apasionado, da [ah-pah-se-o-nah'-do, dah], *a.* 1. Passionate. 2. Affected with pain. 3. Devoted to a person or thing.—*pp.* of APASIONAR.—*m.* Admirer.

Apasionamiento [ah-pah-se-o-nah-mee-en'-to], *m.* Passion, intense emotion, vehemence.

Apasionante [ah-pah-se-o-nahn'-tay], *a.* Exciting. *Una novela apasionante*, A thrilling, exciting novel.

Apasionar [ah-pah-se-o-nar'], *va.* To inspire a passion.—*vr.* To be taken with a person or thing to excess *Apasionarse de*, To dote upon.

Apasturar [ah-pas-too-rar'], *va.* To pasture, to forage.

Apatáu [ah-pah-tahn'], *m.* A dry measure in the Philippine Islands, .094 l.

Apatía [ah-pah-tee'-ah], *f.* Apathy.

Apático, ca [ah-pah'-te-co, cah], *a.* Apathetic, indifferent.

Apatusco [ah-pah-toos'-co], *m.* 1. (Coll.) Ornament, dress. 2. A thing done with precipitation and confusion.

Apazote [ah-pah-tho'-tay], *m.* (Mex. *Epasote*) (Bot.) American basil. Ocimum americanum.

Apea [ah-pay'-ah], *f.* A rope with which the fore feet of horses are fettered.

Apeadero [ah-pay-ah-day'-ro], *m.* An alighting-place; hence: 1, a horse block. 2. A small railway station.

Apeador [ah-pay-ah-dor'], *m.* A land surveyor.

Apeamiento [ah-pay-ah-me-en'-to], *m.* *V.* APEO.

Apear [ah-pay-ar'], *va.* 1. To alight from a horse, or carriage. 2. To measure lands, tenements, or buildings; to set landmarks. 3. To block or scotch a wheel. 4. To prop a building. 5. (Arch.) To take a thing down from its place: to prop, stay, or shore a building, while alterations are in progress. 6. (Met.) To dissuade. 7. (Met.) To remove difficulties. *Apear el río*, To wade or ford a river. *Apear una caballería*, To shackle a horse or mule.—*vr.* To alight. *Apearse por la cola* or *por las orejas*, To give some absurd answer.

Apechugar [ah-pay-choo-gar'], *va.* 1. To push with the breast. 2. (Met.) To undertake a thing with spirit and boldness, without consideration.

Apedazar [ah-pay-dah-thar'], *va.* 1. To patch, to mend, to repair. 2. *V.* DESPEDAZAR.

Apedernalado, da [ah-pay-der-nah-lah' do, dah], *a.* Flinty.

Apedrar [ah-pay-drar'], *va.* (Obs.) *V.* APEDREAR.

Apedreadero [ah-pay-dray-ah-day'-ro], *m.* A place where boys assemble to throw stones at each other.

Apedreado, da [ah-pay-dray-ah'-do, dah], *a.* 1. Stoned, pelted. 2. *Cara apedreada*, A face pitted with the small-pox.—*pp.* of APEDREAR.

Apedreador [ah-pay-dray-ah-dor'], *m.* One who throws stones.

Apedreamiento [ah-pay-dray-ah-me-en'-to], *m.* Lapidation.

Apedrear [ah-pay-dray-ar'], *va.* To stone; to kill with stones.—*vn.* 1. To hail. 2. (Met.) To talk in a rude manner.—*vr.* To be injured by hail.

Apedreo [ah-pay-dray'-o], *m.* A stoning.

Apegadamente [ah-pay-gah-dah-men'-tay], *adv.* Studiously, devotedly.

Apegamiento [ah-pay-gah-me-en'-to], *m.* (Obs.) 1. Adhesion. 2. *V.* APEGO.

Apegarse [ah-pay-gar'-say], *vr.* 1. To abide by. 2. To become attached (to).

Apego [ah-pay'-go], *m.* Attachment, fondness.

Apelable [ah-pay-lah'-blay], *a.* Appealable, subject to appeal.

Apelación [ah-pay-lah-the-on'], *f.* Appeal from an inferior to a superior court. *Médico de apelación*, A physician whose advice is taken in dangerous cases. *No haber* or *no tener apelación*, To be despaired of.

Apelado, da [ah-pay-lah'-do, dah], *a.* Of the same coat or colour; applied to mules or horses.—*pp.* of APELAR.
Apelambrar [ah-pay-lam-brar'], *va.* To steep skins or hides in vats filled with lime-water.
Apelante [ah-pay-lahn'-tay], *pa.* Appellant.
Apelar [ah-pay-lar'], *vn.* 1. To appeal, to transfer a cause from an inferior to a superior court. 2. To have recourse to, to seek remedy. 3. To be of the same colour. *Apelar un tiro de caballos de coche,* To match a set of coach horses. *Apelar el enfermo,* To escape from the jaws of death in a fit of sickness.
Apelativo [ah-pay-lah-tee'-vo], *a.* (Gram.) *Nombre apelativo,* An appellative name, which belongs to a class of beings.
Apeldar [ah-pel-dar'], *vn.* (Coll.) To flee, to set off, to run away, used generally with *las.*
Apelde [ah-pel'-day], *m.* (Coll.) 1. Flight, escape. 2. The first ringing of a bell before daybreak in convents of the Franciscan order.
Apellar [ah-pel-lyar'], *va.* To dress leather; prepare for receiving any colour.
Apellidado, da [ah-pel-lye-dah'-do, dah], *a.* Named.—*pp.* of APELLIDAR.
Apellidamiento [ah-pel-lye-dah-me-en'-to], *m.* The act of giving a name.
Apellidar [ah-pel-lye-dar'], *va.* 1. To call one by his name. 2. To proclaim, to raise shouts. 3. (Obs.) To convene; assemble troops.
Apellido [ah-pel-lyee'-do], *m.* 1. Surname. 2. A peculiar name given to things. 3. A nickname; epithet. 4. (Obs.) The assembling of troops.
Apelmazar [ah-pel-mah-thar'], *va.* 1. To compress, to render less spongy. 2. (Amer.) To be lazy, sluggish.
Apelotonar [ah-pay-lo-to-nar'], *va.* & *r.* To form balls.
Apenar [ah-pay-nar'], *va.* & *vr.* 1. To grieve. 2. To become embarrassed.
Apenas [ah-pay'-nas], *adv.* 1. Scarcely, hardly; with a deal of trouble. 2. No sooner than, as soon as.
Apencar [ah-pen-car'], *vn.* To accept with repugnance.
Apéndice [ah-pen'-de-thay], *m.* Appendix, supplement.
Apendicitis [ah-pen-de-thee'-tis], *f.* (Med.) Appendicitis.
Apenino, na [ah-pay-nee'-no, nah], *a.* Apennine.
Apeo [ah-pay'-o], *m.* 1. Survey, mensuration of lands or buildings. 2. Props, stays, etc., put under the upper parts of a building, while the lower are repaired.
Apeonar [ah-pay-o-nar'], *va.* To walk or run swiftly; used of birds.
Apepsia [ah-pep'-se-ah], *f.* (Med.) Apepsy, indigestion.
Aperador [ah-pay-rah-dor'], *m.* 1. A farmer. 2. A wheelwright.
Aperar [ah-pay-rar'], *va.* To carry on the trade of a wheelwright.
Apercibimiento [ah-per-the-be-me-en'-to], *m.* 1. The act of providing or getting ready. 2. Arrangement. 3. Order, advice, warning. 4. Summons.
Apercibir [ah-per-the-beer'], *va.* 1. To provide, to get ready. 2. To warn, to advise. 3. (Law) To summon.
(*Yo apercibo, yo apercibí,* from *Apercibir. V.* PEDIR.)
Aperción [ah-per-the-on'], *f.* Act of opening. *V.* ABERTURA.
Apercollar [ah-per-col-lyar'], *va.* 1. (Coll.) To seize one by the collar 2. (Met.) To snatch away a thing by stealth. 3. (Coll.) To assassinate.
Aperdigado, da [ah-per-de-gah'-do, dah], *a.* 1. Broiled, toasted. 2. Condemned and burned by the Inquisition; by way of derision.—*pp.* of APERDIGAR.
Aperdigar [ah-per-de-gar'], *va. V.* PERDIGAR.
Apergaminado, da [ah-per-gah-me-nah'-do, dah], *a.* Dry and yellow like parchment.
Aperitivo, va [ah-pay-re-tee'-vo, vah], *a.* Aperitive, that which has the power of opening.
Apernador [ah-per-nah-dor'], *m.* A dog which seizes the game by the legs or hams.
Apernar [ah-per-nar'], *va.* To seize by the ham.
Apero [ah-pay'-ro], *m.* 1. The implements used on a farm. 2. The tools necessary for a trade. 3. A sheepfold.
Aperreado, da [ah-per-ray-ah'-do, dah], *a.* Harassed. *Andar aperreado,* To be harassed or fatigued.—*pp.* of APERREAR.
Aperreador, ra [ah-per-ray-ah-dor', rah], *m.* & *f.* (Coll.) One that is importunate, an intruder.
Aperrear [ah-per-ray-ar'], *va.* To throw one to the dogs.—*vr.* To toil and beat about; to overwork one's self.
Apersonarse [ah-per-so-nar'-say], *vr.* 1. (Law) *V.* COMPARECER. 2. (Obs.) To appear genteel.
Apertura [ah-per-too'-rah], *f. V.* ABERTURA. The calling to order of assemblies, corporations, etc.
Apesadumbrado, da [ah-pay-sah-doom-brah'-do, dah], *a.* Anxious, vexed, mournful.—*pp.* of APESADUMBRAR.
Apesadumbrar [ah-pay-sah-doom-brar'], *va.* To vex, to cause affliction.—*vr.* To grieve.
Apesaradamente [ah-pay-sah-rah-dah-men'-tay], *adv.* Mournfully, grievously.
Apesarar [ah-pay-sah-rar'], *va. V.* APESADUMBRAR.
Apesgamiento [ah-pes-gah-me-en'-to], *m.* The act of sinking under a burden.
Apesgar [ah-pes-gar'], *va.* To overload, to sink under a load.—*vr.* To grow dull; to be aggrieved.
Apestado, da [ah-pes-tah'-do, dah], *a.* Pestered, annoyed. *Estar apestado de alguna cosa,* To have plenty of a thing, even to loathing and satiety. *La plaza está apestada de verduras,* The market-place is full of greens.—*pp.* of APESTAR.
Apestar [ah-pes-tar'], *va.* 1. To infect with the plague. 2. To cause an offensive smell. In this sense it is commonly used as a neuter verb in the third person; e. g. *Aquí apesta,* There is here an offensive smell. 3. (Met.) To corrupt, to turn putrid. 4. To pester, to cause displeasure, nauseate. *Fulano me apesta con su afectación,* He sickens me with his affectation.
Apestoso, sa [ah-pes-to'-so, sah], *a.* Foul-smelling, sickening, nauseating.
Apétalo, la [ah-pay'-tah-lo, lah], *a.* (Bot.) Apetalous, without flower-leaves.
Apetecedor, ra [ah-pay-tay-thay-dor' rah], *m.* & *f.* One who longs for a thing.
Apetecer [ah-pay-tay-therr'], *va.* To long for a thing, to crave.
Apetecible [ah-pay-tay-thee'-blay], *a.* Desirable, worthy of being wished for.
Apetencia [ah-pay-ten'-the-ah], *f.* 1. Appetite, hunger. 2. Natural desire of something.
(*Yo apetezco,* from *Apetecer. V.* ABORRECER.)
Apetite [ah-pay-tee'-tay], *m.* Sauce.
Apetitivo, va [ah-pay-te-tee'-vo, vah], *a.* Appetitive, that does desire.
Apetito [ah-pay-tee'-to], *m.* 1. Appetite, the natural desire for food. 2. Keenness of stomach; hunger. 3. That which excites desire.
Apetitoso, sa [ah-pay-te-to'-so, sah], *a.* 1. Pleasing to the taste, tempting the appetite. 2. (Obs.) Pursuing sensual pleasures.
Apezuñar [ah-pay-thoo-nyar'], *vn.* To tread firm on the hoof.
Apiadador, ra [ah-pe-ah-dah-dor', rah], *m.* & *f.* One who pities.
Apiadarse [ah-pe-ah-dar'-say], *vr.* To pity, to treat with compassion.
Apiaradero [ah-pe-ah-ra-day'-ro], *m.* A shepherd's account of the number of sheep which compose his flock.
Apiario, a [ah-pe-ah'-re-o, ah], *a.* Resembling or relating to the honey-bee.
Apicarado, da [ah-pe-cah-rah'-do, dah], *a.* Roguish, knavish, impudent.
Apicararse [ah-pe-cah-rar'-say], *vr.* To acquire the manners of a rogue.
Ápice [ah'-pe-thay], *m.* 1. Apex, summit, utmost height. 2. The upper part of a thing. 3. (Met.) The most intricate or most arduous point of a question. *Ápices,* Anthers of flowers. *Estar en los ápices,* To have a complete and minute knowledge of a thing.
Apiculado, da [ah-pe-coo-lah'-do, dah], *a.* Apiculate; sharp-pointed.
Apículo [ah-pee'-coo-lo], *m.* A small, keen point.
Apicultura [ah-pe-cool-too'-rah], *f.* Apiculture, raising of bees.
Apilador [ah-pe-lah-dor'], *m.* One who piles the wool up at the sheep-shearing time.
Apilar [ah-pe-lar'], *va.* To heap up, to put one thing upon another.
Apimpollarse [ah-pim-pol-lyar'-say], *vr.* To germinate.
Apiñado, da [ah-pe-nyah-do', dah], *a.* Pyramidal, pine-shaped.—*pp.* of APIÑAR.
Apiñadura [ah-pe-nyah-doo'-rah], *f.*
Apiñamiento [ah-pe-nyah-me-en'-to], *m.* The act of pressing together.
Apiñar [ah-pe-nyar'], *va.* To press together, to join, to unite.—*vr.* To clog, to crowd.
Apio [ah'-pe-o], *m.* (Bot.) Celery. Apium graveolens. *Apio montano* or *levístico,* (Bot.) Common lovage. Ligusticum levisticum. *Apio de risa,* (Bot.) Crow-foot. Ranunculus scelerratus.
Apiolar [ah-pe-o-lar'], *va.* 1. To gyve a hawk. 2. To tie game together by the leg. 3. (Met. Coll.) To seize, to apprehend. 4. (Coll.) To kill, to murder.
Apirético, ca [ah-pe-ray'-te-co, cah], *a.* Apyretic, free from the access of fever.
Apisonadora [ah-pe-so-nah-do'-rah], *f.* Steam roller.
Apisonar [ah-pe-so-nar'], *va.* 1. To roll. 2. To tamp, to drive down.
Apitonamiento [ah-pe-to-nah-me-en'-to], *m.* 1. Putting forth the tenderlings. 2. Passion, anger.
Apitonar [ah-pe-to-nar'], *vn.* 1. To put forth the tenderlings; applied to horned animals. 2. To bud, to germ. —*va.* To pick as chickens in the egg-shell.—*vr.* To treat with abusive language.
Apizarrado, da [ah-pe-thar-rah'-do, dah], *a.* Slate-coloured.
Aplacable [ah-plah-cah'-blay], *a.* Placable, easy to be appeased, meek, gentle.
Aplacación [ah-plah-cah-the-on'], *f.*
Aplacamiento [ah-plah-cah-me-en'-to], *m.* Appeasableness.—*m.* Stay of execution.

Aplacador, ra [ah-plah-cah-dor', rah], *m.* & *f.* One who appeases.

Aplacar [ah-plah-car'], *va.* To appease, to pacify, to mitigate.

(*Me aplace, que aplegue,* from *Aplacer. V.* PLACER.)

Aplacer [ah-plah-therr'], *va.* To please. *V.* AGRADAR.

Aplacerado, da [ah-plah-thay-rah'-do, dah], *a.* 1. (Naut.) Level and not very deep: said of the bottom of the sea. 2. (Amer.) Open, cleared of trees. *Sitio aplacerado,* A clearing (fr. Plaza).

Aplacible [ah-plah-thee'-blay], *a.* Pleasant.

Aplaciente [ah-plah-the-en'-tay], *pa.* Appeasive.

Aplanadera [ah-plah-nah-day'-rah], *f.* 1. A roller for levelling the ground. 2. Beetle, rammer.

Aplanador [ah-plah-nah-dor'], *m.* 1. A leveller. 2. (Mec.) Battledoor, brusher, riveter; ingot hammer; cylinder roller. 3. (Typ.) Planer, planishing mallet.

Aplanamiento [ah-plah-nah-me-en'-to], *m.* Levelling, the act of making level.

Aplanar [ah-plah-nar'], *va.* 1. To level, to make even, to flatten. 2. To terrify, or astonish by some unexpected novelty.—*vr.* 1. To tumble down; applied to a building. 2. To lose animation or vigour.

Aplanático, ca [ah-plah-nah'-te-co, cah], *a.* Aplanatic, free of spherical aberration.

Aplanchado [ah-plan-chah'-do], *m.* 1. Linen which is to be, or has been ironed. 2. Act of smoothing or ironing linen.

Aplanchadora [ah-plan-chah-do'-rah], *f.* A woman whose trade it is to iron linen.

Aplanchar [ah-plan-char'], *va.* To iron linen.

Aplantillar [ah-plan-teel-lyar'], *va.* To adjust or fit stones, timber, or boards, according to the model.

Aplastado, da [ah-plas-tah'-do, dah], *a.* Caked; dispirited.—*pp.* of APLASTAR.

Aplastar [ah-plas-tar'], *va.* 1. To cake, to flatten, or crush a thing, to smash. 2. To confound an opponent.—*vr.* To become flat.

Aplaudir [ah-plah-oo-deer'], *va.* 1. To applaud, to extol with shouts. 2. *Aplaudirse, vr.* To boast of, to be elated by.

Aplauso [ah-plah'-oo-so], *m.* Applause, approbation, praise.

Aplayar [ah-plah-yar'], *vr.* To overflow the banks.

Aplazamiento [ah-plah-thah-me-en'-to], *m.* 1. Convocation, citation. 2. Deferring, postponement.

Aplazar [ah-plah-thar'], *va.* 1. To convene. 2. To invest. 3. To concert, to regulate, to summon. 4. To defer, adjourn, a matter; to treat it later.

Aplebeyar [ah-play-bay-yar'], *va.* (Obs.) To render vile or servile.

Aplegar [ah-play-gar'], *va.* (Prov.) To join, to unite.

Aplicable [ah-ple-cah'-blay], *a.* Applicable.

Aplicación [ah-ple-cah-the-on'], *f.* 1. Application. 2. Assiduity, laboriousness, close study. *Aplicación de bienes* or *hacienda,* The act of adjudging estates or other property.

Aplicado, da [ah-ple-cah'-do, dah], *a.* 1. Studious, intent on a thing. 2. Industrious, laborious, painful.—*pp.* of APLICAR.

Aplicar [ah-ple-car'], *va.* 1. To apply, to put one thing to another; to clap. 2. (Met.) To consider a subject under discussion. 3. (Met.) To attribute or impute. 4. (Law) To adjudge. —*vr.* 1. To study or devote one's self to a thing. 2. To earn a living.

Aplomado, da [ah-plo-mah'-do, dah], *a.* 1. Of the colour of lead. 2. Leaden. 3. (Met.) Heavy, dull, lazy.—*pp.* of APLOMAR.

Aplomar [ah-plo-mar'], *va.* (Obs.) To overload, to crush.—*vn.* To use a plummet and line to see if a wall has been perpendicularly raised.—*vr.* To tumble, to fall to the ground: applied to buildings.

Aplomo [ah-plo'-mo], *m.* 1. Tact, prudence, management, self-possession. 2. Plumb-line, plummet. 3. (Mus.) Exactness in time. 4. Due proportion among the figures of a picture. —*a.* Plumb, perpendicular. *V.* (*á*) PLOMO.

Apnea [ap-nay'-ah], *f.* Want of respiration.

Ápoca [ab'-po-cah], *f.* (Law. Prov.) Receipt, acquittance, discharge.

Apocado, da [ah-po-cah'-do, dah], *a.* 1. Pusillanimous, mean-spirited, cowardly. 2. Narrow-hoofed. 3. Of mean, low extraction.—*pp.* of APOCAR.

Apocador, ra [ah-po-cah-dor', rah], *m.* & *f.* One who lessens or diminishes.

Apocalipsi, Apocalipsis [ah-po-cah-leep'-se, sis], *m.* Apocalypse, the Revelation of St. John.

Apocalíptico, ca [ah-po-cah-leep'-te-co, cah], *a.* Apocalyptical.

Apocamiento [ah-po-cah-me-en'-to], *m.* Abjectness of mind, meanness of spirit, littleness.

Apocar [ah-po-car'], *va.* 1. To lessen. 2. (Met.) To cramp, to contract.—*vr.* To humble one's self, to undervalue one's self.

Apócema, Apócima [ah-po'-thay-mah, ah-po'-the-mah], *f.* (Med.) Apozem, a decoction.

Apocopar [ah-po-co-par'], *va.* To take away the last letter or syllable of a word.

Apócope [ah-po'-co-pay], *f.* (Poet.) A figure, where the last letter or syllable of a word is taken away.

Apócrifamente [ah-po'-cre-fah-men-tay], *adv.* Apocryphally, uncertainly, on a false foundation.

Apócrifo, fa [ah-po'-cre-fo, fah], *a.* Apocryphal, fabulous, of doubtful authority.

Apocrisiario [ah-po-cre-se-ah'-re-o], *m.* A Greek ambassador.

Apodador [ah-po-dah-dor'], *m.* A wag, one who ridicules or scoffs.

Apodar [ah-po-dar'], *va.* To give nicknames, to ridicule.

Apodencado, da [ah-po-den-cah'-do, dah], *a.* Pointer-like.

Apoderado, da [ah-po-day-rah'-do, dah], *a.* 1. Empowered, authorized. 2. (Obs.) Powerful.—*pp.* of APODERAR.

Apoderado [ah-po-day-rah'-do], *m.* Proxy, attorney, agent.

Apoderar [ah-po-day-rar'], *va.* To empower; to grant a power of attorney. —*vr.* 1. To possess one's self of a thing. 2. (Obs.) To become powerful or strong.

Apodíctico, ca [ah-po-deec'-te-co, cah], *a.* Apodictical, demonstrative.

Apodo [ah-po'-do], *m.* A nickname.

Ápodo, da [ah'-po-do, dah], *a.* (Zool.) Apodous, without feet.

Apódosis [ah-po'-do-sis], *f.* Apodosis, the conclusion of a conditional sentence; correlative to protasis.

Apófise, Apófisis [ah-po'-fe-say, ah-po'-fe-sis], *f.* (Med.) The prominent part of some bones, the same as process.

Apoflegmático, ca [ah-po-fleg-mah'-te-co, cah], *a.* Apophlegmatic, drawing away phlegm.

Apogeo [ah-po-hay'-o], *m.* 1. (Ast.) Apogee. 2. Culmination, apex. *En todo su apogeo,* In all its glory, at its peak.

Apógrafo [ah-po'-grah-fo], *m.* Apograph, transcript, or copy of some book or writing.

Apolillado, da [ah-po-leel-lyah'-do, dah], *a.* Moth-eaten, worm-eaten.—*pp.* of APOLILLAR.

Apolilladura [ah-po-leel-lyah-doo'-rah], *f.* A hole eaten by moths in clothes and other things made of wool.

Apolillar [ah-po-leel'-lyar], *va.* To gnaw or eat clothes, or other things.—*vr.* To be moth-eaten.

Apolinar, Apolíneo, nea [ah-po-le-nar', ah-po-lee'-nay-o, ah], *a.* (Poet.) Belonging to Apollo.

Apolinarista [ah-po-le-nah-rees'-tah], *m.* Apollinarian, name given to the followers of a sect of Christians in the fourth century.

Apologético, ca [ah-po-lo-hay'-te-co, cah], *a.* 1. Apologetic, excusatory. 2. Belonging to an apologue or fable. 3. Applied to the writers of apologues.

Apología [ah-po-lo-hee'-ah], *f.* Apology, defence, excuse.

Apológico, ca [ah-po-lo'-he-co, cah], *a.* That which relates to an apologue.

Apologista [ah-po-lo-hees'-tah], *m.* An apologist.

Apólogo [ah-po'-lo-go], *m.* Apologue, a fable or story, to convey moral truth.

Apoltronarse [ah-pol-tro-nar'-say], *vr.* To grow lazy, to loiter.

Apomazar [ah-po-mah-thar'], *va.* 1. To glaze printed linens with pumice-stone for the purpose of painting on them. 2. To burnish a surface with pumice-stone.

Apomeli [ah-po-may'-le], *f.* A decoction prepared of honey-comb dissolved in vinegar and water.

Aponeurosis [ah-po-nay-oo-ro'-sis], *f.* Aponeurosis, fascia.

Aponeurótico, ca [ah-po-nay-oo-ro'-te-co, cah], *a.* Aponeurotic, fascia-like.

Apoplejía [ah-po-play-hee'-ah], *f.* Apoplexy.

Apoplético, ca [ah-po-play'-te-co, cah], *a.* Apoplectic.

Aporcadura [ah-por-cah-doo'-rah], *f.* The act of raising earth around plants; earthing up.

Aporcar [ah-por-car'], *va.* To cover garden-plants with earth for the purpose of whitening them and making them tender; to hill.

Aporisma [ah-po-rees'-mah], *m.* Ecchymosis, an extravasation of blood between the flesh and skin.

Aporismarse [ah-po-ris-mar'-say], *vr* To become an ecchymosis.

Aporracear [ah-por-rah-thay-ar'], *va.* (Prov.) To pommel, to give repeated blows.

Aporrar [ah-por-rar'], *vn.* (Coll.) To stand mute, when silence may be injurious.—*vr.* (Coll.) To become importunate or troublesome.

Aporreado, da [ah-por-ray-ah'-do, dah] *a.* 1. Cudgelled. 2. Dragged along —*pp.* of APORREAR.

Aporreamiento [ah-por-ray-ah-me-en'to], *m.* The act of beating or pommelling.

Aporreante [ah-por-ray-ahn'-tay], *pa.* (Coll.) Cudgeller, applied to bad fencers.

Aporrear [ah-por-ray-ar'], *va.* To beat or cudgel, to knock, to maul.—*vr.* To study with intense application. *Aporrearse en la jaula,* To engage in fruitless toils, to drudge to no purpose.

Aporreo [ah-por-ray'-o], *m.* The act of beating, pommelling, or cudgelling.

Aporrillarse [ah-por-reel-lyar'-say], *vr.* To get swellings in the joints: a term applied to horses.

Aporrillo [ah-por-reel'-lyo], *adv.* (Coll.) Plentifully.

Aportadera [ah-por-tah-day'-rah], *f.* A sort of chest, in which provisions are carried on a horse or mule.

Aportadero [ah-por-tah-day'-ro], *m.* A place where a ship or person may stop.

Aportar [ah-por-tar'], *vn.* 1. To make a port, to arrive at a port. 2. To reach an unexpected place when one is benighted.

Aportellado [ah-por-tel-lyah'-do], *m.* (Obs.) Formerly an officer of justice, a member of the council of large towns, that administered justice to the people of the neighbouring villages.

Aportillar [ah-por-teel-lyar'], *va.* 1. To make a breach in a rampart. 2. To break down, to break open.—*vr.* To tumble down; to fall into ruins.

Aposentador, ra [ah-po-sen-tah-dor', rah], *m.* & *f.* One who lets lodgings; usher in a theatre. *Aposentador de camino*, An officer of the king's household, who goes before the royal family to provide and prepare for their reception.

Aposentamiento [ah-po-sen-tah-me-en'-to], *m.* The act of lodging or affording a temporary habitation.

Aposentar [ah-po-sen-tar'], *va.* To lodge.—*vr.* To take a lodging; to tarry at night.

Aposentillo [ah-po-sen-teel'-lyo], *m. dim.* A small room, a bed-room.

Aposento [ah-po-sen'-to], *m.* 1. A room or apartment. 2. A temporary habitation; an inn. 3. A box or seat in the play-house. *Casas de aposento*, Houses in Spain which are obliged to lodge persons of the king's household. *Aposento de corte*, The apartment or habitation destined for the king's servants. *Huésped de aposento*, A lodger belonging to the king's household.

Aposesionar [ah-po-say-se-o-nar'], *va.* To give possession.—*vr.* To take possession; to possess one's self of a thing.

Aposición [ah-po-se-the-on'], *f.* (Gram.) Apposition, a grammatical term.

Aposiopesis [ah-po-se-o-pay'-sis], *f.* (Rhet.) A figure of speech, in which the speaker breaks off suddenly, as if unable or unwilling to declare his mind.

Apósito [ah-po'-se-to], *m.* Any external medicinal application.

A pospelo [ah-pos-pay'-lo], *adv.* (Obs.) 1. Against the grain. 2. Contrary to the natural order.

Aposta, Apostadamente [ah-pos'-tah, ah-pos-tah-dah-men'-tay], *adv.* Designedly, on purpose. *V.* Adrede.

Apostadero [ah-pos-tah-day'-ro], *m.* 1. A place where soldiers or other persons are stationed. 2. (Naut.) A naval station.

Apostador [ah-pos-tah-dor'], *m.* Better, one that wagers.

Apostal [ah-pos-tahl'], *m.* (Prov.) A convenient fishing-place in a river.

Apostáleos [ah-pos-tah'-lay-os], *m. pl.* (Naut.) Thick planks for gun platforms.

Apostar [ah-pos-tar'], *va.* 1. To bet, to hold a wager, to lay a bet. 2. To place relays. 3. To post soldiers or other persons in a place. *Apostarlas* or *apostárselas*, To contend; to defy. —*vr.* To emulate, to rival, to stand in competition. *Apostar carreras*, To run races.

Apostasía [ah-pos-tah-see'-ah], *f.* 1. Apostasy. 2. (Bot.) A plant of the orchid family.

Apostasis [ah-pos-tah'-sis], *f.* (Med.) 1. A purulent deposit at a distance from the seat of inflammation; metastatic abscess. 2. A splinter of bone.

Apóstata [ah-pos'-tah-tah], *m.* Apostate; forsaker, fugitive.

Apostatar [ah-pos-tah-tar'], *vn.* To apostatize, to fall away.

Apostema [ah-pos-tay'-mah], *f.* An aposteme, abscess.

Apostemación [ah-pos-tay-mah-the-on'], *f.* (Med.) Forming an abscess, apostemation.

Apostemar [ah-pos-tay-mar'], *va.* To form an abscess.—*vr.* To get an abscess; to be troubled with a purulent humour.

Apostemero [ah-pos-tay-may'-ro], *m.* Bistoury, an instrument for opening abscesses.

Apostemilla [ah-pos-tay-meel'-lyah], *f. dim.* 1. A small abscess or pimple. 2. Gum-boil.

Apostemoso, sa [ah-pos-tay-mo'-so, sah], *a.* Relating to abscesses.

Apostilla [ah-pos-teel'-lyah], *f.* A marginal note put to a book or writing; annotation, remark; gloss.

Apostillar [ah-pos-teel-lyar'], *va.* To put marginal notes to a book or writing.—*vr.* To break out in pimples or pustules.

Apóstol [ah-pos'-tol], *m.* Apostle, missionary. *Apóstoles*, (Naut.) Hawse-pieces.

Apostolado [ah-pos-to-lah'-do], *m.* 1. Apostleship. 2. The congregation of the apostles. 3. The images or pictures of the twelve apostles.

Apostólicamente [ah-pos-to'-le-cah-men-tay], *adv.* Apostolically.

Apostólico, ca [ah-pos-to'-le-co, cah], *a.* 1. Apostolical. 2. Apostolic; that which belongs to the Pope, or derives from him apostolical authority.

Apóstolos [ah-pos'-to-los], *m. pl.* (Law. Obs.) Dimissory apostolical letters.

Apostrofar [ah-pos-tro-far'], *va.* To apostrophize, to address one by apostrophe.

Apóstrofe [ah-pos'-tro-fay], *f.* (Rhet.) Apostrophe.

Apóstrofo [ah-pos'-tro-fo], *m.* Apostrophe, the following typographical sign '—disused in Spanish.

Apostura [ah-pos-too'-rah], *f.* 1. Gentleness, neatness in person. 2. Good order and disposition of things; high breeding.

Apoteca [ah-po-tay'-cah], *f.* *V.* Botica.

Apotecario [ah-po-tay-cah'-re-o], *m.* (Prov.) *V.* Boticario.

Apotegma [ah-po-teg'-mah], *m.* Apothegm; maxim.

Apoteosis [ah-po-tay-oh'-sis], *f.* Apotheosis, deification.

Apotome [ah-po-to'-may], *m.* (Alg.) The remainder or difference of two incommensurable qualities.

Apotrerar [ah-po-tray-rar'], *va.* To turn horses out to pasture.

Apotrosis [ah-po-tro'-sis], *f.* (Surg.) 1. A fracture of the skull, with splinters. 2. Extraction of a splinter of bone.

Apoyadero [ah-po-yah-day'-ro], *m.* Prop, support.

Apoyadura [ah-po-yah-doo'-rah], *f.* A flow of the milk when nurses give suck to children.

Apoyar [ah-po-yar'], *va.* 1. To favour, to protect, to patronize, to abet, to countenance, to further. 2. To bear upon the bit: spoken of horses which hang down their heads. *Apoyar las espuelas*, To spur. 3. To confirm, to prove, to corroborate, to hold up; to ground, to found. *Apoya esta sentencia con un texto de la Escritura*, He confirms this sentence by a text of Scripture. *Apoyar una proposición* or *propuesta*, To second a motion.—*vn.* To rest on; to lie. *La columna apoya sobre el pedestal*, The column rests on the pedestal.—*vr.* To lean upon a person or thing. *Apoyarse en los estribos*, To bear upon the stirrups.

Apoyatura [ah-po-yah-too'-rah], *f.* (Mus.) Appoggiatura, leaning or leading note, used to prepare the ear for, or guide it to, the note it precedes.

Apoyo [ah-po'-yo], *m.* 1. Prop, stay, support, fulcrum. 2. (Met.) Protection, patronage, help, countenance, muniment, maintenance.

Apreciable [ah-pray-the-ah'-blay], *a.* 1. Valuable, respectable, worthy of esteem, creditable. 2. That which can fetch a price; marketable.

Apreciación [ah-pray-the-ah-the-on'], *f.* Estimation, valuation, appreciation.

Apreciadamente [ah-pray-the-ah-dah-men'-tay], *adv.* In a valuable, respectable manner.

Apreciador, ra [ah-pray-the-ah-dor', rah], *m.* & *f.* Estimator, appraiser, a person appointed to set a price upon a thing.

Apreciar [ah-pray-the-ar'], *va.* To appreciate, to appraise, to estimate, to value.

Apreciativo, va [ah-pray-the-ah-tee'-vo, vah], *a.* Relating to the value set upon a thing.

Aprecio [ah-pray'-the-o], *m.* 1. Appraisement, appreciation, the value set upon a thing; account. 2. Esteem, approbation, regard.

Aprehender [ah-pray-en-derr'], *va.* 1. To apprehend, to seize. 2. To fancy, to conceive, to form an idea of a thing. *Aprehender la posesión*, To take possession. *Aprehender los bienes*, To seize or distrain goods.

Aprehensión [ah-pray-en-se-on'], *f.* 1. The act of seizing, apprehending, or taking up a criminal. 2. Apprehension, perception, acuteness; a ready and witty saying. 3. Apprehension, fear. 4. Misapprehension. 5. (Ant.) The act of putting the king's arms or seal on a house, until the rights of the different claimants are discussed, or the true owner appears.

Aprehensivo, va [ah-pray-en-see'-vo, vah], *a.* Apprehensive, quick to understand, fearful; sensitive; perceptive.

Aprehensor, ra [ah-pray-en-sor', rah], *m.* & *f.* One who apprehends.

Aprehensorio, ria [ah-pray-en-so'-re-o, ah], *a.* Apprehending, seizing.

Apremiador, ra [ah-pray-me-ah-dor', rah], *m.* & *f.* Compeller, one who compels to do a thing.

Apremiante [ah-pray-me-ahn'-tay], *a.* Urgent, pressing.—*pa.* of Apremiar.

Apremiar [ah-pray-me-ar'], *va.* 1. To press, to urge. 2. To compel, to oblige by a judicial order.

Apremio [ah-pray'-me-o], *m.* 1. Pressure, constriction; constraint, force. 2. Judicial compulsion.

Aprendedor, ra [ah-pren-day-dor', rah], *a.* Learning; apt to learn.

Aprender [ah-pren-derr'], *va.* 1. To learn; to acquire knowledge. 2. To retain in the memory.

Aprendiz, za [ah-pren-deeth', thah], *m.* & *f.* Apprentice or prentice; learner. *Aprendiz de todo, oficial de nada*, A jack of all trades.

Aprendizaje [ah-pren-de-thah'-hay], *m.*

Apprenticeship, the years which an apprentice is to pass under a master to learn a trade.

Aprensador [ah-pren-sah-dor'], *m.* A presser or calenderer.

Aprensar [ah-pren-sar'], *va.* 1. To dress cloth in a press, to calender. 2. To vex, to crush, to oppress. 3. (Naut.) To stow wool, cotton, etc., on board a ship.

Aprensión [ah-pren-se-on'], *f.* 1. Apprehension. 2. False concept, and unfounded fear which it occasions. 3. Mistrust, suspicion: particularly of one believing himself sick, or in dread of contagion.

Aprensivo, va [ah-pren-see'-vo, vah], *a.* Apprehensive, hypochondriac.

Apresador, ra [ah-pray-sah-dor', rah], *m.* & *f.* 1. Privateer, cruiser. 2. Captor.

Apresamiento [ah-pray-sah-me-en'-to], *m.* Capture; clutch, hold.

Apresar [ah-pray-sar'], *va.* 1. To seize, to grasp. 2. (Naut.) To take or capture an enemy's ship.

Aprestar [ah-pres-tar'], *va.* To prepare, to make ready.

Apresto [ah-press'-to], *m.* Preparation for a thing, accoutrement.

Apresuración [ah-pray-soo-rah-the-on'], *f.* Acceleration, the act of quickening motion, or making haste.

Apresuradamente [ah-pray-soo-rah-dah-men'-tay], *adv.* Hastily, forwardly.

Apresurado, da [ah-pray-soo-rah'-do, dah], *a.* 1. Brief, hasty. 2. Acting with precipitation.—*pp.* of Apresurar.

Apresuramiento [ah-pray-soo-rah-me-en'-to], *m.* Eagerness, readiness to act, forwardness. *V.* Apresuración.

Apresurar [ah-pray-soo-rar'], *va.* To accelerate, to hasten, to hurry, to cut off delay, to forward.—*vr.* To accelerate.

Apretadamente [ah-pray-tah-dah-men'-tay], *adv.* Tightly, closely; nearly; close, fast.

Apretadera [ah-pray-tah-day'-rah], *f.* A strap or rope to tie or bind any thing with. *Apretaderas*, Pressing remonstrances.

Apretadero [ah-pray-tah-day'-ro], *m.* Truss or bandage by which ruptures are restrained from relapsing. *V.* Braguero.

Apretadillo, lla [ah-pray-tah-deel'-lyo, lyah], *a. dim.* Somewhat constrained, rather hard put to it. *Apretadillo está el enfermo*, The patient is in great danger.

Apretadizo, za [ah-pray-tah-dee'-tho, thah], *a.* Easily compressible.

Apretado, da [ah-pray-tah'-do, dah], *a.* 1. Mean, miserable, narrow-minded, illiberal; close, close-fisted; costive. 2. Hard, difficult, dangerous.—*pp.* of Apretar.

Apretador [ah-pray-tah-dor'], *m.* 1. One who presses or beats down. 2. An under-waistcoat without sleeves. 3. A sort of soft stays without whalebone for children, to which the "andadores" are fastened. 4. A broad bandage put upon infants. 5. A net for tying up the hair. 6. An instrument which serves for tightening; a rammer, quoin-wedge.

Apretadura [ah-pray-tah-doo'-rah], *f.* Compression.

Apretamiento [ah-pray-tah-me-en'-to], *m.* 1. Crowd, great concourse of people. 2. Conflict. 3. (Obs.) Avarice, closeness; contractedness.

Apretar [ah-pray-tar'], *va.* 1. To compress, to tighten, to press down, to crowd, to constrict, to contract. 2. To constrain, to clutch. 3. To distress, to afflict with calamities. 4. To act with more vigour than usual. 5. To urge earnestly. 6. To darken that part of a painting which is too bright and glaring. *Apretar de soletas*, To run away. *Apretar con uno*, To attack a person. *Apretar la mano*, To correct with a heavy hand, to punish severely.

Apretón [ah-pray-tone'], *m.* 1. Pressure. 2. Struggle, conflict. 3. A short but rapid race. 4. The act of throwing a thicker shade on one part of a piece of painting.

Apretujar [ah-pray-too-har'], *va.* (Coll.) To squeeze, to crowd in a crowd of persons.

Apretura [ah-pray-too'-rah], *f.* 1. A crowd, a multitude crowding. 2. Distress, conflict, anguish. 3. A narrow, confined place; narrowness.

Apriesa [ah-pre-ay'-sah], *adv.* In haste, in a hurry.

Aprieto [ah-pre-ay'-to], *m.* Difficulty, pinch, pressure, stress. *Estar en un aprieto*, To be in a jam, to be in a tight position, under stress.

Aprisa [ah-pree'-sah], *adv.* Swiftly, promptly; fast; in a hurry.

Aprisar [ah-pre-sar'], *va.* (Obs.) To hasten, to hurry, to push forward.

Apriscadero [ah-pris-cah-day'-ro], *m.* (Obs.) *V.* Aprisco.

Apriscar [ah-pris-car'], *va.* To carry to the sheep-fold, to a sure spot.

Aprisco [ah-prees'-co], *m.* Sheep-fold.

Aprisionar [ah-pre-se-o-nar'], *va.* 1. To confine, to imprison. 2. To bind, to subject.

Aproar [ah-pro-ar'], *vn.* (Naut.) To turn the head of a ship toward any part; to trim by the head.

Aprobación [ah-pro-bah-the-on'], *f.* Approbation, concurrence; consent, liking; run.

Aprobado, da [ah-pro-bah'-do, dah], *a.* 1. Approved. 2. Passed (in an examination).—*m.* Passing mark.

Aprobador, ra [ah-pro-bah-dor', rah], *m.* & *f.* Approver, one who approves.

Aprobante [ah-pro-bahn'-tay], *pa.* 1. Approver. 2. One who proves the qualifications of a person for being a member of some corporations.

Aprobar [ah-pro-bar'], *va.* To approve; to like, to be pleased with; to find.

Aprobatorio, ria [ah-pro-bah-to'-re-o, re-ah], *a.* Approbative, approving.

Aproches [ah-pro'-ches], *m. pl.* (Mil.) Approaches, the several works made by besiegers for advancing and getting nearer to a fortress. *Contraaproches*, Counter-approaches. *Las trincheras se llaman líneas de aproches*, The trenches are called lines of approach. (F.)

Aprón [ah-prone'], *m.* (Zool.) A small fresh-water fish resembling a gudgeon.

Aprontar [ah-pron-tar'], *va.* To prepare hastily, to get ready with despatch.

Apronto [ah-pron'-to], *m.* A speedy preparation.

Apropiación [ah-pro-pe-ah-the-on'], *f.* Appropriation, assumption, the act of appropriating or assuming a thing.

Apropiadamente [ah-pro-pe-ah-dah-men'-tay], *adv.* Conveniently, fitly, properly.

Apropiado, da [ah-pro-pe-ah'-do, dah], *a.* Appropriate, fit; official.—*pp.* of Apropiar.

Apropiador [ah-pro-pe-ah-dor'], *m.* Appropriator.

Apropiar [ah-pro-pe-ar'], *va.* 1. To appropriate, to assume. 2. To bring to a resemblance. 3. To accommodate, to apply.—*vr.* To appropriate any thing to one's self, to encroach.

Apropincuación [ah-pro-pin-coo-ah-the-on'], *f.* Approach.

Aprovechable [ah-proh-vay-chah'-blay], *a.* Profitable, useful, or serviceable.

Aprovechado, da [ah-pro-vay-chah'-do, dah], *a.* 1. Improved; taken advantage of. 2. Sparing, parsimonious.—*pp.* of Aprovechar.

Aprovechamiento [ah-pro-vay-chah-me-en'-to], *m.* 1. Profit, utility, advantage. 2. Progress made in an art or science; growth. 3. Lands, commons, houses, etc., belonging to a town or city. *V.* Propios.

Aprovechar [ah-pro-vay-char'], *vn.* To make progress, to become useful, to come forward, to get forward.—*va.* 1. To profit by a thing, to employ it usefully. 2. (Obs.) To protect, to favour. 3. (Obs.) To meliorate.—*vr.* To avail one's self of a thing.

Aproximación [ah-proc-se-mah-the-on'], *f.* Approximation.

Aproximadamente [ah-proc-se-mah-dah-men'-tay], *adv.* Nearly, about.

Aproximar [ah-proc-se-mar'], *va.* To approximate, to approach.

Aproximativo, va [ah-proc-se-mah-tee'-vo, vah], *a.* (Littl. us.) That which approaches to any thing.

(*Yo apruebo, yo apruebe*, from *Aprobar*. *V.* Acordar.)

Apside [ahp'-se-day], *m.* (Astr.) The extremities of the major axis of the orbit of a star. Most used in plural.

Aptamente [ap-tah-men'-tay], *adv.* Conveniently, fitly, commodiously, expediently.

Áptero, ra [ahp'-tay-ro, rah], *a.* (Ent.) Apterous: applied to insects.

Aptitud [ap-te-tood'], *f.* 1. Aptitude or fitness for an employment; ability. 2. Expediency; meetness.

Apto, ta [ahp'-to, tah], *a.* Apt, fit; competent, clever, congruous; good, convenient; meet.

(*Yo apuerco, yo apuerque*, from *Aporcar*. *V.* Acordar.)

Apuesta [ah-poo-ess'-tah], *f.* A bet, a wager. *Ir de apuesta*, To undertake the performance of a thing in competition with others.

Apuesto, ta [ah-poo-ess'-to, tah], *a.* 1. Elegant, genteel. 2. (Obs.) Opportune, fit.

(*Yo apuesto, yo apueste*, from *Apostar*. *V.* Acordar.)

Apuesto [ah-poo-ess'-to], *m.* (Obs.) Epithet, title. *V.* Apostura.

Apulgarar [ah-pool-gah-rar'], *va.* To force with the thumb.—*vr.* (Coll.) To contract black spots from having been doubled up when moist: spoken of linen.

Apunchar [ah-poon-char'], *va.* Among comb-makers, to cut out the teeth of a comb.

Apuntación [ah-poon-tah-the-on'], *f.* 1. Annotation, the act of noting down; memorial. 2. The act of marking musical notes with exactness.

Apuntado, da [ah-poon-tah'-do, dah], *a.* 1. Pointed, marked. 2. *El cañón está apuntado muy bajo*, (Gunn. and Naut.) The gun dips.—*pp.* of Apuntar.

Apuntador [ah-poon-tah-dor'], *m.* 1. Observer, one who notes or marks. 2. (Naut.) Gunner, who points the guns. *Apuntador de comedias*, A prompter to the players. *Apuntador electrónico*, Teleprompter.

Apuntalamiento [ah-poon-tah-lah-me-en'-to], *m.* Propping, pinning. *Apuntalamiento por la base*, Underpinning.

Apuntalar [ah-poon-tah-lar'], *va.* 1. To prop, to support with props. 2. (Naut.) To shore a vessel.

Apuntamiento [ah-poon-tah-me-en'-to], *m.* 1. Remark. 2. Abstract, summary, heads of a law-suit pointed out by the report in a court of justice: a judicial report.

Apuntar [ah-poon-tar'], *va.* 1. To aim; to level, to make after. 2. To point out, to mark, to hint. 3. To put down in writing; to note. 4. To touch lightly upon a point. 5. To fix or fasten provisionally a board or any other thing; (sew) to stitch. 6. To begin to appear or show itself. *Apunta el día*, The day peeps or begins to appear. 7. To sharpen edged tools. 8. To prompt or help players by suggesting the word to them. 9. To offer. *Apuntar y no dar*, To promise readily and not perform.—*vr.* 1. To begin to turn: applied to wine. 2. (Low) To be half-seas over, or half-drunk. *Apuntar los vegetales*, To grow up.

Apunte [ah-poon'-tay], *m.* 1. *V.* Apuntamiento. 2. Annotation, memorandum. (Engin.) Rough sketch. 3. The words suggested by a prompter on the stage; the act of prompting. 4. Stake in some games. *Apunte de cambios*, Exchange-list.

Apuñadar [ah-poo-nyah-dar'], *va.* (Prov.) To strike with the fist.

Apuñalado, da [ah-poo-nyah-lah'-do, dah], *a.* Shaped like a dagger.

Apuñalar [ah-poo-nyah-lar'], *va.* To thrust with a dagger.

Apuñar [ah-poo-nyar'], *va.* (Obs.) To seize with the fist.

Apuñear [ah-poo-nyay-ar'], *va.* (Coll.) To strike with the fist.

Apuracabos [ah-poo-rah-cah'-bos], *m.* A candle-safe; save-all.

Apuración [ah-poo-rah-the-on'], *f.* 1. (Obs.) Investigation. 2. *V.* Apuro. Trouble, misfortune.

Apuradamente [ah-poo-rah-dah-men'-tay], *adv.* 1. At the nick of time. 2. Punctually, exactly. 3. (Obs.) Radically.

Apuradero [ah-poo-rah-day'-ro], *m.* (Obs.) Inquiry, disquisition which ascertains the true nature of a thing.

Apurado, da [ah-poo-rah'-do, dah], *a.* 1. Rushed, in a hurry. 2. Needy. *Estar apurado*, 1. To be in a hurry. 2. To be in need (of money).

Apurador [ah-poo-rah-dor'], *m.* 1. A refiner, purifier. 2. One who spends or consumes. 3. (Prov.) One who gleans and picks up olives left by the first reapers.

Apuramiento [ah-poo-rah-me-en'-to], *m.* Research, inquiry, verification.

Apurar [ah-poo-rar'], *va.* 1. To purify. 2. To clear up, to verify, to investigate minutely, to know a thing radically. 3. To consume, to drain, to exhaust. *Apurar a uno*, To tease and perplex one, to press.—*vr.* 1. To grieve, to be afflicted. 2. To exert one's self. *Verse apurado*, To be hard run for; to be put to. *¡Apure Vd. que es tarde!* Hurry! it is late.

Apurativo [ah-poo-rah-tee'-vo], *a.* Detersive.

Apuro [ah-poo'-ro], *m.* 1. Want. 2. Anguish, pain, affliction. 3. Exigency; gripe.

Aquejar [ah-kay-har'], *va.* 1. To complain, to lament, to grieve. 2. To fatigue, to afflict. 3. (Obs.) To stimulate, to incite. 4. (Obs.) To pin up closely.

Aquel, lla, llo [ah-kel', ah-kel'-lyah, ah-kel'-lyo], *pron. dem.* That; he, she. It denotes persons or objects at a distance from both the speaker and the person addressed. *Aquellos, aquellas*, Those.

Aquelarre [ah-kel-lar'-ray], *m.* Witches' Sabbath. Also applied to any motley and noisy meeting.

Aquende [ah-ken'-day], *adv.* Hither, here.

Aqueno [ah-kay'-no], *m.* Akene, a single, hard pericarp.

Aquerenciarse [ah-kay-ren-the-ar'-say], *vr.* To be fond of a place: applied to cattle.

Aquese, sa, so [ah-kay'-say, sah, so], *pron. dem.* That. *Aquesos, aquesas*, Those. This pronoun is used only in speaking of persons or things not very distant. Hardly used except in poetry.

Aqueste, ta, to [ah-kess'-tay, tah, to]. *pron. dem.* This, that.

Aquí [ah-kee'], *adv.* 1. Here, in this place. 2. To this place. 3. Now, at present. 4. Then, on that occasion. *¡Aquí de Dios!* Assist me, O God! *Aquí fué ello*, Here did it happen. *He aquí*, Look here, behold. *De aquí adelante*, Henceforth. *De aquí para allí*, To and fro, up and down. *De aquí*, From this, hence. *De aquí en adelante*, Henceforth, henceforward. *Aquí alrededor*, Hereabouts. *Aquí dentro*, Herein, hereinto. *Fuera de aquí*, Out of this. *Hasta aquí*, Hitherto.

Aquiescencia [ah-ke-es-then'-the-ah], *f.* (Law) Aquiescence, consent.

Aquietar [ah-ke-ay-tar'], *va.* To quiet, to lull, to pacify; to hush; to allay. —*vr.* To grow calm, to be quiet.

Áquila-alba [ah'-ke-lah-ahl'-bah], *f.* Corrosive sublimate mixed with fresh mercury.

Aquilatar [ah-ke-lah-tar'], *va.* 1. To assay gold and silver. 2. To examine closely, to find out the truth of a thing.

Aquilea [ah-ke-lay'-ah], *f.* (Bot.) Milfoil, yarrow. Achillea millefolium.

Aquileña [ah-ke-lay'-nyah], *f.* (Bot.) Columbine. Aquilegia vulgaris.

Aquilifero [ah-ke-lee'-fay-ro], *m.* Among the Romans, the standard-bearer, he who carried the Roman eagle.

Aquilino, na [ah-ke-lee'-no, nah], *a.* Aquiline, hooked: applied commonly to the nose. *V.* Aguileño.

Aquilón [ah-ke-lone'], *m.* 1. Due north wind. 2. The north point.

Aquilonal, Aquilonar [ah-ke-lo-nahl', ah-ke-lo-nar'], *a.* Northern, northerly. *Tiempo aquilonal*, (Met.) The winter season.

Aquillado, da [ah-keel-lyah'-do, dah], *a.* Keel-shaped.

Aquitibi [ah-ke-tee'-be], *m.* Nickname of priests hired for some processions.

Ara [ah'-rah], *f.* 1. An altar. 2. The consecrated stone, on which a consecrated linen cover is laid during the celebration of the mass. 3. Among plumbers, a cistern-head.

Árabe, Arábigo [ah'-rah-bay, ah-rah'-be-go], *m.* The Arabic language; Arabic.

Arabesco [ah-rah-bess'-co], *m.* (Pict.) Arabesque, whimsical ornaments of foliage in painting; moresque-work.

Arabias [ah-rah'-be-as], *f. pl.* Arabias, a kind of linen so called.

Arábico, ca, or **go, ga** [ah-rah'-be-co, cah], *a.* Arabian. *Estar en arábico*, To be incomprehensible.

Arabismo [ah-rah-bees'-mo], *m.* Arabism: idiom of the Arabic language transferred to some other.

Arabizar [ah-rah-be-thar'], *va.* To Arabicize, to Arabize.

Aracacha [ah-rah-cah'-chah], *f.* An umbelliferous plant of Colombia, having an edible farinaceous root, cultivated in large quantities.

Arácnido, da [ah-rahc'-ne-do, dah], *a.* (Zool.) Arachnid, a class of arthropods; relating to the arachnids.

Aracnoides [ah-rac-no'-e-des], *f.* The arachnoid membrane of the brain and spinal cord, thin and serous, between the dura mater and the pia mater.

Arada [ah-rah'-dah], *f.* (Agr.) 1. Ploughed ground, husbandry. 2. *V.* Aradura, 2d def. 3. Work in the fields.

Arado [ah-rah'-do], *m.* A plough.

Arador [ah-rah-dor'], *m.* 1. A ploughman. 2. A sarcoptic mite that causes itch or scabies. Sarcoptes scabiei. 3. Harvest-mite, or harvest-bug: Leptus.

Aradro [ah-rah'-dro], *m.* (Prov.) *V.* Arado.

Aradura [ah-rah-doo'-rah], *f.* 1. The act or practice of ploughing. 2. (Prov.) Quantity of land which a yoke of oxen can conveniently plough in the course of a day.

Aragonés, esa [ah-rah-go-ness', nay'-sah], *a.* Of Aragon; Aragonese.

Aragonesa [ah-rah-go-nay'-sah]. *Uva aragonesa*, A large black grape very frequent in Aragon.

Aragonito [ah-rah-go-nee'-to], *m.* Aragonite, lime carbonate: named from province of Aragon.

Arambel [ah-ram-bel'], *m.* (Obs.) 1 Drapery, furniture of a room or bed. 2. (Met.) Rag, or piece hanging from cloths.

Arambre [ah-ram'-bray], *m.* (Obs.) *V.* Alambre.

Aramía [ah-rah-mee'-ah], *f.* (Prov.) A piece of ploughed ground fit for sowing.

Arana [ah-rah'-nah], *f.* (Obs.) Imposition, trick, deception.

Aranata [ah-rah-nah'-tah], *f.* An animal of the shape and size of a dog, a native of America.

Arancel [ah-ran-thel'], *m.* 1. The regulations by which the rate and price of bread and other things are fixed. 2. The tariff of duties, fees, taxes, etc., of the custom-house, courts, etc.; the book of rates.

Arancelario, ria [ah-ran-thay-lah'-re-o, re-ah], *a.* Pertaining or referring to the tariff.

Arándano [ah-rahn'-dah-no], *m.* Cranberry. *Arándano azul*, Blueberry.

Arandela [ah-ran-day'-lah], *f.* 1. The pan of the socket of a candlestick. 2. A guard around the staff of a lance. 3. Nave-box of a gun-carriage. (Mech.) Washer, axle-guard; rivet-plate, collar-plate. 4. (Naut.) Half-ports, square boards with a hole in the middle, to which a piece of canvas is nailed, to keep the water out when the cannon is in the port-hole. 5. A tin trough or funnel put around trees, with water, to prevent ants from climbing up. 6. A candelabrum, of glass, to be set upon a table.

Arandillo [ah-ran-deel'-lyo], *m.* (Prov.) Pad or small hoop used by women, which in Castile is called *caderillas.*

Aranero, ra [ah-rah-nay'-ro, rah], *a.* Deceptive, tricky.

Araniego [ah-rah-ne-ay'-go], *a.* Taken in a net, which is called *arañuelo:* applied to a young hawk.

Aranzada [ah-ran-thah'-dah], *f.* A measure of land very different according to the several provinces of Spain; 37.50 ares, 44.7 ares. (Sp. Acad.)

Araña [ah-rah'-nyah], *f.* 1. (Ent.) Spider. 2. (Zool.) Common weaver, sea-spider. Trachinus draco. 3. Chandelier, girandole, sconce. (Bot.) Crow foot. *Es una araña*, He is an industrious man. 4. (Prov.) *V.* Arrebatiña.

Arañador, ra [ah-rah-nyah-dor', rah], *m. & f.* Scratcher, one who scratches.

Arañamiento [ah-rah-nyah-me-en'-to], *m.* The act of scratching.
Arañar [ah-rah-nyar'], *va.* 1. To scratch, to claw. to scrabble. 2. To scrape, to gather by penurious diligence. *Arañar riquezas,* To gather riches with great eagerness. *Arañarse con los codos,* To rejoice in other people's misfortunes. *Arañar la cubierta,* To make great exertions; to get clear of danger.
Arañazo [ah-rah-nyah'-tho], *m. aug.* A long, deep scratch.
Arañero, ra [ah-rah-nyay'-ro, rah], *a. V.* ZAHAREÑO.
Araño [ah-rah'-nyo], *m.* A scratch, any slight wound; nipping.
Arañón [ah-rah-nyone'], *m.* (Prov.) Sloe, the fruit of the blackthorn.
Arañuela [ah-rah-nyoo-ay'-lah], *f. dim.* 1. A small spider. 2. *V.* ARAÑUELO. 3. A plant.
Arañuelo [ah-rah-nyoo-ay'-lo], *m.* 1. A small species of spider; grub or larva, web-spinning, which destroys plants. 2. *V.* CAPARILLA. 3. Fold-net, a very slight net for catching birds.
Arapende [ah-rah-pen'-day], *m.* Ancient measure of 120 square feet.
Arar [ah-rar'], *va.* 1. To plough, to labour. 2. (Poet.) To run or pass through the surface of a liquid. *Arar con el ancla,* (Naut.) To drag the anchor. *No me lo harán creer cuantos aran y cavan,* No man shall ever make me believe it.
Arar [ah-rar'], *m.* An African coniferous tree; its wood was employed in constructing the cathedrals of Seville and Córdoba.
Araucaria [ah-rah-oo-cah'-re-ah], *f.* Araucaria, a tall conifer, of pine family, native of South America.
Arbellón [ar-bel-lyone'], *m.* (Prov.) Gutter for drawing off the water from roads. *V.* ARBOLLÓN.
Arbelo [ar-bay'-lo], *m.* (Geom.) A curvilinear figure composed of three segments of a circle and three acute angles.
Arbitrable [ar-be-trah'-blay], *a.* Arbitrable, depending upon the will.
Arbitración [ar-be-trah-the-on'], *f.* Arbitration.
Arbitrador [ar-be-trah-dor'], *m.* Arbitrator, umpire, referee.
Arbitradora [ar-be-trah-do'-rah], *f.* Arbitress.
Arbitraje, Arbitramento, Arbitramiento [ar be-trah'-hay, ar-be-trah-men'-to, ar-be-trah-me-en'-to], *m.* Arbitration, the award of an arbitrator; arbitrament.
Arbitral, *a. V.* ARBITRATORIO.
Arbitrar [ar-be-trar'], *va.* 1. To adjudge, to award. 2. To judge after one's own feelings and sentiments. 3. To contrive means and expedients.
Abitrariamente [ar-be-trah-re-ah-men'-tay], *adv.* Arbitrarily, in an arbitrary manner; without control.
Arbitrariedad [ar-be-trah-re-ay-dahd'], *f.* Arbitrariness.
Arbitrario, ria, Arbitrativo, va [ar-be-trah'-re-o, ah, ar-be-trah-tee'-vo, vah], *a.* 1. Arbitrary, that which depends upon the will; absolute. 2. (For.) Relating to arbitrators.
Arbitratorio, ria [ar-be-trah-to'-re-o, ah], *a.* That which belongs or relates to arbitrators.
Arbitrio [ar-bee'-tre-o], *m.* 1. Free and uncontrolled will and pleasure; mercy. 2. Means, expedient. 3. Arbitration, bond, compromise. 4. *Arbitrio de juez,* The discretionary power of a judge in cases not clearly decided by law. 5. *Arbitrios,* Duty or taxes imposed on provisions exposed for sale. *Propios y arbitrios,* Ways and means. *No hay arbitrio,* There is no change.
Arbitrista [ar-be-trees'-tah], *m.* Schemer, projector, contriver.
Arbitro [ar'-be-tro], *m.* 1. Arbitrator. 2. Umpire.
Arbol [ar'-bol], *m.* 1. (Bot.) A tree. 2. (Naut.) Mast. *V.* PALO. 3. In some machines, the upright post which serves to give them a circular motion. (Mech.) Arbor, upright shaft; wheel spindle. 4. A drill. 5. Body of a shirt without sleeves. 6. Crown post, upright post, around which winding stairs turn. *Árbol de amor,* (Bot.) Judas-tree. Cercis siliquastrum. *Arbol de clavo,* Clove-tree. Caryophillus aromaticus. *Árbol de fuego* A wooden frame of fireworks. *Arbol del paraíso* or *árbol paraíso,* Flowering-ash. Æleannus angustifolia. *Arbol del pan,* Bread-fruit-tree. Artocarpus incissa domestica. *Árbol marino,* A radiate much resembling the star-fish, but larger. *Arbol pagano,* A wild or uncultivated tree. *En árbol caído todos se suben a las ramas,* Overthrown pride inspires only contempt.
Arbolado, da [ar-bo-lah'-do, dah], *a.* 1. Wooded, woodland; planted with trees. 2. Masted. *Arbolado en la hoya,* Masted hoy-fashion.—*pp.* of ARBOLAR.—*m.* Woodland.
Arboladura [ar-bo-lah-doo'-rah], *f.* (Naut.) A general name for masts, yards, and all sorts of round timber. *Maestre de arboladura,* A master mast-maker.
Arbolar [ar-bo-lar'], *va.* To hoist, to set upright. *Arbolar el navío,* (Naut.) To mast a ship.—*vr. Arbolarse,* To rear on the hind feet: applied to horses.
Arbolario [ar-bo-lah'-re-o], *m.* 1. *V.* HERBOLARIO. 2. Madcap
Arbol de levas [ar'-bol day lay'-vahs], *f.* Camshaft.
Arbolecico, Arbolecillo, Arbolico, Arbolito, Arborcillo [ar-bo-lay-thee'-co, etc.], *m. dim.* Arboret, a small tree.
Arboleda [ar-bo-lay'-dah], *f.* Grove, plantation of trees.
Arbolejo [ar-bo-lay'-ho], *m. dim.* A small tree.
Arbolete [ar-bo-lay'-tay], *m.* Branch of a tree put on the ground, to which bird-catchers fasten their lime-twigs.
Arbolillo [ar-bo-leel'-lyo], *m.* Side of a blast-furnace.
Arbolista [ar-bo-lees'-tah], *m.* A dresser or planter of trees; arborist .
Arbollón [ar-bol-lyone'], *m.* Flood-gate, sluice, conduit, channel.
Arbóreo, rea [ar-bo'-ray-o, ah], *a.* Relating or belonging to trees.
Arborescencia [ar-bo-res-then'-the-ah], *f.* Arborescence, tree-like growth or formation.
Arborescente [ar-bo-res-then'-tay], *a.* Arborescent, having the form of a tree.
Arboricultura [ar-bo-re-cool-too'-rah], *f.* Arboriculture, cultivation of trees.
Arborizado, da [ar-bo-re-thah'-do, dah], *a.* Arborescent, resembling trees and foliage: applied to dendrites or stones having the appearance of foliage.
Arbotante [ar-bo-tahn'-tay], *m.* Arch of stone or brick raised against a wall to support a vault. *Arbotante de pie de campana,* (Naut.) Bell-crank, the place where the ship's bell is hung.
Arbusto [ar-boos'-to], *m.* A shrub.
Arbustillo [ar-boos-teel'-lyo], *m. dim.* Arbuscle, a small shrub.
Arca [ar'-cah], *f.* 1. A chest. *Arcas.* Coffer, iron chest for money. *Hacer arcas,* To open the coffers or treasury-chest. 2. In glass-houses, the tempering oven, in which glassware, just blown, is put to cool. 3. (Met. A reserved person. *Arca de Noé,* (Met.) Lumber-chest. *Arca de fuego,* (Naut.) Fire-chest, a small box, filled with combustibles, used to annoy an enemy who attempts to board a ship. *Ser arca cerrada,* To be yet unknown: applied to persons and things. *Sangrar a uno de 'la vena del arca,* To drain one of his money. *Arca de agua,* Reservoir, cistern. *Arcas,* Cavities of the body under the ribs.
Arcabucear [ar-cah-boo-thay-ar'], *va.* 1. (Obs.) To shoot with the cross-bow. 2. To shoot a criminal by way of punishment.
Arcabucería [ar-cah-boo-thay-ree'-ah], *f.* 1. A troop of archers. 2. A number of cross-bows. 3. Manufactory of bows and arrows.
Arcabucero [ar-cah-boo-thay'-ro], *m.* 1. Archer. 2. Gunsmith. 3. Manufacturer of bows and arrows.
Arcabuco [ar-cah-boo'-co], *m.* (Amer.) A craggy spot full of brambles.
Arcabuz [ar-cah-booth'], *m.* Arquebuse, a fire-arm, a hand-gun.
Arcabuzazo [ar-cah-boo-thah'-tho], *m.* A shot from a gun and the wound it causes.
Arcacil [ar-cah-theel'], *m.* (Bot.) A species of wild artichoke. Cynara horrida.
Arcada [ar-cah'-dah], *f.* 1. Violent motion of the stomach, which excites vomiting. 2. Arcade or row of arches.
Arcade [ar'-cah-day], *a.* Arcadian, belonging to the Roman academy of polite literature called *Arcades.*
Arcadio, dia [ar-cah'-de-o, ah], *a.* Arcadian.
Arcaduz [ar-cah-dooth'], *m.* 1. Conduit or pipe for the conveyance of water. 2. Bucket for raising water out of a draw-well. 3. (Met.) Channel for enforcing a claim, obtaining a place, etc. *Llevar una cosa por sus arcaduces,* To conduct an affair through its proper channel.
Arcaduzar [ar-cah-doo-thar'], *va.* (Obs.) To convey water through conduits.
Arcáico, ca [ar-cah'-e-co, cah], *a.* Archaic, ancient.
Arcaismo [ar-cah-ees'-mo], *m.* Archaism, the mixture of ancient or antiquated words with modern language.
Arcaizar [ar-cah-e-thar'], *vr.* To use archaisms.
Arcam [ar-cahm'], *m.* A very venomous serpent, spotted black and white, which is found in Turkestan.
Arcángel [ar-cahn'-hel], *m.* Archangel.
Arcangelical [ar-can-hay-le-cahl'], *a.* Archangelical.
Arcanidad [ar-cah-ne-dahd'], *f.* (Obs.) A profound secret of great moment.
Arcano [ar-cah'-no], *m.* Arcanum, a secret which is carefully kept.—*a.* Secret, recondite, reserved.
Arcar [ar-car'], *va.* Among clothiers, to beat the wool with a bow of one or two cords.
Arcaza [ar-cah'-thah], *f. aug.* A large chest.
Arcazón [ar-cah-thone'], *m.* 1. Arbuscle. 2. Osier, water-willow. 3. Willow-plot.
Arce [ar'-thay], *m.* (Bot.) Maple-tree. Acer.
Arcedianato [ar-thay-de-ah-nah'-to], *m.* Archdeaconship; archdeaconry.
Arcediano [ar-thay-de-ah'-no], *m.* Archdeacon.
Arcedo [ar-thay'-do], *m.* Maple-grove

Arcén [ar-then'], *m.* 1. (Ant.) Border, brim, edge. 2. (Prov.) Stone laid round the brim of a well.

Arcilla [ar-theel'-lyah], *f.* Argil, white pure earth, alumina, clay.

Arcilloso, sa [ar-theel-lyo'-so, sah], *a.* Clayey, argillaceous.

Arciprestadgo, Arciprestazgo [ar-the-pres-tad'-go, ar-the-pres-tath'-go], *m.* The dignity of an archpriest.

Arcipreste [ar-the-pres'-tay], *m.* Arch-prelate, archpriest, the first or chief presbyter.

Arco [ar'-co], *m.* 1. Arc, a segment of a circle. 2. Arch, arc, a part of a circle not more than the half. 3. Arch of a building, bridge, and other works. 4. Bow for throwing arrows. 5. Fiddle-bow. 6. Hoop, any thing circular with which something else is bound, particularly casks and barrels. 7. (Naut.) Bow of a ship. *Arco Iris, del cielo* or *de San Martín*, Rainbow.

Arcón [ar-cone'], *m. aug.* 1. A large chest, bin, bunker. 2. A great arch or arc.

Arcontado [ar-con-tah'-do], *m.* Archonship.

Arconte [ar-con'-tay], *m.* Archon, a magistrate of Athens.

Árctico, ca [arc'-te-co, cah], *a. V.* Ártico.

Archera [ar-chay'-rah], *f.* Archeress.

Archero [ar-chay'-ro], *m.* Archer.

Archi. Arch-, a prefix from the Greek, meaning pre-eminent.

Archicofradía [ar-che-co-frah-dee'-ah], *f.* A privileged brotherhood or confraternity.

Archidiácono [ar-che-de-ah'-co-no], *m. V.* Arcediano.

Archiducado [ar-che-doo-cah'-do], *m.* 1. Archdukedom, archduchy, the territory belonging to an archduke. 2. The dignity of an archduke.

Archiducal [ar-che-doo-cahl'], *a.* Archducal, that which belongs or relates to an archduke or archduchy.

Archiduque [ar-che-doo'-kay], *m.* Archduke.

Archiduquesa [ar-che-doo-kay'-sah], *f.* Archduchess.

Archilaúd [ar-che-lah-ood'], *m.* A musical instrument shaped and stringed as a lute, but of a larger size.

Archimandrita [ar-che-man-dree'-tah], *m.* Name, in the orient, of the abbot of a monastery.

Archimillonario, ria [ar-che-meel'-lyo-nah'-re-o, ah], *a.* Multimillionaire.

Archipámpano [ar-che-pahm'-pah-no], *m.* (Coll.) A word used to express an imaginary dignity or authority.

Archipiélago [ar-che-pe-ay'-lah-go], *m.* Archipelago, a part of the sea crowded with islands.

Architriclino [ar-che-tre-clee'-no], *m.* (Antiquities) He who ordered and directed banquets.

Archivar [ar-che-var'], *va.* To deposit a thing or writing in an archive.

Archivero, Archivista [ar-che-vay'-ro, ar-che-vees'-tah], *m.* Keeper of the records.

Archivo [ar-chee'-vo], *m.* 1. Archives, the place where public records are kept. 2. (Met.) A person who is intrusted with the most profound secrets, a confidant.

Arda [ar'-dah], *f.* Squirrel. *V.* Ardilla.

Ardalear [ar-dah-lay-ar'], *va.* To make thin or clear. *V.* Ralear.

Ardasas, Ardases [ar-dah'-sas, ar-dah'-ses], *f. pl.* The coarser sort of Persian silk.

Ardasinas, Ardazinas [ar-dah-see'-nas, ar-dah-thee'-nas], *f. pl.* The finer sort of Persian silk.

Ardea [ar-day'-ah], *f.* Bittern. *V.* Alcaraván.

Ardedor [ar-day-dor'], *m.* A species of serpent.

Ardentia [ar-den-tee'-ah], *f.* 1. Heat. 2. (Naut.) Phosphoric sparkling of the sea when it is much agitated.

Ardeola [ar-day-o'-lah], *f.* A small kind of heron.

Arder [ar-derr'], *vn.* 1. To burn, to blaze, to glow. 2. To be agitated by the passions of love, hatred, anger, etc., to heat, to kindle. *Arderse en pleitos*, To be entangled in law-suits.

Ardero, ra [ar-day'-ro, rah], *a.* Squirrel-hunter: applied to dogs.

Ardid [ar-deed'], *m.* Stratagem, artifice, cunning.

Ardido, da [ar-dee'-do, dah], *a.* 1. Heated: applied to grain, olives, tobacco, etc. 2. (Obs.) Bold, intrepid, valiant.—*pp.* of Arder.

Ardiente [ar-de-en'-tay], *pa.* and *a.* 1. Ardent, flagrant, burning. *Calentura ardiente*, A burning fever. 2. Passionate, active, mettlesome, hot, fervent, fiery, fearless; feverish.

Ardientemente [ar-de-en-tay-men'-tay], *adv.* Ardently, flagrantly, fervidly; fearlessly.

Ardilla [ar-deel'-lyah], *f.* 1. Squirrel. Sciurus vulgaris. 2. (Mec.) Granulating machine.

Ardimiento [ar-de-me-en'-to], *m.* 1. (Obs.) Conflagration. 2. (Met.) Valour, intrepidity, undaunted courage.

Ardínculo [ar-deen'-coo-lo], *m.* (Vet.) An inflamed swelling or ulcer on the back of animals.

Ardita [ar-dee'-tah], *f.* A squirrel. *V.* Ardilla.

Ardite [ar-dee'-tay], *m.* An ancient coin of little value, formerly current in Spain. *No vale un ardite*, It is not worth a copper.

Ardor [ar-dor'], *m.* 1. Great heat, hotness, flagrancy. 2. (Met.) Valour, vivacity, spirit, vigour, mettle. 3. Fieriness, fervency. 4. Life.

Ardoroso, sa [ar-do-ro'-so, sah], *a.* Fiery, restless: applied to a horse.

Arduamente [ar-doo-ah-men'-tay], *adv.* Arduously, in a difficult, arduous manner.

Arduo, dua [ar'-doo-o, ah], *a.* Arduous, difficult; high.

Area [ah'-ray-ah], *f.* 1. Area, the surface contained between any lines or boundaries. 2. Area of a building. 3. Halo, a bright circle which surrounds the sun, moon, or stars. 4. A square decametre: equivalent to about 143 square varas.

Areca [ah-ray'-cah], *f.* A palm-tree of the Philippine Islands, used in building huts.

Arefacción [ah-ray-fac-the-on'], *f.* Dryness, extenuation.

Arel [ah-rel'], *m.* A kind of large sieve used to sift the corn.

Arelar [ah-ray-lar'], *va.* To sift the corn with the kind of sieve called *arel.*

Arena [ah-ray'-nah], *f.* 1. Sand, grit. 2. Arena, place where wrestlers and gladiators fought. *Sembrar en arena*, To labour in vain. *Arena de hoya*, Pit-sand. *Arena movediza*, (Naut.) Quicksand. *Arenas*, Gravel formed in the kidneys.

Arenáceo, ea [ah-ray-nah'-thay-o, ah], *a.* Arenaceous, gravelly.

Arenal [ah-ray-nahl'], *m.* A sandy ground, a sandy beach.

Arenalejo, Arenalillo [ah-ray-nah-lay'-ho, ah-ray-nah-leel'-lyo], *m. dim.* 1. A small sandy piece of ground. 2. Small, fine sand.

Arenar [ah-ray-nar'], *va.* To cover with sand; fill with sand.

Arenaria [ah-ray-nah'-re-ah], *f.* (Orn.) Sandpiper.

Arencar [ah-ren-car'], *va.* To salt and dry sardines, etc., like herrings.

Arencón [ah-ren-cone'], *m. aug.* of Arenque.

Arenero [ah-ray-nay'-ro], *m.* One who deals in sand; sand-box.

Arenga [ah-ren'-gah], *f.* Harangue, speech, oration, address.

Arengador [ah-ren-gah-dor'], *m.* A speech-maker.

Arengar [ah-ren-gar'], *vn.* To harangue, to deliver a speech or oration; to hold forth.

Arenícola [ah-ray-nee'-co-lah], *f.* (Zool.) An annelid, used by fishermen for bait; lugworm, or lobworm.

Arenilla [ah-ray-neel'-yah], *f.* 1. Moulding sand; sand. 2. Powder to dry writing.—*pl.* In gunpowder-mills, saltpetre refined, and reduced to grains as small as sand.

Arenisca [ah-ray-nees'-cah], *f.* (Miner.) Sandstone.

Arenisco, ca, Arenoso, sa [ah-ray-nees'-co, cah, ah-ray-no'-so, sah], *a.* Sandy, abounding with sand; gravelly, gritty.

Arenque [ah-ren'-kay], *m.* Herring. Clupea harengus. *Arenque ahumado*, A red herring.

Aréola [ah-ray'-oh-lah], *f.* 1. (Anat.) Areola, circle around the nipple. 2. The reddened area around a pustule.

Areómetro [ah-ray-o'-may-tro], *m.* Areometer, an instrument for measuring the density and gravity of spirituous liquors.

Areopagita [ah-ray-o-pah-hee'-tah], *m.* Areopagite, judge of the supreme court of judicature in Athens.

Areópago [ah-ray-o'-pah-go], *m.* Areopagus, the supreme court of judicature in Athens.

Areóstilo [ah-ray-os'-te-lo], *m.* Aræostyle, the distance from column to column of eight or more modules.

Areotectónica [ah-ray-o-tec-to'-ne-cah], *f.* Areotectonics, a part of the science of fortification.

Arepa [ah-ray'-pah], *f.* (Amer.) A griddle-cake made of soaked maize ground into a paste or dough. *V.* Tortilla.

Aresta [ah-res'-tah], *f.* (Obs.) 1. Coarse tow. 2. *V.* Espina.

Arestin [ah-res-teen'], *m.* (Vet.) Frush, a disease in the heel of horses.

Arestinado, da [ah-res-te-nah'-do, dah], *a.* Afflicted with the disease called the frush.

Arete [ah-ray'-tay], *m. V.* Zarcillo, Pendiente. Ear-drop.

Arfada [ar-fah'-dah], *f.* (Naut.) The pitching of a ship.

Arfar [ar-far'], *va.* (Naut.) To pitch: applied to a ship.

Arfil [ar-feel'], *m. V.* Alfil.

Argadijo, Argadillo [ar-gah-dee'-ho, ar-gah-deel'-lyo], *m.* 1. Reel, bobbin, winder. *V.* Devanadera. 2. (Met.) A blustering, noisy, restless person. 3. (Prov.) Large basket made of twigs of osier.

Argado [ar-gah'-do], *m.* Prank, trick, artifice.

Argal [ar-gahl'], *m.* Argol, crude tartar.

Argalia [ar-gah'-le-ah], *f. V.* Algalia.

Argallera [ar-gal-lyay'-rah], *f.* A saw for cutting grooves; forkstaff plane, reed-plane.

Argamandel [ar-gah-man-del'], *m.* Rag, tatter.

Argamandijo [ar-gah-man-dee'-ho], *m.* (Coll.) Collection of trifling implements used in trade or business. *Dueño* or *señor del argamandijo*, Powerful lord and master.

Argamasa [ar-gah-mah'-sah], *f.* Mortar, a cement for building.

Argamasar [ar-gah-mah-sar'], *va.* 1. To make mortar. 2. To cement with mortar.

Argamasón [ar-gah-mah-sone'], *m.* A large piece of mortar found among the ruins of a building.

Argamula [ar-gah-moo'-lah], *f.* (Bot. Prov.) *V.* AMELO.

Árgana, *f.* **Árgano**, *m.* [ar'-gah-nah]. A machine resembling a crane, for raising stones and other weighty things. *Árganas*, 1. Baskets or wicker vessels in which things are carried on a horse. 2. Large nets in which forage is carried.

Arganel [ar-gah-nel'], *m.* A small brass ring used in the composition of an astrolabe.

Arganeo [ar-gah'-nay-o], *m.* (Naut.) Anchor-ring, a large ring in the anchor to which the cable is fastened.

Argel [ar-hel'], *a.* 1. This adjective is applied to a horse whose right hind foot only is white. 2. (Met.) Unlucky, unfortunate.

Argelino, na [ar-hay-lee'-no, nah], *a.* Algerine; of Algiers.

Argema, Argemón [ar-hay'-mah, ar-hay-mone'], *m.* (Med.) Argema or argemon, a small white ulcer of the globe of the eye.

Argémone [ar-hay'-mo-nay], *f.* (Bot.) Prickly or horned poppy. Argemone mexicana.

Argén [ar-hen'], *m.* (Her.) White or silver colour, argent.

Argentado, da [ar-hen-tah'-do, dah], *a.* This term was formerly applied to a shoe pierced with holes, through which the fine white colour of the stuff was seen with which it was lined.—*pp.* of ARGENTAR.

Argentador [ar-hen-tah-dor'], *m.* One who silvers or covers superficially with silver.

Argentar [ar-hen-tar'], *va.* 1. To plate or cover with silver. 2. To give a silver colour.

Argentería [ar-hen-tay-ree'-ah], *f.* 1. Embroidery in gold or silver. 2. (Met.) An expression more brilliant than solid.

Argentífero, ra [ar-hen-tee'-fay-ro, rah], *a.* Argentiferous; silver-bearing.

Argentifodina [ar-hen-te-fo-dee'-nah], *f.* Silver-mine.

Argentina [ar-hen-tee'-nah], *f.* (Bot.) Satin cinquefoil. Potentilla argentea.

Argentino, na [ar-hen-tee'-no, nah], *a.* 1. Of silver, or like it; argentine. 2. (Geog.) Belonging to the River la Plata: Argentine Republic, southernmost country of South America.

Argento [ar-hen'-to], *m.* 1. (Poet.) Silver. 2. *Argento vivo sublimado*, Sublimate. *V.* SOLIMÁN.

Argilla [ar-heel'-lyah], *f.* *V.* ARCILLA.

Argiritas [ar-he-ree'-tas], *m. pl.* Marcasites, which are found in silver-mines; white pyrites.

Argo [ar'-go], *m.* The ship of Jason and the Argonauts.

Argolla [ar-gol'-lyah], *f.* 1. Large iron ring; buckle, ring, collar; a staple. *Argollas de cureña*, Draught-hooks of a gun-carriage. *Argollas de amarra*, Lashing-rings. 2. Pillory, a public punishment in putting a ring round the neck.

Argolleta, ica, ita [ar-gol-lyay'-tah], *f. dim.* A small staple; a small iron ring.

Argollón [ar-gol-lyone'], *m. aug.* A very large iron ring; a large staple.

Árgoma [ar'-go-mah], *f.* (Bot.) *V.* ALIAGA. Furze. *V.* AULAGA.

Argomal [ar-go-mahl'], *m.* Ground covered with furze.

Argomón [ar-go-mone'], *m. aug.* Large prickly broom.

Argonauta [ar-go-nah'-oo-tah], *m.* 1. One of the Argonauts, the companions of Jason on board the *Argo*. 2. *Argonautas de San Nicolás*, The name of a military order at Naples. 3. (Zool.) The paper nautilus, Argonauta argo. 4. A group of diurnal butterflies.

Argos [ar'-gos], *m.* (Myth.) Argus, fabled to have a hundred eyes, placed by Juno to guard Io. *Ser un argos* or *estar hecho un argos*, To be very vigilant, to be very solicitous.

Argoudán [ar-go-oo-dahn'], *m.* A kind of cotton, manufactured in different parts of India.

Arguajaque [ar-goo-ah-hah'-kay], *m.* Gum-ammoniac.

Argucia [ar-goo'-the-ah], *f.* Subtilty, which degenerates into sophistry.

Argüe [ar'-goo-ay], *m.* 1. Machine for moving large weights; windlass, crane; whim. 2. Machine for drawing fine gold wire.

Argüellarse [ar-goo-ayl-lyar'-say], *vr.* (Prov.) To be emaciated; to be in bad health: applied to children.

Argüello [ar-goo-el'-lyo], *m.* Faintness, want of health.

Argueñas [ar-gay'-nyas], *f. pl.* *V.* ANGARILLAS.

Arguerita [ar-gay-ree'-tah], *f.* (Miner.) Argyrite, or argentite.

Argüir [ar-goo-eer'], *vn.* To argue, to dispute, to oppose.—*va.* To give signs, to make a show of something. *Argüirle a uno su conciencia*, To be pricked by one's conscience.

Arguma [ar'-goo-mah], *f.* *V.* ALIAGA.

Argumentación [ar-goo-men-tah-the-on'], *f.* Argumentation.

Argumentador, ra [ar-goo-men-tah-dor', rah], *m.* & *f.* Arguer, a reasoner, a disputant.

Argumentar [ar-goo-men-tar'], *vn.* To argue, to dispute; to conclude.

Argumentativo, va [ar-goo-men-tah-tee'-vo, vah], *a.* Argumentative.

Argumentillo [ar-goo-men-teel'-lyo], *m. dim.* A slight argument, an unreasonable objection.

Argumento [ar-goo-men'-to], *m.* 1. Argument, a reason alleged for or against a thing. 2. Argument, the subject of a discourse or writing. 3. In the universities, the person who argues or disputes is sometimes called so. 4. Argument, summary of the points treated on in a work, or in a book or chapter of a poem. 5. Indication, sign, token.

Arguyente [ar-goo-yen'-tay], *pa.* Arguer; opponent.

Aria [ah'-re-ah], *f.* 1. Tune or air for a single voice. 2. Verses to be set to music, the last of which in each stanza generally rhyme.

Aribar [ah-re-bar'], *va.* To reel yarn into skeins.

Aribo [ah-ree'-bo], *m.* Reel for making skeins.

Aricar [ah-re-car'], *va.* To plough across the ground sown with corn; to clear it of weeds. *V.* ARREJACAR.

Aridez [ah-re-deth'], *f.* Drought.

Árido, da [ah'-re-do, dah], *a.* 1. Dry, wanting moisture. 2. (Met.) Dry, barren, jejune: applied to style or conversation.

Arienzo [ah-re-en'-tho], *m.* An old coin of Castile.

Aries [ah'-re-es], *m.* Aries or ram, one of the signs of the zodiac.

Arieta [ah-re-ay'-tah], *f. dim.* Arietta, a short air, song, or tune.

Ariete [ah-re-ay'-tay], *m.* Battering-ram, an ancient warlike machine for battering walls.

Arietino, na [ah-re-ay-tee'-no, nah], *a.* Resembling the head of a ram.

Arigue [ah-ree'-gay], *m.* A Philippine timber.

Arije [ah-ree'-hay], *m.* *V.* UVA ARIJE.

Arijo, ja [ah-ree'-ho, hah], *a.* Light, easily tilled: applied to soil.

Arillo [ah-reel'-lyo], *m. dim.* 1. A small hoop 2. Ear-ring.—*pl.* Hoops for ear-rings.

Arimez [ah-re-meth'], *m.* Part of a building which juts or stands out.

Arindajo [ah-rin-dah'-ho], *m.* (Orn.) Jay. Corvus glandarius.

Ario, ia [ah'-re-o, ah], *a.* Aryan, a primitive people and language of Central Asia.

Arisaro [ah-re-sah'-ro], *m.* (Bot.) Wake-robin. Arum arisarum.

Arisco, ca [ah-rees'-co, cah], *a.* 1. Fierce, rude, wild, untractable, stubborn: applied to brutes. 2. (Met.) Harsh, unpolished, churlish, shy: applied to persons.

Arismética [ah-ris-may'-te-cah], *f.* (Obs.) Arithmetic. *V.* ARITMÉTICA.

Arismético [ah-ris-may'-te-co], *a.* (Obs.) *V.* ARITMÉTICO.

Arisnegro, Arisprieto [ah-ris-nay'-gro, ah-ris-pre-ay'-to], *a.* *Trigo arisnegro* or *arisprieto*, Species of wheat with a blackish beard, which yields more flour than the white. It is also called *rubión*.

Arisquillo, lla [ah-ris-keel'-lyo, lyah], *a.* Dim. of ARISCO.

Arista [ah-rees'-tah], *f.* 1. Beard or awn of cereal grains; chaff. 2. Edge of a rough piece of timber in naval architecture. 3. Cant edge, groin, rib, arris.—*pl.* (Mil.) Salient angles.

Aristado, da [ah-ris-tah'-do, dah], *a.* Awned, bearded.

Aristarco [ah-ris-tar'-co], *m.* A severe censurer of another's writings.

Aristino [ah-ris-tee'-no], *m.* *V.* ARESTÍN.

Aristocracia [ah-ris-to-crah'-the-ah], *f.* An aristocracy.

Aristócrata [ah-ris-to'-crah-tah], *m.* Aristocrat, a favourer of aristocracy.

Aristocrático, ca [ah-ris-to-crah'-te-co, cah], *a.* Aristocratical.

Aristoloquia [ah-ris-to-lo'-ke-ah], *f.* (Bot.) Birthwort. Aristolochia.

Aristoso, sa [ah-ris-to'-so, sah], *a.* 1. Having many beards on the ear: spoken of grain.

Aristotélico, ca [ah-ris-to-tay'-le-co, cah], *a.* Aristotelian, belonging to the doctrine of Aristotle.

Aritmancia [ah-rit-mahn'-the-ah], *f.* Arithmancy, foretelling future events by numbers.

Aritmética [ah-rit-may'-te-cah], *f.* Arithmetic.

Aritméticamente [ah-rit-may'-te-cah-men-tay], *adv.* Arithmetically, in an arithmetical manner.

Aritmético [ah-rit-may'-te-co], *m.* Arithmetician, accountant.

Aritmético, ca [ah-rit-may'-te-co, cah], *a.* Arithmetical.

Aritmo [ah-reet'-mo], *a.* Arrhythmic, irregular (used of the pulse).

Arlequín [ar-lay-keen'], *m.* Harlequin, a buffoon who plays tricks to amuse the populace.

Arlequinada [ar-lay-ke-nah'-dah], *f.* A harlequin's trick, or joke; a clownish action.

Arlo [ar'-lo], *m.* (Bot.) Barberry or piperidge bush. Berberis vulgaris.

Arlota [ar-lo'-tah], *f.* Tow of flax or hemp.

Arlote [ar-lo'-tay], *m.* (Obs.) Vagabond, idler.

Arma [ar'-mah], *f.* 1. Weapon, instrument of offence, arms. 2. Alarm or arms. *Arma falsa*, False alarm this expression is used instead of *falsa alarma*. *Arma, arma*, or *a las armas*, To arms. *Arma arrojadiza*, A missile weapon. *Arma de fuego*, Fire-arms; gun. *Arma blanca*, Side-arms, for cutting or thrusting, equivalent of "cold steel."—*pl.* 1. Troops, armies. 2. Armorial ensigns, coat of arms. 3. *Armas de agua*, (Mex.) Skins attached to the pommel of the saddle to protect the thighs and legs from rain. *Armas y dineros buenas manos quieren*, Arms and money ought to be put into wise hands. *Hombre de armas*, A military man. *Maestro de armas*, A fencing-master. *Pasar por las armas*, To be shot as a criminal. *Rendir las armas*, To lay down the arms. *No dejar las armas de la mano*, Not to lay down the arms. *Estar sobre las armas*, To be under arms, and ready for action. *Un hecho de armas*, An achievement, exploit. 3. (Met.) Means, power, reason. *Hacerse a las armas*, To inure one's self to do or perform any thing.

Armada [ar-mah'-dah], *f.* The navy; fleet, squadron, armada. *Armada de barlovento*, (Naut.) The fleet stationed to the windward.

Armadera [ar-mah-day'-rah], *f.* (Naut.) The principal timbers of a ship.

Armadia [ar-mah-dee'-ah], *f.* Raft, a frame or float made by pieces of timber.

Armadijo [ar-mah-dee'-ho], *m.* Trap or snare for catching game.

Armadillo [ar-mah-deel'-lyo], *m.* Armadillo, a small four-footed animal, covered with hard scales like armour. Dasypus.

Armado, da [ar-mah'-do, dah], *a.* 1. Weaponed, armed for offence, furnished with arms. 2. Gold or silver placed on other metal. 3. (Mech.) Mounted, set.—*pp.* of Armar.

Armado [ar-mah'-do], *m.* A man armed with a coat of mail.

Armador [ar-mah-dor'], *m.* 1. One who fits out privateers. 2. Privateer, cruiser. 3. One who recruits sailors for the whale and cod fishery. 4. Outfitter, ship-owner. 5. (Mech.) Framer, adjuster, fitter. 6. Jacket.

Armadura [ar-mah-doo'-rah], *f.* 1. Armour. 2. The union of the integral parts of a thing; framework. 3. (Mech.) Setting, fitting; truss; armature (elec.). 4. Skeleton. 5. Frame of a roof. *Armadura del tejado*, The shell of a building. *Armadura de una mesa*, The frame of a table.

Armajara [ar-mah-hah'-rah], *f.* (Prov.) A plot of ground well dug and dunged for rearing garden plants.

Armamento [ar-mah-men'-to], *m.* Armament, warlike preparation.

Armandijo [ar-man-dee'-ho], *m.* (Obs.) *V.* Armadijo.

Armar [ar-mar'], *va.* 1. To arm, to furnish with arms; to man. 2. To furnish, to fit up. 3. To square with one's opinion. 4. To arm or to plate with anything that may add strength. 5. To set a snare. 6. To place one thing above another. 7. To set up a person in business. 8. (Mech.) To adjust, set, mount; truss, put together. *Armar la cuenta*, To make up an account. *Armarla*, To cheat at cards. *Armarla con queso*, To decoy. *Armar navío* or *bajel*, To fit out a ship. *Armar pleito* or *ruido*, To stir up disturbances; to kick up a dust. *Armar un lazo*, To lay a snare. *Armar una cama*, To set up a bedstead. *Armar una casa*, To frame the timber-work of the roof of a house. *Armar caballero*, To knight. —*vr.* To prepare one's self for war. *Armarse de paciencia*, To prepare one's self to suffer.

Armario [ar-mah'-re-o], *m.* A clothes-press; cabinet, commode.

Armatoste [ar-mah-tos'-tay], *m.* 1. Hulk; any unwieldy machine or piece of furniture which is more cumbersome than convenient. 2. A trap, a snare. *V.* Armadijo. 3. A corpulent person who is shiftless and worthless.

Armazón [ar-mah-thone'], *f.* 1. Frame-work, skeleton, frame. 2. Hulk of a ship.—*m.* 3. Skeleton, of the animal body. *No tener más que la armazón*, To be only skin and bone.

Armelina [ar-may-lee'-nah], *f.* Ermine skin.

Armella [ar-mayl'-lyah], *f.* Staple or ring made of iron or other metal; box staple, bushing, screw-eyes. *Armellas*, (Naut.) Pieces of iron doubled in shape of a II with two large points, that they may be nailed to any part of a ship.

Armelluela [ar-mayl-lyoo-ay'-lah], *f. dim.* A small staple or ring.

Armenio, nia [ar-may'-ne-o, ne-ah], *a.* Armenian, relating to Armenia.

Armería [ar-may-ree'-ah], *f.* 1. Armoury; arsenal. 2. (Obs.) Trade of an armourer or gunsmith. 3. Heraldry.

Armero [ar-may'-ro], *m.* 1. Armourer or gunsmith. 2. Keeper of arms or armour. 3. (Mil.) A rack or stand for fire-arms.

Armígero, ra [ar-mee'-hay-ro, rah], *a.* (Poet.) Warlike.

Armilar [ar-me-lar'], *a.* *Esfera armilar*, Armillary sphere.

Armilla [ar-meel'-lyah], *f.* Principal part of the base of a column.

Armiño [ar-mee'-nyo], *m.* 1. Ermine, a small animal furnishing a valuable fur. Mustela erminea. 2. The fur of the ermine. *Armiños* (Her.), Figures of a white field interspersed with black spots.

Armipotente [ar-me-po-ten'-tay], *a.* (Poet.) Mighty in war.

Armisticio [ar-mis-tee'-the-o], *m.* Armistice, suspension of hostilities.

Armoisín [ar-mo-e-seen'], *m.* A thin silk or taffety manufactured in Italy and the East Indies.

Armón [ar-mone'], *m.* The fore carriage of a piece of artillery.

Armonía [ar-mo-nee'-ah], *f.* 1. Harmony, just proportion or concord of sound; harmoniousness; number. 2. Concord or correspondence of one thing with another. *Hacer* or *causar armonía*, To excite admiration, to produce novelty. 3. Friendship. *Correr con armonía*, To live in peace.

Armónica [ar-mo'-ne-cah], *f.* Harmonica, mouth organ.

Armónico, ca [ar-mo'-ne-co, cah], *a.* Harmonical, adapted to each other, musical, rhythmical.

Armonio [ar-mo'-ne-o], *m.* Harmonium, or reed organ. Strictly, the harmonium has force-bellows and the cabinet organ suction-bellows.

Armoniosamente [ar-mo-ne-o-sah-men'-tay], *adv.* Harmoniously.

Armonioso, sa [ar-mo-ne-o'-so, sah], *a.* 1. Harmonious, sonorous, pleasing to the ear; consonous. 2. (Met.) Adapted to each other, having the parts proportioned to each other.

Armonista [ar mo-nees'-tah], *f.* Harmonist.

Armonizar [ar-mo-ne-thar'], *va.* To harmonize, put in harmony: to produce harmony.

Armuelle [ar-moo-el'-lyay], *m.* (Bot.) Orach. Atriplex.

Arna [ar'-nah], *f.* (Prov.) Bee-hive.

Arnacho [ar-nah'-cho], *m.* 1. (Bot.) Rest harrow. Ononis arvensis. 2. Wild amaranth. 3. Orach.

Arnés [ar-ness'], *m.* 1. Harness, coat of mail or steel net-work for defence; armour. 2. Store-room for the accoutrements of cavalry. *Arneses*, Necessary tools, utensils, furniture used in a house, trade, or kitchen *Arnés de caballo*, Gear, trapping, and furniture of a horse.

Arnica [ar'-ne-cah], *f.* Arnica, a medicinal plant.

Arnilla [ar-neel'-lyah], *f. dim.* (Prov.) A small bee-hive.

Aro [ah'-ro], *m.* 1. Hoop of wood, iron, or other metals; iron staple; hoop-poles. 2. (Bot.) *V.* Yaro. *Meterle a uno por el aro* or *arillo*. To decoy any one.

Aroca [ah-ro'-cah], *f.* A sort of linen somewhat more than three quarters wide.

Aroma [ah-ro'-mah], *f.* Flower of the aromatic myrrh-tree.—*m.* 1. (Chem.) The odorant principle, the volatile spirit of plants. 2. A general name given to all gums, balsams, woods, and herbs of strong fragrance. 3. Perfume, fragrance.

Aromaticidad [ah-ro-mah-te-the-dahd'], *f.* An aromatic or fragrant quality, perfume.

Aromático, ca [ah-ro-mah'-te-co, cah], *a.* Aromatic, fragrant.

Aromatización [ah-ro-mah-te-thah-the-on'], *f.* Aromatization, the act of scenting with aromatics.

Aromatizador [ah-ro-mah-te-thah-dor'], *m.* Aromatizer.

Aromatizar [ah-ro-mah-te-thar'], *va.* To aromatize, to perfume.

Aromo [ah-ro'-mo], *m.* (Bot.) The aromatic myrrh-tree. Mimosa Farnesiana.

Aroza [ah-ro'-thah], *m.* Foreman in iron-works or forges.

Arpa [ar'-pah], *f.* 1. Harp, lyre. 2. (Ast.) Harp, a constellation.

Arpado [ar-pah'-do], *a.* Serrated, toothed.—*pp.* of Arpar.

Arpador [ar-pah-dor'], *m.* (Obs.) Harp-player.

Arpadura [ar-pah-doo'-rah]. *f.* *V.* Araño.

Arpar [ar-par'], *va.* 1. To tear clothes to pieces, to rend to tatters. 2. To claw, to tear with nails or claws.

Arpegio [ar-pay'-he-o], *m.* (Mus.) Arpeggio.

Arpella [ar-payl'-lyah], *f.* (Orn.) Harpy. Falco rufus.

Arpeo [ar-pay'-o], *m.* (Naut.) Grappling iron.

Arpía [ar-pee'-ah], *f.* 1. (Poet.) Harpy, a bird of prey represented by poets. 2. Harpy, a ravenous woman; an ugly, scolding shrew.

Arpillera [ar-peel-lyay'-rah], *f.* Sack-cloth, coarse linen made of tow, pack-cloth.

Arpista [ar-pees'-tah]; *m.* Harper, player on the harp by profession, harpist.

Arpón [ar-pone'], *m.* 1. Harpoon, a harping-iron. 2. (Naut.) Fish-gig.

Arponado, da [ar-po-nah'-do, dah], *a.* Harpooned, like a harpoon.

Arponear [ar-po-nay-ar'], *va.* To throw the harpoon.

Arponero [ar-po-nay'-ro], *m.* Harpooner, he who throws the harpoon.

Arqueada [ar-kay-ah'-dah], *f.* Stroke with the fiddle-bow, whereby sounds are produced from the strings of a musical instrument. *Dar arqueadas*, (Coll.) To show symptoms of nausea.

Arqueador [ar-kay-ah-dor'], *m.* 1. Ship-gauger, an officer whose business is is to measure the dimensions of ships. 2. One who forms arches. 3. Wool-beater.

Arqueaje [ar-kay-ah'-hay], *m.* The gauging of a ship.

Arqueamiento [ar-kay-ah-me-en'-to], *m.* *V.* ARQUEO.

Arquear [ar-kay-ar'], *va.* 1. To arch, to form in the shape of an arch. 2. Among clothiers, to beat the dust out of the wool. 3. (Naut.). To gauge or measure the dimensions of ships. *Arquear las cejas*, To arch the eye-brows: to frown. *Arquear para vomitar*, To retch.

Arqueo [ar-kay'-o], *m.* 1. The act of bending anything into the form of an arch. 2. (Naut.) The tonnage or burden of a ship. *V.* ARQUEAJE. 3. Verification of money and papers in a safe (Com.).

Arqueologia [ar-kay-o-lo-hee'-ah], *f.* Archæology, a discourse on antiquity.

Arqueólogo [ar-kay-o'-lo-go], *m.* Archæologist.

Arquería [ar-kay-ree'-ah], *f.* 1. Series of arches. 2. (Mex.) Aqueduct.

Arquero [ar-kay'-ro], *m.* 1. One whose trade is to make bows for arrows. 2. Treasurer, cashier. 3. Bowman, archer.

Arqueta [ar-kay'-tah], *f. dim.* A little chest, a small trunk.

Arquetipo [ar-kay-tee'-po], *m.* Archetype.

Arquetón [ar-kay-tone'], *m. aug.* A large trunk.

Arquetoncillo [ar-kay-ton-theel'-lyo], *m. dim.* A trunk or chest of a middling size.

Arquibanco [ar-ke-bahn'-co], *m.* A bench or seat with drawers.

Arquiepiscopal [ar-ke-ay-pis-co-pahl'], *a.* Archiepiscopal. *V.* ARZOBISPAL.

Arquifilósofo [ar-ke-fe-lo'-so-fo], *m.* Archphilosopher.

Arquilla, ita [ar-keel'-lyah, kee'-tah], *f. dim.* A little chest.

Arquillo [ar-keel'-lyo], *m. dim.* A small arch or bow.

Arquimesa [ar-ke-may'-sah], *f.* (Prov.) Scrutoire, a case of drawers for writing, with a desk, escritoire.

Arquisinagogo [ar-ke-se-nah-go'-go], *m.* Principal in the synagogue.

Arquitecto [ar-ke-tec'-to], *m.* An architect.

Arquitectónico, ca [ar-ke-tec-to'-ne-co, cah], *a.* Architectonic, architectural.

Arquitectura [ar-ke-tec-too'-rah], *f.* Architecture. *Arquitectura de jardines*, Landscape gardening, landscaping.

Arquitrabe [ar-ke-trah'-bay], *m.* Architrave, that part of a column which lies immediately upon the capital, and is the lowest member of the entablature.

Arrabal [ar-rah-bahl'], *m.* Suburb. *Arrabales*, Suburbs or extremities of a large town.

Arrabalero, ra [ar-rah-bah-lay'-ro, rah], *a.* 1. Belonging to the outskirts; ill-bred, churlish. 2. Coarse in dress or manners.

Arraca [ar-rah'-cah], *f.* (Naut.) Traveller, an iron traveller.

Arracada [ar-rah-cah'-dah], *f.* Ear-ring. *Arracadas*, (Met.) Young children hanging about a widow.

Arracimado, da [ar-rah-the-mah'-do, dah], *a.* Clustered.—*pp.* of ARRACIMARSE. Botryoid, botryoidal.

Arracimarse [ar-rah-the-mar'-say], *vr.* To cluster, or to be clustered together like a bunch of grapes.

Arraclán [ar-rah-clahn'], *m.* *V.* ALISO. Alder-tree.

Arráez [ar-rah'-eth], *m.* Captain or master of a Moorish ship. Used also in the Philippine Archipelago.

Arraigadas [ar-rah-e-gah'-das], *f. pl.* (Naut.) Futtock-shrouds.

Arraigado, da [ar-rah-e-gah'-do, dah]. 1. Possessed of landed property, real estate. 2. Fixed, inveterate, speaking of evils.

Arraigar [ar-rah-e-gar'], *vn.* 1. To root. 2. To give security in land.—*vr.* 1. To establish one's self in a place. 2. To be of long continuance, as a custom, habit, etc.

Arraigo [ar-rah'-e-go], *m.* Landed property. *Es hombre de arraigo*, He is a man of considerable landed property.

Arralar [ar-rah-lar'], *vn.* *V.* RALEAR.

Arramblar [ar-ram-blar'], *va.* 1. To cover with sand and gravel: applied to torrents and rivulets which overflow the adjacent country. 2. To sweep away, to drag along.

Arranca-clavos [ar-rahn'-cah-clah'-vos], *m.* Nail-puller.

Arrancada [ar-ran-cah'-dah], *f.* (Coll.) Sudden departure, violent sally.

Arrancadera [ar-ran-cah-day'-rah], *f.* Large bell worn by those animals which guide the rest of the flocks.

Arrancadero [ar-ran-cah-day'-ro], *m.* 1. (Prov.) The thickest part of the barrel of a gun. 2. Starting-point, course, or route.

Arrancado, da [ar-ran-cah'-do, dah], *a.* 1. (Coll.) Poor, penniless. 2. (Naut.) *Boga arrancada*, Strong uniform rowing. *De boga arrancada*, With long strokes of the oars.—*pp.* of ARRANCAR.

Arrancador, ra [ar-ran-cah-dor', rah], *m. & f.* An extirpator, a destroyer.

Arrancadura [ar-ran-cah-doo'-rah], *f.* (Obs.) **Arrancamiento** [ar-ran-cah-me-en'-to], *m.* Extirpation, the act of pulling up by the roots.

Arrancapinos [ar-ran-cah-pee'-nos], *m.* Nickname for little persons.

Arrancar [ar-ran-car'], *va.* 1. To pull up by the roots, to extirpate. 2. To force out, to wrest. 3. To pull out a nail, to draw out a tooth. 4. To carry off with violence. 5. To force up phlegm, bile, etc. 6. To start and pursue one's course. 7. To begin an arch or vault. 8. (Naut.) To get afloat, or set sail. *Arrancar de raíz*, To root out or up. *Arrancar la espada*, To unsheath the sword. *Arrancársele a uno el alma*, To die broken-hearted.

Arrancasiega [ar-ran-cah-se-ay'-gah], *f.* 1. Poor corn, half mowed and half pulled up. 2. (Prov.) A quarrel or dispute, with injurious language.

Arranciarse [ar-ran-the-ar'-say], *vr.* To grow rancid.

Arrancharse [ar-ran-char'-say], *vr.* To mess together.

Arranque [ar-rahn'-kay], *m.* 1. Extirpation, act of pulling up by the roots. 2. Wrench. 3. Flight of the imagination, sudden, unexpected gesture. 4. Violent fit, impetuousness. 5. Initiative, daring. *Arranque del caballo*, Sudden start of the horse. *Arranque automático*, Self-starter. *Un hombre de mucho arranque*, A man of daring, a man of an enterprising nature.

Arrapar [ar-rah-par'], *va.* To snatch away, to carry off. *V.* ARREBATAR.

Arrapiezo, Arrapo [ar-rah-pe-ay'-tho, ar-rah'-po], *m.* 1. Tatter or rag hanging from old clothes. 2. (Met.) A mean, worthless, despicable person.

Arras [ar'-ras], *f. pl.* 1. Thirteen pieces of money, which the bridegroom gives to the bride, as a pledge, in the act of marriage. 2. Dowry, a sum of money assigned by a husband to his wife, for her maintenance after his death, which according to the Spanish laws cannot exceed the tenth part of his fortune. 3. Earnest-money, handsel. *Arras de la bodega*, (Naut.) Wings of the hold.

Arrasado [ar-rah-sah'-do], *m.* A silk stuff, satin face; satin.

Arrasadura [ar-rah-sah-doo'-rah], *f.* *V.* RASADURA.

Arrasamiento [ar-rah-sah-me-en'-to], *m.* Demolition of a fortress or fortified place.

Arrasar [ar-rah-sar'], *va.* 1. To level, to make even, to smooth the surface of a thing. 2. To destroy, raze, demolish. 3. To obliterate. *Arrasar un bajel*, (Naut.) To cut down a vessel, to cut away part of her dead works.—*vn. & vr.* 1. To clear up, to grow fine: applied to the weather. 2. To fill with tears. *Arrasarse los ojos de lágrimas*, To weep bitterly.

Arrastradamente [ar-ras-trah-dah-men'-tay], *adv.* 1. Imperfectly. 2 Painfully, wretchedly.

Arrastraderas [ar-ras-trah-day'-ras], *f. pl.* (Naut.) Lower studding-sails.

Arrastradero [ar-ras-trah-day'-ro], *m* (Naut.) 1. A place on the seacoast, gently sloping toward the sea, where ships are careened; a careening-place. 2. Road by which logs are dragged. 3. Spot whence dead bulls are taken off.

Arrastrado, da [ar-ras-trah'-do, dah], *a.* 1. Dragged along. 2. Rascally, knavish. 3. Living in abject poverty.—*f.* (Coll.) A fallen woman, prostitute. *Andar arrastrado*, To live in the utmost misery and distress.—*pp.* of ARRASTRAR.

Arrastramiento [ar-ras-trah-me-en'-to], *m.* The act of dragging along the ground.

Arrastrante [ar-ras-trahn'-tay], *m.* Claimant of a degree in colleges.

Arrastrar [ar-ras-trar'], *va. & vn.* 1. To creep, to crawl. 2. To drag along the ground. 3. To bring one over to our opinion. 4. To lead a trump at cards. *Arrastrar la causa, el pleito, los autos*, etc., To move a lawsuit into another court. *Hacer alguna cosa arrastrando*, To do a thing against one's will, to do it ill.

Arrastre [ar-ras'-tray], *m.* 1. The act of leading a trump at cards. 2. The act of dragging; haulage, drayage. 3. Slope of the wall of a shaft. 4. (Amer.) A mill where silver ores are pulverized.

Arrate [ar-rah'-tay], *m.* A pound of sixteen ounces.

Arratonado [ar-rah-to-nah'-do], *a.* Gnawned by mice.

Arrayán [ar-rah-yahn'], *m.* (Bot.) Myrtle. Myrtus communis bœtica.

Arrayanal [ar-rah-yah-nahl'], *m.* Plantation of myrtles.

Arre! [ar'-ray]. Gee, get up; a word used by drivers to horses, mules, etc. *¡Arre, borrico!* Go on, ass!

¡Arre allá! Be off with you!

Arreada [ar-ray-ah'-dah], *f.* (Amer.) 1. Act of herding the grazing flock. 2. Conscription for military service.

Arreador [ar-ray-ah-dor'], *m.* Muleteer

Arrear [ar-ray-ar'], *va.* To drive horses, mules, etc.—*vr.* (Obs.) To be a mule teer.

Arrebañador, ra [ar-ray-bah-nyah-dor', rah], *m. & f.* Gleaner, gatherer.

Arrebañadura [ar-ray-bah-nyah-doo'-rah], *f.* The act of gleaning, picking up, or scraping together.

Arrebañar [ar-ray-bah-nyar'], *va.* To glean, to gather, to scrape together.

Arrebatadamente [ar-ray-bah-tah-dah-men'-tay], *adv.* Precipitately, headlong.

Arrebatado, da [ar-ray-bah-tah'-do, dah], *a.* 1. Rapid, violent. 2. Precipitate, rash, inconsiderate, impetuous. *Muerte arrebatada*, A sudden death. *Hombre arrebatado*, A rash, inconsiderate man.—*pp.* of ARREBATAR.

Arrebatador, ra [ar-ray-bah-tah-dor', rah], *m.* & *f.* One who snatches away, or takes a thing by violence.

Arrebatamiento [ar-ray-bah-tah-me-en'-to], *m.* 1. The act of carrying away by violence or precipitation. 2. Fury, rage, extreme passion. 3. Rapture, ecstasy, fit.

Arrebatar [ar-ray-bah-tar'], *va.* 1. To carry off, to take away by violence. 2. To snatch and seize things with precipitation. 3. To attract the attention, notice, etc.—*vr.* 1. To be led away by passion. 2. To be gathered earlier than usual on account of hot weather; said of crops. 3. To get roasted or scorched. *Arrebatarse el caballo*, Said of a horse which is overheated.

Arrebatiña [ar-ray-bah-tee'-nyah], *f.* The act of carrying off a thing precipitately out of a crowd.

Arrebato [ar-ray-bah'-to], *m.* Surprise, a sudden and unexpected attack upon an enemy; paroxysm, start. *Arrebato de cólera*, Sudden burst of passion.

Arrebol [ar-ray-bole'], *m.* 1. The red appearance of the sky or clouds. 2. Rouge, red paint for ladies. *Arreboles al oriente, agua amaneciente; Arreboles de Portugal, a la mañana, sol serán*, Proverbs relating to forecasting the weather in Spain.

Arrebolar [ar-ray-bo-lar'], *va.* To paint red.—*vr.* To rouge or to lay on rouge.

Arrebolera [ar-ray-bo-lay'-rah], *f.* 1. (Prov.) A woman who sells rouge. 2. Alkanet, a plant of which vegetable rouge is made. 3. A small pot or saucer with red paint. 4. (Bot.) Marvel of Peru, or four-o'clock.

Arrebollarse [ar-ray-bol-lyar'-say], *vr.* (Prov.) To precipitate one's self, to fall headlong.

Arrebozar [ar-ray-bo-thar'], *va.* To overlay meat with a jelly.—*vr.* 1. To muffle or wrap one's self up. 2. To be clustered around the bee-hive: spoken of bees; to swarm: of ants or flies.

Arrebozo [ar-ray-bo'-tho], *m.* *V.* REBOZO.

Arrebujadamente [ar-ray-boo-hah-dah-men'-tay], *adv.* Confusedly, with disorder.

Arrebujar [ar-ray-boo-har'], *va.* To gather up without order; to throw together with confusion, to huddle.—*vr.* To cover and roll one's self in the bed-clothes.

Arrecafe [ar-ray-cah'-fay], *m.* Cardoon. Cynara cardunculus.

Arreciar (ar-ray-the-ar'), *vn.* To become intensified. *Arreció la lluvia*, It rained harder.

Arrecife [ar-ray-thee'-fay], *m.* 1. Causeway, a road paved with stone; mole. 2. (Naut.) A reef, ridge of hidden rocks lying close under the surface of the water.

Arrecil [ar-ray-theel'], *m.* (Prov.) A sudden flood.

Arrecirse [ar-ray-theer'-say], *vr.* To be benumbed with excessive cold, to grow stiff with cold.

Arrechucho [ar-ray-choo'-cho], *m.* 1. A fit of anger. 2. Sudden and passing indisposition.

Arredilar [ar-ray-de-lar'], *va.* To put into the sheep-fold.

Arredomado, da [ar-ray-do-mah'-do, dah], *a.* *V.* REDOMADO.

Arredondar, Arredondear [ar-ray-don-dar', ar-ray-don-day-ar'], *va.* (Obs.) To round. *V.* REDONDEAR.

Arredramiento [ar-ray-drah-me-en'-to], *m.* The act of removing to a greater distance.

Arredrar [ar-ray-drar'], *va.* 1. To remove to a greater distance. 2. To terrify, to cause dread.—*vr.* *V.* ATEMORIZARSE.

Arregazado, da [ar-ray-gah-thah'-do, dah], *a.* Having the point turned up. *Nariz arregazada* or *arremangada*, A cocked nose.—*pp.* of ARREGAZAR.

Arregazar [ar-ray-gah-thar'], *va.* To truss, to tuck up the skirts of clothes.

Arregladamente [ar-ray-glah-dah-men'-tay], *adv.* Regularly.

Arreglado, da [ar-ray-glah'-do, dah], *a.* Regular, moderate.—*pp.* of ARREGLAR.

Arreglador [ar-ray-gla-dor'], *m.* (Com.) Surveyor, valuer (of averages).

Arreglamiento [ar-ray-glah-me-en'-to], *m.* (Obs.) Regulation, instruction in writing.

Arreglar [ar-ray-glar'], *va.* 1. To regulate, to reduce to order, to guide, to moderate. 2. To compound; to frame. (Com.) To arrange, settle; adjust. 3. To adjust the administration of provinces, and enact laws for them.—*vr.* To conform to law.

Arreglo [ar-ray'-glo], *m.* Rule, order. (Com.) Arrangement, settlement. *Con arreglo*, Conformably, according to.

Arregostarse [ar-ray-gos-tar'-say], *vr.* To relish or have a taste for a thing, to be attached to it.

Arrejaca [ar-ray-hah'-cah], *f.* *V.* ARREJAQUE.

Arrejacar [ar-ray-hah-car'], *va.* To plough across a piece of ground, to clear of weeds.

Arrejaco [ar-ray-hah'-co], *m.* (Orn.) Swift, martin. *V.* VENCEJO.

Arrejada [ar-ray-hah'-dah], *f.* (Agr.) Paddle of a plough, paddle-staff.

Arrejaque [ar-ray-hah'-kay], *m.* Fork with three prongs bent at the point.

Arrel, Arrelde [ar-rel', ar-rel'-day], *m.* 1. Weight of four pounds. 2. A bird of a very small size.

Arrellanarse [ar-rel-lyah-nar'-say], *vr.* 1. To sit at ease; to incline one's seat for greater ease. 2. (Met.) To make one's self comfortable. 3. To be satisfied with one's employment.

Arremangado, da [ar-ray-man-gah'-do, dah], *a.* Lifted upward. *Ojos arremangados*, Uplifted eyes.—*pp.* of ARREMANGAR.

Arremangar [ar-ray-man-gar'], *va.* To tuck up the sleeves or petticoats.—*vr.* To be fully resolved.

Arremango [ar-ray-mahn'-go], *m.* The act of tucking up the clothes.

Arremedador, ra [ar-ray-may-dah-dor', rah], *m.* & *f.* (Obs.) A mimic, a ludicrous imitator.

Arremetedor [ar-ray-may-tay-dor'], *m.* Assailant, aggressor.

Arremeter [ar-ray-may-terr'], *va.* 1. To assail, to attack with impetuosity, to make at. 2. To seize briskly. 3. To shock or offend the sight.

Arremetida [ar-ray-may-tee'-dah], *f.* 1. Attack, assault, invasion. 2. Start of horses from a barrier or other place.

Arremolinado, da [ar-ray-mo-le-nah'-do, dah], *a.* Whirled, turned round; (of wheat) blown down by a storm.

Arremolinar [ar-ray-mo-le-nar'], *va.* & *vr.* 1. To eddy, form eddies. 2. To gather together, to form a crowd.

Arrempujar [ar-rem-poo-har'], *va.* (Obs.) *V.* REMPUJAR.

Arremueco [ar-ray-moo-ay'-co], *m.* (Littl. us.) 1. A caress. 2. A movement of the lips expressive of contempt or scorn. *V.* ARRUMACO.

Arrendable [ar-ren-dah'-blay], *a.* Rentable; farmable, tenantable.

Arrendación [ar-ren-dah-the-on'], *f.* The act of renting, or taking at a certain rent.

Arrendadero [ar-ren-dah-day'-ro], *m.* An iron ring fastened to the manger, to which horses are tied.

Arrendado, da [ar-ren-dah'-do, dah], *a.* Obedient to the reins, applied to horses.—*pp.* of ARRENDAR.

Arrendador [ar-ren-dah-dor'], *m.* 1. Landlord, lessor, hirer, tenant, lessee, holder; farmer; copyholder. 2. *V.* ARRENDADERO. *Arrendador de plomo*, A very tiresome person.

Arrendadorcillo [ar-ren-dah-dor-theel'-lyo], *m. dim.* A petty tenant.

Arrendajo [ar-ren-dah'-ho], *m.* 1. (Orn.) The mocking-bird. 2. Mimic, buffoon.

Arrendamiento [ar-ren-dah-me-en'-to], *m.* 1. The act of renting, letting, or hiring to a tenant; lease. 2. The house or lease-rent.

Arrendante [ar-ren-dahn'-tay], *pa.* A tenant.

Arrendar [ar-ren-dar'], *va.* 1. To rent, to hold by paying rent, to let for rent, to lease, to hire. 2. To bridle a horse. 3. To tie a horse by the reins of a bridle. 4. To mimic, to imitate as a buffoon, to ridicule by a burlesque imitation. 5. To thin out plants. *Arrendar a diente*, To rent or let on condition of allowing commonage. *No le arriendo la ganancia*, I would not be bound for the consequences.

Arrendatario, ria [ar-ren-dah-tah'-re-o, ah], *m.* & *f.* 1. One who lets for rent, a lessor. 2. Lessee. 3. Farmer.

Arrentado, da [ar-ren-tah'-do, dah], *a.* Enjoying a considerable income from landed property.

Arreo [ar-ray'-o], *m.* Dress, ornament, decoration.—*pl.* 1. Appendages. 2. Trappings of a horse.

Arreo [ar-ray'-o], *adv.* (Coll.) Successively, uninterruptedly. *Llevar arreo*, To carry on one's shoulders.

Arrepápalo [ar-ray-pah'-pah-lo], *m.* A sort of fritters or buns.

Arrepentida [ar-ray-pen-tee'-dah], *f.* A woman of previous evil life who repents and shuts herself within a convent.

Arrepentido, da [ar-ray-pen-tee'-do, dah], *a.* Repentant.—*pp.* of ARREPENTIRSE.

Arrepentimiento [ar-ray-pen-te-me-en'-to], *m.* 1. Repentance, penitence, contriteness, compunction; conversion. 2. A lock of hair escaping in careless grace. 3. (Painting) Emendation in composition and drawing.

Arrepentirse [ar-ray-pen-teer'-say], *vr.* To repent, to express sorrow for having said or done something.

(*Yo me arrepiento, yo me arrepienta; él se arrepintió, él se arrepintiera;* from *Arrepentirse.* *V.* ASENTIR.)

Arrepistar [ar-ray-pis-tar'], *va.* In paper-mills, to grind or pound rags into a fine pulp.

Arrepisto [ar-ray-pees'-to], *m.* The act of grinding or pounding rags.

Arrepticio, cia [ar-rep-tee'-the-o, ah], *a.* Possessed or influenced by the devil.

Arrequesonarse [ar-ray-kay-so-nar'-say], *vr.* To be curded or coagulated; to curdle.

Arrequife [ar-ray-kee'-fay], *m.* Singeing-iron for burning or taking off the down which remains on cotton goods.

Arrequives [ar-ray-kee'-ves], *m. pl.* 1.

Ornaments, adornments. 2. Circumstances of a case. 3. Requisites.

Arrestado, da [ar-res-tah'-do, dah], *a.* Intrepid, bold, audacious.—*pp.* of ARRESTAR.

Arrestar [ar-res-tar'], *va.* To arrest, to confine, to imprison.—*vr.* To be bold and enterprising, to engage with spirit in an enterprise or undertaking.

Arresto [ar-res'-to], *m.* 1. Spirit, boldness in undertaking an enterprise. 2. Detention. (Mil.) Prison, arrest.

Arretín [ar-ray-teen'], *m.* *V.* FILIPICHÍN.

Arretranca [ar-ray-trahn'-cah], *f.* A broad crupper for mules.

Arrevesado [ar-ray-vay-sah'-do], *a.* Queer, odd.

Arrezafe [ar-ray-thah'-fay], *m.* A place full of thistles, brush-wood, and brambles.

Arria [ar'-re-ah], *f.* Drove of beasts.

Arriada [ar-re-ah'-dah], *f.* (Prov.) Swell of waters, flood, overflowing.

Arrianismo [ar-re-ah-nees'-mo], *m.* Arianism.

Arriano, na [ar-re-ah'-no, nah], *a.* Arian, adherent to the tenets of Arius.

Arriar [ar-re-ar'], *va.* (Naut.) 1. To lower, to strike. *Arriar la bandera,* To strike the colours. *Arriar las vergas y los masteleros,* To strike the yards and top-masts. *Arriar un cabo,* To pay out the cable. *Arriar en banda,* To pay out the whole cable. *Arriar la gavia,* To let go the main-top-sail. 2. *vr.* To destroy by floods or a sudden fall of rain. *¡Arría!* Let go!

Arriata [ar-re-ah'-tah], *f.* *V.* ARRIATE.

Arriate [ar-re-ah'-tay], *m.* 1. A border in gardens where herbs, flowers, etc., are planted. 2. Trellis around beds or walks in a garden. 3. A causeway, a paved road.

Arriaz, Arrial [ar-re-ath', ar-re-ahl'l], *m.* Hilt-bar of a sword.

Arriba [ar-ree'-bah], *adv.* 1. Above, over, up, high, on high, overhead. 2. (Naut.) Aloft. 3. In writings, previously mentioned. 4. (Met.) A high post or station with respect to others. 5. In the hands of the king. *La consulta está arriba,* The business is laid before the king. *Está decretado de arriba,* It is decreed by high authority. *Arriba dicho,* Above mentioned. *De arriba abajo,* From top to bottom. *Arriba de seis varas,* (Coll.) Above six yards. *Ir agua arriba,* (Naut.) To work up the river. *De arriba,* From heaven.

Arribada [ar-re-bah'-dah], *f.* 1. (Naut.) The arrival of a vessel in a port. 2. (Naut.) *Arribada de un bajel a sotavento,* The falling off of a vessel to leeward. *Llega el bajel de arribada,* The ship put into a port by stress of weather.

Arribaje [ar-re-bah'-hay], *m.* 1. Arrival. 2. Spot where a ship may approach land.

Arribar [ar-re-bar'], *vn.* (Naut.) 1. To put into a harbour in distress. 2. To arrive by land at a stopping-place. 3. To fall off to leeward; to bear away. 4. (Met.) To recover from a disease or calamity; to convalesce. 5. (Coll.) To accomplish one's desire. *Arribar todo,* To bear away before the wind. *Arribar a escote larga,* To bear away large. *Arribar sobre un bajel,* To bear down upon a ship.

Arribo [ar-ree'-bo], *m.* Arrival.

Arricete [ar-re-thay'-tay], *m.* Shoal, sand-bank.

Arricises [ar-re-thee'-ses], *m. pl.* The saddle-straps to which the girths are fastened.

Arriendo [ar-re-en'-do], *m.* Ablocation, lease, rental. *V.* ARRENDAMIENTO. (*Yo arriendo, yo arriende,* from *Arrendar.* *V.* ACERTAR.)

Arriería [ar-re-ay-ree'-ah], *f.* The calling of a driver of mules or other beasts of burden.

Arrierico, illo, ito [ar-re-ay-ree'-co, eel'-yo, ee'-to], *m. dim.* One who carries on mule-driving in a petty way.

Arriero [ar-re-ay'-ro], *m.* Muleteer, he who drives mules or other beasts of burden, carrying goods from one place to another.

Arriesgadamente [ar-re-es-gah-dah-men'-tay], *adv.* Dangerously, hazardously.

Arriesgado, da [ar-re-es-gah'-do, dah], *a.* 1. Perilous, dangerous, hazardous. 2. Dangerous to be dealt with; daring. *Hombre arriesgado,* A dangerous man.—*pp.* of ARRIESGAR.

Arriesgar [ar-re-es-gar'], *va.* To risk, to hazard, to expose to danger, to jeopard, to jump.—*vr.* To be exposed to danger; to dare.

Arrimadero [ar-re-mah-day'-ro], *m.* Scaffold, a stage; a stick or support to lean upon.

Arrimadillo [ar-re-mah-deel'-lyo], *m.* A mat or wainscot upon a wall.

Arrimadizo [ar-re-mah-dee'-tho], *a.* & *m.* 1. That which is designed to be applied to any thing. 2. (Met.) Parasite, sponger, one who meanly hangs upon another for subsistence. 3. (Obs.) Support, prop.

Arrimado, da [ar-re-mah'-do, dah], *pp.* of ARRIMAR.—*Tener arrimado* or *arrimados,* To be possessed by evil spirits.

Arrimador [ar-re-mah-dor'], *m.* The back-log in a fire-place.

Arrimadura [ar-re-mah-doo'-rah], *f.* The act of approaching.

Arrimar [ar-re-mar'], *va.* 1. To approach, to draw near, to join one thing to another. 2. (Naut.) To stow the cargo, to trim the hold. 3. To lay a thing aside, to put by; to reject. 4. To lay down a command. 5. To displace, to dismiss. 6. *Arrimar el clavo,* To prick a horse at the time of shoeing him. *Arrimar el clavo a uno,* (Met.) To impose, to deceive.—*vr.* 1. To lean upon a thing. 2. To join others for the purpose of forming a body with them. 3. (Met.) To come to the knowledge of a thing. *Arrimarse al punto de la dificultad,* To come to the point. *Arrimarse al parecer de otro,* To espouse another's opinion.

Arrime [ar-ree'-may], *m.* In the game of bowls, the mark for the balls to arrive at.

Arrimo [ar-ree'-mo], *m.* 1. The act of joining one thing to another. 2. Staff, stick, crutch. 3. (Met.) Protection or support of a powerful person; help. 4. Among builders, an insulated wall which has no weight to support; idle wall.

Arrimón [ar-re-mone'], *m.* (*Hacer el*)—(Coll.) 1. To stagger along a wall, supported by it, in a state of intoxication. 2. *Estar de arrimón,* To stand watch over somebody.

Arrinconado, da [ar-rin-co-nah'-do, dah], *a.* Out of favour, retired from the world.—*pp.* of ARRINCONAR.

Arrinconar [ar-rin-co-nar'], *va.* 1. To put a thing in a corner; to lay aside, to reject. 2. (Met.) To remove one from a trust, to withdraw one's favour or protection.—*vr.* To retire from the world.

Arriscadamente [ar-ris-cah-dah-men'-tay], *adv.* Boldly, audaciously.

Arriscado, da [ar-ris-cah'-do, dah], *a.* 1. Forward, bold, audacious, impudent. 2. Brisk, easy, free. *Caballo arriscado,* A high-mettled horse. 3. Broken or craggy ground.—*pp.* of ARRISCARSE.

Arriscador [ar-ris-cah-dor'], *m.* (Prov.) A gleaner of olives.

Arriscar [ar-ris-car'], *va.* To risk.—*vr.* 1. To hold up the head; to be proud, haughty, or arrogant. 2. To plunge over a cliff: said of flocks. (Acad.) *Quien no arrisca, no aprisca,* Nothing venture, nothing have.

Arristranco [ar-ris-trahn'-co], *m.* (Cuba) Useless furniture; lumber.

Arrizar [ar-re-thar'], *va.* (Naut.) 1. To reef. 2. To stow the boat on deck. *Arrizar el ancla,* To stow the anchor. *Arrizar la artillería,* To house the guns. 3. On board the galleys, to tie or lash one down.

Arroba [ar-ro'-bah], *f.* 1. A Spanish weight of twenty-five pounds; a quarter = 11.5 kilos. 2. A Spanish measure, containing thirty-two pints; about four gallons. *Por arrobas,* By wholesale. *Echar por arrobas,* (Met.) To exaggerate, to make hyperbolical amplifications.

Arrobadizo, za [ar-ro-bah-dee'-tho, thah], *a.* (Coll.) Feigning ecstasy and rapture.

Arrobado [ar-ro-bah'-do], *pp.* of ARROBAR. *Por arrobado,* (Obs.) By wholesale.

Arrobador, ra [ar-ro-bah-dor', rah], *a.* Enchanting, delightful, ecstatic.

Arrobamiento [ar-ro-bah-me-en'-to], *m.* 1. Ecstatic rapture, or elevation of the mind to God. 2. Amazement, astonishment, high admiration. 3. Ecstasy, ravishment.

Arrobar [ar-ro-bar'], *va.* (Obs.) To weigh or measure by arrobas.—*vr.* To be in a state of rapturous amazement, to be out of one's senses.

Arrobero, ra [ar-ro-bay'-ro, rah], *m.* & *f.* (Prov.) 1. About an arroba or quarter in weight. 2. Baker for a community.

Arrobita [ar-ro-bee'-tah], *f. dim.* The weight of an arroba in a small compass.

Arrobo [ar-ro'-bo], *m.* *V.* ARROBAMIENTO and ÉXTASIS.

Arrocabe [ar-ro-cah'-bay], *m.* A wooden frieze.

Arrocero [ar-ro-thay'-ro], *m.* A grower of or dealer in rice.

Arrocinado, da [ar-ro-the-nah'-do, dah], *a.* 1. Dull, stupid, like a worn-out horse or *rocín.* 2. Hack-like: applied to horses.—*pp.* of ARROCINARSE.

Arrocinar [ar-ro-the'-nar], *va.* To reduce to brutish habits, to brutify.—*vr.* To become dull and stupid.

Arrodajarse [ar-ro-dah-har'-say], *vr.* (Costa Rica) To sit upon the ground.

Arrodelado, da [ar-ro-day-lah'-do, dah], *pp.* of ARRODELARSE. Bearing a target, shield, or buckler.

Arrodelarse [ar-ro-day-lar'-say], *vr.* To be armed with a shield or buckler.

Arrodeo [ar-ro-day'-o], *m.* *V.* RODEO.

Arrodilladura [ar-ro-deel-lyah-doo'-rah], *f.* **Arrodillamiento** [ar-ro-deel-lyah-me-en'-to], *m.* The act of kneeling or bending the knee.

Arrodillar [ar-ro-deel-lyar'], *vn.* To bend the knee down to the ground.—*vr.* To kneel to the ground.

Arrodrigar, Arrodrigonar [ar-ro-dre-gar', ar-ro-dre-go-nar'], *va.* (Prov.) To prop vines.

Arrogación [ar-ro-gah-the-on'], *f.* 1. Arrogation, the act of claiming in a proud manner. 2. Adoption of a child which has no father or is independent of him.

Arrogador [ar-ro-gah-dor'], *m.* One who claims in a proud manner.

Arrogancia [ar-ro-gahn'-the-ah], *a.* 1. Arrogance, haughtiness, loftiness, conceit; confidence. 2. Stately carriage of a high-mettled horse.

Arrogante [ar-ro-gahn'-tay], *a.* 1. High-minded, spirited. 2. Haughty, proud, assuming; magisterial, masterly.

Arrogantemente [ar-ro-gan-tay-men'-tay], *adv.* Arrogantly, haughtily, forwardly; highly; magisterially.

Arrogar [ar-ro-gar'], *va.* 1. (Law) To adopt. 2. To arrogate, to claim in a proud manner.—*vr.* To appropriate to one's self, to claim unjustly.

Arrojadamente [ar-ro-hah-dah men'-tay], *adv.* Audaciously, boldly.

Arrojadillo [ar-ro-hah-deel'-lyo], *m.* (Obs.) Handkerchief, or other piece of silk or linen, which women used formerly to tie around the head to keep it warm.

Arrojadizo, za [ar-ro-hah-dee'-tho, thah], *a.* 1. That which can be easily cast, thrown, or darted; missile. 2. (Obs.) Spirited, bold, courageous.

Arrojado, da [ar-ro-hah'-do, dah], *a.* 1. Rash, inconsiderate, forward, foolhardy, hasty, dashing. 2. Bold, intrepid, fearless.—*pp.* of ARROJAR.

Arrojador [ar-ro-hah-dor'], *m.* A thrower, a flinger.

Arrojar [ar-ro-har'], *va.* 1. To dart, launch, or fling any thing, to hurl, to jerk, to dash. 2. To shed a fragrance, to emit light. 3. To shoot, to sprout, to grow up: speaking of plants. 4. (Naut.) To drive or cast on rocks or shoals: applied to the wind. 5. To make red hot, as an oven. 6. To turn away or dismiss in an angry manner.—*vr.* 1. To launch, to throw one's self forward with impetuosity. 2. (Met.) To venture upon an enterprise in an inconsiderate manner.

Arroje [ar-ro'-hay], *m.* 1. The left side of the stage of a theatre. 2. The person who throws himself from this spot, with a rope fastened, to raise the curtain.

Arrojo [ar-ro'-ho], *m.* Boldness, intrepidity, fearlessness. *Arrojo al agua*, or *a la mar*, Jettison, jetsam.

Arrollador [ar-rol-lyah-dor'], *m.* 1. Roller, a kind of cylinder used for moving weighty things. 2. (Obs.) *V.* ARRULLADOR.

Arrollamiento [ar-roh-lyah-me-en'-to], *m.* 1. Winding, coiling. 2. Sweeping, carrying off.

Arrollar [ar-rol-lyar'], *va.* 1. To roll up, to roll any thing round, to wrap or twist round. 2. To carry off, to sweep away: applied to a storm or torrent; to expel. 3. (Met.) To defeat, to rout an enemy. 4. (Met.) To confound an opponent. 5. *Arrollar a un niño*, (Prov.) To dandle a child. 6. (Obs.) To lull to rest.

Arromadizarse [ar-ro-mah-de-thar'-say], *vr.* To catch cold.

Arromanzar [ar-ro-man-thar'], *va.* (Obs.) To translate into the common or vernacular Spanish language.

Arromar [ar-ro-mar'], *va.* To blunt, to dull the edge or point.

Arromper [ar-rom-perr'], *va.* (Obs.) To break up the ground for sowing.

Arrompido [ar-rom-pee'-do], *m.* A piece of ground newly broken.

Arronzar [ar-ron-thar'], *va.* (Naut.) To haul a hawser, without the aid of the capstan, windlass, or tackle.

Arropado, da [ar-ro-pah'-do, dah], *a.* Mixed with must: applied to wine. —*pp.* of ARROPAR.

Arropamiento [ar-ro-pah-me-en'-to], *m.* The act of clothing or dressing.

Arropar [ar-ro-par'], *va.* 1. To cover the body with clothes, to dress. *Arrópate que sudas*, Cover yourself, as you sweat: ironically addressed to a person who has done little and affects to be fatigued. 2. *Arropar el vino*, To mix wine in a state of fermentation with boiled wine, to give it a body. 3. *Arropar las viñas*, To cover the roots of vines with dung and earth.

Arrope [ar-ro'-pay], *m.* 1. Must or new wine boiled until it is as dense as a sirup. 2. A kind of decoction made in imitation of boiled must. 3. Conserve made of boiled honey. *Arrope de moras*, Mulberry sirup.

Arropea [ar-ro-pay'-ah], *f.* Irons, fetters; shackles for horses. In Asturias they are called *farropeas*, and in Galicia *ferropeas*.

Arropera [ar-ro-pay'-rah], *f.* Vessels for holding boiled must, sirup, etc.

Arropía [ar-ro-pee'-ah], *f.* (Prov.) Cake made of flour, honey, and spice. *V.* MELCOCHA.

Arropiero [ar-ro-pe-ay'-ro], *m.* (Prov.) Maker or seller of sweet cakes.

Arrostrar [ar-ros-trar'], *va.* 1. To set about or perform a thing in a cheerful manner. 2. *Arrostrar los peligros, los trabajos, la muerte*, To encounter dangers, fatigues, death.—*vr.* To close with the enemy, to fight him face to face.

Arroyada, *f.* **Arroyadero**, *m.* [ar-ro-yah'-dah, ar-ro-yah-day'-ro]. 1. The valley through which a rivulet runs. 2. The channel of a rivulet.

Arroyar [ar-ro-yar'], *va.* To inundate sown ground; to form gutters, from heavy rain.—*vr.* To be affected with rust: spoken of wheat, and other grain.

Arroyato [ar-ro-yah'-to], *m.* (Obs.) *V.* ARROYO.

Arroyico, Arroyuelo [ar-ro-yee'-co, ar-ro-yoo-ay'-lo], *m. dim.* A rill, a small brook, a rivulet.

Arroyo [ar-ro'-yo], *m.* 1. Rivulet, a small river, current. 2. The water-course of a street; gutter.

Arroz [ar-roth'], *m.* Rice. Oryza sativa. (Coll.) *Arroz y gallo muerto*, a grand dinner, a banquet.

Arrozal [ar-ro-thal'], *m.* Field sown with rice.

Arrozar [ar-ro-thar'], *va.* To ice a liquid, to congeal it a little.

Arruar [ar-roo-ar'], *vn.* To grunt like a wild boar when it sniffs pursuers.

Arrufado, da [ar-roo-fah'-do, dah], *pp.* of ARRUFAR. Sheered, curved. *Navío muy arrufado*, (Naut.) A moon-sheered ship.

Arrufadura [ar-roo-fah-doo'-rah], *f.* (Naut.) Sheer of a ship.

Arrufar [ar-roo-far'], *va.* (Naut.) To incurvate, to form the sheer of a ship.—*vr.* To snarl, show the teeth (of a dog).

Arrufianado, da [ar-roo-fe-ah-nah'-do, dah], *a.* Ruffianly, impudent.

Arrufo [ar-roo'-fo], *m.* *V.* ARRUFADURA.

Arruga [ar-roo'-gah], *f.* 1. Wrinkle, a corrugation. 2. Rumple, or rude plait in clothes, fold, crease.

Arrugación, *f.* **Arrugamiento**, *m.* [ar-roo-gah-the-on', ar-roo-gah-me-en'-to]. Corrugation, the act and effect of wrinkling.

Arrugar [ar-roo-gar'], *va.* 1. To wrinkle, to contract into wrinkles, to corrugate, to constrict, to crumple, to cockle. 2. To rumple, to fold, to gather, to crease, to pleat. *Arrugar la frente*, To knit the brow, to frown.

Arrugia [ah-roo'-hee-ah], *f.* (Obs. Min.) A hole dug in the ground to discover gold.

Arrugón [ar-roo-gone'], *m.* Prominent decoration of carved work.

Arruinador, ra [ar-roo-e-nah-dor', rah], *m.* & *f.* Ruiner, demolisher, a destroyer.

Arruinamiento [ar-roo-e-nah-me-en'-to], *m.* Ruin, destruction, ruinousness.

Arruinar [ar-roo-e-nar'], *va.* 1. To throw down, to demolish, to lay level. 2. To ruin, to confound, to crack; to crush. 3. (Met.) To destroy, to cause great mischief.

Arrullador, ra [ar-rool-lyah-dor', rah], *m.* & *f.* 1. A person who lulls babes to rest. 2. Flatterer, cajoler.

Arrullar [ar-rool-lyar'], *va.* 1. To lull babes. 2. To court, to coo and bill.

Arrullo [ar-rool'-lyo], *m.* 1. The cooing and billing of doves. 2. Lullaby.

Arrumaco [ar-roo-mah'-co], *m.* Caress, the act of endearment, profession of friendship.

Arrumaje [ar-roo-mah'-hay], *m.* (Naut.) Stowage of a ship's cargo.

Arrumar [ar-roo-mar'], *va.* (Naut.) To stow the cargo.

Arrumazón [ar-roo-mah-thone'], *f.* 1. (Naut.) The act and effect of stowing. 2. Horizon overcast with clouds.

Arrumbadas [ar-room-bah'-das], *f. pl.* (Naut.) Wales of a row-galley.

Arrumbador, ra [ar-room-bah-dor', rah], *m.* & *f.* 1. One who heaps or piles. 2. (Naut.) Steersman.

Arrumbamiento [ar-room-bah-me-en'-to], *m.* The direction of a thing as it moves, with respect to another.

Arrumbar [ar-room-bar'], *va.* 1. (Prov.) To put any thing away in a lumber-room. 2. (Met.) To refute one in conversation. 3. To decant wine, to pour it off gently.—*vr.* (Naut.) To resume and steer the proper course.

Arrunflarse [ar-roon-flar'-say], *vr.* To have a flush of cards of the same suit.

Arrurruz [ar-roor-rooth'], *m.* Arrow-root.

Arsáfraga [ar-sah'-frah-gah], *f.* A plant.

Arsenal [ar-say-nahl'], *m.* 1. Ship-yard, dockyard, navy-yard. 2. Arsenal, repository of arms and ammunition. This second definition is not recognized by some of the dictionaries. (Arabic dársena'a.)

Arseniato [ar-say-ne-ah'-to], *m.* (Chem.) Arseniate.

Arsenical [ar-say-ne-cahl'], *a.* (Chem.) Arsenical, relating to arsenic.

Arsénico [ar-say'-ne-co], *m.* (Chem.) Arsenic, a mineral substance, which facilitates the fusion of metals, and proves a violent poison; ratsbane.

Arsenioso [ar-say-ne-o'-so], *a.* Arsenious.

Arsenito [ar-say-nee'-to], *m.* Arsenite.

Arsolla [ar-sol'-lyah], *f.* *V.* ARZOLLA.

Arta [ar'-tah], *f.* *V.* PLANTAINA. Plantain, *Arta de agua.* *V.* ZARAGATONA.

Artal [ar-tahl'], *m.* A kind of pie.

Artalete [ar-tah-lay'-tay], *m.* A sort of tart.

Artanica, Artanita [ar-tah-nee'-cah, ar-tah-nee'-tah], *f.* (Bot.) Sow-bread. Cyclamen Europæum.

Arte [ar'-tay], *m.* & *f.* 1. An art. 2. Art, the power of doing something not taught by nature and instinct. 3. Caution, skill, craft, cunning. 4. Artifice, machine. 5. Everything done by human industry. *No tener arte ni parte en alguna cosa*, To have neither art nor part in a thing, to have nothing to do with the business. *Arte tormentaria*, Art of artillery or military enginery. *Artes, f. pl.* Intrigues, improper means. *Artes mecánicas*, Mechanical arts, occupations, or handicrafts. *Artes liberales*, Liberal arts. *Las bellas artes*, The fine arts. *Buen arte*, Gracefulness of manners and gait. *Mal arte*, Awkward ness of manners and gait.

Artecillo, lla [ar-tay-theel'-lyo, lyah], *m. & f. dim.* Petty art or trade.

Artefacto [ar-tay-fac'-to], *m.* 1. Device, contrivance. 2. Artifact. *Artefacto sideral*, Space artifact.

Artejo [ar-tay'-ho], *m.* Joint or knuckle of the fingers.

Artemisa, Artemisia [ar-tay-mee'-sah, ar-tay-mee'-se-ah], *f.* (Bot.) Mug-wort, feverfew. Artemisia vulgaris.

Artena [ar-tay'-nah], *f.* An aquatic fowl of the size of a goose, found in the island of Tremiti in the Adriatic Gulf.

Artera [ar-tay'-rah], *f.* (Prov.) An iron instrument for marking bread before it is baked.

Arteramente [ar-tay-rah-men'-tay], *adv.* Craftily, fraudulently.

Arteria [ar-tay'-re-ah], *f.* (Anat.) An artery. *Arterias de la madera*, Veins formed in wood and timber by the various ramifications of the fibres. *Áspera arteria* or *traquiarteria*, The wind-pipe.

Artería [ar-tay-ree'-ah], *f.* Artifice, stratagem, cunning; sagacity.

Arterial [ar-tay-re-ahl'], *a.* Arterial, belonging to the arteries.

Arteriola [ar-tay-re-oh'-lah], *f. dim.* Small artery; arteriole.

Arteriosclerosis [ar-tay-re-os-clay-ro'-sis], *f.* Arteriosclerosis, hardening of the arteries.

Arterioso, sa [ar-tay-re-o'-so, sah], *a. V.* Arterial.

Arteriotomía [ar-tay-re-o-to-mee'-ah], *f.* (Anat.) Arteriotomy, the letting blood from an artery.

Artero, ra [ar-tay'-ro, rah], *a.* Dexterous, cunning, artful.

Artesa [ar-tay'-sah], *f.* 1. Trough in which dough of bread is worked. 2. Canoe. *Artesa de panaderos*, Wooden bowl.

Artesano [ar-tay-sah'-no], *m.* Artisan, mechanic, artificer, handicraftsman.

Artesiano, na [ar-tay-se-ah'-no, nah], *a.* Artesian. *Pozo artesiano*, Artesian well.

Artesilla [ar-tay-seel'-lyah], *f.* 1. (Dim.) A small trough. 2. A sort of festive exercise on horseback. 3. A trough for water at a draw-well.

Artesón [ar-tay-sone'], *m.* 1. A round kitchen trough for dishes, plates, etc. 2. Ceiling carved in the shape of a trough; ornamented vaulting; panelled ceiling. *Artesón de lavar*, Wash-tub.

Artesonado, da [ar-tay-so-nah'-do, dah]. *a.* Panelling, trellis-work: applied to ceilings.

Artesoncillo [ar-tay-son-theel'-lyo], *m. dim.* A small trough.

Artesuela [ar-tay-soo-ay'-lah], *f. dim.* A small kneading-trough.

Artético, ca [ar-tay'-te-co, cah], *a.* 1. Afflicted with the arthritis. 2. Arthritic.

Artico, ca [ar'-te-co, cah], *a.* (Astr.) Arctic, northern.

Articulación [ar-te-coo-lah-the-on'], *f.* 1. Articulation, a joint. 2. Articulation, distinct pronunciation of words and syllables. *Articulación universal*, (Mech.) Universal joint.

Articuladamente [ar-te-coo-lah-dah-men'-tay], *adv.* Distinctly, articulately.

Articulado, da [ar-te-coo-lah'-do, dah], *a.* Articulate. provided with a joint. (Zool.) Articulate, belonging to that large division of the animal kingdom, the articulata.

Articular [ar-te-coo-lar'], *va.* 1. To articulate, to pronounce words clearly and distinctly. 2. To form the interrogatories which are put to witnesses examined in the course of law proceedings. 3. (Poet.) To accent.

Articular, Articulario, ria [ar-te-coo-lar', ar-te-coo-lah'-re-o, ah], *a.* Articular, belonging to the joints.

Articulista [ar-te-coo-lees'-tah], *m. & f.* Newspaper or magazine feature writer.

Artículo [ar-tee'-coo-lo], *m.* 1. Article, section; a word or term separately defined in a dictionary. 2. Plea put in before a court of justice. 3. Article, essay, in a periodical. 4. (Gram.) Article, part of speech. 5. Clause, condition, stipulation. 6. (Bot.) Geniculation. 7. (Anat.) Joint of movable bones. *Varios artículos*, (Coll.) Sundry articles, things, knick-knacks. *Formar artículo*, To start an incidental question in the course of a law-suit. *Artículo de la muerte*, Point of death.

Artífice [ar-tee'-fe-thay], *m.* 1. Artificer, artisan, craftsman. 2. Inventor, contriver, maker.

Artificial [ar-te-fe-the-ahl'], *a.* Artificial, made by art. *Fuegos artificiales*, Fireworks.

Artificialmente [ar-te-fe-the-al-men'-tay], *adv.* Artificially.

Artificio [ar-te-fee'-the-o], *m.* 1. Art with which a thing is performed, workmanship, craft. 2. (Met.) Artifice, cunning, trick, guilefulness, contrivance, finesse, craft, fraud. 3. Machine which facilitates the exercise of some art.

Artificiosamente [ar-te-fe-the-o-sah-men'-tay], *adv.* 1. Artificially. 2. Artful, craftily, fraudulently.

Artificioso, sa [ar-te-fe-the-o'-so, sah], *a.* 1. Skilful, ingenious. 2. Artful, crafty, cunning, fraudulent.

Artiga [ar-tee'-gah], *f.* Land newly broken up.

Artigar [ar-te-gar'], *va.* To break and level land before cultivation.

Artillar [ar-teel-lyar'], *va.* To mount cannon.

Artillería [ar-teel-lyay-ree'-ah], *f.* 1. Gunnery. 2. Artillery, cannon, piece of ordnance. 3. The division of the army assigned to this service. *Parque de artillería*, Park of artillery. *Tren de artillería*, Train of artillery. *Poner* or *asestar toda la artillería*, (Met.) To set all engines at work for obtaining something, to leave no stone unturned.

Artillero [ar-teel-lyay'-ro], *m.* 1. Professor of the art of artillery. 2. Gunner, artillery-man.

Artimaña [ar-te-mah'-nyah], *f.* 1. Trap, snare, gin. 2. Device, stratagem, artifice, counterfeit, cunning.

Artimón [ar-te-mone'], *m.* (Naut.) Mizzen-mast; sail of a galley.

Artina [ar-tee'-nah], *f.* (Prov.) The fruit of the box-thorn.

Artista [ar-tees'-tah], *m.* 1. Artist; artisan, tradesman, craftsmaster. 2. He who studies logic, physics, or metaphysics.

Artísticamente, *adv.* Artistically.

Artístico, ca [ar-tees'-te-co, cah], *a.* Artistic, belonging to art.

Artolas [ar-to'-las], *f. pl.* Pannier; a pack-saddle for two persons.

Artólitos [ar-to'-le-tos], *m.* A concave stone of the nature of a sponge.

Artos [ar'-tos], *m.* 1. Various species of thistles. 2. (Prov.) The box-thorn. *V.* Cambronera.

Artrítico, ca [ar-tree'-te-co, cah], *a.* Arthritic, arthritical.

Artritis [ar-tree'-tees], *f.* (Med.) Arthritis.

Artrópodo [ar-tro'-po-do], *m. & a.* (Zool.) Arthropod.

Artuña [ar-too'-nyah], *f.* A ewe whose lamb has perished.

Arturo [ar-too'-ro], *m.* 1. (Astr.) Arcturus, a fixed star of the first magnitude in the constellation Bootes. 2. Proper name, Arthur.

Arugas [ah-roo'-gas], *f.* (Bot.) *V.* Matricaria. Feverfew.

Aruñar [ah-roo'-nyar], *va. V.* Arañar.

Aruñazo [ah-roo-nyah'-tho], *m.* (Obs.) A large scratch. *V.* Arañazo.

Aruño [ah-roo'-nyo], *m. V.* Araño.

Aruñón [ah-roo-nyon'], *m.* 1. (Obs.) A scratcher. 2. Pickpocket.

Arúspice [ah-roos'-pe-thay], *m.* Augurer, soothsayer.

Aruspicina [ah-roos-pe-thee'-nah], *f.* Aruspicy, divining from the intestines of animals.

Arveja [ar-vay'-hah], *f.* (Bot.) Vetch, tare. Lathyrus aphaca.

Arvejal, Arvejar [ar-vay-hahl', ar-vay-har'], *m.* Field sown with vetches.

Arvejo [ar-vay'-ho], *m.* (Bot.) Bastard chick-pea, or Spanish pea. Cicer arietinum.

Arvejón [ar-vay-hone'], *m.* (Bot.) Chickling-vetch. Lathyrus sativa.

Arvejona [ar-vay-ho'-nah], *f.* (Prov.) 1. *V.* Arveja. 2. *V.* Algarroba.

Arvela [ar-vay'-lah], *f.* A blue-feathered bird, the kingfisher.

Arvense [ar-ven'-say], *a.* (Bot.) A term applied to all plants which grow in sown fields.

Arza [ar'-thah], *f.* (Naut.) Fall of a tackle.

Arzobispado [ar-tho-bis-pah'-do], *m.* Archbishopric.

Arzobispal [ar-tho-bis-pahl'], *a.* Archiepiscopal.

Arzobispo [ar-tho-bees'-po], *m.* Archbishop.

Arzolla [ar-thol'-lyah], *f.* (Prov.) *V.* Almendruco. 1. Lesser burdock. 2. Milk thistle.

Arzón [ar-thone'], *m.* Fore and hind bow of a saddle, saddle-tree.

As [ahs], *m.* 1. Ace. 2. Roman copper coin.

Asa [ah'-sah], *f.* 1. Handle, haft. 2. Vault made in the form of the handle of a basket. 3. *Asa dulce*, Gum benzoin, asadulcis. 4. *Asafétida*, Asafœtida, a gum resin. *Amigo del asa* or *ser muy del asa*, A bosom friend. *Dar* or *tomar asa*, To afford or borrow a pretence. *En asas*, Having the hands in the girdle and the elbows turned out. *En asas*, Akimbo.

Asacar [ah-sah-car'], *va.* 1. To impute, defame, vilify. 2. To invent, newly apply.

Asadero, ra [ah-sah-day'-ro, rah], *a.* That which is fit for roasting.—*m.* (Mex.) A small, flat cheese made of the richest of the milk and by beating the curd while making it.

Asado, da [ah-sah'-do, dah], *a.* Roasted; dressed.—*pp.* of Asar.

Asador [ah-sah-dor'], *m.* 1. A spit. 2. Jack, an engine which turns the spit. *Parece que come asadores*, He walks as stiff as if he had swallowed a spit. 3. *Asador de bomba*, (Naut.) The pump-hook.

Asadorazo [ah-sah-do-rah'-tho], *m.* Blow with a spit.

Asadorcillo [ah-sah-dor-theel'-lyo], *m. dim.* Small spit.

Asadura [ah-sah-doo'-rah], *f.* Entrails of an animal, chitterlings. *Asadura de puerco*, Haslet or harslet.

Asaeteador [ah-sah-ay-tay-ah-dor'], *m.* Archer, bow-man.

Asaetear [ah-sah-ay-tay-ar'], *va.* To attack, wound, or kill with arrows.

Asaetinado, da [ah-sah-ay-te-nah'-do, dah], *a.* Like satin: applied to cloths.

Asafétida [ah-sah-fay'-te-dah], *f.* Asafœtida, a gum resin, of fetid odour.

Asainetado, da [ah-sah-e-nay-tah'-do, dah], *a.* That which ought to be serious, but seems farcical.

Asalariar [ah-sah-lah-re-ar'], *va.* To give a fixed salary or pay.

Asalmonado, da [ah-sal-mo-nah'-do, dah], *a.* *V.* Salmonado.

Asaltador [ah-sal-tah-dor'], *m.* 1. Assailant, assaulter. 2. Highwayman.

Asaltar [ah-sal-tar'], *va.* 1. To form an assault, to storm a place. 2. To assail, to surprise, to fall upon. 3. To occur suddenly.

Asalto [ah-sahl'-to], *m.* 1. Assault against a place. 2. Assault, the act of offering violence to a person. 3. (Met.) A sudden gust of passion.

Asamblea [ah-sam-blay'-ah], *f.* 1. Assembly, meeting, congress, junta, congregation, convention, gathering. 2. In the order of Malta, a tribunal established in every grand priory of the order. 3. A beat of the drum directing the soldiers to join their companies, or to assemble in the alarm-place.

Asar [ah-sar'], *va.* To roast.—*vr.* To be excessively hot.

Asarabácara [ah-sah-rah-bah'-cah-rah], **Asáraca** [ah-sah'-rah-cah], *f.* (Bot.) Wild ginger or nard, common asarabacca. Asarum Europæum.

Asarero [ah-sah-ray'-ro], *m.* (Bot.) *V.* Endrino.

Asargado, da [ah-sar-gah'-do, dah], *a.* Serge-like, made in imitation of serge; twilled.

Asarina [ah-sah-ree'-nah], *f.* (Bot.) Bastard asarum. Pseudo-asarum.

Asaro [ah'-sah-ro], *m.* *V.* Asarabácara.

Asativo, va [ah-sah-tee'-vo, vah], *a.* (Pharm.) Dressed or boiled in its own juice, without any other fluid.

Asaz [ah-sath'], *adv.* (Obs. Poet.) Enough, abundantly.

Asbestino, na [as-bes-tee'-no, nah], *a.* Belonging to asbestos.

Asbesto [as-bes'-to], *m.* 1. Asbestos, a mineral, incombustible by fire. 2. A sort of incombustible cloth made of the filaments of asbestos.

Ascalonia [as-cah-lo'-ne-ah], *f.* A seed onion.

Ascárides [as-cah'-re-des], *f.pl.* Ascarides, thread-worms in the rectum.

Ascendencia [as-then-den'-the-ah], *f.* A line of ancestors, as fathers, grandfathers, etc.; family-tree; origin, original.

Ascendente [as-then-den'-tay], *m.* 1. An ascendant. 2. Horoscope, the configuration of the planets at the hour of birth.—*pa.* Ascending.

Ascender [as-then-derr'], *vn.* 1. To ascend, to mount, to climb. 2. To be promoted. 3. *Ascender a*, (Com.) To amount to.

Ascendiente [as-then-de-en'-tay], *m.* & *f.* 1. An ancestor, forefather. 2. *m.* Ascendency, influence, power.

Ascensión [as-then-se-on'], *f.* 1. Ascension, the act of mounting or ascending. 2. Feast of the ascension of Christ. 3. Exaltation to the papal throne. 4. Rising point of the equator.

Ascensional [as-then-se-o-nahl'], *a.* (Astr.) Ascensional, that which belongs to the ascension of the planets, right or oblique.

Ascenso [as-then'-so], *m.* Promotion.

Ascensor [as-then-sor'], *m.* Lift, hoist, elevator.

Asceta [as-thay'-tah], *m.* Ascetic, hermit.

Asceticismo [as-thay-te-thees'-mo], *m.* Asceticism.

Ascético, ca [as-thay'-te-co, cah], *a.* Ascetic, employed wholly in exercises of devotion and mortification.

Ascetismo, *m.* *V.* Asceticismo.

Ascidio [as-thee'-de-o], *m.* (Zool.) An ascidian.

(*Yo asciendo, yo ascienda;* from *Ascender.* *V.* Atender.)

Ascios [as'-the-os], *m. pl.* Ascii, people of the torrid zone, who, at certain times of the year, have no shadow at noon.

Asciro [as-thee'-ro], *m.* (Bot.) St. John's wort, St. Andrew's cross. Hypericum elatum.

Ascitis [as-thee'-tis], *f.* Ascites, dropsy of the abdominal cavity.

Ascítico, ca [as-thee'-te-co, cah], *a.* Belonging to the ascites, ascitic.

Asclepiada [as-clay-pe-ah'-dah], *f.* (Bot.) Swallow-wort. Asclepias.

Asclepiadeo [as-clay-pe-ah-day'-o], *m.* A kind of Latin verse of four feet, containing a spondee, a choriambus, and two dactyles.

Asclepias [as-clay'-pe-as], *f.* Asclepias, milkweed or silkweed; type genus of the Asclepiadæ.

Asco [ahs'-co], *m.* Nausea, loathsomeness, quality of raising disgust. *Es un asco*, It is a mean, despicable thing. *Hacer ascos*, To excite loathsomeness, to turn the stomach.

Ascua [ahs'-coo-ah], *f.* Red-hot coal. *V.* Brasa.

Ascuas [ahs'-coo-as], *int.* (Joc.) How it pains! *Estar en ascuas*, To be very uneasy; to be upon thorns. *Estar hecho un ascua* or *echar ascuas*, To be flushed in the face by agitation or anger.

Aseadamente [ah-say-ah-dah-men'-tay], *adv.* Cleanly, elegantly, neatly.

Aseado, da [ah-say-ah'-do, dah], *a.* Clean, elegant, neatly finished.—*pp.* of Asear.

Asear [ah-say-ar'], *va.* To set off, to adorn, to embellish; polish.

Asechador [ah-say-chah-dor'], *m.* Insnarer, waylayer; plotter.

Asechamiento [ah-say-chah-me-en'-to], *m.* **Asechanza** [ah-say-chahn'-thah], *f.* 1. Waylaying. 2. Artifice, trick, stratagem; plot, intrigue.

Asechar [ah-say-char'], *va.* To waylay, to watch insidiously, to lie in wait, to lie in ambush.

Asechoso, sa [ah-say-cho'-so, sah], *a.* (Obs.) Inclined to insidious artifices, intriguing.

Asedado, da [ah-say-dah'-do, dah], *a.* Silky, that which resembles silk in softness and smoothness.—*pp.* of Asedar.

Asedar [ah-say-dar'], *va.* (Prov.) To work flax and hemp so as to make it feel like silk.

Asedar, *va.* To move or draw from its place. (*a* priv. and Lat. *sedare.*)

Asediador, ra [as-say-de-ah-dor', rah]. *m.* & *f.* Besieger, one who besieges or blockades.

Asediar [ah-say-de-ar'], *va.* To besiege, to lay siege to a strong place or fortress; to blockade.

Asedio [ah-say'-de-o], *m.* A siege, a blockade.

Aseglararse [ah-say-glah-rar'-say], *vr.* To secularize himself, or to make himself worldly: applied to the clergy.

Asegundar [ah-say-goon-dar'], *va.* To repeat with little or no intermission of time.

Asegurable [ah-say-goo-rah'-blay], *a.* Insurable.

Aseguración [ah-say-goo-rah-the-on'], *f.* 1. (Obs.) Security, safety. 2. Insurance.

Asegurado, da [ah-say-goo-rah'-do, dah], *a.* 1. Assured, guaranteed. 2. Decided, fixed; anchored.—*m.* The insured.

Asegurador [ah-say-goo-rah-dor'], *m.* Insurer, underwriter.

Aseguramiento [ah-say-goo-rah-me-en'-to], *m.* 1. The act of securing; security, safe conduct. 2. Insurance.

Asegurar [ah-say-goo-rar'], *va.* 1. To secure, to insure; to fasten, to fix firm. 2. To preserve, to shelter from danger. 3. To bail, to give security. 4. To state, to assert. 5. (Com.) To insure against the dangers of the seas or fire, or other risk. 6. To secure, by mortgage, the fulfilment of an obligation.—*vr.* To escape danger. To be certain of a thing. *Asegurar las velas*, To secure the sails. *Asegurarse de la altura*, To ascertain the degree of latitude in which we find ourselves. *Asegurar la bandera*, To salute the flag when raising it.

Aseidad [ah-say-e-dahd'], *f.* Self-existence, an attribute of God.

Aselarse [ah-say-lar'-say], *vr.* (Prov.) To make ready for passing the night:-said of fowls, etc.

Asemejar [ah-say-may-har'], *va.* To assimilate, to bring to a likeness or resemblance, to favour.—*vr.* To resemble, to be like another person or thing.

Asendereado, da [ah-sen-day-ray-ah'-do, dah], *a.* Beaten, frequented: applied to roads.—*pp.* of Asenderear. Deserted, afflicted.

Asenderear [ah-sen-day-ray-ar'], *va.* 1. To persecute, to pursue with vengeance and enmity. 2. To open a path.

Asengladura [ah-sen-glah-doo'-rah], *f.* (Naut.) A day's run, the way a ship makes in twenty-four hours. = Singladura.

Asenso [ah-sen'-so], *m.* Assent, consent, aquiescence, credence, credit.

Asentada [ah-sen-tah'-dah], *f.* A stone ranged in its proper place. *De una asentada*, At once, at one sitting. *A asentadas*, *V.* A asentadillas.

Asentaderas [ah-sen-tah-day'-ras], *f. pl.* (Coll.) Buttocks, the seat. *V.* Nalgas.

Asentadillas (A) [ah-sen-tah-deel'-lyas], *adv.* Sitting on horseback, like a woman, with both legs on one side.

Asentado, da [ah-sen-tah'-do, dah], *a.* (Obs.) 1. Seated, planted. 2. Clear, serene. *El hombre asentado ni capuz tendido, ni camisón curado*, Idleness is the mother of vice.—*pp.* of Asentar.

Asentador [ah-sen-tah-dor'], *m.* 1. (Obs.) A stone-mason, a stone-cutter. 2. Razor-strop. 3. Grinding slip; turning chisel.

Asentadura [ah-sen-tah-doo'-rah], *f.* **Asentamiento** [ah-sen-tah-me-en'-to], *m.* 1. (Law) Possession of goods given by a judge to the claimant or plaintiff for non-appearance of the defendent. 2. Establishment, settlement, residence. 3. (Obs.) Session. 4. (Obs.) Site.

Asentar [ah-sen-tar'], *va.* 1. To place on a chair, or seat; to cause to sit down. *Asentar el rancho*, To stop in any place or station to eat, sleep, or rest. 2. To suppose, to take for granted. 3. To affirm, to assure. 4. To adjust, to make an agreement. 5

To note, to take down in writing, to register. *Asentar al crédito de*, To place to ——'s credit. 6. To fix a thing in any particular place, to form, to adjust. 7. (Law) To put a claimant or plaintiff in possession of the goods claimed for non-appearance of the respondent or defendant. 8. To assess. *Asentar bien su baza*, To establish one's character or credit. *Asentar casa*, To set up house for one's self. *Asentar con maestro*, To bind one's self prentice to a master. *Asentar plaza*, To enlist in the army. —*vn.* 1. To fit, as clothes. 2. To sit down. 3. To settle, to establish a residence.—*vr.* 1. To subside, as liquors. 2. To perch or settle after flying: applied to birds. 3. (Arch.) To sink, to give way under weight; settle.

Asentimiento [ah-sen-te-me-en'-to], *m.* Assent. *V.* Asenso.

Asentir [ah-sen-teer'], *vn.* To coincide in opinion with another; to acquiesce, to concede, to yield.

Asentista [ah-sen-tees'-tah], *m.* A contractor, one who contracts to supply the navy or army with provisions, ammunition, etc. *Asentista de construcción*, (Naut.) Contractor for ship-building.

Aseo [ah-say'-o], *m.* Cleanliness, neatness, curiosity.

Asequible [ah-say-kee'-blay], *a.* Attainable, obtainable, that which may be acquired.

Aserción [ah-ser-the-on'], *f.* Assertion, affirmation.

Aserradero [ah-ser-rah-day'-ro], *m.* 1. A saw-pit. 2. Horse or wooden machine on which timber or other things are sawed.

Aserradizo, za [ah-ser-rah-dee'-tho, thah], *a.* Proper to be sawed.

Aserrado, da [ah-ser-rah'-do, dah], *a.* Serrate, serrated, dented, like a saw: applied to the leaves of plants.—*pp.* of Aserrar.

Aserrador [ah-ser-rah-dor'], *m.* Sawer or sawyer.

Aserradura [ah-ser-rah-doo'-rah], *f.* Sawing, the act of cutting timber with the saw; saw-cut, kerf. *Aserraduras*, Saw-dust.

Aserrar [ah-ser-rar'], *va.* 1. To saw, to cut with the saw, to cut down. 2. (Met. and coll.) To saw, play the violin badly. *Aserrar piedras en un molino*, To saw stones in a saw-mill.

Aserrido [ah-ser-ree'-do], *m.* Noisy, rasping respiration in diseases of the chest.

Aserrín [ah-ser-reen'], *m.* Saw-dust.

Asertivo, va [ah-ser-tee'-vo, vah], *a.* Assertive. *V.* Afirmativo.

Aserto [ah-ser'-to], *m.* *V.* Aserción.

Asertorio [ah-ser-to'-re-o], *a.* *V.* Juramento. Affirmatory.

Asesar [ah-say-sar'], *vn.* To become prudent, to acquire discretion.

Asesinar [ah-say-se-nar'], *va.* 1. To assassinate, to kill treacherously. 2. To betray the confidence of another, to be guilty of a breach of trust.

Asesinato [ah-say-se-nah'-to], *m.* 1. Assassination, murder. 2. Treachery, deceit, fraud.

Asesino [ah-say-see'-no], *m.* 1. Assassin, murderer, cut-throat. 2. Impostor, cheat, one who practises fraud, and betrays the confidence of another. 3. Small spot of black silk which ladies put near the corner of the eye.

Asesor, ra [ah-say-sor', rah], *m.* & *f.* 1. A counsellor, adviser, conciliator. 2. Assessor, a lawyer appointed to assist the ordinary judge with his advice in the conduct of law proceedings.

Asesorarse [ah-say-so-rar'-say], *vr.* To take the assistance of counsel: used of a judge who takes a lawyer to assist him.

Asesoría [ah-say-so-ree'-ah], *f.* 1. The office or place of an assessor. 2. The pay and fees of an assessor.

Asestadero [ah-ses-tah-day'-ro], *m.* (Prov.) Place where a short sleep is taken after dinner.

Asestador [ah-ses-tah-dor'], *m.* Gunner, who points the cannon.

Asestadura [ah-ses-tah-doo'-rah], *f.* Aim, pointing cannon, or taking aim.

Asestar [ah-ses-tar'], *va.* 1. To aim, to point, to level, to make after. 2. (Met.) To try to do some mischief to others.

Aseveración [ah-say-vay-rah-the-on'], *f.* Asseveration, solemn affirmation.

Aseveradamente [ah-say-vay-rah-dah-men'-tay], *adv.* *V.* Afirmativamente.

Aseverar [ah-say-vay-rar'], *va.* To asseverate; to affirm with great solemnity, as upon oath.

Asfaltar [as-fal-tar'], *va.* To apply or cover with asphalt.

Asfáltico, ca [as-fahl'-te-co, cah], *a.* Of asphaltum; bituminous.

Asfalto [as-fahl'-to], *m.* Asphaltum, a kind of bitumen.

Asfíctico, ca [as-feec'-te-co, cah], *a.* Asphyxial, or asphyctic.

Asfixia [as-feec'-se-ah], *f.* (Med.) Asphyxia, a disease.

Asfixiante [as-fic-se-ahn'-tay], *a.* Asphyxiating. *Calor asfixiante*, Suffocating heat.

Asfixiar [as-fic-se-ar'], *va.* To asphyxiate, suffocate.

Asfódelo [as-fo'-day-lo], *m.* Asphodel, day-lily. *V.* Gamón.

(*Yo asgo, tú ases; yo asga*, from Asir.)

Así [ah-see'], *adv.* 1. So, thus, in this manner. 2. Therefore, so that, also, equally. *Así*, followed by a verb in the subjunctive mood, is translated, Would that—God grant that. = Ojalá. *Así Dios guarde a Vd.* Would that God may preserve you. *Así bien*, As well, as much so, equally. *Así que*, So that, therefore. *Es así, o no es así*, Thus it is, or it is not so. *Así fuera yo santo, como fulano es docto*, If I were as sure of being a saint, as he is learned. 3. Followed immediately by *como*, is equivalent to, in the same manner or proportion, as, *Así como la modestia atrae, así se huye la disolución*, In the same proportion that modesty attracts, dissoluteness deters. But when the particle *como* is in the second part of the sentence, *así* is equal to so much. *Así, así*, So, so; middling. *Así que llegó la noticia*, As soon as the news arrived. *Así como así*, or *así que así*, Any way; it matters not. *Así que asá* or *asado*, Any way; it makes no difference. *Así me estoy*, It is all the same to me. *Como así*, Even so, just so, how so. *Así como así*, By all means.

Asiano, na, *a.* Asian.

Asiático, ca [ah-se-ah'-te-co, cah], *a.* Asiatic.

Asidero [ah-se-day'-ro], *m.* 1. Handle. 2. (Met.) Occasion, pretext. *Asideros*, (Naut.) Ropes with which vessels are hauled along the shore.

Asido, da [ah-see'-do, dah], *pp.* of Asir, Seized, grasped, laid hold of.—*a.* Fastened, tied, attached. *Fulano está asido a su propia opinión*, He is wedded to his own opinion.

Asiduamente, *adv.* fr. Asiduo.

Asiduidad [ah-se-doo-e-dahd'], *f.* Assiduity, assiduousness.

Asiduo, dua [ah-see'-doo-o, ah], *a.* Assiduous, laborious.

Asiento [ah-se-en'-to], *m.* 1. Chair, or other seat. 2. Seat in a tribunal or court of justice. 3. Spot on which a town or building is or was standing; site. 4. Solidity of a building resulting from the reciprocal pressure of the materials upon each other: settling. 5. Bottom of a vessel. 6. Sediment of liquors. 7 Treaty. 8. Contract for supplying an army, town, etc., with provisions, etc. 9. Entry, the act of registering or setting down in writing. 10. Judgment, prudence, discretion. 11. District of the mines in South America. 12. List, roll. 13. Sort of pearls, flat on one side and round on the other. 14. Surfeit, fit of indigestion. 15. The state and order which things ought to take. *Hombre de asiento*, A prudent man. *Asientos de popa*, (Naut.) Stern seats in the cabin. *Asiento de molino*, Bed or lowest stone in a mill. *Dar* or *tomar asiento en las cosas*, To let things take a regular course.

(*Yo asiento, yo asienta*, from *Asentir.* *V.* Asentir.)

(*Yo asiento, yo asiente*, from *Asentar.* *V.* Acertar.)

(*Yo asierro, yo asierre*, from *Aserrar.* *V.* Acertar.)

Asignable [ah-sig-nah'-blay], *a.* Assignable.

Asignación [ah-sig-nah-the-on'], *f.* 1. Assignation. 2. Distribution, partition. 3. Destination.

Asignado [ah-sig-nah'-do], *m.* Assignat: paper money issued by France in 1790.—*pp.* of Asignar.

Asignar [ah-sig-nar'], *va.* To assign, to mark out, to determine, to ascribe, to attribute.

Asignatura [ah-sig-nah-too'-rah], *f.* Each one of the courses of instruction delivered in universities in the course of a year.

Asilo [ah-see'-lo], *m.* 1. Asylum, sanctuary, place of shelter and refuge. 2. Harbourage. 3. (Met.) Protection, support, favour. 4. (Entom.) Asilus, a genus of large and voracious diptera; represented by the bee-killer and robber-fly.

Asilla [ah-seel'-lyah], *f. dim.* 1. A small handle. 2. A slight pretext.—*pl.* 1. The collar-bones of the breast. 2. Small hooks or keys employed in the different parts of an organ.

Asimesmo [ah-se-mes'-mo], *adv.* (Obs.) *V.* Asimismo.

Asimetría [ah-se-may-tree'-ah], *f.* (Littl. us.) Lack of symmetry.

Asimétrico, ca [ah-se-may'-tre-co, cah], *a.* Asymmetrical, out of proportion.

Asimiento [ah-se-me-en'-to], *m.* 1. Grasp, the act of seizing or grasping. 2. Attachment, affection.

Asimilable [ah-se-me-lah'-blay], *a.* Assimilable; capable of assimilation.

Asimilación [ah-se-me-lah-the-on'], *f.* Assimilation.

Asimilar [ah-se-me-lar'], *vn.* To resemble, to be like.—*va.* To assimilate; to convert into living tissue.

Asimilativo, va [ah-se-me-lah-tee'-vo, vah], *a.* Assimilating, having the power of rendering one thing like another.

Asimismo [ah-se-mees'-mo], *adv.* Exactly so, in the same manner, like wise.

Asimplado, da [ah-sim-plah'-do, dah], *a.* Like a simpleton, or silly person.

Asín, Asina [ah-seen', ah-see'-nah], *adv.* (Low) *V.* Así.

Asinarias [ah-se-nah'-re-as], *f. pl.* Birds, in Brazil, which are very ugly, and

whose voice resembles the braying of an ass.
Asindeton [ah-seen'-day-tone], *m.* Asyndeton, a figure of speech in which conjunctions are suppressed to give liveliness to the style.
Asinino, na [ah-se-nee'-no, nah], *a.* Asinine, ass-like.
Asintota [ah-seen'-to-tah], *f.* (Geom.) Asymptote.
Asir [ah-seer'], *va.* & *vn.* 1. To grasp or seize with the hand, to lay hold of. 2. To hold, to gripe, to come upon. 3. To strike or take root.—*vr.* To dispute, to contend, to rival. *Asirse de alguna cosa,* To avail one's self of an opportunity to do or say something.
Asiriano, na, or **Asirio, ria** [ah-se-re-ah'-no, nah, ah-see'-re-o, ah], *a.* Assyrian.
Asisia [as-see'-se-ah], *f.* (Law. Ar.) 1. Part of law proceedings containing the depositions of witnesses. 2. Court of assizes.
Asisón [ah-se-sone'], *m.* (Prov.) Bird belonging to the family of *francolins.*
Asistencia [ah-sis-ten'-the-ah], *f.* 1. Actual presence. 2. Reward gained by personal attendance. 3. Assistance, favour, aid, help, comfort, furtherance. *Asistencia de Sevilla,* Appellation given to the chief magistracy of Seville. *Asistencias,* Allowance made to any one for his maintenance and support; alimony. *Se alquila un cuarto amueblado, con asistencia o sin ella,* To let a furnished room, with or without board. *Hónreme Vd. con su asistencia,* Please to honour me with your company (presence).
Asistencia social [ah-sis-ten'-the-ah so-thee-ahl'], *f.* Social work, social service.
Asistenta [ah-sis-ten'-tah], *f.* 1. The wife of the chief magistrate of Seville. 2. Handmaid. 3. Servant-maid who waits on the maids of honour at court, and also on religious women of any of the military orders in their convents.
Asistente [ah-sis-ten'-tay], *pa.* & *m.* 1. Assistant, helper, helpmate. 2. The chief officer of justice at Seville. 3. The soldier who attends an officer as a servant, an orderly.
Asistir [ah-sis-teer'], *vn.* 1. To be present, to assist. 2. To live in a house, or frequent it much.—*va.* 1. To accompany one in the execution of some public act. 2. To minister, to further, to countenance. 3. To serve or act provisionally in the room of another. 4. To attend a sick person.
Asma [ahs'-mah], *f.* The asthma.
Asmático, ca [as-mah'-te-co, cah], *a.* Asthmatic, troubled with the asthma.
Asna [ahs'-nah], *f.* A she-ass, jenny. *Asnas,* Rafters of a house.
Asnacho [as-nah'-cho], *m.* (Bot.) *V.* Gatuña.
Asnada [as-nah'-dah], *f.* A foolish action.
Asnado [as-nah'-do], *m.* Large piece of timber with which the sides and shafts in mines are secured.
Asnal [as-nahl'], *a.* 1. Asinine. 2. Brutal.
Asnales [as-nah-'les], *m. pl.* (Obs.) Stockings larger and stronger than the common sort.
Asnalmente [as-nal-men'-tay], *adv.* 1. Foolishly. 2. Mounted on an ass.
Asnallo [as-nahl'-lyo], *m.* (Bot.) *V.* Gatuña.
Asnaucho [as-nah'-oo-cho], *m.* A sort of very sharp pepper of South America.
Asnazo [as-nah'-tho], *m. aug.* 1. A large jackass. 2. (Met.) A brutish, ignorant fellow.
Asnería [as-nay-ree'-ah], *f.* (Coll.) Stud of asses. *V.* Asnada.
Asnerizo, Asnero [as-nay-ree'-tho, as-nay'-ro], *m.* (Obs.) Ass-keeper.
Asnico, ca [as-nee'-co, cah], *m.* & *f.* 1. (Dim.) A little ass. 2. (Prov.) Irons at the end of a fire-grate in which the spit turns.
Asnilla [as-neel'-lyah], *f.* Stanchion or prop which supports a ruinous building.
Asnillo, lla [as-neel'-lyo, lyah], *m.* & *f.* *dim.* A little ass. *Asnillo,* Field-cricket.
Asnino, na [as-nee'-no, nah], *a.* (Coll.) Resembling an ass.
Asno [ahs'-no], *m.* 1. An ass. 2. (Met.) A dull, stupid, heavy fellow. *Asno de muchos, lobos le comen,* Everybody's business is nobody's business. *Cada asno con su tamaño,* Birds of a feather flock together. *No se hizo la miel para la boca del asno,* It is not for asses to lick honey, we should not throw pearls before swine.
Asobarcado, da [ah-so-bar-cah'-do, dah], *a.* Having the clothes tucked up to the shoulders: so tucked up.
Asobinarse [ah-so-be-nar'-say], *vr.* To fall down with a burden, so that the head comes between the fore feet: applied to beasts of burden.
Asocarronado, da [ah-so-car-ro-nah'-do, dah], *a.* Crafty, cunning, waggish.
Asociación, *f.* **Asociamiento,** *m.* [ah-so-the-ah-the-on', ah-so-the-ah-me-en'-to]. Association; fellowship, copartnership; knot. Union.
Asociado [ah-so-the-ah'-do], *m.* Associate; comrade. (Com.) Partner.—*pp.* of Asociar.
Asociar [ah-so-the-ar'], *va.* To associate, to unite with another as a confederate, to conjoin.—*vr.* To accompany, to consociate, to consort, to herd.
Asolación, Asoladura [ah-so-lah-the-on', ah-so-lah-doo'-rah], *f.* Desolation, devastation.
Asolador, ra [ah-so-lah-dor', rah], *m.* & *f.* A destroyer, desolater.
Asolamiento [ah-so-lah-me-en'-to], *m.* Depopulation, destruction, havoc.
Asolanar [ah-so-lah-nar'], *va.* To parch or dry up: applied to easterly winds.
Asolapar [ah-so-lah-par']. *V.* Solapar.
Asolar [ah-so-lar'], *va.* To level with the ground, to destroy, to waste, to harrow, to pillage, to devastate.—*vr.* To settle and get clear: applied to liquors.
Asoldar, or **Asoldadar** [ah-sol-dar'], *va.* To hire (chiefly of soldiers).
Asoleado, da [ah-so-lay-ah'-do, dah], *a.* 1. Sunny. 2. Suntanned.
Asolear [ah-so-lay-ar'], *va.* To sun, to expose to the sun.—*vr.* To be sunburnt.
Asolvamiento [ah-sol-vah-me-en'-to], *m.* Stoppage, the act of stopping.
Asolvarse [ah-sol-var'-say], *vr.* To be stopped: spoken of pipes, canals, etc., through which water is running. *V.* Azolvar.
Asomada [ah-so-mah'-dah], *f.* 1. Appearance, apparition. 2. (Obs.) The spot whence any object is first seen or descried.
Asomado, da [ah-so-mah'-do, dah], *a.* Fuddled.—*pp.* of Asomar.
Asomar [ah-so-mar'], *vn.* 1. To begin to appear, to become visible. *Asoma el día,* The day begins to peep. 2. (Naut.) To loom.—*va.* To show a thing, to make it appear. *Asomé la cabeza a la ventana,* I put my head out of the window.—*vr.* To be flustered with wine.
Asombradizo, za [ah-som-brah-dee'-tho, thah], *a.* Fearful, timid, easily frightened.
Asombrador, ra [ah-som-brah-dor', rah], *m.* & *f.* Terrifier, one who frightens.
Asombramiento [ah-som-brah-me-en'-to], *m.* *V.* Asombro.
Asombrar [ah-som-brar'], *va.* 1. To shade, to darken, to obscure, to overshadow. 2. To frighten, to terrify. 3. To astonish, to cause admiration. —*vr.* To take fright.
Asombro [ah-som'-bro], *m.* 1. Dread, fear, terror. 2. Amazement, astonishment, high admiration.
Asombrosamente [ah-som-bro-sah-men'-tay], *adv.* Amazingly, wonderfully, marvellously.
Asombroso, sa [ah-som-bro'-so, sah], *a.* Wonderful, astonishing, marvellous.
Asomo [ah-so'-mo], *m.* 1. Mark, token, sign. 2. Supposition, conjecture, surmise. *Ni por asomo,* Not in the least, by no means.
Asonada [ah-so-nah'-dah], *f.* Tumultuous crowd of people.
Asonadía [ah-so-nah-dee'-ah], *f.* (Obs.) Tumultuous hostility.
Asonancia [as-so-nahn'-the-ah], *f.* 1. Assonance, consonance. A peculiar kind of rhyme, in which the last accented vowel and those which follow it in one word correspond in sound with the vowels of another word, while the consonants differ: as *cálamo* and *plátano.* 2. Harmony or connection of one thing with another.
Asonantar [ah-so-nan-tar'], *va.* (Poet.) To mix assonant with consonant verses in Spanish poetry, which is inadmissible in modern verse.
Asonante [ah-so-nahn'-tay], *a.* Assonant, last word in a Spanish verse whose vowels are the same, beginning with that in which the accent is, as those of the other word, with which it must accord.
Asonar [ah-so-nar'], *vn.* 1. To be assonant, to accord. 2. (Obs.) To unite in riots and tumultuous assemblies.
Asordar [ah-sor-dar'], *va.* To deafen with noise.
Asosegar, *va.* **Asosegarse,** *vr.* *V.* Sosegar.
Asotanar [ah-so-tah-nar'], *va.* To vault, to make vaults or arched cellars.
Aspa [ahs'-pah], *f.* 1. A cross. 2. A reel, a turning frame. 3. Wings of a wind-mill. 4. Cross stud, diagonal stays. (Naut.) Cross gore, bentinck shrouds. Knitting-bar. *Aspa de cuenta,* A clock-reel. *Aspa de San Andrés,* Coloured cross on the yellow cloaks of penitents by the Inquisition.
Aspadera [as-pah-day'-rah], *f.* (Mech.) A reel.
Aspado, da [as-pah'-do, dah], *a.* 1. Having the arms extended in the form of a cross, by way of penance or mortification. 2. (Met.) Having one's arms confined, and their movements obstructed by tight clothes.—*pp.* of Aspar.
Aspador [as-pah-dor'], *m.* A reel.
Aspador, ra [as-pah-dor', rah], *m.* & *f.* Reeler, one who reels yarn, thread, or silk.
Aspalato [as-pah-lah'-to], *m.* (Bot.) Rosewood. Aspalathus.
Aspalto [as-pahl'-to], *m.* 1. Asphalt. 2. *V.* Espalto.
Aspar [as-par'], *va.* 1. To reel, to gather yarn off the spindle, and form it into skeins. 2. To crucify. 3. (Met.) To vex or mortify. *Asparse a gritos,* To hoot, to cry out with vehemence.
Aspaviento [as-pah-ve-en'-to], *m.* 1. Exaggerated dread, fear, consternation. 2. Astonishment, admiration, expressed in confused and indistinct

words. *Aspavientos*, Boasts, brags, bravadoes.

Aspecto [as-pec'-to], *m.* 1. Sight, appearance. 2. Look, aspect, countenance. 3. (Arch.) Situation or position of a building with reference to the cardinal points; outlook. 4. (Ast.) Relative position of stars and planets. *A primer aspecto* or *al primer aspecto*, At first sight. *Tener buen o mal aspecto*, To have a good or bad aspect; to be in a good or bad state.

Asperamente [ahs'-pay-rah-men-tay], *adv.* Rudely, in a harsh manner, grumly, crabbedly, abruptly, obdurately, gruffly, currishly.

Asperear [as-pay-ray-ar'], *vn.* To be rough and acrid to the taste.—*va.* (Obs.) To exasperate, to irritate.

Asperete [as-pay-ray'-tay], *m.* *V.* ASPERILLO.

Aspereza, Asperidad [as-pay-ray'-thah, as-pay-re-dahd'], *f.* 1. Asperity; acerbity, acrimony, gall, keenness. 2. Roughness, ruggedness, inequality or unevenness of the ground, craggedness, gruffness. 3. Austerity, sourness, rigour or harshness of temper, snappishness, moroseness.

Asperges [as-per'-hess], *m.* A Latin word used for *aspersion* or sprinkling. *Quedarse asperges*, To be disappointed in one's expectations; not to understand an iota.

Asperiego, ga [as-pay-re-ay'-go, gah], *a.* Applied to a sour apple of the pippin kind.

Asperilla [as-pay-reel'-lyah], *f.* (Bot.) A plant, perennial, and of agreeable smell.

Asperillo [as-pay-reel'-lyo], *m.* The sourish taste of unripe fruit and other things.

Asperillo, lla [as-pay-reel'-lyo, lyah], *a. dim.* Tart, sourish.

Asperjar [as-per-har'], *va.* To sprinkle.

Áspero, Aspro [ahs'-pay-ro, ahs -pro], *m.* A silver coin current in the Levant, equivalent, about, to a *peseta*.

Aspero, ra [ahs'-pay-ro, rah], *a.* 1. Rough, rugged, cragged, grained, knotty; horrid. 2. (Met.) Harsh and unpleasing to the taste or ear, acerb; hard; crabbed. 3. (Met.) Severe, rigid, austere, gruff, crusty. *Áspera arteria.* *V.* TRAQUIARTERIA.

Asperón [as-pay-rone'], *m.* Grindlestone or grind-stone; flag-stone; holystone.

Aspérrimo, ma [as-per'-re-mo, mah], *a.* Sup. of ÁSPERO.

Aspersión [as-per-se-on'], *f.* Aspersion, the act of sprinkling.

Aspersorio [as-per-so'-re-o], *m.* Water-sprinkler; instrument with which holy water is sprinkled in the church.

Aspid, Áspide [ahs'-pid, ahs'-pe-day], *m.* Asp, aspic, a small kind of serpent. Coluber aspis.

Aspillera [as-pil-lyay'-rah], *f.* Loophole, embrasure, crenel.

Aspiración [as-pe-ra-the-on'], *f.* 1. Aspiration. 2. Inspiration, the act of drawing in the breath. 3. Aspiration, pronunciation of a vowel with full breath. 4. (Mus.) A short pause which gives only time to breathe.

Aspiradora [as-pe-rah-do'-rah], *f.* Vacuum cleaner.

Aspirante [as-pe-rahn'-tay], *pa.* Aspirant, neophyte.

Aspirar [as-pe-rar'], *va.* 1. To inspire the air, to draw in the breath. 2. To aspire, to covet. 3. To pronounce a vowel with full breath.

Aspiratorio, ria [as-pe-ra-to'-re-o, ahl, *a.* Proper to inspiration, or what produces it.

Aspirina [as-pe-ree'-nah], *f.* Aspirin.

Aspisera [as-pe-say'-rah], *f.* *V.* ALPISTERA. (Prov. Andalucia.)

Asquear [as-kay-ar'], *va.* To consider with disgust or dislike, to disdain.

Asquerosamente [as-kay-ro-sah-men'-tay], *adv.* Nastily, nauseously, foully, filthily.

Asquerosidad [as-kay-ro-se-dahd'], *f.* Nastiness, filthiness, foulness, fulsomeness, mawkishness.

Asqueroso, sa [as-kay-ro'-so, sah], *a.* 1. Nasty, filthy, nauseously, impure. 2. Loathsome, fastidious, disgusting, squeamish, fulsome.

Asquia [ahs'-ke-ah], *f.* (Zool.) A kind of grayling or umber, a delicate fresh-water fish.

Asta [ahs'-tah], *f.* 1. Lance. 2. Part of the deer's head which bears the antlers; horn. 3. Handle of a pencil, brush. 4. (Naut.) Staff or light pole erected in different parts of the ship, on which the colours are displayed. 5. (Mas.) Binder, curb-stone. Shank of a tool; shaft, spindle. *Asta de bandera de popa*, Ensign-staff. *Asta de bandera de proa*, Jack-staff. *Asta de tope*, Flag-staff. *Asta de bomba*, Pump-spear. *Astas*, Horns of animals, as bulls, etc. *Darse de las astas*, To snap and carp at each other.

Ástaco [ahs'-tah-co], *m.* Lobster, crayfish, or crawfish.

Astado, Astero [as-tah'-do, as-tay'-ro], *m.* Roman pikeman or lancer.

Astático, ca [as-tah'-te-co, cah], *a.* Astatic, in equilibrium.

Astenia [as-tay-ne-ah], *f.* Asthenia, physical debility.

Asténico, ca [as-tay'-ne-co, cah], *a.* (Med.) Asthenic.

Aster [as-ter'], *m.* (Bot.) Starwort.

Asteria [as-tay'-re-ah], *f.* 1. Star-stone, a kind of precious stone. 2. Cat's-eye, a sort of false opal.

Asterisco [as-tay-rees'-co], *m.* 1. An asterisk, a mark in printing, *. 2. (Bot.) Oxeye. Buphthalmum.

Asteroide [as-tay-ro'-e-day], *m.* Asteroid, a telescopic planet, of a group between Mars and Jupiter.

Astigmatismo [as-tig-mah-tees'-mo], *m* (Med.) Astigmatism.

Astil [as-teel'], *m.* 1. Handle of an axe, hatchet, etc. 2. Shaft of an arrow. 3. Beam of a balance. 4. (Obs.) Any thing which serves to support another.

Astilejos [as-te-lay'-hos], *m. pl.* *V.* ASTILLEJOS.

Astilico [as-te-lee'-co], *m. dim.* A small handle.

Astilla [as-teel'-lyah], *f.* 1. Chip of wood, splinter of timber. 2. (Obs.) Reed or comb of a loom. 3. *Astilla muerta de un bajel*, (Naut.) The dead rising of the floor-timbers of a ship. *De tal palo, tal astilla*, or *astilla del mismo palo*, A chip of the same block. *Sacar astilla*, To profit by a thing.

Astillar [as-teel-lyar'], *va.* To chip.

Astillazo [as-teel-lyah'-tho], *m.* 1. Crack, the noise produced by a splinter being torn from a block. 2. (Met.) The damage which results from an enterprise to those who have not been its principal authors and promoters.

Astillejos [as-teel-lyay'-hos], *m. pl.* (Ast.) Castor and Pollux, two brilliant stars.

Astillero [as-teel-lyay'-ro], *m.* 1. Rack on which lances, spears, pikes, etc., are placed. 2. Shipwright's yard, dockyard. *Poner en astillero*, (Met.) To place one in an honourable post.

Astracán [as-trah-kahn'], *m.* Karakul.

Astragalo [as-trah'-gah-lo], *m.* 1. (Arch.) Astragal, an ornament at the tops and bottoms of columns. 2. (Mil.) A kind of ring or moulding on a piece of ordnance. 3. (Bot.) Milk-vetch. 4. (Anat.) Astragalus, the ankle-bone, articulating with the tibia. 5. Round moulding; beads.

Astral [as-trahl'], *a.* Astral, that which belongs to the stars.

Astrancia [as-trahn'-the-ah], *f.* (Bot.) Master-wort.

Astricción, Astringencia [as-tric-the-on', as-trin-hen'-the-ah], *f.* Astriction, compression.

Astrictivo, va [as-tric-tee'-vo, vah], *a.* Astrictive, styptic.

Astricto, ta [as-treec'-to, tah], *a.* 1. Contracted, compressed. 2. Determined, resolved.—*pp. irr.* of ASTRINGIR.

Astrífero, ra [as-tree'-fay-ro, rah]. (Poet.) Starry, full of stars.

Astringencia [as-trin-hen'-the-ah], *f.* Astringency, constriction.

Astringente [as-trin-hen'-tay], *a.* Astringent.

Astringir [as-trin-heer'], *a.* To astringe, to contract, to compress.

Astro [ahs'-tro], *m.* 1. Luminous body of the heavens, such as the sun, moon, and stars. 2. Illustrious persons of uncommon merit.

Astrobiología [as-tro-be-o-lo-hee'-ah], *f.* Astrobiology.

Astrofísica [as-tro-fee'-se-cah], *f.* Astrophysics.

Astrografía [as-tro-grah-fee'-ah], *f.* Astrography, the science of describing the stars.

Astroite [as-tro'-e-tay], *m.* Astroite, a radiated fossil.

Astrolabio [as-tro-lah'-be-o], *m.* Astrolabe, an instrument chiefly used for taking the altitude of stars at sea, now disused. Sextant.

Astrologia [as-tro-lo-hee'-ah], *f.* Astrology.

Astrológico, ca, Astrólogo, ga [as-tro-lo'-he-co, cah, as-tro'-lo-go, gah], *a.* Astrological, that which belongs to astrology.

Astrólogo [as-tro'-lo-go], *m.* Astrologer.

Astronauta [as-tro-nah'-oo-tah], *m.* Astronaut.

Astronáutica [as-tro-nah'-oo-te-cah], *f.* Astronautics, space travel.

Astronave [as-tro-nah'-vay], *f.* Spaceship.

Astronavegación [as-tro-nah-vay-gah-the-on'], *f.* Astronavigation.

Astronomia [as-tro-no-mee'-ah], *f.* Astronomy.

Astronómicamente [as-tro-no'-me-cah-men-tay], *adv.* Astronomically.

Astronómico, ca [as-tro-no'-me-co, cah], *a.* Astronomical, that which belongs to astronomy.

Astrónomo [as-tro'-no-mo], *m.* Astronomer.

Astucia [as-too'-the-ah], *f.* Cunning, craft, finesse, slyness.

Astur, ra, or **Asturiano, na** [as-too-re-ah'-no, nah], *a.* Asturian.

Asturión [as-too-re-on'], *m.* 1. A pony, a small horse. 2. (Zool.) *V.* SOLLO.

Astutamente [as-too-tah-men'-tay], *adv.* Cunningly, craftily, feigningly, jesuitically.

Astuto, ta [as-too'-to, tah], *a.* Astute, cunning, sly, crafty, fraudulent.

(*Yo asueldo*, from *Asoldar*. *V.* ACORDAR.)

(*Yo asuelo, yo asuele*, from *Asolar*. *V.* ACORDAR.)

(*Yo asueno*, from *Asonar*. *V.* ACORDAR.)

Asueto [ah-soo-ay'-to], *m.* Holiday for school-boys and students; vacation.

Asumir [ah-soo-meer'], *va.* (Obs.) 1. To take to, or for, one's self. 2. To raise by election or acclamation to certain dignities.—*vr. V.* ARROGARSE.

Asunción [ah-soon-the-on'], *f.* 1. Assumption. 2. Elevation to a higher dignity. 3. Ascent of the Holy Virgin to heaven. 4. Assumption, the thing supposed, a postulate.

Asunto [ah-soon'-to], *m.* Subject, the matter or thing treated upon; affair, business.—*pl. Asuntos,* Effects, business, stock.

Asuramiento [ah-soo-rah-me-en'-to], *m.* The act of burning, and the state of being burnt: applied only to ragouts, and to the corn before it is reaped.

Asurarse [ah-soo-rar'-say], *vr.* 1. To be burnt in the pot or pan: applied to meat. 2. To be parched with drought.

Asurcano, na [ah-soor-cah'-no, nah], *a.* Neighbouring: said of lands which adjoin, and their tillers.

Asurcar [ah-soor-car'], *va.* To furrow sown land, in order to kill the weeds.

Asuso [ah-soo'-so], *adv.* (Obs.) Upward, above.

Asustadizo, za [ah-soos-tah-dee'-tho, thah], *a.* Applied to a person easily frightened.

Asustar [ah-soos-tar'], *va.* To frighten, to terrify.—*vr.* To be frightened.

Atabaca [ah-tah-bah'-cah], *f.* (Bot.) Groundsel. *V.* OLIVARDA. Elecampane (?) Inula.

Atabacado, da [ah-tah-bah-cah'-do, dah], *a.* Having the colour of tobacco.

Atabal [ah-tah-bahl'], *m.* 1. Kettle-drum. 2. *V.* ATABALERO.

Atabalear [ah-tah-bah-lay-ar'], *vn.* To imitate the noise of kettle-drums: applied to horses.

Atabalejo, Atabalete, Atabalillo [ah-tah-bah-lay'-ho, etc.], *m. dim.* A small kettle-drum.

Atabalero [ah-tah-bah-lay'-ro], *m.* Kettle-drummer.

Atabanado, da [ah-tah-bah-nah'-do, dah], *a.* Spotted white: applied to horses.

Atabardillado, da [ah-tah-bar-deel-lyah'-do, dah], *a.* Applied to diseases of the nature of spotted fevers.

Atabe [ah-tah'-bay], *m.* A small vent or air-hole left in water-pipes.

Atabernado, da [ah-tah-ber-nah'-do, dah], *a.* Retailed in taverns: applied to liquors.

Atabillar [ah-tah-beel-lyar'], *va.* To fold a piece of cloth so that the selvages are open to view on both sides.

Atabladera [ah-tah-blah-day'-rah], *f.* A kind of roller or levelling board to level land sown with corn.

Atablar [ah-tah-blar'], *va.* To level land sown with corn by means of a levelling board.

Atacadera [ah-tah-cah-day'-rah], *f.* Rammer used in splitting stones with gunpowder.

Atacado, da [ah-tah-cah'-do, dah], *a.* 1. (Met.) Irresolute, inconstant, undecided. 2. (Met.) Close, miserable, narrow-minded. *Calzas atacadas,* Breeches formerly worn in Spain. *Hombre de calzas atacadas,* A strict and rigid observer of old customs.—*pp.* of ATACAR.

Atacador [ah-tah-cah-dor'], *m.* 1. Aggressor, he that invades or attacks. 2. Ramrod or rammer for a gun.

Atacadura, *f.* **Atacamiento,** *m.* [ah-tah-cah-doo'-rah, ah-tah-cah-me-en'-to]. (Obs.) Stricture, act and effect of tightening.

Atacamita [ah-tah-cah-mee'-tah], *f.* (Miner.) Native oxychloride of copper: named from desert of Atacama, where it is found.

Atacar [ah-tah-car'], *va.* 1. To fit clothes tight to the body. 2. To force the charge into fire-arms. 3. To attack, to assault, to fall upon, to come upon. 4. To pin down in argument. *Atacar bien la plaza,* (Coll.) To cram or stuff gluttonously.

Atacir [ah-tah-theer'], *m.* (Astrol.) A division of the celestial arch into twelve parts by circles which pass through points north and south of the horizon.

Atacola [ah-tah-co'-lah], *f.* A strap for a horse's tail.

Ataderas, *f. pl.* **Ataderos,** *m. pl.* [ah-tah-day'-ras, ah-tah-day'-ros]. (Prov.) Garters.

Atadero [ah-tah-day'-ro], *m.* 1. Cord or rope, with which something may be tied. 2. The place where a thing is tied. *No tener atadero,* To have neither head nor tail: applied to a discourse without meaning, and to the person uttering it.

Atadijo, ito [ah-tah-dee'-ho, dee'-to], *m. dim.* (Coll.) An ill-shaped little bundle or parcel.

Atadito, ta [ah-tah-dee'-to, tah], *a. dim* Somewhat cramped or contracted: a little bundle.

Atado [ah-tah'-do], *m.* Bundle, parcel. *Atado de cebollas,* A string of onions.

Atado, da [ah-tah'-do, dah], *a.* Pusillanimous, easily embarrassed, good for nothing.—*pp.* of ATAR.

Atador [ah-tah-dor'], *m.* 1. He who ties. 2. Binder, a man who binds sheaves of corn. 3. The string of a child's bonnet or cap.

Atadura [ah-tah-doo'-rah], *f.* 1. Alligation, the act of tying together. 2. (Obs.) Tie, fastening. 3. (Met.) Union, connection. *Atadura de galeotes y presos,* A number of prisoners tied together, to be conducted to the galleys.

Atafagar [ah-tah-fah-gar'], *va.* 1. To stupefy, to deprive of the use of the senses, especially by strong odours, good or bad. 2. (Met.) To tease, to molest by incessant importunity.

Atafetanado, da [ah-tah-fay-tah-nah'-do, dah], *a.* Taffeta-like, resembling taffeta.

Ataguía [ah-tah-gee'-ah], *f.* Coffer-dam.

Ataharre [ah-tah-ar'-ray], *m.* The broad crupper of a pack-saddle.

Atahona [ah-tah-o'-nah], *f. V.* TAHONA. A mill turned by horse-power. (Arab.)

Atahorma [ah-tah-or'-mah], *f.* (Orn.) Osprey, a kind of sea-eagle. Falco ossifragus.

Ataifor, Ataiforico [ah-tah-e-for', ah-tah-e-fo-ree'-co], *m.* 1. Soup plate or deep dish. 2. (Obs.) A round table formerly used by the Moors.

Atairar [ah-tah-e-rar'], *va.* To cut mouldings in the panels and frames of doors and windows.

Ataire [ah-tah'-e-ray], *m.* Moulding in the panels and frames of doors and windows.

Atajadero [ah-tah-hah-day'-ro], *m.* A sluice-gate.

Atajadizo [ah-tah-hah-dee'-tho], *m.* Partition of boards, linen, etc., by which a place or ground is divided into separate parts. *Atajadizo de la caja de agua,* (Naut.) The manger-board.

Atajador [ah-tah-hah-dor'], *m.* 1. (Obs.) One that intercepts or stops a passage, or obstructs the progress of another. 2. (Mil.) Scout. 3. *Atajador de ganado,* A sheep-thief. 4. (Min.) The lad who unloads the work-horses.

Atajar [ah-tah-har'], *vn.* To go the shortest way; to cut off part of the road.—*va.* 1. To overtake flying beasts or men, by cutting off part of the road, and thus getting before them. 2. To divide or separate by partitions. 3. To intercept, stop, or obstruct the course of a thing. 4. To mark with lines, in a play or writing, the parts to be omitted in acting or in reading. 5. *Atajar ganado* To steal sheep. 6. *Atajar la tierra,* To reconnoitre the ground.—*vr.* To be confounded with shame, dread, or reverential fear.

Atajasolaces [ah-tah-hah-so-lah'-thes], *m.* A disturber of a pleasant reunion.

Atajea, Atajía [ah-tah-hay'-ah, ah-tah-hee'-ah], *f. V.* ATARJEA.

Atajo [ah-tah'-ho], *m.* 1. Cut by which a road or path is shortened; short cut. 2. Ward or guard made by a weapon in fencing. 3. (Obs.) Agreement, expedient, means taken to conclude any difference or dispute. 4. Net with frame. *No hay atajo sin trabajo,* No gains without pains. *Salir al atajo,* To interrupt another's speech, and anticipate in a few words what he was going to say in many.

Ataladrar [ah-tah-lah-drar'], *va.* (Obs.) To bore. *V.* TALADRAR.

Atalajar [ah-tah-lah-har'], *va.* To harness.

Atalaje [ah-tah-lah'-hay], *m.* Breast harness; draft.

Atalantar [ah-tah-lan-tar'], *va.* (Obs.) To stun, to stupefy.—*vn.* To agree, to accord; to be pleased.

Atalaya [ah-tah-lah'-yah], *f.* 1. Watch-tower, which overlooks the adjacent country and sea-coast. 2. Height, whence a considerable tract of country may be overlooked. 3. *m.* Guard, placed in a watch-tower to keep a watchful eye over the adjacent country and sea-coast.

Atalayador, ra [ah-tah-lah-yah-dor', rah], *m. & f.* 1. Guard or sentry stationed in a watch-tower. 2. (Met.) Observer; investigator.

Atalayar [ah-tah-lah-yar'], *va.* 1. To overlook and observe the country and seacoast from a watch-tower or eminence. 2. To spy or pry into the actions of others.

Atalvina [ah-tal-vee'-nah], *f. V.* TALVINA.

Atamiento [ah-tah-me-en'-to], *m.* 1. (Coll.) Pusillanimity, meanness of spirit, want of courage. 2. (Obs.) Embarrassment, perplexity.

Atanasia [ah-tah-nah'-se-ah], *f.* 1. (Bot.) Costmary or alecost. Tanacetum balsamita. 2. Among printers, a size of type named English (14-point).

Atanor [ah-tah-nor'], *m.* (Prov.) A siphon or tube for conveying water.

Atanquía [ah-tan-kee'-ah], *f.* 1. Depilatory, a sort of ointment, to take away hair; mixture of orpiment and lime. 2. Refuse of silk which cannot be spun. 3. *V.* CADARZO.

Atañer [ah-tah-nyerr'], *v. imp.* To belong, to appertain.

Ataque [ah-tah'-kay), *m.* 1. Attack, onset. 2. Fit of apoplexy. 3. Fit of anger. 4. (Mil.) Attack. *Ataque aéreo* or *incursión aérea.* Air raid, air attack. 5. (Med.) Stroke.

Ataquiza [ah-tah-kee'-thah], *f.* The act of layering or laying a branch of a vine in the ground to take root.

Ataquizar [ah-tah-ke-thar'], *va.* To layer or lay a branch of a vine in the ground to take root.

Atar [ah-tar'], *va.* 1. To tie, to bind, to fasten, to knit; to lace. 2. (Met.) To deprive of motion, to stop. *Atar bien su dedo,* To take care of one's self, to be attentive to one's own interest. *Al atar de los trapos,* At the close of the accounts. *Loco de atar.* A fool or a madman that should wear a strait-waistcoat. *Atátela al dedo*, Tie it to the finger: said to ridicule a person led by visionary expectations.—*vr.* 1. To be embarrassed or perplexed, to be at a loss how to extricate one's self from some difficulties. 2. To confine one's self to some certain subject or matter. *Atarse a la letra*, To stick to the letter of the text. *Atarse las manos*, To tie one's self down by promise.

Ataracea [ah-tah-rah-thay'-ah], *f.* Marquetry, checker, checker-work; inlaid work, veneer work.

Ataracear [ah-tah-rah-thay-ar'], *va.* To checker, to inlay or variegate.

Atarantado, da [ah-tah-ran-tah'-do, dah], *a.* 1. Bit by a tarantula. 2. Having a tremulous head and hand, as if bit by a tarantula. 3. (Met.) Surprised, astonished, amazed. 4. Harum-scarum, wild.

Atarazana [ah-tah-rah-thah'-na], *f.* 1. (Obs.) Arsenal, a public dockyard. 2. Shed in rope-walks, for the spinners to work under cover. 3. (Prov.) Cellar, where wine is kept in casks.

Atarazar [ah-tah-rah-thar'], *va.* To bite or wound with the teeth.

Atareado, da [ah-tah-ray-ah'-do, dah], *a.* Busied, occupied; intent.—*pp.* of Atarear.

Atarear [ah-tah-ray-ar'], *va.* To task, to impose a task, to exercise.—*vr.* To overdo one's self, to labour or work with great application.

Atarjea [ah-tar-hay'-ah], *f.* 1. A small vault over the pipes of an aqueduct, to prevent them from receiving hurt. 2. A small sewer or drain.

Atarquinar [ah-tar-ke-nar'], *va.* To bemire, to cover with mire.—*vr.* To be bemired, to be covered with mire.

Atarraga [ah-tar-rah'-gah], *f.* (Bot.) *V.* Olivarda.

Atarragar [ah-tar-rah-gar'], *va.* To fit a shoe to a horse's foot.

Atarrajar [ah-tar-rah-har'], *va.* To form the thread of a screw. *V.* Aterrajar.

Atarraya [ah-tar-rah'-yah], *f.* A cast-net.

Atarugado, da [ah-tah-roo-gah'-do, dah], *a.* (Coll.) Abashed, ashamed.—*pp.* of Atarugar.

Atarugar [ah-tah-roo-gar'], *va.* 1. To fasten or secure with wedges. 2. (Mech.) To plug, to bung; to cram. 3. (Met.) To silence and confound a person.

Atasajado, da [ah-tah-sah-hah'-do, dah], *a.* (Coll.) Stretched across a horse.—*pp.* of Atasajar.

Atasajar [ah-tah-sah-har'], *va.* To cut meat into small pieces, and dry it by the sun, in imitation of hung-beef; to "jerk" beef.

Atascadero, Atascamiento [ah-tas-cah-day'-ro, ah-tas-cah-me-en'-to], *m.* 1. A deep miry place, in which carriages, horses, etc., stick fast. 2. (Met.) Obstruction, impediment.

Atascar [ah-tas-car'], *va.* 1. (Naut.) To stop a leak. 2. (Met.) To throw an obstacle in the way of an undertaking.—*vr.* 1. To stick in a deep miry place. 2. To get stopped up: applied to drains, etc. 3. (Met.) To stop short in a discourse, unable to proceed.

Atasco [ah-tahs'-co], *m.* A barrier, obstruction.

Ataúd [ah-tah-ood'], *m.* 1. Coffin in which dead bodies are put into the ground, casket. 2. (Obs.) A measure for corn.

Ataudado, da [ah-tah-oo-dah'-do, dah], *a.* Made in the shape of a coffin.

Ataujía [ah-tah-oo-hee'-ah], *f.* Damaskeening, the art of adorning metals with inlaid work.

Ataujiado, da [ah-tah-oo-he-ah'-do, dah], *a.* Damaskeened.

Ataviado, da [ah-tah-ve-ah'-do, dah], *a.* Ornamented, ornated.—*pp.* of Ataviar.

Ataviar [ah-tah-ve-ar'], *va.* To dress out, to trim, to adorn, to embellish, to accoutre.

Atavío [ah-tah-vee'-o], *m.* The dress and ornament of a person, accoutrement, finery, gear.

Atavismo [ah-tah-vees'-mo], *m.* Atavism, resemblance to ancestors; the tendency of hybrids to revert to the original type.

Ataxia [ah-tac'-se-ah], *f.* 1. (Med.) Ataxia, ataxy. 2. A graminaceous plant of Java.

Atáxico, ca [ah-tac'-se-co, cah], *a.* Ataxic, in disordered movement.

Ate [ah'-tay], *f.* (Bot.) An orchidaceous plant, resembling habenaria.

Atediar [ah-tay-de-ar'], *va.* To disgust or displease, to consider with disgust. —*vr.* To be vexed, to be tired.

Ateísmo [ah-tay-ees'-mo], *m.* Atheism; denial of God.

Ateísta [ah-tay-ees'-tah], *m.* Atheist; infidel, unbeliever.

Atelaje. *V.* Atalaje. Also a team.

Atemorizar [ah-tay-mo-re-thar'], *va.* To terrify, to strike with terror, to daunt.

Atempa [ah-tem'-pah], *f.* (Asturian) Pasture in plains and open fields.

Atemperación [ah-tem-pay-rah-the-on'], *f.* The act and effect of tempering.

Atemperar [ah-tem-pay-rar'], *va.* 1. To temper, to form metals to a proper degree of hardness. 2. To soften, to mollify, to assuage; to cool. 3. To accommodate, to modify.

Atemporado, da [ah-tem-po-rah'-do, dah], *a.* (Obs.) Alternate, serving by turns. Moderate, temperate.

Atenacear, Atenazar [ah-tay-na-thay-ar'; ah-tay-na-thar'], *va.* To tear off the flesh with pincers.

Atención [ah-ten-the-on'], *f.* 1. Attention, the act of being attentive; heed, heedfulness, mindfulness. 2. Civility, kindness, complaisance, courteousness, observance. 3. In the wool-trade, a contract of sale, whereby the price is not determined. *En atención*, Attending; in consideration.—*pl.* Affairs, business, occupation.

Atender [ah-ten-derr'], *vn.* 1. To attend or be attentive, to mind, or to fix the mind upon a subject. 2. To heed, to hearken. 3. To expect, to wait or stay for; to look at. 4. To meet an emergency with succour or money. 5. To read the "copy" while the corrector reads the proof.

Atendible [ah-ten-dee'-blay], *a.* Meriting attention.

Ateneo [ah-tay-nay'-o], *m.* Athenæum, in its various significations.

Ateneo, a, *adj.* (Poet.) or **Ateniense** [ah-tay-ne-en'-say]. Athenian.

Atener [ah-tay-nerr'], *vn.* (Obs.) 1. To walk at the same pace with another. 2. To guard, to observe.—*vr.* To stick or adhere to one for greater security. *Atenerse a alguna cosa*, To abide.

Atenta [ah-ten'-tah], *f.* (Com.) *Su atenta*, Your favour.

Atentación [ah-ten-tah-the-on'], *f.* (Law) Procedure contrary to the order and form prescribed by the laws.

Atentadamente [ah-ten-tah-dah-men'-tay], *adv.* 1. Prudently, considerately. 2. Contrary to law.

Atentado, da [ah-ten-tah'-do, dah], *a.* 1. Discreet, prudent, moderate. 2. Done without noise, and with great circumspection.—*pp.* of Atentar.

Atentado [ah-ten-tah'-do], *m.* 1. (Law) Proceeding of a judge not warranted by the law. 2. Excess, transgression, offence.

Atentamente [ah-ten-tah-men'-tay], *adv.* 1. Attentively, with attention, mindfully. 2. Civilly, politely, obligingly, observingly.

Atentar [ah-ten-tar'], *va.* 1. To attempt to commit any crime. 2. To try with great circumspection.—*vr.* (Obs.) To proceed with the utmost circumspection in the execution of an enterprise.

Atentatorio, ria [ah-ten-tah-to'-re-o, ah], *a.* (Law) Contrary to the order and form prescribed by the laws.

Atento, ta [ah-ten'-to, tah], *a.* 1. Attentive, bent upon a thing, listful, heedful; observing; mindful. 2. Polite, civil, courteous, mannerly, compliant, complaisant, considerate; notable.—*pp. irr.* of Atender, *adv.* *Atento*, In consideration.

Atenuación [ah-tay-noo-ah-the-on'], *f.* 1. Attenuation, the act of making thin or slender. 2. Maceration. 3. The rhetorical figure litotes.

Atenuante [ah-tay-noo-ahn'-tay], *a.* Attenuating. Extenuating (circumstances), lessening guilt.

Atenuar [ah-tay-noo-ar'], *va.* To attenuate, to render thin and slender; to diminish, to lessen, to macerate, to mince.

Ateo [ah-tay'-o], *m.* *V.* Ateísta.

Atepocate [ah-tay-po-cah'-tay], *m* (Mex.) Frog spawn.

Aterciandо, da [ah-ter-the-ah-nah'-do, dah], *a.* Afflicted with a tertian or intermitting fever.

Aterciopelado, da [ah-ter-the-o-pay-lah'-do, dah], *a.* Velvet-like, resembling velvet.

Aterido, da [ah-tay-ree'-do, dah], *a.* Stiff with cold.—*pp.* of Aterirse.

Aterimiento [ah-tay-re-me-en'-to], *m.* Act of growing stiff with cold.

Aterino [ah-tay-ree'-no], *m.* Atherine, a sand-smelt, about 0.15 metre in length, and presents the rare distinction of being translucent.

Aterirse [ah-tay-reer'-say], *vr.* To grow stiff with cold.

Aternerado, da [ah-ter-nay-rah'-do, dah], *a.* Calf-like.

Ateroma [ah-tay-ro'-mah], *f.* Atheroma, fatty degeneration of an artery.

Aterrador, ra [ah-ter-rah-dor', rah], *a.* Frightful, terrible, dreadful.

Aterrajar [ah-ter-rah-har'], *va.* To cut the thread of a screw; to tap with the die.

Aterramiento [ah-ter-rah-me-en'-to], *m.* 1. Ruin, destruction. 2. Terror, communication of fear. 3. (Naut.) A landing-place.

Aterrar [ah-ter-rar'], *va.* 1. To destroy, to pull or strike down; to prostrate. 2. To terrify, to appal, to cause terror or dismay.—*vr.* (Naut.) To stand inshore, to keep the land on board.

Aterrizaje [ah-ter-re-thah'-hay], *m.* (Aer.) Landing.

Aterrizar [ah-ter-re-thar'], *vn.* (Aer.) To land.

Aterronar [ah-ter-ro-nar'], *va.* To clod, to gather into concretions, to coagulate.

Aterrorizar [ah-ter-ro-re-thar'], *va.* To frighten, to terrify.

Atesador [ah-tay-sah-dor'], *m.* (Mech.) Stretcher, line-tightener, tensor, take-up. Brace-pin.

Atesar [ah-tay-sar'], *va.* 1. To brace, or stiffen a thing. 2. (Naut.) To haul taut.

Atesorador [ah-tay-so-rah-dor'], *m.* A hoarder.

Atesorar [ah-tay-so-rar'], *va.* 1. To treasure or hoard up riches, to lay in, to lay up. 2. To possess many amiable qualities.

Atestación [ah-tes-tah-the-on'], *f.* Attestation, testimony, evidence.

Atestado, da [ah-tes-tah'-do, dah], *a.* 1. Attested, witnessed. 2. *V.* TESTARUDO.—*pp.* of ATESTAR.

Atestados [ah-tes-tah'-dos], *m.pl.* Certificates, testimonials.

Atestadura [ah-tes-tah-doo'-rah], *f.* 1. The act of cramming or stuffing. 2. Must, poured into pipes and butts, to supply the leakage.

Atestamiento [ah-tes-tah-me-en'-to], *m.* (Obs.) The act of cramming, stuffing, or filling.

Atestar [ah-tes-tar'], *va.* 1. To cram, to stuff; to overstock, to clog. 2. To stuff, to crowd. 3. To fill up pipes or butts of wine. 4. To attest, to witness. 5. (Prov.) *V.* ATRACAR.

Atestiguación, *f.* **Atestiguamiento**, *m.* [ah-tes-te-goo-ah-the-on', ah-tes-te-goo-ah-me-en'-to]. Deposition upon oath.

Atestiguar [ah-tes-te-goo-ar'], *va.* To depose, to witness, to attest, to affirm as a witness, to give evidence. *Atestiguar con alguno*, To cite or summon one as a witness.

Atesto [ah-tes'-to], *m.* Certificate, paper. (Com.)

Atetado, da [ah-tay-tah'-do, dah], *a.* Mammillated, mammiform.—*pp.* of ATETAR.

Atetar [ah-tay-tar'], *va.* To suckle, to give suck.

Atetillar [ah-tay-teel-lyar'], *va.* To dig a trench around the roots of trees.

Atezado, da [ah-tay-thah'-do, dah], *a.* Black.—*pp.* of ATEZAR.

Atezamiento [ah-tay-thah-me-en'-to], *m.* The act and effect of blackening.

Atezar [ah-tay-thar'], *va.* To blacken, to make black.—*vr.* To grow black.

Atiborrar [ah-te-bor-rar'], *va.* 1. To stuff or pack up close with locks of wool, tow, etc. 2. To cram with victuals.

Aticismo [ah-te-thees'-mo], *m.* 1. Atticism, elegance and grace in language. 2. Nice, witty, and polite joke.

Ático, ca [ah'-te-co, cah], *a.* 1. Attic, elegant, poignant: applied to wit and humour. 2. (Obs.) Superior to objection or confutation. *Testigo ático*, An irrefragable witness.—*m.* Upper part of a building, attic.

Aticurga [ah-te-coor'-gah], *f.* Base of an attic column.

(*Yo atiendo*, from *Atender*. *V.* ATENDER.)

(*Yo atierro, yo atierre*, from *Aterrar*. *V.* ACERTAR.)

(*Yo atiento*, from *Atentar*. *V.* ACERTAR.)

Atierre [ah-te-err'-ray], *m.* (Mining.) Attle, heap of waste ore.

Atiesar [ah-te-ay-sar'], *va.* To make hard or stiff.

Atifle [ah-tee'-flay], *m.* An instrument in the shape of a trevet, which potters place between earthen vessels, to prevent them from sticking to each other in the kiln or oven.

Atigrado, da [ah-te-grah'-do, dah], *a.* Tiger-coloured, resembling the skin of a tiger.

Atildado, da [ah-teel-dah'-do, dah], *a.* Elegant, neat, fastidious. *Atildado caballero*, Perfect gentleman.

Atildadura [ah-teel-dah-doo'-rah], *f.* 1. (Obs.) Dress, attire, ornament. 2. (Obs.) Culture of the mind, good breeding. 3. Punctuation.

Atildar [ah-teel-dar'], *va.* 1. To put a dash or stroke over a letter. 2. To censure the speeches and actions of others. 3. To deck, to dress, to adorn.

Atillo [ah-teel'-lyo], *m.* Bundle. *V.* HATILLO. *Hacer atillo*, To pack up.

Atinadamente [ah-te-nah-dah-men'-tay], *adv.* 1. Cautiously, judiciously, prudently. 2. Pertinently, appositely, to the purpose. 3. Considerately, consideringly.

Atinar [ah-te-nar'], *vn.* 1. To hit the mark, to reach the point. 2. To hit upon a thing by conjecture, to guess. 3. To find out.

Atincar [ah-teen'-car], *m.* Tincal: when refined, it is the borax of commerce.

Atinconar [ah-tin-co-nar'], *va.* To secure temporarily the walls of an excavation.

Atiplar [ah-te-plar'], *va.* To raise the sound of a musical instrument.—*vr.* To grow very sharp or acute: applied to the sound of a musical instrument.

Atirantar [ah-te-ran-tar'], *va.* (Arch.) To fix collar-beams in a building.

Atisbadero [ah-tis-bah-day'-ro], *m.* Peephole.

Atisbador, ra [ah-tis-bah-dor', rah], *m.* & *f.* A person who pries into the business and actions of others.

Atisbadura [ah-tis-bah-doo'-rah], *f.* The act of prying into the business and actions of others.

Atisbar [ah-tis-bar'], *va.* 1. To scrutinize, to pry, to examine closely. 2. To watch, to waylay.

Atisuado, da [ah-te-soo-ah'-do, dah], *a.* Tissue-like—i. e. like *tisú*, a silk stuff interwoven with gold and silver, presenting a flower pattern.

Atizador, ra [ah-te-thah-dor', rah], *m.* & *f.* 1. One who stirs up or incites others. 2. Poker, an instrument to stir the fire. 3. In oil-mills, the person who puts the olives under the mill-stone. 4. In glass-houses, he who supplies the furnace with wood or coals; feeder.

Atizar [ah-te-thar'], *va.* 1. To stir the fire with a poker. 2. (Met.) To stir up or rouse and incite the passions. *Atizar la lámpara* or *el candil*, To raise the lamp wick, and fill it with oil. *Atizar la lámpara*, (Coll.) To fill the glasses. *Pedro ¿por qué atiza? Por gozar de la ceniza*, Why does Peter sow? Because he expects to reap.

Atizonar [ah-te-tho-nar'], *va.* To join bricks and stones close together, and fill up the chinks in a wall with mortar and brickbats.—*vr.* To be smutted: applied to grain.

Atlante [at-lahn'-tay], *m.* He who bears the weight of government, in allusion to Atlas. *Atlantes*, (Arch.) Figures or half-figures of men, sometimes used instead of columns; atlantes or telamones. *Cf.* CARYATIDES.

Atlántico [at-lahn'-te-co], *a.* Atlantic.

Atlas [at'-las], *m.* 1. Atlas, a collection of maps. 2. (Anat.) Atlas, the name of the first cervical vertebra. 3. (Com.) A kind of rich satin, manufactured in the East Indies.

Atleta [at-lay'-tah], *m.* Athlete, wrestler, gymnast.

Atlético, ca [at-lay'-te-co, cah], *a.* Athletic, belonging to gymnastics; robust.

Atmósfera [at-mos'-fay-rah], *f.* 1. Atmosphere, the air. 2. The space over which the influence of any thing extends, or is exerted. 3. Measure of force founded upon the pressure exerted by the atmosphere.

Atmosférico, ca [at-mos-fay'-re-co, cah], *a.* Atmospherical.

Atoaje [ah-to-ah'-hay], *m.* Towage, warping.

Atoar [ah-to-ar'], *va.* (Naut.) To tow a vessel by the help of a rope.

Atocinado, da [ah-to-the-nah'-do, dah], *a.* (Low) Corpulent, fat, fleshy.—*pp.* of ATOCINAR.

Atocinar [ah-to-the-nar'], *va.* 1. To cup up a pig. To make bacon. 2. (Met.) To assassinate or murder.—*vr.* 1. (Coll.) To swell with anger and rage, to be exasperated. 2. To be violently enamoured.

Atocha [ah-to'-chah], *f.* (Bot.) Tough feather-grass, bass-weed, esparto. Stipa tenacissima.

Atochal, Atochar [ah-to-chahl', ah-to-char'], *m.* A field where bass-weed grows.

Atochar [ah-to-char'], *va.* 1. To fill with bass-weed. 2. To fill a hole, pack in.

Atochón [ah-to-chone'], *m.* (Bot.) Name of the tender panicle of the tough feather-grass.

Atole [ah-to'-lay], or **Atol**, *m.* (Mex. and Cuba) A gruel made by boiling Indian corn, or maize, pounded to flour, in water, and also in milk. In Peru called mazamorra.

Atolón [ah-to-lone'], *m.* Atoll, a coral island.

Atolondrado, da [ah-to-lon-drah'-do, dah], *a.* Hare-brained, thoughtless, mad-brain, giddy, careless, heedless; harum-scarum.—*pp.* of ATOLONDRAR.

Atolondramiento [ah-to-lon-drah-me-en'-to], *m.* Stupefaction, the act and effect of stupefying, consternation.

Atolondrar [ah-to-lon-drar'], *va.* To stun, to stupefy, to confound, to render stupid.—*vr.* To be stupefied, to grow dull or stupid.

Atolladero [ah-tol-lyah-day'-ro], *m.* 1. A deep miry place. 2. (Met.) Obstacle, impediment, obstruction.

Atollar [ah-tol-lyar'], *vn.* To fall into the mire, to stick in the mud.—*vr.* (Met.) To be involved in great difficulties.

Atomico, ca [ah-to'-me-co, cah] *a.* Atomic. *Bomba atómica*, Atomic bomb. *Era* or *edad atómica*, Atomic age.

Atomismo [ah-to-mees'-mo], *m.* Atomism, the atomical philosophy.

Atomista [ah-to-mees'-tah], *m.* Atomist, one who holds the atomical philosophy, or the system of atoms.

Atomístico, ca [ah-to-mees'-te-co, cah], *a.* Atomical, consisting of atoms.

Átomo [ah'-to-mo], *m.* 1. Atom, corpuscle, ace, mote. 2. Any thing extremely small. *No exceder en un átomo*, To stick closely to one's orders and instructions. *Reparar en un átomo*, To remark the minutest actions. *Atomos*, Minute parts seen by a solar ray in any place.

Atondar [ah-ton-dar'], *va.* To spur a horse.

Atónito, ta [ah-to'-ne-to, tah], *a.* Astonished, amazed.

Átono, na [ah'-to-no, nah], *a.* Unaccented; used of a syllable in prosody, a-tonic.

Atontadamente [ah-ton-tah-dah-men'-tay], *adv.* Foolishly, stupidly.

Atontado, da [ah-ton-tah'-do, dah], *a.* Mopish, foolish, stupid.—*pp.* of ATONTAR.

Atontamiento [ah-ton-tah-me-en'-to], *m.* Obstupefaction, the act of stupefying, and state of being stupefied.

Atontar [ah-ton-tar'], *va.* To stun, to stupefy, to flatten, to confound.—*vr.* To be stupid, to grow stupid.

Atora [ah-to'-rah], *f.* (Obs.) Law cf Moses.

Atorarse [ah-to-rar'-say], *vr.* 1. To stick in the mire. 2. To fit closely the bore of a cannon: applied to a ball. 3. To choke, to suffocate.

Atormentadamente [ah-tor-men-tah-dah-men'-tay], *adv.* Anxiously, tormentingly.

Atormentado, da [ah-tor-men-tah'-do, dah], *a.* Painful, full of pain, beset with affliction.—*pp.* of ATORMENTAR.

Atormentador, ra [ah-tor-men-tah-dor', rah], *m.* & *f.* Tormentor.

Atormentar [ah-tor-men-tar'], *va.* 1. To torment, to give pain. 2. (Met.) To cause affliction, pain, or vexation. 3. To rack or torment by the rack.

Atornillar [ah-tor-neel-lyar'], *va.* To screw, to fasten with screws.

Atorozonarse [ah-to-ro-tho-nar'-say], *vr.* To suffer gripes or colic, to be griped: applied to horses, etc.

Atorrante [ah-tor-rahn'-tay], *m.* (Arg.) Vagabond, idler, tramp.

Atortolar [ah-tor-to-lar'], *va.* (Coll.) To confound, to intimidate.—*vr.* To be frightened or intimidated, like a turtle-dove.

Atortorar [ah-tor-to-rar'], *va.* (Naut.) To frap a ship, to strengthen the hull with ropes tied round it.

Atortujar [ah-tor-too-har'], *va.* (Coll.) To squeeze, to make flat.

Atosigamiento [ah-to-se-gah-me-en'-to], *m.* The act of poisoning, and state of being poisoned.

Atosigar [ah-to-se-gar'], *va.* 1. To poison. 2. (Met.) To harass, to oppress.

Atoxicar [ah-toc-se-car'], *va.* To poison.

Atóxico, ca [ah-toc'-se-co, cah], *a.* Poisonous.

Atrabancar [ah-trah-ban-car'], *va.* To huddle, to perform a thing in a hurry, and carelessly.

Atrabanco [ah-trah-bahn'-co], *m.* The act of huddling, or doing a thing hurriedly.

Atrabilis [ah-trah-bee'-lis], *f.* The state of being atrabilarious; black bile.

Atracable [ah-trah-cah'-blay], *a.* Approachable.

Atracadero [ah-trah-cah-day'-ro], *m.* (Naut.) A landing-place for small vessels.

Atracar [ah-trah-car'], *va.* 1. (Naut.) To overtake another ship; to approach land; to come alongside. 2. To cram with food and drink, to glut, to pamper.—*vr.* 1. To be stuffed with eating and drinking, to fill. 2. (Naut.) *Atracarse al costado*, To come alongside of a ship.

Atracción [ah-trac-the-on'], *f.* Attraction, the act or power of attracting.

Atracón [ah-trah-cone'], *m.* Over-eating; gluttony.

Atractivo, va [ah-trac-tee'-vo, vah], *a.* 1. Attractive, having the power of attracting, magnetic, magnetical. 2. Engaging.

Atractivo [ah-trac-tee'-vo], *m.* Charm, something fit to gain the affections; grace; cooing.

Atractriz [ah-trac-treeth'], *a.* Powerful to attract.

Atraer [ah-trah-err'], *va.* 1. To attract, to draw to something; to lead. 2. To allure, to lure, to invite, to make another submit to one's will and opinion; to conciliate.—*vr.* (Obs.) *V.* JUNTARSE and EXTENDERSE.

Atrafagado, da [ah-trah-fah-gah'-do, dah], *a.* 1. Much occupied; laborious.—*pp.* of ATRAFAGAR. 2. Fidgety.

Atrafagar [ah-trah-fah-gar'], *vn.* To toil, to exhaust one's self with fatigue. —*vr.* To fidget.

Atragantarse [ah-trah-gan-tar'-say], *vr.* 1. To stick in the throat or windpipe. 2. (Met.) To be cut short in conversation.

Atraible [ah-trah-ee'-blay], *a.* Attractable, subject to attraction.

Atraidorado, da [ah-trah-e-do-rah'-do, dah], *a.* Treacherous, faithless, perfidious.

(*Yo atraigo*, from *Atraer. V.* TRAER.)

Atraillar [ah-trah-eel-lyar'], *va.* 1. To leash, to bind with a string. 2. To follow game guided by a dog in leash.

Atraimiento [ah-trah-e-me-en' to], *m.* (Obs.) The act of attracting, and state of being attracted.

Atramento [ah-trah-men'-to], *m.* Black colour.

Atramentoso, sa [ah-trah-men-to'-so, sah], *a.* (Obs.) That which has the power of dyeing black.

Atramparse [ah-tram-par'-say], *vr.* 1. To be caught in a snare. 2. To be choked, to be stopped or blocked up. 3. To be involved in difficulties.

Atramuz [ah-trah-mooth'], *m.* (Bot.) Lupine. *V.* ALTRAMUZ.

Atrancar [ah-tran-car'], *va.* 1. To bar a door. 2. (Coll.) To step out, to take long steps. 3. (Met. Coll.) To read hurriedly.

Atranco [ah-trahn'-co], *m.* 1. Mudhole. 2. Jam, difficulty, embarrassment.

Atrapa-moscas [ah-trah'-pa-mos'-cas], *f.* (Bot.) The Venus's fly-trap. Dionæa muscipula.

Atrapar [ah-trah-par'], *va.* 1. To overtake, to nab, to lay hold of one who is running away. 2. To impose upon, to deceive.

Atrás [ah-trahs'], *adv.* 1. Backward, toward the back. 2. Past, in time past. *Hacerse atrás*, To fall back. *Quedarse atrás*, To remain behind. *Volverse atrás*, (Met.) To retract, to unsay. *Hacia atrás*, (Coll.) Far from that, quite the contrary.

Atrasado, da [ah-trah-sah'-do, dah], *pp.* of ATRASAR. *Atrasado de medios*, Short of means, poor. *Atrasado de noticias*, (Coll.) Spoken of a person who does not know what is generally known.

Atrasados [ah-trah-sah'-dos], *m. pl.* Arrears, sums remaining unpaid though due.

Atrasar [ah-trah-sar'], *va.* 1. To leave another behind: in this sense seldom used. 2. To obstruct another person's fortune or advancement. 3. To protract or postpone the execution or performance of something. *Atrasar el reloj*, To retard the motion of a watch, to lose time.—*vr.* 1. To remain behind. 2. To be in debt.

Atraso [ah-trah'-so], *m.* 1. Backwardness. 2. Loss of fortune or wealth. 3. Arrears of money.

Atravesado, da [ah-trah-vay-sah'-do, dah], *a.* 1. Squint-eyed, looking obliquely. 2. Oblique. 3. Cross-grained, perverse, troublesome. 4. Mongrel, of a mixed or cross breed.—*pp.* of ATRAVESAR.

Atravesador [ah-trah-vay-sah-dor'], *m.* (Obs.) Disturber, a violator of peace.

Atravesaño [ah-trah-vay-sah'-nyo], *m.* Cross-timber, timber which crosses from one side to another. *Atravesaño firme de colchar*, (Naut.) A cross-piece for belaying ropes. *Atravesaños de los propaos*, Cross-pieces of the breast-work. *Atravesaños de las latas*, Carlines or carlings, two pieces of timber lying fore and aft from one beam to another, directly over the keel.

Atravesar [ah-trah-vay-sar'], *va.* 1. To lay a beam, piece of timber, or plank, athwart a place. 2. To run through with a sword, to pass through the body. 3. To cross, to cross over, to pass over, to get or go over, to go through, to overpass. 4. (Low) To bewitch by a spell or charm. 5. To bet, to stake at a wager. 6. To lay a trump on a card which has been played. 7. (Naut.) To lie to. *Atravesar el corazón*, (Met.) To move to compassion. *Atravesar los géneros*, To buy goods by wholesale in order to sell them by retail. *Atravesar todo el país*, To overrun or traverse the whole country. *No atravesar los umbrales*, Not to darken one's door.—*vr.* 1. To be obstructed by something thrown in the way. 2. To interfere in other people's business or conversation. 3. To have a dispute. 4. (Naut.) To cross the course of another vessel under her head or stern.

(*Yo atravieso, yo atraviese*, from *Atravesar. V.* ACERTAR.)

Atrayente [ah-trah-yen'-tay], *pa.* Attrahent.

Atrazar [ah-tra-thar'], *va.* (Aragón) To practise artifices, to scheme.

Atreguado, da [ah-tray-goo-ah'-do, dah], *a.* Rash, foolish, precipitate, or deranged.

Atresia [ah-tray'-se-ah], *f.* Closure or absence of a natural passage or channel of the body; atresia.

Atresnalar [ah-tres-nah-lar'], *va.* (Prov.) To collect sheaves of corn into heaps.

Atreverse [ah-tray-verr'-say], *vr.* 1. To be too forward from want of judgment or respect. 2. To dare, to venture.

Atrevidamente [ah-tray-ve-dah-men' tay], *adv.* Audaciously, daringly, boldly, confidently.

Atrevidillo, lla [ah-tray-ve-deel'-lyo, lyah], *a. dim.* Somewhat audacious.

Atrevidísimo, ma [ah-tray-ve-dee'-se mo, mah], *a. sup.* Most audacious.

Atrevido, da [ah-tray-vee'-do, dah], *a.* 1. Bold, audacious, daring, fearless, high-spirited, hardy. 2. Forward, free, confident, insolent.—*pp.* of ATREVERSE.

Atrevido [ah-tray-vee'-do], *m.* A muscle on the shoulder-blade.

Atrevimiento [ah-tray-ve-me-en'-to], *m.* 1. Boldness, audaciousness, daringness, hardihood. 2. Confidence, face, front.

Atriaquero [ah-tre-ah-kay'-ro], *m.* (Obs.) A manufacturer and retailer of treacle.

Atribución [ah-tre-boo-the-on'], *f.* 1. The act of attributing something to another. 2. Attribute.

Atribuir [ah-tre-boo-eer'], *va.* To attribute, to ascribe as a quality, to impute as to a cause, to count, to charge to.—*vr.* To assume, to arrogate to one's self.

Atribular [ah-tre-boo-lar'], *va.* To vex, to afflict.—*vr.* To be vexed, to suffer tribulation.

Atributar [ah-tre-boo-tar'], *va.* (Obs.) To impose tribute.

Atributivo, va [ah-tre-boo-tee'-vo, vah], *a.* Attributive.

Atributo [ah-tre-boo'-to], *m.* Attribute, the thing attributed to another; a quality adherent.

(*Yo atribuyo, atribuya; atribuyó, atribuyeron*, from *Atribuir. V.* INSTRUIR.)

Atricapilla [ah-tre-cah-peel'-lyah], *f.* (Orn.) The Epicurean warbler. Motacilla ficedula.

Atriceses [ah-tre-thay'-ses], *m. pl.* The staples or iron rings to which the stirrup-straps are fastened.

Atrición [ah-tre-the-on'], *f.* 1. Contrition, grief for sin arising from the fear of punishment. 2. (Vet.) Contraction of the principal nerve in a horse's fore leg. 3. Attrition, the wearing away of anything by rubbing, or friction.

Atril [ah-treel'], *m.* 1. Reading-desk, lectern; stand for the missal. 2. A music-stand, or holder.

Atrincheramiento [ah-trin-chay-rah-me-en'-to], *m.* Intrenchment, lodgment, mound. *Atrincheramientos de abordaje,* (Naut.) Close quarters, breast-works on board of merchant ships, from behind which the crew defend themselves when boarded by an enemy.

Atrincherar [ah-trin-chay-rar'], *va.* To intrench, to fortify with a trench, to mound.—*vr.* To cover one's self from the enemy by means of trenches.

Atrio [ah'-tre-o], *m.* 1. Porch, a roof supported by pillars between the principal door of a palace and the staircase. 2. Portico, a covered walk before a church-door. 3. An interior, uncovered courtyard.

Atrípedo, da [ah-tree'-pay-do, dah], *a.* (Zool.) Black-footed.

Atrirrostro, tra [ah-trir-ros'-tro, trah], *a.* Black-beaked: applied to birds.

Atrito, ta [ah-tree'-to, tah], *a.* Contrite through fear.

Atrochar [ah-tro-char'], *vn.* To go by cross paths; to make a short cut.

Atrocidad [ah-tro-the-dahd'], *f.* 1. Atrocity or atrociousness, flagitiousness, foulness, heinousness; grievousness; enormous wickedness. 2. Excess. *Es una atrocidad lo que come o lo que trabaja,* He eats or works to excess.

Atrofia [ah-tro'-fe-ah], *f.* Atrophy, a gradual wasting of the body.

Atrofiarse [ah-tro-fe-ar'-say], *vr.* To waste away, to atrophy.

Atrófico, ca [ah-tro'-fe-co, cah], *a.* Affected with atrophy.

Atrojarse [ah-tro-har'-say], *vr.* (Mex. Coll.) To be stumped; to find no way out of a difficulty.

Atrompetado, da [ah-trom-pay-tah'-do, dah], *a.* Trumpet-like, having the shape of a trumpet. *Tiene narices atrompetadas,* His nostrils are as wide as the mouth of a trumpet.

Atronadamente [ah-tro-nah-dah-men'-tay], *adv.* Precipitately, without prudence or reflection.

Atronado [ah-tro-nah'-do], *m.* Blunderer, wild.—*a.* Acting in a precipitate, imprudent manner.—*pp.* of ATRONAR.

Atronador, ra [ah-tro-nah-dor', rah], *m. & f.* Thunderer, one who makes a thundering noise.

Atronadura [ah-tro-nah-doo'-rah], *f.* 1. Crack or split in wood, from periphery inward, following the medullary rays. 2. *V.* ALCANZADURA.

Atronamiento [ah-tro-nah-me-en'-to], *m.* 1. The act of thundering. 2. Stupefaction caused by a blow. 3. Crepane or ulcer in the feet or legs of horses.

Atronar [ah-tro-nar'], *va.* 1. To make a great noise in imitation of thunder. 2. To stun, to stupefy. 3. To stop the ears of horses, to prevent their fright at noises.—*vr.* 1. To be thunder-struck. 2. To die from effect of a thunder-storm, said of chickens in the egg and of silkworms in the cocoon.

Atronerar [ah-tro-nay-rar'], *va.* To make embrasures in a wall.

Atropado, da [ah-tro-pah'-do, dah], *a.* Grouped, clumped: applied to trees and plants.—*pp.* of ATROPAR.

Atropar [ah-tro-par'], *va.* To assemble in groups without order, to conglomerate, to clutter.

Atropelladamente [ah-tro-pel-lyah-dah-men'-tay], *adv.* Tumultuously, confusedly, helter-skelter.

Atropellado, da [ah-tro-pel-lyah'-do, dah], *a.* Speaking or acting in a hasty, precipitate manner.—*pp.* of ATROPELLAR.

Atropellador, ra [ah-tro-pel-lyah-dor', rah], *m. & f.* 1. Trampler, one who overturns or tramples under foot. 2. Transgressor, violator.

Atropellamiento [ah-tro-pel-lyah-me-en'-to], *m.* Trampling under foot; confusedness.

Atropellar [ah-tro-pel-lyar'], *va.* 1. To trample, to tread under foot. 2. *Atropellar las leyes,* To act in defiance of the law. 3. To insult with abusive language. 4. To hurry, to confuse. *Atropellar al caballo,* To overwork a horse.—*vr.* To hurry one's self too much.

Atropello [ah-tro-payl'-lyo], *m.* 1. Upset, act of upsetting. 2. Abuse, insult, outrage.

Atropina [ah-tro-pee'-nah], *f.* Atropine, an alkaloid extracted from (Atropa) belladonna: highly poisonous.

Atropos [ah-tro'-pos], *f.* 1. One of the three Fates. 2. A species of African viper. 3. *m.* The death's-head moth.

Atroz [ah-troth'], *a.* 1. Atrocious, enormous, heinous, fiend-like. 2. Cruel, flagitious, outrageous. 3. Huge, vast, immense. *Estatura atroz,* Enormous stature.

Atrozar [ah-tro-thar'], *va.* (Naut.) To truss a yard to the mast.

Atrozmente [ah-troth-men'-tay], *adv.* 1. Atrociously, heinously. 2. Excessively, to excess. *Trabajar atrozmente,* To work to excess.

Atruhanado, da [ah-troo ah-nah'-do, dah], *a.* Scurrilous, acting the buffoon, using low jests.

(*Yo atrueno, yo atruene,* from *Atronar. V.* ACORDAR.)

Atuendo [ah-too-enn'-do], *m.* Attire, garb. 2. Pomp, ostentation.

Atufar [ah-too-far'], *va.* To vex, to plague; to inhale noxious vapours. —*vr.* 1. To be on the fret: applied to liquors in a state of fermentation. 2. To be angry.

Atufo [ah-too'-fo], *m.* Vexation.

Atún [ah-toon'], *m.* 1. Tunny or tunny-fish. Scomber thynnus. *Pedazo de atún,* An ignorant, stupid fellow. *Por atún y ver al duque,* To kill two birds with one stone. 2. A shrub of the Moluccas.

Atunara [ah-too-nah'-rah], *f.* A place where tunny-fishes are caught.

Atunera [ah-too-nay'-rah], *f.* A fishing-hook used in the tunny-fishery.

Atunero [ah-too-nay'-ro], *m.* A fisherman engaged in the tunny fishery; a fishmonger who deals in tunny-fish.

Aturar [ah-too-rar'], *va.* 1. (Obs. fr. addurare) To endure; to bear toil. 2. To work with judgment or prudence. 3. (fr. obturare) To stop or close tightly, hermetically.

Aturdido, da [ah-toor-dee'-do, dah], *a.* Hare-brained, mad-brain, giddy, wild, stupid.—*pp.* of ATURDIR.

Aturdimiento [ah-toor-de-me-en'-to], *m.* Perturbation of mind; dulness, drowsiness; consternation.

Aturdir [ah-toor-deer'], *va.* 1. To perturb or perturbate, to confuse, to stun. 2. To stupefy with wonder or admiration.—*vr.* To be out of one's wits; to be perturbed or stupefied.

Aturrullar [ah-toor-rool-lyar'], *va.* (Coll.) To confound, to reduce to silence. *Cf.* TURULATO.

Atusador [ah-too-sah-dor'], *m.* 1. Hair-dresser. 2. One who trims plants in a garden.

Atusar [ah-too-sar'], *va.* 1. To cut the hair even, to comb it smooth and even. 2. To trim the plants in a garden.—*vr.* To dress one's self with too much care.

Atutía [ah-too-tee'-ah], *f.* Tutty, a sublimate of calamine collected in a furnace; crude zinc oxide.

Auca [ah'-oo-cah], *f.* A goose. *V.* OCA. *Cf.* AUK.

(*No hay aución,* (Mex.) *No hay remedio, ni esperanza.* There is no help for it; there is no hope.)

Audacia [ah-oo-dah'-the-ah], *f.* Audacity, boldness.

Audaz [ah-oo-dath'], *a.* Bold, audacious, fearless.

Audibilidad [ah-oo-de-be-le-dahd'], *f.* Audibility.

Audible [ah-oo-dee'-blay], *a.* Audible that may be heard.

Audición [ah-oo-de-the-on'], *f.* Audition, hearing.

Audiencia [ah-oo-de-en'-the-ah], *f.* 1. Audience, a hearing given by men in power to those who have something to propose or represent. 2. Audience-chamber. 3. A court of oyer and terminer. 4. Law-officers appointed to institute some judicial inquiry. 5. *Audiencia de los grados en Sevilla,* A court of appeal in Seville. 6. *Audiencia pretorial en Indias,* A court of judicature in the West Indies.

Audífono [ah-oo-dee'-fo-no], *m.* 1. Earphone, hearing aid. 2. Telephone receiver.

Audiófilo, la [ah-oo-de-o'-fe-lo, lah], *m. & f.* Audiophile.

Audiofrecuencia [ah-oo-de-o-fray-coo-en'-the-ah], *f.* Audiofrequency.

Audiología [ah-oo-de-o-lo-hee'-ah], *f.* Audiology.

Audiómetro [ah-oo-de-o'-may-tro], *m.* Audiometer.

Audión [ah-oo-de-on'), *m.* Audion. (Used in long distance telephony and radio communication.)

Audiovisual [ah-oo-de-o-ve-soo-ahl'], *a.* Audio-visual.

Auditivo, va [ah-oo-de-tee'-vo, vah], *a.* 1. Auditive, auditory, having the power of hearing. 2. Invested with the right of giving an audience.

Auditor [ah-oo-de-tor'], *m.* 1. (Obs.) Auditor, a hearer. 2. A judge. *Auditor de la nunciatura,* A delegate of the Nuncio, appointed to hear and decide appeal causes respecting complaints against bishops. *Auditor de Rota,* One of the twelve prelates who compose the *Rota* at Rome, a court which inquires into and decides appeal causes in ecclesiastical matters.

Auditoría [ah-oo-de-to-ree'-ah], *f.* The place and office of an *auditor.*

Auditorio [ah-oo-de-to'-re-o], *m.* Auditory, an audience; congregation.

Auditorio, ria [ah-oo-de-to'-re-o, ah], *a.* Auditory. *V.* AUDITIVO.

Auge [ah'-oo-hay], *m.* 1. Meridian, the highest point of glory, power, dignity or fortune. 2. (Ast.) Apogee of a planet or star.

Augur [ah-oo-goor'], *m.* Augur, augurer, person who pretends to predict future events by the flight of birds.

Auguración [ah-oo-goo-rah-the-on'], *f.* Auguration, the act of prognosticating by the flight of birds.

Augural [ah-oo-goo-rahl'], *a.* Augurial, belonging to augury.

Augurar [ah-oo-goo-rar'], *va.* To augur.

Augurio [ah-oo-goo'-re-o], *m. V.* AGÜERO.

Augusto, ta [ah-oo-goos'-to, tah], *a.* August, magnificent, majestic.—*m.* Title of the Roman emperors after Octavius Cæsar.

Aula [ah'-oo-lah], *f.* 1. Hall where lectures are given. 2. The court or palace of a sovereign.

Aullador, ra [ah-ool-lyah-dor', rah], *m. & f.* Howler.

Aullar [ah-ool-lyar'], *vn.* To howl, to yell, to cry: applied to wolves and dogs.

Aullido, Aúllo [ah-ool-lyee'-do, ah-ool'-lyo], *m.* Howl, the cry of a wolf or dog; a cry of horror or distress.

Aumentación [ah-oo-men-tah-the-on'], *f.* 1. Augmentation, increase. 2. (Rhet.) Climax.

Aumentado, da [ah-oo-men-tah'-do, dah], *a.* Increased, augmented, onward.—*pp.* of AUMENTAR.

Aumentador, ra [ah-oo-men-tah-dor', rah], *m. & f.* Enlarger, amplifying.

Aumentar [ah-oo-men-tar'], *va.* To augment, to increase, to enlarge.—*vr.* To gather, to grow larger.

Aumentativo, va [ah-oo-men-tah-tee'-vo, vah], *a.* Increasing, enlarging.

Aumento [ah-oo-men'-to], *m.* 1. Augmentation, increase, enlargement. 2. Access, accession; growth. *Aumentos,* Promotion, advancement.

Aun [ah-oon'], *adv.* 1. Yet, as yet, nevertheless, notwithstanding. *V.* TODAVÍA and TAMBIÉN. 2. Still, further, even, further. *El libro es bueno, aun con esas faltas,* The book is good, even with those faults. *Y aun, aun más,* Nay.

Aunar [ah-oo-nar'], *va.* 1. To unite, to assemble. 2. To incorporate, to mix. —*vr.* To be united or confederated for one end.

Aunque [ah-oon-kay'], *adv.* Though, notwithstanding, howsoever.

Aúpa [ah-oo'-pah]. (Coll.) Up, up; a word used to animate children to get up.

Aura [ah'-oo-rah]. *f.* 1. A vulture of Mexico and Cuba. 2. (Poet.) A gentle breeze. *Aura popular,* (Met.) Popularity. 3. Aura, a peculiar premonitory symptom of epilepsy, a feeling as of a breath of air rising from below to the trunk and head.

Auranciáceo [ah-oo-ran-the-ah'-thay-o], *a.* (Bot.) Citrus, citrous.

Áureo, rea [ah'-oo-ray-o, ah], *a.* Golden, gilt, gold.

Aureola, or **Auréola** [ah-oo-ray-o'-lah], *f.* Aureola, a circle of rays of light emblematic of glory.

Aureomicina [ah-oo-ray-o-me-thee'-nah], *f.* (Marca Registrada) Aureomycin.

Aurícula [ah-oo-ree'-coo-lah], *f.* 1. Auricle, one of the two upper cavities of the heart. 2. (Bot.) The bear's-ear. 3. Auricle, the external ear.

Auricular [ah-oo-re-coo-lar'], *a.* 1. Auricular, within the sense or reach of hearing. 2. Auricularis: applied to the little finger of the hand.

Auricular, *m.* 1. Headphone. 2. Earpiece or telephone receiver. *Auricular de casco,* headset.

Aurífero, ra [ah-oo-ree'-fay-ro, rah], *a.* (Poet.) Auriferous, containing or producing gold.

Auriga [ah-oo-ree'-gah], *m.* 1. (Poet.) A coachman. 2. (Ast.) Charioteer or Wagoner, one of the northern constellations.

Aurora [ah-oo-ro'-rah], *f.* 1. The dawn of day. 2. (Poet.) The first appearance of a thing. 3. A beverage, almond-milk and cinnamon-water. 4. (Naut.) The morning watch-gun. 5. *Aurora boreal,* Aurora borealis, or nothern lights.

Auscultar [ah-oos-cool-tar'], *va.* To auscultate, to listen with ear or stethoscope as a means of diagnosis.

Ausencia [ah-oo-sen'-the-ah], *f.* Absence. *Servir ausencias y enfermedades,* To perform the functions of absent or sick persons. *Tener alguno buenas o malas ausencias,* To be ill or well spoken of in one's absence.

Ausentarse [ah-oo-sen-tar'-say], *vr.* To absent one's self.

Ausente [ah-oo-sen'-tay], *a.* Absent, distant.

Auspiciar [ah-oos-pe-the-ar'], *va.* To promote, sponsor, foster.

Auspicio [ah-oos-pee'-the-o], *m.* 1. Auspice, or presage drawn from birds. 2. (Met.) Prediction of future events. 3. Protection, favour, patronage. *Bajo los auspicios de Vd.,* Under your protection or your guidance.

Austeramente [ah-oos-tay-rah-men'-tay], *adv.* Austerely, frowningly.

Austeridad [ah-oos-tay-re-dahd'], *f.* Austerity, severity, rigour.

Austero, ra [ah-oos-tay'-ro, rah], *a.* 1. Harsh, astringent to the taste. 2. Retired, mortified, and penitent. 3. Severe, rigid, harsh, austere.

Austral, Austrino, na [ah-oos-trahl', ah-oos-tree'-no, nah], *a.* Austral, southern.

Australiano, na [ah-oos-trah-le-ah'-no, nah], *a. & m. & f.* Australian.

Austriaco, ca [ah-oos-tre-ah'-co, cah], *a.* Austrian; of Austria.

Austro [ah'-oos-tro], *m.* South wind; notus.

Autarquía [ah-oo-tar-kee'-ah], *f.* 1. Autarchy. 2. Autarky.

Autenticación [ah-oo-ten-te-cah-the-on'], *f.* Authentication.

Auténticamente [ah-oo-ten'-te-cah-men'-tay], *adv.* Authentically.

Autenticar [ah-oo-ten-te-car'], *va.* To authenticate, to attest.

Autenticidad [ah-oo-ten-te-the-dahd'], *f.* Authenticity.

Auténtico, ca [ah-oo-ten'-te-co, cah], *a.* Authentic, genuine, veritable, indisputable, official.

Autillo [ah-oo-teel'-lyo], *m.* 1. (Dim.) A particular act or decree of the Inquisition. 2. (Orn.) The barn-owl.

Auto [ah'-oo-to], *m.* 1. A judicial decree or sentence. 2. A writ, warrant. 3. An edict, ordinance. *Auto de Fe,* The sentence given by the Inquisition. 4. (Obs.) Act, action. *Auto definitivo,* Definitive act, which has the force of a sentence. *Auto sacramental,* An allegorical or dramatical piece of poetry on some religious subject, represented as a play. *Autos,* The pleadings and proceedings in a lawsuit. *Estar en autos* or *en los autos,* To know a thing profoundly. *Auto acordado,* A sentence or decision of a supreme court, to be observed as a precedent.

Auto [ah'-oo-to], *m.* Auto, automobile.

Autobiografía [ah-oo-to-be-o-grah-fee'-ah], *f.* Autobiography.

Autobiográfico, ca [ah-oo-to-be-o-grah'-fe-co, cah], *a.* Autobiographical.

Autobombo [ah-oo-to-bom'-bo], *m.* Self-praise.

Autobús [ah-oo-to-boos'], *m.* Bus, motorbus.

Autocamión [ah-oo-to-cah-me-on'], *m.* Motor truck.

Autoclave [ah-oo-to-clah'-vay], *f.* Autoclave, sterilizer.

Autocracia [ah-oo-to-crah'-the-ah], *f.* Autocracy, absolute sovereignty.

Autócrata [ah-oo-to'-crah-tah], *m.* Autocrat: applied especially to the Emperor of Russia.

Autocrático, ca [ah-oo-to-crah'-te-co, cah], *a.* Autocratical.

Autóctono, na [ah-oo-toc'-to-no, nah], *a.* Autochthonous, native of the country.

Autoescuela [ah-oo-to-es-coo-ay'-lah], *f.* Driving school.

Autogiro [ah-oo-to-hee'-ro], *m.* Autogiro.

Autografía [ah-oo-to-grah-fee'-ah], *f.* The art of copying a writing or drawing by lithography.

Autográfico, ca [ah-oo-to-grah'-fe-co, cah], *a.* Autographical.

Autógrafo [ah-oo-toh'-grah-fo], *m.* Autograph.

Autohotel [ah-oo-to-o-tel'], *m.* Motel.

Autoinducción [ah-oo-to-in-dooc-the-on'], *f.* (Elec.) Self-induction.

Autoinflamación [ah-oo-to-en-flah-mah-the-on'], *f.* Spontaneous combustion.

Autointoxicación [ah-oo-to-in-toc-se-cah-the-on'], *f.* Autointoxication, poisoning from toxic substances in the body.

Autómata [ah-oo-toh'-mah-tah], *m.* 1. A machine containing in itself the power of motion. 2. Automaton, a machine imitating the actions of living animals.

Automático, ca [ah-oo-to-mah'-te-co, cah], *a.* Automatic.

Automatización [ah-oo-to-mah-tee-tha-the-on'], *f.* Automation.

Automatizar [ah-oo-to-mah-te-thar'], *va.* To automate.

Automotor, ra [ah-oo-to-mo-tor', rah], *a.* Self-propelling.

Automotriz [ah-oo-to-mo-treeth'], *a.* Automotive.

Automóvil [ah-oo-to-mo'-veel], *m.* Automobile. *Automóvil acorazado,* Armored car. *Automóvil de plaza,* Taxi, taxicab. *Automóvil de segunda mano,* Used car, second-hand car. *Automóvil de turismo,* Touring car.

Automovilista [ah-oo-to-mo-ve-lees'-tah], *m. & f.* Motorist, automobile rider.

Autonomía [ah-oo-to-no-mee'-ah], *f.* Autonomy, the condition of self-government, independence.

Autónomo, ma [ah-oo-to'-no-mo, mah], *a.* Autonomous, independent, free.

Autopiano [ah-oo-to-pe-ah'-no], *m.* Player piano.

Autopista [ah-oo-to-pees'-tah], *f.* Highway. *Autopista de acceso limitado,* Freeway.

Autoplastia [ah-oo-to-plahs'-te-ah], *f.* Anaplasty, plastic surgery.

Autopropulsión [ah-oo-to-pro-pool-se-on'], *f.* Self-propulsion.

Autopsia [ah-oo-top'-se-ah], *f.* Autopsy.

Autor [ah-oo-tor'], *m.* 1. Author, maker, composer. 2. Writer, one that composes a literary work. 3. Manager of a theatre. 4. (Law) Plaintiff or claimant. *Autor de nota,* A celebrated writer. 5. Speaking of watches, the maker. 6. The cause of anything. *Ser autor de,* to author.

Autora [ah-oo-to'-rah], *f.* Authoress.

Autoridad [ah-oo-to-ree-dahd'], *f.* 1. Authority or power derived from a public station, merit, or birth; credit. 2. Ostentation, display of grandeur. 3. Authority, words cited from a book or writing.

Autoritario, ria [ah-oo-to-re-tah'-re-oh, ah], *m. & f. & a.* Authoritarian.

Autoritativo, va [ah oo-to-re-tah-tee'vo, vah], *a.* Arrogant, assuming.

Autorización [ah-oo-to-re-tha-the-on'], *f.* Authorization.

Autorizadamente [ah-oo-to-re-thah-dah-men'-tay], *adv.* Authoritatively.

Autorizado, da [ah-oo-to-re-thah'-do, dah], *a.* Respectable, commendable. —*pp.* of AUTORIZAR.

Autorizador [ah-oo-to-re-thah-dor'], *m.* He who authorizes.

Autorizar [ah-oo-to-re-thar'], *va.* 1. To authorize, to give power or authority to. 2. To legalize. 3. To exalt.

Autoservicio [ah-oo-to-ser-vee'-the-o], *m.* Self-service.

Auto-stop [ah-oo-to-stop'], *m.* Hitch-hiking.

Autosuficiencia [ah-oo-to-soo-fe-the-en'-the-ah], *f.* Self-sufficiency.

Autosugestión [ah-oo-to-soo-hes-te-on'], *f.* Autosuggestion, self-suggestion.

Autumnal [ah-oo-toom-nahl'], *a.* (Littl. us.) Autumnal.

Auxiliador, ra [ah-ook-se-le-ah-dor', rah], *m.* & *f.* Auxiliary, assistant.

Auxiliar [ah-ook-se-le-ar'], *va.* 1. To aid, to help, to assist. 2. To attend a dying person.

Auxiliar [ah-ook-se-le-ar'], *a.* Auxiliar, auxiliatory, helping, assistant. *Tropas auxiliares,* Auxiliary troops. *Obispo auxiliar,* An assistant bishop. *Verbo auxiliar,* An auxiliary verb.

Auxiliatorio, ria [ah-ook-se-le-ah-to'-re-o, ah], *a.* (Law) Auxiliary.

Auxilio [ah-ook-see'-le-o], *m.* Aid, help, assistance.

Ava-ava [ah'-vah-ah'-vah], *f.* (Bot.) A plant so called by the inhabitants of Otaheite, from the leaves of which they extract an intoxicating liquor.

Avacado, da [ah-vah-cah'-do, dah], *a.* Cow-like, resembling a cow: applied to a big-bellied horse.

Avadarse [ah-vah-dar'-say], *vr.* 1. To become fordable. 2. (Obs.) To subside: applied to passion.

Avahar [ah-vah-ar'], *va.* (Littl. us.) 1. To warm with the breath, or with steam and vapour. 2. To wither: applied to plants.

Aval [ah-vahl'], *m.* Security, guarantee, indorsement (of exchange).

Avalancha [ah-vah-lahn'-chah], *f.* (Neol.) = ALUD. (Falling into disuse, as being a Gallicism.)

Avalar [ah-vah-lar'], *v. imp.* (Prov.) (The earth) trembles.

Avalentado, da [ah-vah-len-tah'-do, dah], *a.* Bragging, boasting.

Avalizar [ah-vah-le-thar'], *va.* To mark the dangerous spots in a channel with buoys.

Avalo [ah-vah'-lo], *m.* (Prov.) 1. A slight movement. 2. An earthquake.

Avalorar [ah-vah-lo-rar'], *va.* 1. To estimate, to value. 2. (Met.) To inspirit, to animate.

Avaluación [ah-vah-loo-ah-the-on'], *f.* Valuation, rate, assessment.

Avaluar [ah-vah-loo-ar'], *va.* To value, to appraise, to estimate.

Avalúo [ah-vah-loo'-oh], *m.* Valuation, official appraisement.

Avallar [ah-val-lyar'], *va.* To inclose a piece of ground with pales or hedges.

Avambrazo [ah vam-brah'-tho], *m.* Piece of ancient armour that served to cover the forearm.

Avampiés [ah-vam-pe-ess'], *m.* (Obs.) Instep of boots, or spatterdashes.

Avance [ah-vahn'-thay], *m.* 1. (Mil.) Advance, attack, assault. 2. Among merchants, an account of goods received and sold. 3. A balance in one's favour.

Avandicho [ah-van-dee'-cho]. (Obs.) *V.* SOBREDICHO. Aforesaid.

Avantal [ah-van-tahl'], *m.* (Obs.) Apron. *V.* DELANTAL.

Avantalillo [ah-van-tah-leel'-lyo], *m. dim.* (Obs.) A small apron.

Avante [ah-vahn'-tay], *adv.* 1. (Naut.) Ahead. *Hala avante,* Pull ahead. 2. (Obs.) *V.* ADELANTE.

Avantrén [ah-van-tren'], *m.* Limbers of a gun-carriage.

Avanzada [ah-van-thah'-dah], *f.* (Mil.) Outpost, reconnoitring body.

Avanzado, da [ah-van-thah'-do, dah], *a.* Advanced; onward. *Avanzado de edad,* or *de edad avanzada,* Advanced in years, stricken in years.—*pp.* of AVANZAR.

Avanzar [ah-van-thar'], *vn.* 1. To advance, to attack, to engage, to come on. 2. To have a balance in one's favour.—*va.* To advance, to push forward.

Avanzo [ah-vahn'-tho], *m.* 1. Among merchants, an account of goods received and sold. 2. A balance in one's favour.

Avaramente [ah-vah-rah-men'-tay], *adv.* Avariciously, in a covetous manner, miserably.

Avaricia [ah-vah-ree'-the-ah], *f.* Avarice, cupidity, covetousness.

Avariciar [ah-va-ree-the-ar'], *va.* & *vn.* (Obs.) To covet, to desire anxiously.

Avariciosamente [ah-vah-re-the-o-sah-men'-tay], *adv.* Greedily, covetously.

Avaricioso, sa [ah-vah-re-the-o'-so, sah], *a.* 1. *V.* AVARIENTO. 2. Anxious to eat or drink.

Avariento, ta [ah-vah-re-en'-to, tah], *a.* Avaricious, covetous, niggard, miserly, miserable, close, narrow.

Avaro, ra [ah-vah'-ro, rah], *a.* *V.* AVARIENTO.

Avasallar [ah-vah-sal-lyar'], *va.* To subdue, to subject, to enslave, to mancipate.—*vr.* To become subject, to become a vassal.

Ave [ah'-vay], *f.* 1. Bird, a general name for the feathered kind. 2. Fowl. *Ave de rapiña,* A bird of prey *Ave brava* or *silvestre,* A wild bird. *Ave fría,* Lapwing, a kind of plover. Vanellus. *Todas las aves con sus pares,* Birds of a feather flock together. *Es un ave,* He is very swift, active. *Ave nocturna,* (Met.) One who rambles about in the night-time. *Ave zonza,* A lazy, half-foolish person.

Avecinar [ah-vay-the-nar'], *va.* 1. (Obs.) To bring near. 2. *V.* AVECINDAR.—*vr.* To come near, to approach.

Avecindamiento [ah-vay-thin-dah-me-en'-to], *m.* 1. Acquisition of the rights of a citizen or freeman. 2. The act of residing in a place invested with the rights of a citizen.

Avecindar [ah-vay-thin-dar'], *va.* To admit to the privileges of a denizen, to enrol in the number of the citizens of a place.—*vr.* 1. To acquire the rights and privileges of a denizen or citizen. 2. To approach, to join.

Avechucho [ah-vay-choo'-cho], *m.* 1. An ugly bird. 2. (Orn.) Sparrow-hawk. Falco nisus, *L.* 2. (Met.) Ragamuffin, a paltry mean fellow.

Avejentado, da [ah-vay-hen-tah'-do, dah], *a.* Appearing old without being really so, oldish.—*pp.* of AVEJENTAR.

Avejentar [ah-vay-hen-tar'], *va.* & *vr.* To look old, to appear older than one really is.

Avejigar [ah-vay-he-gar'], *va.* To produce pimples or small blisters.

Avelar [ah-vay-lar'], *vn.* (Naut.) To set sail.

Avellana [ah-vel-lyah'-nah], *f.* Filbert, hazel-nut. *Avellana índica* or *de la India,* or *nuez ungüentaria.* Myrobalan, or Indian nut, used only in perfumes.

Avellanado, da [ah-vel-lyah-nah'-do, dah], *a.* Nut-brown, of the colour of nuts.—*pp.* of AVELLANARSE.

Avellanador [ah-vel-lyah-na-dor'], *m.* Countersink bit, rose-bit; rimer.

Avellanar [ah-vel-lyah-nar'], *m.* A plantation of hazels or nut-trees.

Avellanarse [ah-vel-lyah-nar'-say], *vr.* To shrivel, to grow as dry as a nut.

Avellanera [ah-vel-lyah-nay'-rah], *f.* *V.* AVELLANO.

Avellanero, ra [ah-vel-lyah-nay'-ro, rah], *m.* & *f.* A dealer in nuts and filberts.

Avellanica [ah-vel-lyah-nee'-cah], *f. dim.* A small filbert.

Avellano [ah-vel-lyah'-no], *m.* (Bot.) The common hazel-nut tree. Corylus avellana. Filbert-tree.

Avemaría [ah-vay-mah-ree'-ah], *f.* Ave Mary, the angel's salutation of the holy Virgin. *Al avemaría,* At the fall of night. *En un avemaría,* In an instant. *Saber una cosa como el avemaría,* To know by heart, thoroughly. *¡ Ave María !* Exclamation denoting surprise. *¡ Ave María purísima !* On entering a house.

Avena [ah-vay'-nah], *f.* (Bot.) 1. Oats. Avena, *L.* *Avena blanca,* Cultivated white oat. Avena sativa alba. *Avena negra,* Cultivated black oat. Avena sativa nigra. *Avena desnuda,* Naked oat. Avena nuda. *Avena estéril, cugua* or *cula,* Bearded oat-grass. Avena esterilis. *Avena estrigosa,* or *afreitas* of the Gallicians, Bristle-pointed oat. Avena estrigosa. *Avena pubescente,* Downy oat-grass. Avena pubescens. *Avena pratense,* Narrow-leaved oat-grass. Avena pratensis. *Avena alpina,* Great alpine oat-grass. Avena alpina. *Avena flavescente,* Yellow oat-grass. Avena flavescens. *Avena loca* or *silvestre,* Wild oat. Avena silvestris. *Avena común,* French oat. Avena communis. *Avena oriental,* Tartarian oat. Avena orientalis. *Avena geórgica,* Potato oat. Avena georgica. 2. (Poet.) A pastoral pipe, made of the stalks of corn, and used by shepherds.

Avenáceo, cea [ah-vay-nah'-thay-o, ah], *a.* Oat-like.

Avenado, da [ah-vay-nah'-do, dah], *a.* 1. (Obs.) Belonging or relating to oats. 2. Lunatic, liable to fits of madness, with lucid intervals.—*pp.* of AVENAR.

Avenal [ah-vay-nahl'], *m.* A field sown with oats.

Avenamiento [ah-vay-nah-me-en'-to], *m.* The act of draining off water.

Avenar [ah-vay-nar'], *va.* To drain or draw off water.

Avenate [ah-vay-nah'-tay], *m.* Water-gruel, oatmeal-gruel.

Avenenar [ah-vay-nay-nar'], *va.* (Obs.) To poison. *V.* ENVENENAR.

Avenencia [ah-vay-nen'-the-ah], *f.* 1. Agreement, compact, bargain. 2. Conformity, union, concord. *Más vale mala avenencia, que buena sentencia,* A bad compromise is better than a good lawsuit.

Avenenteza, Aveninteza [ah-vay-nen-tay'-thah, ah-vay-nin-tay'-thah], *f.* (Obs.) Occasion, opportunity.

(*Yo avengo, yo avine,* from *Avenir.* *V.* VENIR.)

(*Yo me avengo, yo me avine,* from *Avenirse.* *V.* VENIR.)

Aveniceo, cea [ah-vay-nee'-thay-o, ah], *a.* Oaten, belonging to or made of oats.

Avenida [ah-vay-nee'-dah], *f.* 1. Flood, inundation, freshet. 2. (Met.) A concurrence of several things. 3. Agreement, concord. *Avenidas,* 1. Avenues or roads meeting in a certain place. 2. (Naut.) Freshes.

Avenido, da [ah-vay-nee'-do, dah], *a.* Agreed. *Bien* or *mal avenidos,* Living on good or bad terms.—*pp.* of AVENIR.

Avenidor, ra [ah-vay-ne-dor', rah], *m.* & *f.* (Littl. us.) Mediator, one that interferes between two parties to reconcile them.

Avenimiento [ah-vay-ne-me-en'-to], *m.* Convention.

Avenir [ah-vay-neer'], *va.* To reconcile

parties at variance.—*vr.* 1. To settle differences on friendly terms. 2. To join, to unite, to consent; be in harmony with. 3. To compound, to compromise.

Aventadero [ah-ven-tah-day'-ro], *m.* (Prov.) A winnowing-place.

Aventado, da [ah-ven-tah'-do, dah], *a.* *Escotas aventadas*, Flowing sheets. —*pp.* of AVENTAR.

Aventador [ah-ven-tah-dor'], *m.* 1. Fanner, blower, blowing fan, ventilator. (Arch.) Scutcher. (Gas) Bat-wing. 2. Winnower, one who separates chaff from grain. 3. A wooden fork with three or four prongs, used for winnowing corn. 4. A fan, or kind of round mat, used by poor people for blowing the fire.

Aventadura [ah-ven-tah-doo'-rah], *f.* Wind-gall, a disease in horses. *Aventadura de estopa*, (Naut.) A leak.

Aventaja [ah-ven-tah'-hah], *f.* (Obs.) 1. Advantage, profit. 2. (Law. Prov.) Part of the personal estate or chattels of a person deceased, which his or her surviving consort takes before a division of the furniture is made.

Aventajadamente [ah-ven-tah-hah-dah-men'-tay], *adv.* 1. Advantageously, conveniently, opportunely. 2. (Prov.) Exceedingly well.

Aventajado, da [ah-ven-tah-hah'-do, dah], *a.* 1. Advantageous, profitable, convenient. 2. Beautiful, excellent. 3. Having additional pay: applied to common soldiers.—*pp.* of AVENTAJAR.

Aventajar [ah-ven-tah-har'], *va.* 1. To acquire or enjoy advantages. 2. To meliorate, to improve. 3. To surpass, to excel, to cut out.—*vr.* To exceed, to excel.

Aventar [ah-ven-tar'], *va.* 1. To move the air, to fan, to air. 2. To toss something in the wind, such as corn, to winnow it. 3. To expel, to drive away. 4. (Naut.) To work out the oakum: spoken of a ship.—*vr.* 1. To be inflated or puffed up. 2. To escape, to run away. 3. (Prov.) To be tainted; applied to meat.

Aventino [ah-ven-tee'-no], *m.* Aventine, one of the seven hills of Rome.

Aventura [ah-ven-too'-rah], *f.* 1. Adventure, event, incident. 2. Casualty, contingency, chance. 3. Adventure, an enterprise in which something must be left to hazard. 4. Hazard, risk. 5. Duty formerly paid to lords of the manor.

Aventurado, da [ah-ven-too-rah'-do, dah], *a.* *Bienaventurado*, Fortunate. *Malaventurado*, Unfortunate.—*pp.* of AVENTURAR.

Aventurar [ah-ven-too-rar'], *va.* To venture, to hazard, to risk, to endanger, to jump.

Aventurero [ah-ven-too-ray'-ro], *m.* 1. Adventurer; a knight-errant. 2. A soldier who served at his own expense. 3. Adventurer in the bad sense.

Aventurero, ra [ah-ven-too-ray'-ro, rah], *a.* 1. Voluntary; undisciplined: applied to recruits and other soldiers. 2. Applied to a person who voluntarily goes to market to sell any articles. 3. *V.* ADVENEDIZO.

Averamia [ah-vay-rah'-me-ah], *f.* A kind of duck.

Averar [ah-vay-rar'], *va.* (Obs.) To aver, certify, or affirm.

Avergonzado, da [ah-ver-gon-thah'-do, dah], *a.* Ashamed, embarrassed, abashed.

Avergonzar, Avergonar [ah-ver-gon thar', ah-ver-go-nyar'], *va.* To shame, to abash, to confound, or to make ashamed, to put to the blush, to put out of countenance.—*vr.* To shame, or be ashamed, to blush for.

(*Yo avergüenzo, yo avergüence*, from *Avergonzar. V.* ACORDAR.)

(*Yo me avergüenzo, yo me avergüence*, from *Avergonzarse. V.* ACORDAR.)

Avería [ah-vay-ree'-ah], *f.* 1. Average, damage sustained by merchandise; detriment received by ships and their cargoes. *Avería gruesa*, General average. *Avería particular*, Particular average. *Avería ordinaria*, Usual average. 2. In the India trade, a certain duty laid on merchants and merchandise. 3. A collection of birds; an aviary. *Hacer una avería*, To suffer an average.

Averiado, da [ah-vay-re-ah'-do, dah], *a.* Averaged, damaged.—*pp.* of AVERIARSE.

Averiarse [ah-vay-re-ar'-say], *vr.* To make average, to sustain damage, to be damaged.

Averiguable [ah-vay-re-goo-ah'-blay], *a.* Investigable, what may be verified or ascertained.

Averiguación [ah-vay-re-goo-ah-the-on'], *f.* Investigation. *Averiguación judicial*, A judicial inquiry, an inquest.

Averiguadamente [ah-vay-re-goo-ah-dah-men'-tay], *adv.* Certainly, surely.

Averiguador, ra [ah-vay-re-goo-ah-dor', rah], *m.* & *f.* A searcher or examiner.

Averiguar [ah-vay-re-goo-ar'], *va.* To inquire, to investigate, to find out. *Averiguarse con alguno*, To bring one to reason. *Averíguelo Vargas*, It is difficult to investigate.

Averio [ah-vay-ree'-o], *m.* 1. (Prov.) Beast of burden. 2. Flock of birds. 3. Aviary.

Averno [ah-ver'-no], *m.* (Poet.) Hell. Lake of Campania, considered by the ancients as one of the gates of hell.

Averrugado, da [ah-ver-roo-gah'-do, dah], *a.* Having many pimples in the face.

Averrugarse [ah-ver-roo-gar'-say], *vr.* (Med.) To show pimples or warts (used of the skin).

Aversión [ah-ver-se-on'], *f.* 1. Aversion, opposition, dislike. 2. Malevolence, abhorrence, loathing. 3. Fear, apprehension.

Averso, sa [ah-ver'-so, sah], *a.* (Obs.) Averse, hostile; perverse.

Avertir [ah-ver-teer'], *va.* (Obs.) *V.* APARTAR.

Avestruz [ah-ves-trooth'], *m.* (Orn.) Ostrich. Struthio.

Avetado, da [ah-vay-tah'-do, dah], *a.* Veined, seamed: applied to minerals, wood, etc.

Avetarda, *f. V.* AVUTARDA.

Avezar [ah-vay-thar'], *va.* 1. To accustom, to habituate. 2. To train the hawk. *V.* ACOSTUMBRAR.

Aviación [ah-ve-ah-the-on'], *f.* Aviation, flying. *Aviación comercial*, Commercial aviation or flying.

Aviado [ah-ve-ah -do], *m.* (Amer.) One supplied with money and other articles to work a silver-mine.

Aviador [ah-ve-ah-dor'], *m.* 1. Aviator, flyer. 2. Supplier, provider.

Aviar [ah-ve-ar'], *va.* 1. To provide articles for a journey. 2. To accoutre. To furnish one what is lacking for some object, especially money. 3. To hasten the execution of a thing.—*vr.* To get ready, to prepare one's self.

Aviciar [ah-ve-the-ar'], *va.* 1. (Obs.) To render vicious. 2. To give a luxuriant bloom and verdure to plants and trees.

Avicultura [ah-ve-cool-too'-rah], *f.* Aviculture, rearing of birds.

Avidez [ah-ve-deth'], *f.* Covetousness, greediness, avidity.

Ávido, da [ah'-ve-do, dah], *a.* (Poet.) Greedy, covetous; open-mouthed.

Aviejarse [ah-ve-ay-har'-say], *vr.* To grow old. *V.* AVEJENTARSE.

Aviento [ah-ve-en'-to], *m.* A winnowing fork with two or three prongs *V.* BIELDO.

(*Yo aviento, yo aviente*, from *Aventar. V.* ACERTAR.)

(*Yo me aviento, yo me aviente*, from *Aventarse. V.* ACERTAR.)

Aviesamente [ah-ve-ay-sah-men'-tay], *adv.* Sinistrously, perversely.

Avieso, sa [ah-ve-ay'-so, sah], *a.* 1. Fortuitous, irregular. 2. (Met.) Mischievous, perverse.

Avigorar [ah-ve-go-rar'], *va.* To invigorate; to revive.

Avilanado, da [ah-ve-lah-nah'-do, dah], *a.* (Bot.) Villous, downy: said of the seeds of plants. (Zool.) Hairy, feathery: of antennæ of insects.

Avilantez, Avilanteza [ah-ve-lan-teth', ah-ve-lan-tay'-thah], *f.* Forwardness, boldness, audaciousness; shamelessness.

Avillanado, da [ah-veel-lyah-nah'-do, dah], *a.* Having the manners of a peasant, clownish, mean.—*pp.* of AVILLANAR.

Avillanar [ah-veel-lyah-nyar'], *va.* To villanize, to debase.—*vr.* To grow mean or abject, to degenerate.

Avinado, da [ah-ve-nah'-do, dah], *a.* Wine-coloured; bibulous, hard-drinking: said of persons.

Avinagrado, da [ah-ve-nah-grah'-do, dah], *a.* (Met.) Harsh of temper, crabbed, peevish.—*pp.* of AVINAGRAR.

Avinagrar [ah-ve-nah-grar'], *va.* To render sour, to make acid.

Avío [ah-vee'-o], *m.* 1. Preparation, provision. 2. (Amer.) Money and other articles advanced for working silver-mines.—*pl. Avíos de pescar*, Fishing-tackle; the trimmings and other necessary articles for any thing.

Avión [ah-ve-on'], *m.* Airplane, aeroplane, plane. *Avión de bombardeo*, Bomber. *Avión cohete*, Rocket plane. *Avión postal*, Mailplane. *Avión radioguiado*, Drone. *Avión de turbohélice*, Turboprop. *Avión de turborreacción*, Turbojet. *Por avión*, By plane, by air mail.

Avisadamente [ah-ve-sah-dah-men'-tay], *adv.* Prudently.

Avisado, da [ah-ve-sah'-do, dah], *a.* 1. Prudent, cautious. 2. Expert, sagacious, skilful, clever, clear-sighted. *Mal avisado*, Ill-advised, injudicious. —*pp.* of AVISAR.

Avisador [ah-ve-sah-dor'], *m.* Adviser; admonisher.

Avisar [ah-ve-sar'], *va.* 1. To inform, to give notice, to acquaint. 2. To advise, to counsel, to admonish. *Avisar con tiempo, avisar anticipadamente*, To warn or to give warning.

Aviso [ah-vee'-so], *m.* 1. Information, intelligence, notice, legal notice in the newspapers. 2. Prudence, care, attention; counsel. *Estar* or *andar sobre aviso*, To be on one's guard. 3. (Naut.) Advice-boat, a light vessel sent with despatches.

Avispa [ah-vees'-pah], *f.* Wasp. Vespa.

Avispado, da [ah-vis-pah'-do, dah], *a.* Lively, brisk, vigorous.—*pp.* of AVISPAR.

Avispar [ah-vis-par'], *va.* 1. To spur, to drive with the spur. 2. To investigate, to observe closely.—*vr.* To fret, to be peevish.

Avispero [ah-vis-pay'-ro], *m.* 1. Nest made by wasps. 2. Cavities in which wasps lodge their eggs. 3. (Med.) Carbuncle: so named from the numerous perforations resembling the cells of a wasp-nest.

Avispón [ah-vis-pone'], *m.* Hornet, a large wasp.

Avistar [ah-vis-tar'], *va.* To descry at a distance, to see far off.—*vr.* To have an interview to transact business.

Avitar [ah-ve-tar'], *va.* (Naut.) To bitt the cable.

Avitelado [ah-ve-tay-lah'-do], *a.* Vellum-like.

Avituallar [ah-ve-too-al-lyar'], *va.* (Mil.) To victual, to supply with provisions.

Avivadamente [ah-ve-vah-dah-men'-tay], *adv.* In a lively manner, briskly.

Avivador, ra [ah-ve-vah-dor', rah], *m.* & *f.* 1. Enlivener; hastener. 2. Rabbet-plane; panel-plane. 3. (Prov.) Paper full of pin-holes laid over the eggs of silk-worms, that the young worms may creep through it. 4. (Arch.) Groin between mouldings; quirk.

Avivar [ah-ve-var'], *va.* 1. To quicken, to enliven, to encourage, to hasten. *Avivar el paso,* To hasten one's step. 2. To heat, to inflame. 3. To vivify the eggs of silk-worms; to revive. 4. To heighten colours. 5. (Carp.) To rabbet.—*vn.* To revive, to cheer up, to grow gay. *Avivar el ojo,* To be watchful.

Avizorar [ah-ve-tho-rar'], *va.* To watch with attention, to spy, to search narrowly.

Avo [ah'-vo], *m.* 1. One of the fractional parts into which a whole number is divided. Used as a suffix; as, *dozavo,* twelfth. 2. A tree from which Indians make paper.

Avocable [ah-vo-cah'-blay], *a.* Transferable to a superior court.

Avocación, *f.* **Avocamiento,** *m.* [ah-vo-cah-the-on', ah-vo-cah-me-en'-to]. (Law) The act of removing a lawsuit to a superior court.

Avocado [ah-vo-cah'-do], *m.* The fruit of Persea gratissima, "alligator-pear." From Ahuacatl. *V.* AGUACATE.

Avocar [ah-vo-car'], *va.* (Law) To remove a lawsuit to a superior court.

Avoceta [ah-vo-thay'-tah], *f.* Avocet, a wading bird.

Avogalla [ah-vo-gahl'-lyah] *f.* Gall-nut.

Avolcanado, da [ah-vole-cah-nah'-do, dah], *a.* Volcanic.

Avora [ah-vo'-rah], *f.* A kind of medicinal palm.

Avucasta [ah-voo-cahs'-tah], *f.* Widgeon, a kind of wild duck. Anas penelope.

Avucastro [ah-voo-cahs'-tro], *m.* (Obs.) Troubler or importunate person.

Avugés. *V.* AVUGUÉS.

Avugo [ah-voo'-go], *m.* The fruit of the avuguero.

Avuguero [ah-voo-gay'-ro], *m.* (Bot.) A kind of pear-tree.

Avugués [ah-voo-gays'], *m.* (Bot.) *V.* GAYUBA.

Avulsión [ah-vool-se-on'], *f.* (Surg.) A forcible separation, tearing away.

Avutarda [ah-voo-tar'-dah], *f.* Bustard, a wild turkey. Otis tarda.

Avutardado, da [ah-voo-tar-dah'-do, dah], *a.* Bustard-like.

Axil [ac-seel'], *a.* (Bot.) Axial, relating to the axis. (Zool.) Axillary, relating to the base of the wing, or to the thoracic limb of some animals. —*m.* The axil of a plant.

Axila [ac-see'-lah], *f.* 1. (Anat.) Axilla, armpit. 2. (Bot.) Axilla, upper end and inside of the base of leaves or branches.

Axilar [ac-se-lar'], *a.* 1. Axillar, axillary, belonging to the armpit. 2. (Bot.) Axillary.

Axioma [ac-se-oh'-mah], *m.* Axiom, maxim.

Axiomático, ca [ac-se-o-mah'-te-co, cah], *a.* Axiomatic, self-evident.

Axiómetro [ac-se-o'-may-tro], *m.* (Naut.) An instrument which marks the movements of the helm.

Axis [ahc'-sis], *m.* (Anat.) The second vertebra of the neck. 2. (Zool.) Indian deer.

¡ Ay ! [i, or ah'-e], *int.* Alas! an exclamation of pain or grief. *¡ Ay de mí !* Alas, poor me! Woe is me!—*m.* *V.* QUEJIDO and GEMIDO.

Aya [ah'-yah], *f.* Governess, instructress. *V.* AYO.

Ayanque [ah-yahn'-kay], *m.* (Naut.) The main halliard.

Ayate [ah-yah'-tay], *m.* A kind of stuff manufactured of the thread of the agave, or *pita.*

Ayear [ah-yay-ar'], *vn.* (Littl. us.) To repeat the word *ay* in sign of pain or grief.

Aye aye [ah'-yay ah'-yay], *m.* (Zool.) The aye-aye, a nocturnal lemur of Madagascar. Chiromis.

Ayer [ah-yerr'], *adv.* 1. Yesterday. 2. Lately, not long ago. *De ayer acá,* From yesterday to this moment.

¡ Aymé ! [ah-e-may'], *int.* (Littl. us.) *V.* ¡ AY DE MÍ !

Ayo [ah'-yo], *m.* Tutor or governor; a teacher.

Ayocote [ah-yo-co'-tay]. (Mex.) A kidney-bean larger than the common sort.

Ayocuantoto [ah-yo-coo-an-to'-to], *m.* A mountain bird of Mexico.

Ayuda [ah-yoo'-dah], *f.* 1. Help, aid, assistance, comfort; support, succour, friendship. *Ayuda de parroquia,* Chapel of ease. 2. An injection, enema, or clyster. 3. Syringe. 4. (Naut.) Preventer-rope. *Ayuda de costa,* A gratification paid over and above the salary, a gratuity.—*m.* 1. Deputy or assistant of one of the high officers at court. *Ayuda de cámara,* A valet-de-chambre. *Ayuda de cámara del rey,* Groom of the bed-chamber. 2. Helper, a supernumerary servant. *Dios y ayuda,* This cannot be done but with the assistance of God. *Ayuda de oratorio,* Clergyman in an oratory who performs the office of sacristan. *Ayuda de cocinero,* (Naut.) The cook's shifter. *Ayuda de dispensero,* (Naut.) The steward's mate. *Ayuda de virador,* (Naut.) A false preventer.

Ayudador, ra [ah-yoo-dah-dor', rah], *m.* & *f.* Assistant, helper; a shepherd's assistant.

Ayudante [ah-yoo-dahn'-tay], *m.* 1. (Mil.) Adjutant; aide-de-camp. 2. *Ayudante de cirujano,* A surgeon's assistant.

Ayudar [ah-yoo-dar'], *va.* To aid, to help, to favour, to assist. *Ayudar a misa,* To serve the priest at mass.—*vr.* To adopt proper measures to obtain success.

Ayuga [ah-yoo'-gah], *f.* (Bot.) Ground-pine. *V.* PINILLO.

Ayunador, ra [ah-yoo-nah-dor', rah], *m.* & *f.* Faster, one who fasts.

Ayunar [ah-yoo-nar'], *vn.* To fast; to keep the canonical fast. *Ayunar al traspaso,* To fast from holy Thursday to the following Saturday. *Ayunar después de harto,* To fast after a good repast.

Ayunas (En) [ah-yoo'-nas], *adv.* 1. Fasting. 2. Without knowledge. *Quedar en ayunas,* To be ignorant of an affair.

Ayuno [ah-yoo'-no], *m.* Fast, abstinence.

Ayuno, na [ah-yoo'-no, nah], *a.* 1. Fasting, abstaining from food. *Estoy ayuno,* I have not yet broken my fast. 2. Abstaining from certain pleasures. 3. Ignorant of a subject of conversation.

Ayunque [ah-yoon'-kay], *m.* Anvil. *V.* YUNQUE.

Ayuntable [ah-yoon-tah'-blay], *a.* Capable of being joined.

Ayuntador, ra [ah-yoon-tah-dor', rah], *m.* & *f.* One who unites, joins, or assembles.

Ayuntamiento [ah-yoon-tah-me-en'-to], *m.* 1. (Obs.) Union, junction. 2. Municipal government, composed in Spain of a *Corregidor* or *Alcalde,* and *Regidores;* the first corresponding to mayors, and the latter to aldermen in England. *Casa de ayuntamiento,* Town-house, guildhall, senate-house. 3. Carnal copulation, accouplement, coupling.

Ayuntar [ah-yoon-tar'], *va.* (Obs.) *V.* JUNTAR and AÑADIR.

Ayunto [ah-yoon'-to], *m.* (Obs.) *V.* JUNTA.

Ayuso [ah-yoo'-so], *adv.* (Obs.) *V.* ABAJO.

Ayustar [ah-yoos-tar'], *va.* (Naut.) To bend two ends of a cable or rope, to splice. *Ayustar con costura,* To bend with a splice.

Ayuste [ah-yoos'-tay], *m.* (Naut.) Bending or splicing whereby two ends of a rope or cable are joined; scarf, scarfing.

Azabachado, da [ah-thah-bah-chah'-do, dah], *a.* Jetty, black as jet.

Azabache [ah-thah-bah'-chay], *m.* (Min.) Jet, a black shining mineral. Succinum nigrum. *Azabaches,* Trinkets of jet.

Azábara [ah-thah'-bah-rah], *f.* (Bot.) Common aloe. Aloe perfoliata.

Azabra [ah-thah'-brah], *f.* A small coasting vessel in the Cantabrian Seas.

Azacán [ah-thah-cahn'], *m.* (Obs. 1. Water-carrier. 2. *V.* ODRE. *Estar* or *andar hecho un azacán,* To be very busy.

Azacaya [ah-thah-cah'-yah], *f.* (Prov.) Conduit of water, a water-pipe.

Azache [ah-thah'-chay], *a.* Of an inferior quality: applied to silk.

Azada [ah-thah'-dah], *f.* (Agr.) Spade, hoe.

Azadada [ah-thah-dah'-dah], *f.* Blow with a spade.

Azadica, illa, ita [ah-thah-dee'-cah, deel'-lyah, dee'-tah], *f. dim.* A small spade.

Azadón [ah-thah-done'], *m.* Pickaxe, mattock, hoe. *Azadón de peto,* Hand-spike, or lever armed with a kind of chisel.

Azadonada [ah-thah-do-nah'-dah], *f.* Blow with a pickaxe. *A la primera azadonada disteis en el agua,* To detect straightway that one is not worthy of the consideration in which he is held. *A la primera azadonada ¿ queréis sacar agua ?* Do you expect to accomplish a difficult task without effort? *A tres azadonadas sacar agua,* (Met.) To obtain easily the object of one's wishes.

Azadonar [ah-thah-do-nar'], *va.* To dig with a spade or pickaxe.

Azadonazo [ah-thah-do-nah'-tho], *m.* Stroke with a mattock.

Azadoncillo [ah-thah-don-theel'-lyo], *m. dim.* A small pickaxe.

Azadonero [ah-thah-do-nay'-ro], *m.* 1. Digger, one that opens the ground with a spade. 2. (Mil. Obs.) Pioneer.

Azafata [ah-thah-fah'-tah], *f.* 1. Air-line hostess, stewardess. 2. Queen's maid of the wardrobe.

Azafate [ah-thah-fah'-tay], *m.* A low, flat-bottomed basket; a kind of waiter, a tray.

Azafrán [ah-thah-frahn'], *m.* (Bot.) Saffron. Crocus sativus. *Azafrán bastardo* or *azafrán romí* or *romín*, (Bot.) Bastard saffron, dyers' safflower. Carthamus tinctorius. *Azafrán del timón*, (Naut.) After-piece of the rudder. *Azafrán del tajamar*, (Naut.) Fore-piece of the cut-water. *Azafrán de Venus*, (Chem.) Crocus Veneris, the calx or oxide of metals of a saffron colour. *Azafrán de Marte*, Crocus powder; copperas calcined to a red-dish or purple colour, for polishing. (Arabic.)

Azafranado, da [ah-thah-frah-nah'-do, dah], *a.* Saffron-like, croceous.—*pp.* of AZAFRANAR.

Azafranal [ah-thah-frah-nahl'], *m.* A plantation of saffron.

Azafranar [ah-thah-frah-nar'], *va.* To tinge or dye with saffron.

Azafranero [ah-thah-frah-nay'-ro], *m.* Dealer in saffron.

Azagador [ah-thah-gah-dor'], *m.* The path for cattle.

Azagaya [ah-thah-gah'-yah], *f.* Javelin, a spear or half-pike.

Azagayada [ah thah-gah-yah'-dah], *f.* Cast of a javelin.

Azahar [ah-thah-ar'], *m.* Orange or lemon flower. *Agua de azahar*, Orange-flower water. *Azahar bravo*, Narrow-leaved blue lupine. Lupinus angustifolius (Arab. azhâr.)

Azainadamente [ah-thah-e-nah-dah-men'-tay], *adv.* Perfidiously, viciously.

Azalá [ah-thah-lah'], *m.* Prayer, among the Mohammedans.

Azalón [ah-thah-lone'], *m.* (Orn.) A small bird.

Azamboa [ah-tham-bo'-ah], *f.* (Bot.) The fruit of the zamboa-tree; a kind of sweet quince; citron. *V.* ZAMBOA. (Arab. zambo'a.)

Azamboo, or **Azamboero** [ah-tham-bo'-o, ah-tham-bo-ay'-ro], *m.* (Bot.) The zamboa-tree; citron.

Azanca [ah-thahn'-cah], *f.* (Min.) Subterranean spring.

Azándar [ah-thahn'-dar], *m.* (Prov.) *V.* SÁNDALO.

Azanoria [ah-thah-no'-re-ah], *f.* (Bot.) Carrot. *V.* ZANAHORIA.

Azanoriate [ah-thah-no-re-ah'-tay], *m.* (Prov.) 1. Preserved carrots. 2. (Prov.) Fulsome, affected compliments.

Azar [ah-thar'], *m.* 1. Unforeseen disaster, an unexpected accident, disappointment. 2. Unfortunate card or throw at dice. 3. Obstruction, impediment. 4. Hazard. *Tener azar con* or *en alguna cosa*, To be always unfortunate. (Arabic.)

Azarado, da [ah-thah-rah'-do, dah], *a.* & *pp.* of AZARAR. Confused, rattled; used especially of a player. A term much used in billiards.

Azarar [ah-thah-rar'], *va.* To confuse, to bewilder, to rattle.—*vr.* To get rattled in a game. *Azararse una bola*, Said of a ball which loses its direction or effect by striking against a pocket.

Azarbe [ah-thar'-bay], *m.* (Prov.) Trench or drain for irrigation-waters.

Azarbeta [ah-thar-bay'-tah], *dim.* Azarbe, small trench for irrigating.

Azarcón [ah-thar-cone'], *m.* 1. Minium, red lead. 2. Orange colour. 3. Earthen pot.

Azaría [ah-tha-ree'-ah], *f.* A kind of coral.

Azarja [ah-thar'-hah], *f.* Instrument for winding raw silk.

Azarnefe [ah-thar-nay'-fay], *m.* (Obs.) Orpiment. *V.* OROPIMENTE.

Azarolla [ah-thah-rol'-lyah], *f.* (Bot. Prov.) The fruit of the true service-tree. *V.* ACEROLA.

Azarollo [ah-thah-rol'-lyo], *m.* (Bot. Prov.) True service-tree. Sorbus domestica.

Azarosamente [ah-thah-ro-sah-men'-tay], *adv.* Unfortunately.

Azaroso, sa [ah-thah-ro'-so, sah], *a.* Unlucky, unfortunate, ominous.

Azarote [ah-thah-ro'-tay], *m.* (Obs.) *V.* SARCOCOLA.

Azaya [ah-thah'-yah], *f.* 1. Instrument used for reeling silk. 2. (Prov. Gal.) *V.* CANTUESO. French lavender.

Azazel [ah-thah'-thel], *m.* 1. In Mohammedanism, the angels nearest to Allah. 2. The scape-goat of the Mosaic dispensation.

Azcón, *m.* **Azcona**, *f.* [ath-cone' ath-co'-nah]. (Obs.) A dart.

Azenoria [ah-thay-no'-re-ah], *f.* (Prov.) *V.* ZANAHORIA.

Ázer [ah'-ther], *m.* 1. Name of the fire adored by the Magi. 2. A title of Zoroaster.

Ázimo, ma [ah'-the-mo, mah], *a.* Azymous, unleavened.

Azimut [ah-the-moot'], *m.* (Ast.) Azimuth.

Azimutal [ah-the-moo-tahl'], *a.* Relating to the azimuth.

Aznacho, Aznallo [ath-nah'-cho, ath-nahl'-lyo], *m.* (Bot.) 1. Scotch fir. Pinus silvestris. 2. A species of the three-toothed rest-harrow. Ononis tridentata.

Ázoe [ah'-tho-ay], *m.* (Chem.) Azote or nitrogen.

Azofaifa [ah-tho-fah'-e-fah], *f.* *V.* AZUFAIFA.

Azófar [ah-tho'-far], *m.* Brass, latten. *V.* LATÓN.

Azogadamente [ah-tho-gah-dah-men'-tay], *adv.* In a quick and restless manner.

Azogado, da [ah-tho-gah'-do, dah], *a.* (Amer.) Restless, in perpetual movement; trembling.

Azogamiento [ah-tho gah-me-en'-to], *m.* 1. The act of overlaying with quicksilver. 2. Slaking lime. 3. State of restlessness.

Azogar [ah-tho-gar'], *va.* To overlay with quicksilver, to coat a mirror. *Azogar la cal*, To slake lime.—*vr.* 1. To undergo a salivation. 2. To be in a state of agitation.

Azogue [ah-tho'-gay], *m.* 1. (Min.) Mercury, quicksilver. *Es un azogue*, He is restless as quicksilver. *Azogues*, Ships which carry quicksilver. 2. (Obs.) A market-place.

Azoguejo [ah-tho-gay'-ho], *m.* (Obs.) A market-place.

Azoguería [ah - tho - gay - ree'- ah], *f.* (Amer.) The place where quicksilver is incorporated with metals; amalgamating works.

Azoguero [ah-tho-gay'-ro], *m.* 1. Dealer in quicksilver. 2. (Amer.) A workman who incorporates quicksilver, etc., with pounded silver ore, to extract the silver.

Azoico, ca [ah-tho'-e-co, cah], *a.* 1. Nitric. 2. (Geol.) Azoic, antedating life. *Era azoica*, Azoic era.

Azolar [ah-tho-lar'], *va.* To model timber with an adze.

Azolvar [ah-thol-var'], *va.* To obstruct water-conduits.

Azolvo [ah-thol'-vo], *m.* The blocking of pumps or water-pipes.

Azomar [ah-tho-mar'], *va.* (Obs.) To incite animals to fight.

Azor [ah-thor'], *m.* (Orn.) Goshawk. Falco palumbarius.

Azorado [ah-tho-rah'-do], *a.* *Navío azorado*, A ship which sails heavily on account of her cargo being ill-stowed.—*pp.* of AZORAR.

Azoramiento [ah-tho-rah-me-en'-to], *m.* Trepidation, confusion.

Azorar [ah-tho-rar'], *va.* 1. To terrify; to confound. 2. To incite, to irritate.—*vr.* To be restless.

Azorrado, da [ah-thor-rah'-do, dah], *a.* Drowsy, sleepy.—*pp.* of AZORRARSE. (Naut.) Water-logged.

Azorramiento [ah-thor-rah-me-en'-to], *m.* Heaviness of the head.

Azorrarse [ah-thor-rar'-say], *vr.* To be drowsy from heaviness.

Azotacalles [ah-tho-tah-cahl'-lyes], *m.* Street-lounger, idler.

Azotado [ah-tho-tah'-do], *m.* 1. A criminal publicly whipped. 2. He who lashes himself by way of mortification.—*pp.* of AZOTAR.

Azotador, ra [ah-tho-tah-dor', rah], *m.* & *f.* Whipper, one who inflicts lashes with a whip.

Azotaina, Azotina [ah-tho-tah'-e-nah, ah-tho-tee'-nah], *f.* (Coll.) A drubbing, a sound flogging.

Azotalengua [ah-tho-ta-len'-goo-ah], *f.* (Bot.) Goose-grass, cleavers.

Azotamiento [ah-tho-tah-me-en'-to], *m.* (Littl. us.) A whipping.

Azotaperros [ah-tho-ta-per'-ros] *m.* Verger, usher. *V.* PERTIGUERO.

Azotar [ah-tho-tar'], *va.* 1. To whip, to lash, to horsewhip, to flagellate. *Azotar las calles*, To lounge about the streets. 2. (Met.) *Azotar el aire*, To act to no purpose. 3. (Naut.) *Azotar con paleta*, To inflict the punishment called *cobbing* on board English ships. 4. (Naut.) *Azotar la ampolleta*, To flog the glass, when the steersman turns it before the sand has entirely run out.

Azotazo [ah-tho-tah'-tho], *m. aug.* A severe lash or blow on the breech.

Azote [ah-tho'-tay], *m.* 1. Whip. 2. Lash given with a whip. 3. (Met.) Calamity, affliction. 4. The person who is the cause of a calamity. *Pena de azotes*, A public whipping. *Mano de azotes*, or *vuelta de azotes*, The number of lashes a criminal is to receive.

Azotea [ah-tho-tay'-ah], *f.* The flat roof of a house, a platform.

Azótico [ah-tho'-te-co], *a.* *Gas azótico*, (Chem.) Azotic gas.

Azre [ath'-ray], *m.* (Bot.) Maple-tree. Acer. By metathesis fr. *acer*.

Azteca [ath-tay'-cah], *a.* & *m.* Aztec; belonging to the race, dynasty, or language of ancient Mexico.

Azúa [ah-thoo'-ah], *f.* Beverage prepared by the Indians from Indian corn.

Azúcar [ah-thoo'-car], *m.* Sugar. *Azúcar de pilón*, Loaf-sugar. *Azúcar de lustre*, Double loaves, fine powdered sugar. *Azúcar mascabado*, Unclarified sugar. *Azúcar quebrado*, Brown sugar. *Azúcar prieto* or *negro*, Coarse brown sugar. *Azúcar piedra* or *cande*, Sugar-candy. *Azúcar terciado* or *moreno*, Brown sugar. *Azúcar pardo*, Clayed sugar. *Azúcar de plomo*, Calcined sugar of lead. *Azúcar y canela*, Sorrel-gray: a colour peculiar to horses. (Arab. (as-) sukkar.)

Azucarado, da [ah-thoo-ca-rah'-do, dah], *a.* 1. Sugared. 2. Sugary, having the taste of sugar. 3. Sugar coated. 4. (Met.) Affable, pleasing. *Palabras azucaradas*, Soothing, artful words. —*pp.* of AZUCARAR.

Azucarado [ah-thoo-ca-rah'-do], *m.* A kind of paint for ladies.

Azucarar [ah-thoo-ca-rar'], *va* 1. To sugar, to sweeten; to soften 2. To ice with sugar, to coat with sugar.

Azucarero [ah-thoo-ca-ray'-ro], *m.* 1. Sugar-dish, sugar-bowl. 2. (Prov.) Confectioner.

Azucarillo [ah-thoo-ca-reel'-lyo], *m.* Sweetmeat of flour, sugar, and rose-water.
Azucena [ah-thoo-thay'-nah], *f.* (Bot.) White lily. Lilium candidum. *Azucena amarilla*, Yellow amaryllis. Amarillis lutea. *Azucena anteada*, Copper-coloured day-lily. Hemerocallis fulva. *Azucena pajiza*, Yellow day-lily. Hemerocallis flava. *Azucenas*, The military order of the lily, founded by King Ferdinand of Aragón.
Azud [ah-thood'], *f.* A dam with a sluice or flood-gate.
Azuda [ah-thoo'-dah], *f.* Persian wheel. to raise water for irrigation. *Cf.* NORIA.
Azuela [ah-thoo-ay'-lah], *f.* Adze, a carpenter's tool; howell, a cooper's tool. *Azuela de construcción.* A shipwright's adze. *Azuela curva*, A hollow adze.
Azufaifa [ah-thoo-fah'-e-fah], *f.* Jujube or jujubes, the fruit of the jujube-tree. Rhamnus zizyphus.
Azufaifo, Azufeifo [ah-thoo-fah'-e-fo, ah-thoo-fay'-e-fo], *m.* Jujube-tree.
Azufrado, da [ah-thoo-frah'-do; dah], *a.* 1. Whitened or fumigated with sulphur. 2. Sulphureous. 3. Greenish yellow.—*pp.* of AZUFRAR.
Azufrador [ah-thoo-frah-dor'], *m.* 1. Machine for drying linen. 2. Instrument for sulphuring vines.
Azufrar [ah-thoo-frar'], *va.* To bleach, to fumigate with sulphur.
Azufre [ah-thoo'-fray], *m.* Sulphur, brimstone. *Azufre vivo*, Native sulphur.
Azufrón [ah-thoo frone'], *m.* Pyrites in powder.
Azufroso, sa [ah-thoo-fro'-so, sah], *a.* Sulphureous.
Azul [ah-thool'], *a.* Blue. *Azul celeste*, Sky-blue. *Azul oscuro*, Dark blue. *Azul de Prusia*, Prussian blue. *Azul subido*, Bright blue. *Azul turquí* or *turquizado*, Turkish or deep blue; indigo, sixth colour of the spectrum. *Azul de esmalte*, Smalt. *Azul verdemar* or *de costras*, Sea-blue. *Darse un verde con dos azules*, To be highly entertained. (fr. Per.)
Azul [ah-thool'], *m.* Lapis lazuli; a mineral.
Azulado, da [ah-thoo-lah'-do, dah], *pp.* of AZULAR. *Azulado claro*, Azure, azured; bluish.
Azulaque [ah-thoo-lah'-kay], *m.* *V.* ZULAQUE.
Azular [ah-thoo-lar'], *va.* To dye or colour blue.
Azulear [ah-thoo-lay-ar'], *vn.* To have a bluish cast.
Azulejado, da [ah-thoo-lay-hah'-do, dah], *a.* (Prov.) Covered with bluish tiles.
Azulejillo [ah-thoo-lay-heel'-lyo], *m.* Little bluebird.
Azulejo [ah-thoo-lay'-ho], *m.* 1. Glazed tile painted with various colours, or plain white. 2. (Bot.) Blue-bottle, corn-flower. Centaurea cyanus. —*a.* Applied in Spain to several kinds of wheat. 3. (Orn.) The blue jay.
Azulenco, ca [ah-thoo-len'-co, cah], *a.* *V.* AZULADO.
Azulete [ah-thoo-lay'-tay], *m.* Blue colour given to stockings and other garments.
Azulino, na [ah-thoo-lee'-no, nah], *a.* Bluish.
Azumar [ah-thoo-mar'], *va.* To dye the hair.
Azúmbar [ah-thoom'-bar], *m.* (Obs.) *V.* ALISMA.
Azumbrado da [ah-thoom-brah'-do, dah], *a.* Measured by *azumbres.*
Azumbre [ah-thoom'-bray], *f.* A measure of liquids, containing about half an English gallon, 2 litres.
Azur [ah-thoor'], *a.* (Her.) Azure.
Azurita [ah-thoo-ree'-tah], *f.* 1. Blue variety of copper carbonate, azurite. 2. Double phosphate aluminium and magnesium.
Azutero [ah-thoo-tay'-ro], *m.* Sluice-master, he who has the care of dams, sluices, etc.
Azuzador, ra [ah-thoo-thah-dor', rah], *m.* & *f.* Instigator.
Azuzar [ah-thoo-thar'], *va.* 1. To halloo, to set on dogs. 2. To irritate, to provoke.
Azuzón [ah-thoo-thone'], *m.* Instigator, provoker of quarrels. (Vulg. Prov.)

B

B [bay]. The second letter of the Spanish alphabet: it is pronounced in the Spanish as in the English language. But in Spanish the lips only meet and are not pressed together. In this way *b* and *v* are sometimes confounded, chiefly by the illiterate; or as a reminder of an ancient spelling, the latter especially in the Castiles. The learner should make note of this peculiarity, and, not finding a word spelled with one of these consonants, look for it under the other. Thus gabilán, Mexican, is in Spain gavilán. *B por b*, or *C por b*, To know in the smallest details. *B.* at the end of a letter stands for *besa* or *beso.* *B.* stands for Blessed; *B. A.* for Bachelor of Arts; and *B. C.* for *Basso Continuo*, or thorough-bass.
Baba [bah'-bah], *f.* Drivel, slaver, spittle.
Bababuí [bah-bah-boo-ee'], *m.* The mocking-bird. *V.* ARRENDAJO.
Babadero, Babador [bah-bah-day'-ro, bah-bah-dor'], *m.* Bib, chin-cloth.
Babaza [bah-bah'-thah], *f.* 1. Frothy humour from the mouth. 2. Aloe. 3. A viscous worm of the snail kind. Limax. Slug.
Babazorro [bah-bah-thor'-ro], *m.* (Prov.) Clown, an ill-bred man.
Babear [bah-bay-ar'], *vn.* 1. To drivel, to slaver. 2. (Met. and coll.) To be smitten with; to court, woo.
Babeo [bah-bay'-o], *m.* The act of drivelling or slavering.
Babera [bah-bay'-rah], *f.* 1. Fore part of the helmet which covers the cheeks, mouth, and chin. 2. A silly fellow. 3. A bib.
Baberó [bah-bay'-ro], *m.* *V.* BABADOR.
Baberol [bah-bay-role'], *m.* *V.* BABERA, as part of the helmet.
Babia [bah'-bee-ah], *f.* *Estar en babia*, To be absent in mind, heedless, or inattentive.
Babieca [bah-be-ay'-cah], *m.* *Es un babieca*, He is an ignorant, stupid fellow; an idiot.
Babilla [bah-beel'-lyah], *f.* Thin skin about the flank of a horse.
Babilonia [bah-be-lo'-ne-ah], *f.* *Es una babilonia*, There is such a crowd, it is all uproar and confusion.
Babilonico, ca, or onio, nia [bah-be-lo' ne-co, cah, ne-o, ne-ah], *a.* Babylonian.
Babismo [bah-bees'-mo], *m.* Babism, Persian religious doctrine.
Bable [bah'-blay], *m.* The Asturian dialect.
Babor [bah-bor'], *m.* (Naut.) Port, the left-hand side of a ship, looking forward. *A babor del timón*, A-port the helm. *A babor todo*, Head a-port. *De babor a estribor*, Athwart ship.
Babosa [bah-bo'-sah], *f.* 1. A slug. Limax. 2. Aloe. 3. An old onion transplanted. 4. A young onion.
Babosear [bah-bo-say-ar'], *va.* To drivel, to slaver.
Babosilla [bah-bo-seel'-lyah], *f. dim.* Slug.
Babosillo, illa; uelo, uela [bah-bo-seel'-lyo, lyah, oo-ay'-lo, lah], *a. dim.* Somewhat drivelling or slavering.
Baboso, sa [bah-bo'-so, sah], *m.* & *f.* Idiot, simpleton.—*a.* Idiotic.
Babucha [bah-boo'-chah], *f.* A kind of slipper.
Baca [bah'-cah], *f.* (Obs.) 1. Berry. *Baca de laurel*, Bay-berry. 2. Breach in a dike or dam. 3. (Jew.) A kind of pearl. 4. Leather cover of a cart or stage-coach.—*m.* & *f. pl.* Quick tune on the guitar.
Bacalao [bah-cah-lah'-o], *m.* Codfish. *Aceite de hígado de bacalao*, Cod-liver oil. *Bacalao a la vizcaína*, Codfish stew made with olive oil, tomatoes, olives. capers, etc.
Bacanales [bah-cah-nah'-les], *f. pl.* Bacchanals, feasts of Bacchus.
Bacante [bah-cahn'-tay], *f.* 1. Bacchante, bacchant, priestess of Bacchus. 2. Bacchante, a lewd drinking person.
Bácara, Bácaris [bah'-ca-rah, bah'-ca-ris], *f.* (Bot.) Great flea-bane. Baccharis.
Bacelar [bah-thay-lar'], *m.* Land newly planted with vines.
Bacera [ba-thay'-rah], *f.* (Coll.) Obstruction in the milt, a swelling of the belly, in cattle.
Baceta [ba-thay'-tah], *f.* The stock or four remaining cards in the game called *revesino.*
Bacía [ba-thee'-ah], *f.* 1. A metal basin; wash-pot. 2. Barber's basin; shaving-dish.
Báciga [bah'-the-gah], *f.* A game played with three cards.
Bacilo [bah-thee'-lo], *m.* Bacillus, a rod-shaped bacterium.
Bacín [bah-theen'], *m.* 1. A large and very high vase, or basin, which serves as a close-stool. 2. A despicable man.
Bacina [bah-thee'-nah], *f.* 1. (Coll.) Poor-box. 2. *V.* BACÍA. 3. A small basin which serves as a close-stool.
Bacinada [bah-the-nah'-dah], *f.* Filth thrown from a close-stool.
Bacinejo [bah-the-nay'-ho], *m. dim.* A small close-stool.
Bacinero, ra [bah-the-nay'-ro, rah], *m.* & *f.* (Coll.) The person who carries about the poor-box in a church.
Bacineta [bah-the-nay'-tah], *f.* 1. (Dim.) A small poor-box. 2. *Bacineta de arma de fuego*, The pan of a gun-lock.
Bacinete [bah-the-nay'-tay], *m.* 1. A head-piece formerly worn by soldiers, in the form of a helmet. 2. Cuirassier. a horseman.
Bacinica [bah-the-nee'-cah], *f.* 1. A small earthen close-stool for children. 2. Chamber-pot.
Bacinilla [bah-the-neel'-lyah], *f.* 1. A chamber-pot. 2. (Littl. us.) Alms-basin.
Bacitracina [bah-the-trah-thee'-nah], *f.* (Med.) Bacitracin.
Baco [bah'-co], *m.* Bacchus. Wine.
Bacteria [bac-tay'-re-ah], *f.* Bacteria.
Bactericida [bac-tay-re-thee'-dah], *m.* Bactericide, bacteria killer.
Bacteriología [bac-tay-re-o-lo-hee'-ah], *f.* Bacteriology.
Bacteriólogo, ga [bac-tay-re-o'-lo-go, gah], *m.* & *f.* Bacteriologist.
Báculo [bah'-coo-lo], *m.* 1. Walking-stick, a staff. *Báculo de Jacob*, Jacob's staff, a mathematical instrument which serves to take heights

and distances. *Báculo de peregrino*, Pilgrim's staff. *Báculo pastoral*, Bishop's crosier. 2. (Met.) Support, relief, consolation.

Bache [bah'-chay], *m.* 1. A deep hole in a road. 2. A place where sheep are put up to sweat, previously to their being shorn. *V.* SUDADERO. 3. Stick of a hatter for beating felt.

Bachiller [bah-cheel-lyerr'], *m.* 1. Bachelor, one who has obtained the first degree in the sciences and liberal arts. 2. Babbler, prater.

Bachiller [bah-cheel-lyerr'], *a.* Garrulous, loquacious.

Bachillera [bah-cheel-lyay'-rah], *a.* Forward, loquacious woman.

Bachillerato [bah-cheel-lyay-rah'-to], *m.* Bachelorship, the degree and function of a bachelor.

Bachillerear [bah-cheel-lyay-ray-ar'], *vn.* To babble, to prattle.

Bachillerejo [bah-cheel-lyay-ray'-ho], *m. dim.* A talkative little fellow.

Bachillería [bah-cheel-lyay-ree'-ah], *f.* Babbling, prattling.

Bada [bah'-dah], *f.* *V.* ABADA.

Badajada [bah-dah-hah'-dah], *f.* 1. A stroke of the clapper against the bell. 2. Idle talk.

Badajazo [bah-dah-hah'-tho], *m. aug.* A large clapper.

Badajear [bah-dah-hay-ar'], *vn.* (Obs.) To talk nonsense.

Badajo [bah-dah'-ho], *m.* 1. Clapper of a bell. 2. An idle talker.

Badajuelo [bah-dah-hoo-ay'-lo], *m. dim.* A small clapper.

Badal [bah-dahl'], *m.* 1. Muzzle. *Echar un badal a la boca*, To stop one's mouth. 2. (Prov.) Shoulder and ribs of butcher's meat. 3. (Surg.) Instrument for opening the mouth.

Badana [bah-dah'-nah], *f.* A dressed sheep-skin. *Zurrar la badana*, 1. To dress a sheep-skin. 2. (Met.) To give one a flogging.

Badazas [bah-dah'-thas], *f. pl.* (Naut.) Keys of the bonnets, ropes with which the bonnets are laced to the sails. *V.* BARJULETA.

Badea [bah-day'-ah], *f.* 1. Pompion or pumpkin. Cucurbita pepo. 2. (Met.) A dull, insipid being.

Badén [bah-den'], *m.* 1. Channel made by a sudden fall of water. 2. Catch-water, conduit.

Badiana [bah-de-ah'-nah], *f.* (Bot.) Indian aniseed, badiana. Illicium anisatum.

Badil, *m.* **Badila**, *f.* [bah-deel', bah-dee'-lah]. Fire-shovel.

Badilazo [bah-de-lah'-tho], *m.* Blow with a fire-shovel.

Badina [bah-dee'-nah], *f.* (Obs.) Pool of water in the roads.

Badomía [bah-do-mee'-ah], *f.* Nonsense, absurdity.

Badulacada [bah-doo-lah-cah'-dah], *f.* (Peru.) *V.* CALAVERADA.

Badulaque [bah-doo-lah'-kay], *m.* 1. Ragout of stewed-livers and lights. 2. A stupid person. 3. A person not to be relied on.

Bafetas [bah-fay'-tas], *f. pl.* Fabric of white cotton from India.

Baga [bah'-gah], *f.* 1. (Prov.) A rope or cord with which the loads of beasts of burden are fastened. 2. A little head of flax with its seeds.

Bagaje [bah-gah'-hay], *m.* 1. Beast of burden. 2. Baggage, the furniture of an army and the beasts of burden on which it is carried.

Bagajero [bah-gah-hay'-ro], *m.* Driver, he who conducts the beasts which carry military baggage.

Bagar [bah-gar'], *vn.* To yield the seed: applied to flax.

Bagasa [bah-gah'-sah], *f.* A prostitute.

Bagatela [bah-gah-tay'-lah], *f.* Bagatelle, trifle.

Bagazo [bah-gah'-tho], *m.* (Prov.) The remains of sugar-cane, grapes, olives, palms, etc., which have been pressed.

Bagre [bah'-gray], *m.* A delicious fish. Silurus bagre.

Baguio [bah-gee'-o], *m.* A hurricane in the Philippine Islands.

¡**Bah**! *int.* Bah!

Bahari [bah-ah-ree'], *m.* (Orn.) Sparrow-hawk. Falco nisus.

Bahía [bah-ee'-ah], *f.* 1. Bay, an arm of the sea. 2. A city of Brazil.

Bahorrina [bah-or-ree'-nah], *f.* 1. Collection of filthy things. 2. Rabble.

Bahuno, na [bah-oo'-no, nah], *a.* Base, vile. *V.* BAJUNÓ.

Baila [bah'-e-lah], *f.* 1. (Obs.) *V.* BAILE. 2. (Zool.) Sea-trout. *Ser dueño de la baila*, (Prov.) To be the principal of any business.

Bailable [bah-e-lah'-blay], *a.* Danceable.—*m.* A pantomime with dancing. Ballet (recent).

Bailador, ra [bah-e-lah-dor', rah], *m.* & *f.* 1. Dancer. 2. (Low) Thief.

Bailar [bah-e-lar'], *vn.* 1. To dance. 2. To move by a short, brisk gallop: applied to horses. *Bailar el agua adelante*, To dance attendance. *Bailar sin son*, To dance without music; to be too eager for performing any thing to require a stimulus.

Bailarín, na [bah-e-lah-reen', nah], *m.* & *f.* 1. Dancer, caperer. 2. A fiery, high-mettled horse.

Baile [bah'-e-lay], *m.* 1. Dance. 2. Ball, rout. 3. (Prov.) Bailiff, a judge or justice. *Baile de candil* or *de botón gordo*, A rustic dance among the common people. *Baile de disfraces, ó trajes*, Fancy ball. *Baile de San Vito*, St. Vitus's dance, chorea.

Bailete [bah-e-lay'-tay], *m.* A short dance introduced into some dramatic works.

Bailía, *f.* **Bailiazgo**, *m.* [bah-e-lee'-ah, bah-e-le-ahth'-go]. 1. District of the jurisdiction of a *baile* or bailiff. 2. District of a commandery in the order of the Knights of Malta.

Bailiaje [bah-e-le-ah'-hay], *m.* A commandery or dignity in the order of Malta.

Bailío [bah-e-lee'-o], *m.* The knight commander of the order of Malta.

Bailotear [bah-e-lo-tay-ar'], *vn.* To skip and jump in dancing; to dance without grace.

Bailoteo [bah-e-lo-tay'-o], *m.* A mean ball.

Baivel [bah-e-vel'], *m.* In masonry and joinery, bevel, a kind of square, one leg of which is frequently crooked.

Bajá [bah-hah'], *m.* Pasha, bashaw, a Turkish title.

Baja [bah'-hah], *f.* 1. Fall or diminution of price. 2. (Obs.) A dance. 3. (Mil.) Ticket of admission in a hospital. 4. (Mil.) List of casualties in a muster-roll. Places vacant in a company, or regiment. 5. Blackball, adverse vote. *Dar de baja*, To make a return of the casualties which have happened in a military corps.

Bajada [bah-hah'-dah], *f.* 1. Descent, the road or path by which a person descends. 2. Inclination of an arch.

Bajado, da [bah-hah'-do, dah], *a.* Descended, fallen down, lowered. *Bajado del cielo*, Dropped from heaven, uncommonly excellent; unexpected. —*pp.* of BAJAR.

Bajalato [bah-hah-lah'-to], *m.* The dignity and office of a pasha, and the territory belonging thereto.

Bajamar [bah-hah-mar'], *f.* Low water, low tide.

Bajamente [bah-hah-men'-tay], *adv.* Basely, meanly, abjectly, lowly.

Bajar [bah-har'], *vn.* 1. To descend, to come down, to fall. 2. To lower, to lessen, to diminish.—*va.* 1. To lower, to hang down, to let down. 2. To reduce the price in selling. 3. To lessen the value of a thing; to narrow. 4. To humble, to bring down.—*vr.* To crouch, to grovel, to lessen. *Bajar de punto*, To decay, to decline. *Bajar el punto*, To temper. *Bajar la cerviz*, To humble one's self. *Le bajaré los bríos*, I will pull down his courage. *Bajar los humos*, To become more humane. *Bajar los ojos*, To be ashamed. *Bajar la cabeza*, To obey without objection. *Bajar la tierra*, (Naut.) To lay the land. *Bajar por un río*, (Naut.) To drop down a river. *Bajar las velas*, (Naut.) To lower the sails.

Bajel [bah-hel'], *m.* Vessel: a general name for water-craft. *Bajel desaparejado*, A ship laid up in ordinary. *Bajel boyante*, A light ship. *Bajel de bajo bordo*, A low-built ship. *Bajel marinero*, A good sea-boat. *Bajel velero*, a swift sailer.

Bajelero [bah-hay-lay'-ro], *m.* Owner or master of a vessel.

Bajero, ra [bah-hay'-ro, rah], *a.* (Prov.) That which is under, as, *Sábana bajera*, The under sheet.

Bajete [bah-hay'-tay], *m. dim.* 1. A person of low stature. 2. (Mus.) Voice between a tenor and a bass, barytone.

Bajeza [bah-hay'-thah], *f.* 1. Meanness, fawning, paltriness. 2. A mean act. 3. Abjectness, littleness. 4. Lowliness, lowness, mechanicalness. 5. (Obs.) A low, deep place. *Bajeza de ánimo*, Weakness of mind, lowness of spirits. *Bajeza de nacimiento*, Meanness of birth.

Bajillo [bah-heel'-lyo], *m.* (Prov.) Wine-pipe in a vintner's shop.

Bajío [bah-hee'-o], *m.* 1. A shoal, sandbank, shallow, or flat. 2. Decline of fortune or favour.

Bajista [bah-hees'-tah], *m.* 1. (Com.) Bear, a broker who speculates upon the fall of prices or stocks. 2. A double-bass viol, and one who plays it.

Bajo, ja [bah'-ho, hah], *a.* 1. Low. 2. Abject, despicable, faint. 3. Common, ordinary; mechanical, humble. 4. Dull, faint: applied to colours. 5. Mean, coarse, vulgar: applied to language. 6. Bent downward. *Bajo de ley*, Of a base quality: applied to metals. *Con los ojos bajos*, With down-cast eyes.

Bajo [bah'-ho], *adv.* 1. Under, underneath, below. *V.* ABAJO and DEBAJO. 2. Low, with depression of the voice. 3. Low, in a state of subjection. 4. In an humble, submissive manner. *Por lo bajo*, Cautiously, in a prudent manner. *Bajo mano*, Underhand secretly.

Bajo [bah'-ho], *m.* 1. Bass, the lowest part in music. 2. Player on the bass viol or bassoon. 3. Low situation or place. *Bajo relieve*, (Sculp.) Bass-relief. *Cuarto bajo*, Ground-floor.—*pl.* 1. Under-petticoats of women. 2. Hoofs or feet of horses.

Bajoca [bah-ho'-cah], *f.* (Prov.) 1. Green kidney-beans. 2. A dead silk worm.

Bajón [bah-hone'], *m.* 1. Bassoon. 2. A player on the bassoon.

Bajoncillo [bah-hon-theel'-lyo], *m.* Counter-bass.

Bajonista [bah-ho-nees'-tah], *m.* Bassoon player.

Bajorrelieve [bah-hor-ray-le-ay'-vay], *m.* Bas-relief.
Bajovientre [bah-ho-ve-en'-tray], *m* Hypogastrium.
Bajuno, na [bah-hoo'-no, nah], *a.* Vile, low, contemptible: applied to persons.
Bakelita [bah-kay-lee'-tah], *f.* V. BAQUELITA.
Bala [bah'lah], *f.* 1. Bullet, shot. *Bala de metralla,* Grapeshot. *Bala expansiva,* Dumdum bullet. *Como una bala,* Quick as a flash. 2. Bale (of goods or of paper). 3. Small ball of wax to play tricks at carnival time.
Balacear [bah-lah-thay-ar'], *va.* (Mex.) To shoot haphazardly, to shoot at random.
Balacera [bah-lah-thay'-rah], *f.* (Mex.) Haphazard shooting, shooting at random.
Balada [bah-lah'-dah], *f.* Ballad, a song.
Baladí [bah-lah-dee'], *a.* Mean, despicable, worthless.
Balador, ra [bah-lah-dor', rah], *m.* & *f.* Bleating animal.
Baladrar [bah-lah-drar'], *vn.* To cry out, to shout.
Baladre [bah-lah'-dray], *m.* (Bot.) Rose bay. Nerium oleander.
Baladrón [bah-lah-drone'], *m.* Boaster bragger, bully.
Baladronada [ba-lah-dro-nah'-dah], *f.* 1. Boast, brag, fanfaronade, bravado. 2. Rhodomontade.
Baladronear [bah-lah-dro-nay-ar'], *vn.* To boast, to brag, to hector.
Balagar [bah-lah-gar'], *m.* (Prov.) Long straw or hay preserved for winter fodder.
Bálago [bah'-lah-go], *m.* 1. *V.* BALAGAR. 2. Hayrick. 3. Thick spume of soap, of which wash-balls are made. *Sacudir* or *menear a uno el bálago,* To give a sound drubbing.
Balaguero [bah-lah-gay'-ro], *m.* Rick of straw.
Balahú [bah-lah-oo'], *m.* A schooner.
Balaj [bah-lah'], *m.* Balass or spinel ruby.
Balance [bah-lahn'-thay], *m.* 1. Fluctuation, vibration. 2. Libration, swinging, see-saw. 3. Equilibrium or equipoise of a rider on horseback. 4. Balance of accounts, balance-sheet. 5. (Obs.) Doubt. 6. Rolling of a ship. *Balance de comercio,* Balance of trade.
Balancear [bah-lan-thay-ar'], *va.* & *vn.* 1. To balance, to vibrate; to librate, to poise, to hold in equipoise. 2. (Met.) To waver, to be unsettled. 3. To weigh, to examine. 4. To settle accounts.
Balanceo [bah-lan-thay'-o], *m.* Oscillation, rocking motion.
Balancero, *m.* *V.* BALANZARIO.
Balancín [bah-lan-theen'], *m.* 1. Splinter-bar of a carriage, swing-bar of a cart Singletree, whiffletree. (Mech.) Walking-beam, balance-beam. 2. Iron beam for striking coins and medals; minting mill. 3. Poy, a rope-dancer's pole. 4. (Amer.) A sort of gig drawn by three horses abreast. *Balancines,* (Naut.) Lifts, ropes serving to raise or lower the yards. *Balancines de la brújula,* (Naut.) Brass rings by which the compass is suspended in the binnacle.
Balandra [bah-lahn'-drah], *f.* (Naut.) 1. Bilander, a small vessel carrying but one mast. 2. Sloop.
Balandrán [bah-lan-drahn'], *m.* A loose surtout worn by priests, cassock.
Bálano [bah-lah'-no], *m.* 1. Balanus, the glans penis. 2. Barnacle (Balanus balanoides).
Balante [bah-lahn'-tay], *pa.* (Poet.) Bleating.
Balanza [bah-lahn'-thah], *f.* 1. Scale. 2. Balance, a pair of scales. 3. A kind of fishing-net. 4. (Met.) Comparative estimate, judgment. *Fiel de balanza de la romana,* Needle of the balance. *Fiel de balanza,* (in the mints) The weigh-master. *Andar en balanza,* (Met.) To be in danger of losing one's property or place. 5. Gallows, in cant.
Balanzar [bah-lan-thar'], *va.* (Obs.) *V.* BALANCEAR.
Balanzario [bah-lan-thah'-re-o], *m.* Balancer, he who weighs and adjusts the coins in the mint.
Balanzón [bah-lan-thone'], *m.* Copper pan used by silversmiths.
Balaou [bah-lah'-o-oo], *m.* (Zool.) A kind of sprat.
Balar [bah-lar'], *vn.* To bleat. *Andar balando por alguna cosa,* To be gaping after something.
Balasor [bah-lah-sor'], *m.* Balassor, a Chinese stuff made of the bark of trees.
Balastar [bah-las-tar'], *va.* To ballast a railroad track.
Balaste [bah-lahs'-tay], *m.* Ballast, a layer of gravel between the ties.
Balasto [bah-lahs'to], *m.* Ballast.
Balate [bah-lah'-tay], *m.* 1. A boundary mark (heap of stones, etc.). 2. Border of a trench.
Balaustrada, Balaustrería [bah-lah-oos-trah'-dah, oos-tray-ree'-ah], *f.* Balustrade.
Balaustrado, da [bah-lah-oos-trah'-do, dah], **Balaustral,** *a.* Balustered.
Balaustre [bah-lah-oos'-tray], *m.* Baluster. *Balaustres de navío,* (Naut.) Balusters or head-rails of a ship.
Balazo [bah-lah'-tho], *m.* A shot; wound from a ball.
Balboa [bal-bo'-ah], *m.* Balboa, monetary unit of Panama.
Balbucear [bal-boo-thay-ar'], *vn.* To speak and pronounce indistinctly like little children; to stutter, to stammer.
Balbucencia [bal-boo-then'-the-ah], *f.* Stuttering speech.
Balbuceo [bal-boo-thay'o], *m.* Stammering, stuttering.
Balbuciente [bal-boo-the-en'-tay], *a.* Stammering, stuttering.
Balbucir [bal-boo-theer'], *vn.* To lisp.
Balcón [bal-cone'], *m.* Balcony; mirador.
Balconaje [bal-co-nah'-hay], *m.* **Balconería,** *f.* Range of balconies.
Balconazo [bal-co-nah'-tho], *m. aug.* A large balcony.
Balconcillo [bal-con-theel'-lyo], *m. dim.* A small balcony.
Balda [bahl'-dah], *f.* (Obs.) Trifle, a thing of little value. *A la balda,* Living in a heedless, imprudent manner.
Baldar [bal-dar'], *va.* 1. To cripple. 2. (Prov.) To break a set of books, or other things. 3. To trump or win a trick in a game at cards. 4. (Obs.) To obstruct, or hinder.
Balde [bahl'-day], *m.* Bucket, used on board of ships.
Balde (De), *adv.* Gratis, free of cost. *En balde,* In vain, to no purpose.
Baldear [bal-day-ar'], *vn.* (Naut.) To throw water on the deck and sides of a ship for the purpose of cleaning them.
Baldeo [bal-day'-o], *m.* (Naut.) Washing the decks with bucketfuls of water.
Baldés [bal-dess'], *m.* A piece of soft dressed skin for gloves, etc.
Baldío, día [bal-dee'-o, ah], *a.* 1. Untilled, uncultivated: applied to land. 2. Unappropriated. *Los baldíos,* The lay-land, the commons; waste or waste land. 3. (Obs.) Idle, lazy *Hombre baldío,* Vagrant, vagabond.
Baldón [bal-done'], *m.* Affront, reproach, insult, contumely.
Baldonar, Baldonear [bal-do-nar', bal-do-nay-ar'], *va.* To insult with abusive language, to reproach, to stigmatize.
Baldosa [bal-do'-sah], *f.* 1. A fine square tile. 2. Flat paving-stones.
Balduque [bal-doo'-kay], *m.* Narrow red tape, for tying papers.
Baleárico, ca [bah-le-ah'-re-co, cah], **Baleario, ia** [bah-le-ah'-re-o, ah], *a.* Balearic.
Balero [bah-lay'-ro], *m.* A ball-mould.
Baleta [bah-lay'-tah], *f. dim.* A small bale of goods.
Balí [ba-lee'], *m.* 1. A learned language of the Indo-Chinese. 2. One of the five Indian commandments, that of offering food to every animated being.
Balido [bah-lee'-do], *m.* Bleating, bleat.
Balija [bah-lee'-hah], *f.* 1. Portmanteau. 2. Mail, the postman's bag. 3. Post.
Balijero [bah-le-hay'-ro], *m.* A post or post-boy who carries letters out of the post-road.
Balijilla [bah-le-heel'-lyah], *f. dim.* A small bag.
Balijón [bah-lee'-hone], *m. aug.* A large portmanteau.
Balines [bah-lee'-nes], *m. pl.* (Amer.) Mould-shot, buck-shot.
Balista [bah-lees'-tah], *f.* Ballista, engine used in ancient warfare for hurling heavy stones.
Balística [bah-lees'-te-cah], *f.* Ballistics, science that deals with the impact, path, and velocity of projectiles.
Balístico, ca [bah-lees'-te-co, cah], *a.* Ballistic. *Proyectil balístico,* Ballistic missile.
Balneario, *m.* Bathing beach, bathing resort.
Balneario, ria [bal-nay-ah'-re-o, ah], *a.* Of or pertaining to baths and bathing.
Balompié [bah-lom-pe-ay'], *m.* Soccer.
Balón [bah-lon'], *m.* 1. Soccer ball. 2. Glass ball. 3. Balloon. 4. Bale. *Balón medicinal,* Medicine ball.
Baloncesto [bah-lon-thes'-to], *m.* Basketball.
Balonvolea [bah-lon-vo-lay'-ah], *m.* Volleyball.
Balota [bah-lo'-tah], *f.* Ballot, a little ball used in voting.
Balotada [bah-lo-tah'-dah], *f.* Balotade, leap of a horse, in which he shows the shoes of his hinder feet.
Balotar [bah-lo-tar'], *vn.* To ballot, to choose by ballot.
Balsa [bahl'-sah], *f.* 1. Pool, a lake. 2. (Naut.) Raft or float for conveying goods or persons across a river. 3. (Prov.) Half a butt of wine. 4. In oil-mills, the room where the oil is kept. *Estar como una balsa de aceite,* To be as quiet as a pool of oil; spoken of a place or country, or of the sea.
Balsámico, ca [bal-sah'-me-co, cah], *a.* Balsamic, balsamical, balmy.
Balsamina [bal-sah-mee'-nah], *f.* (Bot.) Balsam-apple. Momordica balsamina.
Balsamita mayor [bal-sah-mee'-tah mah-yor']. (Bot.) *V.* ATANASIA. *Balsamita menor,* (Bot.) Maudlin, annual costmary, tansy. Tanacetum annuum.
Bálsamo [bahl'-sah-mo], *m.* 1. Balsam, balm. *Bálsamo de María,* Gum of the calaba-tree. *Bálsamo de copaiba,* Copaiba balsam. *Es un bálsamo,* It is a balsam: applied to generous liquors. 2. (Med.) The purest part of the blood.
Balsar [bal-sar'], *m.* A marshy piece of ground with brambles.
Balsear [bal-say-ar'], *va.* To cross rivers on floats.

Balsero [bal-say'-ro], *m.* Ferry-man.
Balsopeto [bal-so-pay'-to], *m.* (Coll.) 1. A large pouch carried near the breast. 2. Bosom, the inside of the breast.
Baltasar [bal-tah-sar'], *m.* Belshazzar, the last King of Babylon.
Báltico [bahl'-te-co], *m.* The Baltic Sea.
Bálteo [bahl'-tay-o], *m.* (Obs.) Officer's belt.
Baluarte [bah-loo-ar'-tay], *m.* 1. (Fort.) Bastion, formerly bulwark, a mass of earth raised in the angles of a polygon. 2. (Met.) Bulwark, defence, support.
Balumba [bah-loom'-bah], *f.* Bulk or quantity of things heaped together.
Balumbo, Balume [bah-loom'-bo, bah-loo'-may], *m.* A heap of things which take up much room.
Balzo [bahl'-tho], *m.* (Naut.) A bend.
Ballena [bal-lyay'-nah], *f.* 1. Whale. Balæna. 2. Train-oil. 3. Whalebone. 4. (Ast.) One of the northern constellations.
Ballenato [bal-lyay-nah'-to], *m.* Cub, the young of a whale.
Ballener [bal-lyay-nerr'], *m.* (Obs.) A vessel in the shape of a whale.
Ballesta [bal-lyes'-tah], *f.* Cross-bow. *A tiro de ballesta,* (Met.) At a great distance.
Ballestada [bal-lyes-tah'-dah], *f.* Shot from a cross-bow.
Ballestazo [bal-lyes-tah-tho'], *m.* Blow given by or received from a cross-bow.
Ballesteador [bal-lyes-tay-ah-dor'], *m.* Cross bowman, arbalister.
Ballestear [bal-lyes-tay-ar'], *va.* To shoot with a cross-bow.
Ballestera [bal-lyes-tay'-rah], *f.* Loop-holes through which cross-bows were discharged.
Ballestería [bal-lyes-tay-ree'-ah], *f.* 1. Archery, the art of an archer. 2. Number of cross-bows, or persons armed with cross-bows. 3. Place where cross-bows are kept, or arbalists quartered.
Ballestero [bal-lyes-tay'-ro], *m.* 1. Archer, arbalister, cross-bowman. 2. Cross-bow maker. 3. King's archer or armourer. *Ballestero de maza,* Macebearer. *Ballesteros de corte,* The king's porters and the porters of the privy council were formerly so called.
Ballestilla [bal-lyes-teel'-lyah], *f.* 1. (Dim.) Small cross-bow. 2. (Obs.) The instrument for bleeding cattle, at present called a *fleam.* 3. Cross-staff, an instrument for taking heights. 4. (Naut.) Fore-staff, an instrument used for taking the altitude of the sun, stars, etc.
Ballestón [bal-lyes-tone'], *m. aug.* Large cross-bow, arbalet.
Ballestrinque [bal-lyes-treen'-kay], *m.* (Naut.) Clove-hitch, by which one rope is fastened to another.
Ballet [bah-lay'], *m.* Ballet.
Ballico [bal-lyee'-co], *m.* (Bot.) Red or perennial darnal, rye-grass. Lolium perenne.
Ballueca [bal-lyoo-ay'-cah], *f.* (Bot. Prov.) Wild oats. Avena fatua.
Bambalear, Bambanear, *vn.* *V.* BAMBOLEAR.
Bambalina [bam-bah-lee'-nah], *f.* The upper part of the scenes in theatres.
Bambarria [bam-bar'-re-ah], *m.* 1. (Low) A fool, an idiot. 2. An accidental but successful stroke at billiards.
Bambochada [bam-bo-chah'-dah], *f.* **Bamboche** [bam-bo'-chay], *m.* A landscape representing banquets or drunken feasts, with grotesque figures. *Es un bamboche,* or *parece un bamboche,* Applied to a thick, short person with a red, bloated face.
Bambolear, Bambonear [bam-bo-lay-ar', bam-bo-nay-ar'], *vn.* To reel, to stagger, to totter.
Bamboleo, Bamboneo [bam-bo-lay'-o, bam-bo-nay'-o], *m.* Reeling, staggering.
Bambolla [bam-bol'-lyah], *f.* Ostentation, boast, vain show, froth.
Bambú, or **Bambuc** [bam-boo' or bam-book], *m.* Bamboo, the largest of the grass family. Bambusa.
Bambuco [bam-boo'-co], *m.* Popular musical rhythm of Colombia.
Ban [ban], *m.* A sort of fine Chinese muslin.
Banana, *f.* *V.* PLÁTANO.
Banano, *m.* (Bot.) *V.* PLÁTANO.
Banasta [bah-nahs'-tah], *f.* A large basket made of twigs or laths. *Meterse en banasta,* To meddle with things which do not concern one.
Banastero [bah-nas-tay'-ro], *m.* 1. Basket-maker or dealer. 2. (Low) Jailer.
Banasto [bah-nahs'-to], *m.* A large round basket.
Banca [bahn'cah], *f.* 1. Bench. 2. Banking.
Bancada [ban-cah'-dah], *f.* A sort of bench on which to spread cloth to be measured.
Bancal [ban-cahl'], *m.* 1. An oblong plot of ground for raising pulse, roots, and fruit-trees. 2. Terrace in a garden. 3. Cover placed over a bench by way of ornament.
Bancaria, *f.* *V.* FIANZA BANCARIA.
Bancario, ria [ban-cah'-re-o, ah], *a.* Bank, banking, *Cuenta bancaria,* Bank account.
Bancarrota [ban-car-ro'-tah], *f.* Bankruptcy, failure.
Bancaza [ban-cah'-thah], *f.* **Bancazo** [ban-cah'-tho], *m. aug.* A large form or bench.
Banco [bahn'-co], *m.* 1. Form or bench without a back. 2. A strong bench for the use of carpenters. *Banco de acepillar,* A planing-bench. 3. A thwart, or bench for rowers. 4. A bank, a place where money is kept. 5. Company of persons concerned in managing a joint stock of money. 6. The cheeks of the bit of a bridle. 7. A pedestal on which is raised any body of architecture. *Banco de ahorros,* Savings-bank. *Banco de arena,* A sand-bank. *Banco de hielo,* A field of ice. *Banco de río,* Sand-bank in a river. *Banco pinjado,* An ancient warlike machine for battering. *Pasar banco,* To flog the sailors on board a galley. *Razón de pie de banco,* An absurd reason, a groundless motive. *Banco de la paciencia,* (Naut.) Bench on the quarter-deck. *Banco de piedra,* A vein or stratum of a single kind of stone.
Banco de sangre [bahn'-co day sahn'-gray], *m.* Bloodbank.
Banda [bahn'-dah], *f.* 1. Sash formerly worn by military officers when on duty. 2. Ribbon worn by the knights of the military orders. 3. Band or body of troops. 4. Scarf. 5. Party of persons confederated; gang; crew; military band; brass band. 6. Covey, a number of birds together. *V.* BANDADA. 7. Bank, border, edge: side of a ship. 8. Felloe, of wheel. 9. Cushion (billiards). *La banda del norte,* The north side. *La banda izquierda del río,* The left bank of the river. *A la banda,* (Naut.) Heeled or hove down. *En banda,* (Naut.) Amain. *Arriar en banda,* To let go amain. *Caer* or *estar en banda,* To be amain. *Dar a la banda,* To heel. *Bandas del tajamar,* (Naut.) The cheeks of the head. *No ir* or *tirar a ninguna banda,* Not to make any odds. *De banda a banda,* From party to party, from one side to another.
Bandada [ban-dah'-dah], *f.* Covey: flock of birds.
Bandarria [ban-dar'-re-ah], *f.* (Naut.) An iron maul.
Bandear [ban-day-ar'], *va.* (Obs.) To traverse, to pass, to cross from one side to another; to band.—*vn.* (Obs.) To form parties, to unite with a band. —*vr.* To conduct one's self with prudence, to shift for one's self. *Saber bandeárselas,* To know how to look for himself.
Bandeja [ban-day'-hah], *f.* A kind of metallic waiter, tray.
Bandera [ban-day'-rah], *f.* 1. Banner, standard. 2. Flag, ensign, a pair of colours of a regiment of infantry. 3. Infantry. 4. Flag or colours which distinguish the ships of the different nations. *Bandera de popa,* (Naut.) The ensign. *Bandera de proa* (Naut.) The jack. *Bandera blanca* or *de paz,* The flag of truce. *Vuelo de la bandera,* The flag of the ensign. *Arriar la bandera,* To strike the colours *Salir con banderas desplegadas* To get off with flying colours. *Asegurar la bandera,* To fire a cannon-shot with ball at the time of hoisting the colours. *Dar la bandera,* (Met.) To submit to the superior talents or merits of another. *Levantar banderas,* (Met.) To put one's self at the head of a party.
Bandereta [ban-day-ray'-tah], *f. dim.* Banneret, bannerol, a small flag. *Banderetas,* (Mil.) Camp-colours.
Banderica, illa [ban-day-ree'-cah, eel'-lyah], *dim.* Banneret, a small flag.
Banderilla [ban-day-reel'-lyah], *f.* A small dart with a bannerol thrust into the nape of a bull. *Poner a uno una banderilla,* (Met.) To taunt, to ridicule, to revile, to vex.
Banderillear [ban-day-reel-lyay-ar'], *va.* To put *banderillas* on bulls.
Banderillero [ban-day-reel-lyay'-ro], *m.* He who sticks *banderillas* in a bull's nape.
Banderín [ban-day-reen'], *m.* 1. Camp colours. 2. Flag, railway signal. 3. Recruiting post.
Banderizar, *va.* *V.* ABANDERIZAR.
Banderizo, za [ban-day-ree'-tho, thah], *a.* Factious, given to party.
Banderola [ban-day-ro'-lah], *f.* 1. Bannerol, camp colours. 2. Carabine belt. 3. Streamer, a pennant.
Bandido [ban-dee'-do], *m.* 1. Bandit, highwayman, outlaw, freebooter. 2. Fugitive pursued with judicial advertisements.
Bandín [ban-deen'], *m.* (Naut.) Seat in a row-galley.
Bandita [ban-dee'-tah], *f. dim.* A small band.
Bando [bahn'-do], *m.* 1. Proclamation, a public declaration by government. 2. Edict or law solemnly published by superior authority. 3. Faction, party. *Echar bando,* To publish a law.
Bandola, *f.* **Bandolín,** *m.* [ban-do'-lah]. 1. Pandore, a small musical instrument resembling a lute. 2. (Naut.) Jury-mast.
Bandolera [ban-do-lay'-rah], *f.* Carbine belt, cross belt. *Dar* or *quitar la bandolera,* To admit or dismiss one from the king's life-guards in Spain.
Bandolero [ban-do-lay'-ro], *m.* Highwayman, robber, footpad.
Bandolina [ban-do-lee'-nah], *f.* Bandoline, a hair fixative in a pasty mass.
Bandujo [ban-doo'-ho], *m.* (Obs.) Large sausage.

Bandullo [ban-dool'-lyo], *m.* (Vulg.) Belly; the bowels.
Bandurria [ban-door'-re-ah], *f.* Bandore, a musical instrument resembling a fiddle.
Banjo [bahn'ho], *m.* (Mus.) Banjo.
Bánova [bah'-no-vah], *f.* (Prov.) Bed-quilt, bed-cover.
Banquera [ban-kay'-rah], *f.* (Prov.) 1. Small open bee-house. 2. Frame, on which bee-hives are placed in a bee-house.
Banquero [ban-kay'-ro], *m.* Banker, exchanger. *V.* CAMBISTA.
Banqueta [ban-kay'-tah], *f.* 1. A stool with three legs. 2. (Mil.) Banquette or footbank behind the parapet. 3. A sidewalk. *Banquetas de cureña,* (Naut.) Gun-carriage beds. *Banquetas de calafate,* (Naut.) Calking-stools.
Banquete [ban-kay'-tay], *m.* 1. Banquet, a splendid repast. *Banquete casero,* A family feast. 2. Stool.
Banquetear [ban-kay-tay-ar'], *vn.* To banquet, to feast.
Banquillo [ban-keel'-lyo], *m. dim.* A little stool.
Banquito [ban-kee'-to], *m. dim.* (from BANCO). A stool, footstool.
Banzo [bahn'-tho], *m.* Cheek or side of an embroidering or quilting-frame.
Bañadera [ba-nyah-day'-rah], *f.* 1. Bath-tub, bath. 2. Tub, vat. 3. (Naut.) Skeet, a narrow oblong ladle or scoop for wetting the sails, decks, and sides of a ship, or for bailing a boat.
Bañadero [ba-nyah-day'-ro], *m.* Puddle, in which wild beasts wallow; bathing-place, balneary.
Bañado, *m. V.* BACÍN.—*pp.* of BAÑAR.
Bañador, ra [ba-nyah-dor', rah], *m.* & *f.* One who bathes. *Bañador,* Tub with liquid wax, in which wax-chandlers dip their wicks.
Bañar [bah-nyar'], *va.* 1. To bathe, to wash in water, to lave. 2. To water, to irrigate. *El río baña las murallas de la ciudad,* The river washes the walls of the town. 3. To candy biscuits, plums, etc., with sugar. 4. (Art) To wash over a painting with a second coat of transparent colours. 5. To overlay with something shining or pellucid. *Loza bañada* or *vidriada,* Glazed earthenware. *Bañarse en agua de rosas,* To bathe in rose-water, to be highly pleased. 6. To extend or enlarge.
Bañera [bah-nyay'-rah], *f.* Bath-tub.
Bañero [bah-nyay'-ro], *m.* 1. Owner of baths. 2. Bath-keeper or attendant.
Bañil [bah-nyeel'], *m.* A pool in which deer bathe.
Bañista [bah-nyees'-tah], *m.* He who bathes or drinks mineral waters.
Baño [bah'-nyo], *m.* 1. Bath. 2. Bathing. 3. Bath, bathtub. *Cuarto de baño,* Bathroom. *Baño de María,* Cooking in a double boiler. 4. Coat of paint put over another. 5. Basting (in cooking).
Bañuelo [bah-nyoo-ay'-lo], *m. dim.* A little bath.
Bao [bah'-oh], *m.* (Naut.) Beam, the main cross timber. *Baos de las cubiertas altas,* The beams of the upper deck. *Bao maestro,* The midship beam. *Baos del sollado,* Orlop beams. *Baos del saltillo de proa,* The collar beams. *Baos de los palos,* Trestle-trees. *Baos y crucetas de los palos,* Cross and trestle trees.
Baobal [bah-o-bahl'], *m.* (Bot.) Baobab; a great tree of Africa. (Native name.) Adansonia digitata.
Baptismo, *m.* (Obs.) *V.* BAUTISMO.
Baptisterio [bap-tis-tay'-re-o], *m.* Baptistery.
Baptizar [bap-te-thar], *va.* (Obs.) *V.* BAUTIZAR.
Baque [bah'-kay], *m.* 1. The blow which a body gives in falling. 2. A water-trough in glass-houses.
Baquelita [bah-kay-lee'-tah], *f.* Bakelite. (A trade mark for a synthetic resin.)
Baqueriza [bah-kay-ree'-thah], *f.* A cow-house for cattle in winter; a stable.
Baqueta [bah-kay'-tah], *f.* 1. Ramrod, gunstick. 2. Switch used in a riding-house, in breaking in young horses. *Mandar a baqueta, a la baqueta,* To command imperiously. *Tratar a baqueta,* To treat a person in a haughty manner.—*pl.* 1. Drumsticks. 2. Gantlet, gantlope, a military punishment. 3. (Arch.) Beads, reeds, a semicylindric moulding. 4. Rods of hollywood, used in beating wool.
Baquetazo [bah-kay-tah'-tho], *m.* 1. Violent fall, great blow given by the body when falling. 2. A blow with the ramrod. *Tropecé y dí un baquetazo,* I tripped and fell violently.
Baqueteado, da [bah-kay-tay'-ah-do, dah], *a.* Inured, habituated.—*pp.* of BAQUETEAR.
Baquetear [bah-kay-tay-ar'], *va.* 1. (Obs.) To inflict the punishment of the gantlet. 2. To vex. 3. To make to toil heavily. *Baquetear la lana,* To beat wool.
Baqueteo [bah-kay-tay'-o], *m.* Beating of wool.
Baquetón [bah-kay-tone'], *m.* Gun-worm, wiper, cleaning-rod. *V.* SACATRAPOS.
Baquetilla [bah-kay-teel'-lyah], *f. dim.* A little rod.
Báquico, ca [bah'-ke-co, cah], *a.* Bacchanal, relating to Bacchus.
Baquio [bah'-ke-o], *m.* (Poet.) A metrical foot consisting of a short and two long syllables, ⏑ — — .
Baquira [bah-kee'-rah], *f.* (Amer.) A wild hog; peccary.
Bar [bar], *m.* 1. Bar (of a tavern or saloon). 2. Brewery.
Baracutey [bah-ra-coo-tay'-e], *a.* (Amer. Cuba) Morose, sad, retired, fond of solitude.
Baradero [bah-rah-day'-ro], *m.* (Naut.) Skeed or skid. *Baradero de baja mar,* A muddy place in which vessels stick at low water.
Baradura [bah-rah-doo'-rah], *f.* (Naut.) The grounding of a vessel.
Baraha [ba-rah'-ah], *f.* A burlesque song of Indians.
Barahunda, *f. V.* BARAÚNDA.
Baraja [bah-rah'-hah], *f.* 1. A complete pack of cards. 2. (Obs.) A quarrel. *Meterse en barajas,* To seek a quarrel.
Barajador, ra [ba-rah-ha-dor', rah], *m.* & *f.* One who shuffles or jumbles together.
Barajadura [bah-rah-hah-doo'-rah], *f.* 1. Shuffling of cards. 2. Dispute, difference.
Barajar [bah-rah-har'], *va.* 1. To shuffle the cards. 2. (Met.) To jumble things or persons together. *Barajar un negocio,* To entangle or perplex an affair. *Barajarle a alguno una pretensión,* To frustrate one's pretensions. *Barajar una proposición,* To reject a proposal.—*vn.* (Obs.) To wrangle, to contend.
Baranda [bah-rahn'-dah], *f.* Railing of timber, iron, etc. *Barandas de los corredores de popa de un navío,* Stern-rails. *Echar de baranda,* (Met.) To exaggerate something, to boast.
Barandado, daje [bah-ran-dah'-do, dah'-hay], *m.* Balustrade.
Barandal [bah-ran-dahl'], *m.* 1. The upper and under-piece of a balustrade, in which the balusters are fixed. 2. A balustrade or railing.
Barandilla [bah-ran-deel'-lyah], *f. dim.* A small balustrade, a small railing.
Barangay [bah-ran-gah'-el, *m.* 1. An Indian vessel, worked with oars. 2. Each group of forty-five or fifty families of Indians, into which a Philippine village is divided.
Barata [bah-rah'-tah], *f.* 1. (Coll.) Barter, exchange. 2. Low price of things exposed for sale. *V.* BARATURA. *A la barata,* Confusedly, disorderly. *Mala barata,* (Obs.) Profusion, prodigality.
Baratador [bah-rah-tah-dor'], *m.* 1. Barterer. 2. (Obs.) Impostor, deceiver.
Baratar [bah-rah-tar'], *va.* (Obs.) 1. To barter, to traffic by exchanging commodities. 2. To make fraudulent barters, to deceive. 3. To give or receive a thing under its just value.
Baratear [bah-rah-tay-ar'], *vn.* To cheapen; to sell under price.
Baratería [bah-rah-tay-ree'-ah], *f.* 1. Barratry. 2. (Obs.) Fraud, deception.
Baratero [bah-rah-tay'-ro], *m.* 1. He who obtains money from fortunate gamesters. 2. One who provokes quarrels.
Baratijas [bah-rah-tee'-has], *f. pl.* Trifles, toys.
Baratillero [bah-rah-teel-lyay'-ro], *m.* 1. A peddler. 2. A seller of second-hand goods or articles.
Baratillo [bah-rah-teel'-lyo], *m.* 1. A place where new and second-hand furniture, clothing, jewellery, etc., are sold cheap. 2. A heap of trifling articles.
Baratista [bah-rah-tees'-tah], *m.* Barterer, trafficker.
Barato, ta [bah-rah'-to, tah], *a.* 1. Cheap, bought or sold for a low price *De barato,* Gratuitously, gratis. 2. (Met.) Easy.
Barato [bah-rah'-to], *m.* Money given by the winners at a gaming-table to the bystanders. *Hacer barato,* To sell under value in order to get rid of goods, to sell things under cost price. *Dar de barato,* (Met.) To grant for argument's sake, to grant readily, without objection. *Lo barato es caro,* The cheapest goods are dearest. *Ni juega, ni da barato,* To act with indifference, without taking part with a faction.—*adv.* Cheaply.
Báratro [bah'-rah-tro], *m.* (Poet.) Hell, abysm.
Baratura [bah-rah-too'-rah], *f.* Cheapness, little value set upon things.
Baraúnda [bah-rah-oon'-dah], *f.* Noise, hurly-burly, confusion, fluttering.
Barauste, *m.* (Obs.) *V.* BALAUSTRE.
Barba [bar'-bah], *f.* 1. Chin. 2. Beard, the hair which grows on the chin. 3. The first swarm of bees which leaves the hive. *Barba cabruna,* (Bot.) Yellow goat's-beard. Tragopogon pratense. *Barba de Aarón,* (Bot.) Green dragon arum. Arum dracontium. *Barba de cabra* or *cabrón,* Goat's-beard spiræa. Spiræa aruncus. *Amarrado a barba de gato,* (Naut.) Moored by the head. *Temblar la barba,* To shake with fear. *Barba a barba,* Face to face. *A barba regada,* In great plenty. *Barba cabosa,* A noble, earnest fellow. *A la barba, en la barba,* To his face, in his presence. *Por barba,* A head, apiece. *A polla por barba,* Every man his bird.—*m.* 1. Player who acts the part of old men. 2. *pl.* The portion of rays opposite to the tail of a comet; the head. 3 (Bot.) Slender roots of trees or plants; fibres. *Barbas enredadas,* A full

hawse. *Barbas de ballena*, Whalebone. *Barbas de gallo*, Wattle. *Barbas honradas*, A respectable or honourable man. *Cuales barbas, tales tobajas*, Treat every one with due respect. *De tal barba, tal escama*. We must expect people to act in accordance with their condition and education. *Decir a uno en sus barbas alguna cosa*, To tell a man a thing to his face. *Echarlo a las barbas*, To reproach a man with something. *Hacer la barba*, 1. To shave, to take off the beard. 2. (Met.) To speak ill of somebody. *Mentir por la barba*, To tell a barefaced lie. *Pelarse las barbas*, To fly into a violent passion. *Subirse a las barbas*, To fly in one's face. *Tener buenas barbas*, To have a graceful mien: applied to a fine woman. *Echar a la buena barba*, To induce one to pay for what he and his companions have eaten and drunk. *Andar, estar*, or *traer la barba sobre el hombro*, To wear the face on the shoulder, to be alert, to live watchful and careful. *Tener pocas barbas*, To be young or inexperienced. *Hacerse la barba*, To shave one's self. *Hacer la barba a alguno*, (Amer.) To flatter, to cajole.

Barbacana [bar-bah-cah'-nah], *f.* 1. (Mil.) Barbican, an advanced work defending a castle or fortress, or loophole in a fortification to fire missiles through. 2. A low wall around a church-yard.

Barbacoa [bar-ba-co'-ah], *f.* (Amer.) 1. Barbecue, meat roasted in a pit in the earth. 2. A framework suspended from forked sticks.

Barbada [bar-bah'-dah], *f.* 1. Lower part of the lower jaw of a horse (where the bridle-curb rests). 2. Curb or iron chain, made fast to the upper part of the bridle, and running under the beard of the horse. 3. Dab, a small flat fish, related to the codfishes. *Agua de la Barbada*, Barbadoes water, a liquor distilled from sugar-cane.

Barbadamente [bar-bah-dah-men'-tay], *adv.* (Littl. us.) Strongly, vigorously.

Barbadillo, illa [bar-bah-deel'-lyo, lyah], *a. dim.* 1. Having little beard. 2. Having slender filaments: applied to plants.

Barbado, da [bar-bah'-do, dah], *a.* 1. Bearded. 2. Barbed, barbated.—*pp.* of BARBAR.

Barbado [bar-bah'-do], *m.* 1. Full-grown man. 2. Vine or tree transplanted. 3. Shoots issuing from the roots of trees.

Barbaja [bar-bah'-hah], *f.* (Bot.) Cut-leaved viper's grass. Scorzonera laciniata.—*pl.* (Agr.) The first roots of the plants.

Barbar [bar-bar'], *vn.* 1. To get a beard. 2. Among bee-masters, to rear or keep bees. 3. To begin to strike root: applied to plants.

Bárbara [bar'-ba-rah], *f.* *Santabárbara*, (Naut.) Powder-room or magazine on board ships of war.

Bárbaramente [bar'-ba-rah-men-tay], *adv.* 1. Barbarously, savagely. 2. Rudely, without culture.

Barbárico, ca [bar-bah'-re-co, cah], *a.* Barbarous, barbarian.

Barbaridad [bar-bah-re-dahd'], *f.* 1. Barbarity, barbarism, cruelty. 2. Rashness, temerity. 3. Rudeness, want of culture. 4. Barbarous expression or action.

Barbarie [bar-bah'-re-ay], *f.* 1. Barbarousness, incivility of manners; rusticity. 2. Cruelty.

Barbarismo [bar-bah-rees'-mo], *m.* 1. Barbarism, impurity of language; use of words foreign to the language in which they are employed. 2. (Poet.) Crowd of barbarians. 3. Barbarousness. *V.* BARBARIE.

Barbarizar [bar-bah-re-thar'], *va.* To barbarize, to make barbarous, wild, or cruel.

Bárbaro, ra [bar'-bah-ro, rah], *a.* 1. Barbarous, barbarian, fierce, cruel, heathenish, murderous. 2. Rash, bold, daring. 3. Rude, ignorant, unpolished.

Barbarote [bar-bah-ro'-tay], *m. aug.* A great savage or barbarian.

Barbasco [bar-bahs'-co], *m.* A poison from Jacquinia armillaris, an evergreen bush.

Barbato, ta [bar-bah'-to, tah], *a.* Bearded: applied to a comet.

Barbaza [bar-bah'-thah], *f. aug.* A long beard.

Barbear [bar-bay-ar'], *vn.* 1. To reach with the beard or lips. 2. To reach one thing almost to the height of another.

Barbechar [bar-bay-char'], *va.* To prepare ground for sowing; to fallow.

Barbechazón [bar-bay-chah-thone'], *f.* Among farmers, the fallowing-time.

Barbechera [bar-bay-chay'-rah], *f.* 1. Series of successive ploughings. 2. Fallowing season. 3. Act and effect of ploughing or fallowing.

Barbecho [bar-bay'-cho], *m.* 1. First ploughing of the ground. 2. Fallow, ground ploughed in order to be sown. *Como en un barbecho* or *por un barbecho*, With too much confidence or assurance.

Barbel [bar-bel'], *m.* A small barbo; barbel, a river fish.

Barbélula [bar-bay'-loo-lah], *f.* Spiny involucre of certain flowers.

Barbera [bar-bay'-rah], *f.* 1. A barber's wife. 2. Chin-piece of a helmet.

Barbería [bar-bay-ree'-ah], *f.* 1. Trade of a barber. 2. Barber's shop.

Barberito, illo [bar-bay-ree'-to, eel'-lyo], *m. dim.* A little barber.

Barbero [bar-bay'-ro], *m.* 1. Barber. 2. (Zool.) Mutton-fish. Labrus anthias.

Barbeta [bar-bay'-tah], *f.* 1. (Naut.) Rackline, gasket. 2. (Naut.) Ring-rope, a rope occasionally tied to the ringbolts of the deck. *Batería a barbeta*, Barbet-battery, having neither embrasures nor merlons.

Barbiblanco, ca [bar-be-blahn'-co, cah], *a.* Having a beard gray or white with age.

Barbica, ita [bar-bee'-cah, ee'-tah], *f. dim.* A small beard.

Barbicacho [bar-be-cah'-cho], *m.* (Prov.) Ribbon or band tied under the chin; guard ribbon.

Barbicano, na [bar-be-cah'-no, nah], *a.* Graybeard, having a gray beard.

Barbiespeso, sa [bar-be-es-pay'-so, sah], *a.* One who has a thick beard.

Barbihecho, cha [bar-be-ay'-cho, chah], *a.* Fresh shaved.

Barbilampiño, ña [bar-be-lam-pee'-nyo, nyah], *a.* Having a thin beard, or none.

Barbilindo, da [bar-be-leen'-do, dah], *a.* Well-shaved and trimmed; effeminate and pretty.

Barbilucio, cia [bar-be-loo'-the-o, ah], *a.* Smooth-faced, pretty, genteel.

Barbilla [bar-beel'-lyah], *f.* 1. Point of the chin. 2. Morbid tumour under the tongue of horses and cattle. 3. (Dim.) Small beard.

Barbillera [bar-beel-lyay'-rah], *f.* 1. Tuft of tow, put between the staves of a cask or vat to prevent it from leaking. 2. Bandage put under the chin of a dead person.

Barbinegro, gra [bar-be-nay'-gro, grah], *a.* Black-bearded.

Barbiponiente [bar-be-po-ne-en'-tay], *a.* 1. (Coll.) Having the beard growing: applied to a boy or lad. 2. (Met.) Beginning to learn an art or profession.

Barbiquejo [bar-be-kay'-ho], *m.* 1. Handkerchief, which females in some parts of America muffle the chin with, or put round their heads and tie under the chin. 2. A guard-ribbon for a hat. 3. (Naut.) Bobstay. 4. Curb-chain.

Barbiquí, or **Barbiquejo** [bar-be-kee', bar-be-kay'-ho], *m.* A brace and bit.

Barbirrubio, bia [bar-be-roo'-be-o, ah], *a.* Red-bearded.

Barbirrucio, cia [bar-be-roo'-the-o, ah], *a.* Having a black and white beard.

Barbital [bar-be-tahl'], *m.* (Chem.) Barbital.

Barbiteñido, da [bar-be-tay-nyee'-do, dah], *a.* Having a dyed beard.

Barbitúrico [bar-be-too'-ree-co], *m.* (Chem.) Barbiturate.

Barbo [bar'-bo], *m.* (Zool.) Barbel, a river fish. Cyprinus barbus.

Barbón [bar-bone'], *m.* 1. An old man of a grave and austere aspect. 2. A man with a thick, strong beard. 3. A lay brother of the Carthusian order.

Barboquejo [bar-bo-kay'-ho], *m.* 1. Chin-strap. 2. Bandage put under the chin of a dead person.

Barbotar [bar-bo-tar'], *vn.* To mumble, to mutter.

Barbote [bar-bo'-tay], *m.* Fore part of a helmet. *V.* BABERA.

Barbudo, da [bar-boo'-do, dah], *a.* Having a long beard. *A la mujer barbuda de lejos la saluda*, Flee a woman with a beard as you would a bear.

Barbudo [bar-boo'-do], *m.* Vine transplanted with the roots.

Barbulla [bar-bool'-lyah], *f.* Loud, confused noise, made by people talking all at the same time.

Barbullar [bar-bool-lyar'], *vn.* To talk loud and fast, with disorder and confusion.

Barbullón, na [bar-bool-lyone', nah], *a.* Talking loud, fast, and confusedly.

Barca [bar'-cah], *f.* 1. (Naut.) Boat, barge, bark, barkentine. *Barca chata para pasar gente*, A ferry-boat. *Barca longa*, A fishing-boat. *Conduce bien su barca*, He steers his course well. 2. Dyeing trough.

Barcada [bar-cah'-dah], *f.* 1. Passage across a river in a ferry-boat. 2. A boat full of persons or goods. *Barcada de lastre*, A boat-load of ballast.

Barcaje [bar-cah'-hay], *m.* 1. Ferriage. 2. Ferry, passage-boat for carrying goods or persons.

Barcal [bar-cahl'], *m.* (Prov. Gal.) A wooden vessel in which a caldron is put.

Barcarola [bar-cah-ro'-lah], *f.* Barcarolle, the song of an Italian boatman or gondolier.

Barcaza [bar-cah'-thah], *f.* A privilege conceded in some ports of loading and unloading.

Barcazo [bar-cah'-tho], *m.* A large barge.

Barcelonés, sa [bar-thay-lo-ness', sah], *a.* Of Barcelona.

Barceo [bar-thay'-o], *m.* Dry bass or sedge for making mats, ropes, etc.

Barcina [bar-thee'-nah], *f.* (Prov.) 1. Net for carrying straw. 2. Large truss of straw.

Barcinar [bar-the-nar'], *va.* (Prov.) To load a cart or wagon with sheaves of corn.

Barcino, na [bar-thee'-no, nah], *a.* Ruddy, approaching to redness.

Barco [bar'-co], *m.* Boat, barge; bottom. A word comprising every floating craft, of whatever size, strength, or use. *Barco aguador*, A watering-

boat. *Barco chato*, A flat-bottomed boat. *Barco de la vez*, A passage-boat.
Barcolongo, Barcoluengo [bar-co-lon'-go, bar-co-loo-en'-go], *m.* An oblong boat with a round bow.
Barcón, Barcote [bar-cone', bar-co'-tay], *m. aug.* A large boat.
Barchilla [bar-cheel'-lyah], *f.* A Valencian measure for grain; about one-third of a fanega; 0.175 liter.
Barda [bar'-dah], *f.* 1. Bard, ancient armour of horses. 2. Straw, brushwood, etc., laid on fences, etc., to preserve them. *Aun hay sol en bardas*, There are even still hopes of attaining it.
Bardado, da [bar-dah'-do, dah], *a.* Barbed, caparisoned with defensive armour: applied to a horse.
Bárdago [bar'-dah-go], *m.* (Naut.) Pendant; luff-tackle-rope.
Bardaguera [bar-dah-gay'-rah], *f.* Agnus castus; chaste-tree; a willow.
Bardal [bar-dahl'], *m.* Mud wall, covered at the top with straw or brush. *Saltabardales*, A nickname given to mischievous boys.
Bardana [bar-dah'-nah], *f.* Common burdock, or cockle burr. Arctium lappa. *Bardana menor*, (Bot.) Lesser burdock. Xanthium strumarium.
Bardanza [bar-dahn'-thah], *f. Andar de bardanza*, To go here and there.
Bardar [bar-dar'], *va.* To cover the tops of fences or walls with straw or brushwood.
Bardilla [bar-deel'-lyah], *f. dim.* Small brushwood.
Bardiota [bar-de-o'-tah], *a. & m.* Soldier of the Byzantine court.
Bardo [bar'-do], *m.* Bard, poet.
Bardoma [bar-do'-mah], *f.* (Prov. Aragón.) Filth, mud.
Bardomera [bar-do-may'-rah], *f.* (Prov. Mur.) Weeds or small wood carried off by currents.
Barfol [bar-fol'], *m.* A coarse stuff, from the coast of Gambia.
Barga [bar'-gah], *f.* 1. The steepest part of a declivity. 2. (Obs.) Hut covered with straw or thatched.
Barganal [bar-gah-nahl'], *m.* A fence of wooden stakes.
Bárgano [bar'-gah-no], *m.* A stake, six or seven feet high, of split wood.
Barí, or Baril [bah-ree' or bah-reel'], *a.* (Andal.) Excellent.
Bariga [bah-ree'-gah], *f.* A sort of silk which the Dutch bring from India.
Barillo [bah-reel'-lyo], *m.* An inferior sort of silk, which the Portuguese bring from the East Indies.
Barimetría [bah-re-may-tree'-ah], *f.* A treatise on the measure and weight of bodies.
Bario [bah'-re-o], *m.* (Chem.) Barium.
Baripto [bah-reep'-to], *m.* A precious stone of a blackish colour.
Barita [bah-ree'-tah], *f.* (Chem.) Baryta, or barytes.
Baritel [bah-re-tel'], *m.* A hoisting winch, or whim, used in mines.
Barítico, ca [bah-ree'-te-co, cah], *a.* (Chem.) Barytic, belonging to baryta.
Baritina [bah-re-tee'-nah], *f.* Barium sulphate, heavy spar.
Barítono [bah-ree'-to-no], *m.* (Mus.) Voice of a low pitch, between a tenor and a bass; barytone.
Barjuleta [bar-hoo-lay'-tah], *f.* 1. Knapsack, haversack, tool-bag. 2. A sort of double purse used in some of the chapters of Aragón for distributing the dividends of the incumbents. *Ladroncillo de agujeta, después sube a barjuleta*, A young filcher becomes an old robber.
Barloar [bar-lo-ar'], *vn.* (Naut.) To grapple for the purpose of boarding. = ABARLOAR.
Barloas [bar-lo'-as], *f. pl.* (Naut.) Relieving tackles, or relieving tackle pendants.
Barloventear [bar-lo-ven-tay-ar'], *vn.* 1. (Naut.) To ply to windward, to beat about. 2. (Met.) To rove about.
Barlovento [bar-lo-ven'-to], *m.* (Naut.) Weather-gage, the point whence the wind blows. *Costa de barlovento*, The weather shore. *Costado de barlovento*, The weather side. *Ganar el barlovento*, To get to windward.
Barnabita [bar-nah-bee'-tah], *m.* Member of the religious community of St. Paul.
Barnacle [bar-nah'-clay], *m.* Barnacle, a kind of shell-fish.
Barniz [bar-neeth'], *m.* 1. Varnish; japan, lacquer, gloss. 2. Paint or colours laid on the face. 3. Gum of the juniper-tree. 4. Printer's ink.
Barnizar [bar-ne-thar'], *va.* To varnish, to gloss, to lacquer.
Barométrico, ca [bah-ro-may'-tre-co, cah], *a.* Barometrical.
Barómetro [bah-ro'-may-tro], *m.* Barometer, weather-glass.
Barón [bah-rone'], *m.* Baron, a degree of nobility. *Barones del timón*, (Naut.) Rudder pendants and chains.
Baronesa [bah-ro-nay'-sah], *f.* Baroness, a baron's lady.
Baronía [bah-ro-nee'-ah], *f.* 1. Barony, honour or lordship which gives title to a baron. 2. Baronage, the dignity of a baron, and the land which gives his title.
Barosánemo [bah-ro-sah'-nay-mo], *m.* (Littl. us.) Aerometer, an instrument for measuring the air.
Barquear [bar-kay-ar'], *vn.* To cross in a boat.
Barquero [bar-kay'-ro], *m.* Bargeman, waterman, boatman, ferryman.
Barqueta [bar-kay'-tah], *f. dim.* A small boat.
Barquichuelo [bar-ke-choo-ay'-lo], *m. dim.* Small bark or boat.
Barquilla [bar-keel'-lyah], *f.* 1. (Dim.) A little boat, wherry. 2. *Barquilla de la corredera*, (Naut.) The log, a triangular piece of wood which serves to measure the ship's way. 3. Thin boat-formed or conical pastry cake.
Barquillero [bar-keel-lyay'-ro], *m.* 1. One who makes or sells rolled cakes, and the iron mould for making them. 2. Waffle-iron.
Barquillo [bar-keel'-lyo], *m.* 1. Cock-boat, a small boat used on rivers and near a sea-coast. 2. Cot or cott, a little boat. 3. Paste made to close letters. 4. A thin pastry cake rolled up in the form of a tube or cone. 5. A mould with holes, used by wax-chandlers.
Barquín [bar-keen'], *m.* **Barquinera** [bar-ke-nay'-rah], *f.* Large bellows for iron-works or furnaces.
Barquinazo [bar-ke-nah'-tho], *m.* (Coll.) The blow which a body gives in falling.
Barquinero [bar-ke-nay'-ro], *m.* Bellows-maker.
Barquino [bar-kee'-no], *m.* Wine-bag. *V.* ODRE.
Barra [bar'-rah], *f.* 1. Iron crow or lever. 2. Bar or ingot of gold, silver, etc. 3. Bar, rock, or sand-bank at the mouth of a harbour. 4. List or gross-spun thread in cloth. 5. A mould for small (wax) candles. 6. (Mech.) Lever, rod, cross-bar; chase-bar. 7. The shaft of a carriage, thill. 8. (Her.) The third part of a shield. 9. A game or exercise much used among country people in Spain, and the iron bar with which they play. 10. (Naut.) Spar. 11. (Mus.) Bar, or measure. 12. Bar, or railing in a court-room. *Estirar la barra*, (Met.) To make the utmost exertions for attaining some purpose. *Tirar la barra*, (Met.) To enhance the price. *De barra a barra*, From one point to another. *Barras*, Among pack-saddle makers, the arched trees of a pack-saddle. *Barras de cabrestante y molinete*, (Naut.) The bars of the capstan and windlass. *Barras de escotillas*, (Naut.) Bars of the hatches. *Barras de portas*, (Naut.) Gun-port bars. *Estar en barras*, (Met.) To be on the point of settling an affair. *Sin daño de barras*, (Met.) Without injury or danger. *A barras derechas*, Fairly.
Barrabasada [bar-rah-bah-sah'-dah], *f.* (Coll.) Trick, plot, intrigue; a bold action.
Barraca [bar-rah'-cah], *f.* Barrack for soldiers; a cabin, a hut.
Barrachel [bar-rah-chel'], *m.* (Obs.) Head-constable, the principal *alguacil*.
Barraco [bar-rah'-co], *m.* (Prov.) 1. A boar. 2. Spume thrown up by must when in a state of fermentation. 3. An ancient kind of ship guns. 4. (Prov.) Snag, a tooth which grows over another.
Barracuda [bar-ra-coo'-dah], *f.* A Californian food fish; Sphyræna picuda.
Barrado, da [bar-rah'-do, dah], *a.* 1. Among clothiers, corded or ribbed; striped. 2. (Her.) Barred.—*pp.* of BARRAR.
Barragán [bar-rah-gahn'], *m.* 1. (Obs.) Companion. 2. Barracan, a strong kind of camlet.
Barragana [bar-rah-gah'-nah], *f.* (Obs.) 1. A concubine. 2. Married woman or lawful wife, who (being of inferior birth) does not enjoy the civil rights of the matrimonial state.
Barraganería [bar-rah-gah-nay-ree'-ah], *f.* Concubinage.
Barraganía [bar-rah-gah-nee'-ah], *f.* (Obs.) *V.* AMANCEBAMIENTO.
Barraganete [bar-rah-gah-nay'-tay], *m.* (Naut.) Top-timber, timber-head, futtock.
Barral [bar-rahl'], *m.* A large bottle containing an *arroba*, or twenty-five pints.
Barranca, *f.* **Barrancal**, *m.* [bar-rahn'-cah, bar-ran-cahl']. 1. A deep break or hole made by heavy falls of rain. 2. Ravine. 3. A precipice.
Barranco [bar-rahn'-co], *m.* 1. *V.* BARRANCA. 2. Dell, a narrow valley. 3. (Met.) Great difficulty which obstructs the attainment of a purpose.
Barrancoso, sa [bar-ran-co'-so, sah], *a.* Broken, uneven, full of breaks and holes.
Barranquera [bar-ran-kay'-rah], *f.* 1. *V.* BARRANCA. 2. Obstruction, embarrassment.
Barraque [bar-rah'-kay]. *V.* TRAQUE BARRAQUE.
Barraquear [bar-rah-kay-ar'], *vn.* To grunt like a bear.
Barraquilla [bar-rah-keel'-lyah], *f. dim* A little hut.
Barraquillo [bar-rah-keel'-lyo], *m* (Obs.) A short light field-piece.
Barrar [bar-rar'], *va.* 1. (Obs.) To daub, to smear, to paint coarsely. 2. (Obs.) To bar, to barricade.
Barrate [bar-rah'-tay], *m.* A little joist, or rafter.
Barrear [bar-ray-ar'], *va.* 1. To bar, to barricade, to fortify with timbers, fascines, stakes, etc. 2. (Prov.) To cancel a writing. 3. To secure or fasten a thing with a bar of iron.—*vn.* To

graze a knight's armour without piercing it: applied to a lance.—*vr.* 1. *V.* Atrincherarse. 2. (Prov.) To wallow, to roll in mire: applied to wild boars.

Barreda [bar-ray'-dah], *f.* *V.* Barrera.

Barrederas [bar-ray-day'-ras], *f. pl.* (Naut.) Studding-sails.

Barredero [bar-ray-day'-ro], *m.* Mop; generally, the mop used for wiping an oven where bread is baked.

Barredero, ra [bar-ray-day'-ro, rah], *a.* Sweeping along any thing met with. *Red barredera,* Drag-net.

Barredura [bar-ray-doo'-rah], *f.* Act of sweeping.—*pl.* 1. Sweepings. 2. Remains, residue, that which is left.

Barrena [bar-ray'-nah], *f.* 1. Boring bit, auger. *Barrena grande,* Auger, borer. *Barrena pequeña,* Gimlet. *Barrena de gusano,* Wimble. 2. A rock-drill for blasting. *Barrena de diminución,* A taper auger. *Barrena de guía,* A centre-bit.

Barrenado, da [bar-ray-nah'-do, dah], *a.* (Met.) *Barrenado de cascos,* Crack-brained, crazy.—*pp.* of Barrenar.

Barrenador [bar-ray-nah-dor'], *m.* (Naut.) Auger or borer.

Barrenar [bar-ray-nar'], *va.* 1. To bore, to pierce, to make holes, to drill. *Barrenar un navío,* (Naut.) To scuttle or sink a ship. *Barrenar una roca* or *mina,* To blast a rock or a mine. 2. (Met.) To defeat one's intentions, to frustrate one's designs.

Barrendero, ra [bar-ren-day'-ro, rah], *m. & f.* Sweeper, dustman.

Barrenero [bar-ray-nay'-ro], *m.* In the mines of Almadén, the boy that serves with the boring tools.

Barrenillo [bar-ray-neel'-lyo], *m.* 1. An insect which gnaws through the bark and attacks the sap-wood. 2. A disease produced by it in elms and other trees.

Barreno [bar-ray'-no], *m.* 1. A large borer or auger. 2. Hole made with a borer, auger, or gimlet; blast-hole. 3. (Met.) Vanity, ostentation. *Dar barreno,* (Naut.) To bore and sink a ship.

Barreño [bar-ray'-nyo], *m.* 1. Earthen pan. 2. A tub.

Barrer [bar-rerr'], *va.* 1. To sweep. 2. (Met.) To carry off the whole of what there was in a place. *Barrer un navío de popa a proa,* (Naut.) To rake a ship fore and aft. *Al barrer,* On an average. (Com.)

Barrera [bar-ray'-rah], *f.* 1. Clay-pit. 2. Barrier, circular paling within which bull-feasts are performed. 3. Mound or heap of earth from which saltpetre is extracted. 4. Cupboard with shelves where crockery-ware is kept. 5. Barricade, barrier, parapet. 6. Barrier, a bar to mark the limits of a place. 7. Toll-gate, barrier, turnpike. *Barrera antiaérea,* Flak. *Barrera sónica,* Sonic barrier. *Salir a barrera,* (Met.) To expose one's self to public censure.

Barrero [bar-ray'-ro], *m.* 1. Potter. 2. (Prov.) Height, eminence, a high ridge of hills. 3. Clay-pit.

Barreta [bar-ray'-tah], *f.* 1. (Dim.) Small bar. 2. Lining of a shoe. 3. (Obs.) Helmet, casque. *Barretas,* Pieces of iron which hold the bows of a saddle together.

Barretear [bar-ray-tay-ar'], *va.* 1. To fasten a thing with bars. 2. To line the inside of a shoe.

Barretero [bar-ray-tay'-ro], *m.* In mining, one who works with a crow, wedge, or pick.

Barretón [bar-ray-tone'], *m. aug.* Large bar.

Barriada [bar-re-ah'-dah], *f.* Suburb, district or precinct of a city: applied frequently to a part of a suburb.

Barrial [bar-re-ahl'], *m.* *V.* Lodazal. A muddy spot.

Barrica [bar-ree'-cah], *f.* A cask containing sixty gallons.

Barricada [bar-re-cah'-dah], *f.* Barricado, a collection of barrels or beams to form a cover like a parapet.

Barrido [bar-ree'-do], *m.* Sweep, the act of sweeping.—*pp.* of Barrer.

Barriga [bar-ree'-gah], *f.* 1. Abdomen, belly. 2. Pregnancy, state of being pregnant. 3. Middle part of a vessel where it swells out into a larger capacity. 4. *V.* Comba. *Estar, hallarse, con la barriga a la boca,* To be near confinement. *Tener la barriga a la boca,* (Coll.) To be big with child. *Volverse la albarda a la barriga,* To be frustrated in one's wishes and expectations.

Barrigón [bar-re-gone'], *m. aug.* Pot-belly, a big belly.

Barrigudo, da [bar-re-goo'-do, dah], *a.* Big-bellied, pot-bellied.

Barriguilla [bar-re-geel'-lyah], *f. dim.* A little belly.

Barril [bar-reel'], *m.* 1. Barrel. 2. Jug. 3. (Naut.) Water-cask.

Barrilame, *m.* **Barrilería,** *f.* [bar-re-lah'-may, bar-re-lay-ree'-ah]. A number of barrels collected in one place; stock of casks.

Barrilejo [bar-re-lay'-ho], *m.* *dim.* Rundlet, a small barrel.

Barrilero [bar-re-lay'-ro], *m.* One who makes barrels, cooper.

Barrilete [bar-re-lay'-tay], *m.* 1. Hold-fast, dog, clamp. 2. (Naut.) Mouse. 3. (Zool.) A crab covered with prickles. *Barrilete de estay,* The mouse of a stay. *Barrilete de remo,* The mouse of an oar. *Barrilete de virador,* The mouse of a voyol. *Barrilete de banco,* Hold-fast, a tool used by joiners, to keep their stuff steady. 4. (Dim.) Keg. 5. (Prov.) Kite.

Barrilico, illo, ito [bar-re-lee'-co, eel'-lyo, ee'-to], *m. dim.* Keg, rundlet, a small barrel, firkin.

Barrilla [bar-reel'-lyah], *f.* 1. (Dim.) A little bar. 2. A rod. 3. (Bot.) Salt-wort, glass-wort, an herb. *Barrilla fina,* Cultivated salt-wort. Salsola sativa. *Barrilla borde,* Prickly salt-wort. Salsola kali. *Barrilla salicor,* Long fleshy-leaved salt-wort. Salsola soda. *Barrilla carambillo* or *caramillo,* Small-leaved salt-wort. Salsola vermiculata. *Barrilla escobilla,* Tamarisk-leaved salt-wort. Salsola tamariscifolia. *Cavanilles.* 4. Impure soda, called in commerce barilla, a mineral alkali extracted from plants belonging to the genus *Salicornia.* *Barrilla de Alicante,* (Com.) Spanish or Alicante soda.

Barrillar [bar-reel-lyar'], *m.* Barilla-pits, where the plants, from which the barilla is extracted, are burnt, and collected at the bottom in a stony mass, called *rocheta;* it is the barilla ashes of commerce.

Barrio [bar'-re-o], *m.* 1. One of the districts or wards into which a large town or city is divided. 2. Suburb. *Andar de barrio* or *vestido de barrio,* To wear a plain, simple dress.

Barriquita [bar-re-kee'-tah], *f.* A cask.

Barrita [bar-ree'-tah], *f. dim.* 1. A small bar. 2. A small keg.

Barrizal [bar-re-thahl'], *m.* Clay-pit, a place full of clay and mud.

Barro [bar'-ro], *m.* 1. Clay, mud. 2. Earthenware. 3. Drinking-vessel of different shapes and colours, made of sweet-scented clay; sugar-clay. 4. Lock of wool put into the comb. *Dar* or *tener barro a mano,* To have money or the necessary means to do a thing.—*pl.* 1. Red pustules or pimples in the faces of young persons. 2. Fleshy tumours growing on the skin of horses or mules.

Barrocho, *m.* *V.* Birlocho.

Barroso, sa [bar-ro'-so, sah], *a.* 1. Muddy, full of mire. *Camino barroso,* Muddy road. 2. Pimpled, full of pimples called *barros.* 3. Reddish: applied to oxen.

Barrote [bar-ro'-tay], *m.* 1. Iron bar with which tables are made fast. 2. Ledge of timber laid across other timbers. *Barrotes,* (Naut.) Battens, scantlings, or ledges of stuff, which serve for many purposes on board a ship. *Barrotes de las escotillas,* Battens of the hatches.

Barrotines [bar-ro-tee'-nes], *m. pl.* *Barrotines de los baos,* (Naut.) Carlings or carlines. *Barrotines o baos de la toldilla,* (Naut.) Carling knees, or the beams of the stern.

Barrueco [bar-roo-ay'-co], *m.* Pear of irregular form.

Barrumbada [bar-room-bah'-dah], *f.* 1. (Coll.) Great and ostentatious expense. 2. Boastful saying.

Barruntador, ra [bar-roon-tah-dor', rah], *m. & f.* Conjecturer, one who guesses by signs and tokens.

Barruntamiento [bar-roon-tah-me-en'-to], *m.* The act of conjecturing or guessing by signs and tokens.

Barruntar [bar-roon-tar'], *va.* To foresee or conjecture (by signs or tokens); to guess, have a presentiment.

Barrunte [bar-roon'-tay], *m.* *V.* Noticia.

Barrunto [bar-roon'-to], *m.* Conjecture, the act of conjecturing.

Bartola [bar-to'-lah], *f.* (Coll.) Belly. *A la bartola,* On the back, in lazy fashion; careless.

Bartolillo [bar-to-leel'-lyo], *m.* A little meat pie, in triangular form.

Bártulos [bar'-too-los], *m. pl.* (Coll.) Tools, affairs or business.

Baruca [bah-roo'-cah], *f.* Artifice, cunning, deceit.

Barulé [bah-roo-lay'], *m.* (Obs. F. bas roulé.) The upper part of the stockings rolled over the knee, as was anciently the fashion.

Barullo [bah-rool'-lyo], *m.* Confusion, disorder, tumult.

Barzón [bar-thone'], *m.* 1. (Prov.) Idle walk. 2. The strap with which oxen are yoked to the plough-beam.

Barzonear [bar-tho-nay-ar'], *vn.* (Prov.) To loiter about without a certain design.

Basa [bah'-sah], *f.* 1. Basis or pedestal of a column or statue, base. 2. (Met.) Basis or foundation of a thing.

Basácula [bah-sah'-coo-lah], *f.* Locker of the thumb-plate in a stocking-frame.

Basáltico, ca [bah-sahl'-te-co], *a.* Basaltic, of basalt.

Basalto [bah-sahl'-to], *m.* Basalt, basaltes, a kind of stone.

Basamento [bah-sah-men'-to], *m.* (Arch.) Basement, base and pedestal.

Basar [bah-sar'], *va.* 1. To fix, establish, secure upon a base. 2. To rest upon, set up a theory. 3. To start from a fixed base-line.

Basca [bahs'-cah], *f.* Squeamishness inclination to vomit, nausea.

Bascosidad [bas-co-se-dahd'], *f.* Uncleanliness, nastiness, filth.

Báscula [bahs'-coo-lah], *f.* 1. Lever, pole, staff. 2. Platform-scale.

Base [bah'-say], *f.* 1. Base, basis;

ground, foot, footing; groundwork. 2. Chief or ground colour, the principal colour used in dyeing any stuff. *Base de distinción*, Focus of glasses convex on both sides. 3. Base-line in surveying. 4. (Mus.) Bass or base. 5. (Chem.) In any combination the most electro-positive element.

Basilica [bah-see'-le-cah], *f.* 1. Royal or imperial palace. 2. Public hall where courts of justice hold their sittings. 3. (Anat.) Basilica. 4. Basilica, large and magnificent church, especially of Rome.

Basilicón [bah-se-le-cone'], *m.* (Med.) Basilicon, an ointment, resin salve.

Basilio, lia [bah-see'-le-o, ah], *a.* Basilian, monk or nun of the order of St. Basil.

Basilisco [bah-se-lees'-co], *m.* 1. Basilisk, cockatrice, a fabulous kind of serpent. 2. Basilisk, an ancient piece of artillery.

Basketbol [bas-ket-bol'], *m.* Basketball.

Basquear [bas-kay-ar'], *vn.* To be squeamish, or inclined to vomit.

Basquilla [bas-keel'-lyah], *f.* Disease in sheep, arising from plenitude of blood.

Basquiña [bas-kee'-nyah], *f.* Upper petticoat worn by Spanish women.

Basta [bahs'-tah], *adv.* Enough; halt, stop.

Basta [bahs'-tah], *f.* Stitch made by tailors to keep clothes even, basting. *Bastas*, Stitches put into a mattress at certain distances to form a quilt.

Bastaje [bas-tah'-hay], *m.* Porter, carrier.

Bastante [bas-tahn'-tay], *adv.* 1. Sufficient, enough, competent. 2. Not a little.

Bastantemente [bas-tan-tay-men'-tay], *adv.* Sufficiently.

Bastantero [bas-tan-tay'-ro], *m.* In the chancery of Valladolid, and other Spanish courts, an officer appointed to examine into the powers of attorney presented, whether they are sufficient, and drawn up in a legal form.

Bastar [bas-tar'], *vn.* To suffice, to be proportioned to something, to be enough.

Bastarda [bas-tar'-dah], *f.* 1. Bastard file. 2. (Obs.) Piece of ordnance. 3. (Naut.) Bastard, a lateen main-sail. 4. (Print.) Italic, a type. 5. *a.* A pack-saddle.

Bastardear [bas-tar-day-ar'], *vn.* 1. To degenerate, to fall from its kind: applied to animals and plants. 2. (Met.) To fall from the virtues of our ancestors, or the nobleness of our birth. 3. To bastardize, or to bastard.

Bastardelo [bas-tar-day'-lo], *m.* (Prov.) Draft-book of a notary, which contains the minutes or first drafts of acts, deeds, instruments, etc.; blotter. *V.* MINUTARIO.

Bastardia [bas-tar-dee'-ah], *f.* 1. Bastardy, state of being born out of wedlock. 2. (Met.) Speech or action unbecoming the birth or character of a gentleman; meanness.

Bastardilla [bas-tar-deel'-lyah], *f.* 1. (Obs.) A kind of flute. 2. (Print.) Italic, a type.

Bastardo, da [bas-tar'-do, dah], *a.* 1. Bastard, spurious, degenerating from its kind and original qualities. 2. Bastard, illegitimate. 3. Bastard, a type having a face smaller or larger than proper for its body.

Bastardo [bas-tar'-do], *m.* 1. Bastard, a son born out of wedlock. 2. Boa, a short, thick-bodied, and very poisonous snake. *Bastardo de un racamento*, (Naut.) Parrel rope.

Baste [bahs'-tay], *m.* (Prov.) *V.* BASTO.

Bastear [bas-tay-ar'], *va.* To baste, to stitch loosely, to sew slightly.

Bastero [bas-tay'-ro], *m.* One who makes or retails pack-saddles.

Bastida [bas-tee'-dah], *f.* (Obs.) An ancient warlike engine for covering approaches.

Bastidor [bas-te-dor'], *m.* 1. Frame for stretching linen, silk, etc., which is to be painted, embroidered, or quilted. 2. Frame, sash, panel. 3. A frame through which passes the shaft of a screw propeller. 4. Linen stretched in frames: applied to the painted linen used on the sides of the stage to represent the scene. 5. (Phot.) Carrier, for films; plate-holder. *Bastidores*, (Naut.) Frames for canvas bulkheads, provisional cabins, and other temporary compartments. *Bastidos* or *bastidores*, (On the stage) Scenery.

Bastilla [bas-teel'-lyah], *f.* Hem, the edge of cloth doubled and sewed.

Bastillar [bas-teel-lyar'], *va.* To hem.

Bastimentar [bas-te-men-tar'], *va.* To victual, to supply with provisions.

Bastimento [bas-te-men'-to], *m.* 1. Supply of provisions for a city or army. 2. (Obs.) Building, structure 3. (Obs.) Thread with which a mattress is quilted. 4. (Naut.) Vessel. *Bastimentos*, First fruits, in the military order of *Santiago* or St. James.

Bastión [bas-te-on'], *m.* *V.* BALUARTE.

Basto [bahs'-to], *m.* 1. Pack-saddle for beasts of burden. 2. Pad. 3. Ace of clubs in several games of cards. *Bastos*, Clubs, one of the four suits at cards.

Basto, ta [bahs'-to, tah], *a.* 1. Coarse, rude, unpolished, unhewn, clumsy, gross, rugged; cyclopean; linsey-woolsey. 2. Home-spun, clownish.

Bastón [bas-tone'], *m.* 1. Cane or stick with a head or knob to lean upon; gad. 2. Truncheon, a staff of command. 3. (Met.) Military command. 4. Among silk-weavers, the roller of a silk-frame which contains the stuff. 5. Carrot of snuff, weighing about three pounds. 6. (Arch.) Fluted moulding. *Dar bastón*, To stir must with a stick, to prevent its being ropy. *Bastones*, (Her.) Bars in a shield.

Bastonada [bas-to-nah'-dah], *f.* **Bastonazo** [bas-to-nah'-tho], *m.* Bastinado, stroke or blow given with a stick or cane.

Bastoncillo [bas-ton-theel'-lyo], *m.* 1. (Dim.) Small cane or stick. 2. Narrow lace for trimming clothes.

Bastonear [bas-to-nay-ar'], *va.* To stir must with a stick to prevent its becoming ropy.

Bastonero [bas-to-nay'-ro], *m.* 1. Cane-maker or seller. 2. Marshal or manager of a ball, steward of a feast. 3. Assistant jail-keeper.

Basura [bah-soo'-rah], *f.* 1. Sweepings, filth swept away. 2. Dung, manure, ordure, excrement used to manure the ground; off-scouring.

Basurero [bah-soo-ray'-ro], *m.* 1. Dustman, he who carries dung to the field. 2. Dust-pan. 3. Dung-yard, dung-hill.

Bata [bah'-tah], *f.* 1. Dressing-gown, wrapper; a loose gown used for an undress. 2. Refuse of silk. 3. A lady's dress with a train.

Bata [bah'-tah], *m.* An Asiatic of minor age in the Philippine Islands.

Batacazo [bah-tah-cah'-tho], *m.* Violent contusion from a fall.

Batahola [bah-tah-oh'-lah], *f.* Hurley-burley, bustle, clamour, clutter, hubbub.

Batalla [bah-tahl'-lyah], *f.* 1. Battle, the contest, conflict, or engagement of one army with another; fight, combat. 2. (Obs.) Centre of an army, in contradistinction to the van and rear. 3. Fencing with foils. 4. (Met.) Struggle or agitation of the mind. 5. (Art) Battle-piece, a painting which represents a battle. 6. Joust, tournament. *Campo de batalla*, Field of battle. *Cuerpo de batalla de una escuadra*, The centre division of a fleet. *En batalla*, (Mil.) With an extended front.

Batallador, ra [bah-tal-lyah-dor', rah], *m.* & *f.* 1. Battler, combatant; warrior. 2. Fencer with foils.

Batallar [bah-tal-lyar'], *vn.* 1. To battle, to fight, to be engaged in battle. 2. To fence with foils. 3. (Met.) To contend, to argue, to dispute.

Batallón [bah-tal-yone'], *m.* Battalion, a division of infantry.

Batán [bah-tahn'], *m.* Fulling-mill where cloth is fulled, or cleansed from oil and grease. *Batanes*, A boyish play of striking the soles of the feet, hands, etc.

Batanar [bah-tah-nar'], *va.* To full cloth.

Batanear [bah-tah-nay-ar'], *va.* (Coll.) To bang or beat, to handle roughly.

Batanero [bah-tah-nay'-ro], *m.* Fuller, a clothier.

Batanga [bah-tahn'-gah], *f.* An outrigger of bamboo applied to boats in the Philippine Islands.

Batata [bah-tah'-tah], *f.* (Bot.) Spanish potato, or sweet potato of Malaga, yam. Convolvulus batatas, *L.*

Bátavo, va [bah'-tah-vo, vah], *a.* 1. Batavian, relating to ancient Batavia, or the Netherlands, now Holland. 2. Of Batavia, in Java.

Batayola [bah-tah-yo'-lah], *f.* (Naut.) Rail. *Batayolas de los empalletados*, (Naut.) Quarter-netting rails. *Batayolas de las cofas*, (Naut.) Top-rails. *Batayolas del pasamano*, (Naut.) Gangway rails.

Batea [bah-tay'-ah], *f.* 1. Painted tray or hamper of japanned wood which comes from the East Indies. 2. Trough for bathing the hands and feet. 3. Boat made in the form of a trough, punt.

Bateador, ra [bah-tay-ah-dor', rah], *m.* & *f.* 1. (Sports) Batter, hitter. 2. (Mech.) Tamper.—*f.* Power tamper.

Batear [bah-tay-ar'], *va.* & *vn.* (Sports) 1. To bat, to hit. 2. (Mech.) To tamp.

Batei [bah-tay'-e], *m.* (Cuba) 1. A grass-plot. 2. *V.* BATEY.

Batel [bah-tel'], *m.* (Obs.) Small vessel.

Bateo [bah-tay'-o], *m.* *V.* BAUTIZO.

Batería [bah-tay-ree'-ah], *f.* 1. Battery, a number of pieces of ordnance arranged to play upon the enemy; also, the work in which they are placed. *Batería a barbeta*, A barbet battery. *Batería enterrada*, A sunk battery. *Batería a rebote*, A ricochet battery. *Batería cruzante*, Cross battery. *Batería de cocina*, Kitchen furniture. 2. (Naut.) Tier or range of guns on one side of a ship. *Batería entera de una banda*, (Naut.) A broadside. *Navío de batería florada*, (Naut.) A ship which carries her ports at a proper height out of the water. 3. (Met.) Repeated importunities. 4. Battery, the act and effect of battering. 5. (Met.) Any thing which makes a strong impression on the mind.

Batero, ra [bah-tay'-ro, rah], *m.* & *f.* Mantua-maker, one whose trade is to make gowns.

Batey [bah-tay'], *m.* 1. Machinery and appurtenances for sugar-making. 2. Premises surrounding a sugar mill in the West Indies.

Batiborriiio [bah-te-bor-reel'-lyo], *m. V.* BATIBURRILLO.

Baticola [bah-te-co'-lah], *f.* Crupper.

Batida [bah-tee'-dah], *f.* 1. A hunting-party for chasing wild animals; battue. 2. Noise made by huntsmen to cheer the hounds and rouse the game.

Batidera [bah-te-day'-rah], *f.* 1. Beater, an instrument used by plasterers and bricklayers for beating and mixing mortar. 2. An instrument used by glass-makers for stirring the sand and ashes in melting-pots. 3. Batlet. 4. Batting arm, scutcher. 5. Flap of a churn. 6. Small instrument for cutting honey-combs from the hives.

Batidero [bah-te-day'-ro], *m.* 1. Collision, the clashing of one thing against another. 2. Uneven ground, which renders the motion of carriages unpleasant. *Guardar los batideros*, To drive carefully in broken roads. *Guardar batideros*, (Met.) To guard against inconveniences. 3. (Naut.) Wash-board. *Batidero de una vela*, Foot-tabling of a sail. *Batidero de proa*, Wash-board of the cut-water.

Batido, da [bah-tee'-do, dah], *a.* 1. Changeable; shot, chatoyant: applied to silks. 2. Beaten, as roads.—*pp.* of BATIR.

Batido [bah-tee'-do], *m.* Batter of flour and water for making the host, wafers, or biscuits.

Batidor [bah-te-dor'], *m.* 1. Scout, one who is sent to explore the condition of the enemy, and the condition of the roads. 2. Ranger, one who rouses the game in the forest. 3. One of the life-guards, who rides before a royal coach. 4. An out-rider. 5. Leather-beater. 6. Stirring-rod. 7. (Naut.) Strengthening line. *Batidor de cáñamo*, A hemp-dresser. *Batidor de oro o plata*, A gold or silver beater.

Batiente [bah-te-en'-tay], *m.* 1. Jamb or post of a door. 2. Leaf of a folding-door. 3. Port-sill. 4. Hammer of a pianoforte. 5. Spot where the sea beats against the shore or a dike. *Batiente de la bandera*, (Naut.) Fly of an ensign. *Batiente de un dique*, Apron of a dock.—*pa.* of BATIR.

Batifulla [bah-te-fool'-lyah], *m.* (Prov.) *V.* BATIHOJA.

Batihoja [bah-te-o'-hah], *m.* 1. Gold-beater. 2. Artisan who works iron and other metals into sheets. 3. Warp of cloth which crosses the woof.

Batimiento [bah-te-me-en'-to], *m.* (Obs.) 1. The act and effect of beating. 2. The thing beaten.

Batin [bah-teen'], *m.* A morning gown.

Batintin [bah-tin-teen'], *m.* A gong used on Chinese junks.

Bationdeo [bah-te-on-day'-o], *m.* The fluttering of a banner, or curtain, caused by the wind.

Batiportar [bah-te-por-tar'], *va.* (Naut.) To house a gun on board a ship, to secure it by tackles and breechings.

Batiportes [bah-te-por'-tes], *m.pl.* Port-sills.

Batir [bah-teer'], *va.* 1. To beat, to dash, to strike two bodies together. 2. To clash, to clout, to clap. 3. To demolish, to raze, to throw down. 4. To move in a violent manner. 5. In paper-mills, to fit and adjust the reams of paper already made up. 6. To strike or fall on without injury: spoken of the sun or wind. *El cierzo bate a Madrid*, The north wind blows on Madrid. *Batir banderas*, To salute with the colours: (Naut.) to strike the colours. *Batir el campo*, (Mil.) To reconnoitre the enemy's camp. *Batir moneda*, To coin money. *Batir las olas*, To ply the seas. *Batir las cataratas* or *nubes de los ojos*, To couch. *Batir hoja*, To foliate, or to beat metals into leaves or plates.—*vr.* 1. To lose courage, to decline in health or strength. *V.* ABATIRSE. 2. (Met.) *Batirse el cobre*, To toil hard for useful purposes.

Batiscafo [bah-tees'-cah-fo], *m.* Bathyscaphe.

Batista [bah-tees'-tah], *f.* Batiste, the finest cambric or lawn.

Bato [bah'-to], *m.* A rustic, simpleton.

Batojar [bah-to-har'], *va.* (Prov.) To beat down the fruit of a tree.

Batología [bah-to-lo-hee'-ah], *f.* Battology, needless repetition.

Batracios [bah-trah'-the-ose], *m. pl.* Batrachians, aquatic amphibians like the frog.

Batucar [bah-too-car'], *va.* To beat liquors and other things; to mix things by agitation.

Batuecas [bah-too-ay'-cahs], *f.* A district in the southern part of the province of Salamanca; rough and uncultivated.

Batueco, ca [bah-too-ay'-co, cah], *a.* Belonging to Batuecas; simple, ignorant.

Baturrillo [bah-toor-reel'-lyo], *m.* 1. Hodge-podge, hotch-potch, mash, salmagundi, a medley altogether suitable. 2. (Met.) Mixture of unconnected and incongruous ideas.

Batuta [bah-too'-tah], *f.* (It.) A conductor's wand; baton.

Baúl [bah-ool'], *m.* 1. Trunk, a chest for clothes. 2. Belly. *Llenar el baúl*, (Low) To fill the paunch.

Bauprés [bah-oo-press'], *m.* (Naut.) Bowsprit. *Botalón del bauprés*, The bowsprit boom.

Bausán, na [bah-oo-sahn', nah], *m. & f.* 1. Manikin, effigy; image or likeness. 2. Fool, idiot, bayard. 3. (Naut.) Bowsprit. 4. Down, downy hair.

Bautismal [bah-oo-tis-mahl'], *a.* Baptismal.

Bautismo [bah-oo-tees'-mo], *m.* 1. Baptism. 2. (Naut.) Ducking.

Bautisterio [bah-oo-tis-tay'-re-o], *m.* Baptistery.

Bautizante [bah-oo-te-thahn'-tay], *pa.* Baptizing, christening.

Bautizar [bah-oo-te-thar'], *va.* 1. To baptize, to christen. 2. (Naut.) To duck seamen in those seas where they have not been before. *Bautizar un bajel*, To give a name to a ship. *Bautizar el vino*, To mix water with wine.

Bautizo [bah-oo-tee'-tho], *m.* Baptism.

Bauxita [bah-ook-see'-tah], *f.* Bauxite, a mineral.

Bávaro, ra [bah'-vah-ro, rah], *a.* Bavarian.

Baya [bah'-yah], *f.* 1. Berry, any small fruit with seeds or stones. *V.* VAINA. 2. (Prov.) Pole used to separate horses in a stable.

Bayal [bah-yahl'], *a.* Not steeped or soaked: applied to flax.

Bayal [bah-yahl'], *m.* Lever used in raising mill-stones.

Bayeta [bah-yay'-tah], *f.* Baize, a sort of flannel. 2. Blanket in typography. *Bayeta de alconcher*, Colchester baize. *Bayeta fajuela*, Lancashire baize. *Bayeta miniquina*, Long baize. *Bayeta del sur* or *de cien hilos*, White list baize. *Bayeta fina*, Swanskin. *Arrastrar bayetas*, To claim a degree in superior colleges, the claimants whereof are obliged to visit the college in wide loose gowns, with a train of baize. *Arrastrar bayetas*, (Met.) To enforce a claim with care and assiduity.—*pl.* 1. Pall, the covering of he dead. 2. In paper-mills, felts used in the manufacture of paper.

Bayetón [bah-yay-tone'], *m.* Coating. *Bayetón moteado*, Spotted coating. *Bayetón de nubes*, Clouded coating. *Bayetón rayado*, Striped coating. *Bayetón común*, Coarse baize.

Bayo, ya [bah'-yo, yah], *a.* Bay, inclining to a chestnut colour: spoken of a horse.—*m.* Brown butterfly used in angling.

Bayoco [bah-yo'-co], *m.* 1. Copper coin current in Rome and other parts of Italy. 2. (Prov.) Unripe or withered fig.

Bayón [bah-yone'], *m.* Sack of matting for baling.

Bayona (Arda) [ar'-dah bah-yo'nah], *adv.* The little care an exhibition or festival gives to those whom it costs nothing, compared with those whom it costs much.

Bayoneta [bah-yo-nay'-tah], *f.* Bayonet. *Bayoneta calada*, A fixed bayonet.

Bayonetazo [bah-yo-nay-tah'-tho], *m.* Thrust with a bayonet.

Bayuca [bah-yoo'-cah], *f.* Tippling-house; tavern. (Coll.)

Baza [bah'-thah], *f.* 1. Trick at cards *No dejar meter baza*, Not to suffer another to put in a single word. *Tener bien asentada su baza*, To have one's character well established. 2. (Naut.) Oozy ground.

Bazar [bah-thar'], *m.* Bazaar, market-place.

Bazo [bah'-tho], *m.* Spleen or milt.

Bazo, za [bah'-tho, thah], *a.* Brown inclining to yellow. *Pan bazo*, Brown bread.

Bazofia [bah-tho'-fe-ah], *f.* 1. Offal, waste meat. 2. Refuse, thing of no value, remnants. 3. Hogwash.

Bazucar [bah-thoo-car'], *va.* 1. To stir liquids by shaking. 2. To dash.

Bazuqueo [bah-thoo-kay'-o], *m.* The act of stirring liquids by shaking; jumble.

Be [bay'], *m.* Baa, the cry of sheep.—*f.* The name of the second letter, B.

Bearnés, esa [bay-ar-ness', nay'-sah], *a.* Of Berne, in Switzerland, Bernese.

Beata [bay-ah'-tah], *f.* 1. Woman who wears a religious habit, and is engaged in works of charity. 2. Female hypocrite.

Beatería [bay-ah-tay-ree'-ah], *f.* (Iron.) Act of affected piety; bigotry.

Beaterio [bay-ah-tay'-re-o], *m.* House inhabited by pious women.

Beatico, ca [bay-ah-tee'co, cah], *m. & f. dim.* Hypocrite.

Beatificación [bay-ah-te-fe-cah-the-on'], *f.* Beatification.

Beatificamente [bay-ah-tee'-fe-cah-men-tay], *adv.* Beatifically.

Beatificar [bay-ah-te-fe-car'], *va.* 1. To beatify. 2. To render a thing respectable.

Beatífico, ca [bay-ah-tee'-fe-co, cah], *a.* (Theology) Beatific, beatifical.

Beatilla [bay-ah-teel'-lyah], *f.* A sort of fine linen.

Beatísimo, ma [bay-ah-tee'-se-mo, mah], *a. sup. Beatísimo padre*, Most holy father: applied to the Pope.

Beatitud [bay-ah-te-tood'], *f.* 1. Beatitude, blessedness. 2. Holiness, a title given to the Pope.

Beato, ta [bay-ah'-to, tah], *a.* 1. Happy, blessed; beatified. 2. Wearing a religious habit without being a member of a religious community. 3. Devout.

Beato, ta [bay-ah'-to, tah], *m. & f.* 1. A pious person abstaining from public diversions. 2. One who lives in pious retirement, and wears a religious dress.

Beatón, na [bay-ah-tone', nah], *m.* & *f.* Hypocrite, bigot.

Bebedero [bay-bay-day'-ro], *m.* 1. Drinking vessel for birds and domestic animals; drawer of a bird-cage. 2. A drinking trough for beasts. 3. Place whither fowls resort to drink. 4. Gate hole, jet. *Bebederos*, Strips of cloth used by tailors for lining clothes; facing.

Bebedero, ra, Bebedizo, za [bay-bay-day'-ro, rah, bay-bay-dee'-tho, thah], *a.* Potable, drinkable.

Bebedizo [bay-bay-dee'-tho], *m.* 1. Philter or love potion. 2. A physical potion, a drench.

Bébedo, da [bay'-bay-do, dah], *a.* (Prov.) Drunk, intoxicated.

Bebedor, ra [bay-bay-dor', rah], *m.* & *f.* Tippler, toper.

Beber [bay-berr'], *va.* 1. To drink. 2. To pledge, to toast. *Beber a la salud de alguno*, To drink to another's health. *Sin comerlo ni beberlo*, To suffer an injury without having had any part in the cause or motive of it. *Beber de codos*, To drink at leisure and luxuriously *Beber las palabras, los acentos, los semblantes*, or *las acciones a otro*, To listen with the greatest care, to swallow or adopt the speech, accent, features, and actions of another. *Beber los pensamientos a alguno*, To anticipate one's thoughts. *Beber los vientos*, To solicit with much eagerness. *Le quisiera beber la sangre*, I would drink his heart's blood. *Beber como una cuba*, To drink as a fish. *Do entra beber, sale saber*, Excess in drinking dulls the understanding. *Beber en las fuentes*, To obtain information at headquarters, or first hand. *Beber el pilón*, To believe current rumours. *Beber los sesos*, To bewitch. *Beber fresco*, To be tranquil.

Beberrón [bay-ber-rone'], *m.* (Littl. us.) Tippler, malt-worm, low drunkard.

Bebida [bay-bee'-dah], *f.* 1. Drink, beverage, potion. 2. (Prov.) The time allowed to workmen to drink and refresh themselves in the intervals of labour.

Bebido, da [bay-bee'-do, dah], *pp.* of BEBER.—*a.* Applied to an intoxicated person. *Bien bebido*, Drunk.—*m.* & *f.* 1. Drench or physical potion for brutes. 2. (Obs.) *V.* BEBIDA.

Bebistrajo [bay-bis-trah'-ho], *m.* (Coll.) An irregular and extravagant mixture of drinks; cat-lap.

Beborrotear [bay-bor-ro-tay-ar'], *va.* (Coll.) To sip.

Beca [bay'-cah], *f.* 1. Part of a collegian's dress worn over the gown. 2. Fellowship, pension, an establishment in a college. 3. Fellow or member of a college, who shares its revenue. 4. Tippet worn formerly by the dignitaries of the church. *Beca de merced*, Scholarship. *Becas*, Strips of velvet, satin, etc., with which cloaks are faced.

Becabunga [bay-cah-boon'-gah], *f.* (Bot.) Brook-lime. Veronica becabunga.

Becada [bay-cah'-dah], *f.* (Orn.) Woodcock. *V.* CHOCHA.

Becafigo [bay-cah-fee'-go], *m.* (Orn.) Fig-pecker, epicurean warbler. Motacilla ficedula. *Becafigo raro*, (Orn.) Great red-pole, or red-headed linnet. Fringilla cannabina. *V.* PAPAFIGO.

Becardón [bay-car-done'], *m.* (Prov.) Snipe. *V.* AGACHADIZA.

Becerra [bay-therr'-rah], *f.* 1. (Bot.) Snap-dragon. *V.* ANTIRRINO MAYOR. 2. Earth and stones swept down by mountain floods.

Becerril [be-ther-reel'], *a.* Bovine; calf, as adjective.

Becerrillo, illa, ito, ita [bay-ther-reel'-lyo, lyah, ee'-to, ee'-tah], *m.* & *f. dim.* 1. Calf. 2. Tanned and dressed calf-skin.

Becerro, ra [bay-therr'-ro, rah], *m.* & *f.* 1. A yearling calf. 2. Calf-skin tanned and dressed. *Becerros barnizados*, Varnished calf-skins. *Becerros charolados*, Patent leather calf-skins. 3. Register in which are entered the privileges and appurtenances of cathedral churches and convents. 4. Manuscript bound in calf-skin, and found in the archives of Simancas, containing an account of the origin and titles of the Spanish nobility. *Becerro marino*, A sea-calf, the seal.

Becoquín [bay-co-keen'], *m.* Cap tied under the chin.

Becuadrado [bay-coo-ah-drah'-do], *m.* The first property in plain song, or Gregorian mode.

Becuadro [bay-coo-ah'-dro], *m.* (Music) A natural; the sign ♮.

Bedel [bay-del'], *m.* 1. Beadle, an officer in universities, whose business it is to inspect the conduct of the students. 2. Warden. 3. Apparitor of a court of justice.

Bedelía [bay-day-lee'-ah], *f.* Beadleship, wardenship.

Bedelio [bay-day'-le-o], *m.* Bdellium, an aromatic gum.

Beduino, na [bay-doo-ee'-no, nah], *a.* 1. Bedouin, Arab of the desert. 2. Harsh, uncivil.

Befa [bay'-fah], *f.* 1. Irrision, jeer, scoff, mock, taunt.

Befabemí [bay-fah-bay-mee'], *m.* A musical sign.

Befar [bay-far'], *va.* 1. To mock, to scoff, to ridicule, to jeer, to laugh at. 2. To move the lips, and endeavour to catch the chain of the bit: applied to horses.

Befo, fa [bay'-fo, fah], *a.* 1. Blubber-lipped. 2. Bandy-legged.

Befo [bay'-fo], *m.* 1. Lip of a horse or other animal. 2. (Obs.) A person with thick, projecting under lip and bandy legs.

Begardo, da [bay-gar'-do, dah], *m.* & *f.* Beggardus, heretic of the 13th century.

Begonia [bay-go'-ne-ah], *f.* (Bot.) Begonia.

Beguino, na [bay-gee'-no, nah], *m.* & *f.* Beguin, heretic of the 14th century.

Behetría [bay-ay-tree'-ah], *f.* 1. (Obs.) A town whose inhabitants were free from the subjection of any lord. 2. Confusion, disorder. *Lugar de behetría*, A place where perfect equality prevails.

Beisbol [base'-ball], *m.* Baseball.

Bejarano, na [bay-hah-rah'-no, nah], *a.* Of Béjar. (Coll.) Old.

Bejín [bay-heen'], *m.* 1. (Bot.) Puff, common puff-ball, fuzz-ball. Lycoperdon bovista. 2. Whining, peevish child. 3. One who is angry over trifles.

Bejinero [bay-he-nay'-ro], *m.* (Prov.) One who separates the lees or watery sediment from the oil.

Bejucal [bay-hoo-cahl'], *m.* A place where reeds grow.

Bejuco [bay-hoo'-co], *m.* 1. Thin or pliable reed or cane growing in India. 2. Filaments growing on some trees in America.

Bejuquillo [bay-hoo-keel'-lyo], *m.* 1. A small gold chain of Chinese manufacture. 2. Root of a Brazilian plant called ipecacuanha. 3. A rattan.

Belcho [bel'-cho], *m.* (Bot.) Great ephedra, or horsetail-tree. Ephedra listachia.

Beldad [bel-dahd'], *f.* Beauty: at present applied only to the beauty of women. *Una beldad*, Fair, a beauty, elliptically for a fair woman.

Belduque [bel-doo'-kay], *m.* A large heavy knife (Mexico).

Beledín [bay-lay-deen'], *m.* Sort of cotton stuff.

Belemnita [bay-lem-nee'-tah], *f.* Belemnites, arrow-head or finger-stone.

Belén [bay-len'], *m.* 1. Birth. 2. Confusion, bedlam. 3. Bethlehem; hence bedlam.

Beleño [bay-lay'-nyo], *m.* 1. (Bot.) Henbane. Hyoscyamus. *Beleño negro*, Common hen-bane. Hyoscyamus niger. *Beleño blanco*, Hyoscyamus albus. 2. Poison.

Belérico [bay-lay'-re-co], *m.* (Bot.) The fruit and the tree of a kind of myrobalan. *V.* MIRABOLANOS.

Belfo, fa [bel'-fo, fah], *a.* Blob-lipped, or blubber-lipped. *Diente belfo*, Snag tooth, a tooth which projects.

Belfo [bel'-fo], *m.* Thick under lip of a horse.

Belga [bel'-gah], *m.* & *f.* Belgian, a native of Belgium.

Bélgico, ca [bel'-he-co, cah], *a.* Belgic, Belgian.

Bélico, ca [bay'-le-co, cah], *a.* Warlike, martial, military.

Belicoso, sa [bay-le-co'-so, sah], *a.* 1. Warlike, martial, military, belligerent, belligerous. 2. Quarrelsome, irascible, easily irritated.

Belicosidad [bay-le-co-se-dahd'], *f.* Warlike state.

Beligerante [bay-le-hay-rahn'-tay], *a.* Belligerent.

Belígero, ra [bay-lee'-hay-ro, rah], *a.* (Poet.) Warlike, belligerent.

Belitre [bay-lee'-tray], *a.* (Coll.) Low, mean, vile, vulgar; roguish.

Belorta [bay-lor'-tah], *f.* The ring or screw with which the bed of the plough is fastened to the beam.

Beltrán [bel-trahn'], *m.* (Pr. n.) Bertram. *Quien bien quiere á Beltrán bien quiere a su can*, Love me, love my dog.

Belvedere [bel-vay-day'-ray], *m.* (Ital.) Arbour, belvedere.

Bellacada [bel-lyah-cah'-dah], *f.* 1. (Obs.) A nest of rogues, a set of villains. 2. (Low) Knavery, roguery.

Bellacamente [bel-lyah-cah-men'-tay], *adv.* Knavishly, roguishly.

Bellaco, ca [bel-lyah'-co, cah], *a.* 1. Artful, sly. 2. Cunning, roguish, deceitful.

Bellaco [bel-lyah'-co], *m.* Rogue, a villain, a swindler, a knave.

Bellacón, na, Bellaconazo, za [bel-lyah-cone', nah], *m.* & *f. aug.* Great knave, an arrant rogue.

Bellacuelo [bel-lyah-coo-ay'-lo], *m. dim.* Artful, cunning little fellow.

Belladama, Belladona [bel-lyah-dah'-mah], *f.* 1. (Bot.) Deadly nightshade, belladonna, dwale. Atropa belladona. 2. (Zool.) A butterfly whose caterpillar lives in thistles.

Bellamente [bel-lyah-men'-tay], *adv.* Prettily, gracefully, fairly.

Bellaquear [bel-lyah-kay-ar'], *vn.* To cheat, to swindle, to play knavish, roguish tricks.

Bellaquería [bel-lyah-kay-ree'-ah], *f.* Knavery, roguery, the act of swindling or deceiving; cunning, chousing counterfeit.

Belleza [bel-lyay'-thah], *f.* 1 Beauty, fair, fairness, handsomeness, flourish. 2. Decoration or ornament for the front of buildings. *Decir bellezas*

To say things prettily, wittily, or with a grace.

Bello, lla [bel'-lyo, lyah], *a.* Beautiful, handsome, fair, fine; perfect. *Bella pedrería*, Fine jewels. *Bello principio*, An excellent beginning. *De su bella gracia*, Of one's own accord. *Por su bella cara no se le concederá*, It will not be granted for his pretty face's sake, or without peculiar cause or motive.

Bellorio, ia [bel-lyo'-re-o, ah], *a.* Mouse-coloured: applied to the coat of horses.

Bellorita [bel-lyo-ree'-tah], *f.* (Bot.) Primrose, cowslip. Primula. *Bellorita primaveral*, Common cowslip. Primula veris.

Bellota [bel-lyo'-tah], *f.* 1. Acorn. 2. Balsam or perfume box, in the shape of an acorn. *Bellota marina*, Centre-shell, a shell in the shape of an acorn.

Bellote [bel-lyo'-tay], *m.* Large round-headed nail.

Bellotear [bel-lyo-tay-ar'], *vn.* To feed upon acorns: applied to swine.

Bellotera [bel-lyo-tay'-rah], *f.* Season for gathering acorns, and feeding swine with them.

Bellotero, ra [bel-lyo-tay'-ro, rah], *m.* & *f.* One who gathers or sells acorns.

Bellotero [bel-lyo-tay'-ro], *m.* (Obs.) A tree which bears acorns.

Bellotica, illa, ita [bel-lyo-tee'-cah, eel'-lyah, ee'-tah], *f. dim.* Small acorn.

Bemol [bay-mole'], *m.* (Mus.) A flat; the sign ♭.

Bemolado [bay-mo-lah'-do], *a.* Flat(ted), lowered a semitone.

Bemolar [bay-mo-lar'], *va.* To flat.

Ben, Behén [ben', bay-en'], *m.* Fruit of the size of a filbert which yields a precious oil.

Benarriza [bay-nar-ree'-thah], *f.* A savoury bird of the family of ortolans.

Bencina [ben-thee'-nah], *f.* Benzine, a light hydrocarbon fluid.

Bendecir [ben-day-theer'], *va.* 1. To devote to the service of the church; to consecrate. *Bendecir la bandera*, To consecrate the colours. 2. To bless, to praise, to exalt. *Dios te bendiga*, God bless thee.

Bendición [ben-de-the-on'], *f.* 1. Benediction. 2. The marriage ceremony. *Echar la bendición*, (Met.) To give up a business. *Es una bendición* or *es bendición*, (Coll.) It does one's heart good to see what plenty there is. *Miente que es una bendición*, (Iron.) It is a blessing to hear how he lies. *Hijo y fruto de bendición*, A child begotten in wedlock.

(*Yo bendigo, yo bendiga*, from *Bendecir.*)

Bendito, ta [ben-dee'-to, tah], *a.* 1. Sainted, blessed. 2. Simple, silly. *Es un bendito*, He is a simpleton. *El bendito*, A prayer which begins with this word.—*pp. irr.* of Bendecir.

Benedícite [bay-nay-dee'-the-tay], *m.* (Lat.) Permission solicited by ecclesiastics with this word.

Benedicta [bay-nay-deec'-tah], *f.* Benedict, an electuary.

Benedictino, na [bay-nay-dic-tee'-no, nah], *a.* Benedictine, of the order of St. Benet.

Benefactor [bay-nay-fac-tor'], *m.* (Ant. and Amer.) Benefactor. *V.* Bienhechor.

Beneficencia [bay-nay-fe-then'-the-ah], *f.* Beneficence, kindness, well-doing.

Beneficiación [bay-nay-fe-the-ah-the-on'], *f.* Benefaction.

Beneficiado [bay-nay-fe-the-ah'-do], *m.* The incumbent of a benefice which is neither a curacy nor prebend; curate, beneficiary.

Beneficiador, ra [bay-nay-fe-the-ah-dor', rah], *m.* & *f.* 1. Benefactor. 2. Improver. 3. A careful administrator.

Beneficial [bay-nay-fe-the-ahl'], *a.* Relating to benefices or ecclesiastical livings.

Beneficiar [bay-nay-fe-the-ar'], *va.* 1. To benefit. 2. To cultivate the ground. 3. To work and improve mines; to submit ores, etc., to metallurgical processes. 4. (Prov.) To confer an ecclesiastical benefice. 5. To purchase a place or employ. *Beneficiar una compañía de caballería*, To buy the commission of a captain of horse. *Beneficiar los efectos, libranzas y otros créditos*, To resign and make over effects, credits, and other claims.

Beneficiario [bay-nay-fe-the-ah'-re-o], *m.* Beneficiary.

Beneficio [bay-nay-fee'-the-o], *m.* 1. Benefit, favour, kindness, benefaction. 2. The proceeds of a public entertainment given in favour of some person or charity. 3. Right belonging to one either by law or charter. 4. Labour and culture: applied to the ground, trees, mines. 5. Utility, profit. *B. bruto*, Gross profit. *B. neto*, Clear profit. 6. Benefice, ecclesiastical living. *Beneficio curado*, Benefice to which a curacy is annexed. 7. Purchase of public places, employs, or commissions in the army. 8. Act of resigning and making over credits and demands for sums not equal to their amount. *Beneficio de inventario*, Benefit of inventory, the effect whereof is, that the heir is not obliged to pay debts to a larger amount than that of the inheritance. *No tener oficio ni beneficio*, To have neither profession nor property: applied to vagabonds.

Beneficio marginal [bay-nay-fee'-the-o mar-he-nahl'], *m.* (Com.) Fringe benefit.

Beneficioso, sa [bay-nay-fe-the-o'-so, sah], *a.* Beneficial, advantageous, profitable.

Benéfico, ca [bay-nay'-fe-co, cah], *a.* Beneficent, kind.

Benemérito, ta [bay-nay-may'-re-to, tah], *a.* Meritorious, deserving of reward, worthy. *Benemérito de la patria*, Well-deserving of the country.

Beneplácito [bay-nay-plah'-the-to], *m.* Goodwill, approbation, permission, consent.

Benevolencia [bay-nay-vo-len'-the-ah], *f.* Benevolence, goodwill, kindness, humanity, good-nature, courteousness.

Benévolo, la [bay-nay'-vo-lo, lah], *a.* Benevolent, kind, gentle, courteous, favourable, good, kind-hearted, good-natured, gracious.

Bengala [ben-gah'-lah], *f.* 1. Bengal, a sort of thin slight stuff. 2. Cane from which walking-sticks are made.

Bengalí [ben-gah-lee'], *m.* 1. Native of Bengal, or belonging to it. 2. Language of the Bengalese people, Bengalee.

Benignamente [bay-nig-nah-men'-tay], *adv.* Kindly, benevolently, mercifully, favourably, graciously, humanely, clemently.

Benignidad [bay-nig-ne-dahd'], *f.* 1. Benignity, graciousness, mercifulness, kindness, piety, courtesy, lenity. 2. Mildness of the air or weather.

Benigno, na [bay-neeg'-no, nah], *a.* 1. Benign, merciful, gracious, pious, clement, humane. 2. Kind, courteous, favourable. 3. Mild, temperate, gentle.

Benito, ta [bay-nee'-to, tah], *m.* & *f.* & *a.* Benedictine friar or nun.

Benjuí [ben-hoo-ee'], *m.* Benzoin or benjamin, a gum-resin.

Beodo, da [bay-o'-do, dah], *a.* Drunk.

Beorí [bay-o-ree'], *m.* American tapir.

Beque [bay'-kay], *m.* (Naut.) 1. Head of the ship. 2. Privies for sailors in the head gratings.

Bequebo [bay-kay'-bo], *m.* (Orn.) Woodpecker. Picus.

Berám [bay-rahm'], *f.* Coarse cotton stuff brought from the East Indies.

Berberí, isco, or **Bereber** [ber-bay-ree', rees'-co, bay-ray-berr'], *a.* Belonging to Barbary, Berber.

Berberís [ber-bay-rees'], *m.* (Bot.) Barberry, berberry, piperidge-bush.

Berbero [ber-bay'-ro], *m.* A confection made of barberry.

Berbí [ber-bee'], *m.* A sort of woollens.

Berbiquí [ber-be-kee'], *m.* A carpenter's brace. Wimble.

Berceria [ber-thay-ree'-ah], *f.* (Obs.) Green-market, where vegetables are sold.

Bercero, ra [ber-thay'-ro, rah], *m.* & *f.* (Obs.) Green-grocer.

Berenjena [bay-ren-hay'-nah], *f.* (Bot.) Egg-plant, egg-plant night-shade. Solanum melongena.

Berenjenado, da [bay-ren-hay-nah'-do dah], *a.* (Obs.) Having the colour of an egg-plant.

Berenjenal [bay-ren-hay-nahl'], *m.* A bed of egg-plants. *Meterse en un berenjenal*, To involve one's self in difficulties.

Berenjenazo [bay-ren-hay-nah'-tho], *m.* Blow given with an egg-plant.

Bergamasco, ca [ber-ga-mahs'-co, cah], *a.* Proceeding from or belonging to Bérgamo, in Lombardy.

Bergamota [ber-gah-mo'-tah], *f.* 1. Bergamot, a sort of pear. 2. Bergamot, snuff scented with the essence of bergamot.

Bergamote, Bergamoto [ber-gah-mo'-tay], *m.* (Bot.) Bergamot-tree.

Bergante [ber-gahn'-tay], *m.* Brazen-faced villain, a ruffian, rascal.

Bergantín [ber-gan-teen'], *m.* (Naut.) Brig or brigantine, a two-masted vessel with square sail.

Bergantinejo [ber-gan-te-nay'-ho], *m. dim.* Small brig.

Berganton, na [ber-gan-tone', nah], *m.* & *f. aug.* Brazen-faced, impudent person.

Bergantonazo [ber-gan-to-nah'-tho], *m. aug.* Most impudent ruffian.

Berilo [bay-ree'-lo], *m.* Beryl, a precious stone.

Berlina [ber-lee'-nah], *f.* Landau or berlin, an open carriage.

Berlinga [ber-leen'-gah], *f.* 1. (Prov.) Pole driven into the ground, at the top of which is fastened a rope, carried to another pole, which serves to hang clothes upon to be dried. 2. (Naut.) Round timber of six inches in diameter.

Berma [berr'-mah], *f.* (Mil.) Berm, a small space of ground at the foot of the rampart towards the moat, to prevent the earth from falling into the ditch.

Bermejear, Bermejecer [ber-may-hay ar', ber-may-hay-therr'], *vn.* To be of a reddish colour.

Bermejizo, za [ber-may-hee'-tho, thah], *a.* Reddish.

Bermejo, ja [ber-may'-ho, hah], *a.* Of a bright reddish colour.

Bermejón, na [ber-may-hone, nah], *a.* 1. Reddish. 2. *V.* Bermejo. 3. (Obs.) *V.* Bermellón.

Bermejuela [ber-may-hoo-ay'-lah], *f.* 1. (Zool.) Red gurnard, a small river-fish. 2. (Bot.) Heather.

Bermejuelo, la [ber-may-hoo-ay'-lo, lah], *a. dim.* A little reddish.

Bermejura [ber-may-hoo'-rah], *f.* Reddishness, ruddy colour.

Bermellón, Bermillón [ber-mel-lyone'], *m.* Vermilion.
Bermudiana [ber-moo-de-ah'-nah], *f.* (Bot.) Grass-flower, blue-eyed grass. Sisyrinchium bermudiana.
Bernardina [ber-nar-dee'-nah], *f.* (Coll.) Fanfaronade, false boast, lie.
Bernardo, da [ber-nar'-do, dah], *m.* & *f.* & *a.* Bernardine monk or nun.
Bernegal [ber-nay-gahl'], *m.* Bowl, a vessel to hold liquids.
Bernés, sa [ber-ness', sah], *a.* Bernese, relating to Berne.
Bernia [ber'-ne-ah], *f.* 1. Rug, a coarse woollen cloth, of which coverlets are made. 2. Cloak made of rug. 3. (Coll.) A bore.
Bernicla [ber-nee'-clah], *f.* Barnacle, a bird like a goose.
Berniz [ber-neeth'], *m.* (Prov.) *V.* Barniz.
Berra [ber'-rah], *f.* (Bot.) The strong water-cress plant. Nasturtium officinale.
Berraza [ber-rah'-thah], *f.* Water-parsnip. Sium latifolium. *Berraza común* or *nodiflora*, Procumbent water-parsnip. Sium nodiflorum.
Berrear [ber-ray-ar'], *vn.* To cry like a calf, to low, to bellow.
Berrenchín [ber-ren-cheen'], *m.* 1. Foaming, grunting, and blowing of a wild boar. 2. Cry of wayward children.
Berrendearse [ber-ren-day-ar'-say], *vr.* 1. (Prov.) To grow yellow: applied to wheat nearly ripe. 2. To be stained or tinged with two colours.
Berrendo, da [ber-ren'-do, dah], *a.* 1. Stained or tinged with two colours. 2. Ripe wheat which gets a yellow colour. 3. (Prov.) Applied to a silk-worm which has a duskish brown colour.
Berrera [ber-ray'-rah], *f.* (Bot.) *V.* Berraza común.
Berrido [ber-ree'-do], *m.* The bellowing of a calf or other animal.
Berrín [ber-reen'], *m.* Person in a violent passion. *V.* Bejín.
Berrinche [ber-reen'-chay], *m.* Anger, passion, great petulance: applied commonly to children; sulkiness.
Berrinchudo [ber-rin-choo'-do], *a.* Passionate, sulky.
Berrizal [ber-re-thahl'], *m.* Place full of water-cresses.
Berro [ber'-ro], *m.* (Bot.) Water-cress, common water-cress, fen-cress. Nasturtium officinale. Sisymbrium nasturtium. *Andar a la flor del berro*, To stroll and wander about.
Berrocal [ber-ro-cahl'], *m.* A craggy or rocky place.
Berroqueña [ber-ro-kay'-nyah], *a.* *Piedra berroqueña*, Coarse-grained granitic stone.
Berrueco [ber-roo-ay'-co], *m.* 1. (Obs.) Rock. 2. Pin, a small horny induration of the membranes of the eye.
Berrusa [ber-roo'-sah], *f.* Sort of stuff manufactured at Lyons.
Berta [bayr'-tah], *f.* 1. Bertha, proper name. 2. A kind of cape called bertha.
Berza [bayr'-thah], *f.* (Bot.) Cabbage. Brassica. *Berza* or *col común*, Savoy-cabbage. Brassica oleracea bullata. *Berza colinabo*, *V.* Colinabo. *Berza coliflor*, *V.* Coliflor. *Berza bróculi*, *V.* Bróculi. *Berza rizada* or *bretón*, *V.* Bretón. *Berza lombarda*, Red cabbage. Brassica oleracea capitata rubra. *Berza repollo*, *V.* Repollo. *Berza de perro*, (Bot.) Wild mercury, dog's cabbage. Theligonum cynocrambe. *Estar en berza*, To be in the blade: applied to grain.
Berzaza [ber-thah'-thah], *f. aug.* A large head of cabbage.
Besador, ra [bay-sah-dor', rah], *m.* & *f.* & *a.* Kissing; kisser.
Besalamano [bay-sah-lah-mah'-no], *m.* A note with the abbreviation B. L. M. in the third person and unsigned.
Besamanos [bay-sah-mah'-nos], *m.* 1. Levee or court-day, when the nobility assemble at court to kiss the king's hand. 2. Salute performed with the hand.
Besana [bay-sah'-nah], *f.* First furrow opened in the ground with a plough.
Besar [bay-sar'], *va.* 1. To kiss. 2. To touch closely: applied to inanimate things. *A besar*, (Naut.) Home, or block on block. *Besar el azote*, (Met.) To kiss the rod. *Llegar y besar*, No sooner said than done. *Besar la mano* or *los pies*, Expressions of courtesy and respect.—*vr.* To strike heads or faces together accidentally.
Besico, sillo, sito [bay-see'-co, seel'-lyo, see'-to], *m. dim.* A little kiss. *Besicos de monja*, (Bot.) *V.* Farolillos.
Beso [bay'-so], *m.* 1. Kiss. 2. Violent collision of persons or things. 3. Among bakers, kissing-crust, where one loaf touches another. *Beso de monja*, A delicious kind of sweetmeat. *Dar un beso al jarro*, (Low) To toss about the pot, to drink freely.
Bestezuela [bes-tay-thoo-ay'-lah], *f. dim.* A little beast.
Bestia [bes'-te-ah], *f.* 1. Beast, a quadruped. *Bestia de albarda*, A beast of burden. *Bestia de silla*, A saddle mule. *Gran bestia*, An elk, an animal of the stag kind. 2. (Met.) Dunce, idiot, ill-bred fellow. 3. Creature, an animal not human.
Bestiaje, Bestiame [bes-te-ah'-hay, bes-te-ah'-may], *m.* An assembly of beasts of burden.
Bestial [bes-te-ahl'], *a.* Bestial, brutal.
Bestialidad [bes-te-ah-le-dahd'], *f.* *V.* Brutalidad.
Bestialmente [bes-te-al-men'-tay], *adv.* Bestially, brutally.
Bestiaza [bes-te-ah'-thah], *m. aug.* 1. A great beast. 2. An idiot.
Bestiecica, illa, ita, Bestiezuela [bes-te-ay-thee'-cah, eel'-yah, ee'-tah, bes-te-ay-thoo-ay'-lah], *f. dim.* 1. A little beast. 2. An ignorant person.
Béstola [bes'-to-lah], *f.* Paddle, or paddle-staff, for cleaning the coulter of the plough.
Besucador, ra [bay-soo-cah-dor', rah], *m.* & *f.* Kisser.
Besucar [bay-soo-car'], *va.* To give many kisses, kiss repeatedly.
Besucón [bay-soo-cone'], *m.* (Low.) Hearty kiss, buss, smack.
Besugada [bay-soo-gah'-dah], *f.* A luncheon or supper of sea-breams.
Besugo [bay-soo'-go], *m.* (Zool.) Sea-bream, or red gilthead, a fish frequent in the Bay of Biscay. Sparus pagrus. *Ojo de besugo*, Squint-eyed. *Ya te veo, besugo*, (Met.) I can anticipate your design.
Besuguera [bay-soo-gay'-rah], *f.* 1. A pan for dressing *besugos* or breams. 2. *m.* & *f.* One who sells breams.
Besuguero [bay-soo-gay'-ro], *m.* 1. Fishmonger who sells breams. 2. (Prov.) Fishing-tackle for catching breams.
Besuguete [bay-soo-gay'-tay], *m.* (Zool.) Red sea-bream. Sparus erythinus.
Besuqueo [bay-soo-kay'-o], *m.* Hearty and repeated kisses.
Beta [bay'-tah], *f.* (Prov.) 1. A bit or line of thread. 2. The tape with which the people of Aragon tie their hemp-sandals. 3. Beta, the second letter of the Greek alphabet. *Beta de la madera*, The grain of the wood. *Betas*, (Naut.) Pieces of cordage for serving all sorts of tackle.
Betabel [bay-tah-bell'], *m.* (Bot.) (Mex.) Beet.
Betarraga, Betarrata [bay-tar-rah'-gah, bay-tar-rah'-tah], *f.* (Bot.) *V.* Remolacha. Beet.
Betatrón [bay-tah-tron'], *m.* Betatron.
Betel [bay-tel'], *m.* Betel, an Indian shrub.
Bética [bay'-te-cah], *f.* Ancient name of the province now Andalucia.
Bético, ca [bay'-te-co, cah], *a.* Andalusian.
Betlemita [bet-lay-mee'-tah], *m.* Bethlemite, a friar of a religious order established in America.
Betón [be-tone'], *m.* Hydraulic cement.
Betónica [bay-to'-ne-cah], *f.* (Bot.) Betony. Betonica.
Betum, Betume, Betumen [bay-toom', bay-too'-may, bay-too'-men], *m.* (Obs.) *V.* Betún.
Betún [bay-toon'], *m.* 1. Bitumen. 2. Cement made chiefly of lime and oil. 3. Shoe-blacking. 4. (Naut.) Stuff with which the masts and bottoms of ships are payed. *Betún de colmena*, Coarse wax, found at the entrance of a bee-hive. *Betún judaico*, *V.* Asfalto.
Betunar [bay-too-nar'], *va.* (Obs.) To pay or cover a thing with pitch, tar, resin, etc.
Beuna [bay-oo'-nah], *f.* (Prov.) A gold-coloured wine, made of a grape of the same name.
Beut [bay-oot'], *m.* A kind of sea-fish.
Bevatrón [bay-vah-trone'], *m.* (Phy.) Bevatron.
Bey [bay'-e], *m.* Bey, a Turkish governor.
Bezaar, Bezar [bay-thah-ar'], *m.* *V.* Bezoar.
Bezante [bay-thahn'-tay], *m.* (Her.) Round figure on a shield.
Bezo [bay'-tho], *m.* 1. Blubber-lip, a thick lip. 2. (Obs.) A lip in general. 3. Proud flesh in a wound.
Bezoar [bay-tho-ar'], *m.* Bezoar, a calculous concretion found in the intestines of certain ruminant animals, and once considered antidotal to poison.
Bezoárico, ca [bay-tho-ah'-re-co, cah], *a.* 1. Bezoaric. 2. An ancient preparation of the oxide of antimony.
Bezón [bay-thone'], *m.* (Obs.) Battering-ram.
Bezote [bay-tho'-tay], *m.* A ring which the Indians wear in their under lip.
Bezudo, da [bay-thoo'-do, dah], *a.* Blubber-lipped or blob-lipped.
Biambonas [be-am-bo'-nas], *f. pl.* A stuff made in China, of bark.
Biangular [be-an-goo-lar'], *a.* Biangulated, biangulous.
Biasa [be-ah'-sah], *f.* A kind of coarse silk, from the Levant.
Biazas [be-ah'-thas], *f. pl.* Saddle-bags. *V.* Bizaza.
Bibero [be-bay'-ro], *m.* A sort of linen, from Galicia.
Biberón [be-bay-rone'], *m.* A nursing-bottle for infants.
Biblia [bee'-ble-ah], *f.* Bible.
Bíblico, ca [bee'-ble-co, cah], *a.* Biblical.
Bibliófilo [be-ble-o'-fe-lo], *m.* Book-lover, book-worm, bibliophile.
Bibliografía [be-ble-o-grah-fee'-ah], *f.* Bibliography.
Bibliográfico, ca [be-ble-o-grah'-fe-co, cah], *a.* Bibliographical, bibliographic.
Bibliógrafo [be-ble-o'-grah-fo], *m.* Bibliographer.

Bibliomanía [be-ble-o-mah-nee'-ah], *f.* Bibliomania.
Biblíómano, na [be-ble-o'-mah-no, nah], *m.* & *f.* Bibliomaniac.
Biblioteca [be-ble-o-tay'-cah], *f.* Library. Catalogue, collection of authors.
Bibliotecario [be-ble-o-tay-cah'-re-o], *m.* Librarian, bibliothecary.
Biblioteconomía [be-blee-oh-tay-co-no-mee'-ah], *f.* Library science (cataloguing of books, etc.).
Bica [be'-cah], *f.* 1. A sea-fish resembling a bream. 2. (Prov. Gal.) An unleavened cake of maize. (Acad.)
Bicapsular [be-cap-soo-lar'], *a.* (Bot.) Bicapsular.
Bicarbonato [be-car-bo-nah'-to], *m.* Bicarbonate.
Bicentenario [be-then-tay-nah'-re-o], *m.* Bicentenary.
Biceps [be-theps'], *m.* (Anat.) A muscle of two heads or points of origin.
Bicerra [be-ther'-rah], *f.* A kind of wild or mountain goat. Capra ibex.
Bicicleta [be-the-clay'-tah], *f.* Bicycle.
Bicicletista, Biciclista [be-the-clay-tees'-tah, be-the-clees'-tah], *m.* & *f.* Bicyclist.
Bicloruro [be-clo-roo'ro], *m.* (Chem.) Bichloride.
Bicoca [be-co'-cah], *f.* 1. Sentry-box. 2. Thing of little esteem or value; trifle.
Bicolor [be-co-lor'], *a.* Of two colours.
Bicóncavo, va [be-con'-cah-vo, vah], *a.* Biconcave.
Biconvexo, a [be-con-vec'-so, sah], *a.* Double convex.
Bicoquete [be-co-kay'-tay], *m.* A bonnet or head-dress formerly worn.
Bicoquín [be-co-keen'], *m.* Cap. *V.* BECOQUÍN and BIRRETE.
Bicorpóreo, rea [be-cor-po'-ray-o, ah], *a.* Bicorporal.
Bicos [bee'-cos], *m. pl.* Small gold points or lace, formerly put on velvet bonnets.
Bicromato [be-cro-mah'-to], *m.* Bichromate or dichromate.
Bicuadrática [be-coo-ah-drah'-te-cah], *a.* (Alg.) Biquadrate, biquadratic.
Bicúspide [be-coos'-pe-day], *a.* Bicuspid.
Bicha [bee'-chah], *f.* 1. (Naut.) Trail-board. 2. (Arch.) Caryatid in form of a savage. 3. (Ant.) Strumpet, bitch. 4. (Obs.) *V.* BICHO.
Bichero [be-chay'-ro], *m.* (Naut.) Boat-hook. *Asta de bichero*, The shaft of a boat-hook. *Gancho de bichero*, The hook of a boat-hook.
Bicho [bee'-cho], *m.* 1. A general name for small grubs or insects. 2. (Met.) A little fellow of a ridiculous figure and appearance. *Mal bicho*, A mischievous urchin.—*pl.* Vermin. (Hindu.)
Bidente [be-den'-tay], *m.* 1. (Poet.) Two-pronged spade. 2. Sheep. 3. (Bot.) A sort of hemp called water-hemp.
Biela [be-ay'-lah], *f.* 1. Brace-strut. 2. Axle-tree, connecting-rod.
Bielda [be-el'-dah], *f.* Pitchfork with six or seven prongs, and a rack used in gathering and loading straw.
Bieldar [be-el-dar'], *va.* To winnow corn by means of a wooden fork with two or three prongs.
Bieldo, Bielgo [be-el'-do, be-el'-go], *m.* Winnowing-fork.
Bien [be-en'], *m.* 1. Supreme goodness. 2. Object of esteem or love. 3. Good, utility, benefit. *El bien de la comunidad*, The public welfare. *Bienes*, Property, fortune, riches, land. *Bienes de fortuna*, Worldly goods. *Bienes raíces*, Real estate.
Bien [be-en'], *adv.* 1. Well, right. *Ha vivido bien*, He has lived uprightly. 2. Happily, prosperously. *El enfermo va bien*, The patient is doing well. 3. Willingly, readily. 4. Heartily. *Comió bien*, He dined heartily. *Caminó bien*, He walked at a great rate. After a negative, it means, as soon as. *No bien la vió*, As soon as (just as) he saw her. It is used sometimes as a distributive conjunction: *bien . . . bien . . .*; whether . . . or. 5. Well, well: it is all well: often used in an ironical sense. 6. As well as, in the same manner as. 7. *Bien que*, Although. 8. *Bien si*, But if. 9. *Ahora bien*, Now, this being so. *Bien está*, Very well. 10. *Más bien*, Rather. *Si bien me acuerdo*, To the best of my recollection. *Hay bien de eso*, There is plenty of that. *¿Y bien, y qué tenemos con eso?* Well, and what of that? Joined to adjectives or adverbs it is equivalent to *very*, as *bien rico*, very rich; and to verbs, *much*, as, *El bebió bien*, He drank much. *Ser bien*, To be good, useful, or convenient. *De bien a bien* or *por bien*, Willingly, amicably. *Tener a bien*, To be kind enough.
Bienal [be-ay-nahl'], *a.* Biennial.
Bienamado, da [be-en-ah-mah'-do, dah], *a.* Dearly beloved.
Bienandante [be-en-an-dahn'-tay], *a.* Happy, successful, prosperous.
Bienandanza [be-en-an-dahn'-thah], *f.* Felicity, prosperity, success.
Bienaventuradamente [be-en-ah-ven-too-rah-dah-men'-tay], *adv.* Fortunately, happily.
Bienaventurado, da [be-en-ah-ven-too-rah'-do, dah], *a.* 1. Blessed; happy. 2. Fortunate, successful, felicitous. 3. (Iron.) Simple, silly, harmless.
Bienestar [be-en-es-tar'], *m.* Well-being.
Bienfortunado, da [be-en-for-too-nah'-do, dah], *a.* Fortunate, successful.
Bienhablado, da [be-en-ah-blah'-do, dah], *a.* Well and civilly spoken.
Bienhadado, da [be-en-ah-dah'-do, dah], *a.* Lucky, fortunate, happy.
Bienhecho, cha [be-en-ay'-cho, chah], *a.* Well-shaped, well-performed.
Bienhechor, ra [be-en-ay-chor', rah], *m.* & *f.* Benefactor.
Bienio [be-ay'-ne-o], *m.* Term or space of two years.
Bienquerencia [be-en-kay-ren'-the-ah], *f.* Goodwill. *V.* BIENQUERER, as noun.
Bienquerer [be-en-kay-rerr'], *va.* To wish the good of another, to esteem.
Bienquerer [be-en-kay-rerr'], *m.* Esteem, attachment.
Bienquistar [be-en-kees-tar'], *va.* To reconcile.
Bienquisto, ta [be-en-kees'-to, tah], *a.* Generally esteemed and respected.—*pp.* of BIENQUISTAR.
Bienvenida [be-en-vay-nee'-dah], *f.* Welcome
Bienvenido, da [be-en-vay-nee'-do, dah], *a.* Welcome.
Bienventuranza [be-en-ah-ven-too-rahn'-thah], *f.* 1. Beatitude. 2. Prosperity, human felicity. *Bienaventuranzas*, The eight beatitudes mentioned in the Scriptures.
Bierzo [be-err'-tho], *m.* A sort of linen manufactured at Bierzo.
Bifocal [be-fo-cahl'], *a.* Bifocal. *Lentes bifocales*, Bifocals, bifocal glasses.
Biforme [be-for'-may], *a.* (Poet.) Biformed, biform.
Bifronte [be-fron'-tay], *a.* (Poet.) Double-fronted or double-faced.
Bifurcación [be-foor-cah-the-on'], *f.* Branch railroad; bifurcation, forking.
Bifurcado, da [be-foor-cah'-do, dah], *a.* Forked, branched, bifurcate.
Bifurcarse [be-foor-car'-say], *vr.* To branch off, as a river or railway.
Biga [bee'-gah], *f.* (Obs.) Traces or harness of two horses.
Bigamia [be-gah'-me-ah], *f.* 1. Bigamy. 2. (Law) Bigamy, second marriage.
Bigamo [bee'-gah-mo], *m.* 1. Bigamist. 2. (Law) Bigam, he who has married a widow. 3. (Law) A widower who has married again.
Bigardear [be-gar-day-ar'], *vn.* To live licentiously; to wander without an object.
Bigardía [be-gar-dee'-ah], *f.* Jest, fiction, dissimulation.
Bigardo [be-gar'-do], *m.* An opprobrious appellation given to a friar of loose morals and irregular conduct; a lubber.
Bigarrado, da [be-gar-rah'-do, dah], *a.* *V.* ABIGARRADO.
Bigarro [be-gar'-ro], *m.* (Prov.) A large sea-snail.
Bignonia [big-no'-ne-ah], *f.* (Bot.) Trumpet-flower. Bignonia radicans.
Bigorneta [be-gor-nay'-tah], *f. dim.* A small anvil.
Bigornia [be-gor'-ne-ah], *f.* Anvil.
Bigotazo [be-go-tah'-tho], *m. aug.* Large mustache.
Bigote [be-go'-tay], *m.* 1. Mustachio, mustache. 2. Block. (Typ.) Dash rule. *Hombre de bigote*, (Met.) A man of spirit and vigour. *Tener bigotes*, (Met.) To be firm and undaunted; to be obstinate.
Bigotera [be-go-tay'-rah], *f.* 1. Leather cover for mustachios. 2. (Obs.) Ornament of ribbons worn by women on the breast. 3. Folding seat put in the front of a chariot. 4. Bow compass. *Pegar una bigotera*, To play one a trick. *Bigoteras*, Face, mien. *Tener buenas bigoteras*, (Coll.) To have a pleasing face, or graceful mien: applied to women.
Bigotería [be-go-tay-ree'-ah], *f.* Bigotry. (Padre Isla.)
Bigotudo [be-go-too'-do], *a.* Having a large mustache; full-whiskered.
Bija [bee'-hah], *f.* (Bot.) Heart-leaved arnotta or bixa. Bixa orellana. *V.* ACHIOTE.
Bilánder [be-lahn'-der], *m.* (Naut.) Bilander, a small merchant vessel.
Bilateral [be-lah-tay'-rahl], *a.* Bilateral
Biliario, ria [be-le-ah'-re-o, ah], *a.* Biliary.
Bilbaíno, na [beel-bah-ee'-no, nah] *a.* Of Bilbao.
Bilingüe [be-leen'-goo-ay], *a.* Bilingual. Double-tongued, deceitful.
Bilioso, sa [be-le-oh'-so, sah], *a.* Bilious.
Bilis [bee'-lis], *f.* Bile.
Bilítero, ra [be-lee-'tay-ro, rah], *a.* Of two letters.
Bilocarse [be-lo-car'-say], *vr.* To be in two different places at the same time.
Bilorta [be-lor'-tah], *m.* 1. Ring made of a twisted yellow twig. 2. Flying report. 3. (Naut.) Burr, a kind of iron ring used for various purposes on board of ships. 4. A sport among country people, resembling cricket.
Bilorto [be-lor'-to], *m.* Bat having a crooked head.
Biltrotear [beel-tro-tay-ar'], *vn.* (Coll.) To ramble about the streets.
Biltrotera [beel-tro-tay'-rah], *f.* A gossip, gossiping woman.
Billa [beel'-lyah], *f.* In billiards, the pocketing of a ball after it has struck another.
Billalda, or **Billarda** [beel-lyahl'-dah], *f.* A kind of children's play.
Billar [beel-lyar'], *m.* The game of billiards.

Billete [beel-lyay'-tay], *m.* 1. Anciently, an order of the king. 2. Note, a brief letter. 3. A love-letter. 4. A ticket: to theatre, railway, or other public places. 5. (Com.) Bill, note of hand. *Billete de banco*, A bank-note.
Billetero, ra [beel-lyeh-tay'-ro, rah] *m.* & *f.* Vendor of lottery tickets. —*f.* Billfold.
Billón [beel-lyone'], *m.* Billion.
Billonario, ria [beel-lyo-nah'-re-o, ah], *m.* & *f.* Billionaire.
Billonésimo, ma [beel-lyo-nay'-se-mo, mah], *m.* & *f.* & *a.* Billionth, one of a billion equal parts.
Bimano, na [be-mah'-no, nah], *m.* & *f.* & *a.* Bimanous: said only of mankind.
Bimembre [be-mem'-bray], *a.* Having two members.
Bimestral [be-mes-trahl'], *a.* Bimonthly, once in two months. *Publicación bimestral*, Bimonthly, bimonthly publication.
Bimestre [be-mes'-tray], *a.* Of two months' duration.—*m.* Two months' leave of absence or furlough.
Bimotor [be-mo-tor'], *m.* Two-engine plane.
Binar [be-nar'], *va.* To dig or plough ground the second time.
Binario, ria [be-nah'-re-o], *a.* Binary; of two elements or units.
Binocular [be-no-coo-lar'], *a.* Binocular.
Binóculo [be-no'-coo-lo], *m.* Binocle, a dioptric telescope; marine or field glasses.
Binomial, Binominal [be-no-me-ahl', be-no-me-nahl'], *a.* Binomial. *Sistema binomial*, (Math.) Binomial system.
Binza [been'-thah], *f.* Pellicle, lining of the shell of an egg; any thin membrane.
Biodinámica [be-o-de-nah'-me-cah], *f.* Biodynamics, the doctrine of vital force or energy.
Bioecología [be-o-ay-co-lo-hee'-ah], *f.* Bioecology.
Biofísica [be-o-fee'-se-cah], *f.* Biophysics.
Biofísico, ca [be-o-fee'-se-co, cah], *a.* Biophysical.
Biografía [be-o-grah-fee'-ah], *f.* Biography.
Biográfico, ca [be-o-grah'-fe-co, cah], *a.* Biographical.
Biógrafo [be-o'-grah-fo], *m.* Biographer.
Biología [bi-o-lo-hee'-ah], *f.* Biology. *Biología molecular*, Molecular biology.
Biológico, ca [be-o-lo'-he-co, cah], *a.* Biological. *Guerra biológica*, Biological warfare.
Biólogo [be-o'-lo-go], *m.* Biologist.
Biombo [be-om'-bo], *m.* Screen (Chinese word.)
Biónica [be-o'-ne-cah], *f.* (Biol.) Bionics.
Bioquímica [be-o-kee'-me-cah], *f.* Biochemistry.
Bioquímico, ca [be-o-kee'-me-co, cah], *a.* Biochemical.—*m.* Biochemist. —*f.* Biochemistry.
Biosfera [be-os-fay'-rah], *f.* Biosphere.
Biotina [be-o-tee'-nah], *f.* Biotin.
Bióxido [be-ok'-se-do], *m.* (Chem.) Dioxide. *Bióxido* (or *dióxido*) *de carbono*, Carbon dioxide.
Bipartido, da [be-par-tee'-do, dah], *a.* (Poet.) Bipartite.
Bipedal [be-pay-dahl'], *a.* Bipedal.
Bípede, or **Bípedo** [bee'-pay-day, do], *a.* Biped.
Bipétalo, la [be-pay'-tah-lo, lah], *a.* (Bot.) Bipetalous.
Biplano [be-plah'-no], *m.* Biplane.
Biricu [be-re-coo'], *m.* Sword-belt.
Birimbao [be-rim-bah'-o], *m.* (Mus.) A Jew's harp. (Imitative word.)
Birla, *f.* (Prov.) **Birlo,** *m.* [beer-lah, lo], (Obs.) Bowl for playing.
Birlador [beer-lah-dor'], *m.* 1. One who knocks down at a blow; used in the game of nine-pins. 2. Pilferer.
Birlar [beer-lar'], *va.* 1. At the game of nine-pins, to throw a bowl a second time from the same place. 2. To knock down at one blow, to kill at one shot. 3. To snatch away an employment which another was aiming at. 4. To dispossess. 5. To rob, pilfer.
Birlibirloque [beer-le-beer-lo'-kay], *m.* *Por arte de birlibirloque*, (Coll.) To have done any thing by occult and extraordinary means.
Birlocha [beer-lo'-chah], *f.* Paper kite.
Birlocho [beer-lo'-cho], *m.* High open carriage.
Birlón [beer-lone'], *m.* (Prov.) Large middle pin in the game of nine-pins.
Birlonga [beer-lon'-gah], *f.* Mode of playing in the game at cards called *ombre*. *A la birlonga*, In a negligent, careless manner.
Birreme [beer-ray'-may], *a.* Two-oared: applied to a bireme.
Birreta [beer-ray'-tah], *f.* Cardinal's red cap.
Birrete [beer-ray'-tay], *m.* Mortar-board, professional cap.
Bis. *Bis*, a Latin word meaning twice; used in composition.
Bisabuela [be-sah-boo-ay'-lah], *f.* Great-grandmother.
Bisabuelo [be-sah-boo-ay'-lo], *m.* Great-grandfather.
Bisagra [be-sah'-grah], *f.* 1. Hinge. 2. Piece of box-wood, with which shoemakers polish soles of shoes. *Bisagras y pernos*, Hooks and hinges. *Bisagras de la portería*, (Naut.) Port hinges.
Bisanuo, nua [be-sah'-noo-o, ah], *a.* (Bot.) Bisannual.
Bisbisar [bis-be-sar'], *va.* To mutter.
Bisección [be-sec-the-on'], *f.* Bisection.
Bisector, triz [be-sec-tor', treeth], *a.* (Geom.) Bisecting.
Bisel [be-sel'], *m.* The bevel, bevel edge, chamfer. (Coop.) Sloping tool.
Bisemanal [be-say-mah-nahl'], *a.* Semiweekly, twice a week.
Bisemanario [be-say-mah-nah'-re-o], *m.* Semiweekly publication.
Bisiesto [be-se-es'-to], *a.* Bissextile. *Mudar bisiesto* or *de bisiesto*, To change one's ways and means, to alter one's course.
Bisílabo, ba [be-see'-lah-bo, bah], *a.* Consisting of two syllables.
Bismuto [bis-moo'-to], *m.* Bismuth.
Bisnieto, ta [bis-ne-ay'-to, tah], *m.* & *f.* *V.* Biznieto.
Bisojo, ja [be-so'-ho, hah], *a.* Squint-eyed, cross-eyed.
Bisonte [be-son'-tay], *m.* Bison. Bos bison.
Bisoñería [be-so-nyay-ree'-ah], *f.* A rash and inconsiderate speech or action.
Bisoño, ña [be-so'-nyo, nyah], *a.* 1. Raw, undisciplined: applied to recruits or new-levied soldiers. 2. Novice, tyro. 3. Horse not yet broken.
Bispón [bis-pone'], *m.* Roll of oil-cloth, a yard in length, used by sword cutlers.
Bistec [bees-tec'], *m.* Beefsteak.
Bisturí [bees-too-ree'], *m.* Scalpel, surgeon's knife.
Bisulco, ca [be-sool'-co, cah], *a.* Bisulcous, cloven-footed.
Bisulfato [be-sool-fah'-to], *m.* (Chem.) Bisulfate.
Bisulfito [be-sool-fee'-to], *m.* (Chem.) Bisulfite.
Bisunto, ta [be-soon'-to, tah], *a.* (Obs.) Dirty or greasy.
Bisutería [be-soo-tay-ree'-ah], *f.* Imitation jewelry, trinkets.
Bitácora [be-tah'-co-rah], *f.* (Naut.) Binnacle. *Lámpara* or *lantias de la bitácora*, Binnacle-lamp.
Bitadura [be-tah-doo'-rah], *f.* (Naut.) Cable-bitt, a turn of the cable round the bitts. *Bitadura entera de cable*, Weather-bitt of a cable. *Tomar la bitadura con el cable*, To bitt the cable.
Bitas [bee'-tas], *f. pl.* (Naut.) Bitts, large pieces of timber placed abaft the manger, to belay the cable, when the ship rides at anchor. *Forro de las bitas*, Lining of the bitts. *Contrabitas*, Standards of the bitts. *Bita de molinete*, Knight-head of the windlass.
Bitones [be-to'-nes], *m. pl.* (Naut.) Pins of the capstan.
Bitoque [be-to'-kay], *m.* (Prov.) Bung, the wooden stopple of a cask. *Tener ojos de bitoque*, (Coll.) To squint.
Bitor [be-tor'], *m.* (Orn.) Rail, a bird called the king of the quails.
Bitumen [be-too'-men], *m.* *V.* Betún.
Bituminoso, sa [be-too-me-no'-so, sah], *a.* Bituminous.
Bivalvo, va [be-vahl'-vo, vah], *a.* (Conch.) Bivalve, bivalvular.
Biverio [be-vay'-re-o], *m.* 1. *V.* Bíbaro. 2. *V.* Vivero.
Biza [bee'-thah], *f.* (Zool.) Fish belonging to the family of tunnies. Scomber pelamis. *V.* Bonito.
Bizarramente [be-thar-rah-men'-tay], *adv.* Courageously, gallantly, with spirit.
Bizarrear [be-thar-ray-ar'], *vn.* To act in a spirited and gallant manner.
Bizarría [be-thar-ree'-ah], *f.* 1. Gallantry, valour, fortitude; mettle. 2. Liberality, generosity, splendour, gentility.
Bizarro, rra [be-thahr'-ro, rah], *a.* 1. Gallant, brave, high-spirited. 2. Generous, liberal, high-minded.
Bizaza [be-thah'-thah], *f.* Saddle-bag.
Bizcacha [bith-cah'-chah], *f.* An animal with a long tail in Peru, the flesh of which resembles that of a rabbit.
Bizcar [bith-car'], *vn.* To squint.
Bizco, ca [beeth'-co, cah], *a.* *V.* Bisojo.
Bizcochada [bith-co-chah'-dah], *f.* Soup made of biscuit boiled in milk with sugar and cinnamon.
Bizcochar [bith-co-char'], *va.* To make or bake biscuit. To bake bread a second time.
Bizcochero [bith-co-chay'-ro], *m.* 1. Biscuit-cask. 2. One who makes or sells biscuits.
Bizcochito [bith-co-chee'-to], *m. dim.* A small biscuit.
Bizcocho [bith-co'-cho], *m.* 1. Biscuit, hard-tack. 2. Paste made of fine flour, eggs, and sugar. 3. Whiting made of the plaster of old walls.
Bizcochuelo [bith-co-choo-ay'-lo], *m.* 1. Dim. of Bizcocho. 2. (Amer.) Sponge-cake.
Bizma [beeth'-mah], *f.* Cataplasm, poultice.
Bizmar [bith-mar'], *va.* To poultice, to apply a cataplasm.
Bizna [beeth'-nah], *f.* Zest, membrane which quarters the kernel of a walnut.
Biznaga [bith-nah'-gah], *f.* 1. (Bot.) Carrot-like ammi, the sprigs of which are used as tooth-picks. Ammi visnaga. 2. (Coll. and Amer.) A useless, worthless thing.
Biznieta [bith-ne-ay'-tah], *f.* Great-granddaughter.
Biznieto [bith-ne-ay'-to], *m.* Great-grandson.
Bizquear [bith-kay-ar'], *vn.* To squint.

Blanca [blahn'-cah], *f.* 1. Copper coin of the value of half a maravedi; mite. *No tener blanca* or *estar sin blanca*, Not to have a doit to bless one's self with. 2. (Orn.) Magpie. 3. *Blanca morfea*, (Vet.) Alphos, a white scurf, tetter, or ring-worm.

Blanca-espina [blahn'-cah-es-pee'-nah], *f.* Hawthorn, white thorn.

Blancal [blan-cahl'], *a.* & *m.* White wheat.

Blancazo, za [blan-cah'-tho, thah], *a.* 1. (Aug.) Very white. 2. (Coll.) *V.* Blanquecino.

Blanco, ca [blahn'-co, cah], *a.* 1. White, blank, hoar, hoary; fair. 2. Honoured, respected: spoken of persons. *Hombre blanco o mujer blanca*, An honest man or woman. *Hijo de la gallina blanca*, (Low) A lucky fellow. 3. (Naut.) Untarred.

Blanco [blahn'-co], *m.* 1. White star, or any other remarkable white spot in horses. 2. Blank, mark to shoot at. *Dar en el blanco*, To hit the mark. 3. Blank left in writing. 4. (Met.) Aim; object of our desire. 5. First white sheet pulled at a printing-press, after the form is got ready. 6. Interlude: speaking of plays. 7. Interval. 8. White page. 9. (Her.) Argent. 10. Mixture of whiting, lime, etc., to size or lay the first coat for painting. *Blanco de estuco*, Stucco whiting, made of lime and pounded marble. *Blanco de ballena*, Spermaceti. *Blanco de España*, Spanish white. *Blanco de perla*, Pearl white. *Cédula* or *patente en blanco*, A blank paper to be filled up by the person to whom it is sent. *Labor blanca*, Plain work. *Tela* or *ropa blanca*, Linen. *Armas blancas*, Side-arms. *De punta en blanco*, Point-blank. *Dejar en blanco alguna cosa*, To pass over a thing in silence. *El blanco del ave*, The breast of a fowl. *Quedarse en blanco*, To be frustrated in one's expectations, to be left in the lurch. *El blanco de sus deseos*, The object of his desires.

Blancor [blan-cor'], *m.* **Blancura** [blan-coo'-rah], *f.* Whiteness, freedom from colour, hoariness. *Blancura del ojo*, (Vet.) A white spot or film on the eye.

Blandales [blan-dah'-les], *m. pl.* (Naut.) *V.* Brandales.

Blandamente [blan-dah-men'-tay], *adv.* Softly, mildly, gently, sweetly, smoothly.

Blandeador, ra [blan-day-ah-dor', rah], *m.* & *f.* Softener.

Blandear [blan-day-ar'], *va.* 1. To soften, to render mild. 2. To make one change his opinion. 3. To brandish, to flourish.—*vn.* 1. To slacken, to yield, to be softened. 2. To tread tenderly. 3. *Blandear con otro*, To fall in with another's opinion.—*vr.* To be unsteady, to move from one place to another.

Blandengue [blan-den'-gay], *m.* A soldier, armed with a lance, who defended the limits of the province of Buenos Ayres.

Blandeo [blan-day'-o], *m.* The good or bad quality of the soil of forests and pasture-lands.

Blandicia [blan-dee'-the-ah], *f.* (Obs.) Flattery, adulation.

Blandiente [blan-de-en'-tay], *a.* Having a tremulous motion from one side to another.

Blandillo, illa [blan-deel'-lyo, lyah], *a. dim.* Somewhat soft.

Blandimiento [blan-de-me-en'-to], *m.* (Obs.) Adulation, flattery.

Blandir [blan-deer'], *va.* 1. To brandish a sword, pike, lance, etc. 2. To hurtle, to whirl round. 3. (Obs.) To flatter.—*vr.* To quiver, to move tremulously from one side to another.

Blando, da [blahn'-do, dah], *a.* 1. Soft, pliant, smooth to the touch; cottony; milky; flabby; liquid. 2. Lithe. 3. (Met.) Soft, mild, bland, gentle, grateful, pleasing. 4. Mild, moderate: applied to weather. 5. Soft, effeminate, delicate, not bearing fatigue or labour. 6. Tractable, good-natured, kindly; fair. *Blando de ojos*, Tender-eyed. *Blando de boca*, 1. Tender-mouthed: applied to a horse. 2. (Met.) Indiscreet, talkative. *Blando de carona*, 1. (Met.) Soft, not bearing fatigue or labour. 2. (Met.) Fond of women, apt to fall in love. *Blando de corazón*, Tender-hearted. *Hombre blando*, A gentle, mild man. *Llevar blanda la mano*, To carry a gentle hand.

Blandón [blan-done'], *m.* 1. Wax taper with one wick. 2. A large church candlestick, in which wax tapers or flambeaux are placed. (Obs.) Light of the stars.

Blandoncillo [blan-don-theel'-lyo], *m. dim.* A small candlestick for wax tapers.

Blanducho, cha, Blandujo, ja [blan-doo'-cho, chah, blan-doo'-ho, hah], *a.* (Low) Flabby, loose, soft, not firm.

Blandura [blan-doo'-rah], *f.* 1. Softness, litheness. 2. Daintiness, delicacy. 3. (Met.) Gentleness of temper, sweetness of address; favour, lenity. 4. Lenitive or emollient application. 5. Soft, endearing language; blandishing. 6. White paint, used by women. 7. Mild temperature of the air.

Blandurilla [blan-doo-reel'-lyah], *f.* A sort of fine soft pomatum.

Blanqueación [blan-kay-ah-the-on'], *f.* Blanching, the act of blanching metal before it is coined.

Blanqueador, ra [blan-kay-ah-dor', rah], *m.* & *f.* Blancher, whitener, bleacher.

Blanqueadura [blan-kay-ah-doo'-rah], *f.* Whitening, bleaching.

Blanqueamiento [blan-kay-ah-me-en'-to], *m.* (Obs.) *V.* Blanqueadura.

Blanquear [blan-kay-ar'], *va.* 1. To bleach, to whiten, to blanch, to fleece, to clear. 2. To whitewash. 3. To give coarse wax to bees in winter. *Blanquear cera*, To bleach wax.—*vn.* To show whiteness.

Blanquecedor [blan-kay-thay-dor'], *m.* An officer employed in the mint to blanch, clean, and polish the coin.

Blanquecer [blan-kay-therr'], *va.* To blanch coin, to give gold, silver, and other metals their due colours.

Blanquecimiento [blan-kay-the-me-en'-to], *m.* (Obs.) *V.* Blanqueación.

Blanquecino, na [blan-kay-thee'-no, nah], *a.* Whitish, hoary.

Blanqueo [blan-kay'-o], *m.* 1. Whitening, making white or bleaching. 2. Whitewash. *El blanqueo del lienzo*, The bleaching of linen.

Blanquería [blan-kay-ree'-ah], *f.* Bleaching-place, bleach-field.

Blanquero [blan-kay'-ro], *m.* (Prov.) Tanner.

Blanqueta [blan-kay'-tah], *f.* (Obs.) Coarse blanket.

Blanquete [blan-kay'-tay], *m.* Whitewash; paint used by women.

Blanquíbolo [blan-kee'-bo-lo], *m.* (Obs.) *V.* Albayalde.

Blanquición [blan-ke-the-on'], *f.* *V.* Blanqueación.

Blanquilla [blan-keel'-lyah], *f.* 1. Doit, a very small coin. 2. Sort of long yellowish plum. 3. White grape. 4. Blanket, a kind of pear.

Blanquillo, lla [blan-keel'-lyo, lyah], *a. dim.* Whitish, somewhat white.—*m.* A fish of California (Monterey Bay). Caulolatilus anomalus.

Blanquimiento [blan-ke-me-en'-to], *m.* Water mixed with salt of tartar and other things, to bleach wax, linen, etc.

Blanquinoso, sa [blan-ke-no'-so, sah], *a.* (Prov.) *V.* Blanquecino.

Blanquizal, or **Blanquizar** [blan-ke-thahl'], *m.* (Agr.) Whitish clay, pipe-clay. *V.* Gredal.

Blanquizco, ca [blan-keeth'-co, cah], *a.* Whitish.

Blao [blah'-o], *a.* (Her.) Azure, faint blue. (Cf. German blau.)

Blasfemable [blas-fay-mah'-blay], *a.* Blamable, culpable, faulty. *V.* Vituperable.

Blasfemador, ra [blas-fay-mah-dor', rah], *m.* & *f.* Blasphemer.

Blasfemamente [blas-fay-mah-men'-tay], *adv.* Blasphemously, impiously.

Blasfemar [blas-fay-mar'], *vn.* 1. To blaspheme. 2. To curse, to make use of imprecations.

Blasfematorio, ria [blas-fay-mah-to'-re-o, ah], *a.* Blasphemous.

Blasfemia [blas-fay'-me-ah], *f.* 1. Blasphemy. 2. Blaspheming. *Decir blasfemias*, To blaspheme. 3. Gross verbal insult offered to a person.

Blasfemo, ma [blas-fay'-mo, mah], *a.* Blasphemous.—*m.* & *f.* Blasphemer.

Blasón [blah-sone'], *m.* 1. Heraldry, blazon, blazonry, drawing or explaining coats of arms. 2. Figures and devices which compose coats of arms or armorial ensigns. 3. Honour, glory. *Hacer blasón*, To blazon, to boast, to bray.

Blasonador, ra [blah-so-nah-dor', rah], *m.* & *f.* Boaster, bragger.

Blasonante [blah-so-nahn'-tay], *pa.* Vainglorious; boaster.

Blasonar [blah-so-nar'], *va.* 1. To blazon, to draw or explain armorial ensigns. 2. To make a pompous display of one's own merits. *Blasonar del arnés*, To boast of achievements never performed.

Blástema [blahs'-tay-mah], *m.* (Biol.) Blastema, the primitive structureless protoplasm of the embryo.

Blavo, va [blah'-vo, vah], *a.* (Obs.) Yellowish gray and reddish colour.

Ble [blay], *m.* Diversion or play performed with a ball thrown against a wall. *V.* Ple.

Bledo [blay'-do], *m.* (Bot.) Wild amaranth. Amaranthus blitum. *No se me da un bledo*, or *no me importa un bledo*, I don't care a straw. *No vale un bledo*, It is not worth a rush.

Blefaritis [blay-fah-ree'-tis], *f.* Blepharitis, inflammation of the borders of the eyelids.

Blenda [blen'-dah], *f.* (Min.) Blende.

Bleno, Blino [blay'-no, blee'-no], *m.* (Zool.) Hake, blenny. Blennius.

Blenorragia [blay-nor-rah'-he-ah], *f.* (Med.) Blennorrhagia, a disease.

Blenorrea [blay-nor-ray'-ah], *f.* (Med.) Blennorrhœa, gleet, a disease.

Blinda, *f.* **Blindas**, *pl.* *V.* Blindaje.

Blindado, da [blin-dah'-do, dah], *a.* & *m.* Iron-clad, armoured; an armoured war-vessel.

Blindar [blin-dar'], *va.* To apply plates of armour; to armour.

Blindaje [blin-dah'-hay], *m.* 1. (Mil.) Blind, a covering made by the besiegers of a strong place, to protect themselves from the enemy's fire. 2. Armour-plate.

Blonda [blon'-dah], *f.* Broad lace made of silk, blond lace. *Escofieta de blonda*, Head-dress made of silk lace.

Blondina [blon-dee'-nah], *f.* Narrow silk lace, narrow blond lace.

Blondo, da [blon'-do, dah], *a.* Flaxen, flaxy, light, having a fair complexion or flaxen hair.

Bloque [blo'-kay], *m.* 1. Block (of stone). 2. (Mech.) Cylinder block. *En bloque,* (fig.) As a whole, without distinction.

Bloquear [blo-kay-ar'], *va.* (Mil.) To form a blockade. *Bloquear un puerto,* (Naut.) To blockade a port.

Bloqueo [blo-kay'-o], *m.* Blockade.

Blusa [bloo'-sah], *f.* A blouse.

Boa [bo'-ah], *f.* 1. Boa, a large serpent. Boa. 2. Boa, tippet.

Boalaje [bo-ah-lah'-hay], *m.* (Prov.) Pasturage of black cattle.

Boardilla [bo-ar-deel'-lyah], *f.* *V.* BUHARDILLA.

Boarrete [bo-ar-ray'-tay], *m.* (Littl. us.) Storm or tempest at sea.

Boato [bo-ah'-to], *m.* 1. Ostentation, pompous show, habiliment. 2. Shout of acclamation.

Bobada [bo-bah'-dah], *f.* *V.* BOBERÍA.

Bobalias [bo-bah-lee'-as], *m.* (Coll.) A very stupid fellow, a dolt.

Bobalicón, Bobazo [bo-bah-le-cone', bo-bah'-tho], *m.* 1. (Aug.) Great blockhead. 2. Stupid: used commonly in jest, particularly with children.

Bobamente [bo-bah-men'-tay], *adv.* 1. Without trouble or care. 2. Foolishly, stupidly. *Está comiendo su renta bobamente,* He spends his income in a foolish manner.

Bobarrón, na [bo-bar-rone', nah], *a.* (Coll.) Little foolish, little stupid.

Bobatel [bo-bah-tel'], *m.* (Coll.) *V.* BOBO.

Bobático, ca [bo-bah'-te-co, cah], *a.* Silly, foolish, stupid.

Bobazo, za [bo-bah'-tho, thah], *a. aug.* Very foolish: often used as an endearing expression.

Bobear [bo-bay-ar'], *va.* 1. To act or talk in a foolish and stupid manner. 2. To dally, to fribble. 3. To waste one's time in trifles, to loiter about.

Bobería [bo-bay-ree'-ah], *f.* Foolish speech or action; foolery, folly, foolishness.—*pl.* Idle conceits.

Bóbilis [bo'-be-lis], *adv.* *De bóbilis bóbilis,* (Coll.) Without pain or merit.

Bobillo, illa, ito, ita [bo-beel'-lyo, lyah, ee'-to, ee'-tah], *m.* & *f. dim.* A little dolt or fool.

Bobillo [bo-beel'-lyo], *m.* 1. Big-bellied jug with one handle. 2. Modesty-piece, a frill or lace formerly worn by women around the tucker.

Bobina [bo-bee'-nah], *f.* Bobbin, a large sort of spool used in ribbon looms and electrical machines.

Bobísimamente [bo-bee'-se-mah-men-tay], *adv.* Most foolishly.

Bobo, ba [bo'-bo, bah], *m.* & *f.* 1. Dunce, dolt, fool, moon-calf. 2. One who is easily cheated. 3. Sort of ruff formerly worn by women. 4. (Obs.) Stage buffoon. 5. (Orn.) Booby. Pelicanus sula. *El bobo, si es callado, por sesudo es reputado,* A fool that talks little may pass for a wise man. *A bobas,* Foolishly.—*a.* Ample, large.

Bobón, na [bo-bone', nah], *m.* & *f. aug.* Big dolt, great fool.

Boboncillo, lla [bo-bon-theel'-lyo, lyah], *m.* & *f. dim.* A little dolt.

Bobote [bo-bo'-tay], *m. aug.* Great idiot or simpleton.

Boca [bo'-cah], *f.* 1. Mouth. 2. Entrance, opening, hole, nozzle. 3. Muzzle, the mouth of any thing; vulgarly, chops. 4. Chops, the mouth of man, in contempt. 5. Bung-hole. 6. Pincers with which cray-fish hold something. 7. Thin or cutting part of edge-tools. 8. Taste, flavour, relish; one who eats. *Instrumento de boca,* Wind-instrument. 9. (Zool.) Shrimp. *Boca de escorpión,* Calumniator. *Boca del estómago,* Pit of the stomach. *Boca de fuego,* Fire-arm. *Boca de un arma de fuego,* The muzzle of a fire-arm. *Boca de lobo,* 1. (Met.) Dark dungeon. 2. (Naut.) Wolf's mouth, mast-hole, lubbers' hole. *Boca de lobo del tamborete,* Cap-hole for the top-mast. *Boca de la escotilla,* Hatchway. *Boca de risa,* Smiling countenance. *Boca de río o de puerto,* Mouth of a river or of a harbour. *El es la boca del público,* He is a mouthpiece of the public. *Andar de boca en boca,* To be the talk of the town. *Cerrar* or *tapar a uno la boca,* To stop one's mouth. *Coserse la boca,* To shut one's mouth. *Boca de oro,* Mellifluous tongue. *Boca de gacha,* Nickname of a person who mumbles his words. *A boca de jarro,* 1. A hearty draught, drinking without glass or measure. 2. Very near. *Decir alguna cosa con la boca chica,* To offer a thing for mere ceremony's sake. *Andar con la boca abierta,* To go gaping about. *Guardar la boca,* Not to commit any excess in eating or drinking; to be silent. *Hablar por boca de ganso,* To say what any other person has suggested or hinted. *Irse de boca,* To speak much without reflection. *La boca hace juego,* To be as good as one's word. *No decir esta boca es mía,* To keep a profound silence. *No tener boca para negar* or *decir no,* Not to dare to say no. *La boca de V. será medida,* Your taste shall be fitted to a hair. *Punto en boca,* Mum, mum, not a word. *Tener buena o mala boca,* To talk well or ill of others. *A boca de invierno,* About the beginning of winter. *boca de noche,* At the fall of night. *Boca arriba,* Reversed, upside down, on one's back. *Boca abajo,* Face downward. *Boca a boca, adv.* By word of mouth. *Boca con boca,* Face to face. *A boca de costal,* Profusely, without rule or measure. *A boca llena,* Perspicuously, openly. *A pedir de boca,* According to one's desire. *De manos a boca,* Unexpectedly. *De boca,* Verbally; not really; used of boasting or threatening.

Bocacalle [bo-cah-cahl'-lyay], *f.* Entry, end or opening of a street.

Bocacaz [bo-cah-cath'], *m.* Opening left in the weir or dam of a river, sluice, or flood-gate.

Bocací, Bocacín [bo-cah-thee', bo-cah-theen'], *m.* Fine glazed buckram; crimson calico.

Bocada [bo-cah'-dah], *f.* (Obs.) A mouthful.

Bocadear [bo-cah-day-ar'], *va.* To divide into bits or morsels.

Bocadico, illo. ito [bo-cah-dee'-co, eel'-lyo, ee'-to], *m. dim.* Small bit or morsel.

Bocadillo [bo-cah-deel'-lyo], *m.* 1. Thin, middling sort of linen. 2. Narrow ribbon or lace, tape, gimp. 3. Luncheon given to labourers in the field about ten in the morning.

Bocado [bo-cah'-do], *m.* 1. Morsel, a mouthful of food. 2. Gobbet, a mouthful, as much as can be swallowed at once. 3. Modicum, small portion. 4. Bite, a wound made with the teeth. 5. Part of a thing torn off with the teeth or pincers. 6. (Obs.) Poison given in eatables. 7. Bit of a bridle. 8. (Art.) Wad of a large cannon. 9. (Naut.) The hold of a ship. *Bocado sin hueso,* Profitable employment without labour; a sinecure. *Con el bocado en la boca,* Immediately after dinner or supper. *Contarle á uno los bocados,* To watch how another eats. *No tener para un bocado,* To be in extreme distress.—*pl.* 1. Slices of quinces, apples, pumpkins, etc., made up into conserves. 2. (Naut.) Wads of great guns, hawse-plugs. *A bocados* or *bocaditos,* By piecemeals.

Bocaina [bo-cah'-e-nah], *f.* (Naut.) The mouth of a bar.

Bocal [bo-cahl'], *m.* 1. Pitcher. 2. Mouth-piece of a wind instrument. 3. (Naut.) The narrows of a harbour.

Bocamanga [bo-cah-mahn'-gah], *f.* That part of a sleeve which is near the wrist, wristband.

Bocanada [bo-cah-nah'-dah], *f.* 1. A mouthful of liquor. 2. Whiff, puff of smoke. *Bocanada de gente,* Mob, a rout. *Bocanada de viento,* A sudden blast of wind. *Echar bocanadas,* To boast of one's valour, noble birth, etc. *Echar bocanadas de sangre,* 1. To throw up mouthfuls of blood. 2. To vaunt of noble blood.

Bocarán [bo-cah-rahn'], *m.* Fine sort of buckram.

Bocarón [bo-cah-rone'], *m.* Wind-chest of an organ; wind-trunk.

Bocarte [bo-car'-tay], *m.* Ore-crusher, stamp, stamp-mill.

Bocateja [bo-cah-tay'-hah], *f.* The last tile of each line on a tiling.

Bocatijera [bo-ca-te-hay'-rah], *f.* Socket for the pole of a carriage.

Bocaza [bo-cah'-thah], *f. aug.* (Coll.) A large, wide mouth.

Bocel [bo-thel'], *m.* 1. (Arch.) Bowtel, astragal; a fluted moulding, torus. 2. Fluting-plane, an instrument for fluting mouldings.

Bocelar [bo-thay-lar'], *va.* To make fluted mouldings.

Bocelete [bo-thay-lay'-tay], *m. dim.* Small moulding-plane.

Bocelón [bo-thay-lone'], *m. aug.* Large moulding-plane.

Bocera [bo-thay'-rah], *f.* Crumbs, or other remains of eating or drinking, sticking to the outside of the lip.

Boceto [bo-thay'-to], *m.* A sketch, delineation, cartoon.

Bocezar [bo-thay-thar'], *va.* (Vet.) To move the lips from one side to another, as horses and other animals do when they eat.

Bocín [bo-theen'], *m.* 1. Round piece of bass mat put about the nave of a cart, as a cap of defence. 2. The iron, nozzle. 3. Hub of wheel.

Bocina [bo-thee'-nah], *f.* 1. Large trumpet, bugle-horn. *Bocina de cazador,* A huntsman's horn. 2. Hearing trumpet. 3. Automobile horn.

Bocinada [bo-the-nah'-dah], *f.* Empty boast, rant.

Bocinar [bo-the-nar'], *va.* (Obs.) To sound the trumpet, bugle-horn, or huntsman's horn.

Bocinero [bo-the-nay'-ro], *m.* Trumpeter, horn-blower.

Bocio [bo'the-o], *m.* (Med.) Goitre.

Bocón [bo-cone'], *m.* 1. (Aug.) A wide-mouthed person. 2. Braggart, a talkative boaster.

Bocoy [bo-co'-e], *m.* Hogshead.—*pl.* *Bocoyes abatidos,* Shooks of hogsheads.

Bocudo, da [bo-coo'-do, dah], *a.* Large-mouthed.

Bocha [bo'-chah], *f.* 1. Bowl, a wooden ball for playing at bowls. 2. (Prov.) Fold or double in clothes, where they do not fit well, but purse up. *Juego de las bochas,* The game at bowls. *Pan de bochas,* White bread.

Bochar [bo-char'], *va.* To throw a ball so that it hits another, in the game at bowls.
Bochazo [bo-chah'-tho], *m.* Stroke of one bowl against another.
Boche [bo'-chay], *m.* Cherry-pit or chuck-hole. *V.* Bote.
Bochinche [bo-cheen'-chay], *m.* 1. Uproar, disorder, tumult. 2. (Sp. Am.) Mess, quarrel, gossip.
Bochista [bo-chees'-tah], *m.* A good bowler or player at bowls.
Bochorno [bo-chor'-no], *m.* 1. Hot, sultry weather, scorching heat. 2. Blush, flushing, the colour of the cheeks raised by shame or passion.
Bochornoso, sa [bo-chor-no'-so, sah], *a.* 1. Shameful, reproachful, full of indignity, raising shame or confusion. 2. Sultry.
Boda [bo'-dah], *f.* Marriage, nuptials, match, the feast by which it is solemnized, a wedding. *Boda de hongos,* A beggar's wedding. *Perrito de todas bodas,* (Met.) Parasite who runs from wedding to wedding. *Aun ahora se come el pan de la boda,* The honeymoon is not yet over. *De tales bodas tales costras* or *tortas,* A bad beginning a bad end. (Gothic, viden; Anglo-Saxon, wedian.)
Bodaquera [bo-dah-kay'-rah], *f.* A blow-gun in South America.
Bode [bo'-day], *m.* A he-goat.
Bodega [bo-day'-gah], *f.* 1. Wine-vault, a cellar. 2. Abundant vintage or yield of wine. 3. Store-room, warehouse, magazine. . 4. A grocery. 5. (Naut.) Hold of a ship. *Bodega de popa,* After-hold. *Bodega de proa,* Fore-hold.
Bodegón [bo-day-gone'], *m.* 1. Mean chop-house, eating-house, or cook's shop. 2. Sign of a cook's shop or eating-house. 3. Tippling-house, *Bodegón de puntapie,* Stall where cow-heels and black-puddings are sold. *Echar el bodegón por la ventana,* To put one's self into a violent passion. *¿ En qué bodegón hemos comido juntos ?* Where have we eaten together? A rebuke for too much familiarity.
Bodegoncillo [bo-day-gon-theel'-lyo], *m. dim.* Low chop-house.
Bodegonear [bo-day-go-nay-ar'], *va.* To run from one tippling-house to another, to frequent mean eating-houses.
Bodegonero, ra [bo-day-go-nay'-ro, rah], *m. & f.* One who keeps a low chop-house or tippling-house.
Bodeguero, ra [bo-day-gay'-ro, rah], *m. & f.* 1. Butler, one who has the care of a cellar. 2. (Cuba) Grocer.
Bodeguilla [bo-day-geel'-lyah], *f. dim.* Small cellar or vault.
Bodián [bo-de-ahn'], *m.* Sea-fish, resembling a tench.
Bodigo [bo-dee'-go], *m.* Manchet, a small loaf made of the finest flour, and presented as an offering in the church.
Bodijo [bo-dee'-ho], *m.* (Coll.) Unequal match, a hedge-marriage performed with little ceremony or solemnity.
Bodocal [bo-do-cahl'], *a.* (Prov.) Applied to a kind of black grapes.
Bodocazo [bo-do-cah'-tho], *m.* Stroke of a pellet shot from a cross-bow.
Bodollo [bo-dol'-lyo], *m.* (Prov.) Pruning-knife, pruning-hook.
Bodoque [bo-do'-kay], *m.* 1. Pellet, a small ball of clay shot from a cross-bow. 2. Dunce, idiot. *Hacer bodoques,* (Coll.) To be reduced to dust, to be dead.
Bodoquera [bo-do-kay'-rah], *f.* 1. Mould in which pellets are formed. 2. Cradle, or that part of the stock of a cross-bow where the pellet is put. 3. Strings with which the cord of a cross-bow is tied.
Bodoquero, ra [bo-do-kay'-ro, rah], *a.* (Amer.) Contraband, smuggling.
Bodoquillo [bo-do-keel'-lyo], *m. dim.* Small pellet or bullet of clay.
Bodorrio [bo-dor'-re-o], *m.* (Coll.) *V* Bodijo. Banquet (Peru).
Bodrio [bo'-dre-o], *m.* 1. Soup, broken meat, and garden-stuff, given to the poor at the doors of convents. 2. A hash poorly prepared, a medley of broken meat.
Boezuelo [bo-ay-thoo-ay'-lo], *m.* Stalking-ox, which serves to screen fowlers engaged in the pursuit of birds.
Bofada [bo-fah'-dah], *f.* Ragout or fricassee made of the livers and lungs of animals.
Bofe [bo'-fay], *m.* Lung, lights. *Echar el bofe* or *los bofes,* To strain one's lungs; to labour very closely; to be very anxious.
Bofeta [bo-fay'-tah], *f.* **Bofetán** [bo-fay-tahn'], *m.* A sort of thin, stiff linen.
Bofetada [bo-fay-tah'-dah], *f.* Slap, buffet, box, a blow on the face with the hand. *Dar una bofetada,* (Met.) To treat with the utmost contempt.
Bofetón [bo-fay-tone'], *m.* 1. A cuff or violent blow with the hand upon the face. 2. Stage decorations representing folding-doors.
Bofetoncillo [bo-fay-ton-theel'-lyo], *m. dim.* A slight box or slap on the face.
Bofordo [bo-for'-do], *m.* (Obs.) A short lance or spear. *V.* Bohordo.
Boga [bo'-gah], *f.* 1. (Zool.) Ox-eyed cackerel, mendole. Sparus boops. 2. Act of rowing. 3. (Naut.) Rower, one who rows: in this sense it is masculine. 4. (Prov.) Small knife in the shape of a poinard. 5. Vogue, fashion. *V.* Voga. *Boga arrancada,* (Naut.) All hands rowing together with all their strength. *Boga larga,* A long stroke. *Dar la boga,* To give the stroke. *Boga avante,* Strokesman. *Estar en boga alguna cosa,* To be fashionable; to be commonly used.
Bogada [bo-gah'-dah], *f.* 1. Rowing-stroke. 2. Bucking of clothes with lye.
Bogador [bo-gah-dor'], *m.* Rower.
Bogante [bo-gahn'-tay], *pa.* (Poet.) Rower; rowing.
Bogar [bo-gar'], *vn.* To row. *Bogar a cuarteles,* To row by divisions. *Bogar a barlovento,* To row abroad. *Bogar a sotavento,* To row to leeward.
Bogavante [bo-gah-vahn'-tay], *m.* 1. (Naut.) Strokesman of a row galley. 2. Lobster of a large size.
Bogotano, na [bo-go-tah'-no, nah], *a.* Of Bogotá.
(*Yo bogué,* from *Bogar. V.* verbs in *gar.*)
Bohemiano, na, or **Bohemo, ma** [bo-ay-me-ah'-no, nah, bo-ay'-mo, mah], *a.* A Bohemian.
Bohémico, ca [bo-ay'-me-co], *a.* Belonging to Bohemia or its people.
Bohemio, mia [bo-ay'-me-o, ah], *a.* Bohemian, unconventional. *m. & f.* Bohemian, unconventional person.
Bohena, Boheña [bo-ay'-nah, bo-ay'-nyah], *f.* (Obs.) 1. *V.* Bofes. 2. Pork sausages.
Bohio [bo-ee'-o], *m.* Indian hut, a humble hut for the negroes in the West Indies.
Bohordar [bo-or-dar'], *va.* To throw wands, called *bohordos,* in tournaments.
Bohordo [bo-or'-do], *m.* 1. Blade of flag, a water-plant. 2. Wands, the hollow end of which is filled with sand, which tilters threw at each other in tournaments. 3. (Bot.) A scape: flower-peduncle.
Boicoteo [bo-e-co-tay'-o], *m.* Boycott.
Boil [bo-eel'], *m.* Ox-stall, a stand for oxen. *V.* Boyera.
Boina [bo'-e-nah], *f.* Flat, round woollen cap generally worn in Navarre and Biscay.
Boite [bo'-e-tay], *m.* Discotheque, night club, ballroom.
Boj [boh], *m.* 1. Box-tree, box-wood. 2. A box-wood tool, on which shoemakers close their work.
Boja [bo'-hah], *f.* 1. (Obs.) *V.* Buba. 2. (Prov.) Southern-wood.
Bojar [bo-har'], or **Bojear,** *va.* 1. (Naut.) To sail round an island or cape, and measure its circumference. 2. To scrape off the rough integuments, stains, and moisture of leather, that it may the better take the colour.—*vn.* To measure around, to contain.
Bojedal [bo-hay-dahl'], *m.* Plantation of box-trees.
Bojeo, Bojo [bo-hay'-oh, bo'-ho], *m.* (Naut.) The act of sailing round an island or head-land.
Bojeta [bo-hay'-tah], *f.* (Ichth. Prov.) A kind of herring.
Bol [bole], *m.* 1. Bowl. *V.* Ponchera. 2. Bolo, by apocope. 3. Armenian bole, a red earth, used chiefly by gilders.
Bola [bo'-lah], *f.* 1. Ball, globe, pellet; marble, bolus. 2. Game of throwing bullets or bowls. 3. (Coll.) Lie, falsehood, humbug, hoax, fib. 4. (Naut.) Truck, acorn; a round piece of wood at the end of the ensign staffs and vanes. 5. Blacking for shoes. 6. Basin of the glass-grinder. *Escurrir la bola,* To take French leave, to run away. *Ruede la bola,* Colloquial expression, meaning that things are not going on against our wishes. *Pie con bola,* Just enough, as much as is wanted, neither too much nor too little. *Bola de jabón,* Wash-ball. *Juego de bolas,* Bowling-green, bowling-ground; playing marbles.
Bolada [bo-lah'-dah], *f.* Throw or cast of a ball or bowl.
Bolado [bo-lah'-do], *m.* (Prov.) Cake of clarified sugar used in Spain to sweeten water for drinking.
Bolantin [bo-lan-teen'], *m.* Fine sort of pack-thread.
Bolarménico [bo-lar-may'-ne-co], *m. V.* Bol.
Bolazo [bo-lah'-tho], *m.* Violent blow with a bowl.
Bolchaca, *f.* **Bolchaco,** *m.* [bol-chah'-cah, co]. (Prov.) Pocket, purse.
Bolchevique [bol-chay-vee'kay], *m. & f. & a.* Bolshevik.
Bolchevismo [bol-chay-vees'-mo], *m.* Bolshevism.
Bolear [bo-lay-ar'], *vn.* 1. To play at billiards for amusement merely. 2. To throw wooden or iron balls for a wager. 3. (Prov.) To boast, to lie extravagantly.—*va.* 1. To dart, to launch. 2. *Bolear el sombrero,* To fix the hat on the head.
Boleo [bo-lay'-o], *m.* The road or place where balls are thrown.
Bolera [bo-lay'-rah], *f.* Bowling alley.
Bolero [bo-lay'-ro], *m.* 1. Bolero, a Spanish dance and musical rhythm. 2. Bolero, a lady's garment. 3. (Mex.) Bootblack.
Bolero, ra, *a.* 1. Truant. 2. Fibbing, lying.
Boleta [bo-lay'-tah], *f.* 1. Ticket giving the right of admission to a place. 2. Billet or ticket which directs soldiers where they are to lodge. 3. Voucher or warrant for receiving money or other things. 4. (Prov.)

Small paper with tobacco, sold at chandlers' shops.

Boletar [bo-lay-tar'], *va.* (Prov.) To roll up tobacco in small bits of paper for the purpose of selling them.

Boletería [bo-lay-tay-ree'-ah], *f.* (Amer.) Box office, ticket office.

Boletero [bo-le-tay'-ro], *m.* Ticket-agent.

Boletín [bo-lay-teen'], *m.* 1. Warrant given for the payment of money. 2. Ticket for the quartering of soldiers. 3. Ticket granting free admittance at a theatre or other place of amusement. 4. Bulletin of news; official military or medical notice. 5. (Com.) List, statement.

Boleto [bo-lay'-to], *m.* Ticket. *Boleto de ida y vuelta* or *boleto redondo*, Round-trip ticket.

Bolichada [bo-le-chah'-dah], *f.* At one throw, at once. *De una bolichada*, By chance.

Boliche [bo-lee'-chay], *m.* 1. Jack, a small ball which serves as a mark for bowl-players; block. 2. All the small fish caught at once in a drag-net near the shore, and the drag-net with which they are caught. *Juego de boliche*, Pigeon-holes, a game played on a concave table with a ball; troll-madam. *Boliches*, (Naut.) Fore-top bowlines, and top-gallant bowlines. 3. A furnace for lead-smelting. 4. The toy called cup and ball.

Bolichero, ra [bo-le-chay'-ro, rah], *m.* & *f.* One who keeps a pigeon-hole, or troll-madam table.

Bólido [bo'-le-do], *m.* A fiery meteor, shooting-star.

Bolígrafo [bo-lee'-grah-fo], *m.* Ball-point pen.

Bolillo [bo-leel'-lyo], *m.* 1. Dim. of Bolo. 2. Jack, a small ball or bowl to play at trucks. 3. Bobbin, a small pin of box or bone used in making bone-lace. 4. Mould or frame on which the cuffs of linen or gauze, worn on the sleeves of counsellors of state, and formerly of inquisitors, are starched and made up. 5. Bone joined to skull of horses.—*pl.* 1. Paste-nuts, small balls made of sweet paste. 2. Starched cuffs worn by counsellors of state, and formerly by inquisitors.

Bolín [bo-leen'], *m.* Jack, a small ball which serves as a mark for bowl-players. *De bolín, de bolán*, (Coll.) At random, inconsiderately, rashly, thoughtlessly.

Bolina [bo-lee'-nah], *f.* 1. (Coll.) Noise and clamour of a scuffle or dispute. 2. (Naut.) Bowline, a rope fastened to the leech or edge of a square-sail, to make it stand close to the wind. 3. A kind of punishment on shipboard like baqueta, or the gantlet. *Bolina de barlovento*, Weather bowline. *Bolina de sotavento* or *de revés*, Lee bowline. *Bolina de trinquete*, Fore-bowline. *Dar un salto a la bolina*, To ease or check the bowline. *Presentar la bolina*, To snatch the bowline. *Navegar de bolina*, To sail with bowlines hauled. *Ir a la bolina*, To sail with a side wind. *Navío buen bolinador*, A good plyer, a ship which makes great progress against the wind. *Echar de bolina*, (Met.) To make fanfaronades, or idle boasts.

Bolinear [bo-le-nay-ar'], *va.* To haul up the bowline in light winds.

Bolinete [bo-le-nay'-tay], *m.* (Naut.) A movable capstan on deck, in which the whipstaff moves.

Bolisa [bo-lee'-sah], *f.* (Prov.) Embers, hot cinders.

Bolo [bo'-lo], *m.* 1. One of the nine-pins set up to be knocked down by a bowl. 2. (Prov.) Round or oblong cushion on which women make lace. 3. Large piece of timber, in which the shafts and rests of a winding staircase are fitted. 4. Idiot, stupid. 5. Bolus, a very large pill. 6. The game of nine-pins or ten-pins. 7. A large knife, like a machete, used in the Philippines. *Diablos son bolos*, Contingencies cannot be depended on. *Es un bolo*, He is an idiot, an ignorant, stupid fellow. *Juego de bolos*, A game of nine-pins.

Bolones [bo-lo'-nes], *m. pl.* (Naut.) Square bolts or mortar-bed pintles, which serve to fasten the cheeks to the bed.

Bolonio [bo-lo'-ne-o], *m.* An ignorant, rattle-brained fellow.

Boloñés, esa [bo-lo-nyess', sah], *a.* Bolognese; of Bologna.

Bolsa [bol'-sah], *f.* 1. Purse. 2. Purse-net made of silk or worsted, with strings to draw the mouth together. 3. Money. 4. Exchange, the place where merchants meet to negotiate their affairs. *V.* Lonja. 5. Pouch or net used by sportsmen to put game in. 6. Bag in which public papers and despatches are carried by ministers and secretaries of state. 7. Bag for the hair. 8. Bag lined with furs or skins to keep the feet warm. 9. In a gold-mine, the vein which contains the purest gold; a pocket. 10. (Med.) A morbid swelling full of matter. 11. (Anat.) Scrotum. *Bolsa de pastor*, (Bot.) Shepherd's-purse. Capsella bursa pastoris, *Decandolle*. *Bolsa de Dios*, Alms, charity. *Bolsa de hierro*, Avaricious, covetous. *Bolsa rota*, Spendthrift. *Castigar en la bolsa*, To fine. *Dar* or *echar otro nudo a la bolsa*, To become extremely frugal, to lessen one's expense. *Page de bolsa*, A minister's page who carries the official papers. *Tener como en la bolsa alguna cosa*, To be as sure of a thing as if it were in one's pocket. *Tener* or *llevar bien herrada la bolsa*, To have the purse well lined; to have money.

Bolsear [bol-say-ar'], *vn.* (Prov.) To purse up, to pucker: applied to clothes, hangings, and other things.

Bolsería [bol-say-ree'-ah], *f.* Manufactory of purses, and the place where they are sold.

Bolsero [bol-say'-ro], *m.* 1. (Obs.) Cashier, treasurer. 2. Manufacturer of purses, one who makes purses.

Bolsico [bol-see'-co], *m.* Poke, pocket.

Bolsillo [bol-seel'-lyo], *m.* 1. Purse. 2. Pocket. 3. Money. 4. *Dim.* of Bolso. *Buen bolsillo*, or *gran bolsillo*, A large capital, or great sum of money. *Bolsillo de aire*, Air pocket. *Bolsillo para tabaco*, Tobacco pouch. *Bolsillo secreto*, Privy purse. *Hacer bolsillo*, To make or get money. *Tener un gran bolsillo*, To be very rich.

Bolsín [bol-seen'], *m.* Gathering of brokers out of the exchange and the hours observed there.

Bolsista [bol-sees'-tah], *m.* Stock-broker, speculator.

Bolso [bol'-so], *m.* Purse of money, a money-bag.

Bolsón [bol-sone'], *m.* 1. *Aug.* of Bolso. Large purse. 2. Large bar of iron put in vaults or arches to secure the building. 3. In oil-mills, large plank or board with which the oil-reservoir is lined. 4. Stone on which an arch or vault is sprung.

Bolula [bo-loo'-lah], *f.* *V.* Bululú.

Bolla [bol'-lyah], *f.* 1. Duty on woollens and silks retailed for home consumption formerly levied in Catalonia. 2. In South America, great richness of an ore.

Bolladura, [bol-lyah-doo'-rah] *f.* *V.* Abolladura.

Bollar [bol-lyar'], *va.* 1. To put a leaden seal on cloths to indicate their manufactory. 2. To emboss, to raise figures.

Bollero, ra [bol-lyay'-ro, rah], *m.* & *f.* Pastry-cook, seller of sweet cakes.

Bollo [bol'-lyo], *m.* 1. Small loaf or roll made of fine flour; penny loaf. 2. Small biscuit or cake made of sugar, flour, milk, and eggs. 3. Bruise made in metal or any similar matter. *Bollo maimón*, A sort of cake filled with sweetmeats. 4. Morbid swelling. 5. *Bollos*, Ancient head-dress of women, consisting of large buckles. 6. In Peru, bars of silver extracted from the ore by means of fire or quicksilver. *Bollos de relieve*, Embossed or raised work.

Bollón [bol-lyone'], *m.* 1. Brass-headed nail used in coaches and furniture. 2. (Prov.) Button which shoots from a plant, especially from a vine-stock.

Bollonado, da [bol-lyo-nah'-do, dah], *a.* 1. Adorned with brass-headed nails. 2. Furnished with shoots, buds, or buttons.

Bollueio [bol-lyoo-ay'-lo], *m. dim.* of Bollo.

Bomba [bom'-bah], *f.* 1. Pump, pumping engine. 2. Bomb; shell, bomb shell. 3. Lamp chimney. 4. Earthen jar or firkin for skimming oil from water. *¡Bomba!* Your attention, please. *Bomba atómica*, Atomic bomb, A-bomb. *Bomba de alimentación*, Feed pump. *Bomba de apagar incendios*, Fire engine. *Bomba de cadena* or *de rosario*, Chain pump. *Bomba de carena*, Bilge pump. *Bomba de circulación*, Circulating pump. *Bomba de cobalto*, Cobalt bomb. *Bomba de compresión, de impelente*, Force pump. *Bomba de fragmentación*, Fragmentation bomb. *Bomba de fuego* or *de vaho*, Steam engine. *Bomba de guimbalete*, (Naut.) Common pump. *Bomba de hidrógeno*, Hydrogen bomb. *Bomba de mano*, Hand pump. *Bomba de proa*, Head pump. *Bomba de profundidad*, Depth charge. *Bomba de vacío*, Vacuum pump. *Bomba de vapor*, Steam engine. *Bomba incendiaria*, Incendiary bomb. *Bomba inyectora*, Injection pump. *Bomba libre*, Pump in good working order. *Bomba* or *manga marina*, Water spout. *Bomba neutrona*, Neutron bomb. *Cargar la bomba*, To prime the pump. *Estar a prueba de bomba*, To be bomb-proof. *La bomba está atascada*, The pump is clogged. *La bomba llama*, The pump sucks.

Bombardear [bom-bar-day-ar'], *va.* To bombard, to discharge bombs; to shell.

Bombardeo [bom-bar-day'-o], *m.* Bombardment, bombing, *Bombardeo aéreo*, Air raid, air bombing.

Bombardero [bom-bar-day'-ro], *m.* 1. Bomber (plane). 2. Bombardier.

Bombardino [bom-bar-dee'-no], *m.* Saxhorn.

Bombasí [bom-bah-see'], *m.* Bombazine, dimity.

Bombazo [bom-bah'-tho], *m.* Report of a bursting bomb.

Bombé [bom-bay'], *m.* A light two-wheeled carriage open in front.

Bombear [bom-bay-ar'], *va.* *V.* Bombardear.

Bombeo [bom-bay-'o], *m.* Pumping.
Bombero [bom-bay'-ro], *m.* 1. Fireman. 2. Howitzer.
Bombilla [bom-beel'-lyah], *f.* 1. (Amer.) A small silver or gold perforated tube for drinking *Mate.* 2. (Elec.) Light bulb. *Bombilla de destello,* Photoflash bulb.
Bombillo [bom-beel'-lyo], *m.* 1. Lamp chimney. 2. Water-closet trap. 3. Small pump. 4. Tube to draw off liquids.
Bombo [bom'-bo], *m.* 1. Large drum. 2. Player on bass drum. 3. (Naut.) Barge or lighter. 4. Ballyhoo, excessive praise.
Bombo, ba [bom'-bo, bah], *a.* 1. Astonished. 2. (Cuba and Amer.) Tepid.
Bombonaje [bom-bo-nah'-hay], *m.* A screw-pine, Carludovica palmata, used for straw hats.
Bonachón, na [bo-nah-chone', nah], *m.* & *f.* & *a.* Good-natured, easy person.
Bonaerense [bo-nah-ay-ren'-say], *m.* & *f.* Native or resident of Buenos Aires, Argentina.
Bonancible [bo-nan-thee -blay], *a.* Moderate, calm, fair, serene: applied to the weather at sea.
Bonanza [bo-nahn'-thah], *f.* 1. Fair weather at sea. *Ir en bonanza,* (Naut.) To sail with fair wind and weather. 2. Prosperity, success. *Ir en bonanza,* (Met.) To go on prosperously, to do well.
Bonaso [bo-nah'-so], *m.* Bonasus, a kind of buffalo.
Bonazo, za [bo-nah'-tho, thah], *a.* (Coll.) Good-natured, kind.
Bondad [bon-dahd'], *f.* 1. Goodness, either moral or physical; excellence, healthfulness. 2. Goodness, kindness, good-will, graciousness, clemency; frankness, courtesy, suavity, or mildness of temper. 3. Liberality.
Bondadoso, sa [bon-dah-do'-so, sah], *a.* Kind, generous, beautiful. *V.* BENÉVOLO.
Bondón [bon-done'], *m.* Bung, the stopple of a barrel.
Bondoso, sa [bon-do'-so, sah], *a.* *V.* BONDADOSO.
Bonetas [bo-nay'-tas], *f. pl.* (Naut.) Bonnets, pieces of canvas laced to the sails, to make more way in light winds.
Bonetada [bo-nay-tah'-dah], *f.* (Coll.) Salutation made by taking off the hat or bonnet.
Bonete [bo-nay'-tay], *m.* 1. Bonnet or cap used by clergymen, collegians, and doctors or professors of the universities. 2. Secular clergyman who wears a bonnet, in contradistinction to a monk who wears a hood or cowl. 3. Bonnet, a kind of outworks of a fortress. *Tirarse los bonetes,* To pull caps. *Bravo* or *gran bonete,* (Iron.) A great dunce. 4. (Obs.) Wide-mouthed vial for conserves. 5. Second stomach, reticulum, of ruminants. *A tente bonete,* or *hasta tente bonete,* Abundantly, excessively.
Bonetería [bo-nay-tay-ree'-ah], *f.* Shop where bonnets are made or sold.
Bonetero, ra [bo-nay-tay'-ro, rah], *m.* & *f.* 1. One who makes bonnets. 2. (Bot.) Prickwood, gatheridge, or common spindle-tree. Euonymus europæus.
Bonetillo [bo-nay-teel'-lyo], *m.* 1. (Dim.) Small cap or bonnet. 2. Ornament in the shape of a bonnet, which women wear over their head-dress.
Boniato (BUNIATO or MONIATO) [bo-ne-ah'-to], *m.* A sweet potato. Convolvulus batatas.
Bonicamente [bo-ne-cah-men'-tay], *adv.* Prettily, neatly, slyly.
Bonico, ca [bo-nee'-co, cah], *a.* Pretty good, passable. *Andar a las bonicas,* (Met.) To take things easily, to do them at ease, not to burden one's self with business. *Jugar a las bonicas,* To play at ball by passing it from one hand into another.
Bonificación [bo-ne-fe-cah-the-on'], *f.* (Com.) Allowance, discount, bonus.
Bonificar [bo-ne-fe-car'], *va.* 1. (Obs.) To credit, to place to one's credit. 2. To meliorate, to improve.
Bonijo [bo-nee'-ho], *m.* The pit of the olive after having been crushed in the mill.
Bonillo, illa [bo-neel'-lyo, lyah], *a. dim.* (Obs.) 1. Somewhat handsome. 2. Somewhat great, large, or big.
Bonina [bo-nee'-nah], *f.* (Bot.) Ox-eye chamomile. Anthemis tinctoria.
Bonísimo, ma [bo-nee'-se-mo, mah], *a. sup.* of BUENO.
Bonítalo [bo-nee'-tah-lo], *m.* *V.* BONITO. A fish.
Bonitamente [bo-ne-tah-men'-tay], *adv.* (Coll.) *V.* BONICAMENTE.
Bonitillo, illa [bo-ne-teel'-lyo, lyah], *a. dim.* Somewhat handsome.
Bonito [bo-nee'-to], *m.* Sea-fish, resembling a tunny. Scomber pelamis, and Sarda Chilensis (Pacific Ocean). Striped tunny.
Bonito, ta [bo-nee'-to, tah], *a.* 1. Dim. of BUENO. Pretty good, passable. 2. Affecting elegance and neatness. 3. Pretty. 4. Graceful, minion. 5. Soft, effeminate.
Bono [bo'-no], *m.* (Com.) Bond, certificate.
Bonzo [bon'-tho], *m.* Bonze, a priest of Buddha in China, Japan, and other heathen nations.
Boñiga [bo-nyee'-gah], *f.* Cow-dung.
Bootes [bo-o'-tes], *m.* Bootes, a northern constellation.
Boqueada [bo-kay-ah'-dah], *f.* Act of opening the mouth, a gasp. *A la primera boqueada,* Immediately, without delay. *La última boqueada,* The last gasp.
Boquear [bo-kay-ar'], *vn.* 1. To gape, to gasp, to open the mouth wide. 2. To breathe one's last, to expire. 3. (Met.) To end, to terminate.—*va.* To pronounce, to utter a word or expression.
Boquera [bo-kay'-rah], *f.* 1. Sluice made in a canal for irrigating lands. 2. (Prov.) Opening made in inclosures to let in cattle. 3. Eruption of the lips. 4. Ulcer in the mouth of beasts.
Boquerón [bo-kay-rone'], *m.* 1. Wide opening, a large hole. 2. (Zool.) Anchovy. Clupea encrasicolus. 3. (Naut.) Mouth of a channel between shallow bottoms.
Boquete [bo-kay'-tay], *m.* Gap, narrow entrance.
Boquiabierto, ta [bo-ke-ah-be-err'-to, tah], *a.* (Coll.) Having the mouth open; walking about gaping.
Boquiancho, cha [bo-ke-ahn-'cho, chah], *a.* Wide-mouthed.
Boquiangosto, ta [bo-ke-an-gos'-to, tah], *a.* Narrow-mouthed.
Boquiconejuno, na [bo-ke-co-nay-hoo'-no, nah], *a.* Rabbit-mouthed; hare-lipped: applied to horses.
Boquiduro, ra [bo-ke-doo'-ro, rah], *a.* Hard-mouthed: applied to horses.
Boquifresco, ca [bo-ke-fres'-co, cah], *a.* Fresh-mouthed: applied to horses which have a soft salivous mouth.
Boquifruncido, da [bo-ke-froon-thee'-do, dah], *a.* Having the mouth contracted.
Boquihendido, da [bo-ke-en-dee'-do, dah], *a.* Large-mouthed, flewed.
Boquihundido, da [bo-ke-oon-dee'-do, dah], *a.* Having the mouth sunk in, from age or want of teeth.
Boquilla [bo-keel'-lyah], *f.* 1. (Dim.) Little mouth. 2. Opening of breeches at the knees. 3. Opening in a canal for irrigating lands. 4. Chisel for mortising. 5. Mouth-piece of a musical wind instrument. 6. Cigar-holder. 7. (Mas.) Verge, course. 8. (Mech.) Bushing, bush. 9. Bomb-hole.
Boquimuelle [bo-ke-moo-el'-lyay], *a.* 1. Tender-mouthed: applied to a horse. 2. Unwary, easily imposed upon.
Boquín [bo-keen'], *m.* Coarse sort of baize.
Boquinatural [bo-ke-nah-too-rahl'], *a.* Well-mouthed, neither too tender nor too hard: applied to a horse.
Boquinegro, gra [bo-ke-nay'-gro, grah], *a.* Applied to animals whose mouth is black.—*m.* & *f.* A blackish sort of snails.
Boquirrasgado, da [bo-keer-ras-gah'-do, dah], *a.* Deep-mouthed: spoken of a horse.
Boquirroto, ta [bo-keer-ro'-to, tah], *a.* Loquacious, garrulous.
Boquirrubio, bia [bo-keer-roo'-be-o, ah], *a.* Simple, artless, easily imposed upon.
Boquiseco, ca [bo-ke-say'-co, cah], *a.* Dry-mouthed: applied to a horse.
Boquisumido, da [bo-ke-soo-mee'-do, dah], *a.* *V.* BOQUIHUNDIDO.
Boquita [bo-kee'-tah], *f. dim.* Small mouth.
Boquitorcido, da, Boquituerto, ta [bo-ke-tor-thee'-do, dah, bo-ke-too-err'-to, tah], *a.* Wry-mouthed, distorted with crying.
Borácico, ca [bo-rah'-the-co, cah], *a.* Boracic. *V.* BÓRICO.
Borato [bo-rah'-to], *m.* Borate.
Bórax [bo'-rax], *m.* Borax; sodium biborate.
Borbollar, Borbollonear [bor-bol-lyar'], *vn.* To bubble out, to stream or to gush out, to flash.
Borbollón, Borbotón [bor-bol-lyone', bor-bo-tone'], *m.* 1. Bubbling, gushing up of water in large bubbles; flash. 2. (Met.) Flow of language hastily and incorrectly uttered. *A borbollones,* In a bubbling or impetuous manner, in hurry and confusion. *Hirviendo a borbollones* or *a borbotones,* Boiling hot.
Borbónico, ca [bor-bo'-ne-co, cah], *a.* Bourbon.
Borborigmo [bor-bo-reeg'-mo], *m.* Rumbling in the bowels.
Borbotar [bor-bo-tar'], *vn.* (Littl us.) To gush out with violence; to boil over.
Borceguí [bor-thay-gee'], *m.* 1. Buskin, a kind of half-boot. 2. Laced shoes.
Borceguinería [bor-thay-gee-nay-ree'-ah], *f.* A shop where buskins are made or sold.
Borceguinero, ra [bor-thay-gee-nay'-ro, rah], *m.* & *f.* Maker or retailer of buskins.
Borcellar [bor-thel-lyar'], *m.* (Prov.) Brim of a vessel.
Borda [bor'-dah], *f.* 1. (Prov.) Hut, cottage. 2. (Naut.) Gunwale of a ship.
Bordada [bor-dah'-dah], *f.* (Naut.) Board, tack. *Dar una bordada,* To tack, to make a tack.
Bordadillo [bor-dah-deel'-lyo], *m.* Double-flowered taffeta.
Bordado [bor-dah'-do], *m.* Embroidery. *Bordado de pasado,* Plain embroidery, without light or shade.—*pp.* of BORDAR.
Bordador, ra [bor-dah-dor', rah], *m.* & *f.* Embroiderer.

Bordadura [bor-dah-doo'-rah], *f.* 1. Embroidery; variegated needlework. 2. (Her.) Border of the inside of an escutcheon.

Bordaje [bor-dah'-hay], *m.* (Naut.) Side planks of a ship.

Bordar [bor-dar'], *va.* 1. To embroider. 2. To perform a thing according to art. *Baila que lo borda*, He dances charmingly. *Bordar a tambor*, To tambour, to embroider with a tambour needle.

Borde [bor'-day], *m.* 1. Border, the outer edge. 2. Margin, the edge of a thing; verge, fringe. 3. Ledge, a rising or projecting ridge. 4. Hem of a garment. 5. Brim of a vessel. 6. Bastard child. 7. (Obs.) Shoot or bud of a vine. 8. Board, the side of a ship. *A borde*, (Obs.) On the brink; on the eve.—*a.* Wild, savage, uncultivated: applied to trees not ingrafted or cultivated.

Bordear [bor-day-ar'], *vn.* (Naut.) To ply to windward.

Bordelés, sa [bor-day-less', sah], *a.* Of Bordeaux.

Bordo [bor'-do], *m.* 1. (Obs.) Border, the outer edge. 2. Ship or vessel. *Fué a bordo*, (Naut.) He was aboard ship. 3. Board, the side of a ship. *Bordo con bordo*, Board and board, side by side: when two ships are close to each other. *Bordo sobre bordo*, Hank for hank: when two ships tack together, and ply to windward. *Bordo a la tierra*, To stand inshore. *Bordo a la mar*, To stand off. 4. (Naut.) Board, tack. *Bordo corto*, A short board. *Bordo largo*, A long board. *Buen bordo*, A good board. *Dar bordos*, (Naut.) 1. To tack. 2. (Met.) To go frequently to and fro. *Correr sobre el mismo bordo con el enemigo*, (Naut.) To run on the same tack as the enemy.

Bordón [bor-done'], *m.* 1. Jacob's staff, a pilgrim's staff. 2. Bass-string. 3. Bass of an organ. 4. Vicious repetition of words in a discourse. 5. Burden of a song. 6. (Met.) Staff, guide, or support of another. *Bordones*, (Naut.) Shores, out-riggers.

Bordoneado, da [bor-do-nay-ah'-do, dah], *a.* (Her.) Pommelled.—*pp.* of BORDONEAR.

Bordonear [bor-do-nay-ar'], *vn.* 1. To try the ground with a staff or stick. 2. To strike with a staff or cudgel. 3. To rove or wander about, to avoid labour. 4. To play well on the thorough bass. 5. (Aer.) to buzz.

Bordonería [bor-do-nay-ree'-ah], *f.* Vicious habit of wandering idly about, on pretence of devotion.

Bordonero, ra [bor-do-nay'-ro, rah], *m.* & *f.* Vagrant, vagabond, tramp.

Bordura [bor-doo'-rah], *f.* (Her.) *V.* BORDADURA.

Boreal [bo-ray-ahl'], *a.* Boreal, northern

Bóreas [bo'-ray-as], *m.* Boreas, the north wind.

Borgoña [bor-go'-nyah], *f.* Burgundy wine. Burgundy, the district.

Borgoñota [bor-go-nyo'-tah], *f.* Sort of ancient helmet. *A la borgoñota*, In the Burgundy fashion.

Bórico, ca [bo'-re-co, cah], *a.* Boric.

Boricua [bo-ree'-coo-ah], *a.* & *m.* & *f.* Puerto Rican.

Borinqueño, ña [bo-ren-kay'-nyo, nyah], *a.* & *m.* & *f.* Puerto Rican.

Borla [bor'-lah], *f.* 1. Tassel, bunch of silk, gold, or silver lace. 2. Tuft, lock, flaunt. 3. In universities, doctor's bonnet decorated with a tassel. 4. Doctorship.

Borlilla [bor-leel'-lyah], *f.* Anther.

Borlón [bor-lone'], *m.* 1. (Aug.) Large tassel. 2. Napped stuff, made of thread and cotton yarn.

Borne [bor'-nay], *m.* 1. (Obs.) The end of a lance. 2. Kind of oak-tree.

Borneadero [bor-nay-ah-day'-ro], *m.* (Naut.) Berth of a ship at anchor, swinging berth.

Borneadizo, za [bor-nay-ah-dee'-tho, thah], *a.* Pliant, flexible.

Bornear [bor-nay-ar'], *va.* 1. To bend, turn, or twist. 2. (Arch.) To model and cut pillars all round. *Bornear la verdad*, To comment, to explain or expound. *Bornear las palabras*, To turn words into different senses.—*vn.* 1. To edge, to sidle. 2. To warp, to turn. *El navío bornea*, (Naut.) The ship swings or turns round her anchor.

Borneo [bor-nay'-o], *m.* 1. Act of turning or winding a thing. 2. (Naut.) Swinging round the anchor.

Bornera [bor-nay'-rah], *a.* Applied to a blackish sort of mill-stone.

Bornero, ra [bor-nay'-ro, rah], *a.* Ground by a black mill-stone: applied to wheat.

Borní [bor-nee'], *m.* (Orn.) Lanner, a kind of falcon. Falco lanarius.

Boro [bo'-ro], *m.* Boron, one of the chemical elements.

Borona [bo-ro'-nah], *f.* 1. A sort of grain resembling Indian corn. 2. Bread made from this grain.

Boronía [bo-ro-nee'-ah], *f.* Dish made of chopped apples, pumpkins, and green pepper. *V.* ALBORONÍA.

Borra [bor'-rah], *f.* 1. Yearling ewe. 2. The thickest part of the wool. 3. Goat's hair. 4. Nap on the cloth; floss, burl. 5. Tax on sheep. 6. Lees, sediment, waste. 7. Refined borax. *¿ Acaso es borra ?* Do you think that nothing but idle talk? *Borra de castor*, Beaver's hair. *Borra de lana*, Flock wool, waste wool. *Borra de seda*, Floss silk, waste silk.

Borracha [bor-rah'-chah], *f.* (Coll.) Leather bag or bottle for wine.

Borrachear [bor-rah-chay-ar'], *vn.* To be often drunk.

Borrachera, Borrachería [bor-rah-chay'-rah, bor-rah-chay-ree'-ah], *f.* 1. Drunkenness; hard-drinking. 2. Revelry, drunken feast, wassail. 3. (Met.) Madness, great folly.

Borrachero [bor-rah-chay'-ro], *m.* A shrub of South America: the seed ingested causes delirium. Datura arborea.

Borrachez [bor-rah-cheth'], *f.* 1. Intoxication. 2. Perturbation of the judgment or reason.

Borracho, cha [bor-rah'-cho, chah], *a.* 1. Drunk, intoxicated. 2. (Met.) Inflamed by passion. 3. Applied to biscuit baked with wine. 4. Applied to fruits and flowers of a violet colour.

Borrachón, Borrachonazo [bor-rah-chone', bor-rah-cho-nah'-tho], *m. aug.* Great drunkard, a tippler.

Borrachuela [bor-rah-choo-ay'-lah], *f.* (Bot.) Ray-grass. Lolium temulentum: Its seeds, mixed with bread-corn, intoxicate.

Borrachuelo, la [bor-rah-choo-ay'-lo, lah], *m.* & *f. dim.* Little tippler.

Borrador [bor-rah-dor'], *m.* 1. Rough draft of a writing in which corrections are made, foul copy. 2. Waste-book of merchants; blotter.

Borraj [bor-rah'], *m.* *V.* ATÍNCAR and BÓRAX.

Borraja [bor-rah'-hah], *f.* (Bot.) Borage. Borago officinalis.

Borrajear [bor-rah-hay-ar'], *vn.* To scribble, to write carelessly on any subject.

Borrajo [bor-rah'-ho], *m.* (Prov.) *V.* RESCOLDO.

Borrar [bor-rar'], *va.* 1. To cross out, strike out. 2. To blot with ink, to efface. 3. To blur, to erase, rub out, obliterate. 4. To cause to vanish. 5. (Met.) To cloud, to darken, to obscure. *Borrar la plaza*, To abolish a place or employ.

Borrasca [bor-rahs'-cah], *f.* 1. Storm, tempest, violent squall of wind. 2. Barren rock. *Dar o caer en borrasca*, In the mines, a mine that yields nothing, unprofitable. 3. (Met.) Hazard, danger, obstruction.

Borrascoso, sa [bor-ras-co'-so, sah], *a.* Stormy, boisterous, gusty, tempestuous.

Borrasquero, ra [bor-ras-kay'-ro, rah], *a.* & *m.* & *f.* Reveller: applied to a person fond of tumultuous festivities.

Borregada [bor-ray-gah'-dah], *f.* Large flock of sheep or lambs.

Borrego, ga [bor-ray'-go, gah], *m.* & *f.* 1. Lamb not yet a year old. 2. (Met.) Simpleton, a soft, ignorant fellow. *No hay tales borregos*, (Coll.) There is no evidence of its truth, there is not such a thing.

Borreguero [bor-ray-gay'-ro], *m.* Shepherd who tends lambs.

Borreguito [bor-ray-gee'-to], *m. dim.* Little lamb.

Borrén [bor-ren'], *m.* A saddle-cloth; saddle; bolster, straw cushion.

Borriba [bor-ree'-bah], *f.* Engine for raising water.

Borrica [bor-ree'-cah], *f.* A she-ass. *V.* BORRICO.

Borricada [bor-re-cah'-dah], *f.* 1. Drove of asses. 2. Procession on asses. 3. (Met.) Silly or foolish word or action.

Borrico [bor-ree'-co], *m.* 1. Ass, jument. 2. Fool. 3. Trestle-horse of carpenters. *Es un borrico*, He can bear great labour and fatigue. *Puesto en el borrico*, (Met.) Determined to do some business or other. *Poner a alguno sobre un borrico*, To threaten any one with a whipping.

Borricón, Borricote [bor-re-cone', bor-re-co'-tay], *m.* 1. (Aug.) Large jackass. 2. (Met.) Plodder, dull, heavy, and laborious man. 3. Among sawyers, horse, a frame on which timber is sawed.

Borrilla [bor-reel'-lyah], *f.* 1. The downy matter enveloping fruits. 2. Shearing or flue cut from clothes.

Borriqueño, ña [bor-re-kay'-nyo, nyah], *a.* Asinine.

Borriquero [bor-re-kay'-ro], *m.* One who keeps or tends asses.

Borriquete de proa [bor-re-kay'-tay], *m.* (Naut.) Fore-topmast.

Borriquillo, illa; ito, ita [bor-re-keel'-lyo, lyah, bor-re-kee'-to, tah], *m.* & *f dim.* A little ass.

Borriquillos [bor-re-keel'-lyos], *m. pl.* Cross-bars of a table-frame.

Borro [bor'-ro], *m.* 1. Wether not two years old. 2. (Coll.) Dolt, of slow understanding. 3. Duty laid on sheep.

Borrón [bor-rone'], *m.* 1. Blot of ink on paper, blur. 2. Rough draft of a writing. 3. First sketch of a painting. 4. Blemish which tarnishes or defaces. 5. Stigma.

Borronazo [bor-ro-nah'-tho], *m. aug.* Great blot or blur.

Borroncillo [bor-ron-theel'-lyo], *m. dim.* Small blot or stain.

Borronear [bor-ro-nay-ar'], *va.* 1. To sketch. 2. To waste paper by scribbling on it.

Borroso, sa [bor-ro'-so, sah], *a.* 1. Full of dregs and lees: turbid, thick, muddy. 2. Done in a bungling manner. *Letra borrosa*, Letter badly written, and full of blots and corrections.

Borroso [bor-ro'-so], *m.* (Prov.) Bungler, a petty mechanic.

Borrufalla [bor-roo-fahl'-yah], *f.* (Coll. Prov.) Bombast, a pompous show of empty sounds or words.

Borrumbada [bor-room-bah'-dah], *f.* (Obs.) *V.* BARRUMBADA.

Borujo [bo-roo'-ho], *m.* (Obs.) *V.* ORUJO.

Borujón [bo-roo-hone'], *m.* Knob, protuberance.

Borusca [bo-roos'-cah], *f.* Withered leaf. *V.* SEROJA.

Bosar [bo-sar'], *va.* (Obs.) 1. To run over, to overflow. 2. To vomit. 3. (Met.) To utter lofty words.

Boscaje [bos-cah'-hay], *m.* 1. Boscage, cluster of trees, grove. 2. (Pict.) Boscage, landscape.

Bósforo [bos'-fo-ro], *m.* Bosphorus, channel by which two seas communicate.

Bosque [bos'-kay], *m.* Wood, tract of land planted with trees and brushwood; forest, grove; any woody place.

Bosquecillo [bos-kay-theel'-lyo], *m. dim.* Small wood, a coppice, a knoll covered with trees.

Bosquejar [bos-kay-har'], *va.* 1. To make a sketch of a painting. 2. To design or project a work without finishing it. 3. To explain a thought or idea in a rather obscure manner. 4. To make a rough model of a figure, or *basso-relievo*, in clay, plaster, or any soft substance.

Bosquejo [bos-kay'-ho], *m.* 1. Sketch of a painting. 2. Any unfinished work. 3. Unfinished writing or composition. *Estar en bosquejo*, To be in an unfinished state.

Bosquete [bos-kay'-tay], *m.* An artificial grove.

Bostar [bos-tar'], *m.* (Obs.) Ox-stall, or stand for oxen.

Bostezador, ra [bos-tay-thah-dor', rah], *m. & f. & a.* Gaper, yawner.

Bostezante [bos-tay-thahn'-tay], *pa.* Oscitant, yawning.

Bostezar [bos-tay-thar'], *vn.* To yawn, to gape, to oscitate.

Bostezo [bos-tay'-tho], *m.* Yawn, yawning, oscitation, oscitancy.

Bota [bo'-tah], *f.* 1. Small leather wine-bag. 2. Butt or pipe, to contain wine or other liquids. 3. Boot. 4. (Naut.) Water-cask. *Bota fuerte.* Jack-boot, a wide, strong boot. *Estar con las botas puestas*, Ready to perform a journey, or do any thing required. *Cotes de botas*, Boot-legs.

Botabala [bo-tah-bah'-lah], *f.* A kind of ramrod used in a fowling-piece.

Botador [bo-tah-dor'], *m.* 1. Driver, one who drives. 2. Punch, an instrument for driving out nails. 3. Nail set. 4. Crow's bill or pelican, used by dentists to draw teeth. 5. (Naut.) Starting-pole used to shove off a boat from the shore, boat-hook. 6. (Mech.) Furnace-bar, fire-iron; bolt-driver. 7. (Med.) Retractor.

Botafuego [bo-tah-foo-ay'-go], *m.* 1. Linstock, a staff with a match at the end of it, used by gunners in firing cannon. 2. An irritable, quick-tempered person.

Botagueña [bo-tah-gay'-nyah], *f.* Sausage made of pigs' haslets.

Botal [bo-tahl'], *a.* 1. (Anat.) *Agujero botal* or *de botal*, Foramen ovale, formerly called botale foramen, an opening between the two auricles of the heart of the fœtus. 2. (Arch.) Arched buttress.

Botalón [bo-tah-lone'], *m.* (Naut.) Boom, a pole used in setting up studding or stay-sails. *Botalón del foque*, Jib-boom. *Botalones*, Fire-booms.

Botamen [bo-tah'-men], *m.* (Naut.) All the casks on board a ship, which contain wine or water.

Botana [bo-tah'-nah], *f.* 1. Plug or stopple used to stop up the holes made on the leather bags to carry wine. 2. (Coll.) Cataplasm or plaster put on a wound. 3. (Low) Scar remaining after a wound is healed.

Botánica [bo-tah'-ne-cah], *f.* Botany, the science treating of plants.

Botánico, ca [bo-tah'-ne-co, cah], *a.* Botanic, botanical.

Botánico, Botanista [bo-tah'-ne-co, bo-tah-nees'-tah], *m.* Botanist.

Botanomancia [bo-tah-no-mahn'-the-ah], *f.* Botanomancy, superstitious divination by herbs.

Botantes [bo-tahn'-tes], *m. pl.* (Naut.) Shores, out-riggers.

Botar [bo-tar'], *va.* 1. To cast, to throw, to fling, to launch. 2. To bound, to rebound. 3. To squander, to misspend. 4. (Naut.) To shift the helm. *Botar al agua alguna embarcación*, (Naut.) To launch a ship. *Botar en vela*, To fill the sails. *Botar afuera los botalones*, To bear off the booms.

Botaratada [bo-tah-ra-tah'-dah], *f.* A blustering, thoughtless action.

Botarate [bo-ta-rah'-tay], *m.* (Coll.) Madcap, thoughtless, blustering person.

Botarel [bo-tah-rel'], *m.* (Arch.) Buttress, a mass of stone which supports the spring of arches or vaults; abutment, spur, counter pillar.

Botarga [bo-tar'-gah], *f.* 1. Sort of wide breeches formerly worn, gaskins. 2. Motley dress of a harlequin. 3. Harlequin, buffoon. 4. Kind of large sausages. 5. (Prov.) *V.* DOMINGUILLO.

Botasilla [bo-tah-seel'-yah], *f.* (Mil.) Signal given with a trumpet for the cavalry to saddle.

Botavante [bo-tah-vahn'-tay], *m.* (Naut.) Pike used by seamen to defend themselves against an enemy who attempts to board.

Botavara [bo-tah-vah'-rah], *f.* (Naut.) 1. A small boom or pole which crosses the sail of a boat in a diagonal direction, gaff, sprit. 2. Boat-hook. *Botavara de cangreja*, Gaff-sail boom.

Bote [bo'-tay], *m.* 1. Thrust with a pike, lance, or spear. 2. Rebound or bound of a ball on the ground. 3. Gallipot, a small glazed earthen vessel. 4. Toilet-box, in which women keep paint, pomatum, etc. 5. Chuck-farthing, a play in which the money falls with a chuck into the hole beneath. 6. Canister, a tin vessel for tea, coffee, etc. *Bote de tabaco*, Snuff canister. 7. (Naut.) Boat. *Bote de lastre*, Ballast-lighter. *Bota de maestranza* or *minueta*, Shipwright's boat. *Bote en piezas de armazón*, Boat in frame. *Bote de pasaje*, Ferry-boat. *Bote de pescar*, Fishing-boat. *Estar de bote en bote*, To be full of people. *De bote y voleo*, Instantly.—*pl.* 1. In places where wool is washed, heaps of wool piled separately. 2. Frolicsome bounds of a horse.

Botecico, illo, ito [bo-tay-thee'-co, eel'-yo, ee'-to], *m. dim.* 1. Small canister. 2. Skiff.

Botella [bo-tel'-lyah], *f.* Bottle, flask; also the liquor contained in a bottle. *Hemos bebido tres botellas*, We drank three bottles.

Botellón [bo-tel-lyone'], *m.* A demijohn.

Botequín [bo-tay-keen'], *m.* (Naut.) Cog, a small boat.

Botería [bo-tay-ree'-ah], *f.* In ships, collection of leather bags of wine.

Botero [bo-tay'-ro], *m.* 1. One who makes leather bags and bottles for wine. 2. Boatman, wherryman.

Botica [bo-tee'-cah], *f.* 1. Apothecary's shop. 2. Potion given to a sick person. 3. (Obs.) Shop in general. 4. (Obs.) Furnished house or lodging.

Boticario [bo-te-cah'-re-o], *m.* Pharmacist, druggist, apothecary.

Botiguero [bo-te-gay'-ro], *m.* (Prov.) Shopkeeper.

Botiguilla [bo-te-geel'-lyah], *f. dim.* of BOTIGA.

Botija [bo-tee'-hah], *f.* Earthen jug. *Botija para aceite*, An oil-jar.

Botijero [bo-te-hay'-ro], *m.* One who makes or sells jars.

Botijilla, uela [bo-te-heel'-lyah, oo-ay'-lah], *f. dim.* A small jar.

Botijo [bo-tee'-ho], *m.* 1. An earthen jar. 2. (Met.) A plump little child.

Botijón [bo-te-hone'], *m.* 1. (Aug.) A large earthen jar. 2. A plump little child.

Botilla [bo-teel'-lyah], *f.* 1. (Dim.) A small wine-bag. 2. (Obs.) Woman's half-boot.

Botiller [bo-teel-lyer'], *m.* *V.* BOTILLERO.

Botillería [bo-teel-lyay-ree'-ah], *f.* 1. Ice-house, where iced creams, jellies, etc., are prepared or sold. 2. (Naut.) Steward's room and stores. 3. (Obs.) Ancient war tax.

Botillero [bo-teel-lyay'-ro], *m.* One who prepares or sells iced liquids and jellies.

Botillo [bo-teel'-lyo], *m. dim.* A small wine-bag, a leather bottle.

Botín [bo-teen'], *m.* 1. Buskin, a half-boot formerly worn by stage-players. 2. Spatterdash; leggings. 3. Booty taken by soldiers; excoriation. 4. (Naut.) Lashing.

Botina [bo-tee'-nah], *f.* A gaiter.

Botinero [bo-te-nay'-ro], *m.* 1. A soldier who takes care of and sells the booty. 2. One who makes and sells gaiters.

Botinico, illo, ito [bo-te-nee'-co, eel'-lyo, ee'-to], *m. dim.* A little gaiter or spatterdash.

Botiquería [bo-te-kay-ree'-ah], *f.* (Obs.) Perfumer's shop.

Botiquín [bo-te-keen'], *m.* 1. First-aid kit. 2. Medicine chest (in a bathroom, etc.)

Botivoleo [bo-te-vo-lay'-o], *m.* Act of recovering a ball which has just touched the ground.

Boto, ta [bo'-to, tah], *a.* 1. Blunt, round at the point. 2. (Met.) Dull of understanding.

Boto [bo'-to], *m.* (Prov.) Large gut filled with butter, and thus preserved and carried to market.

Botón [bo-tone'], *m.* 1. Sprout, bud, or gem put forth by vines and trees in the spring. 2. Button, of wood or bone. *Botón de metal dorado* or *plateado*, A gilt or plated button. 3. (Fen.) Tip of a foil. 4. Button or knob of doors or windows. *Botón de cerradura*, The button of a lock. 5. Annulet of balusters, and also of keys, serving for ornament. 6. Piece of wood which fastens a fowling-net. 7. Crank-pin. 8. Dowel. 9. Handle, knob (of locks). *Botón de fuego*, Cautery in the form of a button. *Botón de oro*, (Bot.) Creeping double-flowered crow-foot. Ranunculus repens. *Contarle los botones a uno*, (Fen.) To give one as many thrusts as he pleases. *De botones adentro*, Internally.

Botonadura [bo-to-nah-doo'-rah], *f.* Set of buttons for a suit of clothes.

Botonazo [bo-to-nah'-tho], *m.* (Fen.) Thrust given with a foil.

Botoncito [bo-ton-thee'-to], *m. dim.* A small button.

Botonería [bo-to-nay-ree'-ah], *f.* Button-maker's shop.

Botonero, ra [bo-to-nay'-ro, rah], *m.* & *f.* Button-maker; button-seller.

Botones [bo-to'-ness], *m. pl.* Bellboy.

Bototo [bo-to'-to], *m.* Gourd or calabash to carry water. (Amer.)

Botulismo [bo-too-lees'-mo], *m.* Botulism.

Bou [bo'-oo], *m.* A joint casting of a net by two boats, which separate and bring up the haul.

Bóveda [bo'-vay-dah], *f.* 1. Arch or vault. 2. Vault, cave or cavern, a subterraneous habitation. 3. Vault for the dead in churches. *Bóveda de jardín*, Bower.

Bovedar [bo-vay-dar'], *va.* (Obs.) To vault or cover with arches. *V.* ABOVEDAR.

Bovedilla [bo-vay-deel'-lyah], *f.* A small vault in the roof of a house. *Bovedillas*, (Naut.) Counters, arched part of a ship's poop. *Bovedillas costaleras*, Arches two feet wide, more or less. *Subirse a las bovedillas*, (Met.) To be nettled, to be in a passion.

Bovino, na [bo-vee'-no, nah], *a.* Belonging to cattle.

Box [boh], *m.* *V.* BOJ.

Boxeador [boc-say-ah-dor'], *m.* Boxer.

Boxear [boc-say-ar'], *vn.* To box.

Boxeo [boc-say'-o], *m.* Boxing.

Boya [bo'-yah], *f.* 1. (Naut.) Float for a net or submerged rope; beacon, buoy. 2. (Obs.) Butcher. 3. (Obs.) Hangman, executioner. *Boya de barril*, Nun-buoy. *Boya cónica*, Can-buoy. *Boya de palo*, Wooden buoy. *Boya de cable*, Cable-buoy. *Echar afuera la boya a la mar*, To stream the buoy. *La boya nada a la vista*, The buoy floats in sight.

Boyada [bo-yah'-dah], *f.* Drove of oxen.

Boyal [bo-yahl'], *a.* Relating to cattle: applied generally to pasture-grounds where cattle are kept.

Boyante [bo-yahn'-tay], *pa.* Buoyant, floating.—*a.* 1. (Naut.) Light, sailing well: applied to a ship. 2. (Met.) Fortunate, successful.

Boyar [bo-yar'], *vn.* (Naut.) To buoy, to be afloat: applied to ships.

Boyar [bo-yar'], *m.* (Naut.) Kind of Flemish bilander.

Boyazo [bo-yah'-tho], *m. aug.* Large ox.

Boyera, Boyeriza [bo-yay'-rah, bo-yay-ree'-thah], *f.* Ox-stall, ox-house, cow-house, a stand for oxen.

Boyero [bo-yay'-ro], *m.* Oxherd, ox-driver, cowherd.

Boyezuelo [bo-yay-thoo-ay'-lo], *m. dim.* A young or small ox.

Boyuno, na [bo-yoo'-no, nah], *a.* Belonging to cattle; bovine.

Boza [bo'-thah], *f.* (Naut.) One end of a rope made fast in a bolt-ring, till the other brings the tackle to its place. *Bozas*, (Naut.) Stoppers, short ends of cables used to suspend or keep something in its place. *Bozas de la uña del ancla*, Shank-painter. *Bozas de cable* or *cubiertas*, Cable-stoppers. *Bozas de combate* or *de las vergas*, The stoppers of the yards. *Bozas de los obenques*, The stoppers of the shrouds.

Bozal [bo-thahl'], *m.* 1. Muzzle worn by horses, dogs, and calves. 2. A temporary head-stall for a horse.

Bozal [bo-thal'], *a.* 1. Applied to negroes lately imported. 2. Novice, inexperienced in trade or business. 3. Stupid, foolish. 4. Wild, not broken in: applied to horses.

Bozalejo [bo-tha-lay'-ho], *m.* A small muzzle.

Bozo [bo'-tho], *m.* 1. Down, which precedes the beard. 2. Head-stall of a horse.

Brabante [brah-bahn'-tay], *m.* Brabant or Flemish linen.

Brabantés, sa [brah-ban-tess', sah], **Brabantino, na** [brah-ban-tee'-no, nah], *a.* Brabantine, of Brabant.

Brabanzón [brah-ban-thone'], *a.* Native of Brabant.

Brabera [brah-bay'-rah], *f.* Air-hole, ventilator.

Braceada [brah-thay-ah'-dah], *f.* Violent extension of the arms.

Braceaje [brah-thay-ah'-hay], *m.* 1. Coinage, the art and act of coining money. 2. Act of beating the metal for coining in the mint. 3. (Naut.) Bracing of the yards. Depth of water. 4. Brewing.

Bracear [brah-thay-ar'], *vn.* To move or swing the arms.—*va.* 1. (Naut.) To brace. *Bracear las vergas*, To brace the yards. 2. To measure by fathoms. 3. To brew.

Bracero [brah-thay'-ro], *m.* 1. One who walks arm in arm with another. *Ir de bracero*, To walk arm in arm. 2. Day-labourer. 3. A strong-armed man.

Bracete [brah-thay'-tay], *adv.* *De bracete*, Arm in arm.

Bracillo, ito [brah-theel'-lyo, ee'-to], *m. dim.* A little arm.

Bracillo [brah-theel'-lyo], *m.* Branch of the mouth-bit of a horse's bridle.

Bracmán [brac-mahn'], *m.* Brahmin, a Hindu priest.

Braco, ca [brah'-co, cah], *a.* (Obs.) 1. Pointing or setting: applied to a pointer. 2. Broken-nosed, flat-nosed. —*m.* & *f.* A pointer-dog.

Bráctea [brahc'-tay-ah], *f.* (Bot.) Bract.

Bractéola [brahc-tay'-o-lah], *f.* Bractlet.

Bradipepsia [brah-de-pep'-se-ah], *f.* Bradypepsia, slow digestion.

Brafonera [brah-fo-nay'-rah], *f.* (Obs.) 1. Piece of ancient armour for the arm. 2. In clothes, a roller which girded the upper part of the arms; a plaited sleeve.

Braga [brah'-gah], *f.* (Prov.) 1. Child's clout, diaper. 2. *Bragas*, Gaskins, a kind of wide breeches; breeches in general; hose. 3. (Mil.) Breeching, lashing-rope. *Calzarse las bragas*, To wear the breeches: applied to a wife who lords it over her husband. *Vióse el perro en bragas de cerro y no conoció a su compañero*, Set a beggar on horseback and he will ride to the devil.

Bragada [brah-gah'-dah], *f.* 1. The flat of the thigh in beasts, from the flank to the hough. 2. Elbow, throat. *Bragada de una curva*, (Naut.) The throat of a knee. *Madera de bragada*, Compass-timber.

Bragado, da [brah-gah'-do, dah], *a.* 1. Having the flanks of a different colour from the rest of the body: applied to beasts. 2. (Met.) Ill-disposed, of depraved sentiments.

Bragadura [brah-gah-doo'-rah], *f.* 1. Part of the human body where it begins to fork, crotch. 2. Fork of a pair of breeches. 3. Flat of the thigh in beasts, from the flank to the hough.

Bragazas [brah-gah'-thas], *f. pl.* 1. (Aug.) Wide breeches. 2. *m.* (Met.) A person easily persuaded or ruled: generally applied to a hen-pecked husband.

Braguero [brah-gay'-ro], *m.* 1. Truss, bandage for a rupture, brace. 2. *Braguero de cañón*, (Naut.) Breeching of a gun, with which it is lashed to the ship's side. *Braguero de una vela*, Bunt of a sail. 3. Piece put into clothes to make them stronger.

Bragueta [brah-gay'-tah], *f.* Trouser fly.

Braguetazo [brah-gay-tah'-tho], *m. aug.* *Dar braguetazo*, (Coll.) To marry a rich woman.

Braguillas [brah-geel'-lyas], *m.* 1. Boy wearing long pants for the first time. 2. (Coll.) Brat, little whippersnapper.

Brahma [brah'-mah], *f.* Brahma, a deity of the Hindus.

Brahmán, or **Brahmín** = BRACMÁN.

Brahminismo [brah-me-nees'-mo], *m.* Brahminism, the religious system of the Brahmins.

Brahón [brah-on'], *m.* A fold which, in ancient apparel, surrounded the upper part of the arm.

Brama [brah'-mah], *f.* Rut, the season of copulation of deer and other wild animals.

Bramadera [brah-mah-day'-rah], *f.* 1. Rattle. 2. Call or horn used by shepherds to rally and conduct the flock. 3. Horn used by keepers of vineyards and olive plantations, to frighten away cattle.

Bramadero [brah-mah-day'-ro], *m.* Rutting-place of deer and other wild animals.

Bramador, ra [brah-mah-dor', rah], *m.* & *f.* 1. Roarer, brawler, a noisy person. 2. (Poet.) Inanimate things, emitting a sound like roaring or groaning.

Bramante [brah-mahn'-tay], *m.* 1. Pack-thread, a strong thread made of hemp. 2. Bramant or brabant, a linen so called. *Bramante blanco*, White bramant. *Bramante crudo*, Unbleached bramant. 3. Roaring.

Bramar [brah-mar'], *vn.* 1. To roar, to groan, to bellow. 2. (Met.) To roar, to storm, to bluster, to be boisterous: applied to wind and sea. 3. (Met.) To fret, to be in a passion, to be sorely vexed, to cry.

Bramido [brah-mee'-do], *m.* 1. Cry uttered by wild beasts. 2. Clamour of persons enraged. 3. Tempestuous roaring of the elements.

Bramil [brah-meel'], *m.* Chalk-line used by sawyers to mark the place where timbers are to be cut.

Bramín [brah-meen'], *m.* *V.* BRACMÁN.

Bramo [brah'-mo], *m.* Shout, cry. (Slang.)

Bramona [brah-mo'-nah], *f.* *Soltar la bramona*, To break out into injurious expressions, to use foul language: chiefly applied to gamblers.

Bran de Inglaterra [brahn day in-gla-ter'-rah], *m.* An ancient Spanish dance.

Branca [brahn'-cah], *f.* (Obs.) 1. Gland of the throat. 2. Point. *Brancas*, Claws, talons, etc.

Brancada [bran-cah'-dah], *f.* Drag-net or sweep-net, used at the mouth of rivers or in arms of the sea.

Brancaursina [bran-cah-oor-see'-nah], *f.* (Bot.) Bear's-breech, brank-ursine. Acanthus. *Brancaursina blanda*, Smooth bear's-breech. Acanthus mollis. *Brancaursina espinosa*, Prickly leaved bear's-breech. Acanthus spinosus.

Branchas [brahn'-chas], *f. pl.* Gills of a fish.

Brandales [bran-dah'-les], *m. pl.* (Naut.) Back-stays. *Brandales del mastelero de gavia*, The main-top back-stays. *Brandales volantes*, Shifting back-stays.

Brandís [bran-dees'], *m.* Great-coat used formerly. *Brandises*, Collars of ladies' night-gowns.

Brando [brahn'-do], *m.* Tune adapted to a dance.

Brano [brah'-no], *m.* *V.* Estamento.

Branquia [brahn'-kee-ah], *f.* The gill of a fish or other aquatic creature.

Branquiado, da [bran-ke-ah'-do, dah], *a.* Gill-breathing, branchiate.

Branquial [bran-ke-ahl'], *a.* Branchial, relating to gills.

Branquífero, ra [bran-kee'-fay-ro, rah], *a.* Gill-bearing.

Branza [brahn'-thah], *f.* Staple or ring to which the chains of galley-slaves were fastened.

Braña [brah'-nyah], *f.* (Prov.) 1. Summer pasture. 2. Dung, withered leaves, and other remains of fodder, found on summer pasture-grounds.

Braquial [brah-ke-ahl'], *a.* Brachial, belonging to the arm.

Braquíceros [brah-ke-thay'-ros], *m. pl.* The brachycera, a sub-order of the diptera, having short antennæ.

Braquigrafía [brah-ke-grah-fee'-ah], *f.* Brachygraphy, the art of writing in short-hand.

Braquígrafo [brah-kee'-grah-fo], *m.* Brachygrapher, a short-hand writer.

Braquillo, lla [brah-keel'-lyo, lyah], *m.* & *f. dim.* Small pointer.

Braquiocefálico [brah-ke-o-thay-fah'-le-co], *a.* Brachycephalic, in relation with the arm and the head.

Brasa [brah'-sah], *f.* Live coal; burning wood that has ceased to flame; red-hot coal or wood. *Ir, correr* or *pasar como gato por brasas,* To run as light as a cat on burning coals. *Estar hecho unas brasas,* To be all in a blaze; red-faced. *Estar en brasas* or *como en brasas,* (Met.) To be uneasy or restless.

Braserito [brah-say-ree'-to], *m. dim.* A small pan to hold coals; a chafing-dish.

Brasero [brah-say'-ro], *m.* 1. Brasier, a pan to hold coals. 2. Fire-pan. 3. Place where criminals were burnt. 4. Hearth, fire-place. (Mex.)

Brasil [brah-seel'], *m.* 1. (Bot.) Brazilettto. Cæsalpina brasiliensis. 2. Brazil-wood, used by dyers. 3. Rouge, a red paint used by ladies.

Brasilado, da [brah-se-lah'-do, dah], *a.* Of a red or Brazil-wood colour; ruddy.

Brasileño, ña [bra-se-lay'-nyo, nyah], *a.* Brazilian.

Brasilete [bra-se-lay'-tay], *m.* Jamaica-wood, braziletto, an inferior sort of Brazil-wood.

Brasilina [bra-se-lee'-nah], *f.* Brazilin, a red colouring-matter from Brazil-wood.

Brasmología [bras-mo-lo'-he-ah], *f.* The science which treats of the flux and reflux of the sea.

Braulis [brah'-oo-lis], *f.* Cloth or stuff with white and blue stripes, which comes from the coast of Barbary.

Brava [brah'-vah], *f.* (Naut.) Heavy swell of the sea.

Bravada [brah-vah'-dah], *f.* *V.* Bravata.

Bravamente [bra-vah-men'-tay], *adv.* 1. Bravely, gallantly. 2. Cruelly, inhumanly, barbarously. 3. Finely, extremely well. 4. Plentifully, copiously. *Hemos comido bravamente,* We have made a hearty dinner.

Bravata [brah-vah'-tah], *f.* Bravado, boast, or brag, braggardism, an arrogant menace, impudent sally, intended to frighten and intimidate.

Bravato, ta [brah-vah'-to, tah], *a.* (Obs.) Boasting, impudent.

Braveador, ra [brah-vay-ah-dor', rah], *m.* & *f.* Bully, hector.

Bravear [brah-vay-ar'], *vn.* To bully, to hector, to menace in an arrogant manner.

Bravera [brah-vay'-rah], *f.* Vent or chimney of ovens. *V.* Suspirales.

Braveza [brah-vay'-thah], *f.* 1. (Obs.) Bravery, valour. 2. (Obs.) Vigour. 3. Ferocity. 4. Fury of the elements.

Bravillo, illa [brah-veel'-lyo, lyah], *a. dim.* Rather wild, not yet tamed.

Bravío, vía [brah-vee'-o, ah], *a.* 1. Ferocious, savage, wild, untamed. 2. Wild, propagated by nature, not cultivated: applied to plants. 3. Coarse, unpolished: applied to manners.

Bravío [brah-vee'-o], *m.* Fierceness or savageness of wild beasts.

Bravo, va [brah'-vo, vah], *a.* 1. Brave, valiant, strenuous, manful, hardy, fearless. 2. Bullying, hectoring. 3. Savage, wild, fierce: applied to beasts. 4. (Met.) Severe, untractable. 5. (Met.) Rude, unpolished, uncivilized. 6. Sumptuous, expensive. 7. Excellent, fine. *Brava cosa,* (Iron.) Very fine indeed! *El ama brava es llave de su casa,* A severe mistress makes the servants honest. *Mar bravo,* Swollen sea. *¡Bravo! int.* Bravo!

Bravonel [brah-vo-nel'], *m.* (Obs.) Brave, a hector.

Bravosidad [brah-vo-se-dahd'], *f.* (Obs.) *V.* Gallardía.

Bravucón, na [bra-voo-cone', nah], *a.* Boastful, braggart.

Bravura [brah-voo'-rah], *f.* 1. Ferocity, fierceness: applied to wild beasts. 2. Courage, manliness: applied to persons. 3. Bravado, boast, brag.

Braza [brah'-thah], *f.* 1. Fathom, a measure of six feet. 2. (Naut.) Brace which is tied to the yards. *Brazas,* (Naut.) Braces, ropes belonging to the yards of a ship. *Brazas de barlovento,* Weather-braces. *Brazas de sotavento,* Lee-braces. *Brazas de la cebadera,* Sprit-sail braces. *Afirmar las brazas de barlovento,* To secure the weather-braces. *Halar sobre las brazas,* To haul in the braces.

Brazada [brah-thah'-dah], *f.* 1. Movement of the arms out and up. 2. Armful. *Brazada de pecho,* Crawl stroke (in swimming).

Brazado [brah-thah'-do], *m.* An armful. *Un brazado de leña,* An armful of fire-wood. *Un brazado de heno,* A truss of hay.

Brazaje [brah-thah'-hay], *m.* 1. (Naut.) Number of fathoms, depth of water. 2. *V.* Braceaje.

Brazal [brah-thahl'], *m.* 1. (Obs.) Brachial muscle. 2. Bracer, ancient piece of armour for the arms. 3. Bracelet. 4. (Prov.) Ditch or channel from a river or canal, to irrigate lands. 5. Bracer, a wooden instrument for playing balloons. 6. (Naut.) Rail. *Brazales de proa,* Head-rails. *Brazal de medio de proa,* The middle rail of the head.

Brazalete (Vul. Bracelete) [brah-thah-lay'-tay], *m.* 1. Armlet, bracelet. *V.* Manilla, Pulsera. 2. Bracelet, ancient iron piece of armour. *Brazaletes,* (Naut.) Brace pendants.

Brazazo [brah-thah'-tho], *m. aug.* Large or long arm.

Brazo [brah'-tho], *m.* 1. The arm; the entire thoracic limb. 2. The arm, anatomically from the shoulder to the elbow. By extension, arm of a lever, of a balance beam; each half of a yard, etc. 3. The correlative limb in some of the inferior creatures. 4. (Met.) Bough of a tree. 5. (Met.) Valour, strength, power. 6. Each end of a beam or balance. *Brazo de araña,* Curved branch of a girandole or lustre. *Brazo de candelero,* Branch of a chandelier. *Brazo de una trompeta,* Branch of a trumpet. *Brazo de mar,* Arm of the sea. *Brazo de silla,* Arm of a chair. *Brazo a brazo,* Arm to arm, with equal weapons. *A brazo partido,* With the arms only, without weapons; with main force, arm to arm. *Brazos del reino,* States of the realm; that is, the prelates, nobility, and corporations. *A fuerza de brazos,* By dint of merit and labour. *Con los brazos abiertos,* With open arms, cheerfully. *Cruzados los brazos,* With the arms folded, idle. *Dar los brazos a uno,* To embrace one. *Hecho un brazo de mar,* With great show or pomp. *Ser el brazo derecho de alguno,* To be one's right hand, or confidant.

Brazolas [brah-tho'-las], *f. pl.* (Naut.) Coamings of the hatchways.

Brazuelo [brah-thoo-ay'-lo], *m.* 1. (Dim.) Small arm. 2. Shoulder or fore-thigh of beasts. 3. Branch of the mouth-bit of a bridle for a horse or mule.

Brea [bray'-ah], *f.* 1. Pitch. 2. Tar, artificial bitumen composed of pitch, resin, and grease. 3. Coarse canvas for wrapping up wares; sackcloth.

Brear [bray-ar'], *va.* 1. To pitch. 2. To tar, to vex, to plague, to thwart. 3. (Met.) To cast a joke upon one.

Brebaje [bray-bah'-hay], *m.* 1. Beverage, a drink made up of different ingredients harsh to the taste, medicine. 2. (Naut.) Grog.

Breca [bray'-cah], *f.* Bleak or blay, a river fish. *V.* Albur.

Brécol, *m.* **Brecolera,** *f.* [bray'-col, bray-co-lay'rah]. (Bot.) Broccoli. *V.* Bróculi.

Brecha [bray'-chah], *f.* 1. Breach made in the ramparts of a fortress. 2. Opening made in a wall or building. 3. (Met.) Impression made upon the mind. 4. Ball of pebbles. 5. Breccia. *Batir en brecha,* 1. To batter a breach in a fortification. 2. (Met.) To persecute one, and cause his destruction.

Brecho [bray'-cho], *m.* *V.* Escaro.

Bredo [bray'-do], *m.* (Bot.) *V.* Bledo.

Brega [bray'-gah], *f.* 1. Strife, contest, affray. 2. (Met.) Pun, jest, or trick played upon one. *Dar brega,* To play a trick.

Bregar [bray-gar'], *vn.* 1. To contend, to struggle. 2. (Met.) To struggle with troubles, difficulties, and dangers.—*va.* To work up dough with a rolling-pin. *Bregar el arco,* To bend a bow. (*Yo bregué,* from *Bregar.* *V.* verbs in *gar.*)

Bren [brayn], *m.* Bran. *V.* Salvado.

Brenca [bren'-cah], *f.* 1. (Bot. Obs.) Maidenhair. Adiantum capillus Veneris, *L.* *V.* Culantrillo. 2. Sluice-post, one of the posts of a water or flood-gate. 3. Filament, one of the three cristated anthers of saffron.

Breña [bray'-nyah], *f.* Craggy, broken ground, full of brakes and brambles.

Breñal, Breñar [bray-nyahl', bray-nyar'], *m.* Place where the ground is craggy and broken, and full of briers and brambles.

Breñoso, sa [bray-nyo'-so, sah], *a.* Craggy and brambled: applied to ground.

Breque [bray'-kay], *m.* Small river fish. *V.* Breca. *Ojos de breque,* Weak or bloodshot eyes.

Bresca [bres'-cah], *f.* (Prov.) Honey comb.

Brescadillo [bres-cah-deel'-lyo], *m.* A small tube made of gold or silver.

Brescado [bres-cah'-do], *m.* Embroidered with *brescadillo.*

Bretador [bray-tah-dor'], *m.* (Obs.) Call, whistle, or pipe to call birds.

Bretaña [bray-tah'-nyah], *f.* A sort of fine linen; Britannias, or Bretagnes. *Bretañas contrahechas anchas.* Wide

German Britannias. *Bretañas contrahechas angostas*, Narrow German Britannias. *Bretañas legítimas anchas*, Wide French Britannias. *Bretañas legítimas angostas*, Narrow French Britannias.

Brete [bray'-tay], *m.* 1. Fetters, shackles, irons for the feet. 2. Indigence; perplexity, difficulties. *Estar en un brete*, To be hard put to. 3. Kind of food in India.

Bretón [bray-tone'], *m.* 1. (Bot.) Borecole, kale. 2. A native of Brittany.

Breva [bray'-vah], *f.* 1. The early fruit of a variety of the common fig-tree. 2. Early large acorn. *Más blando que una breva*, More pliant than a glove; brought to reason. 3. Pure cigar, rather flat. 4. (Coll.) Any valuable thing or position easily obtained.

Breval [bray-vahl'], *m.* (Prov. Bot.) Early fig-tree. Ficus carica.

Breve [bray'-vay], *m.* 1. Apostolic brief, granted by the Pope or his legates. 2. (Obs.) Card of invitation, ticket, memorandum in a pocket-book. 3. *f.* Breve, the longest note in music, seldom used.

Breve [bray'-vay], *a.* Brief, short, concise, laconic, compact, compendious, close. *En breve*, Shortly, in a little time.

Brevecico, illo, ito [bray-vay-thee'-co, eel'-lyo, ee'-to], *a. dim.* Somewhat short or concise.

Brevedad [bray-vay-dahd'], *f.* Brevity, briefness, shortness, conciseness, compendiousness.

Brevemente [bray-vay-men'-tay], *adv.* Briefly, concisely.

Brevete [bray-vay'-tay], *m.* *V.* MEMBRETE.

Breviario [bray-ve-ah'-re-o], *m.* 1. Breviary, which contains the daily service of the church of Rome. 2. Brevier, a small size of type between minion and bourgeois: of eight points. 3. (Obs.) Memorandum-book. 4. (Obs.) Abridgment, epitome.

Brezal [bray-thahl'], *m.* Heath, place planted with heaths.

Brezo [bray'-tho], *m.* (Bot.) Heath, heather, ling. Erica, *L.*

Briaga [bre-ah'-gah], *f.* Rope made of bass-weed, tied round the shaft or beam of a wine-press.

Brial [bre-ahl'], *m.* Rich silken skirt, formerly worn by ladies.

Briba [bree'-bah], *f.* Truantship, idleness, neglect of business or duty. *A la briba*, In an idle and negligent manner.

Bribia [bree'-be-ah], *f.* A beggar's tale to move compassion. *Echar la bribia*, To go a-begging.

Bribón, na [bre-bone', nah], *m. & f. & a.* Vagrant, impostor; a knave, a scoundrel, a rascal.

Bribonada [bre-bo-nah'-dah], *f.* Knavery, petty villainy, mischievous trick or practice, beggar's trick, mean cunning.

Bribonazo [bre-bo-nah'-tho], *m. aug.* Great cheat, impudent impostor.

Briboncillo [bre-bon-theel'-lyo], *m. dim.* Little gull, young impostor.

Bribonear [bre-bo-nay-ar'], *vn.* To rove and loiter about; to lead a vagabond's life.

Bribonería [bre-bo-nay-ree'-ah], *f.* Life of a vagrant or vagabond, a beggar's trade.

Bribonzuelo [bre-bon-thoo-ay'-lo], *m. dim.* *V.* BRIBONCILLO.

Bricho [bree'-cho], *m.* Spangle, used in embroidery.

Brida [bree'-dah], *f.* 1. Bridle of a horse. 2. The reins of a bridle. 3. Horsemanship, the art of managing a horse by means of a bridle. 4. (Met.) Curb, restraint, check. *Á la brida*, Riding a bur-saddle with long stirrups. 5. Rail coupling, fish-plate. 6. Flange. 7. Clamp, staple (watch-making).

Bridar [bre-dar'], *va.* 1. To put a bridle to a horse, to bridle. 2. To curb, to check, to restrain.

Bridón [bre-done'], *m.* 1. Horseman riding a bur-saddle with long stirrups. 2. Horse accoutred with a bur-saddle and long stirrups. 3. Small bridle used instead of a larger one.

Brigada [bre-gah'-dah], *f.* 1. Brigade, a certain number of battalions or squadrons. 2. A certain number of soldiers in some military bodies. 3. A certain number of beasts of burden to carry the baggage and provisions of an army.

Brigadier [bre-gah-de-err'], *m.* 1. Brigadier or general of brigade. 2. *Brigadier en la real armada*, Officer of the navy, who commands a division of a fleet.

Brigola [bre-go'-lah], *f.* Ram, ancient machine for battering walls.

Brillador, ra [breel-lyah-dor', rah], *a.* Brilliant, sparkling, radiant.

Brilladura [breel-lyah-doo'-rah], *f.* (Obs.) *V.* BRILLO.

Brillante [breel-lyahn'-tay], *a.* 1. Brilliant, bright, shining, sparkling, radiant, fulgent, glossy. 2. Resplendent, golden, lustrous, light, lucid. 3. Glittering, gaudy, gorgeous, gay, holiday, grand, glad.

Brillante [breel-lyahn'-tay], *m.* Brilliant, a diamond cut in triangular faces.

Brillantemente [breel-lyan-tay-men'-tay], *adv.* Brilliantly, brightly, resplendently, splendidly.

Brillantez [breel-lyan-teth'], *f.* *V.* BRILLO.

Brillantina [bril-lyan-tee'-nah], *f.* Brilliantine, hair oil.

Brillar [breel-lyar'], *vn.* 1. To shine, to emit rays of light, to sparkle, to glisten, to glister, to glitter, to gleam. 2. To flare. 3. To glare, to glance. 4. (Met.) To outshine in talents, abilities, or merits.

Brillo [breel'-lyo], *m.* 1. Brilliancy, brilliantness, brightness, luminousness. 2. Lustre, splendour, glitter. 3. Resplendence, resplendency, shining.

Brin [breen'], *m.* 1. (Prov.) Fragments of the stamens of saffron. 2. Sailcloth. *Brin ancho*, Wide Russia sheeting. *Brin angosto*, Raven duck.

Brincador, ra [brin-cah-dor', rah], *m. & f.* Leaper, jumper.

Brincar [brin-car'], *vn.* 1. To leap, to jump, to frisk. 2. To skip, to gambol, to hop, to bounce. 3. (Met.) To step over others in point of promotion. 4. (Met.) To omit something on purpose and pass to another. 5. (Met.) To fling, to flounder, to flounce, to fret, to fly into a passion. *Está que brinca*, He is in a great passion.

Brincho [breen'-cho], *m.* A mode of playing at a game of cards called *Reversi.*

Brincia [breen'-the-ah], *f.* Peel of an onion.

Brinco [breen'-co], *m.* 1. Leap, jump, frisk, hop, jerk, bounce, bound. 2. (Obs.) Small jewel fastened to a spring, formerly worn by ladies in their head-dress.

Brindar [brin-dar'], *vn.* 1. To drink one's health, to toast. 2. To offer cheerfully; to invite. 3. To allure, to entice. (Ger. bringen.)

Brindis [breen'-dis], *m.* Health or the act of drinking the health of another; a toast.

Bringabala [brin-gah-bah'-lah], *f.* (Naut.) Brake or handle of a pump. *V.* GUIMBALETE.

Bringas [breen'-gas], *f. pl.* 1. The osiers which cross the ribs of baskets. 2. The fleshy part of lean meat.

(*Yo brinqué*, from *Brincar*. *V.* verbs in *car.*)

Brinquillo, Brinquiño [brin-keel'-lyo, kee'-nyo], *m.* 1. Gewgaw, a small trinket. 2. Sweetmeat which comes from Portugal. *Estar* or *ir hecho un brinquiño*, To be as spruce and trim as a game-cock.

Brinza [breen'-thah], *f.* 1. Blade, slip. 2. Sprig, shoot.

Brio [bree'-o], *m.* 1. Strength, force, vigour, manliness. 2. (Met.) Spirit, resolution, courage, valour, mettlesomeness. *Es un hombre de bríos*, He is a man of mettle. *Bajar los bríos a alguno*, To pull down one's spirits, to humble.

Briol [bre-ol'], *m.* (Naut.) Bunt-line, line fastened to sails to draw them up to the yards.

Briolín [bre-o-leen'], *m.* (Naut.) Slab-line, fastened to the foot-rope of the main-sail and fore-sail, to draw them up a little.

Brión [bre-on'], *m.* Bryum, wall-moss.

Brionia [bre-oh'-ne-ah], *f.* (Bot.) Briony. Bryonia alba.

Briosamente [bre-o-sah-men'-tay], *adv.* Spiritedly, courageously, mettlesomely, vigorously, lively.

Brioso, sa [bre-o'-so, sah], *a.* Vigorous, spirited, high-minded, mettlesome, courageous, lively.

Brisa [bree'-sah], *f.* 1. Breeze from the northeast. 2. *Brisa carabinera*, A violent gale. 3. (Prov.) Skin of pressed grapes. *V.* ORUJO.

Brisca [brees'-cah], *f.* A game at cards.

Briscado, da [bris-cah'-do, dah], *a.* Mixed with silk: applied to gold and silver twist.—*pp.* of BRISCAR.

Briscar [bris-car'], *va.* To embroider with gold or silver twist mixed with silk.

Británica [bre-tah'-ne-cah], *f.* (Bot.) Great water-dock. Rumex aquaticus.

Británico, ca [bre-tah'-ne-co, cah], *a.* British, English, —*m. & f.* Britisher, Englishman, Englishwoman.

Brizar [bre-thar'], *va.* (Obs.) To rock the cradle.

Brizna [breeth'-nah], *f.* 1. Fragment, splinter, chip. 2. Nervure or filament in the pod of a bean. (Acad.)

Briznoso, sa [brith-no'-so, sah], *a.* Full of fragments or scraps.

Brizo [bree'-tho], *m.* 1. (Obs.) Cradle which is rocked. 2. A species of sea-urchin. Echinus.

Broa [bro'-ah], *f.* 1. (Naut.) A cove of shallow depth and dangerous. 2. Mouth of a river.

Broca [bro'-cah], *f.* 1. Reel for twist, silk, or thread. 2. Drill for boring holes in iron. 3. Shoemaker's tack. 4. (Obs.) Button.

Brocadel, Brocatel [bro-cah-del', tel'], *m.* Brocade, a silk stuff.

Brocadillo [bro-cah-deel'-lyo], *m.* Brocade with gold or silver flowers.

Brocado [bro-cah'-do], *m.* Gold or silver brocade.

Brocado, da [bro-cah'-do, dah], *a.* Embroidered, like brocade.

Brocadura [bro-cah-doo'-rah], *f.* (Obs.) Bite of a bear.

Brocal [bro-cahl'], *m.* 1. Curb-stone of a well. 2. Metal ring of the scabbard of a sword. *Brocal de bota*, Mouth-piece of a leathern wine-bottle.

Brocamanton [bro-cah-man-tone'], *m.* Crochet of diamonds worn by ladies.

Brocatel [bro-cah-tel'], *m.* 1. Stuff made of hemp and silk. 2. Spanish marble with white veins.
Brocato [bro-cah'-to], *m.* (Prov.) Brocado.
Brócula [bro'-coo-lah], *f.* Drill for piercing metals.
Bróculi [bro'-coo-le], *m.* Broccoli, a sort of cabbage. Brassica oleracea, *var.* Botrytis asparagoides.
Brocha [bro'-chah], *f.* 1. Painter's brush. *Brocha de aire* or *rociador de aire,* Airbrush. *De brocha gorda,* Poorly done (applied to painting). 2. Cogged dice used by gamblers.
Brochada [bro-chah'-dah], *f.* Each stroke of the brush made in painting; brushful.
Brochado, da [bro-chah'-do, dah], *a.* Relating to brocade.
Brochadura [bro-chah-doo'-rah], *f.* Set of hooks and eyes.
Broche [bro'-chay], *m.* Clasps; hooks and eyes; locket; hasp; brooch.
Brocheta [bro-chay'-tah], *f.* Skewer.
Brochón [bro-chone'], *m.* 1. (Aug.) Large brush. 2. Whitewash-brush.
Brochura [bro-choo'-rah], *f.* The act of putting a book in boards.
Brodio [bro'-de-o], *m.* 1. (Obs.) *V.* Bodrio. 2. A mixture of things put together without order.
Brodista [bro-dees'-tah], *m.* Poor student who comes to the doors of religious communities, for his portion of *bodrio* or hotch-potch.
Broma [bro'-mah], *f.* 1. Joke, jest. *Broma pesada,* Practical joke. *Dar broma,* To tease, to indulge in jokes applied to anyone present. 2. Clatter, confused noise. 3. Rubbish mixed with mortar formerly used to fill up chinks of foundations of walls.
Bromado, da [bro-mah'-do, dah], *a.* Worm-eaten: applied to the bottom of a ship.—*pp.* of Bromar.
Bromar [bro-mar'], *va.* To gnaw, like the ship-worm called wood-borer.
Bromato [bro-mah'-to], *m.* Bromate.
Brómico [bro'-me-co], *a.* Bromic.
Bromear [bro-may-ar'], *vn.* To droll, to jest.
Bromista [bro-mees'-tah], *m.* A droll, comical, merry fellow.
Bromo [bro'-mo], *m.* 1. (Bot.) Brome grass. Bromus. 2. Bromine, one of the elements.
Bromuro [bro-moo'-ro], *m.* Bromide.
Broncamente [bron-ca-men'-tay], *adv.* Peevishly, morosely, crustily.
Bronce [bron'-thay], *m.* 1. Bronze, brass. 2. (Poet.) Trumpet. 3. Any thing strong and hard. *Ser un bronce,* To be indefatigable. *Escribir en bronce,* To preserve tenaciously the memory either of benefits or injuries. *Ser de bronce* or *tener un corazón de bronce,* To have a heart as hard as steel. (Per. burinj.)
Bronceado [bron-thay-ah'-do], *m.* Brassiness; the act and effect of bronzing.
Bronceado, da [bron-thay-ah'-do, dah], *a.* Brass-paved, brazen.—*pp.* of Broncear.
Broncеadura [bron-thay-ah-doo'-rah], *f.* *V.* Bronceado.
Broncear [bron-thay-ar'], *va.* 1. To bronze, to give a bronze or brass colour. 2. To adorn with pieces of brass, latten, or gilt copper.
Broncería [bron-thay-ree'-ah], *f.* Collection of things made of bronze.
Broncista [bron-thees'-tah], *m.* A worker in bronze.
Bronco, ca [bron'-co, cah], *a.* 1. Rough, coarse, unpolished. 2. Crusty, sturdy, morose, crabbed. 3. Rude, unmannerly, clownish, hard, abrupt. 4. Hoarse: applied to the voice. 5. Applied to musical instruments of a harsh sound.
Bronconeumonía [bron-co-nay-oo-mo-nee'-ah], *f.* (Med.) Bronchopneumonia.
Broncotomía [bron-co-to-mee'-ah], *f.* (Surg.) Bronchotomy.
Broncha [bron'-chah], *f.* (Obs.) 1. Kind of poniard. 2. Jewel. 3. Plasterer's washing-brush.
Bronquedad [bron-kay-dahd'], *f.* 1. (Obs.) Harshness, roughness of sound. 2. Rudeness of manners. 3. Unmalleability, in metals. 4. *V.* Aspereza.
Bronquial [bron-ke-ahl'], *a.* (Anat.) Bronchial, belonging to the throat.
Bronquina [bron-kee'-nah], *f.* (Coll.) Dispute, contention, quarrel.
Bronquio, *m.* **Bronquía,** *f.* [bron'-ke-o, ah]. Bronchia.
Bronquitis [bron-kee'-tis], *f.* Bronchitis.
Brontología [bron-to-lo'-he-ah], *f.* Brontology, a dissertation upon thunder.
Broquel [bro-kel'], *m.* 1. Shield or buckler of wood, iron, etc. 2. (Met.) Support, protection. *Raja broqueles,* Bully, bragger, boaster.
Broquelazo [bro-kay-lah'-tho], *m.* 1. Stroke with a shield or buckler. 2. (Aug.) A large shield or buckler.
Broquelero [bro-kay-lay'-ro], *m.* 1. One who makes shields or bucklers. 2. He that wears shields or bucklers. 3. Wrangler, disputer.
Broquelete [bro-kay-lay'-tay], *m. dim.* A small buckler.
Broquelillo [bro-kay-leel'-lyo], *m.* 1. (Dim.) Small shield. 2. Small earrings worn by women.
Broqueta [bro kay'-tah], *f.* *V.* Brocheta.
Brosquil [bros-keel'], *m.* (Prov.) Sheepfold, or sheep-cot. (Aragón.)
Brota [bro'-tah], *f.* *V.* Brote.
Brotadura [bro-tah-doo'-rah], *f.* Budding, the act of shooting forth buds and germs.
Brótano [bro'-tah-no], *m.* (Bot.) Southern-wood. *V.* Abrótano.
Brotar [bro-tar'], *vn.* 1. To bud, to germinate, to put forth shoots or germs; to come out. 2. To gush, to flow or rush out. 3. To issue, to break out, to appear: applied to the smallpox and other eruptions.
Brote, Broto [bro'-tay, bro'-to], *m.* 1. Germ of vines, bud of trees. 2. (Prov.) Fragment, crumb, chip.
Brotón [bro-tone'], *m.* 1. Large clasp for a kind of wide coat called *sayo.* 2. (Obs.) Shoot, tender twig. 3. (Obs.) Sprout of cabbage.
Broza [bro'-thah], *f.* 1. Remains of leaves, bark of trees, and other rubbish. 2. Thicket, brushwood, on mountains. 3. Useless stuff spoken or written, farrago. 4. Printer's brush, to brush off the ink from types. *Gente de toda broza,* People without trade or employment. *Servir de toda broza,* To do all sorts of work.
Brozar [bro-thar'], *va.* Among printers, to brush the types.
Brozoso, sa [bro-tho'-so, sah], *a.* Full of rubbish.
Brucero [broo-thay'-ro], *m.* Brush-maker.
Bruces [broo'-thes], *adv.* *A bruces* or *de bruces,* With the mouth downward; with the face to the ground. *Caer* or *dar de bruces,* To fall headlong to the ground.
Brueta [broo-ay'-tah], *f.* (Prov.) Wheelbarrow.
Brugo [broo'-go], *m.* (Prov.) A sort of vine-grub, plant-louse.
Bruja [broo'-ha], *f.* 1. Witch, hag, sorceress. *Parece una bruja,* She looks like a witch. —*a.* (Mex. coll.) Broke. out of funds.
Brujear [broo-hay-ar'], *vn.* 1. To practise witchcraft. 2. To rove about in the night-time.
Brujería [broo-hay-ree'-ah], *f.* Witchcraft, hagship.
Brujidor [broo-he-dor'], *m.* Glaziers' nippers used in paring glass.
Brujidura [broo-he-doo'-rah], *f.* Bewitching, casting spells.
Brujir [broo-heer'], *va.* To pare off the corners and edges of panes of glass.
Brujo [broo'-ho], *m.* Sorcerer, conjurer, wizard, warlock, a male witch.
Brújula [broo'-hoo-lah], *f.* 1. (Naut.) Sea-compass. 2. Sight, a small hole which serves as a direction to point a gun. *Mirar por brújula,* (Met.) To pry into other people's affairs.
Brujulear [broo-hoo-lay-ar'], *va.* 1. At cards, to examine the cards for the purpose of knowing one's hand. 2. (Met.) To discover by conjectures the nature and issue of an event.
Brujuleo [broo-hoo-lay'-o], *m.* 1. Act of examining the cards held at a game. 2. Scrutation, close examination. 3. Guess, conjecture.
Brulote [broo-lo'-tay], *m.* 1. (Naut.) Fire-ship, a vessel loaded with combustible matters. 2. Warlike machine of the ancients for throwing darts or fire-arrows.
Bruma [broo'-mah], *f.* 1. (Obs.) Winter season. 2. Mist rising from the sea. 3. Haziness.
Brumador, ra [broo-mah-dor', rah], *m.* & *f.* (Obs.) *V.* Abrumador.
Brumal [broo-mahl'], *a.* Brumal, belonging to winter.
Brumamiento [broo-mah-me-en'-to], *m.* (Obs.) Weariness, lassitude.
Brumar [broo-mar'], *va.* (Obs.) *V.* Abrumar.
Brumazón [broo-mah-thone'], *m.* Thick fog or mist at sea.
Brumo [broo'-mo], *m.* The whitest and finest wax, which wax-chandlers use to polish tapers and wax-candles.
Brumoso, sa [broo-mo'-so, sah], *a.* Foggy.
Brunela [broo-nay'-lah], *f.* (Bot.) Common self-heal or heal-all. Brunella vulgaris.
Bruneta [broo-nay'-tah], *f.* (Obs.) 1. Sort of black cloth. 2. Unwrought silver.
Brunete [broo-nay'-tay], *m.* (Obs.) Coarse black cloth.
Bruno, na [broo'-no, nah], *a.* Of a brown-dark colour; almost black.
Bruno [broo'-no], *m.* (Prov.) 1. A little black plum. 2. Plum-tree.
Bruñido [broo-nyee'-do], *m.* Polish, burnish.—*pp.* of Bruñir.
Bruñidor, ra [broo-nye-dor', rah], *m.* & *f.* Burnisher, polisher.
Bruñidor [broo-nye-dor'], *m.* 1. Burnisher, an instrument used in burnishing. 2. Tool of box-wood, used in finishing leather breeches.
Bruñimiento [broo-nye-me-en' to], *m.* 1. Act of polishing or burnishing. 2. Polish, the effect of burnishing or polishing.
Bruñir [broo-nyeer'], *va.* 1. To burnish, to polish. 2. To put on rouge.
Brusca [broos'-cah], *f.* 1. (Naut.) Bevel, sweep, or rounding of masts, yards, etc., on board a ship. 2. Brushwood, small wood.
Bruscamente [broos-cah-men'-tay], *adv.* Abruptly, peevishly.
Bruscate [broos-cah'-tay], *m.* A sort of hash made of milt, lambs' livers.

chopped up with eggs, and stewed in a pan with almond-milk, herbs, and spice.

Brusco [broos'-co], *m.* 1. (Bot.) Knee-holly, butcher's-broom or prickly pettigree. Ruscus aculeatus. 2. Trifling remains of little value; as, loose grapes dropping at the vintage; fruit blown from the tree, etc. 3. Refuse of wool at shearing-time.

Brusco, ca [broos'-co, cah], *a.* Rude, peevish, forward.

Brusela [broo-say'-lah], *f.* 1. (Bot.) Lesser periwinkle. Vinca minor. 2. *Bruselas,* Pincers used by silversmiths.

Bruseles [broo-say'-les], *m. pl.* Pin or slice used by apothecaries to mix their drugs.

Brusquedad [broos-kay-dahd'], *f.* Brusqueness, rudeness.

Brutal [broo-tahl'], *a.* Brutal, brutish, churlish, currish, savage, ferocious.—*m. V.* Bruto.

Brutalidad [broo-tah-le-dahd'], *f.* 1. Brutality, savageness, brutishness. 2. Brutal action; curship. 3. Clownishness, hoggishness.

Brutalmente [broo-tal-men'-tay], *adv.* Brutally, currishly, churlishly, brutishly.

Brutesco, ca [broo-tes'-co, cah], *a.* (Obs.) Grotesque.

Brutez [broo-teth'], *f.* (Obs.) *V.* Brutalidad.

Bruteza [broo-tay'-thah], *f.* Roughness, want of polish: applied to stones.

Bruto [broo'-to], *m.* 1. Brute. 2. (Met.) An ignorant, rude, and immoral person.

Bruto, ta [broo'-to, tah], *a.* 1. Coarse, unpolished, in a rough state. *Diamante en bruto,* A rough diamond. *Madera en bruto,* Rough timber. 2. Stupid. 3. Gross. *Peso bruto,* Gross weight.

Bruza [broo'-thah], *f.* Round brush for cleaning horses and mules. *Bruzas,* In woollen manufactories, brushes with which the bur of cloth is laid down to show the grain. In printing-offices, brush for cleansing the types. *De bruzas,* (Obs.) *V.* De bruces.

Bruzador [broo-thah-dor'], *m.* Trough in which types are cleansed.

Bu [boo], *m.* Word used by nurses to frighten children into silence.

Búa [boo'-ah], *f.* Pustule, a pimple containing pus.

Buaro, Buarillo [boo-ah'-ro, boo-ah-reel'-lyo], *m.* Buzzard, a bird of prey.

Buba [boo'-bah], *f.* Pustule, small tumour. *Bubas,* Buboes.

Búbalo [boo'-bah-lo], *m.* (Obs.) Búfalo.

Bubático, ca [boo-bah'-te-co, cah], *a.* Having buboes or glandular tumours.

Bubilla [boo-beel'-lyah], *f. dim.* Small pustule, a pimple.

Bubón [boo-bone'], *m.* Morbid tumour, full of matter.

Bubónico, ca [boo-bo'-ne-co, cah], *a.* Bubonic. *Peste bubónica,* Bubonic plague.

Buboso, sa [boo-bo'-so, sah], *a.* Afflicted with pustules or buboes.

Bucanero [boo-cah-nay'-ro], *m.* Buccaneer.

Bucarán [boo-ca-rahn'], *m.* (Prov.) Fine glazed buckram.

Bucare [boo-cah'-ray], *m.* A tree in Venezuela planted to shield plants of coffee and cocoa from the sun.

Bucarito [boo-ca-ree'-to], *m. dim.* Small earthen vessel of odoriferous earth.

Búcaro [boo'-ca-ro], *m.* Vessel made of an odoriferous earth of the same name.

Buccino [book-thee'-no], *m.* Buccinum, whelk, a gasteropod mollusk.

Bucear [boo-thay-ar'], *vn.* To dive, to go under water in search of any thing.

Bucéfalo [boo-thay'-fah-lo], *m.* 1. Bucephalus, horse of Alexander. 2. (Met.) A stupid, dull man.

Bucelario [boo-thay-lah'-re-o], *m.* (Obs.) Vassal or servant.

Buceo [boo-thay'-o], *m.* Diving, the act of going under water in search of any thing.

Bucero [boo-thay'-ro], *a.* Black-nosed: applied to a hound or setting-dog.

Bucle [boo'-clay], *m.* Ringlet, curl, hair crisped and curled.

Buco [boo'-co], *m.* (Obs.) 1. (Naut.) Ship, vessel. 2. Buck, a male goat. 3. Opening, aperture.

Bucólica [boo-co'-le-cah], *f.* 1. Bucolic, a bucolical poem; pastoral or rural poetry. 2. (Coll.) Food.

Bucólico, ca [boo-co'-le-co, cah], *a.* Bucolic, bucolical, relating to pastoral poetry.

Bucha [boo'-chah], *f.* (Obs.) Large chest or box. *V.* Hucha. *Bucha pescadera,* (Naut.) Buss, a vessel employed in the herring-fishery.

Buchada [boo-chah'-dah], *f. V.* Bocanada.

Buche [boo'-chay], *m.* 1. Craw or crop, of birds and fowls. 2. Maw or stomach of quadrupeds. 3. Mouthful of a fluid. 4. Young sucking ass, foal. 5. Purse, wrinkle, or pucker in clothes. 6. Breast, the place where secrets are pretended to be kept. 7. (Coll.) Human stomach. *Ha llenado bien el buche,* (Coll.) He has stuffed his budget well. *Hacer el buche,* (Low) To eat. *Hacer el buche a otro,* To make one dine heartily. *Buche de almizcle,* Musk-bag of the musk-deer; also a bag for perfumes.

Buchear [boo-chay-ar'], *va.* To jest, to mock.

Buchecillo [boo-chay-theel'-lyo], *m. dim.* Little craw.

Buchete [boo-chay'-tay], *m.* Cheek puffed with wind.

Buda [boo'-dah], *m.* Buddha, founder of Buddhism.

Búdico, ca [boo'-de-co, cah], *a.* Buddhic, Buddhistic.

Budismo [boo-dees'-mo], *m.* Buddhism, the religion of the followers of Buddha.

Budista [boo-dees'-tah], *m. & f.* Buddhist, adherent of Buddhism.

Budín [boo-deen'], *m.* Pudding.

Budión [boo-de-on'], *m.* (Zool.) Peacock fish. Labrus pavo.

Buega [boo-ay'-gah], *f.* (Prov.) Landmark.

Buen [boo-en'], *a. V.* Bueno. Used only before a substantive masculine, as *Buen hombre,* A good man, and before a substantive feminine beginning with accented *a*, as *Buen alma,* A good soul.

Buena [boo-ay'-nah], *f.* (Obs.) Property, fortune; inheritance.

Buenaboya [boo-ay-nah-bo'-yah], *m.* Seaman who volunteered to serve on board a galley.

Buenamente [boo-ay-nah-men'-tay], *adv.* 1. Freely, spontaneously, conveniently. 2. Easily, commodiously, without much exertion.

Buenandanza [boo-ay-nan-dahn'-thah], *f.* The good fortune of any one.

Buenaventura [boo-ay-nah-ven-too'-rah], *f.* 1. Fortune, good luck. 2. Prediction of fortune-tellers.

Bueno, na [boo-ay'-no, nah], *a.* 1. Good or perfect in its kind. *El bueno del cura,* (Coll.) The good curate. 2. Simple, fair, plain, without cunning or craft. 3. Fit or proper for something. 4. Sociable, agreeable, pleasant, loving, gracious. *Tener buen día en buena compañía,* To spend a pleasant day in agreeable company. 5. Great, strong, violent. *Buena calentura,* A strong fever. 6. Sound, healthy. 7. Useful, serviceable. 8. (Iron.) Strange, wonderful, notable: used before the verb *ser,* as *Lo bueno es que quiera enseñar a su maestro,* The best of it is, that he wishes to teach his master. *Buenos días,* Good-day: a familiar salute. *Buenas noches,* Good-night. *Buenas tardes,* Good-afternoon or evening. *¿A dónde bueno?* Where are you going? *¿De dónde bueno?* Where do you come from? *Las bellas artes y las buenas letras,* The fine arts and belles-lettres. *De bueno a bueno* or *de buenas a buenas,* Freely, willingly, gratefully. *A buenas,* Willingly.

Bueno [boo-ay'-no], *adv.* Enough, sufficiently. *Bueno* or *bueno está,* Enough, no more.

Buenparecer [boo-en-pah-ray-therr'], *m.* (Coll.) Pleasing aspect.

Buenpasar [boo-en-pah-sar'], *m.* (Prov.) Independent situation, comfortable subsistence.

Bueña [boo-ay'-nyah], *f. V.* Morcilla.

Buera [boo-ay'-rah], *f.* (Prov.) Pustule or pimple near the mouth.

Bueso [boo-ay'-so], *m.* (Obs.) One ridiculously dressed.

Buey [boo-ay'-e], *m.* 1. Ox, bullock. 2. *Buey marino,* Sea-calf. 3. *Buey de cazo,* Stalking-ox. *A paso de buey,* At a snail's gallop. *Buey de agua,* Body of water issuing from a conduit or spring.—*pl.* Oxen.

Bueyazo [boo-ay-yah'-tho], *m. aug.* Big ox.

Bueyecillo, Bueyezuelo [boo-ay-yay-theel'-lyo, thoo-ay'-lo], *m. dim.* Little ox.

Bueyuno, na [boo-ay-yoo'-no, nah], *a.* Belonging to neat cattle.

Buf [boof], *int.* Poh, poh.

Bufado, da [boo-fah'-do, dah], *a.* Bursting with a noise, blown: applied to glass drops blown extremely thin.—*pp.* of Bufar.

Búfala [boo'-fah-lah], *f.* The female of the buffalo or wild ox.

Bufalino, na [boo-fah-lee'-no, nah], *a.* Belonging to buffaloes.

Búfalo [boo'-fah-lo], *m.* 1. Buffalo. 2. Emery stick, buff-stick.

Bufanda [boo-fahn'-dah], *f.* Muffler, comforter.

Bufar [boo-far'], *vn.* 1. To puff and blow with anger, to swell with indignation or pride. 2. To snort.

Bufete [boo-fay'-tay], *m.* 1. Desk or writing-table. 2. An office designed for written documents, as of a lawyer or notary. 3. Bureau, sideboard.

Bufetillo [boo-fay-teel'-lyo], *m. dim.* Small desk or writing-table.

Bufí [boo-fee'], *m.* (Prov.) Kind of watered camlet.

Bufido [boo-fee'-do], *m.* 1. Blowing of an animal, snorting of a horse. 2. Huff, swell of sudden anger or arrogance; expression of anger and passion.

Bufo [boo'-fo], *m.* Harlequin or buffoon on the stage

Bufo, fa [boo'-fo, fah], *a.* *Ópera bufa,* Comic opera.

Bufón [boo-fone'], *m.* 1. Buffoon, harlequin, merry-andrew, mimic, masquerader. 2. Scoffer, jester humorist.

Bufón, na [boo-fone', nah], *a.* Funny, comical.

Bufonada [boo-fo-nah'-dah], *f.* 1. Buffoonery, a low jest, waggery, scurrility. 2. Jesting, mimicry pleasantry.

3. Raillery, sarcastic taunt, ridicule; repartee.

Bufonazo [boo-fo-nah'-tho], *m. aug.* Great buffoon.

Bufoncillo [boo-fon-theel'-lyo], *m. dim.* Little merry-andrew.

Bufonearse [boo-fo-nay-ar'-say], *vr.* To jest, to turn into ridicule.

Bufonería [boo-fo-nay-ree'-ah], *f. V.* BUFONADA.

Bufos [boo'-fos], *m. pl.* Ancient head-dress of women.

Bugada [boo-gah'-dah], *f.* (Obs.) Buck, the lye in which clothes are washed.

Bugaceta, Bugaleta [boo-gah-thay'-tah, lay'-tah], *f.* (Naut.) A small vessel.

Bugalla [boo-gahl'-lyah], *f.* Gall-nut growing on oak leaves.

Buglosa [boo-glo'-sah], *f.* (Bot.) Alkanet; bugloss, ox-tongue. Anchusa.

Búgula [boo'-goo-lah], *f.* (Bot.) Bugle, a British plant of the mint family. Ajuga. *Búgula rastrera,* Common bugle. Ajuga reptans.

Buharda [boo-ar'-dah], *f.* 1. Window in the roof, garret-window, dormer-window. 2. Sky-light, a window placed horizontally in the ceiling of a room. 3. Garret, a room on the highest floor of a house.

Buhardilla [boo-ar-deel'-lyah], *f. dim.* Small garret.

Buharro [boo-ar'-ro], *m.* (Orn.) Eagle-owl. Strix bubo.

Buhedera [boo-ay-day'-rah], *f.* Embrasure, loop-hole. *V.* TRONERA.

Buhedo [boo-ay'-do], *m.* Marl, a kind of calcareous earth.

Buho [boo'-o], *m.* Owl. *Es un buho,* He is an unsocial man, he shuns all intercourse with others.

Buhonería [boo-o-nay-ree'-ah], *f.* 1. Peddler's box, in which his wares are carried and sold. 2. Peddlery, the hardware or other small commodities carried in the peddler's box.

Buhonero [boo-o-nay'-ro], *m.* Peddler or hawker.

Buido, da [boo-ee'-do, dah], *a.* (Met.) 1. Thin, lean, slender. 2. Sharp-pointed (as used of weapons.)

Buir [boo-eer'], *va.* (Obs.) To polish, to burnish.

Buitre [boo-ee'-tray], *m.* Vulture. Vultur.

Buitrera [boo-e-tray'-rah], *f.* Place where fowlers put carrion to catch vultures. *Estar ya para buitrera,* Spoken of a beast so lean as to be fit food for vultures.

Buitrero [boo-e-tray'-ro], *m.* Vulture-fowler; one who feeds vultures.

Buitrero, ra [boo-e-tray'-ro, rah], *a.* Vulturine, belonging to a vulture.

Buitrón [boo-e-trone'], *m.* 1. Osier basket to catch fish. 2. Partridge-net. 3. Furnace where silver ores are smelted. 4. Snare for game.

Buja [boo'-hah], *f.* Chuck (in watch-making).

Bujano [boo'-hah-no], *m. V.* TARANTELA.

Bujarasol [boo-hah-rah-sole'], *m.* (Prov.) Fig, the inside pulp of which is of a reddish colour.

Bujarrón [boo-har-rone'], *m.* (Vul.) *V.* SODOMITA.

Buje [boo'-hay], *m.* Axle-box, bush-box, iron ring; pillow of a shaft.

Bujeda, *f.* **Bujedal, Bujedo,** *m.* [boo-hay'-dah, dahl', do]. Plantation of box-trees.

Bujería [boo-hay-ree'-ah], *f.* Gewgaw, bauble, toy, knick-knack.

Bujeta [boo-hay'-tah], *f.* 1. Box made of box-wood. 2. Perfume-box. 3. Box of any kind of wood.

Bujeto [boo-hay'-to], *m.* Burnisher, a polishing stick used by shoemakers.

Bujía [boo-hee'-ah], *f.* 1. Wax candle. 2. Candlestick for wax candle. 3. Spark plug. 4. Candle, candlepower.

Bujiería [boo-he-ay-ree'-ah], *f.* Office at court where wax-candles are kept, and given out for the use of the palace.

Bujo [boo'-ho], *m* Wooden frame on which painters fix their canvas.

Bula [boo'-lah], *f.* 1. Bull, an instrument despatched from the papal chancery, and sealed with lead. *Echar las bulas a uno,* (Met.) To impose a burden or troublesome duty. *Tener bula para todo,* To take the liberty of acting according to one's fancy. 2. (Obs.) Bubble on water.

Bulario [boo-lah'-re-o], *m.* Collection of papal bulls.

Bulbo [bool'-bo], *m.* (Bot.) Bulb. Bulbus. *Bulbo costaño,* (Bot.) Great earth-nut, pig-nut. Bunium bulbocastanum.

Bulboso, sa [bool-bo'-so, sah], *a.* Bulbous.

Bulero [boo-lay'-ro], *m.* One charged with distributing bulls of crusades, and collecting the alms contributed for them.

Buleto [boo-lay'-to], *m.* Brief or apostolic letter granted by the Pope, or by his legate or nuncio.

Bulevar [boo-lay-var'], *m.* Boulevard.

Búlgaro, ra [bool'-gah-ro, rah], *a.* Bulgarian; native of or belonging to Bulgaria.

Bulimia [boo-lee'-me-ah], *f.* (Med.) Bulimy or bulimia, voracious appetite.

Bulímico, co [boo-lee'-me-co, cah], *a.* Bulimic, relating to voracious appetite.

Bultito [bool-tee'-to], *m. dim.* Little lump or tumour.

Bulto [bool'-to], *m.* 1. Bulk, any thing which appears bulky. 2. Protuberance, tumour, swelling; massiness. 3. Bust, image of the human head and neck. 4. Pillow-case. *Coger* or *pescar el bulto,* (Met.) To lay hold of any one, to seize one. *Figura o imagen de bulto,* Figure or image in sculpture. *Menear* or *tocar a otro el bulto,* To give one a nice drubbing. *A bulto,* Indistinctly, confusedly. *Ser de bulto,* To be as clear as possible; to be a reason or a thing patent and conspicuous by itself. *Comprar las cosas a bulto,* To buy wholesale, or by the lump. 5. (Com.) Package, parcel.

Bululú [boo-loo-loo'], *m.* (Obs.) Strolling comedian, who formerly represented all the characters in a farce, by changing his voice.

Bulla [bool'-lyah], *f.* 1. Noise, any sound made by one or more persons. 2. Clatter, shout, or loud cry. 3. Crowd, mob. *Meterlo a bulla,* To carry off the matter with a joke. *Meter bulla,* To make noise.

Bullaje [bool-lyah'-hay], *m.* Crowd, a multitude confusedly pressed together.

Bullanga [bool-lyahn'-gah], *f.* Tumult, riot.

Bullanguero, ra [bool-lyan-gay'-ro, rah], *m.* & *f.* Rioter, a seditious, turbulent person.

Bullar [bool-lyar'], *va.* To cut the wild-boar's throat while the dogs hold him.

Bullebulle [bool-lyay-bool'-lyay], *m.* (Coll.) Busy-body, bustler, a person of lively and restless disposition, vulgarly smart.

Bullicio [bool-lyee'-the-o], *m.* 1. Bustle, noise, and clamour raised by a crowd. 2. Tumult, uproar, sedition heat.

Bulliciosamente [bool-lye-the-oh-sah-men'-tay], *adv.* In a noisy, tumultuous manner, mutinously.

Bullicioso, sa [bool-lye-the-oh'-so, sah], *a.* 1. Lively, restless, noisy, clamorous, busy. 2. Seditious, turbulent. 3. (Poet.) Boisterous: applied to the sea.

Bullidor, ra [bool-lye-dor', rah], *a. V* BULLICIOSO.

Bullir [bool-lyeer'], *vn.* 1. To boil, as water and other liquids. 2. (Met.) To bustle, to be lively or restless, to fluster. 3. (Met.) To be industrious and active in business. *Bullirle a uno alguna cosa,* To be earnestly desirous of a thing.—*va.* To move a thing from place to place; to manage a business.

Bullón [bool-lyone'], *m.* 1. (Obs.) Kind of knife. 2. Dye bubbling up in a boiler. 3. A metallic ornament for large books. 4. Bouillon, a clear meat broth; particularly used in bacteriology. 5. Puff, in sewing.

Bumerang [boo-may-rahng'], *m.* Boomerang.

Bungo [boon'-go], *m.* A Nicaraguan flat-boat, about 40 by 9 feet.

Buniato [boo-ne-ah'-to], *m. V.* BONIATO.

Bunio [boo'-ne-o], *m.* Sort of earth-nut or pig-nut.

Buñolada [boo-nyo-lah'-dah], *f.* A platter of buns.

Buñolería [boo-nyo-lay-ree'-ah], *f.* A bun-shop; place where fritters are made and sold.

Buñolero, ra [boo-nyo-lay'-ro, rah], *m.* & *f.* One that makes or sells buns.

Buñuelo [boo-nyoo-ay'-lo], *m.* 1. Fritter made of flour and eggs, and fried in oil; pan-cake. *¿Es buñuelo?* Is it nothing? observed to inconsiderate persons who would have things done without the necessary time. 2. (Coll.) Any thing poorly done or spoiled; a failure.

Bupréstidos [boo-pres'-te-dos], *m. pl.* Buprestidans, a family of beetles, destructive of wood in their larval state.

Buque [boo'-kay], *m.* 1. Ship, vessel, boat. 2. Hull of a ship. *Buque de guerra,* War vessel. *Buque de vela,* Sailboat.

Buquinista [boo-ke-nees'-tah], *m.* A collector of old books. (F. bouquiniste.)

Burato [boo-rah'-to], *m.* 1. Canton crape. 2. Cyprus, sort of woollen stuff much worn for mourning, and by clergymen. 3. Transparent veil of light silk, worn by women.

Burbá [boor'-bah], *f.* African coin of small value.

Burbalur [boor-ba-loor'], *m.* Whale of a large kind.

Burbuja [boor-boo'-hah], *f.* Bubble; bleb.

Burbujear [boor-boo-hay-ar'], *vn.* To bubble.

Burbujita [boor-boo-hee'-tah], *f. dim.* Small bubble.

Burcho [boor'-cho], *m.* (Naut.) Large sloop or barge.

Burdas [boor'-das], *f. pl.* (Naut.) Back-stays.

Burdégano [boor-day'-gah-no], *m.* Hinny, offspring of a stallion and a she-ass; mule.

Burdel [boor-del'], *m.* Brothel, brothel-house.—*a.* (Obs.) Libidinous.

Burdelero, ra [boor-day-lay'-ro, rah], *m.* & *f.* (Obs.) *V.* ALCAHUETE.

Burdelés, sa [boor-day-less', sah], *a.* Belonging to Bordeaux.

Burdinalla [boor-de-nahl'-lyah], *f.* (Naut.) Sprit-top-sail-stay.

Burdo, da [boor'-do, dah], *a.* Coarse, common, ordinary.

Burel [boo-rel'], *m.* 1. (Her.) Bar, the ninth part of a shield. 2. (Naut.) Fid, marline-spike.

Bureles [boo-ray'-les], *m. pl.* (Naut.) Pointed wooden rollers. *Bureles de hierro para engarzar motones,* Splicing-fids. *V.* PASADOR.

Burengue [boo-ren'-gay], *m.* (Prov.) Mulatto slave.

Bureo [boo ray'-o], *m.* 1. Court of justice, in which matters are tried relative to persons of the king's household. 2. Entertainment, amusement, diversion. *Entrar en bureo,* To meet for the purpose of inquiring into or discussing a subject.

Bureta [boo-ray'-tah], *f.* Burette, drop-measurer.

Burga [boor'-gah], *f.* (Prov.) Hot spring of mineral waters used for bathing.

Burgalés [boor-gah-less'], *m.* 1. Ancient coin made at Burgos. 2. Wind blowing from Burgos. 3. A native of the province of Burgos.

Burgés [boor-hess'], *m.* (Obs.) Native or inhabitant of a village.

Burgo [boor'-go], *m.* (Obs.) Borough.

Burgomaestre [boor-go-mah-es'-tray], *m.* Burgomaster, magistrate of a Dutch or German city.

Burgueño, ña [boor-gay'-nyo, nyah], *a.* (Obs.) Of Burgos.

Burgués, sa [boor-gess', sah], *a.* Burgess; a citizen of a town of the middle class.

Burguesía [boor-gay-see'-ah], *f.* Burgess-ship; yeomanry.

Burí [boo-ree'], *m.* A palm growing in the Philippine Islands; the pith yields sago.

Buriel [boo-re-el'], *a.* Reddish, dark red.

Buriel [boo-re-el'], *m.* 1. Kersey, a coarse cloth. 2. Rope-walk, manufactory for cordage.

Buril [boo-reel'], *m.* Burin, tool of an engraver. *Buril de punta,* Sharp-pointed burin. *Buril chaple redondo,* Curved burin.

Burilada [boo-re-lah'-dah], *f.* 1. Line or stroke of a burin. 2. Silver taken by an assayer, to test it by the standard.

Buriladura [boo-re-lah-doo'-rah], *f.* Act of engraving with a graver or burin.

Burilar [boo-re-lar'], *va.* To engrave with a burin or graver.

Burjaca [boor-hah'-cah], *f.* Leather bag carried by pilgrims or beggars.

Burla [boor'-lah], *f.* 1. Scoff, flout, mock, mockery, fling, abuse, irrision, sneer. 2. Jest, fun, trick. 3. Jeer, jeering, flirt, gibe. 4. Hoax, low trick. *Burla pesada,* Biting jest, bad trick. *Burla burlando le dijo buenas claridades,* Between joke and earnest he told him some plain truths. *Burlas,* Falsities uttered in a jocular style. *Burlas aparte,* Setting jokes aside. *Hablar de burlas,* To speak in jest. *Hombre de burlas,* He is a plain, honest man. *Decir algunas cosas entre burlas y veras,* To say something between joke and earnest. *De burlas,* In jest.

Burladero [boor-lah-day'-ro], *m.* A narrow doorway in the bull-ring, for escape of the fighter.

Burlador, ra [boor-lah-dor', rah], *m. & f.* 1. Wag, jester, scoffer, mocker, jeerer. 2. Libertine, seducer. (Acad.) 3. Conjurer's cup, a vessel so contrived that the liquor runs out through hidden holes when it is put to the lips. 4. Concealed squirt, which throws out water on those who come near.

Burlar [boor-lar'], *va.* 1. To ridicule, to mock, to scoff, to laugh, to burlesque. 2. To hoax, to gibe, to fetch over, to flout, to abuse, to play tricks, to deceive. 3. To frustrate one's views, to destroy one's hopes.—*vr.* 1. To jest, to laugh at. 2. To fleer, to gibe, to dally, to flout.

Burlería [boor-lay-ree'-ah], *f.* 1. Fun, pun, artifice; drolling. 2. Romantic tale. 3. Deceit, illusion. 4. Derision, reproach.

Burlescamente [boor-les-ca-men'-tay], *adv.* Comically, ludicrously.

Burlesco, ca [boor-les'-co, cah], *a.* Burlesque, jocular, ludicrous, comic, mock, funny.

Burlesco [boor-les'-co], *m.* (Obs.) Burlesquer, wag, jester, scoffer, mimic.

Burleta, illa, ita [boor-lay'-tah, eel'-lyah, ee'-tah], *f. dim.* Little trick, fun, or joke.

Burlete [boor-lay'-tay], *m* Weather-strip; kersey.

Burlón, na [boor-lone', nah], *m. & f.* Great wag, jester, or scoffer.

Buro [boo'-ro], *m.* (Prov.) Chalk, marl.

Buró [boo-roh'], *m.* Bureau; a chest of drawers, with or without conveniences for writing.

Burocracia [boo-ro-crah'-the-ah], *f.* Bureaucracy, a system by which the business of administration is carried on in departments, each under the control of a chief.

Burocrático [boo-ro-crah'-te-co], *a.* Bureaucratic.

Burra [boor'-rah], *f.* 1. A she-ass. *Caer de su burra,* To fall from one's hobby-horse, to become sensible of one's errors. 2. A dirty, ignorant, and unteachable woman. *Cf.* BURRO, 2d def. (Acad.) 3. A laborious woman of much patience.

Burrada [boor-rah'-dah], *f.* 1. Drove of asses. 2. Stupid or foolish action or saying. 3. A play contrary to rule in the game of *burro.*

Burrajo [boor-rah'-ho], *m.* Dry stable-dung to heat ovens.

Burrazo, za [boor-rah'-tho, thah], *m. & f. aug.* Large or big ass.

Burrero [boor-ray'-ro], *m.* 1. Ass-keeper, who sells asses' milk for medicine. 2. Jackass-keeper.

Burrillo [boor-reel'-lyo], *m.* (Coll.) *V.* AÑALEJO.

Burrito [boor-ree'-to], *m. dim.* A little ass.

Burro [boor'-ro], *m.* 1. Ass, jument. 2. Ass, a stupid, ignorant being. *Es un burro cargado de letras,* He is an unmannerly clown, with all his learning. 3. Jack or horse on which sawyers saw boards or timber. 4. Wheel which puts the machine in motion that twists and reels silk. 5. A game at cards. 6. Windlass, in mining. *Caer de su burro,* The same as *caer de su burra. V.* BURRA. *Es un burro en el trabajo,* He works and drudges like an ass. *Burros de la mesana,* (Naut.) Mizzen-bowlines.

Burrucho [boor-roo'-cho], *m.* Young or little ass.

Burrumbada [boor-room-bah'-dah], *f.* *V.* BARRUMBADA.

Bursátil [boor-sah'-teel], *a.* Relating to the bourse or exchange.

Burujo [boo-roo'-ho], *m.* 1. Dregs of pressed olives or grapes. 2. Lump of pressed wood or other matter. 3. Parcel, package.

Burujón, Burullón [boo-roo-hone', boo-rool-lyone'], *m.* 1. (Aug.) Large knob or lump. 2. Protuberance in the head caused by a stroke.

Burujoncillo [boo-roo-hon-theel'-lyo], *m. dim.* Little knob or protuberance.

Busardas [boo-sar'-das], *f. pl.* (Naut.) Breast-hooks, compass-timbers, which serve to strengthen the stem.

Busardo [boo-sar'-do], *m.* Buzzard, a bird of prey.

Busca [boos'-cah], *f.* 1. Search, the act of searching. 2. Pursuit. 3. Terrier or other dog which starts or springs the game. 4. Troop of huntsmen, drivers, and terriers, that overrun a forest to rouse the game.

Buscada [boos-cah'-dah], *f.* Search, research, inquiry, the act of searching.

Buscador, ra [boos-cah-dor', rah], *m. & f.* Searcher, investigator. —*m.* Viewfinder (in a camera or in an optical appliance).

Buscamiento [boos-cah-me-en'-to], *m.* (Obs.) Search, research, inquiry.

Buscapié [boos-cah-pe-ay'], *m.* (Met.) Word dropped in conversation to come at the bottom of something.

Buscapiés [boos-cah-pe-ess'], *m.* Squib running about between people's feet, serpent (pyrotechnic).

Buscar [boos-car'], *va.* 1. To seek, to search, to endeavour to find out. 2. To look, to look after, to look for, or to look out; to hunt or hunt after. *Buscar por todos lados,* To hunt up and down. *Buscar tres pies al gato y él tiene cuatro,* To pick a quarrel. *Quien busca halla,* He that seeks will find. *Buscar el vivo a una pieza* or *cañón,* To take the calibre of a gun.—*vr.* To bring upon one's self.

Buscarruidos [boos-car-roo-ee'-dos], *m.* Restless, quarrelsome fellow.

Buscavidas [boos-cah-vee'-das], *m.* 1. A person prying into the actions of others. 2. One diligent in finding subsistence for himself and his family.

Busco [boos'-co], *m.* (Obs.) Track of an animal.

Buscón, na [boos-cone', nah], *m. & f.* 1. Searcher. 2. Cheat, pilferer, filcher, petty robber.

Busilis [boo-see'-lis], *m.* (Coll.) The point in question where the difficulty lies; a mystery, riddle. *Dar en el busilis,* To hit the mark.

Buso [boo'-so], *m.* (Obs.) Hole. *V.* AGUJERO.

(*Yo busqué,* from *Buscar. V.* verbs in *car.*)

Busqueda [boos-kay'-dah], *f.* Search. *V.* BUSCADA.

Busto [boos'-to], *m.* 1 Bust. 2. (Obs.) Tomb.

Bustrófedon [boos-tro'-fay-done], *m.* A method of writing continuously from left to right, and back vice versa, and so on. It receives its name from the trail of oxen ploughing.

Butaca [boo-tah'-cah], *f.* 1. Arm-chair, easy-chair. 2. Seat in a theatre.

Butifarra [boo-te-far'-rah], *f.* 1. Sort of sausage made in Catalonia. 2. Gaskins, long wide breeches.

Butillo, illa [boo-teel'-lyo, lyah], *a.* (Littl. us.) Of a pale yellowish colour.

Butiondo [boo-te-on'-do], *a.* Fetid, goatish, lustful.

Butiráceo, cea [boo-te-rah'-thay-o, ah], *a.* Butyraceous, of a consistency like butter.

Butírico, ca [boo-tee'-re-co, cah], *a.* Butyric, an acid found in butter, and gives it its odour.

Butorio [boo-to'-re-o], *m.* (Orn.) Bittern. Ardea stellaris.

Butrino [boo-tree'-no], *m.* Fowling-net for catching birds.

Butrón [boo-trone'], *m.* Net for birds. *V.* BUITRÓN.

Butuco [boo-too'-co], *m.* A thick, stumpy plantain.

Buya [boo'-yah], *m.* *V.* CASTOR.

Buyador [boo-yah-dor'], *m.* (Prov.) Brazier. *V.* LATONERO.

Buyo [boo'-yo], *m.* 1. (Prov.) Hut, shepherd's cottage. 2. Boa constrictor. 3. A compound of bonga-fruit, betel-leaves, and lime, for chewing.

Buz [booth], *m.* (Littl. us.) Kiss of respect and reverent regard. *Hacer el buz*, To do homage or pay respect in a servile manner. (Persian.)

Búzano [boo'-thah-no], *m.* (Obs.) 1. Diver. 2. Kind of culverin.

Buzar [boo-thar'], *va.* To dip downward, as a geological stratum.

Buzardas [boo-thar'-das], *f. pl.* (Naut.) Breast-hooks, fore-hooks.

Buzcorona [booth-co-ro'-nah], *f.* A kiss and a blow on the head in fun.

Buzo [boo'-tho], *m.* 1. Diver, one that goes under water in search of things dropped into the sea or rivers. 2. An ancient kind of ship.

Buzón [boo-thone'], *m.* 1. (Arch.) Conduit, canal. 2. (Prov.) Hole through which letters are thrown into the post-office, letter-box, drop-box. 3. Lid or cover of cisterns, ponds, jars, etc. 4. In foundries, hooks to take off the lids of melting-pots. 5. Sluice of a water-course at a mill. 6. Ancient kind of battering-ram.

Buzonera [boo-tho-nay'-rah], *f.* A drain or gutter in a courtyard.

C

C [thay], is the third letter of the alphabet, and before *e* and *i* has generally the sound of the English *th* in *thick;* before *a, o, u, l,* and *r,* it sounds like *k.* It is also a numeral, as, C. 100; IƆ. 500; and CIƆ. 1,000.—The Spanish Academicians consider *ch* as a distinct letter, double in figure but simple in value, and therefore place it after all the other words beginning with a *c.* *Ch* has always the soft sound in Spanish, the same as in the English word *church;* formerly it was pronounced as *k* in words derived from Greek or Hebrew, but in such words the *h* is now omitted, or the orthography changed, as *Cristo*, formerly written *Christo; Querubín*, formerly written *Chêrubín*, etc.

Ca [cah], *conj.* (Obs.) Because, for, the same as. (Lat. quia.)

¡Cá! [cah], *int.* (Coll.) Oh, no! No, indeed! *V.* ¡Quiá!

Cabal [cah-bahl'], *a.* 1. Just, exact: applied to weight or measure. 2. Perfect, complete, accomplished, faultless, consummate; clever. 3. Falling to one's share or dividend. *Por su cabal*, (Obs.) With all his might, most earnestly. *Por sus cabales*, Exactly, perfectly, to the very point; according to rule and order; for its just price, according to what it is worth.

Cábala [cah'-bah-lah], *f.* 1. Cabala, mystical knowledge of the celestial bodies. 2. Secret science of the Hebrew rabbins. 3. Cabal, intrigue, complot, combination. 4. Confederation or confederacy; junta.

Cabalgada [cah-bal-gah'-dah], *f.* 1. Foray. 2. Cavalcade, a procession on horseback. 3. Booty or spoils taken by an incursion into an enemy's country.

Cabalgadero [cah-bal-gah-day'-ro], *m.* Mounting-block.

Cabalgador [cah-bal-gah-dor'], *m.* 1. Rider. 2. Horseman who goes in procession. 3. (Obs.) Horse-block.

Cabalgadura [cah-bal-gah-doo'-rah], *f.* Sumpter, a beast of burden.

Cabalgar [cah-bal-gar'], *vn.* 1. To parade on horseback, to go in a cavalcade. 2. To horse, to get on horseback, to mount on horseback.—*va.* 1. To cover a mare: applied to a stallion. 2. *Cabalgar la artillería*, To mount cannon on their carriages.

Cabalgar [cah-bal-gar'], *m.* (Obs.) Harness.

Cabalgata [cah-bal-gah'-tah], *f.* Cavalcade.

Cabalista [cah-bah-lees'-tah], *m.* Cabalist, one skilled in the traditions of the Hebrews.

Cabalístico, ca [cah-bah-lees'-te-co, cah], *a.* Cabalistic.

Cabalmente [cah-bal-men'-tay], *adv.* Exactly, completely, perfectly, fairly.

Caballa [cah-bahl'-lyah], *f.* Horse-mackerel. Scomber hippos.

Caballada [cah-bal-lyah'-dah], *f.* 1. (Littl. us.) Stud of horses or mares. 2. A number of horses. 3. (Prov.) Any game performed by horsemen on public festivals.

Caballaje [cah-bal-lyah'-hay], *m.* 1. Place where mares and she-asses are served by stallions or jackasses. 2. Money paid for that service.

Caballar [cah-bal-lyar'], *m.* Mackerel. Scomber scombrus.

Caballar [cah-bal-lyar'], *a.* Belonging to or resembling horses, equine.

Caballear [cah-bal-lyay-ar'], *va.* To ride horseback often.

Caballejo [cah-bal-lyay'-ho], *m.* 1. (Dim.) Little horse, nag. 2. Wooden frame for shoeing unruly horses.

Caballerato [cah-bal-lyay-rah'-to], *m.* 1. Right of laymen to enjoy ecclesiastical benefices by virtue of the Pope's dispensation. 2. The benefice enjoyed by virtue of the said dispensation. 3. Privilege of gentleman or esquire, in Catalonia, granted by the Spanish monarchs, and given a middle rank between the nobility and citizens.

Caballerear [cah-bal-lyay-ray-ar'], *vn.* To set up for a gentleman.

Caballerescamente [cah-bal-lyay-res-cah-men'-tay], *adv.* Knightly, cavalierly, gentlemanly.

Caballeresco, ca [cah-bal-lyay-res'-co, cah], *a.* 1. Knightly, befitting a knight; adventurous. 2. Chivalrous. 3. Belonging to or having the appearance of a gentleman.

Caballerete [cah-bal-lyay-ray'-tay], *m. dim.* Spruce young gentleman.

Caballería [cah-bal-lyay-ree'-ah], *f.* 1. A riding beast. *Caballería mayor*, Saddle-horse or mule. *Caballería menor*, Ass. 2. Cavalry horse or horse-troops. 3. Art of managing and mounting a horse. 4. Chivalry, the order of knights, and particularly military order. 5. Knighthood; martialism, nobleness of mind. 6. Assembly of knights of military orders. 7. Chivalry, the institution and profession of knights 8. Body of nobility of a province or place. 9. Service rendered by knights and nobles. 10. Share of spoils given to a knight, according to his rank and merit. 11. A tract of land about thirty-three and one-third acres, U. S. measure. 12. Pre-eminence and privileges of knights. *Libros de caballería*, Books of knight-errantry. *Caballería andante*, The profession of knight-errantry. *Andarse en caballerías*, (Met.) To make a fulsome show of superfluous compliments.

Caballeril [cah-bal-lyay-reel'], *a.* (Obs.) Pertaining to a knight.

Caballerito [cah-bal-yay-ree'-to], *m. dim.* A young gentleman.

Caballeriza [cah-bal-lyay-ree'-thah], *f.* 1. Stable. 2. Number of horses, mules, etc., standing in a stable. 3. Stud of horses. 4. The staff of grooms, coachmen, etc., in any establishment.

Caballerizo [cah-bal-lyay-ree'-tho], *m.* Head groom of a stable. *Caballerizo del rey*, Equerry to the king. *Caballerizo mayor del rey*, Master of the horse to the king.

Caballero [cah-bal-lyay'-ro], *m.* 1 Knight. 2. Cavalier, knight. 3. A nobleman. 4. A gentleman. 5. A rider. 6. Horseman, soldier on horseback. 7. Cavalier, a sort of fortification. 8. An old Spanish dance. 9. (Orn.) Red-legged horseman, gambet. Tringa gambetta. 10. *Caballero andante*, Knight-errant. 11. A poor gentleman strolling from place to place. *A caballero*, Above, in a superior degree. *Armar a uno caballero*, To knight, to create one a knight. *Caballero de industria*, A defrauder, a knave. *Meterse a caballero*, To assume the character of a gentleman or knight. *Ir caballero* or *caballera*, To go on horseback.

Caballero, ra [cah-bal-lyay'-ro, rah], *a.* Applied to a person who goes on horseback. *Ir caballero en burro*, (Coll.) To ride on an ass.

Caballerosamente [cah-bal-lyay-ro-sah-men'-tay], *adv.* 1. Generously, nobly, in a gentleman-like manner. 2. Knightly.

Caballerosidad [ca-bal-lyay-ro-se-dahd'], *f.* Gentlemanliness, behavior of a gentleman. *Caballerosidad deportiva*, Good sportsmanship.

Caballeroso, sa [cah-bal-lyay-ro'-so, sah], *a.* 1. Noble, generous, genteel. 2. Gentleman-like.

Caballerote [cah-bal-lyay-ro'-tay], *m.* 1. A gentleman of an ancient family, and of an unblemished character. 2. (Coll.) Graceless, unpolished gentleman.

Caballeta [cah-bal-lyay'-tah], *f.* Field-cricket. Gryllus campestris.

Caballete [cah-bal-lyay'-tay], *m.* 1. Ridge of a house forming an acute angle; bolster, ridge-piece, hip; carpenter's horse, trestle-horse, bench, trestle. 2. Horse, an instrument of torture. 3. Brake, for dressing hemp and flax. 4. Ridge between furrows, raised by a ploughshare. 5. Cover over the funnel of a chimney in a pyramidal form. 6. Bridge of the nose. 7. Gallows of a printing-press. 8. Easel. 9. (Aer.) Gantry tower. *Caballete de aserrar*, Sawyer's trestle or horse. *Caballete de colchar cabos*, (Naut.) Rope-laying truss. *Caballete de pintor*, Painter's easel.

Caballico, ito [cah-bal-lyee'-co, ee'-to], *m.* 1. (Dim.) Little horse, pony. 2. Hobby or hobby-horse, a rocking-horse; a stick or cane on which children ride.

Caballista [cah-bal-lyees'-tah], *m.* Horseman, connoisseur of horses.

Caballitos [cah-bal-lyee'-tos], *m. pl.* 1. Small horses. 2. Merry-go-round, carrousel.

Caballo [cah-bahl'-lyo], *m.* 1. Horse. *Caballo padre*, A stallion, stone horse. *Caballo de montar* or *silla*, Saddle-horse. *Caballo de carga*, Pack-horse. *Caballo castrado* or *capado*, Gelding. *Caballo de coche*, Coach-horse. *Caballo frisón*, Draught-horse, Flanders horse. *Caballo de guerra*, Charger. *Caballo de albada* or *de regalo*, Sumpter or state horse. *Caballo de arcabuz*, Horse that stands fire. *Caballo de caza*, Hunter. *Caballo de carrera* or *corredor*, Racer, race-horse. *Caballo rabón*, Docked horse, a short-tailed horse. *Caballo desorejado*, Cropped horse. *Caballo de escuela*, Horse well broken in at the manège. *Caballo de* *vara*, Shaft-horse. *Caballo aguililla*, Peruvian horse, very swift. *Caballo de alquiler*, Hack, hackney. *Caballo de tiro*, Draught-horse. *Caballo de mano*, Led horse. *Caballo de posta*, Post-horse. *Caballo espantadizo* or *medroso*, Skittish horse. *Caballo bayo*, Bay horse. *Caballo bayo castaño*, Chestnut bay horse. *Caballo bayo (obscuro)*, Brown bay horse. *Caballo bayo dorado*, Bright bay horse. *Caballo picazo*, Pied horse. *Caballo moro*, Piebald horse. *Caballo rucio rodado*, Dapple gray horse. *Caballo tordo rodado*, Dapple bay horse. *Caballo pardo*, Gray horse. *Caballo alazán*, Sorrel horse. *Caballo alazán tostado*, Dark sorrel horse. *Caballo overo*, White and red spotted horse. *Caballo rubicán*, Speckled white horse. *Caballo retinto*, Shining black horse. *Caballo matado*, A galled horse. *Caballo matado en la cruz*, A horse wrung in the withers. *Caballo aguado*, A foundered horse. *Caballo desbocado*, Runaway horse. *Trabajar un caballo*, To break in a horse, to make him answer to spur and bridle. *Sacar bien su caballo*, (Met.) To extricate one's self decently out of a difficulty. *Caballo de buena boca*, (Met.) A person who accommodates himself readily to circumstances. *Caballo de frisia*, (Mil.) Chevaux-de-frise, hersillon, a military instrument. *Caballo de palo*, 1. (Coll.) Any vessel fit for sea. 2. (Vulg.) Rack for criminals. 3. (Tannery) Tanner's beam. *Caballo marino*, River-horse. Hippopotamus. 2. Pipe-fish, sea-horse. Syngnathus hippocampus. 3. Figure on horseback, equivalent to the queen, at cards. 4. Trestle, bench on which planks or boards are laid for masons and plasterers to work on. 5. Knight in the game of chess. *A caballo*, On horseback. *Caballos*, Horse, cavalry, mounted soldiers. 6. Bubo, tumour in the groin. *V.* Potro. 7. Thread which ravels others. 8. Barren rock in a vein (mining). *Huir a uña de caballo*, To have a hair-breadth escape; to extricate one's self from difficulty by prudence and energy. *Echarle a uno el caballo de cara*, (Coll.) To upbraid roughly. *A caballo regalado no hay que mirarle el diente*, You must not look a gift horse in the mouth. *Caballo de vapor*, A dynamic unit which represents the force necessary to raise seventy-five kilogrammes one metre in one second.

Caballón [cah-bal-lyone'], *m.* 1. (Aug.) Large, clumsy horse. 2. Ridge of ploughed land between two furrows.

Caballuelo [cah-bal-lyoo-ay'-lo], *m. dim.* Little horse.

Caballuno, na [cah-bal-lyoo'-no, nah], *a.* Belonging to a horse.

Cabaña [cah-bah'-nyah], *f.* 1. Shepherd's hut, cottage, cot, cabin. 2. Hole, hovel, mean habitation. 3. Flock of ewes or breeding sheep. 4. Drove of asses for carrying grain. 5. (Prov.) Weekly allowance of bread, oil, vinegar, and salt, for shepherds. 6. Balk, a line drawn on a billiard-table, limiting the players. 7. Landscape representing a shepherd's cottage, with fowls, and other domestic animals. 8. Cabana. *Cabana real*, The whole of the travelling flocks possessed by the members who compose the body of La Mesta in Spain.

Cabañal [cah-bah-nyahl'], *a.* Applied to the road for flocks of travelling sheep and droves of cattle.

Cabañería [cah-bah-nyay-ree'-ah], *f.* Rations for a week, of bread, oil, vinegar, and salt, allowed to shepherds.

Cabañero, ra [cah-bah-nyay'-ro, rah], *a.* Belonging to the drove of mules and asses which go with a flock of travelling sheep.

Cabañil [cah-bah-nyeel'], *a.* Applied to the mules which go with the flocks of travelling sheep.

Cabañil [cah-bah-nyeel'], *m.* Herd or keeper of mules and asses, kept for carrying corn.

Cabañuela [cah-bah-nyoo-ay'-lah], *f, dim.* Small hut or cottage. *Cabañuelas*, Festival of the Jews of Toledo.

Cabaret [cah-bah-ret'], *m.* Cabaret, night club.

Cabaza [cah-bah'-thah], *f.* (Obs.) Large or wide cloak with hood and sleeves.

Cabd. (Obs.) *V.* Cau. For example: Cabdal. *V.* Caudal, etc.

Cabe [cah'-bay], *m.* Stroke given by balls, in the game of *argolla*, whereby the player gains a point. *Dar un cabe al bolsillo, a la hacienda*, etc. (Met.) To give a shake to one's purse, to hurt one in his business, fortune, etc. *Cabe de pala* or *paleta*, A casual stroke of fortune to attain any object.

Cabe [cah'-bay], *prep.* (Obs.) *V.* Cerca and Junto.

Cabecear [cah-bay-thay-ar'], *vn.* 1. To nod with sleep, to hang the head on one side. 2. To shake the head in disapprobation. 3. To raise or lower the head: applied to horses. 4. To incline to one side, to hang over: applied to a load not well balanced. 5. (Naut.) To pitch. 6. To lurch: used of carriages.—*va.* 1. In writing, to give the letters the necessary thick stroke or loop. 2. Among bookbinders, to put the head-band to a book. 3. To garnish cloth with edgings of tape or lace. 4. To cauterize a vein. 5. To head wine, by adding some old to give it strength.

Cabeceo [cah-bay-thay'-o], *m.* Nod of the head.

Cabecequia [cah-bay-thay'-ke-ah], *m.* (Prov.) Inspector of sluices, guardian of water-courses.

Cabecera [cah-bay-thay'-rah], *f.* 1. The beginning or principal part of something. 2. Head or head-board of a bed; also a railing at the head of a bed to prevent pillows from falling. 3. Seat of honour. 4. Head-waters, source of a river. 5. Capital of a province, district, or nation. 6. A fortified point of a bridge. 7. Head-piece or vignette at the beginning of a chapter. 8. Each extremity of the back of a book. 9. A pillow or bolster of a bed. *Estar o asistir a la cabecera del enfermo*, To nurse or wait upon a sick person. 10. The summit of a hill or ridge.

Cabecero [cah-bay-thay'-ro], *m.* 1. Lintel, the upper part of a door-frame. 2. (Obs.) Head of a branch of a noble family. 3. Compress.

Cabeciancho, cha [cah-bay-the-ahn'-cho, chah], *a.* Broad or flat headed: applied to nails.

Cabecica, ita [cah-bay-thee'-cah, ee-tah], *f. dim.* Small head.

Cabecil [cah-bay-theel'], *m.* A pad of cloth which women place on the head for carrying a pail or any thing heavy.

Cabecilla [cah-bay-theel'-lyah], *m.* 1. Wrong-headed person, full of levity, indiscretion, and whims. 2. Leader of rebels. 3. Ringleader.

Cabellazo [cah-bel-lyah'-tho], *m. aug.* Large bush of hair.

Cabellejo [cah-bel-lyay'-ho], *m. dim.* Little hair.

Cabellera [cah-bel-lyay'-rah], *f.* 1. Long hair spread over the shoulders. 2. False hair. 3. Tail of a comet. Any other body which presents a tuft-like appearance, as the branches of willows, etc.

Cabello [cah-bayl'-lyo], *m.* Hair of the head. *Llevar a uno de un cabello*, To lead one by the nose. *No faltar en un cabello*, Not to be wanting in the least thing. *No monta un cabello*, It is not worth a rush. *Hender un cabello en el aire*, To split a hair, to be wonderfully acute. *En cabello*, In a dishevelled manner. *Asirse de un cabello*, To catch at a hair, to adopt any pretext.—*pl.* 1. Large sinews in mutton. 2. Fibres of plants; the silk of maize. *Cabellos de ángel*, Conserve of fruit cut into small threads. *Estar colgado de los cabellos*, To be in anxious expectation of the issue of a critical affair. *Tomar la ocasión por los cabellos.* To take time by the forelock. (Met.) To profit by the occasion. *Traer alguna cosa por los cabellos*, (Met.) To appropriate a phrase, an authority, or a quotation, to a thing which has no relation with it. *Arrancarse los cabellos*, To pull or tear one's hair. *Arrastrar a uno por los cabellos*, To drag one away by the hair.

Cabelludo, da [cah-bel-lyoo'-do, dah], *a.* Hairy. *Cuero cabelludo*, Scalp.

Cabelluelo [cah-bel-lyoo-ay'-lo], *m. dim.* Thin and short hair.

Caber [cah-berr'], *vn.* 1. To be able or capable to contain, or to be contained; to fit. 2. To have room, place, or right of admission. 3. To be entitled to a thing. 4. To fall to one's share. *Honra y provecho no caben en un saco*, Honour and money are seldom found together. *No caber de gozo*, To be overjoyed. *No caber de pies*, To have no room to stand. *No caber en el mundo*, To be elated with excessive pride, to be puffed up with vanity. *No caber en sí*, To be full of one's own merits; to be very uneasy. *Todo cabe*, It is all possible; it may well be so. *Todo cabe en fulano*, He is capable of any thing. *No cabe más*, Nothing more to be desired: applied to any thing that has arrived at its ultimate point.—*va.* To contain, to comprise, to include.

Cabero [cah-bay'-ro], *m.* (Prov.) Maker of handles for tools.

Cabestraje [cah-bes-trah'-hay], *m.* 1. Halter, and other head-tackling for beasts. 2. Money paid to a driver for conducting cattle to market.

Cabestrante [cah-bes-trahn'-tay], *m. V.* Cabrestante.

Cabestrar [cah-bes-trar'], *va.* To halter, to bind with a halter.—*vn.* To fowl with a stalking-ox.

Cabestrear [cah-bes-tray-ar'], *vn.* To follow one willingly who leads by a halter or collar: applied to beasts.

Cabestrería [cah-bes-tray-ree'-ah], *f.* Shop where halters and collars are made and sold.

Cabestrero [cah-bes-tray'-ro], *m.* One who makes or retails halters and collars.

Cabestrero, ra [cah-bes tray'-ro, rah], *a.* (Prov.) Being so tame as to be led by a halter.

Cabestrillo [cah-bes-treel'-lyo], *m.* 1. Sling suspended from the neck, in which a sore arm or hand is carried. 2. Kind of hoop which keeps the cheeks of a saw tight. 3. Gold or silver chain. *Buey de cabestrillo*, Stalking-ox.

Cabestro [cah-bes'-tro], *m.* 1. Halter 2. Bell-ox, a tame bullock that leads the rest of a drove of black cattle. *Traer a alguno de cabestro*, To lead one by the nose. 3. (Obs.) Chain. *V.* CABESTRILLO.

Cabeza [cah-bay'-thah], *f.* 1. Head. 2. Part of the head which comprehends the cranium and forehead. 3. Head, the whole person, and more generally the person as exposed to any danger or penalty. 4. Head, chief, principal person; leader. 5. Head, understanding, faculties of the mind, judgment, talents. 6. Beginning of a thing, e. g. of a book. 7. End or extremity of a thing, e. g. of a beam or bridge. 8. Head, the top of many things, as the head of a nail, of a pin, etc. 9. Head, the upper part of many things. 10. The principal town of a province, district, etc. 11. Head of cattle. *Cabeza mayor*, Head of neat cattle. *Cabeza menor*, Head of sheep, goats, etc. 12. (Naut.) Head of a ship. 13. Diameter of a column. 14. *Cabeza de autos* or *proceso*, Head of a process. *La cabeza de la silla*, (Mex.) The pommel of a saddle. *Cabeza de un muelle*, Pier or mole head. *Cabeza de ajos*, Head of garlic. *Cabeza de monte* or *sierra*, Top of a mountain. *Cabeza de moro*, Moorshead. *Cabeza de perro*, *V.* ANTIRRINO MAYOR and BECERRA. *Cabezas*, Principal parts of a vessel; an equestrian game. *Cabeza torcida*, Wrong-headed fellow. *Cabeza hueca*, *huera* or *vacía*, An addle-pate or addled head. *Cabeza redonda*, (Met.) Blockhead. *Andársele a uno la cabeza*, To get a vertigo or giddiness. *A vuelta de cabeza*, In a trice. *Dar de cabeza*, To fall into misfortunes, to decline in one's fortune, power, or authority. *Hablar de cabeza*, To speak without ground or foundation. *Hacer cabeza*, To be the leader. *Levantar* or *alzar cabeza*, To take courage, to retrieve one's health or fortune. *No levantar* or *no alzar cabeza*, To continue sickly, or unfortunate in business. *Levantar alguna cosa de su cabeza*, To forge a thing out of one's head. *Llevar en la cabeza*, To be frustrated in one's views and expectations. *No tener* or *no llevar pies ni cabeza alguna cosa*, To have neither head nor tail. *Otorgar de cabeza*, To give a nod of approbation. *Perder la cabeza*, To lose one's senses, to be at a loss how to act. *Poner las cosas pies con cabeza*, To jumble things together, to put them topsy-turvy. *Sacar de su cabeza alguna cosa*, To strike out a thing. *Tener una cabeza de hierro* or *de bronce*, To be indefatigable in business. *No tener a quien volver la cabeza*, To have neither money nor friends. *Ser* or *tener mala cabeza*, To be a man of bad principles; to be weak-minded, without judgment or reflection. *Volvérsele la cabeza a alguno*, To lose one's senses. *De cabeza*, 1. From memory. 2. Headlong. *Caer con la cabeza abajo* or *caer de cabeza*, To fall headlong. *Pagar a tanto por cabeza*, To pay so much a piece or so much a head.

Cabezada [cah-bay-thah'-dah], *f.* 1. Headshake, stroke or butt given with the head, or received upon it. 2. Halter, collar. 3. Head-stall of a bridle. 4. Pitching of a ship. 5. Among bookbinders, head-band of a book. 6. Instep of a boot. 7. The part of a piece of ground more elevated than the rest. 8. Nod, of one asleep with the head unsupported. *Dar cabezadas* To nod, to fall asleep. *Darse de cabezddas*, To screw one's wits in the investigation of a thing without success.

Cabezal [cah-bay-thahl'], *m.* 1. Head-piece in a powder-mill. 2. Small square pillow. 3. Compress of folded linen used by surgeons. 4. Long round bolster which crosses a bed. 5. Post of a door. *Cabezales de coche*, Standards of the fore and hind parts of a coach, to which the braces are fastened. 6. Mattress or piece of cloth on which peasants sleep on benches or stones at the fire. 7. Title-page of a book.

Cabezo [cah-bay'-tho], *m.* 1. Summit of a hill. 2. Shirt-collar.

Cabezón [cah-bay-thone'], *m.* 1. Register of the taxes paid to government, and of the names of the contributors 2. Collar of a shirt. 3. Opening of a garment for the head to pass through. 4. Cavesson or nose-band, used in breaking in a horse. *Llevar por los cabezones*, To drag along by the collar. *Entra por la manga, y sale por el cabezón*, Applied to favourites who assume authority and dominion, and originating in the ancient ceremony of adoption, by passing the person through a wide sleeve of a shift.

Cabezorro [cah-bay-thor'-ro], *m. aug.* (Coll.) Large disproportioned head.

Cabezota [cah-bay-thoh'-tah], *m. aug.* 1. Big-headed. 2. Club-headed, having a thick head.

Cabezudo [cah-bay-thoo'-do], *m.* (Zool.) Chub, mullet. Cyprinus cephalus. *V.* MÚJOL. (Acad.)

Cabezudo, da [cah-bay-thoo'-do, dah], *a.* 1. Large-headed. 2. Chubbed. 3. Club-headed. 4. Headstrong, obstinate, morose, stubborn.

Cabezuela [cah-bay-thoo-ay'-lah], *f.* 1. (Dim.) Small head. 2. Blockhead, dolt, simpleton. 3. Coarse flour. 4. Rose-bud, from which rose-water is distilled. 5. Little glass tube in a velvet loom. 6. (Bot.) Eryngo. Eryngium tricuspidatum. 7. (Bot.) Ragwort-leaved centaury. Centaura salmantica. *Escobas de cabezuela*, Brooms made with the ragwort-leaved centaury.

Cabezuelo [cah-bay-thoo-ay'-lo], *m. dim.* Little head or top of any thing.

Cabida [cah-bee'-dah], *f.* Content, space, or capacity of any thing. *Tener cabida con una persona*, To be in high favour, to have a strong influence over one. (Coll.) *Eso no tiene cabida*, That cannot be permitted or allowed.

Cabido [cah-bee'-do], *m.* Knight of the order of Malta, who has the right to claim a commandery.—*Cabido, da, pp.* of CABER.

Cabildada [cah-beel-dah'-dah], *f.* (Coll.) Hasty, ill-grounded proceeding of a chapter or other body.

Cabildear [cah-beel-day-ar'], *vn.* (Littl. us.) 1. To hold a chapter. 2. To carry on private designs.

Cabildeo [cah-beel-day'-o], *m.* Lobbying.

Cabildero [cah-beel-day'-ro], *a.* (Obs.) Belonging to a chapter.

Cabildo [cah-beel'-do], *m.* 1. Chapter of a cathedral or collegiate church. 2. Meeting of a chapter, and the place where the meeting is held. 3. (Prov.) The corporation of a town.

Cabilla [cah-beel'-lyah], *f.* (Naut.) 1. Dowell, round iron bar for securing the knees of a vessel. 2. Tree-nail, belaying-pin.

Cabillo [cah-beel'-lyo], *m.* 1. (Bot.) Flower-stalk. 2. (Dim.) Small end of a rope.

Cabimiento [cah-be-me-en'-to], *m.* 1. Right of claiming a commandery in the order of Malta. 2. *V.* CABIDA.

Cabina [cah-bee'-nah], *f.* **1. Cabin. 2. Cockpit (of a plane). 3. Booth,** encasing. *Cabina a presión*, Pressurized cabin. *Cabina cerrada transparente*, (Aer.) Canopy. *Cabina telefónica*, Telephone booth.

Cabio [cah-bee'-o], *m.* 1. Lintel of a door. 2. A kind of rafter used in building.

Cabito [cah-bee'-to], *m. dim.* The small end of a candle. *V.* CABO, CABILLO. *Cabitos, pl.* Small lines, ends of lines. *De muchos cabitos se hace un cirio pascual*, Many a little makes a mickle.

Cabizbajo, ja [cah-bith-bah'-ho, hah], *a.* 1. Down in the mouth, crest-fallen. 2. Thoughtful, pensive, melancholy. 3. (Bot.) Drooping.

Cabiztuerto, ta [cah-bith-too-er'-to, tah], *m. & f.* Wry-headed; hypocritical.

Cable [cah'-blay], *m.* 1. Cable. *Cable de esperanza*, Sheet-cable, the largest on board a ship. *Cable del ayuste*, Best bower cable. *Cable sencillo* or *de leva*, Small bower cable. *Cable de alambre*, Wire cable. *Cable submarino*, Submarine cable. *Cable telegráfico*, Telegraphic cable. 2. Cable's length, a measure of 120 fathoms.

Cablear [cah-blay-ar'], *va.* To cable.

Cablegráfico, ca [cah-blay-grah'-feco, cah], *a.* By cable. *Dirección cablegráfica*, Cable address. *Mensaje cablegráfico*, Cable message.

Cablegrama [cah-blay-grah'-mah], *m.* A cablegram, message sent by cable.

These two words are really barbarisms, and have not received official sanction.

Cabo [cah'-bo], *m.* 1. Extreme, extremity; end of a thing; tip. 2. Cape, headland, or promontory, foreland. 3. Handle, haft, hold. 4. The extremity of a thing remaining after the principal part has been consumed or destroyed. 5. Lowest card in the game called *revesino*. 6. (Prov.) Paragraph, article, head. 7. Chief, head, commander. 8. (Naut.) Any of the cords employed in a ship. 9. Thread. 10. (Littl. us.) Complement, perfection, completion. 11. At the custom-house a parcel or package smaller than a bale. 12. Place, position, site.—*pl.* 1. The tail and mane of horses. 2. Loose pieces of apparel, as stockings, shoes, hat, etc. 3. Divisions of a discourse. *V.* 6th acceptation. *Cabo de armería*, In Navarre, the original mansion of a noble family. *Cabo de año*, The religious offices performed on the anniversary of a person's death. *Cabo de barras*, Chiselled dollar of Mexico; last payment or balance of an account. *Cabo de forzados*, Overseer of galley-slaves. *Cabo de escuadra*, Corporal. *Cabo de presa*, Prize-master. *Cabo de ronda de alcabalas*, Tide-waiter, custom-house officer. *Coger todos los cabos*, (Met.) To weigh all the circumstances of a case. *Atar cabos*, To collect and examine together divers circumstances bearing on a case. *Dar cabo*, To give occasion, to allow. *Cabos negros en las mujeres*, Black hair, eyes, and eye-brows of a woman. *Cabos blancos*, (Naut.) Untarred cordage. *Dar cabo*, (Naut.) To throw out a rope for another to take hold of. *Al cabo*, At last. *Dar cabo a alguna cosa*, To perfect or complete a thing; to destroy a thing. *De cabo a rabo*, From head to tail. *Estar al cabo de algún negocio*, To be thoroughly acquainted with the nature of an affair. *Estar alguno al cabo* or *muy al cabo*, To be at death's door. *No tener cabo ni cuenta una cosa*, To have neither head nor tail: applied to a perplexed business. *Por cabo* or *por el cabo*, Lastly.

Por ningún cabo, By no means. *Volver a coger el cabo*, To resume the thread of a discourse.
Cabotaje [cah-bo-tah'-hay] *m.* (Naut.) 1. Coasting-trade. 2. Pilotage.
Cabra [cah'-brah], *f.* 1. Goat. Capra, *L.* 2. Engine formerly used to throw stones. 3. *Cabra montés*, Wild goat. Capra ibex. *La cabra siempre tira al monte*, What is bred in the bone will come out in the flesh: a man's acts show what he is.—*pl.* 1. Red marks on the legs caused by fire. 2. Small white clouds floating in the air. *Echar cabras* or *las cabras*, To play for who will pay the reckoning. *Echar las cabras a otro*, To throw the blame upon another. *Piel de cabra*, Goatskin.
Cabrahigadura [cah-brah-e-gah-doo'-rah], *f.* Caprification. (See verb.)
Cabrahigal, Cabrahigar [cah-brah-e-gahl', cah-brah-e-gar'], *m.* Grove or plantation of wild fig-trees.
Cabrahigar [cah-brah-e-gar'], *va.* To improve a fig-tree; that is, to string up some male figs, and hang them on the branches of the female fig-tree, to make it produce better fruit.
Cabrahigo [cah-brah-ee'-go], *m.* The male wild fig-tree, or its fruit which does not ripen.
Cabreia [cah-bray-ee'-ah], *f.* (Obs.) Wooden machine for throwing stones.
Cabreo [cah-bray'-o], *m.* (Prov.) Register, especially of the privileges and charters of cathedral churches.
Cabrería [cah-bray-ree'-ah], *f.* 1. (Obs.) Herd of goats. 2. The place where goat's milk is sold.
Cabreriza [cah-bray-ree'-thah], *f.* A hut for goatherds.
Cabrerizo [cah-bray-ree'tho], *m.* *V.* Cabrero.
Cabrero, ra [cah-bray'-ro, rah], *m.* & *f.* Goatherd.
Cabrestante [cah-bres-tahn'-tay], *m.* (Naut.) Capstan.
Cabria [cah'-bre-ah], *f.* 1. Axle-tree. 2. (Naut.) Sheers, a machine used for setting up and taking out masts. 3. Crane, wheel and axle, winch, windlass, hoist.
Cabrial [cah-bre-ahl'], *m.* (Obs.) Beam. *V.* Viga.
Cabrilla [cah-breel'-lyah], *f.* 1. (Dim.) Little goat. 2. (Zool.) Prawn. Cancer squilla.—*pl.* 1. (Ast.) Pleiades, a constellation. 2. Stones thrown obliquely on the water, called duck and drake. 3. Marks on the legs, produced by being continually too near the fire. 4. (Naut.) White caps on the water.
Cabrillear [cah-breel-lyay-ar'], *vn.* (Littl. us.) To throw stones skippingly along the surface of water.—*va.* To form white caps or wavelets.
Cabrilleo [cah-breel-lyay'-o], *m.* The lapping of the waves when the sea is not high.
Cabrillo [cah-breel'-lyo], *m.* Chabrillion, cheese from goat's milk.
Cabrina [cah-bree'-nah], *f.* (Obs.) Goatskin.
Cabrio [cah'-bree-o], *m.* Rafter, beam, or other timber, used in building.
Cabrío [cah-bree'-o], *a.* Belonging to goats, goatish. *Ganado cabrío*, Goats.
Cabriol [cah-bree'-ol], *m.* Rafter. *V.* Cabrío.
Cabriola [cah-bre-oh'-lah], *f.* 1. Caper, movement made in dancing. 2. Nimble leap, hop, or jump, gambol, skip. *Dar cabriolas*, To leap for joy.
Cabriolar, Cabriolear [cah-bre-o-lar', cah-bre-o-lay-ar'], *vn.* To caper or cut capers, to jump, to curvet, to frisk.
Cabriolé [cah-bre-o-lay'], *m.* 1. Kind of cloak used by ladies. 2. Narrow riding-coat without sleeves. 3. Cabriolet, a kind of open carriage.
Cabrión [cah-bre-on'], *m.* 1. Block or wedge for checking the wheel of a carriage. 2. (Naut.) Quoin, wedge for fastening the wheels of cannon to the decks in a gale.
Cabrita [cah-bree'-tah], *f.* 1. (Dim.) Little she-kid up to one year of age. 2. (Obs.) Kid-skin dressed. 3. (Obs.) Ancient engine to cast stones.
Cabritero [cah-bre-tay'-ro], *m.* 1. Dealer in kids. 2. One who dresses or sells kid-skins.
Cabritilla [cah-bre-teel'-lyah], *f.* A dressed lamb or kid-skin.
Cabritillo [cah-bre-teel'-lyo], *m. dim.* Kid.
Cabrito [cah-bree'-to], *m.* Kid, kidling, up to one year of age.
Cabrituno, na [cah-bre-too'-no, nah], (Obs.) Of the goat kind.
Cabrón [cah-brone'], *m.* 1. Buck, he-goat. 2. One who consents to the adultery of his wife.
Cabronada [cah-bro-nah'-dah], *f.* (Low) Infamous action which a man permits against his own honour.
Cabronazo [cah-bro-nah'-tho], *m. aug.* One who prostitutes his own wife.
Cabroncillo, cito, zuelo [cah-bron-theel-yo, thee'-to, thoo-ay'-lo], *m.* 1. (Dim.) Easy husband. 2. Fetid herb resembling the Celtic spikenard.
Cabronismo [cah-bro-nees'-mo], *m.* Cuckoldism by consent; the state of a husband who consents to the adultery of his wife.
Cabruno, na [cah-broo'-no, nah], *a.* Goatish; goat-like.
Cabu [cah'-boo], *m.* (Prov.) Barren ground.
Cabujón [cah-boo-hone'], *m.* Rough, unpolished ruby.
Cabulla [cah-bool'-lyah], *f.* *V.* Cabuya.
Cabuya [cah-boo'-yah], *f.* 1. (Bot.) Common American agave, a sort of sedge or grass, of which cords are made in America. Agave Americana. 2. (Prov.) Cord or rope made of the aloes-plant. 3. Sisal hemp. *Dar cabuya*, To tie. *Ponerse en la cabuya*, To grasp the trend of a topic.
Cabuyero [cah-boo-yay'-ro], *m.* (Amer.) Ship-chandler.
Cabuyería [cah-boo-yay-ree'-ah], *f.* (Amer.) Ship-chandlery.
Caca [cah'-cah], *f.* 1. Excrements of a child. 2. Word used by children who wish to go to stool. *Descubrir la caca*, (Coll.) To make public some fault or defect.
Cacahual, Cacaotal [cah-cah-oo-ahl', cah-cah-oh-tahl'], *m.* Plantation of chocolate-trees.
Cacahuate, Cacahuete [cah-cah-oo-ah'-tay, cah-cah-oo-ay'-tay], *m.* (Bot.) Arachys hypogea. *V.* Maní. The peanut, or earth-nut; called also goober and pindar.
Cacalote [cah-cah-lo'-tay], *m.* 1. A sweet paste made in Cuba from maize toasted without being ground. 2. (Prov.) A very absurd blunder.
Cacao [cah-cah'-o], *m.* 1. (Bot.) Smooth-leaved chocolate nut-tree. Theobroma cacao. 2. Cocoa, the fruit of the chocolate-tree. *Manteca de cacao*, Cocoa-butter, or butter of cacao.
Cacaotal [cah-cah-o-tahl'], *m.* A cacao orchard.
Cacaraña [cah-cah-rah'-nyah], *f.* Pit, the mark made by the small-pox.
Cacarañado, da [cah-cah-rah-nyah'-do, dah] *m.* & *f.* & *a.* Pitted by the small-pox.
Cacareador, ra [cah-cah-ray-ah-dor', rah], *m.* & *f.* 1. Cackler. 2. Cock that crows, a hen that cackles. 3 Cackler, boaster, braggart.
Cacarear [cah-cah-ray-ar'], *vn.* 1. To crow, to cackle. 2. To exaggerate one's own actions, to brag, to boast. 3. To humbug.
Cacareo [cah-cah-ray'-o], *m.* 1. Crowing of a cock, cackling of a hen. 2. Boast, brag, humbug.
Cacaste [cah-cahs'-tay], *m.* A box or crate to carry fruit.
Cacatoes, or **Cacatue** [cah-cah-to'-es, or cah-cah-too'-ay], *m.* (Zool.) Cockatoo, a bird of the parrot family.
Cacear [cah-thay-ar'], *va.* To toss or shake something with a copper saucepan.
Cacera [cah-thay'-rah], *f.* 1. Canal, channel, or conduit of water, employed in watering lands. 2. Sort of pig-nuts.
Cacería [cah-thay-ree'-ah], *f.* 1. Hunting or fowling party. 2. (Art) Landscape representing field sports.
Cacerilla [cah-thay-reel'-lyah], *f. dim.* Small drain or canal.
Cacerina [cah-thay-ree'-nah], *f.* Cartridge-box or pouch for carrying powder and ball.
Cacerola [cah-thay-ro'-lah], *f.* Stew-pan, sauce-pan.
Caceta [cah-thay'-tah], *f. dim.* Small pan used by apothecaries.
Cacica [cah-thee'-cah], *f.* Wife or daughter of a cacique.
Cacicato, or **Cacicazgo** [cah-the-cath'-go], *m.* The dignity of a chief or cacique and his territory.
Cacillo, ito [cah-theel'-lyo, ee'-to], *m. dim.* Small saucepan.
Cacique [cah-thee'-kay], *m.* 1. Cacique, a prince or nobleman among the Indians. 2. Any leading inhabitant of a small town or village.
Cacle [cah'-clay], *m.* (Mex.) A kind of sandals worn by friars, Indians, and soldiers.
Caco [cah'-co], *m.* 1. Pickpocket. 2. A coward.
Cacófago, ga [cah-co'-fah-go, gah], *a.* Cacophagous, having a depraved appetite.
Cacofonía [cah-co-fo-nee'-ah], *f.* Cacophony, a harsh or unharmonious sound.
Cacografía [cah-co-grah-fee'-ah], *f.* Bad spelling.
Cacomite [cah-co-mee'-tay], *m.* A Mexican plant which produces handsome flowers.
Cacoquimia [cah-co-kee'-me-ah], *f.* Cacochymy, depraved state of the humours of the body.
Cacoquímico, ca [cah-co-kee'-me-co, cah], *a.* Cacochymical.
Cacoquimio [cah-co-kee'-me-o], *m.* He who suffers melancholy, which makes him pale and sorrowful.
Cácteo, ea [cahc'-tay-o, ah], *a.* Cactaceous, relating to cacti.
Cacto [cahc'-to], *m.* The cactus.
Cacumen [cah-coo'-men], *m.* 1. The top, the height. 2. Head, understanding, comprehension.
Cacha [cah'-chah], *f.* 1. Handle of a razor. *Hasta las cachas*, Full to the brim. 2. (Prov.) Tardiness, inactivity.
Cachada [cah-chah'-dah], *f.* Stroke of one top against another, when boys play at tops.
Cachalote [cah-chah-loh'-tay], *m.* The sperm whale. Physeter macrocephalus. *V.* Marsopla.
Cachamarín, *m.* *V.* Cachemarín.
Cachapa [cah-chah'-pa], *f.* Corn-bread with sugar, used in Venezuela.
Cachar [cah-char'], *va.* 1. (Prov.) To break in pieces. 2. To divide a plank in two lengthwise by a saw or axe.

Cacharado [cah-chah-rah'-do], *m.* Kind of linen.

Cacharro [cah-char'-ro], *m.* 1. Coarse earthen pot; also a piece of it. 2. (Met.) Any useless, worthless thing.

Cachaza [cah-chah'-thah], *f.* (Coll.) 1. Inactivity, tardiness; forbearance. 2. (Amer.) Rum. 3. First froth on cane-juice when boiled to make sugar. (Turk. cashasha.)

Cachazudamente, *adv.* from

Cachazudo, da [cah-chah-thoo'-do, dah], *a.* Cool, calm, phlegmatic, tranquil.

Cachemarin [cah-chay-mah-reen'], *m.* A small two-masted craft used in Brittany and on the northern Spanish coast.

Cachemir [cah-chay-meer'], *m.* Cashmere, a fine, soft, costly fabric made in Cashmere and vicinity, especially used for shawls.

Cachemira [cah-che-mee'-rah], *f.* *V.* Cachemir.

Cachera [cah-chay'-rah], *f.* Coarse shagged cloth or baize.

Cachetas [cay-chay'-tas], *f. pl.* Teeth or wards in a lock.

Cachete [cah-chay'-tay], *m.* 1. Cheek. 2. Fist, a blow given with the hand clenched. 3. A cuff on the ear. *Cachetes de un navío*, (Naut.) Bow of a ship.

Cachetero [cah-chay-tay'-ro], *m.* 1. Short and broad knife with a sharp point, used by assassins. 2. A bull-fighter who kills the bulls with the knife called *cachetero.*

Cachetina [cah-chay-tee'-nah], *f.* A hand-to-hand fight.

Cachetón, ona [cah-chay-tone', nah], *a.* Fat-cheeked.

Cachetudo, da [cah-chay-too'-do, dah], *a.* Plump-cheeked, fleshy.

Cachicamo [cah-che-cah'-mo], *m.* An armadillo. South American name.

Cachicán [cah-che-cahn'], *m.* Overseer of a farm.

Cachicuerno, na [cah-che-coo-er'-no, nah], *a.* (Obs.) Having a handle or haft of horn.

Cachidiablo [cah-che-de-ah'-blo], *m.* 1. Hobgoblin. 2. Disguised in a devil's mask. 3. Having an odd and extravagant appearance.

Cachifollar [cah-che-fol-lyar'], *va.* 1. To puff or blow with the cheeks. 2. (Prov.) To play a trick.

Cachigordete, eta, ito, ita [cah-che-gor-day'-tay, tah, dee'-to, tah], *a.* Squat, thick, and plump.

Cachillada [cah-cheel-lyah'-dah], *f.* (Coll.) Litter, young brought forth by an animal at once.

Cachimba [cah-cheem'-bah], *f.* (Cuba) A smoking-pipe.

Cachimbo [cah-cheem'-bo], *m.* A ladle with a long handle. (Sugar-making.)

Cachipolla [cah-che-pol'-lyah], *f.* Day-fly, or May-fly: of very brief life, whence the name. One of the Ephemerids.

Cachiporra, *f.* **Cachiporro,** *m.* [cah-che-por'-rah]. 1. A stick with a big knob used by country people; a cudgel. 2. A fruit-eating bat. 3. An Indian club.

Cachiporra [cah-che-por'-rah], *int.* A vulgar exclamation.

Cachiporro [cah-che-por'-ro], *m.* (Prov. Coll.) Chub-face.

Cachirulo [cah-che-roo'-lo], *m.* 1. Earthen, glass, or tin pot for preserving brandy or other liquors. 2. Bow or rosette worn on the head by women toward the end of the 18th century. 3. (Mex.) Lining of cloth or chamois placed in the seat and legs of trousers for riding.

Cachirulo [cah-che-roo'-lo], *m.* Small three-masted vessel. (Anglo-Saxon, ketoch.)

Cachivache [cah-che-vah'-chay], *m.* 1. Broken crockery, or other old trumpery, laid up in a corner. 2. (Met.) A despicable, useless, worthless fellow.

Cacho [cah'-cho], *m.* 1. Slice, piece: applied to lemons, oranges, melons, etc. 2. Small horn. *Botones de cacho,* Horn buttons. 3. Game of chance at cards. 4. (Zool.) Red surmullet. Mullus barbatus.

Cacho, cha [cah'-cho, chah], *a.* Bent, crooked, inflected. *V.* Gacho.

Cacholas [cah-cho'-las], *f. pl.* (Naut.) Cheeks of the masts.

Cachón [cah'-chone], *m.* 1. A breaker. *V.* Cachones. 2. A fall of water.

Cachondez [cah-chon-deth'], *f.* (Coll.) Sexual appetite.

Cachondo, da [cah-chone'-do, dah], *a.* Ruled by sexual appetite; in heat: applied especially to the bitch. *Cachondas,* (Obs.) Slashed trousers formerly worn.

Cachones [cah-cho'-nes], *m. pl.* Breakers, waves broken by the shore, rocks, or sand-banks.

Cachopo [cah-cho'-po], *m.* 1. (Naut.) Gulf of the sea between rocks. 2. (Prov.) Dry trunk or stump of a tree.

Cachorrenas [cah-chor-ray'-nas], *f. pl.* (Prov.) Sort of soap, made of oil, orange, bread, and salt.

Cachorrillo, ito [cah-chor-reel'-lyo, ree'-to], *m. dim.* 1. A little cub or whelp. 2. A young man: in contempt. 3. A little pistol.

Cachorro, ra [cah-chor'-ro, rah], *m. & f.* 1. Grown whelp or puppy. 2. Cub, the young of a beast. 3. Pocket pistol. 4. A lizard.

Cachucha [cah-choo'-chah], *f.* 1. A well-known Spanish dance in triple measure. 2. Man's cloth or fur cap. 3. An oared boat used in rivers and ports of America, and holding no more than three persons.

Cachucho [cah-choo'-cho], *m.* 1. Oil measure, containing the sixth part of a pound. 2. (Obs.) Cartridge. 3. (Prov.) Clumsy earthen pot. 4. Place for each arrow in a quiver.

Cachuela [cah-choo-ay'-lah], *f.* Fricassee made of the livers and lights of rabbits.

Cachuelo [cah-choo-ay'-lo], *m.* (Zool.) Small river fish resembling an anchovy.

Cachulera [cah-choo-lay'-rah], *f.* (Prov.) Cavern or place where any one hides.

Cachumbo [cah-choom'-bo], *m.* Kind of hard cocoa-wood, of which rosaries, etc., are made.

Cachunde [cah-choon'-day], *f.* Paste made of musk and other aromatics, which the Chinese carry in their mouth to strengthen the stomach.

Cachupín [cah-choo-peen'], *m.* A Spaniard who settles in Mexico or South America. *V.* Gachupín. (Port. *cachopo,* child.)

Cada [cah'-dah], *pron.* Every, every one, each. *Cada uno* or *cada cual,* Every one, each. *Cada vez,* Every time. *Cada día,* Every day. *A cada palabra,* At every word. *Dar a cada uno,* To give to every one. *Cada vez que* or *cada que,* Every time that. *Cada y cuando,* Whenever, as soon as.

Cadalecho [cah-dah-lay'-cho], *m.* Bed made of branches of trees, and much used in the huts of Andalucía.

Cadalso [cah-dahl'-so], *m.* 1. Scaffold raised for the execution of malefactors. 2. (Obs.) Temporary gallery or stage, erected for shows or spectators. 3. (Obs.) Fortification or bulwark made of wood.

Cadañal, Cadañego, ga, Cadañero, ra [cah-dah-nyahl', cah-dah-nyay'-go, gah, cah-dah-nyay'-ro, rah], *a.* Annual. *Mujer cadañera,* A woman who bears every year.

Cadarzo [cah-dar'-tho], *m.* Coarse, entangled silk, which cannot be spun with a wheel.

Cadáver [cah-dah'-ver], *m.* Corpse, corse, cadaver.

Cadavera [cah-dah-vay'-rah], *f.* (Obs.) *V.* Calavera.

Cadavérico, ca [cah-dah-vay'-re-co, cah], *a.* Cadaverous.

Cadejo [cah-day'-ho], *m.* 1. Entangled skein of thread. 2. Entangled hair. 3. Threads put together to make tassels.

Cadena [cah-day'-nah], *f.* 1. Chain. 2. (Met.) Tie caused by passion or obligation. 3. Mortice, a hole cut into wood. 4. (Met.) Series of events. 5. Chain, link, any series linked together. 6. Number of malefactors chained together to be conducted to the galleys: punishment next after the death penalty. 7. Bar of iron with which a way is strengthened. 8. Frame of wood put round the hearth of a kitchen. 9. Treadle of a ribbon-weaver's loom. 10. Turning handle which moves a wheel. *Cadena de rocas,* Ledge or ridge of rocks. *Cadena de puerto,* Boom of a harbour. *Estar en la cadena,* To be in prison. *Balas de cadena,* Chain-shot. *Renunciar la cadena,* To give up all one's effects to get out of prison.

Cadenado [cah-day-nah'-do], *m.* (Obs.) *V.* Candado.

Cadencia [cah-den'-the-ah], *f.* 1. Cadence, fall of the voice. 2. Cadence, number, measure, flow of verses or periods. 3. In dancing, the correspondence of the motion of the body with the music. *Hablar en cadencia,* To affect the harmonious flow of rhyme when speaking in prose.

Cadencioso, sa [cah-den-the-o'-so, sah], *a.* Belonging to a cadence, numerous.

Cadeneta [cah-day-nay'-tah], *f.* 1. Lace or needle-work wrought in form of a chain; chain-stitch. 2. Work put upon the heads of books for security of the sewing.

Cadenilla, ita [cah-day-neel'-lyah, ee'-tah], *f. dim.* Small chain. *Cadenilla y media cadenilla,* Pearls distinguished by their size.

Cadente [cah-den'-tay], *a.* 1. Decaying, declining, going to ruin. 2. Having a correct modulation in delivering prose or verse.

Cadera [cah-day'-rah], *f.* Hip, the joint of the thigh.

Cadereta [cah-day-ray'-tah], *f.* (Mus.) A kind of small organ, manipulated by a second key-board, which imitates the great organ which contains it; echo organ.

Caderillas [cah-day-reel'-lyas], *f. pl.* 1. Hoops worn by ladies to distend the skirts over the hips. 2. Bustle.

Cadete [cah-day'-tay], *m.* 1. Cadet, a volunteer in the army who serves in expectation of a commission. 2. A young man in a military school.

Cadi [cah-dee'], *m.* Cadi, a magistrate among the Turks and Moors.

Cadillar [cah-deel-lyar'], *m.* Place abounding with bur-parsley.

Cadillero, ra [cah-deel-yay'-ro, rah], *a.* (Bot.) Applied to plants bearing fruit covered with hooked bristles or prickles.

Cadillo [cah-deel'-lyo], *m.* (Bot.) A name applied especially to the great bur-parsley, Caucalis latifolia; to the prickly bur-weed, Xanthium spinosum, to the common burdock, Arctium lappa, and finally to different kinds of *Caucalides*, etc. *Cadillos*, Thrum, the first threads or fag-end of a web, or the loose threads of the end of a warp; warp-ends.

Cadiz [cah-deeth'], *m.* (Obs.) Kind of coarse stuff.

Cadmía [cad-mee'-ah], *f.* Calamine. *V.* CALAMINA. Tutty, impure oxide of zinc, collected from a furnace or a crucible.

Cadmio [cahd'-me-o], *m.* Cadmium, a metal, in colour like tin, naturally associated with zinc.

Cado [cah'-do], *m.* (Prov.) Ferret-hole. *V.* HURONERA.

Cadoce [cah-do'-thay], *m.* (Zool. Prov.) Gudgeon. Cyprinus gobio.

Caducamente [cah-doo-cah-men'-tay], *adv.* In a weak, doting manner.

Caducante [cah-doo-cahn'-tay], *pa.* Doting, one who dotes.

Caducar [cah-doo-car'], *vn.* 1. To dote, to have the intellect impaired by age. 2. To be worn out by service, to fall into disuse, to become superannuated. *Caducar el legado o el fideicomiso*, To become extinct: applied to a legacy or fiduciary estate.

Caduceo [cah-doo-thay'-o], *m.* 1. Caduceus or caduce, the wand with which Mercury is depicted. 2. Herald's staff among the ancient Greeks.

Caducidad [cah-doo-the-dahd'], *f.* (Law) Caducity, decrepitude, the state or quality of being worn out by age or labour.

Caduco, ca [cah-doo'-co, cah], *a.* 1. Worn out or broken with fatigue, senile, enfeebled by age, decrepit. 2. Perishable, frail. *Mal caduco*, Epilepsy.

Caduquez [cah-doo-keth'], *f.* Caducity, senility, last stage of life.

C.A.E., Abbreviation of *Cóbrese al entregar*, C.O.D., Cash on delivery.

Caedizo, za [cah-ay-dee'-tho, thah], *a.* 1. Ready to fall, being of short duration, or little consistence. *Hacer caediza una cosa*, To let a thing fall designedly. *Peras caedizas*, Pears dropping from the tree. 2. (Bot.) Deciduous.

Caedura [cah-ay-doo'-rah], *f.* Among weavers, the loose threads dropping from the loom when weaving.

Caer [cah-err'], *vn.* 1. To fall to the ground, to tumble down; to lighten. *Caer a plomo*, To fall flat. 2. To lose one's situation, fortune, or influence. 3. To fall into an error or danger. 4. (Met.) To deviate from the right road, or to take the wrong one. 5. (Met.) To fall due: as instalments or payments of debts. 6. To fall, to decrease, to decline, to come into any state of weakness, misery, etc. 7. To fall to one's lot. 8. To fall, to befall, to happen to, to come to pass. 9. To die. 10. (Mil.) To fall, yield, surrender. 11. To decline, to approach the end: as, *La luz cae*, The light declines; *El día cae*, The day is drawing to a close. 12. To be situated. *Caer a esta parte*, To be situated on this side. *Las ventanas caen al río*, The windows overlook the river. *Caer a la mar*, (Naut.) To fall overboard. *Caer a sotavento*, To drive to leeward. *Caer de espaldas*, To fall backward. *Caer el plazo*, To arrive the fixed time for making payment or answering a demand. *Caer en la cuenta*, To bethink one's self, to see the point, to correct one's habits. *Caer de su asno, de su burra*, To own one's error. *No caer en las cosas*, Not to comprehend a thing. *Caerse de sueño*, To fall asleep. *Caer bien a caballo*, To sit well on horseback. *Caer bien alguna cosa*, To fit, to suit, to become. *Este color cae bien con este otro*, This colour is well matched with the other. *Caer de la gracia de alguno*, To lose one's favour. *Caer en cama* or *en la cama*, To become sick. *Caer en alguna cosa*, To remember or obtain knowledge of a thing. *Caer en falta*, To fail in the performance of one's engagements. *Caer en gracia* or *en gusto*, To please, to be agreeable. *Caer la balanza*, To be partial. *Caerse a pedazos*, To be very fatigued, or very foolish. *Caerse de ánimo*, To be dejected. *Caerse de risa*, To shake with laughter. *Caerse en flor*, To die in the bloom of age. *Al caer de la hoja*, At the fall of the leaf, about the end of autumn. *Dejar caer alguna cosa en la conversación*, To drop something in the course of conversation. *Caer el color*, To fade. *Caer en nota*, To scandalize. *Caer en ello*, To understand or comprehend a thing. *Ya caigo en ello*, Now I have it. *Estar al caer*, About falling, ready to fall. *No caérsele a uno alguna cosa de la boca*, To repeat frequently the same thing. *Caérsele a uno la cara de vergüenza*, To blush deeply with shame.

Caerse [cah-er'-say], *vr.* 1. All the meanings of the active form. 2. To be afflicted, overwhelmed, disconsolate. *Dejarse caer*, To allow one's self to be down-hearted. *Caerse (una cosa) de su peso*, To be very true, or manifest.

Cafa [cah'-fah], *f.* Cotton stuff of various colours and kinds.

Café [cah-fay'], *m.* 1. Coffee tree. 2. Coffee, beverage prepared from the coffee bean.

Café, *m.* Café, restaurant, coffee-house.

Cafeína [cah-fay-ee'-nah], *f.* Caffein, an alkaloid extracted from coffee.

Cafetal [cah-fay-tahl'], *m.* Plantation of coffee-trees.

Cafetán, Caftán [cah-fay-tahn'], *m.* Caftan, embroidered garment worn by the chief Turkish or Persian officers.

Cafetera [cah-fay-tay'-rah], *f.* 1. Coffee-pot. 2. Coffee-service.

Cafetero [cah-fay-tay'-ro], *m.* 1. One who makes or sells coffee. 2. (Bot.) Coffee-tree. Coffea, *L.* *Cafetero árabe*, Arabian coffee-tree. Coffea arabica *Cafetero occidental* or *americano*, Jamaica or western coffee-tree. Coffea occidentalis.

Cafeto [cah-fay'-to], *m.* The coffee-tree.

Cáfila [cah'-fe-lah], *m.* 1. Multitude of people, animals, or other things. 2. Caravan. 3. Single file, one after another.

Cafre [cah'-fray], *a.* 1. Savage, inhuman, belonging or relating to the Caffres. 2. (Prov.) Clownish, rude, uncivil.

Cafúa [cah-foo'-ah], *f.* (Arg. coll.) Jail, arrest. *Ir a la cafúa*, To go to jail, to be arrested.

Cagaaceite [cah-gah-ah-thay'-e-tay], *m.* A little bird, a variety of thrush, whose excrements are of an oily substance.

Cagachín [cah-gah-cheen'], *m.* Kind of gnat or fly, smaller than the ordinary mosquito, and of a reddish colour.

Cagada [cah-gah'-dah], *f.* (Coll.) 1. Excrement. 2. Ridiculous action; unfortunate issue.

Cagadero [cah-gah-day'-ro], *m.* Place to which people resort for the purpose of dejection; a latrine.

Cagadillo [cah-gah-deel'-lyo], *m. dim.* (Low) A sorry little fellow.

Cagado [cah-gah'-do], *a.* (Low) A mean-spirited, chicken-hearted fellow. —*Cagado, da, pp.* of CAGAR.

Cagafierro [cah-gah-fe-er'-ro], *m.* Scoria, dross of iron.

Cagajón [cah-gah-hone'], *m.* 1. Horse-dung. 2. The dung of mules or asses.

Cagalaolla [cah-gah-lah-ol'-lyah], *m.* One who goes dressed in wide trousers and a mask, dancing in processions.

Cagalar [cah-gah-lar'], *m.* *V.* TRIPA. (Anat.) Cæcum.

Cagalera [cah-gah-lay'-rah], *f.* Looseness of the body, diarrhœa.

Cagamelos [cah-gah-may'-los], *m.* Kind of mushroom.

Cagar [cah-gar'], *va.* 1. To go to stool. 2. (Low) To soil, stain, or defile a thing.

Cagarrache [cah-gar-rah'-chay], *m.* 1. One who washes the olives in an oil-mill. 2. Bird of the family of starlings.

Cagarria [cah-gar'-re-ah], *f.* Kind of mushroom, called St. George's agaric. Agaricus, georgii, *Lin.*

Cagarropa [cah-gar-ro'-pah], *m.* *V.* CAGACHÍN.

Cagarruta [cah-gar-roo'-tah], *f.* Dung of sheep, goats, and mice.

Cagatinta [cah-gah-teen'-tah], *m.* 1. Pettifogger. 2. A nickname given in contempt to attorneys' clerks.

Cagatorio [cah-gah-to'-re-o], *m.* *V.* CAGADERO.

Cagón, na [cah-gone', nah], *m.* & *f.* 1. Person afflicted with a diarrhœa. 2. Cowardly, timorous person.

Cague [cah'-gay], *m.* (Naut.) Kaag, a Dutch vessel with one mast, a kind of bilander.

Cahiz [cah-eeth'], *m.* 1. Nominal measure, commonly of twelve *fanegas*, or about twelve English bushels. 2. *V.* CAHIZADA. (Arab. cafīz.)

Cahizada [cah-e-thah'-dah], *f.* Tract of land which requires about one *cahiz* of grain in order to be properly sown.

Cahué [cah-oo-ay'], *m.* Turkish name of coffee and a café (fr. Arabic).

Caída [cah-ee'-dah], *f.* 1. Fall, falling; tumble. 2. Fall, the effect of falling. 3. Fall, downfall; lapse. 4. Fall, diminution, declination, declension. 5. Fall, declivity, descent. 6. Any thing which hangs down, as a curtain or tapestry. 7. Fall, the violence suffered in falling. 8. (Geol.) A land-slip. 9. An interior gallery in houses of Manila, with views upon the courtyard. (See CAER, 12th accept.) 10. (Vulg.) The earnings of a harlot. *Caída de la proa*, (Naut.) Casting or falling off. *Caída de una vela*, Depth or drop of a sail. *Caída de agua*, Waterfall. *Caída incontrolada*, Free fall. *Ir* or *andar de capa caída*, (Met.) To decline in fortune and credit. *A la caída de la tarde*, At nightfall. *A la caída del sol*, At sunset.—*pl.* 1. That part of a head-dress which hangs loose. 2. Coarse wool cut off the skirts of fleece.

Caído, da [cah-ee'-do, dah], *a.* Languid; downfallen.—*pp.* of CAER.

Caídos [cah-ee'-dos], *m. pl.* 1. Rents or annual payments become due and not paid. 2. Arrears of taxes. 3. Sloping lines to show the proper slant in writing.

(*Yo caigo, yo caiga; yo caí, él cayó; yo cayera*, from *Caer*. *V.* CAER.)

Caimán [cah-e-mahn'], *m.* 1. Cayman, alligator, an American crocodile. 2. A cunning man.

Caimiento [cah-e-me-en'-to], *m.* 1. Lowness of spirits; languidness, want of bodily strength. 2. Fall, the act of falling.

Caique [cah-ce'-kay], *m.* (Naut.) Caic, a kind of skiff or small boat.

Cairel [cah-e-rel'], *m.* 1. False hair or wig worn by women to embellish their head-dress. 2. Furbelow, a kind of flounce with which women's dresses are trimmed. 3. Silk threads to which wig-makers fasten the hair of wigs.

Cairelado, da [cah-e-ray-lah'-do, dah], *a.* Adorned with flounces.—*pp.* of CAIRELAR.

Cairelar [cah-e-ray-lar'], *va.* To adorn with flounces.

Caja [cah'-hah], *f.* 1. Box or case of wood, metal, or stone. 2. Coffin. *V.* ATAÚD. 3. Chest in which money is kept; cash-box or safe. (Com.) Cash, funds; cashier's office. 4. A sheath. 5. Drum. 6. Printer's case. 7. Room in post-office where letters are sorted. 8. Portable writing-desk. 9. The well or cavity in which a staircase is raised. 10. Wooden case of an organ. *Caja alta, caja baja,* (Typ.) Upper case, lower case. *Caja de polvo,* Snuff-box. *Cajas en ternos,* Nest of boxes. *Caja de escopeta,* Stock of a firelock. *Caja de brasero,* A wooden case where the brasier is placed on the room. *Caja de coche,* Body of a coach. *Caja de agua,* (Naut.) Manger of a ship. *Caja de balas,* Shot-locker. *Caja de bombas,* (Naut.) Pump-well of a ship. *Caja de lastre,* (Naut.) Ballast-case. *Caja de consulta,* (Law) Counsellor's brief. *Caja de cartuchos,* (Mil.) Cartridge-box. *Caja de mar,* (Naut.) Sea-chest. *Caja de hueso roto,* Cradle for a broken limb. *Libro de caja,* Among merchants, cash-book. *Caja del farol del pañol de pólvora,* (Naut.) Light-room. *Meter las vergas* or *entenas en caja,* To place the yards or lateen-yards in a horizontal position. *Echar con cajas destempladas,* To dismiss from service, to turn away in a harsh manner. *Estar en caja,* To equilibrate, to be in equipoise. *El pulso está en su caja,* (Med.) The pulse is even and natural. *Notario de caja,* (Prov.) Notary public of the city of Saragossa.

Caja de ahorros [cah'-hah day ah-or'-ros], *f.* Savings bank.

Caja de cambios [cah'-hah day cam'-be-os], *f.* Transmission, gear box.

Caja de caudales [cah'-hah day cah-oo-dah'-les], *f.* Strong box.

Caja fuerte [cah'-hah foo-err'-tay], *f.* Safe, vault.

Caja registradora [cah'-hah ray-hes-trah-do'-rah], *f.* Cash register.

Cajero [cah-hay'-ro], *m.* 1. Cashier. 2. Boxmaker.

Cajeta [cah-hay'-tah], *f.* 1. Snuff-box. 2. (Prov.) Poor-box. *Cajetas,* (Naut.) Caburns. 3. (Mex.) Box of jelly.

Cajetazo [cah-hay-tah'-tho], *m.* Blow with a *cajete.*

Cajete [cah-hay'-tay], *m.* (Mex.) A flat bowl of unburnished clay, in which the *pulque* (the juice of the century plant or maguey) is sold to the people.

Cajetilla [cah-hay-teel'lyah], *f.* 1. Wrapper for cigarettes. *Cajetilla de cigarros,* Package of cigarettes. 2. (Arg. coll.) A dude, a dandy.

Cajetín [cah-hay-teen'], *m. dim.* 1. Very small box. 2. (Typ.) Fount-case, letter-case. 3. Spindle-case.

Cajista [cah-hees'-tah], *m.* Compositor (in printing).

Cajo [cah'-ho], *m.* Among bookbinders, groove for the pasteboards in which books are bound.

Cajón [cah-hone'], *m.* 1. Box or chest for goods. 2. Chest of drawers; drawer under a table; locker; money-drawer. 3. Mould for casting the pipes of an organ. 4. Space between the shelves of a bookcase. 5. Tub in which wet cloth is laid. 6. Wooden shed for selling provisions. (Mex.) Dry-goods store. 7. Crib, caisson. *Ser de cajón,* or *una cosa de cajón,* To be a matter of course, or a common thing. *Cosas de cajón,* Common-place things. *Ser un cajón de sastre,* (Met.) 1. To have one's brain full of confused ideas. 2. To know a great many things. *Cajones de cámara,* (Naut.) Lockers in the cabins of ships.

Cajonada [cah-ho-nah'-dah], *f.* (Naut.) Lockers.

Cajoncito [cah-hon-thee'-to], *m. dim.* 1. A small box, chest, or drawer. 2. Compartments or pigeon-holes.

Cajonera [cah-ho-nay'-rah], *f.* A box in which flowers or shrubbery is grown; a wood and glass frame for hot-houses.

Cajonería [cah-ho-nay-ree'-ah], *f.* Chest of drawers.

Cal [cahl], *f.* Lime. *Cal viva,* Quick or unslaked lime. *Pared de cal y canto,* A wall of rough stone and mortar. *Ser de cal y canto,* (Met.) To be as strong as if built with lime and stone.

Cala [cah'-lah], *f.* 1. (Naut.) Creek, a small bay. 2. Small piece cut out of a melon or other fruit to try its flavour. 3. Hole made in a wall to try its thickness. 4. (Med.) Suppository. 5. (Obs.) A probe for wounds. *Hacer cala y cata,* To examine a thing to ascertain its quantity and quality.

Calabacera [cah-lah-bah-thay'-rah], *f.* (Bot.) Pumpkin or gourd-plant. *V.* CALABAZA.

Calabacero [cah-lah-bah-thay'-ro], *m.* Retailer of pumpkins.

Calabacica, illa, ita [cah-lah-bah-thee'-cah, eel'-lyah, ee'-tah], *f. dim.* Small pumpkin.

Calabacilla [cah-lah-bah-theel'-lyah], *f.* 1. Core, piece of wood in the shape of a gourd, around which a tassel of silk or worsted is formed. 2. Ear-ring made of pearls in the shape of a gourd.

Calabacín [cah-lah-bah-theen'], *m.* 1. A small, young, tender pumpkin. 2. (Coll.) Dolt, a silly person.

Calabacinate [cah-lah-bah-the-nah'-tay], *m.* Fried pumpkins.

Calabacino [cah-lah-bah-thee'-no], *m.* Dry gourd or pumpkin scooped out, in which wine is carried; a calabash.

Calabaza [cah-lah-bah'-thah], *f.* 1. (Bot.) The fruit of the pumpkin or gourd. Cucurbita. *Calabaza anaranjada,* Orange-fruited gourd. Cucurbita aurantia. *Calabaza bonetera,* Squash gourd. Cucurbita melopepo. *Calabaza totanera,* Potiron pumpkin. Cucurbita maxima. *Calabaza vinatera,* Bottle gourd or calabash. Cucurbita lagenaria. *Calabaza verruguera* or *verrugosa,* Warted gourd. Cucurbita verrucosa. 2. Calabash. 3. Small button joining the ring of a key. *Dar calabazas,* 1. To reprove, to censure. 2. To give a denial; to give the mitten: applied to a woman who rejects a proposal of marriage. *Llevar calabazas,* To be dismissed, to be sent away. *Salir calabazas,* To be plucked, to fail in an examination. *Tener cascos de calabaza,* To be silly, ignorant, or stupid. *Nadar sin calabazas,* To swim without pumpkins; not to need the support of others.

Calabazada [cah-lah-bah-thah -dah], *f.* 1. Knock with the head against something. *Darse de calabazadas,* (Met.) To labour in vain to ascertain something. 2. Liquor drunk from a calabash.

Calabazar [cah-lah-bah-thar'], *m.* Piece of ground planted with pumpkins.

Calabazate [cah-lah-bah-thah'-tay], *m.* 1. Preserved pumpkin candied with sugar. 2. Piece of a pumpkin steeped in honey or must. 3. Knock of the head against a wall.

Calabazón [cah-lah-bah-thone'], *m. aug.* Large winter pumpkin.

Calabobos [cah-lah-bo'-bos], *m.* Small, gentle, continued rain; drizzle.

Calabozaje [cah-lah-bo-thah'-hay], *m.* Fee paid by prisoners to the jailer.

Calabozo [cah-lah-bo'-tho], *m.* 1. Dungeon, cell, calaboose: generally applied to such as are below ground. 2. (Prov.) Pruning-hook or knife.

Calabrés, sa [cah-lah-bress', bray'-sah], *a.* Calabrian: native of or belonging to Calabria, southeastern Italy.

Calabriada [cah-lah-bre-ah'-dah], *f.* 1. A mixture of different things. 2. A mixture of white and red wine.

Calabrote [cah-lah-bro'-tay], *m.* (Naut.) Stream-cable.

Calacanto [cah-lah-cahn'-to], *m.* (Bot.) Flea-bane.

Calacuerda [cah-lah-coo-er'-dah], *f.* Beat of drums summoning to attack the enemy resolutely.

Calada [cah-lah'-dah], *f.* 1. Rapid flight of birds of prey. 2. Introduction. 3. (Obs.) Narrow, craggy road. 4. Reprimand. *Dar una calada,* To reprimand.

Caladio [cah-lah'-de-o], *m.* (Bot.) Caladium, an ornamental-leaved plant.

Calado [cah-lah'-do], *m.* 1. Open work in metal, stone, wood, or linen; fretwork. 2. (Naut.) Draught, the depth of water which a vessel draws. *Calados,* Lace. *Calado, da, pp.* of CALAR.

Calador [cah-lah-dor'], *m.* 1. Perforator, borer. 2. (Naut.) Calking-iron. 3. A surgeon's probe.

Caladre [cah-lah'-dray], *f.* A bird of the family of larks.

Calafate, Calafateador [cah-lah-fah'tay, cah-lah-fah-tay-ah-dor'], *m.* Calker

Calafateadura [cah-lah-fah-tay-ah-doo' rah], *f.* Calking.

Calafatear, Calafetear [cah-lah-fah-tay-ar'], *va.* (Naut.) To calk.

Calafateo [cah-lah-fah-tay'-o], *m.* Calking.

Calafatería [cah-lah-fah-tay-ree'-ah], *f.* The act of calking.

Calafetín [cah-lah-fay-teen'], *m.* Calker's boy or mate.

Calafraga [cah-lah-frah'-gah], *f.* (Bot.) Saxifrage. Saxifraga.

Calagozo [cah-lah-go'-tho], *m.* Bill or hedging-hook.

Calaguala [cah-lah-goo-ah'-lah], *f.* (Bot.) Calaguala, the root of ferns. *Calaguala fina* or *verdadera,* Genuine calaguala.

Calahorra [cah-lah-or'-rah], *f.* (Prov.) A public office where bread is distributed in times of scarcity.

Calaje [cah-lah'-hay], *m.* (Prov.) Chest, trunk, or coffer.

Calaluz [cah-lah-looth'], *m.* (Naut.) Kind of East Indian vessel.

Calamaco [cah-lah-mah'-co], *m.* Calamanco, woollen stuff. *Calamacos floreados,* Flowered calamancoes. *Calamacos lisos,* Plain calamancoes. *Calamacos rayados,* Striped calamancoes.

Calamar [cah-lah-mar'], *m.* Calamary, squid, or sea-sleeve: a variety of cuttle-fish which has the power of emitting an inky fluid. It contains an internal horny plate shaped much like a quill-pen, and which gives rise to its name. Sepia loligo, *L.*

Calambac [cah-lam-bac'], *m.* (Bot.) Calamba or calambac wood; eagle-wood (fr. Persian).

Calambre [cah-lahm'-bray], *m.* Spasm, cramp.

Calambuco [cah-lam-boo'-co], *m.* (Bot.) Calaba-tree. Callophyllum calaba.

Calambuco, ca [cah-lam-boo'-co, cah], *a.* (Cuba) Pharisaical, hypocritical.

Calamento, *m.* **Calaminta,** *f.* [cah-lah-men'-to, meen'-tah]. (Bot.) Mountain balm or calamint. Melissa calamintha.

Calamidad [cah-lah-me-dahd'], *f.* Misfortune, calamity, misery, grievousness, mishap; oppression.

Calamina, or **Piedra Calaminar** [cah-lah-mee'-nah], *f.* Calamine, zinc ore or lapis calaminaris, a hydrous silicate of zinc. The carbonate, once known as calamine, is now called smithsonite.

Calamís [cah-lah-mees'], *m.* *V.* Cálamo aromático.

Calamita [cah-lah-mee'-tah], *f.* 1. (Obs.) Loadstone. 2. *V.* Calamite. 3. A fossil, equisetaceous plant of coal formations.

Calamite [cah-lah-mee'-tay], *m.* Kind of small green frog. The little green tree-frog. Hyla.

Calamitosamente [cah-lah-me-to-sah-men'-tay], *adv.* Unfortunately, disastrously.

Calamitoso, sa [cah-lah-me-to'-so, sah], *a.* Calamitous, unfortunate, wretched.

Cálamo [cah'-lah-mo], *m.* 1. (Bot.) Sweet-flag. Acorus. *Cálamo aromático,* Calamus, sweet-cane, sweet-flag. Acorus calamus. 2. Pen. *Cálamo currente,* (Lat.) Off-hand, in haste. 3. Sort of flute.

Calamocano [cah-lah-mo-cah'-no], *a.* *Estar* or *ir calamocano,* To be somewhat fuddled; applied also to old men who begin to droop.

Calamoco [cah-lah-mo'-co], *m.* Icicle.

Calamón [cah-lah-mone'], *m.* 1. (Orn.) Purple water-hen or gallinule. Fulica porphyrio. 2. Round-headed nail. 3. Stay which supports the beam of an oil-mill.

Calamorra [cah-lah-mor'-rah], *f.* (Coll.) The head.

Calamorrada [cah-lah-mor-rah'-dah], *f.* Butt of horned cattle.

Calandrajo [cah-lan-drah'-ho], *m.* 1. Rag hanging from a garment. 2. Ragamuffin.

Calandria [cah-lahn'-dre-ah], *f.* 1. (Orn.) Bunting, calendar lark. Alauda calandra. 2. Calender, a clothier's press, beetle mill, rolling-press. 3. A genus of rhyncophorous beetles, very hurtful to seeds and grains. 4. Mangle.

Cálanis [cah'-lah-nees], *m.* (Bot.) *V. Cálamo aromático.*

Calaña [cah-lah'-nyah], *f.* 1. (Obs.) Pattern, sample. 2. Character, quality. *Es hombre de buena* or *mala calaña,* He is a good or ill natured man. *Es una cosa de mala calaña,* It is a bad thing.

Calañés [cah-lah-nyess'], *a.* A native of Calañas; belonging to that town. *Sombrero calañés,* Andalusian hat with a low crown and broad brim, turned up. *V.* Sombrero.

Cálao [cah'-lah-o], *m.* (Orn.) Horn-bill.

Calapatillo [cah-lah-pah-teel'-lyo], *m.* A weevil, or its grub, very destructive to grains, nuts, and roots.

Calar [cah-lar'], *va.* 1. To penetrate, to pierce, to perforate, to plug. 2. (Met.) To discover a design, to comprehend the meaning or cause of a thing. 3. To put, to place. 4. To imitate net or lace work in linen or cotton. 5. (Mech.) To wedge. *Calar el timón,* (Naut.) To hang the rudder. *Calar el palo de un navío,* (Naut.) To step a mast. *Calar el can de un arma de fuego,* To cock a gun. *Calar el melón* or *la sandía,* To tap (or plug) a watermelon to try its flavour. *Calar el puente,* To let down a drawbridge. *Calar la bayoneta,* (Mil.) To fix the bayonet. *Calar la cuerda,* (Mil.) To apply the match to a cannon. *Calar las cubas,* To gauge a barrel or cask. *Calar el sombrero en la cabeza hasta las cejas,* To press the hat down to the eye-brows. *Calar tantos pies,* (Naut.) To draw so many feet water. —*vr.* 1. To enter, to introduce one's self; to insinuate one's self into. 2. To be wet through, to soak, to imbibe. 3. To stoop, to dart down on prey. *Calarse el falcón sobre las aves,* To dart or pounce on the game: spoken of a hawk.

Calar [cah-lar'], *a.* Calcareous.

Calatraveño, ña, or **Calatravo** [cah-lah-trah-vay'-nyo, nyah, or cah-lah-trah'-vo], *a.* Belonging to Calatrava; the city or knighthood.

Calavera [cah-lah-vay'-rah], *f.* 1. Skull. 2. (Met.) Madcap, a wild, hot-brained fellow, rattle-pate.

Calaverada [cah-lah-vay-rah'-dah], *f.* Ridiculous, foolish, or ill-judged action.

Calaverear [cah-lah-vay-ray-ar'], *vn.* To act foolishly, and without judgment or prudence.

Calaverilla, ita [cah-lah-vay-reel'-lyah, ee'-tah], *f. dim.* 1. Little skull. 2. *m.* (Met.) Little crazy fellow.

Calbote [cal-bo'-tay], *m.* (Prov.) Bread made of acorns or chestnuts.

Calcado [cal-cah'-do], *m.* A counter-drawing, tracing.

Calcamar [cal-cah-mar'], *m.* Sea-fowl on the coast of Brazil.

Calcañal, Calcañar [cal-cah-nyahl', cal-cah-nyar'], *m.* Heel, heel-bone. *Tener el seso en los calcañares,* To have one's brains in the heels; to be stupid.

Calcaño [cal-cah'-nyo], *m.* Heel of the foot.

Calcáneo [cal-cah'-nay-o], *m.* (Anat.) Calcaneum, the largest bone in the tarsus, which forms the heel.

Calcañuelo [cal-cah-nyoo-ay'-lo], *m.* A disease of bees.

Calcar [cal-car'], *va.* 1. To counter-draw, or to copy a design by means of pressure, to trace. 2. (Prov.) To trample on.

Calcáreo, rea [cal-cah'-ray-o, ah], *a.* Calcareous.

Calce [cahl'-thay], *m.* 1. The tire of a wheel. 2. A piece of iron or steel added to the coulter of a plough, when it is worn. 3. A wedge. 4. Wheel-shoe, a form of brake. 5. (Naut.) Top. 6. (Obs.) A cup, a chalice. 7. (Obs.) Small canal for irrigation.

Calcedonia [cal-thay-do'-ne-ah], *f.* Chalcedony, a precious stone.

Calcés [cal-thess'], *m.* (Naut.) Mast-head.

Calceta [cal-thay'-tah], *f.* 1. Under-stocking, generally of thread. 2. (Met.) Fetters worn by criminals.

Calcetero, ra [cal-thay-tay'-ro, rah], *m. & f.* 1. One who makes, mends, or sells thread stockings. 2. Knitter of stockings.

Calcetilla, Calcilla [cal-thay-teel'-lyah, cal-theel'-lyah], *f. dim.* Small stocking, sock.

Calcetín [cal-thay-teen'], *m.* *V.* Calcetilla. Half-hose, sock.

Calcetón [cal-thay-tone'], *m. aug.* Large stocking worn under boots.

Calciditos [cal-the-dee'-tose], *m. pl.* Chalcididæ, a family of hymenopterous insects, many parasitic, and useful to the husbandman.

Calcificarse [cal-the-fe-car'-say], *vr.* To calcify, to turn into calcium.

Calcina [cal-thee'-nah], *f.* Mortar.

Calcinación [cal-the-nah-the-on'], *f.* (Chem.) Calcination.

Calcinar [cal-the-nar'], *va.* To calcine. —*vr.* To calcine.

Calcinatorio [cal-the-nah-to'-re-o], *a.* *Vaso calcinatorio,* Calcinatory.

Calcio [cahl'-the-o], *m.* Calcium, a metallic element, never occurring free, but widely distributed in limestone, gypsum, etc.

Calco [cahl'-co], *m.* A counter-drawing copied by means of pressure: a drawing made from another by means of a transparent paper; a tracing.

Calcografía [cal-co-grah-fee'-ah], *f.* 1. Chalcography, art of engraving. 2. Shop where engravings are sold and the place where they are engraved.

Calcógrafo [cal-co'-grah-fo], *m.* Engraver.

Calcomanía [cal-co-mah-nee'-ah], *f.* Decalcomania, a process of transferring prints from paper and making them adhere to porcelain, etc.

Calcopirita [cal-co-pe-ree'-tah], *f.* Copper pyrites, chalcopyrite, native copper sulphide.

Calculable [cal-coo-lah'-blay], *a.* Calculable.

Calculación [cal-coo-lah-the-on'], *f.* Computation, calculation.

Calculador, ra [cal-coo-lah-dor', rah], *m. & f.* Calculator. *Calculador electrónico,* Electronic computer. *Calculadora,* Adding machine.

Calcular [cal-coo-lar'], *va.* To calculate, to reckon.

Calculista [cal-coo-lees'-tah], *m.* Schemer.

Cálculo [cahl'-coo-lo], *m.* 1. Calculation, computation, the result of an arithmetical operation; estimate, count, account. 2. (Med.) Calculus, gravel, stone. 3. Small stone used by the ancients in arithmetical operations. *Cálculo diferencial,* (Mat.) Differential calculus. *Cálculo integral,* Integral calculus.

Calculoso, sa [cal-coo-lo'-so, sah], *a.* Calculose, calculous.

Calda [cahl'-dah], *f.* 1. Warmth, heat. 2. Act of warming or heating. *Caldas,* Natural hot mineral-water baths.

Caldaria [cal-dah'-re-ah], *f.* *Ley caldaria,* Water ordeal.

Caldear [cal-day-ar'], *va.* 1. To weld iron, and render it fit to be forged. 2. To warm, to heat.

Caldeo [cal-day'-o], *m.* Chaldaic.

Caldera [cal-day'-rah], *f.* Caldron, boiler; sugar-kettle. *Caldera de jabón,* Soap-boiler. *Caldera de Pero Botero,* (Coll.) Davy Jones's locker; devil's boiler, hell. *Caldera de vapor,* steam-boiler.

Calderada [cal-day-rah'-dah], *f.* A caldronful, a copperful.

Calderería [cal-day-ray-ree'-ah], *f.* 1. Brazier's shop. 2. Trade of a brazier.

Calderero [cal-day-ray'-ro], *m.* 1. Brazier, coppersmith, blacksmith. 2. Tinker. 3. Among wool-washers, one charged with keeping the fire burning under the boiler.

Caldereta [cal-day-ray'-tah], *f.* 1. (Dim.) Small caldron, a kettle, a pot. *Caldereta de agua bendita,* Holy-water pot.

2. Kettleful. *Caldereta de pescado guisado*, Kettleful of stewed fish. 3. (Mex.) Chocolate-pot. 4. Stew of meat.

Calderico, ica, illo, illa [cal-day-ree'-co, cah, eel'-lyo, lyah], *m.* & *f. dim.* A small kettle.

Calderilla [cal-day-reel'-lyah], *f.* 1. Holy-water pot. 2. Any copper coin. 3. The lowermost part of a well, in the shape of a caldron.

Caldero [cal-day'-ro], *m.* 1. A caldron or boiler in the form of a bucket, a copper. 2. *Caldero hornillo*, Pan, stove. *Caldero de brea*, (Naut.) Pitch-kettle. *Caldero del equipaje*, (Naut.) Mess-kettle.

Calderón [cal-day-rone'], *m.* 1. Copper, large caldron or kettle. 2. Mark of a thousand Ð. 3. (Print.) Paragraph ¶. 4. (Mus.) Sign denoting a suspension of the instruments.

Calderuela [cal-day-roo-ay'-lah], *f.* 1. (Dim.) Small kettle. 2. Small pot or dark-lantern, used by sportsmen to drive partridges into the net.

Caldillo, Caldito [cal-deel'-lyo, cal-dee'-to], *m.* 1. Sauce of a ragout or fricassee. 2. Light broth.

Caldo [cahl'-do], *m.* Broth, beef-tea, bouillon. *Caldo de carne*, Consommé. *Caldos*, Wine, oil, and all spirituous liquors which are transported by sea. *Caldo súlcido*, Pressed juice of herbs. *Revolver caldos*, (Met.) To excite disturbances, to stir up commotions. *Caldo alterado*, Alterative broth, generally made of veal, partridges, frogs, etc.

Caldosito [cal-do-see'-to], *a.* (Coll.) Not too thick.

Caldoso, sa [cal-do'-so, sah], *a.* Having plenty of broth, thin.

Calducho [cal-doo'-cho], *m.* (Coll.) Broth ill-seasoned and without substance, hog-wash.

Calecico [cah-lay-thee'-co], *m. dim.* Small chalice.

Caledonia [cah-lay-do'-ne-ah], *f.* Caledonia, ancient name of Scotland.

Caledonio, ia [cah-le-do'-ne-o, ah], *a.* Caledonian, Scotch.

Calefaciente [cah-lay-fah-the-en'-tay], *a.* (Med.) Heating.

Calefacción [cah-lay-fac-the-on'], *f.* Calefaction, heating.

Calefactorio [cah-lay-fac-to'-re-o], *m.* Stove or place in convents designed for warming.

Calencas [cah-len'-cas], *f.* Kind of East India calico.

Calenda [cah-len'-dah], *f.* The part of the martyrology which treats of the acts of the saints of the day. *Calendas*, Calends, first day of every month. *A las calendas griegas*, i. e. never, because the Greeks had no calends. *A* or *en estas calendas*, At that time.

Calendar [cah-len-dar'], *va.* (Obs.) To date.

Calendario [cah-len-dah'-re-o], *m.* 1. Almanac, calendar. 2. Date. *Hacer calendarios*, (Met.) To make almanacs; to muse, to be thoughtful. *Calendario de Flora*, Floral calendar, a table of the time of flowering of plants. *Calendario Gregoriano*, New style, the calendar as reformed by Gregory XIII, and adopted in 1582. It prevails everywhere except in Russia and Greece. *Formar calendarios*, To build castles in the air.

Calendata [cah-len-dah'-tah], *f.* (Obs.) Date. An Aragón law term.

Caléndula [cah-len'-doo-lah], *f.* (Bot.) Marigold. Calendula. *Caléndula arvense*, Field marigold. Calendula arvensis. *Caléndula oficinal*, Common marigold. Calendula officinalis. *Caléndula pluvial*, Small-cape marigold. Calendula pluvialis.

Calentador [cah-len-tah-dor'], *m.* Heater.

Calentamiento [cah-len-tah-me-en'-to], *m.* 1. (Obs.) Calefaction, warming, heating. 2. Disease incidental to horses.

Calentar [cah-len-tar'], *va.* 1. To warm, to heat; to glow, to calefy, to make warm. 2. To roll and heat a ball in one's hand before it is played. 3. (Met.) To urge, to press forward; to despatch speedily. *Calentar a alguno las orejas*, To chide or reprove one severely. *Calentar alguno el asiento* or *la silla*, To become tiresome by making too long a visit. *No calentar el asiento*, To retain office for but a short time. *Calentar el horno*, (Low) To overheat one's noddle with spirituous liquor.—*vr.* 1. To be in heat: applied to beasts. 2. To mowburn, to ferment and heat in the mow: applied to corn. 3. To grow hot, to calefy, to dispute warmly, to be hurried by the ardour of debate. *Calentársele a uno la boca*, To speak incoherently from excessive ardour.

Calentón [cah-len-tone'], *m.* *Darse un calentón*, (Coll.) To take a bit of a warming.

Calentura [cah-len-too'-rah], *f.* 1. A fever. 2. (Obs.) Warmth, gentle heat. *Calentura de pollo por comer gallina*, A pretended sickness in order to be well treated and excused from work. *El negocio no le da frío ni calentura*, He takes the business coolly, or with great indifference.

Calenturiento, ta [cah-len-too-re-en'-to, tah], *a.* Feverish; fever-sick.

Calenturilla [cah-len-too-reel'-lyah], *f. dim.* Slight fever.

Calenturón [cah-len-too-rone'], *m. aug.* Violent fever.

Calenturoso, sa [cah-len-too-ro'-so, sah], *a.* *V.* CALENTURIENTO.

Calepino [cah-lay-pee'-no], *m.* (Coll.) Vocabulary, dictionary, of Latin.

Calera [cah-lay'-rah], *f.* Lime-kiln; lime-pit.

Calería [cah-lay-ree'-ah], *f.* House, place, or street, where lime is burnt and sold.

Calero, ra [cah-lay'-ro, rah], *a.* Calcareous.

Calero [cah-lay'-ro], *m.* Lime-burner, lime-maker, or seller.

Calesa [cah-lay'-sah], *f.* Calash, a Spanish chaise; gig. (Servian, kolitsa.)

Calesera [cah-lay-say'-rah], *f.* A jacket, parti-coloured, as used by the calash-drivers of Andalucía.

Calesero [cah-lay-say'-ro], *m.* Driver of a calash.

Calesín [cah-lay-seen'], *m.* Single horse-chaise, a gig.

Caleta [cah-lay'-tah], *f.* (Naut.) Cove, creek, fleet, a small bay or inlet.

Caletre [cah-lay'-tray], *m.* 1. (Coll.) Understanding, judgment, discernment. 2. In abusive language, the head.

Cali [cah'-le], *m.* (Chem.) *V.* ÁLCALI.

Calibeado, da [cah-le-bay-ah'-do, dah], *a.* (Med.) 1. Chalybean, relating to steel. 2. Chalybeate, impregnated with iron.

Calibración [cah-le-brah-the-on'], *f.* Calibration.

Calibrador [cah-le-brah-dor'], *m.* Gauge, caliper, calipers.

Calibrar [cah-le-brar'], *va.* To examine the calibre of a ball or fire-arm; to gauge, to size.

Calibre [cah-lee'-bray], *m.* 1. Calibre. 2. Diameter of a column. 3. (Met.) Calibre, sort, kind. *Ser de buen o mal calibre*, To be of a good or bad quality. (Arab. cálib.)

Calicanto [cah-le-cahn'-to], *m.* (Bot.) Allspice. Calycanthus. *Calicanto florido*, Caroline allspice. Calycanthus floridus. *Calicanto fértil*, Fruitful allspice. Calycanthus fertilis.

Calicata [cah-le-cah'-tah], *f.* (Min.) A trial-pit. The test of a piece of ground by auger, or tools, or mere inspection.

Cálice [cah'-le-thay], *m.* (Obs.) *V.* CÁLIZ.

Calicinal [cah-le-the-nahl'], *a.* Relating to a calyx, calycine, or calycinal.

Calicó [cah-le-co'], *m.* Calico.

Calicud, Calicut [cah-le-cood', cah-le-coot'], *f.* Silk stuff from India.

Calicut [cah-le-coot'], *f.* A city in Madras, southern India, whence calico was first imported.

Caliche [cah-lee'-chay], *m.* 1. Pebble or small piece of lime-stone accidentally introduced into a brick or tile at the time of its being burnt. 2. A crust of lime which flakes from a wall. 3. (Peru and Chile) Native saltpetre, or crude sodium nitrate.

Calidad [cah-le-dahd'], *f.* 1. Quality; condition, character; kind or particular nature. 2. Importance or consequence of a thing. 3. Nobility, quality, condition, rank, fashion. 4. Condition, stipulation, requisite. *Dineros son calidad*, (Met.) Money is equal to nobility. *Calidades*, Conditions in playing a game.

Calidez [cah-le-deth'], *f.* *V.* ENCENDIMIENTO.

Cálido, da [cah'-le-do, dah], *a.* 1. Hot, piquant, calid. *La pimienta es cálida*, The pepper is acrid or piquant. 2. Crafty, artful.

Calidoscopio [cah-le-dos-co'-pe-o], *m.* Kaleidoscope; also written *kaleidoscopio*.

Caliente [cah-le-en'-tay], *a.* 1. Warm, hot, calid; scalding. 2. Warm, fiery, feverish, vehement. *Hierro caliente*, Red-hot iron. *Tener la sangre caliente*, (Met.) To face dangers with great spirit. *En caliente*, Piping hot, on the spot, immediately, instantaneously. *Estar caliente*, To be in heat: applied to beasts.

(*Yo caliento, yo caliente*, from *Calentar*. *V.* ACERTAR.

Calieta [cah-le-ay'-tah], *f.* Kind of mushroom.

Califa [cah-lee'-fah], *m.* Caliph, successor: a title assumed by the princes successors of Mohammed.

Califato [cah-le-fah'-to], *m.* Caliphate, the dignity of caliph.

Calificación [cah-le-fe-cah-the-on'], *f.* 1. Qualification. 2. Judgment, censure. 3. Proof. 4. Habilitation.

Calificado, da [cah-le-fe-cah'-do, dah], *a.* Qualified, authorized, competent.—*pp.* of CALIFICAR.

Calificador [cah-le-fe-cah-dor'], *m.* 1. One who is qualified to say and do something. 2. *Calificador del Santo Oficio*, Officer of the Inquisition, appointed to examine books and writings.

Calificar [cah-le-fe-car'], *va.* 1. To qualify. 2. To authorize, to empower. 3. To certify, to attest. 4. To illustrate, to ennoble.—*vr.* To prove one's noble birth and descent according to law.

Californiano, na [cah-le-for-ne-ah'-no, nah], *a.* & *m.* & *f.* Californian, from California.

Californio, ia [cah-le-for'-ne-o, ah], *a.* Native of California.

Caliga [cah-lee'-gah], *f.* A kind of half-boots worn by Roman soldiers.

Caligine [cah-lee'-he-nay], *f.* Mist, obscurity, darkness.

Caliginoso, sa [cah-le-he-no'-so, sah], *a.* 1. Caliginous, dark, dim. 2. Intricate, obscure, difficult to be understood.
Caligrafía [cah-le-grah-fee'-ah], *f.* Caligraphy, elegant penmanship.
Calígrafo [cah-lee'-grah-fo], *m.* One who writes a beautiful hand: a penman.
Calilla [cah-leel'-lyah], *f. dim.* A slight suppository.
Calima [cah-lee'-mah], *f.* 1. *V.* CALINA. 2. A rosary of corks employed in sea-fishing.
Calimaco [cah-le-mah'-co], *m.* (Prov.) *V.* CALAMACO.
Calin [cah-leen'], *m.* A metallic composition resembling lead.
Calina [cah-lee'-nah], *f.* Thick vapour, resembling a mist or fog.
Calinda [cah-leen'-dah], *f.* (Cuba) A popular dance of the creoles.
Calino, na [cah-lee'-no, nah], *a.* Chalky, or containing chalk.
Calio [cah'-le-o], *m.* Kalium or potassium, a metallic element.
Caliope [cah-lee'-o-pay], *f.* Calliope, muse of epic poetry.
Calípedes [cah-lee'-pay-des], *m.* A slow-paced animal.
Calipso [cah-leep'-so], *m.* 1. (Bot.) Calypso. 2. (Mus.) Calypso, musical rhythm from Trinidad.
Calis [cah'-lis], *f.* (Bot.) Alkanet or orchanet.
Calisaya [cah-le-sah'-yah], *f.* (Bot.) Calisaya, a highly prized variety of cinchona bark, indigenous to Peru.
Calisténica [cah-lees-tay'-ne-cah], *f.* Calisthenics, gymnastics.
Calixto [cah-leex'-to], *m.* (Astr. and poet.) The constellation of the Great Bear.
Cáliz [cah'-leeth], *m.* 1. Chalice, a communion cup. 2. Bitter cup of grief and affliction. 3. (Bot.) Calyx of a flower.
Caliza [cah-lee'-thah], *f.* Calcium carbonate in its various forms, whether limestone, marble, gypsum, or other.
Calizo, za [cah-lee'-tho, thah], *a.* Calcareous, limy; calc (spar).
Calma [cahl'-mah], *f.* 1. (Naut.) A calm. 2. Calmness, tranquility, composure. 3. Suspension of business, cessation of pain. *Tierras calmas,* Flat, bleak country, without trees. *En calma,* (Naut.) Smooth sea. *Calma muerta* or *chicha,* (Naut.) Dead calm. 4. Slowness in speaking or doing. (Coll.)
Calmadamente [cal-mah-dah-men'-tay], *adv.* Quietly, calmly.
Calmado, da [cal-mah'-do, dah], *a.* Quiet, calm.—pp. of CALMAR.
Calmante [cal-mahn'-tay], *m.* (Med.) Anodyne; sedative; tranquilizer.
Calmanto [cal-mahn'-tay], *pa. & m. & f.* 1. Mitigating, mitigant. 2. (Med.) Narcotic, anodyne, sedative.
Calmar [cal-mar'], *va.* 1. To calm, to quiet, to compose, to pacify, to still, to hush. 2. To alleviate, to allay, to lay, to mitigate, to lull, to moderate, to soothe, to soften.—*vn.* To fall calm, to be becalmed.—*vr.* (Met.) To be pacified.
Calmia [cahl'-me-ah], *f.* Kalmia, a genus of shrubs of the heath family, indigenous to North America. Kalmia latifolia is the mountain laurel or calico-bush.
Calmo, ma [cahl'-mo, mah], *a.* Uncultivated, untilled; without trees or shrubbery: said of land.
Calmoso, sa [cal-mo'-so, sah], *a.* 1. Calm. 2. (Met.) Tranquil, soothing. 3. Slow, tardy.
Calmuco [cal-moo'-co], *m.* Kalmuck, an inhabitant of Kalmuck Tartary.
Calnado [cal-nah'-do], *m.* *V.* CANDADO, a term still used in some localities, but nearly obsolete.
Caló [cah-lo'], *m.* Cant, the jargon spoken by gipsies and criminals.
Calocar [cah-lo-car'], *m.* Kind of white earth or clay.
Calocha [cah-lo'-chah], *f.* 1. Clog or wooden shoe. 2. Over-shoe, galosh.
Calofillo, lla [cah-lo-feel'-lyo, lyah], *a.* Having handsome leaves.
Calofriado, da [cah-lo-fre-ah'-do, dah], *a.* Chilly, shivering with cold.—*pp.* of CALOFRIARSE.
Calofriarse, Calosfriarse [cah-lo-fre-ar'-say], *vr.* To be chilly, to shudder or shiver with cold; to be feverish or with shiverings.
Calofrío, Calosfrío [cah-lo-free'-o], *m.* Indisposition, attended with shivering and unnatural heat.
Caloma [cah-lo'-mah], *f.* (Naut.) Singing out of sailors when they haul a rope.
Calomel, or **Calomelanos** [cah-lo-may-lah'-nos], *m. pl.* (Med.) Calomel.
Calón [cah-lone'], *m.* 1. Rod for spreading nets. 2. Perch for measuring the depth in shallow water.
Calonjia [cah-lon-hee'-ah], *f.* (Obs.) House of canons. *V.* CANONJÍA.
Caloña [cah-lo'-nyah], *f.* (Obs.) 1. *V.* CALUMNIA. 2. Fine or pecuniary punishment for calumniating.
Calóptero, ra [cah-lop'-tay-ro, rah], *a.* Handsome-winged.
Calor [cah-lor'], *m.* 1. Heat; hotness, calidity; glow. 2. Flagrancy, excandescence. 3. (Met.) Warmth, ardour, fervour, fieriness: applied to sentiments and actions. 4. Brunt of an action or engagement. 5. Favour, kind reception. *Dar calor a la empresa,* To encourage an undertaking. *Dar calor,* Among tanners, to raise the colour of a hide by heating it. *Gastar el calor natural en alguna cosa,* (Met.) 1. To pay more attention to an affair than it is worth. 2. To pay the greatest attention to a business. *Meter en calor,* To incite, to excite, encourage. *Tomar calor,* To become warm, to push an affair warmly.
Caloría [cah-lo-ree'-ah], *f.* Calorie.
Calórico, ca [cah-lo'-re-co, cah], *a.* Caloric.
Calorífero, ra [cah-lo-ree'-fe-ro, rah], *a.* Heat-producing.—*m.* Furnace, heater. *Calorífero de aire caliente,* Hot-air heater.
Calorífico, ca [cah-lo-ree'-fe-co, cah], *a.* Heat-producing, calorific.
Calorífugo, ga [cah-lo-ree'-foo-go, gah], *a.* 1. Heat-resistant. 2. Incombustible.
Calorímetro [cah-lo-ree'-may-tro], *m.* Calorimeter.
Caloroso, sa [cah-lo-ro'-so, sah], *a.* *V.* CALUROSO.
Calostro [cah-los'-tro], *m.* Colostrum.
Calotear [cah-lo-tay-ar'], *va.* (Sp. Am.) To gyp, to swindle.
Caloyo [cah-lo'-yo], *m.* New-born lamb or kid.
Calpense [cal-pen'-say], *a.* From Gibraltar.
Calpul [cal-pool'], *m.* (Sp. Am.) Gathering, get-together.
Calseco, ca [cal-say'-co, cah], *a.* Cured with lime.
Calta [cahl'-tah], *f.* Caltha, marsh marigold.
Calumbrecerse [ca-loom-bray-therr'-say], *vr.* (Obs.) To grow mouldy.
Calumnia [cah-loom'-ne-ah], *f.* Calumny, false charge, slander. *Afianzar de calumnia,* (Law) Applied to an accuser giving security to subject himself to legal penalties if he can not prove his allegations.
Calumniador, ra [cah-loom-ne-ah-dor', rah], *m. & f.* Calumniator, a slanderer.
Calumniar [cah-loom-ne-ar'], *va.* To calumniate, to slander, to accuse falsely.
Calumniosamente [cah-loom-ne-o-sah-men'-tay], *adv.* Calumniously, slanderously.
Calumnioso, sa [cah-loom-ne-o'-so, sah], *a.* Calumnious, slanderous.
Calurosamente, *adv.* Warmly, ardently, hotly.
Caluroso, sa [cah-loo-ro'-so, sah], *a.* 1. Warm, hot. 2. Heating.
Calva [cahl'-vah], *f.* 1. Bald crown of the head, bald pate. 2. Game among country people, in which they knock one stone against another. *Calva de almete,* Crest of a helmet.
Calvar [cal-var'], *va.* 1. To hit a stone in the game of *Calva.* 2. (Obs.) To impose upon one, to deceive.
Calvario [cal-vah'-re-o], *m.* 1. (Met. Coll.) Debts, tally, score. 2. (Obs.) A charnel-house. 3. Calvary, hill or elevation on which are crosses representing the stations at Mount Calvary. Calvary, Golgotha.
Calvatrueno [cal-vah-troo-ay'-no], *m.* 1. Baldness of the whole head. 2. (Met.) A wild person.
Calvaza [cal-vah'-thah], *f. aug.* Large bald pate.
Calvero, Calvijar, Calvitar [cal-vay'-ro, cal-ve-har', tar'], *m.* Barren ground among fruitful lands.
Calvete [cal-vay'-tay], *m. dim.* Little bald pate, when only part of the head is bald.
Calvez, Calvicie [cal-veth', cal-vee'-the-ay], *f.* Baldness.
Calvilla [cal-veel'-lyah], *f. dim.* Little baldness.
Calvinismo [cal-ve-nees'-mo], *m.* Calvinism.
Calvinista [cal-ve-nees'-tah], *m.* Calvinist.
Calvo, va [cahl'-vo, vah], *a.* 1. Bald, without hair. 2. Barren, uncultivated: applied to ground. *Tierra calva,* Barren soil.
Calza [cahl'-thah], *f.* 1. Long, loose breeches, trousers. 2. Hose, stockings. *Calzas acuchilladas,* Slashed trousers. *Calzas bermejas,* Red stockings, formerly worn by noblemen. *Calza de arena,* Bag of sand with which malefactors were formerly chastised. *Medias calzas,* Short stockings, reaching only to the knees. *En calzas y jubón,* (Met.) In an odd or imperfect state. *Echarle una calza a alguno,* To point out a person to be guarded against. *Meter en una calza,* (Met.) To screw up a person, to put him on his mettle. *Tomar calzas* or *las calzas de Villadiego,* To make a precipitate flight or escape. *Hombre de calzas atacadas,* (Met.) A rigid observer of old customs.
Calzada [cal-thah'-dah], *f.* 1. Causeway, a paved highway. 2. The high road. 3. Gravel-walk. 4. Avenue.
Calzadera [cal-thah-day'-rah], *f.* 1. Hempen cord for fastening the *abarcas,* a coarse kind of leathern shoes. 2. Net twine.
Calzadillo, ito [cal-thah-deel'-lyo, dee'-to], *m. dim.* Small shoe.
Calzado, da [cal-thah'-do, dah], *a.* Calceated, shod.—*pp.* of CALZAR.
Calzado [cal-thah'-do], *m.* 1. Footwear of all kinds. 2. Horse with four white feet. *Calzados,* All articles serving to cover the legs and feet. *Tráeme el calzado,* Bring me my stockings, garters, and shoes.

Calzador [cal-thah-dor'], *m.* 1. Shoeing leather, a piece of leather used to draw up the hind quarters of tight shoes. 2. Shoe-horn, a piece of horn used for the same purpose as the shoeing-leather. *Entrar con calzador*, (Met.) To find great difficulties in entering a place.

Calzadura [cal-thah-doo'-rah], *f.* 1. Act of putting on the shoes. 2. Felloe of a cart-wheel.

Calzar [cal-thar'], *va.* 1. To put on shoes. 2. To strengthen with iron or wood. 3. To scot or scotch a wheel. 4. To carry a ball of a determined size; applied to fire-arms. 5. To wedge, chock, key. 6. (Typ.) To overlay, raise, underlay. *Calzar las herramientas*, To put a steel edge to iron tools. *Calzar las espuelas*, To put on spurs. *Calzar espuelas al enemigo*, To pursue the enemy with the utmost vigour. *Calzar los guantes*, To put on gloves. *Calzar las mesas*, To secure tables, to make them stand fast. *Calzar el ancla*, (Naut.) To shoe the anchor. *Calzar los árboles*, To cover the roots of trees with fresh earth. *Calzar ·ancha*, (Met.) Not to be very nice and scrupulous. *Calzarse a alguno*, (Met.) To govern or manage a person. *Calzarse los estribos*, To thrust the feet too far into the stirrups. *El que primero llega, ese la calza*, First come first served.

Calzatrepas [cal-thah-tray'-pas], *f.* (Obs.) Snare, trap.

Calzo [cahl'-tho], *m. V.* Calce. 1. (Typ.) Frisket-sheet, overlay. 2. (r. w.) Block, brake-shoe. 3. (Mech.) Wedge, quoin. 4. Shoe of a felloe. 5. (Naut.) Skid, chock, bed, shoe.

Calzón [cal-thone'], *m.* 1. Ombre, a game at cards. 2. Breeches, small clothes, hose: commonly used in the plural. 3. (Mex.) A disease of the sugar-cane from lack of irrigation. *Calzones marineros*, Trousers worn by sailors.—*pl.* (Naut.) Goose-wings: applied to sails when furled in a peculiar manner.

Calzonarias [cal-tho-nah'-re-ahs], *f.pl.* (Sp. Am.) Suspenders.

Calzonazos [cal-tho-nah'-thos], *m.* (Coll.) Mollycoddle, jellyfish.

Calzoncillos [cal-thon-theel'-lyos], *m.pl.* Shorts, drawers.

Calzoneras [cal-tho-nay'-ras], *f. pl.* (Mex.) Trousers open down both sides and the openings closed by buttons.

Calla callando [cahl'-lyah cal-lyahn'-do], *adv.* Privately, secretly, tacitly.

Callada [cal-lyah'-dah], *f.* Dish of tripe.

Callada [cal-lyah'-dah], *f.* Silence: employed only in certain phrases. *A las calladas* or *de callada*, Without noise, privately, on the quiet. *Dar la callada por respuesta*, To answer by silence.

Calladamente [cal-lyah-dah-men'-tay], *adv.* Silently, tacitly, secretly, privately, in a reserved manner.

Calladaris [cal-lyah-dah'-ris], *f.* A kind of cotton stuff.

Callado, da [cal-lyah'-do, dah], *a.* 1. Silent, reserved, noiseless. 2. Discreet.—*pp.* of Callar.

Callamiento [cal-lyah-me-en'-to], *m.* (Obs.) Imposing or keeping silence.

Callandico, ito [cal-lyan-dee'-co, to], *adv.* In a low voice; silently; without noise, slyly, softly.

Callar [cal-lyar'], *vn.* 1. To keep silence, to be silent. 2. To omit speaking of a thing, to pass it over in silence, to conceal, to hush. 3. To cease singing: said of birds. 4. To dissemble. 5. (Poet.) To abate, to become moderate, to grow calm: applied to the wind or sea. *Callar su pico*, To hold one's tongue, to pretend not to have heard or seen any thing of the matter in question. *Buen callar se pierde*, A phrase applied to one who proclaims the faults of others instead of checking his own. *Mátalas callando*, By crafty silence he obtains his ends. *La mujer y la pera, la que calla es buena*, Silence is very desirable in a woman. *Callarse, cállate y callemos, que sendas nos tenemos*, He who lives in a glass house should not throw stones. *Quien calla, piedras apaña*, He who listens carefully may use or repeat what he has heard. *Quien calla otorga*, Silence implies consent. *Calle el que dió y hable el que tomó*, Let the giver be silent, and the receiver loud with gratitude. *Cortapicos y callares*, Be silent: advice to children not to talk or ask improper questions.—*vr.* (Obs.) To be silent.

Calle [cahl'-lyay], *f.* 1. Street, paved way. 2. Lane, a narrow way between hedges. 3. Lane, a passage between men standing on each side. 4. (Coll.) Gullet. 5. (Cant) Liberty. 6. Pretext, excuse, means for evading a promise. *Calle de árboles*, Alley or walk in a garden. *Boca de calle*, Entrance of a street. *Calle mayor*, Main street. *Calle sin salida*, Alley without egress. *Calle traviesa*, Cross-street. *Alborotar la calle*, To cause an uproar in the street. *Azotar la calle*, To walk the streets, to loiter about. *Calle hita*, To go from house to house. *Dejar a uno en la calle*, To strip one of his all, also to turn one out of doors. *Echar algún secreto en la calle*, To proclaim a secret in the streets. *Hacer calle*, 1. To make way, to clear the passage. 2. (Met.) To overcome difficulties. *Llevarse de calles alguna cosa*, (Met.) To carry everything before one. *Pasear* or *rondar la calle*, To court a woman, flirt on the street. *Pasear las calles*, To loiter about. *Quedar en la calle*, To be in the utmost distress. *Ser buena una cosa sólo para echada a la calle*, Not to be worth keeping. *Calles públicas* or *acostumbradas*, The public streets.—*int.* 1. Strange! wonderful! you don't say so! 2. Way! way! make way!

Callear [cal-lyay-ar'], *va.* To clear the walks in a vineyard of the loose branches.

Calleja [cal-lyay'-hah], *f. V.* Callejuela.

Callejear [cal-lyay-hay-ar'], *vn.* To walk or loiter about the streets, to gad, to ramble.

Callejero, ra [cal-lyay-hay'-ro, rah], *a.* Applied to a loiterer; a gadder.

Callejo, Calleyo [cal-lyay'-ho, cal-lyay'-yo], *m.* (Prov.) Pit into which game falls when pursued.

Callejón [cal-lyay-hone'], *m.* 1. Narrow lane. 2. Narrow pass between mountains. *Callejón sin salida*, 1. Blind alley. 2. Impasse, predicament.

Callejoncillo [cal-lyay-hon-theel'-lyo], *m. dim.* A little narrow passage.

Callejuela [cal-lyay-hoo-ay'-lah], *f.* 1. Lane or narrow passage. 2. (Met.) Shift, subterfuge, evasion. *Dar pan y callejuela*, To help one in his flight. *Todo se sabe, hasta lo de la callejuela*, In time everything comes to light.

Callemandra [cal-lyay-mahn'-drah], *f.* Kind of woollen stuff.

Callialto, ta [cal-lye-ahl'-to, tah], *a.* Having swelling welts or borders: applied to horse-shoes.

Callista [cal-lyees'-tah], *m. & f.* A corn-doctor, chiropodist.

Callizo [cal-lyee'-tho], *m.* (Prov.) *V.* Callejón and Callejuela.

Callo [cahl-lyo'], *m.* 1. Corn, a callous substance on the feet. 2. Wen. 3. (Surg.) Callus. 4. Extremity of a horse-shoe.—*m. & f. pl.* Tripes, the intestines of black cattle, calves, and sheep. *Hacer* or *tener callos*, (Met.) To be hardened by custom against misfortunes, or into vices.

Callón [cal-lyone'], *m.* 1. (Aug.) Big corn or wen. 2. Among shoemakers, rubber, a whetstone for smoothing the blades of awls.

Callosidad [cal-lyo-se-dahd'], *f.* Callosity, callousness.

Calloso, sa [cal-lyo'-so, sah], *a.* Callous: corny, corneous, horny.

Cama [cah'-mah], *f.* 1. Bed, couch, a place of repose. *Cama con ruedas*, A truck-bed. 2. Bed hangings and furniture. 3. Seat or couch of wild animals. 4. Floor or body of a cart. 5. *Cama del arado*, The part of a plough which connects the share with the beam, the sheath. 6. *Cama del melón*, Part of a melon which touches the ground. 7. *V.* Camada. 8. Litter, the straw laid under animals or on plants. 9. Slice of meat put upon another, to be both dressed together. 10. Felloe of a wheel. 11. Branch of a bridle to which the reins are fastened; the cheek. 12. Piece of cloth cut slopewise, to be joined to another, to make a round cloak. 13. Layer of dung and earth for raising plants; a garden-bed. 14. (Mech.) Cam, cog, catch, tooth. 15. Bed plate, base. 16. (Geol.) Layer, stratum. *Hacer cama*, To keep one's bed, to be confined to one's bed on account of sickness. *Hacer la cama*, To make up the bed. *Cama desvencijada*, Crazy bed. *Hacerle la cama a alguno* or *a alguna cosa*, (Met.) To pave the way for a person or thing. *Media cama*, Half the usual bedding; a mattress, a sheet, a coverlet, and a pillow. Also, half of a bed shared by two. *A mala cama, colchón de vino*, If one must watch through the night a little wine is desirable. *Caer en cama*, To fall sick. *No hay tal cama como la de la enjalma*, There is no bed too hard for a tired man.

Camada [cah-mah'-dah], *f.* 1. Brood of young animals, a litter. 2. Layer (of eggs, etc.). *Camada de ladrones*, Den of thieves, nest of rogues.

Camafeo [cah-mah-fay'-o], *m.* Cameo, a gem on which figures are engraved in basso-relievo.

Camal [cah-mahl'] *m.* 1. Hempen halter. 2. (Obs.) Camail, a piece of chain mail depending from a basinet.

Camáldula [cah-mahl'-doo-lah], *f. V.* Camándula.

Camaleón [cah-mah-lay-on'], *m.* 1. Chameleon. Lacerta chamæleon. *Camaleón blanco*, (Bot.) Dwarf carline thistle. Carlina acaulis. *Camaleón negro*, (Bot.) Corymbed carline thistle. Carlina corymbosa. (Mex.) The horned toad, properly lizard, of the U. S. Phrynosoma. 2. A flatterer who changes his language according to the presumed tastes of the person addressed.

Camaleopardo [cah-mah-lay-o-par'-do], *m.* Cameleopard, giraffe.

Camamila, Camomila [cah-mah-mee'-lah, cah-mo-mee'-lah], *f.* (Bot.) Common chamomile. *V.* Manzanilla.

Camándula [cah-mahn'-doo-lah], *f.* Chaplet or rosary of one or three decades. *Tener muchas camándulas*, (Coll.) To make use of many tricks and artifices, to shuffle.

Camandulense [cah-man-doo-len'-say], *a.* Belonging to the religious order of Camandula or reformed Benedictines.

Camandulería [cah-man-doo-lay-ree'-ah], *f.* Hypocrisy, insincerity, dissimulation.

Camandulero, ra [cah-man-doo-lay'-ro, rah], *a.* & *n.* Full of tricks and artifices, dissembling, hypocritical.

Camanonca [cah-mah-non'-cah], *f.* (Obs.) Stuff formerly used for linings.

Cámara [cah'-mah-rah], *f.* 1. Hall or principal apartment of a house. 2. Granary, mow, a store-house of threshed corn. 3. Stool, evacuation by stool, laxity, laxness. 4. *V.* CILLA. 5. (Naut.) Cabin of a ship. 6. *Cámara alta*, (Naut.) Round-house of a ship. 7. Chamber in a mine. 8. Chamber of great guns and other fire-arms. 9. (Obs.) Bed-chamber. 10. Residence of the king and court. *Cámara del rey*, 1. Room in which the king holds a levee for gentlemen of the bed-chamber, etc. 2. Exchequer. 11. The legislative body of foreign nations. 12. A photographic camera. *Cámara plegadiza*, A folding camera. *Cámara de mano*, A hand camera. *Cámara estereoscópica*, Stereoscopic camera. *Pie de la cámara* (*oscura*), Camera-stand. *Cámara de bolsillo*, Pocket-camera. *Cámara con frente de quita y pon*, Removable front camera. *Cámara alta* or *de los pares*, The house of lords. *Cámara baja* or *de los comunes*, The house of commons. *Cámara de ciudad, villa* or *lugar*, (Obs.) *V.* CONCEJO and AYUNTAMIENTO. *Cámara de Castilla*, Supreme council, which consisted of the president or governor, and some other members of the council of Castile. *Moza de cámara*, Chamber-maid. *Coche de cámara*, State coach.

Camarada [cah-mah-rah'-dah], *m.* 1. Comrade, partner, companion, comate, fellow; crony, chum.—*f.* 2. Society or company of people united; assembly. 3. (Obs.) Battery. *Camaradas de rancho*, Messmates. *Camaradas de navío*, Shipmates.

Cámara de Comercio [cah'-mah-rah day co-merr'-the-o], *f.* Chamber of Commerce.

Camaradería [cah-mah-rah-day-ree'-ah], *f.* Comradeship, fellowship.

Camaraje [cah-mah-rah'-hay], *m.* Granary, rent for a granary.

Camaranchón [cah-mah-ran-chone'], *m.* 1. Garret. 2. Retired place, recess.

Camarera [cah-mah-ray'-rah], *f.* 1. Head waiting-maid in great houses. 2. Keeper of the queen's wardrobe. 3. Waitress in hotels and steamers.

Camarería [cah-mah-ray-ree'-ah], *f.* 1. Place and employment of a valet de chambre. 2. A discount of forty maravedis per thousand, which the lord chamberlain used to get from the extraordinary warrants which the king commanded to give.

Camarero [cah-mah-ray'-ro], *m.* 1. Chamberlain, an official of the Pope's residence. 2. Waiter, in hotels, restaurants, and steamers. 3. Steward or keeper of stores.

Camareta [cah-mah-ray'-tah], *f. dim.* (Naut.) Small cabin, deck-cabin, midshipmen's cabin.

Camariento, ta [cah-mah-re-en'-to, tah], *a.* Troubled with a diarrhœa.

Camarilla [cah-mah-reel'-lyah], *f.* 1. (Dim.) Small room. 2. (Obs.) In public schools, the room where boys were flogged. 3. The coterie of private advisers of the king.

Camarín [cah-mah-reen'], *m.* 1. Place behind an altar where the images are dressed, and the ornaments destined for that purpose are kept. 2. Closet. 3. A dressing-room in a theatre.

Camariña [cah-mah-ree'-nyah], *f.* Copse, short wood, a low shrub.

Camarista [cah-mah-rees'-tah], *m.* 1. A member of the supreme council of *la Cámara*. 2. (Obs.) Guest who has a room to himself, without intercourse with the rest of the family.—*f.* 3. Maid of honour to the queen and the *infantas* of Spain.

Camarita [cah-mah-ree'-tah], *f. dim.* Small chamber or room.

Camarlengo [cah-mar-len'-go], *m.* 1. Lord of the bed-chamber of the kings of Aragón. 2. The cardinal who presides over the Apostolic Council at Rome.

Camarógrafo [cah-mah-roh'-grah-fo], *m.* Camera man.

Camarón [cah-mah-rone'], *m.* Shrimp. Cancer crangon.

Camaronero [cah-mah-ro-nay'-ro], *m.* Shrimper.

Camarote [cah-mah-ro'-tay], *m.* (Naut.) Room on board a ship, a berth. *Los primeros* or *mejores camarotes*, State-rooms.

Camasquince [cah-mas-keen'-thay], *m.* Nickname jocularly applied to a meddlesome person.

Camastro [cah-mahs'-tro], *m.* Poor, miserable bed.

Camastrón [cah-mas-trone'], *m.* Sly, artful, cunning fellow.

Camastronazo [cah-mas-tro-nah'-tho], *m. aug.* Great impostor, hypocrite, or dissembler.

Camastronería [cah-mas-tro-nay-ree'-ah], *f.* Cunning, artifice.

Camatones [cah-mah-to'-nes], *m. pl.* (Naut.) Iron fastenings of the shrouds.

Cambalache [cam-bah-lah'-chay], *m.* (Coll.) Barter.

Cambalachear [cam-bah-lah-chay-ar'], *va.* To barter.

Cambalachero [cam-bah-lah-chay'-ro], *m.* Barterer.

Cambaleo [cam-bah-lay'-o], *m.* An ancient company of comedians consisting of five men and a woman; the latter sang.

Cambalés [cam-bah-less'], *a.* Relating to a *cambaleo*.

Cámbaro [cahm'-bah-ro], *m.* The cray-fish. *V.* CANGREJO. (Acad.)

Cambas [cahm'-bas], *f. pl.* Pieces put into a cloak, or other round garment, to make it hang round.

Cambayas [cam-bah'-yas], *f. pl.* Kind of cotton stuff.

Cambiable [cam-be-ah'-blay], *a.* Fit to be bartered or exchanged.

Cambiador [cam-be-ah-dor'], *m.* 1. One who barters. 2. (Obs.) Banker; money-changer, money-broker.

Cambial [cam-be-ahl'], *m.* Bill of exchange.

Cambiamano [cam-be-ah-mah'-no], *f.* A railroad switch.

Cambiante [cam-be-ahn'-tay], *a.* Bartering, exchanging. *Cambiante de letras*, A banker, exchanger.

Cambiante, *m.* Fabrics changeable in colour according to the manner in which the light is reflected.

Cambiar [cam-be-ar'], *va.* 1. To barter, to commute, to exchange one thing for another. 2. To change, to alter. *Cambiar de mano*, To change from the one side to the other: applied to horses. 3. To give or take money on bills, to negotiate bills and exchange them for money. 4. To transfer, to make over, to remove. *Cambiar las velas*, (Naut.) To shift the sails. *Cambiar la comida* (better *vomitar la comida*), To bring up the victuals. *Cambiar el seso*, (Obs.) To lose one's senses. 5. To carry on the business of a banker.—*vr.* (Obs.) To be translated or transferred.

Cámbija [cahm'-be-hah], *f.* Reservoir, basin of water.

Cambio [cahm'-be-o], *m.* 1. Barter, commutation. 2. Giving or taking of bills of exchange. 3. Rise and fall of the course of exchange. 4. Public or private bank. 5. Alteration, change; flux. 6. (Obs.) Compensation. 7. (Vet.) A humour contained in the small veins of an animal. 8. Return of a favour, recompense. *Libre cambio*, Free trade. *Cambio manual*, Note of hand. *Cambio minuto*, Small change. *Cambio seco*, Usurious contract; accommodation bill. *Dar o tomar a cambio*, To lend or borrow money on interest. *Cambio por letras*, Trade in bills of exchange.

Cambista [cam-bees'-tah], *m.* Banker, trader in money, broker, cambist; goldsmith.

Cambiunte [cam-be-oon'-tay], *m.* 1. Changeable silk stuff. 2. A kind of camlet.

Cambogio [cam-bo'-he-o], *m.* The tree which yields gamboge: Garcinia. The name comes from the district in India whence it is imported.

Cambray [cam-brah'-e], *m.* Cambric, fine linen.

Cambrayon [cam-brah-yone'], *m.* Coarse cambric.

Cambrón [cam-brone'], *m.* (Bot.) Common buckthorn. Rhamnus catharticus.

Cambronal [cam-bro-nahl'], *m.* Thicket of briers, brambles, and thorns.

Cambronera [cam-bro-nay'-rah], *f.* (Bot.) Box-thorn, a genus of plants. *Cambronera europea* or *común*, European box-thorn. Lycium europeum. *Cambronera africana*, African box-thorn. Lycium atrum. *Cambronera berberisca*, Willow-leaved box-thorn. Lycium barbarum.

Cambullón [cam-bool-lyone'], *m.* (Peru) Imposition, swindle.

Cambuj [cam-booh'], *m.* 1. Child's cap tied close to its head to keep it straight. 2. Mask, veil.

Cambujo, ja [cam-boo'-ho, hah], *a.* An Indian mestizo; offspring of an Indian woman and a negro, or of a negress and an Indian.

Cambuy [cam-boo'-e], *m.* American myrtle-tree.

Camedrio [cah-may'-dre-o], *m.* (Bot.) Wall germander. Teucrium chamœdrys.

Camedris [cah-may'-dris], *m.* (Bot.) Germander, speedwell, wild germander. Veronica chamœdrys. *Camedris de agua*, Water germander. Teucrium scordium.

Camelar [cah-may-lar'], *va.* 1. To court, to woo. 2. (Coll.) To seduce, deceive by flattering (fr. Gipsy).

Camelea [cah-may-lay'-ah], *f.* (Bot.) Widow-wail, a shrub.

Camelete [cah-may-lay'-tay], *m.* (Obs.) Kind of great gun.

Cameleuca [cah-may-lay'-oo-cah], *f.* (Bot.) Colt's-foot. Tussilago farfara.

Camelia [cah-may'-le-ah], *f.* Camellia, an Asiatic genus of small shrubs, often with smooth leaves, and cultivated for ornament. Camelia Japonica is admired for its showy flowers. The tea-plant is now referred to this genus as Camelia theifera.

Camelina [cah-may-lee'-nah], *f.* (Bot.) *V.* Cantilagua.
Camelo [cah-may'-lo], *m.* 1. Gallant, wooer. 2. (Coll.) A joke, jest.
Camelote [cah-may-lo'-tay], *m.* Camlet.
Camelotillos, Camelloncillos [cah-may-lo-teel'-lyos, cah-mayl-lyon-theel'-lyos], *m.* Light or thin camlets.
Camella [cah-mayl'-lyah], *f.* 1. She-camel. 2. Ridge in ploughed land. 3. A milk-pail. 4. Yoke.
Camellejo [cah-mel-lyay'-ho], *m. dim.* 1. Small camel. 2. Small piece of ordnance, used in former times.
Camellería [cah-mel-lyay-ree'-ah], *f.* 1. Stable or stand for camels. 2. Employment of a camel-driver.
Camellero [cah-mel-lyay'-ro], *m.* Keeper or driver of camels.
Camello [cah-mayl'-lyo], *m.* 1. Camel. 2. Ancient cannon. 3. Engine for setting ships afloat in shoal water. *Camello pardal, V.* Girafa.
Camellón [cah-mel-lyone'], *m.* 1. Ridge turned up by the plough or spade. 2. (Prov.) Long wooden drinking-trough for cattle. 3: Carpenter's horse. 4. Bed of flowers. 5. (Prov.) Camlet. *Camellones listados*, Camleteens.
Camemoro [cah-may-mo'-ro], *m.* (Bot.) Cloud-berry bramble. Rubus chamæmorus.
Camepitios [cah-may-pee'-te-os], *m.* (Bot.) Common ground pine. Teucrium chamæpytis.
Camerododendro [cah-may-ro-do-den'-dro], *m.* (Bot.) Rusty-leaved rhododendron. Rhododendron ferrugineum.
Camero [cah-may'-ro], *m.* 1. Upholsterer. 2. One who lets beds on hire.
Camero [cah-may'-ro], *a.* Belonging to a bed or mattress.
Camilla [cah-meel'-lyah], *f.* 1. (Dim.) Small bed, pallet, or cot; litter, stretcher. 2. Bed on which women repose after childbirth. 3. Horse, on which linen is aired and dried. *Camilla baja*, Low frame, on which cloth-shearers put their work.
Caminada [cah-me-nah'-dah], *f.* (Obs.) *V.* Jornada.
Caminador [cah-me-nah-dor'], *m.* Good walker.
Caminante [cah-me-nahn'-tay], *m.* Traveller, walker.
Caminar [cah-me-nar'], *vn.* 1. To travel; to walk, to go, to march. 2. To move along: applied to rivers and other inanimate things. *Caminar con pies de plomo*, (Met.) To act with prudence. *Caminar derecho*, (Met.) To act uprightly.
Caminata [cah-me-nah'-tah], *f.* (Coll.) 1. Long walk for exercise. 2. Excursion, jaunt.
Camino [cah-mee'-no], *m.* 1. Beaten road; high road. 2. Journey. 3. Turn of a boat or cart, for removing goods from place to place. 4. Gate, way, passage, road. 5. (Met.) Profession, station, calling. 6. (Met.) Manner or method of doing a thing. 7. (Min.) Drift, gait. 8. (Naut.) Ship's way, rate of sailing. *Camino cubierto*, (Mil.) Covert-way. *Camino de herradura*, Path, bridle-road, a narrow road. *Camino carretero*, Road for carriages and wagons. *Camino de Santiago*. (Ast.) Galaxy, the Milky Way. *Camino real*, 1. High-road, highway. 2. (Met.) The readiest and surest way of obtaining one's end. *De un camino* or *de una vía dos mandados*, To kill two birds with one stone. *Ir fuera de camino*, (Met.) To be put out of one's latitude, to act contrary to reason. *Ir su camino*, To pursue one's course, to persist or persevere in one's views. *No llevar alguna cosa camino*, To be without foundation and reason. *Procurar el camino*, To clear the way. *Salir al camino*, 1. To go to meet a person. 2. (Met.) To go on the highway to rob. *De camino*, In one's way, going along. *Fuí a Madrid y de camino hice una visita*, I went to Madrid, and in my way thither I paid a visit. *Echarse al camino*, To take to the roads, to become a highway robber. *Ponerse en camino*, Set out, start off. *Camino de Roma, ni mula coja, ni bolsa floja*, Count the cost before beginning what is difficult.
Camino de acceso [cah-mee'-no day ac-thay'-so], *m.* Access road.
Camión [cah-me-on'], *m.* Truck; lorry.
Camioneta [cah-me-o-nay'-tah], *f.* 1. Station wagon. 2. Small truck.
Camisa [cah-mee'-sah], *f.* 1. Shirt, the undergarment of men. 2. Shift, chemise, the undergarment of women. 3. (Obs.) Alb or surplice, worn by priests and deacons. 4. Thin skin of almonds and other fruit. 5. Slough of a serpent. 6. (Mil.) Chemise, side of a rampart toward the field. 7. Stock of counters used at a game of cards. 8. (Obs.) Catamenia. 9. Rough-casting, or plastering of a wall before it is whitewashed. 10. (St.-e.) Jacket, case, casing, in steam-engines. 11. Internal lining of a furnace. *Camisa alquitranada, embreada* or *de fuego*, (Naut.) Fire-chemise, a piece of canvas thickened by means of a melted composition, and covered with sawdust: used in branders and fire-ships. *Camisa de una vela*, (Naut.) The body of a sail. *Tomar la mujer en camisa*, To marry a woman without money. *¿ Estás en tu camisa ?* Are you in your senses ? *Jugar hasta la camisa*, To play the shirt off one's back. *Meterse en camisa de once varas*, To interfere in other people's affairs; to undertake very difficult or dangerous business, or above one's power or means. *Vender hasta la camisa*, To sell all to the last shirt. *Saltar de su camisa*, (Met.) To jump out of one's skin. *No llegarle a uno la camisa al cuerpo*, To be frightened, to be anxious. *Más cerca está de la carne la camisa que el jubón*, Blood is thicker than water; relatives are to be preferred to acquaintances.
Camisería [cah-me-say-ree'-ah], *f.* Shirt-store.
Camisero [cah-me-say'-ro], *m.* Shirt-maker.
Camiseta [cah-me-say'-tah], *f.* 1. Undershirt. *V.* Elástica. 2. (Obs.) Short shirt or shift with wide sleeves. 3. Chemisette.
Camisola [cah-me-so'-lah], *f.* 1. Ruffled shirt. 2. Dicky. *Camisola de fuerza*. A strait-jacket.
Camisolín [cah-me-so-leen'], *m.* Shirt-front, tucker, wimple.
Camisón [cah-me-sone'], *m.* 1. (Aug.) Long and wide shirt. 2. Frock worn by labourers and workmen. 3. (Amer.) Gown, a woman's upper garment. 4. (Cuba and Puerto Rico) Chemise.
Camisote [cah-me-so'-tay], *m.* Ancient armour.
Camita [cah-mee'-tah], *f. dim.* Small bed, pallet, or cot.
Camón [cah-mone'], *m.* 1. (Aug.) Large bed. 2. A portable throne placed in the chancel when a king is present in the royal chapel. 3. Frame of laths, which serves to form an arch. *Camón de vidrios*, Partition made by a glass frame.—*pl.* 1. Felloes of cart-wheels, shod with evergreen oak instead of iron. 2. Incurvated pieces of timber in the wheels of corn-mills.
Camoncillo [cah-mon-theel'-lyo], *m.* State stool in a drawing-room; a cricket richly garnished.
Camorra [cah-mor'-rah], *f.* (Coll.) Quarrel, dispute.
Camorrear [cah-mor-ray-ar'], *vn.* (Coll.) To dispute often.
Camorrista [cah-mor-rees'-tah], *com.* (Coll.) Noisy, quarrelsome person.
Camote [cah-mo'-tay], *m.* (Bot.) A variety of sweet potato. Convolvulus batatas.
Campal [cam-pahl'], *a.* Belonging to the field and encampments. *Batalla campal*, Pitched battle.
Campamento [cam-pah-men'-to], *m.* Encampment, camp.
Campana [cam-pah'-nah], *f.* 1. Bell. 2. Bell glass, receiver. Any thing which has the shape of a bell. 3. (Met.) Parish church, parish. *Esa tierra está debajo de la campana de tal parte*, That land is situated in the parish of, etc. 4. Bottom of a well made in the form of a bell. 5. In woollen manufactories, iron hoop, serving to keep the yarn from the bottom of the dyeing copper. 6. (Arch.) Drum, corbel. *Campana de vidrio*, A bell-shaped glass vessel. *Campana de chimenea*, Mantel, the funnel of a chimney when made in the form of a bell. *Campaña de rebuzo*, Diving-bell. *Campana de rebato*, Alarm-bell. *A campana herida, á campana tañida* or *a toque de campana*, At the sound of the bell. *Oír campanas y no saber dónde*, To have heard of a fact, but not to be well informed of its true nature and complexion. *No haber oído campanas*, Not to be informed of the most common things.
Campanada [cam-pah-nah'-dah], *f.* Sound produced by the clapper striking against the bell. *Dar campanada*, (Met.) To cause scandal; to make a noise.
Campanario [cam-pah-nah'-re-o], *m.* 1. Belfry. 2. (Coll.) Noddle, head. 3. Rack in velvet-looms.
Campanear [cam-pah-nay-ar'], *va.* 1. To ring the bell frequently. 2. To divulge, to noise about. *Allá se las campaneen*, (Met.) Not to be willing to interfere in affairs foreign to one's self.
Campanela [cam-pah-nay'-lah], *f.* Sudden motion of the feet in dancing.
Campaneo [cam-pah-nay'-o], *m.* 1. Bell-ringing, chime. 2. *V.* Contoneo.
Campanero [cam-pah-nay'-ro], *m.* 1. Bell-founder. 2. Bellman. 3. A bird of Venezuela, so called from the quality of its voice.
Campaneta [cam-pah-nay'-tah], *f. dim.* Small bell.
Campaniforme [cam-pa-ne-for'-may], *a.* (Bot.) Campaniform, bell-shaped. *V.* Campanudo.
Campanil [cam-pah-neel'], *m.* 1. Small belfry.—*a.* 2. *Metal campanil*, Bell-metal.
Campanilla [cam-pah-neel'-lyah], *f.* 1. (Dim.) Small bell, hand-bell. 2. Small bubble. 3. (Anat.) Uvula. 4. Little tassel for ladies' gowns. 5. (Naut.) Cabin-bell. 6. (Bot.) Bell-flower. Narcissus bulbocodium. 7. *Campanillas de otoño*, (Bot.) Autumnal snowflake, garden daffodil. Leucojum autumnale. *De campanillas* or *de muchas campanillas*, Of importance or consideration. *Tener mu-*

chas campanillas, (Met.) To be loaded with honours and titles.

Campanillazo [cam-pah-neel-lyah'-tho], *m.* 1. Violent ringing of a bell. 2. Signal given with a bell.

Campanillear [cam-pah-neel-lyay-ar'], *va.* To ring a small bell often.

Campanillero [cam-pah-neel-lyay'-ro], *m.* Bellman, public crier.

Campanino [cam-pah-nee'-no], *a.* Applied to a kind of marble.

Campante [cam-pahn'-tay], *pa.* 1. Excelling, surpassing. 2. Buoyant, triumphant, cheerful. 3. Intrepid, robust.

Campanudo, da [cam-pah-noo'-do, dah], *a.* 1. Wide, puffed up, bell-shaped: applied to clothes. 2. (Bot.) Bell-shaped, campanulate: spoken of flowers. 3. Pompous, lofty, high-sounding: applied to style.

Campánula [cam-pah'-noo-lah], *f.* (Bot.) Bell-flower, campanula.

Campanulado, da [cam-pah-noo-lah'-do, dah]. *a.* (Bot.) Campanulate, bell-shaped.

Campaña [cam-pah'-nyah], *f.* 1. Campaign, level country. 2. Campaign of an army. *Campaña naval*, (Naut.) Cruise. *Víveres de campaña*, (Naut.) Sea provisions, stores. *Batir* or *correr la campaña*, To reconnoitre the enemy's camp. *Estar* or *hallarse en campaña*, To make a campaign.

Campañola [cam-pah-nyo'-lah], *f.* The water-rat.

Campar [cam-par'], *vn.* 1. To encamp, to be encamped. 2. To excel in abilities, arts, and sciences. *Campar con su estrella*, To be fortunate or successful.

Campeador [cam-pay-ah-dor'], *m.* 1. (Obs.) Combater, warrior. 2. A surname applied particularly to the Cid, Rodrigo Díaz de Vivar.

Campear [cam-pay-ar'], *vn.* 1. To be in the field. 2. To frisk about: applied to brutes. *Campear de sol a sombra*, To be at work from morning to night. 3. To be eminent; to excel.

Campechano, na [cam-pay-chah'-no, nah], *a.* 1. Frank, hearty, ready for amusement. 2. Native of or belonging to Campeachy.

Campeche [cam-pay'-chay], *m.* Campeachy-wood, log-wood. Hematopylon campechianum.

Campeón [cam-pay-on'], *m.* 1. Champion, combatant. 2. Champion, a judicial combatant, either in his own case or another's.

Campero, ra [cam-pay'-ro, rah], *a.* 1. Exposed to the weather in the open field. 2. (Mex.) Having a gait like gentle trotting, pacing.

Campero [cam-pay'-ro], *m.* 1. Friar who superintends a farm. 2. One who inspects another's lands and fields. 3. Pig brought up in the fields.

Campesino, na, Campestre [cam-pay-see'-no, nah, cam-pes'-tray], *a.* Rural, campestral, rustic.—*m.* & *f.* A countryman, countrywoman.

Campillo [cam-peel'-lyo], *m. dim.* Small field.

Campiña [cam-pee'-nyah], *f.* Flat tract of arable land, field, campaign.

Campo [cahm'-po], *m.* 1. Country. 2. Any tract of flat and even country. 3. Field, space, range of things. 4. Crops, trees, plantations. 5. Ground of silks and other stuffs. 6. Camp. 7. Ground on which an army is drawn up. 8. Ground of a painting. 9. *Campo santo*, Burial-ground, cemetery. *Están perdidos los campos*, The crops have failed. *Campo abierto*, Plain, an open country. *Campo volante*, A flying camp. *Campo de batalla*, Field of battle. *Descubrir campo* or *el campo*, 1. To reconnoitre the enemy's camp. 2. (Met.) To inquire how the matter stands. *Hacer campo*, 1. To clear the way. 2. (Obs.) To engage in close combat. *Hacerse al campo*, To retreat, to flee from danger. *Dejar el campo abierto, libre*, etc. To decline an undertaking where there are competitors. *Hombre de campo* or *del campo*, One who leads a country life. *Ir a campo travieso*, To make a short cut. *Partir el campo*, or *el sol*, To mark the ground of the combatants. *Dar campo a la fantasía*, To give free range to one's fancy. *Quedar el campo por uno*, To come off victorious. *Quedar en el campo*, To be killed. *Salir al campo*, To go out to fight a duel. *Campo a campo*, (Mil.) Force to force. *El campo fértil no descansado tórnase estéril*, All work and no play makes Jack a dull boy. (Literally, a fruitful field not fallowed turns unfruitful.)

Campo de concentración [cahm'-po day con-then-trah-the-on'], *m.* Concentration camp.

Camuesa [cah-moo-ay'-sah], *f.* Pippin, an apple. *Camuesa blanca*, White pippin. *Camuesa almizcleña*, A musk-apple.

Camueso [cah-moo-ay'-so], *m.* 1. (Bot.) Pippin-tree. Pyrus malus, *L.* 2. Simpleton, fool.

Camuflaje [cah-moo-flah'-hay], *m.* Camouflage.

Camuza [cah-moo'-thah], *f.* Chamois goat. *V.* Gamuza.

Camuzón [cah-moo-thone'], *m.* *aug.* Large chamois-skin.

Can [cahn], *m.* 1. (Ant.) Dog. 2. (Arch.) Bracket, shoulder, modillion, corbel. 3. (Poet.) Dog-star. *V.* Canícula. 4. (Obs.) Ace in dice. 5. Trigger of guns, etc. 6. Ancient piece of ordnance. *Can rostro*, (Obs.) Pointer or setting-dog. *Can de levantar*, Dog which starts the game. *Can de busca*, Terrier. *Can que mata al lobo*, Wolf-dog. *De hombre que no habla y de can que no ladra, guárdate mucho, porque de ordinario son traidores*, Beware of the man who does not talk, and of the dog which does not bark, for commonly they are both traitors.

Cana [cah'-nah], *f.* 1. Long measure, containing about two ells. 2. Gray hair. *Peinar canas*, To grow old. *No peinar muchas canas*, To die young. *Tener canas*, To be old: it is also applied to things. *Echar una cana al aire*, To divert one's self.

Canaballa [cah-nah-bahl'-lyah], *f.* (Naut.) Fishing-boat.

Canadiense [cah-nah-de-en'-say], *a.* Canadian.

Canado [cah-nah'-do], *a.* (Obs.) *V.* Candado.

Canal [cah-nahl'], *f.* 1. Any of the paths by which the waters and vapours circulate in the bosom of the earth. 2. Drinking-trough for cattle. 3. Gutter, eaves-trough; pantile or pentile. 4. Duct or tube by which secretions of the body are conducted. 5. Comb of the loom, among weavers. 6. A domestic animal killed and dressed; particularly the hog. 7. Hemp which has been once hackled. 8. Front edge of a book. 9. Crease, slot (metal work).—*m.* 10. Canal, an artificial water-way. 11. Channel, a strait between islands or continents. 12. Channel, navigable entrance to a harbour. 13. Channel, bed of a river. 14. Bed of a hot-press. 15. Pole of copper. (Tel.) *En canal*, From top to bottom. *Canal de la Mancha*, (Naut.) British channel. *Canal de tocino*, A hog killed and dressed. *Canal de un brulote*, (Naut.) Train-trough of a fire-ship.

Canalado, da [cah-nah-lah'-do, dah], *a.* *V.* Acanalado.

Canaleja [cah-nah-lay'-hah], *f.* 1. (Dim.) Small drinking-trough for cattle. 2. In corn-mills, small channel to convey grain from the hopper to the mill-stones; mill-spout. 3. A priest's hat shaped like a trough.

Canalera [cah-nah-lay'-rah], *f.* (Prov.) Gutter.

Canalete [cah-nah-lay'-tay], *m.* Paddle, a small oar.

Canalita [cah-nah-lee'-tah], *f. dim.* Small channel or canal.

Canalizar [cah-nah-le-thar'], *va.* To channel, to canalize, provide an outlet.

Canalizo [cah-nah-lee'-tho], *m.* Narrow channel between two islands or sand-banks.

Canalla [cah-nahl'-lyah], *f.* 1. Mob, rabble, multitude, populace, canaille. 2. (Obs.) Pack of hounds.

Canalluza [cah-nal-lyoo'-thah], *f.* Roguery, vagrancy.

Canalón [cah-nah-lone'], *m.* Large gutter or spout, eaves-trough, leader, water-way, rain-conductor.

Canameño [cah-nah-may'-nyo], *m.* A travelling hammock. (Cent. Am.)

Canana [cah-nah'-nah], *f.* 1. A kind of cartridge-belt. 2. Fricassee of chickens.

Canapé [cah-nah-pay'], *m.* 1. Couch or seat with a mattress, to sit or lie on. 2. Settee. 3. Lounge.

Canariense [cah-nah-re-en'-say], *a.* Canary, belonging to the Canary Islands.

Canario [cah-nah'-re-o], *m.* 1. Canary-bird. 2. A dance introduced into Spain by natives of the Canaries. 3. (Naut.) Barge used in the Canary Islands. 4. *¡ Canario ! int.* Zounds!

Canasta [cah-nahs'-tah], *f.* 1. Basket, hamper. 2. Canasta, card game.

Canastero, ra [cah-nas-tay'-ro, rah], *m.* & *f.* Basket-maker.

Canastilla [cah-nas-teel'-lyah], *f.* 1. (Dim.) Small basket. 2. An infant's basket; wardrobe for a baby. 3. A bride's trousseau.

Canastillo [cah-nas-teel'-lyo], *m.* 1. Small tray made of twigs of osier; pannier. 2. Small basket. 3. Maund, a hand-basket.

Canasto, Canastro [cah-nahs'-to, cah-nahs'-tro], *m.* Large basket. *¡ Canastos ! int.* Denoting surprise or annoyance.

Cáncamo [cahn'-cah-mo], *m.* 1. (Naut.) Bolt-ring, to which the breeches and tackle of guns are fixed. *Cáncamos de argolla*, Ring-bolts. *Cáncamos de gancho*, Hook-bolts. *Cáncamos de ojo*, Eye-bolts. 2. A rare gum, or blending of gums resembling myrrh.

Cancamusa [can-cah-moo'-sah], *f.* Trick to deceive. *Ya le entiendo la cancamusa*, I am aware of the device.

Cancán [cahn-cahn'], *m.* Cancan, a French dance of indecent character.

Cáncana [cahn'-cah-nah], *f.* Cricket, a form or stool on which boys are whipped at school.

Cancanilla [can-cah-neel'-lyah], *f.* (Obs.) 1. Thing to play a trick with. 2. Deception, fraud.

Cáncano [cahn'-cah-no], *m.* (Coll.) Louse.

Cancel [can-thel'], *m.* 1. Wooden screen at the doors of churches and halls. 2. Glass-case in chapel behind which the king stands. 3. (Obs.) Limits or extent of a thing.

Cancela [can-thay'-lah], *f.* A grating or screen of open ironwork between the porch and the yard.

Cancelación, Canceladura [can-thay-lah-the-on', can-thay-lah-doo'-rah], *f.* Cancellation, expunging, obliteration, closing up.

Cancelar [can-thay-lar'], *va.* To cancel or annul a writing. *Cancelar de la memoria,* (Met.) To efface from the memory.

Cancelaría, Cancelería [can-thay-lah-ree'-ah, lay-ree'-ah], *f.* Papal chancery, the court at Rome, whence apostolic grants and licenses are expedited.

Cancelario [can-thay-lah'-re-o], *m.* Chancellor in universities who grants degrees.

Cancellería [can-thel-lyay-ree'-ah], *f.* (Obs.) Chancery.

Cáncer [cahn'-ther], *m.* 1. Cancer, virulent ulcer. 2. Cancer, one of the signs of the zodiac.

Cancerarse [can-thay-rar'-say], *vr.* 1. To be afflicted with a cancer. 2. To cancerate or become a cancer.

Cancerbero [can-ther-bay'-ro], *m.* 1. Cerberus, the three-headed dog which guarded the gate of the nether world. 2. (Met.) A severe and incorruptible guard. 3. A worthless gatekeeper.

Cancerígeno, na [can-thay-ree'-hay-no, nah], *a.* Carcinogenic, cancerogenic.

Canceroso, sa [can-thay-ro'-so, sah], *a.* Cancerous.

Cancilla [can-theel'-lyah], *f.* (Prov.) Wicker-door or wicker-gate.

Canciller [can-theel-lyerr'], *m.* Chancellor. *Gran canciller de las Indias,* High chancellor of the Indies.

Cancilleresco, ca [can-theel-lyay-res'-co, cah], *a.* Belonging to the writing characters used in chancery business.

Cancillería [can-theel-lyay-ree'-ah], *f.* (Obs.) *V.* CHANCILLERÍA.

Canción [can-the-on'], *f.* 1. Song, verses set to music. 2. Poem of one or more stanzas, a lay. *Volver a la misma canción,* To return to the old tune, to repeat the old story.

Cancioncica, illa, ita [can-the-on-thee'-cah, eel'-lyah, ee'-tah], *f. dim.* Canzonet, a little song.

Cancionero [can-the-o-nay'-ro], *m.* 1. Song-book. 2. Song-writer.

Cancionista [can-the-o-nees'-tah], *m.* (Obs.) Author or singer of songs.

Canco [cahn'-co], *m.* (Chile) 1. Earthen pot. 2. Flower pot. 3. Big hip. 4. (Bol.) Buttocks, hips.

Cancriforme [can-cre-for'-may], *a.* Cancriform, having the shape of a crab.

Cancrinita [can-cre-nee'-tah], *f.* Cancrinite, a variously coloured silicate, which crystallizes in the hexagonal system.

Cancro [cahn'-cro], *m.* (Obs.) *V.* CÁNCER.

Cancrófago, ga [can-cro'-fah-go, gah], *a.* Crab-eating.

Cancroideo, ea [can-cro-e-day'-o, ah], *a.* Cancroid, resembling cancer.

Cancha [cahn'-chah], *f.* 1. Field, ball park, court. *Cancha de tenis,* Tennis court. 2. Toasted corn. 3. (Peru) Popcorn.

Canchalagua, Canchelagua, Canchilagua [can-chah-lah'-goo-ah], *f.* (Bot.) A medicinal herb growing in Peru. Gentiana canchilagua.

Candado [can-dah'-do], *m.* 1. Padlock. 2. Pendant, ear-ring. *Echar* or *poner candado a los labios,* (Met.) To keep a secret, to be silent. *Candados,* Cavities around the frog of horses' feet.

Cándamo [cahn'-dah-mo], *m.* Ancient rustic dance.

Candar [can-dar'], *va.* (Obs.) To lock, shut.

Cándara [cahn'-dah-rah], *f.* (Prov.) Frame of laths for sifting sand, earth, and gravel.

Cande [cahn'-day], *a.* Sugar-candy. *V.* AZÚCAR.

Candeal [can-day-ahl'], *a.* *Trigo candeal,* White wheat, summer wheat. *Pan candeal,* Bread made of the white wheat.

Candeda [can-day'-dah], *f.* Blossom of the walnut-tree.

Candela [can-day'-lah], *f.* 1. Candle. 2. Flower or blossom of the chestnut-tree. 3. Candlestick. 4. Inclination of the balance-needle to the thing weighed. 5. (Prov.) Light, fire. *Arrimarse a la candela,* (Prov.) To draw near the fire. *Acabarse la candela,* (Met.) To be near one's end. *Acabarse la candela* or *la candelilla en almonedas y subastas,* To sell by inch of candle, to knock down a thing to the highest bidder, the candle being burnt. *Estar con la candela en la mano,* To be dying, it being customary in some parts of Spain to put a *blessed* candle in the hand of a dying person. *La mujer y la tela no la cates a la candela,* Neither a wife nor cloth should be examined by candle-light.

Candelabro [can-day-lah'-bro], *m.* Candlestick. *V.* CANDELERO.

Candelada [can-day-lah'-dah], *f.* (Prov.) Sudden blaze from straw or brushwood. *V.* HOGUERA.

Candelaria [can-day-lah'-re-ah], *f.* 1. Candlemas. 2. (Bot.) Mullein. Verbascum lychnitis. *V.* GORDOLOBO.

Candelejón [can-day-lay-hone'], *a.* (So. Am.) Candid, simple-minded, dumb.

Candelerazo [can-day-lay-rah'-tho], *m.* 1. (Aug.) Large candlestick. 2. Stroke or blow given with a candlestick.

Candelería [can-day-lay-ree'-ah], *f.* (Obs.) Tallow and wax chandler's shop. *V.* VELERÍA.

Candelero [can-day-lay'-ro], *m.* 1. Candlestick. *Candelero con muchos brazos,* Chandelier. 2. (Obs.) Wax or tallow chandler. 3. Lamp. 4. Fishing-torch. *Estar en candelero,* (Met.) To be high in office, to hold an exalted station. *Candelero de ojo,* (Naut.) Eye-stanchion, or iron stay with a ring. *Candelero ciego,* Blind-stanchion, or iron stay without a ring. *Candeleros,* (Naut.) Stanchions or crotches, pieces of timber which support the waist-trees. *Candeleros del toldo,* Awning-stanchions. *Candeleros de los portalones,* Entering-rope stanchions. *Candeleros de trincheras y parapetos,* Quarter-netting stanchions.

Candeletón [can-day-lay-tone'], *m.* Large stanchion.

Candelilla [can-day-leel'-lyah], *f.* 1. (Surg.) Bougie, catheter. 2. Blossom of poplars and other trees. Catkin, ament. *Hacer la candelilla,* To stand on the hands and head, as boys do in play. *Le hacen candelillas los ojos,* (Coll.) He is half-seas over, or his eyes sparkle with the fumes of wine. *Muchas candelillas hacen un cirio pascual,* or *muchos pocos hacen un mucho,* Light gains make a heavy purse.

Candelizas [can-day-lee'-thas], *f. pl.* (Naut.) Brails, small ropes reeved through a block. *Candelizas de barlovento,* Weather-braces. *Candelizas de sotavento,* Lee-braces. *Cargar las mayores sobre las candelizas,* To brail up the courses.

Candencia [can-den'-the-ah], *f.* (Littl. us.) Incandescence, white heat.

Candente [can-den'-tay], *a.* Incandescent, red-hot, tending to a white heat.

Candi [cahn'-de], *a.* *Azúcar candi,* Sugar-candy, rock-candy.

Candial [can-de-ahl'], *a.* *V.* CANDEAL.

Cándidamente [cahn'-de-dah-men-tay], *adv.* Candidly.

Candidato [can-de-dah'-to], *m.* Candidate.

Candidatura [can-de-dah-too'-rah], *f.* 1. Candidacy, soliciting votes. 2. A list of those who aspire to some elective position.

Candidez [can-de-deth'], *f.* 1. Whiteness. 2. Candour, sincerity, purity of mind. 3. Candidness, ingenuousness. 4. Simplicity.

Cándido, da [cahn'-de-do, dah], *a.* 1. White, snowy, gray, pale. 2. Candid, guileless. 3. Simple.

Candil [can-deel'], *m.* 1. A kitchen or stable lamp. 2. (Obs.) Lamp with oil, etc. 3. Cock of a hat. 4. Long irregular fold in petticoats. 5. (Obs.) Fishing-torch. *V.* CANDELERO. 6. (Mex.) A chandelier. *Puede arder en un candil,* It would burn in a lamp: applied to generous wine and to persons of brilliant parts: it is used ironically in the last sense. 7. Top of a stag's horn. *Escoger una cosa a moco de candil,* To examine closely, to choose after a close examination. *Baile de candil,* A ball held by the light of a poor lamp.

Candilada [can-de-lah'-dah], *f.* 1. (Obs.) Small lamp full of oil. 2. Oil spilt from a lamp. 3. Spot of lamp-oil.

Candilazo [can-de-lah'-tho], *m.* (Coll.) Blow or stroke given with a kitchen lamp.

Candileja [can-de-lay'-hah], *f.* 1. Inner part of a kitchen lamp. 2. The footlights of a theatre. 3. (Bot.) Willows, deadly carrot. Thapsia villosa.

Candilejera [can-de-lay-hay'-rah], *f.* (Bot.) Spanish birth-wort. Aristolochia bœtica.

Candilejo [can-de-lay'-ho], *m. dim.* 1. Small kitchen lamp. 2. (Bot.) *V.* LUCÉRNULA.

Candilera [can-de-lay'-rah], *f.* (Bot.) Lamp-wick. Phlomis lychnitis.

Candilón [can-de-lone'], *m. aug.* Large open lamp. *Estar con el candilón en los hospitales,* To be dying. It is used in several hospitals of Spain, where it is customary to put a large lamp near the bed of a dying person.

Candiota [can-de-o'-tah], *f.* 1. Barrel or keg for carrying wine in vintage-time. 2. Large earthen jar, the inside of which is pitched, wherein wine is fermented. 3. *com.* An inhabitant of the island of Candia.

Candiotera [can-de-o-tay'-rah], *f.* A wine-cellar: storage place of casks, tuns, etc.

Candonga [can-don'-gah], *f.* 1. Mean, servile civility, intended to deceive. 2. Merry, playful trick. *Dar candonga* or *chasco,* To play a carnival trick. 3. Old mule unfit for service. 4. An old, ugly woman. 5. (Col.) Earring.

Candongo, ga [can-don'-go, gah], *a.* A cunning, fawning person. *Seda de candongo* or *de candongos,* (Prov.) The finest silk reeled up into three small skeins.

Candonguear [can-don-gay-ar'], *va.* (Coll.) To jeer, to sneer, to turn into ridicule.

Candonguero, ra [can-don-gay'-ro, rah], *a.* (Coll.) Applied to a cunning person who is ludicrously mischievous or plays bad tricks.

Candor [can-dor'], *m.* 1. (Obs.) Supreme whiteness. 2. (Met.) Candour, purity of mind, ingenuousness, fairness, frankness, openness.

Candoroso, sa [can-do-ro'-so, sah], *a.* Ingenuous, frank, honest, straightforward.

Caneca [cah-nay'-cah], *f.* 1. Glazed liquor bottle made of clay. 2. (Arg.) Wooden tub. 3. (Cuba) Hot-water bottle made of earthenware. 4. (Cuba) Liquid measure of 19 liters.

Canecer [cah-nay-therr'], *vn.* (Obs.) *V.* ENCANECER.

Canecillo [cah-nay-theel'-lyo], *m.* (Arch.) Corbel, modillion, truss, cantilever; console.

Canela [cah-nay'-lah], *f.* (Bot.) Cinnamon. Laurus cinnamomum. *Agua de canela*, Cinnamon-water.

Canelado, da [cah-nay-lah'-do, dah], *a.* *V.* ACANELADO.

Canelo [cah-nay'-lo], *m.* (Bot.) Cinnamon-tree or cinnamon laurel. Laurus cinnamomum.

Canelón [cah-nay-lone'], *m.* 1. Gutter. *V.* CANALÓN. 2. Sweetmeat. 3. Icicle. 4. (Bot.) A kind of bastard cinnamon, commonly called *Canelón de Santa Fé*. *Canelones*, End of a cat of nine-tails, thicker and more twisted than the rest.

Canesú [cah-nay-soo'], *m.* 1. A waist for women's wear, short and without sleeves. 2. Upper part of a shirt for either sex.

Caney [cah-nay'-e], *m.* 1. A log-cabin. 2. (Cuban) Bend of a river; a bight.

Canez (cah-neth'], *f.* (Obs.) Hair hoary or gray with age; old age.
(*Yo canezco, yo canezca*, from *Canecer*. *V.* CONOCER.)

Canforero [can-fo-ray'-ro], *m.* The camphor-tree.

Canga [cahn'-gah], *f.* Cangue, a heavy wooden collar or yoke, worn around the neck by convicts in China as a punishment.

Cangalla [can-gahl'lyah], 1. (Salv.) Tattered shred of clothing. 2. (Col.) *m.* or *f.* Thinned-out animal or person. 3. (Arg. & Peru) A coward. 4. (Bol.) Packsaddle. 5. (Arg. & Chile) Mineral wastings.

Cangallar [can-gahl-lyar'], *va.* (Ch. & Arg.) To ransack metal in the mines.

Cangilón [can-he-lone'], *m.* 1. Earthen jar or pitcher. 2. Oblong earthen jar fastened to the rope of a draw-well, or to a wheel for lifting water. 3. Metal tankard for wine or water.

Cangreja [can-gray'-hah], *a.* *Vela cangreja*, (Naut.) Boom-sail, brig-sail, or gaff-sail.

Cangrejal [can-gray-hahl'], *m.* (Amer.) A spot frequented by crabs.

Cangrejo [can-gray'-ho], *m.* 1. (Zool.) Craw-fish, crab. 2. Truckle-cart. 3. Trolley. *Adelantar como el cangrejo*, To retrograde, lose by an enterprise. *Andar como el cangrejo*, To go backward.

Cangrejuelo [can-gray-hoo-ay'-lo], *m.* *dim.* Small craw-fish.

Cangrena [can-gray'-nah], *f.* Gangrene, mortification. *V.* GANGRENA.

Cangrenarse [can-gray-nar'-say], *vr.* To be afflicted with gangrene or mortification. *V.* GANGRENARSE.

Cangrenoso, sa [can-gray-no'-so, sah], *a.* Gangrenous, mortified.

Cania [cah'-ne-ah], *f.* (Bot.) Small nettle. Urtica urens.

Caníbal [ca-nee'-bal], *m.* Cannibal, a man-eater.

Canicas [cah-nee'-cahs], *f. pl.* Marbles.

Canicie [ca-nee'-the-ay], *f.* Whiteness of the hair.

Canícula [ca-nee'-coo-lah], *f.* 1. (Astr.) Dog-star. 2. V. CANICULARES. *Entra la canícula*, The dog-days begin. *Canícula marina*, (Zool.) Lesser spotted dog-fish. Squalus catulus.

Canicular [ca-ne-coo-lar'], *a.* Canicular, belonging to the dog-star.

Caniculares [ca-ne-coo-lah'-res], *m. pl.* Dog-days.

Cánido [ca-nee'-do], *m.* Kind of parrot found in the West Indies.

Canijo, ja [ca-nee'-ho, hah], *a.* & *m.* & *f.* Weak, infirm, sickly. *Fulano es un canijo*, He is a weak, puny being.

Canilla [ca-neel'-lyah], *f.* 1. A long bone of either extremity. *Canilla de la pierna*, Shin-bone. *Canilla del brazo*, Arm-bone. 2. Any of the principal bones of the wing of a fowl. 3. Stop-cock, faucet, spigot. 4. Reel, bobbin, spool; quill put into a shuttle on which the woof is wound. 5. Unevenness or inequality of the woof, in point of thickness or colour. *Irse como una canilla* or *de canillas*, To labour under a violent diarrhœa. *Irse como una canilla*, To let the tongue run like the clapper of a mill.

Canillado, da [ca-neel-lyah'-do, dah], *a.* *V.* ACANILLADO.

Canillera [ca-neel-lyay'-rah], *f.* 1. Ancient armour for the shin-bone. 2. Woman who distributes thread to be wound on spools.

Canillero [ca-neel-lyay'-ro], *m.* 1. Hole in a cask or vat to draw off its contents. 2. Weaver's quill-winder.

Canillita [cah-neel-lyee'-tah], *m.* (Arg.) A newsboy.

Canina [ca-nee'-nah], *f.* Excrement of dogs.

Caninamente [ca-ne-nah-men'-tay], *adv.* In a passionate, snarling manner; like a dog.

Caninez [ca-ne-neth'], *f.* Inordinate appetite. *V.* HAMBRE CANINA.

Canino, na [ca-nee'-no, nah], *a.* Canine. *Hambre canina*, Canine appetite, inordinate hunger. *Dientes caninos*, Eye-teeth or canine-teeth. *Músculo canino*, Canine muscle, which serves to elevate the upper lip.

Canje [cahn'-hay], *m.* Exchange, used only in speaking of prisoners of war, ratified treaties, or the credentials of diplomatists. (It. cangio.)

Canjear [can-hay-ar'], *va.* To exchange prisoners of war, treaties, or credentials.

Cano, na [cah'-no, nah], *a.* 1. Hoary, hoar, frosty, gray-headed. 2. (Met.) Deliberate, prudent, judicious.

Canoa [ca-no'-ah], *f.* Canoe, a boat used by the Indians.

Canoero [ca-no-ay'-ro], *m.* One who conducts a canoe.

Canoi [ca-no'-e], *m.* (Amer.) Basket used by Indians on a fishing party.

Canoita [ca-no-ee'-tah], *m. dim.* Small canoe.

Canon [cah'-non], *m.* 1. Canon, the decision of an ecclesiastical council relative to the doctrines or discipline of the church. 2. Catalogue of the books which compose the Holy Scriptures. 3. (Law) Fee paid in acknowledgment of superiority in a higher lord. 4. Catalogue, list. 5. (Print.) Canon. a large sort of type. *Canon doble*, Double canon, great canon. *Cánones*, Canons or canonical law. 6. (Mus.) Canon. A composition in which the music sung by one part is, after a short rest, sung by another part, note for note.

Canonesa [ca-no-nay'-sah], *f.* Canoness, a woman who lives in a religious house, and observes its rules, without having taken the vows of a monastic life.

Canonical [ca-no-ne-cahl'], *a.* Canonical, relating to canons.

Canónicamente [ca-no'-ne-cah-men-tay] *adv.* Canonically.

Canonicato [ca-no-ne-cah'-to], *m.* *V.* CANONJÍA.

Canónico, ca [ca-no'-ne-co, cah], *a.* 1. Canonical, canonic. *Iglesia o casa canónica*, House or monastery of regular canons. 2. Canonical; applied to the books which compose the Holy Scriptures.

Canóniga [ca-no'-ne-gah], *f.* A siesta, or nap taken before dining.

Canónigo [ca-no'-ne-go], *m.* Canon or prebendary. *Canónigo reglar*, A canon of Pamplona and of the Premonstratensian or Norbertinian order of religious.

Canonista [ca-no-nees'-tah], *m.* Canonist, a professor or student of the canon law.

Canonizable [ca-no-ne-thah'-blay], *a.* Worthy of canonization.

Canonización [ca-no-ne-thah-the-on'], *f.* Canonization, consecration.

Canonizar [ca-no-ne-thar'], *va.* 1. To canonize, to consecrate, to declare one a saint. 2. (Met.) To applaud or praise a thing. 3. (Met.) To prove a thing good.

Canonje [ca-non'-hay], *m.* (Obs.) *V.* CANÓNIGO.

Canonjía [ca-non-hee'-ah], *f.* Canonry, canonship, prebend or benefice of a canon; canonicate.

Canoro, ra [ca-no'-ro, rah], *a.* 1. Canorous, musical. 2. Shrill, loud.

Canoso, sa [ca-no'-so, sah], *a.* 1. Hoary, hoar, frosty, gray-headed. 2. Old.

Cansadamente [can-sah-dah-men'-tay], *adv.* Importunely, troublesomely.

Cansado, da [can-sah'-do, dah], *a.* 1. Weary, wearied, exhausted, tired. 2. Tedious, tiresome, troublesome. *Una pelota cansada*, A spent ball. *Una vista cansada*, An impaired eyesight. *Una lámina cansada*, A worn-out copper-plate. 3. Performed with pain or fatigue.—*pp.* of CANSAR.

Cansado [can-sah'-do], *m.* Bore.

Cansancio [can-sahn'-the-o], *m.* Weariness, lassitude, fatigue.

Cansar [can-sar'], *va.* 1. To weary, to tire, to fatigue, to overcome. 2. To harass, to molest, to bore. 3. To exhaust land.—*vr.* To tire one's self, to be fatigued, to grow weary.

Cansera [can-say'-rah], *f.* Fatigue, weariness. *Fulano es un cansera*, He is a pesterer.

Cansino, na [can-see'-no, nah], *a.* Worn by work: said of beasts.

Cantable [can-tah'-blay], *a.* 1. Tunable, harmonious, musical. 2. Pathetic, affecting.

Cantábrico, ca [can-tah'-bre-co, cah], **Cántabro, bra** [cahn'-tah-bro, brah], *a.* 1. Cantabrian, of Cantabria. 2. Name given to the part of the Atlantic Ocean which washes the northern coast of Spain.

Cantada [can-tah'-dah], *f.* Cantata, a musical composition.

Cantador [can-tah-dor'], *m.* (Obs.) *V.* CANTOR.

Cantaleta [can-ta-lay'-tah], *f.* 1. Charivari, a confused noise of voices or instruments. 2. Pun, jest, joke, humbug. *Dar cantaleta*, To deride, to laugh at, to turn into ridicule.

Cantaloup [can-tah-loop'], *m.* Cantaloup or cantaloupe.

Cantante [can-tahn'-tay], *m.* & *f.* A

singer, especially one who sings for a livelihood.

Cantar [can-tar'], *m.* (Coll.) Song set to music. *Cantares*, Canticles or Song of Solomon. *Cantares de gesta*, Old metrical romances.

Cantar [can-tar'], *va.* 1. To sing. 2. To recite in a poetical manner. 3. (Met. Coll.) To creak, to make a harsh, grinding noise. 4. (Coll.) To divulge a secret. 5. At cards, to announce the trump. *Cantar el gobierno del timón*, (Naut.) To cond or con, to direct the steersman how to steer. *Cantar a libro abierto*, To sing off-hand. *Cantar de plano*, To make a plain and full confession. *Cantar la victoria*, (Met.) To triumph. *Cantarle a uno la potra*, (Met.) To prognosticate a change of weather by bodily pains. *Cantar misa*, To say the first mass. *Ese es otro cantar*, That is another kind of speech. *Cantar mal y porfiar*, To chatter nonsense. *¿ Lo digo cantado o rezado ?* How would you have me say it? *Al fin se canta la gloria*, Do not triumph till all is over (or Don't whistle before you are out of the woods). *Cantar en tinaja*, (Met.) To be fond of one's own praise.

Cántara [cahn'-ta-rah], *f.* 1. Large, narrow-mouthed pitcher. *V.* CÁNTARO. 2. Wine measure containing about thirty-two pints.

Cantaral [can-ta-rahl'], *m.* (Littl. us.) Press or cupboard with drawers.

Cantarcico, illo, ito [can-tar-thee'-co, theel'-lyo, thee'-to], *m. dim.* Little song.

Cantarera [can-ta-ray'-rah], *f.* Shelf for jars, pitchers, etc.

Cantarero, ra [can-ta-ray'-ro, rah], *m.* & *f.* A dealer in earthen jars, pitchers, pans, etc.

Cantárida [can-tah'-re-dah], *f.* 1. Cantharis, Spanish-fly, lytta, the blistering fly. Lytta vesicatoria, *L.* 2. Blistering plaster made with the blistering fly. 3. Blister, the vesicle raised on the skin by the blistering plaster.

Cantarillo [can-ta-reel'-lyo], *m.* 1. (Dim.) Small jar or pitcher. 2. (Bot.) Oval-leaved androsace. Androsace maxima. *Cantarillo que muchas veces va a la fuente, o deja el asa o la frente*, The pitcher which goes often to the well gets broken at last.

Cantarín [can-ta-reen'], *m.* (Coll.) One who sings constantly.

Cantarina [can-ta-ree'-nah], *f.* A woman who sings on the stage.

Cántaro [cahn'-ta-ro], *m.* 1. Large, narrow-mouthed pitcher, and the liquid contained in it. 2. Wine measure of different sizes. 3. Vessel into which votes are put. *Estar en cántaro*, To be proposed for an office. *Entrar en cántaro*, To be liable to be chosen for the army or militia. *Llover a cántaros*, To rain by bucketfuls, to pour. *Moza de cántaro*, Water-girl; fat, bulky woman. *Volver las nueces al cántaro*, To renew a contest.

Cantatriz [can-ta-treeth'], *f.* *V.* CANTARINA.

Cantazo [can-tah'-tho], *m.* Wound given by flinging a stone.

Canteles [can-tay'-les], *m. pl.* (Naut.) Ends of old ropes put under casks to keep them steady.

Cantera [can-tay'-rah], *f.* 1. Quarry where stones are dug. 2. (Met.) Talents or genius. *Levantar una cantera*, To cause disturbances, to raise commotions.

Canterear [can-tay-ray-ar'], *va.* To hang up flitches of bacon, that the brine may run off.

Cantería [can-tay-ree'-ah], *f.* 1. Art of hewing stone, the trade of a stone-cutter. 2. Building made of hewn stone. 3. (Obs.) Quarry. 4. (Obs.) Parcel of hewn stone.

Cantero [can-tay'-ro], *m.* 1. Stone-cutter. 2. The extremity of a hard substance which can be easily separated from the rest. *Cantero de pan*, Crust of bread. *Cantero de heredad*, (Prov.) Piece of ground.

Canterón [can-tay-rone'], *m.* (Prov.) Large tract of land.

Canticio [can-tee'-the-o], *m.* (Coll.) Constant or frequent singing.

Cántico [cahn'-te-co], *m.* Canticle. *Cántico de los cánticos*, The Song of Solomon.

Cantidad [can-te-dahd'], *f.* 1. Quantity. 2. Measure, number, time used in pronouncing a syllable. 3. Quantity, large portion of a thing. *Cantidad continua*, Continued quantity. *Cantidad discreta*, Distinct or separate quantity. *Por una cantidad alzada*, For a sum of money agreed upon. *Hacer buena alguna cantidad*, To pay a sum of money due.

Cantiga [can-tee'-gah], *f.* (Obs.) *V.* CANTAR. A poetical composition divided into strophes; after each follows a refrain.

Cantil [can-teel'], *m.* Steep rock.

Cantilagua [can-te-lah'-goo-ah], *f.* (Prov.) Purging flax. Linum catharticum.

Cantilena [can-te-lay'-nah], *f.* *V.* CANTINELA.

Cantillo [can-teel'-lyo], *m. dim.* A little stone.

Cantimarones [can-te-mah-ro'-nes], *m. pl.* (Naut.) Kind of boats.

Cantimplora [can-tim-plo'-rah], *f.* 1. Siphon, a crooked tube or pipe. 2. Vessel for cooling liquors; liquor-case.

Cantina [can-tee'nah], *f.* 1. Saloon, tavern, bar, barroom. 2. Cellar for wine. 3. Canteen, shop where liquors and provisions are sold in barracks or military camps. 4. Canteen (used to cool wine on a journey or march).

Cantinela [can-te-nay'-lah], *f.* 1. Ballad. 2. Irksome repetition of a subject. *¿ Ahora se viene con esa cantinela ?* Does he come again with that old story?

Cantinero [can-te-nay'-ro], *m.* 1. Bartender. 2. Keeper of a tavern or saloon.

Cantiña [can-tee'-nyah], *f.* A song in Galicia and Asturias.

Cantizal [can-te-thahl'], *m.* Stony ground, place full of stones.

Canto [cahn'-to], *m.* 1. Singing. 2. A short poem, of heroic type. 3. Canto, a division of a long poem. 4. A chant or canticle. (Lat. cantus.) *Al canto del gallo*, At midnight. *Con un canto á los pechos*, With the utmost pleasure, with the greatest alacrity. *Echar cantos*, To be mad.

Canto, *m.* 1. End, edge, or border. 2. Extremity, point. 3. The crust (of a loaf). 4. Thickness of any thing; back of a knife. 5. The front edge of a book. 6. Dimension less than square. *A canto*, Very near. *Al canto*, By the side of. *De canto*, On edge. (Celtic kant, edge.) *El ladrillo está de canto y no de plano*, The brick stands on edge, and not flatwise.

Canto, *m.* 1. A stone, pebble. 2. Game of throwing the stone (duck on a rock). 3. Quarry-stone, block, dressed ashlar.

Cantón [can-tone'], *m.* 1. Corner. 2. (Her.) Part of an escutcheon. 3. Canton, region, tract of land, district.

Cantonada [can-to-nah'-dah], *f.* (Prov.) Corner. *Dar cantonada*, To laugh at a person on turning a corner; to disappoint a person by not taking notice of what he says or does.

Cantonal [can-to-nahl'], *a.* Cantonal, relating to the canton or district.

Cantonar [can-to-nar'], *va.* *V.* ACANTONAR.

Cantonearse [can-to-nay-ar'-say], *vr.* *V.* CONTONEARSE.

Cantoneo [can-to-nay'-o], *m.* *V.* CONTONEO.

Cantonera [can-to-nay'-rah], *f.* 1. Plate nailed to the corners of a chest, etc., to strengthen it. 2. Corner-plate, clip. 3. Angle-iron, corner bracket. 4. Wench, a woman of the town.

Cantonero, ra [can-to-nay'-ro, rah], *a.* (Obs.) Standing idle at the corner of a street.

Cantor, ra [can-tor', rah], *m.* & *f.* 1. Singer; minstrel. 2. (Obs.) One who composes hymns or psalms. 3. Small singing-bird.

Cantorcillo [can-tor-theel'-lyo], *m. dim.* Petty, worthless singer.

Cantoría [can-to-ree'-ah], *f.* (Obs.) Musical canto; singing.

Cantorral [can-tor-rahl'], *m.* Stony ground, place full of stones.

Cantuariense [can-too-ah-re-en'-say], *a.* Canterbury, of or belonging to Canterbury.

Cantuda [can-too'-dah], *f.* (Prov. La Mancha.) Brown-bread.

Cantudas [can-too'-das], *f. pl.* (Prov.) Large coarse knives for poor people.

Cantueso [can-too-ay'-so], *m.* (Bot.) French lavender, spike. Lavandula stœchas.

Canturía [can-too-ree'-ah], *f.* 1. Vocal music. 2. Musical composition. 3. Method of performing musical compositions. *Esta composición tiene buena canturía*, This piece of music may be easily sung.

Canturrear, Canturriar [can-toor-ray-ar', re-ar'], *vn.* To hum, sing in a low voice.

Cantusar [can-too-sar'], *va.* *V.* ENGATUSAR.

Canudo, da [ca-noo'-do, dah], *a.* (Obs.) Hoary, gray; ancient.

Cánula [cah'-noo-lah], *f.* (Med.) Canula, a metal tube for withdrawing fluids; often fitted with a trocar.

Canutillo [cah-noo-teel'-lyo], *m.* *V.* CANUTILLO.

Caña [cah'-nyah], *f.* 1. Cane, reed. Arundo. 2. Stem, stalk. *La caña del trigo*, Stem of corn. 3. Walking-stick. *Caña de cuentas* or *cañacoro*, Common Indian shot, or reed, cane used for walking-sticks. Canna indica. *Caña común*, Cultivated reed. Arundo donax. *Caña dulce* or *de azúcar*, or *cañamiel*, Common sugar-cane. Saccharum officinarum. 4. *V.* CANILLA for a bone. 5. Subterraneous passage in the mines of Almadén. 6. Shaft of a column or pillar. 7. Marrow. 8. Tournament. 9. (Naut.) Helm. *¡ La caña á babor !* Port the helm ! 10. Lever drill, ratchet drill. 11. Glass-blower's pipe. 12. (Carp.) Shank. 13. Reed of wind instruments. *Caña del pulmón*, (Anat.) Windpipe. *Caña de la media*, Leg of a stocking. *Caña del timón*, (Naut.) Tiller. *Caña de pescar*, Fishing-rod. *Caña de vaca*, Shin-bone of beef. *Caña de un cañón*, Chase of a gun. *Cañas de cebadera*, (Naut.) Sprit-sail sheet-blocks. *Hubo toros y cañas*, (Met.) There was the devil to pay. *Pescador de caña, más come que gana*, An angler eats more than he gets. *Parece que es caña*, (Coll.) He is truly very cunning. *¡El hombre es caña!* What a rogue that man is! *Cañas, haber* or *correr cañas*, Equestrian exercises with reed spears.

Cañada [cah-nyah'-dah], *f.* 1. Glen or dale between mountains; glade. 2. *Cañada real*, Sheep-walk for the flocks passing from the mountainous and colder parts of Spain to the flat and warmer parts. 3. (Prov.) Measure of wine. 4. (Amer.) Rivulet, brook.

Cañadicas, Cañaditas [cah-nyah-dee'-cas, dee'-tas], *f. pl.* (Prov.) Small measures for wine.

Cañafistula [cah-nyah-fees'-too-lah], *f.* Cassia fistula, the fruit of the purging cassia. Cassiæ fistulæ fructus.

Cañafistulo [can-nyah-fees'-too-lo], *m.* (Bot.) Purging cassia-tree. Cassia fistula.

Cañaheja, Cañaherla [cah-nyah-ay'-hah, cah-nyah-err'-lah], *f.* (Bot.) Common fennel-giant, or gigantic fennel. Ferula communis.

Cañahuate [cah-nyah-oo-ah'-tay], *m.* A species of lignum-vitæ which grows in Colombia.

Cañal [cah-nyahl'], *m.* 1. Weir or wear for fishing, made of canes or reeds. 2. Plantation of canes or reeds. 3. Small sluice or channel, for catching fish. 4. (Obs.) Conduit of water.

Cañaliega [cah-nyah-le-ay'-gah], *f.* (Obs.) Wear or weir for fishing.

Cáñama [cah'-nyah-mah], *f.* Assessment of taxes, paid by a village or other place. *Casa cáñama*, House exempt from taxes. *Cogedor de cáñama*, Tax-gatherer.

Cañamar [cah-nyah-mar'], *m.* Hemp-field.

Cañamazo [cah-nyah-mah'-tho], *m.* 1. (Obs.) Tow of hemp. 2. Coarse canvas made of hemp-tow. 3. Painted or checkered stuff for table-carpets, made of hemp.

Cañamelar [cah-nyah-may-lar'], *m.* Plantation of sugar-cane. Cane-field.

Cañameño, ña [cah-nyah-may'-nyo, nyah], *a.* Hempen, made of hemp.

Cañamiel [cah-nyah-me-el'], *f.* (Bot.) Sugar-cane. *V.* CAÑA DULCE.

Cañamiz [cah-nyah-meeth'], *m.* Kind of Indian vessel.

Cañamiza [cah-nyah-mee'-thah], *f.* Stalk of hemp; bullen, bun. *V.* AGRAMIZA.

Cáñamo [cah'-nyah-mo], *m.* 1. (Bot.) Hemp. Cannabis. *Cáñamo silvestre*, Bastard hemp. 2. Cloth made of hemp. 3. (Poet.) Slings, nets, rigging, and other things made of hemp. *Cáñamo en rama*, Undressed hemp.

Cañamón [cah-nyah-mone'], *m.* Hemp-seed.

Cañar [cah-nyar'], *m.* 1. Plantation of canes or reeds. 2. Weir for catching fish.

Cañareja [cah-nyah-ray'-hah], *f.* *V.* CAÑAHEJA.

Cañariego, ga [cah-nyah-re-ay'-go, gah], *a. Pellejos cañariegos*, Skins of sheep which die on the road. Applied also to the horses and men who attend the flocks migrating between the north and south of Spain.

Cañarroya [cah-nyar-ro'-yah], *f.* (Bot.) Pellitory, wall-wort. Parietaria officinalis.

Cañavera [cah-nyah-vay'-rah], *f.* (Bot.) Common reed-grass. Arundo phragmites.

Cañaveral [cah-nyah-vay-rahl'], *m.* Plantation of canes or reeds. *Recorrer los cañaverales*, To go from house to house, to get something.

Cañaverear [cah-nyah-vay-ray-ar'], *va.* *V.* ACAÑAVEREAR.

Cañavería [cah-nyah-vay-ree'-ah], *f.* (Obs.) Place where reed-grass or reeds are sold.

Cañaverero [cah-nyah-vay-ray'-ro], *m.* (Obs.) Retailer of canes or reeds.

Cañavete [cah-nyah-vay'-tay], *m.* The knife with which shepherds slaughter their animals.

Cañazo [cah-nyah'-tho], *m.* 1. Hostile blow with a cane. *Dar cañazo*, (Met.) To confound one by a rude communication. 2. Rum. (Peru.)

Cañería [cah-nyay-ree'-ah], *f.* 1. Aqueduct, a water-pipe. 2. Water-main, gas-main. 3. (Naut.) Bilge-holes.

Cañero [cah-nyay'-ro], *m.* 1. (Obs.) Conduit-maker, director of waterworks. 2. (Prov.) Angler.

Cañiger [cah-nyee-herr'], *m.* (Bot.) Kind of wild artichoke which serves for making a fire.

Cañilavado, da [cah-nye-la-vah'-do, dah], *a.* Small-limbed: applied to horses and mules.

Cañilla, ita [cah-nyeel'-lyah, ee'-tah], *f. dim.* Small cane or reed.

Cañillera [cah-nyeel-lyay'-rah], *f.* Ancient armour for the shin-bone.

Cañivete [cah-nye-vay'-tay], *m.* (Obs.) Small knife, penknife.

Cañiza [cah-nyee'-thah], *f.* Coarse linen.

Cañizal, Cañizar [cah-nye-thahl', thar'], *m.* *V.* CAÑAVERAL.

Cañizo [cah-nyee'-tho], *m.* 1. Hurdle, a frame for rearing silk-worms. 2. Hurdle, used by hatters for shearing hats. 3. (Naut.) Flake.

Caño [cah'-nyo], *m.* 1. Tube, pipe, or cylinder, of wood, glass, or metal. 2. Common sewer, gutter. 3. Spring; spout or conduit for spring-water. 4. Cellar or other place for cooling water. 5. (Obs.) Mine. 6. (Obs.) Subterranean passage. 7. (Prov.) Warren or burrow. *V.* VIVAR. *Caños* or *cañones del órgano*, Tubes or pipes of an organ. 8. The channel which forms at the entrance to seaports.

Cañocazo [cah-nyo-cah'-tho], *m.* (Obs.) Coarse flax.

Cañón [cah-nyone'], *m.* 1. Cylindrical tube or pipe. 2. In glass-houses, tube or pipe for blowing glass. 3. Quill. 4. Down, or soft feathers. 5. Hollow folds in clothes. 6. Part of the beard next to the root. 7. Cannon, gun. 8. (Min.) Gallery. 9. (Mech.) Socket. 10. Gorge, ravine, canyon. *V.* CAÑADA. *A boca de cañón*, At the mouth of a cannon. *Cañón de batir*, Battering-piece of ordnance. *Cañón de campaña*, Field-piece. *Cañón de crujía*, Gun of a row-galley. *Cañón de proa*, (Naut.) Bow-chaser. *Cañón reforzado*, A re-enforced cannon. *Cañón de candelero*, Tube of a candlestick. *Cañón de chimenea*, Funnel, flue of a chimney. *Cañón de escalera*, Well of a staircase. 11. One of the four spindles of the bar of a velvet-loom. *Cañones*, Bits of a horse's bridle. *Cañones* or *tubos de vidrio para lámparas*, Glass chimneys.

Cañonazo [cah-nyo-nah'-tho], *m.* 1. (Aug.) Large piece of ordnance. 2. Cannon-shot. 3. Report of a gun or shot.

Cañoncico, illo, ito [cah-nyon-thee'-co, eel'-lyo, ee'-to], *m. dim.* Small cannon; small tube or pipe.

Cañonear [cah-nyo-nay-ar'], *va.* To cannonade.—*vr.* To cannonade each other; to exchange guns.

Cañoneo [cah-nyo-nay'-o], *m.* Cannonade, shell fire.

Cañonera [cah-nyo-nay'-rah], *f.* 1. Embrasure for cannon. 2. Large tent. 3. *V.* PISTOLERA. 4. (Naut.) A gunboat.

Cañonería [cah-nyo-nay-ree'-ah], *f.* The pipes of an organ collectively.

Cañonero, ra [cah-nyo-nay'-ro, rah], *a.* (Naut.) Mounting cannon; a gun boat.

Cañota [cah-nyo'-tah], *f.* (Bot.) Panicled sorghum. Holcus alepensis. *Cañota suave*, Yellow-seeded soft grass. Holcus saccaratus.

Cañucela [cah-nyoo-thay'-lah], *f.* A slender cane or reed.

Cañuela [cah-nyoo-ay'-lah], *f.* (Bot.) Fescue-grass, a genus of grasses. Festuca. *Cañuela descollada*, Tall fescue-grass. Festuca elatior. *Cañuela ovina* or *ovejuna*, Sheep's fescue-grass. Festuca ovina. *Cañuela durilla*, Hard fescue-grass. Festuca duriuscula.

Cañutazo [cah-nyoo-tah'-tho], *m.* (Low) Information, private accusation, suggestion, whisper, tale. *Fué con el cañutazo*, He went to carry his tale.

Cañutería [cah-nyoo-tay-ree'-ah], *f.* 1. *V.* CAÑONERÍA. 2. Gold or silver twist for embroidery.

Cañutillo [cah-nyoo-teel'-lyo], *m.* 1. (Dim.) Small tube or pipe. 2. Bugle, small glass ornamental tubes stitched to the tassels and flounces of women's gowns. *Cañutillo de hilo de oro o de plata para bordar*, Quill of gold or silver twist for embroidery. 3. A mode of grafting. (Acad.)

Cañuto [cah-nyoo'-to], *m.* 1. Part of a cane, from knot to knot, internode. 2. Pipe made of wood or metal. 3. (Prov.) Pin-case. 4. Blast, gust. *V.* SOPLO. 5. Informer, tale-bearer. *V.* SOPLÓN. 6. *Cañutos helados*, (Mex.) Small ice-cream cylinders.

Caoba, Caobana [cah-o'-bah, cah-o-bah'-nah], *f.* (Bot.) Mahogany-tree. Swietenia mahogani.

Caolín [cah-o-leen'], *m.* Kaolin, china-clay.

Caos [cah'-os], *m.* 1. Chaos. 2. Confusion.

Caótico, ca [cah-o'-te-co, cah], *a.* Chaotic; in disorder and confusion.

Caoup [cah-o-oop'], *m.* (Bot.) Caoup, an American tree with fruit like an orange.

Capa [cah'-pah], *f.* 1. Cloak. 2. Mantle. 3. Layer, strata, lamina. 4. Coat or hair of a horse. 5. Cover, any thing laid over another. 6. (Met.) Cloak, pretence or pretext, mask, cover. 7. Hider, harbourer. 8. Property, fortune. *V.* CAUDAL. 9. An American rodent; the spotted cavy. *V.* PACA. 10. Among bell-founders, the third mould used in casting bells. 11. Coat of paint. 12. Bed, stratum, vein, seam, ledge. 13. (Mas.) Bed, course. 14. Wrapper for tobacco. *Capa del cielo*, (Met.) Canopy of heaven. *Capa de rey*, (Obs.) Kind of linen. *Capa magna*, Pontifical cape worn by officiating bishops. *Capa pluvial*, A pluvial or choir-cope, worn by prelates in processions. *Capa del timón*, (Naut.) Rudder-coat, or tarred canvas, put on the head of a rudder. *Capa de fogonaduras*, (Naut.) Mast-coat, or tarred canvas put about the mast. *Capa de los costados, fondos, palos y vergas*, (Naut.) Coat of tar, pitch, resin, tallow, and other materials, with which a ship's bottom, masts, and yards are paid. *Capa y sombrero*, (Naut.) Hat-money, allowance per ton to the captain on his cargo. *Capa rota*, (Met.) Emissary sent in disguise to execute an important commission. *Andar* or *ir de capa caída*, To be down in the mouth, crestfallen. *Defender una cosa a capa y espada*, To defend a thing with all one's might. ***Echar la***

capa al toro, (Met.) To expose one's self to danger. *Estar o estarse a la capa*, (Met.) To have a good or sharp look-out. *Gente de capa parda*, Common country people, whose chief dress is a brown frieze cloak. *Hombre de buena capa*, A man of genteel address. *Gente de capa negra*, Townsmen of decent appearance and situation in life; priests; scholars or students in universities. *Ministro de capa y espada*, Counsellor by brevet, though not brought up to the bar. *Puerto de arrebata capas*, Windy place where cloaks are troublesome. *Jugar hasta la capa*, To gamble the shirt off one's back. *Sacar bien su capa*, (Met.) To disengage one's self from difficulties. *Tirar a uno de la capa*, To pull one by the cloak, to warn him of danger. *A la capa*, (Naut.) Lying to. *De capa y gorra*, In a plain manner.

Capá [cah-pah'], *m.* Capá, a tree which grows in Cuba and Porto Rico; much used in building vessels.

Capacete [cah-pah-thay'-tay], *m.* Helmet, casque.

Capacidad [cah-pah-the-dahd'], *f.* 1. Capacity, capability. 2. Extent, extensiveness of a place. 3. Opportunity or means of executing a thing. 4. (Naut.) Bulk or burden of a ship. 5. (Met.) Talent, genius, mental ability.

Capacha [cah-pah'-chah], *f.* 1. Frail, hamper. *V.* CAPACHO. 2. Frail, a basket made of rushes. 3. (Coll.) The religious order of St. John of God.

Capachazo [cah-pah-chah'-tho], *m.* Blow given with a basket.

Capachero [cah-pah-chay'-ro], *m.* He who carries things in baskets.

Capacho [cah-pah'-cho], *m.* 1. Frail, hamper, large basket. 2. *Capacho de albañil*, Bricklayer's hod. 3. In oil-mills, the bass, or willow frail through which oil is filtered. 4. Mendicant hospitaller, who collects charity for the sick. 5. (Orn.) Common owl, barn-owl. Strix flammea.

Capada [cah-pah'-dah], *f.* 1. Any thing wrapped up and carried in a person's cloak. 2. Lark. *V.* ALONDRA.

Capadociano, na [cah-pah-do-the-ah'-no, nah], or **Capadocio, cia** [cah-pah-do'-the-o, ah], *a.* Cappadocian, belonging to or native of Cappadocia, in Asia Minor.

Capador [cah-pah-dor'], *m.* 1. One whose business is to geld or castrate. 2. A kind of whistle employed by those whose business is to geld.

Capadura [cah-pah-doo'-rah], *f.* 1. Castration. 2. Scar which remains after castration. 3. Leaf of tobacco of the second cutting; used for filling.

Capar [cah-par'], *va.* 1. To geld, to castrate. 2. (Met. Low) To castrate, to take away a part; to curtail, to diminish one's authority, income, etc.

Caparazón [cah-pah-ra-thone'], *m.* 1. Carcass of a fowl. 2. Caparison, a sort of cover over the saddle of a horse. 3. Cover of a coach, or other things, made of oil-cloth. 4. (Prov.) Frail made of grass, in which horses feed when out of the stable.

Caparra [cah-par'-rah], *f.* 1. Sheep-louse. *V.* GARRAPATA. 2. Earnest-money given to confirm a bargain. 3. *V.* ALCAPARRA.

Caparrilla [cah-par-reel'-lyah], *f. dim.* A small tick, which molests bees.

Caparrón [cah-par-rone'], *m.* (Obs.) Bud of a vine or tree.

Caparrós [cah-par-ros'], *m.* (Prov.) *V.* CAPARROSA.

Caparrosa [cah-par-ro'-sah], *f.* Copperas, or vitriol, ferrous sulphate. *Caparrosa azul*, Blue vitriol, copper sulphate. *Caparrosa blanca*, White vitriol, zinc sulphate. *Caparrosa verde*, Green vitriol, copperas.

Capataz [cah-pah-tath'], *m.* 1. Overseer, superintendent. 2. One charged with receiving the marked metal to be coined in the mint. 3. Steward who superintends a farm. 4. Warden of a company or guild. 5. Conductor. 6. Foreman.

Capaz [cah-path'], *a.* 1. Capacious, capable, able to hold other things. 2. Capacious, ample, spacious, roomy, wide. 3. (Met.) Fit, apt, suitable, competent. 4. (Met.) Learned, ingenious, capable, clever. *Capaz de prueba*, Capable of trial; what may be proved. *Hacerse capaz de alguna cosa*, (Met.) To render one's self master of a thing.

Capaza [cah-pah'-thah], *f.* (Prov.) *V.* CAPACHO.

Capazmente [cah-path-men'-tay], *adv.* Capaciously, amply.

Capazo [cah-pah'-tho], *m.* 1. Large frail or basket made of rushes. 2. Blow given with a cloak.

Capazón [cah-pah-thone'], *m. aug.* Very large frail made of bass.

Capción [cap-the-on'], *f.* (Obs.) *V.* CAPTURA.

Capciosamente [cap-the-o-sah-men'-tay], *adv.* Insidiously, captiously, artfully, cunningly.

Capcioso, sa [cap-the-o'-so, sah], *a.* Captious, insidious, artful, cunning, fault-finding.

Capeador [cah-pay-ah-dor'], *m.* 1. A bull-fighter who challenges the bull with his cloak. 2. Cloak-stealer.

Capear [cah-pay-ar'], *va.* 1. To strip or rob one of a cloak in an inhabited place. 2. (Naut.) To try or lay to. 3. To challenge a bull with one's cloak.

Capeja [cah-pay'-hah], *f.* (Dim. of depreciation) A poor or mean cape.

Capel [cah-pel'], *m.* (Prov.) Cocoon or ball of a silk-worm.

Capela [cah-pay'-lah], *f.* (Ast.) Capella, the brightest star in Auriga.

Capelardente [cah-pay-lar-den'-tay], *f.* (Obs.) *V.* CAPILLA ARDIENTE.

Capelete [cah-pay-lay'-tay], *m.* 1. Capulet, a family of Verona. 2. A high hat once in use.

Capelina [cah-pay-lee'-nah], *f.* Capelline, a bandage especially fitted to the head.

Capelo [cah-pay'-lo], *m.* 1. Dues received in ancient times by bishops from their clergy. 2. (Obs.) Hat. *V.* SOMBRERO. 3. Cardinal's hat. 4. Dignity of a cardinal, cardinalate.

Capellada [cah-pel-lyah'-dah], *f.* Toe-piece of a shoe.

Capellán [cah-pel-lyahn'], *m.* 1. Chaplain, a clergyman who has obtained a chaplaincy. *V.* CAPELLANÍA. 2. Chaplain, a clergyman that officiates in domestic worship. *Capellán de navío*, Chaplain of the navy. *Capellán de altar*, The priest who chants the mass. *Capellán de honor*, The king's private chaplain. *Capellán mayor de los ejércitos*, The vicar-general of the army.

Capellanía [cah-pel-lyah-nee'-ah], *f.* Chaplaincy, a capital, the interest of which is required by the Spanish laws for the support of an ecclesiastic. *Capellanía colativa*, The capital and interest of a foundation that requires its possessor to be a clergyman. *Capellanía laica*, The capital and revenue granted to a layman, with the duty of applying a certain part of it to charitable or other pious purposes.

Capellar [cah-pel-lyar'], *m.* A kind of Moorish cloak.

Capellina [cah-pel-lyee'-nah], *f.* 1. Head piece of a helmet or casque. 2. Hood worn by country people. 3. (Obs.) Trooper armed with a helmet.

Capeo [cah-pay'-o], *m.* Act of challenging a bull with a cloak.

Capeón [cah-pay-on'], *m.* (Prov.) Young bull challenged with a cloak.

Capero [cah-pay'-ro] *m.* Priest who carries the cope, or pluvial, in churches.

Caperoles [cah-pay-ro'-les], *m. pl.* (Naut.) *V.* CORONAMIENTO.

Caperuceta, illa [cah-pay-roo-thay'-tah, theel'-lyah], *f. dim.* Small hood.

Caperuza [cah-pay-roo'-thah], *f.* Hood or cap ending in a point, holster-cap. *Caperuza de chimenea*, Covering of the top of a chimney. *Caperuza de fogón*, (Naut.) Hood of the caboose or cook-room. *Caperuza de palo*, Hood of a mast-head when the ship is unrigged. *Dar en caperuza*, (Met.) To frustrate one's views and designs. *Alcalde de caperuza*, An illiterate justice of the peace of a small village.

Caperuzón [cah-pay-roo-thone'], *m. aug.* Large hood.

Capeta [cah-pay'-tah], *f.* A short cape, not reaching below the knee, and without collar.

Capialzado [cah-pe-al-thah'-do], *a.* (Arch.) Applied to an arch; widening outward; arched cap-piece, back arch.

Capibara [cah-pe-bah'-rah], *m.* Capybara, a large South American rodent, about three and a half feet long, related to the guinea-pig; it frequents the borders of lakes and rivers. Called also water-hog. Hydrochœrus capybara. *Cf.* CAPA, 9th accep., and PACA.

Capichola [cah-pe-cho'-lah], *f.* Ribbed silk stuff.

Capidengue [cah-pe-den'-gay], *m.* Small cloak worn by ladies.

Capiello [cah-pe-ayl'-lyo], *m.* (Prov.) *V.* CAPILLO.

Capigorrista [cah-pe-gor-rees'-tah], *m.* (Low) *V.* CAPIGORRÓN.

Capigorrón [cah-pe-gor-rone'], *m.* 1. (Coll.) Vagabond; a parasite. 2. (Prov.) Student who has taken the minor orders.

Capil [cah-peel'], *m.* (Prov.) Little cap or hood.

Capiláceo, cea [cah-pe-lah'-thay-o, ah], *a.* (Bot.) Capillaceous, hair-like.

Capilar [cah-pe-lar'], *a.* Capillary; slender as hair.—*m.* A capillary blood-vessel; capillaries intervene between arteries and veins.

Capilaridad [cah-pe-lah-re-dahd'], *f.* Capillarity, capillary attraction.

Capilla [cah-peel'-lyah], *f.* 1. Hood. 2. Cowl of a monk or friar. 3. Chapel. 4. Chapel, a small church. 5. The priests and others employed in chapel service. 6. Band of musicians; the paid musicians of a church. 7. Chapter or assembly of collegians. 8. Among printers, the proof-sheet. 9. Portable chapel for military corps. *Caja de capilla*, (Naut.) Chest for chapel ornaments. *Capilla ardiente*, Lighted room where a dead body lies in state. *Estar en capilla*, 1. To prepare for death: spoken of criminals. 2. (Coll.) To await with impatience the issue of an affair.

Capillada [cah-peel-lyah'-dah], *f.* A hoodful of any thing.

Capilleja, ita [cah-peel-lyay'-hah, lyee'-tah], *f. dim.* Small chapel.

Capillejo [cah-peel-lyay'-ho], *m.* 1. (Dim.) Small hood. 2. Skein of sewing-silk.

Capiller, Capillero [cah-peel-lyerr', cah-peel-lyay'-ro], *m.* Clerk or sexton of a chapel; a churchwarden.

Capilleta [cah-peel-lyay'-tah], *f.* 1. (Dim. Obs.) Small chapel. 2. Hood used by the knights of Calatrava.

Capillo [cah-peel'-lyo], *m.* 1. Child's cap. 2. Fee given to clergymen for baptizing a child. 3. Apparel of white stuff put on the head of infants after baptism. 4. A tax paid to the factory when the capillo of the church is used. 5. Hood of a hawk. 6. Bud of a rose. 7. Lining under the toe-piece of a shoe. 8. Cap of distaff. *V.* ROCADERO. 9. Net for catching rabbits. 10. Colander through which wax is strained. 11. Cocoon of the silk-worm. *V.* CAPULLO. 12. (Obs.) The covering or cloth which covered the offering of bread which used to be presented to the church. 13. The prepuce. 14. Kind of cowl which formerly served the women for hat and cloak. *Capilla de hierro,* Helmet. *Seda de todo capillo,* Coarse sort of silk. *Lo que en el capillo se toma con la mortaja se deja,* (prov.) The impressions of childhood last through life.

Capilludo, da [cah-peel-lyoo'-do, dah], *a.* Resembling the hood or cowl of a monk.

Capirotada [cah-pe-ro-tah'-dah], *f.* Sort of American paste made of herbs, eggs, etc.

Capirotazo [cah-pe-ro-tah'-tho], *m.* A blow on the nose with the finger; a fillip.

Capirote [cah-pe-ro'-tay], *m.* 1. Hood, ancient cover for the head. 2. Sort of half-gown worn by collegians of Salamanca. 3. Sharp-pointed cap worn in processions. *Tonto de capirote,* Block-head, ignorant fool. 4. *Capirote de colmena,* Cover of a bee-hive when full of honey. *V.* PAPIROTE.

Capirotero [cah-pe-ro-tay'-ro], *a.* Accustomed to carry a hood: applied to a hawk.

Capirucho [cah-pe-roo'-cho], *m.* (Coll.) *V.* CAPIROTE.

Capisayo [cah-pe-sah'-yo], *m.* 1. Garment which serves both as a cloak and riding-coat. 2. A vesture proper to bishops.

Capiscol [cah-pis-col'], *m.* The precentor: sub-chanter.

Capiscolía [cah-pis-co-lee'-ah], *f.* Office and dignity of a precentor.

Capistrato, ta [cah-pis-trah'-to, tah], *a.* Capistrate, epithet applied to animals whose snout appears to have a muzzle or halter.

Capistrato, *m.* A squirrel of Carolina.

Capistro [cah-pees'-tro], *m.* 1. Capistrum, a bandage for the head. 2. Tonic spasm of the muscles of the lower jaw. 3. (Zool.) Capister, the part of a bird's head about the base of the bill.

Capita [cah-pee'-tah], *f. dim.* Small cloak.

Capitación [cah-pe-tah-the-on'], *f.* Poll-tax, head-money.

Capital [cah-pe-tahl'], *m.* 1. Sum of money put at interest. 2. Fortune of a husband at his marriage. 3. Capital stock of a merchant or trading company. 4. (Mil.) Line drawn from the angle of a polygon to the point of the bastion and the middle of the gorge. 5. A capital letter; upper case of printers.—*f.* Capital city (sc. ciudad) of a country.

Capital [cah-pe-tahl'], *a.* 1. Capital, relating to the head. *Remedio capital,* Remedy for the head. 2. Principal, leading; capital, essential. *Enemigo capital,* Mortal enemy. *Error capital,* Capital error. *Pecados capitales,* Deadly sins. *Pena capital,* Capital punishment.

Capitalidad [cah-pe-tah-le-dahd'], *f.* The state of being capital, whether city or thing.

Capitalismo [cah-pe-tah-lees'-mo], *m.* Capitalism.

Capitalista [cah-pe-tah-lees'-tah], *com.* Capitalist.

Capitalización [cah-pe-tah-le-thah-the-on'], *f.* Capitalization, conversion of property into money.

Capitalizar [cah-pe-tah-le-thar'], *va.* To capitalize, convert into capital; to put a value on; to add overdue dividends to the capital stock, in order to obtain increased interest.

Capitalmente [cah-pe-tal-men'-tay], *adv.* Capitally, mortally.

Capitán [cah-pe-tahn'], *m.* 1. Captain, a military officer. 2. (Obs.) Commander-in-chief of an army. 3. Ringleader of a band of robbers. 4. Leader. 5. The commander of a ship of war or merchant vessel. *Capitán a guerra,* The mayor or chief magistrate of a place, invested with military power. *Capitán de bandera,* (Naut.) Captain of the admiral's ship. *Capitán de fragata,* The commander of a frigate, with the rank of lieutenant-colonel. *Capitán de navío,* The commander of a man-of-war, with the rank of colonel. *Capitán de guardias de corps,* A captain in the king's life-guards. *Capitán general de ejército,* Field-marshal. *Capitán general de provincia,* The commander-in-chief of a military district. *Capitán de puerto,* (Naut.) Port-captain. *Capitán del puerto,* (Naut.) Harbour-master, water-bailiff. *Capitán de gallinas de un navío de guerra,* (Naut.) Poulterer of a man-of-war. *Capitán de maestranza en los arsenales,* (Naut.) Store-keeper in a dockyard. *Capitán de llaves en las plazas de armas,* Town-major in strong places. 6. In the wool trade, the overseer, who superintends the washing of wool.

Capitana [cah-pe-tah'-nah], *f.* 1. Admiral's ship. 2. A captain's wife.

Capitanazo [cah-pe-tah-nah'-tho], *m.* (Coll.) Great warrior; an able general.

Capitanear [cah-pe-tah-nay-ar'], *va.* 1. To have the command in chief of an army. 2. To head a troop of people.

Capitanía [cah-pe-tah-nee'-ah], *f.* 1. Captainship, captainry. 2. Company of officers and soldiers commanded by a captain. 3. A tax paid to the port-captain by ships anchored in the harbour. 4. (Obs.) Military government of a province. 5. (Obs.) Chief authority, power, command.

Capitel [cah-pe-tel'], *m.* 1. Spire over the dome of a church. 2. (Arch.) Capital of a column or pilaster. 3. Lid of a refining-furnace.

Capitolino, na [cah-pe-to-lee'-no, nah], *a.* Belonging to the capitol.

Capitolio [cah-pe-to'-le-o], *m.* 1. Capitol, a temple of Jupiter at Rome. 2. The Capitol, legislative building at Rome. 3. Any lofty or majestic public building.

Capitón [cah-pe-tone'], *m.* (Zool.) Pollard, chub. Cyprinus cephalus.

Capitoso, sa [cah-pe-to'-so, sah], *a.* (Obs.) Obstinate, capricious, whimsical.

Capítula [cah-pee'-too-lah], *f.* Part of the prayers read at divine service.

Capitulación [cah-pe-too-lah-the-on'], *f.* 1. Capitulation, stipulation, agreement. *Capitulación de matrimonio,* Articles of marriage. 2. (Mil.) Capitulation, surrender of a place.

Capitulante [cah-pe-too-lahn'-tay], *pa.* Capitulator.

Capitular [cah-pe-too-lar'], *m.* Capitular, member of a chapter.

Capitular [cah-pe-too-lar'], *c.* Capitulary, belonging to a chapter.

Capitular, *va.* 1. To conclude an agreement, to draw up the articles of a contract; to compound. 2. (Mil.) To capitulate, to settle the terms of surrender. 3. (Law) To impeach.—*vn.* To sing prayers at divine service

Capitulario [cah-pe-too-lah'-re-o], *m.* Book of prayers for divine service.

Capitularmente [cah-pe-too-lar-men'-tay], *adv.* Capitulary, according to the rules of a chapter.

Capitulero [cah-pe-too-lay'-ro], *m. & a.* Capitular; capitulary.

Capítulo [cah-pee'-too-lo], *m.* 1. (Prov.) Chapter of a cathedral. 2. A meeting of the prelates of religious orders, and the place where they meet. 3. Meeting of a secular community or corporation. 4. Chapter of a book or other writing. 5. Charge preferred for neglect of duty. 6. *Capítulos matrimoniales,* Articles of marriage. 7. A public reproof for some fault. (Acad.) *Dar un capítulo,* (Met.) To reprimand severely. *Ganar o perder capítulo,* (Met.) To carry or lose one's point.

Capnomancia [cap-no-mahn'-the-ah], *f.* Capnomancy, divination by the flying of smoke.

Capnomante [cap-no-mahn'-tay], *m.* (Obs.) Fortune-teller by smoke.

Capoc [cah-poc'], *m.* **Capoca,** *f.* A sort of cotton so short and fine that it can not be spun: used for mattresses, etc. (East Indian.)

Capolado [cah-po-lah'-do], *m.* (Prov.) 1. Minced meat. *V.* PICADILLO. 2. Act of cutting or tearing into ends and bits.—*Capolado, da, pp.* of CAPOLAR.

Capolar [cah-po-lar'], *va.* (Prov.) 1. To mince or chop meat. 2. To behead, to decapitate.

Capón [cah-pone'], *m.* 1. Eunuch. 2. Gelding. 3. Capon. 4. (Coll.) Fillip on the head. 5. (Prov.) Fagot, a bundle of brush-wood. 6. (Naut.) Anchor-stopper at the cat-head. *Capón de galera,* Kind of salmagundi made in row-galleys. *Capón de ceniza,* Stroke on the forehead with a dust-bag.

Capona [cah-po'-nah], *f.* Shoulder-knot. *Llave capona,* Key worn by a lord of the bed-chamber. *Capona* or *charretera capona,* An epaulet without fringe.

Caponado, da [cah-po-nah'-do, dah], *a.* Tied together, as branches of vines.—*pp.* of CAPONAR.

Caponar [cah-po-nar'], *va.* 1. (Prov.) To tie up the branches of vines. 2. To cut, to curtail, to diminish.

Caponera [cah-po-nay'-rah], *f.* 1. Coop, inclosure to fatten poultry. 2. (Met. Coll.) Place where one lives well at other people's expense. (Met. and coll.) A jail. 3. (Mil.) Caponier, a passage under a dry moat to the outworks. *Estar metido en caponera,* To be locked up in jail. 4. *V.* YEGUA CAPONERA. 5. Stew-pan for dressing fowls.

Capoquero [cah-po-kay'-ro], *m.* (Bot.) Capoc-tree.

Caporal [cah-po-rahl'], *m.* 1. Chief, ringleader. 2. (Obs.) Corporal. 3. (Mex.) Keeper of horned cattle. 4. (Cant) A cock.

Capota [cah-po'-tah], *f.* 1. Car top. 2. Cape without a hood. 3. A light bonnet.

Capote [cah-po'-tay], *m.* 1. Sort of cloak with sleeves to keep off rain. 2. A short cloak, without hood, of bright colour, used by bull-fighters. 3. (Met.) Austere, angry look or mien. 4. (Coll.) Thick cloud or mist over a mountain. 5. In games at cards, capot, when one player wins all the tricks. *Dar capote,* 1. To leave a guest without dinner, for coming late. 2. To win all the tricks at cards. *A mi capote,* In my opinion. *Dije para mi capote,* I said in my sleeve. *Capote de centinela,* A sentinel's great-coat or watch-coat.

Capotear [cah-po-tay-ar'], *va.* 1. To trick a bull with a capote; to hold a cloak before one's self for him to spring at. 2. To wheedle, bamboozle. 3. To evade cleverly difficulties and promises.

Capotero [cah-po-tay'-ro], *m.* (Obs.) One who makes or sells cloaks.

Capotillo [cah-po-teel'-lyo], *m.* Mantelet, short cloak worn by women. *Capotillo de dos faldas,* Short, loose jacket.

Capotón [cah-po-tone'], *m. aug.* Large wide coat.

Capotudo, da [cah-po-too'-do, dah], *a.* Frowning. *V.* CEÑUDO.

Capra-capela [cah'-pra-cah-pay'-lah], *f.* Cobra di capello, A very venomous snake of tropical Asia.

Capricho [cah-pree'-cho], *m.* 1. Caprice, whim, fancy, mood, humour, conceit. 2. (Mus.) Irregular but pleasing composition. 3. (Art) Invention or design of a painting. *Hombre de capricho,* Queer, whimsical fellow. *Capricho extravagante,* A crotchet or odd fancy, a capricious prank.

Caprichosamente [cah-pre-cho-sah-men'-tay], *adv.* Fantastically, fancifully, humorously, moodily, whimsically.

Caprichoso, sa [cah-pre-cho'-so, sah], *a.* 1. Capricious, whimsical, obstinate. 2. Fanciful.

Caprichudo, da [cah-pre-choo'-do, dah], *a.* Obstinate, stubborn, capricious.

Capricornio [cah-pre-cor'-ne-o], *m.* 1. Capricorn, a sign of the zodiac. 2. (Zool.) A capricorn beetle, one of the long-horned cerambycids.

Caprimulga [cah-pre-mool'-gah], *f.* Goat-sucker, a kind of owl.

Caprino, na [cah-pree'-no, nah], *a.* (Poet.) Goatish. *V.* CABRUNO.

Cápsula [cahp'-soo-lah], *f.* 1. (Bot.) Capsule, a seed-vessel in plants. 2. (Anat.) Capsule, a sac enveloping a joint or other region of the body. 3. (Chem.) Capsule, a vessel for the evaporation of liquids. 4. Capsule, a small, gelatinous case for holding a nauseous drug. 5. (Mil.) Cartridge. *Cápsula de emergencia,* (Aer.) Escape capsule. *Cápsula espacial,* Space capsule. *Cápsula fulminante,* Detonator, percussion cap.

Capsular [cap-soo-lar'], *a.* Capsular, capsulary.

Captar [cap-tar], *va.* 1. To captivate, to win, capture. 2. To grasp, to get, to catch.

Captividad [cap-te-ve-dahd'], *f.* (Obs.) *V.* CAUTIVIDAD.

Captura [cap-too'-rah], *f.* (Law) Capture, seizure.

Capuana [cah-poo-ah'-nah], *f.* A whipping.

Capuano, na [cah-poo-ah'-no, nah], *a.* Capuan, relating Capua in southern Italy.

Capucha [cah-poo'-chah], *f.* 1. (Print.) Circumflex (^), an accent. 2. Hood of a woman's cloak. 3. Cowl or hood of a friar.

Capuchina [cah-poo-chee'-nah], *f.* 1. Capuchin nun. 2. (Bot.) Great Indian cress, nasturtium. Tropæolum majus. *Capuchinas,* (Naut.) Crotches and knees. 3. A small lamp of metal with extinguisher in the form of a hood. 4. Confection of yolk of egg. (Acad.)

Capuchino [cah-poo-chee'-no], *m.* Capuchin monk.

Capuchino, na [cah-poo-chee'-no, nah], *a.* Relating to Capuchin friars or nuns. *Chupa capuchina,* Waistcoat.

Capucho [cah-poo'-cho], *m.* Cowl or hood.

Capuchón [cah-poo-chone'], *m.* 1. Aug. of CAPUCHO. 2. A lady's cloak with hood, especially one worn at night.

Capulí [cah-poo-lee'], (Mex.) **Capulín** [cah-poo-leen'], *m.* (Bot.) An American fruit resembling a cherry.

Capullito [cah-pool-lyee'-to], *m. dim.* Small pod of a silk-worm.

Capullo [cah-pool'-lyo], *m.* 1. Cocoon of a silk-worm. 2. Flax knotted at the end; (Com.) a bunch of boiled flax. 3. Germ or bud of flowers. 4. Coarse stuff of spun silk. *Seda de capullos,* Ferret-silk, grogram yarn. 5. Cup of an acorn. 6. Burr of a chestnut. 7. Prepuce.

Capumpeba [cah-poom-pay'-bah], *f.* (Bot.) A Brazil plant.

Capuz [cah-pooth'], *m.* 1. The act of ducking a person. *V.* CHAPUZ. 2. (Obs.) Old-fashioned cloak.

Capuzar [cah-poo-thar'], *va.* *Capuzar un bajel,* (Naut.) To sink a ship by the head. *V.* CHAPUZAR.

Caquéctico, ca [cah-kayc'-te-co, cah], *a.* Cachectical, cachectic, affected by cachexia.

Caquexia [cah-kayc'-se-ah], *f.* (Med.) Cachexia, a condition of general bad health, especially from a specific morbid process, such as cancer or tuberculosis.

Caqui or **kaki** [cah'-ke], *a.* Khaki.

Caquimia [cah-kee'-me-ah], *f.* An imperfect metallic substance.

Car, *f.* (Naut.) Extreme end of the mizzen-yard and mizzen.

Car, *adv.* (Obs.) *V.* PORQUE.

Cara [cah'-rah], *f.* 1. Face, visage, countenance. *Fulano me recibió con buena cara,* He received me with a cheerful countenance. *Fulana me mostró mala cara,* I was received by her with a frown. 2. Base of a sugar-loaf. 3. (Obs.) Presence of a person. 4. Face, front, surface; facing. *Cara de acelga,* Pale sallow face. *Cara de pascua* or *de risa,* Smiling, cheerful countenance. *Cara de pocos amigos,* Churlish look, froward countenance. *Cara de vaqueta* or *de bronce,* Brazen face. *Cara de viernes,* Sad, lean, meagre face. *Cara de cartón,* Wrinkled face. *Cara empedrada, apedreada,* or *cacaraneada,* A face pitted by the small-pox. *Hacer la cara,* In tar manufactories, to make an incision in a pine-tree, to extract the resin. *Cara de cebo,* Pale face. *A cara descubierta,* Openly, plainly. *Andar con la cara descubierta,* To act openly; to proceed with frankness, and without evasion or reserve. *A primera cara,* At first sight. *Cara a cara vergüenza se cata,* That is denied with difficulty which is sought face to face. *Cara sin dientes hace a los muertos vivientes,* ironically denotes that good food restores lost forces, and in a certain manner gives life. *Dar a alguno con las puertas en la cara,* To shut the door in one's face. *Jugar á cara ó cruz,* To toss up a coin and bet on what side it may fall. *Dar en cara,* (Met.) To reproach, to upbraid. *Dar el sol de cara,* To have the sun in one's face. *Decírselo en su cara,* (Met.) To tell one to his face. *Hacer cara,* To face an enemy. *Hombre de dos caras,* Double-dealer, an insidious, artful fellow. *La cara se lo dice,* His face betrays him. *Lavar la cara á alguno,* (Met.) To flatter, to please with blandishments. *Lavar la cara á alguna cosa,* To brush up, to clean; e. g. a painting, house, or coach. *No conocer la cara al miedo* or *á la necesidad,* To be a stranger to fear or distress. *No sabe en dónde tiene la cara,* He does not know his profession or duty. *No tener cara para hacer ó decir alguna cosa,* Not to have the face or courage to make or say a thing. *Quitar la cara,* To threaten any one that he will be punished rigorously. *Saltar á la cara,* To answer reproof or admonition, etc., angrily. *Sacar la cara por otro,* To sustain or defend another. *No volver la cara atrás,* (Met.) To pursue with spirit and perseverance; not to flinch. *Volver á la cara las palabras injuriosas,* To retort or return abusive language. *Salir á la cara el contento, la enfermedad, la vergüenza,* Satisfaction, infirmity, shame, expressed in the face. *Cara á cara,* Face to face. *De cara,* Opposite, over against, regarding in front. *Cara de beato, y uñas de gato,* The face of a devotee and the claws of a cat. *Guardar la cara,* To conceal one's self. *El bien ó el mal, á la cara sal,* The face is the mirror of the soul. *Cruzar la cara,* To give a blow or a cut with a whip on the face. *Echar á la cara,* To throw in one's face; to tell one his faults; also to remind of some benefit done. *Llenar á uno la cara de dedos,* To give a blow in the face with the fist.

Cáraba [cah'-ra-bah], *f.* (Naut.) Vessel used in the Archipelago.

Cárabe [cah'-ra-bay], *m.* Amber.

Carabela [cah-ra-bay'-lah], *f.* 1. (Naut.) Carvel or caravel, a three-masted vessel. 2. (Prov.) Large basket or tray for provisions.

Carabelón [cah-ra-bay-lone'], *m.* (Naut.) Brig or brigantine.

Carabina [cah-ra-bee'-nah], *f.* 1. Fowling-piece. 2. Carbine or carabine. *Carabina rayada,* Rifle carabine. *Es lo mismo que la carabina de Ambrosio,* It is not worth a straw.

Carabinazo [cah-ra-be-nah'-tho], *m.* Report of a carbine, effect of a carbine-shot.

Carabinero [cah-ra-be-nay'-ro], *m* 1. Carabineer. 2. (Obs.) Light horse attached to cavalry.

Cárabo [cah'-ra-bo], *m.* 1. (Zool.) Sort of a crab or cockle. 2. (Orn.) Large horned owl. *V.* AUTILLO. 3. Kind of setter-dog. 4. A ground beetle: a carabid; it is insectivorous. Carabus.

Carabú [cah-ra-boo'], *m.* A handsome tree of India.

Caracoa [cah-ra-co'-ah], *f.* Small row-barge used in the Philippine Islands.

Caracol [cah-ra-col'], *m.* 1. Fusee of a watch or clock. 2. Snail. *Caracol marino,* Periwinkle. 3. Winding staircase. 4. Caracole, the prancing of a horse. 5. A wide though short night-dress, used by women in Mexico. 6. Cochlea, of the ear. *Hacer caracoles,* (Met.) To caracole. *No importa un caracol,* It does not matter, it is not worth a rush.

Caracola [cah-ra-co'-lah], *f.* 1. (Prov.) A small snail with a whitish shell. 2. A conch-shell used as a horn.

Caracolear [cah-ra-co-lay-ar'], *vn.* To caracole.

Caracolejo [cah-ra-co-lay'-ho], *m. dim.* Small snail, or snail-shell.

Caracoleo [cah-ra-co-lay'-o], *m.* The act of caracoling.

Caracolero, ra [cah-ra-co-lay'-ro, rah], *m. & f.* One who gathers snails.

Caracoles! [cah-ra-co'-les], *int. V.* CARAMBA.

Caracolí [cah-ra-co'-lee], *m.* (Min.) Metallic composition resembling pinchbeck.

Caracolilla [cah-ra-co-leel'-lyah], *f. dim.* Small snail-shell.

Caracolillo [cah-ra-co-leel'-lyo], *m.* 1. (Dim.) Small snail. 2. (Bot.) Snail-flowered kidney bean. Phaseolus caracalla. 3. Purple-coloured thread. *Caracolillos,* Shell-work wrought on the edgings of clothes, for ornament. 4. A prized variety of coffee, smaller than the ordinary sort. 5. A much-veined kind of mahogany.

Caracolito [cah-ra-co-lee'-to], *m. dim.* Small snail.

Caracón [cah-ra-cone'], *m.* (Obs.) Small vessel.

Caracosmos [cah-ra-cos'-mose], *m.* Koumiss, fermented mares' milk: a favourite beverage among the Mongolian Tartars.

Carácter [cah-rahc'-ter], *m.* 1. A written sign. 2. Character, condition, mark. 3. Character, consequence, note, adventitious quality impressed by a post or office. 4. Character, handwriting. 5. Character, type, any letter used in writing or printing. 6. Character, personal qualities, particular constitution of mind, humour, manners. 7. Temper, nature, genius. 8. Spiritual stamp impressed upon the soul by the sacraments of baptism and confirmation. (Obs.) Mark put upon sheep; brand. 9. Character, loftiness of soul, firmness, energy. 10. Style of speaking or writing. 11. *Caracteres de imprenta,* Printing types.

Característicamente [cah-rac-tay-rees'-te-cah-men-tay], *adv.* Characteristically.

Característico, ca [cah-rac-tay-rees'-te-co, cah], *a.* Characteristic.

Caracterizado, da [cah-rac-tay-re-thah'-do, dah], *a.* Characterized. *Es hombre muy caracterizado,* He is a man conspicuous either for his qualities or for the posts he fills.—*pp.* of CARACTERIZAR.

Caracterizar [cah-rac-tay-re-thar'], *va.* 1. To characterize, to distinguish by peculiar qualities. *Le caracterizaron de sabio,* He was classed among wise men. 2. To confer a distinguished employment, dignity, or office. 3. To mark, to point out.

Caracumbé [cah-rah-coom-bay'], *m.* Popular Afro-Latin dance.

Caracha [cah-rah'-chah], *f.* or **Carache** [ca-rah'-chay], *m.* Itch, mange, scab.

Caradelante [cah-ra-day-lahn'-tay], *adv.* 1. (Obs.) *V.* EN ADELANTE. 2. (Prov.) Forward.

Carado, da [cah-rah'-do, dah], *a.* Faced. This adjective is always joined to the adverbs *bien* or *mal*—e.g. *Biencarado,* Pretty-faced. *Malcarado,* Ill-faced.

Caraguata [cah-ra-goo-ah'-tah], *f.* A kind of hemp in Paraguay from a plant of the same name.

Caraja [cah-rah'-hah], *f.* A certain sail used by fishermen at Vera Cruz.

Caramallera [cah-ra-mal-lyay'-rah], *f.* A rack, a toothed bar. *Cf.* CREMALLERA.

Caramanchel [cah-ra-man-chel'], *m.* A covering like a shed over the hatchways of ships, fixed or movable.

Caramanchón [cah-ra-man-chone'], *m.* Garret. *V.* CAMARANCHÓN.

¡Caramba! [cah-rahm'-bah], *int.* (Coll.) Hah, strange!

Carámbano [cah-rahm'-bah-no], *m.* Icicle, a shoot of ice.

Carambillo [cah-ram-beel'-lyo], *m.* (Bot.) Salt-wort, a source of barilla.

Carambola [cah-ram-bo'-lah], *f.* 1. Carom, the impact, in billiards, of the cue-ball against two other balls in succession. 2. Device or trick to cheat or deceive. *Lo hizo por carambola,* He accomplished it by a mere chance, through luck, etc.

Carambolear [cah-ram-bo-lay-ar'], *va.* To play the *carambola;* to carom.

Carambolero [cah-ram-bo-lay'-ro], *m.* Player at *carambola.*

Carambú [cah-ram-boo'], *m.* (Bot.) Willow herb, tall jussiena. Jussiena suffruticosa.

Caramel [cah-ra-mel'], *m.* (Zool.) Kind of pilchard or sardine.

Caramelización [cah-ra-may-le-thah-the-on'], *f.* The reduction of sugar to candy by heat.

Caramelo [cah-ra-may'-lo], *m.* Lozenge made of sugar and other ingredients; sugar-candy.

Caramente [cah-ra-men'-tay], *adv.* 1. Dearly. 2. Exceedingly, highly. 3. (Law) Rigorously.

Caramiello [cah-ra-me-ayl'-lyo], *m.* A kind of hat worn by women in the Asturias and Leon.

Caramillar [cah-ra-meel-lyar'], *vn.* (Obs.) To play on the flageolet.

Caramilleras [cah-ra-meel-lyay'-ras], *f. pl.* (Prov.) Pot-hooks.

Caramillo [cah-ra-meel'-lyo], *m.* 1. Flageolet, a small flute. 2. (Bot.) *V.* BARRILLA. 3. Confused heap of things. 4. Deceit, fraudulent trick. 5. Pick-thanking, tale-carrying. *Armar un caramillo,* To raise disturbances. 6. (Bot.) A wild shrub of the rose kind.

Cáramo [cah'-ra-mo], *m.* Wine. (Slang, fr. Arab. chamr, wine.)

Caramuyo [cah-ra-moo'-yo], *m.* Kind of sea-snail. Nerita.

Caramuzal [cah-ra-moo-thahl'], *m.* Transport vessel used by the Moors.

Carángano [cah-rahn'-gah-no], *m.* 1. (Sp. Am.) Louse. 2. (Col.) Native musical instrument.

Carangue [cah-rahn'-gay], *m.* **Caranga** [cah-rahn'-gah], *f.* (Amer.) Kind of flat-fish in the West Indies.

Carantamaula [cah-ran-ta-mah'-oo-lah], *f.* (Coll.) 1. Hideous mask or visor. 2. (Met.) Ugly, hard-featured person.

Carantoña [cah-ran-to'-nyah], *f.* 1. Hideous mask or visor. 2. Old coarse woman, who paints and dresses in style.—*pl.* Caresses, soft words and acts of endearment to wheedle or coax a person.

Carantoñera [cah-ran-to-nyay'-rah], *f.* Coquette.

Carantoñero [cah-ran-to-nyay'-ro], *m.* Flatterer, wheedler, cajoler.

Caraña [cah-rah'-nyah], *f.* Kind of resinous American gum.

Caraos [cah-rah'-os], *m.* (Obs.) Act of drinking a full bumper to one's health.

Carapa [cah-rah'-pah], *f.* Oil of an American nut, which is said to cure the gout.

Carapacho [cah-ra-pah'-cho], *m.* Carapace, shell; as of turtles, crustaceans, etc.

Caraqueño, ña [cah-ra-kay'-nyo, nyah] *a.* Of or relating to Caracas.

Carátula [cah-rah'-too-lah], *f.* 1. Mask of pasteboard. 2. A wire cover for the face to defend it from bees, musquitoes, etc. 3. The title-page of a book. 4. (Met.) The histrionic art.

Caratulero [cah-ra-too-lay'-ro], *m.* One who makes or sells masks.

Cárava [cah'-ra-vah], *f.* (Obs.) Meeting of country people on festive occasions. *Quien no va a Cárava no sabe nada,* He who would know what is going on must mix in the world.

Caravana [cah-ra-vah'-nah], *f.* 1. (Naut.) Sea-campaign performed by the Knights of Malta. 2. Caravan, a company of traders, pilgrims, and the like. A camel-train in the desert. *Hacer* or *correr caravanas,* (Met.) To take a variety of steps for obtaining some end. *Caravana de automóviles,* Autocade, motorcade. (Pers. caruán.)

Caravanera [cah-ra-vah-nay'-rah], *f.* Caravansary.

Caravanero [cah-ra-vah-nay'-ro], *m.* 1. Leader of a caravan. 2. (Prov.) A wild fellow.

Caray [cah-rah'-e], *m.* 1. Tortoise-shell. *V.* CAREY. 2. (Amer.) *int.* An exclamation denoting surprise or impatience, equivalent to *caramba.*

Caraza [cah-rah'-thah], *f. aug.* Broad large face.

Carbohidrato [car-bo-e-drah'-to], *m.* Carbohydrate.

Carbol [car-bole'], *m.* A certain Turkish vessel.

Carbón [car-bone'], *m.* 1. Coal. 2. Charcoal. 3. Black pencil. *Carbón animal,* Animal charcoal. *Carbón de leña* or *carbón vegetal,* Charcoal. *Papel carbón,* Carbon paper. *Al carbón,* Charcoal grilled.

Carbonada [car-bo-nah'-dah], *f.* 1. Load of coal (for a furnace, etc.). 2. A native meat stew. 3. Kind of pancake. 4. Grilled meat ball.

Carbonadilla [car-bo-nah-deel'-lyah], *f. dim.* Small *carbonada.*

Carbonario [car-bo-nah'-re-o], *m.* An individual of a secret society formed to destroy absolutism. (Acad.)

Carbonatado, da [car-bo-nah-tah'-do, dah], *a.* Carbonated.

Carbonato [car-bo-nah'-to], *m.* (Chem.) Carbonate.

Carboncillo [car-bon-theel'-lyo], *m.* 1. (Dim.) Small coal. 2. Black crayon.

Carbonear [car-bo-nay-ar'], *va.* To reduce to charcoal by the action of fire.

Carbonera [car-bo-nay'-rah], *f.* 1. Place where charcoal is made. 2. Coal-house, coal-hole, or coal-cellar. 3. Coal-pit, colliery, coal-mine.

Carbonería [car-bo-nay-ree'-ah], *f.* Coal-yard; coal-shed; coal-mine.

Carbonero [car-bo-nay'-ro], *m.* 1. Charcoal-maker. 2. Collier, coal-man, coal-miner. 3. Coal-merchant, collier. 4. (Naut.) Coal-ship, collier.

Carbónico, ca [car-bo'-ne-co, cah], *a.* (Chem.) Carbonic.

Carbonización [car-bo-ne-thah-the-on'], *f.* Carbonization.

Carbonizado, da [car-bo-ne-thah'-do, dah], *a.* Carbonated.—*pp.* of CARBONIZAR.

Carbonizar [car-bo-ne-thar'], *va.* 1. To combine carbon with another body. 2. To char.

Carbono [car-bo'-no], *m.* (Chem.) Carbon.

Carborundo [car-bo-roon'-do], *m.* Carborundum.

Carbuncal [car-boon-cahl'], *a.* Resembling a carbuncle.

Carbunclo, Carbunco [car-boon'-clo], *m.* 1. Carbuncle, a precious stone. 2. Red pustule or pimple. *V.* CARBÚNCULO.

Carbuncoso, sa [car-boon-co'-so, sah], *a.* Of the nature of a carbuncle.

Carbúnculo [car-boon'-coo-lo], *m.* *V.* RUBÍ.

Carburador [car-boo-rah-dor'], *m.* Carburetor.

Carbureto [car-boo-ray'-to], or **Carburo** [car-boo'-ro], *m.* (Chem.) Carburet, or carbide.

Carcaj [car-cah'], *m.* *V.* CARCAX.

Carcajada [car-ca-hah'-dah], *f.* Loud laughter, hearty laughter, cachinnation.

Carcajú [car-ca-hoo'], *m.* The glutton, wolverene, a ravenous carnivorous animal.

Carcamal [car-ca-mahl'], *m.* Nickname of old people, especially of old women.

Carcamán [car-ca-mahn'], *m.* Tub, a heavy, big, unseaworthy vessel.

Cárcamo [car'-ca-mo], *m.* (Amer.) Riffle, a cleated trough.

Carcañal, Carcañar [car-ca-nyal', car-ca-nyar'], *m.* Heel-bone, calcaneum. *V.* CALCAÑAR.

Carcaño [car-cah'-nyo], *m.* Heel of the foot.

Carcápuli [car-cah'-poo-le], *m.* 1. (Bot.) Indian yellow orange of Java and Malabar. 2. (Bot.) The large carcapulla-tree in America, which produces a fruit resembling a cherry.

Cárcava [car'-ca-vah], *f.* (Obs.) 1. Inclosure, mound, hedge, ditch. 2. Pit or grave for the dead. 3. Gully made by torrents of water.

Carcavera [car-ca-vay'-rah], *f.* A bad woman; a witch.

Cárcavo [car'-ca-vo], *m.* 1. (Obs.) The cavity of the abdomen. 2. The hollow in which a water-wheel turns. 3. The footprint of an animal.

Carcavón [car-ca-vone'], *m.* Large and deep ditch.

Carcavuezo [car-cah-voo-ay'-tho], *m.* A deep pit.

Carcax [car-cahx'], *m.* 1. Quiver. 2. Ribbon with a case at the end, in which the cross is borne in a procession. 3. (Amer.) A leathern case in which a rifle is carried at the saddle-bow. 4. Ornament of the ankle worn by the Moors. *V.* AJORCA.

Cárcel [car'-thel], *f.* 1. Prison, jail. 2. Among carpenters, a wooden clamp to keep glued planks together. 3. Two small cart-loads of fire-wood. 4. Cheek of a printing-press. *Cárceles,* Among weavers, cog-reeds of a loom.

Carcelaje, Carceraje [car-thay-lah'-hay, car-thay-rah'-hay], *m.* Prison-fees, carcelage, jailer's fees, paid on leaving.

Carcelería [car-thay-lay-ree'-ah], *f.* 1. Imprisonment. 2. Bail given for the appearance of a prisoner. 3. (Obs.) Whole number of persons confined in a jail.

Carcelero [car-thay-lay'-ro], *m.* Jail-keeper, jailer. *Fiador carcelero,* One who is bail or surety for a prisoner.

Carcinógeno [car-the-no'-hay-no], *m.* (Med.) Carcinogen.

Carcinoma [car-the-no'-mah], *f.* Carcinoma, cancer.

Carcinomatoso [car-the-no-mah-to'-so], *a.* Carcinomatous, cancerous.

Carcoa [car-co'-ah], *f.* Row-barge used in India.

Cárcola [car'-co-lah], *f.* Treadle of a loom.

Carcoma [car-co'-mah], *f.* 1. Wood-borer, the larva of various beetles which burrow in wood. 2. Dust made by the wood-borer. 3. (Met.) Grief, anxious concern. 4. (Met.) One who runs by degrees through his whole fortune. 5. Cariosity of a bone.

Carcomer [car-co-merr'], *va.* 1. To gnaw, to corrode: applied to the wood-borer. 2. To consume a thing by degrees. 3. (Met.) To impair gradually health, virtue, etc.—*vr.* To decay, to decline in health, virtue, etc.

Carcomido, da [car-co-mee'-do, dah], *a.* 1. Worm-eaten, consumed. 2. (Met.) Decayed, declined, impaired.—*pp.* of CARCOMER.

Carda [car'-dah], *f.* 1. Teasel, for raising the nap on cloth. 2. Card, with which wool is combed. 3. Hatter's jack. 4. (Met.) Severe reprimand or censure. 5. (Naut.) Small vessel built like a galley. *Gente de la carda* or *los de la carda,* Idle street-walkers; wicked, licentious people.

Cardador [car-dah-dor'], *m.* Carder, comber.

Cardadura [car-dah-doo'-rah], *f.* Carding, combing wool.

Cardaestambre [car-dah-es-tahm'-bray], *m.* (Obs.) *V.* CARDADOR.

Cardámine pratense [car-dah'-me-nay], *m.* (Bot.) *V.* CARDÁMINO.

Cardámino pratense or **de prados** [car-dah'-me-no], *m.* (Bot.) Meadow lady's-smock, lady's-smock or cuckoo flower. Cardamine pratensis.

Cardamomo [car-dah-mo'-mo], *m.* (Bot.) Cardamomum, a medicinal seed. Amomum cardamomum.

Cardán [car-dahn'], *m.* (Mech.) Universal joint.

Cardar [car-dar'], *va.* 1. To card or comb wool. 2. To raise the nap on cloth with a teasel. *Cardarle a uno la lana,* (Met.) To win a large sum at play. *Cardarle a alguno la lana,* (Met.) To reprimand severely.

Cardelina [car-day-lee'-nah], *f.* (Orn.) Goldfinch, thistle-finch. Fringilla carduelis. *V.* JILGUERO.

Cardenal [car-day-nahl'], *m.* 1. Cardinal. 2. (Orn.) Virginian nightingale, cardinal grosbeak. Loxia cardinalis. 3. Discoloration from a lash or blow; lividity. *V.* EQUIMOSIS.

Cardenalato [car-day-na-lah'-to], *m.* Cardinalate, cardinalship.

Cardenalicio, cia [car-day-na-lee'-the-o, ah], *a.* Belonging to a cardinal.

Cardencha [car-den'-chah], *f.* 1. (Bot.) Teasel, a genus of plants. Dipsacus. *Cardencha cardadora,* Manured or fuller's teasel. Dipsacus fullonum. *Cardencha silvestre,* Wild teasel. Dipsacus silvestris. *Cardencha laciniada,* Laciniated teasel. Dipsacus laciniatus. *Cardencha pelosa,* Small teasel, shepherd's staff. Dipsacus pilosus. 2. Card or comb, for carding or combing of wool.

Cardenchal [car-den-chahl'], *m.* Place where teasels grow.

Cardenillo [car-day-neel'-lyo], *m.* 1. Verdigris. 2. (Painting) Verditer, a green paint made of verdigris; Paris green.

Cárdeno, na [car'-day-no, nah], *a.* Livid, of a dark purple colour.

Cardería [car-day-ree'-ah], *f.* Cardery, the workshop where combs or cards are made.

Cardero [car-day'-ro], *m.* Card-maker.

Cardiaca [car-dee'-ah-cah], *f.* (Bot.) Common mother-wort. Leonurus cardiaca.

Cardiaco, ca [car-dee'-ah-co, cah], *a.* (Med.) 1. Cardiac: applied to diseases of the heart. 2. Cardiac, cardiacal, cordial, having the quality of invigorating: applied to medicines.

Cardial [car-de-ahl'], *a.* (Obs.) Cardiacal, cardiac.

Cardialgia [car-de-al-hee'-ah], *f.* (Med.) Cardialgia, heart-burn.

Cardias [car'-de-as], *m.* The upper or cardiac orifice of the stomach.

Cardillo [car-deel'-lyo], *m.* 1. (Bot.) Golden thistle. Scolymus. *Cardillo español* or *de comer,* (Bot.) Perennial golden thistle or star-thistle. Scolymus hispanicus. *Cardillo manchado,* Annual golden thistle. Scolymus maculatus. 2. (Mex.) *V.* VISO. 3. Thistle-down.

Cardinal [car-de-nahl'], *a.* Cardinal, principal, fundamental. *Vientos cardinales,* Winds from the four cardinal points. *Virtudes cardinales,* Cardinal virtues. *Números cardinales,* Cardinal numbers.

Cardiógrafo [car-de-o'-grah-fo], *m.* Cardiograph.

Cardiograma [car-de-o-grah'-mah], *m.* Cardiogram.

Cardiología [car-de-o-lo-hee'-ah], *f.* Cardiology.

Carditis [car-dee'-tis], *f.* Inflammation of the muscular tissue of the heart.

Cardizal [car-de-thahl'], *m.* Land covered with thistles.

Cardo [car'-do], *m.* (Bot.) Thistle, a genus of plants. *Cardo silvestre* or *borriqueño,* (Bot.) Spear-plume thistle. Carduus lanceolatus. *Cardo aljonjero,* 1. Stemless, carline thistle. Carline acaulis. 2. Gummy-rooted atractilis. Atractylis gummifera. *Cardo hortense, cardo arrocife, or cardo de comer,* Cardon artichoke. Cinara cardunculus. *Cardo alcachofero,* Garden artichoke. Cynara scolimus. *Cardo corredor* or *setero,* Sea-holly, field eringo. Eryngium campestre. *Cardo bendito* or *santo,* Blessed thistle, centaury, holy thistle, carduus benedictus. Centaurea benedicta. *Cardo de burro* or *crespo,* Curled thistle. Carduus crispus. *Cardo huso,* Woolly carthamus. Carthamus lanatus. *Cardo lechero* or *cardo mariano,* Milk thistle. Carduus marianus. *Más áspero que un cardo,* said of a churlish and sullen person. (Literally, rougher than a thistle.)

Cardón [car-done'], *m.* 1. (Bot.) *V.* CARDENCHA. *Cardón de Canarias,* Canary spurge. Euphorbia canariensis. *Cardón de cochinilla,* Cochineal, fig cactus. Cactus coccinilifer. *Cardón lechal* or *lechar, V.* CARDILLO DE COMER. *Cardón cabezudo,* Turk's-cap cactus. Cactus melocactus. 2. The act and effect of carding.

Cardoncillo [car-don-theel'-lyo], *m.* (Bot.) Mountain carthamus. Carthamus carduncellus.

Carducha [car-doo'-chah], *f.* Large comb for wool.

Cardume, Cardumen [car-doo'-may, car-doo'-men], *m.* Shoal of fishes.

Carduza [car-doo'-thah], *f.* (Obs.) *V.* CARDA.

Carduzador [car-doo-thah-dor'], *m.* Carder. *V.* CARDADOR.

Carduzal [car-doo-thahl'], *m.* *V.* CARDIZAL.

Carduzar [car-doo-thar'], *va.* 1. To card or comb wool. 2. (Obs.) To shear cloth.

Careador [cah-ray-ah-dor'], *a.* *Perro careador,* A shepherd-dog, watch-dog. *V.* CAREAR, 3d def.

Carear [cah-ray-ar'], *va.* 1. (Law) To confront criminals. 2. To compare. 3. To tend a drove of cattle or flock of sheep.—*vr.* To assemble or meet for business.

Carecer [cah-ray-therr'], *vn.* To want, to be in need, to lack.

Careciente [cah-ray-the-en'-tay], *pa.* (Obs.) Wanting.
Carecimiento [cah-ray-the-me-en'-to], *m.* (Obs.) *V.* CARENCIA.
Carena [cah-ray'-nah], *f.* (Naut.) 1. Careening or repairing of a ship. *Media carena*, Boot-hose topping. *Carena mayor*, Thorough repair. 2. (Poet.) Ship. 3. (Obs.) Forty days' penance on bread and water. *Dar carena*, (Met.) To blame, to find fault with, to reprimand; to banter, to joke.
Carenaje [cah-ray-nah'-hay], *m.* *V.* CARENERO.
Carenar [cah-ray-nar'], *va.* To careen a ship, to pay a ship's bottom. *Aparejo de carenar*, Careening gear.
Carencia [cah-ren'-the-ah], *f.* Want, need, lack.
Carenero [cah-ray-nay'-ro], *m.* Careen ing-place
Careo [cah-ray'-o], *m.* 1. (Law) Confrontation, the act of bringing criminals or witnesses face to face. 2. Comparison. 3. (Fort.) Front of a bastion or fortress.
Carero, ra [cah-ray'-ro, rah], *a.* (Coll.) Selling things dear.
Carestía [cah-res-tee'-ah], *f.* 1. Scarcity, want. 2. Famine, famishment; jejuneness. 3. Dearness, or high price originating from scarcity.
Careta [cah-ray'-tah], *f.* 1. Mask made of pasteboard. 2. Wire cover of the face worn by bee-keepers. 3. *V.* JUDÍA.
Careto, ta [cah-ray'-to, tah], *a.* Having the forehead marked with a white spot or stripe: applied to horses.
Carey [cah-ray'-e], *m.* Tortoise-shell. (Malay, cárah.)
Careza [cah-ray'-thah], *f.* (Obs.) *V.* CARESTÍA.
(*Yo carezco, yo carezca*, from *Carecer. V.* CONOCER.)
Carga [car'-gah], *f.* 1. Load, burden, freight, lading. 2. Cargo, the lading of a ship. 3. Charge of a cannon or other fire-arm, and the nozzle of the flask which measures the powder of such charge. *Carga de balas encajonadas*, Case-shot. *Carga muerta*, Overloading, dead load. 4. Corn measure in Castile, containing four *fanegas* or bushels. 5. Medical preparation for curing sprains and inflammation in horses and mules, composed of flour, whites of eggs, ashes, and Armenian bole, all beaten up with the blood of the same animal. 6. Impost, duty, toll, tax. *Carga real*, King's tax, land tax. 7. (Met.) Burden of the mind, heaviness. 8. Load, weight, hinderance, pressure, cumbrance, or encumbrance. *Bestia de carga*, A beast of burden; a mule or sumpter-horse. 9. (Obs.) Discharge of fire-arms. 10. Charge, an attack upon the enemy. *Carga cerrada*, Volley, a general discharge. *Carga concejil*, Municipal office which all the inhabitants of a place must serve in their turn. *Acodillar(se) con la carga*, Not to be able to fulfil one's engagements. *Dar a uno una carga cerrada*, To scold or reprimand one severely. *Dar con la carga en tierra*, or *en el suelo*, (Met.) To sink under fatigue and distress. *Echar la carga á otro*, (Met.) To throw the blame upon another. *Llevar los soldados á la carga*, (Mil.) To lead soldiers to the charge. *Volver á la carga sobre el enemigo*, To return to the charge. *¿Por qué carga de agua?* Why? for what reason? *Sentarse la carga*, To vex and excoriate a beast by a burden badly put on. (Fig.) To make troublesome and burdensome the obligation which one has taken on himself. *Terciar la carga*, To divide a load into parts of equal weight. *Ser alguna cosa de ciento en carga*, To be a thing of little value. *Navío de carga*, (Naut.) Ship of burden, a merchantman *A carga cerrada*, Boisterously, inconsiderately, without reflection. *A cargas*, Abundantly, in great plenty. *A cargas le vienen los regalos*, He receives loads of presents. *A cargas se le va el dinero*, He spends money like water.
Carga útil [car'-gah oo'-teel], *f.* (Aer.) Payload.
Cargadera [car-gah-day'-rah], *f.* (Naut.) Down-hauls, brails. *Cargadera de una vela de estay*, Down-haul of a stay-rail. *Cargaderas de las gavias*, Top-sail brails. *Aparejo de cargadera de racamento*, Down-haul tackle.
Cargadero [car-gah-day'-ro], *m.* Place where goods are loaded or unloaded.
Cargadilla [car-gah-deel'-lyah], *f.* (Coll.) Increase of a debt newly contracted.
Cargado [car-gah'-do], *m.* A Spanish step in dancing.
Cargado, da [car-gah'-do, dah], *a.* Loaded, full: fraught. *Cargado de espaldas*, Round-shouldered, stooping. *Estar cargado de vino*, To be top-heavy, or half-seas over.—*pp.* of CARGAR.
Cargador [cah-gar-dor'], *m.* 1. Freighter, a merchant who ships goods for other markets. 2. Loader, he who loads; porter. 3. Rammer, ramrod. 4. He that loads great guns. 5. A large pitchfork for straw. 6. (Arch.) A post put in a doorway or window.—*pl.* 1. (Naut.) Tackles. *V.* PALANQUINES. 2. Plates of copper or pallets used in gilding.
Cargamento [car-gah-men'-to], *m.* (Naut.) Cargo.
Cargar [car-gar'], *va.* & *vn.* 1. To load, to burden, to freight: to carry a load: applied to men and beasts. 2. To charge, to attack the enemy. 3. To ship goods for foreign markets. *Cargar a flete*, To ship goods on freight. 4. To load or charge a gun. 5. To overload or overburden, to clog; to lay in an abundant stock. 6. To charge in account, to book. 7. To impose or lay taxes. 8. To impute, to arraign, to impeach. 9. To incline with the whole body toward a point or place. 10. To rest, to recline for support. 11. To take a charge, a duty, or any trust. 12. To crowd. 13. In cards, especially in the game named *malilla*, to take a card by playing one higher. *Cargar con*, To carry, take. *Cargar sobre*, To be responsible for another's deficiencies. (Gram.) For one letter or syllable to have more value in prosody than another. *Cargar delantero*, (Met.) To be top-heavy or fuddled. *Cargar arriba una vela*, (Naut.) To clew up a sail. *Cargar la consideración*, (Met.) To reflect with consideration and maturity. *Cargar la mano*, 1. (Met.) To pursue a thing with eagerness. 2. (Met.) To reproach with severity. 3. To extort, *Cargar los dados*, To cog dice. *Cargar sobre uno*, To importune, tease, or molest.—*vr.* 1. To recline, to rest, or to lean against any thing. *El viento se ha cargado al norte*, The wind has veered to the north. 2. To charge one's own account with the sums received. 3. To maintain, to support, or take a new duty upon one's self.
Cargareme [car-ga-ray'-may], *m.* Receipt, voucher. (*Cargaré*, future, and *me*, pronoun.)
Cargazón [car-ga-thone'], *f.* 1. Cargo of a ship. 2. *Cargazón de cabeza*, Heaviness of the head. 3. *Cargazón de tiempo*, Cloudy, thick weather.
Cargo [car'-go], *m.* 1. Burden, loading. 2. (Prov.) Load of stones which weighs forty *arrobas*. 3. A number of baskets piled one on the other and put in the oil-press. 4. A load of pressed grapes. 5. Wood measure in Granada, about a cubic yard. 6. Total amount of what has been received, in a general account. 7. (Met.) Employment, dignity, office, honour; ministry. *Cargo concejil*, A municipal office. 8. Charge, keeping, care. 9. (Met.) Obligation to perform something. 10. (Met.) Command or direction of a thing. 11. Fault or deficiency in the performance of one's duty. 12. Charge, accusation. (Law) Count. *Cargo de conciencia*, Remorse, sense of guilt. *Cargo y data*, (Com.) Creditor and debtor (Cr. and Dr.). *Hacer cargo a alguno de una cosa*, To charge one with a fault, to hold him responsible; to accuse, to impeach. *Hacerse cargo de alguna cosa*, 1. To take into consideration; to reflect. 2. To make one's self acquainted with a thing. *Hacerse uno cargo de algo*, To take upon one's self. *Ser en cargo*, To be debtor.
Cargoso, sa [car-go'-so, sah], *a.* 1. Heavy. 2. Bothersome, annoying.
Cargue [car'-gay], *m.* (Obs.) 1. Loading a vessel. 2. License to load.
Carguero, ra [car-gay'-ro, rah], *a.* He who bears a burden.
Carguica, illa, ita [car-gee'-cah, eel'-lyah, ee'-tah], *f. dim.* Small or light load.
Carguío [car-gee'-o], *m.* 1. Cargo of merchandise. 2. A load.
Cari [cah'-re], *m.* Caraway-seed.
Carí [cah-ree'], *m.* (Amer. Bot.) Blackberry-bush.
Caria [cah'-re-ah], *f.* (Arch.) 1. The shaft (or fust) of a column. 2. *V.* CARIES.
Cariacedo, da [cah-re-ah-thay'-do, dah], *a.* Having a sour-looking countenance.
Cariacontecido, da [cah-re-ah-con-tay-thee'-do, dah], *a.* Sad, mournful, expressive of grief.
Cariacuchillado, da [cah-re-ah-coo-cheel-lyah'-do, dah], *a.* Having the face marked with cuts or gashes.
Cariado, da [cah-re-ah'-do, dah], *a.* Carious, rotten.—*pp.* of CARIARSE.
Cariaguileño, ña [cah-re-ah-gee-lay'-nyo, nyah], *a.* (Coll.) Long-visaged, with an aquiline or hooked nose.
Carialegre [cah-re-ah-lay'-gray], *a.* Smiling, cheerful.
Cariampollado, da [cah-re-am-pol-lyah'-do, dah], *a.* Round-faced, plump-cheeked.
Cariancho, cha [cah-re-ahn'-cho, chah], *a.* Broad-faced, chubby, chub-faced, bull-faced.
Cariarse [cah-re-ar'-say], *vr.* (Med.) To grow carious: applied to the bones.
Cariarú [cah-re-ah-roo'], *m.* A liana of the Antilles yielding a crimson dye.
Cariátide [cah-re-ah'-te-day], *f.* (Arch.) Caryatides, columns or pilasters under the figure of women.
Caribe [cah-ree'-bay], *m.* Cannibal, man-eater, a savage.—*pl.* Caribs, Indians of the Antilles and the adjacent continent, when they were discovered.
Caribito [cah-re-bee'-to], *m.* A river fish of the bream species.
Caribobo, ba [cah-re-bo'-bo, bah], *a.* Having a stupid look.
Carica [cah-ree'-cah], *f.* (Prov.) Sort of kidney beans.

Caricatura [cah-re-cah-too'-rah], *f.* 1. Caricature in art or letters. 2. Cartoon. *Caricatura animada*, Animated cartoon film.

Caricaturar [cah-re-cah-too-rar'], *va.* To caricature.

Caricaturesco, ca [cah-re-cah-too-res'-co, cah], *a.* Caricaturist, caricatural; belonging to caricature.

Caricaturista [cah-re-cah-too-rees'-tah], *m.* Caricaturist.

Caricia [cah-ree'-the-ah], *f.* Caress, act of endearment, endearing expression.

Cariciosamente [cah-re-the-o-sah-men'-tay], *adv.* In a fondling or endearing manner.

Caricioso, sa [cah-re-the-o'-so, sah], *a.* Fondling, endearing, caressing.

Caricuerdo, da [cah-re-coo-err'-do, dah], *a.* Having a serene or composed mien.

Caridad [cah-re-dahd'], *f.* 1. Charity, charitableness, kindness, good-will, benevolence. 2. Alms. 3. Refreshment of bread and wine, which confraternities cause to be given to travellers at the church-door. *Caridad, ¿ sabes cuál es ? Perdona si mal quieres, y paga lo que debes*, Do you know what charity is? Forgive, if you bear ill-will, and pay what you owe. *La caridad empieza por nosotros mismos*, Charity begins at home.

Caridelantero, ra [cah-re-day-lan-tay'-ro, rah], *a.* (Littl. us.) Brazen-faced, impudent.

Caridoliente [cah-re-do-le-en'-tay], *a.* Having a mournful countenance.

Caries [cah'-re-es], *f.* Caries or cariosity, ulceration of bone.

Cariescrito [cah-re-es-cree'-to], *a.* Corrugated, shrivelled.

Cariexento, ta [cah-re-ec-sen'-to, tah], *a.* (Littl. us.) Brazen-faced, impudent.

Carifruncido, da [cah-re-froon-thee'-do, dah], *a.* Having a face contracted into wrinkles.

Carigordo, da [cah-re-gor'-do, dah], *a.* Full-faced.

Carijusto, ta [cah-re-hoos'-to, tah], *a.* Dissembling, hypocritical.

Carilargo, ga [cah-re-lar'-go, gah], *a.* Long-visaged.

Carilla [cah-reel'-lyah], *f.* 1. (Dim.) Little or small face. 2. Mask used by bee-keepers. *V.* CARETA. 3. Silver coin in Aragón worth eighteen *dineros*, or deniers. 4. *V.* LLANA and PÁGINA.

Carilleno, na [cah-reel-lyay'-no, nah], *a.* (Coll.) Plump-faced.

Carillo, lla [cah-reel'-lyo, lyah], *a. dim.* Dear, high-priced.

Carillo [cah-reel'-lyo], *m. dim.* (Obs.) Dear, beloved.

Carilucio, cia [cah-re-loo'-the-o, ah], *a.* Having a shining or glossy face.

Carina [cah-ree'-nah], *f.* 1. (Arch.) Building raised by the Romans in form of a ship. 2. (Bot.) The two lower petals of papilionaceous flowers; the keel, carina.

Carinegro, gra [cah-re-nay'-gro, grah], *a.* Of a swarthy complexion.

Carininfo [cah-re-neen'-fo], *a.* Having a womanish face: applied to men.

Cariñana [cah-re-nyah'-nah], *f.* (Obs.) Ancient head-dress like a nun's veil.

Cariño [cah-ree'-nyo], *m.* 1. Love, fondness, tenderness, affection, kindness; concern. 2. Soft or endearing expression. 3. (Obs.) Anxious desire of a thing.

Cariñosamente [cah-re-nyo-sah-men'-tay], *adv.* Fondly, affectionately; kindly; good-naturedly.

Cariñoso, sa [cah-re-nyo'-so, sah], *a.* 1. Affectionate, endearing, lovely; benevolent, kind, good, good-natured, natural. 2. Anxiously, desirous, longing.

Cariocar [cah-re-o-car'], *m.* (Bot.) A remarkable tree of tropical America, which yields an oil which replaces butter in Guiana. The sonari-tree. Caryocar nuciferum.

Cariofilata [cah-re-o-fe-lah'-tah], *f.* (Bot.) Herb bennet, common avens. Geum urbanum.

Cariofileo, ea [cah-re-o-fee'-lay-o, ah], *a.* Caryophyllaceous; like a pink in structure or habits.

Cariofilo [cah-re-o-fee'-lo], *m.* 1. The pink of gardens. Dianthus caryophyllus. 2. The clove. Caryophyllus aromaticus.

Carioso, sa [cah-re-o'-so, sah], *a.* (Obs.) Carious, liable to corruption.

Cariota [cah-re-oh'-tah], *f.* (Bot.) Wild carrot. Daucus lucidus.

Caripando, da [cah-re-pahn'-do, dah], *a.* (Prov.) Idiot-like, stupid-faced.

Cariparejo, ja [cah-re-pa-ray'-ho, hah], *a. & m. & f.* (Low) Resembling, having a similar face; likeness.

Carirraído, da [cah-rir-rah-ee'-do, dah], *a.* (Coll.) Brazen-faced, impudent.

Carirredondo, da [cah-rir-ray-don'-do, dah], *a.* Round-faced.

Caris [cah'-ris], *m.* Kind of ragout or fricassee.

Carisma [cah-rees'-mah], *m.* (Divin.) Divine gift or favour.

Carita [cah-ree'-tah], *f. dim.* Little or small face.

Caritativamente [cah-re-tah-te-vah-men'-tay], *adv.* Charitably.

Caritativo, va [cah-re-tah-tee'-vo, vah], *a.* Charitable, hospitable.

Cariucho [cah-re-oo'-cho], *m.* An Indian national dish of Ecuador.

Cariz [cah-reeth'], *m.* The face of the sky; the aspect of the atmosphere or of the horizon, or of a business.

Carlán [car-lahn'], *m.* (Prov.) He who owns the duties and jurisdiction of a district.

Carlanca [car-lahn'-cah], *f.* A mastiff's collar. *Tener muchas carlancas*, To be very cunning or crafty.

Carlancón [car-lan-cone'], *m.* (Met. Coll.) Person very subtle and crafty.

Carlanía [car-la-nee'-ah], *f.* Dignity and district of a *carlán*, an ancient magistrate in Aragón.

Carlear [car-lay-ar'], *vn.* To pant. *V.* JADEAR.

Carlín [car-leen'], *m.* An ancient silver coin.

Carlina [car-lee'-nah], *f.* (Bot.) Carline thistle. Carlina. *Carlina acaule*, Stemless carline thistle. Carlina acaulis.

Carlinga [car-leen'-gah], *f.* (Naut.) Step of a mast.

Carlista [car-lees'-tah], *m.* Carlist, a partisan of Don Carlos María Isidro de Borbón, and the latter's claim to the throne of Spain.

Carlovingio, gia [car-lo-veen'-he-o, he-ah], *a.* Carlovingian, relating to Charlemagne.

Carmañola [car-ma-nyo'-lah], *f.* 1. A French republican song, composed in 1792. 2. A kind of jacket with narrow neck and short skirt, much used in the time of the revolution.

Carmel [car-mel'], *m.* (Bot.) Ribwort, plantain, rib-grass. Plantago lanceolata.

Carmelita [car-may-lee'-tah], *m. & f.* 1. Carmelite. 2. *f.* Flower of the great Indian cress.

Carmelitano, na [car-may-le-tah'-no, nah], *a.* Belonging to the Carmelite order.

Carmen [car'-men], *m.* 1. (Prov.) Country-house and garden. 2. Carmelite order. 3. Verse.

Carmenador [car-may-nah-dor'], *m.* Teaser, one who scratches cloth to raise the nap.

Carmenadura [car-may-nah-doo'-rah], *f.* Act of teasing or scratching cloth, to raise the nap.

Carmenar [car-may-nar'], *va.* 1. To prick or card wool. 2. To scratch cloth for the purpose of raising the nap. 3. To pull out the hair of the head. *V.* REPELAR. 4. To win another's money at play.

Carmes [car'-mes], *m.* Kermes, the cochineal insect.

Carmesí [car-may-see'], *m.* Cochineal powder. (Arab. quermezí or qirmiz.)

Carmesí [car-may-see'], *m. & a.* Crimson, bright red, somewhat darkened with blue; purple.

Carmesín, *a.* **Carmeso**, *m.* [car-may-seen', car-may'-so]. (Obs.) *V.* CARMESÍ.

Carmín [car-meen'], *m.* 1. Carmine, the colouring matter of cochineal. *Carmín bajo*, Pale rose colour. 2. (Bot.) Pokeweed; phylotacca. Phytolacca decandra.

Carminante [car-me-nahn' tay], *pa.* (Obs.) *V.* CARMINATIVO.

Carminar [car-me-nar'], *va.* (Obs.) To expel wind.

Carminativo [car-me-nah-tee'-vo], *m.* Carminative, relieving wind.

Carnada [car-nah'-dah], *f.* Bait.

Carnaje [car-nah'-hay], *m.* 1. Salt beef. 2. (Obs.) Carnage, slaughter.

Carnal [car-nahl'], *a.* 1. Carnal, fleshy. 2. Sensual, carnal, fleshly, lustful, lecherous. 3. (Met.) Worldly, outward: opposed to spiritual. 4. United by kindred.

Carnal, *m.* Time of the year in which meat may be eaten: opposed to Lent and other fast-days.

Carnalidad [car-nah-le-dahd'], *f.* Carnality, lustfulness.

Carnalmente [car-nal-men'-tay], *adv.* Carnally, sensually.

Carnaval [car-nah-vahl'], *m.* Carnival, the feast held before Shrovetide. V. CARNESTOLENDAS.

Carnaza [car-nah'-thah], *f.* 1. Fleshy part of a hide or skin. 2. (Coll.) Meal consisting of an abundance of meat.

Carne [car'-nay], *f.* 1. Flesh. 2. Meat or flesh-meat, for food, in contradistinction to fish. 3. Pap, the pulp of fruit. 4. A boyish play with a hollow bone. *Carne de membrillo*, Pulp of quinces, boiled, cooled, and preserved. *Carne de pelo*, Flesh of small quadrupeds, hares, rabbits, etc. *Carne de pluma*, Flesh of fowls. *Carne de gallina*, Mischief sustained by certain woods, characterized by a yellowish white colour of the affected layers. *Carne de sábado*, The remains or scraps of meat allowed by the Roman Church to be eaten on Saturday. *Carne salvajina*, The meat of wild beasts. *Carne sin hueso no se da sino a Don Bueso*, The rich and powerful are always preferred. *Quien come la carne, que roa el hueso*, He who eats the meat must gnaw the bone: equivalent to No rose without a thorn. *Carne momia*, 1. Meat preserved by aromatics and balsams. 2. (Coll.) Flesh of meat without bones. *Carne asada en horno*, Baked meat. *Carne asada en parrillas*, Broiled meat. *Carne fiambre*, Cold meat. *Carne mollar* or *carne magra*, Lean. *Carne nueva*, Meat sold when Lent is over. *Carne sin hueso*, (Met.) Employment of much profit and little trouble. *Carne y sangre*, Flesh and blood, near kindred. *Color de carne*,

Flesh colour. *Caldo de carne*, Flesh broth. *Cobrar carnes*, or *echar carnes*, To grow fat. *Ni es carne ni pescado*, (Met.) He is neither fish nor flesh, an insipid fellow. *Poner toda la carne en el asador*, (Met.) To hazard one's all. *Ser uña y carne*, (Met.) To be hand and glove, to be intimate or familiar. *Ser carne y hueso de alguno*, To be flesh and blood of any one, to be part and parcel of the same thing. *Tomar la mujer en carnes*, To take a wife in her smock. *Temblar las carnes*, (Met.) To shudder with fear or horror. *En carnes*, Naked. *Carne de grajo*, (Met.) Brown, meagre woman. *Tener carne de perro*, To have much fortitude or strength.

Carnecería, Carnescería [car-nay-thay-ree'-ah, car-nes-thay-ree'-ah], *f.*

Carnecilla [car-nay-theel'-lyah], *f.* Small excrescence in some part of the body; caruncle.

Carnerada [car-nay-rah'-dah], *f.* Flock of sheep.

Carneraje [car-nay-rah'-hay], *m.* Tax or duty on sheep.

Carnerario [car-nay-rah'-re-o], *m.* (Prov.) Charnel-house.

Carnereamiento [car-nay-ray-ah-me-en'-to], *m.* Poundage, penalty for the trespass of sheep.

Carnerear [car-nay-ray-ar'], *va.* To fine the proprietor of sheep for damage done.

Carnerero [car-nay-ray'-ro], *m.* Shepherd. *V.* PASTOR.

Carneril [car-nay-reel'], *m.* Sheep-walk, pasture for sheep.

Carnero [car-nay'-ro], *m.* 1. Sheep, mutton. 2. Mutton, the flesh of sheep dressed for food. 3. (Prov.) Sheepskin dressed or tanned. 4. Family vault, burying-place; charnel-house. 5. (Obs.) Larder. *Carnero de cinco cuartos*, The African sheep noted for its very large tail. *Carnero adalid* or *carnero manso para guía*, Bellwether. *Carnero de simiente*, Ram kept for breeding. *Carnero ciclán*, Ridgil or ridgling. *Carnero marino*, (Zool.) White shark. Squalus carcharias. *Carnero verde* Hashed mutton. *No hay tales carneros*, (Coll.) There is no such thing.

Carneruno, na [car-nay-roo'-no, nah], *a.* Resembling or belonging to sheep.

Carnestolendas [car-nes-to-len'-das], *f. pl.* Three carnival days before Shrovetide or Ash-Wednesday.

Carnet [car-net'], *m.* 1. Notebook. 2. Account book. 3. Dance program. 4. Identification card.

Carnicería [car-ne-thay-ree'-ah], *f.* 1. Meat-market. 2. Slaughter-house. 3. Carnage, havoc, slaughter. *Hacer carnicería*, 1. To cut away a great quantity of flesh. 2. To wound in many places. *Parece carnicería*, It is as noisy as the shambles.

Carnicero [car-ne-thay'-ro], *m.* Butcher.

Carnicero, ra [car-ne-thay'-ro, rah], *a.* 1. Carnivorous: applied to animals. 2. Bloodthirsty, sanguinary. 3. Applied to pasture-grounds for cattle. 4. (Coll.) Applied to a person who eats much meat. 5. Belonging to shambles. *Libra carnicera*, Pound for butcher's meat, which varies from twenty-four to thirty-six ounces.

Carnicol [car-ne-cole'], *m.* Hoof of cloven-footed animals. *V.* TABA.

Carnificación [car-ne-fe-ca-the-on'], *f.* Carnification, a morbid change of a tissue to the consistency of flesh, as in hepatization of the lungs.

Carnificarse [car-ne-fe-car'-say], *vr.* To carnify, to breed flesh.

Carnívoro, ra [car-nee'-vo-ro, rah], *a.* Carnivorous: applied to animals.

Carniza [car-nee-thah'], *f.* (Low) 1. Refuse of meat. 2. Cats' or dogs' meat.

Carnosidad [car-no-se-dahd'], *f.* 1. Carnosity, proud flesh, growing on a wound, or a fleshy excrescence of any part of the body. 2. Fatness, abundance of flesh and blood. 3. Fleshiness.

Carnoso, sa [car-no'-so, sah], *a.* 1. Fleshy, carnous, carneous, fleshed. 2. Full of marrow; pulpous, applied to fruit. 3. Papescent, containing pap.

Carnudo, da [car-noo'-do, dah], *a.* *V.* CARNOSO.

Carnuza [car-noo'-thah], *f.* Abundance of meat, producing loathing.

Caro, ra [cah'-ro, rah], *a.* 1. Dear, high-priced, costly. 2. Dear, beloved, affectionate. *Caro bocado*, (Met.) A dear morsel. *Lo barato es caro*, Cheap things are dearest. *Tener en caro*, (Obs.) To estimate highly.

Caró [cah'-ro], *adv.* Dearly, at a high price, at too great a price.

Carobo [ca-ro'-bo], *m.* 1. Weight of the twenty-fourth part of a grain. 2. Kind of Turkish vessel.

Caroca [ca-ro'-cah], *f.* (Coll.) Caress, endearing action or expression made with a selfish purpose. Commonly used in the plural.

Carocha [ca-ro'-chah], *f.* White glutinous secretion (probably from the appendicular glands) of the queen bee, in which she lays her eggs; this with the egg in each cell.

Carochar [ca-ro-char'], *va.* To hatch eggs: applied to the hive-bees.

Cárolus [cah'-ro-loos], *m.* Ancient Flemish coin.

Caromomia [ca-ro-mo'-me-ah], *f.* The dry flesh of a mummy.

Carona [ca-ro'-nah], *f.* 1. Padding of the saddle, which touches the animal's back. 2. Part of the animal's back on which the saddle lies. *Esquilar la carona*, To shear the back of a mule, a custom in Spain. *A carona*, (Obs.) Immediate to the skin or back. *Blando de carona*, (Coll.) 1. Applied to a person very feeble or lazy. 2. Applied to a person who falls in love easily.

Caronada [ca-ro-nah'-dah], *f.* Carronade.

Caroñoso, sa [ca-ro-nyo'-so, sah], *a.* (Obs.) Old, galled, and cast off: applied to beasts of burden.

Caroquero, ra [ca-ro-kay'-ro, rah], *m.* & *f.* Wheedler, flatterer; caressing.

Carosiera [ca-ro-se-ay'-rah], *f.* 1. (Bot.) Species of the palm-tree. 2. Date, the fruit of that species of the palm.

Carotas [ca-ro'-tas], *f. pl.* Rolls of tobacco ground to powder.

Carótida [ca-ro'-te-dah], *f.* (Prov.) The carotid artery.

Carozo [ca-ro'-tho], *m.* 1. (Prov.) Core of a pomegranate, or other fruit. 2. Cob of maize.

Carpa [car'-pah], *f.* 1. (Zool.) Carp, a fresh-water fish. Cyprinus carpio. 2. Part of a bunch of grapes which is torn off. 3. (Peru) A tent of canvas or cloth.

Carpanel [car-pa-nel'], *m.* (Arch.) Arch in a semi-elliptic form.

Carpe [car'-pay], *m.* (Bot.) Common horn-beam tree, witch-hazel. Carpinus betulus.

Carpedal [car-pay-dahl'], *m.* Plantation of common horn-beam trees.

Carpelo [car-pay'-lo], *m.* Carpel.

Carpentear [car-pen-tay-ar'], *va.* (Obs.) *V.* ARREJACAR.

Carpeta [car-pay'-tah], *f.* 1. Table-cover, covering of a table. 2. Portfolio, portable writing-desk. 3. Small curtains before the doors of taverns. 4. Envelope of a letter. 5. Label, or indorsement, upon a bundle of papers; a wrapper.

Carpetazo [car-pay-tah'-tho], *m.* A blow or stroke with a *carpeta*. *Dar carpetazo a una petición, propuesta de ley* or *providencia*, To lay it by, to lay it on the table.

Carpintear [car-pin-tay-ar'], *vn.* To do carpenter's work.

Carpintería [car-pin-tay-ree'-ah], *f.* 1. Carpentry. 2. Carpenter's shop.

Carpintero [car-pin-tay'-ro], *m.* 1. Carpenter, joiner. *Carpintero de blanco*, Joiner who makes utensils of wood. *Carpintero de prieto* or *de carretas*, Cartwright, wheelwright. *Carpintero de obras de afuera*, Carpenter who timbers or roofs houses. *Carpintero de ribera* or *de navío*, Ship-carpenter, shipwright. *Maestro carpintero de remos*, Master oar-maker. *Segundo carpintero*, Carpenter's mate. 2. *Pájaro carpintero*, (Orn.) Woodpecker. *Carpintero real*, Ivory-billed woodpecker.

Carpión [car-pe-on'], *m.* Large carp, resembling a trout.

Carpir [car-peer'], *vn.* (Obs.) To tear, to scrape, to scratch, to scold.

Carpo [car'-po], *m.* (Anat.) Carpus, wrist.

Carpobálsamo [car-po-bahl'-sah-mo], *m.* Carpobalsamum, fruit of the tree which yields the balm of Gilead.

Carpófago [car-po'-fah-go], *m.* One who lives on fruit.

Carqueja, or **Carqueija** [car-kay'-hah, car-kay'-e-hah], *f.* (Bot.) *V.* CARQUESA, for a plant.

Carquesa, Carquesia [car-kay'-sah, car-kay'-se-ah], *f.* 1. In glass-houses, the annealing furnace. 2. (Bot.) Three-toothed leaved genista or rest-harrow, green-weed. Genista tridentata.

Carquexia [car-kek'-se-ah], *f.* A species of broom-plant.

Carraca [car-rah'-cah], *f.* 1. Carack, large and slow-sailing ship of burden. 2. Rattle, an instrument used instead of bells the three last days of the holy week. 3. A rachet brace. 4. The navy-yard in Cadiz.

Carraco, ca [car-rah'-co, cah], *a.* (Obs.) Old, withered, decrepit.

Carracón [car-rah-cone'], *m.* 1. Ship of burden of the largest size. 2. (Aug.) Large rattle. 3. Animal worn out with age and fatigue.

Carral [car-rahl'], *m.* Barrel, butt, vat, pipe for transporting wine in carts and wagons.

Carraleja [car-rah-lay'-hah], *f.* 1. Black beetle with yellow stripes, which when lightly pressed yields an oily substance much used by farriers; the oil-beetle, meloe. 2. Spanish blistering beetle. (Acad.)

Carralero [car-rah-lay'-ro], *m.* Cooper.

Carranclán [car-ran-clahn'], *m.* Gingham.

Carranclo [car-rahn'-clo], *m.* (Prov.) A blue-feathered bird of Estremadura.

Carrancudo, da [car-ran-coo'-do, dah], *a.* (Littl. us.) Starched, stiff, affected, solemn.

Carranque [car-rahn'-kay], *m.* A Peruvian bird resembling a crane.

Carrasca [car-rahs'-cah], *f.* (Bot.) *V.* CARRASCO.

Carrascal [car-ras-cahl'], *m.* Plantation of evergreen oaks.

Carrasco [car-rahs'-co], *m.* (Bot.) Evergreen oak: holm oak. Quercus ilex. *V.* COSCOJA.

Carrascon [car-ras-cone'], *m.* (Bot. Aug.) Large evergreen oak.

Carraspada [car-ras-pah'-dah], *f.* Negus, a beverage made of red wine, honey, and spice.

Carraspante [car-ras-pahn'-tay], *a.* (Prov.) Harsh, acrid, strong.

Carraspera [car-ras-pay'-rah], *f.* 1. Hoarseness. 2. Sore throat, attended with hoarseness.

Carraspique [car-ras-pee'-kay], *m.* (Bot.) Candytuft. Iberis.

Carrasqueño, ña [car-ras-kay'-nyo, nyah], *a.* 1. Harsh, sharp, biting. 2. Rough, rude, sullen. 3. Belonging to the evergreen oak. 4. (Prov.) Strong, nervous.

Carrasquilla [car-ras-keel'-lyah], *f.* (Bot. Prov.) A species of the genus Rhamnus; a buckthorn.

Carrear, Carrejar [car-ray-ar', car-ray-har'], *va.* (Obs.) *V.* ACARREAR.

Carrera [car-ray'-rah], *f.* 1. Running a career, a course, a race. 2. A race-ground for horses. 3. The course of the stars. 4. High-road, from one town to another. 5. In Madrid, a broad and long street, as, *La carrera de San Francisco*, St. Francis street. 6. Alley, a walk in a garden; an avenue leading to a house, planted with trees. 7. Row of things, ranged in a line. 8. Range of iron teeth in combing-cards. 9. Line made by dividing and separating the hair. 10. Girder, in a floor. 11. Stitch in a stocking which has broken or fallen. 12. Course and duration of life. 13. Profession of arms or letters. 14. Course, method of life, train of actions. 15. Course, conduct, manner of proceeding, mode of action. 16. Street or high-road destined for a public procession. 17. Spanish step in dancing. *V.* CARRERILLA. *Carrera de cordelería*, Rope-walk. *Carrera de Indias*, Trade from Spain to South America. *Carrera del émbolo*, Stroke of the piston. *Carrera de válvula*, Travel of a valve. *Estar en carrera*, To be in the way of earning a livelihood. *Poner a uno en carrera*, To provide one with an employment. *No poder hacer carrera con alguno*, Not to be able to bring one to reason. *A carrera abierta*, At full speed. *De carrera*, Without thinking, rashly. *Carrera de armamentos*, Arms race. *Carrera de baquetas*, Gauntlet. *Carrera de relevos*, Relay race. *Carrera de vallas*, Hurdles. *Tomar carrera*, To back up in order to get a running start. *No poder hacer carrera con*, Not to be able to do a thing with, not to make any headway with.

Carrerilla, ta [car-ray-reel'-lyah, ree'-tah], *f.* 1. (Dim.) Small race or course. 2. Rapid motion in a Spanish dance. 3. (Mus.) Rise or fall of an octave.

Carreta [car-ray'-tah], *f.* 1. Long narrow cart. 2. *Carreta cubierta*, Gallery of a siege, or the covered passage to the walls of a fortress.

Carretada [car-ray-tah'-dah], *f.* 1. Cartful, cart-load. 2. Great quantity. *A carretadas*, (Coll.) Copiously, in abundance.

Carretaje [car-ray-tah'-hay], *m.* Cartage, trade with carts.

Carrete [car-ray'-tay], *m.* 1. Spool, bobbin, reel. 2. Small reed for winding silk or gold and silver twist. 3. Reel of a fishing-rod. 4. (Elec.) Bobbin, wire coil.

Carretear [car-ray-tay-ar'], *va.* 1. To cart, to convey in a cart. 2. To drive a cart.—*vr.* To draw unevenly: applied to oxen or mules.

Carretel [car-ray-tel'], *m.* 1. Spool, reel, bobbin. 2. (Prov.) A fishing-reel; line-reel. 3. (Naut.) Log-reel. 4. (Naut.) Spun-yarn winch. 5. Rope-walk reel. 6. *Carretel de carpintero*, Carpenter's marking-line.

Carretela [car-ray-tay'-lah], *f.* Caleche, calash, a four-wheeled carriage on springs.

Carretera [car-ray-tay'-rah], *f.* High-road.

Carretería [car-ray-tay-ree'-ah], *f.* 1. Number of carts. 2. Trade of a carman. 3. Cartwright's yard; wheelwright's shop.

Carretero [car-ray-tay'-ro], *m.* 1. Cartwright. 2. Carman, carrier, carter. *Voz de carretero*, Harsh, loud, and unpleasant voice. *Jurar como un carretero*, To swear like a trooper. 3. (Ast.) Wagoner, a northern constellation.

Carretil [car-ray-teel'], *a.* Suitable for carts.

Carretilla [car-ray-teel'-lyah], *f.* 1. Wheelbarrow. 2. Hand truck. 3. Hand cart. 4. Walker (for babies). 5. Firecracker. 6. Cake decorator. *Carretilla elevadora*, Fork-lift truck. *Saber de carretilla una cosa*, To know something perfectly.

Carretón [car-ray-tone'], *m.* 1. Small cart, in the shape of an open chest. 2. Go-cart. 3. (Obs.) Gun-carriage. 4. *Carretón de lámpara*, Pulley for raising or lowering lamps. 5. In Toledo, stage for religious plays. 6. Truck, dray, van.

Carretoncillo [car-ray-ton-theel'-lyo], *m. dim.* Small go-cart for children.

Carretonero [car-ray-to-nay'-ro], *m.* Driver of the *carretón;* drayman, truckman.

Carricoche [car-re-co'-chay], *m.* 1. (Obs.) Cart with a box like a coach. 2. (Prov.) Old-fashioned coach, wagonette. 3. (Prov.) Muck-cart, dung-cart.

Carrícola [car-ree'-co-lah], *f.* Kind of phaeton.

Carricureña [car-re-coo-ray'-nyah], *f.* (Mil.) Carriage of a light field-piece.

Carriego [car-re-ay'-go], *m.* 1. Osier basket used for fishing. 2. Large rough basket used in bleaching flax-yarn.

Carril [car-reel'], *m.* 1. Rut, cart-way, cart-rut. 2. Narrow road where one cart only can pass at a time. 3. Furrow opened by the plough. 4. A rail of a railway.

Carrilada [cah-re-lah'-dah], *f.* (Obs.) Rut, the track of a cart or coach.

Carrillada [car-reel-lyah'-dah], *f.* Oily or medullar substance of a hog's cheek. *Carrilladas de vaca o carnero*, (Prov.) Cow or sheep's head without the tongue.

Carrillar [car-reel'-lyar], *va.* (Naut.) To hoist light things out of the hold with a tackle.

Carrillera [car-reel-lyay'-rah], *f.* 1. The jaw. 2. Each of two straps, covered with metal scales, used to fasten a soldier's helmet; chin-strap.

Carrillo [car-reel'-lyo], *m.* 1. (Dim.) Small cart. 2. Cheek, the fleshy part of the face. 3. (Naut.) Tackle for hoisting light things. *Carrillos de monja boba, de trompetero*, etc., Bluffy-cheeked. *Correr carrillos*, Horse-racing.

Carrilludo, da [car-reel-lyoo'-do, dah], *a.* Plump or round cheeked.

Carriola [car-re-o'-lah], *f.* 1. Trundle-bed. 2. Small chariot; curricle.

Carrizal [car-re-thahl'], *m.* Land which is full of reed-grass.

Carrizo [car-ree'-tho], *m.* (Bot.) Common reed-grass. Arundo phragmites.

Carro [car'-ro], *m.* 1. Cart, a carriage with two wheels; a chariot, car. *Varas del carro*, Shafts of a cart. *Guardacantones de un carro*, Wheel-iron of a cart. *Estacas del carro*, Staves or rails of the body of a cart. *Arquillo del carro*, Hoops which compose the top of a cart, and support the tilt. *Toldo del carro*; Tilt, the cloth thrown over the hoops of a cart. *Carro de basura*, Offal-cart. *Carro falcado*, A scythe-chariot. 2. A railway car (carriage) (Great Britain). 3. The running gear of a carriage without the body. 4. (Ast.) The Greater Bear, a northern constellation. *Carro menor*, The Lesser Bear. *Carro de Ezequiel*, Sort of woollen stuff manufactured in Languedoc. *Carro de oro*, Brussels camlet, fine camlet. *Carro triunfal*, Triumphal car. 5. (Naut.) Manufactory for cables and other ship cordage. 6. Measure for wood; a cart-load. *Medio carro de leña*, A cord of wood. 7. The bed of a printing-press. *Untar el carro*, (Met.) To bribe, to wheedle. *Cogerle a uno el carro*, To be unlucky or ill-fated.

Carrocilla [car-ro-theel'-lyah], *f. dim.* Small coach.

Carrocín [car-ro-theen'], *m.* Chaise, curricle.

Carrocha [car-ro'-chah], *f.* Seminal substance in bees and other insects. Eggs.

Carrochar [car-ro-char'], *vn.* To shed the seminal substance: applied to bees and other insects. (This definition of the Spanish Academy really means "to lay eggs.")

Carrofuerte [car-ro-foo-er'-tay], *m.* A strong cart or truck for transporting artillery or heavy weights.

Carromatero [car-ro-mah-tay'-ro], *m.* Carter, charioteer, carman.

Carromato [car-ro-mah'-to], *m.* A long, narrow cart with two wheels and tilt, for transporting goods, etc.

Carroña [car-ro'-nyah], *f.* Carrion, putrid flesh.

Carroñar [car-ro-nyar'], *va.* To infect sheep with the scab.

Carroño, ña [car-ro'-nyo, nyah], *a.* Putrefied, putrid, rotten.

Carroza [car-ro'-thah], *f.* 1. Large coach; superb state coach. 2. (Naut.) Awning over a boat, or part of a ship. 3. (Naut.) Kind of cabin on the quarter-deck of a ship.

Carruaje [car-roo-ah'-hay], *m.* All sorts of vehicles for transporting persons or goods.

Carruajero [car-roo-ah-hay'-ro], *m.* Carrier, carter, wagoner.

Carruco [car-roo'-co], *m.* Small cart used in mountainous parts of the country for transporting salt and other things, with solid wheels and turning axle.

Carrucha [car-roo'-chah], *f.* *V.* GARRUCHA.

Carrujado, da [car-roo-hah'-do, dah], *a.* Corrugated, wrinkled. *V.* ENCARRUJADO.

Carsaya [car-sah'-yah], *f.* (Obs.) Kersey, an English woollen stuff.

Carsela [car-say'-lah], *f.* (Arch.) A projecting bracket; commonly carved or ornamented.

Carta [car'-tah], *f.* 1. Letter, an epistle; (Com.) favour. 2. Royal ordinance. 3. Map, chart. 4. Card for playing. 5. A written constitution, charter. 6. (Littl. us.) Any public record. 7. (Obs.) Writing-paper. *Carta de marear*, Sea-chart. *Carta plana*, Plain chart. *Carta blanca;* 1. Letter or commission with a blank for the name to be inserted at pleasure. 2. Carte-blanche, full powers given to one. *Carta acordada*, Letter from a superior to an inferior court, with secret orders or instructions. *Carta abierta*, (Obs.) Open order, addressed to all persons. *Carta certificada*, A registered letter. *Carta con valores declarados*, Money (order) letter. *Carta cuenta*, Bill or account of sale. *Carta credencial* or *de creencia*, Credentials. *Carta de crédito*, Letter of credit. *Carta de dote*, Articles of marriage. *Carta de encomienda*, Letter of safe-conduct. *Carta de espera* or *moratoria*, Letter of respite given to a debtor. *Carta de fletamento*, (Com.) Charter-party. *Carta de guía*, Passport. *Carta de examen*, License granted to a person to exercise his trade or profession. *Carta de horro*, Letters of enfranchisement. *Carta de libre*, Guardian's discharge. *Carta de naturaleza*, Letters of naturalization. *Carta de pago*, Acquittance, receipt, discharge in full. *Carta de pago y lasto*, Acquittance given to a person who has paid money for another. *Carta de portes*, Booking-ticket. *Carta de presentación*, Letter of introduction. *Carta de seguridad*, Safe-guard, protection. *Carta de sanidad*, Bill of health. *Carta de venta*, Bill of sale. *Carta de vuelta*, A dead-letter. *Carta en lista*, Letter "to be kept till called for"; general delivery letter. *Carta forera*, (Obs.) Judicial despatch or decree; royal grant of privileges. *Carta pastoral*, Pastoral letter. *Carta plomada*, Deed or other writing having a seal of lead affixed to it. *Carta receptoria*, Warrant, voucher. *Carta de vecindad*, Burgher-brief. *Carta requisitoria*, Letters requisitorial. *No ver carta*, To have a bad hand at cards. *Pecar por carta de más o de menos*, To have either too much or too little. *Perder con buenas cartas*, (Met.) To fail of success, though possessed of merit and protection. *Traer* or *venir con malas cartas*, (Met.) To attempt to enforce an ill-grounded claim. *Carta canta*, It may be proved by written documents. *Hablen cartas y callen barbas*, Documentary evidence is better than bare assertion. *No firmes carta que no leas, ni bebas agua que no veas*, (prov.) Do not sign a letter which you have not read, nor drink water which you have not seen.

Carta aérea [car'-tah ah-ay'-ray-ah], *f.* Airletter.

Cartabón [car-tah-bone'], *m.* 1. A carpenter's square, rule; an instrument to measure and form angles. *Echar el cartabón*, (Met.) To adopt measures for attaining one's end. *Cartabón de cola*, Small square piece of glue. 2. Shoemaker's slide, size-stick. 3. Quadrant, a gunner's square, or instrument for elevating and pointing guns.

Cartagenero, ra [car-tah-hay-nay'-ro, rah], *a.* Of Carthagena.

Cartaginense [car-tah-he-nen'-say], *a.* Carthaginian: of Carthage.

Cártama [car'-tah-mah], *f.* (Bot.) Officinal carthamus. Carthamus tinctorius. *V.* Alazor.

Cártamo [car'-tah-mo], *m.* (Bot.) 1. A generical name of plants. Carthamus. 2. *V.* Cártama. Safflower.

Cartapacio [car-tah-pah'-the-o], *m.* 1. Memorandum-book. 2. A student's note-book. 3. Satchel.

Cartapartida [car-tah-par-tee'-dah], *f.* Charter-party. *Cartapartida bajo forma*, Memorandum of charter-party.

Cartapel [car-tah-pel'], *m.* 1. Memorandum filled with useless matter. 2. (Obs.) Edict, ordinance.

Cartazo [car-tah'-tho], *m.* (Coll.) Letter or paper containing a severe reprehension.

Cartear [car-tay-ar'], *vn.* To play low cards, in order to try how the game stands.—*va.* 1. (Naut.) To steer by the sea-chart. 2. (Obs.) To turn over the leaves of a book.—*vr.* To correspond by letter.

Cartel [car-tel'], *m.* 1. Placard, hand-bill, poster. 2. Cartel, a written agreement made by belligerent powers relative to the exchange of prisoners. 3. (Obs.) Challenge sent in writing. 4. (Naut.) Cartel-ship or flag of truce. 5. A fishing-net which spreads eighty fathoms.

Cartela [car-tay'-lah], *f.* 1. Slip of paper, piece of wood, or other materials on which a memorandum is made. 2. Console, bracket, or stay on which carved work rests. 3. Iron stay, which supports a balcony.

Cartelear [car-tay-lay-ar'], *va.* (Obs.) To publish libels.

Cartelera [car-tay-lay'-rah], *f.* Bill-board.

Cartelón [car-tay-lone'], *m. aug.* 1. Long edict. 2. Show-bill.

Carteo [car-tay'-o], *m.* Frequent intercourse by letters.

Carter [car'-ter], *m.* Crank case (of an auto).

Cartera [car-tay'-rah], *f.* 1. Wallet. 2. Portfolio, briefcase. 3. Letter-case, letter-box. 4. Portfolio, the office of a cabinet minister.

Carteriana [car-tay-re-ah'-nah], *f.* Sort of silk.

Cartero [car-tay'-ro], *m.* Letter-carrier, postman.

Carteta [car-tay'-tah], *f.* A game at cards. *V.* Parar.

Cartibanas [car-te-bah'-nas], *f.pl.* Pieces of paper glued to the leaves of a book to facilitate the binding; fly-sheets.

Cartica, ita [car-tee'-cah, ee'-tah], *f. dim.* Small letter or note.

Cartilaginoso, sa [car-te-lah-he-no'-so, sah], *a.* Cartilaginous, gristly.

Cartílago [car-tee'-lah-go], *m.* (Anat.) 1. A cartilage, gristle. 2. Parchment. *V.* Ternilla.

Cartilla [car-teel'-lyah], *f.* 1. (Dim.) Small or short letter or note. 2. The first book of children; horn-book; primer. 3. Certificate of a clergyman duly ordained. *Cosa que no está en la cartilla*, Something rather strange or uncommon. *Leerle a uno la cartilla*, (Met.) To give one a lecture. *No saber la cartilla*, (Met.) To be extremely ignorant. 4. *V.* Añalejo.

Cartografía [car-to-grah-fee'-ah], *f.* Chartography, the art of map-drawing.

Cartográfico, ca [car-to-grah'-fe-co, cah], *a.* Chartographic, relative to the drawing of maps.

Cartógrafo [car-to'-grah-fo], *m.* Chartographer, a drawer of maps.

Cartón [car-tone'], *m.* 1. Pasteboard, binders' board. 2. Kind of iron ornament, imitating the leaves of plants. 3. Cartoon, a painting or drawing on strong paper. *Parece de cartón*, He is as stiff as a poker. *Estar hecho un cartón*, To be as thin as a whipping-post.

Cartonera [car-to-nay'-rah], *f.* A paper-making wasp; a social wasp. So called from the appearance of its cells.—*pl.* Pasteboard cases for filing papers.

Cartonero [car-to-nay'-ro], *m.* One whose business is to make pasteboard.

Cartuchera [car-too-chay'-rah], *f.* Cartridge-box or pouch.

Cartucho [car-too'-cho], *m.* 1. Cartouch, a cartridge, a charge of powder contained in paper. *Cartucho de fusil*, Musket-cartridge. 2. Small target. *V.* Tarjeta.

Cartuja [car-too'-hah], *f.* Carthusian order.

Cartujano, na [car-too-hah'-no, nah], *a.* Carthusian.

Cartujo [car-too'-ho], *m.* 1. Carthusian monk. 2. Kind of skin first used by Carthusian monks.

Cartulario [car-too-lah'-re-o], *m.* 1. Archives or registry. 2. The archivist. 3. Coucher, a register book in monasteries.

Cartulina [car-too-lee'-nah], *f.* Bristol-board, card-board. *Cartulina común*, Mill-board. *Cartulina en hojas*, Sheet card. *Cartulina de porcelana*, Enamelled card.

Carúncula [cah-roon'-coo-lah], *f.* 1. Caruncle. 2. Crustaceous excrescence on an ulcer or wound. *Carúncula lagrimal*, The lachrymal caruncle, a reddish elevation at the inner angle of the eye.

Carunculado, da [cah-roon-coo-lah'-do, dah], *a.* Carunculated.—*m. pl.* Applied to birds having caruncles upon the lower mandible or on the head.

Carunculoso, sa [ca-roon-coo-lo'-so, sah], *a.* Relating to or like a caruncle.

Carvallo [car-vahl'-lyo], *m.* (Bot.) Common British oak. Quercus robur.

Carvi [car'-ve], *m.* 1. (Bot.) Common caraway. Carum carvi. 2. Caraway-seed.

Casa [cah'-sah], *f.* 1. House, edifice, dwelling. 2. Home, our own house, the private dwelling. 3. House, household, the family residing in a house. 4. Line or branch of a family. 5. Checkers, or squares, of a chess or draught-board. *Casa a la malicia* or *de malicia*, House which had no upper story, for the purpose of being exempted from court-lodgers. *Casa de aposento*, House obliged to lodge persons belonging to the king's household. *Casa de campo* or *de placer*, Country house. *Casa de contratación de las Indias en Sevilla*, The West Indies or Spanish-American house, in Seville, at the time when there was not free trade between Spain and its American possessions. *Casa cáñama*, *V.* Casa excusada. *Casa excusada* or *dezmera*, That of a landed proprietor chosen to collect tithes of fruits and of flocks. *Casa de socorro*, A receiving or emergency hospital. *Casa de tócame Roque*, A house where many live, not well directed, and in consequent disorder. *Casa de vecindad*, A tenement. *Casa de coima*, (Obs.) Gaming-house, hell. *Casa de locos*, 1. Mad-house. 2. (Met.) Noisy or riotous house. *Casa de moneda*, Mint. *Casa de posada*, *casa de huéspedes* or *casa de pupilos*, Lodging-house, or lodging and boarding-house. *Casa de usted* (in the date of letters), At home, or in my house. *Casa de posta* or *de diligencia*, Stage-house. *Casa de tía*, (Coll.) Jail. *Casa fuerte*, (Obs.) House surrounded with a moat. *Casa llana*, (Obs.) Country-house without a moat or defence. *Casa pública*, Brothel, bawdy-house. *Casa de sanidad*, Office of the board of health. *Casa solariega*, Ancient mansion-house of a family. *A mal decir no hay casa fuerte*, When fortune declares itself against any one, power and riches cannot overcome it. *Toma*, *casa con hogar y mujer que sepa hilar*, A cheerful hearth and a thrifty wife make health and wealth and a happy life. *Apartar casa*, To take a separate house. *Levantar la casa*, To move into another house. *Franquear la casa*, To grant a free access to one's house. *Guardar la casa*, To stay at home. *Hacer su casa*, (Met.) To raise or aggrandize one's own family. *No tener casa ni hogar*, To have neither house nor home. *Poner casa*, To establish house, to begin housekeeping. *Ponerle a uno casa*, To furnish a house for another. *Ser muy de casa*, To be very intimate in a house, to be on familiar terms. *En casa de tía, pero no cada día*, We may visit our relations, yet without being troublesome. *Pues se quema la casa, calentémonos*, Since the house is set on fire, let us warm ourselves. *Casa del Señor*, *de Dios* or *de oración*, Church or temple. *Casa santa*, Church of the Holy Sepulchre at Jerusalem. *En casa de mujer rica, ella manda y ella grita*. (Prov.) In the house where the wife has brought the money, she is the chief, and wears the breeches.

Casaca [ca-sah'-cah], *f.* 1. Coat, upper garment of a man; dress-coat. *Casaca de mujer*, A woman's jacket. *Volver casaca*, To become a turncoat. 2. The marriage contract.

Casación [cah-sah-the-on'], *f.* (Law) Cassation, abrogation, the act of annulling or repealing a law or reversing a judicial sentence.

Casacón [cah-sah-cone'], *m.* 1. Great-coat, worn over other clothes. 2. Cassock.

Casada [cah-sah'-dah], *f.* (Obs. Prov.) Ancient family mansion.

Casadero, ra [cah-sah-day'-ro, rah], *a.* Marriageable, fit for marriage.

Casado [cah-sah'-do], *m.* (typ.) Imposition. *a.* Married.

Casador [cah-sah-dor'], *m.* (Obs.) One who annuls or repeals.

Casal [cah-sahl'], *m.* (Obs.) Country-house of an ancient family.

Casalero [cah-sah-lay'-ro], *m.* (Obs.) One who resides in his country-house.

Casalicio [cah-sah-lee'-the-o], *m.* House, edifice.

Casamata [cah-sah-mah'-tah], *f.* (Mil.) Casemate.

Casamentero, ra [cah-sah-men-tay'-ro, rah], *m.* & *f.* Match or marriage-maker.

Casamiento [cah-sah-me-en'-to], *m.* 1. Marriage, marriage contract; matrimony; match. 2. In games, betting money on a card. 3. A wife's fortune.

Casamuro [cah-sah-moo'-ro], *m.* (Mil. Obs.) Single wall without a terreplein.

Casapuerta [cah-sah-poo-err'-tah], *f.* Porch; entrance of a house.

Casaquilla [cah-sah-keel'-lyah], *f.* Kind of short and loose jacket, worn over other clothes.

Casar [cah-sar'], *m.* 1. Hamlet, a small village. 2. (Prov.) Country-house for labourers to sleep in.

Casar, *va.* 1. To marry, to join a man and woman in marriage or in wedlock: applied to clergymen. 2. To marry, to dispose of in marriage; to couple, to unite in marriage. 3. (Met.) To sort things so as to match one another, to mate, to suit or proportion one thing to another. 4. To repeal, to abrogate, to annul. 5. (Paint.) To blend. 6. (Typ.) To impose. *Casar la pensión*, To relieve a benefice from all incumbrances, by paying the annats at once. *Antes que te cases mira lo que haces*, Look before you leap. *Casarse con su opinion*, To be wedded to one's opinion. *Casarás y amansarás*, Marry, and take the cares and responsibilities of home. *El que se casa, por todo pasa*, Denotes the many cares and vicissitudes of married life.—*vr.* To marry, to take a wife or husband, to enter the conjugal state, to get married. *Por codicia de florín, no te cases con ruin*, Never marry a villain for his money. *Para mal casar, más vale nunca maridar*, Better never marry than marry unwisely.

Casatienda [cah-sah-te-en'-dah], *f* Tradesman's shop.

Casave [cah-sah'-vay], *m.* Cassava, tapioca. Also CASABE and CAZABE.

Casazo [cah-sah'-tho], *m.* (Coll. Aug.) Great event.

Casca [cahs'-cah], *f.* 1. Skins of grapes after the wine has been pressed out. 2. (Prov.) Bad wine or liquor. 3. Bark for tanning leather. 4. Kind of sweet bread.

Cascabel [cas-cah-bel'], *m.* 1. Hawks-bell, bell used for hawks, cats, or dogs, and also for beasts of burden. 2. Knob at the end of the breech of a cannon, cascabel. 3. Rattlesnake. Crotalus. *Echar a uno el cascabel*, (Met.) To throw off a burden and lay it on another. *Echar* or *soltar el cascabel*, (Met.) To drop a hint in conversation, to see how it takes. *Ser un cascabel*, (Met.) To be a crazy or rattle-brained fellow. *Tener cascabel*, (Met.) To be uneasy or unhappy in one's mind.

Cascabelada [cas-cah-bay-lah'-dah], *f.* 1. Jingling with small bells. 2. Inconsiderate speech or action. 3. (Obs.) Noisy feast.

Cascabelear [cas-cah-bay-lay-ar'], *va.* To feed one with vain hopes, to induce one to act on visionary expectations.—*vn.* To act with levity, or little forecast and prudence.

Cascabelero, ra [cas-cah-bay-lay'-ro, rah], *a.* Light-witted.

Cascabelillo [cas-cah-bay-leel'-lyo], *m. dim.* Small black plum.

Cascabillo [cas-cah-beel'-lyo], *m.* 1. Hawk's bell. *V.* CASCABEL. 2. Chaff of wheat or other grain. 3. Husk of an acorn.

Cascaciruelas [cas-cah-the-roo-ay'-las], *m.* Mean, despicable fellow.

Cascada [cas-cah'-dah], *f.* Cascade, water-fall. *Cascadas*, Small plaits or folds in the drapery of paintings.

Cascado, da [cas-cah'-do, dah], *a.* Broken, burst, decayed, infirm; crazy. *Vidrio cascado*, (Met.) Singer who has lost his voice. *Estar muy cascado*, To be in a precarious state of health. *Cascados*, Small, broken pieces of land.—*pp.* of CASCAR.

Cascadura [cas-cah-doo'-rah], *f.* Act of bursting or breaking asunder.

Cascajal [cas-cah-hahl'], *m.* 1. Place full of gravel and pebbles. 2. Place in which the husks of grapes are thrown.

Cascajar [cas-cah'-har], *m.* Place full of gravel and pebbles.

Cascajo [cas-cah'-ho], *m.* 1. Gravel. 2. Fragments of broken vessels. 3. Rubbish. 4. (Littl. us.) Old and useless furniture. 5. Pod or silique; shell of a nut. 6. (Met.) Copper coin. 7. Bit of a bridle. *Estar hecho un cascajo*, To be very old and infirm.

Cascajoso, sa [cas-cah-ho'-so, sah], *a.* Gravelly.

Cascallo [cas-cahl'-lyo], *m.* Brazilian name of a diamond-field.

Cascamajar [cas-cah-ma-har'], *va.* (Prov.) To break, bruise, or pound a thing slightly.

Cascamiento [cas-cah-me-en'-to], *m.* Act of breaking or bruising.

Cascanueces [cas-cah-noo-ay'-thes], *m.* Nut-cracker.

Cascapiñones [cas-cah-pe-nyo'-nes], *m.* One who shells hot pine-nuts and cleans the seed.

Cascar [cas-car'], *va.* 1. To crack, burst, or break into pieces. 2. To crunch. 3. To lick, to beat, or strike. 4. (Prov.) To talk much. *Cascar a uno las liendres*, (Met.) To dress one's jacket, to give one a fine drubbing.—*vr.* To be broken open.

Cáscara [cahs'-ca-rah], *f.* 1. Rind, peel, hull, or husk of various fruits, etc. 2. Bark of trees. *Cáscara sagrada*, Cascara sagrada, dried bark of a tree which is used as a laxative.

Cáscaras! [cahs'-ca-ras], *int.* Oh! exclamation expressive of astonishment or admiration.

Cascarela [cas-ca-ray'-lah], *f.* Lansquenet, a game at cards.

Cascarilla, Cascarita [cas-ca-reel'-lyah, ree'-tah], *f.* 1. (Dim.) Small thin bark. 2. Peruvian bark, Jesuit's bark. 3. Cascarilla bark.

Cascarillero [cas-ca-reel-lyay'-ro], *m.* A gatherer of Peruvian bark.

Cascarrillo [cas-car-reel'-lyo], *m.* The cinchona shrub.

Cascaroja [cas-ca-ro'-hah], *f.* Wood-borer, ship-worm, ship-piercer. Teredo navalis. *V.* BROMA.

Cascarón [cas-ca-rone'], *m.* 1. Egg-shell of a fowl or bird. 2. (Arch.) Arch or vault which contains the fourth part of a sphere; calotte. 3. Niche where the sacrament is placed for adoration in Roman Catholic churches. 4. Trick won in the game of lansquenet. 5. A very thin plate of metal employed in covering various objects. *Aun no ha salido del cascarón y ya tiene presunción*, He is yet a chicken, and assumes the man.

Cascarone [cas-ca-ro'-nay], *m.* An egg-shell filled with coloured paper cut fine, and then broken on one's head. (Mex.)

Cascarrabias [cas-car-rah'-be-as], *com.* A testy, irritable person. *V.* PAPARRABIAS.

Cascarrabieta [cas-car-rah-be-ay'-tah], *com.* *V.* CASCARRABIAS.

Cascarrabio, ia [cas-car-rah'-be-o, ah], *a* Grumbling, testy, irritable.

Cascarrón, na [cas-car-rone', nah], *a.* (Coll.) Rough, harsh, rude. *Vino cascarrón*, Wine of a rough flavour. *Voz cascarrona*, Harsh, unpleasant tone of voice.

Cascarudo, da [cas-ca-roo'-do, dah], *a.* Hully, having a thick rind or shell.

Cascaruleta [cas-ca-roo-lay'-tah], *f.* (Coll.) Noise made by the teeth in consequence of chucking under the chin.

Casco [cahs'-co], *m.* 1. Skull, cranium, the bone which incloses the brain. 2. Potsherd, fragments of an earthen vessel. 3. Quarter of an orange, lemon, or pomegranate. 4. Coat or tegument of an onion. 5. Helmet, casque, or head-piece of ancient armour. 6. (Prov.) Cask, pipe, vat, or other wooden vessel in which wine is preserved. 7. *Casco de un navío*, (Naut.) Hull, or hulk, of a ship. *Casco y quilla*, Bottomry. 8. Crown of a hat. 9. Printer's inking-ball. 10. Sheep-skin stripped of the wool. 11. Hoof of a horse. 12. *Casco* or *tapa de un barril*, The head of a cask. 13. *Casco de una silla de montar*, The tree of a saddle. *Casco de casa*, Shell or carcass of a house.

Casco de lugar, Dimensions of the ground on which a house is built. *Quitar* or *raer del casco*, (Met.) To dissuade or divert one from a preconceived opinion. *Cascos*, Heads of sheep or bullocks without the tongues and brains. *Lavar a uno los cascos*, (Met.) To flatter, to cajole, to coax, to tickle one's vanity. *Levantarle a uno de cascos*, (Met.) To fill one's head with idle notions of grandeur. *Romper los cascos*, (Met.) To disturb, to molest. *Tener los cascos a la jineta*, (Met.) To be on the high horse. *Tener malos cascos*, (Met.) To be crazy or hare-brained.

Cáscol [cahs'-col], *m.* Resin of a tree of Guayaquil which serves to make a kind of black sealing-wax.

Cascolote [cas-co-lo-'tay], *m.* (Mex.) Thick bark of oaks, etc.; a fragment of thick bark.

Cascorvo, va [cas-cor'-vo, vah], *a.* (Mex.) Bowlegged.

Cascote [cas-co'-tay], *m.* Rubbish. rubble, ruins of buildings, fragments of matter used in building.

Cascotería [cas-co-tay-ree'-ah], *f.* (Obs.) Wall or work made of rubbish.

Cascudo, da [cas-coo'-do, dah], *a.* Large-hoofed: applied to beasts.

Caseación [cah-say-ah-the-on'], *f.* (Obs.) Coagulation of milk to form cheese.

Caseína [cah-say-ee'-nah], *f.* Casein, the albuminous proximate principle of milk.

Caseoso, sa [cah-say-o'-so, sah], *a.* Caseous, cheesy.

Casera [cah-say'-rah], *f.* (Prov.) House-keeper, a woman servant that has the care of a single man.

Caseramente [cah-say-rah-men'-tay], *adv.* Homely, in a plain manner.

Casería [cah-say-ree'-ah], *f.* 1. Isolated farm house. 2. Economical household management. 3. (Sp. Am.) Clientele, customers.

Caserío [cah-say-ree'-o], *m.* A series of houses; village or very small town.

Caserna [cah-serr'-nah], *f.* (Mil.) Casern, a bomb-proof vault below a rampart; barracks.

Casero, ra [cah-say'-ro, rah], *m.* & *f.* Landlord or steward of a house.

Casero, ra [cah-say'-ro, rah], *a.* 1. Domestic, homely, in a family way. 2. Home-bred, familiar; house-keeping. *Baile casero*, Family-dance. *Mujer casera*, A woman much attached to her family concerns, a good housewife. *Fulana está muy casera*, She dresses in a very plain and homely manner. *Ejemplo casero*, Domestic example. *Remedio casero*, Domestic medicine. *Pan casero*, Household bread. *Lienzo casero*, Home-spun linen.

Caserón [cah-say-rone'], *m. aug.* 1. A large house. 2. A large house, ill-proportioned and without order.

Caseta [cah-say'-tah], *f. dim.* Small house: used commonly to denominate a hut or cottage.

Casi [cah'-se], *adv.* Almost, nearly, somewhat more or less; just. *Casi que* or *casi casi*, Very nearly.

Casi [cah'-se], *m.* Title which Mohammedans give to the chief of their religion.

Casia [cah'-se-ah], *f.* (Bot.) Bastard cinnamon, cassia. Laurus cassia.

Casica, illa, ita [cah-see'-cah, eel'-lyah, ee'-tah], *f. dim.* Small house, cabin.

Casilla [cah-see'-lyah], *f.* 1. Ticket office. 2. Booth, cockpit, cubby-hole. *Casilla de correos* or *Casilla postal*, Post-office box.

Casillas [cah-seel'-lyas], *f. pl.* 1. Pigeon-holes: ruled columns in accounts, books, or papers. 2. Points or houses of a backgammon table. 3. Square or checkers of a chess or draft-board. *Sacarle a uno de sus casillas*, (Met.) To molest, tease, or harass. *Salir de sus casillas*, To deviate from one's accustomed mode, especially through anger.

Casiller [cah-seel-lyerr'], *m.* In the royal palace, the person appointed to empty the close-stools.

Casillero [cah-seel-lyay'-ro], *m.* A desk fitted with pigeon-holes.—*pl. V.* CASILLAS.

Casillo [cah-seel'-lyo], *m.* 1. (Dim.) Trifling or slight cause. 2. (Iron.) A momentous affair, matter of consequence.

Casimbas [cah-seem'-bas], *f. pl.* (Naut.) Buckets for baling the water made by a ship, which the pumps are unable to discharge.

Casimir [cah-se-meer'], *m.* **Casimira** [cah-se-mee'-rah], *f.* or **Casimiro** [cah-se-mee'-ro], *m.* Cassimere, kerseymere. *Casimir doble*, Double-twilled kerseymere. *Casimir sencillo*, Single-twilled kerseymere.

Casimodo [cah-se-mo'-do], *m.* (Obs.) *V.* CUASIMODO.

Casino [cah-see'-no], *m.* 1. Casino, a room or building used as a public resort, for dancing, social, or club meetings, etc. 2. A club.

Casiopea [cah-se-o-pay'-ah], *f.* Cassiopeia, the name of a northern constellation.

Casis [cah-sees'], *f.* (Bot.) The black currant.—*m.* (Zool.) A mollusk of the Mediterranean and the Indian Ocean.

Casiterita [cah-se-tay-ree'-tah], *f.* Cassiterite, oxide of tin; its chief ore.

Caso [cah'-so], *m.* 1. Event, case, occurrence. 2. Case, contingency, hap, casualty, unexpected accident. 3. Occasion, opportunity. 4. Case stated to lawyers, physicians, etc. 5. (Gram.) Case. *Caso de conciencia*, Case of conscience. 6. Peculiar figure of written characters. *En caso de eso*, In that case. *En todo caso*, At all events. *Estar o no estar en el caso*, To comprehend or not comprehend something. *Hacer caso de una persona*, To esteem or respect a person. *Hacer caso de una cosa*, To take notice. *Hacer o no alguna cosa al caso*, To be material or immaterial. *Ser o no ser al caso*, To be or not to be to the purpose. *Vamos al caso*, Let us come to the point. *No estoy en el caso*, I do not understand the matter. *Caso que*, In that case. *Dado caso* or *demos caso*, Supposing that. *De caso pensado*, Deliberately. *Caso negado*, Proposition admitted only to be refuted.

Caso, sa [cah'-so, sah], *a.* (Law. Obs.) *V.* NULO.

Casoar [cah-so-ar'], **Casobar** [cah-so-bar'], *m.* The cassowary.

Casorio [cah-so'-re-o], *m.* 1. (Coll.) Inconsiderate marriage. 2. The wedding.

Caspa [cahs'-pah], *f.* Dandruff, scurf.

Caspera [cas-pay'-rah], *f.* (Obs.) Comb for dandruff.

Caspio, ia [cahs'-pe-o, ah], *a.* Caspian.

¡Cáspita! [cahs'-pe-tah], *int.* Wonderful!

Casposo, sa [cas-po'-so, sah], *a.* Full of dandruff. lentiginous.

Casquetazo [cas-kay-tah'-tho], *m.* Blow given with the head.

Casquete [cas-kay'-tay], *m.* 1. Helmet, casque; skull-cap, cap. 2. Scull, wig, scratch. 3. Helmet shell. 4. Cataplasm to take the scurf off the heads of children.

Casquiblando, da [cas-ke-blahn'-do, dah], *a.* Soft-hoofed: spoken of horses.

Casquiderramado, da [cas-ke-der-rah-mah'-do, dah], *a.* Wide-hoofed: said of horses.

Casquijo [cas-kee'-ho], *m.* Gravel; ballast material.

Casquilla [cas-keel'-lyah], *f.* Cell of the queen bee.

Casquillo [cas-keel'-lyo], *m.* 1. (Dim.) Small steel helm. 2. Tip, cap, ferule, socket. 3. An iron arrow-head.

Casquilucio, cia [cas-ke-loo'-the-o, ah], *a.* Gay, frolicsome.

Casquimuleño, ña [cas-ke-moo-lay'-nyo, nyah], *a.* Narrow-hoofed like mules: applied to horses.

Casquivano, na [cas-ke-vah'-no, nah], *a.* Impudent, inconsiderate, acting with levity; foolishly conceited.

Casta [cahs'-tah], *f.* 1. Caste, race, generation, lineage, particular breed, clan; offspring, kindred. 2. Kind or quality of a thing. *Hacer casta*, To get a particular breed of horses or other animals.

Castalia [cas-tah'-le-ah], *f.* Castalia, a fountain of Mount Parnassus, and the nymph whose name it received.

Castálidas [cas-tah'-le-das], *f. pl.* A surname of the Muses (fr. Castalia).

Castamente [cas-tah-men'-tay], *adv.* Chastely.

Castaña [cas-tah'-nyah], *f.* 1. (Bot.) Chestnut. 2. Bottle, jug, or jar, in the shape of a chestnut. 3. Club of hair; chignon. 4. An abandoned mine. *Castaña pilonga* or *apilada*, Dried chestnut. *Castaña regoldana*, Wild or horse-chestnut. *Sacar castañas del fuego con la mano del gato*, To make a cat's-paw of any one.

Castañal, Castañar [cas-ta-nyahl', cas-ta-nyar'], *m.* Grove or plantation of chestnut-trees.

Castañazo [cas-ta-nyah'-tho], *m.* Blow from a chestnut.

Castañedo [cas-ta-nyay'-do], *m.* (Prov.) Chestnut-grove or plantation.

Castañera [cas-ta-nyay'-rah], *f.* (Prov.) Country abounding with chestnut-trees.

Castañero, ra [cas-ta-nyay'-ro, rah], *m.* & *f.* Dealer in chestnuts.

Castañeta [cas-ta-nyay'-tah], *f.* 1. Snapping of the fingers. 2. Castanet. *V.* CASTAÑUELA.

Castañetazo [cas-ta-nyay-tah'-tho], *m.* 1. Blow with a castanet. 2. Sound of a chestnut bursting in the fire. 3. Cracking of the joints.

Castañeteado [cas-ta-nyay-tay-ah'-do], *m.* Sound of castanets.—*pp.* of CASTAÑETEAR.

Castañetear [cas-ta-nyay-tay-ar'], *vn.* 1. To rattle the castanets. 2. To crackle, to clack: applied to the knees. 3. To cry: applied to partridges.

Castaño [cas-tah'-nyo], *m.* (Bot.) Common chestnut-tree. Fagus castanea. *Castaño de Indias*, Horse-chestnut-tree. Æsculus hippocastanum.

Castaño, ña [cas-tah'-nyo, nyah], *a.* Hazel, hazelly.

Castañuela [cas-ta-nyoo-ay'-lah], *f.* 1. Castanet. 2. (Bot.) Round tuberous-rooted cyperus. Cyperus rotundus. 3. (Bot. Littl. us.) Prickly ox-eye. Buphthalmum spinosum, *L.* *Estar como unas castañuelas*, To be very gay. *Castañuelas*, (Naut.) Cleats fastened to the yard-arms. *Castañuelas de muescas*, Notched cleats. *Castañuelas de pontón*, Ponton cleats.

Castañuelo, la [cas-ta-nyoo-ay'-lo, lah], *a. dim.* Of a light chestnut colour: applied to horses.

Castellán [cas-tel-lyahn'], *m.* Castellan, governor or warden of a castle.

Castellanía [cas-tel-lyah-nee'-ah], *f.* Castellany, district belonging to a castle.

Castellanizar [cas-tel-lyah-ne-thar'], *va.* To adapt a foreign word for use in Spanish: to castilianize.

Castellano [cas-tel-lyah'-no], *m.* 1. Ancient Spanish coin. 2. Fiftieth part of a mark of gold. 3. Spanish language. 4. (Obs.) Castellan, the governor or warden of a castle. *A la castellana*, In the Castilian fashion.

Castellano, na [cas-tel-lyah'-no, nah], *a.* 1. Castilian. 2. Applied to a mule got by a jackass and a mare. 3. (Prov.) Applied to the foremost mule in a cart or wagon.

Castellar [cas-tel-lyar'], *m.* 1. (Obs.) Place fortified with a castle. 2. (Bot.) St. John's wort, tutsan, park-leaves. Hypericum androsæmum.

Castidad [cas-te-dahd'], *f.* Chastity, continence, honour.

Castigación [cas-te-gah-the-on'], *f.* 1. Castigation. 2. Correction of errors of the press.

Castigadera [cas-te-gah-day'-rah], *f.* 1. Rope with which a bell is tied to a mule, or other beast of burden. 2. Small cord with which the ring of a stirrup is tied to the girth.

Castigador, ra [cas-te-gah-dor', rah], *m.* & *f.* 1. A punisher or chastiser, castigator. 2. (Obs.) One that reproaches.

Castigar [cas-te-gar'], *va.* 1. To chastise, to punish, to castigate. 2. To afflict, to put to pain, to grieve. 3. (Obs.) To advise, to inform. 4. (Met.) To correct proof-sheets or writings.—*vr.* (Obs.) To mend.

Castigo [cas-tee'-go], *m.* 1. Chastisement, punishment, correction, penalty. 2. Censure, animadversion, reproach. 3. (Obs.) Example, instruction. 4. Alteration or correction made in a work. *Castigo de Dios*, God's judgment. *Castigo de la miseria*, A miser, skinflint.

Castilla [cas-teel'-lyah], *f.* Castile. *En Castilla el caballo lleva la silla*, In Castile the son inherits nobility from the father, even though the mother be plebeian.

Castillejo [cas-teel-lyay'-ho], *m.* 1. (Dim.) A small castle. 2. Go-cart.

Castillería [cas-teel-lyay-ree'-ah], *f.* 1. Toll paid on passing through a district which belongs to a castle. 2. (Obs.) Government of a castle.

Castillo [cas-teel'-lyo], *m.* 1. Castle, fort. 2. The mounting of a velvet-loom. 3. Cell of the queen-bee. 4. *Castillo de proa*, (Naut.) Forecastle. *Castillo roquero*, Castle built on a rock. *Hacer castillos en el aire*, (Met.) To build castles in the air. *Jugar a castillo o león*, To play castle or lion, to toss up a coin and bet on what side it may fall.

Castilluelo [cas-teel-lyoo-ay'-lo], *m. dim.* Castlet, a small castle.

Castizo, za [cas-tee'-tho, thah], *a.* Of a noble descent, of a good breed, pure-blooded. *Caballo castizo*, Blood-horse. *Estilo castizo*, A chaste, pure style.

Casto, ta [cahs'-to, tah], *a.* 1. Pure, chaste, honest, modest, continent, cold, clean. 2. Perfect. 3. (Obs.) Pure: applied to style.

Castor [cas-tor'], *m.* 1. Castor, a beaver, an amphibious quadruped. Castor. 2. Beaver, a heavy cloth, of smooth surface, made for overcoats. 3. (Mex.) Fine red baize. *Castor y Pólux*. 1. (Naut.) Castor and Pollux, St. Elmo's fire, or corposant, an electric brush which sometimes appears on the masts and yards of ships in stormy weather. 2. The two brightest stars in the constellation Gemini.

Castorcillo [cas-tor-theel'-lyo], *m.* Kind of rough serge like cloth.

Castóreo [cas-to'-ray-o], *m.* Castoreum, a liquid matter found in the inguinal region of the beaver.

Castra [cahs'-trah], *f.* Act of pruning trees or plants.

Castración [cas-trah-the-on'], *f.* Castration, gelding, spaying.

Castradera [cas-trah-day'-rah], *f.* Iron instrument with which honey is taken from a hive.

Castrado [cas-trah'-do], *m.* A eunuch.

Castrador [cas-trah-dor'], *m.* One that gelds or castrates.

Castradura [cas-trah-doo'-rah], *f.* 1. Castration. 2. Scar which remains after an animal has been castrated.

Castrametación [cas-trah-may-tah-the-on'], *f.* Castrametation, encamping.

Castrapuercas [cas-trah-poo-err'-cas], *m.* Sow-gelder's whistle.

Castrar [cas-trar'], *va.* 1. To geld, to castrate, to spay. 2. To cut away the proud flesh about a wound. 3. To prune trees or plants. 4. *Castrar las colmenas*, To cut the honey-combs from bee-hives.

Castrazón [cas-trah-thone'], *f.* 1. Act of cutting honey-combs out of hives. 2. Castrating or gelding season.

Castrense [cas-tren'-say], *a.* Belonging to the military profession.

Castro [cahs'-tro], *m.* 1. (Obs.) Place where an army is encamped. 2. (Prov.) Ruins of ancient fortified places. 3. Game played by boys. 4. Act of taking honey-combs out of hives.

Castrón [cas-trone'], *m.* Castrated goat; a gelded animal.

Casual [cah-soo-ahl'], *a.* Casual, accidental, contingent, fortuitous, occasional, circumstantial.

Casualidad [cah-soo-ah-le-dahd'], *f.* Casualty, hazard, contingency, occasion, hap, accident.

Casualmente [cah-soo-al-men'-tay], *adv.* Casually, accidentally, contingently, haply.

Casucha [cah-soo'-chah], *f.* (Coll.) Miserable hut or cottage, crib.

Casucho [cah-soo'-cho], *m.* *V.* CASUCHA.

Casuel [cah-soo-el'], *m.* (Orn.) Cassowary, emeu. Struthio casuarius.

Casuista [cah-soo-ees'-tah], *m.* Casuist.

Casuístico, ca [cah-soo-ees'-te-co, cah], *a.* Casuistical.

Casulla [cah-sool'-lyah], *f.* Chasuble, vestment worn by priests.

Casullero [cah-sool-lyay'-ro], *m.* One who makes chasubles and other vestments for priests.

Casus belli [cah'-soos bayl'-lee]. (Lat.) Cause for war: a phrase well known in diplomatic language.

Cata [cah'-tah], *f.* 1. Act of trying a thing by the taste. *Dar a cata*, To give upon trial. *Echar cata*, (Obs.) To make a careful inquiry. 2. (Obs.) Plummet for measuring heights.

Cata [cah'-tah], *adv.* (Coll.) Mark, beware. (Imp. of CATAR.)

Catabolismo [cah-tah-bo-lees'-mo], *m.* (Biol.) Catabolism.

Catabre [cah-tah'-bray], *m.* (Naut.) Sheep-shank.

Catacaldos [cah-tah-cahl'-dos], *m.* Taster of wine, liquors, soup, etc.

Cataclismo [cah-tah-clees'-mo], *m.* Cataclysm, deluge, inundation: a convulsion of nature.

Catacumbas [cah-tah-coom'-bas], *f. pl.* Catacombs.

Catacústica [cah-tah-coos'-te-cah], *f.* Catacoustics.

Catadióptrico, ca [cah-tah-de-op'-tre-co, cah], *a.* Catadioptric, relating to light reflected and refracted.

Catador [cah-tah-dor'], *m.* Taster.

Catadura [cah-tah-doo'-rah], *f.* 1. Trying by the taste, tasting. 2. (Coll.) Gesture, face, countenance. 3. (Obs.) Mode of guarding or inspecting criminals.

Catafalco [cah-tah-fahl'-co], *m.* A temporary cenotaph to celebrate funeral rites, catafalque.

Catalán, na [cah-tah-lahn', lah'-nah], *a.* Catalonian.

Catalejo [cah-tah-lay'-ho], *m.* Telescope.

Cataléctico [cah-tah-layc'-te-co], *a.* (Poet.) Catalectic.

Catalepsia [cah-tah-lep'-se-ah], *f.* Catalepsy, trance.

Catalicón [cah-tah-le-cone'], *m.* Catholicon, universal medicine.

Catalina [cah-tah-lee'-nah], *f.* The balance-wheel of a watch, called Catherine and also St. Catherine's wheel in Spanish.

Catálisis [cah-tah'-le-sis], *f.* (Chem.) Catalysis.

Catalizador [cah-tah-le-thah-dor'], *m.* (Chem.) Catalyst.

Catalogar [cah-tah-lo-gar'], *va.* To catalogue, list.

Catálogo [cah-tah'-lo-go], *m.* Catalogue, roll, file, matricula.

Catalpa [cah-tahl'-pah], *f.* The catalpa, a genus of American and East Indian flowering trees, bearing long, cylindrical pods.

Catalufa [cah-tah-loo'-fah], *f.* (Obs.) Kind of floor-carpet.

Catamiento [cah-tah-me-en'-to], *m.* (Obs.) Observation, inspection.

Catamito [cah-tah-mee'-to], *m.* Catamite. *V.* SODOMITA.

Catán [cah-tahn'], *m.* Indian sabre or cutlass.

Catanance, Catananque [cah-tah-nahn'-thay, kay], *f.* (Bot.) Lion's-foot. Catananche. *Catanance azul*, Blue catananche. Catananche cœrulea.

Cataplasma [cah-tah-plahs'-mah], *f.* Poultice, *Cataplasma de mostaza*, Mustard plaster.

Catapucia menor [cah-tah-poo'-the-ah may-nor'], *f.* (Bot.) Lesser or caper spurge. Euphorbia lathyris. *Cata pucia mayor*, Castor-oil plant, palma christi. Ricinus communis.

Catapulta [cah-tah-pool'-tah], *f.* Catapult, a military engine.

Catar [cah-tar'], *va.* 1. To taste, to try by the taste. 2. To view, to inspect, to inquire, to investigate, to examine 3. To judge, to form an opinion. 4. To esteem, to respect. 5. To bear in mind. 6. To cut the combs out of bee-hives. *Cuando no se cata* or *cuando menos se cata*, (Coll.) When a person thinks least of it.

Catarańa [cah-ta-rah'-nyah], *f.* (Orn.) Sheldrake, a bird resembling a teal. Anas tadorna.

Catarata [cah-ta-rah'-tah], *f.* 1. Cataract, opacity of the crystalline lens of the eye. 2. Cataract, water-fall, cascade. *Abrirse las cataratas del cielo*, To rain heavily, to pour. *Abatir la catarata*, (Surg.) To couch a cataract. *Extraer las cataratas*, To remove or extract cataracts. *Tener cataratas*, (Met.) Not to understand clearly.

Catarral [cah-tar-rahl'], *a.* Catarrhal.

Catarribera [cah-tar-re-bay'-rah], *m.* 1. Man-servant appointed to follow the hawk on horseback, and bring it down with its prey. 2. (Joc.) Lawyer appointed to examine into the proceedings of magistrates charged with the administration of justice.

Catarriento, ta [cah-tar-re-en'-to, tah], *a.* *V.* CATARROSO.

Catarro [cah-tar'-ro], *m.* Catarrh. *Catarro epidémico,* Influenza.

Catarroso, sa [cah-tar-ro'-so, sah], *a.* 1. Catarrhal. 2. Subject to or troubled with a cold.

Catártico, ca [cah-tar'-te-co, cah], *a.* Cathartic, purging.

Catastro [cah-tahs'-tro], *m.* 1. A tax-list of the real property in every district of a country. 2. The office of this tax-list.

Catástrofe [cah-tahs'-tro-fay], *f.* 1. Catastrophe. 2. Catastrophe, dénouement.

Catatán [cah-tah-tahn'], *m.* (Ch.) Punishment.

Cataviento [cah-tah-ve-en'-to], *m.* (Naut.) Dog-vane. Weather-cock.

Catavino [cah-tah-vee'-no], *m.* 1. Small jug or cup used to taste wine. 2. (Prov.) Small hole at the top of large wine-vessels for tasting the wine.—*pl.* Tipplers who run from tavern to tavern to drink.

Catavinos [cah-ta-vee'-nos], *m.* A wine-taster, expert sampler. *V.* CATACALDOS.

Cate [cah'-tay], *m.* A weight, common in the Philippine Islands, equivalent to 1 lb. 6 oz. Spanish, or gm. 632.60.

Catear [cah-tay-ar'], *va.* (Obs.) 1. To inquire after, to investigate, to discover. 2. (Min.) To prospect.

Catecismo [cah-tay-thees'-mo], *m.* Catechism.

Catecú [cah-tay-coo'], *m.* Catechu, an astringent extract from East Indian plants, particularly from an acacia. *V.* CATO.

Catecumeno, na [cah-tay-coo'-may-no, nah], *m.* & *f.* Catechumen.

Cátedra [cah'-tay-drah], *f.* 1. Seat or chair of a professor. 2. Professorship, office and functions of a professor or teacher. *Pedro regentó la cátedra tantos años,* Peter filled the professor's chair so many years. 3. See, the seat of pontifical or episcopal power.

Catedral [cah-tay-drahl'], *a.* & *f.* Cathedral.

Catedrático [cah-tay-drah'-te-co], *m.* 1. Professor in a university, or any other literary establishment. 2. Contribution formerly paid by the inferior clergy to bishops and prelates.

Catedrilla [cah-tay-dreel'-lyah], *f.* 1. (Dim.) Small or poor professor's chair. 2. In some universities, the less important professorship.

Categoría [cah-tay-go-ree'-ah], *f.* 1. Predicament or category. 2. Character of a person. *Ser hombre de categoría,* To be a man of estimable qualities and talents; a man of rank.

Categóricamente [cah-tay-go'-re-cah-men'-tay], *adv.* Categorically.

Categórico, ca [cah-tay-go'-re-co, cah, *a.* Categorical, categoric.

Catequesis [cah-tay-kay'-sis], *f.* A brief and simple explanation of a doctrine.

Catequismo [cah-tay-kees'-mo], *m.* 1. Catechizing, instruction in religious doctrine. 2. (Obs.) *V.* CATECISMO.

Catequista [cah-tay-kees'-tah], *m.* Catechist.

Catequístico, ca [cah-tay-kees'-te-co, cah], *a.* Catechetical, catechetic, catechistical.

Catequizante [cah-tay-ke-thahn'-tay], *pa.* Catechiser, catechist.

Catequizar [cah-tay-ke-thar'], *va.* 1. To catechise, to instruct in the Christian faith. 2. (Met.) To persuade.

Caterva [cah-terr'-vah], *f.* A great number, a swarm, a throng, a crowd; the vulgar.

Catete [cah-tay'-tay], *m.* (Ch. coll.) The devil.

Catéter [cah-tay'-ter], *m.* Catheter, a tube of metal, rubber, or woven material for surgical uses; as for drawing off urine, or for introducing air into the middle ear.

Cateterismo [cah-tay-tay-rees'-mo], *m.* Catheterism, employment of the catheter.

Cateterizar [cah-tay-tay-re-thar'], *va.* To catheterize, to use a catheter remedially.

Cateto [cah-tay'-to], *m.* 1. (Arch.) Cathetus, perpendicular line which intersects the volute by passing through its centre. 2. *pl.* The sides which form the right angle of a right-angled triangle.

Catimbao [cah-teem-bah'-o], *m.* 1. Clown. 2. (Ch.) Someone ridiculously garbed. 3. (Peru) Short and stout person.

Catinga [cah-teen'-gah], *f.* (Sp. Am.) 1. Bad odor exuded by some plants and animals. 2. (Sp. Am.) Body odor attributed to negroes. 3. (Ch.) Name which sailors give to soldiers.

Catire [cah-tee'-ray], *m.* & *f.* (Sp. Am.) Blond mulatto.

Catita [cah-tee'-tah], *f.* (Arg. & Bol.) Type of parrot.

Catite [cah-tee'-tay], *m.* Loaf of the best refined sugar.

Cato [cah'-to], *m.* Japan earth, an extract obtained by the decoction of vegetable substance in water. *V.* CATECÚ.

Catoche [cah-to'-chay], *m.* (Mex.) Bad humour. (Acad.)

Catódico, ca [cah-to'-de-co, cah], *a.* (Phy. & Chem.) Cathodic.

Cátodo [cah'-to-do], *m.* (Phy. & Chem.) Cathode.

Católicamente [cah-to'-le-cah-men-tay], *adv.* In a catholic manner.

Catolicismo [cah-to-le-thees'-mo], *m.* 1. Catholicism. 2. Catholicism, the orthodox faith of the Catholic church.

Católico, ca [cah-to'-le-co, cah], *a.* 1. Catholic. 2. General or universal. 3. True, infallible. *El rey católico,* His catholic majesty. *No estar muy católico,* Not to be in good health, not to be very well.

Católico [cah-to-le-co'], *m.* 1. Catholic, a Roman Catholic. 2. (Chem.) Chemical furnace.

Catolicón [cah-to-le-cone'], *m.* Catholicon, a panacea.

Catón [cah-tone'], *m.* 1. A very wise man or one who affects wisdom. 2. A reading-book for children. 3. (Met.) A severe censor. For proper name, see Appendix.

Catoniano, na [cah-to-ne-ah'-no, nah], *a.* Catonian, relating to Cato.

Catóptrica [cah-top'-tre-cah], *f.* Catoptrics, the science of reflected light.

Catóptrico, ca [cah-top'-tre-co, cah], *a.* Catoptrical.

Catorce [cah-tor'-thay], *a.* Fourteen.

Catorcena [cah-tor-thay'-nah], *f.* The conjunction of fourteen units.

Catorceno, na [cah-tor-thay'-no, nah], *a.* Fourteenth. *V.* PAÑO.

Catorzavo, va [cah-tor-thah'-vo, vah]. One of the fourteen parts of a unit, a fourteenth.

Catre [cah'-tray], *m.* Small bedstead. *Catre de mar,* Hammock or cot. *Catre de tijera a la inglesa,* Field-bed.

Catricofre [cah-tre-co'-fray], *m.* Press-bed which shuts up; a folding-bed, bed-lounge.

Caucáseo, ea [cah-oo-cah'-say-o, ah], **Caucásico, ca,** *a.* Caucasian.

Cauce [cah'-oo-thay], *m* 1. The bed of a river. 2. Trench, acequia, for conveying water to fields, gardens, etc.

Caucera [cah-oo-thay'-rah], *f.* (Obs.) *V.* CACERA.

Caución [cah-oo-the-on'], *f.* 1. Security or pledge given for the performance of an agreement; gage, guarantee. 2. (Law) Bailbond. *Caución juratoria,* Oath taken by a person having no bail to return to prison. 3. Caution, warning, foresight, prevention.

Caucionar [cah-oo-the-o-nar'], *va.* (Law) To guard against an evil or loss; to bail.

Cauchal [cah-oo-chahl'], *m.* Rubber plantation.

Cauchero, ra [cah-oo-chay'-ro, rah], *a.* Pertaining to rubber.—*m.* Rubber worker.—*f.* Rubber plant.

Caucho [cah'-oo-cho], *m.* Rubber. *Árbol del caucho,* Rubber plant. *Caucho sintético,* Synthetic rubber.

Caudal [cah-oo-dahl'], *m.* 1. Property, fortune, wealth, means, fund: especially in money. 2. Capital or principal sum, stock. 3. (Met.) Plenty, abundance. *Hacer caudal de alguna cosa,* To hold a thing in high estimation.

Caudal [cah-oo-dahl'], *a.* (Zool.) Caudal, relating to the tail. *Águila caudal,* The red-tailed eagle.

Caudalejo [cah-oo-dah-lay'-ho], *m. dim.* Middling fortune.

Caudaloso, sa [cah-oo-dah-lo'-so, sah], *a.* 1. Carrying much water: spoken of rivers. 2. (Obs.) Rich, wealthy.

Caudatario [cah-oo-dah-tah'-re-o], *m.* Clergyman who carries the train of an officiating bishop's robe.

Caudato, ta [cah-oo-dah'-to, tah], *a.* 1. Having a tail: applied to a comet. 2. Bearded, hairy.

Caudatrémula [cah-oo-dah-tray'-moo-lah], *f.* (Orn.) The wagtail.

Caudillo [cah-oo-deel'-lyo], *m.* 1. Commander of an armed troop. 2. Chief, leader, or director of a company.

Caudón [cah-oo-done'], *m.* A bird of prey, a kind of falcon. *V.* PEGA REBORDA.

Caulícolo, Caulículo [cah-oo-lee'-co-lo, cah-oo-lee'-coo-lo], *m.* (Arch.) Ornament of the capital of columns.

Causa [cah'-oo-sah], *f.* 1. Cause; occasion. 2. Consideration, motive of action, motive or reason of doing a thing. 3. Causality. 4. Cause, side, or party, affair in which one takes an interest. 5. Lawsuit, trial. 6. Criminal cause or information. *Causa pública,* Public good. *A causa de,* Considering, on account of.

Causable [cah-oo-sah'-blay], *a.* (Littl. us.) Causable.

Causador, ra [cah-oo-sah-dor', rah], *m.* & *f.* Occasioner, causator, causer.

Causal [cah-oo-sahl'], *a.* Causal, ground on which something is done.

Causalidad [cah-oo-sah-le-dahd'], *f.* Causality.

Causante [cah-oo-sahn'-tay], *pa.* & *m.* Occasioner, causer. 2. (Law) The person from whom a right is derived; constituent, principal.

Causar [cah-oo-sar'], *va.* 1. To cause, to produce, to generate, to create, to gender, to make. 2. To sue, to enter an action. 3. To occasion, to originate.

Causativo, va [cah-oo-sah-tee'-vo, vah], *a.* (Littl. us.) Causative.

Causídico [cah-oo-see'-de-co], *m.* Advocate, counsellor.

Causídico, ca [cah-oo-see'-de-co, cah], *a.* (Law) Causidical, forensic.

Castor [cas-tor'], *m.* 1. Castor, a beaver, an amphibious quadruped. Castor.

Cáustico, ca [cah'-oos-te-co, cah], *a.* 1. Caustic, caustical. 2. Applied to a ray of reflected light which unites with others in one point.

Cautamente [cah-oo-tah-men'-tay], *adv.* Cautiously.

Cautchuc [cah-oot-chooc'], **Cauchuco** [cah-oo-choo'-co], *m.* Caoutchouc, the tree and the gum. *Cautchuc vulcanizado,* Vulcanized rubber.

Cautela [cah-oo-tay'-lah], *f.* 1. Caution, prudence, foresight, prevention, precaution and reserve. 2. Heed, heedfulness, guard. 3. Artfulness, craft, cunning.

Cautelar [cah-oo-tay-lar'], *va.* To take the necessary precaution, to proceed with prudence.

Cautelosamente [cah-oo-tay-lo-sah-men'-tay], *adv.* Cautiously, warily, guardedly.

Cauteloso, sa [cah-oo-tay-lo'-so, sah], *a.* Cautious, heedful.

Cauterio [cah-oo-tay'-ree-o], *m.* (Med.) Cautery. *Cauterio actual,* Actual cautery, burning with hot iron. *Cauterio potencial,* Potential cautery procured by chemicals.

Cauterización [cah-oo-tay-re-thah-the-on'], *f.* Cauterization, cauterizing.

Cauterizador [cah-oo-tay-re-thah-dor'], *m.* He who cauterizes.

Cauterizar [cah-oo-tay-re-thar'], *va.* 1. To cauterize. 2. To correct or reproach with severity.

Cautín [cah-oo-teen'], *m.* A soldering-iron.

Cautivar [cah-oo-te-var'], *va.* 1. To make prisoners of war. 2. To imprison. 3. (Met.) To captivate, to charm, to subdue.

Cautiverio, *m.* **Cautividad,** *f.* [cah-oo-te-vay'-re-o, cah-oo-te-ve-dahd']. 1. Captivity. 2. Confinement.

Cautivo, va [cah-oo-tee'-vo, vah], *m.* & *f.* 1. Captive among infidels. 2. Captive, one charmed by beauty.

Cauto, ta [cah'-oo-to, tah], *a.* Cautious, wary.

Cava [cah'-vah], *f.* 1. Digging and earthing of vines. 2. Cellar where wine and water are kept for the use of the royal family. 3. (Obs.) Ditch. 4. (Prov.) Subterraneous vault.

Cavacote [cah-vah-co'-tay], *m.* Mound of earth made with the hoe to serve as a mark or boundary for the time being.

Cavadiza [cah-vah-dee'-thah], *a.* Dug out of a pit: applied to sand.

Cavado, da [cah-vah'-do, dah], *a.* (Obs.) Hollow, concave.—*pp.* of CAVAR.

Cavador [cah-vah-dor'], *m.* 1. Digger. *Cavador de greda,* Chalk-cutter. 2. (Obs.) Grave-digger.

Cavadura [cah-vah-doo'-rah], *f.* Digging.

Cavallillo [cah-val-lyeel'-lyo], *m.* Water-furrow between ridges.

Caván [cah-vahn'], *m.* A measure used in the Philippine Islands equivalent to seventy-five liters.

Cavar [cah-var'], *va.* 1. To dig, to excavate. 2. To paw: applied to horses. —*vn.* 1. To penetrate far into a thing. 2. To penetrate, to think intensely or profoundly.

Cavatina [cah-vah-tee'-nah], *f.* Cavatina, a melody of a more simple form than the aria. A song without a second part and a da capo.

Cavazón [cah-vah-thone'], *f.* (Obs.) Digging.

Caverna [cah-verr'-nah], *f.* 1. Cavern, cave. 2. Hollow inside or depth of wounds; cavity resulting from tuberculous ulceration or from an abscess.

Cavernilla [cah-ver-neel'-lyah], *f. dim.* Small cavern.

Cavernoso, sa [cah-ver-no'-so, sah], *a.* Cavernous, caverned. *Cuerpo cavernoso,* (Anat.) Corpus cavernosum.

Caveto [cah-vay'-to], *m.* (Arch.) Flute, fluting, groove, hollow moulding.

Caví [cah-vee'], *m.* A Peruvian root, called *oca.*

Cavia [cah'-ve-ah], *f.* Circular excavation at the foot of a tree to collect water.

Cavial, or **Caviar** [cah-ve-ahl', cah-ve-ar'], *m.* Caviar, the roe of the sturgeon pressed and salted: a dish of Russian origin.

Cavidad [cah-ve-dahd'], *f.* Cavity, excavation.

Cavidos [cah-vee'-dos], *m.* Portuguese measure of length.

Cavilación [cah-ve-lah-the-on'], *f.* Cavilling.

Cavilar [cah-ve-lar'], *va.* 1. To cavil, find fault. 2. To find subtle excuses to escape from a difficulty.

Cavilosamente [cah-ve-lo-sah-men'-tay], *adv.* Cavillously.

Cavilosidad [cah-ve-lo-se-dahd'], *f.* Captiousness; cavillingness.

Caviloso, sa [cah-ve-lo'-so, sah], *a.* Captious, cavillous.

Cavilla [cah-veel'-lyah], *f.* 1. (Bot.) Sea-holly. Eryngium maritimum. 2. (Naut.) Tree-nail. *V.* CABILLA.

Cavillador [cah-veel-lyah-dor'], *m.* (Naut.) Tree-nail-maker.

Cavillar [cah-veel-lyar'], *va.* (Naut.) To use tree-nails. *Cavillar un bajel,* To drive tree-nails into a ship.

Cavo, va [cah'-vo, vah], *a.* (Obs.) 1. Concave. 2. Having only twenty-nine days: spoken of a month.

Cayadilla [cah-yah-deel'-lyah], *f. dim.* Small shepherd's hook.

Cayado [cah-yah'-do], *m.* 1. Shepherd's hook, crook. 2. Crozier of a bishop. 3. Walking-staff.

Cayán [cah-yahn'], *m.* 1. *V.* TAPANCO. 2. A covering of matting put on certain Philippine boats to protect the persons within.

Cayanto [cah-yahn'-to], *m.* A kind of stuff.

Cayelac [cah-yay-lahc'], *m.* Sweet-scented wood of Siam.

Cayeput [cah-yay-poot'], *m.* Cajeput-oil. Melaleuca leucadendron.

Cayo [cah'-yoh], *m.* A rock, shoal or islet in the sea; key.

Cayote [cah-yo'-tay], *m.* (Bot.) *V.* CIDRACAYOTE.

Cayou [cah-yo'-oo], *m.* Cashew-nut.

Cayuco [cah-yoo'-co], *m.* (Naut.) Small fishing-boat used in Venezuela.

Caz [cath], *m.* Canal, trench, or ditch, near rivers for irrigation; mill-race, conduit (fr. Cauce).

Caza [cah'-thah], *f.* 1. Chase, hunting, fowling, field-sports. 2. Game. 3. (Naut.) Chase, pursuit of a vessel at sea. 4. (Obs.) Thin linen resembling gauze. *Caza mayor,* Hunting wild-boars, stags, wolves, etc. *Caza menor,* Shooting or fowling; chasing hares, rabbits, partridges, etc. *Andar a caza,* To hunt. *Andar a caza de alguna cosa,* (Met.) To go in pursuit of a thing. *Andar a caza de gangas,* To spend one's time uselessly. *Andar a caza con hurón muerto,* (To go rabbit-catching with a dead ferret), To undertake business without adequate means. *Alborotar* or *levantar la caza,* To start the game. *Dar caza,* (Naut.) To give chase to a vessel. *Ponerse en caza,* (Naut.) To manœuvre in order to escape from another vessel. *Espantar la caza,* (Met.) To injure one's claim by an untimely application. *Caballo de caza,* Hunter, hunting-horse. *Trompa de caza,* Hunting horn. *Partida de caza,* Hunting party.

Caza [cah'-thah], *m.* (Aer.) Fighter plane, pursuit plane.

Cazabe [cah-thah'-bay], *m.* (Sp. Am). Cassava bread.

Cazaclavos [cah-thah-clah'-vos], *m.* Nail puller.

Cazadero [cah-thah-day'-ro], *m.* Hunting ground.

Cazador [cah-tha-dor'], *m.* 1. Hunt, hunter, chaser, huntsman, sportsman. 2. Animal which gives chase to another. 3. (Naut.) Vessel which gives chase to another. 4. (Met.) One who prevails upon another, and brings him over to his party. *Cazador de alforja,* One who sports with dogs, snares, and other devices.

Cazadora [cah-tha-do'-rah], *f.* Huntress.

Cazamoscas [cah-tha-mos'-cas], *m.* (Orn.) Fly-catcher, a bird. Muscicapa.

Cazar [cah-thar'], *va.* 1. To chase, to hunt, to fowl, to sport, to course. 2. (Met.) To gain a difficult point by dexterity and skill. 3. (Met.) To gain one's friendship by caresses and deceitful tricks. 4. (Naut.) To give chase to a ship. 5. *Cazar una vela,* (Naut.) To tally a sail, to haul the sheet aft. *Cazar moscas,* (Met.) To waste one's time in idle amusements. *Cazar con perdigones de plata,* To kill with silver shot: applied to those who buy game, instead of killing it.

Cazatorpederos [cah-thah-tor-pay-day'-ros], *m.* Torpedo-boat destroyer.

Cazcalear [cath-cah-lay-ar'], *vn.* 1. (Coll.) To run to and fro with assiduity, without performing any thing important. 2. To fidget.

Cazcarria [cath-car'-re-ah], *f.* Splashings of dirt on clothes: used commonly in the plural.

Cazo [cah'-tho], *m.* 1. Copper saucepan with an iron handle. 2. Copper or iron ladle for taking water out of a large earthen vessel. 3. Large kettle or boiler. 4. (Obs.) Back part of a knife-blade.

Cazoleja, eta [cah-tho-lay'-hah, tah], *f.* 1. (Dim.) Small saucepan. 2. Pan of a musket-lock.

Cazolero [cah-tho-lay'-ro], *m.* (Coll.) Mean person who does women's work in the kitchen.

Cazolero, ra [cah-tho-lay'-ro, rah], *a.* Applied to a person too officious. *V.* COMINERO.

Cazoleta [cah-tho-lay'-tah], *f.* 1. Pan of a musket-lock. 2. Boss or defence of a shield. 3. Hand-guard or languet of a sword. 4. Kind of perfume. 5. *V.* CAZOLEJA.

Cazolilla [cah-tho-leel'-lyah], *f. dim.* Small earthen pan.

Cazolón [cah-tho-lone'], *m. aug.* Large earthen pot or stew-pan.

Cazón [cah-thone'], *m.* 1. (Zool.) Dog-fish or small shark. Squalus galeus. 2. (Obs.) Brown sugar.

Cazonal [cah-tho-nahl'], *m.* (Prov.) Fishing-tackle for the shark-fishery.

Cazonete [cah-tho-nay'-tay], *m.* (Naut.) Toggle, a pin used to fasten a port-rope.

Cazú [cah-thoo'], *m.* An edible African fruit resembling cacao.

Cazudo, da [cah-thoo'-do, dah], *a.* Having a thick back: spoken of knives.

Cazuela [cah-thoo-ay'-lah], *f.* 1. An earthen pan to dress meat in, stewing-pan, crock. 2. Meat dressed in an earthen pan. 3. The gallery of playhouses in Spain reserved for women. 4. *Cazuela mojí* or *mojil,* (Prov.) Tart made of cheese, bread, apples, and honey. 5. Earthen pans for baking pies. *V.* TARTERA.

Cazumbrar [cah-thoom-brar'], *va.* To join staves together with hempen cords.

Cazumbre [cah-thoom'-bray], *m.* Hempen cord with which the staves of wine-casks are joined and tightened.

Cazumbrón [cah-thoom-brone'], *m.* Cooper.

Cazur [cah-thoor'], *m.* (Bot.) *V.* BRIONIA BLANCA.

Cazurro, ra [cah-thoor'-ro, rah], *a.* 1. (Coll.) Taciturn, sulky, sullen. 2. (Obs.) Making use of low language.

Cazuz [cah-thooth'], *m.* (Bot.) Ivy. (Arab. kisūs, fr. Gr. κισσός.)

Ce [thay]. 1. *f.* Name of the third letter of the alphabet. 2. *int.* Hark, here, come hither. *Ce por be*, or *ce por ce*, Minutely, circumstantially. *Por ce o por be*, In one way or other.

Cea [thay'-ah], *f.* Thigh-bone. *V.* CÍA.

Ceanoto [thay-ah-no'-to], *m.* Ceanothus, a genus of American and Oceanic shrubs of the buckthorn family; Jersey tea, redroot, etc.

Ceática [thay-ah'-te-cah], *f.* (Med.) Sciatica, a disease.

Ceático, ca [thay-ah'-te-co, cah], *a* (Med.) Sciatical. *V.* CIÁTICO.

Ceba [thay'-bah], *f.* The fattening of fowls or other domestic animals.

Cebada [thay-bah'-dah], *f.* (Bot.) Barley. Hordeum. *Cebada de abanico*, Battledore barley. Hordeum heocriton. *Cebada común*, Spring barley. Hordeum vulgare. *Cebada común blanca*, A variety of the spring barley with white seeds. *Cebada caballar, de seis hileras* or *romosa*, Winter barley. Hordeum hexastichon. *Cebada ladilla*, Common long-eared barley. Hordeum distichon. *Cebada negra*, Black barley. Hordeum nigrum. *Cebada del milagro*, Necked barley. Hordeum gymnocriton. *Cebada ratonil*, Wall barley. Hordeum murinum. *Cebada perlada*, Pearl barley.

Cebadal [thay-bah-dahl'], *m.* Field sown with barley.

Cebadar [thay-bah-dar'], *va.* To feed barley to horses.

Cebadazo, za [thay-bah-dah'-tho, thah], *a.* Belonging to barley.

Cebadera [thay-bah-day'-rah], *f.* 1. Kind of bag in which feed is given in the field to working cattle. 2. (Naut.) Sprit-sail.

Cebadería [thay-bah-day-ree'-ah], *f.* Barley-market.

Cebadero [thay-bah-day'-ro], *m.* 1. Place where game or fowls are fed. 2. One whose business is to breed and feed hawks. 3. Mule which on a journey carries barley for the rest. 4. Bell-mule which takes the lead. 5. Painting which represents domestic fowls in the act of feeding. 6. Entrance of a tile-kiln. 7. Dealer in barley.

Cebadilla [thay-bah-deel'-lyah], *f.* 1. (Bot.) Indian caustic barley or cevadilla. Veratrum sabbadilla. 2. (Bot.) Sneeze-wort. Achillea ptarmica. 3. (Bot. Prov.) Prickly ox-eye. Buphthalmum spinosum. 4. Hellebore powdered and used as snuff.

Cebado [thay-bah'-do], *a.* (Her.) Ravening: applied to the picture of a wolf with a lamb or kid in its mouth. —*Cebado, da, pp.* of CEBAR.

Cebador [thay-bah-dor'], *m.* 1. One who fattens fowls or other animals. 2. Priming-horn, powder-horn.

Cebadura [thay-bah-doo'-rah], *f.* Act of feeding or fattening fowls or other domestic animals.

Cebar [thay-bar'], *va.* & *n.* 1. To feed animals, to stuff, to cram. 2. To fatten fowls and other domestic animals. 3. (Met.) To keep up a fire. 4. To grapple, or to lay fast hold one thing of another. 5. (Met.) To excite and cherish a passion or desire. 6. To prime a gun. 7. To let off a rocket or squib. 8. *Cebar un anzuelo*, To bait a fish-hook.—*vr.* To be firmly bent upon a thing.

Cebato [thay-bah'-to], *m.* A climbing plant of Arabia.

Cebellina [thay-bel-lyee'-nah], *f.* 1. Sable. Mustela zibellina. 2. Sable, the skin of the sable.

Cebica [thay-bee'-cah], *f.* *V.* CIBICA.

Cebo [thay'-bo], *m.* 1. Food given to animals; fodder. 2. Fattening of fowls and other animals. 3. Bait for wolves and birds of prey. 4. (Met.) That which excites or forments a passion. 5. Kind of monkey. *V.* CEFO. 6. Cart-grease. *Cebo de pescar*, Bait for fishing. 7. Priming of guns. *Cebo* or *ceba fulminante*, Percussion-cap.

Cebolla [thay-bol'-lyah], *f.* 1. (Bot.) Onion. Allium cepa. 2. The bulb of the onion. 3. Every kind of bulbous root. 4. The round part of a lamp into which oil is put. *Cebolla albarrana*, (Bot.) Squill. Scilla maritima. *Cebolla ascalonia*, (Bot.) Shallot garlic or ascalonian garlic. Allium ascalonium.

Cebollana [thay-bol-lyah'-nah], *f.* (Bot.) Three-toothed globularia. Globularia alypum.

Cebollar [thay-bol-lyar'], *m.* Plot of ground sown with onions.

Cebollero, ra [thay-bol-lyay'-ro, rah], *m.* & *f.* Dealer in onions.

Cebolleta [thay-bol-lyay'-tah], *f. dim.* A tender onion.

Cebollino [thay-bol-lyee'-no], *m.* 1. A young onion fit to be transplanted. 2. The onion's seeds. 3. (Bot.) Chive or cive; a plant allied to the leek and the onion. Allium schœnoprasum.

Cebollón [thay-bol-lyone'], *m. aug.* A large onion.

Cebolludo, da [thay-bol-lyoo'-do, dah], *a.* 1. Among gardeners, applied to any plant with a big bulb. 2. (Coll.) Ill-shaped: applied to persons.

Cebón [thay-bone'], *m.* A fat bullock or hog. *Cebones de Galicia*, Stall-fed bullocks.

Ceboncillo [thay-bon-theel'-lyo], *m. dim.* Fatling, a young animal fed for slaughter, particularly a pig.

Cebra [thay'-brah], *f.* Zebra, a kind of ass having the body marked with dark bands. Equus zebra.

Cebratana [thay-brah-tah'-nah], *f.* 1. A long wooden tube or pipe. *V.* CERBATANA. 2. (Art.) Piece of ordnance resembling a culverin.

Cebruno, na [thay-broo'-no, nah], *a.* Having the colour of deer or hares.

Ceburro [thay-boor'-ro], *a.* *V.* MIJO CEBURRO and CANDEAL.

Ceca [thay'-cah], *f.* 1. A mint for the coining of money. 2. *m.* Name of the mosque which the Arabs had in Cordova, the most venerated after Mecca. *Andar de ceca en meca*, To rove, wander about, hither and thither.

Cecear [thay-thay-ar'], *vn.* 1. To pronounce the *s* as *c.* 2. To call one by the word *ce-ce.* 3. To lisp.

Ceceo [thay-thay'-o], *m.* 1. Lisping, lisp. 2. Act of calling any one by the word *ce-ce*, which corresponds to *I say.*

Ceceoso, sa [thay-thay-o'-so, sah], *m.* & *f.* Lisper.—*a.* Lisping.

Cecial [thay-the-ahl'], *m.* Hake or other like fish cured and dried in the air.

Cecias [thay'-the-as], *m.* North-west wind.

Cecina [thay-thee'-nah], *f.* Hung beef. *Echar en cecina*, To salt and dry meat.

Cecinar [thay-the-nar'], *va.* To make hung beef. *V.* ACECINAR.

Ceda [thay'-dah], *f.* *V.* ZEDA.

Cedacería [thay-dah-thay-ree'-ah], *f.* Shop where sieves or cribs are made or sold.

Cedacero [thay-dah-thay'-ro], *m.* One who makes or sells sieves, cribs, etc.

Cedacillo, ito [thay-dah-theel'-lyo, ee'-to], *m. dim.* A small sieve. *Cedacito nuevo tres días en estaca*, A new broom sweeps clean.

Cedazo [thay-dah'-tho], *m.* Hair sieve or strainer; tamis, flour-sieve, bolting-cloth. *Ver* or *mirar por tela de cedazo*, To see through a hair sieve; that is, to see readily other people's faults, but not one's own.

Cedazuelo [thay-dah-thoo-ay'-lo], *m. dim.* A small hair sieve or strainer.

Cedente [thay-den'-tay], *pa.* Ceding, granting. — *m.* Conveyer, assigner, transferrer.

Ceder [thay-derr'], *va.* To grant, to cede, to resign, to yield, to deliver up, to make over, to give up.—*vn.* 1. To yield or yield to, to submit, to comply, to give out, to give over, to give way, to come in, to go back. (Mech.) To sag, slacken. 2. To happen, to turn out ill or well. 3. To abate, to grow less.

Cedilla [thay-deel'-lyah], *f.* Cedilla, the mark ɔ formerly placed under a c to show that it sounded like z (ç). *V.* ZEDILLA.

Cediza [thay-dee'-thah], *a.* Tainted: applied to meat.

Cedo [thay'-do], *adv.* (Obs.) Immediately. *V.* LUEGO.

Cedoaria [thay-do-ah'-re-ah], *f.* Zedoary, a medicinal root.

Cedras [thay'-dras], *f. pl.* Saddle-bags of skin, in which shepherds carry bread and other provisions.

Cedria [thay-dree'-ah], *f.* Cedria, cedrium, a resin distilled from the cedar.

Cédride, Cedrio [thay'-dree-day, thay'-dre-o], *m.* Fruit of the cedar-tree.

Cedrino, na [thay-dree'-no, nah], *a.* Cedrine, cedarn.

Cedro [thay'-dro], *m.* (Bot.) 1. Cedar. *Cedro de América*, Barbadoes bastard cedar. Cedrella odorata. *Cedro del Líbano*, Cedar of Lebanon. Pinus cedrus. 2. (Prov.) Spanish juniper. Juniperus thurifera.

Cédula [thay'-doo-lah], *f.* 1. Slip of parchment or paper written or to write upon. 2. Order, bill, decree. 3. Cedule, a scroll or writing. 4. Lot. 5. Schedule; warrant, share, scrip. *Cédula de aduana*, A permit. *Cédula de abono*, Order to remit a tax in a town or a province. *Cédula de cambio*, Bill of exchange. *Cédula de diligencias*, A warrant which was issued by the Council of the Chamber, commissioning a judge to make some investigation. *Cédula de preeminencias*, 1. A certificate of long and faithful service; an emeritus degree. 2. In the militia, an order whereby a retiring officer retains his military rank. *Cédula personal* or *de vecindad*, An official document declaring the name, occupation, domicile, etc., of each citizen, and to serve for identification. *Dar cédula de vida*, To show bravery by sparing the life of one who is in his opponent's power. *Cédula de* *inválidos*, Warrant for the reception of invalids. *Cédula real*, Royal letters patent. *Cédula de comunión* or *confesión*, Card or certificate of one's having taken the sacrament. *Cédula ante diem*, Secretary's summons of meeting to the members of a society. *Echar cédulas*, To draw or cast lots.

Cedulaje [thay-doo-lah'-hay], *m.* Fees or dues paid for the expedition of decrees or grants.

Cedulilla, ita [thay-doo-leel'-lyah, ee'-tah], *f. dim.* A small slip of paper.

Cedulón [thay-doo-lone'], *m. aug.* A large bill, long edict, a large libellous bill or paper. *Poner cedulones*, To post up bills, edicts, or libels.

Cefalalgia [thay-fah-lahl'-he-ah], *f.* (Med.) Cephalalgia, headache.

Cefalea [thay-fah-lay'-ah], *f.* Violent headache, generally one-sided, like migraine.

Cefálico, ca [thay-fah'-le-co, cah], *a.* Cephalic, belonging to the head; cephalic (vein).

Céfalo [thay'-fah-lo], *m.* (Zool.) Mullet, a kind of perch.

Cefalina [thay-fah-lee'-nah], *f.* The root of the tongue.

Cefalópodo [thay-fah-lo'-po-do], *m.* Cephalopod, the highest class of mollusks.

Cefalotomía [thay-fah-lo-to-mee'-ah], *f.* Cephalotomy, the act of opening or dividing the head of the fœtus, to facilitate delivery.

Cefeo [thay-fay'-o], *m.* Cepheus, a constellation of the northern hemisphere, near Cassiopeia and Draco.

Céfiro [thay'-fe-ro], *m.* Zephyr.

Cefo [thay'-fo], *m.* A large African monkey. Simia cephus.

Cegajo [thay-gah'-ho], *m.* A he-goat, two years old.

Cegajoso, sa [thay-gah-ho'-so, sah], *a.* Blear-eyed.

Cegar [thay-gar'], *vn.* To grow blind. —*va.* 1. To blind, to make blind. 2. (Met.) To darken the light of reason. 3. To shut a door or window. *Cegar los conductos, los pasos o caminos*, To stop up channels, passages, or roads. *Cegar una vía de agua*, (Naut.) To fother a leak.

Cegarra [thay-gar'-rah], *a.* Coll. for CEGATO.

Cegarrita [thay-gar-ree'-tah], *m.* (Coll.) One who contracts the eye to see at a distance. *A cegarritas* or *a ojos cegarritas*, Having the eyes shut.

Cegato, ta [thay-gah'-to, tah], *a.* (Coll.) Short-sighted.

Cegatoso, sa [thay-gah-to'-so, sah], *a.* *V.* CEGAJOSO.

Ceguecillo, Ceguezuelo [thay-gay-theel'-lyo, thay-gay-thoo-ay'-lo], *m. dim.* Little blind fellow.

Ceguedad [thay-gay-dahd'], *f.* 1. Blindness, cecity. 2. (Met.) Blindness, ignorance, intellectual darkness.

Ceguera [thay-gay'-rah], *f.* 1. Disorder in the eye. 2. Absolute blindness.

Cegueríes [thay-gay-ree'-es], *m.* Kind of martens, martens' skins.

Ceguiñuela [thay-gee-nyoo-ay'-lah], *f.* (Naut.) Whip-staff of the helm. *V.* PINZOTE.

Ceiba [thay'-e-bah], *f.* 1. (Bot.) Five-leaved silk-cotton-tree. Bombax ceiba. 2. By the sea-shore, sea-moss, alga.

Ceja [thay'-hah], *f.* 1. Eye-brow. 2. Edging of clothes; projecting part, as in the binding of books. 3. In stringed instruments, bridge on which the cords rest. 4. Summit of a mountain. 5. Circle of clouds round a hill; cloud-cap. 6. (Arch.) Weather-moulding, rim. 7. (Naut.) An opening in a cloudy horizon. *Dar entre ceja y ceja*, (Met.) To tell one to his face unpleasant truths. *Hasta las cejas*, To the utmost, to the extreme. *Tomar a uno entre cejas*, To take a dislike to any one. *Quemarse las cejas*, (Met.) To study with intense application.

Cejadero [thay-hah-day'-ro], *m.* Traces of a harness.

Cejar [thay-har'], *vn.* 1. To retrograde, to go backward. 2. (Met.) To slacken, to relax.

Cejijunto, ta [thay-he-hoon'-to, tah], *a.* Having eye-brows which meet.

Cejo [thay'-ho], *m.* 1. Thick fog which rises from rivers. 2. A cord tied around a bundle of esparto-grass, made of the same. 3. (Obs.) Frown, a look of displeasure.

Cejudo, da [thay-hoo'-do, dah], *a.* Having heavy and long eye-brows.

Cejuela [thay-hoo-ay'-lah], *f. dim.* A small eye-brow.

Celada [thay-lah'-dah], *f.* 1. Helm, helmet. *Celada borgoñona*, Burgundy helmet. 2. Ambuscade, ambush, lurch. 3. Artful trick. 4. Part of the key of the cross-bow. 5. Horse soldier formerly armed with a cross-bow. 6. (Naut.) Decoy or stratagem used by a small ship of war to bring an inferior vessel within gun-shot.

Celadilla [thay-lah-deel'-lyah], *f. dim.* Small helmet.

Celador, ra [thay-lah-dor', rah], *m.* & *f.* 1. Curator. 2. Monitor in schools. 3. Warden.

Celaje [thay-lah'-hay], *m.* 1. Colour of the clouds. 2. Small cloud moving before the wind, scud. 3. Painting which represents the rays of the sun breaking through clouds. 4. Presage, prognostic. 5. Sky-light; upper part of a window; the sky of a picture. *Celajes*, Light swiftly moving clouds, scud.

Celán [thay-lahn'], *m.* A kind of herring.

Celar [thay-lar'], *vn.* & *a.* 1. To fulfil the duties of an office with care. 2. To watch any person's motions from fear. 3. To cover, to conceal. 4. *V.* RECELAR. (Lat. celare, to conceal.) 5. To engrave; to cut in wood. (Lat. cælare, to grave.)

Celda [thel'-dah], *f.* 1. Cell in a convent. 2. Cell in bee-hives. 3. (Naut. Obs.) Small cabin. 4. (Obs.) Small room.

Celdilla [thel-deel'-lyah], *f.* (Bot.) Cell, the part of a pericarp or capsule in which seeds are lodged.

Celebérrimo, ma [thay-lay-ber'-re-mo, mah], *a. sup.* Most celebrated.

Celebración [thay-lay-brah-the-on'], *f.* 1. Celebration, solemn performance. 2. Celebration, praise, applause, acclamation.

Celebrador, ra [thay-lay-brah-dor', rah], *m.* & *f.* Applauder, praiser, celebrator.

Celebrante [thay-lay-brahn'-tay], *m.* 1. Celebrator. 2. A priest celebrating the mass.

Celebrar [thay-lay-brar'], *va.* 1. To celebrate, to perform in a solemn manner. *Celebrar misa*, To say mass. 2. To hold, take place. *Celebrar un contrato*, To draw up a contract. *Celebrar una reunión*, To hold a meeting. 3. To celebrate, to praise, to applaud, to commend.

Celebre [thay'-lay-bray], *a.* 1. Celebrated, famous, renowned, noted. 2. (Met. Coll.) Gay, facetious, agreeable in conversation.

Célebremente [thay'-lay-bray-men-tay], *adv.* 1. Celebriously, with celebrity. 2. Facetiously, merrily.

Celebridad [thay-lay-bre-dahd'], *f.* 1. Celebrity. 2. Celebriousness, renown, fame. 3. Pomp, magnificence, or ostentation, with which a feast or event is celebrated. 4. Public demonstration to commemorate some event.

Celebrillo [thay-lay-breel'-lyo], *m. dim.* Small brains.

Celebro [thay-lay'-bro], *m.* 1. Skull. 2. Brain. *V.* CEREBRO. 3. (Met.) Fancy imagination. 4. Prudence.

Celemín [thay-lay-meen'], *m.* 1. Dry measure, the 12th part of a *fanega*, about an English peck. 2. The quantity of grain contained in a *celemín*.

Celeminero [thay-lay-me-nay'-ro], *m.* (Obs) Hostler who measures grain in inns.

Celerado, Celerario [thay-lay-rah'-do. thay-lay-rah'-re-o], *a.* (Obs.) *V.* MALVADO.

Celerario [thay-lay-rah'-re-o], *m.* (Obs.) Usurer.

Célere [thay'-lay-ray], *a.* Quick, rapid. —*m.* One of the select three hundred knights of ancient Roman nobility.

Celeridad [thay-lay-re-dahd'], *f.* Celerity, velocity.

Celerímetro [thay-lay-ree'-may-tro], *m.* Speedometer.

Celeste [thay-les'-tay], *a.* 1. Celestial. 2. Heavenly. 3. Sky-blue.

Celestial [thay-les-te-ahl'], *a.* 1. Celestial, heavenly. 2. (Met.) Perfect, agreeable, delightful, excellent. 3. (Iron.) Silly, sottish.

Celestialmente [thay-les-te-al-men'-tay], *adv.* Celestially, heavenly; perfectly.

Celfo [thel'-fo], *m.* *V.* CEFO.

Celiaca [thay-lee'-ah-cah], *f.* (Med.) 1. Celiac artery. 2. Cœliac passion, a species of diarrhœa.

Celiaco, ca [thay-lee'-ah-co, cah], *a.* (Med.) 1. Cœliac, relating to the cœliac passion. 2. Applied to a person afflicted with the cœliac passion.

Celibato [thay-le-bah'-to], *m.* 1. Celibacy. 2. A bachelor, a single man.

Célibe [thay'-le-bay], *m.* Bachelor, an unmarried man.

Célico, ca [thay'-le-co, cah], *a.* Celestial, heavenly.

Celidonia [thay-le-do'-ne-ah], *f.* 1. (Bot.) Common celandine, swallow-wort, tether-wort. Chelidonium majus. 2. Swallow-stone, a small stone with various impressions.

Celindrate [thay-lin-drah'-tay], *m.* Ragout made with coriander-seed.

Celita [thay-lee'-tah], *f.* A fish caught in the Straits of Gibraltar.

Celo [thay'-lo], *m.* 1. Zeal, ardour, devotion. 2. Heat, rut, the appetite for generation in animals. 3. Religious zeal, fervour.—*pl.* 1. Jealousy. 2. Suspicions. *Dar celos*, To excite suspicions. *Pedir celos*, To be jealous.

Celofán [thay-lo-fahn'], *m.* Cellophane.

Celosía [thay-lo-see'-ah], *f.* Lattice of a window, Venetian blind.

Celoso, sa [thay-lo'-so, sah], *a.* 1. Jealous. 2. Light and swift-sailing: applied to small vessels. 3. Crank, unsteady, top-heavy: spoken of vessels and boats.

Celotipia [thay-lo-tee'-pe-ah], *f.* Jealousy.

Celsitud [thel-se-tood'], *f.* 1. Celsitude, elevation, grandeur. 2. (Obs.) Highness, a title now expressed by *Alteza*.

Celta [thel'-tah], *com.* Celt, Celtic.—*m.* The Celtic language.

Celtibérico, ca [thel-te-bay'-re-co, cah], *a.* Celtiberian.

Celticismo [thel-te-thees'-mo], *m.* Celticism.

Céltico, ca [thel'-te-co, cah], *a.* Celtic.

Celtista [thel-tees'-tah], *com.* Celtist one who cultivates Celtic language and literature.

Célula [thay'-loo-lah], *f.* (Med.) Cellule.

Celular [thay-loo-lar'], or **Celulario, ia** [thay-loo-lah'-re-o, ah], *a.* 1. (Med.) Cellular. 2. A system of isolation among those imprisoned for grave crimes.

Celulilla [thay-loo-leel'-lyah], *f. dim.* A very small cell or cavity.

Celuloide [thay-loo-lo'-e-day], *m.* Celluloid.

Celulosa [thay-loo-lo'-sah], *f.* Cellulose, woody fibre.

Celuloso, sa [thay-loo-lo'-so, sah], *a.* Cellulose, containing cells.

Cellenco, ca [thel-lyen'-co, cah], *a.* (Coll.) Decrepit.

Cellisca [thel-lyees'-cah], *f.* (Obs.) *V.* Ventisca. Fine rain or snow, sleet, driven by a heavywind.

Cellisquear [thel-lyees-kay-ar'], *vn.* To sleet, to be squally with fine snow or rain.

Cembellina [them-bel-lyee'-nah], *f.* Hartshorn.

Cementación [thay-men-tah-the-on'], *f.* Cementation.

Cementar [thay-men-tar'], *va.* (Obs.) *V.* Cimentar.

Cementerio [thay-men-tay'-re-o], *m.* Cemetery churchyard, grave-yard.

Cemento [thay-men'-to], *m.* 1. Cement, concrete. *Cemento armado*, Reinforced concrete. *Cemento Portland*, Portland cement. 2. (Anat.) Cement (of the teeth).

Cena [thay'-nah], *f.* 1. Supper. 2. (Obs.) Scene, stage. *Jueves Santo* or *de la Cena*, Maundy Thursday, Thursday before Good Friday. *Más mató la cena que sanó Avicena*, Suppers have killed more than Avicenas ever cured. *Cena del rey*, In Navarre and Aragón, a tax paid for the king's table; called *yantar* in Castile.

Cenáculo [thay-nah'-coo-lo], *m.* The dining-hall in which our Lord celebrated the last supper with his disciples.

Cenacho [thay-nah'-cho], *m.* Basket or hamper for fruit and greens.

Cenadero [thay-nah-day'-ro], *m.* 1. (Obs.) A place for supping. 2. Summer-house in a garden.

Cenador [thay-nah-dor'], *m.* 1. One fond of suppers, or who sups to excess. 2. Summer-house in a garden, an arbor, bower. *Cenador chinesco*, Chinese temple.

Cenagal [thay-nah-gahl'], *m.* Quagmire. *Meterse en un cenagal*, (Met.) To be involved in an unpleasant, arduous affair. *Salir de un cenagal*, To get rid of an unpleasant affair.

Cenagoso, sa [thay-nah-go'-so, sah], *a.* Muddy, miry, marshy.

Cenaoscuras [thay-nah-os-coo'-ras], *com.* (Met. and coll.) A misanthrope, miser, man-hater.

Cenar [thay-nar'], *va.* To sup. *Cenar a oscuras*, To sup in the dark to save candle; to be miserly.

Cenata [thay-nah'-tah], *f.* (Col.) Merry banquet or dinner.

Cenceño, ña [then-thay'-nyo, nyah], *a.* 1. Lean, thin, slender. 2. (Obs.) Pure, simple. *Pan cenceño*, Unleavened bread.

Cencerra [then-ther'-rah], *f.* 1. Bell worn by the leading mule. *V.* Cencerro. 2. Clack of a mill which strikes the hopper and promotes the running of the corn. 3. *Señor Cencerra*, Mr. Rattlehead: an appellation given by students of the college of Alcalá to the collegian last arrived. 4. The meat between the throttle and ribs of a saddle of mutton.

Cencerrada [then-ther-rah'-dah], *f.* Noise with bells and horns at the door of an old bridegroom or widower, the right of his marriage; charivari.

Cencerrear [then-ther-ray-ar'], *vn.* 1. To jingle continually: applied to wether, mule, or horse bells. 2. To clack. 3. To play on an untuned guitar. 4. To make a dreadful noise, as of windows and doors shaken by the wind.

Cencerreo [then-ther-ray'-o], *m.* Noise made by mule or horse bells.

Cencerril [then-ther-reel'], *a.* (Obs.) Resembling the noise of horse-bells.

Cencerrilla, illo [then-ther-reel'-lyah, eel'-lyo], *f. & m. dim.* A small wether, horse, or mule bell.

Cencerro [then-ther'-ro], *m.* 1. Bell worn by the leading wether, or mule. 2. Ill-tuned guitar. 3. (Orn.) Wood-crow. Corvus, *L.* *No quiero perro con cencerro*, I do not want a dog with a bell; that is, I do not like to engage in a business that is more troublesome than profitable. *A cencerros tapados*, Privately, by stealth. *Irse a cencerros tapados*, To take French leave, to sneak off.

Cencerrón [then-ther-rone'], *m.* A small bunch of grapes which remains after the vintage.

Cencerruno, na [then-ther-roo'-no, nah], *a.* *V.* Cencerril.

Cencido, da [then-thee'-do, dah], *a.* Untilled, uncultivated: applied to land.

Cencro [then'-cro], *m.* A serpent of Brazil.

Cendal [then-dahl'], *m.* 1. Light thin stuff made of silk or thread; crape. 2. Furbelow, flounce or trimming of gowns, etc. 3. (Poet.) Garter. *Cendales*, Cotton for an inkstand.

Cendea [then-day'-ah], *f.* (Prov.) In Navarre, meeting of the inhabitants of several villages to deliberate on public business.

Cendolilla [then-do-leel'-lyah], *f.* (Obs.) A forward girl acting with little judgment.

Cendra [then'-drah], *f.* 1. Paste used to clean silver. 2. Cupel. *Ser una cendra*, (Met.) To be lively as a cricket.

Cendrar [then-drar'], *va.* (Obs.) *V.* Acendrar.

Cenefa [thay-nay'-fah], *f.* 1. Frame of a picture. 2. Border or list of any kind of stuff. 3. Valance, fringes and drapery of a bed. 4. Trimming. 5. Middle piece of a priest's garment, called chasuble. 6. (Poet.) Bank of a river or lake, the brim of a pond. 7. *Cenefa de un toldo*, (Naut.) Centre of an awning. (Arab.)

Ceni [thay-nee'], *m.* A kind of fine brass or bronze.

Cenicilla [thay-ne-theel'-lyah], *f.* *V.* Oídium.

Cenicero [thay-ne-thay'-ro], *m.* Ash-hole, ash-pit, ash-pan.

Ceniciento, ta [thay-ne-the-en'-to, tah], *a.* Ash-coloured, cinereous.—*m.* Scullion.

Cenit [thay-neet'], *m.* (Ast.) Zenith; vertex.

Cenital [thay-ne-tahl'], *a.* Vertical, relating to the zenith.

Ceniza [thay-nee'-thah], *f.* 1. Ashes, cinders. 2. Coarse ashes, which remain in the strainer when the lye is made. *V.* Cernada. 3. Ashes, the remains of the dead. *Cenizas azules*, Blue paint extracted from various fossils by burning, the most perfect of which is the lapis lazuli. *Cenizas de estaño*, Putty. *Cenizas de vegetales*, Potash. *Cenizas graveladas* or *cenizas de rasuras o heces de vino*, Weed-ashes. *Allegador de la ceniza, y derramador de la harina*, equivalent of Penny wise, pound foolish. *Dar con los huevos en la ceniza*, (Met.) To upset an affair which was in the way of döing well. *Día de ceniza* or *Miércoles de ceniza*, Ash-Wednesday. *Hacerse ceniza* or *cenizas alguna cosa*, (Met.) To be reduced to nothing, to come to nothing. *Poner a uno la ceniza en la frente*, (Met.) To humiliate by reproaches; to overcome one, to surpass in skill, or convince in dispute. (Acad.)

Cenizal [thay-ne-thahl'], *m.* Heap of ashes.

Cenizo [thay-nee'-tho], *m.* 1. (Bot.) White goose-foot. 2. (coll.) Jinx, bearer of ill luck.

Cenizo, za [thay-nee'-tho, thah], *a.* *V.* Ceniciento.

Cenizoso, sa [thay-nee-tho'-so, sah], *a.* Covered with ashes, cineritious.

Cenobio [thay-no'-be-o], *m.* (Obs.) Cenobium. *V.* Monasterio.

Cenobita [thay-no-bee'-tah], *m.* Cenobite, a monk.

Cenobítico, ca [thay-no-bee'-te-co, cah], *a.* (Obs.) Cenobitical.

Cenotafio [thay-no-tah'-fe-o], *m.* Cenotaph, a monument.

Cenote [thay-no'-tay], *m.* Deposit of water found in Mexico and elsewhere in America, generally at a great depth in the center of a cavern. (Acad.)

Censal [then-sahl'], *m. & f. & a.* (Prov.) *V.* Censo and Censual.

Censalista [then-sah-lees'-tah], *m.* (Prov.) *V.* Censualista.

Censatario, Censero [then-sah-tah'-re-o, then-say'-ro], *m.* One who pays an annuity out of his estate to another person.

Censo [then'-so], *m.* 1. An agreement by which a person acquires the right of receiving an annual pension. 2. Quit-rent. 3. Census, censual roll or book, where all the inhabitants of a kingdom or of a state are enumerated. 4. Poll-tax, formerly in use among the Romans. 5. *Censo al quitar* or *reservativo*, A quit-rent or annuity which can be paid at once by a certain sum. *Censo de por vida*, Annuity for one or more lives. *Censo de agua en Madrid*, Money paid in Madrid for the use of water.

Censontli, Censontle [then-son'-tlee, then-son'-tlay], *m.* (Mex.) The Mexican mocking-bird. *Cf.* Sinsonte.

Censor [then-sor'], *m.* 1. Censor, an officer appointed to examine new books and publications, whether they contain any thing contrary to religion and good manners. 2. Critic, reviewer of literary compositions. 3. Censorious person.

Censoría [then-so-ree'-ah], *f.* (Littl. us.) Censorship.

Censorino, Censorio [then-so-ree'-no, then-so'-re-o], *a.* (Littl. us.) Censorian.

Censual [then-soo-ahl'], *a.* 1. Belonging to a quit-rent, annuity, or any other annual rent paid for the possession of land. 2. Belonging to lawful interest, on money advanced or sunk in useful undertakings.

Censualista [then-soo-ah-lees'-tah], *m.* 1. A person in whose favour an annuity has been imposed, and who has the right to enjoy it until his death. 2. A copy-holder.

Censualmente [then-soo-al-men'-tay], *adv.* With a right to enjoy an annuity.

Censuario [then-soo-ah'-re-o], *m.* (Obs.) *V.* Censualista.
Censura [then-soo'-rah], *f.* 1. A critical review of literary productions. 2. Censure, blame, reproach, reprimand, reprehension, objurgation. 3. Reproach without foundation, gossiping. 4. Censure, a spiritual punishment inflicted by an ecclesiastical judge; fulmination or denunciation of censure. 5. (Obs.) Register, list. 6. Censorship, the office of a Roman censor.
Censurable [then-soo-rah'-blay], *a.* Censurable.
Censurador [then-soo-rah-dor'], *m.* Censurer, fault-finder.
Censurante [then-soo-rahn'-tay], *pa.* Censurer, censuring.
Censurar [then-soo-rar'], *va.* 1. To review, to criticise, to judge. 2. To censure, to blame, to find fault with, to expose. 3. To accuse, to note, to reprehend. 4. (Obs.) To record, to enter into a list or register. 5. To correct, to reprove.
Centaura, Centaurea [then-tah'-oo-rah], *f.* (Bot.) Centaury. Centaurea. *Centaurea mayor*, Great centaury. Centaurea centaurium. *Centaurea menor*, Common erythræa. Erithræa centaurium.
Centauro [then-tah'-oo-ro], *m.* 1. Centaur. 2. (Ast.) Centaur, a southern constellation.
Centavo [then-tah'-vo], *m.* The hundredth part of any thing; a cent, as the hundredth of a peso (dollar).
Centella [then-tayl'-lyah], *f.* 1. Lightning. 2. Flash of a flint struck with steel; flake of fire. 3. Remaining spark of passion or discord. *Ser vivo como una centella* or *ser una centella*, To be all fire and tow, to be all life and spirit.
Centellador, ra [then-tel-lyah-dor', rah], *a.* Brilliant.
Centellante [then-tel-lyahn'-tay], *pa.* Sparkling, flashing.
Centellar, Centellear [then-tel-lyar', then-tel-lyay-ar'], *vn.* To sparkle, to throw out sparks.
Centelleo [then-tel-lyay'-o], *m.* Spark, scintillation.
Centellón [then-tel-lyone'], *m. aug.* A large spark or flash.
Centén [then-tayn'], *m.* A Spanish gold coin worth one hundred reals.
Centena [then-tay'-nah], *f.* 1. Hundred. 2. Centenary, the number of a hundred. 3. (Obs.) Stubble of rye.
Centenadas [then-tay-nah'-das], *adv.* *A centenadas* or *a centenares*, By hundreds.
Centenal [then-tay-nahl'], *m.* 1. Field sown with rye. 2. Centenary, the number of a hundred.
Centenar [then-tay-nar'], *m.* 1. A hundred. 2. Field sown with rye. *V.* Centenario.
Centenario, ria [then-tay-nah'-re-o, ah], *a.* 1. Centenary, secular, happening but once in a century. 2. *m.* Centennial, feast celebrated every hundred years.
Centenazo, za [then-tay-nah'-tho, thah], *a.* Belonging to rye. *Paja centenaza*, Rye-straw.
Centeno [then-tay'-no], *m.* (Bot.) Common rye. Secale cereale.
Centeno, na [then-tay'-no, nah], *a.* A numeral adjective which signifies hundred.
Centenoso, sa [then-tay-no'-so, sah], *a.* Mixed with rye.
Centesimo, ma [then-tay'-se-mo, mah], *a.* Centesimal, hundredth.
Centi- [then-te]. A prefix from the Latin, signifying the one one-hundredth.
Centiárea [then-te-ah'-ray-ah], *f.* Centiare, the one one-hundredth of an âre, square measure.
Centigrado, da [then-tee'-grah-do, dah], *a.* Centigrade, a scale divided into one hundred degrees.
Centigramo [then-te-grah'-mo], *m.* Centigramme, 0.01 gramme, about one-sixth of a grain.
Centilitro [then-te-lee'-tro], *m.* Centilitre.
Centiloquio [then-te-lo'-ke-o], *m.* A work divided into a hundred parts or chapters.
Centimano, na [then-tee'-mah-no, nah], *a.* (Poet.) Having a hundred hands.
Centimetro [then-tee'-may-tro], *m.* Centimetre: 0.01 metre.
Céntimo [then'-te-mo], *m.* A French copper coin, centime; the one one-hundredth part of a monetary unit, whether real, peseta, escudo, or peso.
Céntimo, ma [then'-te-mo, mah], *a.* The one-hundredth.
Centinela [then-te-nay'-lah], *com.* 1. (Mil.) Sentry or sentinel. 2. (Met.) One who pries into another's actions. *Centinela avanzada*, Advanced guard. *Centinela a caballo*, Vidette, a sentinel on horseback. *Centinela perdida*, Forlorn hope, a soldier on guard close to the enemy's camp; also a small body of troops detached on some desperate service. *Hacer centinela* or *estar de centinela*, To stand sentry, to be on guard.
Centinodia [then-te-no'-de-ah], *f.* (Bot.) Knot-grass, persicaria. Polygonum aviculare.
Centiplicado, da [then-te-ple-cah'-do, dah], *a.* Centuple, a hundred-fold.
Centiplicar [then-te-ple-car'], *va.* *V.* Centuplicar.
Centola, Centolla [then-to'-lah, then-tol'-lyah], *f.* Centre-fish, a kind of marine crab with spotted scales.
Centon [then-tone'], *m.* 1. Crazy quilt. 2. Cento, a literary composition.
Centrado, da [then-trah'-do, dah], *a.* (Her.) Applied to a globe placed on the centre.
Central [then-trahl'], *f.* Main office (of a telephone company, etc.). *Central telefónica*, Telephone exchange, telephone office. *Central de correos*, Main post office. *Central azucarero* or *azucarera*, Sugar mill.
Central, Centrical [then-trahl', then-tre-cahl'], *a.* Central, centric.
Centralidad [then-trah-le-dahd'], *f.* Centrality.
Centralita [then-trah-lee'-tah], *f.* Telephone exchange.
Centralización [then-trah-le-tha-the-on'], *f.* Centralization.
Centralizar [then-trah-le-thar'], *va.* To centralize.—*vr.* To be centralized.
Centralmente [then-tral-men'-tay], *adv.* Centrally.
Céntrico, ca [then'-tre-co, cah], *a.* Focal. *Punto céntrico*, Object, end of one's views. *V.* Centro.
Centrifugo, ga [then-tree'-foo-go, gah], *a.* Centrifugal.
Centripeto, ta [then-tree'-pay-to, tah], *a.* Centripetal.
Centro [then'-tro], *m.* 1. Centre. 2. Height and depth of a thing. 3. (Met.) The principal object of desire and exertion. 4. (Bot.) Disk of flowers. 5. A short dress of flannel which Indian women and half-breeds use in Ecuador. *Estar en el centro de la batalla*, To be in the centre of the action. *Estar en su centro*, (Met.) To be satisfied with one's fate. *El mando es el centro a que aspira la ambición*, Command is the point to which ambition aspires.
Centroamérica [then-tro-ah-may'-re-cah], *f.* Central America.
Centro comercial [then'-tro co-mer-the-ahl'], *m.* Shopping center.
Centumviro [then-toom-vee'-ro], *m* Centumvir, a civil judge, one of a hundred and five appointed yearly.
Centuplicar [then-too-ple-car'], *va.* To centuplicate.
Céntuplo, pla [then'-too-plo, plah], *a.* Centuple.
Centuria [then-too'-re-ah], *f.* 1. Century. 2. Among the Romans, one hundred soldiers, commanded by a centurion.
Centurión [then-too-re-on'], *m.* Centurion.
Centurionazgo [then-too-re-o-nath'-go], *m.* The office of a centurion.
Cenzalino, na [then-tha-lee'-no, nah], *a.* Pertaining to a *cénzalo*.
Cénzalo [then'-tha-lo], *m.* (Ent.) Gnat.
Ceñido, da [thay-nyee'-do, dah], *a.* 1. Moderate in pleasure or expense. 2. Ringed: applied to bees and other insects.—*pp.* of Ceñir.
Ceñidor [thay-nye-dor'], *m.* Belt, girdle, cest, girdle-belt. *Ceñidor de Venus*, Cestus.
Ceñidura [thay-nye-doo'-rah], *f.* (Obs.) The act of girding.
Ceñiglo [thay-nyee'-glo], *m.* (Bot.) White goose-foot, summer-cypress. Chenopodium album.
Ceñir [thay-nyeer'], *va.* 1. To gird, to surround, to circle, to girdle. 2. To environ, to hem in. 3. (Met.) To reduce, to abbreviate, to contract. *Ceñir espada*, To wear a sword. *Ceñir el viento*, (Naut.) To haul the wind.—*vr.* To reduce one's expenses.
Ceño [thay'-nyo], *m.* 1. Frown, a supercilious look. 2. Ring or ferrule. 3. (Vet.) Circle round the upper part of a horse's hoof. 4. (Poet.) A gloomy aspect, as of the sea, clouds, etc.
Ceñoso, sa [thay-nyo'-so, sah], *a.* 1. Hoof surrounded with rings. 2. *V.* Ceñudo.
Ceñudo, da [thay-nyoo'-do, dah], *a.* Frowning, supercilious; grim; gruff, sour of aspect.
Cepa [thay'-pah], *f.* 1. The stump of a tree. 2. Stock of a vine. 3. (Met.) Stock or origin of a family. 4. (Met.) Bud or root of the horns and tails of animals. 5. Root of the wool. 6. Foundation of columns, pilasters, or arches.
Cepacaballo [thay-pah-ca-bahl'-lyo], *m* (Bot.) Cardoon. Cynara cardunculus. *Cepacaballos de Portugal*, Spiny xanthium. Xanthium spinosum.
Cepeda [thay-pay'-dah], or **Cepedera** [thay-pay-day'-rah], *f.* A spot where heath abounds.
Cepejón [thay-pay-hone'], *m.* The largest part of a branch torn from the trunk.
Cepilladuras [thay-peel-lyah-doo'-ras], *f. pl.* Shavings.
Cepillar [thay-peel-lyar'], *va.* 1. To brush. 2. (Obs.) To plane. *V.* Acepillar.
Cepillo [thay-peel'-lyo], *m.* 1. Plane, carpenter's tool. 2. Brush for clothes. 3. Poor-box; corban. *Cepillo de dientes*, Tooth-brush.
Cepita [thay-pee'-tah], *f. dim.* A small stock of a vine.
Cepo [thay'-po], *m.* 1. Block on which an anvil is put. 2. Stocks, for punishment; on board of ships they are called *bilboes*. 3. Reel on which silk is wound. 4. Trap for wolves or

other animals. 5. Charity-box in churches and public places. 6. *V.* CEFO. 7. The stocks with which a gun is made fast in the carriage. 8. Clamp, joining-press; horse (of shoemakers). *Cepo del ancla,* (Naut.) Anchor-stock. *Cepo de maniguetes,* (Naut.) Cross-piece of the kevel. *Cepo de molinete,* (Naut.) Knighthead of the windlass. *Cepos,* Notched cleats or timbers fixed across other timbers to strengthen or secure them where they are pierced; anchor-stocks. *Cepos quedos,* (Coll.) No more of that.

Cepón [thay-pone'], *m. aug.* The large trunk of a tree or vine-stock.

Ceporro [thay-por'-ro], *m.* An old vine pulled up by the roots.

Cequí, Cequín [thay-kee', thay-keen'], *m.* A gold coin, formerly used by the Moors in Spain.

Cequia [thay'-ke-ah], *f.* (Obs.) *V.* ACEQUIA.

Cequiaje [thay-ke-ah'-hay], *m.* Annual contribution paid for irrigation rights by the towns of a community.

Cera [thay'-rah], *f.* 1. Wax. 2. Tapers and candles of wax. 3. Foot-path in the street. *V.* ACERA. *Cera aleda,* Propolis, bee-glue, a resinous substance, with which bees bedaub the inside of the hive. *Cera virgen,* Virgin wax. *Cera de higos,* A drum of figs. *Cera de dorar,* Gold-size. *Cera de los oídos,* Ear-wax, cerumen. *Hacer de alguno cera y pábilo,* (Met.) To turn a man which way you please. *No hay más cera que la que arde,* There is nothing more than what you see. *No quedar a uno cera en el oído.* (Met.) To have spent the last of one's fortune. *Ser una cera,* or *como una cera,* or *hecho de cera,* (Met.) To be as pliable as wax, to be of a pliant or gentle disposition. *Melar las ceras,* To fill the combs with honey. *Ceras,* The cells of wax and honey formed by bees.

Ceráceo, ea [thay-rah'-thay-o, ah], *a.* Of the consistency of wax.

Ceración [thay-rah-the-on'], *f.* Ceration, preparation of a metal for fusion.

Cerachates [thay-rah-chah'-tes], *f. pl.* Wax-stones, a yellow agate.

Cerafolio [thay-rah-fo'-le-o], *m.* (Bot.) Common chervil. Scandix cerefolium. *V.* PERIFOLLO.

Cerámica [thay-rah'-me-cah], *f.* The ceramic art; ceramics, art of making pottery.

Cerámico, ca [thay-rah'-me-co, cah], *a.* Ceramic, relating to pottery.

Cerapez [thay-rah-peth'], *f.* Cerate, a plaster of wax and pitch.

Cerasina [thay-rah-see'-nah], *f.* Cerasin, the insoluble part of cherry, peach, and similar gums.

Cerasta, *f.* **Ceraste, Cerastes,** *m.* [thay-rahs'-tah, thay-rahs'-tay, thay-rahs'-tes]. Horned serpent.

Cerastio de granada [thay-rahs'-te-o day gra-nah'-dah], *m.* (Bot.) White mouse-ear chickweed. Cerastium tomentosum.

Cerato [thay-rah'-to], *m.* (Pharm.) Cerate.

Ceratófilo, Ceratófilon [thay-rah-to'-fe-lo, thay-rah-to'-fe-lone], *m.* (Bot.) Horn-wort, or pond-weed. Ceratophyllum.

Ceraunia, or **Ceraunita** [thay-rah'-oo-ne-ah, thay-rah-oo-nee'-tah], *f.* Ancient name of jasper or flint; oriental jade.

Cerbatana [ther-bah-tah'-nah], *f.* 1 Blow-gun, popgun, pea-shooter. Acoustic trumpet for the deaf. 3. Ancient culverin of small calibre.

Cerbelo [ther-bay'-lo], *m.* (Obs.) *V* CEREBELO.

Cerbero [ther-bay'-ro], *m.* *V.* CANCERBERO.

Cerca [therr'-cah], *f.* 1. Inclosure, hedge, or wall which surrounds a garden, park, or corn-field; fence. 2. (Obs.) Yard.—*m. pl. Los cercas,* Among painters, objects in the foreground of a painting.

Cerca [therr'-cah], *adv.* Near, at hand, not far off, close by, nigh. Preceding the noun or pronoun to which it refers, it demands the preposition *de.* 1. *Aquí cerca* or *cerca de aquí,* Just by. 2. *Cerca de,* Close, near. 3. (Littl. us.) With regard to, relating or belonging to. 4. *En cerca,* Round about. *Tener buen o mal cerca,* (Coll.) To admit or not admit of a close examination. *Tocar de cerca,* 1. (Met.) To be nearly allied to, or near akin. 2. To be concerned in, to be interested.

Cercado [ther-cah'-do], *m.* A garden or field inclosed with a fence; an inclosure, a lock, a close or small inclosed field.—*Cercado, da, pp.* of CERCAR.

Cercador [ther-cah-dor'], *m.* 1. Hedger, one who incloses. 2. An iron graver marking-iron.

Cercadura [ther-cah-doo'-rah], *f.* (Obs.) Inclosure, wall, fence.

Cercamiento [ther-cah-me-en'-to], *m.* (Obs.) Act of inclosing.

Cercanamente [ther-cah-nah-men'-tay], *adv.* Nigh, nighly; nearly.

Cercanía [ther-ca-nee'-ah], *f.* Proximity, neighbourhood, vicinity.

Cercano, na [ther-cah'-no, nah], *a.* Near, close by, neighbouring, adjoining.

Cercar [ther-car'], *va.* 1. To inclose, to environ, to hem, to circle, to compass, to gird. 2. To fence, to secure by an inclosure; to surround with a hedge or wall; to pale. 3. (Mil.) To invest a town, to block up a fortress. 4. To crowd about a person. 5. (Obs.) To bring or put near. *Cercado de desdichas y trabajos,* Involved in troubles and distress.

Cercén [ther-then'], *adv.* *A cercén,* At the root. *Cercén a cercén,* From end to end, completely.

Cercenadamente [ther-thay-nah-dah-men'-tay], *adv.* In a clipping manner, with retrenchment.

Cercenadera [ther-thay-nah-day'-rah], *f.* Clipping-knife used by wax-chandlers.

Cercenador [ther-thay-nah-dor'], *m.* Clipper.

Cercenadura [ther-thay-nah-doo'-rah], *f.* Clipping, retrenchment.—*pl.* Cuttings.

Cercenar [ther-thay-nar'], *va.* 1. To pare, to retrench, to clip. 2. To lop off the ends or extremities. 3. To lessen: applied to expenses. 4. To curtail, to cut away; to abridge.

Cercera [ther-thay'-rah], *f.* Air-tube of a vault to extract the foul air.

Cerceta [ther-thay'-tah], *f.* 1. (Orn.) Widgeon, garganey, a species of duck. Anas querquedula, *L.* 2. Among sportsmen, the first pearl which grows about the bur of a deer's horn; an antler. 3. (Obs.) *V.* COLETA.

Cercillo [ther-theel'-lyo], *m.* 1. (Obs.) Ear-ring. *V.* ZARCILLO. 2. Tendril of a vine. *V.* TIJERETA. 3. (Obs.) Hoop.

Cercio, Cerción [therr'-the-o, ther-the-on'], *m.* An Indian mocking-bird.

Cerciorar [ther-the-o-rar'], *va.* To assure, to ascertain, to affirm.

Cerco [therr'-co], *m.* 1. Hoop or ring. 2. (Mil.) Blockade of a place. 3. Circular motion. 4. Circle, a private assembly. 5. Frame or case of a door or window. *En cerco,* Round about. *Poner cerco a una plaza,* To block up a place. *Levantar el cerco,* To raise a blockade. *Echar cerco,* To surround game with dogs. *Cerco de puerta o ventana,* The frame of a door or window. *Cerco del sol y de la luna,* Circle round the sun or moon. *Hacer un cerco,* To strike a circle.

Cercopiteco [ther-co-pe-tay'-co], *m.* Cercopithecus, a kind of long-tailed monkey. The baboon is an ally, and the order comprises the tailed monkeys of the Old World.

Cercha [therr'-chah], *f.* A wooden rule for measuring convex or concave objects.

Cerchar [ther-char'], *va.* *V.* ACODAR.

Cerchón [ther-chone'], *m.* *V.* CIMBRIA.

Cerda [therr'-dah], *f.* 1. Strong hair in a horse's tail or mane; a bristle. 2. (Prov.) Corn just cut and formed into sheaves. 3. (Prov.) Bundle of flax broken but not yet hackled. 4. Sow. *Cerda de puerco,* Hog's bristle. *Ganado de cerda,* Herd of swine. *Cerdas,* (Obs.) Snares for birds.

Cerdamen [ther-dah'-men], *m.* Handful of bristles.

Cerdana [ther-dah'-nah], *f.* Kind of dance in Catalonia.

Cerdazo [ther-dah'-tho], *m.* 1. (Aug.) A large hog or pig. 2. (Obs.) Hair sieve. *V.* CEDAZO.

Cerdear [ther-day-ar'], *vn.* 1. To be weak in the fore-quarter: applied to animals. 2. To emit a harsh and inharmonious sound: applied to stringed instruments. 3. To decline a request or demand by subterfuges and evasions.

Cerdillo [ther-deel'-lyo], *m. dim.* A small hog or pig.

Cerdo [therr'-do], *m.* Hog or pig. *Cerdo de muerte,* A pig fit to be killed. *Cerdo de vida,* A pig not old or fat enough to be killed.

Cerdoso, sa, Cerdudo, da [ther-do'-so, sah, ther-doo'-do, dah], *a.* Bristly: applied also to men whose breasts are covered with hair.

Cereal [thay-ray-ahl'], *a.* Cereal, relating to the food-producing grasses.—*m. pl.* Cereals.

Cerebelo [thay-ray-bay'-lo], *m.* (Anat.) Cerebellum, the hindbrain.

Cerebral [thay-ray-brahl'], *a.* Cerebral.

Cerebro [thay-ray'-bro], *m.* 1. Cerebrum, the front brain. 2. The brain entire.

Cerecilla [thay-ray-theel'-lyah], *f. dim.* *V.* GUINDILLA.

Cerecita [thay-ray-thee'-tah], *f. dim.* A small cherry.

Ceremonia [thay-ray-mo'-ne-ah], *f.* 1. Ceremony, outward rite, external form of religion. 2. Ceremony, formality, forms of civility. 3. Ceremony, outward form of state. 4. Course, empty form, an affected compliment paid to a person. *Guardar ceremonia,* To stick to the ancient ceremonies and established customs of society. *Él lo hace de pura ceremonia,* He does it out of mere compliment or ceremony. *De ceremonia,* With all ceremony or pomp. *Por ceremonia* or *de ceremonia,* Out of compliment.—*pl.* Words of course.

Ceremonial [thay-ray-mo-ne-ahl'], *m.* A book of ceremonies for public occasions.

Ceremonial [thay-ray-mo-ne-ahl'], *a.* Ceremonial, ceremonious.

Ceremonialmente [thay-ray-mo-ne-al-men'-tay], *adv.* *V* CEREMONIOSAMENTE.

Ceremoniáticamente [thay-ray-mo-ne-ah'-te-cah-men-tay], *adv.* Ceremoniously.

Ceremoniático, ca [thay-ray-mo-ne-ah'-te-co, cah], *a.* Ceremonious.

Ceremoniosamente [thay-ray-mo-ne-o-sah-men'-tay], *adv.* Ceremoniously.

Ceremonioso, sa [thay-ray-mo-ne-o'-so, sah], *a.* Ceremonious, polite, formal, complimental.

Céreo [thay'-ray-o], *m.* (Bot.) Torch-thistle. Cactus.

Cereolita [thay-ray-o-lee'-tah], *f.* A soft, waxy-looking lava.

Cerería [thay-ray-ree'-ah], *f.* 1. Wax-chandler's shop. 2. Office in the royal palace where wax-candles are kept for use.

Cerero [thay-ray'-ro], *m.* 1. Wax-chandler. 2. (Prov.) An idle person, a vagrant.

Cereza [thay-ray'-thah], *f.* Cherry. *Cereza garrafal*, The large heart cherry, bigaroon.

Cerezal [thay-ray-thahl'], *m.* Plantation of cherry-trees; cherry orchard.

Cerezo [thay-ray'-tho], *m.* (Bot.) Cherry-tree, cherry-wood. Prunus cerasus.

Cergazo [ther-gah'-tho], *m.* (Bot.) Rock-rose, cistus. Cistus.

Ceribón, Ceribones [thay-re-bone', bo'-ness], *m.* (Obs.) Act of an insolvent debtor surrendering his estate to his creditors. *Hacer ceribones*, (Obs.) To make submissive and affected compliments.

Cérico, ca [thay'-re-co, cah], *a.* Ceric, relating to cerium.

Ceriflor [thay-re-flor'], *f.* (Bot.) Honey-wort, honey-flower Cerinthe. *V.* CERINTO.

Cerilla [thay-reel'-yah], *f.* 1. Thin wax tapers rolled up in different forms. 2. Ball of wax and other ingredients used formerly by women as a kind of paint. 3. Wax-tablet. 4. Wax of the ear. 5. A wax-match.

Cerillera [thay-reel-lyay'-rah], *f.* A wax taper for lighting lamps or gas.

Cerina [thay-ree'-nah], *f.* A variety of wax (or wax-like material) extracted from the cork-tree.

Cerinto [thay-reen'-to], *m.* (Bot.) Wax-flower, honey-wort, a plant of the borage family. (Cerinthe major and minor.)

Cerio, Cererio [thay'-re-o, thay-ray'-re-o], *m.* (Chem.) Cerium or cererium. Cerio. An annual solanaceous plant of Cochin China.

Cerita [thay-ree'-tah], *f.* Cerite, a resinous brown silicate of cerium found in copper-mines.

Cermeña [ther-may'-nyah], *f.* A small early pear called the muscadine.

Cermeño [ther-may'-nyo], *m.* (Bot.) Muscadine pear-tree. Pirus communis.

Cernada [ther-nah'-dah], *f.* 1. Coarse ashes which remain in the strainer after the lye is put on. 2. Size laid on canvas to prepare it for painting. 3. Plaster of ashes and other ingredients used by farriers in the cure of horses.

Cernadero [ther-nah-day'-ro], *m.* 1. Coarse linen which serves as a strainer for the lye to buck clothes with. 2. (Obs.) Thread and silk skeins for making ribbon.

Cernedero [ther-nay-day'-ro], *m.* 1. Apron worn in sifting flour. 2. Place for sifting flour.

Cernedor [ther-nay-dor'], *m.* (Littl. us.) Sifter.

Cerneja [ther-nay'-hah], *f.* Fetlock of a horse growing behind the pastern joints.

Cernejudo, da [ther-nay-hoo'-do, dah], *a.* Having large fetlocks.

Cerner [ther-nerr'], *va.* To sift, to bolt.—*vn.* 1. To bud and blossom. 2. To drizzle, to fall in small drops.—*vr.* 1. To waggle, to wiggle, to waddle, to move from side to side. 2. To soar: spoken of birds.

Cernícalo [ther-nee'-cah-lo], *m.* 1. (Orn.) Kestrel, sparrow-hawk, wind-hover. Falco tinnunculus. 2. A person of scanty abilities. *Coger* or *pillar un cernícalo*, To be fuddled, half-seas over.

Cernidillo [ther-ne-deel'-lyo], *m.* 1. Thick mist or small rain; mizzle, drizzle. 2. A short and waddling gait.

Cernido [ther-nee'-do], *m.* 1. Sifting. 2. The flour sifted.—*Cernido, da, pp.* of CERNER.

Cernidura [ther-ne-doo'-rah], *f.* Sifting.

Cernir [ther-neer'], *va.* (Obs.) 1. *V.* CERNER. 2. To examine, to purify.

Cero [thay'-ro], *m.* Zero, cipher, an arithmetical symbol. *Ser un cero*, To be a mere cipher. (Arab. sifr, empty. *Cf.* CIFRA.)

Ceroferario [thay-ro-fay-rah'-re-o], *m.* The acolyte who carries the *cirial* or large candlestick.

Cerografía [thay-ro-grah-fee'-ah], *f.* Cerography, the art or process of engraving or writing on wax.

Cerollo, lla [thay-rol'-lyo, lyah], *a.* Reaped when green and soft: applied to grain.

Cerón [thay-rone'], *m.* Dregs of pressed wax formed into a cake.

Cerote [thay-ro'-tay], *m.* 1. Shoemaker's wax, shoe-blacking. 2. (Coll.) Panic, fear. 3. Cerate, a plaster.

Ceroto [thay-ro'-to], *m.* A soft cerate of oil and wax.

Ceroya [thay-ro'-yah], *f.* Crops of corn which begin to grow yellow.

Cerquillo [ther-keel'-lyo], *m.* 1. (Dim.) A small circle or hoop. 2. The seam or welt of a shoe. 3. The ring of hair or tonsure on the head of a religious person.

Cerquita [ther-kee'-tah], *f. dim.* Small inclosure.

Cerquita [ther-kee'-tah], *adv.* At a small distance, nigh or near in point of time or place. *Aquí cerquita*, Just by.

Cerrada [ther-rah'-dah], *f.* 1. The strongest part of a hide or skin which covers the back-bone of an animal. 2. (Obs.) Shutting or locking up of a thing. *Hacer cerrada*, To commit a gross fault or palpable mistake.

Cerradero [ther-rah-day'-ro], *m.* 1. Staple which receives the bolt of a lock. 2. Any hole made to receive the bolt of a lock. 3. (Obs.) Purse-strings.

Cerradero, ra [ther-rah-day'-ro, rah], *m.* & *f.* & *a.* Applied to the place locked, and to the thing with which it is locked. *Echar la cerradera*, To lend a deaf ear, to refuse.

Cerradizo, za [ther-rah-dee'-tho, thah], *a.* That which may be locked or fastened.

Cerrado [ther-rah'-do], *m.* *V.* CERCADO.

Cerrado, da [ther-rah'-do, dah], *a.* 1. Close, reserved, dissembling. 2. Secreted, concealed. 3. Obstinate, inflexible. *Cerrado como pie de muleto*, As stubborn as a mule. *Cerrado americano*, Downright American. *A ojos cerrados*, Without examination. *A puerta cerrada*, Privately, secretly. —*pp.* of CERRAR.

Cerrador [ther-rah-dor'], *m.* 1. Shutter, one that shuts. 2. Porter or door-keeper. 3. Tie, fastening. 4. (Obs.) Bond, obligation.

Cerradura [ther-rah-doo'-rah], *f.* 1. Closure, the act of shutting or locking up. 2. Lock. *Cerradura de golpe* or *de muelle*, Spring-lock. *Cerradura embutida*, Mortise lock. 3. (Obs.) Park or piece of ground surrounded with an inclosure. *No hay cerradura, donde es de oro la ganzúa*, (prov.) There is no lock proof against a golden picklock.

Cerradurilla, ita [ther-rah-doo-reel'-lyah, ee'-tah], *f. dim.* A small lock.

Cerraja [ther-rah'-hah], *f.* 1. Lock of a door. 2. (Bot.) Common sow-thistle. Sonchus oleraceus. *Todo es agua de cerrajas*, It is all good for nothing, or it is nothing but empty words.

Cerrajear [ther-rah-hay-ar'], *vn.* To carry on the trade of a locksmith.

Cerrajería [ther-rah-hay-ree'-ah], *f.* 1. Trade of a locksmith. 2. Locksmith's shop or forge.

Cerrajero [ther-rah-hay'-ro], *m.* Locksmith.

Cerramiento [ther-rah-me-en'-to], *m.* 1. Closure, occlusion, the act of shutting or locking up. 2. Costiveness. 3. Inclosure. 4. The finishing of the roof of a building. 5. Partition-walls of a house. 6. (Obs. For.) Conclusion of an argument; inference.

Cerrar [ther-rar'], *va.* & *n.* 1. To close so as to prohibit ingress or egress, to occlude, to foreclose, to shut up the inlets or outlets of a place, to obstruct a passage. 2. To fit a door or window in its frame or case. 3. To lock, to fasten with a bolt or latch. 4. To include, to contain. 5. To fence or inclose a piece of ground. 6. (Met.) To terminate or finish a thing. 7. To stop up, to obstruct. 8. To prohibit, to forbid, to interdict. 9. To engage the enemy. *Cerrar la carta*, To fold a letter. *Cerrar la cuenta*, To close an account. *Cerrar la boca*, (Met.) To be silent. *Cerrar la mollera*, (Met.) To begin to get sense. *Cerrar la oreja*, (Met.) Not to listen to one's proposals. *Cerrar la puerta*, (Met.) To give a flat denial. *Cerrar a alguno la puerta para que no entre*, To lock one out, to shut out. *Cerrar los ojos*, 1. To die. 2. To sleep. 3. (Met.) Blindly to submit to another's opinion. *Al cerrar del día*, At the close of day, at nightfall. *A cerrar ojos*, (Met.) Blindly, inconsiderately.—*vn.* *Esta puerta cierra bien*, This door closes tightly.—*vr.* 1. To remain firm in one's opinion. *Cerrarse de campiña*, To adhere obstinately to an opinion. 2. To be shut or locked up. 3. To be cicatrized. 4. To grow cloudy and overcast. 5. To close up: applied to the ranks and files of troops. *Cerrarse todas las puertas*, To be completely destitute. *A puerta cerrada el diablo se huye* (or *se vuelve*), The devil turns away from a locked door; avoid the occasion and you will not sin.

Cerraurgal [ther-rah-oor-gahl'], *m.* (Obs.) Water-conduit.

Cerrazón [ther-rah-thone'], *f.* 1. Fog preceding a storm. 2. Ignorant stubbornness, intolerance, etc.

Cerrejón [ther-ray-hone'], *m.* Hillock.

Cerrero, ra [ther-ray'-ro, rah], *a.* 1. Running wild. *Caballo cerrero*, An unbroken horse. 2. (Obs.) Haughty, lofty.

Cerreta [ther-ray'-tah], *f.* (Naut.) Spar, rough tree. *V.* PERCHA.

Cerril [ther-reel'], *a.* 1. Mountainous, rough, uneven: applied to a country.

2. Wild, untamed: applied to cattle. *Puente cerril*, A small narrow bridge for cattle. 3. (Met.) Rude, unpolished, unmannerly.

Cerrilla [ther-reel'-yah], *f.* A die for milling coins.

Cerrillar [ther-reel'-lyar], *va.* To mill coined metal, or to mark it at the edge.

Cerrillo [ther-reel'-lyo], *m. dim.* A little eminence. *Cerrillos*, The dies for milling coined metal.

Cerrión [ther-re-on'], *m.* 1. Icicle. 2. (Obs.) Fresh cheese.

Cerro [therr'-ro], *m.* 1. Hill or high land. 2. Neck of an animal. 3. Backbone, or the ridge it forms. 4. Flax or hemp which is hackled and cleaned. *Cerro enriscado*, A steep and inaccessible mountain. *En cerro*, Nakedly, barely. *Pasar* or *traer la mano por el cerro*, (Met.) To flatter, to cajole. *Como por los cerros de Úbeda*, (Coll.) Foreign to the purpose, totally different.

Cerrojillo [ther-ro-heel'-lyo], *m.* 1. (Orn.) A wagtail, warbler. Motacilla provincialis. 2. (Dim.) A small bolt.

Cerrojo [ther-ro'-ho], *m.* Bolt. *Tentar cerrojos*, (Met.) To try all ways and means to succeed.

Cerrón [ther-rone'], *m.* Kind of coarse fabric made in Galicia.

Cerrotino [ther-ro-tee'-no], *m.* Carded hemp.

Cerruma [ther-roo'-mah], *f.* Weak or defective quarter in horses.

Cerrumado, da [ther-roo-mah'-do, dah], *a.* Having weak or defective quarters: applied to horses.

Certamen [ther-tah'-men], *m.* 1. (Obs.) Duel; battle. 2. Literary controversy, disputation; competition.

Certanedad [ther-tah-nay-dahd'], *f.* (Obs.) *V.* CERTEZA.

Certería [ther-tay-ree'-ah], *f.* (Obs.) Dexterity. *V.* TINO.

Certero, ra [ther-tay'-ro, rah], *m.* & *f.* 1. Sharp-shooter.—*a.* 2. An excellent shot, well-aimed.

Certeza [ther-tay'-thah], *f.* Certainty, certitude.

Certidumbre [ther-te-doom'-bray], *f.* 1. *V.* CERTEZA. 2. (Obs.) Security, obligation to fulfil a thing.

Certificación [ther-te-fe-cah-the-on'], *f.* 1. Certificate, attesting the truth of a fact or event. 2. Return of a writ. 3. (Obs.) Certainty, security.

Certificado [ther-te-fe-cah'-do], *m.* Certificate. *V.* CERTIFICACIÓN.—*Certificado, da, pp.* of CERTIFICAR.

Certificador, ra [ther-te-fe-cah-dor', rah], *m.* & *f.* Certifier.

Certificar [ther-te-fe-car'], *va.* 1. To assure, to affirm, to certify. *Certificar el pliego* or *la carta*, In the post-office, to assure that a letter will reach its destination; to register a letter. 2. To prove by a public instrument.

Certificativo, va, or **Certificatorio, ria** [ther-te-fe-cah-tee'-vo, vah, ther-te-fe-cah-to'-re-o, ah], *a.* That which certifies or serves to certify.

Certísimo [ther-tee'-se-mo], *a. sup.* of CIERTO. Most certain.

Cerúleo, lea [thay-roo'-lay-o, ah], *a.* Cerulean, sky-blue.

Ceruma [thay-roo'-mah], *f.* (Vet.) *V.* CERRUMA.

Cerumen [thay-roo'-men], *m.* Ear-wax, cerumen.

Ceruminoso, sa [thay-roo-me-no'-so, sah], *a.* Ceruminous, producing cerumen.

Cerusa [thay-roo'-sah], *f.* Ceruse, white-lead.

Cerval [ther-vahl'], *a.* Belonging to a deer. *Miedo cerval*, Great timidity.

Cervantesco, ca [ther-van-tes'-co, cah], **Cervántico** [ther-vahn'-te-co], *a.* In the style of Cervantes.

Cervantista [ther-van-tees'-tah], *a.* Admiring Cervantes.

Cervario, ria [ther-vah'-re-oh, ah], *a.* *V.* CERVAL.

Cervática [ther-vah'-te-cah], *f.* *V.* LANGOSTÓN.

Cervatico, illo [ther-vah-tee'-co, eel'lyo], *m. dim.* A small deer.

Cervato [ther-vah'-to], *m.* A fawn.

Cervecería [ther-vay-thay-ree'-ah], *f.* 1. Brewhouse, brewery. 2. Ale-house.

Cervecero [ther-vay-thay'-ro], *m.* 1. Brewer. 2. Beer-seller.

Cerveda [ther-vay'-dah], *f.* Extremity of the ribs of pork.

Cerveza [ther-vay'-thah], *f.* Beer or ale, malt liquor.

Cervicabra [ther-ve-cah'-brah], *f.* Gazelle.

Cervical [ther-ve-cahl'], *a.* (Anat.) Cervical.

Cervigudo, da [ther-ve-goo-'do, dah], *a.* 1. High or thick-necked. 2. (Obs.) Obstinate, stubborn.

Cerviguillo [ther-ve-geel'-lyo], *m.* Nape of the neck.

Cervino, na [ther-vee'-no, nah], *a.* Resembling a deer.

Cerviolas [ther-ve-oh'-las], *f. pl.* (Naut.) Cat-heads. *V.* SERVIOLAS.

Cerviz [ther-veeth'], *f.* Cervix, nape of the neck. *Ser de dura cerviz*, To be incorrigible. *Doblar* or *bajar la cerviz*, (Met.) To humble one's self. *Levantar la cerviz*, (Met.) To be elated, to grow proud.

Cervuno, na [ther-voo'-no, nah], *a.* 1. Resembling or belonging to a deer. 2. Of the colour of a deer.

Cesacio or **Cesación á Divinis**, [thay-sah'-the-o or thay-sa-the-on' ah de-vee'-nis], *f.* (Lat.) Suspension from religious functions.

Cesación, *f.* **Cesamiento**, *m.* [thay-sah-the-on', thay-sah-me-en'-to]. Cessation, ceasing, pause.

Cesante [thay-sahn'-tay], *m.* A public officer dismissed for economical or political reasons, but left in some cases with a portion of his salary until he obtains a new position; a retired official.—*pa.* Ceasing.

Cesante [thay-sahn'-tay], *a.* Jobless, dismissed from a position.

Cesantía [thay-san-tee'-ah], *f.* The state of being a *cesante*, and the salary he receives.

Cesar [thay-sar'], *vn.* 1. To cease, to give over, to forbear. 2. To leave or leave off, to desist.

César [thay'-sar], *m.* Name of the Roman emperor. *O César o nada*, Neck or nothing.

Cesáreo, rea [thay-sah'-ray-o, ah], *a.* Imperial. *Operacion cesárea*, (Surg.) The Cesarean operation.

Cesariano, na [thay-sah-re-ah'-no, nah], *a.* Relating to Julius Cæsar.

Cesariense [thay-sah-re-en'-say], *a.* Pertaining to Cesarea.

Cese [thay'-say], *m.* Cease: a mark put up against the names of persons who receive payment from the public treasury, that their pay should cease.

Cesible [thay-see'-blay], *a.* (Law) That which may be ceded.

Cesión [thay-se-on'], *f.* Cession, or tranfer of goods or estates made in one's favour; resignation, concession. *Cesión de bienes*, Surrender of the estate of an insolvent debtor into the hands of his creditors.

Cesionario, Cesonario, ria [thay-se-o-nah'-re-o, thay-so-nah'-re-o, ah], *m.* & *f.* Cessionary, one in whose favour a tranfer is made.

Cesionista [thay-se-o-nees'-tah], *m.* Transferer, assigner.

Césped, Céspede [thes'-ped, thes'-pay-day], *m.* 1. That part of the rind of a vine where it has been pruned. 2. Sod, or turf covered with grass, grass-plot. *Césped francés*, (Bot.) Common thrift, sea-gillyflower, sea-pink. Statice armeria.

Cespedera [thes-pay-day'-rah], *f.* Field where green sods are cut.

Cesta [thes'-tah], *f.* Basket, pannier. *Llevar de cesta*, (Met.) To contribute unwillingly to the pleasure of others.

Cestada [thes-tah'-dah], *f.* A basketful.

Cestería [thes-tay-ree'-ah], *f.* Place where baskets are made or sold.

Cestero [thes-tay'-ro], *m.* Basket maker or seller.

Cestica, illa, ita [thes-tee'-cah, eel'-lyah, ee'-tah], *f. dim.* A small basket, hand-basket.

Cestico, illo, ito [thes-tee'-co, eel'-lyo, ee'-to], *m. dim.* A little basket.

Cesto [thes'-to], *m.* A hand-basket, hutch. *Estar hecho un cesto*, To be overcome by sleep or liquor. *Quien hace un cesto hará ciento*, He that steals a pin will steal a pound. *Ser alguno un cesto*, To be ignorant and rude. *Coger agua en cesto*, To labour in vain.

Cestón [thes-tone'], *m.* 1. (Aug.) A large pannier or basket. 2. (Mil.) Gabion.—*pl.* Corbeils.

Cestonada [thes-to-nah'-dah], *f.* Range of gabions.

Cestro [thes'-tro], *m.* (Obs.) *V.* SISTRO.

Cesura [thay-soo'-rah], *f.* Cæsura, a figure or pause in poetry.

Cetáceo, cea [thay-tah'-thay-o, ah], *a.* Cetaceous, of the whale kind.

Cetís [thay-tees'], *m.* An old Galician coin.

Cetra [thay'-trah], *f.* A leather shield formerly used by Spaniards.

Cetre [thay'-tray], *m.* A small brass r copper bucket. *V.* ACETRE.

Cetrería [thay-tray-ree'-ah], *f.* 1. Falconry. 2. Hawking; fowling with falcons.

Cetrero [thay-tray'-ro], *m.* 1. Verger. 2. Falconer, sportsman.

Cetrífero [thay-tree'-fay-ro], *m.* (Poet.) One who bears a sceptre.

Cetrino, na [thay-tree'-no, nah], *a.* 1. Citrine, lemon-coloured, greenish-yellow. 2. (Met.) Jaundiced, melancholy. 3. Belonging to citron.

Cetro [thay'-tro], *m.* 1. Sceptre. 2. (Met.) Reign of a prince. 3. Verge borne by dignified canons on solemn occasions. 4. Wand or staff borne by the deputies of confraternities. 5. Perch or roost for birds.

Ceugma [thay'-oog-mah], *f.* (Rhet.) Zeugma, a figure in rhetoric.

Cía [thee'-ah], *f.* Hip-bone, huckle-bone.

Ciaboga [the-ah-bo'-gah], *f.* (Naut.) The act of putting a row-galley about with the oars. *Hacer ciaboga*, To turn the back, to flee.

Ciaescurre [the-ah-es-coor'-ray], *m.* (Naut.) Putting about and backing a row-galley.

Ciánido [the-ah'-ne-do], *m.* Cyanide, a compound of cyanogen.

Ciano [the-ah'-no], *m.* (Bot.) The blue-bottle. Cyanella, *L.*

Cianógeno [the-ah-no'-hay-no], *m.* Cyanogen, a colourless, poisonous, liquefiable gas (C_2N_2), having an almond-like odour.

Cianosis [the-ah-no'-sis], *f.* Cyanosis, a livid hue resulting from insufficient oxygenation of the blood.

Cianotipia [the-ah-no-tee'-pe-ah], *f.* Blueprint. *Copiar a la cianotipia.* To blueprint.
Cianuro [the-ah-noo'-ro], *m.* Cyanid, a compound of cyanogen.
Ciar [the-ar'], *va.* 1. (Naut.) To hold water, to back a row-galley, to stop with the oars. 2. (Obs.) To retrograde. 3. (Met.) To slacken in the pursuit of an affair.
Ciática [the-ah'-te-cah], *f.* Sciatica, or hip-gout.
Ciático, ca [the-ah'-te-co, cah], *a.* Sciatic, sciatical.
Ciato [the-ah'-to], *m.* (Bot.) A tree-fern of tropical regions.
Cibario, ria [the-bah'-re-o, ah], *a.* Cibarious, relating to food.
Cibéleo, lea [the-bay'-lay-o, ah], *a.* (Poet.) Belonging to the goddess Cybele.
Cibera [the-bay'-rah], *f.* 1. Quantity of wheat put at once in the hopper. 2. All seeds or grains fit for animal subsistence. 3. Coarse remains of grain and fruit, husks, etc. 4. (Littl. us.) Every operation which engages the powers of imagination and fancy. 5. (Prov.) Hopper in a corn-mill.
Cibernética [the-behr-nay'-te-cah], *f.* (Med. & Elec.) Cybernetics.
Cibica [the-bee'-cah], *f.* Clout, the iron plate nailed to an axle-tree, to prevent friction.
Cibicón [the-be-cone'], *m.* A large kind of clout.
Cíbolo, la [thee'-bo-lo, lah], *m.* & *f.* The Mexican bull, with horns turned backward; apparently the bison.
Cibrú [the-broo'], *m.* Peruvian name of the cedar-tree.
Cicaba [the-cah'-bah], *f.* A nocturnal bird of prey.
Cicatear [the-cah-tay-ar'], *vn.* (Coll.) To be sordidly parsimonious.
Cicatería [the-cah-tay-ree'-ah], *f.* Niggardliness, parsimony.
Cicatero, ra [the-cah-tay'-ro, rah], *a.* Niggardly, sordid, parsimonious.
Cicateruelo [the-cah-tay-roo-ay'-lo], *m. dim.* An avaricious or niggardly little fellow, a little miser.
Cicatricera [the-cah-tre-thay'-rah], *f.* A woman who used to follow troops and care for wounds.
Cicatriz [the-cah-treeth'], *f.* 1. Cicatrice or cicatrix, a scar. 2. Gash, mark of a wound. 3. (Met. Obs.) Impression remaining on the mind.
Cicatrización [the-cah-tre-thah-the-on'], *f.* Cicatrization.
Cicatrizal [the-cah-tre-thahl'], *a.* Belonging to a cicatrice or scar.
Cicatrizamiento [the-cah-tre-thah-me-en'-to], *m.* (Obs.) *V.* CICATRIZACIÓN.
Cicatrizante [the-cah-tre-thahn'-tay], *pa.* Cicatrisant.
Cicatrizar [the-cah-tre-thar'], *va.* To cicatrize, to heal a wound.
Cicatrizativo, va [the-cah-tre-thah-tee'-vo, vah], *a.* Cicatrisive.
Cícero [thee'-thay-ro], *m.* (typ.) Pica.
Cicérone [the-thay-ro'-nay], *m.* A paid guide. (Ital.)
Ciceroniano, na [the-thay-ro-ne-ah'-no, nah], *a.* Ciceronian: applied to style.
Cicilaón [the-the-lah-on'], *m.* (Bot.) Bitter vetch. Orobus.
Ciclón [the-the-on'], *m.* (Prov.) An intermittent fever.
Cicindela [the-thin-day'-lah], *f.* (Zool.) 1. A carabid beetle, tiger-beetle; the name is sometimes carelessly used for a fire-fly. 2. (Obs.) Glow-worm.
Ciclada [thee'-clah-dah], *f.* Kind of undress formerly worn by ladies.
Ciclamor [the-clah-mor'], *m.* The sycamore, buttonwood, plane-tree.
Ciclán [the-clahn'], *m.* 1. Ridgel. 2. A cryptorchid (or cryptorchis), an individual whose testicles have not descended into the scrotum. Used of man and the lower animals. 3. (Met.) Single, having no companion.
Ciclatón [the-clah-tone'], *m.* A tunic once used by women.
Cíclico, ca [thee'-cle-co, cah], *a.* Cyclical, belonging to a cycle.
Ciclismo [the-clees'-mo], *m.* Bicycling.
Ciclista [the-clees'-tah], *m.* & *f.* Bicyclist.
Ciclo [thee'-clo], *m.* Cycle, a round of time.
Ciclodiatomía [the-clo-de-ah-to-mee'-ah], *f.* (Mil.) Calculation of the direction of a projectile.
Cicloidal [the-clo'-e-dal], *a.* Cycloidal.
Cicloide [the-clo'-e-day], *f.* (Math.) Cycloid.
Ciclómetro [the-clo'-may-tro], *m.* Cyclometer.
Ciclomotor [the-clo-mo-tor'], *m.* Motorbike.
Ciclón [the-clon'], *m.* 1. Cyclone. 2. Hurricane.
Ciclonal, Ciclónico, ca [the-clo-nahl', the-clo'-ne-co, cah], *a.* Cyclonic, cyclonical.
Cíclope [thee'-clo-pay], *m.* Cyclops.
Ciclópeo, ea [the-clo'-pay-o, ah], *a.* Cyclopean.
Ciclorama [the-clo-rah'-mah], *m.* Cyclorama, pictorial representation.
Ciclotrón [the-clo-trone'], *m.* Cyclotron.
Cicuta [the-coo'-tah], *f.* 1. (Bot.) Hemlock. Conium. *Cicuta acuática,* (Bot.) Water-hemlock. Cicuta virosa. *Cicuta de España,* Spanish hemlock. 2. Pipe or flute made of reed, a flageolet.
Cid [theed], *m.* 1. Word taken from the Arabic signifying chief, commander. 2. Surname of the Spanish hero Rodrigo Díaz de Vivar.
Cidra [thee'-drah], *f.* 1. Citron. 2. (Obs.) Conserve of citrons.
Cidracayote [the-drah-cah-yo'-tay], *f.* (Bot.) The American gourd. Cucurbita citrullus, folio colocynthidis.
Cidrada [the-drah'-dah], *f.* A conserve made of citrons.
Cidral [the-drahl'], *m.* Plantation of citron-trees.
Cidria [thee'-dre-ah], *f.* *V.* CEDRIA.
Cidro [thee'-dro], *m.* (Bot.) Citron-tree. Citrus.
Cidronela [the-dro-nay'-lah], *f.* (Bot.) Common balm. Melissa officinalis.
Ciegamente [the-ay-gah-men'-tay], *adv.* Blindly.
Ciego, ga [the-ay'-go, gah], *a.* 1. Blind. 2. (Met.) Swayed by violent passion. *Ciego de ira,* Blind with passion. 3. Choked or shut up: applied to a passage. *A ciegas,* 1. Blindly, in the dark. 2. Thoughtlessly, carelessly.
Ciego, *m.* 1. (Anat.) Cæcum or blind gut. 2. Large black-pudding. *V.* MORCÓN.
(*Yo ciego, yo ciegue,* from *Cegar. V.* ACERTAR.)
Cieguecico, ica; illo, illa; ito, ita; Cieguezuelo, ela [the-ay-gay-thee'-co, thee'-cah; eel'-lyo, eel'-lyah; ee'-to, tah; theo-ay'-lo, lah], *a.* & *m.* & *f. dim.* A little blind person.
Cielito [the-ay-lee'-to], *m.* Tune and dance of South America.
Cielo [the-ay'-lo], *m.* 1. The sky, firmament, heaven(s). 2. Heaven, the habitation of God and pure souls departed. 3. Heaven, the supreme power, the sovereign of heaven. 4. Climate; atmosphere. *Este es un cielo benigno,* This is a mild climate. *España goza de benigno cielo,* Spain enjoys a salubrious air. *Mudar cielo,* or *de cielo,* To change the air. 5. Roof, ceiling. 6. Glory, felicity: paradise. *El cielo del toldo de un bote.* (Naut.) The roof of a boat's awning. *Cielo raso,* Flat roof or ceiling. *El cielo de la cama,* Tester or cover of a bed. *El cielo de coche,* The roof of a coach. *El cielo de la boca,* The roof of the palate. *Bajado del cielo,* Prodigious, excellent, complete. *Cerrarse el cielo,* To cover over with clouds. *Desgajarse el cielo,* To rain copiously, to storm. *Dormir á cielo raso,* To sleep in the open air. *El cielo aborregado, antes de tres días bañado,* A mackerel sky betokens rain within three days. *Escupir al cielo,* Bad deeds turn against those who commit them. *Estar hecho un cielo,* To be splendid, to be most brilliant. *Tomar el cielo con las manos,* (Met.) To be transported with joy, grief, or passion. *Irse al cielo calzado y vestido,* To gain heaven without passing through purgatory, or to be worthy of such honour. *¡Vaya V. al cielo!* Decrying what another has said. = Get out! *Venirse el cielo abajo,* The sky falling, i. e. to rain heavily. *Ver el cielo abierto,* To find an unforeseen opportunity.
Cielo máximo [the-ay'-lo mahc'-se-mo], *m.* (Aer.) Ceiling.
Ciempiés, *m. V.* CIENTOPIÉS.
Cien [the-en'], *a.* One hundred: used before nouns instead of *ciento,* as, *Cien hombres,* A hundred men. *Cien mujeres,* A hundred women.
Ciénaga [the-ay'-nah-gah], *f.* Marsh moor, a miry place. *V.* CENEGAL.
Ciencabezas [the-en-cah-bay'-thas], *f.* (Bot.) Common eryngo. Eryngium campestre.
Ciencia [the-en'-the-ah], *f.* 1. Science. 2. Knowledge, certainty. *Á ciencia y paciencia,* By one's knowledge and permission. *Ciencias exactas,* The mathematics. *Apostar* or *hacer alguna cosa á ciencia cierta,* To bet, or to do any thing with certainty, knowingly.
Cienmilésimo, ma [the-en-me-lay'-se-mo, mah], *a.* The hundred thousandth.
Cienmilmillonésimo, ma [the-en-mil-mil-lyo-nay'-se-mo, mah], *a.* The hundred thousand millionth.
Cienmillonésimo, ma, *a.* The hundred millionth.
Cieno [the-ay'-no], *m.* Mud, mire, a marshy ground.
Cientemente [the-en-tay-men'-tay], *adv.* (Obs.) In a knowing, sure, and prudent manner.
Científicamente [the-en-tee'-fe-cah-men-tay], *adv.* Scientifically.
Científico, ca [the-en-tee'-fe-co, cah], *a.* Scientific.
Ciento [the-en'-to], *a.* One hundred. *V.* CIEN.
Ciento [the-en'-to], *m.* 1. A hundred. *Un ciento de huevos,* A hundred eggs. 2. A hundred-weight. *Por ciento,* Per cent. *Diez por ciento,* Ten per cent. *Un tanto por ciento,* A percentage.
Cientopiés [the-en-to-pe-ess'], *m.* Woodlouse, milleped, sow-bug. Oniscus asellus.
Cierna [the-err'-nah], *f.* The staminate blossom of vines, corn, and some other plants.
Cierne [the-err'-nay]. *En cierne,* In blossom. *Estar en cierne,* To be in its infancy.
(*Yo cierno, yo cierne,* from *Cerner. V.* ATENDER.)
Cierra España [the-err'-rah es-pah'-

nyah]. The war-whoop of the ancient Spaniards.
Cierre [the-err'-ray], *m.* 1. Closing, shutting, locking. 2. Lock, clasp. *Cierre automático*, Zipper.
Cierro [the-err'-ro], *m.* Inclosure. (*Yo cierro, yo cierre*, from *Cerrar.*
Ciertamente [the-er-tah-men'-tay], *adv* Certainly, forsooth, surely.
Cierto, ta [the-err'-to, tah], *a.* 1. Certain, doubtless, evident, constant. 2. Used in an indeterminate sense, as *Cierto lugar*, A certain place; but in this case it always precedes the substantive. *Ciertos son los toros*, The story is true; it is a matter of fact. *Me dan por cierto que*, I have been credibly informed that. *Por cierto*, Certainly, surely; in truth.—*adv. V.* Ciertamente.
Cierva [the-err'-vah], *f.* Hind, the female stag, or red deer.
Ciervo [the-err'-vo], *m.* Deer, hart, stag.
Ciervo volante [the-err'-vo vo-lahn'-tay], *m.* Stag-beetle. Lucanus cervus, *L.* or Lucanus dama.
Cierzo [the-err'-tho], *m.* A cold northerly wind. *Tener ventana al cierzo*, (Met.) To be haughty, lofty, elated with pride.
Cifac, Cifaque [the-fahc', the-fah'-kay], *m.* (Obs. Anat.) The peritoneum.
Cifra [thee'-frah], *f.* 1. Cipher, the symbol 0. 2. Cipher, a secret or occult manner of writing. 3. Cipher, monogram engraved on seals or stamped upon stationery, etc. 4. Contraction, abbreviation. 5. Any arithmetical mark. 6. Music written with numbers. *En cifra*, Briefly, shortly, in a compendious manner. (Arab.)
Cifrar [the-frar'], *va.* 1. To cipher or write in ciphers. 2. To abridge a discourse. 3. To inclose.
Cigarra [the-gar'-rah], *f.* Balm-cricket, cicada, harvest-fly. Cicada.
Cigarral [the-gar-rahl'], *m.* In Toledo, an orchard or fruit-garden.
Cigarrera [the-gar-ray'-rah], *f.* 1. Cigar-case. 2. Cigarette-maker.
Cigarrero, ra [the-gar-ray'-ro, rah], *m.* & *f.* Cigar-seller.
Cigarrería [the-gar-ray-ree'-ah], *f.* Cigar-shop.
Cigarrillo [the-gar-reel'-lyo], *m.* Cigarette.
Cigarrista [the-gar-rees'-tah], *m.* Person who smokes many cigars.
Cigarro [the-gar'-ro], *m.* Cigar. *Cigarro de papel*, Cigarette.
Cigarrón [the-gar-rone'], *m.* 1. (Aug.) A large cigar. 2. A large balm-cricket.
Cigatera [the-gah-tay'-rah], *f.* (Low) Prostitute.
Cigomático, ca [the-go-mah'-te-co, cah], *a.* Zygomatic, relating to the zygoma.
Cigoñal [the-go-nyahl'], *m.* V. Cigüeñal.
Cigoñino [the-go-nyee'-no], *m.* (Orn.) A young stork.
Cigoñuela [the-go-nyoo-ay'-lah], *f.* (Orn.) A small bird resembling a stork.
Cigoto [the-go'-to], *m.* (Biol.) Zygote.
Ciguatera [the-goo-ah-tay'-rah], *f.* (Amer.) Kind of jaundice, from eating fish diseased with an affection like jaundice.
Ciguato, ta [the-goo-ah'-to, tah], *a.* *V.* Aciguatado.
Cigüente [the-goo-en'-tay], *a.* Applied to a kind of white grape.
Cigüeña [the-goo-ay'-nyah], *f.* 1. (Orn.) White stork, a bird of passage; crane. Ardea ciconia. 2. Crank of a bell, to which a cord is fastened to ring it. 3. *Cigüeña de piedra de amolar*, The iron winch of a grindstone. 4. *Cigüeña de cordelería*, (Naut.) A laying-hook or winch.
Cigüeñal [the-goo-ay-nyahl'], *m.* (Mech.) Crankshaft.
Cigüeño [the-goo-ay'-nyo], *m.* 1. A male stork. 2. (Humorous) Tall, slender, and silly-looking person.
Cigüeñuela [the-goo-ay-nyoo-ay'-lah], *f.* *dim.* Small crank of a bell.
Cigüeñuelo de la Caña del Timón [the-goo-ay-nyoo-ay'-lo]. (Naut.) The goose-neck of the tiller.
Cigzac [theeg-thahk'], *m.* Zigzag, a line in the form of a Z.
Cija [thee'-hah], *f.* 1. (Prov.) Dungeon. 2. (Obs.) Granary.
Cilanco [the-lahn'-co], *m.* A deep pool in bends, or slack water, of rivers.
Cilantro [the-lahn'-tro], *m.* (Bot.) Coriander. Coriandrum sativum. *V.* Culantro.
Ciliado, da [the-le-ah'-do, dah], *a.* Ciliated, provided with cilia.
Ciliar [the-le-ar'], *a.* Ciliary, belonging to the eyelids.
Cilicio [the-lee'-the-o], *m.* 1. Hair-cloth, very rough and prickly. 2. A cilicium or hair covering for the body, worn as penance. 3. Girdle of bristles or netted wire, with points, worn in mortification of the flesh. 4. (Mil. Obs.) Hair-cloth laid on a wall to preserve it.
Cilífero, ra [the-lee'-fay-ro, rah], *a.* *V.* Ciliado.
Ciliforme [the-le-for'-may], *a.* Like an eyelash in form; ciliform.
Cilíndrico, ca [the-leen'-dre-co, cah], *a.* Cylindric or cylindrical.
Cilindro [the-leen'-dro], *m.* Cylinder; a roller. *Cilindro de escarchar*, Silver-smiths' rolls. *Cilindro estriado*, Fluted cylinder.
Cilla [theel'-lyah], *f.* Granary for tithes and other grain.
Cillazgo [theel-lyath'-go], *m.* Store-house fees paid by persons concerned in tithes kept in a granary.
Cillerero [theel-lyay-ray'-ro], *m.* In some religious houses, the cellarist or butler.
Cilleriza [theel-lyay-ree'-thah], *f.* A nun who directs the domestic affairs of the convent.
Cillerizo [theel-lyay-ree'-tho], *m.* Keeper of a granary.
Cillero [theel-lyay'-ro], *m.* 1. Keeper of a granary or store-house for tithes. 2. Granary. 3. Vault, cellar, store-room.
Cima [thee'-mah], *f.* 1. Summit of a mountain or hill. 2. Top of trees. 3. Heart and tender sprouts of cardoons. 4. (Obs.) End or extremity of a thing. 5. (Obs.) Acme. *Por cima*, At the uppermost part, at the very top. *Dar cima*, To conclude happily.
Cimacio [the-mah'-the-o], *m.* (Arch.) Cymatium, gola, ogee, ogive, moulding which is half convex and half concave. *Cimacio del pedestal*, Cornice of a pedestal.
Cimar [the-mar'], *va.* (Obs.) To clip the tops of dry things, as plants, hedges.
Cimarrón, na [the-mar-rone', nah], *a.* (Amer.) Wild, unruly: applied to men and beasts.—*m.* & *f.* A runaway slave, maroon.
Cimbalaria [thim-bah-lah'-re-ah], *f.* Ivy-wort, a plant which grows on old walls.
Cimbalillo [thim-bah-leel'-lyo], *m. dim.* A small bell.
Címbalo [theem'-bah-lo], *m.* 1. Cymbal. 2. A small bell.
Cimbanillo [thim-bah-neel'-lyo], *m.* *V.* Cimbalillo.
Cimbara [theem'-bah-rah], *f.* (Prov.) A large sickle, used to cut shrubs and plants.
Cimbel [thim-bel'], *m.* 1. Decoy-pigeon. 2. Rope with which decoy-pigeons are made fast.
Cimborio, Cimborrio [thim-bo'-re-o, thim-bor'-re-o], *m.* Cupola. *V.* Cúpula.
Cimbornales [thim-bor-nah'-les], *m. pl.* (Naut.) Scupper-holes. *V.* Imbornales.
Cimbra [theem'-brah], *f.* 1. A wooden frame for constructing an arch. 2. *Cimbra de una tabla*, (Naut.) The bending of a board.
Cimbrado [thim-brah'-do], *m.* Quick movement in a Spanish dance.—*Cimbrado, da, pp.* of Cimbrar.
Cimbrar, Cimbrear [thim-brar', thim-bray-ar'], *va.* To brandish a rod or wand. *Cimbrar a alguno*, To give one a drubbing.—*vr.* To bend, to vibrate.
Cimbreño, ña [thim-bray'-nyo, nyah], *a.* Pliant, flexible: applied to a rod or cane.
Cimbreo [thim-bray'-o], *m.* Crookedness, curvature, bending or moulding of a plank.
Cimbria [theem'-bre-ah], *f.* (Obs.) *V.* Cimbra.
Címbrico [theem'-bre-co], *a.* Cimbric, the language of the Cimbri.
Cimbronazo [thim-bro-nah'-tho], *m.* Stroke given with a foil. *V.* Cintarazo.
Cimentado [the-men-tah'-do], *m.* Refinement of gold.—*Cimentado, da, pp.* of Cimentar.
Cimentador [the-men-tah-dor'], *m.* (Obs.) He who lays the foundation of a thing.
Cimental [the-men-tahl'], *a.* (Obs.) *V.* Fundamental.
Cimentar [the-men-tar'], *va.* 1. To lay the foundation of a building, to found, to ground. 2. (Met.) To establish the fundamental principles of religion, morals, and science. 3. To refine metals.
Cimentera [the-men-tay'-rah], *f.* (Obs.) The art of laying the foundation of a building.
Cimenterio [the-men-tay'-re-o], *m.* (Obs.) Cemetery, church-yard. *V.* Cementerio.
Cimento [the-men'-to], *m.* Cement. *V.* Cemento.
Cimera [the-may'-rah], *f.* Crest of a helmet, or coat of arms.
Cimerio, ria [the-may-re-o, ah], *a.* Cimmerian; of a tribe which dwelt on the shores of the sea of Azov.
Cimero, ra [the-may'-ro, rah], *a.* Placed at the height of some elevated spot.
Cimiento [the-me-en'-to], *m.* 1. Foundation of a building. 2. (Met.) Basis, origin. *Cimiento real*, Royal cement, a composition for purifying gold, composed of vinegar, salt, and brick-dust. *Abrir los cimientos*, To make the trenches for laying foundations. (*Yo cimiento, yo cimienta*, from *Cimentar.* *V.* Acrecentar.)
Cimillo [the-meel'-lyo], *m.* Decoy-pigeon.
Cimitarra [the-me-tar'-rah], *f.* Cimeter, falchion.
Cimófana [the-mo'-fah-nah], *f.* Cymofane, the oriental cat's-eye; a variety of chrysoberyl.
Cimorra [the-mor'-rah], *f.* (Vet.) Glanders, a disease in horses.
Cinabrio [the-nah'-bre-o], *m.* 1. Kind of gum, distilled from a tree in Africa. 2. Cinnabar. 3. Vermilion or artificial cinnabar.

Cinamómino [the-nah-mo′-me-no], *m.* (Med.) An aromatic ointment, the chief ingredient of which is taken from the bead-tree.

Cinamomo [the-nah-mo′-mo], *m.* (Bot.) The bead-tree. Melia azedarach.

Cinc [think], *m.* (Acad.) Zinc, a metallic element.

Cinca [theen′-cah], *f.* Any infraction of the rules of the game of nine-pins (ten-pins).

Cincel [thin-thel′], *m.* Chisel.

Cincelador [thin-thay-lah-dor′], *m.* Engraver, sculptor, stone-cutter.

Cincelar [thin-thay-lar′], *va.* To chisel. to engrave, to emboss.

Cincelito [thin-thay-lee′-to], *m. dim.* Small chisel.

Cinco [theen′-co], *m.* & *a.* Five. *Decir cuántas son cinco,* To threaten with reproof or punishment. *Él te dirá cuántas son cinco,* (Met.) He will tell you how many black beans make five; that is, he will oblige you to do it in spite of you. *No sabe cuántas son cinco,* (Coll.) He is a fool.

Cincoañal [thin-co-ah-nyahl′], *a.* Five years old: applied to beasts.

Cincoenrama [theen-co-en-rah′-mah], *f.* (Bot.) Common cinquefoil. Potentilla reptans.

Cincografía [thin-co-grah-fee′-ah], *f.* Zincography, a process of etching printing-plates upon zinc.

Cincomesino, na [thin-co-may-see′-no, nah], *a.* Five months old.

Cincuenta [thin-coo-en′-tah], *m.* & *a.* Fifty.

Cincuentavo [thin-coo-en-tah′-vo], *a.* The one-fiftieth part.

Cincuentén [thin-coo-en-ten′], *m.* A piece of wood, fifty palms in length (50 × 3 × 2).

Cincuenteno, na [thin-coo-en-tay′-no, nah], *a.* Fiftieth.

Cincuentón, na [thin-coo-en-tone′, nah], *a.* Fifty years old.

Cincha [theen′-chah], *f.* Girth, cingle, cinch. *Ir rompiendo cinchas,* To drive on full speed.

Cinchadura [thin-chah-doo′-rah], *f.* The act of girting.

Cinchar [thin-char′], *va.* To girt, to bind with a girth.

Cinchera [thin-chay′-rah], *f.* 1. Girth-place, the spot where the girth is put on a mule or horse. 2. Vein which horses or mules have in the place where they are girted. 3. Disorder incident to horses and mules, which affects the place where they are girted.

Cincho [theen′-cho], *m.* 1. Belt or girdle used by labourers to keep their bodies warm. 2. The tire of a wheel. 3. Vessel of bass-weed, in which cheese is moulded and pressed. 4. Disorder in the hoofs of horses. *V.* CEÑO.

Cinchón [thin-chone′], *m. aug.* A broad girdle.

Cinchuela [thin-choo-ay′-lah], *f.* 1. (Dim.) A small girth. 2. A narrow ribbon.

Cine [thee′-nay], *m.* Motion pictures, movies.

Cinema [the-nay′-mah], *m.* Cinema, moving pictures, movies.

Cinemateca [the-nay-mah-tay′-cah], *f.* Film library.

Cinemática [the-nay-mah′-te-cah], *f.* Kinematics, the study of motion as limited only by space.

Cinematográfico, ca [the-nay-mah-to-grah′-fe-co, cah], *a.* Cinematographic.

Cinematógrafo [the-nay-mah-to′-grah–fo], *m.* Motion pictures, movies, cinema.

Cineración [the-nay-rah-the-on′]. *V.* INCINERACIÓN.

Cinerario, ia [the-nay-rah′-re-o, ah], *a.* 1. *V.* CINÉREO. Ashy. 2. Cinerary.

Cinescopio [the-nes-co′-pe-o], *m.* Kinescope.

Cinético, ca [the-nay′-te-co, cah], *a.* Kinetic, pertaining to motion. *Energía cinética,* Kinetic energy.

Cíngaro, ra [theen′-gah-ro, rah], *m.* & *f.* Gipsy. *V.* GITANO.

Cíngulo [theen′-goo-lo], *m.* 1. Girdle or band with which a priest's alb is tied up. 2. Cordon, band, a wreath. 3. (Obs.) A military badge. 4. Ring or list at the top and bottom of a column.

Cínico, ca [thee′-ne-co, cah], *a.* Cynic, cynical; satirical.

Cínico [thee′-ne-co], *m.* Cynic, a philosopher of the sect of Diogenes.

Cínife [thee′-ne-fay], *m.* The long-shanked buzzing gnat.

Cinismo [the-nees′-mo], *m.* 1. Cynicism, the philosophy of the Cynics. 2. Shamelessness in defending or practising blamable actions or doctrines.

Cinnámico, ca [thin-nah′-me-co, cah], *a.* Cinnamic; derived from cinnamon.

Cinocéfalo [the-no-thay′-fah-lo], *m.* 1. Kind of monkey or baboon. 2. The name of the inhabitants of a fabulous country, who had dogs' heads.

Cinoglosa [the-no-glo′-sah], *f.* (Bot.) Hound's-tongue.

Cinosura [the-no-soo′-rah], *f.* 1. Cynosure, the constellation of the Lesser Bear, which contains the polar star. 2. An object strongly challenging attention.

Cinqueno, na [thin-kay′-no, nah], *a.* (Obs.) *V.* QUINTO.

Cinqueño, Chinquillo [thin-kay′-nyo, thin-keel′-lyo], *m.* Game at cards played among five persons.

Cinta [theen′-tah], *f.* 1. Ribbon, tape. *Cinta de seda,* Silk ribbon. *Cinta de hilo* or *algodón,* Thread or cotton tape. *Cinta de hiladillo,* Ferret ribbon. 2. A strong net used in the tunny-fishery. 3. The lowest part of the pastern of a horse. 4. *Cinta para cinchas,* Girth-web. 5. *Cintas de navío,* (Naut.) Wales. *Cintas galimas,*(Naut.) Bowwales or harpings. 6. (Obs.) Girdle. *V.* CINTO. 7. First course of floor-tiles. *Andar* or *estar con las manos en la cinta,* To be idle. *En cinta,* Under subjection; liable to restraint. *Espada en cinta,* With the sword at one's side. *Estar en cinta,* To be pregnant.

Cintadero [thin-tah-day′-ro], *m.* Part of a cross-bow to which the string is fastened.

Cinta de teletipo [theen′-tah day tay-lay-tee′-po], *f.* (Com.) Ticker tape.

Cintagorda [thin-tah-gor′-dah], *f.* Coarse hempen net for the tunny-fishery.

Cintajos, Cintarajos [thin-tah′-hos, thin-tah-rah′-hos], *m. pl.* 1. Knot or bunch of tumbled ribbons. 2. Tawdry ornaments in female dress.

Cintar [thin-tar′], *va.* (Prov.) To adorn with ribbons.

Cintarazo [thin-tah-rah′-tho], *m.* 1. Stroke or blow with the flat part of a broadsword. 2. Chastisement of a horse with the stirrup-leather.

Cinta transportadora [theen′-tah trans-por-tah-dor′-rah], *f.* (Mech.) Conveyor belt.

Cinteado, da [thin-tay-ah′-do, dah], *a.* Adorned with ribbons.

Cintero [thin-tay′-ro], *m.* 1. One who weaves or sells ribbons. 2. (Obs.) Harness-maker. 3. (Obs.) Belt, girdle. 4. (Prov.) Truss. 5. (Obs.) Rope with a running knot thrown on a bull's head.

Cintilla [thin-teel′-lyah], *f. dim.* 1. A small ribbon. 2. Narrow tape.

Cintillo [thin-teel′-lyo], *m.* 1. Hat-band. 2. Ring set with precious stones.

Cinto [theen′-to], *m.* Belt, girdle. *V.* CINTURA and CÍNGULO.

Cintrel [thin-trel′], *m.* (Arch.) Rule or line placed in the centre of a dome to adjust the ranges of brick or stone.

Cintura [thin-too′-rah], *f.* 1. The waist. 2. (Obs.) Small girdle for the waist. *Meter en cintura,* (Met.) To keep one in a state of subjection. 3. Narrow part of a chimney. *V.* CANAL.

Cinturero [thin-too-ray′-ro], *m.* (Prov.) Girdler.

Cinturica, illa, ita [thin-too-ree′-cah, eel′-lyah, ee′-tah], *f. dim.* 1. A small girdle. 2. Small or delicate waist.

Cinturón [thin-too-rone′], *m.* 1. Belt. 2. Sash. *Cinturón salvavidas,* Life-belt. *Cinturón de seguridad,* Safety belt. *Cinturón Van Allen de radiación,* Van Allen radiation belt.

Cipayo [the-pah′-yo], *m.* Sepoy, a native of India, serving in the British troops.

Cipero [the-pay′-ro], *m.* (Bot.) Cyperus or sedge. Cyperus.

Cipo [thee′-po], *m.* Cippus, a short stone pillar used as a burial monument, as a boundary-mark or as a sign-post or mile-stone.

Ciprés [the-press′], *m.* (Bot.) Cypress-tree. Cupressus semper-virens. *Baya del ciprés,* The cypress nut or berry.

Cipresal [the-pray-sahl′], *m.* Grove or plantation of cypress-trees.

Cipresino, na [the-pray-see′-no, nah], *a.* Resembling or belonging to cypress.

Ciprino, na [the-pree′-no, nah], *a.* Relating to or made of cypress-wood.

Ciprio, ia [thee′-pre-o, ah], *a.* Cyprian; of the island of Cyprus.

Cipripidio [the-pre-pee′-de-o], *m.* (Bot.) Cypripedium, or ladies'-slipper; an orchidaceous plant.

Ciquiricata [the-ke-re-cah′-tah], *f.* (Coll.) Caress, act of endearment; flattery.

Circasiano, na [theer-cah-se-ah′-no, nah], *a.* Circassian.

Circense [theer-then′-say], *a.* Circensial or circensian, relating to the exhibitions in the amphitheatres of Rome.

Circo [theer′-co], *m.* 1. Circus, amphitheatre. 2. (Orn.) The moor-buzzard. Falco Æruginosus.

Circón [theer-cone′], *m.* (Acad.) Zircon, a zirconium silicate, of various colours, transparent to opaque.

Circonio [theer-co′-ne-o], *m.* Zirconium, an earthy metallic element, of no practical application, derived from zircon.

Circuir [theer-coo-eer′], *va.* To surround, to compass, to encircle.

Circuito [theer-coo-ee′-to], *m.* 1. Circuit, circle, extent. 2. Circumference. 3. (Elec.) Circuit. *Corto circuito,* Short circuit. 4. Radio hookup. *En circuito cerrado,* Closed-circuit.

Circulación [theer-coo-lah-the-on′], *f.* Circulation, currency.

Circulante [theer-coo-lahn′-tay], *pa.* & *a.* Circulatory, circling, circulating.

Circular [theer-coo-lar′], *a.* Circular, circulatory, circling. *Carta circular,* A circular letter.

Circular [theer-coo-lar′], *vn.* To circulate, to surround, to travel round, to go from hand to hand.

Circularmente [theer-coo-lar-men′-tay] *adv.* Circularly.

Círculo [theer'-coo-lo], *m.* 1. Circle. 2. Orb, circlet; compass. 3. A superstitious ring or circle. 4. District. 5. Figure of speech, wherein a sentence begins and ends with the same words. *Círculos del imperio*, Circles, provinces or districts of the German empire.
Circumambiente [theer-coom-am-be-en'-tay], *a.* Circumambient, surrounding.
Circumcirca [theer-coom-theer'-cah], *adv.* (Coll. Lat.) About, thereabout; almost.
Circumpolar [theer-coom-po-lar'], *a.* Circumpolar, near the pole.
Circuncidante [theer-coon-the-dahn'-tay], *m.* & *pa.* Circumciser.
Circuncidar [theer-coon-the-dar'], *va.* 1. To circumcise. 2. (Met. Coll.) To diminish, to curtail or modify.
Circuncisión [theer-coon-the-se-on'], *f.* 1. Circumcision. 2. A religious festival celebrated on the 1st of January, or New Year's day.
Circunciso, sa [theer-coon-thee'-so, sah], *pp. irr. of* CIRCUNCIDAR. Circumcised.
Circundar [theer-coon-dar'], *va.* To surround, to circle, to compass.
Circunferencia [theer-coon-fay-ren'-the-ah], *f.* Circumference.
Circunferencial [theer-coon-fay-ren-the-ahl'], *a.* Circumferential, circular, surrounding.
Circunferencialmente [theer-coon-fay-ren-the-al-men'-tay], *adv.* In a circular manner.
Circunflejo, ja [theer-coon-flay'-ho, hah], *a.* *Acento circunflejo*, Circumflex accent (ˆ), composed of the acute and grave.
Circunlocución [theer-coon-lo-coo-the-on'], *f.* Circumlocution, periphrasis, roundabout expression.
Circunloquio [theer-coon-lo'-ke-o], *m.* Circumlocution, circle.
Circunnavegación [theer-coon-nah-ve-gah-the-on'], *f.* Circumnavigation.
Circunnavegar [theer-coon-nah-ve-gar'], *va.* To circumnavigate, sail round the world.
Circunscribir [theer-coons-cre-beer'], *va.* To circumscribe, to inclose.
Circunscripción [theer-coons-crip-the-on'], *f.* Circumscription.
Circunscriptivo, va [theer-coons-crip-tee'-vo, vah], *a.* Circumscriptive, inclosing a superficies.
Circunspección [theer-coons-pec-the-on'], *f.* Circumspection, prudence, watchfulness, general attention.
Circunspectamente [theer-coons-pec-tah-men'-tay], *adv.* Circumspectly.
Circunspecto, ta [theer-coons-pec'-to, tah], *a.* Circumspect, cautious, considerate, judicious, grave.
Circunstancia [theer-coons-tahn'-the-ah], *f.* 1. Circumstance. *Refirió el caso con todas sus circunstancias*, He gave a full and minute account of the case. 2. Incident, event. 3. Condition, state of affairs. *En las circunstancias presentes*, In the actual state of things.
Circunstanciadamente [theer-coons-tan-the-ah-dah-men'-tay], *adv.* Circumstantially, minutely.
Circunstanciado, da [theer-coons-tan-the-ah'-do, dah], *a.* 1. According to circumstances. 2. Circumstantial, minute.—*pp.* of CIRCUNSTANCIAR.
Circunstanciar [theer-coons-tan-the-ar'], *va.* (Littl. us.) To circumstantiate.
Circunstante [theer-coons-tahn'-tay], *a.* Circumstant, surrounding.
Circunstantes [theer-coons-tahn'-tes], *m. pl.* By standers, persons present.
Circunvalación [theer-coon-vah-lah-the-on'], *f.* Circumvallation, the act of surrounding a place.
Circunvalar [theer-coon-vah-lar'], *va.* 1. To surround, to encircle. 2. (Mil.) To circumvallate, to surround with trenches.
Circunvecino, na [theer-coon-vay-thee'-no, nah], *a.* Neighbouring, adjacent, contiguous.
Circunvención [theer-coon-ven-the-on'], *f.* Circumvention, overreaching, deceit.
Circunvenir [theer-coon-vay-neer'], *va.* (Obs.) To circumvent, to overreach.
Circunvolución [theer-coon-vo-loo-the-on'], *f.* Circumvolution.
Circunyacente [theer-coon-yah-then'-tay], *a.* Circumjacent, lying near.
Cirial [the-re-ahl'], *m.* A candlestick set on a pole, used in the Catholic church.
Cirineo [the-re-nay'-o], *m.* (Coll.) Mate, assistant.
Cirio [thee'-re-o], *m.* A thick and long wax-candle. *Cirio pascual*, Paschal candle.
Cirro [theer'-ro], *m.* 1. (Med.) Schirrus. 2. Tuft of mane hanging over a horse's face.
Cirrosis [theer-ro'-sis], *f.* Cirrhosis, a morbid deposit of connective tissue in an organ, especially the liver, resulting in contraction and impaired function.
Cirroso, sa [theer-ro'-so, sah], *a.* 1. Scirrhous. 2. Fibrous. *Raíces cirrosas*, Fibrous roots.
Ciruela [the-roo-ay'-lah], *f.* Plum, prune. Prunum. *Ciruela pasa*, A dried plum; a prune. *Ciruela verdal*, A green gage. *Ciruela de fraile*, The long green plum.
Ciruelar [the-roo-ay-lar'], *m.* A large plantation of plum-trees.
Ciruelica, illa, ita [the-roo-ay-lee'-cah], *f. dim.* A small plum.
Ciruelico, illo, ito [the-roo-ay-lee'-co], *m. dim.* A dwarf plum-tree.
Ciruelo [the-roo-ay'-lo], *m.* (Bot.) Plum-tree. Prunus domestica. *L.*
Cirugía [the-roo-hee'-ah], *f.* Surgery. *Cirugía dental*, Dental surgery. *Cirugía plástica*, Plastic surgery, anaplasty.
Cirujano [the-roo-hah'-no], *m.* Surgeon, chirurgeon. *Primer cirujano de navío*, Surgeon of a ship. *Segundo cirujano de navío*, Surgeon's mate.
Cis. A Latin prefix meaning on this side of, toward Rome.
Cisalpino, na [this-al-pee'-no, nah], *a.* Cisalpine, on this side of the Alps: between the Alps and Rome.
Cisca [thees'-cah], *f.* (Prov.) Reed for roofing huts and cottages. *V.* CARRIZO.
Ciscar [this-car'], *va.* (Coll.) To besmear, to make dirty.—*vr.* To ease nature. *Ciscarse de miedo*, To dirty one's self from fear.
Cisco [thees'-co], *m.* Coal-dust, broken coal.
Cisión [the-se-on'], *f.* Incision. *V.* CISURA OR INCISIÓN.
Cisma [thees'-mah], *m.* 1. Schism. 2. Disturbance in a community.
Cismático, ca [this-mah'-te-co, cah], *a.* 1. Schismatic. 2. Applied to the author of disturbances in a community.
Cismontano, na [this-mon-tah'-no, nah], *a.* Living on this side of the mountains.
Cisne [thees'-nay], *m.* 1. (Orn.) Swan. Anas cygnus. 2. Cygnus, the Swan, a constellation in the northern hemisphere. 3. (Met.) A good poet or musician. 4. (Low) Prostitute.
Cispadano na [this-pa-dah'-no, nah], *a.* Situated between Rome and the river Po.
Cisquero [thees-kay'-ro], *m.* A small linen bag with coal-dust, used by painters and draftsmen.
Ciste [thees'-tay], *m.* (Obs.) Cyst, bladder. *V.* QUISTE.
Cistel, Cister [this-tel', this-terr'], *m.* Cistercian order of St. Bernard.
Cisterciense [this-ter-the-en'-say], *a.* Cistercian.
Cisterna [this-terr'-nah], *f.* 1. Cistern. 2. Reservoir, an inclosed fountain.
Cístico [thees'-te-co], *a.* (Surg.) Cystic.
Cistitis [this-tee'-tis], *f.* Cystitis, inflammation of the bladder.
Cisto [thees'-to], *m.* (Bot.) Cistus, rock-rose.
Cistotomía [this-to-to-mee'-ah], *f.* (Surg.) Cystotomy.
Cistótomo [this-to'-to-mo], *m.* Cystotome; now called lithotome.
Cisura [the-soo'-rah], *f.* Incisure, incision.
Ciszás [this-thahs'], *m.* Word imitative of the crack of a whip and the report of certain fire-arms.
Cita [thee'-tah], *f.* 1. Appointment, engagement, a meeting appointed; rendezvous. 2. Citation, quotation of a passage of a book.
Citable [the-tah'-blay], *a.* Worthy of being cited, quoted.
Citación [the-tah-the-on'], *f.* 1. Citation, quotation. 2. Summons, judicial notice.
Citador, ra [the-tah-dor', rah], *m.* & *f.* Citer.
Citano, na [the-tah'-no, nah], *m.* & *f.* (Coll.) *V.* ZUTANO.
Citar [the-tar'], *va.* 1. To make a business appointment. 2. To convoke, to convene, to cite. 3. To quote, to cite. 4. To cite, to summon before a judge; to give judicial notice. *Dijo que se da por citado*, He declared that he was duly summoned.
Cítara [thee'-ta-rah], *f.* 1. Cithara or cithern, a musical instrument; a guitar strung with wire, zither. 2. (Obs.) Body of troops covering the flanks of those advancing to the charge.
Citara [the-tah'-rah], *f.* Partition-wall of the thickness of a brick.
Citarista [the-ta-rees'-tah], *m.* & *f.* 1. A player of the cithern. 2. A maker or seller of citherns.
Citarístico, ca [the-ta-rees'-te-co, cah], *a.* (Poet. Littl. us.) Belonging to poetry, adapted to the cithara.
Citarizar [the-ta-re-thar'], *vn.* (Obs.) To play the cithara.
Citatorio, ria [the-ta-to'-re-o, ah], *a.* (Law) Citatory: applied to a summons.
Citerior [the-tay-re-or'], *a.* Hither, nearer, toward this part. *España citerior*, The higher or northeastern part of Spain.
Citiso [thee'-te-so], *m.* (Bot.) Shrub-trefoil, cytisus. Cytisus, *L.*
Citocredente [the-to-cray-den'-tay], *a.* (Littl. us.) Credulous.
Cítola [thee'-to-lah], *f.* 1. In corn-mills, clack or clapper, a piece of wood which strikes the hopper and promotes the running of the corn. 2. (Obs.) *V.* CÍTARA. *La cítola es por demás, cuando el molinero es sordo*, Implying that capacity and disposition are necessary in a thing, in order that the measures taken be not fruitless.
Citología [the-to-lo-hee'-ah], *f.* Cytology.
Citote [the-to'-tay], *m.* (Coll.) Summons, a judicial citation.
Citra [thee'-trah], *adv.* (Obs. Lat.) On this side.

Citramontano, na [the-trah-mon-tah'-no, nah], *a.* On this side the mountains.
Citrato [the-trah'-to], *m.* (Chem.) Citrate.
Cítrico [thee'-tre-co], *a.* (Chem.) Citric.
Citrino, na [the-tree'-no, nah], *a.* (Obs.) Lemon-coloured. *V.* CETRINO.
Ciudad [the-oo-dahd'], *f.* 1. City, town. The assemblage of streets and buildings. 2. Corporation, civic body,
Ciudadanía [the-oo-dah-da-nee'-ah], *f.* Citizenship.
Ciudadano, na [the-oo-da-dah'-no, nah], *a.* 1. City, relating to a city. 2. Civil, relating to any man, as member of a community. 3. Citizenlike.
Ciudadano, *m.* 1. Citizen, freeman. 2. Inhabitant of a city. 3. (Obs.) A degree of nobility inferior to that of *caballero*, and superior to the condition of a tradesman.
Ciudadela [the-oo-da-day'-lah], *f.* (Mil.) Citadel, a small fortress.
Civeta [the-vay'-tah], *f.* Civet-cat. *V. Gato de algalia.*
Civeto [the-vay'-to], *m.* Civet, the perfume.
Cívico, ca [thee'-ve-co, cah], *a.* Civic. *V.* DOMÉSTICO.
Civil [the-veel'], *a.* 1. Civil, relating to the community. 2. Civil, relating to a man, as a member of a community. 3. Civil, polite, courteous, gentlemanlike. 4. Civil, not military or ecclesiastical. 5. (Obs.) Of low rank or extraction. 6. In law, civil, not criminal.
Civilidad [the-ve-le-dahd'], *f.* 1. Civility, politeness, urbanity, good manners. 2. (Obs.) Misery, covetousness, vileness, vulgarity.
Civilista [the-ve-lees'-tah], *m.* 1. An attorney skilled in the civil law, especially the Roman law. 2. (Amer.) Partisan of civil government, opponent of militarism.
Civilización [the-ve-le-thah-the-on'], *f.* 1. Civilization. 2. Act of justice by which a criminal process is converted into a civil cause.
Civilizador, ra [the-ve-le-thah-dor', rah], *a.* Civilizing.
Civilizar [the-ve-le-thar'], *va.* To civilize.
Civilmente [the-veel-men'-tay], *adv.* 1. Civilly, courteously, politely. 2. According to the common law. 3. (Obs.) Poorly, miserably, meanly.
Civismo [the-vees'-mo], *m.* Patriotism, zeal for one's country.
Cizalla [the-thahl'-lyah], *f.* Fragments or filings of gold, silver, or other metal; clippings.—*pl. Cizallas*, Cutting-pliers, or strong shears for clipping metal or wire.
Cizallar [the-thahl-lyar'], *va.* To use cutting pliers, or shears, in cutting wire or metal.
Cizaña [the-thah'-nyah], *f.* (Acad.) 1. (Bot.) Darnel. 2. Discord. *V.* ZIZAÑA.
Clac [clahc'], *m.* 1. A clapping of the hands. 2. A hat of tall crown provided with springs for shutting close; opera-hat.
Claco [clah'-co], *m.* *V.* TLACO.
Clacote [clah-co'-tay], *m.* (Mex.) Pimple, pustule.
Claitonia [clah-e-to'-ne-ah], *f.* (Bot.) Claytonia.
Clamar [clah-mar'], *va.* 1. (Obs.) To call. *V.* LLAMAR. 2. To cry out in a mournful tone. 3. (Met.) To show a want of something: applied to inanimate substances, as *La tierra clama por agua*, The ground wants water.
Clámide [clah'-me-day], *f.* A short cape, the chlamys of the Greeks.
Clamor [clah-mor'], *m.* 1. Clamour, outcry, scream, shriek, cry. 2. Sound of passing-bells. 3. (Obs.) The public voice.
Clamorear [clah-mo-ray-ar'], *va.* To clamour, to implore assistance.—*vn.* To toll the passing-bell.
Clamoreo [clah-mo-ray'-o], *m.* Knell.
Clamorosamente [clah-mo-ro-sah-men'-tay], *adv.* Clamorously.
Clamoroso, sa [clah-mo-ro'-so, sah], *a.* Clamorous, loud, noisy. *V.* VOCINGLERO.
Clamoso, sa [clah-mo'-so, sah], *a.* (Obs.) That which calls out, or solicits.
Clan [clan], *m.* Clan.
Clandestinamente [clan-des-te-nah-men'-tay], *adv.* Clandestinely, secretly.
Clandestinidad [clan-des-te-ne-dahd'], *f.* Clandestinity, privacy, or secrecy.
Clandestino, na [clan-des-tee'-no, nah], *a.* Clandestine, secret, private.
Clanga [clahn'-gah], *f.* *V.* PLANGA.
Clangor [clan-gor'], *m.* (Poet.) The sound of a trumpet.
Claque [clah'-kay], *f.* (Th.) Claque, paid applauders.
Clara [clah'-rah], *f.* (Coll.) A short interval of fair weather on a rainy day. *Me aproveché de una clara para salir*, I availed myself of a fair moment to go abroad. *Clara de huevo*, White of an egg. *Claras*, Pieces of cloth ill-woven, through which the light can be seen. *A la clara* or *a las claras*, Clearly, evidently. *Decir cuatro claras*, To tell one's mind bluntly and plainly.
Clarabela [clah-ra-bay'-lah], *f.* Clarabella, an organ-stop of open wood pipes, soft and sweet.
Claraboya [clah-ra-bo'-yah], *f.* Skylight, bull's-eye, window; dormer-window.
Claramente [clah-ra-men'-tay], *adv.* Clearly, openly, manifestly, conspicuously, obviously, fairly.
Clarear [clah-ray-ar'], *vn.* To dawn, to grow light.—*vr.* 1. To be transparent, translucent. 2. (Met.) To be cleared up by conjectures or surmises. *Clarearse de hambre*, To be very hungry.
Clarecer [clah-ray-therr'], *vn.* To dawn, to grow light.
Clarete [clah-ray'-tay], *m.* Claret.—*a. Vino clarete*, Claret wine.
Claridad [clah-re-dahd'], *f.* 1. Clarity, brightness, splendour, light. 2. Clearness, distinctness, freedom from obscurity and confusion. 3. That which is said resolutely, to upbraid. *Yo le dije dos claridades*, I told him my mind very plainly. 4. Glory of the blessed. 5. (Met.) Celebrity, fame. *Salir a puerto de claridad*, (Met.) To get well over an arduous undertaking.
Clarificación [clah-re-fe-cah-the-on'], *f.* Clarification, refining.
Clarificar [clah-re-fe-car'], *va.* 1. To brighten, to illuminate. 2. To clarify, to purify, to refine.
Clarificativo, va [clah-re-fe-cah-tee'-vo, vah], *a.* Purificative or purificatory.
Clarimentos [clah-re-men'-tose], *m. pl.* The lights in a picture.
Clarín [clah-reen'], *m.* 1. Trumpet. 2. In organs, a trumpet or clarion stop.—*V.* CLARÓN. 3. Trumpeter. 4. *Clarín*, or *olan clarín*, Fine cambric.
Clarinada [clah-re-nah'-dah], *f.* 1. Trumpet-call. 2. (Met. and coll.) An extravagant answer.
Clarinado, da [clah-re-nah'-do, dah], *a.* (Her.) Applied to animals with bells in their harness.
Clarinero [clah-re-nay'-ro], *m.* Trumpeter.
Clarinete [clah-re-nay'-tay], *m.* 1. Clarinet. 2. Player on the clarinet, clarinettist.
Clarinetista [clah-re-nay-tees'-tah], *m.* Clarinettist, player upon the clarinet.
Clarión [clah-re-on'], *m.* Crayon.
Clarisa [clah-ree'-sah], *f.* Clare, a nun of the order of St. Clara.
Clarísimo, ma [clah-ree'-se-mo, mah], *a.* Super. of *Claro.* Most illustrious.
Claro, ra [clah'-ro, rah], *a.* 1. Clear, bright, transparent, lightsome. 2. Clear, transparent, pellucid, crystalline, fine, limpid. 3. Clear, thin, rare, not dense. 4. Clear, thin, not close. 5. Clear, free from clouds, serene, fair. 6. Light, not deeply tinged. *Azul claro*, A light blue. 7. Clear, perspicuous, intelligible, not obscure. 8. Clear, obvious, explicit, evident, manifest, indisputable, apparent. *Es una verdad clara*, It is an undeniable truth. 9. Open, frank, ingenuous. 10. Celebrated, illustrious. 11. (Met.) Sagacious, quick of thought.
Claro [clah'-ro], *m.* 1. A kind of skylight. 2. Break in a discourse or writing; spacing in printing. 3. Rays of light falling on a painting. *Claro oscuro*, Chiaroscuro or claro-obscuro, light and shade in painting. 4. Opening or space between the columns of a building or other things. 5. (Naut.) A clear spot in the sky. *Poner* or *sacar en claro*, (Met.) To place a point in its true light, to explain, to expound, or interpret. *Vamos claros*, (Met.) Let us be clear and correct, let us speak frankly or without reserve. *Pasar la noche de claro en claro*, To have not a wink of sleep all night. *De claro en claro*, Evidently, manifestly. *Por lo claro*, Clearly, manifestly, conspicuously.
Claro, *adv.* *V.* CLARAMENTE.
Claro! [clah'-ro], *interj.* Of course! naturally. *¡Claro que sí!* Yes, definitely, of course.
Clarol [clah-rol'], *m.* Inlaid work: applied chiefly to furniture.
Clarón [clah-rone'], *m.* Clarion, a register of the organ.
Claroscuro [clah-ros-coo'-ro], *m.* Monochrome, a painting in one colour.
Clarucho, cha [clah-roo'-cho, chah], *a.* Too watery, too liquid.
Clase [clah'-say], *f.* 1. Class or rank of the people, order of persons. 2. Division of school-boys. 3. Classis, kind, kin, generical class, a set of beings or things. 4. Class, species, family. 5. (Com.) Sort, description, quality. *Clases de navío*, (Naut.) Rates of ships. *Navío de primera clase*, A first-rate ship.
Clase acomodada [clah'-say ah-co-mo-dah'-dah], *f.* Well-to-do class, people of wealth.
Clase media [clah'-say may'-de-ah], *f.* Middle class.
Clásicamente [clah-se-cah-men'-tay], *adv.* Classically.
Clasicismo [clah-se-thees'-mo], *m.* Classic style; classicism.
Clásico, ca [clah'-se-co, cah], *a.* 1. Classical, classic. 2. Principal, remarkable, of the first order or rank. *Error clásico*, A gross error. *Autores clásicos*, Classics.
Clasificación [clah-se-fe-cah-the-on'], *f.* Classification.
Clasificar [clah-se-fe-car'], *va.* To classify, to arrange, to class.
Claudicación [clah-oo-de-cah-the-on'], *f.* Claudication, halting or limping.

Claudicante [clah-oo-de-cahn'-tay], *a.* & *pa.* Claudicant, claudicating, halting, limping.

Claudicar [clah-oo-de-car'], *vn.* 1. To claudicate, to halt or limp. 2. (Met.) To proceed in a bungling manner, without rule or order.

Clauquillador [clah-oo-keel-lyah-dor'], *m.* (Obs. Prov.) Custom-house sealer. (Aragón.)

Clauquillar [clah-oo-keel-lyar'], *va.* (Obs. Prov.) To put the custom-house seal on bales of goods. (Ar.)

Claustra [clah'-oos-trah], *f.* (Obs.) *V.* CLAUSTRO.

Claustral [clah-oos-trahl'], *a.* 1. Claustral. 2. Claustral: applied to monks of the orders of St. Benedict and St. Francis.

Claustrero [clah-oos-tray'-ro], *a.* (Obs.) Applied to members of a cloister.

Claustrico, illo, ito [clah-oos-tree'-co, eel'-lyo, ee'-to], *m. dim.* Small cloister.

Claustro [clah'-oos-tro], *m.* 1. Cloister, piazza, or gallery around the court of a convent. 2. Assembly or meeting of the principal members of a university. 3. Womb. 4. (Obs.) Room, chamber.

Cláusula [clah'-oo-soo-lah], *f.* 1. Period, clause of a discourse. 2. Clause, condition, an article or particular stipulation, proviso.

Clausular [clah-oo-soo-lar'], *va.* To close a period; to terminate a speech.

Clausulilla [clah-oo-soo-leel'-lyah], *f. dim.* A little clause.

Clausura [clah-oo-soo'-rah], *f.* 1. Cloister, the inner recess of a convent. 2. Clausure, confinement, retirement. *Guardar clausura* or *vivir en clausura*, To lead a monastic or retired life.

Clava [clah'-vah], *f.* 1. Club. 2. (Naut.) Scupper.

Clavado [clah-vah'-do], *m.* (Mex.) Fancy dive. *Echarse un clavado*, To dive.

Clavado, da [clah-vah'-do, dah], *a.* 1. Exact, precise. *El reloj está clavado a las cinco*, It is just five by the clock. *Venir clavada una cosa a otra*, To fit exactly. 2. Nailed, armed or furnished with nails. 3. Relating to a club, especially to that of Hercules. —*pp.* of CLAVAR.

Clavador [clah-vah-dor'], *m.* Nail-driver.

Clavadura [clah-vah-doo'-rah], *f.* Nailing, driving a nail to the quick in horse-shoeing.

Clavar [clah-var'], *va.* 1. To nail; to fasten with nails; to fasten in, to force in. 2. To stick, to prick, to gore; to introduce a pointed thing into another. *Se clavó un alfiler*, He pricked himself with a pin. *Me clavé una espina*, I pricked myself with a thorn. *Clavar a un caballo*, To prick a horse in shoeing. *Clavarle a uno el corazón alguna cosa*, To be extremely affected by something. *Clavar la artillería*, To spike, to nail up guns. *Clavar los ojos* or *la vista*, To stare, to look with fixed eyes. 3. To cheat, to deceive. 4. To set in gold or silver. 5. (Mil.) To ground. *Clavar las armas*, To ground the arms.

Clavaria [clah-vah'-re-ah], *f.* *V.* LLAVERA.

Clavario [clah-vah'-re-o], *m.* (Obs.) 1. Treasurer, cashier. 2. A dignitary of the military order of Montesa.

Clavazón [clah-va-thone'], *f.* 1. Set of nails. 2. (Naut.) Assortment of the different nails used in the construction of ships.

Clave [clah'-vay], *f.* 1. Code. *El telegrama está en clave*, The telegram is in code. 2. (Mus.) Key, clef. 3. (Arch.) Keystone of an arch. 4. Harpsichord.

Clavel [clah-vel'], *m.* (Bot.) Pink. Dianthus caryophillus. *Clavel de muerto*, (Bot.) Common marigold.

Clavelina [clah-vay-lee'-nah], *f.* (Bot.) 1. The plant which bears the common pink. 2. Mignonette.

Clavelón [clah-vay-lone'], *m.* (Bot. Aug.) 1. A large pink. 2. A kind of pink. Tagetes erecta. *Clavelón de Indias*, (Bot.) Indian pink.

Clavellina [clah-vel-lyee'-nah], *f.* 1. (Bot.) The pink, carnation. Dianthus. 2. (Obs.) Stopple of tow, put into the vent-hole of a great gun.

Claveque [clah-vay'-kay], *m.* Rock crystal.

Clavera [clah-vay'-rah], *f.* 1. Mould for nail-heads. 2. Hole through which a nail is fastened. 3. Nail-hole in a horse-shoe. 4. (Prov. Ext.) Boundary where landmarks are set up.

Clavería [clah-vay-ree'-ah], *f.* Office and dignity of the key-bearer in the military orders of Calatrava and Alcántara.

Clavero, ra [clah-vay'-ro, rah], *m.* & *f.* 1. Keeper of the keys, treasurer, cashier. 2. (Bot.) Aromatic clove-tree. Caryophyllus aromaticus. 3. Key-bearer, the knight of the orders of Calatrava and Alcantara, who takes care of the castle, convent, and archives.

Clavete [clah-vay'-tay], *m. dim.* Tack, a small nail.

Clavetear [clah-vay-tay-ar'], *va.* 1. To nail, to garnish with brass or other nails. 2. To point or tag a lace.

Clavicordio [clah-ve-cor'-de-o], *m.* Harpsichord, manichord.

Clavícula [clah-vee'-coo-lah], *f.* (Anat.) Clavicle, the collar-bone.

Clavija [clah-vee'-hah], *f.* 1. Pin, peg, or tack of wood or iron, thrust into a hole for rolling or winding something around. 2. A peg for hanging any thing upon. 3. Peg of a stringed instrument. *Clavija maestra*, The fore axle-tree pintle. *Apretar a uno las clavijas*, (Met.) To push home an argument.

Clavijera [clah-ve-hay'-rah], *f.* (Prov.) Opening in mud walls to let in the water. (Aragón.)

Clavijero [clah-ve-hay'-ro], *m.* 1. Bridge of a harpsichord. 2. Rack or perch for clothing or hats.

Clavillo, ito [clah-veel'-lyo, ee'-to], *m. dim.* A small nail. *Clavillo de hebilla*, Rivet of a buckle. *Clavillos*, Cloves.

Claviórgano [clah-ve-or'-gah-no], *m.* An organized harpsichord, composed of strings and pipes, like an organ.

Clavo [clah'-vo], *m.* 1. Nail, an iron spike. *Clavo de herradura*, Hobnail. *Clavo trabadero*, Bolt with a key on the opposite side. *Clavo plateado*, Tinned nail, a nail dipped in lead or solder. 2. Corn, a hard and painful excrescence on the feet. 3. Spot in the eye. 4. Lint for wounds or sores; a tent. (Surg.) 5. *Clavo* or *clavo de especia*, Clove, a valuable spice. 6. (Naut.) Rudder of a ship. 7. (Met.) Severe grief or pain, which thrills the heart. 8. Tumour between the hair and the hoof of a horse. 9. (Prov.) Headache. *V.* JAQUECA. 10. *Clavos romanos*, (Amer.) Curtain knobs. *Clavo*, In the mines of Mexico, a bunch of rich ore. *Es de clavo pasado*, He is utterly abandoned. *Arrimar el clavo a uno*, To impose upon, to deceive. *Arrimar el clavo*, In horse-shoeing, to strike the quick and make the horse limp. *Clavar un clavo con la cabeza*, To be very stubborn. *Por falta de un clavo se pierde una herradura*, For want of a nail the shoe was lost. *Dar en el clavo*, (Met.) To hit the mark, to succeed in a doubtful matter. *Echar un clavo en la rueda de la fortuna*, (Met.) To fix one's fortune. *No importa un clavo*, It does not matter a pin. *Sacar un clavo con otro clavo* (Met.) To cure one excess by another. *Hacer clavo*, To set: applied to mortar.

Clavulina [clah-voo-lee'-nah], *f.* A microscopic shell.

Claxon [klak'-son], *s.* (Mex.) Auto horn.

Clematide [clay-mah'-te-day], *f.* (Bot.) Traveller's-joy, virgin's-bower, or the upright lady's-bower, clematis. Clematis vitalba.

Clemencia [clay-men'-the-ah], *f.* Clemency, mercy, forbearance.

Clemente [clay-men'-tay], *a.* Clement, merciful.

Clementemente [clay-men-tay-men'-tay], *adv.* Mercifully, clemently.

Clementina [clay-men-tee'-nah], *f.* The canons of Pope Clement V, contained in the collection called *Clementinas*, published by Pope John XXII.

Clementísimo, ma [clay-men-tee'-se-mo, mah], *a. sup.* of CLEMENTE.

Clepsidra [clep-see'-drah], *f.* Clepsydra, water-clock, an hour-glass.

Cleptomanía [clep-to-mah-nee'-ah], *f.* Kleptomania.

Cleptómano, na [clep-to'-mah-no, nah], *m.* & *f.* & *a.* Kleptomaniac.

Clerecía [clay-ray-thee'-ah], *f.* 1. Clergy. 2. The body of clergymen who attend with surplices at religious festivals.

Clerical [clay-re-cahl'], *a.* Clerical.

Clericalmente [clay-re-cal-men'-tay], *adv.* In a clerical manner.

Clericato [clay-re-cah'-to], *m.* State and dignity of a clergyman. *Clericato de cámara*, Some distinguished offices in the palace of the Pope.

Clericatura [clay-re-cah-too'-rah], *f.* State of a clergyman.

Clérigo [clay'-re-go], *m.* A clergyman, a cleric, a clerk. *Clérigo de corona*, Roman Catholic clergyman who has received the tonsure. *Clérigo de misa*, A presbyter. *Clérigo de misa y olla*, An unlearned priest.

Clériguillo [clay-re-geel'-lyo], *m. dim.* A little petty clergyman: a term of contempt.

Clerizonte [clay-re-thon'-tay], *m.* 1. One who wears a clerical dress without being ordained. 2. Ill-dressed priest. 3. A clergyman without manners.

Clero [clay'-ro], *m.* Clergy. *Clero secular*, Secular clergy, who do not make the three solemn vows of poverty, obedience, and chastity. *Clero regular*, Regular clergy, who profess a monastic life, and make the above vows.

Cleuasmo [clay-oo-ahs'-mo], *m.* (Rhet.) A figure of speech attributing the speaker's good actions to another, or another's bad actions to himself. Prosopopeia.

Cliente [cle-en'-tay], *com.* Client, a person under the protection and tutorage of another.

Clientela [cle-en-tay'-lah], *f.* 1. A body of clients or dependents; a following; clientele. 2. Protection or patronage. 3. Clientship, condition of a client.

Cliéntulo, la [cle-en'-too-lo, lah], *m.* & *f* (Obs.) *V.* CLIENTE.

Clima [clee'-mah], *m.* Climate, clime. *Clima artificial* or *acondicionamiento del aire*, Air conditioning. *Clima cálido*, Warm climate. *Clima templado*, Temperate climate.

Climatérico, ca [cle-mah-tay'-re-co, cah], *a.* Climacteric, climacterical. *Estar climatérico alguno,* (Coll.) To be ill-humoured.

Climatología [cle-mah-to-lo-hee'-ah], *f.* Climatology, that part of meteorology which treats of climate.

Climatológico, ca [cle-mah-to-lo'-he-co, cah], *a.* Climatological, relating to climate.

Climax [clee'-max], *m.* Climax, a rhetorical figure.

Climeno de España [cle-may'-no day es-pah'-nyah], *m.* (Bot.) Joint-podded pea or lathyrus. Lathyrus articulatus.

Clin [cleen], *f.* (Coll.) *V.* CRIN. The part of a horse's neck from which the mane grows. *Tenerse a las clines,* (Met.) To make every effort not to decline in rank or fortune.

Clínica [clee'-ne-cah], *f.* 1. Clinic, that part of medical instruction imparted by lectures in hospitals about the diseases of the patients who are there. 2. The wards of hospitals where patients are, upon whose diseases the clinical professor makes his lectures.

Clínico, ca [clee'-ne-co, cah], *a.* Clinic, clinical, relating to the bedside.

Clínico, *m.* 1. Clinic, in the primitive church, was he who would not be baptized till he was going to die. 2. The medical student who attends clinical lectures in hospitals.

Clinométrico, ca [cle-no-may'-tre-co, cah], *a.* Clinometric, pertaining to the clinometer.

Clinómetro [cle-no'-may-tro], *m.* Clinometer, generic name of the instruments used for measuring the inclination of any line or plane to the horizontal.

Clinopodio [cle-no-po'-de-o], *m.* (Bot.) Common wild basil, field-basil. Clinopodium vulgare.

Clisado [cle-sah'-do], *m.* Stereotyping, the act and effect.

Clisar [cle-sar'], *va.* To stereotype, to make a cliché or stereotype plate.

Clisé [cle-say'], *m.* 1. The matrix for a stereotype plate. 2. A stereotype plate.

Cliso [clee'-so], *m.* 1. (Med.) Medicament obtained by the vapours of nitre burned with other substances. 2. (Chem.) Product of the distillation of antimony, nitre, and sulphur previously mixed.

Clistel, Clister [clis-tel', clis-tayr'], *m.* Clyster, an injection into the rectum. *V.* AYUDA.

Clistelera [clis-tay-lay'-rah], *f.* (Obs.) A woman who administers clysters.

Clitoria [cle-to'-re-ah], *f.* A leguminous climbing plant of Brazil, the Antilles, and North America.

Clítoris [clee'-to-ris], *m.* Clitoris, a small erectile organ at the summit of the vulva.

Clivoso, sa [cle-vo'-so, sah], *a.* (Poet.) Declivous, gradually descending.

Clo Clo, *m.* Clucking of a hen when she is hatching or calling her chickens.

Cloaca [clo-ah'-cah], *f.* Sewer, a conduit for dirty water, etc.

Clocar [clo-car'], *va.* To cluck. *V.* CLOQUEAR.

Cloque [clo'-kay], *m.* 1. (Naut.) Grapnel, a grappling-iron. *V.* COCLE. 2. Harpoon.

Cloquear [clo-kay-ar'], *vn.* 1. To cluck, to chuck, to make a noise like a hen. —*va.* 2. To angle.

Cloqueo [clo-kay'-o], *m.* Cluck, chuck, the voice of a hen.

Cloquera [clo-kay'-rah], *f.* The state of hatching in fowls.

Cloquero [clo-kay'-ro], *m.* A person who manages the harpoon in the catching of tunny.

Cloral [clo-rahl'], *m.* Chloral.

Cloramfenicol [clo-ram-fay-ne-col'], *m.* (Med.) Chloramphenicol.

Cloremia [clo-ray'-me-ah], *f.* (Med.) Chloremia.

Clorhidrato [clor-e-drah'-to], *m.* Hydrochlorate, clorhydrate.

Clorhídrico [clor-ee'-dre-co], *m.* Clorhydric, hydrochloric.

Clórico [clo'-re-co], *a.* Chloric, pertaining to or obtained from chlorine.

Clorofila [clo-ro-fee'-lah], *f.* Chlorophyll, green coloring matter in plants.

Cloromicetina [clo-ro-me-thay-tee'-nah], *f.* (Med.) Chloromycetin.

Cloris [clo'-ris], *f.* (Orn.) Greenfinch.

Cloro [clo'-ro], *m.* Chlorine, a yellowish green pungent gas; an element allied to iodine and bromine.

Cloroformización [clo-ro-for-me-thah-the-on'], *f.* Chloroformization, anæsthesia by chloroform.

Cloroformizar [clo-ro-for-me-thar'], *va.* To anæsthetize by chloroform; to chloroform.

Cloroformo [clo-ro-for'-mo], *m.* Choloform.

Clorosis [clo-ro'-sis], *f.* (Med.) Chlorosis, green-sickness.

Clorótico, ca [clo-ro'-te-co, cah], *a.* Chlorotic, affected by chlorosis.

Cloruro [clo-roo'-ro], *m.* Chloride, a compound of chlorine.

Club [cloob], *m.* Club, an association of persons. (English.)

Clueca [cloo-ay'-cah], *a.* Clucking and hatching: applied to a hen.

Clueco, ca [cloo-ay'-co, cah], *a.* (Coll.) Decrepit, worn out with age.

Cnico [knee'-co], *m.* (Bot.) Blessed thistle. *V.* CARDO BENDITO.

Co [co], *prep.* equivalent to *con,* with, indicating union or company.

Coa [co'-ah], *f.* 1. (Obs.) *V.* COLA. 2. (Mex.) A kind of hoe.

Coacción [co-ac-the-on'], *f.* Coaction, compulsion.

Coacervar [co-ah-ther-var'], *va.* To coacervate, to heap together.

Coactivo, va [co-ac-tee'-vo, vah], *a.* Coactive, coercive; compulsive.

Coacusar [co-ah-coo-sar'], *va.* (For.) To accuse jointly with another or others.

Coadjutor [co-ad-hoo-tor'], *m.* 1. Coadjutor, assistant. 2. (Obs.) Coadjutor, a person elected or appointed to a prebend without enjoying the benefit thereof until the death of the incumbent. *Obispo coadjutor,* Assistant bishop.

Coadjutora [co-ad-hoo-to'-rah], *f.* Coadjutrix.

Coadjutoría [co-ad-hoo-to-ree'-ah], *f.* 1. Coadjuvancy, help, assistance. 2. Right of survivorship of a coadjutor. 3. Office or dignity of a coadjutor.

Coadministrador [co-ad-me-nis-trah-dor'], *m.* One who governs a diocese by virtue of a bull, or by appointment of a bishop.

Coadunación [co-ah-doo-nah-the-on'], *f.* Coadunition, the conjunction of different substances into one mass.

Coadunamiento [co-ah-doo-nah-me-en'-to], *m.* *V.* COADUNACIÓN.

Coadunar [co-ah-doo-nar'], *va.* To jumble things together.

Coadyudador [co-ad-yoo-dah-dor'], *m.* (Obs.) *V.* COADYUVADOR.

Coadyutor [co-ad-yoo-tor'], *m.* (Obs.) *V.* COADJUTOR.

Coadyutorio, ria [co-ad-yoo-to'-re-o, ah], *a.* That which assists.

Coadyuvador [co-ad-yoo-vah-dor'], *m.* Fellow-helper, assistant.

Coadyuvante [co-ad-yoo-vahn'-tay], *a.* & *pa.* Coadjutant, helper, assistant.

Coadyuvar [co-ad-yoo-var'], *va.* To help, to assist.

Coagulable [co-ah-goo-lah'-blay], *a.* Coagulable.

Coagulación [co-ah-goo-la-the-on'], *f.* Coagulation.

Coagulador, ra [co-ah-goo-lah-dor', rah], *a.* Causing coagulation; coagulatory, coagulative.

Coagulante [co-ah-goo-lahn'-tay], *pa.* Coagulant, that which coagulates.

Coagular [co-ah-goo-lar'], *va.* To coagulate, to curd.—*vr.* To coagulate, to condense, to become concrete, to clod, to curdle.

Coagulativo, va [co-ah-goo-lah-tee'-vo, vah], *a.* Coagulative.

Coágulo [co-ah'-goo-lo], *m.* 1. Coagulum, coagulated blood. 2. Coagulation, the body formed by coagulation. 3. Coagulator, that which causes coagulation.

Coalabar [co-ah-lah-bar'], *va.* To collaud, to join in praising.

Coalescencia [co-ah-les-then'-the-ah], *f.* Coalescence, union of parts.

Coalición [co-ah-le-the-on'], *f.* Coalition, confederacy.

Coalla [co-ahl'-lyah], *f.* (Orn.) Woodcock. *V.* CHOCHA and CODORNIZ.

Coamante [co-ah-mahn'-tay], *a.* (Obs.) A partner or companion in loving.

Coapóstol [co-ah-pos'-tol], *m.* Co-apostle, a fellow-labourer in the gospel.

Coaptación [co-ap-tah-the-on'], *f.* (Obs.) Coaptation, the adjustment of parts to each other.

Coaptar [co-ap-tar'], *va.* (Obs.) To fit, to adjust.

Coarmador [co-ar-mah-dor'], *m.* Part-owner of a vessel.

Coarrendador [co-ar-ren-dah-dor'], *m.* A joint-partner in renting any thing.

Coartación [co-ar-tah-the-on'], *f.* (Law) Obligation to be ordained within a certain time to enjoy a benefice.

Coartada [co-ar-tah'-dah], *f.* Alibi. *Probar la coartada,* To prove an alibi.

Coartado, da [co-ar-tah'-do, dah], *a.* Applied to a slave who has bargained with his master for a sum to obtain freedom and paid in part, in which case the master cannot sell him to any one. (Lat. coarctatus.)

Coartar [co-ar-tar'], *va.* To coarct, to limit, to restrain.

Coatí [co-ah-tee'], *m.* (Zool.) Coati raccoon. Procyon lotor.

Coautor, ra [co-ah-oo-tor', rah], *m.* & *f.* Co-author, joint author.

Coaxial [co-ac-se-al'], *a.* (Mech.) Coaxial.

Coba [co'-bah], *f.* (coll.) Ingenious fib. 2. Flattery. *Dar coba.* To flatter, to soft-soap.

Cobaltífero, ra [co-bal-tee'-fay-ro, rah], *a.* Cobalt-bearing, cobaltiferous.

Cobalto [co-bahl'-to], *m.* Cobalt, a grayish semi-metal.

Cobanillo [co-bah-neel'-lyo], *m.* A small basket used by vintners during the vintage.

Cobarde [co-bar'-day], *a.* Coward, cowardly, timid, fearful, faint-hearted, dastardly, hare-hearted.

Cobardear [co-bar-day'-ar], *vn.* To be a coward, to be timid or fearful.

Cobardemente [co-bar-day-men'-tay], *adv.* Cowardly.

Cobardía [co-bar-dee'-ah], *f.* Cowardice, dastardy, dastardness, abject ness.

Cobayo [co-bah'-yo], *m.* The guinea pig, a familiar rodent. Cavia cobaya.

Cobea [co-bay'-ah], *f.* Coboea, a climbing-plant, having purple bell-shaped flowers; it is a garden plant native of Mexico. Coboea scandens.

Cobejera [co-bay-hay'-rah], *f.* (Obs.) *V.* Encubridora.

Cobertera [co-ber-tay'-rah], *f.* 1. Cover, pot-lid. 2. (Met.) Bawd, procuress. 3. (Prov. Tol.) White water-lily. *V.* Nenúfar. *Coberteras*, The two middle feathers of a hawk's tail.

Cobertero [co-ber-tay'-ro], *m.* (Obs.) Cover or top of any thing.

Cobertizo [co-ber-tee'-tho], *m.* 1. A small roof jutting out from the wall, to shelter people from the rain. 2. A covered passage. *Cobertizo para automóvil*, Carport.

Cobertor [co-ber-tor'], *m.* Coverlet, quilt, cloth, counterpane.

Cobertura [co-ber-too'-rah], *f.* 1. Cover, covering, coverlet. 2. Act of a grandee of Spain covering himself the first time he is presented to the king.

Cobija [co-bee'-hah], *f.* 1. A gutter-tile. 2. (Obs.) A small cloak for women. 3. Fire-screen.

Cobijador, ra [co-be-hah-dor', rah], *a.* Covering, protective.

Cobijadura [co-be-hah-doo'-rah], *f.* (Obs.) The act of covering.

Cobijamiento, Cobijo [co-be-hah-me-en'-to, co-bee'-ho], *m.* 1. The act of covering. 2. Lodging.

Cobijar [co-be-har'], *va.* 1. To cover, to overspread, to shelter. *Quien a buen árbol se arrima, buena sombra le cobija*, (prov.) He who gets under a good tree has a good shelter; that is, he who has powerful protection is in a fair way of doing well. 2. To protect, lodge.

Cobijera [co-be-hay'-rah], *f.* (Obs.) Chamber-maid.

Cobil [co-beel'], *m.* (Obs.) Corner, angle.

Cobra [co'-brah], *f.* 1. (Zool.) Cobra. 2. Rope for yoking oxen. 3. Retrieving (in hunting).

Cobradero, ra [co-brah-day'-ro, rah], *a.* That which may be recovered or collected.

Cobrado, da [co-brah'-do, dah], *a.* & *pp.* of Cobrar. 1. Recovered, received. 2. (Obs.) Complete, undaunted.

Cobrador [co-brah-dor'], *m.* 1. Receiver or collector of rents and other money. 2. Conductor, collector (r. w.). *Perro cobrador*, Kind of dog that fetches game out of the water.

Cobramiento [co-brah-me-en'-to], *m.* (Obs.) 1. Recovery, restoration. 2. Utility, profit, emolument.

Cobranza [co-brahn'-thah], *f.* 1. Recovery or collection of money. 2. Act of fetching game which is killed or wounded.

Cobrar [co-brar'], *va.* 1. To recover, to collect, or receive what is due. 2. To recover what is lost. 3. To fetch game that is wounded or killed. 4. To gain affection or esteem. *Cobrar ánimo* or *corazón*, To take courage. *Cobrar fuerzas*, To gather strength.—*vr.* 1. To recover, to return to one's self. 2. To gain celebrity or fame. *Cóbrese al entregar*, (Com.) C. O. D., collect on delivery. *Cobrar carnes*, To become fat.

Cobratorio, ia [co-bra-to'-re-o, ah], *a.* Belonging to collection of money; collectible.

Cobre [co'-bray], *m.* 1. Copper, a red-coloured metal. 2. Kitchen furniture. 3. (Obs.) String of onions or garlic. 4. *Cobre de cecial*, A pair of cods dried in the sun. *Batir el cobre*, (Met.) To pursue with spirit and vigour.

Cobreño, ña [co-bray'-nyo, nyah], *a.* (Obs.) Made of copper.

Cobrizo, za [co-bree'-tho, thah], *a.* Coppery, cupreous, copperish.

Cobro [co'-bro], *m.* Collection (of debts, etc.). V. Cobranza.

Coca [1] [co'-cah], *f.* 1. The dried leaves of a South American shrub (Erythroxylon coca) of the flax family, chewed by the natives as a stimulant. It yields cocaine, a local anæsthetic. 2. *Coca de Levante*, A moonseed yielding the India fish-berries, cocculus indicus (fr. Gr. κόκκος).

Coca,[2] *f.* (Prov. Gal.) *V.* Tarasca. A bugbear; figure of a serpent borne at the festival of Corpus Christi (fr. Coco).

Coca,[3] *f.* 1. (Naut.) A sort of small vessel. 2. Two puffs of hair of women put back from forehead and fastened behind the ears. 3. A rap with the knuckles on the head. 4. (Obs.) Head. (Lat. concha.)

Coca,[4] *f.* (Prov. Aragón and Val.) Cake, loaf. (Lat. coctus.)

Cocada [co-cah'-dah], *f.* Type of cocoanut candy.

Cocador, ra [co-cah-dor', rah], *a.* Wheedling, coaxing, flattering.

Cocaína [co-cah-ee'-nah], *f.* Cocaine, the alkaloid and active principle of the coca-plant, remarkable for its anæsthetic power locally.

Cocal [co-cahl'], *m.* 1. (Ven.) *V.* Cotal. 2. (Peru.) The cocoa-tree and the spot where it abounds.

Cocar [co-car'], *va.* 1. To make grimaces or wry faces. 2. (Met. Coll.) To coax, to gain by wheedling and flattering.

Cocán [co-cahn'], *m.* Name given in Peru to the breast of a bird.

Cocarar [co-ca-rar'], *va.* To gather the leaves of the plant called coca.

Cocción [coc-the-on'], *f.* Coction.

Coce [co'-thay], *f.* (Obs.) A kick. *V.* Coz.

Coceador, ra [co-thay-ah-dor', rah], *m.* & *f.* Kicker.

Coceadura [co-thay-ah-doo'-rah], *f.* **Coceamiento**, *m.* Kicking.

Cocear [co-thay-ar'], *va.* 1. To kick, to fling out. *V.* Acocear. 2. (Met.) To repugn, to resist. 3. (Obs.) To trample, to tread under foot.

Cocedero, ra [co-thay-day'-ro, rah], *a.* Easily boiled.

Cocedero, *m.* Place where bread is kneaded or baked, or where any thing is boiled.

Cocedor [co-thay-dor'], *m.* A person whose business it is to boil must and new wine.

Cócedra [co'-thay-drah], *f.* (Obs.) Feather-bed. *V.* Cólcedra.

Cocedura [co-thay-doo'-rah], *f.* The act of boiling.

Cocer [co-therr'], *va.* 1. To boil, to dress victuals. 2. To bake bricks, tiles, or earthenware. 3. To digest. —*vn.* 1. To boil; to ferment. 2. To seethe, ferment, without fire, as wine. —*vr.* To suffer intense and continued pain. *Quien cuece y amasa, de todo pasa*, All vocations have their drawbacks. *Vieja fué y no se coció*, Idle excuse for not having done something.

Cocido, da [co-thee'-do, dah], *a.* & *pp.* of Cocer. 1. Boiled, baked. *Carne bien cocida*, Meat well done. 2. (Met.) Skilled, experienced. *Estar cocido en alguna cosa*, To understand business well.

Cocido [co-thee'-do], *m.* *V.* Olla.

Cociente [co-the-en'-tay], *m.* (Math.) Quotient. *Cociente intelectual*, Intelligence quotient, I.Q.

Cocimiento [co-the-me-en'-to], *m.* 1. Coction, decoction. 2. (Med.) Decoction. 3. With dyers, a bath or mordant preparatory to dyeing. 4. (Obs.) A quick, lively sensation. *V.* Escozor.

Cocina [co-thee'-nah], *f.* 1. Kitchen. 2. Cookery, the art of cooking. 3. Range, stove. *Cocina económica*, Stove, cooking range. *Libro de cocina*, Cookbook. *Utensilios de cocina*, Cooking utensils.

Cocinar [co-the-nar'], *va.* 1. To cook or dress victuals. 2. (Met.) To meddle in other people's affairs.

Cocinera [co-the-nay'-rah], *f.* Cook-maid, kitchen-maid.

Cocinería [co-the-nay-ree'-ah], *f.* (Ch. & Peru) Cheap restaurant.

Cocinero [co-the-nay'-ro], *m.* Cook. *Haber sido cocinero antes que fraile*, A guarantee of success in one who directs a thing from having practised it himself.

Cocinilla [co-the-neel'-lyah], *f.* 1. Chafing dish, cooker. 2. Small kitchen.

Cocinita [co-the-nee'-tah], *f.* Small kitchen.

Coole [co'-clay], *m.* (Naut.) Grapnel, a grappling-iron.

Cóclea [co'-clay-ah], *f.* 1. An ancient machine for raising water. 2. An endless screw. 3. The inner cavity of the ear.

Coclear [co-clay-ar'], *va.* To harpoon.—*vn.* To cluck or hatch. *V.* Cloquear.

Coclearia [co-clay-ah'-re-ah], *f.* (Bot.) Common scurvy-grass. Cochlearia officinalis.

Coco [1] [co'-co], *m.* 1. (Bot.) Cocoa-tree; Indian palm-tree. Cocos nucifera. 2. Cocoa-nut. 3. Chocolate-cup made of the cocoa-nut. (Lat. cuci; Gr. κοῦκι.)

Coco,[2] *m.* 1. Worm or grub bred in seeds and fruit. 2. Coccus; scale insect. 3. Coccus, a bacterium of spherical form. (Lat. cœcum; Gr. κόκκος.)

Coco,[3] *m.* Bugbear for frightening children, phantasm. (Gr. κάκος, ugly.) *Ser un coco*, or *parecer un coco*, To be an ugly-looking person.

Coco,[4] *m.* (from Coca, 1st art.). Cocos, India berries from which rosaries are made.

Coco,[5] *m.* Gesture, grimace, a flattering gesture. (Gr. κῆπος.) *Hacer cocos*, (Met.) To flatter, wheedle, gain one's affections. (Coll.) To make signs of affection, to flirt, coquet.

Cocobolo [co-co-bo'-lo], *m.* (Bot.) A species of cocoa-tree, much used by cabinet-makers.

Cocodrilo [co-co-dree'-lo], *m.* Crocodile.

Cocoi [co-co-ee'], *m.* A crested heron, of the size of a stork.

Cocoliste [co-co-lees'-tay], *m.* In New Spain or Mexico, an epidemic fever.

Cócora [co'-co-rah], *com.* An impertinent and annoying person.

Cocoso, sa [co-co'-so, sah], *a.* Worm-eaten, gnawed by grubs.

Cocota [co-co'-tah], *f.* *V.* Cogotera.

Cocotal [co-co-tahl'], *m.* A clump of cocoa-nut-trees.

Cocote [co-co'-tay], *m.* (Prov.) Occiput. *V.* Cogote.

Cocotero [co-co-tay'-ro], *m.* (Bot.) Cocoa-tree. *V.* Coco.[1]

Cocotriz [co-co-treeth'], *f.* (Obs.) *V* Cocodrilo.

Coctel [cok-tell'], *m.* Cocktail.

Cocuyo [co-coo'-yo], or **Cucuyo**, *m.* The fire-fly or fire-beetle of the West Indies, about an inch and a half long. Pyrophorus noctilucus.

Cocha [co'-chah], *f.* In mines, a small reservoir of water.
Cochambre [co-chahm'-bray], *m.* A greasy, dirty, stinking thing.
Cochambrería [co-cham-bray-ree'-ah], *f.* (Coll.) Heap of filthy things.
Cochambroso, sa [co-cham-bro'-so, sah], *a.* (Coll.) Nasty, filthy, stinking.
Cocharro [co-char'-ro], *m.* A wooden dish, cup, or platter.
Cocharse [co-char'-say], *vr.* (Obs.) To hasten, to accelerate.
Cochastro [co-chahs'-tro], *m.* A little sucking wild boar.
Coche [co'-chay], *m.* 1. Coach, carriage. 2. (coll.) Automobile. *Coche dormitorio*, (r.w.) Sleeping car. *Coche comedor*, (r.w.) Dining car. *Coche de plaza* or *coche de alquiler*, Coach for hire, automobile for hire.
Cochear [co-chay-ar'], *vn.* To drive a coach.
Cochecillo [co-chay-thee'-lyo], *m.* Small carriage, child's carriage, baby buggy.
Cochera [co-chay'-rah], *f.* 1. Coach-house. 2. Coachman's wife. 3. *V.* PUERTA COCHERA. Carriage-door; porte-cochère.
Cocheril [co-chay-reel'], *a.* (Coll.) Relating to coachmen.
Cocherillo [co-chay-reel'-lyo], *m. dim.* A little coachman.
Cochero [co-chay'-ro], *m.* 1. Coachman. 2. (Obs.) Coach-maker. 3. Wagoner, a northern constellation.
Cochero, ra [co-chay'-ro, rah], *a.* (Prov.) Easily boiled.
Cocherón [co-chay-rone'], *m.* (Aug.) 1. Large coach-house. 2. Engine-house; round-house.
Cochevira [co-chay-vee'-rah], *f.* Lard.
Cochevís [co-chay-vees'], *m.* The crested shore-lark.
Cochifrito [co-che-free'-to], *m.* Fricassee of lamb, mutton, etc.
Cochigato [co-che-gah'-to], *m.* A bird of Mexico, having the head and neck black, with a red collar and green belly; the bill seven inches long.
Cochina [co-chee'-nah], *f.* Sow.
Cochinada [co-che-nah'-dah], *f.* 1. Herd of swine. 2. Hoggishness; any mean, dirty action.
Cochinamente [co-che-nah-men'-tay], *adv.* 1. Foully, hoggishly, filthily, nastily. 2. Meanly, basely.
Cochinata [co-che-nah'-tah], *f.* (Naut.) Rider, a piece of timber to strengthen a vessel.
Cochinear [co-che-nay-ar'], *vn.* (Littl. us.) To be dirty, to be hoggish.
Cochinería [co-che-nay-ree'-ah], *f.* 1. Dirtiness, foulness, filthiness, nastiness. 2. Meanness, niggardliness.
Cochinero, ra [co-che-nay'-ro, rah], *a.* Used of fruits poor in quality, given to hogs.
Cochinilla [co-che-neel'-lyah], *f.* 1. Wood-louse, a small insect. 2. Cochineal, an insect of commercial value. Coccus cacti. *Cochinilla renegrida*, Brown cochineal.
Cochinillo, illa [co-che-neel'-lyo, lyah], *m. & f. dim.* A little pig. *Cochinillo*, *m.* An animal in Brazil resembling a pig. *Cochinillo de Indias*, Guinea-pig.
Cochino, na [co-chee'-no, nah], *a.* Dirty, nasty, filthy.
Cochino [co-chee'-no], *m.* Pig. *V.* PUERCO.
Cochío, ía, Cochizo, za [co-chee'-o, ah, co-chee'-tho, thah], *a.* (Obs.) Easily boiled.
Cochiquera [co-che-kay'-rah], *f.* Hog-sty.
Cochite hervite [co-chee'-tay er-vee'-tay]. (Coll.) Helter-skelter: applied to any thing done hastily or precipitately.
Cochitril [co-che-treel'], *m.* (Coll.) 1. A pig-sty. 2. A filthy room, quarters.
Cocho, cha [co'-cho, chah], *a.* (Obs.) *V.* COCIDO.
Cochura [co-choo'-rah], *f.* 1. Act of boiling. 2. Dough for a batch of bread.
Coda [co'-dah], *f.* (Prov.) 1. Tail. *V.* COLA. 2. Burden of a song or other piece of music.
Codadura [co-dah-doo'-rah], *f.* Part of an old vine laid on the ground, from which young buds shoot forth.
Codal [co-dahl'], *m.* 1. Piece of ancient armour for the elbow. 2. A short and thick wax-candle, of the size of the elbow. 3. Shoot issuing from a vine. 4. Frame of a hand-saw. *Codales*, A carpenter's square. 5. Prop, shore, stay, strut. Stay-bolt.
Codal [co-dahl'], *a.* Cubital, containing only the length of a cubit. *Palo codal*, A stick of the length of a cubit, hung round the neck as a penance.
Codaste [co-dahs'-tay], *m.* (Naut.) Stern-post.
Codazo [co-dah'-tho], *m.* Blow with the elbow: a hunch.
Codear [co-day-ar'], *vn.* To elbow. *Codearse con*, To rub elbows with.
Codecillar, Codicilar [co-day-theel-lyar', co-de-the-lar'], *vn.* (Obs.) To make a codicil.
Codeína [co-day-ee'-nah], *f.* Codeia, codein, an alkaloid obtained from opium.
Codena [co-day'-nah], *f.* (Obs.) Body or thickness required in cloth.
Codera [co-day'-rah], *f.* 1. Itch or scabbiness on the elbow. 2. A piece reenforcing the elbows of jackets. *Codera en un cable*, (Naut.) A spring on a cable.
Codesera [co-day-say'-rah], *f.* A spot grown over with hairy cytisus.
Codeso [co-day'-so], *m.* (Bot.) Hairy cytisus. Cytisus hirsutus. *Codeso de los Alpes*, Laburnum, ebony of the Alps. Cytisus laburnum.
Códice [co'-de-thay], *m.* Old manuscript, treating on remarkable points of antiquity; codex.
Codicia [co-dee'-the-ah], *f.* 1. Covetousness, cupidity. 2. (Obs.) Sensual appetite, lust. 3. (Met.) Greediness, an ardent desire of good things. *La codicia rompe el saco*, Covet all, lose all. *Por codicia de florín no te cases con ruin*, Never marry a villain for his money.
Codiciable [co-de-the-ah'-blay], *a.* Covetable.
Codiciador [co-de-the-ah-dor'], *m.* Coveter.
Codiciante [co-de-the-ahn'-tay], *pa.* Coveting.
Codiciar [co-de-the-ar'], *va.* To covet.
Codicilar [co-de-the-lar'], *a.* Pertaining to a codicil.
Codicilo [co-de-thee'-lo], *m.* Codicil, a supplement to a last will.
Codiciosamente [co-de-the-o-sah-men'-tay], *adv.* Covetously, greedily.
Codiciosito, ita [co-de-the-o-see'-to, tah], *a. dim.* Somewhat covetous.
Codicioso, sa [co-de-the-o'-so, sah], *a.* 1. Greedy, covetous, avaricious. 2. (Met. Coll.) Diligent, laborious, assiduous.
Codificar [co-de-fe-car'], *va.* To codify laws; reduce to a code.
Código [co'-de-go], *m.* Code (of laws). *Código de comercio*, Mercantile law *Código de señales*, Signal code.
Codillera [co-deel-lyay'-rah], *f.* (Vet.) Tumour on the knee of horses.
Codillo [co-deel'-lyo], *m.* 1. Knee of horses and other quadrupeds. 2. Angle. 3. Codille, a term at ombre. 4. That part of a branch of a tree which joins the trunk. 5. *Codillo de una curva*, (Naut.) Breech of a knee. 6. Stirrup of a saddle. *Jugársela a uno de codillo*, (Met.) To trick or outwit a person. *Codillos*, File used by silversmiths. *Tirar a uno al codillo*, To endeavour to destroy one; doing him all possible damage.
Codo [co'-do], *m.* 1. Elbow. 2. Cubit, a measure of length equal to the distance from the elbow to the end of the middle finger. *Codo real*, Royal cubit, which is three fingers longer than the common. *Codo geométrico*, 418 mm. *Codo real*, 574 mm. *Alzar de codo* or *el codo*, To drink too much wine. *Comerse los codos de hambre*, To be starved with hunger. *Dar de codo*, To elbow, to push with the elbow, to treat with contempt. *Hablar por los codos*, To chatter, to prattle. *Levantar de codo* or *levantar el codo*, (Prov.) Applied to tipplers.
Codón [co-done'], *m.* A leather cover of a horse's tail.
Codoña [co-do'-nyah], *f.* Quince.
Codoñero [co-do-nyay'-ro], *m.* Quince-tree.
Codorniz [co-dor-neeth'], *f.* (Orn.) Quail. Tetrao coturnix.
Coecual [co-ay-coo-ahl'], *a.* (Div.) Coequal.
Coeducación [co-ay-doo-cah-the-on'], *f.* Coeducation.
Coeducacional [co-ay-doo-cah-the-o-nahl'], *a.* Coeducational.
Coeficiente [co-ay-fe-the-en'-tay], *a.* Coefficient.
Coepíscopo [co-ay-pees'-co-po], *m.* Contemporary bishop.
Coercer [co-er-therr'], *va.* To coerce, to check, to restrain.
Coercibilidad [co-er-the-be-le-dahd'], *f.* Coercibility; liability to restraint.
Coercible [co-er-thee'-blay], *a.* Coercible; subject to check.
Coerción [co-er-the-on'], *f.* Coercion, restraint, check.
Coercitivo, va [co-er-the-tee'-vo, vah], *a.* Coercive, restraining.
Coesencial [co-ay-sen-the-ahl'], *a.* (Littl. us.) Coessential, consubstantial.
Coetáneo, nea [co-ay-tah'-nay-o, ah], *a.* Coetaneous, contemporary.
Coeternamente [co-ay-ter-nah-men'-tay], *adv.* (Littl. us.) Coeternally.
Coeternidad [co-ay-ter-ne-dahd'], *f.* (Littl. us.) Coeternity.
Coeterno, na [co-ay-ter'-no, nah], *a.* Coeternal.
Coevo, va [co-ay'-vo, vah], *a.* Coeval.
Coexistencia [co-ek-sis-ten'-the-ah], *f* Coexistence.
Coexistente [co-ek-sis-ten'-tay], *pa.* Coexistent.
Coexistir [co-ek-sis-teer'], *vn.* To coexist.
Coextenderse [co-ex-ten-der'-say], *vr.* To coextend.
Coextensión [co-ex-ten-se-on'], *f.* (Littl. us.) Coextension.
Coextensivamente [co-ex-ten-se-vah-men'-tay], *adv.* (Littl. us.) Coextensively.
Coextensivo, va [co-ex-ten-see'-vo, vah], *a.* (Littl. us.) Coextensive.
Cofa [co'-fah], *f.* (Naut.) Top or round-house of the lower masts.
Cofia [co'-fe-ah], *f.* 1. A net of silk or thread worn on the head; a kind of cowl, head-dress, head-gear, coif. 2. An iron case in which the die is fastened for coining.

Cofiezuela [co-fe-ay-thoo'-lah], *f. dim.* A small net.
Cofin [co-feen'], *m.* A small basket for fruit.
Cofina [co-fee'-nah], *f.* **Cofino**, *m.* (Obs.) *V.* COFÍN.
Cofrade, da [co-frah'-day, dah], *m.* & *f.* Confrier, a member of any confraternity or brotherhood.
Cofradía [co-frah-dee'-ah], *f.* 1. Confraternity, brotherhood, or sisterhood. 2. Association of persons for any purpose.
Cofre [co'-fray], *m.* 1. Trunk for clothes. 2. Fish found in the West Indies. 3. (Mil.) Coffer, a hollow lodgment across a dry moat. 4. (Print.) Coffin of a printing-press. *Pelo de cofre*, Carroty hair.
Cofrecico, illo, ito [co-fray-thee'-co], *m. dim.* A small trunk.
Cofrero [co-fray'-ro], *m.* Trunk-maker or seller of trunks.
Cofundador, ra [co-foon-dah-dor', rah], *m.* & *f.* (Littl. us.) Cofounder, a joint founder.
Cogecha [co-hay'-chah], *f.* (Obs.) *V.* COSECHA.
Cogedera [co-hay-day'-rah], *f.* A sort of bee-hive used to gather a swarm which has quitted the stock.
Cogedero, ra [co-hay-day'-ro, rah], *m.* & *f.* Collector, gatherer.
Cogedizo, za [co-hay-dee'-thoh, thah], *a.* That which can be easily collected or gathered.
Cogedor [co-hay-dor'], *m.* 1. Collector, gatherer. 2. Dust-box or dust-pan. 3. (Obs.) Tax-gatherer. 4. Among velvet-weavers, a box in which the woven velvet is put.
Cogedura [co-hay-doo'-rah], *f.* Act of gathering or collecting.
Coger [co-herr'], *va.* 1. To catch, to seize with the hand, to get, to lay hold of, to come upon. 2. To imbibe, to soak. *La tierra no ha cogido bastante agua*, The earth has not drawn in sufficient water. 3. To gather the produce of the ground. 4. To have room to hold. *Esta cámara coge mil fanegas de trigo*, This granary holds a thousand bushels of wheat. 5. To occupy, to take up. *Cogió la alfombra toda la sala*, The carpet covered the whole room. 6. To find, to procure. *Me cogió descuidado*, He took me unawares. *Procuré cogerle de buen humor*, I endeavoured to see him when in good humour. 7. To surprise, to attack unexpectedly. *La tempestad me cogió*, The storm overtook me unexpectedly. *Coger en mentira*, To catch in a lie. 8. To intercept, to obstruct. *Coger las calles*, To stop the streets. *Coger la calle*, To flee, to escape. *Coger a deseo*, To obtain one's wishes. *Coger un cernícalo, un lobo, una turca* or *una mona*, To be intoxicated.
Cogermano, na [co-her-mah'-no, nah], *m.* & *f.* (Obs.) First cousin.
Cogida [co-hee'-dah], *f.* 1. The gathering or harvesting of fruits. 2. The yield of fruits. 3. The act of the bull's catching the bull-fighter.
Cogido, da [co-hee'-do, dah], *a.* Joined, united.—*m.* Fold, accidental or designed, made in women's clothing, curtains, etc.
Cogimiento [co-he-me-en'-to], *m.* (Obs.) Gathering, collecting, or catching.
Cogitable [co-he-tah'-blay], *a.* (Littl. us.) Cogitable, that which may be thought of.
Cogitabundo, da [co-he-tah-boon'-do, dah], *a.* Pensive, thoughtful, musing.
Cogitación [co-he-tah-the-on'], *f.* Reflection, meditation, cogitation.
Cogitar [co-he-tar'], *va.* To reflect, to meditate, to muse.
Cogitativo, va [co-he-tah-tee'-vo, vah], *a.* Cogitative, given to meditation.
Cogite [co-hee'-tay]. I have caught you; or, There I have you: a familiar phrase, from *Coger*, used in arguing.
Cognación [cog-nah-the-on'], *f.* Cognation, kindred.
Cognado, da [cog-nah'-do, dah], *a.* Cognate, related by consanguinity.
Cognaticio, ia [cog-nah-tee'-the-o, ah], *a.* Order of succession of the collateral relatives by the female line, through lack of male succession.
Cognición [cog-ne-the-on'], *f.* (Obs.) *V.* CONOCIMIENTO.
Cognombre [cog-nom'-bray], *m.* (Obs.) *V.* SOBRENOMBRE.
Cognomento [cog-no-men'-to], *m.* Cognomination, surname.
Cognominar [cog-no-me-nar'], *va.* (Obs.) To give an additional name; to give a surname.
Cognoscer [cog-nos-therr'], *va.* (Obs.) *V.* CONOCER.
Cognoscible [cog-nos-thee'-blay], *a.* (Obs.) Cognoscible, that may be known.
Cognoscitivo, va [cog-nos-the-tee'-vo, vah], *a.* Cognitive, having the power of knowing.
Cogollico, ito [co-gol-lyee'-co, ee'-to], *m. dim.* A small heart or flower of garden plants, such as cabbage, etc.
Cogollo [co-gol'-lyo], *m.* 1. Heart of garden plants, such as lettuce, cabbage, etc. 2. Shoot of a plant. 3. Top, summit. *Cogollos*, Ornaments of the friezes of Corinthian capitals.
Cogolmar [co-gol-mar'], *va.* (Obs.) To fill up a vessel. *V.* COLMAR.
Cogombradura [co-gom-brah-doo'-rah], *f.* (Obs.) Digging and earthing about plants.
Cogombro [co-gom'-bro], *m.* *V.* COHOMBRO.
Cogote [co-go'-tay], *m.* 1. Occiput, hind part of the head. 2. Crest at the back of the helmet. *Ser tieso de cogote*, (Met.) To be stiff-necked, headstrong, obstinate.
Cogotera [co-go-tay'-rah], *f.* (Obs.) The hair combed down on the neck.
Cogucho [co-goo'-cho], *m.* The most inferior sort of sugar.
Cogujada [co-goo-hah'-dah], *f.* (Orn.) Crested lark. Alauda cristata.
Cogujón [co-goo-hone'], *m.* Corner of a mattress or bolster.
Cogujonero, ra [co-goo-ho-nay'-ro, rah], *a.* Pointed, as the corners of mattresses or bolsters.
Cogulla [co-gool'-lyah], *f.* Cowl, monk's hood or habit.
Cogullada [co-gool-lyah'-dah], *f.* *V.* PAPADA DE PUERCO.
Cohabitación [co-ah-be-tah-the-on'], *f.* Cohabitation, the living together as man and wife, whether lawfully or illicitly.
Cohabitar [co-ah-be-tar'], *vn.* To cohabit, to accustom.
Cohecha [co-ay'-chah], *f.* (Agr.) Cultivating the land the last time before sowing the crop.
Cohechador [co-ay-chah-dor'], *m.* 1. Briber, suborner. 2. (Obs.) Bribed judge.
Cohechamiento [co-ay-chah-me-en'-to], *m.* (Obs.) *V.* COHECHO.
Cohechar [co-ay-char'], *va.* 1. To bribe, to gain by bribes, to suborn, to hire, to daub, to fee. 2. (Obs.) To force, to oblige. 3. (Agr.) To plough the ground the last time before it is sown.
Cohechazón [co-ay-chah-thone'], *f.* (Prov.) 1. Act of breaking up the ground for culture. 2. The last ploughing of the ground before it is sown.
Cohecho [co-ay'-cho], *m.* 1. Bribery. 2. (Agr.) Season for ploughing the ground.
Cohén [co-en'], *m.* & *f.* 1. Soothsayer. 2. Procurer, pimp. (Heb. cohén.)
Coheredera [co-ay-ray-day'-rah], *f.* Coheiress, joint-heiress.
Coheredero [co-ay-ray-day'-ro], *m.* Coheir, fellow-heir, joint-heir.
Coherencia [co-ay-ren'-the-ah], *f.* 1. Coherence, the relation of one thing to another; connection. 2. Adhesion of molecules.
Coherente [co-ay-ren'-tay], *a.* Coherent, consistent, cohesive.
Coherentemente [co-ay-ren-tay-men'-tay], *adv.* Cohesively.
Cohermano [co-er-mah'-no], *m.* (Obs.) First cousin. *V.* PRIMO.
Cohesión [co-ay-se-on'], *f.* Cohesion.
Cohete [co-ay'-tay], *m.* 1. Skyrocket; firecracker. 2. Fuse. *Cohete de ignición múltiple*, (Aer.) Multistage rocket. *Cohete de señales*, Flare. *Cohete impulsor*, (Aer.) Booster rocket. *Cohete de cuatro cuerpos*, Four-stage rocket. *Cohete espacial de combustible sólido*, Solid-fueled space rocket.
Cohetería [co-hay-tay-ree'-ah], *f.* Rocketry.
Cohetero [co-hay-tay'-ro], *m.* Rocketeer.
Cohibición [co-e-be-the-on'], *f.* Prohibition, restraint.
Cohibir [co-e-beer'], *va.* To cohibit, to prohibit, to restrain.
Cohita de casas [co-ee'-tah day cah'-sas], *f.* (Obs.) Number of contiguous houses, or part of a street.
Cohobación [co-o-bah-the-on'], *f.* (Obs.) Cohobation, the act of distilling the same liquor over again.
Cohobar [co-o-bar'], *va.* To redistil, cohobate. (Early chemistry.)
Cohombral [co-om-brahl'], *m.* Cucumber-bed.
Cohombrillo [co-om-breel'-lyo], *m. dim.* Gherkin. *Cohombrillo amargo*, The bitter cucumber, squirting cucumber.
Cohombro [co-om'-bro], *m.* 1. Cucumber, or snake cucumber. Cucumbis flexuosus. *Cohombro marino*, or *de mar*, Sea-cucumber, a holothurian. 2. A fritter made of the same mass as used for buns, and after being fried cut into pieces like a cucumber.
Cohonder [co-on-derr'], *va.* (Obs.) To corrupt, to vilify.
Cohondimiento [co-on-de-me-en'-to], *m.* (Obs.) Corruption, reproach, infamy.
Cohonestar [co-o-nes-tar'], *va.* To give an honest or decent appearance to an action.
Cohorte [co-or'-tay], *f.* Cohort, a body of Roman infantry, numbering usually five hundred.
Coi, or **Coy**, *pl.* **Coyes** [co'-e], *m.* (Naut.) Hammock.
Coima [co'-e-mah], *f.* 1. Perquisite received by the keeper of a gaming-table. 2. (Low) A prostitute.
Coime, Coimero [co'-e-may, co-e-may'-ro], *m.* Keeper of a gaming-table:
Coincidencia [co-in-the-den'-the-ah], *f.* Coincidence; concurrence.
Coincidente [co-in-the-den'-tay], *pa.* Coincident, concurrent, consistent.
Coincidir [co-in-the-deer'], *vn.* 1. To fall upon or meet in the same point, to fall in. 2. To concur, to coincide.
Coindicación [co-in-de-cah-the-on'], *f.* (Med.) Coindication.
Coindicante [co-in-de-cahn'-tay], *m.* & *a.* (Med.) Coindicant.

Coinquinarse [co-in-ke-nar'-say], *vr.* (Obs.) To be stained. *V.* MANCHARSE.
Cointeresado, da [co-in-tay-ray-sah'-do, dah], *a.* Jointly interested.
Coitivo, va [co-e-tee'-vo, vah], *a.* (Obs.) Relating to the act of generation or coition.
Coito [co'-e-to], *m.* Coition, carnal copulation,
Coitoso, sa [co-e-to'-so, sah], *a.* (Obs.) *V.* APRESURADO.
Coja [co'-hah], *f.* 1. (Obs.) Back of the knee; popliteal space. 2. A lewd woman.
Cojear [co-hay-ar'], *vn.* 1. To limp, to halt, to hobble. 2. To deviate from virtue. *Cojear del mismo pie,* To have the same defect or passion. *Saber de qué pie cojea,* To know any one's weak side.
Cojera, Cojez [co-hay'-rah, co-heth'], *f.* (Obs.) Lameness, halt, hobble, limp.
Cojijoso, sa [co-he-ho'-so, sah], *a.* Peevish, irritable.
Cojín [co-heen'], *m.* Cushion; soft pad placed on a saddle. *Cojines de bote,* (Naut.) Boat cushions. *Cojines de cámara,* (Naut.) Cabin cushions.
Cojincillo [co-hin-thee'-lyo], *m. dim.* Small cushion or pillow.
Cojinete [co-he-nay'-tay], *m.* Small cushion. *Cojinete de bolas,* (Mech.) Ball bearing. *Cojinete de rodillos,* Roller bearing.
Cojitranco, ca [co-he-trahn'-co, cah], *a.* Applied as a nickname to evil-disposed lame persons.
Cojo, ja [co'-ho, hah], *n.* & *a.* 1. Cripple, halter. 2. Lame, cripple, halt: applied to persons. 3. Applied to a table or chair which does not stand firm. *No ser cojo ni manco,* To have all the necessary requisites to do something: to be very intelligent and skilled in the matter in hand.
Cojón [co-hone'], *m.* (Low) Testicle. *V.* TESTÍCULO.
Cojudo, da [co-hoo'-do, dah], *a.* Entire, not gelt, or castrated.
Cojuelo, ela [co-hoo-ay'-lo, lah], *a. dim.* A small cripple.
Cok [coke], *m.* Coke, retorted coal. (Eng.)
Cokera [co-kay'-rah], *f.* A hod for coke.
Col [cole], *f.* Species of cabbage with large leaves and a short stalk. *Alabaos, coles, que hay nabos en la olla,* A reproach to those who are unreasonably desirous of being preferred to others. *Entre col y col, lechuga,* Variety is pleasing.
Cola [co'-lah], *f.* 1. Tail, cue. 2. Train, the part of a gown that falls upon the ground. 3. Word of reproach among students, in opposition to that of *víctor.* 4. In music, the prolonged sound of the voice at the end of a song. *Colas* or *puntas sueltas de armiños, martas,* etc. Tails or tips of ermine, sable, etc. *Hacer bajar la cola a alguno,* (Coll.) To humble one's pride. *Cubrirse con la cola,* To make use of frivolous evasions. *Castigado de cola,* Deprived of one's place or office. *Cola de golondrina,* (Mil.) Hornwork. *A la cola,* Backwards, behind. *Cola de caballo,* (Bot.) Horse-tail. Equisetum, *L.* *Cola de rata,* Rat-tail file. *De cola de puerco nunca buen virote,* You cannot make a silk purse of a sow's ear. *Llevar (la) cola,* To take the last place. *Menea la cola el can, no por ti, sino por el pan,* The dog wags his tail, not for love of you, but for what you will give him. (Lat. cauda.)
Cola, *f.* (Gr. κόλλα.) Glue. *Cola clara,* A transparent glue used by weavers. *Cola fuerte,* Strong glue made of ox-hides. *Cola de pescado,* Isinglass. *Cola de retazo,* Size used by painters. *Cola de boca,* Lip glue.
Colaboración [co-lah-bo-rah-the-on'], *f.* Collaboration, working together.
Colaboracionista [co-lah-bo-rah-the-o-nees'-tah], *m.* & *f.* (Political) Collaborator.
Colaborador, ra [co-lah-bo-rah-dor', rah], *m.* & *f.* 1. Fellow-labourer. 2. One who is associated with another, especially in literary or scientific work; collaborator.
Colaborar [co-lah-bo-rar'], *va.* To collaborate.
Colación [co-lah-the-on'], *f.* 1. Collation, comparing of one thing with another. 2. Collation, act of bestowing an ecclesiastical benefice, or conferring degrees in universities. 3. Conference or conversation between the ancient monks on spiritual affairs. 4. Collation, a slight repast. 5. Potation, the act of drinking. 6. Sweetmeats given to servants on Christmas eve. 7. Precinct or district of a parish. *Sacar a colación,* To make mention of a person or thing. *Traer a colación,* 1. To produce proofs or reasons to support a cause. 2. To introduce, in conversation, something irrelevant.
Colacionar [co-lah-the-o-nar'], *va.* 1. To collate one thing of the same kind with another, to compare. 2. To collate, to place in an ecclesiastical benefice.
Colada [co-lah'-dah], *f.* 1. The bucking of clothes or linen with lye; buck. 2. The linen thus bucked. 3. Common, an open ground. 4. Road for cattle over a common. 5. One of the swords of the *Cid:* in the jocular style, a good sword. *Todo saldrá en la colada,* The whole fact will be brought to light. *Echar a uno la colada,* (Met.) To scrub or clean one of his filth.
Coladera [co-lah-day'-rah], *f.* 1. Strainer, colander. 2. Sieve or searce used by wax-chandlers.
Coladero [co-lah-day'-ro], *m.* 1. Colander, a sieve through which liquors are poured, a strainer. 2. A narrow passage. 3. (Obs.) Bucking of clothes.
Colador [co-lah-dor'], *m.* 1. Colander. *V.* COLADERO. 2. Collator, one who confers ecclesiastical benefices. 3. (Obs.) In printing-offices, a leach-tub for making lye.
Coladora [co-lah-do'-rah], *f.* (Obs.) A woman who bucks.
Coladura [co-lah-doo'-rah], *f.* Colation, straining, filtration. *Coladuras,* Dregs or lees of clarified wax.
Colaire [co-lah'-e-ray], *m.* (Prov.) Place through which a current of air passes.
Colambre, *f.* *V.* CORAMBRE.
Colanilla [co-lah-neel'-lyah], *f.* A small bolt.
Colaña [co-lah'-nyah], *f.* Joist about twenty palms long and six inches broad.
Colapez, Colapiscis [co-lah-peth', co-lah-pees'-thees], *f.* Isinglass. *V.* COLA DE PESCADO.
Colapso [co-lap'-so], *m.* (Med.) Collapse, prostration.
Colar [co-lar'], *va.* & *vn.* 1. To strain, to filter. 2. To bleach clothing after washing. 3. To collate or confer ecclesiastical benefices. 4. (Obs.) To obtain some difficult matter. 5. (Coll.) To spread false news as certain facts; to pass counterfeit money. 6. To pass through a strait place. 7. To drink wine.—*vr.* 1. To strain or to be filtered. 2. To steal into a place, to creep in by stealth. 3. To be displeased with a jest. *Colar la ropa con la lejía,* To buck linen with lye.
Colateral [co-lah-tay-rahl'], *a.* 1. Collateral. 2. Standing equal in relation to some ancestor.
Colativo, va [co-lah-tee'-vo, vah], *a.* 1. Collative, belonging to ecclesiastical benefices which cannot be enjoyed without a canonical collation. 2. That which can strain or filter.
Colcótar [col-co'-tar], *m.* (Chem.) Colcothar, crocus, rouge.
Colcha [col'-chah], *f.* 1. Coverlet, counterpane. 2. (Naut.) *V.* COLCHADURA.
Colchadura [col-chah-doo'-rah], *f.* 1. Quilting. 2. (Naut.) Laying or twisting ropes.
Colchar [col-char'], *va.* 1. To quilt. *V.* ACOLCHAR. 2. *Colchar cabos,* (Naut.) To lay or twist ropes. *Carro de colchar,* A rope-maker's sledge.
Colchero [col-chay'-ro], *m.* Quilt-maker.
Cólchico [col'-che-co], *m.* (Bot.) Colchicum, meadow saffron. Colchicum montanum, *L.* *V.* CÓLQUICO.
Colchón [col-chone'], *m.* Mattress. *Colchón de pluma,* Feather-bed.
Colchoncico, illo, ito [col-chon-thee'-co], *m. dim.* A small mattress.
Colchonero, ra [col-cho-nay'-ro, rah], *m.* & *f.* Mattress-maker, feather-bed-maker.
Coleada [co-lay-ah'-dah], *f.* Wag or motion of the tail of fishes or other animals.
Coleadura [co-lay-ah-doo'-rah], *f.* 1. Wagging of the tail. 2. Wriggling, a ridiculous motion of women in walking.
Colear [co-lay-ar'], *vn.* 1. To wag the tail (as dogs). 2. To wriggle or move in walking. *Todavía colea,* It's still pending (referring to a business not yet settled).—*va.* (Sp. Am.) 1. To annoy, to nag. 2. To pursue (a person). 3. In bull fights, to take the bull by the tail, and while running, to overturn him.
Colección [co-lec-the-on'], *f.* Collection, an assemblage of things, collation, knot, compilement. *Colección de pus* or *materia en un tumor,* Gathering.
Coleccionar [co-lec-the-o-nar'], *va.* To collect. *Coleccionar sellos de correo,* To collect post stamps.
Colecitas de Bruselas [co-lay-thee'-tahs day broo-say'-lahs], *f. pl.* (Bot.) Brussels sprouts.
Colecta [co-lec'-tah], *f.* 1. Distribution of a tax levied on a town. 2. Collect, a prayer of the mass. 3. Collection of voluntary offerings for pious uses. 4. (Obs.) Assemblage of the faithful in churches for the celebration of divine service.
Colectación [co-lec-tah-the-on'], *f.* Levy, the act of collecting rents, taxes, or other dues. *V.* RECAUDACIÓN.
Colectar [co-lec-tar'], *va.* To collect taxes. *V.* RECAUDAR.
Colecticio, cia [co-lec-tee'-the-o, ah], *a.* Collectitious, applied to troops without discipline.
Colectivamente [co-lec-te-vah-men'tay], *adv.* Collectively.
Colectividad [co-lec-te-ve-dahd'], *f.* Community.
Colectivismo [co-lec-te-vees'-mo], *m.* Collectivism.
Colectivización [co-lec-te-ve-thah-the-on'], *f.* Collectivization.
Colectivizar [co-lec-te-ve-thar'], *va.* To collectivize.
Colectivo, va [co-lec-tee'-vo, vah], *a.* Collective. *Contrato colectivo,* Closed shop (in labor affairs).
Colector [co-lec-tor'], *m.* 1. Collector

gatherer. 2. Tax or rent-gatherer. 3. *Colector de espolios y vacantes*, Collector of the property which Spanish bishops leave when they die. 4. Collector of the contributions for masses or communion alms.

Colecturía [co-lec-too-ree'-ah], *f.* 1. Collectorship. 2. Office of the collector.

Colega [co-lay'-gah], *m.* Colleague; compeer.

Colegatario, ria [co-lay-gah-tah'-re-o, ah], *m.* & *f.* Collegatary, colegatee.

Colegiado [co-lay-he-ah'-do], *a.* Collegiate, a member of a college or corporation, etc.

Colegial [co-lay-he-ahl'], *m.* Collegian, collegiate, a member of a college. *Colegial de baño*, He who takes the tippet, or sash, in a college to decorate himself with it.

Colegial [co-lay-he-ahl'], *a.* Collegial, relating to a college. *Iglesia colegial*, A collegiate church, composed of dignitaries and canons, who celebrate divine service.

Colegiala [co-lay-he-ah'-lah], *f.* A woman who is a member of a college.

Colegialmente [co-lay-he-al-men'-tay], *adv.* In a collegial manner.

Colegiarse [co-lay-he-ar'-say], *vr.* To unite in a college those of the same profession or class.

Colegiata [co-lay-he-ah'-tah], *f.* A collegiate church.

Colegiatura [co-lay-he-ah-too'-rah], *f.* Fellowship or establishment in a college.

Colegio [co-lay'-he-o], *m.* 1. College. 2. College, the house in which collegians reside. 3. A seminary of education for young ladies. 4. College, a society of men of the same profession.

Colegir [co-lay-heer'], *va.* 1. (Obs.) To collect or gather things which are scattered. 2. To collect, to deduce, to infer.

Colegislador, ra [co-lay-his-lah-dor', rah], *a.* Co-legislative (body).

Coleo [co-lay'-o], *m.* (Coll.) *V.* COLEADURA.

Coleóptero, ra [co-lay-op'-tay-ro, rah], *a.* Coleopterous, belonging to the division of insects named coleoptera.—*m. pl.* The coleoptera.

Cólera [co'-lay-rah], *f.* 1. Choler, bile. 2. Choler, anger, fury, rage, passion. *Montar en cólera*, To be angry, to be in a passion. *Tomarse de la cólera*, To fly into a passion.—*m.* 3. *El cólera morbo*, The cholera morbus. *Cólera asiático*, Asiatic cholera.

Colera [co-lay'-rah], *f.* Ornament for the tail of a horse.

Coléricamente [co-lay'-re-cah-men-tay], *adv.* Fumingly, passionately.

Colérico, ca [co-lay'-re-co, cah], *a.* 1. Choleric. 2. Passionate, hasty; hot-headed.

Coleriforme [co-lay-re-for'-may], *a.* Choleriform, like cholera morbus. (Acad.) Like cholera asiatica, as we use the term.

Colerina [co-lay-ree'-nah], *f.* Cholerine, a diarrhœa, sometimes premonitory of cholera.

Colesterina [co-les-tay-ree'-nah], *f.* Cholesterol.

Colesterol [co-les-tay-role'], *m.* Cholesterol.

Coleta [co-lay'-tah], *f.* 1. Cue or queue of the hair. 2. (Coll.) A short addition to a discourse or writing; postscript. 3. (Bot.) Nine-leaved coronilla. Coronilla valentina. 4. Nankin, or nankeen.

Coletáneo, nea [co-lay-tah'-nay-o, ah], *a.* (Obs.) *V.* COLACTÁNEO.

Coletero [co-lay-tay'-ro], *m.* One who makes buff doublets and breeches.

Coletilla [co-lay-teel'-lyah], *f. dim.* A small cue. Narrow nankin.

Coletillo [co-lay-teel'-lyo], *m. dim.* A small doublet of buff or other skins.

Coleto [co-lay'-to], *m.* 1. Buff doublet or jacket. 2. (Coll.) Body of a man. Interior of a person. *Dije para mi coleto*, I said to myself. *Echarse al coleto*, (Coll.) Speaking of a book or a writing, is to read it all over. *Echarse algo al coleto*, To eat or drink something.

Colgadero [col-gah-day'-ro], *m.* Hook to hang things upon.

Colgadero, ra [col-gah-day'-ro, rah], *a.* Fit to be hung up.

Colgadizo [col-gah-dee'-tho], *m.* Shed, a temporary covering from the weather.

Colgadizo, za [col-gah-dee'-tho, thah], *a.* Pendent, suspended.

Colgado, da [col-gah'-do, dah], *a.* Suspended. *Dejar a alguno colgado* or *quedarse alguno colgado*, To frustrate one's hopes or desires.—*pp.* of COLGAR.

Colgador [col-gah-dor'], *m.* Among printers, peel-hanger, y-lintel with which printed sheets are hung up to dry.

Colgadura [col-gah-doo'-rah], *f.* Tapestry, hanging or drapery. *Colgadura de cama*, Bed-furniture. *Colgaduras de papel pintado*, Paper hangings.

Colgajo [col-gah'-ho], *m.* 1. Tatter or rag hanging from clothes. 2. *Colgajo de uvas*, Bunch of grapes hung up to be preserved.—3. *pl.* The fleshy tissues left in some amputations to form the stump.

Colgandero, ra [col-gan-day'-ro, rah], *a.* *V.* COLGANTE.

Colgante [col-gahn'-tay], *pa.* Hanging, pending, clinging. *Colgantes*, Earrings, trinkets.

Colgar [col-gar'], *va.* 1. To hang up, to suspend in the air, to flag, to flow, to hover. 2. To adorn with tapestry or hangings. 3. To hang or kill by hanging.—*vn.* 1. To hang from, to be suspended. 2. (Obs.) To be in a state of dependence. *Colgar los hábitos*, To doff the cassock. *Ella está siempre colgada de la ventana*, She is always fixed at the window. *Colgar a uno*, (Met.) To compliment one on his birthday, or his patron saint's day, by suspending something from his neck.

Colia [co'-le-ah], *f.* **Colias** [co'-le-as], *m.* A small fish resembling a pilchard.

Coliblanca [co-le-blahn'-cah], *f.* (Zool.) An eagle of South America.

Coliblanco, ca [co-le-blahn'-co, cah], *a.* White-tailed.

Colibre, **Colibrí** [co-lee'-bray, co-le-bree'], *m.* (Orn.) Colibri, a beautiful American humming-bird, especially one with a curved beak. Trochilus, *L.*

Cólica [co'-le-cah], *f.* Colic.

Colicano, na [co-le-cah'-no, nah], *a.* Having gray hair in the tail: applied to horses.

Cólico, or **Dolor Cólico** [co'-le-co], *m.* Colic, griping, a disease.

Colicorto, ta [co-le-cor'-to, tah], *a.* Short-tailed.

Colicuable [co-le-coo-ah'-blay], *a.* (Littl. us.) Colliquable, easily dissolved.

Colicuación [co-le-coo-ah-the-on'], *f.* Colliquation, the act of melting or dissolving.

Colicuante [co-le-coo-ahn'-tay], *pa.* Colliquant, colliquative.

Colicuar [co-le-coo-ar'], *va.* To colliquate, to melt, to dissolve.—*vr.* To colliquate, to become liquid.

Colicuativo, va [co-le-coo-ah-tee'-vo, vah], *a.* Colliquative.

Colicuecer [co-le-coo-ay-therr'], *va.* To fuse or melt.

Colicuefacción [co-le-coo-ay-fac-the-on'], *f.* (Littl. us.) Colliquefaction.

Coliculoso, sa [co-le-coo-lo'-so, sah], *a.* (Bot.) Presenting knobs, rounded prominences in a small space.

Colidir [co-le-deer'], *va.* (Obs.) To collide, to dash or knock together.

Colifero, ra [co-lee'-fay-ro, rah], *a.* (Bot.) Cauliferous: said of the ovary of plants when it has a neck.

Coliflor [co-le-flor'], *f.* (Bot.) Cauliflower.—*pl.* Cauliflower excrescences, venereal warts.

Coligación [co-le-gah-the-on'], *f.* 1. Colligation, the binding of things together. 2. Connection of one thing with another. 3. Union, alliance.

Coligado, da [co-le-gah'-do, dah], *m.* & *f.* Leaguer, covenanter.—*a.* Agreed and associated for some purpose.—*pp.* of COLIGARSE.

Coligadura [co-le-gah-doo'-rah], *f.* (Obs.) Combining or connecting of one thing with another.

Coligamiento [co-le-gah-me-en'-to], *m.* (Obs.) *V.* COLIGACIÓN.

Coligancia [co-le-gahn'-the-ah], *f.* (Obs.) Connection, relation, correspondence of one thing with another.

Coligarse [co-le-gar'-say], *vr.* To colligate, to colleague.

(*Yo colijo, yo colija; él colijió*, from *Colegir*. *V.* PEDIR.)

Colilla [co-leel'-lyah], *f.* 1. (Dim.) A small tail. 2. Train of a gown. 3. Stub of a cigar or cigarette thrown away because too short to smoke without burning one.

Colina [co-lee'-nah], *f.* 1. Hill, hillock, hummock. 2. Seed of cabbage. 3. *V.* COLINO.

Colinabo [co-le-nah'-bo], *m.* (Bot.) Turnip. Brassica oleracea caulo rappa.

Colindante [co-lin-dahn'-tay], *a.* Contiguous, adjacent.

Colindar [co-lin-dar'], *vn.* To be contiguous, to be adjacent.

Colino [co-lee'-no], *m.* Small cabbage not transplanted.

Colinsia [co-leen'-se-ah], *f.* Collinsia, a garden plant of the fig-wort family, native of California.

Colirio [co-lee'-re-o], *m.* Collyrium, a wash for the eyes.

Colisa [co-lee'-sah], *f.* A swivel gun.

Coliseo [co-le-say'-o], *m.* Theatre, opera-house, play-house.

Colisión [co-le-se-on'], *f.* 1. Collision, crush, clash. 2. A gall, fretting, chafing. 3. Opposition, clash of ideas.

Colitea [co-le-tay'-ah], *f.* (Bot.) Judas-tree.

Colitigante [co-le-te-gahn'-tay], *m.* One who carries on a lawsuit with another.

Colmadamente [col-mah-dah-men'-tay], *adv.* Abundantly, plentifully

Colmado, da [col-mah'-do, dah], *a* Filled, heaped.—*pp.* of COLMAR.

Colmar [col-mar'], *va.* 1. To heap up to fill to the brim. 2. To fulfil, to make up. *V.* LLENAR. 3. (Met.) To confer great favours.

Colmataje [col-ma-tah'-hay], *m.* A heaping up, brimming.

Colmena [col-may'-nah], *f.* Bee-hive. *Tener la casa como una colmena*, To have one's house well-stocked with provisions.

Colmenar [col-may-nar'], *m.* Apiary.

Colmenero [col-may-nay'-ro], *m.* Bee-keeper, bee-master. *Oso colmenero*, A bear who eats the honey of bee-hives.

Colmenilla [col-may-neel'-lyah], *f.* Mo-rel or moril, a kind of mushroom. Morchella esculenta.

Colmillada [col-meel-lyah'-dah], *f.* An injury made by an eye-tooth.

Colmillazo [col-meel-lyah'-tho], *m.* 1. (Aug.) A large eye-tooth. 2. A wound made by an eye-tooth or fang.

Colmillo [col-meel'-lyo], *m.* 1. Eye-tooth, canine-tooth. 2. Fang, the long tusk of a boar or other animal. *Escupir por el colmillo*, 1. To brag, boast. 2. To exalt one's self above all respect and consideration. *Mostrar los colmillos*, (Met.) To show spirit and resolution. *Tener colmillos, haber nacidos los colmillos*, (to have cut one's eye-teeth) (Met.) To be quick-sighted, not easily imposed upon.

Colmilludo, da [col-meel-lyoo'-do, dah], *a.* 1. Having eye-teeth, fangs, or tusks: applied to persons and animals. 2. Sagacious, quick-sighted, not easily imposed upon.

Colmo [col'-mo], *m.* 1. Heap, that which rises above the brim of a measure of grain, flour, etc. 2. Complement, finishing, completion, crown. 3. Over-measure, full; height. *Ella llegó al colmo de sus deseos*, She attained the summit of her wishes. *No llegará a colmo*, It will not come to perfection. *A colmo*, Abundantly, plentifully.

Colmo, ma [col'-mo, mah], *a.* (Obs.) *V.* COLMADO.

Colo [co'-lo], *m.* A coleopterous, tetramerous, curculionid insect of South America.

Colobo [co-lo'-bo], *m.* 1. A kind of linen tunic worn by Egyptian monks. 2. (Zool.) Colobus, an African monkey, having the thumb absent or rudimentary.

Coloboma [co-lo-bo'-mah], *m.* Coloboma, defect of substance; specifically, of the iris of the eye.

Colocación [co-lo-cah-the-on'], *f.* 1. Employment, place, office. 2. Arrangement of the parts of a building, speech, etc., collocation, location. 3. Position, situation.

Colocar [co-lo-car'], *va.* 1. To arrange, to put in due place or order. 2. To place, to put in any place, rank, condition, or office, to provide one with a place or employment. 3. To collocate, to locate, to lay.

Colocasia [co-lo-cah'-se-ah], *f.* (Bot.) The Egyptian bean, a plant with thick, tuberous rootstocks, large leaves, and rose-coloured blossoms. Arum colocasia.

Colocutor, ra [co-lo-coo-tor', rah], *m.* & *f.* He who holds colloquial intercourse with another; collocutor.

Colodión [co-lo-de-on'], *m.* Collodion.

Colodra [co-lo'-drah], *f.* 1. Milk-pail, a kit; a pailful. 2. A wooden can with which wine is measured and retailed. 3. A wooden can with a handle, used for drinking. 4. A horn with a cork bottom, used as a tumbler. *Ser una colodra*, (Coll.) To be a toper or tippler. 5. (Prov. Sant.) A wooden case tied about the waist, in which the mower carries a whetstone.

Colodrazgo [co-lo-drath'-go], *m.* Tax or excise on wine sold in small quantities.

Colodrillo [co-lo-dreel'-lyo], *m.* Occiput, hind part of the head.

Colodro [co-lo'-dro], *m.* (Obs.) 1. A wooden shoe. 2. (Prov.) Wine measure.

Colofón [co-lo-fone'], *m.* Colophon, an inscription or device put at the end of a book, giving the printer's name and date and place of printing.

Colofonia [co-lo-fo'-nee-ah], *f.* Colophony, a kind of resin.

Colofonita [co-lo-fo-nee'-tah], *f.* A garnet of a light-green or rosy-red colour, the least fusible of all garnets.

Coloide [co-lo'-e-day], *m.* Colloid.

Colombiano, na [co-lom-be-ah'-no, nah], *a.* Columbian, of Colombia.

Colombino na, [co-lom-bee'-no, nah], *a.* Pertaining to Columbus or his family.

Colombroño [co-lom-bro'-nyo], *m.* Namesake. *V.* TOCAYO.

Colon [co'-lone], *m.* 1. Colon (:). *Colon imperfecto*, Semicolon (;). 2. Colon, the largest of the intestines. 3. (Obs.) *V.* CÓLICO and COLONO. 4. (Gram.) Principal part or member of a period.

Colonche [co-lone'-chay], *m.* An intoxicating drink made in Mexico from the sap of the red prickly pear (cactus) and sugar.

Colonia [co-lo'-ne-ah], *f.* 1. Colony. 2. Colony, a plantation. 3. (Mex.) Each subdivision in which cities are divided. *Colonia residencial*, Residential district.

Colonial [co-lo-ne-ahl'], *a.* Colonial.

Colonialismo [co-lo-ne-ah-lees'-mo], *m.* Colonialism.

Colonialista [co-lo-ne-ah-lees'-tah], *a.* & *m.* & *f.* Colonialist.

Colonización [co-lo-ne-thah-the-on'], *f.* Colonization, the making a colony.

Colonizar [co-lo-ne-thar'], *va.* To colonize, form a settlement.

Colono [co-lo'-no], *m.* 1. Colonist, planter. 2. Labourer, who cultivates a piece of ground and lives on it. 3. A farmer.

Coloquintida [co-lo-keen'-te-dah], *f.* (Bot.) Colocynth, or coloquintida, a powerful and useful cathartic; bitter apple or gourd. Citrullus colocynthis.

Coloquio [co-lo'-ke-o], *m.* Colloquy, conversation, talk.

Color [co-lor'], *m.* 1. Colour, hue, dye. 2. Rouge. 3. (Met.) Colour, pretext, pretence; false show or appearance. 4. Colour, the tint of the painter.—*pl.* 1. Colour, the freshness or appearance of blood in the face. 2. (Pict.) Colour, or mixture of paint. *Color lleno* or *cargado*, A deep colour. *Color vivo*, A bright colour. *Color muerto* or *quebrado*, A wan or faded colour. *Color de aire*, A light, delicate colour. *Color de rosa batida*, A mixed rose colour, having the warp of a rose colour and the weft white. *Mudar de colores*, (Met.) To change colour. *Sacarle los colores a una persona*, (Met.) To make a person blush. *So color* or *a color* On pretence, under pretext.

Coloración [co-lo-rah-the-on'], *f.* 1. Coloring, coloration. 2. Blush. *Coloración protectora*, Protective coloring, mimetism.

Coloradamente [co-lo-rah-dah-men'-tay], *adv.* (Obs.) Speciously, under pretext.

Colorado, da [co-lo-rah'-do, dah], *a.* 1. Ruddy, florid, red. 2. Indelicate, smutty: spoken of tales or phrases. 3. Coloured, specious. *Ponerse colorado*, To blush with shame. *Poner a alguno colorado*, To put one to the blush. *A Dios con la colorada*, Farewell, God be with you: used cheerfully.—*pp.* of COLORAR.

Coloramiento [co-lo-rah-me-en'-to], *m.* (Obs.) *V.* ENCENDIMIENTO.

Colorante [co-lo-rahn'-tay], *m.* Dye, coloring.—*a.* Dyeing, coloring. *Materia colorante*, Dyeing matter, coloring substance.

Colorar [co-lo-rar'], *va.* 1. To dye, to colour, or lay on colours. 2. To make plausible.—*vn.* To blush with shame. —*vr.* (Obs.) To be ashamed.

Colorativo, va [co-lo-rah-tee'-vo, vah], *a.* Colorific, tingeing.

Colorear [co-lo-ray-ar'], *va.* To colour, to make plausible, to palliate, to excuse.—*vn.* To redden, to grow red.

Colorete [co-lo-ray'-tay], *m.* Rouge.

Colorido [co-lo-ree'-do], *m.* 1. Colouring or colour. 2. Pretext, pretence.

Colorido, da [co-lo-ree'-do, dah], *a.* Colorate.—*pp.* of COLORIR.

Colorín [co-lo-reen'], *m.* 1. (Orn.) Linnet. 2. Bright, vivid color. *Gustar de colorines*, To like showy colors. *Colorín, colorado, este cuento se ha acabado*, Traditional ending of children's stories.

Colorir [co-lo-reer'], *va.* 1. To colour, to mark with some hue or dye. 2. *V.* COLOREAR.

Colorista [co-lo-rees'-tah], *m.* Colourist.

Colosal [co-lo-sahl'], *a.* Colossal, colossean.

Coloso [co-lo'-so], *m.* Colossus, a statue of enormous magnitude.

Colpa [col'-pah], *f.* A whitish sort of copperas; a flux.

Colpar [col-par'], *va.* (Obs.) *V.* HERIR.

Colpez [col-peth'], *f.* Isinglass; fish glue.

Cólquico [cole'-ke-co], *m.* Colchicum, meadow saffron. Used in medicine as a remedy for gout.

Coludir [co-loo-deer'], *va.* 1. To collude. 2. (Obs.) To collide.

Columbio [co-loom'-be-o], *m.* (Min.) Columbium, a metal.

Columbino, na [co-loom-bee'-no, nah], *a* Dove-like, innocent, candid.

Columbo [co-loom'-bo], *m.* Columbo root. Radix cocculi palmati.

Columbrar [co-loom-brar'], *va.* 1. To discern at a distance, to see afar off. 2. (Met.) To pursue or trace a thing by conjectures.

Columelar [co-loo-may-lar'], *m.* Incisor. *V.* CORTADORES.

Columna [co-loom'-nah], *f.* 1. Column, a round pillar. *Columna ática, compuesta, corintia, dórica, jónica*, etc. Attic, Composite, Corinthian, Doric, Ionic, etc., column. *Columna abalaustrada*, A column broader toward the capital than at the base. *Columna salomónica*, That which rises in spiral form, giving generally six turns. 2. Column of air. 3. *Columna fosfórica*, Light-house, built on a rock. *Columna hueca*, A hollow column, in which is a spiral staircase. *Columna millar* or *miliaria*, A mile-column, or mile-stone. 4. (Met.) Supporter or maintainer. *La justicia, la paz y la religión son las columnas del estado*, Justice, peace, and religion are the supporters of the state. 5. Column, a long file of troops. 6. Column, part of a page.

Columnario, ria [co-loom-nah'-re-o, ah], *a.* Columnar: applied to the money coined in Spanish America, with the impressions of two columns.—*m.* & *f.* (Obs.) *V.* COLUMNATA.

Columnata [co-loom-nah'-tah], *f.* Colonnade.

Columpiar [co-loom-pe-ar'], *va.* To swing.—*vr.* 1. To swing, to fly forward or backward on a rope. 2. (Met.) To waddle, to shake in walking from side to side.

Columpio [co-loom'-pe-o], *m.* 1. A swing. 2. Meritot, a kind of play.

Coluna [co-loo'-nah], *f.* *V.* COLUMNA.

Colunita [co-loo-nee'-tah], *f. dim.* A small column.

Colurión [co-loo-re-on'], *m.* (Orn.) Lesser butcher-bird, flusher. Lanius collurio.

Coluro [co-loo'-ro], *m.* (Ast.) Colure, one of the two great circles of the celestial sphere which pass from the pole through the equinoxes and solstices respectively.

Colusión [co-loo-se-on'], *f.* 1. Collusion, deceitful agreement. 2. Shock, collision.

Colusoriamente [co-loo-so-re-ah-men'-tay], *adv.* Collusively, fraudulently.

Colusorio, ria [co-loo-so'-re-o, ah], *a.* Collusory, collusive.

Colza [cole'-thah], *f.* Colza, summer rape, a variety of turnip, cultivated for its seeds, which yield an oil much employed in northern Europe for lighting.

Colzal [col-thahl'], *f.* Colewort-seed, the seed of the Brassica campestris.

Colla [col'-lyah], *f.* 1. (Obs.) Collet, a piece of ancient armour for the neck. 2. Continuous squalls preceding the monsoons, at times followed by a hurricane. 3. Channel of an auger. 4. Last oakum placed in a seam.

Collación [col-lyah-the-on'], *f.* (Obs.) Precinct or district of a parish.

Collada [col-lyah'-dah], *f.* (Obs.) *V.* Cuello and Collado.

Collado [col-lyah'-do], *m.* Hill, fell, a small eminence.

Collar [col-lyar'], *m.* 1. Necklace. 2. Chain or cord from which hang certain insignia of honour. 3. (Obs.) Collar, collet. 4. *Collar de un estay*, (Naut.) Collar of a stay.

Collarcito [col-lyar-thee'-to], *m. dim.* A small necklace, string of beads, or chain.

Collarín [col-lyah-reen'], *m.* 1. A black collar, edged with white, worn by the Roman Catholic clergy. *V.* Alzacuello. 2. Collar of a coat.

Collarino [col-lyah-ree'-no], *m.* (Arch.) Ring or list at the top and bottom of the shaft of a column; a half round, torus. *V.* Astrágalo.

Collazo [col-lyah'-tho], *m.* Ploughman who tills the ground for a master, for which he gets some small tenement or ground to till for himself. *Collazos*, Poles on which barilla-plants are carried to the pit to be burnt.

Colleja [col-lyay'-hah], *f.* (Bot.) Lamb's-lettuce, or corn-salad. Valerianella olitoria. *Collejas*, Slender nerves found in a sheep's neck.

Coller [col-lyerr'], *va.* (Obs.) *V.* Coger.

Collera [col-lyay'-rah], *f.* 1. Collar, breast-harness of leather, stuffed with hay or straw for draught cattle. 2. Horse collar. 3. Chain gang. 4. Pair (of animals). 5. (Arg.) Cuff links.

Collerón [col-lyay-rone'], *m.* Harness collar, hame.

Colleta [col-lyay'-tah], *f.* (Bot. Prov.) A small kind of cabbage.

Collón [col-lyone'], *m.* (Coll.) Coward, a poltroon, mean fellow.

Collonada [col-lyo-nah'-dah], *f.* Cowardliness.

Collonería [col-lyo-nay-ree'-ah], *f.* 1. Cowardice. 2. (Coll. Vul.) Nonsense.

Com-. Inseparable preposition for con, signifying union.

Coma [co'-mah], *f.* 1. Comma (,). 2. Each of the parts into which a tone is divided. 3. (Obs.) *V.* Crin. *Sin faltar una coma*, or *sin faltar punto ni coma*, Without a tittle being wanting in the account or narrative.

Coma, *m.* Coma, profound insensibility.

Comadre [co-mah'-dray], *f.* 1. Midwife. 2. The name by which the godfather and godmother address the mother of their godson or daughter, and by which she also always addresses the godmother. 3. (Coll.) A gossip. *Ello va en la comadre*, or *Más va en la comadre que en la que lo pare*, Good luck and favour sometimes avail more than merit. *Jueves de comadres*, Gossips' Thursday, the last Thursday before Shrove-Tuesday. *Riñen las comadres y se dicen las verdades*, (Prov.) When gossips fall out, they tell bitter truths.

Comadrear [co-mah-dray-ar'], *vn.* To gossip, tattle.

Comadreja [co-mah-dray'-hah], *f.* Weasel. Mustela vulgaris. *Comadreja marina*, Weasel-blenny. Blennius mustelaris.

Comadrero, ra [co-mah-dray'-ro, rah], *a.* Gossiping from house to house.

Comadrón [co-mah-drone'], *m.* Man-midwife, accoucheur.

Comadrona [co-mah-dro'-nah], *f.* Midwife.

Comal [co-mahl'], *m.* (Mex.) A flat earthenware pan for cooking maize cake.

Comalía, Comalición [co-mah-lee'-ah, co-mah-le-the-on'], *f.* An epizootic disease, not contagious, among the wool-bearing animals, characterized by (chronic) dropsy.

Comandado, da, *a.* (Mil.) Officered. —*pp.* of Comandar.

Comandamiento [co-man-dah-me-en'-to], *m.* (Obs.) *V.* Mando and Mandamiento.

Comandancia [co-man-dahn'-the-ah], *f.* 1. Command, the office of a commander. 2. The province or district of a commander. *Comandancia militar*, A military command. *Comandancia general de Marina*, The High Court of Admiralty.

Comandante [co-man-dahn'-tay], *m.* Commander, a chief, a commandant, a leader. *Comandante en Jefe*, Commander-in-Chief.

Comandar [co-man-dar'], *va.* 1. To command, to govern. 2. (Obs.) To commend, to recommend.

Comandita [co-man-dee'-tah], *f.* A silent partnership.

Comanditario [co-man-de-tah'-re-o], *m.* A sleeping partner.

Comando [co-mahn'-do], *m.* 1. Command. 2. (Mil.) Commando.

Comarca [co-mar'-cah], *f.* 1. Territory, district. 2. Border, boundary, limit.

Comarcano, na [co-mar-cah'-no, nah], *a.* Neighbouring, near, bordering upon.

Comarcar [co-mar-car'], *va.* To plant trees in a straight line, so as to form walks.—*vn.* To border, to confine upon; to be on the borders.

Comato, ta [co-mah'-to, tah], *a.* *Cometa comato*, Hairy or comate comet.

Comatoso, sa [co-ma-to'-so, sah], *a.* Comatose, in a profound stupor.

Comaya [co-mah'-yah], *f.* 1. A large basket, a pannier. 2. (Orn.) The white owl, or barn owl. Strix flammea, *L.* *V.* Zumaya.

Comba [com'-bah], *f.* 1. Curvature or inflexion of timber when warped, or iron when bent; a curve, a bend; convexity. 2. The play of jumping or skipping rope. 3. The skipping-rope itself. *Hacer combas*, To bend and twist the body from one side to the other.

Combadura [com-bah-doo'-rah], *f.* Curvature, convexity, warping, bending.

Combar [com-bar'], *va.* To bend, to curve. — *vr.* To warp, to become crooked, to jut.

Combate [com-bah'-tay], *m.* 1. Combat, conflict, engagement, fray, fight. 2. Agitation of the mind.

Combatidor [com-bah-te-dor'], *m.* Combatant, champion.

Combatiente [com-bah-te-en'-tay], *m.* & *pa.* Combatant, fighter.

Combatir [com-bah-teer'], *va.* & *vn.* 1. To combat, to fight. 2. To contend, to contest, to meet or meet with. 3. To attack, to invade. 4. To contradict, conflict with. 5. (Met.) To agitate the mind, to rouse the passions. *Combatir a la retreta*, (Naut.) To keep up a running fight.

Combatividad [com-ba-te-ve-dahd'], *f.* (Phren.) Combativeness.

Combeneficiado [com-bay-nay-fe-the-ah'-do], *m.* Prebendary of the same church as another.

Combés [com-bess'], *m.* (Naut.) Waist of a ship.

Combinable [com-be-nah'-blay], *a.* Combinable.

Combinación [com-be-nah-the-on'], *f.* 1. Combination. 2. Aggregate of several words which begin with the same syllable. 3. Concurrence. 4. (Chem.) A compound.

Combinar [com-be-nar'], *va.* 1. To combine, to join, to unite, to connect. 2. To compare.

Combinatorio, ria [com-be-nah-to'-re-o, ah], *a.* Combining, uniting.

Combo, ba [com'-bo, bah], *a.* Bent, crooked, warped.

Combo [com'-bo], *m.* Stand or frame for casks.

Combustibilidad [com-boos-te-be-le-dahd'], *f.* Combustibility.

Combustible [com-boos-tee'-blay], *a.* Combustible.

Combustible [com-boos-tee'-blay], *m.* 1. Combustible, a combustible material. 2. Fuel. *Combustible de alta potencia*, Exotic fuel.

Combustión [com-boos-te-on'], *f.* Combustion, burning.

Combusto, ta [com-boos'-to, tah], *a.* (Obs.) Burnt. *V.* Abrasado.

Comedero [co-may-day'-ro], *m.* 1. Dining-room. 2. A feeding-trough for fowls and other animals. *Limpiarle a uno el comedero*, To take away one's means of living.

Comedero, ra [co-may-day'-ro, rah], *a.* Eatable, edible.

Comedia [co-may'-de-ah], *f.* Comedy, *Es una comedia*, It is a complete farce: applied to ridiculous speeches or actions. *Comedia de enredo*, That whose merit consists principally in the ingenuity and complexity of the plot.

Comedianta [co-may-de-ahn'-tah], *f.* *V* Actriz. Comedienne.

Comediante [co-may-de-ahn'-tay], *m.* Player, actor, comedian. *Comediante de la legua*, Strolling player.

Comediar [co-may-de-ar'], *va.* 1. To divide into equal shares. 2. (Obs.) To regulate, to direct.

Comédico ca [co-may'-de-co, cah], *a.* (Obs.) Comical. *V.* Cómico.

Comedidamente [co-may-de-dah-men'-tay], *adv.* Gently, courteously.

Comedido, da [co-may-dee'-do, dah], *a.* 1. Civil, polite, gentle, courteous. 2. Kind, obsequious, obliging.—*pp.* of Comedirse.

Comedimiento [co-may-de-me-en'-to], *m.* 1. Civility, politeness, urbanity. 2. Kindness, obsequiousness.

Comedio [co-may'-de-o], *m.* 1. Middle of a kingdom or place. 2. Intermediate time between epochs.

Comedión [co-may-de-on'], *m.* A poor or long and tedious comedy.

Comedirse [co-may-deer'-say], *vr.* To govern one's self, to regulate one's conduct, to be civil, obliging, kind.

Comedor, ra [co-may-dor', rah], *m.* & *f.* 1. Eater: applied to persons who devour much meat; feeder. 2. *m.* Dining-room.

Comején [co-may-hen'], *m.* 1. Kind of termite or white ant, very destructive to houses and their contents in tropical America. Termes fatale. 2. A sort of wood-borer which pierces pipe-staves.

Comelina [co-may-lee'-nah], *f.* (Bot.) Commelina, a large genus of herbs of the spiderwort family.

Comendable [co-men-dah'-blay], *a.* (Littl. us.) Commendable. *V.* RECOMENDABLE.

Comendador [co-men-dah-dor'], *m.* 1. Knight commander of a military order. 2. Prelate or prefect of religious houses.

Comendadora [co-men-dah-do'-rah], *f.* The superior of a nunnery of a military order, and also of other nunneries.

Comendamiento [co-men-dah-me-en'-to], *m.* (Obs.) *V.* ENCOMIENDA and MANDAMIENTO.

Comendar [co-men-dar'], *va.* (Obs.) *V.* RECOMENDAR.

Comendatario [co-men-dah-tah'-re-o], *m.* Commendator, commendatary, a secular clergyman who enjoys a benefice belonging to a military order.

Comendaticio, cia [co-men-dah-tee'-the-o, ah], *a.* Applied to letters or patents given by prelates recommending their subjects: sometimes used as a substantive.

Comendatorio, ria [co-men-dah-to'-re-o, ah], *a.* Relating to letters of introduction or recommendation.

Comendero [co-men-day'-ro], *m.* He who enjoys a benefice on condition of swearing allegiance to the king of Spain.

Comensal [co-men-sahl'], *com.* Commensal, one that eats at the same table. *V.* CONMENSAL.

Comensalía [co-men-sah-lee'-ah], *f.* Fellowship of house and table.

Comentador, ra [co-men-tah-dor', rah], *m.* & *f.* 1. Commentator, expositor, annotator, expounder, glosser. 2. (Obs.) Inventor of falsehoods.

Comentar [co-men-tar'], *va.* To comment, to explain, to expound, to gloss.

Comentario [co-men-tah'-re-o], *m.* 1. A commentary. 2. Commentary, an historical work written in a familiar manner.

Comento [co-men'-to], *m.* Comment, exposition, or explanation of some writing or circumstance.

Comenzador [co-men-thah-dor'], *m.* (Obs.) One who commences a thing.

Comenzamiento [co-men-thah-me-en'-to], *m.* (Obs.) *V.* PRINCIPIO.

Comenzante [co-men-than'-tay], *pa.* (Obs.) Beginning; beginner.

Comenzar [co-men-thar'], *va.* To commence, to begin.

Comer [co-merr'], *va.* 1. To eat, to chew or swallow any thing, to feed. 2. To dine. 3. (Coll.) To be in possession of an income. *Fulano se come tres mil libras esterlinas de renta,* He has or spends three thousand pounds a year. 4. To run through a fortune. 5. To have an itching all over the body. 6. *vr.* To suppress some letter or syllable in the pronunciation of words. 7. (Met.) To corrode, to consume. *El orín come el hierro,* The rust corrodes the iron. 8. *Comerse una dama,* To take a queen in the game of chess. *Comerse un peón,* To take a pawn in the same game. *Comer á dos carrillos,* 1. To enjoy two places or benefices at the same time. 2. To trim, to please two persons of opposite principles. *Comer de mogollón,* To live at other people's expense. *Comerse de risa,* To refrain from laughing. *Comerse los codos de hambre,* (Met.) To be starved with hunger. *Comerse unos a otros,* (Met.) To be constantly at drawn daggers. *Comerse a uno con los ojos.* To look daggers at any one. *El comer y el rascar, todo es empezar,* (proverb) to encourage one to begin something to which he has a repugnance. *¿En qué bodegón hemos comido juntos?* Where have we eaten together? (a rebuke for undue familiarity). *Tener que comer,* To have a competency to live upon. *Ganar de comer,* To earn a livelihood. *Comer pan con corteza,* (Met.) To be independent; to have a sufficiency. *Comer como un sabañón,* To eat excessively. *Con su pan se lo coma,* (Prov.) As you make your bed, so you must lie; that is his own affair.

Comer [co-merr'], *m.* (Obs.) *V.* COMIDA.

Comerciable [co-mer-the-ah'-blay], *a.* 1. Merchantable, marketable. 2. Sociable, social, affable.

Comercial [co-mer-the-ahl'], *a.* Commercial, trading.

Comercialmente [co-mer-the-al-men'-tay], *adv.* Commercially.

Comerciante [co-mer-the-ahn'-tay], *m.* & *pa.* Trader, merchant, trafficker.

Comerciar [co-mer-the-ar'], *va.* 1. To trade, to traffic. 2. (Met.) To commerce, to have intercourse with: applied to persons and places.

Comercio [co-merr'-the-o], *m.* 1. Trade, commerce, traffic; mart. 2. Communication, intercourse. 3. An unlawful connection between the sexes. 4. Body or company of merchants. 5. The most frequented place in large towns. 6. A kind of game at cards.

Comestible [co-mes-tee'-blay], *a.* Eatable, edible. **Comestibles,** *m. pl.* Provisions, groceries. *Tienda de comestibles,* Grocery store.

Cometa [co-may'-tah], *m.* 1. Comet. *Cometa comado* or *crinito,* Hairy comet.—*f.* 2. Kite, a plaything for boys. 3. Kind of game at cards, in which the nine of diamonds is called *cometa.* 4. (Her.) Allegorical figure in form of a star. 5. (Zool.) A longicorn beetle of Brazil.

Cometario, ia [co-may-tah'-re-o, ah], *a.* Relating to comets, cometary.

Cometedor [co-may-tay-dor'], *m.* 1. Offender, a criminal. 2. Assaulter. *V.* ACOMETEDOR.

Cometer [co-may-terr'], *va.* 1. To commit, to charge, to intrust. 2. To undertake, to attempt. 3. (Obs.) To attack, to assault. 4. To commit some criminal act or error. 5. (Gram.) To use tropes and figures. 6. (Com.) To order.—*vr.* 1. (Obs.) To expose one's self. 2. To take something to one's charge. 3. To commit one's self, make a mistake.

Cometido [co-may-tee'-do], *m.* Commission, charge, trust.

Cometografía [co-may-to-grah'-fee-ah], *f.* Cometography.

Comezón [co-may-thone'], *f.* 1. Itch or itching. 2. (Met.) The anxiety or trouble of mind produced by a longing desire.

Cómicamente [co'-me-cah-men-tay], *adv.* Comically.

Comicial [co-me-the-ahl'], *a.* Pertaining to the Roman comitia; comitial.

Comicios [co-mee'-the-ose), *m. pl.* 1. Comitia, Roman assembly. 2. Government elections, voting.

Cómico, ca [co'-me-co, cah], *a.* 1. Comic, comical, relating to the stage. 2. Comic, comical, ludicrous, funny, mock.

Cómico, *m.* **Cómica,** *f.* 1. Player, actor, comedian. *V.* COMEDIANTE. 2. (Obs.) Comedian, a writer of comedies.

Comida [co-mee'-dah], *f.* 1. Eating, food, dressed victuals. 2. Dinner; fare, feed. 3. The board. *Comida y alojamiento* or *asistencia,* Board and lodging. *Hacer una buena comida,* To make a good meal. *Comida hecha, compañía deshecha,* The meal eaten, the company deserted (i. e. to desert those from whom no more is to be expected).

Comidilla [co-me-deel'-lyah], *f.* 1. (Dim.) A slight repast. 2. Peculiar pleasure afforded by something which strikes our fancy.

Comido, da [co-mee'-do, dah], *a.* Satiate, full to satiety. *Comido por servido,* Meat for work: signifying the small value of any employ.—*pp.* of COMER.

(*Yo me comido, él se comidió,* from *Comedirse. V.* PEDIR.)

Comienzo [co-me-en'-tho], *m.* (Obs.) Origin, beginning, initiation. *A* or *de comienzo,* From the beginning.

(*Yo comienzo, yo comience,* from *Comenzar. V.* ACERTAR.)

Comilitón [co-me-le-tone'], *m.* Parasite, sponger. *V.* CONMILITÓN.

Comilitona, Comilona [co-me-le-to'-nah, co-me-lo'-nah], *f.* (Coll.) A splendid and plentiful repast.

Comilón, na [co-me-lone', nah], *m.* & *f.* A great eater, a glutton.

Comilla [co-meel'-lyah], *f.* Dim. fr. COMA.—*pl.* Quotation-marks (" "). Also guiding-marks („ „ „). (Acad.)

Cominear [co-me-nay-ar'], *vn.* (Coll.) To meddle in trifles or occupations belonging to women: said of a man.

Cominero [co-me-nay'-ro], *a.* Meddlesome, officious.—*n.* Cotquean, one who busies himself in the small matters of women.

Cominillo [co-me-neel'-lyo], *m.* Darnel. *V.* JOYO.

Comino [co-mee'-no], *m.* (Bot.) Cumin plant, cumin-seed. Cuminum cyminum. *Cominos,* Cumin-seed. *No vale* or *no monta un comino,* It is not worth a rush. *No se me da un comino,* (Coll.) I don't value it a rush. *Partir el comino,* To split a hair, to be niggardly.

Comisar [co-me-sar'], *va.* To confiscate, to declare a thing confiscated; to sequestrate, attach.

Comisaría [co-me-sah-ree'-ah], *f.* **Comisariato,** *m.* Commissaryship, commissariat.

Comisario [co-me-sah'-re-o], *m.* Commissary, delegate, deputy, manager. *Comisario de entradas,* In some hospitals, the person charged with taking an account of the patients who enter. *Comisarios de la inquisición,* Commissaries of the inquisition, agents of the inquisitors in the different towns of the kingdom. *Comisario de cuartel* or *de barrio,* Justice of the peace of a ward. *Comisario ordenador,* Quarter-master.

Comisión [co-me-se-on'], *f.* 1. Trust, commission, warrant by which a trust is held. 2. Mandate, charge, precept, or commission sent or transmitted; ministration, ministry. 3. Commission, perpetration, act of committing a crime. *Pecado de comisión,* A sin of commission. 4. Commission, committee. *Comisión de preparativos y disposiciones,* Committee of arrangements.

Comisionado, da [co-me-se-o-nah'-do, dah], *a.* & *pp.* of COMISIONAR. 1. Commissional or commissionary. 2. Commissioned, deputed, empowered. —*m.* & *f.* 1. Commissioner. 2. (Com.) Agent, proxy.

Comisionar [co-me-se-o-nar'], *va.* To commission, to depute, to empower, to appoint.
Comisionista [co-me-se-o-nees'-tah], *m.* 1. Commissioner. 2. Commission merchant. 3. Commission agent.
Comiso [co-mee'-so], *m.* 1. (Law) Confiscation of prohibited goods, and the goods when confiscated. 2. (Com.) Seizure, attachment.
Comisorio, ria [co-me-so'-re-o, ah], *a.* Obligatory for a time or valid for a fixed day.
Comistión [co-mis-te-on'], *f.* *V.* Conmistión.
Comistrajo [co-mis-trah'-ho], *m.* (Coll.) Hodge-podge, a medley of eatables.
Comisura [co-me-soo'-rah], *f.* (Anat.) Commissure, suture.
Comital [co-me-tahl'], *a.* *V.* Condal.
Cómite [co'-me tay], *m.* (Obs.) Count. *V.* Conde.
Comitente [co-me-ten'-tay], *pa.* Constituent.
Comitiva [co-me-tee'-vah], *f.* Suite, retinue, followers.
Cómitre [co'-me-tray], *m.* (Naut.) 1. Boatswain on board a galley. 2. A sea-captain under orders of the admiral of the fleet.
Comiza [co-mee'-thah], *f.* (Zool.) A kind of barbel.
Como [co'-mo], *adv.* 1. How, in what manner, to what degree. *¿ Cómo estamos de cosecha?* How is the harvest? 2. As, in a sense of comparison, e. g. *Es tan fuerte como un león,* He is as strong as a lion. 3. Why? *¿ Cómo no has venido más presto?* Why did you not come sooner? 4. In such a manner. *Hago como tú haces,* I do as you do. 5. In what manner. *Diga Vd. como hemos llegado,* Please to relate in what condition we arrived. 6. If. *Como ello sea bueno,* If it be good. 7. Like, in the same manner, in the same manner as. 8. So that. 9. Used in a causal sense it precedes *que.* 10. Used with the subjunctive it is equivalent to the gerund of the same verb. *Dar como* or *dar un como,* (Coll.) To play a trick, to joke. *Como así me lo quiero,* As easy as I could wish. *Como quiera que sea,* However, at any rate. *Como quiera,* However, notwithstanding, nevertheless, yet: used with the negative *no. Como quiera que,* Notwithstanding that, although, yet, howsoever. *Como* used interrogatively or as an exclamation receives the accent: *cómo.*
Cómoda [co'-mo-dah], *f.* A chest of drawers, bureau.
Comodable [co-mo-dah'-blay], *a.* That which can be lent or borrowed.
Cómodamente [co'-mo-dah-men-tay], *adv.* Conveniently, commodiously, comfortably.
Comodante [co-mo-dahn'-tay], *m.* (For.) One who lends gratuitously for a limited time.
Comodatario [co-mo-dah-tah' re-o], *m.* (Law) 1. Borrower. 2. Pawnbroker.
Comodato [co-mo-dah'-to], *m.* (Law) Loan; a contract of loan and restitution at a stipulated time.
Comodidad [co-mo-de-dahd'], *f.* 1. Comfort, convenience, accommodation. 2. Convenience, ease, or cause of ease, freedom from want. 3. Leisure; opportunity. 4. Profit, interest, advantage.
Comodín [co-mo-deen'], *m.* (Coll.) Something of general utility. In cards, to make a suit.
Cómodo [co'-mo-do], *m.* Utility, profit, convenience.
Cómodo, da [co'-mo-do, dah], *a.* Convenient, commodious, suitable, comfortable.
Comodoro [co-mo-do'-ro], *m.* Commodore (fr. Eng.).
Comorar [co-mo-rar'], *vn.* (Obs.) To cohabit, to live together
Compaciente [com-pah-the-en'-tay], *a.* (Obs.) *V.* Compasivo.
Compacto, ta [com-pac'-to, tah], *a.* Compact, close, dense.
Compadecerse [com-pah-day-therr'-say], *vr.* 1. To pity, to be compassionate. In this sense it is now very often used in an active sense, as *Compadezco a Vd.,* I pity you, I feel for you, I commiserate your distress. 2. To agree with each other.
(*Yo me compadezco, yo me compadezca,* from *Compadecerse. V.* Conocer.)
Compadraje [com-pah-drah'-hay], *m.* A mutual admiration society: generally used in bad part.
Compadrar [com-pah-drar'], *vn.* To become a godfather or mother, to contract a spiritual affinity.
Compadrazgo [com-pah-drath'-go], *m.* Gossipred or compaternity, by the canon law, is a spiritual affinity, or connection contracted by a godfather with the parents of a child for which he stands sponsor.
Compadre [com-pah'-dray], *m.* 1. Godfather, the word by which the godfather and godmother address the father of their godson or daughter, and by which the father and mother address him. 2. Protector, benefactor. 3. Friend: used in Andalusia when casually addressing a person. *Jueves de compadres,* The last Thursday before Shrove-Tuesday. *Arrepásate acá, compadre,* Puss in the corner, a children's game.
Compadrería [com-pah-dray-ree'-ah], *f.* Friendly intercourse between godfathers, friends, or companions.
Compage [com-pah'-hay], *f.* (Obs.) Compages, a system of many parts united.
Compaginación [com-pah-he-nah-the-on'], *f.* Compagination, union, structure.
Compaginador [com-pah-he-nah-dor'], *m.* One who joins, unites, or couples.
Compaginar [com-pah-he-nar'], *va.* To join, to unite, to couple, to compact, to compaginate.
Companage [com-pah-nah'-hay], *m.* A cold lunch; bread, cheese, raisins, etc.
Compango, *m.* *V.* Companage.
Compaña [com-pah'-nyah], *f.* (Obs.) 1. Out-house, office. 2. Company of soldiers. 3. Family. 4. Company.
Compañería [com-pah-nyay-ree'-ah], *f.* *V.* Mancebía.
Compañerismo [com pah-nyay-rees'-mo], *m.* Harmony, good-fellowship.
Compañero, ra [com-pah-nyay'-ro, rah], *m. & f.* 1. Companion, friend, consort, an equal, a match, a compeer, a mate, one with whom a person frequently converses; fellow. 2. *Compañero de cuarto,* Chamber-fellow; chum, a chamber-fellow in the universities. 3. Comrade, colleague, fellow-member, condisciple. 4. Partner, associate, coadjutor. 5. Follower, one who shares the lot and fortune of another. 6. One thing suited to another. *Buen barco compañero,* (Naut.) A ship that does not part company with the convoy.
Compañía [com-pah-nyee'-ah], *f.* 1. Company or society of persons, an assembly or meeting together, fellowship. 2. Partnership, fellowship; copartnership, company. 3. Company, troop, a body of soldiers. 4. Company, a number of players. *Compañía de la legua,* A strolling company of players. 5. Company, conversation of a companion. 6. (Obs.) Family, confederacy. *Compañía de Jesús,* Order of Jesuits, founded by Ignatius de Loyola.
Compaño, Compañón [com-pah'-nyo], *m.* (Obs.) *V.* Compañero.
Compañón [com-pah-nyone'], *m.* Testicle. *V.* Testículo.
Comparable [com-pah-rah'-blay], *a.* Comparable.
Comparación [com-pah-rah-the-on'], *f.* 1. Comparison, conference. 2. Compare; collation, conferring.
Comparador [com-pah-rah-dor'], *m.* An instrument serving to show the smallest difference in the length of two rules; comparing-rule.
Comparanza [com-pah-rahn'-thah], *f.* (Coll.) *V.* Comparación.
Comparar [com-pah-rar'], *va.* To compare, to estimate, to confront, to confer, to collate.
Comparativamente [com-pah-rah-te-vah-men'-tay], *adv.* Comparatively.
Comparativo, va [com-pah-rah-tee'-vo, vah], *a.* 1. Comparative. 2. Comparative, a degree of comparison in grammar.
Comparecencia [com-pah-ray-then'-the-ah], *f.* Appearance before a judge.
Comparecer [com-pah-ray-therr'], *vn.* To appear before a judge.
Compareciente [com-pah-ray-the-en'-tay], *pa.* of Comparecer.
Comparendo [com-pah-ren'-do], *m.* Summons, citation, admonition to appear.
(*Yo comparezco, yo comparezca,* from *Comparecer.*)
Comparición [com-pah-re-the-on'], *f.* (Law) Appearance.
Comparsa [com-par'-sah], *f.* 1. Retinue of personages represented on the stage. 2. A party composed of persons masked and costumed as students, Moors, soldiers, etc.
Comparte [com-par'-tay], *m. & f.* (Law) Joint party or accomplice in a civil or criminal cause.
Compartimiento [com-par-te-me-en'-to], *m.* 1. Compartment, the division of a whole into proportionate parts. 2. Inclosure, department. *Compartimiento interior de un navío,* Accommodations on board a ship. *Compartimiento de guantes,* Glove compartment.
Compartir [com-par-teer'], *va.* 1. To compart or divide into equal parts. 2. (Art) To arrange or dispose the different parts of a painting.
Compás [com-pahs'], *m.* 1. Pair of compasses, a mathematical instrument. *Compás de calibre* or *de puntas curvas,* Calipers or compasses with bowed or arched limbs, to take the diameter of convex or concave bodies. *Compases de grueso,* Calipers. *Compás de proporción,* Proportional compasses. *V.* Pantómetra. *Compás de relojero,* Clock-maker's compass. *Compás de azimuth,* Azimuth compass. 2. A territory and district assigned to a monastery. 3. Power of the voice to express the notes of music. 4. Measure, time in music. *Echar el compás,* To beat time. *A compás,* in right musical time. 5. Motion of the hand of a conductor of an orchestra. 6. Measure, the space upon the staff between two bars. 7. Size, compass. 8. (Met.) Rule of life, principle to be governed by, pattern. *Echar el compás,* (Met.) To direct, to regulate, to govern. *Salir de compás,* (Met. Obs.) To act without rule or measure.

Vivir or *proceder con compás*, To live or act within bounds. 9. *Compás de muelle*, Spring compass. Springs of metal to raise or lower a coach-roof. 10. *Compás de mar*, Mariner's compass. *V.* Brújula and Bitácora. 11. *Compás mixto*, (Fenc.) Mixed movement, partly direct and partly curved; a feint. *Compás trepidante*, (Fenc.) Motion or movement in a right line.

Compasadamente [com-pah-sah-da-men'-tay], *adv.* By rule and measure.

Compasar [com-pah-sar'], *va.* 1. To measure with a rule and compass. 2. (Met.) To regulate things so that there may be neither too much nor too little. 3. (Mus.) To divide a musical composition into equal parts. 4. *Compasar una carta de marear*, (Naut.) To prick the chart—that is, to trace the course of a ship on a chart.

Compasible [com-pah-see'-blay], *a.* 1. Lamentable, deserving pity. 2. Compassionate.

Compasillo [com-pah-seel'-lyo], *m.* Quick musical time.

Compasión [com-pah-se-on'], *f.* Compassion, pity, commiseration, mercifulness.

Compasivo, va [com-pah-see'-vo, vah], *a.* Compassionate, merciful, tender-hearted, humane.

Compaternidad [com-pah-ter-ne-dahd'], *f.* *V.* Compadrazgo.

Compatía [com-pah-tee'-ah], *f.* (Obs.) Sympathy, fellow-feeling.

Compatibilidad [com-pah-te-be-le-dahd'], *f.* Compatibility, consistency, conjuncture.

Compatible [com-pah-tee'-blay], *a.* Compatible, suitable to, fit for, consistent with.

Compatricio [com-pah-tree'-the-o], or **Compatriota** [com-pah-tre-o'-tah], *com.* Countryman or countrywoman, compatriot, fellow-citizen.

Compatrioto [com-pah-tre-oh'-to], *m.* (Obs.) *V.* Compatriota.

Compatrón [com-pah-trone'], *m.* *V.* Compatrono.

Compatronato [com-pah-tro-nah'-to], *m.* Common right of patronage, the right of conferring a benefice in common with another.

Compatrono, na [com-pah-tro'-no, nah], *m.* & *f.* Fellow-patron or patroness, joint-patron.

Compeler, Compelir (Obs.) [com-pay-lerr', com-pay-leer'], *va.* 1. To compel, to constrain. 2. To extort.

Compendiador [com-pen-de-ah-dor'], *m.* Epitomizer, abridger.

Compendiar [com-pen-de-ar'], *va.* To epitomize, to shorten, to abridge, to extract, to contract; to cut short.

Compendiariamente, *adv.* *V* Compendiosamente.

Compendio [com-pen'-de-o], *m.* Compendium, epitome, abridgment, summary, compend, abstract.

Compendiosamente [com-pen-de-o-sah-men'-tay], *adv.* Briefly, compendiously, in a concise manner.

Compendioso, sa [com-pen-de-o'-so, sah], *a.* Brief, abridged, compendious, laconic or laconical, compact.

Compendizar [com-pen-de-thar'], *va.* *V.* Compendiar.

Compensable [com-pen-sah'-blay], *a.* Compensable.

Compensación [com-pen-sah-the-on'], *f.* 1. Compensation, recompense. 2. Handicap (in sports events). 3. (Com.) Clearing. *Bolsa* or *banco de compensación*, Clearing house.

Compensador [com-pen-sah-dor'], *m.* Compensator, a mechanical device of two or more metals to counteract the effect of variations of temperature

Compensar [com-pen-sar'], *va.* & *vn.* 1. To compensate, to recompense, to counterbalance, to countervail. 2. To make amends, to make up. *Los malos años se compensan con los buenos*, Good years make amends for bad ones. 3. To enjoy an equivalent for any loss or injury, to compensate.

Competencia [com-pay-ten'-the-ah], *f.* 1. Competition, rivalry, contest, contention. 2. Competence, cognizance, the power or competency of a court or judge. 3. Incumbency. 4. Aptitude, fitness. *A competencia*, Contentiously, contestingly.

Competente [com-pay-ten'-tay], *a.* Competent, sufficient, fit for, consistent with, applicable to; adequate.

Competentemente [com-pay-ten-tay-men'-tay], *adv.* Competently.

Competer [com-pay-terr'], *vn.* To be one's due, to have a fair claim to something.

Competición [com-pay-te-the-on'], *f.* Competition, corrivalship. *V* Competencia.

Competidor, ra [com-pay-te-dor', rah], *m.* & *f.* Competitor, rival, opponent, contender; competitrix.

Competir [com-pay-teer'], *vn.* 1. To vie, to contest, to contend, to strive. 2. To stand in competition, to rival, to cope. 3. To be on a level or par with another.

Compiadarse [com-pe-ah-dar'-say], *vr.* (Obs.) *V.* Compadecerse.

Compilación [com-pe-lah-the-on'], *f.* 1. Compilation. 2. Compilement.

Compilador, ra [com-pe-lah-dor', rah], *m.* & *f.* Compiler, compilator, collector.

Compilar [com-pe-lar'], *va.* To compile.

Compinche [com-peen'-chay], *m.* (Coll.) Bosom-friend, comrade, confidant, crony.

(*Yo compito, yo compita*, from *Competir.* *V.* Pedir.)

Complacedero, ra [com-plah-thay-day'-ro, rah], *a.* *V.* Complaciente.

Complacencia [com-plah-then'-the-ah], *f.* Pleasure, satisfaction, gratification; complacency, compliance, condescence.

Complacer [com-plah-therr'], *va.* To please, to humour, to content.—*vr.* To be pleased with or take delight in a thing.

Complaciente [com-plah-the-en'-tay], *pa.* Pleasing, one who pleases.

Complañir [com-plah-nyeer'], *vn.* (Obs.) To weep; to be compassionate.

(*Yo complazco, yo complazca*, from *Complacer.* *V.* Conocer.)

Complejo, ja [com-play'-ho, hah], *a.* Complex. *V.* Complexo.

Complementario, ia [com-play-men-tah'-re-o, ah], *a.* Complementary, serving to complete.

Complemento [com-play-men'-to], *m.* Complement, perfection, accomplishment, completion; accomplishment. *Complemento de la derrota*, (Naut.) Complement of the course in navigation.

Completamente [com-play-tah-men'-tay], *adv.* Completely, perfectly, finally.

Completar [com-play-tar'], *va.* To complete, to perfect, to finish, to accomplish, to crown, to consummate, to make up.

Completas [com-play'-tas], *f. pl.* Completory, compline, the last of the canonical hours or evening prayers.

Completivamente, *adv.* *V.* Completivo.

Completivo, va [com-play-tee'-vo, vah], *a.* (Littl. us.) Completive, completory, absolute.

Completo, ta [com-play'-to, tah], *a.* Complete, perfect, finished; concluded; full, absolute; all-out; *Por completo*, Completely, totally.

Complexión [com-plek-se-on'], *f.* Constitution, temperament of the body, habit, nature.

Complexionado, da [com-plek-se-o-nah'-do, dah], *a.* Constituted. *Bien o mal complexionado*, Of a good or bad constitution.

Complexional [com-plek-se-o-nahl'], *a.* Constitutional, temperamental.

Complexo [com-plek'-so], *m.* Complex.

Complexo [com-plek'-so], *a.* 1. Arduous, difficult, complicated. 2. Complex, not simple; of several parts. 3. (Anat.) Applied to one of the muscles of the head.

Complicación [com-ple-cah-the-on'], *f.* Complication, complex, complexure.

Complicadamente, *adv.* *V.* Complicado.

Complicado, da, *a.* Complicate.—*pp.* of Complicar.

Complicar [com-ple-car'], *va.* To complicate, to jumble things together.

Cómplice [com'-ple-thay], *com.* Accomplice, co-operator, associate, complice, abetter, accessory.

Complicidad [com-ple-the-dahd'], *f.* Accessoriness, complicity.

Complidura [com-ple-doo'-rah], *f.* (Obs.) Convenient or correspondent quality or measure.

Complimiento [com-ple-me-en'-to], *m.* (Obs.) 1. Supply of provisions for a journey. 2. *V.* Fin.

Complot [com-plote'], *m.* Plot, conspiracy, a joint agreement to commit crime.

Complutense [com-ploo-ten'-say], *a.* & *n.* Native of or belonging to Alcalá de Henares.

Componedor, ra [com-po-nay-dor', rah], *m.* & *f.* 1. Composer, writer, author. 2. Arbitrator. 3. *m.* (Print.) Composing-stick.

Componenda [com-po-nen'-dah], *f.* Amount of fees paid in the papal chancery at Rome for such bulls and licenses as have no certain tax.

Componente, *pa.* Component.

Componer [com-po-nerr'], *va.* 1. To compose, to compound. 2. To construct. 3. To sum up. 4. To frame, to devise, to invent. 5. To mend, to repair, to heal, to restore. 6. To strengthen, to fortify, to restore. *Esa copa de vino me ha compuesto el estómago*, That glass of wine has strengthened my stomach. 7. To furnish, to fit up, to garnish. 8. To compose, to reconcile, to accommodate, to adjust, to settle, to compose differences. 9. To ward off a danger. 10. To compose, to calm, to quiet. 11. (Mus.) To note, to set down the notes of a tune, to form a tune. 12. To compose or compile a book. 13. To compose or write verses. *Fulano compone muy bien*, He writes very good verses. 14. (Print.) To compose types. *Componer el semblante*, To put on a calm or sedate appearance. *Componer tanto de renta*, To have so much a year.—*vr.* To deck one's self with clothes.

(*Yo compongo, él compuso, yo componga*, from *Componer.* *V.* Poner.)

Componible [com-po-nee'-blay], *a.* Compoundable, accommodable, mendable,

Componimiento [com-po-ne-me-en'-to], *m.* (Obs.) Disposition, order, distribution.

Comporta [com-por'-tah], *f.* (Prov.) A large basket in which grapes are carried during the vintage.
Comportable [com-por-tah'-blay], *a.* Supportable, tolerable.
Comportamiento [com-por-tah-me-en'-to], *m.* (Prov.) Behaviour.
Comportar [com-por-tar'], *va.* 1. (Obs.) To carry or bring together. 2. To suffer, to tolerate.—*vr.* To comport, to behave or conduct one's self.
Comporte [com-por'-tay], *m.* (Obs.) 1. *V.* SUFRIMIENTO. 2. Proceeding, conduct. 3. Air, manner.
Comportilla [com-por-teel'-lyah], *f. dim.* A small basket.
Composible, *a.* (Obs.) *V.* COMPONIBLE.
Composición [com-po-se-the-on'], *f.* 1. Composition, the act of composing something, composure, making up. 2. Composition of a difference, adjustment, agreement, compact. 3. A literary, scientific, or musical work. 4. (Print.) Arrangement of types. 5. Calm, modest, or sedate appearance.
Compositivo, va [com-po-se-tee'-vo, vah], *a.* Compositive, synthetic; used of a preposition or particle forming a compound word.
Compositor [com-po-se-tor'], *m.* 1. Composer of musical compositions. 2. (Print.) Compositor.
Compostura [com-pos-too'-rah], *f.* 1. Composition, composure. 2. Mending or repairing. 3. Cleanliness, neatness of dress. 4. Composition of a difference, composure, accommodation, adjustment, agreement, compact. 5. Modesty, circumspection, sedateness, composure. 6. A mixture with which something is adulterated.
Compota [com-po'-tah], *f.* Preserves, sweetmeats.
Compotera [com-po-tay'-rah], *f.* Vessel in which jams are served up for the table.
Compra [com'-prah], *f.* 1. Purchase. 2. Collection of necessaries bought for daily use. *Dar compra y véndida,* (Obs.) To permit trade.
Comprable [com-prah'-blay], *a.* Purchasable.
Comprada [com-prah' dah], *f.* (Obs.) *V.* COMPRA.
Compradero, ra [com-prah-day'-ro, rah], *a.* *V.* COMPRABLE.
Compradizo, za [com-prah-dee'-tho, thah], *a.* *V.* COMPRABLE.
Comprado, Compradillo [com-prah'-do, com-prah-deel'-lyo], *m.* Kind of play in the game of ombre.
Comprador, ra [com-prah-dor', rah], *m.* & *f.* 1. Buyer, purchaser. 2. Caterer.
Comprante [com-prahn'-tay], *pa.* Buyer, purchaser.
Comprar [com-prar'], *va.* To buy, to purchase; to chop; to lay in.
Compraventa [com-prah-ven'-tah]. *V.* CONTRATO DE COMPRAVENTA.
Comprendedor, ra [com-pren-day-dor', rah], *m.* & *f.* One who comprehends or understands.
Comprender [com-pren-derr'], *va.* 1. To embrace, to encircle, to comprehend. 2. To comprise, to include, to contain. 3. To comprehend, to understand, to conceive, to know.
Comprensibilidad [com-pren-se-be-le-dahd'], *f.* Comprehensibleness, comprehensibility.
Comprensible [com-pren-see'-blay], *a.* Comprehensible, conceivable.
Comprensiblemente, *adv.* (Littl. us.) Comprehensibly.
Comprensión [com-pren-se-on'], *f.* 1. Comprehension, comprisal, conceiving, conception. 2. Comprehensiveness. 3. Act of comprising or containing.
Comprensivo, va [com-pren-see'-vo, vah], *a.* 1. Comprehensive, having the power to comprehend. 2. Comprehensive, having the quality of comprising much.
Comprenso, *pp. irr.* of COMPRENDER.
Comprensor, ra [com-pren-sor', rah], *m.* & *f.* 1. (Theol.) The blessed, one who enjoys the presence of God in the heavenly mansions. 2. One that understands, attains, or embraces a thing.
Compresa [com-pray'-sah], *f.* Compress, folded linen put under a bandage.
Compresibilidad [com-pray-se-be-le-dahd'], *f.* Compressibility.
Compresible [com-pray-see'-blay], *a.* Compressible.
Compresión [com-pray-se-on'], *f.* 1. Compression, pressing together, compressure. 2. (Gram.) *V.* SINÉRESIS.
Compresivamente [com-pray-se-vah-men'-tay], *adv.* Compressibly, contractedly.
Compresivo, va [com-pray-see'-vo, vah], *a.* Compressive, compressing or reducing to a smaller compass.
Compreso, sa [com-pray'-so, sah], *pp. irr.* of COMPRIMIR.
Comprimible [com-pre-mee'-blay], *a.* 1. Compressible. 2. Repressible.
Comprimir [com-pre-meer'], *va.* 1. To compress; to constrain, to constringe; to condense. 2. To repress, to restrain, to keep in awe.—*vr.* To subdue one's passion.
Comprobación [com-pro-bah-the-on'], *f.* 1. Comprobation, attestation. 2. Comparison, verification of printer's proof corrections.
Comprobante [com-pro-bahn'-tay], *pa.* 1. Proving, one who proves. 2. Voucher, schedule, document.
Comprobar [com-pro-bar'], *va.* 1. To verify, to confirm by comparison. 2. To comprobate; to compare. 3. To prove, to give evidence.
Comprofesor [com-pro-fay-sor'], *m.* Colleague.
Comprometedor, ra [com-pro-may-tay-dor', rah], *m.* & *f.* Compromiser, one who compromises.
Comprometer [com-pro-may-terr'], *va.* 1. To compromise. 2. To engage, to bind by an appointment or contract; to render one accountable or answerable. 3. To expose, to put in danger.
Comprometido, da [com-pro-may-tee'-do, dah], *a.* 1. Obligated, obliged. 2. Engaged to be married. —*m.* & *f.* Fiancé, fiancée.
Comprometimiento [com-pro-may-te-me-en'-to], *m.* Compromise, a compact or adjustment.
Compromisario [com-pro-me-sah'-re-o], *m.* Arbitrator, umpire, compromiser, referee.
Compromiso [com-pro-mee'-so], *m.* 1. Compromise. 2. Arbitration bond. 3. Difficulty, embarrassment. 4. An obligation contracted. *Poner en compromiso,* To compromise, to render doubtful.
Compromisorio, ria [com-pro-me-so'-re-o, ah], *a.* (Littl. us.) Compromissorial.
Compropietario, ia [com-pro-pe-ay-tah'-re-o, ah], *m.* & *f.* & *a.* Joint owner, owning jointly with another, or others. *V.* COPROPIETARIO.
Comprotector [com-pro-tec-tor'], *m.* A joint protector.
Comprovincial [com-pro-vin-the-ahl'], *a.* Comprovincial, of the same metropolitan church: applied to a suffragan bishop.
(*Yo compruebo, yo compruebe,* from *Comprobar. V.* ACORDAR.)
Compuerta [com-poo-err'-tah], *f.* 1. Hatch or half-door. 2. Lock or sluice, flood-gate. 3. (Obs.) Curtain before the door of an old-fashioned coach. 4. *Compuerta de marea,* (Naut.) Tide-gate, tide-race. 5. A piece of cloth which formerly bore a knight's badge.
Compuestamente [com-poo-es-tah-men'-tay], *adv.* Regularly, orderly.
Compuesto [com-poo-es'-to], *m.* Compound, commixture, composition.
Compuesto, ta [com-poo-es'-to, tah], *a.* & *pp.* of COMPONER. Composed, compound, complex, made up; fresh, repaired. *Orden compuesto,* The composite order in architecture. *Flores compuestas,* Composite flowers; the family of Compositæ.
Compulsa [com-pool'-sah], *f.* (Law) An authentic or attested copy of some instrument or writing.
Compulsar [com-pool-sar'], *va.* 1. (Obs.) To compel, to force. 2. (Law) To make an authentic copy or transcript. 3. To compare, to collate.
Compulsión [com-pool-se-on'], *f.* 1. Compulsion, forcing. 2. Compulsion,
Compulsivo, va [com-pool-see'-vo, vah], *a.* Compulsive.
Compulso, sa [com-pool'-so, sah], *pp. irr.* of COMPELER.
Compulsorio, ria [com-pool-so'-re-o, ah], *a.* 1. Compulsory, compulsatory, compulsative. 2. Ordering an authentic copy to be made: applied to the decree of a judge or magistrate.
Compunción [com-poon-the-on'], *f.* Compunction, repentance, contrition.
Compungido, da [com-poon-hee'-do, dah], *a.* Compunctious.—*pp.* of COMPUNGIR.
Compungirse [com-poon-heer'-say], *vr.* To feel compunction, to be pierced with remorse.
Compungivo, va [com-poon-hee'-vo, vah], *a.* Compunctive, pricking, stinging.
Compurgación [com-poor-gah-the-on'], *f.* Compurgation.
Compurgador [com-poor-gah-dor'], *m.* Compurgator.
Compurgar [com-poor-gar'], *va.* To prove one's veracity or innocence by the oath of another.
Computable [com-poo-tah'-blay], *a.* (Littl. us.) Computable.
Computación [com-poo-tah-the-on'], *f.* Computation, manner of calculating time.
Computador, ra [com-poo-tah-dor', rah], *m.* & *f.* One who computes; a computer. *Computadora digital,* (Mech.) Digital computer.
Computar [com-poo-tar'], *va.* To compute, to estimate by years or ages.
Computista [com-poo-tees'-tah], *m.* Computist, computer, accountant.
Cómputo [com'-poo-to], *m.* Computation, calculation, account.
Comtos [com'-tose], *m. pl.* In Navarre, the exchequer board.
Comulación [co-moo-lah-the-on'], *f.* Cumulation. *V.* ACUMULACIÓN.
Comulgar [co-mool-gar'], *va.* To administer the holy Eucharist.—*vn.* To communicate or to receive the sacrament.
Comulgatorio [co-mool-gah-to'-re-o], *m.* Communion-altar.
Común [co-moon'], *a.* 1. Common. *Pastos comunes,* Common fields. 2. Common, usual, general, customary, ordinary, familiar, generally received. 3. Common, much used, frequent, current, habitual. 4. Vulgar, mean, low. *Por lo común,* In general, generally.
Común [co-moon'], *m.* 1. Community, public. 2. *V.* SECRETA. *En común,*

Conjointly, collectively. *Por lo común*, Commonly, frequently.

Comuna [co-moo'-nah], *f.* (Prov.) The principal canal of irrigation.

Comunal [co-moo-nahl'], *m.* Commonalty, common people.—*a.* Common, commonable.

Comunaleza [co-moo-nah-lay'-thah], *f.* (Obs.) 1. Mediocrity. 2. Communication, intercourse. 3. Common.

Comunero, ra [co-moo-nay'-ro, rah], *a.* 1. Popular, common, and pleasing to the people. 2. Commoner, one of the common people, as distinguished from the nobility.

Comunero, *m.* 1. A joint holder of a tenure of lands. 2. An individual of the party that upheld Spanish liberty against the encroachments of Charles V.

Comunicabilidad [co-moo-ne-cah-be-le-dahd'], *f.* Communicability.

Comunicable [co-moo-ne-cah'-blay], *a.* 1. Communicable. 2. Sociable, affable.

Comunicación [co-moo-ne-cah-the-on'], *f.* 1. Communication. 2. Communication, intercourse, converse. 3. Junction or union of one thing with another.

Comunicado [co-moo-ne-cah'-do], *m.* An article of a personal nature sent to a periodical for publication.

Comunicante [co-moo-ne-cahn'-tay], *pa.* Communicating; a communicant.

Comunicar [co-moo-ne-car'], *va.* 1. To communicate, to impart, to extend, to discover or make known. 2. To communicate with another either by word or writing. 3. To consult or confer upon a subject. 4. (Obs.) To communicate, to take the Lord's Supper. —*vr.* To be joined, united, or contiguous to each other. *Comunicarse entre sí*, To interchange sentiments or ideas.

Comunicativo, va [co-moo-ne-cah-tee'-vo, vah], *a.* Communicative, liberal, not reserved.

Comunicatorio, ria [co-moo-ne-cah-to'-re-o, ah], *a.* (Littl. us.) That which must be communicated, notified, or published.

Comunidad [co-moo-ne-dahd'], *f.* 1. Commonness. 2. Commonalty, the common people. 3. Community, corporation, guild, society. *De comunidad*, Conjointly, collectively. 4. The cities of Castile, which at the beginning of the reign of Charles V. rose against his government, in support of Spanish liberty.

Comunión [co-moo-ne-on'], *f.* 1. Communion, fellowship, common possession. 2. Familiar intercourse. 3. Communion, the act of receiving the blessed sacrament. 4. Congregation of persons who profess the same religious faith.

Comunismo [co-moo-nees'-mo], *m.* Communism, the doctrine of the community of property.

Comunista [co-moo-nees'-tah], *m.* Communist, an advocate of communism.

Comunistoide [co-moo-nees-toy'-day], *m.* Fellow traveller, communist sympathizer.

Comunmente [co-moon-men'-tay], *adv.* 1. Commonly, customarily, usually, generally. 2. Frequently, often.

Comuña [co-moo'-nyah], *f.* 1. Mixed grain, as wheat and rye, mashlim, or meslin. 2. In Asturias, the dividend or equal share of the produce of lands, and the contracts or agreements between rich proprietors and the poor. *Comuña a armún*, In Asturias, the contract by which a valued herd of cattle is intrusted to another, on condition that he enjoys the milk, butter, and cheese for his trouble of keeping the cattle. *Comuña a la ganancia*, Contract by which a herd of cattle is intrusted to another by a fair appraisement, on condition that, after the capital has been refunded, the profit is to be divided between them. *Comuñas*, Seeds. *V.* Camuñas.

Con [cone], *prep.* 1. With, by. *Con declarar se eximió del tormento*, By confessing, he freed himself from the torture. 2. Although. *Con tal que* or *con que*, So that, provided that, on condition that. *Yo lo haré, con tal que*, etc., I will do it, provided that, etc. 3. *Con que*, Then, so then. *Con que Vd. ha hecho esto*, You have then done this. *Con todo* or *con todo eso*, Nevertheless, notwithstanding. *Con que vámonos*, Well, then, let us go. *Con que, a Dios, señoras*, Then good-by, ladies. *Con que sí, con que no*, Shilly-shally.

Con que, *m.* (Coll.) Condition, stipulation, circumstance.

Conato [co-nah'-to], *m.* 1. Conatus, endeavour, effort, exertion. 2. (Law) Crime attempted but not executed. *Conato de hurto*, Attempt at robbery.

Conaviero [co-nah-ve-ay'-ro], *m.* (Littl. us.) Copartner, or part owner in a ship.

Conca, *f.* (Obs.) *V.* Cuenca.

Concadenar [con-cah-day-nar'], *va.* (Met.) To concatenate; to chain or link together.

Concambio [con-cahm'-be-o], *m.* Exchange. *V.* Cambio.

Concanónigo [con-ca-no'-ne-go], *m.* A fellow-canon.

Concatedralidad [con-cah-tay-drah-le-dahd'], *f.* Union of two cathedral churches.

Concatenación [con-cah-tay-nah-the-on'], *f.* Concatenation.

Concausa [con-cah'-oo-sah], *f.* Concause, joint cause.

Cóncava, Concavidad [con'-cah-vah], *f.* Concavity, hollowness, hollow.

Cóncavo, va [con'-cah-vo, vah], *a.* Concave, hollow.

Cóncavo [con'-cah-vo], *m.* Concavity. *V.* Concavidad.

Concebible [con-thay-bee'-blay], *a.* (Obs.) *V.* Comprensible.

Concebimiento [con-thay-be me-en'-to], *m.* (Obs.) Conception.

Concebir [con-thay-beer'], *va.* & *vn.* 1. To conceive, to become pregnant. 2. To conceive, to imagine, to have an idea of. 3. To conceive, to comprehend, to think, to understand; to look on. *La cláusula está concebida en estos términos*, The clause is expressed in these terms.

Concedente [con-thay-den'-tay], *pa.* Conceding, one who concedes.

Conceder [con-thay-derr'], *va.* 1. To give, to grant, to bestow a boon or gift. 2. To concede, to allow, to grant, to admit.

Concedido, da [con-thay-dee'-do, dah], *a.* & *pp.* of Conceder. Conceded, granted. *Dado y no concedido*, Admitted but not agreed.

Concejal [con-thay-hahl'], *m.* Member of a council or board.

Concejal [con-thay-hahl'], *a.* Relating to public boards or councils.

Concejil [con-thay-heel'], *m.* 1. An alderman, or member of a corporation. 2. (Prov.) Foundling, a child found without parent or owner.

Concejil, *a.* Common, public, belonging to the public.

Concejo [con-thay'-ho], *m.* 1. The civic body of a small town or village, and the house where its members hold their meetings. 2. In Asturias, a district composed of several parishes with one common jurisdiction. 3. Foundling. *Concejo abierto*, A meeting of the inhabitants of a small town or village presided over by the *alcalde*, to deliberate upon public affairs.

Concelebrar [con-thay-lay-brar'], *va.* To celebrate jointly, together.

Concento [con-then'-to], *m.* 1. Concord, a concert of voices; harmony. 2. Metre, verse, cadence.

Concentración [con-then-trah-the-on' *f.* Concentration.

Concentrado, da [con-then-trah'-do, dah], *a.* Concentred, tending to the centre.—*pp.* of Concentrar.

Concentrar [con-then-trar'], *va.* (Littl. us.) To concentrate, to concentre. *V.* Reconcentrar.

Concéntrico, ca [con-then'-tre-co, cah], *a.* Concentric, concentrical.

Concepción [con-thep-the-on'], *f.* 1. Conception, the act of conceiving. 2. Conception, idea, comprehension, conceit, image in the mind, fancy.

Conceptáculo [con-thep-tah'-coo-lo], *m.* 1. Conceptacle, a cavity containing the spores of cryptogamous plants. 2. Fruit, follicle.

Conceptear [con-thep-tay-ar'], *vn.* To give smart repartees, to abound in witty sayings.

Conceptibilidad [con-thep-te-be-le-dahd'], *f.* (Littl. us.) Conceivableness.

Conceptible [con-thep-tee'-blay], *a.* Conceivable, that may be imagined.

Conceptillo [con-thep-teel'-lyo], *m. dim.* A witty trifle, an attempt at wit.

Conceptista [con-thep-tees'-tah], *m.* 1. A wit. 2. A man of genius, a man of fancy. 3. A humorist. 4. Punster.

Concepto [con-thep'-to], *m.* 1. Conceit, thought, idea, conception. 2. (Obs.) Fœtus. *V.* Feto. 3. Sentiment, striking thought, flash of wit, pun. 4. Judgment, opinion. 5. Estimation, favourable opinion.

Conceptualismo [con-thep-too-ah-lees'-mo], *m.* A philosophical system, designed to reconcile nominalism and realism, dating from 12th century.

Conceptuar [con-thep-too-ar'], *va.* To conceive, judge, think, or be of opinion. *Conceptúo que debe hacerse esto.* I am of opinion that this should be done.

Conceptuosamente [con-thep-too-o-sah-men'-tay], *adv.* Ingeniously, wittily.

Conceptuoso, sa [con-thep-too-o'-so, sah], *a.* Witty, conceited.

Concernencia [con-ther-nen'-the-ah], *f.* Concernment, relation, influence.

Concerniente [con-ther-ne-en'-tay], *pa.* Concerning. *Por lo concerniente*, Concerning.

Concernir [con-ther-neer'], *v. imp.* To regard, to concern, to belong or appertain to. *V.* Atañer.

Concertadamente, *adv.* 1. Regularly, orderly, methodically. 2. By agreement.

Concertador [con-ther-tah-dor'], *m.* Regulator, adjuster, expediter.

Concertante [con-ther-tahn'-tay], *a.* (Mus.) Concerted, arranged for two or more voices or instruments.

Concertar [con-ther-tar'], *va.* 1. To concert, to settle by mutual communication, to adjust, to harmonize. 2. To settle the price of things. 3. To bargain, to covenant, to conclude an agreement. 4. To tune musical instruments. 5. To compare, to estimate the relative qualities of things. 6. To beat about the bush, to start or rouse the game.—*vn.* To agree, to accord, to suit one another.—*vr.* 1. (Obs.) To dress or deck one's self.

2. To go hand in hand; to concert, to contrive, to form or design.

Concesión [con-thay-se-on'], *f.* Concession, grant, granting or yielding, acknowledgment.

Concesionario [con-thay-se-o-nah'-re-o], *m.* 1. (Law) Grantee. 2. Concessionary, one to whom a special privilege is granted.

Concia [con'-the-ah], *f.* Prohibited part of a forest.

(*Yo concibo, él concibió*, from *Concebir.* V. PEDIR.)

Concibimiento [con-the-be-me-en'-to], *m.* 1. Conceit, thought, idea, conception. 2. (Obs.) Act of conceiving.

Conciencia [con-the-en'-the-ah], *f.* 1. Conscience. *Ancho de conciencia*, Not scrupulous or delicate with regard to morals or feelings. 2. Scrupulosity, conscientiousness. 3. Consciousness, knowledge of one's personality. *Hacer conciencia de alguna cosa*, To be scrupulous about a thing. *A conciencia*, Conscientiously. *Este aderezo está trabajado a conciencia*, This set of jewels is finished as it ought to be. *En conciencia*, In good earnest, in truth.

Concienzudo, da [con-the-en-thoo'-do, dah], *a.* Conscientious, scrupulous, exactly just: applied generally to a person too scrupulous.

Concierto [con-the-err'-to], *m.* 1. The good order and arrangement of things. 2. Concert, communication of designs; bargain, agreement, or contract between two or three persons. 3. Accommodation. 4. Act of beating the wood with hounds to start the game. 5. Concert, an assembly of musicians performing a musical composition. 6. Concerto, a piece of music composed for a concert. *De concierto*, According to agreement, by common consent.

(*Yo concierto, yo concierte*, from *Concertar.* V. ACERTAR.)

Conciliable [con-the-le-ah'-blay], *a.* Reconcilable, capable of conciliation.

Conciliábulo [con-the-le-ah'-boo-lo], *m.* Conventicle, an unlawful assembly or meeting.

Conciliación [con-the-le-ah-the-on'], *f.* 1. Conciliation. 2. Resemblance or affinity which different things bear to each other. 3. Act of obtaining esteem, friendship, or favour.

Conciliador, ra [con-the-le-ah-dor', rah], *m.* & *f.* Conciliator, peace-maker, reconciler.

Conciliar [con-the-le-ar'], *va.* 1. To conciliate or compose differences. 2. To conciliate, to gain, to win the affection or esteem of others; to reconcile. 3. To accord, to reconcile two or more doctrines or propositions seemingly contraries. *Conciliar el sueño*, To induce sleep. *Conciliar las amistades*, To make friends.

Conciliar [con-the-le-ar'], *a.* Conciliar, relating to councils.

Conciliar [con-the-le-ar'], *m.* Member of a council.

Conciliativo, va [con-the-le-ah-tee'-vo, vah], *a.* Conciliatory.

Concilio [con-thee'-le-o], *m.* 1. Council. 2. Council, an assembly of bishops to deliberate upon points of religion. 3. Collection of decrees of a council. *Hacer* or *tener concilio*, (Coll.) To keep or hold unlawful meetings.

Concinidad [con-the-ne-dahd'], *f.* (Obs.) Harmony, just proportion of sound.

Concino, na [con-thee'-no, nah], *a.* (Obs.) Harmonious, agreeable to number and harmony.

Conción [con-the-on'], *f.* (Obs.) V. SERMÓN.

Concionador, ra [con-the-o-nah-dor', rah], *m.* & *f.* (Obs.) Preacher or reasoner in public.

Concisamente [con-the-sah-men'-tay], *adv.* Concisely, briefly, shortly, laconically.

Concisión [con-the-se-on'], *f.* Conciseness, brevity, terseness.

Conciso, sa [con-thee'-so, sah], *a.* Concise, brief, short, laconic.

Concitación [con-the-tah-the-on'], *f.* Concitation, the act of stirring up.

Concitador [con-the-tah-dor'], *m.* Instigator, inciter to ill.

Concitar [con-the-tar'], *va.* To excite; to stir up commotions.

Concitativo, va [con-the-tah-tee'-vo, vah], *a.* Inciting; stirring up commotions.

Conciudadano [con-the-oo-da-dah'-no], *m.* Fellow-citizen, townsman, countryman.

Conclave [con-clah'-vay], or **Cónclave**, *m.* 1. Conclave, place in which the cardinals meet to elect a pope. 2. Conclave, the meeting held for that purpose by the cardinals. 3. (Obs.) Conclave, a close meeting or assembly.

Conclavista [con-clah-vees'-tah], *m.* Conclavist, a domestic of a cardinal.

Concluir [con-cloo-eer'], *va.* 1. To conclude, to end, to terminate, to finish, to close, to complete, to make up. 2. To complete a thing suddenly. 3. To convince with reason, to make evident. 4. To decide finally, to determine. 5. To infer, to deduce. 6. To close judicial proceedings; to submit to a final decision. 7. (Fenc.) To disarm an adversary by laying hold of the hilt of his sword.

Conclusión [con-cloo-se-on'], *f.* 1. Conclusion. 2. Conclusion, end, fine, close or closure, date, issue. 3. (Fenc.) Act of laying hold of the hilt of an adversary's sword. 4. The conclusion of the proceedings in a suit at law. 5. Conclusion, consequence. 6. Thesis controverted and defended in schools. *En conclusión*, Finally.

Conclusivo, va [con-cloo-see'-vo, vah], *a.* Conclusional, conclusive, final.

Concluso, sa [con-cloo'-so, sah], *a.* 1. Concluded, closed, terminated. 2. (Obs.) Inclosed, contained.—*pp. irr.* of CONCLUIR.

Concluyente [con-cloo-yen'-tay], *pa.* Concluding; concludent, conclusive, conclusional.

Concluyentemente [con-cloo-yen-tay-men'-tay], *adv.* Conclusively.

(*Yo concluyo, yo concluyera, él concluyó*, from *Concluir.* V. INSTRUIR.)

Concofrade [con-co-frah'-day], *m.* He who belongs to the same brotherhood with another.

Concoidal [con-co-e-dahl'], *a.* V. CONCOIDEO.

Concoide [con-co'-e-day], *f.* (Math.) Conchoid.

Concoideo, a [con-co-e-day'-o, ah], *a.* Conchoidal, resembling a shell.

Concolega [con-co-lay'-gah], *m.* Fellow-collegian.

Concomerse [con-co-merr'-say], *vr* To shrug the shoulders.

Concomimiento, Concomio [con-co-me-me-en'-to, con-co'-me-o], *m.* Shrugging of the shoulders.

Concomitancia [con-co-me-tahn'-the-ah], *f.* 1. Concomitance, existence together with some other thing. 2. Circumstantial evidence.

Concomitante [con-co-me-tahn'-tay], *pa.* 1. Concomitant, concurrent, accompanying. 2. Accessory.

Concomitar [con-co-me-tar'], *va.* (Obs.) To concomitate, to attend, to accompany.

Concordable [con-cor-dah'-blay], *a.* Concordant, conformable, agreeable, accommodable, consistent with.

Concordación [con-cor-dah-the-on'], *f.* Co-ordination, combination, conformation.

Concordador [con-cor-dah-dor'], *m.* Conciliator, peacemaker.

Concordancia [con-cor-dahn'-the-ah], *f.* 1. Concordance, concord, agreement between persons and things. 2. Harmony, concord of sounds. 3. A concordance of Scripture texts or words. 4. Grammatical concord.

Concordante [con-cor-dahn'-tay], *pa.* Concordant, agreeing.

Concordar [con-cor-dar'], *va.* 1. To accord, to regulate, to make one thing agree with another; to compromise.—*vn.* 1. To accord, to agree, to comport, to concord. 2. To be congenial, be in accord. *La copia concuerda con su original*, The copy agrees with the original.

Concordata [con-cor-dah'-tah], *f.* (Obs.) V. CONCORDATO.

Concordato [con-cor-dah'-to], *m.* Concordat, a covenant made by a state or government with the Pope upon ecclesiastical matters.

Concorde [con-cor'-day], *a.* Concordant, agreeable, agreeing.

Concordemente [con-cor-day-men'-tay], *adv.* With one accord.

Concordia [con-cor'-de-ah], *f.* 1. Concord, conformity, union, harmony. 2. Agreement between persons engaged in a lawsuit. *De concordia*, Jointly, by common consent.

Concorpóreo, rea [con-cor-po'-ray-o, ah], *a.* Concorporeal, of the same body.

Concreción [con-cray-the-on'], *f.* Concretion.

Concrecionar [cone-cray-the-o-nar'], *vn.* To form concretions.

Concrescencia [con-cres-then'-the-ah], *f.* (Phys.) Concrescence, growing by the union of separate particles.

Concretamente [con-cray-tah-men'-tay], *adv.* Concretely.

Concretar [con-cray-tar'], *va.* To combine, to unite, to concrete.—*vr.* To be reduced to speaking or treating of one subject only.

Concreto, ta [con-cray'-to, tah], *a.* 1. Concrete, in logic, not abstracted: applied to a subject. 2. Concrete, formed by concretion: in this last sense it is used as a substantive.

Concubina [con-coo-bee'-nah], *f.* Concubine, mistress.

Concubinario [con-coo-be-nah'-re-o], *m.* One who keeps a mistress.

Concubinato [con-coo-be-nah'-to], *m.* Concubinage.

Concúbito [con-coo'-be-to], *m.* Coition.

(*Yo concuerdo, yo concuerde*, from *Concordar.* V. ACORDAR.)

Conculcación [con-cool-cah-the-on'], *f.* Trampling.

Conculcar [con-cool-car'], *va.* 1. To trample under foot. 2. To mock, despise, break to pieces, heap abuse upon.

Concuñado, da [con-coo-nyah'-do, dah], *m.* & *f.* Brother or sister-in-law; a term confined to persons who are married to two brothers or sisters.

Concupiscencia [con-coo-pis-then'-the-ah], *f.* 1. Concupiscence, lust, cupidity. 2. Avarice, inordinate desire.

Concupiscible [con-coo-pis-thee'-blay], *a.* Concupiscible; impressing desire.

Concurrencia [con-coor-ren'-the-ah], *f.* 1. Convention or assembly of persons. 2. Concurrence, coincidence. 3.

Conspiracy, tendency of many causes to one event.

Concurrente [con-coor-ren'-tay], *pa.* Concurrent, coincident. *Concurrente cantidad*, The quantity necessary to make up the deficiency of a determinate sum.

Concurrentemente, *adv.* (Littl. us.) Concurrently.

Concurrir [con-coor-reer'], *vn.* 1. To concur, to meet in one point, time, or place. 2. To concur, to contribute, to coincide, to conspire, to agree with or to agree together, to assist.

Concursar [con-coor-sar'], *va.* To lay an injunction on the goods and chattels of an insolvent debtor.

Concurso [con-coor'-so], *m.* 1. Concourse or confluence of persons or things. Crowd, congregation, assembly. 2. Aid, assistance. 3. Contest, competition. 4. Proceedings against an insolvent debtor. *Concurso aéreo*, Air meet. *Concurso de belleza*, Beauty contest. *Concurso deportivo*, Athletic contest.

Concusión [con-coo-se-on'], *f.* Concussion, shaking, the act of shaking. *Concusión violenta*, Concussation.

Concusionario, ia [con-coo-se-o-nah'-re-o, ah], *a.* Concussive, shaking.

Concha [con'-chah], *f.* 1. Shell. 2. Oyster. 3. Tortoise-shell. 4. An ancient copper coin, worth about three farthings, or eight maravedis. *Concha de nácar*, Mother-of-pearl shell. 5. (Arch.) Volute, any ornament in the form of a shell; conch. 6. The external ear. 7. Shell of a dagger or cutlass. 8. The shell-shaped covering of the spike of Indian corn. 9. *Concha de cabrestante*, (Naut.) Socket of the capstan. *Conchas de escobenes*, (Naut.) Navel-woods, or navel-hoods, pieces of stuff fitted into the hawse-holes, to prevent the cable from being galled and the hawse-holes from being worn out. *Tener muchas conchas*, (Met.) To be very reserved, artful, cunning.

Conchabanza [con-chah-bahn'-thah], *f.* 1. The manner of making one's self easy and comfortable. 2. (Coll.) The act of meeting or collecting in unlawful assemblies. 3. Plotting, conspiracy.

Conchabar [con-chah-bar'], *va.* 1. To join, to unite. 2. To mix inferior wool with the superior or middling quality instead of separating it into three kinds at shearing-time.—*vr.* To unite, to join or unite for some evil purpose; to plot, to conspire.

Conchado, da [con-chah'-do, dah], *a.* Scaly, crustaceous, shelly.

Conchal [con-chahl'], *a.* *V.* Seda conchal.

Conchil [con-cheel'], *m.* Rock-shell. Murex, the mollusk which yielded the purple of the ancients. Murex. *Cf.* Púrpura.

Conchilla, ita [con-cheel'-lyah, chee'-tah], *f. dim.* A small shell.

Conchite [con-chee'-tay], *f.* Conchite, a sort of petrified shell.

Conchología [con-cho-lo-hee'-ah], *f.* Conchology.

Conchudo, da [con-choo'-do, dah], *a.* 1. Scaly, crustaceous, ostraceous. 2. Cunning, crafty, close, reserved.

Conchuela [con-choo-ay'-lah], *f. dim.* *V.* Conchilla.

Condado [con-dah'-do], *m.* 1. Earldom, county. 2. Dignity of a count or earl. 3. County, a political division.

Condal [con-dahl'], *a.* Relating to the dignity of an earl or count.

Conde [con'-day], *m.* 1 Earl, count. 2. (Prov.) Overseer. 3. Head or chief of the gipsies, appointed by election.

Condecabo [con-day-cah'-bo], *adv.* (Obs.) Another time, again.

Condecente [con-day-then'-tay], *a.* (Littl. us.) Convenient, fit, proper.

Condecoración [con-day-co-rah-the-on'], *f.* Decoration, embellishing or decorating.

Condecorar [con-day-co-rar'], *va.* To ornament, to adorn, to embellish, to honour, to reward.

Condena [con-day'-nah], *f.* 1. The clerk of the court's attestation of the sentence of a condemned criminal. 2. Sentence.

Condenable [con-day-nah'-blay], *a.* Condemnable, blamable, culpable, damnable.

Condenación [con-day-nah-the-on'], *f.* 1. Condemnation, sentence to punishment. 2. Punishment. *Es una condenación*, (Coll.) It is unbearable, intolerable. 3. (Met.) Eternal damnation.

Condenado, da [con-day-nah'-do, dah], *m. & f.* One condemned to eternal punishment.

Condenado, da [con-day-nah'-do, dah], *a. & pp.* of Condenar. Condemned, damned, sentenced. *Ser* or *salir condenado en costas*, To be sentenced to pay the costs of a suit at law. *Condenado* or *tierra condenada*, The earthy, charry, or saline residue which remains in a vessel after a chemical operation has been performed. *Puerta condenada*, A door shut up and no longer used.

Condenador, ra [con-day-nah-dor', rah], *m. & f.* Condemner, blamer, censurer.

Condenar [con-day-nar'], *va.* 1. To condemn, to pronounce judgment, to sentence. 2. To damn. 3. To condemn, to censure, to blame. 4. To refute a doctrine or opinion, to disapprove. *Condenar una puerta, una ventana* or *un pasadizo*, To stop or shut a door, window, or passage, to nail or wall up a door, etc.—*vr.* 1. To condemn one's self, to acknowledge one's fault. 2. To incur eternal punishment in a future state.

Condenatorio, ria [con-day-nah-to'-re-o, ah], *a.* Condemnatory, damnatory.

Condensabilidad [con-den-sah-be-le-dahd'], *f.* The quality of being condensable.

Condensable [con-den-sah'-blay], *a.* Condensable.

Condensación [con-den-sah-the-on'], *f.* Condensation, compression.

Condensado, da [con-den-sah'-do, dah], *a.* Condensed. *Leche condensada*, Condensed milk.

Condensador, ra [con-den sah-dor', rah], *m. & f.* Condenser.

Condensamiento [con-den-sah-me-en'-to], *m.* *V.* Condensación.

Condensante [con-den-sahn'-tay], *pa.* Condensing.

Condensar [con-den-sar'], *va.* To thicken, to condense.—*vr.* To be condensed, to gather.

Condensativo, va [con-den-sah-tee'-vo, vah], *a.* Condensative.

Condensidad [con-den-se-dahd'], *f.* Condensity, condensation.

Condesa [con-day'-sah], *f.* Countess, the wife of a count or the heiress to an earldom.

Condesar [con-day-sar'], *va.* (Obs.) To spare, to save, to preserve. *Quien come y condesa, dos veces pone la mesa*, A penny saved is a penny gained. (Literally, he who eats and saves sets the table twice.)

Condescendencia [con-des-then-den'-the-ah], *f.* Condescendence, condescension, condescending, compliance, complacency, flexibility.

Condescender [con-des-then-derr'], *vn.* To condescend, to yield, to submit, to comply.

Condescendiente [con-des-then-de-en'-tay], *a. & pa.* Complacent, compliant, acquiescent.

Condescendientemente, *adv.* Condescendingly.

(*Yo condesciendo, yo condescienda*, from *Condescender.* *V.* Atender.)

Condesita [con-day-see'-tah], *f. dim.* A little or young countess.

Condesito [con-day-see'-to], *m. dim.* A little earl, a little count.

Condesil [con-day-seel'], *a.* (Obs.) Belonging to a count or countess.

Condestable [con-des-tah'-blay], *m.* 1. Constable, a lord high constable. 2. *Condestable de arsenales*, (Naut.) Gunner of a dockyard. *Segundo condestable*, Gunner's mate. 3. (Naut.) Sergeant of marine artillery.

Condestablía [con-des-tah-blee'-ah], *f.* Constableship.

Condezmero [con-deth-may'-ro], *m.* (Littl. us.) Part owner of the tithes of a parish.

Condición [con-de-the-on'], *f.* 1. Condition, quality. 2. Condition, state, footing, habit. 3. Condition, natural quality of the mind, natural temper or constitution. 4. Quality, rank, or class in society; fashion, especially implying nobility. 5. Condition, clause, stipulation. *Condición torpe*, That which is directly opposed by law. *Tener mala condición* or *tener condición*, To be of a peevish or irritable disposition; bad-tempered. *Tener* or *poner en condición*, To hazard, to expose to danger. *De condición* or *con condición*, So as, on condition that.

Condicionado, da [con-de-the-o-nah'-do, dah], *a.* 1. Conditioned; well or bad conditioned. 2. *V.* Condicional.—*pp.* of Condicionar.

Condicional [con-de-the-o-nahl'], *a.* Conditional, not absolute.

Condicionalmente [con-de-the-o-nal-men'-tay], *adv.* Conditionally, hypothetically.

Condicionar [con-de-the-o-nar'], *vn.* To agree, to accord, to condition.—*vr.* To be of the same nature, condition, or temper.

Condicionaza [con-de-the-o-nah'-thah], *f. aug.* A violent disposition or temper.

Condicioncilla, ita [con-de-the-on-theel'-lyah, ee'-tah], *f. dim.* 1. A hasty or passionate disposition or temper. 2. A small clause, or stipulation.

Condignamente [con-dig-nah-men'-tay], *adv.* Condignly, deservedly.

Condignidad [con-dig-ne-dahd'], *f.* (Littl. us.) Condignity, condignness, suitableness.

Condigno, na [con-deeg'-no, nah], *a.* Condign, suitable, deserved, merited.

Cóndilo [cone'-de-lo], *m.* (Anat.) Condyle.

Condimentar [con-de-men-tar'], *va.* To dress or season victuals.

Condimento [con-de-men'-to], *m.* Condiment, seasoning, sauce.

Condiscípulo [con-dis-thee'-poo-lo], *m.* Condisciple, school-fellow, fellow-scholar or fellow-student.

Condistinguir [con-dis-tin-geer'], *va.* (Obs.) To distinguish, to make a distinction.

Condolecerse, (Obs.) **Condolerse** [con-do-lay-therr'-say, con-do-lerr'-say], *vr.* To condole, to be sorry for, to be in pain for, to sympathize with.

Condominio [con-do-mee'-ne-o], *m.* 1. Joint ownership. 2. Condominium.

Condómino [con-do'-me-no], *m.* A joint owner.

Condonación [con-do-nah-the-on'], *f.* Condonation, pardoning, forgiving.

Condonar [con-do-nar'], *va.* To pardon, to forgive.

Cóndor [con'-dor], *m.* (Orn.) Condor. Vultur gryphus.

Condrila [con-dree'-lah], *f.* (Bot.) Common gum-succory. Chondrilla juncea.

Condrín [con-dreen'], *m.* A weight for precious metals in the Philippines = 0.3768 gramme, or about one-fourth a pennyweight.

Condritis [con-dree'-tis], *f.* Inflammation of cartilage, chondritis.

Condrografía [con-dro-grah-fee'-ah], *f.* A description of cartilages.

Conducción [con-dooc-the-on'], *f.* 1. Conveyance. 2. Carriage, the act of carrying. 3. The act of conveying or conducting. 4. Leading, guiding, or bringing any thing: conduct. 5. Reward for conducting.

Conducencia [con-doo-then'-the-ah], *f.* The conducing to or promoting any end, conducement.

Conducente [con-doo-then'-tay], *a.* & *pa.* Conducive, conducent, conducible; official.

Conducidor [con-doo-the-dor'], *m.* Conductor, leader.

Conducir [con-doo-theer'], *va.* & *n.* 1. To convey, carry, or conduct a thing from one place to another. 2. To conduct, to guide or direct to a place, to show the way, to lead or lead along. 3. To direct, manage, conduct, or adjust any affair or business. 4. *n.* To conduce, to contribute, to favour, to be fitted for.—*vr.* To behave, to act, to conduct one's self.

Conducta [con-dooc'-tah], *f.* 1. Conduct, management, course, manner of proceeding. 2. Conduct, behaviour, comportment, conversation; managery. 3. Life, conduct. 4. Number of mules or horses carrying money from one place to another. 5. Government, command, direction. 6. Party of recruits conducted to the regiment. 7. In Arragon, a contract made by a town or village with a physician or surgeon to attend their sick. In Castile it is called *partido.*

Conductero [con-duc-tay'-ro], *m.* (Obs.) *V.* Conductor.

Conductibilidad [con-dooc-te-be-le-dahd'], *f.* Conductibility.

Conductible [con-dooc-tee'-blay], *a.* Conveyable, conductible.

Conductivo, va [con-duc-tee'-vo, vah], *a.* Having the power of conveying or transporting.

Conducto [con-dooc'-to], *m.* 1. Conduit, sewer, drain, sink. 2. Channel, mediation. *Por conducto de,* Via, through. *Salvo conducto,* Safe-conduct.

Conductor [con-dooc-tor'], *m.* 1. Conductor, leader, usher, conduct, guide, conveyer. *Conductor de embajadores,* One whose business is to introduce ambassadors. 2. *Conductor eléctrico,* Electric-rod.

Conductora [con-dooc-to'-rah], *f.* Conductress, directress.

(*Yo me conduelo, yo me conduela,* from *Condoler. V.* Mover.)

Condueño [con-doo-ay'-nyo], *m.* (Com.) Joint owner.

Condumio [con-doo'-me-o], *m.* 1. (Coll.) Meat dressed to be eaten with bread. 2. Plenty of food.

Conduplicación [con-doo-ple-cah-the-on'], *f.* The rhetorical figure of reduplication; the repetition of the last word of the clause just preceding.

Conduta [con-doo'-tah], *f.* (Obs.) *V.* Conducta.

Condutal [con-doo-tahl'], *m.* Spout to carry off the rain-water from the houses. *V.* Canal.

(*Yo conduzco, yo conduzca; él condujo, él condujera;* from *Conducir. V.* Conducir.)

Conectar [co-nec-tar'], *va.* (Mech.) To connect, to couple up.

Conectículo [co-nec-tee'-coo-lo], *m.* (Bot.) Connective, elastic ring of ferns.

Coneina [co-nay-ee'-nah], *f.* Conein, coneia, an alkaloid obtained from hemlock.

Coneja [co-nay'-hah], *f.* *V.* Conejo.

Conejal [co-nay-hahl'], *m.* 1. Rabbit-warren. *V.* Conejera. 2. (Met.) Suburb inhabited by the common people.

Conejar [co-nay-har'], *m.* Rabbit-warren.

Conejera [co-nay-hay'-rah], *f.* 1. Warren for breeding rabbits. 2. (Met.) Brothel. 3. (Met.) Den or cavern inhabited by poor people.

Conejero [co-nay-hay'-ro], *m.* Warrener, the keeper of a rabbit-warren.

Conejero [co-nay-hay'-ro, rah], *a.* That which hunts rabbits: commonly applied to a dog.

Conejito [co-nay-hee'-to], *m. dim.* A little rabbit.

Conejo [co-nay'-ho], *a.* *Alambre conejo,* Rabbit-wire, copper wire.

Conejo, ja [co-nay'-ho, hah], *m.* & *f.* Rabbit. Lepus cuniculus. *Es una coneja,* (Met.) She breeds like a rabbit.

Conejuna [co-nay-hoo'-nah], *f.* Rabbit down or fur.

Conejuno, na [co-nay-hoo'-no, nah], *a.* Relating to the rabbit kind.

Cóneo, a [co'-nay-o, ah], *a.* Like a cone; conical.

Conexidades [co-nek-se-dah'-des], *f. pl.* Rights annexed to the principal.

Conexión [co-nek-se-on'], *f.* Connection, conjunction, union, conjucture, cohesion, closeness, coherence.

Conexivo, va [co-nek-see'-vo, vah], *a.* Connective.

Conexo, xa [co-nek'-so, sah], *a.* Connected, united.

Confabulación [con-fah-boo-lah-the-on'], *f.* 1. Confabulation, easy conversation, chat. 2. Leaguing, conspiracy, collusion.

Confabulador, ra [con-fah-boo-lah-dor', rah], *m.* & *f.* A story-teller, gossip; schemer.

Confabular [con-fah-boo-lar'], *vn.* 1. To confabulate, to talk easily together, to chat. 2. (Obs.) To tell stories. 3. *vr.* To league, to enter into conspiracy.

Confalón [con-fah-lone'], *m.* Gonfalon, standard; an ensign.

Confalonier [con-fah-lo-ne-err'], **Confaloniero,** *m.* Gonfalonier, chief standard-bearer.

Confección [con-fec-the-on'], *f.* Confection, making, construction.

Confeccionador, ra [con-fec-the-o-nah-dor', rah], *m.* & *f.* Confectioner.

Confeccionar [con-fec-the-o-nar'], *va.* 1. To make, to prepare, to put together, to complete. 2. To confect, to prepare medicaments according to art. (Acad.)

Confecciones, (Sp. Am.) Ready-made dresses.

Confederación [con-fay-day-rah-the-on'], *f.* 1. Confederacy, league, union, confederation, federation, coalition. 2. Agreement or mutual treaty between monarchs or republics.

Confederado, da [con-fay-day-rah'-do, dah], *a.* & *m.* & *f.* Confederate, allied, conjoint, federate, covenanter, federary, consociate.—*pp.* of Confederar.

Confederar [con-fay-day-rar'], *va.* To confederate, to join in a league.—*vr.* To confederate, to conjoin, to league.

Conferencia [con-fay-ren'-the-ah], *f.* 1. Conference, meeting, conversation, collocution; congress. 2. Daily lecture studied by students in universities.

Conferenciante [con-fay-ren-the-ahn-tay], *m.* & *f.* Lecturer, speaker.

Conferenciar [con-fay-ren-the-ar'], *va.* To confer; to hold a conference.

Conferencista [con-fay-ren-thees'-tah], *m.* & *f.* Lecturer, orator, speaker.

Conferir [con-fay-reer'], *va.* 1. To confer, to compare, to estimate the relative qualities of things. 2. To confer, to deliberate, to commune. 3. To give, to bestow, to confer. *Conferir un beneficio,* To confer a benefice.

Conferva [con-ferr'-vah], *f.* (Bot.) Conferva, a filamentous fresh-water alga.

Confesa [con-fay'-sah], *f.* *V.* Confeso.

Confesado, da [con-fay-sah'-do, dah], *a.* & *pp.* of Confesar, Confessed.—*n.* (Coll.) Penitent, one under the spiritual direction of a confessor.

Confesante [con-fay-sahn'-tay], *pa.* He who confesses by word or writing before a judge.

Confesar [con-fay-sar'], *va.* 1. To manifest or assert one's opinion. 2. To confess, to acknowledge, to own, to avow, to grant. 3. To confess, to hear or receive confessions. 4. To confess to the priest. *Confesar de plano,* To confess plainly or openly. *Confesar sin tormento,* To confess, to acknowledge or avow a fault, a crime, etc., freely and readily.—*vr.* To confess, or make confession; to shrive.

Confesión [con-fay-se-on'], *f.* 1. Confession, acknowledgment. 2. Confession to a priest. *Hijo* or *hija de confesión,* A person who has a certain constant confessor. 3. Declaration of a criminal either denying or confessing the charges against him.

Confesionario [con-fay-se-o-nah'-re-o], *m.* 1. Treatise which lays down rules for confessing or hearing confessions. 2. Confessional.

Confesionera [con-fay-se-o-nay'-rah], or **Confesionariera** [con-fay-se-o-nah-re-ay'-rah], *f.* A nun having the care of confessional books.

Confesionista [con-fay-se-o-nees'-tah], *m.* One professing the confession of faith of Augsburg; a Lutheran.

Confeso, sa [con-fay'-so, sah], *m.* & *f.* 1. Jewish proselyte. 2. (Obs.) A lay-brother; a nun who was before a widow.

Confeso, sa [con-fay'-so, sah], *a.* (Law) Confessed: applied to the person who has acknowledged a crime.—*pp. irr.* of Confesar.

Confesonario [con-fay-so-nah'-re-o], *m.* Confessional.

Confesor [con-fay-sor'], *m.* 1. Confessor, a priest of the Roman church authorized to hear confession of sins and to grant absolution. 2. A title given to holy men by the Roman Catholic church; as, *San Juan Crisóstomo, Doctor, Obispo y Confesor,* St. John Crysostom, B. C. D.

Confeti [con-fay'-te], *m.* Confetti.

Confiable [con-fe-ah'-blay], *a.* Trusty.

Confiadamente [con-fe-ah-dah-men'-tay], *adv.* Confidently.

Confiado, da [con-fe-ah'-do, dah], *a.* Confident, secure, unsuspicious, trusting; presumptuous, arrogant, forward.

Confiador [con-fe-ah-dor'], *m.* 1. A joint surety, a fellow-bondsman. 2. He who confides or expects.

Confianza [con-fe-ahn'-thah], *f.* 1. Confidence, trust, reliance, firm belief. 2. Confidence, honest boldness, firmness of opinion. 3. Confidence, presumptuousness, forwardness, assurance. *En confianza*, Privately, secretly, confidentially.

Confiar [con-fe-ar'], *va.* & *vn.* 1. To confide, to trust in. 2. To confide, to credit, to commit to the care of another. 3. To hope; to feed with hope

Confidencia [con-fe-den'-the-ah], *f.* 1. Confidence. *V.* CONFIANZA. 2. Secret information.

Confidencial [con-fe-den-the-ahl'], *a.* Confidential.

Confidencialmente [con-fe-den-the-al-men'-tay], *adv.* Confidentially.

Confidente [con-fe-den'-tay], *m.* 1. Confident, intimate, neighbour, counsellor. 2. A spy. 3. A settee for two persons: a tête-à-tête.

Confidente [con-fe-den'-tay], *a.* True, faithful, trusty.

Confidentemente [con-fe-den-tay-men'-tay], *adv.* 1. Confidently, fiducially. 2. Faithfully.

(*Yo confiero, yo confiera; él confirió, él confiriera;* from *Conferir.* *V.* ASENTIR.)

(*Yo confieso, yo confiese*, from *Confesar.* *V.* ACERTAR.)

Configuración [con-fe-goo-rah-the-on'], *f.* Configuration.

Configurado, da [con-fe-goo-rah'-do, dah], *a.* Configurated.—*pp.* of CONFIGURAR.

Configurar [con-fe-goo-rar'], *va.* To configure, to dispose into form; to configurate: also used reciprocally.

Confín [con-feen'], *m.* Limit, boundary, confine, border.

Confín, Confinante [con-feen', con-fe-nahn'-tay], *a.* Bordering upon, conterminous, limitaneous.—*Confinante*, *pa.* of CONFINAR.

Confinar [con-fe-nar'], *va.* & *vn.* 1. To banish, to exile. 2. To confine, to imprison or immure. 3. To confine, to border upon, to abut.

Confingir [con-fin-heer'], *va.* To mix ingredients into one mass by means of a liquid: to make conserves, electuaries, etc.

Confirmación [con-feer-mah-the-on'], *f.* 1. Confirmation, corroboration, attestation. 2. Evidence; additional proof. 3. Confirmation, a sacrament of the Catholic church.

Confirmadamente [con-feer-mah-dah-men'-tay], *adv.* Firmly, unalterably.

Confirmador, ra [con-feer-mah-dor', rah], *m.* & *f.* Confirmator, attester, confirmer.

Confirmante [con-feer-mahn'-tay], *pa.* Confirmer.

Confirmar [con-feer-mar'], *va.* 1. To confirm, to corroborate, to fortify. 2. To strengthen or support a person or thing. 3. To confirm, to admit to the full privileges of a Christian by the solemn imposition of hands.

Confirmativamente [con-feer-mah-te-vah-men'-tay], *adv.* Confirmingly.

Confirmatorio, ria [con-feer-mah-to'-re-o, ah], *a.* Confirmatory, confirmative.

Confiscable [con-fis-cah'-blay], *a.* Confiscable, forfeitable.

Confiscación [con-fis-cah-the-on'], *f.* Confiscation, forfeiture.

Confiscado, da [con-fis-cah'-do, dah], *a.* & *pp.* of CONFISCAR. Confiscate, confiscated.

Confiscador [con-fis-cah-dor'], *m.* (Littl. *us.*) Confiscator.

Confiscar [con-fis-car'], *va.* To confiscate, to transfer private property to the public use.

Confitar [con-fe-tar'], *va.* 1. To confect, to candy with melted sugar. 2. To make up into sweetmeats. 3. (Met.) To dulcify, to sweeten.

Confite [con-fee'-tay], *m.* Comfit, sugar-plum. *Morder en un confite*, To be hand and glove, to be intimate and familiar. *Confites*, 1. Dainties, sugar-plums. 2. (Coll.) Whipping given to children and the whip used for the purpose.

Confitente [con-fe-ten'-tay], *a.* *V.* CONFESO.

Confitera [con-fe-tay'-rah], *f.* Candy dish, bonbon dish. V. CONFITERO.

Confitería [con-fe-tay-ree'-ah], *f.* A confectioner's shop.

Confitero, ra [con-fe-tay'-ro, rah], *m.* & *f.* 1. Confectioner. 2. Tray in which sweetmeats are served up.

Confitillo [con-fe-teel'-lyo], *m.* 1. Ornaments in the shape of confitures wrought on coverlets. 2. (Dim.) Small comfit; caraway comfits.

Confitón [con-fe-tone'], *m.* (Aug.) A large comfit.

Confitura [con-fe-too'-rah], *f.* Confiture, comfit, confection, sweetmeats.

Conflación [con-flah-the-on'], *f.* Fusion, melting metals, smelting.

Conflagración [con-flah-grah-the-on'], *f.* 1. Conflagration. 2. A sudden and violent perturbation of towns and nations.

Conflátil [con-flah'-teel], *a.* Fusible.

Conflicto [con-fleec'-to], *m.* 1. Conflict, struggle, a violent combat or contest. 2. (Met.) Struggle, agony, pang.

Confluencia [con-floo-en'-the-ah], *f.* Confluence, conflux, flux.

Confluente [con-floo-en'-tay], *pa.* Con fluent.

Confluir [con-floo-eer'], *vn.* 1. To join or meet: applied to rivers and sea currents. 2. (Met.) To meet or assemble in one place: applied to a mob.

Conformación [con-for-ma-the-on'], *f.* Conformation.

Conformar [con-for-mar'], *va.* To conform, to adjust, to fit.—*vn.* 1. To suit, to fit, to conform, to cohere, to level. 2. To comply with, to agree in opinion.—*vr.* To yield, to submit, to accommodate.

Conforme [con-for'-may], *a.* 1. Conformable, correspondent, suitable, congruent, consonant, convenient, accordant. 2. Consistent, similar. 3. Compliant, resigned. *Conforme a*, Consistent with, agreeable to.

Conforme [con-for'-may], *adv.* 1. In proportion, or according to proportion. 2. Agreeably, according to.

Conformemente [con-for-may-men'-tay], *adv.* Conformably, unanimously.

Conformidad [con-for-me-dahd'], *f.* 1. Similitude, resemblance, likeness, conformity. 2. Agreement, consistence, consonance, congruence. 3. Union, concord, concordance. 4. Symmetry. 5. A close attachment of one person to another. 6. Submission, acquiescence, patience, resignation. *De conformidad*, By common consent; together, in company. *En conformidad*, Agreeably, suitably, according to.

Conformista [con-for-mees'-tah], *m.* Conformist, one belonging to a state church.

Confortación [con-for-tah-the-on'], *f.* Comfort, consolation.

Confortador, ra [con-for-tah-dor', rah], *m.* & *f.* Comforter.

Confortante [con-for-tahn'-tay]. *pa.* Comforting, soothing.—*m.* Calmative, a soothing remedy; stomachic, relating to food.—*pl.* Mitts.

Confortar [con-for-tar'], *va.* 1. To comfort, to corroborate, to strengthen, to enliven, to invigorate. 2. To console.

Confortativo, va [con-for-tah-tee'-vo, vah], *a.* Comfortable, corroborative, cordial. It is frequently used as a substantive.

Confracción [con-frac-the-on'], *f.* Fraction, breaking.

Confraguación [con-frah-goo-ah-the-on'], *f.* The act of mixing, uniting, or incorporating metals with each other.

Confraternidad [con-frah-ter-ne-dahd'], *f.* Confraternity, brotherhood.

Confraternizar [con-frah-ter-ne-thar'], *vn.* To fraternize.

Confricación [con-fre-ca-the-on'], *f.* (Obs.) Confrication, friction.

Confricar [con-fre-car'], *va.* (Obs.) To rub to produce friction.

Confrontación [con-fron-tah-the-on'], *f.* 1. Confrontation. 2. Comparing one thing with another. 3. (Met.) Sympathy, natural conformity.

Confrontante [con-fron-tahn'-tay], *pa.* Confronting, confronter.

Confrontar [con-fron-tar'], *va.* 1. To confer, to collate, to confront. 2. To compare one thing with another.—*vn.* 1. To agree in sentiments and opinion. 2. To border upon.

Confundir [con-foon-deer'], *va.* 1. To confound, to jumble. 2. To confound, to perplex, to confuse, to darken, to throw into disorder. 3. To confute by argument. 4. To abase, humiliate.—*vr.* 1. To be bewildered, perplexed, or confounded. 2. To be ashamed and humbled by the knowledge of one's own character.

Confusamente [con-foo-sah-men'-tay], *adv.* Confusedly, mingledly, helter-skelter.

Confusión [con-foo-se-on'], *f.* 1. Confusion, tumult, disorder, misrule. 2. Confusion, perplexity, perturbation of mind. 3. Confusedness, indistinct combination, obscurity. 4. Humiliation, debasement of mind. 5. Shame, ignominy, reproach. *Echar la confusión a alguno*, (Law. Obs.) To imprecate or curse any one.

Confuso, sa [con-foo'-so, sah], *a.* 1. Confused, mixed, confounded, jumbled together. 2. Obscure, doubtful, indistinct. 3. Fearful, timorous. 4. perplexed. *En confuso*, Confusedly, obscurely, indistinctly.

Confutación [con-foo-tah-the-on'], *f.* Confutation, disproof.

Confutar [con-foo-tar'], *va.* To confute, to disprove, to falsify, to convict.

Congelación [con-hay-lah-the-on'], *f.* Freezing, congealing. *Congelación rápida*, Deep freezing.

Congelador [con-hay-lah-dor'], *m.* or **Congeladora** [con-hay-lah-do'-rah], *f.* Freezer, deepfreeze. *Almacenar en congeladora*, To deepfreeze.

Congelar [con-hay-lar'], *va.* To freeze, to congeal. *Congelar alimentos*, To freeze food.—*vr.* To freeze, to be very cold.

Congelativo, va [con-hay-lah tee'-vo, vah], *a.* Having the power of congealing.

Congénere [con-hay'-nay-ray], **Congenérico, ca** [con-hay-nay'-re-co, cah], *a.* Congeneric, of like kind.

Congenial [con-hay-ne-ahl'], *a.* Congenial, analogous.

Congeniar [con-hay-ne-ar'], *vn.* To be congenial, to sympathize.

Congénito [con-hay'-ne-to], *a.* Congenital, connate.
Congerie [con-hay'-re-ay], *f.* Congeries, heap, mass.
Congestión [con-hes-te-on'], *f.* (Med.) Congestion.
Congestionar [con-hes-te-oh-nar'], *vn.* & *vr.* To congest, become congested.
Congio [con'-he-o], *m.* Ancient Roman liquid measure: gallon.
Conglobación [con-glo-bah-the-on'], *f.* 1. Conglobation; acquired sphericity. 2. Mixture and union of immaterial things, viz. affections, passions, etc. 3. (Rhet.) Accumulation of a number of proofs and arguments crowded together.
Conglobar [con-glo-bar'], *va.* To conglobate; heap together.
Conglomeración [con-glo-may-rah-the-on'], *f.* Conglomeration, heterogeneous mixture.
Conglomerado, da [con-glo-may-rah'-do, dah], *a.* Conglomerate.—*pp.* of CONGLOMERAR.
Conglomerar [con-glo-may-rar'], *va.* To conglomerate.
Congloriar [con-glo-re-ar'], *va.* (Obs.) To fill or cover with glory.
Conglutinación [con-gloo-te-nah-the-on'], *f.* Conglutination, glutination: gluing together.
Conglutinado, da [con-gloo-te-nah'-do, dah], *a.* Conglutinate.—*pp.* of CONGLUTINAR.
Conglutinar [con-gloo-te-nar'], *va.* To conglutinate, to cement, to reunite.—*vr.* To conglutinate.
Conglutinativo, va [con-gloo-te-nah-tee'-vo, vah], **Conglutinoso, sa**, *a.* Viscous, glutinous.
Congoja [con-go'-hah], *f.* Anguish, dismay, anxiety of mind.
Congojar [con-go-har'], *va.* To oppress, to afflict. *V.* ACONGOJAR.
Congojosamente [con-go-ho-sah-men'-tay], *adv.* Anxiously, painfully.
Congojoso, sa [con-go-ho'-so, sah], *a.* 1. Afflictive, painful, tormenting, distressing. 2. Afflicted.
Congoleño, ña [con-go-lay'-nyo, nyah], *a.* Relating to or native of the Congo region, in Africa.
Congraciador, ra [con-grah-the-ah-dor', rah], *m.* & *f.* Flatterer, fawner, wheedler, congratulator.
Congraciamiento [con-grah-the-ah-me-en'-to], *m.* Flattery, false praise, mean obsequiousness.
Congraciar [con-grah-the-ar'], *va.* To ingratiate, to flatter.—*vr.* To get into one's good graces.
Congratulación [con-grah-too-lah-the-on'], *f.* Congratulation, gratulation, felicitation.
Congratular [con-grah-too-lar'], *va.* To congratulate, to compliment upon any happy event, to greet.—*vr.* To congratulate.
Congratulatorio, ria [con-grah-too-lah-to'-re-o, ah], *a.* Congratulatory, congratulant.
Congregación [con-gray-gah-the-on'], *f.* 1. Congregation, a meeting or assembly. 2. Fraternity, brotherhood. 3. Congregation, an assembly met to worship God. 4. In some religious orders, union of many monasteries under the direction of a superior general. *Congregación de los fieles*, The catholic or universal church.
Congregacionalismo [con-gray-gah-the-o-nah-lees'-mo], *m.* Congregationalism.
Congregacionalista [con-gray-gah-the-o-nah-lees'-tah], *com.* Congregationalist.
Congregante, ta [con-gray-gahn'-tay, tah], *m.* & *f.* Member of a congregation, fraternity, or brotherhood.
Congregar [con-gray-gar'], *va.* To assemble, to meet together, to congregate, to collect, to gather.
Congreso [con-gray'-so], *m.* 1. Congress. 2. Consistory, convention, any solemn assembly or congress. 3. Congress, a meeting of commissioners to settle terms of peace between powers at war. 4. Congress, carnal union of man and woman.
Congrio [con'-gre-o], *m.* (Zool.) Conger-eel, or sea-eel. Muræna conger.
Congrua [con'-groo-ah], *f.* A competent sustenance assigned to him who is to be ordained a priest.
Congruamente [con-groo-ah-men'-tay], *adv.* Conveniently, becomingly.
Congruencia [con-groo-en'-the-ah], *f.* Convenience, fitness, congruence.
Congruente [con-groo-en'-tay], *a.* Congruent, agreeing, corresponding.
Congruentemente [con-groo-en-tay-men'-tay], *adv.* Suitably, congruously.
Congruidad [con-groo-e-dahd'], *f.* *V.* CONGRUENCIA.
Congruismo [con-groo-ees'-mo], *m.* Congruism, a religious doctrine which explains the efficacy of grace by its fitness.
Congruista [con-groo-ees'-tah], *m.* A supporter of the foregoing theory.
Congruo, ua [con'-groo-o, ah], *a.* Congruous, apt, fit, suitable.
Conicidad [co-ne-the-dahd'], *f.* Conicity, the figure which the tire of a wheel presents in machines and railroad carriages.
Cónico, ca [co'-ne-co, cah], *a.* Conical or conic.
Conífero, ra [co-nee'-fay-ro, rah], *a.* (Bot.) Coniferous: applied to plants and trees.
Coniza [co-nee'-thah], *f.* (Bot.) Great flea-bane. Conyza squarrosa. *V.* ZARAGATONA.
Conjetura [con-hay-too'-rah], *f.* Conjecture, surmise, guess.
Conjeturable [con-hay-too-rah'-blay], *a.* Conjecturable.
Conjeturador, ra [con-hay-too-rah-dor', rah], *m.* & *f.* Conjecturer, guesser.
Conjetural [con-hay-too-rahl'], *a.* Conjectural.
Conjeturalmente [con-hay-too-ral-men'-tay], *adv.* Conjecturally, guessingly.
Conjeturar [con-hay-too-rar'], *va.* To conjecture, to guess.
Conjuez [con-hoo-eth'], *m.* A judge jointly with another upon the same matter.
Conjugación [con-hoo-gah-the-on'], *f.* 1. Conjugation, the form of inflecting verbs. 2. (Obs.) The act of comparing one thing with another.
Conjugado, da [con-hoo-gah'-do, dah], *a.* & *pp.* of CONJUGAR. Conjugated, inflected; compared. *Nervios conjugados*, (Anat.) Conjugate nerves, those which discharge analogous functions or serve for the same sensation. *Eje conjugado*, Conjugate or minor axis of an ellipse.
Conjugal [con-hoo-gahl'], *a.* (Obs.) *V.* CONYUGAL.
Conjugar [con-hoo-gar'], *va.* 1. To conjugate or inflect verbs. 2. (Obs.) To compare.
Conjunción [con-hoon-the-on'], *f.* 1. Conjunction, union, association, league, conjugation, copulation, the act of coupling or joining together; consolidation. 2. Conjunction, a part of speech. 3. (Ast.) Conjunction of two planets in the same degree of the zodiac.
Conjuntamente [con-hoon-tah-men'-tay], *adv.* Conjunctly, jointly.
Conjuntiva [con-hoon-tee'-vah], *f.* Conjunctiva, the mucous membrane of the eye.
Conjuntivitis [con-hoon-te-vee'-tis], *f.* (Med.) Conjunctivitis.
Conjuntivo, va [con-hoon-tee'-vo, vah], *a.* Conjunctive, copulative, connexive.
Conjuntivo [con-hoon-tee'-vo], *m.* (Obs.) The conjunctive mood of a verb. *V.* SUBJUNTIVO.
Conjunto, ta [con-hoon'-to, tah], *a.* 1. Conjunct, united, connected, conjunctive, contiguous. 2. Allied by kindred or friendship. 3. Mixed or incorporated with another thing.
Conjunto [con-hoon'-to], *m.* The whole, aggregate, entirety.
Conjuntura [con-hoon-too'-rah], *f.* *V.* COYUNTURA and CONJUNCIÓN.
Conjura [con-hoo'-rah], *f.* (Obs.) *V.* CONJURACIÓN.
Conjuración [con-hoo-rah-the-on'], *f.* 1. Conspiracy, conjuration, plot, complot, machination. 2. (Obs.) Conjuration, the form or act of summoning another in some sacred name. 3. (Obs.) *V.* CONJURO.
Conjurado, da [con-hoo-rah'-do, dah], *m.* & *f.* Conspirator; leaguer, covenanter.—*pp.* of CONJURAR.
Conjurador [con-hoo-rah-dor'], *m.* 1. Conjurer, enchanter, impostor. 2. Exorcist. 3. (Obs.) Conspirator.
Conjuramentar [con-hoo-rah-men-tar'], *va.* 1. (Obs.) To bind by an oath. 2. To take an oath to another.—*vr.* To bind one's self by an oath. *V.* JURAMENTARSE.
Conjurante [con-hoo-rahn'-tay], *pa.* Conjuring, conspiring.
Conjurar [con-hoo-rar'], *vn.* 1. To conjure, to conspire, to plot, to hatch or concert treason. 2. To conspire. 3. To join in a conspiracy formed by others. 4. (Obs.) To swear or take an oath improperly with others.—*va.* 1. To exorcise. 2. To conjure, to summon in a sacred name. 3. To entreat, to implore, to ask any thing in a solemn manner. 4. To avert, ward off, a mischief or danger.
Conjuro [con-hoo'-ro], *m.* 1. Conjuration, exorcism. 2. Incantation.
Conllevador [con-lyay-vah-dor'], *m.* Helper, assistant.
Conllevar [con-lyay-var'], *va.* To aid or assist another in his labours; to bear with any one.
Conllorar [con-lyo-rar'], *va.* (Littl. us.) To sympathize with others, to lament their sufferings.
Conmaterial [con-mah-tay-re-ahl'], *a.* (Rare) Of the same material.
Conmemoración [con-may-mo-rah-the-on'], *f.* 1. Remembrance of a person or thing. 2. Commemoration, public celebration. 3. *Conmemoración de los difuntos*, Anniversary celebrated by the Roman Catholic church in memory of the deceased, Nov. 2; All-souls' day.
Conmemorar [con-may-mo-rar'], *va.* To commemorate by public acts.
Conmemorativo, va [con-may-mo-rah-tee'-vo, vah], *a.* (Littl. us.) Commemorative.
Conmemoratorio, ria [con-may-mo-rah-to'-re-o, ah], *a.* (Littl. us.) Commemoratory.
Conmensal [con-men-sahl'], *m.* Commensal, mate, messmate, one who lives and boards with another at his expense.
Conmensalia [con-men-sah-lee'-ah], *f.* Commensality.
Conmensurabilidad [con-men-soo-rah-be-le-dahd'], *f.* Commensurability.
Conmensurable [con-men-soo-rah'-blay], *a.* (Littl. us.) Commensurable.

Conmensuración [con-men-soo-rah-the-on'], *f.* Commensuration.
Conmensurar [con-men-soo-rar'], *va.* To commensurate.
Conmensurativo, va [con-men-soo-rah-tee'-vo, vah], *a.* Commensurable.
Conmigo [con-mee'-go], *pron. pers.* With me, with myself.
Conmilitón [con-me-le-tone'], *m.* Comrade, a fellow-soldier.
Conminación [con-me-nah-the-on'], *f.* Commination, a threat.
Conminar [con-me-nar'], *va.* To threaten or denounce punishment to a criminal in order to make him declare the truth.
Conminatorio, ria [con-me-nah-to'-re-o, ah], *a.* Comminatory, denunciatory, threatening.
Conminuta [con-me-noo'-tah], *a.* Comminuted. *V.* FRACTURA.
Conmiseración [con-me-say-rah-the-on'], *f.* Commiseration, pity, compassion.
Conmistión, Conmistura (Obs.) [con-mis-te-on'], *f.* Commixion.
Conmisto, ta, or **Conmixto, ta** [con-mees'-to, tah], *a.* Mixed, mingled, incorporated.
Conmoción [con-mo-the-on'], *f.* 1. Commotion of the mind or body. 2. Excitement, stirring up; flurry, fretting. 3. Commotion, tumult, disturbance, convulsion.
Conmonitorio [con-mo-ne-to'-re-o], *m.* 1. A written narration of an event. 2. Order from a superior to an inferior judge, reminding him of his duty.
Conmovedor [con-mo-vay-dor'], *m.* (Littl. us.) Disturber, fretter.
Conmover [con-mo-verr'], *va.* To commove, to disturb, to affect.
Conmovimiento [con-mo-ve-me-en'-to], *m.* (Obs.) *V.* CONMOCIÓN.
(*Yo conmuevo, yo conmueva,* from *Conmover. V.* MOVER.)
Conmutabilidad [con-moo-tah-be-le-dahd'], *f.* (Littl. us.) Commutability.
Conmutable [con-moo-tah'-blay], *a.* Commutable.
Conmutación [con-moo-tah-the-on'], *f.* Commutation, exchange.
Conmutador [con-moo-tah-dor'], *m.* Electric switch, telegraph key, cut-out, commutator.
Conmutar [con-moo-tar'], *va.* To commute, to change, to barter.
Conmutativamente [con-moo-tah-te-vah-men'-tay], *adv.* (Littl. us.) Commutatively.
Conmutativo, va [con-moo-tah-tee'-vo, vah], *a.* Commutative.
Connato, ta [con-nah'-to, tah], *a.* 1. (Med.) Connate, congenital, innate. 2. (Bot.) Connate, conjoined.
Connatural [con-nah-too-rahl'], *a.* Connatural, inborn.
Connaturalización [con-nah-too-rah-le-thah-the-on'], *f.* Naturalization, investing aliens with the privileges of native subjects.
Connaturalizar [con-nah-too-rah-le-thar'], *va.* To naturalize, to invest with the privileges of native subjects.—*vr.* To accustom one's self to labour, climate, or food; to inure.
Connaturalmente [con-nah-too-ral-men'-tay], *adv.* Connaturally.
Connexidad [con-nek-se-dahd'], *f. V.* CONEXIDAD.
Connivencia [con-ne-ven'-the-ah], *f.* 1. Connivance. 2. Action of confabulating.
Connosco [con-nohs'-co]. Obs. for *con nosotros.*
Connotación [con-no-tah-the-on'], *f.* 1. Connotation. 2. A distant relation.
Connotado [con-no-tah'-do], *m.* Relationship, kindred.—*Connotado, da, pp.* of CONNOTAR.
Connotar [con-no-tar'], *va.* To connote, to connotate, to imply.
Connotativo, va [con-no-tah-tee'-vo, vah], *a.* (Gram.) Connotative, or connotive, applied to nouns which signify the quality of the object designated by the primitive noun, or the office of the subject from which it is derived, as *aquilino, caballar, bacanal, lírico,* etc.
Connovicio, cia [con-no-vee'-the-o, ah], *m.* & *f.* A fellow-novice.
Connubial [con-noo-be-ahl'], *a.* Connubial, matrimonial, conjugal.
Connubio [con-noo'-be-o], *m.* (Poet.) Matrimony, marriage, wedlock.
Connumeración [con-noo-may-rah-the-on'], *f.* (Littl. us.) Connumeration.
Connumerar [con-noo-may-rar'], *va.* To enumerate; to include in a number.
Connusco [con-noohs'-co]. (Obs.) *V.* CONNOSCO.
Cono [co'-no], *m.* 1. (Geom.) Cone. 2. (Zool.) Genus of mollusks which has the spiral of the shell flattened. 3. (Bot.) Cone, the fruit of the pine family.
Conocedor, ra [co-no-thay-dor', rah], *m.* & *f.* 1. Connoisseur. 2. Judge or critic in matters of taste. 3. In Andalusia, the chief herdsman: in Castile he is called *mayoral.*
Conocer [co-no-therr'], *va.* 1. To know, to be acquainted with. 2. To possess a clear or distinct idea of a person's physiognomy, or the figure of a thing, to feel. 3. To perceive, to comprehend. 4. To experience, to observe. 5. To conjecture, to surmise. 6. To know carnally. 7. (Obs.) To acknowledge a crime, or debt. *Conocer de una causa* or *pleito,* To try a cause; applied to a judge. *Conocer alguno su pecado,* To confess his fault.—*vr.* 1. To know one another. 2. To appreciate one's own good or bad qualities. (*Conocer* and *saber* are distinguished from each other, like the French verbs *connaître* and *savoir,* or the German *kennen* and *wissen.*)
Conocible [co-no-thee'-blay], *a.* Cognoscible, knowable.
Conocidamente [co-no-the-dah-men'-tay], *adv.* Knowingly, evidently, confessedly.
Conocido, da [co-no-thee'-do, dah]. 1. *m.* & *f.* Acquaintance. 2. *a.* Person of family or distinction.—*pp.* of CONOCER.
Conocimiento [co-no-the-me-en'-to], *m.* 1. Knowledge, understanding, skill. 2. Acquaintance, the person with whom we are acquainted. 3. Acquaintance, a slight or initial knowledge, a sort of friendship. 4. Cognizance, judicial notice. 5. (Com.) Bill of lading. 6. A note of identification, relative to business matters. 7. (Amer.) A check for baggage.—*pl.* Accomplishments; science. *Venir en conocimiento,* To remember or recollect a thing distinctly; to comprehend a thing clearly after thinking of it.
Conoidal [co-no-e-dahl'], *a.* Conoidal, conoidical.
Conoide [co-no'-e-day], *f.* Conoid.
Conopial, Conopio [co-no-pe-ahl', co-no'-pe-o], *m.* (Arch.) Ogee arch.
(*Yo conozco, yo conozca,* from *Conocer. V.* ABORRECER.)
Conque [con-kay'], *m.* (Coll.) Condition, quality.
Conquerir [con-kay-reer'], *va.* (Obs.) *V.* CONQUISTAR.
Conquiforme [con-ke-for'-may], *a.* Conchiform, shaped like one-half of a bivalve shell.
Conquiliología, *f. V.* CONCHOLOGÍA
Conquiso, sa [con-kee'-so, sah], *pp. irr.* of CONQUERIR.
Conquista [con-kees'-tah], *f.* 1. Conquest, subjection. 2. Conquest, acquisition by victory; the thing gained. 3. Act of winning another's affections.
Conquistable [con-kees-tah'-blay], *a.* (Littl. us.) Conquerable.
Conquistador [con-kees-tah-dor'], *m.* Conqueror.
Conquistadora [con-kees-tah-do'-rah], *f.* (Littl. us.) Conqueress.
Conquistar [con-kees-tar'], *va.* 1. To conquer, to overcome, to subdue. 2. To acquire, to win another's affections.
Conrear [con-ray-ar'], *va.* 1. In manufactories, to grease wool. 2. To hoe the soil. *V.* BINAR.
Conregnante [con-reg-nahn'-tay], *a.* Reigning with another.
Conreinar [con-ray-e-nar'], *vn.* To reign with another.
Consaber [con-sah-berr'], *vn.* (Littl. us.) To have knowledge of a thing jointly with others.
Consabido, da [con-sah-bee'-do, dah], *a.* Already known; alluded to, in question: applied to persons or things already treated of.—*pp.* of CONSABER.
Consabidor, ra [con-sah-be-dor', rah], *m.* & *f.* One who possesses knowledge jointly with others.
Consagración [con-sah-grah-the-on'], *f.* Consecration.
Consagrado, da [con-sah-grah'-do, dah], *a.* & *pp.* of CONSAGRAR. Consecrate, consecrated, sacred, devoted.
Consagrante [con-sah-grahn'-tay], *m.* & *pa.* Consecrator.
Consagrar [con-sah-grar'], *va.* 1. To consecrate, to hallow, to make sacred. 2. Among the Romans, to deify their emperors. 3. To consecrate, to devote, to dedicate. 4. (Met.) To erect a monument.
Consanguíneo, nea [con-san-gee'-nay-o ah], *a.* Consanguineous, cognate, kindred.
Consanguinidad [con-san-gee-ne-dahd'], *f.* Consanguinity.
Consciencia, *f.* (Obs.) *V.* CONCIENCIA
Consciente [cons-the-en'-tay], *a.* Conscious, in possession of one's faculties, of sound, disposing mind; compos mentis.
Conscripción [cons-crip-the-on'], *f.* Conscription, the enrolling or recruitment of the French armies. (Gallicism.)
Conscripto [cons-creep'-to], *m.* Conscript, taken by lot, or compulsorily enrolled to serve in the army or navy. (Gallicism.)—*a.* Conscript: applied to the Roman senators.
Consectario [con-sec-tah'-re-o], *m.* Consectary, corollary.
Consectario [con-sec-tah'-re-o], *a.* Consectary, consequent.
Consecución [con-say-coo-the-on'], *f.* Attainment of a benefice, employ, or other desirable object.
Consecuencia [con-say-coo-en'-the-ah], *f.* 1. Consequence, conclusion, inference. *Por consecuencia,* Therefore. 2. Result or effect of a cause, issue. 3. Consistence, firmness, coherence. *Guardar consecuencia,* To be consistent. 4. Consequence, importance, moment, concern. matter; consideration, note. *Ser de consecuencia,* To be very important. *En consecuencia,* Consequently, therefore, in consequence of.
Consecuente [con-say-coo-en'-tay], *m.* 1. Consequent, consequence. 2. Effect, that which follows an acting cause.
Consecuente, *a.* 1. Consequent, following by rational deduction. 2. Fol-

lowing, as the effect of a cause. 3. Consistent, coherent. *Ser consecuente en sus operaciones*, To act with consistency.

Consecuentemente [con-say-coo-en-tay-men'-tay], *adv.* 1. Consequently. 2. By consequence, necessarily, inevitably.

Consecutivamente [con-say-coo-te-vah-men'-tay], *adv.* Consecutively.

Consecutivo, va [con-say-coo-tee'-vo, vah], *a.* Consecutive, consequential.

Conseguimiento [con-say-gee-me-en'-to], *m.* Attainment, obtainment. *V.* Consecución.

Conseguir [con-say-geer'], *va.* To attain, to get, to gain, to obtain, to succeed.

Conseja [con-say'-hah], *f.* A fable.

Consejable [con-say-hah'-blay], *a.* (Obs.) Capable of receiving advice.

Consejador [con-say-hah-dor'], *m.* (Obs.) *V.* Aconsejador.

Consejera [con-say-hay'-rah], *f.* Counsellor's wife; woman who gives advice.

Consejero [con-say-hay'-ro], *m.* 1. Counsellor, member of a council. 2. Counsellor, adviser. 3. Any thing which may give warning. 4. *Consejero de estado*, A counsellor of state. *Consejero de capa y espada*, A magistrate not bred to the law.

Consejo [con-say'-ho], *m.* 1. Counsel, advice, opinion. 2. Council, an assembly of magistrates. 3. Council-house. *Consejo directivo*, Board of directors.

Consejuela [con-say-hoo-ay'-lah], *f. dim.* (Obs.) A little tale or story.

Conseminado, da [con-say-me-nah'-do, dah], *a.* (Agr.) Sown with different kinds of grain.

Consenciente [con-sen-the-en'-tay], *pa.* Consenting, conniver.

Consenso [con-sen'-so], *m.* A general assent, agreement of opinion: consensus.

Consentido [con-sen-tee'-do], *a.* 1. Applied to a spoiled child. 2. Applied to a cuckold by his own consent.—*Consentido, da, pp.* of Consentir.

Consentidor, ra [con-sen-te-dor', rah], *m.* & *f.* Complier, conniver.

Consentimiento [con-sen-te-me-en'-to], *m.* 1. Consent, connivance, compliance, acquiescence, concurrence, consenting, acknowledgment. 2. (Med.) Consent.

Consentir [con-sen-teer'], *va.* 1. To consent, to agree. 2. To comply, to acquiesce, to accede, to condescend. 3. To believe for certain, to rely, to depend. 4. To coddle, spoil, over-indulge children or servants. (Acad.)

Conserje [con-serr'-hay], *m.* Keeper or warden of a royal palace, castle, or public building. (*Cf.* Concierge.)

Conserjería [con-ser-hay-ree'-ah], *f.* 1. Wardenship of a royal palace or castle. 2. Warden's dwelling.

Conserva [con-serr'-vah], *f.* 1. Conserve, preserve. 2. Pickles. 3. Fleet of merchantmen under convoy of a ship of war. *Ir* or *navegar de conserva*, To sail under convoy, to navigate in company with other ships.—*pl.* (Coll.) Spectacles, lenses.

Conservación [con-ser-vah-the-on'], *f.* 1. Conservation, preservation. 2. Maintenance, upkeep. *Conservación del suelo*, Soil conservation.

Conservador [con-ser-vah-dor'], *m.* Conservator, preserver.

Conservadora [con-ser-vah-do'-rah], *f.* Conservatrix.

Conservaduría [con-ser-vah-doo-ree'-ah], *f.* A place or dignity in the order of Malta, whose incumbent is obliged to watch over the privileges of the order.

Conservante [con-ser-vahn'-tay], *pa.* Conserving, conserver.

Conservar [con-ser-var'], *va.* 1. To conserve, to maintain, to preserve, to keep, to hold. 2. To guard, to observe, to continue. 3. To preserve or pickle fruit.

Conservativo, va [con-ser-vah-tee'-vo, vah], *a.* Conservative, preservative.

Conservativos [con-ser-vah-tee'-vos], *m. pl.* Spectacles with preservative lenses.

Conservatoría [con-ser-vah-to-ree'-ah], *f.* 1. Place and office of a *Juez conservador*, who is peculiarly charged to preserve and defend the rights and privileges of a community. 2. Indult or apostolical letters granted to communities, by virtue of which they choose their own judges conservators. *Conservatorías*, Letters patent granted by conservatory judges in favour of those under their jurisdiction.

Conservatorio [con-ser-vah-to'-re-o], *m.* Conservatory, a place for instruction in the fine arts.

Conservatorio, ria [con-ser-vah-to'-re-o, ah], *a.* Conservatory, having a preservative quality.

Conservero, ra [con-ser-vay'-ro, rah], *m.* & *f.* Conserver, a preparer of conserves.

Considerable [con-se-day-rah'-blay], *a.* 1. Considerable. 2. Great, large, plentiful.

Considerablemente [con-se-day-rah-blay-men'-tay], *adv.* Considerably.

Consideración [con-se-day-rah-the-on'], *f.* 1. Consideration, regard, notice, sake, account. 2. Consideration; reflection, contemplation, meditation. 3. Consideration, importance, claim to notice, worthiness of regard. 4. Urbanity, respect. *Ser de consideración*, To be of great moment. *En consideración*, Considering, in consideration, in proportion.

Consideracioncilla [con-se-day-rah-the-on-theel'-lyah], *f. dim.* A slight consideration.

Consideradamente [con-se-day-rah-dah-men'-tay], *adv.* Considerately, calmly.

Considerado [con-se-day-rah'-do], *a.* Prudent, considerate.—*Considerado, da, pp.* of Considerar.

Considerador, ra [con-se-day-rah-dor', rah], *m.* & *f.* Considerer, considerator, a person of prudence or reflection.

Considerante [con-se-day-rahn'-tay], *pa.* Considering.

Considerar [con-se-day-rar'], *va.* 1. To consider, meditate. 2. To treat with urbanity, respect, consideration.

(*Yo consiento, yo consienta; él consintió, él consintiera;* from *Consentir. V.* Asentir.)

Consiervo [con-se-err'-vo], *m.* A fellow-slave.

Consigna [con-seeg'-nah], *f.* (Mil.) Watch-word, countersign.

Consignación [con-sig-nah-the-on'], *f.* 1. Consignation. 2. Sum of money destined to serve for a certain time some peculiar purpose. 3. Consignment, cargo of goods.

Consignador [con-sig-nah-dor'], *m.* Consignor, one who consigns goods or merchandise to a foreign correspondent.

Consignar [con-sig-nar'], *va.* 1. To consign, assign, or make over the rent of a house or any other sum for the payment of a debt. 2. To consign, to yield, to intrust, to lay to. 3. To lay by, to deposit. 4. To deliver. 5. To consign goods or merchandise to a foreign correspondent, to be sold for account of the consignors. 6. (Obs.) To sign with the mark of a cross.

Consignatario [con-sig-nah-tah'-re-o], *m.* 1. Trustee, who receives money in trust for another. 2. Mortgagee, who possesses and enjoys the lands or tenements mortgaged, until the debt be paid out of the proceeds. 3. Consignee, a merchant or factor to whom a ship or cargo, or merely a part of the latter, is consigned.

Consigo [con-see'-go], *pro. pers.* With one's self, with himself, herself, themselves, yourself, or yourselves. *Consigo mismo, consigo propio*, or *consigo solo*, Alone, by one's self.

(*Yo consigo, yo consiga*, from *Conseguir. V.* Pedir.)

Consiguiente [con-se-gee-en'-tay], *m.* (Log.) Consequence, result.

Consiguiente [con-se-gee-en'-tay], *a.* Consequent, consecutive, consequential. *De consiguiente, por consiguiente*, or *por el consiguiente*, Consequently, by consequence, pursuantly.

Consiguientemente [con-se-ge-en-tay-men'-tay], *adv.* Consequently.

Consiliario [con-se-le-ah'-re-o], *m.* Counsellor or assistant to the heads of colleges, convents, etc. *V.* Consejero.

Consintiente [con-sin-te-en'-tay], *pa.* Consenting, agreeing.

Consistencia [con-sis-ten'-the-ah], *f.* 1. Consistence, or consistency, degree of density or rarity. 2. Consistency, stability, duration; coherence, conformity. 3. Consistency, firmness, solidity, intellectual strength.

Consistente [con-sis-ten'-tay], *a.* Consistent, firm, solid.

Consistir [con-sis-teer'], *vn.* 1. To consist, to subsist, to continue fixed; to lie. 2. To consist, to be comprised, to be contained. 3. To consist, to be composed. *Consistir en*, To be due to, to be accounted for by.

Consistorial [con-sis-to-re-ahl'], *a.* 1. Consistorial, belonging or relating to an ecclesiastical court. 2. *Casa consistorial*, or *casas consistoriales*, Senate-house, guildhall, town-houses or town-halls, court-house.

Consistorio [con-sis-to'-re-o], *m.* 1. Consistory, a meeting held by the Pope and his cardinals on matters concerning the government and discipline of the Roman Catholic church. 2. In some of the chief towns of Spain, the town-house or town-hall, and the whole civic body, composed of *Corregidor*, or mayor, and aldermen. *Consistorio divino*, The tribunal of God.

Consocio [con-so'-the-o], *m.* Partner, companion, fellow-partner.

Consol [con-sol'], *m.* (Peru) = Consola.

Consola [con-so'-lah], *f.* Console, pier-table, bracket-shelf.

Consolable [con-so-lah'-blay], *a.* Consolable, relievable, comfortable.

Consolablemente, *adv.* Consolably, comfortably.

Consolación [con-so-lah-the-on'], *f.* 1. Consolation, comfort. 2. (Obs.) Charity.

Consolado, da [con-so-lah'-do, dah], *a.* Consoled, comforted.—*pp.* of Consolar.

Consolador, ra [con-so-lah-dor', rah], *m.* & *f.* 1. Consolator, comforter. 2. *m.* Comforter, a name of the Holy Spirit.

Consolador, ra [con-so-lah-dor', rah], *a.* Consolatory, comfortable.

Consolante [con-so-lahn'-tay], *pa.* Comforting, consoling, comfortable.

Consolar [con-so-lar'], *va.* To console, to comfort, to cheer.

Consolativo, va [con-so-lah-tee'-vo, vah], **Consolatorio, ria,** *a.* Consolatory, comfortable.

Consoldamiento, *m.* (Obs.) *V.* CONSOLIDACIÓN.

Consólida [con-so'-le-dah], *f.* (Bot.) *V.* CONSUELDA. *Consólida real,* Larkspur.

Consolidación [con-so-le-dah-the-on'], *f.* Consolidation.

Consolidado, da [con-so-le-dah'-do, dah], *a.* Consolidated.—*pl.* Consolidated annuities, consols, government securities.

Consolidar [con-so-le-dar'], *va.* To consolidate, to compact, to close, to harden, to strengthen.—*vr.* 1. To consolidate, to grow firm, hard, or solid. 2. (Law) To unite the interest with the principal.

Consolidativo, va [con-so-le-dah-tee'-vo, vah], *a.* Consolidant, consolidative.

Consommé [con-so-may'], *m.* Consommé, beef broth. (F.)

Consonancia [con-so-nahn'-the-ah], *f.* 1. Consonance, harmony, accord of sound. 2. Consistency, congruence, consent. 3. (Met.) Conformity.

Consonante [con-so-nahn'-tay], *m.* 1. Rhyme, a word, the last syllable or syllables of which, from the vowel where the accent is, corresponds with that of another. 2. (Mus.) A consonous or corresponding sound. 3. *f.* (Gram.) A consonant.

Consonante [con-so-nahn'-tay], *a.* Consonant, agreeable, consistent, concordant, conformable. *Letras consonantes,* The consonants.

Consonantemente [con-so-nan-tay-men'-tay], *adv.* Consonantly, agreeably.

Consonar [con-so-nar'], *vn.* 1. To make a body sound; to play on musical instruments. 2. To rhyme. 3. (Met.) To agree, to resemble.

Cónsones [con'-so-nes], *m. pl.* (Mus.) Concordant sounds.

Cónsono, na [con'-so-no, nah], *a.* Consonous, harmonious, consonant.

Consorcio [con-sor'-the-o], *m.* 1. Consortion, partnership, society. 2. Friendly intercourse, mutual affection.

Consorte [con-sor'-tay], *com.* 1. Consort, companion, partner; mate. 2. Consort, a person joined in marriage with another. 3. One who enters or defends an action jointly with another.

Conspicuamente [cons-pe-coo-ah-men'-tay], *adv.* (Littl. us.) Conspicuously.

Conspicuo, cua [cons-pee'-coo-o, ah], *a.* 1. Conspicuous, obvious, observable. 2. Conspicuous, eminent, famous, distinguished.

Conspiración [cons-pe-rah-the-on'], *f.* Conspiracy, plot, complot, conjuration, conspiration: an agreement of men to do any thing evil or unlawful.

Conspirado [cons-pe-rah'-do], *m. V.* CONSPIRADOR.—*Conspirado, da, pp.* of CONSPIRAR.

Conspirador [cons-pe-rah-dor'], *m.* Conspirator, complotter, traitor.

Conspirante [cons-pe-rahn'-tay], *pa.* Conspiring. *Fuerzas conspirantes,* Conspiring powers, co-operating mechanical powers which concur in producing the same effect.

Conspirar [cons-pe-rar'], *va.* (Obs.) To implore the assistance or solicit the favour of another.—*vn.* 1. To conspire, to concert a crime, to plot, to complot. 2. To conspire, to agree together, to co-operate, to combine.

Constancia [cons-tahn'-the-ah], *f.* Constancy, steadiness, immutability.

Constante [cons-tahn'-tay], *a.* 1. Constant, firm, unalterable, immutable. 2. Loyal, constant. 3. Manifest, apparent, clear. 4. *m.* & *f.* One who is constant.—*pa.* Composed of, consisting in.

Constantemente [cons-tan-tay-men'-tay], *adv.* 1. Constantly, firmly, unalterably. 2. Evidently, undoubtedly.

Constantinopolitano, na [cons-tan-te-no-po-le-tah'-no, nah], *a.* Of Constantinople.

Constar [cons-tar'], *v. imp.* 1. To be clear, evident, certain. *Consta en autos* or *de autos,* It appears from the judicial proceedings. 2. To be composed of, to consist in. 3. Of verses, to have the measure and accent corresponding to their class.

Constelación [cons-tay-lah-the-on'], *f.* 1. Constellation, a cluster of fixed stars. 2. Climate, temperature of the air. *Corre una constelación,* An epidemic disease prevails.

Consternación [cons-ter-nah-the-on'], *f.* Consternation, perturbation of mind, amazement, horror, distress.

Consternar [cons-ter-nar'], *va.* To terrify, to strike with horror or amazement, to confound.

Constipación [cons-te-pah-the-on'], *f.* 1. Cold, a disease; a stoppage of the cuticular pores, occasioned by cold; want of perspiration. 2. Constipation, costiveness.

Constipado [cons-te-pah'-do], *m.* Cold, a disease.—*Constipado, da, pp.* of CONSTIPAR.

Constipar [cons-te-par'], *va.* To cause a cold, to obstruct the perspiration. —*vr.* 1. To catch cold. 2. To be costive.

Constipativo, va [cons-te-pah-tee'-vo, vah], *a.* Constrictive.

Constitución [cons-te-too-the-on'], *f.* 1. 1. Constitution. 2. Constitution, corporeal frame, temper of body with respect to health or disease, habit of the body. 3. Constitution, established form of government; system of laws and customs. 4. Constitution, particular law or established usage. 5. Any of the by-laws by which a body or corporation is governed.

Constitucional [cons-te-too-the-o-nahl'], *m.* Constitutionalist, constitutionist.

Constitucional, *a.* Constitutional.

Constitucionalidad [cons-te-too-the-o-nah-le-dahd'], *f.* Constitutionality.

Constitucionalismo [cons-te-too-the-o-nah-lees'-mo], *m.* Constitutionalism, love of the constitution of a country.

Constitucionalmente, *adv.* Constitutionally.

Constituidor [cons-te-too-e-dor'], *m.* (Littl. us.) Constituent, constituter.

Constituir [cons-te-too-eer'], *va.* 1. To constitute, to produce. 2. To erect, to establish, to make; to create. 3. To appoint, to depute. 4. *Constituir la dote,* To pay off a woman's portion, either by instalments or in one sum. 5. *Constituirse en obligación de alguna cosa,* To bind one's self to perform any thing.

Constitutivo, va [cons-te-too-tee'-vo, vah], *a.* Constitutive, essential, productive, formal, hypostatical.—*m.* & *f.* Constituent.

Constituto [cons-te-too'-to], *m.* A legal fiction of alienation and transference.

Constituyente [cons-te-too-yen'-tay], *m.* 1. Constituent. 2. *V.* COMITENTE.—*a.* Constituent, that which makes a thing what it is.—*pa.* of CONSTITUIR.

Constreñible [cons-tray-nyee'-blay], *a.* (Littl. us.) Constrainable.

Constreñidamente, *adv.* Compulsively.

Constreñimiento [cons-tray-nyee-me-en'-to], *m.* Constraint or compulsion.

Constreñir [cons-tray-nyeer'], *va.* 1. To constrain, to compel, to force, to constrict. 2. (Med.) To bind or make costive: applied to food.

Constricción [cons-tric-the-on'], *f.* Constriction, contraction.

Constrictivo, va [cons-tric-tee'-vo, vah], *a.* Binding, astringent, or constringent.

Constrictor [cons-tric-tor'], *m.* & *a.* Constrictor.

Constringente [cons-trin-hen'-tay], *a.* & *pa.* Constringent; constrictor.

Constriñir, *va.* (Obs.) *V.* CONSTREÑIR.

(*Yo constriño, yo constriña; él constriñó, constriñera;* from *Constreñir. V.* PEDIR.)

Construcción [cons-trooc-the-on'], *f.* 1. Construction. 2. Construction, the putting of words together. 3. Construction, arranging terms in their proper order; the sense or the meaning. 4. Interpretation, version, translation. 5. Ship-building, naval architecture.

Constructor, ra [cons-trooc-tor', rah], *a.* Building, constructing. *Ingeniero constructor,* Constructing engineer.—*m.* Constructor. *Constructor de caminos,* Road builder.

Construir [cons-troo-eer'], *va.* 1. To form, to build, to construct, to fabricate, to frame. 2. To construe, to range words in their natural order. 3. To translate literally.

Constupración [cons-too-prah-the-on'], *f.* (Littl. us.) Constupration.

Constuprador [cons-too-prah-dor'], *m.* A debaucher, a defiler, a corruptor.

Constuprar [cons-too-prar'], *va.* To constuprate, to defile, to deflour.

Consubstanciación [con-soobs-tan-the-ah-the-on'], *f.* 1. The mingling of one thing with another. 2. Consubstantiation, the doctrine of the Lutherans upon the Eucharist.

Consubstanciador [con-soobs-tan-the-ah-dor'], *a.* Epithet applied by the Catholics to the Lutherans, who hold the doctrine of consubstantiation.

Consubstancial, *a.* Consubstantial: applied to the Holy Trinity; of one and the same substance.

Consubstancialidad [con-soobs-tan-the ah-le-dahd'], *f.* Consubstantiality.

Consuegrar [con-soo-ay-grar'], *vn.* To become joint fathers or mothers-in-law.

Consuegro, gra [con-soo-ay'-gro, grah] *m.* & *f.* The fathers or mothers who marry their children together.

Consuelda [con-soo-el'-dah], *f.* (Bot.) Comfrey. Symphytum officinale. *Consuelda media,* Common bugle, middle consound. Aguja reptans.

Consuelo [con-soo-ay'-lo], *m.* 1. Consolation, comfort, relief, comfortableness. 2. Joy, merriment. 3. (Obs.) Charity. 4. (Coll.) *Sin consuelo,* Out of rule or measure. *Beber sin consuelo,* To drink to excess. *Gastar sin consuelo,* To outrun the constable, to spend in an inconsiderate manner.

(*Yo consuelo, yo consuele,* from *Consolar. V.* ACORDAR.)

(*Yo consueno, yo consuene,* from *Consonar. V.* ACORDAR.)

Consueta [con-soo-ay'-tah], *m.* & *f.* 1. (Prov.) Stage prompter. 2. (Prov.) Directory, which contains the order for divine service. *Consuetas,* Short prayers used on certain days in divine service.

Consuetud [con-soo-ay-tood'], *f.* (Obs.) *V.* Costumbre.

Consuetudinario, ria [con-soo-ay-too-de-nah'-re-o, ah], *a.* 1. Customary, generally practised. 2. (Theol.) In the habit of sinning.

Cónsul [cone'-sool], *m.* 1. Consul, the chief magistrate in ancient Rome. 2. Member of the tribunal of commerce. 3. Consul, an officer commissioned in foreign countries to protect the commerce of his country.

Consulado [con-soo-lah'-do], *m.* 1. Consulate, consulship. 2. Term of office as consul. 3. Tribunal of commerce, appointed to try and decide causes which concern navigation and trade: the president is called in Spain *prior*, and the members *cónsules.* 4. Office of consul and territory of same.

Consulaje [con-soo-lah'-hay], *m.* Fees paid to consuls by all merchant vessels.

Consular [con-soo-lar'], *a.* Consular. *Varón consular,* One who has been consul.

Consulta [con-sool'-tah], *f.* 1. A question proposed, or a proposal made in writing. 2. Consultation, conference, meeting for deliberation. 3. Report made and advice given to the king in council. 4. Advice to the king by the supreme tribunals and officers of state, with regard to persons proposed to fill public employments.

Consultable [con-sool-tah'-blay], *a.* Worthy or necessary to be deliberated upon.

Consultación [con-sool-tah-the-on'], *f.* Consultation, conference, meeting.

Consultante [con-sool-tahn'-tay], *pa.* Consulting, consulter. *Ministro consultante,* Minister who lays before the king the opinion of his council.

Consultar [con-sool-tar'], *va.* 1. To consult, to ask or take another's advice. 2. To advise, to give advice. 3. To consult, to deliberate, to take counsel together. *Consultar con el bolsillo,* To cut the coat according to one's cloth: literally, to consult one's purse. *Consultar con la almohada,* To take into mature consideration: literally, to consult the pillow.

Consultivo, va [con-sool-tee'-vo, vah], *a.* 1. Consultative. 2. Applied to matters which the councils and tribunals are obliged to lay before the king, accompanied with their advice.

Consultor, ra [con-sool-tor', rah], *m.* & *f.* Consultor, adviser, counsel.

Consultorio [con-sool-to'-ryo], *m.* 1. Consulting office. 2. Doctor's office.

Consumación [con-soo-mah-the-on'], *f.* 1. Consummation, perfection, end, finishing, accomplishment. 2. (Littl. us.) Destruction, suppression. *Consumación de los siglos,* Consummation, the end of the present system of things.

Consumadamente, *adv.* Perfectly, completely, consummately.

Consumado, da [con-soo-mah'-do, dah], *a.* Consummate, complete, perfect, accomplished, exquisite—*pp.* of Consumar.

Consumado. *m.* Jelly-broth, a strong broth of sheep and calves' feet; consommé.

Consumador, ra [con-soo-mah-dor', rah], *m.* & *f.* Finisher, one who consummates, perfects, or finishes.

Consumar [con-soo-mar'], *va.* To consummate, to finish, to perfect, to complete.

Consumativo, va [con-soo-mah-tee'-vo, vah], *a.* Consummate, that which consummates or completes: applied to the sacrament.

Consumible [con-soo-mee'-blay], *a.* (Litt. us.) Consumable.

Consumición [con-soo-me-the-on'], *f.* (Com.) *V.* Consumo.

Consumido, da [con-soo-mee'-do, dah], *a.* 1. Lean, meagre, exhausted, spent. 2. Easily afflicted.—*pp.* of Consumir.

Consumidor, ra [con-soo-me-dor', rah], *m.* & *f.* Consumer, destroyer.

Consumiente [con-soo-me-en'-tay], *pa.* (Obs.) Consuming, consumer.

Consumimiento [con-soo-me-me-en'-to], *m.* Consumption.

Consumir [con-soo-meer'], *va.* 1. To consume, to destroy, to waste, to exhaust; to lick up; to obliterate; to melt. *Consumar el caudal,* To run out one's fortune. 2. In the sacrifice of the mass, to swallow the elements of bread and wine in the Eucharist.—*vr.* 1. To be spent, to be exhausted. 2. To fret, to be uneasy, to be vexed. 3. To wear away, to waste away, to languish, to consume, linger, fail.

Consumo [con-soo'-mo], *m.* The consumption of provisions and merchandise. *Consumos,* 1. (Naut.) The consumption of naval stores and provisions in a voyage. 2. A tax upon the traffic in provisions and other merchandise.

Consunción [con-soon-the-on'], *f.* 1. Consumption, waste. 2. Consumption, the state of wasting. 3. (Med.) Consumption, phthisis.

Consuno (De) [con-soo'-no], *adv.* *V.* Juntamente.

Consuntivo, va [con-soon-tee'-vo, vah], *a.* (Obs.) Consumptive.

Consurrección [con-soor-rec-the-on'], *f.* Revival, revivification.

Consustanciación [con-soos-tan-the-ah-the-on'], *f.* *V.* Consubstanciación.

Contabilidad [con-tah-be-le-dahd'], *f.* 1. Calculability. 2. Book-keeping, the art of keeping accounts.

Contacto [con-tac'-to], *m.* 1. Contact, touch, union. 2. Means by which a contagious or epidemic disease is communicated to the healthy: immediate or mediate (fomites). 3. A soft iron guard for bar-magnets. 4. Intersection of two lines.

Contadero, ra [con-tah-day'-ro, rah], *a.* Countable, numerable, that which may be numbered.

Contadero, *m.* A narrow passage where sheep or cattle are counted. *Salir* or *entrar por contadero,* To go in or out through a narrow passage.

Contado, da [con-tah'-do, dah], *a.* 1. Scarce, rare, uncommon, infrequent. *De contado,* Instantly, immediately; in hand. *Al contado,* With ready money, for cash. *Por de contado,* Of course. 2. (Obs.) Designed, marked, or pointed out.—*pp.* of Contar.

Contador, ra [con-tah-dor', rah], *m.* & *f.* 1. Computer, reckoner, one skilled in accounts, accountant. 2. Numberer, numerator. 3. Counter, tell-tale: a device attached to a machine for counting its strokes or revolutions. A meter for gas or water. 4. Counter, the table on which money is told in a shop. 5. Desk. 6. An auditor. 7. (Obs.) Counting-house. 8. Counter, a false piece of money used for marking the game. *Contador de marina,* Purser in the navy. *Contador de nuevas,* Prattler, an idle talker.

Contadorcito [con-tah-dor-thee'-to], *m. dim.* A petty clerk or accountant.

Contador Geiger [con-tah-dor' gay'-ger], *m.* Geiger counter.

Contaduría [con-tah-doo-ree'-ah], *f.* 1. Accountant's or auditor's office at the exchequer. 2. Auditorship, place and employment of a public auditor of receipts.

Contagiar [con-tah-he-ar'], *va.* 1. To infect, to communicate disease, to hurt by contagion. 2. (Met.) To corrupt one's morals by a bad example, to pervert.

Contagio [con-tah'-he-o], *m.* 1. Contagion. 2. (Met.) Contagion, corruption of morals.

Contagión [con-tah-he-on'], *f.* 1. The progressive malignity of a disease, as cancer. 2. (Met.) Propagation of vice and evil habits. 3. (Obs.) *V.* Contagio.

Contagioso, sa [con-tah-he-o'-so, sah], *a.* 1. Contagious, malign, infectious. 2. (Met.) Infectious: applied to dangerous doctrines, mischievous principles, and bad examples. 3. (Coll. Mex.) Odd, particular.

Contal de cuentas [con-tahl' day coo-en'-tas], *m.* A string of beads for counting or reckoning.

Contaminación [con-tah-me-nah-the-on'], *f.* Contamination, pollution, defilement; stain, blot.

Contaminado, da [con-tah-me-nah'-do, dah], *a.* & *pp.* of Contaminar. Contaminated, corrupted, polluted.

Contaminar [con-tah-me-nar'], *va.* 1. To contaminate, to defile, or pollute. 2. To infect by contagion. 3. To corrupt, to vitiate or destroy the integrity of a text or original. 4. (Met.) To profane, to violate any thing sacred.

Contante [con-tahn'-tay], *a.* That can be counted. *Dinero contante y sonante,* Ready cash.

Contar [con-tar'], *va.* 1. To count, to reckon, to number, to enumerate, to relate, to mention. 2. To calculate, to compute. 3. To book, to place to account. 4. To class, to range according to some stated method of distribution. 5. To consider, to look upon. 6. To depend, to rely. *Contar con la amistad de uno,* To rely upon one's friendship. *Mire a quién se lo cuenta,* An expression signifying that he who hears knows more than he who relates the particulars of an event.

Contemperante [con-tem-pay-rahn'-tay], *pa.* Tempering; moderator.

Contemperar [con-tem-pay-rar'], *va.* To temper, to moderate. *V.* Atemperar.

Contemplación [con-tem-plah-the-on'], *f.* 1. Contemplation, meditation. 2. Holy meditation, a holy exercise of the soul. 3. Compliance, complaisance.

Contemplador [con-tem-plah-dor'], *m.* Contemplator. *V.* Contemplativo.

Contemplar [con-tem-plar'], *va.* 1. To contemplate, to consider with continued attention, to study. 2. To view, to behold, to look upon. 3. To contemplate, to meditate, to muse. 4. To assent, to condescend, to yield a point.

Contemplativamente [con-tem-plah-te-vah-men'-tay], *adv.* Attentively, thoughtfully.

Contemplativo, va [con-tem-plah-tee'-vo, vah], *a.* Contemplative, studious, meditative. *Vida contemplativa,* A life spent in contemplation and study.

Contemplativo [con-tem-plah-tee'-vo], *m.* 1. Contemplator; one employed in contemplation and study. 2. A pious devotee.

Contemporáneamente, *adv.* At the same time, contemporaneously.

Contemporaneidad [con-tem-po-rah-nay-e-dahd'], *f.* Contemporariness.

Contemporáneo, nea [con-tem-po-rah'-nay-o, ah], *a.* Contemporary, coetaneous, coeval.

Contemporización [con-tem-po-re-thah-the-on'], *f.* Temporizing, compliance.
Contemporizar [con-tem-po-re-thar'], *vn.* To temporize, to comply with the will and opinion of another.
Contención [con-ten-the-on'], *f.* 1. Contention, emulation. 2. Contest, dispute, strife, fighting.
Contenciosamente, *adv.* (Littl. us.) Contentiously, contestingly.
Contencioso, sa [con-ten-the-o'-so, sah], *a.* 1. Contentious, concertative, contradictious, quarrelsome, disputatious. 2. Being the object of strife or dispute, contestable. 3. Quarrelsome, litigious.
Contendedor [con-ten-day-dor'], *m* *V.* Contendor.
Contender [con-ten-derr'], *vn.* 1. To contend, to strive, to struggle, to contest, to conflict, to debate, to litigate. 2. (Met.) To argue, to discuss, to expostulate.
Contendiente [con-ten-de-en'-tay], *pa.* Disputant, litigant.
Contendor [con-ten-dor'], *m.* Contender, antagonist, opponent.
Contenedor, ra [con-tay-nay-dor', rah], *m. & f.* Holder; a tenant.
Contenencia [con-tay-nen'-the-ah], *f.* 1. Suspension in the flight of birds, especially birds of prey. 2. (For.) A demurrer: a written denial of the cause of action. 3. A peculiar movement in the Spanish dance.
Contener [con-tay-nerr'], *va.* 1. To contain, as a vessel: to comprise, as a writing; to comprehend. 2. To refrain, to curb, to restrain, to coerce. 3. To repress, to check the motion or progress of a thing.—*vr.* 1. To keep one's temper, to refrain, to hold. 2. To contain. *Él no puede contenerse,* He has no command of himself.
(*Yo contengo, yo contuve,* from *Contener.* *V.* Tener.)
Contenido, da [con-tay-nee'-do, dah], *a.* Moderate, prudent, temperate, modest.—*pp.* of Contener.
Contenido [con-tay-nee'-do], *m.* Tenor, contents, context.
Conteniente [con-tay-ne-en'-tay], *pa.* Containing, comprising.
Contenta [con-ten'-tah], *f.* 1. Endorsement. *V.* Endoso. 2. Reception or present which satisfies any one. 3. Certificate of good conduct, given by the magistrate of a place to the commander of troops which have been quartered there; also, a like certificate of attention, given by the commanding officer to the magistrate.
Contentadizo, za [con-ten-tah-dee'-tho, thah], *a.* *Bien contentadizo,* Easily contented. *Mal contentadizo,* Hard to please.
Contentamiento [con-ten-tah-me-en'-to], *m.* Contentment, joy, satisfaction, content.
Contentar [con-ten-tar'], *va.* 1. To content, to satisfy, to gratify, to please, to fill. 2. To indorse. *V.* Endosar. —*vr.* To be contented, pleased, or satisfied. *Ser de buen o mal contentar,* To be easily pleased, or difficult to be pleased.
Contentible [con-ten-tee'-blay], *a.* Contemptible.
Contentivo, va [con-ten-tee'-vo, vah], *a.* Containing, comprising.
Contento, ta [con-ten'-to, tah], *a.* 1. Glad, pleased, full of joy, mirthful. 2. Contented, satisfied, content. 3. (Obs.) Moderate, temperate, prudent.
Contento [con-ten'-to], *m.* 1. Contentment, joy, satisfaction, content, mirth. 2. Receipt, discharge. *A contento,* To one's satisfaction.
Conteo [con-tay'-o], *m.* (Sports) Countdown. Used also in rocket launchings.
Contera [con-tay'-rah], *f.* 1. Chape, a piece of brass, tin, or silver, put at the end of a cane, stick, or scabbard. 2. Button of the cascabel of a gun. 3. (Poet.) Prelude of a song, or other musical composition. *Por contera,* Ultimately, finally.
Contérmino, na [con-terr'-me-no, nah], *a.* Contiguous, bordering upon.
Conterráneo, nea [con-ter-rah'-nay-o, ah], *m. & f.* Countryman, countrywoman.
Contertuliano, na [con-ter-too-le-ah'-no, nah], **or Contertulio,** *a.* Belonging to the same social circle; of the same set.
Contestable [con-tes-tah'-blay], *a.* Contestable, disputable, controvertible.
Contestación [con-tes-tah-the-on'], *f.* 1. Answer, reply. 2. Contestation, the act of contesting: debate, strife. 3. Altercation, disputation, contention.
Contestar [con-tes-tar'], *va.* 1. To confirm the deposition of another. 2. To prove, to attest. 3. To answer, to reply. 4. To plead to an action.—*vn.* To agree, to accord.
Conteste [con-tes'-tay], *a.* Confirming the evidence of another, making the same deposition as another witness.
Contexto [con-tex'-to], *m.* 1. Intertexture, diversification of things mingled or interwoven one among another. 2. Context of a discourse.
Contextura [con-tex-too'-rah], *f.* 1. Contexture. 2. Context, the general series of a discourse. 3. (Met.) Frame and structure of the human body.
Conticinio [con-te-thee'-ne-o], *m.* Dead of the night.
Contienda [con-te-en'-dah], *f.* 1. Contest, dispute, debate, expostulation. 2. Conflict, contention, clashing, fray, jarring.
(*Yo contiendo, yo contienda,* from *Contender.* *V.* Entender.)
Contigo [con-tee'-go], *pron. pers.* With thee.
Contiguamente, *adv.* Contiguously, closely.
Contigüidad [con-te-goo-e-dad'], *f.* Contiguity, closeness.
Contiguo, gua [con-te'-goo-o, ah], *a.* Contiguous, close.
Continencia [con-te-nen'-the-ah], *f.* 1. Continence, self-command. 2. Continence, abstinence from carnal pleasures. 3. Continence, moderation in lawful pleasures. 4. The act of containing. *Continencia de la causa,* (Law) Unity which should exist in every judgment or sentence.
Continental [con-te-nen-tahl'], *a.* Continental.
Continente [con-te-nen'-tay], *m.* 1. Continent, that which contains any thing. 2. Countenance, air, mien, gait. 3. Continent, a large extent of land; mainland.
Continente, *a.* Continent, chaste, abstinent, moderate in pleasures. *En continente,* (Obs.) Immediately.
Continentemente, *adv.* Moderately, abstemiously, chastely.
Contingencia [con-tin-hen'-the-ah], *f.* Contingence or contingency, possibility, risk.
Contingente [con-tin-hen'-tay], *a.* Contingent, fortuitous, accidental.
Contingente, *m.* Contingent, a proportion that falls to any person upon a division.
Contingentemente, *adv.* Casually, accidentally, contingently.
Contino [con-tee'-no], *m.* Ancient office in the royal house of Castile.
Continuación [con-te-noo-ah-the-on'], *f.* 1. Continuation, protraction, an uninterrupted succession, lengthening. 2. Continuity, connection uninterrupted. 3. Continuance, stay.
Continuadamente [con-te-noo-ah-dah-men'-tay], *adv.* Continually.
Continuador [con-te-noo-ah-dor'], *m.* Continuer, continuator.
Continuamente, *adv.* Continually.
Continuamiento, *m.* **Continuanza,** *f.* (Obs.) *V.* Continuación.
Continuar [con-te-noo-ar'], *va. & vn.* 1. To continue, to remain in the same state, to hold. 2. To continue, to last, to endure. 3. To continue, to pursue, to protract, to carry on.
Continuativo, va [con-te-noo-ah-tee'-vo, vah], *a.* Denoting continuation: said of a conjunction; continuative.
Continuidad [con-te-noo-e-dahd'], *f.* Continuity, cohesion, continuance.
Continuo, nua [con-tee'-noo-o, ah], *a.* 1. Continuous, joined together without intervening space; continual. 2. Constant, lasting. 3. Assiduous, persevering; perennial. *A la continua,* Continually.
Continuo, *m.* 1. A whole, composed of united parts. 2. One of the hundred yeomen formerly appointed in Spain to guard the king's person and palace.—*Continuo* or *de continuo, adv.* Continually, constantly.
Contómetro [con-to'-may-tro], *m.* Comptometer, calculating machine.
Contonearse [con-to-nay-ar'-say], *vr.* To walk with an affected air or manner, to waddle.
Contoneo [con-to-nay'-o], *m.* An affected gait or manner of walking.
Contorcerse [con-tor-therr'-say], *vr.* To distort, twist, or writhe one's body.
Contorción [con-tor-the-on'], *f.* *V.* Retorcimiento and Contorsión.
Contornado [con-tor-nah'-do], *a.* (Her.) Applied to the heads of animals turned toward the sinister side of the shield.—*Contornado, da, pp.* of Contornar.
Contornar, Contornear [con-tor-nar', con-tor-nay-ar'], *va.* 1. To trace the contour or outline of a figure. 2. To form according to a proposed model or design.
Contorneo [con-tor-nay'-o], *m.* *V.* Rodeo.
Contorno [con-tor'-no], *m.* 1. Environs or vicinity of a place. 2. Contour, outline. 3. Every line in spiral or volute. *En contorno,* Round about.
Contorsión [con-tor-se-on'], *f.* 1. Contortion, twist, wry motion. 2. A grotesque gesture.
Contra [cohn'-trah], *prep.* 1. Against, in opposition to, counter, contrary to, opposite to. 2. (Obs.) Toward; by favour of. *En contra,* Against or in opposition to another thing. *Ni a favor ni en contra,* Neither pro nor con. *Contra* or *de contra,* (Amer.) A trifling thing or article given to the buyer for his custom. *V.* Ñapa, Pilón, Ganancia.
Contra, *m.* 1. Opposite sense. 2. (Mus.) The pedal organ; the pipes forming the lowest bass. More common in plural.—*f.* 1. Difficulty, inconvenience. 2. Counter, in fencing, a parry in which one foil follows another in a small circle.
Contraabertura [con-trah-ah-ber-too'-rah], *f.* (Med.) Counter-opening.
Contraábside [con-trah-ahb'-se-day], *m. & f.* Western absis.
Contraaletas [con-trah-ah-lay'-tas], *f. pl.* (Naut.) Counter-fashion pieces, the outermost timbers of the stern of the ship on both sides.

Contraalmirante, or **Contralmirante** [con-trah-al-me-rahn'-tay], *m.* Rear-admiral.

Contraamantillas [con-trah-ah-man-teel'-lyas], *f. pl.* (Naut.) Preventer-braces which serve to succour the main or fore-yard of a ship.

Contraamura [con-trah-ah-moo'-rah], *f.* (Naut.) Preventer-tack, which serves to support the tacks.

Contraaproches [con-trah-ah-pro'-chess], *m. pl.* Counter-approaches made by the besieged against the besiegers.

Contraarmiños [con-trah-ar-mee'-nyos], *m. pl.* (Her.) Contrary to ermine, i. e. black field and white spots.

Contraataques [con-trah-ah-tah'-kes], *m. pl.* Counter attacks made by the besieged.

Contrabajo [con-trah-bah'-ho], *m.* 1. Counter-bass, the deepest of all musical sounds. 2. Bass, or base-viol; double bass.

Contrabalancear [con-trah-bah-lan-thay-ar'], *va.* To counterbalance, to counterpoise.

Contrabalanza [con-trah-bah-lahn'-thah], *f. V.* CONTRAPESO and CONTRAPOSICIÓN.

Contrabanda [con-trah-bahn'-dah], *f.* (Her.) 1. A band divided into two of different metals, one coloured. 2. The piece which crosses the shield in a sense contrary to the bend: bend sinister.

Contrabandista [con-trah-ban-dees'-tah], *m.* Smuggler, contrabandist.

Contrabando [con-trah-bahn'-do], *m.* 1. A prohibited commodity. 2. Contraband trade, smuggling. 3. (Met.) Any unlawful action. *Ir* or *venir de contrabando*, To go or come by stealth.

Contrabarrado, da [con-trah-bar-rah'-do, dah], *a.* (Her.) A shield counter-barred.

Contrabasa, *f.* (Arch.) *V.* PEDESTAL.

Contrabatería [con-trah-bah-tay-ree'-ah], *f.* Counter-battery.

Contrabatir [con-trah-bah-teer'], *va.* To fire upon the enemy's batteries.

Contrabitas [con-trah-bee'-tas], *f. pl.* (Naut.) Standards of the bitts.

Contrabolina [con-tra-bo-lee'-nah], *f.* (Naut.) Preventer-bowline.

Contrabovedilla [con-trah-bo-vay-deel'-lyah], *f.* (Naut.) Second counter, upper counter.

Contrabracear [con-trah-brah-thay-ar'], *va.* (Naut.) To counter-brace.

Contrabranque [con-trah-brahn'-kay], *m.* (Naut.) Stemson, a strong piece of timber intended to re-enforce the stem.

Contrabraza [con-trah-brah'-thah], *f.* (Naut.) Preventer-brace.

Contrabrazola [con-trah-brah-tho'-lah], *f.* (Naut.) Head ledge.

Contracalcar [con-trah-cal-car'], *va.* To print backward a drawing, in order to obtain another in the same position as the original.

Contracambiada [con-trah-cam-be-ah'-dah], *f.* Changing of the forefoot by a horse.

Contracambio [con-trah-cahm'-be-o], *m.* 1. Re-exchange, the loss arising from the necessity of redrawing for the amount of a protested bill of exchange. 2. (Met.) *V.* EQUIVALENTE.

Contracanal [con-trah-cah-nahl'], *m.* Channel or conduit leading from another; counter-channel.

Contracarril [con-trah-car-reel'], *m.* Check-rail, guard-rail, safety-rail, wing-rail.

Contracción [con-trac-the-on'], *f.* 1. Contraction, shrinking, shrivelling, contractedness, constriction; corrugation. 2. Contraction, the state of being contracted. 3. Abbreviation, abridgment.

Contracebadera [con-trah-thay-bah-day'-rah], *f.* (Naut.) Sprit-top-sail.

Contracédula [con-trah-thay'-doo-lah], *f.* A decree which reverses or annuls another of an anterior date.

Contraceptivo [con-trah-thep-tee'-vo], *m.* Contraceptive. *Contraceptivo bucal*, Oral contraceptive.

Contracifra [con-trah-thee'-frah], *f.* Countercipher, the key to a secret manner of writing.

Contraclave [con-trah-clah'-vay], *f.* (Arch.) The voussoir next to the keystone.

Contracodaste interior [con-trah-co-dahs'-tay in-tay-re-or'], *m.* (Naut.) The inner stern-post. *Contracodaste exterior*, (Naut.) The back of the stern-post.

Contracorriente [con-trah-cor-re-en'-tay], *f.* (Naut.) Counter-current, stop-water.

Contracosta [con-trah-cos'-tah], *f.* Coast opposite to another.

Contráctil [con-trahc'-teel], *a.* 1. Contractile. 2. Contractible.

Contractilidad [con-trac-te-le-dahd'], *f.* Contractility, contractibility.

Contractura [con-trac-too'-rah], *f.* (Med.) Contracture, rigidity of muscles in a state of flexion, from whatever cause.

Contracuerdas [con-trah-coo-err'-das], *f. pl.* (Naut.) The outward deck-planks or platforms.

Contraculto [con-trah-cool'-to], *m.* (Littl. us.) A plain and natural style, in opposition to an affected manner of writing called *culto*.

Contradancista [con-trah-dan-thees'-tah], *m.* & *f.* A person very fond of dancing country-dances.

Contradanza [con-trah-dahn'-thah], *f.* Square dance, country-dance.

Contradecidor, ra [con-trah-day-the-dor', rah], *m.* & *f. V.* CONTRADICTOR, RA.

Contradecir [con-trah-day-theer'], *va.* To contradict, to gainsay.

Contradicción [con-trah-dic-the-on'], *f.* 1. Contradiction, controversy. 2. Control, controlment. 3. Clashing, oppugnancy, hostile resistance. 4. Contradiction, inconsistency with itself; incongruity in words or thoughts. 5. Contradiction, opposition, gainsaying. *Espíritu de contradicción*, Contradictory temper.

Contradicho, cha, *pp. irr.* of CONTRADECIR.

Contradictor, ra [con-trah-dic-tor', rah], *m.* & *f.* Contradictor, gainsayer.

Contradictoria [con-trah-dic-to'-re-ah], *f.* (Log.) Contradictory.

Contradictoriamente, *adv.* Contradictorily, inconsistently.

Contradictorio, ria [con-trah-dic-to'-re-o, ah], *a.* Contradictory.

(*Yo contradigo, yo contradije, yo contradiga*, from *Contradecir. V.* DECIR.)

Contradique [con-trah-dee'-kay], *m.* Counter-dike, a second dike.

Contradriza [con-trah-dree'-thah], *f.* (Naut.) Second halliard.

Contradurmente, Contradurmiente [con-trah-door-men'-tay], *m.* (Naut.) Clamp.

Contraeje [con-trah-ay'-hay], *m.* A counter-shaft.

Contraemboscada [con-trah-em-bos-cah'-dah], *f.* Counter-ambuscade.

Contraemergente [con-trah-ay-mer-hen'-tay], *a.* (Her.) Counter-salient.

Contraempuñadura [con-trah-em-poo-nyah-doo'-rah], *f.* (Naut.) Preventer ear-ring.

Contraendosar [con-trah-en-do-sar'], *va.* To reindorse, indorse back.

Contraer [con-trah-err'], *va.* & *vn.* 1. To contract, to knit, to furl, to shrink, to join, to unite. 2. To bring two parties together, to make a bargain. 3. To procure, to incur, to get.—*vr.* 1. To contract, to shrink up, as nerves, etc., to crumple. 2. To reduce a discourse to an idea or phrase. *Contraer deudas*, To run in debt. *Contraer enfermedad*, To contract a disease. *Contraer matrimonio*, To marry.

Contraescarpa [con-trah-es-car'-pah], *f.* (Mil.) Counterscarp.

Contraescota [con-trah-es-co'-tah], *f.* (Naut.) Preventer-sheet.

Contraescotín [con-trah-es-co-teen'], *m.* (Naut.) Preventer top-sail sheet.

Contraescritura [con-trah-es-cre-too'-rah], *f.* Counter-deed, instrument granted to protest against what had been previously given.

Contraesmaltar [con-trah-es-mal-tar'], *va.* To enamel the back part.

Contraespaldera [con-trah-es-pal-day'-rah], *f.* A kind of hedge or fence of trees in front of a hedge; a second espalier.

Contraespionaje [con-trah-es-pe-o-nah'-hay], *m.* Counterintelligence, counterespionage.

Contraestay del mayor, or **del trinquete** [con-trah-es-tah'-e del mah-yor', or del treen-kay'-tay], *m.* (Naut.) Preventer-stay of the main or fore-mast.

Contrafajado, da [con-trah-fah-hah'-do, dah], *a.* (Her.) A shield having faces opposed in metal or colour.

Contrafallar [con-trah-fal-lyar'], *va.* At cards, to trump after another.

Contrafaz [con-trah-fath'], *f.* The reverse of every face.

Contrafianza [con-trah-fe-ahn'-thah], *f.* Indemnity-bond.

Contrafigura [con-trah-fe-goo'-rah], *f.* A person or dummy which imitates a personage in the theatre.

Contrafilo [con-trah-fee'-lo], *m.* Back edge (near the point).

Contrafirma [con-trah-feer'-mah], *f.* (Law. Prov.) Inhibition of an anterior decree.

Contrafirmante [con-trah-feer-mahn'-tay], *pa.* (Law. Prov.) The party who obtains an inhibition or injunction.

Contrafirmar [con-trah-feer-mar'], *va.* (Law. Prov.) To obtain a countermanding decree or inhibition.

Contraflorado, da [con-trah-flo-rah'-do, dah], *a.* (Her.) Having flowers opposed in colour and metal.

Contrafoque [con-trah-fo'-kay], *m.* (Naut.) The fore-top stay-sail; also the jib or flying-jib of a smack.

Contraforjar [con-trah-for-har'], *va.* To hammer alike on the flat and on edge.

Contrafoso [con-trah-fo'-so], *m.* Avant-fosse or outer ditch of a fortress.

Contrafractura [con-trah-frac-too'-rah], *f.* A fracture made by counter-stroke or contrecoup.

Contrafuero [con-trah-foo-ay'-ro], *m.* Infringement or violation of a charter or privilege.

Contrafuerte [con-trah-foo-err'-tay], *m.* 1. Counter-fort, a fort constructed in opposition to another. 2. Abutment, buttress, spur, a pillar of masonry serving to prop and support a wall. 3. Strap of leather to secure the girths on a saddle-tree. 4. Stiffener of a shoe.

Contragolpe [con-trah-gole'-pay], *m.* (Med.) A counter-stroke (contrecoup), lesion produced in a part other than that which received the blow.

Contraguardia [con-trah-goo-ar'-de-ah], *f.* Counter-guard, a work erected to cover a bastion or ravelin.
Contraguía [con-trah-gee'-ah], *f.* In a pair of draught animals, the mule which goes forward, to the left.
Contraguiñada [con-trah-gee-nyah'-dah], *f.* (Naut.) Counter-yaw, a movement of the tiller to correct the first.
Contrahacedor, ra [con-trah-ah-thay-dor', rah], *m.* & *f.* (Obs.) Imitator, counterfeiter.
Contrahacer [con-trah-ah-therr'], *va.* 1. To counterfeit. 2. To falsify, to forge. 3. To imitate, to copy. 4. To pirate the works of an author. 5. To mimic.
Contrahacimiento [con-trah-ah-the-me-en'-to], *m.* (Obs.) Counterfeit.
(*Yo contrahago, yo contrahaga*, from *Contrahacer*. *V.* HACER.)
Contrahaz [con-trah-ath'], *m.* The wrong side of cloth and some other things.
Contrahecho, cha [con-trah-ay'-cho, chah], *a.* 1. Humpbacked, deformed. 2. Counterfeit, counterfeited, fictitious.—*pp.* of CONTRAHACER.
Contrahierba [con-trah-e-err'-bah], *f.* 1. (Bot.) Dorstenia contrayerba, a South American medicinal plant. 2. Antidote.
Contrahilera [con-trah-e-lay'-rah], *f.* A second line formed to defend another.
Contrahojas de las ventanas [con-trah-o'-has day las ven-tah'-nas], *f. pl.* (Naut.) Dead-lights of the cabin.
Contrahoradar [con-trah-o-rah-dar'], *va.* To bore on the opposite side.
(*Yo contraigo, yo contraiga*, from *Contraer*. *V.* TRAER.)
Contraindicación [con-trah-in-de-cah-the-on'], *f.* (Med.) Contra-indication.
Contraindicante *m.* (Med.) Contra-indicant.
Contraindicar [con-trah-in-de-car'], *va.* (Med.) To contra-indicate.
Contralizo [con-trah-lee'-tho], *m.* A rod of wood to move the threads in a loom; a back leash.
Contralor [con-trah-lor'], *m.* Comptroller, inspector.
Contraloría [con-trah-lo-ree'-ah], *f.* Comptrollership.
Contralto [con-trahl'-to], *m.* Contralto, counter-tenor, middle voice between the treble and tenor.
Contraluz [con-trah-looth'], *f.* 1. View against the light. 2. Backlight. 3. Bad light. *A contraluz*, Against the light, into the sun.
Contramaestre [con-trah-mah-es'-tray], *m.* 1. (Naut.) Boatswain. 2. Overseer of a manufactory. 3. *Contramaestre de construcción*, The foreman of a dockyard.
Contramalla, Contramalladura [con-trah-mahl'-lyah, con-trah-mahl-lyah-doo'-rah], *f.* A double net for catching fish.
Contramallar [con-trah-mal-lyar'], *va.* To make nets with double meshes.
Contramandar [con-trah-man-dar'], *va.* To countermand.
Contramandato [con-trah-man-dah'-to], *m.* (Littl. us.) Countermand.
Contramangas [con-trah-mahn'-gas], *f. pl.* Over-sleeves.
Contramaniobra [con-trah-mah-ne-o'-brah], *f.* Counter-manœuvre, a sudden change of tactics.
Contramarca [con-trah-mar'-cah], *f.* 1. Countermark, a particular or additional mark. 2. A duty to be paid on goods which have no custom-house mark. 3. A mark added to a medal or other piece of coined metal long after it has been struck, by which the curious know the several changes in value. 4. *Cartas* or *patentes de contramarca*, Letters of marque
Contramarcar [con-trah-mar-car'], *va.* To countermark, to put a second or additional mark on bale goods, etc.
Contramarco [con-trah-mar'-co], *m.* Counter-frame of a glass window.
Contramarcha [con-trah-mar'-cha], *f.* 1. Counter-march, retrocession. 2. Part of a weaver's loom. *V.* VIADERA. 3. (Mil. and naut.) Evolution, by means of which a body of troops or division of ships change their front.
Contramarchar [con-trah-mar-char'], *va.* To counter-march.
Contramarea [con-trah-mah-ray'-ah], *f.* (Naut.) Counter-tide, or spring-tide.
Contramesana [con-trah-may-sah'-nah], *f.* (Naut.) Mizzen-mast.
Contramina [con-trah-mee'-nah], *f.* 1. Countermine, a mine intended to seek out and destroy the enemy's mines. 2. A subterraneous communication between two or more mines of metals or minerals.
Contraminar [con-trah-me-nar'], *va.* 1. To countermine. 2. To counter-work, to defeat by secret measures.
Contramolde [con-trah-mole'-day], *m.* 1. Counter-mould: an enveloping mould. 2. A kind of pasteboard on which is moulded, in relief or depression, what it is desired to represent.
Contramotivo [con-trah-mo-tee'-vo], *m.* (Mus.) A motive or subject opposed to another; counter-subject.
Contramuelle [con-trah-moo-ayl'-lyay], *m.* (Mech.) A duplicate spring.
Contramuralla [con-trah-moo-rahl'-lyah], *f.* (Mil.) Countermure, a low rampart.
Contramuro [con-trah-moo'-ro], *m.* 1. Countermure.
Contranatural [con-trah-nah-too-rahl'], *a.* Counternatural, contranatural, unnatural
Contraofensiva [con-trah-o-fen-see'-vah], *f.* Counteroffensive.
Contraorden [con-trah-or'-den], *f.* Countermand; counter or revoking order.
Contraordenar, *va.* *V.* CONTRAMANDAR.
Contrapares [con-trah-pah'-res], *m. pl.* (Arch.) Counter-rafters in a building.
Contraparte [con-trah-par'tay], *f.* 1. Counterpart. 2. A duplicate copy of a deed.
Contrapartida [con-trah-par-tee'-dah], *f.* In bookkeeping, corrective entry.
Contrapás [con-trah-pahs'], *m.* (Obs.) Kind of dance or step in dancing.
Contrapasamiento [con-trah-pah-sah-me-en'-to], *m.* The act and effect of passing to the opposite side or party.
Contrapasar [con-trah-pah-sar'], *vn.* To join the opposite party.
Contrapaso [con-trah-pah'-so], *m.* 1. A back-step in walking or dancing. 2. (Littl. us.) Counterpace, contrary measure to any scheme. 3. (Obs.) Permutation. 4. (Mus.) Counter-note.
Contrapechar [con-trah-pay-char'], *va.* To strike breast against breast: applied to horses in tilts or tournaments.
Contrapelear [con-trah-pay-lay-ar'], *vn.* (Obs.) To defend one's self in an engagement.
Contrapelo (**Á**) [con-trah-pay'-lo], *adv.* Against the grain.
Contrapesar [con-trah-pay-sar'], *va.* 1. To counterpoise, to counterbalance, to counterweigh. 2. To countervail, to be equivalent to. 3. To act with equal power against any person or cause.
Contrapeso [con-trah-pay'-so], *m.* 1. Counterpoise, equiponderance, counterbalance, countervail. 2. A rope-dancer's pole. 3. (Met.) Equipollence, equivalence of power. 4. Counterpoise in a velvet-loom. 5. An addition of inferior quality thrown to complete the weight of meat, fish, etc.
Contrapeste [con-trah-pes'-tay], *m.* Remedy against pestilence.
Contrapié [con-trah-pe-ay'], *m.* 1. The loss by a dog of the scent or the trail of what it was following. 2. Stratagem, trick.
Contrapilastra [con-trah-pe-lahs'-trah], *f.* 1. (Arch.) Counterpilaster. 2. Moulding on the joints of doors or shutters, to keep out the wind.
Contraponedor [con-trah-po-nay-dor'], *m.* (Obs.) He who compares one thing with another.
Contraponer [con-trah-po-nerr'], *va.* To compare, to oppose.
Contraposición [con-trah-po-se-the-on'], *f.* 1. Contra-position, the placing over against. 2. Counter-view, contrast, a position in which two dissimilar things illustrate each other. 3. An act by which the execution of a sentence is barred.
Contrapresión [con-trah-pray-se-on'], *f.* Counter-pressure, back pressure.
Contraprincipio [con-trah-prin-thee'-pe-o], *m.* Assertion contrary to a principle known as such.
Contraproducente [con-trah-pro-doo-then'-tay], *a.* Self-defeating, counter-productive, defeating its own purpose.
Contrapromesa [con-trah-pro-may'-sah], *f.* 1. Declaration annulling a thing promised. 2. Conflict of one promise with another.
Contraproposición [con-trah-pro-po-se-the-on'], *f.* Counter-proposition.
Contraprueba [con-trah-proo-ay'-bah], *f.* Counterproof, a second impression of a print taken off by printers; counter-drawing.
Contrapuerta [con-trah-poo-err'-tah], *f.* 1. Storm door. 2. Inner large door of a house.
Contrapuesto, ta [con-trah-poo-es'-to, tah], *a.* & *pp.* of CONTRAPONER. Compared.
Contrapunta [con-trah-poon'-tah], *f.* Cutting part of the edge of a sabre's blade.
Contrapuntante [con-trah-poon-tahn'-tay], *m.* He who sings in counter-point.
Contrapuntear [con-trah-poon-tay-ar'], *va.* 1. (Mus.) To sing in counter-point. 2. (Obs.) To compare. 3. To taunt, to revile.—*vr.* To treat one another with abusive language, to wrangle, to dispute.
Contrapuntista [con-trah-poon-tees'-tah], *m.* Contrapuntist, one skilled in counterpoint.
Contrapunto [con-trah-poon'-to], *m.* (Mus.) Counterpoint, harmony.
Contrapunzón [con-trah-poon-thone'], *m.* 1. Puncheon for driving in a nail. 2. Counterpunch, an instrument which serves to open others. 3. The gun-smith's countermark on guns, to prevent their being exchanged for others, or purloined
Contraquerella [con-trah-kay-rayl'-lyah], *f.* A cross-complaint.
Contraquilla [con-trah-keel'-lyah], *f.* (Naut.) False keel. *V.* ZAPATA DE LA QUILLA.
Contrariador [con-trah-re-ah-dor'], *m.* (Obs.) *V.* CONTRADICTOR.
Contrariamente [con-trah-re-ah-men-tay], *adv.* Contrarily, contrariously.
Contrariar [con-trah-re-ar'], *va.* To con-

tradict, to oppose, to counteract, to counter-work; to vex.

Contrariedad [con-trah-re-ay-dahd'], *f.* Contrariety, repugnance, opposition, contradiction

Contrario [con-trah'-re-o], *m.* 1. Opponent, antagonist. 2. Competitor, rival. 3. (Obs.) Impediment, obstacle, obstruction.

Contrario, ria [con-trah'-re-o, ah], *a.* 1. Contrary, repugnant, opposite, contradictory, contrarious. 2. Contrary, adverse, abhorrent, cross. 3. Hurtful, mischievous. *Tiempo contrario*, (Naut.) Foul weather. *Echar al contrario*, To cross the breed. *Al contrario* or *por el contrario*, On the contrary. *En contrario*, Against, in opposition to. *Llevar la contraria*, To contradict, to oppose.

Contrarracamento [con-trar-rah-cah-men'-to], *m.* (Naut.) Preventer-parrel.

Contrarrampante [con-trar-ram-pahn'-tay], *a.* (Her.) Rampant, and face to face.

Contrarreclamación [con-trar-ray-clah-mah-the-on'], *f.* Counterclaim.

Contrarregistro [con-trar-ray-hees'-tro], *m.* Control, a register or account kept to be compared with any other.

Contrarreguera [con-trar-ray-gay'-rah], *f.* A lateral drain, to prevent mischief to the tilled land, and to aid in even distribution of irrigation.

Contrarreparo [con-trar-ray-pah'-ro], *m.* (Mil.) Counterguard, or counter-defence.

Contrarréplica [con-trar-ray'-ple-cah], *f.* Rejoinder, reply to an answer: it is sometimes also rebutter, or an answer to a rejoinder.

Contrarrestar [con-trar-res-tar'], *va.* 1. To strike back a ball, to counter-buff. 2. To resist, to oppose, to check, to counter-check, to counter-work.

Contrarresto [con-trar-res'-to], *m.* 1. A player who is to strike back the ball. 2. Check, opposition, contradiction.

Contrarrevolución [con-trar-ray-vo-loo-the-on'], *f.* Counter-revolution.

Contrarrevolucionario, ria [con-trar-ray-vo-loo-the-o-nah'-re-o, ah], *m.* & *f.* & *a.* 1. Counter-revolutionist. 2. Belonging to a counter-revolution.

Contrarroa, Contrarroda [con-trar-ro'-ah, con-trar-ro'-dah], *f.* (Naut.) Stemson.

Contrarronda [con-trar-ron'-dah], *f.* 1. (Mil.) Counter-round, which follows the first round for greater safety's sake, to visit the different posts. 2. Round made by officers to inspect the posts, guards, and sentinels.

Contrarrotura [con-trar-ro-too'-rah], *f.* (Vet.) Plaster or poultice applied to fractures or wounds by veterinarians.

Contras [cone'-trass], *m. pl.* (Mus.) The bass pipes of a large organ. *V.* CONTRA.

Contrasalida [con-trah-sah-lee'-dah], *f.* Counter-sally; resistance of besiegers to a sally.

Contrasalva [con-trah-sahl'-vah], *f.* (Mil.) Counter-salute.

Contrasellar [con-trah-sayl-lyar'], *va.* To counter-seal, to seal with others.

Contrasentido [con-trah-sen-tee'-do], *m.* 1. Counter-sense, opposed meaning. 2. A deduction opposed to the logical antecedents.

Contraseña [con-trah-say'-nyah], *f.* 1. Countersign or counter-mark. 2. (Mil.) Watchword.

Contrasol [con-trah-sole'], *m.* Sunshade, a tub in green-houses to protect certain plants likely to be injured by full sunlight.

Contrastable [con-tras-tah'-blay], *a.* Contrastable, capable of contrast.

Contrastante [con-tras-tahn'-tay], *pa.* (Obs.) Contrasting.

Contrastar [con-tras-tar'], *va.* 1. To contrast, to place in opposition; to oppose. 2. To resist, to contradict. 3. To assay metals. 4. To examine measures and weights. 5. (Naut.) To endure misfortunes, or contrary winds, and resist them mechanically.

Contraste [con-trahs'-tay], *m.* 1. Assayer of the mint. 2. Assayer's office, where gold and silver are tried and marked. 3. Assayer of weights and measures. 4. (Prov.) A public office where raw silk is weighed. 5. Counterview, contrast, a position in which two dissimilar things illustrate each other. 6. Opposition and strife between persons and things. 7. Contrast, opposition and dissimilitude of figures. 8. (Naut.) Sudden change of the wind, by which it becomes foul or contrary.

Contrata [con-trah'-tah], *f.* 1. Contract, a deed in which the terms of a contract, bargain, or agreement are set forth. 2. (Obs.) Territory, district.

Contratación [con-trah-tah-the-on'], *f.* 1. Trade, commerce, traffic, enterprise, undertaking, business transaction. 2. (Obs.) Familiar intercourse. 3. (Obs.) Writing which contains the terms of a bargain. 4. (Obs.) Reward, recompense. *Casa de contratación* or only *contratación*, A house or place where agreements and contracts are made for the promotion of trade and commerce.

Contratante [con-trah-tahn'-tay], *pa.* Contracting; contractor, one of the parties to a contract.

Contratar [con-trah-tar'], *va.* 1. To trade, to traffic. 2. To contract or bargain. 3. To contract, to stipulate, to covenant.

Contratela [con-trah-tay'-lah], *f.* Second inclosure of canvas, within which game is enveloped or wild boars are fought.

Contratiempo [con-trah-te-em'-po], *m.* Disappointment, misfortune, calamity, trouble, frustration.

Contratista [con-trah-tees'-tah], *m.* Contractor, lessee, patentee, conventionist, covenanter.

Contrato [con-trah'-to], *m.* 1. Contract, convention, or mutual agreement, pact; stipulation, covenant. 2. Contract, a deed in which the terms of a contract or bargain are set forth. *Entrar en contrato*, To make a covenant. *Contrato nominado o innominado*, Definite or indefinite bargain, particular or general agreement. *Contrato a la gruesa* or *a riesgo marítimo*, A kind of marine insurance, respondentia. *Contrato aleatorio*, Aleatory contract, that the subject of which is chance act. *Contrato de compraventa* or *de compra y venta*, A contract of bargain and sale. *Contrato de locación y conducción*, An agreement by virtue of which the owner of a thing, movable or immovable, cedes to another the use thereof for a determined time, in return for a price or service which the latter has to satisfy. *Contrato de retrovendendo*, A side-agreement to a contract of bargain and sale by which the buyer obliges himself to return to the seller the goods sold, the latter returning the price paid, within a certain time, or the terms named in the agreement. *Contrato enfitéutico*, Emphyteusis, a perpetual lease of lands and tenements in consideration of annual rent and improvements thereon; an improving lease.

Contratrancaniles [con-trah-tran-ca-nee'-les], *m. pl.* (Naut.) Inner waterways, serving to carry off the water by the scuppers.

Contratreta [con-trah-tray'-tah], *f.* Counterplot.

Contratrinchera [con-trah-trin-chay'-rah], *f.* (Mil.) Counter-trench, an intrenchment made by the besieged against the besiegers.

Contravalación [con-trah-vah-la-the-on'], *f.* (Mil.) Contravalation.

Contravalar [con-trah-vah-lar'], *va.* To form a line of contravalation.

Contravalor [con-trah-vah-lor'], *m.* Counter-value, equivalent. (Com.)

Contravención [con-trah-ven-the-on'], *f.* Contravention, violation of a law.

Contraveneno [con-trah-vay-nay'-no], *m.* 1. Counter-poison, antidote. 2. (Met.) Precaution taken to avoid some infamy or mischief.

(*Yo contravengo, yo contravenga*, from *Contravenir*. *V.* VENIR.)

Contravenir [con-trah-vay-neer'], *va.* 1. To contravene, to transgress a command, to violate a law. 2. To oppose, to obstruct, to baffle, to countermine.

Contraventana [con-trah-ven-tah'-nah], *f.* 1. Storm window. 2. Outside window shutter.

Contraventor, ra [con-trah-ven-tor', rah], *m.* & *f.* 1. Transgressor, offender. 2. Contravener, he who opposes another.

Contravidriera [con-trah-ve-dre-ay'-rah], *f.* A second glass window, to keep off cold or heat.

Contravirar [con-trah-ve-rar'], *va.* To turn in the opposite direction.

Contray [con-trah'-e], *m.* Sort of fine cloth.

Contrayente [con-trah-yen'-tay], *pa.* Contracting: used of matrimony only.

Contrayugo [con-trah-yoo'-go], *m.* (Naut.) Inner transom.

Contrecho, cha [con-tray'-cho, chah], *a.* Crippled, maimed.

Contrete [con-tray'-tay], *m.* 1. (Naut.) Breast-shore. 2. Crochet, angle-iron, stay. 3. Gusset.

Contribución [con-tre-boo-the-on'], *f.* 1. Contribution. 2. Contribution, tax. *Única contribución*, Income-tax.

Contribuidor, ra [con-tre-boo-e-dor', rah], *m.* & *f.* Contributor.

Contribuir [con-tre-boo-eer'], *va.* 1. To contribute, to pay one's share of a tax. 2. To contribute, to give to some common stock. 3. To contribute, to bear a part in some common design. 4. (Obs.) *V.* ATRIBUIR.

Contribulado, da [con-tre-boo-lah'-do, dah], *a.* Grieved, afflicted.

Contributario [con-tre-boo-tah'-re-o], *m.* Contributor, tax-payer.

Contribuyente [con-tre-boo-yen'-tay], *pa.* Contributing; contributor; co-operative; contributory.

Contrición [con-tre-the-on'], *f.* Contrition, penitence, compunction.

Contrincante [con-trin-cahn'-tay], *m* Competitor, rival, opponent.

Contristar [con-trees-tar'], *va.* To afflict, to sadden.

Contrito, ta [con-tree'-to, tah], *a.* Contrite, compunctious, penitent.

Control [con-trol'], *m.* Control, check, regulation. *Control remoto*, Remote control. *Control de natalidad*, Birth control. *Control de precios*, Price control.

Controlar [con-tro-lar'], *va.* 1. To control, to regulate. 2. To restrain; to hold in check. 3. To monitor, to verify; to check.

Controversia [con-tro-verr'-se-ah], *f.* Controversy, debate.

Controversista [con-tro-ver-sees'-tah], *m.* Controversialist, disputant, controverter.

Controvertible [con-tro-ver-tee'-blay], *a.* Controvertible, disputable, litigious.

Controvertir [con-tro-ver-teer'], *va.* 1. To controvert, to dispute a thing in writing. 2. To discuss, to argue against.

(*Yo controvierto, yo controvierta; él controvirtió, él controvirtiera;* from *Controvertir.* *V.* Asentir.)

Contubernal [con-too-ber-nahl'], *m.* (Obs.) Chamber-fellow, companion in the same apartment.

Contubernio [con-too-berr'-ne-o], *m.* 1. Cohabitation, inhabiting the same place with another. 2. Concubinage, living with a woman not married.

Contumacia [con-too-mah'-the-ah], *f.* 1. Obstinacy; perverseness, stubbornness. 2. (Law) Contumacy, a wilful contempt and disobedience to any lawful summons or judicial order, non-appearance; contempt of court; default.

Contumaz [con-too-math'], *a.* 1. Obstinate, stubborn, perverse. 2. Contumacious, disobedient.

Contumazmente, *adv.* Contumaciously, obstinately.

Contumelia [con-too-may'-le-ah], *f.* Contumely, reproach, contumeliousness, abuse.

Contumeliosamente, *adv.* Contumeliously, reproachfully.

Contumelioso, sa [con-too-may-le-o'-so, sah], *a.* Contumelious, reproachful, sarcastic.

Contundente [con-toon-den'-tay], *pa.* Producing a contusion: applied to weapons which cause a contusion.

Contundir [con-toon-deer'], *va.* To contuse, to contund; to bruise; to cause a contusion.

Conturbación [con-toor-bah-the-on'], *f.* Perturbation, uneasiness of mind.

Conturbado, da [con-toor-bah'-do, dah], *a.* Turbulent, troublesome.—*pp.* of Conturbar.

Conturbador [con-toor-bah-dor'], *m.* Perturber, disturber.

Conturbamiento [con-toor-bah-me-en'-to] *m.* (Obs.) Perturbation, disquietude.

Conturbar [con-toor-bar'], *va.* To perturb, to disquiet, to disturb.

Conturbativo, va [con-toor-bah-tee'-vo, vah], *a.* That which perturbs or disquiets.

Contusión [con-too-se-on'], *f.* Contusion, bruise.

Contuso, sa [con-too'-so, sah], *a.* Bruised.—*pp irr.* of Contundir.

Contutor [con-too-tor'], *m.* Assistant tutor, fellow-tutor.

Conuco, or **Cunuco** [co-noo'-co, coo-noo'-co], *m.* 1. (Amer.) A very small farm or plantation, often given by masters to their slaves to cultivate for themselves. 2. Maize-field.

Conusco, *pron. pers.* (Obs.) With us.

Conusfusorio [co noos-foo-so'-re-o], *m.* A metallic crucible, shaped like an inverted cone, used in smelting.

Convalaria [con-vah-lah'-re-ah], *f.* Lily of the valley. Convallaria majalis.

Convalariado, da, Convalárico, ca, *a.* Resembling the lily of the valley.

Convalecencia [con-vah-lay-then'-the-ah], *f.* Convalescence, recovery from disease. *Casa de convalecencia* or only *convalecencia,* A hospital for convalescent patients.

Convalecer [con-vah-lay-therr'], *vn.* 1. To recover from sickness. 2. (Met.) To recover lost prosperity and power.

Convaleciente [con-vah-lay-the-en'-tay], *pa.* Convalescent.

(*Yo convalezco, yo convalezca,* from *Convalecer.* *V.* Aborrecer.)

Convecino, na [con-vay-thee'-no, nah], *a.* Neighbouring, conterminous.

Convelerse [con-vay-lerr'-say], *vr.* To twitch, to be contracted: applied to muscular fibres, membranes, blood-vessels, etc.

Convencedor, ra [con-ven-thay-dor', rah], *m.* & *f.* One who demonstrates and convinces.

Convencer [con-ven-therr'], *va.* To convince, to convict, to demonstrate. —*vr.* To be assured.

Convencible [con-ven-thee'-blay], *a.* Convincible, convictible.

Convencido, da [con-ven-thee'-do, dah], *a.* Convict.—*pp.* of Convencer.

Convencimiento [con-ven-the-me-en'-to], *m.* Conviction, confutation.

Convención [con-ven-the-on'], *f.* 1. Convention, contract, agreement, pact, composition. 2. Convenience, convening.

Convencional [con-ven-the-o-nahl'], *a.* Conventional, conventionary.

Convencionalmente, *adv.* Conventionally.

(*Yo convengo, yo convenga,* from *Convenir.* *V.* Venir.)

Convenialmente, *adv.* (Obs.) By common consent.

Convenible [con-vay-nee'-blay], *a.* 1. Docile, tractable, compliant, obsequious. 2. (Obs.) Convenient. 3. (Obs.) Of a moderate or reasonable price.

Convenido, da, *a.* & *pp.* of Convenir. Settled by consent, agreed, done.

Conveniencia [con-vay-ne-en'-the-ah], *f.* 1. Conformity, congruity, consistence. 2. Utility, profit, advantage, comfort. 3. Agreement, convention, adjustment. 4. Service, a servant's place in a house or family. *He hallado conveniencia,* I have got a place. *Busco conveniencia,* I am looking out for a place. 5. Convenience, ease, or cause of ease, commodiousness, accommodation, commodity. *Es amigo de conveniencia,* He loves his ease or comfort. 6. Convenience, fitness, expedience. *Conveniencias,* 1. Emoluments, perquisites. 2. Income, property.

Conveniente [con-vay-ne-en'-tay], *a.* 1. Useful, profitable, advantageous, good. 2. Accordant, conformable. 3. Fit, suitable, agreeable. 4. Convenient, expedient, correspondent, opportune. 5. Commodious, timely. 6. Decent.

Convenientemente, *adv.* Conveniently, fitly, suitably, expediently.

Convenio [con-vay'-ne-o], *m.* 1. Convention, contract, agreement, pact, concert, consent. 2. Contrivance. 3. Plot.

Convenir [con-vay-neer'], *vn.* 1. To agree, to be of the same opinion, to coincide, to cohere, to consist, to compromise. 2. To agree, to fit, to harmonize, to comport, to suit. 3. To correspond, to belong to. 4. To assemble, to convene. 5. (Obs.) To cohabit carnally. 6. To litigate.—*v. imp.* To suit, to be to the purpose.—*vr.* To compound, to agree, to close, to suit one's interests. *Convenir en,* To close upon, to close with, to settle. *Conviene a saber,* That is, to wit.

Conventazo [con-ven-tah'-tho], *m. aug.* A large convent or monastery.

Conventículo [con-ven-tee'-coo-lo], *m.* Conventicle, a secret assembly or meeting for some unlawful purpose.

Convento [con-ven'-to], *m.* 1. Convent of monks or nuns, monastery, nunnery. 2. Community of religious men or women.

Conventual [con-ven-too-ahl'], *a.* Conventual, monastic.

Conventual, *m.* 1. Conventual, a monk, one that lives in a convent. 2. Franciscan friar possessing estates or property.

Conventualidad [con-ven-too-ah-le-dahd'], *f.* 1. The state of living together as religious persons in a convent or monastery. 2. Assignment of a monk to a determined convent.

Conventualmente, *adv.* Monastically, reclusely.

(*Yo convenzo, él convenza,* from *Convencer.*)

Convergencia [con-ver-hen'-the-ah], *f.* Convergence.

Convergente [con-ver-hen'-tay], *a.* Convergent, converging.

Converger [con-ver-herr'], *vn.* *V.* Convergir. (Acad.) To converge.

Convergir [con-ver-heer'], *vn.* 1. To converge. 2. To agree in opinions.

Conversa [con-ver'-sah], *f.* (Geom.) Converse.

Conversable [con-ver-sah'-blay], *a.* 1. Conversable, sociable. 2. (Theology) Communicable.

Conversación [con-ver-sah-the-on'], *f.* 1. Conversation, easy talk, chat, converse, conference, communication, colloquy. 2. Conversation, commerce, intercourse, society, company. 3. (Obs.) Room, bed-room. 4. Criminal intercourse. 5. Club, an assembly. *V.* Tertulia. *Casa de conversación,* Assembly-house, club. *La mucha conversación es causa de menosprecio,* Too much familiarity breeds contempt.

Conversar [con-ver-sar'], *vn.* 1. To converse, to discourse familiarly, to commune, to talk together. 2. To live together in the company of others. 3. (Mil.) To change front, wheel.

Conversión [con-ver-se-on'], *f.* 1. Conversion. 2. Conversion, change from one state to another. 3. (Rhet.) Apostrophe. 4. (Mil.) Wheel, wheeling. *Cuarto de conversión,* Quarter-wheeling.

Conversivo, va [con ver-see'-vo, vah], *a.* Having the power of converting or changing one thing into another.

Converso [con-verr'-so], *m.* 1. Convert, a person converted from one religion or opinion to another. 2. Lay-brother, a man admitted for the service of a religious house without being ordained.

Convertibilidad [con-ver-te-be-le-dahd'], *f.* Convertibility, capability of being exchanged.

Convertible [con-ver-tee'-blay], *a.* 1. Convertible. 2. Movable, transferable.

Convertible, *m.* Convertible (automobile).

Convertido, da [con-ver-tee'-do, dah], *a.* & *pp.* of Convertir. Converted, changed, transformed.

Convertidor [con-ver-te-dor'], *m.* Converter, transformer.

Convertir [con-ver-teer'], *va.* 1. To convert, to change into another substance, to permute. 2. To convert, to change from one religion or opinion to another. 3. To convert, to turn from a bad to a good life. 4. To apply things to a use for which they were not intended. 5. To convert, to direct, to appropriate. *Todo lo convierte en substancia,* (Met.) He minds nothing, nothing makes the least impression upon him; he wants nothing but real facts.—*vr.* To be converted, to undergo a change either in religion or life.

Convexidad [con-vek-se-dahd'], *f.* Convexity.

Convexo, xa [con-vek'-so, sah], *a.* Convex, convexed.

Convicción [con-vic-the-on'], *f.* Conviction, convincement.
Convicto, ta [con-veec'-to, tah], *pp. irr. forensic* of CONVENCER. Convicted, guilty.
Convictor [con-vic-tor'], *m.* (Prov.) Boarder, pensioner in a college.
Convictorio [con-vic-to'-re-o], *m.* Among the Jesuits, that part of the college where the pensioners or boarders live and receive their instructions.
Convidada [con-ve-dah'-dah], *f.* An invitation to drink; a treat.
Convidante [con-ve-dahn'-tay], *m.* & *f.* One who invites, host.
Convidado, da [con-ve-dah'-do, dah], *a.* & *pp.* of CONVIDAR. Invited. It is often used as a substantive for a guest, or a person invited to a dinner, party, etc.
Convidador, ra [con-ve-dah-dor', rah], *m.* & *f.* Inviter.
Convidar [con-ve-dar'], *va.* 1. To invite, to bid, to ask or call to any thing pleasing, to treat. 2. To pay the shot, to stand treat. 3. (Met.) To allure, to invite, to persuade.—*vr.* To offer one's services spontaneously.
(*Yo convierto, yo convierta; él convirtió, él convirtiera;* from *Convertir. V.* ASENTIR.)
Convincente [con-vin-then'-tay], *a.* Convincing, convincible.
Convincentemente, *adv.* Convincingly, convictively.
Convite [con-vee'-tay], *m.* 1. Invitation. 2. Feast to which persons are invited.
Conviviente [con-ve-ve-en'-tay], *a.* Living together.
Convocación [con-vo-cah-the-on'], *f.* Convocation.
Convocadero, ra [con-vo-cah-day'-ro, rah], *a.* (Obs.) That is to be convened or convoked.
Convocador, ra [con-vo-cah-dor', rah], *m.* & *f.* Convener, convoker.
Convocar [con-vo-car'], *va.* 1. To convene, to convoke, to call together, to congregate. 2. To shout in triumph or exultation.
Convocatoria [con-vo-cah-to'-re-ah], *f.* Letter of convocation, an edict.
Convocatorio, ria [con-vo-cah-to'-re-o, ah], *a.* That which convokes.
Convoluto, ta [con-vo-loo'-to, tah], *a.* Convolute, wrapped around itself.
Convolvuláceo, cea [con-vol-voo-lah'-thay-o, ah], *a.* Convolvulaceous, of the convolvulus family.
Convólvulo [con-vol'-voo-lo], *m.* 1. (Bot.) Convolvulus, bindweed. 2. A small worm which destroys the vines and wraps itself in their leaves. 3. A vine-fretter.
Convoy [con-vo'-e], *m.* 1. Convoy, conduct, an escort or guard. 2. The things conveyed with an escort or convoy. 3. (Coll.) Retinue, suite. 4. A railway train.
Convoyante [con-vo-yahn'-tay], *pa.* Convoying.
Convoyar [con-vo-yar'], *va.* To convoy, to escort, or guard.
Convulsar [con-vool-sar'], *vn.* (Vet.) To feel an involuntary contraction of the nerves.—*vr.* To be convulsed.
Convulsión [con-vool-se-on'], *f.* Convulsion.
Convulsivamente, *adv.* Convulsively.
Convulsivo, va [con-vool-see'-vo, vah], *a.* Convulsive.
Convulso, sa [con-vool'-so, sah], *a.* Convulsed.
Convusco [con-voos'-co], *pron. pers.* (Obs.) With you.
Conyúdice [con-yoo'-de-thay], *m.* (Obs.) *V.* CONJUEZ.
Conyugal [con-yoo-gahl'], *a.* Conjugal, connubial.
Conyugalmente, *adv.* Conjugally, matrimonially.
Cónyuges [con'-yoo-hess], *m. pl.* A married couple, husband and wife.
Conyunto, ta [con-yoon'-to, tah], *a.* (Obs.) CONJUNTO.
Coñac [co-nyac'], *m.* Cognac.
Cooperación [co-o-pay-rah-the-on'], *f.* Co-operation, conspiracy, co-efficiency.
Cooperador, ra [co-o-pay-rah-dor', rah], *m.* & *f.* Co-operator.
Cooperante [co-o-pay-rahn'-tay], *pa.* & *a.* Co-operating, co-operator, co-operative, coactive, contributive.
Cooperar [co-o-pay-rar'], *va.* To co-operate, to labour jointly with another, to concur.
Cooperario [co-o-pay-rah'-re-o], *m. V.* COOPERADOR.
Cooperativamente, *adv.* Coefficiently.
Cooperativo, va [co-o-pay-rah-tee'-vo, vah], *a.* Co-operative.
Coopositor [co-o-po-se-tor'], *m.* He who is a candidate with another for a prebend, professorship, etc., which is obtained by a public trial of skill; competitor, rival.
Coordinación [co-or-de-nah-the-on'], *f.* Co-ordination; classification; collateralness.
Coordinadamente, *adv.* Co-ordinately.
Coordinado, da [co-or-de-nah'-do, dah], *a.* Co-ordinate.—*pp.* of COORDINAR.
Coordinamiento [co-or-de-nah-me-en'-to], *m.* (Obs.) *V.* COORDINACIÓN.
Coordinar [co-or-de-nar'], *va.* To arrange, to adjust, to class, to classify.
Copa [co'-pah], *f.* 1. Cup, a small drinking vessel; goblet, wine-glass. 2. Meeting of the branches of a tree, a bower. 3. Crown of a hat. 4. Brazier, fire-pan. *Copa del horno,* The roof or vault of an oven or furnace. 5. Gill, liquid measure, the fourth part of a pint; teacupful. 6. Each of the cards with a heart.—*pl.* 1. Hearts, one of the four suits at cards. 2. Bosses of a bridle.
Copado, da [co-pah'-do, dah], *a.* Tufted, copped.—*pp.* of COPAR.
Copaiba [co-pah'-e-bah], *f.* 1. (Bot.) The copaiba-tree, from which the copaiba gum or balsam distils. 2. Balsam copaiba. Copaifera officinalis.
Copal [co-pahl'], *m.* Copal, a transparent resin.
Copaljocol [co-pal-ho-cohl'], *m.* (Bot.) Tree in New Spain resembling a cherry-tree.
Copanete, Cópano [co-pah-nay'-tay, co'-pa-no], *m.* (Obs.) A small bark.
Copar [co-par'], *va.* 1. In monte, to put on a card a sum equal to what there is in the bank. 2. (Met. and coll.) To possess one's self of many persons and things united; to corner. 3. (Mil.) To surprise, cut off the retreat of a military force, making it prisoner.
Copartícipe [co-par-tee'-the-pay], *com.* Participant, copartner.
Copaza [co-pah'-thah], *f. aug.* A large cup or glass with a foot.
Copazo [co-pah'-tho], *m. aug.* 1. Large fleece of wool. 2. Large flake of snow.
Copela [co-pay'-lah], *f.* Cupel or coppel, a vessel used in assaying precious metals.
Copelación [co-pay-lah-the-on'], *f.* Cupellation, the act of refining metals.
Copelar [co-pay-lar'], *va.* To refine or purify metals.
Copera [co-pay'-rah], *f.* Cupboard; closet for glassware.
Coperillo [co-pay-reel'-lyo], *m. dim.* A little cup-bearer or attendant at a feast to serve wine.
Copero [co-pay'-ro], *m.* Cup-bearer, one who serves drink at a feast.
Copeta [co-pay'-tah], *f. dim.* A small cup or drinking-vessel.
Copete [co-pay'-tay], *m.* 1. A crest, a tuft, a pompadour; aigret, toupee. 2. Forelock of a horse. 3. Crown-work of a looking-glass frame, made in the shape of a shell. 4. Top of the shoe which rises over the buckle. 5. Top, summit. 6. The projecting top or cop of sherbets or ice-creams. *Hombre de copete,* A man of respectability and character. *Tener copete* or *mucho copete,* To assume an air of authority, to be lofty, supercilious, and haughty. *Asir la ocasión por el copete,* (Prov.) To profit by the opportunity.
Copetín [co-pay-teen'], *m.* (Arg.) A before-dinner drink.
Copetudo, da [co-pay-too'-do, dah], *a.* 1. Copped, rising to a top or head. 2. High, lofty, supercilious, on account of one's noble descent.
Copey [co-pay'-e], *m.* 1. American tree, of excellent wood for engraving. 2. A bitumen found in Ecuador, and employed in repairing ships.
Copia [co'-pe-ah], *f.* 1. Copiousness, plenty, abundance, fulness; fertility. 2. Copy, transcript; counterpart. 3. Portrait from an original design; copy of a picture. 4. Rate or valuation of tithe. 5. (Gram.) List of nouns and verbs, and the cases they govern.
Copiador [co-pe-ah-dor'], *m.* Copyist, copier, transcriber. *Copiador* or *libro copiador,* Among merchants, book in which letters are copied, a copy-book.
Copiante [co-pe-ahn'-tay], *m.* Copyist, copier, an imitator.
Copiar [co-pe-ar'], *va.* 1. To copy, to transcribe, to exemplify. 2. To imitate, to draw after life. 3. To write on the same subject with another, and nearly in the same manner. 4. (Poet.) To describe, to depict. *Copiar del natural,* To copy from life; among artists, to design from the naked body.
Copilador [co-pe-lah-dor'], *m.* Compiler, collector. *V.* COMPILADOR.
Copilar [co-pe-lar'], *va.* To compile; to collect. *V.* COMPILAR.
Copilla [co-pee'-lyah], *f.* 1. Dim. of COPA. 2. Cigar-lighter.
Copín [co-peen'], *m.* In Asturias, a Spanish measure, equal to half a *celemín,* or the twelfth part of a quintal or *fanega.*
Copina [co-pee'-nah], *f.* (Mex.) A skin taken off whole.
Copinar [co-pe-nar'], *va.* To remove a skin entire.
Copiosamente, *adv.* Copiously, abundantly, plentifully, largely.
Copioso, sa [co-pe-o'-so, sah], *a.* Copious, abundant, full, fruitful, plentiful, fluent, large.
Copista [co-pees'-tah], *m.* 1. Copyist, transcriber. 2. A copying-machine.
Copita [co-pee'-tah], *f. dim.* A small cup or drinking vessel.
Copito [co-pee'-to], *m. dim.* A small fleece or flake.
Copla [co'-plah], *f.* 1. A certain number of consonant verses, a couplet; a stanza of four lines, of eight or eleven syllables, the second and fourth lines rhyming; by extension, short rhymes. 2. A sarcastic hint or remark, a lampoon. 3. (Prov.) Ballad. *Coplas de ciegos,* Vulgar ballads. *Echar coplas de repente,* To talk nonsense. *Andar en coplas,* To be the town-talk. ***Dársele (a uno de una cosa) lo mismo que***

de las coplas de Calaínos, or *de don Gaiferos*, To make light of. *Entenderse a coplas*, To repay in the same coin, return insult for insult.
Copleador [co-play-ah-dor'], *m.* (Obs.) Poetaster, rhymer.
Coplear [co-play-ar'], *vn.* To versify, to make couplets.
Coplero [co-play'-ro], *m.* 1. Poetaster, petty poet. 2. Ballad-seller.
Coplica, illa, ita [co-plee'-cah, eel'-lyah, ee'-tah], *f. dim.* A little couplet.
Coplista [co-plees'-tah], *m. V.* COPLERO.
Coplón [co-plone'], *m. aug.* Low, vile poetry: generally used in the plural number, *Coplones.*
Copo [co'-po], *m.* 1. A small bundle of cotton, hemp, flax, or silk, put on the distaff to be spun. 2. Flake of snow. 3. Thick part of a fishing-net. 4. (Prov.) Odour of the flower of the aromatic myrrh-tree.
Copón [co-pone'], *m.* 1. (Aug.) A large cup or drinking vessel. 2. Cibary, ciborium, a large cup used in Catholic churches. 3. (Naut.) A small cable for weighing the anchor.
Coposo, sa [co-po'-so, sah], *a. V.* COPADO.
Copra [co'-prah], *f.* Copra, dried cocoanut meat.
Copropietario, ia [co-pro-pe-ay-tah'-re-o, ah], *a.* Jointly owning, coproprietor.
Cóptico, ca [cop'-te-co, cah], *a.* Coptic, ancient Egyptian, or from that stock.
Copto [cop'-to], *m.* Coptic, the language of the Copts.
Copudo, da [co-poo'-do, dah], *a.* Tufted, bushy, thick-topped.
Cópula [co'-poo-lah], *f.* 1. The joining or coupling two things together. 2. Copulation, carnal union. 3. (Arch.) *V.* CÚPULA. 4. (Log.) Copula, the word which unites the predicate with the subject.
Copular [co-poo-lar'], *va.* (Obs.) To connect, to join, or unite.—*vr.* (Obs.) To copulate, to come together.
Copulativamente, *adv.* Jointly.
Copulativo, va [co-poo-lah-tee'-vo, vah], *a.* 1. (Gram.) Copulative. 2. Joining or uniting together.
Coqueluche [co-kay-loo'-chay], *f.* Whooping-cough. (F.)
Coqueta [co-kay'-tah], *f.* 1. (Prov.) Feruling or blow with a ferule on the hand by schoolmasters. 2. (Prov.) A small loaf. 3. Coquette, flirt.
Coquetear [co-kay-tay-arr'], *vn.* To coquet, to flirt.
Coquetería [co-kay-tay-ree'-ah], *f.* Coquetry, flirtation.
Coquetismo, *m.* = COQUETERÍA.
Coquetón [co-kay-tone'], *m.* A male flirt, lady-killer.
Coquillo [co-keel'-lyo], *m.* 1. Vine-fretter, an insect which destroys vines. Curculio Bacchus, *L. V.* CONVÓLVULO. 2. Jean, a twilled fabric.
Coquina [co-kee'-nah], *f.* 1. (Prov.) Shell-fish in general. 2. Cockle. Cardium rusticum, *L.*
Coquinario, ria [co-ke-nah'-re-o, ah], *a.* (Obs.) Culinary. *Coquinario del rey*, (Obs.) The king's own cook.
Coquinero [co-ke-nay'-ro], *m.* (Prov.) Fishmonger, one who deals in shell-fish.
Coquito [co-kee'-to], *m.* 1. (Dim.) A small cocoa-nut. 2. Grimace to amuse children. 3. A turtle-dove of Mexico, having a song like the cuckoo's.
Cor, *m.* (Obs.) 1. *V.* CORAZÓN. 2. *V.* CORO. *De cor*, By heart.
Coráceo, cea [co-rah'-thay-o, ah], *a. V.* CORIÁCEO.
Coracora [co-rah-co'-rah], *f.* (Acad.) *V.* CORASCORA.
Coracero [co-rah-thay'-ro], *m.* 1. Cuirassier. 2. (Coll.) A poor cigar.
Coracilla [co-rah-theel'-lyah], *f. dim.* A small coat of mail.
Coracina [co-rah-thee'-nah], *f.* A small breast-plate, anciently worn by soldiers.
Coracha [co-rah'-chah], *f.* A leather bag, used to bring from America cocoa, tobacco, etc.
Corachín [co-rah-cheen'], *m. dim.* A little leather bag.
Corada, Coradela [co-rah'-dah, co-rah-day'-lah], *f. V.* ASADURA.
Coraje [co-rah'-hay], *m.* 1. Courage, bravery, fortitude, mettle. 2. Anger, passion. 3. *Eso me da tanto coraje*, (Met.) That puts me in such a rage.
Corajudo, da [co-rah-hoo'-do, dah], *a.* Angry, passionate, easily irritated.
Coral [co-rahl'], *m.* 1. Coral, a marine calcareous production. *Corales*, Strings of corals. 2. The polyp which produces the substance known as coral; these polyps are mostly anthozoan or hydroid. 3. (Naut.) A large knee which fastens the stern-post to the keel.
Coral [co-rahl'], *a.* Choral, belonging to the choir.
Coralero [co-rah-lay'-ro], *m.* A worker or dealer in corals.
Coralífero, ra [co-rah-lee'-fay-ro, rah], *a.* Coral-bearing.
Coralillo [co-rah-leel'-lyo], *m.* The coral-coloured snake, extraordinarily venemous.
Coralina [co-rah-lee'-nah], *f.* 1. Sea-coralline or white worm-seed. Sertularia. 2. (Naut.) A coral fishing-boat. 3. Every sea-animal resembling coral.
Coralino, na [co-rah-lee'-no, nah], *a.* (Littl. us.) Coralline.
Corambre [co-rahm'-bray], *f.* All hides and skins of animals, dressed or undressed; pelts.
Corambrero [co-ram-bray'-ro], *m.* Dealer in hides and skins.
Coramvobis [co-ram-vo'-bis], *m.* (Coll.) A corpulent person, strutting about with affected gravity.
Corán [co-rahn'], *m.* Koran, the sacred book of the Mohammedans. *V.* ALCORÁN.
Corascora [co-ras-co'-rah], *f.* (Naut.) Corascora, a coasting vessel in India.
Coraza [co-rah'-thah], *f.* 1. Cuirass, an ancient breast-plate. 2. *Coraza* or *caballo coraza*, Cuirassier. 3. A plate of armour, iron or steel, for men-of-war. 4. Shell or carapace of a turtle, or other defensive armour of some reptiles. *Tentar a uno las corazas*, (Met.) To try one's mettle or courage.
Coraznada [co-rath-nah'-dah], *f.* 1. Pith of a pine-tree. 2. Fricassee of the hearts of animals.
Corazón [co-rah-thone'], *m.* 1. Heart, core. 2. Heart, benevolence, affection. 3. Heart, spirit, courage. 4. Will, mind. 5. Heart, the middle or centre of any thing. 6. In a loom, cam. 7. Pith of a tree. 8. *Corazón de un cabo*, (Naut.) Heart-strand. *Llevar* or *tener el corazón en las manos*, To be sincere and candid; to wear one's heart on one's sleeve. *De corazón*, *adv.* 1. Heartily, sincerely. 2. (Obs.) From memory. *Anunciarle el corazón*, To have a presentiment. *A donde el corazón se inclina, el pie camina*, Where there is the will there is a way. *Clavarle (a uno) en el corazón*, To cause or to suffer great affliction. *Helársele (a uno) el corazón*, To be paralyzed by fright.
Corazonada [co-rah-tho-nah'-dah], *f.* 1. Courage, an impulse of the heart to encounter dangers. 2. Presentiment, foreboding. 3. Entrails.
Corazonazo [co-rah-tho-nah'-tho], *m. aug.* A great heart.
Corazoncico, illo, ito [co-rah-thon-thee'-co], *m. dim.* A little heart; a pitiful or faint-hearted person.
Corazoncillo [co-rah-thon-theel'-lyo], *m.* (Bot.) Perforated St. John's wort. Hypericum perforatum.
Corbachada [cor-bah-chah'-dah], *f.* A stroke or lash given with a *corbacho.*
Corbacho [cor-bah'-cho], *m.* The tendon or aponeurosis of an ox or a bull, with which the boatswain of a galley punished the convicts.
Corbás [cor-bahs'], *f. pl.* (Falc.) The four largest feathers of a hawk.
Corbata [cor-bah'-tah], *f.* 1. Cravat, a neck-cloth, neck-handkerchief. 2. A sash or ribbon ornamented with gold or silver fringe tied to banners. 3. Ribbon, insignia of an order.—*m.* Magistrate not brought up to the law; also a layman who has neither studied the civil nor canon law.
Corbatín [cor-bah-teen'], *m.* 1. Cravat. *V.* CORBATA. 2. Stock, a close neck-cloth.
Corbato [cor-bah'-to], *m.* Cooler, a vat filled with water, in which the worm of a still is placed to cool.
Corbatón [cor-bah-tone'], *m.* (Naut.) A small knee used in different parts of a ship.
Corbe [cor'-bay], *m.* An ancient measure for baskets.
Corbeta [cor-bay'-tah], *f.* 1. Corvette, a light vessel with three masts and square-sails. 2. *Corbeta de guerra*, A sloop of war.
Corcel [cor-thel'], *m.* A steady horse, a charger.
Corcesca [cor-thes'-cah], *f.* (Obs.) Ancient pike or spear.
Corcillo, illa [cor-theel'-lyo, lyah], *m. & f. dim.* A small deer or little fawn.
Corcino [cor-thee'-no], *m.* A small deer.
Corcova [cor-co'-vah], *f.* 1. Hump, a crooked back, hunch. 2. Convexity, protuberance, curvature, gibbosity.
Corcovado, da [cor-co-vah'-do, dah], *a.* Hump-backed, gibbous, crooked.—*pp.* of CORCOVAR.
Corcovar, *va.* (Obs.) To crook.
Corcovear [cor-co-vay-ar'], *vn.* To curvet, to cut capers.
Corcoveta [cor-co-vay'-tah], *com.* A crook-backed person.
Corcovilla, ita [cor-co-veel'-lyah], *f. dim.* Little hump or crooked back.
Corcovo [cor-co'-vo], *m.* 1. Spring, or curvet, made by a horse on the point of leaping. 2. A wrong step, unfair proceeding.
Córculo [cor'-coo-lo], *m.* Heart-shell, an aquatic insect.
Corcusido, da [cor-coo-see'-do, dah], *a.* Clumsily mended or sewed on.—*pp.* of CORCUSIR.
Corcusir [cor-coo-seer'], *va.* (Coll.) To darn holes in cloth or stuff, to patch.
Corcha [cor'-chah], *f. V.* CORCHO and CORCHERA.
Corche [cor'-chay], *m.* A sort of sandal or shoe, open at the top, and tied with latchets.
Corchea [cor-chay'-ah], *f.* (Mus.) Crochet, half a minim.
Corchear [cor-chay-ar'], *va.* Among curriers, to grain leather with a cork.
Corchera [cor-chay'-rah], *f.* Vessel of pitched cork or staves, in which a bottle or flask is put with ice or snow, to cool liquor.
Corcheta [cor-chay'-tah], *f.* Eye of a hook or clasp.

Corchete [cor-chay'-tay], *m.* 1. Clasp, a hook and eye: commonly used in the plural. *Corchetes*, Hooks and eyes. 2. Locket, a small lock; crotch. 3. (Coll.) An arresting officer. 4. An iron instrument for flattening tin plates. 5. Brace used to connect lines in writing or printing. 6. Bench-hook of a carpenter's bench.

Corcho [cor'-cho], *m.* 1. Cork, the bark of the cork-tree. 2. Ice-vessel. *V.* CORCHERA. 3. Bee-hive. *V.* COLMENA. 4. Cork, the stopple of a bottle, flask, or jar. 5. Box made of cork, for carrying eatables. 6. Cork-board, put before beds and tables to serve as a shelter. *Nadar sin corcho*, (Met.) Not to need leading-strings, or other people's advice; literally, to swim without cork. *No tener muelas de corcho*, (Met.) Not to be easily imposed upon. *Tener cara de corcho*, (Met.) To have a brazen face, to be impudent.—*pl.* 1. Clogs, a sort of pattens used by women to keep their shoes clean and dry. 2. (Mil.) Guntompions, plugs to stop the mouths of guns and other pieces of ordnance.

Corchoro [cor-cho'-ro], *m.* (Bot.) Corchorus, a genus of plants. Corchorus.

Corchoso, sa [cor-cho'-so, sah], *a.* Like cork in appearance or condition.

Corda [cor'-dah], *f.* *Estar el navío a la corda*, (Naut.) To be close-hauled, or lying to: applied to a ship.

Cordaje [cor-dah'-hay], *m.* (Naut.) Cordage, all sorts of rope used in the rigging of ships.

Cordal [cor-dahl'], *m.* Double tooth. *Cordales*, Grinders.

Cordato, ta [cor-dah'-to, tah], *a.* Wise, prudent, discreet, judicious, considerate.

Cordel [cor-del'], *m.* 1. Cord, a rope of several strands. 2. (Naut.) A thin rope or line used on board a ship; a line. *Cordel alquitranado*, A tarred line. *Cordel blanco*, An untarred line. *Cordel de corredera*, Log-line. *Mozo de cordel*, Porter, one who carries burdens for hire. *Apretar los cordeles*, To oblige one to say or do a thing by violence. *Echar el cordel*, 1. To mark with a line or cord. 2. (Met.) To administer justice impartially. 3. (Met.) To draw lines in order to consider the manner of executing a thing. *Estar a cordel*, To be in a right line.

Cordelado, da [cor-day-lah'-do, dah], *a.* Twisted for ribbons or garters: applied to silk.

Cordelazo [cor-day-lah'-tho], *m.* Stroke or lash with a rope.

Cordelejo [cor-day-lay'-ho], *m.* 1. (Dim.) A small rope. 2. Fun, jest, joke. 3. *Dar cordelejo*, (Met.) Artfully to pump out a secret.

Cordelería [cor-day-lay-ree'-ah], *f.* 1. Cordage, all sorts of ropes. 2. Rope-walk. 3. (Naut.) Rigging.

Cordelero [cor-day-lay'-ro], *m.* Rope-maker, cord-maker.

Cordelito [cor-day-lee'-to], *m. dim.* A small rope, cord, or line.

Cordellate [cor-del-lyah'-tay], *m.* Grogram, a sort of stuff.

Cordera [cor-day'-rah], *f.* 1. Ewe lamb. 2. Meek, gentle, or mild woman.

Cordería [cor-day-ree'-ah], *f.* 1. Cordage. 2. Place where cordage is kept.

Cordérica, illa, ita [cor-day-ree'-cah], *f. dim.* Little ewe lamb.

Corderico, illo, ito [cor-day-ree'-co], *m. dim.* A young or little lamb.

Corderillo [cor-day-reel'-lyo], *m.* Lambskin dressed with the fleece.

Corderina [cor-day-ree'-nah], *f.* Lambskin.

Corderino, na [cor-day-ree'-no, nah], *a.* Of the lamb kind, belonging to lambs.

Cordero [cor-day'-ro], *m.* 1. Lamb. 2. A dressed lambskin. 3. Meek, gentle, or mild man. *Cordero ciclán*, A lamb that never lets down the testicles. *Cordero rencoso*, Lamb with one testicle down and the other concealed. *Cordero de socesto* or *lechal*, House-lamb. *Cordero mueso*, Small-eared lamb. *Cordero de Escitia*, (Bot.) Polypody of Tartary. Polypodium.

Corderuna [cor-day-roo'-nah], *f.* Lambskin.

Cordeta [cor-day'-tah], *f.* (Prov.) A small rope made of the platted strands of bass-weed.

Cordezuela [cor-day-thoo-ay'-lah], *f. dim.* A small rope.

Cordíaco, ca [cor-dee'-ah-co, cah], *a.* *V.* CARDÍACO.

Cordial [cor-de-ahl'], *a.* 1. Cordial, affectionate, sincere. 2. Cordial, invigorating, reviving.

Cordial, *m.* Cordial, a strengthening medicine.

Cordialidad [cor-de-ah-le-dahd], *f.* Cordiality, intimacy.

Cordialmente, *adv.* Cordially, sincerely, affectionately, heartily.

Cordila [cor-dee'-lah], *f.* Spawn of a tunny-fish.

Cordilo [cor-dee'-lo], *m.* An amphibious animal resembling a crocodile.

Cordilla [cor-deel'-lyah], *f.* Guts of sheep, given to cats to eat.

Cordillera [cor-deel-lyay'-rah], *f.* Chain or ridge of mountains. In particular, the Andes.

Cordita [cor-dee'-tah], *f.* Cordite.

Cordobán [cor-do-bahn'], *m.* Cordovan, cordwain, morocco or Spanish leather, tanned goat-skin.

Cordobana [cor-do-bah'-nah], *f.* Nakedness, nudity. *Andar a la cordobana*, To go stark naked.

Cordobés, sa [cor-do-bess', bay'-sah], *f.* Native of or belonging to Córdova.

Cordojo [cor-do'-ho], *m.* (Obs.) Anguish, anxiety, affliction.

Cordón [cor-done'], *m.* 1. Cord or string made of silk, wool, hemp, etc. 2. Twisted or platted lace. 3. Cord or girdle with which monks tie up their habits. 4. A military cordon, formed by a line of troops to prevent any communication. 5. (Naut.) Strand of a cable or rope. *Cabo de tres o cuatro cordones*, A three or four stranded rope or cable. 6. (Mil.) Cordon, a row of stones jutting out between the rampart and the basis of the parapet, where the wall begins to be perpendicular. 7. (Arch.) *V.* BOCEL. 8. The milled edge of coined metal.—*pl.* 1. Silver or gold cords from the right shoulder to the breast, worn by the cadets and other military men. 2. Harness-cords of a velvet-loom.

Cordonazo [cor-do-nah'-tho], *m.* 1. Stroke with a cord or rope. 2. (Aug.) Large cord. *Cordonazo de San Francisco*, A name given by Spanish sailors to the autumnal equinox, on account of the storms which prevail about that time, or Saint Francis's day, the 4th of October.

Cordoncico, illo, ito [cor-don-thee'-co], *m. dim.* A small cord or line.

Cordoncillo [cor-don-theel'-lyo], *m.* 1. A twisted cord, round lace, lacing, braid. 2. Milling round the edge of coin.

Cordonería [cor-do-nay-ree'-ah], *f.* 1. All the work of twisters or lace-makers in general. 2. A lace-maker's shop.

Cordonero, ra [cor-do-nay'-ro, rah], *m.* & *f.* 1. Lace-maker, lace-man, or woman. 2. Rope-maker.

Cordura [cor-doo'-rah], *f.* Prudence, practical wisdom; judgment. *Hacer cordura*, (Obs.) To act in a prudent manner.

Corea [co-ray'-ah], *f.* 1. Dance, accompanied with a chorus. 2. Chorea, St. Vitus's dance. 3. Corea. (Geog.)

Corear [co-ray-ar'], *va.* To sing or play in a chorus. *Música coreada*, Chorus music.

Corecico [co-ray-thee'-co], *m. dim.* of CUERO, Small hide or skin.

Corecillo [co-ray-theel'-lyo], *m.* A roasted sucking pig.

Coreo [co-ray'-o], *m.* 1. A foot in Latin verse; a trochee; a long and a short syllable, — ⌣. 2. Connected harmony of a chorus.

Coreografía [co-ray-o-grah-fee'-ah], *f.* 1. The art of dancing. 2. Choreography, the art of arranging dances and ballets.

Corezuelo [co-ray-thoo-ay'-lo], *m.* 1. (Prov.) Sucking pig. 2. A small roasted pig. 3. (Dim.) Small hide of leather.

Cori or **Coris de Mompeller** [co'-ree], *m.* 1. (Bot.) Montpellier coris, St. John's wort. *V.* CORAZONCILLO. Coris monspeliensis. 2. Cowry, a kind of shells which pass for money in Siam.

Coriáceo, cea [co-re-ah'-thay-o, ah], *a.* Coriaceous, leathery.

Coriámbico, ca [co-re-ahm'-be-co, cah], *a.* Applied to Latin verses written with coriambics.

Coriambo [co-re-ahm'-bo], *m.* Coriambic, a foot of prosody; a trochee and an iambus combined, — ⌣ | ⌣ —.

Coriandro [co-re-ahn'-dro], *m.* (Bot.) Coriander, or common coriander.

Coribante [co-re-bahn'-tay], *m.* Corybantes, priests of Cybele.

Coribantismo [co-re-ban-tees'-mo], *m.* A kind of frenzy accompanied by many contorsions.

Coriceo [co-ree'-thay-o], *m.* A hall for playing ball in ancient gymnasiums.

Córida [co'-re-dah], *f.* 1. A substance which the Arabs use against small-pox. 2. Cowry, a kind of shell used for money by some African tribes. 3. (Bot.) A perennial plant of the cowslip family.

Corifeo [co-re-fay'-oh], *m.* 1. Corypheus, the leader of the ancient dramatic chorus. 2. Corypheus, leader of a sect or party.

Corillo [co-reel'-lyo], *m. dim.* A small choir; an organ-loft.

Corimbífero [co-rim-bee'-fay-ro], *a.* (Bot.) Corymbiferous, bearing fruit or berries in clusters.

Corimbo [co-reem'-bo], *m.* (Bot.) Corymb, a flower-cluster of indeterminate florescence.

Corindón [co-rin-done'], *m.* Corundum, the hardest substance found native, next to the diamond.

Corintio, tia [co-reen'-te-o, ah], *a.* 1. Native of or belonging to Corinth. 2. Corinthian: applied to an order of architecture.

Corion [co'-re-on], *m.* (Anat.) Chorion, the exterior membrane that envelops the fœtus.

Corisanto [co-re-sahn'-to], *m.* (Bot.) Perennial orchidaceous plant cultivated in European botanical gardens, native of Chili and California.

Corista [co-rees'-tah], *com.* Chorist or chorister.

Coristerión [co-ris-tay-re-on'], *m.* An organ secreting the glutinous material with which insects fasten their eggs to one another.

Corito [co-ree'-to], *a.* 1. Timid, pusillanimous. 2. Naked.—*m.* A work-

man who treads grapes in the wine-press.
Coriza [co-ree'-thah], *f.* 1. A kind of shoe of undressed leather, laced from the toe to the instep, worn by the common people in some parts of Spain. 2. Coryza, a copious running from the nose. *V.* ROMADIZO.
Corladura [cor-lah-doo'-rah], *f.* Gold-varnish.
Corlar, Corlear [cor-lar', cor-lay-ar'], *va.* To put on gold-varnish.
Corma [cor'-mah], *f.* 1. The stocks. 2. (Met.) Trouble, uneasiness.
Cormano, na [cor-mah'-no, nah], *m.* & *f.* (Obs.) *V.* COHERMANO.
Cormorán [cor-mo-rahn'], *m.* Cormorant, a water-fowl.
Cornac, or **Cornaca** [cor-nah'-cah], *m.* A keeper of domesticated elephants: native name.
Cornada [cor-nah'-dah], *f.* 1. Thrust with a bull's or cow's horn. 2. Thrust with a foil in a cunning manner, with the vulgar.
Cornadillo [cor-nah-deel'-lyo], *m.* A small piece of money of little value. *Emplear su cornadillo,* To attain one's end by low means.
Cornado [cor-nah'-do], *m.* An old copper coin, mixed with a little silver, and of small value, in the times of the kings of Castile. *No vale un cornado* It is not worth a farthing.
Cornadura [cor-nah-doo'-rah], *f.* Horns.
Cornal [cor-nahl'], *m.* A strap or thong with which oxen are tied to the yoke by the horns.
Cornalina [cor-nah-lee'-nah], *f.* Cornelian, a red variety of chalcedony.
Cornamenta [cor-nah-men'-tah], *f.* Horns of any animal.
Cornamusa [cor-nah-moo'-sah], *f.* 1. Cornemuse, a wind-instrument; a sort of long trumpet (metal). 2. (Naut.) A belaying cleat. *Cornamusas de los palos,* The belaying cleats of the lower masts. *Cornamusas de pontón,* The notched cleats of a pontoon.
Cornas [cor'-nas], *f. pl.* (Naut.) Back-stays. *V.* BRANDALES.
Cornatillo [cor-nah-teel'-lyo], *m.* A kind of olive.
Córnea [cor'-nay-ah], *f.* 1. Cornea, the transparent part of the eye: applied also, in Spanish, to the sclerotic or white of the eye. 2. A stone like jasper.
Corneador, ra [cor-nay-ah-dor', rah], *m.* & *f.* A horned animal, which butts or plays with the horns.
Cornear [cor-nay-ar'], *va.* To butt or play with the horns. *V.* ACORNEAR.
Cornecico, illo, ito [cor-nay-thee'-co], *m. dim.* Cornicle, a small horn.
Corneja [cor-nay'-hah], *f.* (Orn.) Crow, fetlock, dow. Corvus corone, *L.*
Cornejal [cor-nay-hahl'], *m.* A collection of dogwood-trees.
Cornejalejo [cor-nay-hah-lay'-ho], *m.* A kind of pod in which is contained some seed or fruit.
Cornejo [cor-nay'-ho], *m.* (Bot.) Hound-tree or cornel-tree, dogwood. Cornus mascula.
Cornelina [cor-nay-lee'-nah], or **Cornerina,** *f.* *V.* CORNALINA.
Córneo, ea [cor'-nay-o, ah], *a.* Horny, corny, callous.
Cornero [cor-nay'-ro], *m.* *Cornero de pan,* (Prov.) Crust of bread.
Corneta [cor-nay'-tah], *f.* 1. A wind-instrument in the shape of a horn. 2. A French horn. 3. A postillion's horn; hunting-horn. 4. Cornet, an ensign of horse who carries the standard. 5. Troop of horse. 6. (Naut.) Broad pennant; a rear-admiral's flag. 7. Horn used by swineherds to call their hogs.
Cornete [cor-nay'-tay], *m. dim.* A small musical horn, or bugle-horn.—*pl.* 1. (Anat.) Small bony plates of the nasal fossæ. 2. A surgical instrument (bull-dog forceps?).
Cornetín [cor-nay-teen'], *m.* 1. Dim. of CORNETA. 2. Cornet, a brass instrument of the trumpet family, now provided with three valves.
Cornezuelo [cor-nay-thoo-ay'-lo], *m.* 1. Ergot of rye. 2. An instrument for bleeding horses. 3. (Bot.) *V.* CORNICABRA.
Corniabierto, ta [cor-ne-ah-be-err'-to, tah], *a.* Having widespread horns.
Cornial [cor-ne-ahl'], *a.* In the shape of a horn.
Corniapretado, da [cor-ne-ah-pray-tah'-do, dah], *a.* Having horns close-set.
Cornicabra [cor-ne-cah'-brah], *f.* 1. (Bot.) Turpentine-tree, pistachia-tree, of which the *Orihuela* snuff-boxes are made in Spain. Pistacia terebinthus. 2. A sort of olives.
Corniculata [cor-ne-coo-lah'-tah], *a.* Horned, as the new moon.
Cornículo [cor-nee'-coo-lo], *m.* Old name for the antenna of insects.
Corniforme [cor-ne-for'-may], *a.* In the shape of horns.
Cornigacho, cha [cor-ne-gah'-cho, chah], *a.* Having the horns turned slightly downward.
Cornígero, ra [cor-nee'-hay-ro, rah], *a.* (Poet.) Horned, cornigerous.
Cornija [cor-nee'-hah], *f.* (Arch.) Cornice, a horizontal moulding.
Cornijal [cor-ne-hahl'], *m.* Angle or corner of a building.
Cornijamento, Cornijamiento [cor-ne-hah-men'-to], *m.* (Arch.) *V.* CORNIJÓN.
Cornijón [cor-ne-hone'], *m.* (Arch.) The third of the three principal pieces on the tops of columns, consisting of the architrave, frieze, and cornice; the entablature.
Cornil [cor-neel'], *m.* *V.* CORNAL.
Corniola [cor-ne-o'-lah], *f.* *V.* CORNALINA.
Cornisa [cor-nee'-sah], *f.* (Arch.) Cornice.
Cornisamento, Cornisamiento [cor-nee-sah-men'-to], *m.* *V.* CORNIJÓN.
Cornisica, illa, ita [cor-ne-see'-cah], *f. dim.* Small cornice.
Corniveleto, ta [cor-ne-vay-lay'-to, tah], *a.* Having horns turned strongly upward.
Corno [cor'-no], *m.* 1. (Bot.) Cornel-tree. Cornus mascula, *L.* *V.* CORNEJO. 2. Corno, English horn, a reed instrument resembling the oboe, pitched one-fifth lower.
Cornucopia [cor-noo-co'-pe-ah], *f.* 1. Cornucopia, the horn of plenty. 2. Sconce, a branched candlestick. 3. A pier-glass.
Cornudico, illo, ito [cor-noo-dee'-co], *m. dim.* A little cuckold.
Cornudo, da [cor-noo'-do, dah], *a.* Horned.—*m.* Cuckold.
Cornúpeta [cor-noo'-pay-tah], *a.* Attacking with the horns. (Acad.)
Coro [co'-ro], *m.* 1. Choir, a part of a church where the service is sung. 2. Choir, chorus, an assembly or band of singers; also a quartette of voices, or even a trio. 3. Choir, the singers in divine worship. 4. Chorus of a song. 5. Memory. *Decir* or *tomar de coro,* To say or get by heart. 6. Chorus of a Greek tragedy. 7. (Obs.) Dance. 8. (Poet.) Summer solstitial wind. 9. Choir of angels. *Hablar a coros,* To speak alternately. 10. A dry measure of the Hebrews, about six bushels.
Corocha [co-ro'-chah], *f.* 1. (Prov.) Vine-fretter or vine-grub, an insect destructive to vines. 2. (Obs.) Coat.
Corografía [co-ro-grah-fee'-ah], *f.* Chorography, the art of describing particular regions.
Corográficamente, *adv.* Chorographically.
Corográfico, ca [co-ro-grah'-fe-co, cah], *a.* Chorographical.
Corógrafo [co-ro'-grah-fo], *m.* Chorographer.
Coroidea [co-ro-e-day'-ah], *f.* The choroid coat of the eye.
Corola [co-ro'-lah], *f.* (Bot.) Corolla, the envelope of a flower next to the stamens and pistils; usually coloured.
Corolario [co-ro-lah'-re-o], *m.* Corollary, inference, deduction.
Corona [co-ro'-nah], *f.* 1. Crown, the emblem of royalty. 2. Coronet, an inferior crown worn by the nobility. 3. Crown, the top of the head. 4. A clerical tonsure. 5. An old Spanish gold and silver coin. 6. Crown, an English silver coin. 7. Crown, regal power, royalty. 8. Kingdom, monarchy. 9. Crown, reward, distinction. 10. Crown, honour, splendour, ornament, decoration. 11. Aureola with which saints are crowned. 12. Rosary of seven decades offered to the Holy Virgin. 13. End of a work. 14. Corona, a luminous halo about the sun, seen in total eclipses. 15. Crown, completion, reward. 16. (Naut.) Pendant; a rope used for various purposes. *Coronas de los palos,* Main-tackle pendants. *Coronas de quinales,* Preventer-shroud pendants. 17. (Bot.) Appendices of a corolla, resembling a crown; the persistent, dry limb of the calyx of a flower. 18. Glory, triumph. *Eso que se atribuye a mal, es mi corona,* The very thing I am censured for constitutes my glory. *Corona de rosas,* Chaplet of roses. 19. (Mil.) Crown-work. 20. (Arch.) Corona, a large flat member of the cornice, which crowns the entablature. 21. (Her.) The ornament painted in the upper part of a coat of arms, and which denotes the rank of nobility or distinction of the family to which it belongs. *Corona de fraile,* (Bot.) Three-toothed globularia. *V.* CABOLLANA. *Corona de rey,* (Bot.) Common melilot trefoil. Trifolium melilotus officinalis. *Corona real,* (Bot.) Annual sun-flower. Helianthus annuus. *Corona obsidional,* Crown given to the person who compelled an enemy to raise the siege.
Coronación [co-ro-nah-the-on'], *f.* 1 Coronation. 2. The end of any work.
Coronado [co-ro-nah'-do], *m.* A Roman Catholic clergyman who has received the tonsure.—*Coronado, da, pp.* of CORONAR.
Coronador, ra [co-ro-nah-dor', rah], *m.* & *f.* 1. Crowner. 2. Finisher.
Coronal [co-ro-nahl'], *m.* & *f.* & *a.* (Anat.) 1. Os frontis or frontal bone. 2. Belonging to the frontal bone.
Coronamiento [co-ro-nah-me-en'-to], *m.* 1. Ornament placed on the top of a building. 2. (Obs.) Coronation. 3. (Naut.) Taffrail.
Coronar [co-ro-nar'], *va.* 1. To crown, to invest with the crown. 2. (Met.) To crown, to complete, to perfect, to finish. 3. (Met.) To decorate the top of a building. 4. To fill a glass up to the brim.
Coronaria [co-ro-nah'-re-ah], *a.* 1 (Anat.) Coronary. 2. Applied to the crown-wheel of a watch.
Coronario, ria [co-ro-nah'-re-o, ah], *a.* 1. Coronary, relating to a crown. 2.

(Bot.) Coronary. 3. Extremely refined: applied to gold.

Corondel [co-ron-del'], *m.* (Printing) Column-rule; reglet.

Coronel [co-ro-nel'], *m.* 1. Colonel. 2. (Her.) Crown.—*pl.* In paper-mills, the worked little sticks which there are to sustain the mould.

Coronela [co-ro-nay'-lah], *f.* Colonel's wife.

Coronela [co-ro-nay'-lah], *a.* Applied to the company, flag, etc., supposed to belong to the colonel of a regiment.

Coronelía [co-ro-nay-lee'-ah], *f.* Colonelship. *V.* Regimiento.

Corónica, *f.* (Obs.) *V.* Crónica.

Coronilla [co-ro-neel'-lyah], *f.* 1. Crown, top of the head, coxcomb. 2. Among bell-founders, the ear by which a bell is suspended. 3. A genus of plants. Coronilla. *Coronilla juncal,* Rush coronilla. Coronilla juncea. *Coronilla* or *coronilla de rey,* (Bot.) Nine-leaved coronilla. Coronilla Valentina. *Coronilla de fraile,* (Bot.) The French daisy or globularia alypum. Globularia alypum. 4. In Castile, the kingdoms of Arragon, Valentia, Catalonia, and Majorca, which composed the ancient kingdom of Arragon.

Corotos [co-ro'-tos], *m. pl.* (Sp. Am. coll.) Belongings, things.

Coroza [co-ro'-thah], *f.* 1. Coronet of strong paper or pasteboard, worn as a mark of infamy by those on whom punishment is inflicted. 2. A straw cape used by labourers in Galicia as a defence against rain. (Acad.)

Corozo [co-ro'-tho], *m.* (Bot.) A species of high palm-tree in Africa and America. Elais guineensis, *L.*

Corpanchón, Corpazo [cor-pan-chone', cor-pah'-tho], *m. aug.* A very big body or carcass. *Corpanchón de ave,* Carcass of a fowl.

Corpecico, illo, ito, Corpezuelo [cor-pay-thee'-co], *m. dim.* A little or small body, or carcass.

Corpezuelo [cor-pay-thoo-ay'-lo], *m.* An under-waiscoat without sleeves or skirts.

Corpiño [cor-pee'-nyo], *m.* Waist. *V.* Justillo.

Corpo, *m.* (Obs.) *V.* Cuerpo.

Corporación [cor-po-rah-the-on'], *f.* Corporation, guild; community.

Corporal [cor-po-rahl'], *a.* Corporal, belonging to the body. *Castigo corporal,* Corporal punishment.

Corporal *m.* Corporal, altar linen on which the communion bread and wine are put to be consecrated.

Corporalidad [cor-po-rah-le-dahd'], *f.* 1. Corporality, the quality of being embodied. 2. Any corporeal substance.

Corporalmente, *adv* Corporally, bodily.

Corpóreo, rea [cor-po'-ray-o, ah], *a.* Corporeal, corporeous.

Corps, *m.* Corps, a French term, implying body. *Los guardias de corps,* The life-guards. *Sumiller de corps,* Lord chamberlain.

Corpudo, da [cor-poo'-do, dah], *a.* Corpulent, bulky.

Corpulencia [cor-poo-len'-the-ah], *f.* Corpulence, corpulency.

Corpulentamente, *adv* (Littl. us.) Fatly.

Corpulento, ta [cor-poo-len'-to, tah], *a.* Corpulent, fleshy, fat.

Corpus [cor'-poos], *m.* Corpus Christi day, or the procession held on that day in Roman Catholic countries.

Corpuscular [cor-poos-coo-lar'], *a.* Corpuscular.

Corpusculista [cor-poos-coo-lees'-tah], *m.* Atomist.

Corpúsculo [cor-poos'-coo-lo], *m.* Corpuscle, atom, molecule.

Corral [cor-rahl'], *m.* 1. Yard, inclosure; a poultry-yard. 2. (Obs.) Court, open space before a house. 3. Fish-pond. 4. Play-house. 5. Blank left by students in writing the lectures. *Corral de ovejas* or *vacas,* (Met.) Ruins, fragments of walls, a place devastated. 6. (Obs.) Square formed by a body of foot. *Corral de madera,* Timber-yard. *Corral de ganado, corral del concejo,* Pound. (Naut.) Place where cattle are kept on board a ship. *Hacer corrales,* (Met.) To loiter about in school or business hours.

Corralera [cor-rah-lay'-rah], *f.* 1. A brazen-faced impudent woman. 2. Andalusian song in dance rhythm.

Corralero [cor-rah-lay'-ro], *m.* Keeper of a dung-yard.

Corralillo, ito [cor-rah-leel'-lyo], *m. dim.* A small yard.

Corraliza [cor-rah-lee'-thah], *f.* Yard, court.

Corralón [cor-rah-lone'], *m. aug.* A large yard.

Correa [cor-ray'-ah], *f.* 1. Leather strap or thong. 2. Leash. 3. Among saddlers, strap which fastens the holsters to the saddle. 4. Flexibility or extension of any thing. 5. Leather belting, belt, for machinery. *Besar la correa,* (Met.) To be obliged to humble one's self to another. *Tener correa,* To bear wit or raillery without irritation.

Correaje [cor-ray-ah'-hay], *m.* Heap of leather straps or thongs.

Correal [cor-ray-ahl'], *m.* Dressed deer-skin. *Coser correal,* or *labrar de correal,* To sew with small leather thongs instead of thread.

Correar [cor-ray-ar'], *va.* To draw out wool and prepare it for use.

Correazo [cor-ray-ah'-tho], *m.* Blow with a leather strap or thong.

Correcalles [cor-ray-cahl'-lyes], *m.* Idler, lounger.

Corrección [cor-rec-the-on'], *f.* 1. Correction, reprehension, animadversion, lecture. 2. Correction, amendment, alteration to a better state. 3. Correction, that which is substituted in the place of any thing wrong, emendation.

Correccional [cor-rec-the-o-nahl'], *a.* Correctional, corrective.

Correctamente, *adv.* Correctly.

Correctivo, va [cor-rec-tee'-vo, vah], *a.* Corrective.

Correctivo, *m.* 1. Corrective, that which has the power of altering or correcting. 2. (Med.) Corrective, a medicine which abates the force of another.

Correcto, ta [cor-rec'-to, tah], *a.* Exact, correct, conformable to the rules. —*pp. irr.* of Corregir.

Corrector [cor-rec-tor'], *m.* 1. Corrector, amender. 2. Corrector of the press, proof-reader. 3. Superior, or abbot, in the convent of St. Francis de Paula.

Corredentor, ra [cor-ray-den-tor', rah], *m. & f.* One who redeems from captivity, jointly with another

Corredera [cor-ray-day'-rah], *f.* 1. Race-ground. 2. A small wicket or back-door. 3. Runner or upper grinding-stone in a corn-mill. 4. Street. *La corredera de San Pablo en Madrid,* St. Paul's-street in Madrid. 5. (Coll.) Pimp, procuress. 6. (Naut.) Log, or log-line. *Echar la corredera,* To heave the lead. *Carretel de la corredera,* Log-reel. 7. In glass-houses, roller, a metal cylinder for rolling plate-glass. 8. Cockroach. *V.* Cucaracha. 9. (St.-en.) A slide-valve. 10. (Typ.) Track, slide, rail. 11. (Mech.) Tongue, rail, guide, runner. 12. (Mint) A milling-machine. 13. (Ast.) A thread which crosses the field of a lens and serves to measure the apparent diameter of a star.

Corredizo, za [cor-ray-dee'-tho, thah], *a.* Easy to be untied, like a running knot.

Corredor, ra [cor-ray-dor', rah], *m. & f.* 1. Runner. 2. Race-horse. 3. Corridor, a gallery. 4. (Mil.) Corridor, covert-way, lying round a fortress. 5. (Mil.) Scout. 6. Forerunner. 7. Broker, one who does business for another. 8. A certain net, upon some coasts, which drags at the surface of the water, and is drawn into an oared boat. 9. *f.* A name given to certain wandering, non-web-weaving spiders. *Corredor de popa,* (Naut.) Balcony, or stern gallery of a ship. *Corredor de cambios,* Exchange-broker. *Corredor de matrimonios,* Match-maker. *Corredor de oreja,* 1. Exchange-broker. 2. (Met.) Tale-bearer. 3. Pimp, procurer, procuress. 4. In Arragon, the public crier.

Corredorcillo [cor-ray-dor-theel'-lyo], *m. dim.* A small corridor.

Corredura [cor-ray-doo'-rah], *f.* 1. Liquor which flows over the brim of a vessel with which liquids are measured. 2. (Obs.) Incursions into an enemy's country.

Correduría [cor-ray-doo-ree'-ah], *f.* 1. Brokerage. 2. (Coll.) Mulct, fine, penalty.

Correería [cor-ray-ay-ree'-ah], *f.* Trade of a strap-maker.

Correero [cor-ray-ay'-ro], *m.* Strap-maker.

Correjel [cor-ray-hel'], *a.* Relating to English sole-leather, or to an imitation of it.

Corregencia [cor-ray-hen'-the-ah], *f* Co-regency.

Corregente [cor-ray-hen'-tay], *m.* Co-regent.

Corregibilidad [cor-ray-he-be-le-dahd'], *f.* Correctibleness.

Corregible [cor-ray-hee'-blay], *a.* Corrigible, docile.

Corregidor [cor-ray-he-dor'], *m.* 1. Corrector, one who punishes and corrects. 2. Corregidor, a Spanish magistrate; a mayor of a town.

Corregidora [cor-ray-he-do'-rah], *f.* Wife of a *corregidor*

Corregimiento [cor-ray-he-me-en'-to], *m.* The place, office, and district of a *corregidor.*

Corregir [cor-ray-heer'], *va.* 1. To correct, to amend, to mend, to take away faults. 2. To correct, to remark faults, to reprehend, to admonish. 3. To correct, to temper, to mitigate, to make less active. 4. (Obs.) To adorn, to embellish.—*vr.* To mend.

Corregnante [cor-reg-nahn'-tay], *a.* Reigning with another.

Corregüela, or **Correhüela** [cor-ray-goo-ay'-lah], *f.* 1. (Dim.) A small strap or thong. 2. Play among boys with a stick and small strap. 3. (Bot.) Bind-weed. Convolvulus arvensis

Correinante [cor-ray-e-nahn'-tay], *a.* (Acad.) *V.* Corregnante.

Correlación [cor-ray-lah-the-on'], *f.* Correlation, analogy.

Correlativamente, *adv.* Correlatively

Correlativo, va [cor-ray-lah-tee'-vo, vah], *a.* Correlative.

Correligionario, ia [cor-ray-le-he-o-nah'-re-o, ah], *a.* 1. Of the same religion with another, fellow-believer. 2 Of the same politics.

Correncia [cor-ren-the-ah], *f.* (Coll.) Looseness, diarrhœa.

Correndilla [cor-ren-deel'-lyah], *f.* (Coll.) Incursion. *V.* Correría.

Correntía [cor-ren-tee'-ah], *f.* 1. (Prov.) An artificial irrigation of stubble ground, to make the stalks rot, and convert them into manure. 2. *V.* Correncia.

Correntiar [cor-ren-te-ar'], *va.* (Prov.) To irrigate stubble-ground.

Correntío, tía [cor-ren-tee'-o, ah], *a.* 1. Current, running. 2. Light, free, unembarrassed.

Correntón, na [cor-ren-tone', nah], *a.* 1. Gay, fond of company, pleasant, cheerful. 2. Taking a great deal of snuff. 3. A clever fellow.

Correo [cor-ray'-o], *m.* 1. Post, mail. 2. Post office. *Correo aéreo,* Air mail. *Correo marítimo,* Mail via steamer. *Correo ordinario,* Regular mail. *Casilla* or *apartado de correos,* Post-office box.

Correón [cor-ray-on'], *m. aug.* A large leather strap for holding up a carriage-body.

Correoso, sa [cor-ray-o'-so, sah], *a.* Ductile, flexible, easily bent.

Correr [cor-rerr'], *va.* & *vn.* 1. To run, to move at a quick pace. 2. To run, flow, or stream: applied to liquids. 3. To blow: applied to the wind. 4. To run, to pass away: as time and life. 5. To hasten to put any thing in execution. 6. To solicit one's protection. 7. (Met.) To take the proper course, to pass through the proper channel: applied to business. 8. To snatch away. 9. (Coll.) To persecute. 10. To extend, to expand. 11. To put one to the blush. 12. To arrive: said of the time fixed for payments. 13. To receive or admit a thing. 14. To flourish, to prevail for the time. 15. To tend, to guard, to take care of any thing. 16. To be said, be related. 17. Preceded by *con,* To charge one's self with a matter. 18. To travel. 19. To pursue a course. 20. To file right or left. 21. To have relations with, acquaintance with, some one: used with *bueno* or *malo.* 22. To be smooth, fluent in style. *Correr los mares,* (Naut.) To follow the sea, to lead a mariner's life. *Correr a bolina* or *a la trinca,* (Naut.) To run close upon a wind. *Correr del otro bordo,* To stand on the other tack. *Correr por bordos* or *bordear,* To ply to windward. *Correr hacia la tierra,* To stand in shore. *Correr norte,* To stand to the northward. *Correr en el mismo rumbo,* To stand onward in the same course. *Correr a dos puños,* To run before the wind. *Correr viento en popa,* To sail before the wind. *Correr sobre un bajel,* To chase a vessel, to fall down upon a vessel. *Correr la cortina,* To draw the curtain; to discover any thing; to conceal, to quash. *Correr a rienda suelta,* 1. To ride full speed. 2. (Met.) To give a loose rein to one's passions. *Corre la voz,* It is reported, it is said, the story goes. *Correr la voz,* To pass the word, to be divulged. *Correr mal tiempo,* The times are evil. *Correr monte,* To go hunting. *Correr baquetas,* To run the gantlet. *A más correr, a todo correr,* As swiftly as possible. *Correrse,* To be ashamed or confused; to run away *A todo correr,* Happen what may *Correr el gallo,* (Mex.) To pass the night carousing in the streets. *A turbio correr,* If the worst comes to the worst. *Correr a uno,* To put to the blush, to disconcert. *Correr burro alguna cosa,* To disappear. *Correr obligación a alguno,* To be obliged to do something. *El que menos corre, vuela,* He who is observant while pretending indifference. *Quien más corre, menos vuela,* The more haste, the less speed. *Corre la flecha,* The arrow flies (said when Indian tribes agree to make war upon a common enemy). *Correr el velo,* To discover a secret; to take off the mask. *Correr las amonestaciones,* To publish the banns of marriage. *Correr la palabra,* (Mil.) To give the word.

Correría [cor-ray-ree'-ah], *f.* 1. A hostile incursion, a foray. 2. Leather strap.

Correspondencia [cor-res-pon-den'-the-ah], *f.* 1. Correspondence, relation. 2. Correspondence, commerce, intercourse. 3. Correspondence, friendship, interchange of offices or civilities. 4. Proportion, symmetry, congruity. 5. Consentaneousness, consent, agreement.

Corresponder [cor-res-pon-derr'], *va.* & *vn.* 1. To return a favour, to make a suitable return. 2. To correspond, to answer, to fit, to suit, to belong to, to regard. 3. To agree. *-vr.* 1. To correspond, to keep up commerce by alternate letters. 2. To respect or esteem each other. *A todos aquellos a quienes corresponda,* (Met.) To all whom it may concern.

Correspondiente [cor-res-pon-de-en'-tay], *a.* Correspondent, conformable, agreeable, suitable.

Correspondiente [cor-res-pon-de-en'-tay], *m.* *V.* Corresponsal.

Corresponsal, *m.* 1. Correspondent, one with whom intelligence is kept up by messages or letters. 2. One who deals with another that resides in a different place.

Corretaje [cor-ray-tah'-hay], *m.* 1. Brokerage, money paid to a broker for making sales or purchases. 2. (Coll.) Money paid to a pimp or procurer.

Corretear [cor-ray-tay-ar'], *va.* To walk the streets, to rove, to ramble, to go up and down, to jaunt, to gad, to flirt.

Corretera [cor-ray-tay'-rah], *f.* A gadding woman, who runs from house to house.

Corretero [cor-ray'-tay-ro], *m.* Gadder.

Corretora [cor-ray-to'-rah], *f.* In some convents, the nun who directs the choir.

Correvedile, Correveidile [cor-ray-vay-dee'-lay], *m.* (Coll.) 1. Tale-bearer, mischief-maker. 2. Procurer, pimp, go-between.

Correverás [cor-ray-vay-rahs'], *m.* 1. A child's toy, representing a coach or a living figure, and moved by a spring. 2. Something offered to a child to induce it to take medicine, or comply with its parents' wishes. (Acad.)

Corricorriendo [cor-re-cor-re-en'-do], *adv.* (Coll.) In haste, at full speed.

Corrida [cor-ree'-dah], *f.* 1. Course, race, career. 2. (Obs.) Incursion. 3. *Corrida de toros,* Bull-baiting. 4. (Obs.) Flow of any liquid. *De corrida,* At full speed, swiftly, in haste.

Corridamente, *adv.* Currently, easily, plainly.

Corridita [cor-re-dee'-tah], *f. dim.* A small course.

Corrido [cor-ree'-do], *m.* Romance, a merry song, accompanied with a guitar, in the *fandango* style. *Corridos,* (Obs.) Rents due and not paid. *V.* Caídos.

Corrido, da [cor-ree'-do, dah], *a.* 1. Expert, experienced, artful. 2. Abashed, ashamed.—*pp.* of Correr.

Corriente [cor-re-en'-tay], *f.* 1. Course of rivers. 2. Current, a running stream. 3. Current, course, progression. 4. (Elec.) Current. *Corriente de aire,* Draft or draught, current of air.

Corriente [cor-re-en'-tay], *pa.* Runner, running.

Corriente [cor-re-en'-tay], *a.* 1. Current, plain, easy. 2. Current, generally received, uncontradicted. 3. Current, common, general. 4. Current, what is now passing; the present month or year; instant. 5. Fluent: applied to style. 6. Current, running. *Moneda corriente,* Current coin. 7. Marketable, merchantable. *Corriente* or *estamos corrientes,* Done. *Géneros de consumo corriente,* Staple commodities.

Corrientemente, *adv.* Currently.

(*Yo corrijo, yo corrija,* from *Corregir. V.* Pedir.)

Corrillero [cor-reel-lyay'-ro], *m.* Braggadocio, boasting fellow.

Corrillo [cor-reel'-lyo], *m.* A circle of persons standing to talk of the news of the day, or to censure the conduct of others.

Corrimiento [cor-re-me-en'-to], *m.* 1. (Met.) Shame, bashfulness. 2. An acrid humour. 3. (Obs.) Concourse, act of assembling. 4. Act of running; course or flow of waters. 5. (Obs.) *V.* Correría.

Corrincho [cor-reen'-cho], *m.* Meeting of low, vulgar people.

Corrivación [cor-re-vah-the-on'], *f.* A diversion of brooks, and storing their water in a reservoir.

Corro [cor'-ro], *m.* 1. Circle formed by people who meet to talk or see a show.—*Escupir en corro,* To drop in the course of conversation. *Hacer corro,* To clear the way, to make room. 2. Sort of dance.

Corroboración [cor-ro-bo-rah-the-on'], *f.* Corroboration.

Corroborante [cor-ro-bo-rahn'-tay], *m.* & *pa.* Corroborative, corroborant.

Corroborar [cor-ro-bo-rar'], *va.* 1. To corroborate, to strengthen, to fortify, to confirm. 2. (Met.) To give new force to an argument or opinion.

Corroborativo, va [cor-ro-bo-rah-tee'-vo, vah], *a.* *V.* Corroborante.

Corrobra [cor-ro'-brah], *f.* (Obs.) Treat or entertainment given at the conclusion of a bargain or contract. *V.* Alboroque.

Corroer [cor-ro-err'], *va.* To corrode, to eat away by degrees.

Corrompedor, ra [cor-rom-pay-dor', rah], *m.* & *f.* Corrupter.

Corromper [cor-rom-perr'], *va.* 1. To corrupt, to vitiate, to mar, to turn from a sound to a putrescent state, to mortify. 2. To seduce a woman. 3. To corrupt, to bribe, to suborn.—*vn.* To stink, to emit an offensive smell.—*vr.* To corrupt, to rot, to become putrid.

Corrompidamente, *adv.* Corruptly, viciously.

Corrompido, da, *a.* Corrupt, spoiled, unsound.—*pp.* of Corromper.

Corrompimiento [cor-rom-pe-me-en'-to], *m.* 1. Corruption, depravation, depravity. 2. (Obs.) Bribery. *V.* Corrupción.

Corrosca [cor-ros'-cah], *f.* (Col.) Wide straw hat for the sun.

Corrosible [cor-ro-see'-blay], *a.* (Littl. us.) Corrosible.

Corrosión [cor-ro-se-on'], *f.* Corrosion, exulceration.

Corrosivamente, *adv.* (Littl. us.) Corrosively.

Corrosivo, va [cor-ro-see'-vo, vah], *a.* Corrosive, acrid, corrodent, acrimonious.

Corroyente [cor-ro-yen'-tay], *pa.* Corroding, corrodent.

Corroyera [cor-ro-yay'-rah], *f.* A kind of sumac which is employed in tanning.

Corrugación [cor-roo-gah-the-on'], *f.* Corrugation, contraction into wrinkles.

Corrugador [cor-roo-gah-dor'], *m.* Corrugater, a small muscle of the face which wrinkles the skin.

Corrugar [cor-roo-gar'], *va.* (Obs.) *V.* ARRUGAR.

Corrulla [cor-rool'-lyah], *f.* (Naut.) Room under deck in a row-galley.

Corrupción [cor-roop-the-on'], *f.* 1. Corruption, putrefaction, corruptness, corrupting. 2. Corruption, pollution, filth. 3. A spurious alteration in a book or writing. 4. Looseness of the bowels. 5. (Obs.) Destruction. 6. Corruption, depravity, depravation or perversion of manners or principles. 7. Complete disorganization of any substance.

Corruptamente, *adv.* Corruptly, viciously.

Corruptela [cor-roop-tay'-lah], *f.* 1. Corruption, depravation, corruptness. 2. (Law) Bad habit or practice contrary to law; abuse.

Corruptibilidad [cor-roop-te-be-le-dahd'], *f.* Corruptibility, corruptibleness.

Corruptible [cor-roop-tee'-blay], *a.* Corruptible.

Corruptivo, va [cor-roop-tee'-vo, vah], *a.* Corruptive.

Corrupto, ta [cor-roop'-to, tah], *pp. irr.* of CORROMPER, and *a.* (Obs.) Corrupted, corrupt; defiled, perverse.

Corruptor [cor-roop-tor'], *m.* Corrupter, misleader, one who taints or vitiates.

Corrusco [cor-roos'-co], *m.* (Coll.) Offal, broken bread. *V.* MENDRUGO.

Corsa [cor'-sah], *f.* (Naut. Obs.) A coasting voyage, a cruise.

Corsario [cor-sah'-re-o], *m.* Corsair, privateer, pirate.

Corsario, ria [cor-sah'-re-o, ah], *a.* Cruising: applied to a privateer or letter of marque, authorized to cruise against the enemy.

Corsé [cor-say']. Corset, stays for women. (French, corset.)

Corsear [cor-say-ar'], *va.* To cruise against the enemy.

Corsetera [cor-say-tay'-rah], *f.* A woman who makes or sells corsets.

Corsi [cor-see'], *m.* The second of the thrones of God, according to Mohammedan belief, from which he is to judge men at the last day.

Corsia [cor'-se-ah], *f.* Passage between the sails in a row-galley.

Corso [cor'-so], *m.* (Naut.) Cruise, cruising, privateering.

Corta [cor'-tah], *f.* Felling of wood. Said also of reeds.

Cortabolsas [cor-tah-bol'-sas], *m.* Pickpocket, filcher, petty robber.

Cortacésped [cor-tah-thes'-ped], *m.* Lawnmower.

Cortacircuitos [cor-tah-theer-coo-ee'-tose], *m.* (Elec.) Circuit breaker.

Cortadera [cor-tah-day'-rah], *f.* 1. Chisel for cutting hot iron. 2. Knife or instrument used by bee-keepers to cut out the honey-combs.

Cortadero, ra [cor-tah-day'-ro, rah], *a.* Cutting readily; easily cut.

Cortadillo [cor-tah-deel'-lyo], *m.* 1. A small drinking-glass, a tumbler. 2. A liquid measure, about a gill; the quantity which the glass will hold. 3. The block of iron which with others forms grape-shot. 4. A clipped piece of money. *Echar cortadillos,* 1. To speak in an affected manner. 2. To drink wine.

Cortado [cor-tah'-do], *m.* Caper; a leap or jump in dancing.

Cortado, da [cor-tah'-do, dah], *a.* 1. Adapted, proportioned, accommodated, fit, exact. 2. (Obs.) Sculptured. 3. (Her.) Parted in the middle. 4. Confounded. 5. Short, interrupted (of style of writing).—*pp.* of CORTAR. *Quedarse cortado* or *cortarse,* To be out of countenance.

Cortador, ra [cor-tah-dor', rah], *m.* & *f.* 1. Cutter, one who cuts. 2. That which cuts. (Also adj.)

Cortador [cor-tah-dor'], *m.* 1. Butcher. *V.* CARNICERO. 2. Slicing-machine, cutter. 3. (Tel.) Interrupter. 4. (Zool.) Scissor-bill.—*pl.* Incisor teeth.

Cortadora [cor-tah-do'-rah], *f.* Cutting-board in a velvet loom.

Cortadura [cor-tah-doo'-rah], *f.* 1. Cut, the action of a sharp instrument. 2. Cut, the separation of continuity by a sharp instrument; cutting, abscission. 3. Incision, cut, a wound made by cutting. 4. Fissure, or scissure. 5. (Mil.) Parapet with embrasures and merlons, made in a breach to prevent the enemy from taking possession of it. 6. (Mil.) Work raised in narrow passes to defend them. *Cortaduras,* 1. Shreds of cloth, cuttings of paper, parings. 2. Figures cut in paper.

Cortafrío [cor-tah-free'-o], *m.* A cold-chisel; chisel for cutting cold iron.

Cortafuego [cor-tah-foo-ay'-go], *m.* (Arch.) A thick wall, in Spain, between the roofs of adjoining houses, to prevent fire from spreading.

Cortahierro [cor-tah-e-err'-ro], *m.* *V.* CORTAFRÍO.

Cortalápiz [cor-tah-lah'-peeth], *m.* Pencil-sharpener.

Cortamalla [cor-tah-mahl'-lyah], *f.* (Agr.) Alternate pruning of vine-shoots when they are close.

Cortamechas [cor-tah-may'-chas], *m.* A cutting-board or table.

Cortamente, *adv.* Sparingly, frugally, scantily.

Cortamiento [cor-tah-me-en'-to], *m.* (Obs.) The act of cutting or amputating.

Cortán [cor-tahn'], *m.* 1. (Prov.) Measure for grain, containing about a peck. 2. Oil-measure, containing 8 lbs. 5 oz.

Cortante [cor-tahn'-tay], *m.* Cutter, butcher.

Cortante [cor-tahn'-tay], *pa.* Cutting, edged, sharp.

Cortapapel [cor-tah-pa-pel'], *m.* Paper-cutter, paper-knife.

Cortapicos y callares [cor-tah-pee'-cos ee cal-lyah'-res]. (Coll.) Keep still! No more questions! (Used to inquisitive children.)

Cortapiés [cor-tah-pe-ess'], *m.* (Coll.) Thrust made at the legs in fencing.

Cortapisa [cor-tah-pee'-sah], *f.* 1. Obstacle, hindrance, impediment. 2. Elegance and grace in speaking. 3. Condition or restriction with which a thing is given.

Cortaplumas [cor-tah-ploo'-mas], *m.* Penknife.

Cortar [cor-tar'], *va.* 1. To cut, to cut off, to cut out, to curtail. 2. To cut, to disjoin, to separate, to hew, to chop. 3. (Mil.) To cut off part of the enemy's army. 4. To cut, to divide packs of cards in card-playing. 5. To interrupt the course of things. 6. To cut or interrupt a conversation, to cut short. 7. To cut, to form by cutting. 8. To abridge a speech or discourse. 9. To take a short cut, shorten the way. 10. To suspend, to restrain, to keep back. *Cortar el agua,* 1. To cut off the water. 2. (Met.) To navigate or sail through water. 11. To arbitrate or decide. 12. To cut figures in paper. 13. (Naut.) To cut away a mast or cable. *Cortar la corriente,* (Elec.) To break contact. *Cortar la lengua,* To speak a language with propriety and elegance. *Cortar las libranzas,* To stop the payment for goods received. *Cortar de vestir,* 1. To cut and make clothes. 2. (Met.) To murmur or speak evil of any one. *Cortar una pluma,* 1. To make a pen. 2. To mend a pen. *Aire que corta,* A cutting, piercing, or nipping wind. *Cortar a alguno,* (Met.) To put one to the blush.—*vr.* 1. To be daunted, ashamed, or confounded, to stop short, not to know what to say. *Cortarse las uñas con alguno,* To pick a quarrel with any one. 2. To open out the folds or wrinkles in cloth. 3. To separate, as the serous part of milk from the butter. 4. Of geometrical figures, to cross, intersect. 5. To interpose one's forces, dividing those of the enemy. 6. To add to a liquid another to subdue its properties. 7. (Vet.) To injure the forefeet with the shoes, in walking.

Cortavapor [cor-tah-vah-por'], *m.* Cut-off of a steam-engine.

Corte [cor'-tay], *m.* 1. Edge of a sword, knife, or any other cutting instrument. *Ingenio de corte,* A cutting engine. 2. Exsection, abscission, the act of cutting. 3. Cut, the effect of a cutting instrument. 4. Felling of trees. 5. Mediation or reconciliation of persons at variance. 6. Measure, expedient, or step taken in an affair. 7. Notch, hack, a hollow cut in any thing. The stuff necessary for a garment, as *Un corte de chaleco* A vest pattern. *Un corte de vestido* The stuff required for a full dress. 8. The surface which all the edges of the leaves of a book form. 9. (Mining) A shaft made in searching for a vein of mineral. 10. (Arch.) A sectional view of a building. (Acad.) 11. Resolutions which states adopt when they cannot satisfy overdue obligations. (Acad.) 12. Closing an account by a debtor without the assent of the creditor (fr. Cortar).

Corte [cor'-tay], *f.* 1. Court, the town or place where the sovereign resides. 2. Court, persons who compose the retinue of a monarch. 3. Levee. 4. Court, the tribunal of chancery in Spain. 5. Retinue, suite. 6. Yard, court. 7. Court, courtship, art of pleasing, civility. *Hacer la corte,* 1. To court, to endeavour to please. 2. To attend the levees of the sovereign or of men in power, to pay court. 8. Stable for cattle; sheep-fold. 9. (Obs.) District of five leagues round the court.—*pl.* *Cortes,* the senate and congress of deputies of Spain. *Cortes de becerro para botas,* Calf-skin boot-legs. (Lat. cohors.)

Cortecica, illa, ita [cor-tay-thee'-cah], *f. dim.* A small crust, peel, or bark.

Cortedad [cor-tay-dahd'], *f.* 1. Smallness, littleness, minuteness. 2. Dulness, stupidity, want of intellect or instruction. 3. Pusillanimity, timidity, diffidence. *Cortedad de medios,* Poverty, indigence, want of means.

Cortejador [cor-tay-hah-dor'], *m.* Wooer.

Cortejante [cor-tay-hahn'-tay], *pa.* Courting; courtier, he who makes love, gallant.

Cortejar [cor-tay-har'], *va.* 1. To accompany, to assist another. 2. To court, to pay homage. 3. To make love. *Cortejar una dama*, To pay one's addresses to a lady. *Cortejar a alguno*, (Coll.) To stand treat.

Cortejo [cor-tay'-ho], *m.* 1. Court, homage paid to another, courtship. 2. Gift, present, gratification. 3. Gallant, beau, lover, sweetheart. 4. Lady courted or sued for love; paramour.

Cortés [cor-tess'], *a.* Courteous, gentle, mild, civil, complaisant, complacent, gracious, courtly, mannerly, genteel, polite.

Cortesanamente, *adv.* Courteously, politely.

Cortesanazo, za [cor-tay-sa-nah'-tho, thah], *a. aug.* Awkwardly or fulsomely civil.

Cortesanía [cor-tay-sa-nee'-ah], *f.* Courtesy, civility, politeness, complaisance, good manners.

Cortesano, na [cor-tay-sah'-no, nah], *a.* 1. Court-like. 2. *V.* CORTÉS. 3. Courteous, gentle, mild, obliging; courtly. *Cortesana* or *dama cortesana*, Courtesan.

Cortesano [cor-tay-sah'-no], *m.* Courtier.

Cortesía [cor-tay-see'-ah], *f.* 1. Courtesy, an act of civility and respect, obeisance, courteousness; good manners. 2. Compliment, an expression of civility; a title of courtesy. 3. Gift, present gratifications. 4. Days of grace allowed by custom for the payment of a bill of exchange, after it becomes due. 5. Mercy, favour. *Título* or *tratamiento de cortesía*, A title or appellation of honour, not of right, but by courtesy. *Hacer una cortesía*, To drop a courtesy.

Cortesmente, *adv.* Courteously, civilly, genteelly, politely, obligingly.

Corte transversal [cor'-tay trans-ver-sahl'], *m.* Cross section.

Corteza [cor-tay'-thah], *f.* 1. Bark of a tree. 2. Peel, skin, or rind of many things. 3. Crust of bread, pies, etc. 4. A wild fowl of the family of widgeons. 5. *Corteza de palo santo*, Guaiacum bark. 6. (Met.) Outward appearance of things. 7. (Met.) Rusticity, want of politeness, crustiness.

Cortezón [cor-tay-thone'], *m. aug.* Thick bark, rind, crust, or peel.

Cortezoncito [cor-tay-thon-thee'-to], *m. dim.* Thin bark, rind, crust, or peel.

Cortezudo, da [cor-tay-thoo'-do, dah], *a.* 1. Corticose, barky; having a strong rough bark. 2. Rustic, unmannerly, unpolished.

Cortezuela, *f. dim.* *V.* CORTEZONCITO.

Cortical [cor-te-cahl'], *a.* Cortical.

Cortijada [cor-te-hah'-dah], *f.* A collection of houses put up by the labourers or owners of a grange.

Cortijo [cor-tee'-ho], *m.* Farm-house, grange, manse. *Alborotar el cortijo*, (Met. and coll.) To disturb a company by words or actions.

Cortil [cor-teel'], *m.* *V.* CORRAL.

Cortina [cor-tee'-nah], *f.* 1. Curtain, shade, screen, portiere. 2. (Mil.) Curtain, part of a wall or rampart which lies between two bastions. 3. Any veil or covering. *Cortina de hierro*, Iron curtain. *Cortina de humo*, Smoke screen.

Cortinaje [cor-te-nah'-hay], *m.* Set of curtains for a house.

Cortinal [cor-te-nahl'], *m.* A piece of ground near a village or farm-house, which is generally sown every year.

Cortinilla [cor-te-neel'-lyah], *f.* Screen, shade, portiere.

Cortinón [cor-te-none'], *m. aug.* A large curtain to keep out the air.

Cortiña [cor-tee'-nyah], *f.* A plot of vegetables and cereals.

Cortisona [cor-te-so'-nah], *f.* (Med.) Cortisone.

Corto, ta [cor'-to, tah], *a.* 1. Short, not long, scanty, narrow, curt. 2. Small, little. 3. Short, not of long duration. 4. (Met.) Dull, stupid, weak of intellect. 5. (Met.) Timid, pusillanimous, fearful. 6. (Met.) Short of words, concise. 7. Imperfect, defective. *Corto de vista*, Short-sighted. *Corto de oído*, Hard of hearing. *Corto de manos*, Slow at work, unhandy, not handy, not dexterous. *Corto de genio*, Of a diffident character. *A la corta o a la larga*, Sooner or later. *Corta pala*, (Coll.) Unskilful, without knowledge or address. *Corto sastre*, (Met. Coll.) Ignorance of any subject discussed, unskilful, unskilled.

Cortón [cor-tone'], *m.* Worm, ringworm which destroys plants in gardens.

Corulla [co-rool'-lyah], *f.* In galleys, place for the stoppers of cables.

Corundo, *m.* *V.* CORINDÓN.

Coruscante, Corusco, ca [co-roos-cahn'-tay, co-roos'-co, cah], *a.* (Poet.) Coruscant, glittering by flashes, brilliant.

Corva [cor'-vah], *f.* 1. Ham, a part of the leg. 2. Curb, a disease in horses' knees.

Corvadura [cor-vah-doo'-rah], *f.* 1. Curvature, crookedness, inflexion; gibbousness. 2. (Arch.) Bend of an arch or vault.

Corval [cor-vahl'], *a.* Of an oblong shape: applied to olives.

Corvato [cor-vah'-to], *m.* A young crow or rook.

Corvaza [cor-vah'-thah], *f.* Curb, a disease in horses' knees.

Corvecito [cor-vay-thee'-to], *m. dim.* A young little crow or rook.

Corvejón [cor-vay-hone'], *m.* 1. Hough, the joint of the hind leg of beasts. 2. Spur of a cock.

Corvejos [cor-vay'-hose], *m. pl.* An articulation of six bones joined by ligaments with which animals make movements of flexion and extension.

Corveta [cor-vay'-tah], *f.* Curvet, corvetto, leap or bound of a horse.

Corvetear [cor-vay-tay-ar'], *vn.* To curvet, to bound, to leap.

Corvideo, ea [cor-vee'-day-o, ah], *a.* Like or belonging to a crow.

Córvidos [cor'-ve-dose], *m. pl.* (Zool.) The family of crows, jays, etc.; corvidæ.

Corvillo [cor-veel'-lyo], *m.* 1. Bill, a kind of hatchet with a hooked point. 2. *Corvillo de podón*, Pruning-knife. 3. *Corvillo de zapatero*, A shoemaker's paring-knife. 4. A small sickle to cut the thread and form the velvet in velvet-looms. *Miércoles corvillo*, Ash-Wednesday.

Corvina [cor-vee'-nah], *f.* 1. A kind of conger or sea-eel in the Mediterranean. Sciæna lepisma. 2. White sea-bass of California. Cynoscion nobile.

Corvino, na [cor-vee'-no, nah], *a.* (Obs.) Rook-like, belonging to a rook.

Corvo, va [cor'-vo, vah], *a.* 1. Bent, crooked, arched. 2. Stingy, mean.

Corvo [cor'-vo], *m.* 1. (Zool. Prov.) Craw-fish, a kind of sea-fish. 2. Pot-hook.

Corzo, za [cor'-tho, thah], *m.* & *f.* Roedeer, fallow-deer. Cervus capreolus, *L.*

Corzuelo [cor-thoo-ay'-lo], *m.* Wheat left in the husks by the thrashers.

Cosa [co'-sah], *f.* 1. Thing, substance, that which has being or existence. *Cosa de entidad*, An important thing. *Cosa de risa* or *cosa ridícula*, Laughing-stock. *Cosa de ver*, A thing worth seeing. *Fuerte cosa*, A hard task or thing. ***Es fuerte cosa***, It is very hard. *No es cosa*, It does not matter, it is a trifle. ***No hay tal cosa*** or ***no es así***, No such thing. *No vale cosa*, It is not worth a rush. 2. Suit, cause. *Tres cosas demando si Dios me las diese, la tela, el telar, y la que la teje*, Three things I ask of God: the loom, the weaver, and the cloth. (Reproach to those who are never satisfied.) *Cosa del otro jueves*, (Coll.) 1. An extravagant act. 2. Something out of date; a back number. *Cosa de viento*, A vain thing without substance. *¿Qué cosa?* (Coll.) What's the matter? *¿Qué es cosa y cosa?* (Coll.) What means all this? *Quedarle (a uno) otra cosa en el estómago*, To say craftily the opposite of what is felt.

Cosa de, *adv.* About, little more or less. *Cosa de media legua*, Half a league, more or less.

Cosaco, ca [co-sah'-co, cah], *a.* Cossack.

Cosar [co-sar'], *m.* (Com.) Kind of cotton stuff made in India.

Cosario [co-sah'-re-o], *m.* 1. Privateer, corsair, pirate, cruiser. 2. Carrier, one who carries goods. 3. Huntsman by profession. 4. One who is accustomed or in the habit of doing any thing.

Cosario, ria [co-sah'-re-o, ah], *a.* 1. Belonging or relating to privateers or corsairs. 2. Beaten, frequented: applied to roads.

Coscarana [cos-ca-rah'-nah], *f.* (Prov.) Cracknel, a crisp cake.

Coscarse [cos-car'-say], *vr.* (Coll.) *V.* CONCOMERSE.

Coscoja [cos-co'-hah], *f.* 1. (Bot.) Kermes or scarlet-oak. Quercus cocifera, *L.* 2. Dry leaves of the kermes oak. 3. Ring or knob on the cross-bit of a bridle.

Coscojal, Coscojar [cos-co-hahl', cos-co-har'], *m.* Plantation of kermes or scarlet-oaks.

Coscojo [cos-co'-ho], *m.* Scarlet or kermes grain, after the worm or insect (Coccus ilicis, *L.*) has left it. *Coscojos*, Bits of iron composing the chain fastened to the mouth-piece of a horse's bridle.

Coscón, na [cos-cone', nah], *a.* Crafty, sly.

Coscorrón [cos-cor-rone'], *m.* 1. Contusion, a blow or bruise on the head. 2. Bruise in a loaf.

Coscorronera [cos-cor-ro-nay'-rah], *f.* A kind of bonnet put upon children to avoid blows upon the head. *V.* CHICHONERA.

Coscurro [cos-coor'-ro], *m.* Flat loaf.

Cosecante [co-say-cahn'-tay], *m.* (Geom.) Cosecant.

Cosecha [co-say'-chah], *f.* 1. Harvest, harvest-time. 2. Harvest, the corn ripened and gathered. 3. The season of reaping and gathering olives, etc. 4. The act of gathering the harvest. *Cosecha de vino*, Vintage. 5. (Met.) Collection of immaterial things, as virtues, vices, etc. *De su cosecha*, Of one's own invention.

Cosechar [co-say-char'], *va.* (Prov.) To crop, to reap, to gather the corn at harvest-time.

Cosechero [co-say-chay'-ro], *m.* The person who has corn, olives, etc., of his own to reap and gather: commonly used to designate the proprietor of the produce.

Cosederos de los tablones, *m. pl.* (Naut.) Plank seams.

Cosedor [co-say-dor'], *m.* (Littl. us.) Sewer.

Cosedora [co-say-do'-rah], *f.* (Littl. us.) Seamstress, stitcher.

Coselete [co-say-lay'-tay], *m.* 1. Corselet, ancient coat of armour. 2. A light corselet. 3. Pikeman, anciently armed with a corselet. 4. The thorax of insects.

Coseno [co-say'-no], *m.* (Geom.) Cosine. *Coseno verso,* The co-versed sine.

Coser [co-serr'], *va.* 1. To sew. 2. To join and unite things. *Coser un motón,* (Naut.) To lash or seize a block. *Coserse con la pared,* To stick close to a wall. *Coser a puñaladas,* (Coll.) To stab or give wounds with a pointed weapon. *Coser y cantar,* To offer no difficulties; or, more fully: *Ya no queda más que coser y cantar,* What remains to be done is a trifle. *Coserse la boca,* Not to speak a word. *Cosido con hilo gordo,* Badly, carelessly done.

Cosera [co-say'-rah], *f.* (Prov.) Piece of ground which can be irrigated at once.

Cosetada [co-say-tah'-dah], *f.* Race, a violent course.

Cosible [co-see'-blay], *a.* (Obs.) That which may be sewed.

Cosicosa, *f.* *V.* Quisicosa.

Cosido [co-see'-do], *m.* 1. Clothing collectively, and needlework. 2. Action of sewing. *Cosido de cama,* Quilt and blankets of a bed stitched together to prevent their separation.—*Cosido, da, pp.* of Coser, Devoted to, wedded to.

Cosiduras [co-see-doo'-ras], *f. pl.* (Naut.) Lashings, ends of ropes used in ships to secure movable things.

Cosita [co-see'-tah], *f. dim.* A small thing, a trifle.

Cosmético [cos-may'-te-co], *m.* Cosmetic.

Cósmico, ca [cos'-me-co, cah], *a.* 1. Cosmic, belonging to the universe. 2. A rising or setting star, which coincides with the rising of the sun.

Cosmocracia [cos-mo-crah'-the-ah], *f.* Cosmocracy, a system of universal monarchy.

Cosmócrata [cos-mo'-crah-tah], *a.* Cosmocratic, aspiring to universal monarchy.

Cosmocrático, ca [cos-mo-crah'-te-co, cah], *a.* Cosmocratic, relating to cosmocracy.

Cosmogonía [cos-mo-go-nee'-ah], *f.* Cosmogony.

Cosmografía [cos-mo-grah-fee'-ah], *f.* Cosmography.

Cosmográficamente, *adv.* (Littl. us.) Cosmographically.

Cosmográfico, ca [cos-mo-grah'-fe-co, cah], *a.* Cosmographical.

Cosmógrafo [cos-mo'-grah-fo], *m.* Cosmographer.

Cosmología [cos-mo-lo-hee'-ah], *f.* Cosmology.

Cosmológico, ca [cos-mo-lo'-he-co, cah], *a.* (Littl. us.) Cosmological.

Cosmonauta [cos-mo-nah'-oo-tah], *m. & f.* Astronaut, spaceman, cosmonaut.

Cosmopolita [cos-mo-po-lee'-tah], *com.* Cosmopolite.

Cosmorama [cos-mo-rah'-mah], *m.* Cosmorama.

Cosmos [cose'-mose], *m.* The universe.

Cosmotrón [cos-mo-trone'], *m.* Cosmotron.

Coso [co'-so], *m.* 1. (Prov.) Place or square for bull-fights or other public entertainments. 2. Worm which lodges in the trunks of some fruit-trees.

Cospe [cose'-pay], *m.* Chipping with an adze or hatchet.

Cospel [cos-pel'], *m.* A coin blank, in the mint.

Cospillo [cos-peel'-lyo], *m.* Lees of the olive, after expression.

Cosquillas [cos-keel'-lyas], *f. pl.* Tickling, titillation. *Hacer cosquillas alguna cosa,* (Met.) To be tickled by any thing; to excite desire, curiosity, or suspicion. *No consentir* or *no sufrir cosquillas,* (Met.) To understand or suffer no jokes. *Tener malas cosquillas,* (Met.) To be easily offended, to be ill-tempered.

Cosquilleo [cos-keel-lyay'-o], *m.* Sensation of tickling.

Cosquilloso, sa [cos-keel-lyo'-so, sah], *a.* 1. Ticklish. 2. Susceptible, easily offended.

Costa [cos'-tah], *f.* 1. Cost, the price paid for a thing. 2. Cost, charge, expense. 3. Expensiveness. 4. Expense or charges of a lawsuit: in this sense it is almost always used in the plural. *Condenar en costas,* To sentence a party to pay the costs of a suit. 5. (Met.) Labour, expense, fatigue. *A costa de,* At the expense of. *A toda costa,* At all hazards, at all events. 6. Coast; the shore. 7. Wedge used by shoemakers to stretch shoes on the last. *Dar a la costa,* or *en la costa,* To get on shore. *Arrimado a la costa,* Close inshore. *Costa de sotavento,* Lee-shore. *Ir* or *navegar costa a costa,* To coast, to sail along the coast.

Costado [cos-tah'-do], *m.* 1. Side, the lateral part of animals. 2. *V.* Lado. 3. (Mil.) Flank of a body of troops. 4. (Obs.) Hind or back part. 5. Side of a ship. *Presentar el costado a un enemigo,* To bring the broadside to bear upon an enemy's ship. *Navío de costado derecho,* A wall-sided ship. *Navío de costado falso,* A lop-sided ship. *Dar el costado al navío,* To heave down a ship. *Costados,* Race, lineage, succession of ancestors. *Arbol de costados,* Genealogical tree.

Costal [cos-tahl'], *m.* 1. Sack or large bag. 2. Rammer to beat down the earth of a mud-wall or rampart. *No soy costal* or *no tengo boca de costal,* (Coll.) I cannot tell all at once.

Costal cos-tahl'], *a.* Costal, belonging to the ribs.

Costalada [cos-tah-lah'-dah], *f.* A fall flat on the ground.

Costalazo [cos-tah-lah'-tho], *m.* Blow with a sack. *Dar un costalazo,* To fall flat on the ground like a sack; to fail.

Costalero [cos-tah-lay'-ro], *m.* (Prov.) Porter, who carries goods.

Costalito [cos-tah-lee'-to], *m. dim.* A small sack.

Costaneras [cos-tah-nay'-ras], *f. pl.* In building, rafters.

Costanero, ra [cos-tah-nay'-ro, rah], *a.* 1. Belonging to a coast. 2. Declivous, inclining downward. *Buque* or *bajel costanero,* Coaster, a vessel employed in the coasting trade. *Navegación costanera,* Coasting navigation.

Costanilla [cos-tah-neel'-lyah], *f. dim.* Gentle declivity, side of a small hill; a steep street.

Costar [cos-tar'], *vn.* 1. To cost, to be bought for, to be had at a price. *Me cuesta tanto,* It stands me in so much. 2. To suffer detriment or loss. *Costar la torta un pan,* (Coll.) The sprat cost a herring.

Costarricense [cos-tar-re-then'-say], or **Costarriqueño, ña** [cos-tar-re-kay'-nyo, nyah], *a.* Costa Rican; of Costa Rica.

Coste [cos'-tay], *m.* Cost, expense, price paid for a thing. *A coste y costas,* At first or prime cost.

Costeable [cos-tay-ah'-blay], *a.* Financially feasible.

Costear [cos-tay-ar'], *va.* 1. To pay the cost of. 2. To skirt. 3. (Naut.) To sail along the coast of. —*vr.* To pay its own way, to cover the costs involved.

Costeño [cos-tay'-nyo], *a.* *Barco costeño,* A small boat used only in the coasting trade.

Costera [cos-tay'-rah], *f.* 1. Side of a bale of goods. 2. A fisherman's basket. 3. Each of the two parts of the mould into which tubes of lead or tin empty. 4. Time of fishing for surmullets. 5. Outside quire of a ream of paper. 6. Sea-coast.

Costero [cos-tay'-ro], *m.* First plank cut from a pine-tree.

Costero, ra [cos-tay'-ro, rah], *a.* 1. Outward. *Papel costero,* Outside quires. 2. (Obs.) Oblique: applied to a cannon-shot or a declivity.

Costezuela [cos-tay-thoo-ay'-lah], *f. dim.* Slight declivity or coast.

Costífero, ra [cos-tee'-fay-ro, rah], *a.* (Zool.) Ribbed longitudinally.

Costilla [cos-teel'-lyah], *f.* 1. Rib. 2. Stave, the board of a barrel. 3. Furr, a piece of timber which serves to strengthen joists. 4. The rib of a cupola, springer. 5. (Met. Coll.) Property, support, wealth. 6. (Coll.) Rib, for wife. 7. (Bot.) A thick nervure or rib of a leaf. *Hacer costilla,* To bear the brunt. *Costillas de un navío,* (Naut.) Ribs of a ship.—*pl.* 1. Shoulders, back. 2. (Agr.) Wooden strips to which horses are tied in ploughing. 3. (Mech.) Cramp-irons, chimney ties for securing chimney flues. *Medirle à uno las costillas,* To cudgel him.

Costillaje, Costillar [cos-teel-lyah'-hay, cos-teel-lyar'], *m.* 1. The whole of the ribs, and their place in the body. 2. The ribs in a flitch of bacon. 3. (Naut.) The timbers or frame of a ship.

Costilludo, da [cos-teel-lyoo'-do, dah], *a.* (Coll.) 1. Broad-shouldered. 2. Clownish, unmannerly.

Costino, na [cos-tee'-no, nah], *a.* Belonging to the costus-root, which is stomachic and diuretic.

Costípedo, da [cos-tee'-pay-do, dah], *a.* Said of birds which are perfectly balanced upon their legs.

Costo [cos'-to], *m.* 1. Cost, price. 2. Charges, expense. 3. Labour, fatigue. 4. (Bot.) Costus arabicus, or sweet and bitter costus. Costus arabicus. 5. Costus-root. *A costo y costas,* At prime cost.

Costosamente, *adv.* Costly, at a high price, expensively; extravagantly.

Costoso, sa [cos-to'-so, sah], *a.* 1. Costly, dear, expensive. 2. (Met.) Dear, difficult to be obtained. 3. Dear, sad, grievous.

Costra [cos'-trah], *f.* 1. Crust. 2. Crust, scab. 3. Broken biscuit given to the people on board of galleys. 4. An encrusted part of a wick.

Costrada [cos-trah'-dah], *f.* Seed-cake, candied with melted sugar, beaten eggs, and grated bread.

Costribar [cos-tre-bar'], *va.* (Obs.) To indurate, to harden; to make strong.

Costribo [cos-tree'-bo], *m.* (Obs.) *V.* Apoyo and Arrimo.

Costringimiento [cos-trin-he-me-en'-to], *m.* (Obs.) Constraint.

Costringir [cos-trin-heer'], *va.* (Obs.) To constrain, to compel.

Costriñente [cos-tre-nyen'-tay], *pa.* (Obs.) Constringing.

Costroso, sa [cos-tro'-so, sah], *a.* Crusty, covered with a crust.

Costumbrar [cos-toom-brar'], *va.* (Obs.) *V.* ACOSTUMBRAR.

Costumbre [cos-toom'-bray], *f.* 1. Custom, habit, haunt, habitude, familiarity. 2. Custom, a law which has obtained force by usage. 3. Custom, the common way of acting, fashion, established manner. 4. Periodical indisposition of women, catamenia, courses. *Costumbres*, Customs, the characteristic manners and habits of a nation or a person. *A la mala costumbre, quebrarle la pierna*, An evil habit must be overcome. *La costumbre hace ley*, Custom makes law.

Costura [cos-too'-rah], *f.* 1. Seam. 2. Needlework, especially upon white goods: sheets, shirts, etc. 3. (Naut.) Splicing of a rope. (Carp.) A joint between two pieces of wood. *Costuras de los tablones de un navío*, (Naut.) The seams of the planks of a ship. *Costuras abiertas*, Seams of a ship from which the oakum has been washed out. *Saber de toda costura*, To have knowledge of the world and act with all sagacity, and even cheating.

Costurera [cos-too-ray'-rah], *f.* Seamstress.

Costurero [cos-too-ray'-ro], *m.* 1. A lady's work-box. 2. (Obs.) Tailor.

Costurón [cos-too-rone'], *m.* 1. Seam, a coarse suture which joins two edges. 2. A large scar.

Cota [co'-tah], *f.* 1. Coat of mail. 2. Coat of arms, formerly worn by the kings at arms. 3. (Topog.) A number indicating the height of a point above the sea or some other level. (Acad.) 4. Quota, a share assigned to each. 5. The back and callous part of a boar's hide. 6. (Prov.) Mary, a woman's name.

Cotana [co-tah'-nah], *f.* Mortise, mortise-hole.

Cotangente [co-tan-hen'-tay], *f.* (Geom.) Co-tangent.

Cotanza [co-tahn'-thah], *f.* Sort of linen, medium fineness.

Cotar [co-tar'], *va.* (Obs.) *V.* ACOTAR.

Cotarrera [co-tar-ray'-rah], *f.* (Coll.) A gadding woman.

Cotarro [co-tar'-ro], *m.* Charity-hut for the reception of beggars. *Andar de cotarro en cotarro*, To go sauntering about. *Alborotar el cotarro*, To cause disturbance.

Cote [co'-tay], *m.* (Naut.) Half hitch, knot. *Dos cotes*, Clove-hitch.

Cotejar [co-tay-har'], *va.* To compare one thing with another, to confront, to confer.

Cotejo [co-tay'-ho], *m.* Comparison, collation, parallel.

Cotense [co-ten'-say], *m.* (Mex.) Coarse brown linen wrapper.

Coti [co-tee'], *m.* 1. Sort of linen. 2. Ticking used for mattresses.

Cotidianamente [co-te-de-ah-nah-men'-tay], *adv.* Daily.

Cotidiano, na [co-te-de-ah'-no, nah], *a.* Daily, each day; quotidian.

Cotiledón [co-te-lay-done'], *m.* 1. (Bot.) Cotyledon, seed-leaf. 2. (Anat.) Cotyledon, a lobule of the placenta.

Cotiledonado, da, or **Cotiledóneo, ea** [co-te-lay-do-nah'-do, dah, co-te-lay-do'-nay-o, ah], *a.* Cotyledonous.

Cotiliforme [co-te-le-for'-may], *a.* (Bot.) Cotyliform, having a wide cylindrical tube and straight limb.

Cotilo [co-tee'-lo], *m.* (Antiq.) Cotyle, a cup-like cavity.

Cotilóidea [co-te-loi'-day-ah], *f.* The cotyloid cavity which receives the head of the thigh-bone.

Cotilóideo, ea [co-te-loi'-day-o, ah], *a.* Cotyloid, cup-like.

Cotilla [co-teel'-lyah], *f.* Stays, corsets. *Varillas de cotilla*, Whalebones.

Cotillero [co-teel-lyay'-ro], *m.* Staymaker.

Cotillo [co-teel'-lyo], *m.* The peen of a hammer: end opposite to flat surface; claw of hammer.

Cotillón [co-teel-lyone'], *m.* A dance, generally a waltz, at the end of a society ball.

Cotín [co-teen'], *m.* 1. A back stroke given in the air to a ball. 2. Bed-ticking.

Cotiza [co-tee'-thah], *f.* 1. (Her.) Band of a shield, fret. 2. (Mech.) Each of the grooves for the warp of the silk fabric called lustering.

Cotizable [co-te-thah'-blay], *a.* Quotable, valued at.

Cotización [co-te-thah-the-on'], *f.* (Com.) Quotation; price-current, price-list.

Cotizado, da [co-te-thah'-do, dah], *a.* (Her.) Banded, having bands.

Cotizar [co-te-thar'], *va.* To quote prices; to cry out the current prices in the exchange.

Coto [co'-to], *m.* 1. Inclosure of pasture-grounds. 2. Land-mark. 3. (Prov.) Territory, district. 4. Combination among merchants not to sell goods under a certain rate. 5. Measure of a hand-breadth. 6. (Prov.) Fine or mulct. 7. Chub, a small fresh-water fish. 8. Rate or price of a thing. 9. (Amer.) A morbid swelling in the throat, goitre. *V.* PAPERA.

Cotobelo [co-to-bay'-lo], *m.* Opening in the branch of a bridle.

Cotofre [co-to'-fray], *m.* (Obs.) Drinking-glass.

Cotón [co-tone'], *m.* Printed cotton. *Cotón colorado*, (Cant) Punishment by whipping. (Arab.)

Cotona [co-toh'-nah], *f.* (Mex.) Chamois jacket.

Cotonada [co-to-nah'-dah], *f.* Sort of cotton cloth, striped and flowered; calico, prints.

Cotoncillo [co-ton-theel'-lyo], *m.* Button of a maulstick or painter's staff.

Cotonía [co-to-nee'-ah], *f.* Dimity, fine fustian.

Cotopriz [co-to-preeth'], *f.* A fruit of Guiana, of the size and shape of a plum, and the muscat grape in taste.

Cotorra [co-tor'-rah], *f.* 1. (Orn.) A parrot of the smallest kind. 2. (Orn.) Magpie. Corvus pica, *L.* 3. (Met.) A loquacious woman.

Cotorrear [co-tor-ray-ar'], *vn.* To chatter, to gabble.

Cotorreo [co-tor-ray'-o], *m.* Chattering, gossiping.

Cotorrera [co-tor-ray'-rah], *f.* 1. A hen-parrot. 2. (Met.) A prattling woman.

Cotorrería [co-tor-ray-ree'-ah], *f.* (Coll.) Loquacity: speaking of women.

Cotrai [co-trah'-e], *m.* Sort of linen.

Cotral [co-trahl'], *m.* An old worn-out ox, set to graze.

Cotudo, da [co-too'-do, dah], *a.* Hairy, cottony.

Cotufa [co-too'-fah], *f.* 1. (Bot.) Jerusalem artichoke. Helianthus tuberosus. 2. Tid-bits, delicate food. *Pedir cotufas en el golfo*, To require impossibilities.

Cotufero, ra [co-too-fay'-ro, rah], *a.* Producing tid-bits or delicate food.

Cotunio [co-too'-ne-o], *m.* A transparent and viscous fluid which fills the cavities of the internal ear.

Cotunnio, Cotunnito [co-toon'-ne-o, nee'-to], *m.* Cotunnite, a lead chloride found in volcanic craters.

Coturno [co-toor'-no], *m.* Cothurnus, buskin, a kind of high boot worn by the ancient actors of tragedy. *Calzar el coturno*, (Met.) To make use of pompous language in poetry.

Coutelina [co-oo-tay-lee'-nah], *f.* A blue or white cotton cloth imported from India.

Covacha [co-vah'-chah], *f.* A small cave or hollow under ground; a grot or grotto.

Covachuela [co-vah-choo-ay'-lah], *f.* 1. (Dim.) A small cave or grot. 2. (Coll.) Office of secretary of state. *Covachuelas*, Toy-shops kept in the vaults of the royal convent of St. Philip, in Madrid.

Covachuelero [co-vah-choo-ay-lay'-ro], *m.* Shop-keeper in the vaults under the convent of St. Philip, in Madrid.

Covachuelista, or **Covachuelo** [co-vah-choo-ay-lees'-tah], *m.* (Coll.) Clerk in one of the offices of the secretaries of state.

Covanilla, *f. dim* *V.* COVANILLO.

Covanillo [co-vah-neel'-lyo], *m. dim.* Basket with a wide mouth, used for gathering grapes.

Coxalgia [coc-sahl'-he-ah], *f.* Hip-joint disease, coxalgia.

Coxcojilla, ita cox-co heel'-lyah, hee'-tah], *f.* A children's play; hop-scotch.

Coxcoj (Á), or **Coxcojita (Á)** [ah cox-coh, or ah cocs-co-hee'-tah], *adv.* Lamely, haltingly, limpingly.

Coxis [coc'-sees], *m.* The coccyx.

Coy [co'-e], *m.* (Naut.) Hammock, cot, a sailor's bed. *Afuera coys*, All hammocks up.

Coya [co'-yah], *f.* (Peru.) The queen, wife, and sister of the inca.

Coyote [co-yo'-tay], *a.* (Amer.) Native, of the country; domestic; as *cidra coyote, indio coyote.*—*m.* (Mex.) A kind of wolf; coyote.

Coyoteo [co-yoh-tay'-oh], *m.* (Mex. coll.) Lobbying.

Coyunda [co-yoon'-dah], *f.* 1. A strap or cord with which oxen are tied to the yoke. 2. (Met.) Dominion, power. 3. Matrimonial union.

Coyundado, da [co-yoon-dah'-do, dah], *a.* (Obs.) Tied to the yoke with a strap or cord.

Coyundilla [co-yoon-deel'-lyah], *f. dim.* A small strap or cord.

Coyuntura [co-yoon-too'-rah], *f.* 1. Joint, articulation. 2. Occasion, conjuncture, juncture; a critical point of time, a seasonable opportunity.

Coz [coth], *f.* 1. Kicking with the hind leg: applied to beasts. 2. Kick or blow with the foot. 3. Recoil of a gun. 4. Flowing back of a flood. 5. *V.* CULATA. 6. The back of a pistol from the guard to the end of the tip. 7. (Coll.) Churlishness, unprovoked brusqueness. *Coz de mastelero*, (Naut.) Heel of a mast. *A coces*, By dint of kicking. *Tirar coces contra el aguijón*, To kick against the pricks, to spurn at superiority.

Cra [crah], *m.* Caw of the crow.

Crabe [crah'-bay], *m.* Name given by the Americans to one of the woods which are exported to Europe.

Crabrón [crah-brone'], *m.* Hornet. Vespa crabro.

Cralo [crah'-lo], *m.* Slavonian word which in Byzantine history denotes the princes of Servia and Bosnia.

Crambo [crahm'-bo], *m.* Name formerly common to all cabbages and kales.

Crameria [crah-may'-re-ah], *f.* Krameria, rhatany, a medicinal plant of the polygala family indigenous to Peru. It is astringent.

Cran [crahn], *m.* (Typ.) Nick, one of the grooves cast upon the front of the

shank of a type to aid the compositor in rightly placing it.
Craneano, na [crah-nay-ah'-no, nah], *a.* Cranial, relating to the skull.
Cráneo [crah'-nay-o], *m.* The skull; cranium.
Craneología [crah-nay-o-lo-he'-ah], *f.* Craniology, phrenology.
Crápula [crah'-poo-lah], *f.* Inebriation, intoxication, crapulence.
Crapuloso, sa [crah-poo-lo'-so, sah], *a.* 1. Drunken; gluttonous, surfeited. 2. Dissolute, dissipated.
Crasamente, *adv.* Grossly, rudely.
Crascitar [cras-the-tar'], *vn.* To crow, to croak.
Crasicie [crah-see'-the-ay], *f.* (Obs.) Grease, fat.
Crasiento, ta, *a.* Greasy. *V.* GRASIENTO.
Crasino [crah-see'-no], *m.* (Orn.) *V.* Hoco.
Crasitud [crah-se-tood'], *f.* 1. Fatness, corpulency, crassitude, obesity. 2. Ignorance, stupidity, dulness.
Craso, sa [crah'-so, sah], *a.* 1. Fat, greasy, oily, unctuous. 2. Thick, gross, crass. *Ignorancia crasa,* Gross ignorance. *Error craso,* Gross error. *Disparate craso,* Egregious nonsense.
Cráter [crah'-tayr], *m.* Crater of a volcano.
Crátera [crah'-tay-rah], *f.* Krater or crater, amphora, type of Grecian urn.
Craticula [crah-tee'-coo-lah], *f.* A small wicket or window, through which nuns receive the communion.
Craza [crah'-thah], *f.* A receptacle for melted metal.
Crea [cray'-ah], *f.* Linen much used in Spain and Spanish America. *Creas a la Morlaix,* Superfine creas. *Creas finas,* Middling creas. *Creas corrientes,* Common creas. *Creas inglesas,* Scotch creas.
Creable [cray-ah'-blay], *a.* Creative, creatable.
Creación [cray-ah-the-on'], *f.* Creation.
Creado, da [cray-ah'-do, dah], *a.* Created, begotten, made.—*pp.* of CREAR.
Creador [cray-ah-dor'], *m.* The Creator, God.
Crear [cray-ar'], *va.* 1. To create, to make, to cause to exist. 2. (Met.) To institute, to establish; to compose, produce literary or artistic works of relative merit. 3. (Obs.) To nourish, to support.
Crébol [cray'-bol], *m.* (Bot. Prov.) Holly-tree. *V.* ACEBO.
Crecedero, ra [cray-thay-day'-ro, rah], *a.* Able to grow, that which can grow.
Crecer [cray-therr'], *vn.* 1. To grow, to increase. 2. To grow or increase in stature. 3. To become larger 4. To grow, to swell: a sea term. 5. To augment the extrinsic value of money.
Creces [cray'-thes], *f. pl.* 1. Augmentation, increase; excess, in some things. 2. The additional quantity of corn paid by a farmer to a public granary, besides what he borrowed from it.
Crecida [cray-thee'-dah], *f.* Freshet, swollen state of rivers in consequence of heavy falls of rain. *V.* AVENIDA.
Crecidamente, *adv.* Plentifully, copiously, abundantly.
Crecidito, ta [cray-the-dee'-to, tah], *a. dim.* Somewhat increased or grown.
Crecido, da [cray-thee'-do, dah], *a.* 1. Grown, increased. 2. Grave, important. 3. Large, great.—*pp.* of CRECER.
Crecidos [cray-thee'-dos], *m. pl.* Widening stitches with knitting-needles, to enlarge the width of a stocking.
Creciente [cray-the-en'-tay], *pa.* 1. Growing, increasing, crescent. 2. Susceptible of increase. 3. (Her.) A half-moon with points upward.
Creciente, *f.* 1. Swell, freshet of waters. 2. (Prov.) Leaven. 3. Crescent, the moon in her state of increase. *Creciente de la marea,* (Naut.) Flood-tide, flow, flowing.
Crecimiento [cray-the-me-en'-to], *m.* 1. Increase or increment, growing, growth. *Crecimiento de la marejada,* (Naut.) Swell of the sea. 2. Increase of the value of money.
Credencia [cray-den'-the-ah], *f.* 1. Sideboard of an altar, on which all the necessaries are placed for celebrating high mass. 2. (Obs.) Credentials.
Credencial [cray-den-the-ahl'], *f.* Credential, that which gives a title to credit, accreditation. *Credenciales* or *cartas credenciales,* Credentials or credential letters.
Credibilidad [cray-de-be-le-dahd'], *f* Credibility.
Crédito [cray'-de-to], *m.* 1. Acquiescence, assent. 2. Credit, a sum of money due to any one. 3. Credence, credit, belief, faith. 4. Reputation, character, name. 5. Credit, trust, confidence, esteem. 6. Note, bill, order for payment. *Créditos activos,* Assets. *Créditos pasivos,* Liabilities.
Credo [cray'-do], *m.* Creed, articles of faith. *Cada credo,* Every moment. *En un credo,* In a trice, in a moment.
Credulidad [cray-doo-le-dahd'], *f.* 1. Credulity. 2. *V.* CREENCIA.
Crédulo, la [cray'-doo-lo, lah], *a.* Credulous.
Creedero, ra [cray-ay-day'-ro, rah], *a.* Credible. *Tener buenas creederas,* To be easy of belief, to swallow the bait.
Creedor, ra [cray-ay-dor', rah], *a.* Credulous.
Creencia [cray-en'-the-ah], *f.* 1. Credence, belief, credit. 2. Credence, belief of the truths of religion, creed, persuasion. 3. (Obs.) *V.* MENSAJE and SALVA.
Creer [cray-err'], *va.* 1. To believe, to give faith and credit to a thing. 2. To believe, to have a firm persuasion of the revealed truths of religion. 3. To credit, to receive a thing as probable. *Ver y creer,* To believe only what we see. *Creo,* Methinks.
Crehuela [cray-oo-ay'-lah], *f.* Sort of linen, osnaburgs.
Creible [cray-ee'-blay], *a.* Credible, likely.
Creiblemente, *adv.* Credibly.
Crema [cray'-mah], *f.* 1. Cream of milk. *Crema batida,* Whipped cream. 2. Custard. 3. Diaeresis. 4. Cream, the select of society. 5. Cream, cosmetic of creamy consistency.
Cremación [cray-mah-the-on'], *f.* 1. Cremation, the act of burning. 2. Incineration of dead bodies.
Cremallera [cray-mahl-lyay'-rah], *f.* 1. (Mech.) Rack. 2. Zipper. 3. Cog railway.
Cremar [cray-mar'], *va.* To cremate.
Crematística [cray-mah-tees'-te-cah], *f.* Science of acquiring and preserving wealth.
Crematólogo [cray-mah-to'-lo-go], *m.* A political economist.
Crematología [cray-mah-to-lo-he'-ah], *f.* Political economy.
Crematológico, ca [cray-mah-to-lo'-he-co, cah], *a.* Economical, relating to political economy.
Cremonés, sa [cray-mo-ness', sah], *a.* Relating to Cremona.
Crémor [cray'-mor], *m.* *Crémor* or *crémor tártaro,* Cream of tartar.
Crencha [cren'-chah], *f.* The parting of the hair into two equal parts; each of these parts.
Creosota, Creosoto [cray-o-so'-tah, to], *f. & m.* Creasote.
Crepitación [cray-pe-tah-the-on'], *f.* 1. Crepitation, crackling. 2. Crepitus of fractures.
Crepitante [cray-pe-tahn'-tay], *pa.* Crackling, crepitant.
Crepitar [cray-pe-tar'], *vn.* To crackle, crepitate.
Crepuscular [cray-poos-coo-lar'], *a.* Crepuscular.
Crepúsculo [cray-poos'-coo-lo], *m.* Crepuscule, twilight, dawn.
Cresa [cray'-sah], *f.* Fly-blow, the egg of a fly; maggot.
Crespar [cres-par'], *va.* To curl the hair.—*vr.* (Obs.) To grow angry, to be displeased.
Crespilla [cres-peel'-lyah], *f.* An agaric *V.* CAGARRIA.
Crespina [cres-pee'-nah], *f.* (Obs.) Net used by women for holding up their hair.
Crespino [cres-pee'-no], *m.* (Bot.) The barberry-tree.
Crespo, pa [cres'-po, pah], *a.* 1. Crisp, curled, crispy. 2. (Bot.) Crisp-leaved. 3. (Met.) Obscure and bombastic: applied to style. 4. (Amer.) A curl. 5. (Met.) Angry, displeased, vexed.
Crespón [cres-pone'], *m.* Crape. *Crespón de Cantón,* Canton crape.
Cresta [cres'-tah], *f.* 1. Comb, cock's-comb. 2. Crest of birds. 3. Crest of a helmet. 4. Crest or summit of lofty mountains. 5. Cramp iron supporting the runner. (Mill.) *Alzar* or *levantar la cresta,* (Met.) To be elated with pride.
Crestado, da [cres-tah'-do, dah], *a.* Crested.
Crestomatía [cres-to-mah-tee'-ah], *f.* Chrestomathy, a selection of pieces from various authors arranged for study.
Crestón [cres-tone'], *m.* 1. Crest of a helmet in which the feathers are placed. 2. (Min.) An outcropping of a vein, ore.
Creta [cray'-tah], *f.* Chalk.
Cretáceo, cea [cray-tah'-the-o, ah], *a.* Cretaceous, chalky.
Cretense, or **Crético, ca** [cray-ten'-say, cray'-te-co, cah], *a.* Cretan, belonging to Crete.
Crético, *m.* A verse of three syllables, the first and third long, the second short, — ⏑ —.
Cretinismo [cray-te-nees'-mo], *m.* Cretinism, a kind of idiocy, with deformity.
Cretino, na [cray-tee'-no, nah], *a.* A cretin, one affected with cretinism.
Cretona [cray-to'-nah], *f.* Sort of linen, cretonne.
Creyente [cray-yen'-tay], *pa.* Believing, he who believes.
Crezneja [creth-nay'-hah], *f.* Streak of bleached bass-weed.
Cría [cree'-ah], *f.* 1. Brood of animals. 2. Suckling. 3. (Coll.) Child reared by a nurse. 4. (Obs.) A concise and pathetic narrative.
Criada [cre-ah'-dah], *f.* 1. Female servant, maid or maid-servant, handmaid. *Criada de menaje,* House-maid. 2. Wash-bat, pounder, with which washer-women beat clothes.
Criadero [cre-ah-day'-ro], *m.* 1. Plantation of young trees taken from the nursery. 2. Place for breeding animals. 3. Cocoon-bed.
Criadero, ra [cre-ah-day'-ro, rah], *a.* Fruitful, prolific.

Criadilla [cre-ah-deel'-lyah], *f.* 1. Testicle of an animal. 2. A small loaf. 3. (Dim.) A little worthless servant-maid. 4. (Bot.) Truffle, a kind of mushroom. Lycoperdon tuber, *L.*

Criado [cre-ah'-do], *m.* Servant, menial, groom. *Criado capitulado,* A person who, wishing to go to a colony, engages to serve it a certain time in payment for his passage.

Criado, da [cre-ah'-do, dah], *a.* Educated, instructed, bred.—*pp.* of CRIAR.

Criador, ra [cre-ah-dor', rah], *m.* & *f.* 1. One who rears and trains domestic animals and fowls; a breeder. 2. The Creator.

Criadora [cre-ah-do'-rah], *a.* Fruitful, fecund: applied to soil.

Criamiento [cre-ah-me-en'-to], *m.* Renovation and preservation of something.

Criandera [cre-an-day'-rah], *f.* (Amer.) Wet-nurse.

Crianza [cre-ahn'-thah], *f.* 1. Creation, act of creating. 2. Lactation. 3. Breeding, manners, education, nursery. *Dar crianza,* To breed, to educate, to bring up.

Criar [cre-ar'], *va.* 1. To create, to give existence. 2. To breed, to procreate. 3. To rear, to bring up from infancy. 4. To nurse, to suckle, to foster, to nourish. *Criar a sus pechos a alguno,* To inspire and imbue one with his manners and principles; to protect, favour, or patronize one. 5. To rear or fatten fowls and other animals. 6. To breed, to educate, to instruct. 7. To institute a new office or employment. *V.* CREAR. *Criar carnes,* To grow fat and lusty. *Criar molleja,* To grow lazy.

Criatura [cre-ah-too'-rah], *f.* 1. Creature. 2. A new-born child, a baby. 3. An unborn child, a fœtus. 4. Creature, a person who owes his rise or fortune to another. *Es una criatura,* He is but an infant, or like an infant. *Tengo lástima de la pobre criatura,* I pity the poor thing.

Criba [cree'-bah], *f.* Cribble, sieve, crib, riddle, screen.

Cribador, ra [cre-bah-dor', rah], *m.* & *f.* (Littl. us.) Sifter.

Cribadura [cre-bah-doo'-rah], *f.* Cribration, sifting.

Cribar [cre-bar'], *va.* To sift with a sieve, to screen.

Cribo [cree'-bo], *m.* *V.* CRIBA.

Cric [creek], *m.* Jackscrew, lifting-jack. *V.* GATO.

Crica [cree'-cah], *f.* 1. Trench, fissure. 2. (Med.) The female pudenda. (Acad.)

Crimen [cree'-men], *m.* 1. Crime, misdemeanour, offence, guilt. 2. (Theol.) A mortal sin. *Sala del crimen,* A criminal tribunal.

Criminal [cre-me-nahl'], *a.* 1. Criminal, guilty of a crime. 2. Criminal, not civil. 3. Censorious.

Criminalidad [cre-me-nah-le-dahd'], *f.* Criminality, guiltiness.

Criminalista [cre-me-nah-lees'-tah], *m.* An author who has written on criminal matters.

Criminalmente [cre-me-nal-men'-tay], *adv.* Criminally, guiltily.

Criminar [cre-me-nar'], *va.* To accuse, to incriminate.

Criminología [cre-me-no-lo-hee'-ah], *f.* Criminology.

Criminoso, sa [cre-me-no'-so, sah], *m.* & *f.* Delinquent, criminal.

Criminoso, sa, *a.* Criminal.

Crimno [creem'-no], *m.* Sort of coarse flour generally used in making a certain kind of fritters.

Crin [creen], *f.* 1. Mane, horse-hair. 2. A loom, specially constructed for weaving horse-hair. (Also *pl.*)

Crinado, da, Crinito, ta [cre-nah'-do, dah, cre-nee'-to, tah], *a.* Crinite, maned, having long hair. *Cometa crinito,* A long-bearded comet.

Crinífero, ra [cre-nee'-fay-ro, rah], *a.* Mane-bearing; having a mane.

Crinóideo [cre-noi'-day-o], *m.* (Geol.) A crinoid.

Crinolina [cre-no-lee'-nah], *f.* 1. Crinoline, a coarse fabric. 2. Crinoline, a hoop-skirt.

Criogenía [cre-o-hay-nee'-ah], *f.* Cryogenics.

Criógeno, na [cre-o'-hay-no, nah], *a.* Cryogenic.—*m.* Cryogen.

Criollismo [cre-ol-lyees'-mo], *m.* (Amer.) 1. Feature of the New World culture. 2. Inclination for the New World culture.

Criollo, lla [cre-ol'-lyo, lyah], *a.* & *n.* 1. Creole, one born in America or the West Indies, of European parents. 2. The Negro born in America, as opposed to one brought from Africa. —*a.* Indigenous, national.

Crioterapia [cre-o-tay-rah'-pe-ah], *f.* Crymotherapy.

Cripta [creep'-tah], *f.* Crypt.

Criptógamo, ma [crip-to'-gah-mo, mah], *a.* (Bot.) Cryptogamous, of concealed fertilization.

Criptografía [crip-to-grah-fee'-ah], *f.* Cryptography, the art of writing secret characters.

Criptología [crip-to-lo-hee'-ah], *f.* Cryptology, enigmatical language.

Cris [crees], *m.* A dagger of a wavy blade used in the Philippines and Malay peninsula.

Crisálida [cre-sah'-le-dah], *f.* (Ent.) Pupa, the chrysalis of a caterpillar.

Crisantemo [cre-san-tay'-mo], *m.* (Bot.) Chrysanthemum, a genus of plants.

Crisis [cree'-sis], *f.* 1. Crisis, the point in which a disease kills or changes for the better. 2. Judgment passed after mature deliberation; criterion. 3. The decisive moment.

Crisma [crees'-mah], *m.* 1. Chrism, oil mixed with balsam and consecrated by bishops, used in baptism, confirmation, and the consecration of bishops. 2. (Coll.) As synonym of head; in this sense it is feminine. *Romper la crisma,* To break (bruise) the head.

Crismar [cris-mar'], *va.* 1. (Obs.) To perform the rite of confirmation. 2. (Coll.) To break one's skull.

Crismera [cris-may'-rah], *f.* Vial or urn, commonly of silver, in which the chrism or consecrated oil is preserved.

Crisoberilo [cre-so-bay-ree'-lo], *m.* Chrysoberyl, a precious stone.

Crisol [cre-sole'], *m.* 1. Crucible for melting metals, croslet or crosslet. 2. Cruset, a goldsmith's melting-pot.

Crisolada [cre-so-lah'-dah], *f.* Crucible full of metal; a charge.

Crisólito [cre-so'-le-to], *m.* Chrysolite, a precious stone.

Crisopeya [cre-so-pay'-yah], *f.* Alchemy, the transmutation of metals.

Crispamiento [cris-pah-me-en'-to], *m.* Contraction, twitching. *V.* CRISPATURA.

Crispar [cris-par'], *va.* To cause muscles to contract convulsively; to twitch or contract convulsively.

Crispatura [cris-pah-too'-rah], *f.* (Med.) Crispation, a spasmodic contraction of the muscles.

Crispir [cris-peer'], *va.* To spatter with a hard brush, to imitate granite, porphyry, or grained stone.

Crista [crees'-tah], *f.* (Her.) Crest, the ornament of a helmet.

Cristal [cris-tahl'], *m.* 1. (Min.) Crystal. 2. (Chem.) Crystal or crystals, salts congealed in the manner of crystal. 3. Crystal, the best and clearest glass manufactured in glass-houses, flint-glass. 4. Looking-glass. 5. (Poet.) Water. 6. *Cristal tártaro,* Cream of tartar. 7. Fine shining woollen stuff. *Cristal de roca,* Rock crystal, transparent quartz.

Cristalera [cris-tah-lay'-rah], *f.* China closet.

Cristalería [cris-tah-lay-ree'-ah], *f.* 1. Glassware. 2. Repository of glassware.

Cristalino, na [cris-tah-lee'-no, nah], *a.* 1. Crystalline, crystal, transparent, glassy, pellucid, bright. 2. (Anat.) Crystalline lens of the eye.

Cristalizable [cris-tah-le-thah'-blay], *a.* Crystallizable.

Cristalización [cris-tah-le-thah-the-on'], *f.* Crystallization.

Cristalizador [cris-tah-le-thah-dor'], *m.* (Chem.) A vessel in which crystals are made.

Cristalizar [cris-tah-le-thar'], *va.* To crystallize, to cause to congeal in crystals.—*vr.* To crystallize, to coagulate or concrete into crystals.

Cristalografía [cris-tah-lo-grah-fee'-ah], *f.* Crystallography.

Cristel [cris-tel'], *m.* Clyster. *V.* CLISTER.

Cristianamente, *adv.* Christianly.

Cristianar [cris-te-ah-nar'], *va.* (Coll.) To baptize, to christen.

Cristiandad [cris-te-an-dahd'], *f.* 1. Christianity, the body of professing Christians. 2. Christendom. 3. Observance of the law of Christ.

Cristianesco, ca [cris-te-ah-nes'-co, cah], *a.* After the Christian manner: applied to Moorish forms which imitate the Christian manner.

Cristianillo, illa [cris-te-ah-neel'-lyo, lyah], *m.* & *f. dim.* A little Christian: a nickname given to the Spaniards by the Moors.

Cristianísimo [cris-te-ah-nee'-se-mo], *m.* 1. (Sup.) Very Christian. 2. An appellation given by the Pope to the King of France.

Cristianismo [cris-te-ah-nees'-mo], *m.* 1. Christianity. 2. The body of Christians. 3. Christening. *V.* BAUTIZO.

Cristianización [cris-te-ah-ne-thah-the-on'], *f.* Christianization.

Cristianizar [cris-te-ah-ne-thar'], *va.* To Christianize.

Cristiano, na [cris-te-ah'-no, nah], *a.* Christian.

Cristiano, na [cris-te-ah'-no, nah], *m.* & *f.* 1. A Christian. 2. The Spanish language, opposed to Arabic or other foreign tongues. (Acad.) *A ley de cristiano,* Upon the word of a Christian.

Cristífero, ra [cris-tee'-fay-ro, rah], *a.* Bearing the law and love of Christ in one's heart.

Cristino, na [cris-tee'-no, nah], *a.* Supporting the Queen Regent Maria Cristina against the pretender Don Carlos.

Cristo [crees'-to], *m.* 1. Christ, Messiah, our blessed Saviour. 2. Image of Christ crucified. *Ni por un Cristo,* By no means, not for the world. *Haber la de Dios es Cristo,* To have a grand dispute or quarrel. *Ir o ponerse a lo de Dios es Cristo,* To dress one's self to affect gallantry and spirit. *Poner como un Cristo (a alguno),* To flog a person severely, cruelly.

Cristus [crees'-toos], *m.* 1. Cross printed at the beginning of the alphabet. 2. The alphabet; criss-cross row (obs). *No saber el Cristus,* To be very ignorant. *Estar en el Cristus*, (Met.) To be in the rudiments of any thing.

Crisuela [cre-soo-ay'-lah], *f.* The dripping-pan of a lamp.

Criterio [cre-tay'-re-o], *m.* 1. Criterion, a standard by which a judgment can be formed. 2. Judgment, discernment.

Critica [cree'-te-cah], *f.* 1. Criticism. 2. Critique, critic, critical examination of any writing or publication. 3. Censure. 4. Refutation.

Criticable [cre-te-cah'-blay], *a.* (Littl. us.) *V.* CENSURABLE.

Criticador [cre-te-cah-dor'], *m.* Critic, censurer.

Criticar [cre-te-car'], *va.* 1. To criticise, to animadvert. 2. To criticise, to judge.

Criticastro [cre-te-cahs'-tro], *m.* Animadverter, would-be critic.

Crítico [cree'-te-co], *m.* 1. Critic, criticiser. 2. (Coll.) An affected refiner of style and language. 3. Critic, a censurer, a man apt to find fault.

Crítico, ca [cree'-te-co, cah], *a.* 1. Critical, critic, decisive. 2. Hypercritical, nicely judicious. 3. (Med.) Critical, producing a crisis in a disease.

Criticón, ona [cre-te-cone', nah], *a.* Eager to criticize, faultfinding. —*m.* & *f.* Would-be critic, faultfinder.

Critiquear [cre-te-kay-ar'], *va.* To criticise, to play the critic, to censure.

Critiquizar [cre-te-ke-thar'], *va.* (Coll.) To criticise, to censure, to find fault.

Crizneja [crith-nay'-hah], *f.* Trace or rope of hair or osiers.

Croar [cro-ar'], *vn.* To croak like a frog.

Croata [cro-ah'-tah], *a.* Croatian.

Crocante [cro-cahn'-tay], *m.* Brittle. *Crocante de cacahuate o maní*, Peanut brittle.

Crocino, na [cro-thee'-no, nah], *a.* Of crocus, saffron.

Crocodilo [cro-co-dee'-lo], *m.* Crocodile. *V.* COCODRILO.

Cromático, ca [cro-mah'-te-co, cah], *a.* 1. (Mus.) Chromatic, proceeding by semitones. 2. (Opt.) Chromatic, showing prismatic colours; uncorrected.

Cromatismo [cro-mah-tees'-mo], *m.* Chromatic aberration.

Cromato [cro-mah'-to], *m.* Chromate, a salt of chromic acid.

Crómico, ca [cro'-me-co, cah], *a.* Chromic, belonging to chromium.

Cromo [cro'-mo], *m.* 1. Chromium, a metallic element; discovered in 1797. 2. Chromo: a chromolithograph.

Cromolitografía [cro-mo-le-to-grah-fee'-ah], *f.* 1. Chromolithograph, a print in colours. 2. The art of printing in colours; chromolithography.

Cromolitográfico, ca [cro-mo-le-to-grah'-fe-co, cah], *a.* Chromolithographic, printed in colours.

Cromoso, sa [cro-mo'-so, sah], *a.* Relating to chromium; chrome-, chromous.

Cromosoma [cro-mo-so'-mah], *m.* (Biol.) Chromosome.

Crómula [cro'-moo-lah], *f.* The green colouring-matter of leaves, chlorophyll.

Cromurgia [cro-moor'-he-ah], *f.* Treatise on colouring-matters industriously applied.

Cromúrgico, ca [cro-moor'-he-co, cah], *a.* Relating to dyes or colouring-matters.

Crónica [cro'-ne-cah], *f.* Chronicle, a register of events.

Crónico, ca [cro'-ne-co, cah], *a.* Chronic, applied to diseases.

Cronicón [cro-ne-cone'], *m.* Chronicle, a succinct account of events.

Cronista [cro-nees'-tah], *m.* Chronicler, annalist.

Cronografía [cro-no-grah-fee'-ah], *f.* Chronography, the science of time.

Cronógrafo [cro-no'-grah-fo], *m.* Chronograph.

Cronograma [cro-no-grah'-mah], *f.* Chronogram, an inscription including the date of any action.

Cronología [cro-no-lo-hee'-ah], *f.* Chronology.

Cronológicamente [cro-no-lo'-he-cah-men-tay], *adv.* Chronologically.

Cronológico, ca [cro-no-lo'-he-co, cah], *a.* Chronological, chronologic.

Cronologista, Cronólogo [cro-no-lo-hees'-tah, cro-no'-lo-go], *m.* Chronologist, chronologer.

Cronometría [cro-no-may-tree'-ah], *f.* Chronometry, measurement of time.

Cronométrico, ca [cro-no-may'-tre-co, cah], *a.* Chronometric, chronometrical.

Cronometrista [cro-no-may-trees'-tah], *m.* Chronometer-maker.

Cronómetro [cro-no'-may-tro], *m.* 1. Chronometer. 2. Stopwatch.

Croque [cro'-kay], *m.* Hook or crook, used in the tunny-fishery.

Croqueta [cro-kay'-tah], *f.* A croquette.

Croquis [cro'-kees], *m.* 1. A light sketch, made off hand, of some ground or military position. 2. Any sketch, rough draft.

Croscitar [cros-the-tar'], *vn.* *V.* CRASCITAR.

Crotafal [cro-tah-fahl'], *a.* (Anat.) Crotaphite: applied to the elementary bony pieces of the head.

Crotáfico, ca [cro-tah'-fe-co, cah], *a.* Relative to the temples or temporal region; crotaphic.

Crótalo [cro'-tah-lo], *m.* 1. Castanet. 2. The rattlesnake (Crotalus).

Crotalogía [cro-tah-lo-hee'-ah], *f.* The art of playing the castanets.

Crotón [cro-tone'], *m.* A great genus of the spurge family.

Cruce [croo-'thay], *m.* 1. Crossing. 2. Crossroads. *Cruce en trébol*, Highway cloverleaf.

Crucera [croo-thay'-rah], *f.* Withers of a horse. *Cruceras*, The two large pins which fasten the body of a cart or wagon to the axle-tree; bolling pine.

Crucería [croo-thay-ree'-ah], *f.* Gothic architecture.

Crucero [croo-thay'-ro], *m.* 1. Cross-vault or transept of a church under the dome. 2. Cross-bearer, one who carries the cross before the archbishop in a procession. 3. Piece of timber which lies across the rafters in a building. 4. A crossing of two streets or roads; a railway crossing. 5. (Print.) Cross-bar of a chase. 6. (Naut.) Cruising station. 7. (Naut.) Cruiser. 8. (Ast.) Cross, a southern constellation.

Cruceta [croo-thay'-tah], *f.* Cross-piece, head-stick.

Crucial [croo-the-ahl'], *a.* Crucial, making the shape of a cross.

Cruciata [croo-the-ah'-tah], *f.* (Bot.) Cross-wort, vallantia. Vallantia cruciata, *L.*

Cruciferario [croo-the-fay-rah'-re-o], *m.* Cross-bearer.

Crucifero [croo-thee'-fay-ro], *m.* 1. Cross-bearer. 2. Crouched, cruched, or crutched friar, a friar of the order of the Holy Cross.

Crucífero, ra, *a.* 1. Cruciferous or crucigerous, bearing a cross. 2. (Bot.) Having petals in the form of a cross.

Cruciferas, *f. pl.* The cruciferæ, mustard family.

Crucificado, da [croo-the-fe-cah'-do, dah], *pp.* of CRUCIFICAR. Crucified. *El Crucificado*, Jesus Christ.

Crucificar [croo-the-fe-car'], *va.* 1. To crucify. 2. To molest, to vex, to torment.

Crucifijo [croo-the-fee'-ho], *m.* Crucifix.

Crucifixión [croo-the-fik-se-on'], *f.* Crucifixion.

Cruciforme [croo-the-for'-may], *a.* Cruciform.

Crucígero, ra [croo-thee'-hay-ro, rah], *a.* Carrying or bearing the sign of the cross.

Crucigrama [croo-the-grah'-mah], *m.* Crossword puzzle.

Crucillo [croo-theel'-lyo], *m.* Push-pin, a play.

Crudamente [croo-dah-men'-tay], *adv.* Rudely, crudely.

Crudeza [croo-day'-thah], *f.* 1. Crudity, crudeness, unripeness. 2. (Met.) Rudeness, severity, cruelty. 3. (Coll.) Vapour, vain boasting. *Crudezas del estómago*, The crudities or indigestions of the stomach.

Crudo [croo'-do], *m.* Packing or wrapping cloth.

Crudo, da [croo'-do, dah], *a.* 1. Raw, crude. 2. (Prov.) Green, unripe: applied to fruit. 3. Rude, cruel, pitiless, grievous. 4. Crude, unfinished, immature. 5. Crude, hard of digestion. 6. A blustering, hectoring person. 7. (Med.) Unripe, not mature: applied to tumours and abscesses. *Lienzo crudo*, Unbleached linen. *Tiempo crudo*, Bleak, raw weather. *Punto crudo*, A critical moment or juncture. *A punto crudo*, Untimely, unseasonably.

Cruel [croo-el'], *a.* 1. Cruel, hard-hearted. 2. (Met.) Intolerable, insufferable. *Un frío cruel*, An intense cold. *Dolores crueles*, Severe pains. 3. Hard, oppressive. 4. (Met.) Bloody, violent, murderous, merciless, fierce, fiend-like.

Crueldad [croo-el-dahd'], *f.* 1. Cruelty, inhumanity, savageness, mercilessness, ferociousness. 2. Hardness, oppression, acerbity. 3. Cruelty, a barbarous action, outrage.

Cruelmente [croo-el-men'-tay], *adv.* Cruelly, mercilessly.

Cruentamente [croo-en-tah-men'-tay], *adv.* Bloodily, with effusion of blood.

Cruento, ta [croo-en'-to, tah], *a.* Bloody, cruel, inhuman.

Crufia [croo'-fe-ah], *f.* Sign by which obscure passages are marked in literary works, in form of a semicircle with a point in the middle.

Crujía [croo-hee'-ah], *f.* 1. (Naut.) The midship gangway of a galley. 2. A large open hall or passage in a building. *La crujía de un hospital*, The great hall of a hospital, with beds on each side; the aisle of a ward. 3. Passage with rails on each side, from the choir to the high altar, in cathedral churches. *Crujía de piezas*, Flight of rooms one after another. *Pasar crujía*, 1. To run the gantlet. 2. (Met.) To suffer great fatigue and misery.

Crujido [croo-hee'-do], *m.* Crack, noise made by wood, creak, clash, crackling.

Crujidor [croo-he-dor'], *m.* A glass trimmer.

Crujir [croo-heer'], *vn.* 1. To crackle, to rustle. 2. To grind (one's teeth).

Cruor, *m.* 1. Cruor, gore, congealed blood. 2. The colouring-matter of the blood; also the blood-globules.

Cruórico, ca [croo-o'-re-co, cah], *a.* Bloody.
Crup [croop], *m.* Croup, membranous or true croup.
Crupal [croo-pahl'], *a.* Croupal, croupous, belonging to croup. (Acad.)
Crural [croo-rahl'], *a.* Crural, belonging to the leg.
Crustáceo, cea [croos-tah'-thay-o, ah], *a.* Crustaceous, shelly, having jointed shells or carapaces.
Cruz [crooth], *f.* 1. Cross. 2. Cross, a line drawn through another. 3. The sign of the cross, the ensign of the Christian religion. 4. Cross, the badge of some military order. 5. Cross, trial of patience, any thing that thwarts; toil, trouble, vexation. 6. Withers, the upper juncture of the shoulder-bone in beasts. 7. Dagger, in printing; obelisk. *Cruz de las bitas*, (Naut.) Cross-tree of the bitts. *Cruz y botón*, (Naut.) Frapping, the crossing and drawing together the several parts of a tackle. *Cruz tomada con los cables*, (Naut.) A cross in the hawse. *Bracear en cruz*, or *poner las vergas en cruz*, (Naut.) To square the yards. *De la cruz a la fecha*, From beginning to end. *La cruz en los pechos y el diablo en los hechos*, The cross on one's breast and the devil in one's deeds: hypocrites. *Quedarse en cruz y en cuadro*, To be reduced to poverty and distress. *Cruces*, Wings of a reel. *Estar, andar*, or *verse entre la cruz y el agua bendita*, (Coll.) To be in imminent danger of any thing.
Cruzada [croo-thah'-dah], *f.* 1. Crusade. 2. Tribunal of the crusade. 3. Indulgences granted to those who support the crusade.
Cruzado [croo-thah'-do], *m.* 1. Cruzado, an old Spanish coin of gold, silver, or brass. 2. Crusado, a Portuguese coin of gold or silver. 3. Crusader, a soldier enlisted under the banners of the crusade. 4. Knight who wears the badge of some military order. 5. Manner of playing on the guitar. 6. Figure in dancing.
Cruzado, da [croo-thah'-do, dah], *a.* Crucial, transverse, twilled. *Estarse con los brazos cruzados*, To be idle.—*pp.* of CRUZAR.
Cruzador, ra [croo-thah-dor', rah], *a.* (Obs.) Crossing from one side to another.
Cruzamen de una vela [croo-thah'-men day oo'-nah vay'-lah], *m.* (Naut.) Square or width of a sail.
Cruzar [croo-thar'], *va.* 1. To cross, to lay one body across another. 2. To cross a street or road. 3. (Naut.) To cruise. 4. To cross the breed. 5. To twill. *Cruzar la cara a alguno*, To cut and hack one's face.—*vr.* 1. To be knighted, to obtain the cross or badge of a military order. 2. To cross and trip, as horses do which are weak in their pasterns and quarters. *Cruzarse los negocios*, To be overwhelmed with business. *Cruzar los intereses de alguno*, To jar the interests of any one.
Cu [coo], *m.* Name which the ancient historians give to the Mexican temples.
Cuaderna [coo-ah-derr'-nah], *f.* 1. (Prov.) The fourth part of any thing, especially of bread and of money. 2. (Naut.) Frame, the timber-work which forms the ribs of a ship. 3. Double fours, in the game of backgammon. *Cuaderna maestra*, (Naut.) Midship-frame. *Cuaderna del cuerpo popes*, (Naut.) Stern-frame. *Cuadernas de henchimiento*, (Naut.) Filling-timbers. *Cuadernas de la amura*, (Naut.) Loof-frames. *Cuadernas reviradas*, (Naut.) Cant-timber. *Cuadernas a escuadra*, (Naut.) Square-timbers.
Cuadernal [coo-ah-der-nahl'], *m.* (Naut.) Block, a piece of wood with sheaves and pulleys, on which the running rigging is reeved. *Cuadernales de carenar*, (Naut.) Careening gears.
Cuadernalete [coo-ah-der-nah-lay'-tay], *m.* (Naut.) Short and double block.
Cuadernillo [coo-ah-der-neel'-lyo], *m.* 1. Five sheets of paper placed within each other. 2. Clerical directory, containing the daily order of divine service.
Cuadernillo, ito, *m. dim.* Small parcel of paper stitched together.
Cuaderno [coo-ah-derr'-no], *m.* 1. Parcel of paper stitched together. 2. Small memorandum-book. 3. In printing-offices, four printed sheets placed within each other. 4. Chastisement of collegians, depriving them of their pittance. *Cuaderno de bitácora*, (Naut.) Log-book.
Cuadra [coo-ah'-drah], *f.* 1. Hall, saloon; drawing-room. 2. Stable, a house for beasts. 3. (Amer.) A block of houses. 4. (Naut.) Quarter of a ship. *Por la cuadra*, (Naut.) On the quarter.
Cuadradamente, *adv.* Exactly, completely.
Cuadrado, da [coo-ah-drah'-do, dah], *a.* 1. Square, quadrate. 2. Perfect, without defect.—*pp.* of CUADRAR.
Cuadrado, *m.* 1. Square, quadrate. 2. Clock, the flowers or inverted work in stockings. 3. Gusset of a shirt-sleeve. 4. Die. *V.* TROQUEL. 5. (Print.) Quadrat, quad. *De cuadrado*, In front, opposite, face to face; squared.
Cuadragenario, ria [coo-ah-drah-hay-nah'-re-o, ah], *a.* Forty years old, of forty years.
Cuadragésima [coo-ah-drah-hay'-se-mah], *f.* Lent. *V.* CUARESMA.
Cuadragesimal [coo-ah-drah-hay-se-mahl'], *a.* 1. Quadragesimal. 2. Lenten, used in Lent.
Cuadragésimo, ma [coo-ah-drah-hay'-se-mo, mah], *a.* Fortieth.
Cuadral [coo-ah-drahl'], *m.* (Arch.) Piece of timber which crosses two others diagonally.
Cuadrangular [coo-ah-dran-goo-lar'], *a.* Quadrangular.
Cuadrángulo [coo-ah-drahn'-goo-lo], *m. & a.* Quadrangle, a surface with four angles.
Cuadrantal [coo-ah-dran-tahl'], *a.* (Math.) Quadrantal.
Cuadrante [coo-ah-drahn'-tay], *m.* 1. Quadrant, the fourth part of a circle. 2. Quadrant, a mathematical instrument for taking the latitude. 3. Dial-plate of a sun-dial; dial of a clock or a watch. 4. A square board put up in churches, pointing out the order of masses to be celebrated. 5. The fourth part of an inheritance. 6. The smallest coin current in a country. *Hasta el último cuadrante*, To the last farthing.
Cuadrar [coo-ah-drar'], *va. & vn.* 1. To square, to form into a square. 2. To square, to reduce to a square. 3. To square timbers. 4. (Arith.) To multiply a number by itself. 5. (Pict.) *V.* CUADRICULAR. 6. To square, to fit, to suit, to correspond. 7. To regulate, to adjust. 8. To please, to accommodate.
Cuadrática [coo-ah-drah'-te-cah], *f.* Quadratic (equation); containing the square of a quantity.
Cuadratín [coo-ah-drah-teen'], *m.* (Typ.) Quadrat (commonly abbreviated to quad); quotation, piece of type-metal used to fill up blanks.
Cuadratura [coo-ah-drah-too'-rah], *f.* 1. Quadrature. 2. First and last quarter of the moon. 3. Pantograph, an instrument for copyin designs. 4. (Watch) The dial train work; interior works of a watch.
Cuadrete [coo-ah-dray'-tay], *m. dim.* A small square.
Cuadricenal [coo-ah-dre-thay-nahl'], *a.* Done every forty years.
Cuadrícula [coo-ah-dree'-coo-lah], *f.* A series of squares, uniform in size used by painters and sculptors to plot their studies in due proportion.
Cuadricular [coo-ah-dre-coo-lar'], *va.* (Pict.) To copy a drawing with the pantograph; to copy by means of squares.
Cuadrienal [coo-ah-dre-ay-nahl'], *a.* Quadrennial, comprising four years.
Cuadrienio [coo-ah-dre-ay'-ne-o], *m.* Time and space of four years.
Cuadriforme [coo-ah-dre-for'-may], *a.* Four-faced.
Cuadriga [coo-ah-dree'-gah], *f.* Carriage drawn by four horses.
Cuadril [coo-ah-dreel'], *m.* Haunch-bone in beasts.
Cuadrilátero, ra [coo-ah-dre-lah'-tay-ro-rah], *a.* Quadrilateral.
Cuadriliteral [coo-ah-dre-le-tay-rahl'], *a.* (Obs.) Consisting of four letters.
Cuadrilongo [coo-ah-dre-lon'-go], *m.* 1. Rectangle; right-angled parallelogram. 2. Formation of a corps of infantry into an oblong form.
Cuadrilongo, ga [coo-ah-dre-lon'-go, gah], *a.* Having the shape or form of a rectangle.
Cuadrilla [coo-ah-dreel'-lyah], *f.* 1. Meeting of four or more persons, for some particular purpose. 2. Gang, crew, herd, troop. 3. Any one of the four divisions of sheep-masters which form the board of *Mesta*. 4. Band of armed men, sent in pursuit of robbers and highwaymen by the court of *La Santa Hermandad*. *Alcaide de cuadrilla*, Director of one of the four sections of the council of *Mesta*.
Cuadrillero [coo-ah-dreel-lyay'-ro], *m.* 1. Member of the court of *La Santa Hermandad*. 2. The commander of an armed band employed by that court.
Cuadrillo [coo-ah-dreel'-lyo], *m.* 1. (Dim.) A small square. 2. A kind of dart formerly used by the Moors.
Cuadrimestre [coo-ah-dre-mes'-tray], *m* Space of four months.
Cuadringentésimo, ma [coo-ah-drin-hen-tay'-se-mo, mah], *a.* One four-hundredth.
Cuadrinomio [coo-ah-dre-no'-me-o], *m.* (Alg.) Quadrinomial.
Cuadripartido [coo-ah-dre-par-tee'-do], *a.* Quadripartite, divided in four.
Cuádriple [coo-ah'-dre-play], *a.* (Obs.) *V.* CUÁDRUPLE.
Cuadriplicado, da [coo-ah-dre-ple-cah', do, dah], *a.* Quadrupled.
Cuadrisílabo, ba [coo-ah-dre-see'-lah-bo, bah], *a.* Quadrisyllable.
Cuadrivio [coo-ah-dree'-ve-o], *m.* 1. Quadrivium, place where four roads meet. 2. Any thing which may be undertaken four different ways.
Cuadriyugo [coo-ah-dree'-yoo-go], *m.* Cart with four horses.
Cuadro, dra [coo-ah'-dro, drah], *a.* *V.* CUADRADO.
Cuadro, *m.* 1. Square, figure having four equal sides and four angles. *En cuadro*, Squared, in a square form. 2. Picture, painting. 3. A square bed

of earth in a garden. 4. Picture-frame, frame of a window. 5. (Mil.) Square body of troops. 6. (Print.) Platen, part of a printing-press which makes the impression. 7. Scene, a division of an act of a play or of a poem. (Acad.)

Cuadrumano, na [coo-ah-droo-mah'-no, nah], *a.* Quadrumanous; four-handed. —*m. pl.* The quadrumana.

Cuadrupedal [coo-ah-droo-pay-dahl'], *a.* Quadrupedal, four-footed: applied to beasts.

Cuadrupedante [coo-ah-droo-pay-dahn'-tay], *a.* (Poet.) Quadrupedant.

Cuadrúpede, Cuadrúpedo, da [coo-ah-droo'-pay-day], *a.* Quadruped, having four feet.

Cuádruple [coo-ah'-droo-play], *a.* Quadruple, composed of four parts, fourfold.

Cuadruplicación [coo-ah-droo-ple-cah-the-on'], *f.* Quadruplication.

Cuadruplicar [coo-ah-droo-ple-car'], *va.* To quadruplicate.

Cuádruplo, pla [coo-ah'-droo-plo, plah], *a.* Quadruple, fourfold, quadripartite. *Al cuádruplo,* Quadruply.

Cuaga [coo-ah'-gah], *m.* Quagga, a South African animal of the horse tribe.

Cuaja [coo-ah'-hah], *f.* 1. The act of fructifying a tree or plant. 2. In some countries the mire collected after the sun has dried a pond.

Cuajada [coo-ah-hah'-dah], *f.* Curd of the milk separated from the whey.

Cuajadillo [coo-ah-hah-deel'-lyo], *m.* Sort of silk gauze with flowers.

Cuajado [coo-ah-hah'-do], *m.* A dish made of meat, herbs, or fruits, with eggs and sugar, dressed in a pan.—*a.* Immobile, paralyzed with astonishment. (Acad.)—*Cuajado, da, pp.* of CUAJAR.

Cuajaleche [coo-ah-hah-lay'-chay], *f.* (Bot.) Lady's bed-straw, yellow goose-grass, cheese rennet. Galium verum.

Cuajamiento [coo-ah-hah-me-en'-to], *m.* Coagulation.

Cuajar [coo-ah-har'], *m.* Rennet bag, maw or stomach of a calf or sucking animal; the crop of a fowl; the fourth stomach, abomasum, of a ruminant animal.

Cuajar [coo-ah-har'], *va.* 1. To coagulate, to concrete, to curd. 2. To ornament or decorate with too many ornaments. 3. *Cuajar de* or *con azúcar,* To ice with sugar.—*vn.* (Coll.) 1. To succeed, to have the desired effect. 2. To please, to like, to choose.—*vr.* To coagulate, to run into concretions, to curdle.

Cuajarón [coo-ah-hah-rone'], *m.* Grume, clot, gore.

Cuajo [coo-ah'-ho], *m.* 1. A lacteal substance found in the stomach of animals before they feed. 2. Rennet, a liquor made by steeping the stomach of a calf in hot water, and used to coagulate milk for curds and cheese. 3. Concretion, coagulation. *Tener buen cuajo,* To be too dull and patient. *Arrancar de cuajo,* To eradicate, to tear up by the roots. *Hierba del cuajo,* Cheese rennet. Galium verum.

Cuakerismo, or **Cuaquerismo** [coo-ah-kay-rees'-mo], *m.* Quakerism.

Cuákero, ra, or **Cuáquero, ra** [coo-ah'-kay-ro, rah], *m.* & *f.* A Quaker.

Cual [coo-ahl'], *pron.* 1. Which; he who. *V.* EL QUE. *¿ Cuál de los dos quiere Vd.?* Which of the two will you have? 2. Same, like, such. *V.* CUALQUIERA. 3. One, other, partly. *Cual o cual, V.* TAL CUAL. *Cada cual,* Each one.—*adv.* As. *V.* COMO.—*int.* How then.

Cualesquiera, *pl.* of CUALQUIERA, q. v.

Cualidad [coo-ah-le-dahd'], *f.* Quality. *V.* CALIDAD.

Cualitativo, va [coo-ah-le-tah-tee'-vo, vah], *a.* Qualitative. *Análisis cualitativo,* Qualitative analysis.

Cualquier [coo-al-ke-err'], *pron.* Any one: used only before a substantive, with which it is joined.

Cualquiera [coo-al-ke-ay'-rah], *pron.* Any one, some one, either one or the other, whichsoever, whoever.

Cuan [coo-ahn'], *adv.* How, as: used only before nouns. *V.* CUANTO.

Cuando [coo-ahn'-do], *adv.* 1. When, pointing out a certain time. 2. In case that; if. 3. Though, although; even. *Cuando no hubiera más razón,* Were there even no other reason or ground. 4. Sometimes, at times. *Cuando con los criados, cuando con los hijos,* Sometimes with the servants, sometimes with the children. *De cuando en cuando,* From time to time; now and then. *Cuando más* or *cuando mucho,* At most, at best. *Cuando menos,* At least. *Cuando quiera,* When you please, whensoever. *¿ Hasta cuándo?* When shall I see you again? literally, Until when? *¿ De cuándo acá?* Since when? in what time? expression intimating that a thing is extraordinary.

Cuantia [coo-an-tee'-ah], *f.* 1. Quantity. *V.* CANTIDAD. 2. Rank, distinction. *Hombre de gran cuantía,* A man of high rank.

Cuantiar [coo-an-te-ar'], *va.* To estimate or appraise possessions; to fix a price.

Cuantidad [coo-an-te-dahd'], *f.* Quantity; a word especially used by mathematicians. *V.* CANTIDAD.

Cuantimás. (Obs.) *V.* CUANTO MÁS.

Cuantiosamente, *adv.* Copiously.

Cuantioso, sa [coo-an-te-o'-so, sah], *a.* Numerous, copious, rich.

Cuantitativo, va [coo-an-te-tah-tee'-vo, vah], *a.* Quantitive, estimable, according to quantity. (Chem.) *Análisis cuantitativo,* Quantitative analysis.

Cuanto, ta [coo-ahn'-to, tah], *a.* 1. Containing quantity or relating to it, susceptible of quantity. 2. *¿ Cuánto?* How much? *¿ Cuántos?* How many? 3. As many as, as much as, the more; correlative of *tanto.* *Cuanto uno es más pobre, se le debe socorrer más,* The poorer a person is the more should he be supported. *Cuanto Vd. quiera,* As much as you like. 4. All, whatever. 5. Excessive, great in some way. (Note.—*Cuanto,* signifying "how much," receives an accent, thus: *cuánto.* *¡ Cuánta sabiduría!* How much wisdom!)—*adv.* Respecting, whilst. *Cuanto antes,* Immediately, as soon as possible. *Cuanto más,* Moreover, the more as. *En cuanto a,* With regard to, as to, in the meantime. *Cuanto quier,* (Littl. us.) Although. *Por cuanto,* Inasmuch as.

Cuáquero, ra [coo-ah'-kay-ro, rah], *m.* & *f.* & *a.* Quaker.

Cuarango [coo-ah-rahn'-go], *m.* The vulgar name of the *Cinchona* or Peruvian bark tree.

Cuarenta [coo-ah-ren'-tah], *a.* & *m.* Forty. *El año de cuarenta,* The days of yore: an expression used for antiquated things.

Cuarentavo, va [coo-ah-ren-tah'-vo, vah], *a.* The one-fortieth.

Cuarentena [coo-ah-ren-tay'-nah], *f.* 1. Space of forty days, months, or years; the fortieth part. 2. Lent, the forty days of fast prescribed by the Church. 3. (Met.) Suspension of assent to any thing. 4. The number 40 in general. 5. (Naut.) Quarantine, the time when a ship, suspected of infection, is obliged to abstain from intercourse with the inhabitants of a country. *Hacer cuarentena,* (Naut.) To perform quarantine.

Cuarentón, na [coo-ah-ren-tone', nah], *a.* & *m.* & *f.* Person forty years old.

Cuaresma [coo-ah-res'-mah], *f.* 1. Lent, the forty days' fast prescribed by the Church. 2. Collection of Lent sermons.

Cuaresmal [coo-ah-res-mahl'], *a.* Lenten.

Cuarta [coo-ar'-tah], *f.* 1. Fourth, fourth part; a quarter. 2. Funeral part of the masses which belong to the parish where the deceased person was a member. 3. Quadrant, fourth part of a circle. 4. (Naut.) Quarter, point of the compass. 5. Sequence of four cards in the game of piquet. 6. (Fen.) Quart, or carte. 7. Palm, a hand-breadth. 8. Quart, a liquid measure. 9. (Mil.) Quarter of a company of soldiers. 10. (Mus.) A fourth. 11. A piece of timber square in section. 12. (Prov.) A guide-mule. 13. (Mex.) A sort of whip.

Cuartago [coo-ar-tah'-go], *m.* Nag, pony, hack.

Cuartal [coo-ar-tahl'], *m.* 1. Kind of bread weighing the fourth part of a loaf. 2. Quarter, dry measure, fourth part of a fanega.

Cuartán [coo-ar-tahn'], *m.* (Prov.) A grain measure, equal to 18 litres and 8 centilitres.

Cuartana [coo-ar-tah'-nah], *f.* Quartan, an ague which returns every four days.

Cuartanal [coo-ar-tah-nahl'], *a.* Intermittent.

Cuartanario, ria [coo-ar-tah-nah'-re-o, ah], *a.* Labouring under a quartan.

Cuartar [coo-ar-tar'], *va.* To plough the ground the fourth time.

Cuartazo [coo-ar-tah'-tho], *m. aug.* A large room; a large quarter. *Cuartazos,* A coarse, corpulent person; a stroke with a whip.

Cuartear [coo-ar-tay-ar'], *va.* 1. To quarter, to divide into four parts. 2. To bid a fourth more at public sales. 3. To make a fourth person at a game. 4. To zigzag up steep places. —*vr.* To split into pieces.

Cuartel [coo-ar-tell'], *m.* 1. Quarter, the fourth part of a garden or other thing. 2. Quarter, district, ward of a city. 3. Quarter, the place where soldiers are lodged and stationed. 4. Duty imposed on villages for the quartering of soldiers: this, however, is at present generally called *utensilios.* 5. Dwelling, habitation, home. 6. Quarter, remission of life granted by hostile troops. 7. *V.* CUARTETO. 8. (Naut.) Hatch, the lid of a hatchway. *Cuartel de la salud,* A safe place free from hazard and danger. *Cuartel maestre general,* (Mil.) Quartermaster-general.

Cuartelar [coo-ar-tay-lar'], *va.* (Her.) To quarter.

Cuartelero [coo-ar-tay-lay'-ro], *m.* (Mil.) Soldier in each company appointed to keep the apartments clean.

Cuartera [coo-ar-tay'-rah], *f.* A dry measure in Catalonia, containing about fifteen pecks.

Cuartero, ra [coo-ar-tay'-ro, rah], *a.* (Prov.) Applied to those who collect the rents of the grain of farms, which pay the fourth part to the landlords.

Cuarterola [coo-ar-tay-ro'-lah], *f.* Quarter cask of liquors or fluids.

Cuarterón [coo-ar-tay-rone'], *m.* 1. Quartern, quarter, the fourth part of a whole; quarter of a pound. 2. Upper part of windows which may be opened and shut. *Cuarterones*, Squares of wainscot in a door or window-shutter.

Cuarterón, na, *a.* (Amer.) Applied to a child begotten of a creole and a native of Spain; quadroon.

Cuarteta [coo-ar-tay'-tah], *f.* (Poet.) Quatrain, a metrical composition of four lines.

Cuartete, Cuarteto [coo-ar-tay'-tay, coo-ar-tay'-to], *m.* 1. (Poet.) Quatrain, a stanza of four verses. 2. (Mus.) Quartet.

Cuartilla [coo-ar-teel'-lyah], *f.* 1. Fourth part of an *arroba*, or sixteenth part of a quintal. 2. Fourth part of a sheet of paper. 3. Pastern of horses.

Cuartillo [coo-ar-teel'-lyo], *m.* 1. Pint, the fourth part of a pottle in liquids. 2. The fourth part of a peck in grain. 3. Fourth part of a real. *Ir de cuartillo*, To share the profits or losses in any business. *Tumba cuartillos*, Tippler.

Cuartilludo, da [coo-ar-teel-lyoo'-do, dah], *a.* Applied to a horse with long pasterns.

Cuartito [coo-ar-tee'-to], *m. dim.* A small room.

Cuarto [coo-ar'-to], *m.* 1. Fourth part, quadrant, quarter. 2. Habitation, dwelling, room, apartment. *V.* Aposento. *Cuarto bajo*, Room on the ground floor. 3. Copper coin worth four *maravedís*. 4. Series of paternal or maternal ancestors. 5. Crack in horses' hoofs. 6. Quarter of clothes, quarter of animals or of criminals whose body is quartered and exposed in public places. *Cuarto a cuarto*, In a mean, miserable manner. *De tres al cuarto*, Of little moment. *Poner cuarto*, To take lodgings; to furnish apartments. *Cuarto principal*, First floor. *No tener un cuarto*, Not to be worth a farthing. *Cuartos*, 1. Cash, money. 2. Well-proportioned members of an animal's body. *Cuarto de culebrina*, (Mil.) Culverin which carries a five-pound ball.

Cuarto, ta [coo-ar'-to, tah], *a.* Fourth, the ordinal of four.

Cuartogénito, ta [coo-ar-to-hay'-ne-to, tah], *a.* The fourth-born child.

Cuartón [coo-ar-tone'], *m.* 1. Quarter, a large joist or girder, a beam sixteen feet long. 2. (Prov.) Measure of wine and vinegar.

Cuarzo [coo-ar'-tho], *m.* Quartz, a crystallized silicious stone. *Cuarzo citrino*, Occidental topaz.

Cuarzoso, sa [coo-ar-tho'-so, sah], *a.* Quartzose.

Cuasi [coo-ah'-se], *adv.* Almost. *V.* Casi and Como.

Cuasicontrato [coo-ah-se-con-trah'-to], *m.* (Law) Quasi-contract; a contract though not formal, yet effectual. *Cuasidelito*, (Law) Quasi-crime or delict.

Cuasimodo [coo-ah-se-mo'-do], *m.* First Sunday after Easter.

Cuate [coo-ah'-tay], *m.* (Mex.) *V.* Gemelo. *Eso no tiene cuate*, (Coll.) That has no match.

Cuaterna [coo-ah-terr'-nah], *f.* 1. Union of four things. 2. *V.* Cuaderna. 3. Lesson for four.

Cuaternario, ria [coo-ah-ter-nah'-re-o, ah], *a.* Quaternary.

Cuaternidad [coo-ah-ter-ne-dahd'], *f.* Quaternity, quaternary.

Cuaternión [coo-ah-ter-ne-on'], *m.* Union of four things, of four sheets in printing.

Cuatralbo, ba [coo-ah-trahl'-bo, bah], *a.* Having four white feet: applied to a horse or other quadruped.

Cuatralbo, *m.* Commander of four galleys.

Cuatratuo, ua [coo-ah-trah'-too-o, ah], *a.* *V.* Cuarterón for a child.

Cuatrero [coo-ah-tray'-ro], *m.* Thief who steals horses, sheep, or other beasts.

Cuatridial, Cuatridiano, na, Cuatriduano, na, *a.* Lasting four days.

Cuatrienio, *m.* *V.* Cuadrienio.

Cuatrillo [coo-ah-treel'-lyo], *m.* Quadrille, a fashionable game at cards, otherwise called *cascalera* in Spain.

Cuatrimestre [coo-ah-tre-mes'-tray], *a.* Lasting four months.—*m.* The space of four months.

Cuatrin [coo-ah-treen'], *m.* 1. A small coin, formerly current in Spain. 2. (Coll.) Cash in general.

Cuatrinca [coo-ah-treen'-cah], *f.* 1. Union of four persons or things. 2. Four cards of the same print in the game of *báciga*.

Cuatrisílabo, ba, *a.* *V.* Cuadrisílabo.

Cuatro [coo-ah'-tro], *a.* 1. Four, twice two. 2. *V.* Cuarto.

Cuatro, *m.* 1. Character or figure 4. 2. One who votes for four absent persons. 3. Musical composition sung by four voices. 4. Card with four marks. 5. *f.* Four o'clock. *Más de cuatro*, A great number of persons.

Cuatrocientos, tas [coo-ah-tro-the-en'-tos, tas], *a.* Four hundred.

Cuatrodial [coo-ah-tro-de-ahl'], *a.* (Obs.) That which is of four days.

Cuatrodoblar [coo-ah-tro-do-blar'], *va.* To quadruple.

Cuatropea [coo-ah-tro-pay'-ah], *f.* 1. Horse-tax, duty laid on horses which are sold at market. 2. (Obs.) Quadruped.

Cuatropeado, *m.* Step in dancing.

Cuatropear [coo-ah-tro-pay-ar'], *vn.* To run on all fours.

Cuatrotanto [coo-ah-tro-tahn'-to], *m.* (Littl. us.) Quadruple.

Cuba [coo'-bah], *f.* 1. Cask for wine or oil. 2. (Met.) Toper, drunkard. 3. Tub. *Cada cuba huele al vino que tiene*, Every man is to be judged by his actions; literally, every cask smells of the wine it contains.

Cubano, na [coo-bah'-no, nah], *a.* Cuban.

Cubar [coo-bar'], *va.* To cube, to raise to the third power.

Cubaza [coo-bah'-thah], *f. aug.* A large pipe, a hogshead.

Cubazo [coo-bah'-tho], *m.* Stroke received from a pipe or hogshead.

Cubeba [coo-bay'-bah], *f.* (Bot.) Cubeb or cubebs, the berries of the Piper. Cubeba, *L.*

Cubero [coo-bay'-ro], *m.* A cooper.

Cubertura [coo-ber-too'-rah], *f.* Cover, covering. *V.* Cobertura.

Cubeta [coo-bay'-tah], *f.* 1. A small barrel or cask. 2. Tub, pail. 3. Back, vat of brewers. 4. Beck, or trough of dyers. *Cubeta* or *bidón donde se come*, (Naut.) Mess-bucket. *Cubeta para alquitrán*, (Naut.) Tar-bucket.

Cubetilla, ita [coo-bay-teel'-lyah], *f. dim.* A small bucket.

Cubeto [coo-bay'-to], *m.* A small barrel.

Cúbica [coo'-be-cah], *f.* A woollen stuff finer than serge.

Cubicación [coo-be-cah-the-on'], *f.* 1. Measurement of edifices. 2. Act of cubing.

Cúbicamente, *adv.* Cubically.

Cubicar [coo-be-car'], *va.* To cube, to raise to the third power.

Cubichete [coo-be-chay'-tay], *m.* (Naut.) Water-boards or weather-boards, on the upper part of a ship's side, to keep off a rough sea.

Cúbico, ca [coo'-be-co, cah], *a.* Cubical, cubic, cubiform.

Cubiculario [coo-be-coo-lah'-re-o], *m.* Groom of the bed-chamber, valet-de-chambre.

Cubierta [coo-be-err'-tah], *f.* 1. Cover, covering, covert. 2. (Met.) Pretext or pretence. 3. (Naut.) Deck of a ship. *Cubierta primera* or *principal*, The lower or gun-deck. *Segunda cubierta*, The middle deck. *Tercera cubierta*, The upper deck. *Cubierta entera*, A flush deck. *Cubierta arqueada*, A cambering deck. *Cubierta cortada*, A cut or open deck. 4. Cover of a letter, envelope. 5. Casing, coat, facing: roofing. 6. Hood of a carriage.

Cubiertamente, *adv.* Privately, secretly.

Cubierto [coo-be-err'-to], *m.* 1. Cover, part of a table service, consisting of a plate, fork, spoon, knife, and napkin, for every one who sits down to table. 2. Roof of a house, or any other covering from the inclemency of the weather; covert, coverture, cover. 3. Allowance of a soldier billeted in a house. 4. Course, a number of dishes set at once on a table. 5. A meal at a fixed price. (Acad.) *Ponerse a cubierto*, To shelter one's self from an apprehended danger.—*pp. irr.* of Cubrir.

Cubijar, *va.* (Obs.) *V.* Cobijar.

Cubil [coo-beel'], *m.* 1. Lair or couch of wild beasts. 2. (Prov.) Hogsty.

Cubilar [coo-be-lar'], *vn.* To take shelter. *V.* Majadear.

Cubilete [coo-be-lay'-tay], *m.* 1. A copper pan for baking pies and other pastry, and the pie or pastry made on it; used also by jugglers. 2. (Ant.) Tumbler, goblet, a drinking-cup. 3. A cup made of a medicinal wood, such as quassia.

Cubiletero [coo-be-lay-tay'-ro], *m.* 1. Paste-mould. 2. A large mug.

Cubilote [coo-be-lo'-tay], *m.* Cupola smelting furnace, smelting-pot.

Cubilla, *f.* Spanish-fly. *V.* Cubillo.

Cubillo [coo-beel'-lyo], *m.* 1. Spanish-fly, blister-beetle. 2. A piece of table-service for keeping water cool. 3. (Obs.) A small box near the stage. 4. (Naut.) A socket for the flag-pole. *Cubillos*, The ladles or receptacles of a mill-wheel.

Cubismo [coo-bees'-mo], *m.* Cubism.

Cubital [coo-be-tahl'], *a.* Cubital, the length of a cubit.

Cúbito [coo'-be-to], *m.* 1. (Anat.) Ulna, the largest bone of the forearm. 2. The tibia of insects, as named by some zoologists.

Cubo [coo'-bo], *m.* 1. Cube, a solid body of six equal sides. 2. A wooden pail with an iron handle, bucket. 3. Mill-pond. 4. Barrel of a watch or clock. 5. (Mil.) A small tower formerly raised on old walls. 6. Cube, product of the multiplication of a square number by its root. 7. Nave or hub of a wheel. 8. Bayonet socket. 9. Among masons, a hodful of mixed mortar. 10. (Com.) Tongue-way, socket, shaft-case.

Cuboide [coo-bo'-e-day], *m.* 1. Cuboid bone of the tarsus. 2. Rhomboid, little differing from a cube.

Cubreasientos [coo-bray-ah-se-en'-tose], *m.* Seatcover.

Cubrecama [coo-bray-cah'-mah], *f.* Bedspread, coverlet.

Cubrellanta [coo-bray-lyahn'-tah], *m.* Tire covering, tire encasing.

Cubrepán [coo-bray-pahn'], *m.* Sort of fire-shovel, used by shepherds.

Cubriente [coo-bre-en'-tay], *pa.* Covering, hiding.
Cubrimiento [coo-bre-me-en'-to], *m.* 1. Covering, act of covering. 2. Roofing.
Cubrir [coo-breer'], *va.* 1. To cover, to lay, to spread one thing over another. 2. To face, or cover with an additional superficies. 3. (Met.) To cover, to screen, to consent, to palliate. 4. To cover, to disguise, to dissemble, to cloak. 5. To cover or protect a post, to prevent its being attacked by the enemy. 6. To roof a building. 7. To cover, to copulate; to fecundate: applied to animals and to plants. 8. *Cubrir la mesa,* To lay the table. *Cubrir la cuenta,* To balance an account.—*vr.* 1. To take measures to insure one's self against loss. 2. To put a place in a state of defence. 3. To be covered, to put on one's hat. *Cubrírsele a uno el corazón,* To be very melancholy and sorrowful.
Cuca [coo'-cah], *f.* 1. A kind of root-tubercle of a sedge, used in place of coffee. *V.* CHUFA. 2. A Peruvian plant. *V.* COCA. 3. Sort of caterpillar. *V.* CUCO. 4. *Cuca y matacán,* Sort of game at cards. *Mala cuca,* (Coll.) A wicked person. *Cuca de aquí,* (Coll.) Begone!
Cucamonas [coo-ca-mo'-nas], *f. pl.* (Coll.) *V.* CARANTOÑAS.
Cucaña [coo-cah'-nyah], *f.* 1. A public amusement, climbing a greased pole. 2. Any thing acquired with little trouble, and at other people's expense.
Cucañero [coo-ca-nyay'-ro], *m.* Parasite, one who lives at other people's expense.
Cucar [coo-car'], *va.* 1. To wink. 2. To deride, to mock.
Cucaracha [coo-ca-rah'-chah], *f.* 1. Cockroach. Blatta germanica, *L.* 2. Hazel-coloured snuff. *Cucaracha martín,* Nickname formerly given to a brown woman. 3. Scare-crow.
Cucarachera [coo-ca-rah-chay'-rah], *f.* (Vulg.) Luck, good fortune. *Hallarse buena cucarachera,* To be lucky or fortunate.
Cucarda, *f.* *V.* ESCARAPELA.
Cucarro [coo-car'-ro], *m.* Nickname of a boy dressed as a friar. *Cucarros,* (Naut.) Harpings. *V.* CUCHARROS.
Cuceranita [coo-thay-rah-nee'-tah], *f.* (Min.) A certain silicate of aluminum.
Cucioso, sa [coo-the-oh'-so, sah], *a.* Diligent. *V.* SOLÍCITO.
Cucita [coo-thee'-tah], *f.* Lap-dog.
Cuclear [coo-clay-ar'], *vn.* To sing as the cuckoo.
Cuclillas (En) [coo-cleel'-lyas], *adv.* In a cowering manner. *Sentarse en cuclillas,* To squat, to sit cowering, to sit close to the ground.
Cuclillo [coo-cleel'-lyo], *m.* 1. (Orn.) Cuckoo. Cuculus canorus, *L.* 2. (Met.) Cuckold.
Cuco [coo'-co], *m.* 1. Sort of caterpillar. 2. Person of a swarthy complexion. 3. Sort of game at cards. 4. Cuckoo. 5. A gambler. *Reloj de cuco,* Cuckoo-clock. *Cucos,* Nickname given in Castile to the stone-cutters who come from Asturias.
Cuco, ca [coo'-co, cah] *a.* (Coll.) Cunning, crafty, astute, alert for one's own convenience.
Cucú [coo-coo'], *m.* Word imitative of the cuckoo's note.
Cucuiza [coo-coo-ee'-thah], *f.* (Amer.) Thread of the agave.
Cucuma [coo-coo'-mah], *f.* Kind of bread made in Colombia from a root like yucca.
Cucumeráceo, cea [coo-coo-may-rah'-thay-o, ah], *a.* Cucumber-like.
Cuculla [coo-cool'-lyah], *f.* Cowl, a kind of hood formerly worn by men and women.
Cucúrbita [coo-coor'-be-tah], *f.* 1. A retort, for distilling. 2. Scientific name of the gourd.
Cucurbitáceo, cea [coo-coor-be-tah'-thay-o, ah], *a.* (Bot.) Cucurbitaceous.
Cucurucho [coo-coo-roo'-cho], *m.* A paper cone, used by grocers; cornucopia.
Cucúy, Cucuyo, *m.* *V.* COCUYO.
Cucha [coo'-chah], *f.* (Peru.) *V.* LAGUNA.
Cuchar [coo-char'], *f.* 1. Tax or duty on grain. 2. (Prov.) Spoon. 3. Ancient corn measure, the twelfth part of a *celemín* or peck. *Cuchar herrera,* Iron spoon.
Cuchara [coo-chah'-rah], *f.* 1. Spoon. 2. An iron ladle, for taking water out of a large earthen jar. 3. (Mas.) A trowel. *Cuchara para brea,* (Naut.) Pitch-ladle. *Cuchara de cañón,* Gunner's ladle. *Cuchara para sacar el agua de los barcos,* (Naut.) Scoop for baling boats. *Cuchara de pontón para limpiar puertos,* (Naut.) Spoon of a pontoon for cleansing harbours. *Cucharas,* Ladle-boards of a water-wheel in an over-shot mill. *Media cuchara,* A person of mediocre wit or skill.
Cucharada [coo-chah-rah'-dah], *f.* Spoonful, ladleful. *Meter su cucharada,* To meddle in other people's conversation—also, to have a finger in the pie.
Cucharadita [coo-chah-rah-dee'-tah], *f.* Teaspoonful.
Cucharal [coo-chah-rahl'], *m.* Bag in which shepherds preserve their spoons.
Cucharazo [coo-chah-rah'-tho], *m.* Stroke or blow with a spoon.
Cuchareta [coo-chah-ray'-tah], *f. dim.* 1. A small spoon. 2. A variety of wheat in Almeria and Granada. 3. Inflammation of the liver in sheep. (Acad.)
Cucharetear [coo-chah-ray-tay-ar'], *vn.* (Coll.) 1. To stir with a spoon. 2. (Met.) To busy one's self with other people's affairs.
Cucharetero [coo-chah-ray-tay'-ro], *m.* 1. Maker or retailer of wooden spoons. 2. List or linen, nailed to a board, with small interstices to hold spoons. 3. Fringe sewed to under petticoats.
Cucharilla [coo-chah-reel'-lyah], *f.* 1. Liver disease in swine. (Acad.) 2. (Surg.) A scoop.
Cucharita [coo-chah-ree'-tah], *f.* Teaspoon.
Cucharón [coo-chah-rone'], *m.* 1. Ladle for the kitchen, a soup-spoon for the table. 2. (Aug.) A large spoon, dipper.
Cucharro [coo-char'-ro], *m.* 1. (Naut.) Harping. *Tablones de cucharros,* (Naut.) Serving-planks. 2. (Agr.) A vessel made from a gourd used for watering plants by hand.
Cuchichear [coo-che-chay-ar'], *vn.* To whisper.
Cuchicheo [coo-che-chay'-o], *m.* Whisper, whispering.
Cuchichero, ra [coo-che-chay'-ro, rah], *m. & f.* (Coll.) Whisperer.
Cuchichiar [coo-che-che-ar'], *vn.* 1. To call like a partridge. 2. To whisper.
Cuchilla [coo-cheel'-lyah], *f.* 1. A large kitchen-knife; a chopping-knife. 2. Sort of ancient poniard. 3. (Poet.) Sword. 4. Bookbinder's knife. *Gente de cuchilla,* Nickname of the military. *Cuchilla de curtidor para quitar el pelo,* Tanner's knife. *Cuchilla para zurcir* or *pulir,* Currier's knife. *Cuchilla de descarnar,* Drawing-knife.
Cuchillada [coo-cheel-lyah'-dah], *f.* 1. Cut or slash with a knife or other cutting instrument. 2. Gash, a deep wound. *Cuchillada de cien reales,* A large cut or wound. 3. Slash, a cut in cloth, formerly made to let the lining open to view: it was commonly used in the plural. 4. In Madrid, the surplus of the receipt of one play house compared with that of another. —*pl.* Wrangles, quarrels. 5. Galley-stick, side-stick. 6. Truss, girder.
Cuchillar [coo-cheel-lyar'], *a.* Belonging or relating to a knife.
Cuchillejo [coo-cheel-lyay'-ho], *m.* 1. (Dim.) A small knife; a paring-knife (of horse-shoers). 2. (Bot.) Cockle-weed. Agrostemma, *L.*
Cuchillera [coo-cheel-lyay'-rah], *f.* Knife-case or scabbard.
Cuchillería [coo-cheel-lyay-ree'-ah], *f.* Cutler's shop, and the place or street where there are many cutlers' shops; cutlery.
Cuchillero [coo-cheel-lyay'-ro], *m.* Cutler.
Cuchillo [coo-cheel'-lyo], *m.* 1. Knife of one blade, with a handle. 2. Gore, a triangular piece of cloth sewed into a garment. 3. (Met.) Right of governing and putting the laws in execution. 4. A beam, girder. 5. (Naut.) Every plank cut on the bevel. 6. A cut, crevice, fissure. 7. Every triangular sail, leg-of-mutton sail. *Cuchillo de monte,* A hunter's cutlass. *Pasar a cuchillo,* To put to the sword. *Tener horca y cuchillo,* 1. To be lord of a manor, and at the same time invested with the civil and criminal jurisdiction within the circuit of the estate. 2. (Met.) To command imperiously. *Ser cuchillo de alguno,* (Coll.) To torment any one continually; to be very troublesome. *Cuchillo de hoja automática,* Switchblade. *Cuchillo de postres,* Fruit knife. *Cuchillo mantequillero,* Butter knife.
Cuchillón [coo-cheel-lyone'], *m. aug.* A large or big knife.
Cuchipanda [coo-che-pahn'-dah], *f.* A cheerful dinner shared by several persons.
Cuchitril [coo-chee-treel'], *m.* A narrow hole or corner; a very small room; a hut.
Cuchuchear [coo-choo-chay-ar'], *vn.* (Coll.) 1. To whisper, to speak with a low voice. 2. (Met.) To carry tales.
Cuchufleta [coo-choo-flay'-tah], *f.* Joke, jest, fun.
Cudria [coo'-dre-ah], *f.* A flat woven bass-rope.
Cuelga [coo-el'-gah], *f.* 1. Cluster of grapes or other fruit hung up for use. *Cuelga* or *ristra de cebollas,* Bunch of onions. 2. A birth-day present.
Cuelgacapas [coo-el-gah-cah'-pas], *m.* A cloak-hanger.
(*Yo cuelgo, yo cuelgue,* from *Colgar. V.* ACORDAR.)
Cuelmo [coo-el'-mo], *m.* Candle-wood, a piece of pine, or other seasoned wood, which burns like a torch. *V.* TEA.
Cuellicorto, ta [coo-el-lye-cor'-to, tah], *a.* Short-necked.
Cuellierguido, da [coo-el-lyee-er-gee'-do, dah], *a.* 1. Stiff-necked. 2. Elated with pride.
Cuellilargo, ga [coo-el-lyee-lar'-go, gah], *a.* Long-necked.
Cuello [coo-el'-lyo], *m.* 1. The neck. 2. (Met.) Neck of a vessel, the nar-

row part near its mouth. 3. Collar of a priest's garment. 4. Small end of a wax-candle. 5. A large plaited neck-cloth, formerly worn. 6. Collar-band of a cloak, coat, shirt, etc. 7. Collar of a beam in oil-mills. *Levantar el cuello*, (Met.) To be in a state of prosperity.

(*Yo cuelo, yo cuele*, from *Colar. V.* ACORDAR.)

Cuenca [coo-en'-cah], *f.* 1. A wooden bowl. 2. Socket of the eye. 3. The basin of a river. 4. Deep valley surrounded by mountains.

Cuenco [coo-en'-co], *m.* 1. An earthen bowl. 2. (Prov.) Hod.

Cuenda [coo-en'-dah], *f.* 1. End of pack-thread, which divides and keeps together a skein of silk or thread. 2. End of a skein of silk or thread.

Cuenta [coo-en'-tah], *f.* 1. Computation, calculation. 2. Account, count, reckoning. 3. Account, narrative. 4. Obligation, care, duty. (Acad.) 5. One of the beads of a rosary. *Cuentas de ámbar*, Amber-beads. 6. Answerableness; reason, satisfaction. 7. Consideration, merit, importance. (Interj.) *¡ Cuenta !* Take care! *Cuenta* or *caña de cuentas*, (Bot.) Common Indian-shot or Indian-reed. Canna indica, *L.* *Cuenta corriente*, (Com.) Account current. (Com.) *Cuenta de venta*, Account-sales. *Cuenta de resacar recambio*, Return account. *Cuenta simulada*, Pro forma account. *Cuenta a mitad, mutua*, Joint mutual account. *A buena cuenta* or *a cuenta*, On account, in part payment. *A cuenta*, Upon another's word; relying on any thing. *A esa cuenta*, At that rate. *Dar cuenta de su persona*, To answer, or give a justificatory account of what has been intrusted to any one. *Dar cuenta*, To answer, to give account. *Dar cuenta de algo*, (Coll. Iron.) To waste or destroy any thing. *Estar fuera de cuenta*, To have completed the full term of pregnancy. *Hacer cuentas alegres*, To feed one's self with vain hopes of success. *La cuenta es cuenta*, Business is business. *Pasar cuentas*, To pray without devotion. *Tribunal de cuentas*, Exchequer. *Tener cuenta*, To be worthwhile. *Tomar en cuenta*, To take into account. *Tomar por su cuenta*, To take care of. *En resumidas cuentas*, In short. *Perder la cuenta*, To lose track (count).

Cuenta corriente [coo-en'-tah cor-re-en'-tay], *f.* 1. Charge account. 2. Checking account.

Cuentagotas [coo-en-tah-go'-tahs], *m.* Dropper, medicine dropper.

Cuentahilos [coo-en-tah-ee'-los], *m.* Thread counter, linen-prover, weaver's glass.

Cuenta inversa [coo-en-tah in-ver'-sah], *f.* (Aer.) Countdown.

Cuentapasos [coo-en-tah-pah'-sos], *m.* Odometer, an instrument for measuring distances.

Cuentero, ra, *m.* & *f.* & *a.* *V.* CUENTISTA.

Cuentista [coo-en-tees'-tah], *m.* Tale-bearer, informer, misrepresenter.

Cuento [coo-en'-to], *m.* 1. Relation of an event, tale, story. 2. Product of one hundred thousand multiplied by ten, a million; a million of millions. 3. Fable, fictitious story for children. *Cuento de horno*, Vulgar conversation, fire-side tales. *Cuento de viejas*, Old women's stories, idle story. 4. Variance, disagreement between friends. *Andar en cuentos*, To fall to loggerheads; to carry tales, to breed quarrels. 5. Articulation of the wing. 6. Account, number. *A cuento*, To the purpose, seasonably, opportunely. *Ese es el cuento*, There is the rub, that is the difficulty. *Dejarse de cuentos*, or *quitarse de cuentos*, To come to the point. *Cuento de cuentos*, (Met.) Relation or account difficult to explain; a complex detail. *En cuento de*, In place of, instead of. *Hablar en el cuento*, To speak to the point. *No querer cuentos con serranos*, To avoid occasion of quarrelling with evil-disposed persons. *Poner en cuentos*, To expose to risk or peril. *Ser mucho cuento*, To be excessive, exaggerated. *Va de cuento*, Once upon a time (fr. Contar).

Cuento[2] [coo-en'-to], *m.* 1. The butt-end of a pike, spear, or like weapon. 2. Prop, shore, support. (Lat. contus.)

(*Yo cuento, yo cuente*, from *Contar. V.* ACORDAR.)

Cuer [coo-err'], *m.* (Obs.) *V.* CORAZÓN.

Cuera [coo-ay'-rah], *f.* A leather jacket.

Cuerda [coo-err'-dah], *f.* 1. Cord, rope, halter, string, (fishing-) line. 2. A string for musical instruments, catgut or wire. 3. Compass, number of notes which a voice reaches. The four fundamental voices. (Acad.) 4. (Geom.) Chord, a right line which joins the two ends of an arc. 5. Match for firing a gun. 6. Chain of a watch or clock. 7. Cord; a Spanish measure. 8. A number of galley-slaves tied together. 9. (Anat.) Tendon. *Aflojar la cuerda*, To ease up. *Apretar la cuerda*, To crack down. *Bajo cuerda*, Underhandedly. *Cuerda guía*, (Aer.) Dragrope. *Cuerdas vocales*, Vocal cords. *Dar cuerda a*, 1. To wind. 2. (Coll.) To give free rein to. *De cuerda automática*, Self-winding. *De la misma cuerda*, Cut from the same cloth. *Tocar la cuerda sensible*, To get through to.

Cuerdamente, *adv.* Prudently, advisedly, deliberately.

Cuerdecica, illa, ita, Cuerdezuela, *f. dim.* Funicle, a small cord.

Cuerdecito, ita, *a. dim.* Somewhat prudent or discreet.

Cuerdo, da [coo-err'-do, dah], *a.* 1. Prudent, discreet, sensible, judicious. 2. In his senses, not mad.

Cuerezuelo [coo-ay-ray-thoo-ay'-lo], *m.* A sucking pig. *V.* COREZUELO. (Acad.)

Cuerna [coo-err'-nah], *f.* 1. A horn vessel, into which cows or goats are milked. 2. Stag's or deer's horn. 3. Sportsman's horn.

Cuernecico, illo, ito [coo-er-nay-thee'-co], *m. dim.* Cornicle, a small horn.

Cuernezuelo [coo-er-nay-thoo-ay'-lo], *m.* 1. (Dim.) Cornicle, a small horn. 2. A farrier's paring-knife.

Cuerno [coo-err'-no], *m.* 1. Horn, the horn of quadrupeds. 2. Feeler, the horn or antenna of insects. 3. Horn, pointed end of the moon. 4. A button at the end of a rod about which a manuscript was rolled. 5. A huntsman's horn. 6. (Bot.) A spur or outgrowth resembling a horn. 7. (Naut.) An outrigger. 8. (Vet.) A disease of horses, occurring below where the saddle rests; callosity, presumably. 9. *Cuerno de ciervo*, Hart's-horn. *Obra a cuerno*, (Mil.) Horn-work. *Levantar* or *poner u uno sobre los cuernos de la luna*, To exalt one to the stars. *Cuerno de abundancia*, 1. Horn of plenty. 2. Applied to a cuckold whose wife is kept by a rich man. *Verse en los cuernos del toro*, To be in the most imminent danger. *Poner los cuernos*, To cuckold: applied to a wife who wrongs her husband by unchastity. *Cuerno de amón*, (Min.) Cornu ammonis, a fossil shell.

Cuero [coo-ay'-ro], *m.* 1. Pelt, the skin of an animal. 2. Leather. 3. Goat-skin dressed entire, which serves as a bag to carry wine or oil. 4. (Met.) Toper, a great drinker. *Cuero de suela*, Sole-leather. *Cueros al pelo*, Raw hides, skins with the hair on, undressed hides. *De cuero ajeno, correas largas*, To give liberally what is not one's own. *Estirar el cuero*, To make the most of any thing; literally, to stretch the skin. *En cueros* or *en cueros vivos*, Stark-naked. *Entre cuero y carne*, Between skin and flesh. *Cueros*, Hangings or drapery of gilded or painted leather. *Cuero exterior*, Cuticle. *Cuero interior*, Skin.

Cuerpecico, illo, ito, Cuerpezuelo [coo-er-pay-thee'-co], *m. dim.* A small body or carcass.

Cuerpo [coo-err'-po], *m.* 1. Body, material substance. 2. Body of an animal; also more narrowly, the trunk. 3. Cadaver, a corpse, a dead body. 4. Body, matter, opposed to spirit. 5. Body, corporation, guild, any corporate body. 6. (Geom.) Body, any solid figure. 7. (Arch.) Floor or story in a building. 8. Volume, book. *Su librería contiene dos mil cuerpos de libros*, His library contains two thousand volumes. 9. The whole of a book, except the preface and index. 10. (Law) Body, a collection of laws. 11. Degree of thickness of silks, woollens, or cottons. 12. Body, size; strength, thickness of liquids. *El vino de mucho cuerpo*, A strong-bodied wine. 13. Body; a collective mass. Body, in several other senses; as a body of a musical instrument, of ore, of scientific or diplomatic persons, etc. 14. Personal disposition. (Acad.) *Cuerpo de ejército*, The main body of an army. *Cuerpo de reserva*, A corps of reserve. *Cuerpo de batalla de una escuadra*, The centre division of a fleet. *Cuerpo del cabrestante*, (Naut.) Barrel of a capstan. *Cuerpo á cuerpo*, Hand to hand; in single combat. *A cuerpo descubierto*, 1. Without cover or shelter. 2. (Met.) Manifestly. *En cuerpo de camisa*, Half-dressed; having nothing on but the shirt. *Con el rey en el cuerpo*, Despotically; in a despotic manner. *Cuerpo del delito*, Corpus delicti. *Cuerpo de Dios, de mí, de tal*, An exclamation denoting anger or vexation. *Cuerpo de guardia*, A guard-room. *Tratar a cuerpo de rey*, To feast like a king. *Hacer del cuerpo*, To ease the body, to go to stool. *Tomar cuerpo*, To increase, to enlarge. *En cuerpo y alma*, (Coll.) Totally, wholly. *Estar de cuerpo presente*, To be actually present; also, to lie in state after death. *Misa de cuerpo presente*, A mass said while the corpse of the deceased is present in the church. *Cantar cuando lo pide el cuerpo*, To sing when one has a mind to. *Volverla al cuerpo*, To return an injury with another.

Cuerpo aéreo [coo-err'-po ah-ay'-ray-o], *m.* Air corps.

Cuerva [coo-err'-vah], *f.* 1. (Orn.) Crow, rook. Corvus cornix, *L.* 2. A fish very common on the Cantabrian, Biscay, coasts.

Cuervo [coo-err'-vo], *m.* 1. (Orn.) Raven, crow. Corvus corax, *L.* 2. *Cuervo marino*, Cormorant. Pelicanus carbo. 3. (Ast.) A southern constellation. *Venir el cuervo*, (Coll.) To receive repeated relief or succour. *No poder ser el cuervo más negro que las alas*,

The crow cannot be blacker than its wings; greater evil is not to be feared; the worst is over. *¡La ida del cuervo!* He's off! Good riddance!

Cuesa [coo-ay'-sah], *f.* (Obs.) Measure of grain.

Cuesco [coo-es'-co], *m.* 1. Kernel, the stone or core of pulpy fruit. 2. Millstone of an oil-mill. 3. Wind from behind.

Cuesquillo [coo-es-keel'-lyo], *m. dim.* A small kernel or stone of fruit.

Cuesta [coo-es'-tah], *f.* 1. Hill, mount. 2. Any ground rising with a slope. 3. Quest, gathering, charity, money collected by begging. 4. (Obs.) Coast. *Ir cuesta abajo,* To go down hill. *Ir cuesta arriba,* To go up hill. *Cuesta arriba,* Painfully; with great trouble and difficulty. *A cuestas,* 1. On one's shoulders or back. 2. (Met.) To one's charge or care. *Al pie de la cuesta,* (Met.) At the beginning of an undertaking.

Cuestación [coo-es-tah-the-on'], *f.* Petition, solicitation for a charitable purpose.

Cuestero [coo-es-tay'-ro], *m.* One who collects alms or charity.

Cuestión [coo-es-te-on'], *f.* 1. Question, inquiry. 2. Question, dispute, quarrel. 3. Problem. *Cuestión de tormento,* (Law) Torture of criminals to discover their crimes.

Cuestionable [coo-es-te-o-nah'-blay], *a.* Questionable, problematical.

Cuestionar [coo-es-te-o-nar'], *va.* To question, to dispute.

Cuestionario [coo-es-te-o-nah'-re-o], *m.* Questionnaire.

Cuestor [coo-es-tor'], *m.* 1. Questor, a magistrate of ancient Rome. 2. Mendicant, one who collects alms.

(*Yo cuesto, yo cueste,* from *Costar. V.* Acordar.)

Cuestuario, ria, *a. V.* Cuestuoso.

Cuestuoso, sa [coo-es-too-o'-so, sah], *a.* Lucrative, productive.

Cueto [coo-ay'-to], *m.* A lofty place, defended.

Cuetzale [coo-et-thah'-lay], *m.* (Orn.) A large Mexican bird of golden green plumage. *V.* Quetzal.

Cueva [coo-ay'-vah], *f.* 1. Cave, grot, grotto, a subterraneous cavity. 2. Cellar. *Cueva de ladrones,* Nest of thieves. *Cueva de fieras,* Den of wild beasts.

Cuévano [coo-ay'-vah-no], *m.* 1. A basket, or hamper, somewhat wider at the top than below. 2. (Min.) Sump basket. *Después de vendimiar, cuévanos,* The day after the fair; too late.

Cuevero [coo-ay-vay'-ro], *m.* One who makes caves and grottoes.

Cueza [coo-ay'-thah], *f.* Obs.) Ancient measure of grain.

(*Yo cuezo, yo cueza,* from *Cocer. V.* Cocer.)

Cuezo [coo-ay'-tho], *m.* 1. Hod for carrying mortar. 2. (Obs.) Skirt, petticoat. (Acad.) *Meter el cuezo,* To put in an oar, to intrude.

Cúfico, ca [coo'-fe-co, cah], *a.* Cufic, relating to Cufa; said of the characters in which Arabic was written before the 10th century.

Cuguar [coo-goo-ar'], *m.* (Zool.) Puma, cougar.

Cugujada [coo-goo-hah'-dah], *f.* (Orn.) Common field-lark, sky-lark. Alauda arvensis.

Cugulla [coo-gool'-lyah], *f.* Cowl. *V.* Cogulla.

Cuida [coo-ee'-dah], *f.* In ladies' seminaries, a young lady who takes care of another of tender age.

Cuidado [coo-e-dah'-do], *m.* 1. Care, solicitude, attention, heed, heedfulness. 2. Care, keeping, custody, charge or trust conferred. 3. Care, caution, fear, apprehension, anxiety. 4. Followed by prep. *con* and the name of a person. denotes vexation. *Estar de cuidado,* To be in great danger or very ill.—*int. ¡Cuidado!* Mind! stop! beware! *Cuidado ajeno, de pelo cuelga,* Other people's affairs are easily neglected.

Cuidadosamente, *adv.* Carefully, attentively, heedfully, mindfully, cautiously, providently.

Cuidadoso, sa [coo-e-dah-do'-so, sah], *a.* Careful, solicitous; vigilant, heedful, mindful, painstaking, curious, observing.

Cuidaniños [coo-e-dah-nee'-nyos], *m. & f.* Baby-sitter.

Cuidar [coo-e-dar'], *va.* To heed, to care; to execute with care, diligence, and attention; to keep, to mind, to look after.

Cuita [coo-e'-tah], *f.* (1.) Care, grief, affliction, trouble. 2. (Ant.) Ardent desire, craving. *Contar sus cuitas,* To tell one's troubles.

Cuitadamente, *adv.* Slothfully, afflictedly.

Cuitadico, ica, illo, illa, ito, ita [coo-e-tah-dee'-co], *a. dim.* 1. Timid, chicken-hearted. 2. Having some slight trouble or affliction.

Cuitado, da [coo-e-tah'-do, dah], *a.* 1. Anxious, wretched, miserable. 2. Chicken-hearted, pusillanimous, timid.

Cuja [coo'-hah], *f.* 1. Bag, formerly fastened to the saddle, into which a spear or flag-staff was put for easier carriage. 2. Bedstead. 3. (Obs.) Thigh.

Cujarda, *f.* (Bot.) *V.* Coronilla de fraile.

Cuje [coo'-hay], *m.* (Cuba) Withe, each of three slender flexible rods, made of any wood, of which a kind of crane, or gallows, is made for suspending the stems in gathering tobacco. *Cujes, pl.* Hoop-poles.

Culada [coo-lah'-dah], *f.* 1. Stroke with the backside or breech of any thing. 2. Fall on one's backside. *Culadas,* (Naut.) Shocks and rollings of a ship.

Culantrillo, or **Culantrillo de pozo** [coo-lan-treel'-lyo], *m.* Maiden's hair. Adiantum capillus veneris, *L.*

Culantro [coo-lahn'-tro], *m.* (Bot.) Coriander. *V.* Coriandro and Cilantro.

Culata [coo-lah'-tah], *f.* 1. Breech of a gun, butt-end of a musket. 2. Screw-pin, which fastens the breech of a gun to the stock. 3. The back part of any thing. *Dar de culata,* To recoil. Among coachmen and carriage-makers, *dar de culata* means to lift the back of the vehicle in order to remove it without disturbing the front part.

Culatada [coo-lah-tah'-dah], *f.* Kick, recoil of a fire-arm.

Culatazo [coo-lah-tah'-tho], *m.* Recoil of a gun or musket.

Culazo [coo-lah'-tho], *m. aug.* A large backside.

Culcusido [cool-coo-see'-do], *m.* Botchwork, any thing clumsily sewed. *V.* Corcusido.

Culebra [coo-lay'-brah], *f.* 1. Snake. 2. Trick, fun, joke. *V.* Culebrazo. 3. The worm, spiral part of a still. 4. Disorder, confusion suddenly made by a few in a peaceful assembly. *Sabe más que las culebras,* (Coll.) He is very crafty and cunning. *Culebra de cascabel,* A rattlesnake.

Culebrazo [coo-lay-brah'-tho], *m.* Whipping given by jail prisoners to newcomers who have not paid entrance.

Culebrear [coo-lay-bray-ar'], *vn.* To move like a snake; to crankle.

Culebrilla [coo-lay-breel'-lyah], *f.* 1. Tetter, ring-worm; a cutaneous disease. 2. Rocking-staff of a loom. 3. Fissure in a gun-barrel.

Culebrina [coo-lay-bree'-nah], *f.* (Mil.) Culverin.

Culebrino, na [coo-lay-bree'-no, nah], *a.* Snake—as adjective, snaky.

Culebrón [coo-lay-brone'], *m.* A crafty fellow; a double-dealer.

Culebrona [coo-lay-bro'-nah], *f.* An intriguing woman.

Culera [coo-lay'-rah], *f.* 1. Stain of urine in the swaddling-clothes or clouts of children. 2. A patch on the seat of drawers or trousers. (Acad.)

Culero [coo-lay'-ro], *m.* 1. Clout, diaper, a cloth for keeping children clean. 2. Disease in birds.

Culero, ra [coo-lay'-ro, rah], *a.* Slothful, lazy.

Culícidos [coo-lee'-the-dose], *m. pl.* Culicidæ, the family of gnats and mosquitoes.

Culinario, ia [coo-le-nah'-re-o, ah], *a.* Culinary, belonging to the kitchen.

Culito [coo-lee'-to], *m. dim.* A small breech or backside.

Culmífero, ra [cool-mee'-fay-ro, rah], *a.* (Bot.) Culmiferous.

Culminación [cool-me-nah-the-on'], *f.* 1. (Ast.) Culmination, the transit of a planet through the meridian. 2. (Naut.) High tide.

Culminancia [cool-me-nahn'-the-ah], *f.* (Poet.) Height, elevation, peak.

Culminar [cool-me-nar'], *vn.* 1. (Ast.) To culminate, to be in the meridian. 2. To be raised or elevated. 3. (Naut.) To reach high water.

Culo [coo'-lo], *m.* 1. Breech, backside, buttock. 2. Bottom, socket. 3. Anus. 4. The lower or hinder extremity of any thing. *Que lo pague el culo del fraile,* Throwing upon one what ought to be shared by others. *Culo de mona,* Very ugly and ridiculous thing. *Culo de pollo,* Rough, ill-mended part in stockings or clothes.

Culón [coo-lone'], *m.* (Coll.) An invalided or retired soldier.

Culpa [cool'-pah], *f.* Fault, offence, slight crime, failure, guilt. *Culpa lata,* Absence of the simplest precautions. *La culpa del asno echarla a la albarda,* The ass throws the blame on the pack-saddle; laying one's own blame upon another.

Culpabilidad [cool-pah-be-le-dahd'], *f.* Culpability.

Culpable [cool-pah'-blay], *a.* Culpable; faulty, condemnable, accusable.

Culpablemente, *adv.* Culpably.

Culpadamente, *adv.* Culpably.

Culpado, da [cool-pah'-do, dah], *n. & a.* Guilty.—*pp.* of Culpar.

Culpar [cool-par'], *va.* To blame, to impeach, to accuse, to condemn, to reproach.

Cultamente, *adv.* 1. Neatly, genteelly. 2. Affectedly, politely.

Cultedad [cool-tay-dahd'], *f.* (Humorous) Affected elegance and purity of style.

Culteranismo [cool-tay-rah-nees'-mo], *m.* Sect of purists who are affectedly nice in the use of words and phrases.

Culterano, na [cool-tay-rah'-no, nah], *m. & f.* Purist with affectation.

Culterano, na [cool-tay-rah'-no, nah], *a.* Relating to affected elegance and purity of style.

Culteria [cool-tay'-re-ah], *f.* A papilionaceous plant of South America.

Cultero [cool-tay'-ro], *m.* Purist with affectation.
Cultiparlar [cool-te-par-lar'], *vn.* To speak with affected elegance.
Cultiparlista [cool-te-par-lees'-tah], *a.* Speaking much with affected elegance and purity of language.
Cultipicaño, ña [cool-te-pe-cah'-nyo, nyah], *a.* (Humorous) Speaking with affected elegance, and in a jeering manner.
Cultivable [cool-te-vah'-blay], *a.* Cultivable, manurable, capable of cultivation.
Cultivación [cool-te-vah-the-on'], *f.* Cultivation, culture.
Cultivador [cool-te-vah-dor'], *m.* 1. Cultivator. 2. Kind of plough.
Cultivar [cool-te-var'], *va.* 1. To cultivate the soil, to farm, to husband; to manure, to labour. 2. To cultivate, to preserve, to keep up: speaking of friendship, acquaintances, etc. 3. To cultivate, to exercise the memory, the talent, etc. 4. To cultivate the arts or sciences.
Cultivo [cool-tee'-vo], *m.* 1. Cultivation, cultivating and improving the soil. 2. Cultivation, improvement. 3. Act of cultivating one's acquaintance or friendship. 4. Culture of the mind, elegance of manners.
Cultivo de secano [cool-tee'-vo day say-cah'-no], *m.* Dry farming.
Culto, ta [cool'-to, tah], *a.* 1. Pure, elegant, correct: applied to style and language. 2. Affectedly elegant. 3. Polished, enlightened, civilized: applied to a well-informed person, to a nation, etc.
Culto [cool'-to], *m.* 1. Speaking in general, respect or veneration paid to a person, as a testimony of his superior excellence and worth. 2. Worship, adoration, religious act of reverence. *Culto de dulía*, Worship or honour to angels and saints. *Culto de hiperdulía*, Worship of the Virgin Mary. *Culto de latría*, Adoration to God alone. *Culto divino*, Public worship in churches. *Culto externo*, External demonstrations of respect to God and his saints, by processions, sacrifices, offerings, etc. *Culto indebido*, Illegal worship, or superstition of appearing to honour God by false miracles, spurious relics, etc. *Culto sagrado o religioso*, Honour or worship to God and the saints. *Culto superfluo*, Worship by means of vain, useless things. *Culto supersticioso*, Worship paid either to whom it is not due, or in an improper manner.
Cultro [cool'-tro], *m.* (Prov.) Plough with which the first fallow-ploughing is performed.
Cultura [coo-too'-rah], *f.* 1. Culture, improvement or melioration of the soil. 2. Culture and improvement of the mind. 3. Elegance of style or language. 4. Urbanity, polish of manner, politeness.
Cultural [cool-too-rahl'], *a.* Cultural.
Culturar [cool-toor-ar'], *va.* (Prov.) To cultivate. *V.* CULTIVAR.
Cuma [coo'-mah], *f.* (S. Amer.) 1. Godmother. 2. Crony, female friend or neighbour. Apocynaceous plant of Guiana, and its fruit which is sold in Cayenne.
Cumarú [coo-mah-roo'], *m.* The Tonquin or Tonka bean, used for flavouring tobacco and perfuming snuff.
Cumbé [coom-bay'], *m.* Sort of dance among the negroes, and the tune to which it is performed.
Cumbre [coom'-bray], **Cumbrera** [coom-bray'-rah], *f.* 1. Ridge-pole, tie-beam, summit, top. 2. Top, summit, cop, culmination. 3. (Met.) The greatest height of favour, fortune, science, etc.
Cumero [coo-may'-ro], *m.* A tree of Guiana.
Cumia [coo'-me-ah], *f.* Fruit of the cumero-tree, and the resin which is used for incense in the churches of Guiana.
Cumineo, nea [coo-mee'-nay-o, ah], *a.* Cumin-like.
Cuminol [coo-me-nole'], *m.* Oil of cumin.
Cumpa [coom'-pah], *m.* (S. Amer.) 1. Godfather. 2. Comrade, companion.
Cúmplase [coom'-plah-say], *m.* 1. The countersign of a superior officer upon commissions in the army, or certificate of retirement. 2. A permit; "approved."
Cumpleaños [coom-play-ah'-nyos], *m.* Birth-day.
Cumplidamente, *adv.* Completely, complimentally.
Cumplidero, ra [coom-ple-day'-ro, rah], *a.* 1. That which must be fulfilled or executed. 2. Convenient, fit, suitable, accomplishable.
Cumplido, da [coom-plee'-do, dah], *a.* 1. Large, plentiful, high. *Una casaca cumplida*, A full coat. *Una comida cumplida*, A plentiful dinner. 2. Gifted with talents, worthy of esteem, faultless. 3. Polished, polite, civil, courteous.—*pp.* of CUMPLIR.
Cumplido, *m.* 1. Compliment. 2. (Naut.) The length of the thing in question compared with the unit, as a cable's length.
Cumplidor [coom-ple-dor'], *m.* One who executes a commission or trust.
Cumplimentar [coom-ple-men-tar'], *va.* 1. To compliment or congratulate. 2. (Law) To carry out superior orders.
Cumplimentero, ra [coom-ple-men-tay'-ro, rah], *a.* & *n.* 1. (Coll.) Full of compliments, complimental, complaisant. 2. Complimentary.
Cumplimiento [coom-ple-me-en'-to], *m.* 1. Act of complimenting or paying a compliment, complaisance, civility. 2. Compliment, accomplishment, completion, perfection, fulfilling. *Al cumplimiento del tiempo* or *del plazo*, At the expiration of the time. 3. Compliment, an expression of civility, course. *No se ande Vd. en cumplimientos*, Do not stand upon compliments. 4. Complement.
Cumplir [coom-pleer'], *va.* 1. To execute, discharge, or perform one's duty, fulfil. 2. To have served the time required in the militia. *Cumplir años* or *días*, To reach one's birth-day. *Cumplir de palabra*, To offer to do a thing without performing it. *Cumplir por otro*, To do any thing in the name of another. *Cumpla Vd. por mí*, Do it in my name.—*vn.* 1. To be fit or convenient. 2. To suffice, to be sufficient. 3. To mature, be the time (or day) when an obligation, undertaking, ends. 4. To be realized, verified. *Por cumplir*, For mere courtesy, outward show. *El plazo se ha cumplido*, The time has expired.
Cumquibus [coom-kee'-boos], *m.* (Coll.) Cash; money possessions. (Latin.)
Cumulador [coo-moo-lah-dor'], *m.* *V.* ACUMULADOR.
Cumular [coo-moo-lar'], *va.* To accumulate, to compile or heap together. *V.* ACUMULAR.
Cumulativamente, *adv.* In heaps.
Cumulativo, va [coo-moo-lah-tee'-vo, vah], *a.* Cumulative.
Cúmulo [coo'-moo-lo], *m.* 1. Heap or pile; congeries. 2. (Met.) Throng of business; variety of trouble and difficulties.
Cuna [coo'-nah], *f.* 1. Cradle. *Cuna de viento*, Cradle suspended between two upright posts. 2. (Prov.) Foundling hospital. 3. (Met.) The native soil or country. 4. Family, lineage. *De humilde* or *de ilustre cuna*, Of an humble or illustrious family. 5. Origin, beginning of any thing.
Cunar, Cunear [coo-nar', coo-nay-ar'], *va.* To rock a cradle. To move, rock, like a cradle.
Cunasiri [coo-nah-see'-ree], *m.* Peruvian tree of pinkish aromatic wood.
Cuncuna [coon-coo'-nah], *f.* Caterpillar of Chili, resembling the silkworm.
Cunchos [coon'-chose], *m. pl.* Indigenous independent race in Chili.
Cundido [coon-dee'-do], *m.* 1. The provision of oil, vinegar, and salt given to shepherds. 2. Honey or cheese given to boys to eat with their bread.—*Cundido, da, pp.* of CUNDIR.
Cundir [coon-deer'], *va.* (Obs.) To occupy, to fill.—*vn.* 1. To spread: applied to liquids, particularly to oil. 2. To yield abundantly. 3. To grow, to increase, to propagate.
Cuneario, ia [coo-nay-ah'-re-o, ah], *a.* (Bot.) Wedge-shaped.
Cuneiforme [coo-nay-e-for'-may], *a.* Cuneiform, in the form of a wedge.
Cúneo [coo'-nay-o], *m.* 1. (Obs. Mil.) Triangular formation of troops. 2. Space between the passages in ancient theatres.
Cuneo [coo-nay'-o], *m.* 1. Rocking. 2. (Naut.) Rolling, pitching.
Cunera [coo-nay'-rah], *f.* Rocker, a woman appointed to rock the infantas in the royal palace.
Cunero, ra [coo-nay'-ro, rah], *m.* & *f.* (Prov.) A foundling.
Cuneta [coo-nay'-tah], *f.* (Mil.) A small trench, made in a dry ditch or moat of a fortress, to drain off the rain-water; side culvert.
Cuña [coo'-nyah], *f.* 1. Wedge, quoin. 2. Any object employed in splitting or dividing a body. 3. A chip, splinter, driven with a hammer. *Cuñas de mango*, (Naut.) Horsing-irons. *Cuñas de los masteleros*, (Naut.) Fids of the top-masts. *Cuñas de las vasadas o vasón*, (Naut.) Blocks of a ship's cradle. *Cuñas de puntería*, (Mil.) Gun-quoins. *Cuñas de rajar*, Splitting wedges. *No hay peor cuña que la de la misma madera*, or *del mismo palo*, There is no worse enemy than an alienated friend.
Cuñadería [coo-nyah-day-ree'-ah], *f.* Gossipred or compaternity, spiritual affinity contracted by being godfather to a child. (Obs.)
Cuñadía, *f.* **Cuñadío**, *m.* [coo-nyah-dee'-ah, coo-nyah-dee'-o]. Kindred by affinity.
Cuñado, da [coo-nyah'-do, dah], *m.* & *f.* A brother or sister-in-law.
Cuñete [coo-nyay'-tay], *m.* Keg, firkin.
Cuño [coo'-nyo], *m.* 1. Die for coining money. 2. Impression made by the die. 3. Mark put on silver. 4. A triangular formation of troops.
Cuociente [cwo-the-en'-tay], *m.* V. COCIENTE.
Cuodlibético, ca [kwod-le-bay'-te-co, cah], *a.* Quodlibetic, not restricted to a particular subject.
Cuodlibeto [kwod-le-bay'-to], *m.* 1. A debatable point; discussion upon a scientific subject chosen by the author. 2. A thesis, scholastic dissertation in ancient universities. 3. A pungent saying, sharp sometimes, trivial and flat at others, not directed to a useful end.

Cuota [coo-o'-tah], *f.* Quota, contingent, fixed share.

Cupano [coo-pah'-no], *m.* A great tree of the Philippine Islands, the bark yielding a dyestuff and the wood fit for building.

Cupé [coo-pay'], *m.* 1. Landau, a four-wheeled carriage. 2. Coopée, movement in the French dance.

Cupido [coo-pee'-do], *m.* 1. Bit of steel taken out of the eye of a needle. 2. Cupid. 3. A gallant, wooer, lover.

Cupitel [coo-pe-tel']. *Tirar de cupitel,* To throw a bowl archwise.

Cupón [coo-pone'], *m.* Coupon, a voucher for interest attached to a bond.

Cupresino, na [coo-pray-see'-no, nah], *a.* (Poet.) Belonging to the cypress-tree, or made of cypress-wood.

Cúprico, ca [coo'-pre-co, cah], *a.* Cupric, belonging to copper.

Cuproso, sa [coo-pro'-so, sah], *a.* Cuprous, like copper. Cuprous, combining in a lower equivalence than cupric.

Cúpula [coo'-poo-lah], *f.* 1. Cupola, dome. 2. The turret of a monitor. *Cúpula geodésica,* Geodesic dome. 3. (Bot.) Cupule, cup, a sort of involucre.

Cupulifero, ra [coo-poo-lee'-fay-ro, rah], *a.* Cupuliferous, cup-bearing.

Cupulino [coo-poo-lee'-no], *m.* Lantern, a small cupola raised upon another, which serves to light the vault.

Cuquillero [coo-keel-lyay'-ro], *m.* (Prov.) Baker's boy, who fetches the paste of bread, and carries it back when baked.

Cuquillo [coo-keel'-lyo], *m.* 1. (Orn.) Cuckoo. *V.* CUCLILLO. 2. (Ent.) Insect which consumes the vines. Coccus vitis, *Fabr.*

Cura [coo'-rah], *m.* 1. Parish priest, rector, curate. 2. In Castile, it is commonly used to denote any clergyman, priest, or parson.—*f.* 1. Cure, healing, the act and effect of healing or of restoring to health. 2. (Obs.) Guardianship. 3. Parsonage, the benefice of a parish. *Los derechos de cura,* The dues or fees of a rector, parson, or curate, with a parochial charge.

Curable [coo-rah'-blay], *a.* Curable, healable.

Curación [coo-rah-the-on'], *f.* Cure, healing.

Curadero [coo-rah-day'-ro], *m.* Place for bleaching woven goods and other objects.

Curadillo [coo-rah-deel'-lyo], *m.* (Prov.) Cod-fish, ling-fish.

Curado, da [coo-rah'-do, dah], *a.* Rectorial, belonging to the rector of a parish; relating to a rectory or parsonage. *Beneficio curado,* Cure of souls, annexed to a benefice.—*a.* & *pp.* of CURAR. 1. Cured, strengthened, restored to health. 2. Hardened, strengthened, or tanned. 3. Cured, salted.

Curador [coo-rah-dor'], *m.* 1. Overseer. *Curador de lienzo,* Bleacher of linen cloth. *Curador de bacalao,* Cod-salter. 2. Guardian, one who has the care of minors and orphans. 3. (Littl. us.) Physician, surgeon, healer. 4. Curator, administrator. *Curador ad bona,* (Law) Curator of a minor's estate appointed by a court.

Curadora [coo-rah-do'-rah], *f.* Guardianess, a female guardian.

Curaduría [coo-rah-doo-ree'-ah], *f.* Guardianship.

Curalle [coo-rahl'-lyay], *m.* Physic administered to a hawk.

Curandero [coo-ran-day'-ro], *m.* Quack, medicaster, an artful and tricking practitioner in physic.

Curar [coo-rar'], *va.* & *vn.* 1. To cure, to heal, to restore to health, to administer medicines. 2. To prescribe the medicine or regimen of a patient. 3. To salt, to cure meat or fish, to preserve. 4. To bleach thread, linen, or clothes. 5. To season timber. 6. To recover from sickness. 7. (Met.) To remedy an evil. *Curarse en salud,* (Coll.) 1. To guard against evil, when there is little or no danger. 2. To defend one's self, without being accused. 3. To confess a fault, to avoid reproach.

Curare [coo-rah'-ray], *m.* Curare, or woorari, an extract obtained from Strychnos toxifera, a powerful blood-poison, used by South American Indians as an arrow-poison.

Curatela [coo-rah-tay'-lah], *f.* (Law) *V.* CURADURÍA.

Curativo, va [coo-rah-tee'-vo, vah], *a.* Curative.

Curato [coo-rah'-to], *m.* 1. The charge of souls. 2. Parish, the district committed to the care of a rector or parson. *Curato anejo,* A small parish annexed to another.

Curazgo, *m.* (Obs.) *V.* CURATO.

Curbaril [coor-bah-reel'], *m.* A tree of the leguminous family whose wood is used in cabinet-work; it yields a resin employed in varnishes.

Curculiónido, da [coor-coo-leo'-ne-do, dah], *a.* Curculionid, like the curculio.

Cúrcuma [coor'-coo-mah], *f.* 1. Turmeric, a root resembling ginger. 2. Turmeric, the yellow colouring-matter obtained from curcuma, useful in chemistry for testing for alkalies, which turn it brown.

Curcumáceo, cea [coor-coo-mah'-thay-o, ah], *a.* Resembling turmeric.

Curcumina [coor-coo-mee'-nah], *f.* Turmeric yellow, the colouring-matter of curcuma.

Curcusilla, *f.* *V.* RABADILLA.

Cureña [coo-ray'-nyah], *f.* 1. Gun-carriage. 2. Stay of a cross-bow. 3. A gun-stock in the rough. (Acad.) *A cureña rasa,* 1. (Mil.) Without a parapet or breastwork: applied to a barbet battery. 2. (Coll. Met.) Without shelter or defence. *Tirar a cureña rasa,* To fire at random.

Cureñaje [coo-ray-nyah'-hay], *m.* Collection of gun-carriages.

Curesca [coo-res'-cah], *f.* Shear-wool cut off by a clothier with shears when the cloth has been combed.

Curia [coo'-re-ah], *f.* 1. A tribunal, court, more often used of ecclesiastical matters. 2. Care, skill, nice attention. 3. An ancient Roman division of the people.

Curial [coo-re-ahl'], *a.* Relating to the Roman *curia,* or tribunal for ecclesiastical affairs.

Curial, *m.* 1. A member of the Roman *curia.* 2. One who employs an agent in Rome to obtain bulls or rescripts. 3. One in a subaltern employ in the tribunals of justice, or who is occupied with other's affairs.

Curiana [coo-re-ah'-nah], *f.* A cockroach. *V.* CUCARACHA.

Curiosamente, *adv.* 1. Curiously. 2. Neatly, cleanly. 3. In a diligent, careful manner.

Curiosear [coo-re-o-say-ar'], *vn.* To busy one's self in discovering what others are doing and saying.

Curiosidad [coo-re-o-se-dahd'], *f.* 1. Curiosity, inquisitiveness, curiousness. 2. Neatness, cleanliness. 3. An object of curiosity, rarity, curio.

Curioso, sa [coo-re-oh'-so, sah], *a.* 1. Curious, inquisitive, desirous of information. 2. Neat, clean. 3. Careful, attentive, diligent. 4. Odd, curious, exciting attention.

Curruca [coor-roo'-cah], *f.* (Orn.) Linnet, babbling warbler. Motacilla curucca.

Currutaca [coo-roo-tah'-cah], *f.* A woman fond of show, dress, and flutter.

Currutaco [coor-roo-tah'-co], *m.* Beau, fop, dandy, coxcomb, dude.

Currutaco, ca, *a.* Belonging to a person affectedly nice in his or her dress.

Currutaquería [coor-roo-tah-kay-ree'-ah], *f.* Dandyism, coxcombry.

Cursado, da [coor-sah'-do, dah], *a.* Accustomed, habituated, inured.—*pp.* of CURSAR.

Cursante [coor-sahn'-tay], *pa.* 1. Frequenting; assiduous. 2. One who hears lectures in a university; student, scholar.

Cursar [coor-sar'], *va.* 1. To frequent a place, to repeat a thing. 2. To follow the schools, or to follow a course of lectures in the universities.

Curseta [coor-say'-tah], *f.* A snake of the island of Martinique.

Cursi [coor'-se], *a.* Pretentious, vulgar, shoddy. (Arabic, kŭrsi.)

Cursillo [coor-seel'-lyo], *m. dim.* A short course of lectures on any science in a university.

Cursivo, va [coor-see'-vo, vah], *a.* Relating to Italic characters in printing; cursive, script.

Curso [coor'-so], *m.* 1. Course, direction, career. 2. Course of lectures in universities. 3. Course, a collection of the principal treatises used in instruction in some branch in the universities. 4. Course, a series of successive and methodical procedure. 5. Laxity or looseness of the body: generally used in the plural. *Curso de la corriente,* (Naut.) The current's way. *Curso de la marea,* (Naut.) The tide's way.

Cursor [coor-sor'], *m.* (Mech.) Slider, slide.

Curtación [coor-tah-the-on'], *f.* (Ast.) Curtation; curtate distance. *V.* ACORTAMIENTO.

Curtidero [coor-te-day'-ro], *m.* Ground tan-bark.

Curtido, da [coor-tee'-do, dah], *a.* 1. Accustomed; dexterous, expert. 2. Weather-beaten, tanned.

Curtidor [coor-te-dor'], *m.* Tanner, currier, leather-dresser.

Curtidos [coor-tee'-dose], *m. pl.* Tanned leather; sometimes singular.

Curtiduría [coor-te-doo-ree'-ah], *f.* Tanyard, tannery.

Curtiente [coor-te-en'-tay], *a.* A powdery astringent substance serving to tan hides.

Curtimbre [coor-teem'-bray], *f.* 1. Tanning. 2. The total of the hides tanned.

Curtimiento [coor-te-me-en'-to], *m.* Tanning.

Curtir [coor-teer'], *va.* 1. To tan leather. 2. To imbrown by the sun, to tan the complexion: commonly used in its reciprocal sense. 3. To inure to hardships, to harden. *Estar curtido,* (Coll.) To be habituated, accustomed, or inured.

Curto, ta [coor'-to, tah], *a.* (Prov.) Short, dock-tailed. (Arragon.)

Curú [coo-roo'], *m.* (Peru.) Clothes moth.

Curuca, Curuja [coo-roo'-cah, coo-roo'-hah], *f.* (Orn.) Eagle-owl. Stryx bubo.

Curucucú [coo-roo-coo-coo'], *m.* A disease caused by the bite of a certain South American snake.

Curul [coo-rool'], *a.* Curule, belonging to a senatorial or triumphal chair in ancient Rome. Edile.

Curva [coor'-vah], *f.* 1. Curve, a curved line. 2. (Naut.) Knee, timber hewed like a knee. *Curva cuadrada,* Square knee. *Curva capuchina,* Standard of the cut-water. *Curva coral,* Knee of the stern-post. *Curvas a la valona,* Lodging knees. *Curvas verticales de las cubiertas,* Hanging knees of the decks. *Curvas bandas,* Checks of the heads. *Curvas de los yugos,* Transom-knee sleepers.

Curva cerrada [coor'-vah ther-rah'-dah], *f.* Sharp bend (road sign).

Curva doble, curva completa or **curva en U,** *f.* U-turn (road sign).

Curvativo, va [coor-vah-tee'-vo, vah], *a.* (Bot.) Involute, rolling inward.

Curvato [coor-vah'-to], *m.* Bastinado, whipping the feet, an oriental punishment.

Curvatón [coor-vah-tone'], *m.* (Naut.) Little knee or small knee.

Curvatura, Curvidad [coor-vah-too'-rah, coor-ve-dahd'], *f.* 1. Curvature, inflexion. 2. (Naut.) Curvature of any piece of timber.

Curvilíneo, nea [coor-ve-lee'-nay-o, ah], *a.* (Geom.) Curvilinear.

Curvo, va [coor'-vo, vah], *a.* Curved, crooked, bent.

Cusir [coo-seer'], *va.* (Coll.) To sew or stitch clumsily.

Cusita [coo-see'-tah], *a.* Cushite, descended from Cush, son of Ham.

Cúspide [coos'-pe-day], *f.* 1. Cusp, the sharp end of a thing; vertex of a pyramid or cone. 2. Peak of a mountain.

Cuspideo, dea [coos-pee'-day-o, ah], *a.* (Bot.) Cuspidate.

Custodia [coos-to'-de-ah], *f.* 1. Custody, keeping; hold. 2. Monstrance, the casket or reliquary in which the consecrated Host is manifested to public veneration in Catholic churches. 3. Guard, keeper. 4. (Obs.) Tabernacle. 5. In the order of St. Francis, a number of convents not sufficient to form a province.

Custodiar [coos-to-de-ar'], *va.* *V.* GUARDAR.

Custodio [coos-to'-de-o], *m.* Guard, keeper, watchman. *Angel custodio,* Guardian angel.

Cutáneo, nea [coo-tah'-nay-o, ah], *a.* Cutaneous; of the skin.

Cúter [coo'-ter], *m.* (Naut.) Cutter, a small vessel rigged as a sloop.

Cutí [coo-tee'], *m.* Bed-ticking. *V.* COTÍ.

Cutícula [coo-tee'-coo-lah], *f.* The cuticle, epidermis.

Cuticular [coo-te-coo-lar'], *a.* Cuticular. *V.* CUTÁNEO.

Cutio [coo'-te-o], *m.* (Obs.) Labour, work. *Trabajo cutio,* Short work.

Cutir [coo-teer'], *va.* To knock or dash one thing against another.

Cutis [coo'-tis], *m.* & *f.* The skin of the human body. *Piel* and *pellejo* mean hides and pelts.

Cutitis [coo-tee'-tis], *f.* Dermatitis, inflammation of the skin.

Cuto, ta [coo'-to, tah], *a.* (Sp. Am.) Handless, one-handed, maimed.

Cutral [coo-trahl'], *com.* An old worn-out ox, or cow, past usefulness, generally destined to the slaughter-house.

Cutre [coo'-tray], *m.* (Coll.) A pitiful, miserable fellow.

Cuyo, ya [coo'-yo, yah], *pron. pos.* Of which, of whom, whose, whereof.

Cuyo [coo'-yo], *m.* (Coll.) Gallant, lover, wooer, sweetheart.

Cuz, cuz [cooth, cooth], *m.* A term for calling dogs.

Cuzma [cooth'-mah], *f.* (Peru.) A sleeveless shirt used by some forest Indians of Peru. (Kechuan.)

Cuzqueño, ña [cooth-kay'-nyo, nyah], or **Cuzquense,** *a.* Belonging to Cuzco and its inhabitants.

Czar [thar], *m.* *V.* ZAR.

Czarevitz [thah-ray-veets'], *m.* *V.* ZAREVITZ.

Czariano, na [thah-re-ah'-no, nah], *a.* *V.* ZARIANO.

Czarina [thah-ree'-nah], *f.* *V.* ZARINA.

Ch

Ch [chay], *f.* Fourth letter of the Castilian alphabet, double in character, single in value; sounds always as *ch* in chain.

Cha [chah'], *f.* 1. Tea: name given by the Chinese and still preserved in some parts of Spanish America and in the Philippine Islands. (Persian, shā, tea.) 2. A thin and light silk stuff used by the Chinese in summer.

Chabacana [chah-bah-cah'-nah], *f.* An insipid kind of plum.

Chabacanada [chah-bah-ca-nah'-dah, *f.* A very vulgar expression or observation.

Chabacanamente [chah-bah-ca-nah-men'-tay], *adv.* In a bungling manner.

Chabacanería [chah-bah-ca-nay-ree'-ah], *f.* Want of cleanliness and elegance.

Chabacano, na [chah-bah-cah'-no, nah], *a.* Coarse, unpolished, ill-finished. —*m.* (Mex.) A kind of apricot.

Chabán [chah-bahn'], *m.* A month corresponding to May among the ancient orientals.

Chabeta [chah-bay'-tah], *f.* 1. Forelock-key. 2. (Coll.) Judgment, reason. Hence, *Perder la chabeta,* (Met.) To lose one's senses, to run crazy. 3. (Cuba) A kind of knife used by cigar-makers.

Chaborra [chah-bor'-rah], *f.* (Coll. Prov.) A young lass, fifteen to twenty years old.

Chaborreta [chah-bor-ray'-tah], *f. dim.* (Coll. Prov.) A very young lass.

Chacal [chah-cahl'], *m.* Jackal. Canis aureus.

Chácara [chah'-ca-rah], *f.* (S. Amer.) A small plantation. *V.* CHACRA.

Chacina [chah-thee'-nah], *f.* (Prov.) Pork seasoned with spice for sausages and balls.

Chacó [chah-co'], *m.* A high military cap, shako. (Hung. csákó.)

Chacolí [chah-co-lee'], *m.* A light red wine made in Biscay.

Chacolotear [chah-co-lo-tay-ar'], *vn.* To clatter: said of a horse-shoe deficient in nails.

Chacoloteo [chah-co-lo-tay'-o], *m.* The clapping of a loose horse-shoe.

Chacona [chah-co'-nah], *f.* Tune of a Spanish dance of that name; a slow dance in triple, ¾ time.

Chaconá [cha-co-nah'], *m.* **Chaconada** [cha-co-nah'-dah], *f.* Jaconet, a soft cotton cloth for summer dresses.

Chacota [chah-co'-tah], *f.* Noisy mirth. *Echar a chacota alguna cosa,* To carry a thing off with a joke. *Hacer chacota de alguna cosa,* To turn a thing into ridicule.

Chacotear [chah-co-tay-ar'], *vn.* To indulge in noisy mirth, to scoff.

Chacotero, ra [chah-co-tay'-ro, rah], *a.* Waggish, ludicrous, acting the merry-andrew: used as a substantive.

Chacra [chah'-crah], *f.* (Amer.) An Indian rustic habitation, plantation, or farm.

Chacuaco [chah-coo-ah'-co], *m.* (Mex.) A small furnace for melting metals. —*a.* (Coll.) Rustic, boorish, clownish.

Chacual [chah-coo-ahl'], *m.* (Mex.) A gourd-cup.

Chacha [chah'-chah], *f.* Familiar abbreviation of *muchacha.* "Girly." *V.* CHACHO.

Chachal [chah-chahl'], *m.* (Peru.) Graphite, plumbago.

Chachalaca [chah-cha-lah'-cah], *f.* (Mex.) A grouse. A bird which cries continually while flying. (Met.) A chatterer. Also *a.*

Cháchara [chah'-cha-rah], *f.* (Coll.) Chit-chat, idle talk, garrulity. *Todo eso no es más que cháchara,* That is all mere chit-chat.

Chacharear [chah-cha-ray-ar'], *vn.* (Coll.) To prate.

Chacharera [chah-cha-ray'-rah], *f.* & *a.* Forward, talkative woman.

Chacharería [chah-cha-ray-ree'-ah], *f.* (Prov.) Verbosity, verbiage, garrulity.

Chacharero, Chacharón [chah-chah-ray'-ro, chah-cha-rone'], *m.* & *a.* Prater, gabbler.

Chacho [chah'-cho], *m.* 1. (Prov.) Stake at the game of *hombre.* 2. Word of endearment to young persons, particularly in Andalusia, and most generally used in the diminutive, *chachito,* instead of *muchachito,* You, young one.

Chafadura [chah-fah-doo'-rah], *f.* 1. Act of matting velvet. 2. Rumpling, soiling clothes.

Chafaldetes [chah-fal-day'-tes], *m.* (Naut.) Clew-lines.

Chafaldita [chah-fal-dee'-tah], *f.* Joke, fun, repartee.

Chafalonía [chah-fa-lo-nee'-ah], *f.* (Amer. Peru.) Old plate, or broken articles of silver for re-melting.

Chafalla [chah-fahl'-lyah], *f.* (Prov.) A tattered suit of clothes.

Chafallar [chah-fal-lyar'], *va.* To botch, to mend in a clumsy manner.

Chafallo [chah-fahl'-lyo], *m.* Coarse patch, place mended in a botching and clumsy manner.

Chafallón, na [chah-fal-lyone', nah], *m.* & *f.* A botcher.

Chafar [chah-far'], *va.* 1. To make velvet or plush lose its lustre by pressing or crushing the pile. 2. To crease, to rumple, to soil clothing. 3. (Met.) To cut one short in his discourse.

Chafarote [chah-fa-ro'-tay], *m.* A short, broad Turkish sword.

Chafarrinada [chah-far-re-nah'-dah], *f.* 1. Blot or stain in clothes or other things. 2. (Met.) Spot in reputation and character.

Chafarrinar [chah-far-re-nar'], *va.* To blot, to stain.

Chafarrinón [chah-far-re-none'], *m.* Blot, stain. *Echar un chafarrinón,* (Met.) To disgrace one's family by a mean or dishonourable action.

Chaferconeas [chah-fer-co-nay'-as], *f. pl.* (Obs.) Kind of printed linen.

Chaflán [chah-flahn'], *m.* Bevel, obtuse angle; chamfer.

Chaflanar [chah-fla-nar'], *va.* To form a bevel, to cut a slope.

Chagila [chah-hee'-lah], *f.* (Amer.) A slender reed which serves as a weapon among Indians of Ecuador.

Chagra [chah'-grah], *m.* A rustic in Ecuador.

Chair [chah-eer'], *m.* The inner side of a skin, among tanners.

Chaira [chah'-e-rah], *f.* 1. A shoemaker's steel for sharpening. 2. A table steel.

Chal [chahl], *m.* Shawl. *Chal angosto*, Long scarf.

Chala [chah'-lah], *f.* Leaf of maize, serving for fodder, chiefly while green. Corn-husk.

Chalado, da [chah-lah'-do, dah], *a.* Addle-pated, light-witted. (Prov. Andal.)

Chalán, na [chah-lahn', nah], *m.* & *f.* 1. Hawker, huckster. 2. Jockey, a dealer in horses.

Chalana [chah-lah'-nah], *f.* A scow, lighter; square boat.

Chalanear [chah-lah-nay-ar'], *va.* To buy or sell dexterously; to deal in horses.

Chalanería [chah-lah-nay-ree'-ah], *f.* Artifice and cunning used by dealers in buying and selling.

Chalaza [chah-lah'-thah], *f.* 1. Chalaza, one of the ligaments uniting the yolk of an egg to the ends; treadle. 2. (Med.) Chalazion, a sebaceous tumour of the eyelid, resembling a stye.

Chalcosina [chal-co-see'-nah], *f.* Modern name of copper pyrites; chalcopyrite.

Chalchigüite [chal-che-goo-ee'-tay], *m.* (Amer.) Stone of the colour and fineness of the emerald. (Also spelled chalchihuite.)

Chaleco [chah-lay'-co], *m.* A waistcoat, vest.

Chalí [chah-lee'], *m.* (Com.) 1. Mohair: a fabric of goat's hair, which is sometimes mixed with silk. 2. Challis, shalli; delaine.

Chalina [chah-lee'-nah], *f.* Cravat, scarf.

Chalón, Chalún [chah-lone', chah-loon'], *m.* Shaloon, a kind of woollen stuff.

Chalona [chah-lo'-nah], *f.* (Peru.) Mutton cured on ice without salt.

Chalote [chah-lo'-tay], *m.* (Bot.) *V.* CEBOLLA ASCALONIA.

Chalupa [chah-loo'-pah], *f.* 1. (Naut.) Shallop, launch, a small light vessel, a long-boat. 2. (Mex.) A canoe for one or two persons only.

Chalupero [chah-loo-pay'-ro], *m.* A boatman, canoe-man.

Chamada [chah-mah'-dah], *f.* Chips, splinters of wood, to quicken a fire.

Chamagoso, sa [chah-ma-go'-so, sah], *a.* (Mex.) 1. Greasy, filthy. 2. Ill-performed. 3. Applied to things low, vulgar.

Chamaleón [chah-ma-lay-on'], *m.* *V.* CAMALEÓN.

Chamano [chah-mah'-no], *m.* A shrub of the Andes. Croton menthodorum.

Chamarasca [chah-ma-rahs'-cah], *f.* 1. A brisk fire, made of brushwood. 2. (Bot.) Annual costmary. Tanacetum annuum.

Chamaraz [chah-ma-rath'], *m.* (Bot.) Water-germander. Teucrium scordium.

Chamarilero, Chamarillero [chah-ma-re-lay'-ro, chah-ma-reel-lyay'-ro], *m.* 1. Broker who deals in old pictures and furniture. 2. Gambler.

Chamarillón [chah-ma-reel-lyone'], *m.* A bad player at cards.

Chamariz [chah-ma-reeth'], *m.* (Orn. Prov.) Blue tit-mouse. Parus cæruleus.

Chamarón [chah-ma-rone'], *m.* (Orn.) Long-tailed titmouse.

Chamarra [chah-mar'-rah], *f.* Lumber jacket, mackinaw.

Chamarreta [chah-mar-ray'-tah], *f.* A short loose jacket with sleeves.

Chamba [chahm'-bah], *f.* *V.* CHIRIPA.

Chambelán [cham-be-lahn'], *m.* Ant. for *Camarlengo*, chamberlain.

Chamberga [cham-ber'-gah], *f.* 1. A long and wide cassock. 2. A regiment raised in Madrid during the minority of Charles II. 3. Kind of Spanish dance accompanied by a merry song. 4. A narrow silk girdle.

Chambergo, ga [cham-ber'-go, gah], *a.* Slouched, uncocked: applied to a round hat worn by the regiment of *Chamberga*, and ever since a round uncocked hat has retained that name.

Chamberguilla [cham-ber-geel'-yah], *f.* Andal. for *chamberga*.

Chambira [cham-bee'-rah], *f.* A forest palm. Astrocaryum vulgare.

Chambón, na [cham-bone', nah], *a.* Awkward, unhandy (person); botcher.

Chambonada [cham-bo-nah'-dah], *f.* A blunder, piece of stupidity; at billiards, a fluke.

Chambra [cham'-brah], *f.* Morning-jacket, a white short blouse used by women over the chemise.

Chambrana [cham-brah'-nah], *f.* Door-case, jamb-dressing.

Chamelote [chah-may-lo'-tay], *m.* Camlet. *Chamelote de aguas*, Clouded camlet. *Chamelote de flores*, Flowered camlet.

Chamelotina [chah-may-lo-tee'-nah], *f.* Kind of coarse camlet.

Chamelotón [chah-may-lo-tone'], *m.* (Obs.) Coarse camlet.

Chamerluco [chah-mer-loo'-co], *m.* Kind of close jacket with a collar, formerly worn by women.

Chamicera [chah-me-thay'-rah], *f.* A piece of forest where the wood has been scorched by fire.

Chamicero, ra [chah-me-thay'-ro, rah], *a.* Belonging to scorched wood.

Chamiza [chah-mee'-thah], *f.* Kind of wild cane or reed; chamise.

Chamizal [chah-mee-thahl'], *m.* A chamise thicket.

Chamizo [chah-mee'-tho], *m.* A piece of wood half burnt.

Chamorra [chah-mor'-rah], *f.* In the jocular style, a shorn head.

Chamorrada [chah-mor-rah'-dah], *f.* (Low) Butt given with a shorn head.

Chamorrar [chah-mor-rar'], *va.* (Obs.) To cut the hair with shears.

Chamorro, ra [chah-mor'-ro, rah], *a.* Shorn, bald. *Trigo chamorro*, (Bot.) Winter or beardless wheat. Triticum hybernum, *L.*

Champada [cham-pah'-dah], *f.* A large stately tree in Malaga.

Champán [cham-pahn'], *m.* Kind of vessel in South America of seventy or eighty tons burden.

Champaña [cham-pah'-nyah], *m.* Champagne.

Champiñones [cham-pe-nyo'-ness], *m. pl.* Edible muschrooms.

Champú [cham-poo'], *m.* Shampoo.

Champurrado [cham-poor-rah'-do], *m.* (Coll.) 1. Jargon. 2. (Prov.) A mixture of different liquors. (Mex.) Chocolate made in *atole* instead of water. —*Champurrado, da, pp.* of CHAMPURRAR.

Champurrar [cham-poor-rar'], *va.* (Coll.) 1. To mix liquors. 2. (Met.) To speak with a mixture of words of different languages.

Chamuchina [chah-moo-chee'-nah], *f.* (Peru.) Populace, rabble.

Chamuscado, da [chah-moos-cah-do, dah], *a.* 1. Tipsy, flustered with wine; tinged, inclined, addicted to vice. 2. Smitten, scorched, burnt with a passion. (Met.) Contaminated, tainted. —*pp.* of CHAMUSCAR.

Chamuscar [chah-moos-car'], *va.* To singe or scorch; to sear.

Chamusco [chah-moos'-co], *m.* *V.* CHAMUSQUINA.

Chamuscón [chah-moos-cone'], *m. aug.* A large singe or scorch.

Chamusquina [chah-moos-kee'-nah], *f.* 1. Scorching or singeing. 2. (Met.) Scolding, wrangling, high words. *Oler a chamusquina*, (Met.) To come from hot words to hard blows.

Chanada [chah-nah'-dah], *f.* Trick, joke, deceit.

Chanate [chah-nah'-tay], *m.* (Mex.) A blackbird.

Chancaca [chan-cah'-cah], *f.* *Azúcar de chancaca*, The refuse of the sugar in the boiler; raw sugar.

Chancal [chan-cahl'], *m.* The moraine of a glacier.

Chancear [chan-thay-ar'], *vn.* (Littl. us.) To jest, to joke.—*vr.* To jest, to joke, to fool.

Chancellar [chan-thel-lyar'], *va.* (Obs.) *V.* CANCELAR.

Chanceller [chan-thel-lyerr'], *m.* (Obs.) *V.* CANCILLER.

Chancero, ra [chan-thay'-ro, rah], *a.* Jocose, sportful, merry.

Chancica, illa [chan-thee'-cah, eel'-lyah], *f. dim.* A little fun or jest.

Chanciller [chan-theel-lyerr'], *m.* (Ant.) *V.* CANCILLER, chancellor.

Chancilleresco, ca [chan-theel-lyay-res'-co, cah], *a.* Belonging to the court of chancery.

Chancillería [chan-theel-lyay-ree'-ah], *f.* 1. Chancery. 2. (Obs.) Chancellorship. 3. The right and fees of a chancellor.

Chancita [chan-thee'-tah], *f. dim.* A little fun.

Chancla [chahn'-clah], *f.* An old shoe with worn-down heel.

Chancleta [chan-clay'-tah], *f.* Slipper. *V.* CHINELA. *Andar en chancleta*, To go slipshod.

Chancletear [chahn-clay-tay-ar'], *vn.* To go slipshod.

Chanclo [chahn'-clo], *m.* 1. Patten worn under the shoes by women. 2. Strong leather clog worn over shoes to guard against moisture and dirt. 3. Clog, galosh, overshoe.

Cháncharras máncharras [chahn'-char-ras mahn'-char-ras], *f. pl.* (Low) *No andemos en cháncharras máncharras*, Let us not go about the bush, or use subterfuges and evasions.

Chanchullear [chan-chool-lyay-ar'], *va.* 1. To be guilty of sharp practice; to do vile things. 2. (Coll.) To smuggle.

Chanchullo [chan-chool'-lyo], *m.* Unlawful conduct to attain an end, and especially to get gain. (Acad.) Sharp practice, vile trick. (Amer.) Contraband.

Chanfaina [chan-fah'-e-nah], *f.* 1. Ragout of livers and lights. 2. A trifling, worthless thing.

Chanflón, na [chan-flone', nah], *m.* & *f.* Bungler.—*a.* Bungling; made in a bungling manner.

Chanflón [chan-flone'], *m.* Money beaten out to appear larger.

Changa [chahn'-gah], *f.* (Cuba) Jest, joke, diversion.

Changador [chan-gah-dor'], *m.* (S. Amer.) Porter, carrier of burdens.

Changamé [chan-gah-may'], *m.* (Orn.) A thrush of Panama.

Changarro [chan-gar'-ro], *m.* (Agr.) A small cow-bell.

Changote [chan-go'-tay], *m.* An oblong bar of iron.

Changuear [chan-gay-ar'], *vn.* To be jocose with others.

Changüí [chan-goo-ee'], *m.* 1. (Vulg.) Jest, trick: used with *dar*. 2. (Cuba) A dance of the people.

Chantado [chan-tah'-do], *m.* (Prov. Gal.) Wall or fence of slate in upright rows.

Chantaje [chan-tah'-hay], *m.* Blackmail.
Chantajismo [chan-tah-hees'-mo], *m.* Blackmailing.
Chantajista [chan-tah-hees'-tah], *m.* & *f.* Blackmailer.
Chantar [chan-tar'], *va. Chantar a alguno una cosa,* To brave a person to his face. *Se la chantó.*
Chantre [chahn'-tray], *m.* Precentor, a dignified canon of a cathedral church.
Chantría [chan-tree'-ah], *f.* Precentorship.
Chanza [chahn'-thah], *f.* Joke, jest, fun. *Chanza pesada,* A sarcastic taunt, a bad trick. *Hablar de chanza,* To joke, to jest, to speak in jest.
Chanzoneta [chan-tho-nay'-tah], *f.* 1. Joke, jest. 2. A little merry song, a ballad.
Chanzonetero [chan-tho-nay-tay'-ro], *m.* Writer of ballads, a petty poet.
Chapa [chah'-pah], *f.* 1. A thin metal plate which serves to strengthen or adorn the work it covers; scutcheon. 2. A kind of rosy spot on the cheek. 3. Rouge used by ladies. 4. A small bit of leather laid by shoemakers under the last stitches to prevent the binding giving way. 5. *Chapas de freno,* The two bosses on each side of the bit of a bridle. 6. Transom and trunnion plates in gun-carriages; judgment, good sense. *Chapas de caoba,* Mahogany veneers. *Hombre de chapa,* A man of judgment, abilities, and merit.
Chapaja [chah-pah'-hah], *f.* A textile fibre from the stem of Leopoldinia piassaba. (Peru.)
Chapalear [chah-pah-lay-ar'], *va. V.* CHAPOTEAR and CHACOLOTEAR.
Chapaleta [chah-pah-lay'-tah], *f.* (Naut.) A valve of strong leather put at the bottom of a ship's pump, which serves as a sucker.
Chapapote [chah-pah-po'-tay], *m.* A tar natural in Cuba and Santo Domingo.
Chapar [chah-par'], *va.* (Obs.) To plate, to coat.
Chaparra [chah-par'-rah], *f.* 1. Species of oak. *V.* CHAPARRO. 2. A coach with a low roof. 3. (Amer.) Bramble-bush.
Chaparrada [chah-par-rah'-dah], *f. V.* CHAPARRÓN.
Chaparral [chah-par-rahl'], *m.* 1. Plantation of evergreen oaks. 2. (Amer.) Thick bramble-bushes entangled with thorny shrubs in clumps.
Chaparreras [chah-par-ray'-ras], *f. pl.* Leather leggings for horseback riders.
Chaparro [chah-par'-ro], *m.* (Bot.) Evergreen oak-tree. Quercus ilex.
Chaparrón [chah-par-rone'], *m.* A violent shower of rain.
Chapatal [chah-pa-tahl'], *m.* A mire; muddy place. *V.* LODAZAL.
Chapear [chah-pay-ar'], *va.* To adorn with metal plates.—*vn. V.* CHACOLOTEAR.
Chapeleta de una bomba [chah-pay-lay'-tah], *f.* (Naut.) The clapper of a ship's pump. *Chapeletas de los imbornales,* (Naut.) The clappers of the scupper-holes.
Chapelete [chah-pay-lay'-tay], *m.* (Prov.) An ancient cover for the head.
Chapelina [chah-pay-lee'-nah], *f.* An ancient gold coin.
Chapelo [cha-pay'-lo], *m.* Antiquated for *sombrero.*
Chapeo [chah-pay'-o], *m.* (Coll.) Hat.
Chapería [chah-pay-ree'-ah], *f.* Ornament of metal plates.
Chaperón [chah-pay-rone'], *m.* Ancient hood or cowl.
Chapeta [chah-pay'-tah], *f.* A small metal plate. *Chapeta,* 1. Red spot on the cheek. 2. A stud for shirts or other articles.
Chapetón [chah-pay-tone'], *m.* (Amer.) A wheel of silver to adorn a riding harness.
Chapetón, na [chah-pay-tone', nah], *a.* A European lately arrived in America. *V.* POLIZÓN.
Chapetonada [chah-pay-to-nah'-dah], *f.* A disease incident to Europeans in America, before they are accustomed to the climate.
Chapín [chah-peen'], *m.* Clog with a cork sole, worn by women. *Chapín de la reina,* Tax formerly levied in Spain on the occasion of the king's marriage. *Poner en chapines (a una hija),* To marry off a daughter. *Ponerse en chapines,* To raise one's self above one's conditions.
Chapinazo [chah-pe-nah'-tho], *m.* Stroke or blow with a clog or patten.
Chapinería [chah-pe-nay-ree'-ah], *f.* Shop where clogs and pattens are made and sold, and the art of making them.
Chapinero [chah-pe-nay'-ro], *m.* Clog maker or seller.
Chapinito [chah-pe-nee'-to], *m. dim.* A small clog.
Chápiro [chah'-pe-ro], *m.* A word of annoyance or menace used only in the phrases, *¡ Por vida del chápiro (verde) ! ¡ Voto al chápiro !* About equal to " Good gracious !"
Chapitel [chah-pe-tel'], *m.* 1. The upper part of a pillar rising in a pyramidal form. 2. A small movable brass plate over the compass. 3. *V.* CAPITEL.
Chaple [chah'-play], *m.* Graver, the tool used in engraving.
Chapo [chah'-po], *m.* A short, stout person. (Mex.)
Chapodar [chah-po-dar'], *va.* To lop off the branches of trees and vines.
Chapón [chah-pone'], *m.* A great blot of ink.
Chapona [chah-po'-nah], *f. V.* CHAMBRA.
Chapote [chah-po'-tay], *m.* Kind of black glue or wax in America, used for cleaning the teeth.
Chapotear [chah-po-tay-ar'], *va.* To wet with a sponge or wet cloth.—*vn.* To paddle in the water; to dabble.
Chapucear [chah-poo-thay-ar'], *va.* To botch, to bungle, to cobble, to fumble, to clout.
Chapuceramente [chah-poo-thay-rah-men'-tay], *adv.* Fumblingly, clumsily, bunglingly.
Chapucería [chah-poo-thay-ree'-ah], *f.* A clumsy, bungling work.
Chapucero [chah-poo-thay'-ro], *m.* 1. Blacksmith, who makes nails, trivets, shovels, etc.; nailer. 2. Bungler, botcher.
Chapucero, ra [chah-poo-thay'-ro, rah], *a.* Rough, unpolished, clumsy, bungling, rude.
Chapulín [chah-poo-leen'], *m.* 1. (Prov. Mex.) A grasshopper, locust. 2. Trickster.
Chapurrado [chah-poor-rah'-do], *m.* (Coll.) Jargon, broken language.
Chapurrar [chah-poor-rar'], *va.* (Coll.) To speak gibberish. *V.* CHAMPURRAR.
Chapuz [chah-pooth'], *m.* 1. The act of ducking one. 2. A clumsy performance. *Chapuces,* (Naut.) Mast spars.
Chapuzar [chah-poo-thar'], *va.* 1. To duck. 2. To paddle with the oars.—*vn.* & *vr.* To dive; to draggle, to duck.
Chaqueta [chah-kay'-tah], *f.* Jacket.
Chaquete [chah-kay'-tay], *m.* Game resembling backgammon.
Chaquira [chah-kee'-rah], *f.* Seed-glass beads of all colours. (Peru.)
Charada [chah-rah'-dah], *f.* Charade, enigma.
Charadrio [chah-rah'-dre-o], *m.* (Orn.) Common roller. Coracies garrula. *L. V.* GÁLGULO.
Charanchas [cha-rahn'-chas], *f. pl.* (Naut.) Battens used as supporters on board a ship.
Charamusca [chah-ra-moos'-cah], *f.* (Mex.) Twisted candy. 2. (Peru.) *V.* CHAMARASCA.
Charamusquero [chah-ra-moos-kay'-ro], *m.* (Mex.) A seller of twisted candy.
Charanga [chah-rahn'-gah], *f.* A military band of wind instruments only. Fanfare.
Charanguero, ra [chah-ran-gay'-ro, rah], *a.* 1. Clumsy, unpolished, artless. 2. Applied to a bungler or bad workman.
Charanguero [chah-ran-gay'-ro], *m.* (Prov.) 1. Peddler, hawker. 2. A kind of ship for the coast trade. 3. (Coll.) A lucky person.
Charca [char'-cah], *f.* Pool of water collected to make it congeal to ice.
Charcanas [char-cah'-nas], *f.* Stuff of silk and cotton.
Charco [char'-co], *m.* Pool of standing water; small lake. *Pasar el charco,* To cross the seas. *Hacer charcos en el estómago,* To drink too much water.
Charcoso, sa [char-co'-so, sah], *a.* (Prov.) Fenny, moorish, watery.
Charla [char'-lah], *f.* 1. (Orn.) Bohemian chatterer, silk-tail. Ampelis garrulus. 2. Idle chit-chat or prattle, garrulity, gossip, loquaciousness.
Charlador, ra [char-lah-dor', rah], *m.* & *f.* Gabbler, prater, a chattering fellow, a garrulous person, a chatterer.
Charladuría [char-lah-doo-ree'-ah], *f.* Garrulity, gossip.
Charlante [char-lahn'-tay], *m.* & *pa.* Gabbler, chatterer.
Charlantín [char-lan-teen'], *m.* (Coll.) A mean prattler or gossip.
Charlar [char-lar'], *vn.* To prattle, to babble, to chatter, to prate, to gabble, to gossip, to jabber, to clack, to chat.
Charlatán, na [char-lah-tahn', nah], *m.* & *f.* 1. Prater, babbler, idle talker, gabbler. 2. Charlatan, a quack, a mountebank.—*a.* Empirical.
Charlatanear [char-lah-tah-nay-ar'], *vn. V.* CHARLAR.
Charlatanería [char-lah-tah-nay-ree'-ah], *f.* Garrulity, verbosity, charlatanry; quackery.
Charlatanismo [char-lah-tah-nees'-mo], *m.* Charlatanry, quackery, empiricism, verbosity.
Charmilla [char-meel'-lyah], *f.* (Bot.) Common hornbeam-tree. Carpinus betulus.
Charneca [char-nay'-cah], *f.* (Bot.) Mastic-tree, pistachia-tree. Pistacea lentiscus, *L. V.* LENTISCO.
Charnecal [char-nay-cahl'], *m.* Plantation of mastic-trees.
Charnel [char-nel'], *m.* (Cant) 1. Two *maravedís.* 2. Small change.
Charnela [char-nay'-lah], *f.* Hinge; the chape of a buckle; hinge-joint, knuckle.
Charneta [char-nay'-tah], *f.* (Obs.) Iron plate.
Charol [chah-rol'], *m.* 1. Varnish; japan or japan work. 2. Japanned leather, patent leather.
Charolar [chah-ro-lar'], *va.* To varnish, to japan.
Charolista [chah-ro-lees'-tah], *m.* Gilder, varnisher, or japanner.
Charpa [char'-pah], *f.* 1. Leathern belt with compartments for pistols and

poniards. 2. Sling for a broken arm. 3. (Naut.) Sling.
Charpar [char-par'], *va.* To scarf, to lap one thing over another.
Charque, or **Charquí** [char'-kay, char-kee'], *m.* Meat dried in the sun; jerked beef. *V.* Tasajo.
Charquear [char-kay-ar'], *va.* To jerk beef; to dry it in the air.
Charqueo [char-kay'-o], *m.* Act of cleaning holy-water fonts.
Charquicán [char-ke-cahn'], *m.* Sauce prepared with charquí.
Charquillo [char-keel'-lyo], *m. dim.* A small pool or puddle.
Charrada [char-rah'-dah], *f.* 1. Speech or action of a clown. 2. A dance. 3. (Coll.) Tawdriness, tinsel, finery.
Charramente [char-rah-men'-tay], *adv.* Clownishly, tastelessly, ostentatiously fine.
Charrán [char-rahn'], *a.* Rascally, knavish.
Charranear [char-rah-nay-ar'], *vn.* To play the knave, the rascal.
Charranería [char-rah-nay-ree'-ah], *f.* Rascality, knavery.
Charretera [char-ray-tay'-rah], *f.* 1. Strip of cloth, silk, etc., placed on the lower part of trousers to fasten them with a buckle. 2. The buckle with which the strips are fastened. 3. Epaulet. *Charretera mocha*, shoulder-knot.
Charro, ra [char'-ro, rah], *m. & f.* 1. Churl a clownish, coarse, ill-bred person. 2. A tawdry, showy person. 3. A name given to the peasants of the province of Salamanca in Spain.
Charro, ra [char'-ro, rah], *a.* Gaudy, tawdry.
Chas [chas], *m.* A low word, denoting the noise made by the cracking of wood or tearing of linen.
Chasca [chahs'-cah], *f.* (Amer.) Disordered hair.
Chascar [chas-car'], *vn.* To crackle, sputter: said of wood which sends off little pieces from a fire.
Chascarrillo [chas-car-reel'-lyo], *m.* Spicy anecdote, gossipy story.
Chasco [chahs'-co], *m.* 1. Fun, joke, jest, a trick, a sham. 2. Foil, frustration, disappointment. 3. Lash, the thong or point of the whip. *Dar un chasco*, To play a merry trick. *Dar chasco*, To disappoint. *Llevarse chasco*, To be disappointed.
Chasí [chah-see'], *m.* A photographic plate-holder.
Chasis [chah'-sis], *m.* Chassis (of a vehicle).
Chasquear [chas-kay-ar'], *va.* To crack with a whip or lash.—*vn.* 1. To crack as timber at the approach of dry weather: to snap; to crepitate. 2. To fool, to play a waggish trick. 3. To disappoint, to fail, to fall short; to cheat.
Chasqui [chahs'-kee], *m.* (Peru.) Post-boy, or messenger on foot.
Chasquido [chas-kee'-do], *m.* 1. Crack of a whip or lash. 2. Crack, the noise made by timber when it breaks or splits.
Chasquista [chas-kees'-tah], *m.* (Low) A person fond of playing tricks; a sycophant.
Chata [chah'-tah], *f.* (Naut.) A flat-bottomed boat. *Chata alijadora*, Lighter. *Chata de arbolar*, Sheer-hulk. *Chata de carenar*, Careening-hulk.
Chatarrero [chah-tar-ray'-ro], *m.* Junkman.
Chate [chah'-tay], *m.* (Bot.) Round-leaved Egyptian or hairy cucumber. Cucumis chate.
Chato, ta [chah'-to, tah], *a.* Flat, flattish: flat-nosed. *Embarcación chata*, A flat-bottomed vessel.
Chatón [chah-tone'], *m.* 1. Bezel, the bevelled part of a ring in which a diamond is set. 2. Kind of coarse diamond. 3. (Obs.) Ornamental nail or button. 4. *pl.* Knobs which fasten one thing to another.
Chatre [chah'-tray], *a.* (Ecuador) Richly decked out.
Chaúl [chah-ool'], *m.* A kind of blue silk stuff manufactured in China, resembling European grogram.
Chauvinismo [chah-oo-ve-nees'-mo], *m.* Chauvinism.
Chauvinista [chah-oo-ve-nees'-tah], *a. & m. & f.* Chauvinist.
Chaval [chah-vahl'], *a.* Among the common people, young.
Chaveta [chah-vay'-tah], *f.* Bolt, cotter pin. *Perder la chaveta*, To lose one's head, to become rattled.
Chayote [chah-yo'-tay], *m.* (Mex.) Mexican fruit. Scisyos edulis. *V.* Chiote.
Chaza [chah'-thah], *f.* 1. Point where the ball is driven back, or where it stops, in a game at balls. 2. (Naut.) Berth on board a ship. *Hacer chaza*, To walk on the hind feet: applied to a horse that rears.
Chazador [chah-thah-dor'], *m.* A person employed to stop the ball and mark the game.
Chazar [chah-thar'], *va.* 1. To stop the ball before it reaches the winning-point. 2. To mark the point whence the ball was repulsed or driven back.
Checoslovaco, ca [chay-cos-lo-vah'-co, cah], *a.* Czechoslovakian. —*m. & f.* Czechoslovak.
Cheira [chay'-e-rah]. *V.* Chaira.
Chelín [chay-leen'], *m.* Shilling, an English coin worth about twenty-four (24.3) cents of American money or five *reales de vellón*.
Chenil [chay-neel'], *m.* Chenille.
Chepa [chay' pah], *f.* A hump, hunch.
Chepo [chay'-po], *m.* (Vulg.) Pecho.
Cheque [chay'-kay], *m.* Check, cheque. *Cheque de caja*, Cashier's cheque.
Cherna [cherr'-nah], *f.* (Zool. Prov.) Ruffle, a fish resembling a salmon.
Cherva [cherr'-vah], *f.* (Bot.) The castor-oil plant. Palma Christi. Ricinus communis.
Cheurrón [chay-oor-rone'], *m.* (Her.) Chevron, a representation of two rafters of a house in heraldry.
Chevronado, da [chay-vro-nah'-do, dah], *a.* (Her.) Chevroned, coat of arms charged with chevrons.
Chía [chee'-ah], *f.* 1. A short black mantle, formerly worn in mournings. 2. Cowl of fine cloth, formerly worn by the nobility for distinction. 3. A white medicinal earth. 4. (Bot.) Lime-leaved sage. Salvia tiliæfolia.
Chiar [che-ar'], *vn.* To chirp, as birds. *V.* Piar.
Chibcha [cheeb'-chah], *m.* A dweller of the elevated territory about Bogotá.
Chibón [che-bone'], *m.* 1. A young cock-linnet. 2. Sort of gum from America.
Chica [chee'-cah], *f.* A little girl. *Es una linda chica*, (Coll.) She is a pretty girl.
Chicada [che-cah'-dah], *f.* Herd of sickly kids.
Chicalote [che-cah-lo'-tay], *m.* Mexican argemone. Argemone mexicana.
Chicano, na [che-cah'-no, nah], *a.* (Of) Mexican-American. —*m. & f.* Mexican-American, Chicano.
Chicle [chee'-clay], *m.* (Bot.) Chicle, chewing gum.
Chico, ca [chee'-co, cah], *a.* Little, small. *Chico con grande*, Both great and small. *Chico como grande*, Without exception. *Chico pleito*, A trifling matter; of small account.
Chichimeco, ca [che-che-may'-co, cah], *a.* Of Chichimec.
Chichisbeador [che-chis-bay-ah-dor'], *m.* Gallant, wooer.
Chichisbear [che-chis-bay-ar'], *va.* To woo, to court.
Chichisbeo [che-chis-bay'-o], *m.* 1. Court paid to a lady. 2. Cicisbeo, a gallant, an attendant on a lady.
Chichón [che-chone'], *m.* 1. Lump on the head. 2. Bruise. *V.* Abolladura.
Chichoncillo, cito [che-chon-theel'-lyo, thee'-to], *m. dim.* Small lump.
Chichonera [che-cho-nay'-rah], *f.* Tumbling-cap; a sort of wadded hood worn by children to protect the head against falls.
Chichota [che-cho'-tah], *f.* Used only in this phrase: *Sin faltar chichota*, It wants not an iota; it is all complete.
Chico, ca [chee'-co, cah], *m. & f.* A little boy or lad, a little chap, a little girl or lass: dear lad, dear fellow, dear lass. *Es un buen chico*, (Coll.) He is a good man.
Chicolear [che-co-lay-ar'], *va.* To joke or jest in gallantry.
Chicoleo [che-co-lay'-o], *m.* (Coll.) Joke, jest in gallantry.
Chicoria [che-co'-re-ah], *f.* *V.* Achicoria.
Chicorrotico, ca [che-cor-ro-tee'-co, cah], *a. dim.* Very little or small: applied to children.
Chicorrotín [che-cor-ro-teen'], *a.* Very small: applied to children.
Chicote, ta [che-co'-tay, tah], *m. & f.* 1. (Coll.) A fat strong boy or girl. 2. (Naut.) End of a rope or cable. 3. (Coll.) End of a cigar partly smoked.
Chicozapote [che-co-thah-po'-tay], *m.* A delicious American fruit. *V.* Zapote.
Chicha [chee'-chah], *f.* 1. Meat: used only to children. 2. Beverage made of pine-apple rinds, sugar, or molasses. *Ser cosa de chicha y nabo*, To be of little importance. *Tener pocas chichas*, To be very lean or weak.
Chícharo [chee'-chah-ro], *f.* (Bot.) Pea. Pisum sativum.
Chicharra [che-char'-rah], *f.* 1. Balm-cricket, harvest-fly, European cicada. Cicada spumaria. 2. A talkative woman. 3. Kazoo, a child's plaything making a harsh, grating noise. *Cantar la chicharra*, (Coll.) To be scorching hot.
Chicharrar [che-char-rar'], *va.* *V.* Achicharrar.
Chicharrear [che-char-ray-ar'], *vn.* To creak, to chirp: said of the balm-cricket.
Chicharrero [che-char-ray'-ro], *m.* 1. A hot place or climate. 2. One who makes or sells kazoos.
Chicharro [che-char'-ro], *m.* 1. A young tunny-fish. 2. Horse-mackerel. Scomber trachurus.
Chicharrón [che-char-rone'], *m.* Crackles, morsel of fried lard left in the pan.
Chiche [chee'-chay], *m.* (Amer. Prov.) A sauce composed of little fresh-water fishes and eels.
Chichear [chee-chay-ar'], *va.* To sound *ch* or *s* sharply in sign of displeasure; to hiss an actor or speaker.
Chicheo [che-chay'-o], *m.* Hissing a speaker.
Chichería [che-chay-ree'-ah], *f.* Tavern where *chicha* is sold.
Chichigua [che-chee'-goo-ah], *f.* (Mex Vulg.) Wet nurse.

Chifla [chee'-flah], *f.* 1. Whistle. 2. With book-binders, a paring-knife. 3. Hissing in a theatre or public meeting.
Chiflacayote [che-flah-cah-yo'-tay], *m.* A large kind of pumpkin in America.
Chifladera [che-flah-day'-rah], *f.* Whistle.
Chifladura [che-flah-doo'-rah], *f.* 1. Whistling. 2. (Coll.) Craziness.
Chiflar [che-flar'], *va.* With book-binders, to pare leather.—*vn.* 1. To whistle. 2. To mock, to jest. 3. To tipple, to drink to excess.—*vr.* 4. (Coll.) To run mad, to be crazy.
Chiflato [che-flah'-to], *m.* *V.* Silbato.
Chifle [chee'-flay], *m.* 1. Whistle. 2. Call, an instrument used to decoy birds. 3. (Naut.) Priming-horn used by the gunners of the navy. 4. (Naut.) Tide. *Aguas chifles,* Neap-tide.
Chiflete [che-flay'-tay], *m.* *V.* Chifla.
Chiflido [che-flee'-do], *m.* Whistling.
Chiflo [chee'-flo], *m.* *V.* Chifla.
Chiflón [che-flone'], *m.* Draft, draught (current of air).
Chilacayote [che-lah-cah-yo'-tay], *m.* (Bot.) American or bottle gourd. Cucurbita lagenaria.
Chilanco [che-lahn'-co], *m.* Pool or well of water remaining in a river when it has lost its current through drought.
Chilar [che-lar'], *m.* A spot planted with Chile peppers.
Chile [chee'-lay], *f.* (Bot.) American red pepper. Capsicum annuum. *Chile ancho,* Dried-up pepper in a broad shape. *Chile pasilla,* Dried-up pepper in a thin shape or form. *Chile relleno,* (Mex.) Green pepper stuffed with minced meat, coated with eggs, and fried.
Chileno, na, Chileño, ña [che-lay'-nyo, nya], *a.* Chilean; of Chile.
Chilera [che-lay'-rah], *f.* (Naut.) Row-lock hole.
Chilindrina [che-lin-dree'-nah], *f.* 1. (Coll.) Trifle, a thing of little value. *Meterse en chilindrinas,* To meddle in unimportant, but ticklish business. 2. Joke, fun, witticism.
Chilindrinero, ra [che-lin-dre-nay'-ro, rah], *a.* Meddling in trifles.
Chilindrón [che-lin-drone'], *m.* 1. Game at cards for four persons. 2. (Low) Cut in the head.
Chilote [che-lo'-tay], *m.* (Mex.) *V.* Jilote.
Chilla [cheel'-lyah], *f.* Call for foxes, hares, or rabbits. *Clavo de chilla,* Tack, a sort of nail. *Tablas de chilla,* Thin boards. *Chillas,* Kind of East India cotton stuff.
Chillado [cheel-lyah'-do], *m.* (Prov.) Roof of shingles or thin boards.—*Chillado, da, pp.* of Chillar.
Chillador, ra [cheel-lyah-dor', rah], *m.* & *f.* Person who shrieks or screams; a thing that creaks.
Chillante [cheel-lyahn'-tay], *pa.* Screaming, shrieking, screeching.
Chillar [cheel-lyar'], *vn.* 1. To scream, to shriek, to mewl. 2. To crackle, to creak. 3. To imitate the notes of birds. 4. To hiss: applied to things frying in a pan.
Chilleras [cheel-lyay'-ras], *f. pl.* (Naut.) Shot-lockers for balls.
Chillido [cheel-lyee'-do], *m.* 1. Squeak or shriek; a shrill, disagreeable sound. 2. Bawling of a woman or child. *Dar un chillido,* To utter a scream.
Chillo [cheel'-lyo], *m.* Call. *V.* Chilla.
Chillón [cheel lyone'], *m.* 1. (Coll.) Bawler, screamer, shrieker. 2. (Prov.) Common crier. 3. Nail, tack. ***Chillón real,*** Spike used to fasten large timbers or planks. *Clavo chillón,* Tack or small nail.
Chillón, na [cheel-lyone', nah], *a.* Applied to showy or tawdry colours.
Chiltipiquín, Chiltepín [cheel-te-pe-keen', cheel-tay-peen'], *m.* (Mex.) A red pepper, the size of a caper, and very pungent.
Chimate [che-mah'-tay], *m.* *V.* Chancaca.
Chimenea [che-may-nay'-ah], *f.* 1. Chimney. 2. (Met. Coll.) Head. 3. Hearth, fire-place. *Se le subió el humo a la chimenea,* The vapour has mounted to his head: spoken of one affected with drink.
Chimpancé [chim-pan-thay'], *m.* Chimpanzee, an African ape resembling man.
Chimpipe [chim-pee'-pay], *m.* (Nicaragua) Turkey.
China [chee'-nah], *f.* 1. Pebble, a small stone. 2. China-root, a medicinal root. 3. Porcelain, china, china-ware. 4. China silk or cotton stuff. *Media china,* Cloth coarser than that from China. 5. Boyish play of shutting the hands, and guessing which contains the pebble.
Chinampa [che-nahm'-pah], *f.* A small garden tract in lakes near the city of Mexico; anciently a floating garden.
Chinampero [che-nam-pay'-ro], *m.* The tiller of a *chinampa.*
Chinar [che-nar'], *vn.* (Obs.) *V.* Rechinar.
Chinarro [che-nar'-ro], *m.* A large pebble.
Chinateado [che-nah-tay-ah'-do], *m.* Stratum or layer of pebbles.
Chinazo [che-nah'-tho], *m.* 1. (Aug.) A large pebble. 2. Blow with a pebble.
Chincate [chin-cah'-tay], *m.* (Amer.) The last brown sugar which comes from the caldrons.
Chincharrazo [chin-char-rah'-tho], *m.* (Coll.) Thrust or cut with a sword. *V.* Cintarazo.
Chincharrero [chin-char-ray'-ro], *m.* Place swarming with bugs.
Chinche [cheen'-chay], *f.* 1. Bed-bug. 2. Thumbtack.
Chinchero [chin-chay'-ro], *m.* Bug-trap made of twigs.
Chinchilla [chin-cheel'-lyah], *f.* A small quadruped in Peru, well known for its fur.
Chinchín [chin-cheen'], *m.* (Cuba) Drizzling rain, mizzle.
Chincho [cheen'-cho], *m.* (Naut.) A small plumb-line used by constructors of curved timbers.
Chinchón [chin-chone'], *m.* (Obs.) *V.* Chichón.
Chinchorreo [chin-chor-ray'-o], *m.* (Prov.) Tiresome importunity or solicitation.
Chinchorrería [chin-chor-ray-ree'-ah], *f.* 1. (Obs.) Lying jest. 2. (Coll.) Mischievous tale. *V.* Chisme.
Chinchorrero, ra [chin-chor-ray'-ro, rah], *m.* & *f.* 1. (Littl. us.) Insidious tale-teller. 2. *V.* Chincharrero.
Chinchorro [chin-chor'-ro], *m.* 1. Fishing-boat used in America. 2. Kind of fishing-net. 3. A hammock used by Indians, suspended from trees. 4. The smallest rowboat on board a ship.
Chinchoso, sa [chin-cho'-so, sah], *a.* Peevish, fastidious, tiresome.
Chinela [che-nay'-lah], *f.* 1. Slipper. 2. Kind of pattens or clogs worn by women in dirty weather.
Chinero [che-nay'-ro], *m.* A china-closet, or cupboard.
Chinesco, ca [che-nes'-co, cah], *a.* Chinese; relating to China.
Chinflaina [chin-flah'-e-nah], *f.* Felt of a silk hat.
Chingana [chin-gah'-nah], *f.* (Peru, Bol.) 1. A small dram-shop, where low people resort to dance and to get drunk; a "dive." 2. A tunnel, underground gallery.
Chingar [chin-gar'], *va.* To drink protractedly.—*vr.* To get intoxicated.
Chinguirito [chin-ge-ree'-to], *m.* (Mex. and Cuba) 1. Rum from lees of sugar. 2. Draught, swallow.
Chinilla, ita [che-neel'-lyah, ee'-tah], *f. dim.* A small pebble.
Chinita [che-nee'-tah], *f.* (Amer.) *V.* Niña.
Chino, na [chee'-no, nah], *a.* Chinese. *¿Somos chinos?* Do you think me a simpleton?
Chino, *m.* The Chinese language.
Chinoidina [che-no-e-dee'-nah], *f.* Quinoidine, an alkaloid from cinchona bark.
Chipa [chee'-pah], *f.* (Amer.) 1. Wooden basket in which Indians carry fruits. 2. Strap of leather.
Chipichipi [che-pe-chee'-pe], *m.* (Mex.) Mist, drizzle, mizzle.
Chiprino, na [che-pree'-no, nah], *a.* (Poet.) Proper to or proceeding from Cyprus.
Chipriota [che-pre-o'-tah], *a.* Native of Cyprus.
Chiqueadores [che-kay-ah-do'-res], *m. pl.* Rings of tortoise-shell formerly used in Mexico as a feminine ornament.
Chiquero [che-kay'-ro], *m.* 1. Hogsty. 2. (Prov.) Hut for goats and kids. 3. (Prov.) Place where bulls are shut up in bull-feasts.
Chiquichaque [che-ke-chah'-kay], *m.* 1. (Coll.) Sawer, sawyer. 2. Noise made by things rubbing against each other.
Chiquichuite [che-ke-choo-ee'-tay], *m.* (Mex.) A willow basket.
Chiquilicuatro [che-ke-le-coo-ah'-tro], *m.* Dabber, meddler. *V.* Chisgarabís.
Chiquillada [che-keel-lyah'-dah], *f.* A childish speech or action.
Chiquillería [che-keel-lyay-ree'-ah], *f.* A great number of small children.
Chiquillo, illa [che-keel'-lyo], *m.* & *f. dim.* A small child.
Chiquirritico, ica, illo, illa, ito, ita [che-keer-re-tee'-co, ee'-cah], *a. dim.* Very small, very little.
Chiquirritín, Chiquitín [che-keer-re-teen', che-ke-teen'], *m.* (Coll.) A small boy.
Chiquitico, ca, Chiquitillo, lla [che-ke-tee'-co, cah, che-ke-teel'-lyo, lyah], *a. dim.* Very small or little.
Chiquito, ta [che-kee'-to, tah], *a. dim.* Little, small. *Hacerse chiquito,* (Met.) To dissemble or to conceal one's knowledge or power.
Chiribitas [che-re-bee'-tas], *f. pl.* (Coll.) Particles which wander in the interior of the eyes and obscure the sight.
Chiribitil [che-re-be-teel'], *m.* 1. Crib; a narrow and low little hole or corner. 2. A small room or chamber.
Chirigaita [che-re-gah'-e-tah], *f.* (Prov.) Kind of gourd.
Chirimía [che-re-mee'-ah], *f.* Oboe, a musical, wind instrument.—*m.* Oboe-player.
Chirimoya [che-re-mo'-yah], *f.* Most delicious American fruit. Anona Humboltiana, or cherimolia.
Chirimoyo [che-re-mo'-yo], *m.* The tree which yields the *chirimoya.*
Chirinola [che-re-no'-lah], *f.* 1. Game played by boys. 2. Trifle, a thing of little importance or value. ***Estar de chirinola,*** To be in good spirits.

Chiripa che-ree'-pah], *f.* (Coll.) Fortunate chance; windfall, good bargain. In billiards, a lucky stroke; a scratch, a fluke.

Chiripear [che-re-pay-ar'], *va.* 1. To make a lucky hit; to procure a windfall. 2. To make a scratch or fluke at billiards.

Chiripero [che-re-pay'-ro], *m.* A lucky person by chance.

Chirivia [che-re-vee'-ah], *f.* 1. (Bot.) Parsnip. Pastinaca sativa. 2. (Orn.) Wagtail. *V.* AGUZANIEVE.

Chirla [cheer'-lah], *f.* Mussel. *V.* ALMEJA.

Chirlador, ra [chir-lah-dor', rah], *m.* & *f.* A clamorous prattler, a talkative person.

Chirlar [chir-lar'], *vn.* To prattle, to talk much and loud.

Chirle [cheer'-lay], *m.* 1. The dung of sheep and goats. 2. A wild grape.

Chirlo [cheer'-lo], *m.* A large wound in the face, and the scar it leaves when cured.

Chirriado [chir-re-ah'-do], *m.* (Obs.) *V.* CHIRRIDO.—*Chirriado, da, pp.* of CHIRRIAR.

Chirriador, ra [chir-re-ah-dor', rah], *a.* 1. Hissing like hog's lard or other substances when fried. 2. Creaking, as a door. 3. Chirper.

Chirriar [chir-re-ar'], *vn.* 1. To hiss, as hog's lard or oil in which something is fried. 2. To creak as a door or cart. 3. To crepitate; to creep. 4. To chirp, or to chirk. 5. To sing out of tune or time.

Chirrichote [chir-re-cho'-tay], *m.* (Prov.) A presumptuous man. *Chirrichotes*, A nickname for French priests who travel in Spain.

Chirrido [chir-ree'-do], *m.* Chirping of birds; crick; chattering.

Chirrio [chir-ree'-o], *m.* The creaking noise made by carts and wagons; crick; crepitation.

Chirrión [chir-re-on'], *m.* 1. Tumbrel, a strong muck or dung cart; one-horse cart. 2. A whip-handle and lash. 3. Scraping on a violin by one who cannot play rightly.

Chirrionero [chir-re-o-nay'-ro], *m.* Scavenger, dung-cart driver.

Chirumbela [che-room-bay'-lah], *f.* *V.* CHURUMBELA.

Chirumen [che-roo'-men], *m.* Judgment. *V.* CALETRE.

Chischás [chis-chahs'], *m.* (Coll.) Clashing of swords or other side-arms.

Chisgarabís [chis-gah-ra-bees'], *m.* A dabbler, an insignificant, noisy fellow, who meddles and interferes in everything.

Chisguete [chis-gay'-tay], *m.* (Coll.) A small draft of wine; a small spout of any liquid.

Chisguetear [chis-gay-te-ar'], *va.* To drink a small draught.

Chisme [chees'-may], *m.* 1. Misreport, misrepresentation; any account maliciously false; a tale or story intended to excite discord and quarrels. 2. Variety of lumber of little value.

Chismear [chis-may-ar'], *va.* To tattle, to carry tales, to misrepresent, to misreport, to tell tales.

Chismero, ra [chis-may'-ro, rah], **Chismoso, sah** [chis-mo'-so, sah], *a.* Tattling, tale-bearing, propagating injurious rumours.

Chispa [chees'-pah], *f.* 1. Spark emitted by some igneous body, a flake of fire. 2. A very small diamond. 3. (Prov.) A short gun. 4. Small particle. *V.* MIAJA. 5. Penetration, acumen. *Fulano tiene chispa*, Such a one is very acute. *Ser una chispa*, To be all life and spirit. *Echar chispas*, (Met.) To be in a violent passion, to be looking daggers.

Chisparse [chis-par'-say], *vr.* (Amer.) To become intoxicated.

¡Chispas! [chees'-pas], *int.* Fire and tow! Blazes!

Chispazo [chis-pah'-tho], *m.* 1. The flying off of a spark from the fire and the damage it does. 2. (Met.) Tale or story mischievously circulated.

Chispear [chis-pay-ar'], *vn.* 1. To sparkle, to emit sparks. 2. To rain gently or in small drops.

Chispeo [chis-pay'-o], *m.* Sparkle, brilliancy.

Chispero [chis-pay'-ro], *m.* 1. Smith who makes kitchen utensils. 2. A name given to the low people of Madrid.

Chispero, ra [chis-pay'-ro, rah], *a.* Emitting a number of sparks.

Chispo [chees'-po], *m.* 1 (Coll.) Tipsy. 2. *V.* CHISGUETE.

Chisporrotear [chis-por-ro-tay-ar'], *vn.* (Coll.) To hiss and crackle, as burning oil or tallow mixed with water; to sputter.

Chisporroteo [chis-por-ro-tay'-o], *m.* (Coll.) Sibilation, hissing, crackling.

Chisposo, sa [chis-po'-so, sah], *a.* Sparkling, emitting sparks.

Chistar [chis-tar'], *vn.* To mumble, to mutter. *No chistó palabra*, He did not open his lips.

Chiste [chees'-tay], *m.* 1. A fine witty saying. 2. Facetiousness. 3. Fun, joke, jest. *Dar en el chiste*, To hit the nail on the head. *Chiste pesado*, Scurvy trick. *Hacer todo sin chiste*, To take things very seriously.

Chistera [chis-tay'-rah], *f.* 1. A narrow basket for fish. 2. (Coll.) A silk hat, chiefly if old and worn.

Chistosamente [chis-to-sah-men'-tay], *adv.* Facetiously, wittily, merrily, gaily.

Chistoso, sa [chis-to'-so, sah], *a.* Gay, cheerful, lively, facetious, humorous; funny.

Chita [chee'-tah], *f.* 1. The ankle-bone in sheep and bullocks. 2. Game with this bone. *No vale una chita*, It is not worth a rush. *Tirar a dos chitas*, To have two strings to one's bow. *Dar en la chita*, (Met.) To hit the nail on the head. *A la chita callando*, Secretly, very quietly, by stealth.

Chite [chee'-tay], *m.* Kind of cotton stuff; chintzes; India calico.

Chiticalla [che-te-cahl'-lyah], *m.* (Coll.) One who keeps silence and divulges not what he sees.

Chiticallar [che-te-cal-lyar'], *vn.* (Coll.) To keep silence. *Ir* or *andar chiticallando*, To go on one's tiptoes, not to make a noise.

Chito [chee'-to], *m.* A piece of wood, bone, or other substance, on which the money is put in the game of *chita*. *Irse a chitos*, (Coll.) To lead a debauched life.

¡Chito, Chitón! [chee'-to, che-tone'], *int.* Hush! not a word! hist! silence! mum! mum! *Con el rey y la inquisición chitón*, Toward the king and inquisition be silent and respectful.

Chitonisca [che-to-nees'-cah], *f.* Kind of woollen tunic which the Greeks used to wear.

Chiva [chee'-vah], *f.* Kid, a female goat.

Chival [che-vahl'], *m.* (Obs.) Herd of goats.

Chivalete [che-vah-lay'-tay], *m.* Chest of drawers with a desk for writing. *V.* ESCRITORIO.

Chivata [che-vah'-tah], *f.* (Prov.) Shepherd's club or staff.

Chivato [che-vah'-to], *m.* Kid between six and twelve months old; he-goat.

Chivero [che-vay'-ro], *m.* (Amer.) The puma, American lion.

Chivetero, Chivital [che-vay-tay'-ro, che-ve-tahl'], *m.* Fold for kids.

Chivo [chee'-vo], *m.* 1. Kid, he-goat. 2. (Prov.) Pit, a place for the lees of oil.

¡Cho! [cho], *int.* A word used by the drivers of mules or horses to make them stop: whoa!

Choca [cho'-cah], *f.* 1. Part of the game given to a hawk. 2. Stick or paddle used by soap-boilers.

Chocador, ra [cho-cah-dor', rah], *m.* & *f.* (Littl. us.) 1. One that irritates or provokes. 2. Assailant.

Chocallo [cho-cahl'-lyo], *m.* (Obs.) *V.* ZARCILLO.

Chocante [cho-cahn'-tay], *pa.* Provoking, irritating; glaring; gross.

Chocar [cho-car'], *vn.* 1. To strike, to knock, to dash against one another. 2. To jostle, to encounter, to rush against each other. 3. To meet, to fight, to combat.—*va.* To provoke, to vex, to disgust.

Chocarrear [cho-car-ray-ar'], *vn.* To joke, to jest, to act the buffoon.

Chocarrería [cho-car-ray-ree'-ah], *f.* 1. Buffoonery, low jests, scurrilous mirth. 2. Deceiving, cheating at play. *V.* FULLERÍA.

Chocarrero [cho-car-ray'-ro], *m.* 1. Buffoon, low jester, merry-andrew, mimic. 2. (Obs.) Cheat, or sharper at at play. *V.* FULLERO.

Chocarrero, ra [cho-car-ray'-ro, rah], *a.* Practising indecent raillery; scurrilous, buffoon-like.

Chocarresco, ca [cho-car-res'-co, cah], *a.* (Obs.) *V.* CHOCARRERO.

Chocilla [cho-theel'-lyah], *f. dim.* A small hut, a low cottage.

Choclar [cho-clar'], *vn.* 1. In the Spanish game of *argolla*, to drive the ball out by the rings. 2. (Obs.) To bolt into a room.

Choclo [cho'-clo], *m.* 1. *V.* CHANCLO. 2. (Amer.) Green ear of maize in a state fit for eating.

Choclón [cho-clone'], *m.* In the Spanish game of *argolla*, the driving of a ball through the rings.

Choco [cho'-co], *m.* (Prov.) The small cuttle-fish. Sepia sepiola. *V.* JIBIA.

Chocolate [cho-co-lah'-tay], *m.* 1. Chocolate. 2. Chocolate, the liquor made by a solution of chocolate in water, milk, or *atole*. *Esa ni con chocolate*, That pill wants gilding; nothing shall make me believe it.

Chocolatera [cho-co-lah-tay'-rah], *f.* Chocolate-pot.

Chocolatería [cho-co-lah-tay-ree'-ah], *f.* Shop where only chocolate is sold.

Chocolatero [cho-co-lah-tay'-ro], *m.* 1. One who grinds or makes chocolate. 2. The seller of chocolate. 3. (Mex.) A stiff north wind, but not tempestuous like that of winter.

Chocolotear [cho-co-lo-tay-ar'], *vn.* *V.* CHACOLOTEAR.

Chocha, Chochaperdiz [cho'-chah, cho-chah-per-deeth'], *f.* (Orn.) Woodcock. Scolopax rusticola.

Chochear [cho-chay-ar'], *vn.* To dote, to have the intellect impaired by age.

Chochera, Chochez [cho-chay'-rah, cho-cheth'], *f.* Dotage, the speech and action of a dotard.

Chocho, cha [cho'-cho, chah], *a.* Doting, having the intellect impaired by age.

Chocho [cho'-cho], *m.* 1. (Bot.) Lupine. *V.* ALTRAMUZ. 2. A sweetmeat or confection. *Chochos*, All sorts of sweetmeats given to children; dainties.

Chode [cho'-day], *m* (Prov.) Paste of milk, eggs, sugar, and flour.
Chofer [cho-fer'], *m.* Chauffeur, automobile driver.
Chofero [cho-fay'-ro], *m.* *V.* CHOFISTA.
Chofes [cho'-fess], *m. pl.* Lungs. *V.* BOFES.
Chofeta [cho-fay'-tah], *f.* Chafing-dish, fire-pan; a portable grate for coals.
Chofista [cho-fees'-tah], *m.* One who lives upon livers and lights.
Cholo, la [cho'-lo, lah], *a.* (Amer.) 1. Title of contempt which the whites, especially along the seaboard, give to the Indians of the baser sort and to native servants. 2. Half-breed of European and Indian parentage. 3. Familiar diminutive in kindly tone, equivalent to son, deary.
Cholla [chol'-lyah], *f.* 1. (Coll.) Skull. 2. (Met.) Faculty, powers of the mind, judgment. *No tiene cholla,* He has not the brains of a sparrow; he is shallow-pated.
Chonta [chon'-tah], *f.* A kind of palm-tree, the wood of which is harder than ebony and very elastic. Palma chonta. *Cf.* CHORITA.
Chontal [chon-tahl'], *m.* 1. A grove of chonta-trees. 2. (Mex. and C. A.) An Indian with no training.
Chopa [cho'-pah], *f.* 1. (Zool.) Kind of sea-bream. Sparus melanurus. 2. (Naut.) Top-gallant poop, or poop-royal.
Chopo [cho'-po], *m.* (Bot.) Black poplar-tree. Populus nigra.
Choque [cho'-kay], *m.* 1. Shock, clash, dash, collision. 2. Congress, rencounter, occursion. 3. (Mil.) Skirmish, a slight engagement. 4. Difference, dispute, contest; jar. 5. (Naut.) Chock, fur, rush. *Choques de henchimientos,* (Naut.) Filling-pieces. *Choques de entremises,* (Naut.) Faying-chocks.
Choquear [cho-kay-ar'], *va.* To beat the soda-ash with the paddle in order to secure soap in fine pieces.
Choquecilla [cho-kay-theel'-lyah], *f.* *V.* CHOQUEZUELA.
Choqueo [cho-kay'-o], *m.* The act of beating the soap-ashes.
Choquezuela [cho-kay-thoo-ay'-lah], *f.* (Anat.) The knee-pan, patella or rotula, a bone placed at the fore part of the joint of the knee.
Chorca [chor'-cah], *f.* (Prov.) Pit or hole dug in the ground. *V.* HOYO.
Chorcha [chor'-chah], *f.* *V.* CHOCHA.
Chordón, *m.* Raspberry jam. *V.* CHURDÓN.
Choricería [cho-re-thay-ree'-ah], *f.* *V.* SALCHICHERÍA.
Choricero [cho-re-thay'-ro], *m.* Sausage maker or seller.
Chorillo [cho-reel'-lyo], *m.* (Peru.) Mill for coarse fabrics without fulling-stocks.
Chorita [cho-ree'-tah], *m.* (Amer.) A palm-tree, the wood of which is black, solid, and heavier than ebony. Palma chonta. *V.* CHONTA.
Chorizo [cho-ree'-tho], *m.* Pork-sausage.
Chorlito [chor-lee'-to], *m.* 1. (Orn.) Curlew or gray plover. Scolopax arquata. 2. (Orn.) Red shank. Scolopax calidris, *L.* *Cabeza de chorlito,* Hare-brained, frivolous.
Chorlo [chor'-lo], *m.* Schorl, tourmalin, especially the black variety.
Chorote [cho-ro'-tay], *m.* A certain chocolate which the poor people of Venezuela take.
Chorreado, da [chor-ray-ah'-do, dah], *a.* Applied to a kind of satin.—*pp.* of CHORREAR.
Chorreadura [chor-ray-ah-doo'-rah], *f.* Dripping, dropping, welling.
Chorrear [chor-ray-ar'], *vn.* 1. To fall or drop from a spout, to outpour, to gush, to drip. 2. (Met.) To come successively, or one by one. *Está noticia está chorreando sangre,* This news is piping hot.
Chorreo [chor-ray'-o], *m.* The act and effect of dropping, dripping.
Chorrera [chor-ray'-rah], *f.* 1. Spout or place whence liquids drop. 2. Mark left by water or other liquids. 3. Ornament formerly appended to crosses or badges of military orders. 4. Frill of a shirt.
Chorretada [chor-ray-tah'-dah], *f.* (Coll.) Water or other liquid rushing from a spout. *Hablar a chorretadas,* (Met.) To speak fast and thick.
Chorrillo [chor-reel'-lyo], *m.* 1. (Dim.) A small spout of water or any other liquid. 2. The continual coming in and out-going of money. *Irse por el chorrillo,* (Met.) To drive with the current, to conform to custom.
Chorrito [chor-ree'-to], *m. dim.* A small spout of water or any other liquid.
Chorro [chor'-ro], *m.* 1. Water or any other liquid, issuing from a spout or other narrow place, gush. 2. A jet of water. 3. A strong and coarse sound emitted by the mouth. 4. Hole made in the ground for playing with nuts. *Soltar el chorro,* (Met.) To burst out into laughter. *A chorros,* Abundantly, copiously.
Chorro de arena [chor'-ro day ah-ray'-nah], *m.* Sandblast. *Limpiar con chorro de arena, va.* To sandblast.
Chorrón [chor-rone'], *m.* Hackled or dressed hemp.
Chortal [chor-tahl'], *m.* Fountain or spring at the surface of the ground.
Chota [cho'-tah], *f.* 1. A sucking kid. 2. Heifer calf.
Chotacabras [cho-tah-cah'-bras], *f.* (Orn.) Goat-sucker, churn-owl. Caprimulgus.
Chotar [cho-tar'], *va.* (Obs.) To suck. *V.* MAMAR.
Chote [cho'-tay], *m.* *V.* CHAYOTE.
Chotear [cho-tay-ar'], *va.* To tease.
Choteo [cho-tay'-o], *m.* Raillery, badinage, teasing.
Choto [cho'-to], *m.* 1. A sucking kid. 2. A calf.
Chotuno, na [cho-too'-no, nah], *a.* 1. Sucking: applied to young goats or kids. 2. Poor, starved: applied to lambs. 3. Goatish. *Oler a chotuna,* To stink like a goat.
Chova [cho'-vah], *f.* (Orn.) Jay, chough. Corvus glandarius.
Choya [cho'-yah], *f.* (Orn.) Jackdaw, crow. Corvus monedula. *V.* CORNEJA.
Choz [choth], *m.* (Coll.) Sound of a blow or stroke. *Esta especie me ha dado choz,* (Coll.) I was struck with amazement at this affair.
Choza [cho'-thah], *f.* Hut, cottage, hovel.
Chozna [choth'-nah], *f.* Great-grand-daughter.
Chozno [choth'-no], *m.* Great-grandson.
Chozo [cho'-tho], *m.* A small hut, hovel.
Chozuela [cho-thoo-ay'-lah], *f. dim.* A small hut or cottage.
Chual [choo-ahl'], *m.* A wild plant of California; a pig-weed or goose-foot. Chenopodium album, or viride. (Indian.)
Chualar [choo-ah-lar'], *m.* A spot abounding in chual plants.
Chubarba [choo-bar'-bah], *f.* (Bot.) Stone-crop. Sedum album.
Chubasco, Chubazo [choo-bahs'-co, choo-bah'-tho], *m.* (Naut.) Squall, a violent gust of wind and rain. (*Chubazo* is obsolete.)
Chubascoso, sa [choo-bas-co'-so, sah], *a.* Squally, gusty.
Chuca [choo'-cah], *f.* The concave part of a ball used by boys in play.
Chucallo [choo-cahl'-lyo], *m.* (Obs.) *V.* ZARCILLO.
Chucero [choo-thay'-ro], *m.* (Mil.) Pikeman.
Chucha [choo'-chah], *f.* 1. A female dog, bitch. 2. *¡ Chucha !* exclamation to restrain her.
Chucha [choo'-chah], *f.* Opossum, an American animal of the order Feræ. (A Peruvian name.) Didelphis.
Chuchear [choo-chay-ar'], *va.* To fowl with calls, gins, and nets.—*vn.* To whisper. *V.* CUCHICHEAR.
Chuchería [choo-chay-ree'-ah], *f.* 1. Gewgaw, bauble, a pretty trifle, a toy. 2. Tid-bit which is nice, but not expensive. 3. Mode of fowling with calls, gins, and nets.
Chuchero [choo-chay'-ro], *m.* Bird-catcher.
Chucho [choo'-cho], *m.* 1. (Orn.) Long-eared owl. Strix otus, *L.* 2. A dog. 3. *¡ Chucho !* exclamation used to call a dog.
Chuchumeco [choo-choo-may'-co], *m.* A sorry, contemptible little fellow.
Chuchupate [choo-choo-pah'-tay], *m.* A plant of the umbelliferæ, indigenous to the Pacific coast.
Chueca [choo-ay'-cah], *f.* 1. Pan or hollow of the joints of bones. 2. A small ball with which country people play at crickets. 3. (Coll.) Fun, trick. *V.* CHASCO. A soap-maker's paddle.
Chuecazo [choo-ay-cah'-tho], *m.* Stroke given to a ball.
Chufa [choo'-fah], *f.* 1. (Bot.) The edible cyperus; a sedge the root of which is used as a substitute for coffee. Cyperus esculentus. 2. (Obs.) Rhodomontade, an empty boast. *Echar chufas,* To hector, to act the bully.
Chufeta [choo-fay'-tah], *f.* 1. Jest, joke. 2. (Prov.) Small pan used to hold live coals.
Chufleta [choo-flay'-tah], *f.* Taunt, jeer, gibe, fling, scoff.
Chufletear [choo-flay-tay-ar'], *vn.* To sneer, to taunt, to show contempt.
Chufletero, ra [choo-flay-tay'-ro, rah], *a.* Taunting, sneering.
Chulada [choo-lah'-dah], *f.* 1. Droll speech or action, pleasant conversation. 2. Indecorous action of persons of bad breeding or low condition. Contemptuous word or action.
Chuleador [choo-lay-ah-dor'], *m.* (Littl. us.) Punster, jester.
Chulear [choo-lay-ar'], *va.* 1. To jest, to joke. 2. To sneer, to taunt, to ridicule.
Chulería [choo-lay-ree'-ah], *f.* A pleasing manner of acting and speaking.
Chuleta [choo-lay'-tah], *f.* Chop, cutlet.
Chulo, la [choo'-lo, lah], *m.* & *f.* 1. Punster, jester, merry-andrew. 2. An artful, sly, and deceitful person. 3. A funny person. 4. Butcher's mate or assistant. 5. Bull-fighter's assistant. 6. *V.* PÍCARO. A playful term of endearment. (Ital. fanciulo, little boy. Acad.) Lat. puellus, from puer, through plulo (Knapp).
Chulla [chool'-lyah], *f.* (Prov.) Slice of bacon.
Chumacera [choo-mah-thay'-rah], *f.* 1. (Mech.) Bearing, journal bearing, cushion. 2. (Naut.) Rowlock, a strip of wood put on the gunwale of a boat to prevent the oars from wearing it.

Chumbo, or **Higo Chumbo** [choom-bo], *m.* Indian fig.

Chumpipe [choom-pee'-pay], *m.* (Costa Rica and Nicaragua) Turkey.

Chuncaca [choon-cah'-cah], *f.* (Amer.) Cane sirup boiled, but unclarified, of which coarse sugar is made. *V.* CHANCACA.

Chunga [choon'-gah], *f.* Jest, joke. *Estar de chunga*, To be merry or in good-humour.

Chunguear [choon-gay-ar'], *vn.* (Coll.) To be merry, to be in good-humour.

Chunguero, ra [choon-gay'-ro, rah], *a.* Diverting, amusing, humorous, fun-loving.

Chunopa [choo-no'-pah], *f.* (Peru.) *V.* YUCA.

Chuño, Chuno [choo'-nyo, choo'-no], *m.* (Peru.) Dried potatoes cured on ice, for making vegetable soup.

Chupa [choo'-pah], *f.* Waistcoat; jacket (fr. Aljuba).

Chupaderito, or **Chupadorcito**, *m. dim.* Used in the phrase, *Andarse con* or *en chupaderitos*, Ineffective means for difficult tasks.

Chupadero, ra [choo-pah-day'-ro, rah], *a.* Sucking, sucker, drawing out milk or other liquids with the lips; absorbent.

Chupado, da [choo-pah'-do, dah], *a.* (Coll.) Lean, emaciated.—*pp.* of CHUPAR.

Chupador, ra [choo-pah-dor', rah], *m. & f.* 1. Sucker, one who sucks or draws out with the lips. *Chupador de niños*, A sucking-bottle; a child's coral. 2. (Amer.) Tippler, one who gets intoxicated often.

Chupadorcito [choo-pah-dor-thee'-to], *m. dim.* of CHUPADOR.

Chupadura [choo-pah-doo'-rah], *f.* Sucking, exsuction, the act and effect of sucking.

Chupaflores, Chupamiel, Chupamirtos, Chuparomeros [choo-pah-flo'-res, choo-pah-me-el', choo-pah-mir'-tos, choo-pah-ro-may'-ros], *m. & f.* (Orn.) Humming-birds. Trochili.

Chupalandero [choo-pah-lan-day'-ro], *m.* (Prov.) A kind of snail that lives on trees and plants.

Chupar [choo-par'], *va.* 1. To suck. 2. To imbibe moisture: applied to vegetables. 3. (Met. Coll.) To sponge, to hang upon others for subsistence; to fool. *Chuparse los dedos*, To eat with much pleasure, to be overjoyed. *Chupar la sangre*, (Met.) To suck one's blood, to stick to him like a leech, living at his expense.

Chupativo, va [choo-pah-tee'-vo, vah], *a.* Of a sucking nature.

Chupe [choo'-pay], *m.* A savoury stew prepared with potatoes, eggs, cheese, etc.

Chupeno, na [choo-pay'-no, nah], *a.* Attractive, delightsome.

Chupeta, illa, ita [choo-pay'-tah, eel'-lyah, ee'-tah], *f. dim.* A short jacket or waistcoat.

Chupete [choo-pay'-tay], *m.* *Ser alguna cosa de chupete*, To possess great delicacy and good taste.

Chupetada [choo-pay-tah'-dah], *f* *V.* CHUPADURA.

Chupetear [choo-pay-tay-ar'], *va.* To suck gently and by starts, as children do when they are not hungry; to suck over and over.

Chupeteo [choo-pay-tay'-o], *m.* Gentle sucking.

Chupetín [choo-pay-teen'], *m.* A man's inner garment or doublet.

Chupetón [choo-pay-tone'], *m.* The act of sucking a great quantity of liquid at once; exsuction.

Chupilote [choo-pe-lo'-tay], *m.* (Amer.) A vulture.

Chupón [choo-pone'], *m.* 1. Sucker, a young twig. 2. (Obs.) The act of sucking. 3. (Obs.) Doublet. *V.* CHUPETÍN.

Chupón, na [choo-pon', nah], *a.* (Coll.) One who cunningly deprives another of his money.

Chupu [choo'-poo], *m.* (Peru.) Trunk of a tree hacked and cut.

Chuquelas [choo-kay'-las], *m.* A cotton cloth of India.

Chuquiragua [choo-ke-rah'-goo-ah], *f.* A useful shrub of the Andes.

Chura [choo'-rah], *f.* (Peru.) Bee-glue.

Churana [choo-rah'-nah], *f.* (S. Amer.) Quiver which the Indians employ.

Churdón [choor-done'], *m.* Raspberry jam.

Churla, *f.* **Churlo**, *m.* [choor'-lah, choor'-lo]. Bag in which spices are brought from the East Indies.

Churra [choor'-rah], *f.* The little pin-tailed grouse. Tetrao alchata.—*a.* Heifer one year old.

Churrasco [choor-rahs'-co], *m.* (Amer.) Piece of meat broiled over coals.

Churrascón [choor-ras-cone'], *m.* Act and effect of scorching.

Churre [choor'-ray], *m.* (Coll.) Thick dirty grease.

Churrea [choor-ray'-ah], *f.* The Californian grouse. (Imitative.)

Churretada [choor-ray-tah'-dah], *f.* *V.* CHORRETADA.

Churretoso, sa [choor-ray-to'-so, sah], *a.* (Prov.) Gushing spouting: applied to fluids.

Churriburri [choor-re-boor'-re], *m.* (Coll.) 1. A low fellow 2. Rabble. *V.* ZURRIBURRI.

Churriento, ta [choor-re-en'-to, tah], *a.* Greasy.

Churrigueresco, ca [choor-re-gay-res'-co, cah], *a.* In the style of architecture introduced by Churriguera, Ribera, and their followers in the first part of the 18th century; overloaded, rococo.

Churriguerismo [choor-re-gay-rees'-mo], *m.* Overloading, depraved taste in ornamenting architecture.

Churriguerista [choor-re-gay-rees'-tah], *a.* Adopting the style of Churriguera.

Churillero, ra [choor-reel-lyay'ro, -rah], *m. & f.* (Obs.) Tattler, prattler, gossip.

Churro, ra [choor'-ro, rah], *a.* Applied to sheep that have coarse wool, and to their wool. *m.* a sort of fritter.

Churrullero, ra [choor-rool-lyay'-ro, rah], *m. & f.* Tattler, prattler, gossip.

Churrupear [choor-roo-pay-ar'], *vn.* To sip, to drink by small draughts.

Churrús [choor-roos'], *m.* Kind of silk stuff interwoven with a little gold and silver.

Churruscarse [choo-roos-car'-say], *vr.* To be scorched, as bread, etc.

Churrusco [choor-roos'-co], *m.* Bread too much toasted or scorched.

Churruscón [choor-roos-cone'], *m.* *V.* CHURRASCÓN.

Churumbela [choo-room-bay'-lah], *f.* Wind instrument resembling an oboe; shawm.

Churumen, *m.* *V.* CHIRUMEN.

Churumo [choo-roo'-mo], *m.* Juice or substance of a thing. *Hay poco churumo*, There is little cash, little judgment, etc.

Chus ni mus [choos ne moos]. (Coll.) *No decir chus ni mus*, Not to say a word.

Chuscada [choos-cah'-dah], *f.* Pleasantry, drollery, buffoonery, fun, joke.

Chusco, ca [choos'-co, cah], *a.* Pleasant, droll, merry.

Chusma [choos'-mah], *f.* 1. The crew and slaves of a row-galley 2. Rabble, mob.

Chuspa [choos'-pah], *f.* (Amer.) A pouch of skin used among the country folk of the La Plata to carry maté, coca, money, and such like things.

Chuza [choo' thah], *f.* (Mex.) A stroke in the game of pigeon-holes knocking all at once with one ball.

Chuzazo [choo-thah'-tho], *m.* 1. A large pike. 2. The blow or stroke given with it.

Chuzo [choo'-tho], *m.* 1. Pike. 2. (Naut.) Boarding-pike. *Chuzos*, Abundance of rain, snow, or hail. *A chuzos*, Abundantly, impetuously. *Llover a chuzos*, To rain pitch-forks, or bucketfuls. *Echar chuzos*, To brag.

Chuzón, na [choo-thone', nah], *m. & f.* 1. A crafty, artful person. 2. Wag, punster, jester.

Chuzón, *m.* (Aug.) *V* ZUIZÓN.

D

D [day] is the fifth letter of the Spanish alphabet, and the fourth of the consonants. D has the same unvaried sound it has in English in the words *dedicate*, *fed*. In pronouncing this letter the tongue must not touch the palate at all, and but barely come in contact with the teeth. In some provinces of Spain it is wrongly sounded as *th* in *although*, and at the end of a word as *th* lisped in *path*, or as *t*. In Andalusia and some parts of America it is by some made silent in the termination *ado*, *ido*, and they say *compráo*, *vendío*, instead of *comprado*, *vendido*. All these faults should be carefully avoided. D. is a contraction for *Don*, *Doña*, and Doctor; DD., doctors. As a Roman numeral, *D.* is 500.

Dabaji [dah-bah'-he], *m.* An Arabic word used by Cervantes, meaning corporal of a squad.

Dable [dah'-blay], *a.* Possible, feasible, practicable.

Dabna [dahb'-nah], *f.* (Zool.) A kind of African viper, which attacks venomous serpents and destroys injurious insects. The negroes worship it.

Dacá [dah-cah'], *adv.* (Obs.) This here, this side, on this side here. *Dacá*, or *de acá*, From this.

Daca [dah'-cah], *v. def.* Give here. *Daca acá*, Give hither. *En daca las pajas* or *daca esas pajas*, In the snap of scissors, in a trice. *Daca*, or *da acá*, or *dame acá*, Give me here.

Dacio, cia [dah'-the-o, the-ah], *a.* Dacian, relating to Dacia.—*m.* (Obs.) Tribute, tax.

Dación, [dah-the-on'], *f.* (Law) Dedition, yielding or giving up; delivery.

Dacriocistitis [dah-cre-o-this-tee'-tis], *f.* Inflammation of the lachrymal sac; dacryocystitis.

Dacrióideo, dea [dah-cre-o'-i-day-o, day-ah], *a.* Like a tear: applied to seeds.

Dacrón [dah-crone'], *m.* Dacron (trademark); polyester fiber.

Dactílado, da [dac-te-lah'-do, dah], *a.* Finger-shaped.

Dactílico, ca [dac-tee'-le-co, cah], *a.* Dactylic.

Dactilio [dac-tee'-le-o], *m.* (Zool.) A worm parasitic in man, found in the bladder.

Dactilión [dac-te-le-on'], *m.* 1. Webbed fingers or toes, dactylion. 2. An apparatus devised for finger-gymnastics.
Dáctilo [dahc'-te-lo], *m.* 1. Dactyl, a poetic foot, — ⌣ ⌣. 2. (Conch.) Kind of shell. Solon dactylus.
Dactilografía [dac-te-lo-grah-fee'-ah], *f.* Typewriting.
Dactilología [dac-te-lo-lo-hee'-ah], *f.* Dactylology, the art of talking by manual signs.
Dactilóptero [dac-te-lop'-tay-ro], *m.* The flying-fish.
Dactiloscopia [dac-te-los-co'-pe-ah], *f.* Dactyloscopy, identification and classification of fingerprinting.
Dadaísmo [dah-dah-ees'-mo], *m.* Dadaism, a literary movement.
Dádiva [dah'-de-vah], *f.* Gift, present, gratification, grant, keepsake.
Dadivosamente [dah-de-vo-sah-men'-tay], *adv.* Liberally, plentifully, bountifully.
Dadivosidad [dah-de-vo-se-dahd'], *f.* Liberality, magnificence, bounty.
Dadivoso, sa [dah-de-vo'-so, sah], *a.* Bountiful, magnificent, liberal, frank, generous.
Dado [dah'-do], *m.* 1. Die, *pl.* dice. *Dado falso*, Cogged or false dice, filled with quicksilver, with which sharpers play. *A una vuelta de dado*, At the cast of a die. 2. *Dado de la roldana*, (Naut.) Coak of a sheave. 3. (Arch.) Dado. *V.* NETO. 4. (Obs.) *V.* DONACIÓN. *Dados*, Case or grape-shot for large guns. *Dados de las velas*, (Naut.) Tablings of the bow-line cringles.—*pp.* of DAR.
Dador, ra [dah-dor', rah], *m.* & *f.* 1. Donor, giver; one who gives or bestows; God. 2. Drawer of a bill of exchange. 3. *m.* Carrier of a letter from one individual to another, bearer.
Dafnáceo, cea [daf-nah'-thay-o, thay-ah], *a.* Like the daphne, or laurel.
Dafne [dahf'-nay], *m.* (Bot.) Daphne, laurel.
Daga [dah'-gah], *f.* 1. Dagger. 2. Stove or furnace of a brick-kiln.
Daguerrotipia [dah-gher-ro-tee'-pe-ah], *f.* The art of making daguerreotypes.
Daguerrotipo [dah-gher-ro-tee'-po], *m.* Daguerreotype, a portrait made upon a prepared metal plate, and the process by which it was obtained. Important, historically, as the precursor of the photograph.
Daguilla [dah-geel'-lyah], *f.* 1. (Dim.) Small dagger. 2. (Prov.) *V.* PALILLO.
Daifa [dah'-e-fah], *f.* Mistress, concubine. (Arab.)
Daiquirí [dah-e-ke-ree'], *m.* Daiquiri, mixed alcoholic drink.
Dala [dah'-lah], *f.* (Naut.) Pump-dale of a ship.
Dale [dah'-lay], *int.* A word expressive of displeasure at the obstinacy of another. *V.* DAR.
Dalgo. (Obs.) *Hacer mucho dalgo*, To receive any one with great attention and respect.
Dalia [dah'-le-ah], *f.* (Bot.) The dahlia.
Dálmata [dahl'-ma-tah], or **Dalmático, ca** [dal-mah'-te-co, cah], *a.* Dalmatian, belonging to or native of Dalmatia.
Dalmática [dahl-mah'-te-cah], *f.* Dalmatica, vestment worn by the deacons in the Roman Catholic church.
Daltoniano, na [dahl-to-ne-ah'-no, nah], *a.* Affected with daltonism, colour-blind.
Daltonismo [dahl-to-nees'-mo], *m.* Colour-blindness, especially red-blindness; daltonism.
Dallá, *adv.* (Obs.) *V.* DE ALLÁ.
Dallador [dal-lyah-dor'], *m.* (Prov.) A mower of grass.
Dallar [dal-lyar'], *va.* (Prov.) To mow.
Dalle [dahl'-lyay], *m.* Scythe, sickle.
Dallén [dal-lyen'], *adv.* (Obs.) From the other side there; from the other side.
Dama [dah'-mah], *f.* 1. Lady, dame; a noble or distinguished woman. 2. Lady courted by a gentleman. 3. A lady of honour at court. 4. A mistress or concubine. 5. Queen in the game of chess; king in the game of draughts or checkers. *Dama de palacio*, Lady of honour at court. *Dama cortesana*, Courtesan. 6. Any woman affectedly nice. *Es muy dama*, She is excessively nice, difficult, or scrupulous. 7. American fallow deer. Cervus virginianus, *L.* *Juego de damas*, Game of draughts. *Soplar la dama*, To huff a king in the game of draughts. *Soplar la dama*, (Met.) To carry off and marry a lady who was courted by another man. 8. The actress who performs the principal parts: she is also called *primera dama*, or first actress, to distinguish her from *la segunda*, the second, or even *la tercera dama*, the third actress, who acts the secondary female parts in a play.
Damajuana [dah-ma-hoo-ah'-nah], *f.* Demijohn. (Arabic.)
Damasanio, *m.* *V.* ALISMA.
Damascado, da [dah-mas-cah'-do, dah], *a.* *V.* ADAMASCADO.
Damascena [dah-mas-thay'-nah], *f.* Damson, damascene, damask-plum, a small black plum.
Damasceno, na [dah-mas-thay'-no, nah], *a.* Damascene, native of or belonging to Damascus.
Damasco [dah-mahs'-co], *m.* 1. Damask, figured silk stuff. *Damasco de lana*, Woollen damask. 2. The Brussels apricot. 3. Damson, a small black plum.
Damasina [dah-ma-see'-nah], *f.* Silk stuff resembling damask.
Damasquillo [dah-mas-keel'-lyo], *m.* 1. Kind of cloth, of silk or wool, resembling damask. 2. (Prov.) *V.* ALBARICOQUE.
Damasquinar [dah-mas-ke-nar'], *va.* To damaskeen, incrust iron and steel, or decorate with "water" markings.
Damasquino, na [dah-mas-kee'-no, nah], *a.* 1. Damaskeened: applied to iron and steel. 2. Belonging to Damascus. *A la damasquina*, Damascus fashion.
Damero [dah-may'-ro], *m.* Checker-board, draught-board.
Damil [dah-meel'], *a.* (Obs.) Female, feminine.
Damisela [dah-me-say'-lah], *f.* 1. A young gentlewoman: applied to girls that give themselves the air of high ladies. 2. (Coll.) A courtesan.
Damnificador, ra [dam-ne-fe-cah-dor' rah], *m.* & *f.* One who damnifies.
Damnificar [dam-ne-fe-car'], *va.* To hurt, to damage, to injure.
Danchado, da [dan-chah'-do, dah], *a.* (Her.) Dentate, indented.
Danés, sa [dah-ness', sah], *a.* Danish.
Dánico, ca [dah'-ne-co, cah], *a.* Dane, Danish.
Dango, *m.* (Orn.) *V.* PLANGA.
Danta [dahn'-tah], *f.* (Zool.) Tapir. Tapir americanus.
Dante [dahn'-tay], *adv.* (Obs.) Contracted from *de* and *antes;* anterior; before.
Dante [dahn'-tay], *pa.* Giving; he who gives.
Dantellado, da [dan-tayl-lyah'-do, dah], *a.* Dentated, having the form of teeth.
Danza [dahn'-thah], *f.* 1. Dance. 2. A set, or number of dancers. 3 (Coll.) A quarrel. 4. An entangled affair. *Meter en la danza*, (Met.) To involve another in some business or dispute. *¿ Por dónde va la danza?* (Met.) To which side does the wind blow?
Danzador, ra [dan-thah-dor', rah], *m.* & *f.* Dancer.
Danzante, ta [dan-thahn'-tay, tah], *m.* & *f.* 1. Dancer. 2. A knowing person. 3. A fickle, airy person. *Hablar danzante*, To stammer.
Danzar [dan-thar'], *vn.* 1. To dance. 2. To whirl a thing round. *Sacar a danzar*, 1. To invite or engage a lady to dance. 2. To cite or to oblige one to take part in any business. 3. To make public the share which a person has taken in a business. 4. (Coll.) To introduce one's self into any business.
Danzarín, na [dan-thah-reen', nah], *m.* & *f.* 1. A fine dancer. 2. (Met.) Giddy, meddling person.
Dañable [dah-nyah'-blay], *a.* Prejudicial, condemnable.
Dañado, da [dah-nyah'-do, dah], *a.* Eternally damned.—*pp.* of DAÑAR.
Dañador, ra [dah-nyah-dor', rah], *m.* & *f.* Offender.
Dañar [dah-nyar'], *va.* 1. To hurt, to harm. 2. To damage, to injure, to mar, to impair, to spoil. 3. To weaken, to damnify. 4. (Obs.) To condemn.
Dañino, na [dah-nyee'-no, nah], *a.* Noxious, hurtful, injurious, mischievous, harmful.
Daño [dah'-nyo], *m.* Damage, hurt, injury, prejudice, harm, mischief, maim, nuisance, loss, hindrance.
Dañosamente, *adv.* Hurtfully, mischievously, harmfully.
Dañoso, sa [dah-nyo'-so, sah], *a.* Hurtful, noxious, injurious, mischievous, harmful.
Dar [dar], *va.* & *vn.* 1. To give. 2. To give, to supply, to minister, to afford. 3. To minister, to give medicines, to administer a remedy. 4. To give, to deliver, to confer, to bestow. 5. To consign, to give to another in a formal manner. 6. To hit, to strike, to beat, to knock. 7. To give, to impart, to extend, to communicate. 8. To suppose erroneously. *Dar de ojos*, (Met.) To fall into an error. 9. To consider an affair as concluded. 10. To give, to allow, to grant a position, to coincide in opinion. 11. To persist obstinately in doing a thing. 12. To appoint. 13. To sacrifice. 14. To explain, to elucidate. 15. To be situated, to look toward. 16. With *creer*, *imaginar*, and analogous verbs, to simply execute the action implied. *Dar contra alguna cosa*, To hit against. *Dar crédito*, 1. To accredit, to believe. 2. To trust, to sell on trust. *Dar cuenta de*, To account. *Dar de comer*, To feed. *Dar de*, To fall in the manner shown by the noun. *Dar en*, To engage, bind one's self, persist in. *A mal dar*, However bad. *A quien dan no escoge*, Beggars must not be choosers. *Dar bien*, To have good fortune. *Dar consigo*, To cause to fall, to throw down, to stop (trans.). *Dar el texto*, To give the authority. *Dar dado* or *de balde*, To give gratis, or for nothing. *Dar en el blanco*, To hit the mark. *Dar en el hito*, To hit the nail on the head. *Dar en rostro*, To hit in the teeth with, to reproach. *Dar fiado*, To give credit. *Dar que hacer*, To give trouble. *Dar licencia*, To give leave. *Dar memorias*, To give one's

respects. *Dar de ojos*, To meet with an unforeseen obstacle. *Dar razón.* To inform, to give an account of any thing. *Dar prestado*, To lend. *Dar a trompón* or *a bulto*, To give by the lump or bulk. *Dar que reir*, To set a-laughing. *Dar que llorar*, To fall a-crying. *Mi ventana da al campo*, My window overlooks the field. *Dar barro a la mano*, To furnish materials. *Dar culadas*, (Naut.) To strike repeatedly. *Dar de traste*, (Naut.) To run aground. *Dar al traste*, To give up a thing, an undertaking; to lose, to destroy. *Dar golpe*, (Met.) To strike the mind, to astonish. *Dar garrote*, To strangle. *Dar grima*. To strike with terror or horror. *Dar largas*, To prolong an affair. *Dar gana*, To excite a desire, to have a mind to. *Dar punto*, (Com.) To fail, to become insolvent. *Da y ten, y harás bien*, Be liberal, but prudent. *Dar que sentir*, To hurt one's feelings. *Dar que decir*, To give occasion to censure. *Dar de barato*, To allow it for peace' sake. *Darse a jugar*, To be addicted to gaming. *Dar en cara*, To stare in the face, to reproach. *Dar fuego*, (Naut.) To bream a ship. *Dar calda*, To heat the iron. *Dar calle*, To clear the way. *Dar con la entretenida*, To put off with words and excuses. *Dar con uno*, To meet a person one is looking out for. *Dar de comer al diablo*, To wrangle, to quarrel; literally, to prepare food for the devil. *Dar de sí*, To stretch. *Dar el nombre* or *el santo*, (Mil.) To give the watch-word. *Dar el sí*, To grant any thing; to consent to marry a person. *Dar en duro*, To find difficulty or repugnance to the attainment of a thing. *Dar en qué merecer*, To give trouble and uneasiness. *A mal dar, tomar tabaco*, What can't be cured must be endured. *Dar en las mataduras*, To touch one to the quick. *Dar en manías*, To be foolish. *Dar en un bajío*, (Naut.) To strike ground, to get on shore. *Dar fiador* or *fianza*, To find bail, to give security. *Dar el espíritu*, To expire, to die. *Dar guerra*, To wage war; to torment; to be very troublesome. *Dar higa*, To miss fire: applied to fire-arms. *Dar la cara*, To go to the defence of some one. *Dar* or *echar luz*, To recover health. *Dar margen*, To occasion, to cause, to give opportunity. *Dar la enhorabuena*, To rejoice in another's happiness, to congratulate. *Dar la paz*, To give an embrace, to give an image to be kissed as a token of peace and fraternity. *Dar los días*, To congratulate one on his birth-day. *Dar los buenos días*, To wish good-day. *Dar madrugón*, To get up early. *Dar mal rato*, To give uneasiness. *Dar parte*, To share with. *Dar pliego*, To present or lay before a public authority a proposal, with the terms under which a person wishes to make a contract or agreement with the king. *Dar puerta y silla*, To invite a person to come in and sit down. *Dar recados*, To greet absent friends; to invite visitors. *Dar señal*, To give earnest money, in token that a bargain is ratified. *Dar tras uno*, To persecute one. *Dar un raspadillo a un bajel*, (Naut.) To scrape the bottom and sides of a ship slightly. *Dar vez*, To give one his turn. *Dar voces*, To call, cry, or scream. *Dar vuelco a un coche*, To overset a coach. *Dar zapatetas*, To leap with joy. *Dar golpe alguna cosa*, To be surprised or struck with the Beauty or rarity of a thing. *Dar baya*, To tease. *Dar diente con diente*, To shiver with cold so that the teeth chatter. *Dé donde diere*, Inconsiderately, without reflection. *Dar de mano*, To depreciate or despise. *Dar a luz*, 1. To be delivered of a child. 2. To print, to publish. *Andar en dares y tomares*, To dispute, to contend. *Dar de baja*, To dismiss from the army. *Dar poste*, To keep a person waiting. *No dar pie, ni patada*, To take no trouble to gain an end. *Dar entre ceja y ceja*, To strike between the eyes; to make an unpleasant announcement. *Dar para peras*, To strike or punish. *Dar en el busilis*, or *en la yema*, To hit the mark, to hit the nail on the head. *Dar pie con bola*, To guess rightly. *Dar el pésame*. To express condolence. *Dar filo*, To sharpen an instrument. *Dado que*, Supposing that . . ., granted that . . . (used in argument).

Dardabasi [dar-dah-bah-see'], *m.* (Orn.) Hawk, kite.

Dardada [dar-dah'-dah], *f.* Blow with a dart.

Dárdano, na [dar'-dah-no, nah], *a.* Trojan, Dardanian.

Dardo [dar'-do], *m.* 1. Dart, a missile. 2. A fresh-water fish, about a foot long, easy of digestion, but full of spines. *Dardo de pescador*, Fishgig, fizgig, a kind of harpoon.

Dares y tomares, *m. pl.* 1. Quantity given and received. (Acad.) 2. (Coll.) Altercations, disputes.

Dargadandeta [dar-gah-dan-day'-tah], *f.* (Prov.) Nickname given to any poor impudent young girl.

Darse [dar'-say], *vr.* 1. To yield, cease resistance, give in. *Darse a*, with noun or infinitive, to execute quickly or repeatedly the action of the verb. 2. To give one's self up to virtue or vice. 3. *Darse a la vela*, (Naut.) To set sail. 4. *Darse a merced*, (Mil.) To surrender at discretion. In hunting (for birds), to halt fatigued. 5. To concern, to interest. *No se me da nada*. It gives me no concern. *Darse de las astas*, To batter one's brains, to screw one's wits; to dispute or argue pertinaciously. *Darse a perros*, To become enraged or furious. *Darse al diantre*, (Coll.) To despair. *Darse por vencido*, To surrender. *Me doy por vencido*, I give it up. *Darse las manos*, To shake hands. *Darse maña*, To manage one's affairs in an able manner; to contrive. *Darse priesa*, To make haste, to hasten, to accelerate. *Darse una panzada*, (Coll.) To be fed to satiety and sickness. *Darse una panzada de escribir*, (Met.) To get a surfeit of writing. *Darse una vuelta*, To scrutinize one's own conduct, to find out one's own faults. *Darse un repelón*, To gossip, to chat. *No me se da un bledo*, I do not care a straw. *Darse un verde con dos azules*. To have a great amusement or pleasure. *Darse por sentido*, To show resentment, to take offence. *Se me da mucho*, It is very important to me.

Dársena [dar'-say-nah], *f.* Place in a harbour for preserving and repairing ships; dock, basin. (Arab. dar sena'a.)

Data [dah'-tah], *f.* 1. Date the time at which a letter is written, or any instrument drawn up. 2. Item or article in an account. 3. An aperture or orifice made in reservoirs in order to let out a definite quantity. (Acad.) *Estar de mal data*, To be in a bad humour. *La cosa está de mala data*, The affair is in a bad state. 4. (Obs.) Written permission to do any thing.

Datar [dah-tar'], *va.* & *vn.* 1. To date, to note with the time at which any thing is written or done. 2. To date, to reckon.

Dataría [dah-tah-ree'-ah], *f.* Datary, an office of the chancery at Rome where the Pope's bulls are expedited.

Datario [dah-tah'-re-o], *m.* The principal officer of the datary.

Dátil [dah'-teel], *m.* 1. (Bot.) Date, the fruit of the common date-palm. *Dátil de raposa*, The fruit of the dwarf fan-palm. Fructus chamærops humilis. 2. Belemnites, arrow-head or finger stone.

Datilado, da [dah-te-lah'-do, dah], *a* Resembling a date.

Datilera [dah-te-lay'-rah], *f.* (Obs.) Common date-palm. Phœnix dactylifera.

Datililllo [dah-te-leel'-lyo], *m. dim.* A small date.

Dativa, *f.* The thing given.

Dativo [dah-tee'-vo], *m.* Dative, the third case of nouns.

Dato [dah'-to], *m.* 1. Datum, a fact, a truth granted and admitted; the basis of an opinion. 2. A title of high dignity in some oriental countries. *Datos*, Data.

Daturina [dah-too-ree'-nah], *f.* Daturine, the alkaloid of datura. *V.* Atropina.

Dauco [dah'-oo-co], *m.* (Bot.) Carrot. Daucus carota.

Davídico, ca [dah-vee'-de-co, cah]. *a.* Davidic, of David.

Daza [dah'-thah], *f.* 1. (Bot.) Lucern. Medicago sativa. 2. (Bot.) Panic-grass. Panicum.

De [day], *prep.* 1. Of, the sign of a genitive or possessive case, as *La ley de Dios*, The law of God. *El poder de Inglaterra*, England's power. 2. It serves to point out the matter of which a thing is made. *Vaso de plata*, A silver cup. 3. It is the sign of the ablative case. *Vengo de Flandes*, I come from Flanders. 4. It serves sometimes instead of the preposition *con*. *De intento*, On purpose. 5. It is used in place of *por*. *De miedo*, From fear. 6. It is of the same import as *desde*. *Vamos de Madrid a Toledo*, We go from Madrid to Toledo. 7. It sometimes governs the infinitive mood. *Hora de comer*, Dinner-time. 8. It is placed before adverbs of time. *De día*, By day. *De noche*, By night. 9. Sometimes marks an inference. *De aquí se infiere*, Hence it follows. 10. In familiar style it is used to give energy to an expression. *El ladrón del mozo*, The rogue of a boy. 11. It is used after many verbs to denote some, a little, a portion, etc. *Comió del pescado*, He ate some fish. *Bebió del vino*, He drank some wine. 12. It is prefixed to many verbs, nouns, etc., altering their sense, as from *poner*, to put or to place, is formed *deponer*, to depose, etc. 13. (Obs.) To. *Bueno de comer*, Good to eat. *De balde*, For nothing, gratis. (See Knapp, § 631 Ramsey, § 1440.)

Dea [day'-ah], *f.* (Poet.) Goddess. *V* Diosa.

Deal [day-ahl'], *a.* Like a goddess, divine (rare).

Dealbación [day-al-bah-the-on'], *f.* (Chem.) Making white by means of fire.

Deán [day-ahn'], *m.* Dean, an ecclesiastical dignitary.

Deanato, Deanazgo [day-ah-nah'-to, day-ah-nahth'-go], *m.* Deanship.

Debajo [day-bah'-ho], *adv.* Under, underneath, below. *Debajo de mano*,

Underhand, privately.—*prep.* Under, subordinate, dependent.

Debate [day-bah'-tay], *m.* Debate, altercation, expostulation, discussion, contention.

Debatir [day-bah-teer'], *va* 1. To debate, to argue, to discuss. 2. To combat, to engage with arms. 3. To expostulate.

Debe [day'-bay], *m.* (Com.) The debtor side of an account, debit, Dr. *Debe y haber*, Debit and credit.

Debelar [day-bay-lar'], *va.* To debellate, to conquer.

Deber [day-berr'], *m.* 1. Obligation, duty. 2. Debt. *Hacer su deber*, To fulfil one's duty.

Deber [day-berr'], *va.* 1. To owe, not to pay a debt which is due. 2. To be obliged to, to be to, must, ought, would, have to. *Debía ser*, Must have been. *Deber de*, Must. *Deberse*, To be owed, to be due. *Debe de estar frío*, It must be cold.

Debidamente, *adv.* 1. Justly, with moderation and justice. 2. Duly, exactly, perfectly.

Debido, da [day-bee'-do, dah], *a.* Due, proper. *En forma debida*, In due or proper form. *Debido a las circunstancias*, Due to circumstances

Débil [day'-beel], *a.* 1. Feeble, weak, extenuated, debilitated, faintly, sickly, infirm. 2. Feeble, weak. 3. Fragile, frail. 4. Pusillanimous, mean-spirited.

Debilidad [day-be-le-dahd'], *f.* 1. Debility, weakness, languor. 2. Weakness, feebleness, want of strength. 3. (Met.) Pusillanimity, fondness, craziness; frailty.

Debilitación [day-be-le-tah-the-on'], *f.* Debilitation, extenuation.

Debilitar [day-be-le-tar']. *va.* To debilitate, to weaken, to extenuate, to enfeeble, to enervate.

Débilmente [day'-beel-men-tay], *adv.* Weakly, feebly, faintly, lamely.

Débito [day'-be-to], *m.* Debt. *Débito* or *débito conyugal*, Conjugal duty.

Debitorio [day-be-to'-re-o], *m.* Contract of bargain and sale upon credit, by virtue of a partial payment, until settlement of the debt.

Debó [day-bo'], *m.* Instrument used for scraping skins, scraper.

Debut [day-boo'], *m.* Debut.

Debutar [day-boo-tar'], *vn.* To make one's debut, to present for the first time.

Deca [day'-cah]. Greek prefix, meaning ten.

Década [day'-cah-dah], *f* Decade, the number or sum of ten.

Decadencia [day-cah-den'-the-ah], *f.* Decay, decline, fading, failing, decaying. *Ir en decadencia*, To be on the decline.

Decadente, *pa.* Decaying, declining.

Decaédro, dra [day-cah'-ay-dro, drah], *m.* & *f.* Decahedron, a solid of ten faces.

Decaer [day-cah-err'], *vn.* 1. To decay, to decline, to fail, to languish, to grow weak, to fade. 2. (Naut.) To fall to leeward.

(*Yo decaigo, yo decaí, yo decaiga*, from *Decaer.* *V.* Caer.)

Decágono [day-cah'-go-no], *m.* Decagon, a polygon of ten sides or angles.

Decagramo [day-cah-grah'-mo], *m.* Decagramme, the weight of ten grammes

Decaído, da [day-cah-ee'-do, dah], *a.* Crestfallen, dejected, dispirited.

Decaimiento [day-cah-e-me-en'-to], *m.* Decay, failing, decline, weakness.

Decalitro [day-cah-lee'-tro], *m.* Decalitre, ten litres.

Decálogo [day-cah'-lo-go], *m.* Decalogue, the Ten Commandments.

Decámetro [day-cah'-may-tro], *m.* Decametre, the length of ten metres.

Decampamento [day-cam-pah-men'-to], *m.* Decampment, the act of shifting the camp.

Decampar [day-cam-par'], *vn.* To decamp.

Decanato [day-cah-nah'-to], *m.* Dignity of the senior of any community.

Decandrio, dria [day-cahn'-dre-o, ah], *a.* Decandrous, having ten stamens. —*f. pl.* Decandria, plants whose flowers have ten stamens.

Decano [day-cah'-no], *m.* Senior, the most ancient member of a community or corporation.

Decantación [day-can-tah-the-on'], *f.* Decantation, pouring off.

Decantar [day-can-tar'], *va.* 1. To cry up, to exaggerate or magnify a thing. 2. (Obs.) To turn any thing from a right line and give it an oblique direction. 3. To decant, to draw off liquor.

Decapétalo, la [day-cah-pay'-tah-lo, lah], *a.* Having ten petals; decapetalous.

Decapitación [day-cah-pe-tah-thē-on'], *f.* Decapitation, beheading.

Decárea [day-cah'-ray-ah], *f.* Dekâre. ten âres.

Decasílabo [day-cah-see'-lah-bo], *a* (Poet.) Having ten syllables.

Decastilo [day-cas-tee'-lo], *m.* (Arch.) Decastyle, an assemblage of ten pillars.

Deceleración [day-thay-lay-rah-the-on'], *f.* (Phy.) Deceleration.

Decena [day-thay'-nah] *f.* 1. Denary, the number of ten. 2. (Prov.) Company or party of ten persons. 3. (Mus.) Consonance made of an octave and a third; a tenth.

Decenal [day-thay-nahl'], *a.* Decennial, a space of ten years.

Decenar [day-thay-nar'], *m.* A squad or crew of ten.

Decencia [day-then'-the-ah], *f.* 1. Decency, propriety of form or conduct. 2. Decency, reservedness, honesty, modesty.

Decenio [day-thay'-ne-o], *m.* Space of ten years; decennial.

Deceno, na [day-thay'-no, nah], *a* Tenth, ordinal of ten.

Decentar [day-then-tar'], *va.* 1. To commence the use of things not before used. 2. To begin to lose that which had been preserved.—*vr.* To wound, to gall or injure the skin or body; to be bed-ridden.

Decente [day-then'-tay], *a.* 1. Decent, just, honest, becoming, fit, suitable, decorous. 2. Convenient, reasonable. 3. Decent, modest, grave, genteel. 4. Of honest, but not noble parents.

Decentemente, *adv.* 1. Decently, fairly, honourably. 2. Decently, without immodesty, comely. 3. (Iron.) Abundantly.

Decenvirato [day-then-ve-rah'-to], *m.* Decemvirate.

Decepción [day-thep-the-on'], *f.* Deception, illusion; disappointment.

Decepcionar [day-thep-the-o-nar'], *va.* To disappoint; to disillusion.—*vr.* To be disappointed.

Deceso [day-thay'-so], *m.* (Obs.) Decease, a natural death.

Deci [day'-the]. A Latin prefix, signifying one-tenth.

Deciárea [day-the-ah'-ray-ah], *f.* Deciâre, one-tenth of an âre: 10 sq. metres.

Decibel [day-the-bel'], or **Decibelio** [day-the-bay'-le-o], *m.* (Phy.) Decibel.

Decible [day-thee'-blay], *a.* Expressible, that which may be expressed.

Decidero, ra [day-the-day'-ro, rah], *a.* What may be said without inconvenience or impropriety.

Decidido, da [day-the-dee'-do, dah], *a.* Determined, decided.

Decidir [day-the-deer'], *va.* To decide, to determine, to resolve, to conclude. —*vr.* To decide, to be determined.

Decidor, ra [day-the-dor', rah], *m.* & *f.* 1. One who speaks with fluency and elegance. 2. A wit. 3. (Obs.) Versifier, poet.

(*Yo deciento, yo deciente*, from *Decentar.* *V.* Acertar.)

Decigramo [day-the-grah'-mo], *m.* Decigramme, one-tenth gramme.

Decilitro [day-the-lee'-tro], *m.* Decilitre, one-tenth litre.

Décima [day'-the-mah], *f.* 1. (Poet.) A Spanish stanza consisting of ten verses of eight syllables. 2. Tenth, tithe, the tenth part.

Decimal [day-the-mahl'], *a.* 1. Decimal. 2. Belonging to tithes. *Rentas decimales*, Tithe-rents.

Décimanovena [day'-the-mah-no-vay'-nah], *f.* One of the registers of the pipes of an organ.

Decimar [day-the-mar'], *va.* (Obs.) *V.* Diezmar.

Decímetro [day-thee'-may-tro], *m.* Decimetre, one tenth of a metre.

Décimo, ma [day'-the-mo, mah], *a.* Tenth, ordinal of ten.

Décimoctavo, va [day'-the-moc-tah'-vo, vah], *a.* Eighteenth.

Décimocuarto, ta, *a.* Fourteenth.

Décimonono, na [day'-the-mo-no'-no, nah], *a.* Nineteenth.

Décimonoveno, na [day'-the-mo-no-vay'-no, nah], *a.* *V.* Décimonono.

Décimoquinto, ta [day'-the-mo-keen'-to, tah], *a.* Fifteenth.

Décimoséptimo, ma [day'-the-mo-sep'-te-mo, mah], *a.* Seventeenth.

Décimosexto, ta [day'-the-mo-sex'-to, tah], *a.* Sixteenth.

Decimotercio, cia [day'-the-mo-terr'-the-o, ah], *a.* Thirteenth.

Deciochono, na [day-the-o-chay'-no, nah], *a.* 1. Eighteenth. 2. Kind of cloth having a warp of 1,800 threads. 3. *V.* Dieciocheno.

Decir [day-theer'], *va.* 1. To say or utter, to tell, to speak, to express by words. 2. To assure, to persuade. 3. To name, to give a name to a person or place. 4. To be conformable, to correspond. 5. To denote, to mark, to be a sign of. 6. To declare or depose upon oath. 7. (Obs.) To verify. *Decir de repente*, To make verses off hand. *Decir bien*, To speak fluently or gracefully; to explain a thing well. *Decir tijeretas*, To persist stubbornly in a matter of little importance. *¡Digo!* I say; hark; used in calling or speaking to. *Por mejor decir*, More properly speaking. *El decir de las gentes*, The opinion of the people. *Decir que sí*, To affirm any thing *Decir que no*, To deny. *Decir por decir*, To talk for the sake of talking *Dije para mi capote*, I said in my sleeve. *Decir su atrevido pensamiento* or *su dolor*, To make an offer of marriage. *Como dijo el otro*, Used of an unknown author, or when a name cannot be recalled. *Decir alguna cosa con la boca chica*, To offer a thing merely for form's sake. *La misa dígala el cura*, Leave the priest to say mass; reproach to those who undertake what they cannot do. *No dice más la lengua que lo que siente el corazón*, Out of the fulness of the heart the mouth speaketh. *¿Lo he de decir cantado y rezado?* Must I say it in so many words? *No sé qué* *decir*, How can I tell? *¿Qué quiere decir eso?* What does that mean? *Ello dirá*, We shall see. *Sin decir agua va*, Without warning. *Por más que Vd. diga*, You may say what you will.

Decir [day-theer'], *m.* A notable saying. *Decires*, Idle talk, false rumours, scandal, slander.

Decisión [day-the-se-on'], *f.* 1. Decision, determination, resolution, issue. 2. Decision, judgment by court of justice. 3. Verdict by a jury. 4. Disposition.

Decisivamente, *adv.* Decisively.

Decisivo, va [day-the-see'-vo, vah], *a.* Decisive, final, conclusive, decretory.

Decisorio, ria [day-the-so'-re-o, ah], *a.* (Law) Decisive, concluding, decisory.

Declamación [day-clah-mah-the-on'], *f.* 1. Declamation, harangue, oration, discourse. 2. A speech delivered, an oratorial invective. 3. Declamation, a discourse addressed to the passions. 4. Delivery. 5. The manner of reciting theatrical compositions. 6. Panegyric.

Declamador, ra [day-clah-mah-dor', rah], *m.* & *f.* Declaimer, exclaimer.

Declamar [day-clah-mar'], *vn.* To declaim, to harangue.

Declamatorio, ria [day-clah-ma-to'-re-o, ah], *a.* Declamatory.

Declaración [day-clah-rah-the-on'], *f.* 1. Declaration. 2. Declaration, interpretation, exposition. 3. Manifest, manifestation; account. 4. Overture, proposal. 5. (Law) Deposition.

Declaradamente [day-clah-rah-dah-men'-tay], *adv.* Declaredly, avowedly.

Declarado, da [day-clah-rah'-do, dah], *a.* & *pp.* of DECLARAR. 1. Declared. 2. Applied to a person who speaks too plainly.

Declarador, ra [day-clah-rah-dor', rah], *m.* & *f.* Declarer, expositor.

Declarante [day-clah-rahn'-tay], *m.* Declarer, one who declares or explains; a witness in the act of being examined. *Juan declarante*, A talkative person, who speaks his mind too freely

Declarar [day-clah-rar'], *va.* 1. To declare, to manifest, to make known. 2. To expound, to explain, to exemplify. 3. (Law) To determine and decide, to find. 4. (Law) To witness or depose upon oath.—*vr.* To declare one's opinion, to explain one's mind.

Declarativo, va [day-clah-ra-tee'-vo, vah], *a.* Declarative, assertive.

Declaratorio, ria [day-clah-rah-to'-re-o, ah], *a.* Declaratory, explanatory

Declinable [day-cle-nah'-blay], *a.* (Gram.) Declinable, having variety of terminations.

Declinación [day-cle-nah-the-on'], *f.* 1. Declination, descent, decay, fall, decline, falling. 2. (Gram.) Declination, the declension of nouns. 3. (Ast.) Declination, distance of a star or planet from the equator. 4. Deviation of a wall or building from facing one of the cardinal points of the compass. 5. Magnetic variation of the needle from the pole.

Declinante [day-cle-nahn'-tay], *a.* Declining, bending down.

Declinar [day-cle-nar'], *vn.* 1. To decline, to lean downward. 2. To decline, to sink, to be impaired, to decay, to degenerate, to abate, to diminish (of diseases). 3. To be finished or reach the last. 4. (Naut.) To vary from the true magnetic meridian. *Va declinando el día*, It is near twilight.—*va.* 1. (Gram.) To decline a word by various terminations. 2. To challenge a judge, to transfer a cause to another tribunal: in this last sense it is always used with the word *jurisdicción*.

Declinatoria [day-cle-nah-to'-re-ah], *f.* (Law) Plea which attacks the competency of a judge.

Declinatorio [day-cle-nah-to'-re-o], *m.* Declinator, or declinatory, an instrument used in dialing.

Declive, Declivio [day-clee'-vay, day-clee'-ve-o], *m.* Declivity, inclination downward, slope, fall. (Ry.) Gradient, grade.

Declividad [day-cle-ve-dahd'], *f.* Declivity.

Decocción [day-coc-the-on'], *f.* Decoction.

Decoctivo, va [day-coc-tee'-vo, vah], *a.* Digestive.

Decolación [day-co-lah-the-on'], *f.* 1. Separation of the parts of an organ which ought to act together. 2. Decapitation of the fœtus in perilous presentations.

Decoloración [day-co-lo-rah-the-on'], *f.* Decoloration, loss of colour; decolorization, bleaching, blanching.

Decolorar [day-co-lo-rar'], *va.* To remove the colour from any substance, to decolourize.—*vr.* To lose colour.

Decolorímetro [day-co-lo-ree'-may-tro], *m.* Decolorimeter.

Decombustión [day-com-boos-te-on'], *f.* An operation to destroy the oxidation of a body which has undergone combustion.

Decomisar [day-co-me-sar'], *va.* To confiscate, to seize, to forfeit.

Decomiso [day-co-mee'-so], *m.* Confiscation, forfeiture, seizure.

Decoración [day-co-rah-the-on'], *f.* Decoration, ornament.—*pl.* The scenery and curtains of a theatre.

Decorador [day-co-rah-dor'], *m.* (Littl. us.) Decorator.

Decorar [day-co-rar'], *va.* 1. To decorate, to adorn, to embellish, to furnish. 2. To illustrate, to ennoble, to honour, to exalt. 3. To learn by heart. 4. To recite, to repeat.

Decoro [day-co'-ro], *m.* 1. Honour, respect, reverence due to any person. 2. Circumspection, gravity, integrity. 3. Purity, honesty. 4. Decorum, decency, civility.

Decorosamente, *adv.* Decently, decorously.

Decoroso, sa [day-co-ro'-so, sah], *a.* Decorous, decent.

Decorticación [day-cor-te-cah-the-on'], *f.* Decortication, the act of stripping the bark or husk.

Decrecer [day-cray-therr'], *vn.* To decrease, to diminish.

Decremento [day-cray-men'-to], *m.* Decrement, decrease, diminution, declension, wane.

Decrepitación [day-cray-pe-tah-the-on'], *f.* (Chem.) Decrepitation, a crackling noise as made by salt when heated.

Decrepitante [day-cray-pe-tahn'-tay], *pa.* (Chem.) Decrepitant.

Decrepitar [day-cray-pe-tar'], *va.* & *vn.* 1. To decrepitate, to calcine salt until it has ceased to crackle in the fire. 2. To decrepitate, to crackle when put over the fire: applied to salts.

Decrépito, ta [day-cray'-pe-to, tah], *a.* Decrepit, worn with age.

Decrepitud [day-cray-pe-tood'], *f.* Decrepitude, the last stage of decay; old age.

Decretación [day-cray-tah-the-on'], *f.* (Littl. us.) Determination, establishment.

Decretal [day-cray-tahl'], *f.* Decretal, letter or rescript of the Pope. *Decretales*, Decretals, a collection of letters and decrees of the Popes.—*a.* Decretal.

Decretalista [day-cray-tah-lees'-tah], *m.* Decretist, one that draws up or studies the rescripts, letters, and decrees of Popes.

Decretar [day-cray-tar'], *va.* 1. To decree, to determine, to resolve. 2. (Law) To give a decree or a determination in a suit.

Decretero [day-cray-tay'-ro], *m.* 1. Catalogue or list of the names and offences of criminals. 2. Decretal, collection of decrees.

Decretista [day-cray-tees'-tah], *m.* Decretist, one who expounds or explains the decretals.

Decreto [day-cray'-to], *m.* 1. Decree, decision, resolution. 2. Decree, order or determination issued in the king's name. 3. A judical decree. 4. In canon law, decree or ordinance enacted by the Pope with the advice of his cardinals. 5. (Obs.) Opinion, vote, advice. *Decretos de cajón*, Common decrees, not requiring any peculiar formality of the law.

Decretorio, ria [day-cray-to'-re-o, ah], *a.* Decretory, critical: applied to the days when a judgment may be formed on the issue of a fit of illness.

Decúbito [day-coo'-be-to], *m.* 1. (Med.) Decubitus, the position of a patient in bed.

Décuplo, pla [day'-coo-plo, plah], *a.* Decuple, tenfold.

Decuria [day-coo'-re-ah], *f.* 1. Ten Roman soldiers under a decurion. 2. In the Spanish schools, the assembly of ten students to take their lessons.

Decuriato, [day-coo-re-ah'-to], *m.* Any one of the students belonging to a *decuria* in the Spanish schools.

Decurión [day-coo-re-on'], *m.* 1. Decurion, the chief or commander of ten Roman soldiers. 2. In the Spanish schools, the monitor or student who has the care of ten other students, and gives them lessons. *Decurión de decuriones*, A chief monitor who superintends the rest.

Decurrente [day-coor-ren'-tay], *a.* Decurrent, applied to the stem: said of leaves.

Decursas [day-coor'-sas] *f. pl.* (Law) Arrears of rent.

Decurso [day-coor'-so], *m.* Course, succession of movement or time.

Decusación [day-coo-sah-the-on'], *f.* 1. Decussation, intercrossing of nerve-fibres. 2. The spot of intersection of such fibres.

Decusado, da [day-coo-sah'-do, dah], *a.* Decussate, intersected.

Dechado [day-chah'-do], *m.* 1. Sample, pattern, design, standard. 2. Linen, on which young girls perform several sorts of needlework. 3. Example, pattern, or model of virtue and perfection.

Dedada [day-dah'-dah], *f.* 1. That which can be taken up with the finger at once, a pinch. *Dedada de miel*, Adulation, flattery, wheedling. *Dar a uno una dedada de miel*, (Met.) To put a cheat on one, to deceive; literally, to give one a fingerful of honey 2. Triglyph of a Doric frieze.

Dedal [day-dahl'], *m.* 1. Thimble. 2 A leather finger-stall used by calkers on the little finger of the left hand.

Dedalera [day-dah-lay'-rah], *f.* (Bot.) Foxglove. Digitalis purpurea.

Dédalo [day'-dah-lo], *m.* 1. A labyrinth, an entanglement. 2. Proper name, Dædalus.

Dedicación [day-de-cah-the-on'], *f.* Dedication, the act of dedicating, consecration; inscription.

Dedicante [day-de-cahn'-tay], *pa.* Dedicating, dedicator.
Dedicar [day-de-car'], *va.* 1. To dedicate, to devote, to consecrate. 2. To inscribe a literary work to a patron. *Dedicarse a alguna cosa,* To apply one's self to a thing.
Dedicativo, va [day-de-cah-tee'-vo, vah], *a.* *V.* DEDICATORIO.
Dedicatoria [day-de-cah-to'-re-ah], *f.* Dedication, an address by which a literary composition is inscribed to a patron or friend.
Dedicatorio, ria [day-de-cah-to'-re-o, ah], *a.* Dedicatory, containing or serving as a dedication.
Dedición [day-de-the-on'], *f.* Unconditional surrender of a town to ancient Rome.
Dedil [day-deel'], *m.* Thumb-stall of linen or leather used by reapers.
Dedillo, ito [day-deel'-lyo], *m. dim.* A little finger. *Saber una cosa al dedillo,* To know a thing perfectly.
Dedo [day'-do], *m.* 1. Finger. 2. Toe. 3. The forty-eighth part of a Spanish yard, or *vara.* 4. A finger's breadth, a small bit. *Ganar a dedos,* To gain by inches. *Meter los dedos,* To pump one. *Señalarle con el dedo,* To point at another with the finger. *Estar a dos dedos de la eternidad,* To be on the brink of eternity. *Dedo pulgar,* Thumb. *Dedo índice* or *saludador,* The index or fore-finger. *Dedo del corazón, cordial* or *de enmedio,* Middle finger. *Dedo anular,* The ring-finger. *Dedo meñique* or *auricular,* The little finger. *Todo da* or *cae en el dedo malo,* (Prov.) Everything falls on the sore spot. *A dos dedos de,* Very near to. *Chuparse los dedos,* To eat, say, do, or hear something with delight. *Meter a uno los dedos,* To pretend to believe the contrary of what one knows certainly. *Morderse los dedos,* To be revengefully angry. *Mamarse el dedo,* To pretend ignorance or difficulty in understanding what is said. *No mamarse el dedo,* To be awake, not easily deceived. *Poner bien los dedos,* To play an instrument skilfully. *Poner los cinco dedos en la cara,* To strike a person in the face with the open hand. *Tener sus cinco dedos en la mano,* Not to yield to another in valour or power.
Deducción [day-dooc-the-on'], *f.* 1. Deduction, derivation, origin, consequence. 2. Deduction, that which is deducted. 3. (Mus.) The natural progression of sounds.
Deducible [day-doo-thee'-blay], *a.* (Littl. us.) Deducible, inferable.
Deducir [day-doo-theer'], *va.* 1. To deduce, to collect, to infer as a consequence; to fetch, to devise, to draw. 2. To allege in pleading, to offer as a plea. 3. To subtract, to deduct, to extract.
Deductivo, va [day-dooc-tee'-vo, vah], *a.* (Littl. us.) Deducive.
(*Yo deduzco, yo deduzca; yo deduje, yo dedujera;* from *Deducir.* *V.* CONDUCIR.)
Defácile [day-fah'-the-lay], *adv.* Easily.
Defacto [day-fac'-to], *adv.* In fact, actually, effectually. = DE HECHO.
Defalcar, *va.* *V.* DESFALCAR.
Defecación [day-fay-cah-the-on'], *f.* 1. Defecation, purification of a liquid from lees or sediment. 2. Defecation, voiding excrement.
Defecadora [day-fay-cah-do'-rah], *f.* In sugar refining, defecating pan, second boiler.
Defecar [day-fay-car'], *va.* 1. To defecate, purify from lees, dregs, or polluting matter. 2. To defecate, void excrement.
Defección [day-fec-the-on'], *f.* Defection, apostasy; revolt.
Defectible [day-fec-tee'-blay], *a.* Defectible, imperfect, deficient.
Defectillo [day-fec-teel'-lyo], *m. dim.* Slight fault or defect.
Defectivo, va [day-fec-tee'-vo, vah], *a.* Defective, imperfect.
Defecto [day-fec'-to], *m.* 1. Defect, failing, fault. 2. Defect, any natural imperfection.—*pl.* (Print.) Sheets remaining after a day's work in order to complete the full number. *Poner defectos,* To find fault.
Defectuosamente, *adv.* Defectively, faultily, deficiently.
Defectuoso, sa [day-fec-too-oh'-so, sah], *a.* Defective, imperfect, faulty.
Defendedero, ra [day-fen-day-day'-ro, rah], *a.* Defensible.
Defendedor, ra [day-fen-day-dor', rah], *a.* & *m.* & *f.* *V.* DEFENSOR.
Defender [day-fen-derr'], *va.* 1. To defend, to protect, to guard. 2. To defend, to make good, to justify, to assert, to maintain. 3. To defend, to vindicate. 4. To veto, to prohibit, to forbid. 5. To resist, to oppose. 6. To defend a place, a cause, etc.; to fence.
Defendible [day-fen-dee'-blay], *a.* Defensible.
Defendido [day-fen-dee'-do], *m.* A client.
Defenecimiento [day-fay-nay-the-me-en'-to], *m.* (Com. Prov.) Settlement of an account.
Defensa [day-fen'-sah], *f.* 1. Defence, safeguard, arms. 2. Defence, vindication, justification, apology. 3. Defence, guard, shelter, protection; fence. 4. Defence, in law, the defendant's reply. 5. (Sports) Defense. 6. Tusk. 7. Horn. *Legítima defensa,* (For.) Self-defense. *Defensas,* 1. Fortifications, defenses. 2. (Naut.) Skids. 3. (Naut.) Fenders.
Defensa [day-fen'-sah], *m.* (Sports) Back.
Defensa civil [day-fen'-sah the-veel'], *f.* Civil defense.
Defensión [day-fen-se-on'], *f.* Safeguard, defence.
Defensiva [day-fen-see'-vah], *f.* Defensive. *Estar a la defensiva,* or *ponerse sobre la defensiva,* To be upon the defensive, to put one's self upon the defensive.
Defensivo [day-fen-see'-vo], *m.* 1. Defence, safeguard, preservative. 2. Piece of linen steeped in any medicated liquor, and applied to some part of the body, to refresh and strengthen it.
Defensivo, va [day-fen-see'-vo, vah], *a.* Defensive, that which serves as a defence or safeguard; justificatory, defensory.
Defensor, ra [day-fen-sor', rah]. 1. Defender or keeper, maintainer, conservator, protector, supporter. 2. (Law) A lawyer appointed by a court of justice to defend one absent, or one who cannot pay a defender. *V.* ABOGADO DE POBRES.
Defensoria [day-fen-so-ree'-ah], *f.* The duty and office of a lawyer appointed by a judge to defend a person who is absent, or who has no defender.
Defensorio [day-fen-so'-re-o], *m.* Defence, an apologetic writing in favour of any person or thing; a memoir, a manifesto.
Deferencia [day-fay-ren'-the-ah], *f.* Deference, complaisance, condescension.
Deferente [day-fay-ren'-tay], *a.* Assenting, deferring to the opinion of another; deferent.—*m. pl.* The vasa deferentia of the testicles.
Deferir [day-fay-reer'], *vn.* To defer, to pay deference to another's opinion, to yield to another's judgment.—*va.* To communicate, to share in the jurisdiction or power.
Defibríneo, a [day-fe-bree'-nay-o, ah], *a.* Defibrinated.
Deficiencia [day-fe-the-en'-the-ah], *f.* Deficiency, imperfection. (Antiq.)
Deficiente [day-fe-the-en'-tay], *a.* Defective, faulty, deficient.
Déficit [day'-fe-theet], *m.* Deficit.
(*Yo defiendo, yo defienda,* from *Defender.* *V.* ATENDER.)
(*Yo defiero, yo defiera; él defirió, defiriera;* from *Deferir.* *V.* ASENTIR.)
Definible [day-fe-nee'-blay], *a.* Definable.
Definición [day-fe-ne-the-on'], *f.* 1. Definition. 2. Decision, determination. *Definiciones,* Statutes of military orders.
Definido, da [day-fe-nee'-do, dah], *a.* Definite.—*pp.* of DEFINIR.
Definidor [day-fe-ne-dor'], *m.* 1. Definer. 2. In some religious orders, one of the members who compose, under the presidency of their superior, a chapter or assembly to govern the order.
Definir [day-fe-neer'], *va.* 1. To define, to describe, to explain. 2. To decide, to determine. 3. (Pict.) To conclude any work, finishing all its parts, even the least important, with perfection.
Definitivamente, *adv.* Definitively.
Definitivo, va [day-fe-ne-tee'-vo, vah], *a.* Definitive, determinate.
Definitorio [day-fe-ne-to'-re-o], *m.* 1. Chapter or assembly of the chiefs of religious orders, to deliberate on the affairs of the order. 2. House or hall where the above chapters are held.
Deflagración [day-flah-grah-the-on'], *f.* Deflagration, sudden burning.
Deflagrador [day-flah-grah-dor'], *m.* Deflagrator, ignitor.
Deflagrar [day-flah-grar], *va.* To deflagrate, to cause to burn.
Deflegmación [day-fleg-mah-the-on'], *f.* (Med.) Expectoration.
Deflegmar [day-fleg-mar'], *vn.* To become free from water, as spirituous liquors; to dephlegmate, concentrate.
Deflujo [day-floo'-ho], *m.* (Ast.) The recession of the moon from any planet.
Defoliación [day-fo-le-ah-the-on'], *f.* Defoliation, the shedding of leaves.
Deformación [day-for-mah-the-on'], *f.* Deformation; defacing.
Deformador [day-for-mah-dor'], *m.* One who deforms or disfigures.
Deformar [day-for-mar'], *va.* To deform, to disfigure, to misshape.
Deformatorio, ria [day-for-mah-to'-re-o, ah], *a.* Deforming, disfiguring.
Deforme [day-for'-may], *a.* Deformed, disfigured, ugly, hideous.
Deformemente, *adv.* Deformedly.
Deformidad [day-for-me-dahd'], *f.* 1. Deformity, hideousness, ugliness. 2. A gross error.
Defraudación [day-frah-oo-dah-the-on'], *f.* Defraudation, fraud, deceit, usurpation.
Defraudador [day-frah-oo-dah-dor'], *m.* Defrauder, defaulter.
Defraudar [day-frah-oo-dar'], *va.* 1. To defraud, to rob or deprive by wile or trick. 2. To defraud, to cheat, to trick, to usurp what belongs to another. 3. (Met.) To intercept the light of the sun; to spoil the taste; to disturb the sleep.
Defuera [day-foo-ay'-rah], *adv.* Externally, outwardly, on the outside. *Por defuera,* Outwardly.
Defunción [day-foon-the-on'], *f.* (Prov.) 1. Death. 2. Extinction, transition from being to not being.

Degeneración [day-hay-nay-rah-the-on'], *f.* Degeneration, degeneracy.

Degenerado, da [day-hay-nay-rah'-do, dah], *a.* Degenerate.—*pp.* of Degenerar.

Degenerar [day-hay-nay-rar'], *vn.* 1. To degenerate, to fall from its kind, to grow wild or base: applied to plants. 2. To degenerate, to fall from the virtue of our ancestors. 3. (Pict.) To disfigure any thing.

Deglución [day-gloo-the-on'], *f.* (Med.) Deglutition, swallowing.

Deglutir [day-gloo-teer'], *va.* To swallow.

Degollación [day-gol-lyah-the-on'], *f.* Decollation, beheading.

Degolladero [day-gol-lyah-day'-ro], *m.* 1. Throttle, windpipe. 2. Shambles, slaughter-house. 3. In theatres, a place in the pit farthest from the stage, with no seats, where men are admitted at a very low price. It is separated from the pit by a partition as high as one's neck, from which it takes its name. *Degolladero de bolsas,* Cutpurse; also a shop where goods are sold at an extravagant price, or bad measure or weight is given. *Llevar al degolladero,* (Met.) To put one in very great danger.

Degollado [day-gol-lyah'-do], *m.* A dart in women's waists or jackets.

Degollador [day-gol-lyah-dor'], *m.* Headsman, executioner.

Degolladura [day-gol-lyah-doo'-rah], *f.* 1. Cutting of the throat. 2. Interstice between two bricks filled up with mortar. 3. A slope out of women's jackets. 4. Slender part of balusters.

Degollar [day-gol-lyar'], *va.* 1. To behead, to decapitate; to guillotine. 2. (Met.) To destroy, to ruin, to annihilate. 3. (Coll.) To tease, to importune. *Esta persona me degüella,* This person troubles and harasses me. *Degollar a sangrías,* To debilitate by excessive blood-letting.

Degollina [day-gol-lyee'-nah], *f.* (Coll.) Slaughter, butchery.

Degradación [day-grah-dah-the-on'], *f.* 1. Degradation, dismission from an office or dignity; fall. 2. Degradation, degeneracy. 3. (Pict.) Degradation, diminution.

Degradar [day-grah-dar'], *va.* To degrade, to deprive one of his place, dignity, or honours.—*vr.* To degrade or demean one's self.

(*Yo degüello, yo degüelle,* from *Degollar. V.* Acordar.)

Degüello [day-goo-ayl'-lyo], *m.* 1. Decollation, the act of beheading or cutting one's throat. 2. Neck or narrow part of many things. 3. Destruction, ruin. *Tirar a degüello,* To endeavour to destroy a person; to seek one's ruin.

Dehesa [day-ay'-sah], *f.* Pasture-ground. *Dehesa concejil,* Common, a pasture-ground.

Dehesar [day-ay-sar'], *va.* To turn arable land into pasture-ground.

Dehesero [day-ay-say'-ro], *m.* Keeper of a pasture-ground.

Dehiscencia [day-is-then'-the-ah], *f.* (Bot.) Dehiscence.

Deicida [day-e-thee'-dah], *m.* Deicide: a term applied by some writers to those who concurred in the crucifixion of our Saviour.

Deicidio [day-e-thee'-de-o], *m.* Deicide, murder of Christ.

Deidad [day-e-dahd'], *f.* 1. Deity, divinity. 2. Deity, goddess: a term of flattery addressed to women.

Deífero, ra [day-ee'-fay-ro, rah], *m.* & *f.* (Littl. us.) One who carries God in the depths of his heart.

Deificación [day-e-fe-ca-the-on'], *f.* Deification, apotheosis.

Deificar [day-e-fe-car'], *va.* To deify, to praise excessively or extravagantly.

Deífico [day-ee'-fe-co], *a.* Deifical, making divine; belonging to God.

Deiforme [day-e-for'-may], *a.* Deiform, of a godlike form; godlike.

Deípara [day-ee'-pa-rah], *f.* Deiparous, that brings forth a God: applied to the blessed Virgin.

Deisidemonia [day-e-se-day-mo-nee'-ah], *f.* Superstitious fear.

Deísmo [day-ees'-mo], *m.* Deism.

Deísta [day-ees'-tah], *m.* Deist.

Deja [day'-hah], *f.* Prominence between two fissures.

Dejación [day-hah-the-on'], *f.* 1. Act of leaving, relinquishing, or giving up. 2. Abdication, resignation. *Dejación de bienes,* The act of resigning one's property to his creditors.

Dejada [day-hah'-dah], *f. V.* Dejación.

Dejadez [day-hah-deth'], *f.* Slovenliness, neglect, laziness, lassitude.

Dejado, da [day-hah'-do, dah], *a.* 1. Slovenly, idle, indolent. 2. Dejected, low-spirited.—*pp.* of Dejar.

Dejamiento [day-hah-me-en'-to], *m.* 1. Act of leaving, relinquishing, or giving up. 2. Indolence, idleness, carelessness. 3. Languor, decay of spirits. 4. Abdication, resignation.

Dejar [day-har'], *va.* 1. To leave, to let, to relinquish, to quit, to come from, to go from. 2. To omit saying or doing any thing. 3. To permit, to allow, not to obstruct. 4. To leave, to forsake, to desert. 5. To yield, to produce. 6. To commit, to give in charge. 7. To nominate, to appoint. *Dejar cargado,* To debit. *Dejar dicho,* To leave word or orders. *Dejar escrito,* To leave in writing. *Déjale que venga,* Let him come. 8. To fling up, to give up. 9. To lay away. 10. To forbear, to leave off, to cease. 11. To leave a legacy to one absent. *Dejar atrás.* To excel, to surpass. *Dejar a uno a oscuras,* Not to grant a request; to leave one in doubt. *Dejar a uno con tantas narices,* To frustrate another's hopes or plans. *Dejar a uno a la luna,* To leave a service suddenly and without notice. *Dejar a uno a pie,* To deprive a person of an office or employment. *No dejar roso ni velloso,* To leave no stone unturned to insure success. *Dejarse de cuentos,* To come to the point. *Dejar en cueros,* To strip one of his property. *Dejar fresco a alguno,* To frustrate, to baffle. *Dejar para mañana,* To delay, to procrastinate.—*vr.* 1. Not to take care of one's self. 2. To allow or suffer one's self to. 3. To become languid. 4. To abandon one's self to. *Dejarse llevar,* To suffer one's self to be led by another. *Dejarse rogar,* To extend the concession required, that the favour may be more estimable. *Dejarse vencer,* To yield one's self to the opinion of another. *Dejarse caer abajo por un río,* (Naut.) To drop down a river. *Dejarse caer a la popa,* (Naut.) To fall astern. *Dejarse caer a sotavento,* (Naut.) To fall to leeward. *Dejarse alguna cosa en el tintero,* To omit something necessary to the subject.

Dejillo [day-heel'-lyo], *m. dim.* Slight relish or taste which remains after eating or drinking.

Dejo [day'-ho], *m.* 1. End, termination. 2. Negligence, carelessness, laziness. 3. (Obs.) *V.* Abnegación. 4. Relish or taste which remains after eating or drinking. 5. Result, effect, or remains of a passion 6. Particular accentuation on the last syllable of words, of each province or country. 7. Recollection, echo.

Dejugar [day-hoo-gar'], *va.* To extract the juice or substance of any thing.

Del [del]. Of the, a contraction of the preposition *De* and the masculine article *el;* as, *el mérito* del *libro,* instead of *el mérito* de el *libro.*

Delación [day-lah-the-on'], *f.* 1. Delation, accusation, impeachment. 2. Information.

Delantal [day-lan-tahl'], *m.* Apron; dash-board of a carriage.

Delante [day-lahn'-tay], *adv.* 1. Before, in the presence of, in the sight of, in front of. 2. Before, anteriorly, preceding in time. 3. Before, in preference to, prior to.

Delantera [day-lan-tay'-rah], *f.* 1. Fore front, fore end, the fore part of any thing. 2. The front seats, behind the barriers of a place, where bull-feasts are held. 3. Fore skirts of clothes. 4. Advantage obtained over another. 5. (Obs.) Vanguard of an army. *Coger la delantera,* To get the start of a person. *Ir en la delantera,* To take the lead.

Delantero, ra [day-lan-tay'-ro, rah], *a.* Foremost, first.

Delantero [day-lahn-tay'-ro], *m.* The first, one who takes the lead.—*m. pl.* Linemen (in football).

Delatable [day-lah-tah'-blay], *a.* Accusable, blamable.

Delatante [day-lah-tahn'-tay], *pa.* Informer, accuser.

Delatar [day-lah-tar'], *va.* To inform, to accuse, to denounce, to impeach.

Delator [day-lah-tor'], *m.* Accuser, informer, denouncer.

Del crédere [del cray'-day-ray], *m.* A guarantee by a merchant for another's payment. (Ital.)

Dele [day'-lay], *prep.* (Obs.) Now written *Del,* Of the.

Dele [day'-lay], *m.* (Print.) Dele, a mark of erasure; dele, ₰. (Imperat. of Lat. delere, to blot out, destroy.)

Delectación [day-lec-tah-the-on'], *f.* Delectation, pleasure, delight. *Delectación morosa,* The deliberate indulgence of some sensual pleasure.

Delectar [day-lec-tar'], *va.* (Obs.) To delight.

Delecto [day-lec'-to], *m.* (Obs.) Election, choice. *V.* Elección.

Delegación [day-lay-gah-the-on'], *f.* 1. Delegation, substitution. 2. Power conferred upon some one to act in behalf of others; a proxy.

Delegado [day-lay-gah'-do], *m.* Delegate, deputy, commissioner, minister. —*Delegado, da, pp.* of Delegar.

Delegante [day-lay-gahn'-tay], *pa.* Constituent, one that delegates.

Delegar [day-lay-gar'], *va.* To delegate, to substitute.

Deleitabilidad [day-lay-e-tah-be-le-dahd'], *f.* Delectableness, delightfulness.

Deleitable [day-lay-e-tah'-blay], *a.* Delectable, delightful.

Deleitablemente, *adv.* Delightfully.

Deleitación [day-lay-e-tah-the-on'], *f.* Delectation, pleasure, delight.

Deleitamiento [day-lay-e-tah-me-en'-to], *m.* Delight, pleasure.

Deleitante [day-lay-e-tahn'-tay], *pa.* Delighting.

Deleitar [day-lay-e-tar'], *va.* To delight, to please, to content.—*vr.* To delight, to have delight or pleasure in.

Deleite [day-lay'-e-tay], *m.* 1. Pleasure, delight, gratification. *Deleite sensual,* The emotion of any lawful pleasure. 2. Lust, carnal appetite.

Deleitosamente, *adv.* Delightfully, pleasantly, cheerfully.

Deleitoso, sa [day-lay-e-to'-so, sah], *a.* Delightful, agreeable, pleasing.

Deletéreo, ea [day-lay-tay'-ray-o, ah], *a.* (Med.) Deleterious, deletory.

Deletreador [day-lay-tray-ah-dor'], *m.* Speller.

Deletrear [day-lay-tray-ar'], *va.* 1. To spell, to read by spelling. 2. To find out and explain the meaning of what is difficult and obscure; to examine. to scrutinize.

Deletreo [day-lay-tray'-o], *m.* 1. Spelling. 2. Teaching to read by spelling the letters.

Deleznable [day-leth-nah'-blay], *a.* 1. Slippery, smooth. 2. Brittle, fragile.

Deleznadero [day-leth-nah-day'-ro], *m.* A slippery place.

Deleznamiento [day-leth-nah-me-en'-to], *m.* Act of slipping.

Deleznar, *vn.* (Obs.) *V.* Deslizar.

Délfico, ca [del'-fe-co, cah], *a.* Delphic, of Delphi.

Delfín [del-feen'], *m.* 1. Dolphin, a cetaceous animal. Delphinus delphis. 2. Dolphin, a northern constellation. 3. Dauphin, formerly the title of the eldest son of the King of France.

Delfina [del-fee'-nah], *f.* 1. Dauphiness, the wife or widow of the dauphin of France. 2. An alkaloid extracted from larkspur and stavesacre.

Delfinela [del-fe-nay'-lah], *f.* (Bot.) *V.* Delfinio.

Delfinio [del-fee'-ne-o], *m.* (Bot.) Larkspur. Delphinium.

Delgadamente, *adv.* 1. Thinly, delicately. 2. (Met.) Acutely, sharply, finely. 3. Gauntly.

Delgadez [del-gah-deth'], *f.* 1. Thinness, tenuity. 2. (Met.) Acuteness, ingenuity. 3. Slenderness, leanness, smallness.

Delgado, da [del-gah'-do, dah], *a.* 1. Thin, tenuous, delicate, light. 2. Thin, exiguous, slender, lean, lank, gaunt. 3. (Met.) Acute, fine, ingenious. 4. Short, little, scanty, poor, extenuate. *Delgados de un navío,* (Naut.) The narrowing or rising of a ship's floor. *Navío delgado a proa,* (Naut.) A sharp-bowed vessel. *Navío delgado para andar,* (Naut.) A sharp-built vessel for sailing. *Navío de muchos delgados,* (Naut.) A sharp-bottomed ship.

Delgado [del-gah'-do], *m.* A strait place. *Delgados,* Flanks of animals.

Delgaducho, cha [del-gah-doo'-cho, chah], *a.* Thin, delicate (with a sense of depreciation).

Delgazar, *va.* (Obs.) *V.* Adelgazar.

Deliberación [day-le-bay-rah-the-on'], *f.* 1. Deliberation, consideration, reflection. 2. Resolution, determination. 3. (Obs.) Liberation.

Deliberadamente, *adv.* Deliberately.

Deliberador [day-le-bay-rah-dor'], *m.* (Obs.) Deliverer.

Deliberamiento [day-le-bay-rah-me-en'-to], *m.* (Obs.) Deliverance.

Deliberar [day-le-bay-rar'], *vn.* 1. To consider, to deliberate, to discourse. 2. To consult or take counsel together. —*vr.* To have delight or pleasure in. —*va.* 1. To deliberate, to think in order to choose, to ponder. 2. (Obs.) To rescue from captivity. 3. (Obs.) To emancipate.

Deliberativo, va [day-le-bay-rah-tee'-vo, vah], *a.* Deliberative.

Delibrar [day-le-brar'], *va.* (Obs.) 1. To deliberate, to determine. 2. To liberate. 3. *V.* Despachar.

Delicadamente, *adv.* Delicately.

Delicadez [day-le-cah-deth'], *f.* 1. Delicacy, weakness of constitution. 2. (Met.) Delicacy, tenderness, scrupulousness, mercifulness. 3. Gentleness of manners, sweetness of temper.

Delicadeza [day-le-cah-day'-thah], *f.* 1. Delicateness, tenderness, softness, effeminacy; nicety, exquisiteness. 2. Delicacy, nicety in the choice of food, daintiness. 3. Subtlety, dexterity. 4. Fineness, tenuity. 5. (Met.) Acuteness of understanding, refinement of wit; perspicacity; curiosity; mellifluence. 6. Idleness, negligence.

Delicado, da [day-le-cah'-do, dah], *a.* 1. Delicate, sweet, pleasing, tender. 2. Weak, faint, effeminate, finical, feminine, lady-like. 3. Delicate, exquisite, nice, delicious, dainty, pleasing to the taste; of an agreeable flavour. 4. Thin, slender, subtile. 5. Nice, scrupulous, fastidious. 6. Arduous, difficult, perplexing. 7. Captious, easy of annoyance, suspicious.

Delicia [day-lee'-the-ah], *f.* 1. Delight, comfort, satisfaction. 2. A lively sensual pleasure. (Acad.)

Deliciarse [day-le-the-ar'-say], *vr.* (Obs.) To delight, to have delight or pleasure in. (Acad.)

Deliciosamente, *adv.* Deliciously, daintily, delightsomely.

Delicioso, sa [day-le-the-oh'-so, sah], *a.* Delicious, delightful, pleasing.

Delicuescencia [day-le-coo-es-then'-the-ah], *f.* (Chem.) Deliquescence.

Delicuescente [day-le-coo-es-then'-tay], *a.* (Chem.) Deliquescent.

Deligación [day-le-gah-the-on'], *f.* The art of preparing and applying bandages and other external applications.

Delincuencia [day-lin-coo-en'-the-ah], *f.* Delinquency, offence, failure in duty.

Delincuente [day-lin-coo-en'-tay], *pa.* Delinquent, offender.

Delineación [day-le-nay-ah-the-on'], *f.* Delineation, draft, sketch.

Delineador, ra [day-le-nay-ah-dor', rah]. *m.* & *f.* 1. Delineator, draftsman. 2. Pilot practical in drafting sketches.

Delineamento, Delineamiento [day-le-nay-ah-men'-to], *m.* Delineament. *V.* Delineación.

Delinear [day-le-nay-ar'], *va.* 1. To delineate, to draw the first draft of a thing; to sketch, to figure. 2. (Met.) To describe, in prose or verse.

Delinquimiento [day-lin-kee-me-en'-to], *m.* Delinquency, fault, transgression.

Delinquir [day-lin-keer'], *vn.* To transgress the law, to offend.

Delintar, Delinterar, *va.* (Obs.) *V.* Ceder and Traspasar.

Delio [day'-le-o], *m.* Of Delos. (Applied to Apollo.)

Deliquio [day-lee'-ke-o], *m.* 1. Swoon, a fainting-fit, ecstasy. 2. State of a body which has become more or less fluid; deliquescence.

Deliramento [day-le-rah-men'-to], *m.* (Obs.) Delirium.

Delirante, *pa.* Delirious, light-headed; raving.

Delirar [day-le-rar'], *vn.* 1. To delirate, to dote, to rave. 2. (Met.) To rant, to talk nonsense.

Delirio [day-lee'-re-o], *m.* 1. Delirium, alienation of mind, dotage. 2. (Met.) Rant, nonsense, idle talk.

Delírium tremens [day-lee'-re-oom tray'-mens], *m.* Delirium tremens (provoked by excessive alcoholism).

Delitescencia [day-le-tes-then'-the-ah], *f.* 1. Delitescence, a sudden subsidence of a local inflammation. 2. (Chem.) A sudden loss, by a crystallized body, of its water of crystallization, and consequent bursting asunder.

Delito [day-lee'-to], *m.* Transgression of a law; fault, crime, guilt, delinquency.

Della, dello [dayl'-lyah, dayl'-lyo]. (Obs.) Contractions of the words *de ella, de ello,* Of her, of it. *Della con dello,* Reciprocally, alternatively, one with the other, good and bad as they come.

Delta, *f.* Delta, Δ, the fourth letter of the Greek alphabet.—*m.* A triangular island at the mouth of certain rivers, named from resembling the Greek letter of same name.

Deltoides, dea [del-to'-e-des, day-ah], *a.* Deltoid, like a Greek delta.

Delusivo, va [day-loo-see'-vo, vah], *a.* Delusive, fallacious.

Delusor [day-loo-sor'], *m.* (Littl. us.) Cheat, impostor, deluder.

Delusoriamente, *adv.* Delusively, deceitfully.

Delusorio, ria [day-loo-so'-re-o, ah], *a.* Deceitful, fallacious.

Demacración [day-mah-crah-the-on'], *f.* Wasting away in flesh (of men and animals) marasmus.

Demacrado, da [day-mah-crah'-do, dah], *a.* Emaciated. *Rostro demacrado,* Wan, haggard countenance.

Demacrar [day-mah-crar'], *vr.* To waste away.—*va.* To cause wasting.

Demagogia [day-mah-go'-he-ah], *f.* 1. Demagogism, ambition to rule in a popular faction. 2. The predominance of the rabble.

Demagógico, ca [day-mah-go'-he-co, cah], *a.* Demagogical.

Demagogo [day-mah-go'-go], *m.* Demagogue.

Demagrar [day-mah-grar'], *vn.* To waste away. *V.* Demacrar.

Demanda [day-mahn'-dah], *f.* 1. Demand, claim, pretension, complaint. 2. Judicial suit, lawsuit. *Entablar una demanda,* To sue. *Salir a la demanda,* To appear in one's own defense. 3. Request, petition. 4. Interrogation. *La ley de la oferta y la demanda,* The law of demand and supply.

Demandadero, ra [day-man-dah-day'-ro, rah], *m.* & *f.* 1. A servant man or woman who attends at the door of a nunnery or convent, to run errands. 2. A servant in a jail.

Demandado, da [day-man-dah'-do, dah], *m.* & *f.* Defendant, the person accused.—*pp.* of Demandar.

Demandador [day-man-dah-dor'], *m.* 1. One who goes about asking charity for pious uses. 2. Claimant, plaintiff. 3. One who solicits a woman in marriage.

Demandadora [day-man-dah-do'-rah], *f.* (Littl. us.) Demandress, a female plaintiff or petitioner.

Demandante [day-man-dahn'-tay], *pa.* Claimant, complainant, plaintiff.

Demandar [day-man-dar'], *va.* 1. To demand, to ask, to petition. 2. To claim, to enter an action.

Demarcación [day-mar-cah-the-on'], *f.* Demarcation.

Demarcador [day-mar-cah-dor'], *m.* Designator, surveyor.

Demarcar [day-mar-car'], *va.* To mark out confines or limits, to survey. *Demarcar el terreno de un campamento,* To trace out the ground of a camp.

Demarrarse [day-mar-rar'-say], *vr.* (Obs.) To mislead, to deviate from the right way.

Demás [day-mahs'], *adv.* (Obs.) Over and above a certain quantity, measure, or number; besides, moreover.

Demás [day-mahs'], *a.* (Obs.) It is almost always used with the article prefixed to it, except sometimes in the plural. *Lo demás*, The rest. *Los demás* or *las demás*, The rest, the others. *Y así de lo demás*, And so on; so with the rest. *Estar demás*, To be over and above; to be useless or superfluous. *Por demás*, Uselessly, in vain, to no purpose. *V.* Además.

Demases [day-mah'-ses], *m. pl.* (Prov.) Abundance, copiousness.

Demasia [day-mah-see'-ah], *f.* 1. Excess, superabundance. 2. Badness, iniquity, guilt. 3. (Obs.) A bold, arduous undertaking. *En demasía*, Excessively.

Demasiadamente, *adv.* Excessively; too.

Demasiado, da [day-mah-se-ah'-do, dah], *a.* 1. Excessive, more than enough, too much. 2. (Obs.) Bold, daring, enterprising.

Demasiado [day-mah-se-ah'-do], *adv.* Enough, too, sufficiently, excessively.

Dembo [dem'-bo], *m.* A kind of drum which the natives of the Congo use.

Demediar [day-may-de-ar'], *va.* (Obs.) 1. To sunder, to divide into halves. 2. To wear a thing until it has lost half its value. 3. To complete half its age, or course.—*vn.* To reach half the duration of a thing. *Demediar la confesión*, To confess but half one's sins.

Demencia [day-men'-the-ah], *f.* Dementia, loss of mind, insanity.

Dementar [day-men-tar'], *va.* To dementate, to render insane: almost always used in its reciprocal sense.

Demente [day-men'-tay], *a.* Demented, mad, distracted, infatuated, insane.

Demergido [day-mer-hee'-do], *a.* (Obs.) *V.* Abatido.

Demérito [day-may'-re-to], *m.* 1. Demerit, ill desert. 2. The act of demeriting.

Demeritorio, ria [day-may-re-to'-re-o, ah], *a.* Without merit.

Demisión [day-me-se-on'], *f.* Submission, humility.

Demiurgo [day-me-oor'-go], *m.* Demiurge, in Plato's philosophy, a spirit intermediate between God and the creature.

Demo [day'-mo], *m.* (Prov.) Demon, a spirit; generally an evil spirit.

Democracia [day-mo-crah'-the-ah], *f.* Democracy.

Demócrata [day-mo'-cra-tah], *m.* Democrat.

Democráticamente, *adv.* Democratically.

Democrático, ca [day-mo-crah'-te-co, cah], *a.* 1. Democratical, popular, liberal. 2. (Met.) Modest, without pretensions. 3. Rabble.

Democratización [day-mo-crah-te-thah-the-on']. Democratization.

Democratizar [day-mo-cra-te-thar'], *va.* To propagate or spread democratic ideas.

Demografía [day-mo-grah-fee'-ah], *f.* Demography.

Demográfico, ca [day-mo-grah'-fe-co, cah], *a.* Demographic.

Demoler [day-mo-lerr'], *va.* To demolish, to overthrow.

Demolición [day-mo-le-the-on'], *f.* Demolition.

Demonche [day-mone'-chay], *m.* Little devil: a vulgarism in form of the diminutive.

Demoniaco, ca [day-mo-ne-ah'-co, cah], *a.* 1. Demoniacal, devilish. 2. Demoniacal. 3. Demonian.

Demonio [day-mo'-ne-o], *m.* 1. Demon, familiar. 2. The devil. 3. *int.* The deuce! *Estudiar con el demonio*, To show signs of great genius and acuteness for evil, or of great knavery.

Demontre [day-mone'-tray], *m.* *V.* Demonio. Used as an exclamation: The deuce!

Demoñuelo [day-mo-nyoo-ay'-lo], *m. dim.* A little demon or devil.

Demora [day-mo'-rah], *f.* 1. Delay, procrastination, protraction, demurrer. 2. Demurrage, an allowance made for the detention of a ship in a port. 3. (Amer.) The time of eight months, in which miners are obliged to work in the mines. *Sin demora*, Without delay.

Demorar [day-mo-rar'], *vn.* 1. To remain, to continue long in a place. 2. (Naut.) To bear, to be situated in regard to a ship. *La costa demora norte*, The coast bears north. 3. *va.* To retard, delay.

Demostrable [day-mos-trah'-blay], *a.* Demonstrable, manifestable.

Demostrablemente, *adv.* Demonstrably, ostensibly.

Demostración [day-mos-trah-the-on'], *f.* 1. Demonstration; manifestation. 2. (Mil.) Demonstration, a feigned attack upon an enemy, to divert his attention.

Demostrador, ra [day-mos-trah-dor', rah], *m.* & *f.* Demonstrator.

Demostrar [day-mos-trar'], *va.* 1. To demonstrate, to prove, to manifest, to lay open, to make out. 2. To teach.

Demostrativamente, *adv.* Demonstratively.

Demostrativo, va [day-mos-trah-tee'-vo, vah], *a.* Demonstrative.

Demótico, ca [day-mo'-te-co, cah], *a.* Demotic, belonging to the common people: especially used of Egyptian writing.

Demudación [day-moo-dah-the-on'], *f.* Change, alteration.

Demudar [day-moo-dar'], *va.* 1. To alter, to change, vary. 2. To cloak, disguise.—*vr.* To be changed; to change colour suddenly, or the expression of countenance.

(*Yo demuelo*, *yo demuela*, from *Demoler*. *V.* Mover.)

(*Yo demuestro*, *yo demuestre*, from *Desmostrar*. *V.* Acordar.)

Demulcente [day-mool-then'-tay], *a.* & *m.* (Med.) Demulcent, emollient.

Denante, Denantes, *adv.* (Prov. Obs.) *V.* Antes.

Denario [day-nah'-re-o], *m.* 1. Roman denarius, the penny of the New Testament, a small silver coin. 2. Denary, decimal or tenth number. 3. (Obs.) Money paid to labourers for one day's labour.

Denario ria [day-nah'-re-o, ah], *a.* Tenth, containing the number of ten.

Dende [den'-day], *adv.* (Obs.) Hence, from *V.* Desde.

Dendrita, Dendrite [den-dree'-tah, den-dree'-tay], *f.* Dendrite, a mineral representing the figures of plants.

Dendritico, ca [den-dree'-te-co, cah], *a.* Dendritic, showing markings like foliage.

Dendrografia [den-dro-grah-fee'-ah], *f.* Dendrology, a description of trees.

Dendrómetro [den-dro'-may-tro], *m.* (Math.) An instrument which resolves in a graphic manner problems of plane geometry.

Denegación [day-nay-gah-the-on'], *f.* Denial, refusal, denegation.

Denegar [day-nay-gar'], *va.* To deny, to refuse, to denegate.

Denegrecer [day-nay-gray-therr'], *va.* 1. To blacken, to darken, to denigrate. 2. (Obs.) *V.* Denigrar.

Denegrido, da [day-nay-gree'-do, dah], *a.* Blackened, denigrated.—*pp.* of Denegrir.

Denegrir [day-nay-greer'], *va.* *V.* Denegrecer.

Dengoso, sa [den-go'-so, sah], *a.* Fastidious, over-nice, scrupulous.

Dengue [den'-gay], *m.* 1. Fastidiousness. 2. Prudery. 3. A sort of woman's cape with long points. 4. A boat used in the sardine-fishery. 5. Dengue, or break-bone fever. 6. Affectation. *Andar en dengues*, To be over-nice, to be too punctilious. *No andar en dengues*. Not to mind trifles.

Denguero, ra [den-gay'-ro, rah], *a.* Prudish, affected. *V.* Dengoso.

(*Yo deniego*, *yo deniegue*, from *Denegar*. *V.* Acrecentar.)

Denigración [day-ne-grah-the-on'], *f.* Denigration, stigma, disgrace.

Denigrar [day-ne-grar'], *va.* 1. To denigrate or blacken the character of a person, to calumniate, to defame, to expose, to censure. 2. To insult.

Denigrativamente, *adv.* Injuriously, infamously.

Denigrativo, va [day-ne-grah-tee'-vo, vah], *a.* Blackening, stigmatizing.

Denodadamente, *adv.* Boldly, resolutely.

Denodado, da [day-no-dah'-do, dah], *a.* Bold, intrepid, audacious.

Denominable [day-no-me-nah'-blay], *a.* (Littl. us.) Denominable.

Denominación [day-no-me-nah-the-on'], *f.* Denomination.

Denominadamente, *adv.* Distinctly, definitively.

Denominador [day-no-me-nah-dor'], *m.* (Arith.) Denominator.

Denominar [day-no-me-nar'], *va.* To denominate, to give a name.

Denominativo, va, *a.* (Littl. us.) Denominative.

Denostadamente [day-nos-tah-dah-men'-tay], *adv.* Ignominiously, insultingly.

Denostador [day-nos-tah-dor'], *m.* Vilifier, railler, reviler.

Denostar [day-nos-tar'], *va.* To insult a person with foul language, to revile, to abuse.

Denotación [day-no-tah-the-on'], *f.* Designation, denotation.

Denotar [day-no-tar'], *va.* 1. To denote, to signify, to express. 2. To explain.

Denotativo, va [day-no-tah-tee'-vo, vah], *a.* Denoting, denotative.

Densamente, *adv.* Closely, densely.

Densidad [den-se-dahd'], *f.* 1. Density, closeness, compactness, grossness. 2. Obscurity, confusion, darkness.

Densifoliado, da [den-se-fo-le-ah'-do, dah], *a.* Thick-leaved, of crowded foliage.

Densímetro [den-see'-may-tro], *m.* Densimeter, an apparatus for determining the relative density of a substance.

Denso, sa [den'-so, sah], *a.* 1. Dense, thick. 2. Close, compact.

Densuno, *adv.* (Obs.) *V.* Juntamente.

Dentado, da [den-tah'-do, dah], *a.* 1. Furnished with teeth. 2. Denticulated, dentated, toothed. 3. Crenated, indented.—*pp.* of Dentar. *Dentado* is sometimes used as a substantive.

Dentadura [den-tah-doo'-rah], *f.* 1. A set of teeth. 2. Number and quality of the cogs or teeth of a wheel.

Dentagra [den-tah'-grah], *f.* Toothache.

Dental [den-tahl'], *m.* 1. Bed to which the ploughshare is fixed. 2. A wooden fork, used to separate the straw from corn.

Dental [den-tahl'], *a.* 1. Dental, belonging to the teeth. 2. (Gram.) Dental, pronounced principally by the agency of the teeth.

Dentar [den-tar'], *va.* & *vn.* 1. To tooth, to furnish with teeth, to indent; to cut into teeth. 2. To teeth, to cut teeth.

Dentaria [den-tah'-re-ah], *f.* (Bot.) Tooth-wort. Dentaria, *L.*

Dentecillo [den-tay-theel'-lyo], *m. dim.* Small tooth.

Dentejón [den-tay-hone'], *m.* Yoke-tree, with which oxen are yoked to the cart.

Dentelaria [den-tay-lah'-re-ah], *f.* (Bot.) Lead-wort. Plumbago europæa.

Dentelete [den-tay-lay'-tay], *m.* Dentil, or dentel, of a cornice of some Ionic entablatures.

Dentellada [den-tel-lyah'-dah], *f.* 1. Gnashing of teeth. 2. Nip, a pinch with the teeth. 3. Impression made by the teeth. *A dentelladas*, Snappishly, peevishly. *Dar o sacudir dentelladas*, To speak surlily and uncivilly.

Dentellado, da [den-tel-lyah'-do, dah], *a.* 1. Denticulated, dented. 2. Bit or wounded with the teeth.—*pp.* of Dentellar.

Dentellar [den-tel-lyar'], *vn.* To gnash, to grind or collide the teeth.

Dentellear [den-tel-lyay-ar'], *va.* To bite, to fix the teeth in any thing.

Dentellón [den-tel-lyone'], *m.* 1. Moulding or ornament of the Corinthian cornice. 2. Piece of a door-lock which represents a large tooth.

Dentera [den-tay'-rah], *f.* 1. An unpleasant sensation, or tingling pain in the teeth. 2. (Met.) *V.* Envidia.

Dentezuelo [den-tay-thoo-ay'-lo], *m. dim.* A little tooth.

Dentición [den-te-the-on'], *f.* 1. Dentition, cutting the teeth. 2. Dentition, the time at which children's teeth are cut.

Denticular [den-te-coo-lar'], *a.* Like teeth, as a tooth; denticulated, toothed.

Dentículo [den-tee'-coo-lo], *m.* (Arch.) Denticle, dentil.

Dentífrico [den-tee'-fre-co], *m.* Dentifrice, toothpaste.

Dentirrostros [den-teer-ros'-tros], *m. pl.* (Zool.) An order of birds with the upper mandible notched near the tip.

Dentista [den-tees'-tah], *m.* Dentist.

Dentivano, na [den-te-vah'-no, nah], *a.* Having long and large teeth: applied to horses.

Dentolabial [den-to-lah-be-ahl'], *a.* (Gram.) Dentilabial, articulated by placing the lips and teeth together, as f.

Dentón, na [den-tone', nah], *a.* Having large uneven teeth.

Dentón [den-tone'], *m.* (Zool.) 1. Dental, a small shell-fish. Sparus dentex, *L.* 2. A sea-fish of the sparus family, like a bream, remarkable for its strong, conical teeth.

Dentorno, *adv.* (Obs.) *V.* Del rededor.

Dentrambos [den-trahm'-bos]. Contraction of *De entrambos.*

Dentro [den'-tro], *adv.* Within. *Dentro del año*, In the course of the year. *Dentro de poco*, Shortly.

Dentudo, da [den-too'-do, dah], *a.* Having large uneven teeth.

Denudación [day-noo-dah-the-on'], *f.* 1. Denudation, laying bare. 2. (Geol.) Erosion of mineral matters which form beds of auriferous sands.

Denuedo [day-noo-ay'-do], *m.* Boldness, audaciousness, courage, intrepidity.

Denuesto [day-noo-es'-to], *m.* Affront, insult.

(*Yo denuesto*, from *Denostar.* *V.* Acordar.)

Denuncia [day-noon'-the-ah], *f.* 1. Denunciation. 2. Information laid against another person.

Denunciable [day-noon-the-ah'-blay], *a.* Fit to be denounced. *V.* Delatable.

Denunciación [day-noon-the-ah-the-on'], *f.* Denunciation, denouncement. *V.* Denuncia and Delación.

Denunciador [day-noon-the-ah-dor'], *m.* Denunciator, informer, accuser.

Denunciar [day-noon-the-ar'], *va.* 1. To advise, to give notice. 2. To denounce, to lay an information against another. 3. To prognosticate, to foretell. 4. To pronounce, to denunciate, to proclaim, to publish solemnly.

Denunciatorio, ria [day-noon-the-ah-to'-re-o, ah], *a.* Denunciatory.

Denuncio [day-noon'-the-o], *m.* (Prov.) *V.* Denuncia.

Deñar [day-nyar'], *va.* (Obs.) To deign, to deem worthy.

Deo gracias (Lat.) [day'-o grah'-the-ahs], *m.* A term used in Spain in saluting, or in calling in at a house. *Con su deo gracias nos quería engañar*, He tried to deceive us under the cloak of religion, or with his devout countenance.

Deontología [day-on-to-lo-hee'-ah], *f.* Deontology, ethics, the science of moral obligation.

Deontólogo [day-on-toh'-lo-go], *m.* A writer on ethics or deontology.

Deoperculado, da [day-o-per-coo-lah'-do, dah], *a.* (Bot.) Deoperculate, deprived of the operculum.

Deparar [day-pa-rar'], *va.* To offer, to furnish, to present.

Departamento [day-par-tah-men'-to], *m.* 1. Apartment. 2. Department, separate part, office or division. 3. A part or division of the executive government. 4. A province, district, or subdivision of a country.

Departidor, ra [day-par-te-dor', do'-rah], *m. & f.* Distributor, divider.

Departimiento [day-par-te-me-en'-to], *m.* (Obs.) 1. Division, separation. 2. Distance; difference. 3. Dispute.

Departir [day-par-teer'], *vn.* To speak to converse, to commune.—*va.* (Obs.) 1. To divide, to separate. 2. To distinguish by notes of diversity. 3. To argue, to contend, to dispute. 4. To teach, to explain: to mark out, to impede, to obstruct.

Depauperar [day-pah-oo-pay-rar'], *va.* 1. To depauperate, to impoverish. 2. To debilitate, to weaken, to exhaust.

Dependencia [day-pen-den'-the-ah], *f.* 1. Dependence, dependency, the state of dependence on another. 2. Dependence, subordination to superior power. 3. Relations by consanguinity or affinity. 4. Business, affair, trust, charge. *Pedro tiene muchas dependencias*, Peter has a deal of business on his hands. 5. Dependence, relation of one thing to another.

Depender [day-pen-derr'], *vn.* 1. To depend, to rest upon any thing as its cause. 2. To depend, to be in a state of dependence or servitude. 3. To hang, to be dependent on.

Dependiente [day-pen-de-en'-tay], *pa. & m.* 1. A dependent, one subordinate to or at the disposal of another. 2. (Amer.) A clerk.

Dependientemente, *adv.* Dependently.

Depilar [day-pe-lar'], *va.* To strip of hair, to depilate.

Depilatorio, a [day-pe-lah-to'-re-o, ah], *a.* Depilatory, used to remove hair.

Depletivo, va [day-play-tee'-vo, vah], *a.* Depletive, evacuant.

Deplorable [day-plo-rah'-blay], *a.* Deplorable, lamentable, calamitous, hopeless, mournful.

Deplorablemente, *adv.* Deplorably, mournfully, sorrowfully.

Deplorar [day-plo-rar'], *va.* To deplore, to lament, to bewail, to be moan, to condole, to mourn.

Deponente [day-po-nen'-tay], *m. & f.* Deponent, a witness.

Deponente, *a.* Deponent: applied to Latin verbs which have a passive form, but an active meaning.

Deponer [day-po-nerr'], *va.* 1. To lay by, separate, put aside from one's self. 2. To depose, remove from office. 3. To declare judicially, to depose, to declare upon oath. 4. To take down, remove a thing from the place in which it is. 5. To evacuate the bowels.

(*Yo depongo, yo deponga*, from *Deponer.* *V.* Poner.)

Deponible [day-po-nee'-blay], *a.* Declarable, capable of affirmation.

Depopulador [day-po-poo-lah-dor'], *m.* Depopulator, devastator of a country or city.

Deportación [day-por-tah-the-on'], *f.* Deportation, transportation, banishment.

Deportar [day-por-tar'], *va.* To transport, to exile, to banish.—*vr.* (Obs.) 1. To take a diversion. 2. To rest.

Deporte [day-por'-tay], *m.* **1. sports, athletics. 2.** Diversion, **pastime, recreation.**

Deportista [day-por-tees'-tah], *m.* Sportsman, athlete.—*f.* Sportswoman, athlete.

Deportivo, va [day-por-tee'-vo, vah], *a.* Athletic, connected with sports. *Espíritu deportivo.* Sportsmanship.

Deposición [day-po-se-the-on'], *f.* 1. Deposition, testimony upon oath. 2. Declaration, assertion, affirmation. 3. Deposition, degradation from dignity or station. 4. Alvine evacuation. 5. (Med.) Depression.

Depositador [day-po-se-tah-dor'], *m.* One who leaves any thing in trust with another.

Depositante [day-po-se-tahn'-tay], *pa.* Depositor.

Depositar [day-po-se-tar'], *va.* 1. To deposit, to confide, to trust. 2. To commit or put in any place for safekeeping. 3. To put a person in a position where he may freely manifest his will. 4. To inclose, to contain.

Depositaría [day-po-se-tah-ree'-ah], *f.* Depository, the place where a thing is lodged.

Depositario, ria [day-po-se-tah'-re-o, ah], *m. & f.* Depositary, the person with whom a thing is lodged in trust; trustee, receiver.

Depositario, ria [day-po-se-tah'-re-o, ah], *a.* Relating to a depository.

Depósito [day-po'-se-to], *m.* 1. The thing deposited; deposit, trust. 2. Depository, the place where a thing is lodged. 3. The wind-chest and wind-trunks of organs. 4. (Mil.) A recruiting station. 5. (Chem.) Deposit, precipitate. 6. (Geol.) Layers of aqueous rocks formed by sluggish waters. *Depósito de animales perdidos*, Pound. *En depósito*, In bond.

Depravación [day-prah-vah-the-on'], *f.* Depravation, depravity.

Depravado, da [day-prah-vah'-do, dah], *a.* Bad, depraved, lewd.—*pp.* of Depravar.

Depravador [day-prah-vah-dor'], *m.* Depraver, corrupter.

Depravar [day-prah-var'], *va.* To deprave, to vitiate, to corrupt, to contaminate. Used chiefly of immaterial things.

Deprecación [day-pray-cah-the-on'], *f.* Petition, prayer, deprecation, conjuration.

Deprecar [day-pray-car'], *va.* To entreat, to implore, to deprecate.

Deprecativo, va, Deprecatorio, ria [day-pray-cah-tee'-vo, vah], *a.* Deprecative, deprecatory.

Depreciación [day-pray-the-ah-the-on'] *f.* Depreciation, decrease in price.

Depredación [day-pray-dah-the-on'], *f.* 1. Depredation, plundering, laying waste, pillage. 2. Malversation committed by guardians or trustees.

Depredador, ra [day-pray-dah-dor', rah], *m.* & *f.* A robber, destroyer.

Depredar [day-pray-dar'], *va.* To rob, to pillage, to defraud.

Deprensión [day-pren-se-on'], *f.* Abasement, humiliation.

Depresión [day-pray-se-on'], *f.* 1. Depression, pressing down. 2. Depression, abasement.

Depresivo, va [day-pray-see'-vo, vah], *a.* Depressive, lowering.

Depresor [day-pray-sor'], *m.* 1. Depressor, an oppressor. 2. (Anat.) Depressor, a name given to muscles which depress the part on which they act.

Depresorio, ria [day-pray-so'-re-o, ah], *a.* Depressor.

Depreterición [day-pray-tay-re-the-on'], *f.* (Obs. Law) Preterition. *V.* PRETERICIÓN.

Deprimación [day-pre-mah-the-on'], *f.* Act and effect of cropping frost-bitten grass.

Deprimado, da [day-pre-mah'-do, dah], *a.* Applied to the fields or meadow in which the animals have eaten the tips of grass frost-bitten by dews.

Deprimar [day-pre-mar'], *va.* To make horses crop off the ends of grass frost-bitten by the first spring dews.

Deprimido, da [day-pre-mee'-do, dah], *a.* 1. Compressible, disappearing under the pressure of the finger, said of the pulse. 2. Flattened or hollowed at the middle; said of a tumour.

Deprimir [day-pre-meer'], *va.* To depress, to humble, to deject, to sink; to depreciate, to belittle.

De profundis, *m.* That Psalm which begins with these Latin words: the 130th. Used at funerals.

Depuesto, *pp. irr.* of DEPONER.

Depurable [day-poo-rah'-blay], *a.* Purifiable, capable of cleansing.

Depuración [day-poo-rah-the-on'], *f.* Depuration, purification.

Depurado, da [day-poo-rah'-do, dah], *a.* Depurate, cleansed, purified.—*pp.* of DEPURAR.

Depuramiento [day-poo-rah-me-en'-to], *m.* *V.* DEPURACIÓN.

Depurar [day-poo-rar'], *va.* To depurate, to cleanse, to purify, to filter.

Depurativo, va [day-poo-rah-tee'-vo, vah], *a.* Depurant, depurative, purifying; antiscorbutic.

Depuratorio, ria [day-poo-rah-to'-re-o, ah], *a.* Depuratory, purifying.

Deputar, *va.* *V.* DIPUTAR.

Deque [day'-kay], *adv.* Since that, immediately that. (Coll. Acad.)

Derecha [day-ray'-chah], *f.* 1. Right hand, right side. 2. (Obs.) Pack of hounds, or the path they pursue in the chase. *A derechas* or *a las derechas*, Right; well done, as it ought to be: honestly, rightly, justly. *A tuertas o derechas*, Right or wrong, inconsiderately. *Castellano* or *Español a las derechas*, A Castilian or Spaniard to the backbone. *No hacer cosa a derechas*, Not to do any thing right; to do every thing wrong.

Derechamente, *adv.* 1. Directly, full, straight. 2. Rightly, prudently, justly. 3. Expressly, formally, legally.

Derechera [day-ray-chay'-rah], *f.* The direct road.

Derechero [day-ray-chay'-ro], *m.* Clerk appointed to collect taxes.

Derechista [day-ray-chees'-tah], *m.* Rightist (in political tendencies).

Derecho, cha [day-ray'-cho, chah], *a.* 1. Right, even, straight. *Todo derecho*, Straightforward. 2. Just, lawful, well-grounded, reasonable, legitimate. *Hecho y derecho*, Perfect, absolute, complete; true, certain; without doubt. 3. Right, opposite to the left. (Obs.) Certain; directed. *Derecha la caña*, (Naut.) Right the helm, or midships the helm.

Derecho [day-ray'-cho], *m.* 1. Right, justice, law, equity. *Derecho divino, canónico, civil* or *municipal*, Divine, canonical, civil or municipal law. 2. A just claim. 3. Tax, duty, impost, custom, toll. 4. Due, fee, payment claimed by persons in office. In the two last senses it is almost always used in the plural. 5. The right side of cloth. *Según derecho*, According to law. 6. Exemption, freedom, privilege. 7. (Obs.) Road, path. *Derecho administrativo*, A collection of ordinances, regulations, etc. *Derecho cesáreo*, The civil laws. *En derecho de su dedo* or *sus narices*, Selfish care for one's own interest. *Derecho civil* or *común*, The civil (Roman) law. *Derecho de gentes*, Natural law, such as prevails among outside nations, as contrasted with the Roman law. *Derecho no escrito*, Unwritten law, established custom.

Derecho, *adv.* *V.* DERECHAMENTE.

Derecho de vía [day-ray'-cho day vee'-ah], *m.* Right of way.

Derechuelo, Derechuelos [day-ray-choo-ay'-lo], *m.* One of the first seams taught to little girls.

Derechura [day-ray-choo'-rah], *f.* 1. Rectitude; right way. 2. (Obs.) Salary, pay. 3. (Obs.) Right; dexterity. *En derechura*, 1. By the most direct road. 2. Without delay, directly, immediately.

Deriva [day-ree'-vah], *f.* 1. (Naut.) Ship's course. *Ir a la deriva*, To be adrift. 2. (Aer.) Deviation, drift.

Derivable [day-re-vah'-blay], *a.* Derivable, deducible.

Derivación [day-re-vah-the-on'], *f.* 1. Derivation, descent. 2. Derivation, a draining of water, a turning of its course. 3. (Gram.) Derivation, the tracing of a word from its original. 4. (Met.) Derivation, the drawing of a humour from one part of the body to another. 5. The act of separating one thing from another.

Derivado [day-re-vah'-do], *m.* 1. Derivative. 2. By-product.

Derivar [day-re-var'], *va.* 1. To derive, to separate one thing from another. 2. To derive, to deduce, or to trace any thing from its origin.—*vn.* (Naut.) To derive or deflect from the course.—*vr.* To derive, to come from, to descend from.

Derivativo, va [day-re-vah-tee'-vo, vah], *a.* Derivative.

Dermalgia [der-mahl'-he-ah], *f.* Neuralgia of the skin.

Dermatitis [der-mah-tee'-tis], *f.* Dermatitis, inflammation of the skin.

Dermatología [der-mah-to-lo-hee'-ah], *f.* (Anat.) Dermatology, science of skin diseases.

Dermatológico, ca [der-mah-to-lo'-he-co, cah], *a.* Dermatological, skin (as adjective).

Dermatologista, or Dermatólogo [der-mah-to-lo-hees'-tah, der-mah-toh'-lo-go], *m.* Dermatologist, specialist in skin diseases.

Dermatoponte [der-mah-to-pon'-tay], *a.* (Zool.) Breathing by the skin.

Dermestido, da, Dermestino, na, or **Derméstito, ta,** *a.* Dermestid, dermestoid.

Dermesto [der-mes'-to], *m.* Dermestes, a genus including the bacon-beetle and carpet-beetle; very destructive warehouse pests.

Dérmico, ca [dayr'-me-co, cah], *a.* Dermic, relating to the skin.

Dermis [dayr'-mis], *f.* Derm, dermis, the corium or true skin.

Dermitis [der-mee'-tis], *f.* Inflammation of the skin.

Dermodonte [der-mo-don'-tay], *a.* (Zool.) With teeth set below the skin.

Dermografía [der-mo-grah-fee'-ah], *f.* Dermography, a scientific description of the skin.

Dermóideo, a [der-mo'-e-day-o, ah], *a.* Dermoid, resembling skin.

Dermología, Dermologista, etc. *V.* DERMATOLOGÍA, etc.

Dermorrinco, ca [der-mor-reen'-co, cah], *a.* (Zool.) Dermorhynchous, lamellirostrate.

Derogable [day-ro-gah'-blay], *a.* Abolishable, annullable.

Derogación [day-ro-gah-the-on'], *f.* 1. Derogation or abolition of a law, or of one of its clauses. 2. Deterioration, diminution.

Derogado, da [day-ro-gah'-do, dah], *a.* & *pp.* of DEROGAR. Derogate, derogated.

Derogar [day-ro-gar'], *va.* 1. To derogate, to abolish or annul any legal disposition. 2. To reform, to remove.

Derogatorio, ria [day-ro-gah-to'-re-o, ah], *a.* Derogatory, derogative.

Derrabadura [der-rah-bah-doo'-rah], *f.* The wound made in docking the tail of an animal.

Derrabar [der-rah-bar'], *va.* To dock the tail.

Derraigar, *va.* *V.* DESARRAIGAR.

Derrama [der-rah'-mah], *f.* Assessment of a tax, duty, or impost.

Derramadamente, *adv.* 1. Profusely, lavishly. 2. Depravedly, corruptly.

Derramadero, ra [der-rah-mah-day'-ro, rah], *a.* *V.* VERTEDERO.

Derramador [der-rah-mah-dor'], *m.* Prodigal, waster, spendthrift.

Derramamiento [der-rah-mah-me-en'-to], *m.* 1. Pouring out, wasting, or lavishing any thing. 2. Effusion, waste, spilling or shedding. 3. Dispersion, scattering, spreading. *Derramamiento de lágrimas*, Flood of tears.

Derramar [der-rah-mar'], *va.* 1. To pour, to let out of a vessel, as liquids. 2. To leak, to let any liquid in or out. 3. To publish, to spread. 4. To spill, to scatter, to waste, to shed. 5. (Obs.) To assess taxes. *Derramar doctrina*, (Met.) To diffuse a doctrine.—*vr.* 1. To be scattered or spread, to fly abroad. 2. To abandon one's self to sensual pleasures. 3. To disembogue itself, as a river. 4. (Obs.) To escape.

Derrame [der-rah'-may], *m.* 1. The portion of liquor or seed lost in measuring. 2. Leakage, allowance for accidental loss in liquid measures. 3. Bevel of a wall at a window or door, to facilitate the entrance of light. 4. Declivity. 5. Subdivision of a ravine or valley in narrow outlets. 6. (Med.) Accumulation of a liquid in a cavity, or its issuing from the body.

Derramo [der-rah'-mo], *m.* The sloping of a wall in the aperture for a door or window.

Derraspado [der-ras-pah'-do], *a.* Beardless: applied to wheat.

Derredor [der-ray-dor'], *m.* Circumference, circuit; round about: generally used in the plural, or with the article *al*, or the preposition *en*. *Al derredor* or *en derredor*, Round about.

Derrenegar [der-ray-nay-gar'], *vn.* (Coll.) To hate, to detest.

Derrengada [der-ren-gah'-dah], *f.* (Prov.) Step in dancing.

Derrengado, da [der-ren-gah'-do, dah], *a.* Incurvated, bent, crooked, lame, crippled.—*pp.* of DERRENGAR.

Derrengadura [der-ren-gah-doo'-rah], *f.* Weakness in the hip, dislocation of the hip; lameness.

Derrengar [der-ren-gar'], *va.* 1. To sprain the hip, to hurt severely the spine or loins of a person or animal; to cripple. 2. (Prov.) To knock off the fruit of a tree.—*vn.* (Low) To abominate, to detest.

Derrengo [der-ren'-go], *m.* (Prov.) Stick with which fruits are knocked off.

Derretido, da [der-ray-tee'-do, dah], *a.* Enamoured, deeply in love.—*pp.* of DERRETIR.

Derretimiento [der-ray-te-me-en'-to], *m.* 1. Thaw, liquefaction, fusion, melting. 2. Violent affection.

Derretir [der-ray-teer'], *va.* 1. To liquefy, to melt, to dissolve, to fuse. 2. (Coll.) To change money. 3. To consume, to expend.—*vr.* 1. To be deeply in love. 2. To fall in love very easily. 3. To liquefy, to fuse, to melt or to be melted, to become liquid. 4. To melt, to grow tender or loving. 5. To be full of impatience. (Acad.) 6. To smelt, to found.

Derribado [der-re-bah'-do], *a.* Applied to horses having the croup or buttocks rounder and lower than usual. —*pp.* of DERRIBAR.

Derribar [der-re-bar'], *va.* 1. To demolish, to level with the ground. 2. To throw down, to knock down, to fell, to bring to the ground; to flatten; to lay flat, to lodge, to prostrate. 3. To depose, to displace, to divest, make a person lose protection, estimation, or acquired dignity. 4. (Met.) To subject, subdue disordered passions of the mind.—*vr.* To tumble down, to throw one's self on the ground.

Derribo [der-ree'-bo], *m.* 1. Demolition, as of a building. 2. Ruins of a demolished building.

(*Yo derriengo, yo derriengue*, from *Derrengar*. *V.* ACERTAR.)

(*Yo derrito, yo derrita; él dirritió, él dirritiera;* from *Derretir*. *V.* PEDIR.)

Derrisorio, a [der-re-so'-re-o, ah], *a.* Derisive. *V.* IRRISORIO.

Derrocadero [der-ro-cah-day'-ro], *m.* A very rocky and precipitous place, whence there is danger of falling.

Derrocar [der-ro-car'], *va.* 1. To precipitate or fling down from a rock. 2. To pull down, to demolish, to fell, to lay. 3. (Met.) To rob one of his fortune or happiness. 4. To precipitate, to distract any thing spiritual or intellectual.—*vn.* (Obs.) To tumble, to fall down.

Derrochador [der-ro-chah-dor'], *m.* A prodigal, a spendthrift.

Derrochamiento [der-ro-chah-me-en'-to], *m.* (Antiq.) Waste, squandering. *V.* DERROCHE.

Derrochar [der-ro-char'], *va.* To dissipate, to waste or destroy property, to make way with.

Derroche [der-ro'-chay], *m.* Waste, dissipation, destruction.

Derrostrarse [der-ros-trar'-say], *vr.* (Obs.) To have one's face disfigured by blows.

Derrota [der-ro'-tah], *f.* 1. (Naut.) Ship's course, the tack on which a ship sails. *Derrota estimada*, (Naut.) Dead reckoning. *Seguir en directa derrota*, (Naut.) To steer a straight course. 2. Road, path. 3. Rout or defeat of an army; overthrow. 4. (Prov.) Opening made in hedges or fences for the catt e which pasture in the stubbles.

Derrotar [der-ro-tar'], *va.* 1. (Naut.) To cause to drive or fall off: applied to the wind or stormy weather. 2. To destroy health or fortune. 3. To rout, to defeat.—*vn.* To arrive in a place in a ruined state, or in the utmost confusion and disorder.

Derrote [der-ro'-tay], *m.* 1. Defeat, rout, destruction. 2. (Prov.) Dilapidation.

Derrotero [der-ro-tay'-ro], *m.* 1. (Naut.) Collection of sea-charts. 2. (Naut.) Ship's course. 3. (Met.) Course, way or plan of life, conduct, or action.

Derrotismo [der-ro-tees'-mo], *m.* Defeatism.

Derrotista [der-ro-tees'-tah], *m.* & *f.* Defeatist.

Derrubiar [der-roo-be-ar'], *va.* To break the bounds of a river or rivulet insensibly; to undermine or wash away the ground.

Derrubio [der-roo'-be-o], *m.* The insensible overflow of water from a river or rivulet over the level grounds near to its bed, and the earth which falls or moulders away by this means.

Derruir [der-roo-eer'], *va.* To demolish, to destroy, to ruin. *V.* DERRIBAR.

Derrumbadero [der-room-bah-day'-ro], *m.* 1. Precipice; craggy, steep, and broken ground. 2. (Met.) A thorny or arduous affair.

Derrumbamiento [der-room-bah-me-en'-to], *m.* Precipitation.

Derrumbar [der-room-bar'], *va.* To precipitate, to throw down headlong. —*vr.* 1. To precipitate one's self headlong. 2. To sink down, crumble away, tumble down: said of a building.

Derrumbe [der-room-bay'], *m.* 1. A tumbling down, collapse. 2. A landslide.

Derviche [der-vee'-chay], *m.* Dervish, a Mohammedan monk or friar.

Des [dess]. 1. A preposition, corresponding with the Latin *dis;* never used but in compound words. 2. (Obs.) A contraction of *de ese*, of this, of that.

Desabarrancar [des-ah-bar-ran-car'], *va.* 1. To drag, draw, or pull out of a ditch. 2. (Met.) To disentangle from a state of perplexity, to extricate from difficulties.

Desabastecer [des-ah-bas-tay-therr'], *va.* Not to supply a place with provisions, either through neglect or in consequence of a prohibition.

Desabejar [des-ah-bay-har'], *va.* To remove bees from their hive.

Desabido, da [day-sah-bee'-do, dah], *a.* (Obs.) 1. Ignorant, illiterate. 2. Excessive, extraordinary.

Desabillé [des-ah-beel-lyay'], *m.* Dishabille, undress; a loose dress for women.

Desabitar [des-ah-be-tar'], *va.* (Naut.) To unbitt. *Desabitar el cable*, To unbitt a cable; that is, to remove the turns of a cable from the bitts.

Desabollador [des-ah-bol-lyah-dor'], *m.* 1. An instrument used by tin-workers to take bulges out of pewter dishes, plates, or vessels. 2. Tinker.

Desabollar [des-ah-bol-lyar'], *va.* To tinker.

Desabonarse [des-ah-bo-nar'-say], *vr.* To revoke a season-ticket or subscription.

Desabono [des-ah-bo'-no], *m.* Prejudice, injury. *Hablar en desabono de alguno*, To speak to the prejudice of another.

Desabor [day-sah-bor'], *m.* 1. Insipidity, want of taste. 2. (Met. Obs.) Dulness, dejection, lowness of spirits.

Desaborar [day-sah-bo-rar'], *va.* 1. To render a thing tasteless, to make it insipid or disgusting. 2. (Met.) To disgust, to vex.

Desabordarse [des-ah-bor-dar'-say], *vr.* (Naut.) To get clear of a ship which has run foul of one's vessel.

Desaborido, da [day-sah-bo-ree'-do, dah], *a.* 1. Tasteless, insipid. 2. Without substance. (Acad.)

Desabotonar [des-ah-bo-to-nar'], *va.* To unbutton.—*vn.* To blow, to bloom, to blossom.

Desabozar [des-ah-bo-thar'], *va.* (Naut.) To unstopper.

Desabrazar [des-ah-brah-thar'], *va.* To separate one thing from another; to loosen, release what is embraced.

Desabridamente [day-sah-bre-dah-men'-tay], *adv.* Bitterly, rudely, harshly.

Desabrido, da [day-sah-bree'-do, dah], *a.* 1. Tasteless, insipid. 2. Sour, peevish, severe. 3. Hard, difficult: applied to guns that rebound on discharging them. 4. Bleak, sharp: applied to the air and wind. 5. Disgusted, dissatisfied, at variance with.

Desabrigadamente, *adv.* 1. Nakedly, without covering. 2. Without shelter, without harbour.

Desabrigado, da [des-ah-bre-gah'-do, dah], *a.* 1. Uncovered, wanting covering or clothes. 2. Shelterless; harbourless; unsheltered.—*f.* An open roadstead. 3. (Met.) Abandoned, without support.—*pp.* of DESABRIGAR.

Desabrigar [des-ah-bre-gar'], *va.* 1. To uncover, to divest of covering; to strip, or to take off covering. 2. To deprive of shelter or harbour.

Desabrigo [des-ah-bree'-go], *m.* 1. Nudity, nakedness. 2. Want of shelter or harbour. 3. (Met.) Destitution, want of support or protection.

Desabrimiento [day-sah-bre-me-en'-to], *m.* 1. Insipidity, want of taste or flavour, flatness. 2. Severity or asperity of temper, rudeness of manners; acerbity. 3. Despondency, dejection, lowness of spirits. 4. The rebound of guns when discharged.

Desabrir [day-sah-breer'], *va.* To vex, to plague, to torment, to harass.

Desabrochar [des-ah-bro-char'], *va.* 1. To unclasp. 2. To unbutton. 3. To open, to burst open.—*vr.* To unbosom, to reveal in confidence, to disclose.

Desacabalar [des-ah-cah-bah-lar'], *va.* To pilfer. *V.* DESCABALAR.

Desacalorarse [des-ah-cah-lo-rar'-say], *vr.* (Met.) To grow less warm.

Desacatadamente, *adv.* Disrespectfully.

Desacatado, da [des-ah-cah-tah'-do, dah], *a.* Acting in a disrespectful manner. —*pp.* of DESACATAR.

Desacatador, ra [des-ah-cah-tah-dor', rah], *m.* & *f.* An irreverent, uncivil, or disrespectful person.

Desacatamiento [des-ah-cah-tah-me-en'-to], *m.* Disrespect.

Desacatar [des-ah-cah-tar'], *va.* 1. To treat in a disrespectful manner: generally used in its reciprocal sense. 2. To desecrate, to profane, to dishonour.

Desacato [des-ah-cah'-to], *m.* 1. Disrespect, incivility, want of reverence. 2. Desecration, profanation, dishonour.

Desaceitado, da [des-ah-thay-e-tah'-do, dah], *a.* Destitute of the necessary quantity of oil.

Desaceitar [des-ah-thay-e-tar'], *va.* To remove oil from woollen stuffs; to remove fat.

Desacerar [des-ah-thay-rar'], *va.* To unsteel, reduce from the state of steel.

Desacerbar [des-ah-ther-bar'], *va.* 1. To temper, sweeten, take away harshness and bitterness. 2. (Met.) To pacify, tranquillize, calm.

Desacertadamente, *adv.* Inconsiderately.

Desacertado, da [des-ah-ther-tah'-do, dah], *a.* Inconsiderate, imprudent, without reflection.—*pp.* of DESACERTAR.

Desacertar [des-ah-ther-tar'], *va.* To err, to commit a mistake.

Desacidificar [des-ah-the-de-fe-car'], *va.* To remove the acid from a substance, to neutralize an acid state; deacidify.

Desacierto [des-ah-the-err'-to], *m.* Error, mistake, blunder.

(*Yo desacierto*, from *Desacertar. V.* ACERTAR.)

Desacobardar [des-ah-co-bar-dar'], *va.* To remove fear or cowardice, to inspire courage.

Desacollar [des-ah-col-lyar'], *va.* (Prov.) To dig up the ground about vines, to cultivate vines.

Desacomodadamente [des-ah-co-mo-dah-dah-men'-tay], *adv.* Incommodiously, inconveniently.

Desacomodado, da [des-ah-co-mo-dah'-do, dah], *a.* 1. Destitute of the conveniences of life. 2. Out of place or employment; out of service. 3. That which causes trouble or inconvenience.—*pp.* of DESACOMODAR.

Desacomodamiento, *m.* Inconvenience, trouble.

Desacomodar [des-ah-co-mo-dar'], *va.* 1. To incommode, to molest. 2. To deprive of ease or convenience. 3. To turn out of place.—*vr.* To lose one's place, to be out of place: commonly applied to servants.

Desacomodo [des-ah-co-mo'-do], *m.* Loss of a place or position.

Desacompañamiento [des-ah-com-pa-nyah-me-en'-to], *m.* Want of company or society.

Desacompañar [des-ah-com-pa-nyar'], *va.* To leave the company, to retire.

Desaconsejado, da [des-ah-con-say-hah'-do, dah], *a.* Acting without prudence or reflection, inconsiderate, ill-advised. —*pp.* of DESACONSEJAR.

Desaconsejar [des-ah-con-say-har'], *va.* To dissuade, to dehort.

Desacoplar [des-ah-co-plar'], *va.* To unfasten, to separate two similar things.

Desacordadamente, *adv.* Inconsiderately, unadvisedly.

Desacordado, da [des-ah-cor-dah'-do, dah], *a.* (Art) Discordant.—*pp.* of DESACORDAR.

Desacordamiento, *m.* (Obs.) *V.* DESACUERDO.

Desacordanza, *f.* (Obs.) *V.* DISCORDANCIA.

Desacordar [des-ah-cor-dar'], *va.* To untune: said of musical instruments. —*vn.* (Obs.) *V.* DISCORDAR.—*vr.* 1. To be forgetful, or of short memory. 2. To be at variance, to disagree.

Desacorde [des-ah-cor'-day], *a.* Discordant.

Desacordonar [des-ah-cor-do-nar'], *va.* To uncord, remove strings; to untie, to unfasten.

Desacorralar [des-ah-cor-rah-lar'], *va.* 1. To let the flock or cattle out of the penfold. 2. To bring a bull into the open field. 3. (Met. Obs.) To inspirit, to animate, to encourage.

Desacostumbradamente, *adv.* Unusually.

Desacostumbrado, da [des-ah-cos-toom-brah'-do, dah], *a.* Unusual, unaccustomed.—*pp.* of DESACOSTUMBRAR.

Desacostumbrar [des-ah-cos-toom-brar'], *va.* To disuse, to drop or lose the custom.

Desacotar [des-ah-co-tar'], *va.* 1. To lay open a pasture-ground which was before inclosed. 2. To raise or withdraw a prohibition. 3. To relinquish a contract, to withdraw from an agreement. 4. Among boys, to play without conditions or rules.

Desacoto [des-ah-co'-to], *m.* The act of withdrawing the prohibition to enter a pasture-ground.

Desacreditar [des-ah-cray-de-tar'], *va.* 1. To discredit, to impair one's credit or reputation, to cry down. 2. To dissemble or conceal the merits of any thing.

Desactivar [des-ac-te-var'], *va.* To deactivate.

Desacuerdo [des-ah-coo-err'-do], *m.* 1. (Obs.) Forgetfulness, oblivion. 2. Derangement of the mental faculties. 3. Discordance, disagreement, disunion. 4. Error, mistake, blunder. 5. Want of accuracy and exactness.

(*Yo desacuerdo, yo desacuerde*, from *Desacordar. V.* ACORDAR.)

Desacuñador [des-ah-coo-nyah-dor'], *m.* (Typ.) A shooting-stick.

Desacuñar [des-ah-coo-nyar'], *va.* To unwedge, to remove the quoins.

Desachispar [des-ah-chees-par'], *va.* (Coll.) To remove intoxication.

Desaderezar [des-ah-day-ray-thar'], *va.* To undress, to divest of ornaments, to ruffle, to disarrange.

Desadeudar [des-ah-day-oo-dar'], *va.* To pay one's debts.

Desadorar [des-ah-do-rar'], *va.* To cease to worship or love.

Desadormecer [des-ah-dor-may-therr'], *va.* 1. To wake, to rouse from sleep. 2. To rouse from mental stupour.

(*Yo desadormezco, yo desadormezca*, from *Desadormecer. V.* ABORRECER.)

Desadornar [des-ah-dor-nar'], *va.* To divest of ornaments or decorations.

Desadorno [des-ah-dor'-no], *m.* Want of embellishments and charms.

Desadvertidamente, *adv.* Inadvertently, inconsiderately.

Desadvertido, da [des-ad-ver-tee'-do, dah], *a.* Inconsiderate, imprudent.—*pp.* of DESADVERTIR.

Desadvertimiento [des-ad-ver-te-me-en'-to], *m.* Want of prudence and reflection.

Desadvertir [des-ad-ver-teer'], *va.* To act inconsiderately, to proceed without judgment or prudence.

Desafamar, *va.* (Obs.) *V.* DISFAMAR.

Desafear [des-ah-fay-ar'], *va.* 1. To remove, or diminish ugliness. 2. (Obs.) To make ugly.

Desafección [des-ah-fec-the-on'], *f.* Disaffection.

Desafectación [des-ah-fec-tah-the-on'], *f.* (Litt. us.) Unaffectedness.

Desafecto, ta, *a.* Disaffected.

Desafecto [des-ah-fec'-to], *m.* Disaffection, disaffectedness.

Desaferrar [des-ah-fer-rar'], *va.* 1. (Naut.) To raise, weigh the anchors, so that the ship may sail. 2. To loosen any thing which was tied or fastened. 3. To make one change an opinion which he has strenuously maintained.

Desafiadero [des-ah-fe-ah-day'-ro], *m.* A private ground on which duels are fought.

Desafiador [des-ah-fe-ah-dor'], *m.* 1. A challenger, duellist. 2. Darer, one who dares or defies.

Desafianzador, ra [des-ah-fe-ahn-thah-dor', rah], *m.* & *f.* One who withdraws security.

Desafianzar [des-ah-fe-ahn-thar'], *va.* 1. To withdraw the security given in favour of some one. 2. *vr.* To become impaired, to deteriorate.

Desafiar [des-ah-fe-ar'], *va.* 1. To challenge, to defy, to dare. 2. To try one's strength against another. 3. To rival, to oppose, to struggle. 4. (Obs.) To decompose, to dissolve; to rescind; to discharge.

Desafición [des-ah-fe-the-on'], *f.* Disaffection.

Desaficionar [des-ah-fe-the-o-nar'], *va.* To destroy one's desire, wish, or affection for a thing.

Desafijar [des-ah-fe-har'], *va.* (Obs.) 1. *V.* DESFIJAR. 2. To deny the filiation of a son. (Ant.)

Desafinadamente, *adv.* Dissonantly, discordantly.

Desafinar [des-ah-fe-nar'], *va.* & *vn.* 1. To be inharmonious, to be out of tune. 2. To untune.

Desafío [des-ah-fee'-o], *m.* 1. Challenge, duel. 2. Struggle, contest, combat. 3. (Obs.) Dismissal.

Desaforadamente, *adv.* Disorderly, excessively, outrageously, impudently.

Desaforado, da [des-ah-fo-rah'-do, dah], *a.* 1. Huge, uncommonly large. 2. Disorderly, lawless, impudent, outrageous.—*pp.* of DESAFORAR.

Desaforar [des-ah-fo-rar'], *va.* 1. To encroach upon one's rights, to infringe one's privileges. 2. To deprive any one of the rights or privileges belonging to his birth, profession, or character. (Mil.) To cashier. 3. To redeem a property, by annulling the emphyteusis, or perpetual lease.—*vr.* 1. To relinquish one's rights and privileges. 2. To be outrageous or disorderly.

Desaforo [des-ah-fo'-ro], *m.* The act and effect of redeeming a perpetual lease.

Desaforrar [des-ah-for-rar'], *va.* 1 To take off the lining of any thing. 2. *Desaforrar los cables*, (Naut.) To unserve the cables.

Desafortunado, da [des-ah-for-too-nah'-do, dah], *a.* Unfortunate, unlucky.

Desafuero [des-ah-foo-ay'-ro], *m.* Excess; outrage, open violence, downright injustice, infraction of law.

Desagarrar [des-ah-gar-rar'], *va.* (Coll.) To release; to let loose.

Desagitadera [des-ah-he-tah-day'-rah], *f.* (Agr.) An instrument used in separating honey-combs from the hive.

Desagitar [des-ah-he-tar'], *va.* To remove honey-combs from the hive with the *desagitadera*.

Desagotar [des-ah-go-tar'], *va. V.* DESAGUAR.

Desagraciado, da [des-ah-grah-the-ah'-do, dah], *a.* Ungraceful, inelegant. —*pp.* of DESAGRACIAR.

Desagraciar [des-ah-grah-the-ar'], *va.* To deform, to disfigure, to make ungraceful or inelegant.

Desagradable [des-ah-grah-dah'-blay], *a.* Disagreeable, unpleasant; uncomfortable.

Desagradablemente, *adv.* Disagreeably.

Desagradar [des-ah-grah-dar'], *va.* To displease, to offend, to make angry.— *imp.* It does not suit.

Desagradecer [des-ah-grah-day-therr'], *va.* To be ungrateful.

Desagradecidamente, *adv.* Ungratefully.

Desagradecido, da [des-ah-grah-day-thee'-do, dah], *a.* Ungrateful.—*pp.* of DESAGRADECER.

Desagradecimiento [des-ah-grah-day-the-me-en'-to], *m.* Ingratitude.

Desagrado [des-ah-grah'-do], *m.* 1. Asperity, harshness. 2. Discontent, displeasure. *Ser del desagrado del rey,* To have incurred the king's displeasure.

Desagraviamiento, *m.* *V.* DESAGRAVIO.

Desagraviar [des-ah-grah-ve-ar'], *va.* 1. To give satisfaction, or make amends for an injury done; to relieve. 2. To vindicate.

Desagravio [des-ah-grah'-ve-o], *m.* 1. Relief, satisfaction, or compensation for an injury done. 2. Vindication, justice, vengeance.

Desagregación [des-ah-gray-gah-the-on'], *f.* 1. Separation, disintegration. (Min.) Separation of the mineral parts by means of a force which reduces the metal to grains or powder. 2. Separation of the molecules of a body.

Desagregar [des-ah-gray-gar'], *va.* To disjoin, to separate.

Desagriar [des-ah-gre-ar'], *va.* 1. To neutralize acidity. 2. To sweeten, mollify, soften the character of some one. 3. To appease, remove anger.

Desaguadero [des-ah-goo-ah-day'-ro], *m.* 1. Channel, drain for drawing off superfluous water, cesspool. 2. (Met.) Drain of money. *Desaguaderos de la cebadera,* (Naut.) Eyes of the sprit-sail.

Desaguador [des-ah-goo-ah-dor'], *m.* Water-pipe, channel or conduit for water.

Desaguar [des-ah-goo-ar'], *va.* 1. To drain, to draw off water. 2. (Met.) To waste money in extravagant expenses. —*vn.* To empty or flow into the sea: applied to rivers.—*vr.* (Met.) To discharge by vomits or stools.

Desaguazar [des-ah-goo-ah-thar'], *va.* To drain the water from any part.

Desagüe [des-ah'-goo-ay], *m.* 1. Channel, drain, outlet. 2. Extraordinary expense. 3. Drainage.

Desaguisadamente, *adv.* (Obs.) Injuriously; exorbitantly.

Desaguisado, da [des-ah-gee-sah'-do, dah], *a.* (Obs.) 1. Injurious, unjust. 2. Disproportionate, exorbitant. 3. Intrepid, bold.

Desaguisado [des-ah-gee-sah'-do], *m.* Offence, injury, wrong.

Desahijar [des-ah-e-har'], *va.* To wean, to separate the young from the dams.—*vr.* To swarm: applied to bees.

Desahitarse [des-ah-e-tar'-say], *vr.* To relieve indigestion, to unload the stomach.

Desahogadamente, *adv.* 1. Freely, without embarrassment or obstruction. 2. In an impudent or brazen-faced manner.

Desahogado, da [des-ah-o-gah'-do, dah], *a.* 1. Petulant, impudent, brazen-faced, licentious. 2. Having plenty of room, free, unencumbered: applied to places. 3. (Naut.) Having sea-room.—*pp.* of DESAHOGAR.

Desahogamiento, *m.* *V.* DESAHOGO.

Desahogar [des-ah-o-gar'], *va.* To ease pain, to alleviate distress.—*vr.* 1. To recover from fatigue or disease. 2. To unbosom, to disclose one's grief. 3. To expostulate or debate with one against wrong received. 4. To vent, to utter. 5. To extricate one's self from debt. 6. To give a horse liberty, so that he may vent his passion and become obedient to the bridle.

Desahogo [des-ah-o'-go], *m.* 1. Ease, alleviation from pain or affliction. 2. The unbosoming or disclosing one's troubles or grief. 3. Freedom of speech, vent. 4. Laxity. 5. Domestic convenience.

Desahuciado, da [des-ah-oo-the-ah'-do, dah], *a.* Given over, despaired of.—*pp.* of DESAHUCIAR.

Desahuciar [des-ah-oo-the-ar'], *va.* 1. To despair, to take away all hopes of obtaining a thing. 2. To give over, to declare a patient past recovery. 3. To dismiss a tenant or renter, at the expiration of his agreement. 4. To drive away cattle from a pasture-ground, at the expiration of a fixed term.

Desahucio [des-ah-oo'-the-o], *m.* The act of dismissing a tenant, or of driving away cattle from a pasture-ground, at the expiration of the stipulated time.

Desahumado, da [des-ah-oo-mah'-do, dah], *a.* Mild, faded, vapid· applied to liquor which has lost its strength. —*pp.* of DESAHUMAR.

Desahumar [des-ah-oo-mar'], *va.* To free from smoke, to expel smoke.

Desainadura [day-sah-e-nah-doo'-rah], *f.* (Vet.) Disease in horses, occasioned by liquefying their fat through overheating them.

Desainar [day-sah-e-nar'], *va.* To remove the fat of an animal; to lessen or diminish the thickness or substance of any thing.—*vr.* To lose a great quantity of blood. (*De* + *saín.*)

Desairadamente [des-ah-e-rah-dah-men'-tay], *adv.* Unhandsomely, gracelessly.

Desairado, da [des-ah-e-rah'-do, dah], *a.* 1. Unhandsome, graceless. 2. (Met.) Disregarded, slighted, unrewarded.—*pp.* of DESAIRAR.

Desairar [des-ah-e-rar'], *va.* To disregard, to slight, to take no notice, to disrespect, to rebuff.

Desaire [des-ah'-ee-ray], *m.* 1. Slight, rebuff, disdain, disrespect. 2. Awkwardness. 3. (Met.) Frown of fortune or power.

Desaislarse [des-ah-is-lar'-say], *vr.* To cease to be insulated.

Desajustar [des-ah-hoos-tar'], *va.* To mismatch, to unfit, to make unsuitable; not to adjust, not to be fit.—*vr.* 1. To disagree, to withdraw from an agreement. 2. To be out of order; as a door, a shutter, etc.

Desajuste [des-ah-hoos'-tay], *m.* 1. The act of making a thing unfit, unsuitable, or out of order. 2. Disagreement, breaking of a contract.

Desalabanza [des-ah-la-bahn'-thah], *f.* Vituperation, depreciation.

Desalabar [des-ah-lah-bar'], *va.* To dispraise, to censure, depreciate.

Desalabear [des-ah-lah-bay-ar'], *va.* To straighten a warped plank or board.

Desaladamente [des-ah-lah-dah-men'-tay], *adv.* Anxiously, swiftly.

Desaladura [day-sah-lah-doo'-rah], *f.* (Chem.) *V.* DESALAZÓN.

Desalar [des-ah-lar'], *va.* To cut off the wings.—*vr.* 1. (Met.) To run up to one with open arms. 2. To toil with excess to obtain something: to hurry. 3. (Naut.) To take away the stowage or heavy part of the cargo which served as ballast (fr. des + alar, from *ala,* wing).

Desalar [day-sah-lar'], *va.* To take the salt out of fish, meat, etc., by steeping it in fresh water.—*vr.* 1. (Chem.) To precipitate from solutions (as salts), to fall as a precipitate. 2. (Naut.) To make sea-water drinkable (fr. de + salar, from *sal,* salt).

Desalazón [day-sah-lah-thone'], *f.* (Chem.) Removal from a liquid of a part or all of its contained salts.

Desalbardar [des-al-bar-dar'], *va.* To take off the pack-saddle from a beast of burden.

Desalentador, ra [des-ah-len-tah-dor', rah], *a.* Dispiriting, discouraging.

Desalentar [des-ah-len-tar'], *va.* 1. To put one out of breath by dint of labour. 2. (Met.) To discourage, to dismay, to damp.—*vr.* To jade.

Desalfombrar [des-al-fom-brar'], *va.* To remove carpets from a room or house.

Desalforjar [des-al-for-har'], *va.* (Obs.) To take off the saddle-bags from horses or mules.—*vr.* (Met. Coll.) To take off one's accoutrements, to make one's self easy.

Desalhajar [des-al-ah-har'], *va.* To strip a house or room of furniture.

Desaliento [des-ah-le-en'-to], *m.* 1. Dismay, depression of spirits, discouragement, dejection. 2. Faintness, languor.

(*Yo desaliento, yo desaliente,* from *Desalentar.* V. ACERTAR.)

Desalinear [des-ah-le-nay-ar'], *va.* To destroy the lineation, to disorder, to separate from the line.

Desaliñadamente [des-ah-le-nyah-dah-men'-tay], *adv.* Slovenly, uncleanly.

Desaliñar [des-ah-le-nyar'], *va.* To disarrange, to disorder, to ruffle; to make one slovenly or dirty.

Dasaliño [des-ah-lee'-nyo], *m.* 1. Slovenliness, indecent negligence of dress. 2. Carelessness, want of attention. *Desaliños.* An ornament of diamonds that hangs from women's ears down to the breast.

Desalivación [day-sah-le-vah-the-on'], *f.* Salivation, profuse flow of saliva.

Desalivar [day-sah-le-var'], *vn.* To salivate.

Desalmadamente [des-al-mah-dah-men'-tay], *adv.* Soullessly, inhumanly.

Desalmado, da [des-al-mah'-do, dah], *a.* 1. Soulless, inhuman, merciless. 2. Impious, profligate. 3. Inanimate, abject.—*pp.* of DESALMAR.

Desalmamiento [des-al-mah-me-en'-to], *m.* Inhumanity, impiety, profligacy. (Ant.)

Desalmar [des-al-mar'], *va.* (Met.) To speak with ingenuity and candour.—*vr.* To desire any thing very anxiously.

Desalmenado, da [des-al-may-nah'-do, dah], *a.* 1. Stripped of turrets: applied to a castle or fortress. 2. Wanting an ornament or capital.

Desalmidonar [des-al-me-do-nar'], *va.* To take the starch out of linen.

Desalojamiento [des-ah-lo-hah-me-en'-to], *m.* Dislodging.

Desalojar [des-ah-lo-har'], *va.* To dislodge the enemy's troops, to dispossess them of a place or post.—*vn.* To quit one's house or apartments.

Desalquilado, da [des-al-ke-lah'-do, dah], *a.* Untenanted, unrented.

Desalquilar [des-al-kee-lar'], *va.* & *vr.* To leave a room or house for which a rent was paid.

Desalterar [des-al-tay-rar'], *va.* To allay, to assuage, to settle.

Desalumbradamente [des-ah-loom-brah-dah-men'-tay], *adv.* Blindly, erroneously.

Desalumbrado, da [des-ah-loom-brah'-do, dah], *a.* 1. Dazzled, overpowered with light; stricken with astonishment; surprised with splendour. 2. (Met.) Groping in the dark.

Desalumbramiento [des-ah-loom-brah-me-en'-to], *m.* Blindness, want of foresight or knowledge, error.

Desamable [des-ah-mah'-blay], *a.* Unamiable.

Desamador [des-ah-mah-dor'], *m.* One who does not love, or has ceased loving; one who dislikes persons or things.

Desamar [des-ah-mar'], *va.* 1. To love no more, not to love or esteem as formerly. 2. To hate, to detest.

Desamarrar [des-ah-mar-rar'], *va.* 1. (Naut.) To unmoor a ship. 2. To untie. *Desamarrar un cabo,* (Naut.) To unbend a rope.

Desamartelar [des-ah-mar-tay-lar'], *va.* (Ant.) To extinguish love; still used jocosely as reciprocal.

Desamasado, da [des-ah-mah-sah'-do, dah], *a.* Dissolved, disunited, unkneaded.

Desamelgamiento [des-ah-mel-gah-me-en'-to], *m.* Rotation, variation of crops.

Desamelgar [des-ah-mel-gar'], *va.* (Agr.) To rotate crops, to vary the order of cultivation, alternating with lying fallow.

Desamigado, da [des-ah-me-gah'-do, dah], *a.* (Obs.) Unfriendly, unconnected.

Desamistad [des-ah-mis-tahd'], *f.* (Obs.) Unfriendliness.

Desamistarse [des-ah-mis-tar'-say], *vr.* To fall out, to quarrel.

Desamoblar, *va. V.* DESAMUEBLAR.

Desamodorrar [des-ah-mo-dor-rar'], *va.* (Littl. us.) To remove lethargy or drowsiness.—*vr.* To emerge from lethargy or drowsiness; to recover one's self.

Desamoldar [des-ah-mol-dar'], *va.* 1. To unmould, to change as to the form. 2. (Met.) To change the proportion or symmetry of a thing; disfigure.

Desamor [des-ah-mor'], *m.* 1. Disregard, disaffection. 2. Lack of sentiment and affection which certain things generally inspire. 3. Enmity, hatred.

Desamoradamente [des-ah-mo-rah-dah-men'-tay], *adv.* (Obs.) Unfriendly, harshly.

Desamorado, da [des-ah-mo-rah'-do, dah], *a.* 1. Loveless, cold-hearted. 2. Harsh, rude, disdainful.—*pp.* of DESAMORAR.

Desamorar [des-ah-mo-rar'], *va.* To extinguish love, to cease loving.

Desamoroso, sa [des-ah-mo-ro'-so, sah], *a.* Unloving, destitute of regard or love.

Desamorrar [des-ah-mor-rar'], *va.* (Coll.) To cheer up, to make one give up his obstinacy.

Desamortajar [des-ah-mor-tah-har'], *va.* To unshroud, remove the shroud.

Desamortecer [des-ah-mor-tay-therr'], *va.* To remove torpor; to recover from a swoon.

Desamortizar [des-ah-mor-te-thar'], *va.* To disentail, to break an entail.

Desamotinarse [des-ah-mo-te-nar'-say], *vr.* To withdraw from mutiny and sedition.

Desamparador, ra [des-am-pa-rah-dor', rah], *m.* & *f.* Deserter, one who forsakes or abandons.

Desamparar [des-am-pa-rar'], *va.* 1. To forsake, to abandon, to leave, to relinquish, to desert. 2. To quit a place. 3. (Naut.) To dismantle, dismast a ship. *Desamparar la apelación,* To desist from an appeal interposed in a cause. *Desamparar los bienes,* To give up one's property, in order to avoid being molested by creditors.

Desamparo [des-am-pah'-ro], *m.* 1. Abandonment, desertion, want of protection, helplessness, forlornness. 2. Dereliction, the state of being forsaken.

Desamueblado, da [des-ah-moo-ay-blah'-do, dah], *a.* Unfurnished.—*pp.* of DESAMUEBLAR.

Desamueblar [des-ah-moo-ay-blar'], *va.* To unfurnish, to deprive or strip of furniture.

Desanclar, Desancorar [des-an-clar', des-an-co-rar'], *va.* (Naut.) To weigh anchor.

Desandadura [des-an-dah-doo'-rah], *f.* Going back over the same road.

Desandar [des-an-dar'], *va.* To retrograde, to go back the same road by which one came. *Desandar lo andado,* To undo what has been done.

Desandrajado, da [des-an-drah-hah'-do, dah], *a.* Ragged, in tatters.

Desangramiento [day-san-grah-me-en'-to], *m.* (Littl. us.) Bleeding to excess.

Desangrar [day-san-grar'], *va.* 1. To bleed one to excess. 2. To draw a large quantity of water from a river. 3. (Met.) To exhaust one's means, to make poor.—*vr.* To lose much blood.

Desanidar [des-ah-ne-dar'], *vn.* To forsake the nest: applied to birds.—*va.* 1. (Met.) To dislodge from a post. 2. To apprehend fugitives in their place of concealment.

Desanimadamente, *adv.* Spiritlessly.

Desanimado, da [des-ah-ne-mah'-do, dah], *a.* Despondent, dejected, discouraged.

Desanimar [des-ah-ne-mar'], *va.* 1. To dishearten, to dispirit, to discourage; to put a damp upon one's spirits. 2. To damp, to pall, to daunt.—*vr.* To jade.

Desanudar [des-ah-noo-dar'], *va.* 1. To untie, to loosen a knot. 2. (Met.) To extricate, to disentangle, to clear up what was obscure. *Desanudar la voz,* To pronounce clearly and distinctly, to articulate freely.

Desañudadura [des-ah-nyoo-dah-doo'-rah], *f.* The untying or loosening a knot; disentanglement.

Desañudar [des-ah-nyoo-dar'], *va. V.* DESANUDAR.

Desaojadera [des-ah-o-hah-day'-rah], *f.* (Obs.) Woman supposed to cure or dispel charms.

Desapacibilidad [des-ah-pa-the-be-le-dahd'], *f.* Rudeness, churlishness, peevishness.

Desapacible [des-ah-pa-thee'-blay], *a.* Sharp, rough, disagreeable, unpleasant, harsh.

Desapaciblemente [des-ah-pa-the-blay-men'-tay], *adv.* Sharply, disagreeably.

Desapadrinar [des-ah-pah-dre-nar'], *va.* (Met.) To disprove, to contradict.

Desaparear [des-ah-pa-ray-ar'], *va.* To unmatch, to disjoin.

Desaparecer [des-ah-pa-ray-therr'], *va.* To remove out of sight, to hide.—*vn.* & *vr.* To disappear.

Desaparecimiento [des-ah-pa-ray-the-me-en'-to], *m.* The act of disappearing or vanishing out of sight.

Desaparejar [des-ah-pa-ray-har'], *va.* 1. To unharness beasts of draught or burden. 2. (Naut.) To unrig a ship.

Desaparición [des-ah-pah-re-the-on'], *f.* Disappearance, vanishing from sight. (Ast.) Occultation.

(*Yo desaparezco, yo desaparezca,* from *Desaparecer. V.* ABORRECER.)

Desaparroquiar [des-ah-par-ro-ke-ar'], *va.* To remove some one from his parish.—*vr.* 1. To change one's parish, to remove from one parish to another. 2. (Met.) To cease to be a customer of a shop.

Desapasionadamente [des-ah-pah-se-o-nah-dah-men'-tay], *adv.* Impartially.

Desapasionarse [des-ah-pah-se-o-nar'-say], *vr.* To root out a passion, or strong affection for any thing.

Desapegarse [des-ah-pay-gar'-say], *vr.* To be alienated from natural affection.

Desapego [des-ah-pay'-go], *m.* 1. Alienation of love or affection, coolness. 2. Impartiality, disinterestedness, indifference.

Desapercibidamente, *adv.* Inadvertently, carelessly.

Desapercibido, da [des-ah-per-the-bee'-do, dah], *a.* Unprovided, unprepared, unguarded, careless.

Desapercibimiento, Desapercibo [des-ah-per-the-be-me-en'-to, des-ah-per-thee'-bo], *m.* Unpreparedness.

Desapestar [des-ah-pes-tar'], *va.* 1. To cure persons infected with the plague. 2. To disinfect.

Desapiadadamente [des-ah-pe-ah-dah-dah-men'-tay], *adv.* Unmercifully, impiously.

Desapiadado, da [des-ah-pe-ah-dah'-do, dah], *a.* Merciless, impious, inhuman.

Desapilador [des-ah-pe-lah-dor'], *m.* One who takes down the piles of wool in a shearing-place.

Desapiolar [des-ah-pe-o-lar'], *va.* To loose the strings with which game is tied.

Desaplicación [des-ah-ple-cah-the-on'], *f.* Inapplication, indolence.

Desaplicadamente [des-ah-ple-cah-dah-men'-tay], *adv.* Indolently.

Desaplicado, da [des-ah-ple-cah'-do, dah], *a.* Indolent, careless, neglectful.

Desaplomar [des-ah-plo-mar'], *va.* To put out of plumb.

Desapoderado, da [des-ah-po-day-rah'-do, dah], *a.* Furious, impetuous, ungovernable.—*pp.* of DESAPODERAR.

Desapoderamiento [des-ah-po-day-rah-me-en'-to], *m.* 1. The act of depriving or ejecting. 2. (Obs.) Excessive boldness, extreme audacity.

Desapoderar [des-ah-po-day-rar'], *va.* 1. To dispossess, to rob one of his property. 2. To repeal or revoke a power of attorney.

Desapolillar [des-ah-po-leel-lyar'], *va.* To free and clear of moths.—*vr.* (Coll.) To take the air when it is cold and sharp.

Desaporcar [des-ah-por-car'], *va.* To take away from plants earth which had been heaped about them.

Desaposentar [des-ah-po-sen-tar'], *va.* 1. To turn one out of his lodgings, to force him to move. 2. To expel a thing from one's mind.

Desaposesionar [des-ah-po-say-se-o-nar'], *va.* To dispossess.

Desapostura [des-ah-pos-too'-rah], *f.* (Obs.) Inelegance, deformity, indecency.

Desapoyar [des-ah-po-yar'], *va.* To remove the foundation of any thing. *V.* DESAPUNTALAR.

Despreciar [des-ah-pray-the-ar'], *va.* To depreciate, to undervalue, to cry down.

Desaprecio [des-ah-pray'-the-o], *m.* (Prov.) Depreciation, lessening the worth or value of a thing.

Desaprender [des-ah-pren-derr'], *va.* To unlearn, to forget what one has learned by heart.

Desaprensar [des-ah-pren-sar'], *va.* 1. To take away the gloss which clothes or other things obtain in the press. 2. (Met. Obs.) To extricate one's self from a pressing difficulty.

Desapretador [des-ah-pray-tah-dor'], *m.* Screw-driver.

Desapretar [des-ah-pray-tar'], *va.* 1. To slacken, to loosen, to loose. 2.

(Met.) To ease, to free from anxiety and uneasiness.

(*Yo desaprieto, yo desapriete*, from *Desapretar*. *V.* ACERTAR.)

Desaprisionar [des-ah-pre-se-o-nar'], *va.* To release from confinement, to set at liberty.—*vr.* (Met.) To extricate one's self from difficulties, to remove an impediment.

Desaprobación [des-ah-pro-bah-the-on'], *f.* Disapprobation, censure.

Desaprobar [des-ah-pro-bar'], *va.* To disapprove, to censure, to reprove, to condemn, to find fault; to negative.

Desapropiación, *f.* **Desapropiamiento,** *m.* [des-ah-pro-pe-ah-the-on', me-en'-to]. Alienation. *V.* ENAJENAMIENTO.

Desapropiar [des-ah-pro-pe-ar'], *va.* To deprive some one of ownership.—*vr.* To alienate, to transfer one's right and property to another, to expropriate.

Desapropio [des-ah-pro'-pe-o], *m.* Alienation, transfer of property.

Desaprovechadamente, *adv.* Unprofitably.

Desaprovechado, da [des-ah-pro-vay-chah'-do, dah], *a.* 1. Unprofitable, useless. 2. Backward.—*pp.* of DESAPROVECHAR.

Desaprovechamiento [des-ah-pro-vay-chah-me-en'-to], *m.* 1. Backwardness, waste. 2. Inapplication, negligence.

Desaprovechar [des-ah-pro-vay-char'], *va.* To waste, to misspend, to turn to a bad use.—*vn.* To be backward, to make little or no progress.

(*Yo desapruebo, yo desapruebe*, from *Desaprobar*. *V.* ACORDAR.)

Desapteza [des-ap-tay'-thah], *f.* (Obs.) Ineptitude.

Desapuesto, ta [des-ah-poo-es'-to, tah], *a.* (Obs.) Inelegant, unseemly.

Desapuntalar [des-ah-poon-tah-lar'], *va.* To take away the props or supports.

Desapuntar [des-ah-poon-tar'], *va.* 1. To unstitch, to rip up. 2. To lose one's aim, to point or level fire-arms ill. 3. To efface the days of absence from the choir.

Desarbolar [des-ar-bo-lar'], *va.* 1. (Naut.) To unmast a ship, to cut down the masts. 2. *vn.* (Naut) To lose the masts by accident. 3. (Agr.) To root up or cut down the trees of a grove.

Desarbolo [des-ar-bo'-lo], *m.* The act of unmasting a ship or laying her up in ordinary.

Desarenar [des-ah-ray-nar'], *va.* To take away sand, to clear a place of sand.

Desareno [des-ah-ray'-no], *m.* Clearing a place of sand.

Desarmable [des-ar-mah'-blay], *a.* Demountable, collapsible.

Desarmado, da [des-ar-mah'-do, dah], *a.* Unarmed, defenceless, bare.—*pp.* of DESARMAR.

Desarmador [des-ar-mah-dor'], *m.* He who discharges a gun.

Desarmadura, *f.* **Desarmamiento,** *m.* [des-ar-mah-doo'-rah, des-ar-mah-me-en'-to]. Disarming, the act and effect of disarming.

Desarmar [des-ar-mar'], *va.* 1. To disarm. 2. To prohibit the carrying of arms. 3. To undo a thing, to take it asunder. 4. To disband a body of troops. 5. To dismount a cross-bow; to dismount cannon. 6. To butt, to strike with the horns. 7. (Met.) To pacify, to disarm wrath or vengeance.

Desarme [des-ar'-may], *m.* 1. Disarming of ships or troops. 2. Disarmament. *Desarme total,* Total disarmament. *Desarme nuclear,* Nuclear disarmament.

Desarraigar [des-ar-rah-e-gar'], *va.* 1. To eradicate, to root out, to deracinate. 2. (Met.) To extirpate, to destroy, to exterminate. 3. (Law) To expel from the country.

Desarraigo [des-ar-rah'-e-go], *m.* 1. Eradication. 2. (Law) Expulsion from a country.

Desarrancarse [des-ar-ran-car'-say], *vr.* To desert, to separate from a body or association. (Acad.)

Desarrapado, da [des-ar-rah-pah'-do, dah], *a.* Ragged.

Desarrebozar [des-ar-ray-bo-thar'], *va.* 1. To unmuffle. 2. (Met.) To lay open, to manifest, to discover.

Desarrebujar [des-ar-ray-boo-har'], *va.* 1. To unfold, to spread out. 2. To uncover. 3. To explain, to clear up.

Desarregladamente, *adv.* Disorderly.

Desarreglado, da [des-ar-ray-glah'-do, dah], *a.* 1. Immoderate, intemperate. 2. Extravagant, excessive. 3. Lawless, unruly.—*pp.* of DESARREGLAR.

Desarreglar [des-ar-ray-glar'], *va.* To disorder, to discompose; to derange.

Desarreglo [des-ar-ray'-glo], *m.* 1. Disorder, confusion, irregularity, mismanagement. 2. Licentiousness, license, disorder. 3. Derangement.

Desarrendarse [des-ar-ren-dar'-say], *vr.* To shake off the bridle: applied to a horse.

Desarrimar [des-ar-re-mar'], *va.* 1. To remove, to separate. 2. To dissuade, to dehort.

Desarrimo [des-ar-ree'-mo], *m.* Want of props or support

Desarrollar [des-ar-rol-lyar'], *va.* 1. To unroll, to unfold. 2. To develop (photographs).—*vr.* 1. To unfold, develop (as seeds, etc.). 2. To develop, expand, acquire growth and vigor.

Desarrollo [des-ar-rol'-lyo], *m.* Unfolding, development, evolution.

Desarromadizar [des-ar-ro-mah-de-thar'], *va.* (Littl. us.) To cure of a cold.

Desarropar [des-ar-ro-par'], *va.* To uncover, to undress.

Desarrugar [des-ar-roo-gar'], *va.* To take out wrinkles.

Desarrumar [des-ar-roo-mar'], *va.* (Naut.) 1. To unload a ship, to discharge the cargo. 2. To remove the ballast in order to inspect the bottom.

Desarticular [des-ar-te-coo-lar'], *va.* To disarticulate, sever a joint. (Naut.) To loose.

Desartillar [des-ar-teel-lyar'], *va.* To take the guns out of a ship or a fortress.

Desarzonar [des-ar-tho-nar'], *va.* To throw from the saddle, to unhorse.

Desasado, da [des-ah-sah'-do, dah], *a.* 1. Without handles. 2. (Cant) Without ears. (Acad.)

Desaseadamente, *adv.* Uncleanly.

Desasear [des-ah-say-ar'], *va.* To make dirty or unclean; to discompose, to disorder.

Desasegurar [des-ah-say-goo-rar'], *va.* 1. To lose the security of any thing. 2. (Amer.) To cancel life or fire insurance.

Desasentar [des-ah-sen-tar'], *va.* (Met.) To disagree with, to displease, not to suit or not to set well.—*vr.* To stand up.

Desaseo [des-ah-say'-o], *m.* Uncleanliness, dirtiness, carelessness.

Desasimiento [des-ah-se-me-en'-to], *m.* 1. The act of loosening or letting loose. 2. (Met.) Alienation of affection or love, disregard. 3. Disinterestedness.

Desasir [des-ah-seer'], *va.* To loosen, to disentangle, to give up.—*vr.* 1. To disengage or extricate one's self. 2. (Met.) To disregard, to look with indifference or contempt. 3. To give up the possession of property.

Desasnar [des-as-nar'], *va.* (Met. Coll.) To instruct, to polish one's manners.—*vr.* To grow sharp, to learn wit, to become polite.

Desasociable [des-ah-so-the-ah'-blay], *a.* Unsociable.

Desasosegadamente, *adv.* Uneasily.

Desasosegar [des-ah-so-say-gar'], *va.* To disquiet, to disturb.

Desasosiego [des-ah-so-se-ay'-go], *m.* Restlessness, want of tranquillity, uneasiness.

(*Yo desasosiego*, from *Desasosegar*. *V.* ACERTAR.)

Desastradamente, *adv.* Wretchedly, disastrously.

Desastrado, da [des-as-trah'-do, dah], *a.* 1. Wretched, miserable, unfortunate. 2. Ragged, tattered.

Desastre [des-ahs'-tray], *m.* Disaster, catastrophe, misfortune.

Desastroso, sa [des-as-tro'-so, sah], *a.* Unfortunate, disastrous.

Desatacar [des-ah-tah-car'], *va.* To loosen, to untie. *Desatacar la escopeta,* To draw the charge from a gun.

Desatadamente, *adv.* Loosely.

Desatado, da [des-ah-tah'-do, dah], *a.* Loose, unbound, untied.—*pp.* of DESATAR.

Desatador [des-ah-tah-dor'], *m.* He who unties, absolver.

Desatadura, *f.* **Desatamiento,** *m.* [des-ah-tah-doo'-rah, des-ah-tah-me-en'-to]. Untying, loosening.

Desatancar [des-ah-tan-car'], *va.* 1. To clear sewers and conduits.

Desatar [des-ah-tar'], *va.* 1. To untie, to loose, to loosen or unbind, to abstringe, to separate, to detach. 2. To loosen, to separate a compages. 3. To unriddle, to solve, to find out, to unravel. 4. To liquefy, to dissolve.—*vr.* 1. To give a loose rein to one's tongue. 2. To lose all reserve, fear, or bashfulness.

Desatascar [des-ah-tas-car'], *va.* 1. To pull or draw out of the mud or mire. 2. *V.* DESATANCAR. 3. (Met.) To extricate one from difficulties.

Desataviar [des-ah-tah-ve-ar'], *va.* To strip off ornaments and decorations.

Desatavío [des-ah-tah-vee'-o], *m.* Uncleanliness, negligence in dress.

Desate [des-ah'-tay]. *m.* 1. Disorderly proceeding. 2. Loss of fear, of reserve, of bashfulness. *Desate de vientre,* Looseness of the bowels.

Desatención [des-ah-ten-the-on'], *f.* 1 Inattention, absence of mind, abstraction. 2. Disrespect, want of respect 3. Incivility, want of politeness.

Desatender [des-ah-ten-derr'], *va.* 1. To pay no attention to what is said or done. 2. To disregard, to slight, to contemn, to neglect. 3. To take no notice of a person or thing.

Desatentadamente, *adv.* 1. Disorderly, confusedly. 2. Inconsiderately, unadvisedly.

Desatendible [des-ah-ten-dee'-blay], *a.* What ought to be neglected or disregarded; mean, despicable, inconsiderable.

Desatentado, da [des-ah-ten-tah'-do, dah], *a.* 1. Inconsiderate, unadvised; acting in an absurd and unreasonable manner. 2. Excessive, rigorous, disordered.—*pp.* of DESATENTAR.

Desatentamente, *adv.* Disrespectfully, uncivilly.

Desatentar [des-ah-ten-tar'], *va.* To perturb the mind, to perplex the understanding.

Desatento, ta [des-ah-ten'-to, tah], *a.* 1. Inattentive, careless, heedless, thoughtless. 2. Rude, unmannerly, uncivil.

Desatesado, da [des-ah-tay-sah'-do, dah], *a.* (Obs.) Weak, languishing. *V.* FLOJO.

Desatesorar [des-ah-tay-so-rar'], *va.* To remove or spend the treasure.

(*Yo desatiendo, yo desatienda*, from *Desatender. V.* ATENDER.)

Desatestar [des-ah-tes-tar'], *va.* To contradict a testimony.—*vr.* To retract from the testimony given.

Desatiento [des-ah-te-en'-to], *m.* Inconsiderateness, thoughtlessness, absence of mind.

(*Yo desatiento, yo desatiente*, from *Desatentar. V.* ACRECENTAR.)

Desatinadamente, *adv.* 1. Inconsiderately, indiscreetly. 2. Extravagantly, disproportionately.

Desatinado, da [des-ah-te-nah'-do, dah], *a.* Extravagant, nonsensical, crazy, foolish, irregular, wild.—*pp.* of DESATINAR.

Desatinado, *m.* Idiot, fool, madman.

Desatinar [des-ah-te-nar'], *va.* & *vn.* 1. To do foolish things, to act in an incoherent manner. 2. To disorder or derange one's mind. 3. To throw into a violent passion, to make one mad. 4. To talk nonsense. 5. To reel, to stagger, to totter, to dote.

Desatino [des-ah-tee'-no], *m.* 1. Extravagance, irregularity, wildness; headiness. 2. Reeling, staggering. 3. Madness, craziness; nonsense.

Desativar [des-ah-te-var'], *va.* To free a mine from heaps of rubbish. (Acad.)

Desatolondrado, da [des-ah-to-lon-drah'-do, dah], *a.* 1. Recovery from stupor. 2. (Peru.) Extravagant, foolish.—*pp.* of DESATOLONDRAR.

Desatolondrar [des-ah-to-lon-drar'], *va.* To bring one to his senses.—*vr.* To recover one's senses.

Desatollar [des-ah-tol-lyar'], *va.* To pull out of the mud or mire. *V.* DESATASCAR.

Desatontarse [des-ah-ton-tar'-say], *vr.* To recover one's self from stupefaction.

Desatornillar [des-ah-tor-neel-lyar'], *va.* To unscrew, to remove the screws.

Desatrabillar [des-ah-trah-beel-lyar'], *va.* To unstrap, to unbuckle.

Desatracar [des-ah-trah-car'], *va.* (Naut.) To sheer off, to bear away.

Desatraer [des-ah-trah-err'], *va.* To disjoin, to separate, to remove one thing from another.

Desatraillar [des-ah-trah-eel-lyar'], *va.* To uncouple hounds, to untie the leash with which they are coupled.

Desatrampar [des-ah-tram-par'], *va.* 1. To clear a conduit, sink, or sewer. 2. *V.* DESATASCAR.

Desatrancar [des-ah-tran-car'], *va.* 1. To unbar. 2. To clear a well or spring.

Desatufarse [des-ah-too-far'-say], *vr.* To grow calm, to allay one's passion.

Desaturdir [des-ah-toor-deer'], *va.* To rouse from a state of dizziness or stupor, to animate.

Desautoridad [des-ah-oo-to-re-dahd'], *f.* Want of authority.

Desautorizar [des-ah-oo-to-re-thar'], *va.* To disauthorize.

Desavahado, da [des-ah-vah-ah'-do, dah], *a.* (Ant.) Uncovered, free from fogs, clouds, or vapours: applied to places where the sky is commonly very clear. —*pp.* of DESAVAHAR.

Desavahar [des-ah-vah-ar'], *va.* (Ant.) To expose to the air, to evaporate, to send forth a fume or vapour.—*vr.* To grow lively or sprightly.

Desavecindado, da [des-ah-vay-thin-dah'-do, dah], *a.* Deserted, unpeopled: applied to a place abandoned by its inhabitants.—*pp.* of DESAVECINDARSE.

Desavecindarse [des-ah-vay-thin-dar'-say], *vr.* To change one's domicile; to leave the place where one was living.

Desavenencia [des-ah-vay-nen'-the-ah], *f.* Discord, disagreement, misunderstanding, misintelligence.

(*Yo desavengo, yo desavenga*, from *Desavenir. V.* VENIR.)

Desavenido, da [des-ah-vay-nee'-do, dah], *a.* Discordant, disagreeing.—*pp.* of DESAVENIR.

Desavenimiento [des-ah-vay-ne-me-en'-to], *m.* (Obs.) *V.* DESAVENENCIA.

Desavenir [des-ah-vay-neer'], *va.* To discompose, to disconcert, to unsettle. —*vr.* To disagree, to quarrel.

Desaventajadamente, *adv.* Disadvantageously, unprofitably.

Desaventajado, da [des-ah-ven-tah-hah'-do, dah], *a.* Disadvantageous, unprofitable.

Desaventura, *f.* (Obs.) *V.* DESVENTURA.

Desavezar [des-ah-vay-thar'], *va.* (Obs.) *V.* DESACOSTUMBRAR.

Desaviar [des-ah-ve-ar'], *va.* 1. To deviate from the high road, to lead astray. 2. To strip of necessaries or conveniences.—*vr.* 1. To go astray, to miss one's way. 2. To lose the means of acquiring necessaries, conveniences, etc.

Desaviltado, da, *a.* (Obs.) *V.* DESHONRADO.

Desavío [des-ah-vee'-o], *m.* 1. The act of going astray, or losing one's road. 2. Want of the necessary means for attaining some end or purpose.

Desavisado, da [des-ah-ve-sah'-do, dah], *a.* Ill-advised, unadvised, misguided. —*pp.* of DESAVISAR.

Desavisar [des-ah-ve-sar'], *va.* To give a contrary account, to contradict a former advice, to countermand.

Desayudar [des-ah-yoo-dar'], *va.* Not to assist, but oppose one with regard to his claims or rights.—*vr.* To be negligent or careless in the performance of one's duty.

Desayunar [des-ah-yoo-nar'], *va.* To give the first intelligence of any thing unknown.—*vr.* 1. To breakfast. 2. (Met.) To have the first intelligence of any thing.

Desayuno [des-ah-yoo'-no], *m.* Light breakfast.

Desayuntamiento [des-ah-yoon-tah-me-en'-to], *m.* (Agr.) Unyoking, uncoupling.

Desayuntar [des-ah-yoon-tar'], *va.* To disunite, to dissolve, to separate; to uncouple a working span.

Desayustar [des-ah-yoos-tar'], *va.* (Naut.) To unbend a rope or cable.

Desazogar [des-ah-tho-gar'], *va.* To take off the quicksilver from a looking-glass or any other thing.—*vr.* (Peru.) To become unquiet, restless.

Desazón [day-sah-thone'], *f.* 1. Insipidity, want of taste or flavour. 2. Disgust, displeasure. 3. (Met.) Disquietness, uneasiness, affliction, restlessness. 4. Unfitness of a soil for agricultural purposes.

Desazonado, da [day-sah-tho-nah'-do, dah], *a.* 1. Ill-adapted, unfit for some purpose: applied to land. 2. Peevish, impertinent, passionate, ill-humoured. 3. Poorly, indifferent in health.—*pp.* of DESAZONAR.

Desazonar [day-sah-tho-nar'], *va.* 1. To render tasteless, to infect with an unpleasant taste. 2. To disgust, to vex, to mortify.—*vr.* To become indisposed in health, to be sick.

Desazufrar [des-ah-thoo-frar'], *va.* (Chem.) To desulphurize, desulphur.

Desbabador [des-bah-bah-dor'], *m.* A mouthing bit, put on a horse to excite salivation.

Desbabar [des-bah-bar'], *vn.* To drivel, to slaver.—*vr.* (Coll.) To be deeply in love, to regard with excessive fondness, to dote upon.

Desbagar [des-bah-gar'], *va.* To extract the flax-seed from the capsule.

Desbalijamiento [des-bah-le-hah-me-en'-to], *m.* The plundering of a portmanteau.

Desbalijar [des-bah-le-har'], *va.* To plunder a portmanteau of its contents.

Desballestar [des-bal-lyes-tar'], *va.* To unbend a cross-bow, to take it asunder.

Desbancar [des-ban-car'], *va.* 1. To clear a room of the benches, etc. 2. To win all the money staked by a gambler, who holds a basset or faro-table. 3. (Met.) To circumvent one in the friendship and affection of another.

Desbandarse [des-ban-dar'-say], *vr.* To disband, to desert the colours: applied to soldiers.

Desbañado [des-bah-nyah'-do], *a.* Applied to a hawk that has not taken water when required.

Desbarahustar, *va.* *V.* DESBARAJUSTAR.

Desbarajustar [des-bah-rah-hoos-tar'], *va.* To disorder, confuse, mix things

Desbarajuste [des-bah-rah-hoos'-tay], *m.* Disorder, confused medley of things.

Desbaratadamente, *adv.* Disorderly.

Desbaratado, da [des-bah-rah-tah'-do, dah], *a.* Debauched, corrupted with lewdness and intemperance.—*pp.* of DESBARATAR.

Desbaratador, ra [des-bah-rah-tah-dor', rah], *m.* & *f.* 1. Destroyer, confounder, disturber. 2. Debaucher.

Desbaratamiento [des-bah-rah-tah-me-en'-to], *m.* Perturbation, commotion decomposition.

Desbaratar [des-bah-rah-tar'], *va.* 1. To destroy or break up any thing. 2. To defeat or rout an army. 3. To waste, to misspend, to dissipate; to cross. 4. To impede, disturb. *Desbaratar la paz,* To break the peace. *Desbaratar la plática,* To interrupt the conversation.—*vn.* To speak foolishly to talk nonsense.—*vr.* To be confounded, to be disordered in mind, to be deranged.

Desbarate, Desbarato [des-bah-rah'-tay, des-bah-rah'-to], *m.* 1. The act of routing or defeating. 2. Ignorance, folly, madness, misgovernment. *Desbarate de vientre,* Frequent stools, loose bowels.

Desbaraustar, *va.* (Obs.) *V.* DESBARAJUSTAR.

Desbarauste, *m.* (Obs.) *V.* DESBARAJUSTE.

Desbarbado, da [des-bar-bah'-do, dah], *a.* Beardless.—*pp.* of DESBARBAR.

Desbarbar [des-bar-bar'], *va.* 1. (Coll.) To shave. 2. (Met.) To trim, to cut off the filaments of plants, loose threads of stuff, or other things.

Desbarbillar [des-bar-beel-lyar'], *va.* (Agr.) To prune the roots which spring from the stems of young vines.

Desbardar [des-bar-dar'], *va.* To uncover a wall or fence, to remove the brushwood or straw placed on the top of a mud wall to preserve it from injury.

Desbarrar [des-bar-rar'], *vn.* 1. To throw (with an iron bar) as far as the strength permits, without heeding to take aim. 2. To slip, to rove, to go beyond limits. 3. (Met.) To ramble beyond proper bounds; extravagate. 4. To err, mistake in what is said or done.

Desbarretar [des-bar-ray-tar'], *va.* To unbar, to unbolt.

Desbarrigado, da [des-bar-re-gah'-do, dah], *a.* Little-bellied.—*pp.* of DESBARRIGAR.

Desbarrigar [des-bar-re-gar'], *va.* To eventerate, to rip open the belly.

Desbarro [des-bar'-ro], *m.* 1. The act of slipping or falling into fault or error. 2. Nonsense, madness, extravagance, frenzy.

Desbastadura [des-bas-tah-doo'-rah], *f.* The act of planing, trimming, or polishing.

Desbastar [des-bas-tar'], *va.* 1. To plane, to smooth the surface of boards. 2. To trim, to polish. 3. To waste, to consume, to weaken. 4. To purify one's morals and manners.

Desbaste [des-bahs'-tay], *m.* The act of hewing, polishing, or trimming.

Desbastecido, da [des-bas-tay-thee'-do, dah], *a.* Unprovided.

Desbautizarse [des-bah-oo-te-thar'-say], *vr.* 1. (Coll. Met.) To be irritated, to fly into a passion. 2. To change one's name, renounce the baptismal name. 3. (Coll.) To fall from a height and break one's head.

Desbazadero [des-bah-thah-day'-ro], *m.* Humid, slippery place.

Desbeber [des-bay-berr'], *va.* (Coll.) To urinate.

Desbecerrar [des-bay-ther-rar'], *va.* To wean young animals.

Desbituminación [des-be-too-me-nah-the-on'], *f.* Removal of bitumen from a body.

Desbituminizar [des-be-too-me-ne-thar'], *va.* To remove bitumen.

Desblandir [des-blan-deer'], *va.* To remove grease from skins in running water in order to curry them better.

Desblanquecido, da [des-blan-kay-thee'-do, dah], *a.* Blanched. *V.* BLANQUECINO.

Desblanquiñado [des-blan-ke-nyah'-do], *m.* *V.* DESBLANQUECIDO.

Desbocadamente, *adv.* Impudently, ungovernedly.

Desbocado, da [des-bo-cah'-do, dah], *a.* 1. Open-mouthed, wide at the mouth: applied to a piece of ordnance. 2. Wild: applied to a horse. 3. Broken-lipped or mouthed, mouthless. 4. (Met.) Foul-mouthed, indecent.—*pp.* of DESBOCAR.

Desbocamiento [des-bo-cah-me-en'-to], *m.* Impertinence, impudence.

Desbocar [des-bo-car'], *va.* To break the brim of a mug, jar, or other vessel.—*vn.* To disembogue. *V.* DESEMBOCAR.—*vr.* 1. To be hard-mouthed, to be insensible of the bridle. 2. To use injurious or abusive language. 3. To be wild, not to obey the bridle: applied to a horse.

Desbombar [des-bom-bar'], *va.* (Littl. us.) To pump out water.

Desbonetarse [des-bo-nay-tar'-say], *vr.* (Coll.) To take off the cap or bonnet, to be uncovered.

Desboquillar [des-bo-keel-lyar'], *va.* To break the mouth of a vessel.

Desbordamiento [des-bor-dah-me-en'-to], *m.* 1. Inundation. 2. Overflowing.

Desbordar [des-bor-dar'], *vn.* To overthrow, to inundate, to run over the brim of a vessel.

Desboronar [des-bo-ro-nar'], *va.* (Prov.) *V.* DESMORONAR.

Desborrar [des-bor-rar'], *va.* 1. To cut off the loose threads of stuff when it comes out of the loom. 2. (Prov.) To lop off the branches of trees, particularly of the mulberry.

Desboscar [des-bos-car'], *va.* To deforest, to destroy the trees and woods of mountains particularly.

Desbozar [des-bo-thar'], *va.* To take off the relievos, carvings, or mouldings of a statue.

Desbragado, da [des-brah-gah'-do, dah], *a.* Unbreeched.

Desbraguetado, da [des-brah-gay-tah'-do, dah], *a.* 1. Having the fore-part of the breeches unbuttoned and open. 2. Careless, heedless.

Desbravar, Desbravecer [des-brah-var'], *vn.* 1. To tame, to break in: applied to horses. 2. To diminish the strength or force of any thing, to mollify, to moderate; to lose some part of the fierceness.

Desbrazarse [des-brah-thar'-say], *vr.* To extend one's arms, to stretch out the arms violently.

Desbrevarse [des-bray-var'-say], *vr.* To evaporate, to lose body and strength: applied to wine and strong liquors.

Desbridar [des-bre-dar'], *va.* 1. To break or remove a bridle. 2. (Med.) To pare away parts which hinder widening a wound.

Desbriznar [des-brith-nar'], *va.* 1. To chop or mince meat. 2. To cut or divide a thing into small parts. 3. To pluck the stamens of saffron.

Desbroce [des-bro'-thay], *m.* Clippings, cuttings from pruning trees; and the clearing of lands or trenches.

Desbrozar [des-bro-thar'], *va.* To clear away rubbish.

Desbrozo [des-bro'-tho], *m.* The act of clearing away rubbish.

Desbruar [des-broo-ar'], *va.* To clean cloth of grease, to put it in the fulling-mill.

Desbrujar [des-broo-har'], *va.* *V.* DESMORONAR.

Desbuchar [des-boo-char'], *va.* 1. To disclose one's secrets, to tell all one knows. 2. To ease the stomach: applied to birds of prey. 3. *V.* DESAINAR.

Desbulla [des-bool'-lyah], *f.* The part of an oyster that remains on the shell.

Desbullar [des-bool-lyar'], *va.* To extract an oyster from its shell.

Descabal [des-cah-bahl'], *a.* Imperfect, incomplete.

Descabaladura [des-cah-bah-lah-doo'-rah], *f.* Diminution, impairment of a thing.

Descabalar [des-cah-bah-lar'], *va.* 1. To make incomplete, to take away some necessary part; to unmatch. 2. To pilfer; to diminish the weight, quantity, or number of things, by petty thefts. 3. To impair the perfection of any thing.

Descabalgadura [des-cah-bal-gah-doo'-rah], *f.* The act of dismounting or alighting from a horse.

Descabalgar [des-cah-bal-gar'], *vn.* To dismount, to alight from a horse.—*va.* To dismount. *Descabalgar la artillería de las cureñas,* To dismount the guns, to take them from their carriages.

Descaballar [des-cah-bal-lyar'], *va.* Among gardeners, to take away the leaves and superfluous buds of plants.

Descabelladamente, *adv.* Without order or regularity.

Descabellado, da [des-cah-bel-lyah'-do, dah], *a.* 1. Dishevelled: applied to hair. 2. (Met.) Disorderly, out of all rule and order. 3. Lavish, wild, unrestrained. 4. Disproportional. 5. Preposterous, absurd.—*pp.* of DESCABELLAR.

Descabelladura [des-cah-bel-lyah-doo'-rah], *f.* The act and effect of tossing the hair.

Descabellamiento [des-cah-bel-lyah-me-en'-to], *m.* *V.* DESPROPÓSITO.

Descabellar [des-cah-bel-lyar'], *va.* 1. To disorder and undress the hair; commonly used as reciprocal. 2. To kill the bull by pricking it in the back of the neck with the point of the sword.

Descabestrar [des-cah-bes-trar'], *va.* To unhalter. *V.* DESENCABESTRAR.

Descabezado, da [des-cah-bay-thah'-do, dah], *a.* 1. Beheaded. 2. Light-headed, injudicious, void of judgment, giddy.—*pp.* of DESCABEZAR.

Descabezamiento [des-cah-bay-thah-me-en'-to], *m.* 1. The act of beheading. 2. The state of a person who is bewildered, or does not know how to act.

Descabezar [des-cah-bay-thar'], *va.* 1. To behead. 2. To revoke an assessment which towns have made. 3. To cut the upper parts or points of some things; to head, top, poll. 4. To begin, to let the beginning of a thing pass over. 5. (Naut.) To break a mast through its neck. *Descabezar el sueño,* To take a nap. *Descabezar la misa,* To let the beginning of the mass be over, before one enters church.—*vn.* To terminate, to join another property: speaking of the part of an estate or piece of land which adjoins another, belonging to a different person.—*vr.* 1. To screw one's wits, to batter one's brains. 2. To take the grain from the ears of corn. *Descabezarse una vena,* To burst a blood-vessel.

Descabritar [des-cah-bre-tar'], *va.* To wean goats.

Descabullirse [des-cah-bool-lyeer'-say], *vr.* 1. To sneak off, to steal away, to scamper. 2. (Met.) To elude the strength of an argument, to avoid a difficulty by artifice.

Descacilar [des-cah-the-lar'], *va.* (Prov.) To cut the extreme ends of bricks equally.

Descaderar [des-cah-day-rar'], *va.* To hip, to sprain or dislocate the hip.

Descadillar [des-cah-deel-lyar'], *va.* In woollen manufactories, to cut off the loose threads or fag-end of the warp.

Descaecer [des-cah-ay-therr'], *vn.* 1. To decline, to droop, to languish, to decay. 2. (Naut.) To edge away.

Descaecido, da [des-cah-ay-thee'-do, dah], *a.* Weak, feeble, languishing.—*pp.* of DESCAECER.

Descaecimiento, Descaimiento [des-cah-ay-the-me-en'-to], *m.* 1. Weakness, debility, decay. 2. Despondency, lowness of spirits, languor.

Descaer, *vn.* (Obs.) *V.* DECAER.

(*Yo descaezco,* from *Descaecer. V.* ABORRECER.)

Descalabazarse [des-cah-lah-bah-thar'-say], *vr.* (Coll.) To puzzle one's brains, to screw one's wits.

Descalabrado, da [des-cah-lah-brah'-do, dah], *a.* & *pp.* of DESCALABRAR. Injured; wounded on the head. *Salir descalabrado,* To be a loser in any suit, game, or business.

Descalabradura [des-cah-lah-brah-doo'-rah], *f.* 1. Contusion or wound in the head. 2. The scar remaining after such wound.

Descalabrar [des-cah-lah-brar'], *va.* 1. To break or wound the head slightly. 2. To attack or impeach one's character. 3. To hurt, to injure. (Naut.) To cause a ship considerable damage. To occasion losses to the enemy. 4. To cause annoyance. 5. To annoy by screams.—*vr.* To fall from a height and break one's skull. (Peru.) To be ruined, violently destroyed. *Vd. me descalabra con esto,* (Iron.) You will neither do what you offer nor give what you promise. Literally, You break my head with your proposal.

Descalabro [des-cah-lah'-bro], *m.* A calamitous event, a considerable loss; misfortune.

Descalandrajar [des-cah-lan-drah-har'], *va.* To rend or tear one's clothes.

Descalar [des-cah-lar'], *va.* (Naut.) To unship the helm, unhang the rudder.

Descalcador [des-cal-cah-dor'], *m.* (Carp.) Ripping-iron, claw; (naut.) rave-hook.

Descalcar [des-cal-car'], *va.* To take out old oakum from the seams of a boat.

Descalcañalar [des-cal-cah-nyah-lar'], *va.* 1. (Prov.) To smooth, to take out the flutings or furrows. 2. (Coll.) To run shoes down at the heel.

Descalcañar [des-cal-cah-nyar'], *va.* (Littl. us.) To twist the heel of a shoe.

Descalcez [des-cal-theth'], *f.* 1. Nudity of the feet. 2. Barefootedness: applied to those institutions of monks or nuns who are not permitted to wear shoes.

Descalorarse [des-cah-lo-rar'-say], *vr.* (Prov.) *V.* DESACALORARSE.

Descalostrado, da [des-cah-los-trah'-do, dah], *a.* Having passed the days of the first milk: applied to a child suckled by its mother.

Descalzadero [des-cal-thah-day'-ro], *m.* (Prov.) Little door of a pigeon-house.

Descalzado, da [des-cal-thah'-do, dah], *a.* & *pp.* of DESCALZAR. Barefooted.

Descalzador [des-cal-thah-dor']. 1. Boot-jack. 2. (Mas.) Crowbar.

Descalzadura [des-cal-thah-doo'-rah], *f.* Laying bare, the uncovering (of feet, of a foundation, of roots, etc.).

Descalzamiento [des-cal-thah-me-en'-to], *m.* 1. The act of baring the feet. 2. (Agr.) Removal of soil, in part, about the roots of plants.

Descalzar [des-cal-thar'], *va.* 1. To pull off the shoes and stockings. 2. To remove an impediment, to surmount an obstacle: applied only to the impediment or obstacle used to prevent the motion of a wheel. 3. To To take away the bits of thin boards put under tables to make them stand fast. 4. To lose or cast a shoe or shoes: applied to horses.—*vr.* To pull off one's own shoes and stockings. *Descalzarse de risa,* To burst out into a fit of laughter. *Descalzarse los guantes,* To pull off one's gloves.

Descalzo, za [des-cahl'-tho, thah], *a.* 1. Barefoot, barefooted, shoeless. 2. Barefooted: applied to friars or nuns. In this last sense it is frequently used as a substantive.

Descallador, *m.* (Obs.) *V.* HERRADOR.

Descamación [des-cah-mah-the-on'], *f.* 1. Removal of scales or layers from bulbous roots. 2. (Med.) Desquamation of epidermis.

Descambiar [des-cam-be-ar'], *va.* To cancel an exchange or barter. *V.* DESTROCAR.

Descaminadamente, *adv.* Absurdly, unreasonably, out of order.

Descaminado, da [des-cah-me-nah'-do, dah], *a.* & *pp.* of DESCAMINAR. Ill-advised; misguided. *Ir descaminado,* To deviate from rectitude, reason, or truth; to take a wrong way.

Descaminar [des-cah-me-nar'], *va.* 1. To misguide, to mislead, to lead astray. 2. To seduce one from his duty. 3. To seize upon smuggled goods.—*vr.* To go astray.

Descamino [des-cah-mee'-no], *m.* 1. Seizure of smuggled goods. 2. The goods thus seized. 3. Deviation from the high road. 4. Error, blindness; deviation from justice, truth, and reason. 5. (Obs.) Duty imposed on things seized.

Descamisado, da [des-cah-me-sah'-do, dah], *a.* Shirtless, naked: applied commonly to indicate that a person is very poor.—*m. Es un descamisado,* (Coll.) He is a mean, poor fellow, a ragamuffin.

Descampado, da [des-cam-pah'-do, dah], *a.* Disengaged, free, open, clear. *En descampado,* In the open air, exposed to wind and weather.—*pp.* of DESCAMPAR.

Descampar [des-cam-par'], *vn.* (Obs.) *V.* ESCAMPAR.

Descansadamente, *adv.* Easily, without toil or fatigue.

Descansadero [des-can-sah-day'-ro], *m.* Resting-place.

Descansado, da [des-can-sah'-do, dah], *a.* Rested, refreshed. *Vida descansada,* A quiet, easy life.—*pp.* of DESCANSAR.

Descansar [des-can-sar'], *vn.* 1. To rest from labour and fatigue, to recover strength by repose. 2. To have some relief from cares, to give respite (said of evils). 3. To rest, to lean upon, as a joist does upon a beam. 4. To rest, to be satisfied; to trust or place confidence in the power, kindness, activity, etc., of another. 5. To repose, to sleep. *El enfermo ha descansado dos horas,* The patient has slept two hours. *Descansar las tierras,* To lie at rest: applied to lands which lie fallow. 6. To repose in the sepulchre.—*va.* To aid or alleviate another in labour or fatigue.

Descanso [des-cahn'-so], *m.* 1. Rest, repose from labour or fatigue. 2. Quiet, tranquility, peace, stillness, sleep. 3. Cause of tranquility and rest. 4. Landing-place of stairs; seat, bench, or support of any thing. 5. Day of rest, for which the drivers and muleteers receive payment. 6. Parade-rest. 7. (Naut.) A strong chock in which the claw of the anchor rests. 8. (Naut.) Partner of the bowsprit. *Descanso exterior del bauprés,* (Naut.) Pillow of the bowsprit. *Descanso interior del bauprés,* (Naut.) The inner partner of the bowsprit. *Descanso de la caña del timón,* (Naut.) Sweep of the tiller. *La caña tiene juego en el descanso,* (Naut.) The tiller shakes.

Descantar [des-can-tar'], *va.* To clear from stones.

Descantear [des-can-tay-ar'], *va.* To smooth angles or corners.

Descanterar [des-can-tay-rar'], *va.* To take off the crust of any thing: usually applied to bread.

Descantillar, Descantonar [des-can-teel-lyar'], *va.* 1. To pare off, to break off part of a thing. 2. To subtract part from a total. 3. (Met.) To lessen, to speak ill of some one, to murmur at one's neighbour.

Descantillón [des-can-teel-lyone'], *m.* A small line marking the proper scantling to which any thing is to be cut.

Descañar [des-cah-nyar'], *va.* To pull up by the roots the canes from a piece of ground in order to utilize it; to break the stem or branch of any thing.

Descañonar [des-cah-nyo-nar'], *va.* 1. To pluck out the feathers of a bird or fowl. 2. To shave close. 3. (Met.) To trick one out of his money at gambling or otherwise.

Descaperuzar [des-cah-pay-roo-thar'], *va.* To take off the cowl or hood from another's head.—*vr.* To take off one's cowl or hood to salute another; to uncover one's head.

Descaperuzo [des-cah-pay-roo'-tho], *m.* Taking off the cowl, hood, or hunting-cap, in saluting.

Descapillar [des-cah-peel-lyar'], *va.* To take off the hood. *V.* DESCAPERUZAR.

Descapirotar [des-cah-pe-ro-tar'], *va.* To take off the *capirote* or ancient head-cover, now used by doctors of some universities.

Descaradamente, *adv.* Impudently, saucily, barefacedly.

Descarado, da [des-cah-rah'-do, dah], *a.* Impudent, barefaced, saucy, pert, petulant—*pp.* of DESCARARSE.

Descararse [des-cah-rar'-say], *vr.* To behave in an impudent or insolent manner.

Descarburar [des-car-boo-rar'], *va.* To decarbonize, remove carbon from a body containing it.

Descarcañalar [des-car-cah-nyah-lar'], *va.* & *vr.* To run down the heel of a shoe.

Descarga [des-car'-gah], *f.* 1. Unburdening, unloading. 2. The act of mitigating the pressure. 3. Volley, a general discharge of great or small guns, flight, shooting. 4. *Descarga de aduana,* (Com.) Clearance at the custom-house, permit to unload a vessel. *Descarga general del costado del navío,* (Naut.) Broadside of a man-of-war. 5. Unloading or discharge of the cargo of a ship. 6. Exoneration.

Descargadero [des-car-gah-day'-ro], *m.* Wharf, unloading-place.

Descargador [des-car-gah-dor'], *m.* Discharger.

Descargadura [des-car-gah-doo'-rah], *f.* Taking bones out of meat, to render it more useful.

Descargamiento [des-car-gah-me-en'-to], *m.* (Obs.) Discharging, exoneration.

Descargar [des-car-gar'], *va.* 1. To unload, to discharge, to disburden, to ease, to take off or alleviate a burden, to lighten. *Descargar las paredes,* (Arch.) To support walls with buttresses. 2. To take off the flap and bones of meat. 3. To fire, to discharge fire-arms, to unload fire-arms, to draw out the charge of powder and ball. 4. To unload a cargo. (Naut.) 5. To brace a lee, to clear the sails or yards. 6. To put the rudder in the middle or on an even keel, in a line with the keel. 7. To lower slightly the sheets, so as to diminish the surface and angle which the sails present to the wind. 8. To make port by degrees. 9. To acquit, to clear from a charge of guilt. 10. To acquit, to exonerate, to liberate from a charge, obligation, or debt.—*vn.* To disembogue or disgorge waters into the sea. *Descargar o meter en viento una vela,* (Naut.) To fill a sail again.—*vr.* 1. (Law) To give a plea or answer to an impeachment or accusation; to assign or allege a cause of non-appearance when summoned. 2. To resign one's place or employment. 3. In painting, to lose brightness and lustre: applied to colors.

Descargo [des-car'-go], *m.* 1. Exoneration, discharge, acquittal. 2. Acquittance, receipt. 3. Plea or answer to an impeachment or action; acquitted from blame.

Descargue [des-car'-gay], *m.* 1. Unloading. 2. License to discharge vessels. 3. The last and largest metal plate of those which come from the furnace.

Descariñarse [des-cah-ree-nyar'-say], *vr.* To withdraw the love or affection for a thing, to become cool.

Descariño [des-cah-ree'-nyo], *m.* Coolness, indifference.

Descarnador [des-car-nah-dor'], *m.* Scraper, an instrument with which the flesh is removed from a tooth that is to be drawn.

Descarnadura [des-car-nah-doo'-rah], *f.* Excarnification, clearing from flesh.

Descarnar [des-car-nar'], *va.* 1. To excarnate, to clear from flesh. 2. To take away part of a thing. *Descarnar los pellejos,* Among curriers, to scrape hides or skins with the drawing-knife. 3. To remove one from earthly things. —*vr.* 1. To lose flesh, emaciate. 2. (Naut.) To destroy, undermine a spot of ground (said of the sea). 3. To become uncovered: applied to lands or beaches which the sea used to cover over. 4. (Agr.) To prune too severely.

Descaro [des-cah'-ro], *m.* 1. Impudence, barefacedness, effrontery. 2. Sauciness, forwardness; assurance.

Descarriamiento [des-car-re-ah-me-en'-to], *m.* 1. The act of losing one's way or going astray. 2. The act of making any one lose his way.

Descarriar [des-car-re-ar'], *va.* 1. To take out of the right road, to lead astray, to misguide, to mislead. 2. To separate cattle.—*vr.* 1. To be disjoined or separated. 2. (Met.) To deviate from justice or reason. 3. To go astray, to become vitiated, corrupted; to acquire bad habits.

Descarrilamiento [des-car-re-lah-me-en'-to], *m.* Derailment of cars.

Descarrilar [des-car-re-lar'], *va.* & *vr.* To derail a train; to run off the track.

Descarrillar [des-car-reel-lyar'], *va.* To tear the jaws asunder.

Descarrío [des-car-ree'-o], *m.* The act of losing one's way or going astray.

Descartar [des-car-tar'], *va.* To discard, to fling away, to dismiss, to eject, to put aside, to lay out.—*vr.* 1. To discard, or to throw out of the hand such cards as are useless. 2. To excuse one's self; to refuse doing what is solicited or required.

Descarte [des-car'-tay], *m.* 1. The cards discarded or thrown out as useless. 2. The act of discarding. 3. (Met.) Evasion, subterfuge.

Descarzar [des-car-thar'], *va.* 1. To remove fungous matter from the trunks of trees. 2. To remove empty comb from a bee-hive.

Descasamiento [des-cah-sah-me-en'-to], *m.* 1. Unmarrying. 2. Divorce, repudiation.

Descasar [des-cah-sar'], *va.* 1. To unmarry, to divorce: to declare a marriage null. 2. (Met.) To remove or disturb the order of things. 3. (Typ.) To alter the position of the pages of a sheet, in order to suitably rearrange them.

Descascar [des-cas-car'], *va.* To decorticate.—*vr.* To break into pieces.

Descascarador [des-cas-cah-rah-dor'], *m.* Sheller, husker.

Descascarar [des-cas-cah-rar'], *va.* 1. To peel, to decorticate, to flay. 2. (Met.) To boast or talk much, to bluster, to bully.—*vr.* To fall or come off: applied to the last superficies of things.

Descaspar [des-cas-par'], *va.* 1. Among curriers, to scrape off the fleshy parts of a half-dressed hide. 2. To take dandruff from the head.

Descastado, da [des-cas-tah'-do, dah], *a.* Showing little natural affection to relatives, or others to whom it is due.

Descastar [des-cas-tar'], *va.* 1. To lose caste, to deteriorate a race or lineage. 2. To make an end of a caste (applied to ants, bugs, etc.). (Acad.) *V.* Desencastar.

Descaudalado, da [des-cah-oo-dah-lah'-do, dah], *a.* Penniless.

Descebar [des-thay-bar'], *va.* To unprime fire-arms, to take away the priming of guns.

Descendencia [des-then-den'-the-ah], *f.* Descent, origin, offspring, extraction, house.

Descendente [des-then-den'-tay], *pa.* Descending.

Descender [des-then-derr'], *va.* & *vn.* 1. To descend, to get or to go down, to walk downward. 2. To flow or run, as liquids. 3. To descend to, to proceed from, to be derived from. 4. To let down, to lower any thing.

Descendida [des-then-dee'-dah], *f.* (Obs.) 1. Descent. 2. Maritime expedition and disembarkment.

Descendiente [des-then-de-en'-tay], *pa.* & *m.* 1. Descending. 2. Descendant, the offspring of an ancestor. 3. Lineal, allied by lineal descent.

Descendiente, *f.* (Obs.) *V.* Bajada.

Descendimiento [des-then-de-me-en'-to], *m.* 1. Descent. 2. Descension. 3. (Obs.) Defluxion from the head to the breast.

Descensión [des-then-se-on'], *f.* 1. Descension, descent. 2. (Obs.) *V.* Descendencia.

Descenso [des-then'-so], *m.* 1. Descent. 2. The act of putting one from his degree or of reducing from a higher to a lower state; degradation. 3. The rapid flight of a bird of prey in order to fall upon its prey. 4. A conducting tube. 5. (Med.) Hernia, rupture. 6. Prolapse of the womb.

Descentralización [des-then-trah-le-thah-the-on'], *f.* Decentralization.

Descentralizar [des-then-trah-le-thar'], *va.* 1. To decentre. 2. To decentralize, divide the powers and authority of the state. 3. To grant local autonomy.

Desceñidura [des-thay-nye-doo'-rah], *f.* (Obs.) Disjunction, act of untying.

Desceñir [des-thay-nyeer'], *va.* To ungird, to loosen or take off the girdle or belt with which clothes are tied.

Descepar [des-thay-par'], *va.* 1. To eradicate, to pull up by the roots. 2. (Naut.) To remove the anchor-stocks.

Descerar [des-thay-rar'], *va.* To take the empty combs from a bee-hive.

Descercado, da [des-ther-cah'-do, dah], *a.* Open, unfortified, undefended: applied to places.— *pp.* of Descercar.

Descercador [des-ther-cah-dor'], *m.* He that forces the enemy to raise a siege.

Descercar [des-ther-car'], *va.* 1. To destroy or pull down a wall. 2. To oblige the enemy to raise a siege.

Descerco [des-therr'-co], *m.* (Obs.) The act of raising a siege.

Descerrajado, da [des-ther-rah-hah'-do, dah], *a.* Corrupt, vicious, wicked, ill-disposed.—*pp.* of Descerrajar.

Descerrajadura [des-ther-rah-hah-doo'-rah], *f.* The act of taking off locks or bolts.

Descerrajar [des-ther-rah-har'], *va.* 1. To take off the lock of a door, chest, trunk, etc. 2. To discharge fire-arms.

Descerrumarse [des-ther-roo-mar'-say], *vr.* To be wrenched or distorted: applied to the muscles of a beast.

(*Yo desciendo, yo descienda,* from *Descender. V.* Atender.)

Descifrable [des-the-frah'-blay], *a.* Decipherable.

Descifrador [des-the-frah-dor'], *m.* Decipherer.

Descifrar [des-the-frar'], *va.* 1. To decipher, to explain writings in cipher. 2. (Met.) To unravel, to interpret the obscure, intricate, and of difficult understanding. 3. To translate a language or an unknown, strange inscription.

Descinchar [des-thin-char'], *va.* To ungirt a horse.

Desclavador [des-clah-vah-dor'], *m.* Nail-pull, drawer.

Desclavar [des-clah-var'], *va.* To draw out nails; to unnail.

Descoagulable [des-co-ah-goo-lah'-blay], *a.* Redisolvable after coagulation.

Descoagulación [des-co-ah-goo-lah-the-on'], *f.* Solution, liquefaction of a clot or curd.

Descoagular [des-co-ah-goo-lar'], *va.* To liquefy, to dissolve.

Descobajar [des-co-bah-har'], *va.* To pull the stem from a grape.

Descobijar [des-co-be-har'], *va.* To uncover, to undress.

Descocadamente [des-co-cah-dah-men'-tay], *adv.* Impudently, boldly, brazen-facedly.

Descocado, da [des-co-cah'-do, dah], *a.* Bold, impudent, licentious (of women). —*pp.* of Descocar.

Descocar [des-co-car'], *va.* To clean, to clear trees from insects.—*vr.* To be impudent, saucy, or petulant.

Descocer [des-co-therr'], *va.* 1. To digest, to concoct in the stomach. 2. *Descocer los tablones de un bajel,* (Naut.) To rip off the planks of a ship.

Descocho, cha [des-co'-cho, chah], *a.* (Obs.) Very much boiled.

Descoco [des-co'-co], *m.* Barefacedness, impudence, boldness, sauciness.

Descodar [des-co-dar'], *va.* (Prov.) To rip, to unstitch.

Descoger [des-co-herr'], *va.* To unfold, to extend, to spread, to expand.

Descogollar [des-co-gol-lyar'], *va.* To take out the heart or bud of a plant; to strip the summit.

Descogotado, da [des-co-go-tah'-do, dah], *a.* Having the neck naked and exposed.—*pp.* of Descogotar.

Descogotar [des-co-go-tar'], *va.* (Obs.) 1. To kill a beast by one blow on the nape. 2. To knock off with one blow on the nape. 3. To knock off the horns of a stag at one blow.

Descolar [des-co-lar'], *va.* 1. To cut off an animal's tail, to dock. 2. To cut off the fag-end of a piece of cloth.

Descolchar [des-col-char'], *va.* (Naut.) To untwist a cable.

Descolgar [des-col-gar'], *va.* 1. To take down what has been hung up. 2. To unhang, to take down hangings or tapestry.—*vr.* 1. To come down gently, to slip down by means of a rope or any other thing. 2. (Met.) To glide flow, or run down: applied to streams or rivers.

Descolmar [des-col-mar'], *va.* 1. To strike corn in a measure with a strickle. 2. (Met.) To diminish.

Descolmillar [des-col-meel-lyar'], *va.* To pull out or break the eye-teeth.

Descoloración [des-co-lo-rah-the-on'], *f.* 1. Discoloration. 2. (Chem.) Discolourizing.

Descoloramiento [des-co-lo-rah-me-en'-to], *m.* Paleness, discoloration.

Descolorar [des-co-lo-rar'], *va.* To discolour, to pale, to change from the natural hue.—*vr.* To lose the natural hue, to become discoloured or pale.

Descolorido, da [des-co-lo-ree'-do, dah], *a.* Discoloured, pale, colourless, pallid. —*pp.* of Descolorir.

Descolorir [des-co-lo-reer'], *va.* To discolour, to change from the natural hue.

Descolladamente [des-col-lyah-dah-men'-tay], *adv.* Loftily, haughtily; with an air of authority.

Descollamiento, *m.* *V.* Descuello.

Descollar [des-col-lyar'], *vn.* To overtop, to excel, to surpass.—*vr.* To exceed, to outdo, to be superior to others.

Descombrar [des-com-brar'], *va.* To remove obstacles or encumbrances.

Descomedidamente, *adv.* 1. Rudely, coarsely, unmannerly; haughtily. 2. Excessively, immoderately.

Descomedido, da [des-co-may-dee'-do, dah], *a.* 1. Excessive, disproportionate, immoderate. 2. Rude, impudent, insolent.—*pp.* of Descomedirse.

Descomedimiento [des-co-may-de-me-en'-to], *m.* Rudeness, incivility.

Descomedirse [des-co-may-deer'-say], *vr.* To be rude or disrespectful, to act or speak unmannerly.

Descomer [des-co-merr'], *vn.* (Coll.) To ease nature, to go to stool.

(*Yo me descomido*, from *Descomedirse.* *V.* Pedir.)

Descomodidad [des-co-mo-de-dahd'], *f.* Incommodity, inconvenience, uncomfortableness. (Ant.)

Descompadrar [des-com-pah-drar'], *vn.* To disagree, to fall out with one.

Descompás [des-com-pahs'], *m.* Excess, redundance, want of measure or proportion. (Acad.)

Descompasadamente, *adv.* *V.* Descomedidamente.

Descompasado, da [des-com-pah-sah'-do, dah], *a.* 1. Excessive, extravagant, beyond rule and measure, disproportionable. 2. Out of tune or time.—*pp.* of Descompasarse.

Descompasarse [des-com-pah-sar'-say], *vr.* 1. To exceed all rule and measure, to trangress all bounds and proportions. 2. To be out of tune or time. 3. (Met.) To insult a person.

Descomponer [des-com-po-nerr'], *va.* 1. To discompose, to alter the order or composition of a thing. 2. To discompose, to destroy harmony and friendship, to set at odds, to disconcert. 3. To decompound. 4. (Chem.) To decompose bodies.—*vr.* 1. To be out of temper, to transgress the rules of modesty and good behaviour. 2. To be indisposed or out of order. 3. To change for the worse: applied to the weather.

(*Yo descompongo*, from *Descomponer.* *V.* Poner.)

Descomposición [des-com-po-se-the-on'], *f.* 1. Disagreement, disaccord. 2. Discomposure, disorder, confusion. 3. (Chem.) Breakdown, analysis.

Descompostura [des-com-pos-too'-rah], *f.* 1. Disagreement. 2. Discomposure, disorder, confusion, perturbation. 3. Slovenliness, uncleanliness. 4. Forwardness, impudence, want of modesty, disrespectful conduct.

Descompresión [des-com-pray-se-on'], *f.* Decompression.

Descompuestamente, *adv.* Audaciously, impudently, insolently.

Descompuesto, ta [des-com-poo-es'-to, tah], *a.* 1. Audacious, impudent, insolent; immodest; out of order. 2. (Bot.) Branching much at the base (of stems); decompound (of leaves and petals).—*pp.* of Descomponer.

Descomulgado, da [des-co-mool-gah'-do, dah], *a.* Perverse, nefarious, wicked. —*pp.* of Descomulgar.

Descomulgador [des-co-mool-gah-dor'], *m.* Excommunicator. *V.* Excomulgador.

Descomulgar [des-co-mool-gar'], *va.* To excommunicate.

Descomunal [des-co-moo-nahl'], *a.* Extraordinary, monstrous, enormous, colossal.

Descomunalmente, *adv.* Uncommonly, immoderately, extraordinarily.

Descomunión [des-co-moo-ne-on'], *f.* Excommunication. *V.* Excomunión.

Desconcertadamente, *adv.* Disorderly, confusedly.

Desconcertado, da [des-con-ther-tah'-do, dah], *a.* Disorderly, slovenly.—*pp.* of Desconcertar.

Desconcertador [des-con-ther-tah-dor'], *m.* Disturber, disconcerter.

Desconcertante [des-con-ther-tahn'-tay], *a.* Disconcerting.

Desconcertar [des-con-ther-tar'], *va.* 1. To discompose, to disturb the order of things, to confound, to confuse. 2. To disconcert, to defeat machinations, measures, etc.—*vr.* 1. To disagree. 2. To luxate, to put out of joint, to disjoint. 3. To exceed the limits of prudence.

Desconcierto [des-con-the-err'-to], *m.* 1. Discomposure, disagreement of parts. 2. Discomposure, disorder, confusion. 3. Want of prudence and circumspection. 4. Flux, or looseness of the body.

(*Yo desconcierto*, from *Desconcertar.* *V.* Acertar.)

Desconcordia [des-con-cor'-de-ah], *f.* Discord, disagreement, variance, disunion.

Desconchar [des-con-char'], *va.* To strip off a surface of varnish, stucco, plaster, etc.

Desconectar [des-co-nec-tar'], *va.* To disconnect.

Desconfiadamente [des-con-fe-ah-dah-men'-tay], *adv.* Diffidently, mistrustfully.

Desconfiado, da [des-con-fe-ah'-do, dah], *a.* Diffident, distrustful, mistrustful, jealous.—*pp.* of Desconfiar.

Desconfianza [des-con-fe-ahn'-thah], *f.* 1. Diffidence, distrust, mistrust. 2. Jealousy, suspicious fear.

Desconfiar [des-con-fe-ar'], *vn.* 1. To distrust, to have no confidence in. 2. To mistrust, to suspect, to regard with distrust. *¿Desconfía Vd. de mi integridad?* Do you doubt my integrity?

Desconformar [des-con-for-mar'], *vn.* To dissent, to disagree, to differ in opinion.—*vr.* To discord, to disagree, not to suit with.

Desconforme [des-con-for'-may], *a.* 1. Discordant, disagreeing, contrary. 2. Unequal, unlike.

Desconformidad [des-con-for-me-dahd'], *f.* 1. Disagreement, opposition, contrariety of opinion, nonconformity. 2. Inequality, dissimilitude, unlikeness.

Descongelador [des-con-hay-lah-dor'], *m.* Defroster, deicer.

Descongelar [des-con-hay-lar'], *va.* To defrost.—*vn.* To melt.

Desconocer [des-co-no-therr'], *va.* 1. Not to preserve the idea which was held of something. 2. To recognize the notable change which is found in some person or thing. 3. To disown, to disavow. 4. To mistake, to be totally ignorant of a thing, not to know a person. *Desconocer la tierra,* To be unacquainted with a country. *Desconocer a uno por hijo,* Not to own one as a son. *Desconocer el beneficio,* Not to acknowledge a favour received; to be ungrateful.

Desconocidamente, *adv.* 1. Ignorantly. 2. Ungratefully.

Desconocido, da [des-co-no-thee'-do, dah], *a.* Strange, unknown, ungrateful.—*m.* & *f.* Stranger.

Desconocimiento [des-co-no-the-me-en'-to], *m.* 1. Ungratefulness, ingratitude. 2. Ignorance.

(*Yo desconozco*, from *Desconocer.* *V.* Aborrecer.)

Desconsentir [des-con-sen-teer'], *va.* To dissent, to disagree, not to acquiesce.

Desconsideradamente, *adv.* Inconsiderately, rashly.

Desconsiderado, da [des-con-se-day-rah'-do, dah], *a.* Inconsiderate, imprudent, thoughtless, rash.

(*Yo desconsiento*, from *Desconsentir.* *V.* Adherir.)

Desconsolación [des-con-so-lah-the-on'], *f.* Disconsolateness.

Desconsoladamente, *adv.* Inconsolably, disconsolately.

Desconsolado, da [des-con-so-lah'-do, dah], *a.* 1. Disconsolate, hapless, comfortless. 2. Disconsolate, heartsick sorrowful, melancholy.

Desconsolador, ra [des-con-so-lah-dor', rah], *a.* Disconsolate, disappointing, disconcerting, lamentable.

Desconsolar [des-con-so-lar'], *va.* To afflict, to put in pain, to treat rudely. —*vr.* To lose one's cheerfulness; to become low-spirited or afflicted.

Desconsuelo [des-con-soo-ay'-lo], *m.* 1. Affliction, trouble, disconsolateness.

(*Yo desconsuelo*, from *Desconsolar.* *V.* Acordar.

Descontagiar [des-con-tah-he-ar'], *va.* To purify, to disinfect.

Descontaminación [des-con-tah-me-nah-the-on'], *f.* Decontamination.

Descontaminar [des-con-tah-me-nar'], *va.* To decontaminate.

Descontar [des-con-tar'], *va.* 1. To discount. 2. (Met.) To abate, to lessen, to diminish. 3. To detract from merit or virtues.

Descontentadizo, za [des-con-ten-tah-dee'-tho, thah], *a.* Fastidious, too nice.

Descontentamiento [des-con-ten-tah-me-en'-to], *m.* Discontentment, displeasure, grief.

Descontentar [des-con-ten-tar'], *va.* To discontent, to dissatisfy, to displease.

Descontento [des-con-ten'-to], *m.* Discontent, uneasiness, dissatisfaction, disgust, grumbling.

Descontento, ta [des-con-ten'-to, tah], *a.* Discontent, dissatisfied, uneasy, displeased.

Descontinuar [des-con-te-noo-ar'], *va.* To discontinue, to leave off, to forbear, to give over.

Descontinuo, ua [des-con-tee'-noo-o, ah], *a.* Disjoined, discontinued.

Desconveniencia [des-con-vay-ne-en'-the-ah], *f.* Inconvenience, incommodity, disadvantage, prejudice.

Desconveniente [des-con-vay-ne-en'-tay], *pa.* Inconvenient, discording; incongruous.

Desconvenir [des-con-vay-neer'], *vn.* 1. To disagree, to discord. 2. To be unlike or dissimilar; not to suit.

Desconvidar [des-con-ve-dar'], *va.* 1. To disinvite, to retract an invitation. 2. To revoke, to annul, to rescind.

Descopar [des-co-par'], *va.* To lop off the branches of a tree.

Descorazonado, da [des-co-rah-tho-nah'-do, dah], *a.* Depressed, dejected, dispirited.

Descorazonamiento, *m.* Lowness of spirits, depression, dejection.

Descorazonar [des-co-ra-tho-nar'], *va.* 1. To tear out the heart. 2. (Met.) To dishearten, to discourage.

Descorchador [des-cor-chah-dor'], *m.* Uncorker. *Descorchador de colmena*, One who breaks the hive to steal the honey.

Descorchar [des-cor-char'], *va.* 1. To decorticate a cork-tree; to uncork. 2. To break a bee-hive to steal the honey. 3. To break open a chest or trunk to take out the contents. 4. To uncork (bottles, etc.).

Descordar [des-cor-dar'], *va.* To uncord an instrument.

Descorderar [des-cor-day-rar'], *va.* To wean lambs.

Descordonar [des-cor-do-nar'], *va.* To remove or strike off by blows of a hammer the crusty string which sticks to the mallets in a fulling-mill.

Descornar [des-cor-nar'], *va.* To dishorn, to knock off the horns of an animal. *Descornar la flor*, (Met.) To discover a trick or fraud.—*vr.* To break the skull by a fall.

Descoronar [des-co-ro-nar'], *va.* To take away the top or crown from a thing.

Descorrear [des-cor-ray-ar'], *vn.* To loosen the skin that covers the tenderlings of a deer.

Descorregido, da [des-cor-ray-hee'-do, dah], *a.* Incorrect, disarranged.

Descorrer [des-cor-rerr'], *va.* 1. To flow, as liquids. 2. To retrograde. *Descorrer la cortina*, To draw the curtain.

Descorrimiento [des-cor-re-me-en'-to], *m.* The fluxion of any liquid.

Descortés [des-cor-tes'], *a.* Impolite, uncivil, unmannerly, ill-bred, coarse, misbehaved, impudent.

Descortesía [des-cor-tay-see'-ah], *f.* Incivility, impoliteness, churlishness.

Descortesmente, *adv.* Uncivilly, discourteously, rudely.

Descortezador [des-cor-tay-thah-dor'], *m.* One who strips off the bark; decorticator.

Descortezadura, *f.* **Descortezamiento**, *m.* [des-cor-tay-thah-doo'-rah]. Decortication, excortication.

Descortezar [des-cor-tay-thar'], *va.* 1. To decorticate, to divest of the bark or husk. 2. To flay, to take off the crust of bread, to strip off the bark of trees, etc. 3. (Met.) To polish or civilize.—*vr.* To become civil and polite.

Descosedura [des-co-say-doo'-rah], *f.* Ripping, unseaming.

Descoser [des-co-serr'], *va.* 1. To rip, to unseam, to cut open. 2. (Met.) To separate, to disjoin. *No descoser los labios*, To keep a profound silence. —*vr.* 1. (Met.) To give a loose to one's tongue, to babble incessantly and indiscreetly. 2. (Coll.) *V.* Ventosear.

Descosidamente, *adv.* Excessively, immoderately.

Descosido [des-co-see'-do], *m.* 1. Babbler, an idle talker, a teller of secrets. 2. *V.* Descosedura. *Comer o beber como un descosido*, To eat or drink immoderately.

Descosido, da [des-co-see'-doe, dah], *a.* & *pp.* of Descoser. Ripped, unseamed, unstitched.

Descostillar [des-cos-til-lyar'], *va.* 1. To give many blows to any one on the ribs. 2. To take out the ribs; to break the ribs.—*vr.* To fall with violence on one's back.

Descostrar [des-cos-trar'], *va.* To take off the crust.

Descotar [des-co-tar'], *va.* 1. To remove a restriction from the use of any road, boundary, or property. 2. *vr.* To expose the neck and shoulders.

Descote [des-co'-tay], *m.* The nakedness or exposure of the neck and shoulders. *V.* Escote.

Descoyuntamiento [des-co-yoon-tah-me-en'-to], *m.* 1. Luxation, the act of disjointing bones. 2. Dislocation, a joint put out. 3. A pain or uneasiness felt in many parts of the body, in consequence of over-exertion.

Descoyuntar [des-co-yoon-tar'], *va.* 1. To luxate or disjoint bones. 2. To vex, to molest, to displease.—*vr.* To experience some violent motion. *Descoyuntarse de risa*, To split one's sides with laughing.

Descrecencia [des-cray-then'-the-ah], *f.* Decrement, decreasing.

Descrecer [des-cray-therr'], *va.* & *vn.* 1. To decrease, to make less, to diminish. 2. To decrease, to grow less. 3. To fall, to subside: applied to tides and rivers. 4. To grow short: applied to the day.

Descrecimiento [des-cray-the-me-en'-to], *m.* Decrease, diminution, decrement.

Descrédito [des-cray'-de-to], *m.* Discredit, loss of reputation.

Descreer [des-cray-err'], *va.* 1. To disbelieve. 2. To deny due credit to a person; to disown or abjure.

Descreído, da [des-cray-ee'-do, dah], *a.* Incredulous, infidel, miscreant.—*pp.* of Descreer.

Descreimiento [des-cray-ee-me-en'-to], *m.* Infidelity, unbelief, want of religious faith.

Descremar [des-cray-mar'], *va.* To skim (as milk).

Descrestar [des-cres-tar'], *va.* To take off the crest.

Descriarse [des-cre-ar'-say], *vr.* To weaken, to extenuate; to pine with desire or anxiety.

Describir [des-cre-beer'], *va.* 1. To draw, to delineate. 2. To describe, to relate minutely. 3. (Log.) To give a description.

Descripción [des-crip-the-on'], *f.* 1. Delineation, design. 2. Description, narration, account, relation. 3. (Log.) Description, imperfect definition. 4. (Law) *V.* Inventario.

Descriptivo, va [des-crip-tee'-vo, vah], *a.* Descriptive.

Descripto, ta [des-creep'-to, tah], *pp.* of Describir. Described.

Descriptor, ra [des-crip'-tor, rah], *m.* & *f.* Describer, narrator.

Descrismar [des-cris-mar'], *va.* 1. (Coll.) To give one a blow on the head. 2. To remove the crism.—*vr.* To lose patience, to be enraged.

Descristianar [des-cris-te-ah-nar'], *va.* *V.* Descrismar.

Descrito, ta, *pp. irr.* of Describir. Described.

Descruzar [des-croo-thar'], *va.* To undo the form or figure of a cross: used chiefly of the hands.

Descuadernar [des-coo-ah-der-nar'], *va.* 1. To unbind: applied to books. 2. (Met.) To discompose, to disconcert, to disorder.

Descuadrillado [des-coo-ah-dril-lyah'-do], *m.* (Vet.) Sprain in the haunch of animals.

Descuadrillado, da, *a.* Separated from the rank or lines.—*pp.* of Descuadrillar.

Descuadrillarse [des-coo-ah-dril-lyar'-say], *vr.* To be sprained in the haunches: applied to animals.

Descuajado, da [des-coo-ah-hah'-do, dah], *a.* Dispirited, deheartened.

Descuajar [des-coo-ah-har'], *va.* 1. To dissolve, to liquefy. 2. To eradicate, to pluck up weeds. 3. (Met.) To extirpate, to uproot.

Descuajo [des-coo-ah'-ho], *m.* Eradication, destroying or eradicating weeds.

Descuartelado [des-coo-ar-tay-lah'-do]. *A un descuartelado*, (Naut.) Abaft the beam: applied to a wind which blows pretty large.

Descuartelar [des-coo-ar-tay-lar']. 1. To remove troops from winter quarters. 2. (Naut.) To undo the quartering of the sails.

Descuartizar [des-coo-ar-te-thar'], *va.* 1. To quarter. 2. To carve, to cut eatables at the table.

Descubierta [des-coo-be-err'-tah], *f.* 1. Pie without an upper crust. 2. (Mil.) Recognition, inspection made in the morning, before opening the gates of a citadel, or the passes of an encampment, to prevent surprises or ambuscades. 3. (Naut.) Scanning of the horizon at sunrise and sunset. *A la descubierta*, Openly, clearly.

Descubiertamente, *adv.* Manifestly, openly.

Descubierto [des-coo-be-err'-to], *m.* 1. The solemn exposition of the sacrament. 2. Balance of accounts. 3. A deficit. *Al descubierto*, Openly, manifestly. *Dejar en descubierto*, To leave others to pay a debt. *Estar* or *quedar en descubierto*, To be a defaulter.

Descubierto, ta [des-coo-be-err'-to, tah], *a.* Patent, manifest, unveiled. *A descubierto*. (Com.) In blank.—*pp.* of Descubrir.

Descubretalles [des-coo-bray-tahl'-lyes], *m.* (Obs.) Small fan, so called because it did not hide the figure.

Descubridero [des-coo-bre-day'-ro], *m.* Eminence from which the adjacent country can be overlooked.

Descubridor, ra [des-coo-bre-dor', rah], *m.* & *f.* 1. Discoverer, finder, descrier. 2. Investigator, searcher, seeker. 3. (Mil.) Scout, spy. 4. A vessel on a voyage of discovery.

Descubrimiento [des-coo-bre-me-en'-to], *m.* 1. Discovery. 2. Discovery, disclosure. 3. Country or thing discovered.

Descubrir [des-coo-breer'], *va.* 1. To discover, to disclose, to show, to bring to light, to uncover. 2. To discover, to make visible, to expose to view, to lay open. 3. To discover, to find out. 4. To discover, to reveal, to communicate, to make known. 5. To discover things or places before unknown. 6. To expose the sacrament to public adoration or worship. 7. (Mil.) To overlook any place in a fortification. *Descubrir una vía* or *abertura de agua*, (Naut.) To discover a leak. *Descubrir la tierra*, (Naut.) To make the land. *Descubrir el campo*, (Mil.) To reconnoitre. *Descubrir por la popa* or *por la proa*, (Naut.) To descry astern or ahead. *Descubrir su pecho*, To unbosom, to communicate secrets to another. *Descubrir el cuerpo*, 1. To expose to danger any part of the body. 2. (Met.) To favour a perilous undertaking. *Descubrir la hilaza*, (Met.) To manifest the vice or defect which one has, unknown to himself. *Descubrir quién es*, To find out who he is. —*vr.* To uncover one's self, to take off the hat to any one.

(*Yo descuelgo, yo descuelgue*, from *Descolgar*. *V.* Acordar.)

(*Yo descuello, yo descuelle*, from *Descollar*. *V.* Acordar.)

Descuello [des-coo-ayl'-lyo], *m.* 1. Excessive stature or height. 2. (Met.) Pre-eminence, superiority. 3. (Met.) Loftiness, haughtiness.

Descuento [des-coo-en'-to], *m.* 1. Deduction. 2. Discount. 3. Allowance. *Descuento en efectivo*, Cash discount.

(*Yo descuento*, from *Descontar*. *V.* Acordar.)

Descuernacabras [des-coo-er-nah-cah-bras], *m.* Cold north wind.

Descuerno [des-coo-err'-no], *m.* (Coll.) *V.* Desaire.

Descuidadamente [des-coo-e-dah-dah-men'-tay], *adv.* Carelessly, negligently, idly.

Descuidado, da [des-coo-e-dah'-do, dah], *a.* 1. Careless, negligent, thoughtless, heedless, absent, listless, forgetful. 2. Slovenly, unclean. 3. *V.* Desprevenido.—*pp.* of Descuidar.

Descuidar [des-coo-e-dar'], *va.* & *vn.* 1. To neglect, to forget, to overlook, to lay aside. 2. To relieve from care, to make easy. 3. To render careless or indolent; to want attention or diligence.—*vr.* 1. To be forgetful of duty. 2. To make one's self easy. *Descuide Vd.* Make yourself easy.

Descuido [des-coo-ee'-do], *m.* 1. Carelessness, indolence, negligence, omission, forgetfulness. 2. Heedlessness, abstraction, absence. 3. Oversight. 4. Want of attention, incivility, coldness, disesteem. 5. Improper or disgraceful action. 6. Imprudence, immodesty. *Al descuido*, Affectedly or dissemblingly careless. *Al descuido y con cuidado*, Studiously careless, a dissembling carelessness.

Descuitado, da [des-coo-e-tah'-do, dah], *a.* Living without trouble or care. (Acad. Littl. us.)

Desoular [des-coo-lar'], *va.* To break the bottom or end of a thing.

Desculpar, *va.* (Obs.) *V.* Disculpar.

Descultizar [des-cool-te-thar'], *va.* (Littl. us.) To free a writer's style or expressions from affected elegance and nicety.

Descumbrado, da [des-coom-brah'-do, dah], *a.* Level, plain.

Descumplir [des-coom-pleer'], *va.* (Littl. us.) Not to fulfil one's duty.

Descura, *f.* (Obs.) *V.* Descuido.

Descurtir [des-coor-teer'], *va.* To remove tan from the complexion.

Desdar [des-dar'], *va.* Among rope-makers, to untwist a rope.

Desde [des'-day], *prep.* From, since, after, as soon as. *Desde aquí*, From this place. *Desde luego*, Thereupon, immediately. *Desde entonces*, From that time forward, ever since. *Desde niño*, From or since one's childhood. *Desde allí*, Thence, from that period. —*adv.* *V.* Después de.

Desdecir [des-day-theer'], *va.* To give the lie to, to charge with falsehood. —*vn.* 1. To degenerate, to fall from its kind. 2. To differ, to disagree. —*vr.* To gainsay, to retract, to recant.

Desdel (obs.), *contract.* of *Desde él*, Since he.

Desdén [des-dayn'], *m.* 1. Disdain, scorn, contempt, fastidiousness, neglect. *Al desdén*, Affectedly careless. 2. Affront, insult. *Desdenes de la fortuna*, (Met.) The frowns of fortune. *El que no tien* (tiene) *de sus deudos es desdén, y el rico, sin serlo, de todos es deudo*, (prov.) A poor man is never acknowledged by his relatives; but a rich man is claimed as a relation, even when he has not any.

Desdende, *adv.* (Obs.) *V.* Desde entonces.

Desdentado, da [des-den-tah'-do, dah], *a.* Toothless.

Desdentados, *m. pl.* The edentates; mammals having no cutting teeth, e. g. sloths, ant-eaters.—*pp.* of Desdentar.

Desdentar [des-den-tar'], *va.* To draw teeth.

Desdeñable [des-day-nyah'-blay], *a.* Contemptible; despicable.

Desdeñadamente, *adv.* Disdainfully, scornfully.

Desdeñador, ra [des-day-nyah-dor, rah], *m.* & *f.* (Obs.) Scorner.

Desdeñar [des-day-nyar'], *va.* 1. To disdain, to scorn. *La tierra le desdeña*, He is universally despised. 2. To vex, to exasperate.—*vr.* To be disdainful; to be reserved.

Desdeñosamente [des-day nyo-sah-men'-tay], *adv.* Disdainfully, contemptuously.

Desdeñoso, sa [des-day-nyo'-so, sah], *a.* Disdainful; fastidious; contemptuous.

Desdevanar [des-day-vah-nar'], *va.* To unwind or undo a clew.

Desdicha [des-dee'-chah], *f.* Misfortune, calamity, unhappiness, ill-luck, misery, infelicity.

Desdichadamente [des-de-chah-dah-men'-tay], *adv.* Unfortunately, unhappily.

Desdichado, da [des-de-chah'-do, dah], *a.* Unfortunate, unhappy, unlucky, distressed, wretched, miserable, calamitous. *Es un desdichado*, (Coll.) He is a sorry, pitiful creature; he is a good-for-nothing fellow.

Desdicho, cha [des-dee'-cho, chah], *pp. irr.* of Desdecir.

(*Yo desdigo, yo desdiga*, from *Desdecir*. *V.* Decir.)

Desdinerar [des-de-nay-rar'], *va.* (Obs.) To rob of money.

Desdoblar [des-do-blar'], *va.* 1. To unfold, to spread open. 2. (Obs.) To resume the thread of a speech or discourse. 3. (Prov.) To explain, to clear up.

Desdonado, da [des-do-nah'-do, dah], *a.* (Obs.) Graceless, boorish, ungenteel; insipid, foolish.—*pp.* of Desdonar.

Desdonar [des-do-nar'], *va.* (Obs.) To take back a present.

Desdorar [des-do-rar'], *va.* 1. To take off the gilding of a thing. 2. (Met.) To tarnish or sully one's reputation.

Desdoro [des-do'-ro], *m.* Dishonour, blemish, blot, stigma.

Deseable [day-say-ah'-blay], *a.* Desirable.

Deseablemente, *adv.* Desirously.

Deseador, ra [day-say-ah-dor', rah], *m.* & *f.* Desirer, wisher.

Desear [day-say-ar'], *va.* To desire, to desiderate, to wish, to long for, to covet.

Desecación [day-say-cah-the-on'], *f.* Desiccation, exsiccation.

Desecado, da [day-say-cah'-do, dah], *a.* Dry, desiccated.

Desecador [day-say-cah-dor'], *m.* A room destined for drying medicinal substances.

Desecamiento [day-say-cah me-en'-to], *m.* Desiccation.

Desecante [day-say-cahn'-tay], *pa.* & *m.* & *f.* Drying, drier; desiccant.

Desecar [day-say-car'], *va.* 1. To dry, to draw the moisture from any thing, to desiccate. 2. To stop, to detain.

Desecativo, va [day-say-cah-tee'-vo, vah], *a.* Desiccative, exsiccant.—*m.* Healing plaster.

Desechadamente, *adv.* Vilely, despicably.

Desechado, da [des-ay-chah'-do, dah], *a.* & *pp.* of Desechar. Refused, excluded, expelled, rejected; outcast.

Desechar [des-ay-char'], *va.* 1. To exclude, reprobate. 2. To depreciate, undervalue, disesteem. 3. To renounce, not admit. 4. To refuse, not to admit. 5. To put aside sorrow, fear, etc. 6. To lay aside, fling away, not to use or wear; to reject.

Desecho [des-ay'-cho], *m.* 1. Depreciation, renunciation. 2. Residue, overplus, remainder. 3. Refuse, offal. 4. (Met.) Disregard, contempt.

Desedificación [des-ay-de-fe-cah-the-on'], *f.* Scandal, bad example.

Desedificar [des-ay-de-fe-car'], *va.* To scandalize, to offend by some criminal or disgraceful action.

Desegregación [day-say-gray-gah-the-on'], *f.* Desegregation.

Desegregar [day-say-gray-gar'], *va.* To desegregate.

Desejecutar [des-ay-hay-coo-tar'] *va.* (Law) To raise a sequestration, execution, or seizure.

Desselladura [day-sel-lyah-doo'-rah], *f.* Unsealing or taking off the seals.

Desellar [day-sel-lyar'], *va.* To unseal, to take off the seals.

Desembalaje [des-em-bah-lah'-hay], *m.* Unpacking, opening of bales.

Desembalar [des-em-bah-lar'], *va.* To unpack, to open bales of goods.

Desembaldosar [des-em-bal-do-sar'], *va.* To take away the flag-stones or tiles.

Desemballestar [des-em-bal-lyes-tar'], *va.* (Falc.) To dispose to a descent: applied to hawks in the air, when preparing to descend.

Desembanastar [des-em-bah-nas-tar'], *va.* 1. To take out the contents of a basket. 2. (Met.) To talk much and at random. 3. (Coll.) To draw the sword.—*vr.* To break out or break loose: applied to a person or animal that has been confined.

Desembarazadamente [des-em-bah-rah-thah-dah-men'-tay], *adv.* Freely, without embarrassment.

Desembarazado, da [des-sem-bah-ra-thah'-do, dah], *a.* Free, disengaged; unrestrained. *Modales desembarazados*, Easy manners.—*pp.* of Desembarazar.

Desembarazar [des-em-bah-ra-thar'], *va.* 1. To disembarrass, to free, to disengage, to remove an impediment or obstruction. 2. To remove an encumbrance. 3. To extricate. 4. To disencumber. 5. To unburden, to disencumber, to expedite.—*vr.* To be extricated from difficulties or embarrassments.

Desembarazo [des-sem-bah-rah'-tho], *m.* 1. Disembarrassment. 2. Disencumbrance, extrication. 3. Disengagement. 4. Freedom or liberty to do any thing.

Desembarcación, *f.* (Obs.) Disembarkation, landing. *V.* Desembarco.

Desembarcadero [des-em-bar-cah-day'-ro], *m.* Landing-place; dock, quay; platform.

Desembarcar [des-em-bar-car'], *va.* To unship, to disembark.—*vn.* 1. To land, to go on shore. 2. (Met.) To alight from a coach. 3. (Coll.) To be confined, to lie in. 4. To end at a landing place: said of a staircase.

Desembarco [des-em-bar'-co], *m.* 1. Landing, disembarkation, unshipment. 2. Landing-place at the top of stairs.

Desembargador [des-em-bar-gah-dor'], *m.* Chief magistrate and privy councillor in Portugal.

Desembargar [des-em-bar-gar'], *va.* 1. (Law) To raise an embargo or attachment. 2. To remove impediments, or clear away obstructions.

Desembargo [des-em-bar'-go], *m.* (Law) The act of raising an embargo or sequestration: removal of an attachment.

Desembarque [des-em-bar'-kay], *m.*

Landing, the act of coming on shore; clearance.

Desembarrancar [des-em-bar-rahn-car'], *va.* *V.* DESABARRANCAR.

Desembarrar [des-em-bar-rar'], *va.* To clear a thing from mud or clay.

Desembastar [des-em-bas-tar'], *va.* 1. To give a suitable form to any object of metal, filing it to suit. 2. (Mil.) To remove the pack-saddles from the horses which draw the field-pieces.

Desembaste [des-em-bahs'-tay], *m.* Trimming a metallic object.

Desembaular [des-em-bah-oo-lar'], *va.* 1. To empty a trunk, to take out its contents. 2. To empty a box, bag, chest, etc. 3. (Met.) To speak one's mind freely; to disclose one's secret thoughts.

Desembebecerse [des-em-bay-bay-therr'-say], *vr.* To recover the use of one's senses.

Desembelesarse [des-em-bay-lay-sar'-say], *vr.* To recover from amazement or abstraction.

Desemblanza [day-sem-blahn'-thah], *f.* (Obs.) *V.* DESEMEJANZA.

Desembocadero [des-em-bo-cah-day'-ro], *m.* 1. Exit, outlet. 2. The mouth of a river or canal, or the point where it empties into the sea; disemboguement.

Desembocadura [des-em-bo-cah-doo'-rah], *f.* *V.* DESEMBOCADERO.

Desembocar [des-em-bo-car'], *vn.* 1. (Naut.) To disembogue, to sail out of a strait. 2. To disembogue, to flow out at the mouth: said of a river. *Desembocar la calle,* To go from one street into another. ***Todas las calles que desembocan en la plaza estaban empalizadas,*** All the streets that terminate in the square were barricaded.

Desembojadera [des-em-bo-hah-day'-rah], *f.* (Prov.) Woman who takes the cocoons of silk-worms from the southern-wood.

Desembojar [des-em-bo-har'], *va.* To remove silk-cocoons from the southern-wood.

Desembolsar [des-em-bol-sar'], *va.* 1. To empty a purse. 2. To disburse, to expend, to lay out.

Desembolso [des-em-bol'-so], *m.* 1. Disbursement, expenditure. 2. An advance with the object of speculating.

Desemboque [des-em-bo'-kay], *m.* *V.* DESEMBOCADERO.

Desemborrachar [des-em-bor-rah-char'], *va.* To sober, to make sober, to cure of intoxication.—*vr.* To grow sober.

Desemborrar [des-em-bor-rar'], *va.* To take away the nap from wool, silk, cotton, etc.

Desemboscada [des-em-bos-cah'-dah], *f.* 1. The coming out of the game into the open. 2. Sound of horns to give notice that the game has gone into the open.

Desemboscarse [des-em-bos-car'-say], *vr.* To get out of the woods, to get clear of an ambuscade.

Desembotar [des-em-bo-tar'], *va.* To remove dulness from the understanding. (Acad.)

Desembozar [des-em-bo-thar'], *va.* 1. To unmuffle or uncover the face. 2. To unmask, show one's self in one's true colors. Also *vr.*

Desembozo [des-em-bo'-tho], *m.* 1. Uncovering or unmuffling the face. 2. (Littl. us.) Freedom of speech.

Desembragar [des-em-brah-gar'], *va.* 1. To unbind from the cable. 2. (Mech.) To ungear, disconnect.—*pp. Desembragado,* Out of gear.

Desembravecer [des-em-brah-vay-therr'], *va.* To tame, to domesticate.

Desembravecimiento [des-em-brah-vay-the-me-en'-to], *m.* Taming, or reclaiming from wildness.

Desembrazar [des-em-brah-thar'], *va.* 1. To dart or throw weapons; to throw from the arms. 2. To take any thing from the arms.

Desembriagar [des-em-bre-ah-gar'], *va.* To sober, to cure from intoxication.—*vr.* To grow sober, to recover from drunkenness.

Desembridar [des-em-bre-dar'], *va.* To unbridle a horse.

Desembrollar [des-em-brol-lyar'], *va.* To unravel, to disentangle, to clear, to extricate.

Desembuchar [des-em-boo-char'], *va.* 1. To disgorge, to turn out of the maw; said of birds. 2. (Met.) To unbosom, to disclose one's sentiments and secrets.

Desemejable [day-say-may-hah'-blay], *a.* (Obs.) 1. Dissimilar. 2. Strong, large, violent.

Desemejado, da [day-say-may-hah'-do, dah], *a.* & *pp.* of DESEMEJAR.

Desemejante [day-say-may-hahn'-tay], *a.* Dissimilar, unlike.

Desemejantemente, *adv.* Dissimilarly.

Desemejanza [day-say-may-hahn'-thah], *f.* Dissimilitude, unlikeness, dissimilarity.

Desemejar [day-say-may-har'], *vn.* To be dissimilar or unlike.—*va.* *V.* DESFIGURAR.

Desempacar [des-em-pah-car'], *va.* To unpack.—*vr.* (Coll.) To grow calm, to be appeased.

Desempachar [des-em-pah-char'], *va.* To make the stomach discharge crudities or undigested material.—*vr.* (Met.) To grow bold, to lose all bashfulness.

Desempacho [des-em-pah'-cho], *m.* Ease, alleviation. (Acad.)

Desempalagar [des-em-pah-lah-gar'], *va.* 1. To remove nausea or loathing, to restore the appetite. 2. To clear a mill of stagnant or detained water.

Desempañar [des-em-pah-nyar'], *va.* 1. To take away the clouts and swaddling-clothes of children. 2. To clean a glass, looking-glass, or any thing which is tarnished.

Desempapelar [des-em-pah-pay-lar'], *va.* To unwrap, to unfold any thing wrapped up in paper.

Desempaquetar [des-em-pah-kay-tar'], *va.* To unpack, to open a packet.

Desemparejar [des-em-pah-ray-har'], *va.* To unmatch, to make things unequal. —*vn.* 1. To become inimical. 2. To part, to be separated.

Desemparentado, da [des-em-pah-ren-tah'-do, dah], *a.* Without relatives.

Desemparvar [des-em-par-var'], *va.* To gather the thrashed corn in heaps.

Desempastelar [des-em-pas-tay-lar'], *va.* (Print.) 1. To compose disarranged type. 2. To distribute pi, or mixed letters. 3. To undo a secret meeting, political machination. 4. To disentangle, extricate, clear up.

Desempatar [des-em-pah-tar'], *va.* 1. To make unequal, to do away existing equality. 2. (Met.) To explain, to clear up, to facilitate.

Desempedrador [des-em-pay-drah-dor'], *m.* One who unpaves.

Desempedrar [des-em-pay-drar'], *va.* To unpave. *Ir desempedrando la calle,* (Met.) To go very rapidly.

Desempegar [des-em-pay-gar'], *va.* To unglue.

Desempeñado, da [des-em-pay-nyah'-do dah], *a.* & *pp.* of DESEMPEÑAR, Free or clear of debt.

Desempeñar [des-em-pay-nyar'], *va.* 1. To redeem, to recover what was in another's possession, to take out of pawn. 2. To clear or extricate from debt. ***Sus estados están desempeñados,*** His estates are clear of debt. 3. To perform any duty or promise, to discharge, to transact. ***Desempeñar el asunto,*** To prove a subject completely. ***Desempeñó el negocio a satisfacción,*** He accomplished the business satisfactorily. 4. To acquit, to free from an obligation. 5. To disengage from a difficult or arduous affair.—*vr.* 1. To extricate one's self from debt, to pay all debts. 2. In bull-fighting, to disengage one's self from the attack of a bull. *Desempeñarse de la tierra* or *costa,* (Naut.) To claw off, to stand off shore.

Desempeño [des-em-pay'-nyo], *m.* 1. The act of redeeming a pledge. 2. (Met.) Proof or confirmation of a statement. 3. Performance of an obligation or promise; fulfilment, discharge.

Desempeorarse [des-em-pay-o-rar'-say], *vr.* To recover from sickness, to regain health and vigour.

Desemperezar [des-em-pay-ray-thar'], *vn.* To relinquish habits of laziness and indolence.

Desempernar [des-em-per-nar'], *va.* To take out the bolts or spikes.

Desempiolar [des-em-pe-o-lar'], *va.* To remove the leash from falcons.

Desemplomar [des-em-plo-mar'], *va.* To remove a leaden seal placed on goods (by custom-house or otherwise).

Desemplumar [des-em-ploo-mar'], *va.* *V.* DESPLUMAR.

Desempobrecer [des-em-po-bray-therr'], *va.* To relieve from poverty.—*vr.* To extricate one's self from poverty.

Desempolvar [des-em-pol-var'], *va.* To remove dust or powder.

Desempolvoradura [des-em-pol-vo-rah-doo'-rah], *f.* Dusting.

Desempolvorar [des-em-pol-vo-rar'], *va.* To dust, to remove dust.

Desemponzoñar [des-em-pon-tho-nyar'], *va.* 1. To heal from the effects of poison, to expel poison. 2. (Met.) To cure any disordinate passion or affection.

Desempotrar [des-em-po-trar'], *va.* To remove the stays or props which support any thing.

Desempulgadura [des-em-pool-gah-doo'-rah], *f.* The unbending of a bow.

Desempulgar [des-em-pool-gar'], *va.* To unbend a bow.

Desenalbardar [des-ay-nal-bar-dar'], *va.* To take off a pack-saddle.

Desenamorar [des-ay-nah-mo-rar'], *va.* To destroy love or affection.—*vr.* 1. To lose love or affection. 2. To relinquish or yield up one's opinion.

Desenastar [des-ay-nas-tar'], *va.* To remove the handle of a weapon or iron tool.

Desencabalgado, da, *a.* (Obs.) *V.* DESMONTADO.—*pp.* of DESENCABALGAR.

Desencabalgar [des-en-cah-bal-gar'], *va.* (Mil.) To dismount cannon.

Desencabestradura [des-en-cah-bes-trah-doo'-rah], *f.* The disentangling of a beast from the halter.

Desencabestrar [des-sen-cah-bes-trar'], *va.* To disentangle a beast from the halter, in which the fore feet are entangled.

Desencadenar [des-en-cah-day-nar'], *va.* 1. To unchain, to break the chain, to break loose. 2. (Met.) To dissolve all connection or obligation.—*vr.* 1. To break loose, free one's self from chains. 2. To become infuriated: said of persons, passions, and the elements.

Desencajadura [des-en-cah-hah-doo'-rah], *f.* The part or place which remains unjoined, when the connection is removed; unjointing.

Desencajamiento, Desencaje [des-en-cah-hah-me-en'-to, des-en-cah'-hay], *m.* Disjointedness; luxation.

Desencajar [des-en-cah-har'], *va.* 1. To disjoint, to take a thing out of its place; to disfigure. 2. To luxate.

Desencajonar [des-en-cah-ho-nar'], *va.* 1. To unpack, to take out the contents of a box. 2. (Mil.) To separate the wings from the main body in a line of battle.

Desencalabrinar [des-en-cah-lah-bre-nar'], *va.* 1. To remove dizziness, to free from stupidity. 2. To remove wrong impressions.

Desencalcar [des-en-cal-car'], *va.* To loosen or dissolve what was caked, or close pressed.

Desencallar [des-en-cal-lyar'], *va.* (Naut.) To set a ship afloat which has struck on rocky ground.

Desencaminar [des-en-cah-me-nar'], *va.* 1. To lose one's way, to go astray. 2. To deviate from rectitude.

Desencantamiento, *m.* *V.* DESENCANTO.

Desencantar [des-en-can-tar'], *va.* To disenchant, to counter-charm.

Desencantaración [des-en-can-ta-rah-the-on'], *f.* Act and effect of drawing lots or balloting for any thing.

Desencantarar [des-en-can-ta-rar'], *va.* 1. To draw lots for candidates. 2. To be withdrawn as incompetent, to withdraw a name on account of incapacity or privilege.

Desencanto [des-en-cahn'-to], *m.* Disenchantment.

Desencapillar [des-en-cah-pil-lyar'], *va.* (Naut.) To unrig, to take off the rigging.

Desencapotadura [des-en-cah-po-tah-doo'-rah], *f.* Act of stripping off a cloak or a great-coat.

Desencapotar [des-en-cah-po-tar'], *va.* 1. To strip one of his cloak or great-coat. 2. (Met. Coll.) To uncover, to make manifest. 3. (Met.) To raise and keep up the head of a horse. *Desencapotar las orejas,* To cock up the ears.—*vr.* 1. To lay aside frowns; to put on a pleasing countenance. 2. To clear up: said of the sky.

Desencaprichar [des-en-cah-pre-char'], *va.* To dissuade from error or prejudice, to cure one of conceit.—*vr.* To desist, yield, get over a whim.

Desencarcelar [des-en-car-thay-lar'], *va.* 1. To disincarcerate, to release from confinement, to set at liberty. 2. (Met.) To free from oppression, to extricate from difficulties.

Desencarecer [des-en-cah-ray-therr'], *va.* To lower the price of any thing offered for sale.

Desencarnar [des-en-car-nar'], *va.* 1. To prevent dogs from eating game. 2. (Met.) To lose an affection for any thing, or to divert the mind from it. 3. (Art) To soften flesh colour in figures.

Desencasar, *va.* (Obs.) *V.* DESENCAJAR.

Desencastar [des-en-cas-tar'], *va.* To destroy insects, to end their race.

Desencastillar [des-en-cas-til-lyar'], *va.* 1. To expel or drive out of a castle. 2. To manifest, to make appear, to discover.

Desencenagar [des-en-thay-nah-gar'], *va.* 1. *V.* DESATASCAR. 2. To extricate one from a sink of vice or crime.

Desencentrar [des-en-then-trar'], *va.* To take any thing from its centre: to decentre.

Desenceparse [des-en-thay-par'-say], *vr.* To unloosen folds of cable from the anchor-stock.

Desencerrar [des-en-ther-rar'], *va.* 1. To free from confinement. 2. To open, to unclose. 3. To disclose what was hidden or unknown.

(*Yo desencierro,* from *Desencerrar. V.* ALENTAR.)

Desencintar [des-en-thin-tar'], *va.* To untie, to loosen.

Desenclavar [des-en-clah-var'], *va.* 1. To draw out nails. *V.* DESCLAVAR. 2. To put one violently out of his place.

Desenclavijar [des-en-clah-ve-har'], *va.* To take out pins or pegs—e. g. of a musical instrument.

Desencoger [des-en-co-herr'], *va.* To unfold.—*vr.* 1. (Met.) To lay aside bashfulness or reserve, to grow bold. 2. To make merry.

Desencogimiento [des-en-co-he-me-en'-to], *m.* Disembarrassment, freedom from perplexity.

Desencolar [des-en-co-lar'], *va.* To unglue.

Desencolerizarse [des-sen-co-lay-re-thar'-say], *vr.* To grow calm, to be appeased.

Desenconar [des-en-co-nar'], *va.* 1. To remove an inflammation. 2. (Met.) To moderate, to check or appease one's passion. 3. To make mild and benign.—*vr.* To become milder, to be appeased, to forget injuries.

Desencono [des-en-co'-no], *m.* Mitigating anger or passion.

Desencordar [des-en-cor-dar'], *va.* To unstring, to loosen or untie strings.

Desencordelar [des-en-cor-day-lar'], *va.* To loosen, to untie or take away ropes.

Desencorvar [des-en-cor-var'], *va.* To straighten, to untwist.

Desencrespar [des-en-cres-par'], *va.* (Littl. us.) To uncurl, to unfrizzle.

Desencrudecer [des-en-croo-day-therr'], *va.* 1. To prepare silk or thread for receiving the dye. 2. To boil cocoons so as to be able to unwind the silk more readily. 3. To clean fabrics from matter which might alter them.

Desencrudecimiento [des-en-croo-day-the-me-en'-to], *m.* Cleansing of silk (with lye).

Desencuadernar [des-en-coo-ah-der-nar'], *va.* 1. To unbind, to take off the binding of a book. 2. *V.* DESCUADERNAR.

Desende, *adv.* (Obs.) Contraction of *desde* and *ende.* *V.* DESDE.

Desendemoniar, Desendiablar [des-en-day-mo-ne-ar', des-en-de-ah-blar'], *va.* To exorcise, to drive out an evil spirit. *Desendiablarse,* (Met.) To moderate one's fury or passion.

Desendiosar [des-en-de-o-sar'], *va.* To humble vanity, to pull down presumption and haughtiness.

Desenfadaderas [des-en-fah-dah-day'-ras], *f. pl.* *Tener desenfadaderas,* (Coll.) To take means to extricate one's self from difficulties, or liberate one's self from oppression.

Desenfadado, da [des-en-fah-dah'-do, dah], *a.* 1. Free, unembarrassed. 2. Wide, spacious, capacious: applied to places.—*pp.* of DESENFADAR.

Desenfadar [des-en-fah-dar'], *va.* To abate anger, to appease passion.—*vr.* To be entertained or amused.

Desenfado [des-en-fah'-do], *m.* 1. Freedom, ease, facility. 2. Calmness, relaxation.

Desenfaldar [des-en-fal-dar'], *va.* To let fall the train of a gown.

Desenfamar, *va.* *V.* DISFAMAR.

Desenfangar [des-en-fan-gar'], *va.* To cleanse, to clear from mud, mire, or filth.

Desenfardar, Desenfardelar [des-en-far-dar', des-en-far-day-lar'], *va.* To unpack bales of goods.

Desenfardelamiento [des-en-far-day-lah-me-en'-to], *m.* Unpacking of bales.

Desenfardo [des-en-far'-do], *m.* *V.* DESENFARDELAMIENTO.

Desenfatuar [des-en-fah-too-ar'], *va.* (Prov.) To undeceive, to free from error.

Desenfilada [des-en-fe-lah'-dah], *a.* (Mil.) Under cover from fire.—*f.* Part of a fortification protected against being fired upon from adjoining high lands.

Desenfilar [des-en-fe-lar'], *va.* 1. To put the troops under cover from flank fire. 2. To unthread.

Desenfrailar [des-en-frah-e-lar'], *vn.* (Coll.) To leave the monastic life, become secularized.—*vr.* 1. To come out from subjection. 2. To rest from business for a time.—*va.* (Prov. Agr.) To lop off, mutilate trees.

Desenfrenadamente [des-en-fray-nah-dah-men'-tay], *adv.* Ungovernably, licentiously.

Desenfrenado, da [des-en-fray-nah'-do, dah], *a.* & *pp.* of DESENFRENAR. Ungoverned, unbridled, outrageous, licentious, wanton.

Desenfrenamiento [des-en-fray-nah-me-en'-to], *m.* Unruliness, rashness, wantonness, licentiousness, boundless liberty or license; libidinousness.

Desenfrenar [des-en-fray-nar'], *va.* To unbridle.—*vr.* 1. To give loose rein to one's passions and desires. 2. To fly into a violent passion. 3. To be mad or wild.

Desenfreno [des-en-fray'-no], *m.* *V.* DESENFRENAMIENTO. *Desenfreno de vientre,* Sudden and violent looseness.

Desenfundar [des-en-foon-dar'], *va.* To take out of a bag, bolster, pillow-case, etc.

Desenfurecerse [des-en-foo-ray-therr'-say], *vr.* To grow calm or quiet, to lay aside anger.

Desengalanar [des-en-gah-lah-nar'], *va.* To remove trappings or adornments.

Desengalgar [des-en-gal-gar'], *va.* 1. To remove the (wooden) brake of a cart, to unscotch. 2. (Naut.) To remove anchor-stakes.

Desenganchar [des-en-gan-char'], *va.* To unhook, to take down from a hook. *Desenganchen los caballos* (del coche), Let the horses be unharnessed.

Desengañadamente [des-en-gah-nyah-dah-men'-tay], *adv.* 1. Truly, clearly, ingenuously. 2. Awkwardly, without care or address, scurvily.

Desengañado, da [des-en-gah-nyah'-do, dah], *a.* 1. Undeceived, disabused, knowinp by experience. *Él está desengañado de eso,* He is aware of that. 2. Despicable, ill-executed.—*pp.* of DESENGAÑAR.

Desengañador [des-en-gah-nyah-dor'], *m.* Undeceiver.

Desengañar [des-en-gah-nyar'], *va.* 1. To undeceive, to free from error, to disabuse, to set right. 2. (Tech.) To accustom a horse to every kind of noise, and to objects which frighten him.

Desengañilar [des-en-gah-nye-lar'], *va.* To free or disengage from the grasp, claws, or fangs of a person or beast.

Desengaño [des-en-gah'-nyo], *m.* 1. Detection or discovery of an error by which one was deceived: undeceiving, the disabusing or freeing from error. 2. Censure, reproof, reproach upbraiding. 3. Warning, admonition.

Desengarrafar [des-en-gar-rah-far'], *va.* To unfasten or disengage from claws or clinched fingers.

Desengarzar [des-en-gar-thar'], *va.* To unravel, to unstring.

Desengastar [des-en-gas-tar'], *va.* To take a stone out of its setting.

Desengoznar [des-en-goth-nar'], *va.* To unhinge; to disjoint. *V.* DESGOZNAR.

Desengranar [des-en-grah-nar'], *va.* To uncog, separate two cog-wheels; to ungear.—*vr.* To get out of gear.

Desengrasador [des-en-grah-sah-dor'], *m.* A wringing-machine; scourer; wiping clout.

Desengrasar [des-en-grah-sar'], *va.* 1. To take out the grease. 2. To remove the taste of fat.

Desengrase [des-en-grah'-say], *m.* Removal of grease.

Desengrosar [des-en-gro-sar'], *va.* To extenuate, to make lean, to debilitate, to make thin or fine.

Desengrudamiento [des-en-groo-dah-me-en'-to], *m.* The rubbing off of cement or paste.

Desengrudar [des-en-groo-dar'], *va.* To scrape or rub off paste.

(*Yo desengrueso*, from *Desengrosar. V.* ACORDAR.)

Desenhebrar [des-en-ay-brar'], *va.* To unthread.

Desenhornar [des-en-or-nar'], *va.* To take out of the oven.

Desenjaezar [des-en-hah-ay-thar'], *va.* To unharness mules or horses, to unsaddle.

Desenjalmar [des-en-hal-mar'], *va.* To unharness mules or horses; to take off a pack-saddle from a beast of burden.

Desenjaular [des-en-hah-oo-lar'], *va.* 1. To uncage. 2. To remove some one from a jail.

Desenjecutar [des-en-hay-coo-tar'], *va.* (Law) *V.* DESEJECUTAR.

Desenlabonar [des-en-lah-bo-nar'], *va.* To unlink.

Desenlace [des-en-lah'-thay], *m.* 1. (Poet.) Catastrophe of a play or dramatic poem. 2. (Met.) Conclusion, end, unravelling of an affair.

Desenladrillar [des-en-lah-dril-lyar'], *va.* To take up floor-tiles or bricks.

Desenlazar [des-en-lah-thar'], *va.* 1. To unlace, to untie knots; to loose. 2. To distinguish.

Desenlodar [des-en-lo-dar'], *va.* 1. To remove, clean off mud. 2. To separate earthy parts from any mineral or ore.

Desenlosar [des-en-lo-sar'], *va.* To take up a floor made of flags.

Desenlutar [des-en-loo-tar'], *va.* 1. To leave off mourning. 2. To banish sorrow.

Desenmangar [des-en-mahn-gar'], *va.* To unhaft. *V.* DESENASTAR.

Desenmarañar [des-en-mah-ra-nyar'], *va.* 1. To disentangle. 2. (Met.) To extricate from impediments or difficulties, to explain.

Desenmascarar [des-en-mas-cah-rar'], *va.* 1. To remove the mask. 2. To reveal the hidden intentions of some one.

Desenmohecer [des-en-mo-ay-therr'], *va.* 1. To clear from rust. 2. (Met.) To clear up, to make manifest.

Desenmudecer [des-en-moo-day-therr'], *va.* 1. To remove an impediment of speech. 2. To break a long silence.

Desenojar [des-ay-no-har'], *va.* To appease anger, to allay passion.—*vr.* To recreate, to amuse one's self. (Coll.) To make friends.

Desenojo [des-ay-no'-ho], *m.* Reconcilableness, appeasableness.

Desenojoso, sa [des-ay-no-ho'-so, sah], *a.* Appeasing, reconciling.

Desenredar [des-en-ray-dar'], *va.* 1. To disentangle, to free from perplexities, to outwind, to extricate, to loose; to clear. 2. To put in order, to set to rights.—*vr.* To extricate one's self from difficulties.

Desenredo [des-en-ray'-do], *m.* 1 Disentanglement. 2. (Poet.) Catastrophe of a play or poem.

Desenrizar [des-en-re-thar'], *va.* To uncurl the hair, to take out the curls.

Desenrollar [des-en-rol-lyar'], *va.* To unroll. *V.* DESARROLLAR.

Desenroñecer [des-en-ro-nyay-therr'], *va.* 1. To remove rust from metal. 2. (Met.) To polish the manners, to cultivate the mind.

Desenronquecer [des-en-ron-kay-therr'], *va.* To free from hoarseness.

Desenroscar [des-en-ros-car'], *va.* To untwist.

Desensabanar [des-en-sah-ba-nar'], *va.* 1. (Coll.) To change or take off the sheets. 2. (Met. Coll.) To remove an impediment or obstacle.

Desensañar [des-en-sah-nyar'], *va.* 1. To appease, to pacify. 2. To mitigate irritation.

Desensartar [des-en-sar-tar'], *va.* To unthread, to unstring.

Desensebar [des-en-say-bar'], *va.* 1. To strip of fat. 2. (Met.) To change occupation in order to render one's work more endurable, to draw breath. 3. (Met.) To take away the taste of fat of a thing just eaten.

Desensenar [des-en-say-nar'], *va.* To take out of the breast or bosom.

Desenseñado, da [des-en-say-nyah'-do, dah], *a.* Untaught.—*pp.* of DESENSEÑAR.

Desenseñar [des-en-say-nyar'], *va.* (Littl. us.) To make one forget what he had been taught; to unteach.

Desensillar [des-en-sil-lyar'], *va.* To unsaddle.

Desensoberbecer [des-en-so-ber-bay-therr'], *va.* To humble, take away pride.—*vr.* To become humble, to moderate one's pride.

Desensortijado, da [des-en-sor-te-hah'-do, dah], *a.* Dislocated, displaced.

Desentablar [des-en-tah-blar'], *va.* 1. To rip up or off planks or boards. 2. (Met.) To discompose, to disturb, to confuse. 3. To embroil an affair, to break off a bargain, to interrupt friendly intercourse.

Desentalengar [des-en-tah-len-gar'], *va.* (Naut.) To unbend a cable.

Desentarquinar [des-en-tar-ke-nar'], *va.* To free a ditch or trench from mud, mire, or filth.

Desentenderse [des-en-ten-derr'-say], *vr.* 1. To feign not to understand a thing. 2. To pass by a thing without taking notice of it.

Desentendido, da [des-en-ten-dee'-do, dah], *a.* Unmindful, pretending or feigning ignorance.—*pp.* of DESENTENDERSE. *Hacerse el desentendido* or *darse por desentendido*, (Coll.) To wink at a thing; to pretend not to have taken notice, or to be ignorant of it.

Desenterrador [des-en-ter-rah-dor'], *m.* He who disinters or digs up.

Desenterramiento [des-en-ter-rah-me-en'-to], *m.* Disinterment.

Desenterrar [des-en-ter-rar'], *va.* 1. To disinter, to unbury, exhume, to dig up, to unearth. 2. (Met.) To recall to one's memory things forgotten. *Desenterrar los huesos*, (Met.) To verify the ancestors of any one. *Desenterrar los muertos*, (Met.) To slander the dead.

(*Yo me desentiendo*, from *Desentenderse. V.* ENTENDER.)

Desentierramuertos [des-en-te-er-rah-moo-err'-tos], *m.* Calumniator of the dead.

(*Yo desentierro*, from *Desenterrar. V.* ACERTAR.)

Desentoldar [des-en-tol-dar'], *va.* 1. To take away awning. 2. (Met.) To strip a thing of its ornaments.

Desentonación [des-en-to-nah-the-on'], *f.* Dissonance.

Desentonadamente [des-en-to-nah-dah-men'-tay], *adv.* Unharmoniously.

Desentonado, da [des-en-to-nah'-do, dah], *a.* & *pp.* of DESENTONAR. Out of tune, inharmonical, discordant.

Desentonamiento [des-en-to-nah-me-en'-to], *m.* Dissonance, excess in the tone of the voice.

Desentonar [des-en-to-nar'], *va.* To humble, to wound the pride of any one.—*vn.* To be out of tune, to be inharmonious.—*vr.* To be of a coarse address, to be rude or uncouth; to raise the voice in disrespect.

Desentono [des-en-toh'-no], *m.* 1. Disharmony, discord. 2. A harsh, rude tone of voice. 3. Musical discord; false note.

Desentornillar [des-en-tor-nil-lyar'], *va.* To unscrew.

Desentorpecer [des-en-tor-pay-therr'], *va.* To free from torpor; to restore motion to torpid limbs.—*vr.* 1. To be freed from torpor, to be restored from numbness. 2. To become lively, smart, or pert.

(*Yo desentorpezco*, from *Desentorpecer. V.* ABORRECER.)

Desentrampar [des-en-tram-par'], *va.* To free from debts; or to take away traps set for mischievous animals.

Desentrañamiento [des-en-tra-nyah-me-en'-to], *m.* (Ant.) The act of giving any thing as a proof of love and affection.

Desentrañar [des-en-tra-nyar'], *va.* 1. To eviscerate, to disembowel. 2. (Met.) To penetrate or dive into the most hidden and difficult matters. 3. (Naut.) To remove loops, twists, from ropes. —*vr.* (Met.) To give away all one's fortune and property, out of love and affection for a person.

Desentristecer [des-en-tris-tay-therr'], *va.* To banish sadness and grief.

Desentronizar [des-en-tro-ne-thar'], *va.* 1. *V.* DESTRONAR. 2. To deprive any one of his power or authority.

Desentumecer [des-en-too-may-therr'], *va.* *V.* DESENTORPECER.—*vr.* To be freed from numbness.

Desentumir [des-en-too-meer'], *va.* To free from torpor.

Desenvainar [des-en-vah-e-nar'], *va.* 1. To unsheath, as a sword. 2. (Coll.) To expose to view any thing which was hidden or covered. 3. To stretch out the claws: applied to animals having talons.

Desenvelejar [des-en-vay-lay-har'], *va.* (Naut.) To strip a vessel of her sails.

Desenvendar [des-en-ven-dar'], *va.* To take off fillets or bands.

Desenvenenar [des-en-vay-nay-nar'], *va.* To extract, remove poison; to destroy the poisonous qualities of a substance.

Desenvergar [des-en-ver-gar'], *va.* (Naut.) To unbend a sail.

Desenvoltura [des-en-vol-too'-rah], *f.* 1. Sprightliness, cheerfulness. 2. Impudence, effrontery, boldness. 3. A lewd posture or gesture in women. 4. A graceful and easy delivery of one's sentiments and thoughts.

Desenvolvedor [des-en-vol-vay-dor'] *m.* Unfolder, investigator.
Desenvolver [des-en-vol-verr'], *va.* 1. To unfold, to unroll. 2. (Met.) To decipher, to discover, to unravel. 3. (Obs.) To expedite.—*vr.* To be forward, to behave with too much assurance.
(*Yo desenvuelvo,* from *Desenvolver. V.* Absolver.)
Desenvueltamente [des-en-voo-el-tal-men'-tay], *adv.* 1. Impudently, licentiously. 2. Expeditiously.
Desenvuelto, ta [des-en-voo-el'-to, tah], *a.* Forward, impudent, licentious.—*pp.* of Desenvolver.
Desenyesar [des-en-yay-sar'], *va.* To remove plaster from a wall.—*vr.* To fall, as plaster, from a wall.
Desenzarzar [des-en-thar-thar'], *va.* 1. To disentangle from brambles. 2. To appease, reconcile those who quarrel.—*vr.* To get well out of some entangled matter.
Deseñamiento [day-say-nyah-me-en'-to], *m.* (Obs.) Want of instruction.
Deseo [day-say'-o], *m.* Desire, wish, mind, liking. *A medida del deseo,* According to one's wish.
Deseoso, sa [day-say-oh'-so, sah], *a.* 1. Desirous, longing. 2. Greedy, eager.
Desequido, da [day-say-kee'-do, dah], *a.* Dry. *V.* Resequido.
Desequilibrar [des-ay-ke-le-brar'], *va.* To unbalance.
Desequilibrio [des-ay-ke-lee'-bre-o], *m.* Unstable equilibrium; an unbalanced state.
Deserción [day-ser-the-on'], *f.* 1. Desertion. 2. (Law) Abandonment of a suit by plaintiff.
Deserrado, da [des-er-rah'-do, dah], *a.* Free from error.
Desertar [day-ser-tar'], *va.* 1. To desert. 2. To go over to another party. 3. To separate from a body or company. 4. (Law) To abandon a cause. *Desertarse a,* To fall over.
Desertor [day-ser-tor'], *m.* 1. Deserter. 2. Deserter, forsaker, fugitive, he that has forsaken his cause, post, etc.
Deservicio [day-ser-vee'-the-o], *m.* Disservice; fault committed against a person who has a claim to services or devotion.
Deservidor [day-ser-ve-dor'], *m.* He who fails in serving another.
Deservir [day-ser-veer'], *va.* (Ant.) Not to perform one's duty, to disserve.
Desescamar [des-es-cah-mar'], *va.* To scale, to remove scales.
Desescombrar [des-es-com-brar'], *va.* To remove the rubbish.
Deseslabonar [des-es-lah-bo-nar'], *va.* To cut the links of a chain.
Desespaldar [des-es-pal-dar'], *va.* To wound the shoulder.
Desespaldillar [des-es-pal-dil-lyar'], *va.* To wound in the shoulder-blade.—*vr.* To receive a lesion in this bone.
Desesperación [des-es-pay-rah-the-on'], *f.* 1. Despondency, despair, desperation. 2. (Met.) Displeasure, anger, passion, fury. *Es una desesperación,* (Coll.) It is unbearable.
Desesperadamente [des-es-pay-ra-dah-men'-tay], *adv.* 1. Despairingly, hopelessly. 2. Desperately, furiously, madly.
Desesperado, da [des-es-pay-rah'-do, dah], *a.* & *pp.* of Desesperar. 1. Desperate, despaired, hopeless. 2. Desperate, furious.
Desesperado [des-es-pay-rah'-do], *m.* Desperate, despairer, desperado, a desperate man.
Desesperanzar [des-es-pay-ran-thar'], *va.* To deprive one of hope, to make him despair, to deprive of all hope.
Desesperar [des-es-pay-rar'], *vn.* To despair, to be cast down.—*va.* To make one despair, to deprive him of all hope.—*vr.* 1. To sink into the utmost despair, to despond. 2. To fret, to be grievously vexed.
Desespigar [des-es-pe-gar'], *va.* To thrash grain.
Desespigo, Desespigue [des-es-pee'-go, gay], *m.* Thrashing of grain by the trampling of animals, or of suitable instruments.
Desesponjarse [des-es-pon-har'-say], *vr.* To lose porosity or sponginess.
Desestacar [des-es-tah-car'], *va.* To take away stakes or props from vines, after the vintage.
Desestancar [des-es-tan-car'], *va.* To take away a monopoly; to declare an article open to trade.
Desesterar [des-es-tay-rar'], *va.* 1. To take off the mats. 2. (Met.) To lay aside winter clothes. 3. (Coll.) To remove the mustache and beard.
Desestero [des-es-tay'-ro], *m.* The act of taking off the mats, and the time at which it is customary in Spain to do it.
Desestima [des-es-tee'-mah], *f.* (Littl. us.) *V.* Desestimación.
Desestimación [des-es-te-mah-the-on'], *f.* Disesteem, disrespect; crying down.
Desestimador, ra [des-es-te-mah-dor', rah], *m.* & *f.* Contemner, despiser.
Desestimar [des-es-te-mar'], *va.* 1. To disregard, to contemn, to undervalue. 2. To reject, deny.
Desestivar [des-es-te-var'], *va.* (Naut.) To alter the stowage.
Desfacedor [des-fah-thay-dor'], *m.* (Ant.) Destroyer. *Desfacedor de entuertos,* Undoer of injuries.
Desfacer [des-fah-therr'], *va.* (Obs.) *V.* Deshacer.
Desfacimiento [des-fah-the-me-en'-to], *m.* (Obs.) Destruction, undoing.
Desfachatado, da [des-fah-chah-tah'-do, dah], *a.* Impudent, saucy.
Desfachatez [des-fah-chah-teth'], *f.* (Neol. Coll.) Impudence, effrontery.
Desfajar [des-fah-har'], *va.* To ungird.
Desfalcar [des-fal-car'], *va.* 1. To take away part of something, to cut off, to lop. 2. To peculate, defalcate. 3. To oust one from his protection or patronage.
Desfalcazar [des-fal-ca-thar'], *va.* (Naut.) To untwist a rope to make oakum.
Desfalco [des-fahl'-co], m. 1. Defalcation, shortage, deficit. 2. Diminution, diminishing, detracting.
Desfallecer [des-fal-lyay-therr'], *vn.* 1. To pine, to fall away, to grow weak. 2. To swoon, to faint.—*va.* To weaken, to debilitate.
Desfalleciente [des-fal-lyay-the-en'-tay], *pa,* Pining, languishing.
Desfallecimiento [des-fal-lyay-the-me-en'-to], *m.* 1. Languor, fainting, decline; dejection of mind. 2. A swoon, fainting fit.
(*Yo desfallezco,* from *Desfallecer. V.* Aborrecer.)
Desfamar, *va.* (Obs.) To defame. *V.* Difamar.
Desfavor [des-fah-vor'], *m.* Disfavour.
Desfavorable [des-fah-vo-rah'-blay], *a.* Unfavourable, contrary.
Desfavorecedor, ra [des-fah-vo-ray-thay-dor', rah], *m.* & *f.* Disfavourer: contemner.
Desfavorecer [des-fah-vo-ray-therr'], *va.* 1. To disfavour, to discountenance. 2. To despise, to contemn. 3. To injure, to hurt. 4. To contradict, to oppose.
Desfertilizar [des-fer-te-le-thar'], *va.* To destroy fertility.—*vr.* To lose fertility.
Desfiguración, *f.* **Desfiguramiento,** *m.* [des-fe-goo-rah-the-on']. Deformation, disfiguration, disfigurement.
Desfigurar [des-fe-goo-rar'], *va.* 1. To disfigure, to deform, to misshape, to misform. 2. To disguise. 3. To misrepresent, to misstate. 4. (Met.) To cloud, to darken.—*vr.* To be disfigured by passion, or an accident.
Desfijar [des-fe-har'], *va.* To unsettle, to remove a thing from its place.
Desfilachar [des-fe-lah-char'], *va.* *V.* Deshilachar.
Desfilada [des-fe-lah'-dah], *f.* (Mil.) Single file.
Desfiladero [des-fe-lah-day'-ro], *m.* 1. Narrow passage where troops pass, single file. 2. Canyon.
Desfilar [des-fe-lar'], *va.* (Obs.) To ravel, to unweave.—*vn.* (Mil.) 1. To defile; to march off by files; to file off. 2. To march in review before an officer of high rank.
Desfile [des-fee'-lay], *m.* Defiling off, marching by files.
(*Yo desflaquezco,* from *Desflaquecer. V.* Aborrecer.)
Desflecar [des-flay-car'], *va.* To remove the flakes of wool or frettings of cloth.
Desflemación [des-flay-mah-the-on'], *f.* (Chem. Obs.) Dephlegmation.
Desflemar [des-flay-mar'], *va.* To dephlegmate.—*vn.* (Prov.) To brag, to boast.
Desflocar [des-flo-car'], *va.* To ravel out the ends of stuff. *V.* Desflecar.
Desfloración [des-flo-rah-the-on'], *f.* Defloration.
Desfloramiento [des-flo-rah-me-en'-to], *m.* Violation, constupration, ravishment.
Desflorar [des-flo-rar'], *va.* 1. To pull up or cut up flowers. 2. To constuprate, violate, deflower. 3. To tarnish, to stain or sully. 4. To write or speak very superficially.
Desflorecer [des-flo-ray-therr'], *vn.* To lose the flower.—Also *vr.*
Desflorecimiento [des-flo-ray-the-me-en'-to], *m.* Falling of flowers.
(*Yo desflueco,* from *Desflocar. V.* Acordar.)
Desfogar [des-fo-gar'], *va.* 1. To vent, to make an opening for fire. 2. To vent the violence of passion. 3. To temper or moderate passion or desire. 4. To give loose rein to a horse.—*vr.* To vent one's anger.
Desfogonadura [des-fo-go-nah-doo'-rah], *f.* Disproportionate width of the vent of a cannon.
Desfogonar [des-fo-go-nar'], *va.* To widen or burst the vent of a cannon.
Desfogue [des-fo'-gay], *m.* The venting or foaming out of passion.
Desfollonar [des-fol-lyo-nar'], *va.* To strip off useless leaves.
Desfondar [des-fon-dar'], *va.* 1. To break or take off the bottom of a vessel. 2. (Naut.) To penetrate the bottom of a ship.
Desforado, da [des-fo-rah'-do, dah], *a.* Outlawed; unjudicial. *V.* Desaforado.
Desformar [des-for-mar'], *va.* To disfigure, to deform. *V.* Deformar.
Desfortalecer, or **Desfortificar** [des-for-tah-lay-therr'], *va.* (Mil.) To dismantle, to demolish the works of a fortress.
Desfrenar [des-fray-nar'], *va.* To unbridle. *V.* Desenfrenar.
Desfrutar, Desfrute. (Obs.) *V.* Disfrutar, Disfrute.
Desfundar [des-foon-dar'], *va.* *V.* Desenfundar.

Desfusión [des-foo-se-on'], *f.* Dilution, diffusion, attenuation. Quaint and rare form for *Difusión.*
Desgaire [des-gah'-e-ray], *m.* 1. A graceless mien or deportment; slovenliness, affected carelessness in dress. 2. Gesture, indicating scorn or contempt. *Al desgaire,* Affectedly careless, disdainfully, contemptuously.
Desgajadura [des-gah-hah-doo'-rah], *f.* Disruption, tearing off the branch of a tree.
Desgajar [des-gah-har'], *va.* 1. To lop off the branches of trees. 2. To break or tear in pieces.—*vr.* 1. To be separated or disjointed. 2. To be rent or torn in pieces: applied to clothes. *Desgajarse el cielo* or *las nubes,* (Met.) To rain excessively.
Desgalgadero [des-gal-gah-day'-ro], *m.* A rugged declivitous place.
Desgalgado, da [des-gal-gah'-do, dah], *a.* & *pp.* of DESGALGAR. 1. Precipitated. 2. Light, thin, small-waisted.
Desgalgar [des-gal-gar'], *va.* To precipitate; to throw headlong.—*vr.* To flee by rough roads.
Desgalichado, da [des-gah-le-chah'-do, dah], *a.* (Coll.) Ungainly, ungraceful.
Desgana [des-gah'-nah], *f.* 1. Disgust, want of appetite. 2. Aversion, repugnance, reluctance. 3. *V.* CONGOJA.
Desganar [des-gah-nar'], *va.* To deprive of the idea, desire, or pleasure of doing something.—*vr.* 1. To do with reluctance what was before done with pleasure. 2. To lose the appetite or desire for food.
Desganchar [des-gan-char'], *va.* To lop off the branches of trees.
Desgañifarse, Desgañitarse [des-gah-nye-far'-say, des-gah-nye-tar'-say], *vr.* To shriek, to scream, to bawl.
Desgarbado, da [des-gar-bah'-do, dah], *a.* Ungraceful, ungenteel, inelegant, ungainly.
Desgargamillado, da [des-gar-gah-mil-lyah'-do, dah], *a.* (Prov.) *V.* DESIDIOSO and MANDRIA.
Desgargantarse [des-gar-gan-tar'-say], *vr.* (Coll.) To become hoarse with bawling or screaming.
Desgargolar [des-gar-go-lar'], *va.* To shed the seed: applied to ripe and dry hemp.
Desgaritar [des-gah-re-tar'], *vn.* (Naut.) To lose the course: applied to a ship. —*vr.* 1. (Naut.) To lose the course. 2. (Met.) To give up a design or undertaking.
Desgarradamente [des-gar-rah-dah-men'-tay], *adv.* Impudently, barefacedly, shamelessly.
Desgarrado, da [des-gar-rah'-do, dah], *a.* 1. Licentious, dissolute; impudent, shameless, bold.—*pp.* of DESGARRAR. 2. Irregularly segmented upon the border: applied to leaves and to wings of insects.
Desgarrador, ra [des-gar-rah-dor', rah], *m.* & *f.* Tearer.
Desgarradura [des-gar-rah-doo'-rah], *f.* (Prov.) Rent, laceration, break.
Desgarrar [des-gar-rar'], *va.* 1. To rend, to tear; to claw. 2. (Cuba) To expectorate, cough up (phlegm).—*vr.* 1. To withdraw from one's company; to retire. 2. To give a loose rein to one's passions, to lead a licentious life.
Desgarro [des-gar'-ro], *m.* 1. Laceration, rent, break, breach. 2. Impudence, effrontery. 3. Looseness, criminal levity. 4. Fanfaronade, idle boast, brag. 5. Solution of continuity, in a tissue by being overstretched.
Desgarrón [des-gar-rone'], *m.* 1. (Aug.) A large rent or hole. 2. Piece of cloth torn off.
Desgastadoramente, *adv.* (Obs.) Injuriously, prejudicially.
Desgastamiento [des-gas-tah-me-en'-to], *m.* (Obs.) Prodigality, profusion.
Desgastar [des-gas-tar'], *va.* 1. To consume, to waste by degrees. 2. To corrode, to gnaw, to eat away. 3. (Met.) To pervert, to vitiate.—*vr.* To ruin one's self by extravagant expenses; to debilitate one's self.
Desgatar [des-gah-tar'], *va.* 1. (Prov.) To hunt and destroy cats. 2. To root out the herb called catmint.
Desgavilado, da [des-gah-ve-lah'-do, dah], *a.* (Coll.) Unkempt; ungainly. (?) [This word, used by Fernan Caballero, the editor has been unable to fix with certainty.]
Desgaznatarse, *vr.* *V.* DESGAÑITARSE.
Desglosar [des-glo-sar'], *va.* 1. To blot out a note or comment on a thing. 2. To take off, to separate.
Desglose [des-glo'-say], *m.* Act of blotting out a comment or gloss.
Desgobernado, da [des-go-ber-nah'-do, dah], *a.* Ill-governed or regulated, ungovernable: applied to persons.—*pp.* of DESGOBERNAR.
Desgobernadura [des-go-ber-nah-doo'-rah], *f.* (Vet.) Act of confining a vein in animals.
Desgobernar [des-go-ber-nar'], *va.* 1. To disturb or overset the order of government; to misgovern. 2. To dislocate or disjoint. 3. To bar a vein on a horse's leg. 4. (Naut.) Not to steer steadily the right course.—*vr.* To affect ridiculous motions in dancing.
Desgobierno [des-go-be-err'-no], *m.* 1. Mismanagement, misgovernment; misrule, want of conduct and economy; ill administration of public affairs. 2. (Vet.) Act of barring a vein on a horse's leg.
Desgolletar [des-gol-lyay-tar'], *va.* 1. To break off the neck of a bottle or other vessel. 2. To cut off slopingly the fore part of a woman's gown.
Desgonzar [des-gon-thar'], *va.* 1. *V.* DESGOZNAR. 2. To uncase, to unhinge, to discompose, to disjoint.
Desgorrarse [des-gor-rar'-say], *vr.* To pull off one's bonnet, hat, or hunting-cap.
Desgotar [des-go-tar'], *va.* To drain off water. *V.* AGOTAR.
Desgoznar [des-goth-nar'], *va.* To unhinge, to disjoint.—*vr.* 1. To be dislocated or disjointed. 2. To be torn in pieces. 3. To distort the body with violent motions.
Desgracia [des-grah'-the-ah], *f.* 1. Misfortune, adversity, mishap, fatality. 2. Misadventure, mischance, harm. 3. Enmity, unfriendly disposition. 4. Disgrace, state of being out of favour. 5. Unpleasantness, rudeness of language and address. *Correr con desgracia,* To be unfortunate in a design or undertaking. *Caer en desgracia,* To be disgraced or put out of favour.
Desgraciadamente [des-grah-the-ah-dah-men'-tay], *adv.* Unfortunately, unhappily.
Desgraciado, da [des-grah-the-ah'-do, dah], *a.* 1. Unfortunate, unhappy, unlucky, miserable, subject to misfortunes. 2. Misadventured, luckless, hapless. 3. Out of work. 4. Disagreeable, ungrateful.—*pp.* of DESGRACIAR.
Desgraciar [des-grah-the-ar'], *va.* (Obs.) To displease, to disgust, to offend.—*vn.* *V.* MALOGRAR.—*vr.* 1. To disgrace, to fall out with one. 2. To be out of order; not to enjoy good health. 3. To lose the perfection formerly possessed, to degenerate; to die young. *Este negocio se desgració a sus principios,* This business failed at its commencement. *Se desgració con esta acción,* By this action he disgraced himself.
Desgramar [des-grah-mar'], *va.* To pull up the panic-grass by the root.
Desgranadera [des-grah-nah-day'-rah], *f.* An instrument for separating grapes from the stems.
Desgranamiento [des-grah-nah-me-en'-to], *m.* 1. (Agr.) Shaking out grain. 2. (Mil.) Grooves which the expansive force of powder forms on the inner orifice of the vent-hole.
Desgranar [des-grah-nar'], *va.* 1. To shake out the grain from the ears of corn, or other fruits. 2. (Met.) To kill. 3. (Met.) To scatter about.—*vr.* To wear away: applied to the vent of fire-arms.
Desgranzar [des-gran-thar'], *va.* 1. To separate the husks or chaff from the grain. 2. (Pict.) To give colours the first grinding.
Desgrasar [des-grah-sar'], *va.* To remove the fat (from).
Desgreñadura [des-gray-nyah-doo'-rah], *f.* The act and effect of dishevelling.
Desgreñar [des-gray-nyar'], *va.* 1. To dishevel the hair, to pull it out by the roots. 2. To discompose, to disturb.
Desguarnecer [des-goo-ar-nay-therr'], *va.* 1. To strip clothes of trimmings and other ornaments. 2. To deprive any thing of its strength, to strip it of all accessories; to take away what is necessary for the use of some mechanical instrument. 3. To disgarnish, to deprive of ornament or lustre. 4. To disgarrison.

(*Yo desguarnezco, yo desguarnezca,* from *Desguarnecer. V.* CONOCER.)

Desguarnir [des-goo-ar-neer'], *va.* (Naut.) To unrig the capstan.
Desguazar [des-goo-ah-thar'], *va.* To cut asunder timber or wood.
Desguince [des-geen'-thay], *m.* 1. The knife which cuts rags in paper-mills. 2. *V.* ESQUINCE.
Desguindar [des-geen-dar'], *va.* (Naut.) To take and bring down.—*vr.* To slide down a rope.
Desguinzar [des-geen-thar'], *va.* To cut cloth or rags in paper-mills.
Deshabido, da [des-ah-bee'-do, dah], *a.* (Obs.) Unfortunate, unhappy. of DESHABITAR.
Deshabitar [des-ah-be-tar'], *va.* 1. To quit one's house or habitation. 2. To unpeople, to depopulate, to desert a place.
Deshabituación [des-ah-be-too-ah-the-on'], *f.* Disuse, disusage, desuetude.
Deshabituar [des-ah-be-too-ar'], *va.* To disaccustom, to disuse, to destroy the force of habit.
Deshacedor [des-ah-thay-dor'], *m.* *Deshacedor de agravios,* Undoer of injuries.
Deshacer [des-ah-therr'], *va.* 1. To undo or destroy the form or figure of a thing; to undo what has been done. 2. To consume, to diminish. 3. To cancel, to blot or scratch out; to efface. 4. To rout an army; to put to flight. 5. To melt, to liquefy. 6. To cut up, to divide. 7. To dissolve in a liquid. 8. To violate a treaty or agreement. 9. To discharge troops from service.—*vr.* 1. To be wasted or destroyed. 2. To grieve, to mourn. 3. To disappear, to get out of one's sight. 4. To do any thing with vehemence. 5. To grow feeble or meagre. 6. To be crippled, grievously maltreated. 7. To remove a hindrance to the carrying out of a project. 8. To transfer, to sell. *Des-*

hacerse como el humo, To vanish like smoke. *Deshacerse en lágrimas*, To burst into a flood of tears. *Deshacer agravios* or *tuertos*, To revenge or redress injuries or wrongs. *Deshacerse de una cosa*, To give a thing away, to dispose of.

(*Yo deshago, yo deshice, yo deshaga*, from *Deshacer. V.* HACER.)

Desharrapado, da [des-ar-rah-pah'-do, dah], *a.* Shabby, ragged, in tatters.

Desharrapamiento [des-ar-rah-pah-me-en'-to], *m.* Misery, meanness.

Deshebillar [des-ay-bil-lyar'], *va.* To unbuckle.

Deshebrar [des-ay-brar'], *va.* 1. To unthread, to ravel into threads. 2. (Met.) To separate into filaments. 3. (Met.) To shed a flood of tears.

Deshecha [des-ay'-chah], *f.* 1. Simulation, fiction, evasion, shift. 2. A genteel departure, a polite farewell. 3. Step in a Spanish dance. *A la deshecha*, Dissemblingly; deceitfully.

Deshechizar [des-ay-chee-thar'], *va.* To disenchant.

Deshechizo [des-ay-chee'-tho], *m.* Disenchantment.

Deshecho, cha [des-ay'-cho, chah], *a.* & *pp.* of DESHACER. 1. Undone, destroyed, wasted; melted; in pieces. 2. Perfectly mixed; applied to colours. *Borrasca deshecha*, A violent tempest. *Fuga deshecha*, A precipitate flight.

Deshelador [des-ay-lah-dor'], *m.* Deicer.

Deshelar [des-ay-lar'], *va.* 1. To thaw. 2. To overcome one's obstinacy. 3. (Met.) To invite, to inspirit.—*vr.* To thaw, to melt.

Desherbar [des-er-bar'], *va.* To pluck up or extirpate herbs.

Desheredación [des-ay-ray-dah-the-on'], *f.* Disheritance, disinheriting.

Desheredamiento [des-ay-ray-dah-me-en'-to], *m.* Disinheriting.

Desheredar [des-ay-ray-dar'], *va.* 1. To disinherit, to deprive of an inheritance; to disinherit, to cut off from an hereditary right. 2. (Met.) To deprive of influence or favour.—*vr.* To degenerate, to fall from the dignity and virtue of one's ancestors.

Deshermanar [des-er-mah-nar'], *va.* (Met.) To unmatch things which were similar or equal.—*vr.* To violate the love due to a brother.

Desherradura [des-er-rah-doo'-rah], *f.* (Vet.) Surbating, injury done to a horse's foot by being unshod.

Desherrar [des-er-rar'], *va.* 1. To unchain. 2. To rip off the shoes of horses.

Desherrumbrar [des-er-room-brar'], *va.* To clear a thing of rust.

Deshidratado, da [des-e-drah-tah'-do, dah], *a.* Dehydrated.

Deshielo [des-e-ay'-lo], *m.* Thaw.

(*Yo deshielo*, from *Deshelar. V.* ACRECENTAR.)

Deshilachar [des-e-lah-char'], *va.* To ravel, to uncord.

Deshilado [des-e-lah'-do], *m.* Openwork, a kind of embroidery; drawn work.

Deshilado, da [des-e-lah'-do, dah], *a.* Marching in a file. *A la deshilada*, 1. In file, one after another, stealthily. 2. Deceitfully, dissemblingly.—*pp.* of DESHILAR.

Deshiladura [des-e-lah-doo'-rah], *f.* Ripping, ravelling out.

Deshilar [des-e-lar'], *va.* 1. To draw out threads from cloth, to ravel. 2. To reduce, to convert into filaments or lint. 3. To distract bees, in order to lead them from one hive to another.—*vn.* To grow thin, by reason of sickness.

Deshilo [des-ee'-lo], *m.* Obstructing the communication of bees, to get them into a new hive.

Deshilvanar [des-eel-vah-nar'], *va.* To remove the basting-threads.

Deshincadura [des-in-cah-doo'-rah], *f.* Act of drawing out any thing nailed or fixed.

Deshincar [des-in-car'], *va.* To draw a nail, to remove what is fixed.

Deshinchadura [des-in-chah-doo'-rah], *f.* Act of abating a swelling.

Deshinchar [des-in-char'], *va.* 1. To reduce a swelling. 2. To let out the air, or fluid, with which any thing is inflated. 3. To appease anger or annoyance.—*vr.* 1. To be removed: applied to a swelling. 2. (Met.) To abate presumption.

Deshipotecar [des-e-po-tay-car'], *va.* To lift, to satisfy a mortgage.

Deshojador [des-oh-hah-dor'], *m.* A stripper of leaves.

Deshojadura [des-oh-hah-doo'-rah], *f.* (Obs.) Stripping a tree of its leaves.

Deshojar [des-oh-har'], *va.* 1. To strip off the leaves. 2. (Met.) To display rhetorical elegance in discussion. 3. (Met.) To deprive of all hopes.

Deshoje [des-oh'-hay], *m.* The fall of leaves from plants. (Acad.)

Deshollejar [des-ol-lyay-har'], *va.* To peel, to pare, to strip off the husk.

Deshollinador [des-ol-lyee-nah-dor'], *m.* 1. Chimney-sweeper. 2. Any instrument for sweeping chimneys. 3. (Met. Coll.) He who examines and inspects carefully and curiously.

Deshollinar [des-ol-lyee-nar'], *va.* 1. To sweep or clean chimneys. 2. To clean what is dirty. 3. (Met.) To shift, to change clothes. 4. (Met. Coll.) To view and examine with attention.

Deshombrecerse [des-om-bray-therr'-say], *vr.* (Prov.) To shrug up the shoulders.

Deshonestamente [des-o-nes-tah-men-tay], *adv.* 1. Dishonourably, disgracefully. 2. Lewdly, dishonestly.

Deshonestar [des-o-nes-tar'], *va.* 1. To dishonour, to disgrace. 2. (Obs.) To disfigure, to deform.—*vr.* To be insolent, to be saucy.

Deshonestidad [des-o-nes-te-dahd'], *f.* Immodesty, indecency, lewdness in actions or words.

Deshonesto, ta [des-o-nes'-to, tah], *a.* 1. Immodest. lewd, unchaste, libidinous, lustful, dishonest. 2. Unreasonable, not conformable to reason. 3. (Obs.) Saucy, rude, rustic.

Deshonor [des-o-nor'], *m.* 1. Dishonour, disgrace. 2. Injury, insult, affront.

Deshonorar [des-o-no-rar'], *va.* 1. To deprive of office or employ. 2. (Obs.) To dishonour, to disgrace.

Deshonra [des-on'-rah], *f.* 1. Dishonour, discredit. 2. Disgrace or infamy, obloquy, opprobrium. 3. Seduction or defloration of a woman. *Tener a deshonra alguna cosa*, To consider a thing unworthy, and beneath the rank or character of a person.

Deshonrabuenos [des-on-rah-boo-ay'-nos], *com.* 1. Calumniator, libeller. 2. He who degenerates from his ancestors.

Deshonradamente, *adv.* Dishonourably, shamefully, disgracefully.

Deshonrador [des-on-rah-dor'], *m.* 1. Dishonourer, violator of chastity. 2. Disgracer.

Deshonrar [des-on-rar'], *va.* 1. To affront, to insult, to defame; to dishonour, to disgrace. 2. To scorn, to despise. 3. To seduce an honest woman.

Deshonrible [des-on-ree'-blay], *a.* Shameless, despicable. (Acad.)

Deshonroso, sa [des-on-ro'-so, sah], *a.* Dishonourable, indecent, disgraceful, low.

Deshora [des-oh'-rah], *f.* An unseasonable or inconvenient time. *A deshora* or *a deshoras*, Untimely, unseasonably; extemporary.

Deshorado, da [des-o-rah'-do, dah], *a.* Untimely, unseasonable; unpropitious, fatal.

Deshornar [des-or-nar'], *va.* To take out of the oven. *V.* DESENHORNAR.

Deshospedado, da [des-os-pay-dah'-do, dah], *a.* (Obs.) Destitute of lodging.

Deshospedamiento [des-os-pay-dah-me-en'-to], *m.* Inhospitality, the act of refusing strangers a lodging.

Deshuesamiento [des-oo-ay-sah-me-en'to], *m.* Removal of bones.

Deshuesar [des-oo-ay-sar'], *va.* To rid of bones.

Deshumanizar [des-oo-mah-ne-thar'], *va.* To dehumanize.

Deshumano, na [des-oo-mah'-no, nah], *a.* (Littl. us.) Inhuman.

Deshumedecer [des-oo-may-day-therr'], *va.* To dehumidify, to deprive of humidity.—*vr.* To grow dry.

Desiderable [day-se-day-rah'-blay], *a.* Desirable.

Desiderativo, va [day-se-day-rah-tee'-vo, vah], *a.* Desiderative, expressing desire.

Desidia [day-see'-de-ah], *f.* Idleness, laziness, indolence.

Desidiosamente, *adv.* Indolently, idly.

Desidioso, sa [day-se-de-oh'-so, sah], *a.* Lazy, idle, indolent, heavy.

Desierto, ta [day-se-err'-to, tah], *a.* Deserted, uninhabited, lonesome, solitary, desert, waste.

Desierta, *f.* (Law) Withdrawal of an appeal.

Desierto [day-se-err'-to], *m.* Desert, wilderness.

Designación [day-sig-nah-the-on'], *f.* Designation.

Designar [day-sig-nar'], *va.* 1. To design, to purpose, to intend any thing. 2. To appoint a person for some determined purpose. 3. To express, to name.

Designativo, va [day-sig-nah-tee'-vo, vah], *a.* (Littl. us.) Designative.

Designio [day-seeg'-ne-o], *m.* Design, purpose, intention, contrivance, mind.

Desigual [des-e-goo-ahl'], *a.* 1. Unequal, dissimilar, unlike. 2. Uneven, unlevelled, broken, craggy, cragged. 3. Arduous, difficult, perilous. 4. Variable; abrupt. 5. Excessive, extreme.

Desigualar [des-e-goo-ah-lar'], *va.* To make unequal or dissimilar, to mismatch.—*vr.* To excel, to surpass.

Desigualdad [des-e-goo-al-dahd'], *f.* 1. Inequality, odds, dissimilitude. 2. Variableness, levity, inconstancy. 3. Wrong, injury, injustice. 4. Knottiness, unevenness, craggedness, cragginess, unevenness of the ground, anfractuosity.

Desigualmente, *adv.* Unequally, oddly.

Desilusión [des-e-loo-se-on'], *f.* Dis illusion.

Desilusionar [des-e-loo-se-o-nar'], *va.* 1. To destroy an illusion, cause it to vanish. 2. To undeceive.—*vr.* 1. To lose an illusion. 2. To be disabused, undeceived.

Desimaginar [des-e-mah-he-nar'], *va.* To blot out or obliterate in the mind. —*vn.* To be thoughtless or unconcerned about what may happen.

Desimanarse [des-e-mah-nar'-say], *vr.* To lose its magnetism.
Desimpresionar [des-im-pray-se-o-nar'], *va.* To undeceive.
Desinclinar [des-in-cle-nar'], *va.* To disincline.
Desincorporación [des-in-cor-po-rah-the-on'], *f.* Disincorporation, end of corporate existence.
Desincorporar [des-in-cor-po-rar'], *va.* & *vr.* To separate what was before united or incorporated; to disincorporate.
Desinencia [day-se-nen'-the-ah], *f.* (Gram.) Termination, ending.
Desinfatuación [des-in-fah-too-ah-the-on'], *f.* Disinfatuation.
Desinfatuar [des-in-fah-too-ar'], *va.* & *vr.* To disinfatuate, to become freed from infatuation.
Desinfección [des-in-fec-the-on'], *f.* Disinfection, act of disinfecting.
Desinfectante [des-in-fec-tahn'-tay], *pa.* & *m.* Disinfectant; capable of destroying or neutralizing infection.
Desinfectar [des-in-fec-tar'], *va.* To disinfect, to destroy the poison of disease.
Desinficionamiento [des-in-fe-the-o-nah-me-en'-to], *m.* Disinfection.
Desinficionar [des-in-fe-the-o-nar'], *va.* To free from infection.
Desinflación [des-in-flah-the-on'], *f.* 1. Deflation. 2. Depression, dejection.
Desinflamar [des-in-flah-mar'], *va.* To cure or remove an inflammation.
Desinflar [des-in-flar'], *va.* To deflate. *Desinflarse,* (fig.) To be deflated, to come down to earth.
Desintegrable [des-in-tay-grah'-blay], *a.* Fissionable.
Desintegración [des-in-tay-grah-the-on'], *f.* Disintegration. *Desintegración del átomo,* Splitting of the atom.
Desintegrador de átomos [des-in-tay-grah-dor' day ah'to-mos], *m.* (Phy.) Atom smasher.
Desintegrar [des-in-tay-grar'], *va.* To disintegrate, to decompose.
Desinterés [des-in-tay-res'], *m.* Disinterest, indifference.
Desinteresadamente, *adv.* Disinterestedly.
Desinteresado, da [des-in-tay-ray-sah'-do, dah], *a.* Disinterested, impartial.
Desinvernar [des-in-ver-nar'], *vn.* To leave winter quarters: used of troops. (Acad.)
(*Yo desirvo,* from *Deservir.* *V.* PEDIR.)
Desistencia, *f.* *V.* DESISTIMIENTO.
Desistimiento [day-sis-te-me-en'-to], *m.* Desistance, the act of desisting.
Desistir [day-sis-teer'], *vn.* 1. To desist, to cease, to give out, to go back. 2. To leave, to abandon; to flinch. 3. (For.) To abdicate a right.
Desjarretar [des-har-ray-tar'], *va.* 1. To hough, to hamstring. 2. (Met. Coll.) To weaken, to debilitate, to leave powerless.
Desjarrete [des-har-ray'-tay], *m.* Act of houghing.
Desjugar [des-hoo-gar'], *va.* To extract the juice from any thing.
Desjuntamiento [des-hoon-tah-me-en'-to], *m.* Separation, disjunction.
Desjuntar [des-hoon-tar'], *va.* To divide, to separate, to part.
Desjurar [des-hoo-rar'], *va.* To retract an oath, to forswear.
Deslabonar [des-lah-bo-nar'], *va.* 1. To unlink, to separate one link from another. 2. (Met.) To disjoin, to destroy.—*vr.* To withdraw from a company, to retire.
Desladrillar [des-lah-dril-lyar'], *va.* *V.* DESENLADRILLAR.
Deslamar [des-lah-mar'], *va.* To clear of mud.
Deslastrar [des-las-trar'], *va.* To unballast a ship.
Deslatar [des-lah-tar'], *va.* To take the laths or small joists out of a house or other building.
Deslavado, da [des-lah-vah'-do, dah], *a.* Impudent, barefaced.—*pp.* of DESLAVAR.
Deslavadura [des-lah-vah-doo'-rah], *f.* Washing, rinsing.
Deslavar [des-lah-var'], *va.* 1. To wash or cleanse superficially, to rinse. 2. To wet, to spoil by wetting. 3. To take away the colour, force, or vigour of a thing. *Cara deslavada,* A pale, puny face.
Deslavazar [des-lah-vah-thar'], *va.* 1. *V.* DESLAVAR. 2. (Agr.) To expose hay to the action of rain.
Deslave [des-lah'-vay], *m.* Washout, overflowing.
Deslazamiento [des-lah-thah-me-en'-to], *m.* Disjunction, dissolution.
Deslazar [des-lah-thar'], *va.* To unlace, to untie a knot.
Desleal [des-lay-ahl'], *a.* Disloyal; perfidious, faithless; traitorous.
Deslealmente, *adv.* Disloyally, treacherously.
Deslealtad [des-lay-al-tahd'], *f.* Disloyalty, treachery, faithlessness.
Deslechar [des-lay-char'], *va.* (Prov.) To remove the leaves and dirt from silk-worms.
Deslecho [des-lay'-cho], *m.* (Prov.) Act of cleansing silk-worms.
Deslechugador [des-lay-choo-gah-dor'], *m.* Vine-dresser, pruner.
Deslechugar, Deslechuguillar [des-lay-choo-gar'], *va.* (Agr.) To cut and prune the branches of vines.
Desleidura [des-lay-e-doo'-rah], *f.* **Desleimiento,** *m.* Dilution, making thin or weak.
(*Yo deslío, yo desleí; él deslió, él disliera;* from *Desleir.* *V.* PEDIR.)
Desleir [des-lay-eer'], *va.* To dilute, to make thin or weak, to dissolve.
Deslendrar [des-len-drar'], *va.* To clear the hair of nits.
Deslenguado, da [des-len-goo-ah'-do, dah], *a.* Loquacious, impudent, foul-mouthed, scurrilous.—*pp.* of DESLENGUAR.
Deslenguamiento [des-len-goo-ah-me-en'-to], *m.* Loquacity, impudence.
Deslenguar [des-len-goo-ar'], *va.* To cut out the tongue.—*vr.* To talk ill of, to slander.
Desliar [des-le-ar'], *va.* To untie, to loose.
Desligadura, *f.* or **Desligamiento,** *m.* [des-le-gah-doo'-rah]. Disjunction, untying.
Desligar [des-le-gar'], *va.* 1. To loosen, to untie, to unbind. 2. (Met.) To disentangle, to extricate, to unravel something not material. 3. (Met.) To absolve from ecclesiastical censure. 4. To remove from a ship part of its knees, or futtock-timbers, or the spikes which hold them. 5. (Med.) To unfasten bandages or ligatures. 6. (Mus.) To separate notes very clearly. *Desligar el maleficio,* To dissolve a spell which prevented a husband from enjoying the marriage rights.
Deslindable [des-lin-dah'-blay], *a.* Surveyable, capable of demarcation.
Deslindador [des-lin-dah-dor'], *m.* He who marks limits or boundaries.
Deslindamiento [des-lin-dah-me-en'-to], *m.* Demarcation.
Deslindar [des-lin-dar'], *va.* 1. To mark the limits and bounds of a place or district. 2. (Met.) To clear up a thing.
Deslinde [des-leen'-day], *m.* Demarcation.
Deslingar [des-lin-gar'], *va.* To unsling.
Desliñar [des-le-nyar'], *va.* To clean cloth before it goes to the press.
Desliz [des-leeth'], *m.* 1. Slip, the act of slipping or sliding. 2. (Met.) Slip, a false step, frailty, weakness, failure, fault. 3. The mercury which escapes in smelting silver ore.
Deslizable [des-le-thah'-blay], *a.* That which can slip or slide.
Deslizadero [des-le-thah-day'-ro], *m.* A slippery place.—*a.* *V.* DESLIZADIZO.
Deslizadero, ra, or **Deslizadizo, za** [des-le-thah-dee'-tho, thah], *a.* Slippery, slippy, lubricous.
Deslizador [des-le-thah-dor'], *m.* (Aer.) Glider.
Deslizamiento [des-le-thah-me-en'-to], *m.* 1. Slip, slipping. 2. Gliding.
Deslizar [des-le-thar'], *vn.* & *vr.* 1. To slip, to slide, to glide. 2. To act or speak carelessly, to make a slip of the tongue.
Deslodaje [des-lo-dah'-hay], *m.* Cleansing of a mineral substance from mud which enwraps it.
Deslomadura [des-lo-mah-doo'-rah], *f.* Act of breaking the back. (Vet.) Violent extension and even rupture of the fleshy fibres or of the aponeuroses of the muscles of the loins of horses.
Deslomar [des-lo-mar'], *va.* To break the back, to distort or strain the loins, to chine. *No se deslomará,* (Iron.) He is sure not to overwork himself.
Deslucidamente, *adv.* Ungracefully, inelegantly.
Deslucido, da [des-loo-thee'-do, dah], *a.* 1. Unadorned, ungraceful, inelegant, awkward. 2. Useless, fruitless.—*pp.* of DESLUCIR.
Deslucimiento [des-loo-the-me-en'-to], *m.* Disgrace, dishonour, want of splendour.
Deslucir [des-loo-theer'], *va.* 1. To tarnish or impair the lustre and splendour of a thing. 2. (Met.) To obscure one's merit.
Deslumbrador, ra [des-loom-brah-dor', rah], *a.* Dazzling, brilliant, glaring.
Deslumbramiento, Deslumbre [des-loom-brah-me-en'-to], *m.* 1. Glare, overpowering lustre; dazzling. 2. Confusion of sight or mind; hallucination.
Deslumbrar [des-loom-brar'], *va.* 1. To dazzle the sight, to glare. 2. (Met.) To puzzle, to leave in doubt and uncertainty.
Deslustrador, ra [des-loos-trah-dor', rah], *m.* & *f.* Tarnisher.
Deslustrar [des-loos-trar'], *va.* 1. To tarnish or sully the brilliancy of a thing, to take away the lustre. 2. To obscure, to make less beautiful or illustrious. 3. (Met.) To blast one's reputation, to impeach one's character or merit.
Deslustre [des-loos'-tray], *m.* 1. Spot or stain which obscures the lustre or splendour of a thing. 2. Disgrace, ignominy, stigma.
Deslustroso, sa [des-loos-tro'-so, sah], *a.* Unbecoming, ugly.
Desmadejamiento [des-mah-day-hah-me-en'-to], *m.* Languishment, languidness.
Desmadejar [des-mah-day-har'], *va.* To enervate, to produce languor.—*vr.* To languish, to be enervated and weak.
Desmajolar [des-mah-ho-lar'], *va.* 1. To pull up vines by the roots. 2 To loosen or untie the shoe-strings.

Desmallador [des-mal-lyah-dor'], *m.* He who breaks a coat of mail.
Desmalladura [des-mal-lyah-doo'-rah], *f.* Act of ripping up or breaking a coat of mail.
Desmallar [des-mal-lyar'], *va.* To cut and destroy a coat of mail.
Desmamar, *va.* *V.* Destetar.
Desmamonar [des-mah-mo-nar'], *va.* To cut off the young shoots of vines or trees.
Desmamparar, *va.* (Obs.) *V.* Desamparar.
Desmán [des-mahn'], *m.* 1. Misfortune, disaster, mishap, calamity. 2. Misbehaviour. Excess in actions or words. (Acad.) 3. Shrew-mouse.
Desmanarse [des-mah-nar'-say], *vr.* To stray from a flock or herd.
Desmanche [des-mahn'-chay], *m.* Excessive movement in a rider, want of firmness in the saddle.
Desmandado, da [des-man-dah'-do, dah], *a.* *V.* Desobediente.—*pp.* of Desmandar.
Desmandamiento [des-man-dah-me-en'-to], *m.* 1. Act of countermanding or disbanding. 2. Disorder, irregularity, neglect of rule.
Desmandar [des-man-dar'], *va.* 1. To repeal an order, to countermand, to revoke an offer. 2. To revoke a legacy.—*vr.* 1. To transgress the bounds of justice and reason. 2. To disband: applied to troops. 3. To stray from the flock. 4. To go astray.
Desmanear [des-mah-nay-ar'], *va.* To unfetter, to take off fetters or shackles: applied to horses, mules, etc.
Desmangamiento, Desmangue [des-man-gah-me-en'-to], *m.* Taking off the handle of a thing.
Desmangar [des-man-gar'], *va.* To take off the handle of a thing.
Desmanotado, da [des-mah-no-tah'-do, dah], *a.* Unhandy, awkward.
Desmantecar [des-man-tay-car'], *va.* To take off the butter.
Desmantelado, da [des-man-tay-lah'-do, dah], *a.* & *pp.* of Desmantelar. Dismantled, ruinous, dilapidated.
Desmantelar [des-man-tay-lar'], *va.* 1. To dismantle. 2. To abandon, to desert, to forsake. 3. (Naut.) To unmast.
Desmaña [des-mah'-nyah], *f.* 1. Awkwardness, clumsiness. 2. Idleness, laziness.
Desmañado, da [des-mah-nyah'-do, dah], *a.* 1. Unhandy, clumsy, awkward, clownish. 2. Lazy, idle, indolent.
Desmañar [des-mah-nyar'], *va.* (Ant.) To impede, obstruct.
Desmarañar [des-mah-rah-nyar'], *va.* To disentangle. *V.* Desenmarañar.
Desmarcar [des-mar-car'], *va.* To remove, efface, obliterate marks.
Desmaridar [des-mah-re-dar'], *va.* (Obs.) To separate husband and wife.
Desmarojador [des-mah-ro-hah-dor'], *m.* He who takes off the rind of olives.
Desmarojar [des-mah-ro-har'], *va.* To take the glutinous rind from olives.
Desmarrido, da [des-mar-ree'-do, dah], *a.* Sad, languid, dejected, exhausted.
Desmatar, *adv.* *V.* Descuajar.
Desmayadamente, *adv.* Weakly, dejectedly.
Desmayado, da [des-mah-yah'-do, dah], *a.* & *pp.* of Desmayar. 1. Pale, wan, faint of lustre. 2. Dismayed, appalled.
Desmayar [des-mah-yar'], *vn.* To be dispirited or faint-hearted, to want strength and courage.—*vn.* To dismay, to depress, to discourage.—*vr.* To faint, to swoon.
Desmayo [des-mah'-yo], *m.* 1. Swoon, fainting-fit. 2. Decay of strength and vigour. 3. Dismay, discouragement.
Desmazalado, da [des-mah-thah-lah'-do, dah], *a.* Weak, dejected, faint-hearted, spiritless.
Desmedidamente, *adv.* Disproportionably, disproportionately.
Desmedido, da [des-may-dee'-do, dah], *a.* Unproportionable, out of proportion or measure.—*pp.* of Desmedirse.
Desmedirse [des-may-deer'-say], *vr.* *V.* Desmandarse and Excederse.
Desmedrar [des-may-drar'], *vn.* To decrease, to decay.—*va.* To impair, to deteriorate.
Desmedro [des-may'-dro], *m.* Diminution, decay, detriment.
Desmejora [des-may-ho'-rah], *f.* Deterioration, depreciation, diminution, loss.
Desmejorar [des-may-ho-rar'], *va.* To debase, to make worse.—*vr.* To decay, to decline, to grow worse.
Desmelancolizar [des-may-lan-co-le-thar'], *va:* To cheer, to enliven, to gladden.
Desmelar [des-may-lar'], *va.* To take the honey from a hive.
Desmelenar [des-may-lay-nar'], *va.* To dishevel, to disarrange the hair.
Desmembración, Desmembradura [des-mem-brah-the-on', des-mem-brah-doo'-rah], *f.* Dismemberment, division.
Desmembrador, ra [des-mem-brah-dor', rah], *m.* & *f.* Divider, one who dismembers or divides.
Desmembrar [des-mem-brar'], *va.* 1. To dismember, to divide limb from limb, to tear asunder, to curtail. 2. To separate, to divide.
Desmemoriado, da [des-may-mo-re-ah'-do, dah], *a.* Forgetful, having a poor memory.
Desmemoriarse [des-may-mo-re-ar'-say], *vr.* To be forgetful, to forget.
Desmenguar [des-men-goo-ar'], *va.* 1. To lessen; to defalcate. 2. *V.* Menguar.
Desmentida [des-men-tee'-dah], *f.* or **Desmentido,** *m.* The act of giving the lie.
Desmentidor, ra [des-men-te-dor', rah], *m.* & *f.* One who convicts of a falsehood.
Desmentir [des-men-teer'], *va.* 1. To give the lie, to convince of a falsehood. 2. To counterfeit, to conceal, to dissemble. 3. To do things unworthy of one's birth, character, or profession. 4. To lose the right line, to warp or to change from the true situation. 5. To fold a lady's handkerchief so that one point may fall short of the other.—*vr.* 1. To recant, retract. 2. Not to behave in accord with what has been said; to belie.
Desmenuzable [des-may-noo-thah'-blay], *a.* Friable, brittle, crisp, crimp, easily crumbled.
Desmenuzador, ra [des-may-noo-thah-dor', rah], *m.* & *f.* A scrutator or investigator; a purifier.
Desmenuzar [des-may-noo-thar'], *va.* 1. To crumble, to comminute, to crum, to chip, to mill, to fritter. 2. (Met.) To sift, to examine minutely.—*vr.* To crumble, to fall into small pieces.
Desmeollado, da [des-may-ol-lyah'-do, dah], *a.* (Obs.) Silly, simple, crack-brained.
Desmeollamiento [des-may-ol-lyah-me-en'-to], *m.* (Obs.) Act of taking out the marrow.
Desmeollar [des-may-ol-lyar'], *va.* To take out the marrow or pith.
Desmerecedor [des-may-ray-thay-dor'], *m.* An unworthy, undeserving person.
Desmerecer [des-may-ray-therr'], *va.* To demerit, to become unworthy or undeserving of a thing.—*vn.* 1. To lose part of its worth. 2. To grow worse, to deteriorate.
Desmerecimiento [des-may-ray-the-me-en'-to], *m.* Demerit, unworthiness.
Desmesura [des-may-soo'-rah], *f.* 1. Excess, want of moderation and order. 2. Impudence, insolence; rudeness.
Desmesuradamente, *adv.* 1. Immeasurably. 2. Uncivilly, impudently.
Desmesurado, da [des-may-soo-rah'-do, dah], *a.* 1. Immeasurable. 2. Huge, of gigantic stature or size. 3. Unmeasurable.—*pp.* of Desmesurar.
Desmesurar [des-may-soo-rar'], *va.* To disorder, to discompose, to perturbate.—*vr.* To be forward, to act or talk with impudence or insolence, to be rude.
(*Yo desmiembro, yo desmiembre,* from *Desmembrar.* *V.* Acertar.)
(*Yo desmiento, él desmintió, yo desmienta,* from *Desmentir.* *V.* Adherir.)
Desmidia [des-mee'-de-ah], *f.* (Bot.) A desmid; a green, unicellular, fresh-water alga.
Desmidiáceo, cea [des-me-de-ah'-thay-o, the-ah], *a.* Like a desmid, desmidaceous.
Desmigajar [des-me-gah-har'], *va.* To crumble, to comminute.—*vr.* To crumble.
Desmigar [des-me-gar'], *va.* To crumble bread.
Desmilitarización [des-me-le-tah-re-thah-the-on'], *m.* Demilitarization.
Desmilitarizar [des-me-le-tah-re-thar'], *va.* To demilitarize.
Desmirriado, da [des-mir-re-ah'-do, dah], *a.* (Coll.) 1. Lean, extenuated, exhausted. 2. Melancholy.
Desmocha [des-mo'-chah], *f.* 1. Obtruncation, lopping or cutting off. 2. Diminution or destruction of a great part of a thing.
Desmochadura [des-mo-chah-doo'-rah], *f.* *V.* Desmoche.
Desmochar [des-mo-char'], *va.* 1. To lop or cut off, to mutilate. 2. To unhorn: applied to a stag.
Desmoche [des-mo'-chay], *m.* Obtruncation, truncation, mutilation.
Desmocho [des-mo'-cho], *m.* Heap of things lopped or cut off.
Desmogar [des-mo-gar'], *vn.* To cast the horns, as deer.
Desmografía [des-mo-grah-fee'-ah], *f.* Desmography, a description of the ligaments.
Desmogue [des-mo'-gay], *m.* Act of casting the horns, in deer.
Desmolado, da [des-mo-lah'-do, dah], *a.* Toothless, having no grinders.
Desmoldamiento [des-mole-dah-me-en'-to], or **Desmolde** [des-mole'-day], *m.* Removal of a casting from the mould.
Desmoldar [des-mole-dar'], *va.* To remove from the mould, to "strike the frame."
Desmologia [des-mo-lo-hee'-ah], *f.* Desmology, anatomical description of ligaments.
Desmonetizar [des-mo-nay-te-thar'], *va.* 1. To convert money into bullion for other purposes. 2. To demonetize, deprive of legal-tender value.
Desmonta, *f.* *V.* Desmonte.
Desmontador, ra [des-mon-tah-dor', rah], *m.* & *f.* 1. One who fells wood. 2. Dismounter.
Desmontadura [des-mon-tah-doo'-rah], *f.* Felling timber, clearing from shrubbery.
Desmontar [des-mon-tar'], *va.* 1. To fell or cut down wood. 2. To remove

a heap of dirt or rubbish. 3. To uncock fire-arms; to take an instrument to pieces. 4. To dismount a troop of horse; to dismount cannon. 5. *Desmontar el timón*, (Naut.) To unhang the rudder.—*vn.* To dismount, to alight from a horse, mule, etc.

Desmonte [des-mon'-tay], *m.* 1. Felling, the act of cutting down, as timber. 2. The timber remaining on the spot. 3. Clearing a wood from trees, shrubbery, etc.

Desmonterado, da [des-mon-tay-rah'-do, dah], *a.* Without the sort of cap named *montera.*

Desmoñar [des-mo-nyar'], *va.* (Coll.) To undo the toupee of the hair, to loosen the hair.

Desmoralización [des-mo-rah-le-thah-the-on'], *f.* Demoralization, corruption or depravation of morals; depravity.

Desmoralizado, da [des-mo-rah-le-thah'-do, dah], *a.* & *pp.* of DESMORALIZAR. Demoralized, depraved, corrupted.

Desmoralizar [des-mo-rah-le-thar'], *va.* To demoralize, to corrupt, to deprave. —*vr.* (Mil.) To relax the discipline of an army.

Desmoronadizo, za [des-mo-ro-nah-dee'-tho, thah], *a.* Easily mouldered.

Desmoronar [des-mo-ro-nar'], *va.* 1. To destroy by little and little, to ruin by insensible degrees. 2. (Met.) To cause to dwindle or moulder off.—*vr.* To moulder, to fall, to decay.

Desmoso, sa [des-mo'-so, sah], *a.* Ligamentous.

Desmostar [des-mos-tar'], *va.* To separate the must from the grapes.—*vn.* To ferment.

Desmotadera [des-mo-tah-day'-rah], *f.* 1. Woman employed to take off knots and coarse naps from cloth. 2. An instrument used for removing knots from cloth; cloth nipper.

Desmotador, ra [des-mo-tah-dor', rah], *m.* & *f.* Person employed in taking off knots or naps from cloth or wool.

Desmotar [des-mo-tar'], *va.* To clear cloth of knots and coarse naps.

Desmovilizar [des-mo-ve-le-thar'], *va.* To demobilize.

Desmueblar [des-moo-ay-blar'], *va.* *V.* DESAMUEBLAR.

Desmuelo [des-moo-ay'-lo], *m.* Want or loss of grinders.

Desmugrador [des-moo-grah-dor'], *m.* Instrument which serves to clean the wool or cloth of grease.

Desmugrar [des-moo-grar'], *va.* To clean wool or cloth of grease.

Desmuir [des-moo-eer'], *va.* To pick olives.

Desmullir [des-mool-lyeer'], *va.* To discompose any thing soft or bland.

Desmurriar [des-moor-re-ar'], *va.* & *vr.* (Coll.) To take away lowness of spirits or sadness. (Jocose.)

Desnacionalizar [des-nah-the-o-nah-le-thar'], *va.* (Neol.) To denationalize, to cause the loss of national characteristics.

Desnarigado, da [des-nah-re-gah'-do, dah], *a.* & *pp.* of DESNARIGAR. Noseless.

Desnarigar [des-nah-re-gar'], *va.* To cut off the nose.

Desnatadora [des-nah-tah-do'-rah], *f.* Cream separator.

Desnatar [des-nah-tar'], *va.* 1. To skim milk. 2. To take the flower or choicest part of a thing. *Desnatar la hacienda*, To live upon the fat of the land.

Desnaturalización [des-nah-too-rah-le-tha-the-on'], *f.* Expatriation, denaturalization.

Desnaturalizado, da [des-nah-too-rah-le-thah'-do, dah], *a.* Denatured. *Alcohol desnaturalizado*, Denatured alcohol.

Desnaturalizar [des-nah-too-rah-le-thar'], *va.* To divest of the rights of naturalization, to deprive of the privileges of a citizen.—*vr.* To abandon one's country.

Desnegar [des-nay-gar'], *va.* (Obs.) To contradict, to retract.—*vr.* To unsay, to retract, to recant.

Desnervar [des-ner-var'], *va.* To enervate.

Desnevado, da [des-nay-vah'-do, dah], *a.* Thawed, free from snow.—*pp.* of DESNEVAR.

Desnevar [des-nay-var'], *va.* To thaw, to dissolve.

Desnivel [des-ne-vel'], *m.* Unevenness, inequality of the ground.

Desnivelación [des-ne-vay-lah-the-on'], *f.* Making uneven.

Desnivelar [des-ne-vay-lar'], *va.* To make uneven or unequal.—*vr.* To lose its level.

Desnoviar [des-no-ve-ar'], *va.* In jocular style, to separate a newly married couple.

Desnucar [des-noo-car'], *va.* 1. To break the neck, to disjoint the nape. 2. To kill by a blow upon the nape.

Desnudador [des-noo-dah-dor'], *m.* One that denudes.

Desnudamente [des-noo-dah-men'-tay], *adv.* Nakedly; manifestly, plainly.

Desnudar [des-noo-dar'], *va.* 1. To denudate, to denude, to strip off the clothes or coverings; to fleece. 2. (Met.) To discover, to reveal. 3. (Naut.) To unrig.—*vr.* 1. To undress, to take off one's clothes. 2. (Met.) To deprive one's self of a thing.

Desnudez [des-noo-deth'], *f.* Nudity, nakedness.

Desnudismo [des-noo-dees'-moh], *m.* Nudism.

Desnudo, da [des-noo'-do, dah], *a.* 1. Naked, bare, uncovered; ill-clothed. 2. (Met.) Plain, evident, apparent. 3. Empty-handed, destitute of merit, interest, etc. *No está desnudo*, He wants for nothing.

Desnudo [des-noo'-do], *m.* 1. (Pict.) A picture or statue without drapery; the nude. 2. Metal free from all foreign matter.

Desnutrición [des-noo-tre-the-on'], *f.* Malnutrition.

Desobedecer [des-o-bay-day-therr'], *va.* To disobey. *Desobedecer el timón*, (Naut.) To fall off. *Navío que desobedece la virada*, (Naut.) A ship which misses stays.

Desobedecimiento [des-o-bay-day-the-me-en'-to], *m.* 1. Disobedience, incompliance. 2. Contempt of court.

(*Yo desobedezco, yo desobedezca*, from *Desobedecer. V.* CONOCER.)

Desobediencia [des-o-bay-de-en'-the-ah], *f.* Disobedience; lawlessness. *Desobediencia civil*, Civil disobedience.

Desobediente [des-o-bay-de-en'-tay], *pa.* Disobedient.

Desobedientemente, *adv.* Disobediently.

Desobligar [des-o-ble-gar'], *va.* 1. To release from an obligation. 2. To disoblige, to offend; to alienate the affections.

Desobstruir [des-obs-troo-eer'], *va.* 1. To remove obstructions. 2. (Med.) To deobstruct.

Desocupación [des-o-coo-pah-the-on'], *f.* Leisure, want of business or occupation.

Desocupadamente, *adv.* Deliberately, leisurely.

Desocupar [des-o-coo-par'], *va.* To evacuate, to quit, to empty.—*vr.* To disengage one's self from a business or occupation, to withdraw from.

Desodorante [des-o-do-rahn'-tay], *m.* & *a.* Deodorant.

Desofuscar [des-o-foos-car'], *va.* 1. To remove obscurity. 2. (Met.) To remove any one's confusion.

Desoir [des-o-eer'], *va.* To pretend not to hear.

Desojar [des-o-har'], *va.* To break or burst: applied to the eye of a needle, or other instrument with an eye.—*vr.* To strain the sight by looking steadily at a thing; to look intently.

Desolación [day-so-lah-the-on'], *f.* 1. Desolation, destruction, havoc, extermination; fall. 2. Want of consolation or comfort, affliction.

Desolado, da [day-so-lah'-do, dah], *a.* Desolate, disconsolate.—*pp.* of DESOLAR.

Desolador, ra [day-so-lah-dor', rah], *m.* & *f.* (Obs.) *V.* ASOLADOR.

Desolar [day-so-lar'], *va.* To desolate, to lay waste; to harass.

Desolladamente, *adv.* (Coll.) Impudently, petulantly.

Desolladero [des-ol-lyah-day'-ro], *m.* 1. A place where hides are taken off; slaughter-house. 2. An inn or shop, where exorbitant prices are charged.

Desollado, da [day-sol-lyah'-do, dah], *a.* (Coll.) Forward, impudent, insolent. —*pp.* of DESOLLAR.

Desollador [day-sol-lyah-dor'], *m.* 1. Flayer. 2. (Prov.) Slaughter-house, a place where beasts are flayed or skinned. 3. (Met.) Extortioner. 4. Butcher-bird.

Desolladura [day-sol-lyah-doo'-rah], *f.* Excoriation.

Desollar [day-sol-lyar'], *va.* 1. To flay, to skin, to strip off the skin, to excoriate. 2. (Met.) To extort an immoderate price. 3. (Naut.) To pull at the creases of a sail, to reduce them to regular folds. *Desollar la zorra*, or *el lobo*, To sleep while intoxicated.

Desonce [des-on'-thay], *m.* The discount of an ounce or ounces in each pound. (Ant.)

Desonzar [des-on-thar'], *va.* To discount or deduct an ounce or ounces in the pound. (Ant.)

Desopilar [des-o-pe-lar'], *va.* 1. To clear away obstructions. 2. (Med.) To remove retention or suppression of menstruation.

Desopilativo, va [des-o-pe-lah-tee'-vo, vah], *a.* Deobstruent.

Desopinar [des-o-pe-nar'], *va.* To impeach one's character, to defame.

Desoprimir [des-o-pre-meer'], *va.* To free from oppression.

Desorden [des-or'-den], *m.* 1. Disorder, confusion, irregularity. 2. Lawlessness, license, excess, abuse. 3. Lack of symmetry of connection, in which lyric poetry commonly offends; in the phrase, *Bello desorden.*

Desordenadamente [des-sor-day-nah-dah-men'-tay], *adv.* Disorderly, irregularly, confusedly.

Desordenado, da [des-or-day-nah'-do, dah], *a.* 1. Disorderly, irregular, disordered, orderless. 2. Disorderly, lawless, licentious.—*pp.* of DESORDENAR.

Desordenar [des-or-day-nar'], *va.* To disorder, to throw into confusion, to disturb, to confound or confuse.—*vr.* 1. To exceed or go beyond all rule: to be out of order, to be irregular. 2. To get unruly, be unmanageable: said of a horse.

Desorejado, da [des-o-ray-hah'-do, dah], *a.* (Coll.) Licentious, dissolute, degraded.

Desorejador, ra [des-o-ray-hah-dor', rah], *m.* & *f.* One who crops off the ears.

Desorejamiento [des-o-ray-hah-me-en'-to], *m.* Cropping the ears.

Desorejar [des-o-ray-har'], *va.* To crop the ears.

Desorganización [des-or-gah-ne-thah-the-on'], *f.* Disorganization.

Desorganizador [des-or-gah-ne-thah-dor'], *m.* Disorganizer.

Desorganizar [des-or-gah-ne-thar'], *va.* 1. To disorganize. 2. To disconcert in the highest degree. 3. (Chem.) To decompose. 4. (Mil.) To disband an army. 5. To relax discipline.—*vr.* (Med.) To be altered, changed in texture, disorganized.

Desorientado, da [des-o-re-en-tah'-do, dah], *a.* (Littl. us.) Disorientated, turned from the right direction.—*pp.* of DESORIENTAR.

Desorientar [des-o-re-en-tar'], *va.* (Littl. us.) 1. To lose or cause to lose one's bearings so as not to know one's position, geographically or morally. 2. To turn from the right direction, confuse. 3. To lose the way.

Desorillar [des-o-ril-lyar'], *va.* 1. To cut off the selvage of cloth or other things. 2. To stretch skins well, so as not to form folds at the ends.

Desortijado, da [day-sor-te-hah'-do, dah], *a.* (Vet.) Sprained: applied to the muscles or ligaments of mules or horses.—*pp.* of DESORTIJAR.

Desortijar [day-sor-te-har'], *va.* (Agr.) To hoe or weed plants the first time.

Desosado, da [des-o-sah'-do, dah], *a.* (Obs.) Timorous, not bold.—*pp.* of DESOSAR.

Desosar [des-o-sar'], *va.* To deprive of the bones.—*vn.* To be cowardly or fearful.

Desoterrar, *va.* (Obs.) *V.* DESENTERRAR.

Desovar [des-o-var'], *va.* To spawn.

Desove [des-o'-vay], *m.* 1. Spawning. 2. The time in which fishes cast their spawn.

Desovillar [des-o-vil-lyar'], *va.* 1. To unclew. 2. (Met.) To unravel, to disentangle, to clear up. 3. (Met.) To encourage, to animate.

Desoxidación [des-ok-se-dah-the-on'], *f* Deoxydization, removal of oxygen.

Desoxidar [des-ok-se-dar'], *va.* To deoxydize, remove oxygen from any compound.

Desoxigenación [des-ok-se-hay-nah-the-on'], *f.* Deoxydation.

Desoxigenar [des-ok-se-hay-nar'], *va.* To remove from a body the oxygen which it holds; to deoxydize.

Despabiladeras [des-pah-be-lah-day'-ras], *f. pl.* Snuffers.

Despabilado, da [des-pah-be-lah'-do, dah], *a.* & *pp.* of DESPABILAR. 1. Snuffed: applied to candles. 2. (Met.) Watchful, vigilant in sleeping hours. 3. Lively, active, smart.

Despabilador, ra [des-pah-be-lah-dor', rah], *m.* & *f.* Candle-snuffer; he who snuffs.

Despabiladura [des-pah-be-lah-doo'-rah], *f.* Snuff of the candle.

Despabilar [des-pah-be-lar'], *va.* 1. To snuff a candle. 2. (Met.) To cut off a superfluity. 3. (Met.) To despatch briefly or expeditiously. 4. (Met.) To rouse, to enliven. 5. (Coll.) To kill. *Despabilar los ojos,* (Met.) To keep a sharp lookout. *Despabilar el ingenio,* To sharpen the wits.—*vr.* To rouse, to wake from slumber, to be excited. *Vd. le verá despabilarse,* You will see him brighten up.

Despabilo [des-pah-bee'-lo], *m.* (Obs.) *V.* DESPABILADURA.

Despacio [des-pah'-the-o], *adv.* 1. Slowly, leisurely; gently. 2. Insensibly, by little and little. 3. Continually, without interruption.

¡Despacio! *int.* Softly, gently.

Despacito [des-pah-thee'-to], *adv.* 1. Very gently, softly. 2. Leisurely, very slowly.

¡Despacito! [des-pah-thee'-to], *int.* Gently! stop a little!

Despachaderas [des-pah-chah-day'-ras], *f. pl.* Surly words in answer to a question.

Despachado, da [des-pah-chah'-do, dah], *a.* (Coll.) Impudent, bold-faced, brazen.—*pp.* of DESPACHAR.

Despachador. [des-pah-chah-dor'], *m.* Expediter, one who despatches.

Despachar [des-pah-char'], *va.* 1. To despatch, to expedite, abridge, facilitate. 2. To despatch, to pack, to send in a hurry; to lay by. 3. To despatch, to perform a business quickly, to cut off delays. 4. To decide and expedite suits and causes. 5. To dispose of goods and merchandise, to sell. 6. (Met.) To despatch, to send out of the world. *Despachar un barco,* To clear a vessel at the custom-house. *Despachar géneros* or *mercaderías en la aduana,* To clear, or take out goods or merchandise at the custom-house. —*vr.* To accelerate, to make haste.—*vn.* 1. In offices, to carry papers drawn up for the signature of the principal. 2. (Com.) To expend, to let goods go for money or barter. 3. To serve a shop.

Despacho [des-pah'-cho], *m.* 1. Expedient, determination. 2. Despatch, expedition. 3. Custom, application from buyers. 4. Cabinet, office, counting-house. *Despacho de coches de camino, vapores,* etc., Dépôt. 5. Commission, warrant, patent. 6. Despatch, correspondence by telegraph. *Secretario del despacho,* Secretary of state.

Despachurrado, da [des-pah-choor-rah'-do, dah], *a.* Pressed together. *Dejar a uno despachurrado,* (Coll.) To leave one stupefied. *Es un despachurrado,* (Coll.) He is a ridiculous, insipid fellow.—*pp.* of DESPACHURRAR.

Despachurrar [des-pah-choor-rar'], *va.* (Coll.) 1. To press together, to squash, to crush. 2. (Met.) To make a speech, to obscure a subject by a bad explanation. 3. (Met.) To confound one by a smart repartee. *Despachurrar el cuento,* To interrupt a story and prevent its conclusion.

Despagar [des-pah-gar'], *va.* (Obs.) To displease, to disgust.

Despajador, ra [des-pah-hah-dor', rah], *m.* & *f.* One who winnows.

Despajadura [des-pah-hah-doo'-rah], *f.* Winnowing.

Despajar [des-pah-har'], *va.* To winnow.

Despaje [des-pah'-hay], **Despajo** [des-pah'-ho], *m.* Winnowing or cleaning grain.

Despaldar, *va.* & *vr.* *V.* DESPALDILLAR and DESPALDILLARSE.

Despaldillar [des-pal-dil-lyar'], *va.* To dislocate or break the shoulder or back of an animal.—*vr.* To disjoint or dislocate one's shoulder-blade.

Despalillar [des-pah-leel-lyar'], *va.* To remove the stems from raisins; to strip tobacco, etc.

Despalmador [des-pal-mah-dor'], *m.* (Naut.) Careening-place, dockyard.

Despalmadura [des-pahl-mah-doo'-rah], *f.* or **Despalme** [des-pahl'-may], *m.* Calking, paying the bottom.

Despalmar [des-pal-mar'], *va.* 1. (Naut.) To grave, to calk. 2. To pare off a horse's hoof.

Despampanador [des-pam-pah-nah-dor'], *m.* Pruner of vines.

Despampanadura [des-pam-pah-nah-doo'-rah], *f.* Act of pruning vines.

Despampanar [des-pam-pah-nar'], *va.* 1. To prune vines. 2. (Met. Coll.) To unbosom, to give vent to one's feelings. 3. *vr.* (Coll.) To pity much, to be very sorry, to grieve.

Despampanillar [des-pam-pah-nil-lyar'], *va.* To prune grape-vines.

Despamplonador, ra [des-pam-plo-nah dor', rah], *m.* & *f.* One who separates (vine-) stems.

Despamplonar [des-pam-plo-nar'], *va.* To make space between the shoots of the vine or shrub when they are very close.—*vr.* (Met.) To get dislocated: said of the hand.

Despanado, da [des-pah-nah'-do, dah], *a.* (Prov. Coll.) Breadless, in want of bread.—*pp.* of DESPANAR.

Despanar [des-pah-nar'], *va.* (Prov.) To remove the reaped corn from the field.

Despancijar, Despanzurrar [des-pan-the-har', des-pan-thoor-rar'], *va.* (Coll.) To burst the belly.

Despapar [des-pah-par'], *vn.* To carry the head too high: applied to a horse.

Desparcir [des-par-theer'], *va.* (Prov.) To scatter, to disseminate.

Desparear, *va.* (Obs.) To separate.

Desparecer [des-pah-ray-therr'], *vn.* To disappear. *V.* DESAPARECER.—*vr.* To be unlike or dissimilar.

Desparejar [des-pah-ray-har'], *va.* To make unequal or uneven.

Desparpajado, da [des-par-pah-hah'-do, dah], *a.* & *pp.* of DESPARPAJAR. Pert, petulant, garrulous.

Desparpajar [des-par-pah-har'], *va.* 1. To undo in a disorderly manner. 2. (Coll.) To rant, to prattle at random.

Desparpajo [des-par-pah'-ho], *m.* (Coll.) Pertness of speech or action.

Desparramado, da [des-par-rah-mah'-do, dah], *a.* Wide, open.—*pp.* of DESPARRAMAR.

Desparramador, ra [des-par-rah-mah-dor', rah], *m.* & *f.* Disperser, dilapidator; prodigal, waster, spendthrift.

Desparramamiento [des-par-rah-ma-me-en'-to], *m.* Squandering, extravagance, dissipation.

Desparramar [des-par-rah-mar'], *va.* 1. To scatter, to disseminate, to overspread. 2. To squander, to dissipate, to lavish.—*vr.* To give one's self up to pleasures with extravagance and excess, to be dissipated.

Despartidor [des-par-te-dor'], *m.* Pacificator.

Despartir [des-par-teer'], *va.* 1. (Obs.) To dispart, to part, to divide. 2. To conciliate.

Desparvar [des-par-var'], *va.* To take the sheaves of corn out of the stack or rick to be thrashed.

Despasar [des-pah-sar'], *va.* 1. To draw a cord or ribbon from a button-hole or seam. 2. (Naut.) To unreeve a cable from the blocks. 3. When sailing along the coast to keep the course until the wind is received in the same position on the opposite side. *Despasar el virador de combés,* (Naut.) To shift the messenger.

Despasmarse [des-pas-mar'-say], *vr.* (Obs.) To recover one's self from a stupor or spasm.

Despatarrada [des pah-tar-rah'-dah], *f.* Variety in the Spanish dance. *Hacer la despatarrada,* To affect disease or pain; to feign death.

Despatarrado, da [des-pah-tar-rah'-do, dah], *a.* *Quedar* or *dejar a uno despatarrado,* (Coll.) To leave one as tonished, abashed, or stupefied.—*pp.* of DESPATARRAR.

Despatarrar [des-pah-tar-rar'], *va.* To silence, to oblige one to be silent.—*vr.* 1. To slip and fall on the ground. 2. To be stupefied, to remain motionless.

Despatillar [des-pah-til-lyar'], *va.* 1. To cut grooves or mortises in wood. 2. (Naut.) To break off the arm of an anchor by its getting caught in rocks on the bottom. 3. *vr.* (Coll.) To shave one's self.

Despavesadura [des-pah-vay-sah-doo'-rah], *f.* The act of snuffing the candle.

Despavesar [des-pah-vay-sar'], *va.* To snuff the candle.

Despavoridamente [des-pah-vo-re-dah-men'-tay], *adv.* Terrifiedly, aghast.

Despavorir [des-pah-vo-reer'], *vn.* & *vr.* To be terrified, to be frightened, to be aghast. It has only the infinitive termination and past participle.

Despeadura [des-pay-ah-doo'-rah], *f.* Bruising the feet with travel.

Despeamiento [des-pay-ah-me-en'-to], *m.* Act of bruising the feet.

Despearse [des-pay-ar'-say], *vr.* To bruise the feet or make them sore by much walking.

Despectivo, va [des-pec-tee'-vo, vah], *a.* Depreciatory; denoting contempt. (Grammatical term.)

Despechadamente [des-pay-chah-dah-men'-tay], *adv.* Angrily, spitefully.

Despechador [des-pay-chah-dor'], *m.* Extortioner, tormentor, oppressor.

Despechamiento [des-pay-chah-me-en'-to], *m.* Act of enraging or overburdening.

Despechar [des-pay-char'], *va.* 1. To enrage, to excite indignation. 2. To overwhelm with taxes.—*vr.* 1. To fret, to be peevish. 2. To lose all hope, to despair.

Despecho [des-pay'-cho], *m.* 1. Indignation, displeasure, wrath. 2. Asperity, harshness of temper. 3. Despite, spite, defiance. 4. Dejection, dismay, despair. 5. Disrespect, insolence. 6. Deceit, infidelity. 7. Derision, scorn. *A despecho*, In spite of, in defiance of, against one's will.

Despechugadura [des-pay-choo-gah-doo'-rah], *f.* Act of cutting off or uncovering the breast.

Despechugar [des-pay-choo-gar'], *va.* To cut off the breast of a fowl.—*vr.* To uncover the breast, to walk with the breast open.

Despedazador, ra [des-pay-dah-thah-dor', rah], *m.* & *f.* Dissector, lacerator, mangler.

Despedazamiento [des-pay-dah-thah-me-en'-to], *m.* Laceration, dissection, cutting to pieces; mangling.

Despedazar [des-pay-dah-thar'], *va.* 1. To cut into bits, to tear into pieces, to cut asunder, to limb, to claw. 2. (Met.) To lacerate, to destroy, to mangle. *Despedazarse de risa*, To burst into a fit of laughter.

Despedida [des-pay-dee'-dah], *f.* 1. Leave-taking, farewell, leave. 2. The act of turning a lodger out of his lodgings. 3. Dismission, dismissal.

Despedimiento, *m.* *V.* DESPEDIDA.

Despedir [des-pay-deer'], *va.* 1. To emit, to discharge, to dart. 2. To dismiss from office, to discard. 3. To remove, to lay by. 4. To accompany through courtesy a departing guest. 5. To diffuse, disperse odour, rays of light, etc. *Despedir la vida*, To die.—*vr.* 1. To take leave, to say some expression of courtesy. 2. To renounce something temporarily or perpetually. 3. To go out from service, to leave one's occupation.

Despedrar [des-pay-drar'], *va.* (Prov.) *V.* DESPEDREGAR.

Despedregar [des-pay-dray-gar'], *va.* To clear a field or other place of stones.

Despegable [des-pay-gah'-blay], *a.* Dissoluble, dissolvable.

Despegadamente, *adv.* Roughly, harshly, disgustingly.

Despegado, da [des-pay-gah'-do, dah], *a.* & *pp.* of DESPEGAR. Rough, morose, sullen, sour of temper; disgusting, unpleasant, harsh; separated.

Despegadura [des-pay-gah-doo'-rah], *f.* Dissolving, separating.

Despegamiento [des-pay-gah-me-en'-to], *m.* *V.* DESAPEGO.

Despegar [des-pay-gar'], *va.* To unglue, to separate, to disjoin. *Despegar los labios*, To speak, to open one's lips, to break silence. —*vn.* To take off (as a plane). —*vr.* To grow apart, to withdraw one's affections (from someone).

Despego [des-pay'-go], *m.* 1. Asperity, moroseness, coyness. 2. Displeasure, aversion. 3. Coldness, indifference.

Despegue [des-pay'-gay], *m.* (Aer.) 1. Take-off. 2. Blast-off. *Despegue de emergencia*, (Aer.) Scramble. *Despegue vertical*, Vertical takeoff.

Despeinar [des-pay-e-nar'], *va.* To disarrange the hair of.

Despejadamente [des-pay-hah-dah-men'-tay], *adv.* Expeditiously, readily, freely.

Despejado, da [des-pay-hah'-do, dah], *a.* 1. Sprightly, smart, quick, vivacious, sagacious, dexterous, clean. 2. Clear, disengaged.—*pp.* of DESPEJAR.

Despejar [des-pay-har'], *va.* To remove impediments, to surmount obstacles, to clear away obstructions. *Despejen la sala*, Clear the room.—*vr.* 1. To cheer up, to amuse one's self. 2. To acquire or show looseness in behaviour. 3. To be relieved of pain: said of a patient. 4. (Math.) To discover the unknown. *Despejarse el cielo, el día, el tiempo*, To become clear, serene weather.

Despejo [des-pay'-ho], *m.* 1. The act of removing obstacles or clearing away impediments. 2. Sprightliness, smartness, liveliness, vivacity, briskness; grace, ease.

Despelotar [des-pay-lo-tar'], *va.* To dishevel the hair.

Despeluzamiento [des-pay-loo-thah-me-en'-to], *m.* Act of making the hair stand on end, horripilation.

Despeluzar, Despeluznar [des-pay-loo-thar', des-pay-looth-nar'], *va.* To make the hair stand on end: applied to fear or terror.

Despellejadura [des-pel-lyay-hah-doo'-rah], *f.* 1. Scratch, a slight wound. 2. Skinning.

Despellejar [des-pel-lyay-har'], *va.* To skin. *Despellejar un conejo*, To uncase a rabbit.

Despenador, ra [des-pay-nah-dor', rah], *m.* & *f.* One who relieves pain.

Despenar [des-pay-nar'], *va.* 1. To relieve from pain. 2. (Met.) To kill. *Hincar o apretar el codo para despenar a alguno*, To suffocate a dying person in order to relieve him from pain.

Despendedor, ra [des-pen-day-dor', rah], *m.* & *f.* Spendthrift, prodigal.

Despender [des-pen-derr'], *va.* To spend, to expend, to waste, to squander.

Despensa [des-pen'-sah], *f.* 1. Pantry, larder. 2. Store of provisions for a journey. 3. Butlership. 4. The provisions that are bought for daily use; marketing. 5. Contract to provide a horse with hay, straw, and barley, all the year. 6. (Naut.) Steward's room.

Despensería [des-pen-say-ree'-ah], *f.* (Obs.) Office of steward.

Despensero, ra [des-pen-say'-ro, rah], *m.* & *f.* 1. Butler, caterer; (naut.) steward on board of ships. 2. Dispenser, distributer.

Despeñadamente, *adv.* Precipitately.

Despeñadero [des-pay-nyah-day'-ro], *m.* 1. Precipice, crag. 2. (Met.) A bold and dangerous undertaking.

Despeñadero, ra [des-pay-nyah-day'-ro, rah], *a.* Steep, precipitous, headlong.

Despeñadizo, za [des-pay-nyah-dee'-tho, thah], *a.* 1. Steep, precipitous. 2. Glib, slippery.

Despeñar [des-pay-nyar'], *va.* To precipitate, to fling down a precipice.—*vr.* To precipitate one's self, to throw one's self headlong.

Despeño, Despeñamiento [des-pay'-nyo, des-pay-nyah-me-en'-to], *m.* 1. A precipitate fall. 2. Destruction of character or credit. 3. Diarrhœa.

Despepitador [des-pay-pe-tah-dor'], *m.* An instrument for removing cores or stones of fruit.—*va.* To remove the seeds from a melon or other fruit; to stone.

Despepitar [des-pay-pe-tar'], *vr.* To give license to one's tongue, to vociferate, to speak rashly and inconsiderately; to act imprudently.

Despercudir [des-per-coo-deer'], *va.* To clean or wash what is greasy.

Desperdiciadamente, *adv.* Profusely, wastefully.

Desperdiciado, da [des-per-de-the-ah'-do, dah], *a.* & *pp.* of DESPERDICIAR. Wasted, destroyed, squandered.

Desperdiciador, ra [des-per-de-the-ah-dor', rah], *m.* & *f.* Spendthrift, squanderer, lavisher.

Desperdiciar [des-per-de-the-ar'], *va.* 1. To squander, to misspend, to fling away. 2. To lose, not to avail one's self of, not to utilize.

Desperdicio [des-per-dee'-the-o], *m.* 1. Prodigality, profusion, waste. 2. Residuum, relics, remains, garbage. *Desperdicios de cuero*, Furrier's waste.

Desperdigar [des-per-de-gar'], *va.* To separate, to disjoin, to scatter.

Desperecerse [des-pay-ray-therr'-say], *vr.* To crave, to desire eagerly. *Desperecerse de risa*, To laugh heartily.

Desperezarse [des-pay-ray-thar'-say], *va.* To put away sloth.—*vr.* To stretch one's limbs on being roused from sleep.

Desperezo [des-pay-ray'-tho], *m.* *V.* ESPEREZO.

Desperfecto [des-per-fec'-to], *m.* 1. Deterioration, loss. 2. Injury which possessions suffer by the neglect or fault of the owner.

Desperfilar [des-per-fe-lar'], *va.* (Pict.) To soften the lines of a painting.—*vr.* To lose the posture of a profile line or contour.

Despergaminar [des-per-gah-me-nar'], *va.* To hull, decorticate.

Despernada [des-per-nah'-dah], *f.* A motion in dancing.

Despernado, da [des-per-nah'-do, dah], *a.* Weary, fatigued, tired.—*pp.* of DESPERNAR.

Despernar [des-per-nar'], *va.* To maim, cripple, or cut off one's legs.—*vr.* To be worn out, crippled from walking.

Desperpentar [des-per-pen-tar'], *va.* (Prov.) To cut off with one stroke.

Despertador, ra [des-per-tah-dor', rah], *m.* & *f.* 1. Awakener, one who awakes or rouses out of sleep. 2. Alarm-bell in clocks; an alarm-clock. 3. Causing wakefulness, care, or anxiety.

Despertamiento [des-per-tah-me-en'-to], *m.* 1. Awakening. 2. Excitation, the act of rousing or awakening.

Despertar [des-per-tar'], *va.* 1. To awake, to awaken. 2. To awaken, to excite, to put in motion. 3. To enliven, to make lively or sprightly. 4. To call to recollection.—*vn.* 1. To awake, to break from sleep. 2. To revive, to grow lively or sprightly.

Despesar [des-pay-sar'], *m.* (Obs.) Displeasure, aversion, dislike.

Despestañarse [des-pes-tah-nyar'-say], *va.* To pluck out the eye-lashes.—*vr.* 1. To look steadfastly at any thing, to inspect it closely. 2. (Met.) To apply one's self attentively to business.

Despezar [des-pay-thar'], *va.* 1. To dispose and arrange stones at a proper distance. 2. To make thinner at the end. applied to tubes and pipes.

Despezo [des-pay'-tho], *m.* Diminution of one end of a tube or pipe. *Despezos*, Faces of stone, where they join each other.

Despezonar [des-pay-tho-nar'], *va.* 1. To cut off the end of a thing, to break off the stalk of fruit. 2. To divide, to separate.—*vr.* To break off: applied to the stalk of fruit.

Despiadado, da [des-pe-ah-dah'-do, dah], *a.* Impious, cruel. *V.* DESAPIADADO.

Despicar [des-pe-car'], *va.* To satisfy, to gratify.—*vr.* To take revenge.

Despicarazar [des-pe-cah-ra-thar'], *va.* (Prov.) To pick the figs: applied to birds.

Despichar [des-pe-char'], *va.* 1. (Prov.) To pick grapes; to seed grapes before pressing them. 2. To expel or discharge moisture or humour. 3. (Coll.) To die.

Despidida [des-pe-dee'-dah], *f.* (Prov.) Gutter, a passage for water.

Despido [des-pee'-do], *m.* 1. Despatch. 2. Dismissal.

(*Yo despido, él despidió, yo despida*, from *Despedir. V.* PEDIR.)

(*Yo despierno, yo despierne*, from *Despernar. V.* ACERTAR.)

Despiertamente [des-pe-er-tah-men'-tay], *adv.* Acutely, ingeniously, cleverly.

Despierto, ta [des-pe-err'-to, tah], *a.* 1. Awake. 2. Vigilant, watchful, diligent. 3. Brisk, sprightly, lively, smart; clear-sighted.

(*Yo despierto, yo despierte*, from *Despertar. V.* ACERTAR.)

Despiezo [des-pe-ay'-tho], *m.* (Arch.) Juncture or bed of one stone on another.

Despilarar [des-pe-lah-rar'], *va.* (Min.) To take away the pillars of ore-bearing rock.

Despilfarradamente, *adv.* Wastefully; slovenly.

Despilfarrado, da [des-peel-far-rah'-do, dah], *a.* 1. Prodigal, wasteful. 2. Ragged, in tatters.—*pp.* of DESPILFARRAR.

Despilfarrador, ra [des-peel-far-rah dor', rah], *a.* Spendthrift, wasteful.

Despilfarrar [des-peel-far-rar'], *va.* To destroy or waste with slovenliness, or prodigality.

Despilfarro [des-peel-far'-ro], *m.* 1. Slovenliness, uncleanliness. 2. Waste, mismanagement, lavishment. 3. Misgovernment in public affairs.

Despimpollar [des-pim-pol-lyar'], *va.* To prune away useless stems from plants.

Despinces [des-peen'-thes], *m. pl.* Tweezers. *V.* PINZAS.

Despintar [des-pin-tar'], *va.* 1. To blot or efface what is painted. 2. (Met.) To obscure things, or make them less intelligible; to mislead.—*vn.* To degenerate.—*vr.* To be deceived by mistaking one card for another. *No despintársele a uno alguna persona o cosa*, Not to forget the appearance of a person or thing.

Despinzadera [des-pin-thah-day'-rah], *f.* 1. Woman that plucks the knots off cloth.—*pl.* 2. Tweezers.

Despinzar [des-pin-thar'], *va.* To pick off the knots, hair, or straw from clothes.

Despinzas [des-peen'-thas], *f. pl. V.* PINZAS.

Despiojar [des-pe-o-har'], *va.* 1. To louse, to clean of lice. 2. (Met. Coll.) To trim or dress, to relieve from misery.

Despique [des-pee'-kay], *m.* Vengeance, revenge.

Despiritado, da [des-pe-re-tah'-do, dah], *a.* Languid, spiritless.

Despistar [des-pis-tar'], *va.* To turn from the right trail.

Despizcar [des-pith-car'], *va.* To comminute, to break or cut into small bits.—*vr.* To make the utmost exertions, to use one's best endeavours.

Desplacer [des-plah-therr'], *m.* Displeasure, disgust, disobligation.

Desplacer [des-plah-therr'], *va.* To displease, to disgust.

Desplantación [des-plan-tah-the-on'], *f.* Eradication, displantation.

Desplantador, ra [des-plan-tah-dor', rah], *m.* & *f.* One who eradicates; eradicator.—*m.* A trowel, scoop trowel.

Desplantar [des-plan-tar'], *va.* To eradicate. *V.* DESARRAIGAR.—*vr.* To lose one's erect posture in fencing or dancing; to dismount artillery.

Desplante [des-plahn'-tay], *m.* An oblique posture in fencing.

Desplatar [des-plah-tar'], *va.* To separate silver from other substances with which it is mixed.

Desplate [des-plah'-tay], *m.* The act of separating silver from other metals or substances.

Desplayar [des-plah-yar'], *vn.* To retire from the shore, as the tide.—*va.* (Obs.) *V.* EXPLAYAR.

Desplazamiento [des-plah-thah-me-en'-to], *m.* 1. (Obs.) Displacement, change of place. 2. (Naut.) Displacement of a vessel.

Desplazar [des-plah-thar'], *va.* (Ant.) To displace.

(*Yo desplazco, yo desplazca*, from *Desplacer. V.* CONOCER.)

Desplegadura [des-play-gah-doo'-rah], *f.* Explication, unfolding, elucidation.

Desplegar [des-play-gar'], *va.* 1. To unfold, to display, to expand, to spread, to lay out, to lay before. 2. (Met.) To explain, to elucidate. 3. (Naut.) To unfurl. *Desplegar las velas*, To unfurl the sails. *Desplegar la bandera*, To hoist the flag.—*vr.* 1. To open, unfold: used of flowers. 2. To spread out: said of troops. 3. To execute a manœuvre. 4. To acquire ease and freedom in his movements by good teaching: used of the horse.

Despleguetear [des-play-gay-tay-ar'], *va.* (Agr.) To remove the folds from the tendrils of vines.

Despliegue [des-ple-ay'-gay], *m.* 1. Unfurling, unfolding. 2. (Mil.) Change from the order of march to that of battle, or to form in line fronting a given position.

Desplomar [des-plo-mar'], *va.* To make a wall, building, etc., bulge out.—*vr.* 1. To deviate from a perpendicular line, to sag: applied to a wall. 2. (Met.) To fall flat to the ground.

Desplome [des-ploh'-may], *m.* Collapse, downfall, toppling.

Desplomo [des-plo'-mo], *m.* The bulging or jutting out of a wall.

Desplumadura [des-ploo-mah-doo'-rah], *f.* Deplumation.

Desplumar [des-ploo-mar'], *va.* 1. To deplume, to pluck, to strip off feathers. 2. (Met.) To despoil or strip one of his property. 3. (Naut.) To dismast an enemy's ship.—*vr.* To moult the feathers.

Despoblación, Despoblada [des-po-blah-the-on'], *f.* Depopulation.

Despoblado [des-po-blah-do'], *m.* Desert, an uninhabited place.—*Despoblado, da, a.* & *pp.* of DESPOBLAR, Depopulated.

Despoblador, ra [des-po-blah-dor', rah], *m.* & *f.* Depopulator, dispeopler.

Despoblar [des-po-blar'], *va.* 1. To depopulate, to dispeople. 2. To despoil or desolate a place.—*vr.* To depopulate, to become deserted.

Despojador, ra [des-po-hah-dor', rah], *m.* & *f.* Despoiler, spoiler.

Despojar [des-po-har'], *va.* 1. To despoil or strip one of his property. 2. To deprive of, to cut off from, judicially. 3. To dismiss, to turn out of a place or employment.—*vr.* 1. To undress. 2. To relinquish, to forsake. *Despojarse del hombre viejo*, With ascetics, to subdue the evil inclinations of corrupt nature.

Despojo [des-po'-ho], *m.* 1. Despoliation, spoliation. 2. Plunder, spoils. *La hermosura es despojo del tiempo*, Beauty is the spoil of time. 3. Slough, the cast-off skin of a serpent. 4. Head, pluck, and feet of animals.—*pl.* 1. Leavings, scraps of the table. 2. Giblets, the wings, neck, heart, and gizzard of fowls.

Despolarización [des-po-lah-re-thah-the-on'], *f.* Depolarization.

Despolarizar [des-po-lah-re-thar'], *va.* To depolarize.

Despolvar [des-pol-var'], *va.* To remove the dust.

Despolvorear [des-pol-vo-ray-ar'], *va.* 1. To dust. 2. (Met.) To separate, to scatter, to dissipate. (Coll.) To sprinkle.

Desponerse [des-po-nerr'-say], *vr.* To cease laying eggs: applied to fowls.

Despopularizar [des-po-poo-lah-re-thar'], *va.* & *vr.* To deprive of, or lose one's popularity.

Desportillar [des-por-til-lyar'], *va.* To break the neck of a bottle, pot, etc. (Arch.) To splay.

Desposado, da [des-po-sah'-do, dah], *a.* Handcuffed.—*pp.* of DESPOSAR.

Desposar [des-po-sar'], *va.* To marry, to betroth, to mate, to match.—*vr.* 1. To be betrothed or married. 2. (Met.) To be paired or coupled.

Desposeer [des-po-say-err'], *va.* To dispossess, to oust.

Desposeimiento [des-po-say-e-me-en'-to], *m.* Dispossession.

Desposorio [des-po-so'-re-o], *m.* 1. A mutual promise to contract marriage: almost always used in the plural. 2. Betrothal, the act of betrothing.

Déspota [des'-po-tah], *m.* 1. A despot, absolute sovereign. 2. A tyrant.

Despóticamente [des-po'-te-cah-men-tay], *adv.* Despotically.

Despótico, ca [des-po'-te-co, cah], *a.* Despotic, despotical.

Despotismo [des-po-tees'-mo], *m.* Despotism, absoluteness.

Despotricar [des-po-tre-car'], *vn.* (Coll.) To talk inconsiderately.

Despreciable [des-pre-the-ah'-blay] *a.* Contemptible, despicable or despisable, worthless, abject, mean, paltry, miserable, lowly.

Despreciador, ra [des-pray-the-ah-dor', rah], *m. & f.* Depreciator, asperser, despiser, scorner, contemner.

Despreciar [des-pray-the-ar'], *va.* To depreciate, to despise, to scorn, to contemn, to reject, to lay aside, to neglect.

Despreciativo, va [des-pray-the-ah-tee'-vo, vah], *a.* 1. Depreciative, depreciatory. 2. Offensive.

Desprecio [des-pray'-the-o], *m.* 1. Disregard, scorn, contempt, despising, neglect, contumely, irrision. 2. Dispraise.

Desprender [des-pren-derr'], *va.* To unfasten, to loose, to disjoin, to separate.—*vr.* 1. To give way, to fall down. 2. To extricate one's self, to dispossess one's self, give away. 3. To be deduced, to be inferred.

Desprendido, da [des-pren-dee'-do, dah], *a.* Disinterested, generous, uncovetous.

Desprendimiento [des-pren-de-me-en'-to], *m.* 1. Alienation, disinterestedness. 2. A landslide, landslip.

Desprensar [des-pren-sar'], *va.* To remove from the press.

Despreocupación [des-pray-o-coo-pah-the-on'], *f.* Non-prejudice, freedom from bias, enlightenment.

Despreocupado, da [des-pray-o-coo-pah'-do, dah], *a. & pp.* of DESPREOCUPAR. Unconcerned, carefree, unconventional. *Despreocupado en el vestir,* Careless in his attire.

Despreocupar [des-pray-o-coo-par'], *va.* To unprepossess, to unpreoccupy.—*vr.* To be disabused of a prejudice or error; be set right.

Desprestigiar [des-pres-te-he-ar'], *va.* To remove reputation, prestige.

Desprestigio [des-pres-tee'-he-o], *m.* Loss of reputation or prestige.

Desprevención [des-pray-ven-the-on'], *f.* Improvidence, improvision, want of caution.

Desprevenidamente, *adv.* Improvidently.

Desprevenido, da [des-pray-vay-nee'-do, dah], *a.* 1. Unprovided, unprepared. 2. Improvident.

Desproporción [des-pro-por-the-on'], *f.* Disproportion; want of symmetry, disparity; disproportionableness.

Desproporcionadamente [des-pro-por-the-o-nah-dah-men'-tay], *adv.* Disproportionately.

Desproporcionado, da [des-pro-por-the-o-nah'-do, dah], *a. & pp.* of DESPROPORCIONAR. Disproportionate, disproportional, unsymmetrical, unsuitable, unbecoming.

Desproporcionar [des-pro-por-the-o-nar'], *va.* To disproportion, to mismatch things, to misproportion.

Despropositado, da [des-pro-po-se-tah'-do, dah], *a.* Absurd.

Despropósito [des-pro-po'-se-to], *m.* Absurdity, oddity.

Desproveer [des-pro-vay-err'], *va.* To deprive of provisions, to despoil of the necessaries of life.

Desproveidamente, *adv.* Improvidently.

Desproveido, da [des-pro-vay-ee'-do, dah], *a.* Unprovided, unprepared.—*pp.* of DESPROVEER.

Desproveimiento [des-pro-vay-e-me-en'-to], *m.* Penury, poverty.

Desprovisto, ta [des-pro-vees'-to, tah], *a. & pp. irreg.* of DESPROVEER. *V.* DESPROVEÍDO.

Despueble [des-poo-ay'-blay], or **Despueblo** [des-poo-ay'-blo], *m.* Depopulation.

(*Yo despueblo,* from *Despoblar. V.* ACERTAR.)

Después [des-poo-es'], *adv.* After, posterior in time; afterward, next, then. *Después de Dios,* Under or after God. *Después acá,* Ever since. *Primero lo negó y después lo confesó,* He first denied it, then he confessed it.

Despulir [des-poo-leer'], *va.* To tarnish, to frost, to grind (glass). *Vidrio despulido,* Ground glass.

Despulsar [des-pool-sar'], *va.* To leave without vigour or pulse.—*vr.* 1. To be sorely vexed. 2. To be violently affected with any passion; to eagerly desire.

Despumación [des-poo-mah-the-on'], *f.* Despumation, the skimming of liquors.

Despumadera, *f. V.* ESPUMADERA.

Depumar [des-poo-mar'], *va. V.* ESPUMAR.

Despuntadura [des-poon-tah-doo'-rah], *f.* The act of blunting or taking off the point.

Despuntar [des-poon-tar'], *va.* 1. To blunt. 2. To cut away the dry combs in a bee-hive. 3. (Naut.) To double a cape.—*vn.* 1. To advance or make progress in the acquisition of talents and knowledge; to manifest wit and genius. 2. To begin to sprout or bud, as plants. 3. To surpass, excel, morally. 4. To begin to dawn: said of the day or the sun.

Desque [des'-kay], *adv.* (Vulg.) Since, then, presently. *V.* DESDE QUE.

Desquebrajar [des-kay-brah-har'], *va. & vr.* To break, split, crack.

Desquejar [des-kay-har'], *va.* To pluck up a shoot near the root of a plant.

Desqueje [des-kay'-hay], *m.* Pulling up a shoot near the root of a plant.

Desquiciamiento [des-kee-the-ah-me-en'-to], *m.* Unhingeing, disjoining.

Desquiciar [des-ke-the-ar'], *va.* 1. To unhinge. 2. (Met.) To discompose, to disorder. 3. (Met.) To deprive of favour or protection.

Desquijaramiento [des-ke-ha-rah-me-en'-to], *m.* Act of breaking the jaws.

Desquijarar [des-ke-ha-rar'], *va.* 1. To break the jaws. 2. (Naut.) To break the cheek of a block.

Desquijerar [des-ke-hay-rar'], *va.* To cut timber on both sides to make a tenon.

Desquilatar [des-ke-lah-tar'], *va.* To diminish the intrinsic value of gold.

Desquitar [des-ke-tar'], *va.* To retrieve a loss.—*vr.* 1. To win one's money back again. 2. To retaliate, to take revenge; to meet with one.

Desquite [des-kee'-tay], *m.* 1. Compensation, recovery of a loss. 2. Revenge, satisfaction, retaliation.

Desrabotar [des-rah-bo-tar'], *va.* To cut off the tails of lambs or sheep, in order to fatten them.

Desrancharse [des-ran-char'-say], *vr.* To withdraw one's self from a mess.

Desramillar [des-rah-mil-lyar'], *va.* (Agr.) *V.* DESLECHUGAR.

Desraspado [des-ras-pah'-do], *a. V.* CHAMORRO, as a kind of wheat.—*pp.* of DESRASPAR.

Desraspar, *va. V.* RASPAR.

Desrastrojar [des-ras-tro-har'], *va.* (Agr.) To remove the stubble.

Desrastrojo [des-ras-tro'-ho], *m.* Removal, collection of stubble.

Desrayadura [des-rah-yah-doo'-rah], *f.* 1. The last furrow of tillage in a field. 2. A deep boundary furrow between two fields.

Desrayar [des-rah-yar'], *va.* 1. To open furrows for irrigation of a tilled field. 2. To make a boundary furrow to divide one field from another.

Desrazonable [des-rah-tho-nah'-blay], *a.* Unreasonable, idle-headed.

Desregladamente, *adv. V.* DESARREGLADAMENTE.

Desreglado, da [des-ray-glah'-do, dah], *a.* Disorderly, irregular. *V.* DESARREGLADO.

Desreglarse [des-ray-glar'-say], *vr.* To be irregular, or ungovernable.

Desrelingar [des-ray-lin-gar'], *va.* To take away the bolt-ropes from the sails.—*vr.* (Naut.) To be blown from the bolt-rope: applied to a sail.

Desreputación [des-ray-poo-tah-the-on'], *f.* Dishonour, ignominy.

Desrizar [des-re-thar'], *va.* To uncurl.

Desroblar [des-ro-blar'], *va.* To take off the rivets.

Desroñar [des-ro-nyar'], *va.* (Agr.) To lop off decayed branches.

Destacamento [des-tah-cah-men'-to], *m.* 1. Detachment, a body of troops detached on some particular service. 2. Station, or military post.

Destacar [des-tah-car'], *va.* To detach a body of troops from the main army on some particular service.

Destaconar [des-tah-co-nar'], *va.* To wear out, or break, the heels of footwear.

Destajador [des-tah-hah-dor'], *m.* A kind of smith's hammer.

Destajamiento [des-tah-hah-me-en'-to], *m.* (Obs.) 1. (Met.) Diminution, reduction. 2. Current taking a new course.

Destajar [des-tah-har'], *va.* 1. To hire or undertake a work by the bulk, to do task-work. 2. To stipulate the terms and conditions on which an undertaking is to be performed. 3. (Obs.) To prevent, to interrupt, to mislead.

Destajero [des-tah-hay'-ro], *m.* One who undertakes a work by task or by the job.

Destajista, *m. V.* DESTAJERO.

Destajo [des-tah'-ho], *m.* 1. Job. 2. Undertaking the completion of a work within a certain time. *A destajo,* By the job, by the lump; earnestly, diligently. *Hablar a destajo,* To talk much and at random.

Destallar [des-tal-lyar'], *va. V.* DESBORRAR.

Destalonar [des-tah-lo-nar'], *va.* 1. To deprive of talons or heels. 2. (Vet.) To level horses' hoofs.

Destapada [des-tah-pah'-dah], *f.* A kind of pie.

Destapar [des-tah-par'], *va.* To uncover.—*vr.* To be uncovered.

Destapiar [des-tah-pe-ar'], *va.* To pull down mud walls.

Destapo [des-tah'-po], *m.* (Prov.) Act of uncovering or unstopping.

Destaponar [des-tah-po-nar'], *va.* To uncork; to remove the stopper.

Destarar [des-tah-rar'], *va.* To diminish the tare allowed in weighing a thing.

Destartalado, da [des-tar-tah-lah'-do, dah], *a.* Huddled, incompact.

Destazador [des-tah-thah-dor'], *m.* He who cuts dead things in pieces.

Destazar [des-tah-thar'], *va.* To cut a thing in pieces.

Deste, ta, to [des'-tay, tah], *pron.* A contraction formerly used for *De este, de esta, de esto.*

Destechar [des-tay-char'], *va.* To unroof.

Destejar [des-tay-har'], *va.* 1. To untile, to take off the tiles. 2. To leave a thing defenceless.

Destejer [des-tay-herr'], *va.* To unweave, to ravel, to undo a warp prepared for the loom.

Destellar [des-tel-lyar'], *va.* To throw out or scatter rays of light.

Destello [des-tayl'-lyo], *m.* 1. The act of flowing out drop by drop. 2. Sparkle, a glimmering light; scintillation. 3. Brilliancy, ray of light.

Destempladamente [des-tem-plah-dah-men'-tay], *adv.* Intemperately.

Destemplado, da [des-tem-plah'-do, dah], *a.* 1. (Art) Inharmonious, incongruous: applied to paintings. 2. Disharmonious, unharmonious, out of tune. 3. Intemperate.—*pp.* of DESTEMPLAR.

Destemplanza [des-tem-plahn'-thah], *f.* 1. Intemperature, unsteadiness of the weather. 2. Disorder, intemperance; excess in the desires, or in the use of certain things. 3. Indisposition, an alteration in the pulse, not approaching fever symptoms. 4. Disorder, alteration in words or actions, want of moderation.

Destemplar [des-tem-plar'], *va.* 1. To distemper, to alter, to disconcert. 2. To put to confusion. 3. To untune. —*vr.* 1. To be ruffled, to be discomposed. 2. To be out of order: used of the pulse. 3. To grow blunt, to lose the temper: applied to instruments. 4. To act improperly or rashly; to lose moderation in actions or words. 5. To melt glue or other cement. 6. To anneal, take out the temper of metals.

Destemple [des-tem'-play], *m.* 1. Discordance, disharmony. 2. Discomposure, disorder. 3. Intemperance, distemperature. 4. (Pict.) Distemper. 5. Distemper, a slight indisposition.

Destender [des-ten-derr'], *va.* (Prov.) To fold, to double.

Desteñir [des-tay-nyeer'], *va.* To discolour, to change from the natural hue.

Desternillarse [des-ter-nil-lyar'-say], *vr.* To break one's cartilage or gristle. *Desternillarse de risa*, To laugh violently.

Desterradero [des-ter-rah-day'-ro], *m.* A retired part of the town.

Desterrado, da [des-ter-rah'-do, dah], *a.* & *pp.* of DESTERRAR. Banished, outcast.

Desterrado, da [des-ter-rah'-do, dah], *m.* & *f.* Exile, outcast.

Desterrar [des-ter-rar'], *va.* 1. To banish, to transport, to exile. 2. To lay, or put aside. 3. To take the earth from a thing. *Desterrar del mundo*, To be the outcast of the world.

Desterronador, ra [des-ter-ro-nah-dor', rah], *m.* & *f.* Clod-crusher.

Desterronar [des-ter-ro-nar'], *va.* To break clods with a harrow or spade.

Destetadera [des-tay-tah-day'-rah], *f.* Pointed instrument placed on the teats of cows, to prevent the calves from sucking.

Destetar [des-tay-tar'], *va.* To wean, to ablactate.—*vr.* To wean one's self from an evil habit or custom.

Destete [des-tay'-tay], *m.* The act of weaning from the breast.

Desteto [des-tay'-to], *m.* 1. Number of weanlings: applied to cattle. 2. The place where newly weaned mules are kept.

Destiempo [des-te-em'-po], *m.* An unseasonable time. *A destiempo*, Unseasonably, untimely.

Destiento [des-te-en'-to], *m.* (Obs.) Surprise, commotion in the mind.

Destierro [des-te-er'-ro], *m.* 1. Exile, banishment, transportation. 2. The place where the exile lives. 3. Any remote and solitary place. 4. Judicial banishment.

(*Yo destierro, yo destierre*, from *Desterrar*. V. ACERTAR.)

Destilación (des-te-lah-the-on'), *f.* 1. Distillation, act of dropping or falling in drops. 2. Distillation, the act of extracting by the fire or still. 3. Distillation, the substance drawn by the still. 4. Flow of humours in the body.

Destiladera [des-te-lah-day'-rah], *f.* 1. Still, alembic; a vessel for distillation. 2. An ingenious device or stratagem for obtaining one's end.

Destilador [des-te-lah-dor'], *m.* 1. Distiller. 2. Filtering-stone. 3. Alembic, retort.

Destilar [des-te-lar'], *va.* To distil.—*vn.* 1. To distil, to drop, to fall in drops. 2. To distil, to filter through a stone.

Destilatorio [des-te-lah-to'-re-o], *m.* 1. Distillery. 2. Alembic.

Destin [des-teen'], *m.* (Obs.) Will. *V.* TESTAMENTO.

Destinación [des-te-nah-the-on'], *f.* 1. Destination. 2. (Obs.) Destiny, fate.

Destinar [des-te-nar'], *va.* 1. To destine, to appoint for any use or purpose. 2. To destinate, to design for any particular end; to allot, assign. 3. (Naut.) To station ships.

Destino [des-tee'-no], *m.* 1. Destiny. 2. Fate, doom, fortune, force. 3. Destination, appointment for any use or purpose. 4. Profession, business. 5. (Naut.) Station. *Con destino a* —, Bound for —.

Destiño [des-tee'-nyo], *m.* Piece of unfinished yellow or green and dry honeycomb in a bee-hive.

(*Yo destiño, él destiñó*, from *Desteñir*. *V.* PEDIR.)

Destitución [des-te-too-the-on'], *f.* 1. Privation of an employment, office or charge. 2. Destitution, dereliction, abandonment.

Destituido, da [des-te-too-ee'-do, dah], *a.* & *pp.* of DESTITUIR. Destitute, forsaken, friendless, helpless.

Destituir [des-te-too-eer'], *va.* To deprive, to make destitute.

Destocar [des-to-car'], *va.* 1. To uncoif, to pull off the cap or head-dress. 2. (Prov.) To uncover the head.

Destorcedura [des-tor-thay-doo'-rah], *f.* An untwisting, uncurling.

Destorcer [des-tor-therr'], *va.* 1. To untwist, to uncurl. 2. To rectify what was not right.—*vr.* (Naut.) To deviate from the track, to lose the way.

Destorgar [des-tor-gar'], *va.* (Prov.) To break the branches of evergreen oaks, taking off their acorns.

Destornillador [des-tor-nil-lyah-dor'], *m.* Unscrewer, he or that which unscrews; screw-driver, wrench, turn-screw.

Destornillado, da [des-tor-nil-lyah'-do, dah], *a.* Inconsiderate, heedless, rash. —*pp.* of DESTORNILLAR.

Destornillar [des-tor-nil-lyar'], *va.* To unscrew.—*vr.* To act rashly, or without judgment or prudence.

Destoserse [des-to-serr'-say], *vr.* To feign a cough, to cough needlessly.

Destostarse [des-tos-tar'-say], *vr.* To gradually remove the tanning of the skin by the sun.

Destotro, tra, *a.* (Obs.) *V.* DE ESTE OTRO, DE ESTA OTRA.

Destrabar [des-trah-bar'], *va.* 1. To unfetter, to unbind. 2. To untie, to loosen, to separate; to break the barriers.

Destrados [des-trah'-dos], *m. pl.* (Prov.) A coarse sort of woollen carpets, or rugs.

Destraillar [des-trah-il-lyar'], *va.* To unleash the dogs.

Destral [des-trahl'], *m.* A small axe or hatchet.

Destraleja [des-trah-lay'-hah], *f.* A very small hatchet.

Destralero [des-trah-lay'-ro], *m.* One who makes axes and hatchets.

Destramar [des-trah-mar'], *va.* 1. To unweave, to undo the warp. 2. (Mil.) To dissolve a conspiracy or intrigue.

Destrenzar [des-tren-thar'], *va.* To undo a tress of hair.

Destreza [des-tray'-thah], *f.* 1. Dexterity, address, handiness, expertness, mastery, knowledge, cunning. 2. Nimbleness; adroitness. 3. Skill in fencing.

Destrincar [des-trin-car'], *va.* & *vr.* (Naut.) To loose, to unlash.

Destripacuentos [des-tre-pah-coo-en'-tos], *com.* One who interrupts often the person who is talking.

Destripar [des-tre-par'], *va.* 1. To disembowel, to gut, to eviscerate. 2. *V.* DESPACHURRAR. 3. (Met.) To draw out the inside of a thing. *Destripar una botella*, To crack a bottle.

Destripaterrones [des-tre-pah-ter-ro'-nes], *m.* (Coll.) Harrower, day-laborer who harrows the land; clod-beater.

Destripular [des-tre-poo-lar'], *va.* To discharge the crew of a vessel.

Destriunfar [des-tre-oon-far'], *va.* To extract all the trumps in games at cards.

Destrizar [des-tre-thar'], *va.* To mince, to crumble.—*vr.* To break the heart, to wear away with grief.

Destrocar [des-tro-car'], *va.* To return a thing bartered.

Destrocos [des-tro'-cose], *m. pl.* Ruins, remains.

Destrón [des-trone'], *m.* A blind man's guide.

Destronamiento [des-tro-nah-me-en'-to], *m.* Dethronement.

Destronar [des-tro-nar'], *va.* To dethrone, to divest of legality.

Destroncamiento [des-tron-cah-me-en'-to], *m.* Detruncation, amputation, lopping trees.

Destroncar [des-tron-car'], *va.* 1. To detruncate, to lop, to cut short. 2. To maim, to dislocate, to cut a body in pieces. 3. (Met.) To ruin, to destroy any one; obstruct his affairs or pretensions. 4. (Met.) To cut short a discourse.

Destronque [des-tron'-kay], *m.* DESTRONCAMIENTO.

Destroquerio [des-tro-kay'-re-o], *m.* (Her.) The right arm, clothed or bare, but always armed, upon crests of arms.

Destrozador, ra [des-tro-thah-dor', rah], *m.* & *f.* Destroyer, mangler.

Destrozar [des-tro-thar'], *va.* 1. To destroy, to break into pieces. 2. To rout, to defeat, to massacre. 3. (Met.) To spend much inconsiderately.

Destrozo [des-tro'-tho], *m.* 1. Destruction. 2. Havoc, rout, defeat, massacre.

Destrozón, na [des-tro-thone', nah], *m.* & *f.* One who is destructive of apparel, shoes, etc.

Destrucción [des-trooc-the-on'], *f.* 1. Destruction, extermination, extinction, overthrow. 2. Destruction, ruin, havoc, loss.

Destructibilidad, *f.* (Littl. us.) Destructibility.

Destructivamente [des-trooc-te-vah-men'-tay], *adv.* Destructively.

Destructividad [des-trooc-te-ve-dahd'], *f.* Destructiveness, a phrenological term. Its supposed seat is above the auditory canal.

Destructivo, va [des-trooc-tee'-vo, vah], *a.* Destructive, wasteful, consumptive.

Destructor, ra [des-trooc-tor', rah], *m.* & *f.* (Littl. us.) Destructor, destroyer, consumer, harasser.

Destructorio, ria [des-trooc-toh'-re-o, ah], *a.* Destroying.

Destrueco, Destrueque [des-troo-ay'-co, des-troo-ay'-kay], *m.* The mutual restitution of things bartered or exchanged.

(*Yo destrueco, yo destrueque*, from *Destrocar. V.* Acordar.)

Destruible [des-troo-ee'-blay], *a.* Destructible.

Destruidor, ra [des-troo-e-dor', rah], *m. & f.* Destroyer, devastator.

Destruir [des-troo-eer'], *va.* 1. To destroy, to ruin, to lay level. 2. To destroy, to waste or lay waste, to harass; to overthrow. 3. To misspend one's fortune. 4. To deprive one of the means of earning a livelihood.

Destruyente [des-troo-yen'-tay], *pa.* Destroying.

(*Yo destuerzo, yo destuerza*, from *Destorcer. V.* Cocer.)

Desturbar [des-toor-bar'], *va.* (Obs.) To turn out, to drive away. *V.* Echar.

Destutanarse [des-too-tah-nar'-say], *va.* (Amer. Cuba) To kill one's self with work, either physical or mental.

Desubstanciar [day-soobs-tan-the-ar'], *va.* To enervate, to deprive of strength and substance.

Desucación [day-soo-ca-the-on'], *f.* Act of extracting the juice.

Desucar [day-soo-car'], *va. V.* Desjugar. (Lat. succus, juice.)

Desudar [day-soo-dar'], *va.* To wipe off the sweat.

Desuelar [day-soo-ay-lar'], *va.* To take off the sole.—*vr.* To be wrenched off or fall off: applied to the sole of a shoe.

Desuellacaras [day-soo-el-lyah-cah'-ras], *m.* 1. (Prov. Coll.) A bad barber. 2. (Coll.) An impudent, shameless person.

Desuello [des-soo-ay'-lyo], *m.* 1. The act of flaying, fleecing, or skinning. 2. Forwardness, impudence, insolence. 3. Extortion, or an exorbitant price.

(*Yo desuelo, yo desuele* from *Desolar. V.* Acordar.)

(*Yo desuello, yo desuelle*, from *Desollar. V.* Acordar.)

Desulfuración [day-sool-foo-rah-the-on'], *f.* Removal of sulphur from a compound.

Desulfurar [day-sool-foo-rar'], *va.* To desulphurize.

Desuncir [des-oon-theer'], *va.* To unyoke, to abjugate.

Desunidamente, *adv.* Separately, severally.

Desunión [des-oo-ne-on'], *f.* 1. Separation, disunion, disjunction. 2. Discord, disunion, dissension, feud.

Desunir [des-oo-neer'], *va.* To separate, to part, to disunite; to occasion discord.—*vr.* To loosen, to come asunder; to set at odds; to disunite, to become separated.

Desuno, *adv.* (Obs.) *V.* De consuno.

Desuñar [des-oo-nyar'], *va.* 1. To tear off the nails. 2. To pull out the roots of trees.—*vr.* To plunge into vice and disorder.

Desurcar [day-soor-car'], *va.* To remove or undo furrows.

Desurdir [des-oor-deer'], *va.* 1. To unweave cloth. 2. To unravel a plot.

Desús (Al) [day-soos'], *adv.* (Obs.) *V.* Por encima. *Cf.* Fr. au-dessus.

Desusadamente, *adv.* Unusually, out of use, contrary to custom.

Desusado, da [des-oo-sah'-do, dah], *a. & pp.* of Desusar. Disused, obsolete, out of date, archaic.

Desusar [des-oo-sar'], *va.* To disuse, to discontinue the use of.—*vr.* To become disused or obsolete.

Desuso [des-oo'-so], *m.* Disuse, obsoleteness, desuetude.

Desustanciar [day-soos-tan-the-ar'], *va.* 1. To enervate. 2. To deprive of strength and substance.

Desvahar [des-vah-ar'], *va.* (Agr.) To take away the dry or withered part of a plant.

Desvaído, da [des-vah-ee'-do, dah], *a.* 1. Tall and graceless. 2. Dull, lustreless, matt (of colours). 3. (Naut.) Gaping: applied to the sheathing of ships when its joints separate.

Desvainar [des-vah-e-nar'], *va.* 1. To husk, to strip off the outward integument. 2. (Obs.) To unsheath.

Desvalido, da [des-vah-lee'-do, dah], *a.* Helpless, destitute, unprotected. *Niñez desvalida*, Underprivileged children.

Desvalijar [des-vah-le-har'], *va.* 1. To take out the contents of a valise or gripsack. 2. To rob one of what he was carrying in a valise or satchel.

Desvalimiento [des-vah-le-me-en'-to], *m.* Dereliction, abandonment, want of favour or protection.

Desvalorar [des-vah-lo-rar'], *va.* 1. To devalue, to depreciate. 2. To discredit.

Desvalorizar [des-vah-lo-re-thar'], *va.* To devalue, to depreciate.—*vr.* To depreciate.

Desván [des-vahn'], *m.* Garret; loft. *Desván gatero*, Cock-loft, a room over the garret.

Desvanar [des-vah-nar'], *va.* To wind to a skein. *V.* Devanar.

Desvanecer [des-vah-nay-therr'], *va.* 1. To divide into imperceptible parts. 2. To cause to vanish or disappear, to take away from the sight. 3. To undo, to remove. 4. To swell with presumption or pride.—*vr.* 1. To pall, to grow vapid, to become insipid. 2. To vanish, to evaporate, to exhale. 3. To be effected with giddiness or dizziness; to fall.

(*Yo me desvanezco*, or *desvanezca*, from *Desvanecerse. V.* Conocer.)

Desvanecidamente [des-vah-nay-the-dah-men'-tay], *adv.* Vainly, haughtily, proudly.

Desvanecimiento [des-vah-nay-the-me-en'-to], *m.* 1. Pride, haughtiness, loftiness. 2. Giddiness, dizziness.

Desvano [des-vah'-no], *m.* Garret. *V.* Desván.

Desvaporizar [des-vah-po-re-thar'], *va. V.* Evaporar.

Desvarar [des-vah-rar'], *va., vn. & vr.* 1. *V.* Resbalar. 2. (Naut.) To set afloat a ship that was aground.

Desvariadamente, *adv.* 1. Ravingly, foolishly, madly. 2. (Obs.) Differently, diversely, dissimilarly.

Desvariado, da [des-vah-re-ah'-do, dah], *a.* 1. Delirious, raving. 2. Disorderly, irregular. 3. Extravagant, nonsensical. 4. Long, luxuriant: applied to the branches of trees.—*pp.* of Desvariar.

Desvariar [des-vah-re-ar'], *vn.* 1. To rave, delirate, to dote. 2. To make extravagant demands.—*vr.* (Obs.) To deviate, go wrong, go astray.

Desvarío [des-vah-ree'-o], *m.* 1. An extravagant action or speech. 2. Delirium, raving, giddiness. 3. Inequality, inconstancy, caprice. 4. Monstrousness, extravagancy; derangement; disunion.

Desvedado, da [des-vay-dah'-do, dah], *a.* Unprohibited, free from prohibition, having been prohibited before.—*pp.* of Desvedar.

Desvedar [des-vay-dar'], *va.* To remove or revoke a prohibition against a thing.

Desveladamente, *adv.* Watchfully, vigilantly.

Desvelado, da [des-vay-lah'-do, dah], *a.* Watchful, vigilant, careful.—*pp.* of Desvelar.

Desvelamiento [des-vay-lah-me-en'-to], *m.* Watchfulness. *V.* Desvelo.

Desvelar [des-vay-lar'], *va.* To keep awake.—*vr.* To be watchful or vigilant or zealous.

Desvelo [des-vay'-lo], *m.* 1. Watching, want or privation of sleep. 2. Watch, forbearance of sleep. 3. Watchfulness, vigilance. 4. Anxiety, uneasiness.

Desvenar [des-vay-nar'], *va.* 1. To separate or clear the veins of flesh. 2. To extract any thing from the veins of mines or the filaments of plants. 3. To raise the bit of a bridle, so as to form an arch of mouth.

Desvencijado, da [des-ven-the-hah'-do, dah], *a.* Rickety, loose-jointed.

Desvencijar [des-ven-the-har'], *va.* To disunite, to weaken, to divide, to break.—*vr.* 1. To be ruptured; to be relaxed. 2. (Coll.) To be exhausted.

Desvendar [des-ven-dar'], *va.* To take off a bandage, to unbandage.

Desveno [des-vay'-no], *m.* Scatchmouth, arch of mouth; a kind of bridle-bit.

Desventaja [des-ven-tah'-hah], *f.* 1. Disadvantage, misfortune, damage, loss. 2. Disfavour, which results from comparing two persons or things.

Desventajosamente, *adv.* Disadvantageously, unprofitably.

Desventajoso, sa [des-ven-tah-ho'-so, sah], *a.* Disadvantageous, unfavourable, unprofitable, detrimental.

Desventar [des-ven-tar'], *va.* To vent, to let out the air.

Desventura [des-ven-too'-rah], *f.* Misfortune, calamity, mishap, mischance; misery.

Desventuradamente [des-ven-too-rah-dah-men'-tay], *adv.* Unhappily, unfortunately.

Desventurado, da [des-ven-too-rah'-do, dah], *a.* 1. Unfortunate, calamitous, wretched, unlucky, unhappy, miserable. 2. Chicken-hearted, pusillanimous, timid.

Desvergonzadamente [des-ver-gon-thah-dah-men'-tay], *adv.* Impudently, shamelessly.

Desvergonzado, da [des-ver-gon-thah'-do, dah], *a.* Impudent, shameless, immodest.

Desvergonzarse [des-ver-gon-thar'-say], *vr.* To speak or act in an impudent or insolent manner.

Desvergüenza [des-ver-goo-en'-thah], *f.* 1. Impudence, effrontery, assurance, grossness. 2. Shameless word or action.

(*Yo me desvergüenzo, yo me desvergüence*, from *Desvergonzarse. V.* Acordar.)

Desvezar [des-vay-thar'], *va.* (Agr. Prov.) To cut the young shoots of vines near the roots.

Desviación [des-ve-ah-the-on'], *f.* 1. Deviation, deflection, separation. 2. (Med.) Vicious direction of some parts of the body, especially the limbs and the bones: applied also to extravasation of fluids. 3. (Ast.) Wrong position of a telescope out of the plane of the meridian. 4. The quantity by which a body, falling freely, deviates from the perpendicular; and the variation of the magnetic needle. 5. (R. w.) Shunt.

Desviadero [des-ve-ah-day'-ro], *m.* A railway switch, siding, side-track, passing-place.

Desviado, da [des-ve-ah'-do, dah], *a.* Devious, out of the common track askew.—*pp.* of Desviar.

Desviar [des-ve-ar'], *va.* 1. To divert from the right way, to lead off, to avert, to turn aside. 2. To dissuade, to dehort, to put by. 3. (Fen.) To parry a thrust.—*vr.* To deviate, to turn away, to turn off.

Desviejar [des-ve-ay-har'], *va.* Among shepherds, to separate the old ewes or rams from the flock.

Desvigorizar [des-ve-go-re-thar'], *va.* To take away or diminish vigour.

Desvio [des-vee'-o], *m.* 1. Turning away, going astray, deviation, aberrance. 2. The act of diverting or dehorting, dehortation. 3. Aversion, displeasure. 4. Coldness, indifference.

Desvirar [des-ve-rar'], *va.* 1. To pare off the fore part of a sole. 2. In bookbinding, to trim a book. 3. (Naut.) To turn the capstan the other way from that used in winding the cable; to reverse the capstan.

Desvirgar [des-virr-gar'], *va.* (Low) To deflower a maid.

Desvirtuar [des-virr-too-ar'], *va.* To pall, to make insipid or vapid, to take the substance, virtue, or strength from any thing.

Desvivirse [des-ve-veer'-say], *vr.* To love excessively; to desire anxiously.

Desvolvedor [des-vol-vay-dor'], *m.* A screw tap.

Desvolver [des-vol-verr'], *va.* 1. To alter a thing, give it another shape. 2. To plough, to till the ground.

Desyemar [des-yay-mar'], *va.* 1. (Agr.) To remove buds from plants. 2. To separate the yolk from the white of an egg.

Desyerba, *f.* (Obs.) *V.* ESCARDA.

Desyerbar [des-yer-bar'], *va.* To pluck up herbs, to weed, to grub.

Desyuncir [des-yoon-theer'], *va.* 1. To unyoke. 2. To free from oppression or servitude.

Deszafrar [des-thah-frar'], *va.* To carry away the ore from an excavation.

Deszocar [des-tho-car'], *va.* To wound or hurt the foot.

Deszumar [des-thoo-mar'], *va.* To extract the juice or substance.

Detal (En) [day-tahl'], *adv.* In detail, minutely. *V.* MENUDAMENTE.

Detall [day-tahll'], *m.* Detail; account. *Capitán del detall,* Officer charged with the retailing of supplies and provisions.

Detallar [day-tal-lyar'], *va.* To detail, to relate particularly or minutely, to particularize, to enumerate.

Detalle [day-tahl'-lyay], *m.* Detail, enumeration.

Detective [day-tec-tee'-vay], *m. & f.* Detective, sleuth.

Detector [day-tec-tor'], *m.* Detector.

Detención [day-ten-the-on'], *f.* 1. Detention, delay, stopping. 2. (Naut.) Demurrage. 3. Arrest.

Detenedor, ra [day-tay-nay-dor', rah], *m. & f.* Detainer, one that detains.

Detener [day-tay-nerr'], *va.* 1. To stop, to detain, to hinder, to fix. 2. To arrest, to imprison, to constrain. 3. To keep, to keep back, to retain, to reserve.—*vr.* 1. To tarry, to stay, to continue, to forbear, to give over. 2. To be detained, to stop, to be at leisure. 3. To consider a thing maturely.

(*Yo detengo, yo detuve,* from *Detener. V.* TENER.)

Detenidamente [day-tay-ne-dah-men'-tay], *adv.* Dilatorily, cautiously, attentively.

Detenido, da [day-tay-nee'-do, dah], *a.* 1. Sparing, niggardly, parsimonious. 2. Embarrassed, of little resolution, dilatory.—*pp.* of DETENER.

Detenimiento [day-tay-ne-me-en'-to], *m.* 1. *V.* DETENCIÓN. (Acad.) 2. Care, circumspection, reflection, tact.

Detentación [day-ten-tah-the-on'], *f.* (Law) Deforcement, detention, the act of keeping what belongs to another.

Detentar [day-ten-tar'], *va.* To detain, to retain, to keep unlawfully the property or rights belonging to another.

Detentor [day-ten-tor'], *m.* (Com.) Holder.

Detergente [day-ter-hen'-tay], *a.* Detergent. *Jabón detergente,* detergent soap.—*m.* Detergent.

Deterger [day-ter-herr'], *va.* To wash or cleanse an ulcer, a wound, etc.

Deterior [day-tay-re-or'], *a.* Worse, of an inferior quality.

Deterioración [day-tay-re-o-rah-the-on'], *f.* Deterioration, detriment, damage.

Deteriorar [day-tay-re-o-rar'], *va. & vr.* To deteriorate, to impair.

Deterioro [day-tay-re-oh'-ro], *m.* Deterioration, impairment, injury.

Determinable [day-ter-me-nah'-blay], *a.* (Littl. us.) Determinable; conclusible.

Determinación [day-ter-me-nah-the-on'], *f.* 1. Determination, resolution, decision. 2. Conclusion or final decision. 3. Resolution, firmness, boldness, audaciousness.

Determinadamente [day-ter-me-nah-dah-men'-tay], *adv.* 1. Determinately, resolutely. 2. Determinately, definitively, expressly, especially.

Determinado, da [day-ter-me-nah'-do, dah], *a.* 1. Determinate, determined, resolved, decided; fixed, resolute. 2. Determinate, settled, definite, determined.—*pp.* of DETERMINAR.

Determinante [day-ter-me-nahn'-tay], *pa.* Determining.—*a.* Determinate, determinative.

Determinante [day-ter-me-nahn'-tay], *m.* 1. (Gram.) The determining verb. 2. Determiner, determinator, he who determines.

Determinar [day-ter-me-nar'], *va.* 1. To determine, to resolve, to fix in a determination. 2. To distinguish, to discern. 3. To appoint, to assign. 4. To cause, to produce. 5. To classify. 6. To decide; to conclude. *Determinar un pleito,* To decide a lawsuit. —*vr.* To determine, to resolve, to take a resolution, or to come to a resolution.

Determinativo, va [day-ter-me-nah-tee'-vo, vah], *a.* Determinative.

Determinismo [day-ter-me-nees'-mo], *m.* Determinism, fatalism; a philosophy according to which the actions of men obey irresistible motives, mostly not suspected by the individual.

Determinista [day-ter-me-nees'-tah], *m.* A fatalist.

Detersión [day-ter-se-on'], *f.* 1. Detersion, the act of cleansing a sore. 2. Cleansing. 3. The act and effect of cleansing.

Detersivo, va [day-ter-see'-vo, vah], *a.* Detersive, fit for a cleansing surgical application.

Detersorio, ria [day-ter-so'-re-o, ah], *a.* Detersive, cleansing.

Detestable [day-tes-tah'-blay], *a.* Detestable, hateful, heinous, loathsome.

Detestablemente, *adv.* Destestably, hatefully, confoundedly.

Detestación [day-tes-tah-the-on'], *f.* Detestation, hatred, abhorrence, horror, abomination.

Detestar [day-tes-tar'], *va.* To detest, to abhor, to hate, to abominate, to loathe.

Detienebuey [day-te-ay-nay-boo-ay'-e], *m.* (Bot.) Common rest-harrow, cammoc, ground-furze. Ononis spinosa.

Detonación [day-to-nah-the-on'], *f.* Detonation, noise.

Detonador [day-to-nah-dor'], *m.* Detonator.

Detonar [day-to-nar'], *va.* (Chem.) To detonize; to flash, to detonate.

Detorsión [day-tor-se-on'], *f.* Violent extension, wrenching of a muscle, tendon, or ligament.

Detracción [day-trac-the-on'], *f.* 1. Detraction, defamation, slander, obloquy. 2. Detraction, a withdrawing, a taking away.

Detractar [day-trac-tar'], *va.* To detract, to defame, to slander.

Detractor, ra [day-trac-tor', rah], *m. & f.* Detractor, slanderer.

Detraer [day-trah-err'], *va.* 1. To detract, to remove, to take away, to withdraw. 2. To detract, to slander, to vilify.

Detrás [day-trahs'], *adv.* 1. Behind. *Detrás de la puerta,* Behind the door. 2. In the absence.

Detrimento [day-tre-men'-to], *m.* Detriment, damage, loss, harm.

Detrítico, ca [day-tree'-te-co, cah], *a.* Composed of detritus; detrital, detritic.

Detritus [day-tree'-toos], *m.* (Neol.) 1. Detritus, remnants of the destruction of rocks and plants. 2. Inorganic residue replacing tissue in degenerated parts of the body. 3. Filth, excrements.

Detumescencia [day-too-mes-then'-the-ah], *f.* Detumescence, resolution of a swelling.

Detumescente [day-too-mes-then'-tay], *a.* Having power to disperse a swelling.

Deturbadora (Fuerza) [day-toor-bah-do'-rah], *a.* 1. A force perpendicular to the plane of the orbit of the disturbed planet. 2. *V.* PERTURBACIÓN.

Deuda [day'-oo-dah], *f.* 1. Debt, that which one man owes to another. 2. Fault, offence. 3. That which has relationship or affinity. *Deudas activas,* Assets. *Deudas pasivas,* Liabilities. *Deuda común,* Death, the last debt.

Deudo, da [day'-oo-do, dah], *m. & f.* 1. Parent, relative. 2. Kindred, relation. *V.* DESDÉN and PARENTESCO.

Deudor, ra [day-oo-dor', rah], *m. & f.* Debtor.

Deuterio [day-oo-tay'-re-o], *m.* (Chem.) Deuterium.

Deuterogamia [day-oo-tay-ro-gah'-me-ah], *f.* State of second marriage.

Deuterógamo, ma [day-oo-tay-ro'-gah-mo, mah], *a.* One who marries a second time.

Deuteronomio [day-oo-tay-ro-no'-me-o], *m.* Deuteronomy, the fifth book of the Pentateuch.

Devalar [day-vah-lar'], *vn.* (Naut.) To be driven out of the right course by a current: applied to ships.

Devaluar [day-vah-loo-ar'], *va.* To devaluate, to depreciate.

Devanadera [day-vah-nah-day'-rah], *f.* 1. A reel, spool, bobbin. *Devanadera de golpe,* Clock-reel, snap-reel. 2. A movable picture or decoration on the stage. 3. (Naut.) Log-reel.

Devanador, ra [day-vah-nah-dor', rah], *m. & f.* 1. Winder, one who reels yarn. 2. Quill, bit of paper, or other thing, on which yarn is wound; spool.

Devanar [day-vah-nar'], *va.* 1. To reel, as yarn. 2. (Met.) To wrap up one thing in another. *Devanar las tripas,* To importune one with some impertinent affair. *Devanarse los sesos,* To screw one's wits, to fatigue one's self with intense thinking, to hammer one's brains.

Devanear [day-vah-nay-ar'], *vn.* To rave, to talk nonsense; to dote, to be delirious.

Devaneo [day-vah-nay'-o], *m.* 1. Delirium, alienation of mind, giddiness; frenzy. 2. Idle or mad pursuit; dissipation.

Devantal [day-van-tahl'], *m.* Apron. *V.* DELANTAL.

Devastación [day-vas-tah-the-on'], *f.* Devastation, destruction, desolation, waste.

Devastador, ra [day-vas-tah-dor', rah], *m. & f.* Desolator, harasser, spoiler.

Devastar [day-vas-tar'], *va.* To desolate, to waste or to lay waste, to harass.

Develar [day-vay-lar'], *va.* To blockade a port.

Devengar [day-ven-gar'], *va.* To obtain as the reward of labour, to deserve, to acquire a right to a thing as a reward for services, etc.

Devisa [day-vee'-sah], *f.* (Obs.) 1. *V.* DIVISA. 2. Part of the tithes which belong to a plebeian heir. 3. Ancient patrimony in Castile.

Devoción [day-vo-the-on'], *f.* 1. Devotion, piety. 2. Godliness, observance of religious duties. 3. Prayer, act of religion. 4. (Met.) Strong affection, ardent love. 5. (Div.) Devoutness, promptitude in obeying the will of God. *Estar a la devoción de alguno,* To be at one's disposal, to attend his orders.

Devocionario [day-vo-the-o-nah'-re-o], *m.* Prayer-book.

Devocionero, ra [day-vo-the-o-nay'-ro, rah], *a.* Devotional.

Devolución [day-vo-loo-the-on'], *f.* (Law) Devolution, restitution.

Devoluta [day-vo-loo'-tah], *f.* In canonical law, the bestowal by the Pope of a vacant benefice.

Devolutario [day-vo-loo-tah'-re-o], *m.* He who receives from the Pope a benefice by right of devolution.

Devolutivo [day-vo-loo-tee'-vo], *a.* (Law) 1. What may be returned: applied to causes. 2. What may be restored to a former state: applied to rights.

Devolutorio, ria [day-vo-loo-toh'-re-o, ah], *a.* *V.* DEVOLUTIVO.

Devolver [day-vol-verr'], *va.* To return, to refund, to restore. *Devolver el estómago,* (coll.) To vomit.

Devorador, ra [day-vo-rah-dor', rah], *m. & f.* Devourer.

Devorar [day-vo-rar'], *va.* To devour, to swallow up, to consume ravenously, to glut.

Devotamente [day-vo-tah-men'-tay], *adv.* Devoutly, piously.

Devoto, ta [day-vo'-to, tah], *a.* 1. Devout, pious, devotional, religious, godly. 2. Exciting devotion. 3. Strongly attached. *Devoto de monjas,* He who frequently visits and converses with nuns.

Devuelto, ta [day-voo-el'-to, tah], *pp. irr.* of DEVOLVER. Returned, restored. (*Yo devuelvo, yo devuelva,* from *Devolver. V.* MOVER.)

Dexiocardia [dek-se-o-car'-de-ah], *f.* Deviation of the heart to the right side of the thoracic cavity.

Dextrina [dex-tree'-nah], *f.* Dextrine.

Dextrosa [dex-tro'-sah], *f.* (Chem.) Dextrose.

Dey [day'-e], *m.* (Littl. us.) Dey, the title, formerly, of the governor of Algiers.

Dezmable [deth-mah'-blay], *a.* Tithable, subject to tithes.

Dezmar [deth-mar'], *va.* *V.* DIEZMAR.

Dezmatorio [deth-mah-to'-re-o], *m.* 1. Place in which tithes are collected. 2. Tithing.

Dezmero, ra, *a.* Belonging to tithes.

Dezmería, Dezmía [deth-may-ree'-ah, deth-mee'-ah], *f.* Tithe-land.

Dezmero [deth-may'-ro], *m.* 1. One who pays tithes. 2. Tithe-gatherer; a tither.

Dia [dee'-ah], *m.* 1. Day: the space of twenty-four hours. 2. Day: the time between the rising and setting of the sun. 3. Daylight, sunshine. 4. (Obs.) Contraction of *Diego* or *Santiago,* James, a proper name.—*pl.* 1. Certain lapse of time, a certain epoch. 2. Existence, life. *Días caniculares,* Dog-days. *Día de años* or *cumpleaños,* Birthday. *Día de ayuno* or *de vigilia,* Fasting-day or fast-day. *Día de viernes,* Meager-day. *Día de besamanos,* Court-day. *Día de carne,* Day on which it is permitted to eat meat. *Día de trabajo,* Working-day. *Día de descanso,* 1. Day of rest on a journey. 2. The Sabbath-day. *Día del juicio,* Doomsday. *Día diado* or *adiado,* Day appointed for doing any thing. *Día laborable,* (Com.) Clear day. *Día útil,* Working-day. *Día natural* From midnight to midnight. *De día,* By day. *De un día para otro* or *de día en día,* From day to day. *Un día sí y otro no,* or *cada tercer día,* Every other day. *Hasta el día de hoy,* To this day. *El día de hoy* or *hoy en día,* The present day. *El mejor día,* Some fine day. *Día pardo,* A cloudy day, a gray day. *Día pesado,* A dull, gloomy day. *Luz del día,* Daylight. *Entre día,* In the day-time. *En días de Dios,* Never. *Hombre de días,* A man in years. *Jefe de día,* (Mil.) Officer of the day. *Tener días,* (Coll.) 1. To vary in one's physiognomy or countenance. 2. To be full of days, to be old. *De hoy en ocho días,* This day week. *Días complementarios,* Complementary days which the Aztecs added at the end of the year to complete it. *Días y ollas,* (Coll.) Time and patience attain everything. *Días de gracia,* Days of grace allowed for the payment of bills. *Días ha,* It is a long time since. *Buenos días,* Good-morning. *En cuatro días,* In a short time. *En los días de la vida,* Never. *De días,* (Obs.) Some time ago.

Diabetes [de-ah-bay'-tes], *f.* Diabetes, a disease whose chief symptom is the abundant excretion of sugar in the urine.

Diabético, ca [de-ah-bay'-te-co, cah], *a.* Diabetic, relating to diabetes.

Diabla (**A la**) [de-ah'-blah (ah'-lah)], *adv.* Carelessly; rudely.—*f.* 1. A machine for carding wool or cotton. *Cosido a la diabla,* Bound in paper. 2. A truck.

Diablazo [de-ah-blah'-tho], *m. aug.* A great devil.

Diablear [de-ah-blay-ar'], *vn.* (Coll.) To commit deviltries, play pranks.

Diablesa [de-ah-blay'-sah], *f.* (Coll.) A she-devil.

Diablillo [de-ah-bleel'-lyo], *m.* 1. (Dim.) Deviling, devilkin, a little devil. 2. An acute, clever man.

Diablo [de-ah'-blo], *m.* 1. Devil, Satan. 2. Person of a perverse temper. 3. An ugly person. 4. A cunning, subtle person. *Hay mucho diablo aquí,* This business is dreadfully entangled or perplexed. *Ser la piel* or *de la piel del diablo,* To be a limb of the devil. *Diablo cojuelo,* Artful, deceiving devil. *Ese es un diablo encarnado,* (Coll.) That is a most infamous person. *Eso es el diablo,* (Coll.) That is the difficulty. *No valer un diablo,* (Coll.) To be good for nothing.

Diablotín, Diabolín [de-ah-blo-teen', de-ah-bo-leen'], *m.* A sort of sweet-meat.

Diablura [de-ah-bloo'-rah], *f.* A diabolical undertaking, devilishness, deviltry, mischief, wild prank.

Diabólicamente [de-ah-bo'-le-cah-men-tay], *adv.* Diabolically, devilishly.

Diabólico, ca [de-ah-bo'-le-co, cah], *a.* Diabolical, devilish.

Diabrosis [de-ah-bre'-sis], *f.* Ulceration, erosion, corrosion.

Diabrótico, ca [de-ah-bro'-te-co, cah], *a.* Corrosive, erosive.—*m.* *Diabrótico,* a beetle destructive to vegetation.

Diacasis [de-ah-cah'-sis], *m.* A purgative prepared from Cassia fistula (related to senna).

Diacatalicón [de-ah-cah-tah-le-cone'], *m.* Diacatholicion, a universal medicine or purge.

Diacitrón [de-ah-the-trone'], *m.* Lemon-peel preserved in sugar.

Diaco [de-ah'-co], *a. & m.* A cleric of the order of Malta, who reached a chaplaincy only after twelve years of service.

Diaconado, *m.* *V.* DIACONATO.

Diaconal [de-ah-co-nahl'], *a.* Diaconal.

Diaconato [de-ah-co-nah'-to], *m.* Deaconship.

Diaconía [de-ah-co-nee'-ah], *f.* Deaconry.

Diaconisa [de-ah-co-nee'-sah], *f.* Deaconess.

Diácono [de-ah'-co-no], *m.* Deacon, a clergyman next in order below a priest.

Diácope [de-ah'-co-pay], *m.* 1. (Gram.) Hyperbaton. 2. Incision, longitudinal fracture of a bone.

Diacorético, ca [de-ah-co-ray'-te-co, cah], *a.* Having the property of producing evacuations.

Diacrítico, ca [de-ah-cree'-te-co, cah], *a.* Diacritic, diacritical; distinguishing, diagnostic.

Diacroción [de-ah-cro-the-on'], *m.* A collyrium prepared from saffron.

Diacústica [de-ah-coos'-te-cah], *f.* Diacoustics, the doctrine of sounds.

Diadelfia [de-ah-del'-fe-ah], *f.* A plant having the stamens united into two sets.

Diadelfo, fa [de-ah-del'-fo, fah], *a.* Diadelphous, with stamens in two sets.

Diadema [de-ah-day'-mah], *f.* 1. Diadem, crown. 2. Crown, glory, a circle of metal put round the heads of images; represented in pictures by luminous circles.

Diademado, da [dee-ah-day-mah'-do, dah], *a.* (Her.) Diademed, adorned with a diadem.

Diafanidad [de-ah-fah-ne-dahd'], *f.* Diaphaneity, transparency, pellucidness.

Diáfano, na [de-ah'-fah-no, nah], *a.* 1. Transparent, pellucid, clear, lucid, diaphanous. 2. (Amer.) Finical timid, and affected.

Diafiláctico, ca [de-ah-fe-lahc'-te-co, cah], *a.* (Med.) Prophylactic.

Diaforesis [de-ah-fo-ray'-sis], *f.* Diaphoresis, gentle perspiration.

Diaforético, ca [de-ah-fo-ray'-te-co, cah] *a.* (Med.) Diaphoretic.

Diafragma [de-ah-frahg'-mah], *m.* 1. Diaphragm, the midriff. 2. Cartilaginous partition of the nostrils. 3. A perforated disk used to cut off marginal rays in some optical instruments, or the vibrating disk of a telephone. 4. The porous cup of a voltaic cell.

Diafragmático, ca [de-ah-frag-mah'-te-co, cah], *a.* Diaphragmatic, relating to the diaphragm.

Diagnosticar [de-ag-nos-te-car'], *va.* To diagnosticate, form the diagnosis.

Diagnóstico [de-ag-nos'-te-co], *m.* & *a.* (Med.) Diagnostic, a distinguishing symptom; diagnosis.

Diagonal [de-ah-go-nahl'], *a.* Diagonal.

Diagonalmente [de-ah-go-nal-men'-tay], *adv.* Diagonally.

Diagráfica [de-ah-grah'-fe-cah], *f.* Sketch, design.

Diagráfico, ca [de-ah-grah'-fe-co, cah], *a.* Diagraphic, showing by lines.

Diagrafita [de-ah-grah-fee'-tah], *f.* Graphite, from which drawing-pencils are made.

Diagrama [de-ah-grah'-mah], *f.* Diagram.

Dialage [de-ah-lah'-hay], *m.* Diallage, the use of many arguments to prove one proposition.

Dialéctica [de-ah-lec'-te-cah], *f.* Logic, dialectic.

Dialéctico, *m.* Dialectician, logician.

Dialéctico, ca [de-ah-lec'-te-co, cah], *a.* Dialectical, logical.

Dialecto [de-ah-lec'-to], *m.* Dialect, phraseology, speech.

Diálisis [de-ah'-le-sis], *f.* Dialysis.

Dialogal [de-ah-lo-gahl'], *a.* Colloquial.

Dialogar [de-ah-lo-gar'], *vn.* 1. To speak a dialogue. 2. To sing responsively.

Dialogismo [de-ah-lo-hees'-mo], *m.* Dialogism.

Dialogístico, ca [de-ah-lo-hees'-te-co, cah], *a.* Colloquial.

Dialogizar [de-ah-lo-he-thar'], *vn.* To dialogize, to discourse in dialogue.

Diálogo [de-ah'-lo-go], *m.* Dialogue.

Dialoguista [de-ah-lo-gees'-tah], *m.* Dialogist.

Diamantazo [de-ah-man-tah'-tho], *m. aug.* A large diamond.

Diamante [de-ah-mahn'-tay], *m.* 1. Diamond. 2. Hardness, resistance.

Diamantino, na [de-ah-man-tee'-no, nah], *a.* Adamantine, diamantine.

Diamantista [de-ah-man-tees'-tah], *m. V.* Lapidario.

Diametral [de-ah-may-trahl'], *a.* Diametrical.

Diametralmente [de-ah-may-tral-men'-tay], *adv.* Diametrically.

Diámetro [de-ah'-may-tro], *m.* (Geom.) Diameter.

Diana [de-ah'-nah], *f.* (Mil.) 1. Reveille, the beating of the drum at daybreak. 2. The moon.

Dianche, Diantre [de-ahn'-chay, de-ahn'-tray], *m.* & *int.* (Coll.) Deuce, the devil.

Diantero [de-an-tay'-ro, rah], *a.* Having two anthers.

Dianto [de-ahn'-to, tah], *a.* Having two flowers, biflorous.

Diapasón [de-ah-pah-sone'], *m.* 1. Diapason, an octave (from ancient Greek music). 2. A rule provided with scales of equal parts. 3. A tuning-fork, or the standard pitch given by the tuning-fork. 4. Measure, compass.

Diapente [de-ah-pen'-tay], *m.* (Mus.) A perfect fifth.

Diapiema, Diapiesis [de-ah-pe-ay'-mah, de-ah-pe-ay'-sis], *f.* Suppuration.

Diapositiva [de-ah-po-se-tee'-vah], *f.* (Photog.), Plate, slide.

Diaprea [de-ah-pray'-ah], *f.* Sort of round plum.

Diaquea [de-ah-kay'-ah], *f.* A small fungus which grows on decayed wood.

Diaquilón [de-ah-ke-lone'], *m.* Lead plaster, diachylon.

Diaria [de-ah'-re-ah], *f.* (Naut.) Supply of provisions and arms for a fortnight.

Diariamente [de-ah-re-ah-men'-tay], *adv.* Daily.

Diario, ria [de-ah'-re-o, ah], *a.* Daily.

Diario, *m.* 1. Journal, diary; daily newspaper. 2. Diary, a daily account. 3. Daily expense. 4. Log.

Diarista [de-ah-rees'-tah], *com.* Journalist.

Diarrea [de-ar-ray'-ah], *f.* Diarrhœa.

Diasfixia [de-as-feek'-se-ah], *f.* (Med.) Rapid pulse, palpitation of the heart.

Diáspero, Diaspro [de-ahs'-pay-ro, de-ahs'-pro], *m.* Jasper.

Diastasia [de-as-tah'-se-ah], *f.* Diastase, a proximate principle discovered in cereals after germination.

Diastema [de-as-tay'-mah], *m.* 1. Diasteme, name of pores scattered over the surface of bodies, which can be demonstrated only by the penetration of liquids. 2. (Mus.) A simple interval, in contrast to a complex. 3. Interspace between two consecutive teeth.

Diástole [de-ahs'-to-lay], *m.* 1. (Anat.) Diastole, the dilatation of the heart. 2. (Rhet.) Diastole, a figure by which a short syllable is made long.

Diastólico, ca [de-as-toh'-le-co, cah], *a.* Diastolic, relating to the diastole.

Diatérmano, na [de-ah-terr'-mah-no, nah], *f.* Diathermanous, allowing free passage to rays of heat.

Diatermia [de-ah-ter'-me-ah], *f.* Diathermy.

Diatesarón [de-ah-tay-sah-ron'], *m.* 1. The harmony of the four Gospels. 2. (Mus.) Diatessaron, the interval of a fourth.

Diatésico, ca [de-ah-tay'-se-co, cah], *a.* (Med.) Diathetic, belonging to a diathesis.

Diátesis [de-ah'-tay-sis], *f.* (Med.) Diathesis, organic disposition to contract certain diseases.

Diatónico [de-ah-toh'-ne-co], *a.* (Mus.) Diatonic.

Diatriba [de-ah-tree'-bah], *f.* Diatribe, a dissertation or discourse on polemic matters; a severe criticism on works of genius.

Dibujador, ra [de-boo-hah-dor', rah], *m.* & *f.* 1. Delineator. 2. Graver, a tool used in graving.

Dibujante [de-boo-hahn'-tay], *m.* & *pa.* Designer, sketching.

Dibujar [de-boo-har'], *va.* 1. To draw, to design, to delineate, to sketch. 2. (Met.) To paint any passion of the mind.—*vr.* To throw a shadow upon a surface.

Dibujo [de-boo'-ho], *m.* 1. Design, drawing, sketch, draught. 2. Delineation, description. *Es un dibujo,* It is a picture: applied to a handsome face. *No meterse en dibujos,* To relate in a plain manner, not to meddle with arduous affairs.

Dicacidad [de-ca-the-dahd'], *f.* 1. Pertness, sauciness, loquacity. 2. Jesting sarcasm.

Dicaz [de-cath'], *a.* Keen, biting (said of speech).

Dicción [dic-the-on'], *f.* Diction, style, language, expression.

Diccionario [dic-the-o-nah'-re-o], *m.* Dictionary, lexicon.

Diciembre [de-the-em'-bray], *m.* December.

Diciente [de-the-en'-tay], *pa.* of Decir. Saying, talking.

Dicotiledón, Dicotiledóneo, a [de-co-te-lay-done'], *a.* (Bot.) Dicotyledonous, having two seed-leaves.

Dicotomal [de-co-to-mahl'], *a.* Dichotomal.

Dicotomía [de-co-to-mee'-ah], *f.* 1. State of the moon when the sun illuminates no more than half its disk. 2. The angle formed by two dichotomous branches.

Dicotómico, ca, or **Dicótomo, ma,** *a.* (Bot.) Subdividing into two; dichotomous. (Ast.) Half-lighted: applied to the moon, Venus, and Mercury.

Dicroismo [de-cro-ees'-mo], *m.* Dichroism, the property of showing different colours when viewed in different directions.

Dicrónico, ca [de-cro'-ne-co, cah], *a.* Having two epochs or seasons in vegetation.

Dicroto, ta [de-cro'-to, tah], *a.* (Med.) Dicrotic, dicrotous, showing two beats to each systole.

Dictado [dic-tah'-do], *m.* A title of dignity or honour.—*Dictado, da, pp.* of Dictar.

Dictador [dic-tah-dor'], *m.* Dictator, an ancient magistrate of Rome, invested with absolute authority.

Dictadura [dic-tah-doo'-rah], *f.* Dictatorship, dictature.

Dictáfono [dic-tah'-fo-no], *m.* Dictaphone, dictating machine.

Dictamen [dic-tah'-men], *m.* 1. Opinion, sentiments, notion, judgment, mind. 2. Suggestion, insinuation, dictate.

Díctamo [deec'-tah-mo], *m.* (Bot.) Dittany. *Díctamo blanco* or *real,* White flaxinella. Dictamnus albus. *Díctamo crético,* Dittany of Crete, marjoram. Origanum dictamnus. *Díctamo bastardo,* Shrubby-white horehound.

Dictar [dic-tar'], *va.* 1. To dictate, to deliver one's opinions with authority. 2. To dictate, to pronounce what another is to say or write.

Dictatorio, ria [dic-tah-to'-re-o, ah], *a.* Dictatorial.

Dicterio [dic-tay'-re-o], *m.* Sarcasm, taunt, keen reproach, insult.

Dicha [dee'-chah], *f.* Happiness, felicity, fortune, good luck, good fortune. *Dichas,* Honours, riches, dignities, and pleasures. *Por dicha* or *a dicha,* By chance.

Dicharacho [de-chah-rah'-cho], *m.* (Coll.) A vulgar, low, or indecent expression.

Dichido, Dichito [de-chee'-do, de-chee'-to], *m.* (Coll.) A sharp or pert expression, small talk.

Dicho [dee'-cho], *m.* 1. Saying, expression, sentence. 2. Declaration, deposition. 3. Promise of marriage. *Dicho de las gentes,* Gossiping. *Dicho y hecho,* No sooner said than done. *Del dicho al hecho hay gran trecho,* (prov.) Saying and doing are two very different things.—*Dicho, cha, pp. irr.* of Decir.

Dichosamente [de-cho-sah-men'-tay], *adv.* Happily, fortunately, luckily.

Dichoso, sa [de-cho'-so, sah], *a.* Happy, fortunate, prosperous, successful, lucky.

Didáctica [de-dahc'-te-cah], *f.* The art of teaching; pedagogy.

Didáctico, ca, Didascálico, ca [de-dahc'-te-co, cah. de-das-cah'-le-co, cah], *a.* Didactic, didactical, preceptive, giving precepts.

Didascalia [de-das-cah'-le-ah], *f.* Pedagogy, the science and rules of teaching.

Didelfo [de-del'-fo], *m.* The opossum.

Didínamo, ma [de-dee'-nah-mo, mah], *a.* Didynamous: said of stamens arranged in two pairs of different sizes.

Diecinueve [de-ay-the-noo-ay'-vay], *a.* & *m.* Nineteen.

Diecinueveavo, va [de-ay-the-noo-ay-vay-ah'-vo, vah], *a.* Nineteenth.

Dieciochavo, va [de-ay-the-o-chah'-vo, vah], *a.* & *m.* 1. An eighteenth part.

2. (Typ.) 18mo, octodecimo, a sheet folding into 18 parts, or 36 pages.

Dieciocheno, na [de-ay-the-o-chay'-no, nah], *a.* & *m.* 1. Eighteenth. 2. A kind of cloth.

Dieciseisavo [de-ay-the-say-e-sah'-vo], *m.* Decimo-sexto: applied to a book printed on a sheet folded into 16 leaves.

Dieciseiseno, na [de-ay-the-say-e-say'-no, nah], *a.* Sixteenth.

Diecisieteavo, va [de-ay-the-se-ay-tay-ah'-vo, vah], *a.* Seventeenth.

Diedro, dra [de-ay'-dro, drah], *a.* Dihedral, formed by or having two plane faces, as a dihedral angle.

Diente [de-ayn'-tay], *m.* 1. Tooth. 2. Prop used by founders to secure the founding-frame. 3. Fang or tusk of wild boars. *Diente molar*, *V.* MUELA. *Diente incisivo*, Incisor, fore-tooth. 4. Jagg, a protuberance or denticulation. *Diente de lobo*, Burnisher, a burnishing or polishing instrument. 5. *Dientes de elefante*, Elephant's tusks. *Dientes de jabalí*, Wild boar's teeth. 6. *Dientes postizos*, Artificial teeth. 7. *Diente de perro*, Sampler, a piece worked by young girls. 8. *Diente de león*, (Bot.) Dandelion or lion's tooth. Leontodon taraxacum. 9. *Diente de perro*, (Bot.) Dog's-tooth violet. Erythronium.—*pl.* 1. The indented edges of different instruments, jaggs. 2. The prominent parts of wheels. *Dientes de ajo*, Cloves of garlic. *Crujir de dientes*, To grind the teeth. *Aguzar los dientes*, To whet the appetite. *Tomar a uno entre dientes*, To have an antipathy against a person. *Pelear hasta con los dientes*, (Coll.) To fight tooth and nail. *Estar a diente*, Not to have eaten while wishing it. *Estar á diente, como haca de bulero*, To be very hungry. *Primero son mis dientes que mis parientes*, Charity begins at home. *Hablar* or *decir entre dientes*, To mumble, to mutter. *Hincar el diente*, To appropriate property to one's self. (Coll.) To censure, to grumble at. *Mostrar los dientes*, To oppose a person, to growl at him, to show spunk. *No entrar—de los dientes adentro*, To have a repugnance. *A pan duro, diente agudo*, (prov.) Hunger is the best sauce.

Dientecico, illo, ito [de-en-tay-thee'-co, theel'-lyo, ee'-to], *m. dim.* Little tooth.

Diéresis [de-ay'-ray-sis], *f.* 1. (Rhet.) Diæresis, poetical figure. 2. The two points placed over a vowel to show that it does not form a diphthong with the following vowel, as in *argüir*.

Diesi [de-ay'-se], *f.* (Mus.) The smallest and simplest part into which a tone is divided.

Diestra [de-es'-trah], *f.* 1. The right hand. 2. (Met.) Favour, support, protection. *Juntar diestra con diestra*, (Obs.) To shake hands, to make up matters.

Diestramente [de-es-tran-men'-tay], *adv.* Dexterously, cleverly, neatly.

Diestro, tra [de-es'-tro, trah], *a.* 1. Right, dexter. 2. Dexterous, skilful, handy. 3. Sagacious, prudent, knowing, learned. 4. Sly, artful, cunning. 5. Favourable, propitious. *A diestro y siniestro*, Right or wrong. *De diestro a diestro*, Diamond cut diamond. *Llevar del diestro*, To lead a beast by the halter or bridle.

Diestro [de-es'-tro], *m.* 1. A skilful fencer. 2. Halter or bridle for horses.

Dieta [de-ay'-tah], *f.* 1. Diet, regimen, food regulated by the rules of medicine. 2. Diet, the assembly of the ministers of the states of Germany. 3. (Law) One day's journey of ten leagues by land. 4. Daily salary of judges and other officers of the law. *Dietas*, (Naut.) Cattle put on board a fleet, to furnish fresh provisions for the sick.

Dietética [de-ay-tay'-te-cah], *f.* Dietetics, that branch of hygiene which treats of diet.

Dietético, ca [de-ay-tay'-te-co, cah], *a.* Dietetic, dietetical.

Diéxodo [de-ek'-so-do], *m.* Every secretory passage; emunctory. Some use this term as synonymous of dejection, evacuation.

Diez [de-eth'], *m.* Ten. *Diez de bolos*, Pin standing alone in front of the nine-pins. *Diez de rosario*, One of the parts into which a rosary is divided, and a bead larger than the others, which divides one part from another.

Diezma [de-eth'-mah], *f.* (Prov.) *V.* DÉCIMA and DIEZMO.

Diezmador [de-eth-mah-dor'], *m.* (Prov.) *V.* DIEZMERO.

Diezmal [de-eth-mahl'], *a.* Decimal, tenth.

Diezmar [de-eth-mar'], *va.* 1. To decimate, to take the tenth, to tithe. 2. To tithe, to pay the tithe to the church. 3. (Mil.) When there are many offenders, to punish one in ten.

Diezmero [de-eth-may'-ro], *m.* 1. He who pays the tithe. 2. Tither, he who gathers the tithe.

Diezmesino, na [de-eth-may-see'-no, nah], *a.* That which is ten months, or belongs to that time.

Diezmo [de-eth'-mo], *m.* 1. Tithe, the tenth part. 2. Duty of ten per cent paid to the king. 3. Tithe, the tenth part of the fruits of the earth assigned to the maintenance of the clergy. 4. Decimation.

Difamación [de-fah-mah-the-on'], *f.* Defamation, libelling.

Difamador [de-fah-mah-dor'], *m.* Defamer, libeller.

Difamar [de-fah-mar'], *va.* To defame, to discredit; to libel. (Obs.) To divulge.

Difamatorio, ria [de-fah-mah-to'-re-o, ah], *a.* Defamatory, scandalous, calumnious, contumelious, libellous.

Difarreación [de-far-ray-ah-the-on'], *f.* Diffareation, the parting of a cake, a sacrifice performed between man and wife at their divorce, among the Romans.

Diferencia [de-fay-ren'-the-ah], *f.* 1. Difference. 2. Dissimilarity, dissimilitude. 3. Controversy, contrariety, mutual opposition. *Á diferencia*, With the difference.

Diferencial [de-fay-ren-the-ahl'], *a.* Differential, different. *Cálculo diferencial*, Differential calculus. —*m.* (Mech.) Differential, differential gear.—*f.* (Math.) Differential.

Diferenciar [de-fay-ren-the-ar'], *va.* 1. To differ, to make different, to differentiate. 2. To change or alter the use or destination of things.—*vn.* To differ, to dissent, to disagree in opinion.—*vr.* 1. To differ, to be distinguished from. 2. To distinguish one's self.

Diferente [de-fay-ren'-tay], *a.* Different, dissimilar, unlike.

Diferentemente [de-fay-ren-tay-men'-tay], *adv.* Differently, diversely.

Diferir [de-fay-reer'], *va.* To defer, to delay, to put off. *Diferir algo a* or *para otro tiempo*, To defer any thing to another time.—*vn.* 1. To differ, to be different. 2. (Naut.) To remove the gaskets of a sail.

Difícil [de-fee'-theel], *a.* Difficult, arduous, hard, laborious.

Difícilmente [de-fee'-theel-men-tay], *adv.* Difficultly, hardly.

Dificultad [de-fe-cool-tahd'], *f.* 1. Difficulty, embarrassment, hardness. 2. Difficulty, objection, adverse argument.

Dificultador [de-fe-cool-tah-dor'], *m.* One who starts or raises difficulties.

Dificultar [de-fe-cool-tar'], *va.* 1. To start or raise difficulties. 2. To render difficult.

Dificultosamente [de-fe-cool-to-sah-men'-tay], *adv.* Difficultly.

Dificultoso, sa [de-fe-cool-to'-so, sah], *a.* 1. Difficult, hard, troublesome, tiresome, laborious, painful. 2. Ugly, deformed: applied to the face.

Difidación [de-fe-dah-the-on'], *f.* (Obs.) Manifesto, a declaration issued in justification of a war.

Difidencia [de-fe-den'-the-ah], *f.* Distrust, doubtfulness.

Difidente [de-fe-den'-tay], *a.* Disloyal, distrustful.

(*Yo difiero, yo difiera; él difirió, él difiriera;* from *Diferir.* *V.* ASENTIR.)

Difluir [de-floo-eer'], *vn.* To be diffused, spread out; be shed.

Difracción [de-frac-the-on'], *f.* Diffraction.

Difractar [de-frac-tar'], *va.* To diffract a ray of light.

Difractivo, va [de-frac-tee'-vo, vah], *a.* Diffractive, causing diffraction.

Difrige [de-free'-hay], *m.* Dross of melted copper, gathered in the furnace.

Difteria [dif-tay'-re-ah], *f.* Diphtheria, a disease characterized by the formation of false membranes.

Diftérico, ca [dif-tay'-re-co, cah], *a.* Diphtheritic, belonging to diphtheria.

Difugio [de-foo'-he-o], *m.* *V.* EFUGIO.

Difumino [de-foo-mee'-no], *m.* *V.* ESFUMINO.

Difundido, da [de-foon-dee'-do, dah], *a.* & *pp.* of DIFUNDIR. Diffuse, diffused, scattered.

Difundir [de-foon-deer'], *va.* 1. To diffuse, to extend, to outspread. 2. (Met.) To divulge, to publish.

Difunto, ta [de-foon'-to, tah], *a.* 1. Defunct, dead; late. 2. (Met.) Decayed, withered. *Día de los difuntos*, All-souls' Day, celebrated on Nov. 2d by the Roman church. Instituted in 998. *Difunto de taberna*, In the jocular style, a drunken, red faced person.—*m.* *V.* CADÁVER.

Difusamente [de-foo-sah-men'-tay], *adv* Diffusely, diffusedly.

Difusible [de-foo-see'-blay], *a.* Diffusible, of rapid diffusion.

Difusión [de-foo-se-on'], *f.* 1. Diffusion, diffusiveness, dispersion. 2. (Met.) Diffusion, copiousness or exuberance of style.

Difusivo, va [de-foo-see'-vo, vah], *a.* Diffusive.

Difuso, sa [de-foo'-so, sah], *a.* Diffuse, diffusive, copious, ample, wide-spread.

Digástrico, ca [de-gahs'-tre-co, cah], *a.* Digastric, of two muscular bands.

Digerible [de-hay-ree'-blay], *a.* Digestible.

Digerir [de-hay-reer'], *va.* 1. To digest. 2. (Met.) To bear with patience any loss or affront. 3. (Met.) To examine carefully into a thing. 4. (Met.) To digest, to adjust, to arrange methodically in the mind. 5. (Chem.) To digest, to soften by heat, as in a boiler.

Digestible [de-hes-tee'-blay], *a.* Digestible.

Digestión [de-hes-te-on'], *f.* 1. Digestion. 2. Digestion, preparation of matter by chemical heat. *Hombre de mala digestión*, A man of a peevish, fretful temper. *Negocio de mala digestión*, A perplexed affair.

Digestivo [de-hes-tee'-vo], *m.* (Surg.) Digestive, an application which disposes a wound to generate matter.

Digestivo, va [de-hes-tee'-vo, vah], *a.* Digestive, assisting digestion.

Digesto [de-hes'-to], *m.* Digest, the pandect of the civil law, usually cited in writing by the cipher *ff.*

(*Yo digiero, yo digiera ; él digirió, él digiriera ;* from *Digerir. V.* Asentir.)

Digino, na [de-hee'-no, nah], *a.* Digynous, having two pistils.

Digitación [de-he-tah-the-on'], *f.* The art which teaches the use of the fingers upon some instrument.

Digitado, da [de-he-tah'-do, dah], *a.* Digitate, arranged like fingers. (Bot. and Zool.)

Digital [de-he-tahl'], *a.* Digital, belonging to or like fingers. *Huellas digitales*, Fingerprints.—*f.* Digitalis, foxglove, a medicinal plant.

Digitalina [de-he-tah-lee'-nah], *f.* Digitalin, a poisonous alkaloid procured from digitalis.

Digitígrado, da [de-he-tee'-grah-do, dah], *a.* Digitigrade, walking on the toes ; opposed to plantigrade.

Dígito [dee'-he-to], *m.* (Ast.) Digit, the twelfth part of the diameter of the sun or moon.

Dignación [dig-nah-the-on'], *f.* Condescension, voluntary humiliation.

Dignamente [dig-nah-men'-tay], *adv.* Worthily.

Dignarse [dig-nar'-say], *vr.* To condescend, to deign, to vouchsafe.

Dignatario [dig-nah-tah'-re-o], *m.* A dignitary, one who holds high rank, especially ecclesiastical.

Dignidad [dig-ne-dahd'], *f.* 1. Dignity, rank, honour, greatness. 2. Dignity, grandeur of mien, nobleness. 3. Dignity, advancement, high place. 4. Among ecclesiastics, the prebend of a cathedral superior to a simple canonry, and the dignitary who possesses it. 5. The dignity of an archbishop or bishop. 6. (Astrol.) Dignity, the state of a planet being in any sign.

Dignificante [dig-ne-fe-cahn'-tay], *pa.* (Theol.) Dignifying, that which dignifies.

Dignificar [dig-ne-fe-car'], *va.* To dignify.

Digno, na [deeg'-no, nah], *a.* 1. Meritorious, worthy, deserving. 2. Condign, suitable, correspondent. *Digno de alabanza*, Worthy to be praised. *Es digno*, It is worth while.

(*Yo digo, yo diga ; yo dije, yo dijera. V.* Decir.)

Digresión [de-gray-se-on'], *f.* 1. Digression, deviation from the main scope of a speech or treatise. 2. (Ast.) Departure of a planet from the equinoctial line.

Digresivamente, *adv.* Digressively.

Digresivo, va [de-gray-see'-vo, vah], *a.* Digressive.

Dije (or **Dij**) [dee'-hay], *m.* 1. A trinket put upon a child. 2. *pl.* Trinkets, relics, used for personal adornment. *Dije*, 1st pers. sing. past tense, of *decir :* I said.

Dilaceración [de-lah-thay-rah-the-on'], *f.* Dilaceration.

Dilacerar [de-lah-thay-rar'], *va.* To dilacerate, to tear.

Dilación [de-lah-the-on'], *f.* 1. Delay, dilation, procrastination. 2. (Obs.) Dilatation, expansion.

Dilapidación [de-lah-pe-dah-the-on'], *f.* Dilapidation.

Dilapidador [de-lah-pe-dah-dor'], *m.* Dilapidator.

Dilapidar [de-lah-pe-dar'], *va.* To dilapidate, to waste.

Dilatabilidad [de-lah-tah-be-le-dahd'], *f.* (Littl. us.) Dilatability.

Dilatable [de-lah-tah'-blay], *a.* Dilatable.

Dilatación [de-lah-tah-the-on'], *f.* 1. Dilatation, extension, amplification. 2. Evenness, greatness of mind, calmness.

Dilatadamente [de-lah-tah-dah-men'-tay], *adv.* With dilatation.

Dilatado, da [de-lah-tah'-do, dah], *a.* & *pp.* of Dilatar. 1. Large, numerous, great. 2. Prolix, long, not concise. 3. Spacious, extensive, vast.

Dilatador, ra [de-lah-tah-dor', rah], *m.* & *f.* 1. One who dilates or extends. 2. Dilator, an instrument for stretching.

Dilatar [de-lah-tar'], *va.* 1. To dilate, to expand, to enlarge, to lengthen, to spread out. 2. To defer, to retard, to delay, to put off, to protract. 3. (Met.) To comfort, to cheer up.—*vr.* To expatiate or enlarge on any subject.

Dilatativo, va [de-lah-tah-tee'-vo, vah], *a.* That which dilates.

Dilatoria [de-lah-to'-re-ah], *f. V.* Dilación. A term given by a court or judge to a debtor. *Andar con dilatorias*, To waste time by deceiving with false promises.

Dilatorio, ria [de-lah-to'-re-o, ah], *a.* Dilatory, delaying, long.

Dilección [de-lec-the-on'], *f.* Dilection, love, affection.

Dilecto, ta [de-lec'-to, tah], *a.* Loved, beloved.

Dilema [de-lay'-mah], *m.* Dilemma, an argument equally conclusive by contrary suppositions.

Dilemático, ca [de-lay-mah'-te-co, cah], *a.* Belonging to a dilemma, dilemmatic.

Diligencia [de-le-hen'-the-ah], *f.* 1. Diligence, assiduity, laboriousness. 2. Haste, hastiness, speed, diligence, activity, briskness in the performance of a thing. 3. (Coll.) Affair, business, something to be transacted, obligation. *Tengo que ir a una diligencia*, I must go upon some business. 4. Return of a writ, judicial formalties, procedure. *Hacer las diligencias de cristiano*, To perform the duty of a Christian. *Hacer diligencia*, To try, to endeavour. 5. Stage-coach, diligence.

Diligenciar [de-le-hen-the-ar'], *va.* To exert one's self, to endeavour.

Diligenciero [de-le-hen-the-ay'-ro], *m.* 1. Agent, attorney. 2. Apparitor, summoner ; the lowest officer of an ecclesiastical court.

Diligente [de-le-hen'-tay], *a.* 1. Diligent, assiduous, careful, laborious, active. 2. Prompt, swift, ready. *Diligente en aprender*, Diligent to learn.

Diligentemente, *adv.* Diligently, assiduously.

Dilin-dilin [de-leen'-de-leen'], *m.* The sound of a bell ; ding-dong. (Imitative.)

Dilogía [de-lo-hee'-ah], *f.* 1. Ambiguity, double sense. 2. Drama with two actions at once.

Dilucidación [de-loo-the-dah-the-on'], *f.* Elucidation, explanation, illustration.

Dilucidador [de-loo-the-dah-dor'], *m.* Elucidator.

Dilucidar [de-loo-the-dar'], *va.* To elucidate, to explain.

Dilucidario [de-loo-the-dah'-re-o], *m.* Explanatory writing.

Dilución [de-loo-the-on'], *f.* Dilution, solution.

Dilúculo [de-loo'-coo-lo], *m.* (Obs.) The last of the six parts into which the night was divided.

Diluente [de-loo-en'-tay], *pa.* Diluent.

Diluición [de-loo-e-the-on'], *f.* Dilution.

Diluir [de-loo-eer'], *va.* To dilute any thing.

Diluviano [de-loo-ve-ah'-no], *a.* Diluvian, relating to the deluge.

Diluviar [de-loo-ve-ar'], *vn. imp.* To rain like a deluge.

Diluvio [de-loo'-ve-o], *m.* 1. Deluge, overflow, inundation, flood. 2. (Met.) Vast abundance.

Dimanación [de-mah-nah-the-on'], *f.* Act of springing or issuing from, origin.

Dimanante [de-mah-nahn'-tay], *pa.* Springing or proceeding from, originating.

Dimanar [de-mah-nar'], *vn.* To spring or proceed from ; to originate, to flow. *Dimanar de*, To originate from.

Dimensión [de-men-se-on'], *f.* 1. Dimension, extent, capacity, bulk. 2. (Mus.) Compass, range. 3. (Mat.) Either of the three geometrical properties, length, breadth, and depth. 4. Power, or grade of an equation. 5. Quantity which enters as a factor of an algebraic expression.

Dimensional [de-men-se-o-nahl'], *a.* Belonging to the dimension.

Dimes [dee'-mes]. *Andar en dimes y diretes*, To use *ifs* and *ands*, or quibbles and quirks ; to contend, to use altercations.

Dimidiar [de-me-de-ar'], *va.* To dimidiate, to divide into halves. *V.* Demediar.

Diminución [de-me-noo-the-on'], *f.* 1. Diminution, losing ; exhaustion. 2. Contraction of the diameter of a column as it ascends. *Ir en diminución*, 1. To grow tapering to the top. 2. (Met.) To be losing one's character or credit.

Diminuir [de-me-noo-eer'], *va.* To diminish. *V.* Disminuir.

Diminutamente, *adv.* 1. Diminutively. 2. Minutely, by retail.

Diminutivamente, *adv.* (Gram.) Diminutively.

Diminutivo, va [de-me-noo-tee'-vo, vah], *a.* Diminutive.—*m.* A noun which decreases the meaning of the primitive.

Diminuto, ta [de-me-noo'-to, tah], *a.* Defective, faulty, diminute.

Dimisión [de-me-se-on'], *f.* Resignation, the act of resigning a place, employment, or commission. *Hacer dimisión de su empleo*, To resign one's place or employment.

Dimisorias [de-me-so'-re-as], *f. pl.* Dimissory letters, given by the bishop to a candidate for holy orders, that he may be lawfully ordained. *Dar dimisorias*, (Coll.) To dismiss any one, driving him away ungraciously. *Llevar dimisorias*, To get dismissed, packed off.

Dimite [dee'-me-tay], *m.* Dimity. *V.* Cotonía.

Dimitir [de-me-teer'], *va.* To give up, to relinquish, to resign, to abdicate.

Dimoño [de-mo'-nyo], *m.* (Coll.) Demon. *V.* Demonio.

Dimorfismo [de-mor-fees'-mo], *m.* Dimorphism, two different crystallizations.

Dina [dee'-nah], *f.* (Phy.) Dyne.

Dinamarques, sa [de-nah-mar-kes', sah], *a.* Dane, Danish.

Dinamia [de-nah'-me-ah], *f.* 1. Dynam,

a foot-pound; a unit of effective force. 2. (Med.) Dynamia, vigour, robustness.
Dinámica [de-nah'-me-cah], *f.* Dynamics, the science of moving powers.
Dinámico, ca [de-nah'-me-co, cah], *a.* Dynamic.
Dinamita [de-nah-mee'-tah], *f.* Dynamite; nitro-glycerine combined with inert matter, a terrific explosive.
Dinamo [de-nah'-mo], *m.* A dynamo-electric machine; a dynamo.
Dinamómetro [de-nah-mo'-me-tro], *m.* Dynamometer, an instrument for measuring force exerted or power expended.
Dinastía [de-nas-tee'-ah], *f.* Dynasty, sovereignty, race or family of rulers; time of their rule.
Dinerada [de-nay-rah'-dah], *f.* (Coll.) A large sum of money.
Dineral [de-nay-rahl'], *m.* 1. A large sum of money. 2. Weight used by assayers to fix the purity of the precious metals; a gold *dineral* is divided into 24 *quilates* or carats, each of which is 4 grains; a silver *dineral* is divided into 12 *dineros* of 24 grains each.
Dinerillo [de-nay-reel'-lyo], *m.* 1. (Coll.) A round sum of money. 2. A small copper coin, current in Arragon.
Dinero [de-nay'-ro], *m.* 1. Coin, money, gold, coinage. 2. An ancient Spanish copper coin. 3. Standard of silver, the twelfth of a dineral; pennyweight. *Dinero llama dinero*, Money gets money. *Tener dinero*, To be rich. *A dinero, al dinero, a dinero seco*, or *a dinero contante*, In ready money, in cash. *Por el dinero baila* or *salta el perro*, (prov.) Money makes the mare go.
Dineroso, sa [de-nay-ro'-so, sah], *a.* (Obs.) Moneyed, rich.
Dineruelo [de-nay-roo-ay'-lo], *m. dim.* Small coin.
Dinosaurio, or **Dinosauro** [de-no-sah'-oo-re-o], *m.* Dinosaur, a fossil reptile of enormous size.
Dinoterio [de-no-tay'-re-o], *m.* Dinotherium, a gigantic mammal of the miocene epoch.
Dintel [din-tel'], *m.* Lintel, part of a door-frame.
Dintelar [din-tay-lar'], *va.* To make lintels.
Dintorno [din-tor'-no], *m.* (Art) Delineation of the parts of a figure contained within the contour.
Diocesano, na [de-o-thay-sah'-no, nah], *a.* Diocesan.
Diocesano [de-o-thay-sah'-no], *m.* Diocesan, a bishop as he stands related to his own clergy or flock.
Diócesi, Diócesis [de-o'-thay-se, de-o'-thay-sis], *f.* Diocese, the circuit of a bishop's jurisdiction.
Diodón [de-o-don'], *m.* Sea-urchin.
Dióico, ca [de-o'-e-co, cah], *a.* 1. Diœcious, plants whose reproductive organs are borne upon different individuals. 2. Similarly applied to cephalopod mollusks.
Dionea [de-o'-nay-ah], *f.* Dioæna, the Venus's fly-trap of North Carolina.
Dionisia [de-o-nee'-se-ah], *f.* Blood stone, a black stone, variegated with red spots; hematites.
Dióptrica [de-op'-tre-cah], *f.* Dioptrics.
Dióptrico, ca [de-op'-tre-co, cah], *a* Dioptric.
Diorama [de-o-rah'-mah], *m.* Diorama, an optical contrivance consisting of a series of views placed vertically, in which by means of arranged lights objects are seen of natural size and distance without lenses.
Diorámico, ca [de-o-rah'-me-co, cah], *a.* Dioramic, relating to a diorama.
Diorita [de-o-ree'-tah], *f.* Diorite, a crystalline plutonic rock, very esteemed by the ancient Egyptians.
Dios [de-os'], *m.* 1. God, the Supreme Being. 2. God, a false god, an idol. 3. (Met.) God, any person or thing passionately beloved or adored. *A Dios* or *anda con Dios*, Farewell, adieu. *A Dios y a ventura*, At all events, at all risks. *Después de Dios*, Under God. *Vaya Vd. con Dios*, Farewell, God be with you. *Dios dará*, God will provide: used to stimulate alms-giving. *Oh, santo Dios*, Oh, gracious God. *Por Dios*, For God's sake. *No lo quiera Dios*, God forbid. *Quiera Dios* or *plegue a Dios*, Please God. *Sea como Dios quiera*, God's will be done. *A quien Dios quiere bien, uvas le da el laurel*, (prov.) Where God's blessing dwells, prosperity follows (The laurel brings forth grapes to the man whom God loves). *Cuando Dios amanece, para todos aparece*, The sun shines on the just and on the unjust. *Da Dios almendras al que no tiene muelas*, or *Da Dios habas a quien no tiene quijadas*, Prosperity sometimes comes too late for enjoyment. *Da Dios alas a la hormiga para morir mas aína*, Blessings when perverted become curses. *De menos nos hizo Dios*, To imply hope of obtaining an end, though the means seem disproportionate. *Dios los cría y ellos se juntan*, Birds of a feather flock together. *Dios lo quiera* or *lo haga*, God grant. *Irse mucho con Dios*, To go off angrily. *No es Dios viejo*, To indicate a hope of obtaining in the future what was once not obtained. *Ser por alabar a Dios*, To be admirable for its perfection, abundance, etc. *Mediante Dios*, God willing. *¡ Válgame Dios!* Bless me! *¡ Válgate Dios!* God preserve you or bless you. *Que de Dios haya*, To whom may God be merciful: an imprecation in favour of the dead.
Diosa [de-o'-sah], *f.* Goddess.
Diosecillo, Diosecito [de-o-say-theel'-lyo, de-o-say-thee'-to], *m. dim.* A godling, a little divinity.
Diosecita [de-o-say-thee'-tah], *f. dim.* A little goddess.
Diostedé [de-os-tay-day'], *m.* (Amer.) A bird of the toucan family whose note sounds like *¡ Dios te dé!* It abounds in Venezuela, Peru, etc.
Dióxido (or **bióxido**) **de carbono** [de-oc'-se-do, be-oc'-se-do day car-bo'-no], *m.* Carbon dioxide.
Dipétalo, la [de-pay'-tah-lo, lah], *a.* Dipetalous, having two petals.
Diplaco [de-plah'-co], *m.* A scrophulariaceous plant from California, highly esteemed in the gardens of Europe for the beauty of its flowers.
Diplejia espástica [de-play'-he-ah es-pahs'-te-ca], *f.* Cerebral palsy.
Diploe [de-plo'-ay], *m.* Diploe.
Diploma [de-plo'-mah], *m.* 1. Diploma, patent, license. 2. (Chem.) A double-walled vessel in which water is put, and can replace the water-bath.
Diplomacia [de-plo-mah'-the-ah], *f.* 1. Diplomacy, the management of international relations. 2. (Coll.) Simulated and interested courtesy.
Diplomarse [de-plo-mar'-say], *vr.* To graduate, to obtain a diploma.
Diplomática [de-plo-mah'-te-cah], *f.* Diplomatics, the science of diplomas, or of ancient writings, literary and public documents, etc., especially concerned with their authenticity.
Diplomático, ca [de-plo-mah'-te-co, cah], *a.* 1. Diplomatic, relating to diplomas. 2. Diplomatical: applied to negotiations in politics, and to the ambassadors or envoys.—*m.* 3. Diplomatist.
Diplónomo, ma [de-plo'-no-mo, mah], *a.* Obeying two laws simultaneously.
Diplóstomo [de-plos'-to-mo], *m.* A worm found in the eyes of certain fishes, but more often among the whales.
Dipneo, nea, Dipneumóneo, nea [deep'-nay-o, ah, dip-nay-oo-mo'-nay-o, ah], *a.* Having two lungs.
Dípodo, da [dee'-po-do, dah], *a.* Dipodous, biped, having two (hind) feet.
Diprósopo, pa [de-pro'-so-po, pah], *a.* A term applied to fishes having both eyes on the same side.
Dipsaca [dip-sah'-cah], *f.* (Bot.) Teasel. *V.* CONDENCHA.
Dipsas [deep'-sas], *m.* Serpent whose bite is said to produce great thirst.
Díptero, ra [deep'-tay-ro, rah], *a.* 1. (Arch.) Having two wings, or a double colonnade. 2. (Entom.) Dipterous, two-winged.—*m. pl.* The diptera, two-winged insects, embracing the host of flies, mosquitoes, midges, etc.
Dipterólogo [dip-tay-ro'-lo-go], *m.* Dipterologist, a naturalist who devotes himself to the study of the diptera.
Díptica [deep'-te-cah], *f.* Diptych, a register of bishops and martyrs.
Díptico [deep'-te-co], *m.* *V.* DÍPTICA.
Diptongar [dip-ton-gar'], *va.* 1. To unite two vowels. 2. (Met.) To combine two or more things so as to form one whole.
Diptongo [dip-ton'-go], *m.* Diphthong.
Diputación [de-poo-tah-the-on'], *f.* 1. Deputation, the act of deputing on a special commission. 2. Deputation, the body of persons deputed; committee. 3. The object of a deputation.
Diputado [de-poo-tah'-do], *m.* 1. Deputy, one appointed or elected to act for another; a representative, delegate. 2. (Com.) Assignee.—*Diputado, da, pp.* of DIPUTAR.
Diputar [de-poo-tar'], *va.* 1. To depute, to commission; to constitute. 2. To depute, to empower one to act for another.
Dique [dee'-kay], *m.* 1. Dike, dam. 2. Dock. *Dique de carena* or *dique seco*, Dry dock.
Dirección [de-rec-the-on'], *f.* 1. Direction, guiding or directing; tendency of motion. 2. Guidance, direction, government, administration. 3. Direction, order, command, prescription. 4. The board of directors appointed to supervise the management of some business or organization. *De dos direcciones*, Two-way.
Directamente [de-rec-tah-men'-tay], *adv.* Directly, rectilineally. *Directe o indirecte*, (Lat.) Directly or indirectly.
Directiva [de-rec-tee'-vah], *f.* 1. Governing body; management. 2. Directive.
Directivo, va [de-rec-tee'-vo, vah], *a.* Managing, governing.
Directo, ta [de-rec'-to, tah], *a.* 1. Direct, in a straight line, nonstop. 2. Clear, open, apparent, evident.
Director [de-rec-tor'], *m.* 1. Director, one that has authority over others. 2. Conductor, controller, guide, coryphеus. 3. President in some institutions for public business. 4. Director, manager, one who has the management of the concerns of a trading company. 5. Overruler or overseer. *Director* or *director espiritual*, Confessor, who guides the conscience of a person.

Directora [de-rec-to'-rah], *f.* 1. Directress, governess. 2. (Geom.) Directrix, a line determining the motion of another line or point in order to produce a definite curve or surface.
Directorial [de-rec-to-re-ahl'], *a.* Relating to a directory.
Directorio, ria [de-rec-to'-re-o, ah], *a.* Directive, directorial.
Directorio [de-rec-to'-re-o], *m.* 1. Directory, a book which serves as a guide in certain sciences or business matters. 2. The governing body of five men organized in the fourth year of the French republic, Oct., 1795. 3. (Com.) A body of directors, directorate.
Dirigible [de-re-hee'-blay], *m.* Dirigible.—*a.* Pliable, manageable, easily directed.
Dirigir [de-re-heer'], *va.* 1. To direct, to aim, to lead or to drive in a straight line; to level. 2. To guide, to direct, to conduct. 3. To dedicate a work. 4. To direct, to regulate, to head, to govern, to give rules or laws for the management of any thing. 5. *Dirigir el rumbo*, (Naut.) To steer.—*vr.* 6. To address, to apply, to resort to.
Dirimente [de-re-men'-tay], *pa.* Breaking off, dissolving.
Dirimir [de-re-meer'], *va.* 1. To dissolve, to disjoin, to separate. 2. To adjust or accommodate differences. 3. To annul, to declare void.
Dirradiación [dir-rah-de-ah-the-on'], *f.* Radiation of the light proceeding from a body.
Dirradiar [dir-rah-de-ar'], *va.* To radiate, to scatter luminous rays.
Dirruir [dir-roo-eer'], *va.* To ruin, to destroy. *V.* Derruir.
Dis [dees], *prep.* From the Latin, changed often into **Des**; it is used only in compound words; it has the meaning of the English prefixes **Dis** and **Un**, and implies separation, division, but commonly privation or negation; as, *armar*, to arm; *desarmar*, to disarm; *atar*, to tie; *desatar*, to untie; *gusto*, pleasure; *disgusto*, displeasure.
Disafia [de-sah'-fe-ah], *f.* (Med.) Alteration of the sense of touch.
Disanto [de-sahn'-to], *m.* A holy day. (Acad. fr. *día santo.*)
Discantar [dis-can-tar'], *va.* 1. To chant, to sing. 2. To compose or recite verses. 3. To descant, to discourse copiously. 4. To quaver upon a note.
Discante [dis-cahn'-tay], *m.* 1. Treble. *V.* Tiple. 2. Concert, especially of stringed instruments. 3. A small guitar.
Discataposis [dis-cah-tah-po'-sis], *f.* (Med.) Dysphagia, difficulty in swallowing.
Disceptación [dis-thep-tah-the-on'], *f.* Argument, controversy, dispute.
Disceptar [dis-thep-tar'], *va.* To dispute, to argue.
Discernidor [dis-ther-ne-dor'], *m.* Discerner.
Discernimiento [dis-ther-ne-me-en'-to], *m.* 1. Discernment, judgment. 2. Choice, the power of distinguishing. 3. Appointment of a guardian by the proper magistrates.
Discernir [dis-ther-neer'], *va.* 1. To discern, to distinguish, to comprehend, to judge, to know. 2. To appoint a guardian.
Disciforme [dis-the-for'-may], *a.* Disciform, having the shape of a disk.
Discinesia [dis-the-nay'-se-ah], *f.* (Med.) Paralysis of voluntary movements.
Disciplina [dis-the-plee'-nah], *f.* 1. Discipline, education, instruction. 2. Discipline, any art or science taught. 3. Discipline, rule of conduct, order. 4. Correction or punishment inflicted upon one's self. *Disciplinas*, Scourge, a cat-of-nine-tails. 5. Flagellation.
Disciplinable [dis-the-ple-nah'-blay], *a.* Disciplinable, capable of instruction.
Discpilinadamente, *adv.* With discipline.
Disciplinado, da [dis-the-ple-nah'-do, dah], *a.* Marbled, variegated.—*pp.* of Disciplinar.
Disciplinal [dis-the-ple-nahl'], *a.* Relative to discipline, disciplinal.
Disciplinante [dis-the-ple-nahn'-tay], *pa.* Flagellator.
Disciplinar [dis-the-ple-nar'], *va.* 1. To discipline, to educate, to instruct, to bring up. 2. To drill, to teach the manual exercise or the military regulations. 3. To chastise, to correct.—*vr.* To scourge one's self as penance.
Disciplinario, ria [dis-the-ple-nah'-re-o, ah], *a.* Disciplinary, belonging to discipline.
Discipulado [dis-the-poo-lah'-do], *m.* 1. Number of scholars who frequent the same school. 2. Education, instruction.
Discípulo, la [dis-thee'-poo-lo, lah], *m.* & *f.* Disciple, scholar, learner, follower.
Disco [dees'-co], *m.* 1. Disk, a round piece of iron thrown in the ancient sports; a quoit. 2. Face of the sun or moon, as it appears to the eye. 3. A plate of glass, of circular form, which serves for an electric machine, etc. 4. A cylinder whose base is very large as compared with its height: as an unground telescope lens. 5. A railway signal-disk, semaphore.
Discóbolo [dis-co'-bo-lo], *m.* Discus thrower.
Díscolo, la [dees'-co-lo, lah], *a.* Ungovernable; wayward, peevish, froward.
Discontinuar [dis-con-te-noo-ar'], *va.* *V.* Descontinuar.
Discontinuo, a [dis-con-tee'-noo-o, ah], *a.* Discontinued.
Disconveniencia [dis-con-vay-ne-en'-the-ah], *f.* Discord, disunion.
Disconveniente [dis-con-vay-ne-en'-tay], *a.* *V.* Desconveniente.
Discordancia [dis-cor-dahn'-the-ah], *f.* Disagreement, contrariety of opinion; discordance.
Discordante [dis-cor-dahn'-tay], *pa.* & *a.* Dissonant, discordant.
Discordar [dis-cor-dar'], *vn.* To discord, to disagree.
Discorde [dis-cor'-day], *a.* 1. Discordant, contrary, not conformable. 2. (Mus.) Dissonant.
Discordia [dis-cor'-de-ah], *f.* 1. Discord, disagreement, misintelligence. 2. Contrariety of opinion, opposition.
Discoteca [dis-co-tay'-cah], *f.* 1. Record library. 2. Record store. 3. Discotheque.
Discrasia [dis-crah'-se-ah], *f.* (Med.) Dyscrasia, ill-health due to constitutional disease; general bad health.
Discreción [dis-cray-the-on'], *f.* 1. Discretion, prudence, judgment. 2. Acuteness of mind, sharpness of wit, liveliness of fancy. 3. Discretion, liberty of acting at pleasure. *Jugar discreciones*, To play for presents, to be chosen or determined by the loser. *A discreción*, 1. At the discretion or will of another. 2. According to one's own will or fancy.
Discrecional [dis-cray-the-o-nahl'], *a.* Discretional, discretionary.
Discrepancia [dis-cray-pahn'-the-ah], *f.* Discrepancy, difference, contrariety.
Discrepante [dis-cray-pahn'-tay], *pa.* Disagreeing, discrepant. *Nemine discrepante*, Nem. con. (*Nemine contradicente*), Unanimously.
Discrepar [dis-cray-par'], *vn.* To differ, to disagree.
Discretamente [dis-cray-tah-men'-tay], *adv.* Discreetly.
Discretear [dis-cray-tay-ar'], *vn.* To be discreet, to talk with discretion: used ironically.
Discreto, ta [dis-cray'-to, tah], *a.* 1. Discreet, circumspect, considerate, prudent. 2. Ingenious, sharp, witty, eloquent. 3. Discrete, distinct, separate; as, *Viruelas discretas*, Discrete small-pox. *Es más delicado que discreto*, He is more nice than wise.
Discreto, ta [dis-cray'-to, tah], *m.* & *f.* A person elected assistant in the council of some religious houses.
Discretorio [dis-cray-to'-re-o], *m.* Meeting or council of the seniors of religious bodies.
Discriminación [dis-cre-me-nah-the-on'], *f.* Discrimination.
Discriminar [dis-cre-me-nar'], *va.* To discriminate.
Disculpa [dis-cool'-pah], *f.* 1. Apology, excuse, exculpation. 2. (Law) Plea.
Disculpabilidad [dis-cool-pah-be-le-dahd'], *f.* Excusability, palliation, pardonableness.
Disculpable [dis-cool-pah'-blay], *a.* Excusable, pardonable.
Disculpablemente, *adv.* Pardonably, excusably.
Disculpadamente, *adv.* Excusably.
Disculpar [dis-cool-par'], *va.* To exculpate, to excuse, to palliate.
Discurrimiento [dis-coor-re-me-en'-to], *m.* (Obs.) Discourse.
Discurrir [dis-coor-reer'], *vn.* 1. To gad, to ramble about, to run to and fro. 2. To discourse upon a subject. 3. To discuss. *¿Quién tal discurriera?* Who could imagine such a thing?—*va.* 1. To invent, to plan, to contrive, to consult, to meditate, to scheme. 2. To discourse, to infer, to deduce.
Discursar [dis-coor-sar'], *vn.* To discourse, to treat upon, to converse.
Discursista [dis-coor-sees'-tah], *m.* One who discusses a subject.
Discursivo, va [dis-coor-see'-vo, vah], *a.* Discursive, reflective; cogitative.
Discurso [dis-coor'-so], *m.* 1. Discourse. 2. Ratiocination, reasoning. 3. Discourse, conversation. 4. Discourse, dissertation, treatise, tract. 5. Space of time. 6. Ramble.
Discusión [dis-coo-se-on'], *f.* Discussion, argument, dispute.
Discusivo, va [dis-coo-see'-vo, vah], *a.* (Med.) Resolvent.
Discutible [dis-coo-tee'-blay], *a.* Susceptible of discussion or examination; controvertible.
Discutidor, ra [dis-coo-te-dor', rah], *m.* & *f.* Prone to discuss, fond of disputing.
Discutir [dis-coo-teer'], *va.* To discuss, to investigate, to examine.
Disecación [de-say-cah-the-on'], *f.* Dissection, anatomy.
Disecador [de-say-cah-dor'], *m.* Dissector, anatomist.
Disecar [de-say-car'], *va.* 1. To dissect, as animal bodies. 2. To make an autopsy for study. 3. To preserve dead animals with the appearance of life. 4. (Met.) To analyze minutely; to criticise.
Disecativo, va [de-say-cah-tee'-vo, vah], *a.* Desiccative, desiccant, drying.
Disección [de-sec-the-on'], *f.* Dissection, anatomy.
Disector [de-sec-tor'], *m.* Dissector, anatomist.

Diseminable [de-say-me-nah'-blay], *a.* Disseminable, capable of being spread or propagated.

Diseminación [de-say-me-nah-the-on'], *f.* Dissemination, publishing; scattering of ripe seeds.

Diseminador, ra [de-say-me-nah-dor, rah], *m.* & *f.* Disseminator, spreader.

Diseminar [de-say-me-nar'], *va.* To disseminate, to propagate.

Disensión [de-sen-se-on'], *f.* 1. Dissension, misunderstanding, contention, contest, strife. 2. The cause or motive of dissension.

Disenso [de-sen'-so], *m.* Dissent, disagreement.

Disentería [de-sen-tay-ree'-ah], *f.* Dysentery, a disease.

Disentérico, ca [de-sen-tay'-re-co, cah], *a.* Belonging to dysentery.

Disentimiento [de-sen-te-me-en'-to], *m.* Dissent, disagreement, declaration of difference of opinion.

Disentir [de-sen-teer'], *vn.* To dissent, to disagree, or to differ in opinion.

Diseñador [de-say-nyah-dor'], *m.* Designer, delineator.

Diseñar [de-say-nyar'], *va.* To draw, to design.

Diseño [de-say'-nyo], *m.* 1. Design, sketch, draft, plan. 2. Delineation, description. 3. Picture, image. *V.* Designio. 4. Pattern, model.

Disépalo, la [de-say'-pah-lo, lah], *a.* Having two sepals.

Disepimento [de-say-pe-men'-to], *m.* Dissepiment, a partition of a compound ovary.

Disertación [de-ser-tah-the-on'], *f.* Dissertation, a discourse, a disquisition, discussion.

Disertador [de-ser-tah-dor'], *m.* Dissertator, debater.

Disertar [de-ser-tar'], *va.* To dispute, to debate, to argue.

Diserto, ta [de-serr'-to, tah], *a.* (Littl. us.) Eloquent.

Disestesia [dis-es-tay'-se-ah], *f.* Dysæsthesia, numbness, loss of sensation.

Disfagia [dis-fah'-he-ah], *f.* Dysphagia, difficulty in swallowing.

Disfamación [dis-fah-mah-the-on'], *f.* Defamation, slander; censure.

Disfamador, ra [dis-fah-mah-dor', rah], *m.* & *f.* Defamer, detractor, slanderer.

Disfamar [dis-fah-mar'], *va.* 1. To defame, to slander. 2. To discredit.

Disfamatorio, ria [dis-fah-mah-to'-re-o, ah], *a.* Defamatory, calumnious, libellous.

Disfavor [dis-fah-vor'], *m.* 1. Disregard, want of favour. 2. Discountenance, cold treatment.

Disfonía [dis-fo-nee'-ah], *f.* (Med.) Sensible alteration of the voice and speech, dysphonia.

Disformar [dis-for-mar'], *va.* *V.* Deformar and Afear.

Disforme [dis-for'-may], *a.* 1. Deformed, ugly, monstrous, formless. 2. Huge, big.

Disformidad [dis-for-me-dahd'], *f.* Deformity, excessive bigness.

Disfraz [dis-frath'], *m.* 1. Mask, disguise. 2. (Met.) Dissimulation, dissembling.

Disfrazar [dis-frah-thar'], *va.* 1. To disguise, to conceal. 2. To cloak, to dissemble, to cover; to misrepresent. —*vr.* 1. To masquerade, to go in disguise. 2. To feign.

Disfrutar [dis-froo-tar'], *va.* 1. To gain fruit or advantage; to gather the fruit or products. 2. To enjoy, reap benefit from a thing, without caring for its preservation or betterment. 3. To enjoy health, convenience. 4. To avail one's self of, to profit by, the favour, friendship, or protection of some one.

Disfrute [des-froo'-tay], *m.* Use, enjoyment.

Disgregable [dis-gray-gah'-blay], *a.* Separable, segregable.

Disgregación [dis-gray-gah-the-on'], *f.* 1. Separation, disjunction. 2. Dispersion of light-rays.

Disgregar [dis-gray-gar'], *va.* 1. To separate, to disjoin. 2. To disperse the rays of light.

Disgregativo, va [dis-gray-gah-tee'-vo, vah], *a.* Disjunctive.

Disgustadamente, *adv.* Disgustingly.

Disgustar [dis-goos-tar'], *va.* 1. To disgust, to distaste, to disrelish. 2. To disgust, to strike with dislike, to offend.—*vr.* 1. To be displeased, to fall out, to be at variance with another. 2. To get tired, fatigued, to be bored.

Disgustillo [dis-goos-teel'-lyo], *m. dim.* Displeasure, slight disgust.

Disgusto [dis-goos'-to], *m.* 1. Disgust, aversion of the palate, loathing. 2. Ill-humour; offence conceived. 3. Grief, sorrow. *A disgusto,* In spite of, contrary to one's will and pleasure.

Dishérpilo, la [dis-err'-pe-lo, lah], *a.* (Zool.) Creeping slowly and with difficulty.

Disidencia [de-se-den'-the-ah], *f.* Dissidence, nonconformity.

Disidente [de-se-den'-tay], *a.* & *m.* & *f.* Dissident, dissenter, nonconformist, schismatic.

Disidio [de-see'-de-o], *m.* (Poet.) Discord.

Disidir [de-se-deer'], *vn.* 1. To dissent, to separate from a (religious) belief before held. 2. To be of a distinct opinion, especially in matters of belief.

Disilábico, ca [de-se-lah'-be-co, cah], *a.* Dissyllabic, of two syllables. So, too, **Disílabo, ba.**

Disílabo [de-see'-lah-bo], *m.* Dissyllable.

Disímil [de-see'-mil], *a.* Dissimilar.

Disimilar [de-se-me-lar'], *a.* Unequal, dissimilar.

Disimilitud [de-se-me-le-tood'], *f.* Dissimilitude.

Disimulable [de-se-moo-lah'-blay], *a.* What may be dissembled or feigned.

Disimulación [de-se-moo-lah-the-on'], *f.* 1. Dissimulation, the act of dissembling; simulation, hypocrisy, mask, feint. 2. Reserve, reservedness.

Disimuladamente [de-se-moo-lah-dah-men'-tay], *adv.* Dissemblingly; reservedly.

Disimulado, da [de-se-moo-lah'-do, dah], *a.* 1. Dissembling. 2. Reserved, sullen, not open, not frank. 3. Dissembled, sly, cunning.—*pp.* of Disimular. *A lo disimulado,* Dissemblingly; reservedly. *Hacer la disimulada,* To feign ignorance.

Disimulador, ra [de-se-moo-lah-dor', rah], *m.* & *f.* Dissembler.

Disimular [de-see-moo-lar'], *va.* 1. To dissemble, to conceal one's real intentions. 2. To cloak, to conceal artfully any bent of the mind. 3. To hide. 4. To tolerate, to allow so as not to hinder, to overlook, to let pass. 5. To colour, to misrepresent.

Disimulo [de-se-moo'-lo], *m.* 1. Dissimulation, reservedness. *V.* Disimulación. 2. Tolerance.

Disipable [de-se-pah'-blay], *a.* Dissipable, easily scattered, easily dissipated.

Disipación [de-se-pah-the-on'], *f.* 1. Separation of the parts which composed a whole. 2. Resolution of any thing into vapour. 3. Dissolute living. 4. Dissipation, the act of spending one's fortune; licentiousness, extravagance, waste.

Disipado, da [de-se-pah'-do, dah], *a.* 1. Dissipated, devoted to pleasure. 2. Prodigal, lavisher. 3. Licentious, dissolute.—*pp.* of Disipar.

Disipador, ra [de-se-pah-dor', rah], *m.* & *f.* Spendthrift, a prodigal, a lavisher.

Disipar [de-se-par'], *va.* 1. To dissipate, to disperse, to scatter. 2. To misspend, to lavish. 3. To drive away, put to flight.

Disjunto, ta [dis-hoon'-to, tah], *a.* (Mus.) Disjoined, not followed but separated by another interval.

Dislaceración, *f.* *V.* Dilaceración.

Dislacerar [dis-lah-thay-rar'], *va.* To lacerate, violently divide tissues.

Dislate [dis-lah'-tay], *m.* Nonsense, absurdity. *V.* Disparate.

Dislocación, Dislocadura [dis-lo-ca-the-on', dis-lo-ca-doo'-rah], *f.* 1. Dislocation. 2. Dislocation, a luxation, a joint put out. 3. Separation of the different parts which form a machine.

Dislocar [dis-lo-car'], *va.* To dislocate, to displace; to luxate, to disjoint.—*vr.* To be dislocated, to come asunder.

Dismembración, *f.* *V.* Desmembración.

Dismenia [dis-may'-ne-ah], *f.* *V.* Dismenorrea.

Dismenorrea [dis-may-nor-ray'-ah], *f.* Dysmenorrhœa, painful menstruation.

Disminución [dis-me-noo-the-on'], *f.* 1. *V.* Diminución. 2. Disease in horses' hoofs.

Disminuir [dis-me-noo-eer'], *va.* 1. To diminish, to lessen, to lower, to abridge, to cut short. 2. To detract from.—*vr.* To lessen, to lower, to grow less.

Disnea [dis-nay'-ah], *f.* Dyspnœa, difficulty in respiration. (Acad.)

Disociación [de-so-the-ah-the-on'], *f.* Disjunction, separation.

Disociar [de-so-the-ar'], *va.* To dis join, to separate things.

Disodila [de-so-dee'-lah], *f.* (Min.) A papyraceous coal, kind of bituminous earth in plates, found in Sicily.

Disolubilidad [de-so-loo-be-le-dahd'], *f.* (Littl. us.) Dissolubility.

Disoluble [de-so-loo'-blay], *a.* Dissol uble.

Disolución [de-so-loo-the-on'], *f.* 1. Dissolution, the resolution of a body into its constituent elements. 2. Dissoluteness, dissipation, libertinism, lewdness, licentiousness.

Disolutamente [de-so-loo-tah-men'-tay] *adv.* Dissolutely, licentiously.

Disolutivo, va [de-so-loo-tee'-vo, vah], *a* Dissolvent, solvent.

Disoluto, ta [de-so-loo'-to, tah], *a.* Dis solute, loose, licentious, lewd, libidinous, libertine.

Disolvente [de-sol-ven'-tay], *m.* Dissolvent, dissolver.

Disolver [de-sol-verr'], *va.* 1. To loosen, to untie. 2. To dissolve, to separate, to disunite. 3. To melt, to liquefy. 4. To interrupt.—*vr.* To dissolve, to be melted.

Disoma [de-so'-mah], *f.* An arseno sulphide of nickel; grey nickel.

Disón [de-sone'], *m.* (Mus.) Harsh, dissonant tone; discord.

Disonancia [de-so-nahn'-the-ah], *f.* 1. Dissonance. 2. Disagreement, discord. *Hacer disonancia a la razón,* To be contrary to reason.

Disonante [de-so-nahn'-tay], *a.* 1. Dissonant, inharmonious, discrepant. 2. (Met.) Discordant, unsuitable.

Disonar [de-so-nar'], *vn.* 1. To disagree in sound, to be disharmonious.

2. To discord, to disagree. 3. To be contrary or repugnant.

Disono, na [dee'-so-no, nah], *a.* Dissonant, inconstant.

Dispar [dis-par'], *a.* Unlike, unequal.

Disparadamente, *adv. V.* DISPARATADAMENTE.

Disparador [dis-pa-rah-dor'], *m.* 1. Shooter. 2. Trigger of a gun-lock. 3. Ratch, ratchet, or ratchet-wheel, in clock-work. 4. (Naut.) Anchor-tripper. 5. A machine like a musket for setting off rockets.

Disparar [dis-pa-rar'], *va.* & *vn.* 1. To shoot, to discharge a thing with violence. 2. To fire, to discharge firearms; to let off. 3. To cast or throw with violence. 4. (Coll.) To talk nonsense, to blunder.—*vr.* 1. To run headlong. 2. To stoop, to dart down on prey: applied to a hawk or falcon. 3. To run away, disobeying the bridle: said of a riding-horse. 4. (Naut.) To turn violently: said of the capstan. 5. To get loose from the tiller ropes: said of the tiller.

Disparatadamente, *adv.* Absurdly, nonsensically.

Disparatado, da [dis-pa-rah-tah'-do, dah], *a.* Inconsistent, absurd, extravagant, silly, foolish.—*pp.* of DISPARATAR.

Disparatar [dis-pa-rah-tar'], *va.* 1. To act or talk in an absurd and inconsistent manner. 2. To blunder, to talk nonsense.

Disparate [dis-pa-rah'-tay], *m.* Nonsense, blunder, absurdity, extravagance.

Disparatón [dis-pa-rah-tone'], *m. aug.* A great piece of nonsense, a very great blunder.

Disparatorio [dis-pa-rah-to'-re-o], *m.* Speech or discourse full of nonsense.

Disparidad [dis-pa-re-dahd'], *f.* Disparity, inequality, dissimilitude.

Disparo [dis-pah'-ro], *m.* 1. Discharge, explosion. 2. Nonsense, absurdity.

Dispendio [dis-pen'-de-o], *m.* 1. Excessive or extravagant expense. 2. (Met.) Voluntary loss of life, honour, or fame.

Dispendioso, sa [dis-pen-de-o'-so, sah], *a.* Costly, expensive.

Dispensa [dis-pen'-sah], *f.* 1. Dispense, exemption, dispensation. 2. Diploma granting a dispensation.

Dispensable [dis-pen-sah'-blay], *a.* Dispensable.

Dispensación [dis-pen-sah-the-on'], *f.* 1. Dispensation, exemption. 2. *V.* DISPENSA.

Dispensador, ra [dis-pen-sah-dor', rah], *m.* & *f.* 1. One who grants a dispensation. 2. Dispenser, distributor.

Dispensar [dis-pen-sar'], *va.* 1. To dispense, to exempt, to absolve or set free from an engagement. 2. (Coll.) To excuse, to dispense with, to do without. 3. To deal out, to distribute.

Dispensario [dis-pen-sah'-re-o], *m.* 1. Pharmacopœia. 2. Laboratory of medicaments. 3. Dispensary, an institution for relieving the sick poor.

Dispepsia, *f.* Dyspepsia.

Dispéptico, ca [dis-pep'-te-co, cah], *a* Dyspeptic.

Dispermo, ma [dis-perr'-mo, mah], *a.* (Bot.) Having only two seeds.

Dispersar [dis-per-sar'], *va.* 1. To separate the things or persons who were joined. 2. (Mil.) To put to flight, to disperse.

Dispersión [dis-per-se-on'], *f.* Dispersion.

Disperso, sa [dis-perr'-so, sah], *a.* 1. Dispersed, separated. 2. Applied to military men who do not belong to a body of forces, and reside where they please.

Dispertador, ra [dis-per-tah-dor', rah], *m.* & *f.* *V.* DESPERTADOR.

Dispertar [dis-per-tar'], *va.* *V.* DESPERTAR.

(*Yo dispierto, yo dispierte,* from *Dispertar. V.* ACERTAR.)

Displacer [dis-plah-therr'], *va.* *V.* DESPLACER.

Displicencia [dis-ple-then'-the-ah], *f.* Displeasure, discontent, dislike.

Displicente [dis-ple-then'-tay], *a.* 1. Displeasing, unpleasing. 2. Angry, peevish, fretful.

Dispnea, *f.* (Med.) *V.* DISNEA.

Dispondeo [dis-pon-day'-o], *m.* (Poet.) Dispondee, a foot of prosody consisting of four long syllables.

Disponedor, ra [dis-po-nay-dor', rah], *m.* & *f.* Disposer; distributer.

Disponer [dis-po-nerr'], *va.* & *vn.* 1. To arrange, to order, to place things in order. 2. To dispose, to make fit, to prepare. 3. To dispose of, to give, to distribute. 4. To deliberate, to resolve, to direct, to command. 5. To act freely, to dispose of property. *Disponer sus cosas,* To make a last will. *Disponer las velas al viento,* (Naut.) To trim the sails to the wind. *Disponer de bolina ciñendo el viento,* (Naut.) To trim the sails sharp or close to the wind.—*vr.* To prepare one's self, to get ready. To resolve.

(*Yo dispongo, yo dispuse,* from *Disponer. V.* PONER.)

Disponible [dis-po-nee'-blay], *a.* Disposable: applied to property.

Disposición [dis-po-se-the-on'], *f.* 1. Disposition, arrangement or distribution of things, ordering. 2. Disposition, natural fitness. 3. Disposition, tendency to any act or state. 4. Proportion, symmetry, measure. 5. Resolution, order, command. 6. Power, authority. 7. Disposition, inclination, temper of mind. 8. (Naut.) Trim of a ship. 9. Elegance of person. 10. Despatch of business. *A la disposición,* At the disposal or will of another.

Dispositivo, va [dis-po-se-tee'-vo, vah], *a.* Preparatory, readying, preliminary.—*m.* Device, mechanism.

Dispositorio, ria [dis-po-se-to'-re-o, ah], *a.* *V.* DISPOSITIVO.

Dispuesto, ta [dis-poo-es'-to, tah], *a.* 1. Disposed, fit, ready, minded. 2. Comely, genteel, graceful. *Bien dispuesto,* Quite well, with regard to health. *Mal dispuesto,* Indisposed, ill. —*pp. irr.* of DISPONER.

Disputa [dis-poo'-tah], *f.* 1. Dispute, controversy, argument. 2. Dispute, contest, conflict; contention, clash, fray, odds.

Disputable [dis-poo-tah'-blay], *a.* Disputable, controvertible, contestable.

Disputador [dis-poo-tah-dor'], *m.* Disputant, disputer.

Disputar [dis-poo-tar'], *va.* & *vn.* 1. To dispute, to controvert, to contend, to contest. 2. To dispute, to question, to reason about. 3. To dispute, to debate, to argue. 4. To dispute, jar, or clamour. 5. To strive; to resist. *Disputar sobre algo,* To dispute on something. *Disputar sobre frioleras,* To pluck a crow with one. *Disputar el barlovento,* (Naut.) To dispute the weather-gauge.

Disputativamente [dis-poo-tah-te-vah-men'-tay], *adv.* Disputingly.

Disquisición [dis-ke-se-the-on'], *f.* Disquisition, examination.

Distancia [dis-tahn'-the-ah], *f.* 1. Distance, interval of time or place. 2. Remoteness, length. 3. Difference, disparity. 4. (Mil.) Space considered in relation to the depth which troops occupy and respecting their front. (Naut.) *Tomar distancias,* To calculate the longitude of a vessel.

Distante [dis-tahn'-tay], *a.* 1. Distant, remote. 2. (Naut.) Off, offward.

Distar [dis-tar'], *vn.* 1. To be distant or remote with regard to time or place. 2. To be different, to vary.

Distender [dis-ten-derr'], *va.* (Med.) To cause violent stretching in tissues, membranes, etc.

Distensión [dis-ten-se-on'], *f.* Violent stretching.

Distesia [dis-tay'-se-ah], *f.* (Med.) General discomfort and impatience in disease; dysthesia.

Distico [dees'-te-co], *m.* Distich, couplet.

Distilar, *va.* (Obs.) *V.* DESTILAR.

Distilo, la [dis-tee'-lo, lah], *a.* Having two styles or pistils.

Distinción [dis-tin-the-on'], *f.* 1. Distinction, difference, diversity. 2. Prerogative, privilege. 3. Distinction, honourable note of superiority. 4. Order, clarity, precision. *Persona de distinción,* A person of superior rank *A distinción,* In contradistinction.

Distinguible [dis-tin-gee'-blay], *a.* Distinguishable.

Distinguido, da [dis-tin-gee'-do, dah], *a.* & *pp.* of DISTINGUIR. 1. Distinguished, conspicuous.—*m.* 2. *Distinguido* or *soldado distinguido,* A nobleman serving as a private, who was allowed to wear a sword, and exempted from menial labour; he was first in the roll, and, in promotions, was preferred to others of equal merit.

Distinguir [dis-tin-geer'], *va.* 1. To distinguish. 2. To distinguish, to divide by proper notes of diversity. 3. To see clearly, and at a distance. 4. To discern, to discriminate, to know; to judge. 5. To set a peculiar value on things or persons. 6. To clear up, to explain.—*vr.* 1. To distinguish one's self, especially by warlike exploits. 2. To differ, to be distinguished from.

Distintamente [dis-tin-tah-men'-tay], *adv.* Distinctly, diversely.

Distintivo, va [dis-tin-tee'-vo, vah], *a.* Distinctive.

Distintivo, *m.* 1. A distinctive mark, as the badge of a military order. 2. A particular attribute, characteristic feature.

Distinto, ta [dis-teen'-to, tah], *a.* 1 Distinct, different; diverse. 2. Distinct, clear; intelligible.

Distinto, *m.* (Obs.) Instinct. *V* INSTINTO.

Distracción [dis-trac-the-on'], *f.* 1. Distraction, want of attention; heedlessness, absence; ecstasy, reverie. 2. Amusement, pastime, sport. 3. Licentiousness, dissolute living; want of constraint.

Distráctil [dis-trahc'-teel], *a.* (Bot.) Applied to the connective, when it sensibly divides the cells of the anthers, as in the sage; distractile.

Distraer [dis-trah-err'], *va.* 1. To distract, to harass the mind; to perplex, to divert. 2. To seduce from a virtuous life.—*vr.* To muse, to be absent of mind, inattentive.

Distraidamente, *adv.* Distractedly, licentiously.

Distraido, da [dis-trah-ee'-do, dah], *a.* 1. Absent, inattentive, heedless, mopish. 2. Dissolute, licentious.—*pp.* of DISTRAER.

(*Yo distraigo, yo distraje,* from *Distraer. V.* TRAER.)

Distraimiento [dis-trah-e-me-en'-to], *m.* 1. Distraction. *V.* DISTRACCIÓN. 2. A licentious life.

Distribución [dis-tre-boo-the-on'], *f.* 1. Distribution; division, separation. 2. Proper collocation, arrangement. 3. Distribution of type in the printer's cases. 4. (Arch.) The art of economical employment and good selection of building materials. *Tomar algo por distribución*, To do or perform a thing from habit or custom.

Distribuidor, ra [dis-tre-boo-e-dor', rah], *m.* & *f.* Distributer, divider.

Distribuir [dis-tre-boo-eer'], *va.* 1. To distribute, to divide, to deal out. 2. To dispose, to range; to compart; to lot. 3. To allot, to measure. 4. (Print.) To distribute types.

Distributivamente, *adv.* (Littl. us.) Distributively.

Distributivo, va [dis-tre-boo-tee'-vo, vah], *a.* Distributive.

Distributor, ra [dis-tre-boo-tor', rah], *m.* & *f.* Distributer.

Distribuyente [dis-tre-boo-yen'-tay], *pa.* Distributer, giver.

Distrito [dis-tree'-to], *m.* 1. District, circuit of authority, province. 2. District, region, country, territory.

Distrofia muscular [dis-tro'-fe-ah moos-coo-lar'], *f.* Muscular dystrophy.

Disturbar [dis-toor-bar'], *va.* To disturb, to interrupt, perturb.

Disturbio [dis-toor'-be-o], *m.* Disturbance, outbreak, interruption.

Disuadir [de-soo-ah-deer'], *va.* To dissuade, to deter.

Disuasión [de-soo-ah-se-on'], *f.* Dissuasion, determent.

Disuasivo, va [de-soo-ah-see'-vo, vah], *a.* Dissuasive.

(*Yo disuelvo, yo disuelva*, from *Disolver*. *V.* MOVER.)

Disuelto, ta [de-soo-el'-to, tah], *a.* & *pp. irr.* of DISOLVER. Dissolved, melted.

Disuria [dis-oo'-re-ah], *f.* (Med.) Dysuria, difficulty in voiding urine.

Disyunción [dis-yoon-the-on'], *f.* 1. Disjunction, separation. 2. (Gram.) A disjunctive particle.

Disyunta [dis-yoon'-tah], *f.* (Mus.) Change of the voice.

Disyuntivamente, *adv.* Disjunctively, separately.

Disyuntivo, va [dis-yoon-tee'-vo, vah], *a.* 1. Disjunctive. 2. Disjunctive, applied to the insertion of stamens when the petals are united below the receptacle, but not to it.

Disyunto, ta [dis-yoon'-to, tah], *a.* Separated, disjoined, distant.

Disyuntor [dis-yoon-tor'], *m.* (Elec.) Circuit breaker.

Dita [dee'-tah], *f.* 1. Securer, bondsman; security, bond. 2. (Prov. Amer.) Debt.

Ditirámbica [de-te-rahm'-be-cah], *f.* Dithyrambic, a hymn in honour of Bacchus, sung, danced, and played at the same time.

Ditirámbico, ca [de-te-rahm'-be-co, cah], *a.* Dithyrambical.

Ditirambo [de-te-rahm' bo], *m.* 1. (Poet.) Dithyrambic, a dithyramb. 2. Exaggerated eulogy.

Dito [dee'-to], *m.* & *pp. obs.* *V.* DICHO.

Ditono [dee'-to-no], *m.* (Mus.) An interval of two tones, ditone, major third.

Ditorno [de-tor'-no], *m.* A name which engravers give to the intermediate parts of a figure.

Diuresis [de-oo-ray'-sis], *f.* Diuresis.

Diurético, ca [de-oo-ray'-te-co, cah], *a.* (Med.) Diuretic; also used as a substantive.

Diurno, na [de-oor'-no, nah], *a.* Diurnal.—*f. pl.* Butterflies, lepidoptera.—*m. pl.* Insects which live but twenty-four hours; day-flies.

Diurno [de-oor'-no], *m.* Diurnal, a prayer-book, among Roman Catholics, which contains the canonical hours, except matins.

Diuturnidad [de-oo-toor-ne-dahd'], *f.* Diuturnity, long duration.

Diuturno, na [de-oo-toor'-no, nah], *a.* Diuturnal, lasting.

Diva [dee'-vah], *f.* 1. (Poet.) Goddess. 2. (Neol.) A great songstress.

Divagación [de-vah-gah-the-on'], *f.* Wandering, digression.

Divagante [de-vah-gahn'-tay], *pa.* Rambling.

Divagar [de-vah-gar'], *vn.* 1. To ramble. *V.* VAGAR. 2. To digress.

Diván [de-vahn'], *m.* 1. Divan, the supreme council among the Turks. 2. The place of its meetings. 3. By extension, the Sublime Porte, the Ottoman government. 4. Divan, a low, cushioned sofa.

Divaricado, da [de-vah-re-cah'-do, dah], *a.* (Bot.) Divaricate, widely diverging.

Divaricar [de-vah-re-car'], *va.* To separate, cause to diverge or spread.

Divergencia [de-ver-hen'-the-ah], *f.* 1. Divergence. 2. Diversity or difference in opinions.

Divergente [de-ver-hen'-tay], *a.* 1. Divergent. 2. Dissenting, opposed, contrary.

Divergir [de-ver-heer'], *vn.* (Phys.) To diverge.

Diversamente [de-ver-sah-men'-tay], *adv.* Diversely, differently.

Diversidad [de-ver-se-dahd'], *f.* 1. Diversity, dissimilitude, unlikeness. 2. Diversity, distinct being. 3. Diversity, variety of things, abundance, plenty.

Diversificar [de-ver-se-fe-car'], *va.* To diversify, to vary.

Diversión [de-ver-se-on'], *f.* 1. Diversion. 2. Diversion, sport, merriment, fun, amusement. 3. (Mil.) Diversion, an attack made upon the enemy, to withdraw his attention from the real attack.

Diversivo, va [de-ver-see'-vo, vah], *a.* Divertive: applied to medicines which draw off humours.

Diverso, sa, *a.* 1. Diverse, different from another. 2. Diverse, different from itself; various; multiform.—*pl.* Several, sundry, many.

Divertículo [de-ver-tee'-coo-lo], *m.* A blind pouch, a diverticulum; a vertical appendix.

Divertido, da [de-ver-tee'-do, dah], *a.* & *pp.* of DIVERTIR. Amused, amusive, merry, divertive, diverted, festive, funny, absent, inattentive. *Andar divertido*, To be engaged in love affairs.

Divertimiento [de-ver-te-me-en'-to], *m.* 1. Diversion, sport, merriment, fun. 2. Amusement, entertainment of the mind, pastime, sport.

Divertir [de-ver-teer'], *va.* 1. To turn aside, divert, turn away. 2. To amuse, to entertain, to exhilarate, to divert, to make merry. 3. (Mil.) To draw the enemy off from some design, by threatening or attacking a distant part.—*vr.* To sport, to play, to frolic, to wanton, to dally, to fool.

Dividendo [de-ve-den'-do], *m.* 1. (Arith.) Dividend, the number to be divided. 2. Dividend, share, the interest received for money placed in the public stocks or in a partnership.

Divididero, ra [de-ve-de-day'-ro, rah], *a.* Divisible.

Dividir [de-ve-deer'], *va.* 1. To divide, to disjoin, to disunite, to cut. 2. To divide, to distribute, to separate. 3. To divide, to disunite by discord.—*vr.* 1. To divide, to part, to cleave. 2. To divide, or to be of different opinions. 3. To divide, to break friendships, to withdraw one's self from the company and friendship of any one. *Dividir por mitad*, To divide into halves.

Dividuo, dua [de-vee'-doo-o, ah], *a.* (Law) Divisible.

(*Yo divierto, él divirtió*, from *Divertir*. *V.* ASENTIR.)

Divieso [de-ve-ay'-so], *m.* (Med.) Furuncle, boil.

Divinal [de-ve-nahl'], *a.* (Poet.) *V.* DIVINO.

Divinamente [de-ve-nah-men'-tay], *adv* Divinely, heavenly; admirably.

Divinidad [de-ve-ne-dahd'], *f.* 1. Divinity; deity, godhead, godship, divine nature. 2. The Supreme Being. 3. False god. *Decir* or *hacer divinidades*, To say or do admirable things.

Divinizable [de-ve-ne-thah'-blay], *a.* Worthy of being deified.

Divinizado, da [de-ve-ne-thah'-do, dah], *a.* & *pp.* of DIVINIZAR. Deified.

Divinizar [de-ve-ne-thar'], *va.* 1. To deify. 2. (Met.) To sanctify.

Divino, na [de-vee'-no, nah], *a.* 1. Divine. 2. Heavenly, heavenborn, godlike. 3. Excellent, in a supreme degree. *Es un ingenio divino*, He is a man of uncommon talents.

Divino, na [de-vee'-no, nah], *m.* & *f.* *V.* ADIVINO.

Divisa [de-vee'-sah], *f.* 1. Badge, emblem, identifying mark. 2. (Her.) Motto, device. 3. (For.) Share of the paternal inheritance. 4. Foreign exchange.

Divisar [de-ve-sar'], *va.* 1. To descry at a distance, to perceive indistinctly. 2. (Her.) To make a difference, to vary

Divisero [de-ve-say'-ro], *m.* Heir who is not of noble extraction.

Divisibilidad [de-ve-se-be-le-dahd'], *f.* Divisibility.

Divisible [de-ve-see'-blay], *a.* Divisible.

División [de-ve-se-on'], *f.* 1. Division, the act of dividing a thing into parts. 2. Division, partition, distribution, compartment. 3. Division, disunion, difference, diversity of opinion. 4. Hyphen. 5. Division, one of the parts into which a thing is divided: used technically, especially in the army and navy. 6. (Arith.) Division, a rule in arithmetic.

Divisional [de-ve-se-o-nahl'], *a.* Divisional.

Divisivo, va [de-ve-see'-vo, vah], *a.* Divisible, divisive.

Diviso, sa [de-vee'-so, sah], *a.* & *pp. irr.* of DIVIDIR. Divided, disunited.

Divisor [de-ve-sor'], *m.* 1. Divisor. 2. Any thing which divides another.

Divisorio, ria [de-ve-so'-re-o, ah], *a.* Divisive, forming division.

Divo, va [dee'-vo, vah], *a.* (Poet.) Divine, godlike.

Divorciar [de-vor-the-ar'], *va.* To divorce, to separate, to part, to divide. —*vr.* To be divorced.

Divorcio [de-vor'-the-o], *m.* 1. Divorce, separation, disunion. 2. Rupture among friends.

Divulgable [de-vool-gah'-blay], *a.* That which may be divulged.

Divulgación [de-vool-gah-the-on'], *f.* Divulgation, publication.

Divulgador, ra [de-vool-gah-dor', rah], *m.* & *f.* Divulger.

Divulgar [de-vool-gar'], *va.* To publish, to divulge, to report, to give out, to reveal.—*vr.* To go abroad.

Divulsión [de-vool-se-on'], *f.* Divulsion, rupture.
Dixótomo, ma, *a.* *V.* Dicótomo.
Diz [deeth]. Contraction of *dícese* or *dicen.*
Dizambo [de-thahm'-bo], *m.* A foot of Greek and Latin verse consisting of two iambics.
Djerme [dherr'-may], *m.* (Naut.) Skiff or small bark used upon the Nile.
Do [doh], *m.* First note of the musical scale.
Do [doh], *adv.* (Obs.) *V.* Donde. *Do quiera,* In whatever part.
Dobla [do'-blah], *f.* An ancient Spanish gold coin.
Dobladamente [do-blah-dah-men'-tay], *adv.* 1. Doubly. 2. Deceitfully, artfully.
Dobladilla [do-blah-deel'-lyah], *f.* (Obs.) Ancient game of cards. *A la dobladilla,* Doubly, repeatedly.
Dobladillo, lla [do-blah-deel'-lyo, lyah], *a.* Squat and broad, short and thick.
Dobladillo, *m.* 1. Hem, the edge of a garment. 2. A strong thread commonly used to make stockings.
Doblado [do-blah'-do], *m.* 1. Measure of the fold in cloth. 2. (Med.) A sort of asphyxia which attacks those who clean out privies.
Doblado, da [do-blah'-do, dah], *a.* 1. Strong, robust, thick-set. 2. (Met.) Deceitful, dissembling. *Tierra doblada,* A broken, mountainous country.—*pp.* of Doblar.
Doblador [do-blah-dor'], *m.* A machine which serves to pass sugar-cane a second time between the cylinders of the mill.
Dobladura [do-blah-doo'-rah], *f.* 1. Fold, mark of a fold. 2. Anciently, an extra horse, for emergencies, which warriors had to take along. 3. Dish consisting of fried meat, bread, onions, nuts, etc. 4. (Obs.) Malicious fabrication.
Doblamiento [do-blah-me-en'-to], *m.* Doubling, bending, as act and effect.
Doblar [do-blar'], *va.* & *vn.* 1. To double, by addition of the same quantity. 2. To double, to fold. 3. To double, to contain twice the quantity. 4. To bend, to make crooked. to crook. 5. To toll or ring the passing bell. 6. To induce some one to do the contrary of what he had thought. *Doblar la rodilla,* To kneel. *Doblar un cabo* or *promontorio,* (Naut.) To double or weather a cape, to pass round a headland.—*vr.* 1. To bend, to bow, to stoop, to submit. 2. To be led away by the opinion of another. 3. To change one's opinion.
Doble [do'-blay], *a.* 1. Double, twice as much, duplicate; (Chem.) binary. 2. Thick and short. 3. Strong, robust. 4. Double, artful, deceitful. *Al doble,* Doubly. (Mus.) *Espacios dobles* are intervals which exceed octaves.
Doble [do'-blay], *m.* 1. Fold, crease. 2. Dissimulation, double-dealing. 3. Toll of the passing-bell. 4. Step in a Spanish dance.
Doblegable [do-blay-gah'-blay], *a.* 1. Flexible, flexile. 2. Pliant. 3. That which may be doubled.
Doblegar [do-blay-gar'], *va.* 1. To bend, to incurvate, to inflect. 2. To gain by persuasion, to reclaim.—*vr.* 1. To bend, to be incurvated. 2. To bend, to submit, to be submissive.
Doblel [do-blel'], *m.* Bag, sachel.
Doblemano [do-blay-mah'-no], *f.* (Mus.) Octave-coupler.
Doblemente [do-blay-men'-tay], *adv.* Deceitfully, doubly, artfully.
Doblero [do-blay'-ro], *m.* (Prov.) A small loaf of bread.
Doblete [do-blay'-tay], *a.* That which is between double and single.—*m.* 1. Factitious gem. 2. A play in billiards.
Doblez [do-bleth'], *m.* 1. Crease, a mark made by folding; fold; duplication, duplicature. (Anat.) A fold which forms a membrane by being turned back upon itself. 2. Duplicity, doubleness, disingenuity, dissimulation, double-dealing.
Doblo [do'-blo], *m.* (Law) Double.
Doblón [do-blone'], *m.* 1. Doubloon, a Spanish gold coin. *Doblón de oro,* Gold coin of the value of two dollars. *Doblón de a cuatro,* Gold coin of the value of eight dollars. *Doblón de a ocho,* Gold coin of the value of sixteen dollars. *Doblón* or *doblón sencillo,* Nominal money equal to three dollars U. S. currency. 2. *Doblón de vaca,* Tripes of a bullock or cow.
Doblonada [do-blo-nah'-dah], *f.* Heap of doubloons or money. *Echar doblonadas,* To exaggerate one's revenues.
Dobrao [do-brah'-o], *m.* A Portuguese gold coin, corresponding to the doubloon.
Doce [do'-thay], *m.* & *a.* 1. Twelve. 2. Twelfth, as *El doce de Abril,* The 12th of April. *Echarlo a doce,* To pretend to be angry in order to carry one's point; to carry an affair off with a laugh.
Doceañista [do-thay-ah-nyees'-tah], *a.* & *m.* Name given to the authors of the Spanish constitution of 1812 and their partisans.
Docena [do-thay'-nah], *f.* 1. Dozen. 2. Weight of twelve pounds in Navarre. *Docena de fraile,* Baker's dozen. *Entrar en docena,* To consider one's self among the number of persons constituting a certain class. *Meterse en docena,* To meddle in the conversation or business of superiors. *A docenas,* Abundantly, in great quantities.
Docenal [do-thay-nahl'], *a.* That which is sold by dozens.
Docenario, ria [do-thay-nah'-re-o, ah], *a.* Containing twelve or a dozen.
Docente [do-then'-tay], *a.* Teaching. *Iglesia docente,* The body of prelates and clergy.
Doceno, na [do-thay'-no, nah], *a.* Twelfth.
Doceno [do-thay'-no], *m.* & *a.* A kind of cloth, the warp of which consists of twelve hundred threads.
Doceñal [do-thay-nyahl'], *a.* (Obs.) That which consists of twelve years.
Docientos [do-the-en'-tos], *a.* *V.* Doscientos.
Dócil [do'-theel], *a.* 1. Docile, mild, tractable, gentle. 2. Obedient, pliant, flexible, governable. 3. Ductile, pliable, malleable, flexible.
Docilidad [do-the-le-dahd'], *f.* 1. Docility. 2. Flexibleness, compliance, easiness to be persuaded. 3. Manageableness, tractableness. 4. Gentleness, meekness.
Dócilmente [do'-theel-men-tay], *adv.* Tractably.
Docimástica [do-the-mahs'-te-cah], *f.* Assay, the docimastic art, the art of assaying minerals or ores.
Doctamente [doc-tah-men'-tay], *adv.* Learnedly.
Doctilocuo, cua [doc-te-lo'-coo-o, ah], *a.* Fluent and elegant in speech.
Docto, ta [doc'-to, tah], *a.* Learned.
Doctor [doc-tor'], *m.* 1. Doctor in divinity, law, physic, or philosophy. 2. Any able or learned teacher. 3. (Coll.) A physician.
Doctora [doc-to'-rah], *f.* 1. Doctoress, she who professes the skill of a doctor; a vain, impertinent, or assuming woman. 2. The wife of a physician or doctor; a female medical practitioner. 3. Title given to Saint Theresa.
Doctorado [doc-to-rah'-do], *m.* Doctorate, doctorship.
Doctoral [doc-to-rahl'], *a.* Doctoral.
Doctoral [doc-to-rahl'], *f.* The canonry called *doctoral* in the Spanish cathedrals.—*m.* The canon who possesses the *doctoral* canonry; he is one of the dignitaries, and must be LL. D., being *ex officio* councillor of the cathedral.
Doctoramiento [doc-to-rah-me-en'-to], *m.* 1. The act of taking the degree of doctor. 2. Doctorate, doctorship.
Doctorando [doc-to-rahn'-do], *m.* One who is on the point of taking out his degree as doctor.
Doctorar [doc-to-rar'], *va.* To doctorate, to dignify with the degree of a doctor.
Doctorcillo [doc-tor-theel'-lyo], *m. dim.* 1. A little doctor: commonly used in a jocular style. 2. Quack, a petty physician.
Doctorear [doc-to-re-ar'], *vn.* To doctor, to play the doctor.
Doctorismo [doc-to-rees'-mo], *m.* (Hum.) The body of doctors.
Doctrina [doc-tree'-nah], *f.* 1. Doctrine, instruction, lore. 2. Doctrine, the principles or positions of any sect or master. 3. Science, wisdom. 4. Discourse on the tenets of the Christian faith. 5. In America, a curacy, and also an Indian village newly consecrated to the Christian religion. *Niños de la doctrina* or *doctrinos,* Charity children.
Doctrinador, ra [doc-tre-nah-dor', rah], *m.* & *f.* Instructor, teacher.
Doctrinal [doc-tre-nahl'], *m.* Catechism, an abridgment of Christian doctrine.—*a.* Doctrinal, relating to doctrine.
Doctrinar [doc-tre-nar'], *va.* 1. To teach, to instruct. 2. To break in horses.
Doctrinero [doc-tre-nay'-ro], *m.* 1. Teacher of Christian doctrine. 2. Curate or parish priest in America. 3. One who accompanies a missionary in his teaching.
Doctrino [doc-tree'-no], *m.* 1. An orphan child received into some college. 2. (Met.) A person of small talent and too free manners.
Documental [do-coo-men-tahl'], *a.* Documental.—*m.* (Th.) Documentary.
Documentar [do-coo-men-tar'], *va.* 1. To document. 2. To inform, to acquaint.
Documento [do-coo-men'-to], *m.* 1. Instruction, advice to avoid evil. 2. Document; writing, record. 3. Voucher, schedule. 4. (Com.) Any transferable paper, representing value; security.
Dodecaedro [do-day-cah-ay'-dro], *m.* Dodecahedron.
Dodecágono [do-day-cah'-go-no], *m.* Dodecagon.
Dodecasílabo, ba [do-day-cah-see'-lah-bo, bah], *a.* Dodecasyllable, having twelve syllables.
Dodrante [do-drahn'-tay], *m.* (Littl. us.) 1. Drink or beverage, prepared from nine different ingredients, viz.. herbs, water, juice, wine, salt, oil, bread, honey, and pepper. 2. Weight of nine ounces out of the twelve which made a pound among the Romans. 3. Measure of twelve inches.
Dogal [do-gahl'], *m.* 1. Rope tied

round the neck. 2. Halter, a rope to hang malefactors.

Dogma [dog'-mah], *m.* 1. Dogma, established principle. 2. An article of faith.

Dogmáticamente [dog-mah'-te-cah-men-tay], *adv.* Dogmatically, in a dogmatic manner.

Dogmático, ca [dog-mah'-te-co, cah], *a.* Dogmatical or dogmatic.

Dogmático [dog-mah'-te-co], *m.* Dogmatic.

Dogmatismo [dog-mah-tees'-mo], *m.* 1. Dogmatism, disposition to affirm and believe in contrast to scepticism. Dogmatism admits an absolute certainty. 2. Dogmatic assertion, affirmation without proof. 3. Name of an ancient medical theory.

Dogmatista [dog-mah-tees'-tah], *m.* 1. Dogmatist; a teacher of new dogmas. 2. An upholder of dogmatism.

Dogmatizador, Dogmatizante [dog-mah-te-thah-dor', dog-mah-te-thahn'-tay], *m.* Dogmatizer, dogmatist.

Dogmatizar [dog-mah-te-thar'], *va.* To dogmatize, to teach or assert false dogmas.

Dogo [do'-go], *m.* 1. Terrier. 2. A kind of small dog.

Dogre [do'-gray], *m.* A Dutch boat for the herring-fishery, two-masted and like a smack; a dogger.

Doladera [do-lah-day'-rah], *a.* A cooper's adze.

Dolador [do-lah-dor'], *m.* Joiner, one who planes and polishes wood or stone.

Doladura [do-lah-doo'-rah], *f.* Adzing, shavings from planing.

Dolaje [do-lah'-hay], *m.* The wine imbibed by pipe-staves.

Dolamas, *f. pl.* **Dolames**, *m. pl.* [do-lah'-mas, do-lah'-mes]. Hidden vices and defects incident to horses.

Dolar [do-lar'], *va.* To plane or smooth wood or stone.

Dólar [do'-lar], *m.* Dollar, equivalent of a duro or "peso fuerte."

Dolencia [do-len'-the-ah], *f.* 1. Disease, affliction. 2. (Met. Obs.) Danger; dishonour.

Doler [do-lerr'], *vn.* 1. To feel pain, to ache or be in pain. 2. To cause in the mind sorrow or distress.—*vr.* 1. To be in pain about any thing, to be sorry; to repent. 2. To feel for the sufferings of others. 3. To lament, to complain.

Dolerita [do-lay-ree'-tah], *f.* Dolerite, an igneous rock.

Dolerítico, ca [do-lay-ree'-te-co, cah], *a.* Doleritic, containing dolerite or resembling it.

Doliente [do-le-en'-tay], *a.* Suffering or labouring under a complaint or affliction; sorrowful.—*m.* 1. Pall-bearer. 2. Mourner.

Dolimán [do-le-mahn'], *m.* Kind of long robe worn by the Turks.

Dolo [do'-lo], *m.* Fraud, deceit, imposition; vulgarly, humbug. *Poner dolo,* To judge ill of a person.

Dolomía [do-lo-mee'-ah], *f.* Dolomite, a brittle marble, phosphorescent upon rubbing.

Dolomítico, ca [do-lo-mee'-te-co, cah], *a.* Dolomitic.

Dolor [do-lor'], *m.* 1. Pain, sensation of uneasiness, aching, ache. *Dolor de cabeza,* Headache. *Dolor de muelas,* Toothache. *Dolor de tripas,* Griping. 2. Affliction, anguish, grief, painfulness. 3. Repentance, contrition. 4. Pain, the throe of childbirth. *Estar con dolores,* To be in labour.

Dolorcillo, ito [do-lor-theel'-lyo, thee'-to], *m. dim.* A slight pain.

Dolorido, da [do-lo-ree'-do, dah], *a.* Doleful, afflicted, painful, heart-sick. *V.* Doliente.

Dolorido [do-lo-ree'-do], *m.* 1. The chief mourner, the nearest relation of a person deceased. 2. One in pain.

Dolorosamente [do-lo-ro-sah-men'-tay], *adv.* Painfully, sorrowfully, miserably.

Doloroso, sa [do-lo-ro'-so, sah], *a.* Sorrowful, afflicted, dolorous, dismal, doleful; painful.

Dolosamente, *adv.* Deceitfully.

Doloso, sa [do-loh'-so, sah], *a.* Deceitful, knavish.

Domable [do-mah'-blay], *a.* Tamable, conquerable.

Domador, ra [do-mah-dor', rah], *m.* & *f.* 1. Tamer, subduer. 2. Horse-breaker.

Domadura [do-mah-doo'-rah], *f.* Act of taming or subduing.

Domar [do-mar'], *va.* 1. To tame; to break or to break in. 2. To subdue, to overcome, to master, to conquer.

Dombo [dom'-bo], *m.* Dome, cupola.

Domeñar [do-may-nyar'], *va.* To reclaim, to make tractable, to tame, to master, to subdue.

Domesticable [do-mes-te-cah'-blay], *a.* Tamable.

Domésticamente [do-mes'-te-cah-men-tay], *adv.* Domestically.

Domesticar [do-mes-te-car'], *va.* To render gentle, to domesticate.—*vr.* To grow tame.

Domesticidad [do-mes-te-the-dahd'], *f.* Domesticity, affability.

Doméstico, ca [do-mes'-te-co, cah], *a.* 1. Domestic, domestical. 2. Domestic, inhabiting the house, not wild. 3. Domesticant, forming part of the same family.

Doméstico, *m.* Domestic, menial.

Domestiquez [do-mes-te-keth'], *f.* Meekness, tameness.

Domiciliado, da [do-me-the-le-ah'-do, dah], *a.* & *pp.* of Domiciliarse. Received as a denizen or citizen of a place; domiciliated.

Domiciliario, *m.* Inhabitant, citizen.

Domiciliario, ria [do-me-the-le-ah'-re-o, ah], *a.* Domiciliary, intruding into private houses.

Domiciliarse [do-me-the-le-ar'-say], *vr.* To establish one's self in a residence.

Domicilio [do-me-thee'-le-o], *m.* Habitation, abode, domicile, home, dwelling-house.

Dominación [do-me-nah-the-on'], *f.* 1. Dominion, domination, authority, power. 2. (Mil.) Commanding ground.—*pl.* Dominations, some angelic beings.

Dominador, ra [do-me-nah-dor', rah], *m.* & *f.* Dominator.

Dominante [do-me-nahn'-tay], *a.* 1. Dominant, domineering, dictatory, ascendant; prevailing, excelling. 2. Dominative, imperious, masterful. 3. (Mus.) Dominant, the fifth in the scale.

Dominar [do-me-nar'], *va.* 1. To domineer, to rule, to act without control, to oversway. 2. To master, to lord, to lead, to command. 3. (Met.) To moderate one's passions, to correct one's evil habits.—*vr.* To rise above others: applied to hills.

Dominativo, va [do-me-nah-tee'-vo, vah], *a.* Dominative. *V.* Dominante.

Dómine [do'-me-nay], *m.* Appellation given to the master or teacher of Latin grammar, in small towns; dominie.

Domingo [do-meen'-go], *m.* Sunday, the first day of the week, the Christian Sabbath. *Domingo de Adviento,* Advent Sunday. *Domingo de Pasión* or *de Lázaro,* Passion Sunday. *Domingo de Ramos,* Palm Sunday. *Domingo de Resurrección,* Easter Sunday. *Domingo de Cuasimodo,* Low Sunday, the next Sunday after Easter. *Hacer domingo,* To pass a working day idly or in carousing. *Salir con un domingo siete,* (Amer.) To speak out of the purpose.

Dominguero, ra [do-min-gay'-ro, rah], *a.* Belonging to the Sabbath, done or worn on Sunday. *Sayo dominguero,* Sunday clothes.

Dominguillo [do-min-geel'-lyo], *m.* Figure of a boy made of straw, and used at bull-feasts to frighten the bulls. *Hacer a uno su dominguillo,* or *hacer su dominguillo de uno,* (Coll.) To make one a laughing-stock; to sport at some one's expense.

Domínica [do-mee'-ne-cah], *f.* Sunday, in ecclesiastical language. *Domínica in Albis,* Low Sunday. *V.* Domingo.

Dominical [do-me-ne cahl'], *a.* 1. Manorial: applied to feudal rights. 2. Dominical, belonging to the Lord's day. *Oración dominical,* Lord's prayer. 3. A veil used by women in some districts for receiving communion. 4. *f.* Discourse of the Sundays of Advent and Lent.

Dominicano, na, Dominico, ca [do-me-ne-cah'-no, nah], *a.* 1. Dominican, belonging to the Dominican friars. 2. Native of the island of Santo Domingo.

Dominico [do-me-nee'-co, or do-mee'-ne-co], *m.* Jacobin, a friar of the order of Saint Dominic.

Dominicatura [do-me-ne-cah-too'-rah], *f.* (Prov.) Certain duty of vassalage paid to the lord of the manor.

Dominio [do-mee'-ne-o], *m.* 1. Dominion, domination, power, right of possession or use. 2. Dominion, authority. 3. Dominion, territory, region. 4. Domain, possession, estate.

Dominó [do-me-no'], *m.* 1. Domino, a masquerade garment. 2. The game of dominoes.

Dompedro [dom-pay'-dro], *m.* (Bot.) The morning-glory.

Don [don], *m.* 1. Don, the Spanish title for a gentleman. It is equivato *Mr.* in English, but used only before Christian names, as *Don Juan* or *Don Andrés Pérez,* Mr. John or Mr. Andrew Perez. 2. *Don* alone, or with an adjective or epithet, was formerly equivalent to *Señor.* [Generally derived from dominus, which, however, through dom'no makes *dueño.* Possibly, therefore, is the origin from Phœnician don, adon, lord.] *Don Guindo,* One who boasts of learning which he does not possess. *Don Lindo,* A dandy.

Don, *m.* 1. Gift, present. 2. Gift, faculty, dexterity, knack, gracefulness, ability. *Dones sobrenaturales,* Supernatural gifts, as prophecy, etc. *Don de gentes,* An habitual skill to win the good-will of those persons with whom any one is acquainted. *Don de acierto,* Habitual dexterity in doing everything in the most successful manner. *Don de errar,* (Coll.) A knack for doing things wrong. (Lat. donum, gift.)

Dona [do'-nah] *f.* 1. (Obs.) Woman, lady. 2. *pl.* Wedding presents which the groom makes to the bride. (Acad.)

Donación [do-nah-the-on'], *f.* 1. Donation. 2. Donation, gift, grant. *Donación piadosa,* Donary, pious donation.

Donadio [do-nah-dee'-o], *m.* 1. (Obs.)

V. Don. 2. (Prov.) Property derived from royal donations.

Donado, da [do-nah'-do, dah], *m.* & *f.* Lay-brother or lay-sister of a religious community.—*pp.* of Donar.

Donador, ra [do-nah-dor', rah], *m.* & *f.* Donor, bestower, giver.

Donaire [do-nah'-e-ray], *m.* 1. Grace, elegance, gracefulness, gentility. 2. Witty saying, facetiousness. 3. Gracefulness, ease, activity in walking. *Hacer donaire de alguna cosa*, To make little of any thing.

Donairosamente, *adv.* Facetiously, wittily.

Donairoso, sa [do-nah-e-ro'-so, sah], *a.* 1. Pleasant. 2. Graceful, elegant. 3. Witty, facetious.

Donante [do-nahn'-tay], *pa.* Donor; giver.

Donar [do-nar'], *va.* To make free gifts, to bestow.

Donatario [do-nah-tah'-re-o], *m.* Donee, grantee, a person in whose favour a donation is made.

Donatista [do-nah-tees'-tah], *a.* Donatist, follower of Donatus.

Donativo [do-nah-tee'-vo], *m.* Donative.

Doncel [don-thel'], *m.* 1. An appellation formerly given to the king's pages. 2. A man who has not carnally known a woman. 3. (Obs.) The son of noble parents. 4. The youth who was not yet armed as a knight. *Pino doncel*, Timber of young pines without knots.—*adj.* Mild, mellow in flavour. *Vino doncel*, Wine of a mild flavour.

Doncella [don-thayl'-lyah], *f.* 1. Maid, virgin, maiden, lass. 2. Lady's-maid, waiting-maid. 3. *Doncella de Numidia*, (Orn.) The Numidian heron. Ardea virgo. 4. (Zool.) Snake-fish. Ophidium. 5. (Bot.) The sensitive plant, humble plant. Mimosa pudica. *Doncella jamona*, An old maid.

Doncelleja [don-thel-lyay'-hah], *f. dim.* Little maid.

Doncellería [don-thel-lyay-ree'-ah], *f.* (Coll.) Maidenhead, virginity.

Doncellez [don-thel-lyeth'], *f.* Virginity, maidenhood.

Doncellica, ita [don-thel-lyee'-cah, ee'-tah], *f. dim.* A young maid, a girl.

Doncellidueña [don-thel-lye-doo-ay'-nyah], *f.* (Obs.) An old maid who marries.

Doncellona [don-thel-lyo'-nah], *f. aug. coll.* Old maid.

Doncellueca [don-thel-lyoo-ay'-cah, ee'-tah], *f.* (Coll.) An old maid.

Doncelluela [don-thel-lyoo-ay'-lah], *f. dim.* A young maid.

Donde [don'-day], *adv.* 1. *V.* Adonde. 2. Where, in what place? 3. Whither, to what place? *¿De dónde?* From what place? *Donde quiera*, Anywhere. *Donde no*, On the contrary. *¿Hacia dónde?* Toward what place? *¿Por dónde?* By what way or road? by what reason or cause?

Don Diego de día [don de-ay'-go day dee'-ah]. (Bot.) The morning-glory; also written *Dondiego.*

Don Diego de noche [don de-ay'-go day no'-chay], *m.* (Bot.) Jalap, marvel of Peru. Mirabilis jalapa.

Donecillo [do-nay-theel'-lyo], *m. dim.* A small present.

Dongola [don-go'-lah], *f.* A beverage, like beer, made in Ethiopia.

Dongón [don-gone'], *m.* A tree of the Philippine Islands, whose wood is of stony hardness and serves to make keels and other resisting parts of vessels.

Donguindo [don-geen'-do], *m.* A pear-tree of larger fruit than the ordinary.

Donillero [do-nil-lyay'-ro], *m.* Swindler, sharper; a tricking gambler.

Donjuán, *m.* (Bot.) *V.* Dondiego.

Donna [don'-nah], *f.* (Obs.) *V.* Doña.

Donosamente, *adv.* Gracefully, pleasing, comelily.

Donosidad [do-no-se-dahd'], *f.* Gracefulness, wittiness, festivity.

Donosilla [do-no-seel'-lyah], *f.* Piece of plaited muslin, which ladies used to wear around their necks.

Donoso, sa [do-no'-so, sah], *a.* Gay, witty, pleasant.

Donosura [do-no-soo'-rah], *f.* Gracefulness, grace, elegance, gentility.

Donpedro [don-pay'-dro], *m.* Morning glory. *V.* Dompedro.

Doña [do'-nyāh], *f.* Lady, mistress: an appellation of honour prefixed to the Christian names of ladies, as *Don* is to those of gentlemen.—*pl.* Present made every year to the miners in the iron-mines in Spain.

Doñear [do-nyay-ar'], *vn.* (Coll.) To pass the time or converse much with women.

Doñegal, Doñigal [do-nyay-gahl', do-nye-gahl'], *a.* Applied to a kind of figs, red inside.

Doquier, Doquiera [do-ke-err', do-ke-ay'-rah], *adv.* *V.* Donde quiera.

Dorada, Doradilla [do-rah'-dah, do-rah-deel'-lyah], *f.* (Zool.) Gilt-head, gilt-poll. Sparus auratus.

Doradilla [do-rah-deel'-lyah], *f.* 1. (Bot.) Common ceterach. Ceterach officinarum. 2. Gilt-head (fish).

Doradillo [do-rah-deel'-lyo], *m.* 1. Fine brass wire. 2. Wagtail, a small bird.

Dorado, da [do-rah'-do, dah], *a.* Gilt. *Sopa dorada*, A high-coloured soup.—*pp.* of Dorar.

Dorado [do-rah'-do], *m.* 1. Gilding. *V.* Doradura. 2. (Zool.) *V.* Dorada.

Dorador [do-rah-dor'], *m.* Gilder.

Doradura [do-rah-doo'-rah], *f.* Gilding.

Doral [do-rahl'], *m.* (Orn.) Fly-catcher. Muscicapa.

Dorar [do-rar'], *va.* 1. To gild, as with gold. 2. (Met.) To palliate, to excuse. 3. (Poet.) To gild, to illuminate with the rays of the sun, as a mountain-top. 4. To coat pastry with the yolk of egg, to yellow it. *Dorar a sisa*, To gild with gold size. *Dorar a mate*, To lay on a coat of glue size.

Dórico, ca [do'-re-co, cah], *a.* Doric.

Dorífora [do-ree'-fo-rah], *f.* The Colorado potato-beetle, a noxious pest. Doryphora decemlineata.

Doríforo [do-ree'-fo-ro], *m.* A beetle of the chrysomelid group, of equinoctial America, of brilliant colouring.

Dormán [dor-mahn'], *m.* Dolman, a lady's jacket; named from a huzzar's jacket.

Dormida [dor-mee'-dah], *f.* 1. Time during which the silk-worm sleeps and rests before each molt. In general, time spent in sleep. 2. The place where animals repose. 3. (Amer.) Alcove, bed.

Dormidera [dor-me-day'-rah], *f.* (Bot.) Garden-poppy. Papaver somniferum. —*pl.* Sleepiness, drowsiness. *V.* Adormidera.

Dormidero, ra [dor-me-day'-ro, rah], *a.* Sleepy, soporiferous, narcotic, somniferous.—*m.* Place where cattle repose.

Dormidor [dor-me-dor'], *m.* A great sleeper.

Dormidos [dor-mee'-dos], *m. pl.* *V.* Durmientes.

Dormiente [dor-me-en'-tay], *pa.* *V.* Durmiente.

Dormilón, na [dor-me-lone', nah], *m.* & *f.* A dull, sleepy person, one who sleeps much.

Dormir [dor-meer'], *vn.* 1. To sleep. 2. To sleep, to be inattentive, to neglect one's business. *A duerme y vela*, or *entre duerme y vela*, Between sleeping and waking. 3. To be calm or still or torpid. 4. (Naut.) Used of the magnetic needle, to lose its virtue. 5. To be slow and heavy in moving (of ships). 6. To be in the pupa state. 7. Among Freemasons, to cease to be an active member of any lodge. *Dormir en Dios*, or *en el Señor*, To die in the Lord; to sleep in Jesus. *Dormir como una piedra*, To sleep like a top. *Dormir la siesta*, To take a nap after dinner. *Dormir á cortinas verdes*, or *dormir al sereno*, To sleep in the open field. *Dormir a pierna suelta*, *a pierna tendida* or *a sueño suelto*, (Coll.) To sleep carelessly.—*vr.* To be overcome by sleep, to fall asleep.

Dormirlas [dor-meer'-las], *m.* Play among boys, like hide and seek.

Dormitar [dor-me-tar'], *vn.* To doze, to nap, to mope.

Dormitivo [dor-me-tee'-vo], *m.* Dormitive, a soporiferous potion.

Dormitorio [dor-me-to'-re-o], *m.* 1. In convents and colleges, a large room where novices or collegians sleep. 2. Dormitory, bed-room.

Dornajo [dor-nah'-ho], *m.* A trough.

Dornas [dor'-nas], *f. pl.* (Prov.) Small fishing-boats on the coast of Galicia.

Dornillo [dor-neel'-lyo], *m.* *V.* Dornajo and Hortera.

Dorsal [dor-sahl'], *a.* Dorsal, belonging to the back.

Dorsífero, ra [dor-see'-fay-ro, rah], *a.* (Bot.) Dorsiferous, dorsiparous.

Dorso [dor'-so], *m.* The back part of any thing; dorsum. *Al dorso*, On back, on the other side.

Dos [dose], *m.* & *a.* 1. Two. 2. Second, as, *Dos de Abril*, The 2d of April. 3. Deuce. 4. (Obs.) Coin, an *ochavo* or two *maravedís*. *A dos manos*, With both hands, with open arms. *Dos a dos*, Two by two. *A dos por tres*, Inconsiderately, rashly, suddenly, without fear, audaciously. *De dos en dos*, Two by two, by couples. *Dos tanto*, Twice, double. *Aquí para entre los dos*, Between you and me. *En un dos por tres*, In a twinkling.

Dosañal [do-sah-nyahl'], *a.* Biennial, of two years.

Doscientos, tas [dos-the-en'-tos, tas], *a. pl.* & *n.* Two hundred.

Dosel [do-sel'], *m.* A canopy.

Doselera [do-say-lay'-rah], *f.* Valance, the drapery of a canopy.

Doselico [do-say-lee'-co], *m. dim.* A small canopy.

Dosis [do'-sis], *f.* 1. Dose, as of medicine. 2. Quantity.

Dotación [do-tah-the-on'], *f.* 1. Dotation, endowment, foundation, a revenue established for any purpose. 2. Dotation, the act of giving a dowry. *Dotación de navíos*, (Naut.) Fund appropriated to the repairing of ships. 3. *Dotación de un buque*, The complement of a crew. 4. (Prov.) Stock. 5. Munition and garrison of a fortress.

Dotado, da [do-tah'-do, dah], *a.* & *pp.* of Dotar. Dowered, portioned. *Dotado de*, Endowed with, gifted with.

Dotador, ra [do-tah-dor', rah], *m.* & *f.* One who portions or endows; donor, instituter.

Dotal [do-tahl'], *a.* Dotal, relating to a portion or dowry.

Dotar [do-tar'], *va.* 1. To portion, to endow with a fortune, to give a portion. 2. To gift, to endow with powers or talents. 3. To settle a sum for a particular purpose, as for a scholarship; to endow.

Dote [doh'-tay], *m.* & *f.* 1. Dower, dowry, the fortune or portion given with a wife. 2. Stock of counters to play with.—*m. pl.* 1. The choicest gifts of the blessed. 2. Gifts, blessings, talents received from nature. 3. Endowments.

Dovela [do-vay'-lah], *f.* The curved sides of the key-stone of an arch; key-stone.

Dovelaje [do-vay-lah'-hay], *m.* Series of curved stones for an arch.

Dovelar [do-vay-lar'], *va.* To hew a stone in curves for an arch or key-stone.

(*Yo doy, yo dé, yo dí, yo diera.* *V.* Dar.)

Dozavado, da [do-thah-vah'-do, dah], *a.* Twelve-sided.

Dozavo, va [do-thah'-vo, vah], *m.* & *f.* The twelfth part.

Draba [drah'-bah], *f.* (Bot.) Whitlow. Draba.

Dracena [drah-thay'-nah], *f.* Dracæna, a palm-like plant belonging to the lily family.

Dracma [drahc'-mah], *f.* 1. Drachm, the eighth part of an ounce. 2. Greek silver coin.

Draconiano, na [drah-co-ne-ah'-no, nah], *a.* Draconian, hence barbarous and cruel.

Dracúnculo [drah-coon'-coo-lo], *m.* (Ent.) Dracunculus, long worm which breeds between the skin and flesh, guinea-worm.

Draga [drah'-gah], *f.* Dredge, dredger: applied to the machine and the barge which carries it.

Dragaminas [drah-gah-mee'-nas], *m.* (Mil., Naut.) Mine sweeper.

Dragar [drah-gar'], *va.* To dredge, to use the dredging-machine; to deepen a channel.

Dragante [drah-gahn'-tay], *m.* 1. (Bot.) Goat's-thorn. Astragalus tragacantha. 2. Tragacanth, a sort of gum. 3. (Naut.) Pillow of the bowsprit.

Drago [drah'-go], *m.* (Bot.) Dragon-tree, a tree of America and the Canary Islands, from which is obtained the resin called dragon's-blood. Pterocarpus draco.

Dragomán [drah-go-mahn'], *m.* Dragoman, an interpreter among the Turks.

Dragón [drah-gone'], *m.* 1. An old serpent; a fabulous monster. 2. An herb, about three feet high, of red or white flowers, which serves for ornament. 3. (Mil.) Dragoon, a horse-soldier who serves occasionally on foot. 4. White spots in the pupils of horses' eyes. 5. Kind of exhalation or vapour. 6. A chimney of a reverberatory furnace. 7. (Ast.) A constellation of the northern hemisphere, consisting of forty-nine stars. 8. (Head and tail of the dragon.) The two opposite points in which the orbit of the moon cuts the ecliptic.

Dragona [drah-go'-nah], *f.* 1. Shoulder-knot worn by military officers. 2. Female dragon.

Dragonal [drah-go-nahl'], *m.* (Bot.) *V.* Drago.

Dragonazo [drah-go-nah'-tho], *m. aug.* A large dragon.

Dragoncillo [drah-gon-theel'-lyo], *m.* 1. Drake, a kind of ancient gun. 2. (Dim.) A little dragon or dragoon.

Dragonero [drah-go-nay'-ro], *m.* *V.* Dracena.

Dragontea, Dragontía [drah-gon-tay'-ah, drah-gon-tee'-ah], *f.* (Bot.) Common dragon. Arum dracunculus.

Dragontino, na [drah-gon-tee'-no, nah], *a.* Dragonish.

Drama [drah'-mah], *m.* Drama.

Dramática [drah-mah'-te-cah], *f.* The dramatic art.

Dramáticamente, *adv.* Dramatically.

Dramático, ca [drah-mah'-te-co, cah], *a.* Dramatical, dramatic.

Dramaturgo, ga [drah-ma-toor'-go, gah], *m.* & *f.* An author of dramas, especially if tragic.

Drao [drah'-o], *m.* (Naut.) A monkey, ram, pile-driver.

Drapa [drah'-pah], *f.* (Arch.) *V.* Grapa.

Drástico, ca [drahs'-te-co, cah], *a.* Drastic, acting powerfully.

Drecera [dray-thay'-rah], *f.* A row of houses, trees, etc., which form a straight line.

Dreito, *m.* (Obs.) *V.* Derecho.

Drenaje [dray-nah'-hay], *m.* Drainage by means of subterranean pipes; subsoil drainage. (Acad.)

Dríada, Dríade [dree'-ah-dah, dree'-ah-day], *f.* Dryad, wood-nymph.

Dril [dreel], *m.* Drilling, a strong cloth; drill.

Drino [dree'-no], *m.* Kind of venemous serpent.

Drizar [dre-thar'], *va.* (Naut.) To hoist up the yards.

Driza [dree'-thah], *f.* (Naut.) Halliard. *Drizas del foque mayor,* Throat-halliards.

Droga [dro'-gah], *f.* 1. Drug, any ingredient used in physic. 2. (Met.) Stratagem, artifice, deceit.

Drogmán, *m.* Dragoman. (Acad.)

Droguería [dro-gay-ree'-ah], *f.* A druggist's shop; trade in drugs.

Droguero [dro-gay'-ro], *m.* 1. Druggist. 2. Cheat, bad pay-master.

Droguete [dro-gay'-tay], *m.* Drugget, kind of woollen stuff.

Droguista [dro-gees'-tah], *m.* 1. Druggist. 2. Cheat, impostor.

Dromedario [dro-may-dah'-re-o], *m.* 1. Dromedary. 2. (Met.) An unwieldy horse or mule.

Dropacismo [dro-pah-thees'-mo], *m.* Ointment for taking off hairs.

Drope [dro'-pay], *m.* (Coll.) Vile, despicable man.

Druida [droo-ee'-dah], *m.* Druid.

Drupa [droo'-pah], *f.* (Bot.) Drupe, a stone fruit with fleshy exterior and nut within.

Drusa [droo'-sah], *f.* (Min.) A kind of incrustation in a mineral formed of distinct crystals.

Dúa [doo'-ah], *f.* (Obs.) Kind of personal service.

Dual [doo-ahl'], *a.* (Gram.) Dual, belonging to two. *Duales,* Incisors. *V.* Cortadores.

Dualismo [doo-ah-lees'-mo], *m.* 1. A philosophy which recognizes two active principles in the universe, a spirit of good and one of evil, in perpetual conflict. 2. Antagonism.

Duba [doo'-bah], *f.* (Prov.) Wall or inclosure of earth.

Dubio [doo'-be-o], *m.* (Law) Doubt.

Dubitable [doo-be-tah'-blay], *a.* Doubtful, dubitable, dubious.

Dubitación [doo-be-tah-the-on'], *f.* Dubitation, doubt.

Dubitativo, va [doo-be-tah-tee'-vo, vah], *a.* (Gram.) Used to express a doubt, doubtful, dubious: applied to conjunctions.

Ducado [doo-cah'-do], *m.* 1. Duchy, dukedom. 2. Ducat, an ancient gold and silver coin: it is also a nominal money, worth eleven shillings and one maravedi.

Ducal [doo-cahl'], *a.* Ducal.

Ducentésimo, ma [doo-then-tay'-se-mo, mah], *a.* Two-hundredth.

Dúcil [doo'-theel], *m.* (Prov.) *V.* Espita.

Dúctil [dooc'-teel], *a.* Ductile.

Ductilidad [dooc-te-le-dahd'], *f.* Ductility.

Ductivo, va [dooc-tee'-vo, vah], *a.* Conducing. (Acad.)

Ductor [dooc-tor'], *m.* 1. Guide, conductor. 2. (Med.) Probe.

Ductriz [dooc-treeth'], *f.* Conductress.

Ducha [doo'-chah], *f.* 1. List, a strip of cloth. 2. Straight piece of land reaped by a reaper. 3. Douche, a jet of water, used for medicinal effect upon the body. 4. The instrument by which the jet is applied.

Ducho, cha [doo'-cho, chah], *a.* Dexterous, accustomed, skilful.

Duda [doo'-dah], *f.* 1. Doubt, uncertainty of mind, suspense, fluctuation, hesitation, irresolution. 2. Doubtfulness, dubiousness. 3. Doubt, question, point unsettled. *Sin duda* or *sin duda alguna,* Certainly, doubtlessly, without doubt.

Dudable [doo-dah'-blay], *a.* Dubitable, dubious, doubtful.

Dudar [doo-dar'], *vn.* & *va.* 1. To doubt, to hesitate, to be in suspense; to fluctuate. 2. (Obs.) To doubt, to fear. *Dudar de algo,* To doubt any thing.

Dudilla [doo-deel'-lyah], *f. dim.* A slight doubt.

Dudosamente, *adv.* Doubtfully, dubiously.

Dudoso, sa [doo-do'-so, sah], *a.* 1. Doubtful, dubious, uncertain. 2. Dubious, hazardous.

Duela [doo-ay'-lah], *f.* 1. Stave. *Duelas para toneles,* Hogshead staves. *Duelas para pipas,* Pipe staves. *Duelas para barriles,* Barrel staves. 2. Kind of coin of two reals and twenty-two and a half maravedis.

Duelaje [doo-ay-lah'-hay], *m.* *V.* Dolaje.

Duelista [doo-ay-lees'-tah], *m.* 1. Duellist. 2. Duellist, fighter, a single combatant.

Duelo [doo-ay'-lo], *m.* 1. Duel, challenge. 2. Sorrow, pain, grief, affliction. 3. Mourning, funeral; lamentation, condolement. *Duelos,* Troubles, vexations, afflictions. *Sin duelo,* Abundantly. *Los duelos con pan son menos,* Troubles are more bearable if one is not also poor. *Pápenle duelos,* Think of the sorrows and be merciful.

(*Yo me duelo, yo me duela,* from *Dolerse.* *V.* Mover.)

Duende [doo-en'-day], *m.* 1. Elf, fairy, goblin or hobgoblin, ghost. *Tener duende,* To be hypochondriac, to be restless. 2. A kind of glazed silk. *Moneda de duendes,* Small copper coin.

Duendecillo [doo-en-day-theel'-lyo], *m. dim.* A little fairy.

Duendo, da [doo-en'-do, dah], *a.* Domestic, tame: applied to doves.

Dueña [doo-ay'-nyah], *f.* 1. Owner, proprietress, mistress. 2. Duenna, a widowed woman who used to be in the principal houses for authority, respect, and care of the maid-servants. 3. A married lady. 4. (Obs.) A single woman who has lost her virginity. *Dueñas,* Widows, who, in the royal palace, attend on the maids of honour.

Dueña de casa [doo-ay'-nyah day cah'-sah], *f.* 1. Homemaker. 2. Lady of the house.

Dueñaza [doo-ay-nyah'-thah], *f. aug.* A very old duenna, and also the duenna who was very strict.

Dueñesco [doo-ay-nyes'-co], *a.* (Coll.) Belonging to a duenna.

Dueñísima [doo-ay-nyee'-se-mah], *f.* (Joc.) A haughty old duenna.

Dueño [doo-ay'-nyo], *m.* & *f.* Owner.

proprietor, master or mistress.—*m.* Master, with respect to a servant.

(*Yo duermo, yo duerma, yo dormí, yo durmiera,* from *Dormir.* *V.* DORMIR.)

Duermevela [doo-err-may-vay'-lah], *m.* (Acad.) 1. (Coll.) Dozing, a nap. 2. (Coll.) Laboured, interrupted sleep; a cat-nap.

Duerna [doo-err'-nah], *f.* *V.* ARTESA.

Duerno [doo-err'-no], *m.* Double sheet, two sheets of printed paper, one within another.

Dueto [doo-ay'-to], *m.* Duet, a short composition for two voices or two instruments.

Dula [doo'-lah], *f.* (Prov.) 1. Herd of black cattle belonging to different persons. 2. Horses and mules which graze on the same pasture. *Vete a la dula,* (Coll.) Begone, get out of my sight.

Dulcamara [dool-cah-mah'-rah], *f.* (Bot.) Woody nightshade or bittersweet nightshade. Solanum dulcamara.

Dulce [dool'-thay], *a.* 1. Sweet, pleasing to the taste, luscious, honeyed. 2. Sweet, not salt; not sour; fresh; without flavour. 3. Sweet, mild, soft, gentle, meek. 4. Comfortable, pleasing, sweet, pleasant, agreeable. 5. Soft, ductile.—*m.* 1. Comfiture, sweetmeat, confection, candied or dried fruits. *Dulce de almíbar,* Preserves, fruit preserved in sirup. 2. *V.* DULZURA.

Dulcecillo, illa, ito, ita [dool-thay-theel'-lyo], *a. dim.* Sweetish, somewhat sweet.

Dulcedumbre [dool-thay-doom'-bray], *f.* Sweetness. *V.* DULZURA.

Dulcémele [dool-thay'-may-lay], *m.* Dulcimer, a musical instrument.

Dulcemente [dool-thay-men'-tay], *adv.* Sweetly, delightfully, mildly, gently.

Dulcenta [dool-then'-tah], *f.* A large kind of apple, red and savoury, suited for making cider.

Dulcería [dool-thay-ree'-ah], *f.* Confectionery-shop.

Dulcera [dool-thay'-rah], *f.* A preserve dish, generally of glass.

Dulcero, ra [dool-thay'-ro, rah], *m.* & *f.* Confectioner.

Dulcificación [dool-the-fe-cah-the-on'], *f.* Dulcification.

Dulcificante [dool-the-fe-cahn'-tay], *pa.* Dulcifying; sweetener.

Dulcificar [dool-the-fe-car'], *va.* To sweeten, to dulcify.

Dulcinea [dool-the-nay'-ah], *f.* Mistress, beloved one, in allusion to the celebrated character of this name in Don Quixote.

Dulcir [dool-theer'], *va.* To grind plate-glass, to remove the inequalities of the surface, to polish.

Dulcísono, na [dool-thee'-so-no, nah], *a.* Sweet-toned.

Dulero [doo-lay'-ro], *m.* (Prov.) Herdsman.

Dulía [doo-lee'-ah], *f.* Dulia, worship of the saints.

Dulimán [doo-le-mahn'], *m.* Long robe worn by the Turks.

Dulzaina [dool-thah'-e-nah], *f.* 1. A musical wind instrument. 2. (Mex.) A lute. 3. (Coll.) Quantity of sweetmeats.

Dulzamara [dool-thah-mah'-rah], *f.* (Bot.) *V.* DULCAMARA.

Dulzarrón, na [dool-thar-rone', nah], *a.* Cloying, sickening, by being too sweet.

Dulzor [dool-thore'], *m.* *V.* DULZURA.

Dulzorar [dool-tho-rar'], *va.* (Prov.) To sweeten, to dulcify.

Dulzura [dool-thoo'-rah], *f.* 1. Sweetness. 2. Sweetness, meekness, gentleness, graciousness, agreeableness. 3. Comfortableness, pleasure. 4. Forbearance. 5. A grateful and pleasing manner of speaking or writing.

Dulzurar [dool-thoo-rar'], *va.* 1. (Chem.) Free from saltness, to dulcify. 2. (Obs.) To soften, to mitigate.

Dulleta [dool-lyay'-tah], *f.* A loose wrapper, for use in cold weather over the house-dress.

Dunas [doo'-nas], *f. pl.* Downs, banks of sand which the sea forms on a coast; dunes. (Also *sing.*)

Duneta [doo-nay'-tah], *f.* (Naut.) The highest part of the poop.

Dungarra [doon-gar'-rah], *f.* A sort of white cotton stuff, made in Persia.

Dúo [doo'-o], *m.* (Mus.) Duo, duet, a musical composition.

Duodecaedro [doo-o-day-cah-ay'-dro], *m.* (Geom.) Dodecahedron, a solid body of twelve faces.

Duodecágono, na [doo-o-day-cah'-go-no, nah], *a.* & *m.* & *f.* Dodecagon, a polygon of twelve sides.

Duodecasílabo, ba [doo-o-day-cah-see'-lah-bo, bah], *a.* Consisting of twelve syllables.

Duodécima [doo-o-day'-the-mah], *f.* (Mus.) A twelfth, octave of the fifth.

Duodecimal [doo-o-day-the-mahl'], *a.* 1. The last of twelve. 2. Duodecimal, a system of enumeration employing twelve distinct characters, and having more common divisors than the decimal.

Duodécimo, ma [doo-o-day'-the-mo, mah], *a.* Twelfth.

Duodécuplo, pla [doo-o-day'-coo-plo, plah], *a.* Duodecuple, twelve-fold.

Duodenal [doo-o-day-nahl'], *a.* Duodenal, relating to the duodenum.

Duodenario, ria [doo-o-day-nah'-re-o, ah], *a.* 1. Lasting twelve days. 2. Divided into twelve parts.

Duodeno, na [doo-o-day'-no, nah], *a.* Twelfth.

Duodeno [doo-o-day'-no], *m.* & *a.* (Anat.) Duodenum, the first of the small intestines.

Duomesino, na [doo-o-may-see'-no, nah], *a.* Of two months, or relating to that space of time.

Dupa [doo'-pah], *m.* Dupe. (Cant. Acad.)

Dupla [doo'-plah], *f.* In colleges, an allowance of provision larger than usual.

Dúplica [doo'-ple-cah], *f.* A writing in which the defendant replies to the complaint of the plaintiff.

Duplicación [doo-ple-cah-the-on'], *f.* 1. Duplication; the act of multiplying by two. 2. Conduplication, a doubling.

Duplicadamente [doo-ple-cah-dah-men'-tay], *adv.* Doubly.

Duplicado [doo-ple-cah'-do], *m.* Duplicate, counterpart.

Duplicado, da [doo-ple-cah'-do, dah], *a.* & *pp.* of DUPLICAR. Duplicate, doubled.

Duplicador [doo-ple-cah-dor'], *m.* An instrument for estimating the particular state of a given volume of air, and its electricity, positive or negative.

Duplicar [doo-ple-car'], *va.* 1. To double, to duplicate. 2. To repeat, to do or say the same thing twice.

Duplicatura [doo-ple-cah-too'-rah], *f.* *V.* DOBLADURA.

Dúplice [doo'-ple-thay], *a.* Double: applied to ancient monasteries with separate cells for friars and nuns.

Duplicidad [doo-ple-the-dahd'], *f.* Duplicity, deceit, foul dealing, falseness.

Duplo [doo'-plo], *m.* Double, twice as much; duple.

Duque [doo'-kay], *m.* 1. Duke. 2. Fold made by Spanish women in their veils.

Duquecito [doo-kay-thee'-to], *m. dim.* A petty duke; a young duke.

Duquesa [doo-kay'-sah], *f.* 1. Duchess. 2. Species of couch.

Dura [doo'-rah], *f.* Duration, continuance.

Durable [doo-rah'-blay], *a.* Durable, lasting.

Duración, Durada [doo-rah-the-on', doo-rah-dah], *f.* Duration, continuance, durableness, durability.

Duraderamente, *adv.* Durably.

Duraderas [doo-rah-day'-ras], *f. pl.* Lasting; lasting prunella.

Duradero, ra [doo-rah-day'-ro, rah], *a.* Lasting, durable.

Duramáter [doo-rah-mah'-ter], *f.* (Anat.) Dura mater, membrane inclosing the brain.

Duramente [doo-rah-men'-tay], *adv.* Hardy, rigorously.

Durando [doo-rahn'-do], *m.* Kind of cloth formerly used in Spain.

Durante [doo-rahn'-tay], *prep.* During; in the meantime.

Durar [doo-rar'], *vn.* To last, to continue, to endure.

Duraznero [doo-rath nay'-ro], *m.* (Bot.) *V.* DURAZNO for the tree.

Durazno [doo-rath'-no], *m.* 1. (Bot.) Common peach-tree. Amygdalus persica. 2. Peach, the fruit of a peach-tree.

Dureto [doo-ray'-to], *m.* A variety of apple.

Dureza [doo-ray'-thah], *f.* 1. Hardness, solidity, firmness. 2. Acerbity or sharpness of temper, obduracy, hardness of heart, cruelty. 3. Steadiness, perseverance, obstinacy. 4. Want of softness or delicacy in paintings. 5. Tumour or callosity. *Dureza de vientre,* Costiveness. *Dureza de oído,* Dulness of hearing. *Dureza de estilo,* Harshness of style.

Duriagra [doo-re-ah'-grah], *f.* A sort of cotton striped stuff, white and blue.

Durillo, lla [doo-reel'-lyo, lyah], *a. dim.* Rather hard, hardish.—*m.* 1. (Bot.) Common laurestine, viburnum. Viburnum tinus. 2. Callosity upon a horse, arising from the rubbing of some part of the harness or saddle. 3. *Durillo relevante,* Bombast, fustian.

Durmiente [door-me-en'-tay], *pa.* Sleeping, sleeper, dormant.—*m.* 1. In buildings, dormant or dormer, a piece of timber which rests on another; girder, stringer. 2. (R. w.) A cross tie, a sleeper. (Amer.) 3. (Naut.) Clamp, shelf, a thick plank nailed to the ship's side within.

Duro, ra [doo'-ro, rah], *a.* 1. Hard, solid, firm, knotty. 2. Hard, vexatious, unbearable, unjust. 3. Hard, oppressive, rigorous, cruel, hard-hearted, unmerciful. 4. Stubborn, obstinate. 5. Miserable, avaricious. 6. Rude, ill-natured, harsh, peevish, rough, rugged of temper. 7. (Naut.) Carrying a stiff sail: spoken of a ship. 8. (Pict.) Harsh and rough, opposite to delicate and soft. Harsh, unsonorous, in music. *A duras penas,* With difficulty and labour.

Duro [doo'-ro], *m.* 1. Dollar, a silver coin, containing ten silver reals, or twenty reals vellon; equal to eight shillings, British. 2. A low, rough saddle used by Indians. *Pesos duros,* Hard dollars, in contradistinction to dollars of exchange.

Durvillea [door-veel'-lyay-ah], *f.* A fucaceous plant of Chili, which serves as food to poor people.

Dutka [doot'-kah], *f.* A double flute, with three holes in each of the tubes, which are unequal. Used in Russia.

Duunviro [doo-oon-vee'-ro], *m.* Duumvir, one of the duumviri, two Roman judges.

Duunvirato [doo-oon-ve-rah'-to], *m.* Duumvirate.

Dux [doocs], *m.* Doge, magistrate in the republics of Venice and Genoa.

Dzohara [dtho-ah'-rah], *f.* An Arabian divinity, corresponding to Venus.

E

E [A or ay] is the sixth letter of the alphabet, and the second of the vowels. *E* is pronounced in Spanish as in the English words they, eh; when unaccented, much like e in red. *E* was formerly used as a copulative conjunction, corresponding to and, but it is now in general replaced by *y*, yet retained when it precedes a word which begins with the vowel *i* or *hi*; as, *Sabios e ignorantes*, Wise and ignorant men; *Padre e hijo*, Father and son.

Ea [ay'-ah], *m.* A kind of aspiration used to awaken attention. *Ea pues*, An interjection of inference or inquiry, equal to, Well then! Let us see. *Ea sus*, (Obs.) An aspiration of excitement of the same import.

Ebanista [ay-bah-nees'-tah], *m.* Cabinet-maker, ebonist.

Ebanistería [ay-bah-nis-tay-ree'-ah], *f.* Cabinet-work, cabinet-maker's shop.

Ebanizar [ay-bah-ne-thar'], *va.* To ebonize, to give to wood the colour of ebony.

Ébano [ay'-bah-no], *m.* Ebony, a hard, black wood.

Ebonita [ay-bo-nee'-tah], *f.* Vulcanite, ebonite.

Ebriedad [ay-bre-ay-dahd'], *f.* Ebriety. *V.* Embriaguez.

Ebrio, ria [ay'-bre-o, ah], *a.* Inebriated, intoxicated, tipsy.

Ebrioso, sa [ay-bre-o'-so, sah], *a.* Intoxicated, drunken.

Ebulición, Ebullición [ay-boo-le-the-on'], *f.* Ebullition.

Ebúrneo, nea [ay-boor'-nay-o, ah], *a.* (Poet.) Made of ivory, resembling ivory.

Eccehomo [ec-thay-oh'-mo], *m.* Ecce Homo, Behold the man: the name of any painting which represents our Saviour given up to the people by Pilate.

Eccema, *f.* or **Eczema**, *m.* [ec-thay'-mah], (Med.) Eczema, a disease of the skin.

Ecdémico, ca [ec-day'-me-co, cah], *a.* (Med.) Non-contagious.

Ecdora [ec-do'-rah], *f.* (Med.) Excoriation.

Ecfora [ec-fo'-rah], *f.* (Arch.) Ecphora, the projection of any member beyond that immediately below it.

Eclécticamente [ay-clec'-te-cah-men-tay], *adv.* Eclectically.

Eclecticismo [ay-clec-te-thees'-mo], *m.* Eclecticism.

Ecléctico [ay-clec'-te-co], *m.* Eclectic, one of a class of ancient philosophers, who professed to be of no one sect, but to choose what was good from all sects; one of a sect in the Christian church, who considered the doctrine of Plato conformable to the spirit of the Christian doctrine; one of a sect of physicians among the ancients.

Ecléctico, ca [ay-clec'-te-co, cah], *a.* Eclectic.

Eclesiásticamente, *adv.* Ecclesiastically.

Eclesiástico [ay-clay-se-ahs'-te-co], *m.* 1. Clergyman, ecclesiastic, priest. 2. Ecclesiasticus, one of the books of Scripture.

Eclesiástico, ca [ay-clay-se-ahs'-te-co, cah], *a.* Ecclesiastical, ecclesiastic.

Eclesiastizar [ay-clay-se-as-te-thar'], *va.* *V.* Espiritualizar.

Eclipsable [ay-clip-sah'-blay], *a.* That may be eclipsed.

Eclipsar [ay-clip-sar'], *va.* To eclipse, to darken a luminary, to outshine.

Eclipse [ay-cleep'-say], *m.* Eclipse.

Eclipsis [ay-cleep'-sis], *f.* Ellipsis.

Eclíptica [ay-cleep'-te-cah], *f.* Ecliptic, a circle supposed to run obliquely through the equator.

Eclíptico, ca [ay-cleep'-te-co, cah], *a.* Ecliptic, belonging to the eclipse.

Eclisa [ay-clee'-sah], *f.* A rail coupling, fish-plate, shin.

Écloga [ay'-clo-gah], *f.* Eclogue, a pastoral poem. *V.* Égloga.

Eco [ay'-co], *m.* 1. Echo. 2. The repetition of the last syllables of verse. 3. A confused remembrance or idea of the past. 4. Hole or hollow in a horse's sole, occasioned by a frush or other humour. *Hacer eco*, To accord, to agree; to do any thing great or notable.

Ecóico, ca [ay-co'-e-co, cah], *a.* (Poet.) Relating to echoes.

Ecología [ay-co-lo-hee'-ah], *f.* Ecology.

Ecológico, ca [ay-co-lo'-he-co, cah], *a.* Ecological.

Ecólogo, ga [ay-coh'-lo-go, gah], *m.* & *f.* Ecologist.

Ecometría [ay-co-may-tree'-ah], *f.* (Arch.) Echometry.

Ecómetro [ay-co'-may-tro], *m.* Echometer.

Economato [ay-co-no-mah'-to], *m.* Guardianship, trusteeship.

Economía [ay-co-no-mee'-ah], *f.* 1. Economy, prudent management, moderation, frugality. 2. Economy, the disposition of time and many other things. 3. (Pict.) The disposition of figures. 4. Scantiness, niggardliness, misery. 5. Economy, a political science.

Economía doméstica [ay-co-no-mee'-ah do-mes'-te-cah], *f.* Home economics; domestic science.

Económica [ay-co-no'-me-cah], *f.* Economics, household management.

Económicamente, *adv.* Economically.

Económico, ca [ay-co-no'-me-co, cah], *a.* 1. Economical, economic. 2. Economical, frugal; avaricious.

Economista [ay-co-no-mees'-tah], *m.* 1. Economist. 2. One who is a good manager of affairs.

Economizar [ay-co-no-me-thar'], *va.* To economize.

Ecónomo [ay-co'-no-mo], *m.* 1. Curator or guardian, trustee. 2. An administrator of ecclesiastical livings which are under litigation.

Éctasis [ec'-tah-sis], *f.* (Gram.) Ectasis, the lengthening of a short syllable for the due measure of the verse.

Ectipo [ec-tee'-po], *m.* Ectype, copy from an original.

Ectropión [ec-tro-pe-on'], *m.* (Med.) Ectropion, eversion of the eyelids, as a morbid state.

Ecuable [ay-coo-ah'-blay], *a.* 1. Equable, equal to itself. 2. (Obs.) Just, right.

Ecuación [ay-coo-ah-the-on'], *f.* 1. Equation, the difference between the time marked by the sun's apparent motion, and that measured by its real motion. 2. Equation, expression of equality between two algebraic quantities. 3. Equalization.

Ecuador, Ecuator [ay-coo-ah-dor', ay-coo-ah-tor'], *m.* 1. Equator, a great circle of the celestial and terrestrial spheres. 2. The line.

Ecuanimidad [ay-coo-ah-ne-me-dahd'], *f.* Equanimity; evenness of mind.

Ecuatorial [ay-coo-ah-to-re-ahl'], *a* Equatorial, relating to the equator.—*m.* Equatorial telescope.

Ecuatoriano, na [ah-coo-ah-to-re-ah'-no nah], *a.* Ecuadorian, belonging to Ecuador.

Ecuestre [ay-coo-es'-tray], *a.* Equestrian.

Ecuménico, ca [ay-coo-may'-ne-co, cah], *a.* Œcumenical, universal.

Ecuóreo, rea [ay-coo-o'-ray-o, ah], *a.* (Poet.) Belonging to the sea.

Eczema [ec-thay'-mah], *m.* V. Eccema.

Echacantos [ay-chah-cahn'-tos], *m.* (Coll.) A rattle-brained fellow.

Echacorvear [ay-chah-cor-vay-ar'], *vn.* (Coll.) To pimp, to procure.

Echacorvería [ay-chah-cor-vay-ree'-ah], *f.* (Coll.) Profession of a pimp or procurer.

Echacuervos [ay-chah-coo-err'-vos], *m.* (Coll.) 1. Pimp, procurer. *V.* Alcahuete. 2. Cheat, impostor.

Echada [ay-chah'-dah], *f.* 1. Cast, throw. 2. The act of throwing one's self on the ground.

Echadero [ay-chah-day'-ro], *m.* Place of rest or repose.

Echadillo [ay-chah-deel'-lyo], *m.* A foundling.

Echadizo, za [ay-chah-dee'-tho, thah], *m.* & *f.* 1. A spy. 2. One who is employed in cautiously circulating reports. 3. Foundling.

Echadizo, za [ay-chah-dee'-tho, thah], *a.* 1. That which is indirectly reported with the object of discovering some secret. 2. Applied to a person suborned to pry into other people's actions. 3. Supposititious, fictitious.

Echador, ra [ay-chah-dor', rah], *m.* & *f.* Thrower.

Echadura [ay-chah-doo'-rah], *f.* 1. The act of laying one's self down in a place. 2. Brooding, hatching, the act of sitting on eggs.

Echamiento [ay-chah-me-en'-to], *m.* 1. Cast, throw, casting or throwing. 2. Projection, the act of throwing away, rejection. 3. Ejection, casting out, expulsion.

Echapellas [ay-chah-pel'-lyas], *m.* A wool-soaker.

Echar [ay-char'], *va.* 1. To cast, to throw, to dart, to jet. 2. To turn or drive away, to eject, to reject, to cast away, to throw out or expel from an office or profession. 3. To shoot, to bud, to issue, to sprout, burst out. 4. To put, to apply. 5. To lay on or impose as a tax. 6. (Coll.) To eat, to drink. 7. To couple male and female animals for procreating. 8. To impute, to ascribe. 9. To perform for a wager. 10. To deal out, to distribute. 11. To publish, to give out, to issue. 12. With *por* and the name of a calling, to follow it. 13. With the words *rayos*, *centellas*, *fuego*, etc., to show much annoyance, to be very angry. 14. With the name of a punishment, to condemn to it. 15. With the infinitive of a verb and the preposition *á*, it signifies to begin the action denoted by the verb, *echar á reir*, To burst out laughing. 16. *Echar por*, To go by one side or the other. 17. Speaking of horses, coaches, clothing, to use them, put into service. The verb *echar* is well described by a Spanish lexicographer as a verb of general utility. It serves frequently to assist the meaning of another verb, and enters into many phrases. *Echar carnes*, To become fat. *Echar por otra parte*, To differ in opinion from another. *Echar en sal*, To reserve for another occasion. *Echar de menos*, To note, and repair a lack. *Echarse a perder*, To lose its good taste, to spoil. *Echar el pecho al agua*, To undertake a thing resolutely. *Echar fuego*, To be the cause of a dispute. *Echar la pulga tras de la oreja*, To make a person uneasy. *Echar los hígados*, To be very much fatigued. *Echar bando*, To publish a law or edict. *Echar a alguno a patadas*, To kick one out. *Echar a galeras*, To sentence to the galleys. *Echar a borbotones*, To talk much and at random. *Echar al camino*, To take to the road, to become a highway robber. *Echar a fondo* or *a pique*, (Naut.) To sink a vessel. *Echar abajo, en tierra, por tierra* or *por el suelo*, To throw down, to demolish. *Echar agua en el mar*, To give to a person who has a great deal. *Echar el agua a un niño*, To baptize a child. *Echar a la* or *en la piedra*, To throw one's children into the foundling hospital. *Echar a trompa y talega*, To talk nonsense. *Echar bravatas* or *baladronadas*, or *plantas*, To boast, to brag of. *Echarla de bravo, de majo*, or *de grande*, To swagger. *Echar carrillos*, To grow plump and fat in the cheeks. *Echar coche*, To set up a coach. *Echar de manga*, To make a cat's paw of one. *Echar el compás*, To beat time. *Echar el sello*, To give the finishing stroke. *Echar en saco roto*, (Met.) To labour to no purpose: applied to a person who will not heed good advice. *Echar el bofe* or *los bofes*, To labour excessively; to solicit anxiously. *Echar la plática a otra parte*, To cut short the conversation. *Echar la tijera*, To cut up with scissors. *Echar menos una persona* or *cosa*, To miss a person or thing. *Echar piernas*, To boast of beauty or valour; to convalesce. *Echar a uno la pierna encima*, To surpass or outshine a person. *Echar la regla*, To prove correctness by measurement. *Echar buen pelo* or *buena pluma*, To begin to grow rich. *Echar la lanza*, To impugn, to contradict. *Echar tierra a alguna cosa*, To bury an affair in oblivion. *Echar al mundo*, To create, to bring forth. *Echar mano*, To give assistance. *Echar un remiendo a la vida*, (Coll.) To take some little refreshment. *Echar a uno á pasear*, To send one abruptly about his business. *Echar con cajas destempladas* or *enhoramala*, To dismiss one roughly and contemptuously. *Echar suertes*, To draw lots. *Echar a correr*, To run away. *Echar en cara, a la cara* or *en la cara*, To reproach to one's face, to throw any thing in one's teeth. *Echar buen* or *mal lance*, To succeed or fail in an enterprise. *Echar de ver*, To remark, to observe, to perceive. *Echar el cuerpo fuera*, To withdraw from an affair. *Echar la ley a uno*, To judge and condemn a person to the utmost rigour of the law. *Echar a perder*, To spoil, to mar, not to utilize a thing. *Echarlo todo a rodar*, To spoil or mar utterly an affair. *Echar mano*, To lay hold of a thing; to make use of it, to seize, to catch. *Echar pelillos a la mar*, To be reconciled, laying aside all causes of dissension. *Echar por en medio*, To cut short any difference. *Echar el pie adelante*, (Met.) To progress, to be foremost. *Echar el pie atrás*, To retrograde, to be last. *No hay que echar pie atrás*, You must not flinch. *Echar todo el trapo* or *vela*, (Naut.) To crowd all sail. *Echar una mano*, To lend a hand, to assist. *Echar un jarro de agua*, (Met.) To cut short a person's discourse, or throw a damper upon it by an unexpected dry remark. *Echar* or *echarse un borrón*, (Met.) To disgrace one's self. *Echar al contrario*, *V.* 7. To put an ass to a mare, or a horse to a she-ass, in order to raise a mule. *Echar de recio*, To urge on, to incite. *Echar un guante*, (Met.) To make a collection for a distressed person. *Echar el guante*, To arrest a person. *Echar aceite sobre la lumbre para apagarla*, (Coll.) To stir up contentions. *Echar la corredera*, (Naut.) To heave the log. *Echar el escandallo*, (Naut.) To heave the lead, to take soundings. *Echar en tierra*, (Naut.) To land, to disembark. *Echar raíces*. 1. To take root. 2. (Met.) To become fixed or established in a place. 3. To be rooted or confirmed in any thing by inveterate habit or custom.—*vr.* 1. To lie, to rest, to stretch one's self at full length; of birds, to sit on eggs. 2. To throw one's self down. 3. To apply one's self to a business. 4. To yield, to desist; of the wind, to grow calm, to abate. *Echarse sobre áncora*, (Naut.) To drag the anchor. *Echarse a pechos*, To gulp or drink immoderately. *Echarse al coleto*, To eat, to swallow. *Échese y no se derrame*, Spend without extravagance.

Echazón [ay-chah-thon'], *f.* (Law) Jetson or jettison, act of throwing goods overboard.

Echeno [ay-chay'-no], *m.* In foundries, the pouring hole.

Edad [ay-dahd'], *f.* 1. Age, the length of life. 2. Age, a particular generation or epoch of time. 3. Era, the time when a particular group of men or animals lived. *Edad de la aviación*, Air age. *Edad atómica*, Atomic age. *Edad media*, The Middle Ages. *Mayor de edad*, Of age. *Menor edad*, 1. Minority. 2. Infancy. *Ser menor de edad*, To be a minor; to be under age. *Un señor de edad*, An older man. *Tener la edad de diez años*, To be ten years old.

Edecán [ay-day-cahn'], *m.* (Mil.) Aide-de-camp.

Edema [ay-day'-mah], *f.* Œdema, a general puffiness of parts, due to effusion of serum.

Edén [ay-dayn'], *m.* Eden, paradise. (Hebrew.)

Edeografía [ay-day-o-grah-fee'-ah], *f.* Description of the organs of generation.

Éder [ay'-der], *m.* (Zool.) Eider-duck.

Edición [ay-de-the-on'], *f.* Edition.

Edicto [ay-deec'-to], *m.* 1. Edict, a proclamation. 2. Poster, placard.

Edificación [ay-de-fe-cah-the-on'], *f.* 1. Construction, the art of raising any building. 2. Edification, edifying.

Edificador, ra [ay-de-fe-cah-dor', rah], *m. & f.* Edifier, constructor; builder.

Edificante [ay-de-fe-cahn'-tay], *a.* Edifying; erecting.

Edificar [ay-de-fe-car'], *va.* 1. To edify, to build, to raise or construct a building. 2. To edify, to instruct.

Edificativo, va [ay-de-fe-cah-tee'-vo, vah], *a.* Exemplary, instructive.

Edificatorio, ria [ay-de-fe-cah-to'-re-o, ah], *a.* Edificatory.

Edificio [ay-de-fee'-the-o], *m.* Edifice, structure, fabric.

Edil [ay-deel'], *m.* 1. Edile, a Roman magistrate. 2. (Neol.) *V.* CONCEJAL.

Edilidad [ay-de-le-dahd'], *f.* Edileship.

Editor, ra [ay-de-tor', rah], *a.* Publishing.—*m. & f.* 1. Publisher. *Casa editora*, Publishing house. 2. Editor. *Editor responsable*, Editor (of an article).

Editorial [ay-de-to-re-ahl'], *a.* 1. Publishing. 2. Editorial.—*m.* (Article) Editorial.—*f.* Publishing house.

Edredón [ay-dray-done'], *m.* 1. Eider-down, the down of an eider-duck. 2. Feather-pillow.

Educación [ay-doo-cah-the-on'], *f.* Education, instruction, nurture.

Educacionista [ay-doo-cah-the-o-nees'-tah], *m.* (Neol.) Educator.

Educador, ra [ay-doo-cah-dor', rah], *m. & f.* Instructor, educator.

Educando, da [ay-doo-cahn'-do, dah], *m. & f.* Young person that enters a college or convent to be educated.

Educar [ay-doo-car'], *va.* To educate, to instruct, to nourish.

Educativo, va [ay-doo-cah-tee'-vo, vah], *a.* Educational.

Educción [ay-dooc-the-on'], *f.* Eduction, the act of bringing out.

Educir [ay-doo-theer'], *va.* To educe, to extract, to bring out.

Edulcoración [ay-dool-co-rah-the-on'], *f.* Edulcoration, removal of acidity.

Edulcorar [ay-dool-co-rar'], *va.* (Chem.) To sweeten, to remove acidity or acridity.

Efe [ay'-fay], *f.* Spanish name of the letter F.

Efebo, ba [ay-fay'-bo, bah], *a.* Name which the Athenians gave to youths of eighteen to twenty years (arrived at puberty).

Efectivamente [ay-fec-te-vah men'-tay], *adv.* Effectually, powerfully: certainly, actually.

Efectividad [ay-fec-te-ve-dahd'], *f.* Effectiveness.

Efectivo, va [ay-fec-tee'-vo, vah], *a.* 1. Effective, true, certain; effectual. 2. (Com.) Specie, cash, in coin. *Efectivo en caja*, Cash on hand. *Hacer efectiva una letra*, To cash a draft.

Efecto [ay-fec'-to], *m.* 1. Effect; operation. 2. Effect, consequence. 3. Effect, purpose, meaning; general intent.—*pl.* 1. Assets. 2. Effects, goods, movables.—*pl.* (Com.) Drafts. *Efectos públicos*, Public securities. *Efectos en cartera*, Bills in hand. *Efectos á pagar*, Bills payable. *Efectos á recibir*, Bills receivable. *En efecto*, In fact, in truth, actually.

Efectualmente, *adv.* Effectively, effectually.

Efectuar [ay-fec-too-ar'], *va.* To effectuate, to bring to pass, to accomplish, to effect.

Efemérides [ay-fay-may'-re-des], *f. pl.* Ephemeris, a journal; an account of daily transactions.

Efémero [ay-fay'-may-ro], *m.* (Bot.) Iris. Iris sylvestris.

Efervescencia [ay-fer-ves-then'-the-ah], *f.* 1. Effervescence, ebullition. 2. (Met.) Ardour, fervour.

Efervescente [ay-fer-vays-then'-tay], *a.* 1. Effervescent. 2. Seething.

Efetá [ay-fay-tah'], *m.* Word used to signify the pertinacity with which one maintains a position.

Eficacia [ay-fe cah'-the-ah], *f.* Efficacy, activity.

Eficaz [ay-fe-cath'], *a.* Efficacious, active, powerful, forcible, effective.

Eficazmente [ay-fe-cath-men'-tay], *adv.* Efficaciously, actively, effectively.
Eficiencia [ay-fe-the-en'-the-ah], *f.* Efficiency, effectiveness.
Eficiente [ay-fe-the-en'-tay], *a.* Efficient, effective, effectual.
Eficientemente *adv.* Efficiently, effectively.
Efigie [ay-fee'-he-ay], *f.* Effigy, image.
Efimera [ay-fee'-may-rah], *f.* 1. Ephemera, a fever that terminates in one day. 2. Ephemera, ephemerid, day-fly or May-fly, an insect that lives but a day.
Efimeral, *a.* (Obs.) *V.* EFÍMERO.
Efimero, ra [ay-fee'-may-ro, rah], *a.* Ephemeral, ephemerous, diurnal, beginning and ending in one day.
Eflorecer [ay-flo-ray-therr'], *vr.* (Chem.) To effloresce, to fall into powder when exposed to the air.
Eflorescencia [ay-flo-res-then'-the-ah], *f.* (Chem.) Efflorescence.
Eflorescente [ay-flo-res-then'-tay], *a.* (Chem.) Efflorescent.
Efluencia [ay-floo-en'-the-ah], *f.* Effluence, emanation.
Efluente [ay-floo-en'-tay], *f.* Effluent, emanant.
Efluvio [ay-floo'-ve-o], *m.* 1. Effluvium or effluvia. 2. Exhalation.
Efugio [ay-foo'-he-o], *m.* Subterfuge, evasion, shift.
Efundir [ay-foon-deer'], *va.* To effuse, to pour out, to spill.
Efusión [ay-foo-se-on'], *f.* 1. Effusion, efflux. 2. Confidential disclosure of sentiments.
Efuso, sa [ay-foo'-so, sah], *a.* & *pp. irr.* of EFUNDIR. Effused.
Égida [ay'-he-dah], *f.* 1. Egis, the shield of Minerva. 2. (Met.) Protection, defense.
Egilope [ay-hee'-lo-pay], *f.* (Bot.) Wild bastard oat. Ægilops.
Egipciaco, Egipciano, Egipcio [ay-hip-the-ah'-co], *a.* Egyptian.
Egiptólogo [ay-hip-toh'-lo-go], *m.* Egyptologist.
Égira [ay'-he-rah], *f.* Hegira, the Mohammedan epoch.
Égloga [ay'-glo-gah], *f.* Eclogue, a pastoral poem.
Egoismo [ay-go-ees'-mo], *m.* 1. Selfishness, self-love. 2. Egoism.
Egoista [ay-go-ees'-tah], *a.* Selfish, attentive only to one's own interest or ease.—*m.* Egoist, one of a class of philosophers who professed to be sure of nothing but their own existence.
Egotismo [ay-go-tees'-mo], *m.* Egotism, selfishness.
Egotista [ay-go-tees'-tah], *m.* & *a.* Egotist, one who talks too much of himself.
Egregiamente, *adv.* Illustriously, egregiously.
Egregio, gia [ay-gray'-he-o, ah], *a.* Egregious, eminent.
Egrena [ay-gray'-nah], *f.* An iron clamp.
Egreso [ay-gray'-so], *m.* Item of expense, outgo.
Egrisador [ay-gre-sah-dor'], *m.* A box in which lapidaries preserve the powder for grinding diamonds.
Egrisar [ay-gre-sar'], *va.* To grind and polish diamonds.
Eidero [ay-e-day'-ro], *m.* Eider-duck.
Ejarrar [ay-har-rar'], *va.* To scrape the bristles from a hide.
Eje [ay'hay], *m.* 1. Axis. 2. Axle tree, axle. 3. Center. 4. Wrist pin. *Eje de levas,* (Mech.) Camshaft. *Eje vertical,* (Aer.) Vertical axis. *Naciones del Eje,* Axis Nations.
Ejecución [ay-hay-coo-the-on'], *f.* 1. Execution, completion, performance. 2. Execution, the act of the law, by which possession is given of body or goods. 3. Death inflicted by forms of law. 4. (Mus.) Execution, technical skill in playing or singing.
Ejecutable [ay-hay-coo-tah'-blay], *a.* Executable, performable.
Ejecutante [ay-hay-coo-tahn'-tay], *m.* & *a.* One who compels another to pay a debt by legal execution.
Ejecutar [ay-hay-coo-tar'], *va.* 1. To execute, to perform, to make, to do, to act. 2. (Met.) To impel, to urge, to importune, to incite. 3. To oblige one to pay what he owes. 4. To put to death according to the form of justice.
Ejecutivamente [ay-hay-coo-te-vah-men'-tay], *adv.* Executively, promptly.
Ejecutivo, va [ay-hay-coo-tee'-vo, vah], *a.* 1. Executive, active. 2. Executory.
Ejecutor, ra [ay-hay-coo-tor', rah], *m.* & *f.* 1. Executor or executer, one that performs or executes any thing. 2. Officer of justice who serves executions. *Ejecutor* or *ejecutor de la justicia,* Executioner, executer. *V.* VERDUGO.
Ejecutoria [ay-hay-coo-to'-re-ah], *f.* 1. (Law) A writ or decree of execution. 2. Letters patent of nobility, pedigree. 3. Executorship.
Ejecutoria [ay-hay-coo-to-ree'-ah], *f.* The post or office of an executioner.
Ejecutorial [ay-hay-coo-to-re-ahl'], *a.* Applied to the execution of the sentence of an ecclesiastical tribunal.
Ejecutoriar [ay-hay-coo-to-re-ar'], *va.* 1. To obtain a verdict or judgment in one's favour. 2. To establish the truth of a thing.
Ejecutorio, ria [ay-hay-coo-to'-re-o, ah], *a.* (Law) Executory, belonging to an execution or seizure.
Ejemplar [ay-hem-plar'], *m.* 1. Exemplar, a pattern, model; original, prototype. 2. Precedent, example. 3. Copy of a work. 4. An example, warning.—*a.* Exemplary, worthy of imitation. *Sin ejemplar,* 1. Not to be a precedent: used in conceding special grants. 2. Without precedent.
Ejemplarmente, *adv.* 1. Exemplarily. 2. Exemplarily, in a manner to warn others. 3. Edifyingly.
Ejemplificación [ay-hem-ple-fe-cah-the-on'], *f.* Exemplification, illustration by examples.
Ejemplificar [ay-hem-ple-fe-car'], *va.* To exemplify.
Ejemplo [ay-hem'-plo], *m.* 1. Example, precedent, instance; comparison. 2. Pattern, copy; exemplar, exemplarity, footstep. *Por ejemplo,* For instance. *Dar ejemplo,* To set an example for the imitation of others.
Ejercer [ay-her-therr'], *va.* To exercise, to practise, to perform, to use.
Ejercicio [ay-her-thee'-the-o], *m.* 1. Exercise. 2. Employment, exercise, office, task; ministry. 3. Exercise, labour of the body, labour considered as conducive to health. 4. Military evolutions. *Hacer ejercicio,* 1. To drill troops, to train to military operations; to use exercise. 2. To take a walk, to labour for health. *Estar en* or *tomar ejercicios,* To be in a spiritual retreat; to devote some days to meditation, prayer, etc. *El ejercicio hace maestro,* Practice makes perfect.
Ejercitación [ay-her-the-tah-the-on'], *f.* Exercitation, practice.
Ejercitador, ra [ay-her-the-tah-dor', rah], *m.* & *f.* Exerciser, practiser.
Ejercitante [ay-her-the-tahn'-tay], *m.* 1. The person who is in a spiritual retreat. 2. One who maintains a thesis in disputation or for an academic degree.—*pa.* Exerciser, exercising.
Ejercitar [ay-her-the-tar'], *va.* 1. To exercise, to put into practice. 2. To exercise troops, to teach by practice. *Ejercitar la paciencia de alguno,* To try the patience of any one.—*vr.* To practise, to do repeatedly in order to acquire skill.
Ejercitativo, va [ay-her-the-tah-tee'-vo, vah], *a.* That which may be exercised.
Ejército [ay-herr'-the-to], *m.* An army.
Ejido [ay-hee'-do], *m.* Common, a public inclosed space of land.
Ejión [ay-he-on'], *m.* (Arch.) Corbel (piece), purlin.
Ejotes [ay-ho'-tes], *m. pl.* (Mexican) String-beans.
El [el]. An article of the masculine gender. The.
Él, ella, ello [ayl, ayl'-lyah, ayl'-lyo], *pron.* He, she, it.
Elaboración [ay-lah-bo-rah-the-on'], *f.* Elaboration.
Elaborado, da [ay-lah-bo-rah'-do, dah], *a.* Elaborate.—*pp.* of ELABORAR.
Elaborador, ra [ay-lah-bo-rah-dor', rah], *m.* & *f.* One who or that which elaborates.
Elaborar [ay-lah-bo-rar'], *va.* To elaborate, to finish with care.
Elación [ay-lah-the-on'], *f.* 1. Elation, haughtiness, pride. 2. Magnanimity, generosity. 3. Affected elevation or sublimity of style.
Elaina [ay-lah-ee'-nah], *f.* Olein or absolute oil; elain.
Elaiometría [ay-lah-e-o-may-tree'-ah], *f.* The measurement of the density of oils.
Elaiómetro [ay-lah-e-o'-may-tro], *m.* Elæometer, a hydrometer for determining the density of oils.
Elaiso [ay-lah'-e-so], *m.* 1. Greek name of the olive-tree. 2. A kind of palm, from the fruit of which in S. America an oil is obtained.
Elamí [ay-lah-mee'], *m.* The note in music named mi. (Ant.)
Elamita [ay-lah-mee'-tah], *a.* & *m.* Elamite, belonging to Elam.
Elanguero [ay-lan-gay'-ro], *m.* An instrument serving to tie by the head freshly caught codfishes.
Elasticidad [ay-las-te-the-dahd'], *f.* 1. Elasticity. 2. Facility of being adapted to every use and necessity.
Elástico, ca [ay-lahs'-te-co, cah], *a* Elastic, elastical.—*f.* An undershirt —*m.* A spring. (Mech.)
Elaterina [ay-lah-tay-ree'-nah], *f.* Elaterin, a crystallizable principle obtained from elaterium.
Elaterio [ay-lah-tay'-re-o], *m.* Elaterium, violent purge.
Elatine [ay-lah-tee'-nay], *f.* (Bot.) Smooth speedwell. Veronica serpyllifolia.
Elche [el'-chay], *m.* Apostate, renegado.
Eldorado [el-do-rah'-do], *m.* An imaginary paradise of riches and abundance.
Ele [ay'-lay], *f.* Spanish name of the letter L.
Eleborina [ay-lay-bo-ree'-nah], *f.* (Bot.) Helleborine. Serapias.
Eléboro, Elebor [ay-lay'-bo-ro, ay-lay-bor'], *m.* (Bot.) Hellebore. Hellebórus.
Elección [ay-lec-the-on'], *f.* 1. Election, the act of choosing. 2. Election, the ceremony of a public choice. 3. Election, voluntary preference, liberty of action. 4. Election, discernment, choice, distinction, mind.

Electivo, va [ay-lec-tee'-vo, vah], *a.* Elective.

Electo, ta [ay-lec'-to, tah], *a.* & *pp. irr.* of ELEGIR. Elect, chosen.

Electo [ay-lec'-to], *m.* Elect, a person chosen; nominee.

Elector [ay-lec-tor'], *m.* 1. Elector. 2. Elector, a German prince.

Electoral [ay-lec-to-rahl'], *a.* Electoral.

Electricidad [ay-lec-tre-the-dahd'], *f.* Electricity.

Electricista [ay-lec-tre-thees'-tah], *m.* Electrician.

Eléctrico, ca [ay-lec'-tre-co, cah], *a.* Electric or electrical.

Electrificación [ay-lec-tre-fe-cah-the-on'], *f.* Electrification.

Electrificar [ay-lec-tre-fe-car'], *va.* To electrify.

Electrización [ay-lec-tre-tha-the-on'], *f.* (Phys.) Electrification, electrization.

Electrizar [ay-lec-tre-thar'], *va.* 1. To electrify, to make electric, to impart electricity. 2. To fill with enthusiasm.—*vr.* To electrize.

Electro [ay-lec'-tro], *m.* 1. Electron, or amber. 2. Electrum, a mixed metal of gold and silver.

Electrocardiógrafo [ay-lec-tro-car-de-o'-grah-fo], *m.* Electrocardiograph.

Electrocardiograma [ay-lec-tro-car-de-o-grah'-mah], *m.* Electrocardiogram.

Electrocución [ay-lec-tro-coo-the-on'], *f.* Electrocution.

Electrocutar [ay-lec-tro-coo-tar'], *va.* To electrocute.

Electrochoque [ay-lec-tro-cho'-kay], *m.* Electroshock therapy.

Electrodinámica [ay-lec-tro-de-nah'-me-cah], *f.* Electrodynamics.

Electrodinámico, ca [ay-lec-tro-de-nah'-me-co, cah], *a.* Electrodynamic.

Electrodo [ay-lec-tro'-do], *m.* Electrode.

Electrodoméstico, ca [ay-lec-tro-do-mes'-te-co, cah], *a.* *Aparato electrodoméstico*, Home appliance.

Electróforo [ay-lec-tro'-fo-ro], *m.* Electrophorus.

Electrógrafo [ay-lec-tro'-grah-fo], *m.* Electrograph.

Electroimán [ay-lec-tro-ee-mahn'], *m.* Electromagnet.

Electrólisis [ay-lec-tro'-le-sis], *f.* Electrolysis.

Electrólito [ay-lec-tro'-le-to], *m.* Electrolyte.

Electrolizable [ay-lec-tro-le-thah'-blay], *a.* Electrolyzable, decomposable by electricity.

Electrolización [ay-lec-tro-le-thah-the-on'], *f.* Electrolyzation, decomposing by electricity.

Electrolizar [ay-lec-tro-le-thar'], *va.* To electrolyze, to decompose a chemical compound by electricity.

Electromagnético, ca [ay-lec-tro-mag-nay'-te-co, cah], *a.* Electromagnetic.

Electromagnetismo [ay-lec-tro-mag-nay-tees'-mo], *m.* Electro-magnetism.

Electrometría [ay-lec-tro-may-tree'-ah], *f.* Electrometry, the science or art of making electrical measurements.

Electrómetro [ay-lec-tro'-may-tro], *m.* Electrometer, an instrument for measuring electricity.

Electromotor, ra [ay-lec-tro-mo-tor', rah], *a.* Electromotor.—*m.* An electric motor.

Electrón [ay-lec-trone'], *m.* Electron.

Electronegativo, va [ay-lec-tro-nay-gah-te'-vo, vah], *a.* Electro-negative.

Electrónica [ay-lec-tro'-nee-cah], *f.* Electronics.

Electrónico, ca [ay-lec-tro'-nee-co- cah], *a.* Electronic.

Electropositivo, va [ay-lec-tro-po-se-tee'-vo, vah]. Electro-positive.

Electropuntura [ay-lec-tro-poon-too'-rah]. *f.* Electropuncture.

Electroscopio [ay-lec-tros-co'-pe-o], *m.* Electroscope.

Electrotecnia [ay-lec-tro-tec'-ne-ah], *f.* Electrotechnics.

Electroterapia [ay-lec-tro-tay-rah'-pe-ah], *f.* Electrotherapy.

Electrotipia [ay-lec-tro-tec'-pe-ah], *f.* Electrotyping.

Electrotípico, ca [ay-lec-tro-tee'-pe-co, cah]. *a.* Electrotypic, relating to electrotyping.

Electrotipista [ay-lec-tro-te-pees'-tah], *m.* Electrotyper.

Electuario [ay-lec-too-ah'-re-o], *m.* Electuary, a kind of medicinal conserve.

Elefancía [ay-lay-fan-thee'-ah], *f.* Elephantiasis, a species of leprosy.

Elefante, ta [ay-lay-fahn'-tay, tah], *m.* & *f.* Elephant.

Elefantíasis [ay-lay-fan-tee'-ah-sis], *f.* Elephantiasis.

Elefantino, na [ay-lay-fan-tee'-no, nah], *a.* Elephantine.

Elegancia [ay-lay-gahn'-the-ah], *f.* 1. Elegance, beauty of style. 2. Elegance, gracefulness; neatness.

Elegante [ay-lay-gahn'-tay], *a.* Elegant, gallant, fine, accomplished, nice, dainty.

Elegía [ay-lay-hee'-ah], *f.* Elegy.

Elegibilidad [ay-lay-he-be-le-dahd'], *f.* (Littl. us.) Eligibility.

Elegible [ay-lay-hee'-blay], *a.* Eligible, preferable.

Elegido, da [ay-lay-hee'-do, dah], *a.* Elect, chosen.—*pp.* of ELEGIR.

Elegir [ay-lay-heer'], *va.* To choose, to elect, to name, or to nominate.

Élego, ga [ay'-lay-go, gah], *a.* Mournful, plaintive.

Elemental [ay-lay-men-tahl'], *a.* 1. Elemental. 2. Essential, fundamental. 3. Constitutive, constituent.

Elemento [ay-lay-men'-to], *m.* 1. Element. 2. Element, the first or constituent principle of any thing. 3. Element, the proper sphere of any thing, or any thing which pleases the fancy. *Elementos*, Elements, rudiments, as of literature or science.

Elemí [ay-le-mee'], *m.* Elimi, a resin.

Elenco [ay-len'-co], *m.* 1. Table, index. *Elenco de artistas*, Cast of characters (in a play, etc.).

Elevación [ay-lay-vah-the-on'], *f.* 1. Elevation, the act of raising any thing. 2. Highness, loftiness. 3. Elevation, exaltation, dignity, advancement. 4. Elevation, rise, ascent; height. 5. Elevation, exaltation of mind, ecstasy, rapture. 6. Haughtiness, presumption, pride. 7. Altitude, the elevation of the pole above the horizon.

Elevadamente, *adv.* With elevation, loftily.

Elevado, da [ay-lay-vah'-do, dah], *a.* & *pp.* of ELEVAR. 1. Elevate, elevated, exalted, raised aloft. 2. Elevated, sublime, majestic, high, grand, lofty.

Elevador [ay-lay-vah-dor'], *m.* Elevator. *Elevador de granos*, Grain elevator.

Elevamiento [ay-lay-vah-me-en'-to], *m.* Elevation, ecstasy, rapture.

Elevar [ay-lay-var'], *va.* 1. To raise, to elevate, to heave, to lift up. 2. (Met.) To elevate, to exalt to a high station. —*vr.* 1. To be enraptured. 2. To be elated with presumption or pride.

Elidir [ay-le-deer'], *va.* 1. To weaken, to enervate, to debilitate. 2. (Gram.) To elide.
(*Yo elijo, yo elija; él eligió, él eligiera;* from *Elegir.* *V.* PEDIR.)

Elijar [ay-le-har'], *va.* (Pharm.) To seethe or digest vegetable substances.

Eliminacion [ay-le-me-nah-the-on'], *f.* Elimination, exclusion.

Eliminador, ra [ay-le-me-nah-dor', rah], *m.* & *f.* One who or that which eliminates.

Eliminar [ay-le-me-nar'], *va.* 1. To eliminate, to remove one thing from another. 2. To remove a name from a list, a quantity from a calculation, etc.

Elipse [ay-leep'-say], *f.* (Geom.) Ellipse, a conic section.

Elipsis [ay-leep'-sis], *f.* (Gram.) Ellipsis.

Elíptico, ca [ay-leep'-te-co, cah], *a.* Elliptic or elliptical.

Eliseos (**Campos**) [cahm'-pos ay-lee'-say-os], *m. pl.* Elysian fields.

Elisión [ay-le-se-on'], *f.* (Gram.) Elision.

Élitro [ay'-le-tro], *m.* 1. Elytron, a thickened wing-cover. 2. (Bot.) A common conceptacle.

Elixir [ay-lic-seer'], or **Elíxir** [ay-leec'-seer], *m.* Elixir, a medicine.

Elocución [ay-lo-coo-the-on'], *f.* 1. Elocution. 2. Language, expression, style.

Elocuencia [ay-lo-coo-en'-the-ah], *f.* Eloquence.

Elocuente [ay-lo-coo-en'-tay], *a.* Eloquent.

Elocuentemente [ay-lo-coo-en-tay-men'-tay], *adv.* Eloquently.

Elogiador, ra [ay-lo-he-ah-dor', rah], *m.* & *f.* Eulogist, encomiast.

Elogiar [ay-lo-he-ar'], *va.* To praise, to extol, to eulogize, to laud.

Elogio [ay-lo'-he-o], *m.* Eulogy, panegyric.

Elote [ay-lo'-tay], *m.* (Mex.) A tender ear of maize. Also written *Helote.*

Elucidación [ay-loo-the-dah-the-on'], *f.* Elucidation, explanation.

Eludir [ay-loo-deer'], *va.* To elude, to avoid by artifice.

Ella [ayl'-lyah], *pr. f.* She. (It, when referring to things, or neuter in English.)

Elle [ayl'-lyay], *f.* Name of the letter Ll.

Emaciación [ay-mah-the-ah-the-on'], *f.* (Med.) Emaciation, emaceration.

Emanación [ay-mah-nah-the-on'], *f.* 1. Emanation. 2. Emanation, effluvium.

Emanante [ay-mah-nahn'-tay], *pa.* Emanating, emanant, emanative.

Emanar [ay-mah-nar'], *vn.* To emanate, to proceed from.

Emancipación [ay-man-the-pah-the-on'], *f.* Emancipation.

Emancipador, ra [ay-man-the-pah-dor', rah], *m.* & *f.* Emancipator.

Emancipar [ay-man-the-par'], *va.* To emancipate.—*vr.* 1. To recover liberty. 2. To go out from tutelage. 3. To shake off a yoke.

Emasculación [ay-mas-coo-lah-the-on'], *f.* Emasculation, castration.

Emascular [ay-mas-coo-lar'], *va.* To castrate, to emasculate.

Embabiamiento [em-bah-be-ah-me-en'-to], *m.* 1. Stupidity, foolishness. 2. Distraction, absence of mind.

Embachar [em-bah-char'], *va.* To pen sheep to be shorn.

Embadurnar [em-bah-door-nar'], *va.* To besmear, to bedaub.

Embaidor, ra [em-bah-e-dor', rah], *m.* & *f.* Sharper, impostor, swindler.

Embaimiento [em-bah-e-me-en'-to], *m.* 1. Delusion, illusion. 2. Deceit, imposition, imposture.

Embair [em-bah-eer'], *va.* To impose upon, to deceive.

Embajada [em-bah-hah'-dah], *f.* 1. Embassy, a public or solemn message, legation. 2. Embassy, an ambassador's house.
Embajador [em-bah-hah-dor'], *m.* Ambassador.
Embajadora, Embajatriz [em-bah-hah-do'-rah, em-bah-hah-treeth'], *f.* (Poet. Littl. us.) Ambassadress, an ambassador's lady.
Embajatorio, ria [em-bah-hah-to'-re-o, ah], *a.* Belonging to an ambassador.
Embalador [em-bah-lah-dor'], *m.* Packer.
Embalar [em-bah-lar'], *va.* To embale, to make up into bundles, to pack.
Embalaje [em-bah-lah'-hay], *m.* Packing, package, baling.
Embaldosado [em-bal-do-sah'-do], *m.* Tile-floor.—*Embaldosado, da, pp.* of EMBALDOSAR.
Embaldosar [em-bal-do-sar'], *va.* To floor with tiles or flags.
Embalijar [em-bah-le-har'], *va.* To pack up into a portmanteau.
Embalsadero [em-bal-sah-day'-ro], *m.* Pool of stagnant rain-water.
Embalsamador, ra [em-bal-sah-mah-dor', rah], *m.* Embalmer.
Embalsamadura, *f.* **Embalsamamiento,** *m.* Embalming.
Embalsamar [em-bal-sah-mar], *va.* To embalm.
Embalsamiento [em-bal-sah-me-en'-to], *m.* 1. Act of putting any thing into a pool of water. 2. The stoppage of water, forming a pool.
Embalsar [em-bal-sar'], *va.* 1. To put any thing into a pool of still water. 2. To drive cattle into a pool of water to refresh them.
Embalse [em-bahl'-say], *m.* 1. Act of putting any thing into a pool of water. 2. Act of driving cattle into water.
Embalumar [em-bah-loo-mar'], *va.* To load a horse unequally.—*vr.* To embarrass one's self with business.
Emballendor [em-bal-lyay-nah-dor'], *m.* Stay-maker.
Emballenar [em-bal-lyay-nar'], *va.* To stiffen with whalebone.
Emballestado [em-bal-lyes-tah'-do], *m.* Contraction of the nerves in the feet of animals.—*Emballestado, da, pp.* of EMBALLESTARSE.
Emballestarse [em-bal-lyes-tar'-say], *vr.* To be on the point of discharging a cross-bow.
Embanastar [em-bah-nas-tar'], *va.* To put into a basket.
Embancadura [em-ban-cah-doo'-rah], *f.* The benches, collectively, of a row-boat.
Embancar [em-ban-car'], *va.* To move to the centre the spools of the spindles in looms, in order to begin to lay the warp.
Embaracillo [em-bah-rah-theel'-lyo], *m. dim.* A slight embarrassment.
Embarazadamente [em-bah-rah-thah-dah-men'-tay], *adv.* Perplexedly, with embarrassment, awkwardly.
Embarazado, da [em-bah-rah-thah'-do, dah], *a.* Embarrassed, perplexed, mazy.—*pp.* of EMBARAZAR. *Embarazada,* Pregnant.
Embarazador, ra [em-bah-rah-thah-dor', rah], *m. & f.* Embarrasser.
Embarazar [em-bah-rah-thar'], *va.* To embarrass, to perplex, to hinder, to obstruct, to cumber.
Embarazo [em-bah-rah'-tho], *m.* 1. Impediment, embarrassment, vexation, obstruction, obstacle. 2. Confusion, perplexity. 3. Pregnancy, time of gestation.
Embarazosamente, *adv.* Difficultly, cumbersomely.
Embarazoso, sa [em-bah-rah-tho'-so, sah], *a.* Difficult, intricate, entangled, cumbersome, troublesome, vexatious, obstructive.
Embarbascado, da [em-bar-bas-cah'-do, dah], *a.* Difficult, intricate, involved, complicate.—*pp.* of EMBARBASCAR.
Embarbascar [em-bar-bas-car'], *va.* 1. To throw hellebore, mullein, etc., into water, to stupefy fish. 2. (Met.) To perplex, to confound, to embarrass.—*vr.* To be entangled among the roots of plants: applied to a plough.
Embarbecer [em-bar-bay-therr'], *vn.* To have a beard appearing, as at the age of puberty.
Embarbillar [em-bar-beel-lyar'], *va.* To join planks or beams together.
Embarcación [em-bar-cah-the-on'], *f.* 1. Vessel or ship of any size or description. 2. Embarkation. *V.* EMBARCO. 3. Navigation.
Embarcadero [em-bar-cah-day'-ro], *m.* 1. Wharf, quay, or key. 2. Port, harbour.
Embarcador [em-bar-cah-dor'], *m.* One who embarks or ships goods.
Embarcar [em-bar-car'], *va.* 1. To embark, to ship, to put on shipboard. 2. (Met.) To embark, to engage another in an affair or enterprise.—*vr.* 1. To embark, to go on shipboard. *Embarcarse un golpe de mar,* (Naut.) To ship a heavy sea. 2. (Met.) To embark, to engage in an affair. *Embarcarse con poco bizcocho,* (Met.) To embark in an enterprise without the necessary precaution.
Embarco [em-bar'-co], *m.* Embarkation, embarking, shipping (of persons).
Embargador [em-bar-gah-dor'], *m.* One who sequestrates or lays on an embargo; sequestrator.
Embargante [em-bar-gahn'-tay], *pa.* Arresting, impeding, restraining. *No embargante,* Notwithstanding, nevertheless.
Embargar [em-bar-gar'], *va.* 1. (Law) To distrain, to seize, to attach, to lay an embargo upon. 2. (Met.) To impede, to restrain, to suspend.
Embargo [em-bar'-go], *m.* 1. Embargo on shipping, sequestration. 2. (Law) Extent, execution, distraint, seizure, attachment. 3. (Obs.) Embarrassment, impediment. 4. Indigestion. *Sin embargo,* Notwithstanding. *Sin embargo de embargos,* (Coll.) Notwithstanding all the impediments.
Embarnecer [em-bar-nay-therr'], *vn.* (Obs.) To grow plump, full, or fat.
Embarnizador [em-bar-ne-thah-dor'], *m.* (Obs.) Varnisher.
Embarnizadura [em-bar-ne-thah-doo'-rah], *f.* Varnishing.
Embarnizar [em-bar-ne-thar'], *va.* 1. To varnish, to japan, to glaze. 2. (Met.) To adorn, to embellish, to set off.
Embarque [em-bar'-kay], *m.* Putting goods and provisions on shipboard.
Embarrador [em-bar-rah-dor'], *m.* Plasterer, dauber.
Embarradura [em-bar-rah-doo'-rah], *f.* Overlaying with plaster or mortar.
Embarrancarse [em-bar-ran-car'-say], *vr.* To get mired in a deep hole.
Embarrar [em-bar-rar'], *va.* 1. To daub or overlay with plaster, clay, or mortar. 2. (Met.) To confound or perplex an affair. 3. To bedaub or besmear with mud. 4. To parget, to cover with plaster.—*vr.* To collect or mount upon trees, as partridges when pursued.
Embarrilar [em-bar-re-lar'], *va.* To barrel, to put in a barrel.
Embarrotar, *va.* *V.* ABARROTAR.
Embarullar [em-bah-rool-lyar'], *va.* (Coll.) 1. To confuse, mix things in disorder. 2. To act without order or plan.—*vr.* To be confounded, overwhelmed.
Embasamiento [em-bah-sah-me-en'-to], *m.* (Arch.) Basis or foundation of a building.
Embastar [em-bas-tar'], *va.* 1. To baste linen, silk, etc., to secure it in a frame to be embroidered. 2. To put stitches in a mattress. 3. (Prov.) To put a pack-saddle on a beast of burden.
Embaste [em-bahs'-tay], *m.* Basting.
Embastecer [em-bas-tay-therr'], *vn.* To become corpulent; to become fat or gross.—*vr.* To become gross.
Embatada [em-bah-tah'-dah], *f.* (Naut.) A sudden dash of the sea or wind against the course being followed.
Embate [em-bah'-tay], *m.* 1. The dashing of the sea against any thing. 2. A sudden impetuous attack. *Embates,* Sudden reverses of fortune.
Embaucador [em-bah-oo-cah-dor'], *m.* Sharper, impostor, abuser.
Embaucamiento [em-bah-oo-cah-me-en'-to], *m.* Deception, illusion.
Embaucar [em-bah-oo-car'], *va.* To deceive, to delude, to humbug, to impose upon.
Embaular [em-bah-oo-lar'], *va.* 1. To pack in a trunk. 2. (Met. Coll.) To cram with food.
Embausamiento [em-bah-oo-sah-me-en'-to], *m.* Amazement, astonishment, absence of mind.
Embausonar [em-bah-oo-so-nar'], *va.* (Littl. us.) To make one stare with wonder, to strike with amazement.
Embazador [em-bah-thah-dor'], *m.* One who shades or darkens a colour.
Embazadura [em-bah-thah-doo'-rah], *f.* 1. The art of shading or darkening colours. 2. (Met.) Amazement, astonishment.
Embazar [em-bah-thar'], *va.* 1. To tinge, to shade. 2. (Met.) To astonish, to strike with amazement. 3. (Met.) To impede the execution of a thing.—*vn.* To be amazed or astonished, to remain without action.—*vr.* 1. To become tired, disgusted, or satiated. 2. To blush.
Embebecer [em-bay-bay-therr'], *va.* 1. To astonish, to stupefy. 2. To entertain, to amuse.—*vr.* To be struck with amazement.
Embebecidamente, *adv.* Amazedly.
Embebecimiento [em-bay-bay-the-me-en'-to], *m.* Amazement, astonishment.
Embebedor, ra [em-bay-bay-dor', rah], *m. & f.* Imbiber.
Embeber [em-bay-berr'], *va.* 1. To imbibe, to drink in. 2. To imbibe, to drench, to saturate. 3. To incorporate, to introduce, to include. 4. To shrink or make to shrink, to squeeze, to press. 5. Among curriers, to oil a hide.—*vn.* 1. To shrink, to contract itself. 2. To grow thick and close.—*vr.* 1. To be enraptured or ravished, to be wrapt up in thought. 2. To imbibe, to admit or retain firmly in the mind.
Embebimiento [em-bay-be-me-en'-to], *m.* Imbibition.
Embecaduras [em-bay-cah-doo'-ras], *f. pl.* (Arch.) Spandrel.
Embelecador, ra [em-bay-lay-cah-dor', rah], *m. & f.* Impostor, sharper.
Embelecar [em-bay-lay-car'], *va.* To impose upon, to deceive, to humbug.
Embeleco [em-bay-lay'-co], *m.* Fraud, delusion, imposition, humbug.
Embeleñado, da [em-bay-lay-nyah'-do, dah], *a. & pp.* of EMBELEÑAR. 1. Enraptured, ravished. 2. Stupefied, besotted.

Embeleñar [em-bay-lay-nyar'], *va.* To stupefy, to besot.

Embelesamiento [em-bay-lay-sah-me-en'-to], *m.* Amazement, astonishment, rapture.

Embelesar [em-bay-lay-sar'], *va.* 1. To amaze, to astonish. 2. To charm, to subdue the mind by pleasure.—*vr.* To be charmed, ravished, or delighted.

Embeleso [em-bay-lay'-so], *m.* 1. Amazement, astonishment, ravishment. 2. Charm, charmer.

Embellaquecerse [em-bel-lyah-kay-therr'-say], *vr.* To become low-minded or mean-spirited; to have wicked or worthless ideas.

Embellecer [em-bel-lyay-therr'], *va.* To embellish, to adorn, to decorate, to flourish.

Emberar [em-bay-rar'], *vn.* (Prov.) To begin to have a ripe colour: applied to grapes.

Embermejar [em-ber-may-har'], *va.* To give a red colour.

Embermejecer [em-ber-may-hay-therr'], *va.* 1. To dye red. 2. To put to blush, to shame.—*vn.* To blush.

Embermellonar [em-ber-mayl-lyo-nar'], *va.* To apply vermilion, to paint scarlet.

Embere [em-bay'-ray], *m.* (Prov.) Colour of grapes which are ripening.

Emberrincharse [em-ber-rin-char'-say], *vr.* (Coll.) To fly into a violent passion: commonly applied to children.

Embestida [em-bes-tee'-dah], *f.* 1. Assault, violent attack, onset. 2. (Met.) Importunate demand by way of charity, loan, etc.

Embestidor [em-bes-te-dor'], *m.* One who makes importunate demands.

Embestidura [em-bes-te-doo'-rah], *f.* Attack, assault, onset.

Embestir [em-bes-teer'], *va.* 1. To assail, to attack, to offend. 2. To importune with unseasonable demands. 3. (Naut.) To collide against something, or against another vessel.—*va.* & *vr.* 1. To entangle the parts of a harness or to get entangled. 2. (Mil.) To invest a place.

Embetunar [em-bay-too-nar'], *va.* To cover with gum-resin or bitumen.

Embicador [em-be-cah-dor'], *m.* (Amer.) Cup and ball.

Embicar [em-be-car'], *va.* *Embicar las vergas*, (Naut.) To top the yards.—*vn.* 1. To be inclined toward the horizon: said of any thing which has arms. 2. To strike straight upon the shore or beach with the life-boat. 3. To luff, to haul to the wind. 4. (Mil.) To point downward the mouths of cannon as much as possible.

Embijar [em-be-har'], *va.* To paint with minium or red lead.

Embión [em-be-on'], *m.* A shove.

Embioncillo [em-be-on-theel'-lyo], *m.* *dim.* A slight shove.

(*Yo embisto, yo embista; él embistió, él embistiera;* from *Embestir. V.* Pedir.)

Embizarrarse [em-be-thar-rar'-say], *vr.* In the jocular style, to brag, to boast of courage, to bully.

Emblandecer [em-blan-day-therr'], *va.* To moisten, to soften with moisture.—*vn.* (Met.) To soften, or move to pity.

Emblanquecer [em-blan-kay-therr'], *va.* To bleach or whiten.—*vr.* To grow white, to be bleaching.

Emblanquecimiento, Emblanquimiento [em-blan-kay-the-me-en'-to, em-blan-ke-me-en'-to], *m.* (Obs.) Whitening, bleaching.

Emblema [em-blay'-mah], *m.* 1. Emblem. 2. An occult representation, an allusive picture.

Emblemático, ca [em-blay-mah'-te-co, cah], *a.* Emblematic.

Embobamiento [em-bo-bah-me-en'-to], *m.* Admiration, astonishment, enchantment; stupefying.

Embobar [em-bo-bar'], *va.* To amuse, to entertain the mind, to divert from, to distract.—*vr.* To be in suspense, to stand gaping or gazing, to muse.

Embobecer [em-bo-bay-therr'], *va.* To stultify, to stupefy, to make foolish.—*vr.* To become stupefied or stultified.

Embobecimiento [em-bo-bay-the-me-en'-to], *m.* Stupefaction.

Embocadero, Embocador [em-bo-cah-day'-ro, em-bo-cah-dor'], *m.* Mouth of a channel, by which water is conveyed through a mill-dam. *Estar al embocadero*, To be at the point of attaining any thing.

Embocado, da [em-bo-cah'-do, dah], *a.* Applied to wine which is pleasant to the taste.—*pp.* of Embocar.

Embocadura [em-bo-cah-doo'-rah], *f.* 1. The mouth or entrance by a narrow passage. 2. Mouth-piece of a bridle. 3. Mouth-piece of a musical instrument.

Embocar [em-bo-car'], *va.* 1. To enter by the mouth. 2. (Met.) To enter by a pass or narrow passage. 3. To swallow in haste, to cram food. 4. (Met.) To give news agreeable or sad, without preparation or warning.

Embocinado, da [em-bo-the-nah'-do, dah], *a.* *V.* Abocinado.

Embodarse [em-bo-dar'-say], *vr.* (Obs.) To be married.

Embojar [em-bo-har'], *va.* To arrange branches for silk-worms, for forming their webs and cocoons.

Embojo [em-bo'-ho], *m.* The operation of arranging branches for silk-worms, and the branches so arranged.

Embolar [em-bo-lar'], *va.* 1. To put balls on the tips of bulls' horns. 2. To apply the gilding-size.

Embolia [em-bo-lee'-ah], *f.* Embolism, obstruction of a blood-vessel by a clot or plug.

Embolismador, ra [em-bo-lis-mah-dor', rah], *m.* & *f.* & *a.* Detractor, reviler, reviling.

Embolismal [em-bo-lis-mahl'], *a.* Applied to the intercalary year, composed of thirteen lunations.

Embolismar [em-bo-lis-mar'], *va.* To propagate malicious sarcasms and rumours.

Embolismo [em-bo-lees'-mo], *m.* 1. Embolism, intercalation; insertion of days or years to produce regularity and equation of time. 2. The time inserted, intercalary time. 3. Confusion, mixture of things. 4. Maze. 5. Falsehood.

Émbolo [em'-bo-lo], *m.* 1. Embolus, the piston or plunger in a pump. 2. Forcer, the embolus of a force-pump.

Embolsar [em-bol-sar'], *va.* 1. To put money into a purse. 2. To reimburse, to recover money advanced. 3. To imburse.

Embolso [em-bol'-so], *m.* The act of putting money into a purse.

Embonar [em-bo-nar'], *va.* 1. To make good or firm. 2. (Naut.) To cover a ship's bottom and sides with planks.

Embones [em-bo'-nes], *m. pl.* (Naut.) Planks which are employed in covering the ship's bottom.

Embono [em-bo'-no], *m.* 1. (Naut.) The act of doubling a ship's bottom and sides with planks. 2. Lining, stiffening.

Emboñigar [em-bo-nye-gar'], *va.* To plaster with cow-dung.

Emboque [em-bo'-kay], *m.* 1. Passage of a thing through an arch or strait part. 2. Deception, cheat, fraud. *Eso no tiene emboque*, (Amer.) That has not the least appearance of truth.

Emboquillar [em-bo-keel-lyar'], *va.* To make the entrance of a shaft in mines.

Embornal [em-bor-nahl'], *m.* (Naut.) Scupper-hole.

Emborrachador, ra [em-bor-rah-chah-dor', rah], *a.* Intoxicating, producing drunkenness.—*n.* One who makes drunk.

Emborrachamiento [em-bor-rah-chah-me-en'-to], *m.* (Coll.) Intoxication, drunkenness.

Emborrachar [em-bor-rah-char'], *va.* To intoxicate, to inebriate, to fuddle.—*vr.* To inebriate, to be intoxicated, to overdrink one's self. *Emborracharse de cólera*, To be in a violent passion.

Emborrada [em-bor-rah'-dah], *f.* Portion of wool which is passed through the carder.

Emborradura [em-bor-rah-doo'-rah], *f.* 1. Recarding of wool. 2. What serves to recard.

Emborrar [em-bor-rar'], *va.* 1. To stuff with goat's hair. 2. In woollen manufactories, to card the wool a second time.

Emborrascar [em-bor-ras-car'], *va.* & *vr.* To provoke, to enrage.

Emborrazamiento [em-bor-rah-thah-me-en'-to], *m.* Act of basting a fowl while roasting.

Emborrazar [em-bor-rah-thar'], *va.* To tie pieces of pork on a fowl, to serve as basting.

Emborricarse [em-bor-re-car'-say], *vr.* (Coll.) To be stupefied, or to grow stupid.

Emborrizar [em-bor-re-thar'], *va.* To give the first combing to wool.

Emborrullarse [em-bor-rool-lyar'-say], *vr.* In jocular style, to be at variance, to dispute noisily.

Emboscada [em-bos-cah'-dah], *f.* 1. Ambuscade. 2. (Mil.) Ambush, ambuscade.

Emboscadura [em-bos-cah-doo'-rah], *f.* Ambush, ambuscade.

Emboscar [em-bos-car'], *va.* 1. (Mil.) To place in ambush. 2. To emboss. 3. (Met.) To conceal in some secret place.—*vr.* 1. To retire into the thickest part of a forest. 2. To ambush, to lie in ambush.

Embosquecer [em-bos-kay-therr'], *vn.* To become woody, to convert into shrubberies.

Embotado, da [em-bo-tah'-do, dah], *a.* Blunt, dull.—*pp.* of Embotar.

Embotador [em-bo-tah-dor'], *m.* He who blunts the points or edges of swords, etc.

Embotadura [em-bo-tah-doo'-rah], *f.* Bluntness or dulness of swords and other edged weapons.

Embotamiento [em-bo-tah-me-en'-to], *m.* 1. Blunting edged weapons; obtusion. 2. Bluntness, obtuseness, dulness. 3. (Met.) Stupefaction, the act of making dull or stupid.

Embotar [em-bo-tar'], *va.* 1. To blunt, to dull an edge or point, to break off the edges or points of edged tools or weapons, to foil. 2. (Met.) To enervate, to debilitate. 3. To dull, to stupefy.—*vr.* 1. To dull, to become dull. 2. (Coll.) To put on the boots.

Embotellar [em-bo-tel-lyar'], *va.* To bottle wine or other liquors.

Embotijar [em-bo-te-har'], *va.* 1. To lay a stratum of small earthen jars, before a tile flooring is put down. 2. To fill jars with oil or other liquids.—*vr.* 1. To swell, to expand. 2. To be in a passion, to be inflated with arrogance

Embovedado, da [em-bo-vay-dah'-do, dah], *a.* Arched, vaulted.

Embovedar [em-bo-vay-dar'], *va.* To cover with an arch or vault.

Emboza [em-bo'-thah], *f.* Inequalities in the bottom of barrels or casks.

Embozado, da [em-bo-thah'-do, dah], *a.* Covered, involved.—*pp.* of EMBOZAR. *Un embozado*, A person with his face covered, by one side of his cloak being drawn over the left shoulder.

Embozalar [em-bo-thah-lar'], *va.* To muzzle animals.

Embozar [em-bo-thar'], *va.* 1. To muffle the greater part of the face. 2. (Met.) To cloak, to dissemble. 3. To muzzle.—*vr.* To muffle one's self by throwing the right fold of the cape over the left shoulder.

Embozo [em-bo'-tho], *m.* 1. The part of a cloak, veil, or any other thing with which the face is muffled. 2. The act of muffling the greater part of the face. 3. (Met.) An artful way of expressing one's thoughts, so as to keep them in part concealed.

Embozo (De) [em-bo'-tho], *adv.* Incognito, unknown, private.

Embracilado, da [em-brah-the-lah'-do, dah], *a.* (Coll.) Constantly carried about in one's mother's arms

Embragar [em-brah-gar'], *vn.* To let out the clutch.—*va.* 1. (Naut.) To sling. 2. To put in gear, to engage.

Embrague [em-brah'-gay], *m.* 1. Clutch. 2. Letting out the clutch. *Embrague automático*, Automatic transmission.

Embravar, Embravecer [em-brah-var', em-brah-vay-therr'], *va.* To enrage, to irritate, to make furious.—*vn.* To become strong: applied to plants.—*vr.* 1. To become furious, to be enraged. 2. (Naut.) To be extremely boisterous: applied to the sea.

Embravecimiento [em-brah-vay-the-me-en'-to], *m.* Fury, rage, passion.

Embrazadura [em-brah-thah-doo'-rah], *f.* 1. Clasping of a shield or buckler. 2. Embracing, clasping.

Embrazar [em-brah-thar'], *va.* 1. (Obs.) To clasp a shield, as in the posture of fighting. 2. To engage the teeth of two wheels in each other.

Embreado [em-bray-ah'-do], *m.* **Embreadura** [em-bray-ah-doo'-rah], *f.* (Naut.) Paying a ship with pitch.

Embrear [em-bray-ar'], *va.* (Naut.) To pay with pitch, to tar.

Embregarse [em-bray-gar'-say], *vr.* To quarrel, to wrangle, to dispute.

Embreñarse [em-bray-nyar'-say], *vr.* To hide one's self among brambles or in thickets.

Embriagado, da [em-bre-ah-gah'-do, dah], *a.* & *pp.* of EMBRIAGAR. Intoxicated, drunk.

Embriagar [em-bre-ah-gar'], *va.* 1. To intoxicate, to inebriate. 2. To transport, to enrapture.—*vr.* To inebriate, to grow drunk.

Embriaguez [em-bre-ah-geth'], *f.* 1. Intoxication, drunkenness, inebriety. 2. (Met.) Rapture, transport of the mind.

Embriar [em-bre-ar'], *va.* (Littl. us.) To toss in the air.

Embridar [em-bre-dar'], *va.* 1. To bridle, to guide by a bridle. 2. (Met.) To govern, to restrain.

Embriogenia [em-bre-o-hay'-ne-ah], *f.* Formation and development of the fœtus in its intra-uterine existence.

Embriología [em-bre-o-lo-hee'-ah], *f.* Embryology.

Embriólogo, ga [em-bre-o'-lo-go, gah]. *m.* & *f.* Embryologist.

Embrión [em-bre-on'], *m.* 1. Embryo or embryon, the first rudiment of a plant or an animal. 2. The beginning of a thing, still shapeless. 3. (Met.) Assemblage of confused ideas, without method or order. *Esa obra está en embrión*, That work is merely in sketch.

Embrionario, ria [em-bre-o-nah'-re-o, ah], *a.* Embryonal, rudimentary.

Embroca, Embrocación [em-bro'-cah, em-bro-cah-the-on'], *f.* (Pharm.) Embrocation.

Embrocar [em-bro-car'], *va.* 1. To pour out of one vessel into another. 2. With embroiderers, to wind thread or twist upon quills. 3. Among shoemakers, to fasten with tacks to the last. 4. To catch the bull between the horns.

Embrochado, da [em-bro-chah'-do, dah], *a.* Embroidered.

Embrochalar [em-bro-chah-lar'], *va.* To sustain with a cross-piece (breast-summer) or a bar of iron the beams which rest in the walls.

Embrolla [em-brol'-lyah], *f.* (Coll.) *V.* EMBROLLO.

Embrollador, ra [em-brol-lyah-dor', rah], *m.* & *f.* 1. Entangler, confounder. 2. *V.* EMBROLLÓN.

Embrollar [em-brol-lyar'], *va.* 1. To entangle, to twist, to overlace, to cumber. 2. (Met.) To entangle, to insnare, to confound with artful subtleties; to embroil. *Embrollar la bandera*, (Naut.) To waft the ensign.

Embrollo [em-brol'-lyo], *m.* Fraud, imposture, snare, deception; embroiling; knot.

Embrollón, na [em-brol-lyone', nah], *m.* & *f.* 1. Liar, tale-bearer; impostor. 2. Entangler.

Embromado, da [em-bro-mah'-do, dah], *a.* (Prov. Naut.) Misty, hazy, foggy. —*pp.* of EMBROMAR.

Embromador, ra [em-bro-mah-dor', rah], *m.* & *f.* & *a.* 1. Applied to one who is tumultuously merry. 2. Wheedler, one who deceives by artful tricks.

Embromar [em-bro-mar'], *va.* 1. To excite tumultuous mirth. 2. To cajole, to wheedle. 3. To jest, to joke. 4. To repair provisionally the damaged seams of a ship; to chinse.

Embroquelarse, *vr.* *V.* ABROQUELARSE.

Embroquetar [em-bro-kay-tar'], *va.* To skewer the legs of birds, in order to roast them.

Embrosquillar [em-bros-kil-lyar'], *va.* (Prov.) To put cattle into a fold, called, in Spanish, *brosquil.*

Embrujar [em-broo-har'], *va.* To bewitch. *V.* HECHIZAR.

Embrutecer [em-broo-tay-therr'], *va.* To stupefy.—*vr.* 1. To grow stupid, to become brutish. 2. To lose refined manners.

Embrutecimiento [em-broo-tay-the-me-en'-to], *m.* The act of making brutish; stupefaction.

Embuchado [em-boo-chah'-do], *m.* Large sausage made of pork, with salt and spice.—*Embuchado, da, pp.* of EMBUCHAR.

Embuchar [em-boo-char'], *va.* 1. To stuff with minced meat; to make pork sausages. 2. To cram the maw of animals. 3. (Met.) To swallow food without chewing.

Embudador [em-boo-dah-dor'], *m.* Filler, one who fills vessels with a funnel.

Embudar [em-boo-dar'], *va.* 1. To put a funnel into a vessel to pour liquors through. 2. (Met.) To scheme, to insnare.

Embudista [em-boo-dees'-tah], *m.* Intriguer, deceiver.

Embudito [em-boo-dee'-to], *m. dim.* A little funnel.

Embudo [em-boo'-do], *m.* 1. Funnel. 2. Among wax-chandlers, tail of a wax-candle mould. 3. The basin of a water-closet. 4. (Met.) Fraud, deceit, artifice.

Embullarse [em-bool-lyar'-say], *vr.* (Prov. Cuba and Canary Islands.) To carouse, to revel, to be gay.

Embullo [em-bool'-lyo], *m.* Carousal, gaiety, revelry. (Cuba and Canary Islands.)

Emburujar [em-boo-roo-har'], *va.* (Coll.) To jumble, to mix confusedly.

Embuste [em-boos'-tay], *m.* 1. An artful tale; a lie, fiction. 2. Fraud, imposition. 3. (Met.) Pleasing quibble of children. *Embustes*, Gew-gaws, baubles, trinkets.

Embustear [em-boos-tay-ar'], *vn.* 1. To lie, to impose upon, to gab. 2. To make frequent use of frauds, tricks, and deceits.

Embustería [em-boos-tay-ree'-ah], *f.* Deceit, imposture, trick.

Embustero, ra [em-boos-tay'-ro, rah], *m.* & *f.* 1. Liar, tale-bearer, tale-teller. 2. Impostor, cheat. 3. Hypocrite, dissembler. 4. (Coll.) Cajoler, coaxer.

Embusterón, na [em-boos-tay-rone', nah], *a. aug.* *V.* EMBUSTERO.

Embutidera [em-boo-te-day'-rah], *f.* Instrument for riveting tin-work.

Embutido [em-boo-tee'-do], *m.* Inlaid work.—*pl.* Large sausage filled with minced meat.—*Embutido, da, pp.* of EMBUTIR.

Embutidor [em-boo-te-dor'], *m.* A riveting set, a punch.

Embutidura [em-boo-te-doo'-rah], *f.* (Naut.) Worming, filling the grooves of a rope with material.

Embutir [em-boo-teer'], *va.* 1. To inlay, to enchase. 2. To mix confusedly, to jumble, to insert. 3. (Met.) To cram, to eat much. 4. *Embutir un estay*, (Naut.) To worm a stay. 5. (Obs.) To imbue.

Eme [ay'-may], *f.* Spanish name of the letter M.

Emenagogo [ay-may-nah-go'-go], *m.* Emmenagogue, an agent promoting the menstrual flow.

Emendable [ay-men-dah'-blay], *a.* (Ant.) Amendable, corrigible.

Emendación [ay-men-dah-the-on'], *f.* 1. (Obs.) Emendation, amendment, correction. 2. Satisfaction, chastisement.

Emendador [ay-men-dah-dor'], *m.* (Ant.) Emendator.

Emendadura, *f.* **Emendamiento,** *m.* [ay-men-dah-doo'-rah, ay-men-dah-me-en'-to]. (Obs.) *V.* ENMIENDA.

Emendar [ay-men-dar'], *va.* (Ant.) 1. To amend, to correct, to emend. 2. *Emendar un aparejo*, (Naut.) To overhaul a tackle.

Emergencia [ay-mer-hen'-the-ah], *f.* 1. Emergency. 2. Emergence. *Aterrizaje de emergencia*, Forced landing, emergency landing.

Emergente [ay-mer-hen'-tay], *a.* Emergent, resulting, issuing from any thing.

Emérito [ay-may'-re-to], *a.* 1. Emeritus, an epithet applied to a professor in a university, public institution, or religious order, who, having well discharged his duties for a stated time, is allowed to retire, receiving the whole or part of his appointment, and retaining the honours and exemptions belonging to it. 2. A Roman soldier allowed to retire after having done sufficient public service.

Emersión [ay-mer-se-on'], *f.* (Ast.) Emersion.

Emético, ca [ay-may'-te-co, cah], *m.* & *a.* Emetic.—*m.* Tartar emetic; tartrate of antimony and potassa.

Emetina [ay-may-tee'-nah], *f.* Emetin, an alkaloid procured from ipecacuanha.

Emetizar [ay-may-te-thar'], *va.* 1. To add an emetic to any substance whatever. 2. To produce vomiting.

Emienda [ay-me-en'-dah], *f.* (Ant.) *V.* ENMIENDA.

Emigración [ay-me-grah-the-on'], *f.* 1. Emigration, immigration. 2. Sum total of emigrants. 3. Periodical migration of certain animals.

Emigrado [ay-me-grah'-do], *m.* Emigrant, immigrant.

Emigrado, da [ay-me-grah'-do, dah], *a.* & *m.* & *f.* Emigrated, immigrated. —*pp.* of EMIGRAR.

Emigrante [ay-me-grahn'-tay], *m.* An emigrant, one who goes from Europe beyond seas.

Emigrar [ay-me-grar'], *vn.* To emigrate, to immigrate.

Emina [ay-mee'-nah], *f.* 1. Measure containing the fourth part of a Spanish bushel. 2. Ancient tax.

Eminencia [ay-me-nen'-the-ah], *f.* 1. Eminence, eminency, height, a hill. 2. (Met.) Eminence, excellence, conspicuousness. 3. Eminence, greatness, power. 4. Eminence, title given to cardinals. *Con eminencia*, Eminently.

Eminencial [ay-me-nen-the-ahl'], *a.* Eminential.

Eminente [ay-me-nen'-tay], *a.* 1. Eminent, high, lofty. 2. Eminent, eximious, conspicuous.

Eminentemente, *adv.* Eminently, conspicuously.

Eminentísimo [ay-me-nen-tee'-se-mo], *a.* Title of the Romish cardinals.

Emir [ay-meer'], *m.* 1. Emir, or ameer. 2. Prince, lord. 3. A title of dignity among the Turks.

Emisario [ay-me-sah'-re-o], *m.* 1. Emissary, spy. 2. Outlet, discharge. 3. (Med.) Emunctory.

Emisión [ay-me-se-on'], *f.* 1. Emission, vent. 2. Issue of paper money. 3. Scattering of atoms. 4. (Med.) Emission.

Emisivo, va [ay-me-see'-vo, vah], *a.* Having the faculty of spreading or scattering warmth or light.

Emisor, ra [ay-me-sor, rah], *a.* Emitting, issuing.—*f.* (Radio) Broadcasting station.

Emitir [ay-me-teer'], *va.* 1. To emit, to send forth, to let go. 2. To issue, put into circulation, paper money or the like. 3. To show, manifest an opinion; to give a vote.

Emoción [ay-mo-the-on'], *f.* 1. Emotion, agitation of mind.

Emocional [ay-mo-the-o-nahl'], *a.* Emotional.

Emocionalismo [ay-mo-the-o-nah-lees'-mo], *m.* Emotionalism.

Emocionante [ay-mo-the-o-nahn'-tay], *a.* Emotional, thrilling.

Emoliente [ay-mo-le-en'-tay], *m.* & *a.* Emollient, softening, healing.

Emolumento [ay-mo-loo-men'-to], *m.* 1. Emolument, fee, profit, advantage. 2. Perquisite. Most used in the plural.

Emotivo [ay-mo-tee'-vo], *a.* Emotional.

Empacar [em-pah-car'], *va.* To pack up in chests; to wrap up in hides or skins.—*vr.* To be sullen, to be displeased.

Empacón [em-pah-cone'], *a.* (Prov. S. Amer.) Obstinate, stubborn, contumacious.

Empachadamente, *adv.* (Prov.) Cumbersomely.

Empachado, da [em-pah-chah'-do, dah], *a.* & *pp.* of EMPACHAR. 1. Timid, bashful. 2. Surfeited, glutted, fed to satiety. *Navío empachado*, (Naut.) A ship which is overloaded.

Empachar [em-pah-char'], *va.* 1. To impede, to embarrass, to clog, to disturb. 2. To perplex, to confound. 3. To overload, to cram, to cause indigestion. 4. To disguise.—*vr.* 1. To be ashamed, to be confounded. 2. To surfeit, to be fed to satiety.

Empacho [em-pah'-cho], *m.* 1. Bashfulness, timidity. 2. Embarrassment, obstacle. 3. Surfeit, indigestion.

Empachoso, sa [em-pah-cho'-so, sah], *a.* *V.* VERGONZOSO.

Empadronador [em-pah-dro-nah-dor'], *m.* Enroller, census-taker.

Empadronamiento [em-pah-dro-nah-me-en'-to], *m.* 1. Census, an official enumeration of the inhabitants of a country. 2. List or register of persons liable to pay taxes. *V.* PADRÓN.

Empadronar [em-pah-dro-nar'], *va.* 1. To make, or take the census of a country. 2. To enter in a register the names of those who are liable to pay taxes.

Empajar [em-pah-har'], *va.* To cover something or to fill it with straw.

Empalagamiento [em-pah-lah-gah-me-en'-to], *m.* Loathing, surfeit, cloying.

Empalagar [em-pah-lah-gar'], *va.* 1. To loathe, to cause the disgust of satiety, to cloy. 2. To disgust in a high degree, to offend, to trouble.—*vr.* 1. To loathe, to feel abhorrence or disgust. 2. To be cloyed, to be disgusted or displeased.

Empalago [em-pah-lah'-go], *m.* *V.* EMPALAGAMIENTO.

Empalagoso, sa [em-pah-lah-go'-so, sah], *a.* Squeamish, cloying, loathsome, loathful, fastidious, troublesome.

Empalamiento [em-pah-lah-me-en'-to], *m.* Empalement, empaling.

Empalar [em-pah-lar'], *va.* To empale.

Empaliar [em-pah-le-ar'], *va.* (Prov.) To hang with tapestry a church, cloister, or other place, through which a procession passes.

Empalizada [em-pah-le-thah'-dah], *f.* (Mil.) Palisade or palisado.

Empalizar [em-pah-le-thar'], *va.* 1. To palisade, to inclose with palisades. 2. To pale.

Empalmadura [em-pal-mah-doo'-rah], *f.* Dovetailing, the junction of two pieces of wood.

Empalmar [em-pal-mar'], *va.* 1. To scarf, to dovetail. 2. (Naut.) To splice cables. *Empalmar una verga*, To fish a mast.

Empalme [em-pahl'-may], *m.* 1. Scarf, joining, connection. 2. A splicing. 3. Junction of a branch line of railway with the main line.

Empalmillar [em-pal-mil-lyar'], *m.* (Arch.) A wall of stone, unhewed, for procuring the filtering of river water, which is to be turned into irrigating trenches.—*va.* To glue the inner sole of the shoe.

Empalmo [em-pahl'-mo], *m.* Shank, a piece of wood which goes under the head of a beam.

Empalomadura [em-pah-lo-mah-doo'-rah], *f.* (Naut.) Marline.

Empalomar [em-pah-lo-mar'], *va.* (Naut.) To sew the bolt-rope to the sail. *Empalomar los escarpes*, (Naut.) To shift the scarfs.

Empalletado [em-pal-lyay-tah'-do], *m.* (Naut.) A kind of quilting as a defence in fight to those who are on deck.

Empalletar [em-pal-lyay-tar'], *va.* To form the parapet called *empalletado*.

Empamparse [em-pam-par'-say], *vr.* (Amer.) 1. To be absent of mind, be in suspense. 2. To get lost on a pampa, or desert.

Empanada [em-pah-nah'-dah], *f.* Meat pie. *Hacer una empanada*, To conceal part of an affair. *Agua empanada*, Panado; muddy water.

Empanadilla [em-pah-nah-deel'-lyah], *f.* 1. (Dim.) A small pie. 2. (Prov.) Movable footstep put in coaches.

Empanado [em-pah-nah'-do], *a.* (A room) receiving light from another room. *Empanados*, (Naut.) Limber boards; planks laid over the well in a ship.—*Empanado, da*, *pp.* of EMPANAR.

Empanar [em-pah-nar'], *va.* 1. To cover with paste, to bake in paste.—2. To sow grain.—*vr.* To be choked by too much seed having been sown: said of crops. (Acad.)

Empandar [em-pan-dar'], *va.* To bend into an arch.

Empandillar [em-pan-dil-lyar'], *va.* To remove by stealth, to hide.

Empantanar [em-pan-tah-nar'], *va.* 1. To submerge; to make a pond or lake. 2. To bemire. 3. To embarrass the course of an affair.

Empañadura [em-pah-nyah-doo'-rah], *f.* Swaddling of children.

Empañar [em-pah-nyar'], *va.* 1. To swaddle, to wrap in swaddling clothes. 2. (Met.) To soil a glass with one's breath; to darken, to obscure. 3. (Met.) To denigrate, to impeach one's character or reputation.

Empañicar [em-pah-nye-car'], *va.* (Naut.) To hand or furl: applied to sails.

Empapar [em-pah-par'], *va.* To imbibe, to saturate, to soak, to drench.—*vr.* 1. To imbibe, to be soaked; to be surfeited. 2. To imbue one's self with the principles of doctrine, science, etc. 3. To surfeit. 4. To boast of something without reason.

Empapelador [em-pah-pay-lah-dor'], *m.* He who wraps up in paper.

Empapelar [em-pah-pay-lar'], *va.* 1. To wrap up in paper. 2. (Prov.) To waste paper.

Empapirolado, da [em-pah-pe-ro-lah'-do, dah], *a.* (Coll.) Full, satisfied.

Empapirotado, da [em-pah-pe-ro-tah'-do, dah], *a.* (Coll.) Lofty, haughty, puffed up.—*pp.* of EMPAPIROTAR.

Empapirotar [em-pah-pe-ro-tar'], *va.* (Coll.) To adorn carefully, to deck nicely.

Empapujar [em-pah-poo-har'], *va.* To make one eat too much. (Acad.)

Empaque [em-pah'-kay], *m.* 1. Packing. 2. (And. and Amer.) Air, semblance, look: generally in bad part. Appearance and aspect of a person, according to which he pleases us, or displeases, at first sight. (Acad.)

Empaquetador, ra [em-pah-kay-tah-dor', rah], *m.* & *f.* Packer. —*f.* Packing machine.

Empaquetadura [em-pah-kay-tah-doo'-rah], *f.* Packing, gasket.

Empaquetar [em-pah-kay-tar'], *va.* To pack, to bind goods into bales; to clap together.

Emparamentar [em-pah-rah-men-tar'], *va.* To adorn, to set off.

Emparchar [em-par-char'], *va.* To cover with a plaster.

Emparedado, da [em-pah-ray-dah'-do, dah], *m.* & *f.* 1. (Obs.) Cloisterer: applied to a devotee who lives in a cloister without the vows. 2. A sandwich. 3. Confinement.—*pp.* of EMPAREDAR.

Emparedamiento [em-pah-ray-dah-me-en'-to], *m.* 1. Confinement, the act of shutting up between walls. 2. Cloister, religious retirement.

Emparedar [em-pah-ray-dar'], *va.* To confine, to immure, to shut up between walls.

Emparejador [em-pah-ray-hah-dor'], *m.* Matcher, fitter.

Emparejadura [em-pah-ray-hah-doo'-rah], *f.* Equalization.

Emparejamiento [em-pah-ray-hah-me-en'-to], *m.* Act of matching or making equal.

Emparejar [em-pah-ray-har'], *va.* & *vn.* 1. To level, to reduce to a level. 2. To match, to fit, to equal. 3. To put abreast, to put on a level; to be equal.

Emparentar [em-pah-ren-tar'], *vn.* To be related by marriage.

Emparentado, da [em-pah-ren-tah'-do, dah], *a.* & *pp.* of EMPARENTAR. Related by marriage. *Estar bien* or *muy emparentado*, To have respectable relatives.

Emparrado [em-par-rah'-do], *m.* Arbor or bower made with the branches of propped vines.—*Emparrado, da, pp.* of EMPARRAR.

Emparrar [em-par-rar'], *va.* To embower, to form bowers with the branches of vines.

Emparrillar [em-par-reel-lyar'], *va.* To broil on the gridiron.

Emparvar [em-par-var'], *va.* To put grain in order to be thrashed.

Empasma [em-pahs'-mah], *m.* A perfumed toilet powder.

Empastador [em-pas-tah-dor'], *m.* 1. A painter who gives a liberal coat of colour to his works. 2. Paste-brush. 3. (Amer.) Binder of books in leather.

Empastadura [em-pas-tah-doo'-rah], *f.* Dental filling.

Empastar [em-pas-tar'], *va.* 1. To bind (books, etc.) 2. To fill with paste. 3. To fill (a tooth). 4. To cover with paint.

Empastelar [em-pas-tay-lar'], *va.* & *vr.* (Fig. and coll.) 1. To transact a matter without regard to justice in order to get out of a difficulty. 2. (Typ.) To pie, to distribute wrongly, to jumble together.

Empatadera [em-pah-tah-day'-rah], *f.* (Coll.) Checking, impeding; suspension of any thing.

Empatar [em-pah-tar'], *va.* 1. To equal, to make equal: applied commonly to the number of votes. 2. To check, to suspend. 3. To cut short a speech.

Empate [em-pah'-tay], *m.* 1. Equality, equal number of votes. 2. Stop, suspension.

Empatronamiento [em-pah-tro-nah-me-en'-to], *m.* Stamping as standard.

Empatronar [em-pah-tro-nar'], *va.* To stamp a certain mark upon weights and measures, to certify that they are standard.

Empavesada [em-pah-vay-sah'-dah], *f.* (Naut.) Waist clothes, painted linen or close netting spread on the sides of ships to obstruct the enemy's sight. *Empavesadas de las cofas*, The top armour.

Empavesar [em-pah-vay-sar'], *va.* 1. (Naut.) To spread waist clothes on the sides of a ship. 2. (Naut.) To dress ships.

Empecatado, da [em-pay-cah-tah'-do, dah], *a.* Very wily, evil-minded, incorrigible. (Acad.)

Empecer [em-pay-therr'], *va.* 1. To hurt, to offend, to injure. 2. To prevent.

Empecinado [em-pay-the-nah'-do], *m.* (Acad.) 1. *V.* PEGUERO. 2. (Peru.) Stubborn, inexorable, incorrigible.

Empecinar [em-pay-the-nar'], *va.* 1. To fill with mud. 2. *V.* EMPEGAR.—*vr.* (Amer.) To be obstinate, to be given over to vice.

Empedernimiento [em-pay-der-ne-me-en'-to], *m.* Hardness of heart.

Empedernir [em-pay-der-neer'], *va.* To indurate, to harden.—*vr.* 1. To be petrified, to grow hard as stone. 2. (Met.) To be obstinate, to be inflexible.

Empedrado [em-pay-drah'-do], *m.* Pavement.—*Empedrado, da, pp.* of EMPEDRAR.

Empedrador [em-pay-drah-dor'], *m.* Paver or pavier.

Empedrar [em-pay-drar'], *va.* 1. To pave, to floor with stones. 2. To form small holes or cavities in any superficies.

Empega [em-pay'-gah], *f.* 1. Varnish of pitch. 2. Mark of pitch.

Empegadura [em-pay-gah-doo'-rah], *f.* The varnish of pitch which is put on vessels.

Empegar [em-pay-gar'], *va.* 1. To pitch, to cover with pitch. 2. To mark sheep with pitch.

Empego [em-pay'-go], *m.* 1. Marking sheep with pitch. 2. (Amer.) The disagreeable taste which some wines, etc., have.

Empeguntar [em-pay-goon-tar'], *va.* To mark sheep with pitch.

Empeine [em-pay'-e-nay], *m.* 1. The groin. 2. The instep. 3. Hoof of a beast. 4. Tetter, ringworm. 5. (Prov.) Flower of the cotton plant. 6. (Bot. Ant.) Lichen, an order of cryptogamous plants.

Empeinoso, sa [em-pay-e-no'-so, sah], *a.* Full of tetters or ringworms.

Empelar [em-pay-lar'], *vn.* To get hair, to begin to be hairy.

Empelechar [em-pay-lay-char'], *va.* To join or unite marble blocks.

Empelotarse [em-pay-lo-tar'-say], *vr.* 1. To be at variance, to quarrel. 2. To be vexed, to be uneasy.

Empeltre [em-pel'-tray], *m.* (Prov.) Small olive-tree or sapling springing from an old trunk.

Empella [em-pel'-lyah], *f.* 1. The fat of fowls; the lard of swine. 2. Upper leather of a shoe.

Empellar, Empeller [em-pel-lyar', em-pel-lyerr'], *va.* To push, to impel.

Empellejar [em-pel-lyay-har'], *va.* To cover with skins.

Empellón [em-pel-lyone'], *m.* Push, heavy blow. *A empellones*, Rudely, with pushes.

Empenachar [em-pay-nah-char'], *va.* To adorn with plumes.

Empenar [em-pay-nar'], *va.* To feather an arrow, to dress with feathers.

Empenta [em-pen'-tah], *f.* (Obs.) Prop, stay, shore.

Empentar [em-pen-tar'], *va.* (Prov.) To push, to impel. *V.* EMPUJAR.

Empeña [em-pay'-nyah], *f.* (Obs.) Upper leather of a shoe. *V.* PELLA.

Empeñadamente [em-pay-nyah-dah-men'-tay], *adv.* Strenuously, in a courageous or spirited manner.

Empeñar [em-pay-nyar'], *va.* 1. To pawn, to pledge, to gage, to impignorate. 2. To engage, to oblige. *Empeñar la palabra*, To engage one's word.—*vr.* 1. To bind one's self to fulfil a contract or to pay debts. 2. To persist in a determination or resolution. 3. To encounter dangers with courage and spirit. 4. To intercede, to mediate. 5. (Naut.) To be embayed on a lee-shore. *Empeñarse por alguno*, To recommend any one, or to exert one's self in favour of any one. *Empeñarse en algo*, To take a fancy, to undertake a thing eagerly, to be engaged, or bound.

Empeño [em-pay'-nyo], *m.* 1. Obligation contracted by pledging. 2. Engagement, contract. 3. Earnest desire, ardent love. 4. Boldness; courage and perseverance in overcoming difficulties. 5. Firmness, constancy. 6. Protection, favour, recommendation. 7. Recommender, the person who protects or favours. *Con empeño*, With great ardour, diligence, eagerness. *Tengo un empeño con Vd.*, I have a particular favour to ask of you. *Tiene empeño en que su amigo salga bien*, He is bent on his friend's success.

Empeoramiento [em-pay-o-rah-me-en'-to], *m.* Deterioration.

Empeorar [em-pay-o-rar'], *va.* To impair, to deteriorate.—*vn.* To grow worse.

Empequeñecer [em-pay-kay-nyay-therr'], *va.* To make smaller, to diminish.

Emperador [em-pay-rah-dor'], *m.* 1. An emperor. 2. A name given to certain animals on account of their great size and beauty; for example, the golden-crested wren, the emperor moth, etc.

Emperatriz [em-pay-rah-treeth'], *f.* Empress.

Emperchar [em-per-char'], *va.* To suspend on a perch.

Emperdigar [em-per-de-gar'], *va.* *V.* PERDIGAR.

Emperejilar [em-pay-ray-he-lar'], *va.* To adorn, or to dress with a profusion of ornaments.—*vr.* To be adorned, to be dressed out.

Emperezar [em-pay-ray-thar'], *vn.* & *vr.* 1. To be lazy or indolent. 2. To be dilatory, tardy, slow.

Emperícado, da [em-pay-re-cah'-do, dah], *a.* To be dressed in style; to wear false hair.

Emperifollar [em-pay-re-fol-lyar'], *va.* & *vr.* To decorate excessively, to cover with ribbons and bows, to deck with flowers; to ornament a discourse with flowers of rhetoric.

Empernar [em-per-nar'], *va.* 1. To nail, to spike, to peg. 2. (Naut.) To bolt, to fasten with bolts.

Empero [em-pay'-ro], *conj.* Yet, however. *V.* PERO.

Emperrada [em-per-rah'-dah], *f.* A sort of game at cards, also called *renegado*.

Emperrar [em-per-rar'], *va.* To irritate, to enrage.—*vr.* To grow mad or furious; to be obstinate or stubborn.

Empesador [em-pay-sah-dor'], *m.* Handful of rushes used by weavers for trimming their yarn.

Empetro [em-pay'-tro], *m.* (Bot.) Crow-berry. Empetrum. *Empetro blanco*, White-berried crow-berry. Empetrum album. *Empetro negro*, Black-berried crow-berry. Empetrum nigrum.

Empezar [em-pay-thar'], *va.* To begin, to commence. *Obra empezada, medio acabada*, Well begun is half done.

Empicarse [em-pe-car'-say], *vr.* To be too much attached to any thing.

Empicotadura [em-pe-co-tah-doo'-rah], *f.* Act of pillorying.

Empicotar [em-pe-co-tar'], *va.* To pillory, to put in the pillory; to picket.

Empiedro [em-pe-ay'-dro], *m.* Paving: a dry wall.

(*Yo empiedro, yo empiedre*, from *Empedrar*. *V.* ACERTAR.)

Empiema [em-pe-ay'-mah], *m.* 1. A serous, bloody, or purulent accumulation in any part of the body, but especially in the thoracic region. 2. Name of the surgical operation employed to withdraw such fluid; it is called also paracentesis of the thorax.

Empiezo [em-pe-ay'-tho], *m.* (Prov.) Beginning of a thing.

(*Yo empiezo, yo empiece,* from *Empezar. V.* ACERTAR.)

Empinador, ra [em-pe-nah-dor', rah], *m.* & *f.* (Coll.) One who drinks much wine or liquors.

Empinadura [em-pe-nah-doo'-rah], *f.* (Obs.) Exaltation, elevation, raising.

Empinamiento [em-pe-nah-me-en'-to], *m.* Erection, elevation.

Empinar [em-pe-nar'], *va.* 1. To raise, to exalt. 2. (Coll.) To drink much.—*vr.* 1. To stand on tiptoe. 2. To tower, to rise high. *Empinar el puchero,* (Coll.) To have a comfortable subsistence without luxury.

Empingorotar [em-pin-go-ro-tar'], *va.* (Coll.) To raise any thing and put it upón another.

Empino [em-pee'-no], *m.* Elevation, height.

Empiolar [em-pe-o-lar'], *va.* 1. To tie the legs of hawks with jesses. 2. (Met.) To bind, to subject, to imprison. 3. *V.* APIOLAR.

Empireo [em-pee'-ray-o], *m.* 1. Empyrean, the highest heaven. 2. Happiness, paradise.

Empíreo, rea [em-pee'-ray-o, ah], *a.* Empyreal, celestial.

Empireuma [em-pe-ray'-oo-mah], *f.* (Chem.) Empyreum, empyreuma.

Empireumático, ca [em-pe-ray-oo-mah'-te-co, cah], *a.* (Chem.) Empyreumatic, empyreumatical.

Empírico [em-pee'-re-co], *m.* Quack, empiric, medicaster.

Empírico, ca [em-pee'-re-co, cah], *a.* Empiric, empirical.

Empirismo [em-pe-rees'-mo], *m.* 1. Empiricism, quackery. 2. A philosophical doctrine according to which all human knowledge is due to experience.

Empizarrado [em-pe-thar-rah'-do], *m.* The whole slates which cover a building.—*Empizarrado, da, pp.* of EMPIZARRAR.

Empizarrar [em-pe-thar-rar'], *va.* To slate, to roof a building with slates.

Emplastadura, *f.* **Emplastamiento,** *m.* [em-plas-tah-doo'-rah]. Plastering.

Emplastar [em-plas-tar'], *va.* 1. To plaster, to apply plasters. 2. To paint the face. 3. To suspend, to obstruct.—*vr. V.* EMBADURNARSE.

Emplastecer [em-plas-tay-therr'], *va.* (Art) To level the surface in order to paint any thing.

Emplasto [em-plahs'-to], *m.* 1. Plaster or emplaster. *Estar hecho un emplasto,* To be in a bad state of health. 2. A sickly and extremely delicate person.

Emplástrico, ca [em-plahs'-tre-co, cah], *a.* 1. Glutinous, resembling a plaster. 2. (Med.) Suppurative.

Emplazador [em-plah-thah-dor'], *m.* (Law) Summoner; messenger of a court who serves summonses.

Emplazamiento, Emplazo [em-plah-thah-me-en'-to, em-plah'-tho], *m.* (Law) Summons, citation.

Emplazar [em-plah-thar'], *va.* 1. (Law) To summon, to cite. 2. To convene, to summon judicially. *Emplazar la caza,* To arrange or set the chase. 3. (Coll.) To cite to appear before the judgment-seat of God.—*vr.* In bull-fights, for the bull to plant himself in the midst of the ring, and to show no disposition to charge.

Empleado [em-play-ah'-do], *m.* Placeman, one who exercises a public employment or fills a public station.—*Empleado, da, pp.* of EMPLEAR.

Empleador [em-play-ah-dor'], *m.* Employer.

Emplear [em-play-ar'], *va.* 1. To employ, to exercise, to occupy. 2. To employ, to give a place or employment, to commission, to intrust with the management of affairs. 3. To purchase, to lay out, to employ one's money in the purchase of property. 4. To employ, to make use of. 5. To employ, to fill up, to lead, to pass, or spend in a certain manner: applied commonly to time.—*vr.* To be employed; to occupy, to follow business.

Empleita [em-play'-e-tah], *f. V.* PLEITA.

Emplenta [em-plen'-tah], *f.* 1. Piece of mud-wall made at once. 2. (Obs.) Impression.

Emplentar, *va.* (Obs.) To print.

Empleo [em-play'-o], *m.* 1. Employ, employment, business, occupation. 2. Employment or employ, public place or station, office. 3. Employment, calling, vocation, profession. 4. Aim or object of our desires. 5. Lady courted, sweetheart. *Empleo del dinero* or *fondos en algún negocio,* Investment of money or capital in some business.

Empleomanía [em-play-o-mah-nee'-ah], *f.* Rage for public office. (Acad.)

Emplomado [em-plo-mah'-do], *m.* Roof covered with lead.—*Emplomado, da, pp.* of EMPLOMAR.

Emplomador [em-plo-mah-dor'], *m.* Plumber, he who fits with lead in any way.

Emplomar [em-plo-mar'], *va.* To lead, to fit with lead.

Emplumar [em-ploo-mar'], *va.* 1. To feather, or dress in feathers, as a punishment. 2. To feather, to adorn with feathers or plumes.—*vr.* To mew, to moult, to shed the feathers.

Emplumecer [em-ploo-may-therr'], *vn.* To begin to get feathers, to fledge.

(*Yo emplumezco, yo emplumezca,* from *Emplumecer. V.* CONOCER.)

Empobrecer [em-po-bray-therr'], *va.* To impoverish.—*vn.* To become poor.

(*Yo empobrezco, yo empobrezca,* from *Empobrecer. V.* CONOCER.)

Empobrecimiento [em-po-bray-the-me-en'-to], *m.* Impoverishment, depauperation.

Empodrecer [em-po-dray-therr'], *vn.* To corrupt, to reduce to a state of putrefaction.—*vr.* To corrupt, to become putrid.

Empolvar [em-pol-var'], *va.* & *vr.* 1. To cover with dust. 2. To sprinkle powder upon, as the hair; to powder

Empolvoramiento [em-pol-vo-rah-me-en'-to], *m.* (Obs.) The act of covering with dust.

Empolvorizar [em-pol-vo-re-thar'], **Empolvorar** (obs.) [em-pol-vo-rar'], *va.* To cover with dust or powder.

Empollado, da [em-pol-lyah'-do, dah], *a.* 1. Hatched. 2. (Met.) Confined, pent up in the house.—*pp.* of EMPOLLAR.

Empolladura [em-pol-lyah-doo'-rah], *f.* Brood of bees.

Empollar [em-pol-lyar'], *va.* 1. To brood, to hatch. 2. *V.* AMPOLLAR.

Emponzoñador, ra [em-pon-tho-nyah-dor', rah], *m.* & *f.* Poisoner.

Emponzoñamiento [em-pon-tho-nyah-me-en'-to], *m.* Poisoning, the act of administering or killing by poison.

Emponzoñar [em-pon-tho-nyar'], *va.* 1. To poison, to infect with poison. 2. (Met.) To poison, to taint, to corrupt one's morals.

Empopar [em-po-par'], *va.* (Naut.) To give the stern to the wind.—*vn.* & *vr.* To sail before the wind.

Emporcar [em-por-car'], *va.* To soil, to dirty, to foul.

Emporio [em-po'-re-o], *m.* 1. Emporium, a mart for the sale of merchandise. 2. A place which has made itself famous for sciences, arts, etc.

Empotrado, da [em-po-trah'-do, dah], *a.* Built-in. *Muebles empotrados,* Built-in furniture.

Empotramiento [em-po-trah-me-en'-to], *m.* The act of scarfing two timbers together.

Empotrar [em-po-trar'], *va.* 1. To mortise, to join with a mortise. 2. To scarf, to splice. 3. To put bee-hives in a pit (to divide the hives). 4. (Naut.) To fasten the cannon so that they shall not run back on firing. 5. To prevent the turning of the wheels of a gun-carriage.

Empozar [em-po-thar'], *va.* To throw into a well.—*vr.* To be pigeon-holed (said of a formal paper).

Empradizarse [em-prah-de-thar'-say], *vr.* To become meadow.

Emprendedor [em-pren-day-dor'], *m.* 1. Enterpriser, one who undertakes great things. 2. Undertaker, one who engages in projects and affairs.

Emprender [em-pren-derr'], *va.* 1. To undertake, to engage in an arduous undertaking. 2. To attempt, to go about any business. *Emprender a* or *con alguno,* To address or accost one, either to trouble, to reprimand, to supplicate, or to quarrel with him.

Empreñar [em-pray-nyar'], *va.* To impregnate; to beget.

Empresa [em-pray'-sah], *f.* 1. Symbol, motto. 2. Enterprise, undertaking. 3. Design, an intention, a purpose.

Empresario [em-pray-sah'-re-o], *m.* 1 The person who undertakes to do or perform, on his own account, some business of great importance. 2. Manager of a theatre.

Emprestillar [em-pres-til-lyar'], *va.* (Obs.) To borrow frequently, to ask the use of any thing.

Empréstito [em-prays'-te-to], *m.* 1. Lending money on condition of its being repaid. 2. Loan, any thing lent, generally used of government loans.

Emprima, *f. V.* PRIMICIA.

Emprimado [em-pre-mah'-do], *m.* Last combing to wool.—*Emprimado, da, pp.* of EMPRIMAR.

Emprimar [em-pre-mar'], *va.* 1. To print linen or cotton. 2. In woollen manufactories, to card the wool several times, to prepare it for spinning. 3. (Coll.) To abuse one's candour, to deceive, to mock.

Emprimerar [em-pre-may-rar'], *va.* To place one in the first rank at a feast, or on any other occasion.

Empringar [em-prin-gar'], *va. V.* PRINGAR.

Emprisionar [em-pre-se-o-nar'], *vn.* (Obs.) *V.* APRISIONAR.

Empsícosis [emp-see'-co-sis], *f.* (Phil.) 1. Animation. 2. Union of the soul with the body.

Empuchar [em-poo-char'], *va.* To put skeins of thread into a lye, or to buck them before they are bleached.

(*Yo empuerco, yo empuerque,* from *Emporcar.*) *V.* ACORDAR.)

Empués [em-poo-es', *adv.* (Obs.) *V.* DESPUÉS.

Empuesta (De) [em-poo-es'-tah (day)], *adv. V.* POR DETRÁS.

Empujamiento [em-poo-hah-me-en'-to], *m.* (Obs.) 1. The act of pushing away. 2. The force employed for that purpose.

Empujar [em-poo-har'], *va.* 1. To push, to force by constant violence, to press forward. 2. To push away, to shove off.

Empuje [em-poo'-hay], *m.* 1. Impulse, push, driving force. 2. (Aer.) Thrust.

Empujón [em-poo-hone'], *m.* Push, a violent shove. ***Á empujones,* Pushingly, rudely.**

Empulgadura [em-pool-gah-doo'-rah], *f.* The act of stretching the cord of a cross-bow.

Empulgar [em-pool-gar'], *va.* To stretch the cord of a cross-bow.

Empulgueras [em-pool-gay'-ras], *f. pl.* 1. Wings of a cross-bow, through which the ends of the cord run. 2. Instrument with which the thumbs were tied together. *Apretar las empulgueras a uno,* To put one in a difficult situation, to compel him.

Empuntador [em-poon-tah-dor'], *m.* One who makes the points of needles or pins.

Empuntadura [em-poon-tah-doo'-rah], *f.* Pointing of needles or pins.

Empuntar [em-poon-tar'], *va.* To point, form the point of a needle or pin.

Empuñador, ra [em-poo-nyah-dor', rah], *m. & f.* Grasper.

Empuñadura [em-poo-nyah-doo'-rah], *f.* Hilt of a sword. *Empuñaduras,* (Naut.) Ear-rings, thin ropes fastened to the four corners of a sail, in the form of a ring. *Empuñaduras del gratil,* (Naut.) Head-ear-rings. *Empuñaduras de rizos,* (Naut.) Reef-ear, rings. *Empuñadura de las consejas,* Beginning of a discourse or narration.

Empuñar [em-poo-nyar'], *va.* 1. To clinch, to clutch, to grasp, to gripe with the fist. *Empuñar el cetro,* To begin to reign, to seize the sceptre. 2. *Empuñar las escotas y amuras,* (Naut.) To bend the tacks and sheets to the clews of the sails.

Empuñir [em-poo-nyeer'], *va.* (Naut.) To pull on the sheets until the fists touch the block where the top-sail sheet works.

Emulación [ay-moo-lah-the-on'], *f.* Emulation, envy, jealousy.

Emulador, ra [ay-moo-lah-dor', rah], *m.* Emulator, rival.

Emular [ay-moo-lar'], *va.* To emulate, to rival, to contest.

Emulgente [ay-mool-hen'-tay], *a.* Emulgent.

Émulo [ay'-moo-lo], *m.* Competitor, rival, emulator.

Emulsina [ay-mool-see'-nah], *f.* Emulsin or synaptase, an albuminous principle of almonds, which forms an emulsion with water and acts as a ferment.

Emulsión [ay-mool-se-on'], *f.* Emulsion.

Emulsivo, va [ay-mool-see'-vo, vah], *a.* Emulsive.

Emunctorio [ay-moonc-to'-re-o], *m.* Emunctory, excretory gland.

Emundación [ay-moon-dah-the-on'], *f.* Cleansing.

Emuselado, da [ay-moo-say-lah-do', dah], *a.* Muzzled to prevent biting: applied to a bear or other animal.

En [en], *prep.* of time and place. 1. In. *Estar en Londres,* To be in London. *En un año,* In a year's time. 2. For. *En adelante,* For the future. 3. On. *En el otro lado,* On the other side. 4. Upon. *En domingo,* Upon Sunday. *En* going before a gerund is equal to *luego que* or *después que;* as, *En diciendo esto,* Upon or after saying this. Before adjectives it gives them an adverbial signification; as, *En alto,* On high. Before the infinitive of verbs it gives them a participial import; as, *En decir esto,* In saying this. Formerly it was used for *con* and *entre. Juzgar en* or *con todo el rigor del derecho,* To judge according to the letter of the law.

Enaceitarse [ay-nah-thay-e-tar'-say], *vr.* To become oily or rancid.

Enacerar [ay-nah-thay-rar'], *va.* To steel, to edge with steel.

Enaguachar [ay-nah-goo-ah-char'], *va.* To fill or load with water; used only to denote the state of the stomach after drinking a great deal.

Enaguas [ay-nah'-goo-as], *f. pl.* 1. Skirt, petticoat. (In Spanish America it is generally pronounced and written *naguas.*) *Enaguas blancas,* The inner skirt. 2. A gown or tunic of black baize, formerly worn by men as mourning.

Enaguazar [ay-nah-goo-ah-thar'], *va.* To irrigate; to cover with water.

Enagüillas, tas [ay-nah-goo-eel'-lyas, ee'-tas], *f. pl.* 1. (Dim.) Short linen under-petticoats. 2. *V.* ENAGUAS for a gown or tunic.

Enajenable [ay-nah-hay-nah'-blay], *a.* Alienable.

Enajenación, *f.* **Enajenamiento,** *m.* [ay-nah-hay-nah-the-on', ay-nah-hay-nah-me-en'-to]. 1. Alienation, the act of transferring property. 2. Change of affection, want of friendly intercourse. 3. Absence of mind; distress of mind; rapture, astonishment; overjoy. 4. Disorder of the mental faculties.

Enajenar [ay-nah-hay-nar'], *va.* 1. To alienate, to transfer or to give away property. 2. To transport, to enrapture.—*vr.* 1. To withdraw one's affection. 2. To be deprived of reason. 3. To be restless or uneasy.

Enálage [ay-nah'-lah-hay], *f.* (Gram.) Enallage, the use of one part of speech or inflection for another.

Enalbar [ay-nal-bar'], *va.* To heat iron to a white heat.

Enalbardar [ay-nal-bar-dar'], *va.* 1. To lay a pack-saddle on beasts of burden. 2. To cover meat or any other dish with a batter of eggs, flour, and sugar, and fry it afterward in oil or butter.

Enalforjar [ay-nal-for-har'], *va.* To put into a saddle-bag.

Enalmagrado, da [ay-nal-mah-grah'-do, dah], *a. & pp.* of ENALMAGRAR. 1. Coloured with ochre. 2. Vile, despicable.

Enalmagrar [ay-nal-mah-grar'], *va.* To cover with ochre.

Enalmenar [ay-nal-may-nar'], *va.* To crown a wall with indented battlements.

Enaltecer [ay-nal-tay-therr'], *va.* *V.* ENSALZAR.

Enamarillecer [ay-nah-mah-reel-lyay-therr'], *va.* To dye yellow, to make yellow.—*vr.* (Ant.) 1. To become yellow. 2. To grow pale.

Enamorada, *f.* (Obs.) Prostitute.

Enamoradamente [ay-nah-mo-rah-dah-men'-tay], *adv.* Lovingly, in a loving manner.

Enamoradillo, illa [ay-nah-mo-rah-deel'-lyo, deel'-lyah], *a. dim.* *V.* ENAMORADIZO.

Enamoradizo, za [ay-nah-mo-rah-dee'-tho, thah], *a.* Inclined to love, of an amorous disposition.

Enamorado, da [ay-nah-mo-rah'-do, dah], *a. & pp.* of ENAMORAR. In love, enamoured, love-sick. *Un enamorado,* Enamorado. *Es muy enamorado,* (Coll.) He is very susceptible.

Enamorador [ay-nah-mo-rah-dor'], *m.* Lover, wooer.

Enamoramiento [ay-nah-mo-rah-me-en'-to], *m.* Act of enamouring, love-suit.

Enamorar [ay-nah-mo-rar'], *va.* 1. To excite or inspire love. 2. To make love, to woo, to court, to enamour.—*vr.* To fall in love.

Enamoricarse [ay-nah-mo-re-car'-say], *vr.* (Coll.) To be slightly in love.

Enanchar [ay-nan-char'], *va.* (Coll.) To widen, to enlarge.

Enangostar [ay-nan-gos-tar'], *va.* *V.* ANGOSTAR.

Enanito, ita [ay-nah-nee'-to, tah], *a. dim.* Little, minute.

Enano, na [ay-nah'-no, nah], *a.* Dwarfish, low, small, little.

Enano [ay-nah'-no], *m.* Dwarf.

Enante [ay-nahn'-tay], *m.* (Bot.) Water-dropwort. Œnante. *Enante apimpinelado,* Burnet-saxifrage water-dropwort. Œnante pimpineloides. *Enante globuloso* or *de Portugal,* Globe-headed water-dropwort. Œnante globulosa.

Enante, or **Enantes** [ay-nahn'-tay, tes], *adv.* (Obs.) *V.* ANTES.

Enarbolar [ay-nar-bo-lar'], *va.* To hoist, to raise high; to hang out. *Enarbolar la bandera,* (Naut.) To hoist the colours.—*vr.* *V.* ENCABRITARSE.

Enarcar [ay-nar-car'], *va.* 1. To hoop barrels. 2. *V.* ARQUEAR.

Enardecer [ay-nar-day-therr'], *va.* To fire with passion, to kindle, to inflame. —*vr.* To be kindled, inflamed, or animated, with anger.

Enarenación [ay-nah-ray-nah-the-on'], *f.* Lime and sand, or plaster, used to whiten walls before painting them.

Enarenar [ay-nah-ray-nar'], *va.* To fill with sand, to choke with sand.—*vr.* (Naut. Obs.) To run on shore.

Enarme [ay-nar'-may], *m.* (Prov.) A framework in fishing-nets, or the method of fitting them up.

Enarmonar [ay-nar-mo-nar'], *va.* To raise, to rear.—*vr.* To rise on the hind feet.

Enarmonía [ay-nar-mo-nee'-ah], *f.* (Mus.) Enharmonic modulation; a change in notation without a change in sound.

Enarmónico, ca [ay-nar-mo'-ne-co, cah], *a.* Enharmonic, proceeding by quarter tones.

Enarración [ay-nar-rah-the-on'], *f.* Narration, relation.

Enarrar [ay-nar-rar'], *va.* To narrate.

Enastar [ay-nas-tar'], *va.* To put a handle to an instrument.

Enastillar [ay-nas-teel-lyar'], *va.* To put handles to forging-hammers.

Encabalgamiento [en-cah-bal-gah-me-en'-to], *m.* Gun-carriage.

Encabalgar [en-cah-bal-gar'], *vn.* 1. To be upon (something else); to be mounted. 2. (Obs.) To parade on horseback.—*va.* To provide horses.

Encaballadura [en-cah-bal-lyah-doo-rah], *f.* Lapping over.

Encaballar [en-cah-bal-lyar'], *va.* To lap over, to imbricate, to lay so that the object rests upon the end of another, as tiles or shingles upon a roof.

Encabellecer [en-cah-bel-lyay-therr'], *vn. & vr.* To begin to have hair on a part of the head where there was none before.

(*Yo encabellezco, yo encabellezca,* from *Encabellecer. V.* CONOCER.)

Encabestradura [en-cah-bes-trah-doo'-rah], *f.* An injury to a horse by a halter.

Encabestrar [en-cah-bes-trar'], *va.* 1. To put a halter to a beast. 2. (Met.) To force to obedience.—*vr.* To be entangled in the halter.

Encabezador [en-cah-bay-thah-dor'], *m.* Header, a reaping-machine which removes the heads of grain.

Encabezadura, *f.* Scarfing, heading.

Encabezamiento, Encabezonamiento [en-cah-bay-thah-me-en'-to], *m.* 1. List, roll, or register of persons liable to pay a tax; census. 2. The act of enrolling persons liable to pay taxes. 3. Tax, tribute, or imposts. 4. Headline, heading.

Encabezar, Encabezonar [en-cah-bay-thar'], *va.* 1. To make a roll or register of all those subject to any tax or tribute; to take a census of the inhabitants. 2. To register, to enroll, to set down in a list of taxes.—*vr.* 1. To compound for taxes. 2. To compound, to bargain in the lump. 3. To put the beginning of a formula to certain writings, as a will. 4. (Amer.) To put at the head, or in the first line. 5. To strengthen a wine, to add other stronger, or some brandy. 6. *Encabezar un terreno*, (Agr.) To put fresh earth at the top of a slope. 7. (Carp.) To join top and top, to scarf, to head. 8. (Naut.) To mend the furring of a ship. 9. To be content to suffer a small, to avoid a greater evil.

Encabillar [en-cah-beel-lyar'], *va.* (Naut.) To scotch, to pin, to bolt.

Encabrahigar [en-cah-brah-e-gar'], *va.* *V.* CABRAHIGAR.

Encabriar [en-cah-bre-ar'], *va.* To preserve and fashion timber for roofing.

Encabritarse [en-cah-bre-tar'-say], *vr.* To rise on the hind feet: applied to horses.

Encachar [en-cah-char'], *va.* To thrust any thing in a wall or box; to imbed.

Encadenadura, *f.* **Encadenamiento**, *m.* [en-cah-day-nah-doo'-rah, en-cah-day-nah-me-en'-to]. 1. Catenation, the act of linking together. 2. State of being linked or connected; concatenation. 3. Chaining.

Encadenar [en-cah-day-nar'], *va.* 1. To chain, to link, to fetter, to enchain, to shackle. 2. To concatenate, to link together. 3. (Met.) To leave any one without movement or action. 4. To subject, subjugate, oppress. 5. To captivate, to gain the will. 6. To cast the chains which close the entrance of harbours, docks, etc.

Encaecer, *vn.* (Obs.) *V.* PARIR.

Encaja [en-cah'-hah]. Shake hands: a word frequently used by the common people at meeting and shaking hands.

Encajador [en-cah-hah-dor'], *m.* 1. He who enchases or inserts. 2. Instrument for enchasing.

Encajadura [en-cah-hah-doo'-rah], *f.* Enchasing, inserting or inclosing one thing into another.

Encajar [en-cah-har'], *va.* 1. To enchase, to infix, to drive in, to inclose one thing in another, to insert. 2. To thrust with violence one into another. 3. (Met.) To do or say something inopportunely. 4. Of fire-arms, to shoot, fire. *Encajar la suya*, To avail one's self of an opportunity. *Encajar bien*, To be to the purpose, to come to the point, to be opportune. *Encajar las manos*, (Coll.) To join or shake hands.—*vr.* 1. To thrust one's self into some narrow place. 2. To intrude.

Encaje [en-cah'-hay], *m.* 1. The act of adjusting or fitting one thing to another. 2. The place or cavity in which any thing is inlaid or inserted; groove. 3. The measure of one thing to adjust with another. 4. Enchasing. 5. Joining together. 6. Lace. *Encaje de oro, de plata, de hilo*, etc., Gold, silver, thread lace, etc. 7. Inlaid work. *Ley del encaje*, An arbitrary law.

Encajera [en-cah-hay'-rah], *f.* Lacewoman, she who makes lace.

Encajerado, da [en-cah-hay-rah'-do, dah], *a.* (Naut.) Fouled or entangled on the sheave of a block or pulley: applied to a rope.

Encajerarse [en-cah-hay-rar'-say], *vr.* (Naut.) To get caught between the block and the pulley-wheel: said of a rope.

Encajonado [en-cah-ho-nah'-do], *m.* Mud-wall supported by pillars of bricks and stones.—*Encajonado, da*, *pp.* of ENCAJONAR.

Encajonamiento [en-cah-ho-nah-me-en'-to], *m.* Act of packing up in a box.

Encajonar [en-cah-ho-nar'], *va.* To box, to pack up in a box, to lay up in a chest.

Encalabozar [en-cah-lah-bo-thar'], *va.* (Coll.) To put one into a dungeon.

Encalabrinado, da [en-cah-lah-bre-nah'-do, dah], *a.* Headstrong, stubborn, obstinate.—*pp.* of ENCALABRINAR.

Encalabrinar [en-cah-lah-bre-nar'], *va.* To affect the head with some unpleasant smell or vapour.—*vr.* To become headstrong, obstinate, or stubborn; to be confused.

Encalada [en-cah-lah'-dah], *f.* Piece of the trimmings of a saddle.

Encalador [en-cah-lah-dor'], *m.* In tan-yards, lime pit or vat, into which hides are put.

Encaladura [en-cah-lah-doo'-rah], *f.* The act of whitening with lime; whitewashing.

Encalar [en-cah-lar'], *va.* 1. To whitewash. 2. To cover with plaster or mortar. 3. To thrust into a pipe or tube. 4. To put hides into the lime vats or pits.

Encalipto [en-ca-leep'-to], *m.* A kind of moss belonging to the northern hemisphere.

Encalmadura [en-cal-mah-doo'-rah], *f.* A disease in horses occasioned by much work in times of great heat.

Encalmarse [en-cal-mar'-say], *vr.* 1. To be worn out with fatigue. 2. (Naut.) To be becalmed: applied to a ship.

Encalostrarse [en-cah-los-trar'-say], *vr.* To make the young sick by sucking the first milk.

Encalvar, *vn.* (Obs.) *V.* ENCALVECER.

Encalvecer [en-cal-vay-therr'], *vn.* To grow bald.

(*Yo encalvezco, yo encalvezca*, from *Encalvecer.* *V.* CONOCER.)

Encallada [en-cal-lyah'-dah], *f.* V. ENCALLADURA.

Encalladero [en-cal-lyah-day'-ro], *m.* (Naut.) Shoal, sand-bank.

Encalladura [en-cal-lyah-doo'-rah], *f.* (Naut.) Striking on a sand-bank.

Encallar [en-cal-lyar'], *vn.* 1. (Naut.) To run aground, to stand, to hit against. 2. To be checked in the progress of an enterprise, not to be able to proceed.

Encalle [en-cahl'-lyay], *m.* V. ENCALLADURA.

Encallecer [en-cal-lyay-therr'], *vn.* To get corns on the feet. 2. To attain much experience in something.—*vr.* To harden, to be confirmed in wickedness.

Encallecido, da [en-cal-lyay-thee'-do, dah], *a.* & *pp.* of ENCALLECER. 1. Troubled with corns. 2. (Met.) Hardened in wickedness and iniquities.

Encallejonar [en-cal-lyay-ho-nar'], *va.* To enter or put any thing into a narrow street.

(*Yo encallezco, yo encallezca*, from *Encallecer.* *V.* CONOCER.)

Encamación [en-cah-mah-the-on'], *f.* Scaffolding for sustaining the galleries in mines.

Encamarados [en-cah-ma-rah'-dos], *m. pl.* Chambers in cannon and mortars.

Encamarar [en-cah-ma-rar'], *va.* (Coll.) To store up grain in granaries.

Encamarse [en-cah-mar'-say], *vr.* 1. (Coll.) To keep one's self in bed. 2. To lie down, to stretch themselves out to rest: used of beasts. 3. To be lodged by rain, wind, etc: applied to corn.

Encambijar [en-cam-be-har'], *va.* To conduct water by means of arched reservoirs.

Encambrar [en-cam-brar'], *va.* To put in a store.

Encambrillonar [en-cam-breel-lyo-nar'], *va.* To put the first narrow sole, called *encambrillonado*, upon a shoe.

Encambronar [en-cam-bro-nar'], *va.* 1. To inclose with hedges of briers and brambles. 2. To strengthen with iron.

Encaminadura [en-cah-me-nah-doo'-rah], *f.* **Encaminamiento**, *m.* The act of putting in the right road.

Encaminar [en-cah-me-nar'], *va.* 1. To guide, to put in the right road, to show the way. 2. (Met.) To direct or manage an affair or business.—*vr.* To take a road, to proceed in a road, to go to.

Encamisada [en-cah-me-sah'-dah], *f.* 1. (Obs. Mil.) Camisado, an attack or surprise made in the dark. 2. A kind of masquerade which was executed at night.

Encamisarse [en-cah-me-sar'-say], *vr.* To put a shirt over one's clothes, in order to make a camisado.

Encamorrarse [en-cah-mor-rar'-say], *vr.* To embroil one's self in disputes.

Encampanado, da [en-cam-pah-nah'-do, dah], *a.* Bell-shaped: applied to mortars.

Encanalar, Encanalizar [en-cah-nah-lar', en-cah-nah-le-thar'], *va.* To convey through pipes or conduits.

Encanallarse [en-cah-nal-lyar'-say], *vr.* (Acad.) 1. To contract a habit of committing mean and vile acts. 2. To associate with depraved and base people.

Encanarse [en-cah-nar'-say], *vr.* To grow senseless with fear or crying: applied to children.

Encanastar [en-cah-nas-tar'], *va.* 1. To pack up in canisters, baskets or hampers. 2. (Naut.) To put the top-sails in the round-house or top.

Encancerarse [en-can-thay-rar'-say], *vr.* *V.* CANCERARSE.

Encandecer [en-can-day-therr'], *va.* To heat any thing to a white heat.

Encandelar [en-can-day-lar'], *vn.* To bud, as trees, instead of flowering.

Encandiladera, Encandiladora [en-can-de-lah-day'-rah, en-can-de-lah-do'-rah], *f.* Procuress, bawd.

Encandilado, da [en-can-de-lah'-do, dah], *a.* 1. Sharp or high-cocked: applied to hats. *Trae el sombrero muy encandilado*, He wears his hat fiercely cocked. 2. (Naut.) Raised vertically. —*pp.* of ENCANDILAR.

Encandilar [en-can-de-lar'], *va.* 1. To dazzle with the light of a candle or lamp. 2. (Met.) To dazzle or deceive with false appearances. 3. (Coll.) To stir the fire. *Encandilar un sombrero*, To cock a hat.—*vr.* To inflame one's eyes, as with drink, to be dazzled.

Encanecer [en-cah-nay-therr'], *vn.* 1. To grow gray. 2. To mould. 3. To grow old. 4. To possess much experience and knowledge.

(*Yo encanezco, yo encanezca*, from *Encanecer.* *V.* CONOCER.)

Encanijamiento [en-cah-ne-hah-me-en'-to], *m.* Weakness, meagreness; the act of growing weak and lean; extenuation.

Encanijar [en-cah-ne-har'], *va.* To weaken a baby by giving him bad milk.—*vr.* 1. To pine, to be emaciated, to grow weak and thin, to fall away: applied to children badly suckled. 2. To grow weak.

Encanillar [en-cah-nil-lyar'], *va.* To wind silk, wool, or linen on a quill made of cane.

Encantado, da [en-can-tah'-do, dah], *a.* Haunted, enchanted, charmed. *Casa encantada*, A house in which the family lives very retired. *Hombre encantado*, A man who is habitually absent or musing.—*pp.* of ENCANTAR.

Encantador [en-can-tah-dor'], *m.* Enchanter, sorcerer, conjurer; charmer.

Encantadora, *f.* Sorceress, enchantress; charming, bewitching.

Encantamiento [en-can-tah-me-en'-to], *m.* Enchantment, incantation.

Encantar [en-can-tar'], *va.* 1. To enchant, to charm, to conjure, to bewitch. 2. To enchant, to charm, to fascinate, to delight in a high degree.

Encantarar [en-can-tah-rar'], *va.* To put any thing into a jar or pitcher.

Encante [en-cahn'-tay], *m.* Auction, public sale: the place where it is held.

Encanto [en-cahn'-to], *m.* 1. Enchantment, charm, spell. 2. Fascination. *Es un encanto*, It is truly charming, it is bewitching.

Encantorio [en-can-to'-re-o], *m.* (Coll.) Enchantment.

Encantusar [en-can-too-sar'], *va.* To coax, to wheedle, to deceive by flatteries.

Encañado [en-cah-nyah'-do], *m.* 1. Conduit of water. 2. Hedge formed with canes or reeds.—*Encañado, da, pp.* of ENCAÑAR.

Encañador, ra [en-cah-nyah-dor', rah], *m. & f.* One who spools or winds silk on quills made of cane.

Encañadura [en-cah-nyah-doo'-rah], *f.* 1. Hedge made of cane or reeds. 2. Strong rye-straw not broken. 3. (Obs.) Conduit.

Encañar [en-cah-nyar'], *va.* 1. To inclose a plantation with a hedge of cane. 2. To convey water through conduits or pipes. 3. To wind silk on quills of reed or cane.—*vn.* To form or grow into stalks: applied to corn.

Encañizada [en-cah-nye-thah'-dah], *f.* Inclosure made of cane and reeds for catching mullets.

Encañonado [en-cah-nyo-nah'-do], *a.* Applied to the wind blowing through a narrow passage.—*Encañonado, da, pp.* of ENCAÑONAR.

Encañonar [en-cah-nyo-nar'], *va. & vn.* 1. To begin to grow fledged, to get feathers and wings. 2. To put into tubes or pipes. 3. To plait, to fold. 4. To wind silk on quills of cane.

Encañutar [en-cah-nyoo-tar'], *va.* To flute, to mould into the form of tubes and pipes —*vn.* To form straw: applied to corn.

Encapacetado, da [en-cah-pah-thay-tah'-do, dah], *a.* Covered with a helmet.

Encapachadura [en-cah-pah-chah-doo'-rah], *f.* In oil-mills, number of baskets full of olives to be pressed.

Encapachar [en-cah-pah-char'], *va.* 1. To put into a frail or basket. 2. (Agr. Prov.) To guard bunches of grapes from the sun by covering them with the shoots.

Encapado, da [en-cah-pah'-do, dah], *a.* Cloaked, wearing a cloak.

Encapazar [en-cah-pah-thar'], *va.* To collect or put into a basket.

Encaperuzado, da [en-cah-pay-roo-thah'-do, dah], *a.* Hooded, wearing a hood.

Encaperuzarse [en-cah-pay-roo-thar'-say], *vr.* To cover one's head with a hood.

Encapilladura [en-cah-pil-lyah-doo'-rah], *f.* (Naut.) Tie of a shroud or stay; top-rigging.

Encapillar [en-cah-pil-lyar'], *va.* 1. (Naut.) To fix the standing rigging to the mast-head. 2. To rig the yards. *Encapillarse el agua*, (Naut.) To ship a head sea.—*vr.* To put on clothes over the head.

Encapirotado, da [en-cah-pe-ro-tah'-do, dah], *a.* Wearing a cloak or hood.—*pp.* of ENCAPIROTAR.

Encapirotar [en-cah-pe-ro-tar'], *va.* To hood a hawk.

Encapotadura [en-cah-po-tah-doo'-rah], *f.* **Encapotamiento** [en-cah-po-tah-me-en'-to], *m.* Lower, frown, cloudiness of look.

Encapotar [en-cah-po-tar'], *va.* 1. To cloak, to cover with a cloak or great-coat. 2. To cover with a veil, to muffle the face.—*vr.* 1. To lower, to gloom, to be clouded: applied to the sky. 2. Of horses: to lower the head too much and press upon the bit.

Encaprichamiento [en-cah-pre-chah-me-en'-to], *m.* Headstrongness, stubbornness.

Encapricharse [en-cah-pre-char'-say], *vr.* 1. To indulge in whims and fanciful desires; to become obstinate or stubborn. 2. (Coll.) To be somewhat enamoured.

Encapuchar [en-cah-poo-char'], *va.* To cover a thing with a hood.

Encapuzado, da [en-cah-poo-thah'-do, dah], *a.* Covered with a hood or cowl.—*pp.* of ENCAPUZAR.

Encapuzar [en-cah-poo-thar'], *va.* To cover with a long gown.

Encara [en-cah'-rah], *adv.* (Obs.) Yet, even, withal. *V.* AUN.

Encarado, da [en-cah-rah'-do, dah], *a.* 1. Faced. *Bien* or *mal encarado*, Well or ill faced. 2. (Amer.) Haughty, threatening.—*pp.* of ENCARAR.

Encaramadura [en-cah-rah-mah-doo'-rah], *f.* (Obs.) 1. Height, eminence. 2. The act of climbing up an eminence.

Encaramar [en-cah-rah-mar'], *va. & vr.* 1. To raise; to elevate. 2. To extol, to exaggerate. 3. To climb. 4. To reach an eminent post.

Encaramiento [en-cah-rah-me-en'-to], *m.* The act of facing or aiming.

Encarar [en-cah-rar'], *vn.* To face, to front, to be opposite.—*va.* To aim, to point or level a firelock.

Encaratularse [en-cah-rah-too-lar'-say], *vr.* To mask or disguise one's self.

Encaraxis [en-ca-rahk'-sis], *f.* Scarification.

Encarbo [en-car'-bo], *m.* Pointer, a pointer dog.

Encarcajado, da [en-car-cah-hah'-do, dah], *a.* (Obs.) Armed with a quiver.

Encarcavinar [en-car-cah-ve-nar'], *va.* 1. To infect with a pestilential smell. 2. To put one into a ditch.

Encarcelación [en-car-thay-lah-the-on'], *f.* Incarceration.

Encarcelado, da [en-car-thay-lah'-do, dah], *a. & pp.* of ENCARCELAR. Confined, imprisoned.

Encarcelar [en-car-thay-lar'], *va.* 1. To imprison, to commit to prison. 2. To compress newly glued timbers in a clamp. 3. To fasten something with mortar, as a door-casing. 4. (Naut.) To woold; to fasten two cables which cross each other.

Encarcerar [en-car-thay-rar'], *va.* (Obs.) *V.* ENCARCELAR.

Encarecedor [en-cah-ray-thay-dor'], *m.* Praiser, extoller; one who exaggerates.

Encarecer [en-cah-ray-therr'], *va. & vn. & vr.* 1. To raise the price of commodities, to enhance or heighten in price, to overrate, to overvalue. 2. (Met.) To enhance, to exaggerate. 3. To recommend earnestly.

Encarecidamente [en-cah-ray-the-dah-men'-tay], *adv.* Exceedingly, highly, hyperbolically.

Encarecimiento [en-cah-ray-the-me-en'-to], *m.* 1. Enhancement, augmentation of value. 2. Exaggeration, hyperbolical amplification. *Con encarecimiento*, Ardently, earnestly.

(*Yo encarezco, yo encarezca*, from *Encarecer. V.* CONOCER.)

Encargado de negocios [en-car-gah'-do day nay-go'-the-os], *m.* 1. Chargé d'affaires. 2. (Mex.) Agent, attorney, commissioner.

Encargar [en-car-gar'], *va.* To recommend, to charge, to commission, to commit. *Encargarse de alguna cosa*, To take charge of any thing.

Encargo [en-car'-go], *m.* 1. Charge, command, trust conferred, commission, request. 2. Office, place, employ. 3. (Com.) Order.

Encariñar [en-cah-re-nyar'], *va.* To inspire affection, fondness, or love.—*vr.* To become passionately fond of.

Encarna [en-car'-nah], *f.* Act of giving the entrails of dead game to the dogs.

Encarnación [en-car-nah-the-on'], *f.* 1. Incarnation, the act of assuming a body: speaking of our blessed Saviour. 2. Carnation, the natural flesh colour. 3. A certain adhesive cement which serves to repair china-ware, etc. 4. (Med.) Making of tissue in a wound.

Encarnadino, na [en-car-nah-dee'-no, nah], *a.* Incarnadine, of a reddish colour.

Encarnado, da [en-car-nah'-do, dah], *a. & pp.* of ENCARNAR. 1. Incarnate, any thing tinged of a deep-red colour. 2. Dyed flesh colour. 3. Covered with flesh.

Encarnado [en-car-nah'-do], *m.* Flesh colour given to pieces of sculpture.

Encarnadura [en-car-nah-doo'-rah], *f.* 1. The natural state of flesh in living bodies, with respect to the cure of wounds. 2. The effect produced by an edged weapon on the flesh.

Encarnamiento [en-car-nah-me-en'-to], *m.* Incarnation, the act of breeding flesh: applied to a healing wound.

Encarnar [en-car-nar'], *vn.* To incarn, to incarnate, to breed flesh.—*va.* 1. To incarnadine, to give a flesh colour to pieces of sculpture. 2. To make a strong impression upon the mind. 3. To fill a wound with new flesh. 4. To wound, to pierce the flesh with a dart. 5. To embody. 6. To entice or allure dogs; to feed sporting dogs with flesh.—*vr.* To unite or incorporate one thing with another.

Encarnativo [en-car-nah-tee'-vo, vah], *m. & a.* Incarnative, a medicine supposed to generate flesh.

Encarne [en-car'-nay], *m.* First feed given to dogs of the entrails of game.

Encarnecer [en-car-nay-therr'], *vn.* To grow fat and fleshy.

Encarnizado, da [en-car-ne-thah'-do, dah], *a.* Blood-shot, inflamed: commonly applied to the eyes.—*pp.* of ENCARNIZAR.

Encarnizamiento [en-car-ne-thah-me-en'-to], *m.* 1. The act of fleshing or satiating with flesh. 2. Cruelty, rage, fury.

Encarnizar [en-car-ne-thar'], *va.* 1. To flesh, to satiate with flesh. 2. To provoke, to irritate.—*vr.* 1. To be glutted with flesh. 2. To be cruelly bent against one; to fall foul upon one.

Encaro [en-cah'-ro], *m.* 1. The act of viewing steadfastly. 2. (Prov.) Blunderbuss, a wide-mouthed short hand gun. *Encaro de escopeta*, Aiming, the act of levelling a musket or fire-lock, aim.

Encarrilar, or **Encarrillar** [en-car-ril-lyar'], *va.* 1. To direct, to guide, to put in the right road, to conduct a carriage in a proper track, to place in the rails. 2. (Met.) To arrange again what had been deranged.—*vr.* (Naut.) To be fouled or entangled on the sheave of a block: applied to a rope.

Encarroñar [en-car-ro-nyar'], *va.* (Coll.) To infect, to corrupt.—*vr.* To be infected or corrupted.

Encarrujado [en-car-roo-hah'-do], *m.* Ancient kind of silk stuff.—*pp.* of ENCARRUJAR.

Encarrujar [en-car-roo-har'], *va.* To plait, to flute, to mangle.—*vr.* To be corrugated, curled, or wrinkled.

Encartación [en-car-tah-the-on'], *f.* 1. Enrolment. *V.* EMPADRONAMIENTO. 2. Vassalage, the state of a vassal; tenure at will; servitude. 3. The people or places which enter into a state of vassalage, or acknowledge one as a lord.—*pl.* Places adjoining the province of Biscay, which enjoy the same privileges as that province.

Encartado, da [en-car-tah'-do, dah], *a.* Native of, or belonging to the *Encartaciones.*

Encartamiento [en-car-tah-me-en'-to], *m.* 1. Outlawry, proscription. 2. Vassalage. *V.* ENCARTACIÓN.

Encartar [en-car-tar'], *va.* 1. To outlaw, to proscribe. 2. To summon to judgment. 3. To include, to enrol. 4. To enter in the register of taxes.—*vr.* To be unable to discard in a game (of cards).

Encarte [en-car'-tay], *m.* In cards, the fortuitous order in which the cards remain at the close of a hand.

Encartonador [en-car-to-nah-dor'], *m.* One who applies boards to books for binding.

Encartonar [en-car-to-nar'], *va.* 1. To apply (binder's) boards to books. 2. To bind in boards only.

Encartuchar [en-car-too-char'], *va.* To fill cartridges with powder.

Encasamento [en-cah-sah-men'-to], *m.* Niche, place in a wall for a statue.

Encasamiento [en-cah-sah-me-en'-to], *m.* 1. An ornament of fillets and mouldings. 2. Reparation of ruinous houses. 3. Niche.

Encasar [en-cah-sar'], *va.* To set a dislocated bone.

Encascabelado, da [en-cas-cah-bay-lah'-do, dah], *a.* Filled or adorned with bells.

Encascotar [en-cas-co-tar'], *va.* To cover with a layer of rubbish.

Encasillado [en-cah-se-lyah'-do], *m.* Set of pigeonholes.

Encasillar [en-cah-se-lyar'], *va.* 1. To place in pigeonholes. 2. To classify persons or things and assign them to their places.

Encasquetar [en-cas-kay-tar'], *va.* 1. To clap on one's hat close to the head. 2. (Met.) To induce one to adopt an opinion.—*vr.* To persist, to be headstrong.

Encastar [en-cas-tar'], *va.* 1. To improve a race of animals. 2. *V.* PROCREAR.

Encastillado, da [en-cas-til-lyah'-do, dah], *a.* (Met.) Elated, lofty, haughty.—*pp.* of ENCASTILLAR.

Encastillador, ra [en-cas-til-lyah-dor', rah], *m.* & *f.* 1. One who shuts himself up in a castle. 2. A potter's workman who piles up the pieces which ought to be aired before going into the furnace.

Encastillamiento [en-cas-til-lyah-me-en'-to], *m.* Act of shutting up in a castle.

Encastillar [en-cas-til-lyar'], *va.* To fortify with castles.—*vn.* To make the cell of the queen-bee in bee-hives.—*vr.* 1. To shut one's self up in a castle, by way of defence. 2. (Met.) To persevere obstinately in maintaining one's opinion.

Encastrar [en-cas-trar'], *va.* 1. (Naut.) To mortise or scarf pieces of timber. 2. To let in, to imbed.

Encastre [en-cahs'-tray], *m.* Fitting in, groove; socket.

Encatusar [en-cah-too-sar'], *va.* *V.* ENGATUSAR.

Encauchado [en-cah-oo-chah'-do], *m.* An India-rubber poncho.

Encauma [en-cah'-oo-mah], *f.* (Med.) 1. A pustule produced by a burn, and the scar which remains. 2. Corroding ulcer of the cornea.

Encáustico, ca [en-cah'-oos-te-co. cah], *a.* Encaustic, belonging to enamel-painting.

Encausto [en-cah'-oos-to], *m.* 1. (Pict.) Enamelling. 2. *Pintar al encausto,* To paint in colours requiring firing. 3. A red ink with which emperors alone used to write.

Encavarse [en-cah-var'-say], *vr.* To incave one's self; to hide in a hole.

Encebadamiento [en-thay-bah-dah-me-en'-to], *m.* Surfeit, repletion of horses.

Encebadar [en-thay-bah-dar'], *va.* To surfeit with barley, and water drunk immediately after it: applied to beasts.—*vr.* To be surfeited by eating barley and drinking water: applied to horses, mules, etc.

Encebollado [en-thay-bol-lyah'-do], *m.* Fricassee of beef or mutton and onions, seasoned with spice.

Encefálico, ca [en-thay-fah'-le-co, cah], *a.* Encephalic, relating to the brain.

Encefalitis [en-thay-fah-lee'-tis], *f.* Encephalitis, inflammation of the brain. *Encefalitis letárgica,* Sleeping sickness.

Encéfalo [en-thay'-fah-lo], *m.* The encephalon, the brain as a whole; cerebrum, cerebellum, and medulla oblongata.

Encefalóideo, dea [en-thay-fah-lo'-e-day-o, ah], *a.* Encephaloid, resembling brain matter in aspect.—*f.* Encephaloid, a variety of cancer resembling the brain in consistency.

Encelar [en-thay-lar'], *va.* To excite jealousy.—*vr.* To become jealous or suspicious in love.

Encelitis [en-thay-lee'-tis], *f.* (Med.) Intestinal inflammation.

Encellar [en-thel-lyar'], *va.* To mould curds or cheese in a wattle.

Encenagado, da [en-thay-nah-gah'-do, dah], *a.* Mixed or filled with mud.—*pp.* of ENCENAGARSE.

Encenagar [en-thay-nah-gar'], *va.* To mud, to mire.—*vr.* 1. To wallow in dirt or mire, to dirty one's self with mud or mire. 2. (Met.) To wallow in crimes and vices: it is seldom used but in its reflexive sense.

Encencerrado, da [en-then-ther-rah'-do, dah], *a.* Carrying a wether-bell.

Encendedor, ra [en-then-day-dor', rah], *a.* Lighting.—*m.* 1. Lighter. 2. Cigarette lighter.

Encender [en-then-derr'], *va.* 1. To kindle, to light, to make burn. 2. To set fire to, to set on fire. 3. To heat, to produce heat, to glow. 4. (Met.) To inflame, to inspirit, to incite. 5. (Met.) To foment a party, to sow discord.—*vr.* To fire, to take fire, to be kindled. *Encenderse en cólera,* To fly into a passion. *Encenderse en ira,* To kindle with anger.

Encendidamente [en-then-de-dah-men'-tay], *adv.* Vividly, ardently; efficaciously.

Encendido, da [en-then-dee'-do, dah], *a.* & *pp.* of ENCENDER. Inflamed. *Encendido de color,* High coloured.

Encendimiento [en-then-de-me-en'-to], *m.* 1. Incension, the act of kindling and the state of being on fire. 2. Incandescence, excandescency, glow. 3. (Met.) Inflammation. 4. (Met.) Liveliness and ardour of human passions and affections.

Encenizar [en-thay-ne-thar'], *va.* To fill or cover with ashes.

Encensar, Encensuar [en-then-sar', en-then-soo-ar'], *va.* (Obs.) To give or take at lawful interest; to lease.

Encentador [en-then-tah-dor'], *m.* The person who begins to use things not before used.

Encentadura [en-then-tah-doo'-rah], *f.*

Encentamiento, *m.* The act of beginning the use of a thing not before used.

Encentar [en-then-tar'], *va.* 1. To begin the use of a thing not before used, 2. (Obs.) To cut, to mutilate a member. *V.* DECENTAR.

Encepador [en-thay-pah-dor'], *m.* Stocker, gun-stocker.

Encepar [en-thay-par'], *va.* 1. (Coll.) To put in the stocks. 2. To stock a gun; to stock the anchor.—*vn.* To take root.

Encerado [en-thay-rah'-do], *m.* 1. Oilcloth, oil-skin. 2. Window-blind. 3. (Naut.) Tarpauling. 4. Sticking-plaster. 5. A square of oil-skin, used as a slate or blackboard in schools.

Encerado, da [en-thay-rah'-do, dah], *a.* Waxed, like wax. — *p.p. de Encerar.* *Papel encerado,* Wax paper.

Enceramiento [en-thay-rah-me-en'-to], *m.* Act of waxing paper, cloth, etc.

Encerar [en-thay-rar'], *va.* 1. To fasten or stiffen with wax. 2. To fill or stain with wax.

Encernadar [en-ther-nah-dar'], *va.* *V.* ACERNADAR.

Encerotar [en-thay-ro-tar'], *va.* To wax thread.

Encerradero [en-ther-rah-day'-ro], *m.* 1. Place for keeping sheep before or after shearing. 2. *V.* ENCIERRO.

Encerrado, da [en-ther-rah'-do, dah], *a.* (Obs.) Brief, succinct.—*pp.* of ENCERRAR.

Encerrador [en-ther-rah-dor'], *m.* 1. One who shuts or locks up. 2. Driver of black cattle.

Encerradura [en-ther-rah-doo'-rah], *f.* Cloister, enclosure, closure.

Encerramiento [en-ther-rah-me-en'-to], *m.* 1. Cloister, retreat, place of retirement. 2. Prison, jail, dungeon. 3. The locking up of a thing. 4. (Obs.) Inclosure, ground destined for pasture.

Encerrar [en-ther-rar'], *va.* 1. To lock or shut up, to confine, to get in or to close in. 2. To emboss. 3. To contain, to conclude, to comprehend.—*vr.* 1. To retire or withdraw from the world. 2. To be locked or shut up, to be closeted.

Encerrona [en-ther-ro'-nah], *f.* A voluntary retreat, a spontaneous retirement.

Encespedar [en-thes-pay-dar'], *va.* (Mil.) To line or cover the sides of a moat or fosse with sods.

Encestar [en-thes-tar'], *va.* 1. To gather and put in a basket; to toss in a basket, to hamper. 2. (Obs.) To impose upon, to deceive.

Encía [en-thee'-ah], *f.* The gum of the mouth.

Enciclia [en-thee'-cle-ah], *f.* Concentric circles formed in water when a solid and heavy body falls into it.

Encíclica [en-thee'-cle-cah], *f.* An encyclical letter from the Pope to all the world.

Encíclico, ca [en-thee'-cle-co, cah], *a.* Encyclic, circular: applied to pastoral letters.

Enciclopedia [en-the-clo-pay'-de-ah], *f.* Encyclopædia, cyclopædia, the circle of sciences.

Enciclopédico, ca [en-the-clo-pay'-de-co cah], *a.* Encyclopedic.

Enciclopedista [en-the-clo-pay-dees'-tah], *a.* & *n.* Encyclopedist.

(*Yo enciendo, yo encienda,* from *Encender. V.* ATENDER.)

(*Yo encienso. yo enciense,* from *Encensar. V.* ACRECENTAR.)

Encierro [en-the-er'-ro], *m.* 1. Closure, confinement, closeness. 2 Inclosure. 3. Cloister, religious retreat. 4. Prison, close confinement, custody. 5. The act of driving bulls into the pen-fold for the bull-feasts.

(*Yo encierro, yo encierre,* from *Encerrar. V.* ACRECENTAR.)

Encima [en-thee'-mah], *adv.* 1. Above, over. 2. At the top. 3. Over and above, besides. 4. On. 5. Overhead. *Encima de la mesa,* Over the table.

Encimar [en-the-mar'], *va.* (Obs.) To place at the top, to raise high.—*vr.* To raise one's self upon.

Encimero, ra [en-the-may'-ro, rah], *a.* That which is placed over or upon.

Encina [en-thee'-nah], *f.* (Bot.) Evergreen oak, live-oak. Quercus ilex.

Encinal, Encinar [en-the-nahl', en-the-nar'], *m.* Wood, consisting of evergreen oak.

Encinta [en-theen'-tah], *a.* Pregnant.

Encintado [en-thin-tah'-do], *m.* Curb.

Encintar [en-thin-tar'], *va.* 1. To be-ribbon. 2. To curb (a sidewalk).

Encismar [en-this-mar'], *va.* (Coll.) To set a schism or division between.

Encisto [en-thees'-to], *m.* An encysted tumour.

Enclaustrado, da [en-clah-oos-trah'-do, dah], *a.* Shut up in cloisters.

Enclavación [en-clah-vah-the-on'], *f.* (Obs.) Act of nailing or fixing.

Enclavadura [en-clah-vah-doo'-rah], *f.* 1. The part where two pieces of wood are joined. 2. *V.* CLAVADURA.

Enclavar [en-clah-var'], *va.* 1. To nail, to fasten with nails. 2. To prick horses in shoeing. *V.* TRASPASAR. *Enclavar la artillería,* To spike up guns.

Enclavijar [en-clah-ve-har'], *va.* To unite or join closely. *Enclavijar un instrumento,* To put pegs in a musical instrument. (Naut.) *V.* EMPERNAR.

Enclenque [en-clen'-kay], *m.* & *a.* One who is of a weak or feeble constitution, an emaciated person.

Encliquitaje [en-cle-ke-tah'-hay], *m.* Gearing, cogging.

Enclítico, ca [en-clee'-te-co, cah], *a.* Enclitic, appended to a word, as *dícese* (= *dice* + *se*).

Encloclar, Encloquecer [en-clo-clar', en-clo-kay-therr'], *vn.* & *vr.* To cluck, to manifest a desire to hatch eggs.

Encobar [en-co-bar'], *vn.* To cover or hatch eggs.

Encobijar [en-co-be-har'], *va.* *V.* COBIJAR.

Encobrado, da [en-co-brah'-do, dah], *a.* Coppery; copper-coloured, copper-plated.

Encoclar [en-co-clar'], *vn.* To be disposed to cluck: applied to fowls.

Encocorar [en-co-co-rar'], *va.* (Coll.) To molest, to vex, to annoy.

Encofrado [en-co-frah'-do], *m.* (Min.) Plank lining, timbering.

Encofrar [en-co-frar'], *va.* (Min.) To plank, to line with sheeting.

Encoger [en-co-herr'], *va.* 1. To contract, to draw together, to shorten. 2. To shrink, to make to shrink. 3. (Met.) To discourage, to dispirit.—*vr.* 1. To be low-spirited, to be dismayed. 2. To humble one's self, to be dejected. 3. To shrink, to contract itself into less room. *Encogerse de hombros,* To shrink the shoulders with fear; to put an end to a debate, to occasion silence.

Encogidamente, *adv.* Meanly, abjectly.

Encogido, da [en-co-hee'-do, dah], *a.* Pusillanimous, timid, fearful, narrow-minded.—*pp.* of ENCOGER.

Encogimiento [en-co-he-me-en'-to], *m.* 1. Contraction, contracting, drawing together or shortening; constriction, corrugation. 2. Pusillanimity, want of resolution. 3. Lowness of spirits. 4. Humility, submission, resignation. *Encogimiento de los costados,* (Naut.) The tumbling home or housing in of the sides of a ship.

Encohetar [en-co-ay-tar'], *va.* To cover with squibs. (Obsolescent.)

Encojar [en-co-har'], *va.* To cripple, to lame, to make lame.—*vr.* 1. To grow lame. 2. To feign sickness in order to avoid doing some business.

Encoladura [en-co-lah-doo'-rah], *f.* **Encolamiento** [en-co-lah-me-en'-to], *m.* Gluing, the act and effect of gluing.

Encolar [en-co-lar'], *va.* To glue, to fasten with cement; to glutinate.

Encolerizar [en-co-lay-re-thar'], *va.* To provoke, to anger, to irritate.—*vr.* To be in a passion, to be vexed or displeased; to be in a rage.

Encolpismo [en-col-pees'-mo], *m.* (Med.) Vaginal injection.

Encomendable [en-co-men-dah'-blay], *a.* Recommendable, commendable.

Encomendado [en-co-men-dah'-do], *m.* Vassal of a military chief.—*Encomendado, da, pp.* of ENCOMENDAR.

Encomendamiento, *m.* *V.* ENCOMIENDA.

Encomendar [en-co-men-dar'], *va.* 1. To recommend, to commend, to commit, to charge. 2. To praise, to applaud.—*vn.* To hold a commandery in a military order.—*vr.* 1. To commit one's self to another's protection. 2. To send compliments and messages. *Sin encomendarse a Dios ni al diablo,* proverb used to signify foolhardiness in throwing one's self into some desperate affair: literally, without commending one's self to God or the devil.

Encomendero [en-co-men-day'-ro], *m.* 1. Agent, who receives and executes commissions and orders. 2. Pensioner or annuitant. 3. One who holds a commandery in a military order.

Encomiador, ra [en-co-me-ah-dor', rah], *m.* & *f.* One who praises.

Encomiar [en-co-me-ar'], *va.* 1. To offer encomiums or praises. 2. To eulogize, to extol.

Encomiasta, *m.* (Littl. us.) Encomiast.

Encomiástico, ca [en-co-me-ahs'-te-co, cah], *a.* Encomiastic, panegyrical, laudatory.

Encomienda [en-co-me-en'-dah], *f.* 1. Commission, charge. 2. Message, compliment sent to an absent person. 3. Commandery in a military order: land or rent belonging to a commandery. 4. The embroidered cross worn by knights of military orders. 5. Patronage, protection, support. 6. Recommendation. 7. (Com.) Charge or commission for negotiation. *Encomiendas,* Compliments, invitations, respects. *Encomienda de Santiago,* (Bot.) Daffodilly, or jacobæa lily. Amaryllis formosissima.

(*Yo encomiendo, yo encomiende,* from *Encomendar. V.* ACERTAR.)

Encomio [ĕn-co'-me-o], *m.* Praise, encomium, eulogy, commendation.

Encompadrar [en-com-pah-drar'], *vn.* (Coll.) 1. To contract affinity by godfather. 2. To be close friends.

Encompasar, *va.* (Obs.) To encompass. *V.* COMPASAR.

Enconado, da [en-co-nah'-do, dah], *a.* & *pp.* of ENCONAR. 1. Inflamed, swollen. 2. Tainted, stained, spotted.

Enconamiento [en-co-nah-me-en'-to], *m.* 1. Inflammation, a morbid swelling. 2. (Met.) Provocation, the act of exciting passion or anger. 3. (Obs.) Venom.

Enconar [en-co-nar'], *va.* 1. To inflame, to irritate, to provoke. 2. To increase the state of inflammation in a wound.—*vr.* To rankle, to fester: applied to a wound.

Encono [en-co'-no], *m.* Malevolence, rancour, ill-will, steadfast implacability.

Enconoso, sa [en-co-no'-so, sah], *a.* 1. Apt to cause or produce an inflammation. 2. Hurtful, prejudicial, malevolent.

Enconrear [en-con-ray-ar'], *va.* To oil wool that is to be carded.

Encontinente, *adv.* (Obs.) *V.* INCONTINENTI.

Encontrable [en-con-trah'-blay], *a.* That which may be encountered.

Encontradamente, *adv.* Contrarily, in a contrary manner.

Encontradizo, da [en-con-trah-dee'-tho, thah], *a.* That which may be met on the way. *Hacerse encontradizo con alguno,* To go to meet any one as if by chance.

Encontrado, da [en-con-trah'-do, dah], *a.* 1. Opposite, in front. 2. Hostile, opposed. 3. (Naut.) One of the classes of blocks, the contrary course of two vessels, and everything which is moved or is situated opposite to that with which it is compared.—*pp.* of ENCONTRAR.

Encontrar [en-con-trar'], *va.* & *vn.* 1. To meet, to encounter. 2. To meet, to encounter unexpectedly, to hit upon, to find by chance, to fall in with, to light upon. 3. To meet, to assemble, to come together.—*vr.* 1. To meet, to encounter in a hostile manner, to clash. 2. To be of opposite opinions. 3. To meet at the same place, to meet with.

Encontrón [en-con-trone'], *m.* Collision, clash, push, shock, violent concourse, a sudden stroke.

Encopetado, da [en-co-pay-tah'-do, dah], *a.* Presumptuous, boastful.—*pp.* of ENCOPETAR.

Encopetar [en-co-pay-tar'], *va.* (Obs. To raise the hair high, as in a toupee.

Encorachar [en-co-rah-char'], *va.* To put in a leather bag.

Encorado, da [en-co-rah'-do, dah], *a.* & *pp.* of ENCORAR. Wrapped up in leather.

Encorajado, da [en-co-rah-hah'-do, dah] *a.* & *pp.* of ENCORAJAR. 1. Bold, audacious, adventurous. 2. Angry, furious, in a rage.

Encorajar [en-co-rah-har'], *va.* To animate, to give courage, to inflame.—*vr.* To be furious, to be in a rage.

Encoramentar [en-co-rah-men-tar'], *va.* (Naut.) To bolt, to coak, to fay.

Encoramento, Encoramiento [en-co-rah-me-en'-to], *m.* (Naut.) Bolting, coaking, faying.

Encorar [en-co-rar'], *va.* & *vn.* 1. To cover with leather. 2. To wrap up in leather. 3. To get a skin: applied to wounds nearly healed. 4. To skin, to heal the skin.

Encorazado, da [en-co-rah-thah'-do, dah], *a.* 1. Covered with a cuirass. 2. Covered with leather in the cuirass fashion. 3. Iron-clad, armoured. *Acorazado* is more commonly used.

Encorchadura [en-cor-chah-doo'-rah], *f.* 1. The act of hiving bees. 2. The corks or floats, collectively, of fishing nets.

Encorchar [en-cor-char'], *va.* 1. To hive bees, to put them into hives made of cork. 2. To buck: said of a horse.

Encorchetar [en-cor-chay-tar'], *va.* To hook, to put on hooks or clasps.

Encordar [en-cor-dar'], *va.* 1. To string or chord musical instruments. 2. To halter, to lash or bind with cords or ropes.

Encordelar [en-cor-day-lar'], *va.* To bind with cords. *Encordelar una cama,* To cord a bed.

Encordonado, da [en-cor-do-nah'-do, dah], *a.* Adorned with cords.—*pp.* of ENCORDONAR.

Encordonar [en-cor-do-nar'], *va.* To put running strings to a purse or other thing; to tie with strings.

Encorecer [en-co-ray-therr'], *va.* & *vn.* 1. To skin, to heal the skin. 2. To get a skin: applied to wounds.

Encoriación [en-co-re-ah-the-on'], *f.* Act of skinning over a sore, healing a wound.

Encornar [en-cor-nar'], *va.* 1. To inlay with horn. 2. To gore or wound with the horns. 3. (Arch.) To ornament the ends of an arch with tips of horn.

Encornijamento [en-cor-ne-hah-men'-to], *m.* *V.* CORNIJAMENTO.

Encornudar [en-cor-noo-dar'], *vn.* To begin to get horns: applied to black cattle.—*va.* To cuckold, to hornify.

Encorozar [en-co-ro-thar'], *va.* To cover the head with a *coroza,* or cone-shaped cap, worn by criminals as a punishment.

Encorralar [en-cor-rah-lar'], *va.* To inclose and keep in a yard: applied to cattle.

Encortinar [en-cor-te-nar'], *va.* To provide with curtains.

Encorvada [en-cor-vah'-dah], *f.* 1. The act of bending or doubling the body. 2. A graceless and awkward manner of dancing. 3. (Bot.) Hatchet wetch coronilla. Coronilla securidaca. *Hacer la encorvada,* (Met.) To feign disease to avoid something.

Encorvadura, *f.* **Encorvamiento,** *m.* [en-cor-vah-doo'-rah]. 1. Act of bending or reducing to a crooked shape, couching. 2. Crookedness; falcation, hookedness.

Encorvar [en-cor-var'], *va.* To bend, to incurvate, to crook, to curve.—*vr.* To bend, to courb; to go crooked.

Encosadura [en-co-sah-doo'-rah], *f.* (Prov.) The act of sewing or joining fine linen to some of a coarser sort.

Encostarse [en-cos-tar'-say], *vr.* (Naut.) To stand inshore, to near the coast.

Encostradura [en-cos-trah-doo'-rah], *f.* Incrustation, crust.

Encostrar [en-cos-trar'], *va.* 1. To crust, to incrust, to envelope or cover with a crust. 2. To rough-cast with mortar, made of lime and sand.

Encovadura [en-co-vah-doo'-rah], *f.* Act of depositing in a cellar.

Encovar [en-co-var'], *va.* 1. To put or lay up in a cellar. 2. (Met.) To guard, to conceal, to inclose.—*vr.* 1. To go down into a cellar (or cave). 2. To hide one's self (or itself).

Encrasar [en-crah-sar'], *va.* To fatten; to thicken.

Encrespador [en-cres-pah-dor'], *m.* Crisping-pin, crisping-iron, curling-iron.

Encrespadura [en-cres-pah-doo'-rah], *f.* Crispation, the act of curling.

Encrespamiento [en-cres-pah-me-en'-to], *m.* Crispation, crispness, curliness, curledness.

Encrespar [en-cres-par'], *va.* To curl, to frizzle, to crimp.—*vr.* 1. (Naut.) To become rough and boisterous: applied to the sea. 2. To be rude or unpolite. 3. To be involved in quarrels and disputes.

Encrespo [en-cres'-po], *m.* (Obs.) Crispation, the act and effect of curling.

Encrestado, da [en-cres-tah'-do, dah], *a.* & *pp.* of ENCRESTARSE. 1. Adorned with a crest or comb 2. (Met.) Haughty, lofty.

Encrestarse [en-cres-tar'-say], *vr.* 1. To get the crest or comb: applied to a young cock. 2. (Met.) To be proud, elated, or haughty.

Encrinita [en-cre-nee'-tah], *f.* Encrinite, a fossil crinoid.

Encruce [en-croo'-thay], *m.* 1. Crossing of threads. 2. Shed, lease, the plane in which the warp-threads cross.

Encrucijada [en-croo-the-hah'-dah], *f.* Crossway, cross-road.

Encrudecer [en-croo-day-therr'], *va.* 1. To make a wound worse or raw. 2. To exasperate, to irritate.—*vr.* To be enraged, to become furious with passion.

(*Yo me encrudezco, yo me encrudezca,* from *Encrudecerse.* *V.* CONOCER.)

Encruelecer [en-croo-ay-lay-therr'], *va.* To excite to cruelties, to make cruel.

(*Yo me encruelezco, yo me encruelezca,* from *Encruelecer.* *V.* CONOCER.)

Encruzar [en-croo-thar'], *va.* To cross the threads of the warp, to twill.

Encuadernación [en-coo-ah-der-nah-the-on'], *f.* Binding (books, etc.) *Encuadernación en cantoné,* Pasteboard binding.

Encuadernador [en-coo-ah-der-nah-dor'], *m.* Binder or book-binder.

Encuadernar [en-coo-ah-der-nar'], *va.* 1. To bind books, pamphlets, etc. 2. (Met.) To join again what was disjoined. 3. To reconcile.

Encuadrar [en-coo-ah-drar'], *va.* To frame, to encase.

Encubar [en-coo-bar'], *va.* 1. To put liquids into casks, barrels, etc. 2. (Ant.) To put a criminal into a butt, by way of punishment.

Encubertado [en-coo-ber-tah'-do], *m.* (Zool.) A kind of South American armadillo.

Encubertar [en-coo-ber-tar'], *va.* To overspread with a covering of cloth or silk.—*vr.* To dress and arm one's self for defence of the body.

Encubierta [en-coo-be-err'-tah], *f.* Fraud, deceit, imposition.

Encubiertamente, *adv.* 1. Hiddenly, secretly. 2. Deceitfully, fraudulently.

Encubierto, ta [en-coo-be-err'-to, tah], *a.* & *pp.* of ENCUBRIR. 1. Hidden, concealed. 2. *V.* CUBIERTO.

(*Yo encubierto, yo encubierta,* from *Encubertar.* *V.* ACRECENTAR.)

Encubridor, ra [en-coo-bre-dor', rah], *m.* & *f.* Concealer, hider, harbourer. *Encubridor de hurtos,* Receiver of stolen goods.

Encubrimiento [en-coo-bre-me-en'-to], *m.* Concealment, hiding, the act of hiding or concealing.

Encubrir [en-coo-breer'], *va.* To hide, to conceal, to cloak, to mask, to palliate.

Encucar [en-coo-car'], *va.* (Prov.) To gather nuts and filberts, and store them up.

Encuentro [en-coo-en'-tro], *m.* 1. Knock, a sudden stroke, chock, justle, clash. 2. Encounter, accidental congress; sudden meeting. 3. Encounter, fight. 4. The act of going to meet and see any one. 5. Opposition, difficulty. 6. Joint of the wings, in fowls or birds, next to the breast. 7. In the larger quadrupeds, the points of the shoulder-blades. 8. (Arch.) An angle formed by two beams, two walls, etc. *Salir al encuentro,* 1. To go to meet a person in a certain place. 2. To encounter. 3. To prevent a person in what he is to say or observe. *Encuentros,* Temples of a loom.

(*Yo encuentro, yo encuentre,* from *Encontrar.* *V.* ACORDAR.)

(*Yo encuerdo, yo encuerde,* from *Encordar.* *V.* ACORDAR.)

Encuesta, *f.* (Obs.) Inquest. *V.* AVERIGUACIÓN.

Encuitarse [en-coo-e-tar'-say], *vr.* To grieve, to afflict one's self.

Enculatar [en-coo-lah-tar'], *va.* To put on the covering or cap of a hive.

Encumbrado, da [en-coom-brah'-do, dah], *a.* High, elevated, lofty, stately. —*pp.* of ENCUMBRAR.

Encumbramiento [en-coom-brah-me-en'-to], *m.* 1. The act of raising or elevating. 2. Height, eminence.

Encumbrar [en-coom-brar'], *va.* 1. To raise, to elevate. 2. To mount or ascend a height. 3. (Met.) To elevate to dignities or honours.—*vr.* 1. To be raised or elevated. 2. To be proud, to rate himself high.

Encunar [en-coo-nar'], *va.* 1. To put a child in the cradle. 2. (Met.) To catch the bull-fighter between the horns: said of the bull.

Encuñar [en-coo-nyar'], *va.* To coin. *V.* ACUÑAR.

Encureñado, da [en-coo-ray-nyah'-do, dah], *a.* Put into the carriage or stock.

Encurtidos [en-coor-tee'-dos], *m. pl.* Pickles of small cucumbers and peppers.

Encurtir [en-coor-teer'], *va.* To souse in pickle or vinegar.

Encha [en'-chah], *f.* (Obs.) Satisfaction, compensation for damage received in war.

Enchabetar [en-chah-bay-tar'], *va.* *Enchabetar un perno,* (Naut.) To forelock a bolt.

Enchalecar [en-chah-lay-car'], *va.* (Prov. Amer.) To put (insane persons) in the strait-jacket.

Enchamarrado, da [en-chah-mar-rah'-do, dah], *a.* Clothed in coarse frieze or sheepskin.

Enchancletar [en-chan-clay-tar'], *va.* 1. To put on slippers. 2. To wear shoes in the manner of slippers.

Enchapar [en-chah-par'], *va.* To veneer.

Enchapinado, da [en-chah-pe-nah'-do, dah], *a.* 1. Made in the manner of pattens. 2. Built and raised upon a vault or arch.

Encharcada [en-char-cah'-dah], *f.* A pool of water.

Encharcarse [en-char-car'-say], *vr.* To be covered with water, to be inundated.

Enchicar [en-che-car'], *va.* *V.* ACHICAR.

Enchilada [en-che-lah'-dah], *f.* A cake of maize dressed with peppers, a Mexican dish.

Enchiquerar [en-che-kay-rar'], *va.* 1. To shut the bull in the pen called *chiquero.* 2. (Met. Coll.) To imprison.

Enchufar [en-choo-far'], *vn.* To fit, as the orifice of a tube into another.

Enchufe [en-choo'-fay], *m.* 1. Socket joint. 2. Plug. 3. (coll.) Additional job obtained through political influence.

Ende [en'-day], *adv.* (Obs.) *V.* ALLÍ and De ALLÍ. *Facer ende al,* (Law Obs.) To do the contrary of what was desired. *Por ende, V.* POR TANTO.

Endeble [en-day'-blay], *a.* Feeble, weak, flaccid, flimsy, forceless.

Endeblez [en-day-bleth'], *f.* Feebleness, flaccidity, flimsiness.

Endecágono [en-day-cah'-go-no], *m.* Hendecagon, a figure of eleven angles or sides.

Endecasílabo, ba [en-day-cah-see'-lah-bo, bah], *a.* Applied to metrical lines consisting of eleven syllables. *Verso endecasílabo,* Hendecasyllable.

Endecha [en-day'-chah], *f.* Dirge, a doleful ditty.

Endechadera, *f. V.* PLAÑIDERA.

Endechar [en-day-char'], *va.* To sing funeral songs in honour and praise of the dead.—*vr.* To grieve, to mourn.

Endechoso, sa [en-day-cho'-so, sah], *a.* (Obs.) Mournful, doleful.

Endemia [en-day'-me-ah], *f.* Endemia, any disease produced and propagated by local conditions.

Endémico, ca [en-day'-me-co, cah], *a.* Endemic, peculiar to a climate.

Endemoniado, da [en-day-mo-ne-ah'-do, dah], *a.* 1. Possessed with the devil, fiendful. 2. Devilish, extremely bad, perverse or hurtful.—*pp.* of ENDEMONIAR.

Endemoniar [en-day-mo-ne-ar'], *va.* 1. To possess with a devil. 2. (Met.) To irritate, to provoke, to enrage.

Endentar [en-den-tar'], *va.* 1. To join with a mortise. 2. (Naut.) To insert one thing in another. 3. To make the teeth on a wheel.

Endentecer [en-den-tay-therr'], *vn.* To cut teeth, to teeth, to tooth.

(*Yo endentezco, yo endentezca,* from *Endentecer. V.* CONOCER.)

Endeñado, da [en-day-nyah'-do, dah], *a.* Damaged, hurt, inflamed.

Enderezadamente [en-day-ray-thah-dah-men'-tay], *adv.* Justly, rightly; directly.

Enderezador [en-day-ray-thah-dor'], *m.* Guide, director; governor. *Enderezador de tuertos* or *agravios,* A righter, a redresser.

Enderezadura [en-day-ray-thah-doo'-rah], *f.* The straight and right road.

Enderezamiento [en-day-ray-thah-me-en'-to], *m.* Guidance, direction, the act of guiding or setting right.

Enderezar [en-day-ray-thar'], *va.* 1. To erect, to place perpendicularly to the horizon what is not upright, to make straight. 2. To rectify, to set right. 3. To address, to dedicate. 4. To go and meet a person.—*vn.* To take the direct road.—*vr.* 1. To erect, to rise upright. 2. (Met.) To fix or establish one's self in a place or employment. *Enderezar el genio,* To break a bad temper.

Enderezo [en-day-ray'-tho], *m.* (Obs.) The act of directing a letter.

Endérmico, ca [en-derr'-me-co, cah], *a.* Endermic, said of a remedy applied directly to the skin.

Endeudarse [en-day-oo-dar'-say], *vr.* To get in debt, to contract debts. *V.* ADEUDARSE.

Endiablada [en-de-ah-blah'-dah], *f.* Masquerade, a diversion in which the company is dressed in masks.

Endiabladamente, *adv.* Uglily, abominably, devilishly.

Endiablado, da [en-de-ah-blah'-do, dah], *a. & pp.* of ENDIABLAR. 1. Devilish, diabolical, diabolic. 2. Ugly, deformed; perverse, wicked.

Endiablar [en-de-ah-blar'], *va.* 1. (Obs.) To possess with the devil. 2. (Met.) To pervert, to corrupt.—*vr.* 1. To be possessed with a devil. 2. (Met.) To be furious, to be beside one's self.

Endiadis [en-dee'-ah-dis], *f.* (Rhet.) Hendiadys, a figure by which two words are used to express a single idea.

Endibia [en-dee'-be-ah], *f.* (Bot.) Endive, succory. Cichorium endivia.

Endilgador, ra [en-deel-gah-dor', rah], *m. & f.* (Coll.) Pander; inducer, adviser.

Endilgar [en-deel-gar'], *va.* (Coll.) 1. To pander, to induce, to persuade. 2. To procure, to facilitate, to accommodate. 3. To show the way, to direct.

Endiosamiento [en-de-o-sah-me-en'-to], *m.* 1. Haughtiness, loftiness, pride. 2. Ecstasy, abstraction; disregard of worldly concerns.

Endiosar [en-de-o-sar'], *va.* To deify, to adore as a god, to heavenize.—*vr.* 1. To be elated, to be puffed up with pride. 2. To be in a state of religious abstraction or fervent devotion.

Endoblado, da [en-do-blah'-do, dah], *a.* Applied to a lamb that sucks its own mother and another ewe.

Endocardio [en-do-car'-de-o], *m.* Endocardium, the serous lining membrane of the heart.

Endocarditis [en-do-car-dee'-tis], *f.* Endocarditis, inflammation of the lining of the heart.

Endocarpo [en-do-car'-po], *m.* (Bot.) Endocarp, the inner membrane of the pericarp.

Endógeno, na [en-do'-hay-no, nah], *a.* Endogenous, growing by internal additions.

Endorsar, Endosar [en-dor-sar', en-do-sar'], *va.* To indorse a bill of exchange.

Endorso, Endoso [en-dor'-so, en-do'-so], *m.* Indorsement of a bill of exchange.

Endosador, Endosante [en-do-sah-dor', en-do-sahn'-tay], *m.* Indorser.

Endoselar [en-do-say-lar'], *va.* To hang, to make hangings or curtains.

Endósmosis [en-dos'-mo-sis], *f.* Endosmosis, transudation.

Endospermo [en-dos-perr'-mo], *m.* Endosperm, the albumen of a seed.

Endotérmico, ca [en-do-terr'-me-co, cah], *a.* (Chem.) Endothermic.

Endragonarse [en-drah-go-nar'-say], *vr.* In the jocular style, to grow furious as a dragon.

Endriago [en-dre-ah'-go], *m.* A kind of fabulous monster.

Endrina [en-dree'-nah], *f.* Sloe, the fruit of the black-thorn or sloe-tree.

Endrino [en-dree'-no], *m.* (Bot.) Blackthorn, sloe-tree. Prunus spinosa.

Endrino, na [en-dree'-no, nah], *a.* Of a sloe-colour.

Endulzamiento [en-dool-thah-me-en'-to], *m.* **Endulzadura** [en-dool-thah-doo'-rah], *f.* Dulcification, act of sweetening.

Endulzar, Endulzorar [en-dool-thar', en-dool-tho-rar'], *va.* 1. To sweeten, to make sweet. 2. (Met.) To soften, to make mild; to alleviate the toils of life.

Endurador, ra [en-doo-rah-dor', rah], *m. & f. & a.* Miser, a mean, avaricious person.

Endurar [en-doo-rar'], *va.* 1. To harden, to indurate, to make hard. 2. To live in a parsimonious manner. 3. To endure, to bear, to suffer. 4. To delay, to put off.

Endurecer [en-doo-ray-therr'], *va.* 1. To harden, to indurate, to make hard. 2. (Met.) To accustom the body to labour and hardships; to inure. 3. (Met.) To render one steady in his sentiments and opinions. 4. To exasperate, to irritate.—*vr.* 1. To harden, to grow hard, to grow cruel. 2. To hammer metals. 3. In the manufacture of needles, to temper them.

(*Yo endurezco, yo endurezca,* from *Endurecer. V.* CONOCER.)

Endurecidamente [en-doo-ray-the-dah-men'-tay], *adv.* Pertinaciously.

Endurecido, da [en-doo-ray-thee'-do, dah], *a. & pp.* of ENDURECER. 1. Hard, hardy. 2. Indurated, hardened, obdurate. 3. Tutored by experience, inured.

Endurecimiento [en-doo-ray-the-me-en'-to], *m.* Hardness; obstinacy, tenacity, hardness of heart, obdurateness.

Ene [ay'-nay], *f.* Spanish name of the letter N. *Ene de palo,* (Coll.) Gallows.

Enea [ay-nay'-ah], *f.* (Bot.) Cat's-tail, reed-mace, rush. Typha.

Eneágono [ay-nay-ah'-go-no], *m.* A plain figure with nine sides and nine angles.

Eneático, ca [ay-nay-ah'-te-co, cah], *a.* Belonging to the number nine.

Enebral [ay-nay-brahl'], *m.* Plantation of juniper-trees.

Enebrina [ay-nay-bree'-nah], *f.* Fruit of the juniper-tree.

Enebro [ay-nay'-bro], *m.* (Bot.) Common juniper. Juniperus communis.

Eneida [ay-nay'-e-dah], *f.* The Æneid, an epic poem by Virgil.

Enejar [ay-nay-har'], *va.* 1. To put an axle-tree to a cart or carriage. 2. To put any thing in an axle-tree.

Eneldo [ay-nel'-do], *m.* (Bot.) Common dill. Anethum graveolens.

Enema [ay-nay'-mah], *f.* Enema, injection, clyster.

Enemiga [ay-nay-mee'-gah], *f.* Enmity, malevolence, aversion, ill-will.

Enemigamente, *adv.* Inimically, in a hostile manner.

Enemigarse [ay-nay-me-gar'-say], *vr.* (Obs.) To be in a state of enmity.

Enemigo, ga [ay-ne-mee'-go, gah], *a.* Inimical, hostile, contrary, unfriendly, adverse.

Enemigo, ga [ay-nay-mee'-go, gah], *m. & f.* Enemy, antagonist, foe, foeman. *El enemigo,* The fiend, the devil.

Enemistad [ay-nay-mis-tahd'], *f.* Enmity, hatred.

Enemistar [ay-nay-mis-tar'], *va.* To make an enemy.—*vr.* To become an enemy.

Éneo, ea [ay'-nay-o, ah], *a.* (Poet.) Brazen, belonging to brass.

Enerar [ay-nay-rar'], *va.* To kill plants by frost.

Energía [ay-ner-hee'-ah], *f.* 1. Energy, power, vigor. 2. Strength of expression, force of meaning. 3. Comprehensiveness. 4. Pep (coll.). *Energía atómica,* Atomic energy. *Energía solar,* Solar power. *Energía vatimétrica,* (Elec.) Wattage.

Enérgicamente [ay-nerr'-he-cah-men-tay], *adv.* Energetically, expressively.

Enérgico, ca [ay-nerr'-he-co, cah], *a.* Energetic, energetical, energic, forcible, active, vigorous, expressive, lively.

Enero [ay-nay'-ro], *m.* January, the first month in the year.

Enervación [ay-ner-vah-the-on'], *f.* 1. Enervation. 2. (Vet.) Section of two tendons in the head of a horse.

Enervado, da, *a. & pp.* of ENERVAR. Enervate, enervated, weakened.

Enervador, ra [ay-ner-vah-dor', rah], *a.* Weakening, enervating.

Enervamiento [ay-ner-vah-me-en'-to], *m.* 1. Enervation. 2. Effeminacy.

Enervar [ay-ner-var'], *va.* 1. To enervate, to deprive of force. 2. To weaken the reasons or arguments.—*vr.* 1. To grow weak, to lose force. 2. To become effeminate. 3. To become dull: applied to the senses. 4. To cut the tendon of the muscles which raise the upper lip of horses.

Enescar [ay-nes-car'], *va.* (Obs.) 1. To attract by gifts. 2. To set out food.

Enético, ca [ay-nay'-te-co, cah], *a.* Lethal, mortal.

Enfadadizo, za [en-fah-dah-dee'-tho, thah], *a.* Irritable, irascible, peevish, waspish, easily offended, soon angry.

Enfadar [en-fah-dar'], *va.* To vex, to molest, to trouble, to fret, to offend, to make angry, to cut to the heart.—*vr.* To fret, to become angry.

Enfado [en-fah'-do], *m.* 1. Trouble, vexation, molestation, fret, crossness, anger, gall, fastidiousness. 2. *V.* Afán and Trabajo.

Enfadosamente, *adv.* Vexatiously, offensively.

Enfadoso, sa [en-fah-do'-so, sah], *a.* Vexatious, troublesome, heavy, cumbersome, molestful.

Enfaldar [en-fal-dar'], *va.* To lop off the lower branches of trees.—*vr.* To tuck or truss up the skirts of one's clothes.

Enfaldo [en-fahl'-do], *m.* Act of tucking up one's clothes.

Enfangarse [en-fan-gar'-say], *vr.* (Naut.) To touch ground in a miry or muddy place. (Coll.) To get into difficulties.

Enfardador [en-far-dah-dor'], *m.* Packer, he who embales or packs up bales and packages.

Enfardar [en-far-dar'], *va.* To pack, to embale, to make packages.

Enfardelador [en-far-day-lah-dor'], *m.* Packer, one who makes up bales.

Enfardeladura [en-far-day-lah-doo'-rah], *f.* Packing, act of packing merchandise.

Enfardelar [en-far-day-lar'], *va.* To bale, to make up into bales, to pack.

Énfasis [en'-fah-sis], *m.* Emphasis, a remarkable stress laid on a word or sentence.

Enfáticamente [en-fah'-te-cah-men-tay], *adv.* Emphatically.

Enfático, ca [en-fah'-te-co, cah], *a.* Emphatical, emphatic, impressive.

Enfelpar [en-fel-par'], *va.* *V.* Afelpar.

Enfermamente [en-fer-mah-men'-tay], *adv.* Weakly, feebly.

Enfermar [en-fer-mar'], *vn.* To be seized with a fit of illness, to fall ill. —*va.* 1. To make sick. 2. To cause damage or loss. 3. To weaken, to enervate.

Enfermedad [en-fer-may-dahd'], *f.* 1. Infirmity, indisposition, illness, complaint, malady, distemper. 2. Damage, disorder, risk.

Enfermería [en-fer-may-ree'-ah], *f.* Infirmary, lodgings for the sick. *Enfermería del sollado,* (Naut.) Cock-pit, on board of ships of war, where the surgeons attend the wounded. *Estar en la enfermería,* To be in the artisan's shop to be mended.

Enfermero, ra [en-fer-may'-ro, rah], *m.* & *f.* Overseer or nurse, who has the care of the sick.

Enfermizo, za [en-fer-mee'-tho, thah], *a.* 1. Infirm, sickly, morbose, healthless. 2. Morbifical, morbific, causing diseases.

Enfermo, ma [en-ferr'-mo, mah], *a.* 1. Sick, diseased, infirm, indisposed, unhealthy. 2. Weak, feeble. 3. Of little importance or consideration. 4. Corrupted, tainted.

Enfervorizar [en-fer-vo-re-thar'], *va.* To heat, to inflame, to incite.—*vr.* To overheat one's self.

(*Yo enfervorezco, yo enfervorezca,* from *Enfervorecer. V.* Conocer.)

Enfeudación [en-fay-oo-dah-the-on'], *f.* Infeudation, enfeoffment, the act of putting one in possession of a fee or estate.

Enfeudar [en-fay-oo-dar'], *va.* To feoff, to enfeoff, to invest with a right or estate.

Enfielar [en-fe-ay-lar'], *va.* To put in a balance.

Enfierecido, da [en-fe-ay-ray-thee'-do, dah], *a.* (Obs.) Furious, fierce.

Enfilar [en-fe-lar'], *va.* 1. To continue as if united in a file or line. 2. To enfilade, to pierce in a right line; to carry off by a cannon-shot a whole file of the enemy's troops; to keep straight forward. *Enfilar el curso,* (Naut.) To direct the course, to bear to.

Enfintoso, sa [en-feen-toh'-so, sah], *a.* (Obs.) Fraudulent, deceitful.

Enfisema [en-fe-say'-mah], *m.* Emphysema, infiltration of the cellular tissue with air.

Enfisematoso, sa [en-fe-say-ma-to'-so, sah], *a.* Emphysematous, affected by emphysema.

Enfita [en-fee'-tah], *f.* (Obs.) Fraud, deceit.

Enfiteusis, Enfitéosis [en-fe-tay'-oo-sis, en-fe-tay'-o-sis], *m.* & *f.* A species of alienation, by which the use and usufruct are transferred, but not the whole right of property.

Enfiteuta [en-fe-tay'-oo-tah], *m.* A tenant by emphyteusis.

Enfitéutico, ca [en-fe-tay'-oo-te-co, cah], *a.* Emphyteutic, taken on hire.

Enflaquecer [en-flah-kay-therr'], *va.* To weaken, to diminish, to make thin and lean, to extenuate, to fade.—*vr.* To become thin and lean, to fall away or fall off.

Enflaquecidamente [en-flah-kay-the-dah-men'-tay], *adv.* Weakly, feebly, faintly, without strength.

Enflaquecimiento [en-flah-kay-the-me-en'-to], *m.* 1. Extenuation, a general decay in the muscular flesh of the whole body. 2. Attenuation, debilitation, maceration.

(*Yo enflaquezco, yo enflaquezca,* from *Enflaquecer. V.* Conocer.)

Enflautado, da [en-flah-oo-tah'-do, dah], *a.* Turgid, inflated.—*m.* 1. (Naut.) The row of cannon mouths which show upon a vessel's side. 2. (Amer.) The flute-stops of an organ, collectively. 3. A sound which imitates the flute.

Enflautador, ra [en-flah-oo-tah-dor', rah], *m.* & *f.* Procurer, pimp.

Enflautar [en-flah-oo-tar'], *va.* 1. To procure. (Obs.) 2. (Coll.) To trick, to deceive.

Enflechado, da [en-flay-chah'-do, dah], *a.* Applied to a bent bow or arrow ready to discharge.

Enflechastes [en-flay-chahs'-tes], *m. pl.* (Naut.) Ratlines.

Enfocar [en-fo-car'], *va.* 1. To focus. 2. To size up or weigh the aspects (of a problem or a business).

Enfoque [en-fo'-kay], *m.* Focus.

Enfornar, *va.* *V.* Enhornar.

Enfoscado, da [en-fos-cah'-do, dah], *a.* & *pp.* of Enfoscarse. 1. Browbeaten. 2. Confused, entangled.

Enfoscar [en-fos-car'], *va.* & *vr.* 1. To be uneasy, to be troubled or perplexed. 2. To be immersed in business. 3. To be cloudy: applied to the sky. 4. To stop up the holes in a wall after it is constructed.

Enfrailar [en-frah-e-lar'], *va.* & *vr.* To make one a monk or a friar, to induce him to take the vows of a religious order; to become a friar.

Enfranquecer [en-fran-kay-therr'], *va.* To frank, to make free.

Enfrascamiento [en-fras-cah-me-en'-to], *m.* The act of being entangled between brambles and briers.

Enfrascar [en-fras-car'], *va.* To put liquid in a flask or bottle.—*vr.* 1. To be entangled between brambles and briers. 2. (Met.) To be involved in difficulties and troubles, to engage deeply in an object.

Enfrenador [en-fray-nah-dor'], *m.* Bridler, one who puts on a bridle.

Enfrenamiento [en-fray-nah-me-en'-to], *m.* 1. Putting on the brake (of an automobile, etc.). 2. Bridling (a horse).

Enfrenar [en-fray-nar'], *va.* 1. To put on the brake (of an automobile, etc.). 2. To curb, to restrain. 3. To bridle, put on the bridle.

Enfrente [en-fren'-tay], *adv.* Over against, opposite, in front, front to front. *Enfrente de casa,* Opposite to the house.

Enfriadera [en-fre-ah-day'-rah], *f.* Back, cooler or keel-fat, the vessel for cooling any liquid; refrigerator.

Enfriadero, Enfriador [en-fre-ah-day'-ro, en-fre-ah-dor'], *m.* Cooling-place; refrigerator.

Enfriamiento [en-fre-ah-me-en'-to], *m.* Refrigeration, the act of cooling, the state of being cooled.

Enfriar [en-fre-ar'], *va.* 1. To cool, to make cool, to allay, to heat, to refrigerate. 2. (Met.) To cool, to allay the heat of passion, to calm the mind. —*vr.* 1. To cool, to grow less hot. 2. (Met.) To cool, to grow less warm with regard to passion.

Enfundar [en-foon-dar'], *va.* 1. To case, to put into a case. 2. To fill up to the brim, to cram, to stuff.

Enfuñarse [en-foo-nyar'-say], *vr.* (Prov. Cuba) To get excited, worried. *V.* Amohinarse.

Enfurecer [en-foo-ray-therr'], *va.* 1. To irritate, to enrage, to mad, to make furious. 2. *V.* Ensoberbecer.—*vr.* 1. To rage, to grow boisterous or furious: applied to the wind and sea. 2. To become furious or enraged.

(*Yo me enfurezco, yo me enfurezca,* from *Enfurecerse. V.* Conocer.)

Enfurruñarse [en-foor-roon-yar'-say], *vr.* (Coll.) To grow angry, to tiff, to be in a pet, to frown.

Enfurtir [en-foor-teer'], *va.* 1. To full or mill clothes. 2. Among hatters, to felt.

Engabanado, da [en-gah-ba-nah'-do, dah], *a.* Covered with a *gabán* or great-coat, with a hood and close sleeves.

Engace [en-gah'-thay], *m.* Catenation, connection. *V.* Engarce.

Engafar [en-gah-far'], *va.* 1. To bend a cross-bow with a hook or lever. 2. (Prov.) To carry in a hook a gun charged, when travelling in the fields.

Engaitador, ra [en-gah-e-tah-dor', rah], *m.* & *f.* Coaxer, wheedler.

Engaitar [en-gah-e-tar'], *va.* To coax, to wheedle.

Engalanado [en-gah-lah-nah'-do], *m.* The banners and bunting with which a ship is adorned.

Engalanar [en-gah-lah-nar'], *va.* 1. To adorn, to deck. 2. (Naut.) To dress a ship, to display a variety of colours, ensigns, or pendants.

Engalgar [en-gal-gar'], *va.* To pursue closely, not to lose sight of: applied to greyhounds in pursuit of a hare. *Engalgar el ancla,* (Naut.) To back an anchor.

Engallado, da [en-gal-lyah'-do, dah], *a* 1. Erect, upright. 2. Haughty, elated

Engalladura [en-gal-lyah-doo'-rah], *f.* *V.* GALLADURA.

Engallarse [en-gal-lyar'-say], *vr.* To affect gravity.

Enganchador [en-gan-chah-dor'], *m.* One who decoys others into military service, vulgarly a crimp.

Enganchamiento [en-gan-chah-me-en'-to], *m.* 1. Accroachment, the act of drawing as with a hook, hooking. 2. The act of entrapping, alluring, or decoying any one, particularly to make him enlist in the military service.

Enganchar [en-gan-char'], *va.* 1. To hook, to catch with a hook, to accroach. 2. To entrap, to insnare. 3. To decoy into the military service, vulgarly to crimp. 4. To couple, to connect. *Enganchar los caballos al coche,* To harness the horses to the carriage.—*vr.* To engage. To enlist or enroll in military service.

Enganche [en-gahn'-chay], *m.* 1. Enlistment, enrollment. 2. Bounty money. 3. Coupler, coupling, connecting link. 4. (Mex. coll.) Down payment on a purchase.

Engañabobos [en-gah-nyah-bo'-bos], *m.* (Coll.) 1. Impostor. 2. Fool-trap, a snare to catch fools in.

Engañadizo, za [en-gah-nyah-dee'-tho, thah], *a.* Deceptible, easily deceived.

Engañado, da [en-gah-nyah'-do, dah], *a.* & *pp.* of ENGAÑAR. Mistaken, deceived, overseen.

Engañador, ra [en-gah-nyah-dor', rah], *m.* & *f.* Cheat, impostor, deceiver, cozener, colluder, abuser.

Engañadura [en-gah-nyah-doo'-rah], *f.* (Naut.) Seizing truck; shroud, double wall knot.

Engañapastor [en-gah-nyah-pas-tor'], *m.* (Orn.) Wagtail, a bird.

Engañar [en-gah-nyar'], *va.* 1. To deceive, to cheat, to mock, to mislead. 2. To cheat, to delude, to impose upon, to trick, to chouse, to cozen. 3. To fool, to hoax, to abuse, to gull.—*vr.* To be deceived, to mistake, to make a mistake. *Ser malo de engañar,* (Coll.) To be not easily deceived, to be sagacious.

Engañifa [en-gah-nyee'-fah], *f.* (Coll.) 1. Deceit, trick, fraudulent action. 2. A catchpenny.

Engaño [en-gah'-nyo], *m.* 1. Mistake, mistaking, misunderstanding, misapprehension, misconception. 2. Deceit, fraud, imposition, falsehood. 3. Hoax, lure.

Engañosamente, *adv.* Deceitfully, fraudfully, guilefully; mistakenly.

Engañoso, sa [en-gah-nyo'-so, sah], *a.* Deceitful, artful, fallacious, false, fraudulent, mendacious.

Engarabatar [en-gah-ra-bah-tar'], *va.* (Coll.) To hook, to seize with violence.—*vr.* To grow crooked.

Engarabitarse [en-gah-ra-be-tar'-say], *vr.* (Coll.) To climb, to mount, to ascend.

Engarbarse [en-gar-bar'-say], *vr.* To perch on the highest branch of a tree: applied to birds.

Engarbullar [en-gar-bool-lyar'], *va.* (Coll.) To entangle, to involve.

Engarce [en-gar'-thay], *m.* 1. Catenation, link. 2. Close union or connection. 3. Chasing of jewellery.

Engargantar [en-gar-gan-tar'], *va.* 1. To put any thing into the throat. 2. To thrust the foot into the stirrup, quite to the instep. 3. *vn.* To gear, to fit into each other: used of cog-wheels.

Engargolar [en-gar-go-lar'], *va.* To fit the end of one water-pipe into that of another.

Engaripolar [en-gah-re-po-lar'], *va.* (Coll.) To adorn with trifles and baubles.

Engaritado, da [en-gah-re-tah'-do, dah], *a.* 1. Cheated, deceived. 2. Surrounded with sentry-boxes.—*pp.* of ENGARITAR.

Engaritar [en-gah-re-tar'], *va.* 1. To fortify, to adorn with sentry-boxes. 2. To impose upon or deceive in an artful or dexterous manner.

Engarrafador [en-gar-rah-fah-dor'], *m.* Grappler.

Engarrafar [en-gar-rah-far'], *va.* (Coll.) 1. To claw, to seize with the claws or talons. 2. To grapple with hooks.

Engarrotar [en-gar-ro-tar'], *va.* To squeeze and press hard. *V.* AGARROTAR.

Engarzador [en-gar-thah-dor'], *m.* 1. One who links or enchains; stringer of beads. 2. (Obs. Met. Low) Pimp.

Engarzar [en-gar-thar'], *va.* To enchain, to link; to curl.

Engasajar [en-gah-sah-har'], *va.* (Obs.) *V.* AGASAJAR.

Engastador [en-gas-tah-dor'], *m.* Enchaser, incloser.

Engastar [en-gas-tar'], *va.* To inclose one thing in another without being screened, such as a diamond in gold; to enchase.

Engaste [en-gahs'-tay], *m.* 1. The setting of stones, the act of enchasing or infixing. 2. The hoop or envelope. 3. A pearl flat on one side.

Engatado, da [en-gah-tah'-do, dah], *a.* & *n.* A petty robber, a sharper, a petty thief.—*pp.* of ENGATAR.

Engatar [en-gah-tar'], *va.* (Coll.) To cheat in a dexterous manner, to wheedle.

Engatillado, da [en-gah-til-lyah'-do, dah], *a.* Thick, high-necked: applied to horses and bulls.—*pp.* of ENGATILLAR.

Engatillar [en-gah-til-lyar'], *va.* (Arch.) To bind with a cramp-iron.

Engatusador, ra [en-gah-too-sah-dor', rah], *m.* & *f.* One who coaxes; wheedler.

Engatusamiento [en-gah-too-sah-me-en'-to], *m.* (Coll.) Deception, cheat, coaxing.

Engatusar [en-gah-too-sar'], *va.* (Coll.) To trick without intention; to rob or hurt, to coax.

Engavillar, *va.* *V.* AGAVILLAR.

Engazador, ra [en-gah-thah-dor', rah], *m.* & *f.* *V.* ENGARZADOR.

Engazadura [en-gah-thah-doo'-rah], *f.* (Naut.) 1. Splicing in form of a ring. 2. Spot in a cable where a round splice is made.

Engazamiento, *m.* *V.* ENGARCE.

Engazar [en-gah-thar'], *va.* 1. To enchain, to link. 2. (Naut.) To stop or splice an end of a rope in a circular form about a block. 3. To dye in the cloth.

Engendrable [en-hen-drah'-blay], *a.* That may be engendered.

Engendramiento [en-hen-drah-me-en'-to], *m.* Begetting, generating.

Engendrador, ra [en-hen-drah-dor', rah], *m.* & *f.* Engenderer, one who engenders or produces.

Engendrar [en-hen-drar'], *va.* 1. To beget, to engender, to gender, to generate. 2. To produce, to bear fruit: to create.

Engendro [en-hen'-dro], *m.* 1. Fœtus, a shapeless embryo. 2. Abortive. *Mal engendro,* A low breed; a perverse youth.

Engeño, *m.* (Obs.) *V.* INGENIO and MÁQUINA.

Engestado [en-hes-tah'-do], *a.* (Amer.) *Bien* or *mal engestado,* Well or gruff-looking.

Engestarse [en-hes-tar'-say], *vr.* (Amer.) To address abruptly and uncivilly.

Engibar [en-he-bar'], *va.* To crook, to make gibbous.

Engilmar [en-heel-mar'], *va.* (Naut.) To pick up a mast which is floating in the sea.

Engimelgar [en-he-mel-gar'], *va.* (Naut.) To fish a mast, to mend a spar.

Englandado, da [en-glan-dah'-do, dah], *a.* (Her.) Covered with acorns: applied to the oak.

Engolado, da [en-go-lah'-do, dah], *a.* Collared, wearing a collar.

Engolfar [en-gol-far'], *vn.* (Naut.) To enter a gulf or deep bay.—*vr.* 1. To be engaged in arduous undertakings or difficult affairs. 2. To be lost in thought, to be absorbed in meditation.

Engolillado, da [en-go-leel-lyah'-do, dah], *a.* Wearing the ruff or collar which is worn by lawyers in Spain.

Engolondrinarse [en-go-lon-dre-nar'-say], *vr.* 1. (Coll.) To be elated, to be puffed up with pride. 2. (Low) To fall in love, to be smitten with love.

Engolosinar [en-go-lo-se-nar'], *va.* To inspire a longing for any thing, to use to dainties.—*vr.* To delight, or to have delight or pleasure in.

Engollar [en-gol-lyar'], *va.* To make a horse carry his head and neck by means of the bridle.

Engolletado, da [en-gol-lyay-tah'-do, dah], *a.* (Coll.) Elated, puffed up, presumptuous, haughty.—*pp.* of ENGOLLETARSE.

Engolletarse [en-gol-lyay-tar'-say], *vr.* To elate, to become haughty.

Engomadero, ra [en-go-mah-day'-ro, rah], *a.* That may be stiffened with starch or gum.

Engomadura [en-go-mah-doo'-rah], *f.* 1. Gumming, act of gumming. 2. Coat which bees lay over their hives before making the wax.

Engomar [en-go-mar'], *va.* To gum, to stiffen with gum.

Engorar [en-go-rar'], *va.* To addle. *V.* ENHUERAR.

Engordadero [en-gor-dah-day'-ro], *m.* 1. Stall or sty to fatten hogs. 2. Time for fattening them.

Engordador [en-gor-dah-dor'], *m.* One who makes it his sole business to pamper himself.

Engordar [en-gor-dar'], *va.* To pamper, to fatten, to lard, to make fat.—*vn.* 1. To fat, to grow fat, to feed. 2. To grow rich, to amass a fortune. 3. Of waves, to increase in size.

Engorde [en-gor'-day], *m.* Fattening of herds, especially of hogs.

Engorgetado, da [en-gor-hay-tah'-do, dah], *a.* Palisaded breast-high.

Engorrar [en-gor-rar'], *va.* (Obs.) To obstruct, to detain.

Engorro [en-gor'-ro], *m.* (Coll.) Impediment, embarrassment, obstacle.

Engorroso, sa [en-gor-ro'-so, sah], *a.* Troublesome, tiresome, vexatious, cumbersome, cumbrous.

Engoznar [en-goth-nar'], *va.* To hinge, to put hinges on doors and windows.

Engranaje [en-grah-nah'-hay], *m.* 1. Gear, transmission gear. *Caja de engranaje,* Gear case. 2. (fig.) Adjustment, interlocking of ideas, circumstances, etc.

Engranar [en-grah-nar'], *va.* To tooth, to connect; to gear, to throw into gear.

Engrandar, *va.* *V.* AGRANDAR.

Engrandecer [en-gran-day-therr'], *va.* 1. To augment, to aggrandize, to greaten. 2. To promote to a higher station, to exalt, to extol. 3. (Met.) To exaggerate, to magnify.

Engrandecimiento [en-gran-day-the-me-en'-to], *m.* 1. Increase, aggrandizement; aggrandization. 2. Exaggeration, hyperbolical amplification.

(*Yo engrandezco, yo engrandezca,* from *Engrandecer.* V. CONOCER.)

Engranerar [en-grah-nay-rar'], *va.* To inclose in a granary.

Engranujarse [en-grah-noo-har'-say], *vr.* To be covered with pimples.

Engrapar [en-grah-par'], *va.* To secure, to unite or bind with cramp-irons.

Engrasación [en-grah-sah-the-on'], *f.* or **Engrasamiento,** *m.* Lubrication, oiling, greasing.

Engrasador [en-grah-sah-dor'], *m.* Oiler, lubricator.

Engrasar [en-grah-sar'], *va.* 1. To grease, to oil, to fat, to lubricate. 2. To stain with grease. 3. To dress cloth. 4. (Met.) To pickle. 5. (Prov.) To manure, to hearten.

Engravedar [en-grah-vay-dar'], *va.* To assume an air of dignity, to affect gravity.

Engredar [en-gray-dar'], *va.* To bedaub with marl or fuller's earth.

Engreído, da [en-gray-ee'-do, dah], *a.* & *pp.* of ENGREIR. Elate, lofty, haughty; petulant.

Engreimiento [en-gray-e-me-en'-to], *m.* 1. Presumption, vanity, elation. 2. Vain pomp in dress.

Engreir [en-gray-eer'], *va.* To encourage any one's pride and petulance, to make him pert and saucy, to lift, to flush, to pride.—*vr.* 1. *V.* ENSOBERBECERSE and ENVANECERSE. 2. To deck or attire one's self in style, to be extravagant in dress.

Engrifarse [en-gre-far'-say], *vr.* To tiff, to be in a pet, to be displeased.

(*Yo me engrío, yo me engría,* from *Engreirse.* V. PEDIR.)

Engrosar [en-gro-sar'], *va.* 1. To make a thing fat and corpulent, to increase its bulk. 2. To make strong or vigorous. 3. To augment, to make more numerous.—*vn.* To grow strong, to increase in vigour and bulk.—*vr.* 1. To fatten. 2. (Naut.) To increase in cloudiness, to increase in size: said of the waves.

Engrudador [en-groo-dah-dor'], *m.* Paster, one who pastes; gluer.

Engrudamiento [en-groo-dah-me-en'-to], *m.* 1. Act of pasting. 2. Gluing.

Engrudar [en-groo-dar'], *va.* To paste, to fasten with paste.

Engrudo [en-groo'-do], *m.* 1. Paste, flour and water boiled together so as to make a cement. 2. (Naut.) Cement, made chiefly of pounded glass and cow-hair, used to stanch the planks of a ship.

(*Yo engrueso, yo engruese,* from *Engrosar.* V. ACORDAR.)

Engruesar [en-groo-ay-sar'], *va.* *V.* ENGORDAR and ENGROSAR.

Engrumecerse [en-groo-may-therr'-say], *vr.* To clot.

Engualdar [en-goo-ahl-dar'], *va.* To make like woad, or the colour of woad.

Engualdrapar [en-goo-al-drah-par'], *va.* To caparison a horse with rich trappings.

Enguantado, da [en-goo-an-tah'-do, dah], *a.* Wearing gloves.—*pp.* of ENGUANTARSE.

Enguantarse [en-goo-an-tar'-say], *vr.* To put on gloves.

Enguedejado, da [en-gay-day-hah'-do, dah], *a.* 1. Curl-pated, having hair curled or braided, and growing in tufts and locks. 2. Crisped, curled.

Enguijarrar [en-gee-har-rar'], *va.* To pave with pebbles.

Enguillar [en-geel-lyar'], *va.* (Naut.) To wind a thin rope around a thicker one.

Enguirnaldado, da [en-geer-nal-dah'-do, dah], *a.* Adorned with garlands.

Enguirnaldar [en-geer-nal-dar'], *va.* To garland, to engarland, to adorn with garlands.

Enguizgar [en-geeth-gar'], *va.* To excite, to incite, to set on.

Engullidor, ra [en-gool-lye-dor', rah], *m.* & *f.* 1. Devourer, one who swallows without mastication. 2. Gobbler, one who devours in haste.

Engullir [en-gool-lyeer'], *va.* To devour meat without chewing it, to gobble, to glut, to gorge.

Engurriñarse [en-goor-re-nyar'-say], *vr.* (Coll.) To be melancholy: applied to birds.

Enharinar [en-ah-re-nar'], *va.* To cover or besprinkle with flour.

Enhastiar [en-as-te-ar'], *va.* To disgust, to excite disgust, to cloy.

Enhastillar [en-as-til-lyar'], *va.* To put arrows in a quiver.

Enhatijar [en-ah-te-har'], *va.* To cover the mouths of hives with bass-weed, in order to move them from one place to another.

Enhebrar [en-ay-brar'], *va.* 1. To thread a needle. 2. (Met. Coll.) To link, to unite or connect closely.

Enhenar [en-ay-nar'], *va.* To cover with hay, to wrap up in hay.

Enherbolar [en-er-bo-lar'], *va.* To poison with venomous herbs.

Enhestador [en-es-tah-dor'], *m.* He who erects.

Enhestadura [en-es-tah-doo'-rah], *f.* Erection.

Enhestar [en-es-tar'], *va.* 1. To erect, to set upright. 2. (Obs.) To raise a body of troops or an army.—*vr.* To erect, to rise upright.

Enhidro, dra [en-ee'-dro, drah], *a.* (Miner.) Hyaline quartz or fluorine which contains some drops of water.

Enhielar [en-e-ay-lar'], *va.* To mix with gall or bile.

Enhiesto, ta [en-e-es'-to, tah], *a.* & *pp. irr.* of ENHESTAR. Erect, upright, erected.

Enhilado, da [en-e-lah'-do, dah], *a.* Well-arranged, disposed in good order.—*pp.* of ENHILAR.

Enhilar [en-e-lar'], *va.* 1. To thread. 2. To direct, to tend; to take the way or road to any thing or place. 3. To arrange. 4. (Coll.) To enter or go through a long story.

Enhorabuena [en-o-rah-boo-ay'-nah], *f.* Congratulation, felicitation, joy for the happiness or success of another.—*adv.* Well and good; all right.

Enhoramala [en-o-rah-mah'-lah], *f.* A word used to express the act of scorning, despising, or contemning a thing.—*adv.* In an evil hour. *Vete enhora mala,* (Coll.) Go to the devil.

Enhornar [en-or-nar'], *va.* To put into an oven to be baked.

Enhotar, *va.* (Obs.) *V.* AZUZAR.

Enhuecar [en-oo-ay-car'], *va.* *V.* AHUECAR.

Enhuerar [en-oo-ay-rar'], *va.* To lay addle eggs, to addle.

Enhibir, *va.* (Obs.) *V.* INHIBIR.

Enigma [ay-neeg'-mah], *m.* Enigma, a riddle; an obscure question; cross-purpose.

Enigmático, ca [ay-nig-mah'-te-co, cah], *a.* Enigmatical, dark, obscure, ambiguously or darkly expressed.

Enigmatista [ay-nig-mah-tees'-tah], *m.* Enigmatist.

Enigmatizar [ay-nig-mah-te-thar'], *va* To make enigmas.—*vn.* To talk ambiguously.

Enipiotismo [ay-ne-pe-o-tees'-mo], *m.* Magnetic sleep, hypnotism.

Enjabegarse [en-hah-bay-gar'-say], *vr.* (Naut.) 1. To get entangled: said of ropes. 2. Among fishers, to be twisted.

Enjabonadura [en-hah-bo-nah-doo'-rah], *f.* *V.* JABONADURA.

Enjabonar [en-hah-bo-nar'], *va.* 1. To soap, to wash with soap. 2. (Met.) To insult with foul language and blows. 3. (Coll.) To soft-soap one.

Enjaezar [en-hah-ay-thar'], *va.* To caparison a horse with rich trappings; to harness.

Enjagüe [en-hah'-goo-ay], *m.* Adjudication required by the creditors of a ship.

Enjalbegador, ra [en-hal-bay-gah-dor', rah], *m.* & *f.* Whitewasher, a plasterer.

Enjalbegadura [en-hal-bay-gah-doo'-rah], *f.* Act of whitewashing walls.

Enjalbegar [en-hal-bay-gar'], *va.* 1. To whitewash walls. 2. (Met.) To paint, to paint the face.

Enjalbiego [en-hal-be-ay'-go], *m.* Whitewashing.

Enjalma [en-hahl'-mah], *f.* Kind of pack-saddle.

Enjalmar [en-hal-mar'], *va.* 1. To put the pack-saddle on a horse. 2. To make pack-saddles.

Enjalmos [en-hal'-mos], *m.* (Bot.) Crooked-meadow saxifrage. Sesseli tortuosum.

Enjalmero [en-hal-may'-ro], *m.* Pack-saddle-maker.

Enjambradera [en-ham-brah-day'-rah], *f.* 1. (Prov.) Queen-bee of a hive. 2. *V.* CASQUILLA.

Enjambradero [en-ham-brah-day'-ro], *m.* Place where bees collect to form their hives.

Enjambrar [en-ham-brar'], *va.* 1. To gather a scattered swarm of bees. 2. To form a new hive of bees, which left another hive.—*vn.* To breed a new hive of bees, to produce abundantly.

Enjambrazón [en-ham-brah-thone'], *f.* Generation or swarming of bees.

Enjambre [en-hahm'-bray], *m.* 1. Swarm of bees. 2. Crowd, multitude of people.

Enjambrillo [en-ham-breel'-lyo], *m. dim.* A small swarm of bees.

Enjarciadura [en-har-the-ah-doo'-rah], *f.* The act of rigging a ship.

Enjarciar [en-har-the-ar'], *va.* To put the tackle aboard a ship.

Enjardinar [en-har-de-nar'], *va.* 1. To set and trim the trees as they are in gardens. 2. (Fal.) To put a bird of prey into a meadow or green field.

Enjaretado [en-hah-ray-tah'-do], *m.* (Naut.) Gratings, nettings, a kind of lattice-work between the main and fore-mast. *Enjaretado de proa,* The beak or head gratings.

Enjaretar [en-hah-ray-tar'], *va.* 1. To draw through a seam. 2. (Met.) To order, dispose a matter.—*vr.* (Met. Coll.) To creep in by stealth, be introduced subtlely into some place, conversation, etc.

Enjaular [en-hah-oo-lar'], *va.* 1. To cage. 2. (Met.) To imprison, to confine, to mew, to crib, to coop.

Enjebar [en-hay-bar'], *va.* To steep in lye, to buck.

Enjebe [en-hay'-bay], *m.* Lye in which cloth is put to be cleansed or scoured; act of bucking.

Enjergar [en-her-gar'], *va.* (Coll.) To set about a business, to bring a thing on the tapis.

Enjero [en-hay'-ro], *m.* (Prov.) Beam of a plough.
Enjertación [en-her-tah-the-on'], *f.* Insertion, inoculation, budding.
Enjertal [en-her-tahl'], *m.* Nursery of grafted fruit-trees.
Enjertar [en-her-tar'], *va.* *V.* Injertar.
Enjerto [en-herr'-to], *m.* 1. *V.* Injerto. 2. (Met.) Mixture of diverse things.—*pp. irr.* of Enjertar.
Enjorguinar [en-hor-gee-nar'], *va.* To smear or cover with soot.—*vr.* To be blackened with soot.
Enjoyar [en-ho-yar'], *va.* 1. To adorn with jewels. 2. To set a ring with diamonds or other precious stones. 3. (Met.) To heighten the lustre and brilliancy of a thing, to give additional splendour.
Enjoyelado, da [en-ho-yay-lah'-do, dah], *a.* Applied to gold or silver used in jewellery.
Enjoyelador [en-ho-yay-lah-dor'], *m.* Enchaser, he who enchases.
Enjuagadientes [en-hoo-ah-gah-de-en'-tes], *m.* (Coll.) Mouthful of water or wine for rinsing the mouth after a meal.
Enjuagadura [en-hoo-ah-gah-doo'-rah], *f.* Act of rinsing the mouth.
Enjuagar [en-hoo-ah-gar'], *va.* 1. To rinse the mouth and teeth. 2. To rinse clothes.
Enjuagatorio [en-hoo-ah-gah-to'-re-o], *m.* *V.* Enjuague, 1st definition.
Enjuague [en-hoo-ah'-gay], *m.* 1. Water, wine, or other liquid, used to rinse the mouth and teeth, and the act of rinsing the mouth with a liquid. 2. Finger-bowl. 3. (Met.) Plot to obtain an object, which cannot be attained openly.
Enjuanetado, da [en-hoo-ah-nay-tah'-do, dah], *a.* (Prov.) *V.* Juanetudo.
Enjugadero [en-hoo-gah-day'-ro], *m.* 1. *V.* Enjugador, 1st def. 2. A place in which something is dried.
Enjugador, ra [en-hoo-gah-dor', rah]. 1. Drier, one who dries. 2. Round-house for airing linen.
Enjugar [en-hoo-gar'], *va.* 1. To dry in the air or at the fire, to make dry. 2. To wipe off moisture.—*vr.* To dry up; to grow lean.
Enjuiciamiento [en-hoo-ee-the-ah-me-en'-to], *m.* 1. Preparation of a lawsuit. 2. A judge's charge; legal instruction upon the subject of a suit.
Enjuiciar [en-hoo-e-the-ar'], *va.* (Law) 1. To prepare a lawsuit for judgment. 2. To make a pleading. 3. To pass judgment.
Enjulio, or Enjullo [en-hoo'-le-o, en-hool'-lyo], *m.* The cloth-beam of a loom.
Enjuncar [en-hoon-car'], *va.* To tie with rush ropes. *Enjuncar un barco,* To ballast a vessel with kentledge or stones.
Enjundia [en-hoon'-de-ah], *f.* 1. Fat in the ovary of fowls, and also the grease or fat of any animal. 2. Substance, force.
Enjundioso, sa [en-hoon-de-o'-so, sah], *a.* Fat, fatty.
Enjunque [en-hoon'-kay], *m.* (Naut.) The heaviest part of a cargo which serves as ballast.
Enjurar [en-hoo-rar'], *va.* (Obs.) To yield, to transfer.
Enjuta [en-hoo'-tah], *f.* (Arch.) 1. Each of the spaces left by a circle inscribed within a square. 2. *V.* Pechina.
Enjutar [en-hoo-tar'], *va.* To dry.
Enjutez [en-hoo-teth'], *f.* Dryness, aridity.
Enjuto, ta [en-hoo'-to, tah], *a.* & *pp. irr.* of Enjutar. 1. Dried. 2. Lean, spare, slender. ***A pie enjuto,*** **Without pain or labour.**
Enjutos [en-hoo'-tos], *m. pl.* 1. Dry brushwood for lighting a fire. 2. Dry crust of bread.
Enlabiador, ra [en-lah-be-ah-dor', rah], *m.* & *f* Wheedler, cajoler, seducer.
Enlabiar [en-lah-be-ar'], *va.* (Obs.) To wheedle, to cajole, to entice by soft words.
Enlabio [en-lah'-be-o], *m.* (Obs.) Suspension, persuasion, enchantment by eloquence or words.
Enlace [en-lah'-thay], *m.* 1. Connection or coherence of one thing with another; link, lacing. 2. (Met.) Kindred, affinity.
Enlaciar [en-lah-the-ar'], *vn.* To be lax or languid.—*vr.* To wither, to become dry, to decay: applied to plants and fruit.
Enladrillado [en-lah-dril-lyah'-do], *m.* Pavement made of bricks; brickwork. —*Enladrillado, da, pp.* of Enladrillar.
Enladrillador [en-lah-dril-lyah-dor'], *m.* One who bricks or paves with bricks.
Enladrilladura [en-lah-dreel-lyah-doo'-rah], *f.* 1. The act and effect of paving with brick. 2. *V.* Enladrillado.
Enladrillar [en-lah-dril-lyar'], *va.* To pave a floor with bricks.
Enlamar [en-lah-mar'], *va.* To cover land with slime: applied to inundations.
Enlanado, da [en-lah-nah'-do, dah], *a.* Covered or supplied with wool.
Enlardar [en-lar-dar'], *va.* To rub with grease, to baste. *V.* Lardar.
Enlargues [en-lar'-gays], *m. pl.* (Naut.) Rope-ends fastened to the head of a sail, with which it is tied to the yard.
Enlazable [en-lah-thah'-blay], *a.* Which can be bound or fastened together.
Enlazador, ra [en-lah-thah-dor', rah], *m.* & *f.* Binder, uniter.
Enlazadura [en-lah-thah-doo'-rah], *f.* *V.* Enlazamiento.
Enlazamiento [en-lah-thah-me-en'-to], *m.* 1. Connection, binding, uniting. 2. (Met.) *V.* Enlace.
Enlazar [en-lah-thar'], *va.* 1. To bind, to join, to unite; to connect. 2. To knit, to lace.
Enlechuguillado, da [en-lay-choo-gil-lyah'-do, dah], *a.* Applied to one who wears a ruff round the neck.
Enlejiar [en-lay-he-ar'], *va.* To make into lye.
Enligarse [en le-gar'-say], *vr.* To be joined by means of a glutinous substance; to stick, to adhere.
Enlijar [en-le-har'], *va.* (Obs.) To vitiate, to corrupt; to stain, to soil.
Enlistonado [en-lis-to-nah'-do], *m.* Lathing, lath work.
Enlistonar [en-lis-to-nar'], *va.* To lath, to batten.
Enlizar [en-lee-thar'], *va.* To provide a loom with leashes.
Enlodadura [en-lo-dah-doo'-rah], *f.* Act of daubing and filling up with mud.
Enlodar [en-lo-dar'], *va.* 1. To bemire, to mire, to soil or bedaub with mud. 2. To stop up a vessel with loam or clay; to lute. 3. (Met.) To tarnish one's reputation.
Enloquecer [en-lo-kay-therr'], *va.* To enrage, to mad, to madden.—*vn.* or *vr.* 1. To mad, to madden, to become mad, to become enraged. 2. To be vexed, be annoyed. 3. To grow barren: applied to trees.
(*Yo enloquezco, yo enloquezca,* from *Enloquecer.* *V.* Conocer.)
Enloquecimiento [en-lo-kay-the-me-en'-to], *m.* Enraging, immaddening.
Enlosado [en-lo-sah'-do], *m.* Pavement made of flags; flagging.—*Enlosado, da, pp.* of Enlosar.
Enlosar [en-lo-sar'], *va.* To lay a floor with flags.
Enlozanarse [en-lo-thah-nar'-say], *vr.* To boast of one's dexterity or strength.
Enlucido, da [en-loo-thee'-do, dah], *a.* Whitewashed, plastered.—*m.* Whitewash, coat of plaster.
Enlucidor [en-loo-the-dor'], *m.* Whitener.
Enlucimiento [en-loo-the-me-en'-to], *m.* 1. The whitewashing of a wall. 2. The scouring of plate.
Enlucir [en-loo-theer'], *va.* 1. To whitewash a wall. 2. To scour plate with whiting or chalk.
Enlustrecer [en-loos-tray-therr'], *va.* To clean, to brighten, to render bright.
Enlutar [en-loo-tar'], *va.* 1. To put in mourning. 2. To veil, to cover with a veil. 3. To darken.
(*Yo enluzco, yo enluzca,* from *Enlucir.*)
Enllantar [en-lyan-tar'], *va.* To rim, to shoe a wheel.
Enllentecer [en-lyen-tay-therr'], *va.* To soften, to blandish.
Enmachambrar [en-mah-cham-brar'], *va.* To scarf pieces of timber together.
Enmaderamiento, *m.* **Enmaderación,** *f.* [en-mah-day-rah-me-en'-to]. Work or cover of wood; wainscotting.
Enmaderar [en-mah-day-rar'], *va.* To roof a house with timber; to floor with boards.
Enmagrecer [en-mah-gray-therr'], *vn.* To grow lean; to lose fat.
Enmalecer [en-mah-lay-therr'], *vn.* To fall sick.
Enmallar [en-mahl-lyar'], *va.* (Naut.) To put meshes; to border a net.
Enmalletado, da [en-mahl-yay-tah'-do, dah], *a.* (Naut.) Fouled: applied to cables and ropes. *V.* Enredado.
Enmalletar [en-mahl-lyay-tar'], *va.* (Naut.) 1. To set partners; to secure masts. 2. *V.* Endentar.
Enmangar [en-man-gar'], *va.* To put a handle to an instrument.
Enmantar [en-man-tar'], *va.* To cover with a blanket.—*vr.* To be melancholy: applied to birds.
Enmarañamiento [en-mah-ra-nyah-me-en'-to], *m.* Entanglement, perplexity.
Enmarañar [en-mah-ra-nyar'], *va.* 1. To entangle, to perplex, to involve in difficulties. 2. (Met.) To puzzle, to confound.
Enmararse [en-mah-rar'-say], *vr.* (Naut.) To get or take sea-room.
Enmaridar [en-mah-re-dar'], *vn.* To marry, to take a husband.
Enmarillecerse [en-mah-reel-lyay-therr'-say], *vr.* To become yellow.
Enmaromar [en-mah-ro-mar'], *va.* To tie with a rope.
Enmascarar [en-mas-cah-rar'], *va.* 1. To mask, to cover the face with a mask. 2. (Met.) To cloak, to give a false appearance.—*vr.* To masquerade, to go in disguise.
Enmasillar [en-mah-seel-lyar'], *va.* To putty, to cement.
Enmechar [en-may-char'], *va.* (Naut.) To rabbet, to fit and join two pieces of timber.
Enmelar [en-may-lar'], *va.* 1. To bedaub or besmear with honey. 2. (Met.) To sweeten, to give a pleasing taste.
Enmendación [en-men-dah-the-on'], *f.* Emendation, correction.
Enmendadamente [en-men-dah-da-men'-tay], *adv.* Accurately, exactly.
Enmendador [en-men-dah-dor'], *m.* Corrector, emendator, mender.
Enmendadura, *f.* **Enmendamiento,** *m.* [en-men-dah-doo'-rah]. (Obs.) *V.* Enmienda.

Enmendar [en-men-dar'], *va.* 1. To correct, to reform. 2. To repair, to compensate. 3. (Law) To revoke, to abrogate. 4. To put back a thing in the spot which it had before occupied. *Enmendar la plana,* (Met.) To excel, to surpass others in a performance. (Coll.) To alter, to change.—*vr.* To mend, to grow better, to lead a new life.

Enmienda [en-me-en'-dah], *f.* 1. Emendation, correction, amendment. 2. Correction, emendation, that which is substituted in the place of any thing wrong. 3. Reward, premium. 4. (Law) Satisfaction, compensation.

(*Yo enmiendo, yo enmiende,* from *Enmendar. V.* Acrecentar.)

Enmiente [en-me-en'-tay], *f.* (Obs.) *V.* Memoria.

Enmocecer [en-mo-thay-therr'], *vn.* (Obs.) To recover the vigour of youth.

(*Yo enmocezco, yo enmocezca,* from *Enmocecer. V.* Conocer.)

Enmohecer [en-mo-ay-therr'], *va.* To mould, to must, to mildew, to make mouldy.—*vr.* 1. To mould, to grow mouldy or musty. 2. To rust, to gather rust.

Enmohecido, da [en-mo-ay-thee'-do, dah], *a.* & *pp.* of Enmohecer. Musty, mouldy, spoiled with damp.

Enmohecimiento [en-mo-ay-the-me-en'-to], *m.* (Littl. us.) Mustiness, mould, mouldiness.

Enmoldado, da [en-mol-dah'-do, dah], *a.* 1. Moulded, cast in a mould. 2. Figured, modelled.

Enmollecer [en-mol-lyay-therr'], *va.* To soften, to make tender.

Enmondar [en-mon-dar'], *va.* To clear cloth from knots.

Enmordazar [en-mor-dah-thar'], *va.* To gag. *V.* Amordazar.

Enmudecer [en-moo-day-therr'], *vn.* 1. To grow dumb, to be deprived of speech. 2. To be silent, to be still. —*va.* To impose silence, to hush.

(*Yo enmudezco, yo enmudezca,* from *Enmudecer. V.* Conocer.)

Ennatado, da [en-nah-tah'-do, dah], *a.* (Agr.) Recuperated: said of a field which has recovered its fertility by lying fallow.

Ennegrecer [en-nay-gray-therr'], *va.* 1. To blacken, to make black. 2. (Met.) To darken, to obscure.

(*Yo ennegrezco, yo ennegrezca,* from *Ennegrecer. V.* Conocer.)

Ennoblecer [en-no-blay-therr'], *va.* 1. To ennoble, to illustrate, to make noble. 2. (Met.) To adorn, to embellish.

Ennoblecimiento [en-no-blay-the-me-en'-to], *m.* Ennoblement, the act of ennobling.

(*Yo ennoblezco, yo ennoblezca,* from *Ennoblecer. V.* Conocer.)

Ennoviar [en-no-ve-ar'], *vn.* To contract marriage. (Humorous.)

Ennudecer [en-noo-day-therr'], *vn. V.* Anudarse.

Enodación [ay-no-dah-the-on'], *f.* Illustration, explanation.

Enodio [ay-no'-de-o], *m.* Fawn, a young deer.

Enodrida [ay-no-dree'-dah], *a.* Barren: applied to a hen which is past laying eggs.

Enoema [ay-no-ay'-mah], *f.* Fantastic idea, product of simple conception.

Enofobia [ay-no-fo'-be-ah], *f.* Dread of wine.

Enófobo, ba [ay-no'-fo-bo, bah], *m.* & *f.* One who hates wine.

Enóforo [ay-no'-fo-ro], *m.* 1. A vessel for wine. 2. Name of a handsome statue of Praxiteles (the Wine-bearer). 3. One charged with the service of wines or who used to sell them.

Enojadamente [ay-no-hah-dah-men'-tay], *adv.* Fretfully, crossly, peevishly.

Enojadizo, za [ay-no-hah-dee'-tho, thah], *a.* Fretful, peevish, fractious.

Enojado, da [ay-no-hah'-do, dah], *a.* Angry, fretful, peevish, out of humour.—*pp.* of Enojar.

Enojante [ay-no-hahn'-tay], *pa.* He who vexes.

Enojar [ay-no-har'], *va.* 1. To vex, to irritate, to anger, to fret, to make angry. 2. To tease, to molest, to trouble. 3. To offend, to displease, to injure.—*vr.* 1. To be fretful or peevish. 2. To be boisterous. 3. To be offended, displeased.

Enojo [ay-no'-ho], *m.* 1. Fretfulness, peevishness. 2. Anger, choler, passion. 3. (Obs.) Offence, injury.

Enojosamente [ay-no ho-sah-men'-tay], *adv.* Vexatiously, crossly.

Enojoso, sa [ay-no-ho'-so, sah], *a.* Offensive, vexatious, humorsome.

Enojuelo [ay-no-hoo-ay'-lo], *m. dim.* Slight peevishness.

Enología [ay-no-lo-hee'-ah], *f.* The art of making wine; enology.

Enómetro [ay-no'-may-tro], *m.* Œnometer, a hydrometer for determining the alcoholic strength of wines by their specific gravity.

Enorfanecido, da, *a.* (Obs.) *V.* Huérfano.

Enorgullecer [en-or-gool-lyay-therr'], *va.* To make proud or haughty.—*vr.* To be filled with pride or arrogance.

Enorgullecimiento [en-or-gool-lyay-the-me-en'-to], *m.* Arrogance, haughtiness.

Enorgullecido, da [en-or-gool-lyay-thee'-do, dah], *a.* Haughty, arrogant, very proud.

Enorme [ay-nor'-may], *a.* 1. Enormous, vast, huge, mighty, exorbitant. 2. Horrible, crying, grievous. 3. Wicked beyond common measure, highly heinous. *Delito enorme,* Enormity.

Enormemente, *adv.* Immoderately, enormously, hugely, horridly.

Enormidad [ay-nor-me-dahd'], *f.* 1. Enormity, enormousness, monstrousness, exorbitance. 2. Grievousness, horridness, gravity. 3. An enormous deed, an atrocious crime.

Enótera [ay-no'-tay-rah], *f.* (Bot.) Œnothera, a generic name of plants, typical of the evening-primrose family. Œnothera. *Enótera bienal,* The evening-primrose. Œnothera biennis. *Enótera florichica,* Small-flowered œnothera. Œnothera parviflora.

Enquiciado, da [en-ke-the-ah'-do, dah], *a.* 1. Hung upon hinges. 2. (Met.) Built upon a solid foundation.—*pp.* of Enquiciar.

Enquiciar [en-ke-the-ar'], *va.* To hinge, to put on hinges.

Enquillotrarse [en-kil-lyo-trar'-say], *vr.* 1. To be jumbled together. 2. (Coll.) To fall in love, to be enamoured.

Enquimosis [en-ke-mo'-sis], *f.* (Med.) A sudden effusion of blood in the cutaneous vessels.

Enquiridión [en-ke-re-de-on'], *m.* Compendium, summary, abridgment.

Enquistado, da [en-kis-tah'-do, dah], *a.* (Surg.) Cysted, encysted.

Enrabiarse [en-rah-be-ar'-say], *vr.* (Coll.) To grow furious, to become enraged.

Enraigonar [en-rah-e-go-nar'], *va.* (Prov.) To fix bass-weed in the walls of sheds, for the silk-worms to begin to spin.

Enralecer [en-rah-lay-therr'], *va.* (Agr.) 1. To thin plants, to pluck away leaves or branches. 2. To prune.

Enramada [en-rah-mah'-dah], *f.* 1. A decoration formed with the branches of trees. 2. A covering of branches for shade, a bower. 3. (Poet.) A thicket, a wood. 4. Undergrowth.

Enramar [en-rah-mar'], *va.* 1. To cover with branches of trees. 2. To cover the ground with flowers, branches, and aromatic herbs in some festival. 3. (Naut.) To mast a vessel.

Enranciarse [en-ran-the-ar'-say], *vr.* To grow rancid, to be stale.

Enrarecer [en-rah-ray-therr'], *va.* To thin, to rarefy, to extenuate.

Enrarecimiento [en-rah-ray-the-me-en'-to], *m.* Rarefaction.

(*Yo enrarezco, yo enrarezca,* from *Enrarecer. V.* Conocer.)

Enrás [en-rahs'], *m.* 1. (Arch.) Bed, seat. 2. (Mas.) Last or levelling course.

Enrasado, da [en-rah-sah'-do, dah], *a.* & *pp.* of Enrasar. Smoothed, flush. *Puertas enrasadas,* Plain doors.

Enrasar [en-rah-sar'], *va.* 1. To smooth, to plane. 2. To even, make even or level, to flush.—*vn.* To be bald.

Enrastrar [en-ras-trar'], *va.* (Prov.) To string the silk cocoons.

Enrayar [en-rah-yar'], *va.* To fix spokes in a wheel.

Enredadera [en-ray-dah-day'-rah], *f.* (Bot.) 1. A name applied to all twining plants, particularly to the convolvulus, cultivated in gardens. 2. Small bind-weed, bell-bind. Convolvulus arvensis.

Enredado, da [en-ray-dah'-do, dah], *a.* 1. Entangled, matted. 2. (Naut.) Foul: applied to cables and ropes.—*pp.* of Enredar.

Enredador, ra [en-ray-dah-dor', rah], *m.* & *f.* 1. Entangler, one who entangles, insnares, or involves in difficulties. 2. Tattler, tale-bearer; busybody, intermeddler.

Enredar [en-ray-dar'], *va.* 1. To entangle, to insnare, to hamper, to lime, to knot. 2. To confound, to perplex, to involve in difficulties, to puzzle. 3. To catch in the net. 4. To lay snares for birds. 5. To sow discord. 6. To fumble, to play childishly. 7. To coil.—*vr.* 1. To tangle or to be entangled. 2. (Coll.) To live in concubinage.

Enredo [en-ray'-do], *m.* 1. Entanglement, entangling, insnaring. 2. Perplexity, embarrassment, puzzle. 3. Complexity, complicateness. 4. Imposition, falsehood, an intricate or mischievous lie, circumvention. 5. Plot of a play.

Enredoso, sa [en-ray-do'-so, sah], *a.* Full of snares and difficulties.

Enrehojar [en-ray-o-har'], *va.* Among wax-chandlers, to remove the bleached leaves and thin cakes of wax.

Enrejado [en-ray-hah'-do], *m.* 1. Trellis, lattice; grate, grille-work. 2. Kind of open embroidery or lace worn by ladies.—*Enrejado, da, pp.* of Enrejar.

Enrejar [en-ray-har'], *va.* 1. To fix a grating to a window. 2. To fix the ploughshare to the plough. 3. To make a trellis, to grate, to lattice. 4. To wound cattle's feet with a ploughshare.

Enrevesado, da [en-ray-vay-sah'-do, dah], *a. V.* Revesado.

Enriado [en-re-ah'-do], *m.* Maceration, retting of flax or hemp.

Enriador [en-re-ah-dor'], *m.* One who steeps or submerges.

Enriar [en-re-ar'], *va.* To steep hemp and flax in water, in order to macerate its stalky parts; to ret.

Enrielar [en-re-ay-lar'], *va.* To make ingots of gold or silver.

Enripiado [en-re-pe-ah'-do], *m.* Filling, packing, rubble work.
Enripiar [en-re-pe-ar'], *va.* To fill the chinks of a wall with small stones and mortar.
Enriquecedor, ra [en-re-kay-thay-dor', rah], *m.* & *f.* One who enriches.
Enriquecer [en-re-kay-therr'], *va.* 1. To enrich, to aggrandize. 2. To adorn.—*vn.* To gain, to grow rich.
(*Yo enriquezco, yo enriquezca,* from *Enriquecer. V.* CONOCER.)
Enriqueño, ña [en-re-kay'-nyo, nyah], *a.* Belonging to Henry.
Enriscado, da [en-ris-cah'-do, dah], *a.* Mountainous, craggy; full of rocks and cliffs.—*pp.* of ENRISCAR.
Enriscamiento [en-ris-cah-me-en'-to], *m.* Taking refuge among rocks.
Enriscar [en-ris-car'], *va.* To place on the top of mountains or rocks. (Met.) To lift, to raise.—*vr.* To take refuge among rocks.
Enristrar [en-ris-trar'], *va.* 1. To couch the lance, or to fix it in the posture of attack. 2. To range, to file, to string (onions, etc.). 3. (Met.) To go direct to a place, to meet a difficulty. 4. To succeed finally in a difficult matter.
Enristre [en-rees'-tray], *m.* Act of couching a lance.
Enrizamiento [en-re-thah-me-en'-to], *m.* 1. Act of curling. 2. Irritating.
Enrizar [en-re-thar'], *va.* (Ant. and Amer.) 1. To curl, to turn into ringlets. 2. To irritate. *V.* RIZAR.
Enrobrescido, da [en-ro-bres-thee'-do, dah], *a.* Hard and strong, like an oak.
Enrobustecer [en-ro-boos-tay-therr'], *va.* To make robust.
Enrocar [en-ro-car'], *va.* At chess, to castle the king.
Enrodar [en-ro-dar'], *va.* To break on the wheel.
Enrodelado, da [en-ro-day-lah'-do, dah], *a.* Armed with a shield.
Enrodrigonar [en-ro-dre-go-nar'], *va.* To prop vines with stakes.
Enrojar, Enrojecer [en-ro-har', en-ro-hay-therr'], *va.* 1. To tinge, dye, or give a red colour. 2. To put to the blush.
Enrojecido, da [en-ro-hay-thee'-do, dah], *a.* Red.
Enrollar [en-rol-lyar'], *va.* To wrap a thing within another or round about it.
Enromar [en-ro-mar'], *va.* (Littl. us.) To blunt, to dull an edge or point.
Enrona [en-ro'-nah], *f.* (Prov.) Rubbish or refuse.
Enronar [en-ro-nar'], *va.* (Prov.) To throw rubbish in a place.
Enronquecer [en-ron-kay-therr'], *va.* To make hoarse.—*vn.* To grow hoarse.
Enronquecimiento [en-ron-kay-the-me-en'-to], *m.* Hoarseness. *V.* RONQUERA.
Enroñar [en-ro-nyar'], *va.* To fill with scabs or scurf.
Enrosar [en-ro-sar'], *va.* To tinge, dye, or give a rose colour.
Enroscadamente [en-ros-cah-da-men'-tay], *adv.* Intricately.
Enroscadura [en-ros-cah-doo'-rah], *f.* Act of twisting; convolution, sinuosity, twist.
Enroscar [en-ros-car'], *va.* To twine, to twist.—*vr.* To curl or twist itself.
Enrubescer [en-roo-bes-therr'], *va.* (Obs.) To make red.
Enrubiador, ra [en-roo-be-ah-dor', rah] *m.* & *f.* That which has the power of making red.
Enrubiar [en-roo-be-ar'], *va.* To tinge, dye, or give a bright reddish colour.
Enrubio [en-roo'-be-o], *m.* Rubefaction, reddening.
Enrudecer [en-roo-day-therr'], *va.* To weaken the intellect, to make dull.
(*Yo enruedo, yo enruede,* from *Enrodar. V.* ACORDAR.)
Enruinecer, Enruinescer [en-roo-e-nay-therr', en-roo-e-nes-therr'], *vn.* To become vile.
Ensabanar [en-sah-ba-nar'], *va.* To wrap up in sheets.
Ensacar [en-sah-car'], *va.* To sack up, to inclose or put in a sack.
Ensai [en-sah-ee'], *m.* (Naut.) A clear space between the frames.
Ensalada [en-sah-lah'-dah], *f.* 1. Salad, a food of raw herbs, seasoned with salt, oil, vinegar, etc. 2. Hodge-podge, medley.
Ensaladera [en-sah-lah-day'-rah], *f.* Salad-dish or bowl.
Ensaladilla [en-sah-lah-deel'-lyah], *f.* 1. Dry sweetmeats of different sorts and sizes. 2. Jewel made up of different precious stones.
Ensaladista [en-sah-lah-dees'-tah], *m.* Green-grocer, or purveyor of vegetables to the king.
Ensalma [en-sahl'-mah], *f.* (Obs.) *V.* ENJALMA.
Ensalmadera [en-sal-mah-day'-rah], *f.* (Obs.) 1. Sorceress, enchantress. 2. A beautiful woman.
Ensalmador, ra [en-sal-mah-dor', rah], *m.* & *f.* 1. Bone-setter. 2. One who pretends to cure by charms.
Ensalmar [en-sal-mar'], *va.* 1. To set dislocated or broken bones. 2. To enchant, to charm, to bewitch; to lure by spells. *Ensalmar a alguno,* To break the head.
Ensalmo [en-sahl'-mo], *m.* Enchantment, spell, charm.
Ensalobrarse [en-sah-lo-brar'-say], *vr.* To become putrid and corrupt, as stagnant water.
Ensalvajar [en-sal-vah-har'], *va.* To brutalize, to brutify.
Ensalzador [en-sal-thah-dor'], *m.* Exalter, praiser, extoller.
Ensalzamiento [en-sal-thah-me-en'-to], *m.* Exaltation.
Ensalzar [en-sal-thar'], *va.* 1. To extol, to exalt, to aggrandize. 2. To magnify, to exaggerate.—*vr.* To boast, to display one's own worth or actions.
Ensambenitar [en-sam-bay-ne-tar'], *va.* To put on the *sambenito,* a gown worn by penitent convicts of the Inquisition.
Ensamblador [en-sam-blah-dor'], *m.* Joiner, worker in wood.
Ensambladura [en-sam-blah-doo'-rah], *f.* 1. Joinery, the trade of a joiner. 2. Art of joining boards, planks, and timbers together. *Ensambladura de milano,* (Naut.) A swallow-tail scarf.
Ensamblaje [en-sam-blah'-hay], *m.* *V.* ENSAMBLADURA.
Ensamblar [en-sam-blar'], *va.* To join or unite pieces of wood; to scarf, to dovetail, to mortise.
Ensamble [en-sahm'-blay], *m.* *V.* ENSAMBLADURA.
Ensancha [en-sahn'-chah], *f.* Extension, enlargement. *V.* ENSANCHE. *Dar ensanchas,* To give too much license or liberty.
Ensanchador, ra [en-san-chah-dor', rah], *m.* & *f.* One who or that which makes a thing larger; stretcher, widener, expander, reamer.
Ensanchamiento [en-san-chah-me-en'-to], *m.* 1. Widening, enlarging. 2. Dilation, augmentation.
Ensanchar [en-san-char'], *va.* To widen, to extend, to enlarge. *Ensanchar el corazón,* To cheer up, to raise one's spirits, to unburden the mind. *Ensanchar el cuajo,* To solace one's self by weeping.—*vr.* To assume an air of importance, to affect grandeur and dignity.
Ensanche [en-sahn'-chay], *m.* 1. Dilatation, augmentation, widening, extension. 2. Gore, a slip of cloth or linen to widen a garment. 3. Suburbs which are joined to the city. 4. Reaming.
Ensandecer [en-san-day-therr'], *vn.* To grow crazy, to turn mad.
Ensangrentamiento [en-san-gren-tah-me-en'-to], *m.* Bloodiness.
Ensangrentar [en-san-gren-tar'], *va.* To imbrue, to stain with blood.—*vr.* To be too irritated, vexed, in a dispute.
(*Yo ensangriento, yo ensangriente,* from *Ensangrentar. V.* ACRECENTAR.)
Ensañar [en-sah-nyar'], *va.* To irritate, to enrage.
Ensarnecer [en-sar-nay-therr'], *vn.* To get the itch.
Ensarta [en-sar'-tah], *f.* A string (as of pearls). *V.* SARTA.
Ensartar [en-sar-tar'], *va.* 1. To string, to file on a string; to link. 2. (Met.) To make a string of observations; to go through a long story.—*vr.* To be shut up in a narrow place; to be piled one upon another.
Ensay [en-sah'-e], *m.* Assay, trial, proof.
Ensayado, da [en-sah-yah'-do, dah], *a.* Tested, tried, practiced.
Ensayador [en-sah-yah-dor'], *m.* 1. Assayer, an officer of the mint. 2. Rehearser, prompter on the stage.
Ensayar [en-sah-yar'], *va.* 1. To assay precious metals. 2. To instruct, to teach, to make dexterous. 3. To rehearse, to practise. 4. To examine, to prove, to try, to test.—*vr.* To exercise one's self, or to train one's self by use to any act.
Ensaye [en-sah'-yay], *m.* Assay, trial, proof.
Ensayo [en-sah'-yo], *m.* 1. Assay, trial, proof. 2. Rehearsal of a play. 3. Essay, a trial, an experiment, liking. 4. Exercise, preparatory practice. 5. (Com.) Sample.
Ensebar [en-say-bar'], *va.* To grease, to tallow.
Ensedar [en-say-dar'], *va.* To join the thread with the bristle in order to sew shoes.
Enselvado, da [en-sel-vah'-do, dah], *a.* Full of trees.—*pp.* of ENSELVAR.
Enselvar [en-sel-var'], *va.* *V.* EMBOSCAR.
Ensenada [en-say-nah'-dah], *f.* Creek, cove, fleet, a small bay.
Ensenado, da [en-say-nah'-do, dah], *a.* Having the form of a bay, creek, or gulf.—*pp.* of ENSENAR.
Ensenar [en-say-nar'], *va.* (Obs.) To imbosom, to put in one's bosom.—*vr.* (Naut.) To embay.
Enseña [en-say'-nyah], *f.* Standard, colours, ensign.
Enseñable [en-say-nyah'-blay], *a.* Teachable.
Enseñador, ra [en-say-nyah-dor', rah], *m.* & *f.* Teacher, instructor.
Enseñamiento [en-say-nyah-me-en'-to], *m.* *V.* ENSEÑANZA.
Enseñanza [en-say-nyahn'-thah], *f.* 1. Teaching, instruction, doctrine, the act of teaching, the way or manner of teaching. 2. Public instruction.
Enseñar [en-say-nyar'], *va.* 1. To teach, to instruct, to lecture, to lesson. 2. To show the way, to point out the road, to lead.—*vr.* To accustom or habituate one's self; to be inured.
Enseño [en-say'-nyo], *m.* (Coll.) *V.* ENSEÑANZA.
Enseñoreador [en-say-nyo-ray-ah-dor'], *m.* He who domineers.
Enseñorear [en-say-nyo-ray-ar'], *va.* To lord, to domineer.—*vr.* To possess one's self of a thing.

Enserar [en-say-rar'], *va.* To cover with bass-weed.

Enseres [en-say'-res], *m. pl.* Chattels, marketable effects, fixtures, furniture, utensils. *Enseres de cocina,* Kitchen utensils.

Enseriarse [en-say-re-ar'-say], *vr.* (Cuba and Amer.) To become serious, to affect seriousness.

Enserpentado, da [en-ser-pen-tah'-do, dah], *a.* Enraged, furious.

Enserrinar [en-ser-re-nar'], *va.* To varnish.

Ensifoliado, da [en-se-fo-le-ah'-do, dah], *a.* Having sword-shaped or ensiform leaves.

Ensiforme [en-se-for'-may], *a.* Ensiform, having the shape of a sword.

Ensilaje [en-se-lah'-hay], *m.* Ensilage, the process of preserving green fodder in a silo, and the fodder so stored.

Ensilar [en-se-lar'], *va.* To preserve grain in a place under ground.

Ensillado, da [en-sil-lyah'-do, dah], *a.* Hollow-backed: applied to horses.—*pp.* of ENSILLAR.

Ensilladura [en-sil-lyah-doo'-rah], *f.* The part on which a saddle is placed on a horse or mule.

Ensillar [en-sil-lyar'], *va.* 1. To saddle. 2. (Obs.) To raise, to exalt.

Ensimismado [en-se-mis-mah'-do], *a.* 1. Selfish. 2. Absorbed in thought.

Ensimismarse [en-se-mis-mar'-say], *vr.* To be centred in one's self, to be abstracted.

Ensoberbecer [en-so-ber-bay-therr'], *va.* To make proud, to puff up with haughtiness and pride.—*vr.* 1. To become proud and haughty, to be arrogant. 2. (Naut.) To become boisterous: applied to the sea.

Ensoberbecimiento [en-so-ber-bay-the-me-en'-to], *m.* Haughtiness, arrogance, pride.

(*Yo me ensoberbezco, yo me ensoberbezca,* from *Ensoberbecerse. V.* CONOCER.)

Ensogar [en-so-gar'], *va.* To fasten with a rope.

Ensolapar [en-so-lah-par'], *va.* To lap over, to overlap (from *Solapa*).

Ensolerar [en-so-lay-rar'], *va.* To fix stools to bee-hives.

Ensolvedor, ra [en-sol-vay-dor', rah], *m. & f.* (Obs.) Resolver, declarer.

Ensolver [en-sol-verr'], *va.* 1. To jumble, to mix confusedly together. 2. (Med.) To resolve, to discuss, to dissipate.

Ensoñar [en-so-nyar'], *va.* (Obs.) *V.* SOÑAR.

Ensopar [en-so-par'], *va.* To make soup by steeping bread in wine.

Ensordecer [en-sor-day-therr'], *va.* To deafen, to make deaf, to cause deafness.—*vn.* 1. To grow deaf, to be deprived of hearing. 2. To become silent, to observe silence.

Ensordecimiento [en-sor-day-the-me-en'-to], *m.* Deafness, the act of deafening.

Ensortijadura [en-sor-te-hah-doo'-rah], *f.* 1. A ring which looms have in the middle of the netting called *perchado.* 2. (Vet.) Dislocation.

Ensortijamiento [en-sor-te-hah-me-en'-to], *m.* Act of curling the hair, or ringing animals.

Ensortijar [en-sor-te-har'], *va.* 1. To ring, to form into a ring, to encircle; to curl. 2. To ring hogs, buffaloes, or other beasts. *Ensortijar las manos,* To wring the hands in grief.

Ensotarse [en-so-tar'-say], *vr.* To conceal one's self in a thicket.

Ensuciador, ra [en-soo-the-ah-dor', rah], *m. & f.* Stainer, defiler.

Ensuciamiento [en-soo-the-ah-me-en'-to], *m.* Act of dirtying, staining, or polluting.

Ensuciar [en-soo-the-ar'], *va.* 1. To stain, to dirty, to soil, to smear, to file, to daub, to sully, to foul. 2. (Met.) To defile, to pollute with vicious habits.—*vr.* To dirty one's bed, clothes, etc.

Ensueño [en-soo-ay'-nyo], *m.* Sleep, fantasy.

Entablación [en-tah-blah-the-on'], *f.* A register in churches.

Entablado [en-tah-blah'-do], *m.* 1. Floor made of boards. 2. *Entablado de la cofa,* (Naut.) Flooring or platform of the top.—*Entablado, da, pp.* of ENTABLAR.

Entabladura [en-tah-blah-doo'-rah], *f.* Act of flooring with boards; wainscotting.

Entablamento [en-tah-blah-men'-to], *m.* 1. (Arch.) Entablature, entablement. 2. Roof of boards.

Entablar [en-tah-blar'], *va.* 1. To cover with boards, to floor with boards. *Entablar un navío,* (Naut.) To plank a ship. *Entablar con solapadura,* (Naut.) To plank with clincher-work. 2. To bring an affair on the tapis, to take the preparatory steps for attaining one's end. 3. (Coll.) To claim something without right and with pretence. (Amer.)

Entable [en-tah'-blay], *m.* 1. *V.* ENTABLADURA. 2. (Amer.) Exaggerated pretence.

Entablillado [en-tah-ble-lyah'-do], *m.* (Surg.) Splint.

Entablillar [en-tah-blil-lyar'], *va.* To secure with small boards, to bind up a broken leg; to splint.

Entalamado, da [en-tah-lah-mah'-do, dah], *a.* Hung with tapestry.—*pp.* of ENTALAMAR.

Entalamadura [en-tah-lah-mah-doo'-rah], *f.* Awning of a boat, carriage, etc.

Entalegar [en-tah-lay-gar'], *va.* To put in a bag or sack.

Entalingar [en-tah-lin-gar'], *va.* (Naut.) To clinch the cable, to fasten it to the anchor.

Entalpia [en-tal-pee'-ah], *f.* Enthalpy.

Entallable [en-tal-lyah'-blay], *a.* Capable of being sculptured.

Entallado, da [en-tah-lyah'-do, dah], *a.* Close fitting, tight fitting.

Entallador [en-tal-lyah-dor'], *m.* 1. Sculptor, a cutter in wood or stone. 2. Engraver. 3. Carver.

Entalladura [en-tal-lyah-doo'-rah], *f.*

Entallamiento [en-tal-lyah-me-en'-to], *m.* 1. Sculpture, act of sculpturing, carving. 2. Among carpenters, a mortise or groove for receiving a piece. 3. (Med.) A deep incision by a cutting instrument.

Entallar [en-tal-lyar'], *va.* 1. To sculpture, to carve; to cut figures in wood or stone. 2. To engrave, to picture by incisions in copper.—*vn.* To cut or shape a thing so as to fit it to the body.

Entalle [en-tahl'-lyay], *m.* The work of a sculptor or engraver; intaglio.

Entallecer [en-tal-lyay-therr'], *vn.* To shoot, to sprout: applied to plants.

Entamar [en-tah-mar'], *va.* (Prov.) 1. *V.* DECENTAR. 2. In woollen factories, to label the cloth which belongs to a purchaser.

Entapizar [en-tah-pe-thar'], *va.* To hang or adorn with tapestry.

Entarascar [en-tah-ras-car'], *va.* (Coll.) To cover with too many ornaments.

Entarimado [en-tah-re-mah'-do], *m.* Boarded floor; parquetry, inlaid floor. —*Entarimado, da, pp.* of ENTARIMAR.

Entarimar [en-tah-re-mar'], *va.* To cover a floor with boards.

Entarquinar [en-tar-ke-nar'], *va.* To bemire, to cover with mud or mire; to manure land with mud.

Entasis [en'-tah-sis], *m.* The increase of diameter which some columns present in their first third; entasis.

Ente [en'-tay], *m.* 1. Entity, being. 2. Ridiculous man. *Ente de razón,* An maginary and unrealizable thing.

Enteco, ca [en-tay'-co, cah], *a.* 1. Infirm, weak, languid. 2. Timid, pusillanimous.

Entejado, da [en-tay-hah'-do, dah], *a.* (Prov.) Made in the form or shape of tiles.

Entelarañarse [en-tay-lah-ra-nyar'-say], *vr.* (Prov.) To be clouded or overcast: applied to the sky.

Entelequia [en-tay-lay-kee'-ah], *f.* (Phil.) Absolute and relative perfection of being.

Entelerido, da [en-tay-lay-ree'-do, dah], *a.* Fearful, timid.

Entena [en-tay'-nah], *f.* (Naut.) Lateen yard.

Entenada [en-tay-nah'-dah], *f.* A stepdaughter, a daughter of a former marriage.

Entenado [en-tay-nah'-do], *m.* A stepson, a son of a former marriage.

Entenallas [en-tay-nahl'-lyas], *f. pl.* A small hand-vise.

Entendederas [en-ten-day-day'-ras], *f. pl.* (Coll.) Understanding, judgment.

Entendedor, ra [en-ten-day-dor', rah], *m. & f.* Understander, one who understands.

Entender [en-ten-derr'], *va. & vn.* 1. To understand, to comprehend, to conceive, to believe, to hear. 2. To remark, to take notice of. 3. To reason, to think, to judge. 4. To be employed about or engaged in any thing. *Dar en que entender,* To molest, to disturb, to make anxious, to distress. *A mi entender,* In my opinion. *No lo entenderá Galván,* It is an intricate, difficult thing. *Lo mismo se debe entender este artículo,* The same construction is to be given to this article. *Entenderse con alguno,* To address or correspond with one on a certain business. *Tenga V. entendido* I warn you, or, You must be aware, you must keep in mind. *Sólo me he entendido con él,* I have applied only to, or had correspondence only with him. I have known no other person but him.—*vr.* 1. To have some motive for doing a thing. *Él se entiende,* He knows what he is about. 2. To agree or be agreed. 3. To understand each other. *Eso no se entiende conmigo,* That is no affair of mine. *Quien con tosco ha de entender, mucho seso ha menester,* He who has to deal with a blockhead has need of much brains. *Entender de alguna cosa,* To be skilful in any thing. *Entenderse con alguna cosa,* To take the charge or management of an affair. *Ya te entiendo,* I know your intention. *No entender la música,* To pretend to misunderstand an unpleasant remark. *Entenderse en coplas,* To repay in the same coin; to return insult for insult.

Entendidamente [en-ten-de-dah-men'tay], *adv.* Knowingly, prudently.

Entendido, da [en-ten-dee'-do, dah], *a.* Wise, learned, prudent, knowing. *Darse por entendido,* To manifest by signs or words that the thing is understood; to answer any attention or compliment in the customary manner.

Entendimiento [en-ten-de-me-en'-to], *m.* 1. Understanding, knowledge, judgment, mind; conceiving. 2. Explanation, illustration.

Entenebrecer [en-tay-nay-bray-therr'], *va.* To obscure, to darken.
Enténola [en-tay'-no-lah], *f.* (Naut.) A spare spar.
Enteomanía [en-tay-o-mah-nee'-ah], *f.* A kind of religious insanity, which consists in believing one's self inspired by Heaven.
Enteralgia [en-tay-rahl'-he-ah], *f.* Enteralgia, neuralgia of the intestines.
Enteramente [en-tay-rah-men'-tay], *adv.* Entirely, fully, completely, full; clear, clean; quite.
Enterar [en-tay-rar'], *va.* 1. To inform thoroughly, to acquaint, to instruct, to give intelligence. 2. (Amer.) To complete, to make entire.
Entereza [en-tay-ray'-thah], *f.* 1. Entireness, integrity. 2. Rectitude, uprightness; perfection. 3. Fortitude, firmness. *Entereza virginal*, Virginity.
Enteritis [en-tay-ree'-tis], *f.* (Med.) Enteritis, inflammation of the mucous coat of the bowels.
Enterizo, za [en-tay-ree'-tho, thah], *a.* Entire, complete; of one piece.
Enternecedor, ra [en-ter-nay-the-dor', rah], *a.* Compassionate, pitiful.
Enternecer [en-ter-nay-therr'], *va.* 1. To soften, to make tender or soft, to melt, to affect. 2. (Met.) To move to compassion.—*vr.* To be moved to compassion, to pity, to commiserate, to be affected.
Enternecidamente [en-ter-nay-the-dah-men'-tay], *adv.* Compassionately.
Enternecimiento [en-ter-nay-the-me-en'-to], *m.* Compassion, pity, melting.
(*Yo enternezco, yo enternezca*, from *Enternecer*. *V.* CONOCER.)
Entero, ra [en-tay'-ro, rah], *a.* 1. Entire, undiminished. 2. Perfect, complete. 3. Sound, without a flaw. 4. Just, right. 5. Honest, upright, pure, uncorrupted. 6. Strong, robust, vigorous. 7. Informed, instructed. 8. Uncastrated. *Caballo entero*, Stone-horse. 9. Strong, coarse: applied to linen. 10. (Arith.) Whole. *Números enteros*, Whole numbers. 11. Constant, firm. *Por entero*, Entirely, fully, completely.
Enterorrafia [en-tay-ror-rah'-fe-ah], *f.* Enterorraphy, a suture for maintaining the edges of a wound of the intestines.
Enterótomo [en-tay-ro'-to-mo], *m.* Enterotome.
Enterrador [en-ter-rah-dor'], *m.* 1. Grave-digger, burier, sexton. 2. The sexton-beetle; necrophorus.
Enterraje [en-ter-rah'-hay], *m.* In foundries, a bank of earth around a mould.
Enterramiento [en-ter-rah-me-en'-to], *m.* 1. Interment, burial, funeral. 2. Tomb, burying-place.
Enterrar [en-ter-rar'], *va.* 1. To inter, to bury. 2. *V.* SOBREVIVIR. *Enterrar las vasijas en el lastre*, (Naut.) To stow the casks in ballast.
Enterronar [en-ter-ro-nar'], *va.* To cover with clods.
Entesamiento [en-tay-sah-me-en'-to], *m.* The act of stretching, the effect of being stretched; fulness.
Entesar [en-tay-sar'], *va.* To extend, to stretch out. To give greater force or vigour to a thing.
Entestado, da [en-tes-tah'-do, dah], *a.* Obstinate, stubborn.
Entibador [en-te-bah-dor'], *m.* One who shores up mines.
Entibar [en-te-bar'], *vn.* To rest, to lean upon.—*va.* To prop, to shore up mines.
Entibiadero [en-te-be-ah-day'-ro], *m.* Cooler, a bath in which any thing is cooled.
Entibiar [en-te-be-ar'], *va.* 1. To cool to make cool, to damp. 2. To temper to moderate the passions.—*vr.* (Met.) To become cool, to slacken, to relax, to languish.
Entibo [en-tee'-bo], *m.* 1. Stay, prop, shore. 2. Foundation.
Entidad [en-te-dahd'], *f.* 1. Entity, a real being. 2. (Met.) Consideration, estimation, value, moment, consequence, import, matter, importance.
(*Yo entiendo, yo entienda*, from *Entender*. *V.* ATENDER.)
Entierro [en-te-er'-ro], *m.* 1. Burial, interment, funeral. 2. Tomb, grave, sepulture.
(*Yo entierro, yo entierre*, from *Enterrar*. *V.* ACERTAR.)
Entigrecerse [en-te-gray-therr'-say], *vr.* To be as enraged or furious as a tiger.
Entimema [en-te-may'-mah], *f.* Enthymem, a syllogism which consists of two propositions.
Entinar [en-te-nar'], *va.* 1. To tinge, to colour. 2. To put wool into the clearing-bath.
Entintar [en-tin-tar'], *va.* 1. To stain with ink. 2. To tinge or give a different colour.
Entiznar [en-teeth-nar'], *va.* To revile, to defame. *V.* TIZNAR.
Entoldado [en-tol-dah'-do], *m.* An awning.—*Entoldado, da, pp.* of ENTOLDAR.
Entoldamiento [en-tol-dah-me-en'-to], *m.* Act of covering with an awning.
Entoldar [en-tol-dar'], *va.* 1. To cover with an awning. 2. To hang walls with cloths or silks.—*vr.* 1. To dress pompously. 2. To grow cloudy or overcast.
(*Yo entomezco, yo entomezca*, from *Entomecer*. *V.* CONOCER.)
Entomizar [en-to-me-thar'], *va.* To tie bass cords around posts or laths, that the plaster may stick to them.
Entomófago, ga [en-to-mo'-fah-go, gah], *a.* Insectivorous, entomophagous.
Entomófilo, la [en-to-mo'-fe-lo, lah], *a.* Entomophilous, fond of insects.
Entomología [en-to-mo-lo-hee'-ah], *f.* Entomology.
Entomológicamente, *adv.* Entomologically.
Entomológico, ca [en-to-mo-lo'-he-co, cah], *a.* Entomological, relating to the study of insects.
Entomologista [en-to-mo-lo-hees'-tah], *m.* or **Entomólogo**, *m.* An entomologist.
Entomostráceo, cea [en-to-mos-trah'-thay-o, ah], *a.* Entomostracan.—*m. pl.* The entomostracans.
Entonación [en-to-nah-the-on'], *f.* 1. Modulation; intonation. 2. The act of blowing the bellows of an organ. 3. (Met.) Haughtiness, presumption, pride.
Entonadera [en-to-nah-day'-rah], *f.* The blow-lever of an organ.
Entonado [en-to-nah'-do], *m.* The process of toning in photography.
Entonado, da [en-to-nah'-do, dah], *a.* & *pp.* of ENTONAR. Haughty, puffed with pride.
Entonador [en-to-nah-dor'], *m.* 1. Organ-blower. 2. One who tunes the first verse of a psalm. 3. One that sets the tune. 4. (Med.) A tonic.
Entonamiento [en-to-nah-me-en'-to], *m.* 1. *V.* TONO. 2. Intoning. 3. Arrogance, haughtiness.
Entonar [en-to-nar'], *va.* 1. To tune, to modulate, to intonate. 2. To commence or set a tune. 3. (Pict.) To harmonize colours. (Phot.) To tone prints. 4. To blow the bellows of an organ. 5. (Med.) To strengthen the muscular fibres by means of tonic medicines.—*vr.* (Met.) To grow haughty, to be, puffed up with pride; to look big.
Entonatorio [en-to-nah-to'-re-o], *m.* A book of sacred music used in Catholic churches.
Entonces [en-ton'-thes], *adv.* Then, at that time, on that occasion.
Entonelar [en-to-nay-lar'], *va.* To barrel.
Entono [en-toh'-no], *m.* 1. The act of intoning. 2. *V.* ENTONACIÓN. 3. (Met.) Arrogance, haughtiness, pride.
Entontecer [en-ton-tay-therr'], *va.* To mope, to fool, to craze.—*vn.* & *vr.* To grow foolish, to be stupid.
Entontecimiento [en-ton-tay-the-me-en'-to], *m.* Act of growing foolish or stupid.
(*Yo me entontezco, yo me entontezca*, from *Entontecerse*. *V.* CONOCER.)
Entorchado [en-tor-chah'-do], *m.* 1. A twisted gold or silver cord, for embroideries. 2. A sort of twisted fringe used as a mark of distinction by the Spanish general officers. *Entorchados*, Cords for a musical instrument covered with silver wire; bass strings.
Entorchar [en-tor-char'], *va.* 1. To twist a cord. 2. To cover cords for musical instruments with wire.
Entorilar [en-to-re-lar'], *va.* To put the bull in the *toril*, or stall.
Entornar [en-tor-nar'], *va.* To turn.
Entornillar [en-tor-nil-lyar'], *va.* To make any thing in the form of a screw or ring.
Entorpecer [en-tor-pay-therr'], *va.* 1. To benumb, to damp, to render torpid. 2. To stupefy, to obscure the understanding.
Entorpecimiento [en-tor-pay-the-me-en'-to], *m.* 1. Torpor, benumbedness, numbness, stupefaction, dulness. 2. Stupidity, bluntness of intellect.
(*Yo me entorpezco, yo me entorpezca*, from *Entorpecerse*. *V.* CONOCER.)
Entortadura [en-tor-tah-doo'-rah], *f.* Crookedness, curvity.
Entortar [en-tor-tar'], *va.* 1. To bend, to make crooked. 2. To pull out an eye.
Entortijar [en-tor-te-har'], *va.* *V.* ENSORTIJAR.
Entosigar [en-to-se-gar'], *va.* *V.* ATOSIGAR.
Entozoario, ria [en-to-tho-ah'-re-o, ah], *a.* & *n.* Entozoarian, entozoic; entozoa.
Entrada [en-trah'-dah], *f.* 1. Entrance, entry. 2. Entrance, entry, coming in, ingress. 3. Entrance, prerogative of certain authorities to enter places forbidden to the public. 4. Beginning of a musical clause. 5. Entry, the act of publicly entering a city. 6. The act of admitting a person into a community or society. 7. Concourse of people. *Hubo una grande entrada aquel día en la comedia*, The playhouse was crowded on that day. 8. Entrance-fee, admission, ticket. 9. The means or power to do something. 10. Familiar access, intimacy. 11. (Naut.) The rising, beginning, of a wind, a soft breeze, or a storm. 12. A good hand at cards. 13. Each of the more substantial dishes which are served at table. 14. Receipts, property vested in any concern. *Derechos de entrada*, Import duty. *Entradas*, Temples, the upper parts of the sides of the head. 15. *Entrada furtiva en una casa, forzándola para robar*, (Law) Burglary.
Entradero [en-trah-day'-ro], *m.* (Prov.) A narrow entrance.

Entramado [en-tra-mah'-do], *m.* (Carp.) Frame-work, stud-work, bay-work.
Entramar [en-tra-mar'], *va.* To make stud-work, frame-work.
Entrambos, bas [en-trahm'-bos, bas], *pron. pl.* Both. *V.* AMBOS.
Entramiento de bienes, *m.* (Law Obs.) Sequestration.
Entramos, mas, *pron.* (Obs.) Both. *V.* ENTRAMBOS.
Entrampar [en-tram-par'], *va.* 1. To entrap, to insnare, to catch in a trap. 2. (Met.) To involve in difficulties, to perplex. 3. To insnare, to deceive; to noose, to circumvent, to hamper. 4. (Met.) To encumber an estate with debts, to contract debts.—*vr.* To borrow money, to become indebted.
Entrante [en-trahn'-tay], *pa.* 1. Entering, coming in. *El mes entrante,* The coming month.—*m.* 1. One who is entering. 2. The coming month.
Entraña [en-trah'-nyah], *f.* An entrail, a bowel, any principal organ or part which has an appropriate use; very seldom used in the singular in either language.—*pl.* 1. Entrails, bowels. 2. (Met.) Entrails, the internal parts of any thing; centre of a city, heart of a country. 3. (Met.) Mind, affection; disposition; idiosyncrasy. 4. The inmost recess of any thing. *Entrañas mías,* My dear, my love. *Dar las entrañas,* or *dar hasta las entrañas,* To give one's very heart-blood away. *Esto me llega a las entrañas,* That goes to my heart.
Entrañable [en-trah-nyah'-blay], *a.* Intimate, affectionate.
Entrañablemente [en-trah-nyah-blay-men'-tay], *adv.* Affectionately.
Entrañar [en-trah-nyar'], *vn.* To penetrate to the core, to know profoundly. —*vr.* 1. To contract intimacy and familiarity. 2. *V.* EMBUTIR. (Naut.)
Entrapada [en-trah-pah'-dah], *f.* A coarse crimson cloth.
Entrapajar [en-trah-pah-har'], *va.* To tie with rags.
Entrapar [en-trah-par'], *va.* 1. To powder the hair to clean it. 2. (Agr.) To put woollen rags to the roots of plants, as manure.—*vr.* To be covered with dust.
Entrar [en-trar'], *va.* & *vn.* 1. To enter, to go in, to march in, to come in and *fig.*, to penetrate. 2. To inclose one thing in another, to introduce it. 3. To commence, to begin. To win a trick at cards. 4. To undertake. 5. (Geog.) To disembogue, to join (of rivers). 6. To thrust or put one thing upon another. 7. To take possession of a place by force of arms. 8. To set down, or place to account. *Entrar en una partida de trigo, lana,* etc., To purchase a quantity of wheat, wool, etc. 9. To be classed or ranked. To conduce, or be employed for some end: said of a portion or certain number of things. 10. Followed by the prepositions *a* or *en*, it signifies to begin or commence, as, *Entrar a cantar,* To begin to sing in concert. *Entrar en recelo,* To begin to suspect. *Ahora entro yo,* Now I begin: said to one who has engrossed all the conversation. *Entrar de por medio,* To settle a scuffle or fray, to adjust, to reconcile disputants. 11. To dedicate or consecrate one's self to something. 12. To find place, to take possession of the mind: as a passion or affection. 13. In fencing to advance a step. 14. (Naut.) To gain upon a vessel steering the same course. To begin to rise (of the tide) or to blow (of wind). *Lo que entra con el capillo, sale con la mortaja,* That which is learned in infancy can never be forgotten. *Entrar bien alguna cosa,* To come to the point. *Entrar de rondón,* To enter suddenly and familiarly. *Entrar dentro de sí,* or *en sí mismo,* To reflect upon one's own conduct in order to improve it. *No entrar (a alguno) alguna cosa,* Not to believe a thing; to have a repugnance for it. *Entrar a uno,* To prevail upon a person to do as we desire. *Entrar a mates,* To communicate by signs. *Entrar y salir,* To be clever in business or conversation. *Nunca me entró de dientes a dentro,* I never could endure him. *Entrar como por su casa,* To fit loosely. *A la mujer y a la mula, por el pienso les entra la hermosura.* Comfort and kindliness contribute to beauty. *La letra con sangre entra,* Those who would succeed must work with a will. *Entrar con alguno,* To deal with a person.
Entre [en'-tray], *prep.* 1. Between. *Entre año, semana, día,* etc., In the course of the year, week, day, etc. *Entre dos aguas,* Wavering, irresolute. *Traer a uno entre dientes,* To take a dislike to somebody. 2. In, or in the number of things. *Entre tanto,* In the interim. *Entre manos,* In hand. *Traer una cosa entre manos,* To be doing something. *Tomar entre manos,* To take in hand. 3. In composition with another word it weakens or limits the signification, as *entrefino,* middling fine, and others in the list which immediately follows.
Entreabrir [en-tray-ah-breer'], *va.* To half open a door, to leave it ajar.
Entreacto [en-tray-ahc'-to], *m.* Entr'acte, interact.
Entreancho, cha [en-tray-ahn'-cho, chah], *a.* Neither wide nor narrow.
Entrecalle [en-tray-cahl'-lyay], *m.* Clear between two mouldings.
Entrecanal [en-tray-cah-nahl'], *f.* (Arch.) Space between the striæ or flutings of a column.
Entrecano, na [en-tray-cah'-no, nah], *a.* Between black and gray, grayish: applied to the hair or beard.
Entrecava [en-tray-cah'-vah], *f.* A very shallow digging.
Entrecavar [en-tray-cah-var'], *va.* To dig shallow, not to dig deep.
Entrecejo [en-tray-thay'-ho], *m.* 1. The space between the eye-brows. 2. A frowning, supercilious look, show of annoyance.
Entrecerca [en-tray-therr'-cah], *f.* Space between inclosures.
Entrecielo [en-tray-the-ay'-lo], *m.* Awning. *V.* TOLDO.
Entreclaro, ra [en-tray-clah'-ro, rah], *a.* Slightly clear.
Entrecogedura [en-tray-co-hay-doo'-rah], *f.* Act of catching.
Entrecoger [en-tray-co-herr'], *va.* 1. To catch, to intercept. 2. To compel by arguments or threats. (Acad.)
Entrecoro [en-tray-co'-ro], *m.* Space between the choir and the chief altar; chancel.
Entrecortado, da [en-tray-cor-tah'-do, dah], *a.* 1. (Med.) Short of breath, dyspneal. 2. (Geol.) Broken.
Entrecortadura [en-tray-cor-tah-doo'-rah], *f.* Cut made in the middle of any thing without dividing it.
Entrecortar [en-tray-cor-tar'], *va.* To cut a thing in the middle without dividing it.
Entrecorteza [en-tray-cor-tay'-thah], *f.* An imperfection in timbers through the union of the branches to the trunk, with interior defects.
Entrecriar [en-tray-cre-ar'], *va.* To rear plants among others.
Entrecubiertas, Entrepuentes [en-tray-coo-be-err'-tas, en-tray-poo-en'-tes], *m.* & *f. pl.* (Naut.) Between decks.
Entrecuesto [en-trāy-coo-es'-to], *m.* Back-bone.
Entredecir [en-tray-day-theer'], *va.* To interdict, to prohibit.
Entredicho [en-tray-dee'-cho], *m.* 1. Interdiction, prohibition. 2. Ecclesiastical censure or interdict.—*Entredicho, cha, pp. irr.* of ENTREDECIR.
Entredoble [en-tray-do'-blay], *a.* Neither double nor single.
Entredós [en-tray-dose'], *m.* 1. A strip of lace between two hems; insertion. 2. The size of type called long primer. 3. (Arch.) The keystone of an arch. Plancher.
Entrefino, na [en-tray-fee'-no, nah], *a.* Middling fine.
Entreforro [en-tray-for'-ro], *m.* 1. Doublet, waistcoat, jerkin. 2. (Naut.) Parceling, a canvas wrapping, usually tarred, applied to protect a rope.
Entrega [en-tray'-gah], *f.* Delivery, the act of delivering, conveyance.
Entregadamente, *adv.* Really, perfectly.
Entregadero, ra [en-tray-gah-day'-ro, rah], *a.* (Com.) To be supplied; deliverable.
Entregador [en-tray-gah-dore'], *m.* 1. Deliverer. 2. Executor.
Entregamiento [en-tray-gah-me-en'-to], *m.* Delivery.
Entregar [en-tray-gar'], *va.* 1. To deliver, to put into the hands of another, to give, to give way, or to give up; (Com.) to transfer, to pay. 2. To insert, by the point or sidewise, part of one body into another.—*vr.* 1. To deliver one's self up into the hands of another. *Entregarse a vicios,* To abandon one's self to vices. 2. To devote one's self wholly to something. *A entregar,* To be supplied; supply expected.
Entregerir [en-tray-hay-reer'], *va.* To insert, to intermix.
Entrego [en-tray'-go], *m.* Delivery.—*a.* (Obs.) *V.* ÍNTEGRO.
Entrejuntar [en-tray-hoon-tar'], *va.* To nail or join the panels of a door to the cross-bars or ledges.
Entrelazar [en-tray-lah-thar'], *va.* To interlace, to intermix, to interweave, to entwine.
Entreliño [en-tray-lee'-nyo], *m.* Space of ground between the rows of vines or olives.
Entrelistado, da [en-tray-lis-tah'-do, dah], *a.* Striped or variegated.
Entrelucir [en-tray-loo-theer'], *vn.* To glimmer, to shine faintly.

(*Yo entreluzco, yo entreluzca,* from *Entrelucir. V.* DESLUCIR).

Entremedias [en-tray-may'-de-as], *adv.* In the meantime.
Entremés [en-tray-mess'], *m.* 1. A playlet, an interlude, entertainment. 2. Entrée, side-dish.
Entremesar, *va.* (Obs.) *V.* ENTREMESEAR.
Entremesear [en-tray-may-say-ar'], *va.* To act a part in a farce or interlude.
Entremesista [en-tray-may-sees'-tah], *m.* Player of farces or interludes.
Entremeter [en-tray-may-terr'], *va.* 1. To put one thing between others. 2. To put on a clean cloth without undressing children, or taking off the swaddling clothes.—*vr.* 1. To thrust one's self into a place without being called or invited. 2. To take charge of. 3. To intermeddle, to meddle, to pry, to interpose officiously.
Entremetido, *m.* Meddler, obtruder, intermeddler; a busy-body, a go-between.

Entremetido, da [en-tray-may-tee'-do-dah], *a.* & *pp.* of ENTREMETER. Meddling or intermeddling, officious, meddlesome.

Entremetimiento [en-tray-may-te-me-en'-to], *m.* Interposition, interjection intermeddling, meddlesomeness, obtrusion.

Entremezcladura [en-tray-meth-clah-doo'-rah], *f.* Intermixture.

Entremezclar [en-tray-meth-clar'], *va.* To interweave, to intermix.

Entremiche sobre el bauprés, *m.* (Naut.) The chock of the bowsprit. Capstan.

Entremiente, *adv.* (Obs.) *V.* ENTRETANTO.

Entremiso [en-tray-mee'-so], *m.* A long bench on which cheeses are formed.

Entremorir [en-tray-mo-reer'], *vn.* To die away by degrees, to be nearly extinguished: applied to a flame.

Entrenador, ra [en-tray-nah-dor', rah], *m.* & *f.* Coach, trainer, instructor, instructress.

Entrencar [en-tren-car'], *va.* To put rods in a bee-hive.

Entrenervios [en-tray-nerr'-ve-ose], *m. pl.* Among bookbinders the spaces between the bands of the back of a book.

Entrenudos [en-tray-noo'-dos], *m. pl.* (Bot.) Internodes, the spaces between the nodes of a stem.

Entrenzar [en-tren-thar'], *va.* To plait hair.

Entreoir [en-tray-o-eer'], *va.* To hear without perfectly understanding what is said.

(*Yo entreoigo, yo entreoiga; él entreoyó, entreoyera;* from *Entreoir. V.* OIR.)

Entreordinario, ria [en-tray-or-de-nah'-re-o, ah], *a.* Middling, between good and bad.

Entrepalmadura [en-tray-pal-mah-doo'-rah], *f.* (Vet.) Disease in horses' hoofs.

Entrepanes [en-tray-pah'-nes], *m. pl.* Pieces of unsown ground between others that are sown.

Entrepañado, da [en-tray-pa-nyah'-do, dah], *a.* Composed of several panels · applied to doors.

Entrepaño [en-tray-pah'-nyo], *m.* 1. Panel. 2. Space between pilasters. 3. Pier.

Entreparecerse [en-tray-pa-ray-therr'-say], *vr.* 1. To be transparent, to shine through. 2. To have traces of resemblance to some other thing, to be like.

Entrepechuga [en-tray-pay-choo'-gah], *f.* Small piece of flesh on the breast of birds.

Entrepeines [en-tray-pay'-e-nes], *m. pl.* The wool which remains in the comb after combing.

Entrepelado, da [en-tray-pay-lah'-do, dah], *a.* Spotted with white upon a dark ground, pied: used of the colour of horses or mules.

Entrepelar [en-tray-pay-lar'], *va.* To variegate hair, or mix it of different colours.

Entrepernar [en-tray-per-nar'], *vn.* To put the legs between those of others, for ease in sitting.

Entrepiernas [en-tray-pe-er'-nas], *f. pl.* 1. Opening between the legs; the inner surface of the thighs. 2. Pieces put into the fork of a pair of breeches.

Entreponer [en-tray-po-nerr'], *va.* To interpose.

Entrepretado, da [en-tray-pray-tah'-do, dah], *a.* (Vet.) Applied to a mule or horse with a weak breast or shoulder.

Entrepuentes [en-tray-poo-en'-tes], *m. pl.* (Naut.) Between decks.

Entrepunta [en-tray-poon'-tah], *f.* One of the pieces of a crane.

Entrepunzadura [en-tray-poon-thah-doo'-rah], *f.* Pricking pain of an unripe tumour.

Entrepunzar [en-tray-poon-thar'], *va.* (Obs.) To prick slightly.

Entrerenglón [en-tray-ren-glone'], *m.* Interline, space between lines.

Entrerenglonadura [en-tray-ren-glo-nah-doo'-rah], *f.* Any thing inscribed or written within lines: interlineal note.

Entrerenglonar [en-tray-ren-glo-nar'], *va.* To interline.

Entresaca, Entresacadura [en-tray-sah'-cah, en-tray-sah-cah-doo'-rah], *f.* 1. The act of cutting down trees, in order to thin a wood. 2. Selection of branches at the time of pruning.

Entresacar [en-tray-sah-car'], *va.* 1. To pick or choose out of a number or parcel of things. 2. (Agr.) To cut away branches of trees, to make a clearing. 3. To clip hair close to the head.

Entrescuro, ra [en-tres-coo'-ro, rah], *a.* (Prov.) Somewhat obscure.

Entresijo [en-tray-see'-ho], *m.* 1. Mesentery, that round which the bowels are twisted. 2. (Met.) Any thing occult, hidden.

Entresuelo [en-tray-soo-ay'-lo], *m.* A small room between two stories; floor between the ground and first floor, or principal apartment; entresol, mezzanine.

Entresurco [en-tray-soor'-co], *m.* Space between furrows.

Entretalla, Entretalladura [en-tray-tahl'-lyah, en-tray-tal-lyah-doo'-rah], *f.* Sculpture in bas-relief.

Entretallar [en-tray-tal-lyar'], *va.* 1. To sculpture in basso-relievo. 2. To cut, slash, or mangle. 3. (Met.) To intercept or obstruct the passage.

Entretejedura [en-tray-tay-hay-doo'-rah], *f.* Intertexture, a work interwoven with another.

Entretejer [en-tray-tay-herr'], *va.* 1. To tissue, to variegate. 2. To interweave, to intermix, to knit. 3. To insert words, verses, etc., in a book or writing.

Entretejimiento [en-tray-tay-he-me-en'-to], *m.* Intertexture, interweaving; variegation.

Entretela [en-tray-tay'lah], *f.* Interlining (in tailoring).

Entretelar [en-tray-tay-lar'], *va.* To put buckram between the lining and cloth.

Entretenedor [en-tray-tay-nay-dor'], *m.* Entertainer, he that pleases, diverts, or amuses.

Entretener [en-tray-tay-nerr'], *va.* 1. To feed or to keep in hope or expectation. 2. To allay pain, to make less troublesome. 3. To amuse, to entertain. 4. To delay, to put off, to postpone.—*vr.* To amuse one's self.

(*Yo entretengo, yo entretuve; yo entretenga, entretuviera;* from *Entretener. V.* TENER.)

Entretenido, da [en-tray-tay-nee'-do, dah], *a.* 1. Entertaining, pleasant, amusing. 2. Doing business in an office, in hopes of obtaining a place. 3. (Naut.) The prisoner who cannot set foot on land. *Dar a uno con la entretenida,* To put one off with excuses, for not giving what is asked for.—*pp.* of ENTRETENER.

Entretenimiento [en-tray-tay-ne-me-en'-to], *m.* 1. Amusement, entertainment. 2. Pay, allowance, appointment. 3. Delay, procrastination. 4. Game or sport of any kind, fun, jest joke.

Entretiempo [en-tray-te-em'-po], *m.* The middle season between the beginning and end of spring or autumn.

Entreuntar [en-tray-oon-tar'], *va.* To anoint slightly.

Entrevenarse [en-tray-vay-nar'-say], *vr.* To diffuse through the veins.

Entreventana [en-tray-ven-tah'-nah], *f.* Space between windows.

Entrever [en-tray-verr'], *va.* To have a glimpse of, to see imperfectly.

Entreverado, da [en-tray-vay-rah'-do, dah], *a.* Interlined with fat and lean: applied to meat.—*pp.* of ENTREVERAR.

Entreverar [en-tray-vay-rar'], *va.* To intermix, to insert one thing in another, to mix with others.

Entrevía [en-tray-vee'-ah], *f.* Railway gauge, space between rails.

Entrevista [en-tray-vees'-tah], *f.* 1. Interview. 2. Conference. *Entrevista de fondo,* Depth interview, interview in depth.

Entrevistador, ra [en-tray-vees-tah-dor', rah], *m.* & *f.* Interviewer.

Entrevistarse [en-tray-vees-tar'-say], *vr.* To confer. *Entrevistarse con,* To interview, to have an interview with.

Entrincado, da [en-trin-cah'-do, dah], *a.* Intricate. *V.* INTRINCADO.

Entripado, da [en-tree-pah'-do, dah], *a.* Contained in the entrails or intestines.

Entripado [en-tree-pah'-do], *m.* 1. (Coll.) Dissembled anger or displeasure. 2. An indigestion. 3. (Mex.) A game of cards in which that one loses who is left with certain cards in his hand, through not answering to the suit demanded. 4. A dead animal from which the intestines have not been removed.

Entristecer [en-tris-tay-therr'], *va.* To sadden, to grieve, to afflict, to make melancholy.—*vr.* 1. To grieve, to fret, to grow sad or melancholy. 2. To wither, to decay: applied to plants.

Entristecimiento [en-tris-tay-the-me-en'-to], *m.* Gloominess, heaviness of mind, sadness, sorrowfulness; mournfulness, dejection; fretting.

(*Yo entristezco, yo entristezca,* from *Entristecer. V.* CONOCER.)

Entrojar [en-tro-har'], *va.* 1. To gather grain in barns. 2. To mow, to gather the harvest.

Entrometer [en-tro-may-terr'], *va.* & *vr.* *V.* ENTREMETER in all its meanings.

Entrometimiento [en-tro-may-te-me-en'-to], *m.* Intermeddling.

Entronar [en-tro-nar'], *va.* To enthrone. *V.* ENTRONIZAR.

Entroncar [en-tron-car'], *vn.* 1. To be descended from the same stock, to belong to the same family. 2. To contract relationship.

Entronerar [en-tro-nay-rar'], *va.* To drive the ball into the hole of a truck or billiard-table.

Entronización [en-tro-ne-thah-the-on'], *f.* Elevation to a throne.

Entronizar [en-tro-ne-thar'], *va.* 1. To enthrone, to place on the throne. 2. To exalt, to raise to a distinguished rank or station.—*vr.* 1. To be elated or puffed up with pride. 2. To take possession of, to seat one's self in a post.

Entronque [en-tron'-kay], *m.* 1. Cognation, relationship with the chief of a family. 2. A railway junction.

Entropía [en-tro-pee'-ah], *f.* Entropy.

Entruchada [en-troo-chah'-dah], *f.* A clandestine operation, an underhand business. (Coll.) Plot, intrigue.

Entruchar [en-troo-char'], *va.* To decoy, to lure into a snare.

Entruchón, na [en-troo-chone', nah], *m.* & *f.* Decoyer, plotter.

Entruejo [en-troo-ay'-ho], *m.* *V.* ANTRUEJO.

Entruesca [en-troo-es'-cah], *f.* In some mills, the cogged wheel.

Entrujar [en-troo-har'], *va.* 1. To keep olives in the store-room. 2. *V.* ENTROJAR. 3. (Fig. Coll.) To reimburse.

Entuerto [en-too-err'-to], *m.* *V.* AGRAVIO and TUERTO.—*pl.* After-pains.

Entullecer [en-tool-lyay-therr'], *vn.* To be crippled or maimed.—*va.* To stop, to check, to obstruct.

(*Yo entullezco, yo entullezca,* from *Entullecer.* *V.* CONOCER.)

Entumecer [en-too-may-therr'], *va.* 1. To swell, to make tumid. 2. To benumb, to make torpid.—*vr.* To swell, to surge, to rise high.

Entumecimiento [en-too-may-the-me-en'-to], *m.* 1. Swelling. 2. Torpor, deadness, numbness.

Entumescencia [en-too-mes-then'-the-ah], *f.* (Med.) Intumescence, swelling which, according to the infiltration which it produces, takes the names emphysema, œdema, and anasarca.

Entumirse [en-too-meer'-say], *vr.* To become torpid.

Entunicar [en-too-ne-car'], *va.* To give two coats of plaster to a wall before painting it (in fresco).

Entupir [en-too-peer'], *va.* 1. To obstruct, to block up. 2. To compress, to tighten, to press.

Enturbiar [en-toor-be-ar'], *va.* 1. To muddle, to make muddy or turbid. 2. To obscure, to confound.—*vr.* To disorder or derange a thing.

Entusiasmado, da [en-too-se-as-mah'-do, dah], *a.* & *pp.* of ENTUSIASMAR. Enthusiastical, enthusiastic.

Entusiasmar [en-too-se-as-mar'], *va.* To transport, to enrapture.—*vr.* To become enthusiastic, to be enraptured.

Entusiasmo [en-too-se-ahs'-mo], *m.* Enthusiasm, heat of imagination, ardour; fanaticism, caprice.

Entusiasta [en-too-se-ahs'-tah], *m.* & *f.* Enthusiast; a visionary.

Entusiástico, ca [en-too-se-ahs'-te-co, cah], *a.* (Littl. us.) Enthusiastic, fanatical.

Enucleación [ay-noo-clay-ah-the-on'], *f.* 1. Enucleation, extraction of the kernel of a stone-fruit. 2. Enucleation, extirpation of a tumour. 3. Excision of a bone.

Enuclear [ay-noo-clay-ar'], *va.* 1. To enucleate. 2. To excise a bone.

Énula campana [ay'-noo-lah cam-pah'-nah], *f.* (Bot.) Elecampane, a tall herb of the aster family: its root yields a stomachic tonic. Inula helenium.

Enumerable [ay-noo-may-rah'-blay], *a.* Numerable, capable of being counted.

Enumeración [ay-noo-may-ra-the-on'], *f.* 1. Enumeration. 2. Recapitulation of the points of a discourse.

Enumerar [ay-noo-may-rar'], *va.* To enumerate.

Enunciación [ay-noon-the-ah-the-on'], *f.* Enunciation, declaration.

Enunciar [ay-noon-the-ar'], *va.* To enunciate, to declare, to proclaim.

Enunciativamente, *adv.* (Littl. us.) Enunciatively.

Enunciativo, va [ay-noon-the-ah-tee'-vo, vah], *a.* Enunciative.

Enuresis, or **Enuresia** [ay-noo-ray'-sis], *f.* Enuresis, incontinence of urine.

Envagarar, or **Envagrar** [en-vah-ga-rar'], *va.* (Naut.) To set the cross-pawls, or rib-bands, upon the frames of a ship.

Envainador, ra [en-vah-e-nah-dor', rah], *a.* Sheathing. (Bot.) Clasping the stem.

Envainar [en-vah-e-nar'], *va.* To sheathe, as a sword; to plunge.

Envalentonar [en-vah-len-to-nar'], *va.* To encourage, to inspirit, to render bold.—*vr.* To become courageous.

Envanecer [en-vah-nay-therr'], *va.* To make vain; to lift, to swell with pride. —*vr.* To become proud or haughty.

(*Yo envanezco, yo envanezca,* from *Envanecer.* *V.* CONOCER.)

Envarado, da [en-vah-rah'-do, dah], *a.* & *pp.* of ENVARAR. Deadened, benumbed: said of a horse slow in its movements.

Envaramiento [en-vah-rah-me-en'-to], *m.* 1. Deadness, stiffness, numbness. 2. A number of bailiffs or petty officers of justice.

Envarar [en-vah-rar'], *va.* To benumb, to make torpid, to stupefy.

Envasador [en-vah-sah-dor'], *m.* 1. Filler, one whose employment is to fill vessels of carriage. 2. Funnel.

Envasar [en-vah-sar'], *va.* 1. To tun, to put liquor into casks, to barrel. 2. To drink liquor to excess. 3. To put grain into sacks. *Envasar a uno,* To run one through the body.

Envase [en-vah'-say], *m.* The recipient or vessel in which liquids are preserved or transported.

Envedijarse [en-vay-de-har'-say], *vr.* 1. To get entangled. 2. (Coll.) To wrangle.

Envejecer [en-vay-hay-therr'], *va.* To make old, to make a person or thing look old.—*vn.* To grow old.—*vr.* 1. To be of an old date or fashion. 2. To hold out a long time, to be of long duration. 3. To grow out of use.

Envejecido, da [en-vay-hay-thee'-do, dah], *a.* & *pp.* of ENVEJECER. 1. Grown old, looking old. 2. Accustomed, habituated.

Envejecimiento [en-vay-hay-the-me-en'-to], *m.* Oldness, age.

(*Yo envejezco, yo envejezca,* from *Envejecer.* *V.* CONOCER.)

Envenenador, ra [en-vay-nay-nah-dor', rah], *m.* & *f.* A poisoner.

Envenenar [en-vay-nay-nar'], *va.* 1. To envenom, to poison; to infect with poison. 2. To reproach, to judge ill of one. 3. To embitter one's own talk or another's.

Envenenamiento [en-vay-nay-nah-me-en'-to], *m.* Poisoning.

Enverdecer [en-ver-day-therr'], *vn.* To grow green.

(*Yo enverdezco, yo enverdezca,* from *Enverdecer.* *V.* CONOCER.)

Enverdir, *va.* (Obs.) To tinge green.

Enveredar [en-vay-ray-dar'], *va.* To put in the right road, to guide.

Envergadura [en-ver-ga-doo'-rah], *f.* 1. Bending the sails. 2. The rope-bands of a sail collectively. 3. Breadth of the sails. 4. *V.* GRATIL.

Envergar [en-ver-gar'], *va.* (Naut.) To bend the sails.

Envergues [en-ver'-gays], *m. pl.* (Naut.) Rope-bands, used to fasten sails to the yards.

Envés [en-vays'], *m.* 1. The wrong side of any thing, as cloth, etc. *V.* REVÉS. 2. Back, shoulders.

Envesado [en-vay-sah'-do], *m.* Among leather-dressers, the fleshy part of hides.

Envestidura [en-ves-te-doo'-rah], *f.* Act of investing one with an office or place.

Envestir [en-ves-teer'], *va.* 1. To invest, to put in possession of a place or office. 2. To adorn, to set off. 3. To illuminate, to enlighten. 4. To cover. *V.* REVESTIR.—*vr.* 1. To accustom or habituate one's self, to contract a habit. 2. To introduce one's self, or to interfere in any thing. 3. *V.* REVESTIRSE.

Enviada [en-ve-ah'-dah], *f.* 1. Message, errand. 2. Skiff, or smack, for carrying fish to land.

Enviadizo, za [en-ve-ah-dee'-tho, thah], *a.* Missive, designed to be sent.

Enviado [en-ve-ah'-do], *m.* 1. Envoy, a public minister sent from one power to another. 2. Envoy, messenger.

Enviador [en-ve-ah-dor'], *m.* A sender.

Enviajado, da [en-ve-ah-hah'-do, dah], *a.* (Arch.) Oblique, sloped.

Enviar [en-ve-ar'], *va.* 1. To send, to transmit, to convey. 2. To send, to give, to bestow. 3. To exile. *Enviar a pasear,* (Met.) To send any one about his business; to give one his walking-ticket; to dismiss contemptuously. *Enviar enhoramala,* (Coll.) To send one to the devil. *Enviar de vuelta,* (Com.) To return.

Enviciar [en-ve-the-ar'], *va.* To vitiate, to corrupt, to make vicious.—*vn.* To have luxurious foliage and little fruit: applied to plants.—*vr.* To be immoderately addicted to, to be excessively fond of.

Envidador [en-ve-dah-dor'], *m.* He who invites at cards, or opens the game by staking a sum.

Envidar [en-ve-dar'], *va.* Among gamesters, to invite, or to open the game by staking a certain sum.

Envidia [en-vee'-de-ah], *f.* 1. Envy. 2. Emulation.

Envidiable [en-ve-de-ah'-blay], *a.* Enviable.

Envidiador, ra [en-ve-de-ah-dor', rah], *m.* & *f.* Envier, envious person.

Envidiar [en-ve-de-ar'], *vn.* 1. To envy, to feel envy, to grudge, to malign. 2. (Met.) To covet, to desire what is lawful and honourable.

Envidiosamente, *adv.* Enviously.

Envidioso, sa [en-ve-de-oh'-so, sah], *a.* Envious; invidious, jealous, malignant.

Envigotar [en-ve-go-tar'], *va.* (Naut.) To strap dead-eyes.

Envilecer [en-ve-lay-therr'], *va.* To vilify, to debase, to make contemptible. —*vr.* To degrade one's self, to be disgraced.

Envilecimiento [en-ve-lay-the-me-en'-to], *m.* Vilification, debasement.

Envinado, da [en-ve-nah'-do, dah], *a.* Having the taste of wine.—*pp.* of ENVINAR.

Envinagrar [en-ve-nah-grar'], *va.* To put vinegar into any thing.

Envinar [en-ve-nar'], *va.* To mix wine with water.

Envío [en-vee'-o], *m.* Remittance, consignment of goods.

Enviperado, da [en-ve-pay-rah'-do, dah], *a.* In jocular style, viper-like, enraged, furious.

Envirar [en-ve-rar'], *va.* To clasp or unite together cork-wood to form a bee-hive.

Enviscamiento [en-vis-cah-me-en'-to], *m.* Act of gluing.

Enviscar [en-vis-car'], *va.* 1. To glue, to fasten with glue. 2. To irritate, to anger.—*vr.* To be glued with bird-lime: applied to birds and insects.

(*Yo envisto, yo envista, envistiera* or *envistiese,* from *Envestir.* *V.* PEDIR.)

Envite [en-vee'-tay], *m.* 1. The act of inviting at cards, or opening the game by staking a certain sum. 2. Invitation; any kind of polite offer.

Enviudar [en-ve-oo-dar'], *vn.* To become a widower or widow.

Envolcarse [en-vol-car'-say], *vr.* (Obs.) *V.* ENVOLVERSE.

Envoltorio [en-vol-to'-re-o], *m.* 1. Bundle of clothes. 2. Fault in cloth, arising from the mixture of inferior material.

Envoltura [en-vol-too'-rah], *f.* 1. Wrapper, jacket (of a book). 2. Wrapping, covering.

Envolturas [en-vol-too'-ras], *f. pl.* 1. Swaddling-cloth, swaddling-band, cloth wrapped round a baby. 2. (Anat.) The coverings, commonly membranous, which serve as a protection to certain organs.

Envolvedero, Envolvedor [en-vol-vay-day'-ro, en-vol-vay-dor'], *m.* Wrapper, wrapping, envelope, cover.

Envolver [en-vol-verr'], *va.* 1. To wrap up, to wrap around, with paper, cloth, or other analogous thing: to convolve; to inwrap. 2. (Met.) To convince by reasoning. 3. To put things into confusion. 4. (Mil.) To attack an enemy on all sides, to surround, so as to force a surrender.—*vr.* 1. To be implicated in an affair. 2. To be unlawfully connected with women.

Envolvimiento [en-vol-ve-me-en'-to], *m.* 1. Envelopment, inwrapping or enveloping. 2. *V.* Revolcadero.

Envuelto, ta [en-voo-el'-to, tah], *pp. irr.* of Envolver. 1. Wrapped. 2. *Envuelta,* a cord matted.

(*Yo envuelvo, yo envuelva,* from *Envolver. V.* Mover.)

Enyerbarse [en-yer-bar'-say], *vr.* (Amer. Cuba.) To be clothed or covered with grass.

Enyesado [en-yay-sah'-do], *m.* 1. *V.* Enyesadura. 2. *Enyesado de los vinos,* Addition of gypsum to wines, to clarify them and make them stronger.

Enyesadura [en-yay-sah-doo'-rah], *f.* Plastering with gypsum.

Enyesar [en-yay-sar'], *va.* To plaster, to cover with plaster; to whitewash.

Enyugar [en-yoo-gar'], *va.* To yoke cattle.—*vr.* (Met. Obs.) To marry.

Enzainarse [en-thah-e-nar'-say], *vr.* (Coll.) To look sideways; to become insidious, to be treacherous and ostentatious.

Enzamarrado, da [en-thah-mar-rah'-do, dah], *a.* Dressed in a shepherd's great-coat, made of sheep-skins with the wool on.

Enzarzada [en-thar-thah'-dah], *f.* (Mil.) A light fortification; breastworks at the entrance of forests, defiles, and crags, aiding to defend an important pass.

Enzarzado, da [en-thar-thah'-do, dah], *a.* Curled, matted: applied to hair.—*pp.* of Enzarzar.

Enzarzar [en-thar-thar'], *va.* 1. To throw among brambles and briers. 2. (Met.) To sow discord, to excite dissensions. 3. To put hurdles for silk-worms.—*vr.* 1. To be entangled among brambles and briers. 2. (Met.) To be involved in difficulties. 3. To squabble, to wrangle.

Enzima [en-thee'-mah], *f.* Enzyme.

Enzimático, ca [en-the-mah'-te-co, cah], *a.* Enzymic, enzymatic.

Enzimología [en-the-mo-lo-hee'-ah], *f.* Enzymology.

Enzootia [en-tho-o-tee'-ah], *f.* Epizootic, a contagious disease among cattle.

Enzurdecer [en-thoor-day-therr'], *vn* To become left-handed.

Enzurronar [en-thoor-ro-nar'], *va.* 1. To put in a bag. 2. (Met.) To inclose one thing in another.

Eñe [ay'-nyay], *f.* Spanish name of the letter Ñ.

Eoceno, na [ay-o-thay'-no, nah], *a.* (Geol.) Eocene.

Eólico [ay-o'-le-co], *a.* Æolian, Æolic. 2. The Æolian dialect.

Eolio, lia [ay-o'-le-o, ah], *a.* Æolian, Eolian; used of the dialect.

Eolipilo [ay-o-le-pee'-lo], *m.* A ventilator for cleaning chimneys.

Eón [ay-on'], *m.* (Geol.) Eon.

Epacta [ay-pahc'-tah], *f.* 1. Epact, the excess of the solar year over twelve lunar months. 2. *V.* Añalejo.

Epactilla [ay-pac-teel'-lyah], *f.* A small calendar for the performance of divine service, which is published every year.

Epagómeno [ay-pa-go'-may-no], *a.* Epagomenal, intercalary: said of the five days which the Egyptians and Chaldeans added to the 360 of the vague year, after the establishment of the lunar cycle.

Epéntesis [ay-pen'-tay-sis], *f.* (Gram.) Epenthesis.

Eperlano [ay-per-lah'-no], *m.* (Zool.) Smelt, a small sea-fish.

Epi, a Greek preposition signifying on; used as a prefix.

Épicamente, *adv.* In an epic or heroic manner.

Epicarpo [ay-pe-car'-po], *m.* Epicarp, a membrane which covers the pericarp.

Epicedio [ay-pe-thay'-de-o], *m.* Epicedium, elegy, eulogy of the dead.

Epiceno, na [ay-pe-thay'-no, nah], *a.* Epicene, belonging to both genders.

Epicentro [ay-pe-then'-tro], *m.* Epicenter.

Epiciclo [ay-pe-thee'-clo], *m.* Epicycle, a small circle, whose centre is supposed to be upon the circumference of another.

Epicicloide [ay-pe-the-clo'-e-day], *f.* (Geom.) Epicycloid.

Épico, ca [ay'-pe-co, cah], *a.* Epic, narrative, containing narrations. *Poema épico,* Epic, epopee, an epic poem.

Epicúreo, rea [ay-pe-coo'-ray-o, ah], *a.* Epicurean.

Epicureísmo [ay-pe-coo-ray-ees'-mo], *m.* (Littl. us.) Epicurism.

Epidemia [ay-pe-day'-me-ah], *f.* 1. An epidemic disease. 2. A multitude of ills or misfortunes.

Epidémico, ca [ay-pe-day'-me-co, cah], *a.* Epidemical, epidemic.

Epidendro [ay-pe-den'-dro], *m.* Epidendrum, a large genus of tropical American epiphytic orchids often cultivated for their beautiful flowers.

Epidérmico, ca [ay-pe-derr'-me-co, cah], *a.* Epidermic, belonging to the cuticle or outer covering.

Epidermis [ay-pe-derr'-mis], *f.* Epidermis, the scarf-skin, the cuticle.

Epidídimo [ay-pe-dee'-de-mo], *m.* (Anat.) Epididymis.

Epifanía [ay-pe-fah-nee'-ah], *f.* Epiphany.

Epifaringe [ay-pe-fah-reen'-hay], *f.* Epipharynx, a little valve which closes the pharynx of certain hymenoptera.

Epifillo, lla [ay-pe-feel'-lyo, lyah], *a.* (Bot.) Budding and growing upon the surface of leaves.

Epifilospermo, ma [ay-pe-fe-los-perr'-mo, mah], *a.* (Bot.) Epiphyllospermous.

Epífisis [ay-pee'-fe-sis], *f.* (Anat.) Epiphysis.

Epífito, ta [ay-pee'-fey-to, tah], *a.* Epiphytal, growing upon other plants, but not extracting nutriment from them.

Epifonema [ay-pe-fo-nay'-ma], *f.* (Rhet.) Epiphonema, an exclamation made after recounting something.

Epífora [ay-pee'-fo-rah], *f.* 1. Epiphora, watering of the eye. 2. (Rhet.) A kind of amplification.

Epigástrico, ca [ay-pe-gahs'-tre-co, cah], *a.* Epigastric.

Epiglotis [ay-pe-glo'-tis], *f.* Epiglottis, a cartilage of the larynx.

Epígrafe [ay-pee'-grah-fay], *m.* Epigraph, title, inscription; motto.

Epigrama [ay-pe-grah'-mah], *m. & f.* Epigram.

Epigramatario, ria, or **Epigramático, ca** [ay-pe-grah-mah-tah'-re-o, ah], *a.* Epigrammatic.

Epigramático, Epigramatista, Epigramista [ay-pe-grah-mah'-te-co, ay-pe-grah-mah-tees'-tah], *m.* Epigrammatist.

Epilepsia [ay-pe-lep'-se-ah], *f.* Epilepsy.

Epiléptico, ca [ay-pe-lep'-te-co, cah], *a.* Epileptic, epileptical.

Epilogación, *f. V.* Epílogo.

Epilogal [ay-pe-lo-gahl'], *a.* Epilogistic, compendious, summary.

Epilogar [ay-pe-lo-gar'], *va.* To recapitulate, to sum up.

Epilogismo [ay-pe-lo-hees'-mo], *m.* Epilogism, calculation, computation.

Epílogo [ay-pee'-lo-go], *m.* 1. A conclusion or close of a speech 2. Epilogue. 3. Recapitulation, a brief or compendious statement.

Epipedometría [ay-pe-pay-do-may-tree'-ah], *f.* Epipedometry, the mensuration of figures standing on the same base.

Epiqueya [ay-pe-kay'-yah], *f.* A mild and prudent interpretation of the law.

Episcopado [ay-pis-co-pah'-do], *m.* Episcopacy; episcopate, bishopric; the dignity of a bishop.

Episcopal [ay-pis-co-pahl'], *a.* Episcopal, relating to bishops.

Episódico, ca [ay-pe-so'-de-co, cah], *a.* Episodic, episodical.

Episodio [ay-pe-so'-de-o], *m.* 1. Episode, an incidental narrative or digression in a poem. 2. *V.* Digresión.

Epispástico, ca [ay-pis-pahs'-te-co, cah], *a.* Epispastic, blistering, reddening the skin.

Epispermo [ay-pis-perr'-mo], *m.* Episperm, an envelope which inwraps the seed.

Epistaxis [ay-pis-tak'-sis], *f.* Epistaxis, nosebleed.

Epistemología [ay-pis-tay-mo-lo-hee'-ah], *f.* Epistemology.

Epistilo [ay-pis-tee'-lo], *m.* (Arch.) Epistyle.

Epístola [ay-pees'-to-lah], *f.* 1. Epistle, letter. 2. Epistle, a part of the mass. *Epístola* or *orden de epístola,* Subdeaconship, subdeaconry.

Epistolar [ay-pis-to-lar'], *a.* Epistolary.

Epistolario [ay-pis-to-lah'-re-o], *m.* 1. Collection of epistles read or sung at the mass. 2. Volume of letters.

Epistolero [ay-pis-to-lay'-ro], *m.* Epistler, the subdeacon or any priest who sings the epistle.

Epitafio [ay-pe-tah'-fe-o], *m.* Epitaph, inscription on a tomb.

Epitalamio [ay-pe-ta-lah'-me-o], *m.* Epithalamium, a nuptial song; a compliment upon marriage.

Epítasis [ay-pee'-tah-sis], *f.* Epitasis, the most complex part of the plot of a play.

Epitelio [ay-pe-tay'-le-o], *m.* Epithelium, the epidermis of mucous membranes.

Epítema, or **Epítima** [ay-pee'-te-mah] *f.* Epithem, a lotion.

Epíteto [ay-pee'-tay-to], *m.* Epithet.

Epitimar [ay-pe-te-mar'], *va.* To apply an epithem.

Epítimo [ay-pee'-te-mo], *m.* (Bot.) Lesser dodder. Cuscuta epithymum.

Epitomar [ay-pe-to-mar'], *va.* To epitomize, to abstract, to contract into a narrow space.

Epítome [ay-pee'-to-may], *m.* Epitome, abridgment, extract, summary, compend or compendium.

Epizoario, a [ay-pe-tho-ah'-re-o, ah], *a.* (Zool.) Epizoic, epizoan, parasitic on the body of other animals, like lice.

Epizóico, ca [ay-pe-tho'-e-co, cah], *a.* 1. *V.* EPIZOARIO. 2. (Geol.) Denoting upper primitive lands which contain remains of organized bodies.

Epizootia [ay-pe-tho-o'-te-ah], *f.* (Vet.) Epizooty, epidemic influenza.

Época [ay'-po-cah], *f.* 1. Epoch, or epocha. 2. Date of an event.

Épodo [ay'-po-do], *m.* Epode.

Epopeya [ay-po-pay'-yah], *f.* Epopee, an epic poem.

Epoto, ta [ay-po'-to, tah], *a.* (Obs.) Intoxicated. *V.* BEBIDO.

Epsomita [ep-so-mee'-tah], *f.* Epsom salts.

Epulia, Epúlida [ay-poo'-le-ah, ay-poo'-le-dah], *f.* Epulis, a tumour of the gums.

Epulón [ay-poo-lon'], *m.* An epicure or great eater.

Equeno [ay-kay'-no], *m.* A rectangular earthen trough, for pouring melted metal into a mould, used in casting statues.

Equiángulo, la [ay-ke-ahn'-goo-lo, lah], *a.* (Geom.) Equiangular.

Equiáxeo, a [ay-kee-ak'-say-o, ah], *a.* Equiaxe, having equal axes.

Equidad [ay-ke-dahd'], *f.* 1. Equity, equitableness, right, honesty. 2. Equity, impartiality, justice. 3. Conscionableness; conscientiousness. 4. Moderation in the execution of laws, or in the price of things bought or sold.

Equidistancia [ay-ke-dis-tahn'-the-ah], *f.* Equidistance.

Equidistante [ay-ke-dis-tahn'-tay], *pa.* Equidistant.

Equidistar [ay-ke-dis-tar'], *vn.* To be equidistant.

Equidna [ay-keed'-nah], *m.* Echidna, the porcupine ant-eater, a very strange mammal.

Equidnita [ay-keed-nee'-tah], *f.* A kind of agate with spots like those of the viper.

Equilateral [ay-ke-lah-tay-rahl'], *a.* *V.* EQUILÁTERO.

Equilátero, ra [ay-ke-lah'-tay-ro, rah] *a.* Equilateral.

Equilibrado, da [ay-ke-le-brah'-do, dah], *a.* 1. Balanced. 2. Sensible, fair, just. *Dieta equilibrada,* Balanced diet.

Equilibrar [ay-ke-le-brar'], *va.* 1. To equilibrate, to balance in a scale. 2. (Met.) To balance equally. 3. To counterpoise, to counterbalance.

Equilibre [ay-ke-lee'-bray], *a.* Balanced, equilibrious.

Equilibrio [ay-ke-lee'-bre-o], *m.* Equilibrium, equilibrity, equipoise, equality of weight, counterpoise, counterbalance, equilibration.

Equilibrista [ay-ke-le-brees'-tah], *m.* 1. Balancer, tight-rope walker. 2. Turncoat, one who changes political opinions often.

Equimosis [ay-ke-mo'-sis], *m.* (Med.) Ecchymosis, subcutaneous effusion of blood, caused by a blow.

Equinita [ay-ke-nee'-tah], *f.* Sea-urchin, sea-hedgehog, echinus.

Equino, na [ay-kee'-no, nah], *a.* (Poet.) Belonging to a horse, equine.

Equino [ay-kee'-no], *m.* 1. (Zool.) Echinus, a shell-fish set with prickles. 2. (Arch.) Echinus, an ornament.

Equinoccial [ay-ke-noc-the-ahl'], *a.* Equinoctial. *Línea equinoccial,* The equinoctial line.

Equinoccio [ay-ke-noc'-the-o], *m.* The equinox.

Equinodermo, ma [ay-ke-no-derr'-mo, mah], *a.* Echinodermatous.

Equipaje [ay-ke-pah'-hay], *m.* 1. Provision or supply for a voyage or journey; baggage. 2. (Naut.) The crew. 3. (Mil.) Baggage train, supply wagons. 4. Storehouse. *Equipaje de puente,* The pontoons for military bridges.

Equipamento [ay-ke-pah-men'-to], *m.* (Naut.) Fitting out, accoutrement, for navigation and military operations.

Equipar [ay-ke-par'], *va.* 1. To fit out, to supply with every necessary. 2. To equip, to furnish, to accoutre; to gird.

Equiparación [ay-ke-pa-rah-the-on'], *f.* Comparison, collation.

Equiparar [ay-ke-pa-rar'], *va.* To compare, to match.

Equipo [ay-kee'-po], *m.* 1. (Mil.) Fitting out, accoutrement, equipment. 2. Trappings.

Equipolencia [ay-ke-po-len'-the-ah], *f.* Equipollence, equality of force or power.

Equipolente [ay-ke-po-len'-tay], *a.* Equivalent, equipollent.

Equiponderación, or **Equiponderancia** [ay-ke-pon-day-rahn'-the-ah], *f.* Equality of weight, balance. The form in *ción* is obsolescent.

Equiponderante, *pa.* & *a.* Equiponderating; equiponderant.

Equiponderar [ay-ke-pon-day-rar'], *vn.* To equiponderate.

Equis [ay'-kis], *f.* Spanish name of the letter X. *Estar hecho una equis,* To be intoxicated and staggering.

Equitación [ay-ke-tah-the-on'], *f.* Horsemanship; equitation.

Equitativamente [ay-ke-tah-te-vah-men'-tay], *adv.* Equitably.

Equitativo, va [ay-ke-tah-tee'-vo, vah], *a.* 1. Equitable: applied to a just judge. 2. Just, honourable. *A precio muy equitativo,* Very cheap.

Equivalencia [ay-ke-vah-len'-the-ah], *f.* Compensation; equivalence.

Equivalente [ay-ke-vah-len'-tay], *a.* 1. Equivalent. 2. Compensatory, compensative.

Equivalentemente, *adv.* (Littl. us.) Equivalently.

Equivaler [ay-ke-vah-lerr'], *vn.* 1. To be of equal value and price. 2. To equiponderate, to be equal to.

(*Yo equivalgo, yo equivalga; equivaliera, equivaliese, equivaliere;* from *Equivaler.* *V.* VALER.)

Equivocación [ay-ke-vo-cah-the-on'], *f.* 1. Mistake, misconception, error, misapprehension, misunderstanding, oversight. 2. Blunder, hallucination.

Equivocadamente, *adv.* Mistakenly, by mistake.

Equivocado, da [ay-ke-vo-cah'-do, dah], *a.* & *pp.* of EQUIVOCAR. Mistaken.

Equívocamente [ay-kee'-vo-cah-men-tay], *adv.* Ambiguously, equivocally.

Equivocar [ay-ke-vo-car'], *va.* To mistake, to take one thing for another; to conceive wrong.—*vr.* To mistake, to be mistaken, to make a mistake.

Equívoco, ca [ay-kee'-vo-co, cah], *a.* Equivocal, ambiguous.

Equívoco [ay-kee'-vo-co], *m.* 1. Equivocation, equivoke or equivoque, a quibble. 2. (Coll.) Mistake: in this sense it is sometimes pronounced *equivóco.*

Equivoquillo [ay-ke-vo-keel'-lyo], *m. dim.* A quibble, a slight cavil; a sort of pun.

Era [ay'-rah], *f.* 1. Era, computation from any date or epoch. 2. Age, or long space of time. 3. Thrashing-floor. 4. Bed or plot in a garden, sown with salad-seeds, etc.

Eradicación [ay-rah-de-cah-the-on'], *f.* Eradication, thorough cure.

Eradicativo, va [ay-rah-de-cah-tee'-vo, vah], *a.* Eradicative, radically curative.

Eraje [ay-rah'-hay], *m.* (Prov.) Virgin honey.

Eral [ay-rahl'], *m.* A two-year-old ox.

Erar [ay-rar'], *va.* To lay out ground for growing garden-stuff.

Erario [ay-rah'-re-o], *m.* Exchequer public treasury.

Erección [ay-rec-the-on'], *f.* 1. Foundation, erection, establishment. 2. Erection, erectness, elevation.

Eréctil [ay-rayk'-teel], *a.* Erectile, capable of erection.

Erectilidad [ay-rec-te-le-dahd'], *f.* Erectility, power of erection.

Erector, ra [ay-rec-tor', rah], *m.* & *f.* Erecter, founder.

Eremita [ay-ray-mee'-tah], *m.* *V.* ERMITAÑO.

Eremítico, ca [ay-ray-mee'-te-co, cah] *a.* Hermitical, eremitical, solitary.

Eretismo [ay-ray-tees'-mo], *m.* Erethism, abnormal excitability.

Ergio [er'-he-o], *m.* (Phy.) Erg.

Ergotear [er-go-tay-ar'], *vn.* (Coll.) To argue, to debate without reason.

Ergoteo [er-go-tay'-o], *m.* (Coll.) Sophistry, debate on trifling things.

Erguido, da [er-gee'-do, dah], *a.* 1. Erect, straight. 2. Swelled with pride.

Erguir [er-geer'], *va.* To erect, to raise up straight.—*vr.* To be elated or puffed up with pride.

Erial, Eriazo, za [ay-re-ahl', ay-re-ah'-tho, thah], *a.* Unploughed, untilled, uncultivated: it is commonly used as a substantive to express a piece of uncultivated ground.

Erica [ay-ree'-cah], *f.* (Bot.) Heath, heather.

Ericáceo, cea [ay-re-cah'-thay-o, ah], *a.* Ericaceous, of the heath family.

Ericera [ay-re-thay'-rah], *f.* (Prov.) Kind of hut without a roof.

Erigeron [ay-re-hay'-ron], *m.* (Bot.) Erigeron.

Erigir [ay-re-heer'], *va.* 1. To erect, to raise, to build. 2. To erect, to establish anew.

Eringe [ay-reen'-hay], *f.* (Bot.) *V.* ERINGIO.

Eringio [ay-reen'-he-o], *m.* (Bot.) Field eringo. Eryngium campestre.

Erío, ría [ay-ree'-o, ah], *a.* Unploughed, untilled. *V.* ERIAL.

Erísimo [ay-ree'-se-mo], *m.* (Bot.) Hedge-mustard. Erysimum officinale.

Erisipela [ay-re-se-pay'-lah], *f.* (Med.) Erysipelas, a disease.

Erisipelar [ay-re-se-pay-lar'], *va.* To cause erysipelas.

Erisipelatoso, sa [ay-re-se-pay-lah-to'-so, sah], *a.* (Med.) Erysipelatous, belonging to erysipelas.

Eristalo [ay-ris-tah'-lo], *m.* The drone-fly, eristalis; much resembling a drone-bee in appearance.

Eritema [ay-re-tay'-mah], *f.* (Med.) Erythema, congestion of the skin.

Eritematoso, sa [ay-re-tay-ma-to'-so, sah], *a.* Erythematous, relating to or characterized by erythema.

Eritreo, trea [ay-ree-tray'-o, ah], *a.* (Poet.) Erythræan, belonging to the Red Sea.

Erizado, da [ay-re-thah'-do, dah], *a.* Covered with bristles.—*pp.* of ERIZAR.

Erizamiento [ay-re-thah-me-en'-to], *m.* Act of setting on end, as the hair.

Erizar [ay-re-thar'], *va.* To set on end; to bristle.—*vr.* 1. To stand on end: applied to the hair. 2. To bristle, to stand erect.

Erizo [ay-ree'-tho], *m.* 1. Hedgehog. Erináceus europæus. 2. Sea-hedgehog, or urchin. 3. Echinus, the prickly husk of a chestnut and other fruits. 4. (Mec.) In weaving, an urchin, a carding roller; a sprocket wheel, a rag wheel, spar-toothed wheel.

Ermar [er-mar'], *va.* (Obs.) To destroy, to lay waste. *V.* ASOLAR.
Ermita [er-mee'-tah], *f.* 1. Hermitage. 2. (Coll.) Tavern, where wine is sold by retail.
Ermitaña [er-me-tah'-nyah], *f.* Hermitess.
Ermitaño [er-me-tah'-nyo], *m.* Hermit, one who takes care of a hermitage.
Ermitorio [er-me-to'-re-o], *m.* *V.* EREMITORIO.
Ermunia [er-moo'-ne-ah], *f.* A certain kind of earth which needs constant moisture in order to be productive.
Ermunio [er-moo'-ne-o], *m.* Name formerly given to persons exempted from every kind of tribute and service.
Erogación [ay-ro-gah-the-on'], *f.* (Littl. us.) Erogation, distribution, fees, expense.
Erogar [ay-ro-gar'], *va.* To distribute, to divide, to erogate, to spend in fees or judicial proceedings.
Erogatorio [ay-ro-gah-to'-re-o], *m.* Pipe through which liquor is drawn.
Erosión [ay-ro-se-on'], *f.* Erosion, corrosion.
Eróticamente [ay-ro'-te-cah-men-tay], *adv.* Erotically, in an erotic manner.
Erótico, ca [ay-ro'-te-co, cah], *a.* Erotical, erotic, belonging to love ; voluptuous, sensual.
Erótilo [ay-ro'-te-lo], *m.* A beetle of Mexico and South America.
Erótema [ay-ro'-tay-mah], *f.* (Rhet.) Interrogation.
Erotismo [ay-ro-tees'-mo], *m.* 1. A violent love. 2. Sensuality.
Erotomania [ay-ro-to-mah-nee'-ah], *f.* Erotomania, love-madness.
Erpetologia [er-pay-to-lo-hee'-ah], *f.* Herpetology, that branch of zoology which treats of reptiles.
Errabundo, da [er-rah-boon'-do, dah], *a.* Wandering, strolling about.
Errada [er-rah'-dah], *f.* A miss, in billiards.
Erradamente [er-rah-da-men'-tay], *adv.* Erroneously, falsely, faultily, mistakenly, mistakingly, erratically.
Erradicación [er-rah-de-ca-the-on'], *f.* Eradication, extirpation.
Erradicar [er-rah-de-car'], *va.* To eradicate, to pull up by the roots.
Erradizo, za [er-rah-dee'-tho, thah], *a.* Wandering to and fro.
Errado, da, *a.* & *pp.* of ERRAR. Mistaken, erring, erroneous.
Erraj [er-rah'], *m.* Fine coal made from the stones of olives.
Errante [er-rahn'-tay], *pa.* & *a.* Errant, erring, roving, wandering, rambling ; excursive, nomadic.
Errar [er-rar'], *va.* 1. To err, to commit errors. 2. To misjudge, to mistake. 3. (Obs.) Not to perform one's engagements. 4. To offend any one. —*vn.* To wander about without knowing one's way. *Errar el camino,* To miss the right way. *Errar el golpe,* To miss a blow. (Met.) To miss one's aim.
Errata [er-rah'-tah], *f.* Error in writing or printing ; erratum. *Erratas* or *fe de erratas,* Errata, the faults of the printer.
Errático, ca [er-rah'-te-co, cah], *a.* Wandering, vagabond, vagrant, erratic or erratical.
Errátil [er-rah'-teel], *a.* (Coll.) Wavering, not firm or steady.
Erre [er'-ray], *f.* The Spanish name of the letter R. *Erre que erre,* Pertinaciously, obstinately.
Erróneamente [er-ro'-nay-ah-men-tay], *adv.* Erroneously, mistakenly, faultily, falsely.
Erróneo, nea [er-ro'-nay-o, ah], *a.* Erroneous, mistaken, not comformable to truth : applied to doctrines or opinions.
Erronia [er-ro-nee'-ah], *f.* (Coll.) Opposition, hatred.
Error [er-ror'], *m.* 1. Error, mistake, involuntary deviation from truth, misapprehension, misbelief, misconception, hallucination. 2. Mispersuasion, misguidance. 3. Deceit, falsity, illusion. 4. Deficiency, fault, defect.
Erubescencia [ay-roo-bes-then'-the-ah], *f.* Erubescence, the act of blushing.
Eructación [ay-rooc-tah-the-on'], *f.* Eructation, belching.
Eructar [ay-rooc-tar'], *vn.* To belch, to eructate.
Eructo [ay-rooc'-to], *m.* Belching, eructation.
Erudición [ay-roo-de-the-on'], *f.* Erudition, learning, knowledge, letters.
Eruditamente, *adv.* Learnedly.
Erudito, ta [ay-roo-dee'-to, tah], *a.* Erudite, learned, lettered.
Eruginoso, sa [ay-roo-he-no'-so, sah], *a.* That which is thick, coarse, and knotty.
Erupción [ay-roop-the-on'], *f.* Eruption, outbreak, bursting forth.
Eruptivo, va [ay-roop-tee'-vo, vah], *a.* Eruptive.
Erutación [ay-roo-tah-the-on'], *f.* Eructation, belching.
Erutar [ay-roo-tar'], *vn.* *V.* ERUCTAR.
Eruto [ay-roo'-to], *m.* *V.* ERUCTO.
Ervato [er-vah'-to], *m.* (Bot.) Sea sulphur-wort or officinal sulphur-wort, hog's-fennel. Peucedanum officinale.
Ervellada [er-vel-lyah'-dah], *f.* (Bot.) Bean-trefoil. Cytisus hirsutus.
Ervilla [er-veel'-lyah], *f.* (Bot.) Seed of the bitter vetch. *V.* ARBEJA.
Esa [ay'-sah]. A demonstrative pronoun of the feminine gender. That.
Esbatimentar [es-bah-te-men-tar'], *va.* (Art.) To delineate a shadow.—*vn.* To cast the shadow of one body on another.
Esbatimento [es-bah-te-men'-to], *m.* Shade in a picture.
Esbeltez [es-bel-teth'], *f.* Slenderness, gracefulness.
Esbelto, ta [es-bel'-to, tah], *a.* Slender, svelte, graceful.
Esbirro [es-bir'-ro], *m.* Bailiff, apparitor ; a petty officer of courts of justice, a myrmidon.
Esbozar [es-bo-thar'], *va.* To outline, to sketch, to make a plan.
Esbozo [es-bo'-tho], *m.* (Pict.) Sketch, outline ; a rough draught.
Esca [ays'-cah], *f.* 1. Food, nourishment. 2. Bait for hunting or fishing.
Escabechar [es-cah-bay-char'], *va.* To souse, to steep in pickle, to pickle.
Escabeche [es-cah-bay'-chay], *m.* Souse, pickle ; pickled fish.
Escabel [es-cah-bel'], *m.* 1. Foot-stool ; small seat. 2. A small seat of boards, without back.
Escabelillo [es-cah-bay-leel'-lyo], *m. dim.* A small foot-stool.
Escabelón [es-cah-bay-lone'], *m.* (Arch.) A kind of pedestal.
Escabiosa [es-cah-be-o'-sah], *f.* (Bot.) Field-scabious. Scabiosa arvensis.
Escabioso, sa [es-cah-be-o'-so, sah], *a.* (Med.) Scabious ; relating to scabies, or the itch.
Escabro [es-cah'-bro], *m.* 1. A kind of scab, itch, or mange in sheep. 2. The large amphibious crab. 3. A roughness, like mange, which grows upon the bark of trees and vines.
Escabrosamente [es-cah-bro-sah-men'-tay], *adv.* Roughly, ruggedly.
Escabrosearse [es-cah-bro-say-ar'-say], *vr.* (Obs.) To be offended or irritated, to take offence.
Escabrosidad [es-cah-bro-se-dahd'], *f.* 1. Roughness, unevenness. 2. Difficulty, hardness. 3. Sharpness.
Escabroso, sa [es-cah-bro'-so, sah], *a.* 1. Rough, uneven. 2. Very difficult, thorny. 3. Scabrous.
Escabullimiento [es-cah-bool-lyee-me-en'-to], *m.* Evasion, slipping away, act of escaping.
Escabullirse [es-cah-bool-lyeer'-say], *vr.* To escape, to evade ; to slip away, to slip through one's hands.
Escacado, da [es-cah-cah'-do, dah], *a.* (Her.) Checkered, variegated, like a chess-board.
Escachar [es-cah-char'], *va.* (Prov.) To smash, to squash.—*vr.* To prick.
Escacharrar [es-cah-char-rar'], *va.* 1. To break, to smash. 2. (Fig.) To ruin, to wreck.
Escachifollar [es-cah-che-fol-lyar'], *va.* To humiliate.
Escafandra, *f.* **Escafandro,** *m.* [es-cah-fahn'-drah, es-cah-fahn'-dro]. Diving suit. *Escafandra autónoma,* Scuba. *Escafandra espacial,* Space suit. *Escafandra rígida,* Rigid diving suit.
Escafandrero [es-cah-fan-dray'-ro], *m.* Deep-sea diver.
Escafóideo, dea [es-cah-fo'-e-day-o, ah], *a.* Scaphoid, skiff-like.
Escala [es-cah'-lah], *f.* 1. Ladder, scale. 2. Scale, a figure subdivided by lines to measure proportions. 3. Scale, the series of harmonic or musical proportions. 4. Scale, regular graduation. 5. Any port, bay, or road for ships to ride in, in order to get provisions, etc. *Escala del alcázar,* (Naut.) Quarter-deck ladder. *Escala real,* (Naut.) Accommodation ladder. *Escala de la toldilla,* (Naut.) Poop ladder. *Escala de comercio,* A seaport. *Escala franca,* Free port. *A escala vista,* 1. Openly. 2. *V.* ESCALADA.
Escalada [es-cah-lah'-dah], *f.* Escalade, scalado, the act of scaling or storming a place by the help of ladders. *Escalada a escala vista,* A daylight escalade.
Escalado, da [es-cah-lah'-do, dah], *a.* Applied to fish cut open to be salted or cured.—*pp.* of ESCALAR.
Escalador [es-cah-lah-dor'], *m.* Climber, he who scales walls.
Escalafón [es-cah-lah-fon'], *m.* 1. Seniority scale, grade scale. 2. Company roster.
Escalamera [es-cah-lah-may'-rah], *f.* Bar row-lock.
Escalamiento [es-cah-lah-me-en'-to], *m.* Act of scaling walls.
Escálamo [es-cah'-lah-mo], *m.* (Naut.) Thole or thowl, or thowl-pin ; row-lock.
Escalamotes [es-cah-lah-mo'-tes], *m. pl.* (Naut.) Timber-heads, kevel-heads.
Escalante [es-cah-lahn'-tay], *pa.* Scaling, climbing.
Escalar [es-cah-lar'], *va.* To scale, to climb by the help of ladders.
Escaldada [es-cal-dah'-dah], *f.* A woman an very abusive, loose, and lewd in her behaviour.
Escaldado, da [es-cal-dah'-do, dah], *a.* Cautious, suspicious, wary.—*pp.* of ESCALDAR.
Escaldar [es-cal-dar'], *va.* 1. To burn, to scald ; to bathe with very hot water. 2. To make iron red-hot.
Escaldrantes [es-cal-drahn'-tes], *m. pl.* (Naut.) Kevels, wooden pin on which tackle and sails are put to dry.
Escaldrido, da [es-cal-dree'-do, dah], *a.* (Obs.) Cunning, sagacious.
Escaldufar [es-cal-doo-far'], *va.* (Prov.) To take broth out of the pot when it is too full.

Escaleno [es-cah-lay'-no], *a.* (Geom.) Scalene.

Escalentamiento [es-cah-len-tah-me-en'-to], *m.* Inflammation, disease in the feet of animals.

Escalentar [es-cah-len-tar'], *vn.* (Obs.) To foment and preserve the natural heat.

Escalera [es-cah-lay'-rah], *f.* 1. Staircase. 2. Stair. *Escalera de caracol,* A winding stair. 3. Ladder. 4. Sloats of a cart. *Escalera de cabos,* (Naut.) The quarter ladder. *Escalera de costado* or *escalera real,* The quarter-deck ladder.

Escalera mecánica [es-cah-lay'-rah may-cah'-ne-cah], *f.* Escalator.

Escalereja, Escalerilla [es-cah-lay-ray'-hah, es-cah-lay-reel'-lyah], *f.* 1. (Dim.) A small ladder. 2. (Mech.) Rack. 3. Drenching instrument. *En escalerilla,* In degrees.

Escalerón [es-cah-lay-rone'], *m. aug.* A large staircase.

Escaleta [es-cah-lay'-tah], *f.* Engine for raising cannons and mortars on their carriages.

Escalfado, da [es-cal-fah'-do, dah], *a.* Applied to white-washed walls full of blisters.—*pp.* of Escalfar.

Escalfador [es-cal-fah-dor'], *m.* 1. A barber's pan for keeping water warm. 2. Chafing-dish.

Escalfar [es-cal-far'], *va.* 1. To poach eggs. 2. (Obs.) To warm. *Escalfar el pan,* To put bread into an oven which is too hot, and scorches it.

Escalfarote [es-cal-fah-ro'-tay], *m.* A kind of wide boot lined with hay.

Escalfeta [es-cal-fay'-tah], *f.* 1. Small pan, used to hold live coals. 2. Chafing-dish. *V.* Escalfador. 3. Water-dish or water-plate, for keeping meat hot.

Escalimarse [es-cah-le-mar'-say], *vr.* (Naut.) To be split or worked out of the seams of a ship: applied to oakum.

(*Yo escaliento, yo escaliente,* from *Escalentar. V.* Acrecentar.)

Escalinata [es-cah-le-nah'-tah], *f.* A stone staircase in front of an edifice. (It.)

Escalio [es-cah'-le-o], *m.* Land abandoned for tillage.

Escalmo, *m. V.* Escálamo.

Escalofriado, da [es-cah-lo-fre-ah'-do, dah], *a.* Shivering.

Escalofrío [es-cah-lo-free'-o], *m.* Indisposition attended with shivering; cold stage of a fever.

Escalón [es-cah-lone'], *m.* 1. Step of a stair. 2. Degree of dignity. 3. (Mil.) Echelon.

Escalonar [es-cah-lo-nar'], *va.* 1. (Mil.) To echelon. 2. To scale, to place at intervals. 3. To stagger (hours of work, etc.)

Escalpelo [es-cal-pay'-lo], *m.* (Med.) Scalpel, a surgeon's instrument.

Escalplo [es-cahl'-plo], *m.* Currier's knife.

Escaluña [es-cah-loo'-nyah], *f.* (Bot.) Eschalot, shalot, scallion. Allium ascalonicum.

Escama [es-cah'-mah], *f.* 1. Scale, a horny plate, forming the coat of fishes. 2. Scale, any thing exfoliated, a thin lamina. 3. A small scaly piece, many of which, lapping one over another, form a coat of mail. 4. (Met.) Resentment, grudge, deep sense of injury. 5. (Bot.) Scale, an abortive, rudimentary leaf.

Escamada [es-cah-mah'-dah], *f.* Embroidery in figure of scales.

Escamado [es-cah-mah'-do], *m.* Work wrought with the figure of scales.

Escamado, da [es-cah-mah'-do, dah], *a.* & *pp.* of Escamar. Tutored by experience.

Escamadura [es-cah-mah-doo'-rah], *f.* Act of embroidering like scales.

Escamar [es-cah-mar'], *va.* 1. To scale fish. 2. (Met.) To offend, to irritate, to molest.—*vn.* To embroider scale or shell fashion.—*vr.* To be tutored by painful experience, to resent, to take ill.

Escambronal [es-cam-bro-nahl'], *m.* Plantation of buckthorns.

Escamel [es-cah-mel'], *m.* Instrument used by sword-makers; long arm of an anvil on which the sword is laid to beat it out.

Escamilla, ita [es-cah-meel'-lyah, ee'-tah], *f. dim.* A little scale.

Escamochear [es-cah-mo-chay-ar'], *vn.* (Prov.) *V.* Pavordear.

Escamocho [es-cah-mo'-cho], *m.* 1. Broken victuals, leavings. 2. (Prov.) A rickety and languid person.

Escamonda [es-cah-mon'-dah], *f.* The act of pruning trees.

Escamondadura [es-cah-mon-dah-doo'-rah], *f.* Useless branches of trees.

Escamondar [es-cah-mon-dar'], *va.* 1. To prune or clear trees of noxious excrescences. 2. To clean, to cleanse.

Escamondo [es-cah-mon'-do], *m.* Clearing trees of useless branches.

Escamonea [es-cah-mo-nay'-ah], *f.* (Bot.) Scammony. Convolvulus scammonia.

Escamoneado, da [es-cah-mo-nay-ah'-do, dah], *a.* Relating to scammony.—*pp.* of Escamonearse.

Escamonearse [es-cah-mo-nay-ar'-say], *vr.* (Coll.) To resent, to take ill, to be offended.

Escamoso, sa [es-cah-mo'-so, sah], *a.* Scaly, ostraceous, squamous.

Escamotar [es-cah-mo-tar'], *va.* In jugglery, to palm, to make a thing disappear from among the hands.

Escamoteador, ra [es-cah-mo-tay-ah-dor', rah], *m.* & *f.* A juggler, prestidigitateur.

Escamotear [es-cah-mo-tay-ar'], *va. V.* Escamotar.

Escamoteo [es-cah-mo-tay'-o], *m.* Jugglery, sleight of hand.

Escampada [es-cam-pah'-dah], *f.* Stampede.

Escampado, da [es-cam-pah'-do, dah], *a. V.* Descampado.—*pp.* of Escampar.

Escampar [es-cam-par'], *vn.* 1. To cease raining. 2. To leave off working.—*va.* To clean or clear out a place. *Ya escampa,* (Coll.) It is importunate babbling.

Escampavía [es-cam-pa-vee'-ah], *f.* (Naut.) A light craft.

Escamudo, da [es-cah-moo'-do, dah], *a. V.* Escamoso.

Escamujar [es-cah-moo-har'], *va.* To prune olive-trees, to lop off the superfluous branches.

Escamujo [es-cah-moo'-ho], *m.* 1. A lopped-off branch of an olive-tree. 2. Time of pruning olive-trees.

Escanciador, ra [es-can-the-ah-dor', rah], *m.* & *f.* Cup-bearer, the person that serves with wine at feasts.

Escanciar [es-can-the-ar'], *va.* 1. To pour wine from one vessel into another to drink. 2. To drink wine. Much used in poetic style.

Escanda [es-cahn'-dah], *f.* (Bot.) Spelt-wheat. Triticum spelta.

Escandalar [es-can-dah-lar'], *m.* Apartment for the compass.

Escandalizador, ra [es-can-dah-le-thah-dor', rah], *m* & *f.* One who scandalizes.

Escandalizar [es-can-dah-le-thar'], *va.* To scandalize, to offend by a scandalous action.—*vr.* 1. To be scandalized. 2. To be irritated. 3. To be amazed, to wonder (at).

Escandalizativo, va [es-can-dah-le-thah-tee'-vo, vah], *a.* Scandalous.

Escandallar [es-can-dal-lyar'], *va.* (Naut.) To sound.

Escandallo [es-can-dahl'-lyo], *m.* 1. (Naut.) Deep- sea lead. 2. (Met.) Proof, trial.

Escándalo [es-cahn'-dah-lo], *m.* 1. Scandal, offence given by the faults of others. 2. Admiration, astonishment. 3. Tumult, commotion.

Escandalosa [es-can-dah-lo'-sah], *f.* (Naut.) Gaff-sail.

Escandalosamente, *adv.* Scandalously, shamefully.

Escandaloso, sa [es-can-dah-lo'-so, sah], *a.* 1. Scandalous, giving public offence. 2. Scandalous, shameful, disgraceful. 3. Turbulent.

Escandecencia [es-can-day-then'-the-ah], *f.* 1. Candescence, the state of growing hot. 2. Heat, anger, passion. *V.* Excandecencia.

Escandecer [es-can-day-therr'], *va. V.* Excandecer.

Escandelar [es-can-day-lar'], *m.* (Naut.) The second cabin in a row-galley.

Escandelarete [es-can-day-lah-ray'-tay], *m.* (Naut.) A small cabin in a row-galley.

Escandia [es-cahn'-de-ah], *f.* (Bot.) Cienfuegos wheat. Triticum cienfuegos.

Escandinavo, va [es-can-de-nah'-vo, vah], *a.* Scandinavian.

Escandir [es-can-deer'], *va.* (Poet. Obs.) To scan verses.

Escanilla [es-ca-neel'-lyah], *f.* (Prov.) *V.* Cuna.

Escantillado [es-can-teel-lyah'-do], *m. V.* Escantillón.

Escantillar [es-can-til-lyar'], *va.* To trace lines on walls, to make them of different colours.

Escantillón [es-can-teel-lyon'], *m.* 1. Gauge, pattern, templet, rule. 2. Angle formed by two walls. 3. (Mil.) Semi-circular modelling-board to measure the exterior diameters of pieces of artillery.

Escaña [es-cah'-nyah], *f.* (Bot.) Saint Peter's corn, or one-grained wheat. Triticum monococcum.

Escañero [es-cah-nyay'-ro], *m.* Seat-keeper, one who takes care of seats and benches in council-chambers or courts.

Escañillo [es-cah-nyeel'-lyo], *m. dim.* A small bench or form with a back.

Escaño [es-cah'-nyo], *m.* 1. Bench or form with a back. 2. (Naut.) Sheer-rail, which divides the quick works from the dead works.

Escañuelo [es-cah-nyoo-ay'-lo], *m.* Small bench placed at the feet.

Escapada, *f.* **Escapamiento,** *m.* [es-cah-pah'-dah]. Escape, flight, escapade.

Escapar [es-cah-par'], *va.* To liberate from danger; to slip from the memory.—*vn.* & *vr.* To escape, to flee, to get out of danger, to avoid punishment, to flee away or to get away off, to make off, to make one's escape. *Escapar en una tabla,* To have a happy escape.

Escaparate [es-cah-pa-rah'-tay], *m.* 1. Press, case, cupboard. 2. Show-window of a shop.

Escaparatico [es-cah-pa-rah-tee'-co], *m. dim.* A little cupboard.

Escapatoria [es-cah-pa-to'-re-ah], *f.* 1. Escape, flying, flight. 2. Escape, excuse, evasion, subterfuge, loophole.

Escape [es-cah'-pay], *m.* 1. Escape, flight, escaping. 2. Flying, flight. 3. Escape, subterfuge, evasion. *A todo escape,* At full speed. 4. Leak. 5. Exhaust **exhaust valve.**

Escapo [es-cah'-po], *m.* 1. (Arch.) Shaft of a column without base or capital. 2. (Bot.) Scape, a stem rising from the root, and bearing nothing but flowers.

Escápula [es-cah'-poo-lah], *f.* (Anat.) Scapula, shoulder-blade.

Escapular [es-cah-poo-lar'], *va.* (Naut.) To double or clear a cape.—*a.* Scapular, relating to the shoulder-blade.

Escapulario [es-cah-poo-lah'-re-o], *m.* 1. Scapulary, a part of the habit of various religious orders. 2. Two small slips of cloth or flannel, on one of which an image of our Lady of Carmen is engraved, painted, or embroidered, worn by many people in Spain under their clothes. 3. (Med.) Shoulder-strap.

Escaque [es-cah'-kay], *m.* 1. Any of the squares of a chess-board. 2. (Her.) Any of the squares of a coat of arms. —*pl.* 1. Checker-work of a draught or chess-board. 2. Any work resembling the checkers of a draught or chess-board. 3. The game of chess.

Escaqueado, da [es-cah-kay-ah'-do, dah], *a.* Checkered, variegated with alternate colours.—*pp.* of Escaquear.

Escaquear [es-cah-kay-ar'], *va.* (Littl. us.) To divide (a tablet or shield) into squares.

Escara [es-cah'-rah], *f.* (Med.) 1. The scurf or crust of a sore. 2. Eschar, a hard crust or scar made by caustics.

Escarabajear [es-cah-rah-bah-hay-ar'], *vn.* 1. To crawl to and fro like insects. 2. To scrawl, to scribble. 3. (Coll.) To sting, to give pain, to disquiet, to harass.

Escarabajo [es-cah-rah-bah'-ho], *m.* 1. (Ent.) The common black-beetle, tumble-bug, dung-beetle. Scarabæus. 2. Nickname given to a thick, short, ill-shaped person.

Escarabídeo, dea [es-cah-rah-bee'-day-o, ah], *a.* Scarabæid, like a tumble-bug.

Escarafullar [es-cah-rah-fool-lyar'], *vn.* To deceive, to gloss over.

Escaramucear [es-cah-rah-moo-thay-ar'], *vn.* To skirmish.

Escaramujo [es-cah-rah-moo'-ho], *m.* 1. (Bot.) Dog-rose, hep-tree; hep. Rosa canina. 2. (Zool.) A kind of marine small snail which clings to the hull of vessels.

Escaramuza [es-cah-rah-moo'-thah], *f.* 1. Skirmish, slight engagement. 2. (Met.) Skirmish, contest, dispute, quarrel, contention.

Escaramuzador [es-cah-rah-moo-thah-dor'], *m.* 1. Skirmisher. 2. (Met.) Disputer.

Escaramuzar [es-cah-rah-moo-thar'], *vn.* 1. To skirmish, to fight loosely. 2. (Met.) To dispute, quarrel; rarely used in this sense.

Escarapela [es-cah-rah-pay'-lah], *f.* 1. Dispute which terminates in blows: applied commonly to a fray among women. 2. Cockade worn in the hat.

Escarapelar [es-cah-rah-pay-lar'], *vn.* & *vr.* 1. To dispute, to wrangle, to quarrel: generally used of women. 2. *vr.* (Peru. and S. A.) To have the hair stand on end; to cringe upon hearing sharp noises.

Escarbadero [es-car-bah-day'-ro], *m.* Place where boars, wolves, and other animals scrape or scratch the ground.

Escarbadientes [es-car-bah-de-en'-tes], *m.* *V.* Mondadientes.

Escarbador [es-car-bah-dor'], *m.* Scratcher, scraper.

Escarbadura [es-car-bah-doo'-rah], *f.* Act and effect of scratching.

Escarbajuelo [es-car-bah-hoo-ay'-lo], *m.* (Ent.) Vine-fretter. Curculio bacchus.

Escarbaorejas [es-car-bah-o-ray'-has], *m.* Ear-pick.

Escarbar [es-car-bar'], *va.* 1. To scrape or scratch the earth, as fowls. 2. (Met.) To inquire minutely, to investigate.

Escarbo [es-car'-bo], *m.* Act and effect of scraping or scratching.

Escarcela [es-car-thay'-lah], *f.* 1. A large pouch fastened to the girdle; sportsman's net for catching game. 2. Cuish, armour which covers the thigh. 3. Kind of head-dress for women.

Escarceo [es-car-thay'-o], *m.* Small broken waves occasioned by currents. *Escarceos*, Bounds and windings of spirited horses.

Escarcina [es-car-thee'-nah], *f.* 1 A kind of cutlass. 2. A fish like that called *doncella*.

Escarcinazo [es-car-the-nah'-tho], *m.* Blow with a cutlass.

Escarcuñar [es-car-coo-nyar'], *va.* (Prov.) *V.* Escudriñar.

Escarcha [es-car'-chah], *f.* 1. Hoar frost, rime. 2. The frozen watery vapours observable on windows and other articles of glass; frost-work.

Escarchada [es-car-chah'-dah], *f.* (Bot.) Ice-plant, fig marigold. Mesembryanthemum crystallinum, *L.*

Escarchado [es-car-chah'-do], *m.* 1. A kind of gold or silver twist. 2. Frosting upon cakes and confectionery.

Escarchado, da, *a.* & *pp.* of Escarchar. Hoary, white with frost.

Escarchador [es-car-chah-dor'], *m.* Freezing tool, a device in mints for thinning the nibs of ingots so as to make them pass through the gauge-plate.

Escarchar [es-car-char'], *vn.* To be frozen or congealed: applied in particular to dew and watery vapours.—*va.* 1. To dilute potter's clay with water. 2. To put frost-work, shining points, upon confections. 3. To thin nibs of ingots, in mints.

Escarche [es-car'-chay], *m.* A kind of gold or silver flat wire for embroidery.

Escarcho [es-car'-cho], *m.* (Zool.) Red surmullet. Mullus barbatus.

Escarchosa [es-car-cho'-sah], *f.* (Bot.) Ice-plant, fig-marigold. Mesembryanthemum crystallinum.

Escarda [es-car'-dah], *f.* 1. Weed-hook. 2. The act of weeding corn-fields.

Escardadera [es-car-dah-day'-rah], *f.* 1. Woman employed to clear corn-fields of weeds or noxious herbs. 2. A gardener's hoe.

Escardador, ra [es-car-dah-dor', rah], *m.* & *f.* Weeder, a man or woman who weeds corn-fields.

Escardadura [es-car-dah-doo'-rah], *f.* or **Escardamiento**, *m.* Weeding.

Escardar [es-car-dar'], *va.* 1. To weed corn-fields. 2. (Met.) To weed, to part good from bad; to root out vice. *Enviar a escardar*, (Coll.) To refuse harshly.

Escardillar [es-car-deel-lyar'], *va.* *V.* Escardar.

Escardillo, lla [es-car-deel'-lyo, lyah], *m.* & *f.* 1. Small weed-hook. 2. Thistle-down.

Escariador [es-cah-re-ah-dor'], *m.* Kind of punch used by coppersmiths; reamer.

Escariar [es-cah-re-ar'], *va.* To ream, to widen a hole or the interior of a tube, by using the reamer.

Escarificación [es-cah-re-fe-cah-the-on'], *f.* (Med.) Scarification.

Escarificador [es-cah-re-fe-cah-dor'], *m.* (Med.) Scarifier, scarificator; cupping-glass.

Escarificar [es-cah-re-fe-car'], *va.* (Surg.) To scarify.

Escarioso, sa [es-cah-re-o'-so, sah], *a.* (Bot.) Scarious, like a thin scale.

Escarizar [es-cah-re-thar'], *va.* (Surg.) To clean a sore by taking away the scurf or scab.

Escarlador [es-car-lah-dor'], *m.* Iron instrument for polishing combs.

Escarlata [es-car-lah'-tah], *f.* 1. Scarlet, a colour. 2. Scarlet, cloth dyed with a scarlet colour. 3. Scarlet-fever, scarlatina.

Escarlatín [es-car-lah-teen'], *m.* (Obs.) A coarse kind of scarlet.

Escarlatina [es-car-lah-tee'-nah], *f.* 1. (Com.) A red or crimson woollen fabric. 2. (Med.) Scarlatina, scarlet-fever, a contagious eruptive fever.

Escarmenador [es-car-may-nah-dor'], *m.* *V.* Escarpidor.

Escarmenar [es-car-may-nar'], *va.* 1. To comb, to pick wool, silk, etc.; to disentangle what is twisted. 2. To punish any one by depriving him of his money. 3. To cheat.

Escarmentado, da [es-car-men-tah'-do, dah], *a.* Punished (by experience).

Escarmentar [es-car-men-tar'], *vn.* To be tutored by experience, to take warning.—*va.* 1. To correct severely, to inflict an exemplary punishment.

Escarmiento [es-car-me-en'-to], *m.* 1. Warning, caution. 2. Fine, mulct, chastisement.

(*Yo escarmiento, yo escarmiente*, from *Escarmentar*. *V.* Acrecentar.)

Escarnecedor, ra [es-car-nay-thay-dor', rah], *m.* & *f.* Scoffer, scorner, jeerer, giber, mocker, flinger.

Escarnecer [es-car-nay-therr'], *va.* To scoff, to mock, to ridicule, to jeer, to gibe, to laugh at.

(*Yo escarnezco, yo escarnezca*, from *Escarnecer*. *V.* Conocer.)

Escarnecidamente, *adv.* Scornfully.

Escarnecimiento [es-car-nay-the-me-en'-to], *m.* Scoffing; derision.

Escarnido, da [es-car-nee'-do, dah], *a.* *V.* Descarnado.

Escarnio [es-car'-ne-o], *m.* 1. Scoff, contemptuous ridicule. 2. Gibe, jeer, jeering, mock, flout. *A escarnio* or *en escarnio*, (Obs.) Scoffingly.

Escaro [es-cah'-ro], *m.* 1. (Zool.) A kind of mutton fish, abounding between Candia and Rhodes. Labrus scarus. 2. One who has crooked feet.

Escarola [es-cah-ro'-lah], *f.* 1. (Bot.) Endive, garden-succory. Cichorium endivia. 2. Plaited frill round the neck, ruff.

Escarolado, da [es-cah-ro-lah'-do, dah], *a.* 1. Of the endive colour. 2. Curled. —*pp.* of Escarolar.

Escarolar [es-cah-ro-lar'], *va.* *V.* Alechugar.

Escarolero, ra [es-cah-ro-lay'-ro, rah], *m.* & *f.* One who sells endives.

Escarolita [es-cah-ro-lee'-tah], *f. dim.* A small endive.

Escarótico, ca [es-cah-ro'-te-co, cah], *a.* Escharotic, caustic.

Escarpa [es-car'-pah], *f.* 1. Declivity or gradual descent of a place. 2. (Mil.) Scarp, or escarp, the talus or slope on the inside of a ditch toward the rampart.

Escarpado, da [es-car-pah'-do, dah], *a.* Sloped, craggy, rugged, crabbed.—*pp.* of Escarpar.—*m.* (Arch.) *V.* Escarpe.

Escarpar [es-car-par'], *va.* 1. (Naut.) To scarf or join timbers. 2. To rasp or cleanse works of sculpture. 3. (Mil.) To escarp, to slope down.

Escarpe [es-car'-pay], *m.* 1. Declivity, sloped bank. 2. (Arch.) The scarf of a wall, a lapped joint. 3. (Naut.) A scarf-joint.

Escarpelar [es-car-pay-lar'], *va.* (Anat.) To scalp.

Escarpelo [es-car-pay'-lo], *m.* 1. Rasp, a coarse file. 2. (Surg. Obs.) Scalpel.
Escarpia [es-car'-pe-ah], *f.* 1. Tenter-hook. 2. Meat-hook, flesh-hook.
Escarpidor [es-car-pe-dor'], *m.* Comb with large wide teeth.
Escarpin [es-car-peen'], *m.* 1. Sock, half-hose. 2. Shoe with a thin sole and low heel, a pump.
Escarpión (En) [es-car-pe-on'], *adv.* In the form of a tenter or hook.
Escartivana [es-car-te-vah'-nah], *f.* A strip of paper or linen for binding maps or engravings.
Escarza [es-car'-thah], *f.* 1. A sore in the hoofs of horses or mules. 2. An opening for discovering a tumour.
Escarzamiento, *m.* or **Escarzadura,** *f.* [es-car-thah-me-en'-to, es-car-thah-doo'-rah]. Act and effect of removing honey-combs.
Escarzano, na [es-car-thah'-no, nah], *a.* (Arch.) Applied to an arch which is less than a semicircle.
Escarzar [es-car-thar'], *va.* To remove the honey-comb from a hive in February.
Escarzo [es-car'-tho], *m.* 1. Blackish green honey-comb found in the hive without honey. 2. Operation and time of removing honey from a hive. 3. Fungi on the trunks of trees. 4. Floss silk.
Escarzo, za [es-car'-tho, thah], *a.* Lame on account of sores in the hoof: applied to mules and horses.
Escasamente [es-cah-sah-men'-tay], *adv.* 1. Scantily, sparingly, miserably. 2. Hardly, scarcely, difficultly; narrowly.
Escaseada [es-cah-say-ah'-dah], **Escaseadura,** *f.* (Naut.) Lack of wind.
Escasear [es-cah-say-ar'], *va.* 1. To give sparingly and grudgingly. 2. To spare, to live in a frugal manner.—*vn.* 1. To grow less, to decrease, to be wanting. 2. (Naut.) To grow scanty: applied to the wind.
Escasez, Escaseza [es-cah-seth', es-cah-say'-thah], *f.* 1. Scantiness, niggardliness, meagreness; hardiness. 2. Want, lack. 3. Poverty.
Escaso, sa [es-cah'-so, sah], *a.* 1. Small, short, limited; little. 2. Sparing, parsimonious, niggardly. 3. Scanty, defective, narrow; hard; churlish.
Escatimado, da [es-cah-te-mah'-do, dah], *a.* Little, scanty.—*pp.* of ESCATIMAR.
Escatimar [es-cah-te-mar'], *va.* 1. To curtail, to lessen, to clip. 2. To haggle, to be tedious in a bargain. 3. To corrupt the meaning of words. 4. (Obs.) To examine closely.
Escatimosamente, *adv.* Maliciously, viciously.
Escatimoso, sa [es-cah-te-mo'-so, sah], *a.* Cunning, malicious.
Escatofagio, gia [es-cah-to-fah'-he-o, ah], *a.* Scatophagous, dung-eating.
Escaupil [es-cah-oo-peel'], *m.* Armour used by the Mexicans before the conquest.
Escayola [es-cah-yo'-lah], *f.* Paste or composition resembling marble in appearance.
Escena [es-thay'-nah], *f.* 1. The stage. 2. Scene, part of a play. 3. (Met.) Revolution, vicissitude. 4. Bed and shepherd's hut made of branches. 5. A spectacle.
Escenario [es-thay-nah'-re-o], *m.* The stage.
Escénico, ca [es-thay'-ne-co, cah], *a.* Scenic, belonging to the stage.
Escenificación [es-thay-ne-fe-cah-the-on'], *f.* Dramatization, adapting for stage or movies.
Escenificar [es-thay-ne-fe-car'], *va.* To dramatize, to stage.
Escenita [es-thay-nee'-tah], *f. dim.* A short scene.
Escenografía [es-thay-no-grah-fee'-ah], *f.* Scenography, the art of perspective.
Escenográfico, ca [es-thay-no-grah'-fe-co, cah], *a.* Scenographic, perspective.
Escenógrafo [es-thay-no'-grah-fo], *m.* An instrument for representing perspective views.
Escépticamente [es-thep'-te-cah-men-tay], *adv.* Sceptically.
Escepticismo [es-thep-te-thees'-mo], *m.* Scepticism.
Escéptico, ca [es-thep'-te-co, cah], *a.* Sceptic, sceptical.
Esciadofillo, lla [es-the-ah-do-feel'-lyo, lyah], *a.* Having parasol-shaped leaves.
Esciagrafía [es-the-ah-grah-fee'-ah], *f.* 1. (Arch.) Sciagraph, the plan of a building in vertical section. 2. The art of correct shading. 3. (Ast.) Sciagraphy, the art of finding the hour by the shadows of heavenly bodies.
Esciágrafo [es-the-ah'-grah-fo], *m.* Sciagrapher.
Esciarro [es-the-ar'-ro], *m.* A stream of lava.
Esciatérico, ca [es-the-ah-tay'-re-co, cah], *a.* Sciatheric, relative to a sun-dial.
Esciaterio [es-the-ah-tay'-re-o], *m.* 1. Gnomon, triangular piece of a sun-dial. 2. Among quarrymen, a dial-plate.
Esciátero [es-the-ah'-tay-ro], *m.* A kind of sun-dial of the ancients. (Gr. σκιαθῆρον.)
Escibalario, ria [es-the-bah-lah'-re-o, ah], *a.* Living in excrement.
Escible [es-thee'-blay], *a.* Worthy of being known. (Archaic. Late Latin scibile.)
Esciena [es-the-ay'-nah], *f.* (Zool.) A species of craw-fish. Sciæna.
Escientífico, ca [es-the-en-tee'-fe-co, cah], *a.* (Obs.) Scientific. *V.* CIENTÍFICO.
Escífula [es-thee'-foo-lah], *f.* A kind of funnel with which certain lichens are provided.
Escila marítima [es-thee'-lah ma-ree'-te-mah], *f.* (Bot.) Squill.
Esciografía, etc. *V.* ESCIAGRAFÍA, etc.
Escisión [es-the-se-on'], *f.* Scission, splitting, fission.
Esclarecer [es-clah-ray-therr'], *va.* 1. To lighten, to produce light; to illuminate. 2. (Met.) To illustrate, to ennoble.—*vn.* To dawn.
Esclarecidamente, *adv.* Illustriously, conspicuously.
Esclarecido, da [es-clah-ray-thee'-do, dah], *a.* Illustrious, noble, conspicuous, eminent, honourable.—*pp.* of ESCLARECER.
Esclarecimiento [es-clah-ray-the-me-en'-to], *m.* 1. Dawn, the morning dawn. 2. Ennoblement, illustriousness, conspicuousness.
Esclavillo, illa; ito, ita [es-clah-veel'-lyo, lyah, vee'-to, vee'-tah], *m. & f. dim.* A little slave.
Esclavina [es-clah-vee'-nah], *f.* 1. A long robe worn by pilgrims. 2. Pilgrim's pall, to which shells are fixed. 3. Collar worn by priests in Spain. 4. Kind of cloth worn over women's shoulders in winter; tippet. 5. Cape of a cloak.
Esclavista [es-clah-vees'-tah], *a.* Pro-slavery.
Esclavitud [es-clah-ve-tood'], *f.* 1. Slavery, bondage, servitude, enslavement, mancipation, slavishness. 2. (Met.) Brotherhood, congregation. 3. (Met.) Servile subjection of passions and sentiments. 4. Ornament of jewels, worn by women on the breast.
Esclavizar [es-clah-ve-thar'], *va.* 1. To enslave, to reduce to slavery. 2. (Met.) To drive, to overwork.
Esclavo, va [es-clah'-vo, vah], *m. & f.* 1. Slave, captive, helot. 2. Member of a brotherhood or confraternity. 3. Fag, one who works hard. 4. (Met.) Slave of one's own desires and passions.
Esclavón, na [es-clah-vone', nah], *a.* Slavonian, belonging to Slavonia. Slavonic language.
Esclerosis [es-clay-ro'-sis], *f.* (Med.) Sclerosis. *Esclerosis múltiple,* Multiple sclerosis.
Esclerótica [es-clay-ro'-te-cah], *f.* Sclerotic, the exterior, pearly white coat of the eye.
Esclusa [es-cloo'-sah], *f.* Lock, sluice, flood-gate, mill-dam.
Escoa [es-co'-ah], *f.* (Naut.) Rung-head, floor-head, floor-timber of the head.
Escoba [es-co'-bah], *f.* 1. Broom, a besom. 2. A tall shrub resembling the Spanish broom in size and colour, from which brooms are made. *La primera mujer escoba, la segunda señora,* The first wife is a slave, the second a lady. *Escoba* or *escoba de cabezuela,* Rag-wort-leaved centaury. Centaurea salmantica, *L.*
Escobada [es-co-bah'-dah], *f.* The act of sweeping slightly.
Escobadera [es-co-bah-day'-rah], *f.* A woman who sweeps, or cleans, with a broom.
Escobajo [es-co-bah'-ho], *m.* 1. The remains of an old broom. 2. The stalk of a bunch of grapes.
Escobar [es-co-bar'], *m.* A place where broom grows.
Escobar, *va.* To sweep with a broom.
Escobazar [es-co-bah-thar'], *va.* To sprinkle water with a broom or brush.
Escobazo [es-co-bah'-tho], *m.* Stroke or blow with a broom.
Escobera [es-co-bay'-rah], *f. V.* RETAMA.
Escobenes [es-co-bay'-nes], *m. pl.* (Naut.) Hawses or hawse-holes.
Escobero, ra [es-co-bay'-ro, rah], *m. & f.* 1. One who makes or sells brooms. 2. A broom used by masons for cleaning stones.—*f. V.* RETAMA.
Escobeta [es-co-bay'-tah], *f.* 1. A small brush. 2. (Bot.) Sweet sultan centaury. Centaurea moschata.
Escobilla [es-co-beel'-lyah], *f.* 1. Brush. 2. A small broom or besom; a whisk. 3. (Bot.) The head of the plume-thistle with which silk is carded. 4. Sweepings of gold or silver in the workshop of a gold or silversmith. 5. A swab for cleaning the touch-hole of a gun.
Escobillón [es-co-beel-lyone'], *m.* (Mil.) Sponge of a cannon.
Escobina [es-co-bee'-nah], *f.* Chips or dust made in boring any thing.
Escobo [es-co'-bo], *m.* Brushwood, briers, brambles.
Escobón [es-co-bone'], *m.* 1. (Aug.) A large broom. 2. Brush, with which a smith sprinkles the fire in his forge. —*pl.* (Naut.) Hawses.
Escocer [es-co-therr'], *va.* 1. To cause a sharp pain, as if the part had been burnt. 2. (Met.) To make one smart or feel a poignant pain. 3. (Met.) To irritate, to provoke.—*vr.* To smart.
Escocés, sa [es-co-thes', thay'-sah], *a.* Scotch.
Escocia [es-co'-the-ah], *f.* (Arch.) Scotia, a semicircular concave moulding around the base of a column.
Escoda [es-co'-dah], *f.* An edged hammer, used by stone-cutters.

Escodadero [es-co-dah-day'-ro], *m.* Place where cattle rub their horns.

Escodar [es-co-dar'], *va.* To hew stones with an edged hammer.

Escofia, *f.* *V.* Cofia.

Escofiar [es-co-fe-ar'], *va.* To dress the head with a net.

Escofieta [es-co-fe-ay'-tah], *f.* Coif, head-tire, women's head-dress of gauze, etc.

Escofina [es-co-fee'-nah], *f.* 1. Rasp, a coarse file used by carpenters. 2. Nail-file, file for corns.

Escofinar [es-co-fe-nar'], *va.* To rasp, to mould wood with a large file.

Escogedor, ra [es-co-hay-dor', rah], *m.* & *f.* Selecter, chooser.

Escoger [es-co-herr'], *va.* To choose, to select, to pick out, to excerpt, to cull, to elect.

Escogidamente [es-co-he-dah-men'-tay], *adv.* 1. Choicely, selectly. 2. Elegantly, nicely.

Escogido, da [es-co-hee'-do, dah], *a.* 1. Select, choice. 2. Chosen.

Escogimiento [es-co-he-me-en'-to], *m.* (Littl. us.) Choice, selection, choosing.

Escolar [es-co-lar'], *m.* Scholar, student, clerk, learner.—*a.* Scholastic, scholastical.

Escolar [es-co-lar'], *vn.* *V.* Colar.

Escolásticamente [es-co-lahs'-te-cah-men-tay], *adv.* Scholastically.

Escolasticismo [es-co-las-te-thees'-mo], *m.* Scholasticism, Aristotelian philosophy.

Escolástico, ca [es-co-lahs'-te-co, cah], *a.* Scholastic, scholastical, pertaining to schools.

Escolástico [es-co-lahs'-te-co], *m.* A professor of theology.

Escoliador [es-co-le-ah-dor'], *m.* Scholiast, a writer of explanatory notes.

Escoliar [es-co-le-ar'], *va.* To gloss, to explain, to comment.

Escolimado, da [es-co-le-mah'-do, dah], *a.* Weak, delicate.

Escolimoso, sa [es-co-le-mo'-so, sah], *a.* Difficult, severe, hard to please.

Escolio [es-co'-le-o], *m.* 1. Scholion or scholium, a brief explanatory observation. 2. Gloss, commentary. 3. (Geom.) Note which refers to a preceding proposition.

Escoliosis [es-co-le-o'-sis], *f.* (Med.) Scoliosis, lateral curvature of the spinal column.

Escolopendra [es-co-lo-pen'-drah], *f.* 1. (Ent.) Scolopendra, centipede, a myriapod insect. Scolopendra forficata. 2. A fish. 3. (Bot.) Spleenwort, common hart's-tongue. Asplenium scolopendrium.

Escolta [es-col'-tah], *f.* Escort, convoy, guard.

Escoltar [es-col-tar'], *va.* To escort, to convoy, to guard.

Escollera [es-col-lyay'-rah], *f.* (Naut.) Rocky place or cliff.

Escollo [es-col'-lyo], *m.* 1. A shelf in the sea, or a rock under shallow water; a reef. 2. (Met.) Embarrassment, difficulty, danger.

Escombra [es-com'-brah], *f.* Purgation, removal of obstacles.

Escombrar [es-com-brar'], *va.* To remove obstacles, to free from obstructions; to purify.

Escombro [es-com'-bro], *m.* 1. Rubbish, fragments of materials used in building. 2. (Zool.) Mackerel. Scomber scombrus. The Spanish mackerel is Scomberomorus maculatus.

Escomerse [es-co-merr'-say], *va.* To be wasted or worn out with use or time.

Esconce [es-con'-thay], *m.* Corner, angle.

Escondedero [es-con-day-day'-ro], *m.* A hiding or lurking place.

Escondedijo, Escondedrijo [es-con-day-dee'-ho, es-con-day-dree'-ho], *m.* (Obs.) *V.* Escondrijo.

Esconder [es-con-derr'], *va.* 1. To hide, to conceal, to keep in, to keep out of sight. 2. (Met.) To disguise, to dissemble. 3. To include, to contain.—*vr.* To hide, to lie hid, to be concealed, to skulk.

Escondidamente [es-con-de-dah-men'-tay], *adv.* Privately, secretly, hiddenly.

Escondidas (A), A escondidillas [es-con-dee'-das, ah es-con-de-deel'-lyas], *adv.* Privately, in a secret manner.

Escondimiento [es-con-de-me-en'-to], *m.* Concealment, concealing, the act of hiding or concealing any thing.

Escondite [es-con-dee'-tay], *m.* Concealment, hold, a lurking-place, a hiding-place. *Juego de escondite*, Hide and seek.

Escondrijo [es-con-dree'-ho], *m.* Concealment, a hiding or lurking-place.

Escontra, *adv.* (Obs.) *V.* Hacia.

Escontrete [es-con-tray'-tay], *m.* (Naut.) Prop, stay, shore.

Esconzado, da [es-con-thah'-do, dah], *a.* Angular, oblique.

Escopa [es-co'-pah], *f.* A kind of a chisel for chipping or cutting stones.

Escoperada [es-co-pay-rah'-dah], *f.* Gunwale. Old form *Escoperadura.*

Escopero [es-co-pay'-ro], *m.* (Naut.) Pitch-brush for paying the seams of ships; swab.

Escopeta [es-co-pay'-tah], *f.* A firelock, a gun *Escopeta de viento*, An air-gun. *A tiro de escopeta*, 1. Within gun-shot. 2. (Met.) At first view, easily.

Escopetar [es-co-pay-tar'], *va.* To dig out gold-mines.

Escopetazo [es-co-pay-tah'-tho], *m.* 1. Gun or musket-shot. 2. Wound made by a gun-shot.

Escopetear [es-co-pay-tay-ar'], *va.* To discharge a firelock or gun repeatedly.—*vr.* 1. To discharge firelocks at each other. 2. (Met.) To insult each other with foul language.

Escopeteo [es-co-pay-tay'-o], *m.* Act of discharging firelocks.

Escopetería [es-co-pay-tay-ree'-ah], *f.* 1. Infantry armed with muskets. 2. Multitude of gun-shot wounds.

Escopetero [es-co-pay-tay'-ro], *m.* 1. (Obs.) Musketeer. 2. Gunsmith, armourer.

Escopetilla [es-co-pay-teel'-lyah], *f. dim.* A small gun.

Escopetón [es-co-pay-tone'], *m. aug.* A large gun.

Escopleadura [es-co-play-ah-doo'-rah], *f.* Mortise-hole.

Escoplear [es-co-play-ar'], *va.* To chisel, to cut with a chisel.

Escoplillo, ito [es-co-pleel'-lyo, ee'-to], *m. dim.* A small chisel.

Escoplo [es-co'-plo], *m.* Chisel.

Escopo [es-co'-po], *m.* (Obs.) Scope, aim, purpose.

Escora [es-co'-rah], *f.* 1. Stanchion, prop, outrigger. 2. (Naut.) That part of a ship's side which makes the most resistance; the central line of a vessel. *Navío de escora baja*, A ship which carries a stiff sail. *Escoras*, (Naut.) Shores, outriggers.

Escorar [es-co-rar'], *va.* 1. (Naut.) To prop, to shore up. 2. To bank (an airplane). 3. (Naut.) To wedge.—*vn.* To reach low tide.

Escorbútico, ca [es-cor-boo'-te-co, cah], *a.* Scorbutic, scorbutical; it is sometimes used as a substantive for a person affected with scurvy.

Escorbuto [es-cor-boo'-to], *m.* Scurvy, a disease.

Escorchapín [es-cor-chah-peen'], *m.* Passage-boat, ferry.

Escorchar, *va.* *V.* Desollar.

Escorche [es-cor'-chay], *m.* Decrease of a tuberous body.

Escordio [es-cor'-de-o], *m.* (Bot.) Water germander. Teucrium scordium.

Escoria [es-co'-re-ah], *f.* 1. Dross, slags, scoria. 2. Lee. 3. (Met.) Any mean or worthless thing.—*pl.* Scoriæ, volcanic ashes.

Escoriáceo, cea [es-co-re-ah'-thay-o, ah], *a.* Scoriaceous, resembling scoria.

Escoriación [es-co-re-ah-the-on'], *f.* Incrustation, scurf formed on a sore. *V.* Excoriación.

Escorial [es-co-re-ahl'], *m.* 1. Place where a mine has been exhausted. 2. Place where the dross of metals is thrown.

Escoriar [es-co-re-ar'], *va.* *V.* Excoriar.

Escorificación [es-co-re-fe-cah-the-on'], *f.* Scorification, smelting an ore with lead.

Escorificar [es-co-re-fe-car'], *va.* To scorify, to separate (gold and silver) by the process of scorification.

Escorificatorio [es-co-re-fe-cah-to'-re-o], *m.* Scorifier. 1. A small flat dish used for scorifying. 2. A furnace for the same purpose.

Escorodonia [es-co-ro-do'-ne-ah], *f.* (Bot.) Wood sage termander. Teucrium scorodonia, *L.*

Escorpena, Escorpina [es-cor-pay'-nah, es-cor-pee'-nah], *f.* Grouper, a small sea food-fish. Scorpœna.

Escorpiaco [es-cor-pe-ah'-co], *m.* An antidote against scorpion-bites.

Escorpioide [es-cor-pe-o'-e-day], *f.* (Bot.) *V.* Alacranera.

Escorpión [es-cor-pe-on'], *m.* 1. Scorpion. Scorpio. 2. Scorpion, a kind of fish. 3. An ancient warlike machine. 4. Scorpion, a sign in the zodiac. 5. Instrument of torture, a cat-o'-nine-tails armed with metal points.

Escorpiónido, da [es-cor-pe-o'-ne-do, dah], *a.* Scorpion-like.—*m. pl.* Scorpionidea, the scorpion family.

Escorpiuro [es-cor-pe-oo'-ro], *m.* Scorpiurus, an Old World herb of the bean family, so called because the pod resembles a scorpion's tail. Called the caterpillar plant.

Escorroso [es-cor-ro'-so], *m.* (Prov. Cuba) 1. Clamour, vociferation. 2. *V.* Cacareo.

Escorrozo [es-cor-ro'-tho], *m.* (Coll.) Pleasure, enjoyment.

Escorzado [es-cor-thah'-do], *m.* (Art) *V.* Escorzo. *Escorzado, da, pp.* of Escorzar. Foreshortened.

Escorzar [es-cor-thar'], *va.* 1. (Pict.) To contract the size of a figure; to foreshorten. 2. To form a depressed arch.

Escorzo [es-cor'-tho], *m.* (Art) Contraction or decrease of a figure in perspective.

Escorzón [es-cor-thone'], *m.* *V.* Escuerzo.

Escorzonera [es-cor-tho-nay'-rah], *f.* (Bot.) Viper-root or garden vipergrass. Scorzonera hispanica. *Escorzonera laciniada*, Cut-leaved vipergrass. Scorzonera laciniata.

Escoscarse [es-cos-car'-say], *vr.* *V.* Concomerse.

Escota [es-co'-tah], *f.* 1. (Agr. Prov.) A kind of mattock or grubbing axe used in the northern provinces of Spain. 2. (Naut.) Sheet, a rope fastened to the lower corners of a sail, for the purpose of extending or retaining it in a particular situation. *Escotas mayores*, Main-sheets. *Escotas de gavias*, Top-sail sheets. *Escotas de* *las velas de estay*, Stay-sail sheets. *Escotas volantes*, Flowing-sheets. *Escotas de barlovento*, Weather-sheets.

Escotado [es-co-tah'-do], *m.* A sort of dress formerly worn by women, much sloped about the neck.

Escotadura [es-co-tah-doo'-rah], *f.* 1. Sloping of a jacket or a corset. 2. The large trap-door of a theatre or stage. 3. (Mil.) In the breast-plate of armour, the arm-hole (arm-scye) to enable the arms to be moved.

Escotar [es-co-tar'], *va.* 1. To cut out a thing so as to make it fit. 2. To slope. 3. To hollow a garment about the neck. 4. To club, to contribute to a common expense. 5. To draw water from a river or brook by a trench.

Escote [es-co'-tay], *m.* 1. Sloping of a jacket or other garment, especially low neck, decolleté. 2. Tucker, a small piece of lace that shades the breast of women. 3. One's share of a reckoning at a club, feast, etc.

Escotera [es-co-tay'-rah], *f.* (Naut.) Sheet-hole, through which the main and fore-sheets are reeved.

Escotero, ra [es-co-tay'-ro, rah], *a.* Free, disengaged.

Escotilla [es-co-teel'-lyah], *f.* (Naut.) Hatchway. *Escotilla mayor*, The main hatchway. *Escotilla de proa*, Fore-hatchway. *Escotilla de popa*, Magazine-hatchway.

Escotillón [es-co-teel-lyone'], *m.* Scuttle, trap-door.

Escotín [es-co-teen'], *m.* (Naut.) Top-sail-sheet, fastened to the lower corners of top-sails and top-gallant-sails.

Escotista [es-co-tees'-tah], *m.* A follower of Duns Scotus.

Escotomía [es-co-to-mee'-ah], *f.* Dizziness or swimming in the head.

Escoznete [es-coth-nay'-tay], *m.* (Prov.) A nut-pick.

Escozor [es-co-thor'], *m.* 1. A smart pungent pain. 2. (Met.) A lively sensation or perception of the mind.

Escrebidor, Escribidor, *m.* (Obs.) *V.* ESCRITOR.

Escriba [es-cree'-bah], *m.* Scribe, among the Hebrews.

Escribanía [es-cre-bah-nee'-ah], *f.* 1. Office or employment of a notary or scrivener. 2. Office or place where contracts and other notarial deeds and instruments are drawn up. 3. Secretary, escritoire, scrutoire, a case of drawers for writings, with a desk. 4. Portable writing-case.

Escribano [es-cre-bah'-no], *m.* 1. Notary public; scrivener. *Escribano de cámara*, The clerk of a high court of justice, who must be also a notary public. *Escribano de número*, or *del número*, One of a certain number of notaries public, before whom only certain deeds can be executed. 2. Purser of a vessel. 3. (Obs.) Clerk at a public office. 4. (Zool.) An insect, shaped like a small spider, which is in continual movement upon the surface of slow streams or fountains. A (water) skater. Gerris. *Es un gran escribano*, He writes a very neat hand, he writes like copper-plate. *Escribano* or *escribanillo del agua*, Water-skater.

Escribiente [es-cre-be-en'-tay], *m.* 1. Amanuensis, a clerk. 2. (Obs.) Author, writer.

Escribir [es-cre-beer'], *va.* 1. To write. 2. To write, to compose literary works. 3. To write, to tell by letters.—*vr.* 1. To enrol one's self, to enter one's name in a register or roll. 2. To keep up an epistolary correspondence. *Escribir en la arena*, To bury in oblivion.

Escriño [es-cree'-nyo], *m.* 1. Sort of hamper made of straw, and matted together with osier. 2. (Prov.) A jewel-box, casket of jewels.

Escrita [es-cree'-tah], *f.* A kind of fish, having marks like letters upon the back. *V.* ESCUADRO.

Escritillas [es-cre-teel'-lyas], *f. pl.* Lamb's testicles.

Escrito [es-cree'-to], *m.* 1. Book or other literary composition. 2. (Law) Allegation or petition exhibited in a court of justice. 3. (Obs.) A signed receipt.—*Escrito, ta, pp. irr.* of ESCRIBIR.

Escritor [es-cree-tor'], *m.* 1. Writer, author, composer. 2. Copyist.

Escritorcillo [es-cre-tor-theel'-lyo], *m. dim.* A bad writer.

Escritorillo [es-cre-to-reel'-lyo], *m. dim.* A small scrutoire.

Escritorio [es-cre-to'-re-o], *m.* 1. A writing-desk, secretary. 2. Counting-house, office. 3. Press, a large chest of drawers, or sort of cupboard, adorned with inlaid ivory, ebony, etc. 4. At Toledo, a warehouse where goods are sold by wholesale. 5. In printing offices every composing-case.

Escritorzuelo, la [es-cre-tor-thoo-ay'-lo, lah], *m. & f. dim.* A poor writer.

Escritura [es-cre-too'-rah], *f.* 1. Writing, the act of putting any thing on paper. 2. Deed, instrument, bond, contract. 3. Writing, a work or treatise written. *Escritura de seguro*, Policy of insurance. 4. Art of writing.

Escriturar [es-cre-too-rar'], *va.* To bind one's self by a public instrument; to sign articles. *Estar escriturado*, To be under articles.

Escriturario [es-cre-too-rah'-re-o], *m.* One who professes to explain the holy Scripture, a professor of divinity.

Escrófula [es-cro'-foo-lah], *f.* Scrofula, king's evil.

Escrofularia [es-cro-foo-lah'-re ah], *f.* (Bot.) Figwort. Scrophularia.

Escrofuloso, sa [es-cro-foo-lo'-so, sah], *a.* Scrofulous.

Escrotal [es-cro-tahl'], *a.* Scrotal, relating to the scrotum.

Escroto [es-cro'-to], *m.* Scrotum.

Escrudiñar [es-croo-de-nyar'], *va.* *V.* ESCUDRIÑAR.

Escrupulear [es-croo-poo-lay-ar'], *vn.* *V.* ESCRUPULIZAR.

Escrupulete [es-croo-poo-lay'-tay], *m. dim.* (Coll.) A slight doubt or scruple.

Escrupulillo [es-croo-poo-leel'-lyo], *m.* 1. (Dim.) Slight doubt, scruple, or hesitation. 2. Small piece of metal put into a hollow brass globe, to ring as a bell for animals.

Escrupulizar [es-croo-poo-le-thar'], *vn.* To scruple, to doubt, to hesitate.

Escrúpulo [es-croo'-poo-lo], *m.* 1. Doubt, scruple, hesitation. 2. Scrupulosity, a great nicety or tenderness of conscience; conscience. 3. Scruple, a small weight, the third part of a drachm. 4. (Ast.) Minute on a graduated sphere.

Escrupulosamente, *adv.* Scrupulously.

Escrupulosidad [es-croo-poo-lo-se-dahd'], *f.* 1. Scrupulosity, minute and nice doubtfulness. 2. Scrupulosity, conscientiousness.

Escrupuloso, sa [es-croo-poo-lo'-so, sah], *a.* 1. Scrupulous, hard to satisfy in determinations of conscience, conscientious. 2. Scrupulous, nice, cautious, exact; narrow; critical.

Escrutador [es-croo-tah-dor'], *m.* 1. Examiner, scrutator, inquirer, searcher. 2. Inspector of an election.

Escrutar [es-croo-tar'], *va.* 1. To count votes. 2. To search, pry into.

Escrutinio [es-croo-tee'-ne-o], *m.* Scrutiny, inquiry, close examination. *Escrutinio electoral*, Election returns, counting of electoral votes.

Escrutiñador [es-croo-te-nyah-dor'], *m.* Scrutator, censor.

Escuadra [es-coo-ah'-drah], *f.* 1. Square, an instrument for measuring right angles. 2. Socket in which the pivot or spindle of a door turns. 3. A small number of horse or foot soldiers commanded by a corporal; a squad. 4. Squadron, fleet, or more properly a part of a fleet. *A escuadra*, In a square manner. *Jefe de escuadra*, (Naut.) Rear-admiral.

Escuadrador [es-coo-ah-drah-dor'], *m.* Groover, a tool for opening the moulds of wax-candles.

Escuadrar [es-coo-ah-drar'], *va.* 1. To square; to reduce to a square. 2. To fix the trunnions horizontally in a piece of ordnance.

Escuadreo [es-coo-ah-dray'-o], *m.* Dimension, valuation of the square contents of a piece of ground.

Escuadría [es-coo-ah-dree'-ah], *f.* Square, a measure having or forming right angles.

Escuadrilla [es-coo-ah-dree'-lyah], *f.* Escadrille, a squadron of ships or planes.

Escuadro [es-coo-ah'-dro], *m.* 1. Species of dog-fish. 2. (Obs.) *V.* CUADRO.

Escuadrón [es-coo-ah-drone'], *m.* Squadron, troop of horse, a small body of horse. *Escuadrón cuadrado*, A hollow square. *Escuadrón volante*, (Obs.) A flying camp.

Escuadronar [es-coo-ah-dro-nar'], *va.* To draw up troops in rank and file, to form troops in squadrons.

Escuadroncillo, ito [es-coo-ah-dron-theel'-lyo, ee'-to], *m. dim.* A small party of troops.

Escuadronista [es-coo-ah-dro-nees'-tah], *m.* (Mil.) He who forms squadrons.

Escualidez [es-coo-ah-le-deth'], *f.* Squalor, wretchedness.

Escuálido, da [es-coo-ah'-le-do, dah], *a.* 1. Very weak, languid. 2. Squalid, filthy, nauseous. 3. Like the spotted dog-fish.

Escualino, na [es-coo-ah-lee'-no, nah], *a.* *V.* ESCUÁLIDO, 3d def.

Escualo [es-coo-ah'-lo], *m.* The spotted dog-fish; a shark.

Escuatina [es-coo-ah-tee'-nah], *f.* A fish, vulgarly called "sea-angel," of the Mediterranean.

Escucha [es-coo'-chah], *f.* 1. Sentinel, sentry. 2. *Escucha*, or *madre escucha*, A nun who is sent with another to the grate, to listen to what is said. 3. Scout, one who is sent privily to observe the motions of the enemy. 4. A small window, made for hearkening or listening. 5. Servant who sleeps near her mistress, in order to wait on her.

Escuchador, ra [es-coo-chah-dor', rah], *m. & f.* Hearer, hearkener, listener.

Escuchante [es-coo-chahn'-tay], *pa. & m. & f.* Listener; hearkening.

Escuchar [es-coo-char'], *va.* To listen, to hearken, to give ear, to attend, to list, to hear.—*vr.* To hear one's self with complacency, to be highly gratified with one's eloquence.

Escudar [es-coo-dar'], *va.* 1. To shield, to defend with a shield. 2. To guard from danger.—*vr.* (Met.) To depend on some means of evading danger.

Escuderaje [es-coo-day-rah'-hay], *m.* The office and service of a lady's page.

Escuderear [es-coo-day-ray-ar'], *va.* To

perform the service of a page; to perform the functions of a squire.

Escudería [es-coo-day-ree'-ah], *f.* Service of a squire or shield-bearer.

Escuderil [es-coo-day-reel'], *a.* Belonging to the office of a shield-bearer, or to the place of a page.

Escuderilmente, *adv.* In the style and manner of a page, or of a squire or shield-bearer.

Escudero [es-coo-day'-ro], *m.* 1. Shield-bearer, a squire or attendant on a warrior, a custrel. 2. Gentleman descended from an illustrious family. 3. Page who attends a lady. 4. A maker of shields and other defensive armour. *Escudero de a pie*, A servant kept to carry messages.

Escuderón [es-coo-day-rone'], *m.* Squire puffed with vanity and pride.

Escudete [es-coo-day'-tay], *m.* 1. Gusset, a piece of lace sewed on a surplice, under the arm-pit, to strengthen it. 2. A stain on the olive's fruit, from damage received in consequence of falls of rain. 3. Budding or inoculating. 4. (Bot.) White water-lily. *V.* NENÚFAR.

Escudilla [es-coo-deel'-lyah], *f.* Porringer, a crock; a soup-plate.

Escudillar [es-coo-deel-lyar'], *va.* 1. To pour broth into porringers, to distribute broth. 2. (Met.) To lord, to domineer.

Escudillita [es-coo-deel-lyee'-tah], *f. dim.* A small porringer.

Escudillo, ito [es-coo-deel'-lyo, ee'-to], *m. dim.* A small shield.

Escudito [es-coo-dee'-to], *m.* A gold coin formerly worth twenty reals *vellón*, now worth twenty-one reals and a quarter.

Escudo [es-coo'-do], *m.* 1. Shield, buckler. 2. Plate on which arms are engraved. 3. Scutcheon of a lock. 4. Shield, patronage, protection, defense. 5. Back of a wild boar. 6. The bandage used in bleeding. 7. Side-plate of a gun. *Escudo de bote*, (Naut.) The back-board of a boat. *Escudo de popa*, (Naut.) Stern-scutcheon. 8. Crown, a coin of a different value in different countries. In Spain there are gold coins or *escudos* worth two dollars or forty reals, and silver pieces or *escudos* of eight and of ten reals.

Escudriñable [es-coo-dre-nyah'-blay], *a.* Investigable.

Escudriñador, ra [es-coo-dre-nyah-dor', rah], *m.* & *f.* Prier, scrutator; a person who inquires into the secrets of others.

Escudriñamiento [es-coo-dre-nyah-me-en'-to], *m.* Investigation, scrutiny.

Escudriñar [es-coo-dre-nyar'], *va.* To search, to pry into; to inquire after, to examine into; to consult.

Escudriño [es-coo-dree'-nyo], *m.* *V.* ESCUDRIÑAMIENTO.

Escuela [es-coo-ay'-lah], *f.* 1. School, a house of discipline and instruction. 2. School, university, a place of literary education. 3. School, a state of instruction or the instruction given in schools. 4. School, a system of doctrine; style of a teacher. *Escuela de Cristo*, A religious congregation whose members practise charity. *Escuelas*, University, the school where all the faculties are taught and studied.

Escuerzo [es-coo-err'-tho], *m.* Toad. Rana bufo.

Escueto, ta [es-coo-ay'-to, tah], *a.* 1 Disengaged, free from encumbrances. 2. (Amer. Peru.) Solitary, uninhabited.

(*Yo escuezo, yo escueza*, from *Escocer.* *V.* COCER.)

Escueznar [es-coo-eth-nar'], *va.* (Prov.) To extract the kernel of nuts.

Escuezno [es-coo-eth'-no], *m.* (Prov.) Pulp or soft kernel of a nut fit for eating.

Esculina [es-coo-lee'-nah], *f.* Esculin, a principle procured from the horse-chestnut.

Escullador [es-cool-lyah-dor'], *m.* In oil-mills, a vessel for carrying off the oil.

Escullirse [es-cool-lyeer'-say], *vr.* (Prov.) To slip, to slide.

Esculpidor, *m.* (Obs.) *V.* ESCULTOR.

Esculpir [es-cool-peer'], *va.* To sculpture, to engrave in wood or stone.

Esculto, ta [es-cool'-to, tah], *pp. irr. obs.* of ESCULPIR.

Escultor [es-cool-tor'], *m.* Sculptor, carver.

Escultora [es-cool-to'-rah], *f.* Female sculptor, wife of a sculptor; sculptress.

Escultura [es-cool-too'-rah], *f.* 1. Sculpture, the art of cutting wood or stone into images. 2. Carved work, the work made by a sculptor. *Escultura de navíos*, (Naut.) Carved work in ships.

Escultural [es-cool-too-rahl'], *a.* Sculptural; belonging to the art of sculpture.

Escupidera [es-coo-pe-day'-rah], *f.* Spittoon, cuspidor.

Escupidero [es-coo-pe-day'-ro], *m.* 1. Spitting-place. 2. (Met.) Despicable or abject situation.

Escupido [es-coo-pee'-do], *m.* *V.* ESPUTO.—*Escupido, da, pp.* of ESCUPIR.

Escupidor, ra [es-coo-pe-dor', rah], *m.* & *f.* A great spitter.

Escupidura [es-coo-pe-doo'-rah], *f.* 1. The act of spitting. 2. Spittle. 3. Efflorescence, the breaking out of humours in the skin.

Escupir [es-coo-peer'], *va.* 1. To spit. 2. To break out in the skin: applied to morbid humours. 3. (Met. Poet.) To discharge balls from fire-arms. 4. (Met.) To dart, to flash. 5. (Met.) To depreciate, to underrate the value of a thing. *Escupir en la cara*, To deride to the face, to ridicule. *Escupir al cielo*, (Met.) To act rashly. *Escupir doblones*, (Met.) To boast of one's riches. *Escupir sangre*, To boast of nobility. *Escupir sangre en bacín de oro*, (Met. Coll.) To enjoy little happiness in the midst of plenty and wealth: literally, to spit blood in a basin of gold. *Escupir las estopas*, (Naut.) To work out the oakum from the seams: spoken of a ship. *No escupir alguna cosa*, (Coll.) To be attached to any thing.

Escupita, Escupitina [es-coo-pee'-tah, es-coo-pe-tee'-nah], *f.* (Coll.) *V.* SALIVA.

Escurar [es-coo-rar'], *va.* To scour cloth, to cleanse it from grease before it is milled.

Escurialense [es-coo-re-ah-len'-say], *a.* Belonging to the monastery of The Escorial.

Escurina [es-coo-ree'-nah], *f.* (Prov.) Obscurity, darkness.

Escurribanda [es-coor-re-bahn'-dah], *f.* (Humorous) 1. Evasion, subterfuge. 2. Diarrhœa, bowel-complaint. 3. Scuffle, bustle.

Escurrida [es-coor-ree'-dah], *a.* 1. Applied to a woman who wears her petticoats well fitted. 2. She who has narrow hips.

Escurridizo, za [es-coor-re-dee'-tho, thah], *a.* 1. Slippery, not affording firm footing. 2. Hard to hold, hard to keep, easily escaping. *Lazo escurridizo*, A running knot.

Escurriduras, Escurrimbres [es-coor-re-doo'-ras, es-coor-reem'-bress], *f. pl.* Dregs, the sediment of liquors; the lees, the grounds. *Llegar a las escurriduras*, To reach the end of a festival, the remains of a dinner, or other thing.

Escurrimiento, *m.* *V.* DESLIZ.

Escurripa [es-coor-ree'-pah], *f.* (Bot.) Cardinal flower. Lobelia cardinalis

Escurrir [es-coor-reer'], *va.* To drain off liquor to the dregs.—*vn.* 1. To drop, to fall in drops. 2. To slip, to slide. 3. To lapse, to glide slowly.—*vr.* To escape from danger; to slip out, or to slip away; to creep, to skulk.

Escutas, Escutillas [es-coo'-tas, es-coo-teel'-lyas], *f. pl.* (Naut.) Scuttles. *V.* ESCOTILLAS.

Escutelaria [es-coo-tay-lah'-re-ah], *f.* Scutellaria, skull-cap, an herb of the mint family.

Escuteliforme [es-coo-tay-le-for'-may], *a.* (Bot.) Shield-shaped, platter-shaped.

Escutiforme [es-coo-te-for'-may], *a.* Shield-shaped.—*m.* The thyroid cartilage.

Escuyer [es-coo-yerr'], *m.* Purveyor of meat to the palace.

Esdrújulo [es-droo'-hoo-lo], *m.* A Spanish word of more than two syllables, the last two of which are short, e. g. *cántaro.*

Esdrújulo, la [es-droo'-hoo-lo, lah], *a.* Belonging to Spanish words called *esdrújulos.*

Ese [ay'-say], *f.* 1. Spanish name of the letter S. 2. Link of a chain of the figure of this letter. *Eses*, Reeling of a drunken man.

Ese [ay'-say]. A demonstrative pronoun of the masculine gender. That. *Ese, esa, eso.*

Esecilla [ay-say-theel'-lyah], *f. dim.* Small link of a chain.

Esencia [ay-sen'-the-ah], *f.* 1. Essence, formal existence. 2. (Chem. and Phar.) Essence, a volatile oil; a solution in alcohol of an aromatic, or volatile oil. *Quinta esencia*, Quintessence, an extract. *Ser de esencia*, To be indispensably necessary.

Esencial [ay-sen-the-ahl'], *a.* 1. Essential, necessary, constituent. 2. Essential, important in the highest degree, material; principal, main; formal.

Esencialmente, *adv.* Essentially, principally, naturally, materially.

Esenciarse [ay-sen-the-ar'-say], *vr.* To be intimately united, to grow essential.

Esfacelado, da [es-fah-thay-lah'-do, dah], *a.* (Med.) Sphacelated, gangrenous.

Esfacelar [es-fah-thay-lar'], *va.* To cause sphacelus, or gangrene.

Esfacelo [es-fah-thay'-lo], *m.* (Med.) Sphacelus, gangrene of an entire member.

Esfeciforme [es-fay-the-for'-may], *a.* Wasp-shaped, like a sphex (wasp).

Esfenoidal [es-fay-no-ee-dahl'], *a.* Sphenoidal, belonging to the sphenoid bone.

Esfenoides [es-fay-no'-e-days], *m.* The sphenoid bone.

Esfera [es-fay'-rah], *f.* 1. Sphere, a globe or orb. 2. Globe, representing the earth or sky. 3. Quality, character, condition, state, rank. 4. (Poet.) Heaven. *Está fuera de mi esfera*, That is out of my reach or power.

Esferal [es-fay-rahl'], *a.* *V.* ESFÉRICO.

Esféricamente, *adv.* Spherically.

Esfericidad [es-fay-re-the-dahd'], *f* Sphericity, rotundity, orbicularness, globosity.

Esférico, ca [es-fay'-re-co, cah], *a.* Spherical globular, globous, globated.

Esferoidal [es-fay-ro-e-dahl'], *a.* Spheroidical, spheroidal.
Esferoide [es-fay-ro'-e-day], *f.* Spheroid. *Bóveda esferoide,* Elliptical arch.
Esférula [es-fay'-roo-lah], *f.* A rounded conceptacle, whether oblong or conical, which is porous in its upper part.
Esfinge [es-feen'-hay], *f.* Sphinx, a fabulous monster.—*m.* Sphinx, hawk-moth, or humming-bird moth. The larvæ of some are destructive of grape-vines.
Esfingido, da [es-feen'-he-do, dah], *a.* Sphinx-like.
Esfínter [es-feen'-ter], *m.* (Anat.) Sphincter.
Esflorecer [es-flo-ray-therr'], *vn.* (Chem.) To effloresce, to fall into powder when exposed to the air.
Esforrocino [es-for-ro-thee'-no], *m.* Sprig shooting from the trunk of a vine.
Esforzadamente, *adv.* Strenuously, vigorously, valiantly.
Esforzado [es-for-thah'-do], *m.* One of the books of the civil law which treats of testaments and last wills.
Esforzado, da [es-for-thah'-do, dah], *a.* Strong, vigorous, valiant. *Caldo esforzado,* Strong broth, invigorating.—*pp.* of ESFORZAR.
Esforzador, ra [es-for-thah-dor', rah], *m.* & *f.* Exciter, animater.
Esforzar [es-for-thar'], *va.* 1. To strengthen, to invigorate, to exert, to enforce or to force. 2. (Met.) To aid, to corroborate.—*vr.* 1. To exert one's self, to make efforts. 2. To be confident, to assure one's self.
Esfuerzo [es-foo-err'-tho], *m.* 1. Courage, spirit, vigour, heart, manfulness. 2. Effort, strong endeavour, exertion, contention, labouring. 3. Confidence, faith. 4. Help, aid.
(*Yo esfuerzo, yo esfuerce,* from *Esforzar. V.* ACORDAR.)
Esfumado [es-foo-mah'-do], *m.* The first sketch of a painting, drawn with a pencil or charcoal.—*a.* Sfumato, having hazy outlines. *Esfumado, da, pp.* of ESFUMAR.
Esfumar [es-foo-mar'], *va.* (Pict.) To shade over the pencilled outlines of a picture.
Esfumarse [es-foo-mar'-say], *vr.* To disappear, to fade away.
Esfumino [es-foo-mee'-no], *m.* (Art) A stump for shading with charcoal or powdered pigments. *Cf.* DIFUMINO.
Esgarrar [es-gar-rar'], *vn.* (Prov. Amer.) *V.* GARGAJEAR.
Esgarro [es-gar'-ro], *m.* (Amer.) *V.* GARGAJO.
Esgorbia [es-gor'-be-ah], *f.* An auger for tin-workers.
Esgrima [es-gree'-mah], *f.* Fencing, the art of manual defence. *Maestro de esgrima,* Fencing-master.
Esgrimidor [es-gre-me-dor'], *m.* Fencer or fencing-master. *Casa de esgrimidor,* (Met.) House without furniture
Esgrimidura [es-gre-me-doo'-rah], *f* The act of fencing.
Esgrimir [es-gre-meer'], *va.* 1. To practise the use of weapons. 2. To fence, to fight according to art.
Esguazable [es-goo-ah-thah'-blay], *a.* Fordable.
Esguazar [es-goo-ah-thar'], *va.* To ford, as a river.
Esgucio [es-goo'-the-o], *m.* (Arch.) Concave moulding.
Esguin [es-geen'], *m.* Young salmon before entering the sea.
Esguince [es-geen'-thay], *m.* 1. Movement of the body to avoid a blow or a fall. 2. Frown. 3. A twist or sprain of a joint.
Esgüízaro [es-goo-ee'-thah-ro], *a.* A miserable fellow, a ragamuffin.
Eskol [es'-kole], *m.* An enormous wolf which, according to a Scandinavian fable, pursues the moon and is finally to devour it.
Eslabón [es-lah-bone'], *m.* 1. Link of a chain, chain-links. 2. Steel for striking fire with a flint. 3. Steel for sharpening knives. 4. A very poisonous scorpion. 5. *Eslabones de guimbalete,* (Naut.) Swivels, rings made to turn in staples.
Eslabonador [es-lah-bo-nah-dor'], *m.* Chain-maker.
Eslabonamiento [es-la-bo-nah-me-en'-to], *m.* 1. Linking, uniting. 2. A chain, concatenation of various things.
Eslabonar [es-lah-bo-nar'], *va.* 1. To link, to join one ring to another. 2. (Met.) To add, to unite.
Eslavo, va [es-lah'-vo, vah], *a.* Slavic, Slavonic.—*m.* & *f.* Slav.—*m.* Slavic language.
Eslinga [es-leen'-gah], *f.* (Naut.) Sling, a rope with which bales or casks are hoisted. *Eslinga de boya,* (Naut.) Buoy-sling.
Eslingar [es-lin-gar'], *va.* (Naut.) To sling, to throw with a sling.
Eslora [es-lo'-rah], *f.* Length of a ship on the deck from the stem to the stern-post. *Esloras,* Beams running from stem to stern.
Esmaltador [es-mal-tah-dor'], *m.* Enameller.
Esmaltadura [es-mal-tah-doo'-rah], *f.* 1. Enamelling. 2. Enamel work.
Esmaltar [es-mal-tar'], *va.* 1. To enamel, to variegate with colours inlaid. 2. (Met.) To adorn, to embellish.
Esmalte [es-mahl'-tay], *m.* 1. Enamel, any thing enamelled. 2. An azure colour, made of paste. 3. Smalt. *V.* LUSTRE.
Esmarchazo [es-mar-chah'-tho], *m.* A bully.
Esmectita [es-mec-tee'-tah], *f.* Name of some clays like fuller's earth.
Esmeradamente [es-may-rah-dah-men'-tay], *adv.* Nicely, correctly, accurately.
Esmerado, da [es-may-rah'-do, dah], *a.* High-finished, executed with care, nice.—*pp.* of ESMERAR.
Esmeralda [es-may-rahl'-dah], *f.* Emerald, a precious stone.
Esmerar [es-may-rar'], *va.* To polish, to brighten by attrition.—*vr.* To endeavour to attain eminence or excellence, to take great pains.
Esmerejón [es-may-ray-hone'], *m.* 1. (Orn.) Merlin, the yellow-legged falcon. Falco æsalon. 2. Small piece of artillery.
Esmeril [es-may-reel'], *m.* 1. Emery, a mineral used in polishing. 2. Small piece of ordnance.
Esmerilar [es-may-re-lar'], *va.* To burnish, to polish with emery.
Esmerilazo [es-may-re-lah'-tho], *m.* Shot of a gun called *esmeril.*
Esmero [es-may'-ro], *m.* Careful attention, elaborate effort, niceness, correctness, accuracy.
Esmilacina [es-me-lah-thee'-nah], *f.* 1. (Bot.) Smilacina, false Solomon's seal. 2. An alkaloid obtained from the inner pith of the sarsaparilla.
Esmodita [es-mo-dee'-tah], *f.* A pulverulent material produced by volcanoes.
Esmoladera [es-mo-lah-day'-rah], *f.* Whetstone.
Esmuciarse [es-moo-the-ar'-say], *vr.* (Prov.) To slip from the hands.
Esnob or **Snob** [es-nob'], *m.* Snob.
Esnobismo [es-no-bees'-mo], *m.* Snobbery, snobbishness.
Esnón [es-none'], *m.* (Naut.) A spencer mast, trysail mast.
Eso [ay'-so], *demonst. pron.* That. *Esos,* Those. *Eso es,* That is it. *No es eso,* It is not that. *A eso de,* Toward, about.
Esófago [ay-so'-fah-go], *m.* (Anat.) Œsophagus, gullet; the throat.
Esotérico, ca [ay-so-tay'-re-co, cah], *a.* Esoteric; confidential, secret.
Esotro, tra [ay-so'-tro, ay-so'-trah], *pron. dem.* This or that other; pointing out not the first, but the second, third, etc., person or thing.—*pl.* Those others.
Espabiladeras [es-pah-be-lah-day'-ras], *f. pl.* Snuffers.
Espabilar [es-pah-be-lar'], *va.* To snuff a candle. *V.* DESPABILAR.
Espaciador [es-pah-the-ah-dor'], *m.* Spacer (in a typewriter).
Espacial [es-pah-the-ahl'], *a.* Relating to space. *Cápsula espacial,* Space capsule.
Espaciar [es-pah-the-ar'], *va.* 1. To extend, to dilate, to spread. 2. To space, separate the lines in writing or printing. 3. To stagger (hours of work).—*vr.* 1. To expand (either in writing or speaking). 2. To amuse oneself.
Espacio [es-pah'-the-o] *m.* 1. Space, capacity; distance between objects. 2. Space, interval of time. 3. Slowness, delay, procrastination. 4. (Obs.) Recreation, diversion. 5. Musical interval. 6. In printing, space, type which separates words. 7. (Ast.) *V.* DESCAMPADO.
Espacio interastral [es-pah'-the-o in-ter-as-trahl'], *m.* Outer space.
Espaciosamente, *adv.* Deliberately, spaciously.
Espaciosidad [es-pah-the-o-se-dahd'], *f.* Spaciousness, capacity.
Espacioso, sa [es-pah-the-oh'-so, sah], *a.* 1. Spacious, capacious, wide, roomy, large, extensive. 2. Slow, deliberate.
Espada [es-pah'-dah], *f.* 1. Sword. 2. Swordsman. 3. Ace of spades, or any card in the suit of spades. 4. (Zool.) Sword-fish. Xiphias gladius. 5. The bull-fighter who kills the bull with a sword. *Espada blanca,* Sword. *Espada negra* or *de esgrima,* Foil, a blunt sword used in fencing. *Comedia de capa y espada,* A play on every-day business, and not requiring display in the scenery. *Entrar con espada en mano,* To attack sword in hand; to enter upon an affair supporting one's own business strongly. *Hombre de capa y espada,* A person of no profession. *Primer espada,* The head bull-fighter. *Verse entre la espada y la pared,* To be driven to the wall, to be surrounded by danger. *Sacar la espada por alguno,* To uphold the character, name, or opinion of some one. *Es una buena espada,* He is a good or dexterous swordsman. *Espada ancha* or *espada de a caballo,* Broadsword; dragoon's sabre.
Espadachín [es-pah-dah-cheen'], *m.* Bully, hackster, one who affects valour.
Espadada [es-pah-dah'-dah], *f.* (Obs.) Blow with a sword.
Espadadero [es-pah-dah-day'-ro], *m.* Braking-floor, scutch-blade, a table for braking flax or hemp.
Espadado, da [es-pah-dah'-do, dah], *a* Armed with a sword.—*pp.* of ESPADAR.
Espadador [es-pah-dah-dor'], *m.* One who brakes flax or hemp with a swingle.
Espadaña [es-pah-dah'-nyah], *f.* 1. (Bot.) Reed-mace, great cat-tail. Typha latifolia. 2. Spire.

Espadañada [es-pah-dah-nyah'-dah], *f.* Sudden flow of blood, water, etc., from the mouth.

Espadañal [es-pah-dah-nyahl'], *m.* The place where reed-mace is growing.

Espadañar [es-pah-dah-nyar'], *va.* To divide into long thin slips, resembling flags.

Espadar [es-pah-dar'], *va.* To brake hemp or flax with a swingle.

Espadarte [es-pah-dar'-tay], *m.* (Zool.) Sword-fish. *V.* ESPADA.

Espadería [es-pah-day-ree'-ah], *f.* Sword-cutler's shop.

Espadero [es-pah-day'-ro], *m.* Sword-cutler.

Espádice [es-pah'-de-thay], *m.* Spadix, a common receptacle of several flowers inclosed in a spathe.

Espadilla [es-pah-deel'-lyah], *f.* 1. Red insignia of the order of Santiago in the shape of a sword. 2. Swingle used in braking hemp and flax, a scutching handle. 3. (Naut.) A small oar, or helm for boats. 4. Ace of spades. 5. (Bot.) Corn-flag. Gladiolus, *L.* *Espadilla común,* (Bot.) Common corn-flag. Gladiolus communis, *L.*

Espadillar [es-pah-deel-lyar'], *va.* To brake or scutch hemp or flax with a swingle.

Espadillazo [es-pah-dil-lyah'-tho], *m.* Adverse fortune at cards, where the ace is lost.

Espadín [es-pah-deen'], *m.* A small short sword.

Espadita [es-pah-dee'-tah], *f. dim.* A small sword.

Espadón [es-pah-done'], *m.* 1. (Aug.) A large sword, a broadsword. 2. Eunuch, one that is castrated.

Espadrapo [es-pah-drah'-po], *m.* *V.* ESPARADRAPO.

Espagírica [es-pah-hee'-re-cah], *f.* Metallurgy, the art of refining metals.

Espagírico, ca [es-pah-he'-re-co, cah], *a.* Belonging to the art of metallurgy.

Espaí [es-pah-ee'], *m.* Spahi, Turkish horse soldier, or an Algerian cavalryman in the French service.

Espalda [es-pahl'-dah], *f.* 1. Shoulder, the upper part of the back. 2. (Mil.) Shoulder of a bastion. *Espaldas,* 1. Back or back part. 2. (Met.) Aid, protection. *A las espaldas de la iglesia,* At the back part of the church. *A espaldas,* At one's back, in one's absence. *A espaldas vueltas,* Treacherously, behind one's back. *Echar a las espaldas,* To forget designedly, to abandon. *Sobre mis espaldas,* At my expense. *Tornar* or *volver las espaldas,* 1. To avoid any one; to turn one's back in contempt. 2. To fly, to run away.

Espaldar [es-pal-dar'], *m.* 1. Back-piece of an armour, shoulder-piece of a coat of mail. 2. Place where one puts his back to rest against. 3. Espalier in gardens. *Espaldares,* Pieces of tapestry against which chairs lean.

Espaldarazo [es-pal-dah-rah'-tho], *m.* Blow with the flat of a sword, or of the hand, on the shoulders.

Espaldarcete [es-pal-dar-thay'-tay], *m.*

Espaldarón [es-pal-dah-rone'], *m.* Ancient armour for the shoulders.

Espaldear [es-pal-day-ar'], *va.* (Naut.) To break (the waves) with impetuosity against the poop of a vessel.

Espalder [es-pal-derr'], *m.* The first or stern rower in a galley.

Espaldera [es-pal-day'-rah], *f.* Espalier, trees planted and cut so as to join; wall-trees.

Espaldilla [es-pal-deel'-lyah], *f.* 1. Shoulder-blade. 2. Hind quarter of a waistcoat or jacket. 3. (Anat.) Omoplate, scapula.

Espalditendido, da [es-pal-de-ten-dee'-do, dah], *a.* (Coll.) Stretched on one's back.

Espaldón [es-pal-done'], *m.* 1. (Arch.) *V.* RASTRO. 2. Intrenchment or barrier to defend one from an attack. 3. (Naut.) A hawse-piece. 4. A barrier of fagots, baskets, bags, etc., to guard the artillery and sappers during a siege. 5. Half bulwark, generally of one face and one flank.

Espaldonarse [es-pal-do-nar'-say], *vr.* To get under cover, to guard one's self from the fire of the enemy.

Espaldudamente, *adv.* Rudely, unmannerly.

Espaldudo, da [es-pal-doo'-do, dah], *a.* Broad-shouldered.

Espalmadura [es-pal-mah-doo'-rah], *f.* Hoofs of quadrupeds.

Espalmar [es-pal-mar'], *va.* (Naut.) To clean and pay a ship's bottom. *V.* DESPALMAR.

Espalto [es-pahl'-to], *m.* 1. Dark-coloured paint. 2. (Mil.) Esplanade. 3. Spalt, a scaly whitish mineral used as a flux for metals.

Espantable [es-pan-tah'-blay], *a.* 1. Frightful, horrid, terrible. 2. Marvellous, wonderful.

Espantablemente [es-pan-tah-blay-men'-tay], *adv.* Horribly, terribly, frightfully.

Espantadizo, za [es-pan-tah-dee'-tho, thah], *a.* Timid, easily frightened.

Espantador, ra [es-pan-tah-dor', rah], *m. & f.* Bugbear, one that frightens or terrifies.

Espantajo [es-pan-tah'-ho], *m.* 1. Scare-crow, set up to frighten birds. 2. One who cuts grimaces for the purpose of frightening.

Espantalobos [es-pan-tah-lo'-bos], *m.* (Bot.) Bladder or bastard senna. Colutea. *Espantalobos arborescente,* Common bladder senna. Colutea arborescens.

Espantamoscas [es-pan-tah-mos'-cas], *m.* Net put on horses to scare away flies.

Espantanublados [es-pan-tah-noo-blah'-dos], *m.* Rake, vagabond begging in long robes, who is thought by the vulgar to have power over the clouds.

Espantar [es-pan-tar'], *va.* 1. To frighten, to terrify, to fright, to daunt, to shock. 2. To chase or drive away. —*vr.* To be surprised or astonished, to marvel.

Espantavillanos [es-pan-tah-vil-lyah'-nos], *m.* Sort of shining or glittering gaudy stuff.

Espanto [es-pahn'-to], *m.* 1. Fright, consternation, frightfulness. 2. Menace, threat. 3. Admiration, wonder, surprise; horror. 4. Hideousness, grimness.

Espantosamente, *adv.* Dreadfully, marvellously, frightfully, ghastfully.

Espantoso, sa [es-pan-to'-so, sah], *a.* 1. Frightful, dreadful, horrid, horrible; fearful. 2. Marvellous, wonderful.

Español, la [es-pah-nyole', lah], *a.* Spanish, relating to Spain. *A la española,* In the Spanish manner.

Español [es-pah-nyole'], *m.* Spanish language.

Españolado, da [es-pah-nyo-lah'-do, dah], *a.* Applied to a foreigner who in his manners, etc., is like a Spaniard, or who follows Spanish customs.—*pp.* of ESPAÑOLAR.

Españolar [es-pah-nyo-lar'], *va.* *V.* ESPAÑOLIZAR.

Españolería [es-pah-nyo-lay-ree'-ah], *f.* (Obs.) Spanish taste, manners, and customs.

Españoleta [es-pah-nyo-lay'-tah], *f.* Ancient Spanish dance.

Españolismo [es-pah-nyo-lees'-mo], *m.* Love, devotion, to Spain; patriotism.

Españolizado, da [es-pah-nyo-lee-thah'-do, dah], *a. & pp.* of *Españolizar.* *V.* ESPAÑOLADO.

Españolizar [es-pah-nyo-le-thar'], *va.* To make Spanish, to render conformable to the Spanish idiom or Spanish analogies.—*vr.* To adopt the customs and manners of Spain.

Espar [es-par'], *m.* Spar, a kind of aromatic drug.

Esparadrapo [es-pah-rah-drah'-po], *m.* Adhesive plaster, court plaster (sparadrap).

Esparagón [es-pah-rah-gone'], *m.* Grogram, a coarse stuff.

Esparamarín [es-pah-rah-ma-reen'], *m.* Serpent which mounts trees to dart on its prey.

Esparaván [es-pah-rah-vahn'], *m.* 1. (Vet.) Bone-spavin, tumour in the legs of horses; jarde. 2. (Orn.) Sparrow-hawk. Falco nisus, *L.*

Esparavel [es-pah-rah-vel'], *m.* 1. Kind of fishing net. 2. Carpenter's mortarboard.

Esparceta [es-par-thay'-tah], *f.* (Bot.) Saint-foin hedysarum. Hedysarum orobrithys.

Esparciata [es-par-the-ah'-tah], *a.* Spartan.

Esparcidamente, *adv.* Distinctly, separately; gayly.

Esparcido, da [es-par-thee'-do, dah], *a.* 1. Scattered. 2. (Met.) Merry, festive, gay.—*pp.* of ESPARCIR.

Esparcilla [es-par-theel'-lyah], *f.* (Bot.) Spurrey. Spergula. *Esparcilla arvense,* Rough-seeded spurrey. Spergula arvensis.

Esparcimiento [es-par-the-me-en'-to], *m.* 1. Scattering, dissemination. 2. Amusement. 3. (Met.) Frankness, openness. 4. (Met.) Liberality of sentiments, generosity of mind.

Esparcir [es-par-theer'], *va.* 1. To scatter, to disseminate, to fling. 2. (Met.) To divulge, to spread abroad. —*vr.* To amuse one's self, to make merry.

Espardeña [es-par-day'-nyah], *f.* (Prov.) *V.* ESPARTEÑA.

Esparganio [es-par-gah'-ne-o], *m.* (Bot.) Burr-reed. Sparganium.

Esparo [es-pah'-ro], *m.* (Zool.) Gilt-head, a sea-fish. Sparus.

Esparragado [es-par-rah-gah'-do], *m.* A dish of asparagus.

Esparragador [es-par-rah-gah-dor'], *m.* He who collects and takes care of asparagus.

Esparragar [es-par-rah-gar'], *va.* To guard or collect asparagus. *Anda* or *vete a esparragar,* (Coll.) Expression, to dispatch or dismiss one contemptuously or angrily.

Esparragíneo, nea [es-par-ra-hee'-nay-o, ah], *a.* Asparagoid, like asparagus.

Espárrago [es-par'-rah-go], *m.* 1. (Bot.) Sprout of asparagus. Asparagus. *Solo como el espárrago,* (Coll.) As lonely as asparagus; every stalk grow ing by itself. 2. Pole to support an awning.

Esparragón [es-par-rah-gone'], *m.* Silk stuff that forms a cord thicker and stronger than taffeta.

Esparraguera [es-par-rah-gay'-rah], *f.* 1. Asparagus plant; stem of this plant. 2. An asparagus-bed.

Esparraguero, ra [es-par-rah-gay'-ro, rah], *m. & f.* One who gathers and sells asparagus.

Esparrancado, da [es-par-ran-cah'-do.

dah], *a.* Bow-legged, bandy-legged, divaricated.—*pp.* of ESPARRANCARSE.

Esparrancarse [es-par-ran-car'-say], *vr.* (Coll.) To straddle, to bestride.

Espartal [es-par-tahl'], *m.* Field on which feather-grass is growing.

Espartano, na [es-par-tah'-no, nah], *a.* Spartan, belonging to Sparta.

Esparteña [es-par-tay'-nyah], *f.* A sort of sandal made of feather-grass.

Espartería [es-par-tay-ree'-ah], *f.* Place where mats of tough feather-grass are made or sold.

Espartero, ra [es-par-tay'-ro, rah], *m.* & *f.* One who makes and sells articles of feather-grass.

Espartilla [es-par-teel'-lyah], *f.* Handful of feather-grass which serves as a brush for cleaning animals.

Espartizal [es-par-te-thahl'], *m.* Field on which feather-grass is growing.

Esparto [es-par'-to], *m.* (Bot.) Feather-grass; Spanish grass hemp. Stipa. *Esparto tenacísimo* or *esparto de esteras*, Tough feather-grass. Stipa tenacissima. *Esparto basto*, Rush-leaved lygeum. Lygeum spartum. *Cf.* ATOCHA.

Espasmo [es-pahs'-mo], *m.* *V.* PASMO. Spasm.

Espasmódico, ca [es-pas-mo'-de-co, cah], *a.* Spasmodic, convulsive.—*adv.* **Espasmódicamente.**

Espástico, ca [es-pahs'-te-co, cah], *a.* Spastic, spasmodic.

Espata [es-pah'-tah], *f.* (Bot.) Spathe, a large bract sheathing a flower-cluster.

Espático, ca [es-pah'-te-co, cah], *a.* Spathic, of spar.

Espato [es-pah'-to], *m.* Spar, a calcareous mineral.

Espátula [es-pah'-too-lah], *f.* 1. Spatula, or slice used by apothecaries and surgeons. 2. A palette-knife. 3. (Bot.) A kind of fetid iris. 4. (Zool.) The spoonbill, a long-shanked bird common in S. America.

Espaviento [es-pah-ve-en'-to], *m.* *V.* ASPAVIENTO.

Espavorido, da, Espavorecido, da [es-pah-vo-ree'-do, dah, es-pah-vo-ray-thee'-do, dah], *a.* *V.* DESPAVORIDO.

Especería [es-pay-thay-ree'-ah], *f.* The more colloquial form. *V.* ESPECIERÍA. Spicery.

Especia [es-pay'-the-ah], *f.* Spice.—*pl.* 1. Medicinal drugs. 2. (Obs.) Dessert.

Especial [es-pay-the-ahl'], *a.* Special, particular. *En especial*, Specially.

Especialidad [es-pay-the-ah-le-dahd'], *f.* Speciality or specialty, particularity.

Especialista [es-pay-the-ah-lees'-tah], *a.* & *m.* Specialist, one who cultivates or excels in a science.

Especialización [es-pay-the-ah-le-thah-the-on'], *f.* Specialization.

Especializarse [es-pay-the-ah-le-thar'-say], *vr.* To specialize.

Especialmente [es-pay-the-al-men'-tay], *adv.* Especially, in particular, namely, nominally.

Especiar [es-pay-the-ar'], *va.* To spice broth or food.

Especie [es-pay'-the-ay], *f.* 1. Species; a kind, a sort; a sub-division of a general term; nature. 2. Species, any sensible representation. 3. Image or idea of any object in the mind. 4. Event, incident; any thing which has happened. 5. Pretext, show. 6. (Chem.) A collection of properties which only belong to one body. 7. Feint in fencing. 8. *pl.* (Phy.) Luminous rays diversely reflected. 9. *pl. Especies sacramentales*, The accidents of colour, taste, and smell, which remain in the sacrament, after the conversion of the bread and wine into the body and blood of Christ.

Especiería [es-pay-the-ay-ree'-ah], *f.* 1. A grocer's shop, grocery. 2. A shop where spices are sold. 3. Spices and all sorts of aromatic drugs. (Acad.)

Especiero [es-pay-the-ay'-ro], *m.* A dealer in spices and aromatic drugs, a grocer.

Especificación [es-pay-the-fe-ca-the-on'], *f.* Specification, a minute enumeration of things.

Especificadamente, *adv.* Specifically, distinctly, expressly.

Especificar [es-pay-the-fe-car'], *va.* To specify, to state minutely; to name; to show by some particular mark of distinction.

Especificativo, va [es-pay-the-fe-cah-tee'-vo, vah], *a.* That which has the power of specifying or distinguishing.

Especifico [es-pay-thee'-fe-co], *m.* Specific, a remedy for some particular disease.

Especifico, ca [es-pay-thee'-fe-co, cah], *a.* Specific, specifical.

Espécimen [es-pay'-the-men], *m.* (Neol.) Specimen, sample.—*pl.* The known kinds of letters in ancient times.

Especioso, sa [es-pay-the-oh'-so, sah], *a.* 1. Neat, beautiful, gay; finished with care. 2. Superficial, apparent, specious, plausible, colourable; glossy.

Espectáculo [es-pec-tah'-coo-lo], *m.* 1. Spectacle, show; a pageant. 2. Spectacle, any thing to be looked on, or any thing exhibited as eminently remarkable.

Espectador [es-pec-tah-dor'], *m.* Spectator.

Espectral [es-pec-trahl'], *a.* 1. Spectral, phantom-like, ghost-like. 2. (Phy.) Spectral.

Espectro [es-pec'-tro], *m.* 1. Spectre, phantom, ghost, hobgoblin. 2. A vampire bat.

Espectroscópico, ca [es-pec-tros-co'-pe-co, cah], *a.* Spectroscopic, relating to the solar spectrum.

Espectroscopio [es-pec-tros-co'-pe-o], *m.* Spectroscope.

Especulación [es-pay-coo-lah-the-on'], *f.* 1. Speculation, contemplation, mental view. 2. A commercial scheme or adventure. 3. Theory, as opposed to practice.

Especulador, ra [es-pay-coo-lah-dor', rah], *m.* & *f.* Speculator.

Especular [es-pay-coo-lar'], *va.* 1. To behold, to view, to examine by the eye. 2. To speculate, to meditate, to contemplate. 3. To form commercial schemes.

Especular, *adj.* 1. Specular, relating to a mirror. 2. Transparent, diaphanous.

Especulativa [es-pay-coo-lah-tee'-vah], *f.* Faculty of viewing or speculating; understanding.

Especulativamente, *adv.* Speculatively.

Especulativo, va [es-pay-coo-lah-tee'-vo, vah], *a.* Speculative, thoughtful.

Espéculo [es-pay'-coo-lo], *m.* 1. Speculum, an instrument to aid in the inspection of cavities of the body. 2. A code of laws compiled by order of Alonzo the Wise.

Espejado, da [es-pay-hah'-do, dah], *a.* Mirror-like, resembling or consisting of looking-glasses.

Espejería [es-pay-hay-ree'-ah], *f.* 1. Glass-shop. a place where looking-glasses are sold. 2. Glass-house, where plate-glass is made.

Espejero [es-pay-hay'-ro], *m.* One whose trade is to make or sell looking-glasses.

Espejico, illo, ito [es-pay-hee'-co, eel'-lyo, ee'-to], *m. dim.* Little mirror.

Espejismo (or **Espejeo**) [es-pay-hees'-mo, es-pay-hay'-o], *m.* Looming, mirage.

Espejo [es-pay'-ho], *m.* 1. Looking-glass, mirror; a glass which shows forms reflected. *Limpio como un espejo*, As clean as a penny. *Espejo ustorio*, A burning-glass. 2. *Espejo de popa*, (Naut.) Stern-frame.

Espejuela [es-pay-hoo-ay'-lah], *f.* A kind of sharp bit for a horse, forming an arch.

Espejuelo [es-pay-hoo-ay'-lo], *m.* 1. (Dim.) A small looking-glass. 2. Specular stone, selenite, a kind of transparent lamellated gypsum. 3. Transparent leaf of mica. 4. Instrument used by bird-catchers in catching larks. *Espejuelos*, Crystal lenses, of which spectacles are made; spectacles.

Espelta [es-pel'-tah], *f.* (Bot.) 1. *V.* ESCANDIA. 2. *V.* ESCAÑA.

Espélteo, ea [es-pel'-tay-o, ah], *a.* Belonging to spelt.

Espeluznarse [es-pay-looth-nar'-say], *vr.* To have the hair dishevelled, or set on end with fear.

Espeque [es-pay'-kay], *m.* Handspike, wooden lever. *Espeque de la bomba*, (Naut.) The pump brake.

Espera [es-pay'-rah], *f.* 1. Expectation, the act of expecting. 2. Expectance or expectancy, the state of expecting. 3. Stay, the act of waiting. 4. Pause, stop. 5. Stay, restraint, prudence, caution, discreet, steadiness. 6. (Law) Respite, adjournment, pause, interval. 7. A kind of heavy ordnance. 8. A letter of license. *Estar en espera*, To be in expectation of. *Hombre de espera*, A cool, composed man.

Esperable [es-pay-rah'-blay], *a.* That which may be expected or hoped.

Esperador, ra [es-pay-ra-dor', rah], *a.* Expectant.

Esperanza [es-pay-rahn'-thah], *f.* Hope, expectance, expectancy. *Ancora de la esperanza*, (Naut.) Sheet-anchor or anchor of hope. (Coll.) Prospect. *No hay esperanza*, There is no chance.

Esperanzar [es-pay-ran-thar'], *va.* To give hope.

Esperar [es-pay-rar'], *va.* 1. To hope. 2. To expect, to have a previous apprehension of either good or evil. 3. To expect, to stay, to wait for, to attend the coming, to look for. 4. To fear. *Espero la calentura*, I am afraid of the fever.—*vr.* To expect, to wait, to stay.

Esperezarse, or **Desperezarse** [es-pay-ray-thar'-say], *vr.* To stretch one's self.

Esperezo [es-pay-ray'-tho], *m.* The act of stretching one's arms and legs after being roused from sleep.

Esperiego, ga [es-pay-re-ay'-go, gah], *a.* *V.* ASPERIEGA. *Esperiego*, Tart apple-tree, pippin.

Esperlán [es-per-lahn'], *m.* (Zool.) Smelt, a small sea-fish.

Esperma [es-perr'-mah], *f.* Sperm. *V.* SEMEN. *Esperma de ballena*, Spermaceti.

Espermaceti [es-per-ma-thay'-te], *m.* Spermaceti.

Espermático, ca [es-per-mah'-te-co, cah], *a.* Spermatic, seminal, belonging to the sperm.

Espermatorrea [es-per-ma-tor-ray'-ah], *f.* Spermatorrhœa, involuntary loss of semen.

Espermatozoide [es-per-mah-to-thoy'-day], *m.* Spermatozoid.

Espérmido, da [es-perr'-me-do, dah], *a.* Producing seeds.

Espernada [es-per-nah'-dah], *f.* End of a chain.

Espernible [es-per-nee'-blay], *a.* (Prov.) Despicable.
Esperón [es-pay-rone'], *m.* (Naut.) The forecastle head.
Esperonte [es-pay-ron'-tay], *m.* Kind of ancient fortification.
Esperriaca [es-per-re-ah'-cah], *f.* (Prov.) The last must or juice drawn from grapes.
Espesamiento [es-pay-sah-me-en'-to], *m.* (Prov.) Coagulation.
Espesar [es-pay-sar'], *va.* 1. To thicken, to inspissate, to condense what is fluid. 2. To coagulate, to curdle, to concrete. 3. To mass, to assemble. 4. To close, to join, as silk or stuff does.—*vr.* To condensate, to grow thicker.
Espesartina [es-pay-sar-tee'-nah], *f.* Spessartite, or spessartin, a hyacinth-red (or mulberry-coloured) garnet.
Espesativo, va [es-pay-sah-tee'-vo, vah], *a.* That which has the power of thickening.
Espeso, sa [es-pay'-so, sah], *a.* 1. Thick, condensed, dense, gross, crass; curdy. 2. (Obs.) Bulky, heavy, corpulent. 3. Close, contiguous. 4. Frequent, often repeated. 5. Slovenly, dirty.
Espesor [es-pay-sor'], *m.* Thickness, grossness, crassitude; corpulence.
Espesura [es-pay-soo'-rah], *f.* 1. Thickness, density, closeness, crassitude. 2. (Fort.) Thickness, solidity of the works of a fortress. 3. Thicket, a close wood. 4. Slovenliness, negligence of dress.
Espetamiento [es-pay-tah-me-en'-to], *m.* (Coll.) Stiffness, formality, stateliness of mien or deportment.
Espetar [es-pay-tar'], *va.* 1. To spit, to put upon a spit. 2. To run through with a sword. 3. To tell, to relate. *Le espetó fuertes razones,* He gave strong reasons.—*vr.* 1. To be stiff and stately, to be puffed up with pride. 2. (Met. Coll.) To sidle or thrust one's self into some narrow place.
Espetera [es-pay-tay'-rah], *f.* 1. Rack, a board with hooks, on which kitchen utensils are hung. 2. Kitchen furniture.
Espeto, *m.* (Obs.) *V.* ASADOR.
Espetón [es-pay-tone'], *m.* 1. Spit, a long iron prong. 2. A large pin. 3. (Zool.) Sea-pike, spit-fish. Esox sphyræna. 4. Blow given with a spit.
Espia [es-pee'-ah], *m.* & *f.* 1. A spy. *Espía doble,* Person who betrays the secrets of both parties. *Espía del purgatorio,* Nickname of persons very feeble and languid. 2. (Naut.) Warp, a rope used in moving a ship, a tow-rope of twisted bark.
Espiador, *m.* (Obs.) Spy.
Espiar [es-pe-ar'], *va.* 1. To spy, to watch closely. 2. To lurk, to lie in wait. 3. (Naut.) To warp, to move a ship by means of a warp.
Espibia [es-pee'-be-ah], *f.* (Vet.) Incomplete dislocation of the vertebræ.
Espibio, Espibión [es-pee'-be-o, es-pe-be-on'], *m.* (Vet.) Dislocation or contraction in the nape of the neck of animals.
Espicanardi [es-pe-cah-nar'-de], *f.* (Bot.) Spikenard. Andropogon nardus.
Espicifloro, ra [es-pe-the-flo'-ro, rah], *a.* (Bot.) Spicate, having flowers arranged in spikes.
Espicúleo, a [es-pe-coo'-lay-o, ah], *a.* (Bot.) Spiculate, divided into spikelets.
Espiculífero, ra [es-pe-coo-lee'-fay-ro, rah], *a.* (Bot.) Spiculiferous, bearing spikelets.
Espichar [es-pe-char'], *va.* 1. To prick. *V.* PINCHAR. 2. (Coll.) To give up the ghost, to die.
Espiche [es-pee'-chay], *m.* A sharp-pointed weapon. *Espiches,* (Naut.) Pegs, small pointed pieces of wood driven into the holes of the planks of ships, dowel, spile.
Espichón [es-pe-chone'], *m.* Wound with a pointed weapon.
Espiga [es-pee'-gah], *f.* 1. Ear, the spike or head of corn; that part which contains the seed. 2. Tenon, the end of a piece of timber fitted into another. 3. Fuse of a bomb or shell. 4. (Naut.) Distance between the last collar of the top-gallant-masts and the summit or acorn; sail of a galley. 5. *Espiga céltica,* A valerian. 6. *Espiga de agua,* (Bot.) Pond-weed. Potamogeton, *L.* *Quedarse a la espiga,* (Coll.) To remain to the last, to collect the fragments or refuse.
Espigadera [es-pe-gah-day'-rah], *f.* Gleaner, a woman who gathers corn after the reapers.
Espigado, da [es-pe-gah'-do, dah], *a.* 1. Tall, grown: applied to growing persons. 2. Acrospired.—*pp.* of ESPIGAR.
Espigadora [es-pe-gah-do'-rah], *f.* *V.* ESPIGADERA.
Espigar [es-pe-gar'], *vn.* 1. To ear, to shoot into ears. 2. (Met.) To grow, to increase in bulk and stature.—*va.* 1. To glean, to gather corn left by the reapers. 2. (Prov.) To make presents to a bride. 3. To make a tenon.
Espigelia [es-pe-hay'-le-ah], *f.* Spigelia, pink-root, an anthelmintic herb. (Spigelia marilandica.)
Espigón [es-pee-gone'], *m.* 1. Ear of corn. 2. Sting, as of bees, wasps, etc. 3. Point of a dart or javelin. 4. Sharp point of a hill without trees. *Ir con espigón* or *llevar espigón,* (Met.) To retire indignant or irritated.
Espiguilla, ta [es-pe-geel'-lyah, gee'-tah], *f.* 1. Small edging of lace, tape, or inkle. 2. Flower of some trees. 3. (Dim.) A small ear of corn; spikelet.
Espilo [es-pee'-lo], *m.* A small spot upon grasses below the first membrane, at its inner base.
Espilocho [es-pe-lo'-cho], *m.* (Obs.) Poor, destitute person.
Espilorchería [es-pe-lor-chay-ree'-ah], *f.* (Low) Sordid avarice.
Espín [es-peen'], *m.* Porcupine.
Espina [es-pee'-nah], *f.* 1. A thorn. 2. A fish-bone. 3. Spine, the backbone. 4. A small splinter of wood, esparto, etc. 5. (Met.) Scruple, doubt, suspicion. *Espina blanca,* (Bot.) Woolly-cotton thistle. Onopordon acanthium.
Espinaca [es-pe-nah'-cah], *f.* (Bot.) Spinage. Spinacia oleracea.
Espina dorsal [es-pee'-nah dor-sahl'], *f.* Spinal column.
Espinadura [es-pe-nah-doo'-rah], *f.* Act of pricking with a thorn.
Espinal, Espinar [es-pe-nahl', es-pe-nar'], *m.* 1. Place full of thorn-bushes, brambles, and briers. 2. (Met.) A dangerous undertaking, an arduous enterprise.
Espinal [es-pe-nahl'], *a.* Spinal, dorsal.
Espinar [es-pe-nar'], *va.* 1. To prick with thorns. 2. To surround trees with briers and thorn-bushes. 3. (Met.) To nettle, to make uneasy, to abuse, to provoke.
Espinazo [es-pe-nah'-tho], *m.* Spine, the back-bone.
Espinel [es-pe-nel'], *m.* A fishing-line with many hooks, to catch conger-eels and other large fishes.
Espinela [es-pe-nay'-lah], *f.* 1. A piece of Spanish poetry, consisting of ten verses of eight syllables. 2. Spinel-ruby, a precious stone.
Espíneo, ea [es-pee'-nay-o, ah], *a.* (Obs.) Made of thorns.
Espineta [es-pe-nay'-tah], *f.* 1. Spinet, a small harpsichord. 2. The bit of a bridle.
Espingarda [es-pin-gar'-dah], *f.* 1. A small piece of ordnance. 2. A long hand-gun or musket used in Morocco.
Espingardada [es-pin-gar-dah'-dah], *f.* Wound of a ball from an *espingarda.*
Espingardero [es-pin-gar-day'-ro], *m.* (Obs.) Gunner, musketeer.
Espinica, illa [es-pe-nee'-cah, eel'-lyah], *f. dim.* A small thorn.
Espinilla [es-pe-nee'-lyah], *f.* 1. Shin or shin bone. 2. Blackhead.
Espinita [es-pe-nee'-tah], *f. dim.* A little thorn.
Espino [es-pee'-no], *m.* (Bot.) Thorn, a prickly tree of several kinds; hawthorn. *Espino albar* or *blanco, espino majuelo* or *majoletero,* White-thorn. Cratægus oxyacantha, *L.* *Espino amarillo,* Common sea-buckthorn. Hippophæ rhamnoides, *L.* *Espino negro,* Boxthorn like buckthorn. Rhamnus lycioides, *L.* *Espino cerval,* Purging buckthorn. Rhamnus catharticus, *L.*
Espinoso, sa [es-pe-no'-so, sah], *a.* 1. Spiny, thorny. 2. (Met.) Arduous, dangerous.
Espinoso [es-pe-no' so], *m.* (Zool.) Three-spined stickleback. Gasterosteus aculeatus.
Espinulífero, ra [es-pe-noo-lee'-fay-ro, rah], *a.* (Bot.) Spinuliferous, thorn-bearing.
Espinuloso, sa [es-pe-noo-lo'-so, sah], (Bot.) Spinulous, thorny.
Espinzar [es-pin-thar'], *va.* To burl; to dress cloth after it has been milled.
Espión [es-pe-on'], *m.* Spy. *V.* ESPÍA.
Espionaje [es-pe-o-nah'-hay], *m.* Espionage, the action of spying.
Espiote [es-pe-o'-tay], *m.* A sharp-pointed weapon.
Espique [es-pee'-kay], *m.* *V.* ESPICANARDI.
Espira [es-pee'-rah], *f.* 1. A spiral line, a spire, a helix. 2. Spire, a winding staircase. 3. Part of the base of a column, above the plinth. 4. Each turn of a conical shell.
Espiración [es-pe-rah-the-on'], *f.* Expiration, respiration.
Espiráculo [es-pe-rah'-coo-lo], *m.* Spiracle, breathing-pore.
Espiradero [es-pe-rah-day'-ro], *m.* *V.* RESPIRADERO.
Espirador [es-pe-rah-dor'], *m.* He who expires or breathes.
Espiral [es-pe-rahl'], *a.* Spiral, winding, helical, helispherical.
Espiralmente [es-pe-ral-men'-tay], *adv.* Spirally.
Espirante [es-pe-rahn'-tay], *pa.* Expiring, respiring.
Espirar [es-pe-rar'], *vn.* 1. To expire, to breathe the last. 2. To make an emission of the breath, to expire. 3. To finish, to come to an end. 4. To fly out with a blast.—*va.* 1. To exhale. 2. To infuse a divine spirit.
Espirativo, va [es-pe-rah-tee'-vo, vah], *a.* That which can breathe or respire.
Espirea [es-pe-ray'-ah], *f.* (Bot.) Spiræa. Spiræa. *Espirea filipéndula,* Dropwort spiræa. Spiræa filipendula. *Espirea ulmaria,* Meadow sweet spiræa. Spiræa ulmaria. *Espirea opulifolia,* Guelder rose-leaved spiræa. Spiræa opulifolia. *Espirea hojisauceña,* Willow-leaved spiræa. Spiræa salicifolia.
Espiritar [es-pe-re-tar'], *va.* 1. To irritate or agitate. 2. *V.* ENDEMONIAR.

—*vr.* To be possessed with an evil spirit.
Espiritillo [es-pe-re-teel'-lyo], *m. dim.* A little spirit.
Espiritismo [es-pe-re-tees'-mo], *m.* Spiritualism, spiritism, the belief that the spirits of the dead communicate in various ways to men. usually through a medium.
Espiritista [es-pe-re-tees'-tah], *m.* & *f.* A spiritualist.
Espiritosamente, *adv.* Spiritedly, ardently.
Espiritoso, sa [es-pe-re-to'-so, sah], *a.* 1. Spiritous, having the quality of spirit; defecated. 2. (Met.) Spirited, lively, active, ardent.
Espíritu [es-pee'-re-too], *m.* 1. Spirit, an immaterial substance. 2. Soul of man. 3. Genius, vigour of mind; power of mind, moral or intellectual. 4. Spirit, ardour, courage, life, manhood. 5. That which gives vigour or cheerfulness to the mind or body. 6. Inclination, turn of mind. 7. Spirit, inflammable liquor, raised by distillation. 8. True sense or meaning. *El Espíritu Santo,* The Holy Ghost. *Espíritu maligno,* The devil. *Dar el espíritu,* To give up the ghost, to die. *Cobrar espíritu,* To take courage. *Espíritus,* 1. Spirits, demons, hobgoblins. 2. Spirits, subtile vapours, ether.
Espiritual [es-pe-re-too-ahl'], *a.* Spiritual, ghostly.
Espiritualidad [es-pe-re-too-ah-le-dahd'], *f.* 1. Spirituality, incorporality, intellectual nature. 2. Principle and effect of what is spiritual. *Espiritualidades de un obispo,* Revenue of a bishop arising from his jurisdiction.
Espiritualismo [es-pe-re-too-ah-lees'-mo], *m.* Spiritualism, as a philosophic system, opposed to materialism.
Espiritualista [es-pe-re-too-ah-lees'-tah], *m.* He who treats of the vital spirits.
Espiritualizar [es-pe-re-too-ah-le-thar'], *va.* 1. To spiritualize. to purify from the feculencies of the world. 2. To refine the intellect.
Espiritualmente [es-pe-re-too-al-men-tay], *adv.* Spiritually.
Espirituoso, sa [es-pe-re-too-oh'-so, sah], *a.* 1. Spirituous, having the quality of spirit; ardent, inflammable. 2. Spirituous, vivid, airy, lively.
Espirómetro [es-pe-ro'-may-tro], *m.* Spirometer, instrument for measuring the breathing capacity of the lungs.
Espita [es-pee'-tah], *f.* 1. A faucet. 2. Tippler, a drunkard. 3. Span, the space from the end of the thumb to the end of the little finger extended.
Espitar [es-pe-tar'], *va.* To put a faucet in a tub or other vessel.
Espito [es-pee'-to], *m.* Peel, a piece of wood used to hang up paper to dry.
Esplendente [es-plen-den'-tay], *pa.* (Poet.) Shining, glittering, resplendent.
Esplender [es-plen-derr'], *vn.* (Poet. Obs.) To shine, to glitter, to be resplendent.
Espléndidamente, *adv.* Splendidly, nobly, magnificently, gloriously, brightly, glisteringly.
Esplendidez [es-plen-de-deth'], *f.* Splendour, magnificence; ostentation.
Espléndido, da [es-plen'-de-do, dah], *a.* 1 Splendid, magnificent, grand, sumptuous, pompous. 2. (Poet.) Resplendent.
Esplendor [es-plen-dor'], *m.* 1. Splendour, brilliancy, lustre, glory, magnificence, grandeur. 2. Fulgency, glitter, lucidity. 3. Excellence, eminence, nobleness, gallantry. 4. Finery, fineness, gorgeousness. 5. White paint made of pounded egg-shells.
Esplendoroso, sa [es-plen-do-ro'-so, sah], *a.* (Poet.) Brilliant, refulgent, luminous.
Esplenético, ca [es-play-nay'-te-co, cah], *a.* Splenic, belonging to the spleen or milt.
Espliego [es-ple-ay'-go], *m.* (Bot.) Lavender. Lavandula spica. In Andalusia it is called *Alhucema.*
Esplín [es-pleen'], *m.* (Coll.) Spleen, melancholy, hypochondriacal vapours.
Esplique [es-plee'-kay], *m.* Machine for catching birds.
Espodio [es-po'-de-o], *m.* 1. Calx found in copper furnaces. 2. Ashes of burnt ivory or reeds.
Espodito [es-po-dee'-to], *m.* Whitish ashes of volcanoes.
Espodolenco, ca [es-po-do-len'-co, cah], *a.* (Zool.) Ashen in colour, of a mixed gray and white.
Espolada [es-po-lah'-dah], *f.* Prick with a spur. *Espolada de vino,* (Coll.) A large draught of wine.
Espolazo [es-po-lah'-tho], *m.* A violent prick with a spur.
Espoleadura [es-po-lay-ah-doo'-rah], *f.* Wound made with a spur.
Espolear [es-po-lay-ar'], *va.* 1. To spur, to drive with a spur. 2. To spur, to instigate, to incite, to urge forward.
Espoleta [es-po-lay'-tah], *f.* 1. Fuse of a bomb or a hand-grenade. *Espoletas de cubierta,* (Naut.) Fuses of a fire-ship. 2. Small bone between the wings of birds.
Espolín [es-po-leen'], *m.* 1. A small spool for raising flowers on stuff. 2. Silk stuff, on which flowers are raised, like brocade.
Espolinado, da [es-po-le-nah'-do, dah], *a.* Flowered: applied to silk stuffs.—*pp.* of ESPOLINAR.
Espolinar [es-po-le-nar'], *va.* To weave flowers in silk.
Espolio [es-po'-le-o], *m.* The property which a prelate leaves at his death.
Espolique [es-poo-lee'-kay], *m. V.* ESPOLISTA for a servant.
Espolista [es-po-lees'-tah], *m.* 1. A servant who travels on foot before the horse or mule of his master, a running footman. 2. One who farms the fruits of the ecclesiastical benefice of a diseased bishop.
Espolón [es-po-lone'], *m.* 1. Spur, the sharp point on the legs of a cock. 2. The acute angle of the pier of a stone bridge, to break the force of the current. 3. (Arch.) Stay, prop. 4. (Naut.) The ram of a man-of-war. 5. (Naut.) Fender-beam, knee of the head, a curve which is put upon vessels which lack a cutwater, in order to fit the bowsprit to it. 6. Part of a causeway or dock which juts into the sea. 7. (Fort.) Kind of a salient angle. 8. Chilblain.
Espolvorear [es-pol-vo-ray-ar'], *va.* 1. To powder, to sprinkle with powder. 2. To dust, to brush off the dust. 3. (Met.) To separate, to scatter, to dissipate.
Espolvorizar [es-pol-vo-re-thar'], *va.* To scatter powder.
Espondaico, ca [es-pon-dah'-ee-co, cah], *a.* Spondaic, of spondees.
Espondeo [es-pon-day'-o], *m.* Spondee, a foot of verse consisting of two long syllables.
Espondil, *m. V.* VÉRTEBRA.
Espondilitis [es-pon-de-lee'-tis], *f.* (Med.) Spondylitis, inflammation of the spinal column.
Espóndilo [es-pon'-de-lo], *m.* 1. Vertebra. 2. A ball which was used in ancient Greece for elections.
Esponja [es-pone'-hah], *f* 1. Sponge 2. (Met.) Sponger, one who by mean arts lives on others.
Esponjado [es-pon-hah'-do], *m.* (Prov.) A sponge made of sugar which instantly dissolves.—*Esponjado, da, pp.* of ESPONJAR.
Esponjadura [es-pon-hah-doo'-rah], *f.* 1. Act of sponging. 2. Cavity or defect in cast metal.
Esponjar [es-pon-har'], *va.* To sponge, to soak or imbibe.—*vr.* To be puffed up with pride.
Esponjilla, *f.* (Bot.) A fruit of the size of a turkey's egg which abounds in Venezuela, Colombia, and Ecuador.
Esponjilla, ita, uela [es-pon-heel'-lyah], *f. dim.* A small piece of sponge.
Esponjosidad [es-pon-ho-se-dahd'], *f* Sponginess.
Esponjoso, sa [es-pon-ho'-so, sah], *a.* Spongy, porous.
Esponsales [es-pon-sah'-les], *m. pl.* Espousals, betrothal, a mutual promise of marriage.
Esponsalicio, cia [es-pon-sah-lee'-the-o, ah], *a.* Belonging to espousals, nuptial, spousal.
Espontáneamente [es-pon-tah'-nay-ah-men-tay], *adv.* Spontaneously, voluntarily.
Espontanearse [es-pon-tah-nay-ar'-say], *vr.* & *vn.* To avow or declare spontaneously.
Espontaneidad [es-pon-tah-nay-e-dahd'], *f.* Spontaneity, spontaneousness, the state of being spontaneous, voluntariness.
Espontáneo, nea [es-pon-tah'-nay-o, ah], *a.* Spontaneous, voluntary, willing.
Espontón [es-pon-tone'], *m.* Spontoon, a half-pike.
Espontonada [es-pon-to-nah'-dah], *f.* Salute to royal personages or generals with a spontoon.
Esporádico, ca [es-po-rah'-de-co, cah], *a.* Sporadic, isolated (used of disease).—*adv.* **Esporádicamente.**
Espora, *f.* or **Esporo,** *m.* [es-po-rah, roh], (Bot.) Spore.
Esporón [es-po-rone'], *m.* (Obs.) *V* ESPUELA.
Esportear [es-por-tay-ar'], *va.* To carry any thing in frails, panniers, or baskets.
Esportilla [es-por-teel'-lyah], *f. dim.* A small frail, pannier, or wicker vessel.
Esportillero [es-por-til-lyay'-ro], *m.* Porter, one who carries burdens for hire.
Esportillo [es-por-teel'-lyo], *m.* Pannier, frail, a wicker vessel.
Esportón [es-por-tone'], *m. aug.* A large pannier.
Espórtula [es-por'-too-lah], *f.* (Prov.) Judicial fees.
Esposa [es-po'-sah], *f.* Spouse, wife, consort, matron.—*pl.* Manacles, handcuffs, fetters, or chains for the hands.
Esposo [es-po'-so], *m.* Spouse, husband, consort.
Esprilla [es-preel'-lyah], *f* (Bot.) *V.* ESCAÑA.
Espuela [es-poo-ay'-lah], *f.* 1. Spur, a goading instrument worn on a horseman's heel. 2. (Met.) Spur, stimulus, incitement. *Mozo de espuela, V.* ESPOLISTA. *Poner espuela,* (Met.) To incite, to urge on. 3. *Espuela de caballero,* (Bot.) Larkspur or lark's-heel. Delphinium consolida, *L.*
Espuenda [es-poo-en'-dah], *f.* (Naut.) Margin of a river.
Espuerta [es-poo-err'-tah], *f.* Pannier, basket, frail, with two handles.

Espulgadero [es-pool-gah-day -ro], *m.* Place where beggars clean themselves from lice or fleas.
Espulgador, ra [es-pool-gah-dor', rah], *m. & f.* One who cleans off lice or fleas.
Espulgar [es-pool-gar'], *va.* 1. To clean from lice or fleas. 2. To examine closely.
Espulgo [es-pool'-go], *m.* The act of cleaning from lice or fleas.
Espuma [es-poo'-mah], *f.* 1. Froth, spume, foam; the bubbles caused in liquors by agitation. *Espuma de plata*, Litharge of silver. *Espuma de nitro*, Aphronitrum. *Espuma de mar*, A name given on the coast of Spain to polyparies and marine plants which the waves leave on the shores, and are useful for a fertilizer. 2. Scum. 3. Meerschaum.
Espumadera [es-poo-mah-day'-rah], *f.* 1. Skimmer, a sort of ladle with holes. 2. Vessel used by confectioners to clarify sugar. 3. (Naut.) Pitch-skimmer.
Espumajear [es-poo-mah-hay-ar'], *vn.* To froth at the mouth.
Espumajo [es-poo-mah'-ho], *m.* Froth, spume; saliva.
Espumajoso, sa [es-poo-mah-ho'-so, sah], *a.* Foamy, frothy, spumous.
Espumante [es-poo-mahn'-tay], *pa.* Foaming at the mouth, like enraged animals.—*a.* Sparkling.
Espumar [es-poo-mar'], *va.* To skim or to scum, to take off the scum.—*vn.* To froth, to foam.
Espumear [es-poo-may-ar'], *va.* To raise foam.
Espumarajo [es-poo-ma-rah'-ho], *m.* Foam, frothy substance thrown from the mouth. *Echar espumarajos por la boca*, To foam at the mouth with passion.
Espumero [es-poo-may'-ro], *m.* Place where salt water is collected to crystallize.
Espumescente [es-poo-mes-then'-tay], *a.* Spumescent.
Espumilla [es-poo-meel'-lyah], *f.* Thread crape, a sort of thin cloth loosely woven.
Espumillón [es-poo-mil-lyone'], *m.* Silk crape or gauze.
Espumosidad [es-poo-mo-se-dahd'], *f.* Frothiness, foaminess.
Espumoso, sa [es-poo-mo'-so, sah], *a.* Spumy, spumous, frothy, foamy, nappy.
Espundia [es-poon'-de-ah], *f.* (Vet.) A cancerous ulcer.
Espurcílocuo, cua [es-poor-thee'-lo-kwo, kwah], *a.* Of foul, disgusting talk.
Espúreo, rea, or **Espurio, ria** [es-poo'-ray-o, ah, re-o, ah], *a.* 1. Spurious, not legitimate. 2. (Met.) Spurious, adulterated, corrupted, not genuine.
Espurriar, or **Espurrear** [es-poor-re-ar'], *va.* To spurt, to moisten a thing with water.
Espurrir [es-poor-reer'], *va.* To stretch out something; chiefly said of the feet.
Esputo [es-poo'-to], *m.* Spittle, saliva; sputum.
Esquebrajar [es-kay-brah-har'], *va.* To split, to cleave.—*vr.* To become open, to be split or full of chinks, as wood.
Esqueje [es-kay'-hay], *m.* Among gardeners, a cutting, slip.
Esquela [es-kay'-lah], *f.* Billet, a small letter or paper, a note. *Esquela amatoria*, A love-letter.
Esqueleto [es-kay-lay'-to], *m.* 1. Skeleton, the bones of the body preserved in their natural situation. 2. Person very thin and meagre. 3. Watch, the works and movements of which are exposed to view. 4. (Naut.) Carcass or framework of a ship without cover or sheathing. *En esqueleto*, Unfinished, in an incomplete manner.
Esquelita [es-kay-lee'-tah], *f.* 1. A small note, a billet. 2. Tungstate of calcium.
Esquema [es-kay'-mah], *m.* Plan, sketch, outline, diagram. *Esquema del vuelo*, (Aer.) Flight pattern.
Esquematico, ca [es-kay-mah'-te-co, cah], *a.* Schematic.—*m. pl.* Sectarians who believed that the body of Jesus Christ was only apparent.
Esquena [es-kay'-nah], *f.* Spine of fishes.
Esquero [es-kay'-ro], *m.* A leather bag or pouch.
Esquerro, ra [es-ker'-ro, rah], *a.* (Obs.) *V.* Izquierdo.
Esquí [es-kee'], *m.* Ski. *Esquí acuático*, Water ski.
Esquiar [es-ke-ar'], *vn.* To ski.
Esquiciado, da [es-ke-the-ah'-do, dah], *a.* Sketched, traced, delineated.—*pp.* of Esquiciar.
Esquiciar [es-ke-the-ar'], *va.* To sketch, to draw the outlines of a painting; to trace, to delineate.
Esquicio [es-kee'-the-o], *m.* Sketch, outline, line.
Esquifada [es-ke-fah'-dah], *f.* 1. A skiff or boat load. 2. Vault of a cistern.
Esquifar [es-ke-far'], *va.* 1. (Naut.) To arm a boat with oars. 2. To fit out a ship.
Esquifazón [es-ke-fah-thone'], *f.* (Naut.) 1. A boat's crew. 2. A set of sails. Written also **Esquifación.**
Esquife [es-kee'-fay], *m.* 1. A skiff, a small boat. 2. (Arch.) Cylindrical vault.
Esquila [es-kee'-lah], *f.* 1. Hand-bell, a small bell; also a bell carried by cattle. 2. The act and time of sheep-shearing. *V.* Esquileo. 3. (Zool.) Shrimp. Cancer squilla. 4. (Ent.) Water-spider. 5. (Bot.) *V.* Escila.
Esquilada [es-ke-lah'-dah], *f.* (Prov.) *V.* Cencerrada.
Esquilador [es-ke-lah-dor'], *m.* Sheep-shearer, clipper.
Esquilar [es-ke-lar'], *va.* 1. To shear or to fleece sheep, to cut off the wool or hair of animals. 2. (Prov.) To climb a tree with the hands and feet only. *A Dios que esquilan*, An expression used by persons who are in great haste and cannot stop.
Esquileo [es-ke-lay'-o], *m.* Sheep-shearing time; also, the act and place of shearing.
Esquilimoso, sa [es-ke-le-mo'-so, sah], *a.* (Coll.) Fastidious, over nice.
Esquilmar [es-keel-mar'], *va.* To gather and get in the harvest. *Esquilmar la tierra*, To impoverish the earth: applied to trees.
Esquilmeño, ña [es-keel-may'-nyo, nyah], *a.* Fruitful, productive: used of trees or plants.
Esquilmo [es-keel'-mo], *m.* 1. Harvest, the corn garnered. 2. Produce of vines. 3. Produce of cattle.
Esquilo [es-kee'-lo], *m.* 1. Shearing-time; also, the act of shearing. 2. Kind of squirrel.
Esquilón [es-ke-lone'], *m.* 1. A small bell. 2. Large bell worn by cattle.
Esquimal [es-kee-mahl'], *a.* Eskimo.
Esquina [es-kee'-nah], *f.* Corner, the outward angle formed by two lines, coin, edge, angle. *En la esquina de la calle*, In the corner of the street. *Estar de esquina*, (Coll.) To be at variance.
Esquinado, da [es-ke-nah'-do, dah], *a.* Cornered, angled.—*pp.* of Esquinar.
Esquinal [es-ke-nahl'], *m.* Corner plate, angle iron; iron knee, corner casting.
Esquinante, Esquinanto [es-ke-nahn'-tay], *m.* Kind of aromatic or medicinal rush.
Esquinar [es-ke-nar'], *va.* (Prov.) To make a corner, to form into an angle.
Esquinazo [es-ke-nah'-tho], *m.* 1. Corner, a very acute outward angle. 2. (Coll.) Quinsy.
Esquinco [es-keen'-co], *m.* Kind of serpent or crocodile.
Esquinela [es-ke-nay'-lah], *f.* Armour for the legs.
Esquinzador [es-kin-thah-dor'], *m.* Large apartment in paper-mills for putting the rags in, after cutting them.
Esquinzar [es-kin-thar'], *va.* To cut rags in small pieces, in paper-mills.
Esquipado, da [es-ke-pah'-do, dah], *a.* Made boat-fashion.—*pp.* of Esquipar.
Esquipar [es-ke-par'], *va.* (Naut.) To equip, to fit out a ship. *V.* Equipar.
Esquiraza [es-ke-rah'-thah], *f.* Kind of ancient ship.
Esquirla [es-keer'-lah], *f.* (Surg.) Splinter of a bone.
Esquirol [es-ke-rol'], *m.* 1. Squirrel. 2. Strikebreaker.
Esquirro [es-keer'-ro], *m.* (Med.) Scirrhus, hard cancer.
Esquirrogastria [es-kir-ro-gahs'-tre-ah], *f.* Cancerous degeneration of the stomach.
Esquisar [es-ke-sar'], *va.* (Obs.) To search, to investigate.
Esquisto [es-kees'-to], *m.* Schist.
Esquistoso, sa [es-kis-to'-so, sah], *a.* Schistose.
Esquitar [es-ke-tar'], *va.* 1. (Coll.) To pardon, to remit a debt. 2. (Obs.) *V.* Desquitar.
Esquivar [es-ke-var'], *va.* To shun, to avoid, to evade, to escape.—*vr.* To disdain, to scorn, to view with contempt, to coy.
Esquivez [es-ke-veth'], *f.* Disdain, scorn, asperity, coyness, coldness.
Esquivo, va [es-kee'-vo, vah], *a.* 1. Scornful, severe, stubborn, fastidious. 2. Shy, reserved, difficult, coyish, cold, haggard.
Esquizado, da [es-ke-thah'-do, dah], *a.* Applied to spotted marble.
Esquizofrenia [es-ke-tho-fray'-ne-ah], *f.* Schizophrenia.
Esquizofrénico, ca [es-ke-tho-fray'-ne-co, cah], *a. & m. & f.* Schizophrenic.
Esquizomicetes [es-ke-tho-me-thay'-tays], *m. pl.* Schizomycetes, a class of minute unicellular plants allied to the algæ; it comprises the bacteria.
Estabilidad [es-tah-be-le-dahd'], *f.* Stability, duration, permanence, constancy, firmness, consistence, fixedness.
Estabilización [es-tah-be-le-thah-the-on'], *f.* Stabilization.
Estabilizar [es-tah-be-le-thar'], *va.* To stabilize, to hold steady, prevent fluctuations.
Estable [es-tah'-blay], *a.* Stable, permanent, durable, steady, firm, fast, consistent.
Establear [es-tah-blay-ar'], *va.* To tame, to domesticate, to accustom to the stable.
Establecedor [es-tah-blay-thay-dor'], *m.* Founder, he that establishes an institution or law; confirmer.
Establecer [es-tah-blay-therr'], *va.* 1. To enact, to establish by law, to decree, to confirm. 2. To establish, to found, to fix immovably. 3. To fortify; to constitute. 4. To establish, to fix or settle in an opinion, to

ground.—*vr.* To establish or fix one's self in a place.

Estableciente [es-tah-blay-the-en'-tay], *pa.* & *m.* & *f.* Establisher: establishing.

Establecimiento [es-tah-blay-the-me-en'-to], *m.* 1. Statute, law, ordinance. 2. Establishment, foundation, settlement. 3. Establishment, footing, settlement or fixed state of a person. 4. (Coll.) Manufactory, place where handicraft business is carried on.

Establemente, *adv.* Stably, firmly.

Establerizo, Establero [es-tah-blay-ree'-tho, es-tah-blay'-ro], *m.* (Littl. us.) Hostler, groom, horsekeeper.

(*Yo establezco, yo establezca,* from *Establecer. V.* Conocer.)

Establillo [es-tah-bleel'-lyo], *m. dim.* A small stable.

Establo [es-tah'-blo], *m.* Stable for horses and mules.

Estaca [es-tah'-cah], *f.* 1. A stake, picket. 2. Slip of a tree put into the ground to grow. 3. Stick, cudgel, bludgeon.—*pl.* 1. (Naut.) Thowls or tholes. *V.* Toletes. 2. Divisions or partitions made in mines. 3. Clamp-nails, large nails used by carpenters. *Estar a la estaca,* (Coll.) To live very poorly, to be indigent or oppressed with want.

Estacada [es-tah-cah'-dah], *f.* 1. (Mil.) Palisade or stockade. 2. Paling, a kind of fence-work for parks, gardens, and grounds. 3. A place to fight in, place for a duel. *Dejar en la estacada,* To abandon one in peril, to sacrifice him.

Estacado [es-tah-cah'-do], *m.* Place for a duel.—*Estacado, da, pp.* of Estacar.

Estacar [es-tah-car'], *va.* 1. To put stakes into the ground; to inclose a spot with stakes. 2. To tie to a stake. —*vr.* To be inclosed or surrounded with stakes.

Estacazo [es-tah-cah'-tho], *m.* Blow given with a stake.

Estación [es-tah-the-on'], *f.* 1. State, situation, position. 2. Season of the year. 3. Hour, moment, time. 4. Station, a railway stopping-place. 5. Visit to a church in order to pray, especially upon Thursday and Friday of Holy Week, and the prayer itself. *Andar estaciones,* To perform stationary prayers in order to gain indulgences. 6. Apparent motion in the stars. 7. A party of persons posted at some place. 8. Business, duty, one's obligations. *Tornar a andar las estaciones,* (Met.) To return to one's evil ways. *Estación astral,* (Aer.) Space station. *Estación de servicio* Automobile service station. *Estación de vehículos,* Cab stand, parking lot. *Red de estaciones,* Radio network.

Estacional [es-tah-the-o-nahl'], *a.* 1. Pertaining to the seasons. 2. Seasonal, occurring at a specified time. 3. (Ast.) Stationary.

Estacionamiento [es-tah-the-o-nah-me-en'-to], *m.* Parking (of a vehicle).

Estacionar [es-tah-the-o-nar'], *va.* To park (a vehicle).—*vn.* & *vr.* To be motionless or stationary.

Estacionario, ria [es-tah-the-o-nah'-re-o, ah], *a.* Stationary, fixed, not progressive.

Estación astral [es-tah-the-on' as-trahl'], *f.* Space station.

Estacionero, ra [es-tah-the-o-nay'-ro, rah], *a.* 1. One who frequently visits the church to pray, in order to gain indulgences. 2. (Obs.) Bookseller.

Estacte [es-tahc'-tay], *m.* Odoriferous liquor extracted from fresh myrrh.

Estacha [es-tah'-chah], *f.* Rope fastened to a harpoon, to give the whale room to dive.

Estada [es-tah'-dah], *f.* Stay, sojourn, residence.

Estadal [es-tah-dahl'], *m.* 1. Land-measure, containing about three square yards and two thirds, or eleven feet. 2. Kind of ornament or holy ribbon worn at the neck. 3. (Prov.) Fathom of wax taper.

Estadía [es-tah-dee'-ah], *f.* 1. An instrument used for levelling. 2. (Com. and Naut.) Stay, detention; demurrage. Cost of such stay.

Estadio [es-tah'-de-o], *m.* 1. Race-course. 2. Distance or extent of a course which made 125 geometrical paces. 3. Stadium, each period of a disease.

Estadista [es-tah-dees'-tah], *m.* Statist, statesman, politician.

Estadística [es-tah-dees'-te-cah], *f.* Statistics, the science so called.

Estadístico, ca [es-tah-dees'-te-co, cah], *a.* Statistical, statistic, political.

Estadizo, za [es-tah-dee'-tho, thah], *a.* Stagnant, corrupted: applied to water.

Estado [es-tah'-do], *m.* 1. State, the actual condition of a thing. 2. State, condition, circumstances of nature or fortune, footing, station in life. 3. Rank, state, estate, quality, condition. 4. State, the commonwealth. 5. Stature or height of a person. 6. Statement, account, report. 7. Suite, attendants. *Estado general* or *llano,* Community or peasantry of any district, not including the nobles. *Estado honesto,* The state of a maiden woman. *Materias de estado,* State affairs. *Poner a uno en estado* or *darle estado,* To set one up in life; to marry one. *Estado mayor,* (Mil.) Staff, generals and commanders of an army. *Hombre de estado,* Statesman.

Estadounidense, Estadunidense [es-tah-do-oo-nee-denn'-say], *m.* & *f.* Native of United States of America. —*a.* From the United States.

Estafa [es-tah'-fah], *f.* Trick, deceit, imposition.

Estafador, ra [es-tah-fah-dor', rah], *m.* & *f.* Impostor, swindler, chiseler, cheat.—*a.* Chiseling, swindling.

Estafar [es-tah-far'], *va.* 1. To deceive, to defraud. 2. Among sculptors, to size a statue with a white coat in order to gild it.

Estafermo [es-tah-ferr'-mo], *m.* 1. A wooden movable figure of an armed man. 2. (Met.) An idle fellow, who affects importance.

Estafeta [es-tah-fay'-tah], *f.* 1. Courier, express, estafet. 2. General post-office for letters.

Estafetero [es-tah-fay-tay'-ro], *m.* Post-master, director of the post-office.

Estafilea piñada [es-tah-fe-lay'-ah pe-nyah'-dah], *f.* 1. (Bot.) Five-leaved bladder-nut. Staphylea pinnata. 2. *Estafilea,* A nymph converted by Bacchus into a cluster of grapes.

Estafisagra [es-tah-fe-sah'-grah], *f.* (Bot.) Stavesacre, lousewort. Delphinium staphisagria.

Estagnación [es-tag-nah-the-on'], *f.* Stagnation, want of circulation in fluids or in business. *V.* Estancación.

Estala [es-tah'-lah], *f.* 1. Stable. 2. Seaport.

Estalación [es-tah-lah-the-on'], *f.* Class, rank, order.

Estalactita [es-tah-lac-tee'-tah], *f.* Stalactite, a rocky concretion, in form of an icicle, hanging from the vaults of caves.

Estalagmita [es-tah-lag-mee'-tah], *f.* Stalagmite, a cylindrical or conical deposit on the floor of a cavern, formed by a dripping from the roof.

Estalingadura [es-tah-lin-gah-doo'-rah], *m.* (Naut.) The bending of a cable, or fastening it to the ring of the anchor.

Estalingar [es-tah-lin-gar'], *va.* (Naut.) To bend a cable.

Estallar [es-tal-lyar'], *vn.* 1. To crack, to burst into chinks with a loud sound, to creak. 2. (Met.) To break out into fury or rage.

Estallido, Estallo [es-tal-lyee'-do, es-tahl'-lyo], *m.* 1. Crack, crackling, creaking, crashing, the sound of any thing bursting or falling. 2. The report of fire-arms. *Dar un estallido,* To publish, to expose; to make a noise or confusion. (Coll.) To fail dishonestly.

Estambor [es-tam-bor'], *m.* (Naut.) Stern-post.

Estambrado [es-tam-brah'-do], *m.* (Prov.) Kind of cloth made of worsted.

Estambrar [es-tam-brar'], *va.* To twist wool into yarn, to spin worsted.

Estambre [es-tahm'-bray], *m.* 1. Fine worsted or woollen yarn. 2. Fine wool. 3. (Bot.) Stamen of flowers. *Estambre de la vida,* (Poet.) The thread of life. 4. Warp. *V.* Urdimbre.

Estamento [es-tah-men'-to], *m.* 1. Name given to each of the estates of Spain, or to the clergy, nobility, and commons, who composed the assembly of the Cortes. 2. (Obs.) State; degree, sphere of life.

Estameña [es-tah-may'-nyah], *f.* Serge, a kind of woollen stuff.

Estaminal [es-tah-me-nahl'], *a.* Staminal, pertaining to stamens.

Estamíneo, nea [es-tah-mee'-nay-o, ah], or **Estaminífero, ra** [es-ta-me-nee'-fay-ro, rah], *a.* Staminate, having stamens.

Estampa [es-tahm'-pah], *f.* 1. Print, a figure or image printed; stamp; cut. 2. The first sketch or design of a drawing or painting. 3. Press or printing machine for printing books. 4. Track, an impression left by the foot.

Estampado [es-tam-pah'-do], *m.* Impression, act and effect of stamping.

Estampado, da [es-tam-pah'-do, dah], *a.* 1. Stamped: applied to linen, cotton, etc. 2. Embossed, figured: in speaking of printed dry-goods.—*pp.* of Estampar.

Estampador [es-tam-pah-dor'], *m.* 1. One who makes or sells prints. 2. Printer.

Estampar [es-tam-par'], *va.* 1. To print, to stamp. 2. To leave in the ground an impression of the foot. 3. (Met.) To fix in one's mind or memory.

Estampería [es-tam-pay-ree'-ah], *f.* Office for printing or selling prints.

Estampero [es-tam-pay'-ro], *m.* He who makes or sells prints or stamps.

Estampida [es-tam-pee'-dah], *f.* 1. (Amer.) Stampede, a general scamper of animals. 2. (Coll.) *Dar una estampida,* To run away: to run away in debt.

Estampido [es-tam-pee'-do], *m.* 1. Report of a gun or piece of ordinance. 2. Crack, crash, crashing, the sound of any thing bursting or falling. *Dar estampido,* To publish, to propagate, to make a noise.

Estampilla [es-tam-peel'-lyah], *f.* 1. (Dim.) A small print. 2. A small press. 3. Signet, a seal manual, used instead of a signature. 4. (Amer.) A postage-stamp.

Estampita [es-tam-pee'-tah], *f. dim.* A small print or stamp.

Estancación [es-tan-cah-the-on'], *f.* Stagnation of circulating fluids or of business matters.

Estancar [es-tan-car'], *va.* 1. To stop, to check, to stem a current. 2. (Naut.) To fother a leak. 3. To monopolize, to hinder the free sale of merchandise. 4. To interdict, to prohibit, to suspend.

Estancia [es-tahn'-the-ah], *f.* 1. Stay, sojourn, continuance in a place. 2. Mansion, dwelling, habitation; a sitting-room, a bed-room. 3. (Poet.) Stanza, a division of a song or poem. 4. (Amer.) Farm; farm for grazing cattle; a country house. 5. (Amer.) Landed property.

Estanciero [es-tan-the-ay'-ro], *m.* Overseer of a farm, mansion, or domain.

Estanco [es-tahn'-co], *m.* 1. Forestalling, monopoly. 2. Place where privileged goods are sold exclusively. 3. Stop, stay, detention. 4. Repository, archives. 5. Tank.

Estanco, ca [es-tahn'-co, cah], *a.* (Naut.) Stanch, well-repaired: applied to a ship.

Estandardización [es-tan-dar-de-thah-the-on'], *f.* Standardization.

Estandarte [es-tan-dar'-tay], *m.* 1. Banner, standard, colours. 2. *Estandarte real,* (Naut.) Royal standard, used only by the commanding admiral of a fleet. 3. The upper petal of a papilionaceous corolla.

Estangurria [es-tan-goor'-re-ah], *f.* 1. Strangury, difficulty in evacuating urine. 2. Catheter, an instrument to assist in voiding urine.

Estánnico, ca [es-tahn'-ne-co, cah], *a.* Stannic, containing tin. Idem valet **Estannífero, ra.**

Estannolita [es-tan-no-lee'-tah], *f.* Oxide of tin.

Estanque [es-tahn'-kay], *m.* Pond, basin, dam of water.

Estanquero [es-tan-kay'-ro], *m.* 1. Keeper of reservoirs. 2. Retailer of privileged goods, as tobacco and snuff in Spain.

Estanquillero [es-tan-keel-lyay'-ro], *m.* A tobacconist.

Estanquillo [es-tan-keel'-lyo], *m.* (Prov.) Cigar-store, shop where tobacco and snuff are sold, by exclusive privilege.

Estanquito [es-tan-kee'-to], *m. dim.* A small pond or dam of water.

Estantal [es-tan-tahl'], *m.* Buttress. *V.* ESTRIBO.

Estante [es-tahn'-tay], *m.* 1. Shelf, book-shelf. 2. (Prov.) He who carries, in company with others, images in processions. *Estantes,* (Naut.) Props of the cross-beams.—*pa. & a.* 1. Being, existing in a place; extant. 2. Fixed, permanent: applied to sheep which are not driven to the mountains in summer.

Estantería [es-tan-tay-ree'-ah], *f.* 1. A series of book-shelves. 2. Shelving.

Estanterol [es-tan-tay-role'], *m.* Centre of a galley, where the captain stands in an engagement.

Estantigua [es-tan-tee'-goo-ah], *f.* 1. Phantom, vision, hobgoblin. 2. A deformed person in a ridiculous garb.

Estantío, tía [es-tan-tee'-o, ah], *a.* 1. Standing still and immovable on a spot. 2. (Met.) Dull, stupid; without life or spirit.

Estañadera [es-tah-nyah-day'-rah], *f.* Soldering receiver or holder of tin-plate.

Estañado [es-tah-nyah'-do], *m.* Vessel or bath with melted pewter, in which copper or iron plates are immersed to be tinned.—*Estañado, da, pp.* of ESTAÑAR.

Estañador [es-tah-nyah-dor'], *m.* Tinman, a manufacturer of tin or tinned iron.

Estañadura [es-tah-nyah-doo'-rah], *f.* Act of tinning.

Estañar [es-tah-nyar'], *va.* To tin, to cover with tin.

Estañero [es-tah-nyay'-ro], *m.* He who works and sells tin-ware, a metalman.

Estaño [es-tah'-nyo], *m.* 1. Tin, a primitive metal. 2. Tin, iron plates covered with tin.

Estaquero [es-tah-kay'-ro], *m* Buck or doe of a year old.

Estaquilla, ita [es-tah-keel'-lyah, ee'-tah], *f.* 1. In shoemaking a peg. 2. Any wooden pin which fastens one piece of timber to another. 3. Beam of a velvet-loom.

Estaquillador [es-tah-keel-lyah-dor'], *m.* An awl to bore for pegs.

Estaquillar [es-tah-keel-lyar'], *va.* To peg, to fasten with pegs.

Estaquis [es-tah'-kees], *f.* (Bot.) Stachys, hedge-nettle, a plant resembling hoarhound.

Estar [es-tar'], *vn.* 1. To be in a place. 2. To understand or comprehend. *Estoy en lo que Vd. me dice,* I understand what you tell me. 3. To be in favour of, to answer for. *Estoy por fulano,* I will answer for him. 4. To be of opinion. *Estoy en que,* I am of opinion that. 5. To be: an auxiliary verb, derived from the Latin *stare,* to stand, and used always with reference to existing or being in a place. *Estar escribiendo,* To be writing. 6. To undertake, to oblige or subject one's self to. 7. To stand. 8. To cost. *Este vestido me está en veinte doblones,* These clothes cost me twenty doubloons. 9. With the preposition *en,* it signifies cause, motive. *En eso está,* In this it consists, on this it depends. 10. With the preposition *por* and the infinitive of some verbs it sometimes signifies that something is not done, and sometimes that something will be done immediately. *Estar por* or *para partir,* To be ready to set out. 11. With *a* and some nouns it signifies to be obliged or disposed to execute what the noun signifies. *Estar a dos dedos de hacer una cosa,* To be almost decided to do something. 12. With *con* and a person's name, to live in company with. 13. To see another in order to treat with him of a matter. 14. With *de,* to be executing a thing or understanding in it, in whatever way. *Estar de gaita,* To be merry, in high spirits. *Estar algo por suceder,* To expect something to happen. *Estar a erre,* To be doing any thing with the utmost care. *Estar alerta,* To be on the watch, to be vigilant. *Estar bajo de llave* or *cerrado con llave,* To be under lock and key. *Estar de buen humor,* To be in good humour or spirits. *Estar de mal humor,* To sulk, to be angry. *Estar de facción* or *de centinela,* To stand sentry. *Estar de pie* or *en pie; estar levantado* or *derecho,* To stand. *Estar de prisa,* To be in haste, to haste, to hasten. *Estar de por medio,* To interpose, to mediate. *Estar sobre sí,* To be tranquil or serene; to be greatly elated. *Estar para ello,* To be ready, to be disposed to do any thing. *¡Dónde estamos!* An expression of admiration or disgust at what we see or hear. *Estar bien con* ——, To have regard for a person, to be in concord with him. *Estar bien una cosa,* To suit, agree, fit. *Estar en grande,* To live in luxury. *Estar mal con,* To have a bad opinion of. *Estar mal,* Not to suit, to show bad looks. *¿Está Vd.?* or *¿Estamos?* Are you aware? Have you understood well? *Estar con el pie en el aire,* To be unsettled. *Estar a la capa,* (Naut.) To lie to, to lie by. *Estar a la capa con la trinquetilla y la estay mayor,* To try under the fore and main staysail.—*vr.* To be detained; to stay. *Estarse parado* or *quieto,* To stand still.

Estarcido [es-tar-thee'-do], *m.* Stencil.

Estarcir [es-tar-theer'], *va.* To stencil.

Estarna [es-tar'-nah], *f.* (Orn.) Kind of small partridge.

Estatera [es-tah-tay'-rah], *f.* 1. Balance, steel-yard. 2. An ancient Grecian coin.

Estática [es-tah'-te-cah], *f.* (Radio) Static.

Estátice [es-tah'-te-thay], *f.* (Bot.) Sea-lavender. Statice. *Estátice vulgar, V.* CÉSPED FRANCÉS. *Estátice sinuada,* Scallop-leaved sea-lavender. Statice sinuata.

Estático, ca [es-tah'-te-co, cah], *a.* 1. (Radio) Static. 2. Static, motionless. 3. Dumbfounded.

Estatificar [es-tah-te-fe-car'], *va.* To nationalize.

Estatismo [es-tah-tees'-mo], *m.* 1. Static condition. 2. Statism, government control.

Estatua [es-tah'-too-ah], *f.* 1. A statue. 2. A dull, stupid fellow.

Estatuaria [es-tah-too-ah'-re-ah], *f.* Statuary.

Estatuario [es-tah-too-ah'-re-o], *m.* Statuary, one who makes statues.

Estatuir [es-tah-too-eer'], *va.* To establish, to ordain, to enact.

Estatura [es-tah-too'-rah], *f.* Stature, the height of a person.

Estatutario, ria [es-tah-too-tah'-re-o, ah], *a.* Belonging to a statute or law.

Estatuto [es-tah-too'-to], *m.* 1. Statute, law, ordinance. 2. (Littl. us.) Form of government established by laws and customs.

Estay [es-tah'-e], *m.* (Naut.) Stay. *Estay mayor,* The main stay. *Estay de trinquete,* The fore stay. *Estay del mastelero mayor,* The main-top stay.

Este [es'-tay], *m.* East, one of the four cardinal points of the compass. *Este cuarto* or *cuarta al nordeste,* East-by-north. *Este* or *es nordeste,* East-north-east. *Este cuarto al sudeste,* East-by-south. *Este* or *es sudeste,* East-south-east.

Este, ta, to [es'-tay, tah, to], *pron. dem.* This. *En estas y en estotras, (adv.)* In the meanwhile. *En esto,* At this time. *Para estas* or *por estas,* Expression of anger and menace used by fathers to their children.

Estearato [es-tay-ah-rah'-to], *m.* Stearate, a salt of stearic acid.

Esteárico, ca [es-tay-ah'-re-co, cah], *a.* Stearic, relating to stearine. *Bujías esteáricas,* Stearine candles.

Estearina [es-tay-ah-ree'-nah], *f.* (Chem.) Stearine, a white crystalline component of fats.

Estearona [es-tay-ah-ro'-nah], *f.* Stearone, a pearly crystalline compound the ketone of stearic acid.

Esteatita [es-tay-ah-tee'-tah], *f.* Steatite, soap stone, massive talc.

Esteba [es-tay'-bah], *f.* 1. A plant of prickly leaves and stem, growing in ponds and marshy places. 2. A stout pole, used on boats for pushing bales of wool close together. *Cf.* Estiba, 3d def.

Estebar [es-tay-bar'], *va.* With dyers, to put cloth into the caldron to dye it.

Esteclar [es-tay-clar'], *va.* To change the combs of looms for silk fringe, when they can no longer serve.

Esteirosis [es-tay-e-ro'-sis], *f.* (Med.) Barrenness, sterility, steirosis.

Estela [es-tay'-lah], *f.* 1. The wake of a ship. 2. The trail of a meteor. *Estela de vapor,* (Aer.) Contrail.

Estelaria [es-tay-lah'-re-ah], *f.* (Bot.) An old name given to the silvery ladies-mantle. Alchemilla alpina, *L.*

Estelión [es-tay-le-on'], *m.* 1. Stellion, a small spotted lizard. Lacerta stellio. 2. Toad-stone.

Estelionato [es-tay-le-o-nah'-to], *m.* (Law) Stellionate, the crime of maliciously defrauding the unwary.

Estelón [es-tay-lone'], *m.* Toad-stone.

Estelulado, da [es-tay-loo-lah'-do, dah], *a.* Stellular, star-shaped: applied to leaves, pores, or hairs.

Estemenaras [es-tay-may-nah'-ras], *f. pl.* (Naut.) Futtock-timbers. *V.* Ligazones.

Estemple [es-tem'-play], *m.* (Mining.) Stempel, a beam helping to support a platform.

Estenografía [es-tay-no-grah-fee'-ah], *f.* Stenography, short-hand; in particular, phonography.

Estenografiar [es-tay-no-grah-fe-ar'], *va.* To write in stenography.

Estenográfico, ca [es-tay-no-grah'-fe-co, cah], *a.* Stenographic, relating to short-hand.

Estenógrafo, fa [es-tay-no'-grah-fo, fah], *m. & f.* Stenographer, one who writes short-hand.

Estenomecanografía [es-tay-no-may-cah-no-grah-fee'-ah], *f.* Stenotyping.

Estenomecanógrafa [es-tay-no-may-cah-no'-grah-fah], *f.* Stenotypist.

Estenotipía [es-tay-no-te-pee'-ah], *f.* Stenotyping

Estepa [es-tay'-pah], *f.* 1. (Bot.) Rock-rose. Cistus. *Estepa común,* Laurel-leaved rock-rose. Cistus lauriforius. 2. Steppe, an immense uncultivated plain of Russia and certain regions of Asia.

Estepar [es-tay-par'], *m.* Place filled with rock-roses.

Estepilla [es-tay-peel'-lyah], *f.* (Bot.) White-leaved rock-rose. Cistus albidus.

Ester [es'-ter], *m.* (Chem.) Ester.

Estera [es-tay'-rah], *f.* Mat, a texture of sedge, flags, or rushes.

Esterar [es-tay-rar'], *va.* To mat, to cover with mats.—*vn.* (Met. Coll.) To keep one's self warm with clothes.

Estercolar [es-ter-co-lar'], *va.* To dung, to muck, to manure, etc.—*vn.* To void the excrements: applied to animals.

Estercolero [es-ter-co-lay'-ro], *m.* 1. Boy or servant who drives the muck-cart, or carries dung into the fields. 2. Dunghill, muckhill. 3. Laystall, a heap of dung.

Estercorácea [es-ter-co-rah'-thay-ah], *f. adj.* Fistula of the anus.

Estercuelo [es-ter-coo-ay'-lo], *m.* Stercoration, manuring.

Estéreo [es-tay'-ray-o], *m.* (Arith.) Stere, a unit of cubic measurement; one cubic metre.

Estereografía [es-tay-ray-o-grah-fee'-ah], *f.* Stereography, representation of solids on a plane.

Estereofónico, ca [es-tay-ray-o-fo'-ne-co, cah], *a.* Stereophonic. *Sonido estereofónico,* Stereophonic sound.

Estereográfico, ca [es-tay-ray-o-grah'-fe-co, cah], *a.* Stereographic, delineated on a plane.

Estereometría [es-tay-ray-o-may-tree'-ah], *f.* Stereometry, art of measuring solids.

Estereómetro [es-tay-ray-o'-may-tro], *m.* Stereometer, an instrument for measuring the volume of a body.

Estereoscopio [es-tay-ray-os-co'-pe-o], *m.* Stereoscope, an optical instrument, showing two slightly different pictures, blended into one, in relief.

Estereotipa [es-tay-ray-o-tee'-pah], *f.* *V.* Estereotipia.

Estereotipar [es-tay-ray-o-te-par'], *va.* To stereotype or print with solid plates.

Estereotipia [es-tay-ray-o-tee'-pe-ah], *f.* Stereotype, stereotyping

Estereotípico, ca [es-tay-ray-o-tee'-pe-co, cah], *a.* Stereotype, stereotypic, belonging to stereotype.

Esterero [es-tay-ray'-ro], *m.* Mat-maker, mat-seller.

Estéril [es-tay'-reel], *a.* Sterile, barren, unfruitful, unproductive, fruitless.

Esterilidad [es-tay-re-le-dahd'], *f.* 1. Sterility, barrenness, unfruitfulness, jejuneness. 2. Scarcity, the want of crops.

Esterilización [es-tay-re-le-thah-the-on'], *f.* Sterilization, sterilizing.

Esterilizar [es-tay-re-le-thar'], *va.* To sterilize, to make sterile.

Esterilla [es-tay-reel'-lyah], *f.* 1. (Dim.) Small mat. 2. Ferret lace, made of gold, silver, or thread. *Paños de esterilla,* Saved lists. *Esterilla de cerda para forrar sillas,* etc., Hair-cloth.

Estérilmente [es-tay'-reel-men-tay], *adv.* Barrenly, unfruitfully, meagrely.

Esterlino, na [es-ter-lee'-no, nah], *a.* Sterling: applied to money.

Esternón [es-ter-none'], *m.* (Anat.) Sternum, the breast-bone.

Estero [es-tay'-ro], *m.* 1. A large lake near the sea, a salt marsh. 2. Matting, the act of covering with matting; also, the season in which matting is laid down. 3. (Geog.) A small creek, into which the tide flows. 4. A certain fishing-net.

Esteroide [es-tay-ro'-e-day], *m.* Steroid.

Estertor [es-ter-tor'], *m.* Rattle in the throat of agonizing persons; stertor.

Estertoroso, sa [es-ter-to-ro'-so, sah], *a.* Stertorous, accompanied by a snoring sound.

Esteta [es-tay'-tah], *m. & f.* Aesthete or esthete.

Estética [es-tay'-te-cah], *f.* Æsthetics; the science of the beautiful.

Estético, ca [es-tay'-te-co, cah], *a.* Æsthetic.

Estetoscopio [es-tay-tos-co'-pe-o], *m.* (Med.) Stethoscope.

Esteva [es-tay'-vah], *f.* 1. Plough-handle. 2. Curved bar of wood on the bottom of coaches, connected with the shafts.

Estevado, da [es-tay-vah'-do, dah], *a.* Bow-legged.

Estezado [es-tay-thah'-do], *m.* *V.* Correal.

Estiaje [es-te-ah'-hay], *m.* The lowest stage of water in a river, by reason of heat. (Acad.)

Estiba [es-tee'-bah], *f.* 1. Rammer. *V.* Atacador. 2. Stowage, the arrangement of a ship's cargo. 3. Place where wool is compressed.

Estibador [es-te-bah-dor'], *m.* Stevedore, longshoreman.

Estibar [es-te-bar'], *va.* 1. To compress wool. 2. To stow a cargo.

Estibio [es-tee'-be-o], *m.* Antimony stibium.

Estíctico, ca [es-teec'-te-co, cah], *a.* (Biol.) Marked with points, punctate.

Estiércol [es-te-ayr'-col], *m.* 1. Dung, excrement, ordure. 2. Dung or compost to fatten lands, manure.

Estigio, gia [es-tee'-he-o, ah], *a.* Stygian, belonging to the fabulous river Styx.

Estigma [es-teeg'-mah], *m.* 1. Stigma, brand, mark of a slave or criminal. 2. Stigma, every mark of infamy. 3. (Bot.) Stigma, the upper extremity of the pistil for receiving the pollen. 4. A miraculous mark upon the body.

Estigmatizar [es-tig-ma-tee-thar'], *va.* To stigmatize, to mark with a brand.

Estilar [es-te-lar'], *vn. & va.* 1. To use, to be accustomed. 2. To draw up in writing according to the usual style or practice.—*vr.* To be in fashion.

Estilbita [es-teel-bee'-tah], *f.* Stilbite, hydrous aluminum-calcium silicate.

Estilista [es-te-lees'-tah], *m.* Stylist (writer).

Estilito [es-te-lee'-to], *m. dim.* A small style or gnomon.

Estilo [es-tee'-lo], *m.* 1. Style, a pointed iron formerly used to write on tables of wax. 2. Gnomon or style of a dial. 3. Style, the manner of talking or writing, with regard to language. 4. Form or manner of proceeding in suits at law. 5. Use, custom. 6. (Bot.) Style, prolongation of the ovary and support of the stigma. *Estilo castizo,* A correct style.

Estilográfico, ca [es-te-lo-grah'-fe-co, cah], *a.* Stylographic. *Pluma estilográfica* or *pluma fuente,* Fountain pen.

Estilóideo, dea [es-te-lo'-e-day-o, ah], *a.* Styloid, like a style.

Estima [es-tee'-mah], *f.* 1. Esteem, respect. 2. (Naut.) Dead reckoning. *Propasar la estima,* (Naut.) To outrun the reckoning.

Estimabilidad [es-te-mah-be-le-dahd'], *f.* Estimableness.

Estimable [es-te-mah'-blay], *a.* Estimable, valuable, creditable; worthy of honour and esteem; computable.

Estimación [es-te-mah-the-on'], *f.* 1. Estimation, esteem, regard, creditableness. 2. Estimation, estimate, valuation, account. *Estimación propia,* Self-love. 3. (Obs.) Instinct, natural desire or aversion.

Estimador, ra [es-te-mah-dor', rah], *m. & f.* Esteemer, estimator.

Estimar [es-te-mar'], *va.* 1. To estimate, to value; to set a value on a thing; to compute or to computate, to make of. 2. To esteem, to respect, to regard, to honour, to make account of, or to make much of. 3. To judge, to form an opinion. 4. To thank, to acknowledge. 5. To look into.

Estimativa [es-te-mah-tee'-vah], *f.* 1. Power of judging and forming an opinion. 2. Instinct, natural propensity or aversion.

Estimulación [es-te-moo-lah-the-on'], *f.* (Obs.) Stimulation.

Estimulante [es-te-moo-lahn'-tay], *pa. & a.* Stimulating, exciting.—*m.* Stimulant, excitant.

Estimular [es-te-moo-lar'], *va.* 1. To sting, to stimulate, to irritate, to excite, to goad. 2. To incite, to encourage.

Estímulo [es-tee'-moo-lo], *m.* Sting, stimulus; incitement; stimulation, encouragement.

Estinco [es-teen'-co], *m.* Skink, a kind of lizard. Lacerta scincus.

Estío [es-tee'-o], *m.* The summer (Lat. æstivus, fr. æstas.)

Estiomenado, da [es-te-o-may-nah'-do, dah], *a.* Mortified, corrupted.—*pp.* of ESTIOMENAR.
Estiomenar [es-te-o-may-nar'], *va.* To corrode, to mortify.
Estiómeno [es-te-o'-may-no], *m.* Mortification, gangrene.
Estipa [es-tee'-pah], *f.* Stipa, a genus of tall, tufted grasses.
Estipendiar [es-te-pen-de-ar'], *va.* To give a stipend.
Estipendiario [es-te-pen-de-ah'-re-o], *m.* Stipendiary, one who performs a service for a settled payment.
Estipendio [es-te-pen'-de-o], *m.* Stipend, salary, pay, wages, fee.
Estipite [es-tee'-pe-tay], *m.* (Arch.) Plaster in form of a reversed pyramid.
Estipticar [es-tip-te-car'], *va.* To use or apply a styptic.
Estipticidad [es-tip-te-the-dahd'], *f.* 1. Stypticity, the power of stanching blood.
Estiptico, ca [es-teep'-te-co, cah], *a.* 1. Styptic, astringent: having the power of stanching. 2. Costive, bound in the body. 3. (Met.) Miserly, avaricious. 4. (Met.) Difficult to be obtained.
Estiptiquez [es-tip-te-keth'], *f.* 1. Costiveness. 2. Niggardliness.
Estipula [es-tee'-poo-lah], *f.* (Bot.) Stipule, a foliaceous appendage at the base of the petiole.
Estipulación [es-te-poo-lah-the-on'], *f.* Stipulation, promise, clause, covenant, bargain.
Estipulante [es-te-poo-lahn'-tay], *pa.* Stipulator, stipulating.
Estipular [es-te-poo-lar'], *va.* To stipulate, to contract, to bargain, to settle terms, to covenant.
Estique [es-tee'-kay], *m.* Stick, a wooden instrument used by sculptors for modelling in clay.
Estira [es-tee'-rah], *f.* Kind of knife used by curriers.
Estirace [es-te-rah'-thay], *m.* (Bot.) Styrax, the typical genus of the storax family; one species yields benzoin, another storax.
Estiracear [es-te-rah-thay-ar'], *va.* (Coll.) To pull, to tug, to stretch.
Estiráceo, cea [es-te-rah'-thay-o, ah], *a.* Like styrax, styracaceous.
Estiradamente [es-te-rah-dah-men'-tay], *adv.* 1. Scarcely, difficultly. 2. Violently, forcibly.
Estirado, da [es-te-rah'-do, dah], *a.* 1. Extended, dilated, expanded. 2. Excellent. 3. (Met.) Grave, stiff, lofty; full of affected dignity.—*pp.* of ESTIRAR.
Estirador [es-te-rah-dor'], *m.* 1. Stretcher (for curtains, etc.) 2. Drawing table.
Estirar [es-te-rar'], *va.* 1. To dilate, to stretch out, to lengthen. 2. To fit, to adjust. 3. To extend a discourse, to enlarge upon a subject. 4. (Naut.) To row slowly; to continue the tack. *Estirar la barra,* (Met.) To make every possible effort to attain any thing. *Estirar la pierna,* (Coll.) To die.—*vr.* 1. To stretch, to be extended, to bear extension: applied generally to the body, or to a single member of it. 2. To hold up one's head with affected gravity.
Estirón [es-te-rone'], *m.* 1. Pull, the act of pulling; pluck, haul or hauling. 2. Pain produced by the violent extension of any part. 3. (Naut.) The distance gained in the course pursued. *Dar un estirón,* (Coll.) To grow rapidly.
Estirpe [es-teer'-pay], *f.* Race, origin, stock.
Estitico, ca [es-tee'-te-co, cah], *a.* *V.* ESTÍPTICO. (Acad.)
Estitiquez [es-te-te-keth'], *f.* Costiveness. *V.* ESTIPTIQUEZ.
Estivación [es-te-vah-the-on'], *f.* 1. The barrelling of herrings or pilchards. 2. Estivation, the disposition of the parts of a flower within the bud.
Estivador [es-te-vah-dor'], *m.* Packer of wool at shearing.
Estival [es-te-vahl'], *a.* Estival, pertaining to the summer.
Estivo, va [es-tee'-vo, vah], *a.* ESTIVAL.
Esto [es'-to], *pron. dem.* This. *A esto,* Hereto, hereunto. *Con esto,* Herewith. *En esto,* Herein, hereinto. *Sobre esto,* Hereon, hereupon. *Por esto,* Hereby.
Estocada [es-to-cah'-dah], *f.* Stab, a thrust with a pointed weapon. *Estocada de vino,* Breath of a person intoxicated. *Estocada por cornada,* (Coll.) Injury which one receives in striking another.
Estoequiometria [es-to-ay-ke-o-may-tree'-ah], *f.* Stoichiometry, the mathematics of chemistry.
Estoequiométrico, ca [es-to-ay-ke-o-may'-tre-co, cah], *a.* Stoichiometric, belonging to chemical calculations.
Estofa [es-toh'-fah], *f.* 1. Quilted stuff. 2. (Met.) Quality, condition. *Hombre de estofa,* A person of consideration.
Estofado, da [es-to-fah'-do, dah], *a.* & *pp.* of ESTOFAR. 1. Quilted. 2. Stewed.
Estofado, *m.* Stewed meat.
Estofador [es-to-fah-dor'], *m.* Quilter.
Estofar [es-to-far'], *va.* 1. To quilt. 2. To paint relievos on a gilt ground. 3. To stew meat with wine, spice, or vinegar.
Estoicamente [es-to-e-cah-men'-tay], *adv.* Stoically.
Estoicidad [es-to-e-the-dahd'], *f.* Imperturbability.
Estoicismo [es-to-e-thees'-mo], *m.* 1. Stoicism, the doctrine and sect of the Stoics. 2. A philosophical school founded in Athens by Zeno, 308 B. C., and whose motto was, "Suffer and abstain."
Estoico, ca [es-to'-e-co, cah], *a.* Stoic, stoical.—*m.* Stoic.
Estola [es-to'-lah], *f.* 1. Stole, a garment worn by priests. *Derechos de estola,* Surplice fees. 2. Stole, woman's scarf. *Estola de piel,* Fur stole.
Estolidez [es-to-le-deth'], *f.* Stupidity, incapacity.
Estólido, da [es-toh'-le-do, dah], *a.* Stupid, foolish.
Estolón [es-to-lone'], *m. aug.* 1. A large stole. 2. (Bot.) Stolon, a runner or offset.
Estomacacia [es-to-ma-cah'-the-ah], *f.* (Med.) Ulceration of the mouth; also scurvy.
Estomacal [es-to-mah-cahl'], *a.* Stomachic, belonging to the stomach.
Estomagar [es-to-mah-gar'], *vn.* & *va.* 1. To stomach, to resent, to remember with anger or malignity. 2. To enrage, to make angry. 3. (Obs.) To disorder the stomach.
Estómago [es-toh'-mah-go], *m.* The stomach. *Estómago aventurero,* (Coll.) Sponger, one who hangs for a maintenance on others. *Tener buen estómago,* (Coll.) To bear insults patiently. *Ladrar el estómago,* (Coll.) To be hungry.
Estomaguero [es-to-mah-gay'-ro], *m.* Stomacher, a piece of baize applied to the stomach of children.
Estomaguillo [es-to-mah-geel'-lyo], *m.* 1. (Dim.) A small stomach. 2. A weak stomach.
Estomáquico, ca [es-to-mah'-ke-co, cah], *a.* (Med.) Stomachic *V.* ESTOMACAL.
Estomatical [es-to-mah-te-cahl'], *a.* Stomachic.
Estomaticón [es-to-mah-te-cone'], *m.* Stomach-plaster.
Estomatitis [es-to-mah-tee'-tis], *f.* Stomatitis, inflammation of the membranes of the mouth.
Estopa [es-toh'-pah], *f.* 1. Tow, the coarsest part of hemp and flax. 2. Coarse cloth made of tow. 3. (Naut.) Oakum.
Estopada [es-to-pah'-dah], *f.* Quantity of tow for spinning.
Estopear [es-to-pay-ar'], *va.* 1. To calk. 2. (Naut.) To stuff oakum in a sail to catch water.
Estopeño, ña [es-to-pay'-nyo, nyah], *a.* Of tow; belonging to tow.
Estopero [es-to-pay'-ro], *m.* That part of the piston of a pump round which tow is wound.
Estoperol [es-to-pay-role'], *m.* 1. (Naut.) Short, round-headed tarpauling nails. 2. Match or wick made of tow.
Estopilla [es-to-peel'-lyah], *f.* 1. Cheesecloth. 2. Finest part of hemp or flax.
Estopín [es-to-peen'], *m.* Quick-match, to fire off a gun.
Estopón [es-to-pone'], *m.* Coarse tow.
Estoposo, sa [es-to-po'-so, sah], *a.* Belonging to tow; filaceous, filamentous.
Estoque [es-toh'-kay], *m.* 1. Estoc, rapier, a long, narrow sword. 2. (Bot.) *V.* ESPADILLA.
Estoqueador [es-to-kay-ah-dor'], *m.* Thruster: applied to bull-fighters, who use a long, narrow sword.
Estoquear [es-to-kay-ar'], *va.* To thrust with a rapier.
Estoqueo [es-to-kay'-o], *m.* Act of thrusting or stabbing.
Estoraque [es-to-rah'-kay], *m.* 1. (Bot.) Officinal storax. Styrax officinale. 2. Gum of the storax-tree. *Estoraque líquido,* Sweet gum-tree, or sweet gum liquidambar. Liquidambar styraciflua.
Estorbador, ra [es-tor-bah-dor', rah], *m.* & *f.* Hinderer, obstructer.
Estorbar [es-tor-bar'], *va.* To hinder, to impede, to obstruct, to cumber, to hamper, to forbid, to lead off or out of, to be in one's way.
Estorbo [es-tor'-bo], *m.* Impediment, hinderance, obstruction, nuisance.
Estornija [es-tor-nee'-hah], *f.* 1. An iron ring round the end and arms of an axle-tree, which secures the linch-pin holes. 2. (Prov.) Boys' play.
Estornino [es-tor-nee'-no], *m.* (Orn.) Starling. Sturnus, *L.*
Estornudar [es-tor-noo-dar'], *vn.* To sneeze.
Estornudo [es-tor-noo'-do], *m.* Sternutation, sneeze.
Estornutatorio [es-tor-noo-tah-toh'-re-o], *m.* Sternutatory, medicine that provokes sneezing.
Estotro, tra [es-to'-tro, trah]. A compound pronoun of *esto* and *otro,* This other.
Estovar [es-to-var'], *va.* *V.* REHOGAR.
(*Yo estoy, yo esté, estuve, estuviera, estuviere.* *V.* ESTAR.)
Estrabismo [es-trah-bees'-mo], *m.* Cross-eye.
Estracilla [es-trah-theel'-lyah], *f.* Kind of fine brown paper; fine blotting-paper.
Estrada [es-trah'-dah], *f.* Causeway, paved road; turnpike road. *Estrada encubierta,* (Mil.) Covert-way.
Estradiota [es-trah-de-o'-tah], *f.* 1. Ancient mode of riding with long stirrups and stiff legs. 2. Kind of lance.

Estradiote, ta [es-trah-de-oh'-tay, tah], *a.* Relating to riding with long stirrups. *Estradiote,* Soldier mounted with long stirrups.

Estrado [es-trah'-do], *m.* 1. Drawing-room where company is received, guest-chamber. 2. Carpets and other embellishments of a drawing-room. *Estrados,* Halls where courts of justice hold their sittings. 3. Baker's table for holding the loaves to be put into the oven. 4. A platform on which the royal throne is placed.

Estrafalariamente [es-trah-fah-lah-re-ah-men'-tay], *adv.* (Coll.) Carelessly, slovenly; extravagantly, wildly.

Estrafalario, ria [es-trah-fah-lah'-re-o, ah], *a.* 1. Slovenly, uncleanly dressed; indecently neglectful of dress; extravagant, wild. 2. Odd, queer, eccentric.

Estragadamente [es-trah-gah-dah-men'-tay], *adv.* Depravedly.

Estragador, ra [es-trah-gah-dor', rah], *m.* & *f.* Corrupter, destroyer.

Estragamiento [es-trah-gah-me-en'-to], *m.* 1. Ravage, waste, ruin. 2. (Met.) Disorder, corruption of morals.

Estragar [es-trah-gar'], *va.* 1. To deprave, to vitiate, to corrupt, to spoil, to make less pure, to disfigure. 2. (Obs.) To destroy, to ruin, to waste, to harass. *Estragar la cortesía,* To make fulsome compliments.

Estrago [es-trah'-go], *m.* 1. Ravage, waste, ruin, havoc. 2. Wickedness, corruption of morals, depravity.

Estragón [es-trah-gone'], *m.* (Bot.) Tarragon wormwood. Artemisia dracunculus.

Estrambosidad [es-tram-bo-se-dahd'], *f.* Distortion of the eyes.

Estrambote [es-tram-bo'-tay], *m.* Burden of a song.

Estrambótico, ca [es-tram-bo'-te-co, cah], *a.* 1. Strange, extravagant, irregular. 2. Eccentric, eccentrical.

Estramonio [es-trah-mo'-ne-o], *m.* (Bot.) Common thorn-apple; used as a remedy for asthmatic attacks. Datura stramonium.

Estrangol [es-tran-gole'], *m.* (Vet.) Inflammation in a horse's tongue.

Estrangul [es-tran-gool'], *m.* A reed for an oboe or any other wind-instrument, of cane or of metal.

Estrangulación [es-tran-goo-lah-the-on'], *f.* 1. Strangling, as act and effect. 2. Strangulation, constriction of the neck by a circular ligature. 3. Stoppage of a hydraulic apparatus.

Estrangulado, da [es-tran-goo-lah'-do, dah], *a.* (Med.) Strangulated.

Estrangular [es-tran-goo-lar'], *va.* To strangle, to kill by compressing the trachea.

Estrapontina [es-trah-pon-tee'-nah], *f.* Kind of hammock.

Estratagema [es-trah-tah-hay'-mah], *f.* 1. Stratagem in war. 2. Trick, artful deception; craftiness; finesse; fetch.

Estrategia [es-trah-tay'-he-ah], *f.* (Mil.) Strategy, military science.

Estratégico, ca [es-trah-tay'-he-co, cah], *a.* (Mil.) Strategic, strategical, belonging to strategy.

Estratificación [es-trah-te-fe-cah-the-on'], *f.* (Min.) Stratification, arrangement of layers.

Estratificar [es-trah-te-fe-car'], *va.* (Min.) To stratify, to dispose in strata.

Estratiforme [es-trah-te-for'-may], *a.* Stratiform, disposed in strata.

Estratiote [es-trah-te-oh'-tay], *m.* (Bot.) Water-soldier, water-aloe, crab's claw. Stratiotes aloides.

Estrato [es-trah'-to], *m.* (Geol.) Stratum, layer, bed.

Estratosfera [es-trah-tos-fay'-rah], *f.* Stratosphere.

Estrave [es-trah'-vay], *m.* (Naut.) End of a ship's keel.

Estraza [es-trah'-thah], *f.* Rag, fragment of cloth. *Papel de estraza,* Brown paper.

Estrazar [es-trah-thar'], *va.* (Obs.) To tear or break into pieces.

Estrechamente [es-tray-chah-men'-tay], *adv.* 1. Narrowly, tightly, closely, fast, compactly, close; nearly. 2. (Met.) Exactly, punctually. 3. (Met.) Strongly, forcibly. 4. (Met.) Strictly, rigorously. 5. (Met.) Scantily, penuriously.

Estrechamiento [es-tray-chah-me-en'-to], *m.* Act of tightening, tightness, narrowing.

Estrechar [es-tray-char'], *va.* 1. To tighten, to make narrow. 2. To contract, to constringe, to constrict, to curtail, to compress. 3. (Met.) To confine, to pin up. 4. (Met.) To constrain, to compel. 5. (Met.) To restrain, to obstruct.—*vr.* 1. To bind one's self strictly. 2. (Met.) To reduce one's expenses. 3. (Met.) To act in concert with another. 4. (Met.) To relate or communicate in confidence. 5. (Met.) To be dejected. 6. To be intimate with.

Estrechez [es-tray-cheth'], *f.* 1. Straitness, narrowness, compactness, closeness. 2. (Met.) Intimate union. 3. (Met.) Intimacy, friendship. 4. (Met.) Arduous or dangerous undertaking. 5. (Met.) Austerity, abstraction from worldly objects. 6. (Met.) Poverty.

Estrecho [es-tray'-cho], *m.* 1. Strait or frith, a narrow arm of the sea. 2. Pass, a narrow passage between two mountains. 3. (Met.) Peril, danger, risk.

Estrecho, cha [es-tray'-cho, chah], *a.* 1. Narrow, close, dense. 2. Straight, tight. 3. (Met.) Intimate, familiar. 4. (Met.) Rigid, austere. 5. (Met.) Exact, punctual. 6. (Met.) Narrow-minded, illiberal, mean-spirited. 7. (Met.) Poor, indigent, penurious, needy, necessitous. *Al estrecho,* Necessarily, forcedly.

Estrechón [es-tray-chone'], *m.* (Littl. us.) 1. *V.* Apretón. 2. (Naut.) *V.* Socollada.

Estrechura [es-tray-choo'-rah], *f.* 1. Narrowness, straitness; narrowing. 2. (Met.) Austerity, abstraction from the world. 3. (Met.) Distress, danger. 4. Intimate familiarity.

Estregadera [es-tray-gah-day'-rah], *f.* A kind of brush used for rubbing off dirt.

Estregadero [es-tray-gah-day'-ro], *m.* 1. Place where beasts rub themselves against a tree, stone, etc. 2. Place for washing clothes.

Estregadura [es-tray-gah-doo'-rah], *f.* Friction, act of rubbing.

Estregamiento [es-tray-gah-me-en'-to], *m.* Friction.

Estregar [es-tray-gar'], *va.* 1. To rub one thing against another, to scour, to fray, to grind. 2. To scratch.

Estrella [es-trayl'-lyah], *f.* 1. A star. 2. (Met.) A white mark on a horse's face. 3. Asterisk, a mark in printing. 4. (Met.) Fate, lot, destiny. *Tener estrella,* To be fortunate. 5. (Mil.) Star-fort, a work with five or more faces, having salient and re-entering angles. *Tomar la estrella,* (Naut.) To take the altitude of a star. *Estrellas errantes* or *erráticas,* Planets, satellites. *Con estrellas,* After night or before sunrise.

Estrellada [es-trel-lyah'-dah], *f.* (Bot.) Ladies' mantle. *V.* Alquimila.

Estrelladera [es-trel-lyah-day'-rah], *f* Kind of ladle for frying eggs.

Estrelladero [es-trel-lyah-day'-ro], *m.* Kind of frying-pan for dressing eggs without breaking the yolks.

Estrellado, da [es-trel-lyah'-do, dah], *a.* Starry, full of stars. *Caballo estrellado,* Horse with a white mark on the face. *Huevos estrellados,* Eggs fried in oil or butter; fried eggs.—*pp.* of Estrellar.

Estrellamar [es-trel-lyah-mar'], *f.* 1. (Bot.) Buckthorn plantain. Plantago coronopus. 2. Star-fish.

Estrellar [es-trel-lyar'], *a.* Stellated, starry.

Estrellar [es-trel-lyar'], *va.* 1. To dash to bits. 2. To fry (eggs).—*vr.* 1. (Aer. and Naut.) To crash. 2. To brain oneself. 3. (Fig.) To be ruined, to fail utterly. 4. To fill with stars. *Estrellarse con,* To conflict violently with.

Estrellera [es-trel-lyay'-rah], *f.* (Naut.) Plain rigging without runners.

Estrellero [es-trel-lyay'-ro], *m.* Star-gazer; one who wastes his time in looking up to the windows.—*a.* Used of a horse which throws up his head a great deal.

Estrellica, ita [es-trel-lyee'-cah, ee'-tah], **Estrelluela,** *f. dim.* Little star.

Estrellizar [es-trel-lyee-thar'], *va.* (Littl. us.) To embellish or beautify with stars.

Estrellón [es-trel-lyone'], *m.* 1. (Aug.) Large star. 2. Star ball, used in artificial fire-works. *Estrellones,* Cal trops, crow-feet; irons with spikes thrown into breaches and narrow passages to annoy the enemy's horse.

Estremecedor, ra [es-tray-may-thay-dor', rah], *a.* Frightful, terrifying.

Estremecer [es-tray-may-therr'], *va.* 1. To shake, to make tremble. 2. (Naut.) To work or labour hard: applied to a ship.—*vr.* To shake, to tremble, to shudder, to be uncommonly agitated.

Estremecimiento [es-tray-may-the-me-en'-to], *m.* Trembling, quaking, shaking.

Estremeño, ña, *a.* *V.* Extremeño.

(*Yo me estremezco, yo me estremezca.* from *Estremecer.* *V.* Conocer.)

Estremiche [es-tray-mee'-chay], *m.* (Naut.) A piece of timber which is notched into the knees of a ship.

Estrena [es-tray'-nah], *f.* 1. A new year's gift. 2. Handsel, the first act of using any thing; the first act of sale. 3. Treat on wearing a new suit of clothes.

Estrenar [es-tray-nar'], *va.* 1. To handsel, to use or to do any thing the first time. 2. To commence, to begin; to regale.—*vr.* To begin to put any thing in execution.

Estreno [es-tray'-no], *m.* Debut, premier, first presentation.

Estrenque [es-tren'-kay], *m.* (Naut.) Rope made of bass or sedge, much used in America.

Estrenuidad [es-tray-noo-e-dahd'], *f.* Strength, valour, strenuousness. (Acad.)

Estrenuo, nua [es-tray'-noo-o, ah], *a.* Strong, agile, valorous, strenuous. (Acad.)

Estreñido, da [es-tray-nyee'-do, dah], *a.* 1. Close bound, costive, hard bound. 2. Miserable, niggardly—*pp.* of Estreñir.

Estreñimiento [es-tray-nye-me-en'-to], *m.* Obstruction; the act of binding or restraining; costiveness, confinement.

Estreñir [es-tray-nyeer'], *va.* To bind, to tie close, to restrain.—*vr.* To restrain one's self. *Estreñirse el vientre,* To constipate, to be costive.

Estrepa, Estrepilla [es-tray'-pah, es-tray-peel'-lyah], *f.* (Bot.) *V.* ESTEPILLA.

Estrepitarse [es-tray-pe-tar'-say], *vr.* (Coll. Cuba.) To be noisily merry, to carouse wildly.

Estrépito [es-tray'-pe-to], *m.* Noise, clamour, bustle, noisiness, obstreperousness.

Estrepitosamente, *adv.* Clamorously, obstreperously.

Estrepitoso, sa [es-tray-pe-toh'-so, sah], *a.* Noisy, boisterous, loud, clamorous, obstreperous.

Estreptococo [es-trep-to-co'-co], *m.* Streptococcus.

Estreptomicina [es-trep-to-me-thee'-nah], *f.* (Med.) Streptomycin.

Estría [es-tree'-ah], *f.* (Arch.) Fluting, channel cut along half the length of shafts or pilasters. Stria.

Estriadura [es-tre-ah-doo'-rah], *f.* (Arch.) Fluting.

Estriar [es-tre-ar'], *va.* (Arch.) To flute, to cut columns into channels and grooves, to gutter.—*vr.* To be grooved, striated.

Estribadero [es-tre-bah-day'-ro], *m.* Prop, stay.

Estribar [es-tre-bar'], *vn.* 1. To prop, to support with props. 2. (Met.) To found, to build upon; to be supported.

Estribera [es-tre-bay'-rah], *f.* 1. Buttress, arch, pillar. 2. Joiner's bench.

Estribería [es-tre-bay-ree'-ah], *f.* Place where stirrups are kept.

Estriberón [es-tre-bay-rone'], *m.* Prominences made on earth or wood by cross-bars, to serve as steps.

Estribillo [es-tre-beel'-lyo], *m.* 1. Introduction or beginning of a song, chorus, refrain. 2. Tautology, a needless and superfluous repetition of the same words.

Estribo [es-tree'-bo], *m.* 1. Buttress, abutment, arch, pillar. 2. Stirrup. 3. Step on the side of a coach. 4. Staple fixed at the end of a cross-bow. 5. Bone of the ear resembling a stirrup; the stapes. 6. *V.* ESTRIBILLO. 7. (Gunn.) Clasp on the felloes of gun-carriage wheels. *Estribos,* (Naut.) Stirrups of a ship, pieces of timber fastened to the keel with iron plates. *Estribos de guardamancebos de las vergas,* Stirrups of the horses. *Estribos de los pelones de las vergas,* Stirrups of the yard-arms. *Estribos de las cadenas,* Stirrups of the chain-plates.

Estribor [es-tre-bor'], *m.* (Naut.) Starboard.

Estribordarios [es-tre-bor-dah'-re-os], *m. pl.* People on the starboard hand.

Estricnina [es-tric-nee'-nah], *f.* (Med.) Strychnine, an alkaloid obtained from nux vomica; an important medicine and a violent poison.

Estricote (Al) [es-tre-co'-tay], *adv.* Without rule or order. *Tener a uno al estricote,* To amuse one with vain promises.

Estrictamente, *adv.* Strictly.

Estricto, ta [es-treec'-to, tah], *a.* 1. Strict, exact, accurate, rigorously nice. 2. Strict, severe, rigorous, extreme.

Estridente [es-tre-den'-tay], *a.* (Poet.) That which causes noise or creaking; strident.

Estridor [es-tre-dor'], *m.* Noise, creak, screech, stridor.

(*Yo estriego, yo estriegue,* from *Estregar. V.* ACRECENTAR.)

Estrige [es-tree'-hay], *f.* Night-bird, said to be of unlucky omen; screech-owl, vampire.

Estrigila [es-tre-hee'-lah], *f.* Strigil, a scraper of bronze which Roman gladiators used to clean off the oil and dust of combat, and which passed for a specific for certain diseases.

Estrillar [es-tril-lyar'], *va.* (Obs.) To rub, scour, or wash horses.

Estringa [es-treen'-gah], *f. V.* AGUJETA.

(*Yo estriño, yo estriña,* from *Estreñir. V.* PEDIR.)

Estripar [es-tre-par'], *va.* (Prov.) *V.* DESTRIPAR.

Estrobilífero, ra [es-tro-be-lee'-fay-ro, rah], *a.* Cone-bearing, strobiliferous.

Estróbilo [es-tro'-be-lo], *m.* Strobile, cone of the pine family.

Estroboscopio [es-tro-bos-co'-pe-o], *m.* Stroboscope.

Estrofa [es-tro'-fah], *f.* (Poet.) Strophe.

Estrógeno [es-tro'-hay-no], *m.* (Biol.) Estrogen.

Estronciana [es-tron-the-ah'-nah], *f.* Strontia, an alkaline earth.

Estroncio [es-tron'-the-o], *m.* Strontium, a metallic element.

Estropajear [es-tro-pah-hay-ar'], *va.* To clean a wall with a dry brush or rubber.

Estropajeo [es-tro-pah-hay'-o], *m.* Act of rubbing a wall.

Estropajo [es-tro-pah'-ho], *m.* 1. Dish-clout. 2. Brush, made of bass or sedge, to clean culinary vessels. 3. (Met.) A worthless, trifling thing.

Estropajosamente, *adv.* Stammeringly.

Estropajoso, sa [es-tro-pah-ho'-so, sah], *a.* 1. Ragged, despicable, low, mean. 2. (Met.) Troublesome, useless. 3. (Met.) Stuttering, stammering.

Estropalina [es-tro-pah-lee'-nah], *f.* Refuse of wool.

Estropeado, da [es-tro-pay-ah'-do, dah], *a.* & *pp.* of ESTROPEAR. Lame.

Estropeamiento [es-tro-pay-ah-me-en'-to], *m.* Act of maiming, wounding, or laming.

Estropear [es-tro-pay-ar'], *va.* 1. To maim, to cripple, to mutilate, to mangle, to cut. 2. To mix lime and sand.

Estropecillo [es-tro-pay-theel'-lyo], *m. dim.* A slight stumble or impediment.

Estropeo [es-tro-pay'-o], *m.* (Prov.) Maim, hurt, injury.

Estropicio [es-tro-pee'-the-o], *m.* (Acad. Coll.) 1. Crash, destruction, with noise, of table service, etc. 2. By extension, a disturbance of small moment.

Estrovo [es-tro'-vo], *m.* (Naut.) Strap, a piece of rope used for strapping blocks.

Estructura [es-trooc-too'-rah], *f.* 1. Structure, constructure, manner of building or constructing an edifice. 2. Order, method.

Estructurar [es-trook-too-rar'], *va.* 1. To distribute, to organize the parts (of a project, etc.). 2. To construct.

Estruendo [es-troo-en'-do], *m.* 1. Clamour, noise, outcry, clatter. 2. Confusion, bustle. 3. Pomp, ostentation, show. 4. (Obs.) Fame, renown, celebrity.

Estruendoso, sa [es-troo-en-do'-so, sah], *a.* 1. Noisy, clamorous. 2. Pompous, full of ostentation.

Estrujadura [es-troo-hah-doo'-rah], *f.* Pressing, squeezing, pressure, compressing.

Estrujamiento [es-troo-hah-me-en'-to], *m. V.* ESTRUJADURA.

Estrujar [es-troo-har'], *va.* To press, to squeeze the juice. *Estrujar el dinero,* To be avaricious or extremely covetous.

Estrujón [es-troo-hone'], *m.* 1. The last pressing of grapes, which gives a miserable wine. 2. Pressing, squeezing, compression.

Estrupador [es-troo-pa-dor'], *m. V.* ESTUPRADOR.

Estrupar, *va. V.* ESTUPRAR.

Estrupo, Estrupro, *m. V.* ESTUPRO.

Estuación [es-too-ah-the-on'], *f.* (Obs.) Flow of the tide.

Estuante [es-too-ahn'-tay], *a.* Very hot, boiling, scorching.

Estuario [es-too-ah'-re-o], *m.* A low ground, overflowed by the sea at high tides; an estuary.

Estucador [es-too-cah-dor'], *m.* A stucco-plasterer.

Estucar [es-too-car'], *va.* To stucco or whitewash any thing.

Estuco [es-too'-co], *m.* Stucco, a kind of fine plaster.

Estuche [es-too'-chay], *m.* 1. Case for scissors or other instruments; etui. 2. The ace of spades, the deuce of spades or clubs, and ace of clubs in certain games of cards. 3. (Coll.) *Mostrar el estuche,* To show one's teeth, when angry, like a dog. 4. Small comb. 5. (Met.) One who knows a little of every thing, or is capable of any thing. ***Es un estuche*** or ***es un estuche de habilidades,*** (Met. Coll.) He is a very clever fellow.

Estudiador [es-too-de-ah-dor'], *m.* (Coll.) Student.

Estudiantazo [es-too-de-an-tah'-tho], *m.* He who is reputed a great scholar.

Estudiante [es-too-de-ahn'-tay], *m.* 1. Scholar, one who learns of a master: applied generally to those who are learning in the universities; a student. 2. A kind of prompter to players.

Estudiantil [es-too-de-an-teel'], *a.* (Coll.) Scholastic, belonging to a scholar.

Estudiantillo [es-too-de-an-teel'-lyo], *m. dim.* A little scholar.

Estudiantino, na [es-too-de-an-tee'-no, nah], *a.* Belonging to a scholar or student. *A la estudiantina.* In the manner of students.

Estudiantón [es-too-de-an-tone'], *m. aug.* A big student.

Estudiar [es-too-de-ar'], *va.* 1. To study, to acquire knowledge. 2. To muse, to ponder, to contemplate, to commit to memory. 3. To make a drawing after a model or nature. 4. To attend the classes in a university.

Estudio [es-too'-de-o], *m.* 1. Study, application to books and learning. 2. The place where the Latin language is taught. 3. Study, apartment appropriated to literary employment. 4. Hall where models, prints, and plans are kept to be copied or studied. 5. (Met.) Study, attention, meditation, contemplation. *Hacer estudio de alguna cosa,* (Met.) To act with art, cunning, or crafty reflection. *Estudio general,* University. *Juez de estudio* or *de estudios,* A vice-chancellor in some Spanish universities.—*pl.* 1. Time, trouble, and care applied to the study of the sciences. 2. Sciences, letters. *Estudios mayores,* The higher sciences. *Dar estudios a uno,* To maintain one at his studies.

Estudiosamente [es-too-de-o-sah-men'-tay], *adv.* Studiously, with care and reflection.

Estudioso, sa [es-too-de-oh'-so, sah], *a.* 1. Studious, given to study and reflection. 2. (Met.) Studious, careful solicitous, contemplative.

Estufa [es-too'-fah], *f.* 1. A stove. 2. A warm, close room, a hot-house. 3. A drying-chamber, hot closet, dry bath. 4. A small brazier used to warm the feet.
Estufador [es-too-fah-dor'], *m.* Vessel in which meat is stewed.
Estufar [es-too-far'], *va.* (Obs.) 1. To warm any thing. 2. *V.* ESTOFAR.
Estufero [es-too-fay'-ro], or **Estufista**, *m.* He who makes stoves.
Estufilla [es-too-feel'-lyah], *f.* 1. Muff, a cover made of fur to keep the hands warm. 2. A small brasier, used by women to warm the feet on.
Estultamente [es-tool-tah-men'-tay], *adv.* (Coll.) Foolishly, sillily.
Estulticia [es-tool-tee'-the-ah], *f.* (Coll.) Folly, silliness.
Estulto, ta [es-tool'-to, tah], *a.* (Coll.) Foolish, silly.
Estuosidad [es-too-o-se-dahd'], *f.* Burning, excessive hotness.
Estuoso, sa [es-too-oh'-so, sah], *a.* Very hot, ardent, burnt with the heat of the sun.
Estupefacción [es-too-pay-fac-the-on'], *f.* Stupefaction, numbness.
Estupefacientes [es-too-pay-fah-the-en'-tess], *m. pl.* Narcotics, narcotic drugs.
Estupefactivo, va [es-too-pay-fac-tee'-vo, vah], *a.* Stupefying.
Estupefacto [es-too-pay-fahc'-to], *a.* (Coll.) Motionless, petrified, immovable with astonishment.
Estupendamente [es-too-pen-dah-men'-tay], *adv.* Wonderfully, stupendously.
Estupendo, da [es-too-pen'-do, dah], *a.* Stupendous, wonderful, marvellous.
Estúpidamente [es-too'-pe-dah-men-tay], *adv.* Stupidly, dully, lumpishly.
Estupidez [es-too-pe-deth'], *f.* Stupidity, insensibility, dulness, sluggishness, stupidness.
Estúpido, da [es-too'-pee-do, dah], *a.* Stupid, insensible, dull, crack-brained, gross, heavy, mopish.
Estupor [es-too-por'], *m.* 1. Stupour, suspension of sensibility. 2. Amazement, admiration, astonishment.
Estuprador [es-too-prah-dor'], *m.* Ravisher, deflowerer, violator.
Estuprar [es-too-prar'], *va.* To ravish, to violate, to deflower.
Estupro [es-too'-pro], *m.* Ravishment, rape, constupration.
Estuque [es-too'-kay], *m.* *V.* ESTUCO.
Estuquista [es-too-kees'-tah], *m.* Plasterer, stucco-worker.
Esturar [es-too-rar'], *va.* 1. To dry by the force of fire. 2. To overdo meat by the force of fire.
Esturgar [es-toor-gar'], *va.* To polish delft ware.
Esturión [es-too-re-on'], *m.* (Zool.) Sturgeon. Acipenser.
Ésula [ay'-soo-lah], *f.* (Bot.) Leafy-branched spurge. Euphorbia esula.
Esviaje [es-ve-ah'-hay], *m.* (Arch.) 1. The inclination of a vertical with respect to a line which crosses it. 2. Oblique direction of the sides of an arch or vault.
Et [ayt], *conj.* (Obs.) And.
Etanún [ay-tah-noon'], *m.* The seventh month of the Hebrew ecclesiastical year, in which the temple of Solomon was consecrated.
Etapa [ay-tah'-pah], *f.* (Mil.) The ration of necessaries to troops in the field or travelling.
Etcétera [et-thay'-tay-rah], *f.* Et cætera, the rest, and so on. Commonly abbreviated to etc. or &.
Éter [ay'-ter], *m.* 1. (Chem.) Ether, ethyl ether. 2. Ether or æther, a supposed medium, filling all space, through which the vibrations of light, heat, and electricity are propagated. 3. Ether, the upper air, the sky.
Etéreo, rea [ay-tay'-ray-o, ah], *a.* 1. Ethereal, etherous, formed of ether. 2. (Poet.) Ethereal, ethereous, heavenly.
Eterióscopo [ay-tay-re-os'-co-po], *m.* An instrument for measuring the force of solar radiation.
Eterización [ay-tay-re-thah-the-on'], *f.* Etherization, the administration of ether for anæsthesia.
Eterizar [ay-tay-re-thar'], *va.* 1. To etherize, to cause anæsthesia by inhalation of ether. 2. To convert into ether. = Eterificar.
Eternal [ay-ter-nahl'], *a.* Eternal.
Eternalmente, *adv.* Eternally, everlastingly.
Eternamente, *adv.* 1. Eternally, forever, everlastingly, evermore. 2. (Met.) For a long time. 3. Never.
Eternidad [ay-ter-ne-dahd'], *f.* 1. Eternity. 2. Duration or length of continuance, which comprehends many ages.
Eternizar [ay-ter-ne-thar'], *va.* 1. To eternize, to perpetuate. 2. To prolong for a great length of time.
Eterno, na [ay-tayr'-no, nah], *a.* 1. Eternal, endless, never-ending, everlasting. 2. Durable, lasting.
Eteromancia [ay-tay-ro-mahn'-the-ah], *f.* Divination by the flight or song of birds.
Etesio [ay-tay'-se-o], *a.* Applied to wind which begins to blow in April and continues to September on the eastern coast of Spain.
Ética [ay'-te-cah], *f.* Ethics, morals, morality, or the doctrine of morality.
Ético, ca [ay'-te-co, cah], *a.* 1. Ethical, moral, treating on morality. 2. (Coll.) Hectic, labouring under a consumption, consumptive.
Etileno [ay-te-lay'-no], *m.* (Chem.) Ethylene.
Etilo [ay-tee'-lo], *m.* (Chem.) Ethyl.
Etimología [ay-te-mo-lo-hee'-ah], *f.* Etymology, word-formation.
Etimológicamente, *adv.* Etymologically.
Etimológico, ca [ay-te-mo-lo'-he-co, cah], *a.* Etymological.
Etimologista [ay-te-mo-lo-hees'-tah], *m.* Etymologist, etymologer.
Etiope, Etiópico, ca, Etiopio, a [ay-tee'-o-pay, ay-te-o'-pe-co, cah], *a.* Ethiopian.
Etiópide [ay-te-oh'-pe-day], *f.* (Bot.) Clary, Ethiopian mullein. Salvia sclarea.
Etiqueta [ay-te-kay'-tah], *f.* 1. Etiquette, ceremony, formality. 2. Compliments in conversation. 3. (Com.) Label showing price and class of merchandise. In this sense it is a Gallicism.
Etiquetero, ra [ay-te-kay-tay'-ro, rah], *a.* Ceremonious, civil and formal to a fault: it is used frequently as a substantive to express an observer of etiquette, or a very ceremonious person.
Etites [ay-tee'-tes], *f.* Eaglestone, hydroxide of iron.
Etmoides [et-mo'-e-days], *m.* (Anat.) The ethmoid bone.
Étnico, ca [ayt'-ne-co, cah], *a.* Ethnic. *V.* GENTIL.
Etnografía [et-no-grah-fee'-ah], *f.* Ethnography, the study of races of men.
Etnográfico, ca [et-no-grah'-fe-co, cah], *a.* Ethnographic, relating to ethnography.
Etnógrafo [et-no'-grah-fo], *m.* Ethnographer.
Etnología [et-no-lo-hee'-ah], *f.* Ethnology, the science of the natural races or families of men. **Etnólogo**, *m.* Ethnologist.
Etografía [ay-to-grah-fee'-ah], *f.* Ethology, the science of the formation of human character.
Etólico, ca, or **Etolio, lia** [ay-toh'-le-co, cah], *a.* Etolian.
Etrusco, ca [ay-troos'-co, cah], *a.* Etruscan.
Eubolia [ay-oo-bo'-le-ah], *f.* The act of expressing one's thoughts with propriety.
Eucalipto [ay-oo-cah-leep'-to], *m.* Eucalyptus, the Australian blue-gum tree.
Eucaristía [ay-oo-cah-ris-tee'-ah], *f.* The Eucharist.
Eucarístico, ca [ay-oo-cah-rees'-te-co, cah], *a.* 1. Eucharistical, eucharistic. 2. Eucharistical, belonging to works in prose or verse containing acts of thanksgiving.
Euclorina [ay-oo-clo-ree'-nah], *f.* Euchlorine, chlorous oxide gas, an explosive mixture of chlorine dioxide and chlorine.
Eucologio, Eucólogo [ay-oo-co-lo'-he-o, ay-oo-co'-lo-go], *m.* Euchology, book containing the service for all the Sundays and festivals in the year; euchologion.
Eucrasia [ay-oo-crah'-se-ah], *f.* (Med.) Eucrasy, sound health.
Eucrático, ca [ay-oo-crah'-te-co, cah], *a.* Euchratical.
Eudiometría [ay-oo-de-o-may-tree'-ah], *f.* Eudiometry.
Eudiómetro [ay-oo-de-o'-may-tro], *m.* (Chem.) Eudiometer.
Eufemismo [ay-oo-fay-mees'-mo], *m.* Euphemism, a suave style in words and expressions; the toning down of what would otherwise sound harsh or offensive.
Eufonía [ay-oo-fo-nee'-ah], *f.* Euphony.
Eufónico, ca [ay-oo-fo'-ne-co, cah], *a.* Euphonic, euphonious.
Eufono [ay-oo-fo'-no], *m.* Euphonium, a musical instrument composed of 42 glass cylinders.
Euforbio [ay-oo-for'-be-o], *m.* (Bot.) Officinal spurge. Euphorbia officinarum.
Eufrasia [ay-oo-frah'-se-ah], *f.* (Bot.) Eye-bright. Euphrasia. *Euphrasia oficinal*, Common eye-bright. Euphrasia officinalis.
Eugenesia [ay-oo-hay-nay'-se-ah], *f.* Eugenics.
Eumenes [ay-oo-may'-nes], *m.* Eumenes, a genus of solitary wasps.
Eunuco [ay-oo-noo'-co], *m.* Eunuch.
Eupatorio [ay-oo-pah-to'-re-o], *m.* (Bot.) Eupatorium. Eupatorium. *Eupatorio cañameño*, Hemp-agrimony eupatorium. Eupatorium cannabinum.
Euritmia [ay-oo-reet'-me-ah], *f.* 1. (Arch.) Eurythmy, proportion and harmony in an edifice. 2. Happy selection of musical rhythm and movement. 3. Skill in the handling of surgical instruments. 4. Regularity in arterial pulsations, normal pulse.
Euro [ay'-oo-ro], *m.* Eurus, the east wind. *Euro austro* or *Euro noto*, South-east wind. *Euro zefirio*, Motion of the sea from east to west.
Europeo, a [ay-oo-ro-pay'-o, ah], *a.* European.
Éuscaro, ra [ay'-oos-cah-ro, rah], *a.* Pertaining to the Basques or their language.—*n.* A Basque, a native of Biscay.
Eutanasia [ay-oo-tah-nah'-se-ah], *f.* 1. Euthanasia, a painless, peaceful death. 2. A means for producing a gentle, easy death. 3. Death in a state of grace.
Eutaxia [ay-oo-tahc'-se-ah], *f.* (Med.) A perfectly organized constitution.

Eutiquiano, na [ay-oo-te-ke-ah'-no, nah], *a.* Eutychian, belonging to the sect of Eutyches.

Eutrapelia, Eutropelia [ay-oo-trah-pay'-le-ah, ay-oo-tro-pay'-le-ah], *f.* 1. Moderation in jests, jokes, and pleasures. 2. Pastime, sport.

Eutrapélico, ca, Eutropélico, ca [ay-oo-trah-pay'-le-co, cah], *a.* Moderate, temperate.

Evacuación [ay-vah-coo-ah-the-on'], *f.* Evacuation, the act of emptying any vessel or other thing, issue.

Evacuante [ay-vah-coo-ahn'-tay], *pa.* & *a.* Evacuant, evacuating: it is used sometimes as a substantive.

Evacuar [ay-vah-coo-ar'], *va.* 1. To evacuate, to empty. 2. To quit, leave. *Evacuar un negocio,* To finish or complete a business.

Evacuativo, va [ay-vah-coo-ah-tee'-vo, vah], *a.* Evacuative, that which has the power of evacuating.

Evacuatorio, ria [ay-vah-coo-ah-to'-re-o, ah], *a.* That which evacuates.

Evadir [ay-vah-deer'], *va.* 1. To evade, to escape, to flee from danger. 2. To evade, to elude by sophistry, to avoid, to decline by subterfuge.—*vr.* 1. To evade, to escape, to slip away, to make one's escape. 2. To evade, to practise sophistry or evasions.

Evagación [ay-vah-gah-the-on'], *f.* Evagation, the act of wandering; excursion.

Evaluar [ay-vah-loo-ar'], *va.* To evaluate.

Evalúo [ay-vah-loo'-o], *m.* (Com.) Valuation, appraisement.

Evangélicamente, *adv.* Evangelically.

Evangélico, ca [ay-van-hay'-le-co, cah], *a.* Evangelical.

Evangelio [ay-van-hay'-le-o], *m.* Gospel. *Evangelios,* Small book, containing the first chapters of St. John and the other evangelists, placed between relics, and worn at children's necks.

Evangelismo [ay-van-hay-lees'-mo], *m.* (Neol.) 1. Evangelism, the religious and humanitarian system of the Gospel. 2. Spirit of reform among Protestant sects who call themselves evangelical.

Evangelista [ay-van-hay-lees'-tah], *m.* 1. Evangelist. 2. Gospeller, one who chants the gospels in churches.

Evangelistero [ay-van-hay-lis-tay'-ro], *m.* 1. Gospeller, a priest or deacon who chants the books of the evangelists at solemn masses. 2. Gospel book-stand, on which the gospel book is laid to sing the gospel at high mass.

Evangelizar [ay-van-hay-le-thar'], *va.* To evangelize, to preach the gospel.

Evaporable [ay-vah-po-rah'-blay], *a.* Evaporable, that may be evaporated.

Evaporación [ay-vah-po-rah-the-on'], *f.* 1. Evaporation, exhalation of vapour. 2. Act of damping cloth, or placing it over steam, to render the wool softer.

Evaporado, da [ay-vah-po-rah'-do, dah], *a.* Evaporated. *Leche evaporada,* Evaporated milk.

Evaporar [ay-vah-po-rar'], *vn.* To evaporate, to fly off in vapours or fumes. —*va.* To evaporate, to drive away in fumes, to disperse in vapours: to flat, to flatten, to pall, to make vapid.—*vr.* 1. To vanish, to pass away. 2. To pall, to grow vapid.

Evaporatorio [ay-vah-po-rah-toh'-re-o], *a.* Having the power of evaporating.

Evaporizar [ay-vah-po-re-thar'], *vn.* & *va.* To evaporate.

Evasión [ay-vah-se-on'], *f.* Evasion, escape, subterfuge.

Evasiva [ay-vah-see'-vah], *f.* Subterfuge.

Evasivamente [ay-vah-see-vah-men'-tay], *adv.* Evasively.

Evasivo, va [ay-vah-see'-vo, vah], *a.* Evasive, elusive, sophistical.

Evata [ay-vah'-tah], *f.* Kind of black wood resembling ebony.

Evección [ay-vec-the-on'], *f.* (Ast.) Evection, the largest inequality in the motion of the moon, as an effect of solar attraction.

Evento [ay-vayn'-to], *m.* Event, accident, issue.

Eventración [ay-ven-trah-the-on'], *f.* 1. Eventration, ventral hernia, or relaxation of the abdominal walls. 2. Disemboweling.

Eventual [ay-ven-too-ahl'], *a.* Eventual, fortuitous.

Eventualidad [ay-ven-too-ah-le-dahd'], *f.* Contingency.

Eventualmente [ay-ven-too-al-men'-tay], *adv.* Fortuitously.

Eversión [ay-ver-se-on'], *f.* Eversion, destruction, ruin, desolation.

Evicción [ay-vic-the-on'], *f.* Eviction, security, convictiveness.

Evidencia [ay-ve-den'-the-ah], *f.* Evidence, manifestation, proof, obviousness, conspicuity, nakedness, cogency. *Evidencia por pruebas* or *causas concomitantes,* Circumstantial evidence.

Evidenciar [ay-ve-den-the-ar'], *va.* To evidence, to prove, to render evident.

Evidente [ay-ve-den'-tay], *a.* Evident, clear, manifest, open, naked, palpable, obvious, plain, glaring.

Evidentemente, *adv.* Evidently, plainly, clearly, manifestly, glaringly, notoriously.

Evilasa [ay-ve-lah'-sah], *f.* Kind of ebony which grows in the island of Madagascar.

Evisceración [ay-vis-thay-rah-the-on'], *f.* Evisceration, removal of the viscera in an autopsy, or embalming.

Eviscerar [ay-vis-thay-rar'], *va.* To eviscerate, to remove the viscera.

Evitable [ay-ve-tah'-blay], *a.* Avoidable, extricable, evitable.

Evitación [ay-ve-tah-the-on'], *f.* Evitation, act of avoiding.

Evitado, da [ay-ve-tah'-do, dah], *a.* & *pp.* of EVITAR. 1. Avoided. 2. (Obs.) *V.* EXCOMULGADO.

Evitar [ay-ve-tar'], *va.* To avoid, to escape, to forbear, to help; to fly, to shun, to decline.—*vr.* (Obs.) To free one's self from vassalage.

Eviterno, na [ay-ve-terr'-no, nah], *a.* (Theol.) Imperishable, lasting, without end.

Evo [ay'-vo], *m.* 1. (Poet.) Age, a long period of time. 2. (Theol.) Eternity, endless duration.

Evocación [ay-vo-cah-the-on'], *f.* Evocation, pagan invocation.

Evocar [ay-vo-car'], *va.* 1. To call out. 2. To invoke, to solicit a favour, to implore assistance.

Evolución [ay-vo-loo-the-on'], *f.* 1. Evolution, changing the position of troops or ships. 2. Evolution, gradual development of things and of ideas, slow transformation. 3. (Met.) Change of political ideas.

Evolucionar [ay-vo-loo-the-o-nar'], *vn.* (Mil. Naut.) To perform evolutions or tactical movements.

Evoluta [ay-vo-loo'-tah], *f.* 1. (Math.) Volute. 2. (Naut.) A snail-shell.

Evolutivo, va [ay-vo-loo-tee'-vo, vah], *a.* Evolutive.

Evulsión [ay-vool-se-on'], *f.* (Med.) Evulsion, plucking out, forcible extraction.

Ex [ex], *prep.* Used in Spanish only in composition, where it either amplifies the signification, as *exponer,* or serves as a negative, as *exánime.* *Ex-provincial,* Former or late provincial.

Ex abrupto [ex ah-broop'-to], *adv.* Abruptly, violently.

Exacción [ek-sac-the-on'], *f.* 1. Exaction, the act of levying taxes. 2. Impost, tax, contribution, levy. 3. (Obs.) Exactness, punctuality.

Exacerbación [ek-sah-ther-bah-the-on'], *f.* (Med.) Exacerbation, paroxysm.

Exacerbar [ek-sah-ther-bar'], *va.* To irritate, to exasperate, to exacerbate.

Exactamente [ek-sac-tah-men'-tay], *adv.* Exactly, minutely, just, justly, accurately, faithfully, circumstantially, critically, nicely, to a hair.

Exactitud [ek-sac-te-tood'], *f.* Exactness, exactitude, punctuality, accuracy, correctness, justness, niceness.

Exacto, ta [ek-sahc'-to, tah], *a.* Exact, punctual, assiduous, nice, heedful, faithful, observant, critical, just.

Exactor [ek-sac-tor'], *m.* Tax-gatherer, exactor.

Exactora [ek-sac-to'-rah], *f.* Exactress.

Exageración [ek-sah-hay-rah-the-on'], *f.* Exaggeration, hyperbolical amplification.

Exagerador, ra [ek-sah-hay-rah-dor', rah], *m.* & *f.* Amplifier, one that exaggerates.

Exagerante [ek-sah-hay-rahn'-tay], *pa.* & *m.* (Poet.) Amplifier; exaggerating.

Exagerar [ek-sah-hay-rar'], *va.* To exaggerate, to amplify, to heighten by misrepresentation, to magnify, to hyperbolize, to overstate.

Exagerativamente, *adv.* With exaggeration.

Exagerativo, va [ek-sah-hay-rah-tee'-vo, vah], *a.* Exaggerating, exaggeratory.

Exágono, na [ek-sah'-go-no, nah], *a.* Hexagonal. *V.* HEXÁGONO.

Exaltación [ek-sal-tah-the-on'], *f.* 1. Exaltation, elevation. 2. (Chem.) Sublimation.

Exaltado, da [ek-sal-tah'-do, dah], *a.* (Neol.) Exaggerated and violent in political ideas.

Exaltar [ek-sal-tar'], *va.* 1. To exalt, to elevate; to magnify; to lift, to heave. 2. To praise, to extol; to cry up. *Exaltarse la bilis* or *la cólera,* To irritate one's self.

Examen [ek-sah'-men], *m.* 1. Examination, disquisition, exploration, consideration. 2. Trial, inquiry. 3. Examination. 4. Care and diligence in searching out any thing.

Exámetro [ek-sah'-may-tro], *m.* Hexameter verse.

Examinación [ek-sah-me-nah-the-on'], *f.* Examination.

Examinador, ra [ek-sah-me-nah-dor', rah], *m.* & *f.* Examiner, explorator, examinator.

Examinando [ek-sah-me-nahn'-do], *m.* Examinant, he who is to be examined.

Examinante [ek-sah-me-nahn'-tay], *pa.* & *n.* 1. Examining. 2. (Obs.) Examinant.

Examinar [ek-sah-me-nar'], *va.* 1. To examine, to investigate. 2. To consider, to explore, to look into, to look over, to fathom; to feel, to consult. 3. To inquire into books or writings.

Exangüe [ek-sahn'-goo-ay], *a.* 1. Bloodless, without blood; pale from the loss of blood, exsanguious. 2. (Met.) Weak, without strength.

Exángulo, la [ek-sahn'-goo-lo, lah], *a.* Having six angles.

Exanimación [ek-sah-ne-ma-the-on'], *f.* Exanimation.

Exánime [ek-sah'-ne-may], *a.* Spiritless, exanimous, weak, without force or vigour.

Exantema [ek-san-tay'-mah], *f.* Exanthema, an eruptive disease of the skin.

Exantemático, ca, or **Exantematoso, sa** [ek-san-tay-mah'-te-co, cah, ek-san-tay-mah-to'-so, sah], *a.* Exanthematous, or exanthematic.
Exantropía [ek-san-tro-pee'-ah], *f.* (Med.) The last stage of melancholy.
Exápodo, da [ek-sah'-po-do, dah], *a.* Hexapod, six-footed.—*m.pl.* Hexapods, the true insects, with six feet.
Exarcado [ek-sar-cah'-do], *m.* Exarchate or vice-royalty.
Exarco [ek-sar'-co], *m.* 1. Exarch, viceroy. 2. A dignitary in the Greek church.
Exasperación [ek-sas-pay-rah-the-on'], *f.* Exasperation.
Exasperado, da [ek-sas-pay-rah'-do, dah], *a.* & *pp.* of Exasperar. Exasperate, exasperated.
Exasperar [ek-sas-pay-rar'], *va.* To exasperate, to irritate, to offend, to acerbate.
Exastilo [ex-sas-tee'-lo], *m.* (Arch.) Hexastyle, a portico of six columns in front.
Excandecencia [ex-can-day-then'-the-ah], *f.* 1. Candescence, incandescence. 2. Anger, passion.
Excandecer [ex-can-day-therr'], *va.* To irritate, to provoke, to put into a passion.—*vr.* To be in a passion.
Excarcelar [ex-car-thay-lar'], *va.* To remove a prisoner from the jail by command of the judge.
Ex cáthedra. (Acad.) A phrase from the Latin to denote a tone of mastery and finality. To speak, or decide, *ex cáthedra.*
Excava, Excavación [ex-cah'-vah, ex-cah-vah-the-on'], *f.* Excavation.
Excavador, ra [ex-cah-vah-dor'-rah], *a.* Excavating.—*f.* Excavating machine.
Excavar [ex-cah-var'], *va.* To excavate, to dig out, to hollow.
Excavillo [ex-cah-veel'-lyo], *m.* (Prov.) A little spade used in making excavations.
Excedente [ex-thay-den'-tay], *pa.* & *a.* Excessive, exceeding.
Exceder [ex-thay-derr'], *va.* To exceed, to surpass, to excel, to go beyond, to outrun, to outgo, to overtop.—*vr.* To exceed, to overgo. *Excederse a sí mismo,* To surpass one's own actions.
Excelencia [ex-thay-len'-the-ah], *f.* 1. Excellence, eminence, height, exquisiteness, superior worth or merit. 2. Excellency, a title of honour applied in Spain to grandees, councillors of state, etc. *Por excelencia,* (Coll.) Par excellence.
Excelente [ex-thay-len'-tay], *a.* Excellent, exquisite. *Excelente de la granada,* Ancient gold coin worth eleven reals and a maravedi, or 375 maravedis.
Excelentemente, *adv.* Excellently.
Excelentísimo, ma [ex-thay-len-tee'-se-mo, mah], *a. superl.* Most excellent: applied in courtesy to persons receiving the title of excellency.
Excelsamente [ex-thel-sah-men'-tay], *adv.* Sublimely.
Excelsitud [ex-thel-se-tood'], *f.* Excelsitude, loftiness.
Excelso, sa [ex-thel'-so, sah], *a.* Elevated, sublime, lofty.
Excéntrica [ex-then'-tre-cah], *f.* (Mech.) Cam.
Excéntricamente [ex-then'-tre-cah-men-tay], *adv.* Eccentrically.
Excentricidad [ex-then-tre-the-dahd'], *f.* Eccentricity; deviation from the centre; excursion from the proper orb; distance from the centre of an ellipse to one of its foci.
Excéntrico, ca [ex-then'-tre-co, cah], *a.* 1. Eccentric, eccentrical, having a different centre. 2. Extravagant, odd, eccentric.
Excepción [ex-thep-the-on'], *f.* 1. Exception, exclusion from things comprehended. 2. Exception, thing excepted or specified in exception. 3. (Law) Demurrer, exception, a stop or stay to an action.
Excepcional [ex-thep-the-o-nahl'], *a.* Exceptional, unusual, contrary to rule.
Excepcionar [ex-thep-the-o-nar'], *va.* (Law) To except, to object, to demur.
Excepto [ex-thep'-to], *adv.* Except that, besides that, excepting.
Exceptuación [ex-thep-too-ah-the-on'], *f.* *V.* Excepción.
Exceptuar [ex-thep-too-ar'], *va.* To except, to exempt, to exclude, to leave out.
Excerta [ex-therr'-tah], *f.* Excerpt, extract, citation.
Excesivamente, *adv.* Excessively.
Excesivo, va [ex-thay-see'-vo, vah], *a.* Excessive, immoderate, exorbitant, overgreat, extreme.
Exceso [ex-thay'-so], *m.* 1. Excess, overmuch; superfluity, excessiveness, exuberance. 2. Excess, intemperance in eating or drinking. 3. Excess, irregularity, transgression of due limits. 4. Great wickedness, enormity of crime. 5. Excess, violence of passion. *En exceso,* Excessively.
Excipiente [ex-the-pe-en'-tay], *m.* (Med.) Excipient, a substance serving to incorporate, or to dissolve others in a medicine; a vehicle.
Excisión [ex-the-se-on'], *f.* 1. Uprising, mutiny. 2. Altercation, quarrel.
Excitabilidad [ex-the-tah-be-le-dahd'], *f.* Excitability.
Excitable [ex-the-tah'-blay], *a.* Excitable.
Excitación [ex-the-tah-the-on'], *f.* Excitation, exciting, the act of exciting.
Excitante [ex-the-tahn'-tay], *a.* Exciting, stimulating.—*m.* Stimulant, excitant.
Excitar [ex-the-tar'], *va.* 1. To excite, to move, to stimulate. 2. To excite, to stir up, to rouse, to animate, to fire, to flame.
Excitativo, va [ex-the-tah-tee'-vo, vah], *a.* Exciting, stimulative, excitative.
Exclamación [ex-clah-ma-the-on'], *f.* 1. Exclamation, vehement outcry, clamour. *Exclamaciones de regocijo,* Shouts of joy. 2. Exclamation, an emphatical utterance.
Exclamar [ex-clah-mar'], *vn.* To exclaim, to cry out, to clamour, to holla.
Exclamativo, va [ex-clah-mah-tee'-vo, vah], *a.* (Obs.) Exclaiming.
Exclamatorio, ria [ex-clah-mah-to'-re-o, ah], *a.* Exclamatory.
Exclaustrado [ex-clah-oos-trah'-do, dah], *m.* The cleric who has ceased to live in a cloister, chiefly by suppression of his order; a secularized monk.
Excluir [ex-cloo-eer'], *va.* 1. To exclude, to shut out, to expel, to foreclose, to cut out. 2. To exclude, to debar, to hinder from participation.
Exclusión [ex-cloo-se-on'], *f.* 1. Exclusion, shutting out or denying admission, rejection, ejection. 2. Exclusion, exception.
Exclusiva [ex-cloo-see'-vah], *f.* 1. Refusal of place or employment; rejection of an application to become member of a community; exclusion. 2. A special privilege. (Acad.)
Exclusivamente, Exclusive [ex-cloo-se-vah-men'-tay], *adv.* Exclusively.
Exclusivo, va [ex-cloo-see'-vo, vah], *a.* Exclusive.
Excluso, *pp. irr.* from Excluir.
Excogitable [ex-co-he-tah'-blay], *a.* Imaginable, possible to be conceived.
Excogitar [ex-co-he-tar'], *va.* To excogitate, to meditate; to strike out by thinking.
Excomulgación, Excomunicación [ex-co-mool-gah-the-on', ex-co-moo-ne-cah-the-on'], *f.* (Obs.) *V.* Excomunión.
Excomulgado, da [ex-co-mool-gah'-do, dah], *a.* & *pp.* of Excomulgar. Excommunicate, excommunicated, accursed. *Excomulgado vitando,* An excommunicated person, with whom no intercourse can be held.
Excomulgador [ex-co-mool-gah-dor'], *m.* Excommunicator.
Excomulgar [ex-co-mool-gar'], *va.* 1. To excommunicate, to eject from the communion of the church, and the use of the sacraments. 2. To fulminate ecclesiastical censures. 3. (Met.) To treat with foul language, to use ill, to accurse.
Excomunión [ex-co-moo-ne-on'], *f.* Excommunication, exclusion from the fellowship of the church.
Excoriación [ex-co-re-ah-the-on'], *f.* Excoriation, privation of skin, the act of flaying.
Excoriar [ex-co-re-ar'], *va.* (Med.) To excoriate, to flay: it is almost always used in its reciprocal sense.
Excrecencia [ex-cray-then'-the-ah], *f.* Excrescence or excrescency.
Excreción [ex-cray-the-on'], *f.* Excretion.
Excrementar [ex-cray-men-tar'], *va.* To excrementize, to purge, to void by stool.
Excrementicio, cia [ex-cray-men-tee'-the-o, ah], *a.* Excrementitious, excremental.
Excremento [ex-cray-men'-to], *m.* 1. Excrement, flux. 2. Particles separated from plants by putrefaction.
Excrementoso, sa [ex-cray-men-to'-so, sah], *a.* Excremental, excrementitious.
Excretar [ex-cray-tar'], *vn.* To excrete; to eject the excrements.
Excreto, ta [ex-cray'-to, tah], *a.* That which is ejected.
Excretor, ra, or **Excretorio, ria** [ex-cray-to'-re-o, ah], *a.* Excretory, excretive, having the quality of ejecting superfluous parts.
Excursión [ex-coor-se-on'], *f.* 1. Excursion; expedition into the enemy's country. 2. (Law) Liquidation of the estate of a debtor for paying off his debts.
Excursionista [ex-coor-se-o-nees'-tah], *m.* & *f.* Excursionist, traveler.
Excusa [ex-coo'-sah], *f.* 1. Excuse, apology or plea offered in extenuation. 2. Excuse, the act of excusing or apologizing. 3. Excuse, cause for which one is excused. 4. Allowance, excusableness, colour, cloak, loophole. *Excusas,* Exemptions, immunities or emoluments granted to certain persons. *A excusa* or *excusas,* (Obs.) Dissemblingly.
Excusabaraja [ex-coo-sah-ba-rah'-hah], *f.* Basket or pannier with a cover of osiers.
Excusable [ex-coo-sah'-blay], *a.* Excusable, pardonable.
Excusación [ex-coo-sah-the-on'], *f.* *V.* Excusa.
Excusadamente, *adv.* Uselessly, voluntarily, without necessity; not to the purpose.
Excusado, da [ex-coo-sah'-do, dah], *a.* 1. Exempted, privileged. 2. Superfluous, useless. 3. Preserved, laid up as useless.—*pp.* of Excusar. *Lugar excusado,* A privy, closet.

Excusado, *m.* A subsidy levied on his clergy by the Spanish monarch, to assist him in the war against infidels: commonly called *Renta del excusado. Meterse en la renta del excusado,* To meddle in other people's affairs.

Excusador, ra [ex-coo-sah-dor', rah], *m.* & *f.* 1. One who performs another's functions in his stead. 2. Vicar or curate of a parish church. 3. (Law) Excuser, one who excuses the non-appearance of a defendant in court.

Excusali [ex-coo-sah-lee'], *m.* Small apron.

Excusaña [ex-coo-sah'-nyah], *f.* (Obs.) Peasant who used to be employed in watching the enemy in a pass. *A excusañas,* Hiddenly, secretly.

Excusar [ex-coo-sar'], *va.* 1. To excuse, to extenuate by apology, to exculpate, to colour, to palliate. 2. To exempt from taxes. 3. To obstruct, to hinder, to prevent. 4. To shun, to avoid.—*vr.* To decline or reject a request.

Excusión [ex-coo-se-on'], *f.* (Law) 1. Liquidation of the estate of a debtor for paying his debts. 2. (Med.) Concussion, a violent shaking.

Ex diámetro [ex de-ah'-may-tro], *adv.* (Lat.) Diametrically.

Execrable [ek-say-crah'-blay], *a.* Execrable, detestable, hateful, accursed.

Execrablemente, *adv.* Execrably.

Execración [ek-say-crah-the-on'], *f.* Execration, detestation, cursing, abhorrence.

Execrador, ra [ek-say-crah-dor', rah], *m.* & *f.* Execrater.

Execrar [ek-say-crar'], *va.* To execrate, to detest, to curse, to imprecate ill upon.—*vr.* To mutually hate one another.

Execratorio [ek-say-crah-to'-re-o], *a.* *Juramento execratorio,* Execratory.

Exégesis [ek-say'-hay-sis], *f.* Exegesis, explanation in general, and in particular of the Bible.

Exégeta [ek-say'-hay-tah], *m.* (Antiq.) Interpreter, a name which the Athenians gave to those charged by the government to teach foreigners the antiquities of the city.

Exegético, ca [ek-say-hay'-te-co, cah], *a.* Exegetical, explanatory.

Exención [ek-sen-the-on'], *f.* 1. Exemption, immunity, privilege, freedom from imposts. 2. Franchise, exemption from any onerous duty.

Exentado, da [ek-sen-tah'-do, dah], *a.* & *pp.* of Exentar. Exempt, exempted.

Exentamente [ek-sen-tah-men'-tay], *adv.* 1. Freely. 2. Clearly, simply, sincerely.

Exentar [ek-sen-tar'], *va.* 1. To exempt, to grant immunity from, to privilege, to franchise. 2. To absolve, to acquit, to excuse, to disengage from an obligation.—*vr.* To except one's self.

Exento, ta [ek-sen'-to, tah], *a.* 1. Exempt, free, freed, disengaged. 2. Exemptible, exempt, free, privileged. 3. Clear, open, isolated, free from impediment.—*pp. irr.* of Eximir.

Exento [ek-sen'-to], *m.* Officer in the Spanish life-guards, who holds the rank and brevet of a colonel in the army.

Exequátur [ek-say-quah'-toor], *m.* 1. A Latin word signifying the approval which the civil authority of a State gives to pontifical bulls. 2. Authorization given to a foreign consul to exercise the charge with which he has been invested.

Exequial [ek-say-ke-ahl'], *a.* (Obs.) Exequial, relating to funerals.

Exequias [ek-say'-ke-as], *f. pl.* Exequias, funeral rites, obsequies.

Exequible [ek-say-kee'-blay], *a.* Attainable.

Exerción [ek-ser-the-on'], *f.* (Neol. Med.) Irritation, animation, activity, or contraction of fibrous tissues.

Exergo [ek-serr'-go], *m.* Exergue, the space left on the face sides of medals for the inscription.

Exfoliación [ex-fo-le-ah-the-on'], *f.* (Med.) Desquamation, scaling.

Exfoliar [ex-fo-le-ar'], *va.* (Med.) To exfoliate.—*vr.* To become exfoliated.

Exfoliativo, va [ex-fo-le-ah-tee'-vo, vah], *a.* (Surg.) Exfoliative, producing exfoliation.

Exhalación [ex-ah-lah-the-on'], *f.* 1. Exhalation, the act of exhaling. 2. Exhalation, that which rises in vapours. 3. An electrical or other fire accustomed to be seen in the atmosphere; a shooting star.

Exhalador, ra [ex-ah-lah-dor', rah], *m.* & *f.* Exhaler, one who exhales.

Exhalar [ex-ah-lar'], *va.* To exhale, to send or draw out vapours or fumes.—*vr.* 1. To exhale, to evaporate. 2. To be consumed or wasted gradually. 3. To be exhausted by violent exercise of the body. *Exhalarse por alguna cosa,* To covet or desire any thing with anxious eagerness. *Exhalar el espíritu,* To die.

Exhalatorio, ria [ex-ah-lah-to'-re-o, ah], *a.* Exhalant.—*m.* An apparatus for evaporating fresh water in salt-works.

Exhaución [ex-ah-oo-the-on'], *f.* Exhaustion, a method of establishing the equality of two numbers by proving that they differ by less than any assignable quantity.

Exhausto, ta [ex-ah'-oos-to, tah], *a.* Exhausted, totally drained or drawn out.

Exheredación [ex-ay-ray-dah-the-on'], *f.* Disinheritance, privation of an inheritance.

Exheredar [ex-ay-ray-dar'], *va.* To disinherit.

Exhibición [ex-e-be-the-on'], *f.* Exhibition, the act of exhibiting.

Exhibir [ex-e-beer'], *va.* To exhibit, to prevent, to make manifest, to lay.

Exhortación [ex-or-tah-the-on'], *f.* 1. Exhortation, admonition, hortation. 2. A short and familiar sermon.

Exhortador, ra [ex-or-tah-dor', rah], *m.* & *f.* Exhorter, monitor.

Exhortar [ex-or-tar'], *va.* To exhort, to excite by words to any good action.

Exhortatorio, ria [ex-or-tah-to'-re-o, ah], *a.* Exhortatory, hortative.

Exhorto [ex-or'-to], *m.* Letters requisitorial sent by one judge to another.

Exhumación [ex-oo-mah-the-on'], *f.* Exhumation, disinterment.

Exhumar [ex-oo-mar'], *va.* To disinter, to unbury.

Exigencia [ek-se-hen'-the-ah], *f.* Exigence, want, pressing necessity, exaction.

Exigible [ek-se-hee'-blay], *a.* Capable of being demanded or required.

Exigir [ek-se-heer'], *va.* 1. To exact, to demand, to require. 2. To wish for, to desire, to beg of.

Exigüidad [ek-se-goo-e-dahd'], *f.* Exiguity, smallness.

Exiguo, gua [ek-see'-goo-o, ah], *a.* Exiguous, small.

Eximio, mia [ek-see'-me-o, ah], *a.* Eximious, famous, very eminent.

Eximir [ek-se-meer'], *va.* 1. To exempt, to free from an obligation, to clear from a charge. 2. To exempt, to privilege, to excuse, to except.

Exinanición [ek-se-nah-ne-the-on'], *f.* Inanition, want of vigour and strength; debility.

Exinanido, da [ek-se-nah-nee'-do, dah], *a.* Debilitated, very weak, very feeble.

Exir [ek-seer'], *vn.* (Obs.) *V.* Salir.

Existencia [ek-sis-ten'-the-ah], *f.* Existence, existency, state of being; actual possession of being. *Existencias,* Stock in hand; articles or goods remaining unsold.

Existencialismo [ek-sis-ten-the-ah-lees'-mo], *m.* Existentialism.

Existente [ek-sis-ten'-tay], *pa.* & *a.* Existing, extant, existent, on hand.

Existimación [ek-sis-te-ma-the-on'], *f.* Estimation, opinion, esteem.

Existimar [ek-sis-te-mar'], *va.* To hold, to form an opinion, to judge.

Existir [ek-sis-teer'], *vn.* To exist, to be; to have a being.

Éxito [ek'-se-to], *m.* 1. Result, outcome. 2. Success, good fortune.

Exitoso, sa [ek-se-to'-so, sah], *a.* Successful.

Éxodo [ek'-so-do], *m.* Exodus, the second book of Moses.

Exoftalmia [ex-of-tahl-me'-ah], *f.* Exophthalmia, or exophthalmus, abnormal protrusion of the eyeball from the orbit.

Exoneración [ek-so-nay-rah-the-on'], *f.* Exoneration, the act of disburdening.

Exonerar [ek-so-nay-rar'], *va.* To exonerate, to unload; to disburden, to lighten.

Exopilativo, va [ek-so-pe-lah-tee'-vo, vah], *a.* Deobstruent.

Exorable [ek-so-rah'-blay], *a.* Exorable, to be moved by entreaty.

Exorbitancia [ek-sor-be-tahn'-the-ah], *f.* Exorbitance.

Exorbitante [ek-sor-be-tahn'-tay], *a.* Exorbitant, enormous, excessive, extravagant.

Exorbitantemente, *adv.* Exorbitantly, extravagantly.

Exorcismo [ek-sor-thees'-mo], *m.* Exorcism.

Exorcista [ek-sor-thees'-tah], *m.* Exorciser, exorcist.

Exorcizante [ek-sor-the-thahn'-tay], *pa.* & *com.* Exorcising; exorciser.

Exorcizar [ek-sor-the-thar'], *va.* To exorcise, to adjure by some holy name, to drive away by adjuration.

Exordio [ek-sor'-de-o], *m.* Exordium, the proemial part of a composition; origin, beginning.

Exornación [ek-sor-nah-the-on'], *f.* (Rhet.) Exornation, ornaments in writing or speaking.

Exornar [ek-sor-nar'], *va.* To adorn or embellish a discourse with rhetorical figures.

Exortación [ek-sor-tah-the-on'], *f.* Exhortation, familiar admonition to piety; monition.

Exostosis [ek-sos-to'-sis], *f.* 1. Exostosis, a disease of the bones. 2. (Bot.) Excrescence on the trunk of trees of very hard wood, whose fibres cross in all directions.

Exotérico, ca [ek-so-tay'-re-co, cah], *a.* Exoteric, public, common.

Exótico, ca [ek-so'-te-co, cah], *a.* 1. Exotic, foreign, extraneous. 2. Extravagant, odd.

Expalmado, da [ex-pal-mah'-do, dah], *a.* (Littl. us.) Worn out by use: applied to the blade of a razor.

Expansibilidad [ex-pan-se-be-le-dahd'], *f.* Expansibility.

Expansible [ex-pan-see'-blay], *a.* (Littl. us.) Expansible.

Expansión [ex-pan-se-on'], *f.* Expansion, extension.

Expansivo, va [ex-pan-see'-vo, vah], *a.* 1. Expansive, capable of extension. 2. Affable, communicative.

Expanso [ex-pahn'-so], *m.* 1. Expanse, a body widely expanded. 2. Space between the superior sphere of the air and the empyrean or highest heaven.

Expatriación [ex-pah-tre-ah-the-on], *f* Expatriation.
Expatriar [ex-pah-tre-ar], *va.* To expatriate.—*vr.* To be exiled.
Expectable [ex-pec-tah'-blay], *a.* Conspicuous, eminent, illustrious.
Expectación [ex-pec-tah-the-on'], *f.* Expectation, expectance, expectancy, anxious desire, hope, looking. *Joven de expectación*, A hopeful youth. *Hombre de expectación*, A celebrated man.
Expectativa [ex-pec-tah-tee'-vah], *f* 1 Right or claim respecting some future thing. 2. Hope of obtaining a reward, employment, or other thing 3 Expectation, expectance.
Expectoración [ex-pec-to-rah-the-on'], *f.* Expectoration, the act and effect of expectorating; sputum.
Expectorante [ex-pec-to-rahn'-tay], *pa.* Expectorating.—*a.* & *n.* (Med.) Expectorant, a medicine which promotes expectoration
Expectorar [ex-pec-to-rar'], *va* To expectorate, to spit out.
Expectorativo, va [ex-pec-to-rah-tee'-vo, vah], *a.* (Littl. us.) Expectorative, expectorant.
Expedición [ex-pay-de-the-on'], *f* 1 Readiness, facility, or freedom in saying or doing. 2. Expedition, haste, speed, activity, nimbleness. 3. Brevet or bull despatched by the see of Rome. 4. Expedition, a warlike enterprise. 5. Excursion, jaunt, journey.
Expedicionero [ex-pay-de-the-o-nay'-ro], *m.* He who superintends expeditions or despatches.
Expedido, da [ex-pay-dee'-do, dah], *a.* & *pp.* of Expedir. Expedite, quick, prompt, nimble.
Expedidor [ex-pay-de-dor'], *m.* (Com.) Agent, shipper.
Expediente [ex-pay-de-en'-tay], *m.* 1. The collection of all the papers belonging to a business matter. 2. Despatch, course of business. 3. Expedient, measure, means to an end contrived in an exigency or difficulty. 4. Facility or dexterity in the management of affairs.
Expedienteo [ex-pay-de-en–tay'-o], *m.* (coll.) Red tape.
Expedir [ex-pay-deer'], *va.* 1. To expedite, to facilitate, to free from impediment. 2. To despatch, to issue from a public office, to forward, transit.
Expeditamente [ex-pay-de-tah-men'-tay], *adv.* Expeditiously, expeditely, easily.
Expeditivo, va [ex-pay-de-tee'-vo, vah], *a.* Expeditive, performing with speed, expeditious, speedy, quick; apt in expedients.
Expedito, ta [ex-pay-dee'-to, tah], *a.* Prompt, expeditious, speedy, quick.
Expeler [ex-pay-lerr'], *va.* To expel, to eject, to throw with violence.
Expeliente [ex-pay-le-en'-tay], *pa.* & *m.* & *f.* Expelling, expulser.
Expendedor, ra [ex-pen-day-dor', rah], *m.* & *f.* 1. Spendthrift, lavisher. 2. One who sells publicly and disposes of some merchandise. 3. One who passes counterfeit money, knowing it to be so. 4. Agent, commission merchant; one who sells goods for another.
Expendeduría [ex-pen-day-doo-ree'-ah], *f.* A shop in which tobacco and other wares are retailed. (Acad.)
Expender [ex-pen-derr'], *va.* 1. To expend, to spend, to lay out. 2. (For.) To pass counterfeit money or stolen goods in trade.
Expendio [ex-pen'-de-o], *m.* Expense, outlay, consumption. (Acad.)
Expensas [ex-pen'-sas], *f. pl.* Expenses, charges, costs. *Estar a expensas de otro*, To live, by favour, at the cost of another, or to depend upon him
Experiencia [ex-pay-re-en' the-ah], *f* 1. Experience, knowledge gained by practice 2. Experience, experiment, practice, trial.
Experimentado, da [ex-pay-re-men tah'-do, dah], *a.* & *pp.* of Experimentar. Experienced, expert, conversant.
Experimentador, ra [ex-pay-re-men tah-dor', rah], *m.* & *f* Experimenter, experimentalist.
Experimental [ex-pay-re-men-tahl'], *a.* Experimental; attained by experience
Experimentalmente, *adv* Experimentally.
Experimentar [ex-pay-re-men-tar'], *va.* 1. To experience, to learn or know by practice. 2. To experiment, to search out by trial.
Experimento [ex-pay-re-men'-to], *m.* Experiment, trial of any thing.
Expertamente, *adv* Expertly, cunningly
Experto, ta [ex-perr -to, tah], *a.* Expert, able, experienced, conversant, clever, cunning.
Expiación [ex-pe-ah-the-on'], *f.* 1 Expiation, the act of atoning for any crime. 2. Atonement, purification. 3. Reparation, compensation for damage.
Expiar [ex-pe-ar'], *va.* 1. To expiate, to atone for any crime. 2. To purify, to free from profanation.
Expiativo, va [ex-pe-ah-tee'-vo, vah], *a.* That which serves for expiation, expiatory.
Expiatorio, ria [ex-pe-ah-to'-re-o, ah], *a.* Expiatory.
Explanación [ex-plah-nah-the-on], *f.* Explanation, elucidation, exposition.
Explanada [ex-plah-nah'-dah], *f.* (Mil.) 1. A slope. 2. Esplanade, glacis.
Explanar [ex-plah-nar'], *va.* 1. To level. *V.* Allanar. 2. (Met.) To explain, to elucidate, to clear up
Explayamiento [ex-plah-yah-me-en'-to], *m.* The act of dilating or dwelling upon a subject.
Explayar [ex-plah-yar'], *va.* To extend, to dilate, to enlarge.—*vr.* 1 To enlarge or dwell upon a subject. 2. To amuse one's self, by taking a walk or any other amusement. 3. To be extended or enlarged.
Expletivo, va [ex-play-tee'-vo, vah], *a.* Expletive.
Explicable [ex-ple-cah'-blay], *a.* Explicable, explainable.
Explicación [ex-ple-cah-the-on'], *f.* Explanation, explication, elucidation, exposition, interpretation, comment.
Explicadamente [ex-ple-cah-dah-men'-tay], *adv.* Explicitly.
Explicaderas [ex-ple-cah-day'-ras], *f. pl.* (Coll.) Manner in which any thing is explained; facility of explaining. (Ironical.)
Explicador, ra [ex-ple-cah-dor', rah], *m.* & *f.* 1. One who explains. 2. Commentator, glossarist, glossator.
Explicar [ex-ple-car'], *va.* To explain, to elucidate, to clear up, to expound, to comment, to construe.—*vr.* To explain or speak one's mind with propriety and freedom. *Explicar el porqué de una cosa*, To account.
Explicativo, va [ex-ple-cah-tee'-vo, vah], *a.* (Littl. us.) Explicative, explicatory, exegetical.
Explícitamente, *adv.* Explicitly, manifestly.
Explícito, ta [ex-plee'-the-to, tah], *f.* Explicit, clear, distinct, manifest.
Exploración [ex-plo-rah-the-on'], *f.* Exploration.
Explorador, ra [ex-plo-rah-dor', rah], *f.* Explorator, explorer.
Explorar [ex-plo-rar], *va* To explore, to search into, to examine by trial
Exploratorio [ex-plo-rah-to'-re-o], *m* Probe, catheter
Explosión [ex-plo-se-on], *f* Explosion, outburst.
Explosivo, va [ex-plo-see vo, vah], *a* Explosive, capable of producing an explosion
Explotable [ex-plo-tah blay], *a* Workable, minable.
Explotación [ex-plo-tah-the-on'], *f* 1. Exploiting, exploitation, improvement of mines, or of lands. 2. Exploitation, unfair utilization (of someone or something)
Explotar [ex-plo-tar'], *va.* 1. To work or develop mines. 2. To till lands 3. (Met.) To exploit, to get all the benefit possible out of a thing.
Expoliación [ex-po-le-ah-the-on], *f* (Littl. us.) Expoliation.
Expolición [ex-po-le-the-on], *f* Illustration of any saying.
Exponencial [ex-po-nen-the-ahl], *a* (Alg.) Exponential.
Exponente [ex-po-nen -tay], *pa.* & *m.* & *f.* 1. Expositor. 2. (Arith.) Exponent 3. (Com.) Exhibitor; manufacturer, inventor or artist who exhibits a product in public exhibitions.
Exponer [ex-po-nerr'], *va.* 1. To expose, to lay before the public. 2. To expound, to explain. 3. To expose, to lay open, to make bare. 4. To expose, to put in danger, to hazard, to expose to chance. 5. To expose a young child, or to cast him out to chance.—*vr.* To hazard, to adventure, to try the chance.
Exportación [ex-por-tah-the-on], *f* Exportation, sending commodities to other countries.
Exportar [ex-por-tar], *va.* To export, to carry out of a country.
Exposición [ex-po-se-the-on'], *f.* 1. Exposition, explanation, interpretation. 2. Making manifest. 3. Solicitude lifted into petition or allegation. 4. Exposition, a public display of industrial products, agricultural, artistic, etc. 5. Peril, risk.
Expositivo, va [ex-po-se-tee'-vo, vah], *a* Explanatory, expositive.
Expósito, ta [ex-po'-se-to, tah], *a.* Exposed: applied to infants abandoned. *Expósito* or *niño expósito*, Foundling.
Expositor [ex-po-se-tor'], *m.* Expounder, interpeter, explainer, explicator.
Expremijo [ex-pray-mee'-ho], *m.* Cheese-vat, a wooden case in which cheeses are formed and pressed.
Expresado, da [ex-pray-sah'-do, dah], *a.* Before mentioned, cited, aforesaid.
Expresamente [ex-pray-sah-men'-tay], *adv.* Expressly, in direct terms, plainly
Expresar [ex-pray-sar'], *va.* 1. To express, to declare one's sentiments clearly and distinctly. 2. To delineate, to sketch, to design.
Expresión [ex-pray-se-on'], *f.* 1 Expression, declaration of one's sentiments and opinions. 2. Expression, the form of language in which thoughts are uttered. 3. Expression, a phrase, a mode of speech. 4. Expression, the act of squeezing out the juice from succulent fruits. 5. Present, gift. *Envió esa expresión*, He sent this present. 6. Expression, the act of representing any thing.
Expresivamente, *adv.* Expressively.
Expresivo, va [ex-pray-see'-vo, vah], *a.* 1. Expressive: applied to persons or things expressing something in a clear and representative way. 2. Affectionate, kind, gracious.

Expreso, sa [ex-pray'-so, sah], *a.* & *pp irr* of EXPRESAR. Expressed; express, clear, manifest, not dubious.
Expreso [ex-pray'-so], *m* 1 Express, extraordinary messenger, a courier. 2 (Naut.) Packet-boat, advice-boat. 3. A rapid train for passengers and mails
Exprimidera [ex-pre-me-day'-rah], *f.* A small press used by apothecaries to squeeze out the juice of herbs.
Exprimidero [ex-pre-me-day'-ro], *m.* A press or any other thing, by which any thing is crushed or squeezed.
Exprimido, da [ex-pre-mee'-do, dah], *a* & *pp.* of EXPRIMIR Squeezed; dry, extenuated.
Exprimidor [ex-pre-me-dor'], *m.* Wringer, presser, squeezer.
Exprimir [ex-pre-meer'], *va.* 1. To squeeze or press out. 2. To express, to declare clearly and distinctly.
Ex profeso [ex pro-fay'-so], *adv* (Lat.) Avowedly, designedly, on purpose.
Expropiación [ex-pro-pe-ah-the-on'], *f.* Expropriation, dispossession from ownership for public use.
Expropiar [ex-pro-pe-ar'], *va.* To expropriate, to take property from a private owner for public use.
Exprovincial [ex-pro-vin-the-ahl'], *m.* Ex-provincial, a late provincial
Expuesto, ta [ex-poo-es'-to, tah], *a.* & *pp. irr.* of EXPONER. Exposed, liable, obnoxious.
Expugnable [ex-poog-nah'-blay], *a.* Expugnable.
Expugnación [ex-poog-nah-the-on'], *f.* Expugnation.
Expugnador [ex-poog-nah-dor'], *m* Expugner, he who takes by assault.
Expugnar [ex-poog-nar'], *va.* To expugn, to conquer, to reduce a place by force of arms.
Expulsar [ex-pool-sar'], *va.* To expel, to eject, to drive out, to force away.
Expulsión [ex-pool-se-on'], *f.* Expulsion, the act of driving out.
Expulsivo, va [ex-pool-see' vo, vah], *a* Expulsive.
Expulso, sa [ex-pool -so, sah], *a.* & *pp. irr.* of EXPELER and EXPULSAR. (Acad.) Ejected, driven out, expelled; outcast.
Expungir [ex-poon-heer'], *va.* (Littl. us.) To expunge, to rub out.
Expurgación [ex-poor-gah-the-on'], *f.* Expurgation, purification from bad mixture or error.
Expurgar [ex-poor-gar'], *va.* 1 To expurgate, to expunge, to purge away, to cleanse, to purify. 2. (Lit.) To correct, to emend, to remove errors.
Expurgativo, va [ex-poor-gah-tee'-vo, vah], *a.* Expurgatory, expurgatorious.
Expurgatorio [ex-poor-gah-to'-re-o], *m.* Index of the books prohibited by the Inquisition.
Expurgo [ex-poor'-go], *m.* (Prov.) Expurgation, purification from bad mixture.
Exquisitamente, *adv* Exquisitely
Exquisito, ta [ex-ke-see -to, tah], *a.* Exquisite, consummate, excellent, delicious.
Éxtasis [ex -tah-sis], *m.* 1. Ecstasy, enthusiasm. 2. (Med.) Catalepsy, or hypnotic sleep, with the eyes open.
Extático, ca [ex-tah'-te-co, cah], *a.* 1. Ecstatical, absorbed. 2. (Med.) Cataleptic
Extemporáneamente, *adv.* Extemporaneously, extempore, without premeditation.
Extemporáneo, nea [ex-tem-po-rah - nay-o, ah], *a.* Extemporaneous, unpremeditated; out of time
Extendedor [ex-ten-day-dor'], *m* (Littl. us.) Extender
Extender [ex-ten-derr'] *va* 1 To extend, to stretch out or stretch forth, to hold out, to outstretch, to outspread 2. To extend, to expand, to unfold, to unwrap 3 Speaking of a message, writing, etc., to record it in the ordinary form.—*vr.* To be extended or enlarged; to increase in bulk; to propagate.
Extendidamente, *adv.* Extensively
Extendido, da [ex-ten-dee'-do, dah], *a.* & *pp.* of EXTENDER. Extended, stretched out, extent, extensive, spacious, roomy.
Extendimiento [ex-ten-de-me-en -to], *m.* Extension, dilatation.
Extensamente [ex-ten-sah-men -tay], *adv.* Extensively.
Extensible [ex-ten-see'-blay], *a.* Extensible, extensile.
Extensión [ex-ten-se-on'], *f* 1. Extension, the act of extending. 2. Extension, extent, length, space or degree to which any thing is extended; extensiveness.
Extensivamente, *adv.* Amply, extensively, widely, largely.
Extensivo, va [ex-ten-see -vo, vah], *a.* Extensive, ample, wide, large, extensible.
Extenso, sa [ex-ten'-so, sah], *pp. irr.* of EXTENDER, and *a* Extensive. *Por extenso,* At large; clearly and distinctly.
Extensor, ra [ex-ten-sor', rah], *a.* Extending. (Med.) Extensor, as used of certain muscles.
Extenuación [ex-tay-noo-ah-the-on'], *f.* Extenuation, a general decay in the muscular flesh of the whole body; feebleness, wasting.
Extenuado, da [ex-tay-noo-ah'-do, dah], *a.* & *pp.* of EXTENUAR. Extenuated, extenuate, weak.
Extenuar [ex-tay-noo-ar'], *va.* To extenuate, to diminish, to debilitate, to make lean, to wear away.—*vr.* To languish, to grow feeble, to lose strength, to decay.
Extenuativo, va [ex-tay-noo-ah-tee'-vo, vah], *a.* That which extenuates.
Exterior [ex-tay-re-or'], *a.* Exterior, external, formal, extrinsic, extrinsical, outward.
Exterior [ex-tay-re-or'], *m.* Exterior, outside; composure, modest deportment; external man.
Exterioridad [ex-tay-re-o-re-dahd'], *f.* 1. Exteriority, outwardness, outward or external form; outward appearance. 2. Outside, superficies, surface, external part. 3. Pomp, ostentation, pageantry.
Exteriorizar [ex-tay-re-o-re-thar'], *va.* To express, to reveal outwardly.
Exteriormente [ex-tay-re-or-men'-tay], *adv.* 1. Externally, outwardly. 2. Externally, in appearance. 3. Exteriorly.
Exterminación [ex-ter-me-nah-the-on'], *f.* (Littl. us.) *V.* EXTERMINIO.
Exterminador, ra [ex-ter-me-nah-dor', rah], *m.* & *f.* Exterminator.—*a.* Exterminatory.
Exterminar [ex-ter-me-nar'], *va.* 1. To banish, to drive away. 2 To exterminate, to root out, to tear up, to destroy, to confound.
Exterminio [ex-ter-mee'-ne-o], *m.* 1. Expulsion, banishment. 2. Extermination, desolation, extirpation, destruction.
Externo, na [ex-terr'-no, nah], *a.* 1. External, visible, outward. 2. A day-pupil, one who attends classes at a school or college, but does not board there.
Ex testamento [ex tes-tah-men'-to], (Lat.) By will or testament · in contrast to **ab intestato.**
(*Yo extiendo, yo extienda,* from *Extender. V.* ATENDER.)
Extinción [ex-tin-the-on'], *f.* 1. Extinction, quenching or extinguishing. 2. Extinction, suppression. 3. Extinguishment, obliteration.
Extinguible [ex-tin-gee -blay], *a.* Extinguishable.
Extinguir [ex-tin-geer'], *va.* 1. To quench, to extinguish, to put out. 2. To extirpate, to suppress, to destroy.
Extinto, ta [ex-teen'-to, tah], *a.* & *pp. irr.* of EXTINGUIR. Extinguished, extinct.
Extintor [ex-tin-tor'], *m.* Extinguisher, fire extinguisher.
Extirpación [ex-teer-pah-the-on'], *f.* Extirpation, eradication, extermination, excision.
Extirpador [ex-teer-pah-dor'], *m.* Extirpator.
Extirpar [ex-teer-par'], *va.* 1. To extirpate, to root out, to eradicate, to exscind. 2. To destroy.
Extorsión [ex-tor-se-on'], *f* Extortion. (coll.) Shakedown.
Extra [ex -trah], *prep.* Out, without, besides.
Extracción [ex-trac-the-on'], *f.* 1. Exportation. 2. Extraction, the act of drawing one part out of a compound. 3. (Surg.) Extraction, the taking extraneous substances out of the body. 4. Drawing numbers in the lottery *Extracción de fondos,* (Com.) The secreting of effects. 5. (Math.) The process of finding the root of a number.
Extractador [ex-trac-tah-dor'], *m.* Extractor.
Extractar [ex-trac-tar'], *va.* To extract, to abridge, to select an abstract from a longer writing.
Extractivo, va [ex-trac-tee'-vo, vah], *a.* Extractive.
Extracto [ex-trahc'-to], *m.* 1. Extract, an abridgment or compendium of a large work, book, or writing. 2. (Pharm.) Extract, any substance obtained by the evaporation of a vegetable solution. *Extracto de Saturno,* White-lead. *Extractos,* Excerpts. 3. A number drawn in a lottery.
Extractor [ex-trac-tor'], *m.* Extractor.
Extradición [ex-tra-de-the-on'], *f.* Extradition, the delivery of a culprit who has fled to a foreign country by the government of the latter to that to which he belongs upon its demand.
Extraer [ex-trah-err'], *va.* 1. To extract, to remove, to export. 2. To extract, to draw out the chief parts of a compound. 3. (Law) To extract from any document. 4. To discover the root of a number.
(*Yo extraigo, yo extraiga, extraje, extrajera, extrajere,* from *Extraer. V.* TRAER.)
Extrajudicial [ex-trah-hoo-de-the-ahl'], *a.* Extrajudicial.
Extrajudicialmente, *adv.* Extrajudicially.
Extra muros [ex'-trah moo'-ros]. (Lat.) Without the walls of a town.
Extranjería [ex-tran-hay-ree'-ah], *f.* 1. The quality of being a stranger or foreigner. 2. The manner, use, and customs of a foreigner
Extranjerismo [ex-tran-hay-rees'-mo], *m.* Fondness for foreign customs.
Extranjero [ex-tran-hay'-ro], *m.* Any foreign land. *En el extranjero,* Abroad, in a foreign land.
Extranjero, ra [ex-tran-hay'-ro, rah], *m.* & *f.* Stranger, foreigner, alien.—*a.* Foreign, outlandish, exotic.
Extranjía [ex-tran-hee'-ah], *f.* or **Extranjis.** 1. (Coll.) *V* EXTRANJERÍA. *De extranjía* or *de extranjis,* Foreign. 2. (Fig.) A strange or unexpected thing.

Extrañamente [ex-trah-nyah-men'-tay], *adv.* Wonderfully, extraordinarily, oddly.

Extrañamiento [ex-trah-nyah-me-en'-to], *m.* 1. Alienation, rejection, aversion. 2. Expulsion.

Extrañar [ex-trah-nyar'], *va.* 1. To alienate, to banish from one's sight and intercourse. 2. To admire, to wonder. 3. To censure, to chide, to reprimand. *No hay que extrañar*, No wonder.—*vr.* To refuse, to decline; to break off any engagement.

Extrañeza [ex-trah-nyay'-thah], *f.* 1. Alienation or change of affection, aversion. 2. Singularity, irregularity. 3. Admiration, surprise.

Extraño, ña [ex-trah'-nyo, nyah], *a.* 1. Foreign, extraneous. 2. Rare, monstrous, singular, marvelous. 3. Extravagant, irregular, wild. 4. Unwelcome, not well received. *Es muy extraño*, It is very odd.

Extraoficial [ex-trah-o-fe-the-ahl'], *a.* Unofficial.

Extraordinariamente, *adv.* Extraordinarily, uncommonly, remarkably.

Extraordinario [ex-trah-or-de-nah'-re-o, ah], *a.* Extraordinary, uncommon, rare, odd.

Extraordinario [ex-trah-or-de-nah'-re-o], *m.* The dish or dishes which are used only on a particular day or occasion. *Extraordinario* or *correo extraordinario*, An extraordinary courier.

Extrapolar [ex-trah-po-lar'], *va.* & *vn.* (Math.) Extrapolate.

Extrasecular [ex-trah-say-coo-lar'], *a.* 1. Who has lived beyond a century. 2. Of another century, of remote times, antique.

Extrasensorio, ria [ex-tra-sen-so'-re-o, ah], *a.* Extrasensory. *Percepción extrasensoria*, Extrasensory perception.

Extratémpora [ex-trah-tem'-po-rah], *f.* Dispensation for receiving orders out of the time specified by the church.

Extraterritorial [ex-trah-ter-re-to-re-ahl'], *a.* Extraterritorial, outside territorial limits of a jurisdiction.

Extravagancia [ex-trah-vah-gahn'-the-ah], *f.* 1. Extravagance, irregularity, oddness, folly, freak. 2. Extravagance, waste, vain and superfluous expense.

Extravagante [ex-trah-vah-gahn'-tay], *a.* 1. Extravagant, irregular, wild, humorous, frantic, freakish. 2. (Coll.) Odd, out of the way.

Extravagante [ex-trah-vah-gahn'-tay], *f.* Extravagant, a papal constitution not included in the body of the canon law: almost always used in the plural.

Extravagantemente, *adv.* Extravagantly.

Extravasación [ex-trah-vah-sah-the-on'], *f.* (Med.) Extravasation.

Extravasarse [ex-trah-vah-sar'-say], *vr.* To extravasate, to exude.

Extravenado, da [ex-trah-vay-nah'-do, dah], *a.* Extravenate, forced out of the veins.—*pp.* of Extravenarse.

Extravenarse [ex-trah-vay-nar'-say], *vr.* To let out of the veins.

Extraviar [ex-trah-ve-ar'], *va.* To mislead, to lead out of the way; to embezzle, to secrete. *Extraviados*, (Mil.) Men missing.—*vr.* 1. To lose one's way, to deviate from the right or common way. 2. To deviate from rectitude, to err.

Extravío [ex-trah-vee'-o], *m.* 1. Misplacement, loss. 2. Deviation. 3. Irregularity, disorder, misguidance. 4. Frenzy.

Extremadamente, *adv.* Extremely, in the utmost degree, greatly, hugely.

Extremadas [ex-tray-mah'-das], *f. pl.* The time of making cheese.

Extremado, da [ex-tray-mah'-do, dah], *a.* 1. Extreme, absolute, consummate in good or bad. 2. Facetious, cheerful, gay.—*pp.* of Extremar.

Extremamente [ex-tray-mah-men'-tay], *adv.* Extremely, exceedingly, mightily.

Extremar [ex-tray-mar'], *va.* 1. To reduce to an extreme: generally used in a bad sense. 2. To finish, to complete, to give the finishing stroke. 3. (Obs.) To separate.—*vr.* 1. To be punctual or exact in the performance of any thing. 2. To persist obstinately in an undertaking.—*vn.* To winter in Extremadura: applied to sheep.

Extremaunción [ex-tray-mah-oon-the-on'], *f.* Unction or extreme unction.

Extremeño, ña [ex-tray-may'-nyo, nyah], *a.* Native of or belonging to Extremadura.

Extremidad [ex-tray-me-dahd'], *f.* 1. The end or extremity of any thing. 2. The edge, brink, border, or brim of any thing.

Extremismo [ex-tray-mees'-mo], *m.* Extremism.

Extremista [ex-tray-mees'-tah], *a.*, *m.* & *f.* Extremist.

Extremo, ma [ex-tray'-mo, mah], *a.* 1. Extreme, last, that beyond which there is nothing. 2. Extreme, greatest, of the highest degree. 3. Extreme, excessive, utmost. *Con extremo, en extremo, por extremo*, Extremely, in the utmost degree.

Extremo [ex-tray'-mo], *m.* 1. Extreme, utmost point, highest degree. 2. Extreme, the point at the greatest distance from the centre, extremity. 3. (Met.) Extreme care or application. *Hacer extremos*, To caress, to fondle; to manifest grief and displeasure. 4. The winter or summer of migrating flocks.

Extremoso, sa [ex-tray-mo'-so, sah], *a.* Extreme, impassioned, unbridled.

Extrínseco, ca [ex-treen'-say-co, cah], *a.* Extrinsic, outward, external, extern.

Extumescencia [ex-too-mes-then'-the ah], *f.* (Med.) Swelling, tumefaction.

Exuberancia [ek-soo-bay-rahn'-the-ah], *f.* Exuberance, utmost plenty, abundance.

Exuberante [ek-soo-bay-rahn'-tay], *a.* Exuberant, overabundant.

Exuberar [ek-soo-bay-rar'], *vn.* To be exuberant, to exuberate.

Exúbero, ra [ek-soo'-bay-ro, rah], *a.* (Obs.) A weaned (child).

Exudación [ek-soo-dah-the-on'], *f.* Sweating, a critical sweat.

Exudar [ek-soo-dar'], *vn.* To exude, to ooze like sweat.

Exulceración [ek-sool-thay-rah-the-on'], *f.* Exulceration, ulceration.

Exulcerar [ek-sool-thay-rar'], *va.* To exulcerate, to ulcerate, to disease with sores.

Exultación [ek-sool-tah-the-on'], *f.* Exultation, demonstration of joy.

Exutorio [ek-soo-toh'-re-o], *m.* (Med.) Issue, an ulcer artificially made and maintained for a curative purpose.

Exvoto [ex-vo'-to], *m.* (Lat.) Offering to God in consequence of a vow, consisting of relics, pictures, images, etc., hung up in churches.

Eyaculación [ay-yah-coo-lah-the-on'], *f.* (Neol.) 1. (Med.) Ejaculation, the rapid emission of certain secretions. 2. (Zool.) Rapid expulsion of water from the gills of certain fishes (for the purpose of escape). 3. Rapidity with which the chameleon darts its tongue upon the insects which cling to it.

Eyaculador, ra [ay-yah-coo-lah-dor', rah], *a.* Ejaculatory, serving for ejaculation.

Eyacular [ay-yah-coo-lar'], *va.* To ejaculate, to expel fluid secretions.

Eyector [ay-yec-tor'], *m.* Ejector (of a steam-engine).

Ézula [ay'-thoo-lah], *f.* (Bot.) Spurge. *V.* Esula.

F

F [ay'-fay]. Seventh letter of the Spanish alphabet, and fifth of the consonants. Its name is efe. This letter is pronounced in the Spanish, as in the English language; it was formerly used instead of *h*, as *fablar* for *hablar*; and *f* and *h* are still used promiscuously in some words, as *fanega* or *hanega*. In law works, *ff* signifies digest or pandect of the civil law. F stood for 40 in the middle ages, and with a dash above, 40,000. As a Latin abbreviation it had different significations: as, filius, frater, fecit; and before a proper name, Flavius, Flaccus, Fabius. In Spanish it means *Fulano*. In music, *f* stands for *fuerte*, loud. In works of art, *fecit* or *faciebat*.

Fa [fah], *m.* (Mus.) Fourth note in the gamut. In Arabic reckoning it equals 80.

Faba [fah'-bah], *f.* (Prov.) *V.* Haba.

Fabacrasa [fah-bah-crah'-sah], *f.* (Bot.) Common orpine, stone-crop. Sedum telephium.

Fabaraz [fah-bah-rath'], *m.* (Bot. Littl. us.) Lousewort, stavesacre. Delphinium staphisagria.

Fabear [fah-bay-ar'], *va.* (Obs. Prov.) To vote with black and white beans.

Faber [fah-bayr'], *m.* A fish, the gilt-head.

Fábrica [fah'-bre-cah], *f.* 1. Factory, works. 2. Fabrication, manufacture. *Marca de fábrica*, Trade mark. *Trabajo de fábrica*, Factory work.

Fabricación [fah-bre-cah-the-on'], *f.* Manufacture, construction. *Fabricación en serie* or *en gran escala*, Mass production.

Fabricador, ra [fah-bre-cah-dor', rah], *m.* & *f.* 1. *V.* Fabricante. 2. Inventor, contriver, deviser, coiner, framer. 3. (Naut.) Constructor.

Fabricante [fah-bre-cahn'-tay], *m.* 1. Builder, architect, fabricator. 2. Maker, manufacturer, master-workman, artificer. 3. Operative, artisan.

Fabricar [fah-bre-car'], *va.* 1. To build, to construct, to frame, to fabricate. 2. To manufacture. 3. To fabricate, to contrive, to devise. *Fabricar a piedra perdida*, To build upon a false foundation. *Fabricar a juntas encontradas*, (Arch.) To construct by coordinate interpolation of bricks and hewed stones.

Fabril [fah-breel'], *a.* 1. Belonging to manufacturers, artisans, or workmen. 2. Fabrile, belonging to the craft of a smith, mason, or carpenter.

Fabriquero [fah-bre-kay'-ro], *m.* 1. Manufacturer, artisan, artificer. 2. Person charged with the care of cathedrals and church buildings.

Fabuco [fah-boo'-co], *m.* Beech-mast, the fruit of the beech-tree.

Fabueno [fah-boo-ay'-no], *m.* Westerly wind.

Fábula [fah'-boo-lah], *f.* 1. Fable, a feigned story, to enforce some moral precept. 2. Rumour, report, common talk. 3. Fable, a fiction, a lie, a falsehood. 4. Fable, the series of events which constitute a poem: a legend. 5. Mockery, derision. *Está hecho la fábula del mundo*, He is become the laughing-stock of the whole world. 6. *V.* Mitología.

Fabulación [fah-boo-lah-the-on'], *f.* (Obs.) Conversation.

Fabulador [fah-boo-lah-dor'], *m.* Fabulist, author of fables, dealer in fictions.

Fabular [fah-boo-lar'], *va.* To invent fables, or deal in fictions.

Fabulilla, ita [fah-boo-leel'-lyah, ee'-tah], *f. dim.* A little fable.

Fabulista [fah-boo-lees'-tah], *m.* Fabulist, a writer of fables.

Fabulosamente [fah-boo-lo-sah-men'-tay], *adv.* Fabulously.

Fabuloso, sa [fah-boo-lo'-so, sah], *a.* Fabulous, feigned, fictitious, legendary, romantic.

Faca [fah'-cah], *f.* A curved knife much used by sailors.

Facción [fac-the-on'], *f.* 1. Military exploit, engagement, action. 2. Faction, a turbulent party in a state. 3. Party, faction. 4. Feature, countenance, favour: in this last sense it is generally used in the plural. 5. An act of military service, as guard, patrol, etc. *Facción de testamento*, Faculty of testating. *Facciones*, Features; the lineaments, cast or form of the face.

Faccionar [fac-the-o-nar'], *va.* (Obs.) To fashion, to form.

Faccionario, ria [fac-the-o-nah'-re-o, ah], *a.* Belonging to a party or faction.—*m.&f.* Factionary, a party man.

Faccioso, sa [fac-the-o'-so, sah], *a.* Factious, turbulent, unruly, mutinous: it is used as a substantive. *Los facciosos*, The rebels.

Facecia [fah-thay'-the-ah], *f.* (Obs.) Facetiousness, gaiety, mirth, comicalness.

Facecioso, sa [fah-thay-the-o'-so, sah], *a.* (Obs.) Facetious, cheerful, witty.

Facedor, ra, *m.* & *f.* (Obs.) *V.* Hacedor and Factor.

Facer [fah-therr'], *va.* (Obs.) *V.* Hacer.

Faceta [fah-thay'-tah], *f.* Facet, face or side of a precious stone cut into a number of angles.

Faceto, ta [fah-thay'-to, tah], *a.* Merry, witty, gay, lively.

Facial [fah-the-ahl'], *a.* Facial, belonging to the face. *Angulo facial*, The facial angle.

Facie [fah'-the-ay], *f.* (Min.) A face of a crystal.

Facie ecclesiæ (In) [fah'-the-ay ec-clay'-se-ay]. A Latin phrase, used to express that one is legally married.

Facies [fah'-the-es], *m.* (Med.) Facies, physiognomy in disease.

Fácil [fah'-theel], *a.* 1. Facile, easy, light, performable with little trouble. 2. Pliant, flexible, compliant, familiar, easily persuaded. 3. Easy of access: applied to lewd women. 4. Frail, weak of resolution.

Facilidad [fah-the-le-dahd'], *f.* 1. Facility, easiness to be performed; freedom from difficulty. 2. Facility, easiness to be persuaded, vicious ductility, ready compliance.

Facilillo, illa, ito, ita [fah-the-leel'-lyo, eel'-yah, ee'-to, ee'-tah], *a. dim.* Rather easy. *Facilillo es eso*, (Iron.) That is easy enough: meaning that it is extremely difficult.

Facilitación [fah-the-le-tah-the-on'], *f.* (Obs.) Facility, expedition, facilitation.

Facilitar [fah-the-le-tar'], *va.* 1. To facilitate, to make easy, to free from difficulties, to expedite. 2. To supply, to deliver.

Fácilmente [fah'-theel-men-tay], *adv.* Easily, lightly, without difficulty, facilely.

Facilitón, na [fah-the-le-tone', nah], *a.* One who assumes to make everything easy.

Facineroso [fah-the-nay-ro'-so], *a.* Wicked, atrocious, flagitious: it is also used as a substantive, speaking of highwaymen.

Facistol [fah-this-tole'], *m.* 1. Chorister's desk or stand on which choir-books are placed. 2. (Obs.) Bishop's seat.

Facistor, ra [fah-this-tor', rah], *a.* (Cuban). *V.* Fachenda.

Faco [fah'-co], *m.* (Coll.) 1. Pony, a little nag. 2. Francis (nickname).

Facsímile [fac-see'-me-lay], *m.* Facsimile.

Factible [fac-tee'-blay], *a.* Feasible, practicable.

Facticio, cia [fac-tee'-the-o, ah], *a.* Factitious, made by art.

Factor [fac-tor'], *m.* 1. Factor, an agent for another. 2. Factor (in arithmetic). 3. Factor, constituting element. *Factor Rh*, (Med.) Rh factor.

Factoraje [fac-to-rah'-hay], *m.* Factorage, commission for agency in purchasing goods.

Factoría [fac-to-ree'-ah], *f.* 1. Factory, foreign traders in a distant country; also the district where they reside; trading-houses. 2. Factorage, the commission of a factor, agency.

Factorizar [fac-to-re-thar'], *va.* To establish commerce by factors.

Factótum [fac-to'-toom], *m.* 1. Factotum, a man of all work. 2. One who officiously intermeddles in everything.

Factura [fac-too'-rah], *f.* 1. Invoice of merchandise. 2. Among organ-builders, the quality, length, breadth, and thickness of the pipes. 3. (Obs.) Facture, the act and manner of doing any thing.

Facturar [fac-too-rar'], *va.* 1. To note on merchandise the amount of the prime cost. 2. To check baggage.

Fácula [fah'-coo-lah], *f.* (Ast.) Bright spot on the sun's disk.

Facultad [fah-cool-tahd'], *f.* 1. Faculty, power of doing any thing. 2. Faculty, privilege, authority, right to do any thing. 3. Science, art. 4. Faculty, in a university, denotes the body of the professors teaching a science. 5. (Med.) Faculty, the power of performing an action, natural, vital, or animal. 6. License, permission.—*pl.* *Facultades*, Fortune, wealth, means of living. *Facultades del alma*, Powers of the mind. *Facultad mayor*, In universities, divinity, civil and canonical law, or medicine.

Facultado, da [fah-cool-tah'-do, dah], *a.* Authorized, empowered.

Facultador, ra [fah-cool-tah-dor', rah], *m.* & *f.* One who commissions or empowers.

Facultar [fah-cool-tar'], *va.* (Law) To empower, to authorize, to commission.

Facultativamente [fah-cool-tah-te-vah-men'-tay], *adv.* According to the principles, rules, or axioms of a science or art.

Facultativo, va [fah-cool-tah-tee'-vo, vah], *a.* 1. Belonging to some faculty, art, or science. 2. Granting power, faculty, leave, or permission. 3. That which may be done or omitted at pleasure.

Facultativo [fah-cool-tah-tee'-vo], *m.* 1. Master of a science or art. 2 A person skilful, intelligent, or conversant with an art, trade, or business; connoisseur: it is generally used speaking of medical men.

Facundia [fah-coon'-de-ah], *f.* Eloquence, the power of speaking with fluency and elegance.

Facundo, da [fah-coon'-do, dah], *a.* Eloquent, fluent.

Facha [fah'-chah], *f.* (Coll.) Appearance, aspect, look, mien, face. *Facha a facha*, *adv.*, Face to face. *En facha*, (Naut.) Backed. *Vela en facha*, Sail backed, or laid aback. *Ponerse en facha*, (Naut.) To take the sails aback; to bring to. *Ser un facha* or *una facha*, To be ridiculous.

Fachada [fah-chah'-dah], *f.* 1. Façade, face, front, or fore part of a building. 2. (Coll.) *V.* Presencia for figure. 3. (Met.) Broad or plump face. 4. Frontispiece of a book. *Fachada de proa*, (Naut.) Fore front of a ship.

Fachenda [fah-chen'-dah], *a.* (Coll.) Vain, ostentatious: applied to persons who affect great business.—*f.* Vanity, boasting.

Fachendear [fah-chen-day-ar'], *va.* To affect having much important business; to make an ostentatious parade of business.

Fachendista [fah-chen-dees'-tah], *a.* & *m.* & *f.* (Coll.) A vain and ostentatious person, a busy-body.

Fachendón, na [fah-chen-done', nah], *a. aug.* Very vain and ostentatious.

Fachín [fah-cheen'], *m.* (Prov.) Porter carrier.

Fachinal [fah-che-nahl'], *m.* (Prov. Amer.) A salt marsh, tule, place liable to be overflowed.

Fada [fah'-dah], *f.* 1. A small apple of the pippin kind. 2. Witch.

Fadiga [fah-dee'-gah], *f.* (Prov.) Leave granted to sell a fief or feudal estate.

Faena [fah-ay'-nah], *f.* 1. Work, labour, fatigue. 2. (Naut.) Duty on board of ships.

Faetón [fah-ay-tone'], *m.* 1. Phaeton, a kind of open carriage. 2. An omnibus, with seats along the sides.

Fagina [fah-hee'-nah], *f.* 1. Fascine, a small bundle of branches bound up. 2. Fagot, a bundle of sticks or brushwood for fuel. 3. Stock or rick of corn piled up in sheaves. 4. Fatigue, work, labour. *Meter fagina*, To talk much at random. 5. (Mil.) A war-call.

Faginada [fah-he-nah'-dah], *f.* Collection of fascines or fagots.

Fagocitos [fah-go-thee'-tos], *m. pl.* (Biol.) Phagocytes, a type of white corpuscle.

Fagot [fah-gote'], *m.* Bassoon. (It. Fagotto.)

Fagotista [fah-go-tees'-tah], *m.* Bassoon-player.

Faisán, na [fah-e-sahn', nah], *m.* & *f.* Pheasant, a bird.

Faja [fah'-hah], *f.* 1. Band, bandage, roller, fillet; a swathing-band. 2. Border, a line which divides any superficies. 3. (Arch.) Fascia, belt, fillet. 4. A belt, sash, girdle. 5. (Mil.) Scarf, the principal insignia of a general. 6. (Naut.) A reef-band.

Fajadura [fah-hah-doo'-rah], *f.* (Naut.) Patched clothes rolled round a rope to preserve it.

Fajamiento [fah-hah-me-en'-to], *m.* Act of rolling or swathing.

Fajar [fah-har'], *va.* 1. To swathe, to bind a child with bands and rollers; to fillet. 2. To fall on, to attack.

Fajardo [fah-har'-do], *m.* A kind of minced pie.

Fajeado, da [fah-hay-ah'-do, dah], *a.* That which has girdles, bands, or rollers.

Fajero [fah-hay'-ro], *m.* A knitted swaddling-band for children.

Fajín [fah-heen'], *m.* A general's sash of red silk. Other functionaries use a sash of different colours.

Fajo [fah'-ho], *m.* Bundle. *V.* HAZ.—*pl.* Swaddling-clothes.

Fajón [fah-hone'], *m. aug.* A large band or roller.

Fajuela [fah-hoo-ay'-lah], *f. dim.* A small bandage or roller.

Fakir [fah-keer'], *m.* Fakir, a mendicant monk of Hindustan known among Persians and Turks as dervishes.

Falacia [fah-lah'-the-ah], *f.* Fallacy, fraud, sophism, deceitful argument, hollowness, fallaciousness.

Falange [fah-lahn'-hay], *f.* 1. Phalanx, a closely embodied troop. 2. Phalanx, *pl.* phalanges, small bones of the fingers and toes.

Falangia, *f.* **Falangio**, *m.* [fah-lahn'-he-ah, fah-lahn'-he-o]. A venomous spider with a red head and a black body.

Falangista [fah-lan-hees'-tah], *m. & f.* Falangist.

Fálaris [fah'-la-ris], *f.* (Orn. Acad.) *V.* FOJA.

Falaz [fah-lath'], *a.* Deceitful, fraudulent; frustrative, fallacious, disappointing.

Falazmente [fah-lath-men'-tay], *adv.* (Littl. us.) Fallaciously.

Falbalá [fal-bah-lah'], *m.* 1. Flounce, furbelow, an ornament sewed to a garment and hanging loose. *V.* FARFALÁ. 2. Skirt of a gown or coat plaited.

Falca [fahl'-cah], *f.* 1. (Naut.) A waist-board, or wash-board. 2. (Prov.) A small wedge of wood used by carpenters.

Falcada [fal-cah'-dah], *f.* Falcade, a curvet made by horses.

Falcado, da [fal-cah'-do, dah], *a. & pp.* of FALCAR. Hooked, curvated, falcated. A scythed chariot.

Falcar [fal-car'], *va.* (Obs.) 1. To reap, to cut down corn with a sickle or reaping-hook. 2. To cut with a hook or scythe.

Falcario [fal-cah'-re-o], *m.* Roman soldier armed with a falchion.

Falce [fahl'-thay], *f.* 1. Sickle, reaping-hook, scythe, bill-hook. 2. Falchion, a short crooked sword.

Falcidia [fal-thee'-de-ah], *f.* 1. Fourth part of an inheritance. 2. The Roman law which established such division.

Falciforme [fal-the-for'-may], *a.* Falciform, sickle-shaped.

Falcinelo [fal-the-nay'-lo], *m.* (Orn.) Gray ibis, sickle-bill. Tantalus falcinellus.

Falcón [fal-cone'], *m.* 1. Ancient piece of artillery. 2. (Obs.) *V.* HALCÓN.

Falconete [fal-co-nay'-tay], *m.* Falconet, a small piece of ordnance.

Falda [fahl'-dah], *f.* 1. Skirt, the loose edge of a garment; that part which hangs loose below the waist; train; flap. 2. The lap. 3. Brow of a hill, that part of an eminence which slopes into the plain. 4. Loin of beef, mutton, etc. 5. The brim of a brazier where the hinge is fixed. *Cortar faldas,* To backbite. *Perrillo de falda* or *perrillo faldero,* Lap-dog. *Cortar la falda,* To give a kind of ignominious punishment to abandoned women. *Faldas,* Petticoats.

Faldamento [fal-dah-men'-to], *m.* Fold, flap, skirt. *V.* FALDA.

Faldar [fal-dar'], *m.* Tassel, armour for the thighs.

Faldellín [fal-del-lyeen'], *m.* 1. A skirt or under-petticoat used by women. 2. *V.* REFAJO.

Falderillo, illa [fal-day-reel'-lyo, lyah], *a. dim.* 1. Small lap. 2. Little lap-dog.

Faldero, ra [fal-day'-ro, rah], *a.* 1. Belonging to the lap. *Perrillo faldero,* Lap-dog. 2. Fond of being constantly among women, and busy with women's affairs.

Faldeta [fal-day'-tah], *f. dim.* Small skirt.

Faldetes [fal-day'-tes], *f. pl.* 1. Tassels. 2. Fringes, trimmings.

Faldicorto, ta [fal-de-cor'-to, tah], *a.* Having short skirts.

Faldilla [fal-deel'-lyah], *f. dim.* *V.* FALDETA.—*pl.* Small skirts of a jacket.

Faldistorio [fal-dis-to'-re-o], *m.* Stool on which bishops sit during the performance of church functions.

Faldón [fal-done'], *m.* 1. A long flowing skirt, flap. 2. The flap of a saddle. 3. A mill-stone of a horse-mill put upon another to increase the weight. 4. (Arch.) A sloping side, gable; also the cap-piece and walls of the entrance of chimneys.

Faldriquera [fal-dre-kay'-rah], *f.* Pocket. *V.* FALTRIQUERA.

Falena [fah-lay'-nah], *f.* (Zool.) Moth, a nocturnal lepidopterous insect; a noctuid moth; also a tent-caterpillar.

Falencia [fah-len'-the-ah], *f.* Want of security, uncertainty, mistake.

Faleris [fah-lay'-ris], *m.* Coot, a bird of the family of the penguins. It inhabits Behring Strait and adjacent waters.

Falibilidad [fah-le-be-le-dahd'], *f.* Fallibility.

Falible [fah-lee'-blay], *a.* Fallible.

Faliblemente [fah-le-blay-men'-tay], *adv.* (Littl. us.) Fallibly.

Falidamente [fah-le-dah-men'-tay], *adv.* (Obs.) Vainly, without foundation.

Falimiento [fah-le-me-en'-to], *m.* Deception, deceit, falsehood.

Falo [fah'-lo], *m.* 1. Phallus, the generative organ, the penis (or clitoris). 2. Phallus, a genus of fungi.

Falordía [fah-lor-dee'-ah], *f.* (Prov.) Deception, imposition, deceit, fable.

Falsa or **falsa escuadra** [fal'-sah, es-coo-ah'-drah], *f.* Bevel rule, bevel square.

Falsamarra [fal-sah-mar'-rah], *f.* (Naut.) Preventer-rope, employed to support another which suffers an unusual strain.

Falsamente [fal-sah-men'-tay], *adv.* Falsely, deceitfully, lyingly, fallaciously, counterfeitly, untruly.

Falsario, ria [fal-sah'-re-o, ah], *a.* 1. Falsifying, forging, counterfeiting. 2. Accustomed to tell falsehoods.—*m. & f.* Falsary. *V.* FALSEADOR.

Falsarregla [fal-sah-rray'-glah], *f.* Bevel rule, bevel square.

Falseable [fal-say-ah'-blay], *a.* Falsifiable, capable of being counterfeited.

Falseador [fal-say-ah-dor'], *m.* Forger, counterfeiter, falsifier.

Falsear [fal-say-ar'], *va.* 1. To falsify, to adulterate, to counterfeit. 2. To pierce, to penetrate. *Falsear el cuerpo,* To draw back the body to avoid a blow. *Falsear la llave,* To counterfeit a key. *Falsear las guardas* or *centinelas,* To bribe the guards or sentries. —*vn.* 1. To slacken, to lose strength and firmness. 2. Not to agree in sound: applied to musical instruments. 3. To leave a hollow in saddles to make them easy.

Falsedad [fal-say-dahd'], *f.* 1. Falsehood, falsity, untruth, mendacity, fiction, fable, fib. 2. Deceit, malicious dissimulation.

Falsete [fal-say'-tay], *m.* 1. Falsetto voice, the register of head tones. 2. (Prov.) Spigot. *Venir de falsete,* To act in a treacherous manner.

Falsía [fal-see'-ah], *f.* *V.* FALSEDAD.

Falsificación [fal-se-fe-cah-the-on'], *f.* Falsification, falsifying or counterfeiting, forgery, counterfeit.

Falsificador, ra [fal-se-fe-cah-dor', rah], *m. & f.* Falsifier, counterfeiter, forger.

Falsificar [fal-se-fe-car'], *va.* To falsify, to counterfeit, to forge, to foist.

Falsilla [fal-seel'-lyah], *f.* Ruled pattern to guide in writing.

Falsío [fal-see'-o], *m.* (Prov.) Kind of sausage.

Falso, sa [fahl'-so, sah], *a.* 1. False, untrue, uncertain, not real. 2. False, false-hearted, hypocritical, deceitful, treacherous, perfidious, traitorous. 3. False, counterfeit, supposititious, supposed. 4. Feint; mock. *Piedras falsas,* Mock jewellery. 5. Vicious: applied to horses or mules. 6. Producing no fruit: applied to blossoms. 7. Defective, false: applied to weights or honey-combs. *De falso,* Falsely, deceitfully. *En falso,* Without due security. *Falsa acacia,* (Bot.) Common locust; acacia. Robinia pseudo-acacia, *L.* *Falso pimiento,* (Bot.) Peruvian schinus. Schinus molle, *L.* *Falso díctamo, V.* DÍCTAMO BASTARDO. Marrubium pseudictamnus, *L.* *Falso ébano,* Common laburnum cytissus. Cytissus laburnum, *L.* *No levantarás falso testimonio,* Thou shalt not bear false witness against thy neighbour. *Cerrar en falso la puerta,* To miss shutting the door close, or to leave the door purposely unlocked.

Falta [fahl'-tah], *f.* 1. Fault, defect, want, absence, lack. 2. Fault, offence, slight crime, defect, faultiness, failing, misdoing, failure, flaw. 3. Want or stoppage of the catamenia in pregnant women. *Tiene cuatro faltas,* She is in the fifth month of her pregnancy. 4. Deficiency in the weight of coin. 5. Default, non-appearance in court at a day assigned. *Sin falta,* Without fail. *A falta de,* In want or for want of. *Hacer falta,* To be absolutely necessary to any thing; not to be punctual to the fixed time; to be in want of a thing, to disappoint. (Com.) *Falta de aceptación, de pago,* For non-acceptance, for non-payment. *Acusar de falta,* To find fault with.

Faltar [fal-tar'], *vn.* 1. To be deficient, to be wanting. 2. To fail, to falter, to fault, to flinch. 3. To be consumed, to fall short. 4. Not to fulfil one's promise, not to perform one's engagement. 5. To need, to lack, to be in want of. 6. To die. *Faltar a su palabra,* To fall back. *Faltar un cable,* etc., (Naut.) To give way, to break, to split.

Faltilla [fal-teel'-lyah], *f. dim.* A slight fault or defect.

Falto, ta [fahl'-to, tah], *a.* 1. Wanting, deficient, defective, jejune. 2. Miserable, wretched. 3. Mad, insane.

Faltrero, ra [fal-tray'-ro, rah]. Pick-pocket, petty thief.

Faltriquera [fal-tre-kay'-rah], *f.* Pocket, as in clothes.

Falúa, Faluca [fah-loo'-ah, fah-loo'-cah], *f.* (Naut.) Felucca, a small open boat, or a long-boat with oars.

Falucho [fah-loo'-cho], *m.* A small boat with oars, and one lateen sail.

Falla [fahl'-lyah], *f.* 1. (Naut.) Defect, deficiency; lack of wood for the finishing of a certain figure. *V.* Falta. 2. A sort of light loose cover, worn by women over their head-dress at night. 3. (Geol.) Fault, dislocation of a seam or layer.

Fallar [fal-lyar'], *va.* 1. (Law) To give sentence, to judge. 2. To ruff, to trump, to win a trick with trumps.—*v. impers.* To be deficient or wanting.

Falleba [fal-lyay'-bah], *f.* An iron bar for fastening doors and windows.

Fallecedor, ra [fal-lyay-thay-dor', rah], *a.* Perishable.

Fallecer [fal-lyay-therr'], *vn.* To die.

Fallecimiento [fal-lyay-the-me-en'-to], *m.* Decease, death.

(*Yo fallezco, yo fallezca,* from *Fallecer. V.* Aborrecer.)

Fallido, da [fal-lyee'-do, dah], *a.* 1. Deceived, disappointed, frustrated. 2. Bankrupt.

Fallo [fahl'-lyo], *m.* 1. Judgment, decision of a judge in a lawsuit or trial. 2. In some games of cards not to have a card of the suit played. *Echar el fallo,* 1. To pass sentence or judgment on a person. 2. To declare a patient past hope: applied to medical men.

Fama [fah'-mah], *f.* 1. Fame, report, rumour. 2. Fame, reputation, repute, name; glory. *Quien la fama ha perdido, muerto está, aunque vivo,* (Prov.) He who has lost his reputation is as good as dead, though living.

Fame [fah'-may], *f.* (Prov.) Hunger. *V.* Hambre.

Famélico, ca [fah-may'-le-co, cah], *a.* Hungry. *V.* Hambriento.

Familia [fah-mee'-le-ah], *f.* 1. Family, the people who live in the same house together. 2. Family, those that descend from one common progenitor; a race, a generation, a house, a clan; kin. 3. Religious order. 4. Number of servants or retainers.

Familiar [fah-me-le-ar'], *a.* 1. Familiar, domestic, belonging to the family. 2. Familiar, common, frequent. 3. Familiar, well known, well acquainted with. 4. Agreeable, conformable, useful, observant, conversant. *Estilo familiar,* Colloquial, familiar style; an easy, unconstrained style.

Familiar, *m.* 1. Domestic, one belonging to a family, one kept in the same house. 2. Servant, especially of the clergy. 3. College-servant, who waits upon all the collegians collectively. 4. Demon, a familiar spirit. 5. Familiar or intimate friend, one long acquainted. 6. One of the officers of the Inquisition.—*m. pl. Familiares,* Attendants, suite.

Familiarcito [fah-me-le-ar-thee'-to], *m.* 1. (Dim.) Servant-boy, a little servant. 2. One who affects great familiarity or intimacy.

Familiaridad [fah-me-le-ah-re-dahd'], *f.* 1. Familiarity, easiness of conversation or intercourse. 2. Familiarity, acquaintance, habitude. 3. *V.* Familiatura.

Familiarizar [fah-me-le-ah-re-thar'], *va.* To familiarize, to render familiar, to make easy by habitude.—*vr.* To become familiar, to descend from a state of distant superiority.

Familiarmente [fah-me-le-ar-men'-tay], *adv.* Familiarly.

Familiatura [fah-me-le-ah-too'-rah], *f.* 1. Place and employment of a *familiar* of the Inquisition. 2. Place of one of the college-servants called *familiares.*

Famis [fah'-mis], *f.* A kind of gold cloth or brocade from Smyrna.

Famosamente [fah-mo-sah-men'-tay], *adv.* Famously, excellently.

Famoso, sa [fah-mo'-so, sah], *a.* 1. Famous, celebrated, renowned, conspicuous. 2. Noted: applied to robbers and other offenders. 3. Notorious.

Fámula [fah'-moo-lah], *f.* (Coll.) Maid-servant.

Famulato, Famulicio [fah-moo-lah'-to, fah-moo-lee'-the-o], *m.* Servitude.

Fámulo [fah'-moo-lo], *m.* Servant of a college.

Fanal [fah-nahl'], *m.* 1. (Naut.) Poop-lantern of a commodore's ship. 2. Lantern, a light-house to guide ships. 3. A kind of lantern of crystal in the form of a conoid. 4. (Met.) Guide, friend, adviser in difficulties and dangers.

Fanáticamente [fah-nah'-te-cah-men-tay], *adv.* Fanatically.

Fanático, ca [fah-nah'-te-co, cah], *a.* Fanatic, fanatical, enthusiastic, superstitious.

Fanatismo [fah-nah-tees'-mo], *m.* Fanaticism, mysticism, religious frenzy.

Fanatizar [fah-nah-te-thar'], *va.* To spread or instil fanaticism.

Fandango [fan-dahn'-go], *m.* 1. Fandango, a lively Spanish dance; the music to this dance. 2. Festive entertainment; dance with castanets or balls in the hands.

Fandanguear [fan-dan-gay-ar'], *va.* (Coll.) To revel, carouse.

Fandanguero [fan-dan-gay'-ro], *m.* 1. Fandango-dancer. 2. One fond of festive entertainments.

Faneca [fah-nay'-cah], *f.* (Zool.) Pout whiting pout. Gadus barbatus, *L.*

Fanega [fah-nay'-gah], *f.* 1. A measure of grain and seed of about a hundred-weight, or an English bushel: it has been sometimes called faneague in English. 2. The quantity of seed contained in a *fanega* or Spanish bushel, and the vessel containing it. *Fanega de sembradura,* As much tilled ground as is necessary to sow a Spanish bushel of corn. *Fanega de tierra,* Extent of arable land, generally of four hundred fathoms square, and of pasture land five hundred. *Fanega de cacao,* A measure of one hundred and ten pounds of cocoa.

Fanegada [fah-nay-gah'-dah], *f. V.* Fanega de tierra and Fanega de sembradura. *A fanegadas,* In great plenty or abundance.

Faneranto, ta [fah-nay-rahn'-to, tah], *a.* Flowering, having visible flowers.

Fanerocarpo, pa [fah-nay-ro-car'-po, pah], *a.* (Biol.) Having visible fruits or reproductive corpuscles; phanerocarpous.

Fanerógamo, ma [fah-nay-ro'-gah-mo, mah], *a.* Phanerogamous, flowering.

Fanfarrear [fan-far-ray-ar'], *vn.* To bully, to brag. (Arab.)

Fanfarria [fan-far'-re-ah], *f.* (Coll.) Empty arrogance of a bragger.

Fanfarrón [fan-far-rone'], *m.* Fanfaron, a bully, a hector.

Fanfarrón, na [fan-far-rone', nah], *a.* (Coll.) Boasting, vaunting; inflated. *Trigo fanfarrón,* (Bot.) Fanfaron wheat; a sort of flinty wheat cultivated in Andalusia. Triticum fastnosum, *Lag.*

Fanfarronada [fan-far-ro-nah'-dah], *f.* Fanfaronade, boast, brag, a bravado, rhodomontade.

Fanfarronazo, za [fan-far-ro-nah'-tho, thah], *a.* Applied to a great fanfaron, boasting, vaunting.

Fanfarronear [fan-far-ro-nay-ar'], *vn.* To bully, to brag, to gasconade.

Fanfarronería [fan-far-ro-nay-ree'-ah], *f.* Fanfaronade, braggartism.

Fanfarronesca [fan-far-ro-ness'-cah], *f.* Manner of a fanfaron.

Fanfurriña [fan-foor-ree'-nyah], *f.* Passion or displeasure, arising from a slight motive.

Fangal [fan-gahl'], *m.* Slough, a miry place, a fen, a marsh, a place full of mud or mire.

Fango [fahn'-go], *m.* 1. Mire, mud at the bottom of still water. 2. (Naut.) Oozy bottom of the sea.

Fangoso, sa [fan-go'-so, sah], *a.* Muddy, miry.

Fano [fah'-no], *m.* (Obs.) Fane, temple.

Fanón [fah-none'], *m.* 1. (Med.) A cylindrical splint made of barley-straw, and used in fractures of the thigh. 2. (Vet.) The tuft of hairs back of a horse's head. 3. A fold in the lower part of the neck of the ox and the sheep.

Fantasear [fan-tah-say-ar'], *vn.* To fancy, to imagine.

Fantasía [fan-tah-see'-ah], *f.* 1. Fancy, imagination. 2. Fantasy, the power of imagining. 3. Fancy, caprice, humour, whim, conceit. 4. Fancy, an opinion bred rather by the imagination than the reason. 5. Fancy, fiction, conception, image. 6. Presumption, vanity. 7. *pl.* A string of pearls. 8. (Naut.) *V.* Estima. (Mus.) A kind of composition whose origin dates from the 16th century.

Fantasioso, sa [fan-tah-se-o'-so, sah], *a.* (Coll.) Fantastic.

Fantasma [fan-tahs'-mah], *m.* 1. Phantom, a fancied vision. 2. A vain, presumptuous man. 3. Image of some object which remains impressed on the mind.—*f.* 1. Ghost, specter, apparition, a scarecrow to frighten simple folks. 2. (Med.) Lesion or defect of the visual organs.

Fantasmagoría [fan-tas-mah-go-ree'-ah], *f.* Phantasmagoria, an optical illusion.

Fantasmagórico, ca [fan-tas-mah-go'-re-co, cah], *a.* Phantasmagoric.

Fantasmón [fan-tas-mone'], *m. aug.* A presumptuous coxcomb, a vain pretender.

Fantásticamente [fan-tahs'-te-cah-men-tay], *adv.* Fantastically, fallaciously, pompously, conceitedly, grotesquely.

Fantástico, ca [fan-tahs'-te-co, cah], *a.* 1. Fantastic, whimsical, fanciful. 2. Fantastic, imaginary, fantasied, subsisting only in the fancy. 3. Fantastic, unreal. 4. Fantastic, conceited, vain, presumptuous.

Faquín [fah-keen'], *m.* Porter, carrier.

Faquir [fah-keer'], *m.* Fakir. (Acad.)

Far [far], *va.* (Obs.) *V.* Hacer.

Fara [fah'-rah], *f.* A kind of serpent of Africa.

Farachar [fah-rah-char'], *va.* (Prov.) To beat or clean hemp.

Faralá [fah-rah-lah'], *m.* 1. Flounce. *V.* Farfalá, Vuelo. 2. Rufflet, frill.

Farallón [fah-ral-lyone'], *m.* (Naut.) Small rocky island in the sea.

Faramalla [fah-rah-mahl'-lyah], *f.* Bluff, deceitful chatter.—*m.* & *f.* Bluffer, deceitful person.

Faramallear [fah-rah-mahl-lyay-ar'], *va.* To tattle, to babble.

Faramallero, Faramallón [fah-rah-mal-lyay'-ro, -lyon'], *m.* (Coll.) Tattling, deceitful man, busybody.

Farándula [fah-rahn'-doo-lah], *f.* 1. Profession of a low comedian. 2. Artful trick, stratagem.

Farandulero [fah-ran-doo-lay'-ro], *m.* 1. Actor, player. 2. Idle tattler, deceitful talker.

Farandúlico, ca [fah-ran-doo'-le-co, cah], *a.* Relating to a low comedian.

Faraón [fah-rah-on'], *m.* 1. Faro, game at cards. 2. An ancient dance. 3. Pharaoh, the scriptural name of Egyptian kings.

Faraute [fah-rah'-oo-tay], *m.* 1. Messenger, he who carries messages. 2. (Coll.) Principal manager or director. 3. (Coll.) A noisy, meddling fellow. 4. Player who recites the prologue of a play

Farcinador [far-the-nah-dor'], *m.* (Prov.) One who stuffs or fills any thing.

Farda [fahr'-dah], *f.* 1. A kind of tax or tribute formerly paid by foreigners in Spain. 2. Bundle of clothing. 3. Notch in a timber for joining with another. *Pagar la farda,* To gain something at the cost of great sacrifice, to have one's labour for one's pains. (Arab. farda.)

Fardacho [far-dah'-cho], *m.* (Prov.) *V.* Lagarto.

Fardaje [far-dah'-hay], *m.* Equipage, luggage.

Fardar [far-dar'], *va.* To furnish or supply with clothes.

Fardel [far-del'], *m.* 1. Bag, knapsack. 2. Parcel.

Fardelería [far-day-lay-ree'-ah], *f.* (Littl. us.) A collection of bags or sacks.

Fardelillo, lejo [far-day-leel'-lyo, lay'-ho], *m. dim.* A small bag or sack.

Fardería [far-day-ree'-ah], *f.* A collection of bundles or packages, luggage. *V.* Fardaje.

Fardillo [far-deel'-lyo], *m. dim.* A small bundle, a parcel

Fardo [far'-do], *m.* Bale of goods, parcel, bundle, pack, package.

Farellón [fah-rel-lyone'], *m.* 1. Point, cape, headland. 2. Rock, cliff in the sea.

Farfalá [far-fah-lah'], *f.* Flounce, ornament of a gown or curtain; furbelow. *V.* Vuelo.

Farfallás [far-fal-lyahs'], *f. pl.* (Bot. Prov.) *V.* Barbajas.

Farfalloso, sa [far-fal-lyo'-so, sah], *a.* (Prov.) Stammering

Farfán [far-fahn'], *m.* A name given to Christian horsemen who served Mohammedan princes (fr. Germ.).

Farfante, Farfantón [far-fahn'-tay, far-fan-tone'], *m.* A boasting babbler.

Farfantonada, Farfantonería [far-fan-to-nah'-dah], *f.* Idle boast.

Fárfara [far'-fah-rah], *f.* 1. (Bot.) Colt's-foot. Tussilago farfara, *L.* 2. Membrane which covers the white of an egg. *En fárfara,* 1. Immature: applied to an egg without a shell. 2. (Met.) Unfinished, half done.

Farfulla [far-fool'-lyah], *m.* Mumbler a stammering, talkative person.

Farfulladamente, *adv.* Stammeringly.

Farfullador, ra [far-fool-lyah-dor', rah], *m. & f.* Stammerer, mumbler, jabberer.

Farfullar [far-fool-lyar'], *va.* 1 To talk quick and stammeringly; to talk low and quick. 2. (Met.) To do in a hurry and confusion.

Farfullero, ra [far-fool-lyay'-ro, rah], *a.* 1. Mumbling, talking unintelligibly 2. Hurried and confused in action.

Fargallón, na [far-gal-lyone', nah], *a. & m. & f.* (Coll.) Applied to those who are careless or dirty in their dress, and to those who do things hurriedly.

Farigola [fah-re-go'-lah], *f.* Ancient name of thyme, and which is still used in Catalonia.

Farillón [fah-reel-lyone'], *m.* (Naut.) *V.* Farallón.

Farina [fah-ree'-nah], *f.* (Obs.) *V.* Harina.

Farináceo, cea [fah-re-nah'-thay-o, ah], *a.* Farinaceous, mealy, starchy.

Farinetas [fah-re-nay'-tas], *f. pl.* (Prov.) Fritters made of flour, honey, and water

Faringe [fah-reen'-hay], *f.* (Anat.) Pharynx.

Faringeo, gea [fah-reen'-hay-o, ah], *a.* Pharyngeal, relating to the pharynx.

Faringitis [fah-rin-hee'-tis], *f.* (Med.) Pharingitis.

Farisaico, ca [fah-re-sah -e-co, cah], *a.* Pharisaical, pharisaic.

Farisaismo [fah-re-sah-ees -mo], *m.* Pharisaism.

Fariseo [fah-re-say'-o], *m.* 1 A Pharisee.

Farmacéutico, ca [far-mah-thay'-oo-te-co, cah], *a.* Pharmaceutical.—*m.* Pharmacist.

Farmacia [far-mah'-the-ah], *f.* 1. Pharmacy, the art of preparing medicines. 2. Pharmacy, the shop where they are prepared and sold. 3 A collection of medicaments.

Fármaco [far'-mah-co], *m.* *V.* Medicamento.

Farmacología [far-mah-co-lo-hee'-ah], *f.* Pharmacology, the knowledge of medicines.

Farmacológico, ca [far-mah-co-lo'-he-co, cah], *a.* Pharmacological, relating to drugs.

Farmacólogo [far-mah-co'-lo-go], *m.* Pharmacologist, a writer upon medicines.

Farmacopea [far-mah-co-pay'-ah], *f.* Pharmacopœia.

Farmacópola [far-mah-co'-po-lah], *m.* (Coll.) Apothecary, pharmaceutist, pharmacopolist.

Farmacopólico, ca [far-mah-co-po'-le-co, cah], *a.* (Coll.) Pharmaceutical, pharmaceutic.

Farnero [far-nay'-ro], *m.* (Prov.) Receiver of rents.

Faro [fah'-ro], *m.* Pharos, a light-house; beacon.

Farol [fah-role'], *m.* A lantern. *Faroles de señales,* (Naut.) Signal lanterns.

Farola [fah-ro'-lah], *f.* A lantern of great size.

Farolazo [fah-ro-lah'-tho], *m.* 1 A blow given with a lantern. 2. *pl.* (Met.) A dispute coming to blows, a fisticuff.

Farolear [fah-ro-lay-ar'], *vn.* (Coll.) To strut, to make an ostentatious parade.

Farolero [fah-ro-lay'-ro], *m.* 1. One who makes lanterns. 2. Lamp-lighter. (Coll.) *V.* Farolón.

Farolico [fah-ro-lee'-co], *m. dim.* Small lantern. *Farolico de jardín,* Indian heartseed, smooth-leaved heartseed. Cardiospermum halicacabum, *L.*

Farolillo, ito [fah-ro-leel'-lyo, ee'-to], *m. dim.* Small lantern. *Farolillo de jardín,* (Bot.) *V.* Farolico de jardín.

Farolón [fah-ro-lone'], *m.* 1. (Coll.) A boasting person 2. (Aug.) A large lantern

Farota [fah-ro -tah], *f.* (Prov.) A brazen-faced woman, without sense or judgment.

Farotón [fah-roh-tone'], *m.* (Prov.) A brazen-faced, stupid fellow

Farotona [fah-roh-to'-nah], *f* Tall, slovenly woman

Farpa [far'-pah], *f. pl* Any of the notches, hollows, or segments of circles marked on the edge of a thing.

Farpado, da [far-pah'-do, dah], *a.* Scalloped, notched.

Farra [far'-rah], *f.* (Zool.) A kind of salmon.

Fárrago [far'-rah-go], or **Farrago** [far-rah'-go], *m.* Farrago, a confused mass of ingredients; a medley.

Farraguista [far-rah-gees' tah], *m* A pedantic scholar; one vain of useless learning

Farro [far'-ro], *m.* 1. Peeled barley barley freed from the husk. 2. A sort of husked wheat called spelt wheat. Triticum spelta, *L.* *V.* Escanda

Farropea [far-ro-pay'-ah], *f.* (Prov.) *V* Arropea

Farsa [far'-sah], *f.* 1. Farce, a ludicrous dramatical composition, or representation 2. Company of players.

Farsanta [far-sahn'-tah], *f.* An actress.

Farsante [far-sahn'-tay], *m.* 1. An actor, a player. 2. A pretender, a deceiver.

Farsista [far-sees'-tah], *com.* A writer of farces.

Fartal, Farte [far-tahl , far -tay], *m* (Prov.) Fruit-tart or pie.

Fartriquera, *f.* (Prov.) *V* Faltriquera.

Fas (Por) ó por nefas [por fas oh por nay'-fas], *adv.* Justly or unjustly

Fascal [fas-cahl'], *m.* (Prov.) Shock, a pile of sheaves of corn.

Fascas [fahs'-cas], *adv.* (Prov) *V* Hasta and Casi.

Fasces [fahs'-thes], *f. pl.* Fasces, rods anciently carried before the Roman consuls.

Fasciculado, da [fas-the-coo-lah'-do, dah], *a.* Fasciculate, composed of or growing in bundles.

Fascicular [fas-the-coo-lar'], *a.* (Bot.) Fascicular, disposed in bundles

Fascículo [fas-thee'-coo-lo], *m.* 1. A bundle, armful, the quantity of plants which may be carried under the arm. 2. Number, part, a number of printed sheets stitched together.

Fascinación [fas-the-nah-the-on'], *f.* 1 Fascination, the power or act of bewitching; enchantment. 2. Imposition, deceit.

Fascinador, ra [fas-the-nah-dor , rah], *m. & f.* Fascinator, charmer.

Fascinante [fas-the-nahn'-tay], *pa. & m. & f.* Fascinator, fascinating.

Fascinar [fas-the-nar'], *va.* 1. To fascinate, to bewitch, to enchant. 2. To deceive, to impose upon.

Fascismo [fas-thees'-mo], *m.* Fascism

Fascista [fas-thees'-tah], *a. & m. & f.* Fascist.

Fase [fah'-say], *f.* (Ast.) Phase of the moon or planets.

Fasma [fahs'-mah], *f* (Zool.) Walking-stick, phasmá.

Fásoles [fah'-so-les], *m pl.* Kidney-beans, haricots.

Fastial [fas-te-ahl'], *m.* Pyramid placed on the top of an edifice.

Fastidiar [fas-te-de-ar'], *va.* 1. To excite disgust. 2. To loathe, to look on with dislike or abhorrence. 3. To grate, to offend by any thing harsh or vexatious.—*vr.* 1. To loathe, to feel disgust or abhorrence, to weary, to be weary. 2. To suffer damage or loss.

Fastidio [fas-tee -de-o], *m.* 1. Squeamishness, arising from a weak or disordered stomach, or from a bad smell. 2. Weariness, lassitude, fatigue, ennui. 3. Distaste, disgust, fastidiousness. 4. Noisomeness, aptness to disgust. 5 Loathing.

Fastidiosamente [fas-te-de-o-sah-men tay], *adv* Fastidiously

Fastidioso, sa [fas-te-de-o'-so, sah], *a* 1 Fastidious, squeamish, delicate to a vice. 2. Loathsome, nauseous, mawkish 3. Tedious, livelong. 4. Disdainful, disgusted.

Fastigio [fas-tee'-he-o], *m.* (Arch.) 1. Pinnacle, the top of any thing which ends in a point. 2. The top of trees 3. Summit, meridian.

Fasto [fahs'-to], *m.* 1. Haughtiness, pride. 2. Splendour, pageantry, pomp, grandeur. *Fastos*, Feasts or anniversaries among the Romans.

Fastosamente [fas-to-sah-men'-tay], *adv.* Pompously, gaudily, magnificently.

Fastoso, Fastuoso, sa [fas-to'-so, fas-too-o'-so, sah], *a.* Proud, haughty, ostentatious; gaudy.

Fatal [fah-tahl'], *a.* 1. Fatal, ominous, proceeding by destiny. 2. Fatal, deadly, mortal, destructive. 3. Unfortunate.

Fatalidad [fah-tah-le-dahd'], *f.* 1. Fatality, predetermined order of things and events. 2. Fatality, tendency to danger, mischance, ill luck, ill fortune.

Fatalismo [fah-tah-lees'-mo], *m.* Fatalism.

Fatalista [fah-tah-lees'-tah], *m* Fatalist, predestinarian.

Fatalmente [fah-tal-men'-tay], *adv* Fatally, ominously.

Fate-ha [fah'-tay-ah], *m.* 1. Name given by Mohammed to the first chapter of the Koran. 2. A prayer, like the Lord's Prayer, which Mohammedans use. (Arabic, fataha, to open.)

Fatídico, ca [fah-tee'-de-co, cah], *a.* Fatidical, prophetic of gloom.

Fatiga [fah-tee'-gah], *f.* 1 Toil, hard labour, fatigue, lassitude. 2. Hardship, oppression. 3. Anguish, grief, painfulness, importunity.

Fatigadamente [fah-te-gah-dah-men'-tay], *adv.* Difficultly, with toil.

Fatigador, ra [fah-te-gah-dor', rah], *m.* & *f.* Molester.

Fatigar [fah-te-gar'], *va.* 1 To fatigue, to tire, to molest, to weary, to harass, to gall. 2. To desolate or lay waste by warlike incursion or invasion.—*vr.* To tire or be tired, to fail with weariness. *Fatigar la selva*, (Poet.) To employ one's self in hunting or sporting.

Fatigosamente [fah-te-go-sah-men'-tay], *adv.* Painfully, wearisomely, tediously.

Fatigoso, sa [fah-te-go'-so, sah], *a.* 1 Tiresome, troublesome. 2. Anxious, painful.

Fatimita [fah-te-mee'-tah], *a.* Descended from Fátima, only daughter of Mohammed.

Fatuidad [fah-too-e-dahd'], *f.* 1. Fatuity, foolishness, weakness of mind. 2. A stupid speech, a foolish action.

Fatuo, tua [fah'-too-o, ah], *a.* Fatuous, stupid, foolish, coxcombical, foppish, conceited, crazy.

Fauces [fah'-oo-thes], *f pl.* Fauces, gullet.

Fauna [fah'-oo-nah], *f.* 1. Fauna, the whole of the animals belonging to a region or country. 2. A work in which these are described.

Fausto, ta [fah'-oos-to, tah], *a.* Happy, fortunate, prosperous, successful.

Fausto [fah'-oos-to], *m.* Splendour pomp, pageantry, ostentation, gaudiness, gaiety; grandeur, greatness; luxury.

Faustoso, sa [fah-oos-to'-so, sah], *a.* Fastuous, haughty, proud, ostentatious, gaudy.

Fautor, ra [fah-oo-tor', rah], *m.* & *f* Countenancer, abetter, furtherer, favourer, supporter.

Fautoría [fah-oo-to-ree'-ah], *f.* Aid, favour, auxiliary.

Favara [fa-vah'-rah], *f.* Abundant spring of water. From Arabic fawāra; with the article it appears as **Alfaguara.** (Acad.)

Favila [fah-vee'-lah], *f.* (Poet.) Ashes of an extinguished fire.

Favo [fah'-vo], *m* 1 (Obs.) Honeycomb 2. (Med.) *V* Avispero Favus; carbuncle

Favonio [fah-vo'-ne-o], *m* Westerly wind, zephyr

Favor [fah-vor'], *m* 1 Favour, protection, support, countenance, help. 2. Favour, kindness granted, good turn, gift, grace; comfort. 3. Compliment, an expression of civility and kindness. 4. Favour, love-favour, something given by a lady to be worn. *Favor al rey* or *favor a la justicia*, A phrase used to ask assistance, in the king's name, to seize a criminal. *A favor de*, In behalf of, on account of.

Favorable [fah-vo-rah'-blay], *a.* Favourable, advantageous, propitious, kind, friendly, gracious.

Favorablemente [fah-vo-rah-blay-men'-tay], *adv.* Favourably.

Favorcillo [fah-vor-theel'-lyo], *m. dim.* A small favour.

Favorecedor, ra [fah-vo-ray-thay-dor', rah], *m.* & *f.* Favourer, countenancer, friend, helper, well-wisher.

Favorecer [fah-vo-ray-therr'], *va.* 1. To favour, to protect, to help, to countenance, to accredit, to abet. 2. To grant favours. *Favorecerse de alguno* or *de alguna cosa*, To avail one's self of a person's favour or support, or of any other kind of protection.—*vr.* To help one another.

(*Yo favorezco, yo favorezca*, from *Favorecer*. *V.* Aborrecer.)

Favoritismo [fah-vo-re-tees'-mo], *m.* Favouritism, nepotism.

Favorito, ta [fah-vo-ree'-to, tah], *a.* Favourite, beloved, regarded with favour, darling.

Favorito, ta [fah-vo-ree'-to, tah], *m.* & *f.* 1. Favourite, one chosen as a companion by a superior. 2. Favourite, court minion. 3. Favourite, darling, fondling.

Fayado [fah-yah'-do], *m.* (Prov.) A small garret or lumber-room.

Fayanca [fah-yahn'-cah], *f.* Position of the body, in which it does not stand firm and steady.

Fayanco [fah-yahn'-co], *m.* A flat basket made of osier.

Faz [fath], *f.* 1. Face. *V* Rostro. 2. Front, the fore part of a building or any other thing. *V.* Haz. *Faz a faz*, Face to face. *A prima faz*, At first sight. *En faz y en paz*, Publicly and peacefully.

Fazaña, *f.* (Obs.) *V.* Hazaña.

Fe [fay], *f.* 1. Faith, belief of the revealed truths of religion. 2. Faith, trust in God. 3. Faith, testimony, credit, credence, confidence, trust. 4. Promise given. 5. Assertion, asseveration. 6. Certificate, testimony. *Fe de erratas*, Errata, list of the errors of the press. *Dar fe*, To attest, to certify. *Poseedor de buena fe*, A bona fide possessor, one who thinks himself the right owner, although he is not. *De buena fe*, With truth and sincerity. *A fe*, In truth, in good earnest. *A fe mía* or *por mi fe*, Upon my honour. *A la buena fe*, With candour and sincerity, without malice. *En fe*, Consequently. *De mala fe*, Craftily, deceitfully, cunningly, fallaciously *Fe haciente*, Authentic, true on its own face.

Fealdad [fay-al-dahd'], *f.* 1. Ugliness, deformity; disproportion of the parts which compose a whole. 2. Homeliness; hard-favouredness; hideousness. 3. (Met.) Turpitude, dishonesty, foulness, moral depravity.

Feamente [fay-ah-men'-tay], *adv.* 1. Uglily, deformedly 2. (Met.) Brutally, inordinately

Feazo, za [fay-ah'-tho, thah], *a. aug* Very ugly or deformed.

Febeo, bea [fay-bay'-o, ah], *a.* (Poet.) Relating to Phœbus, or the sun.

Feble [fay'-blay], *a.* 1. Weak, faint, feeble. 2. Among jewellers, mint-men, and silversmiths, deficient in weight or quality: applied to silver, diamonds, or money. From the French; antiquated in Spanish.

Feble [fay'-blay], *m.* Light money or coin.

Feblemente [fay-blay-men'-tay], *adv.* Feebly.

Febo [fay'-bo], *m.* (Poet.) Phœbus, the sun.

Febrero [fay-bray'-ro], *m.* February.

Febricitante [fay-bre-the-tahn'-tay], *a* *V.* Calenturiento.

Febrido, da [fay-bree'-do, dah], *a.* (Obs.) Shining, resplendent. *V.* Bruñido.

Febrífugo, ga [fay-bree'-foo-go, gah], *a.* Febrifuge: also used as a substantive.

Febril [fay-breel'], *a.* Febrile.

Fecal [fay-cahl'], *a.* Feculent, excrementitious, fecal.

Fecial [fay-the-ahl'], *m.* The herald among the Romans, who declared war or peace.

Fécula [fay'-coo-lah], *f.* Fecula, a substance obtained by bruising vegetables in water; starch.

Feculencia [fay-coo-len'-the-ah], *f.* Feculence, dregs, lees.

Feculento, ta [fay-coo-len'-to, tah], or **Feculoso, sa,** *a.* Feculent, foul, dreggy.

Fecundación [fay-coon-dah-the-on'], *f* Fecundation, making fruitful or prolific.

Fecundamente [fay-coon-dah-men'-tay], *adv.* Fertilely, fruitfully.

Fecundante [fay-coon-dahn'-tay], *a.* & *pa.* Fructifying, making fruitful.

Fecundar [fay-coon-dar'], *va.* To fertilize, to make fruitful, to fructify.

Fecundativo, va [fay-coon-dah-tee'-vo, vah], *a.* Fertilizing, fructifying.

Fecundidad [fay-coon-de-dahd'], *f.* Fecundity, fertility, fruitfulness.

Fecundizar [fay-coon-de-thar'], *va.* To fecundate, to fertilize, to fructify

Fecundo, da [fay-coon'-do, dah], *a.* Fecund, fruitful, fertile, prolific.

Fecha [fay'-chah], *f.* Date of a letter or other writing. *Larga fecha*, Old date; great age. *De la cruz a la fecha*, From the beginning to the end.

Fechar [fay-char'], *va.* To date, to put the date to a letter or other writing.

Fecho [fay'-cho], *m.* 1. (Obs.) Action, fact, exploit. *V.* Hecho and Hazaña 2. *Fecho de azúcar*, Chest of sugar, containing not more than twelve *arrobas*, or about three hundred-weight. *Fiel de fechos*, Clerk who performs the functions of a notary in small villages.

Fecho, cha [fay'-cho, chah], *pp. irr.* of Facer. Used only in legislative writings.

Fechoría [fay-cho-ree'-ah], *f.* Action, fact, deed, exploit: commonly used in a bad sense.

Fechuría [fay-choo-ree'-ah], *f.* 1. *V* Fechoría. 2. (Obs.) *V.* Hechura

Federación [fay-day-rah-the-on'], *f* Federation, confederation.

Federado [fay-day-rah'-do], *m.* (Littl. us.) Federary, fedary

Federal [fay-day-rahl'], *a.* Federal

Federalismo [fay-day-rah-lees'-mo], *m* Federalism, political autonomy of various provinces or states.

Federativo, va [fay-day-rah-tee'-vo, vah], *a.* Federative.

Feeza [fay-ay'-thah], *f* (Obs.) Ugliness, deformity.

Fehaciente [fay-ah-the-en'-tay], *a.* Authentic.
Feldespato, or **Feldspato** [fel-des-pah'-to, or felds-pah'-to], *m.* Feldspar, a common constituent of rocks; silicate of aluminum and an alkali.
Feldmariscal [feld-mah-ris-cahl'], *m.* (Mil.) Field-marshal.
Felice [fay-lee'-thay], *a.* (Poet.) *V.* FELIZ.
Felicidad [fay-le-the-dahd'], *f.* Felicity, happiness, success, luckiness, blissfulness, blessedness, prosperity.
Felicitación [fay-le-the-tah-the-on'], *f.* Congratulation, felicitation, professing joy for the happiness or success of another.
Felicitar [fay-le-the-tar'], *va.* 1. To congratulate, to compliment upon any happy event, to felicitate. 2. (Littl. us.) To make happy.
Feligrés, sa [fay-le-grays', sah], *m.* & *f.* 1. Parishioner, one who belongs to a parish. 2. (Met. Coll.) A constant visitant at a house.
Feligresía [fay-le-gray-see'-ah], *f.* District of a parish, and the inhabitants of the same.
Feliz [fay-leeth'], *a.* Happy, fortunate, lucky, prosperous, felicitous.
Felizmente, *adv.* Happily, fortunately, luckily, felicitously.
Felonía [fay-lo-nee'-ah], *f.* Treachery, disloyalty, felony.
Felpa [fayl'-pah], *f.* 1. Plush, a silk stuff. 2. In jocular style, a good drubbing.
Felpado, da [fel-pah'-do, dah], *a.* Shaggy, villous.
Felpilla [fel-peel'-lyah], *f.* Corded silk for embroidering; chenille.
Felposo, sa [fel-po'-so, sah], *a.* 1. Felted, with interlaced fibres. 2. Plush-covered.
Felpudo [fel-poo'-do], *m.* Plat made of bass and formed into round or square mats; door mat.
Felpudo, da [fel-poo'-do, dah], *a.* Downy. *V.* FELPADO.
Femenil [fay-may-neel'], *a.* Feminine, womanish, womanly.
Femenilmente, *adv.* Effeminately, womanishly, womanly.
Femenino, na [fay-may-nee'-no, nah], *a.* 1. Feminine, belonging to women, female. 2. Feminine, of the feminine gender.
Fementidamente, *adv.* Falsely, fallaciously.
Fementido, da [fay-men-tee'-do, dah], *a.* False, unfaithful, deficient in the performance of one's promise.
Feminismo [fay-me-nees'-mo], *m.* Feminism, women's liberation.
Feminista [fay-me-nees'-tah], *a.* & *m.* & *f.* Feminist.
Femoral [fay-mo-rahl'], *a.* Femoral, belonging to the thigh.
Fémur [fay'-mor], *m.* Femur, the thigh-bone.
Fenacetina [fay-nah-thay-tee'-nah], *f.* (Med.) Phenacetin.
Fenda [fen'-dah], *f.* A crack in the bark of trees.
Fendiente [fen-de-en'-tay], *m.* Gash, a deep cut or wound.
Fenecer [fay-nay-therr'], *vn.* 1. To terminate, to be at an end. 2. To degenerate, to decline. 3. To die. —*va.* To finish, to conclude, to close.
Fenecimiento [fay-nay-the-me-en'-to], *m.* 1. Close, finish, termination, end. 2. Settling of an account.
(*Yo fenezco, yo fenezca*, from *Fenecer. V.* ABORRECER.)
Fenedal [fay-nay-dahl'], *m.* (Prov.) Hay-loft.
Fenicio, cia [fay-nee'-the-o, ah], *a.* Phœnician.
Fénico [fay'-ne-co], *a.* Phenic, carbolic. *Ácido fénico*, Phenol, carbolic acid (so called).
Fenigeno, na [fay-nee'-hay-no, nah], *a.* (Littl. us.) Having the nature of hay.
Fénix [fay'-nix], *m.* 1. Phœnix, a fabulous bird. 2. (Met.) That which is exquisite or unique of its kind.
Fenogreco [fay-no-gray'-co], *m.* (Bot.) Fenugreek. Trigonella fœnum græcum, *L.*
Fenol [fay-nole'], *n.* Phenol, carbolic acid.
Fenomenal [fay-no-may-nahl'], *a.* Phenomenal.
Fenomenalismo [fay-no-may-nah-lees'-mo], *m.* Phenomenalism, materialism, a doctrine which gives importance only to what can affect our senses.
Fenómeno [fay-no'-may-no], *m.* Phenomenon.
Feo, ea [fay'-o, ah], *a.* 1. Ugly, deformed, hideous, haggard, grim; homely. 2. Causing horror or aversion.
Fer, *va.* 1. (Obs.) *V.* HACER. 2. *m.* Abbreviation of *Fierro (hierro)*, iron.
Feracidad [fay-rah-the-dahd'], *f.* Feracity, fecundity, fruitfulness, fertility.
Feral [fay-rahl'], *a.* Cruel, bloodthirsty.
Feraz [fay-rath'], *a.* 1. Fertile, fruitful, feracious. 2. Abundant, copious, plentiful.
Féretro [fay'-ray-tro], *m.* Bier, coffin, hearse.
Feria [fay'-re-ah], *f.* 1. Any day of the week, excepting Saturday and Sunday, a feria. *Feria segunda* or *lunes*, Monday. 2. Fair, an annual or stated meeting of sellers and buyers. 3. Rest, repose. *Revolver la feria*, To disturb the course of business. *Ferias*, Fairings, presents given at a fair.
Feriado, da [fay-re-ah'-do, dah], *a.* (Law) Applied to the day in which the tribunals are shut.—*pp.* of FERIAR.
Ferial [fay-re-ahl'], *a.* 1. Belonging to fairs. 2. Ferial, relating to the days of the week.—*m.* & *f.* (Obs.) Market, fair.
Feriante [fay-re-ahn'-tay], *m.* (Prov.) One who trades at fairs.
Feriar [fay-re-ar'], *va.* 1. To sell, to buy; to exchange one thing for another. 2. To give fairings, to make presents at a fair. 3. *V.* SUSPENDER.
Ferino, na [fay-ree'-no, nah], *a.* Ferine, wild, savage, ferocious.
Ferir, *va.* (Obs.) *V.* HERIR and MARCAR.
Fermata [fer-mah'-tah], *f.* (Mus.) A pause or hold (𝄐). (Ital.)
Fermentación [fer-men-tah-the-on'], *f.* Fermentation.
Fermentar [fer-men-tar'], *vn.* & *vr.* To ferment. *Hacer fermentar*, To ferment or to cause to ferment, to heat, to rarefy.
Fermentativo, va [fer-men-tah-tee'-vo, vah], *a.* Fermentative.
Fermentescible [fer-men-tes-thee'-blay], *a.* Fermentable, capable of fermentation.
Fermento [fer-men'-to], *m.* 1. Ferment. 2. Leaven, leavening. 3. Ferment, intestine motion, tumult.
Fermosura [fer-mo-soo'-rah], *f.* (Obs.) *V.* HERMOSURA.
Fernambuco [fer-nahm-boo'-co], *m.* A dye-wood of Brazil. (From name of province.)
Fernandina [fer-nan-dee'-nah], *f.* Kind of linen.
Feroce, *a.* (Poet.) *V.* FEROZ.
Ferocidad [fay-ro-the-dahd'], *f.* Ferocity, wildness, ferociousness, fierceness, savageness, fury.
Feróstico, ca [fay-ros'-te-co, cah], *a.* (Coll.) Irritable, wayward.
Feroz [fay-roth'], *a.* Ferocious, cruel, savage, fell, fierce, ravenous, heathenish.
Ferozmente [fay-roth-men'-tay], *adv* Ferociously, felly.
Ferra, *f.* *V.* FARRA.
Ferrada [fer-rah'-dah], *f.* Iron club, used formerly as an offensive and defensive weapon.
Ferrado [fer-rah'-do], *m.* (Prov.) 1. Measure for corn, which makes about the fourth part of a bushel. 2. Measure for land of twelve yards square.
Ferrar [fer-rar'], *va.* 1. To garnish with points of iron; to strengthen with iron plates. 2. *V.* HERRAR.
Ferrarés, sa [fer-rah-rays', fer-rah-ray'-sah], *a.* Native of or belonging to Ferrara.
Férreo, rea [fer'-ray-o, ah], *a.* 1. Ferreous, made of iron or containing iron. 2. Iron: applied to an age. 3. Iron, harsh, stern, severe.
Ferrería [fer-ray-ree'-ah], *f.* Iron works, where iron is manufactured.
Ferrete [fer-ray'-tay], *m.* 1. Burnt copper or brass used to colour glass. 2. Marking-iron.
Ferretear [fer-ray-tay-ar'], *va.* To bind, fasten, mark, or work with iron.
Ferretería [fer-ray-tay-ree'-ah], *f.* Hardware store.
Férrico, ca [fer'-re-co, cah], *a.* 1. Ferric, containing iron. 2. Ferric, pertaining to iron in its higher combinations.
Férridos, das [fer'-re-dos, das], *a. pl.* Simple bodies whose type is iron.
Ferro [fer'-ro], *m.* (Naut.) Anchor.
Ferrocarril [fer-ro-car-reel'], *m.* Railroad. *Ferrocarril funicular*, Cable railroad. *Ferrocarril subterráneo*, Subway.
Ferrocarrilero, ra [fer-ro-car-re-lay'-ro, rah], *a.* Railway.—*m.* Railroad man, railroad worker.
Ferrón [fer-rone'], *m.* (Prov.) 1. Iron manufacturer. 2. Ironmonger.
Ferroso, sa [fer-ro'-so, sah], *a.* Ferrous, obtained from iron; pertaining to iron in its lower combinations.
Ferrotipia [fer-ro-tee'-pe-ah], *f.* Tintype, ferrotype.
Ferroviario, ria [fer-ro-ve-ah'-re-o, re-ah], *a.* Railway, pertaining to a railroad.
Ferrugiento, ta [fer-roo-he-en'-to, tah], *a.* Irony, belonging to or containing iron.
Ferrugíneo, nea [fer-roo-hee'-nay-o, ah], *a.* Ferruginous.
Ferruginoso, sa [fer-roo-he-no'-so, sah], *a.* Ferruginous.
Fértil [fayr'-teel], *a.* Fertile, fruitful, copious, plentiful.
Fertilidad [fer-te-le-dahd'], *f.* Fertility, copiousness, plenty, fruitfulness.
Fertilizantes [fer-te-le-thahn'-tess], *m. pl.* Fertilizers, fertilizing agents.
Fertilizar [fer-te-le-thar'], *va.* To fertilize, to fructify, to make the soil fruitful.
Fértilmente [fayr'-teel-men-tay], *adv* Fertilely.
Férula [fay'-roo-lah], *f.* 1. Ferule, an instrument with which boys are punished. 2. (Met.) Rule, yoke, authority 3. (Bot.) Ferula, a genus of umbelliferous plants.
Feruláceo, ea [fay-roo-lah'-thay-o, ah], *a.* Like a ferule.
Ferventísimo, ma, Fervientísimo, ma [fer-ven-tee'-se-mo, mah], *a. sup.* Very fervent, very ardent in piety, very warm in zeal.
Férvido, da [fayr'-ve-do, dah], *a.* Fervid, ardent.
Ferviente [fer-ve-en'-tay], *a.* Fervent, ardent. *V.* FERVOROSO.

Fervor [fer-vor'], *m.* 1. Fervour, violent heat, warmth. 2. Fervour, fervidness, zeal, ardour, eagerness. 3. Fervour, fervency, ardour of piety. 4. (Obs.) *V.* HERVOR.

Fervorcillo [fer-vor-theel'-lyo], *m. dim.* A slight fervour or zeal of short duration.

Fervorizar [fer-vo-re-thar'], *va.* To heat, to inflame, to incite.

Fervorosamente [fer-vo-ro-sah-men'-tay], *adv.* Fervently.

Fervoroso, sa [fer-vo-ro'-so, sah], *a.* Fervent, ardent in piety, warm in zeal; active, officious.

Fesceninos [fes-thay-nee'-nos], *m. pl.* Fescennines, obscene nuptial verses sung by the Romans.

Festejador, ra [fes-tay-hah-dor', rah], *m. & f.* Feaster, courtier, entertainer.

Festejar [fes-tay-har'], *va.* 1. To entertain, to feast. 2. To court, to woo, to make love. 3. To celebrate or solemnize an event.

Festejo, Festeo [fes-tay'-ho, fes-tay'-o], *m.* 1. An expression of joy for the happiness of another. 2. (Coll.) Courtship, solicitation of a woman in marriage. 3. Feast, entertainment. 4. Obsequiousness.

Festero [fes-tay'-ro], *m.* Director of church music on festive occasions.

Festin [fes-teen'], *m.* Feast, entertainment, banquet.

Festinación [fes-te-nah-the-on'], *f.* Speed, haste, hurry.

Festival [fes-te-vahl'], *a.* (Obs.) *V.* FESTIVO.—*m.* (Neol.) Festival, a great vocal and instrumental concert.

Festivamente [fes-te-vah-men'-tay], *adv.* Festively.

Festividad [fes-te-ve-dahd'], *f.* 1. Festivity, rejoicing, gaiety, merry-making. 2. Solemn manner of celebrating an event.

Festivo, va [fes-tee'-vo, vah], *a.* 1. Festive, gay, joyful, light-hearted. 2. Festival, festal, pertaining to feasts. *Día festivo,* Holiday.

Festón [fes-tone'], *m.* 1. Garland, wreath of flowers. 2. Festoon.

Festonear [fes-to-nay-ar'], *va.* To embellish with festoons.

Festuca [fes-too'-cah], *f.* (Bot.) *V.* CAÑUELA. Fescue-grass, valuable for pasturage.

Fétido, da [fay'-te-do, dah], *a.* Fetid, stinking.

Feto [fay'-to], *m.* Fœtus.

Feúcho, cha [fay-oo'-cho, chah], *a.* Ugly, repulsive.

Feudal [fay-oo-dahl'], *a.* Feudal, feodal.

Feudalidad [fay-oo-dah-le-dahd'], *f.* Feodality, feudality.

Feudalismo [fay-oo-dah-lees'-mo], *m.* Feudalism.

Feudar, *va.* *V.* ENFEUDAR.

Feudatario [fay-oo-dah-tah'-re-o], *m.* Feudatary, feodatary.

Feudatario, ria [fay-oo-dah-tah'-re-o, ah], *a.* Feudatary, feudary.

Feudista [fay-oo-dees'-tah], *m.* Feudist, a writer upon feudal law.

Feudo [fay'-oo-do], *m.* 1. Fief, or fee, all lands or tenements held by an acknowledgment of a superior lord, feod, feud, manor. 2. Tribute or rent paid to a feudal lord.

Fez [feth]. 1. *m.* Fez, a woollen cap, white or red, used in the Orient and in Northern Africa. 2. *f.* (Obs.) *V.* HEZ.

Fiable [fe-ah'-blay], *a.* Trustworthy.

Fiado, da [fe-ah'-do, dah], *a.* & *pp.* of FIAR. Confident, trusting. *Al fiado,* Upon trust. *En fiado,* Upon bail. *Comprar géneros al fiado,* To buy goods on credit. *Dar fiado,* To give credit.

Fiador, ra [fe-ah-dor', rah], *m. & f.* 1. One who trusts another. 2. Bondsman, guarantor, surety, one who becomes security for another. *m.* 3. The loop of a cloak. 4. (Falconr.) Creance. 5. Bolt or instrument with which any thing is made fast; stop, catch, safety catch, ratchet, detent, tumbler of a lock. 6. *pl.* (Coll.) Back-side, where boys are chastised. *Dar fiador,* To give a pledge for security. *Salir fiador,* To stand security.

Fiambrar [fe-am-brar'], *va.* To boil or roast meat, and leave it to cool for eating.

Fiambre [fe-ahm'-bray], *m.* Cold meat preserved for use.—*a.* 1. Cold: applied to meat. 2. (Coll.) Of a long standing.

Fiambrera [fe-am-bray'-rah], *f.* 1. Pannier or basket in which cold meat is carried into the country. 2. (Coll.) Stupid or foolish speech.

Fiambrero [fe-am-bray'-ro], *m.* One who takes care of the larder, or of the cold meat preserved for use.

Fiancilla [f an-theel'-lyah], *f.* Binding-ring of a carriage.

Fianza [fe-ahn'-thah], *f.* 1. Caution, guarantee, security given for the performance of engagements. 2. Reversion. 3. Bond, security, bail. *Fianza bancaria,* Bank security given in Rome to insure pensions charged on ecclesiastical works. *Dar fianza,* To give bail or a pledge.

Fiar [fe-ar'], *va.* 1. To bail, to give bail. 2. To trust, to sell upon trust, to give credit. 3. To place confidence in another, to commit to another, to credit.—*vn.* To confide, to be sure of a thing. *Fiar el pecho,* (Met.) To unbosom. *Yo lo fío,* I warrant it.

Fiasco [fe-ahs'-co], *m.* Failure. *Hacer fiasco,* To result in humiliating failure. Used especially of theatricals. (Ital.)

Fiat [fee'-at], *m.* 1. Consent that something may be done. 2. (Law) Fiat, a word used by courts of justice in Spain to express their consent. 3. The royal document, by which the king appoints a person as a notary public, or royal notary.

Fibra [fee'-brah], *f.* 1. Fibre, filament, staple. 2. Fibre, a delicate root. 3. (Met.) Energy of character, firmness, vigour. 4. (Min.) Vein of ore.

Fibrazón [fe-brah-thone'], *f.* The whole of the ore-veins of a mine.

Fibrila [fe-bree'-lah], *f.* (Bot.) Fibril. a capillary rootlet.

Fibrilar [fe-bre-lar'], *a.* Fibrillar, disposed in fibrils or fine fibres.

Fibrina [fe-bree'-nah], *f.* (Chem.) Fibrin, fibrine.

Fibrinoso, sa [fe-bre-no'-so, sah], *a.* Fibrinous.

Fibroso, sa [fe-bro'-so, sah], *a.* 1. Fibrous. 2. Energetic, firm, or vigorous in character.

Ficción [fic-the-on'], *f.* 1. Fiction, the act of feigning or inventing. 2. Fiction, figment, an invention, and the thing feigned or invented. 3. Fiction, falsehood, lie. 4. Grimace, gesture. 5. Stratagem, artifice.

Fice [fee'-thay], *m.* (Zool.) Whiting. Gadus merlangus, *L.*

Ficticio, cia [fic-tee'-the-o, ah], *a.* Fictitious, fabulous, mock.

Ficto, ta [feec'-to, tah], *a.* 1. Feigned, counterfeited. 2. Vain, useless, of no value.

Ficha [fee'-chah], *f.* Counter, used in reckoning.

Fichero [fe-chay'-ro], *m.* File case.

Fidedigno, na [fe-day-deeg'-no, nah], *a.* Worthy of credit, deserving of belief.

Fideicomisario [fe-day-e-co-me-sah'-re-o], *m.* Trustee, fiduciary, one who holds any thing in trust for another.

Fideicomiso [fe-day-e-co-mee'-so], *m.* Trust, feoffment of any executor.

Fidelidad [fe-day-le-dahd'], *f.* 1. Fidelity, honesty, veracity, faith, constancy, honour. 2. Fidelity, faithful adherence, fealty, loyalty. 3. Punctuality in the execution or performance of any thing.

Fidelísimo, ma [fe-day-lee'-se-mo, mah], *a. sup.* of FIEL.

Fideos [fe-day'-os], *m. pl.* Vermicelli.

Fiducial [fe-doo-the-ahl'], *a.* 1. (Math.) Passing through the centre of graduation, referring to a fixed line. 2. Belonging to faith or credit.

Fiduciario, ria [fe-doo-the-ah'-re-o, ah], *a.* Fiduciary, belonging to a position of trust or confidence.

Fiebre [fe-ay'-bray], *f.* Fever. *Fiebre aftosa,* (Vet.) Hoof-and-mouth disease. *Fiebre amarilla,* Yellow fever. *Fiebre del heno,* Hay fever. *Fiebre mediterránea* or *de Malta,* Undulant fever. *Fiebre del oro,* Gold rush. *Fiebre tifoidea,* Typhoid fever.

Fiebrecilla [fe-ay-bray-theel'-lyah], *f. dim.* Feveret. *V.* CALENTURILLA.

Fiel [fe-el'], *a.* 1. Faithful, honest, loyal, upright. 2. True, right. 3. Faithful, observant of compact or promise.

Fiel [fe-el'], *m.* 1. Clerk of the market, a person appointed to inspect weights and measures. *Fiel de romana,* Magistrate who has the inspection of slaughter-houses and public shambles. 2. Needle of a balance. 3. Pivot of a steel-yard. 4. Pin which keeps the blades of scissors together. *Fiel de muelle,* Wharfinger who has the direction or inspection of a wharf. 5 Catholic Christian who lives in obedience to the Romish Church. 6. (Prov.) *V.* TERCERO. *En fiel,* Equal weight, even balance.

Fieldad [fe-el-dahd'], *f.* Place and employment of the inspector of weights and measures, or of the clerk of the market.

Fielmente [fe-el-men'-tay], *adv.* Faithfully.

Fieltrar [fe-el-trar'], *va.* 1. (Littl. us.) To felt, to unite without weaving. 2. To stuff a saddle with short hair.

Fieltro [fe-el'-tro], *m.* 1. Felt, a stuff used to make hats. 2. A kind of hat used to keep off rain. 3. Surtout, a large great-coat.

Fieme [fe-ay'-may], *m.* (Vet.) Fleam, a heart-shaped lancet.

Fiemo [fe-ay'-mo], *m.* (Prov.) Dung, manure.

Fiera [fe-ay'-rah], *f.* 1. A wild beast. 2. An inhuman, haughty and excessively choleric man, a savage.

Fierabrás [fe-ay-rah-brahs'], *m.* (Coll.) Bully, bragger, blusterer.

Fieramente [fe-ay-rah-men'-tay], *adv.* Fiercely, savagely, ferociously, haughtily.

Fiereza [fe-ay-ray'-thah], *f.* 1. Fierceness, cruelty, ferocity, hardness. 2. Fierceness, heat of temper. 3. (Her.) Attitude of an animal showing its teeth. 4. Deformity, ugliness.

Fiero, ra [fe-ay'-ro, rah], *a.* 1. Fierce, cruel, bloodthirsty; ferocious, fiery. 2. Ugly, deformed. 3. Rough, rude. 4. Great, huge, enormous. 5. Furious, terrible; wild, savage.—*m. pl. Fieros,* Fierce threats and bravadoes.

Fierro [fe-er'-ro], *m.* *V.* HIERRO. Brand, the mark of ownership on an animal, and frequently on other articles. *Fierros,* (Obs.) Irons with which prisoners are chained; imprisonment.

Fiesta [fe-ess'-tah], *f.* 1. Feast, entertainment, rejoicing, feasting, merriment. 2. Feast, festivity, festival, a church-feast holiday; the day of some ecclesiastical festival. *Fiesta de consejo,* Working-day of vacation in the tribunals. *Fiesta de guardar,* Day of obligation to hear mass. *Estar de fiesta,* To be merry, to be in good humour. *Fiesta de pólvora,* Any thing very quick, rapid, and of short duration. *Fiesta doble,* 1. A double feast or festival in the church. 2. (Coll.) A ball and entertainment.—*pl.* 1. Holidays, vacations. *No estar para fiestas,* To be out of humour. *Fiestas reales,* Royal festivals. 2. *Fiestas de pólvora,* Artificial fire-works; a bonfire, a feu de joie. 3. Caresses, acts of endearment. *Hacer fiestas,* To caress, to wheedle, to fawn. 4. (Met. Littl. us.) Money wasted or misspent in a very short time. *Por modo de fiesta,* In fun, for fun.

Figala [fe-gah'-lah], *f.* An East Indian oared boat with one mast.

Figle [fee'-glay], *m.* (Mus.) Ophicleide, a bass brass instrument of several (generally eleven) keys.

Figo [fee'-go], *m.* (Obs.) *V.* HIGO

Figón [fe-gone'], *m.* Eating-house, chop-house.

Figonero [fe-go-nay -ro], *m.* Keeper of an eating-house.

Figuera, *f.* (Obs.) *V.* HIGUERA.

Figueral [fe-gay-rahl'], *m.* Plantation of fig-trees.

Figulino, na [fe-goo-lee -no, nah], *a* Made of potter's clay

Figura [fe-goo'-rah], *f.* 1. Figure, the form of any thing. 2 The shape, the particular external appearance of a thing. 3. Face, mien, countenance. 4. Figure, statue, image, any thing formed in resemblance of something else. 5 (Law) Form, mode. 6. (Mus.) (*a*) A musical note; (*b*) motive, theme, subject. 7 (Gram.) Figure, any deviation from the rules of analogy or syntax. 8. (Geom.) Figure, a space included in certain lines. 9. (Rhet.) Figure, any mode of speaking in which words are distorted from their literal and primitive sense. *Figura de proa,* (Naut.) Figure-head of a ship *Hacer figura,* To figure, to make a figure. *Hacer figuras,* To make grimaces. *Alzar* or *levantar figura,* To assume an air of importance. *Natural* or *genio y figura hasta la sepultura,* (prov.) What is bred in the bone will never come out of the flesh.—*m.* A foolish person assuming an air of importance and dignity.—*com.* Person of a mean or ridiculous appearance.—*f. pl.* In games at cards, the king, queen, and knave.

Figurable [fe-goo-rah'-blay], *a.* Figurable, that which may be figured

Figuradamente [fe-goo-rah-dah-men tay], *adv* Figuratively.

Figurada [fe-goo-rah'-dah], *f.* (Littl. us.) An antic posture, a gesture of affected gravity or importance.

Figurado, da [fe-goo-rah'-do, dah], *a* Figurative, typical; not literal; rhetorical.—*pp.* of FIGURAR.

Figural [fe-goo-rahl'], *a.* Figural, belonging to figures; represented by delineation.

Figuranza [fe-goo-rahn -thah], *f.* (Prov.) Resemblance.

Figurar [fe-goo-rar'], *va.* 1. To figure, to form into a determinate shape. 2. To adorn with figures.—*vr.* To fancy, to imagine, to believe without being able to prove.

Figurativamente [fe-goo-rah-te-vah-men'-tay], *adv.* Figuratively.

Figurativo, va [fe-goo-rah-tee'-vo, vah], *a.* 1. Figurative, typical; not literal, explanatory. 2. Symbolical, emblematic.

Figurería [fe-goo-ray-ree'-ah], *f.* *V.* MUECA.

Figurero, ra [fe-goo-ray'-ro, rah], *m.* & *f.* Mimic, a ludicrous imitator; a buffoon who copies another's actions.

Figurilla [fe-goo-reel'-lyah], *com* A ridiculous little figure.

Figurilla, ita [fe-goo-reel'-lyah, ee'-tah], *f. dim.* A small figure.

Figurín [fe-goo-reen'], *m* Fashion-plate, or small model for dresses; lay-figure.

Figurón [fe-goo-rone'], *m.* 1. (Aug.) A huge or enormous figure of a ridiculous appearance. 2. A low-bred person assuming an air of dignity and importance.

Fija [fee'-hah], *f.* 1. Kind of hinge, bat-hinge. 2. (Obs.) *V* HIJA.

Fijación [fe-hah-the-on'], *f.* 1. Fixation, stability, firmness. 2. The act of posting up printed bills, edicts, etc. 3. Fixation, the act of fixing mercury or any other volatile spirit.

Fijador, ra [fe-hah-dor', rah], *a.* (Phot.) Fixing, fixative.

Fijamente [fe-hah-men -tay], *adv.* 1. Firmly, assuredly. 2. Intensely, attentively. 3. Fixedly, steadfastly.

Fijar [fe-har'], *va.* 1. To fix, to fasten, to make fast, firm, or stable. 2. To fix, to settle, to establish, to clinch. 3 To fix, to direct without variation. 4. To fix, to deprive of volatility.—*vr* 1. To fix or settle itself in a place, to stare at. 2. To fix, to determine, to resolve. *Fijar las plantas,* (Obs.) To confirm one's self in an opinion or idea.

Fijenes [fe-hay'-nes], *m. pl.* Cheeks of a press.

Fijeza [fe-hay -thah], *f* Firmness, stability.

Fijo, ja [fee -ho, hah], *a.* & *pp. irr.* of FIJAR 1 Fixed, firm, secure 2. Settled, permanent.

Fijodalgo [fe-ho-dahl -go], *m.* *V* HIJODALGO

Fil [feel], *m* (Obs.) 1 Needle of a balance, beam of a steel-yard. 2. Equipoise, equality of weight, equilibration *Fil de roda,* (Naut.) Right ahead. *Estar en fil* or *en un fil,* To be in line, to be equal.

Fila [fee'-lah], *f* 1 A long row or series of persons or things. 2. A line of soldiers ranged abreast or side by side *En fila,* In a line, in a row.

Filacteria [fe-lac-tay'-re-ah], *f* Phylactery

Filada [fe-lah -dah], *f* A slaty, schistose, micaceous rock, at times containing other varieties

Filagrama [fe-lah-grah -mah], *f* A wire mould for a water-mark *Cf* FILIGRANA

Filamento [fe-lah-men -to], *m.* Filament Fibre. Thread

Filamentoso, sa [fe-lah-men-to -so, sah], *a.* Filamentous

Filandria [fe-lahn -dre-ah], *f* Worm bred in the intestines of birds of prey.

Filantropía [fe-lan-tro-pee -ah], *f* Philanthropy, good nature.

Filantrópicamente [fe-lan-tro -pe-cah-men-tay], *adv.* Humanely.

Filantrópico, ca, *a.* Philanthropical, philanthropic.

Filántropo [fe-lahn -tro-po], *m.* Philanthropist.

Filar [fe-lar'], *a.* *Triángulo filar,* A mathematical instrument serving as a sector, for various uses.—*va.* (Obs.) 1. *V.* HILAR. 2. (Naut.) To let go, to pay out.

Filarete [fe-lah-ray'-tay], *m.* (Naut.) Netting put on the waist or sides of a ship.

Filariosis [fe-lah-re-o'-sis], *f.* (Med.) Filariasis.

Filarmonía [fe-lar-mo-nee'-ah], *f.* Love of harmony, passion for music.

Filarmónico, ca [fe-lar-mo'-ne-co, cah], *a.* Philharmonic, devoted to music.

Filástica [fe-lahs'-te-cah], *f.* (Naut.) Rope-yarn, yarn made of untwisted ropes. *Filástica fina para maniobras,* Fine rope-yarn for running rigging.

Filatelia [fe-lah-tay'-le-ah], *f.* Philately, stamp collecting.

Filatélico, ca [fe-lah-tay'-le-co cah], *a.* Philatelic.

Filatelista [fe-lah-tay-lees'-tah], *m* & *f.* Philatelist, stamp collector.

Filatería [fe-lah-tay-ree'-ah], *f.* Verbosity, exuberance or superfluity of words.

Filatero [fe-lah-tay'-ro], *m.* A verbose speaker.

Filatura [fe-lah-too'-rah], *f.* The art of spinning wool, cotton, etc.

Filbán [feel-bahn'], *m.* The rough edge of a knife, scissors, etc.

Filderretor [fil-der-ray-tor'], *m.* Sort of superfine camlet.

Fileli [fe-lay-lee'], *m.* A very thin woollen stuff; superfine flannel It came from Barbary.

Fileno, na [fe-lay'-no, nah], *a.* (Coll.) Delicate, effeminate, soft.

Filera [fe-lay'-rah], *f.* 1. A fishing-net apparatus with small weights at the ends 2. Spinneret of weaving spiders.

Filete [fe-lay'-tay], *m.* 1 (Arch.) Fillet, a small member which appears in ornaments and mouldings, otherwise called *listel.* 2. Hem, the edge of a garment doubled and sewed. 3 A thin and small spit for roasting. 4. Welt of a shoe. 5. A twist-like ornament raised on plate. 6. Tenderloin, loin of beef. *Gastar muchos filetes,* To talk very sprucely

Filetear [fe-lay-tay-ar'], *va* To adorn with fillets

Filetón [fe-lay-tone'], *m.* 1 (Aug.) In architecture, a large fillet or listel 2. Kind of embroidery.

Filiación [fe-le-ah-the-on'], *f.* 1 Filiation, the relation of a son to a father 2. Dependence of some things upon others 3. (Mil.) Regimental register of a soldier's height, physiognomy age, etc

Filial [fe-le-ahl'], *a* Filial, befitting a son

Filiar [fe-le-ar'], *vn.* To prove one's descent.—*va* To enrol a soldier.

Filiatra [fe-le-ah -trah], *a.* & *n.* Devoted to the study of medicine. Philiater. (Gr. φιλιατρός.)

Filiatría [fe-le-ah-tree -ah], *f.* Love of the study of medicine

Filibote [fe-le-bo -tay], *m* Fly-boat, a light vessel of 100 tons burden

Filibustero [fe-le-boos-tay ro], *m* 1 Name given to freebooters or buccaneers, who plundered America in the 17th century 2 Filibuster, an armed adventurer invading unlawfully an other's territory.

Filicida [fe-le-thee -dah], *m.* (Littl us.) Murderer of one's own son

Filiforme [fe-le-for -may], *a* Filiform, slender like a thread.

Filigrana [fe-le-grah'-nah], *f.* 1. Filigree, filigrane, fine work made of gold and silver threads. 2. (Met.) Any thing neatly wrought.
Filípica [fe-lee'-pe-cah], *f* Philippic, invective, declamation.
Filipichín [fe-le-pe-cheen'], *m.* Kind of damask, moreen, woollen cloth.
Filipino, na [fe-le-pee'-no, nah], *a.* Philippine, belonging to the Philippine Islands.
Filis [fee'-lis], *f.* 1. Grace, a graceful manner of doing or saying a thing. 2. Gewgaw made of clay.
Filisteo, tea [fe-lis-tay'-o, ah], *m.* & *f.* 1. (Coll.) A very tall and corpulent person. 2. Philistine.
Film, Filme [feelm, feel'-may], *m.* Film, movie.
Filmar [fel-mar'], *va.* To film.
Filo [fee'-lo], *m.* 1. Edge of a sword, or other cutting instrument. *Filo rabioso,* Wire edge. *Darse un filo a la lengua,* To murmur, to detract. *Embotar los filos,* (Met.) To abate one's ardour or energy. *Dar un filo,* V. Afilar or Amolar. 2. (Obs.) V. Hilo 3. (Obs.) The point or line which divides a thing in two equal parts. *Pasar al filo de la espada,* To put to the sword.
Filogenitura [fe-lo-hay-ne-too'-rah], *f.* Philoprogenitiveness.
Filología, Filológica [fe-o-lo-hee'-ah, fe-lo-lo'-he-cah], *f.* Philology, linguistics.
Filológico, ca [fe-lo-lo'-he-co, cah], *a.* Philological.
Filólogo [fe-lo'-lo-go], *m.* Philologist.
Filomena [fe-lo-may'-nah], *f.* Nightingale, philomel, philomela.
Filón [fe-lone'], *m.* (Geol.) Vein, lode, mineral layer; gang(ue).
Filonio [fe-lo'-ne-o], *m.* (Pharm.) Kind of opiate.
Filopos [fe-lo'-pos], *m. pl.* Pieces of linen used to drive game into a place assigned for that purpose
Filoseda [fe-lo-say'-dah], *f.* Vesting, silk and worsted or cotton cloth.
Filosofador, ra [fe-lo-so-fah-dor', rah], *m.* & *f.* Philosopher.
Filosofal [fe-lo-so-fahl'], *a.* *Piedra filosofal,* Philosopher's stone. (Ant.)
Filosofar [fe-lo-so-far'], *va.* 1. To philosophize, to examine as a philosopher. 2. To play the philosopher, to assume the critic.
Filosofastro [fe-lo-so-fahs-tro], *m.* A pretended philosopher, a smatterer in philosophy, philosophaster
Filosofía [fe-lo-so-fee'-ah], *f.* 1. Philosophy, a science which treats of the essence and affections of things and beings. 2. Philosophy, a particular doctrine or system of opinions. *Filosofía moral,* Ethics or moral philosphy. *Filosofía natural,* Physics or natural philosophy
Filosóficamente [fe-lo-so-fe-cah-men tay], *adv.* Philosophically.
Filosófico, ca [fe-lo-so'-fe-co, cah], *a* Philosophical, philosophic.
Filosofismo [fe-lo-so-fees'-mo], *m* (Iron.) Philosophism, sophistry, free-thinking.
Filosofista [fe-lo-so-fees'-tah], *m* (Iron) Philosophist, sophist.
Filósofo [fe-lo'-so-fo], *m.* Philosopher.
Filósofo, fa [fe-lo'-so-fo, fah], *a* 1. Philosophic, philosophical. 2. *V* Afilosofado
Filotimia [fe-lo-tee-me-ah], *f* (Littl us) A moderate desire of honour.
Filoxera [fe-loc-say'-rah], *f.* Phylloxera, an insect of the aphis family, terrible in the destruction it causes to vineyards.
Filtración [fil-trah-the-on'], *f* Filtration.
Filtrar [fil-trar'], *va.* 1. To filter, to filtrate, to defecate. 2. To filter, to strain, to excern.
Filtro [feel'-tro], *m.* 1. Filter, a piece of cloth, linen, or paper, through which liquids are strained. 2. Philter, a love-potion.
Fillo [feel'-lyo], *m.* (Obs.) Son. *Fillos.* Sort of fritters.
Fimbria [feem'-bre-ah], *f.* Edge or lower part of a garment doubled in.
Fimo [fee'-mo], *m.* Manure. *V.* Fiemo.
Fin [feen], *m.* 1. End, close, termination, conclusion, issue. 2. Limit, boundary. 3. End, object, purpose. 4. Goal, the end to which a design tends. *Al fin,* At last, at length, upon the main. *En fin* or *por fin,* Finally, lastly, in fine. *Dar fin,* To die. *Dar fin a alguna cosa,* To finish, to conclude a thing. *Dar fin de alguna cosa.* To destroy a thing completely. *A fin de,* In order that. *Por cualquier fin,* Prompted by any motive, or end.
Finado, da [fe-nah'-do, dah], *a.* & *pp.* of Finar. Dead, deceased. *Día de los finados,* All-Souls' Day.—*m.* & *f.* Person dead.
Final [fe-nahl'], *a.* Final, ultimate, conclusive.
Final [fe-nahl'], *m.* End, termination, conclusion *Por final,* In fine, ultimately, lastly.
Finalizar [fe-nah-le-thar'], *va.* To finish, to conclude.—*vn.* To be finished or concluded.
Finalmente [fe-nal-men'-tay], *adv* Finally, at last, in fine, ultimately, lastly.
Finamente [fe-nah-men-tay], *adv* Finely, nicely, delicately.
Finamiento [fe-nah-me-en'-to], *m.* Death, decease.
Financiamiento [fe-nan-the-ah-me-en'-to), *m.* Financing.
Financiar [fe-nan-the-ar'], *va.* To finance.
Financiero [fe-nan-the-ay-ro], *m.* & *a* Financer, financial.
Finar [fe-nar'], *vn* To die.—*vr* To long for.
Finca [feen-cah], *f.* Any kind of property, but especially land, which yields a regular income; tenement, building, house, real estate.
Fincable [fin-cah'-blay], *a.* (Obs.) *V.* Restante.
Fincar [fin-car'], *vn.* & *va* (Obs.) *V* Quedar and Hincar. 1. To buy real estate. 2. (Fig. Peru.) To lean on, have confidence in something.
Fin de semana [feen day say-mah-nah], *m.* Weekend
Finés, sa [fe-nays, sah], *a* Finnic, or Finnish, relating to the Finns.
Fineza [fe-nay'-thah], *f.* 1. Fineness, goodness, purity, perfection. 2. Kindness, expression of friendship or love. 3 (Obs.) Delicacy, beauty 4. Friendly activity and zeal. 5. A small, friendly gift. a favour.
Fingidamente [fin-he-dah-men-tay], *adv* Feignedly, fictitiously, counterfeitly.
Fingido, da [fin-hee-do, dah], *a.* Feigned, dissembled, false. *Dientes fingidos.* (Coll.) False or artificial teeth. *V* Postizo.—*pp* of Fingir.
Fingidor, ra [fin-he-dor', rah], *m* & *f* Dissembler, simulator, feigner.
Fingimiento [fin-he-me-en'-to], *m* Simulation, deceit, false appearance.
Fingir [fin-heer'], *va* 1. To feign, to dissemble, to counterfeit, to pretend, to affect. 2 To fancy, to imagine what does not really exist.
Finible [fe-nee'-blay], *a.* (Obs.) Capable of being finished.
Finiquitar [fe-ne-ke-tar'], *va.* To give a final receipt, close an account.
Finiquito [fe-ne-kee'-to], *m.* 1. Quittance, close of an account. 2. Final receipt or discharge.
Finítimo, ma [fe-nee'-te-mo, mah], *a.* Bordering, contiguous, near.
Finito, ta [fe-nee'-to, tah], *a* Finite, limited, bounded.
Finlandés, sa [fin-lan-days', sah], *a.* Of Finland, Finnish.—*n.* A Finn.
Fino, na [fee'-no, nah], *a.* 1. Fine, perfect, pure. 2. Delicate, nice. 3. Excellent, eminent in any good quality. 4. Affectionate, true. 5. Acute, sagacious, cunning. 6. Of polished education and choice manners.
Finojo, *m.* (Obs.) *V.* Rodilla.
Finta [feen'-tah], *f.* 1. A tax formerly paid to government. 2. Feint, a deceptive movement in fencing.
Finura [fe-noo'-rah], *f.* 1 Fineness, purity, delicacy. 2. In horsemanship, attention and obedience of a horse to the least wish of the rider.
Fiordo [fe-or'-do], *m.* Fiord or fjord.
Fique [fee'-kay], *m.* A filaceous substance, resembling hemp, made of the leaves of the maguey-tree. Agave americana, *L.*
Firma [feer'-mah], *f.* 1. Sign-manual, signature, subscription. 2. A commercial house and its firm-name. 3. (Law. Prov.) Order or rescript of a tribunal for keeping possession. *Media firma,* Surname, the name of the family. *Buena firma.* A house of standing, solvent.
Firmamento [fir-mah-men'-to], *m.* Firmament, sky, heaven. *V.* Empíreo
Firmán [fir-mahn'], *m.* Firman, a grant or license given by oriental potentates.
Firmante [fir-mahn-tay], *pa.* & *m.* & *f* Supporter, subscriber.
Firmar [fir-mar'], *va.* 1. To sign, to subscribe. 2. (Obs.) To affirm, to attest.—*vr.* To style one's self, to assume a title or appellation.
Firme [feer-may], *a.* 1. Firm, stable, strong, secure, fast, hard, compact. 2 Firm, unshaken, constant, consistent, resolute
Firmemente [fir-may-men-tay], *adv* 1. Firmly, strongly, unmovably. 2 Firmly, faithfully, steadily, constantly.
Firmeza [fir-may'-thah], *f* 1 Firmness, stability, hardness, compactness 2. Firmness, steadiness, constancy 3. Gold or silver clasp, ornament made of a precious stone in a triangular form
Fisalia [fe-sah'-le-ah], *f* (Zool.) Physalia, an acaleph; the Portuguese man of-war
Fiscal [fis-cahl'], *m* 1. Attorney-general, a ministerial officer, who acts for the government by which he is appointed, and who, *ex officio,* personates the king or the people. 2 *Fiscal* or *abogado fiscal,* A public attorney, a prosecutor 3. (Coll.) Censurer, critical.
Fiscal [fis-cahl'], *a* Fiscal, belonging to the exchequer
Fiscalear [fis-cah-lay-ar'], *va* (Coll.) To become a public accuser, to censure.
Fiscalía [fis-cah-lee-ah], *f.* Office and business of the magistrate called *fiscal*
Fiscalizar [fis-cah-le-thar'], *va.* To accuse of a criminal offence, to criticise, to censure.
Fisco [fees-co], *m* National treasury, exchequer.
Fiseter [fe-say-terr'], *m.* (Zool.) The small blunt-headed whale or cachalot. Physeter catodon, *L.*

Fisga [fees'-gah], *f.* 1. Harpoon with three hooks for catching large fish. 2. (Met.) Raillery, jest, scoff. *Hacer fisga de alguno*, To make fun of any one. 3. (Prov.) Wheat of the finest quality; bread of spelt-wheat.

Fisgador, ra [fis-gah-dor', rah], *m.* & *f.* Harpooner; one who burlesques. *V.* Fisgón.

Fisgar [fis-gar'], *va.* 1. To mock, to scoff, to jeer. 2. To fish with a harpoon. 3. To peep, to pry.

Fisgón, ona [fis-gone', nah], *a.* 1. Prying, peeping. 2. Jesting, mocking.—*m.* & *f.* 1. Busybody, Peeping Tom 2. Jester, buffoon.

Fisgonear [fis-go-nay-ar'], *va.* *V.* Fisgar.

Física [fee'-se-cah], *f.* Physics. *Física de altas energías*, High-energy physics. *Física de bajas temperaturas*, Low-temperature physics. *Física del estado sólido*, Solid state physics. *Física del plasma*, Plasma physics.

Físicamente [fee'-se-cah-men-tay], *adv.* Physically; corporeally; really.

Físico, ca [fee'-se-co, cah], *a.* 1. Physical, relating to nature or natural philosophy. 2. Natural, really existing.

Físico [fee'-se-co], *m* 1. Physicist. 2. Physique, constitution. 3. (coll.) Face, appearance.

Fisicoquímico, ca [fee-se-co-kee'-me-co, cah], *a.* Physicochemical.

Fisiografía [fe-se-o-grah-fee'-ah], *f.* Physiography, a description of nature.

Fisiográfico, ca [fe-se-o-grah'-fe-co, cah], *a.* Physiographic.

Fisiología [fe-se-o-lo-hee'-ah], *f.* Physiology, the science of vital phenomena.

Fisiológico, ca [fe-se-o-lo'-he-co, cah], *a.* Physiological.—*adv* **Fisiológicamente.**

Fisiologista [fe-se-o-lo-hees'-tah], *m.* Physiologist.

Fisiólogo [fe-se-o'-lo-go], *m.* Physiologist: used also as adjective.

Fisión [fe-se-on'], *f.* (Phy.) Fission. *Fisión nuclear*. Nuclear fission.

Fisionable [fe-se-o-nah'-blay], *a.* Fissionable.

Fisionomía [fe-se-o-no-mee'-ah]. *V.* Fisonomía. (Acad.)

Fisioterapia [fe-se-o-tay-rah'-pe-ah], *f.* Physiotherapy.

Fisonomía [fe-so-no-mee'-ah], *f.* 1. Physiognomy, lineaments, features. 2. Physiognomy, the art of discovering the temper and talents by the features of the face.

Fisonómico, ca [fe-so-no'-me-co, cah], *a.* Physiognomical.

Fisonomista, Fisónomo [fe-so-no-mees'-tah], *m.* Physiognomist.

Fistol [fis-tole'], *m.* 1. A crafty person, specially a gambler 2. (Mex.) A stickpin.

Fístola [fees'-to-lah] (Obs. and Amer.), *f.* 1. (Surg.) Fistula, a narrow channel not disposed to heal. 2. *V.* Fístula for a pipe. 3. *V* Cañafístula.

Fístula [fees'-too-lah], *f.* 1. Water-pipe or conduit. 2. Musical wind-instrument, resembling a flute or flageolet. 3. (Surg.) Fistula.

Fistular [fis-too-lar'], *a* (Med.) Fistular, fistulous.

Fistuloso, sa [fis-too-lo'-so, sah], *a.* Fistulous.

Fisura [fe-soo'-rah], *f.* 1. (Geol.) Fissure, cleft. 2. (Med.) Fissure, a shallow and narrow break of continuity. 3. Fissure, a longitudinal fracture of a bone.

Fitobiología [fe-to-be-o-lo-hee'-ah], *f.* Phytobiology, the branch of biology which treats of plants.

Fitogenesia [fe-to-hay-nay'-se-ah], *f.* Phytogenesis, the doctrine of the origin of plants.

Fitografía [fe-to-grah-fee'-ah], *f.* Phytography, plant geography; description of plant-life.

Fitología [fe-to-lo-hee'-ah], *f* Phytology, botany.

Fitonisa [fe-to-nee'-sah], *f.* *V.* Pitonisa.

Flabelación [flah-bay-lah-the-on'], *f.* Action of agitating the air to refresh it.

Flabelado, da [flah-bay-lah'-do, dah], *a.* 1. Like a fly-flap. 2. (Bot.) Fan-shaped.

Flacamente [flah-cah-men'-tay], *adv.* Languidly, weakly, feebly

Fláccido, da [flah'-the-do, dah], *a.* (Med.) Flaccid, limber, lax.

Flacidez [flah-the-deth'], *f.* (Med.) Flaccidity, laxity, limberness, want of tension

Flaco, ca [flah'-co, cah], *a.* 1 Lank, lean, meagre, flaccid. 2 Feeble, languid. 3. Dejected, low-spirited. 4. Frail, weak of resolution. *Flaco de memoria*, Weak or short of memory. *Hacer un flaco servicio*, To do or serve an ill turn.

Flacura [flah-coo'-rah], *f.* Meagreness, leanness, weakness.

Flagelación [flah-hay-lah-the-on'], *f.* Flagellation, scourging.

Flagelar [flah-hay-lar'], *va.* To lash, to scourge. *V.* Azotar.

Flagelo [flah-hay'-lo], *m.* 1. Lash, scourge, chastisement. 2. (Biol.) Flagellum, a lash-like locomotive appendage of certain infusoria; a large cilium 3. (Amer.) An epidemic.

Flagicio [flah-hee'-the-o], *m.* Flagitiousness, wickedness; an enormous crime.

Flagicioso, sa [flah-he-the-o'-so, sah], *a.* Flagitious, wicked.

Flagrante [flah-grahn'-tay], *a.* & *pa.* Flagrant, resplendent. *En flagrante*, In the very act.

Flagrar [flah-grar'], *vn.* (Poet.) To flagrate, to burn, to glow, to flame

Flajolé [flah-ho-lay'], *m.* Flagcolet, a beak-flute.

Flama [flah'-mah], *f.* 1. (Obs.) Flame, excessive ardour. 2. An ornament upon the upper part of caps, shakos, etc., in the army.

Flamante [flah-mahn'-tay], *a* 1. Flaming, bright, resplendent. 2. Quite new, spick and span.

Flamear [flah-may-ar'], *vn.* (Naut.) To shiver, to flutter: applied to sails.

Flamenco [flah-men'-co], *m.* (Orn.) Flamingo Phænicopterus ruber, *L.*

Flamenco, ca [flah-men'-co, cah], *a.* Flemish, relating to Flanders.

Flamenquilla [flah-men-keel'-lyah], *f.* (Prov.) 1. Dish of a middling size. 2. Marigold

Flámeo [flah'-may-o], *m.* A kind of yellow veil, with which the face of a bride was formerly covered during the marriage ceremony.

Flameo [flah-may'-o], *m.* Flapping or fluttering of banners, sails, etc.

Flamígero, ra [flah-mee'-hay-ro, rah], *a.* (Poet.) Flammiferous, emitting flames

Flamín [flah-meen'], *m* Flamen, a Roman priest.

Flámula [flah'-moo-lah], *f* 1 (Bot.) Sweet-scented virgin's bower. Clematis flammula, *L* 2. (Naut.) Streamer, pennon

Flan [flahn], *m.* A dessert like a custard.

Flanco [flahn'-co], *m.* 1. (Fort.) Flank, flanker the part of a bastion which reaches from the curtain to the face. 2. (Mil.) Flank of an army. 3 (Naut.) Side of a ship.

Flandes [flahn'-des], *m.* *Es un flandes*, (Obs. Coll.) It is a most valuable thing.

Flanela [flah-nay'-lah], *f.* Flannel.

Flanquear [flan-kay-ar'], *va.* (Fort.) To flank; to defend by lateral fortifications.

Flanqueo [flan-kay'-o], *m* A flank attack.

Flaón [flah-on'], *m.* 1. A custard. 2. Piece of gold or silver ready to be coined.

Flaquear [flah-kay-ar'], *vn.* 1 To flag, to grow feeble, to lose vigour. 2. To grow spiritless or dejected, to be disheartened. 3. To slacken in the ardour with which an enterprise was commenced.

Flaqueza [flah-kay'-thah], *f.* 1. Leanness, extenuation of the body, want of flesh, meagreness, lankness. 2. Feebleness, faintness, languishment. 3. Weakness, frailty, foible. 4. Importunity, molestation.

Flato [flah'-to], *m.* 1. Flatus, wind gathered in a cavity of the body 2. (Littl. us.) Gust of wind.

Flatoso, Flatuoso, sa [flah-to'-so, flah too-o'-so, sah], *a.* Flatuous, windy; full of wind.

Flatulencia [flah-too-len'-the-ah], *f* Flatulency.

Flatulento, ta [flah-too-len'-to, tah], *a.* Flatulent, turgid with air, windy

Flauta [flah'-oo-tah], *f.* A flute.

Flautado, da [flah-oo-tah'-do, dah], *a.* Resembling a flute.

Flautado, *m.* Stop in an organ, which produces the sound of a flute.

Flautero [flah-oo-tay'-ro], *m.* 1 One who makes flutes. 2. (Littl. us.) Player on the flute.

Flautillo [flah-oo-teel'-lyo], *m.* *V* Caramillo.

Flautín [flah-oo-teen'], *m.* Octave flute, piccolo, a small flute of high pitch.

Flautista [flah-oo-tees'-tah], *m.* Player of the flute.

Flautos [flah'-oo-tos], *m. pl.* *Cuando pitos flautos, cuando flautos pitos*, A jocular expression, signifying that things have happened contrary to our wishes, or what they should be.

Flavo, va [flah'-vo, vah], *a.* Of a fallow or honey colour

Flébil [flay'-beel], *a.* Mournful, deplorable, lamentable.

Flebolito [flay-bo-lee'-to], *m.* Phlebolith, a concretion formed in a vein: vein-stone.

Flebotomía [flay-bo-to-mee'-ah], *f* Phlebotomy, blood-letting.

Flebotomiano [flay-bo-to-me-ah'-no], *m.* Phlebotomist, one who lets blood for medical purposes

Flebotomista, *m.* *V* Flebotomiano

Flebotomizar [flay-bo-to-me-thar'], *va* To bleed, to let blood.

Flebótomo [flay-bo'-to-mo], *m* *V* Flebotomiano

Fleco [flay'-co], *m.* 1. Fringe, an ornamental appendage to dress and furniture. 2. Flounce.

Flecha [flay'-chah], *f* 1 Arrow, dart 2. A sign which serves to indicate the north, or the current of rivers, upon a map. 3 (Fort.) A work of two faces and two sides. 4. (Naut.) Front piece of the cutwater 5. The principal piece of those which compose the beakhead of a galley or xebec. 6. (Min.) Variety of hydroxide of iron called "love's dart." 7. Sagitta, a northern constellation *Entrar de flecha*, To enter swiftly, without obstacle.

Flechador [flay-chah-dor'], *m.* Archer.

Flechaduras [flay-chah-doo-ras'], *f. pl.* (Naut.) Ratlines. *V.* FLECHASTES.

Flechar [flay-char'], *va.* 1. To dart, to shoot an arrow or dart. 2. To wound or kill with a bow and arrow. 3. (Prov. Mex.) To point out, without fear, in gambling.—*vn.* To have a bow drawn ready to shoot.

Flechaste [flay-chas'-tay], *m.* (Naut.) Ratline.

Flechazo [flay-chah'-tho], *m.* Blow or stroke given with a dart or arrow.

Flechera [flay-chay'-rah], *f.* (S. Am.) A long, narrow, sharp canoe.

Flechería [flay-chay-ree'-ah], *f.* A number of darts or arrows darted at a time; shower of arrows.

Flechero [flay-chay'-ro], *m.* 1. Archer, bowman. 2. Fletcher, an arrow-maker.

Flegmasía [fleg-mah-see'-ah], *f.* Inflammation, phlegmasia.

Fleje [flay'-hay], *m.* Hoop. *Flejes para aros,* Hoop-poles. *Flejes de hierro* or *fierro,* Iron hoops. *Flejes,* Twigs for barrels.

Flema [flay'-mah], *f.* 1. Phlegm, watery humour of the body. 2. Phlegm, thick spittle ejected from the mouth. 3. Phlegm, coolness, dulness, sluggishness.

Flemático, ca [flay-mah'-te-co, cah], *a.* 1. Phlegmatic, generating phlegm; abounding in phlegm. 2. Phlegmatic, dull, cold, sluggish.

Fleme [flay'-may], *f.* Fleam, an instrument used to bleed cattle.

Flemón [flay-mone'], *m.* 1. Phlegmon, an inflammation of the cellular tissue. 2. A gum-boil, a tumour of the gum ending in suppuration.

Flemoso, sa [flay-mo'-so, sah], *a.* Mucous, consisting of phlegm.

Flemudo, da [flay-moo'-do, dah], *a.* (Prov.) Dull, sluggish, cold, frigid.

Flerecín [flay-ray-theen'], *m.* (Med.) Gout.

Flet, Flez [flet, fleth], *m.* (Zool.) Halibut. Pleuronectes hippoglossus, *L.*

Fletador [flay-tah-dor'], *m.* Freighter, charterer of a ship.

Fletamento [flay-tah-men'-to], *m.* Freightment, the act of freighting a ship; chartering. *Cerrar el fletamento,* To charter, to make out the charter-party. *Fletar redondo,* Out and home freight.

Fletante [flay-tahn'-tay], *m.* 1. Shipowner. 2. Shipper.

Fletar [flay-tar'], *va.* To freight a ship, to charter.

Flete [flay'-tay], *m.* Freight. *Flete aéreo,* Airfreight.

Flexibilidad [flec-se-be-le-dahd'], *f.* 1. Flexibility, pliableness, ductility, flexibleness. 2. Flexibility, easiness to be persuaded, ductility of mind, manageableness, obsequiousness, mildness of temper.

Flexible [flec-see'-blay], *a.* 1. Flexible, ductile, pliant, possible to be bent. 2. Flexible, manageable, docile.

Flexión [flec-se-on'], *f.* Flexion, flexure, act of bending.

Flexor [flec-sor'], *a.* Flexor, used of the muscles which bend a joint.

Flexuoso, sa [flec-soo-o'-so, sah], *a.* (Bot.) Flexuose, changing its direction in a curve from joint to joint or from bud to bud in the stem, or from flower to flower in the peduncle.

Flibote [fle-bo'-tay], *m.* Fly-boat, a small fast-sailing vessel.

Flictena [flic-tay'-nah], *f.* (Med.) Phlyctena, a small blister, or vesicle, filled with a serous or watery fluid.

Flin [fleen'], *m.* Stone used for edging and polishing steel; a kind of emery

Flinflón [flin-flon'], *m.* A fresh-coloured, corpulent man.

Flocadura [flo-cah-doo'-rah], *f.* A trimming made with fringes as an ornament of dress.

Flogosis [flo-go'-sis], *f.* Inflammation, phlegmasia.

Flojamente [flo-hah-men'-tay], *adv.* Slowly, carelessly, laxly.

Flojear [flo-hay-ar'], *vn.* To slacken, to grow weak. *V.* FLAQUEAR.

Flojedad [flo-hay-dahd'], *f.* 1. Weakness, feebleness, laxity. 2. Sloth, laziness, negligence, slackness.

Flojel [flo-hel'], *m.* 1. Wool shorn from cloth by the shearer. 2. Down, soft feathers.

Flojera [flo-hay'-rah], *f.* (Coll.) Weakness. *V.* FLOJEDAD.

Flojo, ja [flo'-ho, hah], *a.* 1. Flexible, lax, slack. *Vino flojo,* Flaggy, insipid wine. *Seda floja,* Soft, untwisted silk. 2. Feeble, weak, flaccid. 3. Slack, remiss, lazy, slothful, negligent, cold, cool, spiritless.

Floqueado, da [flo-kay-ah'-do, dah], *a.* Fringed.

Floquecillo [flo-kay-theel'-lyo], *m. dim.* A small fringe.

Flor [flor'], *f.* 1. Flower, that part of a plant which contains the organs of generation; a blossom. 2. The down of fruits newly gathered. 3. Flower, prime, the most excellent or valuable part of a thing; bloom. 4. Cuticle or thin skin formed on the surface of liquors. 5. (Chem.) Flos, the most subtile part of minerals separated in sublimation. 6. Virginity, maidenhood. 7. The face or surface of the earth. 8. Smart or witty saying: commonly used in plural. 9. Grain, the outside of tanned leather. 10. Trick or artifice among gamesters or gamblers. 11. Flowers or beauties of polite literature, flowers or figures of rhetoric. 12. (Obs.) Catamenia. *Flor de la edad,* Youth, bloom of youth. *Flor de la harina,* Superfine flour. *Flor de especia* or *de nuez de especia,* Mace. *Flor de canela,* Cassia buds. *Flor de oblón,* Hops. *Flor de cobre,* Verdigris. *Flor del cuclillo,* (Bot.) Ragged-robbin lychnis. Lychnis flos cuculi, L. *Flor de la miel,* (Bot.) Great honey-flower. Melianthus major, *L. Flor de lis,* 1. Flower-de-luce. 2. (Bot.) Jacobea lily, amaryllis. Amaryllis formosissima, *L. Flor del sol,* (Bot.) *V.* CORONA REAL. *Flor del tablero,* Checkered fritillary. Fritilaria meleagris, *L. Á flor de agua,* (Naut.) Between wind and water. *A la flor del agua,* Even with the surface of the water. *Flor de viento,* (Naut.) Point of the compass. *Flores de mano,* Artificial flowers. *En flor,* In a state of infancy, imperfect, in blossom, in flower. *Andarse en flores,* To decline entering into a debate. *Tener por flor, tomar la flor,* or *dar en la flor,* To fall into a habit or custom, generally of a bad kind. *En la flor de su edad,* (Met.) In his bloom.

Flora [flo'-rah], *f.* (Bot.) Flora, the description of the plants of some district, region, etc.

Florada [flo-rah'-dah], *f.* (Prov.) The season of flowers with bee-masters.

Florales [flo-rah'-les], *a. pl.* Floral; feasts in honour of Flora.

Florar [flo-rar'], *vn.* To flower. (Acad.)

Flordelisado, da [flor-day-le-sah'-do, dah], *a.* Adorned with iris: applied to crosses in heraldry.—*pp.* of FLORDELISAR.

Floreado, da [flo-ray-ah'-do, dah], *a.* & *pp.* of FLOREAR. 1. Flowered. 2. Applied to things made of the finest flour or meal. *Pan floreado,* Bread made of the finest flour. *Rasos, sedas, u otros efectos* or *géneros floreados,* Silks, or any other figured goods.

Florear [flo-ray-ar'], *va.* 1. To adorn with flowers. 2. To flourish a sword. 3. (Mus.) To flourish, to play the guitar without rule. 4. (Amer.) *V.* FLORAR. *Florar del naipe,* (Coll.) Not to play fair, to cheat at play.

Florecer [flo-ray-therr'], *vn.* 1. To flower, to bloom, to blossom. 2. To flourish, to thrive, to prosper. 3. To flourish in any age.—*vr.* To mould, to become mouldy.

Florecica [flo-ray-thee'-cah], *f. dim.* Floweret.

Floreciente [flo-ray-the-en'-tay], *pa.* & *a.* Flourishing, blossoming, flowery.

Florecilla, ita [flo-ray-theel'-lyah, ee'-tah], *f.* 1. (Dim.) A small flower. 2. (Bot.) The partial or separate little flower of an aggregate flower.

Florentina, *f.* **Florentín,** *m.* [flo-ren-tee'-nah, flo-ren-teen']. A silk stuff first manufactured at Florence; florentines.

Floreo [flo-ray'-o], *m.* 1. Flourish made by fencers before they engage. 2. Flourish on the guitar. 3. A luxuriant redundancy of words. 4. Cross caper, a movement in dancing. 5. Idle pastime.

Florera [flo-ray'-rah], *f.* Flower girl, female flower vendor.

Florero [flo-ray'-ro], *m.* 1. Flower-pot. 2. One who makes or deals in artificial flowers. 3. Painting representing flowers. 4. Case destined for artificial flowers. 5. One who makes use of florid, empty language. 6. A chaplet of flowers.

Florescencia [flo-res-then'-the-ah], *f.* 1. (Bot.) Florescence or the flowering season. 2. Efflorescence, manner of flowering.

Floresta [flo-res'-tah], *f.* 1. Forest, shrubbery, thicket. 2. A delightful, rural place. 3. Collection of fine things pleasing to the taste; beauties.

Florestero [flo-res-tay'-ro], *m.* Forester, keeper of a forest.

Floreta [flo-ray'-tah], *f.* 1. Border of morocco leather on the edge of a girth. 2. In paper mills, pile, heap.

Florete [flo-ray'-tay], *m.* Foil, floret, a blunt sword used in learning to fence.

Florete [flo-ray'-tay], *a.* Very white and fine: applied to paper.

Floretear [flo-ray-tay-ar'], *va.* To garnish with flowers.

Floricultura [flo-re-cool-too'-rah], *f.* Floriculture, cultivation of flowers.

Floridamente [flo-re-dah-men'-tay], *adv.* Elegantly, floridly, flourishingly.

Florideas [flo-ree'-day-as], *f. pl.* Florideæ, a very large class of marine algæ, purple and red. The colour is enhanced upon drying.

Floridez [flo-re-deth'], *f.* Floridity floridness.

Florido, da [flo-ree'-do, dah], *a.* 1. Florid, flowery; full of flowers. 2. Choice, elegant, select. *Día florido,* (Obs.) A clear, cheerful day. *Dinero florido,* Money which has been easily earned.

Florífero, ra [flo-ree'-fay-ro, rah], *a.* Floriferous, bearing flowers.

Florilegio [flo-re-lay'-he-o], *m.* Florilegium, anthology, select writings.

Florín [flo-reen'], *m.* Florin, a silver coin, used elsewhere in Europe, but no longer in Spain.

Floripondio, Floripundio [flo-re-pon'-de-o, flo-re-poon'-de-o], *m.* 1. Magnolia, a tree of great beauty, with very large white fragrant flowers. 2. (Bot.) Floripondium, smooth-stalked brugmansia. Brugmansia candida.

Florisado, da [flo-re-sah'-do, dah], *a.* V. FLORDELISADO.
Florista [flo-rees'-tah], *com.* 1. Florist. 2. One who makes or deals in artificial flowers.
Florón [flo-rone'], *m.* 1. (Aug.) A large flower. 2. Flower-work, an ornament resembling a large flower.
Flósculo [flos'-coo-lo], *m.* (Bot.) The separate little flower of an aggregate one; floscule, floret.
Flosculoso, sa [flos-coo-lo'-so, sah], *a.* (Bot.) Flosculous, composed of flowers or florets.
Flota [flo'-tah], *f.* 1. (Naut.) Fleet of merchant ships. 2. Fleet, squadron. Nowadays the term *escuadra* or *armada* is used.
Flotable [flo-tah'-blay], *a.* 1. Capable of floating. 2. A navigable river. (Acad.)
Flotación [flo-tah-the-on'], *f.* 1. Floating, the act of floating. 2. Friction, rubbing. 3. (Min.) Flotation. *Línea de flotación*, (Naut.) Water-line.
Flotador, ra [flo-tah-dor', rah], *a.* Floating.—*m.* 1. Float. 2. (Aer.) Pontoon.
Flotamiento [flo-tah-me-en'-to], *m.* Stroking, gentle friction.
Flotante [flo-tahn'-tay], *pa.* & *a.* 1. Floating, floaty. 2. (Bot.) Rooted upon the bottom of a stream and whose leaves follow the course of the current.
Flotar [flo-tar'], *vn.* To float.—*va.* (Ant.) To stroke, to rub gently.
Flote [flo-tay'], *m.* V. FLOTADURA. *A flote*, Afloat; (fig.) escaping happily.
Flotilla [flo-teel'-lyah], *f.* 1. Flotilla, a number of small vessels. 2. (Dim.) A small fleet.
Flox [flox], *m.* (Bot.) Phlox.
Fluatado, da [floo-ah-tah'-do, dah], *a.* Fluorid, fluorate.
Fluato [floo-ah'-to], *m.* Fluorate, compound of hydrofluoric acid.
Fluctuación [flooc-too-ah-the-on'], *f.* 1. Fluctuation, motion of the waves. 2. Fluctuation, uncertainty, indetermination, irresolution. 3. (Med.) Fluctuation.
Fluctuamiento, *m.* V. FLUCTUACIÓN.
Fluctuante [flooc-too-ahn'-tay], *pa.* & *a.* Fluctuating, fluctuant.
Fluctuar [flooc-too-ar'], *vn.* 1. To fluctuate, to float backward and forward, to oscillate. 2. To be in danger of being lost or destroyed. 3. To fluctuate, to hesitate, to be irresolute, to vacillate. 4. To fluctuate, to be in an uncertain state.
Fluctícola [flooc-tee'-co-lah], *a.* (Zool.) Inhabiting the waters.
Fluctígena [flooc-tee'-hay-nah], *a.* (Zool.) Born on the water.
Fluctuoso, sa [flooc-too-o'-so, sah], *a.* Fluctuant, wavering.
Fluente [floo-en'-tay], *pa.* & *a.* Fluent, flowing.
Fluidez [floo-e-deth'], *f.* Fluidity, liquidity. *Fluidez de estilo*, Fluency.
Fluidificable [floo-e-de-fe-cah'-blay], *a.* Liquefiable.
Fluidificación [floo-e-de-fe-cah-the-on'], *f.* Liquefaction, rendering fluid.
Fluidificar [floo-e-de-fe-car'], *va.* & *vr.* To convert into fluid, to liquefy.
Fluido, da [floo-ee'-do, dah], *a.* 1. Fluid, not solid. 2. (Met.) Fluent: applied to style.—*pp.* of FLUIR.
Fluido, *m.* 1. Fluid, not solid. 2. (Med.) Fluid, any animal juice.
Fluir [floo-eer'], *vn.* To flow, as water.
Flujo [floo'-ho], *m.* 1. Flux, the motion of liquids. 2. (Med.) Flux, an extraordinary evacuation of humours. 3. Flowing, hæmorrhage. 4. (Naut.) Flow, rising tide. 5. (Chem.) Flux, a substance aiding the fusion of another substance. *Flujo de palabras*, Flow of words, volubility. *Flujo de risa*, Fit of laughter. *Flujo de reir*, Habit of laughing. *Flujo de sangre*, Hæmorrhage. *Flujo de vientre*, Diarrhœa.
Fluor [floo'-or], *m.* Fluorine, a gaseous element.
Fluorescencia [floo-o-res-then'-the-ah], *f.* Fluorescence.
Fluorhídrico, ca [floo-o-ree'-dre-co, cah], *a.* Fluorhydric, hydrofluoric.
Fluórico, ca [floo-o'-re-co, cah], *a.* (Chem.) Fluoric, containing fluorine.
Fluorita, Fluorina [floo-o-ree'-tah, floo-o-ree'-nah], *f.* Fluor(-spar), fluorite.
Fluoroscopio [floo-o-ros-co'-pe-o], *m.* Fluoroscope.
Fluoruración [floo-o-roo-rah-the-on'], *f.* Fluoridation.
Fluvial [floo-ve-ahl'], *a.* Fluvial, pertaining to rivers. *Navegación fluvial*, river navigation.
Flux [floocs], *m.* Flush, a run of cards of the same suit. *Hacer flux*, (Coll.) To spend one's whole fortune without paying a debt.
Fluxión [flooc-se-on'], *f.* 1. A flowing of the humours to some part of the body. 2. (Amer.) A cold, catarrh. 3. (Mex.) A very painful toothache.
Fo. The Chinese name of Buddha.
Foca [fo'-cah], *f.* The fur-bearing seal. Phoca.
Focal [fo-cahl'], *a.* Focal.
Foco [fo'-co], *m.* 1. Focus, the point of convergence. 2. The principal spot where an insurrection has broken out. 3. Centre of action, origin, source. 4. The seat of a purulent process; core or centre of an abscess. 5. (Mil.) Touch-hole of a gun. 6. The focus of an ellipse. 7. (Chem.) Fire-box, furnace; place for combustibles.
Fóculo [fo'-coo-lo], *m.* A small fire-place.
Focha [fo'-chah], *f.* (Zool.) Rail; mud-hen.
Fodolí [fo-do-lee'], *a.* Meddlesome, intrusive.
Fofo, fa [fo'-fo, fah], *a.* Spongy, soft, bland.
Fogaje [fo-gah'-hay], *m.* Hearth-money, a tax formerly laid on houses in Spain.
Fogaril [fo-gah-reel'], *m.* Combustibles which serve for signal lights. (Generally used in the plural.)
Fogata [fo-gah'-tah], *f.* 1. Blaze, the light of a flame. 2. A small mine under some attackable point.
Fogón [fo-gone'], *m.* 1. Hearth, the fireside. 2. Vent or touch-hole of a gun. 3. (Naut.) Caboose, a cooking-stove for a ship. 4. (Naut.) Galley, cook-room, the kitchen in ships.
Fogonadura [fo-go-nah-doo'-rah], *f.* (Naut.) Partner, piece of timber round the holes into which masts are set.
Fogonazo [fo-go-nah'-tho], *m.* Flame of the priming of a gun, a flash in the pan.
Fogonero [fo-go-nay'-ro], *m.* Fireman, stoker.
Fogosidad [fo-go-se-dahd'], *f.* Excessive vivacity, fieriness, heat of temper.
Fogoso, sa [fo-go'-so, sah], *a.* 1. Fiery, vehement, ardent. 2. Fervent, hot in temper; ardent in love, warm in zeal, impetuous, lively, choleric. 3. (Obs.) Fiery, ardent, burning.
Fogote [fo-go'-tay], *m.* A live coal, fagot, match.
Fogueación [foo-gay-ah-the-on'], *f.* Enumeration of hearths or fires.
Foguear [fo-gay-ar'], *va.* 1. To habituate persons or horses to the discharge of fire-arms. 2. To cleanse fire-arms with a charge of gunpowder.
Foja [fo'-hah], *f.* 1. (For.) A sheet of paper. (Obs. V. HOJA.) 2. (Orn.) Coot or common coot. Fulica atra, *L.*
Fole [fo'-lay], *m.* A leather bag, especially of the Galician bagpipe.
Folgo [fol'-go], *m.* Foot-warmer, bag of skin to cover the feet and legs when sitting.
Folía [fo-lee'-ah], *f.* (Obs.) Folly, madness. *Folías*, Kind of merry dance with castanets.
Foliáceo [fo-le-ah'-thay-o], *a.* (Bot.) Foliaceous.
Foliación [fo-le-ah-the-on'], *f.* 1. Numbering the pages of a book. 2. The numeration of the pages of a book. 3. (Bot.) Foliation.
Foliar [fo-le-ar'], *va.* To page, to number the leaves of a book.
Foliatura [fo-le-ah-too'-rah], *f.* 1. Numbering the pages of a book. 2. Numeration of the pages of a book.
Folículo [fo-lee'-coo-lo], *m.* 1. (Bot.) Follicle, a seed-vessel or pericarp. *Folículos de sen*, Senna pods. 2. (Anat.) Follicle, a membraneous sac.
Folijones [fo-le-ho'-nes], *m. pl.* Castilian dance to the guitar and castanets.
Folio [fo'-le-o], *m.* Folio, leaf of a book. *Libro en folio*, A folio. *De a folio*, Jocularly applied to any thing too bulky. *Al primer folio*, At first sight. *Folio índico*, Indian leaf.
Folión [fo-le-on'], *m.* (Prov.) In Galicia, fire-works on the eve of public festivities.
Folklore [foc-lor'], *m.* Folklore.
Folla [fol'-lyah], *f.* 1. An irregular conflict in a tournament. 2. Medley of a variety of things confusedly jumbled together; olio.
Follada [fol-lyah'-dah], *f.* Sort of hollow paste.
Follados [fol-lyah'-dos], *m. pl.* Ancient kind of trousers.
Follaje [fol-lyah'-hay], *m.* 1. Foliage. 2. Leafiness; leafage. 3. Gaudy ornament of trifling value.
Follar [fol-lyar'], *va.* 1. To blow with bellows. 2. To form in leaves.—*vr.* (Coll.) To discharge wind without noise.
Follero [fol-lyay'-ro], *m.* One who makes or sells bellows.
Folleta [fol-lyay'-tah], *f.* Wine measure nearly equal to an English pint.
Folletín [fol-lyay-teen'], *m.* The story, novel, etc., inserted in many periodicals at the lower part of the page, separated by a line from the remaining matter.
Folletinista [fol-lyay-te-nees'-tah], *m.* One who edits *folletines*.
Folletista [fol-lyay-tees'-tah], *m.* Pamphleteer, a writer of pamphlets.
Folleto [fol-lyay'-to], *m.* 1. A pamphlet. 2. (Obs.) A small manuscript newspaper.
Follón, na [fol-lyone', nah], *a.* Feeble, inert, lazy, negligent, mean.
Follón [fol-lyone'], *m.* 1. Rogue, villain, a mean, despicable fellow. 2. Rocket which discharges without noise. 3. Bud or branch from the root or trunk of a tree. 4. Breaking wind without noise.
Follonería [fol-yo-nay-ree'-ah], *f.* Knavishness.
Foma [fo'-mah], *f.* (Bot.) A fungus growing generally in small tubercles upon branches or leaves of plants.
Fomentación [fo-men-tah-the-on'], *f.* Fomentation.
Fomentador, ra [fo-men-tah-dor', rah] *m.* & *f.* Fomenter.

Fomentar [fo-men-tar'], *va.* 1. To foment, to produce warmth by fomentation. 2. (Met.) To foment, to protect, to favour, to patronize, to countenance, to encourage.
Fomento [fo-men'-to], *m.* 1. Fomentation. 2. Fuel. 3. Patronage, protection, support, encouragement.
Fomes [fo'-mes], *m.* 1. Incentive, generally applied to that which excites to sin. 2. Lust, concupiscence.
Fonación [fo-nah-the-on'], *f.* 1. Phonation, emission of the voice. 2. Pronunciation.
Fonas [fo'-nas], *f. pl.* Pieces sewed to a cloak.
Fonda [fon'-dah], *f.* Hotel, inn, tavern, lodging-house.
Fondable [fon-dah'-blay], *a.* That may be sounded with a plummet.
Fondado, da [fon-dah'-do, dah], *a.* Applied to pipes or barrels, the bottoms of which are secured with cords or nails.
Fondeadero [fon-day-ah-day'-ro], *m.* (Naut.) Anchoring-ground.
Fondear [fon-day-ar'], *va.* 1. To sound, to explore the depth of water. 2. To bring up from the bottom of water. 3. (Naut.) To search a ship for prohibited goods. 4. To examine closely. —*vn.* (Naut.) To cast anchor.
Fondeo [fon-day'-o], *m.* The act of searching a ship.
Fondillón [fon-deel-lyone'], *m.* 1. The dregs and lees at the bottom of a cask of liquor. 2. Rancid Alicant wine.
Fondillos [fon-deel'-lyos], *m. pl.* The seat of drawers or wide trousers. (Acad.)
Fondista [fon-dees'-tah], *m.* Innkeeper, hotel-keeper, tavern-keeper.
Fondo [fon'-do], *m.* 1. Bottom of a hollow thing. 2. Bottom, the ground under the water. 3. Bottom of a hill or valley. 4. Ground of silks and other stuffs. 5. Plain or cut velvet. 6. Thickness of a diamond. 7. Bottom, the extent of a man's capacity. *Hombre de fondo,* A man of great talents and abilities. 8. The principal or essential part of a thing. 9. Stock, quantity, store: applied to virtues, vices, etc. 10. Stock, fund, capital, effects. *Fondos públicos,* State securities. 11. Every hollow to be gilded. 12. (Mil.) Space occupied by files of soldiers. *Dar fondo,* (Naut.) To cast anchor. *Dar fondo con codera sobre el ancla,* (Naut.) To anchor with a spring on the cable. *Dar fondo con reguera,* (Naut.) To anchor by the stem. *Echar a fondo,* To sink a vessel. *Irse a fondo,* To go to the bottom, to founder. *A fondo,* Perfectly, completely. *Fondos vitalicios,* Life-annuities. *Fondos de un navío,* (Naut.) The floor or flat of a ship. *Fondos,* Heads of casks. *A fondo,* Deeply. *El fondo,* The background.
Fondón [fon-done'], *m.* 1. *V.* Fondillón. 2. Ground of silk or velvet. *De fondón,* (Obs.) Razed to the foundation; deeply.
Fondona [fon-do'-nah], *a.* Old and ungraceful; (applied to a woman).
Fondura [fon-doo'-rah], *f.* Profundity, depth.
Fonética [fo-nay'-te-cah], *f.* Phonetics.
Fonético, ca [fo-nay'-te-co, cah], *a.* Phonetic, relating to, or representing sounds.
Fónica [fo'-ne-cah], *f.* Phonics, the science of articulate sound.
Fónico, ca [fo'-ne-co, cah], *a.* Phonic, relating to sound; phonetic. (Arch.) An elliptic arch for repeating echoes; the foci are called phonic, and there are placed the speaker and the listener. A whispering gallery.
Fonil [fo-neel'], *m.* (Naut.) Funnel, an instrument for filling hogsheads of water.
Fonje [fon'-hay], *a.* Bland, soft, spongy.
Fonocaptor [fo-no-cap-tor'], *m.* Pick-up of a phonograph.
Fonografía [fo-no-grah-fee'-ah], *f.* Phonography, representation of sound by signs: the chief mode of stenography.
Fonográfico, ca [fo-no-grah'-fe-co, cah], *a.* Phonographic, belonging to phonography.
Fonógrafo [fo-no'-grah-fo], *m.* Phonograph, an apparatus invented by Edison, for fixing and recording sounds.
Fonología [fo-no-lo-hee'-ah], *f.* Phonology, the science of the letters and pronunciation of a language.
Fontal [fon-tahl'], *a.* (Ant.) Main, chief, principal.
Fontana [fon-tah'-nah], *f.* (Poet.) Fountain.
Fontanal [fon-tah-nahl'], *m.* 1. Source or spring of water. 2. Place abounding in springs.—*a.* Belonging to a fountain.
Fontanar [fon-tah-nar'], *m.* A spring of water.
Fontanela [fon-tah-nay'-lah], *f.* Surgeon's instrument for opening issues.
Fontanería [fon-tah-nay-ree'-ah], *f.* 1. The art of conducting water through pipes to make fountains. 2. The collection of pipes and conduits through which water is conducted for a fountain.
Fontanero [fon-tah-nay'-ro], *m.* He that makes fountains, by conducting water through pipes and conduits.
Fontezuela [fon-tay-thoo-ay'-lah], *f. dim.* A small fountain.
Fontícola [fon-tee'-co-lah], or **Fontinal** [fon-te-nahl'], *a.* (Biol.) Living in fountains or on their borders.
Foque [fo'-kay], *m.* (Naut.) Jib. *Foque mayor* or *foque de caza,* The standing jib. *Foque segundo,* The fore-stay-sail. *Petifoque,* The fore-stay gallant-sail. *Botalón del foque,* Jib-boom. *Contra foque,* Standing-jib.
Forajido, da [fo-rah-hee'-do, dah], *a.* 1. Robbing in forests and woods. 2. Wicked, villainous: used as a substantive.
Foral [fo-rahl'], *a.* (Law) Belonging to the statute law of a country, or to the civil rights of its inhabitants. *Bienes forales,* Lands and tenements held by acknowledgment of superiority to a higher lord.
Foralmente [fo-ral-men'-tay], *adv.* In the manner of courts.
Foramen [fo-rah'-men], *m.* Hole in the under stone of a mill.
Foraminíferos [fo-rah-me-nee'-fay-ros], *m. pl.* Foraminifera, microscopic protozoa, having calcareous shells.
Foráneo, nea [fo-rah'-nay-o, ah], *a.* Stranger, foreign.
Forastería [fo-ras-tay-ree'-ah], *f.* Place for strangers, inn for strangers.
Forastero, ra [fo-ras-tay'-ro, rah], *a.* 1. Strange, not living in the town or place. 2. Exotic, not produced in the country.
Forastero, ra [fo-ras-tay'-ro, rah], *m.* & *f.* Stranger, guest: applied to persons belonging to another town, but of the same nation.
Forbante, *m.* *V.* Filibustero.
Forca [for'-cah], *f.* (Obs.) *V.* Horca and Horquilla.
Forcejar [for-thay-har'], or **Forcejear,** *vn.* 1. To struggle, to strive, to labour. 2. To strive, to contest, to contend to struggle in opposition.—*va.* (Obs.) *V.* Forzar.
Forcejo [for-thay'-ho], *m.* Struggling, striving, labouring in opposition.
Forcejón [for-thay-hone'], *m.* Push, effort to disengage one's self from another.
Forcejudo, da [for-thay-hoo'-do, dah], *a.* Strong, robust, of great strength.
Fórceps [for'-theps], *m.* Forceps, ordinary and surgical (or obstetrical).
Forcina [for-thee'-nah], *f.* 1. Swelling of a tree in the angle formed by a thick branch with the trunk. 2. (Obs.) Trident.
Forchina [for-chee'-nah], *f.* War-like instrument in shape of a fork.
Forense [fo-ren'-say], *a.* Forensic, belonging to the courts.
Forero, ra [fo-ray'-ro, rah], *a.* Conformable to the statute law of a country.
Forfícula [for-fee'-coo-lah], *f.* Earwig, an orthopterous insect. Forficula.
Forja [for'-hah], *f.* 1. Forge, the place where silver is beaten into form. 2. Forging, fabricating, manufacturing. 3. Mortar, a cement.
Forjable [for-hah'-blay], *a.* Forgeable.
Forjador [for-hah-dor'], *m.* Smith, gold-beater; framer, forger.
Forjadura [for-hah-doo'-rah], *f.* 1. Forging, beating a metal into form or shape. 2. Trap, snare, imposition. 3. Forgery; falsification.
Forjar [for-har'], *va.* 1. To forge, to hammer, to beat metal into form or shape. 2. To frame, to form or fabricate by orderly construction. 3. To forge, to counterfeit, to falsify. 4. To frame, to invent, to fabricate.
Forlón [for-lone'], *m.* Old kind of chaise with four seats.
Forma [for'-mah], *f.* 1. Form, shape, a figure abstractedly considered, frame, make, fashion. 2. Form, stated method, established practice, ritual, prescribed manner of doing something. 3. Hand, form or cast of writing. 4. Form, the essential modification of matter, by which it has existence. 5. Form, regularity, method, order. 6. Form, particular model or modification, mould, matrix. 7. (Print.) Form, a frame containing the pages arranged for press, as they appear on one side of a printed sheet. 8. The unleavened bread which serves for the communion of the laity. 9. Form, ceremony, external rights. *Forma de zapatero,* Shoemaker's last. *Forma para los quesos,* Cheese-vat, a wooden case in which curds are pressed into cheese. *De forma que,* In such a manner that. *En forma,* Truly, certainly; seriously, in earnest, gravely. *En forma* or *en debida forma,* Formally, according to law or established rules, legally. *En forma* or *en toda forma,* Perfectly, completely, carefully, heedfully, exactly. *Hombre de forma,* A man of merit and distinction; a grave man. *Dar forma,* To regulate or arrange that which was disordered. *Tener buenas formas*: 1. To be of fine figure, well-proportioned, especially said of women. 2. To be polite, affable and discreet in speech and action.
Formable [for-mah'-blay], *a.* That which may be formed.
Formación [for-mah-the-on'], *f.* 1. Formation, the act of forming or generating. 2. Formation, the manner in which any thing is formed; form, shape, figure. 3. (Mil.) Array of troops. 4. Twisted cord of silk, gold silver, etc., used by embroiderers.

Formador, ra [for-mah-dor', rah], *m.* & *f.* Former, one that forms, fashions, or shapes.

Formadura [for-mah-doo'-rah], *f.* (Obs.) Form, shape, figure.

Formaje [for mah'-hay], *m.* Cheese-vat; cheese. *Cf.* Fr. fromage.

Formal [for-mahl'], *a.* 1. Formal, regular, methodical. 2. Proper, genuine. 3. Formal, serious, grave, steady, sedate.

Formalidad [for-mah-le-dahd'], *f.* 1. Formality, the quality by which any thing is what it is. 2. Exactness, punctuality. 3. Formality, ceremony; established mode of behaviour. 4. Gravity, seriousness, solemnity. 5. Established form of judicial proceedings, or legal precedent. *Con formalidad*, In earnest.

Formalismo [for-mah-lees'-mo], *m.* 1. Formalism, a metaphysical system which denies the existence of matter and recognizes only the form. 2. Rigorous application of method, adhesion to routine; red tape.

Formalizar [for-mah-le-thar'], *va.* To form or make complete or perfect: applied to immaterial things.—*vr.* To grow formal, to affect gravity.

Formalmente [for-mal-men'-tay], *adv.* 1. Formally, according to established rules. 2. Formally, seriously.

Formar [for-mar'], *va.* 1. To form, to shape, to fashion, to frame, to make up, to cut out. 2. To form, to make out of materials. 3. To form, to model to a particular shape. 4. To form or draw up troops; to put in order; to arrange in a particular manner.—*vn.* To adjust the edges of embroidery work. *Formar concepto*, To form a judgment. *Formar queja*, To complain.

Formativo, va [for-mah-tee'-vo, vah], *a.* Formative.

Formatriz [for-mah-treeth'], *a.* Forming.

Formejar [for-may-har'], *va.* (Naut.) To arrange things in order on board of ships; to trim the hold.

Formero [for-may'-ro], *m.* (Arch.) Side arch of a vault.

Formicante [for-me-cahn'-tay], *a.* Applied to a low, weak, and frequent pulse.

Formicarios, Formícidos [for-me-cah'-re-os, for-mee'-the-dos], *m. pl.* (Ent.) Hymenoptera which carry a sting; bees, wasps, sand-wasps, etc.

Fórmico [for'-me-co], *m.* 1. Formic, (acid or ether). 2. A certain hard tumour like a wart.

Formicular [for-me-coo-lar'], *a.* Relating to ants.

Formidable [for-me-dah'-blay], *a.* 1. Formidable, dreadful, tremendous, terrific. 2. Uncommonly large.

Formidablemente [for-me-dah-blay-men'-tay], *adv.* Formidably.

Formidoloso, sa [for-me-do-lo'-so, sah], *a.* 1. Timorous, timid, fearful. 2. Dreadful, frightful, horrible.

Formillón [for-meel-lyon'], *m.* A hat-form.

Formón [for-mone'], *m.* 1. Paring chisel, used by carpenters and joiners. 2. Punch, an instrument used to cut wafers for consecration.

Fórmula [for'-moo-lah], *f.* 1. Formula, a prescribed model or rule. 2. Recipe. 3. An algebraical expression. 4. Profession of faith. 5. Formulary.

Formulario [for-moo-lah'-re-o], *m.* Formulary, a book containing models, rules, or formulas.

Formulista [for-moo-lees'-tah], *m.* One who punctually observes the prescribed models.

Fornáceo, cea [for-nah'-thay-o, ah], *a.* (Poet.) Belonging to or like a furnace.

Fornacino, na [for-nah-thee'-no, nah], *a.* (Obs.) 1. The false (ribs). 2. Belonging to bow-making.

Fornaz [for-nath'], *m.* (Poet.) *V.* FRAGUA.

Fornecer [for-nay-therr'], *va.* (Obs.) To furnish, to provide.

Fornecino, na [for-nay-thee'-no, nah], *a.* Bastard, illegitimate: formerly applied to children.

Fornelo [for-nay'-lo], *m.* A portable little oven or furnace.

Fornicación [for-ne-cah-the-on'], *f.* 1. Fornication. 2. In Scripture, sometimes idolatry.

Fornicador, ra [for-ne-cah-dor', rah], *m.* & *f.* Fornicator.

Fornicar [for-ne-car'], *va.* To fornicate, to commit lewdness.

Fornicario, ria [for-ne-cah'-re-o, ah], *a.* Relating to fornication.

Fornicio [for-nee'-the-o], *m.* (Ant.) Fornication.

Fornido, da [for-nee'-do, dah], *a.* Robust, corpulent, lusty, stout.

Fornitura [for-ne-too'-rah], *f.* 1. Leather straps worn by soldiers. 2. (Print.) Types cast to complete sorts.

Foro [fo'-ro], *m.* 1. Court of justice, the hall where tribunals hold their sittings. 2. Bar, the legal profession. 3. Lordship, the right of a superior lord, of whom lands or tenements are held. 4. Background of the stage or theatre. *Por tal foro*, On such conditions.

Forrado [for-rah'-do], *a.* & *pp.* of FORRAR. Lined. (Coll.) *Tonto forrado en lo mismo*, A fool inside and out, a thorough fool.

Forraje [for-rah'-hay], *m.* 1. Forage; grain, hay, or grass for horses; foraging. 2. (Coll.) Abundance of things of little value.

Forrajeador, Forrajero [for-rah-hay-ah-dor'], *m.* Forager, a soldier detached in search of forage; fodderer.

Forrajear [for-rah-hay-ar'], *va.* To forage, to collect forage for the horses of soldiers.

Forrar [for-rar'], *va.* To line, as clothes.

Forro [for'-ro], *m.* 1. Lining. 2. (Naut.) Furring of a ship, double planks laid on the sides, sheathing. 3. Cover of a book. *Forro de cabos*, (Naut.) Service, serving ropes, or covering them with spun-yarn or canvas. *Forro sobrepuesto de cable*, (Naut.) Keckling, rounding. *Forro interior de un navío*, Ceiling or foot-waling of a ship.

Fortachón, na [for-tah-chon', nah], *a.* Applied to a person possessed of uncommon strength.

Fortalecedor, ra [for-tah-lay-thay-dor', rah], *m.* & *f.* Fortifier.

Fortalecer [for-tah-lay-therr'], *va.* 1. To fortify, to strengthen, to corroborate. 2. To fortify a place. 3. To aid, to encourage, to support.

(*Yo fortalezco, yo fortalezca*, from *Fortalecer. V.* ABORRECER.)

Fortalecimiento [for-tah-lay-the-me-en'-to], *m.* 1. Act of fortifying. 2. Works raised for the defence of a place.

Fortaleza [for-tah-lay'-thah], *f.* 1. Fortitude, firmness. 2. Fortitude, valor, courage. 3. Strength, vigor, nerve, force, manhood. 4. Stronghold, fortress. *Fortaleza aérea*, Flying fortress.

Forte [for'-tay], *int.* (Naut.) Avast! —*a.* (Mus.) Loud.

Fortepiano [for-tay-pe-ah'-no], *m.* (Obs.) Pianoforte.

Fortezuelo, la [for-tay-thoo-ay'-lo, lah], *a. dim.* Not very strong.

Fortificable [for-te-fe-cah'-blay], *a.* Fortifiable.

Fortificación [for-te-fe-cah-the-on'], *f.* 1. Fortification, the science of military architecture. 2. Fortification, a place built for strength. 3. Works raised for the defence of a place. *Fortificación de campaña*, Field-fortification.

Fortificador [for-te-fe-cah-dor'], *m.* Fortifier.

Fortificante [for-te-fe-cahn'-tay], *pa.* Fortifying.

Fortificar [for-te-fe-car'], *va.* 1. To strengthen, to fortify, to corroborate, to invigorate. 2. To fortify a place.

Fortín [for-teen'], *m.* 1. (Dim.) Fortin, fortlet, a small fort. 2. Field or temporary fortifications for the defence of troops.

Fortuitamente [for-too-ee-tah-men'-tay], *adv.* Fortuitously.

Fortuito, ta [for-too-ee'-to, tah], *a.* Fortuitous, accidental, unexpected.

Fortuna [for-too'-nah], *f.* 1. Fortune, chance, fate. 2. Good luck, success. 3. Storm, tempest. 4. Chance, unforeseen event. *Fortuna de la Mancha*, Omelet of eggs and chopped bacon. *Moza de fortuna*, A girl of the town. *Probar fortuna*, To try one's fortune. *Al hombre osado la fortuna le da la mano*, (Prov.) Fortune favours the bold.

Fortunal [for-too-nahl'], *a.* (Obs.) Perilous, dangerous.

Fortuno, na, oso, sa [for-too'-no, nah], *a.* (Obs.) Tempestuous.

Fortunón [for-too-none'], *m.* (Aug.) Great fortune, immense riches.

Forzadamente [for-thah-dah-men'-tay], *adv.* Forcibly, violently, forcefully.

Forzado, da [for-thah'-do, dah], *a.* & *pp.* of FORZAR. 1. Forced, constrained, necessitated. 2. (Obs.) Indispensable, necessary. 3. (Obs.) Stormy, boisterous. *Tiempo forzado*, (Naut.) Stress of weather. *Correr un viento forzado*, (Naut.) To sail in a storm.

Forzado [for-thah'-do], *m.* Criminal sentenced to the galleys.

Forzador [for-thah-dor'], *m.* 1. Ravisher. 2. Forcer, one who commits acts of violence to attain some purpose.

Forzal [for-thahl'], *m.* The middle part of a comb between the two rows of teeth.

Forzamiento [for-thah-me-en'-to], *m.* The act of forcing.

Forzar [for-thar'], *va.* 1. To force, to overpower by strength, to draw or push by main strength. 2. To force, to compel, to constrain. 3. To enforce, to urge. 4. To subdue by force of arms. 5. To force, to ravish, to commit a rape. 6. To force, to oblige or enforce, to urge.

Forzosa [for-tho'-sah], *f.* 1. A decisive move at the game of draughts. 2. Necessity of acting against one's will. *Hacer la forzosa*, To compel one to act against his will.

Forzosamente [for tho-sah-men'-tay], *adv.* Forcibly, necessarily; violently, forcedly.

Forzoso, sa [for-tho'-so, sah], *a.* Indispensable, necessary, needful, requisite.

Forzudo, da [for-thoo'-do, dah], *a.* Strong, vigorous, potent, lusty, stout, able-bodied.

Fosa [fo'-sah], *f.* 1. Grave, tomb. 2. (Anat.) Fossa. *Fosa séptica*, Septic tank.

Fosar [fo-sar'], *va.* To make a pit, ditch, or foss round any thing.

Fosca [fos'-cah], *f.* (Prov.) A thick wood or grove.

Fosco, ca [fos'-co, cah], *a.* Brow beaten, frowning. *V.* Hosco.

Fosfático, ca [fos-fah'-te-co, cah], *a.* Phosphatic.

Fosfato [fos-fah'-to], *m.* Phosphate, a salt of phosphoric acid.

Fosfito [fos-fee'-to], *m.* Phosphite, a salt of phosphorous acid.

Fosforado, da [fos-fo-rah'-do, dah], *a.* Phosphated, containing phosphorus.

Fosforera [fos-fo-ray'-rah], *f.* A match-box.

Fosforero, ra [fos-fo-ray'-ro, rah], *m.* & *f.* A vender of matches.

Fosforescencia [fos-fo-res-then'-the-ah], *f.* Phosphorescence.

Fosforescente [fos-fo-res-then'-tay], *a.* Phosphorescent.

Fosforescer [fos-fo-res-therr'], *vn.* To be phosphorescent, to shed a phosphoric light.

Fosfórico, ca [fos-fo'-re-co, cah], *a.* Phosphoric.

Fósforo [fos'-fo-ro], *m.* 1. Phosphorus, one of the elements. 2. A friction match.

Fosforoso, sa [fos-fo-ro'-so, sah], *a.* Phosphorous, relating to the lower equivalents of phosphorus.

Fosfuro [fos-foo'-ro], *m.* Phosphide, a compound of phosphorus, not acid.

Fosgeno [fos-hay'-no], *m.* (Chem.) Phosgene.

Fósil [fo'-seel], *a.* Fossil, dug out of the earth, and mineral in nature.—*m.* Fossil, petrifaction, organic remains.

Fosilizarse [fo-se-le-thar'-say], *vr.* To become fossilized, petrified.

Foso [fo'-so], *m.* 1. Pit, hole dug in the ground. V. Hoyo. 2. Bog, a marshy ground covered with water. 3. Moat, ditch, fosse.

Fotocélula [fo-to-thay'-loo-lah], *f.* Electric eye.

Fotoeléctrico, ca [fo-to-ay-lec'-tre-co, cah], *a.* Photoelectric.

Fotofobia [fo-to-fo'-be-ah], *f.* Photophobia, dread of light (from disease).

Fotogénico, ca [fo-to-hay'-ne-co, cah], *a.* Photogenic, light-producing.

Fotograbado [fo-to-grah-bah'-do], *m.* A photo-engraving, photo-gravure.

Fotografía [fo-to-grah-fee'-ah], *f.* 1. Photography, the art of fixing an image by the chemical rays of light. 2. A photograph, the picture obtained by this process. *Fotografía aérea*, Aerial photography.

Fotografiar [fo-to-grah-fe-ar'], *va.* To photograph.

Fotográfico, ca [fo-to-grah'-fe-co, cah], *a.* Photographic, relative to photography.

Fotógrafo [fo-to'-grah-fo], *m.* Photographer.

Fotolitografía [fo-to-le-to-grah-fee'-ah], *f.* 1. Photolithography, the art of imprinting a photograph upon a lithographic stone. 2. Photolithograph, each of the prints obtained by this process.

Fotometría [fo-to-may-tree'-ah], *f.* Photometry.

Fotométrico, ca [fo-to-may'-tre-co, cah], *a.* Photometric, measuring light.

Fotómetro [fo-to'-may-tro], *m.* Photometer.

Fotosíntesis [fo-to-seen'-tay-sis], *f.* Photosynthesis.

Fotostático, ca [fo-tos-tah'-te-co, cah], *a.* Photostatic.

Fototipia [fo-to-tee'-pe-ah], *f.* Phototypy.

Fovila [fo-vee'-lah], *f.* (Bot.) Fovilla, a substance emitted from the pollen of flowers.

Foya [fo'-yah], *f.* (Prov.) An oven full of charcoal.

Frac [frahc], *m.* A dress-coat; a swallow-tailed coat.

Fracasar [frah-cah-sar'], *vn.* 1. To crumble, to break in pieces: applied commonly to ships. 2. To be lost or destroyed.

Fracaso [frah-cah'-so], *m.* 1. Downfall, ruin, destruction. 2. Calamity, an unfortunate event.

Fracción [frac-the-on'], *f.* 1. Fraction, the act of breaking into parts. 2. Fraction, a broken part of an integral.

Fraccionar [frac-the-o-nar'], *va.* To divide into fractions.

Fraccionario, ria [frac-the-o-nah'-re-o, ah], *a.* Fractional. *Número fraccionario*, A mixed number.

Fracmasón [frac-mah-son'], *m.* Freemason, mason.

Fractura [frac-too'-rah], *f.* 1. Fracture, breach, separation of contiguous parts. 2. (Surg.) Fracture, the separation of the continuity of a bone.

Fracturar [frac-too-rar'], *va.* To fracture, to break a bone.

Fraga, Fragaria [frah'-gah, frah-gah'-re-ah], *f.* Species of raspberry.

Fragancia [frah-gahn'-the-ah], *f.* 1. Fragrance, sweetness of smell. 2. Good name, repute for virtues. 3. Actual commission of a crime.

Fragante [frah-gahn'-tay], *a.* 1. Fragrant, odoriferous. 2. Flagrant, notorious. *En fragante*, In the act itself. *V.* Flagrante.

Fragata [frah-gah'-tah], *f.* 1. A frigate. *Fragata de aviso*, Packet-boat. *Fragata ligera*, A light fast-sailing vessel. 2. The frigate-bird. Fregata (minor).

Frágil [frah'-heel], *a.* 1. Brittle, tangible, fragile. 2. Frail, weak of resolution, liable to error or seduction. 3. Decaying, perishable.

Fragilidad [frah-he-le-dahd'], *f.* 1. Fragility, brittleness. 2. Fragility, frailty, liableness to a fault. 3. Sin of infirmity, sensual pleasure, folly.

Frágilmente [frah'-heel-men-tay], *adv.* Frailly.

Fragmento [frag-men'-to], *m.* 1. Fragment, a small part separated from the whole. 2. Fragment, a part of some book or writing.

Fragor [frah-gor'], *m.* (Archaic) Noise, clamour, crash.

Fragoroso, sa, *a.* (Poet.) Noisy, obstreperous.

Fragosidad [frah-go-se-dahd'], *f.* Unevenness or roughness of the road; imperviousness of a forest; craggedness, cragginess.

Fragoso, sa [frah-go'-so, sah], *a.* Craggy, rough, uneven; full of brambles and briers; noisy.

Fragrancia [frah-grahn'-the-ah], *f.* *V.* Fragancia.

Fragrante [frah-grahn'-tay], *a.* *V.* Fragante.

Fragua [frah'-goo-ah], *f.* 1. Forge, as for iron. 2. Place where intrigues are plotted.

Fraguador [frah-goo-ah-dor'], *m.* Schemer, one who plans an intrigue; one who counterfeits or forges.

Fraguar [frah-goo-ar'], *va.* 1. To forge, to reduce iron or other metal into shape. 2. (Met.) To plan, to plot, to contrive, to brew, to hatch.—*vr.* To unite in a mass: applied to clay and mortar.

Fragura [frah-goo'-rah], *f.* Roughness of the road, imperviousness of a forest.

Fraile [frah'-e-lay], *m.* 1. Friar, brother; appellation of the members of religious orders. *Fraile de misa y olla*, Friar destined to serve in the choir and at the altar, but not in the pulpit or chair. *V.* Religioso. 2. Fold or plait in petticoats. 3. (Print.) That part of a printed page which is pale for want of ink. 4. The upright post of a flood-gate in water-mills.

Frailecillo [frah-e-lay-theel'-lyo], *m.* 1. (Dim.) A little friar, or a child which wears a friar's habit. 2. (Orn.) Lapwing. Tringa vanellus. 3. Wedge securing the spindle of a silk-reel.

Frailecito [frah-e-lay-thee'-to], *m.* A boyish sport with the husk of beans.

Frailería [frah-e-lay-ree'-ah], *f.* (Coll.) Number of friars assembled together.

Frailero, ra [frah-e-lay'-ro, rah], *a.* Very fond of friars.

Frailesco, ca [frah-e-less'-co, cah], *a.* Monkish, belonging to friars, friar-like.

Frailía [frah-e-lee'-ah], *f.* 1. State of monks, monastic life. 2. Regular clergy.

Frailuco [frah-e-loo'-co], *m.* A despicable or contemptible friar.

Frailuno, na [frah-e-loo'-no, nah], *a* Belonging or proper to a friar.

Frambuesa [fram-boo-ay'-sah], *f.* The raspberry.

Frambueso [fram-boo-ay'-so], *m.* (Bot.) Raspberry-bush. Rubus idæus, *L.*

Frámea [frah'-may-ah], *f.* (Obs.) Javelin, dart.

Francachela [fran-cah-chay'-lah], *f.* *V.* Comilona.

Francalete [fran-cah-lay'-tay], *m.* Strap, slip of leather with a buckle.

Francamente [fran-cah-men'-tay], *adv.* Frankly, openly, freely, nakedly.

Francés, sa [fran-thays', sah], *a.* French. —*m.* The French language. *A la francesa*, After the French fashion. *Despedirse a la francesa*, (Coll.) To take French leave. *Mal francés*, Venereal disease.

Francesilla [fran-thay-seel'-lyah], *f.* (Bot.) Common yard crowfoot. Ranunculus asiaticus, *L.* This name is also given to some varieties of the poppy anemone.

Franchipán [fran-che-pahn'], *m.* Frangipani, a perfume.

Franciscano, na [fran-this-cah'-no, nah], *a.* 1. Franciscan, belonging to the order of St. Francis. 2. Gray-coloured, like the dress of the Franciscans.

Francisco, ca [fran-thees'-co, cah], *a.* *V.* Franciscano.

Francmasón [franc-mah-sone'], *m* Freemason, mason.

Francmasonería [franc-mah-so-nay-ree-ah], *f.* Freemasonry, a secret society of mutual protection.

Franco [frahn'-co], *m.* 1. Franc, a French coin, and worth about 10*d.* sterling. 2. Fair-time, when merchandise is sold free of duty.—*pl.* Franks, an appellation given by the Turks, Arabs, and Greeks to the people of the west of Europe.

Franco, ca [frahn'-co, cah], *a.* 1. Frank, open, generous, liberal, open-hearted, bountiful. 2. Free, disengaged. 3. Exempt, privileged. 4. Ingenuous, plain, sincere, fair, generous. 5. Free, exempt from duty. *Lengua franca*, The trading jargon of the Levant. *Puerto franco*, A free port.

Francolín [fran-co-leen'], *m.* (Orn.) Francolin, the African or Indian partridge. Tetrao francolinus, *L.*

Franela [frah-nay'-lah], *f.* Flannel.

Frange [frahn'-hay], *m.* (Her.) Division of the field of a shield.

Frangente [fran-hen'-tay], *m.* Accident, disaster.

Frangible [fran-hee'-blay], *a.* Brittle frangible.

Frangollar [fran-gol-lyar'], *va.* 1. To do a thing carelessly. 2. (Obs.) To shell or grind corn coarse.
Frangollo [fran-gol'-lyo], *m.* 1. Pottage made of wheat boiled in milk. 2. (Peru and Chili) A stew of many ingredients or which is poorly made. 3. (Coll.) Disorder, confusion.
Frangote [fran-go'-tay], *m.* Bale of goods.
Frángula [frahn'-goo-lah], *f.* (Bot.) Berry-bearing alder, alder buckthorn. Rhamnus frangula, *L.*
Franja [frahn'-hah], *f.* Fringe, an ornamental border, stripe.
Franjar [fran-har'], *va.* To fringe, to trim with fringe, to adorn with fringes.
Franjear, *va.* *V.* Franjar.
Franjir [fran-heer'], *va.* (Obs.) To break into several pieces.
Franqueamiento [fran-kay-ah-me-en'-to], *m.* (Obs.) Manumission.
Franquear [fran-kay-ar'], *va.* 1. To exempt, to grant immunity from, to enfranchise. 2. To pay the postage on letters, books, etc. 3. To gratify, to make liberal grants or gifts. 4. To disengage, to extricate; to clear from obstacles or impediments. 5. To free a slave. (Acad.)—*vr.* 1. To give one's self easily to the desire of others. 2. To unbosom one's self, to reveal in confidence one's secrets or thoughts. 3. To become liberal. 4. (Naut.) To be ready for sailing.—*vn.* (Naut.) To be situated at a point whence may be seen clearly and openly a work, harbour-entrance, etc. *Franquearse por encima de un bajo*, (Naut.) To forge over a shoal under a press of sail.
Franqueo [fran-kay'-o], *m.* 1. Franking letters, printed matter, etc. 2. Postage, that which is paid on mail-matter; also postage-stamps.
Franqueza [fran-kay'-thah], *f.* 1. Freedom, liberty, exemption, enfranchisement, freeness. 2. Frankness, generosity, openheartedness; liberality of sentiment. 3. Frankness, ingenuousness, sincerity.
Franquía [fran-kee'-ah], *f.* (Naut.) In the stream. Readiness for sailing.
Franquicia [fran-kee'-the-ah], *f.* 1. Immunity or exemption from taxes, liberty, franchise. 2. A privileged place, which enjoys exemption from taxes and imposts.
Fraque [frah'-kay], *m.* *V.* Frac.
Frasca [frahs'-cah], *f.* (Prov.) Dry leaves or small branches of trees.
Frasco [frahs'-co], *m.* 1. Flask, a bottle with a narrow neck. 2. Powder-horn or flask.
Frase [frah'-say], *f.* 1. Phrase, a mode of speech. 2. Idiomatic expression; style of any writer. 3. An energetic expression, generally metaphorical, signifying more than is expressed.
Frasear [frah-say-ar'], *va.* 1. To phrase, to employ idiomatic expressions. 2. (Mus.) To phrase, to give the proper expression to each musical phrase.
Fraseología [frah-say-o-lo-hee'-ah], *f.* 1. Phraseology, the style of a writer. 2. Verbosity, pomposity.
Frasquera [fras-kay'-rah], *f.* Bottle-case, liquor-case. *Frasquera de fuego*, (Naut.) Fire-case or fire-chest.
Frasquerilla, ita [fras-kay-reel'-lyah, ee'-tah], *f. dim.* Small bottle-case.
Frasqueta [fras-kay'-tah], *f.* Frisket of a printing-press.
Frasquillo, ito [fras-keel'-lyo], *m. dim.* A small flask. *Frasquillos para aguas de olor*, Smelling-bottles.
Fraterna [frah-terr'-nah], *f.* (Coll.) A severe reprimand, lecture, lesson.
Fraternal [frah-ter nahl'], *a.* Fraternal, brotherly.
Fraternalmente [frah-ter-nal-men'-tay], *adv.* Fraternally.
Fraternidad [frah-ter-ne-dahd'], *f.* Fraternity, the state or quality of a brother, brotherhood.
Fraternizar [fra-ter-ne-thar'], *vn.* To live in harmony, to fraternize.
Fraterno, na [frah-terr'-no, nah], *a.* Fraternal, brotherly.
Frates [frah'-tes], *m.* 1. A glass instrument, mushroom-shaped, for polishing stockings after they are washed. 2. A mason's (square) wooden trowel.
Fratesar [frah-tay-sar'], *va.* To polish or smooth with the frates.
Fratricida [frah-tre-thee'-dah], *m.* & *f.* Fratricide, murderer of a brother.
Fratricidio [frah-tre-thee'-de-o], *m.* Fratricide, murder of a brother.
Fraude [frah'-oo-day], *m.* Fraud, deceit, cheat, trick, artifice, imposture, craft, gull.
Fraudulencia [frah-oo-doo-len'-the-ah], *f.* Fraudulence, trickiness, deceitfulness.
Fraudulentamente [frah-oo-doo-len-tah-men'-tay], *adv.* Fraudulently, knavishly.
Fraudulento, ta [frah-oo-doo-len'-to, tah], *a.* Fraudulent, deceitful, artful, knavish.
Fraudulosamente [frah-oo-doo-lo-sah-men'-tay], *adv.* Fraudulently, deceitfully, knavishly.
Fraustina [frah-oos-tee'-nah], *f.* A wooden head for fashioning ladies' head-dresses.
Fraxinela [frac-se-nay'-lah], *f.* (Bot.) White dittany. Fraxinella dictamnus albus, *L.*
Fray [frah'-e], *m.* A contracted appellation of respect addressed to religious men; brother. *V.* Fraile.
Frazada [frah-thah'-dah], *f.* A blanket.
Frazadilla [frah-thah-deel'-lyah], *f. dim.* A small or light blanket.
Frecuencia [fray-coo-en'-the-ah], *f.* Frequency.
Frecuentación [fray-coo-en-tah-the-on'], *f.* Frequentation, frequenting, visiting often.
Frecuentador, ra [fray-coo-en-tah-dor', rah], *m.* & *f.* Frequenter.
Frecuentar [fray-coo-en-tar'], *va.* 1. To frequent, to haunt, to visit often. 2. To repeat an act often.
Frecuentativo [fray-coo-en-tah-tee'-vo], *a.* (Gram.) Frequentative: applied to verbs.
Frecuente [fray-coo-en'-tay], *a.* Frequent, often done or seen, often occurring.—*adv.* *V.* Frecuentemente.
Frecuentemente [fray-coo-en-tay-men'-tay], *adv.* Frequently, often, commonly, oftentimes.
Fregadero [frah-gah-day'-ro], *m.* Kitchen sink.
Fregado [fray-gah'-do], *m.* 1. The act of scouring or cleaning kitchen utensils. 2. A complicated subject or matter. *Mujer de buen fregado*, A buxom girl; sometimes a prostitute. *Mal fregado*, (Met.) Bad business.—*Fregado, da, pp.* of Fregar.
Fregador [fray-gah-dor'], *m.* 1. Scullery. *V.* Fregadero. 2. Dishclout.
Fregadura [fray-gah-doo'-rah], *f.* The act of rubbing or scouring.
Fregajo, *m.* *V.* Estropajo.
Fregamiento [fray-gah-me-en'-to], *m.* *V.* Fricación.
Fregar [fray-gar'], *va.* 1. To rub one thing against another. 2. To scour kitchen utensils.
Fregatriz [fray-gah-treeth'], *f.* Kitchen-maid, kitchen-wench.
Fregona [fray-go'-nah], *f.* Kitchen-maid, kitchen-wench.
Fregoncilla [fray-gon-theel'-lyah], *f. dim.* A little kitchen-maid.
Fregonil [fray-go-neel'], *a.* Belonging to or becoming a kitchen-maid.
Fregonzuela [fray-gon-thoo-ay'-lah], *f. dim.* A little kitchen-girl.
Freidura [fray-e-doo'-rah], *f.* Act of frying or dressing in a pan.
Freila [fray'-e-lah], *f.* A nun or religious woman belonging to military orders.
Freilar [fray-e-lar'], *va.* (Obs.) To receive or admit in a military order.
Freile [fray'-e-lay], *m.* Properly, a knight of a military order, but this name is generally given to the ecclesiastical members of those orders.
Freir [fray-eer'], *va.* To fry or dress in a frying-pan. *Freirse de calor*, To be excessively hot. *Freírsela a alguno*, (Coll.) To deceive one premeditatedly. *Al freir de los huevos lo verás*, The proof of the pudding is in the eating. *Al freir será el reir*, (prov.) Counting chickens before they are hatched.
Freje [fray'-hay], *m.* (Prov.) A hoop of osier to bind things with.
Fréjol [fray'-hole], *m.* French bean, kidney bean. Phaseolus vulgaris, *L.*
Frejol [fray-hole'], *m.* (Amer.) *V.* Fréjol and Frísol.
Frelo, la [fray'-lo, lah], *a.* Delicate, weakly, sickly. (Prov. Andal.)
Frémito [fray'-me-to], *m.* *V.* Bramido.
Frenar [fray-nar'], *va.* (Ant.) *V.* Enfrenar.
Frenería [fray-nay-ree'-ah], *f.* 1. Business of bridle-making. 2. Place in which bridles are made or sold.
Frenero [fray-nay'-ro], *m.* One who makes the bits of a bridle, a bridle-maker.
Frenesí [fray-nay-see'], *m.* 1. Frenzy, madness, distraction. 2. (Met.) Folly, extravagant caprice.
Frenéticamente [fray-nay'-te-cah-men tay], *adv.* Madly, furiously, distractedly, franticly.
Frenético, ca [fray-nay'-te-co, cah], *a.* Mad, distracted, frantic, furious, lunatic.
Frénico, ca [fray'-ne-co, cah], *a.* 1. Phrenic, relating to the diaphragm. 2. Relating to the intelligence or thought (phrenic).
Frenillar [fray-neel-lyar'], *va.* (Naut.) To bridle the oars.
Frenillo [fray-neel'-lyo], *m.* 1. Frenum of the tongue; tongue-tie. 2. (Naut.) Bridle of the oars, a rope with which oars are tied.
Frenitis [fray-nee'-tis], *f.* Inflammation of the diaphragm.
Freno [fray'-no], *m.* 1. Brake (of an automobile, etc.). *Meter el freno*, To put on the brake. 2. Curb, check, restraint. 3. Bridle or bit. 4. Brace (on the teeth).
Frenología [fray-no-lo-hee'-ah], *f.* Phrenology, cranioscopy; doctrine of Gall.
Frenológico, ca [fray-no-lo'-he-co, cah], *a.* Phrenological.
Frenólogo [fray-no'-lo-go], *m.* Phrenologist.
Frental [fren-tahl'], *a.* Frontal: applied to the muscles of the forehead. *V.* Frontal.
Frentaza [fren-tah'-thah], *f. aug.* A broad forehead.
Frente [fren'-tay], *f.* 1. The forehead. *Frente a frente*, Face to face. 2. Blank space at the beginning of a letter or other document. (Acad.) 3. *com.* Front, the forepart of a building or any other thing. *Frente, en frente*, or *frente por frente*, Opposite, over the way.—*m.* 4. (Mil.) Front rank of a body of troops. 5. Face of a bastion.

Navegar de frente, (Naut.) To sail abreast. *A frente*, In front; in a right line. 6. Obverse of coins. *Al frente*, (Com.) Brought or carried forward.

Frentero [fren-tay'-ro], *m.* Band worn on the forehead of children, to save their face in case of falling.

Freo [fray'-o], *m.* (Naut.) 1. A narrow channel between an island and the mainland. 2. (Prov.) Gorge, canyon, ravine between mountains.

Fresa [fray'-sah], *f.* Strawberry, the fruit of the strawberry-plant.

Fresada [fray-sah'-dah], *f.* A dish anciently made of flour, milk and butter.

Fresadora [fray-sah-do'-rah], *f.* Milling or drilling machine.

Fresal [fray-sahl'], *m.* 1. (Bot.) Strawberry-plant. Fragaria, *L.* 2. Ground bearing strawberry-plants.

Fresca [fres'-cah], *f.* 1. *V.* Fresco. *Tomar la fresca*, To take the air. *Salir con la fresca*, To go out during the fresh air in the evening or very early in the morning. 2. (Coll.) That which is said resolutely to upbraid any one. *Le dijo dos* or *cuatro frescas*, He told him his mind freely or bluntly; he was plain with him.

Frescachón, na [fres-cah-chone', nah], *a.* 1. Stout, good-looking. 2. (Naut.) Fresh, cool (of a breeze or wind).

Frescal [fres-cahl'], *a.* (Fish) not entirely fresh, but preserved with little salt. Sardinas frescales.

Frescamente [fres-cah-men'-tay], *adv.* 1. Freshly, recently, lately. 2. Coolly, resolutely, without passion.

Frescar [fres-car'], *vn.* (Naut.) *V.* Refrescar.

Fresco, ca [fres'-co, cah], *a.* 1. Fresh, coolish, rather cool. 2. Fresh, recent, newly come, just made. 3. Plump, ruddy. 4. Fresh, bold in manner. *Dinero fresco*, Ready money, cash paid off-hand. *Viento fresco*, (Naut.) A fresh breeze. *Pintura al fresco*, Painting in fresco, done on plaster not yet dry, and with water colours. *Quedarse fresco*, (Met.) To fail of success in one's expectations; to be disappointed. *Dejar fresco a alguno*, To leave one scoffed at.

Fresco [fres'-co], *m.* 1. Cool, refreshing air. *V.* Frescura. 2. (Peru.) A cold iced drink, prepared from the pine-apple.

Frescón, na [fres-cone', nah], *a. aug.* Very fresh; blooming.

Frescor [fres-cor'], *m.* 1. Cool, refreshing air. 2. *V.* Frescura. 3. (Painting) Flesh-colour.

Frescote, ta [fres-co'-tay, tah], *a.* 1. Aug. of Fresco. 2. Ruddy, youthful, and strong.

Frescura [fres-coo'-rah], *f.* 1. Freshness, coolness, cool, gentle cold. 2. Amenity, agreeableness of situation. 3. Frankness, openness. 4. Freedom, ease, disengagement. 5. Serenity, tranquility, coolness of mind.

Fresera [fray-say'-rah], *f.* A rosaceous plant with fibrous roots, resembling the strawberry and cinquefoil.

Fresita [fray-see'-tah], *f.* The service-berry.

Fresnal [fres-nahl'], *m.* *V.* Fresneda.

Fresneda [fres-nay'-dah], *f.* Grove or plantation of ash-trees.

Fresnillo [fres-neel'-lyo], *m.* *V.* Díctamo blanco. White fraxinella.

Fresno [fres'-no], *m.* 1. (Bot.) Ash-tree. Fraxinus, *L.* 2. (Poet.) Staff of a lance, a spear. *Fresno florido* or *de flor*, (Bot.) Flowering ash-tree. Fraxinus ornus, *L.* *Fresno elevado* or *común*, Common ash-tree.

Fresón, or **Fresón de Chile** [fray-sone'], *m.* (Bot.) Chili strawberry. Fragraria Chilœnsis, *L.*

Fresquecito, ita, Fresquillo, lla [fres-kay-thee'-to, ee'-tah, fres-keel'-lyo, lyah], *a. dim.* *V.* Fresquito.

Fresquista [fres-kees'-tah], *m.* A painter employed in painting in fresco.

Fresquito, ta [fres-kee'-to, tah], *a. dim.* Cool, coolish, approaching to cold.

Fresquito, *m.* Cool, fresh air.

Fresquito, *adv.* Just now, lately.

Frey [fray'-e], *m.* Father, if a religious person; or brother, if a secular man. This is a word of distinction given to the knights commanders, or particularly distinguished knights of the military orders of *St. John* and *Montesa*, in Spain. This word, as well as *Fray*, is always written in abbreviation *Fr.;* but it must be observed that when it is found before the noun *Don* it indicates a knight, and must be pronounced *fray'-e;* and when it comes after it, as *Don Fr. Antonio*, it relates to a religious person of the king's council, and then it is pronounced *frah'-e.*

Frez, Freza [freth, fray'-thah], *f.* Dung, the excrement of animals. (Arab. ferth.)

Freza, *f.* 1. The time in which silk-worms eat. 2. Ground turned up by the snout of a hog or other animal. 3. Track, trace of fish in spawning.

Frezada [fray-thah'-dah], *f.* A blanket. *De frezada*, or *frezadilla*, In deshabille. *V.* Frazada.

Frezar [fray-thar'], *vn.* 1. To eject excrements: applied to animals. 2. To eject the droppings of grubs from hives.

Frezar, *va.* 1. To nibble the leaves of mulberry-trees: applied to silk-worms. 2. To rub in order to spawn: applied to fishes. 3. To turn up the ground, as hogs. 4. To be disposed to rise like worms after moulting.

Fria [free'-ah], *a.* (Prov.) Applied to dead fowls paid as tribute. *A frías*, Heavily, coldly.

Friabilidad [free-ah-be-le-dahd'], *f.* Friability, brittleness.

Friable [free-ah'-blay], *a.* Friable, fragile, brittle.

Frialdad [fre-al-dahd]', *f.* 1. Frigidity, coldness, want of warmth. 2. Frigidity, coldness, unconcern, coolness, lukewarmness, want of affection. 3. Frigidity, insipidity, dulness. 4. A silly observation or saying. 5. (Med.) Impotence, incapacity of generation.

Friamente [free'-ah-men-tay], *adv.* In a heavy, stupid, and graceless manner; coldly, frigidly, coolly; flatly.

Friático, ca [fre-ah'-te-co, cah], *a.* 1. Foolish, graceless, silly. 2. Chilly.

Fricación [fre-cah-the-on'], *f.* Friction, frication.

Fricandó [fre-can-do'], *m.* Scotch collop; veal cut into small pieces and stewed.

Fricar [fre-car'], *va.* To rub, to scour.

Fricasé [fre-cah-say'], *m.* Fricassee.

Fricción [fric-the-on'], *f.* 1. Friction. *V.* Fricación. 2. Embrocation, liniment.

Friega [fre-ay'-gah], *f.* Friction, rubbing with flesh-brush, etc.

(*Yo friego, yo friegue*, from *Fregar*. *V.* Acertar.)

Friera [fre-ay'-rah], *f.* Chilblain.

Frigidez, *f.* *V.* Frialdad.

Frígido, da [free'-he-do, dah], *a.* (Poet.) Cold, frigid.

Frigio, gia [free'-he-o, ah], *a.* Phrygian, relating to the ancient district of Phrygia.

Frigorífero, ra [fre-go-ree'-fay-ro, rah], *a.* Cooling, chilling.

Frigorífico, ca [fre-go-ree'-fe-co, cah], *a.* Cooling, refrigerating, chilling. *Cámara frigorífica*, Cooler, freezer. —*m.* 1. Cold storage. 2. Refrigerator, freezer. 3. Refrigerator van or ship.

Friísimo, ma [fre-ee'-se-mo, mah], *a. sup.* Extremely cold.

Fringilago, *m.* *V.* Monje for a bird.

Frío, ía [free'-o, ah], *a.* 1. Cold, frigid, tepid. 2. Cold, frigid, impotent by nature. 3. Cold, frigid, indifferent, heartless, without warmth of affection. 4. Frigid, dull, graceless, inefficacious.

Frío, *m.* 1. Cold, the effect of coldness. 2. Cool, fresh air. 3. Iced drinks. *Dios da el frío conforme a la ropa*, God tempers the wind to the shorn lamb.

Friolento, ta [fre-o-len'-to, tah], *a.* Chilly; very sensible of cold.

Friolera [fre-o-lay'-rah], *f.* An insignificant speech or act; a trifle.

Friolero, ra [fre-o-lay'-ro, rah], *a.* *V.* Friolento.

Frisa [free'-sah], *f.* Frieze, a coarse woollen stuff.

Frisado [fre-sah'-do], *m.* Silk plush or shag.—*Frisado, da*, *pp.* of Frisar.

Frisador [fre-sah-dor'], *m.* Frizzler, one who frizzles or raises the nap on frieze or cloth.

Frisadura [fre-sah-doo'-rah], *f.* Act of frizzling or shagging.

Frisar [fre-sar'], *va.* To frizzle or frizz, to raise the nap on frieze or other woollen stuff; to rub against the grain—*vn.* To resemble, to be like; to assimilate; to approach.

Friso [free'-so], *m.* 1. (Arch.) Frieze, the part of a column between the architrave and cornice. 2. Wainscot (Arab. ifriz.)

Frisol [free'-sol], *m.* (Bot.) French or kidney-bean. Phaseolus vulgaris, *L.*

Frisón [fre-sone'], *m.* 1. A large draught-horse, a cart or dray-horse. 2. Any animal of a large size.

Frita [free'-tah], *f.* 1. Frit, the ingredients of which glass is made; partially fused sand and fluxes. 2. The time employed in fusing glass. 3. In some factories, slag is so-called.

Fritada [fre-tah'-dah], *f.* Dish of fried meat or fish.

Fritilaria [fre-te-lah'-re-ah], *f.* (Bot.) Fritillary. Fritillaria, *L.* *Fritilaria imperial*, vulgarly *corona imperial*, Crown imperial fritillary. Fritillaria imperialis. *Fritilaria meleágride*, *V* Flor del tablero.

Fritillas [fre-teel'-lyas], *f. pl.* (Prov.) Fritters, pancakes.

Frito [free'-to], *m.* *V.* Fritada.

Frito, ta [free'-to, tah], *pp. irr.* of Freir. Fried.

Frituras [fre-too'-rahs], *f. pl.* Fritters. *Frituras de maíz*, or (Mex.) *Frituras de elote*, Corn fritters.

Frivolamente [free'-vo-lah-men-tay], *adv.* Frivolously, triflingly, without weight.

Frivolidad [fre-vo-le-dahd'], *f.* Frivolity, frivolousness, triflingness, emptiness, frothiness.

Frivolité [fre-vo-le-tay'], *f.* Tatting.

Frívolo, la [free'-vo-lo, lah], *a.* Frivolous, slight, trifling, vain, empty frothy, light, futile.

Froga [fro'-gah], *f.* Brickwork, masonry.

Frogar [fro-gar'], *va.* (Obs.) 1. To make a wall of brick and mortar. 2 To lay a coat of mortar over the joints of bricks.

Fronda [fron'-dah], *f.* (Bot.) Frond, a name given to the leaves of ferns and hepaticæ.

Frondescencia [fron-des-then'-the-ah], *f.* 1. (Bot.) The leafing process, frondescence. 2. (Zool.) Disposition of a polipary in leafy branches.
Frondescente [fron-des-then'-tay], *a.* (Bot.) Frondescent.
Frondífero [fron-dee'-fay-ro], *a.* (Bot.) Frondiferous, bearing leaves.
Frondosidad [fron-do-se-dahd'], *f.* 1. Luxuriance of the branches and leaves of trees; foliage. 2. Redundancy of words or phrases.
Frondoso, sa [fron-do'-so, sah], *a.* Leafy, abounding with leaves, frondose or full of leaves, luxuriant.
Frontal [fron-tahl'], *a.* Frontal, relating to the forehead.—*m.* 1. Frontlet, a fillet with the name of God or a biblical text, which the Jews used to wear upon the forehead. 2. Frontal, a rich hanging for the front of an altar. 3. Chisel used by guitar-makers to finish the frets. 4. Headstall of a bridle. 5. Piece of black baize, put as mourning over a horse's head.
Frontalera [fron-tah-lay'-rah], *f.* Ornament for the front of an altar, and the place where such ornaments are kept.
Frontera [fron-tay'-rah], *f* 1. Frontier, limit, confine, the border, the marches. 2. Fillet of a bridle; binder of a frail-basket. 3. *V.* FACHADA. 4. Ornament for the control of a riding saddle.
Fronterizo, za [fron-tay-ree'-tho, thah], *a.* 1. Limitaneous, belonging to a frontier. 2. Frontier, bounding or bordering upon. 3. Fronting, opposite, over against.
Frontero [fron-tay'-ro], *m.* 1. Governor or magistrate of a frontier town. 2. Frontlet, frontal, or brow-band, worn by children to prevent their heads or faces from being hurt by a fall.—*adv.* In front.
Frontero, ra [fron-tay'-ro, rah], *a.* Frontier, placed in front.
Frontil [fron-teel'], *m.* Bass-weed matting on the foreheads of draught-oxen, to preserve them from injury.
Frontino, na [fron-tee'-no, nah], *a.* Applied to animals marked in the face.
Frontis [fron'-tis], *m.* Frontispiece, façade.
Frontispicio [fron-tis-pee'-the-o], *m.* 1. Front, the fore part of a building, or any other thing which meets the eye. 2. (Coll.) Face, visage. 3. Title-page of a book.
Frontón [fron-tone'], *m.* 1. Jai alai, Basque ball game. 2. Court where Jai alai is played. 3. (Arch.) Pediment, a triangular gable of the principal entrance of a building.
Frontudo, da [fron-too'-do, dah], *a.* Broad-faced.
Frontura [fron-too'-rah], *f.* Front of a stocking-frame.
Frotación, Frotadura [fro-tah-the-on', fro-tah-doo'-rah], *f.* Friction.
Frotador, ra [fro-tah-dor', rah], *m.* & *f.* 1. One who rubs. 2. Kind of old brushes which hatters use to clean the sad-iron.
Frotar [fro-tar'], *va.* 1. To rub one thing against another, to perfricate. 2. To stroke gently with the hand.
Fructescencia [frooc-tes-then'-the-ah], *f.* (Bot.) Frutescence or the fruiting season, the time when vegetables scatter their ripe seeds.
Fructidor [frooc-te-dor'], *m.* Last month of the year in the calendar of the first French republic: 18th August to 16th September.
Fructiferamente [frooc-tee'-fay-rah-men-tay], *adv.* Fruitfully.
Fructífero, ra [frooc-tee'-fay-ro, rah], *a.* Fructiferous, frugiferous, fruit-bearing, fruitful.
Fructificación [frooc-te-fe-cah-the-on'], *f.* (Bot.) Fructification, fertilization.
Fructificador, ra, [frooc-te-fe-cah-dor' rah], *m.* & *f.* Fertilizer.
Fructificar [frooc-te-fe-car'], *va.* 1. To fructify, to fertilize, to make fruitful. 2. (Met.) To profit or give profit, to benefit. 3. (Met.) To edify, to promote piety and morality.
Fructívoro, ra [frooc-tee'-vo-ro, rah], *a.* Frugivorous, fruit-eating.
Fructosa [frook-to'-sah], *f.* Fructose.
Fructuosamente [frooc-too-o-sah-men'-tay], *adv.* Fruitfully.
Fructuoso, sa [frooc-too-o'-so, sah], *a.* Fruitful, fructuous, useful.
Frugal [froo-gahl'], *a.* Frugal, parsimonious, sparing, thrifty.
Frugalidad [froo-gah-le-dahd'], *f.* Frugality, parsimony, thrift, economy.
Frugalmente [froo-gal-men'-tay], *adv.* Frugally, sparingly, thriftily.
Frugívoro, ra [froo-hee'-vo-ro, rah], *a.* Frugivorous, herbivorous, plant-eating.
Fruición [froo-e-the on'], *f.* 1. Fruition, enjoyment of possession. 2. Fruition, satisfaction, gratification, taste.
Fruir [froo-eer'], *vn.* To live in happiness, to enjoy.
Fruitivo, va [froo-e-tee'-vo, vah], *a.* Fruitive, enjoying.
Frumentario, ria [froo-men-tah'-re-o, ah], *a.* Cereal, relating to the cereal grains in respect to their supply and to commerce.—*m.* A Roman official charged with conveying wheat to the army.
Frumenticio, cia [froo-men-tee'-the-o, ah], *a.* (Bot.) Frumentaceous, cereal.
Frunce [froon'-thay], *m.* Plait, fold. (Acad.)
Fruncido, da [froon-thee'-do, dah], *a.* Frizzled, corrugated. *Fruncido de boca*, Hare-lipped—*pp.* of FRUNCIR.
Fruncidor [froon-the-dor'], *m.* Plaiter, folder.
Fruncimiento [froon-the-me-en'-to], *m.* 1. The act of pursing up into corrugations. 2. Fiction, deceit, imposture.
Fruncir [froon-theer'], *va.* 1. To gather the edge of cloth into plaits. 2. (Met.) To reduce to a smaller compass. 3. (Met.) To conceal the truth. 4. To affect modesty and composure. *Fruncir las cejas*, To knit the eyebrows. *Fruncir los labios*, To curl the lips.
Fruslera [froos-lay'-rah], *f.* Brass turnings or clippings.
Fruslería [frus-lay-ree'-ah], *f.* Trifle, a thing of no value, frivolity.
Fruslero, ra [froos-lay'-ro, rah], *a.* Trifling, frivolous, insignificant, futile.
Frustráneo, nea [froos-trah'-nay-o, ah], *a.* Vain, useless, nugatory.
Frustrar [froos-trar'], *va.* To frustrate, to disappoint, to balk, to defeat, to mock, to elude.—*vr.* To miscarry, to fail, to be balked.
Frustratorio, ria [froos-trah-to'-re-o, ah], *a.* *V.* FRUSTRÁNEO.
Fruta [froo'-tah], *f.* Fruitage, fruit, the eatable fruit of a tree or plant. *Fruta de sartén*, Pancake, fritter. *Fruta nueva*, (Met.) Any thing new. *Fruta del tiempo*, 1. Fruit eaten in the season in which it is produced. 2. (Met.) Any thing incident or peculiar to a season. *Uno come la fruta aceda, y otro tiene la dentera*, One man's meat is another man's poison.
Frutaje [froo-tah'-hay], *m.* A painting of fruits and flowers.
Frutal [froo-tahl'], *a.* Fruitful, fruit-bearing: applied to trees.—*m.* Fruit-tree.
Frutar [froo-tar'], *va* (Prov.) To fructify, to fertilize.
Frutería [froo-tay-ree'-ah], *f.* Fruitery, place where fruit is kept or preserved.
Frutero, ra [froo-tay'-ro, rah], *m.* & *f.* 1 Fruiterer, one who deals in fruit. 2 Fruit-basket served up at table. 3 Piece of painting representing various sorts of fruit.
Frutescente [froo-tes-then'-tay], *a.* (Bot.) Frutescent: applied to stems from herbaceous becoming shrubby.
Frútice [froo'-te-thay], *m.* Any perennial shrub.
Fruticoso, sa [froo-te-co'-so, sah], *a.* 1. (Bot.) Fruticant, frutescent; applied to a plant with many branches from its root. 2. Shrubby: applied to vegetables bearing woody stems *Tallo fruticoso*, Shrubby stem.
Frutilla [froo-teel'-lyah], *f.* 1. (Dim.) Small fruit. 2. In Peru, strawberry. 3. Round shell or nut of which rosaries are made.
Frutillar [froo-teel-lyar'], *m.* Strawberry-bed.
Fruto [froo'-to], *m.* 1. Fruit, the product of a tree or plant in which the seeds are contained. 2. Any useful produce of the earth. 3. Fruit, benefice, profit, advantage gained by an enterprise or conduct. *Fruto de bendición*, Children lawfully begotten.—*pl.* 1. Seeds, grain. 2. Produce of an estate, place, or employment.
Fu [foo], *interj.* 1. Of disgust. 2. Sound imitating the snarling of a cat.
Fucáceo, cea [foo-cah'-thay-o, ah], *a.* Fucaceous, relating to fucus, or great sea-weeds.
Fúcar [foo'-car], *m.* A rich, opulent man.
Fucia [foo'-the-ah], *f.* (Obs.) *V.* CONFIANZA.
Fucsia [fooc'-se-ah], *f.* Fuchsia, an ornamental plant with pendent blossoms.
Fucha [foo'-chah], *int.* (Mex.) Exclamation denoting neatness.
Fuego [foo-ay'-go], *m.* 1. Fire, the igneous element. 2. Fire, any thing burning. 3. Fire, a conflagration. 4. Signal given with smoke from the coast; beacon fire. 5. (Met.) Force, life, vigour, animation. 6. Fire; eruption or breaking out of humours in the skin. *Fuego de San Antón*, Erysipelas, as commonly understood; but properly an epidemic gangrene which made great ravages between the 10th and 16th centuries. 7. Firing of soldiers. 8. Hearth, fire-place. *Un lugar tiene tantos fuegos*, A place contains so many hearths or inhabitants. 9. Ardour, heat of an action. *Fuego de San Telmo*, (Naut.) Castor and Pollux, a shining vapour without heat, sometimes observed adhering to ships after a storm. *Fuego fatuo*, (Coll.) Jack-a-lantern. *Dar fuego a un navío*, (Naut.) To bream a ship. *Dar fuego a los tablones*, (Naut.) To heat planks for the purpose of bending them. *Estar hecho un fuego*, (Met.) To burn with heat, to be burning with rage, to be in a great passion. *Fuego greguisco* or *guirgüesco*, (Obs.) *Fuego griego*, Greek or wild-fire. *Fuegos* (Naut.) Lights; light-house. *Fuego graneado*, (Mil.) Successive or incessant firing, effected by small divisions firing together. *A fuego y sangre*. With fire and sword.
¡Fuego! ¡Fuego de Dios! [foo-ay'-go, foo-ay'-go day de-os'], *int.* Bless me!

what is this! *¡Fuego!* the military command to shoot.

Fuellar [foo-el-lyar'], *m.* Paper ornament around wax tapers.

Fuelle [foo-ayl'-lyay], *m.* 1. Bellows. 2. (Coll.) Tale-bearer. 3. Leather curtain of an open chaise. 4. Puff for powdering hair. *Fuelles,* Puckers or corrugations in clothes.

Fuente [foo-en'-tay], *f.* 1. Fountain, fount, a spring of water. 2. Jet, a spout of water. 3. (Met.) Original, first principle, first cause, source. 4. Dish, platter, a broad wide vessel in which food is served up at table. 5. A small ulcer, an issue.

Fuentecica, illa, ita, zuela [foo-en-tay-thee'-cah, eel'-lyah, ee'-tah, thoo-ay'-lah], *f. dim.* A small fountain.

Fuer (A) [foo-ayr'], *adv.* *A fuer de caballero,* Upon the word of a gentleman. *A fuer de más instruído,* Being by the time better informed.

Fuera [foo-ay'-rah], *adv.* 1. Out, speaking of a person or thing which is not in a place. 2. Without, out of the place where one is. 3. *V.* Afuera. 4. Over and above. *Fuera de sí,* Absent of mind; deranged, beside one's self, aghast. *De fuera,* Exteriorly. *Fuera de,* Out of, forth. *Fuera de eso,* Besides, moreover. *Estar fuera,* Not to be at home; not to be in some place. *Fuera de esto,* Short of this; besides this. *Fuera de que,* Besides, over and above.

¡Fuera! [foo-ay'-rah], *int.* Away, get you gone, out of the way, clear the way.

Fuerarropa (Hacer) [foo-ay-rar-ro'-pah]. A command used in the galleys for the rabble to undress.

Fuerecilla, ita [foo-er-thay-theel'-lyah], *f. dim.* Little strength.

Fuero [foo-ay'-ro], *m.* 1. Statute law of a country. 2. Jurisdiction, judicial power. 3. Privilege or exemption granted to a province. 4. A compilation of laws. *Fuero exterior* or *externo,* Canon and civil laws. *A fuero,* According to law. *Fuero de la conciencia, fuero interior* or *fuero interno,* The tribunal of conscience. *De fuero,* Of right, by right or law.

Fuerte [foo-err'-tay], *m.* 1. Fortification, intrenchment, fort, hold.—*f.* 2. Coin over weight. 3. (Mus.) Forte, the loudness of the voice or notes marked *f.* 4. The buckle from which the stirrup hangs.

Fuerte [foo-err'-tay], *a.* 1. Vigorous, able, hardy, lusty, stout, healthy, hale. 2. Strong, fast, impregnable. 3. Strong, firm, compact. 4. Strong, forcible, resistless, cogent, efficacious. 5. Manly, man-like, firm. 6. Hard, not malleable. 7. Terrible, grave.

Fuerte [foo-err'-tay], *adv.* Strongly.

Fuertecico, illo, ito [foo-er-tay-thee'-co, eel'-lyo, ee'-to], *m. dim.* Small fortress, a block-house.

Fuertemente [foo-er-tay-men'-tay], *adv.* Strongly, lustily, firmly, fast, forcible, vehemently.

Fuerza [foo-err'-thah], *f.* 1. Force, strength, might, vigour, cogency. 2. Fortitude, valour, courage, manliness, constancy. 3. Force, violence, coercion, compulsion, constraint. 4. Force, violence, defloration, rape. 5. Force, virtue, efficacy, mental power or strength. 6. Force, moment, impulsive weight, actuating power. 7. Force, armament, warlike preparation: commonly used in the plural. 8. Fortress, a strong place: used commonly in the plural. 9. The natural force power, or faculty of things. 10. *V.* Resistencia. 11. The strongest part of a thing. 12. Proneness, strong propensity. 13. The third of a sword next the hilt. *A fuerza de,* By dint of, by force of. *Por fuerza* or *de por fuerza,* By force, head and shoulders, violently, forcibly; by sheer necessity, necessarily; without excuse. *Hacer fuerza de velas,* (Naut.) To crowd sail, to carry a press of sail. *Hacer fuerza de remos,* (Naut.) To pull hard with the oars. *A viva fuerza,* With great resolution, by main force.

(*Yo fuerzo, yo fuerce,* from *Forzar. V.* Acordar.)

Fuerza aérea [foo-err'-thah ah-ay'-ray-ah], *f.* Air force.

Fuete [foo-ay'-tay], *m.* (Cuba) A whip.

Fufú [foo-foo'], *m.* (Cuba) Mass made of yam, plantain, or other nutritious root, and pounded.

Fuga [foo'-gah], *f.* 1. Flight, escape, elopement. 2. State of the utmost perfection of a thing. 3. (Mus.) Fugue, a musical composition in which a theme introduced by one part is repeated and imitated by the others in succession. 4. (Naut.) Force, violence, velocity of the wind. *Fuga de risa,* Fit of laughter.

Fugacidad [foo-gah-the-dahd'], *f.* Fugacity, volatility, fugitiveness, fugaciousness, brevity.

Fugado, da [foo-gah'-do, dah], *a.* Written in the style of a fugue, without following the strict rules for the latter.

Fugar [foo-gar'], *va.* (Obs.) To cause to fly or escape.—*vr.* To escape, to fly, to run away, to get out of danger.

Fugaz [foo-gahth'], *a.* 1. Fugacious, volatile, apt to fly away. 2. Fugitive, running away. 3. (Met.) Perishable, decaying.

Fúgido, da, *a.* (Poet.) *V.* Fugaz.

Fugitivo, va [foo-he-tee'-vo, vah], *m. & f.* A fugitive.

Fugitivo, va, *a.* 1. Fugitive, running from danger, flying from duty. 2. Fugitive, unsteady, unstable.

Fuina [foo-ee'-nah], *f.* *V.* Garduña.

Fulanito, ta [foo-lah-nee'-to, tah], *m. & f. dim.* Little master, little miss.

Fulano, na [foo-lah'-no, nah], *m. & f.* Such a one; so-and-so. (Arab.)

Fulgecer [fool-hay-therr'], *vn.* (Poet.) To shine, to be resplendent.

Fulgente [fool-hen'-tay], *a.* (Poet.) Refulgent, brilliant.

Fúlgido, da [fool'-he-do, dah], *a.* (Poet.) Resplendent.

Fulgor [fool-gor'], *m.* Fulgency, resplendence, brilliancy.

Fulgora [fool-go'-rah], *f.* Fulgora, the lantern-fly, a homopterous insect, with ocelli and antennæ beneath the compound eyes.

Fulgurante [fool-goo-rahn'-tay], *pa. & a.* (Poet.) Resplendent, shining.

Fulgurar [fool-goo-rar'], *vn.* (Poet.) To fulgurate, to emit flashes of light, to yield splendour and brilliancy.

Fuliginoso, sa [foo-le-he-no'-so, sah], *a.* Fuliginous, dark, obscure.

Fulminación [fool-me-nah-the-on'], *f.* Fulmination, the act of thundering.

Fulminado [fool-me-nah'-do], *a.* Wounded by lightning.—*Fulminado, da, pp.* of Fulminar.

Fulminador [fool-me-nah-dor'], *m.* Thunderer.

Fulminante [fool-me-nahn'-tay], *pa. & a.* Fulminating, thundering. —*m.* Detonator.

Fulminar [fool-me-nar'], *va.* 1. To fulminate, to emit lightning. 2. To throw out as an object of terror, to express wrath. *Fulminar excomuniones* or *censuras,* To issue ecclesiastical censures.

Fulminato [fool-me-nah'-to], *m.* (Chem.) Fulminate, a salt of fulminic acid.

Fulmíneo, nea [fool-mee'-nay-o, ah], *a.* (Poet.) Belonging to thunder and lightning.

Fulmínico [fool-mee'-ne-co], *a.* (Chem.) Fulminic (acid), a compound of cyanogen and oxygen; its salts are explosive in character.

Fulminoso, sa [fool-me-no'-so, sah], *a.* (Poet.) Fulminatory, thundering, striking horror.

Fullería [fool-lyay-ree'-ah], *f.* 1. Cheating at play. 2. Cunning, arts used to deceive. 3. Cogging, cheat, fallacy.

Fullerito [fool-lyay-ree'-to], *m. dim.* A little sharper.

Fullero [fool-lyay'-ro], *m.* Sharper, cheater at play, gamester, gambler.

Fullet [fool-lyet'], *m.* A very small saw.

Fullona [fool-lyo'-nah], *f.* (Coll.) Dispute, quarrel.

Fumada [foo-mah'-dah], *f.* The quantity of smoke taken at once in smoking tobacco; whiff.

Fumadero [foo-mah-day'-ro], *m.* (Coll.) A place particularly used for smoking tobacco; smoking-room.

Fumador, ra [foo-mah-dor', rah], *m. & f.* (Coll.) Smoker, one who smokes tobacco.

Fumante [foo-mahn'-tay], *pa.* Fuming, smoking.

Fumar [foo-mar'], *va.* To disperse in vapours; to smoke: generally used in relation to tobacco.

Fumarada [foo-mah-rah'-dah], *f.* 1. Blast of smoke. 2. A pipeful of tobacco.

Fumaria [foo-mah'-re-ah], *f.* (Bot.) Fumitory. Fumaria. *Fumaria oficinal,* Common fumitory. Fumaria officinalis.

Fumear [foo-may-ar'], *va.* (Prov.) *V.* Humear.

Fumífero, ra [foo-mee'-fay-ro, rah], *a.* (Poet.) Smoking, emitting smoke.

Fumífugo, ga [foo-mee'-foo-go, gah], *a* Smoke-dispersing.

Fumigación [foo-me-gah-the-on'], *f.* 1. Fumigation, fumes raised by fire. 2. Fumigation, application of medicines to the body in fumes.

Fumigador [foo-me-gah-dor'], *m.* Fumigator, one who or that which fumigates.

Fumigar [foo-me-gar'], *va.* 1. To fumigate, to smoke. 2. To fumigate, to medicate or purify by vapours.

Fumigatorio, ria [foo-me-gah-to'-re-o, ah], *a.* Fumigatory.

Fumívoro, ra [foo-mee'-vo-ro, rah], *a.* Smoke-consuming.

Fumorola [foo-mo-ro'-lah], *f.* Cavity in the earth which emits a sulphureous smoke.

Fumosidad [foo-mo-se-dahd'], *f.* Smokiness.

Fumoso, sa [foo-mo'-so, sah], *a.* Full of smoke or fume, fumid, smoky.

Funámbulo, la [foo-nahm'-boo-lo, lah], *m. & f.* Funambulist, a rope dancer.

Función [foon-the-on'], *f.* 1. Function, fulfilling the duties of any employment, profession, or office. 2. (Med.) Function, vital action. 3. Solemnity, festival, feast, party, rout. 4. Festive concourse of people, a public act. 5. Fight, engagement, battle.

Funcionamiento [foon-the-o-nah-me-en'-to], *m.* Functioning, operation, action.

Funcionar [foon-the-o-nar'], *vn.* To work, to perform duly, to functionate: used of machinery or persons.

Funcionario [foon-the-o-nah'-re-o], *m.* Functionary, a public official.

Funda [foon'-dah], *f.* A case, a sheath, a covering, generally of linen or leather. *Funda de almohada,* Pillow-case

Fundación [foon-dah-the-on'], *f.* 1. Foundation, ground-work. 2. Foundation, the act of fixing the basis of an edifice, etc. 3. Foundation, rise, beginning, or origin of a thing. 4. Foundation, revenue established for any purpose.

Fundadamento [foon-dah-dah-men'-tay], *adv.* Fundamentally.

Fundador, ra [foon-dah-dor', rah], *m.* & *f.* Founder.

Fundago [foon-dah'-go], *m.* (Obs.) Magazine, warehouse, storehouse.

Fundamental [foon-dah-men-tahl'], *a.* 1. Fundamental, serving for the foundation. 2. Fundamental, essential, principal. *Hueso f.*, (Anat.) The sacrum; also the sphenoid bone. *Acorde f.*, That concord whose lowest note serves as a base for the chord.

Fundamentalmente [foon-dah-men-tal-men'-tay], *adv.* Fundamentally.

Fundamentar [foon-dah-men-tar'], *va.* 1. To found, to lay the foundation of a building. 2. (Met.) To found, to establish, to fix firm.

Fundamento [foon-dah-men'-to], *m.* 1. Foundation, ground-work. 2. Fundamental, leading proposition. 3. Foundation, ground, the principles on which any notion is raised. 4. Reason, cause, ground or principle. 5. Source, origin, root. 6. Weft, the woof of cloth.

Fundar [foon-dar'], *va.* 1. To found, to lay the foundation of a building 2. To found, to establish. 3. To found, to ground, to raise upon, as on a principle, maxim, or ground. *Fundarse en algo*, To go upon or to take as a principle.

Fundería [foon-day-ree'-ah], *f.* (Littl. us.) Foundry. *V.* FUNDICIÓN.

Fundible [foon-dee'-blay], *a.* Fusible.

Fundibulario [foon-de-boo-lah'-re-o], *m.* In the Roman militia, the soldier who was armed with a sling.

Fundibulo [foon-dee'-boo-lo], *m.* An ancient warlike machine for throwing stones; a sling.

Fundición [foon-de-the-on'], *f.* 1. Fusion, melting of metals. 2. Foundry, a place where melted metal is cast into form; a casting-house. 3. A complete set of printing types; font.

Fundidor [foon-de-dor'], *m.* Founder, melter, one who casts metals.

Fundilario [foon-de-lah'-re-o], *m.* Slinger, Roman soldier who used a sling.

Fundir [foon-deer'], *va.* 1. To found or melt metals. 2. (Met.) To unmake a thing in order to make it anew.

Fundo [foon'-do], *m.* 1. (Law and Amer.) *V.* HEREDAD. 2. A large estate.

Funebre [foo'-nay-bray], *a.* 1. Mournful, sad, lamentable. 2. Funeral, funereal, mourning.

Fúnebremente, *adv.* Mournfully, sorrowfully, lamentably.

Funeral [foo-nay-rahl'], *a.* Funeral. *A la funerala*, Mode of carrying arms by soldiers during holy week, and at funerals.

Funeral [foo-nay-rahl'], *m.* Funeral, the solemnization of a burial; generally used in the plural.

Funeraria [foo-nay-rah'-re-ah], *f.* Funeral parlor.

Funerario, ria [foo-nay-rah'-re-o, ah], *a.* Funeral, funereal.

Funéreo, rea [foo-nay'-ray-o, ah], *a.* (Poet.) Mournful, sad. *V.* FÚNEBRE.

Funestar [foo-nes-tar'], *va.* 1. To blot, stain, to profane. 2. (Obs.) To sadden, to make sad.

Funestamente, *adv.* Mournfully.

Funesto, ta [foo-ness'-to, tah], *a.* Funest, doleful, lamentable, untoward; mournful, sad, dismal.

Fungiforme [foon-he-for'-may], *a.* Fungiform, like a mushroom.

Fungir [foon-heer'], *vn.* (Amer.) To affect importance.

Fungita [foon-hee'-tah], *f.* Fungite, a fossil like a fungioid coral.

Fungívoro, ra [foon-hee'-vo-ro, rah], *a.* Fungivorous, devouring fungi.

Fungo [foon'-go], *m.* (Surg.) Fungus, fleshy excrescence.

Fungóideo, dea [foon-go'-e-day-o, ah], *a.* (Med.) Fungoid, like a fungus.

Fungón [foon-gone'], *m.* (Coll.) A great snuff-taker.

Fungosidad [foon-go-se-dahd'], *f.* (Surg.) Fungosity, excrescence.

Fungoso, sa [foon-go'-so, sah], *a.* Fungous, excrescent, spongy.

Funicular [foo-ne-coo-lar'], *a.* 1. Funicular, consisting of cords or fibres. 2. Funicular machine, a machine with a cord attached at one point and passing over a pulley, weights being added to demonstrate certain mechanical principles. 3. (Naut.) Tackle, rigging.

Funiculo [foo-nee'-coo-lo], *m.* (Bot.) Funicle, or funiculus, a filament which connects the ovule or seed with the placenta.

Funiculoso, sa [foo-ne-coo-lo'-so, sah], *a.* (Zool.) Provided with prominent lines: applied especially to shells.

Funífero, ra [foo-nee'-fay-ro, rah], *a.* (Bot.) Having appendages like cords.

Furacar [foo-rah-car'], *va.* (Obs.) To bore.

Furgón [foor-gone'], *m.* 1. A military covered transport wagon. 2. A freight car or box car. *Furgón entero*, A carload.

Furia [foo'-re-ah], *f.* 1. Fury, rage. 2. Fury, one of the deities of vengeance, and thence a stormy, violent woman. 3. Hurry, velocity and vigour, used in the performance of a thing. *A toda furia*, With the utmost speed. 4. Zeal, ardour. 5. A Roman law which prohibited the manumission of more than one hundred slaves at once.

Furial [foo-re-ahl'], *a.* (Poet.) Belonging to the Furies.

Furibundo, da [foo-re-boon'-do, dah], *a.* Furious, enraged, frantic, raging.

Furiosamente [foo-re-o-sah-men'-tay], *adv.* Furiously.

Furioso, sa [foo-re-o'-so, sah], *a.* 1. Furious, mad, frantic, frenetic. 2. Furious, raging, violent. 3. Very great, excessive.

Furo, ra [foo'-ro, rah], *a.* 1. Shy, reserved. 2. (Prov.) Ferocious, fierce; severe. *Hacer furo*, To conceal a thing with the design of keeping it.

Furor [foo-ror'], *m.* 1. Fury, madness, franticness. 2. Fury, rage, anger, approaching to madness. 3. (Poet.) Fury, enthusiasm, exaltation of fancy.

Furriela, *f.* *V.* FURRIERA.

Furriera [foor-re-ay'-rah], *f.* Place of keeper of the keys of the king's palace.

Furtivamente [foor-te-vah-men'-tay], *adv.* By stealth, clandestinely.

Furtivo, va [foor-tee'-vo, vah], *a.* Furtive, clandestine.

Furúnculo [foo-roon'-coo-lo], *m.* (Surg.) Furuncle, boil.

Furunculoso, sa [foo-roon-coo-lo'-so, sah], *a.* Furunculose, prone to suffer a succession of boils.

Fusa [foo'-sah], *f.* Demisemiquaver, a note in music.

Fusado, da, Fuselado, da [foo-sah'-do, dah], *a.* (Her.) Charged with fusils or spindles.

Fusca [foos'-cah], *f.* A kind of dark-coloured duck.

Fuscar [foos-car'], *va.* (Obs.) To obscure.

Fusco, ca [foos'-co, cah], *a.* Fuscous, brown, of a dim or dark colour.

Fuselaje [foo-say-lah'-hay], *m.* Fuselage (of an airplane).

Fusible [foo-see'-blay], *m.* (Elec.) Fuse.

Fusible, Fúsil [foo-see'-blay, foo'-seel], *a.* Fusible.

Fusiforme [foo-se-for'-may], *a.* Fusiform, spindle-shaped.

Fusil [foo-seel'], *m.* A flint-lock musket; gun, rifle of infantry. *Fusil de boca negra*, (Naut.) Sea-musket. *Fusil rayado*, Rifle gun. *Fusil de retrocarga*, A breech-loader.

Fusilador, ra [foo-se-lah-dor', rah], *m.* & *f.* One who shoots and who commands to shoot.

Fusilamiento [foo-se-lah-me-en'-to], *m.* The act and effect of shooting.

Fusilar [foo-se-lar'], *va.* 1. To kill by shooting. 2. To shoot, pierce by firearms.

Fusilazo [foo-se-lah'-tho], *m.* Musket-shot; blow with a musket.

Fusilería [foo-se-lay-ree'-ah], *f.* Body of fusileers or musketeers.

Fusilero [foo-se-lay'-ro], *m.* Fusileer, musketeer.

Fusión [foo-se-on'], *f.* 1. Fusion, liquation, melting. 2. Alliance, mingling of parties, systems, etc. 3. Liquefaction.

Fusique [foo-see'-kay], *m.* Kind of snuff-box in the shape of a small bottle.

Fuslina [foos-lee'-nah], *f.* Smelting works.

Fuslor [foos-lor'], *m.* Smelting ladle, a vessel for melting.

Fusta [foos'-tah], *f.* 1. Small vessel, with lateen sails. 2. Thin boards of wood. 3 Kind of woollen cloth. 4. Whip.

Fustán [foos-tahn'], *m.* 1. Fustian, a kind of cotton stuff. 2. (Peru.) A woman's white skirt.

Fustanero [foos-tah-nay'-ro], *m.* Fustian manufacturer.

Fuste [foos'-tay], *m.* 1. Wood, timber. 2. Tree and bows of a saddle. 3. (Poet.) A saddle. 4. Shaft of a lance. 5. Foundation of any thing, not material. 6. Substance of any thing. *Hombre de fuste*, Man of weight and importance. 7. (Arch.) Fust or body of a column. 8. An instrument of silversmiths.

Fustero, ra [foos-tay'-ro, rah], *a.* Belonging to a fust, foundation, etc.

Fustero [foos-tay'-ro], *m.* Turner or carpenter.

Fustete [foos-tay'-tay], *m.* (Bot.) Red or Venice sumach-tree. Rhus cotinus. Fustic, a wood from the West Indies, used in dyeing. *V.* FUSTOC.

Fustigar [foos-te-gar'], *va.* To whip, to fustigate.

Fustina [foos-tee'-nah], *f.* Place for fusing metals.

Fustoc [foos-toc'], *m.* Fustic, a yellow dye-wood, Venice sumach.

Futbol [foot-ball'], *m.* Football. *Futbol soccer*, Soccer.

Futesa [foo-tay'-sah], *f.* (Coll.) Trifle, bagatelle.

Fútil [foo'-teel], *a.* Futile, trifling, worthless, flimsy.

Futileza, *f.* *V.* FUTILIDAD.

Futilidad [foo-te-le-dahd'], *f.* Futility, weakness, groundlessness.

Futura [foo-too'-rah], *f.* 1. Survivorship, survival. 2. (Coll.) Intended bride.

Futurismo [foo-too-rees'-mo], *m.* Futurism.

Futurista [foo-too-rees'-tah], *a.* Futuristic.

Futuro, ra [foo-too'-ro, rah], *a.* Future.

Futuro [foo-too'-ro], *m.* 1. Future, futurity. 2. (Gram.) Future tense. *En lo futuro,* For the future.

G

G [hay], before the vowels *a, o* and *u,* has the same sound in Spanish as in English, but before *e* and *i* is the same as the Spanish *j,* or the English *h* strongly aspirated, as in *hay, her, he.* Before the diphthongs *ue, ui,* as in *guerra, guión,* the *u* becomes liquid, and the *g* has the hard sound as in the English word *give*; with a diæresis over the *ü,* both letters have their proper sound as in *agüero.*

Gabacho, cha [gah-bah'-cho, chah], *a.* 1. Applied to the natives of some places at the foot of the Pyrenees; used also in derision to the French. 2. Frenchified, given to Gallicisms.

Gabán [gah-bahn'], *m.* 1. Great-coat with a hood and close sleeves. 2. Overcoat. (Arab. gaftān.)

Gabanzo [gah-bahn'-tho], *m.* (Bot.) Dog-rose. *V.* GAVANZO.

Gabaonita [gah-bah-o-nee'-tah], *a.* & *n.* Gibeonite.

Gabarda [gah-bar'-dah], *f.* (Arragonese) Wild rose.

Gabardina [gah-bar-dee'-nah], *f.* Gabardine, cassock with close-buttoned sleeves.

Gabarra [gah-bar'-rah], *f.* 1. (Naut.) Lighter, a large boat. 2. A ferry-boat. 3. A fishing-boat.

Gabarrero [gah-bar-ray'-ro], *m.* 1. Dealer in wood and timber. 2. (Naut.) Lighterman.

Gabarro [gah-bar'-ro], *m.* 1. A morbid swelling on the pastern of horses. 2. Pip, a horny pellicle on the tongue of fowls. 3. Flaw or defect in cloth. 4. Error or mistake in accounts. 5. Defect discovered in goods after they have been bought. 6. (Met.) Obligation, burdensome change, error in accounts.

Gabasa, *f. V.* BAGASA. (Acad.)

Gábata [gah'-bah-tah], *f.* Bowl, a small wooden basin.

Gabazo [gah-bah'-tho], *m.* In sugar-mills, bruised sugar-cane. *V.* BAGAZO.

Gabela [gah-bay'-lah], *f.* 1. Gabel or gavel, tax or duty paid to government. 2. Load, heavy service.

Gabesina [gah-bay-see'-nah], *f.* Ancient kind of arms.

Gabinete [gah-be-nay'-tay], *m.* 1. Cabinet, a meeting of ministers of state and privy-councillors. 2. Cabinet, a private room for consultation. 3. Cabinet, a closet or small room for retirement. 4. A dressing-room for ladies. 5. Collection of curios, museum. *Gabinete de lectura,* A circulating library.

Gabón [gah-bon'], *m.* 1. (Naut.) Lodging quarters in the hold of a galley. 2. Powder magazine.

Gabote [gah-bo'-tay], *m.* (Prov.) Shuttlecock.

Gacel [gah-thel'], *m.* **Gacela** [gah-thay'-lah] *f.* Gazelle, antelope. (Arab. gazél, gazēla.)

Gaceta [gah-thay'-tah], *f.* Gazette, newspaper; an official publication.

Gacetero [gah-thay-tay'-ro], *m.* 1. Gazetteer, news-writer. 2. A seller of newspapers.

Gacetilla [gah-thay-teel'-yah], *f.* 1. A section of a newspaper devoted to news generally not political. 2. *a.* & *n.* Newsmonger.

Gacetillero [gah-thay-teel-lyay'-ro], *m.* 1. Editor of a *gacetilla.* 2. (derisively) A wretched writer, penny-a-liner.

Gacetista [gah-thay-tees'-tah], *m.* 1. One who delights in reading newspapers. 2. Newsmonger, gossip of news.

Gacha [gah'-chah], *f.* (Amer. Cuba) 1. An unglazed crock for preparing salt, and which the Indians use for eating and drinking. 2. (Naut.) *V.* GATA.

Gachas [gah'-chahs], *f. pl.* 1. Sort of fritters, made of flour, honey, and water. 2. Any sort of soft pap. 3. (Prov. Andal.) Caresses, pettings. *A gachas,* On all-fours. *Hacerse unas gachas,* To manifest extraordinary emotion in the presence or at the recollection of any thing; also, to grant a favour first refused. *¡ Ánimo a las gachas!* Cheer up! take courage!

Gaché [gah-chay'], *m.* (Prov. Andal.) Among vulgar people, beau, "feller."

Gacheta [gah-chay'-tah], *f.* 1. Spring in large locks. 2. (Prov.) *V.* ENGRUDO.

Gacho, cha [gah'-cho, chah], *a.* 1. Curvated, bent downward. 2. Having horns curved downward: applied to cattle. 3. Slouching: applied to hats.

Gachón, na [gah-chone', nah], *a.* & *m.* & *f.* 1. (Coll.) Graceful, sweet, attractive. 2. (Andal.) Pampered, spoiled, petted: applied to children.

Gachondo, da [gah-chon'-do, dah], *a. V.* GACHÓN, second definition.

Gachonería, Gachonada [gah-cho-nay-ree'-ah], *f.* Caress, endearment, fondness.

Gachumbo [gah-choom'-bo], *m.* (Amer.) The woody, tough rind of various fruits, from which cups and other vessels are made.

Gachupín [gah-choo-peen'], *m.* Name given in Mexico to a native of Spain, who in Lima is called *Chapetón* and in Buenos Ayres *Maturrango.*

Gádidos [gah'-de-dos], *m. pl.* Gadidæ, codfishes and allied species.

Gaditano, na [gah-de-tah'-no, nah], *a.* Native of or belonging to Cadiz.

Gaélico, ca [gah-ay'-le-co, cah], *a.* Gaelic.

Gafa [gah'-fah], *f.* A kind of hook, used to bend a cross-bow.—*pl.* 1. (Naut.) Can-hooks, used to raise or lower casks. 2. Spectacles. 3. Spectacle-bows. (Breton, gwaf.)

Gafar [gah-far'], *va.* To hook, to catch with a hook.

Gafedad [gah-fay-dahd'], *f.* 1. Kind of leprosy. 2. Contraction of the nerves.

Gafete [gah-fay'-tay], *m.* Clasp, a hook and eye. *V.* CORCHETE.

Gafo, fa [gah'-fo, fah], *a.* 1. Infected with leprosy. 2. Indisposed with a contraction of the nerves. 3. (Peru.) Paralytic, tremulous.

Gafón [gah-fone'], *m.* (Orn.) Greenfinch. Loxia chloris, *L.*

Gago, ga, *a. V.* TARTAMUDO.

Gaguear [gah-gay-ar'], *vn.* (Peru, Cuba) *V.* TARTAMUDEAR.

Gaillardia [gah-eel-lyar'-de-ah], *f.* (Bot.) Gaillardia, a showy composite flower of the gardens.

Gaita [gah'-ee-tah], *f.* 1. Bagpipe; hornpipe. 2. Flageolet. 3. Hand-organ. 4. (Coll.) The neck. *Estar de gaita,* (Coll.) To be very merry, in high spirits.

Gaitería [gah-e-tay-ree'-ah], *f.* A gay and gaudy dress.

Gaitero [gah-e-tay'-ro], *m.* Piper, one who plays the bagpipe.

Gaitero, ra [gah-e-tay'-ro, rah], *a.* Applied to a person who is more facetious or lively than is proper to his age, character, or profession.

Gaje [gah'-hay], *m.* (Obs.) 1. Challenge, a summons to fight. 2. Salary, pay, wages.—*pl.* Perquisites, fees, above the settled wages: sometimes used in the singular. *Los gajes del oficio,* A jocular manner of expressing the troubles peculiar to any office or employment.

Gajo [gah'-ho], *m.* 1. Branch of a tree. 2. Part of a bunch of grapes torn off. 3. Pyramidal raceme of any fruit.

Gajoso, sa [gah-ho'-so, sah], *a.* Branchy; spreading.

Gala [gah'-lah], *f.* 1. Gala, full, or court-dress. *Día de gala,* Court-day; holiday. 2. Graceful, pleasing address. 3. Parade, ostentation. 4. Choicest part of a thing. 5. In America, the present or premium given to any one as a reward of merit. *Hacer gala,* To glory in having done any thing. *Hacer gala del sambenito,* To boast in one's wickedness.

Galactite [gah-lac-tee'-tay], *f.* Fuller's-earth, alumina.

Galactófago, ga [gah-lac-to'-fah-go, gah], *a.* Living upon milk in the first period of life.

Galactóforo, ra [gah-lac-to'-fo-ro, rah] *a.* 1. Galactiferous, conducting milk. 2. (Med.) Galactogog(ue), increasing the flow of milk. 3. *m.* Breast-pump.

Galactómetro [gah-lac-to'-may-tro], *m.* Galactometer lactometer, an instrument for determining the density of milk.

Galafate [gah-lah-fah'-tay], *m.* 1. An artful thief, a cunning rogue. 2. Hangman, executioner. 3. Porter who carries burdens. 4. (Naut.) Calker. *V.* CALAFATE.

Galafatear. (Naut.) *V.* CALAFATEAR.

Galaico, ca [gah-lah'-e-co, cah], *a. V.* GALLEGO. (Acad.)

Galamero, ra [gah-lah-may'-ro, rah], *a.* Dainty. *V.* GOLOSO.

Galán [gah-lahn'], *m.* 1. Gallant, a spruce, well-made man. 2. Gentleman in full dress. 3. Gallant, courtier; lover, wooer. 4. Actors who perform serious characters in plays are distinguished in order, as first, second, etc., *galán. Galán de noche,* (Bot.) Night-smelling cestrum. Cestrum nocturnum, *L.*

Galán, na [gah-lahn', nah], *a.* 1. Gallant, gay, fine, neat, well-dressed. 2. Elegant, lively, ingenious. 3. Gallant, courtly, with respect to ladies.

Galana [gah-lah'-nah], *f.* 1. (Bot.) Flat-podded lathyrus. Lathyrus cicera, *L.* 2. A woman very showily dressed.

Galanamente [gah-lah-nah-men'-tay], *adv.* Gallantly, elegantly.

Galancete [gah-lan-thay'-tay], *m. dim.* A spruce little man, a buck, a spark, a little gallant.

Galanga [gah-lahn'-gah], *f.* (Bot.) *Galanga mayor,* Officinal galangal. Kæmpferia galanga, *L. Galanga menor,* Smaller galangal. Marauta galanga.

Galano, na [gah-lah'-no, nah], *a.* 1. Gallant, fine, gay, genteel, splendidly dressed. 2. Elegant, ingenious, lively, sprightly.

Galante [ga-lahn'-tay], *a.* 1. Gallant, courtly with respect to ladies. 2. Brave, generous, liberal. 3. Elegant, handsome; witty, facetious.

Galanteador [gah-lan-tay-ah-dor'], *m.* Wooer, lover.

Galantear [gah-lan-tay-ar'], *va.* 1. To court, to woo; to solicit favour. 2 (Obs.) To ornament or deck.

Galantemente [gah-lan-tay-men'-tay], *adv.* Gallantly, civilly.

Galanteo [gah-lan-tay'-o], *m.* 1. The

act of soliciting favour. 2. Gallantry, courtship, refined address to women.

Galantería [gah-lan-tay-ree'-ah], *f.* 1. Gallantness, gallantry, elegance. 2. Splendour of appearance, show, magnificence; a graceful manner. 3. Liberality, munificence, generosity.

Galanto [gah-lahn'-to], *m.* (Bot.) Snowdrop. Galanthus, *L.* *Galanto nivel*, Common snowdrop. Galanthus nivalis, *L.*

Galanura [gah-lah-noo'-rah], *f.* 1. A showy, splendid dress or ornament. 2. Gracefulness, elegance.

Galápago [gah-lah'-pah-go], *m.* 1. Fresh-water tortoise. Testudo lutaria, *L.* 2. Bed of a plough-share. 3. Frame for boring guns. 4. A kind of shed which soldiers once formed with shields joined together. 5. A horse-saddle. 6. A pig of copper, lead, or tin. 7. A convex frame, on which vaults are formed. 8. Cleft in a horse's foot. 9. Ancient military machine. (Turk. kaplūbaga.)

Galapo [gah-lah'-po], *m.* Frame for twisting ropes.

Galardón [gah-lar-done'], *m.* Guerdon, reward, recompense.

Galardonador, ra [gah-lar-do-nah-dor', rah], *m.* & *f.* Remunerator, rewarder.

Galardonar [gah-lar-do-nar'], *va.* To reward, to recompense, to requite.

Gálata [gah'-lah-tah], *a.* Galatian, of Galatia.

Galatea [gah-lah-tay'-ah], *f.* 1. (Bot.) A composite plant common in North America and North Asia. 2. A decapod crustacean of the Mediterranean and of the coasts of Chili.

Galato [gah-lah'-to], *m.* (Chem.) Gallate.

Galatite, *f.* *V.* GALACTITE.

Galavardo [gah-lah-var'-do], *m.* (Obs.) A tall, lean, and weak man.

Galaxia [gah-lac-see'-ah], *f.* 1. (Ast.) Galaxy, the milky way. 2. Soap stone, steatite.

Galbana [gal-bah'-nah], *f.* 1. (Bot.) *V.* GALANA. Lathyrus cicera, *L.* 2. Sloth, laziness, slothfulness, idleness, indolence.

Galbanado, da [gal-bah-nah'-do, dah], *a.* Of the colour of galbanum.

Galbanero, ra [gal-bah-nay'-ro, rah], *a.* (Coll.) Lazy, indolent, careless, inattentive.

Gálbano [gahl'-bah-no], *m.* (Pharm.) Galbanum, a resinous gum.

Galbanoso, sa [gal-bah-no'-so, sah], *a.* Indolent, lazy, shiftless.

Gálbulo [gahl'-boo-lo], *m.* The nut of the cypress-tree.

Galdrope [gal-dro'-pay], *m.* (Naut.) Wheel-rope, the rope of the steering-wheel.

Galdrufa [gal-droo'-fah], *f.* (Prov. Arag.) Top, a child's plaything.

Gálea [gah'-lay-ah], *f.* An ancient morion or helmet.

Galeato, ta [gah-lay-ah'-to, tah], *a.* Applied to the prologue or preface of any work, in which a reply or defence is made to the objections against it.

Galeaza [gah-lay-ah'-thah], *f.* (Naut.) Galeas, a kind of vessel.

Galega [gah-lay'-gah], *f.* (Bot.) Official goat's-rue. Gallega officinalis, *L*

Galena [gah-lay'-nah], *f.* Galena sulphuret of lead.

Galénico, ca [gah-lay'-ne-co, cah], *a.* Galenic, galenical.

Galenismo [gah-lay-nees'-mo], *m.* Galenism, doctrine of Galen.

Galenista [gah-lay-nees'-tah], *m.* Galenist, physician who follows the doctrine of Galen.

Galeo [gah-lay'-o], *m.* (Zool.) Sword-fish. Xiphias gladius, *L.*

Galeón [gah-lay-on'], *m.* (Naut.) Galleon, armed ship of burden, formerly used in Spain for trade in time of war.

Galeota [gah-lay-o'-tah], *f.* (Naut.) Galliot, a smaller galley of sixteen to twenty oars on a side.

Galeote [gah-lay-o'-tay], *m.* Galley-slave.

Galera [gah-lay'-rah], *f.* 1. Galley, a vessel with oars, in use in the Mediterranean. 2. Wagon, a heavy covered carriage for burdens. 3. House of correction for women. 4. (Print.) Galley, an oblong square frame with ledges, to preserve together a column of types as they are composed. 5. (Arith.) Line cutting off the quotient in division. 6. (Mil.) A subterranean gallery under a fortress. 7. A room for keeping the common metals. 8. An organ-builder's plane. 9. A furnace for distilling sulphur.—*pl.* Punishment of rowing on board of galleys. *Estar en galeras*, (Met.) To be in distress or affliction. *Azotes y galeras*, (Met.) Applied to ordinary food never varied.

Galerada [gah-lay-rah'-dah], *f.* (Print.) Galley of types composed, or the proof of a galley for correction.

Galerero [gah-lay-ray'-ro], *m.* A wagoner.

Galería [gah-lay-ree'-ah], *f.* 1. Gallery, lobby. 2. (Fort.) A narrow covered passage across a moat. 3. *Galería de popa*, (Naut.) Stern-gallery or balcony, into which there is a passage out of the great cabin.

Galerilla [gah-lay-reel'-lyah], *f.* *dim.* A small gallery.

Galerín [gah-lay-reen'], *m.* *dim.* A wooden galley in printing offices.

Galerita [gah-lay-ree'-tah], *f.* (Orn.) Crested lark. Alauda cristata, *L.*

Galerna [gah-lerr'-nah], *f.* (Naut.) A stormy north-west wind which blows on hot summer days upon the northern coast of Spain, sometimes very disastrous.

Galfarro [gal-far'-ro], *m.* 1. Rogue, swindler. 2. (Prov. León) *V.* GAVILÁN.

Galga [gahl'-gah], *f.* 1. Greyhound bitch, the female of the *Canis grajus*, *L.* 2. Wheel of the stone of an oil-mill. 3. Kind of itch. 4. (Prov.) Bier with which poor people are buried. 5. (Naut.) Back of an anchor. 6. Drag, Scotch brake for a wheel. 7. *pl.* Ribbons or strings for tying women's shoes.

Galgo [gahl'-go], *m.* Greyhound. Canis grajus, *L.* *El que nos vendió el galgo*, The very man we spoke of. *Vete a espulgar un galgo*, (Coll.) Go to the devil.

Galgo, ga, *a.* (Amer.) Hungry, anxious for something.

Galgueño, ña [gal-gay'-nyo, yah], *a.* Resembling or concerning a greyhound.

Gálgulo [gal'-goo-lo], *m.* (Orn.) Roller. Coracias garrula, *L.*

Galiambo [gah-le-ahm'-bo], *m.* Song of the Gallic priest of Cybele.

Galibar [gah-le-bar'], *va.* (Naut.) To mould.

Gálibo [gah'-lee-bo], *m.* (Naut.) Model of a ship.

Galicado, da [gah-le-cah'-do, dah], *a.* (Coll.) *V.* GALICOSO.

Galicana [gah-le-cah'-nah], *a.* *La iglesia galicana*, The Gallican church.

Galicinio [gah-le-thec'-ne-o], *m.* (Obs.) Cock-crowing time.

Galicismo [gah-le-thees'-mo], *m.* Gallicism, French phraseology.

Gálico [gah'-le-co], *m.* Venereal disease, syphilis.

Galicoso, sa [gah-le-co'-so, sah], *a.* (Coll.) Infected with syphilis.

Galileo, lea [gah-le-lay'-o, ah], *a.* Galilean, of Galilee.

Galillo [gah-leel'-lyo], *m.* Uvula, hanging palate.

Galimatías [gah-le-mah-tee'-ahs], *m.* (coll.) 1. Gibberish, confused speech, jive. 2. A tangled, confused matter.

Galio [gah'-le-o], *m.* 1. (Bot.) Cheese-rennet bed-straw. Galium verum, *L.* 2. (Chem.) Galium.

Galiopsis [gah-le-op'-sis], *f.* (Bot.) Common hedge-nettle. Stachys silvatica, *L.*

Galipodio [gah-le-po'-de-o], *m.* White frankincense, or the white rosin which distils from the pine-tree or fir; galipot.

Galivos [gah-lee'-vos], *m. pl.* Compassings, bevellings, pieces of timber incurvated in the form of an arch.

Galizabra [gah-le-thah'-brah], *f.* Kind of vessel with lateen sails in the Levant trade.

Galo, la [gah'-lo, lah], *a.* Gaul, native of Gaul.

Galocha [gah-lo'-chah], *f.* 1. Galosh, clog, a wooden shoe. 2. Patten, an over-shoe of wood with an iron ring.

Galón [gah-lone'], *m.* 1. Galloon, a texture of silk, thread, gold or silver. 2. Lace. 3. Gallon, a liquid measure. 4. (Naut.) Wooden ornament on the sides of ships. *Galones*, (Naut.) Rails around the quarter-deck.

Galonazo [gah-lo-nah'-tho], *m.* 1. (Aug.) Large galloon. 2. Excessive ornament.

Galoneadura [gah-lo-nay-ah-doo'-rah], *f.* Garnishing with lace or galloons.

Galonear [gah-lo-nay-ar'], *va.* To lace, to adorn with lace.

Galonero [gah-lo-nay'-ro], *m.* Lace or galloon maker.

Galop [gah-lop'], *m.* (Acad.) A Hungarian dance, and the music to which it is set.

Galopada [gah-lo-pah'-dah], *f.* The space over which a horse gallops.

Galopar [gah-lo-par'], *vn.* To gallop.

Galope [gah-lo'-pay], *m.* 1. Gallop, motion of a horse. 2. Hasty execution of a thing. *A galope* or *de galope*, Gallopingly.

Galopeado, da [gah-lo-pay-ah'-do, dah], *a.* & *pp.* of GALOPEAR. Done in a hurry.—*m.* Whipping, flogging.

Galopear [gah-lo-pay-ar'], *vn.* *V.* GALOPAR.

Galopín [gah-lo-peen'], *m.* 1. (Naut.) Swabber, a boy who swabs the deck; a cabin-boy. 2. Scullion, a kitchen-boy. 3. A contemptible rogue. 4. Boy meanly dressed. 5. A clever knave.

Galopo [gah-lo'-po], *m.* Rogue. *V.* GALOPÍN, 3d. def.

Galopinada [gah-lo-pe-nah'-dah], *f.* Action of a cunning, crafty person; knavery.

Galpito [gal-pee'-to], *m.* A weak, sickly chicken.

Galpón [gal-pone'], *m.* (Peru, etc.) A dormitory, or other spacious apartment, which was set aside for the slaves and other labourers of a farm.

Galván (proper name). *No lo entenderá Galván*, An intricate, difficult thing.

Galvánico, ca [gal-vah'-ne-co, cah], *a.* (Phys.) Galvanic.

Galvanismo [gal-vah-nees'-mo], *m.* Galvanism, electricity of metals.

Galvanizar [gal-vah-ne-thar'], *va.* (Phys.) To galvanize.

Galvanómetro [gal-vah-no'-may-tro], *m.* Galvanometer.

Galvanoplastia, or **Galvanoplástica** [gal-vah-no-plahs'-te-ah], *f.* Galvanoplasty, electrotypy.
Galladura [gal-lyah-doo'-rah], *f.* Tread, cicatricula, a ruddy spot in the yolk of an egg.
Gallarda [gal-lyar'-dah], *f.* A kind of airy Spanish dance.
Gallardamente [gal-lyar-dah-men'-tay], *adv.* Elegantly, gracefully, gallantly.
Gallardear [gal-lyar-day-ar'], *vn.* To do any thing with grace or elegance.
Gallardete [gal-lyar-day'-tay], *m.* (Naut.) Pennant, streamer.
Gallardetón [gal-lyar-day-tone'], *m.* (Naut.) Broad pennant.
Gallardía [gal-lyar-dee'-ah], *f.* 1. A graceful air and deportment. 2. Genteelness, elegance, gracefulness. 3. Gallantry, bravery, nobleness. 4. Activity, briskness in the execution or performance of a thing. 5. Liberality of sentiments, disinterestedness. 6. Magnanimity, greatness of mind.
Gallardo, da [gal-yar'-do, dah], *a.* 1. Gay, graceful, elegant, genteel. 2. Magnanimous, great of mind, exalted in sentiments. 3. Generous, disinterested, high-spirited; pleasant, lively. 4. Brave, daring, bold, gallant.
Gallareta [gal-lyah-ray'-tah], *f.* (Orn.) Widgeon. Anas ferina, *L.*
Gallarín [gal-lyah-reen'], *m.* (Obs.) Excessive gain or loss. *Salir al gallarín,* To experience a loss or disgrace, not to succeed.
Gallarón [gal-lyah-ron'], *m.* (Orn.) A kind of bustard.
Gallarito [gal-lyah-ree'-to], *m.* (Bot.) Lousewort. Pedicularis, *L. V.* PEDICULAR.
Gallaruza [gal-lyah-roo'-thah], *f.* A coarse garment, worn by country people.
Gallear [gal-lyay-ar'], *va.* 1. To tread, to copulate as birds. 2. (Met.) To assume an air of importance.—*vn.* 1. To raise the voice with a menace or call; to become irritated. 2. To crow, to bully.
Gallegada [gal-lyay-gah'-dah], *f.* 1. Number of natives of Galicia assembled together. 2. Manners or behaviour of the natives of Galicia. 3. A Galician dance.
Gallego, ga [gah-lyay'-go, gah], *a.* Galician, belonging to the province of Galicia.
Gallego [gal-lyay'-go], *m.* In Castile, the north-west wind.
Gallera [gal-lyay'-rah], *f.* (Sp. Am.) Cockfighting ring.
Galleta [gal-lyay'-tah], *f.* 1. Cracker. 2. Cookie. 3. Sea biscuit. 4. (Coll.) Slap in the face. 5. Small bowl with a spout.
Gallicinio [gal-lye-thee'-ne-o], *m.* (Obs.) Cock-crowing, the time when the cocks crow at night, near dawn.
Gallillo [gal-lyeel'-lyo (generally pronounced gah-leel'-lyo)], *m.* (Anat.) Uvula. *V.* GALILLO.
Gallina [gal-lyee'-nah], *f.* 1. Hen, a domestic fowl. 2. (Met.) Coward, a chicken-hearted fellow. In this sense used as masculine. 3. In some universities, second orator or student destined to deliver the eulogium at graduating. *Gallina ciega,* Blindman's-buff, or hoodman's blind: a play among boys. *Hijo de la gallina blanca,* A lucky, fortunate man. *Gallina de río. V.* GALLINETA. *Acostarse con las gallinas,* (Coll.) To go to bed very early.
Gallináceo, cea [gah-lye-nah'-thay-o, ah], *a.* Gallinaceous, relating to domestic fowls.
Gallinaza [gal-lye-nah'-thah], *f.* 1. Hen-dung. 2. (Orn.) Carrion vulture, kite. Falco brasiliensis, *L.* In Vera Cruz it is called *Zopilote.*
Gallinería [gal-lye-nay-ree'-ah], *f.* 1. (Prov.) Poulterer's shop. 2. Hen-coop or hen-house. 3. (Met.) Cowardice, pusillanimity.
Gallinero, ra [gal-lye-nay'-ro, rah], *a.* (Falc.) Praying or feeding upon fowls.
Gallinero [gal-lye-nay'-ro], *m.* 1. Poulterer, one who deals in poultry. 2. Hen-yard, hen-coop, hen-roost, hen-house. 3. Basket in which fowls are carried to market. 4. (Met.) Place where many women meet. 5. (Coll.) The gallery of a Spanish play-house.
Gallineta [gal-lye-nay'-tah], *f.* 1. (Orn.) Sand-piper. Tringa hypoleucus, *L.* 2. Ruffed grouse.
Gallipavo [gal-lye-pah'-vo], *m.* 1. (Orn.) Turkey. Meleagris gallopavo, *L.* 2. A false, unpleasant note in singing.
Gallipollo [gal-lye-pol'-lyo], *m.* Cockerel, a young cock.
Gallipuente [gal-lye-poo-en'-tay], *m.* (Prov.) Bridge without rails.
Gallito [gal-lyee'-to], *m.* 1. Beau, coxcomb. 2. (Dim.) Small cock. *Gallitos,* Shaggy-leaved toad-flax. Antirrhinum hirtum, *L.* 3. The yellow violet of California.
Gallo [gahl'-lyo], *m.* 1. (Orn.) Cock, rooster, the male to the hen. Gallus. *Gallo inglés* or *de riña,* Game-cock. 2. (Zool.) Dory, a sea-fish. Zeus faber, *L.* 3. (Met.) Chief of a village or parish. 4. Float of cork serving as a mark to fishers, so that they may draw their nets. 5. *V.* GALLIPAVO. 6. (Carp.) Wall-board in the roofing of a house. *Al gallo que canta, le aprietan la garganta,* Strangle the cock that crows (warning to keep a secret). *El que solo come su gallo, solo ensilla su caballo,* He who is selfish in his pleasures must not expect help in his need. *Escarbó el gallo y descubrió el cuchillo,* Inquisitive people sometimes learn unpleasant things. *Pata de gallo,* An artful device. *Salir con una pata de gallo,* To give foolish advice. *Tener mucho gallo,* To be very arrogant and proud. *Hacerse* or *ser el gallo,* To become the ruler in any meeting, body, etc.
Gallobosque [gal-lyo-bos'-kay], *m.* (Orn.) Wood-grouse. Tetrao urogallus, *L.*
Gallocresta [gal-lyo-cres'-tah], *f.* (Bot.) Annual clary sage. Salvia horminum, *L.*
Gallofa [gal-lyo'-fah], *f.* 1. Morsel of bread or other food given to pilgrims. 2. Greens used for salad and pottage. 3. An idle tale. 4. (Prov.) Directory of divine service.
Gallofear [gal-lyo-fay-ar'], *vn.* To saunter about and live upon alms.
Gallofero, ra [gal-lyo-fay'-ro, rah], *a.* Idle, lazy, vagabond: applied to a beggar without a home.
Gallofo, fa [gal-lyo'-fo, fah], *a. V.* GALLOFERO.
Gallón [gal-lyone'], *m.* (Prov.) Green sod, turf; a clod covered with grass. *Gallones,* Festoons, an ornament or carved work.
Gallonada [gal-lyo-nah'-dah], *f.* Wall made of sods.
Galluda [gal-lyoo'-dah], *f.* (Zool.) Tope, dogfish, a small shark. Galeus canis.
Gama [gah'-mah], *f.* 1. Gamut, the scale of musical notes. 2. Doe, the female to a buck.
Gama globulina [gah'-mah glo-boo-lee'-nah], *f.* (Med.) Gammaglobulin.
Gamalote [gah-mah-lo'-tay], *m.* A grass of South America; arrow-grass. Gynerium saccharoides.
Gamarra [gah-mar'-rah]. *f.* Martingale, a strap used to prevent a horse from rearing.
Gamarza [gah-mar'-thah], *f.* (Bot.) Wild Syrian rue, peganum. Peganum harmala, *L.*
Gambaj, or **Gambax** [gam-bah', gambax'], *m.* A quilted jacket of wool.
Gámbalo [gahm'-bah-lo], *m.* (Obs.) Kind of linen.
Gambalúa [gam-bah-loo'-ah], *f.* (Coll.) A tall, ill-shaped man, without life or spirit.
Gámbaro [gahm'-bah-ro], *m.* A kind of small craw-fish.
Gambesina [gam-bay-see'-nah], *f.* or **Gambesón** [gam-bay-son'], *m.* A kind of jacket worn under the armour for comfort.
Gambeta [gam-bay'-tah], *f.* 1. Cross-caper in dancing; ancient dance. 2. Affected language or tone of voice. 3. *Gambeta de mar,* Scaled centre shell. Lepas pollicipes, *L.*
Gambetear [gam-bay-tay-ar'], *vn.* To caper like a horse.
Gambeto [gam-bay'-to], *m.* A quilted great-coat.
Gambo [gahm'-bo], *m.* Cap for a new-born child.
Gambotes [gam-bo'-tes], *m. pl.* (Naut.) Counter-timbers, arched timbers. (Also **Gambotas,** *f.*)
Gambux [gam-boocs'], *m.* A small bonnet or cap for children.
Gamela [gah-may'-lah], *f.* Kind of basket.
Gamelo [gah-may'-lo], *m.* Name given by the Indians to balsam copaiba.
Gamella [gah-mel'-lyah], *f.* 1. Yoke for oxen and mules. 2. A large wooden trough. 3. *V.* CAMELLÓN. 4. She-camel. (Acad.)
Gamelleja [gah-mel-lyay'-hah], *f. dim.* A small yoke.
Gamellón [gah-mel-lyone'], *m.* 1. (Aug.) A large yoke for oxen and mules. 2. (Prov.) Trough in which grapes are trodden.
Gamezno [gah-meth'-no], *m.* Little young buck.
Gamino [gah-mee'-no], *m.* (Vet.) A tumour which attacks sheep and goats.
Gamo [gah'-mo], *m.* 1. Buck of the fallow-deer. Cervus dama, *L.* 2. *V.* GAMINO. 3. An iron hook in a wooden handle for hooking fishes already caught. 4. (Coll.) A restless, quick-moving individual.
Gamogastro [gah-mo-gahs'-tro], *a.* (Bot.) Gamogastrous, having the ovaries united.
Gamón [gah-mone'], *m.* (Bot.) Asphodel. Asphodelus, *L.* Applied to the *asphodelus ramosus, L.*
Gamonal [gah-mo-nahl'], *m.* Place in which asphodels flourish.
Gamoncillo [gah-mon-theel'-lyo], *m.* (Bot.) Onion-leaved asphodel. Asphodelus fistulosus, *L.*
Gamonito [gah-mo-nee'-to], *m.* 1. Young shoots springing round trees or shrubs. 2. (Dim.) Young asphodel. 3. (Bot.) *V.* MARTAGÓN.
Gamonoso, sa [gah-mo-no'-so, sah], *a.* Abounding in asphodels.
Gamopétalo, la [gah-mo-pay'-tah-lo, lah], *a* Gamopetalous.
Gamosépalo, la [gah-mo-say'-pah-lo, lah], *a.* Gamosepalous.
Gamucería [ga-moo-thay-ree'-ah], *f* The factory where chamois skins are curried and prepared.
Gamuno, na [gah-moo'-no, nah], *a.* Applied to the skins of deer.

Gamuza [gah-moo'-thah], *f.* 1. Chamois. Antelope rupicapra, *L.* 2. Chamois or chamois leather. (Arab.)
Gamuzado, da [gah-moo-thah'-do, dah], *a.* Chamois colour.
Gamuzón [gah-moo-thon'], *m. dim.* A kind of coarse chamois.
Gana [gah'-nah], *f.* 1. Appetite, keenness of stomach; hunger. 2. (Prov.) A healthy disposition of body. 3. Inclination, desire, mind, list. *De buena gana*, With pleasure, willingly, voluntarily. *De mala gana*, Unwillingly, with reluctance, with dislike. *Donde hay gana, hay maña*, Where there is a will, there is a way. *De gana*, Designedly, on purpose. *Tener gana*, To have a mind. *Comer con gana*, To eat with an appetite.
Ganada [gah-nah'-dah], *f.* (Obs.) Act of gaining or winning.
Ganadería [gah-nah-day-ree'-ah], *f.* 1. Breeding cattle to sell. 2. Stock of cattle.
Ganadero, ra [gah-nah-day'-ro, rah], *a.* (Obs.) Belonging to cattle.
Ganadero, ra [gah-nah-day'-ro, rah], *m. & f.* Grazier, owner of cattle; dealer in cattle, drover.
Ganado [gah-nah'-do], *m.* 1. Herd of domesticated animals of the same kind; flock, drove. *Ganado mayor*, Cattle: it is also said of mules. *Ganado menor*, Sheep: it is also said of asses. *Ganado churro*, *V.* CHURRO. *Ganado merino*, *V.* MERINO. *Ganado de cerda*, Swine, hogs, pigs. *Ganado de pata hendida*, Oxen, cows, sheep, goats. 2. Cattle, word of contempt applied to men and women. 3. Collection of bees of a bee-hive.—*Ganado, da, pp.* of GANAR.
Ganador, ra [gah-nah-dor', rah], *m. & f.* 1. Winner. 2. Gainer. 3. Earner.
Ganancia [gah-nahn'-the-ah], *f.* 1. Gain, earnings, profit. 2. Winnings. 3. Earning, profiting. *Ganancia bruta*, Gross profit. *Ganancias y pérdidas*, Profit and loss.
Ganancial [gah-nan-the-ahl'], *a.* Lucrative. *Bienes gananciales*, Property acquired during marriage.
Ganancioso, sa [gah-nan-the-o'-so, sah], *a.* Lucrative, gainful.
Ganapán [gah-nah-pahn'], *m.* 1. A porter. 2. A rude, coarse man. (Acad.) A shiftless fellow, a ne'er-do-well.
Ganapierde [gah-nah-pe-err'-day], *m.* A mode of playing draughts, where he who loses all his men wins the game; give-away or losing game.
Ganar [gah-nar'], *va.* 1. To gain, to get or obtain, as profit or advantage. 2. To gain, to win. 3. To gain, to have the overplus in comparative computation. 4. To win, to conciliate, to allure to kindness or compliance. 5. To attain, to acquire. 6. To conquer. 7. To surpass. *Ganar el barlovento*, (Naut.) To get to windward. *Ganar el viento* or *barlovento*, To gain the weather-gage. *Ganar la vida*, To gain a living. *Ganar las albricias*, To get the start in bringing favourable news.
Ganchero [gan-chay'-ro], *m.* Conductor of a raft of timber.
Ganchillo [gan-cheel'-lyo], *m. dim.* A little hook or crotch.
Gancho [gahn'-cho], *m.* 1. Hook, which remains after a branch of a tree has been broken off. 2. Hook, an incurvated piece of iron; a crotch. 3. Crook, a sheep-hook. 4. An allurer, one who insinuates himself into the favour of another to attain some purpose. 5. Pimp, procurer, pander. 6. (Naut.) An iron hook with an eye. *Gancho de bichero*, Boat-hook. *Gancho de botalón*, Gooseneck of a boom. *Gancho de aparejo*, Tackle-hook. *Gancho de las estrelleras del trinquete*, Hook of the fore-tackle. *Gancho de la gata*, Cat-hook. *Gancho de guimbalete de las ostagas*, Swivel-hook of the top-sail-ties. *Ganchos de pescantes de anclas*, Fish-hooks of an anchor. *Ganchos de las arraigadas*, Foot-hooks or futtocks. *Ganchos de revirar maderos*, Cant-hooks.
Ganchoso, sa [gan-cho'-so, sah], *a.* Hooked, curved.
Ganchuelo [gan-choo-ay'-lo], *m. dim.* *V.* GANCHILLO.
Gándara [gahn'-dah-rah], *f.* A low range of mountains, or rough, uncultivated ground. (Acad.)
Gandaya [gan-dah'-yah], *f.* 1. Laziness, idleness. 2. *V.* COFIA. *Andar a la gandaya*, *buscar la gandaya* or *correr la gandaya*, To wander, to gad, to roam.
Gandido, da [gan-dee'-do, dah], *a.* 1. (Prov.) Seduced, led astray. 2. (Amer. Peru.) Hungry, gluttonous.
Gandinga [gan-deen'-gah], *f.* (Cuba) A stew made from the liver of a hog or other animal.
Gandir [gan-deer'], *va.* To eat. (Acad.)
Gandujado [gan-doo-hah'-do], *m.* Ornament or ruffle of a woman's dress. —*Gandujado, da, pp.* of GANDUJAR.
Gandujar [gan-doo-har'], *va.* To bend, to plait, to fold.
Gandul, la [gan-dool', lah], *m. & f.* Vagabond, vagrant, tramp. (Arab. gandur.)
Gandulear [gan-doo-lay-ar'], *vn.* To lounge, to be idle.
Ganfalonero [gan-fah-lo-nay'-ro], *m.* Gonfalonier, Pope's standard-bearer.
Ganfanón [gan-fah-non'], *m.* Gonfalon, ensign of the Romish church, and of some Italian states.
Ganforro, ra [gan-for'-ro, rah], *m. & f.* (Coll.) Vagrant, vagabond.
Ganga [gahn'-gah], *f.* 1. (Orn.) The little pin-tailed grouse. Tetras alchata, *L.* 2. Any thing valuable acquired with little labour. *Andar á caza de gangas*, To spend one's time in looking for some thing that can be had without labour. *Buena ganga es esa*, An ironical expression, meaning that some acquisition is not worth the trouble which had been necessary to obtain it. (Imitative.)
Ganga, *f.* (Min.) Gangue, bed or matrix of minerals. (German, gang.)
Gangarilla [gan-gah-reel'-lyah], *f.* Ancient company of strolling players.
Ganglio [gahn'-gle-o], *m.* 1. (Anat.) Ganglion. 2. (Med.) Ganglion, a small tumour of the sheath of a tendon.
Ganglionar [gan-gle-o-nar'], *a.* Ganglionic, provided with ganglions.
Gangoso, sa [gan-go'-so, sah], *a.* Snuffling, or speaking through the nose.
Gangrena [gan-gray'-nah], *f.* Gangrene, mortification.
Gangrenar [gan-gray-nar'], *va.* To cause gangrene or mortification; to corrupt, to rot.—*vr.* To become gangrenous or mortified.
Gangrenoso, sa [gan-gray-no'-so, sah], *a.* Gangrenous.
Ganguear [gan-gay-ar'], *vn.* To snuffle, to speak through the nose.
Gánguil [gahn'-geel], *m.* 1. A barge used for fishing, or in the coasting-trade; lighter. 2. A fishing-net broader than that called *tartana.*
Ganil [gah-neel'], *m.* A granular, calcareous rock.
Ganoso, sa [gah-no'-so, sah], *a.* Desirous, full of desire; longing after
Gansarón [gan-sah-ron'], *m.* 1. A gosling. 2. A tall, thin man.
Gansería [gan-say-ree'-ah], *f.* Folly, stupidity. (Ger. gans, a goose.)
Ganso, sa [gahn'-so, sah], *m. & f.* 1. (Orn.) Gander, goose. Anas anser, *L.* 2. Tall, slender person, 3. (Coll.) A goose or goose-cap, a silly person.—*pl.* Giblets of a goose.
Gante [gahn'-tay], *m.* A kind of linen manufactured in Ghent.
Ganzúa [gan-thoo'-ah], *f.* 1. Picklock, an instrument with which locks are opened. 2. Thief who picks locks.
Ganzuar [gan-thoo-ar'], *va.* To pick a lock, to open it with a picklock.
Gañán [gah-nyahn'], *m.* Day-labourer; teamster, rustic.
Gañanía [gah-nyah-nee'-ah], *f.* Number of day-labourers.
Gañido [gah-nyee'-do], *m.* Yelping or howling of a dog.—*Gañido, da, pp.* of GAÑIR.
Gañiles [gah-nyee'-les], *m. pl.* The cartilaginous larynx, organ of the voice.
Gañir [gah-nyeer'], *va.* 1. To yelp or howl like a dog. 2. To croak, to cackle, to crow. 3. To talk hoarsely.
Gañón, Gañote [gah-nyon', gah-nyo'-tay], *m.* 1. The throat. 2. (Prov.) Kind of fritters.
Gaón [gah-on'], *m.* 1. A substitute for the oar in the Indian vessels known as barangays and virreys. 2. Title of honour which was once given to rabbis or Jews who distinguished themselves in the sciences.
Garabatada [gah-rah-bah-tah'-dah], *f.* (Coll.) Act of throwing a hook.
Garabatear [gah-rah-bah-tay-ar'], *va.* 1. To hook, to catch with a hook. 2. To scrawl, to scribble. 3. To use tergiversations.
Garabateo [gah-rah-bah-tay'-o], *m.* Act of hooking.
Garabatillo [gah-rah-bah-teel'-lyo], *m.* 1. (Dim.) A small hook. 2. Difficulty of evacuating any peccant matter from the lungs.
Garabato [gah-rah-bah'-to], *m.* 1. Pot-hook; grapnel, creeper. 2. Hook to hang meat on. 3. A graceful gait and deportment. *Tiene garabato*, (Coll.) Said of elegant women who win men's affections by their manner and grace. *Mozo de garabato*, A thief.—*pl.* 1. Ill-formed or scrawling letters or characters; pot-hooks. 2. Improper gestures or movements of the hands and fingers.
Garabatoso, sa [gah-rah-bah-to'-so, sah], *a.* 1. Full of scrawls. 2. (Met.) Elegant, charming, attractive.
Garabeta [gah-rah-bay'-tah], *f.* A stick armed with one or more hooks at the end to catch cuttle-fish.
Garabito [gah-rah-bee'-to], *m.* A linen cover spread over fruit-stalls in a market-place.
Garaje [gah-rah'-hay], *m.* Garage.
Garamón [gah-rah-mone'], *m.* In printing, a small Roman type.
Garante [gah-rahn'-tay], *m.* 1. Guarantee, a power who undertakes to see stipulations performed. 2. Warranter. *V.* FIADOR.
Garantía [gah-ran-tee'-ah], *f.* Warranty, guaranty, the act of securing the performance of articles or stipulations.
Garantir [gah-ran-teer'], *va.* To guarantee.
Garantizar, *va.* *V.* GARANTIR.
Garañón [gah-rah-nyone'], *m.* 1. Jackass kept for breeding. 2. A man much given to lust; lecher. 3. Male breeding camel. (Acad.)
Garapacho [gah-rah-pah'-cho], *m.* Kind of dressed meat.

Garapiña [gah-rah-pee'-nyah], *f.* 1. The congealed particles of any liquid. 2. A kind of black lace. *Bizcochos de garapiña*, Biscuits covered with concreted sugar.

Garapiñado da [gah-rah-pe-nyah'-do, dah], *a.* Glacé, candied.

Garapiñar [gah-rah-pe-nyar'], *va.* To ice, to turn to ice, to cover with ice.

Garapiñera [gah-rah-pe-nyay'-rah], *f.* Vessel in which liquids are congealed; a cooler, refrigerator.

Garapita [gah-rah-pee'-tah], *f.* Fishing-net with small meshes.

Garapito [gah-rah-pee'-to], *m.* Small insect, like a tick.

Garapullo [gah-rah-pool'-lyo], *m.* 1. Dart made of paper. 2. A shuttlecock.

Garatura [gah-rah-too'-rah], *f.* Scraper, an instrument used by curriers of leather. (Ital.)

Garatusa [gah-rah-too'-sah], *f.* 1. A sort of game at cards. 2. (Coll.) Caress, act of endearment.

Garavito [gah-rah-vee'-to], *m.* Stall, a small shed, in which greens, fruit, etc., are sold at market.

Garay [gah-rah'-e], *m.* A Philippine craft, with straight sides and somewhat narrowed toward the bow, with one or two masts and square sail: going out of use.

Garba [gar'-bah], *f.* Sheaf, as of corn. (Bot.) Hairy bastard vetch. Phaca bœtica.

Garbancera [gar-ban-thay'-rah], *f.* (Bot.) *V.* Garbancillo.

Garbancillo [gar-ban-theel'-lyo], *m.*

Garbanzal [gar-ban-thahl'], *m.* A piece of ground sown with chick-peas.

Garbanzo [gar-bahn'-tho], *m.* (Bot.) Chick-pea or common chick-pea. Cicer arietinum. A sort of pulse much esteemed in Spain. *Cuenta garbanzos*, An avaricious person.

Garbanzuelo [gar-ban-thoo-ay'-lo], *m. dim.* 1. (Dim.) Small chick-pea. 2. (Vet.) Disease in horses' feet. *V.* Esparaván.

Garbar [gar-bar'], *va.* (Prov.) To form sheaves, to tie stalks of corn into bundles.

Garbear [gar-bay-ar'], *va.* 1. (Prov.) *V.* Garbar. 2. To seize, to lay hold of any thing eagerly.—*vn.* To affect an air of dignity and grandeur.

Garbeña [gar-bay'-nyah], *f.* (Bot.) Common heath. Erica vulgaris.

Garbias [gar'-be-as], *m. pl.* A ragout, made of herbs, cheese, flour, eggs, sugar, and butter.

Garbillador [gar-beel-lyah-dor'], *m.* Sifter, riddler.

Garbillar [gar-beel-lyar'], *va.* To garble, to sift; to separate the bad from the good.

Garbillo [gar-beel'-lyo], *m.* Riddle, a coarse sieve made of bass or sedge.

Garbín [gar-been'], *m.* Coif made of net-work.

Garbino [gar-bee'-no], *m.* South-west wind. (Arab. garbi.)

Garbo [gar'-bo], *m.* 1. Gracefulness, gentility, elegance of manner, jauntiness; grace. 2. A clever and genteel way of doing things. 3. A gentleman-like air and deportment. 4. Frankness, disinterestedness, generosity; liberality of sentiments; cleverness.

Garbosamente [gar-bo-sah-men'-tay], *adv.* Gallantly, nobly, generously, liberally.

Garboso, sa [gar-bo'-so, sah], *a.* 1. Genteel, graceful, elegant, comely, gallant, sprightly, gay. 2. Liberal, generous, munificent.

Garbullo [gar-bool'-lyo], *m.* Crowd, a multitude confusedly pressed together.

Garcero, ra [gar-thay'-ro, rah], *m.* & *f.* (Orn.) Heron-hawk. Falco, *L.*

Garceta [gar-thay'-tah], *f.* 1. A young heron. 2. Hair which falls in locks on the cheeks and temples. 3. (Naut.) Point or reef-band, a small rope which serves to furl the sails. *Garcetas*, Tenderlings, the first horns of a deer.

Gardenia [gar-day'-ne-ah], *f.* (Bot.) Gardenia.

Garduja [gar-doo'-hah], *f.* Barren stone thrown away in quicksilver mines.

Garduña [gar-doo'-nyah], *f.* Marten. Mustela foina, *L.*

Garduño [gar-doo'-nyo], *m.* 1. He or male marten. 2. (Coll.) Filcher, a petty thief.

Garfa [gar'-fah], *f.* 1. Claw, as of a beast or bird; a hand, in contempt. 2. An ancient tax. *Echar la garfa*, To claw or seize any thing with the nails.

Garfada, Garfiada [gar-fah'-dah, gar-fe-ah'-dah], *f.* Clawing or seizing with the nails.

Garfear [gar-fay-ar'], *vn.* To use a drag-hook for getting any thing out of a well or river.

Garfio [gar'-fe-o], *m.* Hook, drag-hook; gaff.

Gargajeada [gar-gah-hay-ah'-dah], *f.* Spitting, ejecting phlegm.

Gargajear [gar-gah-hay-ar'], *vn.* To spit, to expectorate.

Gargajeo [gar-gah-hay'-o], *m.* Spitting, ejecting phlegm.

Gargajiento, ta [gar-gah-he-en'-to, tah], *a.* Spitting, ejecting expectorated matter.

Gargajo [gar-gah'-ho], *m.* Phlegm or mucus brought up by coughing, expectorated matter, sputum.

Gargajoso, sa [gar-gah-ho'-so, sah], *a.* *V.* Gargajiento.

Garganchón, *m.* *V.* Gargüero.

Garganta [gar-gahn'-tah], *f.* 1. Throat, gullet. 2. The instep. 3. Mountain-flood, torrent. 4. A narrow pass between mountains or rivers. 5. The shaft of a column or balustrade. *Tener buena garganta*, To be a good singer. *Tener el agua a la garganta*, To be in imminent danger.

Gargantada [gar-gan-tah'-dah], *f.* Quantity of water, wine, or blood, ejected at once from the throat.

Gargantear [gar-gan-tay-ar'], *vn.* To quaver, to warble.

Garganteo [gar-gan-tay'-o], *m.* Quavering, a tremulous modulation of the voice.

Gargantilla [gar-gan-teel'-lyah], *f.* Necklace worn by women.

Gárgara [gar'-gah-rah], *f.* Noise made by gargling the throat.

Gargarismo [gar-gah-rees'-mo], *m.* 1. Gargarism, gargle. 2. Gargling.

Gargarizar [gar-gah-re-thar'], *va.* To gargle, to gargarize.

Gárgol [gar'-gol], *m.* Groove. *V.* Ranura. *Gárgoles*, Grooves of casks, where the head and bottom pieces come in; chimes.

Gárgol [gar'-gol], *a.* (Prov.) Empty, addle: applied to eggs.

Gárgola [gar'-go-lah], *f.* 1. Spout of a gutter in the form of a lion or other animal; gargoyle. 2. Linseed.

Gargüero, Garguero [gar-goo-ay'-ro, gar-gay'-ro], *m.* 1. The gullet. 2. Windpipe.

Garico [gah-ree'-co], *m.* A kind of medicinal fungus of Canada which grows among the pines.

Gariofilea [gah-re-o-fe-lay'-ah], *f.* (Bot.) Common avens or herb bennet. Geum urbanum, *L.*

Garita [gah-ree'-tah], *f.* 1. Sentry-box. 2. A porter's lodge. 3. A seat in a privy.

Gariteár [gah-re-tay-ar'], *vn.* (Coll.) To gamble.

Garitero [gah-re-tay'-ro], *m.* 1. Master of a gaming-house. 2. Gamester, gambler.

Garito [gah-ree'-to], *m.* Gaming-house, profits of gaming.

Garla [gar'-lah], *f.* (Coll.) Talk, chatter.

Garlador, ra [gar-lah-dor', rah], *m.* & *f.* (Coll.) Babbler, prattler.

Garlante [gar-lahn'-tay], *pa.* (Coll.) Babbling, prater.

Garlar [gar-lar'], *va.* (Coll.) To babble, to prattle, to chatter.

Garlito [gar-lee'-to], *m.* 1. A wicker snare or trap for fish. 2. Snare, trap, or gin.

Garlocha [gar-lo'-chah], *f.* Goad, with which oxen are driven; ox-goad. *V.* Garrocha.

Garlopa [gar-lo'-pah], *f.* Jack-plane, a long plane.

Garnacha [gar-nah'-chah], *f.* 1. Robe, a dress worn by councillors. 2. Dignity or employment of a councillor. 3. A liquor made of honey and wine. 4. A large red grape and the wine made from it. 5. Company of strolling players. *V.* Gargarilla.

Garo [gah'-ro], *m.* 1. A kind of lobster. 2. Brine for fish or meat.

Garra [gar'-rah], *f.* 1. Claw of a wild beast, talon of a bird of prey, a clutch, a fang. 2. Hand, in contempt. *Gente de la garra*, Filchers, petty thieves. *Navío de media garra*, (Naut.) Vessel which carries no top-sails. *Echarle a uno la garra*, (Coll.) To grasp, to seize, to imprison any one.

Garrafa [gar-rah'-fah], *f.* Vessel for cooling liquors; carafe. (Arab.)

Garrafal [gar-rah-fahl'], *a.* 1. Applied to a kind of cherries larger and sweeter than the common ones. 2. Great, vast, huge.

Garrafilla [gar-rah-feel'-lyah], *f. dim.* A small vessel for cooling liquids.

Garrafiñar [gar-rah-fe-nyar'], *va.* (Coll.) To grapple, to snatch away.

Garrafón [gar-rah-fone'], *m. aug.* 1. A large vessel for cooling liquids. 2. Demijohn, carboy.

Garrama [gar-rah'-mah], *f.* 1. Tax or duty anciently paid by the Moors. 2. Imposition, fraud, robbery.

Garramar [gar-rah-mar'], *va.* 1. To rob, to plunder and pillage. 2. To collect an ancient tax.

Garrancho [gar-rahn'-cho], *m.* Branch of a tree broken off; splinter.

Garrapata [gar-rah-pah'-tah], *f.* 1. Tick, the louse of dogs and sheep. Acarus, *L.* 2. A short, little person.

Garrapatear [gar-rah-pah-tay-ar'], *vn.* To scribble, to scrawl.

Garrapatilla [gar-rah-pah-teel'-yah], *f. dim.* A small tick.

Garrapato [gar-rah-pah'-to], *m.* Pot-hook, ill-formed character or letter.

Garrar, Garrear [gar-rar', gar-ray-ar'], *vn.* (Naut.) To drag, to be driven from the moorings: applied to a ship. *El ancla garra*, The anchor drags.

Garridamente [gar-re-dah-men'-tay], *adv.* Gracefully, neatly.

Garrido, da [gar-ree'-do, dah], *a.* Handsome, neat, graceful.

Garroba, *f.* *V.* Algarroba.

Garrobal [gar-ro-bahl'], *m.* Plantation of carob-trees.

Garrobilla [gar-ro-beel'-lyah], *f.* Chips of carob-trees used to tan leather.

Garrobo [gar-ro'-bo], *m.* (Bot.) Carob-tree, or St. John's bread. Ceratonia siliqua, *L.* *V.* Algarrobo.

Garrocha [gar-ro'-chah], *f.* 1. A sort of javelin with a hooked head. 2. A kind of dart used to prick bulls.
Garrochada [gar-ro-chah'-dah], *f.* or **Garrochazo**, *m.* Prick with a javelin or dart.
Garrocheador [gar-ro-chay-ah-dor'], *m.* Goader, pricker.
Garrochear [gar-ro-chay-ar'], *va.* *V.* AGARROCHAR.
Garrochón [gar-ro-chone'], *m.* Spear, used by bull-fighters on horseback.
Garrofa, or **Garroba** [gar-ro'-fah, gar-ro'-bah], *f.* (Prov.) Fruit of the carob-tree. *V.* ALGARROBA.
Garrofal, *m.* *V.* GARROBAL.
Garrón [gar-rone'], *m.* 1. Spur of cocks and birds. 2. Talon of a bird of prey. 3. *V.* CALCAÑAR. *Tener garrones*, (Coll.) To be experienced, not easily deceived.
Garrotazo [gar-ro-tah'-tho], *m.* 1. Blow with a cudgel. 2. (Aug.) A large cudgel.
Garrotal [gar-ro-tahl'], *m.* A plantation of olive-trees, made with crossed slips of large olive-trees put into the ground to grow.
Garrote [gar-ro'-tay], *m.* 1. Cudgel, a strong stick. 2. A capital punishment used in Spain, consisting in strangling a criminal with an iron collar. 3. The scaffold where the capital punishment called *garrote* is inflicted. 4. *V.* GARROTAZO. 5. The act of tying a rope or cord very tight. 6. (Prov.) Hazel basket or pannier. *Vino de garrote*, The last wine pressed out of grapes.
Garrotear [gar-ro-tay-ar'], *va.* (Obs.) To cudgel.
Garrotillo [gar-ro-teel'-lyo], *m.* Inflammation in the throat, croup, diphtheria.
Garrubia, *f.* *V.* ALGARROBA.
Garrucha [gar-roo'-chah], *f.* 1. Pulley, one of the mechanical powers. 2. Horse or board on which the card is fixed for combing wool.
Garruchón [gar-roo-chone'], *m.* Body of a coach without straps and buckles.
Garrucho [gar-roo'-cho], *m.* (Naut.) Cringle, a sort of rings for a variety of uses on board of ships.
Garruchuela [gar-roo-choo-ay'-lah], *f. dim.* A small pulley.
Garrudo, da [gar-roo'-do, dah], *a.* Nervous, brawny, strong.
Garrulador, ra [gar-roo-lah-dor', rah], *m.* & *f.* A garrulous person.
Garrular [gar-roo-lar'], *vn.* (Obs.) To chatter, to babble, to talk much and idly.
Gárrulo, la [gar'-roo-lo, lah], *a.* 1. Chirping, making a cheerful noise, as birds. 2. Chattering, prattling; garrulous.
Garú [gah-roo'], *m.* A plant of the mezereum family, of disagreeable smell, whose bark is used as a sinapism by moistening it in vinegar.
Garúa [gah-roo'-ah], *f.* (Peru.) Drizzle.
Garuar [gah-roo-ar'], *vn.* (Peru.) To drizzle.
Garuda [gah-roo'-dah], *f.* A marvellous bird which serves Vishnu for riding, and which has the body of an eagle and the head of a man.
Garufo [gah-roo'-fo], *m.* Concrete. *V.* HORMIGÓN.
Garulla [gah-rool'-lyah], *f.* 1. Ripe grapes which remain in the basket. 2. (Coll.) Rabble, assembly of low people. (Per.)
Garullada [gah-rool-lah'-dah], *f.* Gang of rogues.
Garvier [gar-ve-ayr'], *m.* A small pouch anciently in use.

Garza [gar'-thah], *f.* (Orn.) Heron. Ardea, *L.*
Garzo [gar'-tho], *m.* Agaric. Agaricus, *L.*
Garzo, za [gar-tho', thah], *a.* Blue-eyed.
Garzón [gar-thone'], *m.* 1. Lad, boy; stripling. 2. Adjutant in the life-guards of the king of Spain. 3. (Obs.) Wooer, lover.
Garzonear [gar-tho-nay-ar'], *vn.* To make a parade of boyish actions; to solicit, to court.
Garzonía [gar-tho-nee'-ah], *f.* (Obs.) A boyish action.
Garzota [gar-tho'-tah], *f.* 1. (Orn.) Night-heron. Ardea nycticorax, *L.* 2. Plumage worn as an ornament. 3. Crest of a helmet.
Garzul [gar-thool'], *m.* (Prov.) A kind of wheat.
Gas [gahs], *m.* Gas. *Gas de carbón* or *de hulla*, Coal gas. *Gas combustible*, Inflammable gas. *Gas hilarante*, Nitrous oxide. *Gas lacrimógeno*, Tear gas. *Gas mostaza*, Mustard gas. *Gas venenoso*, Poison gas.
Gasa [gah'-sah], *f.* Gauze, a very thin, transparent cloth. *Gasa fina pintada*, Fine printed muslin. *Gasa rayada*, Striped muslin. *Gasa labrada*, Embroidered muslin.
Gasajar [gah-sah-har'], *va.* (Obs.) To divert, to release.
Gascón, na, nés [gas-con', nah, nes'], *a.* Gascon, belonging to or native of Gascony.
Gasconada [gas-co-nah'-dah], *f.* Gasconade, boast, a bravado.
Gaseiforme [gah-say-e-for'-may], *a.* Aeriform, gaseous.
Gaseoso, sa [gah-say-o'-so, sah], *a.* Gaseous, gas.—*f.* Soda water.
Gasífero, ra [gah-see'-fay-ro, rah], *a.* Gas-conducting.
Gasificable [gah-se-fe-cah'-blay], *a.* Convertible into gas.
Gasificación [gah-se-fe-cah-the-on'], *f.* Gasification, conversion into gas.
Gasificar [gah-se-fe-car'], *va.* To gasify, convert into gas.
Gasolina [gah-so-lee'-nah], *f.* Gasoline. *Estación de gasolina*, Gas station.
Gasolinera [gah-so-le-nay'-rah], *f.* 1. Motor launch. 2. Gas station.
Gasómetro [gah-so'-may-tro], *m.* 1. Gasholder, gas-storage tank. 2. Gasometer.
Gasoquimia [gah-so-kee'-me-ah], *f.* Gas chemistry.
Gastable [gas-tah'-blay], *a.* That may be wasted or spent.
Gastadero [gas-tah-day'-ro], *m.* 1. Waster, spender. 2. Wasting, spending.
Gastado, da [gas-tah'-do, dah], *a.* & *pp.* of GASTAR. Worn-out, useless.
Gastador, ra [gas-tah-dor', rah], *m.* & *f.* 1. Spendthrift, prodigal. 2. Pioneer in military operations. 3. Persons sentenced to public labour. 4. (Met.) Corrupter, destroyer.
Gastadura [gas-tah-doo'-rah], *f.* The mark which remains upon any object as an effect of friction.
Gastamiento [gas-tah-me-en'-to], *m.* Consumption of any thing.
Gastar [gas-tar'], *va.* 1. To expend, to lay out money. 2. To waste or make way with, to melt, to consume or wear out gradually. 3. To apply to some purpose. 4. To plunder, to pillage, to sack. 5. To digest, to concoct in the stomach. 6. *Gastar coche*, etc., (Met.) To keep a carriage, etc.: applied to persons who have no means for such expense.—*vr.* 1. To be sold or disposed of. 2. To grow old or useless. 3. To become rotten or corrupted.

Gasterópodo, da [gas-tay-ro'-po-do, dah], *a.* Gasteropod.
Gasto [gahs'-to], *m.* 1. Expenditure, expense, cost, consumption. 2. Act of spending or consuming.—*pl.* Expenses, charges, disbursements, outlay, commission.
Gástrico, ca [gahs'-tre-co, cah], *a.* Gastric, belonging to the stomach.
Gastritis [gas-tree'-tis], *f.* Gastritis, inflammation of the stomach.
Gastrología [gas-tro-lo-hee'-ah], *f.* Gastrology, a treatise on the kitchen and culinary art.
Gastronomía [gas-tro-no-mee'-ah], *f.* Gastronomy, epicurism.
Gastronómico, ca [gas-tro-no'-me-co, cah], *a.* Gastronomic, belonging to epicurism.
Gastrónomo [gas-tro'-no-mo], *m.* 1. Epicure, gourmet, gastronomer, a judge of good eating. 2. A writer on epicurism.
Gastrorrectomía [gas-tror-rec-to-mee'-ah], *f.* Gastrorectomy.
Gastrotomía [gas-tro-to-mee'-ah], *f.* (Surg.) Gastrostomy.
Gástrula [gahs'-troo-lah], *f.* (Surg.) Gastrula.
Gata [gah'-tah], *f.* 1. She-cat, puss. 2. (Bot.) *V.* GATUÑA. 3. (Naut.) A toothed bar from which is suspended the flood-gate of a dam. 4. (Mil.) A machine which served to protect those who were scaling a wall against the besieged. 5. (Naut.) The cross-jack yard. *Gata del ancla*, (Naut.) Cat-tackle. *Tiro del aparejo de la gata*, Cat-fall. *Cuadernal de la gata*, Cat-block. *Enganchar la gata en el ancla*, To cat the anchor. *A gatas*, On all-fours.
Gatada [gah-tah'-dah], *f.* 1. Clawing, wounding with claws. 2. Turn of a hare which is closely pursued. 3. Theft or robbery effected in an artful manner. 4. (Coll.) An artful action or doing; scurvy trick.
Gatafura [gah-tah-foo'-rah], *f.* Cake made of herbs and sour milk.
Gatallón [gah-tal-lyone'], *m.* (Coll.) Rogue, cheat.
Gatatumba [gah-tah-toom'-bah], *f.* (Coll.) Affected civility or submission.
Gatazo [gah-tah'-tho], *m.* 1. (Aug.) A large cat. 2. A clumsy joke. 3. An artful trick.
Gateado, da [gah-tay-ah'-do, dah], *a.* Feline, catlike.—*pp.* of GATEAR.—*m.* A very compact American wood, employed in rich furniture.
Gateamiento [gah-tay-ah-me-en'-to], *m.* Scratching, tearing with the nails.
Gatear [gah-tay-ar'], *vn.* To climb up, to clamber, to go upon all-fours.—*va.* (Coll.) 1. To scratch or claw. 2. To steal, to rob.
Gatera [gah-tay'-rah], *f.* 1. A cat's hole, through which cats go in and out. 2. (Bot.) Common cat-mint. Nepeta cataria, *L.*
Gatería [gah-tay-ree'-ah], *f.* 1. Number of cats brought together in a place. 2. Cringing submission, mean servility. 3. Rabble, assembly of low people; a number of mischievous ill-bred boys brought together.
Gatero, ra [gah-tay'-ro, rah], *a.* Frequented by cats.
Gatesco, ca [gah-tes'-co, cah], *a.* Belonging to cats, feline.
Gatica, illa, ita [gah-tee'-cah, eel'-lyah, ee'-tah], *f. dim.* A little she-cat.
Gaticida [gah-te-thee'-dah], *m.* In the jocular style, cat-killer.

Gatico, illo, ito [gah-tee'-co, eel'-lyo, ee'-to], *m. dim.* A little cat.

Gatillazo [gah-teel-lyah'-tho], *m.* The noise made by a trigger at firing.

Gatillo [gah-teel'-lyo], *m.* 1. (Dim.) A little cat, a kitten. 2. Pelican, an instrument for drawing teeth. 3. Trigger of a gun. 4. Nape of a bull or ox. 5. Cramp-iron. 6. Filcher, a petty thief or robber.

Gato [gah'-to], *m.* 1. Cat, tom-cat. Felis catus, *L.* 2. Skin of a cat used as a purse, and its contents. 3. A pickpocket, petty thief, filcher. 4. Tongs used for hooping casks. 5. Cramp-iron. 6. Instrument used for examining the bore of a cannon. 7. Jack, an engine for raising ponderous bodies. *Gato cornaquí*. Jack-screw used on board of ships for raising great weights. *Gato de algalia*, Civet-cat. Viverra zibetha. *Gato montés* or *de clavo*, Mountain cat. Felis catus agrestis. *Gato maullador, nunca buen cazador*, Great talkers are little doers, or a barking dog never bites: literally, a mewing cat is never a good mouser. *El gato escaldado del agua fría huye*, A burnt child dreads the fire: literally, a scalded cat flees from cold water.

Gatuna, Gatuña [gah-too'-nah, gah-too'-nyah], *f.* (Bot.) Rest-harrow, cammock. Ononis arvensis, *L.*

Gatunero [gah-too-nay'-ro], *m.* (Prov.) He who sells smuggled meat.

Gatuno, na [gah-too'-no, nah], *a.* Cat-like, feline.

Gatuperio [gah-too-pay'-re-o], *m.* 1. Mixture of liquors without art and proportion. 2. Fraud, snare, intrigue.

Gauchada [gah-oo-chah'-dah], *f.* (Rep. Arg.) 1. Artifice. 2. Action of a gaucho.

Gaucho, cha [gah'-oo-cho, chah], *a.* (Arch.) Applied to unlevel superficies.—*m.* & *f.* (Arg.) 1. Rustic, herdsman, or Indian of the pampas of the Argentine Republic. 2. A man of the humble people, of rude manners.

Gaudeamus, Gaudete [gah-oo-day-ah'-moos, gah-oo-day'-tay], *m.* Feast, entertaiment, merrymaking.

Gaulteria [gah-ool-tay'-re-ah], *f.* Gaultheria, a heath-plant of the hot lands of South America.

Gavanza [gah-vahn'-thah], *f.* Flower of the dog-rose.

Gavanzo [gah-vahn'-tho], *m.* Dog-rose. *V.* Escaramujo.

Gaveta [gah-vay'-tah], *f.* Drawer of a desk, locker.

Gavetilla [gah-vay-teel'-lyah], *f. dim.* A small drawer of a desk.

Gavia [gah'-ve-ah], *f.* 1. (Naut.) Maintop-sail. 2. Place where madmen are confined. 3. Pit or hole into which a tree is transplanted with its roots. 4. *V.* Gaviota.—*pl.* (Naut.) Top-sails of the main and fore-mast.

Gavial [gah-ve-ahl'], *m.* A crocodile of the Ganges.

Gaviero [gah-ve-ay'-ro], *m.* (Naut.) Seaman who works at the top-masts. *Gaviero mayor de la cofa del trinquete*, Captain of the fore-top.

Gavieta [gah-ve-ay'-tah], *f.* (Naut.) Scuttle.

Gaviete de las lanchas [gah-ve-ay'-tay], *m.* (Naut.) Davit in a long-boat. *Gaviete del bauprés*, (Naut.) Saddle of the bow-sprit.

Gavilán [gah-ve-lahn'], *m.* 1. (Orn.) Sparrow-hawk. Falco nisus. 2. Fine hair-stroke in letters; either side of the nib of a pen. 3. An iron hook. 4. Among tailors, the point which each trousers-leg forms at the crotch. 5. The part which projects under the chisel in turning with the lathe.—*pl.* 1. (Naut.) Tholes. *V.* Toletes. 2. Dry flowers of artichokes or thistles.

Gavilancillo [gah-ve-lan-theel'-lyo], *m.* 1. (Dim.) A young hawk. 2. The incurvated point of an artichoke leaf.

Gavilla [gah-veel'-lyah], *f.* 1. Sheaf of corn; a bundle of vine-shoots. 2. Gang of suspicious persons.

Gavillero [gah-veel-lyay'-ro], *m.* 1. Place where suspicious persons assemble; a nest of thieves. 2. Place where the sheaves of corn are collected.

Gavina, *f.* (Prov.) *V.* Gaviota.

Gavión [gah-ve-on'], *m.* 1. (Mil.) Gabion, a wicker basket filled with earth to protect against the fire of the enemy. 2. A large hat.

Gavioncillo [gah-ve-on-theel'-lyo], *m. dim.* (Mil.) A small gabion.

Gaviota [gah-ve-o'-tah], *f.* (Orn.) Gull, sea-gull. Larus canus.

Gavitel [gah-ve-tel'], *m.* (Naut.) A small buoy.

Gavota [gah-vo'-tah], *f.* Gavot, a French dance.

Gaya [gah'-yah], *f.* 1. Stripe of different colours on stuffs, silks, ribbons, etc. 2. *V.* Picaza. *Gaya ciencia* or *gaya doctrina*, Poesy, or the art of poetry.

Gayado, da [gah-yah'-do, dah], *a.* & *pp.* of Gayar. Motley, mingled of various colours.

Gayadura [gah-yah-doo'-rah], *f.* Garniture, an ornamental trimming of various colours.

Gayar [gah-yar'], *va.* To garnish or adorn with trimming of a different colour from the stuff; to variegate, to checker.

Gayata [gah-yah'-tah], *f.* (Prov.) Crook, sheep-hook.

Gayo [gah'-yo], *m.* (Orn.) Jay. Corvus glandarius, *L.*

Gayola [gah-yo'-lah], *f.* 1. (Naut.) *V.* Jaula. 2. (Prov.) Kind of hut raised for watching vineyards.

Gayomba [gah-yom'-bah], *f.* (Bot.) White single-seed broom. Spartium monospermum.

Gayuba [gah-yoo'-bah], *f.* (Bot.) Strawberry-tree, red-berried arbutus. Arbutus unedo.

Gayubal [gah-yoo-bahl'], *m.* Place where there is an abundance of the strawberry-tree.

Gaza [gah'-thah], *f.* (Naut.) Strap, spliced in a circular form, and used to fasten blocks to the masts, yards, and rigging. *Gaza de estay*, (Naut.) Collar of a stay. *Gaza de un motón*, (Naut.) Stay of a block.

Gazafatón, Gazapatón [gah-thah-fah-tone', gah-thah-pah-tone'], *m.* Nonsense, foolish talk.

Gazapa [gah-thah'-pah], *f.* (Prov.) Lie, falsehood.

Gazapela [gah-thah-pay'-lah], *f.* Clamorous wrangling or quarrelling.

Gazapera [gah-thah-pay'-rah], *f.* 1. Warren for rabbits. 2. A hiding-place where people meet for unlawful purposes.

Gazapico, illo, ito [gah-thah-pee'-co, eel'-lyo, ee'-to], *m. dim.* A small rabbit.

Gazapina [gah-thah-pee'-nah], *f.* 1. Assembly of vile people. 2. Confusion, disorder, wrangling.

Gazapo [gah-thah'-po], *m.* 1. A young rabbit. 2. A dissembling, artful knave. 3. (Coll.) A great lie.

Gazi [gah-thee'], *a.* Applied formerly to a Moor who changed his religion.

Gazmiar [gath-me-ar'], *va.* To steal and eat tid-bits.—*vn.* (Coll.) To complain, to resent.

Gazmol [gath-mole'], *m.* Kind of cancer on the tongue of hawks.

Gazmoñada, Gazmoñería [gath-mo-nyah'-dah, gath-mo-nyay-ree'-ah], *f.* Hypocrisy, false devotion.

Gazmoñero, ra, Gazmoño, ña [gath-mo-nyay'-ro, rah, gath-mo'-nyo, yah], *a.* Hypocritical, dissembling, hypocrite.

Gaznápiro [gath-nah'-pe-ro], *a.* & *m.* Churlish, a simpleton, booby, clown.

Gaznar, *vn.* *V.* Graznar.

Gaznatada [gath-nah-tah'-dah], *f.* Blow or stroke on the throttle.

Gaznate [gath-nah'-tay], *m.* Throttle, windpipe, gorge. *A gaznate tendido* or *a todo gaznate*, (Coll.) At the top of one's lungs.

Gaznatón [gath-nah-tone'], *m.* 1. Blow on the throat. 2. Pancake, fritter.

Gazofia [gah-tho'-fe-ah], *f.* *V.* Bazofia.

Gazofilacio [gah-tho-fe-lah'-the-o], *m.* Place in which the riches of the temple of Jerusalem were collected.

Gazpachero [gath-pah-chay'-ro], *m.* He who carries dinner to labourers and workmen; maker of the soup called *gazpacho*.

Gazpacho [gath-pah'-cho], *m.* 1. Dish made of bread, oil, vinegar, onions, salt, and red pepper, mixed together in water. 2. Crumbs of bread fried in a pan.

Gazuza [gah-thoo'-thah], *f.* (Coll.) Keenness of stomach, violent hunger.

Ge [hay], *f.* Spanish name of the letter G.

Geato [hay-ah'-to], *m.* (Chem.) Geate, or humate, a salt of humic acid.

Gehena [hay-ay'-nah], *m.* Hell. (Heb.)

Geico, ca [hay'-e-co, cah], *a.* (Chem.) Geic, humic, ulmic.

Geiger, Contador de [gah'-e-ger, con-tah-dor' day], *m.* Geiger counter.

Géiser [hay'-ser], *m.* Geyser, gusher.

Gelasino, na [hay-lah-see'-no, nah], *a.* Seen on laughing: applied to the front teeth.

Gelatina [hay-lah-tee'-nah], *f.* 1. Gelatine, jelly. 2. A compound jelly made of animal substances, with fruit and sugar.

Gelatiniforme [hay-lah-te-ne-for'-may], *a.* Gelatiniform, like gelatine.

Gelatinoso, sa [hay-lah-te-no'-so, sah], *a.* Gelatinous, glutinous.

Gelatinudo, da [hay-lah-te-noo'-do, dah], *a.* (Peru, etc.) 1. Gelatinous. 2. Phlegmatic, lazy, without energy.

Gelberda [hel-bayr'-dah], *f.* An argillaceous variety of ochre belonging to the silicates of iron.

Gelenita [hay-lay-nee'-tah], *f.* (Min.) Stilbite, a hydrous aluminum-calcium-ferrous silicate.

Gelfe [hel'-fay], *m.* A black slave. (Arab. jelf.)

Gélido, da [hay'-le-do, dah], *a.* (Poet.) Gelid, frigid.

Gelosía, *f.* (Obs.) *V.* Celosía.

Gema [hay'-mah], *f.* 1. A short and deep cut in a piece of wood. 2. Gem, precious stone. 3. (Bot.) Bud. *V.* Yema. 4. *Sal gema*, Rock-salt.

Gemación [hay-mah-the-on'], *f.* Gemmation, the first development of the bud.

Gemara [hay-mah'-rah], *f.* Name of the second part of the Talmud, signifying in Hebrew perfection.

Gemebundo, da [hay-may-boon'-do, dah], *a.* (Poet.) Groaning, moaning, howling.

Gemela [hay-may'-lah], *f.* Flower exhaling the odour of orange and jessamine; jasmine.

Gemelo, la [hay-may'-lo, lah], *a.* & *m.* & *f.* Twin.—*m. pl.* 1. Binocular telescope, opera glasses, field glasses. 2. Cuff links.

Gemido [hay-mee'-do], *m.* 1. Groan. 2. Lamentation, moan. 3. Howl, the cry of a wolf or dog.—*Gemido, da, pp.* of GEMIR.

Gemidor, ra [hay-me-dor', rah], *m. & f.* Lamenter, mourner: also used as an adjective, applied to one who groans, or to any thing which makes a noise like a groan.

Gemificación [hay-me-fe-cah-the-on'], *f.* Gemmation, the mode or time of development of the buds of plants.

Geminar [hay-me-nar'], *va.* (Obs.) To double, to repeat.

Geminifloro, ra [hay-me-nee'-flo-ro, rah], *a.* Twin-flowered; bearing flowers set in pairs.

Géminis [hay'-me-nis], *m.* 1. Gemini, a sign of the zodiac. 2. A kind of resolving and healing plaster.

Gemir [hay-meer'], *vn.* 1. To groan, to moan, to grieve. 2. To howl, as a wolf or dog. 3. To roar, to whistle, as the sea or wind. 4. To grunt.

Gen [hen], *m.* (Biol.) Gene.

Genciana [hen-the-ah'-nah], *f.* (Bot.) Gentian. Gentiana, *L.* *Genciana pajiza* or *oficinal*, Yellow gentian. Gentiana lutea.

Gencianáceo, cea [hen-the-ah-nah'-thay-o, ah], *a.* Gentianaceous, belonging to the gentian family.

Genciáneo, a, Gencianoideo, a, *a.* *V.* GENCIANÁCEO.

Gendarme [hen-dar'-may], *m.* 1. Gendarme, French policeman. 2. Policeman.

Gendarmería [hen-dar-may-ree'-ah], *f.* Gendarmery, a military body charged with the police in France.

Genealogía [hay-nay-ah-lo-hee'-ah], *f.* Genealogy, lineage.

Genealógico, ca [hay-nay-ah-lo'-he-co, cah], *a.* Genealogical, heraldic.

Genealogista [hay-nay-ah-lo-hees'-tah], *m.* Genealogist.

Geneantropía [hay-nay-an-tro-pee'-ah], *f.* A treatise on the origin of the human race.

Genearca [hay-nay-ar'-cah], *m.* (Obs.) Head or chief of a family or race.

Geneático, ca [hay-nay-ah'-te-co, cah], *a.* Genethliacal, relating to divination by nativities.

Geneo [hay-nay'-o], *m.* A banana of Peru.

Generable [hay-nay-rah'-blay], *a.* Generable, that may be produced or begotten.

Generación [hay-nay-rah-the-on'] *f.* 1. Generation, act of begetting. 2. Generation, progeny, race, offspring. 3. Generation, age. 4. *V.* NACIÓN. 5. Generation, succession, lineage. 6. Generation, a single succession.

Generador, ra [hay-nay-rah-dor', rah], *m. & f.* 1. Generator. 2. (Math.) Every extension which by its movement produces another. 3. *pl.* The genital organs.

General [hay-nay-rahl'], *a.* 1. General, comprehending many species or individuals. 2. General, universal, relating to a whole class or body of men. 3. General, common, usual. *En general*, Generally, in general. *Las generales de la ley no le tocan*, (Law) He is competent to be a witness, not being comprehended in the general exceptions made by the law to witnesses.

General [hay-nay-rahl'], *m.* 1. Hall or room in a public school where the sciences are taught. 2. A general (officer). 3. (Prov.) Custom-house. 4. General, superior of a religious order.

Generala [hay-nay-rah'-lah], *f.* 1. General, a beat of the drum, which calls troops to arms. 2. The wife of a general. 3. (Naut.) Signal to join convoy.

Generalato [hay-nay-rah-lah'-to], *m.* Generalship, commission or dignity of a general: commonly applied to the generals of religious orders.

Generalero [hay-nay-rah-lay'-ro], *m.* (Prov.) *V.* ADUANERO.

Generalidad [hay-nay-rah-le-dahd'], *f.* 1. Generality, the whole, totality. 2. (Prov.) Community, corporation. 3. (Prov.) Custom duties on goods. *Generalidades*, (Prov.) Custom-house fees; discourse consisting of only general principles.

Generalísimo [hay-nay-rah-lee'-se-mo], *m.* 1. Generalissimo, the commander-in-chief of an army or of a fleet of ships of war. 2. *V.* GENERAL, for a superior of a religious order.

Generalización [hay-nay-rah-le-thah-the-on'], *f.* Generalization.

Generalizar [hay-nay-rah-le-thar'], *va.* To generalize.—*vr.* 1. To become general or usual. 2. To be divulged.

Generalmente [hay-nay-ral-men'-tay], *adv.* Generally.

Generante [hay-nay-rahn'-tay], *pa. & a.* Generating, engendering; generant.

Generativo, va [hay-nay-rah-tee'-vo, vah], *a.* Generative, having the power of propagation.

Generatriz [hay-nay-rah-treeth'], *a.* (Math.) Generatrix.

Genéricamente [hay-nay'-re-cah-men-tay], *adv.* Generically.

Genérico, ca [hay-nay'-re-co, cah], *a.* Generic.

Género [hay'-nay-ro], *m.* 1. Genus, a class comprehending many species. 2. Kin, the same generical class: speaking of the relation between two or more different beings. *Género humano*, Human nature, mankind. 3. Manner, way, kind, sort, or mode of doing any thing. 4. Sex, gender. 5. (Gram.) Gender. 6. Any thing to be bought or sold. *Géneros*, Goods, merchandise, wares, or commodities. *Género para sacos*, German bagging. *Género para chalecos*, Vestings. *Géneros de algodón fino*, Cotton shirtings.

Generosía, *f.* (Obs.) *V.* GENEROSIDAD.

Generosidad [hay-nay-ro-se-dahd'], *f.* 1. Hereditary nobility. 2. Generosity, magnanimity, liberality, frankness, munificence, open-heartedness. 3. Valour and fortitude in arduous undertakings.

Generoso, sa [hay-nay-ro'-so, sah], *a.* 1. Noble, generous, of good extraction. 2. Generous, magnanimous, honourable, free-hearted. 3. Generous, liberal, frank, open-handed, munificent. 4. Generous, strong, vigorous: applied to wines. 5. Excellent.

Genesíaco, ca [hay-ne-see'-ah-co, cah], *a.* 1. Genesiacal, belonging to Genesis. 2. Genesial, belonging to the origin or creation of something.

Génesis [hay'-nay-sis], *m.* 1. Genesis, the first book of the Old Testament. 2. Origin.

Genetica [hay-nay'-te-cah], *f.* (Biol.) Genetics.

Genetivo, *m.* (Obs.) *V.* COMPAÑÓN.

Genetlíaca [hay-net-le-ah'-cah], *f.* Genethliacs, the science of casting nativities.

Genetlíaco, ca [hay-net-le-ah'-co, cah], *a.* Genethliacal, prognosticating by nativities.

Gengibre [hen-hee'-bray], *m.* *V.* JENGIBRE.

Genial [hay-ne-ahl'], *a.* Genial, conformable to the genius or natural disposition. *Días geniales*, Festivals, festive days.

Genialidad [hay-ne-ah-le-dahd'], *f.* Habits or disposition of a person produced by his natural temper.

Genialmente [hay-ne-al-men'-tay], *adv.* Genially.

Geniculación [hay-ne-coo-lah-the-on'], *f.* Geniculation, curvature in the shape of a knee.

Geniculado, da [hay-ne-coo-lah'-do, dah], *a.* Geniculate, bent like a knee-joint.

Genio [hay'-ne-o], *m.* 1. Genius, peculiar mental power or faculties. 2. Genius, the protecting power of men, places, and things; its plural is genii. 3. Nature, genius, peculiar characteristic disposition of a person, temper, character, inclination, humour. 4. (Pict.) Little angel.

Genipa [hay-nee'-pah], *f.* (Bot.) Silky mug-wort or worm-wood. Artemisia glacialis, *L.*

Geniquén (or **Henequén**), *m.* (Mex.) Sisal hemp, the fibre of Agave Ixtli, of Mexico and Yucatan. *V.* HENEQUÉN.

Genista [hay-nees'-tah], *f.* (Bot.) 1. *V.* RETAMA DE OLOR. 2. *V.* GINESTA.

Genital [hay-ne-tahl'], *a.* Genital.—*m.* *V.* TESTÍCULO.

Genitivo, va [hay-ne-tee'-vo, vah], *a.* Having the power of generation.—*m.* (Gram.) The genitive or possessive case.

Genitor [hay-ne-tor'], *m.* (Obs.) Genitor, begetter.

Genitura [hay-ne-too'-rah], *f.* 1. Generation, procreation. 2. (Obs.) Seed or matter of generation. 3. (Ast.) Horoscope.

Genízaro, ra [hay-nee'-thah-ro, rah], *a.* 1. Begotten by parents of different nations. 2. Composed of different species.

Genocidio [hay-no-thee'-de-o], *m.* Genocide, extermination of a racial, political or cultural group.

Génoli, Génuli [hay'-no-le], *m.* A light yellow paste made of sandarach, used by painters.

Genovés, sa [hay-no-vays', sah], *a.* 1. Genoese. 2. (Obs.) A banker.

Gentalla [hen-tahl'-lyah], *f.* Rabble, mob. *V.* GENTUALLA.

Gente [hen'-tay], *f.* 1. People, persons in general, folk. 2. Nation, those who compose a community. 3. (Coll.) A family. 4. Army, troops. *Gente baja* or *del gordillo*, Rabble, mob. *Gente de bien* or *de buen proceder*, Honest people. *Gente común* or *gente vulgar*, Common people. *Gente del bronce*, A people always merry and fond of amusements. *Gente de capa parda*, Villagers, countrymen, rustics. *Gente de la garra*, Thieves, pickpockets. *Gente de la cuchilla*, Butchers. *Gente de la hampa* or *de la vida airada* A debauched set of people. *Gente de modo* or *de traza*, People of fashion. *Gente de paz*, A friend: used in reply to a person asking who knocks at the door, and to a sentinel. *Gente de pluma*, Notaries, attorneys. *Gente principal*, The nobility or gentry. *Gente fina*, Well-educated persons. *Gente de pelo* or *de pelusa*, People of property. *Gente de trato*, Tradesmen, dealers. *Hacer gente*, To raise recruits; to make a party. *Gentes*, Gentiles. *De gente en gente*, From one to another, from generation to generation. *Gente de razón*, Educated persons; white persons in distinction from American Indians. (Lat. gens.)

Gentecilla [hen-tay-theel'-lyah], *f.* Mob, rabble.

Gentil [hen-teel'], *m.* Gentile, pagan, heathen.

Gentil [hen-teel'], *a.* 1. Genteel, elegant, graceful, handsome. 2. Excellent, exquisite. *Gentil necedad*, (Iron. A pretty piece of folly.

Gentil hombre [hen-teel' om'-bray], *m* 1. Fine fellow: my good man. 2. Gentleman, the servant who waits about the person of a man of rank. 3. (Obs.) Person sent to the king with important despatches. *Gentil hombre de cámara*, Lord of the bed-chamber. *Gentil hombre de manga*, Nobleman who attends the princes of Spain when they are children. *Gentil hombre de placer*, (Coll.) Buffoon.

Gentileza [hen-te-lay'-thah], *f.* 1. Gentility, gracefulness of mien, elegance of behaviour, genteel deportment and address. 2. Easiness, freedom from constraint. 3. Ostentation, pageantry. 4. Civility, politeness, genteelness.

Gentilicio, ia [hen-te-lee'-the-o, ah], *a.* 1. Gentilitious, peculiar to a nation. 2. Gentilitious, hereditary, entailed on a family; tribal.

Gentílico, ca [hen-tee'-le-co, cah], *a.* Heathen, gentile, pagan, heathenish, hellenic.

Gentilidad [hen-te-le-dahd'], *f.* Gentilism, gentility, heathenism, paganism, religion of the heathens; the body of heathens or gentiles.

Gentilismo [hen-te-lees'-mo], *m.* *V.* GENTILIDAD.

Gentilizar [hen-te-le-thar'], *vn.* To observe the rites of gentiles or heathens; to gentilize.

Gentilmente [hen-teel-men'-tay], *adv.* Genteelly; heathenishly.

Gentío [hen-tee'-o], *m.* Crowd, multitude.

Gentualla, Gentuza [hen-too-ahl'-lyah, hen-too'-thah], *f.* Rabble, mob.

Genuflexión [hay-noo-flec-se-on'], *f.* Genuflexion, bending the knee.

Genuino, na [hay-noo-ee'-no, nah], *a.* Genuine, pure, real, legitimate, natural, good.

Geocéntrico [hay-o-then'-tree-co], *a.* (Ast.) Geocentric.

Geoda [hay-o'-dah], *f.* Geode, a nodule of stone containing crystals.

Geodesia [hay-o-day'-se-ah], *f.* Geodæsia, the doctrine or art of measuring surfaces; land-surveying.

Geodésico, ca [hay-o-day'-se-co, cah], *a.* Geodesic. *Cúpula geodésica*, Geodesic dome.

Geófago, ga [hay-o'-fah-go, gah], *a.* Geophagous, earth-eating.—*n. f.* Geofagia.

Geofísica [hay-o-fee'-se-cah], *f.* (Geol.) Geophysics.

Geognosia [hay-og-no'-se-ah], *f.* Geognosy, structural geology.

Geografía [hay-o-grah-tee'-ah], *f.* Geography.

Geográficamente [hay-o-grah'-fe-cah-men-tay], *adv.* Geographically.

Geográfico, ca [hay-o-grah'-fe-co, cah], *a.* Geographical.

Geógrafo [hay-o'-grah-fo], *m.* Geographer.

Geología [hay-o-lo-hee'-ah], *f.* Geology.

Geológico, ca [hay-o-lo'-he-co, cah], *a.* Geologic(al), relating to geology.

Geólogo [hay-o'-lo-go], *m.* Geologist.

Geomagnético, ca [hay-o-mag-nay'-te-co, cah], *a.* Geomagnetic.

Geomancia [hay-o-mahn'-the-ah], *f.* Geomancy, foretelling by figures.

Geomántico [hay-o-mahn'-te-co], *m.* Geomancer.—*a.* Geomantic.

Geómetra [hay-o'-may-trah], *m.* Geometer, a geometrician.

Geometral. *a.* *V.* GEOMÉTRICO.

Geometría [hay-o-may-tree'-ah], *f.* Geometry. *Geometría del espacio*, Solid geometry. *Geometría plana*, Plane geometry.

Geométricamente [hay-o-may'-tre-cah-men-tay], *adv.* Geometrically.

Geométrico, ca [hay-o-may'-tre-co, cah], *a.* Geometrical, geometric.

Geometrinos [hay-o-may-tree'-nos], *m. pl.* The geometrid moths, whose larvæ are called measuring-worms.

Geopolítica [hay-o-po-lee'-te-ca], *f.* Geopolitics.

Geopónica [hay-o-po'-ne-cah], *f.* Geoponics, the science of agriculture; gardening.

Georama [hay-o-rah'-mah], *f.* Georama, a large hollow globe, representing within the natural divisions of the earth.

Georgiano, na [hay-or-he-ah'-no, nah], *a.* Georgian, relating to Georgia.

Geórgica [hay-or'-he-cah], *f.* Georgic, a poem upon husbandry.

Geranio [hay-rah'-ne-o], *m.* (Bot.) Crane's-bill. Geranium. *Geranio de malva, olorísimo* or *de olor*, Sweet-scented stork's-bill. Geranium odoratissimum.

Gerapliega [hay-rah-ple-ay'-gah], *f.* (Pharm.) Hierapicra, a bitter purgative medicine.

Gerbo [herr'-bo], *m.* The jerboa.

Gerencia [hay-ren'-the-ah], *f.* 1. Administration. 2. Management (of a business, etc.)

Gerente [hay-ren'-tay], *m.* (Com.) Manager, director.

Geriatra [hay-re-ah'-trah], *m.* Geriatrician.

Geriatría [hay-re-ah-tree'-ah], *f.* (Med.) Geriatrics.

Gericaya [hay-re-cah'-yah], *f.* (Mex.) Custard.

Gerifalte [hay-re-fahl'-tay], *m.* (Orn.) Gerfalcon. Falco gyrfalco.

Germanesco, ca [her-mah-ness'-co, cah], *a.* Belonging to the jargon of the gipsies.

Germanía [her-mah-nee'-ah], *f.* 1. Jargon or cant of the gipsies, thieves, etc.; slang. 2. Concubinage. 3. Faction in Valentia during the days of Charles V.

Germánico, ca [her-mah'-ne-co, cah], *a.* Germanic, German; of Germany.

Germanismo [her-mah-nees'-mo], *m.* Germanism, a German idiom employed in another language.

Germano, na [her-mah'-no, nah], *a.* (Obs.) Pure, genuine, not spurious.

Germen [herr'-men], *m.* 1. Germ. 2. Sprout, shoot.

Germicida [her-me-thee'-da], *a.* Germicidal.—*m.* Germicide.

Germicultura [her-me-cool-too'-rah], *f.* Culture or medium for the growth of bacteria.

Germífugo, ga [her-mee'-foo-go, gah], *a.* Germicidal.

Germinación [her-me-nah-the-on'], *f.* (Bot.) Germination, the first act of vegetation in a seed.

Germinar [her-me-nar'], *vn.* To germinate, to bud.

Germinativo, va [her-me-nah-tee'-vo, vah], *a.* Germinative.

Gerundiada [hay-roon-de-ah'-dah], *f.* (Coll.) An emphatical, pompous, and unmeaning expression.

Gerundio [hay-roon'-de-o], *m.* 1. (Gram.) Gerund, a verbal noun. 2. He who affects to speak or preach in a pompous and emphatical manner.

Gesta [hess'-tah], *f.* (Bot.) *V.* RETAMA. *Gestas*, (Obs.) Actions, feats, achievements.

Gestación [hes-tah-the-on'], *f.* 1. Gestation, the term of pregnancy. 2. An exercise practised among the Romans for the confirmation of health, and the place where it was carried out. 3. Superstition of wearing rings to preserve one's self from evil.

Gestatorio, ria [hes-tah-to'-re-o, ah], *a.* Proper to gestation (state and exercise).

Gestear [hes-tay-ar'], *va.* (Obs.) To gesticulate, to play antic tricks; to make grimaces, to grin.

Gestero, ra [hes-tay'-ro, rah], *a.* Playing antic tricks, making grimaces; it is also used as a substantive for one who distorts his countenance from habit or affectation; a gesticulator.

Gesticulación [hes-te-coo-lah-the-on'], *f.* Gesticulation, gesture.

Gesticular [hes-te-coo-lar'], *va.* To gesticulate, to make gestures or grimaces.

Gesticular [hes-te-coo-lar'], *a.* Relating to gestures or gesticulation; gesticulatory.

Gestión [hes-te-on'], *f.* Conduct; exertion, effort, step; commonly used in the plural.

Gestionar [hes-te-o-nar'], *vn.* To be diligent in attaining what is desired.

Gesto [hess'-to], *m.* 1. Face, visage. 2. Grimace, a distortion of the countenance, a gesture. 3. Aspect, appearance. 4. Likeness, resemblance. *Estar de buen gesto*, To be in good humour. *Ponerse a gesto*, To set one's self off for the purpose of pleasing. *Géstos*, (Obs. Mil.) Feats, achievements, deeds. *Hacer gestos*, 1. To make wry faces or grimaces. 2. To ogle.

Gestor [hes-tor'], *m.* 1. (Com.) Superintendent, manager. 2. (For.) Proxy, representative: one who executes another's business and requires his principal's ratification.

Gestudo, da [hes-too'-do, dah], *a.* Ill-humoured, cross.

Gialomina [he-ah-lo-mee'-nah], *f.* Sort of yellow ochre.

Giba [hee'-bah], *f.* 1. Hump, crooked back, hunch, gibbosity. 2. (Coll.) Importunity, tiresomeness.

Gibado, da [he-bah'-do, dah], *a.* Crooked, hump-backed. *V.* GIBOSO.—*pp.* of GIBAR.

Gibar [he-bar'], *va.* *V.* JIBAR.

Gibelino, na [he-bay-lee'-no, nah], *a.* Ghibelline, siding with the emperors of Germany against the Guelphs. (Ital.)

Gibón [he-bon'], *m.* Gibbon, an anthropoid ape.

Gibosidad [he-bo-se-dahd'], *f.* 1. (Bot.) A hump, gibbosity. 2. (Med.) A hump on the back.

Giboso, sa [he-bo'-so, sah], *a.* Gibbous, crook-backed, hump-backed.

Gicama [hee'-cah-mah], *f.* (Mex.) A palatable root resembling yucca.

Giganta [he-gahn'-tah], *f.* 1. Giantess. 2. (Bot.) Smooth bear's breech. Acanthus mollis, *L.* *V.* GIRASOL.

Gigantazo, za [he-gan-tah'-tho, thah], *m.* & *f. aug.* A huge giant.

Gigante [he-gahn'-tay], *m.* 1. Giant, one unnaturally large. 2. One superior in courage, talents, or virtues.—*a.* Gigantic.

Giganteo, tea, Gigantesco, ca [he-gan-tay'-o, ah], *a.* Gigantic, giant-like.

Gigantez [he-gan-teth'], *f.* Gigantic tallness.

Gigantilla [he-gan-teel'-lyah], *f.* A figure made of paste or paste-board, with a very large head.

Gigantón, na [he-gan-tone', nah], *m.* & *f. aug.* Giant of enormous size. *Gigantones*, Gigantic figures of pasteboard. *Echar a alguno los gigantones*, To reprehend severely.

Gijas [hee'-has], *f. pl.* (Prov.) *V.* GUIJAS.

Gilia [hee'-le-ah], *f.* Gilia, a plant of the phlox family. Many species grow in California. The flowers are often showy and beautiful. (Fr. Philip Gil, a Spanish botanist.)

Gilocopa [he-lo-co'-pah], *f.* *V.* Jilocopo.
Gilvo, va [heel'-vo, vah], *a.* Honey-coloured, or between white and red.
Gimelga [he-mel'-gah], *f.* (Naut.) Fish, a piece of timber used to strengthen masts and yards.
Gimnanto, ta [him-nahn'-to, tah], *a.* (Bot.) Naked, without floral envelopes.
Gimnasia, *f.* *V.* Gimnástica.
Gimnasiarca [him-nah-se-ar'-cah], *m.* Gymnasiarch, head of an academy, college, or school.
Gimnasio [him-nah'-se-o], *m.* 1. School, academy; gymnasium. 2. Gymnasium, a place for athletic training and exercises.
Gimnasta [him-nahs'-tah], *m.* Master of athletic exercises.
Gimnasterio [him-nas-tay'-re-o], *m.* Wardrobe of a gymnasium.
Gimnástica [him-nahs'-te-cah], *f.* Gymnastics.
Gimnástico, ca [him-nahs'-te-co, cah], *a.* Gymnastic, gymnastical.
Gímnica [heem'-ne-cah], *f.* Gymnics, athletic exercises and the art of teaching them.
Gímnico, ca [heem'-ne-co, cah], *a.* Gymnastical.
Gimnobranquio, ia [him-no-brahn'-ke-o, ah], *a.* Having naked gills, gymnobranchiate.
Gimnocarpeo, a [him-no-car'-pay-o, ah], *a.* Gymnocarpous, having naked fruit.
Gimnoclado [him-no-clah'-do], *m.* The Kentucky coffee-tree; gymnocladus.
Gimnópodo, da [him-no'-po-do, dah], *a.* Gymnopodous, naked-footed.
Gimnoto [him-no'-to], *m.* Gymnotus, the electrical eel.
Gimnosofista [him-no-so-fees'-tah], *m.* Gymnosophist, one of a sect of Indian philosophers.
Gimnospermo, ma [him-nos-perr'-mo, mah], *a.* Gymnospermous, having the seeds naked.
(*Yo gimo, yo gima; él gimió, él gimiera;* from *Gemir.* *V.* Pedir.)
Gimotear [he-mo-tay-ar'], *vn.* (Coll.) To be always crying.
Gimoteo [he-mo-tay'-o], *m.* The act of crying very frequently.
Ginantropo [he-nan-tro'-po], *m.* Hermaphrodite (fr. Greek).
Ginebra [he-nay'-brah], *f.* 1. Rattle, an instrument much in use among the Moors. 2. Gin or geneva. 3. (Met.) Confusion, disorder. 4. A confused noise. 5. Game at cards.
Ginebrada [he-nay-brah'-dah], *f.* Sort of puff paste.
Ginebrés, sa, or **Ginebrino, na** [he-nay-brays', sah, he-nay-bree'-no, nah], *a.* Genevan, relating to Geneva.
Gineceo [he-nay-thay'-o], *m.* Gynecеum, the part of an ancient Greek house reserved for women.
Ginecocracia [he-nay-co-crah-thee'-ah], *f.* Gynæcocracy or gynecocracy, gynarchy, female government.
Ginecografía [he-nay-co-grah-fee'-ah], *f.* Gynecology, a treatise on the diseases of women.
Ginecología [he-nay-co-lo-hee'-ah], *f.* (Med.) Gynecology, study of women's diseases.
Ginecólogo, ga [he-nay-co'-lo-go, gah], *m.* & *f.* Gynecologist, specialist in women's diseases.
Gineta [he-nay'-tah], *f.* Genet, a kind of weasel. *V.* Jineta.
Ginete, *m.* *V.* Jinete.
Gingivitis [hin-he-vee'-tis], *f.* (Med.) Gingivitis.
Ginizo [he-nee'-tho], *m.* The moist, viscous surface of the stigma of orchids.
Ginología [he-no-lo-hee'-ah], *f.* Gynecology.
Ginseng [hin-seng'], *m.* (Bot.) Ginseng. Aralia ginseng.
Gipaeto [he-pah-ay'-to], *m.* A diurnal bird of prey resembling the vulture and the eagle.
Gips [heeps], *m.* A bird of the vulture family, of a brownish colour. Habitat Europe, Asia and Northern Africa.
Gipsífero, ra [hip-see'-fay-ro, rah], *a.* Gypseous, containing gypsum.
Gira [hee'-rah], *f.* *V.* Jira.
Girada [he-rah'-dah], *f.* 1. Gyration; pirouette, a turn on one foot in dancing. 2. Reciprocal motion of a tuft of wool from one comb to another in wool-shops.
Girado [he-rah'-do], *m.* (Com.) Drawee.
Girador, Girante [he-rah-dor', he-rahn'-tay], *m.* (Com.) Drawer.
Girafa [he-rah'-fah], *f.* Giraffe, camelopard. Camelopardalis, *L.*
Giralda [he-rahl'-dah], *f.* 1. Vane or weathercock in the form of a statue; derived from the statue of a woman on the spire of the cathedral church of Seville. 2. Common name of this tower.
Giraldete [he-ral-day'-tay], *m.* Rochet or surplice without sleeves.
Giraldilla [he-ral-deel'-lyah], *f. dim.* A small vane or weathercock in the form of a statue.
Girándula [he-rahn'-doo-lah], *f.* 1. In artificial fire-works, box of rockets, which turns swiftly and emits a quantity of rockets. 2. Girandole, a branched candlestick.
Girar [he-rar'], *vn.* 1. To turn round, to make a gyre, to circumgyrate, to hurdle. 2. To remit, by bills of exchange, to draw.
Girasol [he-rah-sole'], *m.* (Bot.) Sunflower. Helianthus annuus, *L.*
Giratorio, ria [he-rah-to'-re-o, ah], *a.* Rotating, gyrating, revolving. *Silla giratoria,* swivel chair.
Girel [he-rel'], *m.* Caparison, trappings for a horse. *V.* Jirel.
Girifalte, *m.* *V.* Gerifalte.
Girimiquiar [he-re-me-ke-ar'], *vn.* (Cuba) To sob.
Girino [he-ree'-no], *m.* 1. Embryo of a frog. 2. Gyrinus, whirligig beetle.
Giro, ra [hee'-ro, rah], *a.* (Obs.) Handsome, perfect.
Giro [hee'-ro], *m.* 1. (Com.) Draft. *Giro a la vista,* Sight draft. *Giro postal,* Money order. 2. Gyration, rotation. 3. Turn, trend, turn of events. *Tomar otro giro,* To change intent or resolution, to change the aspect of the matter. *Giro regular de los negocios,* A fair run of business.
Giromancia [he-ro-mahn'-the-ah], *f.* Gyromancy.
Giroscopio [he-ros-co'-pe-o], *m.* Gyroscope.
Gis [hees], *m.* (Pict.) Crayon.
Gisma, *f.* (Obs.) *V.* Chisme.
Gitanada [he-tah-nah'-dah], *f.* Blandishment, wheedling like gipsies, caress, flattery.
Gitanamente [he-tah-nah-men'-tay], *adv.* In a sly, winning manner.
Gitanear [he-tah-nay-ar'], *va.* To flatter, to wheedle, to caress, to entice by soft words.
Gitanería [he-tah-nay-ree'-ah], *f.* Wheedling, flattery.
Gitanesco, ca [he-tah-ness'-co, cah], *a.* Gipsy-like, gipsy.
Gitanillo, lla [he-tah-neel'-lyo, lyah], *m.* & *f. dim.* Little gipsy.
Gitanismo [he-tah-nees'-mo], *m.* The gipsies taken as a body, gipsyism, customs and manners which characterize gipsies.
Gitano, na [he-tah'-no, nah], *m.* & *f.* 1. Gipsy. 2. A sly, artful fellow, of a genteel, pleasing address.
Gitón [he-tone'], *m.* Ancient copper coin used only as the title of unity. *V.* Guitón.
Glacial [glah-the-ahl'], *a.* Glacial. *Mar glacial,* The frozen sea.
Glaciar [glah-the-ar'], *m.* Glacier.
Glacis [glah'-this], *m.* 1. (Mil.) *V.* Explanada. 2. Ends which join the bar in lace-work. 3. (Painting) Union of colours, scumbling, in a picture to give it tone and harmony. 4. (Arch.) The slope of a cornice to turn off water.
Gladiador [glah-de-ah-dor'], or **Gladiator** [glah-de-ah-tor'], *m.* Gladiator a sword-player; a prize-fighter.
Gladiatorio, ria [glah-de-ah-to'-re-o, ah], *a.* Gladiatorial, gladiatory.
Gladiolo [glah-de-o'-lo], *m.* (Bot.) Common corn-flag. Gladiolus communis, *L.*
Glaglar [glah-glar'], *va.* (Coll.) To gaggle, to talk in a voice resembling the cry of a goose.
Glande [glahn'-day], *m.* The glans penis, or clitoridis.—*f.* (Obs.) Acorn.
Glandífero, ra, Glandígero, ro [glan-dee'-fay-ro, rah], *a.* 1. Glandiferous, bearing acorns. 2. Bearing tubercles in the form of acorns.
Glándula [glan'-doo-lah], *f.* 1. Gland, a soft, spongy substance. 2. (Bot.) Gland, a little tumour discharging a fluid.
Glandular [glan-doo-lar'], *a.* Glandular.
Glandulífero, ra [glan-doo-lee'-fay-ro, rah], *a.* Glanduliferous, gland-bearing.
Glandulilla [glan-doo-leel'-lyah], *f. dim.* Glandule, a small gland.
Glanduloso, sa [glan-doo-lo'-so, sah], *a.* Glandulous, glandular, pertaining to the glands.
Glasé [glah-say'], *m.* Glacé finish.
Glaseado, da [glah-say-ah'-do, dah], *a.* Variegated, embroidered, glossy.
Glasto [glahs'-to], *m.* (Bot.) Woad or common dyers' woad. Isatis tinctoria, *L.*
Glaucio [glah'-oo-the-o], *m.* (Bot.) Celandine. Chelidonium.
Glauco, ca [glah'-oo-co, cah], *a.* (Bot.) Glaucous, sea-green, pale bluish green.
Glauco [glah'-oo-co], *m.* A kind of oyster with equal shells.
Glaucoma [glah-oo-co'-mah], *m.* Glaucoma, a disease of the eye characterized by increased tension, advancing far-sightedness, dimness of vision and ultimate blindness.
Gleba [glay'-bah], *f.* 1. Sod of earth turned up by the plough; glebe; fief; heritage. 2. A slave anciently joined to a piece of land and transferred with it to another owner.
Gleboso, sa [glay-bo'-so, sah], *a.* (Prov.) Glebous, turfy.
Glenóideo, dea [glay-no'-e-day-o, ah], *a.* Glenoid, every deep cavity which receives the head of a bone.
Glera [glay'-rah], *f.* (Obs.) *V.* Cascajal.
Glicerina [gle-thay-ree'-nah], *f.* Glycerine.
Glicónico [gle-co'-ne-co], *m.* A kind of Latin verse.
Glifo [glee'-fo], *m.* (Arch.) Glyph, a concave ornament.
Glíptica [gleep'-te-cah], *f.* Glyptics, the art of engraving fine stones and the like.
Gliptografía [gleep-to-grah-fee'-ah], *f.* Glyptography, a description of the art of engraving upon gems.
Globiforme [glo-be-for'-may], *a.* Globe shaped, globiform, spherical.

Globo [glo'-bo], *m.* 1. Globe, a spherical body. 2 Sphere, a terrestrial or celestial globe on which the various regions of the earth are geographically delineated, or the constellations and stars depicted. 3. Orb. *Hablar en globo*, (Coll.) To speak summarily. *Globo aerostático*, A balloon. *Globo celeste*, A planetarium. *Globo de fuego*, Shooting-star, meteor.

Globoso, sa [glo-bo'-so, sah], *a.* Globular, spherical, orbicular.

Globular [glo-boo-lar'], *a.* Globular spherical.

Glóbulo [glo'-boo-lo], *m.* 1. Globule. 2. Conceptacle of the reproductive bodies of certain lichens.

Globulillo [glo-boo-leel'-lyo], *m. dim.* Little globule.

Globuloso, sa [glo-boo-lo'-so, sah], *a.* Globulous.

Glomérula [glo-may'-roo-lah, *f.* (Bot.) Glomerule, head of flowers.

Glomerulado, da [glo-may-roo-lah'-do, dah], *a.* Glomerulate, in small clusters.

Gloria [glo'-re-ah], *f.* 1. Glory, honour, fame. 2. Paradise, state of blessedness. 3. Pleasure, delight in any thing. 4. Majesty, splendour. 5. Glory, blessedness, that which ennobles or illustrates. 6. A sort of tart or pie. 7. In painting, an opening in the sky, representing angels, splendours, etc.

Gloriarse [glo-re-ar'-say], *vr.* 1. To glory, to boast in, to be proud of, to flourish. 2. To take a delight in any thing.

Glorieta [glo-re-ay'-tah], *f.* Summer-house, bower, arbour.

Glorificación [glo-re-fe-cah-the-on'], *f.* 1 Glorification, giving glory. 2. Praise.

Glorificador [glo-re-fe-cah-dor'], *m.* Glorifier, he that glorifies: an appellation given to God.

Glorificante [glo-re-fe-cahn'-tay], *pa.* & *m.* & *f.* Glorifying; glorifier.

Glorificar [glo-re-fe-car'], *va.* 1. To glorify, to pay honour in worship. 2. To exalt to glory or dignity; to praise, to honour, to extol.—*vr. V.* GLORIARSE.

Gloriosamente [glo-re-o-sah-men'-tay], *adv.* Gloriously.

Glorioso. sa [glo-re-o'-so, sah], *a.* 1. Glorious, excellent, worthy of honour or praise. 2. Enjoying the bliss of heaven, blessed. 3. Glorious, boastful, ostentatious, proud, elate.

Glosa [glo'-sah], *f.* 1. Gloss, a scholium; a comment or commentary. 2. Note added to a document, or inserted in a book of accounts, to explain its contents. 3. (Poet.) Amplification of a verse. 4. (Mus.) Variation in a tune.

Glosador, ra [glo-sah-dor', rah], *m.* & *f.* Commentator, glosser, a writer of glosses.

Glosalgia [glo-sahl'-he-ah], *f.* Glossalgia, neuralgia of the tongue.

Glosantrace [glo-san-trah'-thay], or **Glosántrax**, *m.* Glossanthrax, carbuncle of the tongue.

Glosar [glo-sar'], *va.* 1. To gloss, to explain by comment. 2. To palliate by specious exposition or representation. 3. (Poet.) To amplify the sense of a verse. 4. (Mus.) To vary notes.

Glosario [glo-sah'-re-o], *m.* 1. A glossary; a special lexicon. 2. The mouth-parts of insects.

Glose [glo'-say], *m.* Act of glossing or commentating.

Glosilla [glo-seel'-lyah], *f.* 1. (Dim.) A short gloss, comment, or note. 2. (Print.) Minion type. 7-point.

Glositis [glo-see'-tis], *f.* Glossitis, inflammation of the tongue.

Glotis [glo'-tis], *f.* (Anat.) Glottis, opening of the larynx.

Glotón, na [glo-tone', nah], *m* & *f.* 1. A glutton, gormandizer. 2. Glutton. wolverene. a carnivore.—*a.* Gluttonous, given to excessive feeding.

Glotonazo, za [glo-to-nah'-tho, thah], *m.* & *f. aug.* Great glutton, great eater, gormandizer.

Glotoncillo, illa [glo-ton-theel' lyo, lyah], *m.* & *f. dim.* Little glutton.

Glotonear [glo-to-nay-ar'], *vn.* To indulge too much in eating, to devour, to gormandize.

Glotonería, Glotonía [glo-to-nay-ree' ah], *f.* Gluttony.

Gloxinia [gloc-see'-ne-ah], *f.* Gloxinia, a perennial plant, having large, handsome flowers, coming from South America.

Glucina [gloo-thee'-nah], *f.* Glucina, glucinum oxide.

Glucinio [gloo-thee'-ne-o], *m.* Glucinum (or, beryllium), a hard silver-white metallic element.

Glucosa [gloo-co'-sah], *f.* Glucose, grape-sugar.

Gluma [gloo'-mah], *f.* (Bot.) Glume, the chaff-like bract of the blossom of grasses and sedges.

Glumáceo, cea [gloo-mah'-thay-o, ah], *a.* Glumaceous.

Glumal [gloo-mahl'], *a.* *V.* GLUMÁCEO.

Glumífero. ra [gloo-mee'-fay-ro, rah], *a.* Glumaceous, bearing glumes.

Gluten [gloo'-ten], *m.* Gluten.

Gluteo, tea [gloo-tay'-o, ah], *a.* Gluteal, relating to the buttocks.

Glutinosidad [gloo-te-no-se-dahd'], *f.* Glutinousness, viscosity.

Glutinoso, sa [gloo-te-no'-so, sah], *a.* Glutinous, viscous, mucous.

Gneis [nay'-is], *m.* Gneiss, a rock resembling granite, composed of quartz, feldspar, and hornblende.

Gnómico, ca [no'-me-co, cah], *a.* Sententious, gnomic.

Gnomo [no'-mo], *m.* 1. Aphorism, apothegm. 2. Gnome, a fabulous being.

Gnomon [no'-mon], *m.* 1. Gnomon, the hand of a dial. 2. Bevel square, composed of two movable rules.

Gnomónica [no-mo'-ne-cah], *f.* Gnomonics, the science which teaches the art of making sun-dials.

Gnomónico, ca [no-mo'-ne-co, cah], *a.* Gnomonic, gnomonical, relating to dialing.

Gnosticismo [nos-te-thees'-mo], *m.* Gnosticism, the philosophy of the gnostics, prevailing from the 1st to the 6th century.

Gnóstico [nos'-te-co], *m.* & *a.* Gnostic: applied to one of the earliest heretics.

Goa [go'-ah], *f.* Pig iron.

Gobernación [go-ber-nah-the-on'], *f.* Government. *V.* GOBIERNO.

Gobernado, da [go-ber-nah'-do, dah], *a.* & *pp.* of GOBERNAR. Governed.

Gobernador [go-ber-nah-dor'], *m.* Governor, ruler, master.

Gobernadora [go-ber-nah-do'-rah], *f.* Governess, directress.

Gobernalle [go-ber-nahl'-lyay], *m.* Rudder, helm.

Gobernante [go-ber-nahn'-tay], *m.* (Coll.) A person assuming the management of a thing.—*pa.* Governing.

Gobernar [go-ber-nar'], *va.* 1. To govern, to rule as a first magistrate. 2. To regulate, to govern, to command, to lead, to head, to control, to manage; to guide, to direct. 3. To entertain, to maintain. *Gobernar el timón.* To steer the ship.

Gobernativo, va [go-ber-nah-tee'-vo, vah], *a.* *V.* GUBERNATIVO.

Gobernoso, sa [go-bayr-no'-so, sah], *a.* Methodical, systematic, loving good order.

Gobierno [go-be-ayr'-no], *m.* 1. Government, form of a community with respect to the disposition of the supreme authority. 2. Government, administration of public affairs, executive power. 3. Government, district or province under the command of a governor. 4. The space of time which the administration of a governor lasts, and the manner in which he governs. 5. Government, regularity of behaviour, guidance, conduct, management, direction. *Esto lo digo para gobierno de Vd.*, I say this for your guidance. *Sirva de gobierno.* Let this be a warning to you. *Mujer de gobierno*, 1. House-keeper. 2. (Met.) Any woman skilled in feminine pursuits. *Gobierno de casa*, Household.

(*Yo gobierno, yo gobierne*, from *Gobernar. V.* ACERTAR.)

Gobio [go'-be-o], *m.* (Zool.) Gudgeon.

Goce [go'-thay], *m.* Enjoyment, fruition; possession.

Gociano, na [go-the-ah'-no, nah], *a.* Goth, Gothic.

Gocete [go-thay'-tay], *m.* Ancient armour for the head.

Gocha [go'-chah], *f.* Sow.

Gocho [go'-cho], *m.* Pig, hog.

Godeño, ña [go-day'-nyo, nyah], *a.* (Slang) Rich, renowned.

Godetia [go-day'-te-ah], *f.* Godetia, a genus of showy flowers, belonging to the evening-primrose family (Onagraceæ) of California and Chili.

Godo, da [go'-do, dah], *a.* & *m.* & *f.* Gothic; a Goth.

Gofio [go'-fe-o], *m.* (Cuba) Parched corn-meal, maize, or other cereal.

Gofo, fa [go'-fo, fah], *a.* Stupid, ignorant, rude. *Gofo*, (Pict.) A little figure or image.

Gofrador [go-frah-dor'], *m.* (Neol.) Leaf-marker, a florist's copper tool for stamping in relief the veins of leaves. 2. The one who uses this tool.

Gofrar [go-frar'], *va.* To mark leaves for artificial flowers.

Goja [go'-hah], *f.* (Obs.) Basket in which gleaners put their corn.

Gol [gol], *m.* Goal.

Gola [go'-lah], *f.* 1. Gullet, throat, œsophagus. 2. Gorget, a piece of silver or brass worn by officers of foot when on duty. 3. (Fort.) Gorge, the entrance of a bastion, ravelin, or other work. *Media gola*, (Fort.) Demi-gorge, the line which passes from the angle of the bastion to the capital. 4. (Arch.) Gola, cymatium, a moulding, the profile of which represents an S.

Goldre [gol'-dray], *m.* (Obs.) A quiver.

Goleta [go-lay'-tah], *f.* (Naut.) A schooner.

Golf [golf], *m.* Golf, golf game.

Golfan [gol-fahn'], *m.* *V.* NENÚFAR.

Golfín, *m.* *V.* DELFÍN.

Golfo [gol'-fo], *m.* 1. Gulf, bay. 2. Gulf, abyss. 3. Hoodlum, rake, vagabond.

Golilla [go-leel'-lyah], *f.* 1. A kind of collar, forming part of the dress of the magistrates of some superior courts of justice in Spain. 2. (Coll.) The magistrate of said superior courts. *Ajustar a uno la golilla*, (Met. and Coll.) 1. To oblige one to do his duty. 2. To hang or strangle. *Levantar la golilla.* To become passionate. *Bajar la golilla*, To be pacified.

Golillero, ra [go-leel-lyay'-ro, rah], *m.* & *f.* Collar-maker.

Golmajo, ja [gol-mah'-ho, hah], *a.* (Prov.) *V.* GOLOSO.

Golondrina [go-lon-dree'-nah], *f.* 1. (Orn.) Swallow. Hirundo, *L.* 2. (Zool.) Sapphire gurnard, tub-fish. Trigla hirundo, *L.*

Golondrinera [go-lon-dre-nay'-rah], *f.* (Bot.) Swallow-wort, celandine. Chelidonium majus, *L.*

Golondrino [go-lon-dree'-no], *m.* 1. A male swallow. 2. Vagrant, deserter. 3. Tub-fish. 4. A large tumour in the arm-pit.

Golondro [go-lon'-dro], *m.* Desire, longing. *Campar de golondro,* (Coll.) To live at another's expense. *Andar en golondros,* (Coll.) To feed on vain hopes.

Golosamente [go-lo-sah-men'-tay], *adv.* Daintily.

Golosazo [go-lo-sah'-tho], *m. aug.* Applied to a person extremely fond of dainties or delicacies.

Golosear [go-lo-say-ar'], *va.* *V.* GOLOSINAR.

Golosina [go-lo-see'-nah], *f.* 1. Dainty, something nice or delicate, a tid-bit. 2. Daintiness, fondness of dainties. 3. Any thing more agreeable than useful. 4. Cupidity, desire.—*pl.* Niceties, dainties, delicacies.

Golosinar, Golosinear, Golosmear [go-lo-se-nar', go-lo-se-nay-ar', go-los-may-ar'], *va.* 1. To eat tid-bits, dainties, or sweetmeats, and also to look for them. 2. To be fond of tasting or trying the relish of nice things. 3. To guzzle dainties.

Goloso, sa [go-lo'-so, sah], *a.* & *m.* & *f.* Applied to a person very fond of dainties, niceties, or sweet-meats; sweet-tooth, lickerish.

Golpazo [gol-pah'-tho], *m. aug.* A great blow.

Golpe [gol'-pay], *m.* 1. Blow, stroke, hit; knock, dash; wound, hurt. 2. Action, push, act. 3. Crowd, throng of people; abundance. 4. An unfortunate accident. 5. Spring bolt of a lock. 6. *V.* LATIDO. 7. A pocket-flap (of a coat). 8. Movements of attack in fencing. 9. Admiration, surprise. 10. Opportunity concluding in some business. 11. With gardeners, a hole for planting; also the depth, of a foot or more, to which a thing is planted. 12. (Naut.) Any point which does not follow rigorously the direction of a given line. 13. (Mus.) The action of striking a string, key, etc. *Golpe de arco,* Bowing of a violin. *Golpe de mar,* (Naut.) Surge, a heavy sea. *Golpe de música,* Band of music. *Golpe de remo,* Stroke in rowing. *Golpe de fortuna,* A fortunate event, a jump. *El golpe del reloj,* The tick of the watch, or clock. *De golpe,* Plump, all at once. *De golpe y zumbido,* Unexpectedly, unawares. *De un golpe,* Once, all at once. *Golpe de Estado,* A stroke of policy, coup d'état. *Darse golpes de pecho,* To beat one's breast. *El golpe de la sartén aunque no duele, tizna.* Slander, although known as such, leaves a stain on the reputation. (Literally, the blow of the frying-pan smuts even if it does not ache.)

Golpeadero [gol-pay-ah-day'-ro], *m.* 1. Place much beaten. 2. Noise made by striking a thing repeatedly.

Golpeado, da [gol-pay-ah'-do, dah], *a.* (Painting) Done a stroke, with a free brush and masterfully.

Golpeador, ra [gol-pay-ah-dor', rah], *m.* & *f.* Striker, person or thing that strikes, beater.

Golpeadura [gol-pay-ah-doo'-rah], *f.* Percussion, the act of beating, hammering, or striking.

Golpear [gol-pay-ar'], *va.* 1. To beat, to strike, to hit, to knock, to hammer, to give blows; to bruise. 2. To tick, like a watch.

Golpecico, illo, ito [gol-pay-thee'-co], *m. dim.* A slight blow.

Golpeo [gol-pay'-o], *m.* *V.* GOLPEADURA.

Golpeteo [gol-pay-tay-'o], *m.* Lively and continued striking; constant hammering. (Acad.)

Golusmear, *vn.* *V.* GOLOSINEAR.

Golusmero, ra [go-loos-may'-ro, rah], *a.* *V.* GOLOSO. (Obs.)

Gollería, Golloría [gol-lyay-ree'-ah], *f.* 1. A dainty dish. 2. Delicacy, superfluity, excess. (Acad.)

Gollete [gol-lyay'-tay], *m.* 1. Throttle, the superior part of the throat. 2. The neck of a bottle.

Gollizo [gol-lyee'-tho], *m.* Narrow passage of mountains or rivers.

Goma [go'-mah], *f.* 1. Gum. 2. Rubber. 3. Rubber band. *Goma arábiga,* Gum arabic. *Goma de borrar,* Eraser. *Goma elástica,* Rubber.

Gomal [go-mahl'], *m.* (Sp. Am.) Grove of rubber trees.

Gomero, ra [go-may'-ro, rah], *a.* Rubber.—*m.* & *f.* Rubber plantation worker.

Gomia [go-mee'-ah], *f.* 1. Bugbear to frighten children. 2. Glutton, a voracious eater. *Gomía del caudal,* Spendthrift.

Gomífero, ra [go-mee'-fay-ro, rah], *a.* Bearing or containing gum; gummiferous.

Gomorresina [go-mor-ray-see'-nah], *f.* Gum-resin.

Gomosidad [go-mo-se-dahd'], *f.* Gumminess, viscosity.

Gomos [go'-mos], *m.* A gummatous tumour.

Gomoso, sa [go-mo'-so, sah], *a.* 1. Gummy, productive of gum. 2. Full of viscous humours.

Gomuto [go-moo'-to], *m.* An East Indian palm-tree yielding an edible fruit highly prized.

Gonagra [go-nah'-grah], *f.* (Med.) Gout which attacks the knees.

Gonce [gon'-thay], *m.* *V.* GOZNE.

Góndola [gon'-do-lah], *f.* 1. Gondola, a Venetian flat-boat with an awning. 2. A certain carriage in which several can ride together.

Gondolero [gon-do-lay'-ro], *m.* Gondolier, rower of a gondola.

Gonela [go-nay'-lah], *f.* A tunic or outer garment, sleeveless, and reaching to the calf of the leg, worn over the armour and bearing the arms, in embroidery, of the knight who wore it.

Gonfalón [gon-fah-lon'], *m.* 1. Banner, pennant. 2. (Her.) Standard of the church.

Gonfaloniero [gon-fah-lo-ne-ay'-ro], *m.* 1. Title of the chiefs of some of the small republics in Italy. 2. Standard-bearer.

Gongorino, na [gon-go-ree'-no, nah], *a.* (Coll.) Applied to a pompous, lofty style of writing.

Gongorismo [gon-go-rees'-mo], *m.* (Coll.) Altiloquence, pompous language: commonly applied to poetry.

Gongorista [gon-go-rees'-tah], *f.* One who affects to write poetry in a pompous style.

Gongorizar [gon-go-re-thar'], *vn.* To affect loftiness of style in poetry.

Goniometría [go-ne-o-may-tree'-ah], *f.* Goniometry, art of measuring angles.

Goniométrico, ca [go-ne-o-may'-tre-co, cah], *a.* Goniometric, belonging to goniometry.

Goniómetro [go-ne-o'-may-tro], *m.* Goniometer, instrument for measuring angles.

Gonóideo, dea [go-no'-e-day-o, ah], *a.* Resembling sperm or semen.

Gonorrea [go-nor-ray'-ah], *f.* (Med.) 1. Spermatorrhœa. (Acad.) 2. Gonorrhœa, a venereal disease; specific urethritis.

Gonorreico, ca [go-nor-ray'-e-co, cah], *a.* Gonorrhœal, relating to gonorrhœa.

Gorbión [gor-be-on'], *m.* 1. A kind of edging for embroidering. 2. (Obs.) A kind of flowered taffeta. 3. Gum euphorbium.

Gordal [gor-dahl'], *a.* Fat, big, fleshy.

Gordana [gor-dah'-nah], *f.* Oil extracted in India from the testicles of oxen, and used for wool.

Gordazo, za [gor-dah'-tho, thah], *a. aug.* Very fat and big.

Gordico, ica, illo, illa, ito, ita [gor-dee'-co, cah, etc.], *m.* & *f. dim.* Not very fat, rather plump.

Gordiflón, na [gor-de-flone', nah], *m.* & *f.* A very corpulent, flabby person.

Gordo, da [gor'-do, dah], *a.* 1. Fat, corpulent, full-fed, plump, fleshy, obese. 2. Fat, rich, greasy, oily. *Tocino gordo,* Fat pork. 3. Coarse, thick. *Lienzo gordo,* Coarse linen. 4. Great, large, big. 5. (Obs.) Torpid, stupid. *Mentira gorda,* A gross falsehood. *Hablar gordo,* To speak thick.

Gordo [gor'-do], *m.* Fat, suet, lard.

Gordolobo [gor-do-lo'-bo], *m.* (Bot.) Great-mullein. Verbascum thapsus, *L.*

Gordón, na [gor-done', nah], *a. aug.* (Coll.) Very fat and corpulent.

Gordura [gor-doo'-rah], *f.* 1. Grease, fat. 2. Fatness, corpulence.

Gorfe [gor'-fay], *m.* A deep hole in a river forming a whirlpool or eddy.

Gorga [gor'-gah], *f.* 1. Food of hawks. 2. (Prov.) Whirlpool.

Gorgojarse [gor-go-har'-say], *vr.* *V.* AGORGOJARSE.

Gorgojo [gor-go'-ho], *m.* 1. Grub, weevil. 2. A dwarfish little boy.

Gorgojoso, sa [gor-go-ho'-so, sah], *a.* Full of grubs or weevils.

Gorgona [gor-go'-nah], *f.* 1. Gorgonia, sea-fan, a zoophyte. 2. (Amer.) A whirlpool near the island of this name, S. W. of the coast of Colombia, in lat. 3° N.

Gorgorán [gor-go-rahn'], *m.* Sort of silk grogram.

Gorgorear [gor-go-ray-ar'], *vn.* (Prov.) To cry like a turkey-cock.

Gorgorita [gor-go-ree'-tah], *f.* Bubble formed on water by the fall of rain. *Gorgoritas,* Quavers, trilling.

Gorgoritear [gor-go-re-tay-ar'], *vn.* To warble, to gargle, to quiver the voice.

Gorgoritos [gor-go-ree'-tos], *m. pl.* (Coll.) Quivers of the voice.

Gorgorotada [gor-go-ro-tah'-dah], *f.* The quantity of liquid swallowed at once.

Gorgotero [gor-go-tay'-ro], *m.* Peddler, hawker.

Gorguera [gor-gay'-rah], *f.* 1. A kind of neckcloth, formerly worn by ladies of fashion. 2. Armour of the neck.

Gorguerín [gor-gay-reen'], *f.* Small kind of ruff or frill for the neck.

Gorguz [gor-gooth'], *m.* Javelin, a missile weapon.

Gorigori [go-re-go'-re], *m.* Song with which children mimic the clerk's chant at funerals.

Gorila [go-ree'-lah], *m.* Gorilla.

Gorja [gor'-hah], *f.* 1. Throat, throttle. 2. Rejoicing, merry-making. 3. (Naut.) Head of the keel.

Gorjal [gor-hahl'], *m.* 1. Collar of a doublet. 2. Armour to defend the neck or throat.

Gorjeador, ra [gor-hay-ah-dor', rah], *m.* & *f.* Warbler, modulator.

Gorjear [gor-hay-ar'], *vn.* To warble, to quaver, to shake the voice in a melodious manner; to chirp, to twitter.—*vr.* To gabble: applied to a child which begins to speak.

Gorjeo [gor-hay'-o], *m.* 1. Trilling, quaver; a melodious shake of the voice; chirp, twitter. 2. Chatter of a child which begins to talk.

Gorjería [gor-hay-ree'-ah], *f.* *V.* GORJEO for chatter of a child.

Gormar [gor-mar'], *va.* (Obs.) 1. To vomit. 2. To return what belongs to another.

Gorra [gor'-rah], *f.* 1. Cap, bonnet, a covering of the head. 2. *Gorra de señora*, Lady's hat or bonnet. 3. Hunting-cap. 4. Intrusion at feasts without invitation. 5. Parasite, sponger. *Duro de gorra*, He who waits for others to salute first.

Gorrada [gor-rah'-dah], *f.* *V.* GORRETADA.

Gorrero [gor-ray'-ro], *m.* 1. Cap-maker. 2. Parasite, sponger.

Gorretada [gor-ray-tah'-dah], *f.* Salute with a cap.

Gorrete [gor-ray'-tay], *m. dim.* Small cap.

Gorrica, illa, ita [gor-ree'-cah, eel'-lyah, ee'-tah], *f. dim.* Small cap or bonnet.

Gorrico, illo, ito [gor-ree'-co, eel'-lyo, ee'-to], *m. dim.* Small round cap.

Gorrín, Gorrino [gor-reen', gor-ree'-no], *m.* 1. A small pig, a sucking pig. 2. (Prov.) Pig.

Gorrinada, or **Gorrinera** [gor-re-nah'-dah, gor-re-nay'-rah], *f.* A pigsty.

Gorrinería [gor-re-nay-ree'-ah], *f.* 1. A hogsty. 2. (Met.) Filthiness, bestiality.

Gorrinillo, ito [gor-re-neel'-lyo, ee'-to], *m. dim.* A small sucking pig.

Gorrión [gor-re-on'], *m.* (Orn.) Sparrow. Fringilla domestica, *L.*

Gorrioncillo [gor-re-on-theel'-lyo], *m. dim.* A small sparrow.

Gorrionera [gor-re-o-nay'-rah], *f.* Rendezvous or hiding-place of rogues.

Gorrista [gor-rees'-tah], *m.* Parasite, sponger.

Gorro [gor'-ro], *m.* A night-cap.

Gorrón [gor-rone'], *m.* 1. A poor student who goes from house to house to get his dinner; parasite. 2. Spindle, pivot, or gudgeon of a gate or door; pillow, swing-block. 3. Lazy, unhealthy silkworm. 4. A round, smooth pebble. 5. Man given to debauchery and lewdness. 6. An iron staff which aids in turning the capstan. 7. Peg serving as a hinge in flood-gates.

Gorrona [gor-ro'-nah], *f.* Strumpet, prostitute.

Gorronal [gor-ro-nahl'], *m.* Place full of pebbles or coarse gravel.

Gorronazo [gor-ro-nah'-tho], *m.* (Aug.) A great lecher or rake.

Gorullo [go-rool'-lyo], *m.* A small button or ball of wool, or other matter which sticks together.

Gosipífero, ra [go-se-pee'-fay-ro, rah], *a.* Cotton-producing.

Gosipino, na [go-se-pee'-no, nah], *a.* Of a cottony surface.

Gosipio [go-see'-pe-o], *m.* Gossypium, the cotton-plant.

Gota [go'-tah], *f.* 1. Drop, a globule of moisture which falls at once. 2. A small quantity of any liquor. 3. Gout, a disease. 4. A small portion taken from a smelting of gold or silver for assaying. 5. In clockwork, the small steel plate put at the end of the fuse and sometimes of the barrel arbour. 6. A variety of topaz called "water-drop." *Gota a gota*, Drop by drop—*pl.* (Arch.) Ornaments of the Doric order. *Gota coral* or *caduca*, Epilepsy, falling-sickness. *Gotas amargas*, Bitters.

Goteado, da [go-tay-ah'-do, dah], *a.* & *pp.* of GOTEAR. Guttated, sprinkled, spotted, speckled.

Gotear [go-tay-ar'], *vn.* 1. To drop, to fall drop by drop. 2. To give by driblets or intermittently: to leak.

Goteo [go-tay'-o], *m.* 1. Leak, leakage. 2. Dribbling.

Gotera [go-tay'-rah], *f.* 1. Gutter, a passage made by water on the roofs of houses. 2. Leak, the water which drops or runs through the passage, the place where the water falls, and the mark left by the dropping of rain. 3. Fringe of bed-hangings, valance. 4. (Acad.) Invalidism. *V.* ACHAQUE.

Goterón [go-tay-ron'], *m.* 1. A large drop of rain-water. 2. Throating in a cornice.

Goteroncillo [go-tay-ron-theel'-lyo], *m.* A drop of rain-water not much larger than usual.

Gotica, illa, ita [go-tee'-cah, eel'-lyah, ee'-tah], *f. dim.* Droplet, a small drop.

Gótico, ca [go'-te-co, cah], *a.* Gothic: chiefly applied to the pointed style of building. *Letra gótica*, Gothic characters.

Gotón, na [go-ton', nah], *a.* & *m. pl.* Goth. (Acad.)

Gotoso, sa [go-to'-so, sah], *a.* Gouty.

Goyo [go'-yo], *m.* (Obs.) *V.* Gozo.

Gozador, ra [go-thah-dor', rah], *m.* & *f.* Enjoyer.

Gozante [go-thahn'-tay], *pa.* Enjoying; enjoyer.

Gozar [go-thar'], *va.* To enjoy, to have possession or fruition of.—*vr.* To rejoice.

Gozne [goth'-nay], *m.* Hinge.

Gozo [go'-tho], *m.* 1. Joy, pleasure, satisfaction, glee, merriment, mirth, gladfulness, gladness, cheerfulness. 2. A sudden blaze of dry chips of wood. 3. *pl.* Verses in praise of the Virgin or the saints in which certain words are repeated at the end of every couplet. *No caber de gozo* or *saltar de gozo*, To be in high spirits, to be very merry. *¡El gozo en el pozo!* My illusions have vanished!

Gozosamente [go-tho-sah-men'-tay], *adv.* Joyfully, cheerfully.

Gozoso, sa [go-tho'-so, sah], *a.* Joyful, cheerful, content, glad, festive, mirthful, merry.

Gozque [goth'-kay], *m.* A cur-dog.

Gozquejo [goth-kay'-ho], *m. dim.* A small cur-dog.

Grabado [grah-bah'-do], *m.* 1. Engraving, the art of engraving. 2. Engraving, the copy printed from an engraved plate.—*Grabado, da*, *pp.* of GRABAR.

Grabador, ra [grah-bah-dor', rah], *m.* & *f.* Engraver, a cutter in stone, metal, or wood. *Grabador en hueco*, Punch or die-sinker.

Grabadura [grah-bah-doo'-rah], *f.* Act of engraving, sculpture.

Grabar [grah-bar'], *va.* To engrave, to picture by incisions in stone, wood, or metal; to grave. *Grabar al agua fuerte* or *de agua fuerte*, To etch. *Grabar en hueco*, *en blanco* or *relieve*, To emboss; to sink a die.

Grabazón [grah-bah-thone'], *f.* Engraving, sculpture.

Gracejar [grah-thay-har'], *vn.* (Littl. us.) To joke, to jest.

Gracejo [grah-thay'-ho], *m.* 1. Joke, jest, mirth, facetiousness, cheerful wit. 2. A graceful or pleasing delivery in speaking.

Gracia [grah'-the-ah], *f.* 1. Grace, favourable influence of God in the human mind, and the effect of this influence. 2. Grace, natural excellence; gracefulness, gentility, elegance of mien or manner; cleverness. 3. Grace, favour conferred, gift, benefaction, kindness, concession; graciousness, condescension. 4. Benevolence, courtesy, pleasing manners. 5. Grace, pardon, mercy. 6. Elegance, beauty. 7. Remission of a debt. 8. A witty saying or expression. 9. (Coll.) Name, the discriminative appellation of an individual. *¿Cómo es la gracia de Vd.?* (Low) Pray, what is your name? 10. Gratitude for favours received. *Dar gracias*, To thank, or to give thanks. *Caer en gracia*, To become a favourite. *De gracia*, Gratis, for nothing. *Gracias*, Pontifical grants or concessions. *Decir dos gracias*, To tell home truths. *Gracia de Dios*, (Coll.) The bread. *En gracia de*, For the sake of. *Ella tiene muchas gracias*, She has many accomplishments.—*interj.* *¡Qué gracia!* What a wonder! A fine thing indeed! *De su bella gracia*, Of his own accord. *Golpe de gracia*, Finishing stroke (literally, stroke of mercy).

Graciable [grah-the-ah'-blay], *a.* 1. Good-natured, affable. 2. Easily obtained: applied to favours.

Grácil [grah'-theel], *a.* (Acad.) Gracile, slender, small.

Graciola [grah-the-o'-lah], *f.* (Bot.) Hedge hyssop. Gratiola, *L.* *Graciola oficinal*, Officinal hedge hyssop. Gratiola officinalis, *L.*

Graciosamente [grah-the-o-sah-men'-tay], *adv.* Graciously, gratefully, kindly; gratuitously.

Graciosidad [grah-the-o-se-dahd'], *f.* 1. Gracefulness, beauty, perfection, elegance and dignity of manners. 2. Facetiousness, cheerful wit.

Gracioso, sa [grah-the-o'-so, sah], *a.* 1. Graceful, beautiful, accomplished. 2. Facetious, witty, funny, pleasing. 3. Benevolent, inclined to grant favours, gracious. 4. Gratuitous, granted without claim. 5. Ridiculous, extravagant.

Gracioso, sa [grah-the-o'-so, sah], *m.* & *f.* 1. Merry-andrew, buffoon, harlequin, mime. 2. Comic actor or actress, generally in the character of servants in Spanish plays.

Grada [grah'-dah], *f.* 1. Step of a staircase. 2. In nunneries, a room where the nuns are allowed to hold conversation with their friends through a grate. 3. An order of steps before a church, gradatory. 4. Harrow, to break the clods after ploughing. *Grada de construcción*, (Naut.) Stocks for shipbuilding. *Navío en la grada*, Ship on the stocks.—*pl.* 1. Bar, the place where causes of law are tried. 2. Seats of an amphitheatre.

Gradación [grah-dah-the-on'], *f.* 1. A harmonious gradation or scale of music. 2. (Rhet.) Climax.

Gradado, da [grah-dah'-do, dah], *a.* Applied to the building with an order of steps around it.—*pp.* of GRADAR.

Gradar [grah-dar'], *va.* (Prov.) To harrow, to break with the harrow.

Gradatim [grah-dah'-tim], *adv.* (Lat.) Gradually, by degrees.

Gradería [grah-day-ree'-ah], *f.* Series of seats or steps.

Gradilla [grah-deel'-lyah], *f.* 1. (Dim.) Small step or seat. 2. Tile-mould. 3. A step-ladder, a small portable ladder.

Gradinar [grah-de-nar'], *va.* To cut off with a chisel.

Gradino [grah-dee'-no], *m.* 1. Chisel, an edged tool used by stone-cut ters. 2. Graver, the tool used in graving.

Gradiolo [grah-de-o'-lo], *m.* (Bot.) *V.* GLADIOLO.

Grado [grah'-do], *m.* 1. Step of a staircase. 2. Value or quality of a thing. 3. Degree of kindred, order of lineage. 4. Will, pleasure. 5. Degree, an academical title of honour conferred by universities. 6. (Mil.) Rank. 7. (Geom.) Degree, the three hundred and sixtieth part of the circumference of a circle. 8. Degree, the division of the lines upon mathematical instruments. 9. Degree, grade, the measure of the quality or state of a thing. 10. (Mus.) Degree, the intervals of sounds. *De grado* or *de su grado*, Willingly, with pleasure. *De grado en grado*, Gradually, by degrees, in regular progression. *Mal de su grado*, Unwillingly. *Mal su grado*, In spite of him. *Grados*, Minor orders.

Graduación [grah-doo-ah-the-on'], *f.* 1. The act and effect of measuring or comparing different things. 2. Graduation, regular progression by succession of degrees. 3. Rank, condition or quality of a person. 4. (Mil.) Rank.

Graduado, da [grah-doo-ah'-do, dah], *a.* (Mil.) Brevet: applied to officers enjoying higher rank than they possess.—*pp.* of GRADUAR.—*m.* Graduate, one who has obtained an academical degree.

Graduador [grah-doo-ah-dor'], *m.* Graduator, graduating instrument, gauge.

Gradual [grah-doo-ahl'], *a.* Gradual, proceeding by degrees.

Gradual [grah-doo-ahl'], *m.* A verse read between the epistle and gospel at the celebration of the mass.

Gradualmente [grah-doo-al-men'-tay], *adv.* Gradually, by degrees.

Graduando [grah-doo-ahn'-do], *m.* Candidate for academical degrees.

Graduar [grah-doo-ar'], *va.* 1. To measure or compare different things. 2. To graduate, to dignify with an academical degree. 3. To give military rank. 4. To divide into degrees. (Coll.) To calculate, to appraise.—*vr.* To graduate, to take an academical degree.

Gráfica [grah'-fe-cah], *f.* Diagram, sketch, illustration.

Gráficamente [grah'-fe-cah-men-tay], *adv.* Graphically, in a picturesque manner.

Gráfico, ca [grah'-fe-co, cah], *a.* Graphic, graphical, relating to engravings; well delineated.

Gráfila [grah'-fe-lah], *f.* The little border on the edge of coin.

Grafio [grah'-fe-o], *m.* Graver, a tool used in making grafitto or scratch-work.

Grafioles [grah-fe-o'-les], *m. pl.* Kind of biscuits made in the form of an S.

Grafito [grah-fee'-to], *m.* Graphite, plumbago.

Grafolita [grah-fo-lee'-tah], *f.* Grapholite, a variety of slate suitable for writing on.

Grafología [grah-fo-lo-hee'-ah], *f.* Graphology, study of handwriting.

Grafómetro [grah-fo'-may-tro], *m.* Graphometer, circumferentor, a surveying instrument with sights for measuring angles.

Graja [grah'-hah], *f.* (Orn.) 1. (Acad.) Female jackdaw. 2. Jay. Garrulus glandarius.

Grajal [grah-hahl'], *a.* Belonging to crows, ravens, or magpies.

Grajea [grah-hay'-ah], *f.* A very small sugar-plum.

Grajear [grah-hay-ar'], *vn.* To caw, as crows; to chatter, as magpies. (Acad.)

Grajero, ra [grah-hay'-ro, rah], *a.* Applied to rookeries.

Grajo [grah'-ho], *m.* 1. (Orn.) Jackdaw. Corvus monedula, *L.* 2. (Peru. Coll.) Strong sweat of negroes and other persons, particularly in the armpits.

Grajuelo [grah-hoo-ay'-lo], *m. dim.* A small jackdaw.

Gralario, ria [grah-lah'-re-o, ah], *a.* Grallatory, wading (birds).

Grama [grah'-mah], *f.* (Bot.) Creeping cynodon. Cynodon dactylon, *Pers.* (Bot.) Couch-grass, dog's-grass. Triticum repens, *L.*

Gramal [grah-mahl'], *m.* Place where couch-grass or dog's-grass grows.

Gramalla [grah-mahl'-lyah], *f.* 1. A long scarlet gown anciently worn by the magistrates of Aragon. 2. Coat of mail.

Gramallera [grah-mal-lyay'-rah], *f.* (Prov.) Pot-hanger. *V.* LLARES.

Gramar [grah-mar'], *va.* (Prov.) To knead the dough of bread.

Gramática [grah-mah'-te-cah], *f.* 1. Grammar. 2. Study of the Latin language. *Gramática parda*, Soundness of faculties; strength of natural reason.

Gramatical [grah-mah-te-cahl'], *a.* Grammatical.

Gramaticalmente, *adv.* Grammatically.

Gramático [grah-mah'-te-co], *m.* Grammarian.

Gramaticón [grah-mah-te-cone'], *m.* One who believes himself a great grammarian, or he who knows nothing but grammar.

Gramatícuelo [grah-mah-te-coo-ay'-lo], *m. dim.* Grammaticaster, a smatterer in grammar, a pedant.

Gramatista [grah-mah-tees'-tah], *f.* Teacher of grammar.

Gramil [grah-meel'], *m.* A joiner's marking gauge.

Gramilla [grah-meel'-lyah], *f.* Brake, a wooden instrument for dressing hemp or flax.

Gramíneo, ea [grah-mee'-nay-o, ah], *a.* (Poet.) Gramineous, grassy.

Graminívoro, ra [grah-me-nee'-vo-ro, rah], *a.* Graminivorous, grass-eating, living upon grass.

Gramo [grah'-mo], *m.* Gramme, unit of weight in the metrical system: the weight of a cubic centimetre of distilled water.

Gramófono [grah-mo'-fo-no], *m.* Gramophone, talking machine.

Gramómetro [grah-mo'-may-tro], *m.* A type-gauge.

Grampa [grahm'-pah], *f.* (Naut.) A hook for sustaining light weights.

Gramuro, ra [grah-moo'-ro, rah], *a.* Having a long, slender tail.

Gran, *a.* 1. Great. *V.* GRANDE. It is used only before substantives in the singular, as *Gran cosa*, Great thing; *Gran miedo*, Great fear. 2. Grand, as chief or principal: used also before substantives as *Gran maestre*, Grand-master. *Gran señor*, Grand signior.

Grana [grah'-nah], *f.* 1. Grain, the seed of plants. 2. The time when corn, flax, etc., form their seed. 3. Cochineal. Coccus cacti, *L.* *Grana, grana de coscoja* or *grana quermes*, Kermes dye. 4. Scarlet grain. 5. Fine scarlet cloth. 6. Fresh red colour of the lips and cheeks. *Grana del paraíso*, (Bot.) *V.* AMOMO. *Ponerse como una grana*, (Coll.) To blush up to one's eyes. *Poner a otro como una grana*, To put one to the blush.

Granada [grah-nah'-dah], *f.* 1. Pomegranate. 2. (Mil.) Hand-grenade.

Granadera [grah-nah-day'-rah], *f.* (Mil. A grenadier's pouch.

Granadero [grah-nah-day'-ro], *m.* (Mil.) Grenadier, a foot-soldier, formerly employed to throw grenades.

Granadilla [grah-nah-deel'-lyah], *f.* (Bot.) Passion-flower. Passiflora granadilla vel capsularis, *Lin.*

Granadino, na [grah-nah-dee'-no, nah], *a.* Native of or belonging to Granada, or the U. S. of Colombia, formerly New Granada.—*m.* The flower of the pomegranate-tree.

Granado, da [grah-nah'-do, dah], *a.* 1. Large, remarkable. 2. Principal, chief, illustrious; select. 3. Seedy, abounding with seed.—*pp.* of GRANAR.

Granado [grah-nah'-do], *m.* (Bot.) Pomegranate-tree. Punica granatum, *L.*

Granador [grah-nah-dor'], *m.* A sieve for granulating gunpowder, and the spot destined for this operation.

Granaje [grah-nah'-hay], *m.* The act of granulating powder.

Granalla [grah-nahl'-lyah], *f.* Granulation, grains of metal.

Granar [grah-nar'], *vn.* 1. To seed, to grow to maturity so as to shed the seed. 2. To seed, to shed the seed. 3. To grain, to granulate.

Granate [grah-nah'-tay], *m.* Garnet, a precious stone resembling a ruby.

Granático, ca [grah-nah'-te-co, cah], *a.* Scarlet, garnet; characteristic of cochineal or the garnet.

Granatín [grah-nah-teen'], *m.* Kind of ancient cloth.

Granazón [grah-nah-thone'], *f.* Seeding, shedding the seed.

Gran bestia [gran bes'-te-ah], *f.* Tapir.

Grancé [gran-thay'], *a.* (Acad.) Madder-coloured. (Fr. garance.)

Grandánime [gran-dah'-ne-may], *a.* (Obs.) Magnanimous.

Grande [grahn'-day], *a.* 1. Great, large in bulk or number, extensive, huge. 2. Great, having any quality in a high degree. 3. Grand, principal.

Grande [grahn'-day], *m.* Grandee, a Spanish nobleman of the first rank.

Grandecico, ica, illo, illa, ito, ita, [gran-day-thee'-co], *a.* Growing rather big; pretty large or big.

Grandemente [gran-day-men'-tay], *adv.* Greatly; very well; extremely; grandly.

Grandeza [gran-day'-thah], *f.* 1. Greatness, bigness. 2. Greatness, grandeur, magnificence, grandness, nobleness. 3. Grandeeship, the pre-eminence and dignity of a grandee of Spain. 4. The body of grandees.

Grandilocuencia [gran-de-lo-coo-en'-the-ah], *f.* (Littl. us.) Grandiloquence.

Grandilocuente [gran-dee-lo-coo-en'-tay], *a.* *V.* GRANDÍLOCUO.

Grandílocuo, cua [gran-dee'-lo-coo-o, coo-ah], *a.* Grandiloquent, making use of a lofty or pompous style.

Grandillón, na [gran-deel-lyone', nah], *a. aug.* Excessively large and big.

Grandiosamente [gran-de-o-sah-men'-tay], *adv.* Magnificently.

Grandiosidad [gran-de-o-se-dahd'], *f.* Greatness, grandeur; magnificence; abundance.

Grandioso, sa [gran-de-o'-so, sah], *a.* Grand, great, magnificent, splendid.

Grandor [gran-dor'], *m.* Size and bigness of things, magnitude, greatness, extensiveness.

Grandullón, na [gran-dool-lyone', nah], *a.* Large in proportion to age.

Grandura [gran-doo'-rah], *f.* (Obs.) Magnitude, greatness.

Graneado, da [grah-nay-ah'-do, dah], *a.* 1. Reduced to grains; spotted, granulous. 2. (Peru.) Select, choice—*pp.*

of **Granear**. *Fuego graneado*, *V.* Fuego, ad fin.
Graneador [grah-nay-ah-dor'], *m.* A kind of graver or tool for engraving.
Granear [grah-nay-ar'], *va.* 1. To sow grain in the earth. 2. To engrave.
Granel [grah-nel'], *m.* (Prov.) Heap of corn. *A granel*, 1. In a heap. 2. (Naut.) In bulk. 3. (Amer. Peru.) The *gacetilla* of some periodicals.
Granelar [grah-nay-lar'], *va.* In tanneries, to grain leather.
Graneo [grah-nay'-o], *m.* The act of shedding seed, or sowing seed.
Granero [grah-nay'-ro], *m.* 1. Granary, grange, corn-loft. 2. A fruitful country.
Granete [grah-nay'-tay], *m.* (Mech.) Marking-awl; countersink punch.
Granevano [grah-nay-vah'-no], *m.* (Bot.) Goat's-thorn. Astragalus tragacantha, *L.*
Granguardia [gran-goo-ar'-de-ah], *f.* (Mil.) Grand-guard, an advanced guard in front of an army.
Granico [grah-nee'-co], *m. dim.* Granule, small grain.
Granífero, ra [gra-nee'-fay-ro, rah], *a.* (Bot.) Bearing seeds in the form of grains.
Granilla [grah-neel'-lyah], *f.* Rough nap on cloth.
Granillero, ra [grah-neel-lyay'-ro, rah], *a.* (Prov.) Applied to hogs that feed on what they find in the fields.
Granillo [grah-neel'-lyo], *m.* 1. (Dim.) Granule, small grain. 2. Gain or profit frequently obtained. 3. Pimple growing at the extremity of the rump of canary-birds and linnets.
Granilloso, sa [grah-neel-lyo'-so, sah], *a.* Granulous, granular.
Granítico, ca [grah-nee'-te-co, cah], *a.* Granitic, formed of granite.
Granito [grah-nee'-to], *m.* 1. Granite, a hard stone composed of quartz, feldspar, and mica. 2. Hairs, streaks, or points which diminish the brilliancy and price of diamonds. 3. (Pharmacy) Granule. 4. (Prov. Murcia) Small egg of a silk-worm.
Granitulino, na [grah-ne-too-lee'-no, nah], *a.* (Min.) Nodular; granulous.
Granívoro, ra [grah-nee'-vo-ro, rah], *a.* Granivorous, eating grain, living upon grain.
Granizada [grah-ne-thah'-dah], *f.* 1. Copious fall of hail. 2. (Met.) Multitude of things which fall in abundance.
Granizado, da [grah-ne-thah'-do, dah], *a.* Grandinous, full of hail: destroyed by hail.—*pp.* of Granizar.
Granizar [grah-ne-thar'], *vn.* 1. To hail. 2. To pour down with violence.
Granizo [grah-nee'-tho], *m.* 1. Hail, rain frozen in falling. 2. Cloud or web in the eyes. *V.* Granizada.
Granja [grahn'-hah], *f.* Grange, farm, farm-house; a country-house, a villa, a manse. *Ir de granja*, To go into the country for recreation.
Granjear [gran-hay-ar'], *va.* 1. To gain, to get. to obtain, to win. 2. To conciliate or gain the good-will of another. *Granjear a barlovento*, (Naut.) To gain to windward: applied to a ship.
Granjeo [gran-hay'-o], *m.* 1. The act of getting or acquiring. 2. Gain, profit, advantage, advancement in interest, influence, etc.
Granjería [gran-hay-ree'-ah], *f.* Gain, profit, advantage.
Granjero, ra [gran-hay'-ro, rah], *m.* & *f.* 1. Farmer, husbandman, granger. 2. Dealer in profitable commodities. 3. (Obs.) Broker.
Grano [grah'-no], *m.* 1. Grain, the seed of corn. 2. Grain, a single seed of corn. 3. Grain, any minute particle. 4. Grain, the direction of the fibres of wood or other fibrous matter. 5. (Pharm.) Grain, the smallest weight in physic, twenty of which make an English scruple, and twenty-four a Spanish one. 6. The bushing (or bouching) of a cannon. 7. Pimple, a pustule on the skin, furuncle. *Granos del paraíso*, (Bot.) *V.* Amomo.
Granoso, sa [grah-no'-so, sah], *a.* Granulous, grainy, granular.
Granudo, da [grah-noo'-do, dah], *a.* *V.* Granoso.
Granuja [grah-noo'-hah], *f.* 1. Ripe grapes separated from the branches. 2. Grapestone, the stone or seed contained in the grape. 3. Little rogue, waif, gamin. 4. A boy who follows the troops and serves the stewards.
Granujado, da [grah-noo-hah'-do, dah], *a.* 1. Full of pimples. 2. Full of stones, full of seeds.
Granujiento, ta [grah-noo-he-en'-to, tah], *a.* Grainy, full of grain.
Granujo [grah-noo'-ho], *m.* (Coll.) Pimple or tumour in the flesh.
Gránula [grah'-noo-lah], *f.* (Bot.) Spore, reproductive body of cryptogamous plants.
Granulación [grah-noo-lah-the-on'], *f.* (Chem.) 1. Granulation, the act of being reduced into small particles. 2. Granulation, the act of reducing metal into grains by pouring it, when melted, into cold water.
Granular [grah-noo-lar'], *va.* To granulate, to reduce to small pieces like grains.—*vr.* 1. To granulate. 2. To be covered with granules.
Granular, *a.* Granular.
Gránulo [grah'-noo-lo], *m.* 1. Granule, a small grain. 2. Pellet, a medicated granule.
Granulosidad [grah-noo-lo-se-dahd'], *f.* Granularity, the state of being granular.
Granuloso, sa [grah-noo-lo'-so, sah], *a.* Granulous, granular.
Granza [grahn'-thah], *f.* Madder. *V.* Rubia.—*pl.* 1. Siftings, the refuse of corn which has been winnowed and sifted. 2. Dross of metals.
Granzón [gran-thone'], *m.* Fragment of ore which does not pass through the screen; screenings. (Acad.)—*pl.* Refuse of straw not eaten, but left by the cattle.
Granzoso, sa [gran-tho'-so, sah], *a.* Applied to grain having much refuse.
Grañón [grah-nyone'], *m.* 1. Pap made of boiled wheat. 2. *V.* Grano.
Grao [grah'-o], *m.* Strand, shore.
Grapa [grah'-pah], *f.* 1. Cramp-iron; holdfast. 2. Kind of mangy ulcers in the joints of horses.
Grapón [grah-pone'], *m. aug.* A large cramp-iron.
Graptolita [grap-to-lee'-tah], *f.* Dendrite, generic name of stones exhibiting markings upon the surface.
Grasa [grah'-sah], *f.* 1. Suet, fat; grease; kitchen-stuff. *Grasa de ballena*, Blubber. *Grasa de pescado*, Fish-oil. 2. Gum of juniper-trees. 3. Grease of clothes. 4. (Naut.) Compound of rosin, pitch, and tallow used for preserving masts and yards. 5. Slag of metals. 6. The base of an ointment or pomade.
Grasera [grah-say'-rah], *f.* 1. An ointment jar. 2. Vessel for fat or grease; a dripping-pan.
Grasería [grah-say-ree'-ah], *f.* 1. Tallow-chandler's shop. 2. A disease of silk-worms.
Graseza [grah-say'-thah], *f.* Quality of fat or grease.
Grasiento, ta [grah-se-en'-to, tah], *a* Greasy; filthy, grimy.
Grasilla [grah-seel'-lyah], *f.* 1. Pounce. a powder made of gum sandarach. 2. (Bot.) The odoriferous resin which the juniper produces.
Graso, sa [grah'-so, sah], *a.* Fat, unctuous, lardy.
Graso [grah'-so], *m.* Fat, grease.
Grasones [grah-so'-nes], *m. pl.* Fast-dish, made of flour, milk of almonds, sugar, and cinnamon.
Grasoso, sa, *a.* *V.* Grasiento.
Grasura, *f.* *V.* Grosura.
Grata, Grataguja [grah'-tah, grah-tah-goo'-hah], *f.* Instrument for burnishing silver or silver gilt.
Gratamente [grah-tah-men'-tay], *adv.* Graciously, gratefully, in a kind and benevolent manner.
Gratar [grah-tar'], *va.* To burnish silver or silver gilt.
Gratel [grah-tel'], *m.* A braid, made by hand, with the number of skeins of yarn suited to its use.
Gratificación [grah-te-fe-cah-the-on'], *f.* 1. Gratification, reward, recompense, gratuity, fee; allowance to officers for expenses. 2. Indulgence.
Gratificador, ra [grah-te-fe-cah-dor', rah], *m.* & *f.* Gratifier.
Gratificar [grah-te-fe-car'], *va.* 1. To gratify, to reward, to requite, to recompense. 2. To gratify, to indulge, to delight.
Gratil [grah-teel'], *m.* 1. (Naut.) Head of a sail. 2. Body of the yard where the sail is tied.
Gratis [grah'-tis], *adv.* Gratis, for nothing.
Gratisdato, ta [grah-tis-dah'-to, tah], *a.* Gratuitous.
Gratitud [grah-te-tood'], *f.* Gratitude, gratefulness.
Grato, ta [grah'-to, tah], *a.* 1. Graceful, pleasing, pleasant, luscious; acceptable. 2. Grateful.
Gratonada [grah-to-nah'-dah], *f.* Kind of ragout or fricassee, made of chickens half roasted, bacon, almonds, rich broth, fresh eggs, spice, and greens.
Gratuitamente [grah-too-ee-tah-men'-tay], *adv.* Gratuitously.
Gratuito, ta [grah-too-ee'-to, tah], *a.* Gratuitous, gratis.
Gratulación [grah-too-lah-the-on'], *f.* (Obs.) 1. Cheerful readiness to oblige another. 2. Congratulation.
Gratular [grah-too-lar'], *vn.* To congratulate.—*vr.* To rejoice.
Gratulatorio, ria [grah-too-lah-to'-re-o, ah], *a.* Congratulatory.
Grava [grah'-vah], *f.* Gravel, coarse sand. (Acad.)
Gravamen [grah-vah'-men], *m.* 1. Charge, obligation to perform or execute any thing. 2. Hardship, load, inconvenience, nuisance. 3. Encumbrance, burden. 4. (Law) Mortgage.
Gravar [grah-var'], *va.* To burden, to oppress, to fatigue, to molest.
Gravativo, va [grah-vah-tee'-vo, vah], *a.* Grievous, injurious.
Grave [grah'-vay], *a.* 1. Weighty, ponderous, heavy. 2. Grave, important, momentous, of weight, of great consequence, dangerous. (Met.) Mortal, deadly. 3. Great, huge, vast. 4. Grave, circumspect. 5. Haughty, lofty. 6. Troublesome, vexatious, grievous; arduous, difficult. *Ponerse grave*, To assume an air of importance. 7. (Mus.) Grave tone. 8. (Gram.) Grave accent. *Delito grave*, A heinous crime. *Enfermedad grave*, A dangerous disease.
Gravear [grah-vay-ar'], *vn.* To weigh to gravitate, to sink.

Gravedad [grah-vay-dahd'], *f.* 1. Gravity, weight, heaviness. 2. Gravity, modesty, composure, circumspection. 3. Graveness, seriousness, sobriety of behaviour. 4. Gravity, enormity, atrociousness, 5. Vanity, pride.

Gravedoso, sa [grah-vay-do'-so, sah], *a.* (Obs.) Haughty, vain, elevated.

Gravemente [grah-vay-men'-tay], *adv.* Gravely, seriously.

Gravidez [grah-ve-deth'], *f.* Pregnancy.

Grávido, da [grah'-ve-do, dah], *a.* 1. Full, abundant. 2. Gravid, pregnant.

Gravimetro [gra-vee'-may-tro], *m.* Gravimeter, an instrument for learning specific weight.

Gravitación [grah-ve-tah-the-on'], *f.* Gravitation.

Gravitar [grah-ve-tar'], *va.* To gravitate, to weigh down, to tend to some part slightly.

Gravívolo, la [grah-vee'-vo-lo, lah], *a.* (Zool.) Of heavy flight.

Gravoso, sa [grah-vo'-so, sah], *a.* 1. Grievous, offensive, afflictive, painful, onerous. 2. Unbearable.

Graznador, ra [grath-nah-dor', rah], *m.* & *f.* Croaker; cawing, cackling.

Graznar [grath-nar'], *vn.* To croak, to caw, to cackle.

Graznido [grath-nee'-do], *m.* 1. A croak, caw, or cackle. 2. Croaking.

Greba [gray'-bah], *f.* Ancient armour for the leg; greave(s).

Greca [gray'-cah], *f.* Grecian fret, ornament consisting of a line forming many right angles.

Grecíano, na [gray-the-ah'-no, nah], or **Grecisco** [gray-thees'-co], *a.* Greek, Grecian: applied to the Greek fire.

Grecismo [gray-thees'-mo], *m.* Grecism, Hellenism, Greekism.

Grecizante [gray-the-thahn'-tay], *pa.* Grecianizing, Hellenizing.

Grecizar [gray-the-thar'], *vn.* To Grecianize, to Hellenize, to play the Grecian, to speak Greek.

Greco, ca [gray'-co, cah], *a.* Greek. In the form *Greco* it enters into composition, as: *Grecolatino*, Written in Greek and Latin. *A la greca*, In the Grecian style.

Greda [gray'-dah], *f.* 1. Chalk, marl. 2. Fuller's-earth.

Gredal [gray-dahl'], *m.* Pit where chalk, marl or fuller's-earth is found.

Gredal [gray-dahl'], *a.* Chalky.

Gredoso, sa [gray-do'-so, sah], *a.* Chalky, marly, cretaceous.

Grefier [gray-fe-err'], *m.* Keeper of the rolls; an officer of distinction in the king's palace.

Gregal [gray-gahl'], *m.* North-east wind in the Mediterranean.

Gregal [gray-gahl'], *a.* Gregarious, going in flocks.

Gregalizar [gray-gah-lee-thar'], *vn.* (Naut.) To be north-easting, to drive or decline to north-east.

Gregario, ria [gray-gah'-re-o, ah], *a.* Gregarian, of the common sort, ordinary.

Gregoriano, na [gray-go-re-ah'-no, nah], *a.* Gregorian.

Gregorillo [gray-go-reel'-lyo], *m.* Neckcloth formerly worn by women.

Gregueria [gray-gay-ree'-ah], *f.* 1. Outcry, confused clamour. 2. *V.* GUIRIGAY.

Gregüescos [gray-goo-ays'-cos], *m. pl.* A wide sort of breeches made in the Grecian fashion.

Greguisco, ca [gray-gees'-co, cah], *a.* Greek, belonging to Greece.

Greguizar [gray-gee-thar'], *va.* 1. To Grecianize, to talk Greek. 2. To Grecize, to convert into Greek.

Gremial [gray-me-ahl'], *m.* Lapcloth, used by bishops when they officiate at divine service.

Gremial [gray-me-ahl'], *a.* Belonging or relating to a body, corporation, or guild; it is also used as a substantive for a member of the corporation.

Gremio [gray'-me-o], *m.* 1. The lap. 2. Body, society, company, guild, corporation; fraternity. *El gremio de la iglesia*, The pale of the church. *El gremio de una universidad*, The professors, doctors, and scholars, belonging to a university, considered as a body.

Greña [gray'-nyah], *f.* 1. Entangled or matted hair. 2. Any thing entangled. *Andar a la greña*, To pull one another by the hair. 3. (Prov.) Heap of grain laid to be thrashed. 4. (Prov.) First leaves of a vine-shoot.

Greñudo, da [gray-nyoo'-do, dah], *a.* Dishevelled, having entangled hair.

Greñuela [gray-nyoo-ay'-lah], *f.* (Prov.) The first shoots of a vine.

Gres [grays], *m.* Generic name of every rock of grainy texture.

Gresca [grays'-cah], *f.* 1. Carousal, revelling, clatter. 2. Wrangle, quarrel.

Greuge [gray'-oo-hay], *m.* (Obs.) Grievance, complaints formerly made in the cortes of Arragon.

Grey [gray'-e], *f.* 1. Flock, as of sheep or goats. 2. (Met.) Flock, congregation of the faithful. 3. (Obs.) *V.* REPÚBLICA.

Grial [gre-ahl'], *m.* Grail, the legendary holy chalice of the Last Supper.

Griego, ga [gre-ay'-go, gah], *a.* Greek; belonging to or native of Greece.—*m.* 1. The Greek language. 2. Incomprehensible language.

Griesco, Griesgo [gre-es'-co, go], *m.* (Obs.) Encounter, conflict, battle.

Grieta [gre-ay'-tah], *f.* 1. Crevice, crack, cleft. 2. Chink, fissure, cranny, flaw. 3. Scratch or fissure in the skin. *Grieta en las manos*, Chapped hands.

Grietado, da [gre-ay-tah'-do, dah], *a.* Fissured, cleft, showing flaws.

Grietarse [gre-ay-tar'-say], *vr.* To crack in the form of a star: said of ingots or metal plates.

Grietecilla [gre-ay-tay-theel'-lyah], *f. dim.* A small fissure or scratch; a small crevice.

Grietoso, sa [gre-ay-to'-so, sah], *a.* Full of cracks or crevices, flawy.

Grifa [gree'-fah], *f.* Italics, in printing.

Grifado, da [gre-fah'-do, dah], *a.* Italic (type).

Grifalto [gre-fahl'-to], *m.* Small kind of culverin.

Grifo, fa [gree'-fo, fah], *a.* 1. Applied to the letters invented by Haldus Pius Manutius, which superseded the Gothic characters; Italic. 2. Kinky.

Grifo [gree'-fo], *m.* 1. Griffin or griffon, a fabled animal. 2. (Amer.) The child of a negro and an Indian. *Grifos*, Frizzled hair.

Grifón [gre-fone'], *m.* A stop-cock for water; faucet, spigot.

Gril [greel'], *m.* Grilse, Scotch name of a young salmon on its first return from sea.

Griliforme [gre-le-for'-may], *a.* (Zool.) Shaped like a cricket.

Grilla [greel'-lyah], *f.* 1. Female cricket. *V.* GRILLO. 2. A piece of the mechanism of a stocking-loom. *Esa es grilla*, There is no such a thing: vulgar expression of doubt.

Grillar [greel-lyar'], *vn.* To chirp or squeak: applied to crickets.—*vr.* To shoot, to sprout.

Grillera [greel-lyay'-rah], *f.* Cricket-cage, a place where crickets are kept.

Grillero [greel-lyay'-ro], *m.* He who takes off the irons of prisoners.

Grillete [greel-lyay'-tay], *m.* Shackle, fetter.

Grillo [greel'-lyo], *m.* 1. Cricket, an insect. Gryllus domesticus, gryllus campestris, *L.* 2. Shoot issuing from seed in the earth, germ. *Grillos*, 1. Fetters, irons, gyves, shackles or chains for the feet. 2. Any impediment which prevents motion. *Andar a grillos*, To waste time in useless pursuits.

Grillones [greel-lyo'-nes], *m. pl. aug.* Large fetters or irons.

Grillotalpa [greel-lyo-tahl'-pah], *m.* Mole-cricket, fen-cricket. Gryllus gryllotalpa, *L.*

Grima [gree'-mah], *f.* Fright, horror, astonishment, grimness.

Grimazo [gre-mah'-tho], *m.* A grotesque posture, or contortion of the face.

Grímpola [greem'-po-lah], *f.* (Naut.) Vane, a sort of weather-cock on the top-mast head. 1. Pennant, streamer. 2. *Huso de la grímpola*, Spindle of a vane.

Grinalde [gre-nahl'-day], *m.* Machine of artificial fire-work.

Gringo [green'-go], *a.* (Coll.) Unintelligible, gibberish: applied to language.—*m.* (Vulg.) A nickname given to one who speaks a foreign language. In S. America applied especially to the English and Germans.

Griñón [gre-nyone'], *m.* 1. A wimple worn by nuns and religious women.

Gripe [gree'-pay], *f.* Influenza, flu, grippe.

Gris [grees], *m.* 1. Mixture of white and black, grizzle, gray. 2. Miniver, a grizzle-coloured squirrel or weasel. Sciurus, *L.* 3. (Coll.) Cold, sharp air or weather.

Gris [grees], *a.* Gray, grizzled.

Grisa [gree'-sah], *f.* (Amer.) *V.* CHINCHILLA.

Grisalla [gre-sahl'-yah], *f.* Grisaille, a style of painting in grayish tints in imitation of bass-reliefs.

Grisar [gre-sar'], *va.* To polish the diamond.

Griseta [gre-say'-tah], *f.* 1. Kind of flowered silk. 2. (Neol.) A French grisette.

Grisú [gre-soo'], *m.* A French and Belgian name of fire-damp, or methane gas, which in coal-mines produces an explosive mixture with atmospheric air.

Grita [gree'-tah], *f.* 1. Clamour, outcry, vociferation. 2. Halloo; a word of encouragement to dogs. 3. Exclamations of applause or censure. *Grita foral*, (Prov.) Summons, citation.

Gritador, ra [gre-tah-dor', rah], *m.* & *f.* Clamourer, exclaimer; bawler.

Gritar [gre-tar'], *vn.* 1. To exclaim, to cry out, to clamour, to clatter, to halloo, to shout, to hoot. 2. To talk very loud. 3. To bawl. 4. To shriek.

Gritería [gre-tay-ree'-ah], *f.* 1. Outcry, clamour, confused noise, shout, exclamation, screaming; hooting. 2. Confused cry of many voices.

Grito [gree'-to], *m.* Cry, scream, howling; hoot. *Estar en un grito*, To be in continual pain. *A grito herido*, In a loud voice, with a clamorous cry. *Dar un grito*, To raise an outcry, to set up a shout, a hurrah.

Gritón, na [gre-tone', nah], *a.* Vociferous, clamorous.

Gro, *m.* Grosgrain, a twilled silk fabric; a stout silk.

Groenlandés, sa [gro-en-lan-days', sah] *a.* & *m.* & *f.* Greenlander.

Gromo [gro'-mo], *m.* (Bot.) Leafy bud, young shoot.

Gropos [gro'-pos], *m. pl.* Cotton put in inkstands or inkhorns.
Gros [gros], *m.* Ancient coin of small value. *En gros*, (Obs.) By wholesale. *Gros de Nápoles liso, labrado, de aguas* or *estampado*, Gros de Naples, plain, figured, watered, or printed.
Grosca [gros'-cah], *f.* Kind of venomous serpent.
Grosedad [gro-say-dahd'], *f.* (Obs.) *V.* GROSURA and GROSERÍA.
Grosella [gros-sayl'-lyah], *f.* (Bot.) The fruit of the red currant. *Grosella blanca*, White currant, the fruit of a variety of red currant. *Grosella negra*, Fruit of the black currant.
Grosellero [gros-sel-lyay'-ro], *m.* (Bot.) Currant. Ribes. *Grosellero rojo* or *común*, Red currant. Ribes rubrum. *Grosellero blanco*, White red currant. Ribes rubrum, v. album. *Grosellero negro*, Black currant. Ribes nigrum.
Groseramente, [gro-say-rah-men'-tay], *adv.* Grossly, coarsely, rudely, clownishly, in a rude, unmannerly way.
Grosería [gro-say-ree'-ah], *f.* 1. Grossness, homeliness, plainness, coarseness, churlishness, clumsiness, clownishness, rudeness, ill-breeding. 2. Grossness, shameless word or action.
Grosero, ra [gro-say'-ro, rah], *a.* 1. Gross, coarse, rough, plain, homely, homespun, not elegant, not fine. 2. Gross, thick, fat, bulky. 3. Gross, rude, unpolished, churlish, clownish, uncivil, rough, brutal. 4. Gross, indelicate, indecent, smutty.
Groseza [gro-say'-thah], *f.* (Obs.) Corpulence, bulkiness of body.
Grosísimo, ma [gro-see'-se-mo, mah], superlative of GRUESO. (Acad.)
Groso [gro'-so], *a.* Coarse snuff, badly powdered.
Grosor [gro-sor'], *m.* 1. Thickness, density, closeness, compactness. 2. (Obs.) *V.* GROSURA.
Grosularina, or **Grosulina** [gro-soo-lah-ree'-nah, gro-soo-lee'-nah], *f.* (Chem.) Grossaline, a vegetable jelly found in acid fruits.
Grosura [gro-soo'-rah], *f.* 1. Suet, tallow, fat of animals. 2. Extremities, heart, liver, and lungs of an animal. *Día de grosura*, Saturday, formerly so called in Castille, because on that day the entrails and members of animals were eaten, but not their flesh, nor fish.
Grotesco, ca [gro-tes'-co, cah], *a.* Grotesque, laughable.
Grúa [groo'-ah], *f.* 1. Crane, a machine for raising heavy weights. 2. An ancient military machine. 3. (Naut.) Bend of a curved piece of timber. 4. Hoist, derrick. *Grúa de pórtico*, (Aer.) Gantry tower.
Grúa, *f.* (Obs.) *V.* GRULLA.
Grueras [groo-ay'-ras], *f. pl.* (Naut.) Rope-holes. *Grueras de barbiquejo*, Boy-stay-holes. *Grueras de amura*, The eyes of a tack. *Grueras de las varengas*, A limber hole.
Gruero, ra [groo-ay'-ro, rah], *a.* Belonging to birds of prey, trained to pursue cranes.
Gruesa [groo-ay'-sah], *f.* 1. Gross, twelve dozen. 2. Chief part of a prebend. 3. Bottomry. *Sacar dinero a la gruesa*, (Naut.) To take up money on bottomry.
Gruesamente, *adv.* Grossly, coarsely, by wholesale.
Grueso, sa [groo-ay'-so, sah], *a.* 1. Bulky, corpulent, thick, fleshy, fat, full-fed, plump, gross. 2. Large, great, big. 3. Coarse, plain, home-spun, not fine. 4. Dense, compact. 5. (Met.) Heavy, dull, stupid, dim, not quick in any of the senses.
Grueso [groo-ay'-so], *m.* 1. Corpulence, bulkiness of body. 2. Thickness, density, space taken up by matter interposed. 3. Gross, the main body, the bulk, the chief part. 4. Size, body of type. *El grueso de un ejército*. The main body of an army. *Tratar en grueso* or *vender por mayor*, To deal by wholesale, to sell in the lump.
Gruir [groo-eer'], *vn.* To crank or crankle: to cry like a crane.
Grujidor [groo-he-dor'], *m.* Steel instrument used by glaziers for rounding glass.
Grujir [groo-heer'], *va.* To chip away angles and inequalities of glass with a *grujidor*.
Grulla [grool'-lyah], *f.* 1. (Orn.) Crane. Ardea grus, *L.* 2. Crane, the name of a southern constellation.
Grullada [grool-lyah'-dah], *f.* (Coll.) 1. Crowd of people going together to any place. 2. Crowd of constables or police officers.
Grullero, ra [grool-lyay'-ro, rah], *a.* Applied to falcons or birds of prey in chase of cranes.
Grumete [groo-may'-tay], *m.* (Naut.) Younker, ship's boy.
Grumillo [groo-meel'-lyo], *m. dim.* A small grume, clot, or curd.
Grumo [groo'-mo], *m.* 1. Grume, a thick viscid consistence in a fluid; a clot. *Grumo de leche*, Curd. 2. Cluster, bunch. 3. Heart or pith of trees. *Grumos*, Pinions, the joints of the wings remotest from the body.
Grumoso, sa [groo-mo'-so, sah], *a.* Grumy, grumous, clotty; full of grumes.
Gruñido [groo-nyee'-do], *m.* 1. Grunt, the noise of a hog. 2. Growl, maundering, the murmur of a discontented person.—*Gruñido, da, pp.* of GRUÑIR.
Gruñidor, ra [groo-nye-dor', rah], *m.* & *f.* Grunter, grumbler, murmurer, mutterer.
Gruñimiento [groo-nye-me-en'-to], *m.* Grunting, murmuring, grumbling.
Gruñir [groo-nyeer'], *vn.* 1. To grunt like a hog. 2. To creak: applied to doors, hinges, carts, etc. 3. (Met.) To grumble, to growl, to snarl. *Mamar y gruñir*, (Coll.) To suck and murmur, to be discontented with every thing.
Gruñón, na [groo-nyone', nah], *m.* & *f.* (Coll.) *V.* GRUÑIDOR.
Grupa [groo'-pah], *f.* 1. Croup, the buttocks of a horse. 2. A cavalry call to saddle the horses. *Cargar la grupa*, To pass the tail of a horse through the crupper.
Grupada [groo-pah'-dah], *f.* 1. Squall or gust of wind. 2. Croupade, leap of a horse.
Grupera [groo-pay'-rah], *f.* 1. Cushion at the back of a saddle for carrying a satchel, etc. 2. Crupper, a looped strap for a horse's tail. 3. *V.* RETRANCA.
Grupo [groo'-po], *m.* 1. Group, assemblage. 2. Clump of sprigs growing out of the same root. 3. Cluster.
Gruta [groo'-tah], *f.* Cavern, cavity between rocks; a grotto, a grot. *Gruta de fieras*, Menagerie. *Grutas*, Crypts, vaults, subterranean edifices.
Grutesco [groo-tes'-co], *m.* Grotesque, a kind of ornament in painting, composed of leaves, shells, etc.
Gruyere [groo-yerr'], *m.* A kind of rich cheese, made at Gruyère in France.
¡Gúa! [goo'-ah]. Interjection of surprise and depreciation used in Peru and Bolivia. Come now!
Guaba [goo-ah'-bah], *f.* Abbreviated form of *guayaba*.
Guaca [goo-ah'-cah], *f.* A grave-mound of the ancient Peruvians.
Guacal [goo-ah-cahl'], *m.* (Mex.) An oblong hamper for carrying fruit.
Guacamayo [goo-ah-cah-mah'-yo], *m.* (Orn.) Macao or macaw. Psittacus macao, *L.*
Guacamole [goo-ah-cah-mo'-lay], *m.* (Cuba) Salad of alligator pear.
Guacia [goo-ah'-the-ah], *f.* 1. *V.* ACACIA. 2. Gum-arabic.
Guaco [goo-ah'-co], *m.* (Amer.) A plant of South America, eminent as an antidote for the bite of venomous snakes.
Guachapear [goo-ah-chah-pay-ar'], *va.* To paddle, to play with the feet in water.—*vn.* To clap, as horses' shoes when loose; to clutter.
Guachapelí [goo-ah-chah-pay-lee'], *m.* Solid strong wood, which grows in Guayaquil, used for ships.
Guácharo, ra [goo-ah'-chah-ro, rah], *a.* 1. Sickly, not in health. 2. Dropsical, diseased with a dropsy. 3. (Obs.) Whining, crying. (Arab.)
Guacharrada [goo-ah-char-rah'-dah], *f.* (Obs.) A sudden fall or plunge of a thing into mud or water.
Guachí [goo-ah-chee'], or **Guají** [goo-ah-hee'], *m.* (Mex.) Fool, dolt, simpleton.
Guachinango, ga [goo-ah-che-nahn'-go, gah], *m.* & *f.* A name given by the inhabitants of Cuba to the natives of Mexico, and in Vera Cruz to those of the interior. Also applied to shrewd and brusque persons.
Guacho, cha [goo-ah'-cho, chah], *a.* (W. S. Amer.) 1. Orphan, foundling. 2. Solitary, forlorn.—*m.* Birdling of a sparrow. (Acad.)
Guadafiones [goo-ah-dah-fe-o'-nes], *m. pl.* Fetters with which the legs of horses are shackled.
Guadamacil [goo-ah-dah-mah-theel'], *m.* Printed leather, gilt and adorned with figures. (Arab.)
Guadamacilería [goo-ah-dah-mah-the-lay-ree'-ah], *f.* Manufactory of gilt or printed leather.
Guadamacilero [goo-ah-dah-mah-the-lay'-ro], *m.* Manufacturer of printed leather.
Guadaña [goo-ah-dah'-nyah], *f.* 1. Scythe for mowing. 2. (Met.) Death, as depicted with a scythe. 3. A knife used by manufacturers of leather wine-bags.
Guadañadora [goo-ah-dah-nyah-do'-rah], *f.* Mowing machine.
Guadañar [goo-ah-dah-nyar'], or **Guadañear**, *va.* (Prov.) To mow, to cut grass.
Guadañero [goo-ah-dah-nyay'-ro], *m.* 1. Mower, one who cuts grass. 2. The owner or manager of a *guadaño*.
Guadañil [goo-ah-dah-nyeel'], *m.* Mower who cuts down hay; hay-maker.
Guadaño [goo-ah-dah'-nyo], *m.* 1. A small boat with an awning used in the traffic of the port of Havana. 2. Name given at Cadiz and other sea-ports to transport vessels.
Guadañón [goo-ah-dah-nyone'], *m.* Mower. *V.* GUADAÑERO.
Guadapero [goo-ah-dah-pay'-ro], *m.* 1. (Bot.) Wild common pear. Pyrus communis. 2. A boy who carries victuals to reapers or mowers.
Guadarnés [goo-ah-dar-nays'], *m.* 1. Harness-room, a place where harness is kept. 2. Harness-keeper, an officer of the king's mews.
Guadijeño [goo-ah-de-hay'-nyo], *m.* Poniard, stiletto, knife.—*a.* Belonging to Guadix.
Guadramaña [goo-ah-drah-mah'-nyah], *f.* Trick, deceit, imposition.

Guadua [goo-ah'-doo-ah], *f.* Gadua bamboo-cane of Ecuador and Colombia. Bambusa gadua.

Guadual [goo-ah-doo-ahl'], *m.* Plantation of large reeds.

Guagua [goo-ah'-goo-ah]. 1. *f.*, Nursing baby. (In Ecuad.) Both *f.* and *m.* 2. (Cuba) A kind of insect. 3. (Cuba) A kind of bus. 4. (**De**) *adv.* Free, for nothing.

Guainambi [goo-ah-e-nam-bee'] *m.* (Mex. C. A.) A humming-bird.

Guaira [goo-ah'-e-rah], *f.* (S. Amer.) 1. A triangular sail. 2. A tall furnace which the Peruvians used in smelting metals.

Guairo [goo-ah'-e-ro], *m.* (Ec.) 1. One of the seven faces of certain dice which the Indians of Quito were wont to use in a game called *pasa.* 2. A small two-masted craft with sails called *guairas. V. supra.*

Guajalote, or Guajolote [goo-ah-hah-lo'-tay], *m.* (Mex.) Turkey.

Guajamón, na [goo-ah-hah-mone', nah], *a.* (Cuba) Orange-coloured, speaking of horses.

Guájaras [goo-ah'-hah-ras], *f. pl.* Fastnesses, the roughest part of a range of mountains.

Guaje [goo-ah'-hay], *m.* (Mex.) A calabash which serves for learning to swim. In Peru, called *mate;* in Cuba, *güiro.*

Guajiro, ra [goo-ah-hee'-ro, rah], *a.* (Cuba) 1. Rustic, rural. 2. Rustic, rude, boorish.

Gualá! [goo-ah-lah'], *int.* Assuredly. (Arabic, wallāhi, by God!)

Gualatina [goo-ah-lah-tee'-nah], *f.* Dish made of boiled apples, milk of almonds and broth, and beaten up with spice and rose-water.

Gualda [goo-ahl'-dah], *f.* (Bot.) Weld, wild woad, dyer's weed, reseda, a plant which dyes yellow. Reseda luteola, *L. Cara de gualda,* Pale face.

Gualdado, da [goo-al-dah'-do, dah], *a.* Weld-coloured, yellowish.

Gualderas [goo-al-day'-ras], *f. pl.* The sides, cheeks or brackets of a gun-carriage. *Gualderas de las carlingas,* (Naut.) Checks of the mast-steps.

Gualdo, da [goo-ahl'-do, dah] *a.* Weld, yellow or gold colour.

Gualdón [goo-al-done'], *m.* (Bot.) Base-rocket, reseda. Reseda lutea, *L.*

Gualdrapa [goo-al-drah'-pah], *f.* 1. Horse-cloth, housing, foot-cloth. 2. Tatter, rag hanging from clothes.

Gualdrapazo [goo-al-drah-pah'-tho], *m.* (Naut.) Flap of the sails against the masts.

Gualdrapear [goo-al-drah-pay-ar'], *va.* To put one thing upon another.—*vn.* (Naut.) To flap against the masts: applied to sails.

Gualdrapeo [goo-al-drah-pay'-o], *m.* Flapping of the sails.

Gualdrapero [goo-al-drah-pay'-ro], *m.* Ragamuffin, a ragged fellow.

Gualdrín [goo-al-dreen'], *m.* Weather-strip.

Gualputra [goo-al-poo'-trah], *f.* (Amer.) Name given to the creeping clover.

Guama [goo-ah'-mah], *f.* Fruit of the *guamo.*

Guamo [goo-ah'-mo], *m.* A tall, branching tree of narrow leaves, planted to shade the coffee-tree.

Guambra [goo-ahm'-brah], *f.* (S. Amer.) A child-servant.

Guanábana [goo-ah-nah'-ba-nah]. *f.* 1. Fruit of the *guanábano* tree, very sweet and white. 2. A beverage common in Havana made from same.

Guanábano [goo-ah-nah'-ba-no], *m.* A fruit-tree of America, a variety of chirimoya. Anona.

Guanaco [goo-ah-nah'-co], *m.* (Zool.) Guanaco, So. Am. mammal related to the llama.

Guanajo [goo-ah-nah'-ho], *m.* (Cuba) A turkey.

Guano [goo-ah'-no], *m.* 1. Kind of American palm-tree. 2. Guano, sea-birds' dung, an excellent fertilizing material from Peruvian Islands.

Guantada [goo-an-tah'-dah], *f.* Slap or blow with the palm or inner part of the hand.

Guante [goo-ahn'-tay], *m.* 1. Glove, a cover of the hands. *Guantes surtidos,* Assorted gloves. *Guantes de cabritilla,* Kid gloves. *Guantes de ante,* Buff gloves. 2. Gauntlet, an iron glove used for defence, and thrown down in challenges. 3. Familiarly, the hand. *Echar el guante,* (Coll.) To catch or lay hold on with the hand. *Echar un guante,* To make a collection for charitable purposes. *Echar el guante a otro,* To grasp, to seize, to imprison. *Echar* or *arrojar el guante,* To challenge or to send a challenge. *Poner a uno como un guante,* To render one as pliable as a glove. (Coll.) To abuse one. *Guantes* or *dar para guantes,* To give something extra, or as a remuneration for services. *Salvo el guante,* (Coll.) Excuse me, for giving you my hand with gloves on. (Met.) Excepting things, that of course are not to be included. *Adobar los guantes,* To regale and remunerate any person.

Guantelete [goo-an-tay-lay'-tay], *m.* 1. Gauntlet. 2. A bandage for the hand.

Guantería [goo-an-tay-ree'-ah], *f.* A glover's shop and the art of a glover.

Guantero [goo-an-tay'-ro], *m.* Glover, one who makes gloves.

Guañín [goo-ah-nyeen'], *a.* Applied to gold under legal standard.

Guao [goo-ah'-o], *m.* A tree of the island of Santo Domingo whose smell is fatal.

Guapamente [goo-ah-pah-men'-tay], *adv.* (Coll.) Bravely, courageously.

Guapear [goo-ah-pay-ar'], *vn.* (Coll.) 1. To boast of courage. 2. To take a pride in fine dress.

Guapeza [goo-ah-pay'-thah], *f.* (Coll.) 1. Bravery, courage. 2. Ostentation in dress.

Guapinal [goo-ah-pe-nahl'], *m.* A resin-yielding tree of Central America.

Guapo, pa [goo-ah'-po, pah], *a.* (Coll.) 1. Stout, courageous, valiant, bold, enterprising, good, clever. 2. Spruce, neat, elegant, ostentatious, vain. 3. Gay, sprightly, fond of courting women.

Guaquero [goo-ah-kay'-ro], *m.* Earthenware. Vessel for drinking *chicha* found in ancient Peruvian tombs.

Guaracha [goo-ah-rah'-chah], *f.* 1. A kind of dance. 2. (Mex.) A sandal.

Guarana [goo-ah-rah'-nah], *f.* (Bot.) Paullinia; and the agreeable drink made in Brazil from its seeds.

Guarango [go-ah-rahn'-go], *m.* A shrub used for dyeing; a species of prosopis. (Ecuador.)

Guarapo [goo-ah-rah'-po], *m.* Sub-acid drink made in sugar-mills with the fermented cane-liquor. (Cuba) *Menear el guarapo,* To chastise.

Guarda [goo-ar'-dah], *com.* Guard, keeper; any thing that preserves others from injury.—*f.* 1. Custody, wardship, guard, keeping. 2. Observance of a law or ordinance. 3. Nun who accompanies men through convents. 4. Each of the outside ribs or guards of a fan. 5. Sheet of paper placed at the beginning and end of volumes to guard the printed sheets in binding. 6. The ward of a lock or of a key. *Guarda de la aduana,* An officer of the custom-house. *Guarda brisa,* Glass shade. *Guarda bauprés,* (Naut.) Knight-heads, bollard-timbers. *Guardacalada,* Window in the roof, whence the street may be seen. *Guardabaso,* (Naut.) Thimble or bull's eye, to prevent ropes from being galled by the tackle-hooks *Guardacadenas,* (Naut.) Laths of the chain-wales. *Guardacartuchos,* (Naut.) Cartridge cases. *Guardacosta,* (Naut.) Custom-house cutter, a vessel employed to clear the coast of smugglers. *Guardacuños,* Keeper of the dies in the mint. *Guardadamas,* Officer appointed to keep the apartments of the queen clear of obstruction during a public festival. *Guarda de coto,* Game-keeper. *Guardafuego,* 1. Screen for a chimney-fire. 2. Fender. *Guardainfantes,* (Naut.) Capstan whelps. *Guardajoyas,* Officer of the king's palace, who keeps the jewels and other precious things; also a room where jewels or other precious things are kept. *Guardalobo,* (Bot.) Poet's cassia. Osyris alba, *L. Guardamancebo,* (Naut.) Man-rope, entering-rope. *Guardamancebo de una escala,* Ladder-rope. *Guardamancebos de sondear,* Breast-ropes for sounding. *Guardamancebos de las vergas.* Foot-ropes or horses. *Guardamangier,* Pantry: groom of the pantry. *Guardamayor,* Chief-guard. *Guardamea,* Porter of a palace, person appointed to prevent the commission of any nuisance near the porches of palaces. *Guardamecha,* (Naut.) Match-tub. *Guardapuerta,* Screen or curtain before a door. *Guardasellos,* Keeper of the great seal. *Guardatimones,* (Naut.) Stern-chases. *Guardavela,* (Naut.) A small rope with which the top-sails are furled.

¡**Guarda**! [goo-ar'-dah], *int.* Take care! beware!

Guardaaguja [goo-ar-dah-ah-goo'-hah], *m.* A railway switchman.

Guardaalmacén [goo-ar-dah-al-mah-then'], *m.* Store-keeper.

Guardabosque [goo-ar-dah-bos'-kay], *m.* Keeper of a forest, gamekeeper.

Guardabrazo [goo-ar-dah-brah'-tho], *m.* A part of the armour to defend the arm.

Guardabrisa [goo-ar-dah-bree'-sah] *m.* Windshield.

Guardacabras [goo-ar-dah-cah'-bras], *m.* Goat-herd.

Guardacantón [goo-ar-dah-can-tone'], *m.* A spur-stone, a check-stone.

Guardacostas [goo-ar-dah-cos'-tahs], *m.* Coast-defense ship.

Guardadamente [goo-ar-dah-dah-men'-tay], *adv.* Guardedly.

Guardador, ra [goo-ar-dah-dor', rah], *m.* & *f.* 1. A very careful, watchful, and provident man, one who keeps his property with great care. 2. Keeper. 3. One who observes a law. 4. Miser.

Guardafango [goo-ar-dah-fahn'-go], *m.* Fender (of a vehicle).

Guardafrenos [goo-ar-dah-fray'-nos], *m.* A brakeman.

Guardafuego [goo-ar-dah-foo-ay'-go], *m.* (Naut.) Breaming-board.

Guardainfante [goo-ar-dah-in-fahn'-tay], *m.* Farthingale, ladies' hoop.

Guardaja, *f. V.* GUEDEJA.

Guardalado [goo-ar-dah-lah'-do], *m.* Battlement of a bridge.

Guardamangel [goo-ar-dah-man-hel'], *m.* Pantry, buttery.

Guardamano [goo-ar-dah-mah'-no], *f.* Guard of a sword.

Guardamateriales [goo-ar-dah-mah-tay-re-ah'-les], *m.* Person appointed to purchase bullion and other necessaries for a mint.

Guardameta [goo-ar-dah-may'-tah], *m.* Goalkeeper, goalie.

Guardamonte [goo-ar-dah-mon -tay], *m.* 1. Guard of a gun-lock, sword, etc. 2. Forester, keeper of a forest.

Guardamozo, or **Guardamancebo** [goo-ar-dah-mo'-tho, goo-ar-dah-man-thay'-bo], *m.* (Naut.) Man-rope, entering-rope.

Guardamuebles [goo-ar-dah-moo-ay'-blays], *m.* 1. Store-room for furniture in great houses. 2. Guard over the furniture of a palace.

Guardamujer [goo-ar-dah-moo-herr'], *f.* Servant of the queen, next to the ladies of honour.

Guardapapo [goo-ar-dah-pah'-po], *m.* Ancient piece of armour for the face.

Guardapelo [goo-ar-dah-pay'-lo], *m.* A locket.

Guardapiés [goo-ar-dah-pe-ays'], *m.* 1. A petticoat commonly used under the upper garment. 2. *V.* Brial.

Guardapolvo [goo-ar-dah-pol'-vo], *m.* 1. A piece of cloth or leather to guard against dust. 2. The inner lid of a watch. 3. The dust-guard of a carriage or railway car.

Guardapuerta [goo-ar-dah-poo-err'-tah], *f.* Storm door.

Guardar [goo-ar-dar'], *va.* 1. To keep, to preserve in a state of security, to keep from, to look to, to guard, to protect. 2. To keep, to take care of, to watch, to guard, to preserve from damage. 3. To lay up, to store, to reposit for future use. 4. To lay by, to reserve for some future time, to conserve, to keep back, to maintain. 5. To keep, to hold for another. 6. To observe, to respect. 7. To fulfil one's duty.—*vr.* To be upon one's guard, to avoid, to abstain from, to guard against, to fence. *Guarda, Pablo,* A common phrase to express that the person who speaks will take great care of avoiding any thing supposed to be dangerous. *Guardársela a alguno,* To delay vengeance for a favourable opportunity. *Guardar batideros,* To anticipate and avoid difficulties.

Guardarraya [goo-ar-dar-rah'-yah], *f.* (Cuba) 1. An avenue of trees or shrubs upon a plantation of sugar-cane or coffee. 2. Boundary which marks the end of a drill-hole in mines, after it has been measured.

Guardarrío [goo-ar-dah-ree'-o], *m.* (Orn.) Kingfisher. Alcedo ispida.

Guardarropa [goo-ar-dar-ro'-pah], *f.* Wardroom, checkroom.—*m.* Checkroom attendant.

Guardarruedas [goo-ar-dar-roo-ay'-das], *m.* *V.* Guardacantón.

Guardasol, *m.* *V.* Quitasol.

Guardavajilla [goo-ar-dah-vah-heel'-yah], *f.* A room for keeping the (royal) plate or table-service.

Guardaventana [goo-ar-dah-ven-tah'-nah], *f.* Storm window.

Guardería [goo-ar-day-ree'-ah], *f.* 1. Occupation of a guard. 2. Day nursery.

Guardia [goo ar'-de-ah], *f.* 1. Guard, a body of soldiers or armed men to watch by way of defence. *Cuerpo de guardia,* Guard-room. 2. (Naut.) Watch. *Guardia de babor,* Larboard-watch. *Guardia de estribor,* Starboard watch. *Guardia de la madrugada,* Morning-watch. *Guardia del tope,* Masthead look-out. (Mil.) *Estar de guardia,* To be on duty. *Montar la guardia,* To mount guard. *Mudar la guardia,* To relieve the guard. *Salir de guardia,* To come off guard. —*m.* Soldier belonging to the guards. *Guardia de corps,* Life-guard. *Guardia marina,* Midshipman.

Guardián, na [goo-ar-de-ahn', nah], *m.* & *f.* 1. Keeper, one who has the charge of any thing. 2. Guardian, one to whom the care and preservation of any thing is committed.—*m.* 1. The local superior of convents of the order of St. Francis. 2. (Naut.) Keeper of the arms and store-room. *Guardián del contramaestre,* (Naut.) Boatswain mate.

Guardianía [goo-ar-de-ah-nee'-ah], *f.* 1. Guardianship. 2. The district assigned to every convent to beg in.

Guardilla [goo-ar-deel'-lyah], *f.* 1. Garret, skylight. 2. With seamstresses, ornament and guard of a seam.

Guardín de la caña [goo-ar-deen' day lah cah'-nyah], *m.* (Naut.) Tiller-rope.

Guardoso, sa [goo-ar-do'-so, sah], *a.* 1. Frugal, parsimonious. 2. Niggardly, stingy.

Guare [goo-ah'-ray], *m.* (Ec.) Raft made of great rushes, with a square sail.

Guarecer [goo-ah-ray-therr'], *va.* 1. To aid, to succour, to assist. 2. To guard, to preserve; to cure.—*vn.* (Obs.) To grow well, to recover.—*vr.* To take refuge, to escape from danger.

Guarentigio, gia [goo-ah-ren-tee'-he-o, ah], *a.* (Law) Applied to a contract, writing, or clause, which empowers the justices to cause it to be executed.

Guarida [goo-ah-ree'-dah], *f.* 1. Den, the cave or couch of a wild beast. 2. Haunt, the place where one is frequently found. 3. Protection, aid, shelter, a lurking-place, a cover.

Guarín [goo-ah-reen'], *m.* Young pig, last born of a litter.

Guarir [goo-ah-reer'], *va.* & *vn.* To subsist. (Obs.) *V.* Curar and Sanar.

Guarismo [goo-ah-rees'-mo], *m.* Figure, cipher, an arithmetical character.

Guarismo, ma [goo-ah-rees'-mo, mah], *a.* Arithmetical.

Guarne [goo-ar'-nay], *m.* (Naut.) Each turn of a cable or tackle.

Guarnecedor [goo-ar-nay-thay-dor'], *m.* 1. Hatter who cocks hats. 2. One who garnishes or surrounds a thing with ornamental appendages.

Guarnecer, Guarnescer [goo-ar-nay-therr'], *va.* 1. To garnish, to surround with ornamental appendages. 2. To set a diamond or stone in gold, silver, etc. 3. To trim, to adorn. 4. To harness horses or mules. 5. To garrison a town or other place.

Guarnés [goo-ar-ness'], *m.* Harness-room. *V.* Guadarnés.

(*Yo guarnezco, yo guarnezca,* from *Guarnecer.* *V.* Conocer.)

Guarnición [goo-ar-ne-the-on'], *f.* 1. Flounce, furbelow, trimming. 2. Setting of any thing in gold or silver. 3. Guard of a sword. 4. Garrison, a body of soldiers in a fortified town to defend it. 5. Garniture, garnish, any ornamental hem, lace, or border. *Guarnición de trama y figura,* Garniture of figured satin ribbons. *Guarnición de tafetán labrado,* Garniture of taffety ribbon. *Guarnición de velillo bordado,* Garniture of figured gauze ribbons. 6. Marines, naval troops. 7. *Guarnición de la bomba,* (Naut.) The upper or spear-box of a pump.—*pl.* 1. Ancient steel armour of defence. 2. Gears or traces of mules and horses; harness.

Guarnicionería [goo-ar-ne-the-o-nay-ree'-ah], *f.* Shop of a harness-maker.

Guarnicionero [goo-ar-ne-the-o-nay'-ro], *m.* Harness-maker.

Guarniel [goo-ar-ne-el'], *m.* 1. Leather purse used by carriers, with divisions for paper, money, and other things. 2. (Mex.) A powder-flask.

Guarnir [goo-ar-neer'], *va.* To reeve, to pass a rope through the eyes of blocks, to form a tackle. *Guarnir el cabrestante,* To rig the capstan.

Guaro [goo-ah'-ro], *m.* A small, very talkative parrot. (Acad.)

Guarra [goo-ar'-rah], *f.* A sow.

Guarrillo [goo-ar-reel'-lyo], *m. dim.* A small pig.

Guarro [goo-ar'-ro], *m.* Hog, pig, whether large or small.

Guaruba [goo-ah-roo'-bah], *f.* 1. An American parrot with a red neck. 2. A howling ape.

Guasa [goo-ah'-sah], *f.* (Coll.) 1. Jest, satire, irony. 2. Insipidity, dulness.

Guasanga [goo-ah-sahn'-gah]. (Cuba) Noisy mirth.

Guasanguero, ra [goo-ah-san-gay'-ro, rah], *a.* (Cuba) Jolly, merry, noisy.

Guasca [goo-ahs'-cah], *f.* (Peru.) Cord, thong, whip. *Dar guasca,* To whip, to scourge.

Guaso [goo-ah'-so], *m.* 1. *V.* Gaucho. 2. Lasso.

Guasón, na [goo-ah-sone', nah], *a.* (Coll. Andal.) Jocose, witty, satirical.

Guasquear [goo-as-kay-ar'], *va.* (Amer.) To whip, to scourge.

Guastar [goo-as-tar'], *va.* (Obs.) *V.* Consumir.

Guataca [goo-ah-tah'-cah], *f.* (Cuba) 1. Spade. 2. Applied ironically to a large ear.

Guataquear [goo-ah-tah-kay-ar'], *va.* (Cuba) To spade, to clear sowed ground with the spade.

Guatemalteco, ca [goo-ah-tay-mal-tay'-co, cah], *a.* Guatemalan, of Guatemala.

Guatuse [goo-ah-too'-say], *m.* A Nicaraguan animal with reddish-brown fur. Inga pachycarpa.

¡Guay! [goo-ah'-e], *int.* Oh! an exclamation of pain or grief. *V.* Ay. *Tener muchos guayes,* To labour under many afflictions.

Guaya [goo-ah'-yah], *f.* Grief, sorrow, affliction.

Guayaba [goo-ah-yah'-bah], *f.* Fruit of the guava-tree. *Guayaba blanca,* White guava. Psydium pyriferum. *Guayaba roja,* Red guava. Psydium pomiferum, *L.*

Guayabal [goo-ah-yah-bahl'], *m.* An orchard of guava-trees.

Guayabo [goo-ah-yah'-bo], *m.* (Bot.) Guava-tree.

Guayacán [goo-ah-yah-cahn'], *m.* (Bot.) *V* Guayaco.

Guayacana [goo-ah-yah-cah'-nah], *f.* (Bot.) Date-plum. Diospyros. *Guayacana loto,* European date-plum. Diospyros lotus.

Guayaco [goo-ah-yah'-co], *m.* (Bot.) Lignum-vitæ tree, guaiacum. Guaiacum. *Guayaco oficinal,* Officinal guaiacum, or lignum-vitæ tree. Guaiacum officinale.

Guayapil, Guayapin [goo-ah-yah-peel', goo-ah-yah-peen'], *m.* A loose Indian dress for women.

Guayusa [goo-ah-yoo'-sah], *f.* A tall shrub of the Napo River, Ecuador; an ilex. The leaves are used for tea.

Gubán [goo-bahn'], *m.* Kind of large boat used in the Philippines. It is made without nails, clinker-built, is rowed rapidly and is easily taken on land.

Gubernamental [goo-ber-nah-men-tahl'], *a.* Governmental.

Gubernativo, va [goo-ber-nah-tee'-vo, vah], *a.* Administrative, relating to government; gubernative.

Gubia [goo'-be-ah], *f.* Gouge, a round hollow chisel.
Gubiadura [goo-be-ah-doo'-rah], *f.* (Naut.) Notch, channel.
Gubilete [goo-be-lay'-tay], *m.* (Prov.) Kind of vase. *V.* CUBILETE.
Guedeja [gay-day'-hah], *f.* 1. Lock of hair falling on the temple, forelock. 2. Lion's mane.
Guedejar [gay-day-har'], *va.* (Littl. us.) To dress the hair, to adorn the head with locks of hair.
Guedejilla [gay-day-heel'-lyah], *f. dim.* A small lock of hair.
Guedejón, na, Guedejoso, sa [gay-day-hone', nah], *a. V.* GUEDEJUDO.
Guedejudo, da [gay-day-hoo'-do, dah], *a.* Bushy, clotted: applied to hair.
Guelde [gayl'-day], *m.* (Bot.) Water-elder, guelder-rose, viburnum. Viburnum opulus.
Güelfo, fa [goo-el'-fo, fah], *a.* Guelph, partisan of the popes, and opponents of the Ghibellines.
Gueltre [gayl'-tray], *m.* A cant word for money or cash.
Güembé [goo-em-bay'], *m.* Manila-hemp. *V.* ABACÁ.
Guerindola [gay-rin-do'-lah], *f.* 1. *V.* GUIRINDOLA. 2. A kind of flannel (baize) cape worn by the women of the Cantabrian coast.
Güérmeces [goo-ayr'-may-thes], *m.* A morbid swelling in the throat of hawks, and other birds of prey.
Güero, ra [goo-ay'-roh, rah], *a.* & *m.* & *f.* (Mex.) Blond, blonde.
Guerra [gayr'-rah], *f.* 1. War. 2. Art of war, military science. 3. War, profession of arms. 4. War, hostility, conflict of passions. *Guerra fría*, Cold war. *Estado de guerra*, State of war. *Hacer guerra*, To wage war. *En buena guerra*, By fair and lawful means. *Guerra mundial*, World war. *Guerra nuclear*, Nuclear war. *Guerra química*, Chemical warfare. *Guerra relámpago*, Blitzkrieg. *Guerra de escaramuzas*, Brushfire war. *Guerra de guerrillas*, Guerilla warfare. *Dar guerra*, To be troublesome, to annoy (usually said of a child).
Guerreador, ra [gayr-ray-ah-dor', rah], *m.* & *f.* Warrior, one passionately fond of military fame.
Guerreante [gayr-ray-ahn'-tay], *pa.* & *m.* & *f.* Warrior, warring.
Guerrear [gayr-ray-ar'], *va.* 1. To war, to wage war, to fight. 2. To oppose, to be in a state of hostility.
Guerrera [gayr-ray'-rah], *f.* Military jacket.
Guerreramente [gayr-ray-rah-men'-tay], *adv.* Warlikely.
Guerrero [gayr-ray'-ro], *m.* 1. Warrior. *V.* GUERREADOR. 2. A soldier, a military man.
Guerrero, ra [gayr-ray'-ro, rah], *a.* Martial, warlike.
Guerrilla [gayr-reel'-lyah], *f. dim.* 1. Band of guerrillas. *Guerra de guerrillas*, Guerrilla warfare. 2. Game of cards between two persons, each with twenty cards.
Guerrillear [gayr-reel-lyay-ar'], *vn.* To take part in guerrilla warfare.
Guerrillero [gayr-reel-yay'-ro], *m.* 1. The commander of a skirmish force. 2. A civilian who serves in guerilla warfare.
Guía [gee'-ah], *m.* & *f.* 1. Guide, one who directs another in his way. 2. Guide, conductor, leader, director, regulator, one who directs another in his conduct.—*f.* 3. Permit, cocket, docket; a writing or letter of safe-conduct, proving that the customs and duty are paid at the custom-house. 4. A young shoot or sucker of a vine. 5. A certain timber in the water-wheels called norias. 6. An instrument of jewellers for guiding drills. *En guía* or *en la guía*, (Obs.) Guiding. 7. (Naut.) Guy, a small rope, to keep weighty things in their places. 8. Earth which indicates the vein of a mine. 9. Guard of a fan. 10. *m.* Sergeant or corporal who attends to dressing the line. *Guía de falsa amarra*, (Naut.) Guest-rope. *Guía de forasteros*, Court-guide.—*pl.* 1. Trains of powder in rockets or fire-works. 2. Horses or mules which go before the wheel horses or mules; leaders. 3. Guide-lines, reins for controlling the leader horses. *A guías*, Driving four in hand: applied to a coachman driving four horses.
Guiadera [gee-ah-day'-rah], *f.* Guide or conductor in mills. *Guiaderas*, Two upright pieces of wood in oil-mills.
Guiado, da [gee-ah'-do, dah], *a.* & *pp.* of GUIAR. Guided.
Guiador, ra [gee-ah-dor', rah], *m.* & *f.* Guide, director.
Guiamiento [gee-ah-me-en'-to], *m.* Guidance, the act of guiding, security.
Guiar [gee-ar'], *va.* 1. To guide, to conduct, to show the way. 2. To guide, to govern by counsel, to lead, to teach, to direct. 3. To lead a dance. *Guiar el agua a su molino*, To bring grist to one's mill.
Guienés, sa [gee-ay-nays', sah], *a.* Of Guienne.
Guija [gee'-hah], *f.* 1. Pebble, pebble-stone, cobble, coarse gravel. 2. (Bot.) *V.* ALMORTA.—*pl.* (Coll.) Strength, force, vigour. *Ser de pocas guijas* or *tener pocas guijas*, To be short and thin; to be very weak.
Guijarral [gee-har-rahl'], *m.* Heap of pebble-stones, a place abounding in pebbles.
Guijarrazo [gee-har-rah'-tho], *m.* Blow with a pebble-stone.
Guijarreño, ña [gee-har-ray'-nyo, nyah], *a.* 1. Pebbly, gravelly. 2. Hardy, strong and rude.
Guijarrillo, ito [gee-har-reel'-lyo, ee'-to], *m. dim.* A small pebble.
Guijarro [gee-har'-ro], *m.* Pebble or smooth stone, cobble-stone.
Guijarroso, sa [gee-har-ro'-so, sah], *a.* Pebbly.
Guijeño, ña [gee-hay'-nyo, nyah], *a.* 1. Full of pebbles or coarse gravel. 2. Hard, sour, difficult.
Guijo [gee'-ho], *m.* Small pebbles or gravel for roads.
Guijón [gee-hone'], *m. V.* NEGUIJÓN.
Guijoso, sa [gee-ho'-so, sah], *a.* 1. Gravelly. 2. *V.* GUIJEÑO.
Guilalo [gee-lah'-lo], *m.* A Philippine bark, intended for the postal service.
Guilla [geel'-lyah], *f.* A plentiful harvest.
Guillame [geel-lyah'-may], *m.* Rabbet-plane, a carpenter's tool.
Guilledin [geel-lyay-deen'], *m.* Gelding.
Guillemote [geel-lyay-mo'-tay], *m.* (Zool.) A puffin.
Guillote [geel-lyo'-tay], *m.* 1. Husbandman who enjoys the produce of a farm. 2. Tree-nail or iron pin. 3. Vagrant, sponger, an idle fellow. 4. (Coll.) A simpleton.
Guillotina [geel-lyo-tee'-nah], *f.* Guillotine, a machine for decapitating.
Guillotinar [geel-lyo-te-nar'], *va.* To guillotine.
Guimbalete [geem-bah-lay'-tay], *m.* (Naut.) Brake or handle of a pump.
Guimbarda [geem-bar'-dah], *f.* 1. An ancient dance. 2. A plane like a rabbet-plane. 3. A jew's-harp.
Guinchar [geen-char'], *va.* To prick; to stimulate.
Guincho [geen'-cho], *m.* 1. Goad, pike. 2. (Cuba) Sea-gull.
Guinda [geen'-dah], *f.* 1. Cherry, a fruit. 2. Height of the masts (and top-masts). *Échele Vd. guindas a la tarasca*, What you say is devoid of common sense.
Guindado, da [geen-dah'-do, dah], *a.* Hoisted, set up. *Los masteleros están guindados*, (Naut.) The top-masts are on end.—*pp.* of GUINDAR.
Guindajos [geen-dah'-hos], *m. pl* Fringe or small tassels for ornament.
Guindal [geen-dahl'], *m.* (Bot.) Cherry-tree. *V.* GUINDO.
Guindalera [geen-dah-lay'-rah], *f* Cherry-orchard, a plantation of cherry-trees.
Guindaleta [geen-dah-lay'-tah, *f.* 1. Crank-rope, a rope used to raise materials to the top of a building. 2. Fulcrum of a balance.
Guindaleza [geen-dah-lay'-thah], *f.* (Naut.) Hawser.
Guindamaina [geen-dah-mah'-e-nah], *f.* (Naut.) Salute between ships or squadrons.
Guindar [geen-dar'], *va.* 1. To lift, to elevate, to raise, to hoist. 2. To procure in concurrence with others. 3. (Coll.) To hang. *V.* AHORCAR.—*vr.* To be suspended, to hang by or on any thing.
Guindastes [geen-dahs'-tes], *m. pl.* (Naut.) Gears or jeers, an assemblage of tackles.
Guindilla [geen-deel'-lyah], *f.* 1. Small kind of red pepper. 2. (Dim.) A small cherry.
Guindillo [geen-deel'-lyo], *m.* Indian cherry-tree.
Guindo [geen'-do], *m.* (Bot.) Cherry-tree. Prunus cerasus. *Guindo griego*, Large cherry-tree. *Don Guindo*, (Joc.) Coxcomb.
Guindola [geen'-do-lah], *f.* (Naut.) A triangular hanging stage.
Guinea [gee-nay'-ah], *f.* Guinea, an English gold coin. *Pimiento de Guinea*, Guinea-pepper. *Cochino de Guinea*, Guinea-pig.
Guineo [gee-nay'-o], *m.* Dance used amongst negroes. *Plátano guineo*, A short kind of banana.—*a.* Native of or belonging to Guinea.
Guinga [geen'-gah], or **Guingans** [geen-gahns'], *f.* Ginghams.
Guinja, *f.* **Guinjo,** *m.* [geen'-hah, ho], *V.* AZUFAIFA and AZUFAIFO.
Guinjolero [geen-ho-lay'-ro], *m. V.* AZUFAIFO.
Guiñada, Guiñadura [gee-nyah'-dah, gee-nyah-doo'-rah], *f.* 1. Wink, a hint given by the eye. 2. (Naut.) Yaw, the deviation of a ship from her course.
Guiñador, ra [gee-nyah-dor', rah], *m.* & *f.* Winker.
Guiñapo [gee-nyah'-po], *m.* 1. Tatter, rag. 2. Ragamuffin, tatterdemalion; a ragged fellow.
Guiñaposo, sa, Guiñapiento, ta [gee-nyah-po'-so, sah, gee-nyah-pe-en'-to, tah], *a.* Ragged, tattered, torn. (Acad.)
Guiñar [gee-nyar'], *va.* 1. To wink, to hint or direct by a motion of the eye-lids. 2. (Naut.) To yaw or make yaws; not to steer in a steady manner.
Guión [gee-on'], *m.* 1. Hyphen, division in writing. 2. Cross, the standard carried before prelates and corporations or communities. 3. Repeat, in music. 4. Scenario of a play, etc.
Guionaje [gee-o-nah'-hay], *m.* (Obs.) 1. Guide or conductor. 2. An ancient tax for the safe transit of goods.

Guipar [gee-par'], *va.* (Coll. and vulgar) To see.

Guirigay [gee-re-gah'-e], *m.* Gibberish; unmeaning words, jargon.

Guirindola [gee-rin-do'-lah], *f.* Bosom of a shirt, frill.

Guirlache [geer-lah'-chay], *m.* Roast almond caramel.

Guirnalda [geer-nahl'-dah], or **Guirlanda**, *f.* 1. Garland, a wreath or open crown interwoven with flowers. 2. (Naut.) Puddening, a wreath of cordage put around a variety of things on board of ships. *Guirnalda del ancla*, Puddening of the anchor-ring.

Guirnaldar [geer-nal-dar'], *va.* (Prov.) To surround a thrashing-place with trees.

Güiro [goo-ee'-ro], *m.* (Cuba) Fruit of disagreeable odour and harsh taste, much like a gourd. *Cf.* GUAJE.

Guirre [geer'-ray], *m.* (Prov. Canaries) Vulture.

Guisa [gee'-sah], *f.* (Obs.) Guise, mode, manner, class, species.

Guisado [gee-sah'-do], *m.* 1. A stew, or made dish; ragout, fricassee. 2. (Met. Coll.) Action or deed performed under very remarkable circumstances. *Estar uno mal guisado*, To be disgusted and discontent.

Guisador, ra [gee-sah-dor', rah], *m.* & *f.* *V.* GUISANDERO.

Guisandero, ra [gee-san-day'-ro, rah], *m.* & *f.* A cook.

Guisantal [gee-san-tahl'], *m.* A pea-patch; ground planted with pease.

Guisante [gee-sahn'-tay], *m.* (Bot.) Pea. Pisum sativum. *Guisante de olor* or *oloroso*, Sweat-pea, lathyrus. Lathyrus odoratus. *Guisante florigrande* or *grandiflora*, Perennial lathyrus. Lathyrus grandiflorus. *V.* CHÍCHARO.

Guisar [gee-sar'], *va.* 1. To cook or dress victuals; to cure meat. 2. (Met.) To arrange, to adjust.

Guiso [gee'-so], *m.* The seasoning of a dish; sauce of meat, or any other victuals; condiment.

Guisopillo [gee-so-peel'-lyo], *m.* *V.* HISOPILLO.

Guisote [gee-so'-tay], *m.* Dish of meat dressed country-fashion.

Guita [gee'-tah], *f.* Pack-thread, a small hempen cord.

Guitar [gee-tar'], *va.* To sew with pack-thread.

Guitarra [gee-tar'-rah], *f.* 1. Guitar, a stringed musical instrument played with the fingers. 2. Pounder, a pestle for pounding gypsum or whiting. *Ser buena guitarra*, (Met. Coll.) To be very artful and cunning. (Arab. gitār, fr. Gr. κιθάρα.

Guitarrear [gee-tar-ray-ar'], *vn.* To play the guitar.

Guitarrero, ra [gee-tar-ray'-ro, rah], *m.* & *f.* 1. Guitar-maker. 2. Player on the guitar.

Guitarresco, ca [gee-tar-res'-co, cah], *a.* (Joc.) Belonging to the guitar.

Guitarrillo [gee-tar-reel'-lyoh], *m. dim.* A small guitar. (= TIPLE.)

Guitarrista [gee-tar-rees'-tah], *m.* Player on the guitar.

Guitarrón [gee-tar-rone'], *m.* 1. (Aug.) A large guitar. 2. (Coll.) An acute knave.

Guito, ta [gee'-to, tah], *a.* Treacherous, vicious: applied to mules.

Guitón, na [gee-tone', nah], *m.* & *f.* Mendicant, vagrant, vagabond.

Guitonazo [gee-to-nah'-tho], *m. aug.* A great vagabond.

Guitonear [gee-to-nay-ar'], *vn.* To loiter or idle about, to lead a vagabond life; to tramp it.

Guitonería [gee-to-nay-ree'-ah], *f.* Idleness; a vagrant or vagabond life.

Guizgar [geeth-gar'], *va.* To excite, to invite.

Guizque [geeth'-kay], *m.* 1. (Prov.) Hook of a hanging lamp. 2. (Prov.) Sting of a wasp.

Guja [goo'-hah], *f.* Arm used by archers.

Gula [goo'-lah], *f.* Gluttony, inordinate desire of eating and drinking.

Gulchenita [gool-chay-nee'-tah], *a.* & *n.* A member of one of the Mussulman monastic orders.

Gules [goo'-les], *m. pl.* (Her.) Gules, red.

Guloso, sa [goo-lo'-so, sah], *a.* Gluttonous, greedy.

Gulusmear [goo-loos-may-ar'], *vn.* (Coll.) *V.* GOLOSINEAR.

Gullería [gool-lyay-ree'-ah], *f.* Dainty. *Pedir gullerías*, To wish or look for something unreasonable or out of purpose.

Gullería [gool-lyo-ree'-ah], *f.* 1. (Orn.) A kind of lark. 2. *V.* GOLLERÍA.

Gúmena [goo'-may-nah], *f.* Cable.

Gumeneta [goo-may-nay'-tah], *f. dim.* A small cable.

Gumía [goo-mee'-ah], *f.* Kind of dagger or poniard. (Arab.)

Gumífero, ra [goo-mee'-fay-ro, rah], *a.* Gum-producing, gummiferous.

Gur [goor], *m.* A white cotton fabric which comes from India.

Gurbión [goor-be-on'], *m.* 1. Twisted silk, of a coarse quality. 2. Silk stuff resembling grogram. 3. Gum-resin extracted from the officinal spurge. Euphorbium officinarum.

Gurbionado, da [goor-be-o-nah'-do, dah], *a.* Made of twisted coarse silk.

Gurdo, da [goor'-do, dah], *a.* (Obs.) Silly, simple.

Gurrar [goor-rar'], *vn.* 1. (Naut.) To get clear of another ship. 2. To retrograde, to fall back.

Gurrufalla [goor-roo-fahl'-lyah], *f.* (Obs.) A worthless trifle, a thing of no value.

Gurrufero [goor-roo-fay'-ro], *m.* A deformed nag or horse.

Gurrumina [goor-roo-mee'-nah], *f.* (Coll.) Uxoriousness, unbecoming submission to a wife.

Gurrumino [goor-roo-mee'-no], *m.* (Coll.) Henpecked husband.

Gurullada [goo-rool-lyah'-dah], *f.* 1. A crowd of people. 2. Crowd of constables or police officers.

Gurullo [goo-rool'-lyo], *m.* Lump or knot. *V.* BURUJO.

Gurullón [goo-rool-lyone'], *m.* A knot of wool in cloths.

Gurumete [goo-roo-may'-tay], *m.* Ship's boy. *V.* GRUMETE.

Gurupa [goo-roo'-pah], *f.* Croup of a horse. *V.* GRUPA.

Gurupera [goo-roo-pay'-rah], *f.* Crupper. *V.* GRUPERA.

Gurupetín [goo-roo-pay-teen'], *m. dim.* A small crupper.

Gurvio, a [goor'-ve-o, ah], *a.* Curved, arched, incurvated.

Gusanear [goo-sah-nay-ar'], *vn.* To itch. *V.* HORMIGUEAR.

Gusanera [goo-sah-nay'-rah], *f.* 1. Place or spot where maggots or vermin are bred. 2. (Met.) The passion which reigns most in the mind.

Gusanico, ito [goo-sah-nee'-co, ee'-to], *m. dim.* A small worm or maggot.

Gusaniento, ta [goo-sah-ne-en'-to, tah], *a.* Troubled with maggots or vermin, maggoty, worm-eaten.

Gusanillo [goo-sah-neel'-lyo], *m.* 1. (Dim.) A small worm or maggot. 2. A kind of embroidery. 3. Bit of a gimlet or auger.

Gusano [goo-sah'-no], *m.* 1 Maggot. worm, grub, caterpillar. 2. A meek person. 3. Distemper among sheep. *Gusano de seda*, Silk-worm. *Gusano de luz*, *V.* LUCIÉRNAGA. *Gusano de San Antón*, Gray grub. *V.* COCHINILLA, 1st def. *Gusano de la conciencia*, Worm of conscience, remorse. (Sanscrit.)

Gusanoso. sa, *a.* *V.* GUSANIENTO.

Gusarapa, *f.* (Prov.) *V.* GUSARAPO.

Gusarapiento, ta [goo-sah-rah-pe-en'-to, tah], *a.* Wormy, corrupted.

Gusarapillo, ito [goo-sah-rah-peel'-lyo, ee'-to], *m. dim.* A small water-worm.

Gusarapo [goo-sah-rah'-po], *m.* Water-worm, an aquatic insect.

Gusil [goo-seel'], *m.* A kind of harp of horizontal strings in use among the Russians.

Gustable [goos-tah'-blay], *a.* 1. Tastable, gustable, capable of being tasted or relished. 2. (Obs.) *V.* GUSTOSO.

Gustadura [goos-tah-doo'-rah], *f.* Gustation, tasting.

Gustar [goos-tar'], *va.* 1. To taste. 2. To perceive by the taste.—*vn.* 3. To like, to love. 4. To enjoy a thing. 5. To experience, to examine. 6. To take pleasure or delight in a thing, to be pleased with.

Gustativo [goos-tah-tee'-vo], *a.* Lingual: applied to a branch of the inferior maxillary nerve.

Gustazo [goos-tah'-tho], *m. aug.* A great pleasure.

Gustillo [goos-teel'-lyo], *m.* 1. Relish. 2. (Dim.) Agreeable, delicate taste.

Gusto [goos'-to], *m.* 1. Taste, the sense of tasting. 2. The sensation of tasting. 3. Pleasure, delight, gratification, complacence, contentment. 4. Liking, mind, gust. 5. One's own will and determination. 6. Election, choice. 7. Taste, intellectual relish or discernment. 8. Caprice, fancy, diversion. *Artículos* or *cosas de gusto*, Fancy articles. *Zarazas de gusto*, Calicoes of good patterns. *Por dar gusto a*, For the sake or gratification of, to please. *Gustos*, Sensual pleasures; evil habits; vices. *Dar gusto*, To gratify.

Gustosamente, *adv.* Tastefully, fain, gladly, acceptably.

Gustoso, sa [goos-to'-so, sah], *a.* 1. Gustable, dainty, pleasing to the taste. 2. Tasty. 3. Cheerful, merry, content, joyful. 4. Pleasing, pleasant, entertaining.

Gutagamba, Gutiámbar [goo-tah-gahm'-bah, goo-te-ahm'-bar], *m.* Gamboge. (Malay.)

Gutapercha [goo-tah-perr'-chah], *f.* 1. Gutta-percha. 2. Caoutchouc, India-rubber.

Gutífero, ra [goo-tee'-fay-ro, rah], *a.* Guttiferous, gum-yielding.

Gutiforme [goo-te-for'-may], *a.* Guttiform, in the shape of a drop.

Gutural [goo-too-rahl'], *a.* 1. Guttural, pronounced in the throat. 2. Guttural, belonging to the throat.

Guturalmente [goo-too-ral-men'-tay], *adv.* Gutturally.

Guturoso, sa [goo-to-ro'-so, sah], *a.* 1. (Bot.) Throated: said of certain mosses. 2. (Zool.) Throaty, having a large or capacious throat. 3. Pouter pigeon, vulgarly called *buchona.*

Guzla [gooth'-lah], *f.* 1. A soft, harmonious musical instrument among the Greeks and the Asiatics. 2. A fiddle with a single string.

Guzmán [gooth-mahn'], *m.* Nobleman who formerly served as midship man in the navy or cadet in the army.

Guzpatarra [gooth-pah-tar'-rah], *f.* Ancient play of boys.

H

H [ah'-chay], ninth letter of the Castilian alphabet, is now treated as a mere aspiration. The moderns use *h* to soften the pronunciation of many words, as *facer*, *fijo*, are now written *hacer*, *hijo*. For the same purpose it is placed before *u*, followed by *e*, in many words derived from the Latin; as *huevo*, from *ovum*, an egg; *hueso*, from *os*. The *h* is never sounded in the Spanish language except by the common people in Andalusia, Extremadura, and the former Spanish possessions in America. The words in which *h* was preceded by a *p*, and took the sound of *f*, are now written as pronounced, thus: *fenómeno*, phenomenon. After *r* and *t* the *h* is entirely omitted, as in *reuma*, rheum, *teatro*, theatre; but it is retained, but not aspirated, in all words which originally began with *h*, or between two vowels, as *honor*, *almohaza*.—*H*. 1. In German musical notation H denotes B natural. 2. Symbol of hydrogen.

¡Ha! [ah], *int.* 1. Ha! 2. Ah, alas! 3. (Naut.) Haul away!

Haba [ah'-bah], *f.* 1. (Bot.) Bean, a kind of pulse. *Haba común*, Garden beach vetch. Vicia faba. *Haba común caballar*, Horse-bean. Vicia faba, varietas equina. *Haba loca* or *haba narbonense*, Broad-leaved vetch. Vicia narbonensis. *Haba de perro*, (Bot.) Dog's-bane. Apocynum. 2. A kind of mange in horses and oxen. *Habas*, White and black balls used in voting. *Esas son habas contadas*, A thing clear and manifest.

Habanero, ra [ah-bah-nay'-ro, rah], *a.* Havanese, of Havana.

Habano, na [ah-bah'-no, nah], *a.* Applied to Havana tobacco.

Habar [ah-bar'], *m.* Bean-field.

Habascón [ah-bas-cone'], *m.* A kind of root, like parsnip, in use as a food in almost all South American towns.

Habeas corpus [ah'-bay-as cor'-poos], *m.* (*for.*) Habeas corpus.

Habenaria [ah-bay-nah'-re-ah], *f.* Habenaria, rein-orchid, a large genus of American orchids.

Haber [ah-berr'], *va.* 1. To possess. 2. To have, an auxiliary verb. 3. To take, to recover. 4. To happen, to fall out, to befall. 5. To exist.—*v. impers.* *V.* Acaecer. *Más vale saber que haber*, It is better to be wise than to be rich, or, knowledge is preferable to wealth. *Haberlas* or *habérselas con alguno*, To dispute, to contend with any one.—*vr.* To behave, to act, to conduct one's self; to become, to pretend, to feign. *Hay*, There is, there are. *Había, hubo*, There was, there were. So also with other tenses. *Ha*, It is, since, ago. *Ha más de — que*, It is more than — since. *Poco ha*, A little while ago, whilom, quondam. *Ha de*, Is to, ought, must, etc. *Haber que*, To be to. *Hay que*, It is necessary. *No hay de qué*, You are welcome; don't mention it. (Literally, there is no cause why.) *Haber de*, With an infinitive, expresses a probable futurity. *¿Y por qué hemos de rehusar los goces que se hallan esparcidos en el difícil camino de la vida?* And why are we to refuse the pleasures which are scattered along life's difficult road? *No haber más que pedir*, It leaves nothing to be desired. *No haber tal*. To be no such thing.

Haber [ah-berr'], *m.* Property, income, fortune, assets. Cr.

Háber [ah'-berr], *m.* Doctor of the law among the Jews; a title inferior to rabbi.

Haberío [ah-bay-ree'-o], *m.* A work animal, or beast of burden. (Acad.)

Habichuela [ah-be-choo-ay'-lah], *f.* (Bot.) French-bean or kidney-bean. Phaseolus. *Habichuela común*, Common kidney-bean. Phaseolus vulgaris. *Habichuela común negra*. Black common kidney-bean. Phaseolus vulgaris semine nigro. *Habichuela multiflora*, Scarlet bean. Phaseolus multiflorus. *Habichuela enana*, Common dwarf kidney-bean. Phaseolus manus. *V.* Fríjol.

Hábil [ah'-beel], *a.* 1. Clever, skilful, dexterous, expert, knowing, cunning. 2. Capable, intelligent, learned, able to understand. 3. Agile, active, ready. 4. Apt, fit, handy, able, qualified for.

Habilidad [ah-be-le-dahd'], *f.* 1. Ability, ableness, dexterity in performing. 2. Cleverness, expertness, mastery, knowledge, talent; cunning. 3. Nimbleness, quickness, speed. 4. Instinct.—*pl.* Accomplishments.

Habilidoso, sa [ah-be-le-do'-so, sah], *a.* (Andal. and Amer. coll.) Accomplished.

Habilitación [ah-be-le-tah-the-on'], *f.* 1. Habilitation, qualification. 2. Fitting out, equipment.

Habilitado, da [ah-be-le-tah'-do, dah], *a. & pp.* of Habilitar. Habilitate, qualified.

Habilitado [ah-be-le-tah'-do], *m.* An officer in every Spanish regiment charged with the agency of his regiment; a paymaster.

Habilitador, ra [ah-be-le-tah-dor', rah], *m. & f.* Qualifier, one who makes fit or able.

Habilitar [ah-be-le-tar'], *va.* 1. To qualify, to enable. 2. To provide, to supply. 3. To fit out, to equip, to furnish means.

Hábilmente [ah'-beel-men-tay], *adv.* Dexterously, ably, knowingly, cleverly.

Habitable [ah-be-tah'-blay], *a.* Habitable, lodgeable.

Habitación [ah-be-tah-the-on'], *f.* 1. Habitation, abode, lodging. 2. Set of rooms, that part of a house intended to be inhabited.

Habitáculo [ah-be-tah'-coo-lo], *m.* (Coll.) A cramped, inconvenient dwelling.

Habitador, ra [ah-be-tah-dor', rah], *m. & f.* Inhabitant, resident, dweller, abider.

Habitante [ah-be-tahn'-tay], *pa.* Inhabiting.—*m. & f.* Inhabitant or habitant, dweller.

Habitar [ah-be-tar'], *va.* To inhabit, to live, to reside, to lodge or lie in a place.

Habitico, illo, ito [ah-be-tee'-co], *m. dim.* A small dress or habit.

Hábito [ah'-be-to], *m.* 1. Dress, habit, habiliment, garment. *Hábitos*, Dress of ecclesiastics. 2. Habit, habitude, custom, customariness. 3. The robes of the military orders. *Caballero del hábito de Santiago*, A knight of the military order of Saint James. *Colgar los hábitos*, (Coll.) To throw off the cowl.

Habituación [ah-be-too-ah-the-on'], *f.* Habitude, custom.

Habitual [ah-be-too-ahl'], *a.* Habitual, accustomed, inveterate, customary, common, frequent.

Habitualidad [ah-be-too-ah-le-dahd'], *f.* (Littl. us.) Custom, use.

Habitualmente [ah-be-too-al-men'-tay], *adv.* Habitually, customarily, by habit.

Habituar [ah-be-too-ar'], *va.* To accustom, to habituate, to inure.—*vr.* To become accustomed, to accustom one's self.

Habitud [ah-be-tood'], *f.* Habitude, the respect or relation which one thing bears to another.

Habla [ah'-blah], *f.* 1. Speech, idiom, language. 2. Discourse, argument. 3. Talk, conversation. *Estar en habla*, To talk about a matter. *Estar sin habla* or *perder el habla*, To be speechless. *Negar* or *quitar el habla*, To refuse speaking to a person. *Ponerse al habla*, 1. To come within speaking distance (used of two ships). 2. (Coll.) To talk with any one by means of the telephone.

Hablador, ra [ah-blah-dor', rah], *m. & f.* An impudent prattler; a trifling talker, a gabbler, a prattler, a chattering fellow.

Habladorcillo, lla [ah-blah-dor-theel'-lyo, lyah], *m. & f. dim.* A babbling dandiprat.

Habladuría [ah-blah-doo-ree'-ah], *f.* An impertinent speech.

Hablantín, na, Hablanchín, na [ah-blan-teen', nah, ah-blan-cheen', nah], (Coll.) A talkative person.

Hablar [ah-blar'], *va.* 1. To speak, to express thoughts by words. 2. To talk, to speak in conversation, to commune, to reason, to converse. 3. To harangue, to address, to make a speech. 4. To advise, to admonish. *Hablar Dios a alguno*, To be inspired. *Hablar a bulto* or *a tiento*, To talk at random. *Hablar disparates* or *necedades*, To talk nonsense. *Hablar al aire*, To talk to the air, to speak vaguely. *Hablar al alma*, To speak one's mind. (Met.) To speak things that touch the quick. *Hablar al caso*, To speak to the point. *Hablar alto*, To talk loud. *Hablar con el dedo*, To speak as a master, with authority. *Hablar en plata*, To speak clearly, without ambiguity. *Hablar en romance*, To speak out, to speak plainly. *Hablar por hablar*, To talk for the sake of talking. *Hablen cartas y callen barbas*, We must have less talking and more doing. *Hablar lobos*, There is risk in it. *Hablar entre dientes*, To mutter, to mumble. *Hablar de talanquera*, To find fault with an absent person. *Hablar desde la talanquera*, To speak with impunity. *Habló el buey y dijo "mú,"* When the ox spoke he said "moo"; when fools talk they talk nonsense. *Hablar por boca de ganso*, To echo what another has said (to speak by the mouth of a goose). *Hablar de burlas* or *de chanza*, To jeer, to mock. *Hablar de la mar*, To talk on an endless subject. *Hablar de memoria*, To talk without reflection, without knowledge of the matter. *No dejar que hablar*, To convince any one, to impose silence. *Hablar de veras*, To speak in earnest. *Hablar paso, quedo* or *bajo*, To talk low. *Hablar con los ojos*, To indicate one's sentiments by looks. *Hablar de hilván*, To speak too rapidly and confusedly. *Hablar de vicio*, To be loquacious. *No hablarse*, Not to speak to each other, from enmity or aversion. *Hablar de* or *en bóveda*, To speak pompously or arrogantly. (Lat. fabulari.)

Hablatista [ah-blah-tees'-tah], *m.* (Joc.) A trifling prattler, an idle talker.

Hablilla [ah-bleel'-lyah], *f.* 1. Rumour, report, little tale. 2. Babbling, a foolish talk.

Hablista [ah-blees'-tah], *m.* A person who speaks or writes with great correctness.

Habón [ah-bone'], *m. aug.* Large kind of bean.

Habrotamno [ah-bro-tahm'-no], *m.* Habrothamnus, a solanaceous shrub, native of Mexico.

Haca [ah'-cah], *f.* Pony, pad, a small horse. *¿ Qué haca ?* or *¿ qué haca morena ?* For what good ? to what purpose ?

Hacán [ah-cahn'], *m.* A learned man among the Jews.

Hacanea [ah-cah-nay'-ah], *f.* Nag, a small horse somewhat bigger than a pony.

Hace [ah'-thay], *m.* (Obs.) *V.* HAZ.

Hacecico, illo, ito [ah-thay-thee'-co], *m. dim.* A small sheaf.

Hacedero, ra [ah-thay-day'-ro, rah], *a.* Feasible, practicable ; easily effected.

Hacedor, ra [ah-thay-dor', rah], *m.* & *f.* 1. Maker, author; factor. 2. Steward, one who manages the estate of another. 3. A good workman, an able performer.

Hacendado [ah-then-dah'-do], *m.* A land-holder, a farmer.

Hacendado, da [ah-then-dah'-do, dah], *a.* & *pp.* of HACENDAR. 1. Acred, landed, having a fortune in land, having a real property. 2. Rich.

Hacendar [ah-then-dar'], *va.* To transfer or make over the property of an estate.—*vr.* To make a purchase of land in order to settle in a place.

Hacendeja [ah-then-day'-hah], *f. dim.* A small farm.

Hacendera [ah-then-day'-rah], *f.* Public work, at which all the neighbourhood assists.

Hacendero, ra [ah-then-day'-ro, rah], *a.* Industrious, laborious, sedulous.

Hacendilla, Hacenduela [ah-then-deel'-lyah, ah-then-doo-ay'-lah], *f. dim.* 1. A small farm. 2. A trifling work.

Hacendoso, sa [ah-then-do'-so, sah], *a.* Assiduous, diligent.

Hacer [ah-therr'], *va.* & *vn.* 1. To make, to form, to produce. 2. To do, to practise, to act any thing good or bad, to make, to perform. 3. To put in execution, to carry into effect ; to effect. 4. To make, to cause to have any quality, to bring into any new state or condition, to prepare, to dispose, to compose. 5. To make up a number, to complete. 6. To make, to raise as profit from any thing, to gain. 7. To make, to turn to some use. 8. To habituate, to accustom. 9. To give, to grant. 10. To include, to contain. 11. To cause, to occasion. 12. To resolve, to determine, to judge, to consider. 13. To assemble, to convoke : to correspond. 14. To make, to compel, to force, to constrain, to oblige : in this sense it is followed by an infinitive verb. *Hacer venir,* To oblige to come. 15. To dress : applied to hawks or cocks for fighting.—*vn.* 16. To grow, to increase or receive any thing. 17. To matter, to import. 18. To be, to exist. *Hace frío,* It is cold. 19. To accord, to agree, to fit, to answer, to suit. 20. Joined with the particle *a,* it signifies to be ready or disposed. *Hacer a todo,* To be ready or disposed to do any thing. 21. Joined with the particle *de,* and the names of offices or professions, it signifies to perform their duties ; as *Hacer de escribano,* To act as a scrivener or notary. *Hacer de portero,* To act as a porter. 22. Joined with *de, se, el, la, lo,* it signifies to represent, to counterfeit, or to show what is not in reality. *Hacer de bobo.* To counterfeit an idiot. 23. With *por* or *para,* joined to an infinitive verb, it signifies taking pains and care in executing the import of such verb ; as *Hacer por llegar,* To endeavour to arrive : *Hacer para* or *por salvarse,* To strive to save one's self. 24. Followed by substantives it gives them a verbal signification ; as *Hacer estimación,* To esteem. *Hacer almanaques,* To be very pensive and silent, to be musing. *Hacer ánimo,* To mean, to mind, intend, to make up one's mind. *Hacer aguas,* (Coll.) To make water. *V.* ORINAR. *Hacer pensar,* To put in mind, to give cause to suspect. *Hacer acordarse,* To put in mind, to make one remember. *Hacer avergonzar,* To put one to the blush, to frown any one down. *Hacer bajar los ojos,* To make one abashed. *Hacer bajar las orejas,* To humble any one. *Hacer calceta,* (Coll.) To knit. *Hacer labor,* To sew. *Hacer el capitán,* To personate or act the captain. *Hacer diligencia,* To try, to endeavour, to take measures. *Hacer de negocio y deuda ajena, suyo propio,* (Law) To take as one's own the debt or concern of another person. *Hacer hacer,* To cause to be made, to order a thing to be made. *Comida hecha, compañía deshecha,* The meal eaten, the company deserted (*i. e.* to desert those from whom no more is to be expected). *De menos nos hizo Dios,* The desire for something great or difficult to attain. *Hacer a dos palos,* To derive benefit from two sources at the same time. *Hacer buen tercio,* To do good to a person. *Hacer tercio,* To join an association. *Haz bien, y guárdate,* Be kind, but also on your guard. *Hacer honor a una letra,* To honour or protect a draft. *Hacer su casa,* To aggrandize one's family. *Haz por venir,* Try to come. *No hace tanto la zorra en un año como paga en una hora,* Craft and crime may succeed temporarily, but the day of retribution is sure to come. *Hacer estómago a alguna cosa,* To make up one's mind to bear what may come. *Hacer calceta* or *malla,* To knit. *Lo que no se hace a la boda, no se hace a toda hora,* If you must ask a favour of a person, do it when he is in a happy mood. *Hacer cuerpo presente,* To attend a meeting without taking part in it. *Hacer venir,* To order an article to be brought or sent. *Hacer presente,* (Law) To show, to state, to remonstrate. *Hacer a uno con alguna cosa,* (Coll.) To procure a thing for any one. *No hacer alto,* To overlook, not to mind. *No hagas caso,* Never mind. *Hacer el papel,* To personate or act the part of another person. *Hacer la vista gorda,* To wink at, to connive at. *Hacer orejas de mercader,* To give one a deaf ear. *Hacer plato de alguno,* (Met.) To make one the object of ridicule or censure. *Hacer antesala,* To attend in a hall in order to speak to a person of consequence in passing. *Hacer alarde,* To muster ; to boast of. *Hacer aire,* To blow : speaking of the wind. *Hacer aire a alguno,* To vex, to plague or torment any one. *Hacer alguna cosa a la moda,* To fashion. *Hacer a uno perder los estribos,* To make any one lose his temper : literally, to make a man lose his stirrups. *Hacer bancarrota,* To fail, to break, to become bankrupt. *Hacer caso de,* To pay attention to, to mind, to care. *Hacer correrías,* To make incursions. *Hacer cara,* To make head against, to face, to resist. *Hacer chacota,* To ridicule, to turn into ridicule. *Hacer costilla* or *costillas,* To bear with patience, to suffer. *Hacer del cuerpo,* To go to stool. *Hacer de tripas corazón,* To pluck up courage, to bluster and show much boldness when one is afraid, to pluck up heart. *Hacer de necesidad virtud,* To make a virtue of necessity. *Hacer de figura* or *hacer figura,* To make a figure or cut a figure. *Hacer espaldas,* To bear, to endure. *Hacer estrados,* To give a hearing : applied to judges and magistrates. *Hacer fermentar,* To heat. *Hacer frente a,* To make head against, to face, to resist. *Hacer fiesta,* To make a holiday. *Hacer fiestas,* To fondle, to endear, to flatter, to cajole, to fawn. *Hacer gasto,* To spend. *Hacer gente,* To raise soldiers. *Hacer hombre a alguno,* To make one's fortune. *Hacer humo,* 1. To smoke. 2. (Met.) To continue long in a place. *Hacer honras,* To honour, to pay honours ; to hold in esteem. *Hacer libro nuevo,* To turn over a new leaf, to improve one's habits. *Haces mal, espera otro tal,* Sow the wind, and reap the whirlwind. *No hacemos moneda falsa,* Our conversation is not private: you may listen if you like. *No hacer moneda falsa,* To say what is true. *Hacer opinión,* To form an opinion, to be an authority. *Hacer placer* or *por hacer placer,* To oblige, or please. *Hacer plaza,* To sell at retail. *Hacer por la vida,* To eat something. *Hace ocho días,* Eight days ago. So with other phrases of time. *Hacer intención,* To intend, to mean, to mind. *Hacer juego,* To be well matched. *Hacer la comida,* To dress the dinner. *Hacer limosna,* To give alms. *Hacer la barba,* To shave, to get shaved. (Mex.) To flatter. *Hacer la cuenta sin la huéspeda,* To reckon without the hostess. *Hacer las amistades,* To make it up. *Hacer las cosas por arte de birlibirloque,* To do things by virtue of hocus-pocus. *Hacer la mamona,* To pull one's nose, to scoff or ridicule. *Hacer mal de ojo,* (Coll.) To fascinate. *Hacer merced* or *mercedes,* To confer honours or employments. *Hacer memoria,* To recollect, to remember. *Hacer milagros,* To do wonders. *Hacer morisquetas,* To play pranks. *Hacer niebla,* To haze. *Hacer papel,* To act a part ; to make or to cut a figure ; to acquit one's self well. *Hacer penitencia con alguno,* To take pot-luck or a family dinner, to dine with one on whatever he chances to have. *Hacer plato,* To carve. *Hacer por,* To try, to do one's best. *Hacer prenda,* To take a pledge or security for a debt. *Hacer progresos,* To gain ground, to improve. *Hacer pedazos,* To pull to pieces. *Hacer pucheros,* To make wry faces, as children are used to do before they begin to cry. *Hacer pie,* To find the bottom of water without swimming ; to be firm and secure in any thing ; to stop, to reside in a place. *Hacer punta,* To be the first, to lead. *Hacer que hacemos,* To act officially, to affect doing some business, to fidget about for no purpose. *Hacer saber,* To acquaint, to make known. *Hacer sombra,* (Met.) To protect, to support ; to impede, to obscure. *Hacer su agosto,* To make hay while the sun shines : literally, to make one's harvest. *Hacer ventaja,* To exceed, to surpass. *Hacer agua,* (Naut.) To leak or spring a leak, to water or to make water ; speaking of a ship which is leaky. *Hacer el bastardo,* (Naut.) To veer or tack, so as to bring the ship before the wind. *Hacer fanal,* (Naut.) To carry the poop-lantern lighted : applied to the headmost ship which leads the van. *No hay que hacer* or *eso no tiene que hacer,* It is only to act, it is easily done. *Hacer vela*, (Naut.) To set sail. *Hacer fuerza de vela*, (Naut.) To crowd sail, to carry a press of sail. *Hacer poca vela*, (Naut.) To carry an easy sail. *Hacer derrota*, (Naut.) To stand on the course. *Hacer buen bordo*, (Naut.) To make a good tack. *Hacer camino para avante*, (Naut.) To have headway. *Hacer camino para popa*, (Naut.) To make sternway. *Hacer cabeza*, (Naut.) To head. *Hacer la rueda a alguno*, To flatter a person for a purpose, to wheedle. *Hacer que*, To feign, to pretend, to affect. *Hágame Vd. el favor*, Pray. *Haga buen o mal tiempo*, Rain or shine. *La boca hace juego*, To be as good as one's word.

Hacerse [ah-therr'-say], *vr.* 1. To recede, to separate. 2. To become, to enter into some new state or condition. 3. To accustom one's self. *Hacerse de miel*, To treat one gently, not to be very severe. *Hacerse con algo* or *de algo*, To acquire, to attain; to purchase any thing which is wanting. *Hacerse lugar*, To gain a name or reputation. *Hacerse memorable*, To become memorable, famous, notorious, etc. *Hacerse tortilla*, To fall down as flat as a cake. *Hacerse a la vela*, (Naut.) To set sail. *Hacerse añicos*, To take great pains in doing any thing. *Hacerse una zarpa*, To get very wet. *Hacerse unas gachas*, To grant a favour first refused; to show great emotion. *Hacerse chiquito*, To pretend to be modest; to conceal one's knowledge. *Se hace noche*, Night falls. *Hacerse las narices*, To receive an unexpected blow in the face. *Hacerse con una cosa*, To obtain a thing rightly or wrongly. *Hacerse de nuevas*, To affect ignorance.

Hacerir, *va.* (Obs.) *V.* ZAHERIR.

Hacezuelo [ah-thay-thoo-ay'-lo], *m. dim.* of HAZ.

Hacia [ah'-the-ah], *adv.* Towards, in a direction to, near to, about. *Hacia adelante*, Forward. *Hacia acá* or *hacia esta parte*, Hitherward, hitherwards. *Hacia dónde*, Whither, toward which, to what place, to where. *Hacia casa, hacia su país*, Homeward, homewards.

Hacienda [ah-the-en'-dah], *f.* 1. Landed property, lands, tenements. 2. Estate, fortune, wealth. 3. Farm. 4. Domestic work done by the servants of the house. *Hacer hacienda*, To mind one's business, to do what is to be done. *Haciendas apalabradas*, Goods already bespoken. *Real hacienda* Exchequer. *Ministro de hacienda* (in Spain), and *Secretario de hacienda* (in Spanish America), The Secretary of the Treasury, or Chancellor of the Exchequer. *Hacienda pública*, Public treasury, finances. *Hacienda de beneficio*, (Mex.) Reduction works.

Hacina [ah-thee'-nah], *f.* 1. Stack or rick of corn piled up in sheaves. 2. Any collection of things placed one over another.

Hacinador, ra [ah-the-nah-dor', rah], *m. & f.* Stack-maker, one who piles up the sheaves of corn. *Hacinador de riquezas*, Hoarder of riches.

Hacinamiento [ah-the-nah-me-en'-to], *m.* 1. Accumulation, act of heaping or hoarding up. 2. Acervation, coacervation, heaping together.

Hacinar [ah-the-nar'], *va.* 1. To stack or pile up sheaves of corn. 2. To hoard, to make hoards. 3. To cumulate; to coacervate.

Hacino, na [ah-thee'-no, nah], *a.* *V.* AVARO and TRISTE. (Arab. hazin.)

Hacha [ah'-chah], *f.* 1. A large taper with four wicks. *Hacha de viento*, Flambeau, torch, link. *Pajè de hacha*, Link-boy. 2. An axe or hatchet. *Hacha de armas*, Battle-axe. 3. Ancient Spanish dance.

Hachazo [ah-chah'-tho], *m.* Blow or stroke with an axe.

Hache [ah'-chay], *f.* Name of the letter H.

Hachear [ah-chay-ar'], *va.* To cut with an axe; to hew.—*vn.* To strike with an axe.

Hachero [ah-chay'-ro], *m.* 1. Torch-stand, a large candlestick for tapers or torches. 2. (Mil.) *V.* GASTADOR. 3. (Obs.) Person appointed for making signals in a watch-tower or lighthouse. 4. Wood-cleaver or wood-cutter; a labourer employed to fell wood and cut timber. 5. (Prov.) Carpenter.

Hacheta [ah-chay'-tah], *f. dim.* 1. A small hatchet. 2. A small torch or link.

Hachich [ah-cheech'], *m.* Hasheesh, a preparation of Indian hemp.

Hacho [ah'-cho], *m.* Fagot, or bundle of straw or feather-grass, covered with pitch or resin.

Hachón [ah-chone'], *m.* 1. A large torch made of bass and pitch. 2. Kind of altar, on which bonfires are lighted for illuminations.

Hachuela [ah-choo-ay'-lah], *f. dim.* A small hatchet or axe. *Hachuela de abordar*, (Naut.) Boarding-axe.

Hada [ah'-dah], *f.* Fairy. *Cuento de hadas*, Fairy tale. *Hada encantada*, Enchanted fairy.

Hadado, da [ah-dah'-do, dah], *a. & pp.* of HADAR. Fortunate, lucky.

Hadador, ra [ah-dah-dor', rah], *m. & f.* (Obs.) Sorcerer, fortune-teller.

Hadar [ah-dar'], *va.* (Obs.) 1. To divine, to foretell future events. 2. To enchant.

Hado [ah'-do], *m.* Fate, destiny, inevitable doom. (Lat. fatum.)

Haftara [af-tah'-rah], *f.* Haphtarah, or haftarah, a selection from the prophets read in the synagogue equivalent to the "ite, missa est," of the Roman Catholics.

Hagiógrafo [ah-he-o'-grah-fo], *m.* Hagiographer, a writer of lives of the saints.

(*Yo hago, yo hice, él hizo, hiciera. V.* HACER.)

Haitiano, na [ah-e-te-ah'-no, nah], *a.* Haytian, relating to Hayti.

Haje [ah'-hay], *f.* The African cobra or asp: it has the power of inflating the neck. (Arab.)

Halacabullas, Halacuerdas [ah-lah-cah-bool'-lyas, ah-lah-coo-err'-das], *m.* (Coll.) Fresh-water sailors.

Halagador, ra [ah-lah-gah-dor', rah], *m. & f.* Cajoler, flatterer.

Halagar [ah-lah-gar'], *va.* To cajole, to flatter; to caress, to dandle, to coax, to coy, to allure, to make much of, to wheedle, to hug, to fondle, to treat with tenderness. (Arab. halāwa. something sweet.)

Halago [ah-lah'-go], *m.* Cajolery, flattery, caress, adulation; cooing.

Halagüeñamente [ah-lah-goo-ay-nyah-men'-tay], *adv.* Endearingly, flatteringly.

Halagüeño, ña [ah-lah-goo-ay'-nyo, nyah], *a.* Endearing, attractive, alluring, fawning, flattering, meek, gentle.

Halar [ah-lar'], *va.* (Naut.) To haul. to pull by a rope. *Halar al viento*. To haul the wind.

Halcón [al-cone'], *m.* (Orn.) Falcon, a hawk trained for sport. Falco.

Halconado, da [al-co-nah'-do, dah], *a.* Falcon or hawk-like.

Halconcico, illo, ito [al-con-thee'-co, eel'-lyo, ee'-to], *m. dim.* Jashawk, a young falcon or hawk.

Halconear [al-co-nay-ar'], *va.* (Coll.) 1. To look and inveigle: applied to women of the town. 2. (Obs.) To look about as haughty as a falcon; to view with contempt.

Halconera [al-co-nay'-rah], *f.* Place where falcons are kept.

Halconería [al-co-nay-ree'-ah], *f.* Falconry.

Halconero [al-co-nay'-ro], *m.* Falconer, one who rears or trains hawks for sport.

Halda [ahl'-dah], *f.* 1. Bag or sack made of sack-cloth. 2. Skirt of a garment. *V.* FALDA. *Haldas en cinta*, (Coll.) Disposed and ready for any thing. *De haldas o de mangas*, (Coll.) Justly or unjustly, with good or ill will, in any way.

Haldada [al-dah'-dah], *f.* Skirt full of any thing.

Haldear [al-day-ar'], *vn.* To run along with the skirts flying loose.

Haldica, illa, ita [al-dee'-cah], *f. dim.* A small skirt.

Haldudo, da [al-doo'-do, dah], *a.* Having flying skirts.

Haleche [ah-lay'-chay], *m.* Horsemackerel, a kind of mackerel. *V.* ESCOMBRO.

Halia [ah-lee'-ah], *f.* 1. (Bot.) A papilionaceous plant of the Cape of Good Hope. 2. (Ent.) A European moth. 3. A nereid, a sea-nymph.

Haliéntica [ah-le-en'-te-cah], *f.* Angling, the art of fishing.

Haliéntico, ca [ah-le-en'-te-co, cah], *a.* Angling, belonging to the art of angling.

Halieto [ah-le-ay'-to], *m.* Sea-eagle.

Halinatrón [ah-le-nah-tron'], *m.* Native soda.

Haliquedón [ah-le-kay-don'], *a.* Like the sea-swallows.

Hálito [ah'-le-to], *m.* 1. The breath. 2. Vapour. 3. (Poet.) Soft air.

Halo, Halón [ah'-lo, ah-lone'], *m.* (Ast.) Halo, a red circle round the sun or moon.

Halodendro, dra [ah-lo-den'-dro, drah]. *a.* (Bot.) Growing in earth impregnated with salts.

Halógeno, na [ah-lo'-hay-no, nah], *a.* (Chem.) Halogen, producing saline compounds.

Halografía [ah-lo-grah-fee'-ah], *f.* (Chem.) The section of chemistry which treats of salts, halography.

Halomancia [ah-lo-mahn'-the-ah], *f.* Halomancy, divination with salt.

Haloquimia [ah-lo-kee'-me-ah], *f.* The branch of chemistry which treats of salts and their properties.

Halotecnia [ah-lo-tec-ne-ah'], *f.* (Littl. us.) The science which treats of salts.

Haloza [ah-loh'-thah], *f.* Wooden shoe.

Haltera [al-tay'-rah], *f.* Barbell, dumbbell.

Halterofilia [al-tay-ro-fee'-le-ah], *f.* Weight lifting.

Halurgia [ah-loor'-he-ah], *f.* Preparation of salts and the art of preparing them.

Hallado, da [ah-lyah'-do, dah], *a.* Found. *Bien hallado*, Very familiar, welcome, easy, contented. *Mal hallado*, Uneasy, not at ease, constrained.—*pp.* of HALLAR.

Hallador, ra [al-lyah-dor', rah], *m. & f.* 1. Finder, discoverer. 2. (Obs.) Inventor.

Hallar [al-lyar'], *va.* 1. To find, to obtain by searching or seeking. 2. To find, to hit on, to hit upon by chance, to perceive by accident. 3. To find, to meet with, to fall upon. 4. To find out, to discover. 5. To find, to gain by any mental endeavour, to invent, to excogitate. 6. To find, to remark, to observe, to note, to compare, to verify. 7. To find, to discover something hidden. 8. To find, to detect, to catch, to understand, to comprehend. 9. To manifest, to show any thing unexpected.—*vr.* 1. To meet occasionally in any place, to light, to happen to find, to fall upon by chance. 2. To be content or pleased in any place. 3. To be somewhere. 4. To find one's self, to be, to fare with regard to ease or pain.

Hallazgo [al-lyath'-go], *m.* 1. The act of finding or recovering any thing lost. 2. Reward given for finding any thing lost. 3. Thing found.

Hallulla [al-lyool'-lyah], *f.* 1. A kind of paste made and used to feed fowls. 2. *V.* HALLULLO.

Hallullo [al-lyool'-lyo], *m.* Cake baked on or under cinders.

Hamaca [ah-mah'-cah], *f.* Hammock, a kind of suspended bed.

Hamaquero [ah-mah-kay'-ro], *m.* Person who carries a hammock.

Hamano [ah-mah'-no], *m.* A kind of pink cotton stuff from the Levant.

Hambre [ahm'-bray], *f.* 1. Hunger, appetite; the pain felt from fasting. *Tener hambre,* To be hungry, to have an appetite. 2. Scarcity and dearth of provisions, famine. 3. Greediness, eagerness of appetite or desire. *Acosado de hambre,* Pinched with hunger. *Muerto de hambre,* Starved with hunger.

Hambrear [am-bray-ar'], *vn.* To hunger, to be hungry—*va.* 1. To hunger, to cause hunger. 2. To starve, to famish, to kill with hunger, to subdue by famine.

Hambrientamente [am-bre-en-tah-men'-tay], *adv.* Hungrily.

Hambriento, ta [am-bre-en'-to, tah], *a.* 1. Hungry, starved, greedy, ravenous. 2. Greedy, eager, vehemently desirous.

Hambrón, na [am-brone', nah], *m.* & *f.* (Coll.) A hungry person, one who is often hungry.

Hamburgués, sa [am-boor-gays', sah], *a.* Pertaining to the city Hamburg.

Hamburguesa [am-boor-gay'-sah], *f.* Hamburger.

Hamez [ah-meth'], *f.* A distemper in hawks or falcons which makes them lose their feathers. (Arab.)

Hampa [ahm'-pah], *f.* 1. Underworld, skid row. 2. Life of vagrancy and rowdyism.

Hampesco, ca [am-pes'-co, cah], *a.* Vagabond, villainous, vainglorious.

Hampo, Hampón [ahm'-po, am-pone'], *a.* Bold, valiant, licentious.

Hanega [ah-nay'-gah], *f.* A dry measure. *V.* FANEGA.

Hanegada [ah-nay-gah'-dah], *f.* Quantity of land sown with a *fanega* of corn.

Hangar [an-gar'], *m.* (Aer.) Hangar.

Hanquilla [an-keel'-lyah], *f.* A kind of boat.

Hansa [ahn'-sah], *f.* *V.* ANSA. A commercial league between various free German cities in the 15th century.

Hanseático, ca [an-say-ah'-te-co, cah], *a.* Hanseatic, belonging to the league named Hansa.

Hao [ah'-o], *interj.* 1. (Obs.) Holloa, a vulgar word used in calling to any one at a distance. 2. *m.* Noise.

Haquilla, ita [ah-keel'-lyah, ee'-tah], *f. dim.* Very little pony.

Haragán, na [ah-rah-gahn', nah], *m.* & *f.* & *a.* 1. Idler, loiterer, lingerer, lounger, lubbard, an idle, lazy person. 2. Idle, slothful, inactive, indolent.

Haraganamente [ah-rah-gah-nah-men'-tay], *adv.* Idly, lazily, slothfully, indolently.

Haraganazo, za [ah-rah-gah-nah'-tho, thah], *a. aug.* Very idle.

Haraganear [ah-rah-gah-nay-ar'], *vn.* To lead an idle life, to be lazy, to act the truant, to lounge, to idle, to loiter.

Haraganería [ah-rah-gah-nay-ree'-ah], *f.* Idleness, laziness, sluggishness, inactivity, slothfulness.

Haraldo, Haraute [ah-rahl'-do, ah-rah'-oo-tay], *m.* (Obs.) Herald, king at arms.

Harapo [ah-rah'-po], *m.* Rag hanging from torn clothes; fringe.

Haraposo, sa [ah-rah-po'-so, sah], *a.* Ragged, tattered. (Gr. ἄῤῥαφος.)

Harbar [ar-bar'], *va.* (Obs.) To huddle, to perform in a hurry.

Harem, Harén [ah-rem', ah-ren'], *m.* Harem, Turkish seraglio.

Harija [ah-ree'-hah], *f.* Mill-dust, the flour which flies about in a corn-mill.

Harina [ah-ree'-nah], *f.* 1. Flour, the edible part of corn and meal. 2. (Met.) Powder, dust.

Harinado [ah-re-nah'-do], *m.* Flour dissolved in water.

Harinero [ah-re-nay'-ro], *m.* 1. Mealman, one who deals in flour. 2. Place where meal or flour is kept.

Harinero, ra [ah-re-nay'-ro, rah], *a.* Made of flour, belonging to flour.

Harinoso, sa [ah-re-no'-so, sah], *a.* Mealy, containing meal.

Harkisa [ar-kee'-sah], *f.* Nickel sulphide.

Harma [ar'-mah], *f.* (Ant. Bot.) Wild rue. *V.* GAMARZA.

Harmaga [ar-mah'-gah], *f.* (Bot.) *V.* GAMARZA and ALHÁRGAMA.

Harmonía [ar-mo-nee'-ah], *f.* Harmony. *V.* ARMONÍA and its adjuncts.

Harmonista [ar-mo-nees'-tah], *m.* Musician.

Harnerico, illo, ito [ar-nay-ree'-co], *m. dim.* A small sieve.

Harnero [ar-nay'-ro], *m.* Sieve; properly, of fine meshes and small diameter. *V.* CRIBA. *Estar hecho un harnero,* To be covered with wounds.

Harón, na [ah-ron', nah], *a.* 1. Slow, inactive, sluggish. 2. Balky.

Haronear [ah-ro-nay-ar'], *vn.* 1. To dawdle, move sluggishly; to be tardy or slow. 2. To balk, to stop short (of a horse).

Haronía [ah-ro-nee'-ah], *f.* Sluggishness, laziness, idleness.

Harpado, da [ar-pah'-do, dah], *a.* *V.* ARPADO.

Harpía [ar-pee'-ah], *f.* Harpy. *V.* ARPÍA.

Harpillera [ar-peel-lyay'-rah], *f.* A coarse tow fabric like burlap.

Harria [ar'-re-ah], *f.* (Amer.) Drove of beasts of burden.

Hartada, *f.* *V.* HARTAZGO.

Hartar [ar-tar'], *va.* 1. To stuff with eating and drinking, to glut. 2. To satiate, to gratify desire. 3. To satiate, to satisfy, to cloy, to fill to uneasiness, to fill beyond natural desire. Joined with *de* and any nouns, it signifies to give or cause an abundance or excess of the things expressed by the nouns.

Hartazgo [ar-tath'-go], *m.* Satiety, the act of glutting or filling beyond natural desire.

Harto [ar'-to], *adv.* Enough.

Harto, ta [ar'-to, tah], *a.* & *pp. irr.* of HARTAR. 1. Satiate, satiated, glutted, full of satiety. 2. Sufficient, full, complete.

Hartura [ar-too'-rah], *f.* 1. Satiety, fulness beyond desire or pleasure, glut. 2. Plenty, abundance.

Hasiz [ah-seeth'], *m.* Guard or keeper of silk.

Hasta [ahs'-tah], *prep.* Until, as far as; also, even. *Hasta no más,* To the highest pitch. *Hasta ahora, hasta aquí,* Hitherto. *Hasta el fin de la calle,* Down to the end of the street.

Hastial [as-te-ahl'], *m.* 1. A gable end. 2. (Fig.) A coarse, rude man. 3. Lateral face of an excavation, in mining. (Acad.)

Hastiar [as-te-ar'], *va.* To loathe, to create disgust.

Hastío [as-tee'-o], *m.* Loathing, want of appetite; disgust, abhorring.

Hataca [ah-tah'-cah], *f.* 1. A large kind of wooden ladle. 2. Rolling-pin, with which paste is moulded.

Hatajar [ah-tah-har'], *va.* To divide cattle into flocks or herds.

Hatajo [ah-tah'-ho], *m.* 1. A small herd of cattle. 2. Assemblage, collection; abundance.

Hatear [ah-tay-ar'], *vn.* To collect one's clothes necessary for travelling, when on a journey.

Hatería [ah-tay-ree'-ah], *f.* Allowance of provisions and clothes for shepherds, when travelling with their flocks.

Hatero [ah-tay'-ro], *m.* 1. Shepherd or other person who carries provisions to those who attend a flock of sheep. 2. (Cuba) Cow-boy, herder of cattle, or keeper of a cattle-farm.

Hatero, ra [ah-tay'-ro, rah], *a.* Applied to the animals that carry the shepherd's baggage.

Hatijo [ah-tee'-ho], *m.* Covering of straw or feather-grass over bee-hives.

Hatillo [ah-teel'-lyo], *m. dim.* A small bundle; a few clothes. *Echar el hatillo al mar,* To irritate, to vex one's self. *Coger* or *tomar su hatillo* or *el hatillo,* To go away, to leave a place.

Hato [ah'-to], *m.* 1. A large herd of cattle. *Un hato de carneros,* A flock or fold of sheep. (Amer.) A farm for rearing cattle. 2. Fold, place chosen by shepherds to eat and sleep near their flocks. 3. Provisions for shepherds, for some days' consumption. 4. Clothes, wearing apparel. 5. Heap, cluster, number driven together. 6. Herd, in contempt, a company of men; a crowd, multitude, or meeting of suspicious people. 7. Assemblage, collection, abundance. 8. (Coll.) *V.* CORRILLO.

Hay [ah'-ee]. Impersonal form, from *Haber,* there is, there are. (Contraction of *ha,* with obsolete *y,* there, *ha-y,* it has there, there is.)

Haya [ah'-yah], *f.* (Bot.) Beech-tree. Fagus. *Haya común* or *silvática,* Common beech. Fagus silvatica.

Hayal, Hayedo [ah-yahl'], *m.* Plantation of beech-trees.

Hayeno, na [ah-yay'-no, nah], *a.* (Obs.) Beechen.

Hayo [ah'-yo], *m.* (Cuba) Coca, the shrub and its leaves.

Hayucal [ah-yoo-cahl'], *m.* (Prov.) Grove of beech-trees.

Hayuco [ah-yoo'-co], *m.* Beech-mast, fruit of the beech.

Haz [ahth'], *m.* 1. Fagot, fascine, a bundle of brush-wood or sticks; a bundle of hay or grass; a sheaf of corn. (Lat. fascis.) 2. (Obs.) A file of soldiers, also troops arranged in divisions.

Haz [ahth], *f.* 1. Face, visage. 2. Right side or outside of cloth. 3. (Arch.) Facing. *V.* PARAMENTO. *Sobre la haz de la tierra,* Upon the face of the earth. *A sobre haz*, Apparently, exteriorly, at first view. *En haz y en paz*, With common consent and approbation. *Ser de dos haces*, To be double-faced, to say one thing and think another. (Lat. facies.)

Haza [ah'-thah], *f.* Piece of cultivable land.

Hazada [ah-thah'-dah], *f.* *V.* AZADA.

Hazadón, *m.* *V.* AZADÓN.

Hazaleja [ah-thah-lay'-hah], *f.* (Prov.) A towel.

Hazán [ah-thahn'], *m.* The cantor of a synagogue.

Hazaña [ah-thah'-nyah], *f.* 1. Exploit, achievement, an heroic feat. 2. (Iron.) Ignoble action.

Hazañería [ah-thah-nyay-ree'-ah], *f.* Show or affectation of scrupulosity.

Hazañero, ra [ah-thah-nyay'-ro, rah], *a.* Prudish, affectedly grave and scrupulous.

Hazañero, ra [ah-thah-nyay'-ro, rah], *m. & f.* Affected, prudish person.

Hazañosamente [ah-thah-nyo-sah-men'-tay], *adv.* Valorously.

Hazañoso, sa [ah-thah-nyo'-so, sah], *a.* Valient, courageous, heroic.

Hazcona [ath-co'-nah], *f.* Dart. *V.* DARDO.

Hazmerreír [ath-may-ray-eer'], *m.* Ridiculous person, laughing-stock, gazing-stock, or jesting-stock.

Hazteallá [ath-tay-al-lyah'], *m.* Roughness or austerity in behaviour or disposition.

He! [ay], *int.* 1. Ho! hey! a sudden exclamation to give notice of any thing. 2. Hark! list! hear! listen! Behold! look here. 3. What? Eh? It is used with pronouns, as *te*, *lo*, *los*, etc., and *aquí* or *allí*.

Hebdómada [eb-do'-mah-dah], *f.* 1. Hebdomad, a week, seven days. 2. Seven years.

Hebdomadario, ria [eb-do-mah-dah'-re-o, ah], *m. & f.* Hebdomadary, a member of a chapter or convent, whose week it is to officiate in the choir.—*a.* Weekly.

Hebe [ay'-bay], *f.* 1. The down which grows upon the pubis. 2. The age of puberty. 3. An asteroid of this name. 4. A very pretty moth.

Hebén [ay-ben'], *a.* 1. Applied to white grapes, like muscatels. 2. (Obs.) Empty, futile: applied to persons.

Hebepétalo, la [ay-bay-pay'-tah-lo, lah], *a.* Downy-petaled.

Hebetina [ay-bay-tee'-nah], *f.* Willemite, silicate of zinc.

Hebilla [ay-beel'-lyah], *f.* A buckle, a clasp. (Lat. fibula.)

Hebillaje [ay-beel-lyah'-hay], *m.* Collection of buckles, or mounting of horses, accoutrements.

Hebillita [ay-beel-lyee'-tah], *f. dim.* Small buckle.

Hebillar [ay-beel-lyar'], *va.* To buckle.

Hebillón [ay-beel-lyone'], *m. aug.* A large buckle.

Hebillona, ota [ay-beel-lyo'-nah, oh'-tah], *f. aug.* *V.* HEBILLÓN.

Hebra [ay'-brah], *f.* 1. A needleful of thread of linen, yarn, worsted, or silk. 2. Pistil of the flower or blossom of saffron and other plants. 3. Fibre, filament, thread. 4. Vein, layer, stratum. 5. *pl.* (Poet.) Hair. *Cortar la hebra*, To cut the thread of life. *Ser* or *estar de buena hebra*, To be strong and robust.

Hebraico, ca [ay-brah'-e-co, cah], *a* Belonging to the Hebrews.

Hebraísta [ay-brah-ees'-tah], *m.* Hebraist, one who is proficient in Hebrew.

Hebreo [ay-bray'-o], *m.* 1. A Hebrew. 2. (Coll.) A merchant, a tradesman.

Hebreo, ea [ay-bray'-o, ah], *a.* Hebraic, Judaical. *A la hebrea*, In the Hebrew manner.—*m.* 1. Hebrew language. 2. (Coll.) Trader. 3. (Coll.) Usurer.

Hebrero [ay-bray'-ro], *m.* (Obs.) February. *V.* FEBRERO.

Hebroso, sa [ay-bro'-so, sah], *a.* Fibrous, filaceous; consisting of many fibres and threads.

Hecatombe [ay-cah-tom'-bay], *f.* 1. Hecatomb. 2. Massacre, slaughter.

Heciento, ta [ay-the-en'-to, tah], *a.* (Obs.) Full of lees.

Hectárea [ec-tah'-ray-ah], *f.* Hectare, a measure of surface.

Héctico, ca [ec'-te-co, cah], *a.* Hectic. *Cf.* HÉTICO.

Hecto [ec'-to], *m.* Greek prefix, signifying one hundred.

Hectógrafo [ec-to'-grah-fo], *m.* Hectograph.

Hectogramo [ec-to-grah'-mo], *m.* Hectogramme, the weight of 100 grammes.

Hectolitro [ec-to-lee'-tro], *m.* Hectolitre. 100 litres.

Hectómetro [ec-to'-may-tro], *m.* Hectometre, 100 metres.

Hectóreo, ea [ec-to'-ray-o, ah], *a.* Belonging to Hector.

Hecha [ay'-chah], *f.* (Obs.) 1. *V.* HECHO. 2. (Prov. Arag.) Land-tax. *De esta hecha*, From this time.

Hechiceresco, ca [ay-che-thay-res'-co, cah], *a.* Relating to witchcraft.

Hechicería [ay-che-thay-ree'-ah], *f.* 1. Witchcraft, the practices of witches. 2. Witchery, enchantment. 3. Charmingness, the power of pleasing.

Hechicero, ra [ay-che-thay'-ro, rah], *m. & f. & a.* 1. Witch, wizard; hag. 2. Charmer, enchanter, bewitcher. 3. Charming, bewitching, attractive in the highest degree.

Hechizar [ay-che-thar'], *va.* 1. To bewitch, to enchant, to injure by witchcraft. 2. To charm, to fascinate.

Hechizo [ay-chee'-tho], *m.* 1. Bewitchment, fascination. 2. Enchantment, irresistible power of pleasing, enchanter, charmer. 3. Entertainment. amusement.

Hechizo, za [ay-chee'-tho, thah], *a.* Made or done on purpose; artificial, factitious, imitated, well-adapted.

Hecho, cha [ay'-cho, chah], *pp. irr.* of HACER. 1. Made, done. 2. Accustomed, inured, used. *Hecho al trabajo*, Inured to labour and hardship. *Hecho un león*, Like a lion, furiously angry. *A lo hecho pecho*, (Prov.) We must make the best of what we have done. *De hecho y de derecho*, By act and right. *Hombre hecho*, A man of experience. *Tiempo hecho*, (Naut.) Settled weather. *Viento hecho*, (Naut.) Steady wind.

Hecho [ay'-cho], *m.* 1. Action, well or ill performed. 2. Act, feat. 3. Event, incident. 4. Subject or matter discussed. 5. (Law) Point litigated. *De hecho*, In fact, actually, effectually. *En hecho de verdad*, In truth. *Hombre de hecho*, A man of his word. *Hecho y derecho*, Perfect, absolute, complete; right.

Hecho a la medida [ay'-cho ah lah may-dee'-dah], *a.* Tailor-made, custom-made, custom-built.

Hechura [ay-choo'-rah], *f.* 1. Act of performing or doing any thing. 2. The work done or made, and the price of making it. 3. Form, cut, shape, fashion make, figure or form given to a thing. 4. (Obs.) Effigy, statue. 5. Workmanship. 6. Creature, client, a person who owes his rise or fortune to another.

Hedentina [ay-den-tee'-nah], *f.* Stench, stink.

Heder [ay-derr'], *vn.* 1. To stink, to emit an offensive smell. 2. (Met.) To vex, to fatigue, to be intolerable.

Hederáceo, cea [ay-day-rah'-thay-o, ah], *a.* Hederaceous, relating to ivy.

Hediondamente [ay-de-on-dah-men'-tay], *adv.* Stinkingly.

Hediondez [ay-de-on-deth'], *f.* A strong stench or stink; thing stinking; fetidness.

Hediondo, da [ay-de-on'-do, dah], *a.* 1. Fetid, mephitical, stinking. 2. Irascible, pettish, unpleasant. *Este es un hediondo*, He is a stinkard.

Hediondo [ay-de-on'-do], *m.* (Bot.) *V.* GAMARZA.

Hedonismo [ay-do-nees'-mo], *m.* Hedonism, theory of living for pleasure.

Hedor [ay-dor'], *m.* Stench, stink, fetor.

Hedrar [ay-drar'], *va.* (Prov.) To dig a second time about the vines.

Hegemonía [ay-hay-mo-nee'-ah], *f.* Hegemony, pre-eminence, leadership (of Athens, Sparta, and Thebes).

Hégira [ay'-he-rah], *f.* Hegira, the Mohammedan epoch.

Hegueliano, na [hay-gay-le-ah'-no, nah] *a.* Hegelian, relating to the philosopher Hegel. (Note.—The h is sounded in this word.)

Hejotes, or **Ejotes** [ay-ho'-tes], *m. pl.* (Mex.) String-beans.

Helable [ay-lah'-blay], *a.* Congealable.

Helada [ay-lah'-dah], *f.* Frost; nip.

Heladería [ay-lah-day-ree'-ah], *f.* Ice-cream parlor.

Heladizo, za [ay-lah-dee'-tho, thah], *a.* Easily congealed.

Helado, da [ay-lah'-do, dah], *a. & pp.* of HELAR. 1. Gelid, frigid. 2. Frozen, congealed, frost-bitten, glacial, icy. 3. Frozen, chill in affection, indifferent. 4. Astonished, astounded.

Helado [ay-lah'-do], *m.* 1. Ice-cream, frozen custard. 2. In Andalusia, pink sugar.

Helamiento [ay-lah-me-en'-to], *m.* Congelation, frostiness.

Helar [ay-lar'], *va. & vn.* 1. To congeal, to ice, or to turn to ice. 2. To freeze, to congeal or be congealed with cold. 3. To freeze, to chill by the loss of power or motion. 4. To astound, to astonish, to amaze. 5. To dispirit, to discourage.—*vr.* 1. To freeze, to be congealed with cold, to be frozen. 2. To glaciate, to turn into ice. 3. To congeal, to concrete, to gather into a mass by cold; to be coagulated. 4. To grow motionless, to remain without action; to be stupefied; to be dispirited. *Se me heló la sangre* or *se me heló la sangre en las venas*, (Met.) My blood curdled.

Héle, Hétele, aquí [ay'-lay, ay'-tay-lay, ah-kee'], *int.* Behold it, look here. *V.* HE.

Helear [ay-lay-ar'], *va.* (Prov.) To point with the finger.

Helechal [ay-lay-chahl'], *m* A fernery.

Helecho [ay-lay'-cho], *m.* (Bot.) Fern. Filix. *Helecho macho*, Male fern. Tectaria filix mas. *Helecho hembra*, Female fern. Tectaria filix fœmina.

Helena [ay-lay'-nah], *f.* (Naut.) Castor and Pollux, a meteor, called also night-fire, or jack-with-a-lantern.

Helénico, ca [ay-lay'-ne-co, cah], *a.* Hellenic, Greek.

Helenismo [ay-lay-nees'-mo], *m.* 1. Hellenism, Greek idiom. 2. Imitation, or study of Greek civilization.

Helenista [ay-lay-nees'-tah], *m.* Hellenist, a name given to the Jews of Alexandria, who spoke Greek, or to the Greeks who embraced Judaism.

Helenístico, ca [ay-le-nees'-te-co, cah], *a.* 1. Hellenistic, pertaining to the Hellenists. 2. The Alexandrine Greek dialect, and particularly that of the Septuagint.

Helera [ay-lay'-rah], *f.* Pip, disease in fowls.

Helgado, da [el-gah'-do, dah], *a.* Jag-toothed.

Helgadura [el-gah-doo'-rah], *f.* Irregularity of the teeth.

Heliaco, ca [ay-le-ah'-co, cah], *a.* Heliacal, rising or setting of a star.

Helianto [ay-le-ahn'-to], *m.* (Bot.) Sun-flower.

Hélice [ay'-le-thay], *f.* 1. Propeller (of ships or planes). 2. (Ast.) Northern constellation of Ursa Major. 3. (Geom.) Helix, spiral.

Helicóptero [ay-le-cop'-tay-ro], *m.* Helicopter.

Helio [ay'-le-o], *m.* Helium.

Heliocéntrico, ca [ay-le-o-then'-tre-co, cah], *a.* (Ast.) Heliocentric, appearing from the centre of the sun.

Heliograbado [ay-le-o-grah-bah'-do], *m.* Photogravure.

Heliografía [ay-le-o-grah-fee'-ah], *f.* Blueprint.

Heliómetro [ay-le-oh'-may-tro], *m.* Heliometer.

Helioscopio [ay-le-os-co'-pe-o], *m.* Helioscope, telescope fitted for viewing the sun.

Helioterapia [ay-le-o-tay-rah'-pe-ah], *f.* Heliotherapy, treating of disease by sunbaths.

Heliotropio, Heliotropo [ay-le-o-tro'-pe-o], *m.* 1. (Bot.) Turnsol, heliotrope. Heliotropium. 2. Heliotrope, bloodstone, a precious stone. 3. Heliotrope, an instrument for reflecting solar light to an observer at a long distance.

Helmíntico, ca [el-meen'-te-co, cah], *a.* Helminthic: applied to medicines against worms.

Helota [ay-lo'-tah], *a.* & *n.* Helot, a bondman of Sparta.

Helote [ay-lo'-tay], *m.* (Mex.) Green maize.

Helvecio, cia [el-vay'-the-o, ah], *a.* Helvetian, Swiss.

Helvético, ca [el-vay'-te-co, cah], *a.* Helvetic, Swiss (used of persons).

Hemacrimo, ma [ay-mah-cree'-mo, mah], *a.* Cold-blooded.

Hemafobia [ay-mah-fo'-be-ah], *f.* Dread of blood.

Hematemesis [ay-mah-tay-may'-sis], *f.* Hematemesis, vomiting of blood.

Hemafóbico, ca [ay-mah-fo'-be-co, cah], *a.* Hæmaphobic, having an aversion to blood.

Hematina [ay-mah-tee'-nah], *f.* 1. Hematoxylin, the colouring matter of logwood. 2. Hematine, the colouring matter of the blood. **Hematino,** *m.* = Hematina.

Hematites [ay-mah-tee'-tes], *f.* Hematites, ore of iron.

Hematosis [ay-mah-to'-sis], *f.* Hæmatosis, conversion of venous blood into arterial.

Hematuria [ay-mah-too'-re-ah], *f.* Hematuria, blood in the urine.

Hembra [em'-brah], *f.* 1. Female of animals or plants. 2. Nut of a screw. 3. Eye of a hook. 4. *Hembra del timón,* Gudgeon of the rudder. 5. *V.* Mujer.

Hembrear [em-bray-ar'], *vn.* 1. To be inclined to females: applied to males. 2. To generate or produce females only, or chiefly.

Hembrilla [em-breel'-lyah], *f.* 1. A sort of wheat of very fine grain. 2. (Mech.) Any piece into which another is fitted. 3. (Prov.) Leather trace of horses for ploughing.

Hembruno, na [em-broo'-no, nah], *a.* (Obs.) Feminine, female, belonging to the female sex.

Hemicarpo [ay-me-car'-po], *m.* The half of a fruit divided naturally, as seen in the umbelliferæ.

Hemiciclo [ay-me-thee'-clo], *m.* *V.* Semicírculo.

Hemicilindrico,ca [ay-me-the-leen'-dre-co, cah], *a.* Semi-cylindrical.

Hemicránea [ay-me-crah'-nay-ah], *f.* Hemicrania, megrim, headache of one side of the head.

Hemina [ay-mee'-nah], *f.* 1. A measure containing the third part of a fanega. 2. Hemina, a Greek liquid measure.

Hemiope [ay-me-o'-pay], *a.* & *n.* Hemiope, one who is affected with hemiopia.

Hemiopía [ay-me-o-pee'-ah], *f.* Hemiopia, partial obliteration of the field of vision.

Hemiplejía [ay-me-play'-he-ah], *f.* (Med.) Hemiplegia, paralysis of one side of the body.

Hemíptero, ra [ay-meep'-tay-ro, rah], *a.* Hemipterous.—*m. pl.* The hemiptera; true bugs.

Hemisférico, ca [ay-mis-fay'-re-co, cah], *a.* Hemispheric, hemispherical, half-round.

Hemisferio [ay-mis-fay'-re-o], *m.* Hemisphere.

Hemisferoidal [ay-mis-fay-ro-e-dahl'], *a.* Hemispheroidal.

Hemistiquio [ay-mis-tee'-ke-o], *m.* Hemistich, half a verse.

Hemofilia [ay-mo-fee'-le-ah], *f.* (Med.) Hemophilia.

Hemoglobina [ay-mo-glo-bee'-nah], *f.* Hemoglobin.

Hemómetro [ay-mo'-may-tro], *m.* Hemometer, an instrument for measuring the tension of a blood-vessel.

Hemopatía [ay-mo-pah-tee'-ah], *f.* (Med.) Disease of the blood.

Hemoptisis [ay-mop-tee'-sis], *f.* Hæmoptysis; spitting of blood.

Hemorragia [ay-mor-rah'-he-ah], *f.* Hemorrhage, flux of blood.

Hemorrágico [ay-mor-rah'-he-co], *a.* Hemorrhagic, relating to bleeding.

Hemorroida [ay-mor-ro'-e-dah], *f.* 1. *V.* Hemorroide. 2. *V.* Hemorroo.

Hemorroide [ay-mor-ro'-e-day], *f.* (Med.) Piles, hemorrhoids, a disease.

Hemorroidal [ay-mor-ro-e-dahl'], *a.* Hemorrhoidal.

Hemostático, ca [ay-mos-tah'-te-co, cah], *a.* Hemostatic, serving to stanch bleeding.

Henal [ay-nahl'], *m.* Haymow.

Henar [ay-nar'], *m.* Meadow of hay.

Henchidor, ra [en-chee-dor', rah], *m.* & *f.* Filler, satiator, one who fills.

Henchidura [en-chee-doo'-rah], *f.* Repletion, act of filling.

Henchimiento [en-chee-me-en'-to], *m.* Abundance, repletion. *Henchimientos,* (Naut.) Filling timbers, used to fill up the vacant part of the ship's frame.

Henchir [en-cheer'], *va.* 1. To fill up. 2. To stuff or fill with mingled ingredients, to farce. 3. To sow discord, to produce mischief.—*vr.* To fill one's self. *Henchirse de lepra,* To be covered with the leprosy.

Hendedor, ra [en-day-dor', rah], *m.* & *f.* Divider, one who divides or splits any thing.

Hendedura [en-day-doo'-rah], *f.* Fissure, crack, rent, chink, cleft, cranny, crevice, cut.

Hender [en-derr'], *va.* 1. To chink, to break into apertures or chinks, to crack, to flaw, to break, to fissure, to cleave, to split. 2. To go through: to open a passage. 3. To break into pieces.—*vr.* To gape, to open in fissures or holes. (Lat. findĕre.)

Hendible [en-dee'-blay], *a.* Fissile, capable of being split.

Hendido, da [en-dee'-do, dah], *a.* & *pp.* of Hender. Crannied, full of chinks, cleft.

Hendiente [en-de-en'-tay], *m.* (Obs.) Down-stroke of a sword or edged tool.

Hendrija [en-dree'-hah], *f.* (Prov.) A small fissure or crack.

Henequén [ay-nay-ken'], *m.* (Mex.) 1. Maguey, American agave. 2. Fibre of this plant, applied to making hammocks, etc. There are two varieties, called "white" and "green."

Henil [ay-neel'], *m.* Hay-loft.

Heno [ay'-no], *m.* 1. Hay. 2. (Amer.) Moss, used for filling mattresses.

Heñir [ay-nyeer'], *va.* To knead dough. *Hay mucho que heñir,* (Coll.) There is much to do. *Tiene mucho que heñir,* (Coll.) It is very difficult.

Heparina [ay-pah-ree'-nah], *f.* Heparin.

Hepática [ay-pah'-te-cah], *f.* (Bot.) Liverwort. Anemone hepatica.

Hepático, ca [ay-pah'-te-co, cah], *a.* Hepatic, hepatical, belonging to the liver. (Gr., fr. ἧπαρ, liver.)

Hepatitis [ay-pah-tee'-tis], *f.* (Med.) Hepatitis, inflammation of the liver.

Hepatización [ay-pah-te-thah-the-on'], *f.* Hepatization.

Hepatizarse [ay-pah-te-thar'-say], *vr.* To become hepatized; to be transformed into a liver-like substance.

Heptacordo [ep-tah-cor'-do], *m* Heptachord, a musical instrument.

Heptagonal [ep-tah-go-nahl'], *a.* (Math.) Heptagonal. *V.* Heptágono, which is more used.

Heptágono, na [ep-tah'-go-no, nah], *a.* Heptagonal, having seven angles or sides.

Heptágono [ep-tah'-go-no], *m.* Heptagon, a figure of seven sides and angles.

Heptamerón [ep-tah-may-ron'], *m.* A literary work divided into seven parts (acts or volumes).

Heptámetro [ep-tah'-may-tro], *m.* Heptameter, verse of seven feet.

Heptanemo [ep-tah-nay'-mo], *a.* Having seven tentacles.

Heptangular [ep-tan-goo-lar'], *a.* Having seven angles.

Heptapétalo, la [ep-tah-pay'-tah-lo], *a.* Seven petaled, heptapetalous.

Heptarquía [ep-tar-kee'-ah], *f.* Heptarchy, a seven-fold government.

Heráldica [ay-rahl'-de-cah], *f.* Heraldry, the art and office of a herald.

Heráldico, ca [ay-rahl'-de-co, cah], *a.* Heraldic, relating to a herald.

Heraldo [ay-rahl'-do], *m.* Herald, an officer who registers genealogies and adjusts armorial ensigns.

Heraprica [ay-rah-pree'-cah], *f.* (Pharm.) Hierapicra, a bitter purgative medicine.

Herbáceo, cea [er-bah'-thay-o, ah], *a.* 1. Herby, having the nature of herbs. 2. Herbaceous, belonging to herbs.

Herbajar [er-bah-har'], *va.* To put flocks to graze, to pasture.—*vn.* To graze, to browse.

Herbaje [er-bah'-hay], *m.* 1. Herbage, grass, pasture, feeding. 2. Payment for pasturage. 3. (Prov.) Tribute to a new king for cattle. 4. Kind of ancient coarse cloth made of herbs.

Herbajero [er-bah-hay'-ro], *m.* One who rents meadows or pastures; one who lets pasturage.

Berbar [er-bar'], *va.* To dress skins with herbs.
Herbario [er-bah'-re-o], *m.* 1. *V.* Botánico. 2. Herbarium, a hortus siccus, collection of dried plants.
Herbario, ria [er-bah'-re-o, ah], *a.* Herbaceous, of or belonging to herbs.
Herbazal [er-bah-thahl'], *m.* A place herbaged or covered with herbs or grass; a pasture-ground for cattle.
Herbecer [er-bay-therr'], *vn.* To begin to grow: applied to herbs or grass.
Herbífero, ra [er-bee'-fay-ro, rah], *a.* Herbiferous, bearing herbs.
Herbívoro, ra [er-bee'-vo-ro, rah], *a.* Herbivorous, herbaceous, feeding on herbs.
Herbolado, da [er-bo-lah'-do, dah], *a.* Applied to things poisoned with the juice of plants, as daggers, darts.
Herbolario [er-bo-lah'-re-o], *m.* 1. Herbalist, herbarist, herbist, a person skilled in herbs. 2. Herbman, he who sells herbs. 3. A ridiculous, extravagant man. 4. (Obs.) *V.* Botánico.
Herborización [er-bo-re-thah-the-on'], *f.* Herborization, botanizing.
Herborizador, Herborizante [er-bo-re-thah-dor'], *m.* Herbalist, herbarist, one who herborizes.
Herborizar [er-bo-re-thar'], *vn.* To herborize, to go in search of herbs and plants.
Herboso, sa [er-bo'-so, sah], *a.* Herbous, herby, grassy, abounding in herbs.
Hercúleo, ea [er-coo'-lay-o, ah], *a.* 1. Herculean. 2. (Obs.) Epileptic.
Hércules [err'-coo-les], *m.* 1. A man of great strength. 2. (Ast.) A northern constellation. 3. Name of a gigantic beetle. 4. (Obs.) Epilepsy, a convulsive disease.
Heredad [ay-ray-dahd'], *f.* 1. Piece of ground which is cultivated and bears fruit. 2. (Obs.) Hereditament.
Heredado, da [ay-ray-dah'-do, dah], *a.* *V.* Hacendado. *Estar heredado,* To be in possession of one's family property.—*pp.* of Heredar.
Heredamiento [ay-ray-dah-me-en'-to], *m.* Landed property, lands, tenements.
Heredar [ay-ray-dar'], *va.* 1. To inherit, to heir. 2. To make over property to another, to be possessed by himself and his heirs or successors. 3. To possess the disposition or temperament of their fathers: applied to children.
Heredero, ra [ay-ray-day'-ro, rah], *m.* & *f.* 1. Heir, heiress, inheritor to any thing left by a deceased person. 2. Heir, one possessing the same propensities as his predecessors. 3. (Prov.) Vintager, one who gathers the vintage. *Heredero forzoso,* General heir. *Heredero presuntivo,* Heir-apparent.
Heredípeta [ay-ray-dee'-pay-tah], *com.* Legacy-seeker; one who artfully plots to procure legacies or inheritances. (Acad.)
Hereditario, ria [ay-ray-de-tah'-re-o, ah], *a.* Hereditary, derived from ancestors; entailed on a family.
Hereje [ay-ray'-hay], *com.* A heretic. *Cara de hereje,* Hideous or deformed aspect.
Herejía [ay-ray-hee'-ah], *f.* 1. Heresy. 2. Literary error, contrary to the principles of a science. 3. Injurious expression against any one.
Herejote, ta [ay-ray-ho'-tay, tah], *m.* & *f.* (Coll.) A great heretic.
Herén [ay-ren'], *m.* (Bot.) Vetch. *V.* Yero.
Herencia [ay-ren'-the-ah], *f.* Inheritance, hereditament, heritage, heirship, heirdom.
Heresiarca [ay-ray-se-ar'-cah], *m.* Heresiarch, a leader in heresy.
Heresiólogo [ay-ray-se-o'-lo-go], *m.* (Littl. us.) Writer on heresies.
Heretical [ay-ray-te-cahl'], *a.* Heretical, containing heresy.
Hereticar [ay-ray-te-car'], *va.* (Obs.) To believe and defend a heresy.
Herético, ca [ay-ray'-te-co, cah], *a.* Heretical.
Hergoma [er-go'-mah], *f.* An Irish linen made with threads of a spider's web.
Heria [ay'-re-ah], *f.* 1. Strolling vagrant. *V.* Hampa.
Herida [ay-ree'-dah], *f.* 1. Wound. 2. Affliction, any thing which afflicts the mind. 3. Injury, outrage, mischief. 4. Place where the game perches when pursued by the hawk.
Herido, da [ay-ree'-do, dah], *a.* & *pp.* of Herir. 1. Wounded. *Mal herido,* Dangerously wounded. 2. (Obs.) Bloody, cruel. *A grito herido,* With loud cries. *A pendón herido,* Urgently, with all speed. *Bienes heridos,* Encumbered inheritances.
Heridor, ra [ay-re-dor', rah], *m.* & *f.* Wounder, striker.
Herimiento [ay-re-me-en'-to], *m.* 1. Act of wounding. 2. Conjunction of vowels in a syllable; elision.
Herir [ay-reer'], *va.* 1. To wound, to break the continuity of any part of the body. 2. To wound, to hurt by violence, to cause either bodily or mental pain, to harm, to mischief. 3. To shine upon, to cast his beams upon, to irradiate: applied to the sun. 4. To knock, to dash together, to strike, to collide. 5. To strike, or to make an impression upon the mind or upon the senses, to affect, to touch, to move. 6. To play on a stringed instrument. 7. To offend, to pique, to irritate: applied generally to words and writings.—*vr.* *V.* Agraviarse. *Herir las letras,* To pronounce the letters. *Herir el casco de un navío,* (Naut.) To hull a ship, to wound her hull.
Hermafrodita, Hermafrodito [er-mah-fro-dee'-tah, to], *m.* Hermaphrodite, androgyne, an animal or plant uniting two sexes.
Hermana [er-mah'-nah], *f.* 1. Sister. 2. Sister-in-law. *V.* Hermano.
Hermanable [er-mah-nah'-blay], *a.* Fraternal, brotherly.
Hermanablemente [er-mah-nah-blay-men'-tay], *adv.* Fraternally.
Hermanal [er-mah-nahl'], *a.* Brotherly, belonging to a brother. (Obs.)
Hermanar [er-mah-nar'], *va.* 1. To match, to suit, to proportion, to fellow, to pair, to harmonize. 2. To own for a brother.—*vn.* To fraternize, to join, to unite.—*vr.* To love one another as brothers.
Hermanastro, tra [er-mah-nahs'-tro, trah], *m.* & *f.* Step-brother, step-sister.
Hermanazgo [er-mah-nath'-go], *m.* Fraternity, brotherhood.
Hermandad [er-man-dahd'], *f.* 1. Fraternity, the state or quality of a brother. 2. Conformity, resemblance. 3. Amity, friendship. 4. Brotherhood, confraternity, an association of men; fraternity. *La santa hermandad,* A kind of court of justice, which had the right of trying and punishing without appeal persons who had committed offences or misdemeanours in fields and roads.
Hermanear [er-mah-nay-ar'], *va.* To treat as a brother.
Hermanita [er-mah-nee'-tah], *f. dim.* A little sister.
Hermanito [er-mah-nee'-to], *m. dim.* A little brother.
Hermano, na [er-mah'-no, nah], *a.* Matched, suitable, having resemblance.
Hermano [er-mah'-no], *m.* 1. Brother, one born of the same parents with another. 2. Brother-in-law. 3. Similarity; as among the members of a religious community. *Hermano carnal,* Brother by the same father and mother. *Hermano consanguíneo,* A brother having the same father, but not the same mother. *Hermano uterino,* A brother of the same mother, but not of the same father. *Hermano de leche,* Foster-brother. *Hermano de trabajo,* (Prov.) *V.* Ganapán. *Hermano político,* Brother-in-law. *Medio hermano,* Half-brother.—*pl.* 1. Members of the same religious confraternity. 2. Lay-brothers of a religious order.
Hermanuco [er-mah-noo'-co], *m.* Name given in contempt to lay-brothers of some religious orders.
Herméticamente [er-may'-te-cah-men-tay], *adv.* Hermetically.
Hermético, ca [er-may'-te-co, cah], *a.* Hermetical, chemical.
Hermodátiles [er-mo-dah'-te-les], *m. pl.* Hermodactyl, a bulbous root formerly used as a cathartic. Colchicum variegatum, probably.
Hermosamente [er-mo-sah-men'-tay], *adv.* Beautifully, handsomely, lovely; perfectly, properly.
Hermoseador, ra [er-mo-say-ah-dor', rah], *m.* & *f.* Beautifier.
Hermosear [er-mo-say-ar'], *va.* 1. To beautify, to embellish, to adorn. 2. To glamorize, to add glamor or luster.
Hermoso, sa [er-mo'-so, sah], *a.* Beautiful, handsome, graceful, lovely, comely, neat, goodly, fine, beauteous, fair.
Hermosura [er-mo-soo'-rah], *f.* 1. Beauty, that assemblage of graces which pleases the eye or the ear. 2. Handsomeness, goodliness, fineness, fairness, freshness. 3. Symmetry, agreement of one part with another. 4. Beauty, a beautiful person.
Hernia [ayr'-ne-ah], *f.* Hernia, rupture.
Herniario [er-ne-ah'-re-o], *a.* Hernial, relating to hernia. *Saco herniario,* Hernial sac.
Hernista [er-nees'-tah], *m.* Surgeon who applies himself to the cure of ruptures.
Herodiano, na [ay-ro-de-ah'-no, nah], *a.* Herodian, belonging to Herod. *Herodianos,* Herodians, a Jewish sect.
Héroe [ay'-ro-ay], *m.* 1. Hero, a man eminent for bravery and valour. 2. Hero, the principal person in a poem. 3. Among the ancient pagans, one whom they believed to be born of a god or goddess and a human being.
Heroicamente [ay-ro-e-cah-men'-tay], *adv.* Heroically.
Heroicidad [ay-ro-e-the-dahd'], *f.* Quality or character which constitutes an heroic action. *V.* Heroísmo.
Heroico, ca [ay-ro'-e-co, cah], *a.* 1. Heroic, eminent for bravery. 2. Heroical, befitting a hero. 3. Reciting the acts of heroes. *A la heroica,* In the fashion of heroic times.
Heroína [ay-ro-ee'-nah], *f.* A heroine.
Heroína [ay-ro-ee'-nah], *f.* Heroin, a narcotic.
Heroísmo [ay-ro-ees'-mo], *m.* Heroism.
Herpe [err'-pay], *m.* or *f.* Herpes, tetter, a cutaneous disease: commonly used in the plural.
Herpético, ca [er-pay'-te-co, cah], *a.* Herpetic.
Herpil [er-peel'], *m.* Sack of esparto netting with wide meshes, made for carrying straw, melons, etc. (Acad.)

Herrada [er-rah'-dah], *f.* A pail.

Herrada [er-rah'-dah], *a.* Applied to water in which red-hot iron has been cooled.

Herradero [er-rah-day'-ro], *m.* 1. Place destined for marking cattle with a hot iron. 2. Marking cattle with a hot iron.

Herrador [er-rah-dor'], *m.* Farrier, a shoer of horses.

Herradura [er-rah-doo'-rah], *f.* 1. Shoe: speaking of animals. *Herradura de caballo*, Horse-shoe. 2. Collar or necklace in the form of a horseshoe. 3. The horse-shoe shape commonly given to the galleries of a theatre, or like audience-chamber.

Herraj [er-rah'], *m.* Stones of olives after extracting the oil. *V.* Errax.

Herraje [er-rah'-hay], *m.* 1. Ironwork, pieces of iron used for ornament and strength. *Herraje de un navío*, Ironwork of a ship. 2. Horse-shoe. 3. *V.* Herraj.

Herramental [er-rah-men-tahl'], *m.* & *a.* Bag with instruments for shoeing horses.

Herramienta [er-rah-me-en'-tah], *f.* 1. Set of tools or instruments. 2. Ironwork. 3. Horns of a beast. 4. (Coll.) Teeth, grinders.

Herrar [er-rar'], *va.* 1. To garnish with iron. 2. To shoe horses. 3. To brand cattle with a hot iron.

Herrén [er-ren'], *m.* 1. Maslin, mixed corn for feeding horses. 2. *V.* Herrenal.

Herrenal, or **Herreñal** [er-ray-nahl', er-ray-nyahl'], *m.* Piece of ground in which meslin is sown.

Herrería [er-ray-ree'-ah], *f.* 1. Ironworks, where iron is manufactured and moulded into pigs or bars. 2. Forge. 3. Clamour, confused noise.

Herrerico, Herrerillo [er-ray-ree'-co, eel'-lyo], *m.* Small bird.

Herrero [er-ray'-ro], *m.* Smith, one who forges iron.

Herrerón [er-ray-rone'], *m.* A bad smith.

Herreruelo [er-ray-roo-ay'-lo], *m.* 1. (Orn.) Wagtail, a bird whose note resembles the sound of hammering and betokens rain. Motacilla provincialis, *L.* 2. *V.* Ferreruelo. 3. (Dim.) *V.* Herrerico.

Herrete [er-ray'-tay], *m.* Tag, point of metal at the end of a cord.

Herretear [er-ray-tay-ar'], *va.* To tag a cord, string, or ribbon.

Herretero, ra [er-ray-tay'-ro, rah], *m.* & *f.* Tag-maker.

Herrezuelo [er-ray-thoo-ay'-lo], *m.* Light piece of iron.

Herrial [er-re-ahl'], *a.* Applied to a kind of large black grapes, and to the vines which bear them.

Herrín [er-reen'], *m.* Rust of iron.

Herrón [er-rone'], *m.* 1. A ring, in the middle of which is a hole, which boys pitch at a stake; a quoit. 2. A washer.

Herronada [er-ro-nah'-dah], *f.* 1. A violent blow or stroke. 2. (Met.) Blow with a bird's beak.

Herrugiento, ta [er-roo-he-en'-to, tah], *a.* Rusty.

Herrumbre [er-room'-bray], *f.* Rust of iron; irony taste.

Herrumbroso, sa [er-room-bro'-so, sah], *a.* 1. Rusty, drossy, scaly. 2. Participating of the qualities of iron.

Herventar [er-ven-tar'], *va.* To boil any thing.

Hervidero [er-ve-day'-ro], *m.* 1. Ebullition, the agitation of a boiling fluid. 2. Kind of water-clock or small spring, whence water bubbles out. 3. Rattling in the throat. 4. Multitude, great quantity or number.

Hervir [er-veer'], *vn.* 1. To boil. 2. (Met.) To swarm with vermin, to be crowded with people. 3. To be fervent, vehement. *Hervir el garbanzuelo*, To be too solicitous and clamorous.

Hervor [er-vor'], *m.* 1. Ebullition, the agitation of boiling fluids. 2. Fervour, heat, vigour; fret. 3. (Met.) Noise and movement of waters. *Alzar* or *levantar el hervor*, To begin to boil. 4. *Hervor de sangre*, Rash. *V.* Sarpullido.

Hervoroso, sa [er-vo-ro'-so, sah], *a.* *V.* Fogoso.

Hesitación [ay-se-tah-the-on'], *f.* (Littl. us.) Hesitation, doubt, perplexity, hesitancy.

Hesitar [ay-se-tar'], *vn.* (Obs.) To hesitate, to doubt.

Hespéride, Hespérido, da [es-pay'-re-day, es-pay'-re-do, dah], *a.* 1. Relating to the Pleiades. 2. (Poet.) Western.

Hespérides [es-pay'-re-des], *f. pl.* *V.* Pléyades.

Héspero [ays'-pay-ro], *m.* The planet Venus, as evening star.

Heteróclito, ta [ay-tay-ro'-cle-to, tah], *a.* 1. (Gram.) Heteroclite, inflected irregularly. 2. Irregular, abnormal.

Heterodino, na [ay-tay-ro-dee'-no, nah], *a.* Heterodyne.

Heterodoxia [ay-tay-ro-doc'-se-ah], *f.* Heterodoxy, misbelief.

Heterodoxo, xa [ay-tay-ro-doc'-so, sah], *a.* Heterodox, not orthodox.

Heterodromo [ay-tay-ro-dro'-mo], *m.* A lever whose fulcrum is between the power and the weight.

Heterogamia [ay-tay-ro-gah'-me-ah], *f.* Heterogamy.

Heterógamo, mah [ay-tay-ro'-gah-mo, mah], *a.* Heterogamous, bearing flowers of two sexual kinds.

Heterogeneidad [ay-tay-ro-hay-nay-e-dahd'], *f.* Heterogeneousness, heterogeneity.

Heterogéneo, nea [ay-tay-ro-hay'-nay-o, ah], *a.* Heterogeneous, dissimilar in nature, heterogene, heterogeneal.

Heteromorfo, fa [ay-tay-ro-mor'-fo, fah], *a.* Heteromorphic, or -morphous; of diverse form in several of its parts.

Heterónomo, ma [ay-tay-ro'-no-mo, mah], *a.* Heteronymous, differing from the common type.

Heterópsido, da [ay-tay-rop'-se-do, dah], *a.* (Metals) in a state of alkaline earth.

Hética, Hetiquez [ay'-te-cah, ay-te-keth'], *f.* Phthisis, consumption, hectic.

Hético, ca [ay'-te-co, cah], *a.* Hectic, hectical, affected with a hectic fever; languid: used also as a substantive, applied to a person affected with a hectic fever, and to a person or animal that is very thin.

Heu [ay'-oo], *m.* Sloop, with one sail, of 300 tons, used in northern seas.

Hexacordo [ec-sah-cor'-do], *m.* (Mus.) Hexachord.

Hexaedro [ec-sah-ay'-dro], *m.* Hexahedron, a cube.

Hexágono [ec-sah'-go-no], *m.* Hexagon, a figure of six sides.

Hexágono, na [ec-sah'-go-no, nah], *a.* Hexagonal, having six sides.

Hexámetro [ec-sah'-may-tro], *m.* Hexameter, a verse of six feet.

Hexápeda, *f.* *V.* Toesa.

Hexástilo [ec-sahs'-te-lo], *m.* (Arch.) Hexastyle, a building with six columns in front.

Hez [eth], *f.* 1. Scum, lee, the dregs of liquors. 2. Dross of metals. 3. Grains of malt. *La hez del pueblo*, The scum of the people. *Heces*, Fæces, excrements.

Hi, hi, hi [hee, hee, hee], *int.* Expression of merriment or laughter.

Hi [ee'], *adv.* (Obs.) *V.* Allí.

Hi [e], *m.* (Obs.) Used for *hijo*, son, in *Hidalgo*, and the vulgar phrases, *Hi de puta*, *Hi de perro*.

Hiadas, Hiades [ee'-ah-das, ee'-ah-des], *f. pl.* *V.* Pléyades.

Hialino, na [e-ah-lee'-no, nah], *a.* Hyaline, transparent.

Hialitis [e-ah-lee'-tis], *f.* Hyalitis, inflammation of the vitreous body.

Hialóideo, dea [e-ah-lo'-e-day-o, ah], *a.* Vitreous, glass-like.

Hialoides [e-ah-lo'-e-des], *f.* Hyaloid membrane, inclosing the vitreous body of the eye.

Hialosomo, ma [e-ah-lo-so'-mo, mah], *a.* (Zool.) Transparent in body; hyaline.

Hialurgia [e-ah-loor'-hee-ah], *f.* The art of making glass.

Hialúrgico, ca [e-ah-loor'-he-co, cah], *a.* Glass-working, belonging to glass-making.

Hiante [e-ahn'-tay], *a.* Applied to a verse with a hiatus.

Hiato [e-ah'-to], *m.* Hiatus, pause or cacophony, by the succession of an initial to a final vowel.

Hibernal, Hibernizo, za [e-ber-nahl', e-ber-nee'-tho, thah], *a.* Hibernal, wintry.

Hibernar [e-ber-nar'], *vn.* (Prov.) To winter, to live in a place during winter.

Hibernés, sa [e-ber-nays', sah], *a.* Hibernian, Irish.

Hibierno [e-be-err'-no], *m.* Winter. *V.* Invierno.

Hibisco [e-bees'-co], *m.* (Bot.) Syrian mallow. Hibiscus syriacus, *L.*

Hibleo, blea [e-blay'-o, ah], *a.* (Poet.) Abundant; pleasant; belonging to Mount Hybla.

Híbrido, da [ee'-bre-do, dah], *m.* & *f.* Hybridous animal, as a mule; hybridous words.—*a.* Hybridous, hybrid.

Hibridación [e-bre-dah-the-on'], *f.* Hybridization, hybridism.

Hicocervo [e-co-therr'-vo], *m.* Fabulous animal; chimera, a wild fancy.

Hidalgamente [e-dal-gah-men'-tay], *adv.* Nobly, in a gentlemanlike manner.

Hidalgarse [e-dal-gar'-say], *vr.* (Coll.) To assume the nobleman, to affect the gentleman.

Hidalgo, ga [e-dahl'-go, gah], *a.* Noble, illustrious, excellent, exalted.

Hidalgo, ga [e-dahl'-go, gah], *m.* & *f.* Hidalgo, a noble man or woman, a person of noble descent, one who is ennobled. *Hidalgo de bragueta*, One who enjoys the privileges of nobility from being the father of seven sons without an intervening female child. *Hidalgo de gotera*, He who enjoys the rights of nobility in one place or town only.

Hidalgón, na, Hidalgote, ta [e-dal-gone', nah], *m.* & *f. aug.* An old noble man or woman, proud of the rights and privileges of their class.

Hidalguejo, ja, Hidalguete, ta, Hidalguillo, lla [e-dal-gay'-ho, hah], *m.* & *f. dim.* A petty country squire, a poor gentleman or lady.

Hidalguía [e-dal-gee'-ah], *f.* 1. Nobility, the rights and privileges of noblemen. 2. Nobleness of mind, liberality of sentiments.

Hidátide [e-dah'-te-day], *f.* 1. Hydatid, a cyst containing a larval tapeworm. 2. (Min.) A stone esteemed as precious by the ancients: used also as an adjective.

Hidatidiforme [e-da-te-de-for'-may], *a.* Hydatidiform, bladder-shaped.

Hidra [ee'-drah], *f.* 1. Hydra, a fabulous monster. 2. A poisonous serpent. 3. (Met.) Seditions, plots. 4. Hydra, a fresh-water polyp.
Hidragogo [e-drah-go'-go], *m.* & *a.* (Med.) Hydragogue.
Hidrargirido, da [e-drar-hee'-re-do, dah], *a.* Resembling mercury.
Hidrargirio [e-drar-hee'-re-o], *m.* An amalgam of mercury with another metal.
Hidrárgiro [e-drar'-he-ro], *m.* Ancient name of mercury (hydrargyrum); entering into composition.
Hidratado, da [e-drah-tah'-do, dah], *a.* Hydrate(d), containing water in composition.
Hidratar [e-drah-tar'], *va.* To hydrate, to combine with water.
Hidrato [e-drah'-to], *m.* Hydrate, a compound with water or hydrogen peroxide.
Hydráulica [e-drah'-oo-le-cah], *f.* Hydraulics, a branch of hydrodynamics.
Hidráulico, ca [e-drah'-oo-le-co, cah], *a.* Hydraulical, hydraulic.
Hidráulico [e-drah'-oo-le-co], *m.* Professor of hydraulics.
Hidrazina [e-drah-thee'-nah], *f.* Hydrazine (fuel).
Hidremia [ey-dray'-me-ah], *f.* Hydræmia, an excess of water in the blood.
Hidria [ee'-dre-ah], *f.* Jar or pitcher for water.
Hidro [ee'-dro], *m.* The combining form of the Greek word ὕδωρ, water.
Hidroavión [e-dro-ah-ve-on'], *m.* Hydroplane.
Hidrocarburo [e-dro-car-boo'-ro], *m.* (Chem.) Hydrocarbon.
Hidrocéfalo [e-dro-thay'-fah-lo], *m.* (Med.) Hydrocephalus, dropsy in the head.
Hidrocerámico, ca [e-dro-thay-rah'-me-co, cah], *a.* Hydroceramic, porous.
Hidroclórico, ca [e-dro-clo'-re-co, cah], *a.* Hydrochloric.
Hidrodinámica [e-dro-de-nah'-me-cah], *f.* Hydrodynamics, science which relates to the motion of fluids.
Hidroeléctrico, ca [e-dro-ay-lec'-tre-co, cah], *a.* Hydroelectric.
Hidrofilacio [e-dro-fe-lah'-the-o], *m.* Great cavern full of water.
Hidrófilo, la [e-dro'-fe-lo, lah], *a.* Water-loving.
Hidrofobia [e-dro-fo'-be-ah], *f.* Hydrophobia, a disease; rabies.
Hidrófobo [e-dro'-fo-bo], *m.* Person suffering hydrophobia.
Hidrófugo, ga [e-dro'-foo-go, gah], *a.* (Zool.) Hydrofuge, shedding water.
Hidrogenar [e-dro-hay-nar'], *va.* To hydrogenate.
Hidrógeno [e-dro'-hay-no], *m.* (Chem.) Hydrogen. *Hidrógeno líquido,* Liquid hydrogen.
Hidrogogia [e-dro-go-hee'-ah], *f.* The art or science of taking the level of water.
Hidrografía [e-dro-grah-fee'-ah], *f.* Hydrography, the description of the watery part of the globe.
Hidrográfico, ca [e-dro-grah'-fe-co, cah], *a.* Hydrographical.
Hidrógrafo [e-dro'-grah-fo], *m.* Hydrographer.
Hidrólisis [e-dro'-le-sis], *f.* Hydrolisis.
Hidrolizar [e-dro-le-thar'], *va.* To hydrolize.
Hidrología [e-dro-lo-hee'-ah], *f.* Hydrology, description of the nature and properties of water.
Hidromático, ca [e-dro-mah'-te-co, cah], *a.* Hydromatic.
Hidromel, Hidromiel [e-dro-mel', me-el'], *m.* Hydromel, mead, metheglin.
Hidrómetra [e-dro'-may-trah], *m.* Professor of hydrometry.
Hidrometría [e-dro-may-tree'-ah], *f.* Hydrometry.
Hidrómetro [e-dro'-may-tro], *m.* Hydrometer, instrument for measuring the weight of fluids.
Hidrónica [e-dro'-ne-cah], *f.* Hydronics.
Hidrópata [e-dro'-pah-tah], *m.* Hydropath, follower of hydropathy.
Hidropatía [e-dro-pah-tee'-ah], *f.* Hydropathy, hydrotherapy.
Hidropático, ca [e-dro-pah'-te-co, cah], *a.* Hydropathic.
Hidropesía [e-dro-pay-see'-ah], *f.* Dropsy.
Hidrópico, ca [e-dro'-pe-co, cah], *a.* Hydropic, hydropical, dropsical.
Hidroplano [e-dro-plah'-no], *f.* Hydroplane.
Hidrópota [e-dro'-po-tah], *a.* & *n.* Who drinks water only: a water-drinker.
Hidróscopo [e-dros'-co-po], *m.* One who detects the presence of water under ground.
Hidrosita [e-dro-see'-tah], *f.* A geode of chalcedony which contains water.
Hidrostática [e-dros-tah'-te-cah], *f.* Hydrostatics.
Hidrostáticamente, *adv.* Hydrostatically.
Hidrostático, ca [e-dros-tah'-te-co, cah], *a.* Hydrostatical.
Hidrosulfúrico, ca [e-dro-sool-foo'-re-co, cah], *a.* Hydrosulphuric, or sulphhydric.
Hidrotecnia [e-dro-tec'-ne-ah], *f.* Hydraulics, hydraulic engineering.
Hidroterapia [e-dro-tay-rah'-pe-ah], *f.* Hydrotherapeutics.
Hidrotórax [e-dro-to'-rax], *f.* Hydrothorax, dropsy of the chest.
Hiedra [e-ay'-drah], *f.* 1. (Bot.) Ivy. Hedera helix. 2. (Local) Poison-vine. *Hiedra terrestre,* Ground ivy. Nepeta glechoma.
(*Yo hiedro, yo hiedre,* from *Hedrar.* V. Acrecentar.)
Hiel [e-el'], *f.* 1. Gall, bile, an animal juice. 2. (Met.) Bitterness, asperity. *Echar la hiel,* To labour excessively. *No tener hiel,* To be meek, simple, and gentle. *Estar hecho de hieles,* To be as bitter as gall. *Hieles,* Calamities, misfortunes, toils. *Dar a beber hieles,* To make one live a most wretched life.
Hiel de la tierra [e-el' day lah te-ay'-rah], *f.* 1. (Bot.) Common fumitory or earth-smoke. Fumaria officinalis. 2. Common erythræa centaurium.
Hielo [e-ay'-lo], *m.* 1. Ice. 2. Frost. 3. Congealment. *Hielo seco,* Dry ice. 4. (fig.) Coolness, indifference.
Hiena [e-ay'-nah], *f.* Hyena, a fierce animal. Canis hyena.
(*Yo hiero, él hirió, hiriera,* from *Herir.* V. Asentir.)
Hierarca [e-ay-rar'-cah], *m.* Hierarch, among the Greeks, the chief of a sacred order.
Hierático, ca [e-ay-rah'-te-co, cah], *a.* Hieratic, sacerdotal.
Hierba [e-err'-bah], *f.* 1. Herb, a plant not possessing a woody stem, but dying down to the ground after flowering. 2. Green food for cattle, herbage, grass (chiefly in plural). 3. Flaw in the emerald which tarnishes its lustre.—*pl.* 1. Poison given in food; a poisonous plant. 2. Among the clergy, greens, garden-stuff. 3. Grass, pasturage. *Otras hierbas* (humorous), And so forth. *Crecer como la mala hierba,* To grow like weeds. Modern spelling of Yerba, q. v. (Lat. herba.)
Hierbabuena, *f.* (Acad.) Peppermint, mint. *V.* Yerbabuena.
Hierogenia [e-ay-ro-hay'-ne-ah], *f.* Origin of different religions and the science which treats of such origin.
Hieroglífico, ca [e-ay-ro-glee'-fe-co, cah], *a.* Hieroglyphic, hieroglyphical, emblematical.—*m.* (Acad.) *V.* Jeroglífico.
Hierología [e-ay-ro-lo'-he-ah], *f.* (Littl. us.) Hierology, discourse on sacred things.
Hieromancia [e-ay-ro-mahn'-the-ah], *f.* (Littl. us.) Hieromancy, divination by sacrifices.
Hieroscopia [e-ay-ros-co'-pe-ah], *f.* *V.* Aruspicina.
Hierro [e-er'-ro], *m.* 1. Iron, a malleable metal. 2. Any iron tool. 3. Brand, a mark made by burning with a hot iron. 4. An iron instrument to wound with. *Hierro de la grímpola,* (Naut.) Spindle of the vane. *Hierro albo,* Red-hot iron. *Hierro colado* or *fundido,* Cast-iron. *Hierro forjado,* Forged iron. *Hierro de fragua,* Wrought iron. *Hierro cuadrillado,* Square iron. *Hierro varilla,* Round iron. *Es de hierro,* He is indefatigable, or as hardy as steel. *Machacar* or *majar en hierro frío,* To labour in vain. *Tienda de hierro,* An ironmonger's shop. *Hierros,* Irons, fetters; jail. *Le echaron hierros,* They put him in irons. *El me ha puesto un hierro* or *fierro,* (Met.) He has done me a favour or benefit, by which I am bound to be his slave.
(*Yo hierro, yo hierre,* from *Herrar.* V. Acrecentar.)
(*Yo hiervo, él hirvió, hirviera;* from *Hervir.* V. Asentir.)
Hietómetro [e-ay-to'-may-tro], *m.* Hyetometer, rain-gauge, or pluviometer.
Higa [ee'-gah], *f.* 1. Amulet, charm, hung about the neck for preventing or curing disease. 2. Method of shutting the hand. 3. Ridicule, derision. *Dar higa la escopeta,* To hang fire. *Dar higas,* To despise a thing. *No dar por una cosa dos higas,* Not to value a thing at all.
Higadillo [e-gah-deel'-lyo], *m. dim.* A small liver; the liver of birds, fishes, and other small animals.
Hígado [ee'-gah-do], *m.* 1. Liver, one of the entrails. 2. (Met. Coll.) Courage, valour, bravery. *Tener malos hígados,* 1. To be white-livered, to be ill-disposed. 2. (Met.) To hate. *Echar los hígados,* To be very tired or fatigued. *Echar los hígados por alguna cosa,* (Coll.) To desire anxiously. *Malos hígados,* (Coll.) Ill-will. *Hasta los hígados,* (Coll.) To the heart. *Lo que es bueno para el hígado, es malo para el bazo,* What is one man's meat is another man's poison.
Higate [e-gah'-tay], *m.* Pottage, formerly made of figs, pork, and fowl, boiled together, and seasoned with sugar, ginger, cinnamon, pimento, and other spices.
Higiene [e-he-ay'-nay], *f.* (Med.) Hygiene.
Higiénicamente [e-he-ay'-ne-cah-men-tay], *adv.* Hygienically.
Higiénico, ca [e-he-ay'-ne-co, cah], *a.* Hygienic.
Higo [ee'-go], *m.* 1. Fig, the fruit of the fig-tree. *Higo chumbo* or *de pala,* Fruit of the nopal or Indian fig-tree. *Pan de higos,* Cake made of figs. 2. A kind of piles. *Higo maduro,* (Orn.) Green woodpecker.
Higrometría [e-gro-may-tree'-ah], *m.* Hygrometry.
Higrométrico, ca [e-gro-may'-tre-co, cah], *a.* Hygrometric, measuring moisture.
Higrómetro [e-gro'-may-tro], *m.* Hy-

grometer, an instrument for measuring the degrees of moisture.

Higroscopia [e-gros-co'-pe-ah], *f.* Hygroscopy, hygrometry.

Higroscopio [e-gros-co'-pe-o], *m.* Hygroscope, a device for indicating the humidity of the air.

Higuera [e-gay'-rah], *f.* (Bot.) Fig-tree. Ficus carica. *Higuera infernal*, Castor-oil plant. Ricinus communis. *Higuera de Indias* or *de las Indias*, Indian fig-tree, prickly-pear cactus. Opuntia.

Higueral [e-gay-rahl'], *m.* Plantation of fig-trees.

Higuerón [e-gay-rone'], *m.* Large tree in America.

Higuito [e-gee'-to], *m. dim.* A small fig.

Hija [ee'-hah], *f.* 1. Daughter. 2. Daughter-in-law. *V.* Hijo, ja.

Hijar [e-har'], *m.* *V.* Ijar.

Hijastro, tra [e-hahs'-tro, trah], *m.* & *f.* Step-child.

Hijezna [e-heth'-nah], *m.* The young of any bird.

Hijito, ita [e-hee'-to, tah], *m.* & *f. dim.* Little child, little dear.

Hijo [ee'-ho], *m.* 1. Son. 2. Son-in-law.

Hijo, ja [ee'-ho, hah], *m.* & *f.* 1. Child. 2. Young of all animals. 3. Son or native of a place. 4. Child, son, daughter, any thing which is the product or effect of another. *Hijo de familia*, 1. A minor. 2. A son of noble parents. 5. Bud or root of the horns of animals. *Hijo del agua*, A good sailor, a good swimmer. *Hijo de la piedra*, Foundling. *Hijo de leche*, Foster-child. *Hijo bastardo*, *hijo de ganancia* or *hijo de su madre*, (Coll.) Bastard.

Hijodalgo, Hijadalgo [e-ho-dahl'-go, e-hah-dahl'-go], *m.* & *f.* *V.* Hidalgo.

Hijuela [e-hoo-ay'-lah], *f.* 1. Piece of cloth or linen joined to another which is too short or narrow. 2. A small mattress, put between others, to make the bed even. 3. Pall, a square bit of linen or pasteboard put over the chalice. 4. A small drain for drawing off water from an estate. 5. Schedule or inventory delivered in Spain to parties entitled in distribution to the estate of a person deceased, containing an exact account of their distributive share. 6. An inventory, a catalogue of the articles which belong to the estate of a deceased person. 7. Cross-road. 8. Postman who delivers letters from the office. 9. Palm-seed. 10. (Prov. Andal.) Fascine of wood. 11. (Prov. Murcia) Cord made of the gut of silk-worms.

Hijuelo, la [e-hoo-ay'-lo, lah], *m.* & *f. dim.* 1. A young child. 2. (Bot.) Sucker.

Hila [ee'-lah], *f.* 1. Row, line. *V.* Hilera. 2. Thin gut. 3. Act of spinning. 4. Lint to lay on sores. 5. Small trench for dividing the water destined for the irrigation of different pieces of ground. *A la hila*, (Prov.) In a row or line, one after another.

Hilacha [e-lah'-chah], *f.* Filament or thread ravelled out of cloth.

Hilachoso, sa [e-lah-cho'-so, sah], *a.* Filamentous.

Hilada [e-lah'-dah], *f.* 1. Row or line of bricks or stones in a building. 2. *V.* Hilera.

Hiladillo [e-lah-deel'-lyo], *m.* 1. Ferret silk. 2. Narrow ribbon or tape.

Hilado [e-lah'-do], *m.* Spun flax, hemp, wool, silk, or cotton.—*Hilado, da, pp.* of Hilar.

Hilador, ra [e-lah-dor', rah], *m.* & *f.* Spinner, spinster.

Hilandera [e-lan-day'-rah], *f.* Spinster, woman who spins.

Hilandería [e-lan-day-ree'-ah], *f.* Place where hemp is spun.

Hilandero [e-lan-day'-ro], *m.* 1. Spinner. 2. Spinning-room, a rope-walk.

Hilanderilla [e-lan-day-reel'-lyah], *f. dim.* A little spinster.

Hilanza [e-lahn'-thah], *f.* (Prov.) Thread, line, mode of spinning.

Hilar [e-lar'], *va.* 1. To spin, to draw silk, cotton, etc., into thread. 2. To argue, to discuss. *Hilar delgado*, To handle a subject in too subtile and nice a manner. 3. To spin a cocoon: applied to silk-worms.

Hilaracha [e-lah-rah'-chah], *f.* Filament. *V.* Hilacha.

Hilarante [e-lah-rahn'-tay], *a.* Nitrous oxide gas; so-called laughing-gas.

Hilaridad [e-lah-re-dahd'], *f.* Hilarity, laughter, jollity.

Hilaza [e-lah'-thah], *f.* 1. Any thing spun or drawn out into thread. *V.* Hilado. 2. Yarn. *Hilazas*, Filaments of plants.

Hilera [e-lay'-rah], *f.* 1. Row, line. 2. (Mech.) Wiredrawer. 3. Fine thread. 4. (Mil.) File, single file. 5. (Arch.) Ridgepole. 6. (Zool.) Spinneret. 7. (Mas.) Course. 8. Fine yarn.

Hilero [e-lay'-ro], *m.* 1. Sign of currents in the sea. 2. Thread-seller.

Hilete [e-lay'-tay], *m. dim.* of Hilo.

Hilo [ee'-lo], *m.* 1. Thread, a small line of cotton, silk, etc. 2. Wire, metal drawn into threads. 3. A slender thread, formed by liquids falling in drops. 4. (Met.) Continuation, series. 5. Fine thread of spiders or silk-worms. 6. V. Filo. *Hilo a hilo*, Drop by drop. *Hilo de palomar*, or *hilo bramante*, Pack-thread. *Hilo acarreto*, Twine. *Hilo de velas*, Sail-maker's twine. *Hilo de zapatero*, Shoemaker's thread. *Hilo de oro* or *de plata*, Gold or silver thread. *Hilo para sastre*, Tailors' thread. *Hilo en carreteles*, Thread in spools. *Hilo en ovillos*. Thread in balls. *Hilo de torzal* or *de pelas*, Cotton yarn. *Hilo de perlas*, String of pearls. *Hilo de una corriente*, (Naut.) Direction of a current. *A hilo*, Successively, one after another. *Ir al hilo del mundo*, To follow the opinion of the world. *De hilo*, Directly, instantly.

Hilván [eel-vahn'], *m.* Basting, long stitches set in clothes to keep them in order for sewing.

Hilvanar [eel-vah-nar'], *va.* 1. To baste, to sew slightly. 2. To act or perform in a hurry.

Himen [ee'-men], *m.* Hymen, the virginal membrane.

Himeneo [e-may-nay'-o], *m.* 1. (Poet.) Marriage, matrimony. 2. Epithalamium, hymeneal, hymenean. 3. Hymen, the god of marriage.

Himenocarpo, pa [e-may-no-car'-po, pah], *a.* (Bot.) Bearing a membranous fruit.

Himenófilo [e-may-no'-fe-lo], *m.* Hymenophyllum, filmy fern, lace fern.

Himenópteros [e-may-nop'-tay-ros], *m. pl.* The hymenoptera: the order of insects which contains those of the highest intelligence, as bees and ants, and others which are indirectly beneficial to husbandmen.

Himnario [im-nah'-re-o], *m.* Hymnal, hymnary.

Hímnico, ca [eem'-ne-co, cah], *a.* Hymnic, pertaining to hymns; lyric.

Himnista [im-nees'-tah], *m.* (Coll.) Composer of hymns.

Himno [eem'-no], *m.* Hymn.

Himnología [im-no-lo-hee'-ah], *f.* Hymnology, the study of hymns; a treatise on hymns.

Himplar [im-plar'], *vn.* To roar or bellow: applied to the panther and ounce.

Himpón [im-pon'], *m.* Name of one of the tribunals of the Chinese empire.

Hin [een or heen], *m.* Sound emitted by mules or horses; whinny.

Hincadura [in-cah-doo'-rah], *f.* Act of fixing any thing.

Hincapié [in-cah-pe-ay'], *m.* An effort made with the foot by fixing it firmly on the ground. *Hacer hincapié*, To make a strenuous attempt.

Hincar [in-car'], *va.* 1. To thrust in, to drive into, to nail one thing to another. *Hincar la rodilla*, To kneel down. 2. (Prov.) To plant. *Hincar el diente*, To appropriate property to one's self; to censure, to calumniate.

Hincón [in-cone'], *m.* Post to which cables are fastened on the banks of rivers.

Hincha [een'-chah], *f.* (Coll.) Hatred, displeasure, enmity.

Hinchadamente [in-chah-dah-men'-tay], *adv.* Haughtily, loftily.

Hinchado, da [in-chah'-do, dah], *a.* & *pp.* of Hinchar. 1. Swollen, tumefied, swelled. 2. Vain, arrogant, presumptuous. 3. Inflated, turgid, tumid: applied to a pompous style.

Hinchar [in-char'], *va.* 1. To inflate, to swell with wind. 2. To fill a musical instrument with air. 3. To swell, to raise to arrogance.—*vr.* 1. To swell, to grow turgid, to be tumefied. 2. To be elated with arrogance or anger.

Hinchazón [in-chah-thone'], *m.* 1. Swelling, tumefaction, a tumid inflammation. 2. Ostentation, vanity, pride; inflation.

Hinchir, *va.* (Obs.) *V.* Henchir.

Hiniesta [e-ne-es'-tah], *f.* (Bot.) Spanish broom. Spartium junceum.

Hiniestra [e-ne-es'-trah], *f.* (Prov.) Window. *V.* Ventana.

Hinnible [in-nee'-blay], *a.* Capable of neighing.

Hinojal [e-no-hahl'], *m.* Bed or place full of fennel.

Hinojar [e-no-har'], *vn.* & *vr.* (Obs.) *V.* Arrodillar and Arrodillarse.

Hinojo [e-no'-ho], *m.* 1. Knee. *V.* Rodilla. 2. (Bot.) Fennel. Anethum fœniculum. 3. *Hinojo marino*, (Bot.) Samphire. Crithmum maritimum. *Hinojos fitos*, (Obs.) On bended knees.

Hintero [in-tay'-ro], *m.* Table on which bakers knead their dough.

Hiñir [e-nyeer'], *va.* (Prov.) *V.* Heñir. (*Yo hiño, yo hiña; él hiñó, hiñera*; from *Heñir*. *V.* Pedir.)

Hióideo, dea [e-o'-e-day-o, ah], *a.* Hyoid, like a Y in shape.

Hipar [e-par'], *vn.* 1. To hiccough. 2. To be harassed with anxiety and grief. 3. To pant, to desire eagerly, to be anxious. 4. To follow the chase by the smell: spoken of pointers.

Hiparca [e-par'-cah], *m.* Name given by the Greeks to the satraps and their lieutenants.

Hipear [e-pay-ar'], *vn.* To hiccough. *V.* Hipar.

Hipecoo [e-pay-co'-o], *m.* (Bot.) Horned cumin. Hypecoum.

Hipérbola [e-per'-boh-lah], *f.* (Geom.) Hyperbola, section of a cone.

Hipérbole [e-per'-boh-lay], *f.* Hyperbole, a figure in rhetoric.

Hiperbólicamente [e-per-bo'-le-cah-men-tay], *adv.* Hyperbolically.

Hiperbólico, ca [e-per-bo'-le-co, cah], *a.* Hyperbolical.

Hiperbolizar [e-per-bo-le-thar'], *vn.* To use hyperboles.

Hiperboloide [e-per-bo-lo'-e-day], *f.* Hyperboloid

Hiperbóreo, rea [e-per-bo'-ray-o, ah], *a.* Hyperborean.

Hipercrítico, ca [e-per-cree'-te-co, cah], *a.* Hypercritical, censorious.

Hiperdulía [e-per-doo-lee'-ah], *f.* Hyperdulia, worship of the Virgin Mary.

Hiperemesia, or **Hiperemesis** [e-per-ay-may'-se-ah], *f.* Hyperemesis, excessive vomiting.

Hipergólico, ca [e-per-go'-le-co, cah], *a.* Hypergolic.

Hipérico, Hipéricon [e-pay'-re-co, e-pay'-re-cone], *m.* (Bot.) St. John's-wort. Hypericum.

Hipersónico, ca [e-per-so'-ne-co, cah] *a.* Hypersonic.

Hipertensión [e-per-ten-se-on'], *f.* Hypertension, high blood pressure.

Hipertrofia [e-per-tro'-fe-ah], *f.* Hypertrophy, undue growth.

Hipertrofiarse [e-per-tro-fe-ar'-say], *vr.* To hypertrophy, become hypertrophied.

Hipertrófico, ca [e-per-tro'-fe-co, cah], *a.* Hypertrophic, relating to hypertrophy.

Hípico, ca [ee'-pe-co, cah], *a.* Relating to horses.

Hipio [ee'-pe-o], *m.* Surname of Mars and Neptune, meaning *equestrian.*

Hipnal [ip-nahl'], *m.* Kind of serpent said to occasion sleep.

Hipnosis [ip-no'-sis], *f.* Hypnosis.

Hipnótico, ca [ip-no'-te-co, cah], *a.* & *m.* (Med.) Hypnotic.

Hipnotismo [ip-no-tees'-mo], *m.* Hypnotism, mesmerism, hypnotic suggestion.

Hipnotizar [ip-no-te-thar'], *va.* To hypnotize.

Hipo [ee'-po], *m.* 1. Hiccough. 2. Wish, desire, anxiety. 3. Anger, displeasure, fury.

Hipocampo [e-po-cahm'-po], *m.* Hippocampus, sea-horse.

Hipocentauro [e-po-then-tah'-oo-ro], *m.* Hippocentaur, a fabulous monster.

Hipocondría [e-po-con-dree'-ah], *f.* Hypochondria, melancholy, hypochondriasis, hypochondriac affection or passion.

Hipocondriaco, ca [e-po-con-dre-ah'-co, cah], *a.* Hypochondriasis, hypochondriacal, melancholy, fanciful.

Hipocondriaco, ca, *m.* & *f.* Hypochondriac, melancholist.

Hipocóndrico, ca [e-po-con'-dre-co, cah], *a.* Hypochondriac, hypochondriacal.

Hipocondrio [e-po-con'-dre-oh], *m.* (Anat.) Hypochondrium, that part of the body which lies under the cartilages of the false ribs: more generally used in its plural, hypocondres.

Hipocrás [e-po-crahs'], *m.* Hippocras, medicated wine.

Hipocrático, ca [e-po-crah'-te-co, cah], *a.* Hippocratic, relating to Hippocrates. Cadaveric countenance.

Hipocrénides [e-po-cray-nee'-des], *f. pl.* (Poet.) Epithet applied to the muses of Parnassus.

Hipocresía [e-po-cray-see'-ah], *f.* Hypocrisy, dissimulation.

Hipócrita [e-po'-cre-tah], *a.* Hypocritical, dissembling, insincere.

Hipócrita [e-po'-cre-tah], *com.* Hypocrite, a dissembler.

Hipócritamente [e-po'-cre-tah-men-tay], *adv.* Hypocritically.

Hipocritilla [e-po-cre-teel'-lyah], *f. dim.* A sly hypocrite.

Hipócrito, ta [e-po'-cre-to, tah], *a.* Feigned, dissembled, hypocritical.

Hipocritón, na [e-po-cre-tone', nah], *a. aug.* Extremely hypocritical or dissembling.

Hipodérmico, ca [e-po-der'-me-co, cah], *a.* Hypodermic.

Hipódromo [e-po'-droh-mo], *m.* Hippodrome, race track, arena.

Hipofosfito [e-po-fos-fee'-to], *m.* Hypophosphite, a salt of hypophosphorous acid.

Hipofosforoso, sa [e-po-fos-fo-ro'-so, sah], *a.* Hypophosphorous (acid).—H^3PO^2.

Hipogástrico, ca [e-po-gahs'-tre-co, cah], *a.* Hypogastric.

Hipogastro [e-po-gahs'-tro], *m.* Hypogastrium, the lower part of the belly.

Hipogeo [e-po-hay'-o], *m.* 1. Subterranean vault where the ancient Greeks, etc., kept their dead without cremating them. 2. Hypogeum, an underground chapel or structure.

Hipogloso, sa [e-po-glo'-so, sah], *a.* Hypoglossal.

Hipogrifo [e-po-gree'-fo], *m.* Hippogriff, a winged horse.

Hipohema [e-po-ay'-mah], *m.* Hyphæmia, effusion of blood in the eye.

Hipomanes [e-po-mah'-nes], *m.* A vaginal discharge from the mare when in heat. (Acad.)

Hipomoclio, Hipomoclión [e-po-mo'-cle-o, e-po-mo-cle-on'], *m.* Fulcrum of a lever; part on which the beam of a balance revolves.

Hiponitrato [e-po-ne-trah'-to], *m.* Subnitrate.

Hipopión [e-po-pe-on'], *m.* (Med.) Hypopyon, a collection of pus in the chambers of the eye.

Hipopo, pa [e-po'-po, pah], *a.* Hoofed like a horse.

Hipopótamo [e-po-po'-tah-mo], *m.* Hippopotamus, a river-horse.

Hipóstasis [e-pos'-tah-sis], *f.* (Theol.) Hypostasis, any one of the persons of the Holy Trinity.

Hipostático, ca [e-pos-tah'-te-co, cah], *a.* Hypostatical.

Hiposulfato, furo. fito [e-po-sool-fah'-to, foo'-ro, fee'-to], *m.* (Chem.) Hyposulphite. Hyposulphite of soda, so called (properly thiosulphate), is important in photography.

Hipoteca [e-po-tay'-cah], *f.* Mortgage, pledge; security given for the performance of an engagement. *Buena hipoteca,* A phrase used to express that a person or thing is worthless and not to be relied upon.

Hipotecable [e-po-tay-cah'-blay], *a.* Capable of being pledged.

Hipotecar [e-po-tay-car'], *va.* To hypothecate, to pledge, to mortgage.

Hipotecario, ria [e-po-tay-cah'-re-o, ah], *a.* Belonging to a mortgage.

Hipotensión [e-po-ten-se-on'], *f.* (Med.) Hypotension.

Hipotenusa [e-po-tay-noo'-sah], *f.* Hypotenuse.

Hipótesis [e-po'-tay-sis], *f.* Hypothesis, a supposition.

Hipotético, ca [e-po-tay'-te-co, cah], *a.* Hypothetic, hypothetical, conditional.

Hipsómetro [ip-so'-may-tro], *m.* Hypsometer, an instrument for measuring altitude above the sea-level by comparison of the boiling-point of water.

Hipúrico [e-poo'-re-co], *a.* (Chem.) Hippuric (acid).

Hirma [eer'-mah], *f.* Edge of cloth.

Hirsuto, ta [ir-soo'-to, tah], *a.* 1. Hirsute, covered with rough hairs. 2. (Poet.) Rough, rugged.

Hirundinaria [e-roon-de-nah'-re-ah], *f.* (Bot.) *V.* CELIDONIA and GOLONDRINERA.

Hirviente [ir-ve-en'-tay], *pa.* Boiling.

Hisca [ees'-cah], *f.* Bird-lime, a glutinous substance by which the feet of birds are entangled.

Hiscal [is-cahl'], *m.* A rope of three strands made of esparto.

Hisopada [e-so-pah'-dah], *f.* Water sprinkled with a water-sprinkler.

Hisopear [e-so-pay-ar'], *va.* To sprinkle water with a sprinkler.

Hisopillo [e-so-peel'-lyo], *m.* 1. A small water-sprinkler. 2 Bit of soft linen at the end of a stick, used to wash and refresh the mouth of a sick person. 3. (Bot.) Winter-savory.

Hisopo [e-so'-po], *m.* 1. (Bot.) Hyssop. Hyssopus, *L.* 2. Water-sprinkler, with which holy water is sprinkled, made of a lock of horse-hair fastened to the end of a stick. *Hisopo húmedo,* (Pharm.) Grease collected in washing fleeces of wool.

Hispalense [is-pah-len'-say], *a.* Native of or belonging to Seville.

Hispánico, ca [is-pah'-ne-co, cah], *a.* Spanish.

Hispanidad [is-pah-ne-dahd'], *f.* 1. Spanish culture, Spanish spirit. 2. Spanish-speaking world.

Hispanismo [is-pah-nees'-mo], *m.* A Spanish idiom.

Hispanizado, da [is-pah-ne-thah'-do, dah], *a.* & *pp.* of HISPANIZAR. *V.* ESPAÑOLIZADO.

Hispanizar [is-pah-ne'-thar], *va.* *V* ESPAÑOLIZAR.

Hispano, na [is-pah'-no, nah], *a.* Spanish.—*m.* & *f.* (Poet.) A Spaniard.

Hispanoamericano, na [is-pah-no-ah-may-re-cah'-no, nah], *m.* & *f.* & *a.* Spanish American.

Híspido, da [ees'-pe-do, dah], *a.* Bristly, like hogs.

Histerectomía [is-tay-rec-to-mee'-ah], *f.* (Med.) Hysterectomy, surgical removal of the uterus.

Histeria [is-tay'-re-ah], *f.* Hysteria, hysterics.

Histérico [is-tay'-re-co], *m.* Hysterics. *V.* HISTERISMO.

Histérico, ca [is-tay'-re-co, cah], *a.* Hysteric, hysterical; relating to the womb, or to hysteria.

Histerismo [is-tay-rees'-mo], *m.* Hysteria.

Histología [is-to-lo-hee'-ah], *f.* Histology, the science of the tissues, or a treatise upon them.

Histológico, ca [is-to-lo'-he-co, cah], *a* Histological.

Histólogo, *m.* Histologist.

Historia [is-to'-re-ah], *f.* 1. History, a narration of events. 2. (Coll.) Tale, story; fable. 3. History-piece, an historical painting. *Meterse en historias,* To meddle in things without possessing sufficient knowledge thereof, or being concerned in them.

Historiado, da [is-to-re-ah'-do, dah], *a.* Applied to a painting consisting of various parts harmoniously united. *Libro historiado,* Book illustrated with plates.— *pp.* of HISTORIAR.

Historiador, ra [is-to-re-ah-dor', rah], *m.* & *f.* Historian, historiographer, chronicler, a writer of history or of facts and events.

Historial [es-to-re-ahl'], *a.* Historical, historic.—*m.* 1. Background, history. 2. Employment record.

Historialmente [is-to-re-al-men'-tay], *adv.* Historically.

Historiar [is-to-re-ar'], *va.* 1. To historify, to record in history. 2. To represent historical events in paintings or tapestry.

Históricamente [is-to'-re-cah-men-tay], *adv.* Historically.

Histórico, ca [is-to'-re-co, cah], *a.* Historical, historic.—*m.* (Obs.) Historian.

Historieta [is-to-re-ay'-tah], *f. dim.* Short story or tale, short novel or anecdote, mixed with fact and fable. *Historieta cómica,* Comic strip.

Historiografía [is-to-re-o-grah-fee'-ah], *f.* Historiography.

Historiógrafo [is-to-re-oh'-grah-fo], *m.* Historiographer, historian.
Historión [is-to-re-on'], *m.* A tedious, long-winded story.
Histrión [is-tre-on'], *m.* 1. Actor, player; used only in contempt. 2. Buffoon, juggler.
Histriónico, ca [is-tre-o'-ne-co, cah], *a.* Histrionic, histrionical.
Histrionisa [is-tre-oh-nee'-sah], *f.* An actress.
Histrionismo [is-tre-o-nees'-mo], *m.* In contempt, histrionism, the art and profession of an actor or player.
Hita [ee'-tah], *f.* A sort of nail without a head; stub-nail.
Hito, ta [ee'-to, tah], *a.* 1. (Obs.) Black. 2. Fixed, firm; importunate.
Hito [ee'-to], *m.* 1. Landmark, any thing set up to mark boundaries. 2. Guide-post; mile-stone. 3. Pin, or mark at which quoits are cast; mark to shoot at. *A hito*, Fixedly, firmly. *Mirar de hito en hito*, To view with close attention, to fix the eyes on an object. *Dar en el hito* or *dar en el hito de la dificultad*, To hit the nail on the head, to come to the point.
Hitón [e-tone'], *m.* A large square nail without a head. (Acad.)
Hobachón, na [o-bah-chone', nah], *a.* Sluggish, fat, and lazy.
Hobechos [o-bay'-chos], *m. pl.* Soldiers armed with pikes; pike-men.
Hoblonera [o-blo-nay'-rah], *f.* Hop-ground, hop-yard, hop-garden, any place where hops are cultivated.
Hocicada [o-the-cah'-dah], *f.* 1. A blow given with the snout of a beast, and sometimes also with the mouth. 2. Fall upon the face, or headlong on the ground. 3. (Coll.) A smart reprimand.
Hocicar [o-the-car'], *va.* To break up the ground with the snout.—*vn.* 1. To fall headlong with the face to the ground. 2. To stumble or slide into errors.
Hocico [o-thee'-co], *m.* 1. Snout, the nose of a beast. 2. Mouth of a man who has very prominent lips. 3. Any thing disproportionably big or prominent. 4. Gesture of thrusting out the lips, pouting. 5. (Met.) The face. *Meter el hocico en todo*, To meddle in everything. *De hocicos*, By the nose upon the face. *Poner tanto hocico*, (Coll.) To pout. *Estar de hocico*, To be at variance.
Hocicudo, da, or **Hocicón, na** [o-the-coo'-do, dah, o-the-cone', nah], *a.* 1. Long-snouted. 2. Blubber-lipped, flap-mouthed. 3. Looking sullen by thrusting out the lips.
Hocino [o-thee'-no], *m.* 1. Bill, a sort of hatchet with a hooked point. 2. The narrow bed of a river which flows between mountains.
Hociquillo, ito [o-the-keel'-lyo, ee'-to], *m. dim.* A little snout.
Hodometría [o-do-may-tree'-ah], *f.* Odometry, mechanical measurement of distance.
Hodómetro [o-do'-may-tro], *m.* Odometer, an instrument for measuring distance travelled.
Hogañazo, *adv.* (Coll.) *V.* Hogaño.
Hogaño [o-gah'-nyo], *adv.* (Coll.) This present year; in this epoch.
Hogar [o-gar'], *m.* 1. Hearth, fire-place; the pavement of a room where fire is kindled. 2. (Met.) House, residence, home.
Hogaza [o-gah'-thah], *f.* 1. A large loaf of household bread. 2. Any large loaf.
Hoguera [o-gay'-rah], *f.* 1. Bonfire. 2. Any blaze produced by burning things heaped together.
Hoja [o'-hah], *f.* 1. Leaf of trees and plants. 2. Leaf, any thing foliated or thinly beaten; scales of metal. 3. *Hoja de puerta*, Leaf, one side of a double door. *Hoja de ventana*, Shutter. 4. Blade of a sword or knife. 5. Ground cultivated one year, and lying at rest for another. 6. Half of each of the principal parts of a coat, etc. *Hoja de servicios*, (Mil.) A certificate setting forth the rank and services of a military officer. *Hoja de lata*, Tin-plate. *Hoja de lata negra*, Iron plate. *Hoja de papel*, Leaf of paper. *Hoja de un libro*, Leaf of a book. *Hoja de tocino*, Flitch of bacon. *Hoja de estaño*, Sheet of bismuth, tin, and quicksilver, laid on the back of a looking-glass. *Hoja volante*, A printed sheet, as a supplement of a newspaper; an "extra." *Vivir* or *ser de la hoja*, In Mexico means to lead a bad life. *Hoja seca*, The leaf-insect. *Doblemos la hoja*, No more of that; Let us change the subject. *Volver la hoja*, To turn over a new leaf, to alter one's sentiments and proceedings.—*pl.* 1. Leaves, greens. 2. Lamina, thin plates, one coat laid over another. *Vino de dos, tres* or *más hojas*, Wine two, three, or more years old.
Hoja de ruta [o'-hah day roo'-tah], *f.* (Aer.) Flight plan.
Hoja de trébol [o'-hah day tray'-bol], *f.* 1. (Bot.) Cloverleaf. 2. Clover leaf, highway intersection.
Hojalata or **Hoja de lata** [o-hah-lah'-tah, o'-hah day lah'-tah], *f.* Tin plate.
Hojalatería [o-ha-lah-tay-ree'-ah]. 1. The art of making tin-plate, or utensils of it. 2. A tin-shop.
Hojalatero [o-hah-lah-tay'-ro], *m.* Tinman, a manufacturer of tin.
Hojaldrado [o-hal-drah'-do], *a.* Laminated, foliated, resembling thin cakes. —*Hojaldrado, da, pp.* of Hojaldrar.
Hojaldrar [o-hal-drar'], *va.* To make any thing of puff paste.
Hojaldre [o-hahl'-dray], *m.* or *f.* A sort of pancake or paste. *Quitar la hojaldre al pastel*, (Coll.) To detect any fraud, to discover a plot.
Hojaldrista [o-hal-drees'-tah], *m.* Maker of buttered cakes.
Hojarasca [o-hah-rahs'-cah], *f.* 1. Withered leaves; redundancy of leaves; foliage. 2. Useless trifles. (Frequentative of Hoja.)
Hojear [o-hay-ar'], *va.* To turn the leaves of a book.—*vn.* To form metal into sheets; to foliate.
Hojica, illa, ita [o-hee'-cah, eel'-lyah, ee'-tah], *f. dim.* A small leaf.
Hojoso, sa, Hojudo, da [o-ho'-so, sah, o-hoo'-do, dah], *a.* Leafy, full of leaves.
Hojuela [o-hoo-ay'-lah], *f.* 1. (Dim.) A small leaf, a leaflet. 2. Puff paste, composed of thin flakes lying one on another. 3. Flat gold or silver thread in spools for embroidery. 4. Skins of olives after pressing.
¡Hola! [oh'-lah], *int.* 1. A word used in calling to any one at a distance. 2. Ho! ho! a sudden exclamation of wonder or astonishment. 3. (Naut.) Hoy! Ahoy!
Holán, Holán batista [o-lahn'], *m.* (Coll.) Cambric: the finest cambric, batiste.
Holanda [o-lahn'-dah], *f.* Holland, fine Dutch linen.
Holandés, sa [o-lan-days', sah], *a.* Dutch, Hollandish.
Holandilla, Holandeta [o-lan-deel'-lyah, o-lan-day'-tah], *f.* 1. A lead-coloured glazed linen, used for lining. 2. Tobacco of inferior quality. (Acad.)
Holgachón, na [ol-gah-chone', nah], *a.* Fond of ease and little work.
Holgadamente [ol-gah-dah-men'-tay] *adv.* 1. Widely, amply, fully, loosely. 2. Quietly, carelessly.
Holgado, da [ol-gah'-do, dah], *a.* & *pp.* of Holgar. 1. Loose, lax, disproportionably wide or broad. 2. Loose, disengaged, at leisure. 3. Well off, in easy circumstances, free from want. *Andar* or *estar holgado*, To be well off
Holganza [ol-gahn'-thah], *f.* 1. Repose, ease, tranquility of mind, quiet. 2. Diversion, recreation, amusement, entertainment. 3. *V.* Asueto.
Holgar [ol-gar'], *vn.* 1. To rest, to cease from labour, to lie at rest. 2. To spend one's time free from business. 3 (Acad.) To take pleasure or satisfaction in.—*vr.* To sport, to dally, to trifle, to idle, to toy, to play the fool.
Holgazán, na [ol-gah-thahn', nah], *m.* & *f.* Idler, loiterer, vagabond, lounger. —*a.* Idle, lazy, slothful, inactive, indolent.
Holgazanear [ol-gah-thah-nay-ar'], *vn.* To idle or to be idle, to lead an idle life, to be lazy, to loiter, to lounge.
Holgazanería [ol-gah-thah-nay-ree'-ah], *f.* Idleness, laziness, sluggishness slothfulness, inactivity, indolence.
Holgín, na [ol-heen', nah], *a.* *V.* Hechicero.
Holgorio [ol-go'-re-o], *m.* (Coll.) Mirth, jollity, noisy merriment.
Holgueta [ol-gay'-tah], *f.* (Coll.) A feast, a merry-making.
Holgura [ol-goo'-rah], *f.* 1. Country-feast, an entertainment in the country. 2. Width, breadth. 3. Ease, repose.
Holocausto [ol-o-cah'-oos-to], *m.* 1. Holocaust, a burnt sacrifice. 2. *V.* Sacrificio.
Hológrafo, fa [o-lo'-grah-fo, fah], *a.* Holographic, holograph, written entirely by the testator.
Holómetro [o-lo'-may-tro], *m.* Holometer, an instrument for making all kinds of angular measurements.
Holoturias [o-lo-too'-re-as], *a.f.pl.* Holothurian(s), belonging to the Holothuridea; a division of echinoderms, including sea-cucumbers, etc.
Holladura [ol-lyah-doo'-rah], *f.* 1. Act of trampling. 2. Duty paid for the run of cattle.
Hollar [ol-lyar'], *va.* 1. To tread upon, to trample under foot. 2. To trample on or to tread in contempt, to pull down, to humble, to depress.
Holleca [ol-lyay'-cah], *f.* (Orn.) *V.* Herrerillo.
Hollejico, illo, ito, uelo [ol-lyay-hee'-co], *m. dim.* A small pellicle or peel of grapes and some other fruits.
Hollejo [ol-lyay'-ho], *m.* Pellicle, peel, the thin skin which covers grapes and other fruit.
Holli [ol-lyee'], *m.* Balsam or resinous liquor which distils from a tree of Mexico and which is used mixed with chocolate.
Hollín [ol-lyeen'], *m.* Soot, condensed smoke. (Lat. fuligo.)
Holliniento, ta [ol-lye-ne-en'-to, tah], *a.* Fuliginous, sooty.
Homarrache [o-mar-rah'-chay], *m.* Buffoon, jack-pudding, a merry-andrew.
Hombracho [om-brah'-cho], *m.* A squat and square thick man.
Hombrachón [om-brah-chone'], *m. aug.* A very tall, square, thick man.
Hombrada [om-brah'-dah], *f.* 1. A manly action. 2. It is used also in an ironical sense for a ridiculous action.
Hombrazo [om-brah'-tho], *m. aug.* A large man.
Hombre [om'-bray], *m.* 1. Man, mankind. 2. Man, a male human being, as distinguished from woman. 3. Man

not a boy: one who has reached adult age. 4. Man, one of uncommon qualifications, qualified in a particular manner. 5. Man, a word of familiarity bordering on contempt. 6. Husband, among the populace. 7. Ombre, game at cards. *Hombre bueno*, Any one of the community who is not an ecclesiastic or nobleman. *Hombre al agua, a la mar*, A man who gives no hope of improvement in health or conduct. *Buen hombre, pero mal sastre*, A man of good heart but small ability. *Hombre de bien*, An honest man. *Hombre de bigote*, A grave and spirited man. *Hombre de bigote al ojo* or *de peso*, A sensible man. *Hombre de buena capa*, A well-dressed man. *Hombre de burlas*, An empty jester. *No es hombre de burlas*, He is not a jesting person. *Hombre de calzas atacadas*, A rigid observer of old customs; a very rigid and upright man. *Hombre de capa y espada*, A person of no profession. *Hombre de capricho*, A fanciful man, a whimsical fellow. *Hombre de corazón* or *de gran corazón*, A courageous man. *Hombre de chapa*, A man of judgment, abilities, and merit. *Hombre de días*, An old man. *Hombre de pro* or *de provecho*, A worthy, useful man. *Hombre de puños*, A very strong man. *Hombre hecho*, A grown man. *Hombre honrado*, An honest, worthy man. *Hombre de negocios*, Man of business. *Hombre seco*, 1. A thin and spare man. 2. An austere man, one of no conversation. *No tener hombre*, To be without protection. *Hombre sin dolo*, A plain-dealing man. *Hombre de su palabra*, A man of his word. *Ser muy hombre*, To be a man of spirit and courage. *Hombre de cabeza*, A talented man. *¡Hombre!* an exclamation of surprise. *¡Hombre al agua!* Man overboard!

Hombrear [om-bray-ar'], *vn.* To assume the man before the time.—*vn. & vr.* To vie with another; to put one's self upon a level with.

Hombrecillo [om-bray-theel'-lyo], *m. dim.* Manikin, manling, a pitiful little fellow. *Hombrecillos*, (Bot.) Hops. Humulus lupulus.

Hombrecito [om-bray-thee'-to], *m.* Youth, a young man.

Hombrera [om-bray'-rah], *f.* Piece of ancient armour for the shoulders.

Hombre rana [om'-bray rah'-nah], *m.* Frogman.

Hombría de bien [om-bree'-ah day be-en'], *f.* Probity, honesty. *Ricahombría de España*, A name formerly given to the ancient nobility of Spain.

Hombrillo [om-breel'-lyo], *m.* Gusset, an angular piece of cloth.

Hombro [om'-bro], *m.* The shoulder. *Hombro con hombro*, Cheek by jowl. *Encogerse de hombros*, To shrug up the shoulders. *A hombro* or *sobre los hombros*, On the shoulders. *Llevar en hombros*, To support, to protect. *Arrimar el hombro*, To work with a will; to lend a hand. *Echar al hombro*, To shoulder, to become responsible for. *Mirar sobre el hombro*, To cast a contemptuous look.

Hombrón [om-brone'], *m.* 1. (Aug.) A big, lusty man. 2. A man distinguished for talents, knowledge, and valour.

Hombronazo [om-bro-nah'-tho], *m. aug.* A huge, vulgar man.

Hombruno, na [om-broo'-no, nah], *a.* 1. Manlike, virile; belonging to man. 2. Relating to the shoulders.

Home [o'-may], *m.* (Obs.) *V.* Hombre.

Homecillo [o-may-theel'-lyo], *m.* (Bot.) Hops. Humulus lupulus, *L.*

Homecillo, Homecio, *m.* (Obs.) *V.* Homicidio.

Homenaje [o-may-nah'-hay], *m.* Homage, service and fealty to a superior lord; obeisance. *Rendir homenaje*, To pay homage, to profess fealty. *Torre de homenaje*, Tower in a castle where the governor took the oath of fidelity.

Homeópata [o-may-o'-pah-tah], *m.* Homœopath(ist).

Homeopatía [o-may-o-pah-tee'-ah], *f.* Homœopathy, the medical system of Hahnemann.

Homeopático, ca [o-may-o-pah'-te-co, cah], *a.* Homœopathic, relating to homœopathy.

Homérico, ca [o-may'-re-co, cah], *a.* Homeric.

Homicida [o-me-thee'-dah], *com.* Murderer, homicide.

Homicida [o-me-thee'-dah], *a.* Homicidal, murderous.

Homicidio [o-me-thee'-de-o], *m.* 1. Murder, homicide. 2. Ancient tribute.

Homilía [o-me-lee'-ah], *f.* Homily, a discourse read in a congregation.

Homilista [o-me-lees'-tah], *m.* Author or writer of homilies.

Homocéntrico, ca [o-mo-then'-tre-co, cah], *a.* Homocentric, having a common centre.

Homófono, na [o-mo'-fo-no, nah], *a.* Of like sound, homophonous.

Homógamo, ma [o-mo'-gah-mo, mah], *a.* Homogamous, having flowers of one sex only.

Homogeneidad [o-mo-hay-nay-e-dahd'], *f.* Homogeneity, homogeneousness.

Homogeneizar [o-mo-hay-nay-thar'], *va.* To homogenize (milk, etc.).

Homogéneo, nea [o-mo-hay'-nay-o, ah], *a.* Homogeneous.

Homógrafo, fa [o-mo'-grah-fo, fah], *a.* Homonymous, written alike. *Cf.* Homófono.

Homologación [o-mo-lo-gah-the-on'], *f.* (Littl. us.) Homologation, publication, or confirmation of a judicial act, to render it more valid.

Homólogo, ga [o-mo'-lo-go, gah], *a.* Homologous, having the same ratio; synonymous.

Homonimia [o-mo-nee'-me-ah], *f.* Homonymy, sameness of name where there is difference of meaning; ambiguity, equivocation.

Homónimo, ma [o-mo'-ne-mo, mah], *a.* Homonymous, equivocal.

Homosexual [o-mo-sek-soo-ahl'], *a. & m.* Homosexual.

Honda [on'-dah], *f.* 1. Sling, a stringed instrument for casting stones. 2. *Honda y precinta*, (Naut.) Parbuckle, a rope used to slip and unship casks, pieces of ordnance, and other heavy articles.

Hondable [on-dah'-blay], *a.* (Naut.) Soundable.

Hondamente [on-dah-men'-tay], *adv.* 1. Deeply, profoundly, to a great depth. 2. Deeply, profoundly, with deep concern; with deep insight.

Hondarras [on-dar'-ras], *f. pl.* (Prov.) Dregs or lees of any liquor remaining in the vessel which contained it.

Hondazo [on-dah'-tho], *m.* Cast or throw with a sling.

Hondear [on-day-ar'], *va.* To unload a vessel.

Hondero [on-day'-ro], *m.* Slinger, a soldier armed with a sling.

Hondica, illa, ita [on-dee'-cah], *f. dim.* A small sling to cast stones.

Hondijo [on-dee'-ho], *m.* *V.* Honda.

Hondillo [on-deel'-lyo], *m.* Any of the pieces of cloth or linen which forms the seats of breeches or drawers.

Hondo, da [on'-do, dah], *a.* 1. Profound, deep, far below the surface. 2. Profound, low with respect to neighbouring places. 3. (Met.) *V.* Profundo.

Hondo [on'-do], *m.* (Prov.) *V.* Fondo for bottom.

Hondón [on-done'], *m.* 1. Bottom of a vessel or jar where the dregs of liquor settle. 2. Any deep or broken ground. 3. A deep hole. 4. Eye of a needle.

Hondonada [on-do-nah'-dah], *f.* 1. Dale, ravine, bottom of a steep place. 2. Comb, a valley surrounded by hills.

Hondura [on-doo'-rah], *f.* Depth, profundity.

Honestad [o-nes-tahd'], *f.* (Obs.) Honesty. *V.* Honestidad.

Honestamente [o-nes-tah-men'-tay], *adv.* Honestly; modestly.

Honestar [o-nes-tar'], *va.* 1. To honour, to dignify. 2. To excuse, to palliate.

Honestidad [o-nes-te-dahd'], *f.* 1. Honesty, composure, modesty, moderation. 2. Honesty, purity of sentiments and principles, honourableness; urbanity.

Honesto, ta [o-nes'-to, tah], *a.* 1. Honest, decent, honourable, creditable, handsome, grave. 2. Honest, comely, pure, chaste, virtuous. 3. Honest, reasonable, just. *Mujer de estado honesto*, A spinster.

Hongo [on'-go], *m.* 1. (Bot.) Mushroom. Fungus, *L.* 2. Fungus, an excrescence which grows upon the bark of trees, and serves for tinder. 3. A fleshy excrescence growing on the lips of wounds.

Hongoso, sa [on-go'-so, sah], *a.* (Obs.) Fungous, spongy. *V.* Fungoso.

Honor [o-nor'], *m.* 1. Honour, a public mark of respect to virtue or merit. 2. Honour, reputation, fame, celebrity. 3. Honour, chastity in women. 4. Honour, dignity, rank, employment: more commonly used in the plural. *Palabra de honor*, Word of honour. *Señoras de honor*, Maids of honour. *Honores*, 1. Honours, privileges of rank or birth. 2. Honours, or privileges conferred without gain. 3. Public marks of respect to a person of rank.

Honorable [o-no-rah'-blay], *a.* Honourable, illustrious, noble.

Honorablemente [o-no-rah-blay-men'-tay], *adv.* Honourably, creditably.

Honorar [o-no-rar'], *va.* (Obs.) *V.* Honrar.

Honorario, ria [o-no-rah'-re-o, ah], *a.* 1. Honorary, bestowing honour without gain. *Consejero honorario*, Honorary counsellor, one who has the rank and title of a counsellor without the pay.

Honorario [o-no-rah'-re-o], *m.* 1. Salary or stipend given for labour. 2 Fees of counsellors, notaries, or physicians.

Honorcillo [o-nor-theel'-lyo], *m. dim.* V. Honrilla.

Honoríficamente [o-no-ree'-fe-cah-men-tay], *adv.* Honourably.

Honorificencia [o-no-re-fe-then'-the-ah], *f.* The act of honouring or doing honour.

Honorífico, ca [o-no-ree'-fe-co, cah], *a.* Creditable, honourable, liberal, that which gives honour.

Honra [on'-rah], *f.* 1. Honour, reverence, respect. 2. Honour, reputation, celebrity, fame, glory. 3. Honour, chastity in woman. 4. Honour, mark of respect, favour conferred or received. *Honras*, Funeral honours. *De honra* *y provecho*, (Coll.) For both interior and exterior qualities: not for a glossy surface, but for good wear.

Honradamente [on-rah-dah-men'-tay], *adv.* Honourably, reputably, honestly.

Honradez [on-rah-deth'], *f.* Honesty, probity, integrity, fairness, faithfulness.

Honrado, da [on-rah'-do, dah], *a.* 1. Honest, honourable, reputable, just, fair. 2. Honest, exact in the performance of engagements. 3. In an ironical sense, refined in point of roguery and fraud.

Honrador, ra [on-rah-dor', rah], *m.* & *f.* Honourer, one that honours.

Honramiento [on-rah-me-en'-to], *m.* Act of honouring.

Honrar [on-rar'], *va.* 1. To honour, to reverence, to respect. 2. To cajole, to caress, to fondle. 3. To dignify, to illustrate, to exalt, to glorify. 4. To praise, to applaud. 5. To credit, to grace, to adorn.

Honrilla [on-reel'-lyah], *f. dim.* Nice point of honour: almost always used with the adjective *negra*, black. *Por la negra honrilla he omitido hacerlo*, I have left it undone from some little point of honour or bashfulness.

Honrosamente [on-ro-sah-men'-tay], *adv.* Honourably, honestly, creditably.

Honroso, sa [on-ro'-so, sah], *a.* 1. Honourable, decent, decorous, creditable. 2. Just, equitable, honest. 3. Jealous of one's honour.

Honrudo, da [on-roo'-do, dah], *a.* Firm in maintaining one's honour, and acting conformably to it.

Hontana [on-tah'-nah], *f.* (Obs.) Fountain, spring.

Hontanal [on-tah-nahl'], *m.* *V.* Hontanar. *Hontanales*, Feasts of the ancients held at fountains.

Hontanar [on-tah-nar'], *m.* Place in which water rises, source of springs and rivers.

Hopa [oh'-pah], *f.* 1. A long cassock with sleeves. 2. The sack of those who are executed for crime.

Hopalanda [o-pah-lahn'-dah], *f.* Tail or train of a gown worn by students.

Hopear [o-pay-ar'], *vn.* To wag the tail: applied to animals.

Hopeo [o-pay'-o], *m.* (Coll.) Volatile coxcomb.

Hopo [o'-po], *m.* Tail with a tuft of hair, similar to that of a fox or squirrel. *Seguir el hopo*, To dog, to pursue closely. *Sudar el hopo*, To cost much trouble and toil in attainment. *Volver el hopo*, To escape, to run away.

Hoque [o'-kay], *m.* Treat given to celebrate the completion of a bargain or contract.

Hora [o'-rah], *f.* 1. Hour, the twenty-fourth part of a day. 2. Hour, particular time for doing any thing. 3. Hour, the time as marked by the clock. 4. (Prov.) Way made in an hour, a league. 5. Time between twelve and one o'clock on the day of the ascension, during which that mystery is celebrated in Catholic churches. *Hora horada*, Hour passed over. *Hora menguada*, Fatal moment. *A la hora de esta* or *a la hora de ahora*, (Coll.) At this moment. *Cada hora*, Every hour, continually. *A buena hora*, At a seasonable time. *A la hora*, At the nick of time; then. *En hora buena*, It is well. *Vete en hora mala*, (Coll.) Begone, get out of my sight. *Por hora*, Each hour. *Por horas*, By instants.—*pl.* 1. Hours or canonical hours, the stated times of devotion of the Catholic church. 2. Book which contains the office of the blessed Virgin and other devotions.

Hora [o'-rah], *adv.* Now, at this time, at present.—*conj.* *V.* Ora.

Horacar [o-rah-car'], *va.* (Obs.) *V.* Horadar.

Horadable [o-rah-dah'-blay], *a.* Capable of being pierced.

Horadación [o-rah-dah-the-on'], *f.* Act of boring or piercing.

Horadado [o-rah-dah'-do], *m.* Silkworm's cocoon bored through.—*Horadado, da, pp.* of Horadar.

Horadar [o-rah-dar'], *va.* To bore or pierce from side to side.

Horado [o-rah'-do], *m.* 1. Hole bored from side to side. 2. Cavern, grotto; niche or cavity in a wall.

Horambre [o-ram'-bray], *m.* Hole in the cheeks of mills.

Horario, ria [o-rah'-re-o, ah], *a.* Horary, horal, relating to an hour, continuing for an hour.

Horario [o-rah'-re-o], *m.* Hour-hand of a clock or watch.

Horca [or'-cah], *f.* 1. Gallows, on which malefactors are hanged. *Señor de horca y cuchillo*, Lord of the manor, who is invested with civil and criminal jurisdiction within the circuit of his estate. 2. Sort of yoke for dogs or hogs, to prevent them from doing mischief; also used formerly as a punishment. 3. Fork with two wooden prongs, used by husbandmen for lifting straw, corn, hay, etc. 4. Rope or string of onions or garlic.

Horcado, da [or-cah'-do, dah], *a.* Forked into different branches; forky.

Horcadura [or-cah-doo'-rah], *f.* Fork of a tree.

Horcajadas (A), or **A horcajadillas** [ah or-cah-hah'-das], *adv.* Astride on horseback.

Horcajadura [or-cah-hah-doo'-rah], *f.* Fork formed by the two thighs.

Horcajo [or-cah'-ho], *m.* 1. Yoke or collar put on the neck of mules, when employed in drawing. 2. In oil-mills, the Y-shaped division of the beam. 3. Confluence of two streams.

Horcate [or-cah'-tay], *m.* 1. A yoke or collar of a horse. 2. Hame, collar of a draught-horse.

Horco [or'-co], *m.* Rope or string of onions or garlic.

Horcón [or-cone'], *m.* A forked pole set upright, to support the branches of fruit-trees.

Horchata [or-chah'-tah], *f.* An emulsion, commonly made of melon or pumpkin seeds, or of almonds.

Horchatero, ra [or-chah-tay'-ro, rah], *m.* & *f.* One who makes or sells almond-emulsion.

Horchilla [or-cheel'-lyah], *f.* True dyer's orchil rocella, archil. Roccella tinctoria.

Horda [or'-dah], *f.* Horde, clan, tribe. *V.* Aduar.

Hordeáceas [or-day-ah'-thay-as], *f. pl.* (Bot.) Pertaining to barley, hordeaceous.

Hordeina [or-day-ee'-nah], *f.* 1. The finest bran of barley. 2. Hordein, a proximate principle from barley.

Hordeolo [or-day-o'-lo], *m.* Hordeolum, stye.

Hordiate [or-de-ah'-tay], *m.* 1. Beverage of barley-water. 2. *f.* (Bot.) Barley without awns or beard. 3. (Bot.) Spring naked barley. Hordeum vulgare, *B.* Cæleste, *L.*

Horizontal [o-re-thon-tahl'], *a.* Horizontal, parallel to the horizon; on a level.

Horizontalmente [o-re-thon-tal-men'-tay], *adv.* Horizontally, flatly.

Horizonte [o-re-thon'-tay], *m.* 1. Horizon, the line which terminates the view. 2. (Geog.) Horizon, the largest circle of the sphere, which divides it into two equal parts.

Horma [or'-mah], *f.* Mould, model in which anything is cast, formed or modeled. *Horma de zapatero*, Shoemaker's last. *Horma para zapato*, Shoe tree. *Horma de sombrerero*, Hatter's block. *Hallar la horma de su zapato*, 1. (coll.) To meet one's wishes, to accommodate or satisfy anyone. 2. To meet with his match, someone who understands his artifices and can oppose his designs. *Horma* or *pared horma*, A dry wall, built without lime or mortar.

Hormazo [or-mah'-tho], *m.* 1. (Prov.) House and garden. 2. (Obs.) *V.* Pared horma.

Hormero [or-may'-ro], *m.* Last-maker.

Hormiga [or-mee'-gah], *f.* 1. Ant, pismire, or emmet. 2. A cutaneous eruption, producing an itching which resembles the biting of an ant.

Hormigón [or-me-gone'], *m.* Concrete. *Hormigón armado*, reinforced concrete. *Hormigón para bloques*, Block concrete.

Hormigonera [or-me-go-nay'-rah], *f.* Concrete mixer.

Hormigos [or-mee'-gos], *m. pl.* 1. Dessert of hazelnuts and honey. 2. Coarse remains of sifted wheat.

Hormigoso, sa [or-me-go'-so, sah], *a.* Relating to ants.

Hormigueamiento [or-me-gay-ah-me-en'-to], *m.* Formication, act of itching or moving like ants.

Hormiguear [or-me-gay-ar'], *vn.* 1. To itch. 2. To run about like ants.

Hormigueo [or-me-gay'-o], *m.* Formication, a sensation like that of the creeping or stinging of ants.

Hormiguero [or-me-gay'-ro], *m.* 1. Ant-hill or hillock, formicarium. 2. Place where there are a crowd of people moving. 3. *pl.* Piles of weeds covered with earth in which ants breed, and after being burned serve as manure. 4. An ant-eater.

Hormiguero, ra [or-me-gay'-ro, rah], *a.* Relating to the cutaneous eruption called *hormiga*.

Hormiguita [or-me-gee'-tah], *f. dim* A small ant.

Hormiguilla [or-me-geel'-lyah], *f.* A distemper which affects the hoofs of horses.

Hormiguillo [or-me-geel'-lyo], *m.* 1. Distemper which affects the hoofs of horses. 2. People ranged in a line, who pass from hand to hand the materials for a work to be raised. 3. In Mexico, a beverage made of pounded biscuit, sugar, and spice, boiled together. 4. Mixture of salts with silver. 5. (Prov.) *V.* Hormigueo.

Hormilla [or-meel'-lyah], *f.* 1. (Dim.) A small last.

Hormona [or-moh'-nah], *f.* Hormone.

Hornabeque [or-nah-bay'-kay], *m.* (Fort.) Hornwork, an outwork, composed of a front and two demi-bastions, joined by a curtain.

Hornacero [or-nah-thay'-ro], *m.* Person who watches crucibles with silver and gold in the furnace.

Hornacina [or-nah-thee'-nah], *f.* Vaulted niche in the wall of an altar.

Hornacho [or-nah'-cho], *m.* 1. Shaft of a mine, an excavation formed in a hill. 2. Furnace in which metal is melted for casting statues.

Hornachuela [or-nah-choo-ay'-lah], *f.* Hole made in a wall.

Hornada [or-nah'-dah], *f.* Batch, the bread baked at one time.

Hornaguear [or-nah-gay-ar'], *va.* To

open the ground in search of pit-coals.
Hornaguera [or-nah-gay'-rah], *f.* Pit-coal, hard coal.
Hornaguero, ra [or-nah-gay'-ro, rah], *a.* 1. Wide, spacious. 2. Coaly: applied to ground containing coals.
Hornaje [or-nah'-hay], *m.* (Prov.) Money paid to a baker for baking bread.
Hornaza [or-nah'-thah], *f.* 1. A small furnace, used by gold and silver-smiths, and other founders, to melt and cast metal. 2. A light yellow colour, in painting; a yellow glazing.
Hornazo [or-nah'-tho], *m.* 1. Cake made with a batter of eggs and butter. 2. Present given on Easter Sunday by the inhabitants of a village to the friar or clergyman who has preached the Lent sermons.
Hornblenda [orn-blen'-dah], *f.* Hornblende, a greenish-black variety of amphibole.
Hornear [or-nay-ar'], *va.* To carry on the trade of a baker.
Hornería [or-nay-ree'-ah], *f.* Trade of a baker.
Hornero, ra [or-nay'-ro, rah], *m.* & *f.* Baker.
Hornija [or-nee'-hah], *f.* Brushwood burnt in an oven, to heat it for baking bread.
Hornijero [or-ne-hay'-ro], *m.* Person who supplies the oven with fuel.
Hornilla [or-neel'-lyah], *f.* 1. Small furnace, stew-hole, a small stove in a kitchen-hearth on which any thing is put to boil or stew. 2. Pigeon-hole, a hole for pigeons to make their nests and breed in.
Hornillo [or-neel'-lyo], *m.* 1. (Dim.) A small stove. 2. (Mil.) Chamber of a mine. 3. A portable furnace. 4. (Mil.) Fougade, a small mine dug under some work or fortification, in order to blow it up.
Hornito [or-nee'-to], *m.* (Mex.) A mud-volcano.
Horno [or'-no], *m.* 1. Oven. 2. Kiln. 3. (Fig.) Furnace. *Alto horno*, Blast furnace. *Horno de cuba*, Shaft furnace. *No estar el horno para bollos*, Not to be the right moment (to make one's move).
Horología [o-ro-lo-hee'-ah], *f.* Horology.
Horón [o-rone'], *m.* (Prov.) Large round hamper or frail.
Horópter, Horóptero [o-rop'-tayr, tay-ro], *m.* A straight line through the point where the optical axes meet.
Horóscopo [o-ros'-co-po], *m.* Horoscope, the configuration of the planets at the hour of birth.
Horqueta [or-kay'-tah], *f.* 1. (Dim. of HORCÓN.) A little fork. 2. (Naut.) *V.* HORQUILLAS.
Horquilla [or-keel'-lyah], *f.* 1. Forked stick, for hanging up and taking down things from an elevated place. 2. Disease which causes the hair of the head to split. 3. A hair-pin. 4. A pitchfork. 5. The upper extremity of the sternum. 6. (Anat.) The fourchette, inferior commissure of the labia majora. 7. Instrument for operating on tongue-tie. 8. (Mil.) An instrument which arquebusiers used to sustain the weapon and fix the aim. 9. (Vet.) The frog of a horse's foot. *Horquillas*, (Naut.) Crotches or crutches, curbs, the crooked timbers which are placed upon the keel in the fore and hind part of a ship. *Horquillas del fondo*, Fore crotches. *Horquillas de sobre-pluro*, Crotches of the riders. *Horquillas de dar fuego*, Breaming-forks.
Horquilladura [or-keel-lyah-doo'-rah], *f.* (Prov.) Forkedness.
Horra [or'-rah], *a.* Among graziers, applied to females not with young; also to the head of cattle given to herds to keep at the expense of their owners.
Horrendamente [or-ren-dah-men'-tay], *adv.* Dreadfully.
Horrendo, da [or-ren'-do, dah], *a.* 1. Vast, enormous; dreadful, hideous, monstrous, fearful, horrible, grim. 2. Extraordinary, uncommon.
Hórreo [or'-ray-o], *m.* A kind of granary built upon pilasters, to prevent rats and mice from injuring the grain.
Horrero [or-ray'-ro], *m.* One who has the care of a granary; store-keeper.
Horribilidad [or-re-be-le-dahd'], *f.* Horribleness, dreadfulness.
Horrible [or-ree'-blay], *a.* Horrid, dreadful, hideous, horrible, heinous.
Horriblemente [or-re-blay-men'-tay], *adv.* Horribly, heinously, horridly, formidably, damnably.
Hórrido, da [or'-re-do, dah], *a.* Horrid, vast, enormous, hideous.
Horrífico, ca [or-ree'-fe-co, cah], *a.* (Poet.) Horrific, causing horror.
Horripilación [or-re-pe-lah-the-on'], *f.* (Med.) Horripilation, a symptom of the approach of fever.
Horripilante [or-re-pe-lahn'-tay], *pa.* Horrifying, harrowing.
Horripilar [or-re-pe-lar'], *va.* 1. To cause bristling of the hair. 2. To inspire horror.—*vr.* To feel horripilation.
Horripilativo, va [or-re-pe-lah-tee'-vo, vah], *a.* (Med.) Causing horripilation, or belonging to it.
Horrísono, na [or-ree'-so-no, nah], *a.* (Poet.) Horrisonous, sounding dreadfully.
Horro, ra [or'-ro, rah], *a.* 1. Enfranchised, set at liberty. 2. Free, disengaged. *Ovejas horras*, Barren ewes.
Horror [or-ror'], *m.* 1. Horror, consternation, fright. 2. Horror, hate, abhorrence. 3. Horridness, enormity, hideousness, grimness, frightfulness, the cause of fright or astonishment. *¡ Es un horror !* (Coll.) It is a wonder; that is to say, a great deal of any thing.
Horrorizar [or-ro-re-thar'], *va.* To cause horror, to terrify.—*vr.* To be terrified.
Horrorosamente [or-ro-ro-sah-men'-tay], *adv.* Horribly.
Horroroso, sa [or-ro-ro'-so, sah], *a.* 1. (Coll.) Horrid, hideous, frightful, haggish. 2. Horrid, dreadful, shocking, offensive.
Horrura [or roo'-rah], *f.* 1. Scoria, dross, recrement. 2. Dreariness of a thicket or close wood. 3. Filth, dirt, obscenity. 4. (Obs.) Terror, horror.
Hortaliza [or-tah-lee'-thah], *f.* Garden stuff, pot-herbs, all sorts of esculent plants produced in a garden.
Hortatorio, ria, *a.* *V.* EXHORTATORIO.
Hortelanear [or-tay-lah-nay-ar'], *vn.* (Prov.) To cultivate an orchard.
Hortelana [or-tay-lah'-nah], *f.* A gardener's wife.
Hortelano [or-tay-lah'-no], *m.* Gardener, horticulturist. *Hortelano*, (Orn.) Ortolan. Emberiza hortulana.
Hortense [or-ten'-say], *a.* Hortensial, hortulan, relating to gardens.
Hortensia [or-ten'-se-ah], *f.* (Bot.) Hydrangea. Hydrangea hortensia.
Hortera [or-tay'-rah], *f.* A wooden bowl.—*m.* Nickname of shop-boys in Madrid.
Hortícola [or-tee'-co-lah], *a.* Horticultural.
Horticultor [or-te-cool-tor'], *m.* Horticulturist.
Horticultura [or-te-cool-too'-rah], *f.* Horticulture, culture of orchards.
Hosco, ca [os'-co, cah], *a.* 1. Dark brown, liver-coloured. 2. Sullen, gloomy. 3. Boastful, ostentatious, vainglorious, arrogant.
Hoscoso, sa [os-co'-so, sah], *a.* Crisp, rough.
Hospedable [os-pay-dah'-blay], *a.* (Obs.) Hospitable.
Hospedado, da [os-pay-dah'-do, dah], *a.* Applied to a house receiving guests. —*pp.* of HOSPEDAR.
Hospedador, ra [os-pay-dah-dor', rah], *m.* & *f.* One who kindly entertains guests and strangers.
Hospedaje [os-pay-dah'-hay], *m.* 1. Kind reception of guests and strangers. 2. (Obs.) Inn, a house of entertainment for travellers. 3. (Acad.) Price paid for lodging.
Hospedamiento [os-pay-dah-me-en'-to], *m.* Reception of guests.
Hospedar [os-pay-dar'], *va.* To receive, to lodge and entertain strangers and travellers, to harbour.—*vr.* To host, to take up entertainment; to lodge or take a temporary residence.—*vn.* To lodge collegians who have finished their studies, though they live in the college, but at their own expense.
Hospedería [os-pay-day-ree'-ah], *f.* 1. Hospice, a house close to a monastery, a convent or a college, for the reception and accommodation of travellers and strangers. 2. Hospitium, a house kept in some places, at the expense of communities, to lodge their members. 3. *V.* HOSPEDAJE.
Hospedero [os-pay-day'-ro], *m.* 1. One who kindly receives guests and strangers. 2. Hospitaller, he whose trade is to receive and accommodate travellers and strangers.
Hospiciano, na [os-pe-the-ah'-no, nah], *m.* & *f.* Poor person who lives in a house of charity.
Hospicio [os-pee'-the-o], *m.* 1. Hospitium, charitable institution, house of charity. 2. Work-house. 3. (Prov.) House of correction. 4. Kind reception to guests and strangers. 5. In monasteries, the same as *hospedería*.
Hospital [os-pe-tahl'], *a.* Hospitable, affable.
Hospital [os-pe-tahl'], *m.* Hospital, infirmary, a place for the reception of the sick or support of the poor. *Hospital de sangre*, A field hospital for first aid to the wounded.
Hospitalario [os-pe-tah-lah'-re-o], *m.* Hospitaller, one of a religious community whose office was to relieve the poor, etc.
Hospitalario, ria [os-pe-tah-lah'-re-o, ah], *a.* Applied to the religious communities which keep hospitals.
Hospitalero, ra [os-pe-tah-lay'-ro, rah], *m.* & *f.* 1. Person intrusted with the care and direction of a hospital. 2. Any hospitable person.
Hospitalidad [os-pe-tah-le-dahd'], *f.* 1. Hospitality, hospitage, the practice of kindly entertaining travellers and strangers. 2. Hospitableness, kindness to strangers. 3. The days which a person remains in an hospital.
Hospitalización [os-pe-tah-le-thah-the-on'], *f.* Hospitalization.
Hospitalizar [os-pe-tah-le-thar'], *va.* To hospitalize.
Hospitalmente [os-pe-tal-men'-tay], *adv.* Hospitably.
Hosquillo, lla [os-keel'-lyo, lyah], *a. dim.* Darkish, somewhat gloomy.
Hostal, *m.* *V.* HOSTERÍA.
Hoste [os'-tay], *m.* (Obs.) 1. Enemy. 2. Host, army. *Hoste puto*, (Coll.)

Expression of repugnance to any thing disagreeable.
Hostelero, ra [os-tay-lay'-ro, rah], *m.* & *f.* An inn-keeper, tavern-keeper.
Hostería [os-tay-ree'-ah], *f.* Inn, tavern, hostry.
Hostia [os'-te-ah], *f.* 1. Host, victim, sacrifice offered on the altar. 2. Host, the wafer prepared for the sacrifice of the mass.
Hostiario [os-te-ah'-re-o], *m.* Wafer-box, in which the bread is preserved that is to be consecrated.
Hostiero [os-te-ay'-ro], *m.* Person who prepares the host.
Hostigamiento [os-te-gah-me-en'-to], *m.* Chastisement, vexation, molestation.
Hostigar [os-te-gar'], *va.* To vex, to trouble, to harass, to molest, to gall, to tire.
Hostigo [os-tee'-go], *m.* 1. That part of a wall which the rain and winds beat on. 2. The beating of rain and winds against a wall.
Hostil [os-teel'], *a.* Hostile, adverse.
Hostilidad [os-te-le-dahd'], *f.* Hostility, opposition in war.
Hostilizar [os-te-le-thar'], *va.* To commit hostilities; to hostilize.
Hostilmente [os-teel-men'-tay], *adv.* Hostilely.
Hotel [o-tel'], *m.* (Neol.) Hotel.
Hotentote, ta [o-ten-to'-tay], *m.* & *f.* & *a.* Hottentot.
Hoto, *m.* (Obs.) *V.* Confianza.
Hoy [oh'-e], *adv.* 1. To-day, this present day. 2. The present time, the time we live in. *Hoy día, hoy en el día* or *hoy en día,* Nowadays. *Hoy por hoy,* This very day. *De hoy en adelante* or *de hoy más,* Henceforward, in future. *Antes hoy que mañana,* Rather to-day than to-morrow, the sooner the better.
Hoya [oh'-yah], *f.* 1. Hole, cavity, pit in the earth. 2. *V.* Sepultura. 3. (Amer. Peru.) Bed of a river.
Hoyada [o-yah'-dah], *f.* The lowest part of a field.
Hoyito [o-yee'-to], *m. dim.* A small hole, cavity, pit, or excavation.
Hoyo [o'-yo], *m.* 1. Hole, pit, excavation. 2. *V.* Sepultura. 3. Inequality or unevenness of a surface.
Hoyoso, sa [oh-yo'-so, sah], *a.* Pitted, full of holes.
Hoyuelo [oh-yoo-ay'-lo], *m.* 1. (Dim.) A little hole, a dimple in the chin or cheek. 2. A boy's play.
Hoz [oth], *f.* 1. Sickle, a reaping-hook, with which corn is cut. 2. Defile, ravine; a narrow pass. 3. (Anat.) Every membranous fold of a sickle shape. *De hoz y de coz,* Headlong. *La hoz en el haza, y el hombre en la caza,* The work waiting and the workmen idling.
Hozadero [o-thah-day'-ro], *m.* Place where hogs turn up the ground.
Hozadura [o-thah-doo'-rah], *f.* Rooting, turning up the ground, as hogs do with their snouts.
Hozar [o-thar'], *va.* To root, to turn up the ground, as hogs.
Hu [oo], *adv.* (Obs.) *V.* Donde.
Huaca [oo-ah'-cah], *f.* (Peru.) Burial-place, ruins, etc., of the ancient Indians of Peru. *V.* Guaca.
Huacal [oo-ah-cahl'], *m.* (Amer.) 1. Crate for crockery or fruit. 2. (Mex.) A small hen-coop, carried on the back. *V.* Guacal.
Huaquero [oo-ah-kay'-ro], *m.* (Peru.) A pitcher of fine earthenware found in the huacas.
Huasicama [oo-ah-se-cah'-mah], *m.* (S. Amer. Indian) A door-keeper.
Huasipongo [oo-ah-se-pon'-go], *m.* (Ec.) An Indian hut.
Huaso [oo-ah'-so], *m.* *V.* Guaso. (Vulgar.)
Hucia [oo'-the-ah], *f.* (Obs.) *V.* Confianza.
Hucha [oo'-chah], *f.* 1. A large chest, in which labouring people keep their clothes, money, and other valuable articles. 2. Money-box. 3. Money kept and saved.
Huchear [oo-chay-ar'], *va.* (Littl. us.) 1. To hoot, to shout at in derision. 2. To cry out, to call.
Húchoho [oo'-cho-o], *m.* Word used to call birds.
Huebra [oo-ay'-brah], *f.* 1. Extent of ground which a yoke of oxen can plough every day. 2. Pair of mules with a ploughman hired or let out for a day's work. 3. (Prov.) *V.* Barbecho.
Huebrero [oo-ay-bray'-ro], *m.* Ploughman, who attends a pair of mules labouring by the day.
Hueca [oo-ay'-cah], *f.* Notch at the small end of a spindle.
Hueco, ca [oo-ay'-co, cah], *a.* 1. Hollow, empty, concave. 2. Empty, vain, ostentatious. 3. Tumid, resonant, inflated. *Voz hueca,* Sonorous and hollow voice. 4. Soft, spongy: applied to ground, or to short wool fit only for carding. *Se ha puesto muy hueco,* He is become very vain or ostentatious.
Hueco [oo-ay'-co], *m.* 1. Notch or nick of a wheel, into which the leaves of a pinion or the teeth of a wheel hitch, and set it in motion. 2. Interval of time or place. 3. Hollowness. 4. Hollow, gap, hole. 5. Any vacant space or aperture in a house or other building. 6. *V.* Muesca. 7. (Met.) Office or post vacant. *Huecos de las olas,* (Naut.) Trough of the sea.
Huélfago [oo-el'-fah-go], *m.* Difficulty of breathing in beasts and hawks, or other birds.
Huelga [oo-el'-gah], *f.* 1. Rest, repose; relaxation from work. 2. Recreation, merry-making. 3. Fallow, ground lying at rest. 4. (Neol.) Strike, the quitting of work by a body of labourers to enforce compliance with some demand. 5. *Huelga de la bala,* (Gunn.) Windage of a piece of ordnance, being the difference between the diameter of the bore and that of the ball.
Huelgo [oo-el'-go], *m.* 1. Breath, respiration. *Tomar huelgo,* To breathe, to respire. 2. *V.* Holgura.
(*Yo huelgo, yo huelgue,* from *Holgar. V.* Acordar.)
Huella [oo-el'-lyah], *f.* 1. Track, footstep; the print of the foot of a man or beast. 2. The horizontal width of the steps of a stair-case. 3. Act and effect of treading or trampling. 4. Impression of a plate or other thing on paper. 5. An impression morally or physically speaking.
Huellas digitales [oo-el'-lyahs de-he-tah'-less], *f. pl.* Finger prints.
Huello [oo-el'-lyo], *m.* 1. Ground, the floor or level of a place. 2. Step, pace. 3. Lower part of an animal's hoof.
(*Yo huello, yo huelle,* from *Hollar. V.* Acordar.)
Huembe [oo-em'-bay], *m.* (Amer.) A liana so tough as to sustain great weights. *Cf.* Güembé.
Huequecito [oo-ay-kay-thee'-to], *m. dim.* A small cavity or space.
Huérfago, *m.* (Vet.) *V.* Huélfago.
Huerfanito, ita [oo-er-fah-nee'-to, tah], *m.* & *f. dim.* A little orphan.
Huérfano, na [oo-err'-fah-no, nah], *m.* & *f.* Orphan, a child who has lost a father or mother, or both. *Huérfano de padre,* Fatherless.—*a.* Orphan, bereft of parents.
Huérgano, *m.* (Obs.) *V.* Órgano.
Huero, ra [oo-ay'-ro, rah], *a.* 1. Empty, addle. 2. (Met.) Addle, empty, void.—*m.* (Mex.) A person with light-coloured hair.
Huerta [oo-err'-tah], *f.* 1. A large orchard, fruit-garden, or kitchen-garden. 2. (Prov.) Land which can be irrigated.
Huerto [oo-err'-to], *m.* A small orchard or kitchen-garden, generally near the house.
Huesa [oo-ay'-sah], *f.* Grave, sepulture.
Huesarrón [oo-ay-sar-rone'], *m. aug.* A large bone.
Huesecico, illo, ito [oo-ay-say-thee'-co], *m. dim.* A little bone.
Hueso [oo-ay'-so], *m.* 1. Bone. 2. Stone, core, the case which contains the seeds and kernels of fruit. 3. The part of a lime-stone which remains unburnt in the kiln. 4. Any thing which produces more pains than profit. 5. Any useless or unprofitable thing. 6. Piece of ground of little value and bad quality. *Estar con los huesos en punta,* To stand up. *La sin hueso,* The tongue.
Huesoso, sa [oo-ay-so'-so, sah], *a.* Bony, osseous.
Huésped, da [oo-ays'-ped, dah], *m.* & *f.* 1. Guest, lodger, one entertained in the house of another. 2. (Obs.) Host, hostess, he who entertains others in his house. 3. Inn-keeper, tavern-keeper. 4. Stranger.
Hueste [oo-ays'-tay], *f.* Host, army in campaign. *Huestes,* Hosts, armies.
Huesudo, da [oo-ay-soo'-do, dah], *a.* Bony, having large bones.
Hueva [oo-ay'-vah], *f.* Egg or spawn of fishes.
Huevar [oo-ay-var'], *vn.* To lay eggs.
Huevecico, illo, ito, zuelo [oo-ay-vay-thee'-co], *f. dim.* A small egg.
Huevera [oo-ay-vay'-rah], *f.* 1. Ovarium of birds. 2. Egg-stand.
Huevero, ra [oo-ay-vay'-ro, rah], *m.* & *f.* Dealer in eggs.
Huevo [oo-ay'-vo], *m.* 1. Egg. 2. Spawn, sperm. 3. Hollow piece of wood used by shoemakers for shaping shoes. 4. Small waxen vessel filled with scented drops. *Huevo de juanelo,* Applied to any thing which appears difficult to do, but when tried and known seems easy. *A huevo,* For a trifle, at a low price. *Huevos espirituales,* Egg-nog. *Huevos de faltriquera,* Candied yolks of eggs. *Huevos estrellados,* Fried eggs. *Huevos pasados por agua,* Soft-boiled eggs. *Huevos escalfados,* Poached eggs. *Huevos hilados,* The yolks of eggs, beaten with sugar to the consistency of jelly, and thrown into different forms. *Huevos moles,* The yolks of eggs, made up with pounded almonds and sugar. *Huevos revueltos,* Buttered eggs. *Huevos y torreznos,* Collops and eggs.
Hugonote, ta [oo-go-no'-tay, tah], *m.* & *f.* & *a.* Huguenot, a French Protestant.
Huida [oo-ee'-dah], *f.* 1. Flight, escape, outleap. *V.* Fuga. 2. Hole made to put in or draw out any thing with facility.—*pl.* Evasions, subterfuges.
Huidero [oo-ee-day'-ro], *m.* 1. Place of retreat, whither game retires. 2. Labourer in quicksilver mines, who opens the holes in which the beams of the mine are fixed.
Huidizo, za [oo-e-dee'-tho, thah], *a.* Fugitive, fleeing.
Huiñapu [oo-e-nyah'-poo], *m.* (Amer.) Maize moistened and spread upon a

bed of straw until it begins to germinate for making chicha.

Huir [oo-eer'], *vn.* 1. To flee, to escape; to pack, to go, to flinch or get away, to get off. 2. To give the slip, to slip away, to pass; with words denoting time, to pass rapidly, to fly. 3. To shun, to avoid doing a bad thing, to flee from.—*vr.* To run away, to escape, to take to one's heels, to pack off one's tools, to make one's escape. *Huir el cuerpo*, To avoid or decline.

Huito [oo-e'-to], *m.* (Ec.) A vegetable dye used for skin diseases.

Hulanos [oo-lah'-nos], *m. pl.* Uhlans, name of a light Asiatic cavalry introduced into Europe.

Hule [oo'-lay], *m.* 1. Rubber. 2. Oil cloth. *Hule espuma*, Foam rubber. *Zapatos de hule*, Rubber shoes.

Hulero [oo-lay'-ro], *m.* A collector of rubber or caoutchouc.

Hulla [ool'-lyah], *f.* Pit-coal, hard coal.

Hullera [ool-yay'-rah], *f.* A coal-mine.

Humada, *f.* *V.* AHUMADA.

Humanado, da [oo-mah-nah'-do, dah], *a.* & *pp.* of HUMANAR. Humanate, invested with humanity: applied to the Son of God.

Humanamente [oo-mah-nah-men'-tay], *adv.* 1. Humanely, kindly, mercifully. 2. Humanly, in the power of men. *Eso humanamente no se puede hacer*, That cannot possibly be done.

Humanar [oo-mah-nar'], *va.* 1. To humanize, to soften. 2. (Poet.) To transform or convert into man.—*vr.* 1. To become man: applied to the Son of God. 2. To become humane or meek: to grow familiar; to be humbled, to be lowered.

Humanidad [oo-mah-ne-dahd'], *f.* 1. Humanity, the nature of man. 2. Humanity, human kind, the collective body of mankind. 3. Humanity, benevolence, tenderness, kindness, benignity. 4. (Coll.) Corpulence, bulkiness of body, fleshiness. 5. Human weakness.—*pl.* Philology, grammatical studies.

Humanista [oo-mah-nees'-tah], *m.* Humanist, philologer, grammarian.

Humanitario, ria [oo-mah-ne-tah'-re-o, ah], *a.* 1. Humanitarian, philanthropic. 2. Interesting to the generality of mankind, or tending toward their well-being.

Humanizar, *va.* & *vr.* *V.* HUMANAR.

Humano, na [oo-mah'-oo, nah], *a.* 1. Human, peculiar to man. 2. Humane, kind, merciful, benevolent, gracious. *En lo humano*, As regards human power or agency.

Humareda [oo-mah-ray'-dah], *f.* 1. A great deal of smoke. 2. Confusion, perplexity.

Humazga [oo-math'-gah], *f.* Hearth-money, fumage, tax paid on fire-places.

Humazo [oo-mah'-tho], *m.* Smoke; fume proceeding from burning paper which is doubled and twisted. *Humazo de narices*, (Met.) Displeasure, disdain, vexation.

Humeante [oo-may-ahn'-tay], *va.* Fuming, fumant.

Humear [oo-may-ar'], *vn.* 1. To smoke, to emit smoke. 2. To vapour, to emit or exhale fumes or vapours. 3. (Met.) To inflame, to fire: applied to the passions. 4. (Met.) To kindle or stir up a tumult, quarrel, or lawsuit.

Humectación [oo-mec-tah-the-on'], *f.* 1. (Obs.) Humectation, dampening. 2. Preparation of a medicine by moistening with water. 3. Dampness of the surface. 4. (Med.) Action of fomentations.

Humectante [oo-mec-tahn'-tay], *pa.* (Med.) Moistening.

Humectar [oo-mec-tar'], *va.* (Med.) To moisten, to humectate, to wet.

Humectativo, va [oo-mec-tah-tee'-vo, vah], *a.* Humective, causing moisture.

Humedad [oo-may-dahd'], *f.* Humidity, moisture, dampness, moistness.

Humedal [oo-may-dahl'], *m.* Humid soil, a marsh.

Humedecer [oo-may-day-therr'], *va.* To moisten, to wet, to soak, to steep, to humectate, to dampen.

(*Yo humedezco, yo humedezca*, from *Humedecer.* *V.* CONOCER.)

Humedecido, da [oo-may-day-thee'-do, dah], *a.* Dampened, moistened, humidified.

Húmedo, da [oo'-may-do, dah], *a.* Humid, wet, moist, watery, damp.

Humeral [oo-may-rahl'], *a.* (Anat.) Humeral, belonging to the humerus.

Húmero [oo'-may-ro], *m.* Humerus, a bone situated between the scapula and fore-arm.

Humero [oo-may'-ro], *m.* Tunnel, funnel, the shaft of a chimney; the passage for the smoke.

Humildad [oo-meel-dahd'], *f.* 1. Humility, modesty, meekness. 2. Lowliness, meanness, lowness of mind or birth; submission. *Humildad de garabato*, Feigned humility.

Humilde [oo-meel'-day], *a.* 1. Humble, modest, submissive, meek. 2. Humble, low, not high, not great, not tall. 3. Base, ignoble, of little worth or account.

Humildemente [oo-meel-day-men'-tay], *adv.* Humbly, submissively; modestly, meekly.

Humildito, ita [oo-meel-dee'-to, tah], *a. dim.* Very humble or modest.

Humillación [oo-meel-lyah-the-on'], *f.* 1. Humiliation, submission, abatement of pride. 2. Humiliation, act of humility, abjectness, humbling; obsequiousness. 3. Humiliation, mortification, self-contempt.

Humilladero [oo-meel-lyah-day'-ro], *m.* A small chapel, in the roads and near villages.

Humillador, ra [oo-meel-lyah-dor', rah], *m.* & *f.* Humiliator.

Humillante [oo-meel-yahn'-tay], *pa.* & *a.* Humbling, indecorous, unbecoming, degrading.

Humillar [oo-meel-lyar'], *va.* 1. To humble, to lower; to bend, to bow. 2. To humble, to crush, to subdue, to bring down from loftiness and pride, to degrade, to depreciate. *Humillar a alguno*, To frown down.—*vr.* To humble one's self, to become humble or submissive.

Humillo [oo-meel'-lyo], *m.* 1. (Dim.) Smoke or vapour which is not dense. 2. Vanity, petty pride: commonly used in the plural. 3. Disease of sucking pigs.

Humita [oo-mee'-tah], *f.* (Amer. Peru.) 1. A small cake made of tender maize and sugar. It is wrapped in maize leaves and cooked in an oven or a water-bath. 2. A rocky substance found in small crystals, in material from Vesuvius.

Humo [oo'-mo], *m.* 1. Smoke, the visible effluvium from any thing burning. 2. Vapour, steam, fume. 3. Thin, clear, black silk stuff.—*pl.* 1. Families or houses in a town or village. 2. (Met.) Vanity, petty pride, haughtiness, presumption.

Humor [oo-mor'], *m.* 1. Humour, a general name for any fluid of the body. 2. Humour, the disposition of a person to act in any way. 3. Humour, general turn or temper of mind, mood. *Buen humor*, Good-nature, pleasant disposition. *Mal humor*, Ill-temper. *Hombre de buen humor*, A good-humoured man. *Estar de buen humor*, To be in humour, to be gay.

Humorada [oo-mo-rah'-dah], *f.* 1. Graceful sprightliness. 2. A witty saying, stroke of wit.

Humorado, da [oo-mo-rah'-do, dah], *a.* 1. Full of humours. 2. Well or ill disposed.

Humoral [oo-mo-rahl'], *a.* Humoral, proceeding from the humours.

Humorcico, illo, ito [oo-mor-thee'-co], *m. dim.* of HUMOR. Generally used to denote a bad-tempered person.

Humorismo [oo-mo-rees'-mo], *m.* Humor, humorousness.

Humorista [oo-mo-rees'-tah], *m.* & *f.* Humorist.

Humorosidad [oo-mo-ro-se-dahd'], *f.* Copiousness of humours.

Humoroso, sa [oo-mo-ro'-so, sah], *a.* Watery, containing fluid.

Humoso, sa [oo-mo'-so, sah], *a.* Smoky, fumy.

Humus [oo'-moos], *m.* Vegetable mould; humus.

Hundible [oon-dee'-blay], *a.* Sinkable, capable of submersion or destruction.

Hundimiento [oon-de-me-en'-to], *m.* 1. Submersion, immersion, the act of sinking. 2. Downfall, destruction of fabrics.

Hundir [oon-deer'], *va.* 1. To submerge, to immerge, to put under water. 2. To sink, to crush, to overwhelm, to beat down. 3. To refute, to confound. 4. To sink, to make to fall, to pull or bear down, to destroy, to ruin.—*vr.* 1. To sink, to fall down, to fall to a level. 2. To sink, to go to the bottom. 3. (Coll.) To hide, to lie hid: applied to things which cannot be found. 4. To have dissensions and quarrels.

Húngaro, ra [oon'-gah-ro, rah], *a.* Hungarian, pertaining to Hungary.

Huno, na [oo'-no, nah], *a.* Hun, one of an obscure Asiatic warlike race.—*m. pl.* The Huns.

Hupa [oo'-pah]. A word used by children, either to ask of any one to lift them up, or to complain of some harm.

Hupe [oo'-pay], *f.* A white spongy substance which results from the decomposition of certain woods, and serves as tinder.

Hura [oo'-rah], *f.* 1. Furuncle, an angry pustule on the head. 2. A tree of the Antilles, known as the American walnut. 3. A carbuncle.

Huracán [oo-rah-cahn'], *m.* Hurricane, a violent storm. (Carib.)

Hurañamente [oo-rah-nyah-men'-tay], *adv.* 1. Wildly, in a savage and intractable manner. 2. Diffidently, disdainfully.

Huraño, ña [oo-rah'-nyo, nyah], *a.* 1. Shy, diffident; intractable. 2. Disdainful. 3. Cold-hearted, loveless.

Hurción, *f.* *V.* INFURCIÓN.

Hurgar [oor-gar'], *va.* 1. To stir, to move with a stick or iron. 2. To stir up disturbances, to excite quarrels.

Hurgón [oor-gone'], *m.* 1. Poker for stirring the fire; a fire-fork. 2. Thrust in fencing.

Hurgonada [oor-go-nah'-dah], *f.* *V* ESTOCADA.

Hurgonazo [oor-go-nah'-tho], *m.* A violent thrust.

Hurgonear [oor-go-nay-ar'], *va.* 1. To stir the fire with a poker. 2. To make a thrust in fencing.

Hurgonero [oor-go-nay'-ro], *m.* Poker. *V.* Hurgón.
Huri [oo-ree'], *f.* Houri, a Mohammedan nymph of paradise.
Hurón, na [oo-rone', nah], *m.* & *f.* 1. Ferret. Mustela furo, *L.* 2. Ferreter, one who pries into others' secrets.—*a.* Cold-hearted, loveless, shy, intractable, disdainful.
Huronear [oo-ro-nay ar'], *va.* 1. To ferret, to hunt with a ferret. 2. To hunt another in his privacies.
Huronera [oo-ro-nay'-rah], *f.* 1. Ferret-hole. 2. Lurking-place.
Huronero [oo-ro-nay'-ro], *m.* Ferret-keeper.
¡ Hurra ! [oor'-rah], *int.* 1. War-whoop of the Cossacks. 2. Hurrah! (English.)
Hurraca [oor-rah'-cah], *f.* (Orn.) Magpie. Corvus pica, *L.*
Hurtable [oor-tah'-blay], *a.* Capable of being stolen.
Hurta cordel (A) [oor-tah cor-del'], *adv.* 1. Spinning a top on the palm of the hand. 2. (Met.) Suddenly, insidiously, unexpectedly.
Hurtadas (A), *adv.* (Obs.) *V.* Á hurtadillas.
Hurtadillas (A) [oor-tah-deel'-lyas], *adv.* By stealth, slyly, artfully, privately, in a hidden manner.
Hurtadineros [oor-tah-de-nay'-ros], *m.* (Prov.) *V.* Alcancía.
Hurtador, ra [oor-tah-dor', rah], *m.* & *f.* Robber, thief.
Hurtagua [oor-tah'-goo-ah], *f.* (Prov.) *V.* Regadera.
Hurtamano (De) [oor-tah-mah'-no], *adverbial phrase.* Without consideration or pity.
Hurtar [oor-tar'], *va.* 1. To steal, to rob, to make way with. 2. To cheat in weight or measure. 3. To recover a piece of ground from the sea or a river. 4. To separate, to part. *Hurtar el cuerpo,* To flee, to avoid a difficulty. 5. To commit plagiarism.—*vr.* To remove or withdraw, to abscond.
Hurtarropa [oor-tar-ro'-pah], *f.* Boy's play.
Hurto [oor'-to], *m.* 1. Theft, robbery, stealing. 2. Theft, the thing stolen. 3. In mines, passage between the principal apartments. *A hurto,* By stealth.
Husada [oo-sah'-dah], *f.* A spindleful of thread or worsted.
Husaño [oo-sah'-nyo], *m.* A large spindle.
Húsar [oo'-sar], *m.* Hussar, originally a Hungarian horse soldier.
Husillero [oo-seel-lyay'-ro], *m.* One who attends the spindle in oil-mills.
Husillo [oo-seel'-lyo], *m.* 1. (Dim.) A small spindle. 2. A hollow cylinder running round in a spiral nut; a screw-pin.—*pl.* Drains, small channels for draining fens.
Husita [oo-see'-tah], *m.* Hussite, a follower of John Huss.
Husma [oos'-mah]. *Andar a la husma,* (Coll.) To peep narrowly in order to discover secrets.
Husmeador, ra [oos-may-ah-dor', rah], *m.* & *f.* Scenter, smeller.
Husmeadorcillo, lla [oos-may-ah-dor-theel'-lyo, lyah], *m.* & *f. dim.* Little smeller.
Husmear [oos-may-ar'], *va.* 1. To scent, to find out by smelling. 2. To pry, to peep, or inspect curiously, officiously, or impertinently.—*vn.* To begin to smell bad: applied to flesh.
Husmo [oos'-mo], *m.* Smell of meat somewhat tainted. *Estar al husmo,* To be upon the scent; to watch a favourable opportunity for obtaining one's end.
Huso [oo'-so], *m.* Spindle, the pin by which the thread is formed, and on which it is wound.
Huta [oo'-tah], *f.* Hut, kind of shed in which huntsmen hide, in order to start their dogs at the chase.
Hutia [oo-tee'-ah], *f.* Cuban rat.
¡ Huy ! [oo'-e]. Interjection of surprise, astonishment, grief, on seeing or hearing something.
Huyuyo, ya [oo-yoo'-yo, yah], *a.* (Cuba) Untractable, shy, diffident.

I

I [ee], the third of the Spanish vowels, called the Latin *i*, to distinguish it from the *y* called Greek. *I* in Spanish is sounded like the English *e* in *even*, or *i* in *idiotism*. When it should be a capital letter, in manuscript, *y* is often used instead of it, as *Ygnacio, Yglesia,* which in printing would be *Ignacio, Iglesia.* As a numeral, it stands for one. In chemistry, it is the symbol for iodine. (I.)
Iberia [e-bay'-re-ah], *f.* 1. An ancient region of Asia, now transcaucasian Georgia. 2. Name given by the ancient Greeks to Spain and Portugal.
Ibérico, ca [e-bay'-re-co, cah], *a.* or
Ibero [e-bay'-ro], *m.* Spaniard.—*a.* Spanish, Iberian.
Íbice [ee'-be-thay], *m.* Ibex, kind of goat. Capra ibex, *L.*
Ibidem [e-bee'-dem]. Latin word, meaning in the same place. In the same writing of an author.
Ibis [ee'-bis], *f.* (Orn.) Ibis, a kind of bird. Tantalus, *L.*
Icaco [e-cah'-co], *m.* (Bot.) West Indian cocoa-plum. Chrysobalanus icaco, *L.*
Icneumón [ic-nay-oo-mon'], *m.* 1. Ichneumon, a small animal; a mongoose. The Egyptian ichneumon devours the eggs of the crocodile, and was held sacred by the ancient Egyptians. 2. The ichneumon-fly, a hymenopterous insect predatory upon other insects.
Icnografía [ic-no-grah-fee'-ah], *f.* 1. Ichnography, ground-plan, a delineation of the length, breadth, angles, and lines of a fortification or building. 2. Ground-plot, the ichnography of a building.
Icnográfico, ca [ic-no-grah'-fe-co, cah], *a.* Ichnographical.
Icónico, ca [e-co'-ne-co, cah], *a.* Exactly conformable to the model; a perfect image.
Iconoclasta, Iconómaco [e-co-no-clahs'-tah, e-co-no'-mah-co], *m.* Iconoclast, image-breaker, heretic who denies the worship due to holy images.
Iconoclástico, ca [e-co-no-clahs'-te-co, cah], *a.* (Littl. us.) Iconoclastic.
Iconografía [e-co-no-grah-fee'-ah], *f.* Iconography, the art of describing by pictures.
Iconográfico, ca [e-co-no-grah'-fe-co, cah], *a.* Relating to iconography.
Iconólatra [e-co-no'-lah-trah], *m.* Iconolater, a worshipper of images.
Iconología [e-co-no-lo-hee'-ah], *f.* Iconology, representation by figures.
Iconoscopio [e-co-nos-co'-pe-o], *m.* Iconoscope.
Icoroso, sa [e-co-ro'-so, sah], *a.* Ichorous, serous.
Icosaedro [e-co-sah-ay'-dro], *m.* Icosahedron, a solid bounded by twenty plane faces.
Ictericia [ic-tay-ree'-the-ah], *f.* Jaundice, a disease.
Ictericiado, da, Ictérico, ca [ic-tay-re-the-ah'-do, dah, ec-tay'-re-co, cah], *a.* Icterical, jaundiced.
Ictiofagia [ic-te-o-fah'-he-ah], *f.* Ichthyophagy, diet of fish.
Ictiófago, ga [ic-te-o'-fah-go, gah], *a.* Fish-eating, relating to the ichthyophagists.—*m.* & *f.* Ichthyophagist.
Ictiología [ic-te-o-lo-he'-ah], *f.* Ichthyology, the science of the nature of fishes.
Ictiopetra [ic-te-o-pay'-trah], *f.* A petrified fish.
Ictiosauro [ic-te-o-sah'-oo-ro], *m.* Ichthyosaurus.
Ictiosis [ic-te-o'-sis], *f.* Ichthyosis, a scaly disease of the skin.
Ictita [ic-tee'-tah], *f.* A stone which preserves the impression of a fish.
Icho, or Ichu [ee'-cho, ee'-choo], *m.* The grass which grows spontaneously on the heaths of the Andes. (Peru.)
Ida [ee'-dah], *f.* 1. Departure, act of going from one place to another. 2. (Met.) Impetuosity; rash, inconsiderate, or violent proceeding; sally. 3. Act of driving a ball out of the truck-table. 4. Mark or impression of the foot of game on the ground. *Ida del humo,* Departure never to return. *Idas,* Frequent visits. *Darse dos idas y venidas,* (Coll.) To talk a matter over very briefly, to transact business expeditiously. *En dos idas y venidas,* Briefly, promptly. *Ida y vuelta,* Out and home, round-trip, excursion. *¡ La ida del cuervo !* He's off (good riddance, expression of gladness).
Idalio, lia [e-dah'-le-o, ah], *a.* Idalian, of Idalia, an ancient city of Cyprus.
Idea [e-day'-ah], *f.* 1. Idea, a mental image. 2. Notion, conception. 3. Contrivance, design, intention, plan, project, scheme. 4. Thread of a discourse. 5. Model, example. 6. Genius, talent. 7. Fancy, conceit, extravagant notion, impression: in this sense it is used commonly in the plural.
Ideal [e-day-ahl'], *a.* Ideal, mental, intellectual, imaginary, notional: not physical.
Idealidad [e-day-ah-le-dahd'], *f.* 1. Ideality; the ideal. 2. Ideality, the sentiment of the beautiful, the poetic, the eloquent.
Idealismo [e-day-ah-lees'-mo], *m.* 1. Idealism, generic name of the philosophic systems which consider the idea as the essence of things. 2. Aptitude of the artist, poet, orator, etc., to raise above reality the objects which he describes.
Idealista [e-day-ah-lees'-tah], *a.* Idealistic, striving after the ideal.—*n.* Idealist, believer in idealism.
Idealizar [e-day-ah-le-thar'], *va.* To idealize.
Idealmente [e-day-al-men'-tay], *adv.* Ideally, intellectually.
Idear [e-day-ar'], *va.* 1. To form or conceive an idea. 2. To think, to contrive, to invent, to imagine, to plan, to scheme, to meditate. 3. To discuss a subject on futile grounds, to indulge in airy conceptions.
Ídem [ee'-dem], *pron.* (Lat.) Idem, the same. (Abbrev. id.)
Idénticamente [e-den'-te-cah-men-tay], *adv.* Identically.
Idéntico, ca [e-den'-te-co, cah], *a.* Identic, identical, congenerous, the same, implying the same thing.
Identidad [e-den-te-dahd'], *f.* Identity, sameness, identicalness.
Identificación [e-den-te-fe-cah-the-on'], *f.* Identification.
Identificar [e-den-te-fe-car'], *va.* To identify; to ascertain the sameness of two objects.—*vr.* To become the same.

Ideo, ea [ee-day'-o, ah], *a.* (Poet.) Belonging to Mount Ida.

Ideográfico, ca [e-day-o-grah'-fe-co, cah], *a.* Ideographic, presenting ideas by symbolic characters.

Ideografía [e-day-o-gra-fee'-ah], *f.* Ideography, representation of thought by signs, especially phonetic.

Ideología [e-day-o-lo-hee'-ah], *f.* Ideology, ideas.

Ideológico, ca [e-day-o-lo'-he-co, cah], *a.* Ideological.

Idílico, ca [e-dee'-le-co, cah], *a.* Idyllic, having the qualities of an idyl.

Idilio [e-dee'-le-o], *m.* (Poet.) Idyl, a pastoral poem.

Idioma [e-de-o'-mah], *m.* 1. Idiom, the language peculiar to a nation or country. 2. Idiom, mode of speaking peculiar to a dialect or language. 3. Sounds with which brutes express their wants or sensations.

Idiomático, ca [e-de-o-mah'-te-co, cah], *a.* Idiomatic, proper to a language.

Idiopatía [e-de-o-pah-tee'-ah], *f.* Idiopathy, a primary disease distinctive in character.

Idiopático, ca [e-de-o-pah'-te-co, cah], *a.* Idiopathic, primary, independent: applied to diseases.

Idiosincrasia [e-de-o-sin-crah'-se-ah], *f.* Idiosyncrasy, a peculiar disposition.

Idiota [e-de-o'-tah], *m.* Idiot, a fool, an ignorant person.

Idiotez [e-de-o-teth'], *f.* Idiotism, silliness, ignorance, idiocy.

Idiótico, ca [e-de-o'-te-co, cah], *a.* Idiotic, belonging to idiocy.

Idiotismo [e-de-o-tees'-mo], *m.* 1. Idiom, idiotism, peculiarity of expression. 2. Idiocy, folly, natural imbecility of mind.

Ido, da [ee'-do, dah], *pp.* of Ir. Gone.

Idólatra [e-do'-lah-trah], *a.* Idolatrous; heathen, paganish.

Idólatra [e-do'-lah-trah], *m.* 1. Idolater, a worshipper of idols. 2. One who idolizes a woman, or loves her with excessive fondness.

Idolatradamente [e-do-lah-trah-dah-men'-tay], *adv.* Idolatrously.

Idolatrar [e-do-lah-trar'], *va.* 1. To idolatrize. 2. To idolize, to love with excessive fondness.

Idolatría [e-do-lah-tree'-ah], *f.* 1. Idolatry. 2. Inordinate love, excessive fondness.

Idolátrico, ca [e-do-lah'-tre-co, cah], *a.* (Obs.) Idolatrous, idolish.

Idolito, illo [e-do-lee'-to], *m.* (Dim.) 1. A little idol. 2. Darling, favourite, the object of fondness.

Idolo [ee'-do-lo], *m.* 1. Idol, an image worshipped as God. 2. (Coll.) Idol, a person or thing loved with the utmost affection.

Idoneidad [e-do-nay-e-dahd'], *f.* Aptitude, fitness, capacity.

Idóneo, nea [e-doh'-nay-o, nah], *a.* Fit, convenient, proper, meet.

Idus [ee'-doos], *m.* Ides, last of the three parts into which the Romans divided the month.

Iglesario [e-glay-sah'-re-o], *m.* The total of the lands which used to belong to the edifices of churches.

Iglesia [e-glay'-se-ah], *f.* 1. Church, the collective body of Christians. 2. Church, body of Christians adhering to some particular form of worship. 3. Church, place which Christians consecrate to the worship of God. 4. Temple, place either of Christian or heathen worship. 5. Ecclesiastical state; chapter; diocese. *Hombre de iglesia*, An ecclesiastic. 6. Right of immunity enjoyed in churches. *Iglesia fría*, Church where a malefactor does not enjoy protection against the laws of his country. *Iglesia me llamo*, I am called the church: expression of delinquents when they do not wish to tell their name, but seek the immunity of the church.

Ignaro, ra [ig-nah'-ro, rah], *a.* Ignorant, unlearned, uninstructed.

Ignavia [ig-nah'-ve-ah], *f.* Idleness, laziness, carelessness. (Acad.)

Ígneo, ea [eeg'-nay-o, ah], *a.* Igneous, fiery.

Ignescente [ig-nes-then'-tay], *a.* Scintillating, burning, ignescent.

Ignición [ig-ne-the-on'], *f.* Ignition, the act of kindling or setting on fire.

Ignícola [ig-nee'-co-lah], *m.* Fire-worshipper.

Ignífero, ra [ig-nee'-fay-ro, rah], *a.* (Poet.) Igniferous, ignifluous, containing or emitting fire.

Ignipotente [ig-ne-po-ten'-tay], *a.* (Poet.) Ignipotent, powerful over fire.

Igniscencia [ig-nis-then'-the-ah], *f.* Incandescence.

Igniscente [ig-nis-then'-tay], *a.* Incandescent, glowing with heat.

Ignoble, *a.* (Ant.) *V.* Innoble.

Ignografía, *f.* *V.* Iconografía.

Ignominia [ig-no-mee'-ne-ah], *f.* Ignominy, infamy, public disgrace, opprobrium.

Ignominiosamente [ig-no-me-ne-o-sah-men'-tay], *adv.* Ignominiously, opprobriously.

Ignominioso, sa [ig-no-me-ne-o'-so, sah], *a.* Ignominious, opprobrious, reproachful, disgraceful.

Ignorado, da [ig-no-rah'-do, dah], *a.* & *pp.* of Ignorar. Unknown, occult, fameless.

Ignorancia [ig-no-rahn'-the-ah], *f.* Ignorance, unlearnedness, want of knowledge, illiterateness; idiotism; folly; darkness.

Ignorante [ig-no-rahn'-tay], *pa.* & *a.* 1. Ignorant, stupid, unlearned, uninstructed. 2. Ignorant, without knowledge of some particular.—*m.* Ignorant.

Ignorantemente [ig-no-ran-tay-men'-tay], *adv.* Ignorantly.

Ignorantón, na [ig-no-ran-tone', nah], *a. aug.* Grossly ignorant.

Ignorar [ig-no-rar'], *va.* To be ignorant of, not to know.

Ignoto, ta [ig-no'-to, tah], *a.* Unknown, undiscovered.

Igorrote [e-gor-ro'-tay], *m.* Name of a tribe of savage Indians of the island of Luzón (Philippines), and of their language.

Igual [e-goo-ahl'], *a.* 1. Equal, similar, fellow, coequal, like another in any quality that admits comparison. 2. Level, even, flat. 3. Like, resembling, similar; uniform, equable. 4. Constant, firm, determined, equanimous, consistent.—*m.* The sign of equality, viz. =. *En igual de*, Instead of, in lieu of. *Al igual*, Equally. *No tiene igual*, He has not his like; it is matchless. *Por igual* or *por un igual*, Equally, with equality. *Sin igual*, Not to be equalled.

Iguala [e-goo-ah'-lah], *f.* 1. Agreement, convention, stipulation, contract, commutation. 2. Equalizing, equalling, the act of equalling. 3. Level, an instrument with which masons adjust their work. 4. Stipend or gratuity given in settlement, and especially a yearly or monthly stipend given in rural districts to doctors and apothecaries for the right to services and medicines. *A la iguala*, Equally. *Él tiene iguala con* or *está igualado con*, He serves, attends, etc., for a stipulated sum.

Igualación [e-goo-ah-lah-the-on'], *f.* 1. Equalling, equalizing, equalization, levelling, the act and effect of making equal or even. 2. Agreement, stipulation, contract. 3. (Alg.) Equation. 4. Counter-gauge, a trimming of one piece of wood into another.

Igualado, da [e-goo-ah-lah'-do, dah], *pp.* of Igualar. Equalled. Said of some birds which have shed the down and have even plumage. *Dejar a uno igualado*, (Coll.) To give one a severe drubbing.

Igualador, ra [e-goo-ah-lah-dor', rah], *m.* & *f.* 1. Equalizer, leveller. 2. A kind of sieve of fine skin for refining the grain of powder.

Igualamiento [e-goo-ah-lah-me-en'-to], *m.* Equalizing, equalization, act of equalling.

Igualar [e-goo-ah-lar'], *va.* 1. To equalize, to match, to mate. 2. To judge without partiality, to hold in equal estimation. 3. To flatten, to make even or level, to level the ground. *Igualar las mercaderías*, To put a fair price upon merchandise. 4. To rake the ground. 5. To adjust differences, to agree upon.—*vn.* To be equal.—*vr.* To level, to efface distinction or superiority, to place one's self upon a level with others. *Igualar la sangre*, (Coll.) 1. To bleed a second time. 2. (Met.) To give a second blow.

Igualdad [e-goo-al-dahd'], *f.* 1. Equality, similitude. 2. Conformity, consimilitude, likeness. 3. Levelness, evenness, equality of surface. 4. Equality, uniformity. *Igualdad de ánimo*, Evenness of mind; constancy, equability.

Igualmente [e-goo-al-men'-tay], *adv.* Equally, uniformly, equably, evenly; likewise; constantly.

Iguana [e-goo-ah'-nah], *f.* Iguana, a kind of lizard, a native of America. Lacerta iguana, *L.*

Iguarandi [e-goo-ah-rahn'-de], *m.* (Amer.) Pellitory.

Iguarias [e-goo-ah'-re-as], *f. pl.* Viands dressed and served up. (Obs.)

Igüedo [e-goo-ay'-do], *m.* *V.* Cabrón. (Acad.)

Ijada [e-hah'-dah], *f.* 1. Flank, the lateral part of the lower belly. 2. Pain in the side, colic. *Tener su ijada*, (Met.) To have a weak side.

Ijadear [e-hah-day-ar'], *vn.* To pant, to palpitate.

Ijal [e-hahl'], *m.* (Cuba) *V.* Ijada.

Ijar [e-har'], *m.* Flank. *V.* Ijada. *Caballo de pocos ijares*, A light-flanked horse.

Ilación [e-lah-the-on'], *f.* Inference, illation, conclusion drawn.

Ilativo, va [e-lah-tee'-vo, vah], *a.* Illative, that which denotes illation or conclusion.

Ilécebra [e-lay'-thay-brah], *f.* (Obs.) Allurement, enticement, temptation.

Ilegal [e-lay-gahl'], *a.* Illegal, unlawful.

Ilegalidad [e-lay-gah-le-dahd'], *f.* Illegality, unlawfulness.

Ilegalmente [e-lay-gal-men'-tay], *adv.* Illegally, lawlessly, unlawfully.

Ilegible [e-lay-hee'-blay], *a.* Illegible.

Ilegítimamente [e-lay-hee'-te-mah-men-tay], *adv.* Illegitimately, foully.

Ilegitimar [e-lay-he-te-mar'], *va.* To illegitimate, to render or prove a person illegitimate.

Ilegitimidad [e-lay-he-te-me-dahd'], *f.* Illegitimacy.

Ilegítimo, ma [e-lay-hee'-te-mo, mah], *a.* 1. Illegal, contrary to law. 2. Illegitimate, unlawfully begotten.

Ileo [e'-lay-o], *m.* Ileus, severe colic due to intestinal obstruction. Called also iliac passion.

Ileon [ee'-lay-on], *m.* Ileum, the third division of the small intestines.
Ileosía [e-lay-o-see'-ah], *f.* *V.* Íleo.
Ileso, sa [e-lay'-so, sah], *a.* Unhurt, free from damage, harmless.
Ilíaco, ca [e-lee'-ah-co, cah], *a.* Iliac, relating to the ilium.
Iliaco, ca [e-lee'-ah-co, cah], *a.* Belonging or relating to Ilium or Troy.
Iliberal [e-le-bay-rahl'], *a.* Illiberal.
Ilícitamente [e-lee'-the-tah-men-tay], *adv.* Illicitly, forbiddenly.
Ilícito, ta [e-lee'-the-to, tah], *a.* Illicit, unlawful.
Ilimitable [e-le-me-tah'-blay], *a.* (Littl. us.) Illimitable.
Ilimitado, da [e-le-me-tah'-do, dah], *a.* Unlimited, boundless, limitless; unconditional.
Ilion [ee'-le-on], *m.* Ilium, the upper part of the innominate bone.
Ilíquido, da [e-lee'-ke-do, dah], *a.* Unliquidated: applied to accounts or debts.
Iliterato [e-le-tay-rah'-to], *a.* Illiterate, unlearned.
Ilógico, ca [e-lo'-he-co, cah], *a.* Illogical.
Ilota [e-lo'-tah], *m.* 1. A slave of Lacedemonia; a Helot. 2. One deprived of the rights and privileges of a citizen.
Iludir [e-loo-deer'], *va.* *V.* Burlar.
Iluminación [e-loo-me-nah-the-on'], *f.* 1. Illumination, the act of supplying with light. 2. Illumination, festive lights, hung out as a token of joy. 3. Illumination, infusion of intellectual light, knowledge, or grace.
Iluminado, da [e-loo-me-nah'-do, dah], *a.* & *pp.* of Iluminar. Illuminate, enlightened: commonly applied in a bad sense. *Estampas iluminadas*, Coloured plates.
Iluminado [e-loo-me-nah'-do], *m.* Illuminate, in the plural, illuminati: a name given to certain heretics of the sixteenth century, and to a sect of philosophers of our own times. A visionary.
Iluminador [e-loo-me-nah-dor'], *m.* Illuminator, one who illumines; one who adorns with colours.
Iluminar [e-loo-me-nar'], *va.* 1. To illumine or illuminate, to light, to fill with light, to supply with light. 2. To illuminate, to adorn with festal lamps or bonfires. 3. To illuminate, to enlighten intellectually, to infuse knowledge or grace. 4. To give light and shade to a painting; to colour, to illumine books. 5. To render transparent.
Iluminativo, va [e-loo-me-nah-tee'-vo, vah], *a.* Illuminative.
Ilusión [e-loo-se-on'], *f.* 1. Illusion, false show, counterfeit appearance; fallaciousness. 2. A sort of smart and lively irony. 3. (Coll.) Apprehension.
Ilusionar [e-loo-se-o-nar'], *va.* 1. To cause illusion. 2. To fascinate.—*vr.* To suffer illusions.
Ilusivo, va [e-loo-see'-vo, vah], *a.* Delusive, illusive, false, deceitful.
Iluso, sa [e-loo'-so, sah], *a.* 1. Deluded, deceived, ridiculed. 2. Bigoted.
Ilusoriamente [e-loo-so-re-ah-men'-tay], *adv.* Illusively.
Ilusorio, ria [e-loo-so'-re-o, ah], *a.* 1. Delusive, illusory, deceptive. 2. (Law) Null, void of effect of no value.
Ilustración [e-loos-trah-the-on'], *f.* 1. Illustration, explanation, elucidation, exposition, explication. 2. *pl.* The engravings of a book or periodical.
Ilustrado, da [e-loos-trah'-do, dah], *a.* Wise, intelligent, of abundant knowledge.
Ilustrador, ra [e-loos-trah-dor', rah], *m.* & *f.* Illustrator, explicator.
Ilustrar [e-loos-trar'], *va.* 1. To illustrate, to clear up, to explain, to enlighten, to elucidate. 2. To inspire, to infuse supernatural light. 3. To aggrandize, to ennoble, to illustrate, to heighten. 4. To provide printed matter with plates or engravings. (Acad.)—*vr.* 1. To acquire knowledge. 2. To become celebrated.
Ilustre [e-loos'-tray], *a.* Illustrious, noble, celebrated, conspicuous, glorious, honourable, magnificent.
Ilustremente [e-loos-tray-men'-tay], *adv.* Illustriously, greatly.
Ilustrísimo, ma [e-loos-tree'-se-mo, mah], *a.* Appellation of honour given to bishops and other persons of a certain dignity.
Illutar [eel-lyoo-tar'], *va.* To cover a part of the body with mud or mineral sediment; to illutate; to take a mud bath.
Imadas [e-mah'-das], *f. pl.* (Naut.) Ways, sliding planks used in launching ships.
Imagen [e-mah'-hen], *f.* 1. Image, figure, any corporeal representation, imagery, statue, effigy. 2. Image, show, appearance, fancy, conception. 3. (Rhet.) Picture or lively description.
Imagencita, illa [e-mah-hen-thee'-tah, theel'-lyah], *f. dim.* A little image.
Imaginable [e-mah-he-nah'-blay], *a.* Imaginable, contrivable, conceivable.
Imaginación [e-mah-he-nah-the-on'], *f.* 1. Imagination, fancy; the power of forming ideal pictures. 2. Imagination, conception, image of the mind. 3. Conceit, fantasy; any unsolid or fanciful opinion or idea.
Imaginar [e-mah-he-nar'], *vn.* 1. To imagine, to fancy, to image, to paint in the mind. 2. To imagine, to scheme, to contrive, to excogitate, to conceive; to find out. 3. To form erroneous suppositions.—*va.* (Obs.) To adorn with images.—*vr.* *V.* Figurarse.
Imaginaria [e-mah-he-nah'-re-ah], *f.* (Mil.) Reserve guard.
Imaginariamente [e-mah-he-nah-re-ah-men'-tay], *adv.* In a visionary manner.
Imaginario [e-mah-he-nah'-re-o], *m.* Painter or sculptor of images.
Imaginario, ria, *a.* Imaginary, fancied, visionary.
Imaginativa [e-mah-he-nah-tee'-vah], *f.* Imagination, fancy.
Imaginativo, va [e-mah-he-nah-tee'-vo, vah], *a.* Imaginative, fantastic, fanciful.
Imaginería [e-mah-he-nay-ree'-ah], *f.* Imagery, an embroidery representing flowers, birds, or fishes.
Imán [e-mahn'], *m.* 1. Loadstone, the magnet. 2. The mariner's compass. 3. Charm, attraction. 4. Electromagnet. 5. The Mohammedan leader of prayer. (Arab. imām.)
Imanación [e-ma-nah-the-on'], *f.* *V.* Imantación.
Imanar [e-mah-nar'], *va.* To magnetize, to communicate the property of a loadstone.
Imantación [e-man-tah-the-on'], *f.* Magnetization. *V.* Magnetización.
Imantar [e-man-tar'], *va.* To touch the mariner's compass needle with loadstone. 2. To magnetize. (Not recognized by the Spanish Academy.)
Imbécil [im-bay'-theel], *a.* 1. Weak, feeble, imbecile. 2. Simple, silly.
Imbecilidad [im-bay-the-le-dahd'], *f.* 1. Imbecility, weakness, debility. 2. Simplicity, silliness.
Imbele [im-bay'-lay], *a.* (Poet.) Feeble, weak; unfit for war.
Imberbe [im-bayr'-bay], *m.* Beardless youth.
Imbibición [im-be-be-the-on'], *f.* Imbibition.
Imbornal [im-bor-nahl'], *m.* (Naut.) Scupper-hole. *Imbornal de bomba*, Pump scupper-hole. *Imbornales de varengas*, Limber-holes. *Imbornales de la caja de agua*, Scuppers of the manger.
Imborrable [im-bor-rah'-blay], *a.* Indelible.
Imbricación [im-bre-cah-the-on'], *f.* Imbrication, overlapping of scales.
Imbricado, da [im-bre-cah'-do, dah], *a.* Imbricated, indented with concavities: applied to shells that are waved.
Imbricativo, va [im-bre-cah-tee'-vo, vah], *a.* (Bot.) Imbricate, overlapping in the bud.
Imbuir [im-boo-eer'], *va.* To imbue, to admit into the mind, to infuse into the mind, to instruct.
Imbursación [im-boor-sah-the-on'], *f.* (Prov.) Act of putting into a sack.
Imbursar [im-boor-sar'], *va.* (Prov.) To put into a sack or bag.
Imilla [e-meel'-lyah], *f.* (S. Amer.) The girl sent by each settlement of Indians to the curate, to serve him for a week.
Imitable [e-me-tah'-blay], *a.* Imitable.
Imitación [e-me-tah-the-on'], *f.* 1. Imitation, the act of copying. 2. Imitation, that which is offered as a copy. *A imitación*, After the example, in imitation of.
Imitado, da [e-me-tah'-do, dah], *a.* & *pp.* of Imitar. Copied, imitated, imitative.
Imitador, ra [e-me-tah-dor', rah], *m.* & *f.* Imitator, follower.
Imitante [e-me-tahn'-tay], *pa.* of Imitar. Imitator.
Imitar [e-me-tar'], *va.* To imitate, to copy, to follow; to counterfeit.
Imitativo, va [e-me-tah-tee'-vo, vah], *a.* Imitative, aiming at resemblance.
Imóscapo [e-mos'-cah-po], *m.* (Arch.) Apophyge, a concave curve in a column where the shaft rises from the base.
Impaciencia [im-pah-the-en'-the-ah], *f.* 1. Impatience, inability to suffer pain; rage under suffering. 2. Impatience, inability to suffer delay, eagerness, hastiness. 3. Impatience, peevishness, vehemence of temper, heat of passion.
Impacientar [im-pah-the-en-tar'], *va.* To vex, to irritate, to make one lose all patience.—*vr.* To become impatient, to lose all patience.
Impaciente [im-pah-the-en'-tay], *a.* Impatient, fidgety, restless, peevish, not able to endure delay.
Impacientemente [im-pah-the-en-tay-men'-tay], *adv.* Impatiently, longingly, peevishly, eagerly, ardently, with great desire.
Impacto, ta [im-pahc'-to, tah], *a.* Impacted, thrust into, packed tight.
Impalpabilidad [im-pal-pa-be-le-dahd'], *f.* Impalpability.
Impalpable [im-pal-pah'-blay], *a.* Impalpable, not to be perceived by the touch.
Impar [im-par'], *a.* 1. Unequal, dissimilar, odd. 2. Uneven, not divisible into equal numbers.
Imparcial [im-par-the-ahl'], *a.* 1. Impartial, equitable. 2. Impartial, indifferent, disinterested, just. 3. Unprejudiced, imprejudicate.
Imparcialidad [im-par-the-ah-le-dahd'], *f.* Impartiality, equitableness, justice; indifference.

Imparcialmente [im-par-the-al-men'-tay], *adv.* Impartially, equitably, justly, honestly.

Imparidad [im-pa-re-dahd'], *f.* Inequality, imparity, dissimilarity.

Impartibilidad [im-par-to-be-le-dahd'], *f.* (Littl. us.) Indivisibility, impartibility.

Impartible [im-par-tee'-blay], *a.* 1. Indivisible. 2. (Law) Impartible, communicable, what can be bestowed or conferred.

Impartir [im-par-teer'], *va.* 1. To demand or require assistance; chiefly applied to courts of judicature, which demand one another's assistance for the effectual administration of justice. 2. To grant, to impart.

Impasable [im-pah-sah'-blay], *a.* Impassable.

Impasibilidad [im-pa-se-be-le-dahd'], *f.* Impassibility, impassiveness, insusceptibility of suffering, exemption from pain.

Impasible [im-pa-see'-blay], *a.* 1. Impassible, incapable of suffering. 2. Impassible, exempt from external impression, insensible of pain.

Impastar [im-pas-tar'], *va.* To reduce a ground material to paste.

Impávidamente [im-pah'-ve-dah-men-tay], *adv.* Intrepidity, undauntedly.

Impavidez [im-pah-ve-deth'], *f.* Intrepidity, courage, boldness.

Impávido, da [im-pah'-ve-do, dah], *a.* Dauntless, intrepid, undaunted.

Impecabilidad [im-pay-cah-be-le-dahd'], *f.* Impeccability, impeccancy, incapacity for sin.

Impecable [im-pay-cah'-blay], *a.* Impeccable, exempt from possibility of sin.

Impedido, da [im-pay-dee'-do, dah], *a.* Invalid, impeded, sick, valetudinarian, crippled; having lost the use of the limbs.—*pp.* of IMPEDIR.

Impedidor, ra [im-pay-de-dor', rah], *m.* & *f.* Obstructer, one who impedes.

Impediente [im-pay-de-en'-tay], *pa.* Hindering, that which impedes.

Impedimento [im-pay-de-men'-to], *m.* Impediment, obstacle, hinderance, obstruction, let, clog, cumbrance, cumbersomeness, impeachment. (Met.) Shackles.

Impedir [im-pay-deer'], *va.* 1. To impede, to hinder, to obstruct, to prevent. (Obs.) To clog, to keep back from, to forbid. 2. To constrain, to restrain, to cohibit; to counteract, to preclude. 3. (Poet.) To suspend.

Impeditivo, va [im-pay-de-tee'-vo, vah], *a.* Impeding, hindering, impeditive.

Impeler [im-pay-lerr'], *va.* 1. To impel, to give an impulse. 2. To incite, to stimulate, to move. 3. To impel, to press on, to urge forward, to propel.

Impenetrabilidad [im-pay-nay-trah-be-le-dahd'], *f.* Impenetrability, impenetrableness.

Impenetrable [im-pay-nay-trah'-blay], *a.* 1. Impenetrable, impervious, that cannot be pierced or penetrated. 2. Impenetrable, incomprehensible, not to be conceived by the mind; fathomless.

Impenetrablemente, *adv.* (Littl. us.) Impenetrably, imperviously.

Impenitencia [im-pay-ne-ten'-the-ah], *f.* Impenitence.

Impenitente [im-pay-ne-ten'-tay], *a.* Impenitent, obdurate, hard-hearted.

Impensa [im-pen'-sah], *f.* (For.) Expense.

Impensadamente [im-pen sah-dah-men'-tay], *adv.* Unexpectedly.

Impensado, da [im-pen-sah'-do, dah], *a.* Unexpected, unforeseen, fortuitous.

Imperante [im-pay-rahn'-tay], *pa.* Commanding.—*a.* (Astrol.) Ruling: applied to a star. Formerly it was used as a substantive.

Imperar [im-pay-rar'], *vn.* To command, to reign.—*va.* (Obs.) To command a person, to direct his actions.

Imperativamente [im-pay-rah-te-vah-men'-tay], *adv.* Imperatively, author itatively.

Imperativo, va [im-pay-rah-tee'-vo, vah], *a.* Imperative, commanding, expres sive of command; a mood in grammar.—*f.* The tone or gesture of command. *Tomar la imperativa,* To assume authority.

Imperatoria [im-pay-rah-to'-re-ah], *f.* (Bot.) Masterwort. Imperatoria ostruthium, *L.*

Imperatorio, ria [im-pay-rah-to'-re-o, ah], *a.* 1. Imperial, royal, belonging to an emperor or monarch. 2. Eminent, possessed of superior qualities.

Imperceptible [im-per-thep-tee'-blay], *a.* Imperceptible.

Imperceptiblemente [im-per-thep-te-blay-men'-tay], *adv.* Imperceptibly.

Impercuso, sa [im-per-coo'-so, sah], *a.* Unstruck: used of coins where a side remains blank.

Imperdible [im-per-dee'-blay], *a.* (Coll.) Imperdible, not to be lost or destroyed.

Imperdonable [im-per-do-nah'-blay], *a.* (Coll.) Impardonable, irremissible.

Imperecedero, ra [im-pay-ray-thay-day'-ro, rah], *a.* Imperishable, unforgettable.

Imperfección [im-per-fec-the-on'], *f.* Imperfection, fault, slight failure or defect.

Imperfectamente [im-per-fec-tah-men'-tay], *adv.* Imperfectly, faultily, lamely, inadequately.

Imperfecto, ta [im-per-fec'-to, tah], *a.* 1. Imperfect, not complete; defective, faulty, crippled, broken. 2. Imperfect, in grammar: referring to past time.

Imperforación [im-per-fo-rah-the-on'], *f.* (Med.) Imperforation, the state of being closed.

Imperforado, da [im-per-fo-rah'-do, dah], *a.* (Med.) Imperforate, closed up.

Imperial [im-pay-re-ahl'], *f.* 1. Roof of a coach or carriage. 2. (Naut.) Poop-royal, a platform which serves as a covering of the poop-gallery of a ship.

Imperial [im-pay-re-ahl'], *a.* 1. Imperial, belonging to an emperor or monarch. 2. Applied to a kind of small black plum.

Imperiales [im-pay-re-ah'-les], *m. pl.* Imperialists, a name given to the troops of the Emperor of Austria.

Imperialismo [im-pay-re-ah-lees'-mo], *m.* Imperialism, government by empire.

Imperialista [im-pay-re-ah-lees'-tah], *m.* Imperialist.

Impericia [im-pay-ree'-the-ah], *f.* Unskilfulness, want of knowledge or experience.

Imperio [im-pay'-re-o], *m.* 1. Empire, dominion, command. 2. Dignity of an emperor. 3. Empire, the dominions of an emperor. 4. Kind of linen made in Germany. *Alto* or *bajo imperio,* Upper or lower empire.

Imperiosamente [im-pay-re-o-sah-men'-tay], *adv.* Imperiously, lordly, masterly.

Imperiosidad [im-pay-re-o-se-dahd'], *f.* Imperiousness.

Imperioso, sa [im-pay-re-o'-so, sah], *a.* 1. Imperious, commanding, arrogant, haughty. 2. Powerful, overbearing, magisterial.

Imperitamente [im-pay-re-tah-men'-tay], *adv.* Unskilfully, ignorantly.

Imperito, ta [im-pay-ree'-to, tah], *a.* Unlearned, unskilled; deficient in the knowledge of art and science.

Impermeabilidad [im-per-may-ah-be-le-dahd'], *f.* Impermeability.

Impermeable [im-per-may-ah'-blay], *a.* Waterproof.—*m.* Raincoat.

Impermutable [im-per-moo-tah'-blay], *a.* Immutable.

Impersonal [im-per-so-nahl'], *a.* 1. Impersonal: applied to verbs. 2. Mode of speaking impersonally. *En* or *por impersonal,* Impersonally.

Impersonalmente [im-per-so-nal-men'-tay], *adv.* Impersonally.

Impersuasible [im-per-soo-ah-see'-blay], *a.* Impersuasible, not to be moved by persuasion.

Impertérrito, ta [im-per-tayr'-re-to, tah], *a.* Intrepid, unterrified, dauntless.

Impertinencia [im-per-te-nen'-the-ah], *f.* 1. Impertinence, folly, nonsense. 2. Peevishness, humorousness. 3. Impertinence, troublesomeness, intrusion. 4. Minute accuracy in the performance of a thing.

Impertinente [im-per-te-nen'-tay], *a.* 1. Impertinent, intrusive, importunate, meddling. 2. Impertinent, nonsensical, trifling. 3. Peevish, fretful, cross, froward, ill-humoured.

Impertinentemente, *adv.* Impertinently.

Imperturbabilidad [im-per-toor-bah-be-le-dahd'], *f.* (Littl. us.) Imperturbability.

Imperturbable [im-per-toor-bah'-blay], *a.* Imperturbable, not to be disturbed.

Imperturbablemente, *adv.* Imperturbably.

Imperturbar [im-per-toor-bar'], *va.* (Ven.) To disturb.

Impervio, via [im-payr'-ve-o, ah], *a.* Impervious, impassable, impenetrable.

Impetra [im-pay'-trah], *f.* 1. Diploma, license, permission. 2. Bull by which dubious benefices are granted.

Impetrable [im-pay-trah'-blay], *a.* (Law) Impetrable, possible to be obtained.

Impetración [im-pay-trah-the-on'], *f.* Impetration, the act of obtaining by prayer or entreaty.

Impetrado, da [im-pay-trah'-do, dah], *a.* & *pp.* of IMPETRAR. Impetrate, impetrated, granted.

Impetrador, ra [im-pay-trah-dor', rah], *m.* & *f.* One who impetrates.

Impetrante [im-pay-trahn'-tay], *pa.* Impetrating.—*m.* (Law) Grantee; impetrator.

Impetrar [im-pay-trar'], *va.* To impetrate, to obtain by entreaty.

Ímpetu [eem'-pay-too], *m.* 1. Impetus, a violent tendency to any point; a violent effort. 2. Impetuosity, fit, impulse, sally, start, violence or vehemence of passion.

Impetuosamente, *adv.* Impetuously, vehemently, violently.

Impetuosidad [im-pay-too-o-se-dahd'], *f.* Impetuosity, vehemence.

Impetuoso, sa [im-pay-too-o'-so, sah], *a.* 1. Impetuous, violent, forcible, fierce. 2. Impetuous, vehement, passionate, heady.

Impia or **Flor impia** [im-pee'-ah], *f.* Scarlet-flowered pentapetes, an herb like rosemary. Pentapetes phœnicea, *L.*

Impiedad [im-pe-ay-dahd'], *f.* 1. Impiety; irreligion, contempt of religion. 2. Impiety, any act of wickedness, impiousness; cruelty.

Impío, pía [im-pee'-o, ah], *a.* Impious. irreligious, wicked, profane, godless.
Impla [eem'-plah], *f.* Woman's veil anciently used, and the fabric of which it was made (fr. wimple).
Implacabilidad, *f.* Implacability.
Implacable [im-plah-cah'-blay], *a.* Implacable, not to be pacified; inexorable.
Implantación [im-plan-tah-the-on'], *f.* Implantation, act of implanting.
Implantar [im-plan-tar'], *va.* To implant, to set for growth; to inculcate.
Implaticable [im-plah-te-cah'-blay], *a.* Intractable, unmanageable.
Implexo, a [im-plec'-so, sah], *a.* Said of epic or dramatic poems which present vicissitudes in the fortune of the heroes.
Implicación [im-ple-cah-the-on'], *f.* 1. Implication; contradiction; implicitness. 2. Complicity.
Implicado, da [im-ple-cah'-do, dah], *a.* & *pp.* of IMPLICAR. Implicit, entangled, implicated.
Implicar [im-ple-car'], *vn.* To oppose, to contradict one another: applied to terms and propositions.—*va.* To implicate, to involve; to entangle, to embarrass.
Implicatorio, ria [im-ple-cah-to'-re-o, ah], *a.* Implicative.
Implícitamente [im-plee'-the-tah-men-tay], *adv.* Implicitly.
Implícito, ta [im-plee'-the-to, tah], *a.* Implicit, inferred; tacitly comprised, not expressed.
Imploración [im-plo-rah-the-on'], *f.* Entreaty, imploration, the act of imploring.
Implorar [im-plo-rar'], *va.* 1. To implore, to call upon in supplication, to solicit. 2. To implore, to ask with eagerness, to crave, to entreat, to beg.
Impolítica [im-po-lee'-te-cah], *f.* 1. Incivility, want of courtesy, clownishness, rudeness coarseness. 2. Impolicy.
Impolíticamente, *adv.* (Coll.) Impolitically, impoliticly.
Impolítico, ca [im-po-lee'-te-co, cah], *a.* 1. Impolitic or impolitical, indiscreet, imprudent. 2. Impolite, rude, coarse, unpolished.
Impoluto, ta [im-po-loo'-to, tah], *a.* Unpolluted, pure, free from stain, clean.
Imponderabilidad [im-pon-day-rah-be-le-dahd'], *f.* Imponderability (of heat, etc.).
Imponderable [im-pon-day-rah'-blay], *a.* Inexpressible, unutterable, imponderable.
Imponedor [im-po-nay-dor'], *m.* He who imposes or charges.
Imponente [im-po-nen'-tay], *a.* Imposing, awe-inspiring.
Imponer [im-po-nerr'], *va.* 1. To lay, put, or set in or upon. 2. To impose or lay a tax, a duty, etc. 3. To impose, to lay on as a burden or penalty. 4. To charge upon or impute falsely. 5. To advise, to give notice, to acquaint, to instruct some one. 6. To infuse respect or fear. 7. (Print.) To impose, to arrange pages of types for the press.
Impopular [im-po-poo-lar'], *a.* Unpopular.
Impopularidad [im-po-poo-lah-re-dahd'], *f.* Unpopularity.
Imporosidad [im-po-ro-se-dahd'], *f.* Imporosity, state of being without pores.
Imporoso, sa [im-po-ro'-so, sah], *a.* Imporous, without pores, solid.
Importable [im-por-tah'-blay], *a.* What can be imported from abroad: importable.
Importación [im-por-tah-the-on'], *f.* Importation.
Importador [im-por-tah-dor'], *m.* Importer.
Importancia [im-por-tahn'-the-ah], *f.* 1. Importance, import, consequence, moment, concern. 2. Importance, considerableness, a claim to notice; claim to respect.
Importante [im-por-tahn'-tay], *a.* Important, momentous, weighty, material, considerable.
Importantemente, *adv.* Importantly, usefully, materially, essentially.
Importar [im-por-tar'], *v. imp.* 1. To import, to be of moment, to be important or convenient, to concern, to matter. 2. To amount, or amount to. *No importa,* No matter, it is no matter, it matters not. *¿ Qué importa ?* or *¿ qué importa eso ?* What matters it? what of that? what does it signify? *Importa mucho,* It matters much.—*va.* 1. To import, to carry into any country from abroad. 2. To carry along with, to be a consequence of.
Importe [im-por'-tay], *m.* Amount or gross amount, value. *Importe medio,* Average amount.
Importunación [im-por-too-nah-the-on'], *f.* Importunity, incessant solicitation.
Importunadamente, *adv.* Importunately.
Importunador, ra [im-por-too-nah-dor', rah], *m.* & *f.* Importunator, importuner.
Importunamente, *adv.* 1. Importunely, with importunity. 2. Importunely, unseasonably.
Importunar [im-por-too-nar'], *va.* 1. To importune, to disturb by reiteration of the same request; to crave. 2. To vex, to molest, to harass, to tease, to disturb by reiteration of the same request.
Importunidad [im-por-too-ne-dahd'], *f.* Importunity, importunacy, importunateness.
Importuno, na [im-por-too'-no, nah], *a.* 1. Importune, importunate, unseasonable, happening at a wrong time. 2. Importune, troublesome, vexatious, heavy.
Imposibilidad [im-po-se-be-le-dahd'], *f.* Impossibility, impracticability, impracticableness.
Imposibilitado [im-po-se-be-le-tah'-do], *a.* & *pp.* of IMPOSIBILITAR. 1. Helpless, without means, poor. 2. Disabled, weakened, unfit for service.
Imposibilitar [im-po-se-be-le-tar'], *va.* To disable, to render impossible, to weaken, to unfit for service.
Imposible [im-po-see'-blay], *a.* 1. Impossible, impracticable, unfeasible. 2. Extremely difficult. *Los imposibles,* A kind of Spanish dance. *Imposible de toda imposibilidad,* (Coll.) Altogether impossible.
Imposiblemente, *adv.* Impossibly.
Imposición [im-po-se-the-on'], *f.* 1. Imposition, the act of laying any thing on another. 2. Imposition, the act of laying, putting, or setting in or upon. 3. Imposition, the act of imposing taxes or duties, and the tax, charge, or duty imposed. 4. Injunction of any thing as a law or duty. 5. Among printers, imposition, the arrangement of pages for the press.
Imposta [im-pos'-tah], *f.* (Arch.) Impost, that part of a pillar in vaults and arches on which the weight of the whole building lies.
Impostor, ra [im-pos-tor', rah], *m.* & *f.* Impostor, juggler.
Impostura [im-pos-too'-rah], *f.* 1. A false imputation or charge. 2. Imposture, fiction, deceit, cheat, fraud.
Impotable [im-po-tah'-blay], *a.* Impotable, not drinkable, unpotable.
Impotencia [im-po-ten'-the-ah], *f.* 1. Impotence or impotency, inability, weakness. 2. Impotence, frigidity, incapacity of propagation.
Impotente [im-po-ten'-tay], *a.* 1. Impotent, weak, feeble, wanting force. 2. Impotent, frigid, without power of propagation.
Impracticable [im-prac-te-cah'-blay], *a.* 1. Impracticable, impossible, unfeasible. 2. Impassable applied to roads.
Imprecación [im-pray-cah-the-on'], *f.* Imprecation, curse.
Imprecar [im-pray-car'], *va.* To imprecate, to curse.
Imprecatorio, ria [im-pray-cah-to'-re-o, ah], *a.* Imprecatory.
Imprecaución [im-pray-cah-oo-the-on'], *f.* Imprevision, want of foresight.
Impregnación [im-preg-nah-the-on'], *f.* Impregnation.
Impregnar [im-preg-nar'], *va.* To impregnate, to saturate with any matter or quality.—*vr.* To be impregnated.
Impremeditación [im-pray-may-de-tah-the-on'], *f.* Unpremeditation, absence of plan.
Impremeditado, da [im-pray-may-de-tah'-do, dah], *a.* Unpremeditated, unforeseen.
Impremir, *va.* (Obs.) *V.* IMPRIMIR.
Imprenta [im-pren'-tah], *f.* 1. Printing, the art of printing. 2. Printing-office. 3. Print, the form, size, etc., of the types used in printing books.
Imprescindible [im-pres-thin-dee'-blay], *a.* That which cannot be prescinded or put aside.
Imprescriptible [im-pres-crip-tee'-blay], *a.* Imprescriptible, without the compass of prescription.
Impresión [im-pray-se-on'], *f.* 1. Impression, the act of pressing one body upon another. 2. Impression, impress, mark made by pressure, stamp. 3. Print, the form, size, etc., of the types used in printing books. 4. Impression, edition, number printed at once. 5. Impression, efficacious agency, influence, or operation of one body upon another. 6. Impression, impress, image fixed in the mind. 7. (Astrol.) Influence of the stars; impression or effect.
Impresionable [im-pray-se-o-nah'-blay], *a.* Emotional, impressionable.
Impresionante [im-pray-se-o-nahn'-tay], *a.* Impressive, awe-inspiring.
Impresionar [im-pray-se-o-nar'], *va.* To imprint or fix on the mind or memory.
Impresionismo [im-pray-se-o-nees'-mo], *m.* (Lit. & Art) Impressionism.
Impreso [im-pray'-so], *m.* Pamphlet, a short treatise.
Impreso, sa [im-pray'-so, sah], *pp. irr.* of IMPRIMIR. Printed.
Impresor [im-pray-sor'], *m.* Printer.
Impresora [im-pray-so'-rah], *f.* Wife of a printer; a female proprietor of a printing-office.
Imprestable [im-pres-tah'-blay], *a.* That cannot be lent.
Imprevisión [im-pray-ve-se-on'], *f.* Imprevision, improvidence.
Imprevisto, ta [im-pray-vees'-to, tah], *a.* Unforeseen, unexpected, unprovided against.
Imprimación [im-pre-mah-the-on'], *f.* Priming, the act of laying on the first colours on canvas or boards to be painted; stuff for priming.
Imprimadera [im-pre-mah-day'-rah], *f.* The instrument used in priming, or laying on the first colours in painting.

Imprimador [im-pre-mah-dor'],*m.* One who lays the first colours on a piece of linen or board to be painted.

Imprimar [im-pre-mar'],*va.* To prime, to lay the first colours on in painting.

Imprimir [im-pre-meer'],*va.* 1. To print, to stamp. 2. To imprint, to fix an idea on the mind or memory. 3. To put a work to press, to get it printed.

Improbabilidad [im-pro-bah-be-le-dahd'],*f.* Improbability, unlikelihood, difficulty to be believed.

Improbable [im-pro-bah'-blay], *a.* Improbable, unlikely, difficult to be proved.

Improbablemente, *adv.* Improbably.

Improbar [im-pro-bar'], *va.* To disapprove, to dislike, to censure.

Improbidad [im-pro-be-dahd'], *f.* Improbity, dishonesty.

Improbo, ba [eem'-pro-bo, bah], *a.* 1. Corrupt, wicked. 2. Laborious, painful.

Improductivo, va [im-pro-dooc-tee'-vo, vah], *a.* 1. Unproductive, unfruitful. 2. Useless.

Impronta [im-pron'-tah], *f.* Cast, or reproduction in any soft substance, like wax, papier-maché, etc., of images in relief or intaglio. (Acad.)

Improperar [im-pro-pay-rar'], *va.* To upbraid, to gibe, to taunt.

Improperio [im-pro-pay'-re-o], *m.* Contemptuous reproach, injurious censure.

Impropiamente [im-pro-pe-ah-men'-tay], *adv.* Improperly.

Impropiar [im-pro-pe-ar'],*vr.* (Obs.) To twist or distort the true sense of a law, injunction, or word.

Impropiedad [im-pro-pe-ay-dahd'], *f.* Impropriety, unfitness, want of justness.

Impropio, pia [im-pro'-pe-o, ah], *a.* 1. Improper, unfit; not conducive to the right end; unqualified. 2. Improper, unbecoming.

Improporción [im-pro-por-the-on'], *f.* Disproportion.

Improporcionado, da [im-pro-por-the-o-nah'-do, dah], *a.* Disproportionate, unsymmetrical, unsuitable in point of quality or quantity.

Impropriedad [im-pro-pre-ay-dahd'], *f.* (Obs.) Impropriety.

Impropio, ria [im-pro'-pre-o, ah], *a.* (Obs.) *V.* Impropio.

Improrrogable [im-pror-ro-gah'-blay], *a.* That which cannot be prorogued.

Impróspero, ra [im-pros'-pay-ro, rah], *a.* Unfortunate, unprosperous, unhappy.

Impróvidamente [im-pro'-ve-dah-men-tay], *adv.* Improvidently.

Impróvido, da [im-pro'-ve-do, dah], *a.* Improvident, wanting forecast or care to provide, thoughtless.

Improvisación [im-pro-ve-sah-the-on'], *f.* (Littl. us.) Extemporaneous, improvisation.

Improvisamente [im-pro-ve-sah-men'-tay], *adv.* Unexpectedly, improvidently.

Improvisar [im-pro-ve-sar'], *va.* To extemporize, to speak extempore.

Improviso, sa [im-pro-vee'-so, sah], **Improvisto, ta,** *a.* Unexpected, unforeseen, not provided against. *De improviso* or *a la improvista,* Unexpectedly, on a sudden.

Imprudencia [im-proo-den'-the-ah], *f.* Imprudence, indiscretion, heedlessness; impolicy; improvidence.

Imprudente [im-proo-den'-tay], *a.* Imprudent, indiscreet, improvident.

Imprudentemente, *adv.* Imprudently.

Impúber [im-poo'-ber], *a.* *V.* Impúbero.

Impúbero, ra [im-poo'-bay-ro, rah], *a.* Impuberal, not having reached puberty.

Impudencia [im-poo-den'-the-ah], *f.* Impudence, shamelessness, immodesty.

Impudente [im-poo-den'-tay], *a.* Impudent, shameless.

Impúdicamente [im-poo'-de-cah-men-tay], *adv.* Lewdly, impudently.

Impudicicia [im-poo-de-thee'-the-ah], *f.* Unchastity, lewdness, incontinence, lustfulness, impudicity.

Impúdico, ca [im-poo'-de-co, cah], *a.* 1. Unchaste, lewd, lustful, obscene. 2. Impudent, shameless.

Impuesto [im-poo-ays'-to], *m.* 1. Tax. 2. Duty, impost. *Impuesto sobre la renta,* Income tax.

Impuesto, ta [im-poo-ays'-to, tah], *a.* & *pp. irr.* of Imponer. Imposed. *Estar* or *quedar impuesto de alguna cosa,* To have full knowledge of some business or command.

Impugnable [im-poog-nah'-blay], *a.* Impugnable.

Impugnación [im-poog-nah-the-on'], *f.* Opposition, contradiction, refutation, impugnation.

Impugnador, ra [im-poog-nah-dor', rah], *m.* & *f.* One who refutes, attacks or contradicts; impugner, objector.

Impugnar [im-poog-nar'], *va.* To impugn, to contradict, to oppose, to confute.

Impugnativo, va [im-poog-nah-tee'-vo, vah], *a.* Impugning.

Impulsar [im-pool-sar'], *va.* To impel, to give an impulse, to urge on.

Impulsión [im-pool-se-on'], *f.* 1. Impulsion, impulse, communicated force, the effect of one body acting upon another. 2. Impulsion, impulse, influence acting upon the mind, motive.

Impulsivo, va [im-pool-see'-vo, vah], *a.* Impulsive.

Impulso [im-pool'-so], *m.* Impulsion; impulse. *V.* Impulsión.

Impulsor, ra [im-pool-sor', rah], *m.* & *f.* Impeller.

Impune [im-poo'-nay], *a.* Exempt from punishment, unpunished.

Impunemente [im-poo-nay-men'-tay], *adv.* With impunity.

Impunidad [im-poo-ne-dahd'], *f.* Impunity, freedom from punishment.

Impuramente [im-poo-rah-men'-tay], *adv.* Obscenely, impurely.

Impureza [im-poo-ray'-thah], *f.* 1. Impurity, foul with extraneous mixtures. 2. Impurity, dishonesty, unchastity. 3. Obscenity, obsceneness, foulness.

Impuridad [im-poo-re-dahd'], *f.* (Obs.) *V.* Impureza.

Impuro, ra [im-poo'-ro, rah], *a.* Impure, foul.

Imputable [im-poo-tah'-blay], *a.* Imputable, chargeable.

Imputabilidad [im-poo-tah-be-le-dahd'], *f.* Imputableness.

Imputación [im-poo-tah-the-on'], *f.* Imputation, attribution of any thing, generally of ill.

Imputador, ra [im-poo-tah-dor', rah], *m.* & *f.* Imputer.

Imputar [im-poo-tar'], *va.* To impute, to charge upon, to attribute, to father.

In [een], *prep. Lat.* Used only in composition, where it has generally a negative signification, as *incapaz,* incapable. *In albis, V.* Quedar.

Inabarcable [in-ah-bar-cah'-blay], *a.* Not capable of being embraced.

Inacabable [in-ah-cah-bah'-blay], *a.* Interminable, inconsumptible, that cannot be brought to an end.

Inaccesibilidad [in-ac-thay-se-be-le-dahd'], *f.* Inaccessibility.

Inaccesible [in-ac-thay-see'-blay], *a.* Inaccessible, not to be approached.

Inaccesiblemente, *adv.* Inaccessibly.

Inacción [in-ac-the-on'], *f.* Inaction cessation from labour.

Inactividad [in-ac-te-ve-dahd'], *f.* Inactivity.

Inactivo, va [in-ac-tee'-vo, vah], *a.* Inactive.

Inadaptable [in-ah-dap-tah'-blay], *a.* Not adaptable.

Inadecuado, da [in-ah-day-coo-ah'-do, dah], *a.* Inadequate.

Inadherente [in-ad-ay-ren'-tay], *a.* Unadherent.

Inadmisible [in-ad-me-see'-blay], *a.* Inadmissible.

Inadvertencia [in-ad-ver-ten'-the-ah], *f.* Inadvertence, carelessness, inattention, heedlessness.

Inadvertidamente [in-ad-ver-te-dah-men'-tay], *adv.* Inadvertently.

Inadvertido, da [in-ad-ver-tee'-do, dah], *a.* 1. Inadvertent, inconsiderate, careless. 2. Unseen, unnoticed.

Inafectado, da [in-ah-fec-tah'-do, dah], *a.* Natural, free from affectation.

Inagotable [in-ah-go-tah'-blay], *a.* 1. Inexhaustible, exhaustless. 2. Unexhausted: applied to the powers of the mind. 3. Never-failing.

Inaguantable [in-ah-goo-an-tah'-blay], *a.* Insupportable.

Inajenable [in-ah-hay-nah'-blay], *a.* Inalienable, that cannot be alienated.

Inalámbrico, ca [in-ah-lahm'-bre-co, cah], *a.* Wireless. *Telegrafía inalámbrica,* Wireless telegraphy.

Inalienable [in-ah-le-ay-nah'-blay], *a.* Inalienable.

Inalterable [in-al-tay-rah'-blay], *a.* Inalterable.

Inalterablemente, *adv.* Unalterably.

Inalterado, da [in-al-tay-rah'-do, dah], *a.* Unchanged, stable.

Inamisible [in-ah-me-see'-blay], *a.* Inamissible, not to be lost.

Inamovible [in-ah-mo-vee'-blay], *a.* Immovable.

Inamovibilidad [in-ah-mo-ve-be-le-dahd'], *f.* Immovability.

Inane [in-ah'-nay], *a.* (Littl. us.) Empty, void, inane.

Inanición [in-ah-ne-the-on'], *f.* (Med.) Inanition, extreme weakness from want of nourishment.

Inanidad [in-ah-ne-dahd'], *f.* 1. Emptiness. 2. Vanity, uselessness.

Inanimado, da [in-ah-ne-mah'-do, dah], *a.* Inanimate, lifeless.

Inánime [in-ah'-ne-may], *a.* *V.* Inanimado.

Inapagable [in-ah-pah-gah'-blay], *a.* Inextinguishable, unquenchable.

Inapeable [in-ah-pay-ah'-blay], *a.* 1. That cannot be lowered or levelled. 2. Incomprehensible, inconceivable. 3. Obstinate, stubborn.

Inapelable [in-ah-pay-lah'-blay], *a.* Without appeal, not admitting appeal.

Inapetencia [in-ah-pay-ten'-the-ah], *f.* Inappetence or inappetency, want of appetite or desire of food.

Inapetente [in-ah-pay-ten'-tay], *a.* 1. Having no appetite or desire of food. 2. Disgusted.

Inaplacable [in-ah-plah-cah'-blay], *a.* Implacable, unappeasable.

Inaplicable [in-ah-ple-cah'-blay], *a.* Inapplicable.

Inaplicación [in-ah-ple-ca-the-on'], *f.* Indolence, inapplication.

Inaplicado, da [in-ah-ple-cah'-do, dah], *a.* Indolent, careless, inactive.

Inapreciable [in-ah-pray-the-ah'-blay], *a.* Inestimable, invaluable, inappreciable.

Inaptitud [in-ap-te-tood'], *f.* (Prov.) *V.* Ineptitud.

Inarticulado, da [in-ar-te-coo-lah'-do, dah], *a.* Inarticulate, not uttered with distinctness.

Inasequible [in-ah-say-kee'-blay], *a.* That which cannot be followed.

Inasimilable [in-ah-se-me-lah'-blay], *a.* Unassimilable.

Inastillable [in-as-te-lyah'-blay], *a.* Shatterproof.

Inatacable [in-ah-tah-cah'-blay], *a.* (Coll.) Which cannot be attacked.

Inaudible [in-ah-oo-dee'-blay], *a.* (Littl. us.) Inaudible.

Inaudito, ta [in-ah-oo-dee'-to, tah], *a.* Unheard of, strange, most extraordinary.

Inauguración [in-ah-oo-goo-rah-the-on'], *f.* 1. Inauguration, investiture by solemnities. 2. Exaltation or elevation to royal dignity. 3. Auguration, the practice of augury.

Inaugural [in-ah-oo-goo-rahl'], *a.* Inaugural.

Inaugurar [in-ah-oo-goo-rar'], *va.* 1. To divine by the flight of birds. 2. To inaugurate, to invest with a new office by solemnities.

Inaveriguable [in-ah-vay-re-goo-ah'-blay], *a.* That cannot be ascertained, that cannot be easily proved.

Inbab [in-bahb'], *f.* A sort of stuff which comes from Cairo.

Inca [een'-cah], *m.* Inca, title of the sovereigns of Peru in the 15th and 16th centuries.

Incalculable [in-cal-coo-lah'-blay], *a.* Incalculable.

Incalificable [in-cah-le-fe-cah'-blay], *a.* Unqualifiable, downright.

Incamerar [in-cah-may-rar'], *va.* To unite to the Apostolic Chamber, or ecclesiastical dominion.

Incandescencia [in-can-des-then'-the-ah], *f.* Incandescence, white heat.

Incandescente [in-can-des-then'-tay], *a.* Incandescent, glowing with heat.

Incansable [in-can-sah'-blay], *a.* Indefatigable, unwearied.

Incansablemente, *adv.* Indefatigably.

Incantable [in-can-tah'-blay], *a.* That cannot be sung.

Incantación [in-can-tah-the-on'], *f.* (Obs.) *V.* Encanto.

Incapacidad [in-cah-pah-the-dahd'], *f.* 1. Incapacity, inability, want of power or strength. 2. Incapability, incapableness, natural inability, want of comprehensiveness of mind. 3. Incapability, legal disqualification.

Incapacitar [in-cah-pah-the-tar'], *va.* To incapacitate, to render incapable.

Incapaz [in-cah-path'], *a.* 1. Incapable, unable, not equal to any thing. 2. Incapable, wanting power to do any thing. 3. Incapable, wanting understanding; wanting talent. *Incapaz de sacramentos*, (Coll.) Applied to a very weak, silly person.

Incardinación [in-car-de-nah-the-on'], *f.* (Law) Administration of church revenues without ownership.

Incasable [in-cah-sah'-blay], *a.* 1. Unmarriageable. 2. Averse or opposed to marriage.

Incautamente [in-cah-oo-tah-men'-tay], *adv.* Unwarily, incautiously.

Incauto, ta [in-cah'-oo-to, tah], *a.* Incautious, unwary, heedless.

Incendiar [in-then-de-ar'], *va.* To kindle, to set on fire, to inflame. *El acto de incendiar maliciosamente una casa*, (Law) Arson.

Incendiario, ria [in-then-de-ah'-re-o, ah], *m.* & *f.* 1. Firebug, incendiary, one who sets fires compulsively. 2. Firebrand, agitator, one who inflames factions or promotes quarrels.

Incendio [in-then'-de-o], *m.* 1. Fire, conflagration, burning. 2. Inflammation, the act of setting on flame; the state of being in flame.

Incensación [in-then-sah-the-on'], *f.* The act of perfuming with incense.

Incensar [in-then-sar'], *va.* 1. To perfume, to incense, to offer incense on the altar. 2. To bestow fulsome praise or adulation.

Incensario [in-then-sah'-re-o], *m.* Incensory, thurible, the vessel in which incense is burnt.

Incensor, ra [in-then-sor', rah], *a.* (Obs.) *V.* Incendiario.

Incensurable [in-then-soo-rah'-blay], *a.* Unblamable, not culpable.

Incentivo [in-then-tee'-vo], *m.* Incentive, incitement, spur; encouragement.

Inceptor [in-thep-tor'], *m.* (Obs.) Beginner, he that commences any thing.

Inceración [in-thay-rah-the-on'], *f.* Inceration, the act of covering with or mixing with wax.

Incertidumbre [in-ther-te-doom'-bray], *f.* Incertitude, uncertainty, doubtfulness, hesitancy, fluctuation.

Incertitud [in-ther-te-tood'], *f.* (Obs.) *V.* Incertidumbre.

Incesable [in-thay-sah'-blay], *a.* Incessant, unceasing.

Incesablemente, *adv.* Incessantly, without intermission.

Incesante [in-thay-sahn'-tay], *a.* Incessant, unceasing, continual, uninterrupted.

Incesantemente, *adv.* Incessantly, continually.

Incestar, *va.* (Obs.) To commit incest.

Incesto [in-thes'-to], *m.* Incest.

Incestuosamente [in-thes-too-o-sah-men'-tay], *adv.* Incestuously.

Incestuoso, sa [in-thes-too-o'-so, sah], *a.* Incestuous.

Incidencia [in-the-den'-the-ah], *f.* 1. Incidence or incidency, an accident, hap, casualty. 2. Incidence, the direction with which one body strikes upon another.

Incidental [in-the-den-tahl'], *a.* Incidental, dependent, subsidiary.

Incidente [in-the-den'-tay], *a.* Incident, casual, incidental, happening by chance.

Incidente [in-the-den'-tay], *m.* Incident, hap, accident, casualty, occurrence, accidental event.—*pl.* (Com.) Appurtenances. *Incidentes de comercio*, Lease and good-will.

Incidentemente, *adv.* Incidentally.

Incidir [in-the-deer'], *vn.* To fall in or upon, to meet with.

Incienso [in-the-en'-so], *m.* 1. Incense, an aromatic gum used to perfume the altar. 2. Peculiar reverence and veneration paid to a person. 3. Court paid to a person out of flattery or interested views. *Incienso hembra*, Impure frankincense, that which is obtained by incision. *Incienso macho*, Pure frankincense, that which flows from the trees spontaneously.

Inciente [in-the-en'-tay], *a.* (Obs.) Ignorant.

Inciertamente, *adv.* Uncertainly.

Incierto, ta [in-the-ayr'-to, tah], *a.* 1. Untrue, false, contrary to reality. 2. Uncertain, doubtful. 3. Unstable, inconstant; unknown.

Incineración [in-the-nay-rah-the-on'], *f.* Incineration, the act of burning a thing to ashes.

Incinerar [in-the-nay-rar'], *va.* To incinerate or burn to ashes.

Incipiente [in-the-pe-en'-tay], *a.* Beginning, incipient, inceptive, inchoative.

Incircunciso, sa [in-theer-coon-thee'-so, sah], *a.* Uncircumcised.

Incircunscripto, ta [in-theer-coons-creep'-to, tah], *a.* Uncircumscribed.

Incisión [in-the-se-on'], *f.* 1. Incision a cut; a wound with a sharp instrument. 2. *V.* Cesura.

Incisivo, va [in-the-see'-vo, vah], *a.* Incisive. *Dientes incisivos*, Incisors, cutting teeth.

Inciso [in-thee'-so], *m.* 1. Comma. *V.* Coma. 2. Partial meaning of a clause.

Inciso, sa [in-thee'-so, sah], *a.* Incised. *V.* Cortado.

Incisorio, ria [in-the-so'-re-o, ah], *a.* Incisory, that which cuts.

Incitación [in-the-tah-the-on'], *f.* Incitation, incitement.

Incitador, ra [in-the-tah-dor', rah], *m.* & *f.* Instigator, inciter, exciter.

Incitamento, Incitamiento [in-the-tah-men'-to], *m.* Incitement, impulse, inciting power, incentive.

Incitar [in-the-tar'], *va.* To incite, to excite, to spur, to stimulate.

Incitativa [in-the-tah-tee'-vah], *f.* (Law) Writ from a superior tribunal to the common judges, that justice may be administered.

Incitativo, va [in-the-tah-tee'-vo, vah], *a.* 1. Incentive, inciting, incensive. 2. (Law) *V.* Aguijatorio.

Incitativo, *m.* Incitement.

Incivil [in-the-veel'], *a.* Uncivil, unpolished, incivil.

Incivilidad [in-the-ve-le-dahd'], *f.* Incivility, rudeness, coarseness, grossness.

Incivilmente [in-the-veel-men'-tay], *adv.* Uncivilly, rudely, incivilly.

Inclasificable [in-clah-se-fe-cah'-blay], *a.* Unclassifiable, difficult of classification.

Inclemencia [in-clay-men'-the-ah], *f.* 1. Inclemency, severity, harshness, rigour, unmercifulness. 2. Inclemency of the weather. *A la inclemencia*, Openly, without shelter.

Inclemente [in-clay-men'-tay], *a.* Inclement, cruel.

Inclinación [in-cle-nah-the-on'], *f.* 1. Inclination, the act of inclining and the state of being inclined. 2. Inclination, propension of mind, favourable disposition, love, affection, liking, fancy. 3. Inclination, tendency toward any point. 4. A bow, an act of reverence. 5. (Math.) Inclination, the angle between two lines or planes; in gunnery, the angle between the axis of the piece and the horizon. *Inclinación magnética*, The angle of magnetic dip.

Inclinado, da [in-cle-nah'-do, dah], *a.* & *pp.* of Inclinar. 1. Inclined to any part. 2. (Met.) Inclined, disposed, affected, minded.

Inclinador, ra [in-cle-nah-dor', rah], *m.* & *f.* One who inclines.

Inclinante [in-cle-nahn'-tay], *pa.* Inclining, bending, drawing nigh to.

Inclinar [in-cle-nar'], *va.* 1. To incline, to bend; to give a tendency or direction to any place or state. 2. To incline, to influence, to turn the desire toward any thing.—*vn.* To resemble, to be alike.—*vr.* 1. To incline, to lean, to bend to, to tend toward any part. 2. To incline, to lean, to be favourably disposed to. 3. To bend the body, to bow. 4. To have a particular reason to follow some opinion or do something. 5. (Naut.) To heel. *Ser inclinado a*, To be apt to, to be accustomed to, to propend.

Inclinativo, va [in-cle-nah-tee'-vo, vah], *a.* Inclinatory.

Ínclito, ta [een'-cle-to, tah], *a.* Famous, renowned, conspicuous, illustrious.

Incluir [in-cloo-eer'], *va.* 1. To include, to comprise, to inclose; to

comprehend, to contain. 2. To allow one a share in a business.
Inclusa [in-cloo'-sah], *f.* 1. Foundling hospital. 2. (Obs.) *V.* ESCLUSA.
Inclusero, ra [in-cloo-say'-ro, rah], *m.* & *f.* & *a.* Foundling.
Inclusión [in-cloo-se-on'], *f.* 1. Inclusion, the act of inclosing or containing a thing. 2. Easy access, familiar intercourse.
Inclusivamente, Inclusive, *adv.* Inclusively.
Inclusivo, va [in-cloo-see'-vo, vah], *a.* Inclusive.
Incluso, sa [in-cloo'-so, sah], *a.* & *pp. irr.* of INCLUIR. Inclosed.
Incluyente [in-cloo-yen'-tay], *pa.* Including.
Incoado, da [in-co-ah'-do, dah], *a.* & *pp.* of INCOAR. Inchoate, begun, commenced.
Incoagulable [in-co-ah-goo-lah'-blay], *a.* Incoagulable, uncoagulable.
Incoar [in-co-ar'], *va.* To commence, to begin, to inchoate.
Incoativo, va [in-co-ah-tee'-vo, vah], *a.* Inchoative, inceptive, noting inchoation or beginning.
Incobrable [in-co-brah'-blay], *a.* Irrecoverable, irretrievable.
Incoercible [in-co-er-thee'-blay], *a.* 1. Incoercible, which cannot be forced or restrained. 2. Incoercible, used of imponderable agents, as light, heat, electricity, magnetism.
Incógnito, ta [in-cog'-ne-to, tah], *a.* Unknown. *De incógnito*, 1. Incog or incognito. 2. Hiddenly, or clandestinely.—*f.* (Math.) An unknown quantity, the quantity sought. *Despejar la incógnita*, To clear the unknown quantity of coefficients, exponents, or divisor.
Incognoscible [in-cog-nos-thee'-blay], *a.* Imperceptible.
Incoherencia [in-co-ay-ren'-the-ah], *f.* Incoherence.
Incoherente [in-co-ay-ren'-tay], *a.* Incoherent, inconsistent.
Íncola [een'-co-lah], *m.* Inhabitant.
Incoloro, ra [in-co-lo'-ro, rah], *a.* Free of colour, colourless.
Incólume [in-co'-loo-may], *a.* Sound, safe, unharmed.
Incolumidad [in-co-loo-me-dahd'], *f.* Security, safety.
Incombinable [in-com-be-nah'-blay], *a.* Uncombinable, which cannot be combined.
Incombustibilidad [in-com-boos-te-be-le-dahd'], *f.* Incombustibility.
Incombustible [in-com-boos-tee'-blay], *a.* Incombustible.
Incomerciable [in-co-mer-the-ah'-blay], *a.* 1. Contraband, unlawful, prohibited: applied to articles of trade. 2. (Obs.) Impassable: applied to roads.
Incómodamente [in-co'-mo-dah-men-tay], *adv.* Incommodiously.
Incomodar [in-co-mo-dar'], *va.* To incommode.
Incomodidad [in-co-mo-de-dahd'], *f.* 1. Incommodiousness, inconvenience. 2. Weariness; annoyance. (Acad.)
Incómodo, da [in-co'-mo-do, dah], *a.* Incommodious, inconvenient.
Incomparable [in-com-pa-rah'-blay], *a.* Incomparable, matchless.
Incomparablemente, *adv.* Incomparably.
Incomparado, da [in-com-pa-rah'-do, dah], *a.* *V.* INCOMPARABLE.
Incompartible [in-com-par-tee'-blay], *a.* Indivisible.
Incompasible [in-com-pa-see'-blay], *a.* *V.* INCOMPASIVO.
Incompasivo, va [in-com-pa-see'-vo, vah], *a.* Uncompassionate, void of pity
Incompatibilidad [in-com-pah-te-be-le-dahd'], *f.* Incompatibility, inconsistency, contrariety
Incompatible [in-com-pah-tee'-blay], *a.* Incompatible, inconsistent.
Incompensable [in-com-pen-sah'-blay], *a.* Incompensable, that cannot be compensated.
Incompetencia [in-com-pay-ten'-the-ah], *f.* Incompetency, inability.
Incompetente [in-com-pay-ten'-tay], *a.* 1. Incompetent, not proportionate, not adequate. 2. (Law) Unqualified. 3. Unsuitable.
Incompetentemente, *adv.* Incompetently, unduly, unsuitably.
Incomplejo, ja [in-com-play'-ho, hah], *a.* Incomplex, simple.
Incompletamente, *adv.* Incompletely.
Incompleto, ta [in-com-play'-to, tah], *a.* Incomplete, inconsummate.
Incomplexo, xa [in-com-plec'-so, sah], *a.* (Acad.) Disunited, without connection, non-adherent.
Incomponible [in-com-po-nee'-blay], *a.* Incompoundable.
Incomportable [in-com-por-tah'-blay], *a.* Intolerable, unbearable.
Incomposibilidad [in-com-po-se-be-le-dahd'], *f.* Incompossibility, quality of being not possible, but by the negation or destruction of something.
Incomposible [in-com-po-see'-blay], *a.* Incompossible, not possible together.
Incomposición [in-com-po-se-the-on'], *f.* 1. Want of proportion, or defective comparison. 2. (Obs.) *V.* DESCOMPOSTURA.
Incomprehensible [in-com-pray-en-see'-blay], *a.* (Acad.) *V.* INCOMPRENSIBLE.
Incomprensibilidad [in-com-pren-se-be-le-dahd'], *f.* Incomprehensibility.
Incomprensible [in-com-pren-see'-blay], *a.* 1. Incomprehensible, that cannot be comprehended. 2. Incomprehensible, expressing thoughts in an obscure or confused manner.
Incomprensiblemente, *adv.* Inconceivably, incomprehensibly.
Incomprimible [in-com-pre-mee'-blay], *a.* Incompressible.
Incompuesto, ta [in-com-poo-es'-to, tah], *a.* (Obs.) Simple, uncomposed; unadorned.
Incomunicabilidad [in-co-moo-ne-cah-be-le-dahd'], *f.* Incommunicability.
Incomunicable [in-co-moo-ne-cah'-blay], *a.* Incommunicable.
Incomunicado, da [in-co-moo-ne-cah'-do, dah], *a.* Incommunicated, incommunicating; having no intercourse.—*m.* A prisoner deprived of intercourse with any one.
Incomunicar [in-co-moo-ne-car'], *va.* To deprive a prisoner of intercourse with any one.
Inconcebible [in-con-thay-bee'-blay], *a.* Inconceivable.
Inconciliable [in-con-the-le-ah'-blay], *a.* *V.* IRRECONCILIABLE.
Inconcino, na [in-con-thee'-no, nah], *a.* Disordered, disarranged.
Inconcusamente, *adv.* Certainly, indubitably
Inconcuso, sa [in-con-coo'-so, sah], *a.* Incontrovertible, incontestable.
Incondicional [in-con-de-the-o-nahl'], *a.* Unconditional, absolute, without restriction.
Incondicionalmente [in-con-de-the-o-nal-men'-tay], *adv.* Unconditionally.
Inconducente [in-con-doo-then'-tay], *a.* Incongruous.
Inconexión [in-co-nec-se-on'], *f.* 1. Incoherency, incongruity, want of dependence of one part upon another. 2. Inconnection, want of connection contrariety to itself.
Inconexo, xa [in-co-nec'-so, sah], *a.* 1. Unconnected, incoherent, inconsequential, having no dependence of one part upon another. 2. Independent, not supported by any other.
Inconfeso, sa [in-con-fay'-so, sah], *a.* Unconfessed: applied to a criminal who does not confess his guilt.
Inconfidencia [in-con-fe-den'-the-ah], *f.* 1. Distrust, mistrust, want of confidence. 2. Disloyalty, want of fidelity to the sovereign.
Incongruamente [in-con-groo-ah-men-tay], *adv.* Incongruously.
Incongruencia [in-con-groo-en'-the-ah], *f.* Incongruence, want of symmetry or proportion; unsuitableness, want of adaptation
Incongruente [in-con-groo-en'-tay], *a.* Incongruous, incongruent.
Incongruentemente, *adv.* Incongruously, incompatibly.
Incongruidad [in-con-groo-e-dahd'], *f.* (Obs.) Incongruity.
Incongruo, grua [in-con'-groo-o, ah], *a.* 1. Incongruous, disproportionate, unsuitable. 2. Applied to ecclesiastical livings which do not yield a competent income, and to the priests who perform the duties of those livings.
Inconjugable [in-con-hoo-gah'-blay], *a.* Inconjugable, that cannot be conjugated.
Inconmensurable [in-con-men-soo-rah'-blay], *a.* Incommensurable, not to be reduced to any measure.
Inconmovible [in-con-mo-vee'-blay], *a.* Unshakable, inflexible, relentless.
Inconmutabilidad, *f.* *V.* INMUTABILIDAD
Inconmutable [in-con-moo-tah'-blay], *a.* 1. Incommutable, that cannot be exchanged, commuted, or bartered 2 *V.* INMUTABLE.
Inconquistable [in-con-kis-tah'-blay], *a.* 1. Unconquerable, impregnable, inexpugnable; invincible. 2. Incorruptible: applied to persons.
Inconsciencia [in-cons-the-en'-the-ah], *f.* 1. Unconsciousness. 2 Irresponsibility.
Inconsciente [in-cons-the-en'-tay], *a* 1. Unconscious. 2. Irresponsible
Inconsecuencia [in-con-say-coo-en'-the-ah], *f.* Inconsequence, inconclusiveness, want of just inference; unsteadiness, changeableness.
Inconsecuente [in-con-say-coo-en'-tay], *a.* Inconsequent, changeable.
Inconservable [in-con-ser-vah'-blay], *a* Unpreservable.
Inconsiderable [in-con-se-day-rah'-blay], *a.* Valueless, worthless
Inconsideración [in-con-se-day-rah-the-on'], *f.* Inconsideration, want of thought, inattention, inadvertency, abruptness.
Inconsideradamente, *adv* Inconsiderately, thoughtlessly.
Inconsiderado, da [in-con-se-day-rah'-do, dah], *a.* Inconsiderate, thoughtless, inattentive.
Inconsiguiente [in-con-se-gee-en'-tay], *a.* Inconsequent, without just conclusion, without regular inference. contradictory.
Inconsistencia [in-con-sis-ten'-the-ah], *f.* 1. Inconsistency, self-contradiction, incongruity, contrariety. 2. Inconsistence, unsteadiness, changeableness.
Inconsistente [in-con-sis-ten'-tay], *a.* Inconsistent, incongruous, absurd.
Inconsolable [in-con-so-lah'-blay], *a.* Inconsolable.
Inconsolablemente, *adv* Inconsolably.
Inconstancia [in-cons-tahn'-the-ah], *f* Inconstancy, fickleness, unsteadiness. levity, lightness. frailty

Inconstante [in-cons-tahn'-tay], *a.* Inconstant, changeable, mutable, variable, fickle.

Inconstantemente, *adv.* Inconstantly, fickly, giddily.

Inconstitucional [in-cons-te-too-the-o-nahl'], *a.* Unconstitutional.

Inconstitucionalidad [in-cons-te-too-the-o-nah-le-dahd'], *f* Unconstitutionality.

Inconstitucionalismo [in-cons-te-too-the-o-nah-lees'-mo], *m.* Disobedience to the principles of the constitution.

Inconstruible [in-cons-troo-ee'-blay], *a.* 1. (Coll.) Whimsical, fantastical, fanciful, variable, fickle. 2. (Gram.) Obscure, unintelligible, difficult to be construed.

Inconsulto, ta [in-con-sool'-to, tah], *a.* (Obs.) Unadvised, indeliberate.

Inconsútil [in-con-soo'-teel], *a.* Seamless, having no seam.

Incontable [in-con-tah'-blay], *a.* Innumerable.

Incontaminado, da [in-con-tah-me-nah'-do, dah], *a.* Undefiled, uncontaminated.

Incontestable [in-con-tes-tah'-blay], *a.* Incontestable, indisputable, incontrovertible.

Incontestablemente, *adv* Incontestably.

Incontinencia [in-con-te-nen'-the-ah], *f.* Incontinence or incontinency; unchastity, lewdness. *Incontinencia de orina,* (Med.) Incontinence of urine, a disease.

Incontinente [in-con-te-nen'-tay], *a.* 1. Incontinent: applied to one who has no command of his passions. 2. Incontinent, unchaste.

Incontinente [in-con-te-nen'-tay], *adv.* Instantly, immediately, incontinently.

Incontinentemente, *adv.* 1. Incontinently, unchastely. 2. (Obs.) *V* INCONTINENTI.

Incontinenti [in-con-te-nen'-te], *adv.* Incontinently, instantly, immediately.

Incontrastable [in-con-tras-tah'-blay], *a.* 1. Insurmountable, irresistible, incontrollable, insuperable. 2. Inexpugnable, unconquerable. 3. Inconvincible.

Incontratable, *a.* *V.* INTRATABLE.

Incontrovertible [in-con-tro-ver-tee'-blay], *a.* Incontrovertible, indisputable.

Inconvencible [in-con-ven-thee'-blay], *a.* 1. Inconvincible, not capable of conviction. 2. *V.* INVENCIBLE.

Inconvenible [in-con-vay-nee'-blay], *a.* 1. Discordant, inconsistent, opposite. 2. (Obs.) Inconvenient.

Inconveniencia [in-con-vay-ne-en'-the-ah], *f.* 1. Inconvenience, incommodity, unfitness. 2 Incongruence, unsuitableness.

Inconveniente [in-con-vay-ne-en'-tay], *a.* Inconvenient, incommodious, troublesome.

Inconveniente [in-con-vay-ne-en'-tay], *m.* Difficulty, obstacle, obstruction, impediment.

Inconversable [in-con-ver-sah'-blay], *a.* Unsociable, incommunicative.

Inconvertible [in-con-ver-tee'-blay], *a.* Inconvertible, that cannot be converted or changed.

Incordio [in-cor'-de-o], *m.* Bubo, a tumour in the groin.—*a.* (Vul.) Wearisome, vexing.

Incorporable [in-cor-po-rah'-blay], *a.* (Obs.) *V.* INCORPÓREO.

Incorporación [in-cor-po-rah-the-on'], *f.* Incorporation, the act of uniting in one mass.

Incorporadero [in-cor-po-rah-day'-ro], *m* The spot where mercury is mixed with metals.

Incorporal [in-cor-po-rahl'], *a.* Incorporeal.

Incorporalmente, *adv.* Incorporeally. incorporally.

Incorporamiento [in-cor-po-rah-me-en'-to], *m.* *V.* INCORPORACIÓN.

Incorporar [in-cor-po-rar'], *va.* 1. To incorporate, to unite in one mass, to embody. 2. To incorporate, to form into a corporation or body politic. 3. To raise or to make a patient sit up in his bed.—*vr.* 1. To incorporate, to mingle. 2. To become incorporated or united in one mass or body. *Incorporarse en la cama,* To sit up in bed. 3. (Naut.) To sail in company, to join the convoy.

Incorporeidad [in-cor-po-ray-e-dahd'], *f.* Incorporeity, incorporality, immateriality.

Incorpóreo, rea [in-cor-po'-ray-o, ah], *a.* Incorporeal, immaterial, unbodied.

Incorporo, *m.* *V.* INCORPORACIÓN.

Incorrección [in-cor-rec-the-on'], *f.* Incorrectness, inaccurately.

Incorrectamente, *adv.* Inaccurately.

Incorrecto, ta [in-cor-rec'-to, tah], *a.* Incorrect, inaccurate.

Incorregibilidad [in-cor-ray-he-be-le-dahd'], *f.* Incorrigibleness, hopeless depravity.

Incorregible [in-cor-ray-hee'-blay], *a.* Incorrigible, froward.

Incorregiblemente, *adv.* (Coll.) Incorrigibly, obstinately.

Incorrupción [in-cor-roop-the-on'], *f.* 1. Incorruption, incapacity of corruption. 2. Incorruptness, purity of manners, integrity, honesty.

Incorruptamente [in-cor-roop-tah-men'-tay], *adv.* Incorruptly.

Incorruptible [in-cor-roop-tee'-blay], *a.* Incorruptible.

Incorrupto, ta [in-cor-roop'-to, tah], *a.* 1. Incorrupt, free from depravation. 2. Uncorrupt or uncorrupted, pure of manners, honest, good, incorruptible. *Incorrupta,* Applied to a virgin.

Incrasar [in-crah-sar'], *va.* To inspissate, to thicken, to incrassate: applied to humours.

Increado, da [in-cray-ah'-do, dah], *a.* Uncreated, increate: a divine attribute.

Incredibilidad [in-cray-de-be-le-dahd'], *f.* Incredibility, incredibleness, the quality of surpassing belief.

Incredulidad [in-cray-doo-le-dahd'], *f.* Incredulity, incredulousness.

Incrédulo, la [in-cray'-doo-lo, lah], *a.* Incredulous, hard of belief, refusing credit.—*m.* & *f.* A miscreant.

Increíble [in-cray-ee'-blay], *a.* Incredible, not to be credited.

Increíblemente, *adv.* Incredibly

Incrementar [in-cray-men-tar'], *va.* To increase, to intensify.

Incremento [in-cray-men'-to], *m.* Increment, increase, act of growing greater, cause of growing more.

Increpación [in-cray-pah-the-on'], *f.* Increpation, reprehension, chiding, reproach.

Increpador, ra [in-cray-pah-dor', rah], *m.* & *f.* Chider, rebuker, scolder.

Increpar [in-cray-par'], *va.* To chide, to reprehend, to scold, to reproach, to rebuke.

Incriminar [in-cre-me-nar'], *va.* 1. To incriminate. 2. To exaggerate a fault or defect. *V.* ACRIMINAR.

Incristalizable [in-cris-tah-le-thah'-blay], *a.* Uncrystallizable.

Incruento, ta [in-croo-en'-to, tah], *a.* Unstained with blood, bloodless.

Incrustación [in-croos-tah-the-on'], *f.* Incrustation.

Incrustar [in-croos-tar'], *va.* To incrust or incrustate, to cover with an additional coat

Incuartación [in-coo-ar-tah-the-on'], *f.* Inquartation, or quartation, the adding of silver to a button of gold (usually in the proportion of three-fourths to one-fourth) in the process of refining gold.

Incubación [in-coo-bah-the-on'], *f.* 1. Incubation, the process of hatching eggs. 2. Incubation, the time intervening between exposure and the outbreak of a disease. 3. (Met.) Secret preparation of a design.

Incubadora [in-coo-bah-do'-rah], *f.* 1. Incubator. 2. Brooder.

Incubar [in-coo-bar'], *va.* To incubate, to hatch eggs. *V.* ENCOBAR.

Íncubo [een'-coo-bo], *m.* 1. Incubus, the nightmare. 2. Incubus, a pretended fairy or demon.

Inculcación [in-cool-ca-the-on'], *f.* 1. Inculcation, enforcing. 2. (Print.) Act of binding or wedging in a form.

Inculcar [in-cool-car'], *va* 1. To inculcate, to impress by frequent admonitions. 2. To make one thing tight against another. 3. (Print.) To lock up types.—*vr.* To be obstinate, to conform one's self in an opinion or sentiment.

Inculpabilidad [in-cool-pah-be-le-dahd'], *f* Inculpableness, unblamableness.

Inculpable [in-cool-pah'-blay], *a.* Inculpable, unblamable.

Inculpablemente, *adv* Inculpably.

Inculpadamente, *adv.* Faultlessly.

Inculpado, da [in-cool-pah'-do, dah], *a* Faultless.—*pp.* of INCULPAR.

Inculpar [in-cool-par'], *va.* To accuse, to blame.

Incultamente [in-cool-tah-men'-tay], *adv.* Rudely, without culture.

Incultivable [in-cool-te-vah'-blay], *a.* Incapable of cultivation, inarable, uncultivable.

Inculto, ta [in-cool'-to, tah], *a.* 1 Incult, uncultivated, untilled. 2. Uncivilized, unpolished, unrefined, clownish, clumsy.

Incultura [in-cool-too'-rah], *f.* Inculture, want or neglect of culture.

Incumbencia [in-coom-ben'-the-ah], *f.* 1. Incumbency. 2. Duty imposed upon a person; ministry. *Eso no es de la incumbencia de Vd.,* That does not concern you; it is not your business.

Incumbir [in-coom-beer'], *vn.* To be, incumbent upon any one, to have any thing imposed as a duty.

Incunable [in-coo-nah'-blay], *m.* & *a.* Printing done in the 15th century before the invention of movable types; incunabula.

Incurable [in-coo-rah'-blay], *a.* Incurable, immedicable; irremediable, hopeless.

Incuria [in-coo'-re-ah], *f* Negligence, indolence, inaccuracy.

Incurioso, sa [in-coo-re-o'-so, sah], *a.* Negligent, indolent, incurious, inattentive.

Incurrimiento [in-coor-re-me-en'-to], *m.* Act of incurring.

Incurrir [in-coor-reer'], *vn.* To incur, to become liable to punishment or reprehension: to deserve.

Incursión [in-coor-se-on'], *f.* 1. Incurring. 2. Incursion, raid, over-running an enemy's country. *Incursión aérea* or *ataque aéreo.* Air raid, air attack.

Incurso, sa [in-coor'-so, sah]. *pp. irr.* of INCURRIR.

Incurvación, *f.* *V.* ENCORVADURA.

Incusar [in-coo-sar'], *va.* (Obs.) To accuse. *V.* ACUSAR.

Indagación [in-dah-gah-the-on'], *f.* Indagation, search, inquiry, examination, inquest.

Indagador, ra [in-dah-gah-dor', rah], *m.* & *f.* Investigator, inquirer, indagator, an examiner.

Indagar [in-dah-gar'], *va.* To search, to indagate, to inquire, to examine into; to investigate.

Índar [een'-dar], *m.* A kind of mattock for clearing out shrubs, grubbing of the ground and like uses.

Indebidamente, *adv.* Unjustly, illegally.

Indebido, da [in-day-bee'-do, dah], *a.* Undue, illegal, unlawful, void of equity and moderation.

Indecencia [in-day-then'-the-ah], *f.* 1. Indecency, indecorum, obscenity. 2. Nuisance.

Indecente [in-day-then'-tay], *a.* Indecent, dishonest, unbecoming.

Indecentemente, *adv.* Indecently, fulsomely.

Indecible [in-day-thee'-blay], *a.* Inexpressible, unutterable.

Indeciblemente, *adv.* Inexpressibly.

Indecisamente [in-day-the-sah-men'-tay], *adv.* Irresolutely.

Indecisión [in-day-the-se-on'], *f.* Irresolution, indecision, want of firmness of mind.

Indeciso, sa [in-day-thee'-so, sah], *a.* 1. Irresolute, indecisive, not constant in purpose. 2. Undecided, not settled.

Indeclinable [in-day-cle-nah'-blay], *a.* 1. Incapable of decline or decay, firm, unshaken. 2. (Gram.) Indeclinable, not varied by terminations.

Indecoro [in-day-co'-ro], *m.* Indecorum, indecorousness, indecency.

Indecorosamente, *adv.* Indecorously, indecently.

Indecoroso, sa [in-day-co-ro'-so, sah], *a.* Indecorous, indecent, unbecoming.

Indefectibilidad [in-day-fec-te-be-le-dahd'], *f.* Indefectibility, quality of suffering no decay or defect.

Indefectible [in-day-fec-tee'-blay], *a.* Indefectible, unfailing.

Indefectiblemente, *adv.* Indefectibly.

Indefendible [in-day-fen-dee'-blay], *a.* Indefensible, that cannot be defended.

Indefensable, Indefensible [in-day-fen-sah'-blay, see'-blay], *a.* Indefensible.

Indefenso, sa [in-day-fen'-so, sah], *a.* Defenceless, indefensive.

Indeficiente [in-day-fee-the-en'-tay], *a.* Indefectible, unfailing.

Indefinible [in-day-fe-nee'-blay], *a.* Indefinable.

Indefinidamente, *adv.* Indefinitely.

Indefinido, da [in-day-fe-nee'-do, dah], *a.* 1. Indefinite, not defined. 2. Indefinite not determined. 3. Indefinite, large beyond the comprehension of man. 4. Indefinite, not limited.

Indefinito, ta [in-day-fe-nee'-to, tah], *a.* Indefinite, without limits.

Indehescencia [in-day-es-then'-the-ah], *f.* (Bot.) Indehiscence, lack of the power to open spontaneously.

Indehiscente [in-day-es-then'-tay], *a.* Indehiscent, not splitting spontaneously.

Indeleble [in-day-lay'-blay], *a.* Indelible, not to be blotted out.

Indeleblemente, *adv.* Indelibly.

Indeliberación [in-day-le-bay-rah-the-on'], *f.* 1. Indetermination, irresolution. 2. Inadvertency.

Indeliberadamente, *adv.* Inadvertently, indeliberately.

Indeliberado, da [in-day-le-bay-rah'-do, dah], *a.* Indeliberate or indeliberated, unpremeditated; done without sufficient consideration.

Indemne [in-dem'-nay], *a.* Undamaged, unhurt.

Indemnidad [in-dem-ne-dahd'], *f.* Indemnity, exemption from damage.

Indemnizable [in-dem-ne-thah'-blay], *a.* What can be made good, or indemnified.

Indemnización [in-dem-ne-thah-the-on'], *f.* Indemnification, reimbursement.

Indemnizar [in-dem-nee-thar'], *va.* To indemnify, to secure against loss; to maintain unhurt, to make amends, to compensate, to make good to one.

Indemostrable [in-day-mos-trah'-blay], *a.* Indemonstrable, incapable of demonstration.

Independencia [in-day-pen-den'-the-ah], *f.* Independence, freedom from reliance or control.

Independiente [in-day-pen-de-en'-tay], *a.* Independent, free: it is sometimes used as a substantive. *Independiente de eso*, Independent of that, besides that.

Independientemente, *adv.* Independently.

Indescifrable [in-des-the-frah'-blay], *a.* Undecipherable.

Indescribible [in-des-cre-bee'-blay], or **Indescriptible,** *a.* Indescribable.

Indesignable [in-day-sig-nah'-blay], *a.* That which cannot be designed.

Indestructibilidad [in-des-trooc-te-be-le-dahd'], *f.* Indestructibility.

Indestructible [in-des-trooc-tee'-blay], *a.* Indestructible, imperishable.

Indeterminable [in-day-ter-me-nah'-blay], *a.* 1. Indeterminable. 2. Irresolute, undecided.

Indeterminación [in-day-ter-me-nah-the-on'], *f.* Indetermination or indeterminateness, irresolution.

Indeterminadamente, *adv.* Indeterminately.

Indeterminado, da [in-day-ter-me-nah'-do, dah], *a.* 1. Indeterminate, not defined. 2. Undetermined, irresolute, doubtful. 3. Pusillanimous, chicken-hearted. 4. Indefinite, general; loose.

Indevoción [in-day-vo-the-on'], *f.* Indevotion, want of devotion.

Indevoto, ta [in-day-vo'-to, tah], *a.* Indevout, irreligious.

India [een'-de-ah], *f.* (Met. Coll.) Great wealth, abundance of money and other precious things.

Indiana [in-de-ah'-nah], *f.* Chintz.

Indianismo [in-de-ah-nees'-mo], *m.* 1. Interest in or knowledge of West Indian culture. 2. East Indian idiom.

Indianista [in-de-ah-nees'-tah], *m.* & *f.* 1. Indianist. 2. Person versed in West Indian cultures.

Indiano, na [in-de-ah'-no, nah], *a.* & *m.* & *f.* 1. East Indian. 2. West Indian. 3. Spanish or Latin American.—*m.* Nabob, person returning rich from America.

Indicación [in-de-ca-the-on'], *f.* 1. Indication, any mark, token, sign or note. 2. (Med.) Indication, the sign or symptom which indicates what is to be done.

Indicador [in-de-ca-dor'], *m.* 1. Indicator, pointer. 2. The forefinger. 3. Electrical indicator. *Indicador de dirección*, (Aer.) Direction indicator.

Indicante [in-de-cahn'-tay], *pa.* Indicating.—*m.* (Med.) Indicant, any thing from which an indication is drawn in a disease.

Indicar [in-de-car'], *va.* 1. To indicate, to show, to point out. 2. (Med.) To indicate, to point out a remedy.

Indicativo, va [in-de-cah-tee'-vo, vah], *a.* Indicative, pointing.

Indicativo, *m.* (Gram.) Indicative, one of the modes of verbs.

Indicción [in-dic-the-on'], *f.* Indiction, the convening of a synod, council, etc. *Indicción Romana*, Roman indiction: a manner of computing time.

Índice [een'-de-thay], *m.* 1. Mark, sign, index. 2. Hand of a watch or clock. 3. Pin that casts the shade on a sun-dial. 4. Index, table of contents to a book. 5. Index, forefinger. *Índice expurgatorio*, Catalogue of books prohibited by the Inquisition. *Congregación del índice*, A papal commission at Rome, to examine the contents of books.

Indiciado, da [in-de-the-ah'-do, dah], *a.* Suspected of a crime or vice.—*pp.* of Indiciar. Suspicious, liable to be suspected.

Indiciador, ra [in-de-the-ah-dor', rah], *m.* & *f.* 1. One who entertains suspicions. 2. Informer, one who discovers offenders to the magistrates.

Indiciar [in-de-the-ar'], *va.* (Law) 1. To give reasons to suspect or surmise. 2. To discover offenders to the magistrates. 3. *V.* Indicar.

Indicio [in-dee'-the-o], *m.* Indication, mark, sign, token. *Indicios vehementes.* (Law) Circumstantial evidences.

Índico, ca [een'-de-co, cah], *a.* Indian.

Indicolita [in-de-co-lee'-tah], *f.* A variety of tourmaline of indigo-blue colour, found in Sweden.

Indiferencia [in-de-fay-ren'-the-ah], *f.* 1. Indifference, incuriosity. 2. Neglect, unconcern, coldness, lukewarmness, listlessness. 3. Neutrality, suspension.

Indiferente [in-de-fay-ren'-tay], *a.* 1. Indifferent, neutral. 2. Unconcerned, inattentive, regardless. 3. Lukewarm, cool, frigid, listless. *Eso es indiferente*, (Coll.) That is immaterial, that makes no difference.

Indiferentemente, *adv.* Indifferently, impartially, coolly.

Indígena [in-dee'-hay-nah], *a.* Indigenous, native.—*m.* & *f.* An Indian.

Indigencia [in-de-hen'-the-ah], *f.* Indigence, want, penury, poverty, need.

Indigenismo [in-de-hay-nees'-mo], *m.* Study of or interest in West Indian culture.

Indigenista [in-de-hay-nees'-tah], *a.* Treating of or defending West Indian culture.—*m.* & *f.* Supporter of West Indians and their culture.

Indigente [in-de-hen'-tay], *a.* Indigent, necessitous, poor, needy.

Indigerible [in-de-hay-ree'-blay], *a.* Not possible of digestion.

Indigestible [in-de-hes-tee'-blay], *a.* Indigestible, hard to digest.

Indigestión [in-de-hes-te-on'], *f.* 1. Indigestion. 2. Rudeness of temper, ill-nature.

Indigesto, ta [in-de-hes'-to, tah], *a.* 1. Indigest or undigested, not concocted in the stomach. 2. Indigest, confused, not separated into distinct parts, not methodized, not well considered. 3. (Coll.) Rude, ill-natured.

Indigete [in-de-hay'-tay], *m.* (Obs.) Indigite, native demi-god or hero of antiquity.

Indignación [in-dig-nah-the-on'], *f.* Indignation, anger.

Indignado, da [in-dig-nah'-do, dah], *a.* & *pp.* of Indignar. Provoked, teased, indignant, angry.

Indignamente, *adv.* Unworthily, unsuitably.

Indignante [in-dig-nahn'-tay], *pa.* Indignant, irritating.

Indignar [in-dig-nar'], *va.* To irritate, to provoke, to tease.—*vr.* To be inflamed with anger and disdain, to become angry or indignant.

Indignidad [in-dig-ne-dahd'], *f.* 1. Indignity, want of merit. 2. An unworthy action, meanness. 3. Indignation, passion.

Indigno, na [in-deeg'-no, nah], *a.* 1. Unworthy, undeserving. 2. Unbecoming, incongruous, unsuitable. 3. Unworthy, bringing indignity, disgraceful, vile, mean, despicable.

Índigo [een'-de-go], *m.* (Bot.) *V.* AÑIL.

Indiligencia [in-de-le-hen'-the-ah], *f.* Indiligence, want of diligence, carelessness.

Indio, ia [een'-de-o,ah]. *a.* 1. East or West Indian. 2. Blue, azure.—*m.* & *f.* East or West Indian.—*m.* (Chem.) Indium.

Indirecta [in-de-rec'-tah], *f.* Innuendo, an oblique hint, a cue, a surmise. *Indirecta del Padre Cobos*, A broad hint.

Indirectamente, Indirecte, *adv.* 1. Indirectly, obliquely. 2. Indirectly, not in express terms.

Indirecto, ta [in-de-rec'-to, tah], *a.* Indirect, not direct; oblique.

Indiscernible [in-dis-ther-nee'-blay], *a.* (Littl. us.) Indiscernible, inconspicuous.

Indisciplina [in-dis-the-plee'-nah], *f.* Want of discipline, insubordination.

Indisciplinable [in-dis-the-ple-nah'-blay], *a.* Indisciplinable, incapable of discipline.

Indisciplinado, da [in-dis-the-ple-nah'-do, dah], *a.* Untaught, undisciplined.

Indiscreción [in-dis-cray-the-on'], *f.* Indiscretion, imprudence, rashness, inconsideration, folly.

Indiscretamente [in-dis-cray-tah-men'-tay], *adv.* Indiscreetly.

Indiscreto, ta [in-dis-cray'-to, tah], *a.* Indiscreet, imprudent, incautious, foolish; injudicious, inconsiderate.

Indisculpable [in-dis-cool-pah'-blay], *a.* Inexcusable.

Indiscutible [in-dis-coo-tee'-blay], *a.* Unquestionable, beyond discussion, beyond peradventure.

Indisolubilidad [in-de-so-loo-be-le-dahd'], *f.* Indissolubility, indissolubleness.

Indisoluble [in-de-so-loo'-blay], *a.* Indissoluble, indissolvable.

Indisolublemente, *adv.* Indissolubly.

Indispensable [in-dis-pen-sah'-blay], *a.* Indispensable, needful.

Indispensablemente, *adv.* Indispensably, necessarily.

Indisponer [in-dis-po-nerr'], *va.* 1. To disable, to indispose, to render unfit. 2. To indispose, to disincline, to make averse or unfavourable. 3. To indispose or disorder slightly with regard to health: commonly used in its reciprocal sense.—*vr.* 1. To be indisposed, to grow ill. 2. To become peevish or fretful.

Indisponible [in-dis-po-nee'-blay], *a.* (Law) That which cannot be bequeathed.

Indisposición [in-dis-po-se-the-on'], *f.* 1. Indisposition, disinclination, dislike. 2. Indisposition, slight disorder.

Indisposicioncilla [in-dis-po-se-the-on-theel'-lyah], *f. dim.* Slight indisposition.

Indispuesto, ta [in-dis-poo-ays'-to, tah]. *a.* & *pp. irr.* of INDISPONER. 1. Indisposed, disordered in health. 2. Indisposed, at variance.

Indisputable [in-dis-poo-tah'-blay], *a.* Indisputable, incontrovertible.

Indisputablemente, *adv.* Indisputably.

Indistinción [in-dis-tin-the-on'], *f.* Indistinction, indiscrimination.

Indistinguible [in-dis-tin-gee'-blay], *a.* Undistinguishable, indistinguishable.

Indistintamente [in-dis-tin-tah-men'-tay], *adv.* Indistinctly, indiscriminately.

Indistinto, ta [in-dis-teen'-to, tah], *a.* Indistinct, indiscriminate.

Individuación [in-de-ve-doo-ah-the-on'], *f.* *V.* INDIVIDUALIDAD.

Individual [in-de-ve-doo-ahl'], *a.* Individual.

Individualidad [in-de-ve-doo-ah-le-dahd'], *f.* Individuality.

Individualismo [in-de-ve-doo-ah-lees'-mo], *m.* Individualism.

Individualista [in-de-ve-doo-ah-lees'-tah], *a.* Individualistic.—*m.* & *f.* Individualist.

Individualizar [in-de-ve-doo-ah-le-thar'], *va.* To individualize.

Individualmente, *adv.* 1. Individually, numerically. 2. Individually, not separably.

Individuar [in-de-ve-doo-ar'], *va.* To individuate, to distinguish; to particularize, to specify individually.

Individuo [in-de-vee'-do-o], *m.* Individual, a single person or thing.

Individuo, dua [in-de-vee'-doo-o, ah], *a.* Individual, indivisible, inseparable.

Indivisamente [in-de-ve-sah-men'-tay], *adv.* Indivisibly.

Indivisibilidad [in-de-ve-se-be-le-dahd'], *f.* Indivisibility.

Indivisible [in-de-ve-see'-blay], *a.* Indivisible.

Indivisiblemente, *adv.* Inseparably, indivisibly.

Indiviso, sa [in-de-vee'-so, sah], *a.* Undivided, individuate, not separated into parts. *Pro indiviso*, (Law) Applied to an inheritance when the partitions are not made.

Indiyudicable [in-de-yoo-de-cah'-blay], *a.* (Obs.) Not to be judged.

Indo, da [een'-do, dah], *a.* Indian. (Acad.) *V.* INDIO.—*m.* The river Indus, now the Sind.

Indócil [in-do'-theel], *a.* 1. Indocile, unteachable. 2. Inflexible, not to be prevailed upon; headstrong, froward.

Indocilidad [in-do-the-le-dahd'], *f.* 1. Indocility, refusal of instruction. 2. Inflexibility, stubbornness of mind.

Indócilmente [in-do'-theel-men-tay], *adv.* Inflexibly.

Indocto, ta [in-doc'-to, tah], *a.* Ignorant, uninstructed, unlearned.

Indoeuropeo, a [in-do-ay-oo-ro-pay'-o, ah], *a.* Indo-European.

Indogermánico, ca [in-do-her-mah'-ne-co, cah], *a.* Indo-Germanic.

Índole [een'-do-lay], *f.* Disposition, temper, inclination, peculiar genius, idiosyncrasy, humour.

Indolencia [in-do-len'-the-ah], *f.* Indolence, indifference, laziness; insensibility to grief or pain.

Indolente [in-do-len'-tay], *a.* Indolent, indifferent.

Indolentemente, *adv.* Indolently, inertly.

Indomable [in-do-mah'-blay], *a.* 1. Undamable, indomitable, unmanageable: applied to wild animals. 2. Inflexible, unconquerable: applied to the passions.

Indomado, da [in-do-mah'-do, dah], *a.* Untamed.

Indomesticable [in-do-mes-te-cah'-blay], *a.* Untamable.

Indoméstico, ca [in-do-mays'-te-co, cah], *a.* Untamed, fierce, intractable.

Indómito, ta [in-do'-me-to, tah], *a.* Untamed, ungoverned, wild.

Indostánico, ca [in-dos-tah'-ne-co, cah], *a.* Hindu or Hindoo, belonging to Hindustan

Indostano, na [in-dos-tah'-no, nah], *m.* & *f.* Hindu, a native of Hindustan.

Indotación [in-do-tah-the-on'], *f.* (Law) Want of a wife's portion.

Indotado, da [in-do-tah'-do, dah], *a.* 1. Unendowed, wanting endowments or talents. 2. Portionless: applied to women.

Indri [in-dree'], *m.* (Zool.) A mammal of the lemur family, greatly resembling an anthropoid ape.

Indubitable [in-doo-be-tah'-blay], *a.* Indubitable, unquestioned, irrefutable, unquestionable.

Indubitablemente, *adv.* Undoubtedly, indubitably, unquestionably.

Indubitado, da [in-doo-be-tah'-do, dah], *a.* Undoubted, indubitate.

Inducción [in-dooc-the-on'], *f.* 1. Induction, inducement, persuasion. 2. Induction, the act of inferring a general proposition from several particular ones. *Por inducción*, Inductively.

Inducidor, ra [in-doo-the-dor', rah], *m.* & *f.* Inducer, persuader.

Inducimiento [in-doo-the-me-en'-to], *m.* Inducement, motive to any thing.

Inducir [in-doo-theer'], *va.* To induce, to persuade, to influence, to attract.

Inductancia [in-dooc-tahn'-the-ah], *f.* (Elec.) Inductance.

Indúctil [in-dooc'-teel], *a.* Not ductile.

Inductivo, va [in-dooc-tee'-vo, vah], *a.* Inductive.

Indudable [in-doo-dah'-blay], *a.* (Prov.) *V.* INDUBITABLE.

Indulgencia [in-dool-hen'-the-ah], *f.* 1. Indulgence, forbearance, tenderness, clemency, forgiveness. 2. Fond kindness. 3. Indulgence, release of the penalty due to sin.

Indulgente [in-dool-hen'-tay], *a.* Indulgent, kind, mild, gentle.

Indulgentemente, *adv.* Indulgently.

Indultar [in-dool-tar'], *va.* 1. To pardon, to forgive. 2. To free, to exempt.

Indultario [in-dool-tah'-re-o], *m.* He who in virtue of a pontifical privilege can dispense ecclesiastical benefices.

Indulto [in-dool'-to], *m.* 1. Pardon, forgiveness, amnesty. 2. Indult, privilege, exemption. 3. Impost, tax or duty on merchandise imported into Spain.

Indumentaria [in-doo-men-tah'-re-ah], *f.* The study of ancient apparel.

Indumento [in-doo-men'-to], *m.* (Obs.) Wearing apparel.

Induración [in-doo-rah-the-on'], *f.* (Med.) Induration, a morbid hardness of any part.

Industria [in-doos'-tre-ah], *f.* 1. Industry, diligence, assiduity. 2. Ingenuity, subtilty, acuteness. *De industria*, Designedly, purposely, intentionally. *Caballero de industria*, A man who lives by infamous expedients.

Industrial [in-doos-tre-ahl'], *a.* Industrial. **-mente,** *adv.*

Industrialismo [in-doos-tre-ah-lees'-mo], *m.* Industrialism, a social system which considers industry as the principal and most important of the objects of mankind. (Neol.)

Industrialista [in-doos-tre-ah-lees'-tah], *a.* Industrialist.

Industrialización [in-doos-tre-ah-le-thah-the-on'], *f.* Industrialization.

Industrializar [in-doos-tre-ah-le-thar'], *va.* To industrialize.

Industriar [in-doos-tre-ar'], *va.* To teach, to instruct.

Industriosamente [in-doos-tre-o-sah-men'-tay], *adv.* 1. Industriously. 2. (Obs.) Designedly.

Industrioso, sa [in-doos-tre-o'-so, sah], *a.* 1. Industrious, skilful, dexterous; painstaking, laborious, assiduous. 2. Made with ingenuity, skilfully or finely done.

Inebriativo, va [in-ay-bre-ah-tee'-vo, vah], *a.* Inebriating. (Obs.) *V.* EMBRIAGADOR.

Inedia [in-ay'-de-ah], *f.* Fast, abstinence from food.

Inédito, ta [in-ay'-de-to, tah], *a.* Not published, unedited, inedited.

Inefabilidad [in-ay-fah-be-le-dahd'], *f.* Ineffability, unspeakableness; impossibility of being explained.
Inefable [in-ay-fah'-blay], *a.* Ineffable. unspeakable.
Inefablemente [in-ay-fah-blay-men-'tay], *adv.* Ineffably.
Ineficacia [in-ay-fe-cah'-the-ah], *f.* Inefficacy, want of effect, ineffectualness, inefficiency.
Ineficaz [in-ay-fe-cath'], *a.* Inefficacious, ineffectual, ineffective, inefficient.
Ineficazmente, *adv.* Inefficaciously.
Inegual [in-ay-goo-ahl'], *a.* (Obs.) *V.* DESIGUAL.
Inelegancia [in-ay-lay-gahn'-the-ah], *f.* Inelegance.
Inelegante [in-ay-lay-gahn'-tay], *a.* Inelegant.
Ineluctable [in-ay-looc-tah'-blay], *a.* Inevitable, irresistible.
Inenarrable [in-ay-nar-rah'-blay], *a.* Inexplicable, inexpressible.
Inepcia [in-ep'-the-ah], *f.* (Rare) *V.* NECEDAD.
Ineptamente [in-ep-tah-men'-tay], *adv.* Unfitly, ineptly.
Ineptitud [in-ep-te-tood'], *f.* Ineptitude, inability, unfitness.
Inepto, ta [in-ep'-to, tah], *a.* Inept. unfit, useless; foolish.
Inequívoco, ca [in-ay-kee'-vo-co, cah]. *a.* Unequivocal, unmistakable.
Inercia [in-ayr'-the-ah], *f.* 1. Inertia, the passive principle in matter; inertness, want of motion. 2. Inactivity, inertia, dulness, indolence.
Inerme [in-ayr'-may], *a.* Disarmed. without arms.
Inerrable [in-er-rah'-blay], *a.* Inerrable, exempt from error.
Inerrante [in-er-rahn'-tay], *a.* (Ast. Fixed: applied to the stars.
Inerte [in-ayr'-tay], *a.* 1. Inert, dull, sluggish. 2. Unskilful. 3. (Med.) Paralytic, paralyzed.
Inerudito, ta [in-ay-roo-dee'-to, tah], *a.* Inerudite, unlearned.
Inervación [in-er-vah-the-on'], *f.* Innervation, the act of giving nervous stimulus and control to an organ.
Inescrutable [in-es-croo-tah'-blay], *a.* Inscrutable, unsearchable. **-mente,** *adv.*
Inescudriñable [in-es-coo-dree-nyah'-blay], *a.* Inscrutable.
Inesperadamente [in-es-pay-rah-dah-men'-tay], *adv.* Unexpectedly, suddenly.
Inesperado, da [in-es-pay-rah'-do, dah], *a.* Unexpected, unforeseen.
Inestabilidad [in-es-tah-be-le-dahd'], *f.* Instability, inconstancy, fickleness, mutability, giddiness.
Inestimabilidad [in-es-te-mah-be-le-dahd'], *f.* Inestimableness.
Inestimable [in-es-te-mah'-blay], *a.* Inestimable, invaluable.
Inestimado, da [in-es-te-mah'-do, dah], *a.* (Law) That which has not been rated or valued.
Inevitable [in-ay-ve-tah'-blay], *a.* Inevitable, unavoidable, fatal.
Inevitablemente, *adv.* Inevitably.
Inexactitud [in-ec-sahc-te-tood'], *f.* Inaccuracy, want of exactness.
Inexacto, ta [in-ec-sahc'-to, tah], *a.* Inexact, inaccurate.
Inexcusable [in-ex-coo-sah'-blay], *a.* 1. Inexcusable. 2. Inevitable, indispensable 3. Excuseless.
Inexcusablemente [in-ex-coo-sah-blay-men'-tay], *adv.* Inexcusably.
Inexhausto, ta [in-ec-sah'-oos-to, tah], *a.* 1. Unexhausted, unemptied, unspent. 2. Full, abundant, plentiful.
Inexistencia [in-ec-sis-ten'-the-ah], *f.* 1. Inexistence. 2. (Obs.) Existence of one thing in another.
Inexistente [in-ec-sis-ten'-tay], *a.* Inexistent, non-existent.
Inexorable [in-ec-so-rah'-blay], *a.* Inexorable, relentless, hard-hearted.
Inexperiencia [in-ex-pay-re-en'-the-ah], *f.* Inexperience.
Inexperto, ta [in-ex-per'-to, tah], *a.* Inexpert, unskilful, inexperienced.
Inexpiable [in-ex-pe-ah'-blay], *a.* Inexpiable.
Inexplicable [in-ex-ple-cah'-blay], *a.* Inexplicable, inexplainable.
Inexplorado, da [in-ex-plo-rah'-do, dah], *a.* Unexplored.
Inexpugnable [in-ex-poog-nah'-blay], *a.* 1. Inexpugnable, impregnable. 2. Firm, constant; obstinate, stubborn.
Inextenso, sa [in-ex-ten'-so, sah], *a.* (Littl. us.) Unextended.
Inextinguible [in-ex-tin-gee'-blay], *a.* Inextinguishable, unquenchable; perpetual.
Inextricable [in-ex-tre-cah'-blay, *a.* Inextricable.
In facie Ecclesiæ (Latin phrase) Publicly and duly celebrated: said of a marriage.
Infacundo, da [in-fah-coon'-do, dah], *a.* Ineloquent, not persuasive, not oratorical.
Infalibilidad [in-fah-le-be-le-dahd'], *f.* Infallibility.
Infalible [in-fah-lee'-blay], *a.* Infallible.
Infaliblemente, *adv.* Infallibly.
Infamable [in-fah-mah'-blay], *a.* Capable of infamy; calumnious.
Infamación [in-fah-mah-the-on'], *f.* Slander, calumny, defamation; the defaming of another.
Infamador, ra [in-fah-mah-dor', rah], *m. & f.* Defamer, libeller.
Infamante [in-fah-mahn'-tay], *pa. & a.* Defaming; opprobrious.
Infamar [in-fah-mar'], *va.* To defame, to make infamous, to dishonour by reports.
Infamativo, va [in-fah-mah-tee'-vo, vah], *a.* That which defames.
Infamatorio, ria [in-fah-mah-to'-re-o, ah], *a.* Defamatory, libellous, foul-spoken.
Infame [in-fah'-may], *a.* Infamous, vile, despicable, damnable.
Infamemente [in-fah-may-men'-tay], *adv.* Infamously, vilely.
Infamia [in-fah'-me-ah], *f.* Infamy, dishonour, public reproach or opprobrium; meanness, baseness.
Infancia [in-fahn'-the-ah], *f.* 1. Infancy, the first part of life. 2. Infancy, the first age of any thing; beginning, commencement.
Infando, da [in-fahn'-do, dah], *a.* Infandous, so abominable as not to be expressed, too bad to be mentioned.
Infant [in-fahnt'], *m.* (Obs.) *V* INFANTE.
Infanta [in-fahn'-tah], *f.* 1. Infant, a female child under seven years of age. 2. Infanta, a princess of the royal blood of Spain. 3. Wife of a prince royal.
Infantado [in-fan-tah'-do], *m.* Territory assigned to a prince of the royal blood of Spain.
Infante [in-fahn'-tay], *m.* 1. Infant, a male child under seven years of age. 2. Infante, a title given to all the sons and some of the nephews of the King of Spain, except the heir-apparent to the crown. 3. A foot-soldier.—*pl.* Choristers, boys brought up to sing in cathedral churches.
Infantería [in-fan-tay-ree'-ah], *f.* Infantry, foot-soldiers.
Infanticida [in-fan-te-thee'-dah], *com.* Infanticide, the murderer of an infant.
Infanticidio [in-fan-te-thee'-de-o], *m.* Infanticide, the murder of a child or infant.
Infantil [in-fan-teel'], *a.* Infantile, infantine.
Infanzón [in-fan-thone'], *m.* Nobleman.
Infanzonado, da [in-fan-tho-nah'-do, dah], *a.* Pertaining to a noble.
Infanzonazgo [in-fan-tho-nath'-go], *m.* Territory of a nobleman.
Infanzonía [in-fan-tho-nee'-ah], *f.* Nobility.
Infartación [in-far-tah-the-on'], *f.* Infarction, the stoppage of a channel.
Infarto [in-far'-to], *m.* Infarct, that which composes an infarction.
Infatigable [in-fah-te-gah'-blay], *a.* Indefatigable, unwearied.
Infatigablemente, *adv.* Indefatigably.
Infatuación [in-fah-too-ah-the-on'], *f.* (Littl. us.) 1. Infatuation. 2. *En materias de religión,* Bigotry.
Infatuado, da [in-fah-too-ah'-do, dah], *a. & pp.* of INFATUAR. Infatuate, infatuated, stupefied; infatuating.
Infatuar [in-fah-too-ar'], *va.* To infatuate, to deprive of understanding. —*vr.* 1. To become stupefied. 2. In religious matters, to be or become a bigot.
Infaustamente [in-fah-oos-tah-men tay], *adv.* Unluckily.
Infausto, ta [in-fah'-oos-to, tah], *a.* Unlucky, unhappy, unfortunate, accursed.
Infección [in-fec-the-on'], *f.* 1 Infection, the act of catching a disease through the medium of an atmosphere charged with poisonous miasma or effluvia, and the same miasma or effluvia. 2. Infection, that which propagates mischief or disease.
Infecir [in-fay-theer'], *va.* (Obs.) *V* INFECTAR.
Infectar [in-fec-tar'], *va.* 1. To infect, to hurt by infection. 2. To corrupt, to vitiate, to pervert.—*vr.* To catch, to take by infection.
Infectivo, va [in-fec-tee'-vo, vah], *a.* Infective, infectious.
Infecto, ta [in-fec'-to, tah], *a. & pp. irr* of INFECIR. Infected, tainted.
Infecundarse [in-fay-coon-dar'-say], *vr* (Obs.) To become sterile.
Infecundidad [in-fay-coon-de-dahd'], *f.* Infecundity, sterility, infertility.
Infecundo, da [in-fay-coon'-do, dah], *a.* Infecund, barren, unfruitful, infertile.
Infelice [in-fay-lee'-thay], *a.* (Poet.) *V.* INFELIZ.
Infelicidad [in-fay-lee-the-dahd'], *f* Misfortune, calamity, disgrace, misery, unhappiness, infelicity.
Infeliz [in-fay-leeth'], *a.* 1. Unhappy, unfortunate, luckless, miserable. 2. (Coll.) Applied to a man of excessive softness and good-nature.
Infelizmente, *adv.* Unhappily, unluckily, unfortunately.
Inferaxilar [in-fay-rac-se-lar'], *a.* (Bot.) Infra-axillary, situated below the axil
Inferencia [in-fay-ren'-the-ah], *f* Inference, illation.
Inferior [in-fay-re-or'], *a.* 1 Inferior lower in place. 2. Inferior, lower in value or excellency. 3. Inferior, lower in station or rank. 4. Inferior, subordinate, subject.
Inferioridad [in-fay-re-o-re-dahd'], *f* Inferiority, subjection.
Inferir [in-fay-reer'], *va.* To infer, to deduce, to draw conclusions, to collect, to gather.—*vr.* To follow, to be consequential, as inference to premises.

Infernáculo [in-fer-nah'-coo-lo], *m.* A Kind of boyish play, called in America *rayuela;* hop-scotch.
Infernal [in-fer-nahl'], *a.* 1. Infernal, hellish. 2. Extremely hurtful. *Máquina infernal,* A machine arranged to throw many projectiles at once. *Pie dra infernal,* Lapis infernalis, vulgar name of nitrate of silver in sticks.
Infernalmente, *adv.* (Coll.) Hellishly, infernally.
Infernar, *va.* 1. To damn, to doom to eternal torments. 2. To tease, to vex, to provoke.
Inferno, na [in-fer'-no, nah], *a.* (Poet.) Infernal.
Ínfero, ra [een'-fay-ro, rah], *a.* Combining form of inferior; and in botany and poetry for inferior.
Infestación [in-fes-tah-the-on'], *f.* Act of harassing, infestation, annoyance.
Infestar [in-fes-tar'], *va.* 1. To infest, to overrun, to harass an enemy by incursions. 2. *V.* INFICIONAR. 3. *V.* APESTAR.
Infeudar [in-fay-oo-dar'], *va.* *V* ENFEUDAR.
Infición [in-fe-the-on'], *f.* Infection. *V.* INFECCIÓN.
Inficionar [in-fe-the-o-nar'], *va.* 1. To infect, to hurt by infection. 2. To corrupt, to defile, to pervert by bad maxims or bad example. 3. To defile the honours of a noble descent, to taint the purity of noble blood; to vitiate.
Infidelidad [in-fe-day-le-dahd'], *f.* 1. Infidelity, treachery, deceit, faithlessness. 2. Miscreance, unbelief, want of faith, disbelief of Christianity. 3. The whole body of infidels.
Infidelísimo, ma [in-fe-day-lee'-se-mo, mah], *a. super.* of INFIEL.
Infidencia [in-fe-den'-the-ah], *f.* 1. Unfaithfulness, faithlessness; treason. 2. (Law) Misfeasance.
Infidente [in-fe-den'-tay], *a.* Unfaithful.
Infiel [in-fe-el'], *a.* Unfaithful, infidel; faithless, disloyal; godless; pagan: it is also used as a substantive.
Infielmente [in-fe-el-men'-tay], *adv.* Unfaithfully.
Infiernillo, Infernillo [en-fe-er-neel'-lyo, en-fer-neel'-lyo], *m.* Chafing dish.
Infierno [in-fe-err'-no], *m.* 1. Hell, the place of the devil and wicked souls; torment of the wicked. 2. Limbo. 3. Any thing which causes confusion, pain, or trouble; discord, dispute. 4. Refectory or eating-room in some convents. 5. A large retort or other chemical vessel.
Infigurable [in-fe-goo-rah'-blay], *a.* That which cannot be represented by any figure.
Infiltración [in-feel-trah-the-on'], *f.* (Med.) Infiltration.
Infiltrarse [in-feel-trar'-say], *vr* To infiltrate, to insinuate by filtration
Ínfimo, ma [een'-fe-mo, mah], *a.* 1. Lowest, lowermost, most inferior; the least. 2. Abject, vile, low-bred.
Infingidor, ra [in-fin-he-dor', rah], *m.* & *f.* (Obs.) Dissembler.
Infinidad [in-fe-ne-dahd'], *f.* 1. Infinity, infiniteness, immensity, boundlessness. 2. Infinity, endless number.
Infinitamente [in-fe-ne-tah-men'-tay], *adv.* Infinitely, immensely.
Infinitesimal [in-fe-ne-tay-se-mahl'], *a.* (Mat.) Infinitesimal: applied to fractions.
Infinitésimo, ma [in-fe-ne-tay'-se-mo, mah], *a.* (Coll.) Infinitely small.
Infinitivo [in-fe-ne-tee'-vo], *m.* (Gram.) Infinitive, one of the modes of verbs.
Infinito, ta [in-fe-nee'-to, tah], *a* Infinite, unbounded, unlimited, immense. 2. Infinite, very numerous, excessive.
Infinito [in-fe-nee'-to], *adv.* Infinitely, immensely.
Inflación [in-flah-the-on'], *f.* 1. Inflation, the state of being swelled with wind; flatulence. 2. Inflation, conceit, vanity, haughtiness, vaingloriousness.
Inflamabilidad [in-flah-mah-be-le-dahd'], *f.* Inflammability.
Inflamable [in-flah-mah'-blay], *a.* Inflammable, easy to be set on flame.
Inflamación [in-flah-mah-the-on'], *f.* 1. Inflammation, setting on flame; the state of being in flame. 2. (Med.) Inflammation, a morbid state characterized by heat, pain, etc. 3. Inflammation, excitement of passions or of fervour of mind.
Inflamar [in-flah-mar'], *va.* 1. To inflame, to kindle, to set on fire. 2. To inflame, to kindle desire.—*vr.* To become red, to become inflamed or heated.
Inflamatorio, ria [in-flah-mah-to'-re-o, ah], *a.* Inflammatory.
Inflar [in-flar'], *va.* 1. To inflate, to swell with wind. 2. (Met.) To elate, to inflate, to puff up with pride.—*vr.* To jet, to strut.
Inflexibilidad [in-flec-se-be-le-dahd'], *f.* 1. Inflexibility, stiffness, the quality of resisting flexure. 2. Inflexibility, inflexibleness, obstinacy, quality of the temper not to be bent, inexorability.
Inflexible [in-flec-see'-blay], *a.* 1. Inflexible, not to be bent. 2. Inflexible, not to be prevailed upon, immovable; contumacious.
Inflexiblemente, *adv.* Inflexibly, inexorable; invariably.
Inflexión [in-flec-se-on'], *f* 1. Inflection, the act of bending or turning. 2. (Gram.) Inflection, variation of a noun or verb. 3. Inflection, modulation of the voice.
Inflictivo, va [in-flic-tee'-vo, vah], *a.* (Law) Inflictive, used as punishment.
Infligir [in-fle-heer'], *va.* To inflict, to condemn.
Inflorescencia [in-flo-res-then'-the-ah], *f.* Inflorescence; habit or axis of flowering.
Influencia [in-floo-en'-the-ah], *f.* 1. (Ant.) Influence, the power of the celestial bodies upon terrestrial bodies and affairs. 2. (Met.) Influence, influx, influencing, credit, consequence, holding ascendent power, power of directing or satisfying. 3. (Met.) Inspiration of divine grace.
Influente [in-floo-en'-tay], *pa.* & *a.* Influencing, influential.
Influenza [in-floo-en'-thah], *f* Flu, influenza.
Influir [in-floo-eer'], *va.* 1. To influence; to modify; to prevail upon, to guide. 2 To interfere; to inspire with grace.
Influjo [in-floo'-ho], *m.* Influx, influence, power, credit.
Influyente [in-floo-yen'-tay], *a.* Influential, effective.
Infolio [in-fo'-le-o], *m.* A book in folio form. (Acad.)
Inforciado [in-for-the-ah'-do], *m.* Second part of the digest or pandects of Justinian.
Información [in-for-mah-the-on'], *f.* 1. Information, account, intelligence given; instruction: hint. 2. Information, charge or accusation exhibited. 3. Judicial inquiry and process. 4. Brief, the writing given to the pleaders, containing the case. 5 Inquiry, investigation.
Informal [in-for-mahl'], *a.* 1. Informal, irregular. 2. Applied to persons who do not keep their word, or who have no regard for the established forms of society.
Informalidad [in-for-mah-le-dahd'], *f.* Informality, want of attention to established forms.
Informante [in-for-mahn'-tay], *pa.* Informing, instructing.—*m.* 1. Informant, informer, one who gives information. 2. Informant, one who is peculiarly charged to collect information respecting the descent and quality of a person.
Informar [in-for-mar'], *va.* 1. To inform, to instruct, to supply with intelligence or knowledge, to acquaint, to report. 2. To inform, to animate, to actuate by vital powers. 3. To state a case to a counsellor or judge. —*vr.* To take cognizance, to make an inquiry, to ask for information.
Informativo, va [in-for-mah-tee'-vo, vah], *a.* 1. Instructive, that which informs. 2. Animative, informative, having power to animate.
Informe [in-for'-may], *m.* 1. Information, the act of communicating intelligence or imparting knowledge; account; a report. 2. Brief. 3. *V* INFORMACIÓN.
Informe [in-for'-may], *a.* 1. Informous, shapeless, formless. 2. Not performed in a regular manner.
Informidad [in-for-me-dahd'], *f.* (Littl. us.) Informity, shapelessness.
Infortificable [in-for-te-fe-cah'-blay], *a.* That which cannot be fortified.
Infortuna [in-for-too'-nah], *f.* (Astrol.) Sinistrous influence of the stars.
Infortunado, da [in-for-too-nah'-do, dah], *a.* Unfortunate, unlucky, unhappy.
Infortunio [in-for-too'-ne-oh], *m.* Misfortune, ill luck, calamity, mischance; misery; fatality.
Infosura [in-fo-soo'-rah], *f.* Surfeit in cattle and other animals.
Infracción [in-frac-the-on'], *f.* 1. Infraction, the act of breaking. 2. Infraction, breach, contravention, infringement, violation of a compact; misdemeanour, trespass.
Infracto, ta [in-frahc'-to, tah], *a.* Steady, not easily moved.
Infractor, ra [in-frac-tor', rah], *m.* & *f.* Violator.—*a.* Violating.
Infraestructura [in-frah-es-trooc-too'-rah], *f.* 1. Substructure, foundation. 2. (Aer.) Ground installations. 3. (R.W.) Roadbed and installations. 4. (Mil.) Infrastructure. 5. Groundwork, base, underpinnings.
In fraganti [in frah-gahn'-tee], *adv.* *V* EN FLAGRANTE.
Infrangible [in-fran-hee'-blay], *a.* Infrangible, not to be broken; inviolable.
Infranqueable [in-fran-kay-ah'-blay], *a.* Unsurmountable, inextricable.
Infraoctava [in-frah-oc-tah'-vah], *f.* Six days comprehended in any church festival of eight days, not counting the first and the last.
Infrarrojo, ja [in-frar-ro'-ho, hah], *a.* Infrared.
Infrascripto, ta [in-fras-creep'-to, tah], or **Infrascrito, ta** [in-fras-cree'-to, tah], *a.* Underwritten, undersigned applied to names.
Infringir [in-frin-heer'], *va.* To infringe, to violate or break; to infract.
Infrucción [in-frooc-the-on'], *f* *V* INFURCIÓN.
Infructífero, ra, Infrugífero, ra [in-frooc-tee'-fay-ro, rah], *a.* Unfruitful, not producing fruit: useless.
Infructuosamente, *adv.* Unfruitfully, fruitlessly

Infructuoso, sa [in-frooc-too-oh'-so, sah], *a.* Fruitless, unproductive, unprofitable, gainless, abortive; unsuccessful.
Ínfulas [een'-foo-las], *f. pl.* 1. Ornaments or marks of a sacerdotal or pontifical dignity. 2. Presumption, ostentation.
Infundadamente, *adv.* Groundlessly, without reason or cause.
Infundado, da [in-foon-dah'-do, dah], *a.* Groundless, void of reason.
Infundible [in-foon-dee'-blay], *a.* Infusible, incapable of fusion.
Infundibuliforme [in-foon-de-boo-le-for'-may], *a.* Infundibuliform, funnel-shaped. (Bot.)
Infundíbulo [in-foon-dee'-boo-lo], *m.* 1. Infundibulum, a funnel-shaped prolongation from the base of the brain to the pituitary body. 2. The expanded end of the ureter, of the Fallopian tube, etc.
Infundir [in-foon-deer'], *va.* 1. To infuse, to pour liquor into a vessel. 2. To infuse, to make an infusion with any ingredient. 3. To infuse, to inspire with. 4. To infuse, to pour into the mind, to instil.
Infurción, Infulción [in-foor-the-on'], *f.* Tribute formerly paid in Spain to the lord of the manor for the ground of houses.
Infurcioniego, ga [in-foor-the-o-ne-ay'-go, gah], *a.* Subject to pay the ground rent of a house.
Infurtir [in-foor-teer'], *va.* *V.* ENFURTIR.
Infuscar [in-foos-car'], *va.* (Obs.) To obscure.
Infusibilidad [in-foo-se-be-le-dahd'], *f.* Infusibility, resistance to melting.
Infusible [in-foo-see'-blay], *a.* Infusible, incapable of being melted.
Infusión [in-foo-se-on'], *f.* 1. Infusion, the act and effect of infusing. 2. (Med.) Infusion, the act of pouring water of any required degree of temperature on substances of a loose texture, and suffering it to stand a certain time; and the liquor obtained by the above process. 3. The act of sprinkling water on the person baptized. 4. Infusion, influxion, inspiration; the act of pouring into the mind. *Estar en infusión para alguna cosa,* (Coll.) Said of persons who are going to obtain what they wish.
Infuso, sa [in-foo'-so, sah], *a.* & *pp.* of INFUNDIR. Infused, introduced: applied solely to the grace of God in the soul.
Infusorio, ria [in-foo-so'-re-o, ah], *a.* (Zool.) Infusorian.—*pl.* The infusoria, protozoans occurring in infusions.
Inga, *m.* (Obs.) Inca.
Ingenerable [in-hay-nay-rah'-blay], *a.* Ingenerable, not to be produced or brought into being.
Ingeniador, ra [in-hay-ne-ah-dor', rah], *m.* & *f.* Inventor, contriver.
Ingeniar [in-hay-ne-ar'], *va.* To conceive, to contrive, to strike out.—*vr.* To work in the mind, to endeavour to find out, to try by all means to obtain or do any thing; to manage skilfully.
Ingeniatura [in-hay-ne-ah-too'-rah], *f.* (Coll.) 1. Ingenuity, subtilty, acuteness; skilful management. 2. (Amer.) Engineering.
Ingeniería [in-hay-ne-ay-ree'-ah], *f.* Engineering. *Ingeniería civil,* Civil engineering. *Ingeniería eléctrica,* Electrical engineering. *Ingeniería mecánica,* Mechanical engineering.
Ingeniero [in-hay-ne-ay'-ro], *m.* 1. (Obs.) Contriver, inventor. 2. Engineer, one versed in engineering, the science and art of making or using machines and public works. Civil, military, mining, electrical, hydraulic, engineers.
Ingenio [in-hay'-ne-o], *m.* 1. Genius, talent, skill, cleverness, creative ability. 2. Ingenuity. 3. Engine, any mechanical complication in which various movements and parts concur to one effect. *Ingenio de azúcar,* Sugar mill. *Ingenio de pólvora,* Powder mill.
Ingeniosidad [in-hay-ne-o-se-dahd'], *f.* Ingenuity, ingeniousness, invention.
Ingenioso, sa [in-hay-ne-o'-so, sah], *a.* 1. Ingenious, inventive. 2. Made with ingenuity.
Ingénito, ta [in-hay'-ne-to, tah], *a.* 1. Unbegotten, not generated. 2. Innate, inborn, ingenerate, ingenite.
Ingente [in-hen'-tay], *a.* Very large, huge, prodigious.
Ingenuamente [in-hay-noo-ah-men'-tay], *adv.* Ingenuously, fairly.
Ingenuidad [in-hay-noo-e-dahd'], *f.* Ingenuousness, candour, frankness, openness, open-heartedness.
Ingenuo, nua [in-hay'-noo-o, ah], *a.* 1. Ingenuous, open, candid, fair, open-hearted. 2. (Law) Ingenuous, free-born, not of servile extraction.
Ingerencia [in-hay-ren'-the-ah], *f.* Interference, intermeddling.
Ingeridor [in-hay-re-dor'], *m.* A grafting-knife.
Ingeridura [in-hay-re-doo'-rah], *f.* 1. Grafting. 2. The place where a tree is grafted.
Ingerir [in-hay-reer'], *va.* 1. To insert, to place in or among other things. 2. To introduce, to inclose within another. 3. To graft.—*vr.* To interfere officiously, to intermeddle.
Ingerto, ta [in-her'-to, tah], *a.* & *pp. irr.* of INGERIR. Grafted, ingrafted.
Ingestión [in-hes-te-on'], *f.* (Med.) Ingestion, taking in or introducing into the stomach.
Ingina, *f.* *V.* QUIJADA.
Ingle [een'-glay], *f.* Groin, the part next the thigh.
Inglés, sa [in-glays', sah], *a.* English, belonging to or native of England. *A la Inglesa,* In the English fashion.
Inglés, *m.* English language.
Inglesar [in-glay-sar']. 1. *va.* & *vr.* To anglicize, to acquire English tastes. 2. *va.* To dock a horse's tail.
Inglete [in-glay'-tay], *m.* Diagonal, oblique line which divides a square into two triangles.
Inglosable [in-glo-sah'-blay], *a.* That admits no gloss or comment.
Ingobernable [in-go-ber-nah'-blay], *a.* Ungovernable.
Ingraduable [in-grah-doo-ah'-blay], *a.* (Coll.) That cannot be graduated.
Ingramatical [in-grah-mah-te-cahl'], *a.* Ungrammatical. **-mente,** *adv.*
Ingratamente, *adv.* Ungratefully.
Ingratitud [in-grah-te-tood'], *f.* Ingratitude.
Ingrato, ta [in-grah'-to, tah], *a.* 1. Ungrateful. 2. Unpleasant, disagreeable. 3. Unproductive, harsh.
Ingravidez [in-grah-ve-deth'], *f.* Weightlessness.
Ingrávido, da [in-grah'-ve-do, dah], *a.* Weightless.
Ingrediente [in-gray-de-en'-tay], *m.* Ingredient.
Ingresar [in-gray-sar'], *vn.* To enter.—*va.* To deposit, to place.
Ingreso [in-gray'-so], *m.* 1. Ingress, entrance. 2. Commencement of a work. 3. Entry, any sum of money received which is to be charged in accounts. 4. Surplice-fees. *Derechos de ingreso,* *V.* DERECHOS DE ENTRADA.
Inguinal, *a.* (Med.) *V.* INGUINARIO.
Inguinario, ria [in-gee-nah'-re-o, ah], *a.* Inguinal, belonging to the groin.
Ingurgitación [in-goor-he-tah-the-on'], *f.* 1. Ingurgitation. 2. (Obs.) Fulness of the stomach. 3. Introduction of fluids by a tube or syringe.
Ingurgitar [in-goor-he-tar'], *va.* (Obs.) To ingurgitate, to swallow.—*vr.* To get filled: used of a cavity.
Ingustable [in-goos-tah'-blay], *a.* (Obs.) 1. Ingustable, not perceptible by the taste. 2. Tasteless, having no taste.
Inhábil [in-ah'-beel], *a.* 1. Unable, incapable, unqualified; disqualified, unfit. 2. Unskilful, clumsy, awkward.
Inhabilidad [in-ah-be-le-dahd'], *f.* Inability, unskilfulness, incapacity, unfitness.
Inhabilitación [in-ah-be-le-tah-the-on'], *f.* 1. Act of disabling or disqualifying. 2. Disqualification; disability.
Inhabilitar [in-ah-be-le-tar'], *va.* 1. To disqualify, to make unfit, to disable by some natural or legal impediment. 2. To disqualify, to deprive of a right or claim.—*vr.* To lose a right or claim.
Inhábilmente, *adv.* Unskilfully.
Inhabitable [in-ah-be-tah'-blay], *a.* Uninhabitable.
Inhabitado, da [in-ah-be-tah'-do, dah], *a.* Uninhabited.
Inhabituado, da [in-ah-be-too-ah'-do, dah], *a.* Unhabituated, unaccustomed.
Inhalación [in-ah-lah-the-on'], *f.* (Med.) Inhalation.
Inhalar [in-ah-lar'], *va.* To inhale, to absorb.
Inhallable [in-al-lyah'-blay], *a.* (Littl. us.) Not to be found.
Inhartable [in-ar-tah'-blay], *a.* Insatiable.
Inherencia [in-ay-ren'-the-ah], *f.* Inherence or inherency.
Inherente [in-ay-ren'-tay], *a.* Inherent.
Inherentemente, *adv.* (Littl. us.) Inherently.
Inhestar [in-es-tar'], *va.* *V.* ENHESTAR.
Inhibición [in-e-be-the-on'], *f.* Inhibition, prohibition. *Orden de inhibición,* Writ to forbid a judge from further proceeding in the cause before him.
Inhibir [in-e-beer'], *va.* 1. To inhibit, to prohibit. 2. (Law) To prohibit an inferior court from proceeding further in a cause depending before them.
Inhibitorio, ria [in-e-be-to'-re-o, ah], *a.* Prohibitory.
Inhiesto, ta [in-e-ays'-to, tah], *a.* Entangled, perplexed. *V.* ENHIESTO.
Inhonestamente [in-o-nes-tah-men'-tay], *adv.* Dishonestly.
Inhonestidad [in-o-nes-te-dahd'], *f.* Dishonesty; indecency.
Inhonesto, ta [in-o-nays'-to, tah], *a.* 1. Dishonest. 2. Indecent, immodest.
Inhonorar [in-o-no-rar'], *va.* *V.* DESHONRAR.
Inhospedable, Inhospitable [in-os-pay-dah'-blay], *a.* Inhospitable, repulsive.
Inhospital, *a.* *V.* INHOSPITALARIO.
Inhospitalario, ria [in-os-pe-tah-lah'-re-o, ah], *a.* Unhospitable, reluctant to entertain guests.
Inhospitalidad [in-os-pe-tah-le-dahd'], *f.* Inhospitality, inhospitableness, want of courtesy to strangers.
Inhumanamente [in-oo-mah-nah-men'-tay], *adv.* Inhumanly.
Inhumanidad [in-oo-mah-ne-dahd'], *f.* Inhumanity, cruelty.
Inhumano, na [in-oo-mah'-no, nah], *a.* Inhuman, savage, cruel.
Iniciación [e-ne-the-ah-the-on'], *f.* Initiation, introduction.
Inicial [e-ne-the-ahl'], *a.* Initial, placed at the beginning. *Letras iniciales* or *las iniciales,* Initials.

Iniciar [e-ne-the-ar'], *va.* To initiate, to instruct in the rudiments of an art, to put into a new society.—*vr.* To be initiated, to receive the first orders.

Iniciativo, va [e-ne-the-ah-tee'-vo, vah], *a.* Initiating or producing initiation, initiatory.—*f.* Initiative, the right of proposing laws, etc. *Tomar la iniciativa,* To be first in doing or saying something.

Inicuamente [in-e-coo-ah-men'-tay], *adv.* Iniquitously.

Inicuo, cua [in-ee'-coo-o, ah], *a.* Iniquitous, wicked, unjust.

Inimaginable [in-e-mah-he-nah'-blay], *a.* Unimaginable, inconceivable.

Inimicicia [in-e-me-thee'-the-ah], *f.* (Obs.) *V.* Enemistad.

Inimitable [in-e-me-tah'-blay], *a.* Inimitable, above imitation; not to be copied.

Inimitablemente, *adv.* (Littl. us.) Inimitably.

Ininteligible [in-in-tay-le-hee'-blay], *a.* Unintelligible, that cannot be understood.

Iniquidad [in-e-ke-dahd'], *f.* Iniquity, injustice, unrighteousness.

Iniquísimo, ma [e-ne-kee'-se-mo, mah], *a.* Superlative of Inicuo.

Injeridura [in-hay-re-doo'-rah], *f.* *V.* Ingeridura.

Injerir [in-hay-reer'], *va.* *V.* Ingerir.

Injertar [in-her-tar'], *va.* To ingraft a tree, to graft, to inoculate.

Injerto [in-her'-to], *m.* 1. Grafting, the action of transplanting a section of one plant to another. 2. Graft, the part transplanted. *Injerto de órganos.* (Med.) Medical transplant.

Injuria [in-hoo'-re-ah], *f.* 1. Injury, offence, wrong, insult, outrage. 2. Injury, annoyance, hardship, contumely, mischief. 3. Injury, contumelious language, reproachful appellation.

Injuriado, da [in-hoo-re-ah'-do, dah], *a.* & *pp.* of Injuriar. Injured, wronged.

Injuriador, ra [in-hoo-re-ah-dor', rah], *m.* & *f.* Aggressor, injurer, wrongdoer.

Injuriante [in-hoo-re-ahn'-tay], *pa.* Injuring, injurer.

Injuriar [in-hoo-re-ar'], *va.* To injure, to wrong, to annoy, to harm or hurt unjustly, to offend.

Injuriosamente, *adv.* Injuriously, offensively, hurtfully.

Injurioso, sa [in-hoo-re-oh'-so, sah], *a.* Injurious, contumelious, reproachful, hurtful, opprobrious, offensive.

Injustamente [in-hoos-tah-men'-tay], *adv.* Unjustly.

Injusticia [in-hoos-tee'-the-ah], *f.* Injustice, iniquity, wrong.

Injustificable [in-hoos-te-fe-cah'-blay], *a.* Unjustifiable.

Injusto, ta [in-hoos'-to, tah], *a.* Unjust, wrongful.

Inlegible [in-lay-hee'-blay], *a.* Illegible.

Inllevable [in-lyay-vah'-blay], *a.* Insupportable.

Inmaculadamente, *adv.* Immaculately.

Inmaculado, da [in-mah-coo-lah'-do, dah], *a.* Immaculate, holy, pure, spotless.

Inmadurez [in-mah-doo-reth'], *f.* Immaturity.

Inmaduro, ra [in-mah-doo'-ro, rah], *a.* Immature, unripened, unmellowed.

Inmaleable [in-mah-lay-ah'-blay], *a.* Unmalleable.

Inmanejable [in-mah-nay-hah'-blay], *a.* Unmanageable; intractable.

Inmanente [in-mah-nen'-tay], *a.* Immanent, inherent.

Inmarcesible [in-mar-thay-see'-blay], *a.* Unfading, unwithering, imperishable.

Inmaterial [in-mah-tay-re-ahl'], *a.* Immaterial, incorporeal.

Inmaterialidad [in-mah-tay-re-ah-le-dahd'], *f.* Immateriality.

Inmaturo, ra [in-mah-too'-ro, rah], *a.* Immature.

Inmediación [in-may-de-ah-the on'], *f.* Contiguity, contact.

Inmediatamente, *adv.* Contiguously; immediately, forthwith.

Inmediate [in-may-de-ah'-tay], *adv.* (Obs.) Immediately; contiguously.

Inmediato, ta [in-may-de-ah'-to, tah], *a.* Contiguous, meeting so as to touch, close, hard by, next. *Llegar a las inmediatas,* To arrive at the critical moment of a dispute or contest.

Inmedicable [in-may-de-cah'-blay], *a.* Incurable.

Inmejorable [in-may-ho-rah'-blay], *a.* Unimprovable, not capable of improvement, unsurpassable.

Inmemorable [in-may-mo-rah'-blay], *a.* Immemorable.

Inmemorablemente, *adv.* Immemorably.

Inmemorial [in-may-mo-re-ahl'], *a.* Immemorial, past time, out of memory; so ancient that the beginning cannot be traced.

Inmensamente [in-men-sah-men'-tay], *adv.* Immensely, infinitely, hugely.

Inmensidad [in-men-se-dahd'], *f.* Immensity, unbounded greatness; infinity.

Inmenso, sa [in-men'-so, sah], *a.* Immense, unlimited, unbounded, infinite.

Inmensurable [in-men-soo-rah'-blay], *a.* Immensurable, measureless; not to be counted.

Inmergir [in-mer-heer'], *va.* To submerge, to souse (implying immediate withdrawal of the body acted on).

Inméritamente [in-may'-re-tah-men-tay], *adv.* Unmeritedly.

Inmérito, ta [in-may'-re-to, tah], *a.* (Obs.) Undeserved, undeserving.

Inmeritorio, ria [in-may-re-to'-re-o, ah], *a.* Immeritorious, undeserving.

Inmersión [in-mer-se-on'], *f.* 1. Immersion. 2. The entry of a planet into the shadow of another during an eclipse.

Inmigración [in-me-grah-the-on'], *f.* Immigration.

Inmigrante [in-me-grahn'-tay], *m.* Immigrant.

Inmigrar [in-me-grar'], *vn.* To immigrate.

Inminente [in-me-nen'-tay], *a.* Imminent, impending, at hand.

Inmiscible [in-mis-thee'-blay], *a.* Immiscible, incapable of being mixed.

Inmiscuir [in-mis-coo-eer'], *va.* To mix.—*vr.* To interfere in, to intermeddle.

Inmoble [in-mo'-blay], *a.* 1. Unmovable, immovable, motionless. 2. Unmovable, immovable, unshaken, unaffected, constant.

Inmoblemente, *adv.* (Littl. us.) Immovably.

Inmoderación [in-mo-day-rah-the-on'], *f.* Immoderation, immoderateness; excess.

Inmoderadamente [in-mo-day-rah-dah-men'-tay], *adv.* Immoderately.

Inmoderado, da [in-mo-day-rah'-do, dah], *a.* Immoderate, excessive.

Inmodestamente [in-mo-des-tah-men'-tay], *adv.* Immodestly.

Inmodestia [in-mo-days'-te-ah], *f.* Immodesty, indecency, indelicacy.

Inmodesto, ta [in-mo-days'-to, tah], *a.* Immodest.

Inmódico, ca [in-mo'-de-co, cah], *a.* (Littl. us.) Superfluous, excessive.

Inmodificable [in-mo-de-fe-cah'-blay], *a.* Unmodifiable.

Inmolación [in-mo-lah-the-on'], *f.* Immolation, the act of sacrificing; a sacrifice offered.

Inmolador, ra [in-mo-lah-dor', rah], *m.* & *f.* Immolator.

Inmolar [in-mo-lar'], *va.* To immolate, to sacrifice.

Inmorigerado, da [in-mo-re-hay-rah'-do, dah], *a.* Of bad habits: not self-controlled.

Inmortal [in-mor-tahl'], *a.* 1. Immortal, exempt from death. 2. Immortal, endless.

Inmortalidad [in-mor-tah-le-dahd'], *f.* Immortality, exemption from death and oblivion.

Inmortalizar [in-mor-tah-le-thar'], *va.* 1. To immortalize, to make immortal. 2. To exempt from oblivion, to perpetuate.

Inmortalmente [in-mor-tal-men'-tay], *adv.* Immortally.

Inmortificación [in-mor-te-fe-cah-the-on'], *f.* Immortification, want of subjection of the passions; licentiousness.

Inmortificado, da [in-mor-te-fe-cah'-do, dah], *a.* Unmortified, free from mortification.

Inmotivado, da [in-mo-te-vah'-do, dah], *a.* Without reason or cause.

Inmóto, ta [in-mo'-to, tah], *a.* Unmoved.

Inmovible, Inmóvil [in-mo-vee'-blay, in-mo'-veel], *a.* Immovable. *V.* Inmoble.

Inmovilidad [in-mo-ve-le-dahd'], *f.* 1. Immobility, unmovableness, resistance to motion. 2. Immovability, incapacity of being removed. 3. Immovableness, the state or quality of being immovable; firmness, constancy.

Inmudable [in-moo-dah'-blay], *a.* Inmutable. *V.* Inmutable.

Inmueble [in-moo-ay'-blay], *a.* Immovables or inmovable estate: applied to landed, opposed to chattel property.

Inmundicia [in-moon-dee'-the-ah], *f.* 1. Uncleanliness, nastiness, dirtiness, filthiness. 2. Uncleanness, impurity.

Inmundo, da [in-moon'-do, dah], *a.* 1. Unclean, filthy, dirty. 2. Obscene, unchaste.

Inmune [in-moo'-nay], *a.* 1. Free, exempt. 2. Enjoying immunity.

Inmunidad [in-moo-ne-dahd'], *f.* Immunity, privilege, exemption, franchise, freedom; liberty.

Inmunizar [in-moo-ne-thar'], *va.* To immunize, render immune.

Inmutabilidad [in-moo-tah-be-le-dahd'], *f.* Immutability, immutableness.

Inmutable [in-moo-tah'-blay], *a.* Immutable, invariable, unalterable.

Inmutación [in-moo-tah-the-on'], *f.* Change, alteration.

Inmutar [in-moo-tar'], *va.* To change, to alter.—*vr.* To change one's appearance.

Inmutativo, va [in-moo-tah-tee'-vo, vah], *a.* That which changes or causes alterations.

Innatismo [in-nah-tees'-mo], *m.* Philosophical system of those who claim that ideas are innate.

Innato, ta [in-nah'-to, tah], *a.* Innate, innated, ingenite, inborn, natural.

Innavegable [in-nah-vay-gah'-blay], *a.* 1. Innavigable, not to be passed by sailing. 2. Unfit for sea, unseaworthy: applied to ships.

Innecesario, ria [in-nay-thay-sah'-re-o, ah], *a.* Unnecessary.

Innegable [in-nay-gah'-blay], *a.* Incontestable, incontrovertible.

Innervación [in-ner-vah-the-on'], *f.* Innervation, the nervous control of an organ.

Innoble [in-no'-blay], *a.* Ignoble, mean of birth; not of noble descent.
Innocivo, va [in-no-thee'-vo, vah], *a.* Innoxious.
Innocuo, ua [in-no'-coo-o, ah], *a.* Innocuous, harmless.
Innominado, da [in-no-me-nah'-do, dah], *a.* Nameless. *Hueso innominado,* Innominate bone.
Innovación [in-no-vah-the-on'], *f.* Innovation.
Innovador, ra [in-no-vah-dor', rah], *m.* & *f.* Innovator.
Innovar [in-no-var'], *va.* 1. To innovate, to bring in something not known before. 2. To pursue a cause while an appeal or decree of inhibition is pending.
Innumerabilidad [in-noo-may-rah-be-le-dahd'], *f.* Innumerability, innumerableness.
Innumerable [in-noo-may-rah'-blay], *a.* Innumerable, numberless, countless
Innumerablemente, *adv.* Innumerably.
Innutrición [in-noo-tre-the-on'], *f.* Innutrition, failure of nourishment.
Innutritivo, va [in-noo-tre-tee'-vo, vah], *a.* Innutritious, not nourishing.
Inobediencia [in-o-bay-de-en'-the-ah], *f.* Disobedience.
Inobediente [in-o-bay-de-en'-tay], *a.* 1. Disobedient. 2. Inflexible: applied to inanimate things.
Inobservable [in-ob-ser-vah'-blay], *a.* Unobservable, inobservable.
Inobservancia [in-ob-ser-vahn'-the-ah], *f.* Inadvertency, neglect, inobservance.
Inobservante [in-ob-ser-vahn'-tay], *a.* Inobservant.
Inocencia [e-no-then'-the-ah], *f.* 1. Innocence, untainted integrity. 2. Innocence, harmlessness, guilelessness, innocuousness. 3. Innocence, freedom from guilt imputed. 4. Innocence. sincerity, simplicity.
Inocentada [e-no-then-tah'-dah], *f.* (Coll.) A simple or silly speech or action.
Inocente [e-no-then'-tay], *a.* 1. Innocent, pure, candid, harmless, lamblike, just. 2. Innocent, free from particular guilt. 3. Innocent, simple, easily imposed upon.
Inocentemente, *adv.* Innocently, guiltlessly, harmlessly, innocuously, innoxiously.
Inocentón, na [e-no-then-tone', nah], *a. aug.* Very simple and credulous.
Inoculación [e-no-coo-lah-the-on'], *f.* 1. Inoculation. 2. Vaccination.
Inoculador [e-no-coo-lah-dor'], *m.* Inoculator.
Inocular [e-no-coo-lar'], *va.* 1. To inoculate, to propagate by incisions or insertions. 2. To contaminate, pervert by bad examples or doctrines.
Inodoro, ra [in-o-do'-ro, rah], *a.* Odorless.—*m.* 1. Deodorizer. 2. Toilet, water-closet.
Inofensivo, va [in-o-fen-see'-vo, vah], *a.* Inoffensive.
Inoficioso, sa [in-o-fe-the-oh'-so, sah], *a.* (Law) Done at an improper time, and not in the manner prescribed by the law; irregular; inofficious.
Inojeta [in-o-hay'-tah], *f.* Top of a boot.
Inolvidable [in-ol-ve-dah'-blay], *a.* Unforgettable, not to be forgotten.
Inoperable [in-o-pay-rah'-blay], *a.* (Med.) Inoperable, not admitting operation.
Inopia [in-o'-pe-ah], *f.* Indigence, poverty, penury.
Inopinable [in-o-pe-nah'-blay], *a.* 1. Unthought of, not to be foreseen or expected. 2. Indisputable, incontrovertible.
Inopinadamente [in-o-pe-nah-dah-men'-tay], *adv.* Unexpectedly.
Inopinado, da [in-o-pe-nah'-do, dah], *a.* Inopinate, unexpected, unforeseen.
Inoportuno, na [in-o-por-too'-no, nah], *a.* Inopportune.
Inoportunamente, *adv.* (Littl. us.) Inopportunely.
Inordenadamente, *adv.* Inordinately.
Inordenado, da, Inordinado, da [in-or-day-nah'-do, dah], *a.* Inordinate, irregular, disorderly.
Inorgánico, ca [in-or-gah'-ne-co, cah], *a.* (Med.) Inorganic.
Inoxidable [in-oc-se-dah'-blay], *a.* 1. Stainless. 2. Rustproof. *Acero inoxidable,* Stainless steel.
In partibus infidelium. Latin phrase applied to a bishop without a diocese, whose jurisdiction is merely nominal. Literally, in the regions of unbelievers.
In promptu [in promp'-too], *adv.* Off hand, impromptu, extempore.
Inquebrantable [in-kay-bran-tah'-blay], *a.* 1. Inviolable, irrevocable. 2. Unswerving. *Fe inquebrantable,* Unswerving faith.
Inquietador, ra [in-ke-ay-tah-dor', rah], *m.* & *f.* Disturber.
Inquietamente [in-ke-ay-tah-men'-tay], *adv.* Disquietly, uneasily.
Inquietar [in-ke-ay-tar'], *va.* 1. To disquiet, to trouble, to disturb. 2. To molest, to vex, to pain. 3. To stir up or excite disturbances.—*vr.* To become uneasy or restless.
Inquieto, ta [in-ke-ay'-to, tah], *a.* 1. Restless, turbulent. 2. Noisy, troublesome, clamorous. 3. Anxious, solicitous, uneasy, fidgety, disquiet.
Inquietud [in-ke-ay-tood'], *f.* Inquietude, restlessness, uneasiness, vexation, anxiety.
Inquilinato [in-ke-le-nah'-to], *m.* (Law) Right acquired by the tenant of a house.
Inquilino, na [in-ke-lee'-no, nah], *m.* & *f.* 1. Tenant, the inhabitant of a house that is hired from another. 2. One that has temporary possession and use of the property of another; an inmate, a lodger.
Inquina [in-kee'-nah], *f.* (Coll.) Aversion, hatred.
Inquinar [in-kee-nar'], *va.* (Obs.) To inquinate, to pollute.
Inquiridor, ra [in-ke-re-dor', rah], *m.* & *f.* Inquirer, inquisitor.
Inquirir [in-kee-reer'], *va.* 1. To inquire, to look for carefully or anxiously, to look after. 2. To ascertain by research and inquiry, to explorate.
Inquisición [in-ke-se-the-on'], *f.* 1. Inquisition, examination, judicial inquiry. 2. Inquisition, a court for the detection of heresy. 3. Building where the Inquisition held its sittings. *Hacer inquisición,* To examine papers or books in order to burn the useless ones.
Inquisidor, ra [in-ke-se-dor', rah], *m.* & *f.* 1. Inquirer, examiner. 2. Inquisitor, a member of the tribunal of Inquisition.
Inquisitivo, va [in-ke-se-tee'-vo, vah], *a.* Inquisitive, curious; busy in search
Inquisitorial [in-ke-se-to-re-ahl'], *a.* Inquisitorial, inquisitorious.
Insaciabilidad [in-sah-the-ah-be-le-dahd'], *f.* Insatiableness, greediness.
Insaciable [in-sah-the-ah'-blay], *a.* Insatiable, greedy beyond measure, craving.
Insaciablemente, *adv.* Insatiably.
Insaculación [in-sah-coo-lah-the-on'], *f.* (Law) Act of casting lots or balloting for names.
Insaculador [in-sah-coo-lah-dor'], *m.* (Law) Balloter.
Insacular [in-sah-coo-lar'], *va.* To ballot, to vote by ballot.
Insalivación [in-sah-le-vah-the-on'], *f.* Insalivation, the mixing of saliva with food.
Insalivar [in-sah-le-vahr'], *va.* To mix with saliva in the mouth.
Insalubre [in-sah-loo'-bray], *a.* Insalubrious, unhealthy.
Insalubridad [in-sah-loo-bre-dahd'], *f.* Insalubrity, unhealthfulness.
Insanable [in-sah-nah'-blay], *a.* Incurable, irremediable.
Insania [in-sah'-ne-ah], *f.* Insanity. *V* LOCURA.
Insano, na [in-sah'-no, nah], *a.* Insane, mad.
Inscribir [ins-cre-beer'], *va.* 1. To inscribe, to mark with writing. 2. (Geom.) To inscribe, to draw a figure within another.
Inscripción [ins-crip-the-on'], *f.* Inscription.
Inscripto, ta [ins-creep'-to, tah], *pp. irr* of INSCRIBIR.
Inscrito, ta [ins-cree'-to, tah], *pp. irr.* of INSCRIBIR.
Inscrutable [ins-croo-tah'-blay], *a.* *V* INESCRUTABLE.
Insculpir [ins-cool-peer'], *va.* To insculp, to engrave, to cut.
Insecable [in-say-cah'-blay], *a.* (Prov.) Not to be dried, that cannot be dried.
Insección [in-sec-the-on'], *f.* (Littl. us.) Incision, cut; a wound with an edged instrument.
Insecticida [in-sec-te-thee'-dah], *m.* Insecticide, insect-killer.
Insectil [in-sec-teel'], *a.* Insectile.
Insectívoro [in-sec-tee'-vo-ro], *a.* (Nat. Hist.) Insectivorous.
Insecto [in-sec'-to], *m.* Insect.
Insectólogo, ga [in-sec-to'-lo-go, gah], *m.* & *f.* Entomologist.
Insectología, *f.* Entomology.
Inseguridad [in-say-goo-re-dahd'], *f.* Insecurity, uncertainty.
Inseguro, ra [in-say-goo'-ro, rah], *a.* Insecure, uncertain.
Insembrado, da [in-sem-brah'-do, dah], *a.* Unsowed or unsown.
Insenescencia [in-say-nes-then'-the-ah], *f.* Quality of not becoming old.
Insensatamente [in-sen-sah-tah-men'-tay], *adv.* Madly, stupidly.
Insensatez [in-sen-sah-teth'], *f.* Insensateness, stupidity, folly.
Insensato, ta [in-sen-sah'-to, tah], *a.* Insensate, stupid, mad, fatuous, out of one's wits.
Insensibilidad [in-sen-se-be-le-dahd'], *f.* 1. Insensibility, inability to perceive, dulness of mind. 2. Insensibility, want of feeling, hard-heartedness.
Insensible [in-sen-see'-blay], *a.* 1. Insensible, void of feeling, either mental or corporeal; callous, stupid. 2. Imperceptible, not discoverable by the senses. 3. Hard, stupid, unfeeling, obdurate, cold, cold-hearted, loveless. *Insensible al honor* or *a la gloria,* Inglorious.
Insensiblemente, *adv.* Insensibly.
Inseparabilidad [in-say-pa-rah-be-le-dahd'], *f.* Inseparableness, inseparability.
Inseparable [in-say-pa-rah'-blay], *a.* Inseparable, not easily separated or disjoined.
Inseparablemente, *adv.* Inseparably.
Insepulto, ta [in-say-pool'-to, tah], *a.* Unburied, uninterred, graveless.
Inserción [in-ser-the-on'], *f.* Insertion.
Inserir [in-say-reer'], *va.* (Obs.) To insert, to plant.
Insertar [in-ser-tar'], *va.* To insert, to introduce.
Inserto, ta [in-ser'-to, tah], *a.* & *pp. irr.* of INSERTAR. Inserted. *V.* INGERTO.

Inservible [in-ser-vee'-blay], *a.* Unserviceable, useless.

Insidia [in-see'-de-ah], *f.* Ambush, snare, contrivance.

Insidiador, ra [in-se-de-ah-dor', rah], *m.* & *f.* Plotter, waylayer, insidiator.

Insidiar [in-se-de-ar'], *va.* To plot, to waylay.

Insidiosamente, *adv.* Insidiously, guilefully.

Insidioso, sa [in-se-de-oh'-so, sah], *a.* Insidious, sly, circumventive, guileful.

Insigne [in-seeg'-nay], *a.* Notable, remarkable, flagrant, noted.

Insignemente, *adv.* Notably, signally, conspicuously.

Insignia [in-seeg'-ne-ah], *f.* A distinctive mark of honour, a badge. *Insignias,* Insignia, distinguishing marks of office or honour.

Insignificación [in-sig-ne-fe-cah-the-on'], *f.* Insignificance.

Insignificancia [in-sig-ne-fe-cahn'-the-ah], *f.* (Littl. us.) Insignificance.

Insignificante [in-sig-ne-fe-cahn'-tay], *a.* Insignificant, unimportant.

Insignificativo, va [in-sig-ne-fe-cah-tee'-vo, vah], *a.* Insignificant; insignificative.

Insinuación [in-se-noo-ah-the-on'], *f.* 1. Insinuation, innuendo. 2. Insinuation, power of pleasing, or stealing upon the affections. 3. (Law) Exhibition of a public instrument before a judge. 4. (Rhet.) Kind of exordium.

Insinuante [in-se-noo-ahn'-tay], *pa.* & *a.* Insinuant, insinuating, having the power to gain favour,

Insinuar [in-se-noo-ar'], *va.* 1. To insinuate, to hint. 2. To touch slightly on a subject.—*vr.* 1. To insinuate, to ingratiate, to wheedle, to gain on the affections by gentle degrees; to gain another's favour by artful means. 2. To insinuate, to get in, to creep in, to steal into imperceptibly: speaking of the insinuation of a virtue or vice into the mind.

Insipidamente [in-see'-pe-dah-men-tay], *adv.* Insipidly, without taste; without spirit.

Insipidez [in-se-pe-deth'], *f.* Insipidity, insipidness.

Insípido, da [in-see'-pe-do, dah], *a.* Insipid, tasteless, unpleasant; spiritless, flat.

Insipiencia [in-se-pe-en'-the-ah], *f.* Ignorance, want of knowledge or taste.

Insipiente [in-se-pe-en'-tay], *a.* Ignorant, tasteless, uninformed.

Insistencia [in-sis-ten'-the-ah], *f.* Persistence, steadiness, constancy, obstinacy.

Insistir [in-sis-teer'], *vn.* 1. To insist, to persist. 2. To insist, to dwell upon in discourse.

Ínsito, ta [een'-se-to, tah], *a.* Ingrafted, natural.

Insociabilidad [in-so-the-ah-be-le-dahd'], *f.* Unsociability, unsociableness.

Insociable [in-so-the-ah'-blay], *a.* Unsociable, averse to conversation and society.

Insocial [in-so-the-ahl'], *a.* *V.* INSOCIABLE.

Insolación [in-so-lah-the-on'], *f.* 1. Insolation, exposure to the sun. 2. (Med.) Sun-stroke, heat-stroke, thermic fever.

Insolar [in-so-lar'], *va.* To insolate, to dry in the sun; to expose to the action of the sun.—*vr.* To disease one's self by the heat of the sun.

Insoldable [in-sol-dah'-blay], *a.* 1. That cannot be soldered. 2. Irreparable, irretrievable.

Insolencia [in-so-len'-the-ah], *f.* 1. Insolence, impudence, effrontery, malapertness, haughtiness, frowardness. 2. Effrontery, barefacedness. 3. Insulting.

Insolentar [in-so-len-tar'], *va.* To make bold.—*vr.* To become insolent.

Insolente [in-so-len'-tay], *a.* 1. Insolent, impudent, froward, haughty. 2. Performing uncommon things. 3. Unusual, uncommon; unaccustomed: it is also used as a substantive, for a barefaced or shameless man.

Insolentemente, *adv.* Insolently, haughtily, insultingly.

In sólidum [in so'-le-doom], *adv.* (Law) Jointly, so as to be answerable for the whole.

Insólito, ta [in-so'-le-to, tah], *a.* Unusual, unaccustomed, insolite.

Insolubilidad [in-so-loo-be-le-dahd'], *f.* Insolubility.

Insoluble [in-so-loo'-blay], *a.* 1. Indissoluble, insoluble. 2. Insolvable, that cannot be paid.

Insolutundación [in-so-loo-toon-dah-the-on'], *f.* (Law) Assignment of goods or effects in payment of a debt.

Insolvencia [in-sol-ven'-the-ah], *f.* Insolvency.

Insolvente [in-sol-ven'-tay], *a.* Insolvent.

Insomne [in-some'-nay], *a.* Insomnious, sleepless.

Insomnio [in-some'-ne-o], *m.* Insomnia, sleeplessness.

Insondable [in-son-dah'-blay], *a.* 1. Unfathomable, not to be sounded, fathomless. 2. Inscrutable, unsearchable. 3. Abysmal.

Insonoro, ra [in-so-no'-ro, rah], *a.* Insonorous, not clear.

Insoportable [in-so-por-tah'-blay], *a.* Insupportable, intolerable.

Insoportablemente, *adv.* (Littl. us.) Insupportably.

Insostenible [in-sos-tay-nee'-blay], *a.* (Coll.) Indefensible.

Inspección [ins-pec-the-on'], *f.* 1. Inspection, survey; superintendence; control. 2. The house or office of an inspector. 3. Union of five consistorial churches forming an ecclesiastical district in the French organization of the Protestant worship.

Inspeccionar [ins-pec-the-o-nar'], *va.* To inspect, to examine, to oversee.

Inspector, ra [ins-pec-tor', rah], *m.* & *f.* Inspector, a careful examiner; superintendent, controller.

Inspiración [ins-pe-rah-the-on'], *f.* 1. Inspiration, the act of drawing in the breath. 2. (Met.) Inspiration, infusion of ideas into the mind by a superior power.

Inspirador, ra [ins-pe-rah-dor', rah], *m.* & *f.* Inspirer, one who inspires.

Inspirante [ins-pe-rahn'-tay], *pa.* Inspiring.

Inspirar [ins-pe-rar'], *va.* 1. To inspire, to draw air into the lungs, to inhale. 2. To infuse with fortitude, courage, etc. 3. To inspire, to infuse into the mind, to instil, to induce. 4. To inspire, to animate by supernatural infusion.—*vn.* (Poet.) To blow.

Inspirativo, va [ins-pe-rah-tee'-vo, vah], *a.* Inspiratory, producing inspiration.

Instabilidad [ins-tah-be-le-dahd'], *f.* *V.* INESTABILIDAD.

Instable [ins-tah'-blay], *a.* Unstable, inconstant, changing, mutable, fickle.

Instalación [ins-tah-lah-the-on'], *f.* Installation, instalment; induction.

Instalar [ins-tah-lar'], *va.* (Law) 1. To instal, to give possession of a rank or employment. 2. To induct, to put into actual possession of a benefice.

Instancia [ins-tahn'-the-ah], *f.* 1. Instance or instancy, importunity, persistency, urgency. 2. Instance, prosecution or process of a suit. 3. Instance, pressing argument. *De primera instancia,* Instantly, on the first impulse; first, in the first place. *V* JUEZ and JUZGADO.

Instantáneamente, *adv.* Instantly, instantaneously.

Instantanea [ins-tan-tah'-nay-ah], *f.* Snapshot.

Instantáneo, nea [ins-tan-tah'-nay-o, ah], *a.* Instantaneous.

Instante [ins-tahn'-tay], *m.* Instant, a point in duration, a moment. *Al instante,* Immediately. *Por instantes,* Incessantly, continually.

Instante [ins-tahn'-tay], *pa.* & *a.* Instant, pressing, urgent.

Instantemente, *adv.* Instantly, with urgent importunity.

Instar [ins-tar'], *va.* 1. To press or urge a request or petition. 2. In schools, to impugn the solution of a question.—*vn.* To urge the prompt execution of any thing.

Instauracion [ins-tah-oo-rah-the-on'], *f.* Instauration, restoration.

Instaurar [ins-tah-oo-rar'], *va.* To renew, to re-establish, to rebuild.

Instaurativo, va [ins-tah-oo-rah-tee'-vo, vah], *a.* Restorative.

Instigación [ins-te-gah-the-on'], *f.* Instigation, incitement, impulse, encouragement.

Instigador, ra [ins-te-gah-dor', rah], *m.* & *f.* Instigator, abetter.

Instigar [ins-te-gar'], *va.* To instigate, to incite, to provoke, to urge to ill.

Instilación [ins-te-lah-the-on'], *f.* Instillation, pouring in by drops.

Instilar [ins-te-lar'], *va.* 1. To instil, to infuse by drops. 2. To instil, to insinuate imperceptibly into the mind.

Instintivo, va [ins-tin-tee'-vo, vah], *a.* Instinctive, determined by natural impulse. **-amente,** *adv.*

Instinto [ins-teen'-to], *m.* 1. Instinct, natural desire or aversion; natural tendency. 2. Instinct, the power determining the will of brutes. 3. Divine inspiration. 4. Encouragement, incitement, impulse. *Por instinto,* Instinctively.

Institución [ins-te-too-the-on'], *f.* 1. Institution, establishment, settlement. 2. Institution, education, instruction. 3. Collation or bestowing of a benefice. *Instituciones,* Institutes of any science.

Institucional [ins-te-too-the-o-nahl'], *a.* Institutional.

Institucionalizar [ins-te-too-the-o-nah-le-thar'], *va.* To institutionalize.

Instituente [ins-te-too-en'-tay], *pa.* Instituting; founder.

Instituidor, ra [ins-te-too-e-dor', rah], *m.* & *f.* Institutor, founder.

Instituir [ins-te-too-eer'], *va.* 1. To institute, to establish, to found. 2. To institute, to teach, to instruct. 3. To nominate, to appoint; to determine or resolve.

Instituta [ins-te-too'-tah], *f.* Institute, a part or section of the Roman law.

Instituto [ins-te-too'-to], *m.* Institute, established law; settled order; design, object, end.

Institutor, ra [ins-te-too-tor', rah], *m* & *f.* *V.* INSTITUIDOR.

Institutriz [ins-te-too-treeth'], *f.* Governess, child's private instructress.

Instituyente [ins-te-too-yen'-tay], *pa.* Institutor; foundling.

Instridente [ins-tre-den'-tay], *a.* (Obs.) Squeaking, creaking.

Instrucción [ins-trooc-the-on'], *f.* 1 Instruction, the art of teaching; lesson. 2. Precepts conveying knowledge; lore, knowledge. *Instruccio*

nes, Instructions, directions, orders. *Instrucciones breves*, (Mil.) Briefing.
Instructivamente [ins-trooc-te-vah-men'-tay], *adv.* Instructively.
Instructivo, va [ins-trooc-tee'-vo, vah]. *a.* Instructive.
Instructor [ins-trooc-tor'], *m.* Instructor, teacher, lecturer, monitor.
Instructora [ins-trooc-to'-rah], *f.* Instructress.
Instruir [ins-troo-eer'], *va.* 1. To instruct, to teach, to lecture, to acquaint. 2. To civilize. 3. To inform authoritatively. 4. (Law) To instruct, to model a cause according to established rules.
Instrumentación [ins-troo-men-tah-the-on'], *f.* Instrumentation.
Instrumental [ins-troo-men-tahl'], *a.* 1. Instrumental, produced by instruments, not vocal. 2. (Law) Belonging to legal instruments.
Instrumentalmente, *adv.* Instrumentally.
Instrumentista [ins-troo-men-tees'-tah], *m.* Player on an instrument of music.
Instrumento [ins-troo-men'-to], *m.* 1. Instrument, a tool; an engine or machine. 2. Instrument, the agent or means of any thing. 3. (Law) Instrument, a writing containing a contract, or serving as proof or evidence. 4. (Mus.) Instrument, any musical instrument. 5. (Coll.) Instrument, one who acts merely for another. *Instrumento de viento*, A wind instrument. *Instrumento de cuerda*, A stringed instrument. *Aproximación por instrumentos*, (Aer.) Instrument approach. *Tablero de instrumentos*, Instrument panel. *Vuelo con instrumentos*, (Aer.) Blind flying.
Insuave [in-soo-ah'-vay], *a.* Unpleasant, disagreeable.
Insubordinación [in-soo-bor-de-nah-the-on'], *f.* Insubordination, disorder, want of obedience.
Insubordinado, da [in-soo-bor-de-nah'-do, dah], *a.* & *pp.* of INSUBORDINARSE. Insubordinate, rebellious, resisting authority.
Insubordinar [in-soo-bor-de-nar'], *va.* To incite to resist authority.—*vr.* To rebel against authority: commonly applied to military men.
Insubsistencia [in-soob-sis-ten'-the-ah], *f.* Instability, inconstancy.
Insubsistente [in-soob-sis-ten'-tay], *a.* 1. Unable to subsist, incapable of duration. 2. Instable, inconstant, changing.
Insubstancial [in-soobs-tan-the-ahl'], *a.* Unsubstantial, of little substance or worth, or of none.
Insuficiencia [in-soo-fe-the-en'-the-ah], *f.* Insufficiency, inadequateness.
Insuficiente [in-soo-fe-the-en'-tay], *a.* Insufficient, inadequate; wanting abilities.
Insuficientemente, *adv.* Insufficiently.
Insuflación [in-soo-flah-the-on'], *f.* Insufflation, the blowing into the air-passages of air, a powder, etc.
Insuflar [in-soo-flar'], *va.* 1. (Obs.) To blow. *V.* SOPLAR. 2. To suggest, to prompt. 3. (Med.) To insufflate, to blow or breathe into.
Insufrible [in-soo-free'-blay], *a.* Intolerable, insufferable, overbearing, insupportable.
Insufriblemente [in-soo-fre-blay-men'-tay], *adv.* Insufferably.
Ínsula [een'-soo-lah], *f.* (Archaic) 1. Isle. *V.* ISLA. 2. (Joc.) A petty state or government (in allusion to Sancho Panza).
Insular, Insulano, na [in-soo-lar', in-soo-lah'-no, nah], *a.* Insular *V.* ISLEÑO.
Insulina [in-soo-lee'-nah], *f.* Insulin.
Insulsamente [in-sool-sah-men'-tay], *adv.* Insipidly.
Insulsez [in-sool-seth'], *f.* Insipidity, flatness, want of taste.
Insulso, sa [in-sool'-so, sah], *a.* 1. Insipid, tasteless. 2. (Met.) Dull, heavy; flat; cold.
Insultador, ra [in-sool-tah-dor', rah], *m.* & *f.* Insulter.
Insultante [in-sool-tahn'-tay], *pa.* Insulting, insulter.
Insultar [in-sool-tar'], *va.* To insult, to treat with insolence or contempt.—*vr.* (Coll.) To meet with an accident, to be suddenly attacked with disease.
Insulto [in-sool'-to], *m.* 1. Insult, act of insulting. 2. A sudden and violent attack. 3. A sudden fit of illness.
Insumable [in-soo-mah'-blay], *a.* Incalculable, unnumberable.
Insumergible [in-soo-mer-hee'-blay], *a.* Insubmergible, incapable of being submerged.
Insuperable [in-soo-pay-rah'-blay], *a.* Insuperable, insurmountable; overbearing, not to be overcome.
Insupurable [in-soo-poo-rah'-blay], *a.* That which cannot suppurate or form pus.
Insurgente [in-soor-hen'-tay], *m.* Insurgent, one who rises in rebellion against the government of his country: it is also used as an adjective
Insurrección [in-soor-rec-the-on'], *f.* Insurrection, a seditious rising, a rebellious commotion.
Insurreccional [in-soor-rec-the-o-nahl'], *a.* (Littl. us.) Insurrectionary, suitable to an insurrection.
Insurreccionar [in-soor-rec-the-o-nar'], *va.* To promote an insurrection.—*vr.* To rebel against the constituted authorities.
Insurrecto, ta [in-soor-rec'-to, tah], *a.* Rebellious.—*m.* & *f.* Rebel, insurgent.
Insustancial [in-soos-tan-the-ahl'], *a.* *V.* INSUBSTANCIAL.
Intáctil [in-tahc'-teel], *a.* Intangible, intactible, not perceptible to touch.
Intacto, ta [in-tahc'-to, tah], *a.* 1. Untouched, not touched. 2. Untouched, not meddled with, not spoken of. 3. Pure, unmingled; entire; intact.
Intachable [in-tah-chah'-blay], *a.* Uncensurable, unexceptionable, not deserving blame.
Intangible [in-tan-hee'-blay], *a.* Intangible, not to be touched.
Integérrimo, ma [in-tay-her'-re-mo, mah], *a. super.* Very sincere.
Integración [in-tay-grah-the-on'], *f.* Integration.
Integral [in-tay-grahl'], *a.* Integral, whole.
Integralmente [in-tay-gral-men'-tay], *adv.* Integrally.
Íntegramente [een'-tay-grah-men-tay], *adv.* *V.* ENTERAMENTE.
Integrante [in-tay-grahn'-tay], *a.* Integral, integrant.
Integrar [in-tay-grar'], *va.* 1. To integrate, to make up a whole. 2. To find the integral of a differential quantity.
Integridad [in-tay-gre-dahd'], *f.* 1. Integrality, wholeness, completeness. 2. Integrity, honesty, purity of manners, uprightness. 3. Virginity, maidenhead. 4. Confidence, honour.
Íntegro, gra [een'-tay-gro, grah], *a.* 1. Integral, entire, complete, not fractional. 2. Candid, upright, honest, disinterested, just.
Intelección [in-tay-lec-the-on'], *f.* Intellection, the act of understanding.
Intelectiva [in-tay-lec-tee'-vah], *f.* Intellect, the power of understanding.
Intelectivo, va [in-tay-lec-tee'-vo, vah], *a.* Intellective, having power to understand.
Intelecto [in-tay-lec'-to], *m.* (Ant.) Intellect, understanding.
Intelectual [in-tay-lec-too-ahl'], *a.* Intellectual, relating to the understanding: mental, ideal, belonging to the mind.
Intelectualmente, *adv* Intellectually, mentally, ideally
Inteligencia [in-tay-le-hen'-the-ah], *f.* 1. Intelligence, commerce of information: mutual communication, comprehension, knowledge, knowing. 2. Intelligence, direction or government, understanding, skill, ability, experience. 3. Intelligence, commerce of acquaintance, friendly intercourse. 4. Sense, signification of a passage. 5. Intelligence, spirit, unbodied mind. *En inteligencia*. In the understanding, suppositively.
Inteligenciado, da [in-tay-le-hen-the-ah'-do, dah], *a.* (Coll.) Instructed, informed.
Inteligente [in-tay-le-hen'-tay], *a.* Intelligent, skilful, clever, learned, knowing.
Inteligibilidad [in-tay-le-he-be-le-dahd'], *f.* Intelligibility, capacity of being understood.
Inteligible [in-tay-le-hee'-blay], *a.* Intelligible, conceivable, perspicuous, to be perceived by the senses.
Inteligiblemente, *adv* Intelligibly.
Intemperancia [in-tem-pay-rahn-the-ah], *f.* Intemperance, want of moderation; excess.
Intemperante [in-tem-pay-rahn'-tay], *a.* Intemperate. *V.* DESTEMPLADO.
Intemperie [in-tem-pay'-re-ay], *f.* Intemperateness, unseasonableness of weather; inclemency.
Intempesta [in-tem-pays'-tah], *a.* (Poet.) Excessively dark, dreary: applied to the dead of night.
Intempestivamente, *adv.* Unseasonably, abortively, intempestively.
Intempestivo, va [in-tem-pes-tee'-vo, vah], *a.* Unseasonable, not suited to the time or occasion: abortive.
Intención [in-ten-the-on'], *f.* 1. Intention, design, meaning, mind, view. 2. Instinct of brutes. *Hombre de intención*, A dissembler.
Intencionadamente [in-ten-the-o-nah-dah-men'-tay], *adv.* Designedly.
Intencionado, da [in-ten-the-o-nah'-do, dah], *a.* Inclined, disposed.
Intencional [in-ten-the-o-nahl'], *a* Intentional, designed.
Intencionalmente, *adv* Intentionally.
Intendencia [in-ten-den'-the-ah], *f* 1. Administration, management. 2. Place, employment, or district of an intendant.
Intendenta [in-ten-den'-tah], *f* Lady of an intendant.
Intendente [in-ten-den'-tay], *m.* Intendant, an officer of high rank who over sees any particular allotment of the public business. *Intendente de provincia*, The governor of a province under a viceroy or captain-general. *Intendente de ejército*, Quarter-master general. *Intendente de marina*, The commandant of a navy-yard. *Intendente de matrículas*, Intendant or commissary-general of the impress service.
Intensamente [in-ten-sah-men'-tay], *adv.* Intensely

Intensidad [in-ten-se-dahd'], *f.* Intensity: vehemence.

Intensificar [in-ten-se-fe-car'], *va.* To intensify, to heighten, deepen.

Intensión [in-ten-se-on'], *f.* Intenseness, vehemence, ardency; earnestness, great attention.

Intensivo, va, Intenso, sa [in-ten-see'-vo, vah, in-ten'-so, sah], *a.* Intense, intensive, vehement, ardent, lively.

Intentar [in-ten-tar'], *va.* 1. To try, to attempt, to endeavour. 2. To intend, to mean, to design. 3. To enter an action, to commence a lawsuit.

Intento [in-ten'-to], *m.* 1. Intention, intent, object. 2. Attempt. *De intento,* Intentionally. *Intento golpista,* Attempted coup.

Intentona [in-ten-to'-nah], *f.* Foolhardy attempt.

Inter [een'-ter], *adv.* (Obs.) 1. In the meanwhile. *V.* INTERIN. 2. A prepositive particle used in composition. 3. *m.* (Peru.) The substitute of a curate.

Interacción [in-ter-ac-the-on'], *f.* Interaction.

Interamericano, na [in-ter-ah-may-re-cah'-no, nah], *a.* Inter-American.

Interarticular [in-ter-ar-te-coo-lar'], *a.* Interarticular, between joints.

Interbranquial [in-ter-bran-ke-ahl'], *a.* (Zool.) Interbranchial, between the branchiæ or gills.

Intercadencia [in-ter-cah-den'-the-ah], *f.* 1. Interruption, interposition. 2. Inconstancy. 3. (Med.) Intermission or inequality of the pulse.

Intercadente [in-ter-cah-den'-tay], *a.* Changeable, variable.

Intercadentemente, *adv.* Changeably.

Intercalación [in-ter-cah-lah-the-on'], *f.* Intercalation, the act of inserting amongst other things.

Intercalar [in-ter-cah-lar'], *va.* To intercalate, to insert among other things.

Intercalar, *a.* Intercalary.

Intercambiable [in-ter-cam-be-ah'-blay], *a.* Interchangeable.

Intercambio [in-ter-cahm'-be-o], *m* Interchange, mutual exchange, reciprocity.

Interceder [in-ter-thay-derr'], *vn.* 1. To intercede, to mediate, to entreat for another. 2. To intercede, to interpose, to place between.

Intercelular [in-ter-thay-loo-lar'], *a.* Intercellular.

Interceptación [in-ter-thep-tah-the-on'], *f.* Interception, stoppage, the act of intercepting. (Acad.)

Interceptar [in-ter-thep-tar'], *va.* To intercept, to cut off, to obstruct.

Intercesión [in-ter-thay-se-on'], *f.* Intercession, mediation, interposition, interceding.

Intercesor, ra [in-ter-thay-sor', rah], *m.* & *f.* Intercessor, interceder, mediator, excuser, solicitor.

Intercesorio, ria [in-ter-thay-so'-re-o, ah], *a.* Intercessory, intervening between two parties; entreating for another.

Intercolumnio [in-ter-co-loom'-ne-o], *m.* Intercolumniation, the space between pillars or columns.

Intercostal [in-ter-cos-tahl'], *a.* Intercostal, between the ribs.

Intercurrente [in-ter-coor-ren'-tay], *a.* Intercurrent, intervening.

Intercutáneo, nea [in-ter-coo-tah'-nay-o, ah], *a.* Intercutaneous, between the skin and flesh.

Interdecir [in-ter-day-theer'], *va.* To interdict, to prohibit.

Interdentario, ria [in-ter-den-tah'-re-o ah], *a.* Interdental, between the teeth.

Interdicción [in-ter-dic-the-on'], *f.* Interdiction, prohibition; interdict.

Interdicto [in-ter-deec'-to], *m.* 1. A judgment of summary possession. 2. Prohibition, interdiction.

Interés [in-tay-ress'], *m.* 1. Interest, concern, advantage, concernment. 2. Interest, share or participation in any profit. 3. Interest, any surplus of advantage. 4. Interest, money paid for the use of money. 5. Interest, part taken for or against any person. 6. (Poet.) Pathos or interest of dramatic incidents. *Interés de interés,* Compound interest. *Dar a interés,* To put on interest. *Llevar cinco por ciento de interés,* To bear five per cent. interest.

Interesable [in-tay-ray-sah'-blay], *a.* Avaricious, mercenary.

Interesadamente, *adv* (Littl. us.) Selfishly.

Interesado, da [in-tay-ray-sah'-do, dah], *a.* & *pp.* of INTERESAR. 1. Interested, concerned. 2. Interested, selfish, sordid, mercenary, avaricious.

Interesado, da [in-tay-ray-sah'-do, dah], *m.* & *f.* A person concerned in any undertaking or business, a partner. *Los interesados,* The concern, persons connected in business, or their affairs in general.

Interesante [in-tay-ray-sahn'-tay], *a.* Interesting, useful, convenient.

Interesar [in-tay-ray-sar'], *vn.* & *vr.* To be concerned or interested in, to have a share in or to take a part in any concern.—*va.* 1. To interest, to concern, to give a share in. 2. To interest, to concern, to engage by feeling or sentiment. 3. (Poet.) To interest, to affect or touch with passion: speaking of a poem.

Interescolar [in-ter-es-co-lar']. *a.* Interscholastic. interschool.

Interesencia [in-tay-ray-sen'-the-ah], *f.* (Obs.) Personal assistance at any thing.

Interesillo [in-tay-ray-seel'-lyo], *m. dim.* A slight interest.

Interferencia [in-ter-fay-ren'-the-ah], *f.* (Opt.) Interference of rays of light; crossing.

Interfoliar [in-ter-fo-le-ar'], *va.* To interleave a book.

Ínterin [een'-tay-rin], *m.* *V.* INTERINIDAD.

Ínterin, or **En el ínterin** [een'-tay-rin], *adv.* In the interim, in the meantime. *V.* INTERINAMENTE.

Interinamente [in-tay-re-nah-men'-tay], *adv.* In the intervening time, in the interim, meantime, provisionally

Interinidad [in-tay-re-ne-dahd'], *f.* Quality of holding a temporary charge or office.

Interino, na [in-tay-ree'-no, nah], *a.* Provisional, appointed provisionally, having the temporary charge of an employ or office.

Interior [in-tay-re-ore'], *a.* Interior, internal, inward, inner.

Interior, *m.* 1. The interior, inside, inner part. 2. Mind, soul. 3. That which is only felt in the soul. 4. In coaches with three compartments, the middle one. *Interiores,* Entrails, intestines.

Interioridad [in-tay-re-o-re-dahd'], *f.* 1. Inside, interior part. 2. The act of concealing any thing, and the thing hidden.

Interiormente [in-tay-re-or-men'-tay], *adv.* In the interior, internally, inwardly, interiorly.

Interjección [in-ter-hec-the-on'], *f.* (Gram.) Interjection, a part of speech.

Interlineación [in-ter-le-nay-ah-the-on'], *f.* Interlineation.

Interlineal [in-ter-le-nay-ahl'], *a.* Interlineal.

Interlinear [in-ter-le-nay-ar'], *va.* *V.* ENTRERRENGLONAR.

Interlocución [in-ter-lo-coo-the-on'], *f.* Interlocution, dialogue, interchange of speech.

Interlocutor, ra [in-ter-lo-coo-tor', rah], *m.* & *f.* 1. Interlocutor, one who speaks in the name of another. 2. Collocutor, colloquist, one of the speakers in a dialogue.

Interlocutorio, ria [in-ter-lo-coo-to'-re-o, ah], *a.* Interlocutory, preparatory to a definitive decision.

Intérlope [in-ter'-lo-pay], *a.* Interloping, defrauding in commerce between a nation and the colonies of another.

Interlunio [in-ter-loo'-ne-o], *m.* Time when the moon, being about to change, is invisible.

Intermediar [in-ter-may-de-ar'], *va.* To interpose, to be in the middle.

Intermedio, dia [in-ter-may'-de-o, ah], *a.* Intermediate, intervening, interposed, intermedial.

Intermedio [in-ter-may'-de-o], *m.* 1. Interval, intermedium, time passing between; interim. 2. Interlude, an entertainment between the acts of a play; farce; interval; middle.

Interminable [in-ter-me-nah'-blay], *a.* Interminable, endless.

Intérmino, na [in-ter'-me-no, nah], *a.* (Obs.) Interminable, immense.

Intermisión [in-ter-me-se-on'], *f.* Intermission, interruption, forbearance.

Intermitencia [in-ter-me-ten'-the-ah], *f.* Discontinuance of an intermittent fever; the interval between the fits.

Intermitente [in-ter-me-ten'-tay], *a.* Intermittent, intermissive, coming by fits.

Intermitir [in-ter-me-teer'], *va.* To intermit, to discontinue.

Intermundo [in-ter-moon'-do], *m.* Space between the worlds.

Intermuscular [in-ter-moos-coo-lar'], *a.* Intermuscular, between the muscles.

Internación [in-ter-nah-the-on'], *f.* Importation. *Derechos de internación,* Importation duties.

Internacional [in-ter-nah-the-o-nahl'], *a.* International.

Internacionalizar [in-ter-nah-the-o-nah-le-thar'], *va.* To internationalize.

Internado, da [in-ter-nah'-do, dah]. *a.* Interned.—*m.* Boarding school. boarding pupils.

Internamente [in-ter-nah-men'-tay], *adv.* Internally. *V.* INTERIORMENTE.

Internar [in-ter-nar'], *va.* To pierce, to penetrate beyond the surface; to penetrate into the interior of a country.—*vr.* To insinuate, to gain upon the affections by gentle degrees; to wheedle.

Interno, na [in-ter'-no, nah], *a.* Interior, internal, inward, intern.

Internuncio [in-ter-noon'-the-o], *m.* Internuncio, an agent of the court of Rome; interlocutor.

Interpelación [in-ter-pay-lah-the-on'], *f.* 1. (Law) Interpellation, summons. 2. Interpellation, an earnest address, a demand for an official statement.

Interpelar [in-ter-pay-lar'], *va.* 1. To appeal to, to implore the aid of. 2. (Law) To summon, to cite. 3. To interrogate as to the truth or falsity of an act. 4. To interpellate, to officially interrogate a member of a government, as in continental legislatures.

Interplanetario, ria [in-ter-plah-nay-tah'-re-o, ah], *a.* Interplanetary.

Interpolación [in-ter-po-lah-the-on'], *f.* 1. Interpolation, something added to

the original. 2. Act of adding something to the original.
Interpoladamente, *adv* In an interpolating manner.
Interpolar [in-ter-po-lar'], *va.* 1. To interpolate, to foist in. 2. To interpose, to intermix, to intermit. 3. To interpose, to interrupt.
Interponer [in-ter-po-nerr'], *va.* 1. To interpose, to place between. 2. (Obs.) To refer. 3. To thrust in as an interruption or obstruction. 4. *Interponer la autoridad,* (Law) To sanction, approve, or confirm by the authority of the law.—*vr.* To go between, to interpose.
Interposición [in-ter-po-se-the-on'], *f.* 1. Interposition, the state of being placed between other things or persons. 2. Interposition, intervenient agency, interference, mediation, meddling. 3. Interval, time passing between.
Interpósita persona [in-ter-po'-se-tah per-so'-nah]. (Lat. exp. Law) Intermediary, agent, one who acts for another.
Interpresa [in-ter-pray'-sah], *f.* Military enterprise, a sudden undertaking or attempt.
Interpretable [in-ter-pray-tah'-blay], *a.* (Coll.) Interpretable.
Interpretación [in-ter-pray-tah-the-on'], *f.* 1. Interpretation, the act of interpreting. 2. Interpretation, elucidation, explanation, exposition, construction, commentary; the sense given by an interpreter. *Interpretación de lenguas,* A secretary's office, where writings of other languages are translated into Spanish. (Spain.)
Interpretador, ra [in-ter-pray-tah-dor', rah], *m.* & *f.* Interpreter, translator.
Interpretante [in-ter-pray-tahn'-tay], *pa.* & *m.* & *f.* Interpreting, translator.
Interpretar [in-ter-pray-tar'], *va.* 1. To interpret, to explain, to expound. 2. To translate, to interpret, to construe. 3. To interpret, to take or understand the meaning in a particular sense or manner. 4. To attribute.
Interpretativamente, *adv.* Interpretatively.
Interpretativo, va [in-ter-pray-tah-tee'-vo, vah], *a.* Interpretative.
Intérprete [in-ter'-pray-tay], *com.* Interpreter, expounder, translator; indication, sign.
Interpuesto, ta [in-ter-poo-ays'-to, tah], *a.* & *pp. irr.* of INTERPONER. Interposed, intervening, placed between, mediate.
Interregno [in-ter-reg'-no], *m.* Interreign, interregnum, the time in which a throne is vacant; vacancy of the throne.
Interrogación [in-ter-ro-gah-the-on'], *f.* 1. Question. 2. Questioning. 3. Question marks.
Interrogante [in-ter-ro-gahn'-tay], *a.* Questioning.—*m.* & *f.* Questioner. *La gran interrogante,* The real issue. *Punto interrogante,* Question marks.
Interrogar [in-ter-ro-gar'], *va.* To question, to interrogate.
Interrogativamente, *adv* Interrogatively.
Interrogativo, va [in-ter-ro-gah-tee'-vo, vah], *a.* Interrogative.
Interrogatorio [in-ter-ro-gah-to'-re-o], *m.* Interrogatory, questionnaire.
Interrumpidamente, *adv* Interruptedly.
Interrumpido, da [in-ter-room-pee'-do, dah], *a.* & *pp.* of INTERRUMPIR. Interrupted, broken.
Interrumpir [in-ter-room-peer'], *va.* 1. To interrupt, to hinder or obstruct the continuance of a thing. 2. To interrupt, to hinder from proceeding, to cut off, to cut short.
Interrupción [in-ter-roop-the-on'], *f.* Interruption, interpellation, discontinuance.
Intersecar [in-ter-say-car'], *va.* (Obs.) To cross-cut.—*vr* (Geom.) To intersect each other.
Intersección [in-ter-sec-the-on'], *f.* 1. Intersection, the point where lines cross each other 2. A line common to two surfaces which cut one another.
Intersectario, ria [in-ter-sec-tah'-re-o, ah], *a.* Interdenominational.
Intersticio [in-ters-tee'-the-o], *m.* Interstice, interval.
Intertropical [in-ter-tro-pe-cahl'], *a.* Intertropical, placed or produced between the tropics.
Interuniversitario, ria [in-ter-oo-ne-ver-se-tah'-re-o, ah], *a* Intercollegiate.
Intervalo [in-ter-vah'-lo], *m.* 1. Interval, space between places. 2. Interval, time passing between two assignable points, interlapse. *Claro* or *lúcido intervalo,* Remission of delirium or madness; a lucid interval.
Intervención [in-ter-ven-the-on'], *f.* Intervention, supervision, assistance, mediation, interposition; knowledge, consent.
Intervenir [in-ter-vay-neer'], *vn.* 1. To intervene, to come between things or persons; to mediate; to intercur, to intermediate. 2. To assist, to attend, to supervise, to superintend.—*v. impers. V.* ACONTECER.
Interventor, ra [in-ter-ven-tor', rah], *m.* & *f.* Comptroller, supervisor, inspector, superintendent.
Intervertebral [in-ter-ver-tay-brahl'], *a.* Invertebral, between the vertebræ.
Interyacente [in-ter-yah-then'-tay], *a.* Interjacent, intervening, lying between.
Intestable [in-tes-tah'-blay], *a.* 1. Intestable, legally disqualified to make a will. 2. Legally disqualified to testify.
Intestado, da [in-tes-tah'-do, dah], *a.* Intestate, dying without a will.
Intestinal [in-tes-te-nahl'], *a.* Intestinal.
Intestino, na [in-tes-tee'-no, nah], *a.* Intestine, internal; civil, domestic.
Intestino [in-tes-tee'-no], *m.* Intestine, the gut; the bowels.
Intimación [in-te-mah-the-on'], *f.* Intimation, hint.
Íntimamente [een'-te-mah-men-tay], *adv.* Intimately.
Intimar [in-te-mar'], *va.* To intimate, to hint, to make known.—*vr.* 1. To pierce, to penetrate. 2. To gain on the affections, to insinuate.
Intimidación [in-te-me-dah-the-on'], *f.* (Littl. us.) Intimidation.
Intimidad [in-te-me-dahd'], *f.* Intimacy, close familiarity or connection, friendship, consociation, inwardness.
Intimidar [in-te-me-dar'], *va.* To intimidate, to daunt, to fright.
Íntimo, ma [een'-te-mo, mah], *a* 1. Internal, innermost. 2. Intimate, familiar, conversant, near, closely acquainted.
Intitular [in-te-too-lar'], *va.* 1. To entitle, to prefix a title to a book or writing. 2. To entitle, grace, or dignify with a title or honourable appellation. —*vr.* To use a title or honourable appellation.
Intitulata [in-te-too-lah'-tah], *f.* (Obs.) Title prefixed to a book or writing.
Intolerabilidad [in-to-lay-rah-be-le-dahd'], *f.* Intolerableness.
Intolerable [in-to-lay-rah'-blay], *a* Intolerable, insufferable
Intolerancia [in-to-lay-rahn'-the-ah], *f* Intolerance.
Intolerante [in-to-lay-rahn'-tay], *a.* Intolerant, not favourable to toleration.
Intonso, sa [in-tone'-so, sah], *a.* (Poet.) 1. Unshorn, having the hair uncut. 2. Ignorant, unpolished 3 A book bound with uncut leaves
Intorsión [in-tor-se-on'], *f.* (Bot.) Intortion, turning of a plant out of the vertical position.
Intoxicación [in-toc-se-cah-the-on'], *f* (Med.) Intoxication, poisoning caused voluntarily or involuntarily
Intoxicar [in-toc-se-car'], *va* (Med.) To poison
Intradós [in-trah-dos'], *m.* The concave face of an arch or vault; intrados.
Intraducible [in-trah-doo-thee'-blay], *a* Untranslatable.
Intramitable [in-trah-me-tah'-blay], *a.* (Law) Not capable of advancement upon the calendar
Intramuros [in-trah-moo -ros], *adv* Within the walls.
Intranquilizar [in-tran-ke-le-thar'], *va* Disquiet, make uneasy —*vr* To worry.
Intranquilo, la [in-tran-kee'-lo, lah], *a.* 1. Uneasy, restless. 2. Worried, discomfited.
Intransitable [in-tran-se-tah'-blay], *a* Impassable, impenetrable.
Intransitivo, va [in-tran-se-tee' vo, vah], *a.* (Gram.) Intransitive.
Intrasmutabilidad [in-tras-moo-tah-be-le-dahd'], *f.* Immutability.
Intrasmutable [in-tras-moo-tah'-blay], *a.* Intransmutable.
Intratable [in-trah-tah'-blay], *a.* 1. Intractable, ungovernable, stubborn, obstinate, unmanageable. 2. Intractable, unsociable, rude, hard to deal with 3. Impassable.
Intrauterino, na [in-trah-oo-tay-ree'-no, nah], *a.* Intrauterine, existing or occurring in the uterus.
Intrépidamente [in-tray'-pe-dah-men tay], *adv.* Intrepidly, fearlessly
Intrepidez [in-tray-pe-deth'], *f.* 1. Intrepidity, courage, boldness, fearlessness, dauntlessness, hardiness. 2. Temerity.
Intrépido, da [in-tray'-pe-do, dah], *a.* Intrepid, daring, fearless, courageous, dauntless, gallant, hardy.
Intriga [in-tree'-gah], *f.* 1. Intrigue, a (complicated) plot or scheme. 2. Entanglement, embroilment.
Intrigante [in-tre-gahn'-tay], *m.* Intriguer, cunning meddler.
Intrigar [in-tre-gar'], *vn.* To intrigue, to form plots.
Intrincable [in-trin-cah'-blay], *a.* Intricate, perplexed, easily entangled.
Intrincación [in-trin-cah-the-on'], *f* Intricacy, intricateness.
Intrincadamente [in-trin-cah-dah-men tay], *adv.* Intricately.
Intrincado, da [in-trin-cah'-do, dah], *a.* & *pp.* of INTRINCAR. Intricate, entangled, perplexed, knotty, obscure
Intrincamiento [in-trin-cah-me-en'-to], *m.* Intricateness, intrication.
Intrincar [in-trin-car'], *va.* To perplex, to intricate, to entangle, to knot, to involve, to confound, to obscure.
Intríngulis [in-treen'-goo-lis], *m.* 1 (Coll.) Crafty intention, hidden motive. 2. (Peru.) Mystery, enigma.
Intrínsecamente [in-treen'-say-cah meh-tay], *adv* Intrinsically, essentially.
Intrínseco, ca [in-treen'-say-co, cah], *a* 1. Intrinsic, intrinsical, internal, hidden. 2 Close, habitually silent *V* ÍNTIMO. 3. (Law) *V* JUDICIAL
Introducción [in-tro-dooc-the-on'], *f* 1 Introduction, the art of conducting or

ushering to any place or person, intromission. 2. Access, intercourse. 3. Introduction, the act of bringing any new thing into notice or practice. 4. Introduction, the preface of a book.

Introducir [in-tro-doo-theer'], *va.* 1. To introduce, to conduct or usher into a place, to lead in. 2. To introduce, to bring into notice or practice. 3. To induce, to facilitate, to conciliate.—*vr.* To insinuate, to gain on the affections: to interfere, to find one's way, to get into.

Introductor, ra [in-tro-dooc-tor', rah], *m.* & *f.* 1. Introducer, any one who brings a thing into notice. 2. Introductor, introducer, one who introduces another to a person or place.

Introductivo, va [in-tro-dooc-tee'-vo, vah], *a.* Introductory, introductive.

Introductorio, ria [in-tro-dooc-to'-re-o, rah], *a.* (For.) Introductory.

Introito [in-tro'-e-to], *m.* 1. Entrance, entry. 2. Introit, the beginning of the mass; the commencement of public devotions.

Intromisión [in-tro-me-se-on'], *f.* Introduction, inserting, intromission.

Introspección [in-tros-pec-the-on'], *f.* Introspection, examination of the interior.

Introspectivo, va [in-tros-pec-tee'-vo, vah], *a.* Introspective.

Introversión [in-tro-ver-se-on'], *f.* Introversion.

Introverso, sa [in-tro-vayr'-so, sah], *a.* Introverted, self-contemplating.

Intrusamente, *adv.* Intrusively.

Intrusarse [in-troo-sar'-say], *vr.* To obtrude one's self in a place or office.

Intrusión [in-troo-se-on'], *f.* Intrusion, obtrusion, the act of intruding or obtruding one's self into any place, state, or office, without right or welcome.

Intruso [in-troo'-so], *m.* Intruder, obtruder, one who forces himself into any place, office, company, etc., without right or welcome; squatter.

Intruso, sa [in-troo'-so, sah], *a.* Intruded, intrusive, obtrusive.

Intuición [in-too-e-the-on'], *f.* Intuition, knowledge not obtained by deduction of reason.

Intuitivamente [in-too-e-te-vah-men'-tay], *adv.* Intuitively.

Intuitivo, va [in-too-e-tee'-vo, vah], *a.* Intuitive, evident; perceived without ratiocination.

Intumescencia [in-too-mes-then'-the-ah], *f.* *V.* HINCHAZÓN.

Intumescente [in-too-mes-then'-tay], *a.* Intumescent, swollen.

Intususcepción [in-too-soos-thep-the-on'], *f.* (Med.) Introsusception, intussusception.

Inulina [in-oo-lee'-nah], *f.* Inulin, a substance like starch obtained from the root of elecampane and other plants.

Inulto, ta [in-ool'-to, tah], *a.* (Poet.) Unrevenged, unpunished.

Inundación [in-oon-dah-the-on'], *f.* 1. Inundation, overflow of waters; flood, deluge. 2. Confluence of any kind.

Inundante [in-oon-dahn'-tay], *pa.* Inundating; inundant, that which inundates.

Inundar [in-oon-dar'], *va.* 1. To inundate, to overflow, to deluge, to flood. 2. To overrun with numbers. *Se le inundaron los ojos en lágrimas,* A flood of tears fell from her eyes.

Inurbanamente [in-oor-bah-nah-men'-tay], *adv.* Incivilly, uncivilly.

Inurbanidad [in-oor-bah-ne-dahd'], *f.* Incivility, want of education, inurbanity.

Inurbano, na [in-oor-bah'-no, nah], *a.* Uncivil, rude, unpolished, inurbane.

Inusitadamente [in-oo-se-tah-dah-men tay], *adv.* Unusually.

Inusitado, da [in-oo-se-tah'-do, dah], *a.* Unusual, not in use, not accustomed.

Inútil [in-oo'-teel], *a.* Useless, unprofitable, inutile, fruitless, needless, frivolous, idle.

Inutilidad [in-oo-te-le-dahd'], *f.* Inutility, uselessness, unprofitableness, needlessness.

Inutilizar [in-oo-te-le-thar'], *va.* To render useless.

Inútilmente, *adv.* Uselessly, idly.

In utroque. Latin phrase. Graduated in both civil and canonical law.

Invadeable [in-vah-day-ah'-blay], *a.* Not fordable, impassable without swimming.

Invadir [in-vah-deer'], *va.* To invade, to attack a country.

Invaginación [in-vah-he-nah-the-on'], *f.* Invagination.

Invalidación [in-vah-le-dah-the-on'], *f.* Invalidation, invalidity.

Inválidamente [in-vah'-le-dah-men-tay], *adv.* Invalidly.

Invalidar [in-vah-le-dar'], *va.* To invalidate, to deprive of force or efficacy, to irritate, to nullify.

Inválido, da [in-vah'-le-do, dah], *a.* Invalid, without force; feeble, weak, null.

Inválido [in-vah'-le-do], *m.* 1. (Mil.) Invalid, a soldier who has retired from the service in consequence of age or disability. *Dar* or *conceder inválidos,* To give pensions to veteran soldiers, to invalid soldiers. 2. (Coll.) Invalid, any person weakened by sickness.

Invariabilidad [in-vah-re-ah-be-le-dahd'], *f.* Invariability.

Invariable [in-vah-re-ah'-blay], *a.* Invariable, constant.

Invariablemente [in-vah-re-ah-blay-men'-tay], *adv.* Invariably.

Invariación [in-vah-re-ah-the-on'], *f.* (Obs.) Immutability invariableness.

Invariado, da [in-vah-re-ah'-do, dah], *a.* Unvaried, constant, invaried.

Invasión [in-vah-se-on'], *f.* Invasion, hostile entrance, attack.

Invasor, ra [in-vah-sor', rah], *m.* & *f.* Invader.

Invectiva [in-vec-tee'-vah], *f.* Invective, harsh censure.

Invencible [in-ven-thee'-blay], *a.* Invincible, insuperable, unconquerable.

Invenciblemente [in-ven-the-blay-men'-tay], *adv.* Invincibly.

Invención [in-ven-the-on'], *f.* 1. Invention, excogitation, the act or power of inventing. 2. Invention, discovery, the thing invented. 3. Invention, contrivance, fiction, artifice. *Hacer invenciones,* To make wry faces. *Vivir de invenciones,* To live by tricks and cunning.

Invencionero, ra [in-ven-the-o-nay'-ro, rah], *m.* & *f.* 1. Inventor. 2. Plotter. 3. Boaster, decider. 4. (Coll.) Gesticulator, mimic.

Invendible [in-ven-dee'-blay], *a.* Unmerchantable; not marketable, unsalable.

Inventar [in-ven-tar'], *va.* 1. To invent, to discover, to find out, to excogitate. 2. To invent, to forge, to frame, to contrive falsely.

Inventariar [in-ven-tah-re-ar'], *va.* 1. To make an inventory, to inventory, to register. 2. (Coll.) To commemorate the doings of a person.

Inventario [in-ven-tah'-re-o], *m.* Inventory, catalogue, stock.

Inventiva [in-ven-tee'-vah], *f.* The faculty of invention.

Inventivo, va [in-ven-tee'-vo, vah], *a.* Inventive, quick at contrivance, ready at expedients; inventful.

Invento [in-ven'-to], *m.* Invention, discovery.

Inventor, ra [in-ven-tor', rah], *m.* & *f.* Inventor, contriver, framer.

Inverecundo, da [in-vay-ray-coon'-do, dah], *a.* Shameless, impudent.

Inverisímil [in-vay-re-see'-meel], *a.* V. INVEROSÍMIL.

Invernaculo [in-ver-nah'-coo-lo], *m.* Green-house, hot-house, conservatory.

Invernada [in-ver-nah'-dah], *f.* Winter season.

Invernadero [in-ver-nah-day'-ro], *m.* 1. Winter-quarters: applied generally to wintering-places for sheep. 2. *V* INVERNÁCULO.

Invernal [in-ver-nahl'], *a.* Hibernal, wintry.

Invernar [in-ver-nar'], *vn.* To winter, to pass the winter; to be in the winter season, to hyemate.

Invernizo, za [in-ver-nee'-tho, thah], *a.* 1. Winterly, suited to the winter: hibernal. 2. Winter-beaten, harassed by frost and severe weather.

Inverosímil [in-vay-ro-see'-meel], *a.* Unlikely, improbable.

Inverosimilitud [in-vay-ro-se-me-le-tood'], *f.* Improbability, unlikelihood.

Inversamente [in-ver-sah-men'-tay], *adv.* Inversely; contrariwise.

Inversión [in-ver-se-on'], *f.* 1. Inversion; change of order, time, or place. 2. Investment, the act of employing or spending a sum of money.

Inversionista [in-ver-se-on-ees'-tah], *m.* & *f.* Investor.

Inverso, sa [in-ver'-so, sah], *a.* & *pp. irr.* of INVERTIR. Inverse, inverted, reciprocal. *A* or *por la inversa,* On the contrary.

Invertebrado, da [in-ver-tay-brah'-do, dah], *a.* Invertebrate, without a backbone.—*m. pl.* The invertebrata.

Invertir [in-ver-teer'], *va.* 1. To invert, to turn upside down; to change the order of time or place. 2. To employ, to spend, or lay out money, to invest.

Investidura [in-ves-te-doo'-rah], *f.* Investiture, the act of giving possession of a manor, office, or benefice.

Investigable [in-ves-te-gah'-blay], *a.* Investigable.

Investigación [in-ves-te-gah-the-on'], *f.* Investigation, research; inquest.

Investigador, ra [in-ves-te-gah-dor', rah], *m.* & *f.* Investigator.

Investigar [in-ves-te-gar'], *va.* To investigate, to search out; to look after.

Investir [in-ves-teer'], *va.* To invest, to confer some dignity.

Inveterado, da [in-vay-tay-rah'-do, dah], *a.* & *pp.* of INVETERARSE. Inveterate, old, chronic, obstinate.

Inveteradamente [in-vay-tay-rah-dah men'-tay], *adv.* Inveterately.

Inveterarse [in-vay-tay-rar'-say], *vr.* To become antiquated, to grow old, to become chronic: it has been used, though seldom, as an active verb.

Invictamente [in-vic-tah-men'-tay], *adv.* Unconquerably, valiantly.

Invicto, ta [in-veec'-to, tah], *a.* Unconquerable, unconquered.

Invierno [in-ve-er'-no], *m.* Winter.

Invigilancia [in-ve-he-lahn'-the-ah], *f.* 1. Want of vigilance. 2. Watching, observant attention.

Invigilar [in-ve-he-lar'], *vn.* To watch, to be observant, to be attentive.

Inviolabilidad [in-ve-o-lah-be-le-dahd'], *f.* Inviolability, inviolableness.

Inviolable [in-ve-o-lah'-blay], *a.* Inviolable.

Inviolablemente, *adv.* Inviolably holily; infallibly.

Inviolado, da [in-ve-o-lah'-do, dah], *a.* Inviolate, unhurt, uninjured.
Invisibilidad [in-ve-se-be-le-dahd'], *f.* Invisibility.
Invisible [in-ve-see'-blay], *a.* Invisible, not perceptible. *En un invisible,* (Coll.) In an instant.
Invisiblemente, *adv.* Invisibly.
Invitación [in-ve-tah-the-on'], *f.* Invitation.
Invitado, da [in-ve-tah'-do, dah], *m.* & *f.* Guest.—*a.* Invited.
Invitador, ra [in-ve-tah-dor', rah], *m.* & *f.* One who invites, an inviter.
Invitar [in-ve-tar'], *va.* 1. To invite. 2. To excite, to stimulate, to execute a thing.
Invitatorio [in-ve-tah-to'-re-o], *m.* Invitatory, psalm or anthem sung at the beginning of matins or morning worship.
Invocación [in-vo-cah-the-on'], *f.* 1. Invocation, the act of calling upon in prayer. 2. (Poet.) Invocation, the form of calling for the assistance or presence of any being.
Invocador, ra [in-vo-cah-dor', rah], *m.* & *f.* One who invokes.
Invocar [in-vo-car'], *va.* To invoke, to implore, to cry unto.
Invocatorio, ria [in-vo-cah-to'-re-o, ah], *a.* That which invocates.
Involucela [in-vo-loo-thay'-lah], *f.* (Bot.) Involucel.
Involución [in-vo-loo-the-on'], *f.* (Bot.) State of being rolled in; involution.
Involucral [in-vo-loo-crahl'], *a.* (Bot.) Involucral, relating to an involucre.
Involucrar [in-vo-loo-crar'], *va.* 1. To wrap up, to cover. 2. To mingle, to confuse, to upset. 3. To insert in writings questions or subjects foreign to their principal object.
Involucro [in-vo-loo'-cro], *m.* (Bot.) Involucre. *Involucro parcial, V.* INVOLUCELA.
Involuntariamente, *adv.* Involuntarily.
Involuntariedad [in-vo-loon-tah-re-ay-dahd'], *f.* Involuntariness.
Involuntario, ria [in-vo-loon-tah'-re-o, ah], *a.* Involuntary.
Involuta [in-vo-loo'-tah], *f.* (Arch.) Volute. *V.* VOLUTA.
Invulnerabilidad [in-vool-nay-rah-be-le-dahd'], *f.* Invulnerability.
Invulnerable [in-vool-nay-rah'-blay], *a.* Invulnerable.
Inyección [in-yec-the-on'], *f.* 1. Injection, the art of injecting. 2. The liquid injected, shot. *Inyección estimulante,* (Med.) Booster shot.
Inyectador, ra [in-yec-tah-dor', rah], *m.* & *f.* 1. One who injects. 2. (Med.) Any instrument which serves for making injections.
Inyectar [in-yec-tar'], *va.* To inject.
Inyector [in-yec-tor'], *m.* (Mech.) Injector. *Inyector del combustible,* (Aer.) Afterburner.
Ion [e-on'], *m.* (Chem. & Phy.) Ion.
Iónico, ca [e-o'-ne-co, cah], *a.* Ionic.
Ionización [e-o-ne-thah-the-on'], *f.* Ionization.
Ionizar [e-o-ne-thar'], *va.* To ionize.
Ionosfera [e-o-nos-fay'-rah], *f.* Ionosphere.
Iota [e-o'-tah], *f.* Ninth letter of the Greek alphabet. (*Cf.* Jot.)
Ipil [e-peel'], *m.* A large, handsome tree of the Philippine Islands with opposite compound leaves; flowers in a panicle, gamopetalous, with ten stamens; a coriaceous pod, sickle-shaped, few-seeded. The wood is hard, heavy, yellowish, growing darker with age, very durable, and esteemed for cabinet work and like uses.
Ipomea [e-po-may'-ah], *f.* Ipomea, a large genus of the bindweed family.
Ipso facto [eep'-so fahc'-to]. (Law) An adverbial phrase; immediately, without delay; also, by the very fact.
Ipsojure [eep'-so yoo'-ray]. (Law) An adverbial phrase used in courts of law, to denote that a thing does not require the declaration of the judge, as it constitutes the law itself.
Ir [eer], *vn.* 1. To go, to move, not to stand still. 2. To go, to walk, to move step by step. 3. To be, to exist. 4. To bet, to lay a wager. *Van cien doblones que es cierto,* I lay a hundred pistoles that it is true. 5. To consist, to depend on. 6. To import, to concern. *Nada se me va en ello,* I have no concern in it, I do not care for it. 7. To differ, to be different, to be distant. 8. To lead: applied to a road. 9. To devote one's self to a calling, to follow a profession: in this last sense it is used with *por.* 10. To proceed, to act. 11. To decline a noun or conjugate a verb for another. *Ir* joined to present participles implies the existence or actual execution of the action designated; joined with past participles it signifies to suffer their action; with the preposition *a* and infinitive mode, it implies disposition toward, as *ir a oir misa,* to go to hear mass; followed by *con,* it gives the noun an adverbial import, as *ir con tiento,* to go on softly; and accompanied by the preposition *contra* or *fuera de,* it signifies to persevere, or act contrary to.—*vr.* 1. To go, to go off or go away, to depart or remove from a place. 2. To be dying. 3. To go off, to go out of life, to be gone. 4. To leak, to ooze. 5. To exhale, to evaporate. 6. To discharge wind. 7. To break: to grow old. *Ir a caballo,* To ride. *Ir a la mano a alguno,* To restrain or moderate any one. *Ir al amor del agua,* To temporize. *Ir a medias,* To go halves. *Ir agua arriba,* To work up stream. *A gran ir, a más ir,* At the utmost speed. *Ir a una,* To act with one accord, harmoniously. *Allá se va,* It is all the same, it amounts to the same thing. *A ir sordo,* Silently, quietly. *Ir y venir,* To revolve a thing in one's mind. *Írsele a uno el alma por alguna cosa,* To long for. *Irse de boca,* To speak without reflection. *Írsele a uno la mula,* To speak unadvisedly from carelessness or anger. *Ir* (or *andar*) *de capa caída,* To be crestfallen; to decline in fortune or credit. *Ir de manga,* To conspire. *Ni va, ni viene,* Indecision, want of resolution. *Ir de campo,* To go to a picnic. *Ir a campo travieso,* To make a short cut. *Ir en alcance,* In a printing-office, to divide the (original) copy among various compositors. *Ir con espigón* (or *llevar espigón*), To retire indignant or irritated. *Ir* or *irse a pique* or *por ojo,* (Naut.) To founder, to go to the bottom. *Ir adelante,* To go on. *Ir a pie,* To walk. *Ir de una parte a otra,* To go up and down. *Ir en contra de,* To go against. *Ir en decadencia* or *ir empobreciendo,* To go down the wind. *Ir en demanda de,* (Naut.) To be on the look-out for. *Ir en busca de* or *ir por algo,* To go for. *Ir otra vez,* To go back or to go again. *Ir separadamente,* To go asunder. *Ir sobre seguro,* To go upon sure grounds. *Ir tras la corriente,* To go down the stream. *Ir a los alcances,* To pursue very closely. *Ir bien* or *mal,* Speaking of a business, it means that it is going on prosperously or unprosperously. *Ir con alguno,* 1. To be of the same opinion as another. 2. To be of the same party as another. 3. To accompany. *Irse a la mano,* To become moderate, or restrain one's self. *Irse a leva y monte,* To escape, to retire. *Irse con Dios* or *irse con su madre de Dios,* To absent one's self; to despatch with disgust or disapprobation. *Írsele a alguno la cabeza,* To perturb the mind, to confuse the reason. *¿ Quién va ?* or *¿ quien va allá ?* Who is there, or who goes there? *Vaya Vd.* or *vete con Dios,* Farewell; God be with you. *Vaya Vd. al cielo* or *al rollo* or *a pasear,* etc., Go to, expressions of contempt for what another says. *Ir pagando,* (Coll.) To pay by degrees. *Ir pasando* or *mejorando,* To be recovering by degrees *El se mete en lo que no le va, ni le viene,* He meddles in what does not concern him at all. *Ir delante* or *por delante,* To go ahead. *No hay que irse atrás,* Flinch not. (Met.) To treat or discuss, to look for. *Mucho va de Pedro a Pedro,* (prov.) There is a wide difference between man and man. *A donde fueres, haz lo que vieres,* When you are at Rome, do as the Romans do. *Irse los ojos tras de una persona* or *cosa,* To have an admiring eye, or longing after a person or thing; to look after it with anxiety. *Irse por sus pies,* To run away, to escape. *Por la calle de " después " se va a la casa de " nunca,"* By the street of " By and by " one arrives at the house of " Never."
Ira [ee'-rah], *f.* 1. Ire, anger, passion, indignation, wrath, fury, choler, rage. 2. Ire, desire of vengeance, chastisement threatened or executed. 3. (Met.) Violence of the elements or weather. *¡ Ira de Dios !* Expression of aversion used when the bad effects of something are feared. Zounds!
Iracundia [e-rah-coon'-de-ah], *f.* Irascibility, ire, irascibleness.
Iracundo, da [e-rah-coon'-do, dah], *a.* 1 Passionate, ireful. 2. (Poet.) Enraged, furious: applied to the winds.
Iranio, nia [e-rah'-ne-o, ah], *a.* Iranian, relating to Persia or Iran.
Irascencia [e-ras-then'-the-ah], *f.* (Obs.) *V.* IRACUNDIA.
Irascible [e-ras-thee'-blay], *a.* Irascible, impetuous, determined.
Irenarca [e-ray-nar'-cah], *m.* Irenarch, an officer of the Greek empire, employed to preserve public tranquility
Iridáceo, cea [e-re-dah'-thay-o, thay-ah], *a.* Iridaceous, iris-like.
Íride [ee'-re-day], *f* (Bot.) *V* EFÉMERO.
Iridectomia [e-re-dec-to-mee'-ah], *f.* Iridectomy, excision of a portion of iris.
Irideo, dea [e-ree'-day-o, ah], *a.* Irideous, like the iris or flower-de-luce.
Iridescente [e-re-des-then'-tay], *a.* Iridescent, rainbow-hued.
Iridio [e-ree'-de-o], *m.* (Min.) Iridium, a metallic element.
Iris [ee'-ris], *m.* 1. Iris, the rainbow. 2. Iris, the circle round the pupil of the eye. 3. Mediator, peace-maker. 4. (Bot.) *V.* LIRIO PAJIZO or ESPADAÑAL. 5. Prism.
Irisado, da [e-re-sah'-do, dah], *a.* Rainbow-hued.
Irisar [e-re-sar'], *va.* To throw out rainbow-hued scintillations.
Irlanda [ir-lahn'-dah], *f.* 1. Cloth made of cotton and woollen yarn. 2. Fine Irish linen.
Irlandés, esa [ir-lan-days', sah], *a.* Irish, relating to Ireland.—*m.* The Irish language.
Ironía [e-ro-nee'-ah], *f.* Irony, the use of words designed to convey a meaning opposite to the literal sense. A rhetorical figure.

Irónicamente [e-ro'-ne-cah-men-tay], *adv.* Ironically.
Irónico, ca [e-ro'-ne-co, cah], *a.* Ironical.
Irracional [ir-rah-the-o-nahl'], *a.* Irrational, void of reason, absurd: sometimes used as a substantive for an irrational animal.
Irracionalidad [ir-rah-the-o-nah-le-dahd'], *f.* Irrationality, absurdness.
Irracionalmente, *adv.* Irrationally, absurdly.
Irradiación [ir-rah-de-ah-the-on'], *f.* 1. Irradiation, the act of emitting light; irradiance. 2. Illumination, intellectual light.
Irradiar [ir-rah-de-ar'], *va.* To irradiate, to emit beams of light.
Irrazonable [ir-rah-tho-nah'-blay], *a.* Unreasonable.
Irrealizable [ir-ray-ah-le-thah'-blay], *a.* Unrealizable.
Irrebatible [ir-ray-bah-tee'-blay], *a.* Indisputable.
Irreconciliable [ir-ray-con-the-le-ah'-blay], *a.* Irreconciliable, unappeasable.
Irreconciliablemente, *adv.* Irreconcilably.
Irreconocible [ir-ray-co-no-thee'-blay], *a.* Unrecognizable.
Irrecuperable [ir-ray-coo-pay-rah'-blay], *a.* Irrecoverable, irretrievable.
Irrecusable [ir-ray-coo-sah'-blay], *a.* 1. Not to be refused or declined, unimpeachable. 2. Inevitable.
Irredimible [ir-ray-de-mee'-blay], *a.* Irredeemable, irrepleviable.
Irreducible [ir-ray-doo-thee'-blay], *a.* 1. Irreducible. 2. Stubborn, obstinate.
Irreemplazable, Irremplazable [ir-ray-em-plah-thah'-blay, ir-rem-plah-thah'-blay], *a.* Irreplaceable.
Irreflexión [ir-ray-flec-se-on'], *f.* Rashness, indiscretion, inconsideration.
Irreflexivo, va [ir-ray-flec-see'-vo, vah], *a.* Inconsiderate, indiscreet, unreflecting.
Irreformable [ir-ray-for-mah'-blay], *a.* Not to be reformed or reclaimed.
Irrefragable [ir-ray-frah-gah'-blay], *a.* Irrefragable, irrefutable.
Irregular [ir-ray-goo-lar'], *a.* 1. Irregular, disorderly, abnormal. 2. Irregular, immethodical.
Irregularidad [ir-ray-goo-lah-re-dahd'], *f.* Irregularity, deviation from rule, disorder, misgovernance, abnormity.
Irregularmente, *adv.* Irregularly, loosely.
Irreligión [ir-ray-le-he-on'], *f* Irreligion, impiety, unbelief.
Irreligiosidad [ir-ray-le-he-o-se-dahd'], *f.* Irreligiousness, impiety.
Irreligioso, sa [ir-ray-le-he-o'-so, sah], *a.* Irreligious, impious.
Irremediable [ir-ray-may-de-ah'-blay], *a.* Irremediable, incurable: helpless.
Irremediablemente, *adv.* Irremediably, helplessly, irrecoverably.
Irremisible [ir-ray-me-see'-blay], *a.* Irremissible, unpardonable.
Irremisiblemente, *adv* Unpardonably, irremissibly.
Irremunerado, da [ir-ray-moo-nay-rah'-do, dah], *a.* Unremunerated
Irreparable [ir-ray-pah-rah'-blay], *a* Irreparable, irretrievable.
Irreparablemente, *adv.* Irreparably, irretrievably, irrecoverably
Irreprensible [ir-ray-pren-see'-blay], *a.* Irreprehensible, irreproachable, irreprovable.
Irreprensiblemente, *adv.* Irreprehensibly, irreproachably
Irresistibilidad [ir-ray-sis-te-be-le-dahd'], *f.* Irresistibility.
Irresistible [ir-ray-sis-tee'-blay], *a.* Irresistible.

Irresistiblemente, *adv.* Irresistibly.
Irresoluble [ir-ray-so-loo'-blay], *a.* 1. Indeterminable, not to be defined; not to be resolved, irresoluble. 2. Irresolute, not constant in purpose.
Irresolución [ir-ray-so-loo-the-on'], *f.* Irresolution, want of firmness, irresoluteness, hesitation.
Irresolutamente, *adv.* (Littl. us.) Irresolutely.
Irresoluto, ta, Irresuelto, ta [ir-ray-so-loo'-to, tah, ir-ray-soo-el'-to, tah], *a.* Irresolute, unsteady.
Irrespetuoso, sa [ir-res-pay-too-o'-so, sah], *a.* Unrespectful, wanting in respect.
Irrespirable [ir-res-pe-rah'-blay], *a.* Irrespirable, not fit to be breathed.
Irresponsabilidad [ir-res-pon-sah-be-le-dahd'], *f.* Irresponsibility.
Irresponsable [ir-res-pon-sah'-blay], *a.* Irresponsible.
Irreverencia [ir-ray-vay-ren'-the-ah], *f.* Irreverence, want of respect or veneration.
Irreverente [ir-ray-vay-ren'-tay], *a.* Irreverent.
Irreverentemente, *adv.* Irreverently.
Irrevocabilidad [ir-ray-vo-cah-be-le-dahd'], *f.* Irrevocability.
Irrevocable [ir-ray-vo-cah'-blay], *a* Irrevocable, irreversible.
Irrevocablemente, *adv.* Irrevocably.
Irrisible [ir-re-see'-blay], *a.* Risible, laughable.
Irrisión [ir-re-se-on'], *f.* Irrision, the art of laughing at another, mockery.
Irrisoriamente [ir-re-so-re-ah-men'-tay], *adv.* Laughingly, derisively.
Irrisorio, ria [ir-re-so'-re-o, ah], *a.* Derisive, risible.
Irritabilidad [ir-re-tah-be-le-dahd'], *f.* Irritability
Irritable [ir-re-tah'-blay], *a.* 1. That can be rendered void or annulled. 2. Irritable, easily provoked. 3 Irritable, easily irritated.
Irritación [ir-re-tah-the-on'], *f.* 1. Irritation, commotion, agitation. 2. Invalidation, abrogation. 3. (Med.) Irritation, morbid action of the organs.
Irritador, ra [ir-re-tah-dor', rah], *m.* & *f.* Irritator, stimulator.
Írritamente [eer'-re-tah-men-tay], *adv.* Invalidly, vainly.
Irritamiento [ir-re-tah-me-en'-to], *m.* Irritation; abrogation.
Irritante [ir-re-tahn'-tay], *a.* & *pa.* 1. Annulling or making void 2. Irritative, irritant, stimulating.
Irritante, *m.* (Med.) Stimulant, irritant.
Irritar [ir-re-tar'], *va.* 1. To annul, to render void. 2. To irritate, to exasperate, to agitate violently, to nettle, to offend, to make angry. 3. To alter, to produce a change.
Írrito, ta [eer'-re-to, tah], *a.* Null, void.
Irrogar [ir-ro-gar'], *va.* To cause, to occasion (damage).
Irrompible [ir-rom-pee'-blay], *a* Unbreakable.
Irrupción [ir-roop-the-on'], *f.* Irruption, inroad.
Isabelino, na [e-sah-bay-lee'-no, nah], *a.* Stamped with the bust of Isabella II., or defending her.
Isagoge [e-sah-go'-hay], *f.* Introduction, preliminary remarks.
Isagógico, ca [e-sah-go'-he-co, cah], *a.* Isagogical, introductive, introductory.
Iságono [e-sah'-go-no], *m.* (Geom.) Isagon.
Isanto, ta [e-sahn'-to, tah], *a.* (Bot.) Having floral envelopes just alike.
Isatina [e-sah-tee'-nah], *f.* Isatin, a crystalline compound obtained by oxydizing indigo.

Isocofonía [is-co-fo-nee'-ah], *f.* (Med.) A defect of the voice, difficulty in pronouncing certain consonants.
Isla [ees'-lah], *f.* 1. Isle, island. 2 A remote or retired spot. *En isla,* Insulated. 3. Square, an area of four sides, with houses on each side. *Islas de barlovento,* Windward Islands. *Islas de sotavento,* Leeward Islands.
Islam [is-lahm'], *m.* Islamism, the believers in Mohammedanism.
Islámico, ca [es-lah'-me-co, cah], *a.* Islamic.
Islamismo [is-lah-mees'-mo], *m.* Mohammedanism.
Islán [is-lahn'], *m.* A kind of veil anciently worn by women.
Islandés, sa [is-lan-days', sah], *a.* Icelandic, relating to Iceland.
Isleño, ña [is-lay'-nyo, nyah], *m.* & *f.* Islander. (Cuba) A native of the Canary Islands.
Isleo [is-lay'-o], *m.* Island formed by rocks.
Isleta [is-lay'-tah], *f. dim.* A small isle, islet.
Islilla [is-leel'-lyah], *f.* Flank, part of the body from the hip to the armpit.
Islote [is-lo'-tay], *m.* A small barren island.
Ismaelita [is-mah-ay-lee'-tah], *a.* Ishmaelite, Mohammedan, Arab.
Isobárico, ca [e-so-bah'-re-co, cah], *a.* (Phy.) Isobaric.
Isócrono, na [e-so'-cro-no, nah], *a.* Isochronal, having equal times.
Isoglos [e-so'-glos], *m.* Isoglos.
Isógono, na [e-so'-go-no, nah], *a.* Having two equal angles.
Isomérico, ca [e-so-may'-re-co, cah], *a* Isomeric, relating to isomerism.
Isomerismo [e-so-may-rees'-mo], *m.* (Chem.) Isomerism, the condition of having different properties, but the same molecular composition, or same atomic weight
Isómero, ra [e-so'-may-ro, rah], *a.* 1 Isomerous, equal in number 2 Isomeric.
Isometría [e-so-may-tree'-ah], *f.* Isometrics.
Isométrico, ca [e-so-may'-tre-co, cah], *a.* Isometric.
Isomorfismo [e-so-mor-fees'-mo], *m.* Isomorphism, identical crystallization.
Isomorfo, fa [e-so-mor'-fo, fah], *a.* Isomorphous, isomorphic, of the same construction.
Isonomía [e-so-no-mee'-ah], *f.* Equality of civil rights, isonomy.
Isónomo, ma [e-so'-no-mo, mah]; *a.* Governed by the same law.
Isoperimétrico, ca [e-so-pay-re-may'-tre-co, cah], *a.* Isoperimetrical.
Isósceles [e-sos'-thay-les], *a.* (Geom.) Isosceles, a triangle having two sides equal.
Isotermo, ma [e-so-ter'-mo, mah], *a.* Isothermal, of equal temperature.
Isótopo [e-so'-to-po], *m.* (Phy & Chem.) Isotope.
Isquiático, ca [is-ke-ah'-te-co, cah], *a.* Ischiatic, relating to the ischium.
Israelí [is-rah-ay-lee'], *a.* & *m.* & *f.* Israeli.
Israelita [is-rah-ay-lee'-tah], *m* Israelite, Jew.
Israelítico, ca [is-rah-ay-lee'-te-co, cah], *a.* Israelitish, Jewish.
Ístmico, ca [eest'-me-co, cah], *a.* Isthmian, belonging to the isthmus: used especially of certain Greek games.
Istmo [eest'-mo], *m.* Isthmus.
Italianismo [e-tah-le-ah-nees'-mo], *m* Italianism, an Italian idiom or expression.
Italianizar [e-tah-le-ah-ne-thar'], *va.* To Italianise.

Italiano [e-tah-le-ah'-no], *a.* Italian.—*m.* The Italian language.

Itálico, ca [e-tah'-le-co, cah], *a.* Italic.—*f.* Italic type.

Item [ee'-tem], *m.* Item, new article.—*adv.* Also, moreover.

Iterar [e-tay-rar'], *va.* To iterate, to repeat. *V.* REPETIR.

Iterativo, va [e-tay-rah-tee'-vo, vah], *a.* Iterative, repeating, redoubling.

Itinerario [e-te-nay-rah'-re-o], *m.* Itinerary, book of travels; guide for travelling; march, route.

Itinerario, ria [e-te-nay-rah'-re-o, ah], *a.* Itinerary.

Itria [ee'-tre-ah], *f.* (Min.) Yttria, a white insoluble earth.

Itrio [ee'-tre-o], *m.* Yttrium, a rare element belonging to the cerium group.

Iza [ee'-thah], *f.* (Naut.) Hoisting, hauling up.

Izaga [e-thah'-gah], *f.* Place abounding in rushes and reeds.

Izamiento [e-thah-me-en'-to], *m.* Hoisting, raising (of the flag, etc.)

Izar [e-thar'], *va.* (Naut.) To hoist, to raise up on high.

Izquierdear [ith-ke-er-day-ar'], *vn.* To degenerate, to fall from its kind; to grow wild.

Izquierdista [ith-ke-er-dees'-tah], *a.* & *m.* & *f.* Leftist.

Izquierdo, da [ith-ke-er'-do, dah], *a.* 1. Left-handed; left; sinister. *A la izquierda,* To the left. 2. Crooked, not right or straight. 3. Applied to horses which turn out their toes in travelling.

Izquierdo, da [ith-ke-er'-do, dah], *m.* & *f.* A left-handed person.

J

J [ho'-tah], in the Spanish language, is always a consonant, and its pronunciation is guttural, or like the sound of *h* strongly aspirated, as in *ham, her, him, home, who.* J is at present used in some cases in preference to G to represent the guttural sound before *e*, thus: *mujer* instead of *muger.*

Jaba [hah'-bah], *f.* (Cuba) A basket made of the leaves of *yarey. Llevar* or *tener la jaba,* (Coll.) To be unpolished, uneducated, a boor.

Jabalcón [hah-bal-cone'], *m.* Bracket, purlin.

Jabalconar [hah-bal-co-nar'], *va.* To support the roof of a house with brackets.

Jabali [hah-bah-lee'], *m.* Wild boar. Sus. (Arabic.)

Jabalina [hah-bah-lee'-nah], *f.* 1. Sow of a wild boar. 2. Javelin, a kind of spear for hunting wild boars.

Jabalonar [hah-bah-lo-nar'], *va.* *V.* JABALCONAR.

Jabardear [hah-bar-day-ar'], *va.* To swarm, to rise as bees in a body.

Jabardillo [hah-bar-deel'-lyo], *m.* *V.* JABARDO for a crowd.

Jabardo [hah-bar'-do], *m.* 1. A small swarm of bees. 2. Any crowd or assembly of low people; mob, rabble.

Jabato [hah-bah'-to], *m.* A young wild boar.

Jábeca [hah'-bay-cah], *f.* 1. Sweep-net, a large net for fishing. 2. *V.* JÁBEGA.

Jábega [hah'-bay-gah], *f.* A Moorish wind instrument, somewhat like a flute.

Jabeguero [hah-bay-gay'-ro], *m.* Fisherman who fishes with a sweep-net.

Jabeguero, ra [hah-bay-gay'-ro, rah], *a.* Belonging to a sweep-net for fishing.

Jabeque [hah-bay'-kay], *m.* (Naut.) 1. Xebec, a small three-masted vessel, navigated in the Mediterranean, and on the coasts of Spain and Portugal. 2. A wound made in the face with a knife or other cutting weapon. (Used most with the verb *pintar.*) (Turk.)

Jabi [hah-bee'l, *m.* 1. Small wild apple or crab. 2. Small kind of grapes. 3. A hard-wood tree of Yucatan.

Jabladera [hah-blah-day'-rah], *f.* Crozer, a cooper's tool.

Jable [hah'-blay] *m.* Croze, the groove in the staves of casks which receives the heads.

Jabón [hah-bone'], *m.* 1. Soap. 2. (Met.) Any saponaceous mass or matter. *Jabón de Palencia,* (Coll.) Batlet used by washer-women to wash linen. *Jabón de piedra* or *de Castilla,* Castile soap. 3. (Coll.) Smart stroke with a batlet. *Dar un jabón,* To reprimand severely. *Bola de jabón,* 1. Wash-ball. 2. Soap-bubble.

Jabonado, da [hah-bo-nah'-do, dah], *a.* & *pp.* of JABONAR. Soaped, cleansed with soap.

Jabonado [hah-bo-nah'-do], *m.* 1. Wash, the act of washing with soap. 2. Parcel of linen washed with soap.

Jabonadura [hah-bo-nah-doo'-rah], *f.* The act of washing. *Jabonaduras,* 1. Suds or soapsuds. 2. Lather. *Echarle* or *darle a uno una jabonadura,* (Coll.) To reprimand one.

Jabonamiento [hah-bo-nah-me-en'-to], *m.* *V.* JABONADURA.

Jabonar [hah-bo-nar'], *va.* 1. To soap, to cleanse with soap. 2. (Coll.) To reprimand severely.

Jaboncillo, Jabonete, or **Jabonete de olor** [hah-bon-theel'-lyo, hah-bo-nay'-tay], *m.* Wash-ball; shaving soap.

Jaboncillo, *m.* 1. Soapstone or French chalk used by tailors. 2. Mixture of oils and alkali, especially ammonia, hardly saponified.

Jabonera [hah-bo-nay'-rah], *f.* 1. Box or case for a wash-ball. 2. (Bot.) Soapwort. Saponaria.

Jaboneria [hah-bo-nay-ree'-ah], *f.* Soap-manufactory, soap-house.

Jabonero [hah-bo-nay'-ro], *m.* Soap maker or seller.

Jabonoso, sa [hah-bo-no'-so, sah], *a.* (Littl. us.) Soapy.

Jabuco [hah-boo'-co], *m.* (Cuba) A round basket in the form of a very large decanter with a narrow neck.

Jaca [hah'-cah], *f.* 1. Nag, pony. *V.* HACA. 2. A name of the bread-fruit tree.

Jacal [hah-cahl'], *m.* (Mex.) 1. An Indian hut, a wigwam. 2. (Zool.) Jackal. *V.* CHACAL.

Jacamar [hah-cah-mar'], *m.* Jacamar, an insectivorous bird of South America, notable for its beauty.

Jacana [hah-cah'-nah], *f.* A tropical South American wading bird. Parra jacana.

Jácara [hah'-cah-rah], *f.* 1. A sort of romance. 2. A kind of rustic tune for singing or dancing; a kind of dance. 3. Company of young men who walk about at night-time singing *jácaras.* 4. Molestation, vexation. 5. Idle talk or prattle, story, tale; fable, lie, vainglorious fiction.

Jacarandina, Jacarandana [hah-cah-ran-dee'-nah, hah-cah-ran-dah'-nah], *f.* 1. Low, foul language, slang; the language of ruffians and prostitutes' bullies. 2. Singing of *jácaras* or boastings. 3. (Low) Assembly of ruffians and thieves.

Jacarear [hah-cah-ray-ar'], *vn.* 1. To sing *jácaras.* 2. To go about the streets with singing and noise. 3. To be troublesome and vexatious.

Jacarero [hah-cah-ray'-ro], *m.* 1. Ballad-singer. 2. Wag or merry droll, a facetious person.

Jacarilla [hah-cah-reel'-lyah], *f. dim.* of JÁCARA.

Jácaro [hah'-cah-ro], *m.* Boaster, bully.

Jácaro, ra [hah'-cah-ro, rah], *a.* Belonging to boasters or noisy singers. *A lo jácaro,* In a boastful or bragging manner.

Jacena [hah-thay'-nah], *f.* Girder, a beam on which joists rest.

Jacerina [hah-thay-ree'-nah], *f.* Mail, a coat of steel net-work for defence.

Jacilla [hah-theel'-yah], *f.* Mark which a thing leaves upon the ground where it has been for some time. (Acad.) (*Cf.* YACER, fr. Lat. jacēre.)

Jacinto [hah-theen'-to], *m.* 1. (Bot.) Hyacinth; harebell. Hyacinthus, *L.* 2. Hyacinth, a precious stone.

Jacio [hah'-the-o], *m.* (Naut.) A dead calm.

Jaco [hah'-co], *m.* 1. Nag, pony. 2. A short jacket, formerly used by soldiers. 3. *V.* JAQUE.

Jacobinico, ca [hah-co-bee'-ne-co, cah], *a.* Jacobin, Jacobinical, belonging to Jacobins.

Jacobinismo [hah-co-be-nees'-mo], *m.* Jacobinism, the principles of a Jacobin.

Jacobino [hah-co-bee'-no], *m.* Jacobin, one of a faction in the French revolution; a downright democrat; an infidel.

Jacobita [hah-co-bee'-tah], *f.* Jacobite, one attached to the cause or family of James the Second, after his abdication.

Jacra, or **Jagra** [hah'-crah], *f.* A kind of sugar obtained from the wine of the palm-tree or the cocoanut.

Jactancia [hac-tahn'-the-ah], *f.* Jactancy, boasting, arrogance, ostentation.

Jactanciosamente [hac-tan-the-o-sah-men'-tay], *adv.* Boastingly.

Jactancioso, sa [hac-tan-the-o'-so, sah], *a.* Boastful, vainglorious; arrogant, glorious, ostentatious.

Jactarse [hac-tar'-say], *vr.* To vaunt, to boast, to display with ostentation, to glory, to flourish, to brag, to gasconade.

Jaculatoria [hah-coo-lah-to'-re-ah], *f.* Ejaculation, a short prayer.

Jaculatorio, ria [hah-coo-lah-to'-re-o, ah], *a.* Jaculatory.

Jachali [hah-chah-lee'], *m.* The custard-apple, Anona reticulata, a tropical shrub or low tree valued for its hard wood.

Jada [hah'-dah], *f.* (Prov.) *V.* AZADA.

Jade [hah'-day], *m.* Jade, a mineral.

Jadeante [hah-day-ahn'-tay], *a.* Panting, breathless, gasping.

Jadear [hah-day-ar'], *vn.* To pant, to palpitate, to have the breast heaving as for want of breath; to jade.

Jadeo [hah-day'-o], *m.* Pant, palpitation.

Jadiar [hah-de-ar'], *va.* (Prov.) To dig up with a spade.

Jaecero, ra [hah-ay-thay'-ro, rah], *m.* & *f.* Harness-maker.

Jaén [hah-en'], *m.* A kind of large white grape, with thick rind.

Jaenés, sa [hah-ay-nays', sah], *a.* Native of or belonging to the city of Jaen.

Jaez [hah'-eth], *m.* 1. Harness, the traces of draught-horses. 2. Manner or quality in which several things resemble each other. *Jaeces,* Ornaments or harness of horses in processions. (Arab. jahāz.)

Jafético, ca [hah-fay'-te-co, cah], *a.* Japhetic, Indo-Germanic, descended from Japhet.

Jaga [hah'-gah], *f.* (Obs.) Wound. *V.* LLAGA.

Jagua [hah'-goo-ah], *f.* Fruit of the custard-apple, of a sweet, agreeable taste. (Cuba.)

Jaguar, or **Jaguarete** [hah-goo-ar', or hah-goo-ah-ray'-tay], *m.* The jaguar, a ferocious beast resembling the leopard.

Jagüey [hah-goo-ay'-e], *m.* 1. In Peru and Mexico, a large pool or lake. Also, a reservoir for rain-water, when no spring water is at hand. 2. (Cuba) The matador liana, a climbing plant which kills the tree which it clasps.

Jaharrar [hah-ar-rar'], *va.* To plaster, to overlay or make even with plaster.

Jaharro [hah-ar'-ro], *m.* Plaster, the act of plastering.

Jai alai [hah-e ah-lah'-e], *m.* Jai alai, Basque ball game.

Jaiba [hah'-e-bah], *f.* (Cuba & Mex.) Certain type of crab.

Jaibol [hah-e-bol'], *m.* (Mex.) Highball.

Jaique [hah'-e-kay], *m.* An Arabic cape with a hood. (Arab. hāik.)

Jairar [hah-e-rar'], *va.* To carry the knife inclined outward in trimming shoes.

Jaire [hah'-e-ray], *m.* 1. The curved line made in a timber which is joined to another for greater solidity. 2. Among shoemakers, the outward inclination of the knife in splitting leather.

¡Ja, ja, ja! [hah, hah, hah], *int.* Exclamation, denoting laughter.

Jalapa [hah-lah'-pah], *f.* (Bot.) 1. Jalapa. Convolvulus jalapa, *L.* 2. Jalap, the root of the jalap, plant frequently used in medicine.

Jalbegar [hal-bay-gar'], *va.* 1. To whiten, to whitewash. 2. To paint excessively, to lay too much white on the face.

Jalbegue [hal-bay'-gay], *m.* 1. Whitewash. 2. Whitewashing, whitening a wall with lime. 3. Whitewash, a paint or wash to make the skin seem fair.

Jaldado, da, Jaldo, da [hal-dah'-do, dah, hahl'-do, dah], *a.* Of a bright yellow colour.

Jalde [hahl'-day], *a.* Bright yellow, crocus-coloured.

Jaldre [hahl'-dray], *m.* A bright yellow colour, peculiar to birds.

Jalea [hah-lay'-ah], *f.* Jelly, the inspissated juice of fruit, boiled with sugar. *Hacerse una jalea*, (Met.) To love with excessive fondness. *Jalea del agro*, Conserve of citron.

Jalear [hah-lay-ar'], *va.* 1. To encourage hounds to follow the chase. 2. To animate dancers, by clapping hands. 3. To quaver the voice, to use the vibrato.

Jaleo [hah-lay'-o], *m.* (Coll.) Genteelness, jauntiness.

Jaletina [hah-lay-tee'-nah], *f.* 1. Calf's foot jelly. 2. Gelatine.

Jalma [hahl'-mah], *f.* A kind of pack-saddle.

Jalmero [hal-may'-ro], *m.* One whose trade is to make pack saddles and harness for mules.

Jaloque [hah-lo'-kay], *m.* South-east wind. *V.* SIROCO.

Jallulo [hal-lyoo'-lo], *m.* (Prov.) Bread toasted in the ashes.

Jamaicano, na [hah-mah-e-cah'-no, nah], *a.* Jamaican, pertaining to Jamaica.

Jamaiquense, Jamaiqués, sa [hah-mah-e-ken'-say, kays', sah], *a.* & *m.* & *f.* Jamaican.

Jamás [hah-mahs'], *adv.* 1. Never, at no time. 2. (Obs.) Once. *Para siempre jamás*, Forever. (Vulg.) For ever and a day. *Jamás, por jamás* or *nunca jamás*, Never, nevermore.

Jamba [hahm'-bah], *f.* (Arch.) Door-jamb, window-post, which supports the lintel or head-piece.

Jambaje [ham-bah'-hay], *m.* (Arch.) Collection of jambs.

Jámbico, ca [hahm'-be-co, cah], *a.* Iambic. *V.* YÁMBICO.

Jamerdana [hah-mer-dah'-nah], *f.* Sewer which runs from a slaughter-house.

Jamerdar [hah-mer-dar'], *va.* 1. To clean the guts of animals. 2. To wash hastily.

Jamete [hah-may'-tay], *m.* A sort of stuff, formerly worn in Spain.

Jametería [hah-may-tay-ree'-ah], *f.* (Prov.) *V.* ZALAMERÍA.

Jamilla [hah-meel'-lyah], *f.* *V.* ALPECHÍN.

Jamón [hah-mone'], *m.* Ham, the salted thigh of a hog.

Jamona [hah-mo'-nah], *a.* A stout middle-aged woman. (Coll.) *Doncella jamona*, Old maid.

Jamuga, or **Jamugas** [hah-moo'-gah], *f.* A kind of side-saddle for women.

Jándalo, la [hahn'-dah-lo, lah], *a.* Having the gait and dialect of an Andalusian; particularly in giving the *h* a strong guttural sound.

Jangada [han-gah'-dah], *f.* Raft, a frame or float. *Jangada de perchas para arboladura*, (Naut.) Raft of spars for masting.

Jántio [hahn'-te-o], *m.* (Bot.) Lesser burdock. Xantium strumarium, *L.*

Japonense [hah-po-nen'-say], *a.* Japanese (person).

Japonés, sa [hah-po-nays', sah], *a.* Japanese, relating to Japan.

Jaque [hah'-kay], *m.* 1. Braggart, boaster. 2. Check, in the game of chess. *Jaque mate*, Checkmate. 3. Saddle-bag. 4. Sort of smooth combing of the hair. *Jaque de aquí*, Away from here, avaunt!

Jaquear [hah-kay-ar'], *va.* To give or make check at chess.

Jaqueca [hah-kay'-cah], *f.* Migrain headache, a severe headache.

Jaquel [hah-kayl'], *m.* Chessboard.

Jaquelado, da [hah-kay-lah'-do, dah], *a.* Checkered: applied to cut diamonds or precious stones.

Jaquero [hah-kay'-ro], *m.* Fine-toothed comb.

Jaqués, sa [hah-kess', sah], *a.* Applied to an ancient Spanish coin, struck at Jaca.

Jaqueta [hah-kay'-tah], *f.* Jacket, a short, loose coat, formerly worn in Spain.

Jaquetilla [hah-kay-teel'-lyah], *f. dim.* A small *jaqueta.*

Jaquetón [hah-kay-tone'], *m. aug.* 1. A large, wide coat. 2. Great swaggerer, boaster.

Jáquima [hah'-ke-mah], *f.* Headstall of a halter. (Arab.)

Jaquimazo [hah-ke-mah'-tho], *m.* 1. Stroke with the headstall of a halter. 2. Displeasure; an unfair trick, ill turn.

Jara [hah'-rah], *f.* 1. (Bot.) Cistus or rock-rose, labdanum-tree. Cistus ladamiferus. 2. A kind of dart or arrow. *Jara cerval*, (Bot.) Round-leaved cistus. Cistus globularifolius.

Jarabe [hah-rah'-bay], *m.* 1. Sirup, vegetable juice with sugar. 2. Any very sweet mixed drink, especially if not very cool. *Ser todo jarabe de pico*, To be readier with words than deeds. (Arab.)

Jarabear [hah-rah-bay-ar'], *va.* To prescribe sirups very often.—*vr.* To take sirups or sweet beverages frequently.

Jaraiz [hah-rah'-eeth], *m.* Pit for pressing grapes. (Arab. shawārif.)

Jaral [hah-rahl'], *m.* 1. Place planted with the cistus or labdanum shrub. 2. A very intricate or puzzling point.

Jaramago [hah-rah-mah'-go], *m.* (Bot.) All the species of cruciferous plants bearing yellow flowers; mustards.

Jarameño, ña [hah-rah-may'-nyo, nyah], *a.* Applied to bulls reared on the banks of the Jarama, a river in Spain.

Jaramugo [hah-rah-moo'-go], *m.* Small fish used as bait for others.

Jarana [hah-rah'-nah], *f.* 1. Carousal, revelry, romping. 2. (Coll.) Scuffle, contest. 3. Outcry. *No querer meterse en jaranas*, Not to like to get into scrapes.

Jarano [hah-rah'-no], *m.* Mexican wide-brimmed felt hat.

Jarapastroso, sa [hah-rah-pas-tro'-so, sah], *a.* Dialectic for *zarrapastroso* ragged.

Jarapote [hah-rah-po'-tay], *m.* (Prov.) *V.* JAROPEO.

Jarapotear [hah-rah-po-tay-ar'], *va.* (Prov.) To stuff or fill with medicinal drugs.

Jarazo [hah-rah'-tho], *m.* Blow or wound with a dart.

Jar[illegible]ia [har'-the-ah], *f.* 1. Parcel or b[illegible] of a variety of things laid by f[illegible] 2. A multitude of thingz w[illegible]er. 3. (Naut.) Tackle, rig[illegible]rdage belonging to a ship[illegible]ouds. 4. A complete fishing-tackle. *Jarcia de primera suerte*, Cordage of the first quality. *Almacén de jarcias*, Rigging-house, store-house for rigging. *Jarcias de respeto*, Spare rigging. *Tablas de jarcia*, Suit or set of rigging. *Jarcia viva*, The running rigging. *Jarcia muerta*, The standing rigging. *Jarcia mayor*, The main shrouds. *Jarcia de trinquete*, The fore shrouds. *Jarcia de mesana*, The mizzen shrouds. *Jarcia de gavia* or *del mastelero mayor*, The main-top shrouds. *Jarcia del juanete mayor*, The main-top-gallant shrouds.

Jardín [har-deen'], *m.* 1. A garden. 2. Spot which disfigures an emerald. 3. Privy on board of ships.

Jardincito, Jardinito [har-din-thee'-to, har-de-nee'-to], *m. dim.* A small garden.

Jardinería [har-de-nay-ree'-ah], *f.* Gardening, the art of cultivating gardens.

Jardinero, ra [har-de-nay'-ro, rah], *m.* & *f.* Gardener.—*f.* 1. Flower-stand, jardinière. 2. A basket carriage.

Jareta [hah-ray'-tah], *f.* 1. Seam made by doubling the edge of cloth, through which a string or lace may be drawn. 2. (Naut.) Netting, harpings. *Jaretas del pie de las arraigadas*, Cat harpings.

Jaretera [hah-ray-tay'-rah], *f.* *V.* JARRETERA.

Jarife [hah-ree'-fay], *m.* *V.* JERIFE.

Jarifo, fa [hah-ree'-fo, fah], *a.* Showy, full-dressed, adorned.

Jaripeo [ha-re-pay'-o], *m.* Rodeo.

Jaro, ra [hah'-ro, rah], *a.* Resembling a wild boar: applied to hogs.

Jarocho [hah-ro'-cho], *m.* 1. (Mex. Coll.) A rough, stout countryman. 2. Mulatto or negro.

Jaropar, Jaropear, or **Jaropotear** [hah-ro-par', hah-ro-po-tay-ar'], *va.* To stuff or fill with medicinal drugs; to give any liquor as a medical draught, to medicine.

Jarope [hah-ro'-pay], *m.* 1. Medical draught or potion. 2. Any kind of bitter beverage. 3. Sirup.

Jaropeo [hah-ro-pay'-o], *m.* The excessive and frequent use of bitters or medical potions; the drug habit.

Jarra [har'-rah], *f.* 1. Jug, jar, pitcher, of earthenware. 2. (Prov.) Ancient equestrian order. *En jarra* or *de jarras,* Akimbo. *Ponerse en jarras,* To set one's arms akimbo.

Jarrear [har-ray-ar'], *vn.* (Coll.) To take out often water or wine with a jug; to drink often.

Jarrero [har-ray'-ro], *m.* Vender or maker of jugs or jars.

Jarreta, illa, ita [har-ray'-tah, eel'-lyah, ee'-tah], *f. dim.* 1. A small jar. 2. (Naut.) Gratings.

Jarrete [har-ray'-tay], *m.* Ham, the upper part of the leg. *Tener bravos jarretes,* To have strong hams.

Jarretera [har-ray-tay'-rah], *f.* 1. Garter. 2. Garter, the highest order of English knighthood.

Jarrito [har-ree'-to], *m. dim.* A small jug or pot with one handle.

Jarro [har'-ro], *m.* 1. Jug or pot with one handle only, pitcher. 2. (Prov.) A chatterer.

Jarrón [har-rone'], *m. aug.* A large jug or pitcher, an urn.

Jaspe [hahs'-pay], *m.* Jasper, a precious stone.

Jaspeado, da [has-pay-ah'-do, dah], *a.* & *pp.* of JASPEAR. Spotted, like jasper; marbled, mottled, variegated.

Jaspeadura [has-pay-ah-doo'-rah], *f.* Marbling, the act of marbling.

Jaspear [has-pay-ar'], *va.* To marble, to paint, to vein or speckle with variegated colours in imitation of jasper.

Jasteo, tea [has-tay'-o, ah], *a.* Chasing the fox: applied to fox-dogs.

Jastial [has-te-ahl'], *m.* Façade of an edifice.

Jato, ta [hah'-to, tah], *m.* & *f.* *V.* BECERRO.

¡Jau! [hah'-oo], *int.* Exclamation to incite animals, especially bulls. Repeated signifies noisy applause.

Jauja [hah'-oo-hah], *pr. n.* *¿Estamos aquí, o en Jauja?* A rebuke or caution: take care!

Jaula [hah'-oo-lah], *f.* 1. Cage, an inclosure for birds. 2. Cell for insane persons.

Jaulón [hah-oo-lone'], *m. aug.* A large cage for birds.

Jauría [hah-oo-ree'-ah], *f.* Pack of hounds.

Jauto, ta [hah'-oo-to, tah], *a.* (Prov.) *V.* Soso.

Javanés, sa [hah-vah-nays', sah], *a.* Javanese, relating to Java.

Javo, va [hah'-vo, vah], *a.* Javan, native of or belonging to the island Java.

Javia, or **Javio arenillero** [hah'-ve-ah, or hah'-ve-o ah-ray-neel-lyay'-ro], *m.* The sand-box tree.

Jayán, na [hah-yahn', nah], *m.* & *f.* A tall, strong, and robust person.

Jayanazo [hah-ya-nah'-tho], *m. aug.* A huge, big fellow.

Jazilla [hah-theel'-lyah], *f.* Vestige, mark, trace. *V.* JACILLA.

Jazmín [hath-meen'], *m.* (Bot.) Jessamine or jasmine, a fragrant flower. Jasminum, *L.* *Jazmín real,* Catalonian jessamine. Jasminum grandiflorum. *Jazmín amarillo.* Italian jessamine. Jasminum humile. *Jazmín de Virginia,* Ash-leaved trumpet-flower. Bignonia radicans. *Jazmín oficinal* or *común,* Common white jessamine. Jasminum officinale. *Jazmín horro, V.* JAZMINORRO.

Jazminorro [hath-me-nor'-ro], *m.* (Bot.) Common yellow jessamine. Jasminum fructicans, *L.*

Jazz [yath], *m.* (Mus.) Jazz. *Jazz progresivo,* Progressive jazz.

Jea [hay'-ah], *f.* Import duty formerly paid for all goods imported from the Moorish dominions.

Jebe [hay'-bay], *m.* 1. (Prov.) Rock-alum. (Acad.) 2. (Peru.) Caoutchouc, India-rubber.

Jedive [hay-dee'-vay], or **Kedive,** *m.* Khedive, Viceroy of Egypt.

Jeera [hay-ay'-rah], *f.* Piece of drained marshy ground.

Jefatura [hay-fah-too'-rah], *f.* 1. The dignity of a chief, or governor of a province. 2. The place where the different offices of that government are kept.

Jefe, fa [hay'-fay, fah], *m.* & *f.* Chief, head, superior, leader. *Jefe de las caballerizas,* Master of the horse. *Jefe de escuadra,* (Naut.) Rear-admiral.

Jehová [hay-o-vah']. Hebrew word for God. Properly Yahweh.

Jeja [hay'-hah], *f.* In eastern Spain, white wheat.

¡Je, je, je! [hay], *int.* denoting laughter.

Jema [hay'-mah], *f.* The part of a beam which is badly squared.

Jemal [hay-mahl'], *a.* Of the length of a *jeme.*

Jeme [hay'-may], *m.* 1. The distance from the end of the thumb to the end of the forefinger (both extended). 2. (Coll.) A woman's face.

Jemoso, sa, *a.* Badly squared, with bark upon it.

Jenabe, Jenable [hay-nah'-bay, hay-nah'-blay], *m.* Mustard. *V.* MOSTAZA.

Jengibre [hen-hee'-bray], *m.* Ginger, the pungent, spicy rootstock of Zingiber officinale. Used as medicine and as a spice.

Jeniquén [hay-ne-ken'], *m.* Sisal hemp. *V.* HENEQUÉN.

Jeque [hay'-kay], *m.* 1. An old man; a governor or chief among the Moors. 2. Portmanteau.

Jera [hay'-rah], *f.* (Prov.) Extent of ground which can be ploughed in a day with a pair of oxen.

Jerapellina [hay-rah-pel lyee'-nah], *f.* An old ragged suit of clothes.

Jerarca [hay-rar'-cah], *m.* Hierarch: used of the Pope.

Jerarquía [hay-rar-kee'-ah], *f.* 1. Hierarchy, order among the various choirs of angels and ranks of the church. 2. By extension, a rank or grade of importance.

Jerárquico, ca [hay-rar'-ke-co, cah], *a.* Hierarchical, belonging to a hierarchy.

Jerezano, na [hay-ray-thah'-no, nah], *a.* & *m.* & *f.* Native of or belonging to Jerez de la Frontera.

Jerga [herr'-gah], *f.* 1. Coarse frieze, any coarse cloth. 2. Jargon, gibberish, unintelligible talk. *V.* JERIGONZA. 3. Large sack. *Estar* or *poner una cosa en jerga,* (Met.) To block out, to be begun, but not finished.

Jergón [her-gone'], *m.* 1. Large coarse mattress or sack, filled with straw or paper cuttings. 2. Suit of clothes ill made. 3. An ill-shaped person. 4. Kidderminster carpeting. 5. (Coll.) Paunch, belly. *Llenar el jergón,* To eat heartily.

Jerguilla [her-geel'-lyah], *f.* A sort of serge made of silk or worsted.

Jerife [hay-ree'-fay], *m.* Title of honour among the Moors.

Jerigonza [hay-re-gon'-thah], *f.* 1. Jargon, gibberish, especially of gipsies. 2. Language difficult to understand. 3. Strange and ridiculous action. *Andar en jerigonzas,* To quibble, to cavil.

Jeringa [hay-reen'-gah], *f.* Syringe, an instrument for injecting liquids into animal bodies, wounds, etc.

Jeringación [hay-rin-gah-the-on'], *f.* Syringing, the action and effect of the syringe; the liquid injected by this action.

Jeringar [hay-rin-gar'], *va.* To syringe, to inject by means of a syringe; to wash and cleanse by injections from a syringe.

Jeringazo [hay-rin-gah'-tho], *m.* 1. The act of injecting a liquid with the syringe. 2. Clyster, injection, the liquid substance injected with a syringe.

Jeringuilla [hay-rin-geel'-lyah], *f. dim.* A little syringe. *Jeringuilla,* A white flower of a very pungent odour.

Jeroglífico [hay-ro-glee'-fe-co], *m.* Hieroglyph, the symbol for a word; an ideograph, especially the sacred writing of the Egyptians.

Jeroglífico, ca, *a.* Hieroglyphic, hieroglyphical.

Jerosolimitano, na [hay-ro-so-le-me-tah'-no, nah], *a.* Native of Jerusalem.

Jerpa [herr'-pah], *f.* Sterile shoot of a vine.

Jerricote [her-re-co'-tay], *m.* A pottage of almonds, sugar, sage and ginger, in chicken broth.

Jerviguilla [her-ve-geel'-lyah], *f.* (obs.), or **Jervilla** [her-veel'-yah]. A kind of short boot.

Jesucristo [hay-soo-crees'-to], *m.* Jesus Christ.

Jesuita [hay-soo-ee'-tah], *m.* 1. Jesuit. 2. (Met. and Coll.) Hypocrite, one keen and astute in his own affairs.

Jesuítico, ca [hay-soo-ee'-te-co, cah], *a.* Jesuitical, relating to the Jesuits.

Jesuíticamente [hay-soo-ee'-te-cah men-tay], *adv.* Jesuitically.

Jesuitismo [hay-soo-e-tees'-mo], *m.* Jesuitism.

Jesús [hay-soos'], *m.* Jesus. *Decir los Jesuses,* To assist dying persons. *En un decir Jesús,* In an instant. *¡Jesús mil veces!* Good God! *No saber ni el Jesús,* Not to know even the alphabet, to be quite illiterate, uneducated.

Jesusear [hay-soo-say-ar'], *vn.* To repeat often the name of Jesus.

Jeta [hay'-tah], *f.* 1. Thick, heavy lips; blobber-lip. 2. A hog's snout.

Jeto [hay'-to], *m.* (Prov.) An empty bee-hive rubbed with honey to attract the bees.

Jetudo, da [hay-too'-do, dah], *a.* Thick-lipped.

Jiba [hee'-bah], *f.* 1. A hump. 2. Bother, tiresomeness.

Jibado, da [he-bah'-do, dah], *a.* Hump-backed, crooked.

Jibar [he-bar'], *va.* (Coll.) To vex, molest, annoy.

Jíbaro, ra [hee'-bah-ro, rah], *a.* (Cuba) 1. Run wild. 2. Rustic, rude.—*m.* Countryman.

Jibia [hee'-be-ah], *f.* (Zool.) Cuttle-fish. Sepia, *L.*

Jibión [he-be-on'], *m.* Cuttle-fish bone used by gold and silversmiths.

Jiboso, sa [he-bo'-so, sah], *a.* Gibbous, hump-backed.

Jícama [hee'-ca-mah], *f.* (Amer.) A farinaceous root. Bumelia solscifolia.

Jícara [hee'-ca-rah], *f.* 1. Chocolate-cup. 2. Gourd-tree. Crescentia cujete. (Aztec xicalli.)

Jicarazo [he-ca-rah'-tho], *m. aug.* A large chocolate cup. (Amer. Coll.) *Dar un jicarazo,* To give poison to a person.

Jicotea [he-co-tay'-ah], *f.* (Amer.) A mud-turtle.

Jifa [hee'-fah], *f.* Refuse of slaughtered beasts.

Jiferada [he-fay-rah'-dah], *f.* Stroke with a butcher's knife

Jifería [he-fay-ree'-ah], *f.* Slaughtering, the act of killing beasts for the shambles.

Jifero, ra [he-fay'-ro, rah], *a.* Belonging to the slaughter-house.

Jifero, *m.* 1. Butcher's knife. 2. Butcher.

Jifia [hee'-fe-ah], *f.* (Zool.) Xiphias, the sword-fish. Xiphias gladius, *L.*

Jiga [hee'-gah], *f.* Jig, a lively dance and tune.

Jigote [he-go'-tay], *m.* 1. Minced meat, stewed and dressed with butter; a hash. 2. Any other dish minced.

Jiguilete [he-gee-lay'-tay], *m.* Name given in India to the indigo-plant.

Jijallar [he-hal-lyar'], *m.* A place full of broom or cytisus.

Jijallo [he-hahl'-lyo], *m.* (Bot.) Prickly broom, hairy cytisus. Cytisus hirsutus.

Jijene [he-hay'-nay], *m.* (S. Amer.) Sand-fly.

Jijona [he-ho'-nah], *f.* A variety of flinty wheat. Triticum gærtnerianum jijona, *Lag.*

Jilguero [heel-gay'-ro], *m.* (Orn.) Linnet.

Jilocopo [he-lo-co'-po], *m.* The carpenter bee: xylocopa.

Jilote [he-lo'-tay], *m.* *V.* HELOTE.

Jimagua [he-mah'-goo-ah], *m.* & *f.* (Cuba) Twin.

Jimelga [he-mel'-gah], *f.* (Naut.) The fish of a mast. *Jimelgar un palo,* To fish a mast.

Jimenzar [he-men-thar'], *va.* (Prov.) To ripple flax or hemp.

Jinestada [he-nes-tah'-dah], *f.* Sauce made from milk, rice-flour, dates, spices and other things (figs and raisins).

Jineta [he-nay'-tah], *f.* 1. A kind of short lance anciently used. 2. Art of horsemanship. 3. The office of a sergeant. 4. Ancient tribute imposed upon cattle. *Andar a la jineta,* To go at a short trot. *Cabalgar a la jineta,* To ride with very short stirrups. *Tener los cascos a la jineta,* To be hare-brained, wild, giddy.

Jinete [he-nay'-tay], *m.* 1. Trooper, cavalryman. 2. One mounted on horseback, a horseman, cavalier.

Jinetear [he-nay-tay-ar'], *va.* (Mex.) To tame wild horses by riding them. 2. To ride on horseback, publicly, with ostentation.

Jinglar [hin-glar'], *vn.* To move from one side to another as if hung in a swing.

Jingoísmo [hin-go-ees'-mo], *m.* Jingoism, exaggerated patriotism.

Jingoísta [hin-go-ees'-tah], *a.* Jingoistic.—*m.* & *f.* Jingoist, ardent patriot.

Jinjol [heen-hole'], *m.* Jujube. *V.* AZUFAIFA.

Jipato, ta [he-pah'-to, tah], *a.* (Cuba) 1. Pale, of sickly countenance. 2. Full, replete with eating.

Jipijapa [he-pe-hah'-pah], *f.* 1. Fine straw, flexible and durable, used in weaving hats, cigar cases, dippers, etc. 2. Panama hat. *Sombrero de jipijapa,* Panama hat.

Jira [hee'-rah], *f.* 1. Strip of cloth. 2. Shred, tatter, scrap. 3. Picnic, outing. 4. Tour, excursion.

Jirafa [he-rah'-fah], *f.* 1. Giraffe. 2. Boom (for a microphone).

Jirapliega [he-rah-ple-ay'-gah], *f.* A purgative confection.

Jirasal [he-rah-sahl'], *f.* Fruit of the lac-tree.

Jirel [he-rel'], *m.* Rich trappings, caparison, for a horse.

Jiride [hee'-re-day], *f.* (Bot.) *V.* LIRIO HEDIONDO.

Jirofina [he-ro-fee'-nah], *f.* A kind of sauce or gravy.

Jiroflé [he-ro-flay'], *m.* The clove-tree.

Jirón [he-rone'], *m.* 1. Facing of a skirt. 2. Piece torn from a gown or other clothing. 3. Banner, pennant. 4. Small part of any whole. 5. (Peru) A long street, a row of houses.

Jironado, da [he-ro-nah'-do, dah], *a.* 1. Torn into strips or fragments. 2. Garnished with triangular pieces of cloth.

Jirpear [heer-pay-ar'], *va.* To dig about vines.

Jisca [hees'-cah], *f.* (Bot.) Cylindrical sugar-cane. *V.* CARRIZO.

Jiste [hees'-tay], *m.* Yeast, barm, leaven. Froth of beer. (Acad.)

Jitar [he-tar'], *va.* (Prov.) To emit, to turn out.

Jito [hee'-to], *m.* The channel by which melted metal runs, and the hole where it enters the mould.

¡Jo! [ho], *int.* Whoa!

Jobero, ra [ho-bay'-ro, rah], *a.* (Peru and Cuba) One who has a skin spotted with white and green: applied to negroes and horses. Among educated persons the word *overo* is used.

Jocó [ho-co'], *m.* *V.* ORANGUTÁN.

Jocosamente [ho-co-sah-men'-tay], *adv.* Jocosely, jocularly, waggishly, humorously, ludicrously, good humouredly.

Jocoserio, ria [ho-co-say'-re-o, ah], *a.* Jocoserious, partaking of mirth and seriousness.

Jocosidad [ho-co-se-dahd'], *f.* Jocularity, jocoseness, jocosity, waggery.

Jocoso, sa [ho-co'-so, sah], *a.* Jocose, jocular, waggish, facetious, ludicrous, good-humoured.

Jocoyote [ho-co-yo'-tay], *m.* (Amer.) The youngest child, best loved by the parents.

Jofaina [ho-fah'-e-nah], *f.* A china bowl. *V.* ALJOFAINA.

Jojoto [ho-ho'-to], *m.* (Ven.) Maize in the milk. (Acad.)

Jolgorio [hol-go'-re-o], *m.* (Coll.) 1. Recreation, relaxation. 2. Mirth, jollity.

Joliez [ho-le-eth'], *f.* (Obs.) Jollity, juvenile merriment.

Jolito [ho-lee'-to], *m.* Rest, leisure, calm. *Haber jolito,* (Naut.) To be becalmed; applied to a ship.

Jónico, ca, Jonio, nia [ho'-ne-co, cah, ho'-ne-o, ah], *a.* (Arch.) Ionic: applied to an order of architecture.—*m.* A foot in poetry.

Jonuco [ho-noo'-co], *m.* (Mex.) A dark, damp corner under a staircase.

Jordan [hor-dahn'], *m.* (Prov.) Any thing which revives, or gives a fresh bloom.

Jorfe [hor'-fay], *m.* 1. A wall made of dry stones only. 2. A high, solitary rock; a tor.

Jorfear [hor-fay-ar'], *va.* To form a floor without arches.

Jorguin [hor-geen'], *m.* (Prov.) Soot, condensed smoke.

Jorjina [hor-hee'-nah], *f.* Witch, sorceress, whose charms consist in soporiferous draughts.

Jornada [hor-nah'-dah], *f.* 1. March or journey performed in one day. 2. Journey, travel by land. 3. A military expedition. 4. Opportunity, occasion, circumstance. 5. Passage through life. 6. Act, one of the parts into which Spanish plays are divided. 7. Number of sheets printed off in a day. *A grandes* or *a largas jornadas,* With celerity and promptness, by forced marches. *Al fin de la jornada,* (Met.) At the end, at last.

Jornal [hor-nahl'], *m.* 1. Day-work, day-labour or journey-work, the work done by a workman hired by the day. 2. Day-wages, or wages paid to day-labourers for one day's work. *Mujer que trabaja a jornal,* Char-woman. *A jornal,* By the day. 3. (Com.) Journal, diary, a book used by merchants; it is a modern word.

Jornalero [hor-nah-lay'-ro], *m.* Day-labourer, journeyman.

Joroba [ho-ro'-bah], *f.* 1. Hump, a prominence on the back. 2. (Coll.) Importunity, incessant, troublesome solicitation.—*m.* & *f.* A worry, a bore.

Jorobado, da [ho-ro-bah'-do, dah], *a.* Crooked, gibbous, hump-backed or crook-backed.—*pp.* of JOROBAR.

Jorobar [ho-ro-bar'], *va.* (Coll.) To importune, to worry, to tease or harass by frequent repetition of the same request.

Jorro [hor'-ro], *m.* (Cuba) Bad tobacco.

Josa [ho'-sah], *f.* Piece of ground planted with vines and fruit-trees.

Jostrado, da [hos-trah'-do, dah], *a.* Round-headed: applied to a foil, shaft, or dart.

Jota [ho'-tah], *f.* 1. Name of the letter J. 2. Jot, tittle. 3. Spanish dance. *No saber una jota,* To be very ignorant of any thing.

Jovada [ho-vah'-dah], *f.* (Prov.) Ground which may be tilled by a pair of mules in one day.

Joven [ho'-ven], *a.* Young, youthful, juvenile.—*m.* & *f.* Youth, a stripling, a young man; a young woman; a young person.

Jovenado [ho-vay-nah'-do], *m.* The time or place in which young persons, after taking the vows, are under the direction of a master in convents.

Jovencillo, illa [ho-ven-theel'-lyo, eel'-lyah], *m.* & *f. dim.* Youngster.

Jovial [ho-ve-ahl'], *a.* 1. Jovial, under the influence of Jupiter. 2. Jovial, gay, airy, merry, cheerful.

Jovialidad [ho-ve-ah-le-dahd'], *f.* Joviality, jollity, mirth, merriment, gaiety, good-humour, festivity.

Joya [ho'-yah], *f.* 1. Jewel, a precious stone set in gold or silver. 2. Any thing well polished and finished. 3. Present, gift. 4. Astragal, a convex architectural moulding.—*pl.* Jewels, trinkets; all the wearing apparel and ornaments of women, especially of brides.

Joyante [ho-yahn'-tay], *a.* Extremely glossy: applied to silks. *Pólvora joyante,* Refined gunpowder.

Joyel [ho-yel'], *m.* A small jewel.

Joyera [ho-yay'-rah], *f.* Woman who keeps a jeweller's shop.

Joyería [ho-yay-ree'-ah], *f.* Jeweller's shop.

Joyero [ho-yay'-ro], *m.* Jeweller.

Joyita [ho-yee'-tah], *f. dim.* *V.* JOYUELA.

Joyo [ho'-yo], *m.* (Bot.) Bearded darnel, darnel-grass. Lolium temulentum, *L.*

Joyuela [ho-yoo-ay'-lah], *f. dim.* Jewel of small value.

Juaguarzo [hoo-ah-goo-ar'-tho], *m.* (Bot.) Montpellier rock-rose. Cistus monspeliensis, *L.*

Juan [hoo-ahn'], *m.* John. *Buen Juan* or *Juan de buena alma,* A poor, silly fellow. *Hacer San Juan,* To leave a place before the expiration of the time agreed upon: applied to servants. *Juan Lanas,* (Low) A simpleton.

Juanete [hoo-ah-nay'-tay], *m.* 1. The knuckle-bone of the great toes, especially when it sticks out more than usual. A bunion. 2. Prominent check-bones. 3. (Naut.) A gallant sail. *Juanete mayor*, Main-top-gallant sail. *Juanete de sobremesana*, Mizzen-top-gallant sail.

Juanetero [hoo-ah-nay-tay'-ro], *m.* A young marine apprentice who is occupied in furling and loosening the top-gallant sails.

Juanetudo, da [hoo-ah-nay-too'-do, dah], *a.* Applied to persons who have the knuckle-bone of the great toes very protuberant.

Juarda [hoo-ar'-dah], *f.* Stain in cloth, occasioned by the wool having imbibed too much oil before it was carded and spun.

Juardoso, sa [hoo-ar-do'-so, sah], *a.* Stained, spotted: applied to woollen cloth.

Jubarba [hoo-bar'-bah], *f.* Houseleek.

Jubertar [hoo-ber-tar'], *va.* (Naut.) To hoist the boat on board.

Jubetería [hoo-bay-tay-ree'-ah], *f.* Shop where jackets and doublets are sold; a slop-shop.

Jubetero [hoo-bay-tay'-ro], *m.* One who makes and sells jackets and doublets.

Jubilación [hoo-be-lah-the-on'], *f.* The act and effect of pensioning off or of superannuating a placeman; an exemption from the duties of a professorship, charge, etc., without losing all the salary belonging to it.

Jubilar [hoo-be-lar'], *va.* 1. To pension off; to superannuate; to exempt any one from the duties of a charge. 2. To exempt from toil and labour. 3. To lay aside as useless.—*vn.* To become a pensioner in consequence of having been exempted from the labour or burden of a charge, office, or ministry.

Jubileo [hoo-be-lay'-o], *m.* Jubilee, a public festivity; concession of plenary indulgence; an ecclesiastical solemnity, celebrated by the Jews every fifty years. *Por jubileo*, Rarely, happening seldom.

Júbilo [hoo'-be-lo], *m.* Glee, joy, merriment, rejoicing, festivity, hilarity, mirth.

Jubiloso, sa [hoo-be-lo'-so, sah], *a.* Gleeful, joyful.

Jubón [hoo-bone'], *m.* 1. Doublet, jacket. 2. The waist in female dress. *Jubón de azotes*, (Coll.) A public whipping.

Juboncito [hoo-bon-thee'-to], *m. dim.* A small jupon or jacket, a doublet of little value.

Jubonero [hoo-bo-nay'-ro], *m.* Maker of jackets, doublets, or jupons.

Jucla [hoo'-clah], *f.* A sign which the Arabs place over consonants to replace the vowels which they lack.

Judaico, ca [hoo-dah'-e-co, cah], *a.* Judaical, Jewish, relating to the Jews.

Judaísmo [hoo-dah-ees'-mo], *m.* Judaism, religion of the Jews.

Judaizante [hoo-dah-e-thahn'-tay], *pa.* & *m.* Judaizing, Judaizer, one who Judaizes.

Judaizar [hoo-dah-e-thar'], *va.* To Judaize, to observe the rites of the Jews.

Judas [hoo'-das], *m.* 1. One that treacherously deceives his friend, an impostor, traitor. 2. Silk-worm that does not spin. 3. Effigy of Judas burnt in the streets in the Spanish towns during Lent.

Judería [hoo-day-ree'-ah], *f.* Jewry; a quarter of the town where the Jews live; tax on Jews.

Judía [hoo-dee'-ah], *f.* 1. (Bot.) French bean, kidney-bean. Phaseolus vulgaris, *L. Judía de careta*, Kind of small spotted French beans. 2. Jewess, a Hebrew woman.

Judiada [hoo-de-ah'-dah], *f.* 1. An inhuman action. 2. Excessive and scandalous profit.

Judicante [hoo-de-cahn'-tay], *m.* (Prov.) Judge appointed to inquire into the conduct and proceedings of officers of justice.

Judicar [hoo-de-car'], *va.* (Obs.) *V.* JUZGAR.

Judicatura [hoo-de-cah-too'-rah], *f.* 1. Judicature, the power and act of administering justice. 2. Dignity of a judge.

Judicial [hoo-de-the-ahl'], *a.* Judicial, juridical, practised in the distribution of justice or used in courts of justice.

Judicialmente [hoo-de-the-al-men'-tay], *adv.* Judicially.

Judiciaria [hoo-de-the-ah'-re-ah], *f.* Judiciary astrology.

Judiciario, ria [hoo-de-the-ah'-re-o, ah], *a.* Astrological, professing the art of foretelling future events.

Judicioso, sa [hoo-de-the-o'-so, sah], *a.* (Obs.) Judicious. *V.* JUICIOSO.

Judiega [hoo-de-ay'-gah], *f.* Kind of olives, good for making oil, but not for eating.

Judihuelo, la [hoo-de-oo-ay'-lo, lah], *m.* & *f.* 1. A young Jew or Jewess. 2. French bean.

Judío, día [hoo-dee'-o, ah], *a.* Judaical, Jewish.

Judío [hoo-dee'-o], *m.* 1. Jew. 2. Appellation given by boys to the trumpeters who attend the processions in the holy week. 3. Word of contempt used by angry persons. *Judío de señal*, Converted Jew, who, living among Christians, wears a mark on his shoulder.

Judión [hoo-de-on'], *m.* A large sort of French beans. Dutch kidney-beans. Phaseolus multiflorus, *L.*

Juego [hoo-ay'-go], *m.* 1. Play, amusement, diversion, sport. 2. Game, gaming, gambling. *Juego de suerte y ventura*, Game of hazard or chance. 3. A set of good cards. 4. Manner of acting of an engine. 5. Set, a number of things suited to each other; or a number of things of which one cannot conveniently be separated from the rest. *Juego de cajoncitos*, A nest of small boxes. 6. Disposition, ability, or artfulness to obtain or prevent any end or object. 7. Method, convenient order. 8. Running gear of a vehicle. *Juego de palabras*, A pun, a quibble. *Juego de bochas*, A bowling alley. *Juego de bolos*, Nine-pins. *Juego de manos*, Juggling feat, legerdemain. *Juego de pelota*, Tennis court. *Juego de velas*, A set or complete suit of sails. *Juego de niños*, Play-game. *Juego de prendas*, Forfeits. *Tener juego*, (Naut.) To have fetched way; not to be firm or steady. *El palo mayor tiene juego en su fogonadura*, The main-mast has fetched way in its partners. *Juegos*, Public feasts, exhibitions, or rejoicings. *Juego trasero*, Hind part of a four-wheeled carriage. *Por juego* or *por modo de juego*, In jest, in joke, in fun. *Entrar en juego*, To come in play. *Hacer juego*, To match, to suit, to fit. *Conocer el juego*, (Met.) To discover any one's designs.

(*Yo juego, yo juegue*, from *Jugar. V.* JUGAR.)

Jueguecico, illo, ito [hoo-ay-gay-thee'-co, eel'-lyo, ee'-to], *m.* A little game, a bit of play.

Juerga [hoo-er'-gah], *f.* (coll.) Carousal, revel, spree.

Jueves [hoo-ay'-ves], *m.* Thursday. *Cosa del otro jueves*, Something that is seldom seen. *Jueves de comadres*, The penultimate Thursday before carnival. *Jueves de compadres*, The antepenultimate Thursday before Lent.

Juez [hoo-eth'], *m.* 1. Judge, one invested with power and authority to decide and determine causes and lawsuits. 2. Judge, one who has sufficient skill to form a correct opinion or judgment of the merit of any thing. *Juez árbitro*, Arbitrator, umpire. *Juez de enquesta*, In Arragon, a judge whose duty was to investigate the conduct and decisions of judges, ministers of justice, notaries, solicitors, etc., and to punish them if guilty, by virtue of his office, and not at the instance of others. *Juez de letras* or *juez letrado*, A justice of the peace of a small district, who, being a counsellor at law, has more authority in certain cases than other justices. *Juez de primera instancia*, Judge of the primary court of claims.

Jugada [hoo-gah'-dah], *f.* 1. Play, the act of playing, a throw. 2. The act of playing a card. 3. Ill turn, wicked trick.

Jugadera [hoo-gah-day'-rah], *f.* Shuttle used to make net-work. *V.* LANZADERA.

Jugador, ra [hoo-gah-dor', rah], *m.* & *f.* 1. Player, one who plays. 2. Gamester, gambler. *Jugador de manos*, Juggler, one who practises sleight of hand, or plays tricks by legerdemain.

Jugano [hoo-gah'-no], *m.* (Ec.) A solid wood of Guayaquil employed in ship-building.

Jugar [hoo-gar'], *va.* & *vn.* 1. To play, to sport, to frolic, to trifle, to toy. 2. To play, to game, to contend at some game. 3. To gamble, to game, to play extravagantly for money, to lose at play. 4. To put in action or motion: speaking of a part of the body. 5. To make use of weapons. 6. To move on joints or hinges. 7. To intervene; to take an active part in an affair, to exercise. 8. To mock, to make game of. *Jugar los años*, To play without gambling. *Jugársela de codillo*, To outwit a person. *Jugar a cara o lis*, or *a cara o cruz*, To bet on the toss of a coin. *Ni juega, ni da de barato*, (Fig. and coll.) Indifferent, not taking sides.

Jugarreta [hoo-gar-ray'-tah], *f.* (Coll.) Bad play, unskilful manner of playing.

Juglándeo, dea [hoo-glahn'-day-o, ah], *a.* Belonging to the walnut family.

Juglar [hoo-glar'], *m.* Buffoon, mimic, juggler, mountebank.

Juglara, Juglaresa [hoo-glah'-rah, hoo-glah-ray'-sah], *f.* A female buffoon or mimic.

Juglería [hoo-glay-ree'-ah], *f.* (Obs.) Buffoonery, mimicry.

Jugo [hoo'-go], *m.* 1. Sap, juice of plants. 2. Juice, moisture. 3. (Met.) Marrow, pith, substance of any thing.

Jugosidad [hoo-go-se-dahd'], *f.* Sappiness, succulence, juiciness.

Jugoso, sa [hoo-go'-so, sah], *a.* Sappy, juicy, succulent.

Juguete [hoo-gay'-tay], *m.* 1. Toy, plaything, gewgaw, trinket. 2. Jest, joke. *Por juguete*, Jestingly. 3. Carol, a song of joy and exultation.

Juguetear [hoo-gay-tay-ar'], *vn.* To trifle, to fool, to toy, to frolic, to sport, to dally, to wanton, to play childish tricks.

Juguetón, na [hoo-gay-tone', nah], *a.* Playful, acting the buffoon, wanton, playsome.

Juicio [hoo-ee'-the-o], *m.* 1. Judgment, the power of judging; the act of judging. 2. Sense, soundness of faculties, strength of natural reason. 3. Judgment, notion, opinion. 4. Prudence, wisdom: applied to practice. 5. Judgment, the act of exercising judicature. 6. Forecast of the events of a year made by astrologers. *Pedir en juicio*, To sue at law. *Ser un juicio*, (Coll.) To be a confused multitude of persons or things. *No estar en su juicio*, To be out of one's senses. *Tener mucho juicio*, To be sedate, steady, well-behaved. *No tener juicio*, To be wild; to be a harum-scarum fellow. *Sano de juicio*, (Law) Perfectly sound in mind. *Asentar el juicio*, To begin being sensible and judicious. *Cargar el juicio*, To reflect attentively.

Juiciosamente [hoo-e the-o-sah-men'-tay], *adv.* Judiciously, considerately.

Juicioso, sa [hoo-e-the-o'-so, sah], *a.* Judicious, prudent, mature, clear-sighted.

Julepe [hoo-lay'-pay], *m.* 1. Julep, a sirup-like medical potion. 2. (Fig. and coll.) Reprimand, punishment. (Arab., fr. Per.)

Juliano, na [hoo-le-ah'-no, nah], *a.* Julian, relating to Julius Cæsar, or instituted by him.

Julio [hoo'-lee-o], *m.* July, the seventh month of the year.

Julo [hoo'-lo], *m.* 1. Bell-mule, that takes the lead of a sumpter's or carrier's mules. 2. Male which guides the flocks of goats, sheep, or cattle. 3. Iulus, a myriapod.

Jumá [hoo-mah'], *m.* Mohammedan name of Friday (*i. e.*, day of assembly).

Jumenta [hoo-men'-tah], *f.* Female ass.

Jumental, or **Jumentil** [hoo-men-tahl', teel'], *a.* Belonging to the ass.

Jumentillo, illa, ito, ita [hoo-men-teel'-lyo, lyah, ee'-to, tah], *m.* & *f. dim.* A little ass or beast of burden.

Jumento [hoo-men'-to], *m.* 1. Beast of burden. 2. Ass, jument. 3. A stupid person. *V.* Asno.

Juncáceas [hoon-cah'-thay-as], *f. pl.* Juncaceæ, the rush family of plants.

Juncada [hoon-cah'-dah], *f.* 1. Kind of fritters. 2. A horse medicine against the glanders.

Juncago [hoon-cah'-go], *m.* (Bot.) Bastard rush.

Juncal, Juncar [hoon-cahl'], *m.* Marshy ground full of rushes.

Júnceo, a [hoon'-thay-o, ah], *a.* Rush-like.—*f. pl.* The rush family.

Juncia [hoon'-the-ah], *f.* (Bot.) Cyperus, a sedge, the root of which serves for fumigation. *Vender juncia*, To boast, to brag. *Juncia olorosa*, Sweet cyperus, English galangal. Cyperus longus. *Juncia avellanada* or *redonda*, Round-rooted cyperus, the round cyperus. Cyperus rotundus. *Juncia comestible*. *V.* Chufas.

Junciana [hoon-the-ah'-nah], *f.* Brag, boast.

Junciera [hoon-the-ay'-rah], *f.* An earthen vessel with a perforated lid, in which aromatics are kept.

Juncino, na [hoon-thee'-no, nah], *a.* Rushy, consisting of rushes.

Juncir [hoon-theer'], *va.* (Obs.) *V.* Uncir.

Junco [hoon'-co], *m.* 1. (Bot.) Rush. Juncus. *Junco de esteras*, Soft rush. Juncus effusus. *Junco de flor* or *florido*, Umbelled flowering rush. Butomus umbellatus. 2. Junk, Chinese ship.

Juncoso, sa [hoon-co'-so, sah], *a.* Full of rushes, resembling rushes; juncous.

Junio [hoo'-ne-o], *m.* June, the sixth month of the year.

Junior [hoo'-ne-or], *m.* In convents, one still subject to instruction.

Junípero [hoo-nee'-pay-ro], *m.* *V.* Enebro.

Junquera [hoon-kay'-rah], *f.* (Bot.) Rush.

Junqueral [hoon-kay-rahl'], *m.* *V.* Juncal.

Junquillo [hoon-keel'-lyo], *m.* 1. (Bot.) Jonquil. Narcissus junquilla, *L.* 2. A small round moulding.

Junta [hoon'-tah], *f.* 1. Junta or junto, a congress, an assembly, a council, a convention, a tribunal. 2. Any meeting of persons to speak about business. 3. Conjunction, union, junction, concession, fraternity. 4. Each lateral surface of a square hewed stone. *Junta de médicos*, A consultation. *Junta de comercio*, Board of trade. *Junta de sanidad*, Board of health.

Juntador, ra [hoon-tah-dor', rah], *m.* & *f.* Joiner, one who joins.

Juntamente, *adv.* Jointly; at the same time, conjunctively.

Juntar [hoon-tar'], *va.* 1. To join, to conjoin, to combine, to coalesce, to connect, to unite. 2. To join, to convoke, to couple; to associate, to consociate, to congregate. 3. To amass, to collect, to heap, to gather, to lay up.—*vr.* 1. To join, to meet, to assemble, to concur. 2. To be closely united. 3. To copulate. *Juntar meriendas*, (Coll.) To unite interests.

Juntera [hoon-tay'-rah], *f.* Carpenter's plane, jointer.

Junterilla [hoon-tay-reel'-lyah], *f. dim.* Small plane.

Junto, ta [hoon'-to, tah], *a.* & *pp. irr.* of Juntar. United, conjoined, annexed.

Junto [hoon'-to], *adv.* Near, close to, at hand, near at hand; at the same time. *Por junto* or *de por junto*, In the bulk, by the lump, wholesale. *En junto*, Together, in all.

Juntorio [hoon-to'-re-o], *m.* (Obs.) Kind of tribute.

Juntura [hoon-too'-rah], *f.* 1. Juncture, the part at which two things are joined together, joining. 2. Joint, articulation of limbs; juncture of movable bones in animal bodies. 3. (Naut.) Scarf. *Juntura de las plantas*, Knuckle.

Júpiter [hoo'-pe-ter], *m.* 1. Jupiter, a planet. 2. Among chemists, tin.

Jura [hoo'-rah], *f.* 1. Oath, an affirmation, negation, or promise, corroborated by the attestation of the Divine Being. 2. Oath of allegiance.

Jurado [hoo-rah'-do], *m.* 1. Jury, a certain number of persons sworn to declare the truth upon such evidence as shall be given before them. 2. Juror, juryman, one serving in a jury. 3. Jurat, a magistrate in some corporations.

Jurador, ra [hoo-rah-dor', rah], *m.* & *f.* Swearer, profane swearer.

Juraduría [hoo-rah-doo-ree'-ah], *f.* Office of a jurat.

Juramentar [hoo-rah-men-tar'], *va.* To swear, to put to an oath.—*vr.* To bind one's self by an oath, to obtest by an oath.

Juramento [hoo-rah-men'-to], *m.* 1. Oath, an affirmation, negation, or promise, corroborated by the attestation of the Divine Being. 2. Oath, curse, imprecation: commonly used in the plural in this last sense. *Juramento asertorio*, Declaratory oath.

Jurar [hoo-rar'], *va.* To obtest some superior power; to attest the great name; to promise upon oath; to swear, to make oath.

Jurásico, ca [hoo-rah'-se-co, cah], *a.* Jurassic, relating to the mountains of Jura.

Juratoria [hoo-rah-to'-re-ah], *f.* (Prov.) Plate of silver containing the holy evangelists, on which magistrates lay their hands in taking an oath.

Juratoria [hoo-rah-to' re-ah], *a.* *Caución* or *fianza juratoria*, Juratory security, an oath taken by a poor person to return to prison when called, having no bail.

Juratorio [hoo-rah-to'-re-o], *m.* Instrument setting forth the oaths taken by Arragonese magistrates.

Jurdía [hoor-dee'-ah], *f.* Kind of fishing-net.

Jurel [hoo-rel'], *m.* A spiny sea-fish of the mackerel family.

Jurguina, or **Jurgina** [hoor-gee'-nah, hoor-hee'-nah], *f.* Witch, sorceress.

Jurídicamente [hoo-ree'-de-cah-men-tay], *adv.* Lawfully, legally, juridically.

Jurídico, ca [hoo-ree'-de-co, cah], *a.* Lawful, legal, juridical; done according to law.

Jurisconsulto [hoo-ris-con-sool'-to], *m.* 1. Jurisconsult, one who gives his opinion in law. 2. Civilian, civilist. 3. Jurist, a lawyer.

Jurisdicción [hoo-ris-dic-the-on'], *f.* 1. Jurisdiction, legal authority, extent of judicial power; power, authority. 2. Jurisdiction, district to which any judicial authority extends. 3. Boundary of some place or province.

Jurisdiccional [hoo-ris-dic-the-o-nahl'], *a.* Jurisdictional, relating to jurisdiction.

Jurisperito [hoo-ris-pay-ree'-to], *m.* A professor of jurisprudence.

Jurisprudencia [hoo-ris-proo-den'-the-ah], *f.* Jurisprudence, law, or the science of law.

Jurisprudente [hoo-ris-proo-den'-tay], *m.* *V.* Jurisconsulto.

Jurista [hoo-rees'-tah], *m.* 1. Jurist, lawyer, a man who professes the science of law. 2. Pensioner, one who has an annuity assigned to him upon the revenue of the crown.

Juro [hoo'-ro], *m.* 1. Right of perpetual property. 2. Annuity assigned upon the revenue of the crown. *De juro*, Certainly.

Jusbarba [hoos-bar'-bah], *f.* (Bot.) Field myrtle. Ruscus aculeatus, *L.*

Jusello [hoo-sel'-lyo], *m.* Pottage made of broth, parsley, grated cheese, eggs, and spice.

Jusi [hoo'-se], *m.* A delicate vegetable fibre of the Philippine Islands used for dresses.

Justa [hoos'-tah], *f.* 1. Joust, tilt, tournament. 2. Literary contest in poetry or prose.

Justador [hoos-tah-dor'], *m.* Tilter, one who plays at jousts.

Justamente [hoos-tah-men'-tay], *adv.* Justly, just, exactly; precisely, fairly.

Justar [hoos-tar'], *vn.* To joust, to tilt.

Justicia [hoos-tee'-the-ah], *f.* 1. Justice, giving to every man his due. 2. Justice, the attribute of God according to which he arranges all things. 3. Reason, honesty; equity; right. 4. Retribution, punishment.—*m.* Justice, magistrate or tribunal. *Justicia de Aragón*, (Obs.) The chief magistrate of Arragon. *Justicia mayor*, (Obs.) The lord chief-justice of Spain. *De justicia*, According to justice, duly, meritedly.

Justiciero, ra [hoos-te-the-ay'-ro, rah], *a.* One who rigorously observes justice; one who chastises crimes with rigid justice.

Justificación [hoos-te-fe-cah-the-on'], *f.* 1. Justification, defence, maintenance, support. 2. Production of the documents or instruments tending to establish a claim or right. 3. Equity conformity with justice. 4. Sanctification by grace. 5. (Print.) Adjustment of lines in a page of types.

Justificadamente [hoos-te-fe-cah-dah-men'-tay], *adv.* Justly, correctly, justifiably.

Justificado, da [hoos-te-fe-cah'-do, dah], *a.* Equal, justified; conformable to justice.—*pp.* of JUSTIFICAR.

Justificador [hoos-te-fe-cah-dor'], *m* Justifier, justificator. *V.* SANTIFICADOR.

Justificante [hoos-te-fe-cahn'-tay], *pa.* Justifying; justifier.

Justificar [hoos-te-fe-car'], *va.* 1. To justify, to free from past sin, to render just. 2. To justify, to clear from imputed guilt; to absolve from an accusation; to exculpate. 3. To prove or establish a claim in a court of judicature. 4. To prove or show by argument or testimony. 5. To justify, to rectify, to adjust, to arrange, to regulate exactly. 6. (Print.) To justify or equalize the spaces between the words in a line of types.—*vr.* To vindicate one's character, to clear one's self from imputed guilt.

Justificativo, va [hoos-te-fe-cah-tee'-vo, vah], *a.* Justificative, justifying, justificatory.

Justillo [hoos-teel'-lyo], *m.* Jacket without sleeves; inner waist of a dress; corset-cover.

Justipreciar [hoos-te-pray-the-ar'], *va.* To estimate any thing.

Justipreciador [hoos-te-pray-the-ah-dor'], *m.* Appraiser, a person appointed to set a price upon things.

Justiprecio [hoos-te-pray'-the-o], *m.* Appraisement, just valuation.

Justo, ta [hoos'-to, tah], *a.* 1. Just, conformable to justice, rightful, lawful; fair. 2. Just, upright. 3. Just, honest, honourable, good, faithful. 4. Just, exact, strict, punctual. 5. Just, fit, tight, close, exactly proportioned. 6. Just, good, pious.

Justo [hoos'-to], *m.* A just and pious man. *En justos y en verenjustos,* (Coll.) Right or wrong, with reason or without.

Justo [hoos'-to], *adv.* Tightly, straitly. *Al justo,* Fitly, duly; completely, punctually.

Juta [hoo'-tah], *f.* (Orn.) A kind of American goose.

Jutía [hoo-tee'-ah], *f.* *V.* HUTÍA.

Juvenco, ca [hoo-ven'-co, cah], *m.* & *f.* (Obs.) *V.* NOVILLO.

Juvenil [hoo-vay-neel'], *a.* Juvenile, young, youthful; girlish.

Juventud [hoo-ven-tood'], *f.* Youthfulness, youth, juvenility.

Juzgado [hooth-gah'-do], *m.* Tribunal, court of justice; judicature.

Juzgador, ra [hooth-gah-dor', rah], *m.* & *f.* Judge, one who judges.

Juzgamundos [hooth-gah-moon'-dos], *m.* & *f.* One who censures the actions of every one but himself.

Juzgante [hooth-gahn'-tay], *pa.* Judging; judge.

Juzgar [hooth'-gar'], *va* & *vn.* 1. To judge, to pass sentence upon, to give judgment. 2. To judge, to apprehend, to form or give an opinion, to opine, to hold, to find.

K

K, twelfth letter of the alphabet, and ninth of the consonants. It was used anciently, but has no longer any use in Spanish except in words taken from other languages. It has the same sound as in English. **K** in chemistry is the symbol of potassium. (Kalium.)

Ka [kah], *f.* Name of the letter K.

Kabila [kah-bee'-lah], *f.* A tribe of Barbary, living in the Atlas region.

Kahué [kah-oo-ay'], *m.* Arabic name of coffee.

Káiser [kah'-e-ser], *m.* Kaiser,

Kaki or **caqui** [kah'-ke], *a.* Khaki.

Kaleidoscopio [ka-lay-e-dos-co'-pe-o], *m.* *V.* CALIDOSCOPIO.

Kalenda [ka-len'-dah], *f.* Kalends. V. CALENDA.

Kalmuco, ca [kal-moo'-co, cah], *a.* & *n.* Kalmuck, a race of Western Mongols. *V.* CALMUCO.

Kan [kahn], or **Khan**, *m.* Khan, chief or prince among the Tartars. (Per. khān.)

Kanna [kahn'-nah], *f.* Canna, a root very esteemed by the Hottentots as the best of stomachics. It resembles ginseng.

Kantiano, na [kan-te-ah'-no, nah], *a.* Kantian, relating to the philosophy of Kant.

Kantismo [kan-tees'-mo], *m.* Kantism, the philosophic system of Kant.

Keralila [kay-rah-lee'-lah], *f.* (Mex.) Horny flint.

Kermes [kerr'-mes], *m.* 1. *V.* QUÉRMES. 2. Kermes mineral, an impure antimony sulphide.

Kilo [kee'-lo], *m.* A prefix from the Greek signifying a thousand-fold.—*m.* (Com.) Kilogramme, an abbreviation.

Kilociclo [ke-lo-thee'-clo], *m.* Kilocycle

Kilográmetro [ke-lo-grah'-may-tro], *m.* Kilogrammeter, the unit of force required to raise a kilogramme one metre in one second (7.2 foot-pounds).

Kilogramo [ke-lo-grah'-mo], *m.* Kilogram(me), a metric unit of weight, 1,000 grammes (2⅕ lbs.).

Kilolitro [ke-lo-lee'-tro], *m.* Kilolitre, the measure of 1,000 litres.

Kilometraje [ke-lo-may-trah'-hay], *m.* Length or distance in kilometers, mileage.

Kilométrico, ca [ke-lo-may'-tre-co, cah], *a.* Kilometric. *Discurso kilométrico,* long-winded speech

Kilómetro [ke-lo'-may-tro], *m.* Kilometre, the distance of 1,000 metres, chief unit of long distance in the metric system; about five-eighths of a mile. A Spanish league slightly exceeds five and a half kilometres.

Kilotón [ke-lo-ton'], *m.* or **Kilotonelada** [ke-lo-to-nay-lah'-da], *f.* Kiloton.

Kilovatio [ke-lo-vah'-te-o], Kilowatt.

Kilovoltamperio [ke-lo-vol-tam-pay'-re-o], m. Kilovolt-ampere.

Kilovoltio [ke-lo-vol'-te-o], *m.* Kilovolt.

Kinoscopio [ke-nos-co'-pe-o], *m.* Kinescope.

Kiosco [ke-os'-co], *m.* 1. Kiosk, an open, small pavilion, designed, according to the custom of orientals, for taking refreshment in the middle of the day. 2. Kiosk, a news-stand, etc., in imitation of the foregoing. (Turk.)

Kirie [kee'-re-ay], *m.* Kyrie (eleison) the first movement in the mass, after the introit. (Greek Κύριε.)

Kirieleisón [ke-re-ay-lay-e-sone'], *m.* 1. *V.* KIRIE. 2. (Coll.) Funeral chant.

Kirsch (or **Kirschwasser**), *m.* Kirschwasser, a cordial distilled from the European wild cherry. (Ger.)

Kopú [ko-poo'], *m.* A Chinese fabric.

Krausismo [krah-oo-sees'-mo], *m.* Krausism, the philosophic system of Krause.

Kremlín [krem-leen'], *m.* A Slavic word which signifies fortress. In particular. the citadel of this name in Moscow (Russian kremli.)

Kurdo, da [koor'-do, dah], *a.* Kurdish, or Kurd; native of or belonging to Kurdistán.

L

L [ay'-lay] is in the Spanish language a semi-vowel, and sometimes becomes a liquid when a mute letter precedes it; *e. g.* in the words *claustro, gloria, flueco.* The *l* always keeps the same sound as in English. **L** as a numeral stands for fifty.

La [lah], *def. art. fem. sing.* The.

La [lah], *pron. pers. acc. f. sing.* Her, it.

La [lah], *m.* (Mus.) La, the sixth sound of the hexachord.

L.A.B., Abbreviation of *Libre a bordo.* F.O.B. Free on board.

Laberinto [lah-bay-reen'-to], *m.* 1. Labyrinth, maze. 2. An intricate and obscure matter, hard to be understood; maze, uncertainty, perplexity. 3. (Anat.) Labyrinth of the ear.

Labia [lah'-be-ah], *f.* (Coll.) Sweet, winning eloquence.

Labiado, da [lah-be-ah'-do, dah], *a.* (Bot.) Labiate.

Labial [lah-be-ahl'], *a.* Labial, uttered by the lips: applied to letters.

Labiérnago [lah-be-ayr'-nah-go], *m.* A shrub with lanceolate, shining leaves.

Labihendido, da [lah-be-en-dee'-do, dah], *a.* Hare-lipped.

Labio [lah'-be-o], *m.* 1. The lip. 2. Lip, the edge of any thing. *Labio hendido,* Hare-lip.

Labiodental [lah-be-o-den-tahl'], *a.* Labiodental.

Labionasal [lah-be-o-nah-sahl'], *a.* Labio-nasal.

Labor [lah-bor'], *f.* 1. Labour, task, the act of doing what requires an exertion of strength. 2. Labour, work to be done, work done. 3. Symmetry, adaptation of parts to each other; design. 4. A seamstress's work, any kind of needle-work, embroidery. *Labor de retacitos* or *de taracea,* Patch-work. *Labor blanca,* White work. *Ir a la labor,* To go to school: speaking of girls. *Sacar la niña de la labor,* To take a child from her needle. 5. A thousand tiles or bricks. 6. Cultivation, husbandry, tillage. *V.* LABRANZA. 7. (Prov.) Egg of a silkworm. *Labores,* Figures raised upon a ground; variegated needle-work; diaper. 8. (Amer.) The works of a mine. *Campo de labor,* A cultivated field.

Laborable [lah-bo-rah'-blay], *a.* Tillable, workable.

Laborador [lah-bo-rah-dor'], *m* *V* TRABAJADOR and LABRADOR

Laborar [lah-bo-rar'], *va.* To work, to till (the soil, etc.).—*vn.* To scheme, to plot.

Laborativo, va [lah-bo-rah-tee'-vo, vah]. *Día laborativo,* (Com.) Clear day.

Laboratorio [lah-bo-rah-to'-re-o], *m.* Laboratory, a chemist's work-room.

Laborcica, illa, ita [lah-bor-thee'-cah], *f. dim.* 1. An insignificant work or task. 2. Pretty needle-work.

Laborear [lah-bo-ray-ar'], *va.* 1. To cultivate, to till the ground. 2. (Naut.) To work a ship, to direct her movements. *V.* MANIOBRAR.

Laboreo [lah-bo-ray'-o], *m.* 1. (Prov.) Culture, labour. 2. The working of mines.

Laborera [lah-bo-ray'-rah], *a.* (Obs.) Clever, skilful: applied to a good workwoman.

Laborio [lah-bo-ree'-o], *m.* (Littl. us.) *V.* LABOR.

Laboriosamente [lah-bo-re-o-sah-men'tay], *adv.* Laboriously, painfully.

Laboriosidad [lah-bo-re-o-se-dahd], *f.* Laboriousness, industry, assiduity.

Laborioso, sa [lah-bo-re-o'-so, sah], *a.* 1. Laborious, assiduous, industrious. 2. Laborious, requiring much toil and labour; tiresome, painful.

Labra [lah'-brah], *f.* 1. The action of working or chiselling stone. 2. Carving, or other work given to materials before placing them, especially if rough stone.

Labrada [lah-brah'-dah], *f.* Land ploughed and fallowed to be sown the ensuing season.

Labradero, ra [lah-brah-day'-ro, rah], *a.* Suited to labour, capable of labour.

Labradío, dia [lah-brah-dee'-o, ah], *a.* *V.* LABRANTÍO.

Labrado, da [lah-brah'-do, dah], *a.* Worked: applied to figured cloth.—*pp.* of LABRAR.

Labrado [lah-brah'-do], *m.* Land cultivated: commonly used in the plural.

Labrador, ra [lah-brah-dor', rah], *a.* Industrious, laborious, fit for work.—*m.* & *f.* 1. Labourer, one who works at the plough or spade. 2. Cultivator, farmer, a husbandman or woman. 3. Rustic, peasant.

Labradoresco, ca [lah-brah-do-ress'-co, cah], *a.* Belonging or relating to a labourer; rustic, clownish.

Labradorita [lah-brah-do-ree'-tah], *f.* (Min.) Labradorite.

Labrandera [lah-bran-day'-rah], *f.* Seamstress, embroiderer.

Labrante [lah-brahn'-tay], *m.* Stone-cutter, sculptor.

Labrantin [lah-bran-teen'], *m.* A petty farmer, who cultivates a small farm.

Labrantío, tia [lah-bran-tee'-o, ah], *a.* Producing grain: applied to arable land fit for the culture of grain.

Labranza [lah-brahn'-thah], *f.* 1. Tillage, the cultivation of the ground, ploughing, farming. 2. Husbandry, the employment of a cultivator or farmer. 3. Farm, land let to a tenant; tilled land; an estate applied to the purposes and pursuits of agriculture.

Labrar [lah-brar'], *va.* 1. To work, to labour. 2. To till, to cultivate the ground. *V.* ARAR. 3. To build, to construct buildings. 4. To do needle-work, to embroider. 5. To inform, to instruct. 6. To finish, to polish to the degree of excellence intended or required. 7. To make designs in fabrics, stones, arms, etc.—*vn.* To make a strong impression on the mind.

Labrero, ra [lah-bray'-ro, rah], *a.* Applied to a kind of fishing-net.

Labriego [lah-bre-ay'-go], *m.* Peasant.

Labro [lah'-bro], *m.* The upper lip, labrum, of the mouth of animals.

Labrusca [lah-broos'-cah], *f.* A wild grape-vine.

Laburno [lah-boor'-no], *m.* (Bot.) Laburnum. Cytisus laburnum.

Laca [lah'-cah], *f.* 1. Lac, or gum-lac, a red, brittle, resinous substance, brought from India, and used for dyeing and making sealing-wax. *Laca en palillos*, Stick lac. *Laca en grano*, Seed-lac. *Laca en tablillas*, Shellac. 2. Red colour, lake, a pigment; *e. g.* madder lake. 3. Lacquer, a kind of varnish. (Per.)

Lacayo [lah-cah'-yo], *m.* 1. Lackey, footman, servant, foot-boy. 2. Knot of ribbons worn by women.

Lacayuelo [lah-cah-yoo-ay'-lo], *m. dim.* Foot-boy.

Lacayuno, na [lah-cah-yoo'-no, nah], *a.* Belonging to a lackey or foot-boy.

Lacear [lah-thay-ar'], *va.* 1. To adorn with ribbons tied in bows; to lace. 2. To pin up the game or drive it into an appointed place.

Lacedemónico, ca [lah-thay-day-mo'-ne-co, cah], or **Lacedemonio, a** [lah-thay-day-mo'-ne-o, ah], *a.* Lacedemonian, relating to Lacedemonia.

Laceración [lah-thay-rah-the-on'], *f.* Laceration, lancination, tearing.

Lacerado, da [lah-thay-rah'-do, dah], *a.* 1. Unfortunate, unhappy. 2. Leprous.—*pp.* of LACERAR.

Lacerar [lah-thay-rar'], *va.* To mangle, to tear in pieces, to lacerate.

Laceria [lah-thay'-re-ah], *f.* 1. Misery, poverty, wretchedness. 2. Labour, fatigue, trouble.

Lacería [lah-thay'-ree-ah], *f.* A set of nets.

Lacerioso, sa [lah-thay-re-o'-so, sah], *a.* Miserable: scrofulous.

Lacinia [lah-thee'-ne-ah], *f.* (Bot.) 1. Lacinia, a narrow, deep, slender lobe. 2. The fringe of a Roman toga.

Laciniado, da [lah-the-ne-ah'-do, dah], *a.* (Bot.) Laciniate, slashed irregularly.

Lacio, cia [lah'-the-o, ah], *a.* Faded, withered, dried up; flaccid, languid.

Lacónicamente [lah-co'-ne-cah-men-tay], *adv.* Laconically, concisely.

Lacónico, ca [lah-co'-ne-co, cah], *a.* Laconic, brief, concise.

Laconismo [lah-co-nees'-mo], *m.* Laconism, conciseness, brevity, concise expression or style.

Lacra [lah'-crah], *f.* 1. Mark left by some wound or disorder. 2. Fault, vice, wickedness.

Lacrar [lah-crar'], *va.* 1. To injure or impair the health. 2. To hurt or injure in point of property or money. 3. To seal with sealing-wax.

Lacre [lah'-cray], *m.* Sealing-wax.

Lacrimacion [lah-cre-mah-the-on'], *f.* (Obs.) Effusion of tears, lachrymation.

Lacrimal [lah-cre-mahl'], *a.* Lachrymal.

Lacrimatorio, ria [lah-cre-mah-to'-re-o, ah], *a.* & *m.* & *f.* Lachrymatory.

Lacrimógeno [lah-cre-mo'-hay-no], *a.* Tear-producing. *Bomba lacrimógena*, Tear bomb.

Lacrimoso, sa [lah-cre-mo'-so, sah], *a.* Weeping, shedding tears, lachrymose.

Lacris [lah'-cris], *m.* Fruit of rosemary.

Lactación [lac-tah-the-on'], *f.* Lactation, the act of suckling.

Lactancia [lac-tahn'-the-ah], *f.* Lactation, the act or time of giving suck.

Lactante [lac-tahn'-tay], *m.* Sucker, one who sucks milk.

Lactar [lac-tar'], *va.* To suckle, to give suck.

Lactario, ria [lac-tah'-re-o, ah], *a.* Lactary, lacteous, lactescent.

Lactato [lac-tah'-to], *m.* (Chem.) Lactate.

Lácteo, tea [lac'-tay-o, ah], *a.* Lacteous, milky, lacteal, lactean, lactescent. *Via láctea*, (Ast.) Galaxy, the milky way.

Lactescente [lac-tes-then'-tay], *a.* Lactescent, having a milky juice.

Lacticinio [lac-te-thee'-ne-o], *m.* Milk-pottage, and, in general, all sorts of food prepared with milk.

Lacticinoso, sa [lac-te-the-no'-so, sah], *a.* *V.* LÁCTEO.

Láctico, ca [lahc'-te-co, cah], *a.* Lactic, relating to milk.

Lactífago, ga [lac-tee'-fah-go, gah], *a.* Feeding upon milk, galactophagous.

Lactífico, ca [lac-tee'-fe-co, cah], *a.* Lactific, yielding milk.

Lactífero, ra [lac-tee'-fay-ro, rah], *a.* Lactiferous, lacteal, milky.

Lactómetro [lac-to'-may-tro], *m.* Lactometer, a hydrometer for determining the density of milk.

Lactosa [lac-to'-sah], *f.* Lactose, milk sugar.

Lactumen [lac-too'-men], *m.* Scab breaking out on the head of sucking children.

Lacustre [lah-coos'-tray], *a.* Marshy, belonging to lakes.

Lacha [lah'-chah], *f.* *V.* HALECHE.

Lada [lah'-dah], *f.* *V.* JARA.

Ládano [lah'-dah-no], *m.* Labdanum, a resin which exudes from a shrub.

Ladeado, da [lah-day-ah'-do, dah], *a.* & *pp.* of LADEAR. Turned to one side, inclined, lopsided.

Ladeamiento [lah-day-ah-me-en' to], *m.* *V.* LADEO.

Ladear [lah-day-ar'], *va.* To move or turn to one side; to go side by side; to go along rails.—*vn.* 1. (Naut.) To incline: applied to the needle of the mariner's compass. 2. To go by the side, to incline to one side.—*vr.* To incline to an opinion or party.

Ladeo [lah-day'-o], *m.* Inclination or motion to one side.

Ladera [lah-day'-rah], *f.* Declivity, gradual descent.—*pl.* 1. Rails or staves of a common cart. 2. Cheeks of a gun-carriage.

Laderica, illa, ita [lah-day-ree'-cah, eel'-lyah, ee'-tah], *f. dim.* A small declivity of the ground.

Ladierno [lah-de-err'-no], *m.* (Bot.) Buckthorn. Rhamnus alaternus.

Ladilla [lah-deel'-lyah], *f.* 1. Crab-louse. Pediculus pubis, *L.* 2. (Bot.) Common barley. Hordeum distichum, *L.*

Ladillo [lah-deel'-lyo], *m.* Shifting panel placed in the sides of coaches.

Ladinamente [lah-de-nah-men'-tay], *adv.* Sidewise, artfully, sagaciously.

Ladino, na [lah-dee'-no, nah], *a.* 1. (Obs.) Versed in an idiom, speaking different languages fluently. 2. Sagacious, cunning, crafty. 3. *Negro ladino*, (Amer.) A negro that speaks Spanish so as to be understood.

Lado [lah'-do], *m.* 1. Side, that part of the human body which extends from the arm-pit to the hip-bone. 2. Side or half of an animal. 3. Side, the right or left. 4. Side, part of any body opposed to another part. 5. Side, any part placed in contradistinction or opposition to another. 6. Side, the margin, edge, or verge of any thing. 7. (Met.) Side, party, faction, interest. 8. (Met.) Companion, comrade. 9. Mat used to cover carts, etc. 10. (Met.) Patron, protector. 11. Course, manner; mode of proceeding. 12. Side: it is used to note consanguinity. *Al lado*, Just by, at hand, or near at hand. *De lado*, Incidentally. *A un lado*, Clear the way.

Ladón [lah-don'], *m.* *V.* LADA. (Gr.)

Ladra [lah'-drah], *f.* 1. Barking. 2. Cry of hounds after the game.

Ladrador, ra [lah-drah-dor', rah], *m.* & *f.* 1. Barker, one that barks or clamours. 2. (Coll.) Talker, one who talks much and to no purpose.

Ladrante [lah-drahn'-tay], *pa.* Barking, latrant; barker.

Ladrar [lah-drar'], *vn.* 1. To bark, howl, or cry like a dog. 2. To use empty threats. 3. To clamour, to vociferate, to make outcries. *Ladrar el estómago*, To be hungry.

Ladrear [lah-dray-ar'], *vn.* To bark often and without object.

Ladrería [lah-dray-ree'-ah], *f.* 1 Lazaretto, a hospital for the treatment of lepers. 2. Elephantiasis, or leprosy of the Arabs. 3. (Vet.) A certain disease of swine and another of horses.

Ladrido [lah-dree'-do], *m.* 1. Barking or howling of a dog. 2. Vociferation, outcry; calumny; incitement.

Ladrillado [lah-dreel-lyah'-do], *m.* Floor made with bricks.

Ladrillador, *m.* *V.* ENLADRILLADOR.

Ladrillal, Ladrillar [lah-dreel-lyahl' lah-dreel-lyar'], *m.* Brick-field, brick kiln, a place where bricks are made

Ladrillazo [lah-dreel-lyah'-tho], *m.* Blow with a brickbat.

Ladrillejo [lah-dreel-lyay'-ho], *m.* 1. (Dim.) Little brick. 2. Boy's amusement of knocking at doors with a piece of brick.

Ladrillera [lah-dreel-lyay'-rah], *f.* Brick-kiln.

Ladrillero [lah-dreel-lyay'-ro], *m.* Brick-maker.

Ladrillo [lah-dreel'-lyo], *m.* A brick. *Ladrillo de chocolate,* Cake of chocolate.

Ladrilloso, sa [lah-dreel-lyo'-so, sah], *a.* Made of brick.

Ladrón, na [lah-drone', nah], *m.* & *f.* 1. Thief, robber, highwayman, cutpurse. 2. Lock, sluice-gate. 3. Snuff of a candle that makes it melt.

Ladronamente, *adv.* Thievishly, dissemblingly.

Ladroncillo [lah-dron-theel'-lyo], *m. dim.* of LADRÓN. Petty thief, filcher. *Ladroncillo de agujeta, después sube a barjuleta,* A young filcher becomes an old robber.

Ladronera [lah-dro-nay'-rah], *f.* 1. Nest of rogues, den of robbers. 2. Filching, stealing; defrauding, extortion. 3. Sluice-gate in a mill. 4. Money-box. *V.* ALCANCÍA.

Ladronería [lah-dro-nay-ree'-ah], *f.* *V.* LADRONICIO.

Ladronesco, ca [lah-dro-nes'-co, cah], *a.* (Coll.) Belonging to thieves, thievish.

Ladronicio [lah-dro-nee'-the-o], *m.* Larceny, theft, robbery. *V.* LATROCINIO.

Lafria [lah-free'-ah], *f.* A robber-fly, encountered in most of the world.

Laga [lah'-gah], *f.* A large black bean of the Orient which serves for weighing gold.

Lagaña [lah-gah'-nyah], *f.* A slimy humour running from the eyes.

Lagañoso, sa [lah-gah-nyo'-so, sah], *a.* Blear-eyed, troubled with a running from the eyes.

Lagar [lah-gar'], *m.* 1. Place where grapes are pressed. 2. Wine-press, an engine for squeezing the juice from grapes.

Lagarada [lah-gah-rah'-dah], *f.* A wine-pressful; each filling of a wine-press.

Lagarejo [lah-gah-ray'-ho], *m.* A small wine-press.

Lagarero [lah-gah-ray'-ro], *m.* 1. Wine-presser, one employed in pressing grapes. 2. One employed in expressing the juice of olives.

Lagareta [lah-gah-ray'-tah], *f.* Small wine-press.

Lagarta [lah-gar'-tah], *f.* Female lizard.

Lagartado, da [lah-gar-tah'-do, dah], *a.* *V.* ALAGARTADO.

Lagartera [lah-gar-tay'-rah], *f.* Lizard-hole, a place under ground where lizards breed.

Lagartero, ra [lah-gar-tay'-ro, rah], *a.* Catching lizards: applied to animals fond of devouring lizards.

Lagartija [lah-gar-tee'-hah], *f.* Eft, newt, a small lizard.

Lagartijero, ra [lah-gar-te-hay'-ro, rah], *a.* Catching efts: applied to animals.

Lagartillo [lah-gar-teel'-lyo], *m. dim.* A small lizard.

Lagarto [lah-gar'-to], *m.* 1. Lizard. 2. A large muscle of the arm. 3. A sly, artful person.

Lago [lah'-go], *m.* A lake; a large quantity of any liquid. *Lago de leones,* A den of lions.

Lagostín [lah-gos-teen'], *m.* *V.* LANGOSTÍN.

Lagotear [lah-go-tay-ar'], *vn.* (Coll.) To flatter, to wheedle, to cajole.

Lagotería [lah-go-tay-ree'-ah], *f.* (Coll.) Flattery, adulation.

Lagotero, ra [lah-go-tay'-ro, rah], *a.* (Coll.) Flattering, soothing.

Lágrima [lah'-gre-mah], *f.* 1. A tear. 2. Any moisture trickling in drops; a drop or small quantity. 3. (Bot.) Gray-mill, gromwell. Lithospermum. *Lágrima de Moisés* or *de Job,* (Bot.) Job's-tears. Coix lacryma Jobi. 4. Wine extracted from the grape by very slight pressure, in order to have the purest juice. *Lágrimas de S. Pedro,* Pebbles, stones thrown at any person. *Lágrimas de Batavia* or *de Holanda,* Prince Rupert's drops, glass globules.

Lagrimable [lah-gre-mah'-blay], *a.* Lachrymable, lamentable; worthy of tears.

Lagrimal [lah-gre-mahl'], *m.* Corner of the eye near the nose.

Lagrimar, Lagrimear [lah-gre-mar'], *vn.* To weep, to shed tears.

Lagrimeo [lah-gre-may'-o], *m.* The act of shedding tears.

Lagrimón [lah-gre-mone'], *m. aug.* A large tear.

Lagrimoso, sa [lah-gre-mo'-so, sah], *a.* 1. Weeping, shedding tears. 2. Watery: applied to humours running from the eye; lachrymary.

Laguna [lah-goo'-nah], *f.* 1. Pond, lake, a large diffusion of stagnant water, marsh. 2. An uneven country, full of marshes. 3. Blanks in a book or writing.

Lagunajo [lah-goo-nah'-ho], *m.* Small pool of water in a field after rain.

Lagunar [lah-goo-nar'], *m.* Timber-roof.

Lagunero, ra [lah-goo-nay'-ro, rah], *a.* Belonging to marshes or lakes.

Lagunoso, sa [lah-goo-no'-so, sah], *a.* Marshy, fenny, abounding in lakes; laky.

Laical [lah-e-cahl'], *a.* Laical, belonging to the laity or people, as distinct from the clergy.

Laicismo [lah-e-thees'-mo], *m.* Laicism, exclusion of the clergy from teaching and all positions of the state.

Laico, ca [lah'-e-co, cah], *a.* *V.* LEGO.

Laido, da [lah'-e-do, dah], *a.* (Obs.) *V.* IGNOMINIOSO and FEO.

Lairén [lah-e-ren'], *a.* Applied to a kind of grapes, and to the vines which produce them.

Laja [lah'-hah], *f.* A thin flat stone.

Lama [lah'-mah], *f.* 1. Mud, slime, ooze. 2. *Lama de oro* or *de plata,* Lama, gold or silver cloth. 3. (Prov.) A flat even country. 4. (Prov.) Fine sand used for mortar. 5. Foam on the surface of water. 6. Dust of ores in mines.

Lamar [lah-mar'], *va.* (Obs.) *V.* LLAMAR.

Lambel [lam-bel'], *m.* (Her.) Lambel, label, a bar with three pendants.

Lambrequines [lam-bray-kee'-nes], *m. pl.* (Her.) Ornaments which hang from helmets.

Lambrija [lam-bree'-hah], *f.* 1. Worm bred in the human body. *V.* LOMBRIZ. 2. (Coll.) Meagre, slender person.

Lamedal [lah-may-dahl'], *m.* A musty, miry place.

Lamedero [lah-may-day'-ro], *m.* A salt-lick.

Lamedor, ra [lah-may-dor', rah], *m.* & *f.* 1. Licker, one that laps and licks. 2. (Pharm.) Loch, a soft medicine between a sirup and an electuary. 3. (Met.) Enticement, allurement, wheedling. *Dar lamedor,* To feign losing at play in order to insure greater success.

Lamedura [lah-may-doo'-rah], *f.* Act of licking.

Lamelar [lah-may-lar'], *va.* To roll copper into sheets.

Lamelibranquio [lah-may-le-brahn'-ke-o], *a.* Lamellibranchiate, having lamellate gills.

Lamelicornios [lah-may-le-cor'-ne-os], *a.* & *m. pl.* Lamellicorn beetles.

Lameliforme [lah-may-le-for'-may], *a.* Lamelliform, in thin layers or plates.

Lamentable [lah-men-tah'-blay], *a.* Lamentable, deplorable.

Lamentablemente [lah-men-tah-blay-men'-tay], *adv.* Lamentably.

Lamentación [lah-men-tah-the-on'], *f.* Lamentation, lamenting, groaning.

Lamentador, ra [lah-men-tah-dor', rah], *m.* & *f.* Lamenter, weeper, mourner, complainer.

Lamentar [lah-men-tar'], *va.* To lament, to mourn, to bewail, to moan. —*vn.* & *vr.* To lament, to grieve, to wail, to complain, to cry.

Lamento [lah-men'-to], *m.* Lamentation, lament, moan, groaning, mourning, cry.

Lamentoso, sa [lah-men-to'-so, sah], *a.* Lamentable, mournful, to be lamented.

Lameplatos [lah-may-plah'-tos], *m.* Lick-plate, nickname given to the servants who attend at table.

Lamer [lah-merr'], *va.* 1. To lick, to pass over with the tongue. 2. To lick, to lap, to take in by the tongue. 3. To touch slightly.

Lamerón, na [lah-may-rone', nah], *m.* & *f.* (Coll.) A person very fond of dainties or delicacies.

Lameronazo, za [lah-may-ro-nah'-tho, thah], *m.* & *f. aug.* (Coll.) A person extremely fond of dainties.

Lamia [lah'-me-ah], *f.* 1. Lamia, a fabulous monster. 2. Kind of shark. 3. A longicorn beetle of Europe.

Lamido, da [lah-mee'-do, dah], *a.* Deformed, worn out with use.—*pp.* of LAMER.

Lamiente [lah-me-en'-tay], *a.* 1. Licking. 2. Lapping.

Lámina [lah'-me-nah], *f.* 1. Thin sheet. 2. Plate, engraving. 3. Print, illustration. 4. Thin layer. 5. (Bot. & Zool.) Lamina. *Tener buena lámina,* To look good.

Laminable [lah-me-nah'-blay], *a.* Capable of lamination, laminable.

Laminación [lah-me-nah-the-on'], *f.* 1. Rolling. 2. Lamination.

Laminado, da [lah-me-nah'-do, dah], *a.* Laminated, laminate.—*m.* 1. Rolling. 2. Lamination.

Laminador, ra [lah-me-nah-dor', rah], *a.* 1. Laminating. 2. Rolling.—*m.* 1. Rolling mill. 2. Laminator.

Laminar [lah-me-nar'], *va.* 1. To roll (metals). 2. To laminate.—*a.* Laminar, laminal.

Laminaria [lah-me-nah'-re-ah], *f.* (Bot.) Laminaria.

Laminería [lah-me-nay-ree'-ah], *f.* Tidbit, choice morsel.

Laminero, ra [lah-me-nay'-ro, rah], *m.* & *f.* 1. Laminator. 2. Decorator of containers for religious objects.—*a.* Fond of sweets.

Laminoso, sa [lah-me-no'-so, sah], *a.* Laminose, laminous.

Lamiscar [lah-mes-car'], *va.* (Coll.) To lick up greedily.

Lamoso, sa [lah-mo'-so, sah], *a.* Muddy, slimy.

Lampa [lahm'-pah], *f.* (Peru. Agr.) Shovel for grain.

Lampacear [lam-pa-thay-ar'], *va.* (Naut.) To swab, to clean the decks with a swab.

Lampar [lam-par'], *vn.* & *vr.* *V.* ALAMPAR. To be eager for any thing.

Lámpara [lahm'-pa-rah], *f.* 1. Light, a luminous body. 2. An oil lamp. 3. An electric light or lamp. 4. A spot of grease or oil. 5. Branch of a tree placed at the door on festival days. *Lámpara de arco*, Arc light. *Lámpara de bitácora*, (Naut.) Binnacle lamp. *Lámpara de intermitencia*, Flashlight. *Lámpara portátil*, Emergency light. *Lámpara de radio*, Radio tube. *Lámpara de rayos ultravioletas*, Sunlamp. *Lámpara de seguridad*, Miner's safety lamp. *Lámpara de soldar*, Blowtorch. *Lámpara de tungsten*, Mazda lamp.

Lamparero, ra [lam-pa-ray'-ro, rah], *m.* & *f.* Lamp-lighter.

Lamparilla [lam-pa-reel'-lyah], *f.* 1. (Dim.) A small lamp. 2. A night-taper. 3. A sort of coarse camlet.

Lamparín [lam-pa-reen'], *m.* Case into which a glass lamp is put.

Lamparista [lam-pa-rees'-tah], *n. com.* Lamp-lighter.

Lamparón [lam-pa-rone'], *m.* 1. (Aug.) A large grease-spot. 2. King's-evil, a scrofulous tumour in the neck.

Lamparonoso, sa [lam-pa-ro-no'-so, sah], *a.* Scrofulous.

Lampatán [lam-pah-tahn'], *m.* A Chinese plant.

Lampazo [lam-pah'-tho], *m.* 1. (Bot.) Burdock. *V.* BARDANA. 2. (Naut.) Swab, a mop used to clean the decks and cabin of a ship. *Paños de lampazo*, Tapestry on which landscapes are represented. *Lampazos*, Pimples on the face.

Lampiño, ña [lam-pee'-nyo, nyah], *a.* Beardless; having little hair.

Lampión [lam-pe-on'], *m.* A large lantern.

Lampíride, Lampiro [lam-pee'-re-day, lam-pee'-ro], *m.* (Zool.) Lampyris, the glow-worm, a serricorn beetle. Also the fire-fly.

Lampote [lam-po'-tay], *m.* Cotton cloth made in the Philippine Islands.

Lamprea [lam-pray'-ah], *f.* (Zool.) Lamprey. Petromyzon, *L.*

Lamprear [lam-pray-ar'], *va.* 1. To marinate, to prepare a stew. 2. (Mex.) To dip in flour and beaten egg (before cooking).

Lamprehuela, Lampreilla [lam-pray-oo-ay'-lah, lam-pray-eel'-lyah], *f.* Kind of small lamprey.

Lana [lah'-nah], *f.* 1. Wool, the fleece of sheep. 2. Short curled hair of some animals. 3. Woollen manufacture in general. 4. (Coll.) Cash, money. *A costa de lanas*, At another man's expense. *Lana burda* or *churla*, Coarse wool. *Lana de gorjales*, Wool of the third sort. *Lana en rama*, Uncombed wool. *Lana peladiza*, Glovers' wool. *Lana fieltrada*, Felt wool. *Lana de camello*, Camel's hair. *Lana de chinchorra*, (Mex.) Best Querétaro wool. *Ir por lana y volver trasquilado*, To go for wool and come back shorn.

Lanada [lah-nah'-dah], *f.* Sponge for cleaning cannons.

Lanado, da [lah-nah'-do, dah], *a.* *V.* LANUGINOSO.

Lanar [lah-nar'], *a.* Woolly, clothed with wool: applied to sheep.

Lanaria [lah-nah'-re-ah], *f.* (Bot.) Cudweed, used in cleaning wool.

Lance [lahn'-thay], *m.* 1. Cast, throw. 2. Casting of a net to catch fish. 3. A favourable opportunity, critical moment. 4. Chance, casualty, accident, fortuitous event, occurrence. (Met.) Transaction. 5. Sudden quarrel or dispute. 6. Skill and industry of a player. *De lance*, Cheap, at second hand.—*pl.* 1. Missile weapons. 2. Plot or intrigues of a play. *A pocos lances*, In a short time and with little labour.

Lancear [lan-thay-ar'], *va.* To wound with a lance.

Lancéola [lan-thay'-o-lah], *f.* (Bot.) Rib-grass plantain. Plantago lanceolata, *L.*

Lanceolado, da [lan-thay-o-lah'-do, dah], *a.* Lance-shaped, lanceolate.

Lancera [lan-thay'-rah], *f.* Hooks in an armoury, on which arms are placed.

Lancero [lan-thay'-ro], *m.* 1. Pikeman, lancer. 2. Maker of pikes. —*pl.* Type of square dance.

Lanceta [lan-thay'-tah], *f.* 1. Lancet. 2. Potter's knife.

Lancetada, *f.* **Lancetazo**, *m.* [lan-thay-tah'-dah, lan-thay-tah'-tho]. Act of opening or wounding with a lancet.

Lancetero [lan-thay-tay'-ro], *m.* A case for carrying lancets.

Lancita [lan-thee'-tah], *f. dim.* A small lance.

Lancurdia [lan-coor'-de-ah], *f.* Small trout.

Lancha [lahn-chah], *f.* 1. Barge, launch, lighter. *Lancha de motor*, Motorboat. *Lancha de socorro*, Lifeboat. 2. A thin and flat piece of stone. 3. Snare for partridges.

Lanchada [lan-chah'-dah], *f.* A lighter full of goods; as much as a lighter carries at once

Lanchaje [lan-chah'-hay], *m.* Lighterage.

Lanchar [lan-char'], *m.* A quarry from which flat stones are procured.

Lanchazo [lan-chah'-tho], *m.* Blow with a flat stone.

Lanchero [lan-chay'-ro], *m.* A bargeman.

Lanchón [lan-chone'], *m.* (Naut.) Lighter. *Lanchón de lastrar*, Ballast-lighter.

Lanchonero [lan-cho-nay'-ro], *m.* Lighterman.

Landgrave [land-grah'-vay], *m.* Landgrave, a German title.

Landó [lan-doh'], *m.* Landau, a kind of carriage.

Landre [lahn'-dray], *f.* 1. A morbid swelling of the glands. 2. A purse concealed in the clothes. 3. Acorn.

Landrilla [lan-dreel'-lyah], *f.* Small grain which grows under the tongues of hogs.

Lanería [lah-nay-ree'-ah], *f.* Shop where washed wool is sold.

Lanero [lah-nay'-ro], *m.* 1. Dealer in wool. 2. Warehouse for wool.

Langaruto, ta [lan-gah-roo'-to, tah], *a.* (Coll.) Tall, lank, ill-shaped.

Langor [lan-gor'], *m.* (Littl. us.) Languor, faintness; a decay of spirits.

Langosta [lan-gos'-tah], *f.* 1. Locust, a devouring insect. Gryllus. 2. Lobster, a marine crustacean. Homarus. 3. One who extorts money.

Langostera [lan-gos-tay'-rah], *f.* Name of a fishing-net.

Langostín [lan-gos-teen'], *m.* Prawn, a shrimp-like crustacean, esteemed as food.

Langostino [lan-gos-tee'-no], *m.* Prawn *V.* LANGOSTÍN.

Langostón [lan-gos-tone'], *m.* The large green locust.

Langrave [lan-grah'-vay], *m.* *V.* LANDGRAVE.

Langüente [lan-goo-en'-tay], *a.* Infirm, weak.

Lánguidamente [lahn'-gee-dah-men-tay], *adv.* Languidly, languishingly.

Languidecer [lan-gee-day-ther'], *vn.* To languish, to pine, wither.

Languidez, Languideza [lan-gee-deth'], *f.* 1. Languishment, languidness, languishing, heaviness, languor, weariness, faintness. 2. Decay of spirits, melancholy.

Lánguido, da [lahn'-gee-do, dah], *a.* 1. Languid, faint, weak, languishing, feeble. 2. Dull, heartless.

Lanífero, ra [lah-nee'-fay-ro, rah], *a.* (Poet.) Laniferous, woolly.

Lanificio [lah-ne-fee'-the-o], *m.* Woollen manufacture, the art of manufacturing wool.

Lanilla [lah-neel'-lyah], *f.* 1. Nap of cloth, down, villous substance. 2. Swan-skin, a very fine flannel. 3. (Naut.) Bunting, a thin woollen stuff, of which flags are made. 4. (Bot.) Down.

Lanío, a [lah-nee'-o, ah], *a.* Woolly. *V.* LANAR. (Obsolescent.)

Lanosidad [lah-no-se-dahd'], *f.* Down of the leaves of plants.

Lanoso, sa [lah-no'-so, sah], *a.* *V.* LANUDO.

Lanteja [lan-tay'-hah], *f.* Lentil. *V.* LENTEJA.

Lantejuela [lan-tay-hoo-ay'-lah], *f.* 1. Spangle, a small plate of shining metal. 2. Scurf left on the skin after a sore.

Lanudo, da [lah-noo'-do, dah], *a.* Woolly, consisting of wool, clothed with wool, lanigerous, fleecy.

Lanuginoso, sa [lah-noo-he-no'-so, sah], *a.* Lanuginous, lanigerous, downy; covered with soft hair.

Lanza [lahn'-thah], *f.* 1. Lance, spear, javelin. 2. Pole of a coach or wagon. 3. Pikeman, soldier armed with a pike. *Lanza en ristre*, Ready for action. *A punta de lanza*, Strenuously, with all one's might. *Echar la lanza*, To impugn, to contradict, to distrust an assertion. *Echar lanzas en la mar*, To toil in vain. *Romper lanzas*, (Fig.) To remove hindrances and obstacles to the accomplishment of a thing. *Lanzas*, Duty paid to the Spanish government by the grandees and nobility of the realm, in lieu of military services.

Lanzabombas [lan-thah-bom'-bahs], *m.* Bomber, bomb thrower, bomb release.

Lanzacohetes [lan-thah-co-ay'-tes], *m.* Rocket launcher.

Lanzada [lan-thah'-dah], *f.* Stroke with a lance, thrust with a spear.

Lanzadera [lan-thah-day'-rah], *f.* Shuttle, a weaver's instrument.

Lanzado, da [lan-thah'-do, dah], *a.* (Naut.) Raking, overhanging.—*pp.* of LANZAR.

Lanzador, ra [lan-thah-dor', rah], *m.* & *f.* Thrower, ejecter.

Lanzafuego [lan-thah-foo-ay'-go], *m.* *V.* BOTAFUEGO.

Lanzallamas [lan-thah-lyah'-mas], *m.* Flame thrower.

Lanzamiento [lan-thah-me-en'-to], *m.* 1. Launch, launching. 2. Cast, throw. 3. Flinging, hurling. 4. Throwing off. 5. Publication. 6. (For.) Eviction. *Lanzamiento del disco*, Discus throw. *Lanzamiento del martillo*, Hammer throw. *Lanzamiento del peso*, Shot put. *Lanzamiento de la jabalina*, Javelin throw.

Lanzaminas [lan-thah-mee'-nas], *m.* Mine layer, mine thrower.

Lanzar [lan-thar'], *va.* 1. To lance, to throw, to dart, to launch, to fling. 2. To cast up, to vomit. 3. (Law) To eject, to dispossess. 4. To let loose. —*vr.* 1. To rush or dart upon; to launch. 2. (Com.) To engage or embark on. *Lanzarse en paracaídas*, (Aer.) To bail out.

Lanzatorpedos [lan-thah-tor-pay'-dos], *m.* Torpedo boat.

Lanzón [lan-thone'], *m. aug.* A short and thick lance.

Laña [lah'-nyah], *f.* 1. Cramp or cramp-iron. 2. Green cocoanut.

Lañar [lah-nyar'], *va.* 1. To cramp, to fasten two things together with a cramp-iron. 2. (Prov.) To open and gut fish.

Lapa [lah'-pah], *f.* 1. Scum or pellicle raised on the surface of some liquors. 2. (Zool.) A kind of shell-fish. Lepas. 3. (Bot.) Goose-grass, cleavers. Galium aparine.

Lapachar [lah-pah-char'], *m.* Hole full of mud and mire.

Lápade [lah'-pah-day], *f.* (Zool.) Acorn shell-fish. Lepas.

Lapaza [lah-pah'-thah], *f.* (Prov.) Rough panic-grass. Panicum verticillatum.

Lapicero [lah-pe-thay'-ro], *m.* 1. A metal pencil case. 2. Pencil holder. 3. Mechanical pencil.

Lapida [lah'-pe-dah], *f.* A flat stone, on which inscriptions are engraved.

Lapidación [lah-pe-dah-the-on'], *f.* Lapidation, stoning to death.

Lapidar [lah-pe-dar'], *va.* 1. To throw stones. 2. To stone to death.

Lapidaria [lah-pe-dah'-re-ah], *f.* The art or profession of a lapidary, who deals in stones and gems.

Lapidario [lah-pe-dah'-re-o], *m.* Lapidary, lapidist, one who deals in stones and gems.

Lapidario, ria [lah-pe-dah'-re-o, ah], *a.* Lapidary.

Lapídeo, dea [lah-pee'-day-o, ah], *a.* Lapideous, stony of the nature of

Lapidificación [lah-pe-de-fe-ca-the-on'], *f.* Petrification, lapidification.

Lapidífico, ca [lah-pe-dee'-fe-co, cah], *a.* Lapidescent, lapidific, growing or turning to stone.

Lapidoso, sa [lah-pe-do'-so, sah], *a.* Lapideous, stony.

Lapilla [lah-peel'-lyah], *f.* (Bot.) Hound's-tongue.

Lapislázuli [lah-pis-lah'-thoo-le], *m.* Lapis-lazuli, an azure stone, of which the ultra-marine colour is prepared by calcination.

Lápiz [lah'-pith], *m.* Pencil, lead pencil, crayon. *Lápiz de labios* or *lápiz labial*, Lipstick.

Lapizar [lah-pe-thar'], *m.* Black-lead mine.

Lapizar [lah-pe-thar'], *va.* To draw or delineate with black chalk or black lead.

Lapo [lah'-po], *m.* (Coll.) Blow with the flat side of a sword.

Lapón, na [lah-pone', nah], *a.* & *m.* & *f.* Laplander, relating to Lapland, Laplandish.

Lapso [lahp'-so], *m.* (Law) Lapse or course of time.

Lapsus linguæ [lap'-soos leen'-goo-ay], *m.* Slip of the tongue.

Lar [lahr], *m.* A household god. *V.* LARES.

Larario [lah-rah'-re-o], *m.* Place where the pagans worshipped their house-gods.

Lardar, Lardear [lar-dar', lar-day-ar'], *va.* 1. To baste meat on the spit. 2. To beat with a stick.

Lardero [lar-day'-ro], *a.* Applied to the Thursday before Lent.

Lardo [lar'-do], *m.* Lard, the fat of swine and other animals.

Lardón [lar-done'], *m.* A marginal note, observation, or addition, in a book or in a proof. Also a piece of paper clinging to the frisket and preventing the impression of some part of a sheet.

Lardosico, ica, illo, illa, ito, ita [lar-do-see'-co, ee'-cah], *a. dim.* Greasy dirty with grease.

Lardoso, sa [lar-do'-so, sah], *a.* Greasy fatty.

Lares [lah'-res], *m. pl.* 1. House-gods of the ancient Romans. 2. Home.

Larga [lar'-gah], *f.* 1. An added piece which shoemakers put to a last, in order to lengthen a shoe. 2. Delay, procrastination: commonly used in the plural.

Largamente [lar-gah-men'-tay], *adv.* Largely, copiously; completely; liberally, frankly; for a long time.

Largar [lar-gar'], *va.* 1. To loosen, to slacken. 2. To let go, to set at liberty. 3. (Naut.) To loosen a sail, to ease a rope. *Larga las brazas de la gavia*, (Naut.) Let go the main top-sail braces. *Larga el lof*, (Naut.) Up tack-sheets. *Toda vela larga*, (Naut.) All sails out. *Largar el cable por el chicote* or *por ojo*, To pay out the cable end for end. *Largar las velas*, (Naut.) To set sail.—*vr.* 1. (Coll.) To go off, to pack away, to pack off one's tools. 2. (Naut.) To set sail.

Largo, ga [lar'-go, gah], *a.* 1. Long, of a certain measure in length. 2. Long, not short: applied to space and to time. 3. Long, protracted, not soon ceasing or at an end. 4. Large, generous, free, liberal. 5. Copious. 6. Prompt, expeditious. *Largo de lengua*, Too free and unguarded with the tongue; to be mordacious. *Largo de uñas*, Light-fingered. *De largo a largo*, From one end to the other, lengthwise. *Navegar a lo largo de la costa*, (Naut.) To navigate along the coast. *Pasar de largo*, To pass by without stopping. *A la corta o a la larga*, Sooner or later. *A la larga*, At length, slowly; in the long run; in course of time. *A lo largo*, 1. At a distance. 2. The long way, lengthwise. *Hacerse a lo largo*, (Coll.) To keep at a distance. *Gastar largo y tendido*, To spend lavishly. *Pasar de largo*, To pass by a person without taking notice of him. *Ese es cuento largo*, That is a long story.—*adv.* Largely, profusely.

Largo [lar'-go], *m.* 1. *V.* LONGITUD. 2. (Mus.) Largo.

Largomira [lar-go-mee'-rah], *f.* Telescope.

Largón, na [lar-gone', nah], *a. aug.* Very long.

Largor [lar-gor'], *m.* Length, the extent of any thing from end to end.

Largueado, da [lar-gay-ah'-do, dah], *a.* Striped. *V.* LISTADO.

Larguero [lar-gay'-ro], *m.* Jamb-post of a door or window. *V.* CABEZAL.

Largueza [lar-gay'-thah], *f.* 1. Length, extent, largeness, width. 2. Liberality, generosity, munificence, frankness.

Larguito, ita [lar-gee'-to, tah], *a.* Not very long.

Largura [lar-goo'-rah], *f.* Length, longness, stretch, extent.

Lárice [lah'-re-thay], *m.* (Bot.) Larch-tree. Larix.

Laricino, na [lah-re-thee'-no, nah], *a.* Belonging to the larch-tree.

Larige [lah-ree'-hay], *a.* Applied to a kind of very red grapes.

Laringa [lah-reen'-gah], *f.* Turpentine extracted from the larch-tree; Venice turpentine.

Laringe [lah-reen'-hay], *f.* (Anat.) Larynx, the upper part of the trachea, where the voice is formed.

Laringeo, gea [lah-reen'-hay-o, ah], *a.* Laryngeal, relating to the larynx.

Laringitis [lah-rin-hee'-tis], *f.* Laryngitis, inflammation of the larynx.

Laringologia [lah-rin-go-lo-hee'-ah], *f.* Laryngology, scientific knowledge of the larynx.

Laringoscopia [lah-rin-gos-co'-pe-ah], *f.* Laryngoscopy, use of the laryngoscope; inspection of the larynx.

Laringoscopio [lah-rin-gos-co'-pe-o], *m.* Laryngoscope, a reflecting mirror for examining the larynx.

Laringotomia [lah-rin-go-to-mee'-ah], *f.* (Surg.) Laringotomy.

Laro [lah'-ro], *m.* (Orn.) Gull, sea-gull. Larus.

Larva [lar'-vah], *f.* 1. Mask. *V.* MÁSCARA and FANTASMA. 2. (Ent.) Larva, grub-state of an insect. *Larvas*, Hobgoblins; lemures.

Larvado, da [lar-vah'-do, dah], *a.* (Med.) Larvate, masked.

Larval [lar-vahl'], *a.* 1. Frightful, ghastly. 2. Larvated, like a mask.

Las [lahs], *pron.* of third person plural feminine. It does not admit a preposition, and should not be used for the dative.

Lasaña [lah-sah'-nyah], *f.* A sort of paste fried in a pan.

Láscar [lahs'-car], *m.* Lascar, a native seaman or gunner in India.

Lascar [las-car'], *va.* (Naut.) To ease off, to slacken. *Lascar el virador de combés*, To surge the capstan.

Lascivamente [las-the-vah-men'-tay], *adv.* Lasciviously, lustfully, libidinously.

Lascivia [las-thee'-ve-ah], *f.* 1. Luxuriance, luxury; excess in delicious fare. 2. Lasciviousness, lewdness, lust.

Lascivo, va [las-thee'-vo, vah], *a.* 1. Lascivious, lewd, lustful, libidinous. 2. Luxuriant, exuberant.

Láser [lah'-ser], *m.* (Bot.) Benzoin.

Laserpicio [lah-ser-pee'-the-o], *m.* (Bot.) Laserwort. Laserpitium.

Lasitud [lah-se-tood'], *f.* Lassitude, weariness, faintness.

Laso, sa [lah'-so, sah], *a.* 1. Weary, tired with labour, subdued by fatigue. 2. Lax, flaccid.

Lastar [las-tar'], *va.* To pay, answer, or suffer for another.

Lástima [lahs'-te-mah], *f.* 1. Grief, compassion, pity, condolence. 2. Object of compassion or pity. *Es lástima*, It is a pity.

Lastimar [las-te-mar'], *va.* 1. To hurt, to wound, to offend. 2. To move to compassion, to excite pity, to pity.—*vr.* To be moved to compassion, to grieve, to be sorry for; to complain.

Lastimeramente [las-te-may-rah-men'-tay], *adv.* Sadly, sorrowfully.

Lastimero, ra [las-te-may'-ro, rah], *a.* Sad, doleful, mournful, miserable, moving, lamentable, grievous.

Lastimosamente [las-te-mo-sah-men'-tay], *adv.* Miserably, pitifully, grievously, lamentably.

Lastimoso, sa [las-te-mo'-so, sah], *a.* Doleful, sad. *V.* LASTIMERO.

Lasto [lahs'-to], *m.* Receipt given or belonging to him who has paid for another.

Lastra [lahs'-trah], *f.* (Naut.) Boat, lighter. *V.* LANCHA.

Lastrar [las-trar'], *va.* 1. (Naut.) To ballast a ship. 2. To keep any thing steady by means of a weight. *Vela de lastrar*, (Naut.) Port-sail. *Lancha de lastrar*, (Naut.) Ballast-lighter.

Lastre [lahs'-tray], *m.* 1. Rough stones used to ballast ships or build walls. 2. Ballast, a weight put at the bottom of ships to keep them steady, lastage. *Lastre grueso*, Heavy ballast. *Lastre lavado*, Washed ballast. *Ir en lastre*, To go in ballast. *El lastre se corre*,

The ballast shifts. 8. Weight, motive, judgment.
Lata [lah'-tah], *f.* 1. Tin can. 2. (coll.) Annoyance, boredom. *Dar lata,* To annoy, to bother, to bore.
Lata, *f.* Lath, ledge, batten. *Poner latas en las techumbres,* To lath.
Latamente [lah-tah-men'-tay], *adv.* Largely, amply.
Latastro [lah-tahs'-tro], *m.* (Arch.) *V.* PLINTO.
Latente [lah-ten'-tay], *a.* Latent, obscure, hidden. *Colórico latente,* Latent heat.
Lateral [lah-tay-rahl'], *a.* Lateral, belonging to the side.
Látex [lah'-teks], *m.* (Bot.) Latex.
Latido [lah-tee'-do], *m.* 1. Pant, palpitation; motion of the heart. 2. Howling or barking of a dog after game.—*pp.* of LATIR.
Latiente [lah-te-en'-tay], *pa.* Palpitating, fluttering.
Latigadera [lah-te-gah-day'-rah], *f.* (Prov.) Strap or thong by which the yoke is fastened to the pole of a cart.
Latigazo [la-te-gah'-tho], *m.* 1. Lash, crack of a whip, a jerk. 2. Unexpected offence; a harsh or unlooked-for reproof. *Dar latigazos,* To lash.
Látigo [lah'-te-go], *m.* 1. Whip; thong, or point of a whip. 2. Rope with which any thing to be weighed is fastened to the steel-yard. 3. The end of every strap which must be passed through a buckle. 4. Mast of a boat when it is extremely tall.
Latiguear [lah-te-gay-ar'], *vn.* To smack or crack with the lash of a whip, to lash or ply the whip.
Latiguera [lah-te-gay'-rah], *f.* Cord with which a girth is fastened.
Latiguero [lah-te-gay'-ro], *m.* Maker or seller of whip thongs or lashes.
Latiguillo [lah-te-geel'-lyo], *m. dim.* A small whip.
Latín [lah-teen'], *m.* 1. Latin, the Latin tongue. 2. A Latin word or clause interposed in a Romance text. *Saber mucho latín,* To be full of wit and cunning.
Latinajo [lah-te-nah'-ho], *m.* (Coll.) Latin jargon.
Latinamente [lah-te-nah-men'-tay], *adv.* In pure Latin, Latinly.
Latinidad [lah-te-ne-dahd'], *f.* Latinity, the Latin tongue.
Latinismo [lah-te-nees'-mo], *m.* Latinism, a mode of speech peculiar to the Latin idiom.
Latinizar [lah-te-ne-thar'], *va.* To Latinize, to give names a Latin termination. —*vn.* To use words borrowed from the Latin.
Latino, na [lah-tee'-no, nah], *a.* 1. Latin, written or spoken in the language of the old Romans. 2. Belonging to the Latin language, or to the country of Latium. 3. Applied to the Western church, opposed to the Greek. *A la latina,* In a lateen or triangular fashion. *Vela latina,* Lateen sail, of a triangular shape, and used chiefly in the Mediterranean. *Unión latina,* Latin union, a monetary convention among certain Latin countries in regard to silver coins.
Latino, na [lah-tee'-no, nah], *m.* & *f.* 1. Latinist, one who knows the Latin language. 2. A native of Latium.
Latinoamericano, na [lah-te-no-ah-may-re-cah'-no, nah], *a.* & *m.* & *f.* Latin American.
Latir [lah-teer'], *vn.* 1. To palpitate, to beat at the heart; to flutter. 2. To yelp, to bark as a hound in pursuit of game.
Latiro [lah-tee'-ro], *m.* (Bot.) Vetch, tare. *V.* ARVEJA.
Latitud [lah-te-tood'], *f.* 1. Breadth, width, latitude, extent. 2. (Geog.) Latitude, the distance of any point from the equator. *Latitud corregida,* (Naut.) Corrected latitude. *Latitud por encima,* (Naut.) Latitude by dead reckoning. *Latitud arribada,* (Naut.) Latitude come to.
Latitudinal [lah-te-too-de-nahl'], *a.* Relating to the latitude.
Lato, ta [lah'-to, tah], *a.* Large, diffuse, extensive.
Latón [lah-tone'], *m.* Brass, latten, orichalch. *Latón en hojas* or *planchas,* Latten brass; sheet brass.
Latonería [lah-to-nay-ree'-ah], *f.* 1. The art of working in brass. 2. A brass-worker's shop.
Latonero [lah-to-nay'-ro], *m.* Brazier, a manufacturer who works in brass.
Latones [lah-to'-nes], *m. pl.* (Naut.) Laths or ledges, used on board of ships.
Latoso, sa [lah-to'-so, sah], *a.* (coll.) Boring, annoying.
Latría [lah-tree'-ah], *f.* Latria, worship, adoration due to God only.
Latrina [lah-tree'-nah], *f.* Privy-house. *V.* LETRINA.
Latrocinio [lah-tro-thee'-ne-o], *m.* Robbery, frequent and repeated theft.
Laúd [lah-ood'], *m.* 1. Lute, a stringed musical instrument. 2. Merchant vessel, craft.
Lauda [lah'-oo-dah], *f.* (Obs.) Tombstone. *V.* LAUDE, 1st def.
Laudable [lah-oo-dah'-blay], *a.* Laudable, praiseworthy.
Laudablemente [lah-oo-dah-blay-men'-tay], *adv.* Laudably.
Láudano [lah'-oo-dah-no], *m.* Laudanum, a tincture from opium.
Laudar [lah-oo-dar'], *va.* 1. (Obs.) To praise. 2. To render a decision as an arbitrator or umpire. (Acad.)
Laudatorio, ria [lah-oo-dah-to'-re-o, ah], *a.* Laudatory, acclamatory.
Laude [lah'-oo-day], *f.* 1. A tombstone with an epitaph engraved on it. 2. *pl.* Lauds, that part of the divine service which is said after matins, and consists in praise of the Almighty. *A laudes,* At all hours, frequently. *Tocar a laudes,* To praise one's self.
Laudemio [lah-oo-day'-me-o], *m.* (Law) Dues paid to the lord of the manor on all transfers of landed property, within the manor.
Launa [lah'-oo-nah], *f.* 1. Lamina, a thin plate of metal. 2. Schistose clay for covering houses.
Laura [lah'-oo-rah], *f.* Solitary situation where the ancient monks had their detached cells.
Lauráceo, cea [lah-oo-rah'-thay-o, ah], *a.* Laurel-like.
Láurea [lah'-oo-ray-ah], *f.* A laurel leaf or crown.
Laureado, da [lah-oo-ray-ah'-do, dah], *a.* & *pp.* of LAUREAR. Laureate, laurelled.
Laureando [lah-oo-ray-ahn'-do], *m.* He who is soon to receive a degree in a university.
Laurear [lah-oo-ray-ar'], *va.* 1. To crown with laurel. 2. To graduate, to dignify with a degree in the universities.
Lauredal [lah-oo-ray-dahl'], *m.* Plantation of laurel-trees.
Laurel [lah-oo-rel'], *m.* 1. (Bot.) Laurel. Laurus. 2. A crown of bays as a reward.
Lauréola [lah-oo-ray'-o-lah], *f.* 1. A crown of laurel. *Lauréola hembra,* Mezereon daphne. Daphne mezereum. *Lauréola macho,* Spurge laurel. Daphne laureola. 2. Diadem.
Laurífero, ra [lah-oo-ree'-fay-ro, rah], *a.* (Poet.) Lauriferous, producing or carrying laurel.
Laurineo, nea [lah-oo-ree'-nay-o, ah], *a.* (Bot.) Laurel-like.
Laurino, na [lah-oo-ree'-no, nah], *a.* Belonging to laurel.
Lauro [lah'-oo-ro], *m.* 1. Glory, honour, fame, triumph. 2. (Bot.) *V.* LAUROCERASO.
Lauroceraso, Lauroreal [lah-oo-ro-thay-rah'-so, lah-oo-ro-ray-ahl'], *m.* (Bot.) Cherry-laurel or laurel plum-tree. Prunus lauruscerasus.
Lautamente [lah-oo-tah-men'-tay], *adv.* Splendidly. (Acad.)
Lauto, ta [lah'-oo-to, tah], *a.* Rich, wealthy.
Lava [lah'-vah], *f.* 1. Washing of metals in mines. 2. Lava, a volcanic production.
Lavabo [lah-vah'-bo], *m.* 1. A wash-hand-stand and its belongings. 2. A part of the sacrifice of the mass, and the tablet on which are these words: *lavabo inter innocentes,* etc. 3. The napkin on which the priest dries his hands after washing.
Lavacaras [lah-vah-cah'-ras], *m.* (Met.) A flatterer.
Lavación [lah-vah-the-on'], *f* Lotion, wash.
Lavada [lah-vah'-dah], *f* A large drawnet for fishing.
Lavadero [lah-vah-day'-ro], *m.* 1. Washing-place, where wool and other things are washed. 2. Vat or pit in which tanners clean their skins. 3. Laundry, the room in which clothes are washed.
Lavado [lah-vah'-do], *m.* Wash, washing. *Lavado bucal,* Mouth wash. *Lavado intestinal,* Enema. *Lavado en seco,* Dry cleaning.
Lavador, ra [lah-vah-dor', rah], *m.* & *f.* 1. Washer, one who washes wool. 2. Burnisher, an instrument which serves to clean and brighten fire-arms.
Lavadora [lah-vah-do'-rah], *f.* Electric dishwashing machine or clothes washer. *Lavadora de platos,* Dishwasher (machine or woman). *Lavadora de ropa,* Clotheswasher (machine or woman).
Lavadura [lah-vah-doo'-rah], *f.* 1. Wash, washing, lavation, the act of washing any thing. 2. Composition of water, oil, and eggs, beat together, in which glove-leather is prepared. 3. *V.* LAVAZAS.
Lavaje [lah-vah'-hay], *m.* Washing of wools.
Lavajo [lah-vah'-ho], *m.* Pool where cattle go to drink; morass.
Lavamanos [lah-vah-mah'-nos], *m.* A washing-stand, lavatory.
Lavanco [lah-vahn'-co], *m.* A kind of wild duck.
Lavandera [lah-van-day'-rah], *f.* 1 Laundress, a washer-woman. 2. (Zool.) Wagtail. *V.* AGUZANIEVE.
Lavandería [lah-van-day-ree'-ah], *f.* 1. Laundry, laundering establishment. 2. Washing, laundering. *Lavandería automática,* Laundromat.
Lavandero [lah-van-day'-ro], *m.* 1. Washer, he who washes, launderer. 2. One who carries and brings foul linen to be washed.
Lavaojos [lah-vah-o'-hose], *m.* Eye-cup.
Lavaplatos [lah-vah-plah'-tose], *m.* Dishwasher.
Lavar [lah-var'], *va.* 1. To wash, to cleanse by ablution, to lave, to launder. 2. To clear from an imputation or charge of guilt. 3. To white-wash a wall with lime or chalk. *Lavar de*

lana a alguno, (Obs.) To dive into the truth of any thing.
Lavativa [lah-vah-tee'-vah], *f.* 1. Clyster, a medicinal injection. 2. A clyster-pipe; a syringe. 3. (Met.) Vexation, annoyance.
Lavatorio [lah-vah-to'-re-o], *m.* 1. Lavation, the act of washing. 2. Medicinal lotion with which diseased parts are washed. 3. Ceremony of washing the feet on Holy Thursday. 4. Lavatory. *V.* LAVAMANOS.
Lavazas [lah-vah'-thas], *f. pl.* Foul water running from a washing-place.
Lave [lah'-vay], *m.* Washing of metals in mines.
Lavotear [lah-vo-tay-ar'], *va.* & *vr.* (Coll.) To wash hurriedly and poorly. (Acad.)
Lavoteo [lah-vo-tay'-o], *m.* Washing hurriedly and poorly performed.
Laxación [lac-sah-the-on'], *f.* Loosening, laxation, slackening.
Laxamiento [lac-sah-me-en'-to], *m.* Laxation, laxity, laxness, loosening.
Laxante [lac-sahn'-tay], *pa.* Loosening, softening.—*n.* & *a.* (Med.) Laxative.
Laxar [lac-sar'], *va.* To loosen, to soften.
Laxativo, va [lac-sah-tee'-vo, vah], *a.* & *m.* Laxative, lenitive.
Laxidad [lac-se-dahd'], *f.* *V.* LAXITUD.
Laxitud [lac-se-tood'], *f.* 1. Lassitude, weariness. 2. Laxity, laxness.
Laxo, xa [lac'-so, sah], *a.* 1. Lax, slack, not tense, feeble. 2. (Met.) Lax, vague; loose in opinions or morals.
Laya [lah'-yah], *f.* 1. Quality, nature. 2. (Prov.) A two-pronged instrument, with which the ground is turned up.
Layador [lah-yah-dor'], *m.* He who cultivates the soil with a two-pronged instrument.
Layar [lah-yar'], *va.* To turn up the ground with a *laya.*
Lazada [lah-thah'-dah], *f.* 1. Slip-knot formed with a ribbon, cord, thread, etc. 2. Any ornament made in the form of a knot. (Amer.) The knot or slip made with a *lazo* on an animal's horns or neck, to keep him fast.
Lazador [lah-thah-dor'], *m.* He who catches with the lasso.
Lazar [lah-thar'], *va.* (Mex.) To catch with a lasso.
Lazareto [lah-thah-ray'-to], *m.* Lazaretto, lazaret, a public building for the reception of persons coming from places suspected of being infected with the plague, to perform quarantine.
Lazarillo [lah-thah-reel'-lyo], *m.* Boy who guides a blind man; a blind person's guide.
Lazarino, na [lah-thah-ree'-no, nah], *a.* Leprous, lazar-like, lazarly.
Lázaro [lah'-thah-ro], *m.* Lazar, a person deformed and nauseous with filthy and pestilential diseases.
Lazo [lah'-tho], *m.* 1. Bow, a slip knot. 2. Any knot or complication of thread, ribbon, string, etc. 3. Ornament in the shape of a knot. 4. Snare, trick, scheme. 5. Tie, bond, chain. 6. The act of decoying or driving the game to a certain spot. 7. (Arch.) Interlaced lines and flower-work. 8. Pattern made with box and other plants in a garden bed. 9. Cord with which a load is fastened. 10. (Amer.) Lasso, a line or rope for catching wild animals. —*pl.* Figures in dancing.
Lazulita [lah-thoo-lee'-tah], *f.* Lazulite.
Le [lay], *pron.* Him or her, to him, to her, dat. and accus. sing. of the personal pronoun *él*, he or it; and of its feminine, *ella*, she.
Leal [lay-ahl'], *a.* 1. Loyal, true to government. 2. Faithful, gentle, tame; applied to animals.
Leal [lay-ahl'], *m.* Loyalist.
Lealmente [lay-al-men'-tay], *adv.* Loyally, faithfully.
Lealtad [lay-al-tahd'], *f.* 1. Loyalty, fidelity, attachment to the laws and government, fealty. 2. Gentleness toward a master: applied to beasts.
Lebrada [lay-brah'-dah], *f.* Fricassee made of hare.
Lebratico, illo, ito [lay-brah-tee'-co, eel'-lyo, ee'-to], *m. dim.* A young hare, a leveret.
Lebrato [lay-brah'-to], or **Lebratón** [lay-brah-tone'], *m.* Young hare.
Lebrel [lay-brel'], *m.* Greyhound.
Lebrela [lay-bray'-lah], *f.* Greyhound bitch.
Lebrero, ra [lay-bray'-ro, rah], *a.* Applied to dogs for hunting hares.
Lebrillo [lay-breel'-lyo], *m.* A glazed earthenware tub or pan.
Lebrón [lay-brone'], *m.* 1. A large hare. 2. Coward, poltroon.
Lebroncillo [lay-bron-theel'-lyo], *m.* *V.* LEBRATO.
Lebruno, na [lay-broo'-no, nah], *a.* Leporine, of the hare kind.
Lección [lec-the-on'], *f.* 1. Art of reading; reading. 2. Lesson, any thing read or repeated to a teacher. 3. Lecture, a discourse upon any subject. 4. Lection, the letter or text of a work. 5. Warning, admonition, example.
Leccionario [lec-the-o-nah'-re-o], *m.* Lesson-book of the matins.
Leccioncita [lec-the-on-thee'-tah], *f. dim.* A short lecture or lesson.
Leccionista [lec-the-o-nees'-tah], *m.* One who gives lessons in private houses; a private tutor.
Lectisternio [lec-tis-terr'-ne-o] *m.* Banquet of the heathen gods.
Lectivo, va [lec-tee'-vo, vah], *a.* Applied to the time of lecture in universities.
Lector, ra [lec-tor', rah], *m.* & *f.* 1. Reader. 2. In monastic orders, a lecturer, teacher, or professor. 3. In the Roman Catholic church, the second of the four minor orders.
Lectorado [lec-to-rah'-do], *m.* Institution of lecturer.
Lectoral [lec-to-rahl'], *f.* 1. A prebendary, dignity in cathedral churches of Spain. 2. *m.* The person who enjoys the prebend called *lectoral.*
Lectoral [lec-to-rahl'], *a.* Applied to the prebend or canonry called *lectoral* in Spain, and to the prebendary who enjoys it.
Lectoria [lec-to-ree'-ah], *f.* Lectureship, in monastic orders; the place and office of a lecturer.
Lectura [lec-too'-rah], *f.* 1. Reading, lecture, the act of reading. 2. The act of teaching by way of lectures. 3. Among printers, small pica, 11-point.
Lecha, Lechaza [lay'-chah, le-chah'-thah], *f.* 1. Seminal fluid of fishes. 2. Each of the two sacs which contain it. (Acad.)
Lechada [lay-chah'-dah], *f.* 1. Lime slaked in water, whitewash. 2. Pulp for making paper. 3. Lime-water.
Lechal [lay-chahl'], *a.* 1. Sucking: applied to all mammiferous animals. 2. Lactiferous, milky.
Lechar [lay-char'], *a.* 1. *V.* LECHAL. 2. Nursing: applied to a woman who has milk in her breasts. 3. Promoting the secretion of milk in female mammals.
Lechaza, *f.* *V.* LECHA.
Lechazo [lay-chah'-tho], *m.* 1. A suckling, an unweaned mammal. 2. A weaned lamb.
Leche [lay'-chay], *f.* 1. Milk. 2. Milk or white fluid in plants. *Cochinillo de leche*, Sucking pig. *Vaca de leche*, Milch cow. *Leche de canela*, Oil of cinnamon dissolved in wine. *Leche de gallina* or *leche de ave*, Common star of Bethlehem. Ornithogalum umbellatum, *L.* *Hermano de leche*, Foster-brother. *Leche de los viejos*, (Coll.) Old wine. *Estar alguna cosa en leche*, Not to have attained a state of maturity. *Estar la mar en leche*, The sea being calm and smooth. *Mamarlo en la leche*, To imbibe in one's infancy. *Leche de tierra*, Magnesia. *Como una leche*, (Coll.) Applied to any thing very soft and tender. *Leche crema* or *quemada*, Custard. *Estar con la leche en los labios*, To lack experience. *Lo que en la leche se mama, en la mortaja se derrama*, Habits acquired in childhood last till death.
Lechecillas [lay-chay-theel'-lyas], *f. pl.* 1. Sweetbread of calves, lambs, and kids. 2. Livers and lights.
Lechera [lay-chay'-rah] *f.* 1. Milkwoman, milkmaid, dairymaid. 2. Milk-pan, or vessel for serving milk.
Lechera, *a.* Milch: applied to animals kept for giving milk.
Lechería [lay-chay-ree'-ah], *f.* Cow-house, dairy, lactary.
Lechero, ra [lay-chay'-ro, rah], *a.* (Coll.) Milky; containing milk.
Lechero [lay-chay'-ro], *m.* 1. Milkman. 2. Tan-pit, where the ooze of bark is prepared.
Lecherón [lay-chay-rone'], *m.* (Prov.) 1. Milk-pail, milk-vessel. 2. Flannel in which new-born infants are rolled
Lechetrezna [lay-chay-treth'-nah], *f.* (Bot.) Spurge. Euphorbia.
Lechigada [lay-che-gah'-dah], *f.* 1. Litter, a number of animals produced at a single birth. 2. A company of persons of the same kind of life or the same calling.
Lechín [lay-cheen'], *m.* 1. Tent, pledget. 2. (Prov.) Olives rich in oil.
Lechino [lay-chee'-no], *m.* 1. Tent, a roll of lint put into a sore. 2. Small tumour in horses.
Lecho [lay'-cho], *m.* 1. Bed, a couch. 2. Litter, straw laid under animals. *Lecho de lobo*, Haunt of a wolf. *Lecho de respeto*, Bed of state. 3. Bed of a river; horizontal surface of a seat. 4. Layer, a stratum or row.
Lechón [lay-chone'], *m.* 1. A sucking pig; pig of any size. 2. A dirty fellow in point of dress or manner of living.
Lechona [lay-cho'-nah], *f.* 1. Sucking female pig. 2. (Coll.) A dirty woman in point of dress.
Lechoncico, illo, ito [lay-chon-thee'-co], *m. dim.* A very young pig.
Lechoso, sa [lay-cho'-so, sah], *a.* (Bot.) Having a milky juice.—*m.* (S. Amer.) The papaw-tree; the juice has remarkable digestive properties.
Lechuga [lay-choo'-gah], *f.* 1. (Bot.) Lettuce. Lactuca. 2. *V.* LECHUGUILLA for a frill.
Lechugado, da [lay-choo-gah'-do, dah], *a.* Having leaves like lettuce.
Lechuguero, ra [lay-choo-gay-ro, rah], *m.* & *f.* Retailer of lettuce.
Lechuguilla [lay-choo-geel'-lyah], *f.* 1. (Dim.) Small lettuce. 2. Frill formerly worn around the neck.
Lechuguino [lay-choo-gee'-no], *m.* Plot of small lettuces. (Coll.)—*m.* & *f.* Dandy, dandizette.
Lechuza [lay-choo'-thah], *f.* Owl, barn-owl. Strix passerina.
Lechuzo, za [lay-choo'-tho, thah], *a.* 1. Suckling: applied to mule colts less than a year old. 2. Collecting debts in trust for another. 3. Owl-like; a nickname applied to persons.

Lechuzo [lay-choo'-tho], *m.* 1. Nickname of an agent, collector, or commissioner who collects money or debts. 2. Nickname of persons resembling owls in any of their qualities.

Ledamente [lay-dah-men'-tay], *adv.* (Poet.) Merrily, cheerfully.

Ledo, da [lay'-do, dah], *a.* (Poet.) Gay, merry, cheerful, glad, joyful.

Leer [lay-err'], *va.* 1. To read. 2. To lecture, to instruct publicly. 3. To read one's thoughts.

Lega [lay'-gah], *f.* A lay-sister who serves the community.

Legacía, Legación [lay-gah-thee'-ah, lay-gah-the-on'], *f.* 1. Embassy, legation, deputation. 2. Legateship, office of a legate. 3. Message sent by an ambassador or deputy. 4. Province of the ecclesiastical states governed by a legate. 5. Duration of a legate's embassy or government.

Legado [lay-gah'-do], *m.* 1. Legacy, a particular thing given by last will and testament. 2. Deputy, ambassador, legate. *Legado a látere*, Legate, an ambassador from the Pope to a foreign power, generally a cardinal or bishop. 3. Commander of a Roman legion.

Legador [lay-gah-dor'], *m.* (Prov.) Daylabourer, who ties the feet of sheep, for shearing them.

Legadura [lay-gah-doo'-rah], *f.* (Ant.) Ligature, cord, or strap for tying or binding.

Legajico, illo, ito [lay-gah-hee'-co], *m. dim.* A small bundle of loose papers tied together.

Legajo [lay-gah'-ho], *m.* Bundle of loose papers tied together.

Legal [lay-gahl'], *a.* 1. Legal, lawful, constitutional. 2. Loyal, true, faithful in the performance of duty, punctual.

Legalidad [lay-gah-le-dahd'], *f.* Legality, fidelity, punctuality; lawfulness, legitimateness.

Legalización [lay-gah-le-thah-the-on'], *f.* 1. Attestation of a signature or subscription by which an instrument or writing is legalized. 2. Notarial certificate.

Legalizar [lay-gah-le-thar'], *va.* To legalize, to authorize, to make lawful.

Legalmente [lay-gal-men'-tay], *adv.* Legally, lawfully; faithfully.

Legamen [lay-gah'-men], *m.* (Obs.) Ambassador, legate.

Legamente [lay-gah-men'-tay], *adv.* Ignorantly, in an illiterate manner.

Légamo [lay'-gah-mo], *m.* Slime, mud, or clay left by water.

Legamoso, sa [lay-gah-mo'-so, sah], *a.* Slimy, greasy.

Legaña [lay-gah'-nyah], *f.* Lippitude, blearedness of eyes.

Legar [lay-gar'], *va.* 1. To depute, to send on an embassy. 2. To bequeath, to leave by last will or testament.

Legatario, ria [lay-gah-tah'-re-o, ah], *m.* & *f.* Legatee, a person to whom a legacy is left, legatory.

Legatina [lay-gah-tee'-nah], *f.* A stuff made of silk and wool.

Legenda [lay-hen'-dah], *f.* Legend, traditionary history of saints. (Acad.)

Legendario [lay-hen-dah'-re-o], *m.* 1. Legend, a chronicle or register of the lives of saints. 2. Legendary, author of a legend.

Legible [lay-hee'-blay], *a.* Legible, such as may be read.

Legiblemente, *adv.* (Littl. us.) Legibly.

Legión [lay-he-on'], *f.* 1. Legion, a Roman corps. 2. Legion, an indefinite number.

Legionario, ria [lay-he-o-nah'-re-oh, ah], *a.* Legionary, belonging to a legion.

Legislación [lay-his-lah-the-on'], *f.* 1. Legislation, collection of the laws of a country. 2. Enactment of laws.

Legislador, ra [lay-his-lah-dor', rah], *m.* & *f.* 1. Legislator, law-giver, lawmaker. 2. Censor, censurer, he that blames or censures.

Legislar [lay-his-lar'], *va.* 1. To legislate, to enact laws. 2. To censure, to criticise.

Legislativo, va [lay-his-lah-tee'-vo, vah], *a.* Legislative, law-giving: constitutive.

Legislatura [lay-his-lah-too'-rah], *f.* Legislature, the power that makes laws.

Legisperito [lay-his-pay-ree'-to], *m.* V. JURISPERITO.

Legista [lay-hees'-tah], *m.* Legist, one skilled in law; a professor of laws; a student of jurisprudence.

Legítima [lay-hee'-te-mah], *f.* Portion or share of the paternal or maternal estate, which belongs to the children, according to law.

Legitimación [lay-he-te-mah-the-on'], *f.* Legitimation, the act of investing with the privileges of lawful birth.

Legítimamente [lay-hee'-te-mah-men-tay], *adv.* Legitimately, lawfully.

Legitimar [lay-he-te-mar'], *va.* 1. To prove, to establish in evidence. 2. To legitimate, to procure to any the rights of legitimate birth. 3. To make legitimate or adequate; to legalize.

Legitimidad [lay-he-te-me-dahd'], *f.* Legitimacy, legitimateness; legality, lawfulness.

Legitimista [lay-he-te-mees'-tah], *a.* & *m.* & *f.* Legitimist, upholding the divine right of kings, and of succession to the crown by rigorous order of primogeniture.

Legítimo, ma [lay-hee'-te-mo, mah], *a.* 1. Legitimate, legal, lawful, authentic. 2. True, certain.

Lego [lay'-go], *m.* 1. Layman, laic, one of the people distinct from the clergy. 2. Lay-brother or lay-friar, a person admitted for the service of a religious body. *Carta de legos*, Decree which excludes an ecclesiastic judge from the cognizance of civil causes.—*a.* 1. Laical, lay, laic. 2. Ignorant, illiterate.

Legón [lay-gone'], *m.* Spade.

Legra [lay'-grah], *f.* Trepan, surgeon's instrument; a cylindrical saw, trephine.

Legración, Legradura [lay-grah-the-on', lay-grah-doo'-rah], *f.* Act of trepanning.

Legrar [lay-grar'], *va.* To trepan, to perforate the skull with a trepan; to trephine.

Legua [lay'-goo-ah], *f.* League, a linear measure: 17½ Spanish leagues make a geographical degree; 8,000 Spanish yards make a Spanish league, or nearly four English miles. *A legua, a la legua, a leguas, de cien leguas, de muchas leguas* or *desde media legua*, Very far, at a great distance.

Leguilla [lay-geel'-lyah], *f.* V. LIGUILLA.

Legumbre [lay-goom'-bray], *f.* 1. Pulse, leguminous plants. 2. Vegetables, garden-stuff, legume or legumen.

Legúmina [lay-goo'-me-nah], *f.* Legumin, a proteid compound called also vegetable casein.

Leguminoso, sa [lay-goo-me-no'-so, sah], *a.* (Bot.) Leguminous: applied to plants which bear legumes or pods.

Leíble [lay-ee'-blay], *a.* Legible, readable.

Leído, da [lay-ee'-do, dah], *a.* Having read much, book-learned.—*pp.* of LEER.

Leijar, Lejar [lay-e-har', lay-har'], *va.* (Obs.) *V.* DEJAR.

Leila [lay'-e-lah], *f.* A Moorish dance.

Leima [lay'-e-mah], *m.* Interval of music.

Lejanía [lay-hah-nee'-ah], *f.* Distance, remoteness in place.

Lejano, na [lay-hah'-no, nah], *a.* Distant, remote, far.

Lejía [lay-hee'-ah], *f.* 1. Lye, water boiled with ashes. 2. (Met.) Severe reprehension.

Lejío [lay-hee'-o], *m.* Among dyers, lye.

Lejivial [lay-he-ve-ahl'], *a.* Lixivial.

Lejos [lay'-hos], *adv.* At a great distance, far off. *Buen lejos*, Looking best at a distance.

Lejos [lay'-hos], *m.* 1. Perspective, distant prospect, background. 2. (Met.) Similarity, appearance, resemblance. *A lo lejos, de lejos, de muy lejos* or *desde lejos*, At a great distance.

Lejos, jas [lay'-hos, has], *a.* Distant very remote: generally used in the feminine.

Lejuelos [lay-hoo-ay'-los], *adv. dim.* At a little distance.

Lelilí [lay-le-lee'], *m.* War-whoop of the Moors.

Lelo, la [lay'-lo, lah], *a.* Stupid, ignorant, crazy.

Lema [lay'-mah], *m.* 1. Argument of a poem explained in the title; motto. 2. Lemma, a proposition previously assumed.

Leme [lay'-may], *f.* (Obs. Naut.) Tiller, helm. (Eng. helm.)

Lemosín, na [lay-mo-seen', nah], *a.* Relating to the Lemosin language, or that of the troubadours.

Lemosín [lay-mo-seen'], *m.* The Lemosin language; langue d'oc.

Len [len], *a.* Applied to soft, untwisted silk.

Lena [lay'-nah], *f.* Spirit, vigour. (Acad.)

Lencera [len-thay'-rah], *f.* A woman who deals in linen; the wife of a linen-draper.

Lencería [len-thay-ree'-ah], *f.* 1. An assortment of linen; plenty of linen. 2. Linen-draper's shop; linen-hall, where linen is sold. 3. Linen trade.

Lencero, ra [len-thay'-ro, rah], *m.* & *f.* Linen-draper, linen merchant.

Lendel [len-del'], *m.* Circle described by a horse turning a wheel to raise water out of a well.

Lendrera [len-dray'-rah], *f.* A close comb for taking out nits.

Lendrero [len-dray'-ro], *m.* Place full of nits.

Lendroso, sa [len-dro'-so, sah], *a.* Nitty, full of nits.

Lene [lay'-nay], *a.* 1. Mild, soft, bland. 2. Mild, pleasant, benevolent. 3. Light, of small weight or consideration.

Lengua [len'-goo-ah], *f.* 1. The tongue. 2. Language, idiom. 3. Information, advice. 4. Speech, discourse. 5. Tongue or needle of a balance. 6. Clapper of a bell. *Lenguas*, In the order of Malta, the provinces into which the possessions of the order are divided. *Lengua del agua*, At the edge of the water. *Lengua de tierra*, Neck of land running out into the sea. *Con la lengua de un palmo*, or *con un palmo de lengua*, With great anxiety or eagerness. *Tener algo en el pico de la lengua*, To have any thing at the tongue's end. *Len-*

gua sabia, Learned language. *Lengua canina* or *de perro*; (Bot.) Hound's-tongue. Cynoglossum. *Lengua de buey*, (Bot.) Common bugloss. Anchusa officinalis. *Lengua cerval*, Hart's-tongue or common hart's-tongue. Asplenium scolopendrium. *Lengua de vaca*, Neat's tongue. *De lengua en lengua*, From mouth to mouth. *Poner la lengua en alguno*, (Met.) To backbite, to speak ill of a person. *Irse la lengua*, To give a loose rein to one's tongue. 7. (Antiq.) Interpreter. *Andar en lenguas*, To be much talked of. *Morderse la lengua*, (Met.) To curb one's speech sharply. *Tomar lengua* or *lenguas*, To seek information.

Lenguado [len-goo-ah'-do], *m.* (Zool.) Sole, flounder.

Lenguaje [len-goo-ah'-hay], *m.* 1. Language, idiom, speech. 2. Language, style, manner of speaking or writing. *Lenguaje bajo* or *obsceno*, Ribaldry.

Lenguaraz [len-goo-ah-rath'], *a.* 1. Languaged, having various languages. 2. Fluent, voluble. 3. Forward, petulant. 4. Talkative, free-tongued. It is sometime used as a substantive for a linguist.

Lenguaz [len-goo-ath'], *a.* Loquacious, garrulous.

Lengüecica, illa, ita [len-goo-ay-thee'-cah, eel'-yah], *f. dim.* A small tongue.

Lengüeta [len-goo-ay'-tah], *f.* 1. (Dim.) A small tongue. 2. Languet, any thing cut in the form of a tongue; a free reed in wind instruments. 3. (Anat.) Epiglottis. 4. Needle of a balance. 5. Bookbinder's cutting-knife. 6. (Mech.) Feather, a thin wedge. 7. (Arch.) Buttress; moulding. 8. Borer used by saddlers and chair-makers.

Lengüetada [len-goo-ay-tah'-dah], *f.* The act of licking.

Lengüetería [len-goo-ay-tay-ree'-ah], *f.* The reed-work of an organ.

Lengüezuela [len-goo-ay-thoo-ay'-lah], *f. dim.* A small tongue.

Lenidad [lay-ne-dahd'], *f.* Lenity, mildness, favour.

Lenificar [lay-ne-fe-car'], *va.* To lenify, to soften. *V.* Suavizar.

Lenificativo, va [lay-ne-fe-cah-tee'-vo, vah], *a.* Mollifying, softening.

Lenir [lay-neer'], *va.* (Obs.) To mollify, to assuage. *V.* Lenificar.

Lenitivo, va [lay-ne-tee'-vo, vah], *a.* Lenitive, assuasive, lenient, mitigant.

Lenitivo [lay-ne-tee'-vo], *m.* Emollient, mitigator, lenient.

Lenocinio [lay-no-thee'-ne-o], *m.* Pimping, pandering. *V.* Alcahuetería.

Lenón [lay-none'], *m.* (Obs.) *V.* Alcahuete.

Lentamente [len-tah-men'-tay], *adv.* Slowly, heavily, lazily, lingeringly.

Lente [len'-tay], *com.* 1. Lens. 2. Eye-glass. *Lente gran angular*, Wide-angle lens. *Lente telefotográfico*, Telephoto lens. *Lentes bifocales*, Bifocals, bifocal glasses. *Lentes de contacto*, Contact lenses. *Lentes contra resplandores*, Sun glasses; heat glasses.

Lentecer [len-tay-therr'], *vn.* & *vr.* To grow soft or tender. (Acad.)

Lenteja [len-tay'-hah], *f.* (Bot.) Lentil. Cicer lens. *Lenteja de agua*, Gibbous duck-weed. Lemna gibba.

Lentejuela [len-tay-hoo-ay'-lah], *f.* Spangle, a small plate of shining metal.

Lenteza [len-tay'-thah], *f.* (Obs.) Slowness.

Lenticular [len-te-coo-lar'], *a.* Lenticular, in the form of a lentil. *Hueso lenticular*, The smallest bone of the ear; stapes.

Lentiforme [len-te-for'-may], *a.* (Anat.) Lens-shaped, lentiform.

Lentisco [len-tees'-co], *m.* (Bot.) Mastich-tree. Pistacia lentiscus.

Lentitud [len-te-tood'], *f.* Slowness, sluggishness, coldness.

Lento, ta [len'-to, tah], *a.* 1. Slow, sluggish, tardy, heavy, long, lingering. 2. (Met.) Glutinous. 3. (Mus.) Largo. 4. (Med.) Slow, hectic.

Lentor [len-tor'], *m.* Lentor, a viscous humour.

Leña [lay'-nyah], *f.* 1. Wood, fire-wood. 2. (Coll.) Stick, beating. (Acad.) *Llevar leña al monte*, or *hierro a Vizcaya*, To carry coals to Newcastle. *Del árbol caído todos hacen leña*, Of a fallen tree, all make fire-wood; contempt of humbled pride. *Echar leña al fuego*, (Met.) To foment discord.

Leñador, ra [lay-nyah-dor', rah], *m.* & *f.* Woodman, wood-cutter, dealer in wood.

Leñar [lay-nyar'], *va.* To cut wood.

Leñera [lay-nyay'-rah], *f.* Place for fire-wood.

Leñazgo [lay-nyath'-go], *m.* Pile of wood or timber.

Leñero [lay-nyay'-ro], *m.* 1. Dealer in wood, timber-merchant. 2. Timber-yard. 3. A logman.

Leño [lay'-nyo], *m.* 1. Block, a heavy piece of timber; a log; the trunk of a tree cut down. 2. (Poet.) Ship, vessel. 3. (Met.) Person of little talent or ability. 4. (Bot.) Woody fibre. *Leño hediondo*, (Bot.) *V.* Hediondo. *Leño blanco*, (Amer.) Bignonia leucoxylum. *Leño jabón*, *V.* Palomanteca.

Leñoso, sa [lay-nyo'-so, sah], *a.* Woody, ligneous.

León [lay-on'], *m.* 1. Lion. Felis leo. *León pardo*, *V.* Leopardo. 2. (Ast.) Leo, the fifth sign of the zodiac. 3. (Met.) An irritable and cruel person. 4. A neuropterous insect, dragon-fly.

Leona [lay-o'-nah], *f.* Lioness.

Leonado, da [lay-o-nah'-do, dah], *a.* Lion-coloured, tawny.

Leoncico, illo, ito [lay-on-thee'-co], *m.* Whelp of a lion.

Leonera [lay-o-nay'-rah], *f.* Cage or place where lions are shut up; a menagerie.

Leonero [lay-o-nay'-ro], *m.* 1. Keeper of lions. 2. Master of a gambling-house.

Leonés, sa [lay-o-nays', sah], *a.* Belonging to or native of Leon, a province of Spain.

Leónica [lay-o'-ne-cah], *f.* Vein or gland under the tongue: chiefly used of horses.

Leonino, na [lay-o-nee'-no, nah], *a.* 1. Leonine, belonging to lions. 2. Leonine verses, the end of which rhymes to the middle.

Leonina [lay-o-nee'-nah], *f.* Elephantiasis, a kind of leprosy.

Leopardo [lay-o-par'-do], *m.* Leopard, panther. Felis pardus.

Lépero, ra [lay'-pay-ro, rah], *a.* (Mex.) Of the lowest kind of people, ragged and wretched.

Lepidio [lay-pee'-de-o], *m.* (Bot.) Pepper-grass. Lepidium.

Lepidóptero, ra [lay-pe-dop'-tay-ro, rah], *a.* Lepidopterous, belonging to the lepidoptera.—*m. pl.* The lepidoptera, a class of insects having wings covered with dust-like scales. It includes butterflies, moths, and sphinxes.

Lepisma [lay-pees'-mah], *f.* Lepisma, the bristle-tail, silver-fish, or sugar louse.

Leopoldina [lay-o-pol-dee'-nah], *f.* Watch fob.

Leporino, na [lay-po-ree'-no, nah], *a.* Like a hare. *Labio leporino*, Harelip.

Lepra [lay'-prah], *f.* Leprosy.

Leprosería [lay-pro-say-ree'-ah], *f.* A hospital for lepers.

Leprosidad [lay-pro-se-dahd'], *f.* (Med.) Leprousness.

Leproso, sa [lay-pro'-so, sah], *a.* Leprous, leperous.—*m.* & *f.* Leper.

Lercha [lerr'-chah], *f.* (Prov.) A reed passed through the gills of fishes to hang them up.

Lerdamente [ler-dah-men'-tay], *adv.* Slowly, heavily, lumpishly, obtusely.

Lerdez [ler-deth'], *f.* Slowness, tardiness, heaviness.

Lerdo, da [layr'-do, dah], *a.* Slow, heavy; dull of comprehension, lumpish, obtuse.

Lerdón [ler-done'], *m.* (Vet.) Tumour in a horse's pastern.

Lesbiano, na, Lesbio, bia [les-be-ah'-no, nah, les'-be-o, ah], *a.* & *f.* & *m.* Lesbian.

Lesbio, bia [les'-be-o, ah], *a.* Lesbian, of Lesbos.

Lesión [lay-se-on'], *f.* Hurt, damage, wound; injury, wrong.

Lesivo, va [lay-see'-vo, vah], *a.* Prejudicial, injurious.

Lesna [les'-nah], *f.* Awl, a pointed instrument to bore holes.

Lesnordeste [les-nor-des'-tay], *m.* (Naut.) East-north-east wind.

Leso, sa [lay'-so, sah], *a.* Wounded, hurt, damaged; perverted. *Lesa majestad*, Leze-majesty; high treason.

Leste [les'-tay], *m.* East wind, east.

Lesueste [lay-soo-es'-tay], *m.* (Naut.) East-south-east wind.

Letal [lay-tahl'], *a.* Mortal, deadly, destructive, lethal.

Letanía [lay-tah-nee'-ah], *f.* 1. Litany, a form of prayer. *Letanías*, Supplicatory processions. 2. (Coll.) List or enumeration of things.

Letárgico, ca [lay-tar'-he-co, cah], *a.* Lethargic, lethargical.

Letargo [lay-tar'-go], *m.* Lethargy, a morbid drowsiness.

Letargoso, sa [lay-tar-go'-so, sah], *a.* Causing lethargy, deadening.

Leteo, a [lay-tay'-o, ah], *a.* (Poet.) Lethean.

Leticia [lay-tee'-the-ah], *f.* (Obs.) Joy, mirth.

Letífero, ra [lay-tee'-fay-ro, rah], *a.* Lethiferous, deadly, that which is the cause or sign of death.

Letificante [lay-te-fe-cahn'-tay], *pa.* Exhilarating.

Letificar [lay-te-fe-car'], *va.* (Littl. us.) 1. To rejoice, to make merry. 2. To animate, cheer.

Letífico, ca [lay-tee'-fe-co, cah], *a.* Cheering, bringing joy.

Letra [lay'-trah], *f.* 1. Letter, a character of the alphabet. 2. Hand, character, or peculiar manner of writing. 3. Type, a printing letter. 4. Motto, inscription. 5. Letter, the verbal expression, the literal meaning, the grammatical sense of a phrase. 6. A kind of Spanish poetical composition. 7. Words of a song. 8. An arithmetical character, a figure. *Letra* or *letra de cambio*, Bill of exchange. *A la letra*, Literally, punctually, entirely. *Tener mucha letra*, To be very artful and cunning. *Letras*, 1. Letters, learning; the learned professions. 2. Rescript, despatch. 3. (Prov.) Certification, testimony. *Letras humanas*, *V.* Humanidades. *Letras sagradas*, The Bible, the sacred Scriptures. *Seguir las letras*, To study or devote oneself to the sciences. *Tener las letras gordas*, To be dull or ignorant in point of sciences and learning.

Letrada [lay-trah'-dah], *f.* (Coll.) Lawyer's wife.
Letradería, Letraduría [lay-trah-day-ree'-ah], *f.* 1. (Low) Body or society of lawyers, inn. 2. A foolish speech pompously uttered.
Letrado, da [lay-trah'-do, dah], *a.* 1. Learned, erudite, lettered. 2. (Coll.) Vain, presumptuous. *A lo letrado,* As a lawyer, like a counsellor.
Letrado [lay-trah'-do], *m.* Lawyer, professor of law; advocate, counsellor.
Letrero [lay-tray'-ro], *m.* An inscription, a title, sign, label; a legend on medals or coins.
Letrilla [lay-treel'-lyah], *f.* 1. (Dim.) A small letter. 2. A short poem adapted to music.
Letrina [lay-tree'-nah], *f.* Privy, water-closet, latrine.
Letrón [lay-trone'], *m. aug.* A large letter.
Letrones [lay-tro'-nes], *m. pl.* Capital letters or large characters written at the door of churches.
Leucemia [lay-oo-thay'-me-ah], *f.* Leukemia.
Leucocito [lay-oo-co-thee'-to], *m.* (Anat.) Leucocyte.
Leucoma [lay-oo-co'-mah], *f.* (Med.) Leucoma, disease of the cornea.
Leucorrea [lay-oo-cor-ray'-ah], *f.* Leucorrhœa; colloquially, whites.
Leucoris [lay-oo-co'-ris], *f.* Generic name of diseases which attack the lymphatic vessels.
Leudar [lay-oo-dar'], *va.* To ferment dough with leaven; to raise bread.
Leudo, da [lay'-oo-do, dah], *a.* Fermented, leavened: applied to bread.
Leva [lay'-vah], *f.* 1. (Naut.) Act of weighing anchor. *Pieza de leva,* Shot fired as a signal for weighing anchor. 2. Levy, the act of raising men for military service; press. *Ronda* or *piquete de leva* or *matrícula,* Press-gang. 3. (Naut.) Swell of the sea. *Hay mar de leva,* There is a swell in the offing. 4. Cog, tooth, cam, wiper. 5. Play of a piston.—*pl.* Tricks, artful devices.
Levada [lay-vah'-dah], *f.* 1. Silk-worm which moves from one place to another. 2. Salute or flourish made with the foil by fencers before they set to. *V.* Llevada.
Levadero, ra [lay-vah-day'-ro, rah], *a.* That which is demanded.
Levadizo, za [lay-vah-dee'-tho, thah], *a.* That can be lifted or raised.
Levadura [lay-vah-doo'-rah], *f.* 1. Ferment, leaven, yeast. 2. (Med.) Ferment, septic matter, humour vitiated and capable of causing disorders.
Levantada [lay-van-tah'-dah], *f.* (Coll.) Rise, the act of rising.
Levantadamente, *adv.* In an elevated or exalted manner.
Levantador, ra [lay-van-tah-dor', rah], *m. & f.* 1. One who raises or lifts up. 2. Disturber, rioter. 3. (Surg.) Levator, elevator.
Levantamiento [lay-van-tah-me-en'-to], *m.* 1. Elevation, the act of raising; sublimity. 2. Insurrection, revolt, rebellion, commotion. 3. (Prov.) Balance of accounts.
Levantar [lay-van-tar'], *va.* 1. To raise, to lift or lift up, to heave, to get up, to hold up, to hang up, to mount, to set upright. 2. To build up, to raise, to erect a building. 3. To raise, to excite to tumult or war, to stir up. 4. To impute or attribute falsely. 5. To rouse, to raise, to excite to action. 6. To elevate, to aggrandize, to promote. 7. To rouse or start game. 8. To cut the cards. 9. To levy, to raise men for military service. 10. To increase, to enlarge. 11. To raise the voice, to utter loudly. 12. To cause, to occasion; to begin.—*vr.* 1. To rise, to change a jacent or recumbent for an erect posture, to get up from a fall. 2. To rise, to get up from a bed. 3. To stand up. 4. To rise, to have more elevation than some other thing. 5. To rise, to break in commotions or insurrections. 6. To start or to rise suddenly: applied to game. *Levantar un plano, mapa,* etc., To draw the sketch of a place. *Levantar falso testimonio,* To accuse falsely. *Levantar la cabeza,* To retrieve one's fortunes; to take courage. *Levantar el pensamiento,* To conceive the idea of something heroic. *Levantarse las piedras contra uno,* To be unpopular and unfortunate. *Levantar la casa,* To break up housekeeping. *Levantar velas,* (Met.) To abandon one's residence. *Levantar la cerviz,* (Met.) To exalt; to extol one's self. *Levantar polvareda,* To raise a dust, to excite disturbances. *Levantar el caballo,* To drive a horse at the gallop. *Levantar la mesa,* To clear the table. *Levantarse con algo,* To take possession of any thing.
Levante [lay-vahn'-tay], *m.* 1. Levant, particularly the coasts of the Mediterranean east of Italy. 2. East; east wind. *Estar de levante,* To be ready to set sail. *Comercio de Levante,* The Levant trade.
Levantin [lay-van-teen'], *m.* Levantine: generally used in the plural.
Levantino, na [lay-van-tee'-no, nah], *a.* Levantine, relating to the Levant.
Levantisco, cah [lay-van-tees'-co, cah], *a.* 1. Turbulent, restless. 2. *V.* Levantino.
Levar [lay-var'], *va.* 1. (Obs.) To carry, to transport. 2. (Naut.) To weigh anchor.—*vr.* To set sail.
Leve [lay'-vay], *a.* Light, of little weight; trifling.
Leveche [lay-vay'-chay], *m.* (Naut.) The south-west wind. (Acad.)
Levedad [lay-vay-dahd'], *f.* Lightness, levity; inconstancy.
Levemente [lay-vay-men'-tay], *adv.* Lightly, gently; venially.
Leviatán [lay-ve-ah-tahn'], *m.* Leviathan, a monstrous water animal.
Levigación [lay-ve-gah-the-on'], *f.* Levigation, separation by washing of a finer powder from a coarser; elutriation.
Levigar [lay-ve-gar'], *va.* To levigate, to free from grit, to elutriate.
Levita [lay-vee'-tah], *m.* 1. Levite, one of the tribe of Levi. 2. *V.* Diácono.
Levita [lay-vee'-tah], *f.* Frock-coat, Prince Albert coat. *Gente de levita,* Middle classes. *Señor de levita,* Gentleman, respectable person.
Levítico [lay-vee'-te-co], *m.* 1. Book of Leviticus. 2. (Coll.) Ceremonial used at a festival.
Levítico, ca [lay-vee'-te-co, cah], *a.* (Coll.) Levitical, priestly.
Levitón [lay-ve-tone'], *m.* A long overcoat, like a frock-coat.
Levulosa [lay-voo-lo'-sah], *f.* Fructose.
Léxico, or Lexicón [lec'-se-co, or lec-se-cone'], *m.* 1. Lexicon, an abridged or special dictionary, principally Greek or Latin. 2. Glossary, vocabulary. (Gr.)
Lexicografía [lec-se-co-grah-fee'-ah], *f.* Lexicography, the art of writing dictionaries.
Lexicográfico, ca [lec-se-co-grah'-fe-co, cah], *a.* Lexicographic, relating to compiling a lexicon or dictionary.
Lexicógrafo [lec-se-co'-grah-fo], *m.* Lexicographer, author or writer of a dictionary.
Lexicología [lec-se-co-lo-hee'-ah], *f.* Lexicology, the systematic study of the words of a language.
Lexicólogo [lec-se-co'-lo-go], *m.* Lexicologist.
Ley [lay'-e], *f.* 1. Law, an ordinance, constitution or statute publicly established. 2. Law, a rule of action. 3. Loyalty, faithful attachment to a superior or master. 4. Religion. 5. A legal standard of quality, weight or measure. 6. A principle, or universal property. *Ley del encaje,* (Coll.) Dictamen of a judge without regard to the laws. *Ley de la trampa,* Fraud, deceit. *A la ley,* With propriety and neatness. *A toda ley,* Perfectly, according to rule.—*pl.* 1. Body or collection of laws. 2. Study and profession of the law. *Ley escrita,* Statute law, as opposed to custom or unwritten law. *Ley antigua,* The law of Moses. *A ley de caballero,* or *de cristiano,* On the word of a gentleman or a Christian. *Echar la ley a alguno,* To judge with the utmost rigour of the law. *Ley del embudo,* Severity for others, indulgence for ourselves.
Leyenda [lay-yen'-dah], *f.* 1. Reading, lecture, legend, what is read. 2. Inscription on coins or medals.
Lezda [leth'-dah], *f.* Ancient tax on merchandise.
Lezna [leth'-nah], *f.* *V.* Lesna.
Lía [lee'-ah], *f.* 1. A thin bass-rope. 2. Husk of pressed grapes. *Estar hecho una lía,* (Coll.) To be tipsy.
Liana [le-ah'-nah], *f.* Liana, a twining or climbing plant of the tropical forest.
Liar [le-ar'], *va.* To tie, to bind, to fagot.—*vr.* To contract an alliance. *Liarlas,* (Met. Coll.) To elope, to die.
Liaza [le-ah'-thah], *f.* Collection of hoops used by coopers.
Libación [le-bah-the-on'], *f.* Libation, pouring out wine for a sacrifice.
Libamiento [le-bah-me-en'-to], *m.* The offering in ancient sacrifices.
Libar [le-bar'], *va.* 1. To suck, to sip, to extract the juice; to taste. 2. To perform a libation. 3. To sacrifice.
Libelar [le-bay-lar'], *va.* To petition, to sue at law.
Libelático, ca [le-bay-lah'-te-co, cah], *a.* Applied to the Christians who renounced the Christian religion in a written declaration, for which the Roman emperors exempted them from persecution.
Libelo [le-bay'-lo], *m.* 1. Petition, libel; a declaration of charge in writing against a person in court. 2. A defamatory writing, lampoon, libel.
Libélula [le-bay'-loo-lah], *f.* Libellula, the dragon-fly, a neuropterous insect of the greater part of the globe.
Líber [lee'-ber], *m.* Bast, liber, or inner bark of exogenous plants.
Liberación [le-bay-rah-the-on'], *f.* 1. Setting at liberty, liberation. 2. (Law) Remission of a debt.
Liberal [le-bay-rahl'], *a.* 1. Liberal, generous, free, open, large, munificent, open-hearted. 2. Quick in the performance of a thing; brisk, active. 3. Liberal: applied to the arts, as opposed to mechanics.
Liberalidad [le-bay-rah-le-dahd'], *f.* Liberality, generosity, largeness, munificence, frankness, open-heartedness; gallantry.
Liberalismo [le-bay-rah-lees'-mo], *m.* Liberalism, profession of liberal doctrines favourable to political and religious liberty.

Liberalizar [le-bay-rah-lee-thar'], *va.* To liberalize: modern word.

Liberalmente [le-bay-ral-men'-tay], *adv.* Liberally, expeditiously; largely, munificently, generously, frankly.

Liberamente, *adv.* (Obs.) *V.* LIBREMENTE.

Libérrimo, ma [le-ber'-re-mo, mah], *a. sup.* Most free.

Libertad [le-ber-tahd'], *f.* 1. Liberty, freedom, the power of doing without inconvenience what is not contrary to the laws or established customs. 2. Liberty, freedom, as opposed to slavery. 3. Liberty, freedom, the state of one who is not a prisoner. 4. Liberty, freedom, license, assumed familiarity, relaxation of restraint. 5. Liberty, freedom, exemption, privilege, immunity. 6. Freedom, agility, address; independence, unconventionality. 7. Ransom. *Libertad académica*, Academic freedom. *Libertad de comercio*, Free trade. *Libertad de estado*, The unmarried state. *Libertad provisional*, Freedom on bail.

Libertadamente, *adv.* Freely, impudently.

Libertado, da [le-ber-tah'-do, dah], *a.* 1. Libertine, impudent. 2. Free, ungoverned. 3. Idle, disengaged.—*pp.* of LIBERTAR.

Libertador, ra [le-ber-tah-dor', rah], *m.* & *f.* Deliverer, liberator.

Libertar [le-ber-tar'], *va.* 1. To free, to set at liberty, to liberate. 2. To exempt, to free, to excuse, to clear from an obligation or debt, to acquit. 3. To free, to rid from, to clear from any thing ill. 4. To preserve.

Liberticida [le-ber-te-thee'-dah], *m.* Liberticide, a destroyer of liberty.

Libertinaje [le-ber-te-nah'-hay], *m.* Libertinism, licentiousness of opinion or practice; libertinage, license, irreligion.

Libertino, na [le-ber-tee'-no, nah], *m.* & *f.* Child of a freed man.—*a.* Libertine, irreligious, dissolute, impudent, licentious, lewd.

Liberto [le-ber'-to], *m.* A freed man, an emancipated slave.

Libi [lee'-be], *m.* A kind of linseed of Mindanao (P. I.), from which oil is obtained.

Libidine [le-bee'-de-nay], *f.* Lewdness, lust.

Libidinosamente [le-be-de-no-sah-men'-tay], *adv.* Libidinously.

Libidinoso, sa [le-be-de-no'-so, sah], *a.* Libidinous, lewd, lustful.

Libitum (Ad) [lee'-be-toom], *adv.* (Lat.) At will.

Libra [lee'-brah], *f.* 1. Pound, a weight of sixteen ounces. *Libra medicinal*, Pound troy, of twelve ounces, apothecaries' weight, troy weight. *Libra carnicera*, Flesh-pound of thirty-six ounces. 2. *Libra esterlina*, A pound sterling. *Libra tornesa*, A French livre. 3. (Ast.) Libra, sign of the zodiac.

Libración [le-brah-the-on'], *f.* Libration, the state of being balanced.

Libraco [le-brah'-co], *m.* (Coll.) An old worm-eaten book or pamphlet; a bad book.

Librado [le-brah'-do], *m.* (Com.) Drawee.

Librador, ra [le-brah-dor', rah], *m.* & *f.* 1. Deliverer. 2. The drawer of a bill of exchange. 3. Store-keeper of the king's stables. 4. Metal scoop for handling dry sweetmeats, vegetables, etc.

Libramiento [le-brah-me-en'-to], *m.* 1. (Littl. us.) Delivery, the act of delivering. 2. Warrant, order of payment.

Librancista [le-bran-thees'-tah], *m.* One who holds a warrant or order of payment.

Libranza [le-brahn'-thah], *f.* Bank draft.

Librar [le-brar'], *va.* 1. To free, to deliver, to extricate, to exempt; to preserve from ill. 2. To give a warrant or order for paying a certain sum. 3. To despatch, to expedite. 4. (Obs.) To give leave to converse in the parlour: applied to nuns. 5. To commit, to intrust. *Librar bien* or *mal*, To get over a thing well or ill. *A bien* or *a buen librar*, The best that could possibly happen.

Libratorio [le-brah-to'-re-o], *m.* *V.* LOCUTORIO.

Librazo [le-brah'-tho], *m.* 1. (Aug.) A large book. 2. Blow with a book.

Libre [lee'-bray], *a.* 1. Free, uncumbered, unrestrained; independent; unembarrassed. 2. Free, at liberty, not enslaved, not a prisoner. 3. Free, exempt, privileged. 4. Free, innocent, guiltless. 5. Single, unmarried. 6. Free, libertine, loose, unrestrained, frank, licentious, impudent. 7. Rash, bold, forward, thoughtless. 8. Independent. 9. Free, clear from distress. 10. Isolated, alone. *Libre cambio*, Free trade. *Libre a bordo*, Free on board.

Librea [le-bray'-ah], *f.* Livery, clothes given to servants.

Librear [le-bray-ar'], *va.* To weigh, to sell or distribute by pounds.

Librecambista [le-bray-cam-bees'-tah], *m.* Free-trader.—*a.* Advocating free trading.

Librejo [le-bray'-ho], *m. dim.* A little book, a pamphlet.

Libremente [le-bray-men'-tay], *adv.* Freely; boldly; audaciously; impudently.

Librería [le-bray-ree'-ah], *f.* Bookstore, bookseller's shop.

Librero [le-bray'-ro], *m.* Bookseller.

Libreta [le-bray'-tah], *f.* 1. The troy-weight pound. 2. Loaf of bread which weighs sixteen ounces. 3. Small memorandum-book. 4. The book in which each private keeps his account with the sergeant.

Librete [le-bray'-tay], *m.* 1. (Dim.) A small book. 2. Small vessel with coals, used by women for warming their feet; foot-warmer.

Libreto [le-bray'-to], *m.* (Mus.) Libretto (of an opera, etc.)

Librico, ito [le-bree'-co, ee'-to], *m. dim.* A small book.

Librilla [le-breel'-lyah], *f. dim.* A small pound.

Librillo [le-breel'-lyo], *m.* 1. Small book. 2. Cigarette paper. *Librillo de cera*, A wax taper for carrying light.

Libro [lee'-bro], *m.* 1. A book. 2. Book, a division or part of a work. 3. (Met.) Contribution, impost, tax. *Libro becerro*, Dooms-day-book. *Libro de caja*, A cash-book. *Libro de asiento* or *libro de cuentas*, Account-book. *Libro de facturas*, Invoice-book. *Libro del diario*, (Naut.) Journal. *Libro en blanco*, A paper-book. *Libro mayor*, Ledger. *Libro de memoria*, Memorandum-book. *Libro de las cuarenta hojas*, (Coll.) Pack of cards. *Libro verde*, (Coll.) Book for topographical and genealogical remarks; also the compiler of such writings.

Librote [le-bro'-tay], *m. aug.* Large book: applied in general to a bad book.

Licantropia [le-can-tro-pee'-ah], *f.* Lycanthropy, insanity in which the patient imagines himself transformed into a wolf. *V.* ZOANTROPÍA.

Licantrópico, ca [le-can-tro'-pe-co, cah], *a.* Lycanthropic, relating to or affected by lycanthropy.

Licencia [le-then'-the-ah], *f.* 1. Permission, leave, license, liberty. (Mil.) Furlough. 2. Licentiousness, contempt of just restraint, looseness, wantonness. 3. Degree of licentiate.

Licenciadillo [le-then-the-ah-deel'-lyo], *m.* Nickname given to a little ridiculous person dressed in clerical habits.

Licenciado [le-then-the-ah'-do], *m.* 1. Licentiate, a degree in Spanish universities, and the person who has taken that degree. 2. (Coll.) Any scholar in the Spanish universities. 3. A title given to lawyers.

Licenciado, da [le-then-the-ah'-do, dah], *a.* & *pp.* of LICENCIAR. Licensed; vainglorious.

Licenciamiento [le-then-the-ah-me-en'-to], *m.* 1. The act of taking the degree of licentiate. 2. The disbandment of troops.

Licenciar [le-then-the-ar'], *va.* 1. To permit, to allow; to license; to licentiate. 2. To license, to dismiss, to send away. 3. To make a licentiate. (Mil.) To break off, to disband.—*vr.* To become dissolute.

Licenciatura [le-then-the-ah-too'-rah], *f.* The degree of licentiate, and the act of receiving it.

Licenciosamente [le-then-the-o-sah-men'-tay], *adv.* Licentiously.

Licencioso, sa [le-then-the-o'-so, sah], *a.* Licentious, dissolute, free, loose.

Liceo [le-thay'-o], *m.* 1. Lyceum, a public school. 2. Name of certain literary societies.

Licio [lee'-the-o], *m.* (Bot.) Box-thorn. Lycium.

Licitación [le-the-tah-the-on'], *f.* Selling by auction.

Licitamente [lee'-the-tah-men-tay], *adv.* Lawfully, justly, licitly.

Licitante [le-the-tahn'-tay], *m.* Bidder or buyer at auction.

Licitar [le-the-tar'], *va.* To sell at auction.

Licito, ta [lee'-the-to, tah], *a.* Licit, lawful; just.

Licnomancia [lic-no-mahn'-the-ah], *f.* Superstitious divination by means of flames.

Licor [le-cor'], *m.* 1. Liquor, any thing liquid. 2. Liquor, strong drink, spirits.

Licorera [le-co-ray'-rah], *f.* Liqueur bottle.

Licorista [le-co-rees'-tah], *m.* (Com.) A manufacturer or dealer in spirituous liquors.

Licoroso, sa [le-co-ro'-so, sah], *a.* Applied to generous wine.

Lictor [lic-tor'], *m.* Lictor, a minister of justice in ancient Rome.

Licuable [le-coo-ah'-blay], *a.* Liquable, that may be melted.

Licuación [le-coo-ah-the-on'], *f.* Liquation, liquefaction, the act of melting.

Licuante [le-coo-ahn'-tay], *pa.* of LICUAR. Liquefying, dissolving, melting.

Licuar [le-coo-ar'], *va.* To liquefy, to dissolve, to melt.

Licuefacción [le-coo-ay-fac-the-on'], *f.* Liquefaction, conversion into the liquid state.

Licuefacer [le-coo-ay-fah-therr'], *va.* & *vr.* *V.* LICUAR. (Acad.)

Licuefactible [le-coo-ay-fac-tee'-blay], *a.* Liquefiable.

Licuescencia [le-coo-es-then'-the-ah], *f.* Liquescence, aptness to melt.

Licuescente [le-coo-es-then'-tay], *a.* Liquescent, melting.

Lichera [le-chay'-rah], *f.* (Prov.) Woollen cover of a bed.
Lid [leed], *f.* Conflict, contest, fight; dispute, argument.
Líder [lee'-der], *m.* Leader.
Lidiador [le-de-ah-dor'], *m.* Combatant; one who publicly disputes or argues.
Lidiar [le-de-ar'], *vn.* 1. To fight, to oppose, to contend. 2. (Met.) To deal with annoying, vexing persons. 3. (Archaic) To plead before a court. —*va.* To run or fight bulls.
Lidio [lee'-de-o], *a.* (Mus.) Lydian, a species of ancient music.
Liebrastón [le-ay-bras-tone'], *m.* Leveret, a small or young hare.
Liebratico [le-ay-brah-tee'-co], *m.* Young hare.
Liebre [le-ay'-bray], *f.* 1. Hare. Lepus. 2. Coward, poltroon. *Coger una liebre,* To fall into mud or mire.—*pl.* 1. (Naut.) Racks or ribs. 2. (Naut.) Dead-eyes.
Liebrecica, illa, ita [le-ay-bray-thee'-cah, eel'-lyah, ee'-tah], *f. dim.* A young or small hare.
Liebrecilla [le-ay-bray-theel'-lyah], *f.* (Bot.) *V.* Azulejo.
Liebrezuela [le-ay-bray-thoo-ay'-lah], *f. dim.* *V.* Liebrecica.
Lienecico, illo, ito [le-en-thay-thee'-co, eel'-lyo, ee'-to], *m. dim.* Little linen cloth.
Liendre [le-en'-dray], *f.* Nit, the egg of a louse. *Cascar a uno las liendres,* (Vul.) To give one a severe drubbing.
Lientera, Lientería [le-en-tay'-rah, le-en-tay-ree'-ah], *f.* Lientery, diarrhœa which carries off the food undigested.
Lientérico, ca [le-en-tay'-re-co, cah], *a.* Lienteric.
Liento, ta [le-en'-to, tah], *a.* Damp, moist.
Lienza [le-en'-thah], *f.* A narrow strip of any cloth.
Lienzo [le-en'-tho], *m.* 1. Linen, cloth made of flax or hemp; canvas. *Lienzo encerado,* Glazed linen. *Lienzo curado,* Bleached linen. 2. Handkerchief. 3. Painting on linen. 4. (Fort.) Curtain, part of a wall lying between the two bastions. 5. Face or front of a building.
Lifara [le-fah'-rah], *f.* (Prov. Ar.) *V.* Alifara.
Liga [lee'-gah], *f.* 1. A garter. 2. Bird-lime. 3. League, coalition, confederacy, combination, alliance. 4. Alloy for gold and silver.
Ligación [le-gah-the-on'], *f.* 1. Ligation, act of tying. 2. Union, mixture.
Ligada [le-gah'-dah], *f.* (Print.) Ligature, logotype.
Ligado, da [le-gah'-do, dah], *a. & pp.* of Ligar. Tied, bound, leagued, confederate.
Ligado, *m.* (Mus.) Slur.
Ligadura [le-gah-doo'-rah], *f.* 1. Ligature, any thing tied round another. 2. Ligation, ligature, the act of binding. 3. Subjection. 4. (Mus.) A tie, a slur. 5. (Arch.) All the arcs made by cross-timbers in arches. 6. (Mech.) An iron wire which binds the strands of a wire cable. 7. (Naut.) Seizing, the fastening of two ropes with a thin line; lashing. *Dar una ligadura,* (Naut.) To seize.
Ligagamba [le-gah-gahm'-bah], *f.* (Obs.) Garter. *V.* Liga.
Ligamaza [le-gah-mah'-thah], *f.* Viscous or glutinous matter around fruits.
Ligamento [le-gah-men'-to], *m.* 1. (Anat.) Ligament; a cord. 2. Ligament, bond, chain, entanglement.
Ligamentoso, sa [le-gah-men-to'-so, sah], *a.* Ligamentous, ligamental.
Ligamiento [le-gah-me-en'-to], *m.* 1. Union, act of tying or uniting. 2. Union, concord. 3. (Obs.) Ligament.
Ligar [le-gar'], *va.* 1. To tie, to bind, to fasten, to knit. 2. To alloy gold or silver for coinage. 3. To league, to coalesce, to confederate. 4. To render impotent by charms or spells. 5. To exorcise, to purify from the influence of malignant spirits.—*vr.* 1. To league, to conspire, to conjoin, to be leagued, to be allied. 2. To bind one's self to the performance of a contract.
Ligazón [le-gah-thone'], *f.* 1. Union, contexture, confixture, connection, ligament, bond. 2. (Naut.) Futtock-timbers. *Navío que carece de ligazones,* A ship slightly built.
Ligeramente [le-hay-rah-men'-tay], *adv.* Swiftly, lightly, easily; giddily.
Ligereza [le-hay-ray'-thah], *f.* 1. Lightness, celerity, fleetness, agility, nimbleness. 2. Levity, unsteadiness, inconstancy, fickleness, flippancy, flirtation. 3. Lightness, want of weight. *Ligereza de manos,* Legerdemain, juggle.
Ligero, ra [le-hay'-ro, rah], *a.* 1. Light, of little weight. 2. Light, thin: applied to stuff or cloth. 3. Swift, light, active, nimble, fleet. 4. Light, gay, airy, unsteady, giddy. 5. Light, trifling 6. Easily digestible: applied to food. 7. Unsound, not calm: applied to sleep. *Ligero de dedos,* Light-fingered. *A la ligera,* Lightly, expeditiously. *De ligero,* Rashly; easily.
Ligeruela [le-hay-roo-ay'-lah], *a.* Applied to early grapes.
Ligio, a [lee'-he-o, ah], *a.* Liege, bound by some feudal tenure.
Lignito [lig-nee'-to], *m.* Lignite, brown coal.
Lignívoro, ra [lig-nee'-vo-ro, rah], *a.* Wood-eating.—*m. pl.* The longicorn beetles.
Lignum crucis [lig-noom croo'-this], *m.* Relic of the cross of Christ.
Ligomela [le-go-may'-lah], *a.* *V.* Ligeruela.
Liguilla [le-geel'-lyah], *f.* Kind of narrow ribbon.
Lígula [lee'-goo-lah], *f.* 1. (Anat.) Epiglottis, the cartilage which covers the larynx. 2. (Bot.) Ligule, a scarious appendage at the summit of a sheathing petiole in grasses.
Ligulado, da [le-goo-lah'-do, dah], *a.* (Bot.) Ligulate, strap-shaped.
Ligurino, na [le-goo-ree'-no, nah], or **Ligústico, ca** [le-goos'-te-co, cah], *a.* Ligurian.
Ligústico [le-goos'-te-co], *m.* (Bot.) Lovage. Ligusticum.
Ligustro [le-goos'-tro], *m.* (Bot.) Privet. *V.* Alheña.
Lija [lee'-hah], *f.* 1. Dog-fish, a small variety of shark. 2. Skin of the dog-fish used, dry, for polishing wood, lining boxes, etc.
Lijar [le-har'], *va.* 1. To smooth, to polish. 2. (Prov.) *V.* Lastimar.
Lila [lee'-lah], *f.* 1. (Bot.) Lilac-tree. Syringa vulgaris. 2. Lilac flower. 3. A kind of light woollen stuff of various colours.
Lilaila [le-lah-ee'-lah], *f.* 1. Thin woollen stuff. 2. Artifice, trick, wile.
Liliáceo, cea [le-le-ah'-thay-o, ah], *a.* Liliaceous, of the lily family.
Lilili [le-le-lee'], *m.* War-whoop of the Moors.
Lima [lee'-mah], *f.* 1. (Bot.) Lime-tree. Citrus limetta. 2. Lime, the fruit of the lime-tree; also, the sweet lime, another variety of small lemon. 3. File, an instrument for smoothing metals. 4. (Met.) Correction, finish, polish. 5. Channel in the roof of a house for the water to pass to the eaves. *Lima sorda,* (Met.) That which imperceptibly consumes any thing.
Limación [le-mah-the-on'], *f.* The process of filing roughnesses of the teeth.
Limadura [le-mah-doo'-rah], *f.* 1 Act of filing. 2. Filing, limature, metallic fragment rubbed off by the file.
Limalla [le-mahl'-lyah], *f.* Filings.
Limar [le-mar'], *va.* 1. To file, to cut with a file. 2. To file, to polish; to give the finishing stroke to literary productions.
Limatón [le-mah-tone'], *m.* Coarse round file.
Limaza [le-mah'-thah], *f.* 1. Snail. Limax. 2. Archimedes' screw. 3. A disease of the feet of cattle.
Limazo [le-mah'-tho], *m.* Viscosity, sliminess.
Limazón [le-mah-thone'], *m.* Slug, a snail or slimy animal without a shell.
Limbo [leem'-bo], *m.* 1. Limbo, a region assigned to the souls of unbaptized children. 2. (Ast.) Limb, edge or border of the sun or moon. 3. Limb, exterior graduated border of a quadrant. 4. (Zool.) Circumference, or edge of a bivalve shell.
Limen [lee'-men], *m.* (Poet.) *V.* Umbral.
Limeño, ña [le-may'-nyo, nyah], *a.* Belonging to or native of the city Lima.
Limera [le-may'-rah], *f.* 1. Shop-woman who sells files or limes. 2. (Naut.) Helm-port, where the tiller is fastened to the rudder of the ship.
Limero [le-may'-ro], *m.* 1. Shopkeeper who sells files or limes. 2. (Bot.) Lime-tree. Citrus limetta.
Limeta [le-may'-tah], *f.* 1. Vial, a small bottle. 2. (Amer.) Medium-sized wine-bottle.
Limiste [le-mees'-tay], *m.* Cloth made of Segovia wool; cloth of the first quality.
Limitación [le-me-tah-the-on'], *f.* 1. Limitation, restriction, modification, circumscription, corrective; conditionality. 2. Limit, district.
Limitadamente [le-me-tah-dah-men'-tay], *adv.* Limitedly, finitely.
Limitado, da [le-me-tah'-do, dah], *a.* Limited, possessed of little talent.—*f.* (Com.) Of limited liability (fr. Eng. limited).—*pp.* of Limitar.
Limitador, ra [le-me-tah-dor', rah], *m. & f.* One who limits, circumscriber.
Limitáneo, nea [le-me-tah'-nay-o, ah], *a.* 1. Limitary, placed on the boundaries. 2. Limitaneous, belonging to limits.
Limitar [le-me-tar'], *va.* 1. To limit, to confine within bounds, to narrow. 2. To form boundaries, to establish limits. 3. To restrain, to circumscribe; to reduce expense.
Límite [lee'-me-tay], *m.* Limit, boundary, bound, border, confine.
Limítrofe [le-mee'-tro-fay], *a.* Limiting, bounding, conterminous, limitary: applied to frontier provinces.
Limnea [lim-nay'-ah], *f.* Limnæa, the common pond-snail.
Limo [lee'-mo], *m.* Slime, mud.
Limón [le-mone'], *m.* 1. Lemon, the fruit of the lemon-tree. 2. (Bot.) Lemon-tree. Citrus medica. 3. *V.* Limonera. (Per.)
Limonada [le-mo-nah'-dah], *f.* Lemonade. *Limonada de vino,* Lemonade mixed with wine.
Limonado, da [le-mo-nah'-do, dah], *a.* Lemon-coloured.
Limonar [le-mo-nar'], *m.* Plantation of lemon-trees.
Limoncillo [le-mon-theel'-lyo], *m. dim.* A small lemon.

Limonera [le-mo-nay'-rah], *f.* Shaft of a cart.

Limonero [le-mo-nay'-ro], *m.* (Bot.) Lemon-tree. Citrus medica.

Limonero, ra [le-mo-nay'-ro, rah], *m.* & *f.* Dealer in lemons.—*a.* Applied to the shaft horses in carriages, etc.

Limonza [le-mon'-thah], *f.* The citron, or the bitter lemon.

Limoscapo [le-mos-cah'-po], *m.* (Arch.) The part of the shaft of a column nearest the base, apophyge.

Limosidad [le-mo-se-dahd'], *f.* 1. Sliminess. 2. Foul matter between teeth.

Limosna [le-mos'-nah], *f.* Alms, charity.

Limosnero [le-mos-nay'-ro], *m.* Almoner.—*a.* Charitable.

Limoso, sa [le-mo'-so, sah], *a.* Slimy, muddy, limose.

Limpia [leem'-pe-ah], *f.* 1. Cleansing, freeing from dirt. 2. Dredging of harbours. 3. A certain tax paid by ships in harbours where dredging is required.

Limpiabotas [lim-pe-ah-bo'-tas], *m.* A boot-black.

Limpiachimeneas [leem'-pe-ah-che-may-nay'-as], *m.* Chimney-sweeper.

Limpiadera [lim-pe-ah-day'-rah], *f.* 1. A clothes-brush. 2. Comb-brush; a plough-cleaner.

Limpiadientes [lim-pe-ah-de-en'-tes], *m.* Toothpick.

Limpiador, ra [lim-pe-ah-dor', rah], *m.* & *f.* Cleanser, scourer.

Limpiadura [lim-pe-ah-doo'-rah], *f.* Cleansing.—*pl.* Dirt thrown away in cleansing any thing.

Limpiamente [lim-pe-ah-men'-tay], *adv.* Cleanly, neatly; purely; sincerely, faithfully.

Limpiamiento [lim-pe-ah-me-en'-to], *m.* Act of cleansing.

Limpiaoidos [lim-pe-ah-o-ee'-dos], *m.* Earspoon, earpick.

Limpiaojos [lim-pe-ah-o'-hos], *m.* An eye-stone.

Limpiaplumas [lim-pe-ah-ploo'-mas], *m.* A pen-wiper.

Limpiar [lim-pe-ar'], *va.* 1. To clean, to scour, to cleanse. 2. To purify, to clear from guilt. 3. To pursue, to persecute. 4. (Coll.) To steal. *Limpiar las faldriqueras a uno,* To pick one's pockets.—*vr.* To clear one's self from imputed guilt.

Limpiauñas [lim-pe-ah-oo'-nyas], *m.* Fingernail cleaner.

Limpidez [lim-pe-deth'], *f.* Transparency, limpidity.

Limpido, da [leem'-pe-do, dah], *a.* Limpid, crystal-clear, transparent.

Limpieza [lim-pe-ay'-thah], *f.* 1. Cleanness, cleanliness, neatness, purity, limpidness. 2. Chastity, purity of morals. 3. Integrity, rectitude; disinterestedness. 4. Purity of blood. *Limpieza de bolsa,* Emptiness of the purse.

Limpio, pia [leem'-pe-o, ah], *a.* 1. Clean, free from stain; cleanly, limpid. 2. Neat, elegant. 3. Pure: applied to families unconnected with Moors or Jews. 4. Pure, unmingled: commonly applied to corn. 5. Pure, free, clear. 6. Clear of all charges, net. *Limpio de polvo y paja,* Clear or free from all charges. *Jugar limpio,* To deal fair, to act uprightly. *Poner en limpio,* To make a fair copy. *Tierra limpia,* Even, flat country. *Costa limpia,* (Naut.) Clear coast, without shoals, sand-banks, or shallows. *En limpio,* In substance; net price; clearly.

Limpión [lim-pe-on'], *m.* A hasty cleaning. *Date un limpión,* (Coll.) Ironical phrase telling some one he will not get what he wishes.

Limulo [lee'-moo-lo], *m.* Limulus, king-crab.

Lináceas [le-nah'-thay-as], *a.* & *f. pl.* Linaceous, of the flax family.

Linaje [le-nah'-hay], *m.* 1. Lineage, race, progeny, offspring, family, house, kin, extraction, generation. 2. Class, condition. 3. (Prov.) Nobless, nobility.

Linajista [le-nah-hees'-tah], *m.* Genealogist, a writer of pedigrees.

Linajudo, da [le-nah-hoo'-do, dah], *m.* & *f.* & *a.* 1. One who boasts of his origin or family. 2. *m.* Genealogist.

Lináloe [le-nah'-lo-ay], *m.* Aloes. *V.* Áloe.

Linar [le-nar'], *m.* Flax-field, land on which flax is grown.

Linaria [le-nah'-re-ah], *f.* (Bot.) Wild flax, yellow toad flax. Antirrhinum linaria.

Linaza [le-nah'-thah], *f.* Linseed, the seed of flax. *Aceite de linaza,* Linseed oil.

Lince [leen'-thay], *m.* 1. Lynx. Felis lynx. 2. Person of great acuteness and perspicacity.

Lince [leen'-thay], *a.* 1. Sharp-sighted, quick-sighted. 2. Acute, penetrating.

Lincear [lin-thay-ar'], *va.* (Coll.) To discover, to note what may be seen with difficulty.

Linches [leen'-chays], *m. pl.* (Mex.) Saddle-bags made from the fibre of the maguey.

Lindamente [lin-dah-men'-tay], *adv.* Neatly, elegantly.

Lindar [lin-dar'], *vn.* To be contiguous.

Linde [leen'-day], *m.* & *f.* Landmark, boundary, limit.

Linde [leen'-day], *a.* Contiguous, bordering upon.

Lindero, ra [lin-day'-ro, rah], *a.* Contiguous, bordering upon.

Lindero [lin-day'-ro], *m.* *V.* Linde.

Lindeza [lin-day'-thah], *f.* 1. Neatness, elegance, prettiness. 2. *pl.* (Iron.) Improprieties, insults.

Lindo, da [leen'-do, dah], *a.* 1. Neat, handsome, pretty, fine, genteel. 2. Complete, perfect. *De lo lindo,* Perfectly, wonderfully.

Lindo [leen'-do], *m.* Beau, coxcomb, minion.

Lindón [lin-done'], *m.* Ridge, ground thrown up between asparagus-beds.

Lindura [lin-doo'-rah], *f.* *V.* Lindeza.

Linea [lee'-nay-ah], *f.* 1. Line, longitudinal extension. 2. *V.* Raya. 3. *V.* Renglón. 4. Line, lineage, progeny, family ascending or descending. 5. Line, equator, equinoctial line. 6. Line, boundary, limit. 7. Class, order. 8. (Mil.) Trench or intrenchment. 9. (Mil.) Rank of soldiers. 10. Line, twelfth part of an inch. *Línea de agua de mayor carga* or *del fuerte,* (Naut.) Load-water line. *Línea* or *arrufo de la astilla muerta,* (Naut.) The cutting-down line. *Línea de los reveses del costado,* (Naut.) The top timber lines.

Lineal [le-nay-ahl'], *a.* Lineal, composed of lines.

Lineamento [le-nay-ah-men'-to], *m.* Lineament, exterior feature of a body.

Lineamiento [le-nay-ah-me-en'-to], *m.* Lineament, feature.

Linear [le-nay-ar'], *va.* To draw lines, to form with lines.

Linero, ra [le-nay'-ro, rah], *m.* & *f.* (Obs.) Dealer in flax or linen.

Linfa [leen'-fah], *f.* 1. Lymph, a fluid of the body. 2. (Poet.) Water.

Linfático, ca [lin-fah'-te-co, cah], *a.* Lymphatic, pertaining to lymph: applied to vessels and glands.

Linfoquicia [lin-fo-kee'-the-ah], *f.* (Med.) Serous diarrhœa.

Lingote [lin-go'-tay], *m.* (Min.) Ingot, a mass of gold or silver, lingot, a pig of metal.

Lingual [lin-goo-ahl'], *a.* Lingual, relating to the tongue.

Linguete [lin-gay'-tay], *m.* A pawl; a ratchet.

Lingüista [lin-goo-ees'-tah], *m.* Linguist, one versed in languages.

Lingüística [lin-goo-ees'-te-cah], *f.* Linguistics, the science of languages, comparative philology.

Lingüístico, ca [lin-goo-ees'-te-co, cah], *a.* Linguistic, relating to language or linguistics.

Linimento [le-ne-men'-to], *m.* (Med.) Liniment.

Linio [lee'-ne-o], *m.* *V.* Liño.

Lino [lee'-no], *m.* 1. (Bot.) Flax. Linum. 2. Linen. 3. Sail-cloth, canvas.

Linóleo [le-no'-lay-o], *m.* Linoleum.

Linón [le-non'], *m.* Lawn.

Linotipia [le-no-tee'-pe-ah], *f.* Linotype machine.

Linotípico, ca [le-no-tee'-pe-co, cah], *a.* Linotype.

Linotipista [le-no-te-pees'-tah], *m.* & *f.* Linotype operator.

Linotipo [le-no-tee'-po], *m.* Linotype.

Lintel [lin-tel'], *m.* Lintel.

Linterna [lin-terr'-nah], *f.* 1. Lantern. 2. (Arch.) Small tower, cupola. 3. (Mech.) Lantern pinion. 4. (Arg.) Firefly. *Linterna de proyección,* Slide projector. *Linterna eléctrica,* Flashlight. *Linterna mágica,* Magic lantern. *Linterna sorda,* Dark lantern.

Linternazo [lin-ter-nah'-tho], *m.* 1. Blow with a lantern. 2. (Coll.) Wallop, crack.

Linternero [lin-ter-nay'-ro], *m.* Lantern-maker.

Linternilla [lin-ter-neel'-lyah], *f dim.* A small lantern.

Linueso [le-noo-ay'-so], *m.* *V.* Linaza.

Liño [lee'-nyo], *m.* 1. Row of trees or plants. 2. Ridge between furrows in ploughed land.

Liñuelo [le-nyoo-ay'-lo], *m.* Rope, cord.

Lío [lee'-o], *m.* 1. Bundle, parcel, pack. 2. (coll.) Entanglement, row. *Armar un lío,* To start a fight. *Hacerse uno un lío,* To become entangled, to get all confused.

Liorna [le-or'-nah], *f.* (Coll.) Uproar, hullabaloo, confusion.

Lipia [lee'-pe-ah], *f.* Lippia, a plant of the verbena family. Lipia citriodora is the lemon-scented verbena.

Lipis [lee'-pis], *f.* Blue vitriol, copper sulphate.

Lipitud [le-pe-tood'], *f.* (Med.) Lippitude, bleareduess of the eyes.

Liquen [lee'-ken], *m.* Lichen, a low cryptogamic plant.

Liquidable [le-kee-dah'-blay], *a.* Liquefiable.

Liquidación [le-kee-dah-the-on'], *f.* 1. Liquidation, settlement. 2. Balance.

Liquidámbar [le-ke-dahm'-bar], *m.* Liquidambar, a resinous substance, obtained by incision from the *Liquidambar styraciflua, L.*

Liquidamente [lee'-ke-dah-men-tay], *adv.* In a liquid manner.

Liquidar [le-kee-dar'], *va.* To liquefy, to melt, to dissolve. *Liquidar cuentas,* To clear accounts, to liquidate debts.—*vr.* 1. To liquefy, to liquate, to grow liquid. 2. To become liquid: used of letters.

Liquidez [le-kee-deth'], *f.* Liquidness, fluidity.

Liquidificar [le-ke-de-fe-car'], *va.* To dissolve, to liquefy.

Líquido, da [lee'-ke-do, dah], *a.* 1. Liquid, fluid, fluent. 2. Evident, clear. 3. Net, neat.

Lira [lee'-rah], *f.* 1. Lyre, a harp; a lyric poem. 2. Lyra, a northern constellation.

Liria [lee'-re-ah], *f.* *V.* LIGA, birdlime.

Lírico, ca [lee'-re-co, cah], *a.* Lyric, lyrical.

Lirio [lee'-re-o], *m.* The lily. *Lirio blanco*, *V.* AZUCENA. *Lirio florentino*, Orris, Florentine iris. *Lirio de los valles*, Lily of the valley. *V.* MUGUETE. *Lirio hediondo*, Gladwyn. Iris fœtidissima.

Lirón [le-rone'], *m.* 1. Dormouse. Myoxus glis. 2. (Bot.) *V.* ALISMA. 3. (Naut.) Jack-screw.

Lirondo, da [le-ron'-do, dah], *a.* Pure, clean, neat. *Mondo y lirondo*, (Coll.) Pure, unmixed.

Lis [lees], *f.* Flor de lis, flower-de-luce, iris.

Lisa [lee'-sah], *f.* 1. A smooth stone for polishing paper. 2. A mixture for moulding the letters of a bell.

Lisamente [le-sah-men'-tay], *adv.* Smoothly, plainly. *Lisa y llanamente*, Openly and frankly; without dispute or contention.

Lisbonense [lis-bo-nen'-say], or **Lisbonés, sa** [lis-bo-nays', sah], *a.* Belonging to or native of Lisbon.

Lisera [le-say'-rah], *f.* Large cane used in silk-worm sheds.

Lisiado, da [le-se-ah'-do, dah], *a.* (Poet.) Lamed, injured, hurt. (Prov.) Anxiously desirous.—*pp.* of LISIAR.

Lisiar [le-se-ar'], *va.* To lame; to hurt a limb.

Lisimaquia [le-se-mah'-ke-ah], *f.* (Bot.) Loose strife. Lysimachia.

Lisis [lee'-sis], *f.* Lysis, the gradual abatement of disease, opposed to crisis. (Gr., from λύω, to loose.)

Liso, sa [lee'-so, sah], *a.* 1. Plain, even, flat, glib, smooth. 2. Clear, evident. *Hombre liso*, A plain-dealing man.

Lisonja [le-son'-hah], *f.* 1. Adulation, flattery, fawning, coaxing. 2. (Her.) Lozenge. 3. (Geom.) Rhomb or rhombus.

Lisonjado, da [le-son-hah'-do, dah], *a.* (Her.) Lozenged; rhombic.

Lisonjeador, ra [le-son-hay-ah-dor', rah], *m.* & *f.* Flatterer.

Lisonjear [le-son-hay-ar'], *va.* 1. To flatter, to praise deceitfully, to coax, to wheedle, to fawn. 2. To delight, to please.

Lisonjeramente [le-son-hay-rah-men'-tay], *adv.* Flatteringly, fawningly.

Lisonjero, ra [le-son-hay'-ro, rah], *m.* & *f.* A flatterer, a fawner, a parasite.—*a.* 1. Parasitical, wheedling, fawning. 2. Flattering, pleasing, agreeable.

Lista [lees'-tah], *f.* 1. Slip of paper, shred of linen, a list or strip of cloth. 2. Selvage, the edge of cloth. 3. List, catalogue. (Law) Docket. *Lista del equipaje*, (Naut.) Muster-book of the ship's company. *Pasar lista*, To call over; to muster, to review troops, to call the roll. *Lista de gastos*, Bill of expense and charges. *Lista de manjares* or *lista de platos*, Bill of fare, menu.

Listadillo [lis-tah-deel'-lyo], *m.* (Amer.) 1. Cotton cloth striped white and blue. 2. Striped gingham.

Listado, da [lis-tah'-do, dah], *a.* Striped, listed.—*pp.* of LISTAR.—*m. pl. Listados*, Striped checks, plaid.

Listadura [lis-tah-doo'-rah], *f.* 1. The action of listing or applying strips. 2. The thing so listed.

Listar [lis-tar'], *va.* 1. To list, to cover with strips of cloth. 2. *V.* ALISTAR.

Listeado, da [lis-tay-ah'-do, dah], *a.* *V.* LISTADO.

Listel, Listelo [lis-tel', lis-tay'-lo], *m.* (Arch.) *V.* FILETE.

Listo, ta [lees'-to, tah], *a.* Ready, diligent, prompt, active, clever.

Listón [lis-tone'], *m.* 1. Ribbon. 2. Ferret, tape. 3. Lath, cleat. 4. (Arch.) Fillet. *Listones*, (Naut.) Battens. *Listones de las escotillas*, (Naut.) Battens of the hatchways.

Listonado, da [lis-to-nah'-do, dah], *a.* (Arch.) Barred, striped, filleted.

Listonar [lis-to-nar'], *va.* To batten, to lath.

Listonería [lis-to-nay-ree'-ah], *f.* 1. Parcel of ribbons, tapes, and inkles. 2. A ribbon-store; ribbon-manufactory.

Listonero, ra [lis-to-nay'-ro, rah], *m.* & *f.* Ribbon-maker.

Lisura [le-soo'-rah], *f.* 1. Smoothness, evenness, glibness, flatness. 2. Sincerity, candour.

Lita [lee'-tah], *f.* Larva of an insect which fixes itself under the tongue of certain quadrupeds. =Landrilla.

Litación [le-tah-the-on'], *f.* Sacrificing.

Litagogo, ga [le-tah-go'-go, gah], *a.* Lithagogue, solvent of urinary calculi; also, lithontriptic, destroying calculi: applied to surgical instruments.

Litar [le-tar'], *va.* To sacrifice to the divinity.

Litarge, Litargirio [le-tar'-hay, le-tar-hee'-re-o], *m.* Litharge. *V.* ALMÁRTAGA.

Lite [lee'-tay], *f.* Lawsuit, process. *V.* PLEITO.

Litera [le-tay'-rah], *f.* Litter, stretcher, bed. *Litera alta*, Upper berth (in a sleeping car). *Litera baja*, Lower berth.

Literal [le-tay-rahl'], *a.* Literal.

Literalmente, *adv.* Literally.

Literario, ria [le-tay-rah'-re-o, ah], *a.* Literary.

Literatillo [le-tay-rah-teel'-lyo], *m. dim.* of LITERATO: commonly used in contempt.

Literato, ta [le-tay-rah'-to, tah], *a.* Learned, lettered literate, versed in sciences and letters.

Literato [le-tay-rah'-to], *m.* A learned man, a literary man.—*pl.* Literati, the learned.

Literatura [le-tay-rah-too'-rah], *f.* Literature, learning; skill in sciences and letters.

Literero [le-tay-ray'-ro], *m.* One who drives a litter.

Litiasis [le-te-ah'-sis], *f.* (Med.) Lithiasis, the formation of stones or gravel in the human body, especially in the urinary passages.

Litigante [le-te-gahn'-tay], *pa.* & *n.* Litigating; litigant; a party concerned in a lawsuit.

Litigar [le-te-gar'], *va.* 1. To litigate, to manage a suit at law. 2. To contend, to dispute.

Litigio [le-tee'-he-o], *m.* 1. Litigation, lawsuit. 2. Dispute, contest.

Litigioso, sa [le-te-he-o'-so, sah], *a.* Litigious, contentious.

Litina [le-tee'-nah], *f.* Lithia, lithium oxide.

Litio [lee'-te-o], *m.* Lithium, an alkaline metal, the lightest solid element.

Litis [lee'-tis], *f.* *V.* LITE.

Litisconsorte [le-tis-con-sor'-tay], *com.* Associate in a lawsuit.

Litiscontestación [le-tis-con-tes-tah-the-on'], *f.* (Law) Answer to a juridical command.

Litisexpensas [le-tis-ex-pen'-sas], *f. pl.* (Law) Costs of suit.

Litispendencia [le-tis-pen-den'-the-ah], *f.* The state of a lawsuit which is under judgment or pending.

Litocálamo [le-to-cah'-lah-mo], *m.* Petrified or fossil reed.

Litoclasto [le-to-clahs'-to], *m.* Lithoclast, an instrument for crushing stone in the bladder.

Litocola [le-to-co'-lah], *f.* Lithocolla, lapidary's cement, composed of marble dust, glue, and white of egg.

Litófago, ga [le-to'-fah-go, gah], *a.* Rock-consuming.

Litófilo, la [le-to'-fe-lo, lah], *a.* (Bot.) Growing on or attached to rocks.

Litófito [le-to'-fe-to], *m.* Lithophyte, a stone plant; coral.

Litofotografía, *f.* *V.* FOTOLITOGRAFÍA.

Litografía [le-to-grah-fee'-ah], *f.* Lithography, printing from prepared stone. Inv. 1799, by Senefelder.

Litografiar [le-to-grah-fe-ar'], *va.* To lithograph.

Litográfico, ca [le-to-grah'-fe-co, cah], *a.* Lithographic.

Litógrafo [le-to'-grah-fo], *m.* Lithologist.

Litoideo, dea [le-to-ee'-day-o, ah], *a.* Lithoid, having the appearance of stone.

Litolapaxia [le-to-lah-pahc'-se-ah], *f.* Litholapaxy, crushing of a stone and washing out at one operation.

Litología [le-to-lo-hee'-ah], *f.* Lithology, natural history of stones.

Litológico, ca [le-to-lo'-he-co, cah], *a.* Lithological, mineralogical.

Litólogo [le-to'-lo-go], *m.* Lithologist.

Litoral [le-to-rahl'], *a.* Littoral, pertaining to the shore.—*m.* Coast line.

Litoscopio [le-tos-co'-pe-o], *m.* Lithoscope.

Litosfera [le-tos-fay'-rah], *f.* Lithosphere.

Litote [le-to'-tay], *f.* Litotes, a rhetorical figure: denial of the opposite.

Litotricia [le-to-tree'-the-ah], *f.* Lithotrity, the crushing of a stone within the bladder.

Litotritor [le-to-tre-tor'], *m.* Lithotrite, instrument for crushing vesical calculi.

Litoxilo [le-toc-see'-lo], *m.* Petrified wood.

Litrámetro [le-trah'-may-tro], *m.* Litrametre, an instrument for measuring the specific gravity of liquids.

Litro [lee'-tro], *m.* Liter, litre, a unit of capacity in the decimal system. One cubic decimetre.

Lituano, na [le-too-ah'-no, nah], *a.* Lithuanian.

Lituo [lee'-too-o], *m.* 1. Ancient military instrument of music. 2. Lituus, augur's staff.

Liturgia [le-toor'-he-ah], *f.* Liturgy, form of prayers; manner of celebrating the mass.

Litúrgico, ca [le-toor'-he-co, cah], *a.* Liturgical, liturgic, belonging to the liturgy.

Livianamente [le-ve-ah-nah-men'-tay], *adv.* Licentiously; with levity; lightly.

Liviandad [le-ve-an-dahd'], *f.* 1. Lightness, want of weight. 2. Levity, imprudence. 3. Incontinence, libidinousness.

Liviano, na [le-ve-ah'-no, nah], *a.* 1. Light, of little weight. 2. Imprudent, light, unsteady. 3. Incontinent, unchaste, libidinous.

Livianos [le-ve-ah'-nos], *m. pl.* Lungs. *V.* BOFES.

Lividez [le-ve-deth'], *f.* 1. Lividity, lividness. 2. The black and blue colour of a bruise.

Lívido, da [lee'-ve-do, dah], *a.* Livid. *V.* AMORATADO.

Lixiviación [lec-se-ve-ah-the-on'], *f.* Leaching, or lixiviation of an alkali.

Liza [lee'-thah], *f.* 1. Skate, a sea fish. 2. Arena for tournaments, prize ring.
Lizo [lee'-tho], *m.* Skein of silk.
Lizón [le-thone'], *m.* (Bot.) Water plantain. Alisma plantago.
Lo, *indef. pron.* It: placed before or after verbs. It is used before adjectives, when by an ellipsis they are used in a general sense, referring to a thing either masculine or feminine, singular or plural. It is used also with reference to whole sentences.
Loa [lo'-ah], *f.* 1. Prologue of a play. 2. Praise.
Loable [lo-ah'-blay], *a.* Laudable, praiseworthy.
Loablemente, *adv.* Laudably, commendably.
Loador, ra [lo-ah-dor', rah], *m.* & *f.* Praiser, lauder.
Loán [lo-ahn'], *m.* A land measure of the Philippine Islands, equal to 3,600 square feet (2.79 âres).
Loanda [lo-ahn'-dah], *f.* Kind of scurvy.
Loar [lo-ar'], *va.* To praise; to approve.
Loasa [lo-ah'-sah], *f.* Loasa, a genus of South American climbing plants of elegant flowers.
Loba [lo'-bah], *f.* 1. Ridge between furrows. 2. Long gown worn by clergymen and students. 3. She-wolf.
Lóbado [lo'-bah-do], *m.* Morbid swelling incident to horses.
Lobanillo [lo-bah-neel'-lyo], *m.* Wen, a callous excrescence.
Lobato [lo-bah'-to], *m.* Young wolf.
Lobelia [lo-bay'-le-ah], *f.* (Bot.) Lobelia.
Lobera [lo-bay'-rah], *f.* Thicket where wolves make their lair.
Lobero, ra [lo-bay'-ro, rah], *a.* Relating to wolves.
Lobero [lo-bay'-ro], *m.* *V.* Espantanublados.
Lobezno [lo-beth'-no], *m.* A young wolf.
Lobina [lo-bee'-nah], *f.* Striped bass.
Lobo [lo'-bo], *m.* 1. Wolf. Canis lupus. 2. Lobe, a division of the lungs, liver, etc. 3. (Joc.) Intoxication, inebriation. *Fulano cogió un lobo*, He was tipsy. 4. Iron instrument for defending or scaling walls. *Son lobos de la misma camada*, They are all chips of the same block. *Quien con lobos anda a aullar se enseña*, (prov.) The friend of the wicked is made like unto them. *Ver las orejas del lobo*, (Met.) To find one's self in the greatest danger.
Lobo marino [lo'-bo mah-ree'-no], *m.* Seal, sea-calf.
Loboso, sa [lo-bo'-so, sah], *a.* Full of wolves: applied to countries or forests.
Lóbrego, ga [lo'-bray-go, gah], *a.* Murky, obscure, sad, mirk.
Lobreguecer [lo-bray-gay-therr'], *vn.* To grow dark, to be dark.—*va.* To make dark.
Lobreguez [lo-bray-geth'], *f.* Obscurity, darkness.
Lóbulo [lo'-boo-lo], *m.* Lobe or lobule, a division or distinct part of the lungs, liver, etc.
Lobuno, na [lo-boo'-no, nah], *a.* Wolfish, resembling a wolf.
Locación y conducción [lo-ca-the-on' ee con-dooc-the-on'], *f.* (Law) Contract of letting on lease.
Local [lo-cahl'], *a.* Local, relating to a particular place.
Localidad [lo-cah-le-dahd'], *f.* Locality, existence in place; location.
Localización [lo-cah-le-thah-the-on'], *f.* Localization, fixing in a definite place.
Localizar [lo-cah-le-thar'], *va.* To localize, to fix in a determined place.
Localmente, *adv.* Locally.
Locamente [lo-cah-men'-tay], *adv.* Madly; immoderately, extravagantly; fondly.
Locarias [lo-cah'-re-as], *m.* (Coll.) A madcap, a wild, hot-brained fellow.
Loción [lo-the-on'], *f.* 1. Lotion, a medicine used to wash any part with. 2. Wash, lavation, the act of washing.
Loco, ca [lo'-co, cah], *a.* 1. Mad, crack-brained. 2. Fool. 3. Abundant, fertile. *A tontas y a locas*, Inconsiderately, without reflection. *Estar loco de contento*, (Coll.) To be mad with joy. *A palabras locas, orejas sordas*, A silly question deserves no answer.
Loco [lo'-co], *m.* A madman, crazy-man.
Locomoción [lo-co-mo-the-on'], *f.* (Phys.) Locomotion, power of moving.
Locomotivo, va [lo-co-mo-tee'-vo, vah], *a.* Locomotive, possessed of the power of moving.
Locomotor, ra [lo-co-mo-tor', rah], *a.* Locomotor, having the power of producing motion.
Locomotora [lo-co-mo-to'-rah], *f.* A locomotive engine.
Locomotriz [lo-co-mo-treeth'], *a.* Locomotive.
Locomóvil [lo-co-mo'-veel], *a.* Locomotive.—*f.* Traction engine.
Locro [lo'-cro], *m.* (Peru, Ec.) A stew composed chiefly of winter squash, potatoes, tender maize, meat or fish, etc.
Locuacidad [lo-coo-ah-the-dahd'], *f.* Loquacity, talkativeness, garrulity, flippancy.
Locuaz [lo-coo-ath'], *a.* Loquacious, talkative, garrulous, flippant.
Locuazmente, *adv.* (Littl. us.) With loquacity, flippantly.
Locución [lo-coo-the-on'], *f.* Locution, manner of speech; phrase, expression.
Locuela [lo-coo-ay'-lah], *f.* 1. Each one's particular mode of speaking. 2. Name commonly given to a giddy and conceited young girl.
Locura [lo-coo'-rah], *f.* 1. Madness, frenzy, lunacy, craziness. 2. Fury; folly, absurdity. *Hacer locuras*, To act in an absurd, foolish manner.
Locutor [lo-coo-tor'], *m.* Speaker, announcer. *Locutor de radio*, Radio announcer, radio commentator. *Locutor de televisión*, Television announcer or commentator.
Locutorio [lo-coo-to'-re-o], *m.* Parlour, place in monasteries for receiving visits.
Locha, *f.* **Loche**, *m.* [lo'-chah, lo'-chay]. (Zool.) Loach, groundling, a small fish.
Locho, cha [lo'-cho, chah], *a.* (Amer. coll.) Red-bearded, bright red.
Lodazal, Lodazar [lo-dah-thahl', lo-dah-thar'], *m.* A muddy place.
Lodo [lo'-do], *m.* Mud, mire.
Lodoñero [lo-do-nyay'-ro], *m.* (Bot.) Guaiac, lignum-vitæ tree.
Lodoso, sa [lo-do'-so, sah], *a.* Muddy, miry.
Logarítmico, ca [lo-gah-reet'-me-co, cah], *a.* Logarithmic, logarithmical.
Logaritmo, *m.* Logarithm.
Logia [lo'-he-ah], *f.* Lodge, assembly of Freemasons and the place where they meet.
Lógica [lo'-he-cah], *f.* Logic, dialectics.
Lógicamente, *adv.* Logically.
Lógico, ca [lo'-he-co, cah], *a.* Logical.
Lógico [lo'-he-co], *m.* Logician, dialectician, a professor of logic.
Logístico, ca [lo-hees'-te-co, cah], *a.* Logistic.—*f.* Logistics.
Logografía [lo-go-grah-fee'-ah], *f.* Shorthand.
Logogrifo [lo-go-gree'-fo], *m.* Logogriph, an enigma in which the different parts of a word are taken in divers meanings.
Logomaquia [lo-go-mah'-ke-ah], *f.* Logomachy, dispute about words.
Lograr [lo-grar'], *va.* 1. To gain, to obtain, to succeed, to procure, to compass. 2. To possess, to enjoy. 3. To avail one's self of. 4. To hit upon, to manage, to do well.—*vr.* To reap the benefit of one's labour and exertions.
Lograr [lo-gray-ar'], *vn.* To borrow or lend on interest.
Logrería [lo-gray-ree'-ah], *f.* Dealing in interest, usury.
Logrero, ra [lo-gray'-ro, rah], *m.* & *f.* Lender at interest, usurer.
Logro [lo'-gro], *m.* 1. Gain, benefit. 2. Attainment of some purpose. 3. Interest; usury. *Dar a logro*, To put out money at usurious interest.
Loma [lo'-mah], *f.* 1. Rising ground in the midst of a plain, a little hill or hillock. 2. Slope.
Lombarda [lom-bar'-dah], *f.* 1. Lombardy gun. 2. (Bot.) Red cabbage. Brassica capitata rubra.
Lombardada [lom-bar-dah'-dah], *f.* Shot from a Lombardy gun.
Lombardear [lom-bar-day-ar'], *va.* To discharge Lombardy guns.
Lombardería [lom-bar-day-ree'-ah], *f.* Park of Lombardy guns.
Lombardero [lom-bar-day'-ro], *m.* Soldier appointed to Lombardy guns.
Lombárdico, ca [lom-bar'-de-co, cah], *a.* Lombard, belonging to Lombardy.
Lombardo, da [lom-bar'-do, dah], *a.* Lombard, belonging to Lombardy.
Lombriguera [lom-bre-gay'-rah], *f.* 1. Hole made by worms. 2. (Bot.) Southernwood wormwood. Artemisia abrotanum.
Lombriz [lom-breeth'], *f.* Worm bred in the body, or in the earth.
Lombrizal [lom-bre-thahl'], *a.* (Anat.) Vermiform.
Lomear [lo-may-ar'], *vn.* To yerk or move the loins of horses in a circular manner.
Lomento [lo-men'-to], *m.* (Bot.) Loment, a kind of legume falling in pieces when ripe.
Lomera [lo-may'-rah], *f.* 1. Strap of harness which crosses the loins. 2. (Prov.) Ridge of a house.
Lomiancho, a [lo-me-ahn'-cho, chah], *a.* Strong or broad-backed.
Lomica, illa, ita [lo-mee'-cah], *f. dim.* A very little hill or hillock.
Lomillo [lo-meel'-lyo], *m.* 1. (Dim.) A small loin. 2. A kind of needle-work.
Lominhiesto, ta [lo-min-e-es'-to, tah], *a.* 1. High-cropped. 2. Presumptuous, arrogant.
Lomo [lo'-mo], *m.* 1. Loin. 2. Chine, a piece of the back of an animal. 3. Back of a book or cutting tool; double of any cloth, crease. 4. Ridge between furrows. *Llevar* or *traer a lomo*, To carry on the back. *Jugar de lomo*, To be idle and lascivious.—*pl.* Ribs; loins.
Lomudo, da [lo-moo'-do, dah], *a.* Large in the loins, broad-backed.
Lona [lo'-nah], *f.* Canvas. *Lona para hacer velas*, Duck-canvas, sail-cloth. *Lona para encerados*, Tarpauling canvas or glazing.
Loncha [lone'-chah], *f.* 1. Thin flat stone. 2. Thin slice of meat.
Lóndiga [lon'-de-gah], *f.* Alhóndiga.
Londinense [lon-de-nen'-say], *a.* Of London, Londonese.
Londó [lon-do'], *m.* (Com.) A fabric made in Brittany.
Londrina [lon-dree'-nah], *f.* A sort of woollen cloth from London.
Loneta [lo-nay'-tah], *f.* Ravens' duck sail-cloth.

Longa [lone-gah], *f.* Long musical note.
Longanimidad [lon-gah-ne-me-dahd'], *f.* Longanimity, forbearance.
Longánimo, ma [lon-gah'-ne-mo, mah], *a.* Forbearing, generous, magnanimous.
Longaniza [lon-gah-nee'-thah], *f.* A kind of long sausage.
Longar [lon-gar'], *a.* Applied to a long piece of honey-comb in the hive.
Longazo, za [lon-gah'-tho, thah], *a. aug.* Very long.
Longevidad [lon-hay-ve-dahd'], *f.* Longevity.
Longevo [lon-hay'-vo], *a.* Longeval, long-lived.
Longicornios [lon-he-cor'-ne-ose], *a.* & *m. pl.* Longicorn; the longicorn beetles have very long antennæ, sometimes surpassing the entire length of the body. The larvæ burrow in the hardest woods.
Longifloro, ra [lon-he-flo'-ro, rah], *a.* Long-flowered, longiflorous.
Longimetría [lon-he-may-tree'-ah], *f.* (Geom.) Longimetry, the art of measuring distances.
Longincuo, cua [lon-heen'-coo-o, ah], *a.* Distant, remote.
Longípedo, da [lon-hee'-pay-do, dah], *a.* Long-footed.
Longirrostros [lon-hir-ros'-trose], *m. pl. a.* Longirostres, a family of birds, including snipes, etc. As adjective, longirostral, long-billed.
Longísimo, ma [lon-hee'-se-mo, mah], *a. sup.* of LUENGO. Longest. So, too, LONGUÍSIMO.
Longitud [lon-he-tood'], *f.* 1. Length, longness. 2. Longitude.
Longitudinal [lon-he-too-de-nahl'], *a.* Longitudinal.
Longitudinalmente, *adv.* Longitudinally, lengthwise.
Longuera [lon-gay'-rah], *f.* Long and narrow strip of land.
Longura [lon-goo'-rah], *f.* 1. Length. 2. Long lapse of time. 3. Delay.
Lonja [lone'-hah], *f.* 1. Exchange, a public place where merchants meet. 2. Slice or steak of ham, or any other eatable. 3. Grocer's shop; warehouse, sale-room. *Lonja cerrada* or *abierta*, Shut or open shop or exchange. 4. Entrance hall of an edifice. 5. Leather strap, used in falconry.
Lonjero [lon-hay'-ro], *m.* Grocer.
Lonjista [lon-hees'-tah], *com.* Shopkeeper who deals in groceries.
Lontananza [lon-tah-nahn'-thah], *f.* (Art) Distance, background.
Loor [lo-or'], *m.* (Poet.) Praise.
Lopigia [lo-pee'-he-ah], *f.* Disease which makes the hair fall off.—*V.* ALOPECIA.
Loquear [lo-kay-ar'], *vn.* 1. To act the fool, to talk nonsense. 2. To rejoice, to exult, to revel, to frolic.
Loquero, ra [lo-kay'-ro, rah], *m.* & *f.* 1. Keeper of a mad-house. 2. Physician to a mad-house.
Loquesca [lo-kes'-cah], *f.* The frantic demeanour of mad people.
Loquillo, illa, ito, ita [lo-keel'-lyo], *a. dim.* Wild, almost mad.
Loquios [lo'-ke-ose], *m. pl.* Lochia, the evacuations following childbirth for two to three weeks.
Loran [lo'-rahn], *m.* Loran, contraction of LOng RAnge NAvigation.
Lord, *m.* (*pl.* **Lores**). Lord, a title of honour given to the highest nobility in England.
Lorenzana [lo-ren-thah'-nah], *f.* A sort of coarse linen.
Loriga [lo-ree'-gah], *f.* 1. Coat of mail, cuirass. 2. Naveband, the hoop which surrounds the nave of a coach-wheel.
Lorigado, da [lo-re-gah'-do, dah], *a.* Armed with a coat of mail, loricate.
Loriguillo [lo-re-geel'-lyo], *m.* Shrub used by dyers.
Loro, ra [lo'-ro, rah], *a.* Tawny, dark brown.
Loro [lo'-ro], *m.* 1. Parrot. Psittacus. 2. (Bot.) Portugal laurel. Prunis lusitanica.
Losa [lo'-sah], *f.* 1. Flag, a square stone used for pavements. 2. Painter's block of marble on which colours are ground. 3. Trap for catching birds or rats.
Losado [lo-sah'-do], *m.* *V.* ENLOSADO. —*Losado, da, pp.* of LOSAR.
Losanje [lo-sahn'-hay], *m.* (Her.) Lozenge; rhomb.
Losar [lo-sar'], *va.* *V.* ENLOSAR.
Losica, ita [lo-see'-cah, ee'-tah], *f. dim.* A small flag or stone.
Loseta, Losilla [lo-say'-tah, lo-seel'-lyah], *f.* 1. A small trap or snare. 2. *V.* LOSICA. *Coger en la loseta* or *losilla*, To deceive one cunningly.
Lote [lo'-tay], *m.* Lot, fortune, chance.
Lotería [lo-tay-ree'-ah], *f.* 1. Lottery. 2. The game lotto.
Loto [lo'-to], *m.* (Bot.) 1. Lotus, the Egyptian and Indian water-lily. 2. The lote-tree, or nettle-tree. *V.* ALMEZ. 3. Jujube-tree.
Loza [lo'-thah], *f.* China, fine earthenware. *Loza refractaria*, Pyrex ware.
Lozanamente [lo-thah-nah-men'-tay], *adv.* Luxuriantly.
Lozanear [lo-thah-nay-ar'], *vn.* To affect pomp and ostentation in words and actions.
Lozanía [lo-thah-nee'-ah], *f.* 1. Luxuriance of verdure, exuberant growth of plants. 2. Elegance; lustiness.
Lozano, na [lo-thah'-no, nah], *a.* 1. Luxuriant. 2. Sprightly.
Lúa [loo'-ah], *f.* 1. Esparto glove (with no separation for the fingers) for cleaning horses. (Obs.) Glove. 2. (Prov.) A sort of crane for raising weights. 3. (Naut.) Lee. 4. (Prov.) Saffron-bag. *Tomar por la lúa*, (Naut.) To bring to the lee.
Lubricación [loo-bre-cah-the-on'], *f.* Lubrication.
Lubricador, ra [loo-bre-cah-dor', rah], *a.* Lubricating.
Lubricar, Lubrificar [loo-bre-car', loo-bre-fe-car'], *va.* To lubricate.
Lubricativo, va [loo-bre-cah-tee'-vo, vah], *a.* Lubricant, lubricative.
Lubricidad [loo-bre-the-dahd'], *f.* 1. Lubricity, slipperiness. 2. Lewdness.
Lúbrico, ca [loo'-bre-co, cah], *a.* Slippery; lubricous; lewd.
Lubrificación [loo-bre-fe-cah-the-on'], *f.* Lubrication.
Lubrificador, ra [loo-bre-fe-cah-dor', rah], *a.* Lubricating.
Lubrificante [loo-bre-fe-cahn'-tay], *a.* Lubricating.
Lucano [loo-cah'-no], *m.* The stag-beetle, commonly called *cometa.*
Lucas [loo'-cas], *m. pl.* (Cant.) Playing-cards.
Lucerna [loo-therr'-nah], *f.* 1. Glow-worm. 2. Lamp.
Lucérnula [loo-therr'-noo-lah], *f.* (Bot.) Lucern, lucerne, alfalfa.
Lucero [loo-thay'-ro], *m.* 1. Morning star, Venus, day-star, Lucifer. 2. Splendour. 3. Part of a window where light enters. 4. White spot on the forehead of certain quadrupeds. (Acad.)—*pl.* (Poet.) Eyes.
Lucible [loo-thee'-blay], *a.* (Obs.) Resplendent.
Lucidamente [loo-the-dah-men'-tay], *adv.* Lucidly, brightly.
Lucidar [loo-the-dar'], *va.* To copy a picture on transparent paper.
Lucidez [loo-the-deth'], *f.* Brilliancy, brightness.
Lucido, da [loo-thee'-do, dah], *a.* Magnificent, splendid, brilliant in performance.—*pp.* of LUCIR.
Lúcido, da [loo'-the-do, dah], *a.* 1. Lucid, clear in reason. 2. Brilliant, shining.
Lucidura [loo-the-doo'-rah], *f.* (Coll.) Whiteness of white-washed walls.
Luciente [loo-the-en'-tay], *pa.* Shining, lucid, luminous, bright.
Luciérnaga [loo-the-err'-nah-gah], *f.* Glow-worm, fire-fly. Lampyris.
Luciérnago, *m.* (Obs.) *V.* LUCIÉRNAGA.
Lucifer [loo-the-ferr'], *m.* 1. Lucifer, Satan. 2. A very proud and wicked man. 3. *V.* LUCERO for the morning star.
Luciferino, na [loo-the-fay-ree'-no, nah], *a.* Luciferian, devilish.
Lucífero, ra [loo-thee'-fay-ro, rah], *a.* (Poet.) Resplendent, shining, luciferous.—*m.* (Obs.) *V.* LUCERO.
Lucífugo, ga [loo-thee'-foo-go, gah], *a.* Avoiding the light, lucifugous.
Lucillo [loo-theel'-lyo], *m.* Tomb; sarcophagus.
Lucimiento [loo-the-me-en'-to], *m.* 1. Lucidity, brightness. 2. Splendour, lustre, applause.
Lucio, cia [loo'-the-o, ah], *a.* Lucid, bright.
Lucio [loo'-the-o], *m.* (Zool.) Common pike, luce. Esox lucius.
Lucir [loo-theer'], *va.* 1. To emit light, to glitter, to gleam, to glow. 2. To illuminate, to enlighten. 3. To outshine, to exceed.—*vn.* & *vr.* 1. To shine, to be brilliant. *Le luce el trabajo*, He enjoys the fruits of his labour. 2. To dress to advantage. *Lucirlo*, (Coll.) To dash away, to sport.
Lucrarse [loo-crar'-say], *vr.* To get gain or profit from a business or charge.
Lucrativamente, *adv.* Profitably, lucratively.
Lucrativo, va [loo-crah-tee'-vo, vah], *a.* Lucrative, productive of gain.
Lucro [loo'-cro], *m.* Gain, profit, lucre.
Lucroso, sa [loo-cro'-so, sah], *a.* Lucrific, gainful, profitable.
Luctuosa [looc-too-o'-sah], *f.* Ancient tax paid to lords and bishops for the dead.
Luctuosamente, *adv.* Mournfully, sorrowfully.
Luctuoso, sa [looc-too-o'-so, sah], *a.* Sad, mournful.
Lucubración [loo-coo-brah-the-on'], *f.* Lucubration, nocturnal study.
Lucubrar [loo-coo-brar'], *va.* To lucubrate, to study by night.
Lúcuma [loo'-coo-mah], *f.* Fruit of the *lúcumo*, a tree of Peru and tropical America. Achras mammosa, *L.*
Lucha [loo'-chah], *f.* 1. Struggle, strife, contest, wrestle. 2. Dispute, argument.
Luchador, ra [loo-chah-dor', rah], *m.* & *f.* Wrestler.
Luchar [loo-char'], *va.* 1. To wrestle to contend, to struggle. 2. To discuss, to debate.
Lucharniego, ga [loo-char-ne-ay'-go, gah], *a.* Applied to dogs used for catching hares at night.
Luchillo [loo-cheel'-lyo], *m.* (Naut.) Gering, goring cloth.
Ludia [loo'-de-ah], *f.* (Prov.) Ferment yeast.
Ludiar [loo-de-ar'], *va.* & *vr.* (Prov.) To ferment.

Ludibrio [loo-dee'-bre-o], *m.* Mockery, derision, scorn.

Ludimiento [loo-de-me-en'-to], *m.* (Prov.) *V.* Colisión.

Ludir [loo-deer'], *va.* To rub, to waste by friction, to collide.

Ludria [loo'-dre-ah], *f.* *V.* Nutria.

Lúe [loo'-ay], *f.* Infection. (Acad.) (Lat. lues, pox.)

Luego [loo-ay'-go], *adv.* 1. Presently, immediately, outright, out of hand. *Desde luego*, From the present moment; in hand. 2. Soon afterward.—*conj.* Then, therefore.

Luengo, ga [loo-en'-go, gah], *a.* (Obs.) *V.* Largo.

Lueñe [loo-ay'-nyay], *adv.* (Obs.) *V.* Lejos.

Lugano [loo-gah'-no], *m.* A linnet. *V.* Jilguero.

Lugar [loo-gar'], *m.* 1. Place, spot, situation, position. 2. City, town, village: properly speaking, it is applied to a village or a very small town. 3. Employment, office, dignity. 4. Time, opportunity, occasion. 5. Leisure, convenience of time. 6. Cause, motive, reason. 7. Text, authority or sentiment of an author. *Lugar común*, Privy-house, water-closet. *Lugar muy pasajero*, A thoroughfare. *Lugares comunes*, Commonplace topics. *Lugares de un combate*, (Naut.) Quarters in a sea-fight. *En lugar de*, Instead of, in lieu of.

Lugarcico, illo, ito [loo-gar-thee'-co] *m. dim.* *V.* Lugarillo.

Lugarillo, Lugarejo [loo-gah-reel'-lyo, loo-gah-ray'-ho], *m. dim.* Hamlet, a small village.

Lugareño, ña [loo-gah-ray'-nyo, nyah], *m. & f. & a.* 1. Belonging to a village. 2. Inhabitant of a village.

Lugarete [loo-gah-ray'-tay], *m. dim.* *V.* Lugarillo.

Lugarón [loo-gah-rone'], *m. aug.* *V.* Lugarazo.

Lugarote [loo-gah-ro'-tay], *m. aug.* *V.* Lugarazo.

Lugartenencia [loo-gar-tay-nen'-the-ah], *f.* Lieutenancy.

Lugarteniente [loo-gar-tay-ne-en'-tay], *m.* 1. Deputy, substitute, delegate. 2. Lieutenant.

Lugre [loo'-gray], *m.* Lugger, a small two or three-masted vessel.

Lugo [loo'-go], *m.* Kind of linen.

Lúgubre [loo'-goo-bray], *a.* Sad, mournful, gloomy, melancholy, lugubrious, dismal.

Luir [loo-eer'], *vn.* (Naut.) To gall, or be galled or fretted, to wear away by friction.—*va.* (Prov.) *V.* Redimir censos.

Lujación [loo-hah-the-on'], *f.* *V.* Luxación.

Lujar [loo-har'], *va.* (Cuba) 1. To rub. *V.* Ludir. 2. To smooth the sole of a shoe. 3. (Med.) To luxate, to dislocate.

Lujo [loo'-ho], *m.* Profuseness, extravagance or excess in pomp, dresses, fare, etc.; superfluity, luxury, finery.

Lujoso, sa [loo-ho'-so, sah], *a.* Showy (in dress), sumptuous, luxurious; profuse, lavish.

Lujuria [loo-hoo'-re-ah], *f.* 1. Lechery, lubricity, lust, carnal pleasure. 2. Excess, profuseness, lavishness.

Lujuriante [loo-hoo-re-ahn'-tay], *pa.* Lusting.—*a.* Luxuriant, exuberant.

Lujuriar [loo-hoo-re-ar'], *vn.* 1. To be lecherous or libidinous, to lust. 2. To couple together: speaking of animals.

Lujuriosamente, *adv.* Lecherously, lustfully, voluptuously.

Lujurioso, sa [loo-hoo-re-o'-so, sah], *a.* Lecherous, lustful, voluptuous, lewd, libidinous.

Lumbago [loom-bah'-go], *m.* (Med.) Lumbago, lumbar rheumatism.

Lumbar [loom-bar'], *a.* Lumbar, lumbary.

Lumbrada, Lumbrarada [loom-brah'dah, loom-brah-rah'-dah], *f.* A great fire; a fierce conflagration.

Lumbre [loom'-bray], *f.* 1. Fire, any thing burning. 2. Spark from a flint. 3. Splendour, brightness, lucidity, clearness. 4. (Obs.) *V.* Vista. *A lumbre de pajas*, (Coll.) Very swiftly.—*pl.* 1. Tinder-box, with the materials for striking fire. 2. Hammer, that part of a gun-lock which strikes fire from the flint. 3. Fore-part of horse-shoes. *A lumbre mansa*, On a slow fire. *Ni por lumbre*, By no means. *Lumbre del agua*, Level, or surface of the water.

Lumbrera [loom-bray'-rah], *f.* 1. Luminary, any body which emits light. 2. Sky-light. 3. Luminary, he who from his transcendent abilities is fit to instruct mankind.

Luminar [loo-me-nar'], *m.* 1. Luminary, any body which emits light. 2. Among painters, light, as opposed to shade. 3. Luminary, a man eminent in science.

Luminaria [loo-me-nah'-re-ah], *f.* 1. Illumination, festival lights. 2. Lamp which is kept burning in Roman Catholic churches before the sacrament.—*pl.* Money paid for illuminations.

Lumínico, ca [loo-mee'-ne-co, cah], *a.* *V.* Luminoso.—*m.* Light.

Luminosamente, *adv.* Luminously.

Luminoso, sa [loo-me-no'-so, sah], *a.* Luminous, shining.

Luna [loo'-nah], *f.* 1. The moon. 2. Glass plate for mirrors, glass for optical instruments. 3. Effect of the moon upon lunatic people. 4. *Media luna*, (Mil.) Half-moon, a ravelin built before the angle or curtain of a bastion. 5. (Prov.) Open, uncovered court or hall. *Luna llena* or *menguante*, Full or waning moon.

Lunación [loo-nah-the-on'], *f.* Lunation, the period of revolution of the moon.

Lunado, da [loo-nah'-do, dah], *a.* Lunated, formed like a half-moon.

Lunanco, ca [loo-nahn'-co, cah], *a.* Applied to animals with one quarter higher than another.

Lunar [loo-nar'], *m.* 1. Mole, a natural spot or discoloration of the body. *Lunar postizo*, Patch which ladies wear on the face as an ornament. 2. Note or stain of infamy.—*a.* Lunar, lunary.

Lunaria [loo-nah'-re-ah], *f.* (Bot.) Moonwort, honesty.

Lunario [loo-nah'-re-o], *m.* *V.* Calendario.

Lunático, ca [loo-nah'-te-co, cah], *a.* Lunatic, moonstruck, mad.

Lunecilla [loo-nay-theel'-lyah], *f.* Crescent worn by women.

Lunes [loo'-nes], *m.* Monday.

Luneta [loo-nay'-tah], *f.* 1. The two or three rows of cushioned seats in the pit of a play-house, immediately behind the orchestra. 2. The spot where olives are pressed. 3. A saddler's knife, leather knife. 4. (Ant.) A spectacle lens. 5. Ornament in the shape of a half moon which women used to wear on the head and children on the shoes. 6. (Arch.) *V.* Bocateja and Luneto.

Luneto [loo-nay'-to], *m.* A skylight, of half-moon shape, in an arch, lunette.

Lunista [loo-nees'-tah], *m.* (Obs.) Lunatic, a mad person.

Lúnula [loo'-noo-lah], *f.* 1. A crescent, a figure formed by two arcs of a circle. 2. (Opt.) Meniscus, a lens or glass convex on one side and concave on the other.

Lupa [loo'-pah], *f.* Magnifying glass.

Lupanar [loo-pah-nar'], *m.* Brothel, a bawdy-house.

Lupanario, ia [loo-pah-nah'-re-o, ah], *a.* Belonging to a brothel.

Lupia [loo'-pe-ah], *f.* Encysted tumour

Lupino, na [loo-pee'-no, nah], *a.* (Littl. us.) Wolfish.

Lupino [loo-pee'-no], *m.* (Bot.) Lupine or lupin. *V.* Altramuz.

Lupulina [loo-poo-lee'-nah], *f.* Lupulin, the active principle of hops.

Lúpulo [loo'-poo-lo], *m.* (Bot.) Hops. Humulus lupulus.

Luquete [loo-kay'-tay], *m.* 1. Zest, a slice of orange with the peel thrown into wine. 2. Match, a card, rope, or small chip dipped in melted sulphur.

Luquetera [loo-kay-tay'-rah], *f.* Match-girl.

Lurte [loor'-tay], *m.* (Prov. Arragon.) *V.* Alud.

Lusitano, na [loo-se-tah'-no, nah], *a.* Lusitanian, Portuguese.

Lustración [loos-trah-the-on'], *f.* Lustration, purification by water.

Lustrador [loos-trah-dor'], *m.* 1. Hot-press, mangler, a machine which gives a gloss to clothes. 2. Hot-presser. 3. Mirror-polisher.

Lustral [loos-trahl'], *a.* Lustral: applied to water used in purifications.

Lustramiento [loos-trah-me-en'-to], *m.* Action of decorating or honouring some one. (Acad.)

Lustrar [loos-trar'], *va.* 1. To expiate, to purify. 2. To illustrate, to make brilliant. 3. To mangle; to fine. 4. To wander.

Lustre [loos'-tray], *m.* 1. Gloss, lustre, fineness. 2. Clearness, nobleness, splendour, glory. 3. Shoe-polish.

Lústrico, ca [loos'-tre-co, cah], *a.* (Poet.) Belonging to a lustrum, or to lustration.

Lustro [loos'-tro], *m.* 1. Lustrum, the space of five years. 2. Lamp or chandelier for illumination.

Lustrosamente, *adv.* Brilliantly, splendidly, glitteringly.

Lustroso, sa [loos-tro'-so, sah], *a.* Bright, brilliant, lustrous, shining, glossy, golden.

Luten [loo'-ten], *m.* (Chem.) Lute, a kind of paste to make vessels air-tight.

Lúteo, tea [loo'-tay-o, ah], *a.* Miry, muddy. (Acad.)

Luteranismo [loo-tay-rah-nees'-mo], *m.* Lutheranism.

Luterano, na [loo-tay-rah'-no, nah], *a.* & *m. & f.* Lutheran.

Luto [loo'-to], *m.* 1. Mourning, the dress of sorrow. *Medio luto*, Half-mourning. 2. Mourning, sorrow, condolement.

Lutria [loo'-tre-ah], *f.* *V.* Nutria.

Luxación [looc-sah-the-on'], *f.* Luxation, dislocation of a joint.

Luz [looth'], *f.* 1. Light. 2. Daylight. 3. Guiding light, inspiration. *Dar a luz*, 1. To give birth. 2. To bring out, to publish. *Luz blanca para marcha atrás*, Back-up light. *Luz intermitente*, 1. Directional signal. 2. Blinker. *Luz negra*, Black light. *Luz roja*, Stop light. *Luz trasera*, Taillight. *Salir a luz*, 1. To come out, to be published. 2. To come to light. *Ver la luz*, To see the light of day. *Luces*, 1. Windows, openings. 2. Cultural attainments. *A todas luces*, obviously. *En-*

tre dos luces, 1. At dawn. 2. At dusk. 3. (Coll.) Tipsy. *Luces de carretera*, High beams, brights. *Luces de cruce*, Low beams, dims. *Luces de población*, Parking lights. *Luces de posición*, (Aer.) Navigation lights. *Traje de luces*, Bullfighter's costume.

Luzbel [looth-bel'], *m.* Lucifer, Satan.

(*Yo luzco, yo luzca*, from *Lucir. V.* Deslucir.)

Ll

LL [el'-lyay], *f.*, is the fourteenth letter of the Spanish alphabet; and though double in figure, it is considered simple in its sound. It should not, therefore, be divided at the end of a line, but added to the succeeding vowel, with which it forms a complete syllable: as *ha-llar, seguidi-lla.* It has the liquid sound of *lli* in halliard.

Llábana [lyah'-bah-nah], *f.* (Prov.) A natural flagstone, smooth and commonly slippery from the action of water. An Asturian word.

Llaga [lyah'-gah], *f.* 1. An ulcer. 2. Wound, sore. 3. Prick, thorn, tormenting thought. 4. Crack between the bricks of a wall.

Llagar [lyah-gar'], *va.* To wound, to hurt, to injure.

Llama [lyah'-mah], *f.* 1. Flame, light emitted from fire. 2. Flame, force and violence of passion. 3. *V.* Alpaca. In this sense (*lama*), though feminine in America, it is masculine according to the Spanish Academy. 4. (Prov.) Marshy ground.

Llamada [lyah-mah'-dah], *f.* 1. Call, the act of calling. 2. Marginal note. 3. Any motion or sign to call attention. 4. (Mil.) A call by drum or trumpet; chamade. 5. (Com.) Notice, entry. *La última llamada*, The last peal.

Llamador, ra [lyah-mah-dor', rah], *m. & f.* 1. Caller, he who calls. 2. Beadle, messenger. 3. Knocker of a door. 4. Servant of a salesman, vulgarly called barker, clicker, or drummer.

Llamamiento [lyah-mah-me-en'-to], *m.* 1. Calling, call, the act of calling. 2. Convocation, the act of convening the members of an assembly or corporation. 3. Calling, call, inspiration, divine vocation. 4. Attraction of humours to one part of the body.

Llamar [lyah-mar'], *va.* 1. To call to one. 2. To call, to summon, to cite. 3. To call, or call upon, to invoke, to appeal to. 4. To call, to invoke with ardour of piety. 5. To call, to name, to denominate. 6. To incline. 7. To call, to attract. 8. To excite thirst. *Llamar a la puerta*, To knock or rap at the door. *Llaman*, Some one is knocking. *Llamar por los nombres*, To call the roll. *Llamar a Cortes*, To convoke parliament. *Bolsa sin dinero, llámola cuero*, Like a purse without money (*i. e.* useless). *Iglesia me llamo*, I am called the church (said by criminals who seek asylum in the church). *Llamarse nones*, To deny a thing. *Cuando fueres a casa ajena, llama a la puerta*, Do not be too familiar in the houses of others. *Llamar* or *dar voces para que se haga alguna cosa*, To call out orders to have something done. *El viento llama a popa*, (Naut.) The wind veers aft. *El viento llama a proa*, (Naut.) The wind hauls forward.—*vr.* To bear such a name. *Llamarse andana* or *antana*, (Coll.) To deny obstinately that which one has said or offered.

Llamarada [lyah-mah-rah'-dah], *f.* 1. A sudden blaze of fire, a flash. 2. Flash, a sudden burst of wit. 3. Sudden flush of the face.

Llamativo, va [lyah-mah-tee'-vo, vah], *a.* 1. Exciting thirst. 2. Showy.

Llamazar [lyah-mah-thar'], *m.* Swamp.

Llambria [lyahm'-bre-ah], *f.* Steep face of a rock difficult to pass. (Acad.)

Llamear [lyah-may-ar'], *vn.* To blaze.

Llana [lyah'-nah], *f.* 1. Trowel, a tool for spreading mortar. 2. Page of a book or writing. 3. Plain.

Llanada [lyah-nah'-dah], *f.* A plain, a tract of level ground.

Llanamente, *adv.* Ingenuously, simply, sincerely; homely; plainly.

Llanero, ra [lyah-nay'-ro, rah], *m. & f.* Plainsman or plainswoman, inhabitant of the plains.

Llaneza [lyah-nay'-thah], *f.* 1. (Obs.) Evenness, equality. 2. Plainness, sincerity, simplicity. 3. Want of attention and respect, familiarity. 4. Uncultivated style.

Llano, na [lyah'-no, nah], *a.* 1. Plain, even, level, smooth, flat. 2. Meek, homely, affable. 3. Unmannerly, uncivil. 4. Plain, open, honestly rough. 5. Plain, simple, void of ornament. 6. Plain, clear, evident, discernible. 7. Plain, simple, not varied by art: applied to style. 8. *V.* Pechero. *Carnero llano*, A wether. *A la llana*, Simply, sincerely, candidly.

Llano [lyah'-no], *m.* A level field, an even ground.

Llanta [lyahn'-tah], *f.* 1. (Bot.) *V.* Berza llanta. 2. Tire, the iron hoop or band of a wheel.

Llantén [lyan-ten'], *m.* (Bot.) Plantain. Plantago, *L. Llantén de agua*, *V.* Lizón.

Llantina [lyan-tee'-nah], *f.* A violent fit of crying, especially in children.

Llanto [lyahn'-to], *m.* Flood of tears, crying, weeping.

Llanura [lyah-noo'-rah], *f.* 1. Evenness, equality; flatness, level. 2. A vast tract of level ground, a prairie.

Llapa [lyah'-pah], *f.* 1. An additional portion of mercury added to metal for working in a smelting furnace. 2. (Peru.) A gratuity given to the buyer.

Llapar [lyah-par'], *va.* To add an additional portion of quicksilver in extracting metals.

Llares [lyah'-res], *m.pl.* Pot-hanger, an iron chain, on which pots are hung over the fire.

Llave [lyah'-vay], *f.* 1. Key. 2. Wrench. 3. Spigot, faucet, tap. 4. Lock, gunlock. 5. Bracket. 6. Hold (in wrestling). 7. (Mus.) Clef. *Debajo de llave*, Under lock and key. *Echar la llave a*, 1. To lock. 2. (Fig.) To put the finishing touches on. *Llave de la mano*, Span of the hand. *Llave del paso*, Valve. *Llave del pie*, Distance from heel to instep. *Llave de percusión*, Percussion lock. *Llave inglesa*, Monkey wrench. *Llave maestra*, Master key.

Llavero, ra [lyah-vay'-ro, rah], *m. & f.* 1. Keeper of the keys. 2. Ring in which keys are kept. 3. (Prov.) Housekeeper.

Lle, *pron. obs. V.* Le.

Llegada [lyay-gah'-dah], *f.* Arrival, coming.

Llegar [lyay-gar'], *vn.* 1. To arrive, to come to any place. 2. To reach, to arrive at, to go as far as, to fetch. 3. To last, to continue. 4. To attain a purpose. 5. To suffice, to be enough. 6. To ascend; to amount to.—*va.* 1. To approach, to bring near to. 2. To join.—*vr.* 1. To approach, to draw near. 2. To proceed to some neighbouring place. 3. To unite. *Llegar a las telas del corazón*, To offend a person in his most tender point. *No llegará a colmo*, It will not come to perfection. *Llegar a*, To come to, to get to be, to succeed in. *Llegar a ser*, To come to be. *Llegar y besar*, No sooner said than done. *Llegar a los anises*, To come the day after the fair. *Llegar a las aceitunas*, To arrive at a banquet when it is nearly over. *No llegar a uno la camisa al cuerpo*, To be terrified and anxious. *Llegar a las manos*, To come to blows, to fight. *Llegar a oir*, To hear. *Llegar a saber*, To find out, to be informed of. *No llegar*, To fall short, not to reach. (Met.) To be inferior.

Lleira [lyay'-e-rah], *f.* (Prov.) Place full of pebbles or gravel.

Llena [lyay'-nah], *f.* Alluvion, overflow of rivers.

Llenamente, *adv.* Fully, copiously.

Llenar [lyay-nar'], *va.* 1. To fill, to stuff. 2. To occupy a public place. 3. To fill, to satisfy, to content. 4. To make up a number. 5. To beget young.—*vr.* 1. To feed gluttonously. 2. To be irritated after having suffered long. *Llenar la luna*, To be full moon. *Llenar completamente*, To fill up.

Llenero, ra [lyay-nay'-ro, rah], *a.* (Law) Full, complete, absolute.

Lleno [lyay'-no], *m.* 1. Glut, plenty, abundance, full. 2. Perfection, completeness. 3. Full moon. 4. An organ-stop.

Lleno, na [lyay'-no, nah], *a.* Full, replete, complete. *Lleno de bote en bote*, Brimful, full to the brim. *Hombre lleno*, A learned man. *De lleno* or *de lleno en lleno*, Entirely, totally. *Llena la luna*, The moon is full.

Llenura [lyay-noo'-rah], *f.* Fulness, plenty, copiousness, abundance.

Lleta [lyay'-tah], *f.* Stalk of plants bearing fruit.

Lleudar [lyay-oo-dar'], *va.* To ferment bread with leaven.

Llevada [lyay-vah'-dah], *f.* or **Lleva.** Carriage, transport, act of carrying.

Llevadero, ra [lyay-vah-day'-ro, rah], *a.* Tolerable, light.

Llevador, ra [lyay-vah-dor', rah], *m. & f.* Carrier, conductor.

Llevar [lyay'-var], *va.* 1. To carry, to convey, to transport. 2. To carry, to bear, to wear, to have about one. 3. To carry, to take, to have with one. 4. To exact, to demand, to ask a price for a thing. 5. To bear, to produce. 6. To excel, to exceed. 7. To bear, to suffer, to endure. 8. To lead, to guide. 9. To manage a horse. 10. To cut off. 11. To induce, to bring to any opinion. 12. To introduce. 13. To gain, to obtain. 14. To obtain possession. 15. To fetch away or fetch off. 16. To carry in accounts. 17. With the preposition *por*, it signifies to exercise whatever may be the import of the following noun. *Llevár(se) lo de calle*, To overpower another in argument. *Llevar la suya adelante*, To carry one's point. *Llevar de sobreojo a uno*, To keep a watchful eye on one. *Llevar calabazas*, To be dismissed; to be sent away. *Llevar mosca*, To go away offended and angry. *Llevar en peso*, To carry in the air. *Llevar salida*, (Naut.) To be under way (weigh). *Llevar por cortesanía*, To be polite, courteous. *Llevar consigo*, To carry along with, to be attached to, to be a consequence of. *Llevar una caída, golpe, porrazo, chasco*, etc. (Coll.) To get a fall or blow; to be disappointed. *Llevar y conllevar*, To bear and forbear. *Llevar de conformidad*, (Com.) To find correct.—*vn.* To be reprimanded, to suffer chastisement. *Llevar la proa al nordoeste*, (Naut.) To stand to the north-west. *Llevar las velas a buen viento*, (Naut.) To fill the sails. *Llevar las velas llenas*, (Naut.) To keep the sails full. *Llevar los juanetes viados*, (Naut.) To have the top-gallant sails set. *Llevar a cuestas*, 1. To carry on one's shoulders or back. 2. (Coll.) To burden one's self with others' affairs. —*vr.* 1. To suffer one's self to be led away by passion. 2. *Llevarse el día*. To carry the day. *Llevarse bien* or *mal*, To be on good or bad terms. *Llevárselo la trampa*, To be entirely spoiled. *No llevarlas todas consigo*, To be suspicious, to be afraid. *Llevarse calzones*, To lose all the tricks at cards. *Llevarse los ojos*, To call the attention of bystanders. *Llevar el compás*, To beat time in music.

Lloica, *f. V.* PECHICOLORADO. Robin redbreast.

Lloradera [lyo-rah-day'-rah], *f.* Weeping from slight motives.

Llorador, ra [lyo-rah-dor', rah], *m. & f.* Weeper, one who sheds tears.

Lloraduelos [lyo-rah-doo-ay'-los], *m.* (Coll.) Weeper, mourner.

Llorar [lyo-rar'], *vn.* 1. To weep, to cry. 2. To mourn, to lament, to bewail. 3. To affect poverty and distress. 4. (Met.) To fall drop by drop. *Llorar la aurora*, (Poet.) To fall dew at sunsetting.

Lloriquear [lyo-re-kay-ar'], *vn.* To be constantly crying.

Lloro [lyo'-ro], *m.* Act of weeping or crying.

Llorón [lyo-rone'], *m.* 1. Weeper, one apt to shed tears, mourner. 2. A weeping willow (Babylon willow).

Llorón, na [lyo-rone', nah], *a.* Crying with little cause.

Lloronas [lyo-ro'-nas], *f. pl.* Weepers, mourners.

Llorosamente, *adv.* Weepingly.

Lloroso, sa [lyo-ro'-so, sah], *a.* Mournful, sorrowful, tearful.

Llovediza (Agua) [lyo-vay-dee'-thah], *a.* Rain-water.

Llover [lyo-verr'], *vn.* 1. To rain. 2. To pour down as rain. 3. To shower, to abound, to come in abundance, as troubles.—*vr.* To penetrate the roof with rain. *Llover a cántaros* or *a chorros*, To rain bucketfuls. *Llover chuzos*, To rain pitchforks. *Llueva o no*, Rain or shine.

Llovido [lyo-vee'-do], *m.* Man who secretly steals on board a ship for the West Indies, and does not discover himself till on the high seas; a stowaway.—*Llovido, da, pp.* of LLOVER.

Llovioso, sa, *a. V.* LLUVIOSO.

Llovizna [lyo-veeth'-nah], *f.* Mist, a fine rain.

Lloviznar [lyo-veeth-nar'], *vn.* To drizzle.

Llueco, ca [lyoo-ay'-co, cah], *a. V.* CLUECO.

(*Llueve, llueva*, from *Llover V.* ABSOLVER.)

Lluvia [lyoo'-ve-ah], *f.* 1. Rain, shower, water from the clouds. 2. Shower, abundance, copiousness. 3. Shower, storm. *Lluvia de oro*, (Bot.) *V.* FALSO ÉBANO.

Lluvioso, sa [lyoo-ve-o'-so, sah], *a.* Rainy, wet, showery.

M

M [ay'-may], *f.*, has in the Spanish language the same sound as in English. *M* is never doubled in Spanish. M. 1. Sign for one thousand. 2. Abbr. for midday, noon. 3. Abbr. for misce, mix. 4. Abbr. for majesty, *merced* (grace), *mano* (hand), and in recipes for *manipulus* (handful).

Mabre [mah'-bray], *f.* Marver, a plate of iron used to shape a ball of glass upon.

Maca [mah'-cah], *f.* 1. Bruise in fruit. 2. Spot, stain. 3. Deceit, fraud, trick.

Macabro, bra [mah-cah'-bro, brah], *a.* Macabre, gruesome.

Macaco, ca [mah-cah'-co, cah], *m. & f.* 1. Macaque, or macaco, a flat-headed monkey. 2. (Mex.) Hobgoblin, bogie for frightening children.—*a.* Ugly, ill-shaped, squat.

Macádam [mah-cah'-dam], *m.* Macadam, macadam paving.

Macadamizar [mah-cah-dah-me-thar'], *va.* To macadamize (a road).

Macagua [mah-cah'-goo-ah], *f.* An American bird of prey whose hoarse cry resembles a laugh.

Macaisa [mah-cah'-e-sah], *f.* (Bot.) A tree of the Philippine Islands, of very light wood.

Macana [mah-cah'-nah], *f.* 1. A wooden weapon in use among the ancient Indians of Mexico and Peru, generally edged with sharp flint.

Macanudo, da [mah-cah-noo'-do, dah], *a.* (Sp. Am. coll.) 1. Extraordinary, terrific. 2. Glaring, conspicuous.

Macareno, na [mah-cah-ray'-no, nah], *a.* (Coll.) Applied to a bragging, boasting person.

Macarrón [mah-car-rone'], *m.* 1. Macaroni, a kind of paste. 2. (Naut.) Awning-stanchions. *V* CANDELEROS.

Macarrónico, ca [mah-car-ro'-ne-co, cah], *a.* Macaronic.

Macarronismo [mah-car-ro-nees'-mo], *m.* The macaronic style of poetry.

Macarse [mah-car'-say], *vr.* To rot, to be spoiled in consequence of a bruise or hurt: applied to fruit.

Macayo [mah-cah'-yo], *m.* (Centr. Amer.) Macaw.

Maceador [mah-thay-ah-dor'], *m.* Beater, hammerer.

Macear [mah-thay-ar'], *va.* To beat or drive with a mallet, to knock, to hammer down.—*vn.* To repeat frequently the same demand.

Maceración [mah-thay-rah-the-on'], *f.* 1. Maceration, steeping, infusion. 2. Mortification, maceration, corporeal severity.

Macerar [mah-thay-rar'], *va.* 1. To macerate, to soften by steeping or by blows. 2. To mortify, to macerate, to harass with corporeal hardships. 3. (Chem.) To bruise plants, to extract their juice.

Macerina [mah-thay-ree'-nah], *f.* A kind of saucer with a round cavity in the middle to hold the chocolate-cup when served.

Macero [mah-thay'-ro], *m.* Mace-bearer.

Maceta [mah-thay'-tah], *f.* 1. Flower-pot. 2. Handle of a stick used at Spanish truck-tables. 3. Handle of many kinds of tools. 4. Haunch of mutton. 5. Two-clawed hammer. 6. (Naut.) Maul, mallet. *Maceta de aforra*, A serving-mallet. *Maceta de calafate*, A calking-mallet. *Maceta de ajustar*, A driving-mallet. *Macetas*, Mallets or beetles, with which rope-ends are beaten to make oakum.

Macetón [mah-thay-tone'], *m. aug.* of MACETA.

Mach [mahk], *m. V.* Número Mach.

Macicez [mah-the-theth'], *f.* (Prov.) Solidity, compactness.

Macilento, ta [mah-the-len'-to, tah], *a.* Lean, extenuated; withered, decayed.

Macis [mah'-this], *f.* Mace, a kind of spice.

Macizamente, *adv.* In a firm and solid manner.

Macizar [mah-the-thar'], *va.* 1. To close an opening or passage, to form into a compact body. 2. To support a proposition by argument.

Macizo, za [mah-thee'-tho, thah], *a.* 1. Compact, close, solid, massive. 2. Firm, certain.

Macizo [mah-thee'-tho], *m.* Massiveness, bulk.

Macla [mah'-clah], *f.* 1. (Bot.) Water-caltrops. Trapa natans, *L.* 2. Wooden instrument to scotch flax or hemp.

Macle [mah'-clay], *m.* (Her.) Mascle, a perforated lozenge.

Macoca [mah-co'-cah], *f.* A large sort of early figs.

Macolla [mah-col'-lyah], *f.* Bunch of flowers, etc., growing on one stalk.

Macona [mah-co'-nah], *f.* (Prov.) Basket without handles.

Macrocéfalo, la [mah-cro-thay'-fah-lo, lah], *a.* Macrocephalous, of a large head.

Macrocomo, ma [mah-cro-co'-mo, mah], *a.* (Biol.) Long-haired.

Macrocosmo [mah-cro-cos'-mo], *m.* Macrocosm, the whole world, or visible system, in opposition to the microcosm, or little world of man.

Macrogloso, sa [mah-cro-glo'-so, sah], *a.* Macroglossate, having a long tongue.

Macruros [mah-croo'-rose], *m. pl.* Macruros, a division of the decapods, including lobsters and shrimps.

Macsura [mac-soo'-rah], *f.* Precinct in a mosque reserved for the caliph or leader of prayer, or to contain the sepulchre of one held as sacred.

Macuache [mah-coo-ah'-chay], *m.* A newly arrived Mexican Indian who has not yet had any teaching.

Macuba [mah-coo'-bah], *f.* Tobacco from the north of Martinique. (*m.* in America.)

Macuca [mah-coo'-cah], *f.* (Bot.) Kind of wild pear or pear-tree.

Mácula [mah'-coo-lah], *f.* Stain, spot, blemish, macula.

Macular [mah-coo-lar'], *va.* To mackle or make a double impression in printing, with types or copper-plates.

Maculatura [mah-coo-lah-too'-rah], *f.* (Print.) Sheet which has received a double impression in printing.

Maculca [mah-cool'-cah], *f.* (Amer.) *V.* AGUJETAS.

Macuquino, na [mah-coo-kee'-no, nah], *a.* Applied to coin with the milled edges cut away.

Macuteno [mah-coo-tay'-no], *m.* (Mex.) An infamous man, a petty thief. (Acad.)

Machaca [mah-chah'-cah], *com.* (Coll.) A bore, tiresome person.

Machacadera [mah-chah-cah-day'-rah], *f.* Instrument for pounding or breaking.

Machacador, ra [mah-chah-cah-dor', rah], *m. & f.* Pounder, beetler, bruiser.

Machacar [mah-chah-car'], *va.* To pound or break any thing into small pieces, to crush, to contuse.—*vn.* To importune, to harass, to molest. *Machacar en hierro frío*, To hammer

cold iron: phrase indicating inutility. (Coll.) To brood upon a thing.
Machacón, na [mah-chah-cone', nah], *a.* Heavy, monotonous, importunate.
Machada [mah-chah'-dah], *f.* 1. Flock of he-goats. 2. (Coll.) *V.* NECEDAD.
Machado [mah-chah'-do], *m.* A hatchet. —*Machado, da, pp.* of MACHAR.
Machaque [mah-chah'-kay], *m.* The act of pounding or breaking.
Machaquería [mah-chah-kay-ree'-ah], *f.* (Coll.) Importunity, insistence.
Machar [mah-char'], *va.* To pound. *V.* MACHACAR. *A macha martillo,* Firmly, strongly; in a solid manner. *Creer en Dios a macha martillo,* To believe in God firmly and sincerely.
Machear [mah-chay-ar'], *vn.* To beget more males than females.
Machetazo [mah-chay-tah'-tho], *m.* Blow or stroke with a cutlass.
Machete [mah-chay'-tay], *m.* Cutlass chopping-knife, cane-knife.
Machetear [mah-chay-tay-ar'], *va.* 1. To wound or cut with a machete. 2. (Naut.) To make slow headway against a heavy sea.
Machetero [mah-chay-tay'-ro], *m.* One who clears away bushes with a cutlass.
Machial [mah-che-ahl'], *m.* A wooded hill availed of for pasturing goats.
Machiega [mah-che-ay'-gah], *a.* *V* ABEJA MACHIEGA.
Machihembrar [mah-che-em-brar'], *va.* To join or dovetail pieces of wood in a box with grooves.
Machina [mah-chee'-nah], *f.* 1. Sheers. a machine for masting or unmasting a vessel. 2. A cutting compass for cutting out the brims of hats.
Machismo [mah-chees'-mo], *m.* Manliness, male chauvinism.
Macho[1] [mah'-cho], *m.* 1. A male animal; in particular, a he-mule or a he-goat. 2. A masculine plant. 3. A piece of some instrument which enters into another. 4. Hook to catch hold in an eye. 5. Screw-pin. 6. An ignorant fellow. 7. *Machos del timón,* (Naut.) Rudder-pintles.
Macho[2] *m.* 1. Pillar of masonry to support a building. 2. Sledge hammer. 3 Block on which a smith's anvil is fixed. 4. A square anvil.
Macho [mah'-cho], *a.* Masculine, vigorous, robust; male.
Machón [mah-chone'], *m.* (Arch.) Buttress, an arched pillar to support a wall or building.
Machorra [mah-chor'-rah], *f.* 1. A barren ewe. 2. A barren woman.
Machota, *f.* **Machute,** *m.* [mah-cho'-tah, mah-choo'-tay]. A kind of beetle or mallet.
Machucadura [mah-choo-cah-doo'-rah], *f.* The act of pounding or bruising.
Machucamiento [mah-choo-cah-me-en'-to], *m.* *V.* MACHUCADURA.
Machucar [mah-choo-car'], *va.* To pound, to bruise. *V.* MACHACAR.
Machucho, cha [mah-choo'-cho, chah], *a.* Mature, ripe of age and understanding; judicious.
Machuelo [mah-choo-ay'-lo], *m.* 1. (Dim.) A small he-mule. 2. Heart of an onion.
Madama [mah-dah'-mah], *f.* Madam. *V.* SEÑORA. (F.)
Madamisela [mah-dah-me-say'-lah], *f.* An appellation given in Spain to young women who are over-nice in point of dress, and affect the lady. (F.)
Madapolán [mah-dah-po-lahn'], *m.* A fine white percale which takes its name from a town of India.
Madeja [mah-day'-hah], *f.* 1. Hank or skein of thread, worsted, silk, or cotton. 2. Lock of hair 3. A weak, lazy person. *Madeja sin cuenda,* Confused, disordered, irregular person or thing. *Hacer madeja,* To be ropy: said of liquors.
Madejeta, ica, illa, ita [mah-day-hay'-tah], *f. dim.* A small skein.
Madera [mah-day'-rah], *f.* 1. Wood, timber, lumber. *Madera de construcción,* Timber for ship-building. *Madera de sierra,* Lumber, stuff. *Madera de vuelta,* Compass-timber. *Madera del aire,* Horn of animals. *A media madera,* Said of scarfed timbers. 2. Hoof of a horse or other beast. 3. Said of green or unripe fruit. *Descubrir la madera,* (Coll.) To manifest any unknown vice or defect. *Ser de mala madera* or *tener mala madera,* To be lazy.
Madera, *m.* Madeira wine.
Maderable [mah-day-rah'-blay], *a.* Bearing timber, timber producing.
Maderada [mah-day-rah'-dah], *f.* Raft, a wooden frame or float.
Maderaje; Maderamen [mah-day-rah'-hay, mah-day-rah'-men], *m.* The timber necessary for a building; a house in frame.
Maderamen [mah-day-rah'-men], *m.* Lumber for construction.
Madera terciada [mah-day'-rah ter-the-ah'-dah], *f.* Plywood.
Maderería [mah-day-ray-ree'-ah], *f.* Timber-yard.
Maderero [mah-day-ray'-ro], *m.* 1. Timber-merchant, lumber-dealer. 2. Carpenter.
Maderero, ra [mah-day-ray'-ro, rah], *a.* Pertaining to the lumber industry. *Industria maderera,* Lumber industry.
Maderista [mah-day-rees'-tah], *m.* (Prov.) Conductor of a raft or float.
Madero [mah-day'-ro], *m.* Beam, any large piece of timber: sometimes applied to any piece of timber. *Maderos de cuenta,* The main timbers of a vessel.
Madia [mah'-de-ah], *f.* A plant of Chili, from the seed of which an edible oil is extracted.
Madona [mah-do'-nah], *f* Madonna. (It.)
Madraza [mah-drah'-thah], *f. aug.* A very fond mother.
Madrastra [mah-drahs'-trah], *f.* 1. Stepmother. 2. (Met.) Any thing disagreeable.
Madre [mah'-dray], *f.* 1. A mother. 2. Mother, that which has produced any thing. 3. The most efficacious means for the attainment or intelligence of a thing. 4. Mother, a title given to religious women. 5. Matron in an hospital. 6. Basis, foundation, origin. 7. Matrix, womb. 8. Bed of a river. 9. Sewer, sink. 10. Mother, a substance concreted in liquors, or the lees or scum concreted. 11. Mother, a familiar term of address to an old woman. 12. The principal irrigating ditch whence small branches issue. *Madre de leche,* A wet-nurse. *Mal de madre,* 1. Mother or hysterical passion. 2. The state of children spoiled by their mother. *Madre del timón,* (Naut.) Main-piece of the rudder. *Madre de la rueda del timón,* (Naut.) Barrel of the steering-wheel. *Madres,* (Naut.) Gallows-beams.
Madrear [mah-dray-ar'], *va.* To construct sewers.
Madrecilla [mah-dray-theel'-lyah], *f.* 1. Ovary of birds. 2. (Dim.) *V.* MADRECITA.
Madrecita [mah-dray-thee'-tah], *m. dim.* of MADRE. Used as an endearing expression instead of mother.
Madreclavo [mah-dray-clah'-vo], *m.* Clove, a spice which has remained on the tree two years.
Madreperla [mah-dray-perr'-lah], *f.* Mother-of-pearl; pearl-oyster. Mytilus margaritiferus, *L.*
Madrépora [mah-dray'-po-rah], *f.* Madrepore, white coral.
Madrero, ra [mah-dray'-ro, rah], *a.* (Prov. Coll.) Fondling, caressing a mother.
Madreselva [mah-dray-sel'-vah], *f.* (Bot.) Honey-suckle. Lonicera.
Madrigada [mah-dre-gah'-dah], *a.* Applied formerly to a woman twice married.
Madrigado, da [mah-dre-gah'-do, dah], *a.* 1. Practical, experienced. 2. Applied to a bull that has been a sire.
Madrigal [mah-dre-gahl'], *m.* Madrigal, a light airy song.
Madrigaleja, Madrigalete [mah-dre-gah-lay'-hah, mah-dre-gah-lay'-tay], *m. dim.* A short madrigal.
Madriguera [mah-dre-gay'-rah], *f.* 1. Burrow, the holes made in the ground by rabbits or conies. 2. Den, lurking-place.
Madrileño, ñah [mah-dre-lay'-nyo, nyah], *a.* Native of or belonging to Madrid.
Madrilla [mah-dreel'-lyah], *f.* (Prov.) A small river fish. *V.* BOGA.
Madrillera [mah-dreel-yay'-rah], *f.* (Prov.) Instrument for catching small fish.
Madrina [mah-dree'-nah], *f.* 1. A godmother. 2. Bridesmaid. 3. Protectress. 4. Prop, stanchion. 5. Straps or cords which yoke two horses.
Madriz [mah-dreeth'], *f.* 1. (Obs.) *V.* MATRIZ. 2. Place where quails nest or sea-urchins grow.
Madrona [mah-dro'-nah], *f.* 1. Mother over-fond of her children, who spoils them by excessive tenderness. 2. (Bot.) Clandestine toothwort. Lathræa clandestina, *L.*
Madroncillo [mah-dron-theel'-lyo], *m.* Strawberry.
Madroñal [mah-dro-nyahl'], *m.* A grove of madrone-trees.
Madroñero, rah [mah-dro-nyay'-ro, rah], *m. & f.* One who sells silk tassels; also a seller of madrones.—*f. V.* MADROÑAL.—*m.* (Bot. Prov. Mur.) Madrone-tree.
Madroño [mah-dro'-nyo], *m.* 1. The madrone, or strawberry-tree. Arbutus unedo. 2. Fruit of the strawberry-tree. 3. Silk tassel.
Madrugada [mah-droo-gah'-dah], *f.* 1. Dawn, the first appearance of light. 2. The act of rising early in the morning. *De madrugada,* At break of day.
Madrugador, ra [mah-droo-gah-dor', rah], *m. & f.* Early riser.
Madrugar [mah-droo-gar'], *vn.* 1. To rise early. 2. To contrive, to premeditate. 3. To anticipate, to be beforehand.
Madrugón [mah-droo-gone'], *m.* 1. Act of rising early in the morning. 2. Early riser.
Maduración [mah-doo-rah-the-on'], *f.* Ripeness, maturity.
Maduradero [mah-doo-rah-day'-ro], *m.* Place for ripening fruits.
Madurador, ra [mah-doo-rah-dor', rah], *a.* That which matures or ripens.
Maduramente, *adv.* Maturely, prudently, considerately.
Madurante [mah-doo-rahn'-tay], *va.* Maturing, ripening.
Madurar [mah-doo-rar'], *va.* To ripen, to mature, to mellow. (Med.) To maturate.—*vn.* 1. To ripen, to grow ripe. 2. To attain the age of maturity.—*vr.* To ripen, to grow ripe.

Madurativo, va [mah-doo-rah-tee'-vo, vah], *a.* Maturative.

Madurativo, *m.* 1. Any thing that matures. 2. Means employed to induce a person to yield to a request.

Madurero, *m.* *V.* MADURADERO.

Madurez [mah-doo-reth'], *f.* 1. Maturity, mellowness, ripeness. 2. Prudence, wisdom.

Madurillo, lla [mah-doo-reel'-lyo, lyah], *a.* Beginning to ripen.

Maduro, ra [mah-doo'-ro, rah], *a.* 1. Ripe, mature, perfect, mellow, full-grown. 2. Prudent, judicious.

Maelstrom [mah'-els-trom], *m.* Maelstrom, Norwegian whirlpool.

Maesa [mah-ay'-sah], *f.* *V.* ABEJA MAESTRA.

Maese [mah-ay'-say], *m.* (Obs.) Master. *V.* MAESTRO. *Maese coral,* A kind of game played with balls.

Maesil [mah-ay-seel'], *m.* *V.* MAESTRIL.

Maesillas [mah-ay-seel'-lyas], *f. pl.* Cords which serve in making trimmings or passementerie to raise or lower the skeins.

Maestra [mah-es'-trah], *f.* 1. Mistress, school-mistress. 2. Master's wife in all trades and professions. 3. Queen-bee. 4. Whatever instructs. *La historia es maestra de la vida,* History is the instructress of life. 5. Among masons, a guide line for evening the surface.

Maestral [mah-es-trahl'], *a.* 1. Suiting or relating to a grand-master of a military order, or to his dignity or jurisdiction. 2. (Obs.) *V.* MAGISTRAL. 3. North-west: applied to the wind. *Mesa maestral,* The sheep-walk board.—*m.* Cell of the queen-bee.

Maestralizar [mah-es-trah-le-thar'], *vn.* (Naut.) To vary or decline to west or north-west: applied to the compass-needle (in the Mediterranean).

Maestrante [mah-es-trahn'-tay], *m.* Any of the members of one of the societies called *maestranzas.*

Maestranza [mah-es-trahn'-thah], *f.* 1. Society of noblemen in Spain for practising equestrian exercises. 2. All the workmen of a navy-yard. 3. Workshop of naval furniture. 4. Factory or workshops for making weapons of war. 5. Spot which the workshops occupy; navy-yard, arsenal.

Maestrazgo [mah-es-trath'-go], *m.* Dignity or jurisdiction of a grand-master of a military order.

Maestrazo [mah-es-trah'-tho], *m. aug.* A great master.—*a.* Masterly, skilled, highly intelligent.

Maestre [mah-es'-tray], *m.* 1. Grand-master of a military order: also called *gran maestre.* 2. (Naut.) Mate of a merchant-ship. *Maestre de raciones,* (Naut.) Purser.

Maestrear [mah-es-tray-ar'], *vn.* (Coll.) To domineer, to act the master.—*va.* 1. To lop vines. 2. (Prov.) To adulterate, to falsify. 3. To level the surface of a wall.

Maestresala [mah-es-tray-sah'-lah], *m.* The chief waiter at a nobleman's table in Spain.

Maestrescolia [mah-es-tres-co-lee'-ah], *f.* Dignity of a *maestrescuela* in the Spanish cathedral churches.

Maestrescuela [mah-es-tres-coo-ay'-lah] *m.* 1. A dignitary in the Spanish cathedral churches, whose duty formerly was to teach divinity. 2. Chancellor in some universities.

Maestría [mah-es-tree'-ah], *f.* 1. Mastery, mastership, complete knowledge. 2. In regular orders, the dignity or degree of a master. 3. (Obs.) Artifice, stratagem.

Maestril [mah-es-treel'], *m.* Cell in which the queen-bee is bred; a queen-cell.

Maestrillo [mah-es-treel'-lyo], *m. dim.* A little master. *Cada maestrillo tiene su librillo,* (prov.) Every one has his hobby.

Maestro [mah-es'-tro], *m.* 1. Master, teacher, professor. 2. Master, a man eminently skilful in practice or science. 3. A title of respect in monastic orders. 4. Master, a title of dignity in some universities. 5. The main-mast of a vessel. 6. *Maestro de capilla,* A choir-master, one who composes and directs church music. (Ger. Kapellmeister.) *Maestro de obra prima,* A shoemaker (one who *makes* shoes, in contrast to a cobbler). *Maestro de obras,* A contractor, or builder; superintendent of construction. *Maestro de armas* or *de esgrima,* Fencing-master. *El ejercicio hace maestro,* Practice makes perfect.

Maestro, tra [mah-es'-tro, trah], *a.* Masterly, principal, first, main.

Maestro de ceremonias [mah-es'-tro day thay-ray-mo'-ne-ahs], *m.* Master of ceremonies.

Magallánico, ca [mah-gahl-lyah'-ne-co, cah], *a.* Magellanic, relating to the Straits of Magellan.

Maganto, ta [mah-gahn'-to, tah], *a.* Spiritless, dull, faint, languid.

Magaña [mah-gah'-nyah], *f.* 1. Honey-comb, a flaw in the bore of a gun. 2. (Coll.) Cunning artifice, stratagem. (Acad.)

Magarzuela [mah-gar-thoo-ay'-lah], *f.* Stinking chamomile. Anthemis lotula, *L.*

Magdalena [mag-dah-lay'-nah], *f.* 1. A paste composed of sugar, lemon-juice, flour, eggs, almonds, and other ingredients. 2. Magdalen, a repentant woman.

Magdaleón [mag-dah-lay-on'], *m.* Sticks of plaster, made up in small cylindrical rolls for use.

Magia [mah'-he-ah], *f.* 1. Magic, the art of producing effects by the secret agency of natural powers: in this sense it is also called *magia blanca* or *magia natural.* 2. Magic, the pretended science of putting in action the power of spirits: in this sense it is generally called *magia negra.*

Magiar, or **Magyar** [mah-he-ar'], *a.* & *n.* 1. Magyar, of the race predominant in Hungary and Transylvania. 2. Their language.

Mágicamente, *adv.* Magically.

Mágico, ca [mah'-he-co, cah], *a.* Magic, magical, necromantic.

Mágico, ca [mah'-he-co, cah], *m.* & *f.* Magician, one who professes magic.

Magín [mah-heen'], *m.* (Coll.) Fancy, idea. *V.* IMAGINACIÓN. *Se le ha metido en el magín,* He has taken it into his head.

Magisterial [mah-his-tay-re-ahl'], *a.* Magisterial.

Magisterio [mah-his-tay'-re-o], *m.* 1. Mastery, rule of a master. 2. Mastership, the title and rank of a master in universities. 3. Teaching profession, body of teachers in a nation, city, etc. 4. (fig.) Affected gravity.

Magistrado [mah-his-trah'-do], *m.* 1. A magistrate. 2. Magistracy, the office or dignity of a magistrate. 3. Court, tribunal.

Magistral [mah-his-trahl'], *a.* 1. Magisterial, masterly, oracular. 2. Applied to a prebend in Catholic cathedrals, called *magistral,* and to the person who enjoys it. 3. (Med.) Magistral or magistralia: applied to such medicines as are extemporaneous or in common use.—*f.* Title of a prebendary, in the Roman Catholic church, whose functions consist in teaching and preaching.

Magistralmente, *adv.* Magisterially, masterly.

Magistratura [mah-his-trah-too'-rah], *f.* Magistracy, judicature, judgeship.

Magnánimamente [mag-nah'-ne-mah-men-tay], *adv.* Magnanimously, bravely; generously.

Magnanimidad [mag-nah-ne-me-dahd'], *f.* Magnanimity, fortitude, greatness.

Magnánimo, ma [mag-nah'-ne-mo, mah], *a.* Magnanimous, heroic, generous; honourable.

Magnate [mag-nah'-tay], *m.* Magnate, a person of rank, opulence, etc.

Magnesia [mag-nay'-se-ah], *f.* Magnesia, a medicinal powder: magnesium oxide.

Magnesiano, na [mag-nay-se-ah'-no, nah], *a.* Magnesian, containing magnesia.

Magnesio [mag-nay'-se-o], *m.* Magnesium, a light, grayish-white metal.

Magnesita [mag-nay-see'-tah], *f.* Meerschaum, hydrous magnesium silicate.

Magnético, ca [mag-nay'-te-co, cah], *a.* Magnetic, magnetical, attractive.

Magnetismo [mag-nay-tees'-mo], *m.* Magnetism.

Magnetizable [mag-nay-te-thah'-blay], *a.* Magnetizable.

Magnetización. [mag-nay-te-thah-the-on'], *f.* Magnetizing.

Magnetizar [mag-nay-te-thar'], *va.* To magnetize.

Magneto [mag-nay'-to], *m.* Magneto.

Magnetoeléctrico, ca [mag-nay-to-ay-lec'-tre-co, cah], *a.* Magneto-electric.

Magnetofónico, ca [mag-nay-to-fo'-ne-co, cah], *a.* Tape-recording.

Magnetófono, Magnetofón [mag-nay-to'-fo-no, mag-nay-to-fon'], *m.* Tape recorder.

Magnetohidrodinámica (mag-nay-to-e-dro-de-nah'-me-cah], *f.* Magneto-hydrodynamics.

Magnetómetro [mag-nay-to'-may-tro], *m.* Magnetometer.

Magnetrón [mag-nay-tron'], *m.* Magnetron.

Magníficamente [mag-nee'-fe-cah-men-tay], *adv.* Magnificently, loftily, nobly.

Magnificar [mag-ne-fe-car'], *va.* To magnify, to extol, to exalt.

Magníficat [mag-nee'-fe-cat], *m.* The song of the blessed Virgin. *Criticar* or *corregir el Magníficat,* To criticise without reason or judgment.

Magnificencia [mag-ne-fe-then'-the-ah], *f.* Magnificence, grandeur, splendour; gorgeousness.

Magnífico, ca [mag-nee'-fe-co, cah], *a.* 1. Magnificent, splendid, grand, costly; gaudy. 2. A title of honour.

Magnitud [mag-ne-tood'], *f.* 1. Magnitude, comparative bulk. 2. Magnitude, greatness, grandeur.

Magno, na [mahg'-no, nah], *a.* Great: used as an epithet in the Spanish language; e. g. *Alejandro el Magno,* Alexander the Great.

Magnolia [mag-no'-le-ah], *f.* (Bot.) Magnolia.

Mago, ga [mah'-go, gah], *m.* & *f.* 1. A title formerly given in the east to philosophers, kings, or wise men, called magi. 2. Magician, one skilled in magic; a necromancer.

Magra [mah'-grah], *f.* Rasher, slice of pork, bacon, or ham with eggs.

Magro, gra [mah'-gro, grah], *a.* Meagre lean.

Magrura [mah-groo'-rah], *f.* Leanness. thinness.
Magua [mah'-goo-ah], *f.* (Cuba) Jest, joke.
Magüer, Magüera [mah-goo-err', mah-goo-ay'-rah], *conj.* (Obs.) Although. *V.* AUNQUE.
Magüeto, ta [mah-goo-ay'-to, tah], *m.* & *f.* Young steer or heifer.
Maguey [mah-gay'-e], *m.* (Bot.) American agave, the century plant. Agave Americana. (Synonyms: *Ixtle, henequén, jeniquén* and *pita.*)
Maguillo [mah-geel'-lyo], *m.* Wild apple-tree, used as grafting-stock in southern Spain.
Magujo [mah-goo'-ho], *m.* (Naut.) Rave-hook, an instrument with a crooked point, which serves to pick old oakum out of the seams of the ship's sides and decks.
Magulladura [mah-gool-lyah-doo'-rah], *f.* Bruise, contusion; a hurt with something blunt and heavy.
Magullamiento [mah-gool-lyah-me-en'-to], *m.* Act of bruising: contusion.
Magullar [mah-gool-lyar'], *va.* To bruise, to mangle.
Maguntino, na [mah-goon-tee'-no, nah], *a.* Of the city Mentz or Mayence; in Spanish, Maguncia.
Maharón, na [mah-ah-rone', nah], *a.* (Obs.) Unhappy, unlucky. (Arab.)
Maharrana [mah-ar-rah'-nah], *f.* (Prov. Andal.) Fresh bacon.
Mahometano [mah-o-may-tah'-no], *n.* & *a.* Mohammedan.
Mahometismo [mah-o-may-tees'-mo], *m.* Mohammedanism.
Mahometizar [mah-ho-may-te-thar'], *vn.* To profess Mohammedanism.
Mahón [mah-on'], *m.* Nankeen or nankin, a kind of light cotton. (Name derived from Port Mahón, in the Balearic Islands.)
Mahona [mah-o'-nah], *f.* Turkish transport vessel.
Maido [mah-ee'-do], *m.* Mewing. *V.* MAULLIDO.
Maimona [mah-e-mo'-nah], *f.* Beam of a horse-mill in which the spindle runs.
Maimonetes [mah-e-mo-nay'-tes], *m. pl.* (Naut.) Pins, placed near the main and foremast, to which ropes are fastened; belaying-pins.
Maitinante [mah-e-te-nahn'-tay], *m.* Priest whose duty is to celebrate or attend matins.
Maitinario [mah-e-te-nah'-re-o], *m.* Book containing the matins.
Maitines [mah-e-tee'-nes], *m. pl.* Matins, earliest of the canonical hours in the Catholic church.
Maiz [mah-eeth'], *m.* (Bot.) Maize, Indian corn. Zea mays. *Maíz machacado*, Hominy.
Maizal [mah-e-thahl'], *m.* Indian cornfield.
Maja [mah'-hah], *f.* Pestle of a mortar.
Majá [mah-hah'], *m.* A thick-bodied snake of Cuba.
Majada [mah-hah'-dah], *f.* 1. Sheep-cot. sheep-fold. 2. Dung of animals. (Acad.)
Majadal [mah-hah-dahl'], *m.* Land which has been used for a sheep-fold and has been improved by the manure of the flock.
Majadear [mah-hah-day-ar'], *vn.* To take shelter in the night: applied to a flock of sheep.
Majadería [mah-hah-day-ree'-ah], *f.* Absurd speech, nonsense; lumpishness.
Majaderico, ca, Majaderillo, lla [mah hah-day-ree'-co, cah, eel'-lyo, lyah], *a. dim.* Rather dull, somewhat silly gawkish.
Majaderillo [mah-hah-day-reel'-lyo], *m* Bobbin for lace.
Majadero, ra [mah-hah-day'-ro, rah], *a* Dull, foolish, doltish, silly, sottish.
Majadero, *m.* 1. Gawk, a foolish. troublesome fellow, a bore. 2. Pestle. an instrument with which any thing is broken in a mortar. *Majaderos*, Bobbins for making bone-lace.
Majaderón [mah-hah-day-rone'], *m. aug.* A great gawk, a great fool, a great bore.
Majador, ra [mah-hah-dor', rah], *m.* & *f.* Pounder, bruiser.
Majadura [mah-hah-doo'-rah], *f.* The act of pounding or bruising.
Majagranzas [mah-hah-grahn'-thas], *m.* (Coll.) A stupid brute: nickname for an ignorant, troublesome fellow.
Majagua [mah-hah'-goo-ah], *f.* A tree of Cuba and parts of South America. from the bark of which the strongest and most durable cordage is made. Hibiscus tiliaceus.
Maja martillo (Á), *adv. exp.* Hammer and tongs; strongly.
Majamiento [mah-hay-me-en'-to], *m. V.* MAJADURA.
Majano [mah-hah'-no], *m.* A small heap of stones serving as a landmark.
Majar [mah-har'], *va.* 1. To pound, to break in a mortar. 2. To importune, to vex, to molest.
Majarete [mah-hah-ray'-tay], *m.* (Cuba) Corn-pudding, a dessert made from grated maize, milk, and sugar.
Majarrana [mah-har-rah'-nah], *f.* (Prov.) Fresh pork.
Majenca [mah-hen'-cah], *f.* (Prov.) Digging of vines. (Murcia.)
Majencar [mah-hen-car'], *va.* (Prov.) To dig the earth about vines, and clear them of weeds.
Majencia [mah-hen'-the-ah], *f.* (Prov. Coll.) Spruceness or fineness in one's dress.
Majestad [mah-hes-tahd'], *f.* 1. Majesty, dignity; grandeur of appearance, loftiness; gravity. 2. Majesty, royalty, the title of emperors, kings, empresses, and queens. 3. Power, kingship, sovereignty, elevation.
Majestoso, sa [mah-hes-to'-so], *a. V.* MAJESTUOSO.
Majestuosamente [mah-hes-too-o-sah-men'-tay], *adv.* Majestically, kingly.
Majestuosidad [mah-hes-too-o-se-dahd'], *f.* Majesty, dignity.
Majestuoso, sa [mah-hes-too-o'-so, sah], *a.* 1. Majestic, majestical, august, grand. 2. Stately, pompous, lofty. 3. Grave, solemn.
Majeza [mah-hay'-thah], *f.* (Coll.) Spruceness, fineness in dress.
Majo, ja [mah'-ho, hah], *m.* & *f.* Boaster, bragger.
Majo, ja [mah'-ho, hah], *a.* Gallant, gay, spruce, fine.
Majojo [mah-ho'-ho], *m.* Dry, half-thrashed straw and trodden stubble used as fodder.
Majolar [mah-ho-lar'], *va.* To put straps to the shoes, to tie them tight.
Majorca [mah-hor'-cah], *f. V.* MAZORCA.
Majuela [mah-hoo-ay'-lah], *f.* 1. Fruit of the white hawthorn. 2. Strap with which shoes are tied, shoe-lacing.
Majuelo [mah-hoo-ay'-lo], *m.* 1. Vine newly planted. 2. The white hawthorn.
Mal [mahl], *m.* 1. Evil, harm, hurt, injury, mischief. 2. Illness, disease, complaint. 3. Imperfection. 4. Fault, trespass.—*a. V.* MALO: it is used only before masculine substantives.—*adv.* Badly, injuriously, ill. *Anda mal*, He is a bad walker. *Mal caduco*, Epilepsy. *Mal hecho*, 1. Badly done, ill finished. 2. Unjust, contrary to equity and justice. *Mal de mi grado, mal de tu grado* or *mal de su grado*, In spite of me, of you, or of him or her; maugre; notwithstanding. *Mal que bien*, With good or ill will. *Mal por mal*, For want of something better. *Del mal el menos*, The least of two evils. *De mal en peor*, Worse and worse. *Mal francés*, Venereal disease. *Mal de ojo*, Evil eye. *Mal de ojos*, Eye-sore. *Mal de ánimo*, Heart-sore. *¡Que mal haya!* May he repent it! *¡Mal haya quien mal piense!* Evil to him who evil thinks! *¡Mal haya Vd. que no me lo ha dicho!* God forgive you for not having told me! *Mal que le pese*, In spite of him. *Bien vengas, mal, si vienes solo*, Misfortunes never come singly.
Mala [mah'-lah], *f.* 1. Mail: in Spain a bag for letters from France. 2. Deuce of spades. 3. (Amer.) A mail-steamer.
Malacate [mah-lah-cah'-tay], *m.* Hoisting machine in mines.
Malacología [mah-lah-co-lo-hee'-ah], *f.* Malacology, the science which treats of mollusks, especially their soft parts.
Malaconsejado, da [ma-lah-con-say-hah'-do, dah], *a.* Ill-advised.
Malaconsejar [ma-lah-con-say-har'], *va.* 1. To advise badly. 2. To incline to evil.
Malacostumbrado, da [mah-lah-cos-toom-brah'-do, dah], *a.* Having bad habits or customs.
Malacuenda [mah-lah-coo-en'-dah], *f.* Coarse cloth made of tow.
Malagaña [mah-lah-gah'-nyah], *f.* (Prov.) Pole set up with dry furze to catch bees swarming.
Malagradecido, da [mal-ah-grah-day-thee'-do, dah], *a.* Unappreciative, ungrateful.
Malagradecimiento [mal-ah-grah-day-the-me-en'-to], *m.* Ungratefulness, lack of appreciation.
Malagueño, na [mah-lah-gay'-nyo, nyah], *a.* Native of or belonging to Malaga.—*f.* A song popular in the province of Malaga.
Malagueta [mah-lah-gay'-tah], *f.* Tabasco pepper.
Malamente [mah-lah-men'-tay], *adv.* Badly, wickedly.
Malandante [mah-lan-dahn'-tay], *a.* Calamitous, unfortunate.
Malandanza [mah-lan-dahn'-thah], *f.* Misfortune, calamity.
Malandar [mah-lan-dar'], *m.* (Prov.) Wild hog.
Malandrín [mah-lan-dreen'], *m.* Highwayman.—*a.* Malign, perverse.
Malanga [mah-lahn'-gah], *f.* A farinaceous root of great consumption in Cuba. Arum sagitæ folium.
Malaquita [mah-lah-kee'-tah], *f.* (Min.) Malachite, precious stone: green copper carbonate.
Malar [mah-lar'], *a.* Malar, relating to the cheek.
Malatia [mah-lah-tee'-ah], *f.* 1. Leprosy. 2. (Obs.) Disease in general. (Acad.)
Malato, ta [mah-lah'-to, tah], *a.* 1. Leprous. 2. (Obs.) Sick, diseased. (Acad.) Also noun.
Malato, *m.* (Chem.) Malate.
Malavenido, da [mah-lah-vay-nee'-do, dah], *a.* & *n.* Quarrelsome person, a sower of discord; curst, mischievous.
Malaventura [mah-lah-ven-too'-rah], *f.* Calamity, misfortune.
Malaventurado, da [mah-lah ven-too-rah'-do, dah], *a.* Unfortunate, ill-fated, luckless.

Malaventuranza [mah-lah-ven-too-rahn'-thah], *f.* Infelicity, unhappiness.

Malayo, a [mah-lah'-yo, yah], *a.* 1. Malay, belonging to Malacca. 2. The Malay tongue.

Malbaratador, ra [mal-bah-rah-tah-dor', rah], *m.* & *f.* Spendthrift, prodigal.

Malbaratar [mal-bah-rah-tar'], *va.* 1. To misspend, to lavish. 2. To disorder.

Malbaratero, ra [mal-bah-rah-tay'-ro, rah], *a.* *V.* MALBARATADOR.

Malbaratijar [mal-bah-rah-te-har'], *va.* *V.* MALBARATAR.

Malbaratijo [mal-bah-rah-tee'-ho], *m.* Bad sale, sale in a second-hand shop.

Malbaratillar [mal-bah-rah-teel-lyar'], *va.* *V.* MALBARATAR.

Malbaratillo [mal-bah-rah-teel'-lyo], *m.* A cheap, second-hand shop.

Malcarado, da [mal-cah-rah'-do, dah], *a*, Grim-faced, foul-faced.

Malcasado, da [mal-cah-sah'-do, dah], *a.* & *pp.* of MALCASAR. Not well married.

Malcasar [mal-cah-sar'], *va.* To make any one marry against his or her will: applied to parents, guardians, etc.—*vr.* To contract an improper or unfortunate marriage.

Malcaso [mal-cah'-so], *m.* Treason, turpitude, crime.

Malcocinado [mal-co-the-nah'-do], *m.* 1. Tripes, liver, and lights of a quadruped. 2. Place where tripes are sold.

Malcomido, da [mal-co-mee'-do, dah], *a.* Hungry, destitute of wholesome food.

Malcontento, [mal-con-ten'-to], *m.* 1. Malcontent; grumbler. 2. A game at cards.

Malcontento, ta [mal-con-ten'-to, tah], *a.* Discontented, malcontent.

Malcorte [mal-cor'-tay], *m.* Transgression of the mountain laws in cutting wood or making charcoal.

Malcriado, da [mal-cre-ah'-do, dah], *a.* Ill-bred, unmannerly, impolite, clownish; spoiled: commonly applied to children.

Maldad [mal-dahd'], *f.* 1. Wickedness, iniquity, corruption, abomination. 2. Guiltiness, criminality, mischievousness.

Maldecidor, ra [mal-day-the-dor', rah], *m.* & *f.* Detractor; swearer.

Maldecimiento [mal-day-the-me-en'-to], *m.* (Obs.) Backbiting, privy calumny; censure of the absent.

Maldecir [mal-day-theer'], *va.* 1. To curse, to accurse, to execrate. 2. To detract.

Maldiciente [mal-de-the-en'-tay], *pa.* & *m.* & *f.* Cursing; curser; mordacious.

Maldición [mal-de-the-on'], *f.* 1. Malediction, curse, execration; imprecation. 2. Divine chastisement.

Maldicho, cha [mal-dee'-cho, chah], *pp. irr. obs.* of MALDECIR. Accursed; calumniated.

(*Yo maldigo, yo maldiga,* from *Maldecir.* *V.* BENDECIR.)

Maldita [mal-dee'-tah], *f.* (Coll.) The tongue. *Soltar la maldita,* (Coll.) To give a loose rein to one's tongue, to tell one's mind very freely.

Maldito, ta [mal-lee'-to, tah], *a.* 1. Perverse, wicked. 2. Chastised by Divine justice. 3. Damned, cursed, confounded. 4. (Coll.) None, not one.—*pp. irr.* of MALDECIR, Accursed.

Maleabilidad [mah-lay-ah-be-le-dahd'], *f.* Malleability, malleableness.

Maleable [mah-lay-ah'-blay], *a.* Malleable.

Maleante [mah-lay-ahn'-tay], *m.* Corrupter, injurer.—*pa.* Corrupting.

Malear [mah-lay-ar'], *va.* To pervert, to corrupt, to injure, to damnify.

Malecón [mah-lay-cone'], *m.* Dike, embankment, levee, jetty.

Maledicencia [mah-lay-de-then'-the-ah], *f.* Slander, calumny, obloquy.

Maleficencia [mah-lay-fe-then'-the-ah], *f.* Mischievousness, the habit of doing mischief.

Maleficiador, ra [mah-lay-fe-the-ah-dor', rah], *m.* & *f.* Adulterator, corrupter.

Maleficiar [mah-lay-fe-the-ar'], *va.* 1. To adulterate, to corrupt, to vitiate. 2. To bewitch, to injure by witchcraft.

Maleficio [mah-lay-fee'-the-o], *m.* 1. (Obs.) Hurt, damage, injury. 2. Witchcraft, charm, enchantment.

Maléfico, ca [mah-lay'-fe-co, cah], *a.* Mischievous, malicious, injurious to others, especially by witchcraft.

Maleolar [mah-lay-o-lar'], *a.* Malleolar, relating to the ankle.

Maléolo [mah-lay'-o-lo], *m.* Malleolus, each bony prominence of the ankles.

Malestar [mah-les-tar'], *m.* 1. Discomfort, uneasiness. 2. Indisposition, physical disorder.

Maleta [mah-lay'-tah], *f.* Portmanteau, valise, gripsack. *Hacer la maleta,* To make preparations for a journey.

Maletero [mah-lay-tay'-ro], *m.* Harness-maker, saddler; portmanteau-maker.

Maletilla [mah-lay-teel'-lyah], *f.* Satchel, small handbag.

Maletin [mah-le-teen'], *m. dim.* A satchel.

Maletón [mah-lay-tone'], *m. aug.* A large leather bag, portmanteau.

Malevolencia [mah-lay-vo-len'-the-ah], *f.* Malevolence, ill-nature, ill-will, malignancy.

Malévolo, la [mah-lay'-vo-lo, lah], *a.* Malevolent, malignant, mischievous, hateful.

Maleza [mah-lay'-thah], *f.* 1. Piece of ground, rendered unfruitful by brambles and briers. 2. Undergrowth, thicket, coppice.

Malfechor [mal-fay-chor'], *m.* (Obs.) *V.* MALHECHOR.

Malgama, *m.* (Chem.) *V.* AMALGAMA.

Malgastador, ra [mal-gas-tah-dor', rah], *m.* & *f.* Spendthrift, squanderer.

Malgastar [mal-gas-tar'], *va.* To misspend, to waste, to lavish, to lose, to throw away.

Malhablado, da [mal-ah-blah'-do, dah], *a.* Bold, impudent in speaking, foul-mouthed.

Malhadado, da [mal-ah-dah-do, dah], *a.* Wretched, unfortunate.

Malhecho [mal-ay'-cho], *m.* Flagitious action; an evil deed.

Malhecho, cha [mal-ay'-cho, chah], *a.* Ill-shaped: applied to persons who are humpbacked or otherwise deformed.

Malhechor, ra [mal-ay-chor', rah], *m.* & *f.* Malefactor, offender, misdoer.

Malherido, da [mal-ay-ree'-do, dah], *a.* & *pp.* of MALHERIR. Badly wounded.

Malherir [mal-ay-reer'], *va.* To wound badly.

Malhojo [mal-o'-ho], *m* (Ant.) Vegetable refuse. (Acad.)

Malhumorado, da [mal-oo-mo-rah'-do, dah], *a.* Ill-humoured, peevish; having gross humours.

Malicia [mah-lee'-the-ah], *f.* 1. Malice, perversity, wickedness, malignity. 2. Malice, maliciousness, mischievousness, intention of mischief to another. 3. Suspicion, apprehension. 4. Cunning, artifice. 5. Dissimulation, hypocrisy. 6. Gall, rancour, animosity.

Maliciar [mah-le-the-ar'], *va.* To corrupt, to adulterate.—*vn.* To put a malicious construction on a thing; to discourse in a malicious manner; to suspect maliciously.

Maliciosamente [mah-le-the-o-sah-men'-tay], *adv.* Maliciously.

Maliciosico, ica, illo, illa, ito, ita [mah-le-the-o-see'-co], *a. dim.* A little malicious.

Malicioso, sa [mah-le-the-o'-so, sah], *a.* Malicious, suspicious, wicked, knavish, mischievous.

Málico, ca [mah'-le-co, cah], *a.* Malic, belonging to or derived from apples.

Malignamente [mah-lig-nah-men'-tay], *adv.* Malignantly, mischievously, hatefully, malevolently.

Malignar [mah-lig-nar'], *va.* To vitiate, to corrupt, to deprave.—*vr.* 1. To become sore. 2. To grow worse.

Malignidad [mah-lig-ne-dahd'], *f.* Malignity, malice; perverseness; mischievousness, hatred.

Maligno, na [mah-leeg'-no, nah], *a.* Malignant, perverse, malicious, ill-disposed, hateful.

Malilla [mah-leel'-lyah], *f.* 1. Manille the deuce of spades or clubs, or the seven of hearts or diamonds, in the game of ombre. 2. A game of cards like whist. 3. (Coll.) Person full of wickedness and malice.

Malintencionado, da [mal-in-ten-the-o-nah'-do, dah], *a.* Bearing ill-will, ill disposed, with bad intentions.

Malmandado, da [mal-man-dah'-do, dah], *a.* (Coll.) Disobedient, obstinate.

Malmeter [mal-may-terr'], *vn.* (Coll.) To incline, to induce to evil; to make one differ with another; to breed quarrels.

Malmirado, da [mal-me-rah'-do, dah], *a.* 1. Impolite, inconsiderate. 2. Indiscreet, imprudent.

Malo, la [mah'-lo, lah], *a.* 1. Bad, evil, not good. 2. Bad, vicious, wicked, perverse, naughty. 3. Imperfect, defective. 4. Artful, cunning, crafty, mischievous. 5. Sickly, disordered, ill. *Estar malo,* To be ill, to be sick. *Ser malo,* To be wicked. 6. Unhealthy, prejudicial to health. 7. Difficult, inquiet. *De mala,* Deceitfully, in an insidious manner. *Andar a malas,* To go in enmity.

Malo [mah'-lo], *int.* Bad; so much the worse.

Malogramiento [mah-lo-grah-me-en'-to], *m.* Disappointment.

Malograr [mah-lo-grar'], *va.* 1. To disappoint, to disconcert. 2. (Com.) To waste or spoil goods.—*vr.* To be disappointed, to fail of success.

Malogro [mah-lo'-gro], *m.* Disappointment, miscarriage, failure.

Maloja [mah-lo'-hah], *f.* (Cuba) The leaves and stalks of Indian corn, used only for fodder.

Malojo [mah-lo'-ho], *m.* (Acad.) *V.* MALOJA. (Venezuela.)

Maloler [mah-lo-lerr'], *vn.* To stink.

Maloliente [mah-lo-le-en'-tay], *pa.* Stinking, foul-smelling.

Malolor [mah-lo-lor'], *m.* Stench, stink, pestiferous smell. (These three words are not recognized by the Academy.)

Malón [mah-lone'], *m.* (Chili) A hostile, predatory incursion of Indians.

Maloquear [ma-lo-kay-ar'], *vn.* (Mex.) 1. To make a predatory raid (by Indians). 2. To trade with Indians for stolen goods.

Maloquero, ra [mah-lo-kay'-ro, rah], *a.* & *n.* (Amer.) 1. An Indian thief. 2. One who trades with Indian thieves.

Malordenado, da [mah-lor-day-nah'-do, dah], *a.* Badly contrived, ill arranged.

Malparado, da [mal-pah-rah'-do, dah] *a.* & *pp.* of MALPARAR. Ill-conditioned, impaired, useless.

Malparar [mal-pah-rar'], *va.* (Obs.) To ill-treat, to impair, to damage, to hurt to blemish.

Malparecido, da [mal-pah-ray-thee'-do dah], *a.* Of evil aspect or countenance ugly.

Malparida [mal-pah-ree'-dah], *f.* Woman who has miscarried.

Malparir [mal-pah-reer'], *vn.* To miscarry.

Malparto [mal-par'-to], *m.* Abortion. miscarriage.

Malpaso [mal-pah'-so], *m.* 1. Exigency. tight place, grievous difficulty. 2. Reprehensible fault.

Malponer [mal-po-nerr'], *va.* 1. To indispose. 2. To excite quarrels.

Malquerencia [mal-kay-ren'-the-ah], *f.* Ill-will, hatred.

Malquerer [mal-kay-rerr'], *va.* To abhor, to hate, to bear ill-will.

Malquistar [mal-kis-tar'], *va.* To excite disputes and quarrels among friends and others.—*vr.* To incur hatred and displeasure.

Malquisto, ta [mal-kees'-to, tah], *a.* Hated, detested, abhorred.

Malrotador, ra [mal-ro-tah-dor', rah], *m.* & *f.* Squanderer, spendthrift.

Malrotar [mal-ro-tar'], *va.* To misspend, to lavish, to waste one's fortune.

Malsano, na [mal-sah'-no, nah], *a.* 1. Unhealthy, sickly, infirm. 2. Unwholesome, insalubrious, injurious to health.

Malsín [mal-seen'], *m.* Tale-bearer, mischief-maker. (Obsolescent.)

Malsonante [mal-so-nahn'-tay], *a.* Applied to doctrines offensive to pious or virtuous ears.

Malsonar [mal-so-nar'], *vn.* (Obs.) To sound bad; to make a disagreeable sound.

Malsufrido, da [mal-soo-free'-do, dah], *a.* Impatient of suffering.

Malta [mahl'-tah], *f.* 1. A bandage in the shape of a Maltese cross. 2. Asphalt, mineral pitch.

Maltés, sa [mal-tays', sah], *a.* Maltese, of Malta.

Maltosa [mal-to'-sah], *f.* Maltose.

Maltrabaja [mal-trah-bah'-hah], *com.* (Coll.) Idler, lounger.

Maltraer [mal-trah-err'], *va.* To treat ill. *V.* MALTRATAR.

Maltratadamente [mal-trah-tah-dah-men'-tay], *adv.* Ill-used, in an abused manner.

Maltratamiento [mal-trah-tah-me-en'-to], *m.* Ill treatment, bad usage; affliction.

Maltratar [mal-trah-tar'], *va.* 1. To treat ill, to abuse, to maltreat, to misuse. 2. To spoil, to destroy.

Maltrato [mal-trah'-to], *m.* Ill treatment.

Malucho, cha [mah-loo'-cho, chah], *a.* 1. (Coll.) A sickly person. 2. Naughty, wayward.

Malva [mahl'-vah], *f.* (Bot.) Mallows. Malva. *Malva blanca*, Walteria hibiscus. *Malva rosa*, Hibiscus mutabilis. *Malva te*, Corcorus siliquosus (Cuba), used as a substitute for tea.

Malvadamente [mal-vah-dah-men'-tay], *adv.* Wickedly, naughtily, mischievously; hellishly; lewdly.

Malvado, da [mal-vah'-do, dah], *a.* Malicious, wicked, insolent, vicious, nefarious.

Malvar [mal-var'], *m.* Place covered with mallows.—*va.* (Obs.) To vitiate, to corrupt.

Malvasía [mal-vah-see'-ah], *f.* Malmsey or Malvoisie grape; malmsey wine.

Malvavisco [mal-vah-vees'-co], *m.* (Bot.) Marsh-mallows. Althæa officinalis.

Malversación [mal-ver-sah-the-on'], *f.* Misapplication or maladministration of money; malversation.

Malversador, ra [mal-ver-sah-dor', rah], *m.* & *f.* Person who misapplies property.

Malversar [mal-ver-sar'], *va.* To misapply, to apply money to wrong purposes.

Malvís, Malviz [mal-vees', mal-veeth'], *m.* Bird resembling a thrush; redwing.

Malla [mahl'-lyah], *f.* 1. Mesh, space between the threads of a net. *Hacer malla*, To knit. 2. (Naut.) Net-work of a ship. 3. Coat of mail.

Mallar [mahl-lyar'], *va.* 1. To make net-work. 2. (Obs.) To mail, to arm with a coat of mail.

Mallero [mah-lyay'-ro], *m.* Armourer, maker of coats of mail.

Malletes [mal-lyay'-tes], *m. pl.* Partners, strong pieces of timber bolted to the beams, encircling the masts, to keep them steady in their steps.

Mallo [mahl'-lyo], *m.* 1. Pall-mall, game of bowls, skittles, or nine-pins. 2. Mall, bowling-green, skittle-ground. 3. Mallet.

Mallorquín, na [mal-lyor-keen', nah], *a.* Native of or belonging to Majorca; Mallorcan.

Mamá [mah-mah'], *f.* Ma, mamma: a fond word for mother.

Mama [mah'-ma], *f.* 1. The mammary gland, breast. 2. (Prov. Andal.) Mamma, mother.

Mamacallos [mah-mah-cahl'-lyos], *m.* (Coll.) Dolt, simpleton.

Mamada [mah-mah'-dah], *f.* (Coll.) Time which a child takes in sucking.

Mamadera [mah-mah-day'-rah], *f.* Breast-pump.

Mamador, ra [mah-mah-dor', rah], *m.* & *f.* Sucker, suckling, one who sucks. —*n.* Feeding-bottle, nursing-bottle for artificial lactation.

Mamahigos [mah-mah-ee'-gose], *a.* Silly, booby.

Mamalón [mah-mah-lon'], *m.* (Cuba) Idler who tries constantly to live at another's expense; parasite.

Mamante [mah-mahn'-tay], *a.* Sucking. *Piante ni mamante*, Not one, none: it is accompanied with the verb *quedar* and a negative.

Mamantón, na [mah-man-tone', nah], *a.* Sucking: applied to animals.

Mamar [mah-mar'], *va.* 1. To suck, to draw milk from the breast. 2. (Coll.) To cram and devour victuals. 3. To acquire in infancy. 4. (Coll.) To get, obtain.

Mamario, ria [mah-mah'-re-o, ah], *a.* Mammary: relating to the breast.

Mamarrachada [mah-mar-rah chah'-dah], *f.* 1. A collection of rude or ridiculous figures. 2. A foolish action or speech.

Mamarrachista [mah-mar-rah-chees'-tah], *m.* (Littl. us.) Dauber, bad painter.

Mamarracho [mah-mar-rah'-cho], *m.* An ill-drawn figure of a man; a grotesque ornament.

Mamayuca [mah-mah-yoo'-cah], *f.* Crust of bread put into a frying-pan or dish where many eat, to set bounds to or suspend a meal.

Mambla [mahm'-blah], *f.* Isolated rounded hillock. (Word of Old Castile.)

Mamey [mah-may'-e], *m.* (Bot.) 1. American mammee-tree of the gamboge family. 2. Its fruit, used medicinally and for making oil. Mammea Americana.

Mamelón [mah-may-lon'], *m.* (Anat.) 1. Teat, nipple. 2. Any teat-shaped tubercle.

Mameluco [mah-may-loo'-co], *m.* 1. Mameluke, Egyptian soldier. 2. Leotard, practice costume for dancing. 3. Child's rompers. 4. A fool, an idiot.

Mamella [mah-mayl'-lyah], *f.* 1. Small teat, nipple. 2. A small teat-shaped appendage on the neck of goats, etc. *V.* MARMELLA.

Mamellado, da [mah-mel-lyah'-do, dah], *a.* Mammellated: applied to animals having loose skins on their necks.

Mamífero, ra [ma-mee'-fay-ro, rah], *a.* Mammiferous, having mammary glands: mammalian.—*m. pl.* Mammals.

Mamiforme [mah-me-for'-may], *a.* Having the shape of a mammary gland. *V.* MASTÓIDEO.

Mamila [mah-mee'-lah], *f.* 1. The chief part of a woman's breast round the nipple. 2. The nipple in men. (Acad.)

Mamilar [mah-me-lar'], *a.* Mamillary.

Mammuth [mam-moot'], *m.* Mammoth, fossil elephant.

Mamola [mah-mo'-lah], *f.* Chuck under the chin.

Mamón, na [mah-mone', nah], *m.* & *f.* 1. A sucking animal. 2. A child that sucks too much, or for too long a time. 3. Sucker, young twig.

Mamoso, sa [mah-mo'-so, sah], *a.* 1. Sucking. 2. Applied to panic grass.

Mamotreto [mah-mo-tray'-to], *m.* Memorandum-book.

Mampara [mam-pah'-rah], *f.* Screen before a door or any other place.

Mamparar [mam-pah-rar'], *va.* (Obs.) To shelter, to protect.

Mamparo [mam-pah'-ro], *m.* (Naut.) Bulkhead, partition in a ship. *Mamparos de quita y pon*, (Naut.) Ship and unship bulkheads.

Mampostear [mam-pos-tay-ar'], *va.* To raise mason-work, to cement with mortar.

Mampostería [mam-pos-tay-ree'-ah], *f.* 1. Rubble-work masonry. 2. The employment of collecting alms or tithes.

Mampostero [mam-pos-tay'-ro], *m.* 1. Mason, stone mason. 2. Collector of alms or tithes.

Mampresar [mam-pray-sar'], *va.* (Prov.) To begin to break horses.

Mampuesta [mam-poo-es'-tah], *f.* Row of bricks.

Mampuesto [mam-poo-es'-to], *m.* Rubble, rough stone. *De mampuesto*, Provisionally.

Mamujar [mah-moo-har'], *va.* To play with the breast, to have no inclination to suck: applied to children.

Mamullar [mah-mool-lyar'], *va.* To eat or chew as if sucking; to mutter; to mumble.

Mamut [mah-moot'], *m.* Mammoth, primitive elephant now extinct.

Man [mahn], *f.* (Obs.) Hand. *Á man salva*, Without risk or danger; very easily.

Maná [mah-nah'], *m.* 1. Manna, food of the Israelites. 2. Manna, a gum obtained from ash-trees. 3. Tart made of blanched almonds, sugar, spice, etc. 4. Kind of small sugar-plums.

Manada [mah-nah'-dah], *f.* 1. Flock, herd; drove of cattle. 2. Handful of corn, etc., or any other thing; tuft, cluster. 3. Crowd, fry, multitude. *A manadas*, In troops or crowds.

Manadera [mah-nah-day'-rah], *f.* Strainer, an instrument for filtration.

Manadero [mah-nah-day'-ro], *m.* 1. Source, spring. 2. Shepherd, herdsman.

Manadero, ra [mah-nah-day'-ro, rah], *a.* Springing, that which issues.

Manadilla [mah-nah-deel'-lyah], *f. dim.* A small flock.

Manante [mah-nahn'-tay], *pa.* Proceeding, issuing.
Manantial [mah-nan-te-ahl'], *m.* 1. Source, spring. 2. Source, origin, principle, head.
Manantial, *a.* Flowing, running: applied to water.
Manar [mah-nar'], *va.* 1. To spring from; to distil from, as a liquor. 2. To drop or distil from. 3. To proceed, to issue, to arise. 4. To abound.
Manati, Manato [mah-nah-tee', mah-nah'-to], *m.* 1. Manati, manatee, sea-cow. 2. A whip made of the manati's hide.
Manaza [mah-nah'-thah], *f. aug.* A large hand, a mutton-fist.
Manca [mahn'-cah], *f.* *V.* MANCO.
Mancamiento [man-cah-me-en'-to], *m.* Want, defect, privation, deficiency, maimedness.
Mancar [man-car'], *va.* 1. To maim, to render useless an arm or hand. 2. (Obs.) To fail of the desired effect. 3. To disable a man for business.
Manceba [man-thay'-bah], *f.* Mistress, concubine.
Mancebia [man-thay-bee'-ah], *f.* 1. (Obs.) Youth. *V.* JUVENTUD. 2. Brothel, bawdy-house.
Mancebico, illo, ito [man-thay-bee'-co], *m. dim.* A little young man.
Mancebo, ba [man-thay'-bo, bah], *m.* & *f.* 1. Young person, under forty years of age. *Mancebo de mercader*, Shop-man, shop-boy, clerk. 2. Journeyman, a hired workman.
Mancer [man-therr'], *m.* Son of a prostitute.
Mancera [man-thay'-rah], *f.* Plough-tail, handle of a plough.
Mancerina [man-thay-ree'-nah], *f.* (Prov.) Saucer. *V.* MACERINA.
Mancilla [man-theel'-lyah], *f.* Spot, blemish. ***Más vale mancha en la frente que mancilla en el corazón***, Better be ugly and good, rather than handsome and bad.
Mancillar [man-theel'-lyar], *va.* To spot, to stain. *V.* AMANCILLAR.
Mancipar [man-the-par'], *va.* To subject, to enslave, to mancipate.
Manco, ca [mahn'-co, cah], *a.* 1. Handless, one-handed, lacking one or both hands, or without the use of them. 2. Maimed, defective, faulty, imperfect.
Manco, ca [mahn'-co, cah], *m.* & *f.* A handless or a one-handed person.
Mancomún [man-co-moon'], *m.* Concurrence of two or more persons in the execution of a thing; it is now used only in the adverbial phrase, *de mancomún*, Jointly, by common consent.
Mancomunadamente, *adv.* Conjointly, by common consent.
Mancomunar [man-co-moo-nar'], *va.* 1. To associate, to unite. 2. (Law) To make two or more persons pay jointly the costs of a lawsuit.—*vr.* To act together, to join in the execution of a thing.
Mancomunidad [man-co-moo-ne-dahd'], *f.* Union, conjunction, fellowship.
Mancornar [man-cor-nar'], *va.* 1. To throw a young steer with his horns fixed in the ground, leaving him motionless. 2. To tie two head of cattle by the horns, so as to make them go together.
Mancuerda [man-coo-err'-dah], *f.* One of the implements of torture.
Mancuerna [man-coo-err'-nah], *f.* 1. Pair of animals or things. 2. Thong for throwing a steer. 3. (Cuba) Stem with two or three leaves, which is cut from the plant in collecting tobacco.
Mancha [mahn'-chah], *f.* 1. Stain, spot, discoloration; blot, macula. 2. Stigma. mark of infamy. 3. Piece of ground distinct from those which adjoin it. 4. (Met.) Stigma, blemish, dishonour, either from mean birth or an ignominious act. *No es mancha de judío*, (Coll.) It is but a trifling thing. 5. A spot on the sun or other heavenly body.
Manchado, da [man-chah'-do, dah], *a.* Spotted, speckled.—*pp.* of MANCHAR.
Manchar [man-char'], *va.* 1. To stain, to corrupt, to soil, to contaminate; to daub; to darken, to cloud. 2. To defile one's character, to tarnish one's name and reputation. *Manchar papel*, To scribble, to write much, and nothing to the purpose. 3. (Pict.) To lay in spots of light colour before defining the figure.
Manchega [man-chay'-gah], *f.* Garter of different colours, made of worsted, especially in La Mancha.
Manchego, ga [man-chay'-go, gah], *a.* Native of or belonging to La Mancha, a province of Spain.
Manchica, illa, ita [man-chee'-cah], *f. dim.* A small stain, spot, or macula.
Manchón [man-chone'], *m.* 1. Spot where grain grows rank or thick. 2. (Aug.) A large stain or spot.
Manchú [man-choo'], *a.* Belonging to Manchuria or its inhabitants; Manchurian.
Manda [mahn'-dah], *f.* 1. Offer, proposal. 2. Legacy or donation left by virtue of a last will. *Manda forzosa*, A forced bequest or legacy, which every testator must make in Spain, for certain objects.
Mandadera [man-dah-day'-rah], *f.* *V.* DEMANDADERA.
Mandadero, ra [man-dah-day'-ro, rah], *m.* & *f.* 1. Porter, messenger; one engaged to run errands. 2. *V.* DEMANDADERO.
Mandado [man-dah'-do], *m.* 1. Mandate, precept, command. 2. Errand, message; advertisement, notice. *Muchacho de mandados*, Errand-boy.—*Mandado, da, pp.* of MANDAR.
Mandamiento [man-dah-me-en'-to], *m.* 1. Mandate, precept, order, command. 2. Commandment, one of the ten precepts of the Decalogue. 3. Peremptory order issued by a judge, respecting the execution of his sentence.—*pl.* (Coll.) The five fingers of the hand. *Mandamientos de la ley de Dios*, The ten commandments. *Mandamientos de la Iglesia* or *de la Santa Madre Iglesia*, Commandments of the church.
Mandante [man-dahn'-tay], *pa.* Commanding.
Mandar [man-dar'], *va.* 1. To command, to give orders, to order, to ordain, to enact. 2. To lead, to head. 3. To leave or bequeath in a last will or testament. 4. (Prov.) To send, to transmit. 5. To offer, to promise. *Mandar hacer*, (Coll.) To have made, to order or cause to be made, to bespeak.—*vr.* 1. In buildings, to communicate with. 2. To have free use of one's limbs, to manage one's self without the aid of others: applied to the infirm. ***Mandar a alguno a puntapiés, a puntillazos*** or ***a zapatazos***, To have complete ascendency over any one. ***Mandar a coces***, To command harshly.
Mandarin [man-dah-reen'], *m.* Mandarin, a Chinese magistrate.
Mandarina [man-dah-ree'nah], *f.* 1. (Bot.) Tangerine. 2. Mandarin language, Chinese dialect.
Mandarria [man-dar'-re-ah], *f.* (Naut.) Iron maul, a large hammer or sledge.
Mandatario [man-dah-tah'-re-o], *m.* 1. Attorney, agent. 2. Mandatory; mandatary. 3. (Mex.) Collector of religious confraternities.
Mandato [man-dah'-to], *m.* 1. Mandate, precept, injunction, order, ordinance 2. Charge, trust, commission. 3. Ecclesiastical ceremony of washing the feet of twelve persons on Maundy Thursday.
¡ Mande ! [mahn'-day], *int.* (Naut.) Holla! a word of command on shipboard, enjoining attention.
Mandíbula [man-dee'-boo-lah], *f.* Jawbone, mandible.
Mandibular [man-de-boo-lar'], *a.* Mandibular, belonging to the jaw.
Mandil [man-deel'], *m.* 1. Coarse apron used by men or women. 2. (Low) Servant to a pimp or prostitute.
Mandilada [man-de-lah'-dah], *f.* 1. An apronful. 2. (Low) A number of ruffians. (Acad.)
Mandilar [man-de-lar'], *va.* To wipe a horse with a coarse apron or cloth.
Mandilejo [man-de-lay'-ho], *m.* 1. (Dim.) A small apron, a ragged apron. 2. (Low) Servant of a rogue or prostitute; pimp, pander.
Mandilete [man-de-lay'-tay], *m.* (Mil.) Door of the port-hole of a battery.
Mandilón [man-de-lone'], *m.* (Coll.) Coward, a mean, dastardly fellow.
Mandioca [man-de-o'-cah], *f.* The Brazilian name of the yucca (manioc) or cassava, yielding tapioca.
Mando [mahn'-do], *m.* Command, authority, power, dominion, rule.
Mandoble [man-do'-blay], *m.* 1. A two-handed blow. 2. A severe reprimand.
Mandolina [man-do-lee'-nah], *f.* Mandolin, a stringed instrument played with a plectrum.
Mandón, na [man-done', nah], *a.* Imperious, domineering.—*n.* An imperious, haughty person.
Mandrachero [man-drah-chay'-ro], *m.* Proprietor of a gaming-table.
Mandracho [man-drah'-cho], *m.* (Prov.) Gambling-house.
Mandrágora [man-drah'-go-rah], *f.* (Bot.) Mandrake. Atropa mandragora.
Mandria [mahn'-dre-ah], *m.* Coward, poltroon.
Mandril [man-dreel'], *m.* 1. (Zool.) Mandrill, a West African baboon. 2. Mandrel, chuck, spindle of a lathe, for holding the object in work.
Mandrín [man-dreen'], *m.* 1. Mandrel. 2. A hollow iron instrument which serves to join the ends of a metallic rod or to support the arms of a wheel.
Manducación [man-doo-cah-the-on'], *f.* (Coll.) Manducation, act of chewing or eating.
Manducar [man-doo-car'], *va.* (Coll.) To manducate, to eat, to chew.
Manducatoria [man-doo-cah-to'-re-ah], *f.* Dining-room, refectory.
Manea [mah-nay'-ah], *f.* Shackles, fetters, hopple. *V.* MANIOTA.
Manear [mah-nay-ar'], *va.* To hobble, to fasten with fetters or shackles: applied to horses, asses, etc.
Manecica, ita [mah-nay-thee'-cah, ee'-tah], *f. dim.* A small hand.
Manecilla [mah-nay-theel'-lyah], *f.* 1. (Dim.) A small hand. 2. A mark ☞ or index, in grammar. 3. Book-clasp. 4. Hand of a clock or watch.
Manejable [mah-nay-hah'-blay], *a.* Manageable, tractable.
Manejado [mah-nay-hah'-do], *a.* (Pict.) Handled.—*pp.* of MANEJAR.
Manejar [mah-nay-har'], *va.* 1. To manage, to wield, to move with the hand. 2. To manage, to train a horse to graceful action. 3. To manage, to

conduct, to govern, to contrive. 4. To handle, to hand, to palm. 5. To manage, to carry on.—*vr.* 1. To know how to conduct one's self. 2. To be able to move after having been deprived of motion.

Manejo [mah-nay'-ho], *m.* 1. Employment of the hands to any purpose, handling. 2. Management, conduct, administration. 3. Horsemanship, manège. 4. Handling, cunning, trick; intrigue, device. *Manejos de corte,* Court intrigues. *Manejo doméstico,* Household.

Maneota [mah-nay-o'-tah], *f.* Shackles, hobbles, fetters. *V.* MANIOTA.

Manera [mah-nay'-rah], *f.* 1. Manner, form, figure; method, mode, kind, guise; manner of style. 2. Manner, or style, in painting, or carving in stone. 3. Ceremonious behaviour, deportment. 4. Fore part or fall of breeches. 5. (Ant.) Quality, class of persons. *De manera* or *por manera,* So as, in such a manner.

Manero, ra [mah-nay'-ro, rah], *a.* Tame: applied to hawks in falconry.

Manes [mah'-nes], *m. pl.* Manes, ghost of the dead.

Manezuela [mah-nay-thoo-ay'-lah], *f.* 1. (Dim.) A small hand. 2. A clasp, a buckle.

Manfla [mahn'-flah], *f.* (Coll.) 1. A concubine. 2. (Prov.) Old sow.

Manga [mahn'-gah], *f.* 1. Sleeve, part of a garment. 2. Arm of an axletree, on which the nave turns. 3. Kind of cloak-bag or portmanteau. 4. Stripe of cloth hanging from the shoulder of clerical cloaks. 5. Hose for water, fire-hose. (Acad.) 6. Body of troops in a line. 7. Fishing-net. 8. Bag made of woollen, linen, or paper, in the form of a sleeve, used to strain and clarify liquors; Hippocrates' sleeve. 9. *Manga* or *manga marina,* Hurricane, whirlwind, water-spout. 10. (Mex.) Blanket or oblong piece of cloth, round at the ends, with a slit in the middle to put the head through, used as a covering when travelling on horseback. *V.* PONCHO. 11. *Manga de granaderos,* (Coll.) A picket of grenadiers. *Manga del navío,* (Naut.) Extreme breadth of a ship. *Mangas,* Conveniences. *Estar* or *ir de manga,* To join in the execution of some wicked or malicious design. *Manga de ángel,* Women's wide sleeves. *Manga de cruz,* A case of silk that hangs on a cross. *Manga de pica,* The spear of a pike. *Manga de viento,* Whirlwind. *Andar manga por hombro,* To be very careless in domestic affairs. *Buenas son mangas después de pascua,* Better late than never; good things are always welcome. *Pegar mangas,* To intermeddle, to intrude.

Manga, *f.* A variety of mango (tree and fruit).

Manga de aire [mahn'-gah day ah'-e-ray], *f.* (Aer.) Jet stream.

Mangana [man-gah'-nah], *f.* Lasso lariat. (Acad.)

Manganear [man-gah-nay-ar'], *va.* (Amer. Mex.) To throw a lasso at a running animal.

Manganeo [man-gah-nay'-o], *m.* Sport in which lassoing is the chief diversion.

Manganato [man-gah-nah'-to], *m.* Manganate, a salt of manganic acid.

Manganesa, or **Manganesia** [man-gah-nay'-sah], *f.* Peroxide of manganese, used in the manufacture of glass and paints, and in medicine.

Manganeso [man-gah-nay'-so], *m.* Manganese, a hard, brittle, grayish-white metallic element.

Mangánico, ca [man-gah'-ne-co, cah], *a.* Manganic, relative to manganese.

Manganilla [man-gah-neel'-lyah], *f.* 1. Sleight of hand, a juggling trick. 2. (Prov.) Pole for gathering acorns.

Manganoso [man-gah-no'-so], *a.* Manganous.

Mangla [mahn'-glah], *f.* Gum which exudes from the rock-rose or dwarf sun-flower.

Manglar [man-glar'], *m.* Plantation of mangrove trees.

Mangle [mahn'-glay], *m.* (Bot.) Mangrove tree. Rhizophora Mangle.

Mango [mahn'-go], *m.* 1. Handle, haft, heft; helve, the handle of an axe. 2. (Bot.) Indian mango-tree. Mangifera indica, *L.*

Mangonada [man-go-nah'-dah], *f.* Push with the arm.

Mangonear [man-go-nay-ar'], *vn.* (Coll.) 1. To wander about; to rove idly. 2. To intermeddle; to pry.

Mangorrero, ra [man-gor-ray'-ro, rah], *a.* 1. Wandering, roving, rambling. 2. Hafted: applied to a knife.

Mangosta [man-gos'-tah], *f.* Mongoos, a quadruped noted for its ability to kill the most venomous snakes. Herpestes mungo.

Mangote [man-go'-tay], *m.* (Coll.) A large and wide sleeve.

Mangual [man-goo-ahl'], *m.* Weapon consisting of a pole with iron chains terminated by balls attached to it.

Manguardia [man-goo-ar'-de-ah], *f.* Buttress of a bridge.

Manguera [man-gay'-rah], *f.* 1. Hose, a tube for conveying liquids. 2. (Naut.) Piece of canvas tarred for various uses.

Mangueta [man-gay'-tah], *f.* 1. Bladder and pipe for administering clysters. 2. Jamb of a glass-door. 3. Lever.

Manguilla [man-geel'-lyah], *f. dim.* A small sleeve.

Manguita [man-gee'-tah], *f.* 1. Sheath. *V.* FUNDA. 2. (Dim.) *V.* MANGUILLA.

Manguitero [man-gee-tay'-ro], *m.* 1. Muff-maker, muff-seller. 2. Leather-dresser, one who dresses fine skins or white leather.

Manguito [man-gee'-to], *m.* 1. Muff, a cover for the hands. 2. Sleeve which is tight from the elbow to the wrist.

Maní [mah-nee'], *m.* (Cuba, Peru, Chili) Pea-nut. *V.* CACAHUATE.

Manía [mah-nee'-ah], *f.* 1. Mania, frenzy, madness. 2. Extravagance, whimsical obstinacy. 3. Inordinate desires.

Maníaco, ca [mah-ne-ah'-co, cah], *a.* Maniac, manical, mad, frantic.—*n.* Maniac, a mad person.

Manialbo [mah-ne-ahl'-bo], *a.* White-footed: applied to a horse.

Maniatar [mah-ne-ah-tar'], *va.* To manacle, to handcuff.

Maniático, ca [mah-ne-ah'-te-co, cah], *a.* *V.* MANIACO.

Manicero [mah-ne-thay'-ro], *m.* (Cuba) Peanut vendor.

Manicomio [mah-ne-co'-me-o], *m.* Asylum or hospital for the insane. (Acad.)

Manicordio [mah-ne-cor'-de-o], *m.* Manichord, a musical instrument: a clavichord.

Manicorto, ta [mah-ne-cor'-to, tah], *a.* Illiberal, parsimonious.

Manicurista [mah-ne-coo-rees'-tah], *m. & f.* Manicurist.

Manicuro, ra [mah-ne-coo'-ro, rah], *m. & f.* Manicurist.

Manida [mah-nee'-dah], *f.* Resort, abode, nest, any place where persons or animals take shelter. *Manida de pícaros,* Nest of thieves.

Manido, da [mah-nee'-do, dah], *a.* 1. Hidden, concealed. 2. (Peru) Said of meats which smell bad; "high."—*pp.* of MANIR.

Manifacero, ra [mah-ne-fah-thay'-ro, rah], *a.* (Prov.) Intriguing, meddlesome, intrusive.

Manifactura [mah-ne-fac-too'-rah], *f.* 1. *V.* MANUFACTURA. 2. Form in which a thing is made.

Manifestación [mah-ne-fes-tah-the-on'], *f.* 1. Manifestation, declaration, explication. 2. In Arragon, a writ resembling the English habeas corpus.

Manifestador, ra [mah-ne-fes-tah-dor', rah], *m. & f.* Discoverer, publisher.

Manifestante [mah-ne-fes-tahn'-tay], *com.* Demonstrator.

Manifestar [mah-ne-fes-tar'], *va.* To manifest, to make known.

Manifiestamente, *adv.* Clearly.

Manifiesto, ta [mah-ne-fe-es'-to, tah], *a.* Manifest, plain, open, obvious, clear, overt.—*pp. irr.* of MANIFESTAR.

Manifiesto [mah-ne-fe-es'-to], *m.* 1. Act of exposing the Holy Sacrament to public adoration. 2. Manifest or manifesto, public protestation or declaration. *Poner de manifiesto,* To manifest, to make public, to expose, to lay open.

(*Yo manifiesto, yo manifieste,* from *Manifestar. V.* ACRECENTAR.)

Manigua [mah-nee'-goo-ah], *f.* (Cuba) 1. Thicket, jungle. 2. Monte played for diversion.

Manigueta [mah-ne-gay'-tah], *f.* Handle, clasp.

Manija [mah-nee'-hah], *f.* 1. Handle of an instrument or working tool. 2. Shackles, handcuffs. 3. Ring, brace.

Manilargo, ga [mah-ne-lar'-go, gah], *a.* 1. Large-handed, that is, having long hands. 2. Prone to fisticuffs, pugilistic.

Maniluvio [mah-ne-loo'-ve-o], *m.* Bath for the hands used as a remedy.

Manilla [mah-neel'-lyah], *f.* 1. (Dim.) Small hand. 2. Bracelet for the arm or wrist. 3. Manacle, handcuff.

Maniobra [mah-ne-o'-brah], *f.* 1. Work with the hand, handiwork. 2. Handling, artifice for obtaining a thing. 3. (Mil.) Manœuvre, evolution, movement of troops. 4. (Naut.) Working of a ship. *Navío que maniobra bien,* Ship that works freely. 5. (Naut.) Gear, rigging. *Maniobras de combate,* Preventer rigging.

Maniobrar [mah-ne-o-brar'], *va.* 1. To work with the hands. 2. (Naut.) To work a ship. 3. (Met.) To seek the means of effecting any thing. 4. (Mil.) To manœuvre troops. Also, *vn.*

Maniobrista [mah-ne-o-brees'-tah], *m.* (Naut.) A skilful naval tactician.

Maniota [mah-ne-o'-tah], *f.* Hobble or cord tied about the feet of beasts to prevent running away.

Manipodio [mah-ne-po'-de-o], *m.* (Coll.) Bawdry, pollution.

Manipulación [mah-ne-poo-lah-the-on'], *f.* Manipulation: used in speaking of minerals.

Manipulante [mah-ne-poo-lahn'-tay], *m.* (Coll.) Administrator, negotiator.

Manipular [mah-ne-poo-lar'], *va.* (Coll.) To manipulate, to handle, to manage business in a peculiar manner; to meddle with everything.

Manípulo [mah-nee'-poo-lo], *m.* 1. Maniple, a fanon worn by the officiating priests of the Roman Catholic church. 2. Maniple, a division of the Roman army. 3. A handful, expressed in recipes by an M.

Maniqueísmo [mah-ne-kay-ees'-mo], *m.* Manicheism.

Maniqueo, a [mah-ne-kay'-o, ah], *a.* Manichean.

Maniquí [mah-ne-kee'], *m.* 1. Puppet, one governed by another's caprice. 2.

Manikin, a movable figure, which can be put in different postures, for the study of drapery.

Manir [mah-neer'], *va.* To keep meat until it grows tender; to mellow.—*vr.* To become tender or mellow: applied to meat.

Manirroto, ta [mah-nir-ro'-to, tah], *a.* Extravagant, wasteful.

Manita [mah-nee'-tah], *f.* The hour-hand of a watch or clock.

Manivacío, cía [mah-ne-vah-thee'-o, ah], *a.* (Coll.) Empty-handed; idle, lazy.

Manivela [mah-ne-vay'-lah], *f.* Winch, handle, crank.

Manjar [man-har'], *m.* 1. Food, victuals. 2. (Met.) Refection or entertainment which recruits the spirits. 3. Any of the four suits of a pack of cards. *Manjar blanco,* (1) Dish made of the breast of fowl mixed with sugar, milk, and rice flour. (2) Blancmange. *Manjar de ángeles,* Dish composed of milk and sugar. *Manjar imperial,* Dish made of milk, yolks of eggs, and rice flour.

Manjarria [man-har'-re-ah], *f.* (Cuba) The driving beam of a cane-mill.

Manjelin [man-hay-leen'], *m.* Weight used for diamonds: carat.

Manjolar [man-ho-lar'], *va.* To carry a hawk in the hand, in a basket or a cage.

Manjorrada [man-hor-rah'-dah], *f.* Abundance of ordinary victuals.

Manlieva [man-le-ay'-vah], *f.* 1. (Obs.) Tax levied in haste, and collected from house to house. 2. *V.* GASTOS and EXPENSAS.

Mano [mah'-no], *f.* 1. The hand. 2. Fore foot of a quadruped. 3. Among butchers, the feet of cattle after being cut off. 4. Proboscis, the snout or trunk of an elephant. 5. Hand, side, right or left. 6. Hand of a clock or watch. 7. Pestle. 8. A long cylindrical stone, with which cocoa is ground, to make chocolate. 9. Quire of paper. 10. Command, power. 11. Reprimand, censure. 12. The musical scale. 13. First hand at play. 14. Workmanship, power or means of making or attaining something. 15. Hand, time or turn in correcting something. 16. Cover, or varnish, colours, coat, laid over a thing. 17. Industry. 18. *V.* PATROCINIO. 19. *V.* SOCORRO. —*pl.* 1. Handicraft, handiwork. 2. Works of the hand considered by themselves. *Mano en el juego,* Deal, in a game. *A la mano,* At hand, near at hand. *A mano,* At hand; with the hand; studiously. *Mano de gato,* Ladies' paint; correction of a writing by a superior hand. *Manos de carnero,* Sheep's trotters. *Manos de vaca,* Cow-heels. *¡Manos a la obra!* (Naut.) Bear a hand! to work! *Manos libres,* Emoluments annexed to an office or place. *Manos muertas,* Mortmain, an unalienable estate. *A dos manos,* Willingly, readily. *A manos llenas,* Liberally, abundantly, copiously. *A mano salva,* Without risk. *De ruin mano, ruin dado,* Meanness works its own punishment. *Ser sus pies y sus manos,* To be one's chief support and consolation in distress. *Venir con sus manos lavadas,* To usurp the fruit of another's labour. *Untar las manos,* To bribe. *Mano a mano,* In company, familiarly; alone. *Bajo mano* or *de mano,* Underhandedly, secretly. *Estar a mano,* To be square, to be quits. *Yo lo tengo de buena mano,* I have it on good authority. *Mano* enters into very numerous phrases, of which but few are given here; others must be looked for under the respective verbs. *De mano a boca,* Suddenly, unexpectedly. *Alzar la mano,* (Met.) (1) To lift the hand, threatening to strike. (2) To cease protecting an individual. (3) To leave off attending to a business which one had begun to care for. *Mano de jabón,* Soaping of clothes before washing. *Mano certera,* A steady hand. *Uno mano lava la otra y ambas la cara,* (Fig.) Denotes mutual dependence and reciprocal aid. *Llevar blanda la mano,* To have a gentle touch. *Llevar la mano ligera* or *blanda,* To treat kindly, indulgently.

Manobra [mah-no'-brah], *f.* (Prov.) Raw material.

Manobre [mah-no'-bray], *m.* (Prov.) A hodman, hod-carrier.

Manojico, illo, ito [mah-no-hee'-co], *m. dim.* A small bundle, a small fagot.

Manojo [mah-no'-ho], *m.* 1. A bundle of herbs or other things which may be held in the hand. 2. A fagot or bundle of twigs bound together for the fire. *Manojo de llaves,* Bunch of keys. *Un manojo de apio,* A bunch of celery. *A manojos,* Abundantly.

Manolo, la, *a.* & *n.* *V.* MAJO.

Manómetro [mah-no'-may-tro], *m.* (Phys.) Manometer, an instrument for ascertaining the tension of gases; pressure-gauge.

Manopla [mah-no'-plah], *f.* 1. Gauntlet, a glove for defence. 2. Coachman's whip. *Tela de manoplas,* A sort of silk with large flowers.

Manosear [mah-no-say-ar'], *va.* 1. To handle, to touch, to feel. 2. To rumple clothes.

Manoseo [mah-no-say'-o], *m.* Handling.

Manotada, *f.* **Manotazo,** *m.* [mah-no-tah'-dah, mah-no-tah'-tho]. Blow with the hand, a cuff.

Manotear [mah-no-tay-ar'], *va.* To strike with the hand.—*vn.* To wring the hands from emotion.

Manoteo [mah-no-tay'-o], *m.* 1. A blow with the hand. 2. Manual gesticulation.

Manquear [man-kay-ar'], *vn.* To affect the cripple, to pretend to be maimed.

Manquedad [man-kay-dahd'], *f.* or **Manquera,** *f.* 1. Lameness, a hurt which prevents the use of the hands or arms. 2. Defect, imperfection.

Mansalva, A [ah man-sahl'-vah], *adv.* Unsportsmanly, cowardly. *Tiro a mansalva,* Pot shot.

Mansamente [man-sah-men'-tay], *adv.* Meekly, gently, quietly.

Mansedumbre [man-say-doom'-bray], *f.* Meekness, gentleness, peacefulness, mildness, manageableness.

Mansejón, na [man-say-hone', nah], *a.* Tame: applied to animals.

Mansera [man-say'-rah], *f.* (Cuba) A vat placed below the hammers of a sugar-mill, which receives the cane-juice.

Mansión [man-se-on'], *f.* 1. Stay, sojourn, residence. 2. Habitation, mansion, abode, home.

Mansito [man-see'-to], *adv.* *V.* MANSAMENTE.

Manso, sa [mahn'-so, sah], *a.* 1. Tame: applied to horses and other animals. 2. Meek, gentle, tractable; soft, quiet, mild, gentle, lamblike. *A lumbre mansa,* By a mild light.

Manso [mahn'-so], *m.* Male, which guides the flocks of goats, sheep, or cattle; bell-wether.

Manta [mahn'-tah], *f.* 1. A woollen blanket; in some parts of America, domestic cotton shirting. *Manta blanca,* Bleached cotton. *Manta prieta,* Unbleached cotton. 2. A horse-blanket. 3. (Mil.) Mantelet, a movable parapet. 4. Thrashing, drubbing. 5. (Min.) A bag of agave for loading ore in clearings. 6. The devil-fish, octopus. 7. (S. Amer.) A mantle. 8 A game of cards resembling *tresillo* or *ombre. A manta* or *a manta de Dios,* (Coll.) Copiously, plentifully. *Tomar la manta,* To undergo salivation. *Dar una manta, V.* MANTEAR.

Mantalona [man-tah-lo'-nah], *f.* A cotton stuff used for boat-sails in the Philippines and all through India.

Mantaterilla [man-tah-tay-reel'-lyah], *f.* Coarse hempen cloth for horse-blankets.

Manteador, ra [man-tay-ah-dor', rah], *m.* & *f.* Tosser, one who tosses in a blanket.

Manteamiento [man-tay-ah-me-en'-to], *m.* Tossing in a blanket.

Mantear [man-tay-ar'], *va.* To toss in a blanket.—*vn.* (Prov.) To gad frequently abroad in a mantle: spoken of women.

Manteca [man-tay'-cah], *f.* 1. Lard, fat; pomatum. 2. Butter. 3. Pulpy and oily parts of fruits. 4. A name given to certain metallic chlorides, as of antimony, bismuth, and zinc.

Mantecada [man-tay-cah'-dah], *f.* Buttered toast and sugar.

Mantecado [man-tay-cah'-do], *m.* 1. Butter-cake. 2. Ice-cream.

Mantecón [man-tay-cone'], *m.* Milk-sop; sweet-tooth, a dainty person.

Mantecoso, sa [man-tay-co'-so, sah], *a.* Buttery, consisting of butter, mellow.

Manteista [man-tay-ees'-tah], *m.* Student in universities.

Mantel [man-tel'], *m.* 1. Table-cloth: commonly used in the plural. *Juego de manteles adamascados,* Damask service; a table-cloth with a dozen napkins. 2. Altar-cloth. *Levantar los manteles,* To clear the table.

Mantelería [man-tay-lay-ree'-ah], *f.* Table-linen.

Manteleta [man-tay-lay'-tah], *f.* Mantelet, a small mantle, cloak, or scarf worn by ladies.

Mantelete [man-tay-lay'-tay], *m.* 1. Mantelet, a short mantle worn by bishops. 2. Mantelet, a movable parapet. 3. (Her.) Mantling, the representation of a mantle or any drapery drawn about a coat of arms.

Mantellina [man-tel-lyee'-nah], *f.* A short cloak worn by women.

Mantenedor [man-tay-nay-dor'], *m.* 1. (Obs.) Maintainer. 2. The principal in a tournament.

Mantener [man-tay-nerr'], *va.* 1. To maintain, to support, to keep up with the hand; to hold up. 2. To maintain, to support life, to nourish, to keep, to feed. 3. To maintain, to continue, to keep up. 4. To be the first challenger at a tournament. 5. To persevere, to persist in a design. 6. To support a weight. 7. To pursue, to continue. 8. To maintain, to hold out, to defend or sustain an opinion. 9. To support any one in the possession of a thing. *Mantener correspondencia,* To keep up a correspondence. —*vr.* 1. To continue residing in a place. 2. To continue in the same condition without alteration. 3. To nourish or gain nourishment, to maintain one's self. *Mantenerse firme,* To stand one's ground. *Mantenerse en lo dicho,* To abide by. *Mantenerse á la mar,* To keep the sea.

Manteniente [man-tay-ne-en'-tay], *m.* A violent blow with both hands. *A manteniente,* With all one's might, firmly.

Mantenimiento [man-tay-ne-me-en'-to], *m.* Maintenance, sustenance, subsist ence; a supply of the necessaries of life; livelihood, living.

(*Yo mantengo, yo mantuve, mantuviera*, from *Mantener. V.* TENER.)

Manteo [man-tay'-o], *m.* 1. A long cloak or mantle worn by priests and formerly by students. 2. Sort of woollen petticoat.

Mantequera [man-tay-kay'-rah], *f.* 1. A churn. 2. A butter-dish or bowl.

Mantequero, ra [man-tay-kay'-ro, rah], *m. & f.* One who sells butter; dairy-man, dairy-maid.

Mantequilla [man-tay-keel'-lyah], *f.* 1. Hard-sauce, a paste of butter and sugar. 2. In America, butter.

Mantequillera [man-tay-keel-lyay'-rah], *f.* Butter dish.

Mantera [man-tay'-rah], *f.* Mantua-maker, one who makes or sells mantles.

Mantero, ra [man-tay'-ro, rah], *m. & f.* One who sells or manufactures blankets.

Mántide [mahn'-te-day], *f.* (Zool.) The praying mantis, an orthopterous insect.

Mantilla [man-teel'-lyah], *f.* 1. Mantilla, or veil, for women, made of silk or other stuff. *Mantillas de tul, fondo tafetán con velo, de una a tres blondas*, Sarcenet mantillas with lace trimmings, veil, and one to three flounces. 2. Housing, saddle-cloth.—*pl.* The outer (long) clothes of little children. 3. (Typ.) A blanket. *Estar en mantillas*, To be in a state of infancy.

Mantillo [man-teel'-lyo], *m.* Humus, dung, organic portion of soil.

Mantillón, na [man-teel-lyone', nah], *a.* (Prov.) Dirty, slovenly.

Manto [mahn'-to], *m.* 1. Silken veil for ladies, a mantle, a kirtle. 2. Cloak, robe; a mantle of state. 3. Mantel-piece of a chimney. 4. In mines, a horizontal vein. 5. Veil, cover.

Mantón [man-tone'], *m.* 1. (Aug.) A large cloak or mantle. 2. A kind of shawl; in Cuba, a woman's mantilla.

Manuable [mah-noo-ah'-blay], *a.* Tractable, manageable.

Manual [mah-noo-ahl'], *a.* 1. Manual, handy, performed by the hand. 2. Easily handled or performed with the hand. 3. Tractable, pliant; light, prompt.

Manual [mah-noo-ahl'], *m.* 1. Manual, a portable book. 2. Book in which the heads of matters are set down; note-book, account-book. 3. Ritual, a book of rites. 4. Old name of the journal, a book of accounts recorded so as to be easily posted in the ledger. (Acad.) 5. *pl.* Extra fees given to the priests for being present in the choir.

Manubrio [mah-noo'-bre-o], *m.* Handlebar (of a bicycle, etc.)

Manucodiata [mah-noo-co-de-ah'-tah], *f.* Bird of paradise.

Manuella [mah-noo-el'-lyah], *f.* Hand-spike.

Manufactura [mah-noo-fac-too'-rah], *f.* Manufacture, any mechanical work.

Manufacturar [mah-noo-fac-too-rar'], *va.* To manufacture: a modern word.

Manufacturero, ra [mah-noo-fac-too-ray'-ro, rah], *a.* Belonging to manufacture.

Manumisión [mah-noo-me-se-on'], *f.* Manumission.

Manumiso, sa [mah-noo-mee'-so, sah], *pp. irr.* of MANUMITIR. Emancipated. —*a.* Free, disengaged.

Manumisor [mah-noo-me-sor'], *m.* (Law) Liberator.

Manumitir [mah-noo-me-teer'], *va.* To manumit, to emancipate.

Manuscrito, ta [mah-noos-cree'-to, tah], *a.* Manuscript, not printed.

Manuscrito [mah-noos-cree'-to], *m.* Manuscript, a book written and not printed.

Manutención [mah-noo-ten-the-on'], *f.* 1. Maintaining. 2. Maintenance, supply of the necessaries of life. 3. Maintenance, support, protection. 4. Conservation.

Manutener [mah-noo-tay-nerr'], *va.* (Law) To maintain, to support.

Manutisa [mah-noo-tee'-sah], *f.* (Bot.) *V.* MINUTISA.

Manvacío, a [man-vah-thee'-o, ah], *a. V.* MANIVACÍO.

Manzana [man-thah'-nah], *f.* 1. An apple. 2. Block of houses bounded on every side by a street; square. 3. (Ant.) Knob of a sword. *La manzana podrida pierde a su compañía*, Evil communications corrupt good manners.

Manzanal [man-thah-nahl'], *m.* 1. *V.* MANZANAR. 2. *V.* MANZANO.

Manzanar [man-thah-nar'], *m.* Orchard, a garden of apple-trees.

Manzanil [man-thah-neel'], *a.* Like an apple.

Manzanilla [man-thah-neel'-lyah], *f.* 1. (Bot.) Common chamomile. Anthemis. *Manzanilla fina*, Golden cotula. Cotula aurea. *Manzanilla hedionda*, *V.* MAGARZUELA. 2. Small ball or knob at the top of coaches, bedsteads, etc. 3. Kind of small olive. 4. Lower part of the chin. 5. The pad, or cushion, of the feet of animals having claws. 6. (Dim.) A small apple.

Manzanillo, ito [man-thah-neel'-lyo, ee-to], *m.* (Bot.) Little apple-tree. *Olivo manzanillo*, A kind of olive-tree.

Manzanillo, *m.* Manchineel, a tropical American tree, having an apple-like fruit reputed to be poisonous. Hippomane mancinella.

Manzanita [man-thah-nee'-tah], *f.* 1. (Dim.) Little apple. 2. Name of a California shrub, or small tree, related to the *madroño*. Named from its fruit. Arctostaphylos. *Manzanita de dama*, *V.* ACEROLA.

Manzano [man-thah'-no], *m.* (Bot.) Apple-tree. Pyrus malus.

Maña [mah'-nyah], *f.* 1. Handiness, skill, contrivance, dexterity, cleverness, expertness, ability, faculty. 2. Cunning, craftiness, artifice, craft. 3. An evil habit or custom. 4. Bundle of hemp or flax when reaped. *Darse maña*, To contrive, to bring about, to manage.

Mañana [mah-nyah'-nah], *f.* 1. Morning, morrow, forenoon. 2. The part of the day from twelve o'clock at night to twelve o'clock at noon. *De mañana*, In the morning.—*adv.* 1. To-morrow. 2. Soon, ere long, immediately. 3. Expression of negation. 4. In time to come. *Tomar la mañana*, (1) To rise very early. (2) (Coll.) To drink liquor before breakfast. *Muy de mañana*, Very early.

Mañanear [mah-nyah-nay-ar'], *vn.* To rise early habitually.

Mañanica, ita [mah-nyah-nee'-cah], *f.* Break of day.

Mañear [mah-nyay-ar'], *va.* To act with craft and address to attain one's end.

Mañería [mah-nyay-ree'-ah], *f.* 1. Sterility. 2. Right of succeeding to the possessions of those who die without legitimate succession.

Mañero, ra [mah-nyay'-ro, rah], *a.* 1. Dexterous, skilful, artful. 2. Meek, tractable. 3. (Obs.) Charged to pay for another.

Mañosamente [mah-nyo-sah-men'-tay], *adv.* Dexterously, neatly, handily, cleverly; subtly; maliciously, craftily.

Mañoso, sa [mah-nyo'-so, sah], *a.* Dexterous, skilful, handy, clever.

Mañuela [mah-nyoo-ay'-lah], *f.* Low cunning, mean trick. *Mañuelas*, An artful, cunning person.

Mapa [mah'-pah], *m.* Map, a geographical picture. *Mapamundi*, A map of the world.—*f.* Anything excellent and prominent in its line.

Mapache [mah-pah'-chay], *m.* (Zool.) Racoon.

Mápula [mah'-poo-lah], *f.* (Min.) A precious stone mined near Popayán in Colombia.

Mapurite [mah-poo-ree'-tay], *m.* (Amer. Ven.) A skunk.

Maque [mah'-kay], *m.* (Mex.) A certain varnish or lacquer; sumac lacquer.

Maquear [mah-kay-ar'], *va.* To varnish or lacquer with *maque.*

Maquí [mah-kee'], *m.* 1. Kind of ginger. 2. A lemur of Madagascar.

Maquiavélico, ca [mah-ke-ah-vay'-le-co, cah], *a.* Machiavelian.

Maquiavelismo [mah-ke-ah-vay-lees'-mo], *m.* Machiavelism.

Maquiavelista [mah-ke-ah-vay-lees'-tah], *m.* Machiavelian.

Maquila [mah-kee'-lah], *f.* 1. Toll-corn, corn which the miller takes for grinding. 2. Toll in general. 3. Corn-measure, the 24th part of a *fanega.*

Maquilar [mah-ke-lar'], *va.* 1. To measure and take the miller's dues for grinding corn. 2. To clip, to retrench, to cut off.

Maquilero, Maquilón [mah-ke-lay'-ro, mah-ke-lone'], *m.* One who measures or takes the miller's dues for grinding corn.

Maquillaje [mah-keel-lyah'-hay], *m.* Make-up, cosmetics.

Máquina [mah'-ke-nah], *f.* 1. Machine. 2. Engine. 3. A vast structure. 4. Project, imaginative scheme. 5. (Cuba) An automobile. *Máquina calculadora digital*, Digital computer. *Máquina de coser*, Sewing machine. *Máquina de escribir*, Typewriter. *Máquina de vapor*, Steam engine. *Máquina electoral*, Voting machine.

Maquinación [mah-ke-nah-the-on'], *f.* Machination, artifice, contrivance.

Maquinador, ra [mah-ke-nah-dor', rah], *m. & f.* Contriver, schemer, machinator; plotter.

Maquinal [mah-ke-nahl'], *a.* Machinal, relating to machines; mechanical.

Maquinalmente, *adv.* Mechanically: undesignedly.

Maquinar [mah-ke-nar'], *va.* To machinate, to plan, to contrive, to hatch, to conspire, to compass.

Maquinaria [mah-ke-nah'-re-ah], *f.* 1. Applied mechanics, the art of contriving and building machines. 2. Machinery. 3. Mechanics.

Maquinista [mah-ke-nees'-tah], *m.* Machinist, mechanician, mechanist.

Mar [mar], *com.* (Mar was formerly feminine; the masculine use is comparatively modern.) 1. The sea, the water, opposed to the land. 2. Sea, some large lakes. 3. Sea, proverbially for any large quantity. 4. Swell of the sea. *Alta mar* or *mar ancha*, The main sea, the high sea. *De mar a mar*, Copiously, excessively; in the extreme of fashion. *Baja mar*, Low-water, ebb-tide. *Mar llena* or *plena, plea mar*, High-water. *Correr con la mar en popa*, To scud before the sea. *Correr los mares*, To follow the seas. *Echar lanzas en el mar*, To labour in vain. *Meter el mar en el pozo*, To attempt the impossible. *Mar de través*, A sea on the beam. *La mar arde*, The sea sparkles. *Estre-*

cho de mar, Narrow sea. *Mar de leva*, High swelling sea. *Salir a la mar*, To put to sea. *La mar está muy crecida*, The sea runs very high. *Quien no se arriesga, no pasa la mar*, (prov.) Nothing venture, nothing have.

Marabú [mah-rah-boo'], *m.* Marabou, an African bird of the stork family and the white plumes from it.

Maranata, *f.* Maranatha, a form of anathematizing.

Maranta [mah-rahn'-tah], *f.* An American plant which yields arrow-root.

Maraña [mah-rah'-nyah], *f.* 1. Place rendered impassable by brambles or briers. 2. Entanglement of a skein of silk, thread, cotton, etc. 3. Silk waste and stuff made from it. 4. Perplexity, puzzle. 5. Fraud, imposition. 6. Intrigue, plot.

Marañado, da [mah-rah-nyah'-do, dah], *a.* Entangled, perplexed.

Marañero, ra [mah-rah-nyay'-ro, rah], **Marañoso, sa**, *a.* Entangling, insnaring, perplexing.

Marañón [mah-rah-nyone'], *m.* (Cuba) The common cashew (Anacardium occidentale); also its fruit, the cashew-nut.

Marasmo [mah-rahs'-mo], *m.* (Med.) Consumption, marasmus, wasting.

Maratro [mah-rah'-tro], *m.* *V.* Hinojo.

Maravedí [mah-rah-vay-dee'], *m.* (*pl.* Maravedis, Maravedises and formerly Maravedies.) Maravedi, an old Spanish coin of the smallest value; worth about one-sixth of a cent or one-third of a farthing. (Arab. morabiti.)

Maravilla [mah-rah-veel'-lyah], *f.* 1. Wonder, an uncommon event; a marvel, admiration. 2. (Bot.) Common marigold. Calendula officinalis. *A las (mil) maravillas*, Uncommonly well; exquisitely. *A maravilla*, Marvellously. *Por maravilla*, Very seldom. *Maravilla mejicana, maravilla de noche* or *maravilla de Indias*, Common marvel of Peru. Mirabilis jalapa.

Maravillar [mah-rah-vil-lyar'], *va.* To admire, to regard with wonder.—*vr.* To wonder, to marvel, to be astonished, to be struck with admiration.

Maravillosamente, *adv.* Wonderfully, marvellously, miraculously.

Maravilloso, sa [mah-rah-vil-lyo'-so, sah], *a.* Wonderful, marvellous, monstrous, astonishing, admirable, miraculous; strange.

Marbete [mar-bay'-tay], *m.* 1. Stamp, the manufacturer's mark on cloth. 2. Label.

Marca [mar'-cah], *f.* 1. A frontier province. 2. The due measure or weight of any thing. 3. Marker, stamp, an instrument used for marking. 4. Landmark, light-house. 5. A mark made upon a person or thing to distinguish it from another. 6. The act of marking. *De marca*, Excellent of its kind. *De más de marca*, or *de marca mayor*, Something very superior. *Palos de marca*, Buoys.

Marcadamente [mar-cah-dah-men'-tay], *adv.* Markedly, notably.

Marca de fábrica [mar'-cah day fah'-bre-cah], *f.* Trade mark.

Marcador [mar-cah-dor'], *m.* Marker. assay-master.

Marcar [mar-car'], *va.* 1. To mark, to brand; to embroider initials. *Marcar el campo*, To mark the ground for a camp. 2. To mark, to observe, to note; to designate.

Marcasita [mar-cah-see'-tah], *f.* Marcasite, a dimorphous iron sulphide, called white pyrites. (Arab.)

Marcear [mar-thay-ar'], *va.* To shear the wool, hair, or fur of animals.

Marceo [mar-thay'-o], *m.* Trimming away of the lower soiled parts of honey-combs in spring by bee-keepers.

Marcial [mar-the-ahl'], *m.* Aromatic powder used anciently for dressing gloves.

Marcial [mar-the-ahl'], *a.* 1. Martial, warlike. 2. (Pharm.) Martial, having iron. 3. Frank, unceremonious.

Marcialidad [mar-the-ah-le-dahd'], *f.* 1. Martialness. 2. Freedom, assumed familiarity or liberty.

Marco [mar'-co], *m.* 1. Door-case, window-case. 2. Picture-frame. 3. Mark, a weight of eight ounces. 4. An instrument for measuring the length of shoes, etc. 5. A measure for liquids. 6. The necessary size of timber for being felled. 7. Model, archetype. 8. Measure of ground which should have a *fanega* of grain. 9. Mark, the unit of German money-values.

Márcola [mar'-co-lah], *f.* Pruning-hook for trimming trees.

Marcha [mar'-chah], *f.* 1. March, a solemn movement of troops; a journey of soldiers. *Marchas forzadas*, Forced marches. 2. March, signal to move. 3. Marching tune. 4. (Prov.) Bonfire. 5. The movement of a watch. 6. Regularity, working-order of a machine. *Sobre la marcha*, Off-hand, on the spot. *Tocar la marcha*, To strike up a march. *A largas marchas*, With celerity, speedily.

Marchamar [mar-chah-mar'], *va.* To mark goods at the custom-house.

Marchamero [mar-chah-may'-ro], *m.* Custom-house officer who marks goods.

Marchamo [mar-chah'-mo], *m.* Mark put on goods at the custom-house.

Marchante [mar-chahn'-tay], *m.* 1. Shop-keeper, dealer. 2. (Prov. Andal.) Customer, buyer. 3. (Cuba) Sharper, trickster.—*a.* 1. *V.* Mercantil. 2. Merchantable.

Marchantear [mar-chan-tay-ar'], *va.* To trade, especially in live-stock.

Marchar [mar-char'], *vn.* & *vr.* 1. To go, to go away, to go off, to depart from a place. 2. To march, to walk gravely. 3. (Mil.) To march, in military form. 4. (Naut.) To have much headway, to sail fast.

Marchaucha [mar-chah'-oo-chah], *f.* (Chili) The catching by boys of coins (vulgarly called *chauchas*), or other things thrown to them.

Marchazo [mar-chah'-tho], *m.* Braggadocio, boaster, bragger.

Marchitable [mar-che-tah'-blay], *a.* Perishable, liable to wither.

Marchitamiento [mar-che-tah-me-en'-to], *m.* The act of withering or fading (in both active and passive senses).

Marchitar [mar-che-tar'], *va.* 1. To wither, to make to fade. 2. To fade, to wear away, to deprive of vigour.—*vr.* 1. To wither, to fade, to fall away; to dry up. 2. To pine away, to grow lean.

Marchitez [mar-che-teth'], *f.* Withering, fading, marcidity.

Marchito, ta [mar-chee'-to, tah], *a.* Faded, withered, decayed, marcid.

Marea [mah-ray'-ah], *f.* 1. The tide. 2. Sea-shore; tidal area. 3. Soft wind. 4. Collection of street dirt. *Marea creciente*, Flood-tide. *Marea menguante*, Ebb-tide. *Dirección de las mareas*, Setting of the tide. *Establecimiento de marea*, Time of high-water. *Ir contra marea*, To sail against the tide. *Navegar con la marea*, To tide it up or down. *Marea parada*, Slack-tide. *Mareas vivas*, Spring-tides. *La marea mengua*, The tide ebbs. *La marea crece*, The tide flows. *Canal de marea*, Tide-way.

Mareaje [mah-ray-ah'-hay], *m.* Art of navigating a ship.

Mareamiento [mah-ray-ah-me-en'-to], *m.* Sea-sickness.

Mareante [mah-ray-ahn'-tay], *a.* Skilled in navigating a ship.

Marear [mah-ray-ar'], *va.* 1. To work a ship. 2. To molest and harass by impertinent questions. 3. To sell goods at auction. 4. *Marear las velas*, (Naut.) To trim the sails.—*vr.* 1. To be seasick. 2. To be damaged at sea; to be averaged: applied to goods or merchandise.

Marecanita [mah-ray-cah-nee'-tah], *f.* (Min.) Marekanite, a variety of obsidian occurring in rounded globules.

Marejada [mah-ray-hah'-dah], *f.* Swell of the sea, head sea, surf. *Tuvimos una marejada del noroeste*, We had a great sea from the north-west.

Mare magnum [mah'-ray mahg'-noom], *m.* (Lat.) Expressing the abundance or magnitude of any thing; also confusion, disorder.

Mareo [mah-ray'-o], *m.* 1. Sea-sickness. 2. (Coll.) Molestation, vexation.

Mareógrafo [mah-ray-o'-grah-fo], *m.* Mareograph, a recording tide-gauge.

Marero [mah-ray'-ro], *a.* Sea-breeze, wind coming from the sea.

Mareta [mah-ray'-tah], *f.* (Naut.) Slight commotion of the sea.

Maretazo [mah-ray-tah'-tho], *m.* Surge of the sea.

Márfaga, or **Márfega** [mar'-fah-gah], *f.* 1. A coarse woollen frieze, or sackcloth, anciently used for mourning. 2. (Prov.) Rug, a bed coverlet.

Marfil [mar-feel'], *m.* Ivory. *Marfil vegetal*, Vegetable ivory, the fruit of a palm-tree of equatorial America. (Arab. 'adm-alfil.)

Marfileño, ña [mar-fe-lay'-nyo, yah], *a.* (Poet.) Belonging to ivory.

Marfuz [mar-footh'], *a.* 1. Repudiated, rejected. 2. Fallacious, deceitful. (Ar.)

Marga, Marega [mar'-gah, mah-ray'-gah], *f.* 1. Marl, loam, clay-marl. 2. A coarse cloth, formerly used for mourning.

Margaita [mar-gah-ee'-tah], *f.* Marl in which either the limestone or clay exceeds eighty parts. (Acad.)

Margajita [mar-gah-hee'-tah], *f.* Iron pyrites.

Margal [mar-gahl'], *m.* Soil chiefly clayey.

Margallón [mar-gal-lyone'], *m.* *V.* Palmito.

Margar [mar-gar'], *va.* To manure with marl.

Margarato [mar-gah-rah'-to], *m.* (Chem.) Margarate.

Margárico, ca [mar-gah'-re-co, cah], *a.* *Acido margárico*, Margaric acid.

Margarina [mar-gah-ree'-nah], *f.* Margarine.

Margarita [mar-gah-ree'-tah], *f.* 1. Daisy. 2. Pearl. 3. Periwinkle. *Echar margaritas a puercos*, To cast pearls before the swine.

Margen [mar'-hen], *com.* 1. Edge, border. 2. Margin. 3. Marginal notation. 4. (Fig.) Latitude. 5. (Fig.) Chance. *A media margen*, With a center margin. *Andarse por las márgenes*, To beat around the bush. *Dar margen para*, To bring about. *Margen bruto de ganancia*, (Com.) Gross margin.

Margenar [mar-hay-nar'], *va.* 1. *V.* Marginar. 2. To leave a margin on paper.

Marginado, da [mar-he-nah'-do, dah], *a.* & *pp.* of Marginar. Marginated, having a margin.

Marginal [mar-he-nahl'], *a.* Marginal, belonging to the margin.

Marginar [mar-he-nar'], *va.* To make annotations on the margin.
Margoso, sa [mar-go'-so, sah], *a.* Marly, loamy.
Margrave [mar-grah'-vay], *m.* Margrave, a German title of sovereignty.
Marguera [mar-gay'-rah], *f.* Marl-pit.
María [mah-ree'-ah], *f.* 1. (Coll.) A white wax-taper, placed in the middle of eight shorter yellow wax-candles, in Roman Catholic churches. 2. An old silver coin worth twelve reals vellon. 3. Mary, a proper name. *Árbol de maría*, Balsam of tolu tree. Toluifera balsamum.
Mariachi [mah-re-ah'-che], *m.* 1. Mariachi, Mexican street band. 2. Member of a mariachi. 3. Mariachi music.
Marial [mah-re-ahl'], *a.* Praising the Virgin Mary.
Marianismo [mah-re-ah-nees'-mo], *m.* Mariolatry.
Mariano, na [mah-re-ah'-no, nah], *a.* Marian. *Año mariano*, Marian Year.
Marica [mah-ree'-cah], *f.* 1. Magpie. 2. Jack of diamonds.—*m.* Sissy.
Maricastaña [mah-re-cas-tah'-nyah], *f. En tiempo de Maricastaña*, Ages ago, in days of yore.
Maricón [mah-re-con'], *m.* 1. Sissy. 2. (Coll.) Fairy, queer.
Maridable [mah-re-dah'-blay], *a.* Conjugal, matrimonial, connubial, marital.
Maridaje [mah-re-dah'-hay], *m.* 1. Marriage, conjugal union. 2. Intimate connection or union.
Maridanza [mah-re-dahn'-thah], *f.* (Prov.) Treatment of a wife.
Maridar [mah-re-dar'], *vn.* To marry. —*va.* To unite, to join.
Maridazo [mah-re-dah'-tho], *m.* *V.* Gurrumino.
Maridillo [mah-re-deel'-lyo], *m.* 1. A sorry, pitiful husband. 2. A brazier, used by women to warm the feet.
Marido [mah-ree'-do], *m.* Husband, a married man.
Mariguana or **marihuana** [mah-re-goo-ah'-nah, mah-re-oo-ah'-nah], *f.* Marihuana or marijuana.
Marimacho [mah-re-mah'-cho], *m.* Virago, a robust, masculine woman.
Marimanta [mah-re-mahn'-tah], *f.* Bugbear, a phantom.
Marimba [mah-reem'-bah], *f.* (Mus.) Marimba.
Marimbula [mah-reem'-boo-lah], *f.* The jew's-harp. *V.* Birimbao.
Marimorena [mah-re-mo-ray'-nah], *f.* (Coll.) Dispute, difference, quarrel.
Marina [mah-ree'-nah], *f.* 1. Shore, seacoast. 2. (Pict.) Sea-piece. 3. Seamanship, nautical art, marine, sea affairs. 4. The navy. *Soldados de marina*, Marines. *Departamento de marina*, Naval department.
Marinada [mah-re-nah'-dah], *f.* 1. A stew much in favour among sailors. 2. A ship's provisions and the brine (marinade) with which it is prepared.
Marinaje [mah-re-nah'-hay], *m.* 1. Seamanship, the art of working a ship. 2. Sailors, considered as a body.
Marinar [mah-re-nar'], *va.* 1. To marinate, to salt fish. 2. To man a ship taken from the enemy.
Marinear [mah-re-nay-ar'], *va.* To be a mariner.
Marinerado, da [mah-re-nay-rah'-do, dah], *a.* Manned, equipped. *V.* Tripulado.
Marinería [mah-re-nay-ree'-ah], *f.* 1. Seamanship. 2. Profession of seafaring men. 3. The body of seamen. *Me ha salido mal esta marinería*, (Coll.) That speculation has turned out unfortunately.
Marinero [mah-re-nay'-ro], *m.* Mariner seaman, sailor. *A lo marinero*, In a seamanlike manner.
Marinero, ra, *a.* Ready to sail.
Marinesco, ca [mah-re-nes'-co, cah], *a.* Nautical. *A la marinesca*, In a seamanlike manner, ship-shape.
Marino, na [mah-ree'-no, nah], *a.* Marine, belonging to the sea.
Marino [mah-ree'-no], *m.* Mariner, seaman, seafaring man.
Marión, Marón [mah-re-on', mah-rone'], *m.* Sturgeon.
Mariona [mah-re-oh'-nah], *f.* Spanish dance.
Maripérez [mah-re-pay'-reth], *f.* 1. Last hand at cards. 2. Servant-maid.
Mariposa [mah-re-po'-sah], *f.* 1. Butterfly. 2. A night-taper.
Mariposear [mah-re-po-say-ar'], *vn.* To flit like a butterfly; to be fickle and capricious.
Mariquita [mah-re-kee'-tah], *f.* Lady-bird, lady-cow, or lady-fly, a hemispherical beetle.
Marisabidilla [mah-re-sah-be-deel'-lyah], *f.* Blue-stocking, a woman who presumes on being learned.
Mariscal [mah-ris-cahl'], *m.* 1. Marshal, a general officer of high rank in some armies. 2. Farrier, blacksmith. *Mariscal de campo*, Field-marshal, major-general, a rank inferior to lieutenant-general.
Mariscalato [mah-ris-cah-lah'-to], *m.* *V.* Mariscalía.
Mariscalía [mah-ris-cah-lee'-ah], *f.* Marshalship, the dignity or office of a marshal.
Mariscar [mah-ris-car'], *va.* To gather shell-fish on the strand.
Mariscos [mah-rees'-cos], *m. pl.* Seafood.
Marisma [mah-rees'-mah], *f.* Lake formed by the overflow of the tide.
Marismo [mah-rees'-mo], *m.* (Bot.) *V.* Orzaga.
Marital [mah-re-tahl'], *a.* Marital, pertaining to a husband.
Marítimo, ma [mah-ree'-te-mo, mah], *a.* Maritime, maritimal, marine.
Maritornes [mah-re-tor'-nes], *f.* (Coll.) An ill-shaped, awkward woman.
Marjal [mar-hahl'], *m.* Fen, marsh, moor, moorland, marshy ground. In Murcia it is called *armajal.*
Marjoleta [mar-ho-lay'-tah], *f.* (Prov.) *V.* Majuela.
Marjoleto [mar-ho-lay'-to], *m.* *V.* Majuelo or Espino majuelo.
Marlo [mar'-lo], *m.* (Amer.) An ear of Indian corn.
Marlota [mar-lo'-tah], *f.* Robe, a kind of Moorish gown.
Marmatita [mar-mah-tee'-tah], *f.* (Min.) Marmatite, a ferriferous variety of sphalerite.
Marmella [mar-mel'-lyah], *f.* Each of two long oval warts which some goats have under the neck.
Marmellado, da [mar-mel-lyah'-do, dah], *a.* Having warts (*marmellas*) under the throat.
Marmita [mar-mee'-tah], *f.* Kettle, flesh-pot, porridge-pot, a small copper. *Marmita de Papín*, A Papin's digester.
Marmitón [mar-me-tone'], *m.* Scullion, one who is engaged to wash the dishes and plates in the kitchen.
Mármol [mahr'-mol], *m.* 1. Marble. *Mármol pintado*, Spotted marble. *Mármol rayado*, Streaked marble. 2. Pillar, column. 3. Marver, flatting-table. 4. (Typ.) Imposing-stone.
Marmolejo [mar-mo-lay'-ho], *m.* A small pillar or column of marble.
Marmoleño, ña [mar-mo-lay'-nyo, yah], *a.* Made of marble, resembling marble.
Marmolería [mar-mo-lay-ree'-ah], *f.* Any work made of marble.
Marmolista [mar-mo-lees'-tah], *m.* Worker in marble, sculptor.
Marmoración [mar-mo-rah-the-on'], *f.* *V.* Estuco.
Marmóreo, ea, Marmoroso, sa [mar-mo'-ray-o, ah, mar-mo-ro'-so, sah], *a.* Marbled, marble, marmorean, made of marble.
Marmosete [mar-mo-say'-tay], *m.* Among printers, a vignette, or ornamental cut, at the end of a chapter, or of a volume.
Marmota [mar-mo'-tah], *f.* 1. (Zool.) Marmot, groundhog, woodchuck. 2. (fig.) Sleepyhead.
Marmote, *m.* *V.* Marmosete.
Maro [mah'-ro], *m.* (Bot.) Germander. common marum, catthyme germander. Teucrium marum, *L.*
Marojo [mah-ro'-ho], *m.* (Prov. Andal.) *V.* Muérdago.
Maroma [mah-ro'-mah], *f.* Rope, a thick cord made of bass or hemp. *Andar en la maroma*, 1. To dance on a rope. 2. (Met.) To engage in a perilous undertaking. (Arab. mabróm.)
Marón, *m.* 1. *V.* Marión. 2. Title of nobility and name of the governors of the provinces of ancient Etruria. Vergil was a *marón.*
Maronitas [mah-ro-nee'-tas], *m. pl.* Christians of Mount Lebanon.
Marota [mah-ro'-tah], *f.* (Amer. Mex.) *V.* Marimacho.
Marqués [mar-kays'], *m.* Marquis, marquess.
Marquesa [mar-kay'-sah], *f.* 1. Marchioness, the lady of a marquis. 2. *V.* Marquesina.
Marquesado [mar-kay-sah'-do], *m.* Marquisate.
Marquesica, illa, ita [mar-kay-see'-cah], *f. dim.* A little marchioness, a young marchioness.
Marquesico, illo, ito, *m. dim.* A little or young marquis.
Marquesina [mar-kay-see'-nah], *f.* Marquee, tilt over an officer's tent, serving more effectually to keep out the rain.
Marquesita [mar-kay-see'-tah], *f.* Marcasite, pyrite, mundic, a metallic sulphide.
Marquesote [mar-kay-so'-tay], *m.* (Mex.) Caramel, burnt sugar.
Marqueta [mar-kay'-tah], *f.* Crude cake of wax.
Marquetería [mar-kay-tay-ree'-ah], *f.* 1. Cabinet-manufactory. 2. Marquetry, checkered or inlaid work.
Marquida, Marquisa, *f.* (Cant; low Prostitute.
Marquito [mar-kee'-to], *m. dim.* A photographic kit; holder for a smaller plate.
Marra[1] [mar'-rah], *f.* 1. Want, deficiency, defect. 2. *V.* Almadana.
Marra.[2] *f.* Club, knobbed stick.
Márraga [mar'-rah-gah], *f.* *V.* Marga, 2d def.
Marrajo [mar-rah'-ho], *m.* White shark. Squalus carcarias.
Marrajo, ja [mar-rah'-ho, hah], *a.* Sly, cunning, crafty, artful, wily.
Marrana [mar-rah'-nah], *f.* Sow, a female pig.
Marranada [mar-rah-nah'-dah], *f.* 1. Hoggish action. 2. Swinishness, brutishness, filthiness; dirty, low act.
Marranalla [mar-rah-nahl'-lyah], *f.* *V.* Canalla.
Marranamente [mar-rah-nah-men'-tay], *adv.* Piggishly, swinishly.
Marranchón, na, *a.* *V.* Marrano.
Marranería [mar-rah-nay-ree'-ah], *f.* 1. *V.* Marranada. 2. Trade in hogs.

Marraneta [mar-rah-nay'-tah], *f.* (Prov.) A young sow.
Marrano [mar-rah'-no], *m.* 1. Pig, hog. 2. Rafter or wood-work which supports a floor or cistern.
Marrano, na, *a.* Dirty, indecent.
Marrar [mar-rar'], *vn.* 1. To deviate from truth or justice. 2. *V.* Errar.
Marras [mar'-ras], *adv.* (Coll.) Long ago, long since.
Marrasquino [mar-ras-kee'-no], *m.* Maraschino, a cordial.
Márrega, *f.* *V.* Márfaga.
Marregón], *m.* (Prov.) Straw-sack. *V.* Jergón.
Marrido, da, *a.* (Obs.) *V.* Amarrido.
Marrilla [mar-reel'-lyah], *f.* A rather slender club.
Marrillo [mar-reel'-lyo], *m.* (Prov.) Thick, short stick.
Marro [mar'-ro], *m.* 1. Kind of game, quoits. 2. Slip given by a deer or hare in the course of the chase. 3. Disappointment, failure. 4. Crooked bat for striking a ball.
Marrojar [mar-ro-har'], *va.* To lop off the useless branches of trees.
Marrón [mar-rone'], *m.* 1. Quoit, pitcher. 2. (Cuba) A runaway negro, or domestic animal. 3. (Mil.) Metal plate on which, in a garrison, is engraved the hours of service which the officers have to fulfil, and which these leave at the posts which they visit by night. (Fr.)
Marroquí [mar-ro-kee'], **Marroquín, na** [mar-ro-keen', nah], *a.* Morocco, belonging to Morocco.
Marrubio [mar-roo'-be-o], *m.* (Bot.) Common white horehound. Marrubium vulgare.
Marrueco, ca [mar-roo-ay'-co, cah], *a.* Moroccan, belonging to Morocco.
Marrullería [mar-rool-lyay-ree'-ah], *f.* Cunning, craft; artful tricks.
Marrullero, ra [mar-rool-lyay'-ro, rah], *a.* Crafty, cunning.
Marsellés [mar-sel-lyess'], *m.* A kind of short jacket.
Marsellés, sa [mar-sel-lyess', sah], *a.* Relating to Marseilles.—*f.* Marseillaise, the French national hymn.
Marsopa, or **Marsopla** [mar-so'-plah], *f.* Blunt-headed cachalot, spermaceti-whale. Physeter macrocephalus.
Marsupiales [mar-soo-pe-ah'-less], *a. m. pl.* The marsupial animals, as opossums and kangaroos.
Marta [mar'-tah], *f.* Pine marten. Mustela martes. *Martas,* Martens, dressed marten-skins.
Martagón, na [mar-tah-gone', nah], *m. & f.* 1. (Coll.) Cunning, artful person. 2. *m.* (Bot.) Wild lily, Turk's-cap lily. Lilium martagon.
Marte [mar'-tay], *m.* Mars; iron.
Martellina [mar-tel-lyee'-nah], *f.* Marteline, a marble-worker's hammer having a surface presenting rows of teeth (pointed peen).
Martes [mar'-tes], *m.* Tuesday, the third day of the week. *Martes de carnestolendas,* Shrove Tuesday.
Martillada [mar-til-lyah'-dah], *f.* Stroke with the hammer.
Martillador, ra [mar-til-lyah-dor', rah], *m. & f.* Hammerer.
Martillar [mar-til-lyar'], *va.* To hammer, to malleate. *Martillar el caballo.* To spur a horse.
Martillejo [mar-til-lyay'-ho], *m. dim.* A small hammer.
Martilleo [mar-til-lyay'-o], *m.* Noise caused by hammering.
Martillo [mar-teel'-lyo], *m.* 1. A hammer; claw-hammer. 2. Person who perseveres in any thing. 3. Tuning hammer. 4. Malleus (hammer), the largest of the ossicles of the ear. *A martillo,* With strokes of a hammer. *De martillo,* Wrought metal. *A macha martillo,* Strongly, roughly made.
Martín del río, *m.* (Orn.) *V.* Martinete. Swift.
Martín pescador [mar-teen' pes-cah dor'], *m.* (Orn.) Kingfisher. Alcedo ispida.
Martinete [mar-te-nay'-tay], *m.* 1. A swift or martin. 2. The crest of the kingfisher. 3. Jack in a harpsichord; hammer of a pianoforte. 4. Hammer in copper-works. 5. A pile-driver, drop-hammer.
Martingala [mar-tin-gah'-lah], *f.* 1. Martingale, a strap fastened to the girth and noseband of a horse. 2. Ancient kind of breeches.
Martini [mar-tee'-ne], *m.* Martini, mixed alcoholic drink.
Martinico [mar-te-nee'-co], *m.* (Coll.) *V.* Duende.
Martiniega [mar-te-ne-ay'-gah], *f.* Tax payable on St. Martin's day.
Mártir [mar'-teer], *com.* A martyr.
Martirio [mar-tee'-re-o], *m.* Martyrdom.
Martirizador, ra [mar-te-re-thah-dor', rah], *m. & f.* One who commits martyrdom.
Martirizar [mar-te-re-thar'], *va.* 1. To martyr, to put to death as a martyr. 2. To inflict great sufferings; to martyrize.
Martirologio [mar-te-ro-lo'-he-o], *m.* Martyrology, a register of martyrs.
Marxismo [mark-sees'-mo], *m.* Marxism, marxianism.
Marxista [mark-sees'-tah], *a. & m. & f.* Marxist.
Marzal [mar-thahl'], *a.* Belonging to the month of March.
Marzo [mar'-tho], *m.* March, the third month of the year.
Mas [mahs], *conj.* But, yet. *Mas que,* Although, even if. *Mas si,* Perhaps, if.
Más [mahs], *adv.* 1. More, to a greater degree. 2. Plus; the sign +. 3. Besides, moreover. *A más correr,* With the utmost speed. *A más tardar,* At latest. *A más y mejor,* Greatly, highly, at best; excellently. *De más a más,* Still more and more. *Por lo más,* At most. *Por más que,* However much. *Más que* or *de,* More than, but. *Más de tres años,* More than three years. *A más de esto,* Besides this. *Sin más ni más,* Without more ado, heedlessly. *Más vale doblarse que quebrarse,* Better to bow than to break. *Más bien,* Rather. *Los más,* The largest number. *Lo más antes,* As soon as possible. *Más vale* or *más valiera si . . .* It is better or would be better if . . . *Sin más acá ni más allá,* Without ifs or ands.
Mas [mahs], *m.* 1. (Prov.) Farm-house and stock. 2. A weight for gold and silver used in the Philippines equal to 3.768 gm. or 58 grains.
Masa [mah'-sah], *f.* 1. Dough. 2. Mortar. 3. Mass of gold, silver, or other metal. 4. The whole mass of a thing; the lump. 5. Mass, congeries, the union or concurrence of many things. 6. A gentle disposition. 7. (Prov.) Farm-house, with all necessary tools and utensils. 8. Estate of a bankrupt.
Masadero [mah-sah-day'-ro], *m.* (Prov.) Neighbour.
Masaje [mah-sah'-hay], *m.* Massage.
Masajista [mah-sah-hees'-tah], *m.* or *f.* Masseur, masseuse.
Masar [mah-sar'], *va.* *V.* Amasar.
Masato [mah-sah'-to], *m.* A fermented liquor made from the yuca or plantain-tree by Indians bordering on the branches of the Amazon river.
Mascabado, da [mas-cah-bah'-do, dah], *a.* Applied to inferior sugar; raw, unrefined, muscovado.
Mascada [mas-cah'-dah], *f.* (Mex.) 1. A silk handkerchief. 2. The iron ring by which the neck of criminals condemned to death by the *garrote* is broken.
Mascador, ra [mas-cah-dor', rah], *m. & f.* Chewer, masticator.
Mascadura [mas-cah-doo'-rah], *f.* Mastication, manducation.
Mascar [mas-car'], *va.* 1. To chew, to masticate. 2. To pronounce or talk with difficulty.
Máscara [mahs'-cah-rah], *f.* 1. Mask, a cover to disguise the face. 2. Masquerade. 3. Mask, any pretence or subterfuge. 4. A face-mask used by bee-keepers. 5. *com.* Masker, masquerader, mummer; a person in a mask.
Mascarada [mas-cah-rah'-dah], *f.* Masquerade, mummery.
Mascarero [mas-cah-ray'-ro], *m.* Dealer in masks.
Mascarilla [mas-cah-reel'-lyah], *f.* 1. (Dim.) A small mask which covers only the forehead and eyes. *Quitarse la mascarilla,* To take off the mask, to declare one's sentiments boldly. 2. Mould taken from the face of a dead person; death-mask.
Mascarón [mas-cah-rone'], *m.* (Aug.) 1. A large hideous mask. 2. Hideous or grotesque forms: *e. g.,* satyrs' faces, used to adorn fountains and buildings. 3. Person ridiculously grave and solemn. *Mascarón de proa,* Figure-head of a vessel.
Mascota [mas-co'-tah], *f.* Mascot.
Masculinidad [mas-coo-le-ne-dahd'], *f.* Masculinity, manhood.
Masculino, na [mas-coo-lee'-no, nah], *a.* 1. Masculine, male, virile. 2. (Gram.) Masculine: applied to the gender.
Mascullar [mas-cool-lyar'], *va.* To falter in speaking.
Masecoral, Masejicomar [mah-say-co-rahl', mah-say-he-co-mar'], *m.* Sleight of hand, legerdemain.
Masera [mah-say'-rah], *f.* A kneading-trough.
Masería, Masía [mah-say-ree'-ah, mah-see'-ah], *f.* Farm-house. *V.* Masada.
Masetero [mah-say-tay'-ro], *m.* Masseter, a muscle of the lower jaw.
Masica [mah-see'-cah], *f.* The bread-nut tree of Central America.
Masicote [mah-se-co'-tay], *m.* Massicot, oxide of lead prepared without fusion by the dry method.
Masiliense [mah-se-le-en'-say], *a.* Of Marseilles.
Masilla [mah-seel'-lyah], *f.* 1. Glaziers' putty. 2. (Dim.) A little mass.
Masita [mah-see'-tah], *f.* Pittance retained for providing a soldier with shoes, etc.
Maslo [mahs'-lo], *m.* 1. Root of the tail of quadrupeds. 2. Shaft or stem of some plants.
Masón [mah-sone'], *m.* 1. Mess of dough given to fowls. 2. (Aug.) A large mass. 3. *V.* Francmasón.
Masonería [mah-so-nay-ree'-ah], *f.* Freemasonry.
Masónico, ca [mah-so'-ne-co, cah], *a.* Masonic.
Masoquismo [mah-so-kees'-mo], *m.* Masochism.
Masora [mah-so'-rah], *f.* Masorah, a Hebrew work on the Bible. The tradition relied on by the Jews to preserve the text of the Old Testament from corruption.
Masorético, ca [mah-so-ray'-te-co, cah], *a.* Masoretic.
Masque [mahs'-kay], *adv.* (Mex.) No matter, let it be so. (*mas* and *que.*)

Mastelero [mas-tay-lay'-ro], *m.* (Naut.) Top-mast. *Masteleros de respeto*, Spare top-masts. *Masteleros de juanete*, Top-gallant masts. *Mastelero mayor* or *de gavia*, Main top-mast. *Mastelero de juanete mayor*, Fore top-mast. *Mastelero de proa*, Fore top-gallant-mast. *Mastelero de sobremesana*, Mizzen top-gallant-mast.

Masticación [mas-te-cah-the-on'], *f.* Mastication.

Masticar [mas-te-car'], *va.* 1. To masticate, to chew. 2. To ruminate or meditate.

Masticatorio, ria [mas-te-cah-to'-re-o, ah], *a.* Masticatory.

Mastigador [mas-te-gah-dor'], *m.* Instrument put into horses' mouths to prevent their chewing.

Mástil [mahs'-teel], *m.* 1. *V.* MASTELERO. 2. Upright post of a bed or loom. *Mástil de barrena*, Shank of an auger. 3. Trunk or stem of a tree. 4. Wide breeches worn by Indians. 5. The handle of some musical instruments.

Mastín, na [mas-teen', nah], *m.* & *f.* 1. Mastiff, a dog of the largest size; bull-dog. 2. A clumsy fellow; clown.

Mastinazo [mas-te-nah'-tho], *m. aug.* A large mastiff.

Mastinillo [mas-te-neel'-lyo], *m. dim.* A little mastiff.

Masto [mahs'-to], *m.* (Prov. Ar'n) Stock into which a scion is grafted.

Mastodonte [mas-to-don'-tay], *m.* The mastodon, a fossil mammal like the elephant.

Mastoideo, dea [mas-to-e-day'-o, ah], *a.* Mastoid, nipple-shaped. (Gr.)

Mastoides [mas-to'-e-days], *m.* The mastoid prominence of the temporal bone.

Mastoiditis [mas-toy-dee'-tis], *f.* (Med.) Mastoiditis, mastoid inflammation.

Mastranto, Mastranzo [mas-trahn'-to, mas-trahn'-tho], *m.* (Bot.) Round-leaved mint. Mentha rotundifolia.

Mastuerzo [mas-too-err'-tho], *m.* (Bot.) Common-cress. Lapidium sativuni, *L.*

Masturbación [mas-toor-bah-the-on'], *f.* Masturbation.

Masturbarse [mas-toor-bar'-say], *vr.* To masturbate.

Masvale [mas-vah'-lay], *m.* *V.* MALVASÍA.

Mata [mah'-tah], *f.* 1. Small bush, shrub, under-shrub. Suffrutex. 2. Sprig, blade. 3. Grove, a cluster of trees of one species; copse. 4. The mastic-tree. 5. Lock of matted hair. 6. Piece of ore only partly fused. 7. *Mata parda*, Young evergreen oak. *De mala mata, nunca buena caza*, or *buena zarza*, One cannot make a silken purse out of a sow's ear. *Saltar de la mata*, To make one's self known, to come out into the open.

Mata, *f.* 1. Game at cards. *V.* MATARRATA. 2. (Obs.) Slaughter. (From MATAR.)

Matacán [mah-tah-cahn'], *m.* 1. A poisonous composition for killing dogs. 2. (Bot.) *V.* NUEZ VÓMICA. 3. A hare previously hunted. 4. Stone which may be grasped in the hand and thrown.

Matacandelas [mah-tah-can-day'-las], *f.* Extinguisher.

Matacandil [mah-tah-can-deel'], *m.* (Prov. Murcia) Lobster.

Matacía [mah-tah-thee'-ah], *f.* (Prov. Ar'n) Slaughter, death.

Matachín [mah-tah-cheen'], *m.* 1. Merry-andrew, jack-pudding. 2. Dance performed by grotesque figures. 3. Slaughterman, butcher. *Dejar a alguno hecho un matachín*, To make any one a laughing-stock.

Matadero [mah-tah-day'-ro], *m.* Slaughter-house; severe labour.

Matador [mah-tah-dor'], *m.* 1. Murderer. 2. A card in the game of ombre.—*a.* Mortal; murderous, homicidal.

Matadora, *f.* Murderess.

Matadura [mah-tah-doo'-rah], *f.* Wound on a horse's back made by the harness; gall. *Dar (a uno) en las mataduras*, (Coll.) To tread on one's corns, to hurt one's tender spot.

Matafuego [mah-tah-foo-ay'-go], *m.* 1. Fire-engine, fire-extinguisher. 2. Fireman.

Matagallina [mah-tah-gal-lyee'-nah], *f.* (Prov. Log.) *V.* TORVISCO.

Matahambre [mah-tah-ahm'-bray], *m.* (Cuba) Marchpane, dainty made of yucca flour, sugar, etc.

Matahormigas [mah-tah-or-mee'-gas], *a.* & *m.* & *f.* (Coll.) Half-witted, doltish.

Matalobos [mah-tah-lo'-bos], *m.* (Bot.) Wolf's-bane, aconite. Aconitum lycoctonum.

Matalón, Matalote [mah-tah-lone', mah-tah-lo'-tay], *m.* An old worn-out horse.

Matamoros [mah-tah-mo'-ros], *m.* Braggart, boaster. *V.* MATASIETE.

Matanza [mah-tahn'-thah], *f.* 1. The action of slaughtering. 2. Cattle to be slaughtered. 3. Massacre, butchery; slaughter in the field of battle. 4. Obstinacy, eagerness of pursuit.

Mataperros [mah-tah-per'-ros], *m.* (Met. and coll.) A mischievous, street-lounging boy.

Matapolvo [mah-tah-pol'-vo], *m.* Light rain which scarcely settles the dust.

Matar [mah-tar'], *va.* 1. To kill, to put to death; to make away with; to execute. 2. To murder. 3. To put out a light, to extinguish the fire. 4. To slake lime. 5. To worry, to vex, to molest. *Matar a pesadumbres*, (Coll.) To break one's heart. 6. To make a horse's back sore by the rubbing of the harness. *Matar de un golpe*, To knock on the head. *Matar de hambre*, To famish, to starve, to kill with hunger. *A mata caballo*, In the utmost hurry. *Vender a mata candelas*, To sell at public auction by inch of candle.—*vr.* 1. To commit suicide. 2. To make the utmost exertions to obtain a thing. 3. To be extremely concerned at a failure or disappointment. *Matarse con otro*, To be at drawn daggers. *Matarse un caballo*, To be saddle-galled. *Mátalas callando*, (Coll.) By crafty silence, or under-hand means, he obtains his end.

Matarife [mah-tah-ree'-fay], *m.* (Prov.) Slaughterman. *V.* MATACHÍN.

Matarrata [mah-tar-rah'-tah], *f.* Game at cards.

Matasanos [mah-tah-sah'-nos], *m.* Quack, charlatan; empiric.

Matasellos [mah-tah-sayl'-lyos], *m.* Postmark.

Matasiete [mah-tah-se-ay'-tay], *m.* Bully, braggadocio.

Mate [mah'-tay], *m.* 1. Checkmate in chess. *Dar mate*, To scoff at any one. 2. Size, used by painters and gilders; gold or silver sizing. 3. The leaves of a shrub of that name, used in South America as a substitute for tea. 4. Unpolished ore. 5. (Amer.) A dry gourd. *Dar mate*, (Coll.) To make fun of a person by laughing. *Entrar a mates*, (Prov. Mex.) To correspond or understand each other by signs: applied to lovers.—*Dar mate ahogado*, 1. To give smothered mate. 2. To wish things immediately, on the spot, without taking reflection.—*a.* Unpolished, rough, matt; faded.

Matear [mah-tay-ar'], *vn.* 1. (Prov.) To grow up into stalks: applied to wheat and barley. 2. (Amer.) To take mate-tea.

Matemáticamente, *adv.* Mathematically.

Matemáticas [mah-tay-mah'-te-cas], *f.* Mathematics. (Less used in the singular.)

Matemático, ca [mah-tay-mah'-te-co, cah], *a.* Mathematical.

Matemático [mah-tay-mah'-te-co], *m.* Mathematician.

Materia [mah-tay'-re-ah], *f.* 1. Matter, substance extended. 2. Materials of which any thing is composed. *Prima* or *primera materia*, Raw material. 3. Matter, subject, thing treated; cause, occasion. 4. Matter, question considered, point discussed. 5. Matter, pus. 6. Matter, corporeal substance; opposed to spirit.

Material [mah-tay-re-ahl'], *a.* 1. Material, not spiritual. 2. Rude, uncouth, ungenteel.—*m.* Ingredient, component portion of which any thing is made.

Materialidad [mah-tay-re-ah-le-dahd'], *f.* 1. Materiality, corporeity. 2. Surface or appearance of things; sound of words. 3. (Theol.) Materiality, physical fact of actions done in ignorance of right and wrong.

Materialismo [mah-tay-re-ah-lees'-mo], *m.* Materialism.

Materialista [mah-tay-re-ah-lees'-tah], *com.* Materialist.

Materialmente, *adv.* Materially, corporeally.

Maternal [mah-ter-nahl'], *a.* Maternal. *V.* MATERNO.

Maternalmente, *adv.* Maternally.

Maternidad [mah-ter-ne-dahd'], *f.* 1. Maternity, the condition of being a mother. 2. (Amer.) Maternity, a hospital for women lying-in.

Materno, na [mah-terr'-no, nah], *a.* Maternal, motherly.

Mático [mah'-te-co], *m.* (Acad.) Matico, a shrub of the pepper family, native of Peru and Bolivia, the leaves containing an astringent, aromatic oil. Pronounced mah-tee'-co in Peru.

Matigüelo, Matihuelo [mah-te-goo-ay'-lo], *m.* Figure of a boy, made of straw, used as a plaything at bull-feasts.

Matinal [mah-te-nahl'], *a.* (Poet.) *V.* MATUTINAL.

Matiné [mah-te-nay'], *f.* (Th.) Matinee, morning or afternoon performance.

Matiz [mah-teeth'], *m.* Shade of colours; mixture of a variety of colours.

Matizado, da [mah-te-thah'-do, dah], *a.* & *pp.* of MATIZAR. Variegated.

Matizar [mah-te-thar'], *va.* 1. To mix colours agreeably. 2. To embellish, to adorn, to beautify.

Mato [mah'-to], *m.* *V.* MATORRAL.

Matojo [mah-toh'-ho], *m.* 1. (Acad.) A barrilla-producing bush about two feet high which grows in Spain. 2. (Cuba) Shoot which trees put out after being cut.

Matón [mah-tone'], *m.* Bully, a noisy, quarrelsome fellow.

Matorral [mah-tor-rahl'], *m.* 1. Field full of brambles and briers, a bushy place. 2. A thicket, copse.

Matoso, sa [mah-to'-so, sah], *a.* Bushy, covered with copse or bushes.

Matraca [mah-trah'-cah], *f.* 1. A wooden rattle. 2. Jest, contemptuous joke. *Dar matraca*, To banter.

Matraquear [mah-trah-kay-ar'], *va.* To jest, to scoff, to mock, to ridicule.

Matraquista [mah-trah-kees'-tah], *com.* Wag, jester, punster.

Matraz [mah-trath'], *f.* Matrass, vessel used by apothecaries.

Matrería [mah-tray-ree'-ah], *f.* (Mex. Cuba) Penetration, shrewdness, suspiciousness.

Matrero, ra [mah-tray'-ro, rah], *a.* Cunning, sagacious, knowing.—*m.* Artful knave; cunning, knavish soldier.

Matriarcado [mah-tre-ar-cah'-do], *m.* Matriarchy.

Matricaria [mah-tre-cah'-re-ah], *f.* (Bot.) Common feverfew. Matricaria parthenium.

Matricida [mah-tre-thee'-dah], *com.* Matricide, murderer of one's mother.

Matricidio [mah-tre-thee'-de-o], *m.* Matricide, slaughter of a mother.

Matrícula [mah-tree'-coo-lah], *f.* 1 Register, list. 2. Matriculation.

Matriculación [mah-tre-coo-lah-the-on'], *f.* (Littl. us.) Matriculation.

Matriculador [mah-tre-coo-lah-dor'], *m.* He who matriculates.

Matricular [mah-tre-coo-lar'], *va.* To matriculate, to register, to enrol, to enter a list.

Matrimonial [mah-tre-mo-ne-ahl'], *a.* Matrimonial, connubial, nuptial.

Matrimonialmente, *adv.* Matrimonially.

Matrimonio [mah-tre-mo'-ne-o], *m.* 1. Marriage, matrimony. 2. (Coll.) Husband and wife, couple. *Matrimonio rato,* Legal marriage not consummated. *Matrimonio morganático* or *de la mano izquierda,* A morganatic or left-handed marriage; one of a prince with a woman of lower rank.

Matriz [mah-treeth'], *f.* 1. Mother church, metropolitan church. 2. Matrix, womb. 3. Mould, form, matrice. 4. The original draft of a writing. 5. A female screw. *Lengua matriz,* Mother-tongue.—*a.* First, principal, chief.

Matrona [mah-tro'-nah], *f.* 1. A matron. 2. A midwife.

Matronaza [mah-tro-nah'-thah], *f. aug.* A corpulent, respectable matron.

Maturrango, ga [mah-too-rahn'-go, gah], *m.* & *f.* Appellation given to a European in Buenos Ayres. It means a bad horseman or bad horse.

Matusalén [mah-too-sah-layn'], *a.* (Coll.) Old as Methuselah.

Matute [ma-tooh'-tay], *m.* 1. Smuggling. 2. Smuggled goods, a prohibited commodity.

Matutear [mah-too-tay-ar'], *va.* To smuggle goods.

Matutero, ra [mah-too-tay'-ro, rah], *m.* & *f.* Smuggler, contrabandist.

Matutinal [mah-too-te-nahl'], *a.* Belonging to the morning; morning.

Matutino, na [mah-too-tee'-no, nah], *a.* Matutinal, belonging to the morning.

Maula [mah'-oo-lah], *f.* 1. Any thing worthless; rubbish, trumpery, trash. 2. Cunning, craft; deceitful tricks, imposition.—*com.* (Coll.) Cheat, bad paymaster. *Es una buena maula,* (Coll.) He is a good-for-nothing fellow. *Ella es buena maula,* She is a hussy: used jocularly.

Maulería [mah-oo-lay-ree'-ah], *f.* 1. Frippery, old clothes-shop; a piece-broker's shop. 2. Craft, cunning.

Maulero [mah-oo-lay'-ro], *m.* 1. Piece-broker, seller of old clothes. 2. Impostor, cheat, swindler.

Maullador, ra [mah-ool-lyah-dor', rah], *a.* Applied to a mewing cat.

Maullar [mah-ool-lyar'], *vn.* To mew, as a cat.

Maullido, Maúllo [mah-ool-lyee'-do, mah-ool'-lyo], *m.* Mew, cry of a cat.

Mauraca [mah-oo-rah'-cah], *f.* (Prov. Andal.) Act of roasting chestnuts, acorns, or ears of Indian corn over coals in the open air.

Mauritano, na [mah-oo-re-tah'-no, nah] *a.* Mauritanian.

Mauseolo [mah-oo-say-o'-lo], *m.* *V* MAUSOLEO.

Mausoleo [mah-oo-so-lay'-o], *m.* Mausoleum.

Maxilar [mac-se-lar'], *a.* Maxillary, maxillar.

Máxima [mahc'-se-mah], *f.* 1. A maxim, an axiom. 2. Sentence, apothegm. 3. Idea, thought. 4. Musical point.

Máximamente and **Máxime** [mahc'-se-may], *adv.* Principally.

Máximo, ma [mahc'-se-mo, mah], *a. sup.* Chief, principal; very great.

Máximum [mac'-se-moom], *m.* Maximum, extreme limit.

Maya [mah'-yah], *f.* 1. (Bot.) Common daisy. Bellis perennis, *L.* 2. May-queen, a little girl adorned with flowers and placed in the street to collect money. 3. Name of the native language of Yucatan and of its ancient civilization.

Mayador, ra [mah-yah-dor', rah], *a.* Mewing.

Mayal [mah-yahl'], *m.* 1. Flail, a thrashing instrument. 2. Lever in oil-mills.

Mayar [mah-yar'], *vn.* To mew. *V.* MAULLAR.

Mayo [mah'-yo], *m.* 1. May, the fifth month. 2. May-pole.

Mayólica [mah-yo'-le-cah], *f.* Majolica ware.

Mayonesa [mah-yo-nay'-sah], *f.* Mayonnaise dressing; oil and yelks of eggs beaten together.

Mayor [mah-yor'], *a.* Greater, larger. *Hombre mayor,* An elderly man; also, a man of great age.—*m.* 1. Superior, mayor or chief of a community. 2. Major, a field officer. 3. (Geog.) Lake Maggiore, in northern Italy. 4. (Arch.) *V.* SILLAR.—*f.* (Log.) Major, first proposition in a syllogism.—*pl.* 1. Ancestors, forefathers. 2. Superiors. 3. (Naut.) Three principal sails of a ship. 4. In grammar-schools, the higher class. *Mayor* or *mayor de edad,* Person of age. *Hermano mayor,* Eldest brother. *Ganado mayor,* Cattle and larger sort of beasts of burden, as mules and horses. *Por mayor,* By wholesale, by the lump; summarily.

Mayora [mah-yo'-rah], *f.* Mayoress.

Mayoral [mah-yo-rahl'], *m.* 1. Head shepherd; leader. 2. Overseer, steward. 3. (Obs.) Chief person of a corps or society.

Mayorana [mah-yo-rah'-nah], *f.* *V.* MEJORANA.

Mayorazga [mah-yo-rath'-gah], *f.* 1. The wife of a person possessing an entailed estate. 2. She who possesses an entailed estate.

Mayorazgo [mah-yo-rath'-go], *m.* 1. Right of succession in family estates, vested in the first-born son. 2. First-born son, possessing the right of primogeniture. 3. Family estate, which devolves to the first-born son, by right of inheritance; an entailed estate.

Mayorazguista [mah-yo-rath-gees'-tah], *m.* (Law) Author who treats on entails.

Mayordoma [mah-yor-do'-mah], *f.* Steward's wife.

Mayordomía [mah-yor-do-mee'-ah], *f.* Administration, stewardship, controllership.

Mayordomo [mah-yor-do'-mo], *m.* Steward, the principal servant of a nobleman or gentleman; major-domo, superintendent. *Mayordomo de propios,* City steward.

Mayoría [mah-yo-ree'-ah], *f.* 1. Advantage, excellence, superiority. 2. Major's commission. *Mayoría de plaza,* A town-major's place. 3. Majority, full age.

Mayoridad [mah-yo-re-dahd'], *f.* Superiority.

Mayorista [mah-yo-rees'-tah], *m.* Student of the highest classes in grammar-schools.

Mayormente, *adv.* Principally, chiefly.

Mayúscula [mah-yoos'-coo-lah], *a.* Capital (upper case) letter; used also as a substantive.

Maza [mah'-thah], *f.* 1. Club, a stick shod with iron. 2. Mace, an ensign of authority. 3. Engine or pile-engine. 4. Nave or hub of a wheel. 5. Rag pinned to men or women's clothes to make a laughing-stock of them. 6. Beetle for flax or hemp. 7. An importunate or troublesome fellow. 8. The thick end of a billiard-cue. 9. Something noisy tied to a dog's tail (in carnival time). *Maza de fraga,* Hammer. *Maza sorda, V.* ESPADAÑA. *La maza y la mona,* (Coll.) Applied to two persons who constantly walk together.

Mazacote [mah-thah-co'-tay], *m.* 1. Kali, barilla. 2. Mortar, cement. 3. Dry, tough mass. 4. Injurious nickname for a peevish person. 5. (Amer.) Antimony.

Mazada [mah-thah'-dah], *f.* Blow with a mallet; offensive expression.

Mazagatos [mah-thah-gah'-tos], *m.* Noise, dispute, contention.

Mazamorra [mah-thah-mor'-rah], *f.* 1. Bread-dust; biscuit spoiled and broken in pieces. 2. Any thing broken into small bits. 3. Sort of pap, made of the flour of Indian corn, honey, and sugar, much used in Peru.

Mazaneta [mah-thah-nay'-tah], *f.* Apple-shaped ornament in jewels.

Mazapán [mah-thah-pahn'], *m.* Marchpane, a sweet paste of almonds, sugar, etc. (Ital.)

Mazar [mah-thar'], *va.* (Prov.) To churn milk.

Mazarí [mah-thah-ree'], *m.* A tile-shaped brick.

Mazmorra [math-mor'-rah], *f.* Moorish dungeon, underground.

Mazo [mah'-tho], *m.* 1. Mallet, a wooden hammer. 2. Bundle, a quantity of ribbons or other things tied together. *Mazo de llaves,* Bunch of keys. 3. An importunate, tiresome person.

Mazonería [mah-tho-nay-ree'-ah], *f.* 1. Masonry, brickwork. 2. Relief or relievo-work.

Mazorca [mah-thor'-cah], *f.* 1. Spindle full of thread, spun from the distaff in the shape of a cone. 2. Ear of corn, the spike or cob of corn. 3. Spindle-shaped work upon a balustrade. (Acad.)

Mazorral [mah-thor-rahl'], *a.* Rude, uncouth, clownish.

Mazote [mah-tho'-tay], *m.* 1. A kind of cement or mortar. 2. A block-head.

Mazotear [mah-tho-tay-ar'], *va.* To strike with a club or mallet.

Mazurca [mah-thoor'-cah], *f.* Mazurka.

Me [may], *pron.* Me, the dative and accusative case of the pronoun I, placed either before or after a verb.

Mea [may'-ah], *f.* Term used by children wishing to make water.

Meada [may-ah'-dah], *f.* 1. The quantity of urine made at one time. 2. Spot or mark left by making water.

Meadero [may-ah-day'-ro], *m.* Place for making water.

Meados, *m.pl.* *V.* Orines.
Meajuela [may-ah-hoo-ay'-lah], *f.* Small piece attached to the bits of a bridle.
Mear [may-ar'], *vn.* To urinate, to make water.
Meato [may-ah'-to], *m.* Passage or channel of the body; meatus.
Meauca [may-ah-oo'-cah], *f.* A seafowl, so called from its cry; a gull.
Meca [may'-cah], *f.* *Casa de meca*, House of noise and confusion. *Andar de Ceca en Meca*, To wander about.
Mecánica [may-cah'-ne-cah], *f.* 1. Mechanics. *V.* Maquinaria. 2. (Coll.) A mean, despicable action or thing. 3. (Mil.) Management of soldiers' affairs.
Mecánicamente, *adv.* Meanly, sordidly, mechanically.
Mecánico, ca [may-cah'-ne-co, cah], *a.* 1. Mechanical, done by machinery. 2. Mean, servile; of mean occupation. *Potencias mecánicas*, Mechanical powers.
Mecánico [may-cah'-ne-co], *m.* 1. Mechanician, mechanic, manufacturer, handicraftsman.
Mecanismo [may-cah-nees'-mo], *m.* Mechanism, action performed according to mechanical laws.
Mecanización [may-cah-ne-thah-the-on'], *f.* Mechanization.
Mecanizar [may-cah-ne-thar'], *va.* To mechanize.
Mecanografía [may-cah-no-grah-fee'-ah], *f.* Typewriting.
Mecanógrafo, fa [may-cah-no'-grah-fo, fah], *m.* & *f.* Typist.
Mecapal [may-cah-pahl'], *m.* (Mex.) A kind of leather band with two cords attached, serving porters to carry a load more conveniently.
Mecate [may-cah'-tay], *m.* (Mex.) Rope or cord made of the maguey or American agave.
Mecatito [may-cah-tee'-to], *m.* Small cord, twine.
Mecedero [may-thay-day'-ro], *m.* *V.* Mecedor.
Mecedor, ra [may-thay-dor', rah], *m.* & *f.* 1. Rocker, one who rocks any thing to and fro. 2. *m.* Stirrer, a pole with which wine is stirred in a hogshead, wort in a vat, and soap in a boiler. *Mecedora*, *f.* Rocking-chair.
Mecedura [may-thay-doo'-rah], *f.* Act of rocking any thing.
Mecer [may-therr'], *va.* 1. To stir, to agitate, to jumble, to mix. 2. To rock, to shake. 3. To dandle a child.
Mecereón [may-thay-ray-on'], *m.* (Bot.) Mezereon. Daphne mezereum.
Mecida [may-thee'-dah], *f.* *V.* Mecedura.
Meco, ca [may'-co, cah], *a.* (Mex.) Blackish red; copper-coloured: used of animals.—*m.* & *f.* (Mex.) Savage Indian.
Mecónico, ca [may-co'-ne-co, cah], *a.* Meconic acid, a white solid discovered in opium.
Mecha [may'-chah], *f.* 1. Wick, for candles, tapers, and torches. 2. Roll of lint put into a sore. 3. Match, match-cord, for firing ordnance. 4. Bacon, with which fowls and meat are larded. 5. A lock of hair; a bundle of threads or fibres. *Alargar la mecha*, To augment a salary; to protract a business; to allow a debtor time to discharge a debt.
Mechar [may-char'], *va.* To lard fowls, game, or meat, with bacon; to force or stuff.
Mechazo [may-chah'-tho], *m.* Burning of a slow-match (fuse) without setting off the blast.
Mechera [may-chay'-rah], *f.* Larding-pin.
Mechero [may-chay'-ro], *m.* Tube for the wick of a lamp; socket of candlesticks.
Mechificar [may-che-fe-car'], *va.* (Peru Ven. coll.) To annoy, to make fun of.
Mechinal [may-che-nahl'], *m.* Square stones left projecting in a wall to be continued.
Mechoacán [may-cho-ah-cahn'], *m.* (Bot.) Mechoacan bind-weed, an inferior kind of jalap. Convolvulus mechoacan, *L.*
Mechón [may-chone'], *m. aug.* 1. Large lock of hair; large match. 2. A large bundle of threads or fibres separated from the rest.
Mechoso, sa [may-cho'-so, sah], *a.* Full of matches or wicks.
Medalla [may-dahl'-lyah], *f.* 1. A medal. *Medalla anepígrafa*, Medal without a title. 2. (Sculpt.) A round or oval target on which a figure is carved in relief. 3. (Coll.) Gold coin weighing an ounce.
Medallón [may-dal-lyon'], *m. aug.* 1. Medallion. 2. (Arch.) Round or oval bas-relief placed on buildings. 3. A locket for a portrait or some souvenir.
Médano, Medaño [may'-dah-no, may-dah'-nyo], *m.* 1. Sand-bank on the seashore; dune. 2. A mound of sand covered by shallow water.
Media [may'-de-ah], *f.* 1. Stocking, hose. *Medias lisas*, Plain hose. *Medias labradas* or *bordadas*, Figured or embroidered hose. *Medias rayadas*, Ribbed hose. *Medias-medias*, Socks, half-hose. 2. Measure of about half a hundred-weight.
Mediacaña [may-de-ah-cah'-nyah], *f.* 1. (Arch.) A concave moulding. 2. A strip of wood with mouldings. 3. A gouge, a chisel with a curved cutting edge. 4. A half-round file. 5. Curling-tongs for the hair.
Mediación [may-de-ah-the-on'], *f.* Mediation, intervention, interposition, intercession.
Mediador, ra [may-de-ah-dor', rah], *m.* & *f.* Mediator, intercessor.
Mediana [may-de-ah'-nah], *f.* 1. Flesh of the shoulder near the neck of animals. 2. Household bread. 3. (Prov.) Top of a fishing-rod. 4. *V.* Barzón.
Medianamente, *adv.* Middlingly, moderately, meanly.
Mediados de (A), *adv.* (Coll.) About the midst of, in the midst of.
Medianejo, ja [may-de-ah-nay'-ho, hah], *a.* (Coll.) Barely middling or moderate; hardly mediocre.
Medianería [may-de-ah-nay-ree'-ah], *f.* 1. A wall common to two contiguous houses. 2. Moiety of land or rent equally divided and enjoyed by halves.
Medianero, ra [may-de-ah-nay'-ro, rah], *a.* 1. Mediating, interceding, mediatory. 2. Intermediate; having the moiety. *Pared medianera*, Partition-wall.
Medianero [may-de-ah-nay'-ro], *m.* 1. Mediator, go-between. 2. Owner of a house which has a common wall.
Medianía, Medianidad [may-de-ah-nee'-ah, may-de-ah-ne-dahd'], *f.* 1. Moderation or temperance in the execution of a thing. 2. Mediocrity, mean, middle state; moderate means.
Medianil [may-de-ah-neel'], *m.* (Agr.) Middle-piece of ground.
Medianista [may-de-ah-nees'-tah], *m.* Student of the fourth class in grammar.
Mediano, na [may-de-ah'-no, nah], *a.* Moderate, middling, mediocre.
Medianos [may-de-ah'-nos], *m. pl.* In grammar-schools, the class in syntax.
Mediante [may-de-ahn'-tay], *adv.* By means of, by virtue of.
Mediar [may-de-ar'], *vn.* 1. To come to the middle of a thing, to be at the middle. 2. To intercede for another, to mediate. 3. To intervene. *Si no mediara su respeto*, (Coll.) Were it not for respect to him.
Mediastino [may-de-as-tee'-no], *m.* (Anat.) 1. Mediastinum, the intervening space between the lungs. 2. (Bot.) Delicate septum of the silique of the mustard family.
Mediatamente, *adv.* Mediately.
Mediato, ta [may-de-ah'-to, tah], *a.* Mediate.
Mediator [may-de-ah-tor'], *m.* Ombre, game at cards.
Médica [may'-de-ca], *f.* 1. Doctor's wife. 2. Doctress, female physician.
Medicable [may-de-cah'-blay], *a.* Curable, medicable.
Medicamento [may-de-cah-men'-to], *m.* Medicament, medicine, physic.
Medicar [may-de-car'], *va.* (Obs.) *V.* Medicinar.
Medicastro [may-de-cahs'-tro], *m.* Quack, empiric in physic.
Medicina [may-de-thee'-nah], *f.* Medicine, the healing arts. 2. Medicine, a remedy. *Medicina espacial*, Space medicine.
Medicinal [may-de-the-nahl'], *a.* Medicinal, healing, belonging to physic.
Medicinar [may-de-the-nar'], *va.* To medicine, to administer medicines, to apply medicaments.
Medición [may-de-the-on'], *f.* Measurement, mensuration, measuring.
Medicucho [may-de-coo'-cho], *a.* Quackish, quack (used adjectively).
Médico [may'-de-co], *m.* Physician.
Médico, ca [may'-de-co, cah], *a.* Medical, medicinal.
Medida [may-dee'-dah], *f.* 1. Measure, that by which any thing is measured; standard, gauge. 2. Mensuration, measuring, measurement. 3. Height, length, breadth, or quantity measured. 4. Proportion, relation, correspondence. 5. (Arith.) Root, a number which, repeated various times, exactly produces another. 6. Measure, syllables metrically numbered. 7. Measure, means to an end. 8. Measure, moderation, prudence. 9. Girdle on the statues of saints bearing their name. *A medida del deseo*, According to one's wishes. *A medida* or *a sabor de su paladar*, To his heart's content. *A medida que*, According as, in proportion; at the same time that, whilst. *Llenar*, or *henchir las medidas*, (1) To express a candid opinion. (2) To flatter excessively. *Llenarse la medida*, To drain a cup of sorrow.
Medidamente, *adv.* Moderately.
Medidor, ra [may-de-dor', rah], *m.* & *f.* Measurer, evaluator.—*m.* Meter, gauge. *Medidor de franqueo*, Postage meter. *Medidor del gas*, Gas meter.
Medeiro [may-de-ay'-ro], *m.* 1. Hosier, dealer in stockings. 2. Knitter of stockings. 3. Sharecropper, copartner in the cultivation of lands, etc.
Medieval [may-de-ay-vahl'], *a.* & *m.* Mediæval, pertaining to the Middle Ages. (Neol.)
Medio, dia [may'-de-o, ah], *a.* Half, in part. *Media noche*, Midnight, twelve at night. *Medio día*, Midday, noon. *Medio hermano*, Half-brother or half-blood. *Medio borracho*, Half-seas over. *Media naranja*, *V.* Cúpula. *A medio-nao*, (Naut.) Midships. *A medias*, By halves. *Ir a medias*, To go halves with one.

Medio [may'-de-o], *m.* 1. Middle. 2. Medium. 3. Step, measure. 4. Means. 5. Surroundings, environment. 6. (Math.) Half. 7. Middle finger. 8. (Sports) Lineman.—*pl.* 1. Means, resources. 2. Center of the bullring.—*adv.* Half. *A medio cocer*, Half cooked. *Corto de medios*, Short of funds. *De medio a medio*, 1. Right in the middle. 2. Absolutely. *De por medio*, 1. Halfway. 2. In the middle. *Echar por en medio*, To face the issue, to take the bull by the horns. *En medio de*, 1. In the middle of. 2. Despite. *Estar de por medio*, To mediate. *Por medio de*, By means of, through. *Medios de publicidad*, Advertising media.

Mediocre [may-de-o'-cray], *a.* Middling, mean, moderate, mediocre.

Mediocridad [may-de-o-cre-dahd'], *f.* Mediocrity, small degree, middle rate, middle state.

Mediodia [may-de-o-dee'-ah], *m.* 1. Noon, mid-day, noonday, noontide, meridian. 2. South. 3. South wind.

Mediopaño [may-de-o-pah'-nyo], *m.* Thin woollen cloth.

Mediquillo [may-de-keel'-lyo], *m.* Indian of the Philippine Islands, having medical experience, but no title.

Medir [may-deer'], *va.* 1. To measure, to ascertain the length, magnitude, or quantity of a thing. 2. To measure or examine the number or syllables of a verse. 3. To compare, to measure, to estimate the quality of things. 4. *Medir el suelo*, (Coll.) To measure the ground with one's body, to fall flat on the ground.—*vr.* To be moderate, to act with prudence.

Meditabundo, da [may-de-tah-boon'-do, dah], *a.* Pensive, musing, thoughtful.

Meditación [may-de-tah-the-on'], *f* Meditation, cogitation, deep thought contemplation.

Meditar [may-de-tar'], *va.* To meditate, to contemplate, to consider.

Mediterráneo, nea [may-de-ter-rah'-nay-o, ah], *a.* Mediterranean, encircled with land, midland.

Médium [may'-de-oom], *m.* Medium, a person fit for spiritualistic communications.

Medo, da [may'-do, dah], *a.* Mede, belonging to ancient Media.

Medra [may'-drah], *f.* Proficiency, progress, melioration, improvement.

Medrar [may-drar'], *vn.* To thrive, to prosper, to grow rich; to improve.

Medriñaque [may-dre-nyah'-kay], *m.* 1. A Philippine stuff for lining and stiffening women's garments. 2. A short petticoat.

Medro [may'-dro], *m.* *V.* Medra.—*pl.* Progress, improvement.

Medrosamente, *adv.* Timorously, fearfully, faintly.

Medroso, sa [may-dro'-so, sah], *a.* 1. Fearful, timorous, faint-hearted, cowardly. 2. Terrible, inspiring fear.

Medula, or **Médula** [may-doo'-lah, may'-doo-lah], *f.* 1. Marrow, medulla. 2. The substance or essence of any thing.

Medular [may-doo-lar'], *a.* Medullar, medullary.

Meduloso, sa [may-doo-lo'-so, sah], *a.* Full of marrow, marrowish.

Megaciclo [may-gah-thee'-clo], *m.* Megacycle.

Megáfono [may-gah'-fo-no], *m.* Megaphone.

Megalomanía [meh-gah-lo-mah-nee'-ah], *f.* Megalomania, delusions of grandeur.

Megalómano, na [me-gah-lo'-mah-no, nah], *a.* Megalomaniacal.—*m.* & *f.* Megalomaniac.

Mego, ga [may'-go, gah], *a.* Gentle, mild, meek, peaceful.

Mejana [may-hah'-nah], *f.* Islet in the middle of a river.

Mejicano, na [may-he-cah'-no, nah], *a.* Mexican, native of or belonging to Mexico.—*m.* The Mexican language, Aztec.

Mejido, da [may-hee'-do, dah], *a.* Beaten up with sugar and water: applied to the yolk of eggs.

Mejilla [may-heel'-lyah], *f.* The cheek.

Mejillón, Mijillón [may-hil-lyone'], *m.* A kind of cockle.

Mejor [may-hor'], *a.* Better, *comp.* of Bueno.—*adv.* Better; more exactly. *A lo mejor*, When least expected. *El mejor día*, Some fine day. *A cual mejor*, To a wish. *Llevar lo mejor*, To come off victorious. *Mejor que mejor*, Much better. *Lo mejor será*, The better way will be. *Tanto mejor*, So much the better.

Mejora [may-ho'-rah], *f.* 1. Improvement, melioration, addition, growth. 2. Appeal to a superior court. 3. The act of leaving by will to a legatee a larger share than the legatee by law had a right to. 4. Outbidding at a public sale.

Mejorable [may-ho-rah'-blay], *a.* Improvable.

Mejoramiento [may-ho-rah-me-en'-to], *m.* Improvement, melioration.

Mejorana [may-ho-rah'-nah], *f.* (Bot.) Sweet marjoram. Origanum majorana.

Mejorar [may-ho-rar'], *va.* 1. To improve, to meliorate, to heighten, to cultivate, to mend. 2. To outbid, or bid over. 3. To leave, by will, to a son or grandson an increased share beyond his legal right.—*vn.* To recover from a disease or calamity.—*vr.* To improve, to grow better.

Mejoría [may-ho-ree'-ah], *f.* 1. Improvement, melioration, mending. 2. Repairs. 3. The state of growing better in health. 4. Advantage; superiority.

Mejunje [may-hoon'-hay], *m.* (Coll.) *V.* Menjurje.

Melada [may-lah'-dah], *f.* A slice of toasted bread soaked in honey.

Melado, da [may-lah'-do, dah], *a.* Of the colour of honey.—*pp.* of Melar.

Meladucha [may-lah-doo'-chah], *f.* A coarse, mealy apple.

Meladura [may-lah-doo'-rah], *f.* (Cuba) Purified sap of the sugar-cane; sirup, treacle.

Meláfiro [may-lah'-fe-ro], *m.* Melaphyre, a pre-tertiary basalt.

Melaina [may-lah-ee'-nah], *f.* 1. Black colouring matter of cephalopod mollusks. 2. Pigment of the skin of negroes.

Melancolía [may-lan-co-lee'-ah], *f.* Melancholy, gloomy madness, gloom, gloominess.

Melancólico, ca [may-lan-co'-le-co, cah], *a.* Melancholy, sad, gloomy, fanciful, cloudy, mournful, hypochondriacal.

Melancolizar [may-lan-co-le-thar'], *va.* To affect with melancholy, to render gloomy and dejected, to dispirit.

Melandro [may-lahn'-dro], *m.* (Prov. Ast.) Badger.

Melanesiano, na [may-lah-nay-se-ah'-no, nah], *a.* Melanesian, relating to the islands between New Guinea and the Fijis, called collectively Melanesia.

Melanuro, ra [may-lah-noo'-ro, rah], *a.* Black-tailed.

Melapia [may-lah'-pe-ah], *f.* Kind of apple, related to the pippin.

Melar [may-lar'], *vn.* 1. In sugar-works, to boil down the juice of the sugar-cane a second time, until it obtains the consistency of honey. 2. To deposit honey as bees.

Melaza [may-lah'-thah], *f.* 1. Molasses 2. (Prov.) Dregs of honey.

Melca, *f.* *V.* Zahina.

Melcocha [mel-co'-chah], *f.* Paste made of honey, flour, and spice; molasses candy.

Melcochero [mel-co-chay'-ro], *m.* Molasses-candy maker or seller; gingerbread baker.

Melecina [may-lay-thee'-nah], *f.* (Obs.) *V.* Medicina.

Melele [may-lay'-lay], *a.* Foolish, silly. *V.* Meliloto.

Melena [may-lay'-nah], *f.* 1. Dishevelled hair hanging loose over the eyes. 2. Fore-top hair or mane that falls on a horse's face; also a lion's mane. 3. A soft, fleecy skin put on the forehead of working oxen to prevent their being hurt by the yoke. *Traer a la melena*, To compel one to execute a thing against his will.

Melena [may-lay'-nah], *f.* Black stools from intestinal hemorrhage. (Gr. μέλαινα.)

Melenudo, da [may-lay-noo'-do, dah], *a.* Hairy, having bushy hair.

Melera [may-lay'-rah], *f.* 1. State of melons spoiled by rain. 2. (Bot.) *V.* Buglosa.

Melero [may-lay'-ro], *m.* 1. Dealer in honey. 2. Place destined to preserve honey.

Melgacho [mel-gah'-cho], *m.* Dog-fish. Squalus catulus.

Melgar [mel-gar'], *m.* Patch of wild alfalfa.

Melgarejo [mel-gah-ray'-ho], *m.* The helmsman's post. *V.* Timonera.

Mélico, ca [may'-le-co, cah], *a.* Lyrical, belonging to song, or to lyric poetry. (Acad.)

Melífero, ra [may-lee'-fay-ro, rah], *a.* Melliferous, productive of honey.

Melificado, da [may-le-fe-cah'-do, dah], *a.* Mellifluous, mellificent.—*pp.* of Melificar.

Melificar [may-le-fe-car'], *va.* & *vn.* To make honey as bees.

Melifluamente, *adv.* Mellifluently.

Melifluidad [may-le-floo-e-dahd'], *f.* Mellifluence, suavity, delicacy.

Melifluo, flua [may-lee'-floo-o, ah], *a.* Mellifluous, mellifluent, honey-mouthed; flowing with honey.

Meliloto [may-le-lo'-to], *m.* (Bot.) Bird's-foot trefoil; melilot, a sweet clover. Melilotus officinalis.

Meliloto, ta, *a.* Silly, stupid. (Used also as a noun.)

Melindre [may-leen'-dray], *m.* 1. A sort of fritters made of honey and flour. 2. Prudery, overmuch nicety in conduct. 3. Fastidiousness.

Melindrear [may-lin-dray-ar'], *vn.* To act the prude.

Melindrero, ra [may-lin-dray'-ro, rah]. *V.* Melindroso.

Melindrillo [may-lin-dreel'-lyo], *m.* (Prov.) Ferret, narrow tape.

Melindrizar [may-lin-dre-thar'], *vn.* (Coll.) *V.* Melindrear.

Melindroso, sa [may-lin-dro'-so, sah], *a.* Prudish, precise, finical, too nice, too formal, fastidious, dainty, very particular.

Melisa [may-lee'-sah], *f.* Balm. *Agua de melisa*, Balm-water distilled from the fresh leaves. *V.* Toronjil.

Melocotón [may-lo-co-tone'], *m.* 1. (Bot.) Common peach-tree. Amygdalus persica. 2. Peach, fruit of that tree.

Melocotonero [may-lo-co-to-nay'-ro], *m.* 1. Peach-tree. 2. Vender of peaches.

Melodía [may-lo-dee'-ah], *f.* 1. Melody, harmony, melodiousness. 2. Melody, sweetness of sound.

Melodiosamente, *adv.* Melodiously, harmoniously.

Melodioso, sa [may-lo-de-o'-so, sah], *a.* Melodious, musical, harmonious.
Melodrama [may-lo-drah'-mah], *m.* Melodrama.
Melodramático, ca, *a.* Melodramatic.
Meloe [may-lo'-ay], *m.* Meloe, oil-beetle, blister-beetle. *V.* also CANTÁRIDA.
Melografía [may-lo-grah-fee'-ah], *f.* The art of writing music.
Meloja [may-lo'-hah], *f.* Metheglin, honey boiled with water and fermented: mead.
Melojo [may-lo'-ho], *m.* Plant like the white oak.
Melomanía [may-lo-mah-nee'-ah], *f.* Melomania, a mania for music.
Melómano, na [may-lo'-mah-no, nah], *a.* Music-mad, excessively fond of music.
Melón [may-lone'], *m.* (Bot.) 1. Melon-vine. 2. Musk-melon, cantaloupe. Cucumis melo. *Melón de agua,* Water-melon. (Used in some parts. The Castilian name is *Sandía.*) *Catar el melón,* To sound or pump one. *Decentar el melón,* To cut into the melon, to run risk of loss, to be in for it.
Melonar [may-lo-nar'], *m.* Field or bed of melons.
Melonero, ra [may-lo-nay'-ro, rah], *m.* & *f.* One who raises or deals in melons.
Melonífero, ra [may-lo-nee'-fay-ro, rah], *a.* 1. Melon-bearing. 2. Melon-shaped.
Melosidad [may-lo-se-dahd'], *f.* 1. Sweetness arising from honey, lusciousness. 2. Meekness, gentleness of behaviour.
Meloso, sa [may-lo'-so, sah], *a.* 1. Having the taste or qualities of honey; mellow. 2. Gentle, mild, pleasing.
Melote [may-lo'-tay], *m.* 1. Molasses, treacle. 2. (Prov.) Conserve of honey.
Melsa [mel'-sah], *f.* 1. (Prov.) *V.* BAZO. 2. Phlegm, lentor, slowness.
Melusa [may-loo'-sah], *f.* (Cuba) Portion of honey, or of fruit-juices which sticks to clothing or to the fingers.
Mella [mel'-lyah], *f.* 1. A hollow or crack made in something by a blow which it has received. Notch, nick, in edged tools. 2. Gap, empty space. *Hacer mella,* To make an impression upon the mind by reproach or advice.
Mellado, da [mel-lyah-do, dah], *a.* & *pp.* of MELLAR. 1. Notched, hacked. 2. Toothless, wanting teeth.
Mellar [mel-lyar'], *va.* 1. To notch, to hack, to cut in small hollows. 2. To deprive of lustre and splendour. *Mellar la honra,* To wound one's character and honour.
Mellica [mel-lyee'-cah], *f.* (Prov.) *V.* MELLIZA.
Melliza [mel-lyee'-thah], *f.* Kind of sausage made of lean pork, almonds, pine-apple kernels, and honey.
Mellizo, za [mel-lyee'-tho, thah], *a.* *V.* GEMELO.
Mellón [mel-lyone'], *m.* A handful of straw lighted as a torch.
Membrado, da [mem-brah'-do, dah], *a.* (Her.) Membered: applied to the beak and legs of a bird, when of a different tincture from the body.
Membrana [mem-brah'-nah], *f.* 1. Membrane, a thin skin; a caul. 2. (Anat.) Membrane.
Membranáceo, cea [mem-brah-nah'-thay-o, ah], *a.* Membranaceous, membrane-like.
Membranoso, sa [mem-brah-no'-so, sah], *a.* Membranous, filmy.
Membrete [mem-bray'-tay], *m.* 1. Short annotation or note written to remember a thing. 2. In letters or notes, a line in which the person's name is inserted to whom it is written. 3. A note or small bit of paper given as a memorandum to a person in office, to put him in mind of any one's pretentions. 4. A card of invitation.
Membrilla [mem-breel'-lyah], *f.* (Prov.) The tender bud of a quince-tree.
Membrillar [mem-bril-lyar'], *m.* Plantation of quince-trees.
Membrillero, Membrillo [mem-bril-lyay'-ro, mem-breel'-lyo], *m.* 1. (Bot.) Quince-tree. Pyrus cydonia, *L.* 2. Quince, the fruit of the quince-tree.
Membrudamente, *adv.* Robustly, strongly.
Membrudo, da [mem-broo'-do, dah], *a.* Strong, robust, corpulent; membered.
Mementos [may-men'-tose], *m. pl.* The two parts of the mass, in which the sacrifice is offered for the quick and the dead.
Memo, ma [may'-mo, mah], *a.* Silly, foolish. *Hacerse memo,* To pretend not to understand.
Memorable, Memorando, da [may-mo-rah'-blay, may-mo-rahn'-do, dah], *a.* Memorable, commemorable, notable, famous.
Memorablemente, *adv.* Memorably.
Memorándum [may-mo-rahn'-doom], *m.* 1. Memorandum, note-book. 2. Memorandum, diplomatic note of informal character, often not signed, set down for reference or explanation.
Memorar [may-mo-rar'], *va.* To remember, to record, to mention.
Memoratísimo, ma [may-mo-rah-tee'-se-mo, mah], *a. sup.* Worthy of eternal memory.
Memoria [may-mo'-re-ah], *f.* 1. Memory, reminiscence, recollection. 2. Fame, glory. 3. Memory, memorial, monumental record. 4. An anniversary or pious work which any one founds to preserve his memory. 5. Memoir, an account of transactions familiarly written: commonly used in the plural. 6. Bill, account. 7. Memorandum, a note to help the memory. 8. Codicil. *Hacer memoria,* To remember, to put in mind. *De memoria,* By heart. *Hablar de memoria,* To talk at random.—*pl.* 1. Compliments, expression of kindness and civility. 2. Memorandum-book. 3. Two or more rings put on the finger as a memorandum.
Memorial [may-mo-re-ahl'], *m.* 1. Memorandum-book. 2. Memorial, brief.
Memorialista [may-mo-re-ah-lees'-tah], *m.* An amanuensis; a person who writes petitions for others.
Memorión [may-mo-re-on'], *m. aug.* A strong memory.
Memorioso, sa [may-mo-re-o'-so, sah], *a.* Mindful, retentive: applied to the memory.
Mena [may'-nah], *f.* 1. Small sea-fish, kind of anchovy. 2. A mineral vein; ore. 3. *V.* VITOLA. Ball-gauge. 4. (Naut.) Size of cordage.
Ménade [may'-nah-day], *f.* 1. Bacchante, priestess of Bacchus. 2. A woman beside herself, in a frenzy.
Menador, ra [may-nah-dor', rah], *m.* & *f.* (Prov.) Winder, one who turns a wheel to wind silk.
Menaje [may-nah'-hay], *m.* Furniture, movables, house-stuff.
Menar [may-nar'], *va.* (Prov. Murcia.) To wind silk on a reel or spinning-jenny.
Mención [men-the-on'], *f.* Mention, oral or written recital of any thing.
Mencionar [men-the-o-nar'], *va.* To mention, to name.
Mendicación, *f.* *V.* MENDIGUEZ.
Mendicante [men-de-cahn'-tay], *a.* Mendicant, begging.
Mendicante, *m.* Mendicant, one of a begging fraternity.
Mendicidad [men-de-the-dahd'], *f.* Mendicity, mendicancy, beggary.
Mendigante, ta [men-de-gahn'-tay, tah], *m.* & *f.* Mendicant, beggar.
Mendigar [men-de-gar'], *va.* To ask charity, to live upon alms, to beg, to mendicate; to crave, to entreat.
Mendigo [men-dee'-go], *m.* Beggar.
Mendiguez [men-de-gheth'], *f.* Beggary, indigence, mendicancy.
Mendosamente, *adv.* Falsely, erroneously, equivocally.
Mendoso, sa [men-do'-so, sah], *a.* False, mendacious.
Mendrugo [men-droo'-go], *m.* Broken bread given to beggars.
Mendruguillo [men-droo-geel'-lyo], *m. dim.* A small bit of bread.
Meneador, ra [may-nay-ah-dor', rah], *m.* & *f.* Mover, manager, director.
Menear [may-nay-ar'], *va.* 1. To move from place to place. 2. To manage, to direct.—*vr.* 1. To be brisk and active, to stir about. 2. To wriggle, to waddle; to move from side to side. *Menear las manos,* To fight; to work expertly.
Meneo [may-nay'-o], *m.* 1. A wriggling or waddling motion of the body. 2. (Obs.) Trade, business.
Menester [may-nes-terr'], *m.* 1. Necessity, need, want. *Ser menester,* To be necessary, to be wanting. 2. Employment, business, occupation, office.—*pl.* (Coll.) 1. Natural or corporal necessities. 2. Implements, necessary tools of a workman.
Menesteroso, sa [may-nes-tay-ro'-so, sah], *a.* Needy, necessitous.
Menestra [may-nes'-trah], *f.* 1. Pottage made of different pulse and roots. 2. Vegetable soup.
Menestral [may-nes-trahl'], *m.* Mechanic, handicraftsman, workman.
Mengano, na [men-gah'-no, nah], *m.* & *f.* Such a one; so and so (the second of two) (fr. MENGUE).
Mengua [men'-goo-ah], *f.* 1. Decay, decline. 2. Poverty, indigence. 3. Disgrace arising from cowardly conduct.
Menguadamente, *adv.* Ignominiously.
Menguado [men-goo-ah'-do], *m.* 1. Coward, a silly, mean-spirited fellow. 2. An avaricious, miserable wretch. 3. Decrease, narrowing of stockings, etc.
Menguado, da [men-goo-ah'-do, dah], *a.* 1. Diminished, impaired, stunted. 2. Cowardly, pusillanimous; foolish. *Hora menguada,* Fatal moment.—*pp.* of MENGUAR.
Menguante [men-goo-ahn'-tay], *m.* 1. Ebb-tide, low-water, neap-tide. 2. Decline, decay. 3. Decrease of the moon.
Menguar [men-goo-ar'], *va.* 1. To decay, to decline, to fall off. 2. To fail, to be deficient. 3. To narrow stockings.
Mengue [men'-gay], *m.* (Coll.) The deuce, the devil.
Menhir [men-eer'], *m.* Menhir, a great megalithic vertical stone.
Menina [may-nee'-nah], *f.* A young lady who in childhood enters the service of the royal family of Spain, by waiting upon the queen.
Meninge [may-neen'-hay], *f.* Meninges membranes enveloping the brain and spinal cord.
Meningitis [may-neen-hee'-tis], *f.* Meningitis, inflammation of the membranes of the brain.
Menino [may-nee'-no], *m.* 1. Page of the queen and *infantas* of Spain. 2. (Prov.) An affected, spruce little fellow.
Menipea [may-ne-pay'-ah], *f.* Kind of satire in prose and verse.
Menique [may-nee'-kay], *a.* Applied to the little finger of the hand: it is

also used as a substantive. *V.* MENIQUE.

Menisco [may-nees'-co], *m.* Meniscus. glass concave on one side and convex on the other.

Menjuí [men-hoo-ee'], *m.* *V.* BENJUÍ.

Menjunje, Menjurje [men-hoon'-hay. men-hoor'-hay], *m.* (Coll.) Beverage composed of different ingredients, and of an unpleasant taste.

Menologio [may-no-lo'-he-o], *m.* Menology, the martyrology of the Greeks divided into the months of the year.

Menopausia [may-no-pah'-oo-se-ah], *f.* Menopause, cessation of menstruation. the change of life in women.

Menor [may-nor'], *m.* & *f.* 1. Minor. one under age. 2. Minor premise, the second proposition in a syllogism. 3. Minor, minorite, a Franciscan friar or nun.—*pl.* 1. The third class in a grammar-school. 2. Minor orders.

Menor [may-nor'], *a. comp.* 1. Less, smaller, minor. 2. Minor, in music. *Menor edad*, Minority, under age. *Hermano menor*, Younger brother. *Por menor*, By retail, in small parts; minutely.

Menorete [may-no-ray'-tay], *a. dim. coll.* *Al menorete* or *por el menorete*, At least.

Menoría [may-no-ree'-ah], *f.* Inferiority, subordination.

Menorista [may-no-rees'-tah], *m.* Student of grammar in the third class.

Menorquín, na [may-nor-keen', nah], *a.* Native of or belonging to the island Minorca.

Menorragia [may-nor-rah'-he-ah], *f.* (Med.) Menorrhagia, excessive menstrual flow.

Menos [may'-nos], *adv.* 1. Less, in a lower degree. *Menos valer*, Less worthy 2. Except, with the exception of. *A lo menos* or *por lo menos*, At least, however. *Mucho menos*, Much less. *Poco más o menos*, A little more or less. *Venir a menos*, To decay, to grow worse; to become poor. *Ni más, ni menos*, Neither more nor less, just equal.

Menoscabador, ra [may-nos-cah-bah-dor', rah], *m.* & *f.* Detracter, lessener.

Menoscabar [may-nos-cah-bar'], *va.* 1. To impair, to lessen, to make worse. 2. To reduce, to deteriorate.

Menoscabo [may-nos-cah'-bo], *m.* Diminution, deterioration, loss.

Menoscuenta [may-nos-coo-en'-tah], *f.* Discount.

Menospreciable, *a.* Despicable, contemptible.

Menospreciablemente, *adv.* Contemptuously.

Menospreciador, ra [may-nos-pray-the-ah-dor', rah], *m.* & *f.* Contemner, despiser.

Menospreciar [may-nos-pray-the-ar'], *va.* To underrate, to undervalue; to despise, to contemn, to neglect, to overlook, to make light of.

Menosprecio [may-nos-pray'-the-o], *m.* Contempt, scorn; the act of undervaluing a thing, neglect, contumely.

Mensaje [men-sah'-hay], *m.* 1. Message, despatch, errand. 2. Petition or congratulation which the Cortes addressed to the king. 3. An official communication between the legislative and the executive power. (Acad.

Mensajero, ra [men-sah-hay'-ro, rah], *m.* & *f.* 1. Messenger. 2. The secretary-bird. 3. (Naut.) Bull's-eye traveller. a wooden thimble.

Ménsola, *f.* (Arch.) *V.* MÉNSULA.

Menstruación [mens-troo-ah-the-on'], *f.* Menstruation

Menstrual [mens-troo-ahl'], *a.* Menstrual.

Menstrualmente, *adv.* Monthly, menstrually.

Menstruante [mens-troo-ahn'-tay], *a.* Menstruating.

Menstruar [mens-troo-ar'], *vn.* To menstruate.

Menstruo [mens'-troo-o], *m.* 1. Menses, catamenia, courses. 2. (Chem.) Menstruum, any liquor used as a solvent.

Menstruo, a [mens'-troo-o, ah], *a.* Menstruous, monthly, menstrual.

Menstruosa [mens-troo-o'-sah], *a.* (Med.) Applied to a female menstruating.

Mensual [men-soo-ahl'], *a.* Monthly, menstrual.

Mensualidad [men-soo-ah-le-dahd'], *f.* A month's pay; monthly salary.

Mensualmente. *adv.* Monthly.

Ménsula [men'-soo-lah], *f.* (Arch.) Cantilever, bracket.

Mensura [men-soo'-rah], *f.* Measure.

Mensurabilidad [men-soo-rah-be-le-dahd'], *f.* Mensurability.

Mensurable [men-soo-rah'-blay], *a.* Mensurable.

Mensurador, ra [men-soo-rah-dor', rah], *m.* & *f.* Measurer, meter.

Mensural [men-soo-rahl'], *a.* Applied to any thing used to measure.

Mensurar [men-soo-rar'], *va.* *V.* MEDIR and JUZGAR.

Menta [men'-tah], *f.* (Bot.) Mint. Mentha officinalis.

Mentado, da [men-tah'-do, dah], *a.* Famous, celebrated, renowned.—*pp.* of MENTAR.

Mental [men-tahl'], *a.* Mental, intellectual, ideal.

Mentalidad [men-tah-le-dahd'], *f.* Mentality, mind.

Mentalmente, *adv.* Mentally, intellectually, ideally.

Mentar [men-tar'], *va.* To mention, to record.

Mentastro [men-tahs'-tro], *m.* (Bot.) *V.* MASTRANZO.

Mente [men'-tay], *f.* 1. Mind, understanding; intellectual power. 2. Sense, meaning; will, disposition.

Mentecatada, *f.* *V.* MENTECATERÍA.

Mentecatería [men-tay-cah-tay-ree'-ah], *f.* Folly, absurdity, nonsense.

Mentecatez [men-tay-cah-teth'], *f.* (Littl. us.) Foolishness, silliness.

Mentecato, ta [men-tay-cah'-to, tah], *a.* Silly, foolish, stupid, crack-brained.—*n.* Fool.

Mentecatón, na [men-tay-cah-tone', nah], *a. aug.* Very silly.

Mentidero [men-te-day'-ro], *m.* Talking corner, where idlers meet to tattle.

Mentir [men-teer'], *va.* 1. To lie, to utter falsehoods. 2. To disappoint, to frustrate, to deceive, to feign. 3. To gainsay, to retract; to equivocate, to falsify.

Mentira [men-tee'-rah], *f.* 1. Lie, falsehood, mendacity. 2. Error, mistake in writing.

Mentirilla, ita [men-te-reel'-lyah, ee'-tah], *f. dim.* Falsehood told in jest. *De mentirillas*, In jest.

Mentirón [men-te-rone'], *m. aug.* Great lie.

Mentirosamente, *adv.* Falsely, deceitfully, lyingly.

Mentirosito, ta [men-te-ro-see'-to, tah] *a. dim.* A little false, deceitful.

Mentiroso, sa [men-te-ro'-so, sah], *a.* 1. Lying, mendacious. 2. Erroneous, equivocal, incorrect.

Mentís [men-tees'], *m.* You lie, or thou liest. Term of insult.

Mentol [men-tole'], *m.* Menthol.

Mentolado, da [men-to-lah'-do, dah], *a.* Mentholated.

Mentón [men-tone'], *m.* Chin.

Mentor [men-tor'], *m.* Mentor, counsellor, guide.

Menú [may-noo'], *m.* Menu, bill of fare.

Menudear [may-noo-day-ar'], *va.* To repeat, to detail minutely.—*vn.* To relate or describe little things. (Com.) To sell by retail.

Menudencia [may-noo-den'-the-ah], *f.* Trifle, littleness; minuteness, minute accuracy.

Menudeo [may-noo-day'-o], *m.* Act of repeating minutely; retail.

Menudero, ra [may-noo-day'-ro, rah], *m.* & *f.* Dealer in tripes, giblets, sausages, etc.

Menudico, ica, ito, ita [may-noo-dee'-co, cah], *a.* Somewhat small.

Menudillo [may-noo-deel'-lyo], *m.* Extremities of animals. *Menudillos*, Giblets of fowls.

Menudo, da [may-noo'-do, dah], *a.* 1. Small, slender of body; minute. 2. Of no moment or value, worthless. 3. Common, vulgar. 4. Examining minutely into things. 5. Small money, change. 6. Exact, scrupulous. *Hombre menudo*, A mean, miserable fellow. *A menudo*, Repeatedly, frequently, continually, often. *Por menudo*, Minutely; by retail.

Menudo [may-noo'-do], *m.* 1. Intestines, viscera. 2. Tithe of fruits. *Menudos*, Copper coin.

Menura, or **Menura-lira** [may-noo'-rah-lee'-rah], *f.* Lyre-bird. Menura superba.

Meñique [may-nyee'-kay], *a.* 1. Applied to the little finger of the hand: in this sense it is used as a substantive. 2. (Coll.) Very small.

Meollar [may-ol-lyar'], *m.* (Naut.) Thin line of spun-yarn made of oakum or untwisted ropes.

Meollo [may-ol'-lyo], *m.* 1. Marrow. 2. Judgment, understanding. 3. Soft part of bread, crumb. 4. The substance or essential part of any thing.

Meón, na [may-on', nah], *a.* (Coll.) Continually making water.

Meona [may-o'-nah], *f.* (Coll.) New-born female infant, in distinction from the male.

Mequetrefe [may-kay-tray'-fay], *m.* Insignificant, noisy fellow, jackanapes, coxcomb.

Meramente [may-rah-men'-tay], *adv.* Merely, solely, nakedly.

Merar [may-rar'], *va.* To mix liquors: generally applied to the mixture of wine and water.

Merca [merr'-cah], *f.* (Coll.) A purchase. *V.* COMPRA.

Mercachifle [mer cah-chee'-flay], *m.* Peddler, hawker.

Mercadantesco, ca [mer-cah-dan-tes'-co, cah], *a.* Mercantile.

Mercadear [mer-cah-day-ar'], *vn.* To trade, to traffic.

Mercader [mer-cah-derr'], *m.* Dealer, trader, shopkeeper.

Mercadera [mer-cah-day'-rah], *f.* Shopkeeper's wife, tradeswoman.

Mercadería [mer-cah-day-ree'-ah], *f.* 1. Commodity, merchandise. Trade, the business of a trader.—*pl.* Goods.

Mercado [mer-cah'-do], *m.* 1. Market, marketing. 2. Market, market place, mart. *Mercado negro*, Black market.

Mercadotecnia [mer-cah-do-tec'-ne-ah], *f.* Marketing, marketing techniques.

Mercaduría [mer-cah-doo-ree'-ah], *f.* Merchandise, trade.

Mercal [mer-cahl'], *m.* Ancient Spanish copper coin.

Mercancía [mer-can-thee'-ah], *f.* 1. Trade, traffic. 2. Merchandise, salable goods.

Mercante [mer-cahn'-tay], *m. & a.* Dealer, trader; mercantile, commercial. *Buque mercante*, A trading-vessel.

Mercantil [mer-can-teel'], *a.* Commercial, mercantile, merchant-like.

Mercantilizar [mer-can-te-le-thar'], *va.* To commercialize.

Mercantilmente, *adv.* Merchantly, in a commercial or mercantile manner.

Mercar [mer-car'], *va. V.* COMPRAR.

Merced [mer-thed'], *f.* 1. Gift, favour, grace, mercy. 2. Wages, pay for service, especially to day-labourers. 3. Will, pleasure. 4. Appellation of civility, with which untitled persons are addressed. *Vuestra* or *vuesa merced*, Your honour, your worship, sir: in abbreviation V., or Vd.; the latter preferred. 5. A religious military order, whose chief object is to redeem captives. 6. *Merced de tierra*, A grant of land. *Estar a merced*, To live at another's expense. *Muchas mercedes*, Many thanks for the favours received. *Hágame Vd. la merced*, Do me the favour. *No estar hoy para mercedes*, Not to be in an obliging temper.

Mercenario [mer-thay-nah'-re-o], *m.* 1. Day-labourer. 2. Mercenary, hireling.

Mercenario, ria [mer-thay-nah'-re-o,ah], *a.* 1. Mercenary, hired, hireling. 2. Applied to a friar or nun of the religious order of *la Merced*: in this sense it is also used as a substantive.

Mercería [mer-thay-ree'-ah], *f.* 1. Trade of a haberdasher, who deals in small wares, mercery. 2. (Amer.) Fine hardware store.

Mercerizado, da [mer-thay-re-thah'-do, dah], *a.* Mercerized.

Mercero [mer-thay'-ro], *m.* 1. Haberdasher. 2. The keeper of a fine hardware store.

Mercurial [mer-coo-re-ahl'], *m. & a.* 1. (Bot.) All good, mercury. Mercurialis. *Mercurial añal* or *medicinal*, Annual mercury. Mercurialis annua. 2. Mercurial.

Mercúrico [mer-coo'-re-co], *a.* Mercuric, of the higher combining equivalence of mercury.

Mercurio [mer-coo'-re-o], *m.* 1. Mercury, quicksilver. 2. Planet Mercury. 3. A periodical publication so called.

Mercurioso, sa [mer-coo-re-o'-so, sah], *a.* Mercurous, relative to mercury, especially in its lower valence.

Mercurocromo [mer-coo-ro-cro'-mo], *m.* (Med.) Mercurochrome.

Merchante [mer-chahn'-tay], *m.* Merchant, who buys and sells goods without keeping an open shop.—*a.* Merchant: applied to a trading-vessel. *V.* MERCANTE.

Merdellón, na [mer-del-lyone', nah], *a.* (Low) Slovenly, unclean, dirty.

Merdoso, sa [mer-do'-so, sah], *a.* Nasty, filthy.

Mere [may'-ray], *adv.* (Obs.) Merely. *V.* MERAMENTE.

Merecedor, ra [may-ray-thay-dor', rah], *m. & f.* One who deserves reward or punishment.

Merecer [may-ray-therr'], *vn.* 1. To deserve, to merit. 2. *V.* LOGRAR. 3. To owe, to be indebted for. *He merecido a mi hermano aquella honra*, I am indebted to my brother for that honour. —*va.* To do any thing deserving reward or censure. *Merecer el trabajo*, To be worth the while.

Merecidamente, *adv.* Worthily, meritoriously, condignly.

Merecido, da [may-ray-thee'-do, dah], *a.* Meritorious, condign.—*pp.* of MERECER.

Merecido [may-ray-thee'-do], *m.* Condign punishment.

Merecimiento [may-ray-the-me-en'-to], *m.* Condignity, merit, desert.

Merendar [may-ren-dar'], *vn.* 1. To take a collation between dinner and supper. 2. (Prov.) To eat the principal meal at noon.—*va.* 1. To pry into another's writings or actions. 2. To anticipate, to be in advance of another.

Merendero, ra [may-ren-day'-ro, rah], *a.* Picking up the seeds in corn-fields: applied to crows.

Merendilla [may-ren-deel'-lyah], *f. dim.* of MERIENDA. A light lunch.

Merendona [may-ren-do'-nah], *f. aug.* A plentiful or splendid collation.

Merengue [may-ren'-gay], *m.* Kiss, sugar-plum, a confection of sugar and white of eggs; meringue.

Meretricio, cia [may-ray-tree'-the-o, ah], *a.* Meretricious, harlot, lustful.

Meretricio [may-ray-tree'-the-o], *m.* Carnal sin.

Meretriz [may-ray-treeth'], *f. V.* RAMERA.

Merey [may-ray'-e], *f.* (Bot.) Cashew-tree. Anacardium occidentale.

(*Yo merezco, yo merezca*, from *Merecer. V.* ABORRECER.)

Mergánsar [mer-gahn'-sar], *m.* (Orn.) Goosander, merganser. Mergus merganser.

Mergo [merr'-go], *m.* (Orn.) Diver.

Merián [may-re-ahn'], *com.* (Zool.) Merian-opossum of South America, a marsupial without a pouch.

Meridiana [may-re-de-ah'-nah], *f.* Meridional line. *A la meridiana*, At midday, noon.

Meridiano [may-re-de-ah'-no], *m.* Meridian, a large circle of the celestial sphere. *Meridianos.* Gladiators who fought naked.—*a.* Meridional, noon.

Meridional [may-re-de-o-nahl'], *a.* Southern, southerly, meridional.

Merienda [may-re-en'-dah], *f.* 1. Luncheon, collation between dinner and supper. 2. (Prov.) Principal meal eaten at noon. 3. (Coll.) Hump-back. *Hacer merienda de negros*, To make a hodge-podge of any thing to the prejudice of the right owner's just claim.

(*Yo meriendo, yo meriende*, from *Merendar. V.* ACERTAR.)

Merindad [may-rin-dahd'], *f.* District of the jurisdiction of a *merino*, or judge of the sheep-walks.

Merino [may-ree'-no], *m.* 1. Royal judge and superintendent of sheep-walks. 2. Shepherd of merino sheep. 3. Merino wool.

Merino, na [may-ree'-no, nah], *a.* 1. Moving from pasture to pasture: applied to sheep. 2. Applied to thick, curled hair.

Méritamente, *adv. V.* MERECIDAMENTE.

Mérito [may'-re-to], *m.* Merit, desert, excellence, virtue.

Meritoriamente, *adv.* Meritoriously.

Meritorio, ria [may-re-to'-re-o, ah], *a.* 1. Meritorious. 2. Employed in an office, without salary; emeritus.

Merla [merr'-lah], *f.* (Orn.) Blackbird, merle. Turdus merula.

Merlán [merr-lahn'], *m.* The European whiting, a small fish of the cod family. Merlangus merlangus.

Merlín [mer-leen'], *m.* (Naut.) Marline, a loosely twisted hempen line.

Merlín, *m.* Merlin, name of a famous enchanter. *Saber más que Merlín*, To be very shrewd or keen.

Merlo [merr'-lo], *m.* (Zool.) A sea-fish very frequent in the Mediterranean. Labrus merula.

Merlón [mer-lone'], *m.* (Mil.) Merlon the solid part of a parapet between the embrasures.

Merluza [mer-loo'-thah], *f.* Hake, merluce, a fish of the cod family. Merlucius smiridus.

Merma [merr'-mah], *f.* Waste, leakage, soakage.

Mermar [mer-mar'], *vn.* To waste, to diminish, to dwindle, to lessen.

Mermelada [mer-may-lah'-dah], *f.* Marmalade, a conserve. *Brava mermelada*, A fine hodge-podge, in contempt.

Mero [may'-ro], *m.* Pollack, a Mediterranean food-fish of delicate flavour. Pollachius. (Note.—This fish belongs to the perch family; hence the name pollack is probably incorrect, the latter belonging to the cod-fishes.)

Mero, ra [may'-ro, rah], *a.* Mere, pure, simple, naked.

Merodeador [may-ro-day-ah-dor'], *m.* Marauder, pillager.

Merodear [may-ro-day-ar'], *vn.* To pillage, to maraud.

Merodeo [may-ro-day'-o], *m.* The act of pillaging or marauding.

Merodista [may-ro-dees'-tah], *m.* Pillager, marauder.

Merovingio, gia [may-ro-veen'-he-o, ah], *a.* Merovingian.

Mes [mess], *m.* 1. Month. 2. Catamenia, menses, courses. 3. Monthly wages. *Meses mayores*, 1. Last months of pregnancy. 2. Months immediately preceding harvest. *Al mes*, In a month's time, by the month, at the expiration of a month.

Mesa [may'-sah], *f.* 1. Table, an article of furniture. 2. Table, the fare or viands put on a table. *El general tiene buena mesa*, The general keeps a good table. 3. Table, a flat surface on the top of hills or mountains. 4. Landing-place of a staircase. 5. In printing offices, a case for types. 6. The table of accounts of the rents of cathedral churches, prelates, or dignitaries in Spain. 7. Set or rubber, any one of the games played at a truck-table. 8. Spanish truck-table, or the hire of it. 9. The flat of a sword, of a shoemaker's awl, etc. 10. Communion table. *Mesa de cambios*, Bank. *Levantar la mesa*, To take away the cloth. *Mesa franca*, Open table. *Sentarse a mesa puesta*, To live at other people's expense. *Mesas de guarnición*, (Naut.) Channels to which the shrouds are fastened. *Mesas de guarnición del palo mayor*, Main channels. *Mesas de guarnición del trinquete*, Fore channels. *Mesa de milanos*, Scanty table. *Mesa redonda*, (1) Round table, that which has no preference or distinction in the seats. (2) Table d'hote in a hotel. *Media mesa*, Second table; lower-priced or servants' table. *Mesa traviesa*, Cross-table in the refectory of a convent where the superior sits.

Mesada [may-sah'-dah], *f.* Monthly pay, wages, or allowance; stipend.

Mesana [may-sah'-nah], *f.* (Naut.) Mizzen-mast or sail.

Mesar [may-sar'], *va.* To pluck off the hair with the hands.

Mescal, *m. V.* MEZCAL.

Meseguero [may-say-gay'-ro], *m.* 1. Keeper of the fruits of the harvest. 2. (Prov.) The guard of the vineyard.

Meseguero, ra [may-say-gay'-ro, rah], *a.* Relating to the harvest fruits.

Mesentérico, ca [may-sen-tay'-re-co, cah], *a.* Mesenteric, relating to the mesentery.

Mesenterio [may-sen-tay'-re-o], *m.* Mesentery, a fold of the peritoneum enveloping the small intestine and connecting it to the abdominal wall posteriorly.

Meseraica [may-say-rah'-e-cah], *a.* Mesenteric (vein). The portal vein with its branches.

Mesero [may-say'-ro], *m.* Journeyman who works for monthly wages.

Meseta [may-say'-tah], *f.* Landing-place of a staircase. *Meseta de guarnición,* (Naut.) Backstay stool.

Mesías [may-see'-as], *m.* Messiah, Jesus Christ.

Mesilla [may-seel'-lyah], *f.* 1. (Dim.) Small table; sideboard. 2. Screw. 3. Board-wages. 4. Censure by way of a jest. *Mesilla corrida,* A landing-place between two staircases.

Mesillo [may-seel'-lyo], *m.* First menses after parturition.

Mesinés, sa [may-se-nays', sah], *a.* Of or belonging to Messina, a city of Sicily.

Mesino, na [may-see'-no, nah], *a.* Native of or belonging to Metz.

Mesita [may-see'-tah], *f. dim.* 1. A small table. 2. *Mesita de un pie,* Stand.

Mesmedad [mes-may-dahd'], *f.* Nature, actuality, used only in the pleonastic phrase: *Por su misma mesmedad,* By the very fact.

Mesmerismo [mes-may-rees'-mo], *m.* Mesmerism, hypnotism.

Mesmo, ma [mes'-mo, mah], *a.* (Obs.) *V.* MISMO. *Eso mesmo, V.* TAMBIÉN.

Mesnadero [mes-nah-day'-ro], *m.* (Obs.) Commander of a body of armed men.

Mesocracia [may-so-crah'-the-ah], *f.* Mesocracy, government by the middle class.

Meson [may-sone'], *m.* 1. Inn, hostelry. 2. (Phy. & Chem.) Meson.

Mesonaje [may-so-nah'-hay], *m.* Street or place which contains numerous inns and public-houses.

Mesoncillo [may-son-theel'-lyo], *m. dim.* A little inn.

Mesonero, ra [may-so-nay'-ro, rah], *m. & f.* Inn-keeper, publican, landlord of an inn, host, hostess.

Mesonero, ra [may-so-nay'-ro, rah], *a.* Waiting, serving in an inn.

Mesonista [may-so-nees'-tah], *com.* Waiter in an inn or public-house.

Mesopotámico, ca [may-so-po-tah'-me-co, cah], *a.* Mesopotamian, relating to Mesopotamia.

Mesta [mes'-tah], *f.* 1. The proprietors of cattle and sheep, considered as a body. 2. Annual meeting of shepherds and owners of flocks, which bears the title of *El honrado concejo de la Mesta,* The honorable board of *Mesta.*

Mestal [mes-tahl'], *m.* (Obs.) A piece of barren, uncultivated ground.

Mesteño, ña [mes-tay'-nyo, yah], *a.* 1. Belonging to the *mesta* or graziers. 2. *V.* MOSTRENCO.

Mester [mes-terr'], *m.* (Obs.) *V.* MENESTER.

Mestizar [mes-te-thar'], *va.* To cross breeds or races of animals. (Acad.)

Mestizo, za [mes-tee'-tho, thah], *a.* 1. Of a mongrel breed, hybrid, hybridous. 2. (Amer.) Mestee or mustee, the offspring of a white man and an Indian woman, or vice versâ.

Mesto [mes'-to], *m.* (Bot.) 1. Large, prickly oak. Quercus ægylops. 2. Turkey oak. *V.* REBOLLO.

Mestura [mes-too'-rah], *f.* (Prov.) Mashlin, mixed wheat and rye.

Mesura [may-soo'-rah], *f.* 1. A grave deportment, a serious countenance. 2. Civility, politeness. 3. Moderation; measure.

Mesuradamente, *adv.* Gently, prudently, measurably.

Mesurado, da [may-soo-rah'-do, dah], *a.* Moderate, circumspect, modest; regular, temperate, regulated.—*pp.* of MESURAR.

Mesurar [may-soo-rar'], *va.* To assume a serious countenance, to act with solemn reserve.—*vr.* To behave with modesty and prudence.

Meta [may'-tah], *f.* 1. Boundary, limit.

Metábola [may-tah'-bo-lah], *f.* 1. (Med.) Transformation of one disease into another. 2. Metabolism, the sum of the assimilative and destructive processes in the body. 3. (Rhet.) Pleonasm, bringing together several synonymous expressions to set forth a single idea.

Metabolismo [may-tah-bo-lees'-mo], *m.* Metabolism. *Metabolismo basal,* Basal metabolism.

Metacarpiano, na [may-tah-car-pe-ah'-no, nah], *a.* Metacarpal, relating to the metacarpus.

Metacarpo [may-tah-car'-po], *m.* (Anat.) Metacarpus, the part of the hand between the wrist and the fingers.

Metacronismo [may-tah-cro-nees'-mo], *m.* Metachronism, anachronism.

Metafísica [may-tah-fee'-se-cah], *f.* 1. Metaphysic, metaphysics, ontology. 2. The art of subtilizing in any matter.

Metafísicamente, *adv.* Metaphysically.

Metafísico, ca [may-tah-fee'-se-co, cah], *a.* Metaphysical, abstract, obscure.

Metafísico [may-tah-fee'-se-co], *m.* Metaphysician, ontologist.

Metáfora [may-tah'-fo-rah], *f.* Metaphor, a rhetorical figure.

Metafóricamente, *adv.* Metaphorically, figuratively.

Metafórico, ca [may-tah-fo'-re-co, cah], *a.* Metaphorical.

Metaforizar [may-tah-fo-re-thar'], *va.* To use metaphors.

Metal [may-tahl'], *m.* 1. Metal. 2. Brass, latten. 3. The sound or tone (tone-colour) of the voice. 4. Quality, nature or condition of a thing.

Metalario, Metálico, Metalista [may-tah-lah'-re-o, may-tah'-le-co, may-tah-lees'-tah], *m.* Workman or dealer in metal, metallist, metallurgist.

Metalescente [may-tah-les-then'-tay], *a.* Metallic in lustre.

Metálica [may-tah'-le-cah], *f.* *V.* METALURGIA.

Metálico, ca [may-tah'-le-co, cah], *a.* 1. Metallic. 2. Medallic, pertaining to medals.—*m.* Bullion. *Metálico en caja,* (Com.) Cash on hand.

Metalífero, ra [may-tah-lee'-fay-ro, rah], *a.* (Poet.) Metalliferous.

Metalistería [may-tah-lis-tay-ree'-ah], *f.* Metalworking.

Metalizar [may-tah-le-thar'], *va.* To make a body acquire metallic properties.—*vr.* 1. To be converted into or impregnated with metal. 2. (Met.) To be controlled by love of money.

Metalografía [may-tah-lo-grah-fee'-ah], *f.* Metallography.

Metaloide [may-tah-lo'-e-day], *m.* Metalloid, a simple body resembling the metals in some of its properties, such as sulphur, carbon, phosphorus.

Metalurgia [may-tah-loor'-he-ah], or **Metalúrgica,** *f.* Metallurgy.

Metalúrgico, ca [may-tah-loor'-he-co, cah], *a.* Relating to metallurgy.

Metalúrgico, *m.* Metallurgist.

Metalla [may-tahl'-lyah], *f.* Small piece of gold leaf used to cover parts imperfectly gilt.

Metamorfosear [may-tah-mor-fo-say-ar'], *va.* To metamorphose, to transform.

Metamórfico, ca [may-tah-mor'-fe-co, cah], *a.* (Geol.) Metamorphic, igneous: applied to rocks.

Metamorfosi, Metamorfosis [may-tah-mor-fo'-sis], *f.* Metamorphosis, transformation.

Metaplasmo [may-tah-plahs'-mo], *m.* (Gram.) The changing, taking away, or adding to the letters of a word; metaplasm.

Metástasis [may-tahs'-tah-sis], *f.* (Med.) Metastasis, translation or removal of a disease from one place to another.

Metasticizar [may-tahs-te-the-thar'], *vn.* To metastasize.

Metatarsiano, na [may-tah-tar-se-ah'-no, nah], *a.* (Anat.) Metatarsal.

Metatarso [may-tah-tar'-so], *m.* (Anat.) Metatarsus, the part of the foot or pelvic limb between the ankle and the toes; in man it consists of five bones.

Metate [may-tah'-tay], *m.* (Mex.) A curved stone, in the shape of an inclined plane, resting on three feet, used for grinding maize for *tortillas,* or cocoa for chocolate (fr. Aztec, *metlatl*).

Metátesis [may-tah-tay'-sis], *f.* (Rhet.) Metathesis, a transposition.

Metedor, ra [may-tay-dor', rah], *m. & f.* 1. He who puts one thing into another. 2. Smuggler. 3. Clout of new-born children.

Metedur ía [may-tay-doo-ree'-ah], *f.* Smuggling.

Metemuertos [may-tay-moo-err'-tose], *m.* 1. Attendant in a play-house. 2. Busy-body, a vain, meddling person.

Meteórico, ca [may-tay-o'-re-co, cah], *a.* Meteoric, meteorous.

Meteorismo [may-tay-o-rees'-mo], *m.* (Med.) Meteorism, distension of the abdomen by gases.

Meteorita [may-tay-o-ree'-tah], *f.* Meteorite.

Meteorizar [may-tay-o-re-thar'], *va.* To cause meteorism or tympanites.—*vr.* To suffer it.

Meteoro [may-tay-o'-ro], *m.* An atmospheric phenomenon.

Metéoro [may-tay'-o-ro], *m.* *V.* METEORO.

Meteorología [may-tay-o-ro-lo-hee'-ah], *f.* Meteorology.

Meteorológico, ca [may-tay-o-ro-lo'-he-co, cah], *a.* Meteorological. *Informe* or *boletín meteorológico,* Weather report.

Meteorologista [may-tay-o-ro-lo-hees'-tah], *m.* Meteorologist.

Meter [may-terr'], *va.* 1. To place or to put in, to include one thing within another, to get on. 2. To smuggle goods into a country. 3. To make, to occasion, to urge, to move. 4. To engage, to prevail upon, to induce. 5. To stake, to put to hazard. 6. To cram down victuals. 7. To put things close together, to cram or heap them together. 8. To impose upon, to deceive. 9. To compress, to straighten, to reduce. 10. (Coll.) To eat. *V.* COMER. *Meter bulla,* To make a noise. *Meter a voces,* To reduce the affair to a bustle. *Meter en calor,* To excite, to incite. *Meter cizaña,* To sow discord, to breed disturbances. *Meter el cuezo,* To introduce one's self to any thing with little ceremony. *Meter paz,* To accommodate matters between contending parties. *Meter priesa,* To urge, to hasten.—*vr.* 1. To meddle, to intermeddle, to interfere. 2. To be on terms of familiarity with a person. 3. To choose a profession or trade. 4. To be led astray, to plunge into vice. 5. To empty into the sea: applied to rivers. 6. To attack sword in hand. *Meterse con alguno,* To pick a quarrel.

Meterse donde no le llaman, To thrust one's self where he is not called. *Meterse en vidas ajenas*, To dive into other people's affairs. *Meterse en todo*, To be jack of all trades. *Meterse en sí mismo*, To revolve in the mind; to follow one's own opinion. *Meterse soldado*, To become a soldier. *Meterse a sabio*, To affect learning and knowledge. (Naut.) To stave in.

Metesillas [may-tay-seel'-lyas], *m.* *V.* METEMUERTOS.

Meticuloso, sa [may-te-coo-lo'-so, sah], *a.* Meticulous, scrupulous, finicky.

Metido [may-teè'-do], *m.* Strong lye used by washerwomen.

Metido, da [may-tee'-do, dah], *a.* & *pp.* of METER. Placed or put in or into; engaged; deceived. *Estar muy metido en algún negocio*, To be deeply engaged in any affair.

Metileno [may-te-lay'-no], *m.* (Chem.) Methylene, an organic radical known only in combination.

Metilo [may-tee'-lo], *m.* (Chem.) Methyl.

Metimiento [may-te-me-en'-to], *m.* Inclusion, the act and effect of putting one thing into another.

Metódicamente, *adv.* Methodically, orderly.

Metódico, ca [may-to'-de-co, cah], *a.* Methodical, formal.

Metodismo [may-to-dees'-mo], *m.* 1. Systematic method. 2. Methodism, the belief of Methodists.

Metodista [may-to-dees'-tah], *n. com.* 1. Methodist, a religious sectary, follower of John Wesley. 2. *a.* *V.* METÓDICO.

Método [may'-to-do], *m.* Method, manner, mode, custom, order, form.

Metonimia [may-to-nee'-me-ah], *f.* Metonymy, a rhetorical figure.

Metonímico, ca [may-to-nee'-me-co, cah], *a.* Metonymical, relating to metonymy.

Metopa [may-to'-pah], *f.* (Arch.) Metope, the space between the triglyphs in the Doric order.

Metraje [may-trah'-hay], *m.* Length in meters. *Película de largo metraje*, Full length film.

Metralla [may-trahl'-lyah], *f.* Grape-shot, case-shot, canister-shot.

Metrallar [may-tral-lyar'], *va.* To canister, to attack with grape-shot.

Metreta [may-tray-tah], *f.* A Greek and Roman measure of liquids.

Métrica [may'-tre-cah], *f.* Metrical art, poesy.

Métricamente, *adv.* Metrically.

Métrico, ca [may'-tre-co, cah], *a.* Metrical, composed in verse.

Metrificar [may-tre-fe-car'], *va.* *V.* VERSIFICAR.

Metritis [may-tree'-tis], *f.* (Med.) Metritis, inflammation of the womb.

Metro [may'-tro], *m.* 1. Metre, unit of measure in the decimal system. 2. Metre, verse. 3. Subway train.

Metrología [may-tro-lo-hee'-ah], *f.* A treatise on weights and measures.

Metrónomo [may-tro'-no-mo], *m.* Metronome.

Metrópoli [may-tro'-po-le], *f.* 1. Metropolis, the chief city of a country. 2. Archiepiscopal church.

Metropolitano [may-tro-po-le-tah'-no], *m.* 1. Metropolitan, archbishop. 2. Subway train.

México. (Amer. Mex.) *V.* MÉJICO.

Meya [may'-yah], *f.* Kind of large crab; maia, spider-crab.

Meyor [may-yor'], *a.* (Obs.) *V.* MEJOR.

Mezcal [meth-cahl]', *m.* (Mex.) 1. A species of maguey, or American agave. 2. An intoxicating liquor prepared from this plant.

Mezcla [meth'-clah], *f.* 1. Mixture, commixture, compound, composition, medley. 2. Mortar. 3. Mixed cloth.

Mezcladamente, *adv.* In a mixed or promiscuous manner.

Mezcladillos [meth-clah-deel'-lyos], *m. pl.* A kind of paste made by confectioners.

Mezclador, ra [meth-clah-dor', rah], *m.* & *f.* One who mixes, mingler, compounder.

Mezclar [meth-clar'], *va.* 1. To mix, to mingle, to unite, to commix. 2. To spread false reports, to sow discord, to excite disturbances.—*vr.* 1. To mix, to be united into a mass. 2. To marry a person of inferior rank. 3. To introduce one's self into any thing.

Mezclilla [meth-clee'-lyah], *f.* Denim, coarse cotton drill.

Mezcolanza [meth-co-lahn'-thah], *f.* (Coll.) Bad mixture of colours, mishmash.

Mezquinamente [meth-ke-nah-men'-tay], *adv.* Miserably, avariciously.

Mezquindad [meth-keen-dahd'], *f.* 1. Penury, poverty, indigence. 2. Avarice, covetousness, paltriness, currishness, meanness.

Mezquino, na [meth-kee'-no, nah], *a.* 1. Poor, indigent, penurious; diminutive. 2. Avaricious, covetous, niggardly, mean, paltry; miserable, lean. 3. Petty, minute, puny. (Arab. meskin.)

Mezquita [meth-kee'-tah], *f.* Mosque, a Mohammedan temple or place of worship. (Arab. masjid.)

Mezquite [meth-kee'-tay], *m.* The mezquite shrubs of Mexico. 1. The honey-mezquite. Prosopis juliflora, yielding the algarroba pods. 2. The screw bean, Prosopis pubescens.

Mi [mee], *pro.* Me; the oblique case of the pronoun *yo* when it is governed by any preposition other than *con*: as, *de mí*, from me.

Mi [mee], *pro. pos.* My; placed before substantives, as *mío* is placed after them; thus, *Mi amor* or *amor mío*, My love. *V.* Mío.—*pl.* My relatives, my family.

Mi. *m.* Mi, the third note of the scale.

Miaja [me-ah'-hah], *f.* Crumb, minute portion.

Miar [me-ar'], *vn.* To mew, as a cat.

Miasma [me-ahs'-mah], *m.* (Med.) Miasm or miasma.—*pl.* Miasmata.

Miasmático, ca [me-as-mah'-te-co, cah], *a.* Miasmatic, producing miasm.

Miau [me-ah'-oo], *m.* Mew of a cat.

Mica [mee'-cah], *f.* Mica, a mineral cleaving in thin scales, transparent to translucent. Called also isinglass.

Micáceo, cea [me-cah'-thay-o, ah], *a.* Micaceous, mica-like.

Micasquisto [me-cas-kees'-to], *m.* Mica-schist.

Micción [mic-the-on'], *f.* Micturition, the act of urinating.

Micer [me-therr'], *m.* Ancient title of respect, in Arragon.

Mico [me co], *m.* 1. Monkey, an ape with a long tail. 2. (Coll.) Libidinist. 3. An ugly, ill-shaped man.

Micología [me-co-lo-hee'-ah], *f.* Mycology, the science of fungi.

Micra [mee'-crah], *f.* Micron (unit of length).

Micro [me-cro], *a.* A Greek word, signifying small, much used in combination.

Micro [mee'-cro], *m.* (Coll.) Mike.

Microamperio [me-cro-am-pay'-re-o], *m.* Microampere.

Microbiano, na [me-cro-be-ah'-no, nah], *a.* Microbial, microbic.

Microbicida [me-cro-be-thee'-dah], *m.* Microbicide.—*a.* Microbicidal.

Microbilanza [me-cro-be-lahn'-thah], *f.* Microbalance.

Microbio [me-cro'-be-o], *m.* Microbe.

Microbiología [me-cro-be-o-lo-hee'-ah], *f.* Microbiology.

Microbiológico, ca [me-cro-be-o-lo'-he-co, cah], *a.* Microbiological.

Microbiólogo [me-cro-be-o'-lo-go], *m.* Microbiologist.

Microcéfalo, la [me-cro-thay'-fah-lo, lah], *a.* Microcephalous, microcephalic, having an unusually small skull.

Microcircuito [me-cro-theer-coo-ee'-to], *m.* Microcircuit.

Micrococo [me-cro-co'-co], *m.* Micrococcus.

Microcosmo [me-cro-cos'-mo], *m.* Microcosm.

Microfilm [me-cro-feelm'], *m.* Microfilm.

Microfísica [me-cro-fee'-se-cah], *f.* Microphysics.

Micrófono [me-cro'-fo-no], *m.* Microphone.

Microfotografía [me-cro-fo-to-grah-fee'-ah], *f.* 1. Microphotography. 2. Microphotograph.

Micrografía [me-cro-grah-fee'-ah], *f.* Micrography.

Micrómetro [me-cro'-may-tro], *m.* Micrometer.

Microómnibus, Microbús [me-cro-om'-ne-boos, me-cro-boos'], *m.* Microbus.

Microonda [me-cro-on'-dah], *f.* Microwave.

Microorganismos [me-cro-or-gah-nees'-mos], *m. pl.* Microorganisms.

Microscópico, ca, *a.* Microscopic, microscopical.

Microscopio [me-cros-co'-pe-o], *m.* Microscope. *Microscopio electrónico*, Electron microscope.

Microsurco [me-cro-soor'-co], *m.* Migrogroove.

Michito [me-chee'-to], *m. dim.* Kitten, a young cat.

Micho, cha [mee'-cho, chah], *m.* & *f.* Puss, name of a cat.

Mida [mee'-dah], *m.* Mida, bean-fly, worm that breeds in vegetables.

(*Yo mido, yo mida; él midió, midiera*; from *Medir.* *V.* PEDIR.)

Miedo [me-ay -do], *m.* Fear, dread, apprehension. *Morirse de miedo*, To die for fear. *No haya miedo*, There is nothing to be apprehended.

Miedoso, sa [me-ay-do'-so, sah], *a.* Fearful, timorous, easily afraid.

Miel [me-el'], *f.* Honey. *Miel de caña*, Molasses. *Dejar a uno con la miel en los labios*, To deprive one of what he was just beginning to enjoy. *Miel sobre hojuelas* (honey on leaflets), A phrase signifying that something adds lustre to another thing. *Miel en la boca, y guarde la bolsa*, If you can not give, refuse courteously. *Quedarse (uno) a media miel*, To be deprived of something one was beginning to enjoy.

Mielga [me-el'-gah], *f.* 1. (Bot.) Lucerne, when it grows wild. Medicago. 2. A kind of dog-fish. Squalus centrina. 3. Rake, an instrument for raking hay, etc. 4. Stripe of ground.

Mielitis [me-ay-lee'-tis], *f.* Myelitis, inflammation of the spinal cord.

Miembro [me-em'-bro], *m.* 1. Member, a limb of the body. 2. Member, one of a community or corporation. 3. Member, any branch or part of an integral. 4. Member, a head, a clause of a discourse or period.

Mienta [me-en'-tah], *f.* (Bot.) Mint. Mentha. *V.* HIERBABUENA.

(*Yo miento, yo miente,* from *Mentar.* *V.* ACRECENTAR.)
(*Yo miento, yo mienta,* from *Mentir.* *V.* ASENTIR.)

Mientra, Mientre, *adv.* (Obs.) *V.* MIENTRAS.

Mientras [me-en'-tras], *adv.* In the meantime, in the meanwhile; when. *Mientras que,* Whilst, during the time that, as long as, so long as. (Lat. (du)m interim.)

Miera [me-ay'-rah], *f.* 1. Juniper oil. 2. Resin.

Miércoles [me-err'-co-les], *m.* Wednesday. *Miércoles de ceniza,* Ash Wednesday.

Mierda [me-err'-dah], *f.* (Coll.) 1. Excrement, fæces, ordure. 2. Dirt, grease.

Mierdacruz [me-er-dah-crooth'], *f.* (Bot. Prov.) Ciliate sparrow-wort. Passerina ciliata.

Mierla [me-err'-lah], *f.* (Orn.) Blackbird. *V.* MERLA.

Mierra, *f.* *V.* NARRIA.

Mies [me-ess'], *f.* 1. Wheat and other grain of which bread is made, corn. 2. Harvest, the time of reaping. 3. (Met.) Multitude converted or ready for conversion.

Miga [mee'-gah], *f.* 1. Crumb, the soft part of bread. 2. A small fragment of any thing. 3. Marrow, substance, or principal part. *Migas,* Crumbs of bread fried in a pan, with oil, salt, and pepper. *Hacer buenas* or *malas migas,* (Coll.) To agree or disagree readily with one.

Migaja [me-gah'-hah], *f.* 1. A small particle, scrap, or bit of bread. 2. Scrap, crumb, small particles of bread, meat, etc., left at the table. 3. A small bit of any thing, ace. 4. (Coll.) Nothing, little or nothing. *No tiene migaja de juicio,* He has not a grain of sense.—*pl.* Offals, leavings; broken victuals.

Migajada [me-gah-hah'-dah], *f.* A small particle.

Migajica, illa, ita, uela [me-gah-hee'-cah], *f. dim.* A very small particle of bread or any other thing.

Migajón [me-gah-hone'], *m.* Crumb, without crust; marrow core.

Migala [mee'-gah-lah], *f.* Mygale, bird-spider, a very large species of spider.

Migar [me-gar'], *va.* To crumble, to break into small bits.

Migración [me-grah-the-on'], *f.* Migration.

Migratorio, ria [me-grah-to'-re-o, ah], *a.* Migrating, migratory.

Miguelete [me-gay-lay'-tay], *m.* *V.* MIQUELETE.

Miguero, ra [me-gay'-ro, rah], *a.* Crummy, relating to crumbs fried in a pan. *Lucero miguero,* The morning star, so called by pastors, because on seeing it they prepare their dish of fried crumbs.

Mijar [me-har'], *m.* A millet-field.

Mijero [me-hay'-ro], *m.* Mile-stone.

Mijo [mee'-ho], *m.* 1. (Bot.) Millet or millet panic-grass. Panicum miliaceum. *Mijo italiano,* Italian panic-grass. Panicum italicum. *Mijo alemán,* German panic-grass. Panicum germanicum. *Mijo ceburro,* White wheat. *V.* TRIGO CANDEAL. 2. (Bot.) Turkey-millet. Holcus sorghum. 3. (Local) Maize.

Mikado [me-kah'-do], *m.* Mikado, the sovereign of Japan.

Mil [meel], *m.* One thousand or ten hundred. *Sala de mil y quinientas,* Former supreme court of appeals in Spain. *Perdió muchos miles de pesos,* He lost several thousand dollars. *Mil y quinientas,* (Coll.) Lentils. *Milenrama,* Milfoil. yarrow. Achillea microphylla. *V.* MILENRAMA.

Milagrero, ra [me-lah-gray'-ro, rah], *m.* & *f.* Person fond of considering natural events as miracles, and publishing them as such; a miracle-monger.

Milagro [me-lah'-gro], *m.* 1. Miracle, wonder, something above human power. 2. Offering of wax or any other substance, hung up in churches in commemoration of a miracle. *Vida y milagros,* (Coll.) Life, character, and behaviour.

Milagrón [me-lah-grone'], *m.* (Coll.) Dread, astonishment; extreme.

Milagrosamente, *adv.* Miraculously, marvellously.

Milagroso, sa [me-lah-gro'-so, sah], *a.* Miraculous, done by miracle; marvellous, admirable.

Milamores [meel-ah-mo'-res], *f.* Perennial plant, a species of valerian.

Milán [me-lahn'], *m.* 1. The city Milan. 2. Kind of linen cloth, so called from being made in Milan.

Milanés, sa [me-la-nays', sah], *a.* Native of or belonging to Milan, Milanese.

Milano [me-lah'-no], *m.* 1. (Orn.) Kite, glede, a bird of prey. Falco milvus. *Mesa de milanos,* Keen hunger and little to eat. 2. Bur or down of the thistle.

Milenario, ria [me-lay-nah'-re-o, ah], *a.* Millenary, consisting of a thousand.

Milenario [me-lay-nah'-re-o], *m.* 1. Millenary, the space of a thousand years. 2. Millennium. 3. Millenary, one who expects the millennium.

Mileno, na [me-lay'-no, nah], *a.* Applied to cloth, the warp of which contains a thousand threads.

Milenrama [me-len-rah'-mah], *f.* (Bot.) Common milfoil or yarrow. Achillea millefolium.

Milésimo, ma [me-lay'-se-mo, mah], *a.* 1. Thousandth, millesimal, the ordinal of a thousand. 2. The thousandth part of any thing.—*Milésima, f.,* Mill, the thousandth part of the monetary unit.

Milesio, ia [me-lay'-se-o, ah], *a.* 1. Milesian, of Miletus. 2. Milesian: applied to ridiculous tales for pastime.

Milhojas [mil-o'-has], *f.* (Bot.) Yarrow. *V.* MILENRAMA.

Miliar [me-le-ar'], *a.* Miliary, having the size or form of a millet-seed.

Miliárea [me-le-ah'-ray-ah], *f.* Milliare, one-thousandth of an âre.

Milicia [me-lee'-the-ah], *f.* 1. Art and science of war, warfare. 2. Military men in general, the militia or soldiery. 3. Militia, the trained bands of the inhabitants of a country: in this last sense it is almost always used in the plural.

Miliciano [me-le-the-ah'-no], *m.* Militia-man.

Miliciano, na, *a.* Military, militar.

Miligramo [me-le-grah'-mo], *m.* Milligramme, the thousandth part of a gramme.

Mililitro [me-le-lee'-tro], *m.* Millilitre, the thousandth part of a litre.

Milímetro [me-lee'-may-tro], *m.* Millimetre, the thousandth part of a metre, 25·4 to the inch.

Militante [me-le-tahn'-tay], *a.* Militant; military.

Militar [me-le-tar'], *m.* Soldier, a military man.—*pl.* Military, the soldiery. —*a.* Militar, military, soldierly, warlike, martial.

Militar [me-le-tar'], *vn.* 1. To serve in the army, to follow the profession of arms. 2. To hold, to militate, to stand good, to go against: applied to argument and reasons.

Militarismo [me-le-tah-rees'-mo], *m.* Militarism, predominance in the government of state of the military spirit.

Militarización [me-le-tah-re-thah-the-on'], *f.* Militarization.

Militarizar [me-le-tah-re-thar'], *va.* To militarize.

Militarmente, *adv.* Militarily, in a military style.

Milite [mee'-le-tay], *a.* (Obs.) Soldier. military man.

Milmillonésimo, ma [mil-meel-lyo-nay'-se-mo, mah], *a.* Thousand millionth, billionth.

Milo [mee'-lo], *m.* (Prov. Ast.) Earth-worm.

Milocha [me-lo'-chah], *f.* (Local) Kite, a toy.

Milpa [meel'-pah], *f.* (Mex.) A maize-field (planted or unplanted).

Milpiés [mil-pe-ays'], *m.* Centipede, millipede.

Milréis [mil-rays'], *m.* Milreis, Brazilian and Portuguese coin.

Milla [meel'-lyah], *f.* 1. Mile, a linear measure; eight stadia, or one thousand geometric steps. 2. (Obs.) Quarter of a league. 3. (Naut.) Knot.

Millar [mil-lyar'], *m.* 1. Number of a thousand. 2. Thousand, proverbially a great number: in this last sense it is almost always used in the plural. 3. A certain quantity of cocoa, which in some parts is three pounds and a half, and in others more.

Millarada [mil-lyah-rah'-dah], *f.* Several thousands. *Echar millaradas,* To brag of wealth and riches. *A millaradas,* Innumerable times.

Millo [meel'-lyo], *m.* (Prov.) In the Canary Islands, and in Galicia, maize.

Millón [mil-lyone'], *m.* 1. Million, ten hundred thousand. 2. Million, any very great number. *Millones,* Excise or duty levied in Spain on wine, vinegar, oil, meat, soap, and tallow candles, to defray the expenses of the army. *Sala de millones,* Board of excise, which regulated the duty called *Millones.*

Millonario [mil-lyo-nah'-re-o], *m.* Millionaire, a person very rich in money.

Millonésimo, ma [mil-lyo-nay'-se-mo, mah], *a.* Millionth.

Mimado, da [me-mah'-do, dah], *a.* Spoiled, humoured.

Mimador [me-mah-dor'], *m.* (Littl. us.) Coaxer.

Mimar [me-mar'], *va.* To coax, to wheedle, to flatter, to fondle, to caress, to indulge, to humour, to pet.

Mimbral [mim-brahl'], *m.* Plantation of osiers.

Mimbre [meem'-bray], *m.* (Bot.) 1. Twig of an osier. 2. Osier, willow.

Mimbrear [mim-bray-ar'], *vn.* *V.* CIMBRAR.

Mimbrera [mim-bray'-rah], *f.* (Bot.) Osier. Salix viminalis.

Mimbreral [mim-bray-rahl'], *m.* Plantation of osiers.

Mimbroso, sa [mim-broh'-so, sah], *a.* Made of osiers.

Mimeografiar [me-may-o-grah-fe-ar'], *va.* To mimeograph.

Mimeógrafo [me-may-o'-grah-fo], *m.* Mimeograph.

Mimetismo [me-may-tees'-mo], *m.* Mimetism, protective coloring.

Mímica [mee'-me-cah], *f.* Pantomime, sign-language.

Mímico, ca [mee'-me-co, cah], *a.* Mimic.

Mimo [mee'-mo], *m.* 1. Buffoon, merry-andrew, mime, mimic. 2. Endearingness, fondness, indulgence. 3. Prudery, delicacy. 4. Ancient mimes or farcical representations.

Mimología [me-mo-lo-hee'-ah], *f.* Mimology, act of imitating the voice and actions of others.

Mimosa [me-mo'-sah], *f.* (Bot.) Mimosa, the sensitive-plant.

Mimoso, sa [me-mo'-so, sah], *a.* Delicate, endearingly soft, fond, foolishly nice or tender.

Mina [mee'-nah], *f.* 1. Conduit, mine, a subterraneous canal or cavity in the ground. 2. Mine, a place which contains metals or minerals. *Mina amparada*, A mine worked to a sufficient extent to prove a legal title. 3. Spring, source of water. 4. Business which yields great profit and demands but little exertion. 5. (Coll.) A large quantity of money. 6. (Mil.) Mine under a fortress.

Minador, ra [me-nah-dor', rah], *m.* & *f.* Miner, one who works in mines; one who makes military mines; engineer.

Minal [me-nahl'], *a.* Belonging to a mine.

Minar [me-nar'], *va.* 1. To mine, to dig mines and burrows. 2. To mine, to sap, to ruin by mines. 3. To make uncommon exertions to attain some end or collect information.

Minarete [me-nah-ray'-tay], *m.* Minaret, a spire in Saracen architecture.

Mineraje [me-nay-rah'-hay], *m.* Labour of mining.

Mineral [me-nay-rahl'], *a.* Mineral, consisting of inorganic bodies.

Mineral [me-nay-rahl'], *m.* 1. Mineral, an inorganic substance; matter dug out of the earth, ore. 2. A spring of water, the mineral source or origin of fountains. 3. A source or origin which produces a plenty of any thing. 4. Mine which contains metals, minrals, or precious stones.

Mineralización [me-nay-rah-le-thah-the-on'], *f.* (Phys.) Mineralization, the state of a metal in combination with another body.

Mineralogía [me-nay-rah-lo-hee'-ah], *f.* Mineralogy.

Mineralógico, ca [me-nay-rah-lo'-he-co, cah], *a.* Belonging to mineralogy, mineralogical.

Mineralogista [me-nay-rah-lo-hees'-tah], *m.* Mineralogist.

Mineralurgia [me-nay-rah-loor'-he-ah], *f.* Metallurgy.

Mineralurgista [me-nay-rah-loor-hees'-tah], *m.* Metallurgist.

Minería [me-nay-ree'-ah], *f.* 1. The art of mining. 2. Force of miners; the whole body of workers in a mine. 3. Body of mine-operators.

Minero [me-nay'-ro], *m.* 1. Mine, place in the earth which contains metals or minerals. 2. Miner, one who digs for metals, or makes military mines. 3. Source, origin.

Mingo [meen'-go], *m.* One of the three balls in the game of billiards, which is never struck by a cue, but by another ball: the red ball.

Minguito [min-gee'-to], *m.* Piece of bread, one-quarter of a loaf.

Miniar [me-ne-ar'], *va.* To paint in miniature.

Miniatura [me-ne-ah-too'-rah], *f.* Miniature, a painting on vellum, ivory, or paper.

Miniaturista [me-ne-ah-too-rees'-tah], *com.* Painter of miniatures.

Miniaturización [me-ne-ah-too-re-thay-the-on'], *f.* Miniaturization.

Mínima [mee'-ne-mah], *f.* (Mus.) Minim; half-note.

Minimista [me-ne-mees'-tah], *m.* Student of the second class in grammar.

Mínimo, ma [mee'-ne-mo, mah], *a.* Least, smallest.—*m.* Minim, religious of the order of St. Francis de Paula. *Mínimos*, (Coll.) Second class in grammar-schools.

Minino, Mino [me-nee'-no, mee'-no], *m.* Word used for calling a cat.

Minio [mee'-ne-o], *m.* Minium, red-lead, an oxide of lead.

Ministerial [me-nis-tay-re-ahl'], *a.* Ministerial.

Ministerialmente, *adv.* Ministerially.

Ministerio [me-nis-tay'-re-o], *m.* 1. Ministry, office, public place, employment. 2. Manual labour. 3. Ministry, administration, the principal officers of government. 4. Ministry, the charge or office of a minister or secretary of state, and the time which he is in office. *Ministerio de Fomento, de la Gobernación, de Gracia y Justicia, etc.*, *V.* Ministro.

Ministra [me-nees'-trah], *f.* 1. Ministress, she who serves. 2. Wife of a cabinet minister.

Ministrador, ra [me-nis-trah-dor', rah], *m.* & *f.* One who ministers.

Ministrante [me-nis-trahn'-tay], *pa.* Serving, ministrating.

Ministrar [me-nis-trar'], *va.* & *vn.* 1. To minister, to serve an office or employment, to perform the functions of a public place. 2. To minister, to supply, to furnish.

Ministril [me-nis-treel'], *m.* 1. Apparitor, tipstaff; a petty officer of justice. 2. Minstrel, one who plays the flute and other musical wind-instruments. *Ministriles*, Musical wind-instruments.

Ministro [me-nees'-tro], *m.* 1. Minister, agent. 2. Minister employed in the administration of justice. 3. Secretary of state. *Ministro de Estado*, or *de relaciones exteriores*, The secretary of state or minister of foreign affairs. *Ministro de la Gobernación*, or *de relaciones interiores*, Minister of the home department, or of the interior. *Ministro de Hacienda*, Secretary of the exchequer or treasury. *Ministro de Gracia y Justicia*, Attorney-general. *Ministro de Fomento*, Secretary of the public works and instruction. *Ministro de capa y espada*, A member of the supreme council, though not bred to the bar. 4. Minister or agent of a foreign power. 5. A petty officer of justice. 6. One of the heads of some religious communities.

Minoración [me-no-rah-the-on'], *f.* Minoration.

Minorar [me-no-rar'], *va.* To lessen, to reduce to a smaller compass, to diminish, to clip.—*vr.* To lower, to fall.

Minorativo, va [me-no-rah-tee'-voh, vah], *a.* Lessening, that decreases or lessens.

Minoría [me-no-ree'-ah], *f.* Minority, the smaller number.

Minoridad [me-no-re-dahd'], *f.* Minority, nonage.

Minotauro [me-no-tah'-oo-ro], *m.* Minotaur, fabulous monster.

Minucia [me-noo'-the-ah], *f.* 1. Minuteness, smallness; mite, atom, any thing of very little value. 2. Small tithes paid of wool, lambs, etc.—*pl.* Minutiæ.

Minuciosidad [me-noo-the-o-se-dahd'], *f.* 1. Minute explanation of a thing. 2. A trifle.

Minucioso, sa [me-noo-the-o'-so, sah], *a.* Superfluously exact, nice, scrupulously and minutely cautious.

Minué, Minuete [me-noo-ay', me-noo-ay'-tay], *m.* Minuet, a kind of grave and stately dance.

Minuendo [me-noo-en'-do], *m.* (Arith.) Minuend.

Minúscula [me-noos'-coo-lah], *a.* Small, lower-case letters.

Minuta [me-noo'-tah], *f.* 1. Minute, first draft of an agreement in writing; an enumeration of the principal heads of a contract. 2. Papers containing brief notes or memorandums. *Libro de minutas*, Minute-book, memorandum-book, a commonplace book.

Minutar [me-noo-tar'], *va.* To take down the principal heads of an agreement; to make the first draft of a contract, to minute.

Minutario [me-noo-tah'-re-o], *m.* The book in which public notaries keep a memorandum of the documents they authorize.

Minutero [me-noo-tay'-ro], *m.* Minute-hand of a watch or clock.

Minutisa [me-noo-tee'-sah], *f.* (Bot.) Sweet-william pink. Dianthus barbatus.

Minuto [me-noo'-to], *m.* 1. Minute, the sixtieth part of a hour; the sixtieth part of a degree. 2. Minute, moment, any small space of time.

Miñón [me-nyone'], *m.* 1. Name given to some troops of light infantry in Spain. 2. Minion, scoriæ of iron ore.

Miñona [me-nyo'-nah], *f.* (Typ.) Minion, 7-point type; that of the present line.

Mío, Mía [mee'-o, mee'-ah], *pron. poss.* My, mine. *Es muy mío*, He is much my friend. *Soy mío*, I am my own master. *Con lo mío me ayude Dios*, Live and let live (I want only what legitimately belongs to me). *De mío*, By myself; by my own efforts or resources. *V.* Mi.

Miocardio [me-o-car'-de-o], *m.* Myocardium.

Mioceno, na [me-o-thay'-no, nah], *a.* (Geol.) Miocene.

Miografía [me-o-grah-fee'-ah], *f.* Myography. *V.* Miología.

Miología [me-o-lo-hee'-ah], *f.* Myology. part of anatomy which treats of the muscles; a treatise on muscles.

Miope [me-o'-pay], *a.* Myopic, near sighted. Also *n.*

Miopía [me-o-pe'-ah], *f.* Myopia, nearsightedness.

Miosota [me-o-so'-tah], *f.* (Bot.) Myosotis, forget-me-not, a plant of the borage family.

Miquelete [me-kay-lay'-tay], *m.* Miquelet, mountain soldier belonging to the militia of Catalonia and the Pyrenees.

Mira [mee'-rah], *f.* 1. The sight of a gun. 2. A point of mathematical instruments to direct the sight. 3. Care: vigilance; expectation, design. *Estar a la mira*, To be on the look-out, to be on the watch. *Mira de bombadero*, Bombsight. *Miras de proa*, (Naut.) Bow chasers. *A la mira y a la maravilla*, Excellently, admirably.

¡ Mira ! [mee'-rah], *int.* Look ! behold ! take care ! see ! lo !

Mirabel [me-rah-bel'], *m.* 1. (Bot. Summer cypress goose-foot. Chenopodium scoparia. 2. (Prov.) Sun flower.

Mirabolano [me-rah-bo-lah'-no], *m.* (Bot.) Myrobalan, a dried astringent prune-like fruit of India, used as a cathartic.

Mirada [me-rah'-dah], *f.* 1. Glance, a transient view. 2. Gaze, steadfast look.

Miradero [me-rah-day'-ro], *m.* Place exposed to view on all sides; watch-tower, or any elevated spot which commands an extensive prospect.

Mirado, da [me-rah'-do, dah], *a.* Considerate, circumspect, prudent. moderate.—*pp.* of Mirar.

Mirador, ra [me-rah-dor', rah], *m.* & *f.* 1. Spectator, looker-on. 2. *m.* Mirador, gallery which commands an extensive view. 3. *m.* A kind of balcony. 4. A boat used in the tunny-fishery.

Miradura [me-rah-doo'-rah], *f.* Act of looking. *V.* MIRADA.

Miraje [me-rah'-hay], *m.* Mirage, looming.

Miramamolin [me-rah-mah-mo-leen'], *m.* Appellation given to the sovereign of the Moors: it means "prince of the believers."

Miramiento [me-rah-me-en'-to], *m.* 1. Awe, reverence, dread. 2. Consideration, reflection; expectation. 3. Circumspection, prudence. 4. Reverential civility.

Mirar [me-rar'], *va.* 1. To behold, to look or look at, to look upon or toward, to give a look. 2. To respect, to have regard for, to esteem, to appreciate, to look on. 3. To have some private end, to aim at, to have in view. 4. To look, to be directed with regard to any object. 5. To observe, to watch, to spy. 6. To take notice, to notice. 7. To look, to consider, to reflect, to meditate. 8. To inquire, to collect information. 9. To look, to take care, to attend, to protect. *Mirar aspera y orgullosamente,* To browbeat. *Mirar de hito en hito,* To look steadfastly at an object. *Mirar a uno con malos ojos,* To look at one with an evil eye. *Mirar al rededor,* To look about. *Mirar por uno,* To take care of, to look after. *Mirar de través,* To squint. *Mirarse en ello,* To reflect seriously. *Mirarse a los pies,* To examine into one's own failings and imperfections. *Mirar por encima,* To examine slightly. *Mirar sobre el hombro,* To cast a contemptuous look or frown. *Mirarse las uñas,* (Met.) To be idle; to play at cards. *Antes que ates, mira que desates,* (prov.) Look before you leap. *Quien adelante no mira, atrás se queda,* He who does not look forward, remains behind.

Mirasol [me-rah-sole'], *m.* (Bot.) Turnsol, sunflower. *V.* GIRASOL.

Miriagramo [me-re-ah-grah'-mo], *m.* Myriagramme, ten thousand grammes.

Miriámetro [me-re-ah'-may-tro], *m.* Myriametre, ten thousand metres.

Miriápodos [me-re-ah'-po-dos], *a.* & *m. pl.* Myriapods, centipedes, articulates which have a great number of feet.

Mirífico, ca [me-ree-fe-co, cah], *a.* Marvellous, wonderful.

Miriñaque [me-re-nyah'-kay], *m.* 1. Bauble, gewgaw, trifling articles. 2. Manila grass-cloth. 3. Hoop-skirt.

Miristica [me-rees'-te-cah], *f.* The nutmeg-tree. Myristica.

Mirla [meer'-lah], *f.* (Orn.) Blackbird. *V.* MIRLO.

Mirlamiento [meer-lah-me-en'-to], *m.* Air of importance, affected gravity.

Mirlarse [meer-lar'-say], *vr.* To assume an air of importance, to affect gravity.

Mirlo [meer'-lo], *m.* 1. (Orn.) Blackbird. Turdus merula. 2. Air of importance, affected gravity.

Mirmego, ga [meer-may'-go, gah], *a.* Like an ant.

Mirón, na [me-rone', nah], *m.* & *f.* 1. Spectator, looker-on, bystander. 2. Prier, busybody, gazer.

Mirra [meer'-rah], *f.* Myrrh, a resinous gum.

Mirrado, da [mir-rah'-do, dah], *a.* Composed of myrrh, perfumed with myrrh; myrrhine.

Mirrauste [mir-rah'-oos-tay], *m.* Pigeon-sauce, made of bread, almonds, and other ingredients.

Mirrino, na [mir-ree'-no, nah], *a.* Myrrhine, of or like myrrh. (Acad.)

Mirtáceo, cea [meer-tah'-thay-o, ah], *a.* Myrtaceous, pertaining to the myrtle family.

Mirtidano [meer-te-dah'-no], *m.* Sprout which springs at the foot of a myrtle.

Mirtiforme [meer-te-for'-may], *a.* Myrtiform, having the shape of myrtle.

Mirtino, na [meer-tee'-no, nah], *a.* Resembling myrtle.

Mirto [meer'-to], *m.* (Bot.) Myrtle. Myrtus. *V.* ARRAYÁN.

Misa [mee'-sah], *f.* 1. Mass, the service of the Roman church. 2. Music composed for a solemn mass. *Misa del gallo,* Midnight mass. *Misa mayor,* High mass.

Misacantano [me-sah-can-tah'-no], *m.* 1. Priest who is ordained and says the mass. 2. Priest who celebrates the first mass.

Misal [me-sahl'], *m.* 1. Missal, the mass-book. 2. (Typ.) Two-line pica.

Misantropia [me-san-tro-pee'-ah], *f.* Misanthropy.

Misantrópico, ca [me-san-tro'-pe-co, cah], *a.* Misanthropic, misanthropical, hating mankind.

Misántropo [me-sahn'-tro-po], *m.* Misanthropist.

Misar [me-sar'], *vn.* (Coll.) To say mass; to hear mass. (Acad.)

Misario [me-sah'-re-o], *m.* Acolyte, one who attends on the priest during mass.

Miscelánea [mis-thay-lah'-ne-ah], *f.* Miscellany, mixture, medley.

Miscibilidad [mis-the-be-le-dahd'], *f.* Miscibility, capacity for being mixed.

Miscible [mis-thee'-blay], *a.* Miscible, such as can be mixed.

Miserable [me-say-rah'-blay], *a.* 1. Miserable, wretched, hapless, unhappy, lamentable. 2. Exhausted, dejected. 3. Covetous, avaricious, niggard; hard.

Miserablemente, *adv.* Miserably, unhappily, covetously, sordidly.

Miseramente [mee'-say-rah-men-tay], *adv.* Meanly. *V.* MISERABLEMENTE.

Miserear [me-say-ray-ar'], *vn.* To act penuriously.

Miserere [me-say-ray'-ray], *m.* 1. The Psalm *miserere* (the 50th in the Roman psalter, 51st in English). 2. A solemn Lenten service in which this psalm is sung. 3. (Med.) Volvulus, the iliac passion.

Miseria [me-say'-re-ah], *f.* 1. Misery, miserableness, calamity, wretchedness, forlornness, need; oppression. 2. Covetousness, avariciousness, niggardness, niggardliness, narrowness, hardness, stinginess, meanness. 3. Trifle, a very small matter.

Misericordia [me-say-re-cor'-de-ah], *f.* Mercy, mercifulness, clemency, loving-kindness.

Misericordiosamente, *adv.* Piously, clemently, mercifully.

Misericordioso, sa [me-say-re-cor-de-oh'-so, sah], *a.* Pious, humane, compassionate, merciful.

Misero, ra [me-say'-ro, rah], *a.* 1. Mass-loving. 2. Applied to a priest who says mass very often.

Mísero, ra [mee'-say-ro, rah], *a.* *V.* MISERABLE.

Misérrimo, ma [me-ser'-re-mo, mah], *a. sup.* Very miserable.

Misio, sia [mee'-se-o, ah], *a.* Mysian, native of or belonging to Mysia in ancient Asia Minor.

Misión [me-se-on'], *f.* 1. Mission, the act of sending. 2. Mission, travel undertaken by priests and other religious persons to propagate religion. 3. Country or province where missionaries preach the gospel among infidels. 4. Missionary discourse or sermon. 5. Charges, cost, expense. 6. Money and victuals allowed to reapers during the harvest.

Misionar [me-se-o-nar'], *va.* & *vn.* To preach as a missionary. (Coll.) To reprimand.

Misionero, Misionario [me-se-o-nay'-ro], *m.* Missionary, one sent to propagate religion.

Misivo, va [me-see'-vo, vah], *a.* Missive: applied to a letter or small note sent to any person.

Mismísimo, ma [mis-mee'-se-mo, mah], *a. sup.* Very same.

Mismo, ma [mees'-mo, mah], *a.* Same, similar, equal, self-same, like. *Yo mismo lo hago,* I myself do it.

Misoginia [me-so-hee'-ne-ah], *f.* Misogyny, hatred of women.

Misógino, na [me-so'-he-no, nah], *a.* Misogynous, hating women.

Mistamente, *adv.* *V.* MIXTAMENTE.

Mistar [mis-tar'], *vn.* To speak or make a noise with the mouth: used generally with a negative.

Mistela [mis-tay'-lah], *f.* Drink made of wine, water, sugar, and cinnamon.

Misterio [mis-tay'-re-o], *m.* 1. Mystery, something above human intelligence. 2. Mystery, any thing artfully made difficult; abstruseness, abstrusity. *No ser sin misterio,* Not to be without a meaning.

Misteriosamente, *adv.* Mysteriously, secretly.

Misterioso, sa [mis-tay-re-o'-so, sah], *a.* Mysterious, dark, obscure, mysterial, mystic, mystical.

Mistica [mees'-te-cah], *f.* Mysticalness, mystical theology.

Misticamente *adv.* Mystically; spiritually; emblematically.

Misticismo [mis-te-thees'-mo], *m.* Mysticism, the doctrine of a sect of philosophers: a modern word.

Místico, ca [mees'-te-co, cah], *a.* 1. Mystic, mystical, sacredly obscure. 2. Mystical, emblematical. 3. Mystical, spiritual, belonging to mystical divinity, or to the contemplation of spiritual things.

Mistico [mees'-te-co], *m.* 1. A mystic, a person devoted to religious contemplation; a writer in mystical divinity. 2. Small coasting vessel in the Mediterranean.

Misticón [mis-te-cone'], *m. aug.* A great mystic man; a person who affects a mystical or holy life in a high degree.

Mistifori, *a.* *V.* MIXTIFORI.

Mistilineo, nea [mis-te-lee'-nay-o, ah], *a.* (Geom.) *V.* MIXTILÍNEO.

Mistión, Misto, Mistura, Misturar. *V.* MIXTIÓN, MIXTO, MIXTURA, and MIXTURAR.

Misturera [mis-too-ray'-rah], *f.* (Mex. Peru) Flower-girl who sells bouquets or mixed flowers.

Mita [mee'-tah], *f.* The number of Indians subjected to compulsory labour by terms, in conformity with the law of that name.

Mitad [me-tahd], *f.* Moiety, half. *Por mitades,* By halves. *Mitad y mitad,* By equal parts. *Cuenta de mitad,* (Com.) Joint account.

Mitán [me-tahn'], *m.* A kind of glazed linen for lining. (Obs.)

Mitayo [me-tah'-yo], *m.* Indian serving his turn of compulsory labour.

Mítico, ca [mee'-te-co, cah], *a.* Mythical.

Mitigación [me-te-gah-the-on'], *f.* Mitigation, moderation, extenuation.

Mitigador, ra [me-te-gah-dor', rah], *m.* & *f.* Mitigator, mollifier.

Mitigar [me-te-gar'], *va.* 1. To mitigate, to soften, to mollify, to lull. 2 To quench, to assuage.

Mitigativo, va, Mitigatorio, ria [me-te-gah-tee'-vo, vah], *a.* Lenitive, mitigant, mitigative.
Mitin [mee'-tin], *m.* Political or labor meeting.
Mito [mee'-to], *m.* Myth, allegorical fiction, chiefly about a religious subject.
Mitocondrio [me-to-con'-dre-o], *m.* Mitochondrion.
Mitologia [me-to-lo-hee'-ah], *f.* Mythology, the history of the fabulous gods of antiquity.
Mitológico, ca [me-to-lo'-he-co, cah], *a.* Mythological.—*m.* Mythologist.
Mitologista, Mitólogo, *m.* Mythologist.
Mitón [me-tone'], *m.* Mitt, a sort of ladies' glove without fingers.
Mitosis [me-to'-sis], *f.* (Biol.) Mitosis.
Mitote [me-to'-tay], *m.* 1. An Indian dance. 2. (Amer.) Household festival. 3. (Amer.) Fastidiousness, affectedness. 4. (Mex. Coll.) Riot, uproar, disturbance, confusion.
Mitotero, ra [me-to-tay'-ro, rah], *a.* & *n.* (Mex. Amer.) 1. Precise, finical, dainty, fastidious. 2. Jolly, fond of diversion.
Mitra [mee'-trah], *f.* Mitre, an ornament for the head, worn by bishops; the dignity of a bishop.
Mitrado [me-trah'-do], *a.* Mitred: applied to a person bearing a mitre at festivals.—*pp.* of Mitrar.
Mitrar [me-trar'], *vn.* (Coll.) To be mitred or wear a mitre.
Mitridato [me-tre-dah'-to], *m.* Mithridate, antidote.
Mixtamente, *adv.* Belonging to both ecclesiastical and civil courts.
Mixtifori [mix-te-fo'-re], *a.* (Lat. Law) Applied to a crime that may be tried either in ecclesiastical or secular courts.
Mixtilineo, nea [mix-te-lee'-nay-o, ah], *a.* (Geom.) Mixtilinear.
Mixtión [mix-te-on'], *f.* Mixtion, mixture, commixture.
Mixto, ta [meex'-to, tah], *a.* 1. Mixed, mingled. 2. Mixed, composed of various simples. 3. Half-breed, of a crossbreed: of mixed breed, mongrel.—*m. V.* Mixtura.
Mixtura [mix-too'-rah], *f.* Mixture, a mass formed by mingled ingredients. 2. Meslin, mixed corn, as rye and wheat.
Mixturar [mix-too-rar'], *va.* To mix, to mingle.
Mixturero, ra [mix-too-ray'-ro, rah], *a.* 1. Mixing, which mixes. 2. (Obs.) Firebrand, provoking quarrels.
Miz [meeth], *m.* Puss, the common appellation of cats.
Mizo, za [mee'-tho, thah], *m.* & *f. V.* Micho, cha.
Moaré [mo-ah-ray'], *m.* Moiré, watered silk.
Mobiliario, ria [mo-be-le-ah'-re-o, ah], *a.* House-furnishing, relating to furniture.—*m.* Furniture, fitment.
Moblar [mo-blar'], *va.* (Obs.) To furnish, to decorate with furniture.
Moca, *f.* Mocha coffee.
Mocadero, Mocador [mo-cah-day'-ro, mo-cah-dor'], *m.* (Prov.) Pocket-handkerchief.
Mocarro [mo-car'-ro], *m.* 1. Mucus of the nose, not cleaned away (vulgarly, snot). 2. Money or treat given by a journeyman to his companions the first day he works at a shop.
Mocasín [mo-ca-seen'], *m.* 1. Moccasin, an Indian shoe of soft leather. 2. The moccasin snake.
Mocear [mo-thay-ar'], *va.* To act as a boy; to revel, to rake.
Mocedad [mo-thay-dahd'], *f.* 1. Juvenility, youthfulness. 2. Light and careless kind of living.
Mocetón, na [mo-thay-tone', nah], *m.* & *f.* A young, robust person.
Moción [mo-the-on'], *f.* 1. Motion, movement. 2. Leaning, inclination of mind. 3. Divine inspiration. 4. (Neol.) Motion, a proposal to be voted on in an assembly.
Mocito, ta [moth-ee'-to, tah], *a. dim.* Juvenile, youthful.—*m.* & *f.* A very young person.
Moco [mo'-co], *m.* 1. Mucus, a viscid fluid secreted by mucous membranes. 2. Any viscid, glutinous matter. 3. Snuff of a lamp or candle. 4. Candle drippings. 5. Slag of iron. *Moco de pavo,* 1. Crest which hangs over the forehead of a turkey. 2. Any worthless thing. *¿Es moco de pavo?* Do you call that nothing? *No sabe quitarse los mocos,* The fellow does not know how to blow his nose. *Quitar a uno los mocos,* To knock off one's nose with a blow. *A moco de candil,* By candle-light: applied to things hastily or inconsiderately done.
Mocora [mo-co'-rah], *f.* A tree of Ecuador from which hats are sometimes made.
Mocosidad [mo-co-se-dahd'], *f.* Mucosity, mucousness, viscosity.
Mocoso, sa [mo-co'-so, sah], *a.* 1. Snivelly: running from the nose. 2. Despicable, worthless. 3. Ignorant, thoughtless.
Mocoso, sa [mo-co'-so, sah], *m.* & *f.* An ignorant, thoughtless person; an inexperienced youth.
Mocosuelo, la [mo-co-soo-ay'-lo, lah], *m.* & *f. dim.* A thoughtless, inexperienced youth.
Mochada [mo-chah'-dah], *f.* Butt, a stroke with the head of a horned animal.
Mochar [mo-char'], *va.* To cut, to lop off. *V.* Desmochar.
Mochazo [mo-chah'-tho], *m.* Blow with the butt-end of a musket.
Mochil [mo-cheel'], *m.* Farmer's boy.
Mochila [mo-chee'-lah], *f.* Knapsack, a bag in which soldiers carry their linen and provisions. *Hacer mochila,* To provide provisions for a journey.
Mochilera [mo-che-lay'-rah], *a.* Pouched. *Zorra mochilera,* The opossum.
Mochilero [mo-che-lay'-ro], *m.* One who carries the baggage of soldiers.
Mochin [mo-cheen'], *m.* Young shoot of a tree. *V.* Verdugo.
Mocho, cha [mo'-cho, chah], *a.* 1. Dishonoured. 2. Cropped, shorn. 3. Lopped, having the branches cut off. 4. Maimed, mutilated. 5. (Mex. Coll.) Hypocritical.
Mochuelo [mo-choo-ay'-lo], *m.* (Orn.) Red owl. Strix. *Tocar el mochuelo,* To get always the worst part of a thing.
Moda [mo'-dah], *f.* Fashion, form, mode, custom; especially in dress.
Modales [mo-dah'-les], *m. pl.* Manners, breeding, education.
Modalidad [mo-dah-le-dahd'], *f.* 1. Modality, method. 2. Character, nature. 3. (Mus.) Mode and tone.
Modelar [mo-day-lar'], *va.* To model, to form.
Modelo [mo-day'-lo], *m.* Model, pattern, standard, copy, exemplar, paragon, rule.
Moderación [mo-day-rah-the-on'], *f.* Moderation, temperance, frugality, abstemiousness, circumspection, continence.
Moderadamente, *adv.* Moderately, temperately, reasonably, measurably.
Moderado, da [mo-day-rah'-do, dah], *a.* 1. Moderate, temperate, abstemious, abstinent, considerate; gentle. 2. In politics, conservative.
Moderador [mo-day-rah-dor'], *m.* Moderator.
Moderadora [mo-day-rah-do'-rah], *f.* Moderatrix.
Moderante [mo-day-rahn'-tay], *m.* Moderator, in some colleges, he who presides over the studies of pupils.
Moderantismo [mo-day-ran-tees'-mo], *m.* Conservatism in politics.
Moderar [mo-day-rar'], *va.* To moderate, to regulate, to adjust, to restrain, to curb, to repress.—*vr.* To become moderate, to refrain from excesses.
Moderativo, va [mo-day-rah-tee'-vo, vah], *a.* Moderating.
Moderatorio, ria [mo-day-rah-to'-re-o, ah], *a.* That which moderates.
Modernamente, *adv.* Recently, lately, newly, freshly.
Modernismo [mo-der-nees'-mo], *m.* Modernism.
Modernización [mo-der-ne-thah-the-on'], *f.* Modernization.
Modernizar [mo-der-ne-thar'], *va.* To modernize.
Moderno, na [mo-derr'-no, nah], *a.* Late, recent, modern, new, novel.
Modestamente, *adv.* Modestly, comelily, meekly, maidenly, honestly.
Modestia [mo-des'-te-ah], *f.* Modestly, decency, chastity; meekness, maidenliness; coyness; humility.
Modesto, ta [mo-des'-to, tah], *a.* Modest, decent, pure, chaste, maidenly, unpretending, unassuming.
Módico, ca [mo'-de-co, cah], *a.* Moderate in price.
Modificación [mo-de-fe-cah-the-on'], *f.* Modification, the act of modifying.
Modificador, ra [mo-de-fe-cah-dor', rah], *m.* & *f.* Modifier.
Modificar [mo-de-fe-car'], *va.* To modify, to moderate.
Modificativo, va [mo-de-fe-cah-tee'-vo, vah], *a.* Modificative, that which modifies.
Modillón [mo-dil-lyone'], *m.* (Arch.) Modillion, bracket.
Modio [mo'-de-o], *m.* Roman dry measure.
Modiolo [mo-de-o'-lo], *m.* (Arch.) Intermodillion, the quadrangular space between the modillions of a column.
Modismo [mo-dees'-mo], *m.* Particular phraseology in a language deviating from the rules of grammar; mannerism.
Modista [mo-dees'-tah], *f.* 1. (Obs.) A person fond of dress, fashionable, fashion-monger. 2. Milliner, dressmaker, mantua-maker.
Modo [mo'-do], *m.* 1. Mode, method, manner, form. 2. Moderation, temperance. 3. Civility, urbanity. 4. Mode or mood in grammar. 5. (Mus.) A system of dividing the intervals of an octave; a Greek or Gregorian mode. *Del modo, del mismo modo que* or *al modo que,* In the same manner as. *A modo,* After a similar manner. *De modo,* So that. *Sobre modo,* Extremely.
Modorra [mo-dor'-rah], *f.* 1. Drowsiness, heaviness. 2. Dawn or approach of day. 3. Flabby softness of the pulp of fruit. 4. A disease in sheep arising from plethora: sturdy.
Modorrar [mo-dor-rar'], *va.* To drowse, to render heavy with sleep.—*vr.* To become flabby: applied to the pulp of fruit.
Modorrilla [mo-dor-reel'-lyah], *f.* The third night-watch.

Modorro, ra [mo-dor'-ro, rah], *a.* 1. Drowsy, sleepy, heavy. 2. Drowsy, dull, stupid.

Modoso, sa [mo-doh'-so, sah], *a.* Temperate, sedate, in manner and gestures.

Modrego [mo-dray'-go], *m.* Dunce, dolt, thick-skull.

Modulación [mo-doo-lah-the-on'], *f.* Modulation, agreeable harmony.

Modulador, ra [mo-doo-lah-dor', rah], *m.* & *f.* Modulator.

Modulante [mo-doo-lahn'-tay], *a.* Modulating.

Modular [mo-doo-lar'], *vn.* To modulate, to sing with harmony and variety of sound.

Módulo [mo'-doo-lo], *m.* 1. (Arch.) Module, measure of columns. 2. Modulation of voice. 3. Unit of measure of running water for household use, irrigation, and manufacturing application. 4. Size of coins and medals.

Mofa [mo'-fah], *f.* Mockery, jeer, scoff, ridicule, sneer.

Mofador, da [mo-fah-dor', rah], *m.* & *f.* Scoffer, scorner, jeerer, jester, mocker.

Mofadura [mo-fah-doo'-rah], *f.* Jeer, scoff, scorn, jesting.

Mofar [mo-far'], *va.* To deride, to jeer, to scoff, to mock, to ridicule, to flout.—*vr.* To sneer, to scoff, to behave with contempt.

Mofeta [mo-fay'-tah], *f.* 1. Mephitis, a pestilential exhalation in mines or other deep places. 2. (Zool.) Skunk or polecat.

Moflete [mo-flay'-tay], *m.* Chub-cheek.

Mofletudo, da [mo-flay-too'-do, dah], *a.* Chub-cheeked.

Mogate [mo-gah'-tay], *m.* Varnish, glazing which covers any thing. *A medio mogate*, Carelessly, heedlessly.

Mogato, ta [mo-gah'-to, tah], *a.* *V.* Mojigato.

Mogol, la [mo'-gol, go'-lah] (Acad.), or **Mongol, la,** *a.* Mongolian. *Gran mogol*, Grand mogul, title of the ancient Emperor of the Mongolians.

Mogólico, ca [mo-go'-le-co, cah], *a.* Relating to Mongolia.

Mogollón [mo-gol-lyone'], *m.* A hanger-on, a trencher friend, a parasite. *Comer de mogollón*, To sponge upon others.

Mogote [mo-go'-tay], *m.* 1. An insulated rock or cliff with a flat crown, appearing at sea. 2. Pointed stack of corn. *Mogotes*, Tendrils, the soft tops of the horns of deer when they begin to shoot.

Mogrollo [mo-grol'-lyo], *m.* 1. Parasite, sponger. 2. Clown, rustic.

Moharra [mo-ar'-rah], *f.* The point in which an ensign or flag-staff terminates.

Moharrache, Moharracho [mo-ar-rah'-chay, mo-ar-rah'-cho], *m.* Jack-pudding, merry-andrew; a low jester.

Mohatra [mo-ah'-trah], *f.* The act of selling for high prices and buying on the lowest terms, in order to overreach the buyer or seller.

Mohatrar [mo-ah-trar'], *va.* To buy under price and sell above it; to make a deceitful sale.

Mohatrero, ra [mo-ah-tray'-ro, rah], *m.* & *f.* Extortioner.

Mohatrón [mo-ah-trone'], *m.* Extorter.

Mohecer [mo-ay-therr'], *va.* To moss, to cover with moss.

Mohiento, ta [mo-e-en'-to, tah], *a.* *V.* Mohoso.

Mohín [mo-een'], *m.* Grimace.

Mohina [mo-ee'-nah], *f.* Animosity, desire of revenge.

Mohino, na [mo-ee'-no, nah], *a.* 1. Fretful, peevish. 2. Begotten by a stallion and she-ass: applied to mules. 3. Black: applied to horses, mules, etc. 4. Sad, mournful.

Mohino, *m.* One who plays alone against several others. *Tres al mohino*, Three against one.

Moho [mo'-o], *m.* 1. (Bot.) Moss. 2. Mould, concreted matter; rust; mouldiness. 3. Bluntness occasioned for want of application.

Mohoso, sa [mo-o'-so, sah], *a.* Mouldy, musty, rusty, mossy.

Mojada [mo-hah'-dah], *f.* 1. The act of wetting or moistening; dampening. 2. Sop, a piece of bread steeped in liquor. 3. (Coll.) Stab, a wound with a pointed weapon.

Mojado, da [mo-hah'-do, dah], *a.* Wet.

Mojador, ra [mo-hah-dor', rah], *m.* & *f.* Wetter, moistener.

Mojadura [mo-hah-doo'-rah], *f.* Act of moistening or wetting.

Mojama [mo-hah'-mah], *f.* Salt tunny-fish, dried or smoked.

Mojar [mo-har'], *va.* 1. To wet, to moisten, to damp. 2. To meddle, to interfere.—*vn.* To be immersed in any business.

Mojarra [mo-har'-rah], *f.* 1. Sea-fish, small and very broad. 2. (Amer.) A heart-shaped, or short and broad dagger.

Mojarrilla [mo-har-reel'-lyah], *m.* (Coll.) Punster, jester.

Moje [mo'-hay], *m.* (Coll.) Sauce of fricassee, ragout, or any other dressed meat.

Mojeles [mo-hay'-less], *m. pl.* (Naut.) Blocks, pulleys.

Mojicón [mo-he-cone'], *m.* 1. Blow in the face with the clinched fist. 2. Kind of biscuit.

Mojiganga [mo-he-gahn'-gah], *f.* A morrice or morris dance; masquerade, mask, mummery.

Mojigatería [mo-he-gah-tay-ree'-ah], *f.* Hypocrisy, religious fanaticism.

Mojigatez [mo-he-gah-teth'], *f.* Bigotry. *V.* Mojigatería.

Mojigato, ta [mo-he-gah'-to, tah], *m.* & *f.* Dissembler, hypocrite, a person who affects humility and servile submission to obtain his end.—*a.* Deceitful, hypocritical, hypocritic.

Mojí, Mojil [mo-hee', mo-heel'], *a.* *V.* Cazuela.

Mojón [mo-hone'], *m.* 1. Landmark. 2. Heap, pile. 3. Kind of play, like pitching. 4. Solid excrement.

Mojona [mo-ho'-nah], *f.* 1. Duty on wine sold by retail. 2. Survey of land; the setting up of landmarks.

Mojonación, *f.* *V.* Amojonamiento.

Mojonar, *va.* *V.* Amojonar.

Mojonera [mo-ho-nay'-rah], *f.* Landmark.

Mojonero [mo-ho-nay'-ro], *m.* Gauger, a person appointed by government to measure wine.

Mola [mo'-lah], *f.* 1. Mole, a formless concretion in the uterus, false conception, commonly called *mola-matriz.* 2. Barley or flour mixed with salt and used in sacrifices.

Molada [mo-lah'-dah], *f.* Quantity of colours ground at once.

Molar [mo-lar'], *a.* Molar, belonging to a mill-stone, or any other thing for grinding, as the teeth.

Molcajete, or **Morcajete** [mol-cah-hay'-tay], *m.* (Mex.) A mortar, either of burnished clay or stone, used to pound spices and small seeds.

Moldar [mol-dar'], *va.* To mould. *V.* Amoldar.

Molde [mol'-day], *m.* 1. Mould, the matrix in which any thing is cast or receives its form: pattern, mould, block. 2. A form ready for printing. 3. A person who has reached the highest grade in any thing; example, model. *De molde*, In print, printed or published; fitting, to the purpose.

Moldeador [mol-day-ah-dor'], *m.* (Prov.) Moulder.

Moldear [mol-day-ar'], *va.* To mould, to make moulds.

Moldura [mol-doo'-rah], *f.* Moulding, an ornamental cavity in wood or stone. *Molduras de proa de un navío*, (Naut.) The carved work of a ship's head.

Moldurar [mol-doo-rar'], *va.* To make a moulding or ornament of any thing.

Mole [mo'-lay], *a.* Soft, mild.—*f.* Vast size or quantity; massiness.

Mole, *m.* Mexican stew of meat or fowl with a special hot sauce.

Molécula [mo-lay'-coo-lah], *f.* Molecule, invisible particle of bodies.

Molecular [mo-lay-coo-lar'], *a.* Molecular, relating to molecules.

Moledera [mo-lay-day'-rah], *f.* (Coll.) Botheration. *V.* Cansera.

Moledero, ra [mo-lay-day'-ro, rah], *a.* That which is to be ground.

Moledor, ra [mo-lay-dor', rah], *m.* & *f.* 1. Grinder, one who grinds and prepares colours. 2. Bore, a tiresome fellow. 3. A tool employed by powder-makers for reducing powder to small grains. 4. Each of the crushing cylinders in a sugar-mill.

Moledura [mo-lay-doo'-rah], *f.* The act of grinding. *V.* Molienda.

Molendero [mo-len-day'-ro], *m.* 1. Miller, grinder. 2. Chocolate manufacturer, one who grinds the cocoa and beats it up with sugar and flavouring.

Moler [mo-lerr'], *va.* 1. To grind, to pound, to pulverize, to mill. 2. To vex, to molest; to fatigue. 3. To waste, to consume by use. 4. To masticate, to chew. *Moler a azotes*, To lash, to whip.

Molero [mo-lay'-ro], *m.* Maker or seller of mill-stones.

Molestador, ra [mo-les-tah-dor', rah], *m.* & *f.* Disturber, vexer, molester.

Molestamente, *adv.* Troublesomely, vexatiously, grievously.

Molestar [mo-les-tar'], *va.* To vex, to disturb, to molest, to trouble, to hurry, to tease, to grate, to cut to the heart.

Molestia [mo-les'-te-ah], *f.* Injury, molestation, hardship, grievance, nuisance, excruciation.

Molesto, ta [mo-les'-to, tah], *a.* Grievous, vexatious, oppressive, molestful, heavy.

Moleta [mo-lay'-tah], *f.* 1. Muller, a stone flat at the bottom and round at the top, used by painters to grind colours on marble. 2. An apparatus for smoothing and polishing flint glass. 3. Muller, grinder for printing-ink on the ink-table.

Moletón [mo-lay-tone'], *m.* Milled flannel, canton or cotton flannel, swan's-down.

Molibdato [mo-lib-dah'-to], *m.* Molybdate.

Molibdeno [mo-lib-day'-no], *m.* Molybdenum, a white, brittle, lustreless metal.

Molíbdico [mo-leeb'-de-co], *a.* Molybdic, relating to, derived from, or compounded with molybdenum.

Molicie [mo-lee'-the-ay], *f.* 1. Tenderness, softness, effeminacy. 2. An unnatural crime.

Molido, da [mo-lee'-do, dah], *a.* & *pp.* of Moler. Ground; fatigued; flogged.

Molienda [mo-le-en'-dah], *f.* 1. The act of grinding or pounding. 2. Quantity pounded or ground at once; grist. 3. Weariness, fatigue, lassitude. 4. Season of grinding sugar-cane or olives. (Acad.)

Moliente [mo-le-en'-tay], *pa.* Grinder, grinding. *Moliente y corriente,* (Coll.) Right, justly, exactly.

Molificable [mo-le-fe-cah'-blay], *a.* (Littl. us.) Mollifiable.

Molificación [mo-le-fe-cah-the-on'], *f.* Mollification.

Molificar [mo-le-fe-car'], *va.* To mollify, to soften, to mitigate.

Molificativo, va [mo-le-fe-cah-tee'-vo, vah], *a.* That which mollifies, lenitive.

Molimiento [mo-le-me-en'-to], *m.* 1. The act of grinding, pounding, or beating up. 2. Fatigue, weariness, lassitude.

Molina [mo-lee'-nah], *f.* Oil-mill of large capacity. (Recent.)

Molinar [mo-le-nar'], *m.* Place where there are mills; milling-plant.

Molinejo [mo-le-nay'-ho], *m. dim.* A small mill.

Molinera [mo-le-nay'-rah], *f.* 1. Miller's wife. 2. Woman who tends or works in a mill.

Molinería [mo-le-nay-ree'-ah], *f.* (Littl. us.) Collection of mills.

Molinero [mo-le-nay'-ro], *m.* Miller, grinder.

Molinero, ra [mo-le-nay'-ro, rah], *a.* Any thing which is to be ground or pounded; any thing belonging to a mill.

Molinete [mo-le-nay'-tay], *m.* 1. (Naut.) Windlass. 2. *Molinete del cabrestante,* The barrel of the capstan. 3. Turnstile. 4. (Dim.) A little mill. 5. Brandish, twirl about the head in fencing. 6. (Mech.) Friction roller; sway-plate of a vehicle; smoke dispeller.

Molinillo [mo-le-neel'-lyo], *m.* 1. (Dim.) A little mill; a hand-mill. 2. Churn-staff, chocolate-mill, a stick with which chocolate is beat up in a chocolate-pot.

Molinismo [mo-le-nees'-mo], *m.* Molinism or quietism, principles of a sect.

Molinista [mo-le-nees'-tah], *m.* Molinist, a follower of the doctrines of Molinism.

Molinito [mo-le-nee'-to], *m. dim.* A small mill.

Molino [mo-lee'-no], *m.* 1. Mill, an engine in which corn is ground into meal, or any other body comminuted; corn-mill. *Molino de viento,* Windmill. *Molino de sangre,* Mill turned by men or animals, in contradistinction to such as are turned by wind, water, or steam. *Molino de agua,* Water-mill. *Molino de herrería* or *fragua,* A forge-mill. *Molino de mano,* Hand-mill. *Molino de papel,* Paper-mill. *Molino de estampar,* Stamping-mill. *Molino de corteza de roble,* Tan or bark-mill. *Molino de aserrar,* Saw-mill. *Molino de seda,* A throw-mill for twisting and winding silk. 2. A restless, noisy fellow. 3. (Coll.) Mouth.

Molitivo, va [mo-le-tee'-vo, vah], *a.* Mollient.

Molondro, Molondrón [mo-lon'-dro, mo-lon-drone'], *m.* A sluggish, mean-spirited and ignorant fellow, poltroon.

Moloquita [mo-lo-kee'-tah], *f.* (Min.) A variety of agate of dull-green hue.

Moloso [mo-lo'-so], *m.* Molossus, a foot of Latin verse, consisting of three long syllables (— — —).

Moltura [mol-too'-rah], *f.* 1. *V.* Molienda. (Acad.) 2. (Prov. Arag.) *V.* Maquila.

Molusco [mo-loos'-co], *m.* Mollusk, one of the mollusca, invertebrates having an unsegmented body, and usually a calcareous shell.

Molla [mol'-lyah], *f.* 1. Lean meat without bone. 2. (Prov.) Crumb of bread.

Mollar [mol-lyar'], *a.* 1. Soft, tender, pappy, pulpous. 2. Fleshy, lean, without bone.

Mollear [mol-lyay-ar'], *vn.* To grow soft and pliable, to soften or to grow less hard, to yield easily.

Molledo [mol-lyay'-do], *m.* 1. The fleshy part of a limb. 2. Crumb of bread.

Molleja [mol-lyay'-hah], *f.* 1. Gland, particularly that which is seated at the root of the tongue. 2. Gizzard, the strong muscular stomach of a fowl; maw.

Mollejón [mo-lyay-hone'], *m.* 1. (Aug.) A large gland. 2. A big, corpulent person.

Mollejuela [mol-lyay-hoo-ay'-lah], *f. dim.* A small gland.

Mollera [mol-lyay'-rah], *f.* Crown or top of the head. *Ser duro de mollera,* To be obstinate. *Cerrado de mollera,* Rude, ignorant.

Mollero [mol-lyay'-ro], *m.* (Prov.) Fleshy part of the arm.

Molleta [mol-lyay'-tah], *f.* 1. Snuffers. 2. Bread made of the finest flour.

Mollete [mol-lyay'-tay], *m.* Manchet, a small loaf made of the finest flour. *Molletes,* Plump or round cheeks.

Mollina, Mollizna [mol-lyee'-nah, mol-lyeeth'-nah], *f.* Mist, small rain.

Molliznar, Molliznear [mol-lyeeth-nar'], *vn.* To drizzle, to mizzle, to fall in small, slow drops.

Moma [mo'-mah], *f.* (Mex.) Blind-man's-buff. (Acad.)

Momentáneamente, *adv.* 1. Instantly. 2. Momentarily.

Momentáneo, nea [mo-men-tah'-nay-o, ah], *a.* Momentous, momentary, of short duration.

Momento [mo-men'-to], *m.* 1. Moment, the least space of time. 2. Moment, consequence, momentum, weight, importance. 3. (Math.) Difference. 4. (Mech.) Power, force. *Al momento,* In a moment, immediately. *Por momentos,* Successively, continually.

Momería [mo-may-ree'-ah], *f.* Mummery, a farcical entertainment, in which masked persons play frolics and antic tricks.

Momia [mo'-me-ah], *f.* Mummy, a dead body preserved by embalming.

Momificar [mo-me-fe-car'], *va.* To mummify, to convert into a mummy. —*vr.* To resemble a mummy.

Momio, mia [mo'-me-o, ah], *a.* Meagre, lean. *De momio,* Gratis, for nothing.

Momo [mo'-mo], *m.* Buffoonery, low jests, scurrile mirth, wry faces, grimaces.

Momórdiga [mo-mor'-de-gah], *f.* (Bot.) *V.* Balsamina.

Momperada [mom-pay-rah'-dah], *f.* A kind of glazed woollen stuff.

Mona [mo'-nah], *f.* 1. Female monkey or ape. 2. (Coll.) A mimic, a ludicrous imitator. 3. In jocular style, drunkenness and drunkard. 4. (Prov.) Cake made of flour, eggs, and milk. 5. Iron plate worn for protection on the right leg by bull-fighters on horseback. *Aunque la mona se vista de seda, mona se queda,* (prov.) Dress a monkey as you will, it remains a monkey still.

Monacal [mo-nah-cahl'], *a.* Monachal, monastic, monkish, belonging to monks.

Monacalmente, *adv.* Monastically.

Monacato [mo-nah-cah'-to], *m.* Monkhood, monachism.

Monacillo [mo-nah-theel'-lyo], *m.* Acolyte, acolithe, or acolotist, a boy who serves in a church.

Monacordio [mo-nah-cor'-de-o], *m.* Spinet, an old-fashioned stringed musical instrument with keys.

Monada [mo-nah'-dah], *f.* 1. Grimace, a ludicrous or ridiculous distortion of the countenance. 2. Monkeyism, monkey-shine, behaviour characteristic of a monkey. 3. Fawning, flattery. (Acad.)

Mónada [mo'-nah-dah], *f.* 1. Monad, an indivisible thing. 2. A microscopic infusorian, monad.

Monadelfo, fa [mo-nah-del'-fo, fah], *a.* Monadelphous, (stamens) united into one cluster.

Monago, Monaguillo [mo-nah'-go, mo-nah-geel'-lyo], *m.* *V.* Monacillo.

Monaquismo [mo-nah-kees'-mo], *m.* Monachism, monasticness.

Monarca [mo-nar'-cah], *m.* Monarch, king, sovereign, lord.

Monarquía [mo-nar-kee'-ah], *f.* Monarchy, the government of a single person, kingdom, empire, kingship.

Monárquico, ca [mo-nar'-ke-co, cah], *a.* Monarchical, monarchal, kingly, kinglike.

Monasterial [mo-nas-tay-re-ahl'], *a.* Monastic.

Monasterillo [mo-nas-tay-reel'-lyo], *m. dim.* A small monastery.

Monasterio [mo-nas-tay'-re-o], *m.* Monastery, a house of religious retirement; convent, minster; cloister.

Monásticamente, *adv.* Monastically.

Monástico, ca [mo-nahs'-te-co, cah], *a.* Monastic, monastical, monachal, monkish.

Monazo, za [mo-nah'-tho, thah], *m. & f. aug.* Large monkey or ape.

Monda [mon'-dah], *f.* Pruning of trees; the pruning season.

Mondadientes [mon-dah-de-en'-tays], *m.* Toothpick.

Mondador, ra [mon-dah-dor', rah], *m. & f.* Cleaner, purifier.

Mondadura [mon-dah-doo'-rah], *f.* Cleaning, cleansing, the act of freeing from filth. *Mondaduras,* Parings, peelings, any thing which comes off by cleaning.

Mondaoídos [mon-dah-o-ee'-dose], or **Mondaorejas** [mon-dah-o-ray'-has], *m.* Ear-spoon.

Mondar [mon-dar'], *va.* 1. To clean, to cleanse, to free from filth. 2. To husk, to strip off the husks of fruit, to peel, to decorticate; to deprive of money. 3. To cut the hair. *Mondar los huesos,* To pick bones quite clean.

Mondejo [mon-day'-ho], *m.* Paunch or belly of a pig or sheep stuffed with minced meat.

Mondo, da [mon'-do, dah], *a.* Neat, clean, pure, unadulterated. *Mondo y lirondo,* (Coll.) Pure, without any admixture.

Mondonga [mon-don'-gah], *f.* In contempt, a kitchen-wench or a maid-servant.

Mondongo [mon-don'-go], *m.* Paunch, tripes, black pudding. *Hacer el mondongo,* *V.* Mondongonizar.

Mondongonizar [mon-don-go-ne-thar'], *va.* To dress tripe, to make black puddings.

Mondonguero, ra [mon-don-gay'-ro, rah], *m. & f.* One who makes black puddings or deals in them.

Mondonguil [mon-don-geel'], *a.* (Coll.) Relating to tripes or puddings.

Monear [mo-nay-ar'], *vn.* To act in an affected, ridiculous, or preposterous manner; to monkey.

Moneda [mo-nay'-dah], *f.* Money, pieces of gold, silver, or copper, coined for the purpose of trade; coinage. *Moneda corriente,* Current coin. *Moneda de vellón,* 1. Inferior silver coin. 2.

Copper coin, token money. *Batir moneda,* To coin money. *Casa de moneda,* Mint. *Moneda sonante,* Hard money, specie. *No hacemos moneda falsa,* Our conversation is not private (you may listen if you like). *No hacer moneda falsa,* To say what is true. *Pagar en buena moneda,* To give full satisfaction.

Monedaje [mo-nay-dah'-hay], *m.* Coinage, seigniorage, the charges paid for coining money.

Monedar, Monedear [mo-nay-dar'], *va.* To coin.

Monedería [mo-nay-day-ree'-ah], *f.* Mint, factory of money.

Monedero [mo-nay-day'-ro], *m.* Officer of the mint who coins money, coiner, moneyer. *Monedero falso,* Coiner or maker of base money.

Monedilla, ita [mo-nay-deel'-lyah], *f. dim.* A small piece of money.

Monería [mo-nay-ree'-ah], *f.* 1. Grimace, a ludicrous or ridiculous distortion of the countenance; mimicry. 2. Trifle, gewgaw, bauble.

Monesco, ca [mo-nes'-co, cah], *a.* Apish, having the qualities of a monkey.

Monetario [mo-nay-tah'-re-o], *m.* 1. Cabinet of ancient coins and models. 2. Collection of coins and medals; the whole number of cases, tables or drawers which contain them. 3. Treasury-chamber, museum or place which holds such a collection.

Monetario, ria, *a.* Monetary, pertaining to money or finance.

Monetización [mo-nay-te-thah-the-on'], *f.* Monetization, the act of legally declaring to be money.

Monetizar [mo-nay-te-thar'], *va.* To monetize, to legalize as money.

Monfí [mon-fee'], *m.* Name formerly given to Moorish highwaymen.

Mongol, la, *a. V.* Mogol.

Moniato [mo-ne-ah'-to], *m.* A farinaceous root of which a kind of bread is made in some parts of South America.

Monicaco, Monicongo [mo-ne-cah'-co], *m.* A conceited, thoughtless person. *V.* Chuchumeco.

Monición [mo-ne-the-on'], *f.* Admonition, publication of the bans of marriage.

Monigote [mo-ne-go'-tay], *m.* (Coll.) 1. Lay-brother of religious orders. 2. A person who is considered without knowledge or skill in his own profession. 3. (Met. and coll.) A poorly made painting or statue.

Moniliforme [mo-ne-le-for'-may], *a.* Moniliform, like a string of beads.

Monillo [mo-neel'-lyo], *m.* Waist, bodice, a jacket without sleeves, worn by women.

Monipodio [mo-ne-po'-de-o], *m.* Any combination or agreement among several persons with an unlawful object.

Monismo [mo-nees'-mo], *m.* (Phil.) Monism.

Mónita [mo'-ne-tah], *f.* 1. Artifice, artfulness, affected flattery. 2. (Peru. Coll.) Severe reproof.

Monitor [mo-ne-tor'], *m.* 1. *V.* Admonitor. 2. Monitor, an armour-clad vessel sitting very low in the water and with one or two deck-turrets carrying heavy guns.

Monitoria [mo-ne-to'-re-ah], *f.* Summons issued by an ecclesiastical judge to command the personal appearance and deposition of a witness.

Monitorio, ria [mo-ne-to'-re-o, ah], *a.* Monitory, admonitory.

Monja [mon'-hah], *f.* Nun, a religious woman confined in a cloister.—*pl.* Appellation given to sparks in burned papers.

Monje [mon'-hay], *m.* 1. Monk: also, recluse, anchoret. 2. Brown peacock

Monjía [mon-hee'-ah], *f.* Prebend, enjoyed by a monk in his convent.

Monjil [mon-heel'], *m.* 1. Habit or dress of a nun. 2. Mourning-dress or weeds of a widow.

Monjío [mon-hee'-o], *m.* The day and ceremony of a lady's taking the veil.

Mono, na [mo'-no, nah], *a.* (Coll.) Cute, pretty.—*m.* 1. Monkey. 2. (Fig.) Mimic. 3. Coveralls. *Estar de monos,* (Coll.) To be on the outs. *Meter los monos a,* (Sp. Am.) To scare the daylights out of.

Monoceronte, Monocerote [mo-no-thay-ron'-tay], *m.* Unicorn.

Monocordio [mo-no-cor'-de-o], *m.* Monochord, an instrument of one string anciently used.

Monocotiledóneo, ea [mo-no-co-te-lay-do'-nay-o, ah], *a.* (Bot.) Monocotyledonous.

Monocromático, ca [mo-no-cro-mah'-te-co, cah], *a.* Monochromatic, of one colour: applied to yellow light, and also to a painting done in one colour.

Monócromo [mo-no'-cro-mo], *m.* Monochrome, a painting done in one colour. Used also as adjective.

Monóculo, la [mo-no'-coo-lo, lah], *a.* Monoculous, monocular, one-eyed.

Monóculo [mo-no'-coo-lo], *m.* 1. Monocle. 2. Bandage for only one eye.

Monodonte [mo-no-don'-tay], *m.* (Zool.) Narwhal, sea-unicorn.

Monogamia [mo-no-gah'-me-ah], *f.* Monogamy, marriage of one wife only.

Monógamo [mo-no'-gah-mo], *m.* He who marries only once.

Monogástrico, ca [mo-no-gahs'-tre-co, cah], *a.* (Zool.) Monogastric, having a single stomach.

Monografía [mo-no-grah-fee'-ah], *f.* Monograph, a description of one genus, one species, etc.; an extended essay upon a single topic.

Monográfico, ca [mo-no-grah'-fe-co, cah], *a.* (Litt. us.) Monographic, drawn in plain lines.

Monograma [mo-no-grah'-mah], *m.* Monogram, a cipher or character compounded of several letters and standing for some name.

Monoico, ca [mo-no'-e-co, cah], *a.* Monœcious, bearing distinct male and female flowers upon one stem.

Monolito [mo-no-lee'-to], *m.* Monolith, a stone monument in a single piece.

Monólogo [mo-no'-lo-go], *m.* Monologue, soliloquy, monology.

Monomanía [mo-no-mah-nee'-ah], *f.* Monomania, insanity upon one subject.

Monomaniaco, ca [mo-no-mah-ne-ah'-co, cah], *a.* Monomaniac.

Monomio [mo-no'-me-o], *m.* (Alg.) Monomial; expression consisting of a single term.

Monona [mo-no'-nah], *a.* (Coll.) (A woman) graceful and pretty, especially if very young.

Monopastos [mo-no-pahs'-tose], *m.* Pulley with one wheel.

Monopétalo, la [mo-no-pay'-tah-lo, lah], *a.* Monopetalous, having only one flower-leaf; gamopetalous.

Monoplano [mo-no-plah'-no], *m.* Monoplane.

Monópodo, da [mo-no'-po-do, dah], *a.* Monopode, having but one foot.

Monopolio [mo-no-po'-le-o], *m.* Monopoly, the exclusive privilege of selling any thing, and the combination or agreement among tradesmen for selling a thing at a certain price.

Monopolista [mo-no-po-lees'-tah], *m.* Monopolist, forestaller, monopolizer.

Monopolizar [mo-no-po-le-thar'], *va.* To monopolize, to forestall.

Monosilábico, ca [mo-no-se-lah'-be-co, cah], *a.* Monosyllabic, consisting of one syllable.

Monosílabo, ba [mo-no-see'-lah-bo, bah] *m. & f.* Monosyllable.

Monospermo, ma [mo-nos-perr'-mo mah], *a.* (Bot.) Monospermous, single seeded.

Monóstrofe [mo-nos'-tro-fay], *f.* A poetical composition of a single strophe; monostrophe.

Monoteísmo [mo-no-tay-ees'-mo], *m.* Monotheism, belief in only one God.

Monoteísta [mo-no-tay-ees'-tah], *a.* Monotheistic, holding or relating to monotheism.—*n.* Monotheist.

Monotipia [mo-no-tee'-pe-ah], *f.* (typ.) Monotyping.

Monotipo [mo-no-tee'-po], *m.* Monotype.

Monotonía [mo-no-to-nee'-ah], *f.* Monotony, uniformity of sound.

Monótono, na [mo-no'-to-no, nah], *a* Monotonous, monotonic.

Monseñor [mon-say-nyor'], *m.* A title of honour given to the Dauphin of France, and to Italian and French prelates.

Monserga [mon-serr'-gah], *f.* (Coll.) Gabble, confused language.

Monstruo [mons'-troo-o], *m.* Monster, a production contrary to the order of nature.

Monstruosamente, *adv.* Monstrously.

Monstruosidad [mons-troo-o-se-dahd'], *f.* Monstruosity, monstrosity, excessive ugliness, monstrousness.

Monstruoso, sa [mons-troo-o'-so, sah], *a.* 1. Monstrous, contrary to or deviating from the stated order of nature. 2. Monstrous, too irregular, enormous; shocking.

Monta [mon'-tah], *f.* 1. Amount, sum total. 2. Value, worth, price. 3. Signal given with a trumpet for the cavalry to mount their horses.

Montacargas [mon-tah-car'-gas], *m.* Elevator hoist, freight elevator.

Montada [mon-tah'-dah], *f.* The elevation given to the bit of a bridle.

Montadero [mon-tah-day'-ro], *m.* One who mounts; mounting-stone.

Montado [mon-tah'-do], *a.* 1. Applied to a horse ready for being mounted. 2. Applied to a trooper or horseman. —*pp.* of Montar.

Montador [mon-tah-dor'], *m.* 1. Mounter. 2. Mounting block. 3. Film editor.

Montadura [mon-tah-doo'-rah], *f.* 1. Mounting. 2. Setting (of a gem). 3. Harness, trappings.

Montaescaleras [mon-tah-es-cah-lay'-ras], *m.* Chair lift.

Montaje [mon-tah'-hay], *m.* 1. Assembly. 2. Editing (of a film).

Montanera [mon-tah-nay'-rah], *m.* The feeding of hogs with acorns, driven for that purpose into groves of oak.

Montanero [mon-tah-nay'-ro], *m.* Forester, keeper of a forest.

Montano, na [mon-tah'-no, nah], *a* Mountainous.

Montantada [mon-tan-tah'-dah], *f.* 1. Ostentation, boasting. 2. Multitude.

Montante [mon-tahn'-tay], *m.* 1. A broadsword used by fencing-masters. 2. A kind of fireworks which, when lighted, forms this figure. 3. (Naut.) Flood tide. 4. (Arch.) Upright, standard, a piece of wood, stone, or metal which divides a window into various parts. 5. (Mil.) Stempel, an upright timber used for support in a mine.

Montantear [mon-tan-tay-ar'], *vn.* 1. To wield the broadsword in a fencing-school. 2. To vaunt, to brag.

Montantero [mon-tan-tay'-ro], *m.* He who fights with a broadsword.

Montaña [mon-tah'-nyah], *f.* Mountain, mount. *V.* MONTE.—*pl.* Highlands; a ridge of mountains.

Montaña rusa [mon-tah'-nyah roo'-sah], *f.* Roller coaster.

Montañés, sa [mon-tah-nyes', sah], *a.* 1. Mountain, pertaining to the mountains. 2. Mountainous, inhabiting mountains, highlandish.

Montañés, sa [mon-tah-nyes', sah], *m.* & *f.* Mountaineer, mountainer, an inhabitant of the mountains, a highlander.

Montañeta, Montañuela [mon-tah-nyay'-tah, nyoo-ay'-lah], *f. dim.* A small mountain.

Montañoso, sa [mon-tah-nyo'-so, sah], *a.* Mountainous, hilly.

Montar [mon-tar'], *vn.* 1. To mount or go on horseback. 2. To amount to, to be worth. 3. To cock a gun. 4. To be of importance. *Montar un navío,* To take the command of a ship. *Montar el timón,* To hang the rudder. *Montar en cuidado,* To be on one's guard, to be careful.—*va.* 1. To impose a penalty for cattle entering a forest. 2. To mount, to set, to provide with a setting. 3. To mount, to set up, to put in place the parts of a machine or apparatus. 4. To cover, to copulate with: said of a horse or ass. 5. To mount, to carry, or be equipped with. 6. (Mar.) To double a cape or headland. 7. To edit (a film). *Montar en cólera,* To get angry. *Tanto monta,* It's all the same. *Vestido* or *traje de montar,* Riding habit. *Montar un reloj,* To wind a watch or clock. *Montar en pelo,* To mount an animal bareback.

Montaraz [mon-tah-rath'], *m.* Forester, guard of woods or farms.

Montaraz [mon-tah-rath'], *a.* 1. Mountain, mountainous. 2. Wild, untamed, haggard.

Montazgar [mon-tath-gar'], *va.* To levy or collect the toll for cattle passing from one province into another.

Montazgo [mon-tath'-go], *m.* 1. Toll to be paid for cattle passing from one province into another. 2. Place through which the cattle pass.

Monte [mon'-tay], *m.* 1. Mountain, mount, a large hill, a vast protuberance of the earth. 2. Wood, forest, a woody place. 3. Difficulty, obstruction. 4. A bushy head of hair much entangled. 5. Stock of cards which remain after each player has received his share. 6. (Amer.) A game at cards. *Monte alto* or *de árboles,* A lofty grove or wood. *Monte bajo* or *de malezas,* Copse, a low or short wood, a brush wood, a thicket. *Monte de piedad,* A certain office where money is lent to the poor for a certain time on security. *Monte pío,* A pension to widows and orphans. *Andar a monte,* To skulk, to lurk in hiding-places.

Montea [mon-tay'-ah], *f.* 1. Art or trade of cutting or hewing stone. 2. Plan or profile of a building. 3. (Arch.) Convexity of an arch.

Montear [mon-tay-ar'], *va.* 1. To beat a wood in pursuit of game, to hunt. 2. To draw the plan or profile of a building. 3. To vault, to form arches.

Montecillo [mon-tay-theel'-lyo], *m. dim.* 1. A small wood or forest. 2. Hillock, hummock, a small mount.

Montepío or **Monte de piedad,** *m.* Charitable pawnshop.

Montera [mon-tay'-rah], *f.* 1. A kind of cap made of cloth, used by common people in Spain. 2. Skylight, covering of glass over a gallery, court, etc. 3. Receiver, condenser of a still or alembic. 4. (Naut.) Skysail, skyscraper. 5. Hunter's wife.

Montereria [mon-tay-ray-ree'-ah], *f.* Shop or place where caps are made or sold.

Monterero [mon-tay-ray'-ro], *m.* One who makes or sells those caps called *monteras* in Spain.

Montería [mon-tay-ree'-ah], *f.* 1. Hunting, hunt, chase. 2. Place where hunting-caps are made or sold.

Montero [mon-tay'-ro], *m.* Huntsman, hunter.

Monteruca [mon-tay-roo'-cah], *f.* An ugly cap.

Monterrey [mon-ter-ray'-e], *m.* A kind of thin paste rolled up into spiral tubes.

Montés, sa [mon-tes', sah], *a.* Montigenous, mountain, bred or found in a forest or mountain.

Montesa [mon-tay'-sah], *f.* One of the military orders of Spain.

Montescos [mon-tes'-cos], *m. pl. Haber Montescos y Capeletes,* To have great disputes and contentions (to be Montagues and Capulets).

Montesino, na [mon-tay-see'-no, nah], *a.* Montigenous, bred or found in a forest or mountain.

Monto [mon'-to], *m.* Amount, sum.

Montón [mon-tone'], *m.* 1. Heap, pile. *Montón de gente,* Crowd, multitude. 2. Congeries, mass, cluster. 3. A dirty, lazy fellow. *Montón de tierra,* Very old, infirm person. *A montones,* Abundantly, by heaps.

Montuosidad [mon-too-o-se-dahd'], *f.* (Prov.) Mountainousness.

Montuoso, sa [mon-too-o'-so, sah], *a.* Full of woods and thickets, mountainous, hilly.

Montura [mon-too'-rah], *f.* 1. Horses and mules intended for the saddle. 2. Saddle, trappings and accoutrements of horses.

Monuelo [mo-noo-ay'-lo], *m. dim.* A coxcomb, a fop.

Monumental [mo-noo-men-tahl'], *a.* Monumental, belonging to monuments.

Monumento [mo-noo-men'-to], *m.* 1. Monument, any thing by which the memory of persons or things is preserved, such as a statue, a tomb, a cenotaph, etc. 2. Altar raised in churches on Holy Thursday to resemble a sepulchre. *Monumentos,* Monuments or remains of antiquity.

Monzón [mon-thone'], *m.* Monsoon, a periodical wind in the East Indian Ocean.

Moña [mo'-nyah], *f.* 1. Lay-figure of a woman to show a style of dress. 2. Peevishness, fretfulness. 3. An ornament of ribbons used on the head by bull-fighters. 4. (Coll.) Drunkenness. 5. Very elaborate cap for nursing infants as used sometimes in Andalusia.

Moño [mo'-nyo], *m.* 1. Hair on the crown of the head tied together; tuft. 2. Tuft of feathers on the heads of birds. 3. A bow of ribbons.

Moñudo, da [mo-nyoo'-do, dah], *a.* Crested, topped.

Moquear [mo-kay-ar'], *vn.* To snivel, to run at the nose; to blow the nose.

Moquero [mo-kay'-ro], *m.* (Coll.) Pocket-handkerchief.

Moqueta [mo-kay'-tah], *f.* Moquette, a woollen stuff, with a woof of hemp, from which carpets and rugs are made.

Moquete [mo-kay'-tay], *m.* Blow on the face or nose.

Moquetear [mo-kay-tay-ar'], *vn.* To discharge much mucus from the nose.—*va.* To give blows in the face.

Moquillo [mo-keel'-lyo], *m.* 1. (Dim.) A little mucus. 2. Pip, a disease in fowls.

Moquita [mo-kee'-tah], *f.* Snivel, running from the nose in cold weather.

Mora [mo'-rah], *f.* 1. (Law) Delay, procrastination. 2. Mulberry, the fruit of the mulberry-tree.

Morabita [mo-rah-bee'-tah], *m.* Member of a sect formed by a son-in-law of Mohammed.

Morabito [mo-rah-bee'-to], *m.* 1. A Mohammedan hermit. 2. *V.* MORABITA.

Moracho, cha [mo-rah'-cho, chah], *a.* Dark purple.

Morada [mo-rah'-dah], *f.* Habitation, abode, residence, mansion, lodging, home; continuance.

Morado, da [mo-rah'-do, dah], *a.* Violet, mulberry-coloured.

Morador, ra [mo-rah-dor', rah], *m.* & *f.* Inhabitant, lodger.

Moraga [mo-rah'-gah], *f.* Handful or bundle formed by female gleaners.

Morago, *m. V.* MORAGA.

Moral [mo-rahl'], *m.* (Bot.) Mulberry tree.

Moral, *f.* 1. Morale, buoyant spirits despite danger. 2. Moral ethics, morality.—*a.* Moral. *Apoyo moral,* Moral support.

Moraleja [mo-rah-lay'-hah], *f.* A brief moral observation.

Moralidad [mo-rah-le-dahd'], *f.* 1. Morality, the doctrine of the duties of life. 2. Morality, form of an action, which makes it the subject of reward or punishment.

Moralista [mo-rah-lees'-tah], *m.* Moralist, one who teaches the duties of life.

Moralizador, ra [mo-rah-le-thah-dor', rah], *m.* & *f.* Commentator, critic, moralizer.

Moralizar [mo-rah-le-thar'], *va.* & *vn.* 1. To moralize, to apply to moral purposes; to explain in a moral sense. 2. To moralize, to speak or write on moral subjects.

Moralmente, *adv.* Morally, in the ethical sense; according to the rules of virtue; popularly, by common sense.

Morar [mo-rar'], *vn.* To inhabit, to dwell, to reside, to lodge, to live; to continue.

Morato, ta [mo-rah'-to, tah], *a.* (Poet. Obs.) Relating to manners and morals.

Moratoria [mo-rah-to'-re-ah], *f.* 1. Letters of license granted to a debtor. 2. (Com.) Delay (for payment).

Moravo, va [mo-rah'-vo, vah], *a.* Moravian.

Morbidez [mor-be-deth'], *f.* Softness, delicacy.

Mórbido, da [mor'-be-do, dah], *a.* 1. Morbid 2. Soft, delicate.

Morbilidad, Morbididad [mor-be-le-dahd', mor-be-de-dahd'], *f.* 1. Morbidity. 2. Sickness rate.

Morbo [mor'-bo], *m.* Disease.

Morboso, sa [mor-bo'-so, sah], *a.* Diseased, morbid.

Morcajo [mor-cah'-ho], *m.* A low grade wheat cultivated in Old Castile.

Morcella [mor-thel'-lyah], *f.* Spark from a lamp.

Morcilla [mor-theel'-lyah], *f.* Black pudding, hog's pudding.

Morcillero, ra [mor-theel-lyay'-ro, rah], *m.* & *f.* One who makes or deals in black puddings.

Morcillo, lla [mor-theel'-lyo, lyah], *a.* Entirely black: applied to horses.

Morcillo [mor-theel'-lyo], *m.* The fleshy part of the arm from the shoulder to the elbow.
Morcón [mor-cone'], *m.* 1. A large black pudding made of the blind gut; a large sausage. 2. (Coll.) A short, plumpy fellow.
Mordacidad [mor-dah-the-dahd'], *f.* 1. Mordacity, biting quality. 2. Roughness, asperity, acrimony in unripe fruit. 3. Mordacity, a nipping, sarcastic language.
Mordante [mor-dahn'-tay], *m.* (Print.) Guide; container: a frame used by compositors to keep their copy secure, and mark the place up to which their work is completed.
Mordaz [mor-dath'], *a.* Corrosive, biting, nipping; sarcastic; acrimonious, satirical; keen.
Mordaza [mor-dah'-thah], *f.* 1. Gag, to prevent speaking or crying. 2. Sort of nippers or pincers.
Mordazmente, *adv.* Acrimoniously, nippingly.
Mordedor, ra [mor-day-dor', rah], *m.* & *f.* 1. Biter, one who bites. 2. One who satirizes.
Mordedura [mor-day-doo'-rah], *f.* Bite, wound made by biting; mordication.
Mordente [mor-den'-tay], *m.* 1. Mordant, a substance used in dyeing for fixing the colours. 2. (Mus.) Mordent, or double appoggiatura, a musical embellishment. 3. (Mus.) Turn.
Morder [mor-derr'], *va.* 1. To bite, to seize with the teeth, to nip. 2. To be sharp or pungent to the taste; to make rough to the touch. 3. To seize or stick fast one thing in another. 4. To bite, to gnaw, to wear away gradually. 5. (Met.) To nip, to carp at, to taunt, to nibble, to find fault with, to satirize. *No morderse los labios,* (Coll.) To speak one's opinions frankly and openly. *Morderse los dedos,* To be irritated and vexed from desire of revenge. *Morder la tierra,* To bite the dust. *Morder en un confite con otro,* To be hand and glove with any one; to be intimate. *Esa te muerda,* Your proposition is declined. *Morderse la lengua,* To refrain from saying what one is tempted to say.
Mordicante [mor-de-cahn'-tay], *pa.* & *a.* Biting, pungent, acrid.
Mordicar [mor-de-car'], *va.* To gnaw, to nibble; to smart, to sting.
Mordicativo, va [mor-de-cah-tee'-voh, vah], *a.* Biting, gnawing, mordicant.
Mordida [mor-dee'-dah], *f.* 1. Bite. 2. (Mex. coll.) Bribe.
Mordido, da [mor-dee'-do, dah], *a.* Diminished, wasted away.—*pp.* of Morder.
Mordido [mor-dee'-do], *m.* Bit, mouthful of meat.
Mordiente [mor-de-en'-tay], *m.* 1. Gold size, mordant, used by painters. 2. Mordant. *V.* Mordente. 3. Mordant, the acid or other corrosive by which etching is done.
Mordihuí [mor-de-oo-ee'], *m.* Weevil, a grub bred in wheat.
Mordimiento [mor-de-me-en'-to], *m.* Bite, mordication, biting.
Mordiscar [mor-dis-car'], *va.* 1. To nibble. 2. *V.* Morder.
Mordisco, Mordiscón [mor-dees'-co], *m.* Bite, the act of seizing with the teeth; the piece bitten off.
Morel de sal [mo-rel' day sahl], *m.* (Art.) Purple red used for painting in fresco.
Morena [mo-ray'-nah], *f.* 1. Brown bread. 2. Moray, a murænoid eel.
Morenilla, Morenita [mo-ray-neel'-lyah], *f.* A brunette.
Morenillo [mo-ray-neel'-lyo], *m.* A black powder, used by sheep-shearers for the wounds of sheep.
Morenillo, illa, ito, ita [mo-ray-neel'-lyo], *a. dim.* of Moreno; brunette: used always as endearing.
Moreno, na [mo-ray'-no, nah], *a.* 1. Brown, inclining to black. 2. Swarthy: applied to the complexion. *Ponerse moreno,* To become sunburned. *Sobre ello, morena,* If you do not, you will be punished; a menace.
Morera [mo-ray'-rah], *f.* (Bot.) White mulberry-tree. Morus alba.—*pl. V.* Moreral.
Moreral [mo-ray-rahl'], *m.* Plantation of white mulberry-trees.
Morería [mo-ray-ree'-ah], *f.* 1. Suburb or quarter where Moors reside. 2. A Moorish province or lands.
Moretón [mo-ray-tone'], *m.* (Coll.) Bruise, ecchymosis.
Morfa [mor'-fah], *f.* Scale, disease produced by scale-insects on orange and lemon-trees. (Lat. morbus.)
Morfeo [mor-fay'-o], *m.* (Myth.) Morpheus.
Morfina [mor-fee'-nah], *f.* Morphine, the chief alkaloid of opium.
Morfología [mor-fo-lo-hee'-ah], *f.* Morphology, the science of organic forms.
Morfológico, ca [mor-fo-lo'-he-co, cah], *a.* Morphologic(al).
Morga [more'-gah], *f.* Indian berries. Cocculus Indicus.
Morganático [mor-gah-nah'-te-co], *a.* Morganatic. *V.* Matrimonio.
Moribundo, da [mo-re-boon'-do, dah], *a.* Dying, near death.
Moriche [mo-ree'-chay], *m.* An American tree, like the cocoanut, useful to mankind.
Moriego, ga [mo-re-ay'-go, gah], *a.* (Prov.) Moorish.
Morigeración [mo-re-hay-rah-the-on'], *f.* Morigeration, obedience, obsequiousness, temperance.
Morigerar [mo-re-hay-rar'], *va.* To endeavour to curb or restrain one's affections and passions; to moderate.
Morillo [mo-reel'-lyo], *m.* 1. (Dim.) A little Moor. 2. Andiron.
Morir [mo-reer'], *vn.* 1. To die, to expire. 2. To die, to perish, to come to nothing. 3. To hanker, to desire excessively. 4. To perish or be lost for want of any thing. *Morir de sed,* To die with thirst. *Morir de frío,* To perish with cold. *Morir al mundo,* To quit the world. *Morir vestido,* To die a violent death; to die suddenly; not to die in bed.—*vr.* 1. To go out, to be extinguished or quenched: applied to fire or light. 2. To be benumbed: applied to a limb. *Morirse por,* To be excessively fond of. *Morir de pesadumbre,* To die broken-hearted. *Irse muriendo,* To die away gradually.
Morisco, ca [mo-rees'-co, cah], *a.* Moorish, belonging to the Moors.—*m.* & *f.* Name given to the Moors who remained in Spain after its restoration, and to their descendants, till they were expelled by Philip III.
Morisma [mo-rees'-mah], *f.* Mohammedan sect; multitude of Moors.
Morisqueta [mo-ris-kay'-tah], *f.* (Coll.) 1. Moorish trick. 2. Deception, fraud, trick. 3. Rice boiled, and without salt, the ordinary food of the Indian natives of the Philippines.
Morlaco, ca [mor-lah'-co, cah], *a.* Affecting ignorance and stupidity.
Morlés [mor-less'], *m.* A sort of linen loosely woven, made at Morlaix; lawn. *Morlés de morlés,* 1. (Coll.) All of a piece. 2. The finest linen.
Morlón, na, *a. V.* Morlaco.
Mormones [mor-mo'-nes], *m. pl.* Mormons, Latter-day Saints, a sect founded by Joseph Smith in 1830.
Mormullo, Mormureo [mor-mool'-lyo, mor-moo-ray'-o], *m.* Mutter, murmur; a low noise. *V.* Murmullo.
Mormuración [mor-moo-rah-the-on'], *f. V.* Murmuración.
Mormurador [mor-moo-rah-dor'], *m.* Murmurer, detractor.
Mormurar [mor-moo-rar'], *va.* To murmur. *V.* Murmurar.
Moro, ra [mo'-ro, rah], *a.* 1. Moorish, belonging to the Moors. 2. In jocular style, it is applied to wine not mixed with water or christened.—*m.* & *f.* Moor, a native of Africa. *Haber moros y cristianos,* To have a great scuffle or dispute.
Morocada [mo-ro-cah'-dah], *f.* Blow given by a ram with its horn, butt.
Morocho, cha [mo-ro'-cho, chah], *a.* (Amer.) 1. Fresh, vigorous, well preserved: said of persons. 2. Applied to a hard kind of Indian corn. 3. *V.* Gemelo.
Morón [mo-rone'], *m.* Hill, hillock.
Moroncho, cha [mo-ron'-cho, chah], *a. V.* Morondo.
Morondanga [mo-ron-dahn'-gah], *f.* (Coll.) Hodge-podge, medley.
Morondo, da [mo-ron'-do, dah], *a.* Bald, leafless.
Moronía [mo-ro-nee'-ah], *f.* A dish made of a variety of vegetables. *V.* Alboronía.
Morosamente, *adv.* Slowly, tardily.
Morosidad [mo-ro-se-dahd'], *f.* Slowness, tardiness, detention, delay.
Moroso, sa [mo-ro'-so, sah], *a.* Slow, tardy, heavy. *Juro moroso,* Law giving the king any property till a just claim is made of it.
Morquera [mor-kay'-rah], *f.* (Bot.) Spanish thyme. Thymus zygis.
Morra [mor'-rah], *f.* 1. Upper part of the head, top, crown. 2. Vulgar play with the fingers; odd or even. *Andar a la morra,* To come to blows.
Morrada [mor-rah'-dah], *f.* Butting with the heads by two persons.
Morral [mor-rahl'], *m.* 1. A bag hung to the mouths of mules or horses, out of which they eat when travelling. 2. Game-bag.
Morralla [mor-rahl'-lyah], *f.* 1. Small fry, little fish. 2. Heap or medley of useless things. 3. Rabble.
Morrillo [mor-reel'-lyo], *m.* 1. Pebble. 2. Fat of the nape of a sheep.
Morriña [mor-ree'-nyah], *f.* 1. Murrain, a disease among cattle. 2. Sadness, melancholy.
Morrión [mor-re-on'], *m.* 1. Morion, steel helmet. 2. Vertigo, a disease in hawks.
Morro [mor'-ro], *m.* 1. Any thing that is round like the head. 2. Headland, head, bluff. 3. A prominent, overhanging lip. *Andar al morro,* To come to blows.
Morro, rra, *a.* Purring: applied to a cat.
Morrocotudo, da [mor-ro-co-too'-do, dah], *a.* 1. Strong, stout, solid. 2. Of much importance or difficulty.
Morroncho, cha [mor-ron'-cho, chah], *a.* (Prov.) Mild, meek, tame.
Morrudo, da [mor-roo'-do, dah], *a.* Blobber-lipped, flap-mouthed, having prominent lips.
Morsa [mor'-sah], *f.* Walrus, morse, a large marine seal-like mammal (fr. Danish).
Mortadela [mor-tah-day'-lah], *f.* Bologna sausage.
Mortaja [mor-tah'-hah], *f.* 1. Shroud, winding-sheet, grave-clothes. 2. Mortise, a hole cut into wood. 3. (Amer.)

Cigarette paper. (Acad.) *Mortajas de molinete*, (Naut.) Pawl-plates.

Mortal [mor-tahl'], *a.* 1. Mortal, subject to death. 2. Mortal, fatal, deadly, destructive. 3. Mortal, deadly, implacable. 4. One who has the appearance or symptoms of death.

Mortal [mor-tahl'], *m.* Mortal, human being: commonly used in the plural.

Mortalidad [mor-tah-le-dahd'], *f.* Mortality, liability to death.

Mortalmente, *adv.* Mortally.

Mortandad [mor-tan-dahd'], *f.* Mortality, frequency of death; massacre, butchery.

Mortecino, na [mor-tay-thee'-no, nah], *a.* 1. Dying a natural death: applied to an animal that dies of itself, and to its flesh. 2. Dying away or extinguishing; on the point of dying. 3. (Low) Weak, exhausted. *Hacer la mortecina*, To feign death. *Color mortecino*, A pale or deadly colour.

Morterada [mor-tay-rah'-dah], *f.* 1. Sauce made at once in a mortar. 2. Quantity of stones thrown out at once by a stone mortar.

Morterete [mor-tay-ray'-tay], *m.* 1. (Dim.) A small mortar. 2. Piece of wax in shape of a mortar, with a wick in it, to serve as a lamp: it is placed in a glass with water. 3. (Met.) Hollow piece of iron used for firing gunpowder at rejoicings.

Morterico, illo, ito [mor-tay-ree'-co], *m. dim.* A small mortar.

Mortero [mor-tay'-ro], *m.* 1. Mortar, a piece of ordnance. 2. Mortar, a vessel in which materials are pounded with a pestle. 3. Mortar, a building cement. *Mortero de una bomba de agua*, (Naut.) Pump-box of a ship's pump. *Mortero de brújula*, An inner compass-box.

Morteruelo [mor-tay-roo-ay'-lo], *m.* 1. (Dim.) A small mortar. 2. A kind of play of boys. 3. Fricassee of hog's liver.

Mortífero, ra [mor-tee'-fay-ro, rah], *a.* Death-dealing, fatal.

Mortificación [mor-te-fe-cah-the-on'], *f.* 1. Mortification of the body, by hardships and macerations. 2. Mortification, gangrene. 3. Mortification, vexation, trouble.

Mortificar [mor-te-fe-car'], *va.* 1. To mortify, to destroy vital qualities. 2. To mortify, to subdue inordinate passions. 3. To mortify, to afflict, to disgust, to vex.—*vr.* 1. To mortify, to gangrene. 2. To mortify, to practise religious severities; to conquer one's passions.

Mortuorio [mor-too-o'-re-o], *m.* Burial, funeral.—*a.* Mortuary, belonging to the dead. *Casa mortuoria*, House of the deceased.

Morueca [mo-roo-ay'-cah], *f.* Heap of loose stones.

Morueco [mo-roo-ay'-co], *m.* Ram, a male sheep.

Moruno, na [mo-roo'-no, nah], *a.* Moorish, belonging to the Moors.

Morusa [mo-roo'-sah], *f.* (Coll.) Cash, specie; money in hand.

Mosa [mo'-sah], *f.* (Zool.) Moose.

Mosaico, ca [mo-sah'-e-co, cah], *a.* Mosaic. *Obra mosaica*, Mosaic work.

Mosaismo [mo-sah-ees'-mo], *m.* The Mosaic law or civilization.

Mosca [mos'-cah], *f.* 1. Fly, a two-winged insect; the house-fly. 2. (Coll.) Cash, specie; money in hand. *Tener mucha mosca*, To be very rich. 3. An impertinent intruder. 4. Vexation, trouble. 5. *pl.* Sparks from a light. 6. *pl.* Exclamation of complaint or surprise. *Mosca de burro*, Horse-fly. Œstrus equi. *Mosca en leche*, Brown or black woman dressed in white. *Mosca jorobada*, The dung-fly. *Mosca muerta*, Applied to persons apparently spiritless, but not so in reality. *Andar con mosca*, To fly into a passion. *Llevar mosca*, (Coll.) To go away offended and in a passion. *Moscas blancas*, Falling snowflakes. *Papar moscas*, To gape with astonishment. *Picarle la mosca*, To spend a bad quarter of an hour; to be disquieted. *Sacudir las moscas*, To shake off an incumbrance. *Soltar* or *aflojar la mosca*, To give or spend money by force.

Moscada, *a.* *V.* Nuez moscada.

Moscarda [mos-car'-dah], *f.* 1. Gad-fly, Horse-fly. Œstrus. 2. (Prov.) Eggs of bees.

Moscardear [mos-car-day-ar'], *vn.* (Prov.) To lay eggs as bees in the cells of their combs.

Moscardón [mos-car-done'], *m.* 1. Large gad-fly or horse-fly. 2. A hornet. 3. An importuning, sly fellow, a cheat.

Moscareta [mos-cah-ray'-tah], *f.* (Orn.) Fly-catcher. Muscicapa.

Moscatel [mos-cah-tel'], *a.* 1. Muscat or muscatel; musk-flavoured: applied to a kind of grape and to the wine made from them. 2. A tiresome, ignorant fellow.

Moscella, *f.* *V.* Morcella.

Mosco [mos'-co], *m.* *V.* Mosquito.

Moscón [mos-cone'], *m.* 1. A large fly, a blow-fly. 2. A hanger-on, a crafty, deceitful fellow.

Moscovita [mos-co-vee'-tah], *a.* Muscovite, Russian.

Mosén [mo-sen'], *m.* Sir: title given in Arragon and Valencia to ecclesiastics.

Mosqueado, da [mos-kay-ah'-do, dah], *a.* Spotted, painted.—*pp.* of Mosquear.

Mosqueador [mos-kay-ah-dor'], *m.* 1. Fly-trap, flap for killing flies. 2. (Coll.) Tail of animals.

Mosquear [mos-kay-ar'], *va.* 1. To flap, to frighten flies away with a flap; to catch flies. 2. To retort a joke, to make a smart repartee. *Mosquear las espaldas*, (Coll.) To flog the shoulders.—*vr.* To repel embarrassments with violence. (Coll.) To become angry or vexed.

Mosqueo [mos-kay'-o], *m.* The act of catching flies or driving them away with a flap.

Mosquero [mos-kay'-ro], *m.* Fly-trap.

Mosqueruela [mos-kay-roo-ay'-lah], *f.* Muscadine pear.

Mosqueta [mos-kay'-tah], *f.* White musk-rose.

Mosquetazo [mos-kay-tah'-tho], *m.* Musket-shot.

Mosquete [mos-kay'-tay], *m.* Musket, blunderbuss, an ancient fire-arm, which was rested upon a crotch to fire it.

Mosquetería [mos-kay-tay-re'-ah], *f.* 1. A body of musketeers. 2. The company in the pit of a play-house.

Mosqueteril [mos-kay-tay-reel'], *a.* (Coll.) 1. Belonging to musketeers. 2. Belonging to the crowd in the pit of a theatre.

Mosquetero [mos-kay-tay'-ro], *m.* 1. Musketeer, a foot-soldier. 2. Person who frequents the pit in a play-house.

Mosquil, Mosquino, na [mos-keel', mos-kee'-no, nah], *a.* Belonging to flies.

Mosquita [mos-kee'-tah], *f.* A small bird of Sardinia in whose nest the cuckoo lays an egg.

Mosquitero, ra [mos-ke-tay'-ro, rah], *m.* & *f.* Mosquito bar or net, a gauze cover hung over a bed, to keep off gnats and mosquitoes.

Mosquito [mos-kee'-to], *m.* 1. Gnat, mosquito. 2. Tippler.

Mostacera [mos-tah-thay'-rah], *f.* Mustard-pot.

Mostacilla [mos-tah-theel'-lyah], *f.* 1. Sparrow-shot, the smallest kind of bird-shot. 2. Seed bugle; very small glass, gold, silver, or steel beads.

Mostacho [mos-tah'-cho], *m.* 1. *V.* Bigote. 2. Spot in the face, gloom in the countenance. *Mostachos*, (Naut.) Standing lifts. *Mostachos del bauprés*, (Naut.) Bowsprit-shrouds.

Mostachón [mos-tah-chone'], *m.* A kind of ginger-bread.

Mostachoso, sa [mos-tah-cho'-so, sah], *a.* Wearing a mustache.

Mostajo [mos-tah'-ho], *m.* (Bot.) White beam-tree; Cumberland hawthorn. Cratægus aria.

Mostaza [mos-tah'-thah], *f.* 1. (Bot.) Mustard. Sinapis. 2. Mustard-seed. 3. Fine shot. *Hacer la mostaza*, To make the nose bleed with a blow.

Mostazo [mos-tah'-tho], *m.* (Bot.) Mustard; a plant. 2. (Aug.) Strong, thick must.

Mostear [mos-tay-ar'], *vn.* 1. To yield must: applied to grapes. 2. To put must into vats or earthen jars to ferment. 3. To mix must with old wine, in order to revive it. *V.* Remostar.

Mostela [mos-tay'-lah], *f.* (Prov.) Sprig or twig of vines.

Mostelera [mos-tay-lay'-rah], *f.* Place where the sprigs or twigs of vines are laid up.

Mostellar [mos-tel-lyar'], *m.* A tree having a white hard wood and a fleshy-red fruit.

Mostén, Mostense, *a.* *V.* Premonstratense.

Mostillo [mos-teel'-lyo], *m.* 1. Cake made of must and other ingredients. 2. Sauce made of must and mustard.

Mosto [mos'-to], *m.* 1. Must, the pressed juice of the grape not yet fermented. 2. Stum, must, new wine. *Mosto agustín*, A kind of cake.

Mostrable [mos-trah'-blay], *a.* That which may be shown.

Mostrado, da [mos-trah'-do, dah], *a.* Accustomed, habituated, inured.—*pp.* of Mostrar.

Mostrador, ra [mos-trah-dor', rah], *m.* & *f.* 1. Demonstrator, one who demonstrates, one who shows.—*m.* 2. Pointer, hand of a clock or watch. 3. Counter, the table of a shop.

Mostrar [mos-trar'], *va.* 1. To show, to exhibit to view, to point out, to lay before. 2. To show, to establish, to prove, to explain, to expound, to demonstrate. 3. To show or make a thing appear what it is not, to feign, to dissemble. 4. To show any quality of the mind. *Mostrar las suelas de los zapatos*, To run away.—*vr.* To appear, to show one's self.

Mostrenco, ca [mos-tren'-co, cah], *a.* 1. Strayed, having no owner. 2. Vagabond, vagrant: applied to a stroller without house or home. 3. Dull, ignorant, stupid. 4. (Prov.) Fat, bulky. *Bienes mostrencos*, Goods which have no known owner.

Mota [mo'-tah], *f.* 1. A small knot on cloth, which is taken off with burling irons or scissors. 2. A bit of thread or any thing similar sticking to clothes. 3. Mote, small particle of matter. 4. A slight defect or fault. 5. Bank or mound of earth. 6. Quota of each sailor to a common fund for subsistence stores, when the crew of a merchant vessel join together in trading.

Motacilla [mo-tah-theel'-lyah], *f.* *V.* Aguzanieve.

Mote [mo'-tay], *m.* 1. Motto or sentence added to a device, or prefixed to any thing written. 2. Nickname. 3. (Peru, Bol.) Pop-corn.

Motear [mo-tay-ar'], *vn.* To speckle, to mark with spots.

Motejador, ra [mo-tay-hah-dor', rah], *m.* & *f.* Mocker, scoffer, censurer.

Motejar [mo-tay-har'], *va.* To censure, to ridicule, to nickname.

Motete [mo-tay'-tay], *m.* Motet or motetto, a short musical composition to be sung in church.

Motil [mo-teel'], *m.* *V.* Mochil.

Motilar [mo-te-lar'], *va.* To cut the hair, to crop.

Motilón, na [mo-te-lone', nah], *a.* Poor, indigent.—*m.* (Coll.) Lay-brother of a religious order.

Motín [mo-teen'], *m.* Mutiny, insurrection, riot.

Motita [mo-tee'-tah], *f.* A small bit of thread or any other thing sticking to cloths.

Motivar [mo-te-var'], *va.* To give a reason for any thing, to assign a motive.

Motivo [mo-tee'-vo], *m.* 1. Motive, cause, reason, occasion, impulse. 2. Motif, motive, or theme in a musical composition.

Motivo, va, *a.* Motive, moving, causing motion; having the power to move. *De su motivo*, Of one's own accord. *Con motivo de*, Owing to, by reason of.

Motocicleta [mo-to-the-clay'-tah], *f.* Motorcycle.

Motolita [mo-to-lee'-tah], *f.* *V.* Aguzanieve.

Motolito, ta [mo-to-lee'-to, tah], **Motolótico, ca,** *a.* Easily deceived, ignorant.

Motón [mo-tone'], *m.* (Naut.) Block, pulley, tackle for ropes to run in. *Motón ciego*, Dead-block. *Motón sencillo*, Single-block. *Motón de gancho*, Hook-block. *Motón de aparejo*, Tackle-block. *Motón de amantillo*, Lift-block. *Motón de la gata*, Catblock. *Motón del virador del tamborete*, Top-block. *Motones*, (Naut.) Pulleys with sheaves. *Motones herrados*, Iron-bound blocks. *Motones de retorno*, Leading-blocks. *Motones de aparejo de combés*, Winding-tackle-blocks. *Motones de las cañas de la cebadera*, Sprit-sail sheet-blocks. *Motones de la driza mayor*, Main gear-blocks. *Motones de los palanquines de las velas mayores*, Clew-garnet-blocks.

Motonave [mo-to-nah'-vay], *f.* Motorship.

Motonería [mo-to-nay-ree' ah], *f.* (Naut.) Blocks and pulleys in ships.

Motonero [mo-to-nay'-ro], *m.* Blockmaker.

Motor, ra [mo-tor', rah], *a.* Motor, motive causing motion.—*m.* Motor, a prime mover, particularly an electrical machine.

Motorista [mo-to-rees'-tah], *m.* Motorman.

Motril, *m.* *V.* Mochil.

Motriz [mo-treeth'], *a.* Motor, motive, moving cause. *Fuerza motriz*, Moving cause.

Motu proprio [mo'-too pro'-pre-o]. (Lat.) By his own will.

Movedizo, za [mo-vay-dee'-tho, thah], *a.* 1. Movable, easily moved. 2. Variable, unsteady, inconstant, shifting.

Movedor, ra [mo-vay-dor', rah], *m.* & *f.* Mover, motor, exciter, occasioner.

Movedura, *f.* *V.* Movimiento.

Mover [mo-verr'], *va.* 1. To move, to put in motion. 2. To move, to prevail upon, to persuade, to induce. 3. To move, to stir passion, to touch pathetically, to cause or give occasion to. 4. To move, to stir up, to put into commotion. 5. To move, to excite, to commence a thing. 6. To move, to inspire.—*vn.* 1. (Arch.) To spring an arch. 2. To bud, to begin to sprout. 3. To miscarry, to have an abortion. —*vr.* 1. To move, to be in a state of changing place, to walk. 2. To move, to have vital action. 3. To move, to go forward.

Movible [mo-vee'-blay], *a.* 1. Movable, locomotive. 2. Variable.

Moviente [mo-ve-en'-tay], *pa.* & *a.* Moving, motory.

Móvil [mo'-veel], *a.* Movable, capable of moving or of being moved.—*m.* Mover, motor. *Primer móvil*, Primum mobile; prime motor.

Movilidad [mo-ve-le-dahd'], *f.* 1. Mobility, movableness, aptitude to be moved. 2. Mobility, inconstancy, unsteadiness, levity.

Movilización [mo-ve-le-thah-the-on'], *f.* Mobilization.

Movilizar [mo-ve-le-thar'], *va.* 1. To put in movement. 2. To mobilize, to make ready for active service.—*vr.* 1. To be set in motion. 2. To be mobilized, to go into active service.

Movimiento [mo-ve-me-en'-to], *m.* 1. Movement, motion, moving. 2. Commotion, disturbance, sedition, revolt. 3. (Arch.) *V.* Arranque.

Moya [mo'-yah], *f.* (Amer. Colom.) A small, unglazed jar for boiling salt.

Moyana [mo-yah'-nah], *f.* 1. A small culverin. 2. (Coll.) Lie, falsehood. 3. Bread made of bran for feeding dogs.

Moyo [mo'-yo], *m.* 1. Liquid measure of about 32 gallons or 129 litres. 2. Number of tiles fixed at 110.

Moyuelo [mo-yoo-ay'-lo], *m.* Grits, pollard, coarse meal.

Moza [mo'-thah], *f.* 1. Girl, a maidservant engaged to do all kinds of work. *Moza de cámara*, Chambermaid. *Moza de cántaro*, Girl to carry water. *Moza de fortuna*, Prostitute. 2. A clothes-pounder, used to beat linen when it is washing. 3. Last or conquering game.

Mozalbete, Mozalbillo [mo-thal-bay'-tay, mo-thal-beel'-lyo], *m.* A lad, a beardless youth.

Mozallón [mo-thal-lyone'], *m.* A young, robust labourer.

Mozcorra [moth-cor'-rah], *f.* (Vulg.) A common prostitute.

Mozo, za [mo'-tho, thah], *a.* 1. Young, youthful. 2. Applied to any unmarried person.

Mozo [mo'-tho], *m.* 1. Youth, a young man, a lad. 2. Man-servant engaged to do all kinds of work in the house. 3. Bachelor, a man unmarried. 4. (Coll.) Fellow. 5. Waiter. *Mozo de caballos*, Groom, horse-boy. *Mozo de paja y cebada*, Hostler at an inn. 6. Dumbwaiter. *Mozo de mulas*, Muleteer, who walks at the head of his mules; feeder of mules. *Mozo de espuela* or *de espuelas*, *V.* Espolista. *Mozo de bomba*, Fireman. *Mozo de cordel* or *de esquina*, Porter in the street. *V.* Ganapán.

Mozón [mo-thone'], *m. aug.* A robust young man.

Mozuela [mo-thoo-ay'-lah], *f. dim.* 1. A very young lass or woman: sometimes applied in contempt. 2. (Vulg.) A prostitute.

Mozuelo [mo-thoo-ay'-lo], *m. dim.* A very young man or lad.

Mozuelo, la [mo-thoo-ay'-lo, lah], *a. dim.* Young, youthful.

Mu [moo], *f.* A child's word for sleep. *¡ Vamos a la mu !* Go to sleep! (said to children).—*m.* Lowing of cattle. (Imitative.)

Muaré, *m.* (Acad.) *V.* Moaré.

Mucamuca [moo-cah-moo'-cah], *f.* (Peru.) *V.* Zorra mochilera.

Muceta [moo-thay'-tah], *f.* 1. Part of the dress worn by bishops when officiating. 2. A short cape worn by doctors.

Mucilaginoso, sa [moo-the-lah-he-no'-so, sah], *a.* Mucilaginous, slimy.

Mucílago (Acad.), or **Mucilago** [moo-thee'-lah-go], *m.* Mucilage, a solution of gum; any viscous or slimy body.

Mucina [moo-thee'-nah], *f.* Mucin, an alkaline glutinous fluid.

Muciparo, ra [moo-thee'-pah-ro, rah], *a.* Muciparous, secreting mucus.

Mucol [moo-cole'], *m.* Mucilage considered as an excipient.

Mucor [moo-cor'], *m.* Mucor, mouldiness.

Mucosidad [moo-co-se-dahd'], *f.* Mucosity, mucilaginousness.

Mucoso, sa [moo-co'-so, sah], *a.* Mucous, slimy, viscous, mucilaginous.

Mucronato, ta [moo-cro-nah'-to, tah], *a.* Mucronate, tipped with a sharp point.

Múcura [moo'-coo-rah], *f.* A kind of pitcher or ewer used in Venezuela among Indians.

Muchachada [moo-chah-chah'-dah], *f.* A boyish trick, a girlish trick, gaiety.

Muchachear [moo-chah-chay-ar'], *vn.* To act in a boyish or childish manner, to fumble or play childishly.

Muchachería [moo-chah-chay-ree'-ah], *f.* 1. Boyish trick. 2. Clamorous noise made by a crowd of boys.

Muchahez [moo-chah-cheth'], *f.* Childhood; puerility; boyhood.

Muchacha [moo-chah'-chah], *f.* Girl; lass, child.

Muchacho [moo-chah'-cho], *m.* Boy, lad.

Muchacho, cha [moo-chah'-cho, chah], *a.* Boyish, girlish, childish.

Muchedumbre [moo-chay-doom'-bray], *f.* Multitude, many, a great number; plenty, abundance, much.

Muchísimo, ma [moo-chee'-se-mo, mah], *a.* Superlative of Mucho. Very much, very large; a great deal.

Mucho, cha [moo'-cho, chah], *a.* Much, large in quantity, long in time, many in number; abundant, plentiful. *No ha mucho*, Not long since. *No es mucho*, It is no wonder.—*adv.* Much, in a great degree; excessively, by far, often, long; to a certain degree.

Muda [moo'-dah], *f.* 1. Change, alteration. 2. Change of linen. 3. The act and time of moulting and shedding feathers. 4. A transition of the voice in boys who come to maturity. 5. Roost of birds of prey. 6. A cosmetic. *Estar en muda*, To keep silence in company.

Mudable [moo-dah'-blay], *a.* Changeable, variable, mutable, fickle, light.

Mudamente, *adv.* Silently, tacitly, mutely.

Mudanza [moo-dahn'-thah], *f.* 1. Alteration, change; mutation, commutation. 2. Removal from place to place. 3. Inconstancy, levity. 4. Certain number of motions in a dance.

Mudar [moo-dar'], *va.* 1. To change, to put one thing in place of another, to remove, to deviate. 2. To change, to cause alteration, to vary, to alter. 3. To change one thing for another, or to quit any thing for the sake of another. 4. To shed the feathers, to moult. 5. To change the voice: applied to boys who come to maturity. 6. To change, to vary in a moral sanse; to mend the disposition.—*vr.* 1. To change, to undergo change. 2. To change the sentiments and manners. 3. To shift, to dress in fresh linen or clothes. 4. To move into another house. 5. (Coll.) To wander from the topic of conversation.

Mudéjar [moo-day'-har], *a.* & *m. pl.* Used of a Mohammedan who, without changing his religion, became a subject of Christian sovereigns.

Mudez [moo-deth'], *f.* Dumbness; impediment of speech.

Mudo, da [moo'-do, dah], *a.* Dumb, silent, still, mute.

Mué, Muer [moo-ay', moo-err'], *m.* Tabby, moiré, watered silk.

Mueblaje [moo-ay-blah'-hay], *m.* Fitment, collection of furniture.

Mueble [moo-ay'-blay], *m.* Any movable piece of furniture—*pl.* Movable goods, chattels, furniture, household stuff.

Mueblista [moo-ay-blees'-tah], *m.* Furniture dealer, furniture maker.

Mueca [moo-ay'-cah], *f.* Grimace, wry face, grin.

Muedín [moo-ay-deen'], *m.* Muezzin, one who calls the Mohammedan faithful to prayer. (Ar.) *V.* ALMUÉDANO.

Muela [moo-ay'-lah], *f.* 1. In corn-mills, runner, the upper mill-stone. 2. Grindstone, whetstone. 3. Water sufficient to set a mill in motion. 4. Hill, hillock; any artificial mound. 5. Track or circle made with any thing. 6. Grinder, one of the back teeth, molar teeth. *Muelas de gallo,* As toothless as a cock. *Muela cordal,* Wisdom tooth. *Al que le duele la muela, que se la saque,* It is none of my business. *Entre dos muelas cordales* (or *molares*), *nunca metas* (or *pongas*) *tus pulgares,* Avoid meddling in family quarrels.

Muellaje [moo-el-yah'-hay], *m.* Wharfage, dockage, a harbour tax.

Muelle [moo-el'-lyay], *a.* 1. Tender, delicate, soft. 2. Licentious, luxurious.—*m.* 1. Spring, an elastic body. 2. Regulator, a small spring which regulates the movements of a watch. 3. (Naut.) Mole, pier; jetty; quay, wharf; a place in a seaport for shipping goods, etc. 4. (Obs.) Gewgaw, trinket worn by women of distinction.

Muellear [moo-el-yay-ar'], *vn.* To bear against, to prop. A word much used by type-founders.

Muellemente, *adv.* Tenderly, gently, softly.

Muérdago [moo-err'-dah-go], *m.* (Bot.) Mistletoe. Viscum album.

(*Yo muerdo, yo muerda,* from *Morder. V.* MOVER.)

Muermera [moo-er-may'-rah], *f.* (Bot.) Common virgin's-bower; traveller's-joy. Clematis vitalba.

Muermo [moo-err'-mo], *m.* Glanders, a contagious disease in horses, affecting the nose and accompanied by a pustular eruption.

Muermoso, sa [moo-er-mo'-so, sah], *a.* Snoring, breathing with difficulty; glandered.

(*Yo muero, yo muera; el murió, muriera,* from *Morir. V.* DORMIR.)

Muerte [moo-err'-tay], *f.* 1. Death, the extinction of life. 2. Death, murder, assassination, the act of killing unlawfully. 3. Death, image of mortality, represented by a skeleton. 4. A violent affection that cannot be borne, labour, difficulty, severe affliction. *Muerte civil,* (1) (Law) Civil death. (2) (Coll.) A miserable and painful life. *Buena muerte,* A good end. the contrite death of a person. *Bajo pena de muerte,* On pain of death. *Hasta la muerte,* Until death. *A muerte o a vida,* Kill or cure; at all risks. *Estar a la muerte,* To be at death's door. *Sentir de muerte,* To regret exceedingly (to be sorry to death). *Tomarse la muerte por su mano,* To imperil one's life, health, or welfare against good advice.

Muerto [moo-err'-to], *m.* 1. Corpse, a dead body. 2. (Naut.) The standing part of a running rope.—*pl.* 1. Stripes, strokes, blows. 2. (Naut.) Ground-ways.

Muerto, ta [moo-err'-to, tah], *a.* & *pp. irr.* of MORIR. 1. Dead, extinguished, lifeless. 2. Languid, faded: applied to spirits or colours. 3. Slaked: applied to lime. *Manos muertas,* Mortmain.

Muesca [moo-ays'-cah], *f.* 1. Groove cut in the staves of casks and baskets, in which the bottoms and head-pieces are fixed; hack, nick, mortise. 2. An empty or void space. *V.* MELLA. 3. Dove-tail scarf.

Muestra [moo-ays'-trah], *f.* 1. A small sample of cloth. 2. Outer piece of cloth where the stamp of the maker is put. 3. A shop sign. 4. Any indicative sign or demonstration of a thing. 5. Specimen, design, model, copy. 6. (Mil. Obs.) Muster-roll. 7. Clock which does not strike. *Muestra de faltriquera,* Watch.

(*Yo muestro, yo muestre,* from *Mostrar. V.* ACORDAR.)

(*Yo muevo, yo mueva. V.* MOVER.)

Muestrario [moo-es-trah'-re-o], *m.* Samples, set of samples.

Mufla [moo'-flah], *f.* Muffle, an earthen cover placed over tests and coppels in the assaying of metals. *Muflas,* Thick winter gloves, which serve instead of a muff.

Mufti [moof'-te], *m.* Mufti, the high-priest of the Mohammedans.

Mugido [moo-hee'-do], *m.* The lowing of an ox, cow, or bull.

Múgil [moo'-heel], *m.* Mullet. *V.* MÚJOL.

Mugir [moo-heer'], *vn.* To low, to bellow like an ox.

Mugre [moo'-gray], *f.* Grime, dirt, or filth which sticks to clothes and other things.

Mugriento, ta [moo-gre-en'-to, tah], *a.* Greasy, dirty, filthy, grimy.

Mugrón [moo-grone'], *m.* Sprig or shoot of a vine.

Muguete [moo-gay'-tay], *m.* Lily of the valley. (Fr. muguet.)

Muharra [moo-ar'-rah], *f.* The steel point at the top of the staff of a pair of colours.

Muito [moo'-e-to], *a.* & *adv.* (Obs.) *V.* MUCHO.

Mujer [moo-herr'], *f.* 1. Woman, the female of the human race. *Ser mujer,* To be a woman, to have attained the age of puberty. 2. Wife, mate. *Mujer de su casa* or *mujer de gobierno,* Housewife, a woman skilled in female business. *Mujer varonil,* A manly woman. *Mujer pública* or *mundana,* A prostitute, a street-walker. *Mujer de bigotes,* Clever, commanding woman. *A la mujer y a la mula, por el pico* (or *pienso*) *les entra la hermosura,* Comfort and kindness contribute to beauty. *La mujer y la pera, la que calla es buena,* Silence is very desirable in a woman. *La primera mujer escoba, y la segunda señora,* The first wife is a drudge, the second a lady. *La mujer y la sardina, de rostros en la ceniza,* The fireside duties are best for a woman.

Mujeracha [moo-hay-rah'-chah], *f.* (Coll.) A coarse woman of the lowest class.

Mujercilla [moo-her-theel'-lyah], *f.* A worthless woman; jade, hussy; a strumpet.—*m.* Hilding, a sorry, paltry, cowardly fellow.

Mujeriego, ga [moo-hay-re-ay'-go, gah], *a.* 1. Feminine, womanly, belonging to women. 2. Womanish, given to women.—*m.* Womankind; all the women of a place.

Mujeril [moo-hay-reel'], *a.* Womanish, womanly, feminine.

Mujerilmente, *adv.* Effeminately.

Mujerío [moo-hay-ree'-o], *m.* A gathering of women.

Mujerona [moo-hay-ro'-nah], *f. aug.* A stout woman; a matron.

Mula [moo'-lah], *f.* 1. She-mule. 2. A kind of thick-soled shoe. 3. A certain Moorish vessel.

Muladar [moo-lah-dar'], *m.* 1. Place where the dirt and sweepings of houses are put. 2. Dung-heap; rubbish heap. 3. Any thing very dirty or infectious.

Muladí [moo-lah-dee'], *a.* Renegade Spanish Christian who lived among the Moors.

Mular [moo-lar'], *a.* Belonging to mules.

Mulatero [moo-lah-tay'-ro], *m.* Muleteer, mule-driver; a mule-boy.

Mulato, ta [moo-lah'-to, tah], *a.* Mulatto, tawny.—*n.* Mulatto, the offspring of a white person and a black person.

Múleo, Muléolo [moo'-lay-o, moo-lay'-o-lo], *m.* Name of a pointed, purple-coloured footwear used among the Roman patricians.

Muleque [moo-lay'-kay], *n.* (Cuba) A newly arrived negro of seven to ten years.

Mulero [moo-lay'-ro], *m.* Mule-boy, who takes care of mules employed in agriculture; a muleteer.—*a.* Applied to a horse fond of mules.

Muleta [moo-lay'-tah], *f.* 1. A young she-mule, not yet trained to work. 2. Crutch, prop, support. 3. An instrument of rope-makers. *Muleta de filar filástica,* (Naut.) Winch for making spun-yarn. 4. *V.* MULETILLA.

Muletada [moo-lay-tah'-dah], *f.* Herd of mules.

Muletero [moo-lay-tay'-ro], *m.* Muleteer, mule-driver.

Muletilla [moo-lay-teel'-lyah], *f.* 1. Word or phrase often repeated inadvertently in talking. 2. A wand or rod. 3. A rod with a cape (commonly red) which the bull-fighter uses to provoke the bull when he is about to kill it. 4. A passementerie button. 5. A cane, the head of which forms a kind of crutch.

Muleto [moo-lay'-to], *m.* A young he-mule not yet broken.

Mulilla [moo-leel'-lyah], *f. dim.* of MULA.

Mulo [moo'-lo], *m.* Mule.

Mulso, sa [mool'-so, sah], *a.* Of mixed honey and sugar.

Multa [mool'-tah], *f.* 1. Mulct, fine, forfeit, a pecuniary penalty. 2. A wild fruit-tree of Puerto Rico.

Multar [mool-tar'], *va.* To mulct, to fine, or impose a fine.

Multicaule [mool-te-cah'-oo-lay], *a.* (Bot.) Multicauline, having many stems.

Multicoloro, ra [mool-te-co-lo'-ro, rah], *a.* Many-hued, many-coloured.

Multifacético, ca [mool-te-fah-thay'-te-co, cah], *a.* With many phases.

Multifloro, ra [mool-te-flo'-ro, rah], *a.* Many-flowered.

Multiforme [mool-te-for'-may], *a.* Multiform.

Multígrafo [mool-tee'-grah-fo], *m.* Multigraph.

Multilátero, ra [mool-te-lah'-tay-ro, rah], *a.* Multilateral.

Multimillonario, ria [mool-te-mil-lyo-nah'-re-o, ah], *m.* & *f.* Multi-millionaire.

Multinomio, mia [mool-te-no'-me-o, ah], *a.* (Alg.) Polynomial.

Múltiple [mool'-te-play], *a.* Multiple, complex; opposed to simple.

Multiplicable [mool-te-ple-cah'-blay], *a.* Multiplicable, multipliable.

Multiplicación [mool-te-ple-cah-the-on'], *f.* Multiplication.

Multiplicador, ra [mool-te-ple-cah-dor', rah], *m.* & *f.* Multiplier; multiplicator.

Multiplicando [mool-te-ple-cahn'-do], *m.* (Arith.) Multiplicand.

Multiplicar [mool-te-ple-car'], *va.* & *vr.* To increase, to multiply.

Multíplice [mool-tee'-plee-thay], *a.* Multiple; multiplex.

Multiplicidad [mool-te-ple-the-dahd'], *f.* Multiplicity.

Múltiplo, pla [mool'-te-plo, plah], *a.* Multiple; exactly divided by another quantity. *V.* MULTÍPLICE.

Multitud [mool-te-tood'], *f.* Multitude, a great number. *V.* MUCHEDUMBRE.

Multivalvo, va [mool-te-vahl'-vo, vah], *a.* (Con.) Multivalve: applied to a class of shell-fish.

Mulla [mool'-lyah], *f.* The act of digging around vines.

Mullida [mool-yee'-dah], *f.* Ridge of soil between furrow and furrow.

Mullido [mool-yee'-do], *m.* A soft cushion, or pillow.

Mullidor, ra [mool-lye-dor', rah], *m.* & *f.* 1. Bruiser, mollifier. 2. *V.* MUÑIDOR.

Mullir [mool-lyeer'], *va.* 1. To beat up any thing, in order to make it soft and spongy. *Mullir la cama,* To beat up the bed. 2. To call, to convene. *V.* MUÑIR. 3. To adopt proper measures for attaining one's purpose. 4. To dig about the roots of vines and trees.

Mumiforme [moo-me-for'-may], *a.* Mummiform; like a mummy.

Mundanalidad [moon-dah-nah-le-dahd'], *f.* Worldliness.

Mundano, na [moon-dah'-no, nah], *a.* Mundane, worldly. *Mujer mundana,* Common prostitute.

Mundial [moon-de-ahl'], *a.* World-wide.

Mundificar [moon-de-fe-car'], *va.* To cleanse, to make clean.

Mundificativo, va [moon-de-fe-cah-tee'-vo, vah], *a.* Mundificant, cleansing.

Mundillo [moon-deel'-lyo], *m.* 1. An arched frame put over braziers to dry or air linen. 2. Cushion on which bone-lace is made. 3. Warming-pan.

Mundinovi, Mundonuevo [moon-de-no'-ve], *m.* Raree-show, magic lantern.

Mundo [moon'-do], *m.* 1. World, the collective idea of all bodies whatever; terrestrial sphere, globe. 2. (Coll.) Great multitude, great quantity. 3. (Met.) The manners of men; worldly desires and practices. 4. A dissipated life. *El nuevo mundo,* North and South America. *El otro mundo,* The next world, the world to come. *No ser de este mundo,* To live retired from the world; to be very innocent and simple. *Ver mundo,* To travel. *Medio mundo,* Many people. *Desde que el mundo es mundo,* From the beginning of time. *Echar al mundo,* To create. *Echarse al mundo,* To plunge into dissipation. *Echar del mundo,* To banish from society, to send to Coventry. *No caber en el mundo,* To be inflated with pride. *Ponerse el mundo por montera,* To care nothing for what people will say. *Tener mundo* or *mucho mundo,* To be acute, not easily deceived.

Munición [moo-ne-the-on'], *f.* 1. Munition or ammunition, materials for war; warlike stores. 2. Charge of fire-arms. *De munición,* Done in a hurry, and therefore badly. *Pan de munición,* Brown bread for soldiers.

Municionar [moo-ne-the-o-nar'], *va.* To supply with ammunition or warlike stores.

Municipal [moo-ne-the-pahl'], *a.* Municipal, corporate.

Municipalidad [moo-ne-the-pah-le-dahd'], *f.* Municipality; town council, the governing board of a city.

Munícipe [moo-nee'-the-pay], *m.* Citizen, denizen; member of a corporation.

Municipio [moo-ne-thee'-pe-o], *m.* Place which enjoys the rights and privileges of a city.

Munificencia [moo-ne-fe-then'-the-ah], *f.* Munificence, liberality.

Munificentísimo, ma [moo-ne-fe-then-tee'-se-mo, mah], *a. super.* of MUNÍFICO.

Munífico, ca [moo-nee'-fe-co, cah], *a.* Munificent, liberal.

Muñeca [moo-nyay'-cah], *f.* 1. The wrist. 2. A doll. 3. A small bundle of medicinal ingredients put into a decoction.—*pl.* In the mint, the screws that pinch the coin, and give it the due thickness. *Menear las muñecas,* (Met.) To work rapidly at any thing, to labour hard.

Muñeco [moo-nyay'-co], *m.* 1. Puppet, representing a male figure. 2. A soft, effeminate fellow.

Muñeira [moo-nyay'-e-rah], *f.* A popular dance of Galicia.

Muñequear [moo-nyay-kay-ar'], *va.* To play with the wrist in fencing.

Muñequera [moo-nyay-kay'-rah], *f.* Bracelet, an ornament for the wrist of dolls.

Muñequería [moo-nyay-kay-ree'-ah], *f.* Excessive fondness of dress and ornaments.

Muñidor [moo-nye-dor'], *m.* 1. Beadle of a corporation or confraternity; apparitor, messenger. 2. (Amer.) Undertaker.

Muñir [moo-nyeer'], *va.* To summon, to call to a meeting.

Muñón [moo-nyone'], *m.* 1. Brawn, the fleshy part of the body. 2. Stump of an amputated arm or leg. 3. Trunnion of a cannon; gudgeon, lug, swing-block.

Muñonera [moo-nyo-nay'-rah], *f.* Trunnion-plate, trunnion-socket; (Mech.) gudgeon-socket.

Murajes [moo-rah'-hes], *m.* A medicinal herb of pungent taste.

Mural [moo-rahl'], *a.* Mural, belonging to walls.

Muralla [moo-rahl'-lyah], *f.* Rampart which surrounds a place; wall.

Murar [moo-rar'], *va.* To wall, to surround with a rampart.

Murciano, na [moor-the-ah'-no, nah], *a.* Murcian, of Murcia.

Murciélago [moor-the-ay'-lah-go], *m.* (Zool.) The bat. Vespertilio.

Murecillo [moo-ray-theel'-lyo], *m.* (Anat. Obs.) *V.* MÚSCULO.

Murena [moo-ray'-nah], *f.* A kind of eel. *V.* MORENA.

Murga [moor'-gah], *f.* 1. *V.* ALPECHÍN. 2. In Madrid, strolling street musicians who play for a gratuity.

Muriático, ca [moo-ree-ah'-te-co, cah], *a.* (Chem.) Muriatic.

Muriato, *m.* (Chem.) Muriate.

Múrice [moo'-re-thay], *m.* 1. Porcelain shell-fish; generic name of sea-shells which end in a straight canal; murex, Tyrian purple. 2. (Poet.) Purple.

Múrido, da [moo'-re-do, dah], *a.* Mouse-like.

Murmujear [moor-moo-hay-ar'], *va.* To murmur, to mutter.

Murmullar [moor-mool-lyar'], *vn.* (Prov.) *V.* MURMURAR, 2d def.

Murmullo [moor-mool'-lyo], *m.* 1. Muttering, mumbling in speaking. 2. Murmuring, purling.

Murmuración [moor-moo-rah-the-on'], *f.* Backbiting, privy calumny, slander, gossiping, obloquy.

Murmurador, ra [moor-moo-rah-dor', rah], *m.* & *f.* Murmurer, detractor, backbiter.

Murmurar [moor-moo-rar'], *va.* 1. To murmur, to purl, to flow gently: applied to streams. 2. To murmur, to grudge, to grumble, to mutter. 3. To backbite, to censure an absent person.

Murmurio [moor-moo'-re-o], *m.* The purling or murmuring of a stream.

Muro [moo'-ro], *m.* Wall. *V.* PARED and MURALLA.

Murria [moor'-re-ah], *f.* 1. Heaviness of the head, lowness of spirits, melancholy, mumps, reverie, spleen. 2. A former astringent medicament.

Murrino, na [moor-ree'-no, nah], *a.* Applied to a cup or vase much esteemed in old times.

Murrio, ria [moor'-re-o, ah], *a.* Sad, melancholy.

Murta [moor'-tah], *f.* Myrtle. *V.* ARRAYÁN and MIRTO.

Murtal [moor-tahl'], *m.* Grove of myrtles.

Murtilla, Murtina [moor-teel'-lyah, moor-tee'-nah], *f.* (Bot.) 1. A shrub growing in Chili. 2. The fruit of the same shrub. 3. The fruit of the myrtle.

Murtón [moor-tone'], *m.* Myrtle-berry the fruit of myrtle.

Murucuya [moo-roo-coo'-yah], *f.* (Bot.) Purple passion-flower. Passiflora murucuja.

Murueco, *m.* *V.* MORUECO.

Musa [moo'-sah], *f.* 1. Muse, the goddess of poetry. 2. Poetic genius. 3. Musa, Latin name of the plantain and banana trees.

Musaraña [moo-sah-rah'-nyah], *f.* 1. Fetid shrew-mouse. Sorex araneus. 2. Spirit, ghost, hobgoblin. 3. Any insect or small animal; vermin.

Muscardina [moos-car-dee'-nah], *f.* Muscardin(e), a disease of silk-worms due to a fungus.

Muscaria, or **Muscícapa** [moos-cah'-re-ah, moos-thee'-cah-pah], *f.* (Orn.) Fly-catcher. Muscicapa.

Múscido, da [moos'-the-do, dah], *a.* Like a fly.

Muscívoro, ra [moos-thee'-vo-ro, rah], *a.* Devouring flies; fly-catching.

Musco [moos'-co], *m.* 1. Moss. 2. (Obs.) Musk. *Musco de Islanda,* Iceland moss.

Musco, ca [moos'-co, cah], *a.* Chestnut colour.

Muscosidad [moos-co-se-dahd'], *f.* Mossiness.

Musculado, da [moos-coo-lah'-do, dah], *a.* (Pict.) Muscular, brawny.

Muscular [moos-coo-lar'], *a.* Muscular.

Musculatura [moos-coo-lah-too'-rah], *f.* Musculature, the entire muscular system.

Músculo [moos'-coo-lo], *m.* 1. Muscle, a fleshy fibre susceptible of contraction and relaxation. 2. Whale of a prodigious size.

Musculoso, sa [moos-coo-lo'-so, sah], *a.* Muscular, full of muscles.

Muselina [moo-say-lee'-nah], *f.* Muslin, fine cotton cloth. *Muselina fina estampada,* French jaconet muslin.

Museo [moo-say'-o], *m.* 1. Museum, a place set apart for the study of the sciences and arts. 2. Repository of learned curiosities.

Muserola [moo-say-ro'-lah], *f.* The nose-band of a horse's bridle.

Musgaño [moos-gah'-nyo], *m.* 1. Shrew-mouse. *V.* MUSARAÑA. 2. Large field-spider.

Musgo [moos'-go], *m.* Moss. Muscus.

Musgoso, sa [moos-go'-so, sah], *a.* 1. Mossy. 2. Moss-covered.

Música [moo'-se-cah], *f.* 1. Music, the science of harmonical sounds. 2. Music, instrumental or vocal harmony. 3. Harmony, or melody; modulated sound. 4. Company of musicians. 5. A musical composition. 6. Written sheets of music. 7. Music: applied by antiphrasis to a dissonant sound. *Música de campanas,* Chimes. *Música ratonera,* Harsh music, produced by bad voices or instruments.

Musical [moo-se-cahl'], *a.* Musical.

Músico, ca [moo'-se-co, cah], *m.* & *f.* Musician, one skilled in harmony, harmonist; one who performs upon instruments of music.—*a.* Musical, harmonious, relating to music.

Musicómano, na [moo-se-co'-mah-no, nah], *a.* Music-mad. *V.* MELÓMANO.

Musitación [moo-se-tah-the-on'], *f.* Muttering, or whispering of a sick person, generally accompanying delirium.

Musitar [moo-se-tar'], *vn.* To mumble, to mutter; also, to whisper.

Muslera [moos-lay'-rah], *f.* Cuish, ancient armour for the thigh.

Muslime [moos-lee'-may], *a.* Moslem.

Muslímico, ca [moos-lee'-me-co, cah], *a.* Moslem, Mohammedan.

Muslo [moos'-lo], *m.* Thigh, which includes all between the buttocks and the knee. *Muslos,* (Coll.) Breeches. *V.* CALZONES.

Musmón [moos-mone'], *m.* 1. Mouflon, a wild sheep with very large curved horns, native of Corsica and Sardinia, considered by some as the original type of the domestic sheep. Ovis musimon.

Musquerola [moos-kay-ro'-lah], *f.* Muscadine pear.

Mustela [moos-tay'-lah], *f.* (Obs.) Weasel.

Mustelino, na [moos-tay-lee'-no, nah], *a.* Weasel-like.

Mustelo [moos-tay'-lo], *m.* (Zool.) Fish without scales, having a hard rough skin, and of about five feet in length.

Mustiamente, *adv.* In a sad and melancholy manner.

Mustio, tia [moos'-te-o, ah], *a.* Parched, withered; sad, sorrowful.

Musulmán [mo-sool-mahn'], *m.* Mussulman.

Muta [moo'-tah], *f.* Pack of hounds.

Mutabilidad [moo-tah-be-le-dahd'], *f.* Mutability, inconstancy, fickleness.

Mutación [moo-tah-the-on'], *f.* 1. Mutation, change. *V.* MUDANZA. 2. A change of scene in a theatre. 3. Unseasonable weather.

Mutanza [moo-tahn'-thah], *f.* (Obs.) 1. Change. 2. In ancient sol-fa, change of register of the voice.

Mutila [moo-tee'-lah], *f.* Mutilla, a solitary ant.

Mutilación [moo-te-lah-the-on'], *f.* Mutilation, maimedness.

Mutilar [moo-te-lar'], *va.* To mutilate, to maim, to cripple, to mangle.

Mútilo, la [moo'-te-lo, lah], *a.* Maimed. (Acad.)

Mutis [moo'-tees], *m.* A word used by theatrical prompters to signify that one or all of those in the scene are to go off. *¡ Mutis ! int.* Silence!

Mutual [moo-too-ahl'], *a.* Mutual, reciprocal. *V.* MUTUO.

Mutualidad [moo-too-ah-le-dahd'], *f.* 1. Mutuality, state of being mutual. 2. (Com.) System of mutual insurance companies or societies.

Mutuamente, *adv.* Mutually converse-ly, reciprocally.

Mutuante [moo-too-ahn'-tay], *com.* Lender, loaner.

Mutuo, tua [moo'-too-o, ah], *a.* Mutual, reciprocal, commutual.

Mutuo [moo'-too-o], *m.* Loan.

Muy [moo'-e], *adv.* Very; a particle which, being joined to a positive adjective, converts it into a superlative one; greatly. *Muy ilustre,* Most illustrious. *Muy mucho,* (Coll.) Very much. *Soy muy de Vd.,* I am entirely yours. In political phraseology, or connected with a negative, it is somewhat less than a superlative; as *muy ilustre* is less than *ilustrísimo,* and *no estoy muy bueno,* I am not very well.

Muz [mooth], *m.* (Naut.) Extremity of the cut-water.

Muzárabe [moo-thah'-rah-bay], *a.* *V.* MOZÁRABE.

Muzo [moo'-tho], *m.* Wood of a tree of Columbia, veined black and red, much esteemed for handsome furniture.

My [me], *f.* Mu, twelfth letter of the Greek alphabet, corresponding to M.

N

N [ay'-nay], sixteenth letter of the alphabet, has the same pronunciation in the Spanish as in the English language. *N* in Spanish stands for some proper name unknown, or not wished to be expressed; as, *N. me dijo esto,* Such a one told me this. In maritime or geographical charts, N stands for north; and on medals and inscriptions, for Number or *Número.* With the preposition *de,* it signifies that a thing or action is very common, or that it is as it ought to be, of course, or by settled rule.

Na [nah], *art. fem.* (Obs.) *V.* LA.

Naba [nah'-bah] *f.* (Bot.) 1. Rutabaga, Swedish turnip. 2. The root of this plant.

Nabal, Nabar [nah-bahl', nah-bar'], *m.* Turnip field.– *a.* Belonging to turnips, made of turnips, pottage made of turnips.

Nabería [nah bay-ree'-ah], *f.* Turnip-pottage or heap of turnips.

Nabillo [nah-beel'-lyo], *m. dim.* A small turnip.

Nabina [nah-bee'-nah], *f.* Rape and turnip seed.

Nabiza [nah-bee'-thah], *f.* (Bot.) 1. The lateral branches of the root of turnips. 2. The young shoots from the root or stem of turnips.

Nabla [nah'-blah], *f.* Ancient instrument of music like a psaltery.

Nabo, Nabo común [nah'-bo], *m.* 1. (Bot.) Rape, turnip; the plant and the root. Brassica. 2. Cylindrical timber, spindle, newel.

Naboria [nah-bo'-re-ah], *a.* & *n.* Free Indian who used to be employed in domestic service.

Nácar [nah'-car], *m.* 1. Mother-of-pearl, nacre. 2. Pearl-colour.—*a.* (Amer.) Scarlet.

Nacarado, da [nah-cah-rah'-do, dah], *a.* Set with mother-of-pearl; of a pearl colour.

Nacáreo, rea [nah-cah'-ray-o, ah], *a.* *V.* NACARINO.

Nacarino, na [nah-cah-ree'-no, nah], *a.* Like nacre, nacreous.

Nacarón [nah-cah-rone'], *m.* Large pearl shell of inferior quality.

Nacencia [nah-then'-the-ah], *f.* (Obs.) 1. Birth. 2. Swelling, tumour, outgrowth.

Nacer [nah-therr'], *vn.* 1. To be born, to come into the world. 2. To flower, to blossom. 3. To bud, to shoot, to grow: speaking of plants. 4. To rise, to appear on the horizon. 5. To take its rise, to have its beginning from. 6. To spring, to take its rise, to flow from. 7. To be reared in some habit. 8. To infer one thing from another. 9. To appear or start up of a sudden. 10. Followed by a preposition, it signifies natural propensity or destiny; as, *Nació para ser gran general,* He was born to be a great general. *Nacer de cabeza,* To be born to wretchedness. *Nacer de pies,* To be born to good luck. *No le pesa de haber nacido,* He is very proud of his merits and talents. *Haber nacido tarde,* To be deficient in experience or intelligence. *Nacer en tal día,* To escape from peril. *No con quien naces, sino con quien paces,* Association is stronger than blood relationship (or, a man is known by the company he keeps). *Al sol que nace,* To flatter the rising sun.—*vr.* To be propagated by nature, not sown, as grass.

Nacido, da [nah-thee'-do, dah], *a.* Proper, apt, fit, connate.—*pp.* of NACER.

Nacido [nah-thee'-do], *m.* 1. A living man: generally used in the plural. 2. Pimple, pustule, tumour. *Hacer ver por sus obras que uno es bien* or *mal nacido,* (Met.) To show by one's actions that he is of a noble or a mean family.

Naciente [nah-the-en'-tay], *pa.* & *a.* 1. Growing, which grows or springs up; very recent. 2. (Her.) Naissant.

Nacimiento [nah-the-me-en'-to], *m.* 1. Birth, nativity. 2. Growing of plants. 3. Beginning of a thing. 4. Nativity, the place of birth. 5. Rising of the planets. 6. Nativity, the coming of our Lord into the world. 7. Origin, descent, lineage. 8. The origin or the physical or moral cause of a thing. *Nacimiento de un río,* Head of a river. *De nacimiento,* From its birth.

Nación [nah-the-on'], *f.* 1. (Coll.) Birth, issue into life. 2. A nation. 3. (Coll.) Foreigner. 4. (Amer.) A race, or tribe of Indians. *De nación,* Native of.

Nacional [nah-the-o-nahl'], *a.* National, gentile.

Nacionalidad [nah-the-o-nah-le-dahd'], *f.* National manners and customs, nationality.

Nacionalismo [nah-the-o-nah-lees'-mo], *m.* Patriotism, love of country.

Nacionalización [nah-the-o-nah-le-thah-the-on'], *f.* Nationalization.

Nacionalizar [nah-the-o-nah-le-thar'], *va., vn.,* & *vr.* To nationalize, to become nationalized, to become a citizen (of a country).

Nacionalmente, *adv.* Nationally.

Nacionalsocialismo, Partido [nah-the-oh-nahl-so-the-ah-lees'-mo, par-tee'-do], *m.* Nazi party (National Socialist German Workers' Party).

Nacrita [nah-cree'-tah], *f.* Variety of talc with a nacreous lustre.

Nacho, cha [nah'-cho, chah], *a.* *V.* ROMO and CHATO.

Nada [nah'-dah], *f.* Nothing, nothingness, naught; nonentity; little, or very little. *En menos de nada* or *en una nada*, In an instant. *Ser un para nada*, (Coll.) To be a good-for-nothing fellow. *Nada entre dos platos*, (Coll.) Great show and nothing else. *Enfadarse por nada*, To be vexed by the most insignificant thing. *Más vale algo que nada*, (prov.) Half a loaf is better than no bread.

Nada [nah'-dah], *adv.* In no degree, by no means. *Nada menos*, Nothing less: a particular negation.

Nadaderas [nah-dah-day'-ras], *f. pl.* Corks or bladders used in learning to swim.

Nadadero [nah-dah-day'-ro], *m.* Swimming-place.

Nadador, ra [nah-dah-dor', rah], *m.* & *f.* Swimmer.

Nadadora [nah-dah-do'-rah], *f.* Dragon-fly. Libellula.

Nadante [nah-dahn'-tay], *pa.* 1. (Poet.) Natant, swimming. 2. (Her.) Naiant.

Nadar [nah-dar'], *vn.* 1. To swim. 2. To float on the water, not to sink. 3. To be wide or loose. *Se me nadan los pies en los zapatos*, My shoes are quite loose. 4. (Met.) To abound, to be plentiful.

Nadie [nah'-de-ay], *indef. pron.* Nobody, no one, none.

Nadir [nah-deer'], *m.* Nadir, the point opposite to the zenith. (Arab.)

Nado (A) [nah'-do]. 1. Afloat. *Poner un bajel a nado*, To set a ship afloat. *Pasó el río a nado*, He swam across the river. 2. With difficulty and great toil. *Salir a nado*, To save one's self by swimming; to effect something with great difficulty and labour. *Echarse a nado*, To hazard, to undertake something boldly.

Nafta [nahf'-tah], *f.* Naphtha, fluid bitumen.

Naftalina [naf-tah-lee'-nah], *f.* Naphthalene, a solid crystalline body obtained from coal-tar by distillation.

Naguaclato, Naguatate [nah-goo-ah-clah'-to], *m.* (Mex.) Interpreter.

Naguas [nah'-goo-as], *f. pl.* Under-petticoat. *V.* ENAGUAS.

Naife [nah'-ee-fay], *m.* A rough, unwrought diamond.

Naipe [nah'-ee-pay], *m.* Playing-card. *Dar el naipe para una cosa*, To be very skilful or dexterous. *Naipes españoles*, Spanish playing-cards. *Dar (a uno) el naipe*, To have good luck in playing cards. *Estar como el naipe*, To be as thin as a shadow. *Tener el naipe*, To have good luck, to have the deal.

Naire [nah'-e-ray], *m.* Elephant-keeper.

Nalga [nahl'-gah], *f.* Buttock, hip, rump.

Nalgada [nal-gah'-dah], *f.* 1. Ham, the cured thigh of a hog. 2. Blow on the rump.

Nalgado, da [nal-gah'-do, dah], *a.* Having round and fleshy posteriors.

Nalgatorio [nal-gah-to'-re-o], *m.* (Coll.) Seat, posteriors, nates.

Nalguear [nal-gay-ar'], *vn.* To shake the posteriors in walking.

Nalguilla [nal-geel'-lyah], *f.* The thick part of the hub of a wheel.

Nana [nah'-nah], *f.* (Mex. Coll.) 1. A child's nurse. 2. A slumber song.

Nancito [nan-thee'-to], *m.* A yellow berry of Nicaragua.

Nandú [nan-doo'], *m.* The American ostrich. Rhea.

Nanquín [nan-keen'], *m.* Nankeen. *V.* MAHÓN.

Nansa [nahn'-sah], *f.* Fish-pond.

Nao [nah'-o], *f.* Ship, vessel. *V.* NAVE.

Naonato, ta [nah-o-nah'-to, tah], *a.* Born on board ship.

Napa [nah'-pah], *f.* 1. A cord for drawing in the tunny-nets. 2. (Low) Backside. (N. B.—Napa, a proper name of California, is of Indian origin, and has no relation with this word.)

Napea [nah-pay'-ah], *f.* Wood-nymph.

Napelo [nah-pay'-lo], *m.* (Bot.) Monk's-hood, wolf's-bane. Aconitum napellus.

Napoleón [nah-po-lay-on'], *m.* A French silver five-franc piece.

Napolitano, na [nah-po-le-tah'-no, nah], *a.* Neapolitan, relating to Naples.

Naque [nah'-kay], *m.* Ancient company of two comedians.

Naranja [nah-rahn'-hah], *f.* 1. Orange, the fruit of the orange-tree. *Media naranja*, (Arch.) Cupola. 2. A cannon-ball of the size of an orange. (Arab. fr. Persian.)

Naranjada [nah-ran-hah'-dah], *f.* 1. Conserve of oranges. 2. Orange-water, orangeade. 3. A rude saying or deed.

Naranjado, da [nah-ran-hah'-do, dah], *a.* Orange-coloured.

Naranjal [nah-ran-hahl'], *m.* Orangery, grove or plantation of orange-trees.

Naranjazo [nah-ran-hah'-tho], *m.* Blow with an orange.

Naranjero, ra [nah-ran-nay'-ro, rah], *m.* & *f.* 1. One who sells oranges. 2. (Prov.) Orange-tree.

Naranjero, ra [nah-ran-hay'-ro, rah], *a.* 1. Applied to pieces of artillery which carry balls of the size of oranges. 2. Applied to a blunderbuss with a mouth of the size of an orange.

Naranjilla [nah-ran-heel'-lyah], *f.* Small green orange used in making a conserve.

Naranjo [nah-rahn'-ho], *m.* (Bot.) 1. Orange-tree. Citrus aurantium. 2. (Coll.) A booby, a noodle, an ignorant fellow.

Narciso [nar-thee'-so], *m.* 1. (Bot.) Daffodil. Narcissus. *Narciso junquillo*, Jonquil narcissus. Narcissus jonquilla. *Narciso poético*, Poet's narcissus. Narcissus poeticus. 2. Narcissus flower. 3. A precious stone of the colour of daffodil. 4. Fop, coxcomb.

Narcosis [nar-co'-sis], *f.* 1. Narcosis. 2. Narcotization.

Narcótico, ca [nar-co'-te-co, cah], *a.* Narcotic, narcotical, producing stupor.

Narcotina [nar-co-tee'-nah], *f.* Narcotine, an inodorous, insipid alkaloid of opium.

Narcotismo [nar-co-tees'-mo], *m.* Narcotism, a state of stupor produced by narcotics.

Nardino [nar-dee'-no], *a.* Made of spikenard.

Nardo [nar'-do], *m.* (Bot.) Spikenard, nard, a plant of India, bulbous-rooted; and the ointment or confection prepared from it.

Narguile [nar-gee'-lay], *m.* Narghile, hookah, an oriental pipe for smoking tobacco in which the smoke passes through perfumed water.

Narigón [nah-re-gone'], *m. aug.* A large nose, a large-nosed person.

Narigón, na, Narigudo, da [nah-re-gone', nah], *a.* Having a large and long nose.

Narigueta, Nariguita [nah-re-gay'-tah, nah-re-gee'-tah], *f. dim.* A small nose.

Nariz [nah-reeth'], *f.* 1. The nose. 2. The nostril. *Nariz de tomate*, Copper-nose. *Caballete de la nariz*, Bridge of the nose. *Nariz chata*, Flat or pug-nose. *Dar en las narices*, (Coll.) To smell or perceive a thing at a distance. (Met.) To find out what another person is about. *Tener largas narices*, (1) To be keen-scented. (2) To be cautious, on one's guard. *Ser hombre de buenas narices*, To be prudent, cautious, provident. *Meter la nariz en todas partes*, To be a busy-body. 3. Sense of smelling. 4. The projecting point of a bridge or pier which breaks the violence of the current. 5. The tube or pipe of an alembic or other similar thing. 6. (Naut.) Cut-water, break of a ship's head. *Narices* or *ventanas de la nariz*, Nostrils. *Hinchar las narices*, To be excessively irritated. *No ver* (uno) *más allá de sus narices*, Not to see beyond one's nose, to be half-witted. *Tener narices de perro perdiguero*, (1) To be keen-scented. (2) To foresee what is to come.

Narizado, da [nah-re-thah'-do, dah], *a.* Having a large nose.

Narra [nar'-rah], *f.* A tree of the Philippines whose wood is employed in boat-building; it tinges water a blue colour and exhales an agreeable smell.

Narración [nar-rah-the-on'], *f.* Narration, account, relation, legend.

Narrador [nar-rah-dor'], *a.* (Littl. us.) Narrator. Also used as a noun.

Narrar [nar-rar'], *va.* To narrate, to relate, to recite, to tell.

Narrativa [nar-rah-tee'-vah], *f.* 1. Narrative, relation, history, account. 2. Art or talent of relating things past.

Narrativo, va, Narratorio, ria [nar-rah-tee'-vo, vah], *a.* Narrative, narratory.

Narria [nar'-re-ah], *f.* 1. Sledge, a carriage without wheels. 2. A fat, heavy, bulky woman.

Narval [nar-vahl'], *m.* (Zool.) Narwhal, sea-unicorn.

Nasa [nah'-sah], *f.* 1. Fyke, a fish-trap (used in the Mediterranean) with a conical mouth; a bag-net. 2. Round, narrow-mouthed net; bow-net. 3. A wicker basket for holding fish; a kipe (provincial name). 4. (Acad.) Basket or jar for keeping bread, flour or such things.

Nasal [nah-sahl'], *a.* Nasal, relating to the nose.

Nasardo [nah-sar'-do], *m.* Nasard, one of the registers of an organ.

Nasturcio [nas-toor'-the-o], *m.* (Bot.) Nasturtium.

Nata [nah'-tah], *f.* 1. Cream. 2. The most esteemed or principal part of a thing; the cream. *Ser la nata de alguna cosa*, (Met.) To be the cream, the spice of any thing. 3. *pl.* Whipped cream with sugar. 4. *V.* NATILLA.

Natación [nah-tah-the-on'], *f.* 1. The art of swimming. 2. The act of swimming.

Natal [nah-tahl'], *a.* Natal, native.—*m.* Birth, birth-day.

Natalicio, cia [nah-tah-lee'-the-o, ah], *a.* & *m.* & *f.* Natal; nativity, birth-day.

Natalidad [nah-tah-le-dahd'], *f.* Birth rate.

Natatorio, a [nah-tah-to'-re-o, ah], *a.* Natatory, relating to swimming.

Naterón [nah-tay-rone'], *m.* Second curds after the first cheese is made. *V.* REQUESÓN.

Natillas [nah-teel'-lyas], *f. pl.* Custard, a composition of milk, eggs, and sugar boiled together; it may be thickened with flour or starch, making a batter.

Natio [nah-tee'-o], *m.* (Prov.) Birth; sprouting: used of plants.—*a.* Native. *Oro natío*, Native gold.

Natividad [nah-te-ve-dahd'], *f.* Nativity.

Nativitate (A) [nah-te-ve-tah' tay] (Lat.) *V.* DE NACIMIENTO.

Nativo, va [nah-tee'-vo, vah], *a.* 1. Native, produced by nature, natal; not artificial. 2. Fit, proper, apt. 3. Vernacular.

Nato [nah'-to]. *Ex officio nato*, By reason or virtue of office: adverbial expression, denoting the power of doing certain things by virtue of one's office.

Natrón [nah-trone'], *m.* 1. Natron, native carbonate of soda. 2. A saline substance which separates from crucibles in glass-works.

Natura [nah-too'-rah], *f.* 1. (Ant.) Nature. 2. The genital parts. 3. In music, a major scale.

Natural [nah-too-rahl'], *m.* 1. Temper, genius, natural disposition. 2. Instinct of brutes. 3. Native of a place or country.—*a.* 1. Natural, according to nature. 2. Natural, native, not artificial. 3. Native, pertaining to the place of birth. 4. Common, usual, regular, resembling nature. 5. Natural, ingenuous, without art or craft, unaffected. 6. Natural, not performed by industry or art. 7. Natural, that which imitates nature, and treats of her secrets and operations. 8. Natural, produced by the sole power of nature. *Al natural*, Without art or affectation.

Naturaleza [nah-too-rah-lay'-thah], *f.* 1. Nature, aggregate, order, and disposition of all created beings; often personified. 2. Nature, the native state or property of things. 3. Nature, constitution of an animated body; complexion, constitution. 4. Nature, the property, virtue, or quality of things. 5. Nature, the regular course of things, the quality, order, and disposition of affairs. 6. Nature, instinct, property, or inclination. 7. Sex, genitals, especially the female. 8. Species, kind. 9. The state of a native with respect to the place where he was born. 10. Naturalization. 11. Nature, genius, temperament.

Naturalidad [nah-too-rah-le-dahd'], *f.* 1. State of being born in a certain place or country; birthright. 2. Naturalness, conformity to nature and truth. Ingenuity, candour.

Naturalismo [nah-too-rah-lees'-mo], *m.* 1. Naturalism, mere state of nature. 2. Realism, in a literary and artistic sense, strict copying of nature, without concealing its deformities.

Naturalista [nah-too-rah-lees'-tah], *m.* Naturalist, one versed in the knowledge of nature, or natural philosophy, more especially of natural history.

Naturalización [nah-too-rah-le-thah-the-on'], *f.* Naturalization, the act of investing aliens with the rights of native subjects.

Naturalizar [nah-too-rah-le-thar'], *va.* To naturalize, to invest with the rights of native subjects.—*vr.* To be accustomed, to grow fit for any purpose.

Naturalmente, *adv.* Naturally, natively, by nature; humanly; plainly, without fiction, ingenuously, frankly.

Naufragar [nah-oo-frah-gar'], *vn.* 1. To be stranded or shipwrecked, to suffer shipwreck. 2. To suffer wreck or ruin in one's affairs, to fail in one's purposes.

Naufragio [nah-oo-frah'-he-o], *m.* 1. Shipwreck. 2. Miscarriage, disappointment, calamity, heavy loss.

Náufrago, ga [nah'-oo-frah-go, gah], *a.* Relating to shipwreck, wrecked.

Naumaquia [nah-oo-mah'-ke-ah], *f.* Naumachy, a mock sea-fight.

Náusea [nah'-oo-say-ah], *f.* Nauseousness, squeamishness, nausea, disposition to vomit. (Most used in the plural.)

Nauseabundo [nah-oo-say-ah-boon'-do], *a.* Nauseous, loathsome, exciting nausea.

Nausear [nah-oo-say-ar'], *vn.* To nauseate, to loathe, to become squeamish; to suffer nausea.

Nauseativo, va [nah-oo-say-ah-tee'-vo, vah], *a.* Nauseous.

Nauseoso, sa [nah-oo-say-o'-so, sah], *a.* *V.* NAUSEABUNDO.

Nauta [nah'-oo-tah], *m.* Mariner, a seafaring man.

Náutica [nah'-oo-te-cah], *f.* Navigation, the art of conducting ships over the ocean.

Náutico, ca [nah'-oo-te-co, cah], *a.* Nautical.

Nautilo [nah-oo-tee'-lo], *m.* Nautilus, a cephalopod mollusk.

Nava [nah'-vah], *f.* A plain or level piece of ground.

Navaja [nah-vah'-hah], *f.* 1. Clasp-knife, folding-knife. 2. Razor. 3. Tusk of a wild boar. 4. Tongue of backbiters. *Navajas de gallo*, Cock-spurs.

Navajada [nah-vah-hah'-dah], *f.* A thrust or gash with a knife.

Navajazo [nah-vah-hah'-tho], *m.* *V.* NAVAJADA.

Navajero [nah-vah-hay'-ro], *m.* 1. Razor-case. 2. A piece of linen on which a barber cleans his razor.

Navajita [nah-vah-hee'-tah], *f. dim.* A small clasp-knife.

Navajo, *m.* *V.* NAVAZO.

Navajón [nah-vah-hone'], *m. aug.* A large knife.

Navajonazo [nah-vah-ho-nah'-tho], *m.* Gash or wound made with a large knife.

Naval [nah-vahl'], *a.* Naval, consisting of ships; belonging to ships. *Armada naval*, Royal navy, royal fleet.

Navarro, rra [nah-var'-ro, rah], *a.* Belonging to or native of Navarre.

Navazo [nah-vah'-tho], *m.* 1. Kitchen-garden in Sanlúcar upon a sandy shore. 2. Level piece of ground where the rains make a pool.

Nave [nah'-vay], *f.* 1. Ship, a vessel with decks and sails. 2. Nave, the middle part or body of a church. *Nave de San Pedro*, The Roman Catholic Church. *Nave espacial*, Spacecraft.

Navecilla [nah-ve-theel'-yah], *f.* A vessel for incense.

Navegable [nah-vay-gah'-blay], *a.* Navigable.

Navegación [nah-vay-gah-the-on'], *f.* 1. Navigation, the act or practice of passing by water. 2. Passage, time which a ship takes in going from one place to another. 3. Navigation, art of navigating.

Navegador, ra [nah-vay-gah-dor', rah], *a.* Navigating.—*m.* Navigator.

Navegante [nah-vay-gahn'-tay], *pa.* & *m.* Navigator; navigating.

Navegar [nah-vay-gar'], *vn.* 1. To navigate, to sail, to pass by water. 2. To go from place to place for the purpose of trade. 3. (Ant.) To carry wares by sea from one part to another for trade.—*va.* To sail, to go, to travel (e. g. ten knots per hour).

Naveta [nah-vay'-tah], *f.* 1. Vessel for incense in the church. 2. Small drawer.

Navicular [nah-ve-coo-lar'], *a.* Applied to the middle bone of the foot; the scaphoid.

Navichuelo, la [nah-ve-choo-ay'-lo, lah], *m.* & *f.* (Naut.) A small vessel.

Navidad [nah-ve-dahd'], *f.* 1. Nativity. 2. Christmas day.

Navideño, ña [nah-ve-day'-nyo, nyah], *a.* Belonging to the time of nativity.

Naviero, ra [nah-ve-ay'-ro, rah], *a.* Shipping. *Empresa naviera*, Steamship concern.

Navío [nah-vee'-o], *m.* A ship, especially a large ship, or a ship of war. *Navío de guerra*, A ship of war, a man-of-war. *Navío de línea* or *de alto bordo*, Ship of the line. *Navío mercante*, Merchant ship. *Navío de almacén*, Store-ship. *Navío de transporte*, Transport. *Lastrar un navío*, To ballast a ship. *Recorrer un navío*, To repair a ship. *Navío guardacosta*, Guard-ship. *Navío de carga*, Ship of burden. *Navío pesado*, A bad sailer. *Navío de tres puentes*, Three-decked ship.

Náyade [nah'-yah-day], *f.* Naïad, water-nymph.

Nazareno, na [nah-thah-ray'-no, nah], *a.* 1. Nazarene, native of Nazareth. 2. Nazarite, one who neither shaved the beard, cut the hair, nor drank strong drinks.—*m.* He who goes in processions in Passion Week, dressed in a long brown robe.

Nazareo, ea [nah-thah-ray'-o, ah], *a.* Nazarite, among the Jews.

(*Yo nazco, yo nazca*, from *Nacer. V.* CONOCER.)

Nazi [nah'the], *m.* & *f.* & *a.* Nazi. *Partido Nazi*, Nazi Party. V. NACIONALSOCIALISMO, PARTIDO.

Nebeda [nay'-bay-dah], *f.* Catmint, an aromatic herb. Nepeta cataria.

Nebladura [nay-blah-doo'-rah], *f.* Damage which crops receive from mist.

Neblí [nay-blee'], *m.* (Zool.) Falcon gentle.

Neblina [nay-blee'-nah], *f.* 1. Mist, small rain. 2. Confusion, obscurity.

Nebrina [nay-bree'-nah], *f.* Juniper-berry.

Nebuloso, sa [nay-boo-lo'-so, sah], *a.* Misty, cloudy, nebulous, foggy, hazy.

Necear [nay-thay-ar'], *vn.* To talk nonsense, to play the fool.

Necedad [nay-thay-dahd'], *f.* Gross ignorance, stupidity; imprudence; foolishness, folly, foppery, idiocy.

Necesaria [nay-thay-sah'-re-ah], *f.* Privy, necessary, water-closet.

Necesariamente, *adv.* Necessarily, indispensably, consequently, needfully.

Necesario, ria [nay-thay-sah'-re-o, ah], *a.* Necessary, requisite, needful. *Si fuere necesario*, If need be. *Lo necesario*, What is needful.

Neceser [nay-thay-serr'], *m.* A case of necessary articles, as for the dressing-table. (F.)

Necesidad [nay-thay-se-dahd'], *f.* Necessity, need, want; cogency, extremity, constraint. *La necesidad carece de ley*, Necessity has no law. *Necesidad mayor* or *menor*, Evacuation of the body by stool or water.

Necesitado, da [nay-thay-se-tah'-do, dah], *a.* Necessitous, poor, needy.—*pp.* of NECESITAR.

Necesitado, da [nay-thay-se-tah'-do, dah], *m.* & *f.* A poor person, a needy man or woman.

Necesitar [nay-thay-se-tar'], *va.* To necessitate, to constrain, to compel.—*vn.* To want, to need, to lack.

Neciamente, *adv.* Ignorantly, stupidly, foolishly.

Necio, cia [nay'-the-o, ah], *a.* 1. Ignorant, stupid, idiotic, foolish. 2. Imprudent, injudicious.—*m.* & *f.* Fool.

Necróforo [nay-cro'-fo-ro], *m.* Necrophorus, the sexton or burying beetle, noted for its keenness of smell.

Necrolatría [nay-cro-lah-tree'-ah], *f.* Worship of the dead.

Necrología [nay-cro-lo-hee'-ah], *f.* Necrology, a register of persons deceased.
Necrológico, ca [nay-cro-lo'-he-co, cah], *a.* Necrological, belonging to necrology.
Necrologio [nay-cro-lo'-he-o], *m.* Necrology, mortuary, register of bishops.
Necropsia, or **Necroscopia**, *f.* Necropsy, autopsy, post-mortem examination.
Necrosis [nay-cro'-sis], *f.* Necrosis, mortification of the bones.
Nectar [nec'-tar], *m.* 1. Nectar, the supposed drink of the gods. 2. Any very pleasant drink. 3. Nectar, the honey of plants.
Nectáreo, rea [nec-tah'-ray-o, ah]. *a.* Nectareal, nectarean, sweet as nectar.
Nectarífero, ra [nec-tah-ree'-fay-ro, rah], *a.* Nectar-bearing.
Nectarino, na [nec-tah-ree'-no, nah], *a.* *V.* NECTÁREO.
Nectario [nec-tah'-re-o], *m.* (Bot.) Nectary, the part of a plant which secretes nectar or honey.
Neerlandés, sa [nay-er-lan-days', sah], *a.* Netherlandish, Flemish, Dutch.
Nefandamente, *adv.* Basely, nefariously, abominably.
Nefando, da [nay-fahn'-do, dah], *a.* Base, nefarious, abominable, heinous. *Pecado nefando*, An unnatural crime.
Nefario, ria [nay-fah'-re-o, ah], *a.* Nefarious, abominable, extremely wicked.
Nefas [nay'-fas], *adv.* *Por fas o por nefas*, Right or wrong.
Nefasto [nay-fahs'-to], *a.* Applied to days of rest among the Romans.
Nefrítico, ca [nay-free'-te-co, cah], *a.* 1. Nephritic, belonging to the kidneys; troubled with the gravel. 2. Applied to a kind of jasper.
Nefritis [nay-free'-tis], *f.* (Med.) Nephritis, Bright's disease.
Negable [nay-gah'-blay], *a.* That which may be denied.
Negación [nay-gah-the-on'], *f.* 1. Negation, the act of denying, denial. 2. Want or total privation of any thing. 3. Negative particle.
Negado, da [nay-gah'-do, dah], *a.* Incapable, inapt, unfit.—*pp.* of NEGAR.
Negador, ra [nay-gah-dor', rah], *m.* & *f.* Denier, disclaimer.
Negar [nay-gar'], *va.* 1. To deny, to contradict. 2. To deny, to refuse, not to grant, to gainsay. 3. To forbid, to prohibit, to hinder, to oppose. 4. To deny, to contradict an accusation. 5. To deny, to disown, to disclaim. 6. To deny, to disregard, to forget what one has previously held in esteem, to withdraw from a company frequented before. 7. To hide, to conceal. 8. To dissemble. 9. To refuse to acknowledge the obligations a person has contracted.—*vr.* 1. To decline doing any thing. 2. To desire to be denied to persons who call to see one. *Negarse a sí mismo*, To govern one's passions and appetites. *Negar una cosa de plano*, To deny a thing flatly.
Negativa [nay-gah-tee'-vah], *f.* Negation; repulse; negative, refusal.
Negativamente, *adv.* Negatively.
Negativo, va [nay-gah-tee'-vo, vah], *a.* Negative, implying negation or denial, negatory.—*f.* Negative, a developed photographic plate or film, showing reversed lights and shadows.
Negligencia [nay-gle-hen'-the-ah], *f.* Negligence, neglect, heedlessness, forgetfulness, habit of acting carelessly.
Negligente [nay-gle-hen'-tay], *a.* Negligent, careless, heedless, absent, thoughtless, listless.
Negligentemente, *adv.* Negligently, neglectfully, giddily, loosely, listlessly, heedlessly.
Negociabilidad [nay-go-the-ah-be-le-dahd'], *f.* (Neol. Com.) Negotiability, particularly of bills of exchange.
Negociable [nay-go-the-ah'-blay], *a.* Negotiable.
Negociación [nay-go-the-ah-the-on'], *f.* Negotiation, management; commerce.
Negociado [nay-go-the-ah'-do], *m.* 1. Each separate division or section in the official departments. 2. *V.* NEGOCIO.—*Negociado, da, pp.* of NEGOCIAR.
Negociador [nay-go-the-ah-dor'], *m.* 1. A man of business. 2. Negotiator, one employed to treat with others.
Negociante [nay-go-the-ahn'-tay], *pa.* & *m.* Trader, dealer; negotiating, trading.
Negociar [nay-go-the-ar'], *vn.* 1. To trade, to buy and sell goods. 2. To negotiate bills of exchange; to negotiate political affairs.
Negocio [nay-go'-the-o], *m.* 1. Occupation, employment, management, business. 2. Affair, pretension, treaty, agency, concern. 3. Negotiation, trade, commerce. *Fingir negocios*, To affect the man of business. 4. Utility or interest in trading.—*pl.* Business, commercial transactions.
Negocioso, sa [nay-go-the-o'-so, sah], *a.* Diligent, prompt, careful.
Negozuelo [nay-go-thoo-ay'-lo], *m. dim.* Any insignificant affair or business.
Negra [nay'-grah], *f.* 1. A foil for fencing. 2. Negress, black woman.
Negrada [nay-grah'-dah], *f.* (Cuba, Peru) A collection of Negroes.
Negrear [nay-gray-ar'], *vn.* To grow black, to appear black.
Negrecer [nay-gray-therr'], *vn.* To blacken, to become black.
Negrero [nay-gray'-ro], *m.* 1. Trafficker in slaves. *Negrero* or *barco negrero*, A slaver. 2. (Cuba) The white man who is fond of Negresses.
Negreta [nay-gray'-tah], *f.* (Orn.) Coot, a kind of duck of a blackish colour. Anas fusca.
(*Yo negrezco, yo negrezca*, from *Negrecer*. *V.* CONOCER.)
Negrilla [nay-greel'-lyah], *f.* 1. (typ.) Boldface type. 2. (Zool.) Conger eel.
Negrillera [nay-gril-lyay'-rah], *f.* Plantation of black poplar.
Negrillo [nay-greel'-lyo], *m.* 1. (Dim.) A young Negro 2. Black silver ore, stephanite. 3. (Bot.) *V.* OLMO.
Negrito, ta [nay-gree'-to, tah], *a.* (Mex.) *V.* NEGRO, 6th def.
Negro, gra [nay'-gro, grah], *a.* 1. Black; jetty. 2. Brown or gray; not well bleached. 3. Blackish; of a dark-brown colour. 4. Gloomy, black, dismal, melancholy. 5. Unfortunate, wretched. 6. (Coll. Amer.) An endearing expression, equivalent to my dove, my dear.
Negro, gra, *m.* & *f.* Negro, a blackamoor; Negress. *Negro de humo*, Lamp-black. *Negro de hueso*, Bone-black. *Negro de marfil*, Ivory-black. *Negro de plomo*, Ochre-black. *Negro de carbón*, Blue-black. 2. (Met.) The least of any thing. *Boda de negros*, (Coll.) Any noisy rout and confusion.
Negrura [nay-groo'-rah], *f.* Blackness.
Negruzco, ca [nay-grooth'-co, cah], *a.* Blackish, nigrescent, dark brown.
Neguijón [nay-gee-hone'], *m.* Caries, rottenness of the teeth.
Neguilla [nay-geel'-lyah], *f.* 1. (Bot.) Fennel-flower, love-in-a-mist. Nigella. 2. Obstinate denial.
Nema [nay'-mah], *f.* Seal or sealing of a letter.
Nematócero, ra [nay-mah-to'-thay-ro, rah], *a.* Nematocerous, nemocerous, of thread-like antennæ.
Nemeo, mea [nay-may'-o, ah], *a.* Nemæan: applied to some ancient games.
Némine discrepante [nay'-me-nay dis. cray-pahn'-tay]. (Lat.) Unanimously: no one dissenting.
Nemoroso, sa [nay-mo-ro'-so, sah], *a.* Woody, nemorous, consisting of wood; relating to wood.
Nene, Nena [nay'-nay, nay'-nah], *m.* & *f.* (Coll.) An infant, a baby.
Nenúfar [nay-noo'-far], *m.* (Bot.) White water-lily. Nymphæa alba.
Neófito [nay-o'-fe-to], *m.* 1. Neophyte, one regenerated; a convert. 2. Novice, beginner.
Neografía [nay-o-grah-fee'-ah], *f.* Neography, a new system of writing.
Neografismo [nay-o-grah-fees'-mo], *m.* (Littl. us.) Neography, new method of writing; contrary to the received custom.
Neógrafo, fa [nay-o'-grah-fo, fah], *a.* Applied to one who uses a new and peculiar mode of writing.
Neolatino, na [nay-o-lah-tee'-no, nah], *a.* Neo-Latin, Romanic: used of the languages derived from Latin.
Neología [nay-o-lo-hee'-ah], *f.* Neology, introduction or use of new words and phrases.
Neológico, ca [nay-o-lo'-he-co, cah], *a.* Neological, employing new words and phrases.
Neologismo [nay-o-lo-hees'-mo], *m.* Neologism, a new and yet unsanctioned expression.
Neólogo [nay-o'-lo-go], *m.* Neologist, a coiner of words.
Neomenia [nay-o-may'-ne-ah], *f.* Neomenia, first day of new moon.
Neón [nay-on'], *m.* & *a.* Neon. *Luces de Neón*, Neon lights.
Neoplasma [nay-o-plahs'-mah], *m.* (Med.) Neoplasm, a new growth due to morbid action.
Neorama [nay-o-rah'-mah], *m.* Panorama upon a cylindrical surface, the observer being placed at the centre.
Neoyorquino, na [nay-o-yor-kee'-no, nah], *a.* from New York.—*m.* & *f.* New Yorker.
Nepente [nay-pen'-tay], *m.* Nepenthe, a drug supposed to drive away all pain.
Nepote [nay-po'-tay], *m.* *V.* SOBRINO. A privileged relative of the Pope. (Ital.)
Nepotismo [nay-po-tees'-mo], *m.* Nepotism; favoritism exercised towards nephews or other relatives.
Neptuno [nep-too'-no], *m.* 1. The planet Neptune. 2. (Poet.) The sea.
Nequicia [nay-kee'-the-ah], *f.* Perversity.
Nereida [nay-ray'-e-dah], *f.* Nereid, a sea-nymph.
Nervado, da [ner-vah'-do, dah], *a.* (Bot.) Nervate, nerved.
Nervadura [ner-vah-doo'-rah], *f.* Nervation, or nervature of leaves; arrangement of nerves.
Nervino, na [ner-vee'-no, nah], *a.* Calming and fortifying the nerves; nervine.
Nervio [nerr'-ve-o], *m.* 1. A nerve. 2. The main and most powerful part of any thing. 3. String of a musical instrument. 4. (Naut.) A small rope, the middle of which is fixed to a stay. 5. Nerve, energy, vigour. 6. In botany, the perfect and unbranched vessels extending from the base towards the tip; nerve. 7. Tendon, or aponeurosis.
Nerviosidad [ner-ve-o-se-dahd'], *f.* *V.* NERVOSIDAD.

Nervioso, sa [ner-ve-o'-so, sah], *a.* 1. Nervous, relating to the nerves. 2. Nervous, vigorous: applied to a discourse, phrase, or word. 3. (Bot.) Nerved.
Nervosamente, *adv.* Nervously.
Nervosidad [ner-vo-se-dahd'], *f.* 1. Strength, nervousness. 2. Efficacy, vigour. 3. Flexibility.
Nervoso, sa [ner-vo'-so, sah], *a.* 1. Nervous, relating to the nerves. 2. Nervous, strong, vigorous, robust.
Nervudo, da [ner-voo'-do, dah], *a.* Nervous, well strung, strong, vigorous.
Nesciencia [nes-the-en'-the-ah], *f.* Ignorance, nescience, want of knowledge.
Nesciente [nes-the-en'-tay], *a.* Ignorant, foolish.
Nesga [nes'-gah], *f.* Gore, a triangular piece of linen or stuff sewn upon cloth. (Arab. nasj, weaving.)
Nestorianismo [nes-to-re-ah-nees'-mo], *m.* Nestorianism, a heresy of the fifth century.
Nestoriano [nes-to-re-ah'-no], *m.* Nestorian, one of the followers of Nestorius.
Netezuelo, la [nay-tay-thoo-ay'-lo, lah], *m.* & *f. dim.* A little grandchild.
Neto, ta [nay'-to, tah], *a.* Neat, pure, clean, unadulterated; net, clear, genuine; without foreign mixture. *Producto neto,* Net produce. *En neto,* Purely. *Peso neto,* Net weight.
Neto [nay'-to], *m.* (Arch.) Naked pedestal of a column.
Neuma [nay-oo'-mah], *m.* Expression by signs of what one wishes or thinks. (Gr.)
Neumático, ca [nay-oo-mah'-te-co, cah], *a.* Pneumatic. *Perforación neumática,* Pneumatic drilling. —*m.* Automobile tire. *Neumático balón,* Balloon tire. *Neumático de repuesto,* Spare tire. *Neumático recauchado,* Retread.
Neumococo [nay-oo-mo-co'-co], *m* Pneumococcus.
Neumonía [nay-oo-mo-nee'-ah], *f.* Pneumonia, lung fever, inflammation of the lungs.
Neumónico, ca [nay-oo-mo'-ne-co, cah], *a.* Pneumonic, relating to the lungs, or to pneumonia.
Neuralgia [nay-oo-rahl'-he-ah], *f.* Neuralgia, pain along a nerve, without fever.
Neurálgico, ca [nay-oo-rahl'-he-co, cah], *a.* Neuralgic, relating to neuralgia.
Neurastenia [nay-oo-ras-tay'-ne-ah] *f.* (Med.) Neurasthenia.
Neurasténico, ca [nay-oo-ras-tay'-ne-co, cah], *a.* Neurasthenic, suffering from nervous exhaustion. (Neol.)
Neurítico, ca [nay-oo-ree'-te-co, cah], *a.* (Med.) Neurotic.—*pl.* Neurotica: applied to medicines supposed to strengthen the nerves.
Neuritis [nay-oo-ree'-tis], *f.* (Med.) Neuritis.
Neurología [nay-oo-ro-lo-hee'-ah], *f.* Neurology, a description of the nerves.
Neuroma [nay-oo-ro'-mah], *m.* Neuroma, a tumour of a nerve.
Neurona [nay-oo-ro'-nah], *f.* (Anat.) Neuron, neurone.
Neuropatía [nay-oo-ro-pah-tee'-ah], *f.* A nervous disorder; neuropathy.
Neuróptero, ra [nay-oo-rop'-tay-ro, rah], *a.* Neuropterous.
Neurosis [nay-oo-ro'-sis], *f.* Neurosis, functional nervous disease.
Neurotomía [nay-oo-ro-to-mee'-ah], *f.* (Med.) 1. Neurotomy, dissection of nerves. 2. Section or division of a nerve.
Neutral [nay-oo-trahl'], *a.* Neutral, neuter, indifferent; it has been used as a substantive, especially in the plural.
Neutrino [nay-oo-tree'-no], *m.* (Phy. & Chem.) Neutrino.
Neutralidad [nay-oo-trah-le-dahd'], *f.* 1. Neutrality, a state of indifference. 2. Neutrality, state of peace with belligerent nations.
Neutralizar [nay-oo-trah-le-thar'], *va.* (Chem.) To neutralize.
Neutralmente, *adv.* (Littl. us.) Neutrally, indifferently.
Neutro, tra [nay'-oo-tro, trah], *a.* 1. Neutral, neuter, not engaged on either side. 2. (Gram.) Neuter, a noun that implies no sex; a verb that is neither active nor passive, intransitive.
Neutrón [nay-oo-trone'], *m.* (Phy. & Chem.) Neutron.
Nevada [nay-vah'-dah], *f.* 1. Snowfall, descent of snow. 2. Snowfall, the quantity of snow which falls at one time; a heavy fall of snow. 3. (Bot.) *V.* NEVADILLA.
Nevadilla [nay-vah-deel'-lyah], *f.* (Bot.) Whitlow-wort, any species of Paronychia with dry silvery stipules and clustered flowers. It belongs to the Illecebraceæ or knot-wort family.
Nevado, da [nay-vah'-do, dah], *a.* White as snow.—*pp.* of NEVAR.
Nevar [nay-var'], *vn.* To snow; to fall in snow. —*va.* To make white as snow.
Nevasca [nay-vahs'-cah], *f.* 1. Fall of snow; snow and wind. 2. Snowstorm.
Nevatilla [nay-vah-teel'-yah], *f.* (Zool.) Wag-tail. *V.* AGUZANIEVE.
Nevera [nay-vay'-rah], *f.* 1. Ice-house. 2. Applied to any very cold room or place. 3. Icebox.
Nevereta, *f.* *V.* AGUZANIEVE.
Nevería [nay-vay-ree'-ah], *f.* Ice-house, a place where ice is sold.
Nevero, ra [nay-vay'-ro, rah], *m.* & *f.* One who sells ice.
Nevisca [nay-vees'-cah], *f.* *V.* NEVASCA.
Neviscar [nay-vis-car'], *vn.* To snow lightly.
Nevoso, sa [nay-vo'-so, sah], *a.* 1. Snowy, abounding with snow, nival, niveous. 2. Snowy: applied to weather indicating snow.
Nexo [nek'-so], *m.* Knot, string, union.
Nexo, *adv.* (Cant or low) No. (*Cf.* nix and Ger. nichts.)
Ni [nee], *conj.* Neither, nor. *Ni fuí, ni tengo intención de ir,* I did not go, nor do I intend to go. *Ni le amo, ni le temo,* I neither love nor fear him. *Ni siquierá,* Not even. *Ni Vd. lo sabe,* Even you do not know it. *Él no dice ni sí ni no,* He is neither *pro* nor *con.*
Niacina [ne-ah-thee'-nah], *f.* Niacine.
Nícalo [nee'-cah-lo], *m.* *V.* NISCALO.
Nicaragüense [ne-cah-rah-goo-en'-say], *m.* & *f.* & *a.* Nicaraguan.
Nicerobino [ne-thay-ro-bee'-no], *a.* Applied to a precious ointment used by the ancients.
Nicotina [ne-co-tee'-nah], *f.* Nicotine, a highly poisonous alkaloid of tobacco.
Nictálope [nic-tah'-lo-pay], *m.* Nyctalops, one who sees best at night.
Nictalopía [nic-tah-lo'-pe-ah], *f.* Nyctalopy, a disease of the eye; day-blindness.
Nicho [nee'-cho], *m.* 1. Niche, a recess in a wall to place a statue in. 2. Any hole or corner to put something in. 3. Any employment or destination in which a person ought to be placed according to his merits.
Nidada [ne-dah'-dah], *f.* Nestful of eggs, on which a hen sits; brood, covey.
Nidal [ne-dahl'], *m.* 1. A nest, place where a hen or other bird lays her eggs. 2. Nest-egg. 3. Basis, foundation, motive. 4. Haunt.
Nidificar [ne-de-fe-car'], *vn.* To nest, to build nests.
Nidito [ne-dee'-to], *m. dim.* A small nest.
Nido [nee'-do], *m.* 1. Nest, the bed formed by the bird for incubation. 2. Nest, any place where animals are produced. 3. Nest, habitation, abode, residence. *Nido de ladrones,* Nest of thieves.
Niebla [ne-ay'-blah], *f.* 1. Fog, mist, haze, damp. 2. Disease of the eyes, which dims the sight. 3. Mildew which blasts. 4. Mental obscurity, confusion of ideas.
Niego [ne-ay'-go], *a.* New-born: applied to a falcon. *V.* HALCÓN.
(*Yo niego, yo niegue,* from *Negar. V.* ACERTAR.)
Niel [ne-el'], *m.* Embossment, relief; raised work.
Nielar [ne-ay-lar'], *va.* To form with a protuberance, to carve in relief, or raised work on plate; to engrave, to enamel.
Nieta [ne-ay'-tah], *f.* Grand-daughter, grandchild.
Nieto [ne-ay'-to], *m.* 1. Grand-son, grandchild. 2. Descendant.
(*Nieva, nieve,* from *Nevar. V.* ACERTAR.)
Nietro [ne-ay'-tro], *m.* In Arragon, a measure for wine, about equal to the *moyo* of Castile.
Nieve [ne-ay'-vay], *f.* 1. Snow. 2. Snowy weather: commonly used in the plural. 3. (Obs.) Fall of snow. 4. Extreme whiteness.
Nigromancia [ne-gro-mahn'-the-ah], *f.* Necromancy; black art.
Nigromante [ne-gro-mahn'-tay], *m.* Necromancer, conjurer, magician.
Nigromántico, ca [ne-gro-mahn'-te-co, ca], *a.* Necromantic.—*m.* & *f.* *V.* NIGROMANTE.
Nigua [nee'-goo-ah], *f.* Chigoe, jigger flea, an insect found in tropical America, which burrows under the nails. Sarcopsylla penetrans.
Nihilismo [ne-he-lees'-mo], *m.* 1. Nihilism, denial of all belief. 2. Russian anarchism, antagonism to religion, society, and government.
Nihilista [ne-he-lees'-tah], *m.* Nihilist, anarchist.
Nimiamente, *adv.* Excessively.
Nilad [ne-lahd'], *m.* A shrub of about six feet high which grows in the Philippine archipelago. The leaves are opposite, thick, ovate or obovate, entire, and smooth; the flowers axillary in an umbel; the fruit is a drupe of six or eight acute angles, and the stone may be divided in two. The city of Manila received its name from its site having been covered with these shrubs.
Niliaco, ca [ne-lee'-ah-co, cah], *a.* Belonging to the Nile.
Nilómetro [ne-lo'-may-tro], *m.* Nilometer, a column or gauge for measuring the height of water in the Nile.
Nimiedad [ne-me-ay-dahd'], *f.* 1. Superfluity, excess, nimiety. 2. Niceness, extravagant nicety. 3. (Coll.) A ridiculous sparingness, or frugality.
Nimio, mia [nee'-me-o, ah], *a.* Excessive, too much, prolix.
Ninfa [neen'-fah], *f.* 1. Nymph. 2. A young lady. 3. Pupa, the chrysalis of a caterpillar.
Ninfea [nin-fay'-ah], *f.* (Bot.) Water-lily. Nymphæa. *Ninfea blanca,* White water-lily. Nymphæa alba

Ninfo [neen'-fo], *m.* A beau, a young effeminate fop, a dude.

Ninfomania [nin-fo-mah-nee'-ah], *f.* Nymphomania, morbid, insane sexual desire in women.

Ningún [nin-goon'], *a.* None, not one: used before masculine nouns. *De ningún modo,* In no manner, by no means.

Ninguno, na [nin-goo'-no, nah], *a.* None, not one, no, neither. *De ninguna manera,* By no means, in no manner. *Ninguna cosa,* Nothing.

Nini nana [nee'-ne nah'-nah]. Words without meaning for humming a tune.

Ninivita [ne-ne-vee'-tah], *a.* Ninevite, of Nineveh.

Niña [nee'-nyah], *f.* 1. Pupil of the eye. 2. Girl, a female child. *Niña de los ojos,* Darling.

Niñada [ne-nyah'-dah], *f.* Puerility, childishness, a childish speech or action.

Niñato [ne-nyah'-to], *m.* Calf found in the belly of a cow which has been killed.

Niñear [ne-nyay-ar'], *vn.* To act like a child, to behave in a childish manner.

Niñera [ne-nyay'-rah], *f.* Nursemaid, servant employed to take care of children. 2. Baby-sitter.

Niñería [ne-nyay-ree'-ah], *f.* 1. Puerility, childish action. 2. Bauble, gewgaw, plaything. 3. Trifle, thing of no moment.

Niñero, ra [ne-nyay'-ro, rah], *a.* & *m.* & *f.* One who is fond of children, or who delights in childish tricks; a dandler.

Niñeta [ne-nyay'-tah], *f.* The small pupil of the eye.

Niñez [ne-nyeth'], *f.* 1. Childhood, infancy. 2. Infancy, the first age of any thing; beginning, commencement.

Niñita [ne-nyee'-tah], *f. dim.* Babe, infant.

Niño, ña [nee'-nyo, nyah], *a.* Childish, child-like, puerile: applied to an infant.

Niño [nee'-nyo], *m.* 1. Child, infant. 2. Person of little experience or prudence. *Desde niño,* From infancy, from a child. *No es niño,* He is no more a child.

Nioto [ne-o'-to], *m.* *V.* Cazón.

Nipa [nee'-pah], *f.* A kind of palm-tree in the Philippine Islands; from the leaves are made mats and thatches for roofs, and from the roots a spirituous drink.

Nipe, or **Nipis** [nee'-pay, nee'-pis], *m.* (Com.) A fabric made from the fibres of the *nipa* in the Philippines and in Madagascar.

Nipón, na [ne-pone', nah], *m.* & *f.* & *a.* Nipponese, Japanese.

Niquel [nee'-kel], *m.* Nickel, a silvery white metal.

Niquelado [ne-kay-lah'-do], *a.* (Ore) Holding nickel; also nickel-plated.

Niquelar [ne-kay-lar'], *va.* To nickel-plate.

Niquiscocio [ne-kis-co'-the-o], *m.* Trifle, a thing of little moment.

Niscalo [nees'-cah-lo], *m.* A non-poisonous mushroom.

Nispera [nees'-pay-rah], *f.* A Nicaraguan timber-tree. Achras sapota. *V.* Zapote.

Níspero [nees'-pay-ro], *m.* (Bot.) Medlar-tree. Mespilus germanica, *L.*

Níspola [nees'-po-lah], *f.* Fruit of the medlar-tree.

Nítido, da [nee'-te-do, dah], *a.* (Poet.) Bright, shining, lustrous, nitid, neat.

Nito [nee'-to], *m.* A brake found in the Philippine Islands, from the petioles of which is obtained a fibre used in making hats and cigar-cases.

Nitos [nee'-tos], *m.* Insignificant word, meaning nothing, in reply to an impertinent question, or to conceal any thing.

Nitral [ne-trahl'], *m.* Place where nitre is formed; nitre-bed.

Nitrato [ne-trah'-to], *m.* (Chem.) Nitrate.

Nitrería [ne-tray-ree'-ah], *f.* Saltpetre-works, where saltpetre is prepared and refined.

Nítrico [nee'-tre-co], *a.* Nitric, applied to an acid; consisting of nitre.

Nitrito [ne-tree'-to], *m.* Nitrite, a compound of nitrous acid.

Nitro [nee'-tro], *m.* Nitre, saltpetre; nitrate of potassium.

Nitrobencina [ne-tro-ben-thee'-nah], *f.* (Chem.) Nitrobenzene.

Nitrocelulosa [ne-tro-thay-loo-lo'-sah], *f.* Nitrocellulose, nitrated cellulose.

Nitrógeno [ne-tro'-hay-no], *m.* (Chem.) Nitrogen, azote.

Nitroglicerina [ne-tro-gle-thay-ree'-nah], *f.* Nitro-glycerine, a powerful explosive, basis of dynamite.

Nitroso, sa [ne-tro'-so, sah], *a.* Nitrous, nitry, impregnated with nitre.

Nivel [ne-vel'], *m.* 1. Level, instrument for ascertaining the level of a surface. 2. Level, a plane or surface without inequalities, levelness. *A nivel,* Perfectly level, in a line or row.

Nivelación [ne-vay-lah-the-on'], *f.* 1. Act of levelling. 2. Levelling, the operation of obtaining comparative elevations in surveying.

Nivelador [ne-vay-lah-dor'], *m.* One who ascertains the level of a surface, leveller.

Niveladora [ne-vay-lah-do'-rah], *f.* (Mech.) Bulldozer.

Nivelar [ne-vay-lar'], *va.* 1. To ascertain the level of a surface. 2. To make even, to level. 3. To observe equity and justice.

Níveo, ea [nee'-vay-o, ah], *a.* (Poet.) Snowy, like snow.

Nizardo, da [ne-thar'-do, dah], *a.* Native of or belonging to Nice.

No [no], *adv.* No or not, nay. *No importa nada,* It signifies nothing. *No vale nada,* It is worth nothing. *Decir que no,* To give a flat denial. *No sino,* Not only so. *No sino no,* It cannot be otherwise. *Pues no,* But no, not so. *No sé qué,* I know not what, an inexplicable something. *Por sí o por no,* At any rate. *Sin faltar un sí ni un no,* Without an iota wanting. *No sea que,* Lest.

Nobiliario [no-be-le-ah'-re-o], *m.* A genealogical account of the peerage of a country, nobiliary.

Noble [no'-blay], *a.* 1. Noble, of noble extraction, high-born. 2. Illustrious, eminent, conspicuous, magnific, magnifical, generous. 3. Honourable, respectable. *Estado noble,* Nobility.—*m.* Nobleman.

Noblemente, *adv.* Nobly, generously, magnanimously.

Nobleza [no-blay'-thah], *f.* 1. Nobleness, nobility, antiquity of family with lustre of pedigree. 2. Nobility, the body of noblemen. 3. Gentility, elegance of behaviour. 4. Nobleness, nobility, dignity, greatness, generousness, magnanimity, worth; stateliness. 5. Fine damask silk.

Nocedal. *m.* *V.* Nogueral.

Noción [no-the-on'], *f.* 1. Notion, idea. 2. Acceptation, meaning of a word.

Nocional [no-the-o-nahl'], *a.* Notional.

Nocir [no-theer'], *va.* (Obs.) To hurt, to do mischief.

Nocivamente [no-the-vah-men'-tay], *adv.* Mischievously, hurtfully, harmfully.

Nocivo, va [no-thee'-vo, vah], *a.* Noxious, hurtful, mischievous, malignant.

Noctambulismo [noc-tam-boo-lees'-mo], *m.* The act of walking in sleep. *V.* Somnambulismo.

Noctámbulo, la [noc-tahm'-boo-lo, lah], *m.* & *f.* Somnambulist, one who walks in his sleep.

Noctiluca [noc-tee'-loo-cah], *f.* Glow worm, noctiluca.

Noctiluco [noc-tee'-loo-co], *m.* Noctiluca, a microscopic infusorian, a usual cause of phosphorescence in the ocean.

Noctuinos [noc-too-ee'-nose], *m. pl.* Moths, nocturnal lepidoptera.

Nocturlabio [noc-toor-lah'-be-o], *m.* Nocturnal, an antiquated instrument for measuring the altitude of the pole by night.

Nocturnal [noc-toor-nahl'], *a.* Nocturnal, nightly; done or doing by night.

Nocturnancia, *f.* (Obs.) The dead of the night.

Nocturno, na [noc-toor'-no, nah], *a.* 1. Nocturnal, nightly. 2. Lonely, melancholy, mournful. *Ave nocturna,* Night-bird, such as owls. *Arco nocturno,* (Ast.) The nocturnal arch described by the sun in the night.

Nocturno [noc-toor'-no], *m.* 1. Nocturn, one of the three parts into which matins are divided. 2. (Mus.) Nocturn, a serenade; a dreamy sentimental composition appropriate to the evening or night.

Noche [no'-chay], *f.* 1. Night. 2. (Poet.) Night, death. 3. Night, state of obscurity, confusion, or ignorance. *Noche toledana,* A restless night. *A noche* or *ayer noche,* Last night. *Noche y día,* Night and day, always, constantly. *Quedarse a buenas noches,* (Mex. Coll.) To be left in the dark respecting the knowledge of an affair; also, to be disappointed.

Nochebuena [no-chay-boo-ay'-nah], *f.* Christmas eve.

Nochecita [no-chay-thee'-tah], *f.* (Amer.) Twilight.

Nochielo, la [no-che-ay'-lo, lah], *a.* (Obs.) Darkish, of a dark colour.

Nochizo [no-chee'-tho], *m.* (Bot.) Wild common hazel-nut tree.

Nodal [no-dahl'], *a.* Nodal, referring to the nodes of a vibrating surface.

Nodo [no'-do], *m.* 1. Node, a morbid swelling on the bone. 2. (Ast.) Node, the point where the orbit of a heavenly body intersects the ecliptic.

Nodriza [no-dree'-thah], *f.* Nurse, a woman that has the care of another's child.

Nódulo [no'-doo-lo], *m.* Nodule, a concretion formed in bodies; a small node.

Nogada [no-gah'-dah], *f.* Sauce made of pounded walnuts and spice.

Nogal [no-gahl'], *m.* (Bot.) 1. Common walnut-tree. Juglans. 2. The wood of the common walnut-tree.

Nogueña [no-gay'-nyah], *f.* Flower or blossom of a walnut-tree. (Rare, or of local use.)

Noguera [no-gay'-rah], *f.* (Bot.) Walnut-tree.

Noguerado, da [no-gay-rah'-do, dah], *a.* Of a walnut colour.

Nogueral [no-gay-rahl'], *m.* Plantation of walnut-trees.

Nolición [no-le-the-on'], *f.* Nolition, unwillingness; opposed to *volition.* (Theology.)

Noli me tángere [no-le may tahn'-hay-ray], *m.* Nolimetangere, a malignant ulcer on the face or nose.

Nómada, or **Nómade** [no'-mah-dah, day], *a.* Nomad, nomadic, having no fixed abode.

Nombradamente, *adv.* Namely, expressly.

Nombradía [nom-brah-dee'-ah], *f.* Fame, reputation, conspicuousness, credit.

Nombrado [nom-brah'-do], *m.* Nominee, a person nominated to a place or office.

Nombrador [nom-brah-dor'], *m.* Nominator, appointer.

Nombramiento [nom-brah-me-en'-to], *m.* 1. Nomination, naming, or mentioning by name. 2. Appointment, creation, commission.

Nombrar [nom-brar'], *va.* 1. To name, to mention by name. 2. To nominate, to appoint.

Nombre [nom'-bray], *m.* 1. Name, the discriminative appellation of an individual; title. *Nombre de pila,* Christian name. 2. Fame, reputation, credit. 3. Nickname. *Poner nombres a uno,* To call one names. 4. Power by which any one acts for another. 5. (Gram.) Noun. 6. (Mil.) Countersign; watch-word. *Nombre apelativo,* (1) Surname. (2) Generic name. *Nombre colectivo,* Collective noun. *Dar el nombre,* To give the watch-word (to the sentries). *Decirse los nombres de las fiestas* (or *pascuas*), To use contumelious language. *Hacer nombre de Dios,* To begin or start a thing. *Poner nombre,* To fix a price *En el nombre,* In the name of God.

Nomenclador [no-men-clah-dor'], *m.* 1. Nomenclator, a list of names; glossary; vocabulary of terms. 2. Nomenclator, one who assigns names in a science.

Nomenclátor, *m.* Nomenclator.

Nomenclatura [no-men-clah-too'-rah], *f.* 1. A catalogue. 2. Nomenclature, technical glossary.

Nomeolvides [no-may-ol-vee'-des], *f.* (Bot.) Forget-me-not.

Nómina [no'-me-nah], *f.* 1. Catalogue, an alphabetical list of things or persons. 2. (Obs.) Relic of saints.

Nominación [no-me-nah-the-on'], *f.* 1. Nomination, the act of mentioning by name. 2. Power of presenting to a benefice.

Nominador, ra [no-me-nah-dor', rah], *m.* & *f.* Nominator, appointing power; one who appoints another to a position.

Nominal [no-me-nahl'], *a.* Nominal, belonging to a name; relating to names rather than things; titular.

Nominal [no-me-nahl'], *m.* Nominal, nominalist, one of a sect of scholastical philosophers.

Nominalmente, *adv.* Nominally.

Nominar [no-me-nar'], *va.* To name. *V.* NOMBRAR.

Nominativo [no-me-nah-tee'-vo], *m.* (Gram.) Nominative: applied to the first case of nouns. *Nominativos,* Elements, rudiments.

Nominilla [no-me-neel'-lyah], *f.* A warrant or certificate enabling a pensioner of an office to draw his dues.

Nómino [no'-me-no], *m.* Nominee, a person appointed or nominated to any office or employment.

Nomocanon, *m.* Nomocanon, collection of imperial constitutions and canons.

Nomografía [no-mo-grah-fee'-ah], *f.* Nomography, a treatise on laws.

Nomógrafo [no-mo'-grah-fo], *m.* Nomographer, a writer on laws.

Nomología [no-mo-lo-hee'-ah], *f.* Nomology, the science of laws and their interpretation.

Nomológico, ca [no-mo-lo'-he-co, cah], *a.* Nomological.

Nomparell [nom-pah-rayl'], *f.* (Typ. Nonpareil, a size of type next smaller than the present line; six-point.

Non, *a.* Odd, uneven.

Non, *m.* An odd number. *Quedar de non,* To be or remain quite alone. *Andar de nones,* To be idle, to have nothing to do. *Estar de non,* To serve for nothing. (Coll.) *Pares y nones,* Even or odd. *Llamarse nones,* To deny a thing, to retract, to flinch.

Nona [no'-nah], *f.* None, last of the minor canonical hours, answering to three o'clock P. M.

Nonada [no-nah'-dah], *f.* Trifle, little or nothing, nothingness.

Nonadilla [no-nah-deel'-lyah], *f. dim.* of NONADA.

Nonagenario, ria [no-nah-hay-nah'-re-oh, ah], *a.* Ninety years old, nonagenarian.

Nonagésimo, ma [no-nah-hay'-se-mo, mah], *a.* Ninetieth, nonagesimal.

Nonagonal [no-nah-go-nahl'], *a.* Enneagonal, nine-sided.

Nonágono, *m.* Nonagon.

Nonato, ta [no-nah'-to, tah], *a.* Not naturally born, but extracted from the mother's womb by Cesarean section.

Nono, *a.* Ninth. *V.* NOVENO.

Non plus ultra, *m.* (Lat.) 1. Nonpareil. 2. Pearl, a small printing type; five-point. 3, The utmost of a thing.

No obstante [no obs-tahn'-tay], *conj.* Nevertheless, notwithstanding, however.

Nopal [no-pahl'], *m.* (Bot.) Nopal, cochineal fig-tree, prickly Indian pear-tree. Cactus opuntia. It is vulgarly called in Castile, *higuera chumba.*

Nopalera [no-pah-lay'-rah], *f.* (Amer.) Cochineal plantation.

Noque [no'-kay], *m.* 1. A tan-pit or vat in which the ooze is kept for tanning hides. 2. Heap or basket of bruised olives.

Noquero [no-kay'-ro], *m.* Currier, leather-dresser.

Norabuena [no-rah-boo-ay'-nah], *f.* Congratulation. *V.* ENHORABUENA.

Noramala [no-rah-mah'-lah], *f.* A term of contempt or displeasure. Also *adv. V.* ENHORAMALA.

Nord, *m.* (Naut.) North wind.

Nordest, Nordeste [nor-dest', nor-des'-tay], *m.* North-east. *Nordest cuarto al norte,* North-east-by-north. *Nordeste cuarto al este,* North-east-by-east.

Nordestear [nor-des-tay-ar'], *vn.* (Naut.) To be north-easting.

Nórdico, ca [nor'-de-co, cah], *m.* & *f.* & *a.* Nordic.

Nordovest, *m.* North-west.

Nordovestear, *vn.* (Naut.) To decline to north-west.

Noreste [no-rays'-tay], *m.* North-east.

Noria [no'-re-ah], *f.* 1. An irrigating wheel. 2. Wheel for drawing water from a well; a chain-pump. 3. Draw-well, a deep well. (Ar. na'ora.)

Norial [no-re-ahl'], *a.* Relating to the well called *noria.*

Norma [nor'-mah], *f.* 1. Square, a rule or instrument by which workmen form or measure their angles. 2. Model, a standard or rule to guide and govern all operations.

Normal [nor-mahl'], *a.* 1. Normal, according to an established law. 2. Model, serving as a standard. *Escuela normal,* Normal school.—*f.* Normal, a perpendicular. **-mente,** *adv.*

Normando, da [nor-mahn'-do, dah], *a.* Norman, relating to Normandy.

Nornodeste [nor-no-des'-tay], *m.* (Naut.) North-north-east.

Nornorueste [nor-no-roo-es'-tay], *m.* North-north-west.

Noroeste [no-ro-ess'-tay], *m.* North-west.

Nortada [nor-tah'-dah], *f.* Strong, continued north wind.

Norte [nor'-tay], *m.* 1. North, the arctic pole. 2. North, the northern part of the sphere. 3. North or north wind. 4. Rule, law, guide, clew, direction.

Norteamericano, na [nor-tay-ah-may-re-cah'-no, nah], *m.* & *f.* & *a.* North American (generally from U.S.)

Nortear [nor-tay-ar'], *va.* (Naut.) To steer or stand to the northward.

Noruego, ga [no-roo-ay'-go, gah], *m.* & *f.* & *a.* Norwegian.

Norueste [no-roo-es'-tay], *m.* North-west.

Noruestear [no-roo-es-tay-ar'], *vn.* To decline to the north-west: applied to the magnetic needle.

Nos, *pron.* We: commonly used in an authoritative style, instead of I.

Nosabo (Hacer el). (Prov. Coll.) To make believe, to feign ignorance.

Nosografía [no-so-grah-fee'-ah], *f.* (Med.) Nosography, description of diseases.

Nosología [no-so-lo-hee'-ah], *f.* (Med.) Nosology, classification of diseases.

Nosotros, tras [no-so'-tros, tras], *pron.* We, ourselves.

Nostalgia [nos-tahl'-he-ah], *f.* Nostalgia, inordinate homesickness.

Nota [no'-tah], *f.* 1. Note, mark, or token put upon any thing to make it known; schedule. 2. Note, explanatory annotation in a book or writing. 3. Censure, notice, remark upon one's actions; critique. *Incurrir en la nota,* To incur the imputation. 4. Style, manner of writing. 5. Memorandum or note taken down to help the memory; (Com.) account, statement. 6. Official communication of a government or a foreign minister. 7. Note, reproach. stigma. *Buena* or *mala nota,* Good or bad standing or reputation in society. 8. (Mus.) Musical character; a single sound.—*pl.* The collection of minutes of proceedings taken by a notary. *Autor de nota,* Author of repute.

Notabilidad [no-tah-be-le-dahd'], *f.* Notability. (Neol.)

Notabilísimo, ma [no-tah-be-lee'-se-mo, mah], *a.* Super. of *Notable.*

Notable [no-tah'-blay], *a.* 1. Notable, remarkable, noteworthy, conspicuous. 2. Very great.

Notable [no-tah'-blay], *m.* Introductory observation.

Notablemente, *adv.* Notably, observably, notedly.

Notación [no-tah-the-on'], *f.* 1. An algebraic sign. 2. Notation, the art of representing the written sign in music. 3. Part of prosody which treats of the accentuation of syllables.

Notar [no-tar'], *va.* 1. To note, to mark. 2. To remark, to observe, to note, to heed, to notice, to take notice of, to mind. 3. To take short notes on a subject. 4. To comment, to expound. 5. To annotate a writing or book. 6. To dictate what another may write. 7. To find fault, to censure, to criticise; to reprehend.

Notaría [no-tah-ree'-ah], *f.* 1. Employment or profession of a notary. 2. A notary's office.

Notariado [no-tah-re-ah'-do], *m.* Profession of a notary.

Notariato [no-tah-re-ah'-to], *m.* Title of a notary.

Notario [no-tah'-re-o], *m.* 1. Notary, an officer whose business is to take notes of protests and other transactions, to draw and pass public instruments, and to attest and legalize private dealings and writings: it is now commonly applied to those officers who transact ecclesiastical affairs. 2. Amanuensis. *Entre dos amigos un notario y dos testigos,* (prov.) Even among friends legal vouchers and warranties should not be omitted.

Notho, tha [no'-to, tah], *a.* Bastard, illegitimate. (Acad.)

Noticia [no-tee'-the-ah], *f.* 1. Notice, knowledge, information, note, light. 2. News, intelligence. *Noticias alegres,* Glad tidings. *Poner en la noticia de,* To bring to one's knowledge, to advise, inform. *Noticia remota,* A confused memory. *Atrasado de noticias,* Behind the times.

Noticiar [no-te-the-ar'], *va.* To give notice, to communicate intelligence.

Noticiario [no-te-the-ah'-re-oh], *m.* 1. Newsreel. 2. Newscast.

Noticiero [no-te-the-ay'-ro], *m.* (Mex.) 1. Newsreel. 2. Newscast.

Noticioso, sa [no-te-the-o'-so, sah], *a.* Informed; knowing, learned, instructed.

Notificación [no-te-fe-cah-the-on'], *f.* Notification, judicial intimation.

Notificado, da [no-te-fe-cah'-do, dah], *a.* & *pp.* of NOTIFICAR. Notified: applied to a person who has received a judicial notification.

Notificar [no-te-fe-car'], *va.* To notify, to make known, to intimate; to inform.

Notilla, ita [no-teel'-lyah], *f. dim.* A short note, memorandum, etc.

Noto, ta [no'-to, tah], *a.* 1. Known, notorious. *En noto,* (Obs.) Knowingly. 2. Illegitimate, not born in wedlock. *Terciana nota,* An irregular ague.

Noto [no'-to], *m.* South wind, notus.

Notoriamente, *adv.* Notoriously, manifestly, glaringly.

Notoriedad [no-to-re-ay-dahd'], *f.* Notoriety, notoriousness, public knowledge.

Notorio, ria [no-to'-re-o, ah], *a.* Notorious, publicly known, glaring, flagrant.

Nóumeno [no'-oo-may-no], *m.* (Phil.) Being or essence which every phenomenon declares or reveals; noumenon, "the thing in itself."

Novación [no-vah-the-on'], *f.* (Law) Renovation of an obligation formerly contracted.

Noval [no-vahl'], *a.* Applied to land newly broken up and converted into arable ground, and to the fruits it produces.

Novar [no-var'], *va.* (Law) To renew an obligation formerly contracted.

Novato, ta [no-vah'-to, tah], *a.* (Coll.) New, commencing in any thing.

Novator [no-vah-tor'], *m.* Innovator, an introducer of novelties; novator.

Novecientos, tas [no-vay-the-en'-tos, tas], *s.* & *a.* Nine hundred.

Novedad [no-vay-dahd'], *f.* 1. Novelty, a new state of things; newness, modernness. 2. Admiration excited by novelties or any extraordinary thing. 3. (Coll.) Remarkable occurrence, danger, trouble. *Estar* or *quedar sin novedad,* To be in a good state of health. *Los negocios continúan sin novedad,* Business goes on as usual. *No hacer novedad,* Not to make any change.

Novedoso [no-vay-doh'-so], *a.* Original, novel.

Novel [no-vel'], *a.* New, inexperienced.

Novela [no-vay'-lah], *f.* 1. Novel, a fictitious story, a tale. 2. Falsehood, fiction. 3. (Law) Novel, any new law added to the Justinian codes.

Novelador [no-vay-lah-dor'], *m.* Novelist, a writer of novels.

Novelar [no-vay-lar'], *vn.* 1. To compose, write, or publish novels. 2. To relate stories.

Novelería [no-vay-lay-ree'-ah], *f.* 1. Narration of fictitious stories. 2. Taste for novels and novelties.

Novelero, ra [no-vay-lay'-ro, rah], *a.* 1. Fond of novels and fictitious tales. 2. Fond of hearing and telling news. *Un novelero,* A newsmonger. 3. Newfangled. 4. Inconstant, wavering, unsteady.

Novelesco, ca [no-vay-les'-co, cah], *a.* Novelistic, pertaining to novels.

Novelista [no-vay-lees'-tah], *m.* & *f.* Novelist, a writer of novels.

Novena [no-vay'-nah], *f.* 1. Term of nine days appropriated to some special worship. 2. Offering for the dead.

Novenario [no-vay-nah'-re-o], *m.* Novenary, nine days' condolence for the deceased, or nine days of public worship offered to some saint.

Novendial [no-ven-de-ahl'], *a.* Applied to any day of the novenary, or worship offered for the souls of the faithful.

Noveno, na [no-vay'-no, nah], *a.* Ninth, the ordinal number of nine; ninthly.

Noveno [no-vay'-no], *m.* One of the nine parts into which tithes are divided.

Noventa [no-ven'-tah], *m.* & *a.* Ninety.

Noventón, na [no-ven-tone', nah], *a.* Ninety years old.—*m.* A nonagenarian.

Novia [no'-ve-ah], *f.* 1. Bride, a woman newly married. 2. Woman betrothed.

Noviaje [no-ve-ah'-hay], *m.* Term of betrothal.

Noviazgo [no-ve-ath'-go], *m.* Engagement, betrothal.

Noviciado [no-ve-the-ah'-do], *m.* 1. Novitiate, the time spent in a religious house by way of trial before the vow is taken. 2. House or apartment in which novices live. 3. Novitiate, the time in which the rudiments of a science or art are learned; noviceship.

Novicio [no-vee'-the-o], *m.* 1. Novice, one who has entered a religious house, but not yet taken the vow; a probationer. 2. Novice, a freshman, one in the rudiments of any knowledge.

Novicio, cia [no-vee'-the-o, ah], *a.* Probationary: applied to a novice or probationer.

Noviembre [no-ve-em'-bray], *m.* November.

Novilunio [no-ve-loo'-ne-o], *m.* New moon, conjunction of the moon.

Novilla [no-veel'-lyah], *f.* Cow between three and six years of age; heifer.

Novillada [no-veel-lyah'-dah], *f.* 1. Drove of young bulls or bullocks. 2. Fight of young bulls or bullocks.

Novillejo, eja [no-veel-lyay'-ho, hah] *m.* & *f. dim.* A young bull, a heifer

Novillero [no-veel-lyay'-ro], *m.* 1. Stable in which young cattle are kept. 2. Herdsman who attends young cattle. 3. Piece of pasture ground where calves are put, separate from other cattle, to be weaned. 4. Truant, idler.

Novillico, ito, *m. dim.* *V.* NOVILLEJO.

Novillo [no-veel'-lyo], *m.* 1. A young bull or ox, particularly one not trained to the yoke. 2. (Low) Cuckold. *Hacer novillos,* (Coll.) To play truant.

Novio [no'-ve-o], *m.* 1. Bridegroom. 2. A man betrothed to a woman. 3. One new to some dignity or state.

Novísimo, ma [no-vee'-se-mo, mah], *a.* Newest, most recent; last in the order of things.—*m.* Each of the four last incidents of mankind: death, judgment, heaven, and hell.

Novocaína [no-vo-cah-ee'-nah], *f.* Novocaine.

Nubada, Nubarrada [noo-bah'-dah], *f.* 1. Shower of rain. 2. Plenty, abundance.

Nubado, da, Nubarrado, da [noo-bah'-do, dah], *a.* Clouded, figured like clouds.

Nubarrón [noo-bar-rone'], *m.* A heavy shower of rain, a large cloud.

Nube [noo'-bay], *f.* 1. A cloud. 2. Cloud, a crowd, a multitude, any thing that spreads wide so as to interrupt the view. 3. Film which obstructs the sight. 4. Cloud or shade in precious stones. *Andar* or *estar por las nubes,* (1) *V. Subir a las nubes.* (2) To run mountain high: said of waves. (3) To be extremely annoyed. *Levantar* (or *subir*) *a* or *hasta las nubes,* To praise to the skies. *Levantarse a las nubes* (or *las estrellas*), To be lifted up with pride, or excited with anger. *Poner en* or *sobre las nubes,* To extol to the skies. *Subir a las nubes,* To raise or increase prices very much.

Nubífero, ra [noo-bee'-fay-ro, rah], *a.* (Poet.) Cloud-bringing.

Nubiloso, sa, *a.* *V.* NUBLOSO.

Núbil [noo'-beel], *a.* Nubile, marriageable.

Nublado [noo-blah'-do], *m.* 1. A large cloud. 2. Perturbation of the mind, gloominess. 3. Dread or fear of impending danger.

Nublado, da [noo-blah'-do, dah], *a.* & *pp.* of NUBLAR. Cloudy, misty, nebulous.

Nublar, Nublarse [noo-blar'], *va.* & *vr.* *V.* ANUBLAR.

Nubloso, sa [noo-blo'-so, sah], *a.* 1. Cloudy, dark, overcast. 2. Gloomy, ill-fated.

Nuca [noo'-cah], *f.* Nape of the neck, nucha.

Nuclear [noo-clay-ar'], *a.* Nuclear. *Energía nuclear,* Nuclear energy. *Física nuclear,* Nuclear physics.

Nucleico, ca [noo-clay'-e-co, cah], *a.* Nucleic.

Núcleo [noo'-clay-o], *m.* 1. Kernel of a nut, nucleus. 2. Nucleus, a centre of union or of development.

Nudifloro, ra [noo-de-flo'-ro, rah], *a.* Nudiflorous, having naked flowers.

Nudifoliado, da [noo-de-fo-le-ah'-do, dah], *a.* Having smooth or bare leaves; nudifolious.

Nudillo [noo-deel'-lyo], *m.* 1. Knuckle, the joint of the fingers. 2. (Arch.) Wooden abutment to roofing-timbers. 3. Small knot in stockings. 4. Nodule.

Nudo, da [noo'-do, dah], *a.* (Obs.) Naked. *V.* DESNUDO.

Nudo [noo'-do], *m.* 1. Knot, complication of a cord or string. 2. Knot, node, articulation or joint of plants. 3. Joint in animal bodies. 4. The principal difficulty or doubt in certain matters. 5. Tie, union, bond of association. 6. Node, a swelling on nerves or bones. 7. Knot, intricacy, difficulty. 8. The crisis of a drama. *Nudos del cordel de la corredera,* (Naut.) Knots of the logline. *Echamos doce nudos por hora,* We ran twelve knots an hour. *Nudo gordiano,* Gordian knot, insuperable difficulty. *Atravesársele a uno un nudo en la garganta,* To have a lump in one's throat, to be speechless on ac-

count of violent emotion. *Dar* or *echar otro nudo a la bolsa*, To draw tight the purse-strings, to be miserly.
Nudoso, sa [noo-do'-so, sah], *a.* Knotty, nodous, knotted, knaggy.
Nuégados [noo-ay'-gah-dose], *m. pl.* A sort of paste of flour, honey, and nuts.
Nuera [noo-ay'-rah], *f.* Daughter-in-law.
Nuestramo [noo-es-trah'-mo], *f.* Our master, contracted from *nuestro amo.*
Nuestro, tra [noo-es'-tro, trah], *a.* Our, pertaining to us. *Los nuestros*, The persons of the same party or profession as the speaker.
Nueva [noo-ay'-vah], *f.* News, fresh account of any thing.
Nuevamente, *adv.* Newly, recently, freshly.
Nueve [noo-ay'-vay], *m.* & *a.* 1. Nine, an arithmetical character by which the number nine is denoted. 2. A card with nine marks. 3. Ninth. *El nueve de Enero*, The ninth of January. *El libro nueve*, The ninth book.
Nuevecito [noo-ay-vay-thee'-to], *a. dim.* Quite new, fresh, very lately made.
Nuevo, va [noo-ay'-vo, vah], *a.* 1. New, not old; novel, modern, fresh. *Nuevo flamante*, Spick and span, brand-new. 2. New, having the effect of novelty, not known before. 3. New, renovated, repaired. 4. New, not being before. 5. Recently arrived in a country or place. 6. Inexperienced, not habituated, not familiar. 7. Beginning. *De nuevo*, Anew, recently, of late. *¿ Qué hay de nuevo ?* What is the news ? Is there any news ?
Nuez [noo-eth'], *f.* 1. Walnut, the fruit of the walnut-tree. 2. Fruit of some trees in the shape of a nut. 3. Adam's apple, the prominent part of the throat. *Apretar a uno la nuez*, (Low) To strangle one. 4. Plummet. 5. *Nuez moscada* or *de especia*, (Bot.) Nutmeg. Myristica aromatica. *Nuez métel*, (Bot.) Thorn-apple. Datura metel. *Nuez del país* or *nuez chiquita*, Butter-nut. *Nuez grande*, Madeira-nut. *Nuez dura*, Hickory-nut. *Nuez de San Juan*, Black walnut. *Nuez vómica*, (1) (Bot.) Nux vomica or poison-nut; strychnos. Strychnos nux vomica. (2) The fruit of the poison-nut strychnos.
Nueza [noo-ay'-thah], *f.* (Bot.) Briony. Bryonia. *Nueza blanca*, White-berried briony. Bryonia alba. *Nueza negra*, Common black briony. Tamus communis.
Núfar [noo'-far], *f.* The spatterdock, or yellow water-lily.
Nugatorio, ria [noo-gah-to'-re-o, ah, *a.* Nugatory, futile, deceitful.
Nulamente [noo-lah-men'-tay], *adv.* Invalidly, ineffectually.
Nulidad [noo-le-dahd'], *f.* 1. Nullity, want of force or efficacy. 2. Defeasance, a condition annexed to an act or deed, which, when performed by the obligee, renders the act or deed void. 3. (Coll.) Insignificance.
Nulo, la [noo'-lo, lah], *a.* Null, void of effect, of no force.
Numen [noo'-men], *m.* 1. Divinity, deity. 2. Genius, talent: commonly applied to poetical genius.
Numerable [noo-may-rah'-blay], *a.* Numerable.
Numeración [noo-may-rah-the-on'], *f.* Numeration, the art of numbering: first part of arithmetic.
Numerador [noo-may-rah-dor'], *m.* 1. Numerator, numberer, he who numbers. 2. Numerator, the upper term of a common fraction.
Numeral [noo-may-rahl'], *a.* Numeral, relating to numbers.
Numerar [noo-may-rar'], *va.* 1. To number, to enumerate, to numerate, to calculate, to cipher. 2. To page, to mark the pages of a book. 3. To number, to reckon as one of the same kind.
Numerario, ria [noo-may-rah'-re-o, ah], *a.* Numerary, belonging to a certain number.—*m.* Hard cash, coin.
Numerata pecunia [noo-may-rah'-tah pay-coo'-ne-ah], *adv.* (Lat.) In ready money.
Numéricamente, *adv.* Individually, numerically.
Numérico, ca [noo-may'-re-co, cah], *a.* Numerical, individual, numeral; denoting number.
Numerista [noo-may-rees'-tah, *m.* (Littl. us.) Numerist.
Número [noo'-may-ro], *m.* 1. Number, an aggregate of units. 2. Character, cipher, or figure which denotes the number. 3. Number, comparative multitude. 4. Number, harmony, proportional measure or cadence in music or poetry. 5. (Gram.) Number; singular or plural. 6. Determinate number of persons of any company or society. 7. Verse. *Académico de número*, One of the appointed number of Spanish academicians.—*pl.* Numbers, one of the five books of the Pentateuch. *Número uno*, Number one, one's own selfish interests. *Mirar por el número uno*, To look out for number one. *Sin número*, Numberless, innumerable.
Número Mach [noo'-may-ro mahk], *m.* Mach number; ratio of the velocity of a moving body to the speed of sound.
Numerosamente, *adv.* Numerously.
Numerosidad [noo-may-ro-se-dahd'], *f.* Numerosity, numerousness.
Numeroso, sa [noo-may-ro'-so, sah], *a.* 1. Numerous, containing many. 2. Harmonious, melodious; consisting of parts rightly numbered, rhythmical, harmonical.
Númida [noo'-me-dah], *a.* Numidian, of Numidia.
Numidico, ca [noo-mee'-de-co, cah], *a.* *V.* Númida.
Numisma [noo-mees'-mah], *m.* Coin. (Gr.)
Numismática [noo-mis-mah'-te-cah], *f.* Numismatics, science of medals and coins.
Numismático, ca [noo-mis-mah'-te-co, cah], *a.* Numismatical.
Numismatografía [noo-mis-mah-to-grah-fee'-ah], *f.* Numismatography, description of ancient medals.
Numo [noo'-mo], *m.* Money, coin.
Numularia [noo-moo-lah'-re-ah], *f.* (Bot.) Money-wort. Lysimachia nummularia.
Numulario [noo-moo-lah'-re-o], *m.* A banker.
Nunca [noon'-cah], *adv.* Never, at no time. *Nunca jamás*, Never, never more.
Nunciatura [noon-the-ah-too'-rah], *f.* Nunciature, the office or house of a nuncio.
Nuncio [noon'-the-o], *m.* 1. Messenger. 2. Nuncio, envoy or ambassador from the Pope to Roman Catholic princes. 3. *El Nuncio* or *la casa del Nuncio*, The mad-house in Toledo.
Nuncupativo, va [noon-coo-pah-tee'-vo, vah], *a.* Nuncupative, nominal; verbally pronounced.
Nuncupatorio, ria [noon-coo-pah-to'-re-o, ah], *a.* Nuncupatory.
Nupcial [noop-the-ahl'], *a.* Nuptial, pertaining to marriage, hymeneal.
Nupcias [noop'-the-as], *f. pl.* Nuptials, wedding, marriage.
Nusco [noos'-co], *pron.* (Obs.) We, ourselves. *V.* Nosotros.
Nutación [noo-tah-the-on'], *f.* 1. Direction of plants towards the sun. 2. (Ast.) Nutation, movement of the earth's axis, by which it inclines more or less to the plane of the ecliptic.
Nutante [noo-tahn'-tay], *a.* (Bot.) Nodding.
Nutra, Nutria [noo'-trah, noo'-tre-ah], *f.* 1. Otter. Mustela lutra. 2. A kind of small sea-otter, the fur of which is so called.
Nutricio, cia [noo-tree'-the-o, ah], *a.* Nutritious, nourishing, nutritive.
Nutrición [noo-tre-the-on'], *f.* 1. Nutrition, the act or quality of nourishing. 2. (Pharm.) A certain preparation of medicines.
Nutrimental [noo-tre-men-tahl'], *a.* Nutrimental, having the quality of food.
Nutrimento [noo-tre-men'-to], *m.* 1. Nutriment, food, aliment, nourishment. 2. Nutrition.
Nutrir [noo-treer'], *va.* 1. To nourish, to fatten, to feed. 2. To nourish, to encourage, to foment, to support.
Nutritivo, va [noo-tre-tee'-vo, vah], *a.* Nutritive, nourishing.
Nutriz [noo-treeth'], *f.* Nurse.
Nutual [noo-too-ahl'], *a.* Irremovable: said of chaplains and other ministers not removable at pleasure of the grantor.
Ny [nee], *f.* Nu, thirteenth letter of the Greek alphabet, corresponding to N.

Ñ [ay'-nyay] is the seventeenth letter in the Spanish alphabet. The ancient Spanish writers used *nn* in words derived from the Latin having *gn*, as from *lignum* was written *lenno*, and now *leño*, the *n* with a *tilde*, or circumflex, being substituted in their place. *Ñ* has a strong nasal sound, resembling that of *n* in the English word *poniard*, and exactly similar to that of *gn* in the French word *poignard.*
Ñagaza [nyah-gah'-thah], *f.* Bird-call, a decoy. *V.* Añagaza.
Ñame [nyah'-may], *m.* Yam.
Ñandú [nyan-doo'], *m.* An Argentine variety of the American ostrich. *V.* Nandú.
Ñapa [nyah'-pah], *f.* (Amer.) That which is thrown in gratis, at the end of a bargain. *Dar de ñapa*, To give a thing gratis. *V.* Contra and Pilón.
Ñaque [nyah'-kay], *m.* Heap of useless trifles.
Ñigua [nyee'-goo-ah], *f.* *V.* Nigua.
Ñiquiñaque [nye-kee-nyah'-kay]. An expression used by the vulgar to depreciate any thing; folderol.
Ñoclo [nyo'-clo], *m.* A kind of macaroon, or round sweetmeat.
Ñoña [nyo'-nyah], *f.* (Coll.) Excrement.
Ñoñería [nyo-nyay-ree'-ah], *f.* Decrepitude, second childhood.
Ñoño, ña [nyo'-nyo, nyah], *a.* (Coll.) 1. Delicate, plaintive, timid. 2. Decrepit, impaired by age.
Ñorbo [nyor'-bo], *m.* A certain flower of Peru.
Ñurumé [nyoo-roo-may'], *m.* (Zool.) An ant-eater of Paraguay.

O

O [oh], the eighteenth letter in the Spanish alphabet, is pronounced like the English *o* in cone. *O*, in arithmetic, serves for naught or cipher; it is also used as a circle, of which there is no end, and therefore emblematic of eternity. *O*, in sea-charts, signifies west; Oeste. The seven anthems sung in the church, the seven days before the nativity of our Lord, are called *OO*, because they all commence with this letter.

O, *conj.* Or, either. *O rico o pobre*, Either rich or poor. When followed by another *o* the conjunction *u* is used instead of *o*, to avoid cacophony; as, *Siete u ocho*, Seven or eight.

¡O! *int.* *V.* ¡Ohr!

Oasis [o-ah'-sis], *m.* Oasis, a fertile spot in a desert.

Obcecación [ob-thay-cah-the-on'], *f.* Obduracy, blindness.

Obcecado, da [ob-thay-cah'-do, dah], *a.* Blind.—*pp.* of Obcecar.

Obcecar [ob-thay-car'], *va.* To blind, to darken or obscure.

Obduración [ob-doo-rah-the-on'], *f.* Hardness of heart, obstinacy, obduracy.

Obedecedor, ra [o-bay-day-thay-dor', rah], *m.* & *f.* Obeyer, one who obeys or submits.

Obedecer [o-bay-day-therr'], *va.* To obey, to yield to. *El hierro obedece, el acero no*, Iron bends, steel does not.

Obedecimiento [o-bay-day-the-me-en'-to], *m.* Obedience, obsequiousness.

(*Yo obedezco, yo obedezca*, from *Obedecer.* *V.* Conocer.)

Obediencia [o-bay-de-en'-the-ah], *f.* 1. Obedience, submission. 2. Obsequiousness, pliancy, flexibility; docility in animals. *A la obediencia*, At your service, your most obedient.

Obediencial [o-bay-de-en-the-ah'], *a.* Obediential, according to the rules of obedience.

Obediente [o-bay-de-en'-tay], *a.* Obedient, obsequious, compliant, submissive. *Navío obediente al timón*, (Naut.) Ship which answers the helm readily.

Obedientemente, *adv.* Obediently.

Obelisco [o-bay-lees'-co], *m.* Obelisk, a slender stone pyramid. 2. Dagger, mark for reference, thus:†.

Obelo [o-bay'-lo], *m.* Obelisk. *V.* Obelisco.

Obencadura [o-ben-cah-doo'-rah], *f.* (Naut.) A complete set of shrouds; shrouds in general.

Obenques [o-ben'-kes], *m. pl.* (Naut.) Shrouds. *Obenques mayores.* The main shrouds.

Obertura [o-ber-too'-rah], *f.* (Mus.) Overture.

Obesidad [o-bay-se-dahd'], *f.* Obesity, corpulence.

Obeso, sa [o-bay'-so, sah], a. Obese, fat, corpulent.

Óbice [o'-be-thay], *m.* Obstacle, impediment, hinderance, opposition.

Obispado [o-bis-pah'-do], *m.* 1. Bishopric, the diocese of a bishop. 2. Episcopate, the office and dignity of a bishop.

Obispal [o-bis-pahl'], *a.* Episcopal, belonging to a bishop.

Obispalía [o-bis-pah-lee'-ah], *f.* Palace of a bishop; bishopric, diocese.

Obispar [o-bis-par'], *vn.* 1. To be made a bishop, to obtain a bishopric. 2. (Coll.) To die, to expire.

Obispillo [o-bis-peel'-lyo], *m. dim.* 1. Boy-bishop, a chorister boy dressed like a bishop, and allowed to imitate a bishop. 2. A large black pudding; a pork or beef sausage. 3. Rump or croup of a fowl.

Obispo [o-bees'-po], *m.* 1. Bishop. *Obispo de anillo* or *de título*, Bishop *in partibus*. *Obispo auxiliar*, Assistant bishop. *Obispo sufragáneo*, Suffragan or assistant bishop. *Obispo in partibus*, or *in partibus infidelium*, A titular bishop of the Roman church whose territory is occupied by infidels, and where he cannot consequently reside. 2. A large black pudding.

Obito [o'-be-to], *m.* (Law and religion) Death of a person.

Obituario [o-be-too-ah'-re-o]. *m.* Obituary, a register of burials.

Objeción [ob-hay-the-on'], *f.* Objection, opposition, exception.

Objetar [ob-hay-tar'], *va.* To object, to oppose, to remonstrate.

Objetivamente, *adv.* Objectively.

Objetivar [ob-hay-te-var'], *va.* To make objective.

Objetividad [ob-hay-te-ve-dahd'], *f.* Objectivity.

Objetivismo [ob-hay-te-vees'-mo], *m.* 1. Objectivity. 2. Objectivism.

Objetivo, va [ob-hay-tee'-vo, vah], *a.* Objective.—*m.* 1. Lens. 2. Objective.

Objeto [ob-hay'-to], *m.* 1. Object. 2. Subject.

Objetor [ob-hay-tor'], *m.* Objector. *Objetor de conciencia*, Conscientious objector.

Oblación [o-blah-the-on'], *f.* Oblation, offering, gift.

Oblada [o-blah'-dah], *f.* Funeral offering of bread for the souls of the deceased.

Oblata [o-blah'-tah], *f.* 1. Host and chalice offered before being consecrated in the celebration of the mass. 2. Sum of money given to the church to defray the expense of bread, wine, candles, etc., for celebrating mass.

Oblato, ta [o-blah'-to, tah], *a.* & *n.* 1. One who, on becoming a monk, donated his property to the community. 2. Anciently, a child offered to God to make him embrace the clerical profession. 3. A lay monk of certain orders. 4. A certain tax anciently paid. 5. An invalided soldier, who had a right of receiving a living and clothing from some abbey or priory.

Oblea [o-blay'-ah], *f.* Wafer, paste made to close letters.

Obleero [o-blay-ay'-ro], *m.* 1. One who sells wafers about the streets.

Oblicuángulo [o-ble-coo-ahn'-goo-lo], *a.* Oblique-angled.

Oblicuidad [o-ble-coo-e-dahd'], *f.* Obliquity, deviation from physical rectitude.

Oblicuo, cua [o-blee'-coo-o, ah], *a.* Oblique, not direct, not perpendicular, not parallel, crooked.

Obligación [o-ble-gah-the-on'], *f.* 1. Obligation, the binding power of an oath, vow or duty; contract. 2. (For.) Obligation, bond; written security for the carrying out of something. 3. Obligation, duty of acknowledging a benefit received. 4. Obligation, bond, of a public debt or of a company, bearing interest. 5. (Acad.) Provision office, the place where provisions are sold, pursuant to a previous contract.—*pl.* 1. Character and integrity which a man must possess to be worthy of esteem. *Es hombre de obligaciones*, He is a man of integrity and honour. 2. Family which one is obliged to maintain. 3. Engagements.

Obligado [o-ble-gah'-do], *m.* 1. Contractor who engages to supply a city with some kind of provisions. 2. (Law) Obligee, one bound by a contract. 3. Obligato, properly obbligato, an accompaniment indispensable to the proper performance of a piece of music.

Obligante [o-ble-gahn'-tay], *pa.* Obligating, imposing.

Obligar [o-ble-gar'], *va.* 1. To oblige, to compel, to bind, to constrain, to necessitate. 2. To oblige, to confer favors, to lay obligations of gratitude.—*vr.* To oblige or bind one's self.

Obligatorio, ria [o-ble-gah-to'-re-o, ah], *a.* Obligatory, binding, coercive.

Obliteración [o-ble-tay-rah-the-on'], *f.* Obliteration.

Obliterar [o-ble-tay-rar'], *va.* 1. To blot out, to obliterate, to make disappear. 2. (Med.) To obstruct or close some channel of the body.

Oblongo, ga [o-blon'-go, gah], *a.* Oblong, longer than broad.

Obnoxio, xia [ob-nok'-se-o, ah], *a.* Obnoxious, hurtful.

Oboe [o-bo'-ay], *m.* 1. Oboe or hautboy, a musical wind-instrument with a double reed. 2. Player on the oboe.

Óbolo [o'-bo-lo], *m.* 1. Obolus, Athenian money. 2. Obole, a weight of twelve grains. 3. A small gift for charity.

Obra [o'-brah], *f.* 1. Work, anything made. 2. Work, writings of an author. 3. Work, a new building on which men are at work. 4. The repairs made in a house. 5. Work, every moral action. 6. Means, virtue, power. 7. Toil, work, labor, employment. *Obras pías*, Charitable funds or establishments. *Obra de retacitos*, Patchwork. *Obra de cada día*, Something made according to the exigencies of the day. *Hacer mala obra*, To cause a loss of time. *Obra de arte mayor*, Masterly piece of work. *Poner por obra*, To set at work. *Obras de marea*, (Naut.) Graving, calking and paying a ship's bottom. *Obras muertas*, (Naut.) Upper works of a ship. *Obras vivas*, (Naut.) Quick or lower works, the part of a ship which is under water when loaded. *Obra de* or *a obra de*, Nearly, about, more or less.

Obrada [o-brah'-dah], *f.* As much ground as two mules or oxen can plough in a day.

Obrador, ra [o-brah-dor', rah], *m.* & *f.* 1. Workman or workwoman, artificer, mechanic. 2. Workshop. *Obradores*, (Naut.) Workshop or working-places in a dock-yard.

Obradura [o-brah-doo'-rah], *f.* That which is expressed at every pressful in oil-mills.

Obraje [o-brah'-hay], *m.* 1. Manufacture, anything made by art. 2. Manufactory, workshop. (Amer.) A manufactory of coarse cloth, baize, and other woollen stuffs. It is used as a house of correction, where persons guilty of small offences are confined, and obliged to work hard for a certain time.

Obrajero [o-brah-hay'-ro], *m.* Foreman, overseer, superintendent.
Obrar [o-brar'], *va.* 1. To work, to manufacture. 2. To operate, to produce effects; to act, to have agency. 3. To operate, to produce the desired effect: applied to medicines. 4. To put into practice, to execute; to construct, to build. 5. To ease nature. *En chica hora Dios obra,* God's power is not limited to time or place. *Quien obra mal, para sí hará,* The wicked work their own ruin.
Obrepción [o-brep-the-on'], *f.* Obreption, false narration to obtain some end.
Obrepticiamente, *adv.* Falsely, deceitfully.
Obrepticio, cia [o-brep-tee'-the-o, ah], *a.* Obreptitious, obtained by a false statement of matters of fact, by deceit or surprise.
Obrería [o-bray-ree'-ah], *f.* 1. Task of a workman. 2. Money destined for the repairs of a church.
Obrero, ra [o-bray'-ro, rah], *m.* & *f.* 1. Worker, workman, day-laborer. 2. Missionary. 3. Prebendary who superintends the repairs of church buildings. 4. Person who collects money for the building of churches.
Obreropatronal [o-bray-ro-pah-tro-nahl'], *a.* Relating to capital and labor. *Relaciones obreropatronales,* Capital and labor relations.
Obrita [o-bree'-tah], *f. dim.* Small or little work.
Obrizo, za [o-bree'-tho, thah], *a.* Pure, refined: applied to gold.
Obscenidad [obs-thay-ne-dahd'], *f.* Obscenity, impurity, unchastity, lewdness.
Obsceno, na [obs-thay'-no, nah], *a.* Obscene, impure, lewd, lustful.
Obscuramente, *adv.* 1. Obscurely, darkly, faintly, abstrusely. 2. Obscurely, privately. 3. Obscurely, confusedly, not plainly.
Obscurantismo [obs-coo-ran-tees'-mol, *m* Obscurantism.
Obscuras (A) [obs-coo'-ras, ah], *adv.* Obscurely, darkly.
Obscurecer [obs-coo-ray-therr'], *va.* 1. To obscure, to darken. 2. To impair the lustre of things. 3. To fill with gloom or darkness. 4. To cloud, to confuse the reason. 5. To render a subject less intelligible. 6. (Pict.) To use deep shades.—*v. impers.* To grow dark.—*vr.* 1. To cloud over. 2. To disappear.
Obscurecimiento [obs-coo-ray-theme-en'-to], *m.* 1. Obscuration, act of darkening. 2. Blackout (during war, etc.)
Obscuridad [obs-coo-re-dahd'], *f.* 1. Obscurity, darkness. 2. Cloudiness, gloominess, opacity, density. 3. Obscurity, darkness of meaning, abstruseness, confusedness. 4. The humbleness of a stock whence a family or any other thing proceeds. 5. Retired, private life.
Obscuro, ra [obs-coo'ro, rah], *a.* 1. Obscure, dark, gloomy. 2. Obscure, unintelligible, confused, abstruse. 3. Obscure, little known, unknown. 4. (Pict.) Dark, deep, heavy. *Andar a obscuras* or *a escuras,* (Met.) To grope in the dark, to proceed in a business without understanding its nature or principles.
Obsecración [ob-say-crah-the-on'], *f.* Obsecration, entreaty, supplication.
Obsecuente [ob-say-coo-en'-tay], *a.* Obsequious, obedient.
Obsequiador, ra [ob-say-ke-ah-dor', rah], *a.* & *n.* (Littl. us.) *V.* OBSEQUIANTE.
Obsequiante [ob-say-ke-ahn'-tay], *pa.* & *n.* Obsequious; courtier, gallant.
Obsequiar [ob-say-ke-ar'], *va.* To court, to wait upon, to serve, to obey.
Obsequio [ob-say'-ke-o], *m.* Obsequiousness, complaisance, civility, desire of pleasing. *En* or *por obsequio de,* For the sake of, out of respect to.
Obsequioso, sa [ob-say-ke-o'-so, sah], *a.* Obsequious, obedient, compliant, obliging, attentive.
Observación [ob-ser-vah-the-on'], *f.* 1. Observation, the act of observing; remark, note. *Observaciones sueltas,* Desultory remarks. 2. Observance, careful obedience.
Observador, ra. [ob-ser-vah-dor', rah], *m.* & *f.* 1. Observer, remarker. 2. Observer, one who keeps any law, custom, or practice.—*m.* An astronomer.
Observancia [ob-ser-vahn'-the-ah], *f.* 1. Observance, respect, reverence, regard. 2. Attentive practice, obedience, observation, ritual practice. 3. The original state of some religious orders, in contradistinction to their reformed condition. *Poner en observancia,* To execute punctually whatever is ordered.
Observante [ob-ser-vahn'-tay], *pa.* & *a.* Observant, respectfully obedient; observing.—*m.* Monk of certain branches of the order of St. Francis.
Observar [ob-ser-var'], *va.* 1. To observe, to regard attentively. 2. To observe, to notice, to mind, to heed. 3. To observe, to keep religiously or ritually, to follow. 4. To obey, to execute with punctuality and exactness. *Observar la altura,* (Naut.) To take the meridian altitude.
Observatorio [ob-ser-vah-to'-re-o], *m.* Observatory, a place for astronomical or meteorological observations.
Obsesión [ob-say-se-on'], *f.* Obsession.
Obsesionar [ob-say-se-o-nar'], *va.* & *vr.* To obsess, to be obsessed (with an idea, etc.)
Obseso, sa [ob-say'-so, sah], *a.* Beset, tempted, as with evil spirits.
Obsidiana [ob-se-de-ah'-nah], *f.* Obsidian, a glassy, volcanic rock.
Obsistente [ob-sis-ten'-tay], *a.* (Arch.) Resonant, resounding: applied to a wall or building. (Obs.)
Obstáculo [obs-tah'-coo-lo], *m.* Obstacle, impediment, obstruction, clog, hinderance.
Obstante [obs-tahn'-tay], *pa.* Withstanding: seldom used except in the phrase, *no obstante,* Notwithstanding, nevertheless.
Obstar [ob-star'], *vn.* To oppose, to obstruct, to hinder, to withstand.
Obstetrical [obs-tay-tre-cahl'], *a.* Obstetrical.
Obstetricia [obs-tay-tre'-the-ah], *f.* Obstetrics, midwifery.
Obstétrico, ca [obs-tay'-tre-co, cah], *a.* Obstetrical, relating to childbirth.—*f.*
Obstinación [obs-te-nah-the-on'], *f.* Obstinacy, stubbornness, obduracy.
Obstinado, da [obs-te-nah'-do, dah], *a.* Obstinate, obdurate, headstrong, opinionated.—*pp.* of OBSTINARSE.
Obstinarse [obs-te-nar'-say], *vr.* To be obstinate.
Obstrucción [obs-trooc-the-on'], *f.* 1. (Med.) Obstruction in the vessels of the body. 2. Obstruction, closure of any passage.
Obstructivo, va [obs-trooc-tee'-vo, vah], *a.* Obstructive, obstruent.
Obstruir [obs-troo-eer'], *va.* To obstruct or block up the natural passages of the body.—*vr.* To be obstructed or choked: applied to an opening or aperture.
Obtemperar [ob-tem-pay-rar'], *va.* (Ant.) To obey, to assent (used with prep. *a*).
Obtención [ob-ten-the-on'], *f.* Attainment, obtainment, the act of attaining or obtaining.
Obtener [ob-tay-nerr'], *va.* 1. To attain, to obtain, to procure. 2. To preserve, to maintain.
(*Yo obtengo, obtenga; obtuve, obtuviera;* from *Obtener. V.* TENER.)
Obtento [ob-ten'-to], *m.* 1. Benefice, prebend, living. 2. Attainment.
Obtentor [ob-ten-tor'], *m.* One who obtains a living on being ordained priest.
Obtestación [ob-tes-tah-the-on'], *f.* Obtestation, protestation; a rhetorical figure in which the speaker calls to witness God, Nature, men, or inanimate things.
Obturador, triz [ob-too-rah-dor', treeth'], *a.* Serving to stop up or plug.—*m.* 1. Plug, stopper; breechblock. 2. Obturator, a surgical plate for closing a fissure. 3. Gas-check, a circular plate of glass placed over the mouth of vessels filled with gas, for carrying them. 4. A photographic shutter.
Obturar [ob-too-rar'], *va.* To stop up, to plug, to obturate.
Obtusángulo [ob-too-sahn'-goo-lo], *m.* & *a.* Obtuse angle; obtusangular.
Obtuso, sa [ob-too'-so, sah], *a.* 1. Obtuse, blunt, not pointed; not shrill. 2. Obtuse, dull.
Obué [o-boo-ay'], *m.* Oboe and oboe-player. *V.* OBOE.
Obús [o-boos'], *m.* 1. Howitzer, a kind of mortar used for firing shells and grapeshot. 2. (Neol.) A conical shell.
Obusero, ra [o-boo-say'-ro, rah], *a.* (Mil.) Shell-throwing: used of cannons and of a vessel provided with howitzers.
Obvención [ob-ven-the-on'], *f.* A casual profit, obvention.
Obviar [ob-ve-ar'], *va.* To obviate, to prevent.—*vn.* To oppose.
Obvio, via [ob'-ve-o, ah], *a.* Obvious, evident.
Obyecto, ta [ob-yec'-to, tah], *m.* (Met.) Interposed.
Oc, *m.* A kind of arrow which the ancient Turks made use of. *Lengua de oc* (from *oc,* yes), A dialect spoken in southern France and in Catalonia in the thirteenth century. From it is derived modern Provençal and Catalonian.
Oca [o'-cah], *f.* 1. (Orn.) Goose. Anas anser. 2. (Bot.) Oca oxalis, with yellow flowers. Oxalis oca. 3. Kind of game called royal goose. It has sixty-three divisions painted in a spiral upon a cardboard and which represent different objects; each ninth space depicts a goose, and some of them rivers, wells, etc. Dice are thrown for the moves.
Ocal [o-cahl'], *m.* 1. Cocoon of silk formed by two silk-worms together, and the silk made from it. —*a.* Applied to very delicate sweet pears and apples.

Ocalear [o-cah-lay-ar'], *vn.* To make ocals: applied to silk-worms.
Ocarina [o-cah-ree'-nah], *f.* (Mus.) Ocarina.
Ocasión [o-cah-se-on'], *f.* 1. Occasion, opportunity, juncture, convenience. 2. Occasion, accidental cause or motive. 3. Danger, risk. *Ponerse en ocasión*, To expose one's self to danger; to put one in jeopardy. *Asir la ocasión por la melena* or *por los cabellos*, (Coll.) To take time by the forelock. *Por ocasión*, By chance. *Quien quita la ocasión, quita el pecado*, He who avoids temptation, avoids sin.
Ocasionado, da [o-cah-se-o-nah'-do, dah], *a.* Provoking, vexatious, insolent; perilous.—*pp.* of OCASIONAR.
Ocasionador, ra [o-cah-se-o-nah-dor', rah], *m.* & *f.* Occasioner, one that causes or promotes.
Ocasional [o-cah-se-o-nahl'], *a.* Occasional, extemporaneous.
Ocasionalmente, *adv.* Occasionally.
Ocasionar [o-cah-se-o-nar'], *va.* 1. To cause, to occasion; to move, to excite. 2. To endanger.
Ocasioncilla, ita [o-cah-se-on-theel'-lyah, thee'-tah], *f. dim.* of OCASIÓN.
Ocaso [o-cah'-so], *m.* 1. The setting of the sun or any heavenly body. 2. Occident, the west. 3. Death.
Occidental [oc-the-den-tahl'], *a.* Occidental, western.
Occidente [oc-the-den'-tay], *m.* 1. Occident, the west. 2. Europe, in contrast to Asia or the Orient. 3. (Met.) Age, decadence.
Occiduo, dua [oc-thee'-doo-o, ah], *a.* Occidental. (Acad.)
Occipital [oc-the-pe-tahl'], *a.* Occipital, a bone in the hinder part of the head.
Occipucio [oc-the-poo'-the-o], *m.* Occiput, the back part of the head, where it joins the spine.
Occiso, sa [oc-thee'-so, sah], *a.* (Obs.) Murdered, killed. *Tañer de occiso*, To blow the bugle-horn, indicating the death of the game.
Oceánico, ca [o-thay-ah'-ne-co, cah], *a.* 1. Oceanic, belonging to the ocean. 2. Living or growing in the ocean.
Océano [o-thay'-ah-no], *m.* 1. The ocean. 2. Any vast expanse.
Oceanografía [o-thay-ah-no-grah-fee'-ah], *f.* Oceanography, oceanic geography.
Ocelotl (or **Ocelote**), *m.* Ocelot, a leopard-like cat of Mexico and South America.
Ociar [o-the-ar'], *va.* (Obs.) To disturb one in the performance of a business.—*vn.* To loiter, to spend time carelessly.
Ocio [o'-the-o], *m.* 1. Leisure, freedom from business; vacancy of mind. 2. Pastime, diversion.
Ociosamente, *adv.* Idly, uselessly.
Ociosidad [o-the-o-se-dahd'], *f.* Idleness, laziness, sluggishness, leisure.
Ocioso, sa [o-the-o'-so, sah], *a.* Idle, lazy, fruitless, unprofitable; foppish.
Oclocracia [o-clo-crah'-the-ah], *f.* Ochlocracy, government by the multitude.
Oclusión [o-cloo-se-on'], *f.* Occlusion, obliteration.
Ocote [o-co'-tay], *m.* A very resinous pine-tree of Mexico; pitch-pine.
Ocozoal [o-co-tho-ahl'], *m.* Mexican serpent, like a viper.
Ocre [o'-cray], *m.* Ochre, a brown or yellow earth.
Ocropira [o-cro-pee'-rah], *f.* Yellow fever.
Ocroso, sa [o-cro'-so, sah], *a.* Ochreous, of the nature or colour of ochre.
Octaedro [oc-tah-ay'-dro], *m.* (Geom.) Octahedron, a solid bounded by eight plane triangles.
Octagonal [oc-tah-go-nahl'], *a.* Octagonal.
Octágono, na [oc-tah'-go-no, nah], *a.* Having eight sides and angles.
Octágono [oc-tah'-go-no], *m.* An octagon.
Octangular [oc-tan-goo-lar'], *a.* Octangular.
Octano [oc-tah'-no], *m.* (Chem.) Octane.
Octante [oc-tahn'-tay], *m.* Octant, an instrument containing the eighth part of a circle.
Octava [oc-tah'-vah], *f.* 1. Octave, a space of eight days comprising a church festival. 2. A poetical composition of eight lines of eleven syllables, rhyming thus: 1, 3, 5; 2, 4, 6; 7 and 8. 3. (Mus.) Octave. 4. *V.* OCTAVARIO.
Octavar [oc-tah-var'], *vn.* 1. To form octaves on stringed instruments. 2. To deduct the eighth part.
Octavario [oc-tah-vah'-re-o], *m.* 1. Book which contains the office for an octave festival. 2. Festival lasting a week.
Octavilla [oc-tah-veel'-lyah], *f.* 1. Half-pint for excise taken on the retail of vinegar, oil, and wine. 2. (Mus.) Octave.
Octavín [oc-tah-veen'], *m.* 1. A piccolo flute. 2. Flageolet.
Octavo [oc-tah'-vo, *m.* 1. An eighth. 2. In America, an octoroon.
Octavo, va, *a.* Eighth; octave, octonary. *Un libro en octavo*, An octavo volume.
Octeto [oc-tay'-to], *m.* (Mus.) Octet.
Octogenario, ria [oc-to-hay-nah'-re-o, ah], *a.* Octogenary, eighty years old.
Octogentésimo [oc-to-hen-tay'-se-mo], *a.* Eight hundredth.
Octogésimo [oc-to-hay'-se-mo], *a.* Eightieth.
Octógono, na [oc-toh'-go-no, nah], *a.* *V.* OCTÁGONO.
Octopétala [oc-to-pay'-tah-lah], *a.* (Bot.) Octopetalous, of eight petals.
Octosilábico, ca, Octosílabo, ba [oc-to-se-lah'-be-co, cah], *a.* Octosyllabic.
Octubre [oc-too'-bray], *m.* October.
Octuplicar [oc-too-ple-car'], *va.* To multiply by eight, to increase eight-fold.
Óctuplo, pla [oc'-too-plo, plah], *a.* Octuple, eight-fold.
Ocular [o-coo-lar'], *a.* Ocular. *Testigo ocular*, Eye-witness. *Dientes oculares*, Eye-teeth.—*m.* Eye-glass, ocular, eye-piece.
Oculista [o-coo-lees'-tah], *m.* Oculist; eye specialist.
Ocultación [o-cool-tah-the-on'], *f.* 1. Concealment, hiding. 2. (Ast.) Occultation of a star or planet. 3. Wrongful silence.
Ocultador, ra [o-cool-tah-dor', rah], *m.* & *f.* Hider, concealer.
Ocultamente, *adv.* Secretly, hiddenly.
Ocultar [o-cool-tar'], *va.* 1. To hide, to conceal, to disguise, to secrete, to mask, to hoodwink, to cloak. 2. To keep back, to keep secret what ought to be said.
Ocultismo [o-cool-tees'-mo], *m.* Occultism.
Oculto, ta [o-cool'-to, tah], *a.* Hidden, concealed, occult, secret, clandestine. *De oculto*, Incog, incognito. *En oculto*, Secretly, in secret.
Ocupación [o-coo-pah-the-on'], *f.* 1. Occupation; business, concern; employment, office, pursuit; action. 2. Prolepsis, a rhetorical figure.
Ocupado, da [o-coo-pah'-do, dah], *a.* Busy, occupied, engaged.
Ocupador [o-coo-pah-dor'], *m.* Occupier, possessor, occupant.
Ocupante [o-coo-pahn'-tay], *pa.* & *n.* Occupant; an actual possessor of lands
Ocupar [o-coo-par'], *va.* 1. To occupy to take possession of. 2. To hold an employ, to fill a public station. 3. To occupy, to busy, to employ, to give employment. 4. To disturb, to interrupt, to obstruct. 5. To inhabit a house. 6. (Met.) To occupy or gain the attention. —*vr.* To occupy, to follow business.
Ocurrencia [o-coor-ren'-the-ah], *f.* 1. Occurrence, accident, incident, occasion. *Ocurrencia de acreedores*, Meeting of creditors to divide the debtor's effects. 2. Bright thought or original idea which occurs to the mind. *Ocurrencia* or *ocurrencia salada*, (Coll.) A witty sally.
Ocurrente [o-coor-ren'-tay], *a.* Off hand, original, bright, witty.—*pa.* of OCURRIR.
Ocurrir [o-coor-reer'], *vn.* 1. To meet, to go to meet, to anticipate. 2. To occur, to happen, to fall on the same day: applied to two feasts of different solemnities. 3. To obviate, to make opposition to. 4. To repair, to proceed. *Me ocurre una idea*, (Coll.) A thought strikes me.—*v. impers.* To occur, to be presented to the memory or attention.
Ochava [o-chah'-vah], *f.* The eighth part of any thing. *Ochavas del molinete*, (Naut.) The whelps of the windlass.
Ochavado, da [o-chah-vah'-do, dah], *a.* Octagonal, eight-sided.—*pp.* of OCHAVAR.
Ochavar [o-chah-var'], *va.* To form an octagon.
Ochavear [o-chah-vay-ar'], *va.* To be divided into eighths.
Ochavo [o-chah'-vo], *m.* 1. A small Spanish brass coin, valued at two maravedies. 2. Any thing octagonal.
Ochenta [o-chen'-tah], *a.* & *m.* Eighty.
Ochentavo, va [o-chen-tah'-vo, vah], *a.* The one-eightieth part.
Ochentón, na [o-chen-tone', nah], *a.* Eighty years old.
Ochete [o-chay'-tay], *m.* Bore or empty part of hollow projectiles.
Ocho [o'-cho], *a.* & *m.* 1. Eight. 2. Eight, the figure 8. 3. A card with eight marks. *El ocho de Marzo*, The eighth of March.
Ochocientos [o-cho-the-en'-tos], *a.* & *m.* Eight hundred.
Ochosén [o-cho-sen'], *m.* The smallest coin among the ancient Spaniards.
Oda [o'-dah], *f.* 1. Ode, a lyric poem. 2. Ode, a poem written to be set to music.
Odalisca [o-dah-lees'-cah], *f.* Odalisk, a woman of the harem of the Sultan of Turkey; a servant of his sisters, daughters, and wives, and often a concubine.
Odiar [o-de-ar'], *va.* To hate, to abhor, to detest.—*vr.* To hate one another.
Odio [o'-de-o], *m.* Hatred, abhorrence, detestation, malevolence.
Odiosamente, *adv.* Odiously, hatefully.
Odiosidad [o-de-o-se-dahd'], *f.* Hatefulness, odiousness, odium.
Odioso, sa [o-de-oh'-so, sah], *a.* Odious, hateful, detestable.
Odisea [o-de-say'-ah], *f.* The Odyssey, a poem written by Homer.
Odómetro [o-do'-may-tro], *m.* Instrument for measuring the road passed over; odometer.
Odontalgia [o-don-tahl'-he-ah], *f.* Odontalgia, toothache.
Odontálgico [o-don-tahl'-he-co], *m.* Odontalgic, remedy for toothache.
Odontecnia [o-don-tec'-ne-ah], *f.* Dental surgery.

Odontina [o-don-tee'-nah], *f.* 1. A remedy for curing toothache. 2. A dentifrice.
Odontología [o-don-to-lo-hee'-ah], *f.* Odontology, the science of dentistry.
Odontólogo [o-don-to'-lo-go], *m.* Odontologist, dentist.
Odontotecnia [o-don-to-tec'-ne-ah], *f.* Practical art of dentistry.
Odorífero, ra [o-do-ree'-fay-ro, rah], *a.* Odoriferous, fragrant, perfumed.
Odorífico, ca [o-do-ree'-fe-co, cah], *a.* Odour-producing. *Órgano odorífico,* The organ which, in the hemiptera, secretes the smell which they emit at will.
Odre [o'-dray], *m.* 1. Bag generally used for wine, oil, and other liquids, commonly made of a dressed goat-skin; a leather bottle lined with pitch. 2. (Humorous) Drunkard.
Odrería [o-dray-ree'-ah], *f.* Shop where leather bottles are made or sold.
Odrero [o-dray'-ro], *m.* One who makes or deals in leather bottles.
Odrina [o-dree'-nah], *f.* Ox-skin bag.
Oenas [o-ay'-nas], *f.* Stock-dove, wood-pigeon.
Oenate [o-ay-nah'-tay], *f.* (Orn.) Fallow-finch, stone-chatter.
Oesnorueste [o-es-no-roo-es'-tay], *m.* West-north-west.
Oessudueste [o-es-soo-doo-es'-tay], *m.* West-south-west.
Oeste [o-es'-tay], *m.* 1. West. 2. The west wind. *Oeste cuarta al norte,* West-by-north. *Oeste cuarta al sur,* West-by-south.
Ofendedor, ra [o-fen-day-dor', rah], *m.* & *f.* *V.* OFENSOR.
Ofender [o-fen-derr'], *va.* To offend, to harm, to injure, to make angry.—*vr.* To be vexed or displeased; to take offence. *Ofenderse del aire,* To be of an irritable disposition.
Ofensa [o-fen'-sah], *f.* 1. Offence, injury, transgression, crime. 2. Offence; attack. 3. Offence, breaking the law of God.
Ofensión [o-fen-se-on'], *f.* (Obs.) Offence, grievance; injury.
Ofensivamente, *adv.* Offensively, injuriously.
Ofensivo, va [o-fen-see'-vo, vah], *a.* 1. Offensive, displeasing, disgusting. 2. Assailant, not defensive.—*f. Tomar la ofensiva,* To take the offensive; to prepare for attack, and to attack in fact.
Ofensivo, *m.* Any thing which serves as a defence or remedy.
Ofensor, ra [o-fen-sor', rah], *m.* & *f.* Offender.
Oferente [o-fay-ren'-tay], *m.* Offerer, one who offers.
Oferta [o-ferr'-tah], *f.* 1. Offer, promise, offering. 2. Supply. *La ley de la oferta y la demanda,* The law of supply and demand.
Ofertorio [o-fer-to'-re-o], *m.* 1. Offertory, the act of offering; the thing offered; the part of the mass where the priest offers up the host and wine. 2. The anthem belonging to this service.
Oficial, la [o-fe-the-ahl', lah], *m.* & *f.* 1. Workman, workwoman, artificer, tradesman; journeyman. *Buen oficial,* A first-rate hand, a good operative. *Oficial de guarnicionero,* A journeyman harness-maker. 2. Officer who holds a commission in the army or navy. 3. Clerk in a public office. *Oficial mayor de la secretaría de estado,* First under secretary of the state department. *Oficial mayor,* Chief clerk. 4. Hangman, executioner. 5. (Prov.) Butcher, one who cuts up and retails meat. 6. Municipal magistrate. *Oficial de la sala,* Actuary in criminal causes. *Oficial general de mar,* (Naut.) Flag-officer. *Oficiales de la mayoría,* Adjutants. *Es buen oficial,* He is a clever workman; he is a good officer.
Oficial [o-fe-the-ahl'], *a.* Official, pertaining to a public charge.
Oficialazo [o-fe-the-ah-lah'-tho], *m. aug.* A skilful workman.
Oficialejo [o-fe-the-ah-lay'-ho], *m. dim.* A petty workman.
Oficialía [o-fe-the-ah-lee'-ah], *f.* 1. Clerk's place in a public office. *Oficialía mayor,* Chief clerkship. 2. Artist's working-room.
Oficialidad [o-fe-the-ah-le-dahd'], *f.* Body of officers of an army or regiment.
Oficialmente [o-fe-the-al-men'-tay], *adv.* Officially, in an official manner.
Oficiar [o-fe-the-ar'], *va.* To officiate, commonly in worship; to minister.
Oficina [o-fe-thee'-nah], *f.* 1. Workshop. 2. Office, counting-house. *Oficinas,* Offices, the lower apartments in houses, such as cellars.
Oficinal [o-fe-the-nahl'], *a.* Officinal: applied to the drugs prepared by apothecaries.
Oficinesco, ca [o-fe-the-nes'-co, cah], *a.* Departmental, relating to the offices of state, in a derogatory sense; "red-tape."
Oficinista [o-fe-the-nees'-tah], *m.* Any one employed in a public or a secretary's office.
Oficio [o-fee'-the-o], *m.* 1. Office, employ, work, occupation, ministry. 2. Function, operation. 3. Official letter. 4. Trade, business; craft. 5. Notary's office. 6. Benefit, service. *Correr bien el oficio,* To make the most of a place or office. *De oficio,* Officially, by duty, not by request. *Mozo de oficio,* An under-servant in the king's palace. *Tomarlo por oficio,* To do a thing frequently. *Oficio de boca* or *de la boca,* Purveyor to the king. *Oficios,* Solemn church service or divine service.
Oficiosamente, *adv.* Officiously.
Oficiosidad [o-fe-the-o-se-dahd'], *f.* 1. Diligence, application to business. 2. Officiousness.
Oficioso, sa [o-fe-the-o'-so, sah], *a.* 1. Officious, diligent, attentive to business, compliant, accommodating. 2. Officious, meddling, forward. *Mentira oficiosa,* Falsehood, useful to some and injurious to none.
Oficleido [o-fe-clay'-e-do], *m.* Ophicleide, a brass wind-instrument, deep-toned, of open mouth-piece, and nine (or eleven) keys.
Ofidios [o-fee'-de-ose], *m. pl.* Ophidia, the serpents or snakes.
Ofiólatra [o-fe-o'-lah-trah], *a.* Ophiolatrous, relating to serpent-worship.
Ofita [o-fee'-tah], *f.* Ophite, a kind of greenish porphyry.
Ofrecedor [o-fray-thay-dor'], *m.* Offerer.
Ofrecer [o-fray-therr'], *va.* 1. To offer, to make an offer, to hold out. 2. To present. 3. To exhibit, to manifest. 4. To dedicate, to consecrate. —*vr.* To offer, to occur, to present itself. *Ofrecer (una cosa) con la boca chica,* To make a complimentary offer without intending fulfilment. *¿Se le ofrece a usted algo?* At your service (can any thing be offered to you?).
Ofrecimiento [o-fray-the-me-en'-to], *m.* 1. Offer, promise, offering. 2. Occurrence, incident. 3. Extemporary discourse.
Ofrenda [o-fren'-dah], *f.* Offering, oblation, gift.
Ofrendar [o-fren-dar'], *va.* 1. To present offerings to God. 2. To contribute toward some end or purpose.
(*Yo ofrezco, yo ofrezca,* from *Ofrecer.* *V.* CONOCER.)
Oftalmía [of-tal-mee'-ah], *f.* Ophthalmia, a disease of the eyes.
Oftálmico [of-tahl'-me-co], *a.* Ophthalmic.
Oftalmografía [of-tal-mo-grah-fee'-ah], *f.* Ophthalmography, a minute description of the eye.
Oftalmología, *f.* Ophthalmology, discourse upon the eye.
Oftalmólogo [of-tal-mo'-lo-go], *m.* Ophthalmologist, oculist.
Oftalmómetro [of-tal-mo'-may-tro], *m.* Ophthalmometer, an instrument for examining the refraction of the eye.
Oftalmoscopia [of-tal-mos-co'-pe-ah], *f.* Ophthalmoscopy, examination of the eye.
Oftalmcsoopio [of-tal-mos-co'-pe-o], *m.* Ophthalmoscope, a mirror with a central aperture for viewing the interior of the eye.
Ofuscación, *f.* **Ofuscamiento,** *m.* [o-foos-cah-the-on', o-foos-cah-me-en'-to]. Obfuscation, dimness of the sight; confused reason.
Ofuscar [o-foos-car'], *va.* To obfuscate, to darken, to render obscure. *Ofuscar la razón* or *el entendimiento,* To disturb the mind, to confuse the judgment. (Met.) To dazzle.
Ogro [o'-gro], *m.* Ogre, a fabulous monster.
¡Oh! *int.* O! Oh! *¡Oh, quiera Dios!* God grant! *¡Oh, qué hermosa casa!* Oh, what a fine house! (Naut.) Ho! *¡Oh, el barco!* Ho! ship ahoy!
Ohmio [o'-me-o], *m.* (Elec.) Ohm.
Oíble [o-ee'-blay], *a.* Audible, that can be heard.
Oída [o-ee'-dah], *f.* Act and effect of hearing.
Oído, da [o-ee'-do, dah], *pp.* of OIR. Heard. *De oídas* or *por oídas,* By hearsay.
Oído [o-ee'-do], *m.* 1. The sense of hearing. 2. Ear, organ of hearing. 3. Ear, power of judging of harmony. 4. Touch-hole of a gun. *Está sordo de un oído,* He is deaf of one ear. *Lisonjear el oído,* To tickle the ear, to flatter. *Negar los oídos,* To refuse a hearing. *Hablar al oído,* To whisper in one's ear. *Dolor de oídos,* Ear-ache. *Hacer* or *tener oídos de mercader.* (Met.) To lend a deaf ear. *Tener buen oído,* To have a quick ear. *Llegar a oídos,* or *a sus oídos,* To come to one's ears or knowledge. *De oídos,* By hearsay. *¡Oídos que tal oyen!* Exclamation of surprise about equal to You don't say so! or Well, I never!
Oidor, ra [o-e-dor', rah], *m.* & *f.* 1. Hearer, one who hears. 2. One of the judges of the *Audiencia,* or supreme court, in several provinces of Spain, who, together with the other members of said court, is authorized to hear pleadings and decide lawsuits.
Oidoría [o-e-do-ree'-ah], *f.* Office or dignity of an *oidor.*
(*Yo oigo, oiga, oyera; él oyó.* *V.* OIR.)
Oil [o-eel'], *m.* Yes. *Lengua de oil,* A language spoken in the middle ages in France, north of the river Loire.
Oir [o-eer'], *va.* 1. To hear, to listen. *Oir campanas y no saber dónde,* To hear without understanding. 2. To understand, to comprehend. 3. To attend the lectures on some science or art, in order to study it. *Oir misa,* To attend at or hear mass. *Por oir*

misa y dar cebada nunca se perdió jornada, The fulfilment of duty can never be superfluous. *No haber oído la campana*, To be unobservant or ignorant of com. on things. *Quien no oye más que una campana, no oye más que un sonido*, Never judge a cause before hearing both sides. *¿ Oyes ?* or *¿ oye Vd. ?* I say, do you hear ? *Oígase* or *oigámonos*. Silence, attention. *Oiga* or *oigan*, Exclamation of surprise. *Oye, oye*, Hear ! hear ! *Oír, ver, y callar*, Mind your own business.

Oislo [o-ees'-lo], *m.* Person beloved, wife (or husband). Very ancient word.

Ojal [o-hahl'], *m.* 1. Button-hole. 2. Hole through any thing.

Ojalá [o-hah-lah'], *int.* Would to God ! God grant ! *Ojalá que él viva*, May he live. *Ojalá que vaya*, I wish he may go. (Arab. or Heb.)

Ojaladera [o-hah-lah-day'-rah], *f.* A woman who works button-holes.

Ojaladura [o-hah-lah-doo'-rah], *f.* The set of button-holes in a garment.

Ojalar [o-hah-lar'], *va.* To make button-holes.

Ojazo [o-hah'-tho], *m. aug.* A large eye.

Ojeada [o-hay-ah'-dah], *f.* Glance, glimpse, ogle.

Ojeador [o-hay-ah-dor'], *m.* One who starts game for the chase.

Ojeadura [o-hay-ah-doo'-rah], *f.* Act of glazing clothes.

Ojear [o-hay-ar'], *va.* 1. To eye, to view with attention, to glance at. 2. To start game by hallooing. 3. To startle any thing.

Ojeo [o-hay'-o], *m.* The act of starting game for the chase by hallooing. *Echar un ojeo*, To start and drive game toward the sportsmen. *Irse á ojeo*, To go in search of any thing.

Ojera [o-hay'-rah], *f.* 1. Bluish circle under the lower eye-lid, indicative of indisposition. 2. An eye-bath or eye-cup, a glass vessel for bathing the eye.

Ojeriza [o-hay-ree'-thah], *f.* Spite, grudge, ill-will.

Ojeroso, sa, Ojerudo, da [o-hay-ro'-so, sah], *a.* Applied to persons with blackish circles under the eyes.

Ojete [o-hay'-tay], *m.* 1. Eyelet-hole in clothes. 2. (Coll.) Anus.

Ojetear [o-hay-tay-ar'], *va.* To make eyelet-holes in clothes.

Ojetera [o-hay-tay'-rah], *f.* 1. Piece of whalebone sewed near the eyelet-holes in clothes. 2. A woman or a machine which makes eyelet-holes.

Ojialegre [o-he-ah-lay'-gray], *a.* Having lively, sparkling eyes.

Ojiazul [o-he-ah-thool'], *a.* Blue-eyed. (Neol. Amer.)

Ojito [o-hee'-to], *m. dim.* A small eye.

Ojienjuto, ta [o-he-en-hoo'-to, tah], *a.* Dry-eyed.

Ojimiel, Ojimel [o-he-me-el'], *m.* Oxymel, a mixture of honey and vinegar.

Ojimoreno, na [o-he-mo-ray'-no, nah], *a.* Brown-eyed.

Ojinegro, gra [o-he-nay'-gro, grah], *a.* Black-eyed.

Ojiva [o-hee'-vah], *f.* 1. Diagonal rib of a vaulted arch. 2. Ogive, a pointed arch.

Ojival [o-he-vahl'], *a.* Ogival, belonging to an ogive.

Ojizaino, na [o-he-thah-ee'-no, nah], *a.* Squint-eyed, moon-eyed.

Ojizarco, ca [o-he-thar'-co, cah], *a.* Blue or gray-eyed.

Ojo [o'-ho], *m.* 1. The eye. 2. Eye, sight, ocular knowledge. 3. Eye of a needle. 4. Eye, any small perforation. 5. Head formed on liquors; drop of oil or grease which swims on liquors. *Ojo de gallo*, Red sparkling wine. 6. Arch of a bridge. 7. Eye or socket, for receiving a handle. 8. Attention, care, notice. 9. Key-hole. 10. Lather, formed from soap. 11. *Ojo marginal, ojo al canto* or *al margen*, Marginal note, formed of *oo*, with a stroke across them ; a sign for calling attention. 12. (Typ.) Face of a printing type. 13. Mesh of a net. 14. Eye or hollow in bread or cheese. 15. Expression of ardent affection or endearment, or the object of it. *Abrir tanto ojo*, To stare with joy. *A cierra ojos* or *a ojos cerrados*, Without hesitation ; at all events. *En un abrir y cerrar de ojos*, In the twinkling of an eye. *A ojo*, (1) By the bulk or lump. (2) At the discretion of another. *A ojo. a los ojos de alguno* or *a sus ojos*, Face to face, in presence of any one. *Al ojo*, At sight, at hand. *A ojos vistos*, Visibly, publicly. *Ojos de bitoque*, Goggle eyes. *Avivar el ojo*, To be on one's guard. *Ojo alerta*, Look sharp. *Costar un ojo*, To be excessively dear. *Cuan lejos de ojo, tan lejos de corazón*, Out of sight, out of mind. *Escalera de ojo*, A winding stair-case. *Tener sangre en el ojo*, To be prompt and honorable in fulfilling engagements. *Hacer ojo*, To overbalance, to outweigh. *Hacer del ojo*, To wink at one another, to have a secret understanding. *Hacerse ojos*, To be very vigilant, to look with sharp eyes. *Estar empeñado hasta los ojos*, To be deeply in debt. *No tener donde volver los ojos*, (Met.) To be friendless and entirely destitute. *Ojos que te vieron ir, no te volverán a ver*, An opportunity lost never returns. *Ojos que no ven, corazón que no siente*, (prov.) Out of sight, out of mind. *Mal de ojo*, Fascination, enchantment. *Mal de ojos*, Sore eyes. *De medio ojo*, Lurkingly, concealedly. *Niñas de los ojos*, Apple of one's eye ; darling, treasure. *Ojo de la caña del ancla*, (Naut.) Eye of the anchor. *Ojo de gaza*, (Naut.) Eye of a strap. *Ojo de la cuña del mastelero*, (Naut.) The fifth hole of a mast. *Ojo de buey*, (1) (Bot.) Ox-eye. Buphthalmum. (2) (Coll.) Doubloon of eight dollars. *Dichosos los ojos que ven a usted*, Delighted to see you again ! (expression used on meeting another after a considerable interval). *Entrar a ojos cerrados*, To begin a thing blindly, without reflection. *Entrarle (a uno) una cosa por el ojo* or *por los ojos*, To delight, to charm one. The reader is referred to the Dictionary of the Spanish Academy for one hundred or more other phrases containing the word *ojo*.

Ojo eléctrico [o'-ho ay-lec'-tre-co] *m.* Electric eye.

Ojoso, sa [o-ho'-so, sah], *a.* Full of eyes.

Ojota [o-ho'-tah], *f.* A kind of shoe worn by Indian women. (Peru.)

Ojuelo [o-hoo-ay'-lo], *m. dim.* A small eye.—*pl.* 1. Sparkling eyes, smiling eyes. 2. (Prov.) Spectacles.

Ola [o'-lah], *f.* 1. A wave. 2. A sudden, violent commotion.

Olaje [o-lah'-hay], *m.* Succession of waves, surge.

Olán [o-lahn'], *m.* Holland, Dutch linen, batiste.

Ole [o'-lay], *m.* Andalusian dance. *¡ Ole ! int.* Bravo !

Oleáceo, cea [o-lay-ah'-thay-o, ah], *a.* Of the olive family (ash, etc.).

Oleada [o-lay-ah'-dah], *f.* 1. Surge, swell of the sea. 2. A plentiful produce of oil. 3. Surging of crowded people.

Oleaginosidad [o-lay-ah-he-no-se-dahd'], *f.* Oleaginousness, oiliness.

Oleaginoso, sa [o-lay-ah-he-no'-so, sah], *a.* Oleaginous, oily.

Oleaje [o-lay-ah'-hay], *m.* *V.* OLAJE.

Olear [o-lay-ar'], *va.* To administer extreme unction.

Oleario, ria [o-lay-ah'-re-o, ah], *a.* Oily.

Oleato [o-lay-ah'-to], *m.* Oleate, a compound of oleic acid.

Oleaza [o-lay-ah'-thah], *f.* (Prov.) The watery dregs which remain in the mill after the oil has been extracted.

Oledero, ra [o-lay-day'-ro, rah], *a.* Odorous, fragrant.

Oledor, ra [o-lay-dor', rah], *m.* & *f.* 1. Smeller, one who smells. 2. (Obs.) Smelling-bottle.

Oleico, ca [o-lay'-e-co, cah], *a.* Oleic, pertaining to oil.

Oleina [o-lay-ee'-nah], *f.* Olein, a colorless oily substance, the base of fatty oils.

Óleo [o'-lay-o], *m.* 1. Oil. *V.* ACEITE. *Al óleo*, In oil colours. 2. Extreme unction ; the holy oil ; act of anointing.

Oleoducto [o-lay-o-dooc'-to], *m.* Pipeline (for conveying oil).

Oleolato [o-lay-o-lah'-to], *m.* Essential oils.

Oleomargarina [o-lay-o-mar-gah-ree'-nah], *f.* Oleomargarine.

Oleosidad [o-lay-o-se-dahd'], *f.* Oiliness.

Oleoso, sa [o-lay-o'-so, sah], *a.* Oily, oleaginous.

(*Yo huelo, huela ; olí.* *V.* OLER.)

Oler [o-lerr'], *va.* 1. To smell, to scent. 2. To smell, to find out, to search, to scent, to discover. 3. To pry, to inspect curiously.—*vn.* 1. To smell, to strike the nostrils. 2. To smell, to have a particular tincture or smack of any quality. *Oler la casa a hombre*, A man should be master in his own house. *Oler a soga*, To deserve to be hanged. *Oler a chamusquina*, To come from hot words to hard blows. *Oler el poste*, To have a premonition of evil. *Cada cuba huele al vino que tiene*, Character is shown by one's actions (literally, every cask smells of the wine it holds). *Huele a hereje*, He smells of heresy. *Olió a petardo*, It savoured of imposition or fraud. *Huélele el pescuezo a cáñamo*, The neck savours of the halter. *No oler bien alguna cosa*, (Met.) To be a suspicious thing.

Olfacción [ol-fac-the-on'], *f.* (Med.) Olfaction, the act or the sense of smelling.

Olfatear [ol-fah-tay-ar'], *va.* To smell, to scent.

Olfato [ol-fah'-to], *m.* Scent, the sense or organ of smell.

Olfatorio, ria [ol-fah-to'-re-o, ah], *a.* Olfactory.

Olíbano [o-lee'-bah-no], *m.* (Bot.) Incense, a gum-resin produced by the Lycian juniper.

Oliente [o-le-en'-tay], *pa.* Smelling, odorous.

Oliera [o-le-ay'-rah], *f.* Vessel in which holy oil is kept.

Oligarca [o-le-gar'-cah], *m.* Oligarch, a member of an oligarchy.

Oligarquía [o-le-gar-kee'-ah], *f.* Oligarchy, a form of government by the few.

Oligárquico, ca [o-le-gar'-ke-co, cah], *a.* Oligarchical.

Olimpiada [o-lim-pe-ah'-dah], *f.* Olympiad, period of four years.

Olímpico, ca [o-leem'-pe-co, cah], *a.* Olympic.

Olimpo [o-leem'-po], *m.* 1. Height, eminence. 2. (Poet.) Heaven.

Oliscar [o-lis-car'], *va.* 1. To smell, to scent. 2. To investigate, to ascertain. —*vn.* To stink.

Olisquear [o-lis-kay-ar'], *va.* V. OLISCAR.

Oliva [o-lee'-vah], *f.* 1. Olive-tree. *V.* OLIVO. 2. (Obs.) The olive itself.

Olivar [o-le-var'], *m.* Plantation of olive-trees, olive-grove, olive-yard.

Olivarse [o-le-var'-say], *vr.* To form bubbles: applied to bread.

Olivastro de Rodas [o-le-vahs'-tro], *m.* (Bot.) *V.* LINÁLOE.

Olivera [o-le-vay'-rah], *f.* Olive-tree. *V.* OLIVO.

Olivífero, ra [o-le-vee'-fay-ro, rah], *a.* (Poet.) Producing olives, olive-bearing.

Olivo [o-lee'-vo], *m.* (Bot.) Olive-tree. Olea europea.

Olmeda [ol-may'-dah], *f.* **Olmedo**, *m.* Elm-grove.

Olmo [ol'-mo], *m.* (Bot.) Elm-tree. Ulmus.

Ológrafo [o-lo'-grah-fo], *a.* Holographic, written in the hand of the testator.

Olor [o-lor'], *m.* 1. Odour, scent. 2. Stink, stench. 3. Hope, promise, offer. 4. Cause or motive of suspicion. 5. (Met.) Fame, reputation. *Agua de olor*, Sweet-scented water.

Oloroso, sa [o-lo-ro'-so, sah], *a.* Odoriferous, fragrant, perfumed.

Olote [o-lo'-tay], *m.* (Amer.) Corn-cob.

Olvidadizo, za [ol-ve-dah-dee'-tho, thah], *a.* Short of memory, forgetful, oblivious.

Olvidado, da [ol-ve-dah'-do, dah], *a.* & *pp.* of OLVIDAR. Forgotten, forsaken, forlorn.

Olvidar [ol-ve-dar'], *va.* To forget, to neglect, to omit.

Olvido [ol-vee'-do], *m.* Forgetfulness, carelessness, heedlessness; neglect, oblivion. *Echar al olvido* or *en olvido*, To forget designedly, to cast in oblivion.

Olla [ol'-lyah], *f.* 1. A round earthen pot, or wide-mouthed jar. 2. Olla, an olio, a dish made of boiled meat and vegetables. 3. Any gulf in which are whirlpools; a whirlpool. *Olla ciega*, *V.* ALCANCÍA. *Olla carnicera*, Boiler, a kettle in which large pieces of meat may be boiled. *Olla fétida*, (Gunn.) Stink-pot, an earthen shell charged with combustible materials, emitting a suffocating smell. *Olla podrida*, Dish composed of different sorts of meat and vegetables boiled together. *Olla de campaña*, Copper vessel with a cover for carrying dressed meat.

Olla a presión [ol'-lyah ah pray-se-on'], *f.* Pressure cooker.

Olla express [ol'-lyah ex-press'], *f.* (Mex.) Pressure cooker.

Ollao [ol-lyah'-o], *m.* (Naut.) Eyelet-hole, round hole in sails. *Ollaos de los rizos*, Reef-eyelet holes.

Ollar [ol-lyar'], *a.* Soft, readily workable: applied to stone.

Ollaza [ol-lyah'-thah], *f. aug.* A large pot or boiler.

Ollazo [ol-lyah'-tho], *m.* Blow with an earthen pot or jar.

Ollería [ol-lyay-ree'-ah], *f.* Pottery; a shop where earthenware is sold.

Ollero [ol-lyay'-ro], *m.* 1. Potter. 2. Dealer in earthenware.

Ollita [ol-lyee'-tah], *f. dim.* Pipkin, a small pot.

Olluela [ol-lyoo-ay'-lah], *f.* Pit or hollow under the Adam's apple.

Ombligada [om-ble-gah'-dah], *f.* Part corresponding to the navel, in skins of animals.

Ombligo [om-blee'-go], *m.* 1. The navel, umbilicus. 2. Navel-string, the umbilical cord. 3. Centre or middle of a thing. *Ombligo de Venus*, Venus navel-wort, or penny wort navel-wort. Cotyledon umbilicus.

Ombliguera [om-ble-gay'-rah], *f.* (Bot.) *V.* OREJA DE ABAD, or MONJE.

Ombliguero [om-ble-gay'-ro], *m.* Bandage put upon the navel of new-born children.

Ombría [om-bree'-ah], *f.* Shade, place secluded from the sun.

Ombú [om-boo'], *m.* (Argen. Cuba) Tree with a wood so spongy that it burns at once to ashes.

Omega [o-may'-gah], *f.* Omega, last letter in the Greek alphabet: long O.

Omental [o-men-tahl'], *a.* Belonging to the omentum; omental.

Omento [o-men'-to], *m.* Omentum, the caul or covering of the bowels.

Ómicron [o'-me-crone], *f.* Name of the Greek short O, fifteenth of their alphabet.

Ominosamente, *adv.* Ominously, with good or bad omen.

Ominoso, sa [o-me-no'-so, sah], *a.* Ominous, foreboding ill.

Omisión [o-me-se-on'], *f.* Omission, carelessness, neglect, negligence, heedlessness.

Omiso, sa [o-mee'-so, sah], *a.* Neglectful, remiss, heedless, careless.

Omitir [o-me-teer'], *va.* To omit, to neglect.

Ómnibus, *m.* Omnibus, a public carriage for a number of persons.

Omnímodamente, *adv.* Entirely, by all means.

Omnímodo, da [om-nee'-mo-do, dah], *a.* Entire, total.

Omnipotencia [om-ne-po-ten'-the-ah], *f.* Omnipotence.

Omnipotente [om-ne-po-ten'-tay], *a.* Omnipotent, almighty.

Omnipotentemente, *adv.* Omnipotently.

Omnipresencia [om-ne-pray-sen'-the-ah], *f.* Omnipresence.

Omniscencia [om-nis-then'-the-ah], *f.* Omniscience.

Omniscio, ia [om-nees'-the-o, ah], *a.* Omniscient.

Omnívoro, ra [om-nee'-vo-ro, rah], *a.* Omnivorous, living upon foods of all kinds.

Omoplato [o-mo-plah'-to], *m.* (Anat.) Omoplate, the shoulder-blade, scapula.

Onagra [o-nah'-grah], *f.* (Bot.) A genus of the evening-primrose family, now referred to Œnothera.

Onagro [o-nah'-gro], *m.* Wild ass.

Once [on'-thay], *a.* & *m.* Eleven; figure eleven. *El once de Enero*, The eleventh of January. *El libro once*, The eleventh book. *Hacer las once*, (Coll.) To take a lunch about noon. *Estar a las once*, (Low) To be on one side: applied to clothes.

Oncear [on-thay-ar'], *va.* To weigh out by ounces.

Oncejera, Oncijera [on-thay-hay'-rah], *f.* A small snare for catching birds.

Oncejo [on-thay'-ho], *m.* (Prov.) String, band, tie.

Onceno, na [on-thay'-no, nah], *a.* Eleventh. *El onceno no estorbar*, Obstruct not industrious persons at their business.

Onda [on'-dah], *f.* 1. A wave. 2. Fluctuation, agitation. *Radio de onda corta*, Short-wave radio. *Longitud de onda*, Wave length. *Onda de choque*, Shock wave. *Onda etérea*, Ether wave. *Onda marina*, Ocean wave. *Onda sonora*, Sound wave.

Onde [on'-day], *conj.* (Obs.) Wherefore.—*adv.* (Obs.) *V.* DONDE.

Ondeado [on-day-ah'-do], *m.* & *a.* Any thing in waves.

Ondear [on-day-ar'], *vn.* 1. To undulate. 2. To fluctuate.—*vr.* To float backward and forward.

Ondina [on-dee'-nah], *f.* Undine, water-sprite.

Ondulación [on-doo-lah-the-on'], *f.* Waving, undulation.

Ondulado, da [on-doo-lah'-do, dah], *a.* Waved, wavy. *Ondulado permanente*, Permanent wave. *Cabello ondulado*, Wavy hair.

Ondular [on-doo-lar'], *vn.* To ripple, to wave, to undulate.

Oneiromancia [o-nay-ee-ro-mahn'-the-ah], *f.* Oneiromancy, divination by means of dreams.

Oneroso, sa [o-nay-ro'-so, sah], *a.* Burdensome, troublesome, onerous.

Onfacino, na [on-fah-thee'-no, nah], *a.* Extracted from green olives: applied to oil.

Onice, *m.* **Onique**, *f.* **Ónix**, *m.* [o'-ne-thay, o'-ne-kay]. Onyx, a precious stone.

Onomatopéyico, ca [o-no-mah-to-pay'-ye-co, cah], *a.* Onomatopeic, imitative in sound.

Onomatopeya [o-no-mah-to-pay'-yah], *f.* Onomatopœia, the selection of words to imitate natural sounds.

Onoquiles [o-no-kee'-les], *f.* (Bot.) Dyer's bugloss, alkanet. Anchusa tinctoria.

Ontología [on-to-lo-hee'-ah], *f.* Ontology, metaphysics.

Ontologista [on-to-lo-hees'-tah], *m.* Ontologist, metaphysician.

Onza [on'-thah], *f.* 1. Ounce, the twelfth part of a pound, troy weight, or sixteenth of a Castilian pound. 2. Ounce, lynx. Felis uncia. *Por onzas*, With a sparing hand.

Onzavo, va [on-thah'-vo, vah], *a.* Eleventh.—*m.* Eleventh part.

Opa [o'-pah], *f.* A hole left in a newly-built wall on removing the scaffold. —*a.* (Amer.) 1. Dumb, silent. 2. Silly, foolish.

Opacamente, *adv.* Obscurely, darkly.

Opacidad [o-pah-the-dahd'], *f.* Opacity, cloudiness, darkness.

Opaco, ca [o-pah'-co, cah], *a.* 1. Opacous, opaque. 2. Melancholy, gloomy.

Opalino, na [o-pah-lee'-no, nah], *a.* Opaline, opalescent.

Ópalo [o'-pah-lo], *m.* Opal, a precious stone.

Opción [op-the-on'], *f.* 1. Option, choice. 2. Right to an office or dignity.

Ópera [o'-pay-rah], *f.* Opera, a musical drama.

Operable [o-pay-rah'-blay], *a.* 1. Capable of operating. 2. Operable, practicable.

Operación [o-pay-rah-the-on'], *f.* 1 Operation, the act of exercising some power or faculty. 2. Operation, agency, effect or action produced. 3. (Surg.) Operation. (Com.) Transaction, venture. *Operaciones de banco*, Banking business. *Operaciones marítimas*, Shipping trade or business. 4. A chemical process.—*pl.* 1. Operations of an army. 2. Works, deeds, actions.

Operador [o-pay-rah-dor'], *m.* 1. Surgical operator. 2. (Min.) Prospector.

Operante [o-pay-rahn'-tay], *pa.* & *n.* Operator; operating.

Operar [o-pay-rar'], *vn.* To operate, to act.

Operario [o-pay-rah'-re-o], *m.* 1. Operator, labourer. 2. Friar who assists sick or dying persons.

Operativo, va [o-pay-rah-tee'-vo, vah], *a.* Operative.

Operculado, da [o-per-coo-lah'-do, dah], *a.* Operculate, covered with a lid.

Opercular [o-per-coo-lar'], *a.* Opercular, serving as a lid.
Opérculo [o-perr'-coo-lo], *m.* Operculum, lid, cover of a pore or cell.
Opereta [o-pay-ray'-tah], *f.* Operetta, a light opera.
Operista [o-pay-rees'-tah], *com.* Opera-singer.
Operoso, sa [o-pay-ro'-so, sah], *a.* Laborious, operose.
Opiado, da [o-pe-ah'-do, dah], *a.* Opiate, narcotic.
Opiata [o-pe-ah'-tah], *f.* Opiate.
Opiato, ta [o-pe-ah'-to, tah], *a.* & *n.* Opiate narcotic.
Opilación [o-pe-lah-the-on'], *f.* 1. Oppilation, obstruction of the vessels of the body. 2. (Coll.) Amenorrhœa, abnormally scanty or obstructed menstruation.
Opilar [o-pe-lar'], *va.* To oppilate, to obstruct.
Opilativo, va [o-pe-lah-tee'-vo, vah], *a.* Obstructive, oppilative.
Opimo, ma [o-pe'-mo, mah], *a.* Rich, fruitful, abundant.
Opinable [o-pe-nah'-blay], *a.* Disputable, problematical.
Opinante [o-pe-nahn'-tay], *pa.* & *a.* Arguing; opinionated.
Opinante [o-pe-nahn'-tay], *m.* Arguer.
Opinar [o-pe-nar'], *vn.* To argue, to judge, to form an opinion, to opine.
Opinativo, va [o-pe-nah-tee'-vo, vah], *a.* Opinionative, opinative.
Opinión [o-pe-ne-on'], *f.* 1. Opinion, persuasion of the mind, judgment. 2. Reputation, character. *Andar en opiniones*, To render any one's credit doubtful. *Hacer opinión*, To form an opinion, to be a man whose opinion is an authority.
Opinioncilla, ita [o-pe-ne-on-theel'-lyah], *f. dim.* Opinion founded on slight grounds.
Opio [o'-pe-o], *m.* Opium.
Opíparo, ra [o-pee'-pah-ro, rah], *a.* Opiparous, sumptuous: applied to an entertainment.
Oploteca [o-plo-tay'-cah], *f.* Museum of ancient, rare, or valuable weapons.
Ópol [o'-pol], *m.* Juice, sap of a plant, in general. (Gr.)
Oponer [o-po-nerr'], *va.* 1. To oppose, to go against, to contradict. 2. To oppose, to object in a disputation.—*vr.* 1. To oppose, to be adverse, to act against, to be contrary. 2. To front, to be opposite to. 3. To stand in competition with another.

(*Yo opongo, oponga; opuse, opusiera; opondré;* from *Oponer. V.* PONER.)
Opopónaca, Opopónace [o-po-po'-nah-cah, o-po-po'-nah-thay], *f.* (Bot.) Rough parsnip. Pastinaca opoponax.
Opopónaco, Opopónax [o-po-po'-nah-co], *m.* Opoponax, a gum resin obtained from the rough parsnip.
Oportunamente, *adv.* Opportunely, conveniently.
Oportunidad [o-por-too-ne-dahd'], *f.* Opportunity, convenience, fitness of time or circumstances.
Oportunismo [o-por-too-nees'-mo], *m.* Opportunism.
Oportunista [o-por-too-nees'-tah], *m.* & *f.* Opportunist.
Oportuno, na [o-por-too'-no, nah], *a.* Convenient, seasonable, opportune.
Oposición [o-po-se-the-on'], *f.* 1. Opposition, situation so as to front something opposed, counterview. 2. Opposition, contrariety of affection, of interest, of party, of measures, of meaning, etc. 3. Opposition, the members of a legislative house who oppose the measures of the ministry. 4. (Fine arts) Contrast. 5. Competition among competitors for a prebend, professorship, etc. 6. (Ast.) Opposition between two heavenly bodies.
Opositor, ra [o-po-se-tor', rah], *m.* & *f.* Opposer, opponent.
Opresión [o-pray-se-on'], *f.* 1. Oppression, cruelty, severity, coercion, hardship. 2. Oppression, pressure.
Opresivamente, *adv.* Oppressively, overwhelmingly.
Opresivo, va [o-pray-see'-vo, vah], *a.* 1. Oppressive, cruel. 2. Oppressive, heavy, overwhelming.
Opresor [o-pray-sor'], *m.* Oppressor; extortioner.
Oprimir [o-pre-meer'], *va.* 1. To oppress by hardship or severity. 2. To overpower, to overwhelm, to subdue. 3. To crush, to press, to squeeze.
Oprobio [o-pro'-be-o], *m.* Opprobrium, ignominy, shame, injury.
Oprobioso, sa [o-pro-be-o'-so, sah], *a.* Opprobrious, reproachful.
Oprobrio, *m.* (Obs.) *V.* OPROBIO.
Optar [op-tar'], *va.* To choose, to elect.
Optativo [op-tah-tee'-vo], *m.* (Gram.) Optative, one of the modes of verbs.
Óptica [op'-te-cah], *f.* Optics, the science of light and vision.
Óptico, ca [op'-te-co, cah], *a.* Optic, optical, visual.—*m.* Optician.
Óptimamente [op'-te-mah-men-tay], *adv.* In the best way, perfectly.
Optimismo [op-te-mees'-mo], *m.* Optimism.
Optimista [op-te-mees'-tah], *com.* Optimist.
Óptimo, ma [op'-te-mo, mah], *a.* Best, eminently good.
Optómetra [op-to'-may-trah], *m.* Optometrist.
Optometría [op-to-may-tree'-ah], *f.* Optometry.
Opuestamente, *adv.* Oppositely.
Opuesto, ta [o-poo-es'-to, tah], *a.* Opposite, contrary, adverse.—*pp. irr.* of OPONER.
Opugnación [o-poog-nah-the-on'], *f.* Oppugnancy, opposition.
Opugnador [o-poog-nah-dor'], *m.* Oppugner, opposer.
Opugnar [o-poog-nar'], *va.* To oppugn; to impugn, to attack, to resist, to contradict.
Opulencia [o-poo-len'-the-ah], *f.* Opulence, wealth, affluence.
Opulentamente, *adv.* Opulently.
Opulento, ta [o-poo-len'-to, tah], *a.* Opulent, wealthy, rich, affluent.
Opuncia [o-poon'-the-ah], *f.* Prickly-pear cactus. Opuntia.
Opúsculo [o-poos'-coo-lo], *m.* A short, compendious treatise.
Oquedal [o-kay-dahl'], *m.* Plantation of lofty trees.
Ora [o'-rah], *adv.* At present. *V.* AHORA.—*conj.* Whether.
Oración [o-rah-the-on'], *f.* 1. Oration, harangue, declamation. 2. Orison, a prayer, supplication. 3. Sentence: in grammar, an expression composed of one or more words, which makes perfect sense. *Partes de la oración*, The parts of speech. 4. Position, a proposition which denies or affirms a thing. 5. A part of the mass. *Las oraciones*, Sun-setting, the Angelus, when the angel's salutation to the Virgin is repeated by the people; also, the bell which calls to this prayer. *A la oración en punto*, (Coll.) At early candle-light. *La oración breve sube al cielo*, Short prayers find their way to heaven (hint to be brief and avoid giving annoyance in asking a favour).
Oracional [o-rah-the-o-nahl'], *m.* Prayer-book.
Oracionero [o-rah-the-o-nay'-ro], *m.* He who goes praying from door to door.
Oráculo [o-rah'-coo-lo], *m.* 1. Oracle something delivered by supernatural wisdom. 2. Oracle, the place where, or person of whom, the determinations of heaven are inquired. 3. Oracle, person famed for wisdom.
Orada [o-rah'-dah], *f. V.* DORADA.
Orador, ra [o-rah-dor', rah], *m.* & *f.* 1. Orator, a public speaker. 2. Panegyrist, encomiast, preacher.
Oral [o-rahl'], *a.* Oral, delivered by the mouth.
Oralmente [o-ral-men'-tay], *adv.* Orally, by mouth.
Orangután [o-ran-goo-tahn'], *m.* Orang-utan (orang-outang), an anthropoid ape of Borneo.
Orar [o-rar'], *vn.* & *a.* 1. To harangue. 2. To pray. 3. To ask, to demand.
Orate [o-rah'-tay], *com.* Lunatic, madman. *Casa de orates*, A mad-house.
Oratoria [o-rah-to'-re-ah], *f.* Oratory, eloquence.
Oratoriamente, *adv.* Oratorically.
Oratorio [o-rah-to'-re-o], *m.* 1. Oratory, a private place for prayer. 2. Oratorio, a dramatic musical composition upon a sacred subject. It receives its name from the Oratory in Rome. 3. A congregation of presbyters.
Oratorio, ria [o-rah-to'-re-o, ah], *a.* Oratorial, rhetorical, oratorical.
Orbe [or'-bay], *m.* 1. Orb, sphere. 2. Orb, terrestrial sphere; celestial body. 3. Orb, circle described by any of the mundane spheres. 4. Globe-fish.
Orbicular [or-be-coo-lar'], *a.* Orbicular, circular.
Órbita [or'-be-tah], *f.* 1. Orbit, the path of a planet. 2. Cavity in which the eye is placed, orbit.
Orbitales [or-be-tah'-less], *a.* & *m. pl.* Orbital: used of the bones which form the orbit of the eye.
Orca [or'-cah], *f.* Grampus, orca. Delphinus orca.
Orcaneta [or-cah-nay'-tah], *f.* (Bot.) Dyer's bugloss, alkanet. Anchusa tinctoria.
Orco [or'-co], *m.* 1. (Zool.) Grampus. *V.* ORCA. 2. Hell.
Orcotomía [or-co-to-mee'-ah], *f.* Orchotomy, castration.
Orchilla [or-cheel'-lyah], *f.* (Bot.) Archil, roccella, true dyer's orchil. Rocella tinctoria.
Ordalía [or-dah-lee'-ah], *f.* Ordeal, a trial by fire or water.
Ordeata [or-day-ah'-tah], *a.* 1. Peeled barley. 2. Ptisan, a medical drink.
Orden [or'-den], *com.* 1. Order, regularity, settled mode. 2. Order, method, course, rule, regulation. 3. Order, class. 4. Order, a society of dignified persons. 5. Order, a religious fraternity. 6. The sixth sacrament of the Roman Catholic church. 7. Arrangement of chords in a musical instrument. 8. Order, mandate, precept command. 9. Relation of one thing to another. 10. Order of architecture. *En orden*, In an orderly manner; with regard to. *Por su orden*, In its turn; successively. *No haber orden de conseguir algo*, (Coll.) To be no means or possibility of obtaining a thing.
Ordenación [or-day-nah-the-on'], *f.* 1. Methodical arrangement; disposition, ordination. 2. Edict, ordinance. 3. Clerical ordination. 4. Part of architecture which treats of the capacity which every room should have. 5. Part of the composition of a picture.
Ordenada [or-day-nah'-dah], *f.* (Math.) Ordinate, a line drawn perpendicular to the axis of a curve.
Ordenadamente, *adv.* Orderly.

Ordenado, da [or-day-nah'-do, dah], *a.* Ordained, ordinate, orderly, just.—*pp.* of ORDENAR.
Ordenador, ra [or-day-nah-dor', rah], *m. & f.* One who ordains, ordainer; orderer. *V.* COMISARIO.
Ordenamiento [or-day-nah-me-en'-to], *m.* 1. The act and effect of ordaining, regulating, or putting in order. 2. Law, edict, ordinance.
Ordenando, Ordenante [or-day-nahn'-do, or-day-nahn'-tay], *m.* He who is ready to receive holy orders.
Ordenanza [or-day-nahn'-thah], *f.* 1. Method, order. 2. Law, statute, ordinance; command; ordination. 3. *m.* Orderly man, a corporal or soldier who attends a commanding officer. *Estar de ordenanza,* To be on duty, to be in waiting.
Ordenar [or-day-nar'], *va.* 1. To arrange, to put in order, to class, to dispose. 2. To order, to command, to enact. 3. To ordain, to regulate; to direct. 4. To order, to confer holy orders.—*vr.* To be ordained, to receive holy orders.
Ordeñadero [or-day-nyah-day'-ro], *m.* Milk-pail.
Ordeñador, ra [or-day-nyah-dor', rah], *m. & f.* Milker, one who milks animals.
Ordeñar [or-day-nyar'], *va.* 1. To milk animals. 2. To pick olives with the hand.
Ordinal [or-de-nahl'], *a.* Ordinal, noting order.—*m.* Ordinal, ritual; a book containing orders.
Ordinariamente, *adv.* Frequently; ordinarily; customarily; rudely.
Ordinariez [or-de-nah-re-eth'], *f.* 1. (Coll.) Low rank of a person; common stock. 2. Rough manners, rude behaviour.
Ordinario, ria [or-de-nah'-re-o, ah], *a.* 1. Ordinary, common, usual, customary, familiar. 2. Coarse, mean, of low rank, vulgar. *Juez ordinario,* Judge who takes cognizance of causes in the first instance. *Decreto, provisión* or *auto ordinario,* Decree given by a judge at the instance of one of the contending parties. *Justicia ordinaria,* The court or judge where causes are first seen and tried.
Ordinario [or-de-nah'-re-o], *m.* 1. Ordinary, settled establishment of daily expense: commonly applied to the expenses of the table. 2. Ordinary, established judge of ecclesiastical causes. 3. Ordinary, a bishop. 4. Mail, post, or courier, who goes and arrives at stated times. 5. The carrier, muleteer, or driver of beasts of burden, who usually goes and comes from one place to another. 6. Ordinary, a book containing the prayers of the mass. *De ordinario,* Regularly, commonly.
Orear [o-ray-ar'], *va.* 1. To cool, to refresh: applied to the wind. 2. To dry, to air, to expose to the air.—*vr.* To take the air, to take an airing.
Orégano [o-ray'-gah-no], *m.* (Bot.) Wild marjoram. Origanum vulgare.
Oreja [o-ray'-hah], *f.* 1. Auricle, the external ear. 2. Ear, the organ of hearing. 3. Flap of a shoe for adjusting to the instep. 4. Flatterer, tale-bearer. 5. (Mech.) Lug, flange, ear, a projecting piece of certain instruments, as the claw of a hammer, the barb of an arrow, the head of a nail. *Oreja de un ancla,* (Naut.) Fluke of an anchor. *Orejas de mercader,* Deaf ear. *Con las orejas caídas,* Crestfallen, down in the mouth; dejected. *Pan de orejas,* (Prov.) Small indented bread. *Apearse por las orejas,* To give an absurd answer. *Bajar las orejas,* To yield; to humble one's self. *Calentar a alguno las orejas,* To chide or reprove a person severely. *Con las orejas tan largas,* With great care and attention. *Animal de cuatro orejas,* Horned animals, especially the bull. *Mojar la oreja,* (Met.) To conquer or excel another. *Poner las orejas coloradas,* To make one blush to the ears. *Vino de dos orejas,* (Coll.) A strong-bodied wine. *Oreja de abad* or *monje,* (Bot.) Venus navel-wort, or penny wort navel-wort. Cotyledon umbilicus. *Oreja de ratón,* (Bot.) Mouse-ear. Myosotis.
Orejano, na [o-ray-hah'-no, nah], *a.* (Amer.) Ownerless, unbranded: said of animals. In Spain, motherless: said of a calf.
Orejeado, da [o-ray-hay-ah'-do, dah], *a.* Informed, advised, instructed.—*pp.* of OREJEAR.
Orejear [o-ray-hay-ar'], *vn.* 1. To shake the ears: applied to horses and mules. 2. To act with reluctance. 3. (Prov.) To whisper in the ear.
Orejera [o-ray-hay'-rah], *f.* Earmuff.
Orejeta [o-ray-hay'-tah], *f.* Each of the two wooden languets which the scabbard of a sword carries within.
Orejita [o-ray-hee'-tah], *f. dim.* A small auricle or external ear.
Orejón [o-ray-hone'], *m.* 1. Slice of dried apple or other fruit. as *Orejones de durazno,* Dried peaches. 2. Pull by the ear. 3. A young nobleman of Peru, educated for public employments.
Orejudo, da [o-ray-hoo'-do, dah], *a.* Flap-eared, long-eared.
Orellana [o-rel-lyah'-nah], *f.* (Bot.) Arnatto or arnotto, a drug or dyestuff, prepared from the seeds of the arnotta. Bixa orellana.
Oreo [o-ray'-o], *m.* Breeze, fresh air.
Orfandad, Orfanidad [or-fan-dahd'], *f.* Orphanage, state of orphans; want of friends or support.
Orfebrería [or-fay-bray-ree'-ah], *f.* Gold or silver twist or braid. (Fr. orfévrerie.)
Órfico, ca [or'-fe-co, cah], *a.* Orphean, relating to Orpheus.
Organdí [or-gan-dee'], *m.* Organdy.
Organero [or-gah-nay'-ro], *m.* Organ-maker, organ-builder.
Orgánicamente, *adv.* Organically.
Orgánico, ca [or-gah'-ne-co, cah], *a.* 1. Organic, organical, consisting of various parts. 2. Organic, relating to the organs. 3. Harmonious.
Organillero [or-gah-nil-lyay'-ro], *m.* Organ grinder.
Organillo [or-gah-neel'-lyo], *m. dim.* Barrel-organ, hand-organ.
Organismo [or-gah-nees'-mo], *m.* 1. Organism, an organized or living being. 2. Social organization.
Organista [or-gah-nees'-tah], *com.* (Mus.) Organist. *Tener malos dedos para organista,* To be incompetent.
Organizable [or-gah-ne-thah'-blay], *a.* Organizable, capable of organization.
Organización [or-gah-ne-thah-the-on'], *f.* 1. Organization, construction. 2. Order, arrangement.
Organizador, ra [or-gah-ne-thah-dor', rah], *a.* Organizing. *Comité organizador,* Organizing committee. —*m. & f.* Organizer.
Organizar [or-gah-ne-thar'], *va.* 1. To tune an organ. 2. To organize, to form organically.
Órgano [or'-gah-no], *m.* 1. Organ, a musical wind instrument, a pipe-organ. 2. Organ, natural instrument, as the tongue is the organ of speech. 3. Machine for cooling liquors. 4. (Amer.) The high round fluted cactus, called so because it resembles an organ-pipe. 5. (Met.) Organ or medium by which a thing is communicated.
Organografía [or-gah-no-grah-fee'-ah], *f.* Description of organs; organography.
Orgasmo [or-gahs'-mo], *m.* (Med.) Orgasm.
Orgía [or-hee'-ah], *f.* Frantic revel.—
Orgullo [or-gool'-lyo], *m.* 1. Pride, haughtiness, loftiness. 2. Activity, briskness.
Orgullosamente, *adv.* Haughtily.
Orgulloso, sa [or-gool-lyo'-so, sah], *a.* 1. Proud, haughty, lofty, lordly. 2. Brisk, active.
Orientación [o-re-en-tah-the-on'], *f.* 1. Orientation, position, exposure. 2. Bearings. 3. Orientation, guidance. *Orientación por inercia,* (Aer.) Inertial guidance. *Orientación profesional,* Vocational guidance.
Oriental [o-re-en-tahl'], *a.* Oriental, eastern.—*m.* An oriental.
Orientar [o-re-en-tar'], *va.* 1. To turn a thing to the eastward. 2. To orientate, to orient, to find the position of with regard to the cardinal points. *Orientar una vela,* (Naut.) To trim a sail. *Navío bien orientado a la bolina* or *a la trinca,* (Naut.) A close-hauled ship.—*vr.* 1. To know the place which is occupied, to find one's bearings. 2. To consider the course to be taken.
Oriente [o-re-en'-tay], *m.* 1. Orient, the east; the Levant. 2. Source, origin. 3. Youth, juvenile age. 4. East wind. 5. Orient; Asia, and the contiguous regions of Europe and Africa.
Orificación [o-re-fe-cah-the-on'], *f.* Filling of a tooth (with gold, silver, etc.)
Orificar [o-re-fe-car'], *va.* To fill a tooth (with gold, silver, etc.)
Orífice [o-ree'-fe-thay], *m.* Goldsmith.
Orificia [o-re-fee'-the-ah], *f.* Art and profession of a goldsmith.
Orificio [o-re-fee'-the-o], *m.* Orifice, mouth, aperture.
Origen [o-ree'-hen], *m.* 1. Origin, source, motive, fountain, original. 2. Natal country; family, lineage, extraction. 3. Beginning or moral cause of things.
Original [o-re-he-nahl'], *a.* 1. Original, primitive. 2. (Coll.) Extravagant.
Original [o-re-he-nahl'], *m.* 1. Original, first copy, archetype. 2. Source, fountain.
Originalidad [o-re-he-nah-le-dahd'], *f.* (Coll.) Originality.
Originalmente, *adv.* Originally, radically.
Originar [o-re-he-nar'], *va.* To originate, to bring into existence.—*vr.* To originate, to take existence, to descend, to derive existence from, to cause, to occasion.
Originariamente, *adv.* Radically, originally.
Originario, ria [o-re-he-nah'-re-o, ah], *a.* Originary, primary, primitive.
Originario [o-re-he-nah'-re-o], *m.* Native, descendent.
Orilla [o-reel'-lyah], *f.* 1. Limit, extent, border, margin. 2. Edge of stuff or cloth. 3. Bank of a river, shore of the sea. 4. Extent, limit of something not material. 5. (Ant.) Foot-path in a street, avoiding mud. *A la orilla,* Near a place, on the brink. *Salir a la orilla,* To overcome difficulties.
Orilla, *f.* A brisk wind or fresh

breeze. *Hacer buena* or *mala orilla*, Andalusian expressions for good or bad weather.

Orillar [o-reel-lyar'], *va.* 1. To arrange, to conclude, to expedite, to put in order. 2. To leave a selvage on cloth. 3. To adorn the border of some fabric or garment.—*vr.* & *vn.* To approach or reach the shore.

Orillo [o-reel'-lyo], *m.* Selvage or list of cloth.

Orín [o-reen'], *m.* 1. Rust, the red oxide of iron. 2. Stain, taint of guilt; defect. 3. *pl. V.* ORINA.

Orina [o-ree'-nah], *f.* Urine.

Orinal [o-re-nahl'], *m.* Urinal, chamber-vessel, chamber-pot (of glass, earthenware or metal).

Orinar [o-re-nar'], *vn.* To urinate, to make water.

Oriniento, ta [o-re-ne-en'-to, tah], *a.* Rusty, mouldy.

Orinque [o-reen'-kay], *m.* (Naut.) Buoy-rope.

Oriol [o-re-ole'], *m.* Golden oriole or thrush. Oriolus galbula.

Orión [o-re-on'], *m.* (Ast.) Orion, a conspicuous constellation.

Oriundo, da [o-re-oon'-do, dah], *a.* Originated, derived from.

Orla [or'-lah], *f.* 1. List, selvage, border, fringe, trimming. 2. (Her.) Orle. 3. (Typ.) An ornamental border.

Orlador, ra [or-lah-dor', rah], *m.* & *f.* Borderer, one who makes borders.

Orladura [or-lah-doo'-rah], *f.* Border, edging, list.

Orlar [or-lar'], *va.* To border, to garnish with an edging.

Orlo [or'-lo], *m.* An organ-stop, named after an ancient reed-instrument.

Orlón [or'-lone'], *m.* Orlon (trade-mark).

Ormesí [or-may-see'], *m.* A kind of silk stuff.

Ornadamente, *adv.* Ornamentally.

Ornado, da [or-nah'-do, dah], *a.* & *pp.* of **Ornar**. Ornamented, ornate.

Ornamentar [or-nah-men-tar'], *va.* To adorn, to embellish, to ornament, to bedeck.

Ornamento [or-nah-men'-to], *m.* Ornament, embellishment, decoration.—*pl.* 1. Sacred vestments. 2. Frets, mouldings, etc., in architectural works. 3. The moral qualities of any person.

Ornar [or-nar'], *va.* To adorn, to embellish, to garnish.

Ornato [or-nah'-to], *m.* Dress, apparel; ornament, decoration.

Ornis [or'-nees], *m.* A sort of muslin from India.

Ornitolito [or-ne-to-lee'-to], *m.* Part of a bird petrified.

Ornitología [or-ne-to-lo-hee'-ah], *f.* Ornithology.

Ornitológico, ca [or-ne-to-lo'-he-co, cah], *a.* Ornithological.

Ornitólogo [or-ne-to'-lo-go], *m.* Ornithologist.

Ornitomancia [or-ne-to-mahn'-the-ah], *f.* Ornithomancy, divination by the flight of birds.

Oro [o'-ro], *m.* 1. Gold. 2. Gold colour: applied generally to women's hair. 3. Ornaments, or trinkets made of gold. 4. Gold, money, wealth, riches. 5. *pl.*—Diamonds, a suit at cards. *A peso de oro*, To succeed by means of money. *Como oro en paño*, We show our value of things by the care we take of them. *Oro batido*, Leaf-gold. *Oro en pasta, bruto* or *virgen*, Bullion. *Oro en libritos*, or *libritos de oro fino*, Gold-leaf. *Oro en polvo*, Gold-dust. *Oro mate*, Gold-size. *Como un oro* or *como mil oros*, As clean and beautiful as gold. *De oro y azul*, Dressed in one's best. *Es otro tanto oro*, So much the better. *No es oro todo lo que reluce*, (prov.) All is not gold that glitters. *Oro es lo que oro vale*, Gold is worth what it will buy; other things than money have value. *Oro majado luce*, Broken gold glitters; i. e. that is most esteemed which is tried and approved. *Poner (a uno) de oro y azul*, (Coll.) To teach one his p's and q's; to give one fits; to reprove bitterly.

Orobanquia [o-ro-bahn'-ke-ah], *f.* Broom-rape; a parasitic, gamopetalous plant which sometimes destroys a whole crop, especially of beans. Commonly called *hierba tora*. Orobanche.

Orografía [o-ro-grah-fee'-ah], *f.* Orography, description of mountains.

Orología [o-ro-lo-hee'-ah], *f.* Orology, a treatise on mountains.

Orondo, da [o-ron'-do, dah], *a.* Pompous, showy; hollow.

Oropel [o-ro-pel'], *m.* 1. A thin plate of brass, latten-brass. 2. Tinsel, any thing showy and of little value.

Oropelero [o-ro-pay-lay'-ro], *m.* Brass-worker.

Oropéndola [o-ro-pen'-do-lah], *f.* Loriot, golden oriole.

Oropimente [o-ro-pe-men'-tay], *m.* Orpiment, a sulphide of arsenic.

Oroya [o-ro'-yah], *f.* (Amer. Peru) Hanging basket or sling for carrying passengers and goods over rope bridges; it is generally made of leather.

Orozuz [o-ro-thooth'], *m.* (Bot.) Licorice or liquorice. Glycyrrhiza.

Orquesta [or-kes'-tah], *f.* 1. Orchestra, a body of musicians using stringed and wind-instruments. 2. Orchestra, place in a play-house for musicians.

Orquestación [or-kes-tah-the-on'], *f.* Orchestration.

Orquide [or'-ke-day], *f.* (Bot.) Orchid.

Orquídeo, dea [or-kee'-day-o, ah], *a.* Orchidaceous.

Orquitis [or-kee'-tis], *f.* Orchitis, inflammation of the testicle.

Orraca [or-rah'-cah], *f.* A kind of spirit distilled from the cocoanut.

Ortega [or-tay'-gah], *f.* Hazel-grouse. Tetrao bonasia.

Ortiga [or-tee'-gah], *f.* (Bot.) Nettle. Urtica. *Ser como unas ortigas*, To be as cross as a bear.

Ortigaje [or-te-gah'-hay], *m.* A disease of grape-vines marked by the yellow colour of the leaves.

Ortivo, va [or-tee'-vo, vah], *a.* (Ast.) Oriental, eastern, ortive.

Orto [or'-to], *m.* Rising of a star.

Ortodóntico [or-to-don'-te-co], *m.* (Med.) Orthodontist.

Ortodoxia [or-to-dok'-se-ah], *f.* Orthodoxy: (Catholicism).

Ortodoxo, xa [or-to-dok'-so, sah], *a.* Orthodox, not heretical.

Ortografía [or-to-grah-fee'-ah], *f.* Orthography.

Ortográficamente, *adv.* Orthographically.

Ortográfico, ca [or-to-grah'-fe-co, cah], *a.* Orthographical.

Ortógrafo [or-to'-grah-fo], *m.* Orthographer.

Ortología [or-to-lo-hee'-ah], *f.* Orthoepy, art of pronunciation.

Ortopedia [or-to-pay'-de-ah], *f.* Orthopedia, art of correcting deformities in the human body, especially in children.

Ortopédico, ca [or-to-pay'-de-co, cah], *a.* Orthopedic, relating to orthopedia.

Ortopedista [or-to-pay-dees'-tah], *m.* (Med.) Orthopedist.

Ortóptero [or-top-tay-ro], *a.* Orthopterous.—*m. pl.* The orthoptera, an order of insects, having wings folded lengthwise, as the common locust.

Oruga [o-roo'-gah], *f.* 1. (Bot.) Rocket, an herb of the mustard family. Brassica eruca. 2. Caterpillar.

Orujo [o-roo'-ho], *m.* Skin or peel of pressed grapes.

Orvalle [or-vahl'-lyay], *m.* (Bot.) *V.* GALLOCRESTA.

Orza [or'-thah], *f.* 1. Gallipot, a jar for sweetmeats, small earthen pot, crock. 2. (Naut.) Luff. *Orza a la banda*, (Naut.) Hard a-lee. *A orza*, (Naut.) Luff, luff.

Orzaderas [or-thah-day'-ras], *f. pl.* (Naut.) Lee-boards.

Orzaga [or-thah'-gah], *f.* (Bot.) Orach. Atriplex. Mountain spinach.

Orzar [or-thar'], *vn.* (Naut.) To luff, to steer closer to the wind.

Orzuelo [or-thoo-ay'-lo], *m.* 1. Sty, a small inflamed swelling on the eyelid; a hordeolum. 2. Snare to catch birds; a trap for catching wild beasts. (Lat. hordeolus.)

Os [osc], *pron.* You or ye. It is placed before and after verbs, and used instead of *vos*.

Osa [o'-sah], *f.* She-bear. *Osa mayor*, Ursa major.

Osadamente, *adv.* Boldly, daringly.

Osadía [o-sah-dee'-ah], *f.* 1. Courage, boldness, intrepidity, hardiness. 2. Zeal, fervour, ardour.

Osado, da [o-sah'-do, dah], *a.* Daring, bold, high-spirited, high-mettled.—*pp.* of OSAR.

Osambre [o-sahm'-bray], *m.* **Osamenta** [o-sah-men'-tah], *f.* A skeleton.

Osar [o-sar'], *vn.* 1. To dare, to venture, to outdare. 2. To imagine, to fancy.

Osario [o-sah'-re-o], *m.* 1. Charnel-house. 2. Any place where there are bones.

Oscilación [os-the-lah-the-on'], *f.* Oscillation, vibration of a pendulum.

Oscilador [os-the-lah-dor'], *m.* Oscillator.

Oscilar [os-the-lar'], *vn.* To oscillate, to vibrate as a pendulum.

Oscilatorio, ria [os-the-lah-to'-re-o, ah], *a.* Oscillatory, vibratory.

Oscitante [os-the-tahn'-tay], *a.* (Med.) Oscitant, gaping, yawning.

Osco, ca [os'-co, cah], *a.* Oscan, belonging to this ancient region of Italy.

Osculación [os-coo-lah-the-on'], *f.* (Geom.) Osculation.

Osculatorio, ria [os-coo-lah-to'-re-o, ah], *a.* (Geom.) Osculatory.

Ósculo [os'-coo-lo], *m.* Kiss. *V.* BESO.

Oscuramente, *adv. V.* OBSCURAMENTE.

Oscurantismo [os-coo-ran-tees'-mo], *m.* Antiquated ideas; "old fogyism."

Oscuras (A) [ah os-coo'-ras], *adv. V.* Á OBSCURAS.

Oscurecer [os-coo-ray-therr'], *va.* & *vn. V.* OBSCURECER.

Oscurecimiento [os-coo-ray-the-me-en'-to], *m. V.* OBSCURECIMIENTO.

Oscuridad [os-coo-re-dahd'], *f. V.* OBSCURIDAD.

Oscuro, ra [os-coo'-ro, rah], *a. V.* OBSCURO.

Osecico, illo, Osezuelo [o-say-thee'-co], *m. dim.* Small bone.

Óseo, a [oh'-say-o, ah], *a.* Osseous, bony.

Osera [o-say'-rah], *f.* Den of bears.

Osezno [o-seth'-no], *m.* Whelp or cub of a bear.

Osfresia [os-fray'-se-ah], *f.* The sense of smell.

Osfrésico, ca [os-fray'-se-co, cah], *a.* Olfactory, relating to the sense of smell.

Osículo [o-see'-coo-lo], *m. dim.* Ossicle, a diminutive bone.

Osificación [o-se-fe-cah-the-on'], *f.* Ossification.

Osificarse [o-se-fe-car'-say], *vr.* To ossify.

Osífico, ca [o-see'-fe-co, cah], *a.* Ossific.

Osmazoma [os-mah-tho'-mah], *f.* or **Osmazomo,** *m.* Osmazome, a substance contained in meat, imparting taste and odour to broths.
Ósmico [os'-me-co], *a.* Osmic, relating to osmium.
Osmio [os'-me-o], *m.* (Min.) Osmium.
Oso [o'-so], *m.* Bear. Ursus. *Oso hormiguero,* Ant-eater. Myrmecophaga. *Oso colmenero,* Bear that robs bee-hives. *Manteca de oso,* Bear's-grease. *Piel de oso,* Bear-skin.
Ososo, sa [o-soh'-so, sah], *f.* Osseous, bony.
Ostaga [os-tah'-gah], *f.* (Naut.) Tie, runner. *Ostaga de gavia,* The main-top-sail tie.
Oste, *int.* (Ant.) *V.* Oxte.
Ostealgia [os-tay-ahl'-he-ah], *f.* Bone-ache, ostalgia.
Osteitis [os-tay-ee'-tis], *f.* Osteitis, inflammation of bone.
Ostensible [os-ten-see'-blay], *a.* Ostensible, apparent.
Ostensiblemente, *adv.* Ostensibly.
Ostensión [os-ten-se-on'], *f.* Show, manifestation.
Ostensivo, va [os-ten-see'-vo, vah], *a.* Ostensive, showing, betokening.
Ostentación [os-ten-tah-the-on'], *f.* 1. Ostentation, appearance. 2. Ambitious display, vain show, flourish, parade.
Ostentador, ra [os-ten-tah-dor', rah], *m.* & *f.* Boaster, ostentator.
Ostentar [os-ten-tar'], *va.* To show, to demonstrate.—*vn.* To boast, to brag; to be fond of vain shows.
Ostentativo, va [os-ten-tah-tee'-vo, vah], *a.* Ostentatious.
Ostento [os-ten'-to], *m.* Portent, prodigy.
Ostentosamente, *adv.* Ostentatiously, boastfully; gaudily.
Ostentoso, sa [os-ten-to'-so, sah], *a.* Sumptuous, ostentatious, boastful, jaunty, gaudy, garish.
Osteócopo [os-tay-o'-co-po], *a.* (Med.) Osteocopic, bone-breaking (pain).
Osteografía [os-tay-o-grah-fee'-ah], *f.* Osteography, description of the bones.
Osteolita [os-tay-o-lee'-tah], *f.* Osteolite, fossil bone.
Osteología [os-tay-o-lo-hee'-ah], *f.* Osteology, that part of anatomy which treats of the bones.
Osteólogo [os-tay-o'-lo-go], m. Osteologer, a describer of the bones.
Osteópata [os-tay-o'-pah-tah], *m.* Osteopath.
Osteopatía [os-tay-o-pah-tee'-ah], *f.* Osteopathy.
Ostiario [os-te-ah'-re-o], *m.* Ostiary, door-keeper, one of the minor orders of the Roman Catholic church.
Ostiatim [os-te-ah'-tim], *adv.* From door to door.
Ostión [os-te-on'], *m.* (Prov. Andal.) An oyster larger and coarser than the common one.
Ostra [os'-trah], *f.* Oyster. Ostrea.
Ostracismo [os-trah-thees'-mo], *m.* Ostracism, a method of banishment practised by the Athenians.
Ostracita [os-trah-thee'-tah], *f.* Ostracite, the common oyster in its fossil state.
Ostral [os-trahl'], *m.* Oyster-bed.
Ostrera [os-tray'-rah], *f.* 1. *V.* Ostral. 2. Oyster-wench, oyster-woman. 3. Oyster-plover.
Ostrero [os-tray'-ro], *m.* Dealer in oysters.
Ostrífero, ra [os-tree'-fay-ro, rah], *a.* Producing oysters, ostriferous.
Ostro [os'-tro], *m.* 1. Oyster; large oysters are denominated in the masculine gender; they are also called *Ostrones.* 2. South wind. 3. Purple anciently obtained from a mollusk: Tyrian purple.
Ostrogodo, da [os-tro-go'-do, dah], *a.* Ostrogothic.
Ostugo [os-too'-go], *m.* Piece, part.
Osudo, da [o-soo'-do, dah], *a.* Bony.
Osuno, na [o-soo'-no, nah], *a.* Bear-like, bearish.
Otacústico [o-tah-coos'-te-co], *a.* Otacoustic, assisting the sense of hearing.—*m.* Otacousticon, instrument to assist hearing.
Otalgia [o-tahl'-he-ah], *f.* Otalgia, ear-ache.
Otálgico, ca [o-tahl'-he-co, cah], *a.* Otalgic, suitable for allaying earache.
Otáñez [o-tah'-nyeth], *m.* (Hum.) An old squire who courts or attends a lady; an old beau. *Iba con su Don Otáñez,* She went with her old beau.
Oteador, ra [o-tay-ah-dor', rah], *m.* & *f.* Spy, sly observer.
Otear [o-tay-ar'], *va.* To observe, to examine, to pry into, to discover by artifice; to inspect.
Otero [o-tay'-ro], *m.* Hill, eminence, height, in a plain.
Ótico, ca [oh'-te-co, cah], *a.* (Med.) Otic, aural, employed in treating the ear.
Otitis [o-tee'-tis], *f.* Otitis, inflammation of the ear.
Oto [o'-to], *m.* (Zool.) Bustard, otis. *V.* Avutarda.
Otología [o-to-lo-hee'-ah], *f.* (Med.) Otology, study of ear diseases.
Otólogo, [o-to'-lo-go], *m.* Otologist, ear specialist.
Otomana [o-to-mah'-nah], *f.* Ottoman, a cushioned seat, like a sofa.
Otomano, na [o-to-mah'-no, nah], *a.* Ottoman, relating to the Turkish empire.
Otona [o-to'-nah], *f.* (Bot.) Ragwort.
Otoñada [o-to-nyah'-dah], *f.* Autumn season.
Otoñal [o-to-nyahl'], *a.* Autumnal.
Otoñar [o-to-nyar'], *vn.* 1. To spend the autumn season. 2. To grow in autumn: applied to plants.—*vr.* To be seasoned, to be tempered: applied to earth after rain.
Otoño [o-to'-nyo], *m.* 1. Autumn. 2. Aftermath, second crop of grass.
Otorgador, ra [o-tor-gah-dor', rah], *m.* & *f.* Consenter, granter, stipulator.
Otorgamiento [o-tor-gah-me-en'-to], *m.* 1. Grant, license. 2. The act of making an instrument in writing.
Otorgancia [o-tor-gahn'-the-ah], *f.* (Law) Authorization. *Auto de otorgancia,* Act of empowering or authorizing.
Otorgante [o-tor-gahn'-tay], *pa.* & *m.* & *f.* 1. Granter; authorizing. 2. The party that signs and executes any public instrument.
Otorgar [o-tor-gar'], *va.* 1. To consent, to agree to, to condescend. *Otorgar de cabeza,* To nod assent. 2. To covenant, to stipulate. 3. (Law) To declare, to execute, to do. *Quien calla otorga,* Silence gives consent.
Otorrea [o-tor-ray'-ah], *f.* Otorrhœa, a discharge from the ear.
Otoscopio [o-tos-co'-pe-oh], *m.* (Med.) Otoscope.
Otre, Otri, Otrie, *a.* (Obs.) *V.* Otro.
Otro, tra [o'-tro, trah], *a.* Another, other. *Otro que tal,* (Coll.) Another such. *Esa es otra,* (Coll.) That is another impertinence of the same kind.
Otro, Otra, *int.* Again! exclamation of disgust.
Otrosi [o-tro-see'], *adv.* Besides, moreover.—*m.* (Law) Every petition made after the principal.
Ova [o'-vah], *f.* (Bot.) Sea-lettuce, laver. Ulva.—*pl.* (Prov.) Eggs. *V.* Huevas.
Ovación [o-vah-the-on'], *f.* Ovation, a lesser triumph among the Romans.
Ovado, da [o-vah'-do, dah], *a.* & *pp.* of Ovar. 1. Oval. 2. Fecundated by the male bird.
Oval [o-vahl'], *a.* Oval, oblong.
Ovalado, da [o-vah-lah'-do, dah], *a.* Egg-shaped, oval-formed.
Óvalo [o'-vah-lo], *m.* Oval, a body or figure in the shape of an egg.
Ovar [o-var'], *vn.* To lay eggs.
Ovárico, ca [o-vah'-re-co, cah], *a.* Ovarian.
Ovario [o-vah'-re-o], *m.* 1. Ovary, the organ in a female by which impregnation is performed. 2. (Bot.) Ovarium, ovary, the seed-vessel of plants, the lowest part of the pistil. 3. Ornament in architecture in the form of an egg.
Ovecico [o-vay-thee'-co], *m. dim.* A small egg.
Oveja [o-vay'-hah], *f.* Ewe, a female sheep. *Cada oveja con su pareja,* Like seeks like. *Encomendar las ovejas al lobo,* To set the wolf to guard the sheep. *Ovejas y abejas en tus dehesas,* Keep your sheep and your bees in your own grounds, if you would profit by them.
Ovejero [o-vay-hay'-ro], *m.* Shepherd.
Ovejuela [o-vay-hoo-ay'-lah], *f. dim.* A young ewe.
Ovejuno, na [o-vay-hoo'-no, nah], *a.* Relating to ewes.
Overa [o-vay'-rah], *f.* Ovary of oviparous animals.
Overo, ra [o-vay'-ro, rah], *a.* Dappled: applied to animals speckled, or trout-coloured.—*pl.* (Coll.) Eyes which look quite white, as if without a pupil.
Ovezuelo [o-vay-thoo-ay'-lo], *m. dim.* A small egg.
Oviforme [o-ve-for'-may], *a.* Egg-shaped.
Ovil, *m.* Sheep-cot. *V.* Redil.
Ovillar [o-vil-lyar'], *vn.* To wind into a clew, to hank.—*vr.* To shrug or contract one's self into a ball or clew.
Ovillejo [o-vil-lyay'-ho], *m.* 1. (Dim.) A small clew or ball. 2. A kind of metrical composition. *Decir de ovillejo,* To make verses extempore.
Ovillo [o-veel'-lyo], *m.* 1. Clew, thread wound upon a bottom. 2. Any confused heap or multitude of things.
Ovino, na [o-vee'-no, nah], *a.* Ovine, pertaining to sheep. *Ganado ovino,* Sheep.
Ovíparo, ra [o-vee'-pah-ro, rah], *a.* Oviparous, bringing forth eggs.
Ovoide [o-vo'-e-day], *a.* Ovoid, egg-shaped.
Ovolo [o'-vo-lo], *m.* (Arch.) Ovolo, a quarter-round; a convex moulding.
Ovoso, sa [o-vo'-so, sah], *a.* Full of sea-weeds.
Óvulo [o'-voo-lo], *m.* Ovule, germ contained in an ovary before impregnation.
¡ Ox ! [oks], *int.* A word used to frighten away fowls, birds, and other animals; shoo!
Oxalato [ok-sah-lah'-to], *m.* (Chem.) Oxalate, salt formed with oxalic acid.
Oxálico [ok-sah'-le-co], *a.* Oxalic: applied to acid made from sorrel.
Oxálide [ok-sah'-le-day], *f.* (Bot.) Oxalis.
Oxalme [ok-sahl'-may], *m.* Acid brine.
Oxear [ok-say-ar'], *va.* To shoo or scare away fowls.
Oxidacion [ok-se-dah-the-on'], *f.* (Chem.) Oxidation.
Oxidar [ok-se-dar'], *va.* To oxidate, to oxidize.—*vr.* To absorb oxygen.
Oxido [ok'-se-do], *m.* Oxide. *Óxido de cinc,* Zinc oxide.

Oxigenable [ok-se-hay-nah'-blay], *a.* (Chem.) Oxygenizable.

Oxigenación [ok-se-hay-nah-the-on'], *f.* Oxygenation, combining with oxygen.

Oxigenado, da [ok-se-hay-nah-do, dah], *a.* Oxygenated. *Rubia oxigenada*, Peroxide blond.—*pp.* of OXIGENAR.

Oxigenar [ok-se-hay-nar'], *va.* To oxygenate, to saturate with oxygen.—*vr.* To oxygenate, to be oxygenated.

Oxígeno [ok-see'-hay-no], *m.* (Chem.) Oxygen. *Oxígeno líquido*, Lox, liquid oxygen.

Oxigonio [ok-se-go'-ne-o], *a.* Acute-angled.

Oxígono, na [ok-see'-go-no, nah], *a.* Acute-angled; having all the angles acute.

Oximaco [ok-se-mah'-co], *m.* A bird of prey with a curved black bill.

¡Oxte! [ox'-tay], *int.* Keep off, begone. *Sin decir oxte ni moxte*, (Coll.) Without asking leave or saying a word. *¡Oxte puto!* Exclamation on touching any thing very hot or burning.

Oyamel [o-yah-mel'], *m.* Mexican fir.

Oyente [o-yen'-tay], *pa.* Hearing; auditor, hearer.

Ozena [o-thay'-nah], *f.* (Med.) Ozæna, an ulceration of the nostrils, producing a fetid pus.

Ozono [o-tho'-no], *m.* Ozone, considered an allotropic form of oxygen, generally produced by electricity.

Ozonómetro [o-tho-no'-may-tro], *m.* Ozonometer, an instrument for measuring the amount of ozone in the air.

P

P [pay], nineteenth letter of the alphabet, is pronounced in the Spanish as in the English language; joined with an *h*, it had formerly the sound of *f*, but now all those words are written with *f*. *P.* is a contraction for father; in the complimentary style, for feet; in petitions, for powerful. *PP.* fathers. (Com.) Put on bills of exchange *p.* means protested. *B. p. p.*, Bills payable, (*Billetes por pagar*). *P.* in pharmacy stands for *parte*, part. *P.* in the Italian music signifies soft; *PP.* softer; and *PPP.* softest.

Pabellón [pah-bel-lyone'], *m.* 1. Pavilion, a kind of tent; field-bed. 2. Curtain hanging in the form of a tent. 3. *Pabellón de armas.* (Mil.) Bell tent. 4. (Naut.) National colours, flag. 5. Summer-house in the shape of a pavilion.

Pábilo [pah'-be-lo], *m.* 1. Wick, as of a torch or candle. 2. Snuff of a candle.

Pablar [pah-blar'], *va.* (Coll.) Word used for consonance, as *Ni hablar, ni pablar*, Not to speak.

Pábulo [pah'-boo-lo], *m.* Pabulum, nourishment, food, provender, support, nutriment.

Paca [pah'-cah], *f.* 1. The spotted cavy. Cavia paca. 2. Bale of goods, bundle, package.

Pacal [pah-cahl'], *m.* Bundle, parcel.

Pacana [pah-cah'-nah], *f.* Pecan, an American tree like a walnut-tree, with an olive-shaped nut.

Pacato, ta [pah-cah'-to, tah], *a.* Pacific, quiet, tranquil, mild, gentle.

Pacedero, ra [pah-thay-day'-ro, rah], *a.* Pasturable, fit for pasture: applied to the ground.

Pacedura [pah-thay-doo'-rah], *f.* Pasture-ground.

Pacer [pah-therr'], *vn.* 1. To pasture, to graze. 2. To gnaw, to corrode, to feed.

Paciencia [pah-the-en'-the-ah], *f.* 1. Patience, endurance. 2. Patience, the quality of expecting long without rage or discontent. 3. Patience, forbearance, long-suffering. 4. Slowness, tardiness in action. 5. Exhortatory exclamation to have patience.

Paciente [pah-the-en'-tay], *a.* 1. Patient, calm under affliction or pain, forbearing. 2. Consenting, accommodating: spoken of a contented cuckold.

Paciente [pah-the-en'-tay], *m.* 1. Patient, sufferer, that which receives impressions from external agents. 2. (Coll.) Patient; a sick person.

Pacientemente, *adv.* Patiently, tolerantly.

Pacienzudo, da [pah-the-en-thoo'-do, dah], *a.* (Coll.) Patient, tolerant.

Pacificación [pah-the-fe-cah-the-on'], *f.* Pacification, the act of making peace; quietness, peace of mind.

Pacificador, ra [pah-the-fe-cah-dor', rah], *m.* & *f.* Pacificator, pacifier, peacemaker, reconciler.

Pacíficamente [pah-thee'-fe-cah-men-tay], *adv.* Pacifically.

Pacificar [pah-the-fe-car'], *va.* To pacify, to appease.—*vn.* To treat for peace.

Pacífico, ca [pah-thee'-fe-co, cah], *a.* Pacific, peaceful; desirous of peace; tranquil, undisturbed; mild, gentle.

Pacifista [pah-the-fees'-tah], *m.* & *f.* Pacifist.

Paco [pah'-co], *m.* 1. Paco, a kind of vicuña: alpaca. 2. (Chili) Police force. 3. Diminutive of Francisco. 4. *pl.* Silver ores containing chlorides, etc., and iron.

Pacotilla [pah-co-teel'-lyah], *f.* Venture, goods embarked in a ship on the private account of an individual. *Ser de pacotilla*, Of poor quality. (Acad.)

Pactar [pac-tar'], *va.* To covenant, to contract, to stipulate.

Pacto [pahc'-to], *m.* Pact, covenant, agreement. *Pacto de caballeros*, Gentleman's agreement.

Pácul [pah'-cool], *m.* A wild plantain of the Philippines which yields a textile fibre less good than abacá.

Pachamanca [pah-chah-mahn'-cah], *f.* (Peru) Barbecue, meat roasted out-of-doors, by covering with hot stones; barbecue feast.

Pachón [pah-chone'], *m.* 1. A peaceful, phlegmatic man. 2. Pointer, pointer-dog.

Pachona [pah-cho'-nah], *f.* Pointer-bitch.

Pachorra [pah-chor'-rah], *f.* Sluggishness, a slow and phlegmatic disposition.

Pachorrudo, da [pah-chor-roo'-do, dah], *a.* Sluggish, tardy, phlegmatic.

Padecer [pah-day-therr'], *va.* 1. To suffer corporal affliction. 2. To sustain an injury. 3. To be liable to.

Padecimiento [pah-day-the-me-en'-to], *m.* Suffering, sufferance.

(*Yo padezco, yo padezca*, from *Padecer.* V. CONOCER.)

Padilla [pah-deel'-lyah], *f.* 1. A small frying-pan. 2. A small oven.

Padrastro [pah-drahs'-tro], *m.* 1. Stepfather. 2. Obstacle, impediment. 3. Height, eminence which commands a tower or other place. 4. Hang-nail.

Padrazo [pah-drah'-tho], *m. aug.* of PADRE. An indulgent parent.

Padre [pah'-dray], *m.* 1. Father. 2. Father, the appellation of the first person of the adorable Trinity. 3. Male of all animals. 4. Father, ancestor. 5. Source, origin, principal author. 6. Father, one who acts with paternal care. 7. Father, an ecclesiastical writer of the first centuries. 8. Father, the appellation of a religious man. 9. Father, the title of a confessor. *Padre de familia*, Householder, housekeeper. *Padre santo*, The Pope. *Padre de menores*, The alderman who, *ex officio*, is the guardian of orphan minors, and public administrator. *Nuestros padres a pulgadas, y nosotros á brazadas*, (prov.) After a gatherer comes a scatterer. *Padre nuestro*, The Lord's prayer; the large bead in the rosary over which the Lord's prayer is to be said.—*pl.* 1. Parents, the father and mother. 2. Ancestors. 3. The members of a religious congregation taken as a body. *¡Mi padre!* No, indeed! never! *Un padre para cien hijos, y no cien hijos para un padre*, The love of parents for their children is greater than that of children for their parents.

Padrear [pah-dray-ar'], *vn.* 1. To resemble the father in features or habits. 2. To be kept for procreation: applied to cattle.

Padrina [pah-dree'-nah], *f.* (Obs.) Godmother. *V.* MADRINA.

Padrinazgo [pah-dre-nath'-go], *m.* Compaternity, act of assisting at baptism; title or charge of a god-father.

Padrino [pah-dree'-no], *m.* 1. God-father, the sponsor at the font. 2. Second, in a duel. 3. Protector, assistant. *Padrino de boda*, (Coll.) A groom's-man.

Padrón [pah-drone'], *m.* 1. Poll, a register of persons in a place who pay taxes. 2. A kind of public monument among the Romans. 3. Mark or note of infamy. 4. An indulgent parent.

Paella [pah-el'-lyah], *f.* Rice and chicken dish originating in Valencia, Spain.

Pafio, na [pah'-fe-o, ah], *a.* Paphian, of Paphos.

Paflón [pa-flone'], *m.* (Arch.) Soffit, the under side of a cornice or archway. *Cf.* PLAFÓN.

Paga [pah'-gah], *f.* 1. Payment, fee, salary. 2. Satisfaction for a fault or error committed. 3. Sum or fine paid. 4. Monthly pay of a soldier. 5. Friendly intercourse, mutual friendship. *En tres pagas*, Bad payment; badly or never paid.

Pagadero, ra [pah-gah-day'-ro, rah], *a.* Payable.

Pagadero [pah-gah-day'-ro], *m.* Time and place of payment.

Pagado, da [pah-gah'-do, dah], *a.* Peaceful, agreeable, pleased.—*pp.* of PAGAR.

Pagador, ra [pah-gah-dor', rah], *m.* & *f.* 1. Payer, one who pays. 2. Paymaster.

Pagaduría [pah-gah-doo-ree'-ah], *f.* Paymaster's office.

Pagamento [pah-gah-men'-to], *m.* Payment.

Paganismo [pah-gah-nees'-mo], *m.* Paganism, heathenism.

Pagano [pah-gah'-no], *m.* 1. Heathen, pagan. 2. Peasant, rustic. 3. (Coll.) One who pays his share.

Pagano, na [pah-gah'-no, nah], *a.* Heathenish, unchristian, paganish.

Pagar [pah-gar'], *va.* 1. To pay, to discharge a debt, to acquit. 2. To be liable for customs duties; used of merchandise. 3. To pay, to atone, to make amends. 4. To please, to give pleasure. 5. To pay, to reward, to requite, to fee.—*vr.* To be pleased (with one's self); to be fond of (another). *Pagar la visita*, To return a visit. *Pagar con el pellejo*, (Coll.) To die. *Pagar el pato*, (Coll.) To receive unmerited punishment, or to pay for another man's misconduct. *Está muy pagado de sí mismo*, He entertains a high opinion of himself.

Pagaré [pah-gah-ray'], *m.* A note of hand, a promissory note.
Pagaya [pa-gah'-yah], *f.* A Philippine oar, tied about with a twining stem.
Página [pah'-he-nah], *f.* Page of a book.
Pago [pah'-go], *m.* 1. Payment, discharge of a debt. 2. Payment, reward, the thing given in discharge of a debt or promise. *Suspender el pago,* To stop payment. 3. Lot of land: especially of vineyards. *Pronto pago,* Prompt payment. *Dar cuenta con pago,* To close or balance an account. *En pago,* In payment, as a recompense, in return.—*a.* (Coll.) Paid.
Pagoda [pah-go'-dah], *f.* Pagoda, Indian temple.
Pagodita [pa-go-dee'-tah], *f.* An earth which the Chinese employ for making figures.
Pagote [pah-go'-tay], *m.* (Coll.) One who is charged with the faults of others, and pays or suffers for them all.
Pagua [pah'-goo-ah], *f.* (Mex.) Avocado, alligator pear.
Paguro [pah-goo'-ro], *m.* Small crab.
Paila [pah'-e-lah], *f.* 1. A large pan of copper, brass, or iron. 2. A boiler.
Pailón [pah-e-lone'], *m.* A large copper.
Pairar [pah-e-rar'], *vn.* (Naut.) To bring to, to lie to. *V.* Capear.
Pairo [pah'-e-ro], *m.* (Naut.) Act of lying to with all sail set. *Al pairo,* Lying to.
País [pah-ees'], *m.* 1. Country, land, region, ground. 2. In painting, landscape. 3. (Met.) Field, subject: applied to scientific researches.
Paisaje [pah-e-sah'-hay], *m.* Landscape.
Paisana [pah-e-sah'-nah], *f.* 1. Countrywoman, a woman of the same country as another person. 2. A kind of country-dance.
Paisanaje [pah-e-sah-nah'-hay], *m.* 1. The lay inhabitants of a country, in contradistinction to the military men and clergy; the peasantry. 2. Quality of being of the same country.
Paisano, na [pah-e-sah'-no, nah], *a.* Of the same country.
Paisano [pah-e-sah'-no], *m.* 1. Fellow-countryman, one of the same country as another. 2. Countryman: appellation given by soldiers to those who are not military men; a civilian.
Paja [pah'-hah], *f.* 1. Straw, the stalk on which corn grows; haum. 2. Straw, the stalk of corn after being thrashed. 3. Beard of grain, blade of grass. 4. Straw, chaff, any thing proverbially worthless, froth. *A lumbre de pajas,* In a trice, speedily. *Paja pelaza,* Barley-straw cut small. *Paja trigaza,* Wheat-straw. *Echar pajas,* To draw lots with straw. *Todo eso es paja,* That is all nonsense. *En quítame allá esas pajas,* In the twinkling of an eye. *Por quítame allá esas pajas,* To quarrel for a straw. *No dormirse en las pajas,* (Met.) To be very vigilant; to profit by the occasion. *No haberle echado a alguno paja ni cebada,* To have nothing to do with a person. *¡ Pajas!* Exclamation denoting equality. *Pedro es valiente, pues Juan ¡ pajas!* Peter is valiant, while John is not less so.
Pajada [pah-hah'-dah], *f.* Straw boiled with bran.
Pajado, da [pah-hah'-do, dah], *a.* Pale, straw-coloured.
Pajar [pah-har'], *m.* Place where straw is kept.
Pájara [pah'-hah-rah], *f.* 1. The female of any bird, hen-bird. 2. (Prov.) Paper kite. *Pájara pinta,* A game of forfeits.
Pajarear [pah-hah-ray-ar'], *va.* 1. To go bird-catching. 2. To loiter about. 3. (Mex.) To be skittish: speaking of horses.
Pajarel [pah-hah-rel'], *m.* *V.* Jilguero.
Pajarera [pah-hah-ray'-rah], *f.* Aviary.
Pajarería [pah-hah-ray-ree'-ah], *f.* 1. Abundance of sparrows or little birds. 2. Place where straw is sold.
Pajarero [pah-hah-ray'-ro], *m.* 1. Bird-catcher. 2. One who idles about.
Pajarero, ra [pah-hah-ray'-ro, rah], *a.* 1. Merry, cheerful, gay. 2. Shy: applied to horses. 3. Gaudy, ill-matched: applied to colours.
Pajaril [pah-hah-reel'], *m.* (Naut.) Passaree or passarado, a rope fastened to the corner of a sail.
Pajarilla [pah-hah-reel'-lyah], *f.* 1. (Dim.) A small bird, hen or female of a bird. 2. Milt of a hog. 3. (Prov.) *V.* Palomilla (as insect). *Abrasarse, caerse* or *asarse las pajarillas,* To be intolerably hot.
Pajarito, ta [pah-hah-ree'-to, tah], *m.* & *f. dim.* A small bird.
Pájaro [pah'-hah-ro], *m.* 1. Bird, a general name for the feathered kind: used generally for the smaller birds. 2. Sparrow. *Adiestrar pájaros,* To teach birds to sing. 3. (Met.) A conspicuous person; a sly fellow. *Pájaro mosca,* The humming-bird. *Pájaro solitario,* Man who shuns company.—*pl.* The song-birds. (Lat. *passer.*) *Pájaro del sol,* The bird of paradise. *Pájaro niño,* The penguin. *Pájaro polilla,* Kingfisher. *¡ Chico pájaro para tan gran jaula!* A small bird for so large a cage! (ridicule of pretension). *Más vale pájaro en mano que buitre* (or *ciento*) *volando,* A bird in the hand is worth two in the bush.
Pajarota [pah-hah-ro'-tah], *f.* A false, idle report, a hoax.
Pajarraco [pah-har-rah'-co], *m.* 1. A large bird. 2. (Coll.) A low, cunning, designing fellow.
Pajaza [pah-hah'-thah], *f.* Refuse of straw left by horses in the manger.
Pajazo [pah-hah'-tho], *m.* Prick of stubbles received in a horse's face when feeding among them.
Paje [pah'-hay], *m.* 1. Page, a young boy attending on a great personage. 2. (Naut.) Cabin-boy. *Paje de guión,* The oldest page of the Spanish monarch, who carries the king's arms in the absence of the arm-bearer.—*pl.* (Coll.) Whippings inflicted at school.
Pajear [pah-hay-ar'], *vn.* (Coll.) To behave, conduct one's self.
Pajel [pah-hel'], *m.* (Zool.) Red sea-bream. Sparus erythinus.
Pajera [pah-hay'-rah], *f.* A place where straw is kept.
Pajero [pah-hay'-ro], *m.* One who deals in straw, and carries it about for sale.
Pajica, Pajilla [pah-hee'-cah, pah-heel'-lyah], *f.* Cigar made of a maize-leaf.
Pajizo, za [pah-hee'-tho, thah], *a.* 1. Made of straw, thatched with straw. 2. Straw-colour.
Pajón [pah-hone'], *m.* 1. Coarse straw. 2. (Coll.) An unpolished, ill-bred man.
Pajoso, sa [pah-ho'-so, sah], *a.* Made of straw.
Pajote [pah-ho'-tay], *m.* Straw interwoven with a bulrush, with which gardeners cover fruit-trees and plants.
Pajuela [pah-hoo-ay'-lah], *f.* 1. Short, light straw. 2. Match for lighting.
Pajuelero [pah-hoo-ay-lay'-ro], *m.* Match-maker.
Pajujero [pah-hoo-hay'-ro], *m.* (Prov.) Place where straw is deposited to rot and become manure.
Pajuncio [pah-hoon'-the-o], *m.* (Prov.) 1. Booby, ninny, fool. 2. In contempt, rush, worthless thing.
Pajuz [pah-hooth'], *m.* (Prov.) Refuse of straw in the manger or stable.
Pajuzo [pah-hoo'-tho], *m.* (Prov.) Bad straw, designed for manure.
Pala [pah'-lah], *f.* 1. A wooden shovel for grain; shovel. *Palas con mango,* Shovels with handles. 2. Peel used by bakers. 3. Blade of an oar. 4. Upper-leather of a shoe. 5. The breadth or flat surface of the teeth. 6. Craft, cunning, artifice. 7. Dexterity, cleverness. 8. (Bot.) Common name of a spathe. 9. Leaf of the prickly pear. 10. Smooth part of an epaulet from which the fringe hangs. *Corta pala,* (Coll.) He who is ignorant of a thing. *Meter su media pala,* To have a share in the business. *Higuera de pala,* (Bot.) *V.* Nopal.
Palabra [pah-lah'-brah], *f.* 1. Word, a single part of speech. 2. Word, affirmation, confirmation. 3. Word, promise, offer. 4. (Div.) The Word, or only-begotten Son. *Palabra de matrimonio,* Promise of marriage. *Se han dado palabra,* They are engaged. *Palabras mayores,* Offensive or insulting words; also, things that require great expense. *Soltar la palabra,* Not to oblige a person to keep his word. *Dar palabra y mano,* To celebrate one's betrothal. *Dejar a uno con la palabra en la boca,* To turn away without listening to one who is speaking. *Empeñar la palabra,* To bind one's self to a contract. *Decir a uno cuatro palabritas al oído,* (Coll.) To intimidate a person by informing him that his character is known; also, to obtain a thing by secret flattery. *Palabra preñada,* A word which means more than it expresses. *Palabras libres,* Indecent expressions. *A media palabra,* At the least hint. *De palabra,* By word of mouth. *Mi palabra es prenda de oro,* My word is as good as a bond. *Pedir la palabra,* To ask for the floor. *Tomar la palabra,* To take a man at his word; to speak first. *A la primera palabra,* At the first word (meaning quick apprehension). *Remojar la palabra,* (Coll.) To drink at a dram-shop. *Palabra,* Superstitious words used by sorcerers; sentence extracted from any work; formula of the sacraments, table on which the words of consecration are written. (Lat. *parabola.*)
¡ Palabra ! [pah-lah'-brah], *int.* I say, a word with you.
Palabrada [pah-lah-brah'-dah], *f.* Low, scurrilous language.
Palabrería [pah-lah-bray-ree'-ah], *f.* Wordiness, much talk, emptiness of meaning.
Palabrero, ra [pah-lah-bray'-ro, rah], *a.* Talkative, loquacious.
Palabrimujer [pah-lah-bre-moo-herr'], *m.* Man who has an effeminate voice.
Palabrista [pah-lah-brees'-tah], *com.* One who is full of idle talk, a loquacious person.
Palabrita [pah-lah-bree'-tah], *f.* 1. (Dim.) A short word: it is commonly used for an endearing expression. 2. Word full of meaning. *Palabritas mansas,* Soft, winning expressions.
Palabrota [pah-lah-bro'-tah], *f. aug.* A coarse expression.
Palaciego, ga [pah-lah-the-ay'-go, gah], *a.* Pertaining to the palace.—*m.* Courtier.
Palacio [pah-lah' the-o], *m.* 1. Palace, a royal residence; a house eminently splendid. 2. Castle, the mansion of the ancient nobility. *Hacer palacio,*

To develop, to discover what was concealed.

Palacra, Palacrana [pah-lah'-crah, pah-lah-crah'-nah], *f.* A piece of native gold; ingot of pure gold.

Palada [pah-lah'-dah], *f.* 1. A shovelful. 2. (Naut.) Every stroke of an oar.

Paladar [pah-lah-dar'], *m.* 1. Palate, the roof of the mouth. 2. Palate, the instrument of taste and the taste itself. 3. Taste, relish; longing desire. *A medida* or *a sabor de su paladar,* According to the taste of any one.

Paladear [pah-lah-day-ar'], *va.* 1. To rub the palate of a new-born child with any sweet substance. 2. To amuse, to divert. 3. To clean the mouth or palate of animals.—*vn.* To manifest a desire of sucking: applied to a new-born child.—*vr.* To get the taste of a thing by little and little; to relish.

Paladeo [pah-lah-day'-o], *m.* The act of tasting or relishing.

Paladial [pah-lah-de-ahl'], *a.* Palatal, pronounced by the palate, as y, r.

Paladin [pah-lah-deen'], *m.* Paladin, a knight.

Paladinamente, *adv.* Publicly, clearly.

Paladino, na [pah-lah-dee'-no, nah], *a.* Manifest, clear, apparent, public. *A paladinas,* (Obs.) Publicly.

Paladio [pa-lah'-de-o], *m.* (Min.) Palladium, a metal.

Paladión [pah-lah-de-on'], *m.* Palladium, safeguard.

Palafrén [pah-lah-fren'], *m.* Palfrey, a small horse for ladies; a servant's horse.

Palafrenero [pah-lah-fray-nay'-ro], *m.* Groom, hostler.

Palahierro [pah-lah-e-er'-ro], *m.* Bushing for the spindle of the upper millstone.

Pala mecánica [pah'-lah may-cah'-ne-cah], *f.* Power shovel, steam shovel.

Palamenia [pah-lah-may'-ne-ah], *f.* The oars of a row-galley, *Estar debajo de la palamenia,* To be at the beck of any one.

Palanca [pah-lahn'-cah], *f.* 1. Lever. 2. A staff or pole by which a burden is supported between two men. 3. Exterior fortification with stakes. *Palanca de impulsión,* Operating lever. *Palanca de mano,* Hand lever. *Palanca de retroceso,* Return lever. *Mecanismo de palanca,* Lever system.

Palancada [pah-lan-cah'-dah], *f.* Stroke with a lever.

Palancana, Palangana [pah-lan-gah'-nah], *f.* A basin.

Palanganero [pa-lan-gah-nay'-ro], *m.* Wash-stand, usually resting on three feet.

Palangre [pah-lahn'-gray], *m.* A line from which several fish-hooks are suspended.

Palanquera [pah-lan-kay'-rah], *f.* Inclosure with stakes or poles.

Palanquero [pah-lan-kay'-ro], *m.* Driver of stakes, pile-driver.

Palanqueta [pah-lan-kay'-tah], *f.* 1. (Mil.) Bar-shot or cross-bar-shot, two balls joined by a bar. 2. (Dim.) A small lever.

Palanquin [pah-lan-keen'], *m.* 1. Porter who carries burdens. 2. (Naut.) Double-tackle, clew-garnet. 3. Palanquin, a covered carriage or litter used in the east.

Palastro [pah-lahs'-tro], *m.* Iron plate, sheet of hammered iron.

Palatina [pah-lah-tee'-nah], *f.* Tippet, neckcloth for women in winter.

Palatinado [pah-lah-te-nah'-do], *m.* 1. Palatinate; dignity of a palatine. 2. A county palatine.

Palatino, na [pah-lah-tee'-no, nah], *a.* Palatial, belonging to the palace or the courtiers.

Palay [pah-lah'-ee], *m.* (Phil. Is.) Rice with its husk.

Palazo [pah-lah'-tho], *m.* Blow with a shovel or stick.

Palazón [pah-lah-thone'], *m.* (Naut.) Masting, the masts of vessels.

Palco [pahl'-co], *m.* 1. (Th.) Box, box seat. 2. Scaffold raised for spectators.

Paleador [pah-lay-ah-dor'], *m.* Man who works with a shovel.

Palear, *va.* *V.* Apalear.

Palenque [pah-len'-kay], *m.* 1. Palisade, inclosure made with piles; paling. 2. Passage from the pit to the stage in a play-house.

Paleografía [pah-lay-o-grah-fee'-ah], *f.* Paleography, art of reading ancient MSS.

Paleolítico [pah-lay-o-lee'-te-co], *a.* Paleolithic.

Paleología [pah-lay-o-lo-hee'-ah], *f.* Paleology, the study of ancient languages.

Paleontología [pah-lay-on-to-lo-hee'-ah], *f.* Paleontology, the science which treats of organic fossil remains and of the ancient life of the globe.

Paleozoico [pah-lay-o-tho'-e-co], *a.* (Geol.) Paleozoic.

Palería [pah-lay-ree'-ah], *f.* Art and business of draining low wet lands.

Palero [pah-lay'-ro], *m.* 1. One who makes or sells shovels. 2. Ditcher, drainer; pioneer.

Palestina [pah-les-tee'-nah], *f.* Two-line small pica; type of 22 points.

Palestra [pah-les'-trah], *f.* 1. A place for wrestling and other athletic exercises; a palæstra. 2. A place for disputations or debates. 3. (Poet.) Art of wrestling.

Paléstrico, ca [pah-les'-tre-co, cah], *a.* Relating to a place for wrestling or other exercises; palestric, palestrical, belonging to the exercise of wrestling.

Palestrita [pah-les-tree'-tah], *m.* One versed in athletic or logical exercises.

Paleta [pah-lay'-tah], *f.* 1. Fire-shovel. 2. Palette, a painter's tablet. 3. Iron ladle, used in public kitchens to distribute viands. 4. (Dim.) A small shovel. 5. Blade-bone of the shoulder. 6. Trowel, a mason's tool. 7. *pl.* Chop-sticks to eat with. *Paleta de azotar,* (Naut.) Cobbing-board, used to punish mariners. *De paleta,* Opportunely. *En dos paletas,* (Coll.) Shortly, briefly.

Paletada [pah-lay-tah'-dah], *f.* Trowelful of mortar.

Paletilla [pah-lay-teel'-lyah], *f.* 1. (Dim.) A little fire-shovel. 2. A shoulder-blade. 3. *V.* Palmatoria. 4. A cartilage under the pit of the stomach (the xiphoid).

Paleto [pah-lay'-to], *m.* 1. Fallow-deer. *V.* Gamo. 2. Clown, rustic.

Paletón [pah-lay-tone'], *m.* Bit, the part of a key in which the wards are formed.

Paletoque [pah-lay-to'-kay], *m.* Kind of dress like a scapulary which hangs to the knees.

Pali [pah'-le], *a.* & *m.* An ancient language of India, derived from the Sanscrit.

Palia [pah'-le-ah], *f.* 1. Altar-cloth. 2. Veil which hangs before the tabernacle; square piece of linen put over the chalice.

Paliación [pah-le-ah-the-on'], *f.* Palliation, extenuation.

Paliadamente, *adv.* Dissemblingly in a palliative manner.

Paliar [pah-le-ar'], *va.* To palliate, to extenuate, to excuse.

Paliativo, va [pah-le-ah-tee'-vo, vah], **Paliatorio, ria,** *a.* Palliative, mitigating; that may be palliated.

Palidecer [pah-le-day-therr'], *vn.* To grow pale.

Palidez [pah-le-deth'], *f.* Paleness, wanness, pallor, ghastliness.

Pálido, da [pah'-le-do, dah], *a.* Pallid, pale, ghastly.

Palillero [pah-leel-lyay'-ro], *m.* 1. One who makes or sells tooth-picks. 2. Tooth-pick case.

Palillo [pah-leel'-lyo], *m.* 1. (Dim.) A small stick. 2. Knitting-needle case, a utensil which women carry fastened to the waist by the apron-strings. 3. Tooth-pick. 4. Bobbin, a wooden implement for making net-work or laces. 5. Drum-stick. 6. Peruvian plant similar to the guava-tree.—*pl.* 1. After-dinner table-talk. 2. Small pins put on the billiard-table in certain games. 3. (Coll.) Trifles, things of no moment. *Palillos de tabaco,* Tobacco-stalks.

Palimpsesto [pa-limp-ses'-to], *m.* Palimpsest, an ancient parchment twice written upon, the first writing more or less erased.

Palindromo [pah-lin-dro'-mo], *m.* Palindrome, a word, line, or sentence, which, read either from left to right, or vice versâ, has the same meaning.

Palio [pah'-le-o], *m.* 1. Cloak, short mantle. 2. Pallium, a pontifical ornament, worn by patriarchs and archbishops. 3. Any thing in the form of a canopy. 4. Premium or plate given as a reward in racing. *Recibir con palio,* To receive under a pall, as kings, etc.

Palique [pah-lee'-kay], *m.* (Coll.) Trifling conversation, chit-chat, small talk.

Palito [pah-lee'-to], *m. dim.* A little stick.

Palitroque, Palitoque [pah-le-tro'-kay], *m.* A rough, ill-shaped stick.

Paliza [pah-lee'-thah], *f.* Cudgelling, caning, cowhiding.

Palizada [pah-le-thah'-dah], *f.* 1. Palisade or palisado. 2. Paling, *V.* Estacada.

Palma [pahl'-mah], *f.* 1. (Bot.) Date palm-tree. Phœnix dactylifera. *Palma real,* Royal palm. *Palma criolla,* Cabbage palm. *Palma indiana,* Cocoanut-tree. 2. Leaf of a palm-tree. 3. Palm of the hand. 4. Quick sole of a horse's hoof. 5. Insignia of victory. 6. Insignia of virginity. *Llevarse la palma,* To carry the day. *Andar en palmas,* To be universally applauded. *Palma brava,* A fan-palm of the Philippine Islands, resembling the sago palm; the wood and the leaves are both made use of by the natives.

Palmacristi [pal-mah-crees'-te], *f.* Palma Christi, the castor-oil plant. Ricinus communis.

Palmada [pal-mah'-dah], *f.* Slap with the palm of the hand.—*pl.* Clapping of hands, applause.

Palmadilla [pal-mah-deel'-yah], *f.* A kind of dance.

Palmar [pal-mar'], *a.* 1. Measuring a palm, or three inches. 2. Relating to palms. 3. Clear, obvious, evident.

Palmar [pal-mar'], *m.* 1. Plantation or grove of palm-trees. 2. Fuller's thistle.—*pl.* (Amer.) Woods of dwarf palms, a kind of palmetto.

Palmario, ria [pal-mah'-re-o, ah], *a.* Clear, obvious, evident.

Palmatoria [pal-mah-to'-re-ah], *f.* 1. A rod with which boys at school are beaten on the hand. 2. A small candlestick with a handle.

Palmeado, da [pal-may-ah'-do, dah], *a.* 1. Palmiped, web-footed, palmated: applied to fowls. 2. (Bot.) Palmate: applied to the leaves and roots of plants.—*pp.* of PALMEAR.

Palmear [pal-may-ar'], *va.* To slap with the open hand.

Palmejar [pal-may-har'], *m.* (Naut.) Thick stuff, thick plank nailed to the inner sides of ships.

Palmera [pal-may'-rah], *f.* Palm-tree. *V.* PALMA.

Palmero [pal-may'-ro], *m.* Palmer, a pilgrim, a crusader who bore a palm in his hand.

Palmeta [pal-may'-tah], *f.* 1. Ferule. *V.* PALMATORIA. 2. Slap on the palm of the hand. *Ganar la palmeta,* (1) To reach school before the other children. (2) To get ahead of (literally or figuratively).

Palmífero, ra [pal-mee'-fay-ro, rah], *a.* (Poet.) Palmiferous.

Palmillà [pal-meel'-lyah], *f.* A blue woollen cloth manufactured chiefly in Cuenca.

Palmípedo, da [pal-mee'-pay-do, dah], *a.* Web-footed, palmiped.

Palmitieso [pal-me-te-ay'-so], *a.* Hard-hoofed horse.

Palmito [pal-mee'-to], *m.* 1. Dwarf fan-palm; palmetto. Chamærops humilis. 2. Its root. *Como un palmito,* Neat, clean, genteel. 3. Little face: applied to women and damsel-like youths. *Buen palmito,* A pretty face. 4. (Cuba) Top of a palm-tree containing a bud which is palatable and nutritious.

Palmo [pahl'-mo], *m.* 1. Palm, a measure of length from the thumb to the end of the little finger extended; hand, handbreadth. *En un palmo de tierra,* In a short space of ground. 2. Game, commonly called span-farthing. *Palmo a palmo,* Inch by inch. *Medir a palmos,* (Met.) To have complete knowledge of any thing. *Dejar a uno con un palmo de narices.* To disappoint one in an affair in which he expected to succeed. *Venir* or *andar con un palmo de lengua,* (Vul.) To be over-heated.

Palmotear [pal-mo-tay-ar'], *va.* To slap with the hand. *V.* PALMEAR.

Palmoteo [pal-mo-tay'-o], *m.* Clapping of hands, clap.

Palo [pah'-lo], *m.* 1. Stick, cudgel. 2. Timber, log. 3. Wood of some American trees which serves for medicine or dyes. 4. Blow given with a stick; whack. 5. Execution on the gallows. 6. Suit at cards. 7. Stalk of fruit, pedicle. 8. In writing, a line which projects above or below. 9. (Her.) Pale, a vertical band one-third the width of the shield. *Dar palo,* To turn out contrary to one's expectations. *Dar de palos,* Caning, cowhiding. *Un alcalde de palo,* A wooden justice or *alcalde,* an ignorant, stupid *alcalde.* *Tener el mando y el palo,* To have absolute power over any thing. *Palo de bañón* or *palo mesta,* (Bot.) Alatern buck-thorn. Rhamnus alaternus. 10. (Naut.) Mast. *Palo de una sola pieza,* Pole-mast. *Palo reforzado,* Fished mast. *Palo en bruto,* Rough mast. *A palo seco,* Under bare poles. *Palo mayor,* Main-mast. *Palo de trinquete,* Fore-mast. *Palo de mesana,* Mizzen-mast. *Palos principales,* Lower or standing masts. *Palos de marca,* Buoys. *Palo de tinte* or *de Campeche,* Log-wood. *Palos,* Fillers; speaking of tobacco.

Palo dulce [pah'-lo dool'-thay], *m.* (Bot.) Licorice. V. OROZUZ. *Palo amarillo* or *moralete,* Fustic.

Palo santo [pah'-lo sahn'-to], *m.* (Bot.) Lignum-vitæ. Guaiacum officinale.

Paloma [pah-lo'-mah], *f.* 1. Pigeon, dove. *Paloma mensajera,* Homing pigeon. *Paloma torcaz,* Ring-dove. *Paloma zorita,* A wood-pigeon. 2. A meek, mild, dove-like person. 3. (Ast.) Columba, one of the southern constellations.

Palomaduras [pah-lo-mah-doo'-ras], *f.pl.* (Naut.) Seams of the sails, where the bolt-rope is sewed to them.

Palomar [pah-lo-mar'], *a.* Applied to hard-twisted linen or thread.—*m.* Pigeon-house, dove-cot.

Palomariego, ga [pah-lo-mah-re-ay'-go, gah], *a.* Applied to domestic pigeons in the fields.

Palomear [pah-lo-may-ar'], *vn.* 1. To shoot pigeons. 2. To care for them.

Palomera [pah-lo-may'-rah], *f.* 1. A bleak place. 2. Small dove-cot.

Palomería [pah-lo-may-ree'-ah], *f.* Pigeon-shooting.

Palomero [pah-lo-may'-ro], *m.* One who deals in doves or pigeons.

Palomero, *a.* Applied to arrows with long iron points.

Palomilla [pah-lo-meel'-lyah], *f.* 1. (Dim.) A young pigeon. 2. A sort of ashy moth reared in barley. 3. Back-bone of a horse. 4. Peak of a pack-saddle. 5. Horse of a milk-white colour. 6. A wall-bracket; a galley-rack (among printers). 7. Brass box of the axis of a wheel. 8. Chrysalis or pupa. 9. (Bot.) Common fumitory. Fumaria officinalis.

Palomina [pah-lo-mee'-nah], *f.* 1. Pigeon-dung. 2. (Bot.) Fumitory. 3. A kind of black grape.

Palomino [pah-lo-mee'-no], *m.* 1. A young pigeon. 2. (Coll.) Stain of excrements upon the shirt.

Palomita [pah-lo-mee'-tah], *f.* 1. Squab, pigeon. *Palomitas de maíz,* Popcorn.

Palomo [pah-lo'-mo], *m.* Cock-pigeon. *Juan palomo,* An idle, useless fellow.

Palón [pah-lone'], *m.* (Her.) Guidon, an ensign resembling a flag.

Palotada [pah-lo-tah'-dah], *f.* Stroke with a battledoor. *No dar palotada,* Not to have hit on the right thing in all that is said or done; not to have begun a line or tittle of what was undertaken or ordered; not to answer any thing to the purpose.

Palote [pah-lo'-tay], *m.* 1. Stick of a middling size; drum-stick. 2. Rule or line used by scholars in writing.—*pl.* The first lines formed by boys in writing.

Paloteado [pah-lo-tay-ah'-do], *m.* 1. Rustic dance performed with sticks. 2. Noisy scuffle or dispute, in which they come to blows.—*Paloteado, da, pp.* of PALOTEAR.

Palotear [pah-lo-tay-ar'], *vn.* To scuffle, to clash, to strike sticks against one another; to contend or dispute loudly.

Paloteo [pah-lo-tay'-o], *m.* Fight with sticks.

Palpable [pal-pah'-blay], *a.* 1. Palpable, perceptible to the touch. 2. Palpable, plain, evident, clear.

Palpablemente, *adv.* Palpably, evidently.

Palpadura [pal-pah-doo'-rah], *f.* or **Palpamiento** [pal-pah-me-en'-to], *m.* Palpation, the act of feeling, touching, palpableness.

Palpar [pal-par'], *va.* 1. To feel, to touch. 2. To grope in the dark. 3. To know positively, as if one had felt it. *Palpar la ropa,* To be near death, to be confused and irresolute.

Pálpebra [pahl'-pay-brah], *f.* Eyelid. *V.* PÁRPADO.

Palpebral [pal-pay-brahl'], *a.* Palpebral, belonging to the eyelid.

Palpitación [pal-pe-tah-the-on'], *f.* Palpitation, as of the heart: panting, heaving.

Palpitante [pal-pe-tahn'-tay], *pa.* Vibrating, palpitating.

Palpitar [pal-pe-tar'], *vn.* To palpitate, to pant, to flutter, to heave.

Palpo [pahl'-po], *m.* Palpus, an organ of touch in insects, accessory to the mouth.

Palta [pahl'-tah], *f.* (Bot. Peru.) Alligator-pear. *V.* AGUACATE.

Palto [pahl'-to], *m.* (Bot.) Alligator-pear tree.

Palude [pah-loo'-day], *f.* Lake, pool. *V.* LAGUNA.

Palúdico, ca [pah-loo'-de-co, cah], *a.* 1. Malarial, afflicted with malaria. 2. Paludal, marshy.

Paludismo [pah-loo-dees'-mo], *m.* (Med.) Malaria.

Paludoso, sa [pah-loo-do'-so, sah], *a.* Marshy, swampy.

Palumbario [pah-loom-bah'-re-o], *a.* Dove-hunting: applied to a goshawk.

Palurdo [pah-loor'-do], *m.* A clown, a churl, a rustic.

Palurdo, da [pah-loor'-do, dah], *a.* Rustic, clownish, rude.

Palustre [pah-loos'-tray], *a.* Marshy, fenny, boggy.—*m.* Trowel.

Palustrillo [pah-loos-treel'-lyo], *m.* Angle-float, a plasterer's trowel.

Pallaco [pal-lyah'-co], *m.* (Amer.) Piece of ore of good quality found in a waste-heap.

Pallaquear [pal-lyah-kay-ar'], *va.* (Peru) *V.* PALLAR.

Pallar [pal-lyar'], *va.* To extract the richest metallic part of minerals.

Pallete [pal-lyay'-tay], *m.* (Naut.) Fender, paunch-mat.

Pallón [pal-lyone'], *m.* 1. The quantity of gold or silver resulting from an assay. 2. Assay of gold when incorporated with silver.

Pamandabuán [pah-man-dah-boo-ahn'], *m.* A Philippine craft like a dug-out, but larger; it carries oars and sometimes a mast, with a sail of matting.

Pamema [pa-may'-mah], *f.* Trifle, bagatelle to which it was desired to give importance; folderol.

Pampa [pahm'-pah], *f.* 1. (S. Amer.) An extensive plain. 2. *m.* A tree of the Philippine Islands. The wood is used for making chests and for sheathing boats.

Pámpana [pahm'-pah-nah], *f.* Vine-leaf. *Tocar* or *zurrar la pámpana,* (Coll.) To threaten, to chastise.

Pampanada [pam-pah-nah'-dah], *f.* Juice of tendrils or vine-shoots.

Pampanaje [pam-pah-nah'-hay], *m.* 1. Abundance of vine-shoots. 2. Vain parade.

Pampanilla [pam-pah-neel'-lyah], *f.* A covering of foliage, used by Indians to screen their nakedness.

Pámpano [pahm'-pah-no], *m.* 1. Young vine-branch or tendril. 2. (Zool.) *V.* SALPA. 3. (Amer.) A delicious steel-blue harvest-fish. Stromateus similibus. (In this sense erroneously written *pompano* in English.)

Pampanoso, sa [pam-pah-no'-so, sah], *a.* Abounding with foliage, tendrils, and clusters of grapes.

Pampero [pam-pay'-ro], *m.* (Arg.) A violent wind from the south-west; so called because it blows from the pampas.

Pampero, ra [pam-pay'-ro, rah], *m.* & *f.* & *a.* A dweller on the pampas.

Pampirolada [pam-pe-ro-lah'-dah], *f.* 1. Sauce made of garlic, bread, and water, pounded in a mortar. 2. (Coll.) Any silly thing without substance.

Pamplemusa [pam-play-moo'-sah], *f.* (Bot.) The shaddock and its fruit; grape-fruit.

Pamplina [pam-plee'-nah], *f.* 1. (Bot.) Duck-weed. Lemna arhiza. 2. (Bot.) Mouse-ear. 3. A plant yielding food to canary birds. 4. (Coll.) Futility, trifle, a worthless thing.

Pamporcino [pam-por-thee'-no], *m.* (Bot.) Cyclamen.

Pamposado, da [pam-po-sah'-do, dah], *a.* Lazy, idle, cowardly.

Pampringada [pam-prin-gah'-dah], *f.* 1. *V.* PRINGADA. 2. (Met. Coll.) Frivolous, futile thing.

Pan [pahn], *m.* 1. Bread, a loaf. 2. Pie-crust. 3. Mass of figs, salt, sugar, etc., in the shape of a loaf. 4. Food in general. 5. Wheat. *Este año hay mucho pan*, This year there is plenty of wheat. 6. A wafer or bread for the Eucharist, baked with baking-irons. 7. Leaf of gold or silver. 8. Greek prefix, signifying "all." 9. In Galicia, all grains, except wheat, of which bread is made. *Pan de la boda*, Honeymoon; wedding-cake. *Pan de cera virgen*, White wax in cakes. *Pan de azúcar*, Loaf sugar. *Pan de munición*, Ammunition bread, made of unsifted flour, for soldiers' use. *Pan perdido*, (Met.) He who leaves his house and becomes a vagrant. *No comer el pan de balde.* Not to eat the bread of idleness. *A pan y cuchillo*, Familiarly, assiduously, frequently. *A pan y manteles*, At bed and board. *Con su pan se lo coma*, That is his own affair. *Pan y quesillo*, (Bot.) Shepherd's-purse. Bursa pastoris. *Pan de flor*, The best wheat bread. *Pan de perro*, Very bad bread; chastisement or injury to any one. *Pan casero* or *bazo*, Household bread. *Pan por pan, vino por vino*, The plain unvarnished truth. *Pan porcino*, (Bot.) *V.* ARTANITA. *Pan de oro*, Gold-leaf. *El pan comido, la compañía deshecha*, The meal eaten, the company deserted (i. e. to desert those from whom no more is to be expected).

Pana [pah'-nah], *f.* 1. Velveteen, corduroy. 2. *pl.* (Naut.) Limber-boards, which form part of the lining of the ship's floor.

Panacea [pah-nah-thay'-ah], *f.* Panacea, universal medicine.

Panada [pah-nah'-dah], *f.* Panada or panado.

Panadear [pah-nah-day-ar'], *va.* To make bread for sale.

Panadeo [pah-nah-day'-o], *m.* Baking bread.

Panadería [pah-nah-day-ree'-ah], *f.* 1. Trade or profession of a baker. 2. Baker's shop, bake-house.

Panadero, ra [pah-nah-day'-ro, rah], *m.* & *f.* Baker, maker or seller of bread, kneader.—*f.* Baker's wife.

Panadizo, Panarizo [pah-nah-dee'-tho], *m.* 1. Whitlow, felon. 2. (Coll.) Pale-faced, sickly person.

Panado, da [pah-nah'-do, dah], *a.* Applied to bread macerated in water for sick persons.—*m.* Panada or panado.

Panal [pah-nahl'], *m.* 1. Honey-comb. 2. Any thing pleasing to the taste.

Panameño, ña [pah-nah-may'-nyo, nyah], *m.* & *f.* & *a.* Panamanian, from Panama.

Panamericanismo [pah-nah-may-re-cah-nees'-mo], *m.* Pan Americanism.

Panamericano, na [pahn-ah-may-re-cah'-no, nah], *a.* Pan-American, of both Americas.

Panarra [pah-nar'-rah], *m.* Dolt, simpleton.

Panática [pah-nah'-te-cah], *f.* Provision of bread.

Panca [pahn'-cah], *f.* 1. The husk of an ear of maize. 2. A Philippine fishing-boat. It is provided with outriggers and with paddles, and is steered by a *pagaya.*

Pancarpia [pan-car'-pe-ah], *f.* A garland.

Pancera [pan-thay'-rah], *f.* Armour which covers the belly.

Páncreas [pahn'-cray-as], *m.* (Anat.) Pancreas, sweetbread.

Pancromático, ca [pan-cro-mah'-te-co, cah], *a.* (Photog.) Panchromatic.

Panda [pahn'-dah], *m.* (Zool.) Panda.

Panda [pahn'-dah], *f.* Gallery in a cloister.

Pandear [pan-day-ar'], *vn.* To bend, to be inclined, to belly, to bulge out.

Pandeo [pan-day'-o], *m.* Bulge, any thing that bulges out in the middle.

Panderada [pan-day-rah'-dah], *f.* 1. Number of timbrels joined in concert. 2. Stroke with a timbrel. 3. (Coll.) A silly, untimely, or unreasonable proposition.

Panderazo [pan-day-rah'-tho], *m.* Blow with a timbrel.

Pandereta [pan-day-ray'-tah], *f.* Tambourine.

Panderetear [pan-day-ray-tay-ar'], *vn.* To play on the timbrel.

Pandereteo [pan-day-ray-tay'-o], *m.* The act of beating the timbrel.

Panderetero, ra [pan-day-ray-tay'-ro, rah], *m.* & *f.* 1. One who beats the timbrel. 2. A maker or seller of timbrels.

Panderillo [pan-day-reel'-lyo], *m. dim.* A small timbrel.

Pandero [pan-day'-ro], *m.* 1. Timbrel, a musical instrument. 2. (Coll.) Silly person who talks at random. 3. (Prov.) Paper kite.

Pandilla [pan-deel'-lyah], *f.* 1. Plot, league, party, faction. 2. Party of persons joined together for recreation in the country or for mischief.

Pandillador, pandillero, pandillista [pan-dil-lyah-dor', lyay'-ro, lyis'-tah], *m.* Gangster, member of a rowdy gang.

Pando, da [pahn'-do, dah], *a.* 1. Bulged. 2. Slow of motion: applied to deep waters. 3. Heavy, bulky (of persons).

Pandorga [pan-dor'-gah], *f.* 1. Concert of musical instruments. 2. (Coll.) Fat, bulky woman. 3. (Prov.) Kite.

Panecico, illo, ito [pah-nay-thee'-co], *m.* A small loaf of bread, a roll of bread.

Panegírico, ca [pah-nay-hee'-re-co, cah], *a.* Panegyrical.

Panegírico [pah-nay-hee'-re-co], *m.* Panegyric, eulogy.

Panegirista [pah-nay-he-rees'-tah], *m.* Panegyrist, encomiast, eulogist.

Panela [pah-nay'-lah], *f.* 1. (Colom.) Brown sugar. 2. (Her.) A heart-shaped shield.

Panera [pah-nay'-rah], *f.* 1. Granary. 2. Pannier, a bread-basket.

Panes [pah'-nes], *m. pl.* 1. Corn or grain in the field. 2. Fauns, satyrs.

Panetela [pah-nay-tay'-lah], *f.* 1. Panada, soup made by boiling bread and water. 2. (Amer.) Sponge-cake. 3. A long and slender cigar of Havana.

Panetería [pah-nay-tay-ree'-ah], *f.* Room or office in the palace of the Spanish monarch, where bread and table-linen are kept for use; pantry.

Panetero [pah-nay-tay'-ro], *m.* Pantler, the officer in the palace who keeps the bread.

Pánfilo [pahn'-fe-lo], *m.* 1. A slow, sluggish, heavy person. 2. A jesting game, extinguishing a small candle in pronouncing this word.

Pangelín [pan-hay-leen'], *m.* Angelin-tree, forty or fifty feet high, with leaves like the walnut and a nut with a bitter and sourish taste.

Pangolín [pan-go-leen'], *m.* Pangolin, the scaly ant-eater.

Paniaguado [pah-ne-ah-goo-ah'-do], *m.* 1. Table-fellow, one who receives board and lodging from a friend. 2. Comrade, an intimate friend.

Pánico, ca [pah'-ne-co, cah], *a.* Panic, struck with groundless fear. Also *m.*

Panículo [pah-nee'-coo-lo], *m.* Panicle, pellicle, a membrane.

Paniego, ga [pah-ne-ay'-go, gah], *a.* Eating or yielding much bread.

Paniego [pah-ne-ay'-go], *m.* Bag of coarse cloth, in which charcoal is carried and sold.

Panificar [pan-ne-fe-car'], *va.* To convert pasture-land into arable ground or corn-fields.

Panilla [pah-neel'-lyah], *f.* 1. A small measure of oil (¼ lb.). 2. (Prov. Andal.) *V.* ABACERÍA.

Panizal [pah-ne-thahl'], *m.* A maize-field.

Panizo [pah-nee'-tho], *m.* 1. (Bot.) Panic-grass; panic. Panicum. 2. (Prov.) Maize, Indian-corn.

Panoja [pah-no'-hah], *f.* (Bot.) Panicle, a species of inflorescence, consisting of a branched raceme or corymb. Grasses present spikes arranged in panicles.

Panorama [pah-no-rah'-mah], *m.* Panorama.

Pansofía [pan-so-fee'-ah], *f.* Universal science.

Pantaletas [pan-tah-lay'-tahs], *f. pl.* Panties.

Pantalón [pan-tah-lone'], *m.* *V.* PANTALONES.

Pantalones [pan-tah-lo'-ness], *m. pl.* Trousers, pants, slacks. *Ponerse los pantalones*, (coll.) To show who is boss (generally applied to the man of the house). *Llevar los pantalones*, (coll.) To wear the pants, to be the head of a household.

Pantalla [pan-tahl'-lyah], *f.* 1. Lamp-shade. 2. Any screen or shelter. *Pantalla de chimenea*, Fire-screen. 3. A person who puts himself before a thing to shelter and conceal it. *Pantallas*, Coverings of straw, etc., to preserve plants.

Pantano [pan-tah'-no], *m.* 1. Pool of stagnant water, fen, moor, marsh, morass. 2. A reservoir or lake for the purpose of irrigation. 3. Hindrance, obstacle, difficulty.

Pantanoso, sa [pan-tah-no'-so, sah], *a.* 1. Marshy, fenny, boggy. 2. Full of difficulties, obstacles, and obstructions.

Panteísmo [pan-tay-ees'-mo], *m.* Pantheism, belief that the universe is God.

Panteísta [pan-tay-ees'-tah], *com.* Pantheist.

Panteología [pan-tay-o-lo-hee'-ah], *f.* Pantheology.

Panteón [pan-tay-on'], *m.* Pantheon, a temple of ancient Rome, now consecrated to the Holy Virgin, under the title of Our Blessed Lady of the

Rotunda. Hence, a splendid mausoleum for kings and other celebrities.

Pantera [pan-tay'-rah], *f.* 1. Panther. Felis pardus. 2. A mineral crystal inclosing foreign bodies.

Pantógrafo [pan-to'-grah-fo], *m.* Pantograph, a mathematical instrument for copying a drawing.

Pantómetro [pan-to'-may-tro], *m.* Pantometer; proportional compasses for measuring heights and angles.

Pantomima [pan-to-mee'-mah], *f.* Pantomime, a dumb show.

Pantomímico, ca [pan-to-mee'-me-co, cah], *a.* Pantomimic, pantomimical.

Pantomimo [pan-to-mee'-mo], *m.* Pantomime, a mimic, one who expresses his meaning by signs.

Pantoque [pan-to'-kay], *m.* (Naut.) Bilge or flat of the ship.

Pantorrilla [pan-tor-reel'-lyah], *f.* Calf of the leg.

Pantorrillera [pan-tor-reel-lyay'-rah], *f.* A stocking used to make the calf look big.

Pantorrilludo, da [pan-tor-reel-lyoo'-do, dah], *a.* Having large or thick calves.

Pantuflazo [pan-too-flah'-tho], *m.* Blow given with a slipper.

Pantuflo [pan-too'-flo], *m.* Slipper.

Panza [pahn'-thah], *f.* 1. Belly, paunch. 2. The projecting part of certain artificial bodies. *Panza en gloria*, (Coll.) One who is too placid and feels nothing. *Panza al trote*, (Coll.) Sponger, a parasite.

Panzada [pan-thah'-dah], *f.* 1. Belly-ful. 2. Push with the belly.

Panzón [pan-thone'], *m.* Large-bellied person.

Panzudo, da [pan-thoo'-do, dah], *a.* Big-bellied.

Pañal [pah-nyahl'], *m.* 1. Swaddling-clout or cloth. 2. Cloth in which any thing is wrapped up. 3. Tail of a shirt. *Pegarse el pañal*, To be too much smitten with any one.—*pl.* 1. Swaddling-clothes. 2. (Met.) The elements of education and instruction. *Estar en pañales*, To have little knowledge of any thing. 3. Childhood, infancy. 4. Diaper.

Pañalico, illo, ito [pah-nyah-lee'-co], *m. dim.* A small swaddling-cloth.

Pañalón [pah-nyah-lone'], *m.* One who has part of his clothes always falling off.

Pañero [pah-nyay'-ro], *m.* Woollen-draper, clothier.

Pañete [pah-nyay'-tay], *m.* 1. *dim.* of PAÑO. 2. Cloth of inferior quality or light body.—*pl.* 1. A kind of trousers worn by fishermen and tanners. 2. Linen attached to the crucifix below the waist.

Pañito, Pañizuelo [pah-nyee'-to], *m. dim.* A small cloth. (Mex. Small handkerchief; also, a Madras pocket-handkerchief.

Paño [pah'-nyo], *m.* 1. Cloth, woollen stuff. 2. Any woven stuff, whether of silk, flax, hemp, wool, or cotton. *Paño listado para pantalones*, Striped cloth for pantaloons. *Paño de seda negro*, Strong black silk serge. *Paño de tierra*, (Prov.) A small parcel of land. 3. The breadth of any stuff made of wool, silk, etc. 4. *Paños de corte*, Very fine pieces of Flemish tapestry. 5. The red colour of a bloodshot eye; livid spot on the face; a ring-worm. 6. Spot in looking-glasses, crystals, or precious stones. 7. (Naut.) Canvas, sail-cloth. *El barco va con poco paño*, The vessel carries but little sail. *Paños*, Clothes, garments. *Paños menores*, Small-clothes, under-garments; dishabille. *Paños calientes*, (Met.) Exertions to stimulate one to do what is desired; efforts to moderate any one's rigour. *Al paño*, Peeping: applied to a person looking through the drop-curtain of a theatre or listening. *Paño de sol*. (Mex.) A large square handkerchief embroidered with coloured silk, thrown over the head and shoulders as a protection from the sun, when travelling. *Paño catorceno*, A coarse kind of cloth. *Paño de encantos*, or *de rebozo*, or simply *rebozo*, A long, plain, or embroidered cotton shawl, manufactured in the country.

Pañol [pah-nyole'], *m.* (Naut.) Room in a ship where stores are kept. *Pañol de pólvora*, (Naut.) Magazine. *Pañol de proa*, (Naut.) Boatswain's store-room. *Pañol de las velas*, (Naut.) Sail-room. *Pañol del condestable*, (Naut.) Gunner's room.

Pañolero de Santa Bárbara [pah-nyo-lay'-ro], *m.* (Naut.) The gunner's yoeman. *Pañolero del pañol de proa*, (Naut.) The boatswain's yoeman.

Pañolón [pah-nyo-lone'], *m.* A long square shawl.

Pañoso, sa [pah-nyo'-so, sah], *a.* Ragged, dressed in rags.

Pañuelo [pah-nyoo-ay'-lo], *m.* Handkerchief, kerchief, hand-cloth. *Pañuelos de merino*, Merino shawls. *Pañuelos de olán batista bordados*, Cambric pocket-handkerchiefs embroidered. *Pañuelos estampados*, Printed handkerchiefs. *Pañuelo de sol*, *V.* PAÑO.

Papa [pah'-pah], *m.* 1. The Pope. 2. *f.* (Prov. and Amer.) Potato. Solanum tuberosum. 3. (Peru.) A piece of silver found where there are no mines of this metal. 4. (Zool.) The yellow-bird; American goldfinch or yellow wabbler. 5. *pl.* Pap, a soup for infants; any sort of pap; any kind of food. *V.* PUCHAS.

Papá [pah-pah'], *m.* (Coll.) Papa, a fond name for father.

Papada [pah-pah'-dah], *f.* Double-chin; gill. *Papada de buey* or *toro*, Dew-lap of oxen. *Papada de puerco*, Neck of a hog or pig.

Papadilla [pah-pah-deel'-lyah], *f.* The fleshy part under the chin.

Papado [pah-pah'-do], *m.* Popedom, pontificate, papacy.

Papafigo [pah-pah-fee'-go], *m.* The fig-pecker, beccafico, the European garden-warbler. Sylvia hortensis.

Papagaya [pah-pah-gah'-yah], *f.* Female parrot.

Papagayo [pah-pah-gah'-yo], *m.* 1. Parrot. Psittacus. 2. Red fish full of venomous prickles. *Hierba del papagayo*, Three-coloured amaranth. *Amaranthus tricolor*.

Papahigo [pah-pah-ee'-go], *m.* 1. Cap, head-gear covering the face and neck. 2. *V.* PAPAFIGO. 3. (Naut.) Course, the lower sail.

Papahuevos [pah-pah-oo-ay'-vos], *m.* Simpleton, clodpoll.

Papal [pah-pahl'], *a.* Papal, papistical. *Zapatos papales*, Clogs.

Papalina [pah-pah-lee'-nah], *f.* Cap with flaps which cover the ears.

Papalote [pah-pah-lo'-tay], *m.* (Cuba) Kite. *V.* COMETA.

Papalmente, *adv.* In a papal manner.

Papamoscas [pah-pah-mos'-cas], *m.* 1. (Orn.) *V.* MOSCARETA. 2. Ninny.

Papanatas [pah-pah-nah'-tas], *m.* Oaf, simpleton, ninny.

Papandujo, ja [pah-pan-doo'-ho, hah], *a.* (Coll.) Too soft: applied to over-ripe fruit.

Papar [pah-par'], *va.* 1. To swallow soft food without chewing. 2. (Coll.) To eat. 3. To pay little attention to things which claim much notice. *Papar moscas* or *viento*, To go with the mouth open like a fool, to gape.

Páparo [pah'-pah-ro], *m.* Gawk, gump, a rustic who stares stupidly.

Paparrabias [pah-par-rah'-be-as], *m.* & *f.* (Coll.) A testy, fretful person.

Paparrasolla [pah-par-rah-sol'-lyah], *f.* Hobgoblin, a bugbear for children.

Paparrucha [pah-par-roo'-chah], *f.* (Coll.) 1. Silliness, folly, impertinence. 2. Hoax, humbug. 3. *V.* PATRAÑA. *Contar grandes paparruchas*, To tell incredible tales.

Papasal [pah-pah-sahl'], *m.* Play among boys; any trifling amusement.

Papaya [pah-pah'-yah], *f.* Papaw, the fruit of the *Papayo*.

Papayo [pah-pah'-yo], *m.* (Bot.) Papaw tree. Carica papaya.

Pápaz [pah'-path], *m.* Christian priest, so called in Africa.

Papazgo [pah-path'-go], *m.* Popedom, pontificate.

Papel [pah-pel'], *m.* 1. Paper. 2. Paper, writing, treatise, discourse. 3. Part acted in a play; actor, actress. 4. Any thing written or printed which does not form a book. 5. A figure; a person of importance. 6. (Com.) Document; obligation.—*pl.* 1. Manuscripts. 2. Wry faces, gesticulations. *Hacer papel*, To cut a figure, to play a part, to personate. *Papel jaspeado*, Marbled paper. *Papel de estraza*, Brown paper. *Papel sellado*, Stamped paper, stamp. *Papel que se cala*, Paper which sinks. *Papel pintado*, Stained paper; paper-hanging. *Papel marquilla*, Card paper, Bristol-paper. *Papel avitelado*, Vellum paper. *Papel moneda*, Paper-money. *Papel piedra*, Artificial lithographic stone. *Papel reactivo*, Test-paper, litmus paper. *Papel marca mayor*, Royal; *marquilla*, medium; *marca*, regular, demy. *Papel de seda*, Tissue-paper. *Papel viejo*, Waste paper. *Papel de lija*, Sand-paper. *Papel secante* or *de estracilla*, Blotting-paper. *Papelucho*, A contemptible pamphlet. *Hoja de papel*, Leaf of paper. *Pliego de papel*, Sheet of paper. *Mano de papel*, Quire of paper. *Resma de papel*, Ream of paper. *Papel volante*, A small pamphlet. *Papel continuo*, Endless paper. *Papel chupón* or *teleta*, Bibulous paper. *Papel esmeril*, Emery-paper. *Papel de entapizar*, Wall-paper, paper-hanging. *Papel para excusados*, Toilet paper. *Papel majado*, Papier-maché.

Papeleador [pah-pay-lay-ah-dor'], *m.* Searcher of papers; scribbler.

Papelear [pah-pay-lay-ar'], *vn.* 1. To run over papers. 2. (Coll.) To figure, or make a figure.

Papeleo [pah-pay-lay'-o], *m.* (coll.) Red tape.

Papelera [pah-pay-lay'-rah], *f.* 1. A number of written papers placed together. 2. Writing-desk, scrutoire, paper-case.

Papelería [pah-pay-lay-ree'-ah], *f.* 1. Heap of papers without order. 2. A stationery shop.

Papelero [pah-pay-lay'-ro], *m.* Paper-maker.

Papeleta [pah-pay-lay'-tah], *f.* 1. Slip of paper on which any thing is written. 2. Case of paper in which money or sweetmeats are kept.

Papelillo [pah-pay-leel'-lyo], *m. dim.* *V.* PAPELEJO.

Papelina [pah-pay-lee'-nah], *f.* 1. A small wine-glass with a foot. 2. A very thin sort of cloth; poplin.

Papelista [pah-pay-lees'-tah], *m.* One

who is always employed about papers and writings.

Papelito [pah-pay-lee'-to], *m. dim.* A small paper, paper for a hair-curl.

Papelón [pah-pay-lone'], *m.* 1. (Aug.) A large piece of paper posted up, such as edicts and proclamations; prolix writing. 2. Pamphlet. 3. Boaster. *Escritor de papelones sueltos*, Pamphleteer.

Papelonear [pah-pay-lo-nay-ar'], *vn.* To be boastful or presumptuous.

Papera [pah-pay'-rah], *f.* 1. Wen on the throat. 2. Mumps.

Papero [pah-pay'-ro], *m.* Pot in which a child's pap is made.

Papialbillo [pah-pe-al-beel'-lyo], *m.* Weasel. Mustela, *L.*

Papila [pah-pee'-lah], *f.* (Med.) Papilla, the fine termination of nerves in some organs.

Papilar [pah-pe-lar'], *a.* Papillary, papillous, very small eminences on the skin.

Papilla [pah-peel'-lyah], *f.* 1. Pap, food for infants. 2. Guile, deceit, artifice. *Dar papilla*, To deceive by insidious caresses.

Papilonáceo, a [pah-pe-lo-nah'-thay-o, ah], *a.* Papilionaceous, butterfly-like.

Papión [pah-pe-on'], *m.* A kind of large monkey. *V.* Cefo.

Papiráceo, cea [pah-pe-rah'-thay-o, ah], *a.* Papyraceous, papery, dry and thin.

Papiro [pah-pee'-ro], *m.* (Bot.) Egyptian papyrus or paper-tree. Cyperus or papyrus.

Papirolada [pah-pe-ro-lah'-dah], *f.* Sauce made of garlic and bread. *V.* Pampirolada.

Papirotada [pah-pe-ro-tah'-dah], *f.* Fillip on the neck or face; rap at the nose.

Papirote [pah-pe-ro'-tay], *m.* (Coll.) Fillip.

Papista [pah-pees'-tah], *a.* Papist, Roman Catholic. *Más papista que el papa*, More papist than the Pope, more royalist than the king.

Papo [pah'-po], *m.* 1. The fleshy part which hangs from the chin. 2. Quantity of food given to a bird of prey at once. 3. Down of thistles. *Papo de viento*, (Naut.) A small sail. *Hablar de papo*, To speak big. *Papos*, Furbelow.

Papudo, da [pah-poo'-do, dah], *a.* Double-chinned.

Papujado, da [pah-poo-hah'-do, dah], *a.* 1. Full gorged: applied to birds and fowls. 2. Swollen, thick, elevated.

Pápula [pah'-poo-lah], *f.* Papula, a scrofulous tumour on the throat.

Paquebote [pah-kay-bo'-tay], *m.* Packet or packet-boat, a vessel appointed to carry the mail.

Paquete [pah-kay'-tay], *m.* 1. A small packet, a little bale, a parcel. 2. Bundle of letters sealed or tied up together. *Paquete de duelas*, Shooks. 3. A packet-boat.

Paquidermo, ma [pah-ke-derr'-mo, mah], *a.* Thick-skinned, pachydermatous.—*m. pl.* (Zool.) The pachydermata.

Par, *a.* 1. Equal, alike, on a par, even. *Sin par*, Matchless.—*adv.* Near. *V.* Cerca or Junto. *Par Dios* or *par diez*, A minced oath instead of *Por Dios*, By God.

Par, *m.* 1. Pair, couple. 2. Peer of the realm. 3. Handle of a bell. *Pares y nones*, Odd or even; a play. *A la par*, Jointly, equally; at par, without discount. *A pares*, By pairs, two and two. *De par en par*, Broad, open: applied to the door; openly, clearly, without obstruction. *Ir a la par*, To go halves, To have an equal share in the business. *A par de*, Near, joining; like. *Sentir a par de muerte una cosa*, To be extremely sorry for a thing. *A pares*, By pairs. *Números pares*, Round or even numbers.—*f. Las pares*, The placenta or after-birth.

Para [pah'-rah], *prep.* For, to, in order to, toward, wherefore, to the end that. *Ese hombre es para todo* or *es para nada*, That man is fit for everything or he is fit for nothing. *Para entre los dos*, Between us both. *Para evitar*, To avoid. *Dar para nieve* or *fruta*, To buy snow or fruit or to give money for snow or fruit. *¿Para qué?* Why? *Leer para sí*, To read to one's self. *Para conmigo*, Compared with me. *Para siempre*, For ever. *Para eso*, For that, for so much: used in contempt. *Para en uno*, To one and the same end. *Para esta*, You will pay me for this: uttered as a menace. *Sin qué ni para qué*, Without motive, without rhyme or reason. *Para con él no vale nada*, According to him it is worth nothing.

Parabás [pah-rah-bahs'], *m.* Thick border of a palm mat on the step of an altar.

Parabién [pah-rah-be-en'], *m.* Compliment of congratulation, felicitation. *Dar el parabién*, To congratulate, to compliment.

Parabienero [pah-rah-be-ay-nay'-ro], *m.* (Coll.) One who congratulates; a person full of compliments.

Parábola [pah-rah'-bo-lah], *f.* 1. Parable. 2. (Geom.) Parabola.

Parabólico, ca [pah-rah-bo'-le-co, cah], *a.* Parabolical, parabolic, relating to parables or parabolas.

Parabrisas [pah-rah-bree'-sahs], *m.* Windshield.

Paracaídas [pah-rah-cah-ee'-das], *m.* Parachute. *Paracaídas de frenado*, (Aer.) Drag chute.

Paracaidista [pah-rah-cah-ee-dees'-tah), *m.* Parachutist, parachute jumper. (Mex. coll.) Squatter.

Paracéntrico, ca [pah-rah-then'-tre-co, cah], *a.* Paracentric, deviating from circularity.

Paracleto, Paráclito [pah-rah-clay'-to, pah-rah'-cle-to], *m.* Paraclete, name given to the Holy Ghost.

Paracronismo [pah-rah-cro-nees'-mo], *m.* Parachronism.

Parachoques [pah-rah-cho'-kays], *m.* Fender (of an automobile).

Parada [pah-rah'-dah], *f.* 1. Halt, halting, the place where one halts. 2. The end of the motion of any thing. 3. Stop, suspension, pause. 4. Fold for cattle. 5. Relay of mules or horses. 6. Dam, bank. 7. Stakes, set, bet; any thing staked. 8. Parade, a place of parade for troops. *Doblar la parada*, (1) To double the bet or stake. (2) To double the former price. *Llamar de parada*, To hold the game at bay (in hunting).

Paradera [pah-rah-day'-rah], *f.* 1. Sluice, flood-gate. 2. A kind of fish-net.

Paradero [pah-rah-day'-ro], *m.* 1. Halting-place. 2. Term or end of any thing. *Paradero de los carros*, An inn where carts or wagons put up. *No saber el paradero de alguno*, Not to know the whereabouts of a person; not to know what has become of him.

Paradigma [pah-rah-deeg'-mah], *m.* Example, instance, paradigm.

Paradisiaco, ca [pah-rah-de-see'-ah-co, cah], *a.* Paradisiacal, relating to paradise.

Paradislero [pah-rah-dis-lay'-ro], *m.* 1. Sportsman waiting for his game. 2. Newsmonger.

Parado, da [pah-rah'-do, dah], *a.* 1. Remiss, careless, indolent, cold, inactive. 2. Without business or employment. *Coche parado*, (Met. Coll.) A balcony from which those who pass may be seen. *A lo bien parado*, A phrase indicating that a person, to avoid trouble, selects what is easier to be had, or what is better.—*pp.* of Parar.

Paradoja [pah-rah-do'-hah], *f.* Paradox.

Paradójico, ca [pah-rah-do'-he-co, cah], *a.* Paradoxical.

Paradojo, ja [pah-rah-do'-ho, hah], *a.* Paradoxical, extravagant.

Parador [pah-rah-dor'], *m.* 1. Sojourner, lodger. 2. Inn, hostelry. *Parador para turistas*, Tourist court, motel.

Parafernales (**Bienes**), [pah-rah-fer-nah'-les], *a. & m. pl.* Paraphernalia, goods which a wife brings, independent of her portion, and which are at her disposal.

Parafina [pah-rah-fee'-nah], *f.* Paraffin, a translucent solid mixture of hydrocarbons, used in candles, and in other industrial applications.

Parafrasear [pah-rah-frah-say-ar'], *va.* To paraphrase.

Paráfrasis [pah-rah'-frah-sis], *f.* Paraphrase, explanation in more intelligible terms.

Parafraste [pah-rah-frahs'-tay], *m.* Paraphrast, expounder.

Parafrástico, ca [pah-rah-frahs'-te-co, cah], *a.* Paraphrastic, paraphrastical.

Paragoge [pah-rah-go'-hay], *f.* (Gram.) Addition of a letter or syllable at the end of a word.

Paragonar [pah-rah-go-nar'], *va.* To paragon, to compare, to equal.

Paraguas [pah-rah'-goo-as], *m.* Umbrella.

Paraguay [pah-rah-goo-ah'-ee], *m.* A species of parrot.

Paraguayano, na [pah-rah-goo-ah-yah'-no, nah], *a.* Of Paraguay.

Paraíso [pah-rah-ee'-so], *m.* 1. The garden of Eden. 2. Paradise, any delightful place. 3. Paradise, heaven. *Paraíso de bobos*, Imaginary pleasures.

Paraje [pah-rah'-hay], *m.* 1. Place, residence. 2. Condition, disposition.

Paral [pah-rahl'], *m.* 1. Wooden trough in which the keel of a ship runs in launching. 2. A scaffolding-pole.

Paraláctico, ca [pah-rah-lahc'-te-co, cah], *a.* Parallactic.

Paralaje [pah-rah-lah'-hay], *f.* (Ast.) Parallax. So, too, **Paralaxi.**

Paralelepipedo [pah-rah-lay-lay-pee'-pay-do], *m.* (Geom.) Parallelepiped.

Paralelismo [pah-rah-lay-lees'-mo], *m.* Parallelism.

Paralelizar [pah-rah-lay-le-thar'], *va.* To parallel, to compare.

Paralelo, la [pah-rah-lay'-lo, lah], *a.* Parallel, similar, correspondent.

Paralelo [pah-rah-lay'-lo], *m.* Parallel, resemblance, comparison.

Paralelogramo, ma [pah-rah-lay-lo-grah'-mo, mah], *a.* Parallelogramical.

Paralelogramo, *m.* Parallelogram.

Paralipómenos [pah-rah-le-po'-may-nos], *m.* Two books of the Bible, 1st and 2d Chronicles.

Parálisis [pah-rah'-le-sis], *f.* Paralysis. *Parálisis cerebral*, Cerebral palsy. *Parálisis infantil*, Infantile paralysis, poliomyelitis.

Paralítico, ca [pah-rah-lee'-te-co, cah] *a.* *V.* Perlático.

Paralizar [pah-rah-le-thar'], *va.* 1. To paralyze, to palsy. 2. To impede moral action.

Paralogismo [pah-rah-lo-hees'-mo], *m* Paralogism, false reasoning.

Paralogizar [pah-rah-lo-he-thar'], *vn.* To paralogize, to reason sophistically.

Paramentar [pah-rah-men-tar'], *va.* To adorn, to embellish.

Paramento [pah-rah-men'-to], *m.* 1. Ornament, embellishment, facing. 2. Cloth, with which any thing is covered.

Paramera [pah-rah-may'-rah], *f.* A great extent of territory where bleak deserts abound.

Paramilitar [pah-rah-me-le-tar'], *a.* Paramilitary.

Parámetro [pah-rah'-may-tro], *m.* (Geom.) Parameter.

Páramo [pah'-rah-mo], *m.* 1. Paramo, an Alpine plain open to the winds. 2. Any place extremely cold.

Parancero [pah-ran-thay'-ro], *m.* Bird-catcher.

Parangón [pah-ran-gone'], *m.* Paragon, model, comparison.

Parangona [pah-ran-go'-nah], *f.* (Print.) Paragon type; about 20-point.

Parangonar, Parangonizar [pah-ran-go-nar'], *va.* To paragon, to match, to compare.

Paraninfico [pah-rah-neen'-fe-co], *a.* (Arch.) Applied to a style of building having statues of nymphs instead of columns.

Paraninfo [pah-rah-neen'-fo], *m.* 1. Paranymph, he who conducts the bride to the marriage solemnity; a harbinger of felicity. 2. He who announced the commencement of a course in a university.

Paranoia [pah-rah-noy'-ah], *f.* Paranoia.

Paranoico, ca [pah-rah-noy'-co, cah], *m.* & *f.* & *a.* Paranoiac.

Paranza [pah-rahn'-thah], *f.* Hut in which sportsmen lie in ambush for game.

Parao [pah-rah'-o], *m.* Large vessel in the Philippines, resembling a casco, but larger, and carrying a high cabin at the poop.

Parapeto [pah-rah-pay'-to], *m.* 1. (Mil.) Parapet, breast-work. 2. Rails or battlements on bridges and quays. *Parapetos de combate*, (Naut.) Netting, parapets in the waist of the ship.

Paraplegia [pah-rah-play'-he-ah], *f.* Paraplegia.

Parapléjico, ca [pah-rah-play'-he-co, cah], *a.* Paraplegic.

Parapoco [pah-rah-po'-co], *com.* A numskull, a blockhead.

Parapsicología [pah-rah-pse-co-lo-hee'-ah], *f.* Parapsychology.

Parar [pah-rar'], *m.* Lansquenet, a game at cards.

Parar [pah-rar'], *vn.* To stop, to halt, to desist, to give over.—*va.* 1. To stop, to detain, to put an end to the motion or action of a thing. 2. To get ready, to prepare. 3. To end, to bring to a close. 4. To treat or use ill. 5. To stake at cards. 6. To point out the game: applied to pointers. 7. To devolve, to come to the possession of. 8. To happen, to fall out. 9. To come to an end, to finish. 10. To change one thing into another. *Parar la consideración*, To take into consideration. *Parar en mal*, To end ill. *Ir a parar*, To come to, to end this or that way. *No poder parar*, Not to rest; to be uneasy. *Sin parar*, Instantly, without delay.—*vr.* 1. To stop, to halt. 2. (Littl. us.) To be prompt, to be ready. 3. To assume another character.

Pararrayo [pah-rar-rah'-yo], *m.* A lightning-rod or conductor.

Parasca [pah-rahs'-cah], *f.* A portion of the Scriptures assigned to be read in the synagogue.

Paraselene [pah-rah-say-lay'-nay], *f.* (Met.) Mock-moon.

Parasema [pah-rah-say'-mah], *f.* Figure-head of a vessel.

Parasismo [pah-rah-sees'-mo], *m.* Paroxysm, a fit.

Parasítico, ca [pah-rah-see'-te-co, cah], *a.* Parasitic, living upon another.

Parásito, ta [pah-rah'-se-to, tah], *a.* Parasitic.—*m.* Parasite. *Ruidos parásitos*, Interference, static.

Parasitología [pah-rah-se-to-lo-hee'-ah], *f.* Parasitology.

Parasol [pah-rah-sole'], *m.* Parasol. *V.* Quitasol.

Paratesis [pah-rah-tay'-sis], *f.* Prayer which the Greek bishop makes at the ceremony of confirmation.

Paratifoidea [pah-rah-tee-foy-day'-ah], *f.* (Med.) Paratyphoid, paratyphoid fever.

Parauso [pah-rah'-oo-so], *m.* Drill for metals; a mandrel.

Parazonio [pah-rah-tho'-ne-o], *m.* Broadsword without a point.

Parca [par'-cah], *f.* Fate, death.

Parcamente, *adv.* Sparingly, parsimoniously.

Parce [par'-thay], *m.* Written excuse or pardon given to grammar scholars.

Parcero [par-thay'-ro], *m.* Partner, copartner.

Parcial [par-the-ahl'], *a.* 1. Partial, inclined to favour without reason. 2. Partial, partisan, inclined to favour a party or side of the question. 3. Partial, affecting only one part; subsisting only in a part. 4. Partial, friendly, familiar. 5. Sociable, communicable.

Parcialidad [par-the-ah-le-dahd'], *f.* 1. Partiality, prejudice against or in favour of a person. 2. Friendship, familiar intercourse, sociability. 3. Party, faction.

Parcializar [par-the-ah-le-thar'], *va.* To partialize, to render partial.

Parcialmente, *adv.* Partially, familiarly, friendly.

Parcidad [par-the-dahd'], *f.* Parsimony, frugality.

Parcionero [par-the-o-nay'-ro], *m.* Partner in a business.

Parco, ca [par'-co, cah], *a.* 1. Sparing, scanty. 2. Sober, moderate.—*m.* (Prov.) *V.* Parce.

Parchazo [par-chah'-tho], *m.* 1. (Augm.) A large plaster. 2. (Met. Coll.) Deception, jest.

Parche [par'-chay], *m.* 1. A plaster for a wound or sore. 2. Parchment with which a drum is covered. 3. (Poet.) Drum. 4. Patch on the face. *Pegar un parche*, (Coll.) To serve a scurvy trick; to swindle an amount of money; to disappoint.

Pardal [par-dahl'], *a.* Clownish, rustic; cunning.—*m.* 1. (Orn.) A sparrow. 2. A leopard. 3. A crafty fellow. 4. Pardillo. 5. (Bot.) Aconite, wolf's-bane.

Pardear [par-day-ar'], *vn.* To grow gray or brownish; to become dusky.

Par diez [par de-eth']. Kind of jocular oath. *V.* Par Dios. (F.)

Pardillo [par-deel'-lyo], *m.* 1. Greater redpoll, linnet. Fringilla cannabina. 2. Robin-redbreast. 3. A kind of grape, and the wine made from it.—*a.* Grayish, brown: applied to coarse cloth.

Pardo, da [par'-do, dah], *a.* 1. Gray, drab, brown; a mixture of black and white containing some yellow or red. 2. Cloudy. *Pardo blanquizco*, Silver gray. *Oso pardo*, Brown bear. *De noche todos los gatos son pardos*, All cats are gray after dark; dim light favours the concealment of blemishes.

Pardo [par'-do], *m.* Leopard.

Pardusco, ca [par-doos'-co, cah], *a.* Light brown, grayish, grizzly.

Parear [pah-ray-ar'], *va.* To match, to pair, to couple.

Parecer [pah-ray-therr'], *m.* 1. Opinion, advice, counsel. 2. Countenance, air, mien: look.

Parecer [pah-ray-therr'], *vn.* 1. To appear, to be visible. 2. To seem 3. To form a judgment of a thing, to seem. 4. To appear, to be found: applied to a thing which was lost. 5. To judge, to approve or disapprove. *Al parecer*, Seemingly, to all appearance. *Por el bien parecer*, To save appearances, for form's sake.—*vr.* To present one's self to view; to assimilate or conform to; to be like, to resemble.

Pareciente [pah-ray-the-en'-tay], *a.* Similar, apparent.

Parecido, da [pah-ray-thee'-do, dah], *a.* & *pp.* of Parecer. 1. Appeared, found. 2. Resembling, like. 3. Good or ugly-looking, well or ill-favoured, with the adverbs *bien* or *mal*.

Pared [pah-red'], *f.* 1. Wall of bricks or stones. 2. Surface of a field of barley which is close and even. *Pared medianera*, Party-wall. *Paredes*, House or home. *Entre cuatro paredes*, Confined, retired: imprisoned. *Arrimarse a las paredes*, (Fig.) To be intoxicated. *Darse contra* or *por las paredes*, To butt against the wall, to struggle ineffectively. *Las paredes oyen*, Walls have ears. *Pegado a la pared*, Put to shame, confounded or dumfounded; used with *dejar* or *quedarse*.

Paredaño, ña [pah-ray-dah'-nyo, nyah], *a.* Having a wall between.

Paredilla [pah-ray-deel'-lyah], *f. dim.* A slight wall.

Paredón [pah-ray-done'], *m. aug.* A thick wall.

Paregórico [pah-ray-go'-re-co], *a.* Paregoric, anodyne.

Pareja [pah-ray'-hah], *f.* Pair, couple, brace; match; coupling.

Parejo, ja [pah-ray'-ho, hah], *a.* Equal, similar. *Por parejo* or *por un parejo*, On equal terms, on a par.

Parejura [pah-ray-hoo'-rah], *f.* Equality, similitude, uniformity.

Parénesis [pah-ray'-nay-sis], *f.* Admonition, precept, instruction.

Parentación [pah-ren-tah-the-on'], *f.* (Obs.) Parentation, something done or said in honour of the dead.

Parental [pah-ren-tahl'], *a.* Parental.

Parentela [pah-ren-tay'-lah], *f.* Parentage, kindred, kinsfolk.

Parentesco [pah-ren-tes'-co], *m.* 1. Cognation, kindred, relationship. 2. Union, chain, link.

Paréntesis [pah-ren'-tay-sis], *m.* 1. Parenthesis, a short digression included in a sentence. 2. Interruption or suspension of things. *Entre* or *por paréntesis*, Parenthetically, by parenthesis. *Entre paréntesis*, (Coll.) By-the-bye. 3. Parenthesis, the character ( ).

Pareo [pah-ray'-o], *m.* The act of pairing, coupling, or matching.

Parergón [pah-rer-gone'], *m.* Additional ornament.

(*Yo parezco, yo parezca*, from *Parecer*. *V.* Conocer.)

Pares [pah'-res], *f. pl.* *V.* Secundinas.

Paresia [pah-ray'-se-ah], *f.* (Med.) Paresis, slight paralysis.

Parhelia [par-ay'-le-ah], *f.* **Parhelio**, *m.* Parhelion, a mock sun.

Parhilera [par-e-lay'-rah], *f.* (Arch.) Ridge-pole, ridge-piece.

Paria [pah'-re-ah], *m.* Pariah, a Hindu outcast: one of the lowest caste.

Parias [pah'-re-as], *f.* 1. Tribute paid by one prince to another. 2. Placenta.

Parición [pah-re-the-on'], *f.* Child-bearing, parturition; season of bringing forth young.

Parida [pah-ree'-dah], *f* Woman lately delivered. *V.* PARIDO.

Paridad [pah-re-dahd'], *f.* Parity, the act of comparing; equality.

Paridera [pah-re-day'-rah], *a.* Fruitful, prolific: applied to females.—*f.* 1. Place where cattle bring forth their young. 2. Act of bringing forth young.

Parido, da [pah-ree'-do, dah], *a.* & *pp.* of PARIR. *Parida,* 1. Delivered, brought to bed. 2. Lately delivered.

Pariente, ta [pah-re-en'-tay, tah], *m.* & *f.* 1. Relation, by birth or marriage; kinsman, kinswoman. 2. Any thing resembling another. 3. (Coll.) Appellation given by husband and wife to each other.

Parietal [pah-re-ay-tahl'], *a.* Relating to a wall. (Anat.) Parietal (bone).

Parietaria [pah-re-ay-tah'-re-ah], *f.* (Bot.) Pellitory. Parietaria.

Parificar [pah-re-fe-car'], *va.* To exemplify.

Parihuela [pah-re-oo-ay'-lah], *f.* Hand-barrow, litter; stretcher.

Pario (mármol) [pah-re-o], *a.* Parian marble.

Parir [pah-reer'], *va.* 1. To bring forth a fœtus, to give birth. 2. To lay eggs, to spawn. 3. To produce, to cause. 4. To explain, to clear up; to publish. *Poner a parir,* To oblige one to perform a thing against his will; to put one to his trumps.

Parisién, siense [pah-re-se-en', se-en'-say], *m.* & *f.* & *a.* Parisian.

Parla [par'-lah], *f.* Easy delivery, loquacity, gossip.

Parladillo [par-lah-deel'-lyo], *m.* An affected style.

Parlador, ra [par-lah-dor', rah], *m.* & *f.* A chattering person.

Parladuría [par-lah-doo-ree'-ah], *f.* An impertinent speech; loquacity.

Parlamental [par-lah-men-tahl'], *a.* Parliamentary.

Parlamentar, Parlamentear [par-lah-men-tar'], *vn.* 1. To talk, to converse. 2. To parley, to treat for the surrender of a place.

Parlamentario [par-lah-men-tah'-re-o], *m.* 1. Member of parliament. 2. A person who goes to parley with an enemy. 3. A flag of truce, a cartel. 4. Parliamentarian, one who adhered to the English parliament in the time of Charles I.

Parlamentario, ria [par-lah-men-tah'-re-o, ah], *a.* Parliamentary, parliamentarian.

Parlamento [par-lah-men'-to], *m.* 1. Speech or harangue in a public assembly. 2. Parliament, the legislative assembly of Great Britain. 3. Parley. 4. A flag of truce.

Parlanchín, na [par-lan-cheen', nah], *a.* & *n.* Chatterer, jabberer.

Parlante [par-lahn'-tay], *pa.* Speaking; a talker.

Parlar [par-lar'], *va.* 1. To chatter. 2. To disclose what ought to be kept secret. *Parlar en balde,* To talk nonsense.

Parlatorio [par-lah-to'-re-o], *m.* 1. Converse, parley. 2. Parlour, the place in convents where nuns are allowed to converse with their friends.

Parlera, Parlantina [par-lay'-rah, par-lan-tee'-nah], *f.* (Coll.) A talkative little woman.

Parlería [par-lay-ree'-ah], *f.* 1. Loquacity, garrulity, gossip; tale, jest. 2. Singing or chirping of birds: purling of brooks and rivers.

Parlerito, ita [par-lay-ree'-to, tah], *a. dim.* (Coll.) Talkative, garrulous.

Parlero, ra [par-lay'-ro, rah], *a.* Loquacious, talkative.

Parlero, *m.* 1. Tale-bearer, tattler. 2. Bird that chirps and chatters. 3. Purling brook or rill. 4. Interesting conversation.

Parleta [par-lay'-tah], *f.* Conversation on the weather, or on trifling subjects.

Parlón, na [par-lone', nah], *a.* Loquacious, garrulous.

Parlotear [par-lo-tay-ar'], *vn.* To prattle, to prate, to chatter, to gossip.

Parloteo [par-lo-tay'-o], *m.* Prattle, talk.

Parmesano, na [par-may-sah'-no, nah], *a.* Parmesan, of Parma.

Parnaso [par-nah'-so], *m.* 1. (Poet.) Parnassus, Helicon. 2. A collection of selected poems. 3. An assemblage of poets.

Paro [pah'-ro], *m.* 1. Lockout, suspension of work. *Paro forzoso,* Layoff (in a factory, etc.) 2. (Orn.) Titmouse.

Parodia [pah-ro-de-ah], *f.* Parody.

Parodiar [pah-ro-de-ar'], *va.* To parody.

Paródico, ca [pah-ro'-de-co, cah], *a.* Parodical.

Parola [pah-ro'-lah], *f.* 1. (Coll.) Eloquence, fluency, volubility. 2. Chat, idle talk.

Pároli [pah'-ro-lee], *m.* Double of what was laid in stakes at the game of bank.

Parolina, *f.* *V.* PAROLA.

Parónimo, ma [pah-ro'-ne-mo, mah], *a.* Paronymous; words cognate or alike.

Paronomasia [pah-ro-no-mah'-se-ah], *f.* Paronomasia, a rhetorical figure.

Parótida [pah-ro'-te-dah], *f.* 1. A parotid gland. 2. Swelling of the parotid glands, mumps.

Paroxismal [pah-rok-sis-mahl'], *m.* Paroxysmal.

Paroxismo [pah-rok-sees'-mo], *m.* Paroxysm. *V.* PARASISMO.

Parpadear [par-pah-day-ar'], *vn.* To wink, to open and shut the eyes by turns.

Párpado [par'-pah-do], *m.* The eye-lid.

Parpalla [par-pahl'-lyah], *f.* A milled copper piece, valued at two cuartos, or one halfpenny English.

Parpar [par-par'], *m.* Quacking, the cry of a duck.

Parque [par'-kay], *m.* 1. Park, an inclosed wood or ornamental grounds. 2. Park of artillery, park of provisions.

Parquedad [par-kay-dahd'], *f.* Parsimony.

Parra [par'-rah], *f.* 1. Vine raised on stakes or nailed to a wall. 2. Earthen jar or pot, broad and low, with handles.

Párrafo [par'-rah-fo], *m.* Paragraph, a distinct part of a discourse; a mark (§) in printing; ¶ in English.

Parragón [par-rah-gone'], *m.* Standard silver for assayers.

Parral [par-rahl'], *m.* 1. Vine abounding with shoots for want of dressing, and the place where there are such vines. 2. A large earthen jar for honey.

Parrar [par-rar'], *vn.* To extend, to spread out in branches and bowers.

Parricida [par-re-thee'-dah], *com.* Parricide, one who kills his father or mother, or any other person to whom he owes reverence.

Parricidio [par-re-thee'-de-o], *m.* Parricide, murder of a father or mother, or of any person to whom reverence is due.

Parrilla [par-reel'-lyah], *f.* An earthen jug with broad base and narrow neck. —*pl.* Gridiron, broiler, toaster; grate, furnace grating.

Parriza [par-ree'-thah], *f.* Wild vine.

Párroco [par'-ro-co], *m.* Rector or incumbent of a parish; a parson.

Parrón, *m.* *V.* PARRIZA.

Parroquia [par-ro'-ke-ah], *f.* 1. Parish, the parochial church. 2. Parish, the precinct or territory of a parochial church. 3. The spiritual jurisdiction of a rector or parson in his parish. 4. The clergy of a parish.

Parroquial [par-ro-ke-ahl'], *a.* Parochial.—*f.* Parochial church.

Parroquialidad [par-ro-ke-ah-le-dahd'], *f.* Parochial right, the right of a parishioner.

Parroquiano [par-ro-ke-ah'-no], *m.* 1. Parishioner. 2. Customer, an accustomed buyer or patron.

Parroquiano, na [par-ro-ke-ah'-no, nah], *a.* Belonging to a parishioner. *V.* PARROQUIAL.

Parsi [par'-se], *a.* & *m.* 1. Parsee, a Zoroastrian. 2. The sacred language of Persia (before being mixed with Arabic).

Parsimonia [par-se-mo'-ne-ah], *f.* Economy, frugality, husbandry, temperance.

Parte [par'-tay], *f.* 1. Part, a portion of some whole. 2. Part, a determinate quantity of some aggregate number. *Parte alicuanta* or *alícuota,* Aliquant or aliquot part. 3. Part, portion, share, lot. 4. District, territory, place. 5. Part, the right or left side. 6. Part, side, every one of two or more things opposite to each other. 7. Part, the sense given to words or acts. *Echar una cosa a buena* or *mala parte,* To take a thing in a good or bad sense. 8. Party, a person concerned in a business with others. 9. (Law) Party, one of two litigants. 10. It is used for the time present with reference to the past. *De ocho días a esta parte,* Within these last eight days. 11. Part, character in a play.—*m.* 1. Royal or official communication. 2. Receiving-house for the post-office. 3. Official notice of mails. 4. Despatch, telegram, urgent message. *Parte por parte,* Part by part, distinctly. *A partes* or *en partes,* By parts, or in parts. *De parte a parte,* From side to side, through. *De parte,* By orders, by command. *En parte,* Partly, in part. *Ir a la parte,* To go halves, to share alike.—*f. pl.* 1. Parts, talents, endowments. 2. Privy parts. 3. Party, faction. *Por todas partes,* On all hands, on all sides.—*adv.* In part, partly.

Partear [par-tay-ar'], *va.* To deliver or assist women in childbirth.

Partenópeo, pea [par-tay-no'-pay-o, ah], *a.* Parthenopean, Neapolitan.

Partera [par-tay'-rah], *f.* Midwife.

Partería [par-tay-ree'-ah], *f.* Midwifery, obstetrics.

Partero [par-tay'-ro], *m.* Obstetrician, man-midwife, accoucheur.

Partesana [par-tay-sah'-nah], *f.* Partizan; a kind of halberd.

Partesanero [par-tay-sah-nay'-ro], *m.* Pikeman.

Partible [par-tee'-blay], *a.* Divisible, separable, partible.

Partición [par-te-the-on'], *f.* Partition, division, distribution, lot.

Particionero, ra [par-te-the-o-nay'-ro, rah], *a.* Participant, having a part in a business.

Participable [par-te-the-pah'-blay], *a.* (Littl. us.) Participable.

Participación [par-te-the-pah-the-on'], *f.* 1. Participation, sharing in common. (Com.) Copartnership. *Cuenta en participación*, Joint account. 2. Participation, communication, conversation.

Participante [par-te-the-pahn'-tay], *pa.* Sharing; participant.

Participar [par-te-the-par'], *va.* & *n.* 1. To give notice, to inform. 2. To participate, to partake, to share. 3. To partake, to participate, to have something of the property, nature, claim, right, etc.

Partícipe [par-tee'-the-pay], *a.* Participant, sharing.

Participial [par-te-the-pe-ahl'], *a.* (Gram.) Participial.

Participio [par-te-thee'-pe-o], *m.* (Gram.) Participle.

Partícula [par-tee'-coo-lah], *f.* 1. Particle, small part. 2. (Gram.) Particle. 3. Molecule. *Partícula beta*, Beta particle.

Particular [par-te-coo-lar'], *a.* 1. Particular, peculiar, special. 2. Particular, odd, distinguished from others. 3. Particular, individual, single, not general. 4. Applied to a play represented in a private theatre. *En particular*, Particularly, in particular.

Particular [par-te-coo-lar'], *m.* 1. A private gentleman. 2. A peculiar matter or subject treated upon; topic.

Particularidad [par-te-coo-lah-re-dahd'], *f.* 1. Particularity, peculiarity. 2. Friendship, intimacy.

Particularizar [par-te-coo-lah-re-thar'], *va.* To particularize, to detail.—*vr.* To singularize, to be particular.

Particularmente, *adv.* Particularly, especially, namely.

Partida [par-tee'-dah], *f.* 1. Departure, going away from a place. 2. Death, decease. 3. Party of soldiers. 4. Item in an account, charge, entry, record, annotation. 5. Parcel, lot. 6. Game at play. 7. (Naut.) Crew of a ship, gang. *¡Buena partida!* Excellent conduct! *Partida doble*, (Com.) Double entry. *Partida simple*, Single entry (in book-keeping). *Partida serrana*, Unjust and disloyal behaviour.—*pl.* 1. Parts, talents, accomplishments. 2. The laws of Castile, compiled by King Alphonso the Tenth.

Partidamente, *adv.* Separately, distinctly.

Partidario [par-te-dah'-re-o], *m.* 1. Partisan, the commander of a party of troops. 2. Party-man, adherent to a faction.—*a.* Having the care of a certain district: applied to physicians and surgeons.

Partido, da [par-tee'-do, dah], *a.* 1. Free, liberal, munificent. 2. (Her.) Party, parted, or parti per pale.—*pp.* of PARTIR.

Partido [par-tee'-do], *m.* 1. Party, a number of persons confederated. 2. Advantage, profit, utility. 3. Favour, protection, interest. 4. A game, a contest, a match. 5, Odds given to one in a game; party engaged to play a game. 6. Treaty, agreement; terms proposed for adjusting a difference. 7. One of the districts into which provinces are divided in Spain. 8. District intrusted to the care of a physician or surgeon. 9. Proper means for the performance of what is to be done. 10. Interest or one's own convenience. *Mujer del partido*, Woman of the town, strumpet. *Tomar partido*, (1) To embrace a resolution; to resolve. (2) To engage or enlist in a party.

Partidor [par-te-dor'], *m.* 1. Parter, divider. *Partidor de leña*, Cleaver, the instrument and the workman employed in cleaving wood. 2. Bodkin to divide the hair. 3. (Arith.) *V.* DIVISOR.

Partija [par-tee'-hah], *f.* *V.* PARTICIÓN.

Partil [par-teel'], *a.* Applied to the astrological aspects.

Partimento, Partimiento [par-te-men'-to], *m.* *V.* PARTICIÓN.

Partir [par-teer'], *va.* 1. To part, to divide, to sever, to disunite, to separate, to cut, to cleave. 2. To break by violence. 3. To part, to share, to divide, to distribute. 4. To crack the stones of fruit. 5. To attack in combat or battle. 6. To resolve. 7. (Arith.) To divide. 8. To divide a bee-hive in two, at the proper season. —*vn.* To part, to depart, to march, to set out on a journey.—*vr.* To be divided in opinion. *Partir la diferencia*, To split the difference. *Partir al puño*, (Naut.) To gripe, to carry a weatherly helm. *Partir las amarras*, (Naut.) To part the cable. *Partir por entero*, To carry off the whole: to divide a number. *Partir mano*, To desist, to abandon. *Partirse el alma*, To die; to die broken-hearted. *Partir abierto*, To uncover a bee-hive that it may swarm. *Partir cerrado*, To divide a bee-hive when it is full.

Partitivo, va [par-te-tee'-vo, vah], *a.* (Gram.) Partitive.

Partitura [par-te-too'-rah], *f.* The musical score. *Partitura de una ópera*, The full score of an opera.

Parto [par'-to], *m.* 1. Childbirth, parturition. 2. Newborn child. 3. Any natural production. 4. Any literary composition. 5. Any particular thing that may happen, and is hoped to be of importance.

Parturiente [par-too-re-en'-tay], *a.* Parturient.

Párulis [pah'-roo-lis], *m.* Gumboil, an abscess of the gums.

Parva [par'-vah], *f.* 1. Unthrashed corn laid in heaps to be thrashed. 2. Multitude, large quantity. 3. *V.* PARVEDAD, 2d def.

Parvada [par-vah'-dah], *f.* (Prov.) Place for unthrashed corn.

Parvedad, Parvidad [par-vay-dahd'], *f.* 1. Littleness, minuteness. 2. Snack, bite of food taken in the morning of a fast day.

Parvificencia [par-ve-fe-then'-the-ah], *f.* (Obs.) Parsimony, sordid avarice.

Parvo, va [par'-vo, vah], *a.* Small, little.

Parvulez [par-voo-leth'], *f.* Smallness, small size.

Parvulico, ica, illo, illa, ito, ita [par-voo-lee'-co], *a. dim.* Very little.

Párvulo, la [par'-voo-lo, lah], *a.* Very small; innocent; humble, low.—*n.* A child.

Pasa [pah'-sah], *f.* 1. Raisin, dried grape. 2. Passage of birds.—*pl.* The curled hair of negroes.

Pasabalas [pah-sah-bah'-las], *m.* (Mil.) Ball calibre-gauge.

Pasacalle [pah-sah-cahl'-lyay], *m.* Music played on the guitar and other instruments in the streets. An ancient dance.

Pasacampana [pah-sah-cam-pah'-nah], *f.* (Vet.) A tumour which forms on the calcaneum of horses.

Pasada [pah-sah'-dah], *f.* 1. Passage, the act of passing. 2. Pace, step; measure of five feet. 3. A malicious action to some one's hurt. 4. (Ant.) Competency, sufficiency. *Dar pasada*, To tolerate, to permit. *De pasada*, On the way, in passing, hastily, cursorily.

Pasadera [pah-sah-day'-rah], *f.* 1. A stepping-stone. 2. Sieve, strainer. 3. (Naut.) Furling-line of spun-yarn.

Pasaderamente, *adv.* Passably.

Pasadero, ra [pah-sah-day'-ro, rah], *a.* 1. Supportable, sufferable. 2. Passable, tolerably good.—*m.* *V.* PASADERA.

Pasadillo [pah-sah-deel'-lyo], *m.* A small embroidery on both sides of a piece of stuff.

Pasadizo [pah-sah-dee'-tho], *m.* A narrow passage or covered way. *Pasadizo continuado de cuartos*, A row of rooms contiguous to each other.

Pasado, da [pah-sah'-do, dah], *pp.* of PASAR. *Lo pasado pasado*, What is past is forgotten and forgiven.—*m.* 1. Past time. 2. A (military) deserter. —*pl.* Ancestors. *V.* ASCENDIENTES and ANTEPASADOS.

Pasador [pah-sah-dor'], *m.* 1. One who carries a thing from one place to another. 2. A smuggler, one who deals in contraband goods. 3. Bolt of a lock. 4. A woman's brooch. 5. Cylinder which founders use for making tubes without soldering. 6. A clock peg. 7. Bolt-pin, linch-pin, cotter. 8. A shoemaker's tool for smoothing the inside of a shoe. 9. A sieve. 10. A piece of a loom, snecket.—*pl.* 11. Irons placed between the tympanum and the frisket. 12. Cord straps. 13. (Naut.) Marline-spike.

Pasagonzalo [pah-sah-gon-thah'-lo], *m.* (Coll.) Flip, a slight blow, briskly given.

Pasahilo [pah-sah-ee'-lo], *m.* Thread-guide.

Pasaje [pah-sah'-hay], *m.* 1. Passage, the act of passing. 2. Road, way, the place of passing. 3. Passage-money. 4. (Coll.) Event, accident, a piece of business. 5. (Mus.) Transition or change of voice. 6. Passage of a book or writing.

Pasajeramente, *adv.* Transiently, going along, without detention.

Pasajero, ra [pah-sah-hay'-ro, rah], *a.* 1. Applied to a common thoroughfare. 2. Transient, transitory, fugitive. 3. Applied to birds of passage.

Pasajero, ra [pah-sah-hay'-ro, rah], *m.* & *f.* Traveller, passenger. *Pasajero de cámara*, Cabin passenger. *Pasajero de proa, de bodega* or *combés*, Steerage passenger.

Pasamanar [pah-sah-mah-nar'], *va.* To make ribbons, trimmings, lace, etc.

Pasamanera [pah-sah-mah-nay'-rah], *f.* Lace-woman, lace-maker.

Pasamanería [pah-sah-mah-nay-ree'-ah], *f.* The trade of a lace-man; the profession of a fancy-trimming maker, twister, or ribbon-weaver, and the place where those things are sold; passementerie work.

Pasamanero [pah-sah-mah-nay'-ro], *m.* Lace-maker, lace-man, a fancy-trimming maker, a twister, a ribbon-maker.

Pasamanillo [pah-sah-mah-neel'-lyo], *m. dim.* A narrow lace; a small twist for the edge of a coat.

Pasamano [pah-sah-mah'-no], *m.* 1. Balustrade. 2. Kind of lace or edging for clothes; passementerie. 3. (Naut.) Gangway.

Pasamiento [pah-sah-me-en'-to], *m.* (Obs.) Passage, transit.

Pasante [pah-sahn'-tay], *m.* 1. Assistant or student of a physician or lawyer. 2. A student who acts the teacher or lecturer to beginners. 3. (Her.) Passant: applied to animals in a shield appearing to walk. 4. Game at cards. *Pasante de pluma*, An attorney's or barrister's clerk who is learning the profession.

Pasantia [pah-san-tee'-ah], *f.* Profession of a student of the law or medicine, who practises under the direction of another.

Pasapán [pah-sah-pahn'], *m.* (Coll.) *V.* GARGÜERO.

Pasapasa [pah-sah-pah'-sah], *m.* Legerdemain, slight of hand, hocus-pocus.

Pasaporte [pah-sah-por'-tay], *m.* 1. Passport. 2. (Mil.) Furlough. 3. A free license to do any thing.

Pasar [pah-sar'], *vn.* 1. To pass, to move from place to place. 2. To go or pass in any manner or to any end, to go through. 3. To go to any determinate place. 4. To make way for a person, inviting him to come forward. 5. To be in motion, or to steer from one place to another: speaking of immaterial things. 6. With the preposition *a* and some infinitives, to proceed to. 7. To ascend, to be promoted to a higher post. 8. To pass away, to elapse: speaking of time. 9. To travel through a place or country. 10. To die. 11. To pass, to become current, as money. 12. To be marketable: speaking of goods. 13. To pass, to be in a certain state, speaking of health, conveniences of life, etc. 14. To pass, to be spent, to go away progressively. 15. To be executed before a notary.—*va.* 1. To convey from one place to another. 2. To send or carry a thing from one part to another. 3. To pierce, to penetrate, to go through. 4. To pass beyond the limit of the place of destination. 5. To change for better or worse, from one thing to another. 6. To pass or advance from one class to another. 7. To exceed in number, quantity, quality, or abilities. 8. To depart, to decease. 9. To suffer, to bear, to undergo. 10. To strain or percolate liquor, to clarify it. 11. Not to censure or find fault with any thing. 12. To pass over in silence, to omit. 13. To dissemble, to overlook. 14. To stop, to terminate. 15. To run over one's lesson, to rehearse; to run over a book. 16. To carry one thing above another, so as to touch it lightly. 17. To teach privately; to study privately with some professor. 18. To present an act, charter, or privilege to be confirmed. 19. To handle an affair with judgment and prudence. 20. To draw up an instrument. 21. To dry by the sun or in an oven.—*v. imp.* To pass, to happen, to turn out.—*vr.* 1. To go over to another party. 2. To cease, to finish; to lose its force. 3. Not to shut well. 4. To be spoiled: applied to fruit. 5. To pass unimproved: applied to a favourable opportunity. *El papel se pasa,* The paper blots. 6. To surpass, to exceed. *Pasar a cuchillo.* To put to the sword, to kill. *Pasar muestra* or *revista,* To muster. *Pasar de largo,* (1) To pass by without stopping. (2) (Met.) Not to reflect upon what one reads. *Pasar por las armas,* To shoot a soldier. *Pasa al frente,* (Coll.) This sum is carried forward. *Pasa a la vuelta,* This sum is carried over. *Pasar el dinero,* To count over money. *Pasar el tiempo,* To loiter, to pass away time. *Pasar los ojos* or *la vista,* To run over a writing carelessly. *Pasar por alto,* To overlook, to overpass, not to take notice. *Pasar algo por uno,* To have experienced a thing. *Pasar en claro alguna cosa,* To omit any mention of a thing. *Pasar por encima,* To overcome difficulties. *Ir pasando,* To be about the same, neither better nor worse. *Pasar plaza,* To be reputed something which one is not. *¿ Cómo lo pasa Vd.?* How do you do? *Pasar un cabo,* (Naut.) To reeve a rope, to pass it through a block or hole. *Pasarse con poco,* To be satisfied with a little. *Pasarse de bueno,* To be too good. *Pasarse de cortés,* To be over-polite. *Un buen pasar,* A competency or maintenance.

Pasatiempo [pah-sah-te-em'-po], *m.* Pastime, diversion, amusement, game.

Pasaturo, *m.* (Obs.) A student with whom another repeated lectures on any art or science.

Pasavante [pah-sah-vahn'-tay], *m.* 1. Safe-conduct furnished to a ship by the commander of the enemy's forces. 2. A permit for articles of commerce.

Pasavolante [pah-sah-vo-lahn'-tay], *m.* An inconsiderate speech or action.

Pasavoleo [pah-sah-vo-lay'-o], *m.* Ball which passes the line in bowling.

Pascasio [pas-cah'-se-o], *m.* Student who goes to pass the holidays at home.

Pascua [pahs'-coo-ah], *f.* 1. Passover, a feast among the Jews. 2. Easter, the day on which the Saviour's resurrection is commemorated. 3. (Met.) Christmas. 4. (Coll.) Any festival of the church which lasts three days. *Decir los nombres de las pascuas,* To use injurious language. *Estar como una pascua,* To be as merry as a cricket. *Hacer pascua,* To begin to eat meat after Lent. *Santas pascuas,* Be it so.

Pascual [pas-coo-ahl'], *a.* Paschal, relating to Easter.

Pascuilla [pas-coo-eel'-lyah], *f.* The first Sunday after Easter.

Pase [pah'-say], *m.* 1. An act of a court of justice which orders a decree to be expedited and carried into effect. 2. A written permission to sell or carry goods freely from place to place. 3. A kind of passport.

Paseadero [pah-say-ah-day'-ro], *m.* Walk, avenue, public walk.

Paseador, ra [pah-say-ah-dor', rah], *m.* & *f.* A walker: applied to one who walks much, or to a horse.

Paseante [pah-say-ahn'-tay], *m.* & *f.* **1. Walker, one who goes for a walk. 2. Idler, lazy vagabond.**

Pasear [pah-say-ar'], *va.* & *vn.* 1. To walk, to take the air, to exercise. 2. To be at the walk, to be in the field. 3. To move at the slowest pace: applied to a horse. 4. To walk about, to bring out to walk. 5. To take the air or exercise on horseback or in a coach.—*vr.* 1. To walk for exercise or amusement. 2. To loiter, to wander idly, to gape about. *Pasear la calle,* To court a lady in the street. *Pasear las calles,* To be whipped through the streets by order of a magistrate. *Anda, ande Vd.* or *váyase Vd. a pasear* Go along: an expression of displeasure.

Paseata [pah-say-ah'-tah], *f.* (Coll.) A walk, airing, drive.

Paseo [pah-say'-o], **1. Ride, drive. 2. Walk, outing.** ***Paseo al aire libre,*** **Outdoor walk.** ***Paseo campestre,*** **Picnic.** ***Ir de paseo,*** **To go walking, to go on an outing.**

Pasera [pah-say'-rah], *f.* (Prov.) Place where raisins are dried, and the act of drying them.

Pasibilidad [pah-se-be-le-dahd'], *f.* Passibleness, susceptibility to impressions from external agents.

Pasible [pah-see'-blay], *a.* Passible, capable of suffering.

Pasicorto, ta [pah-se-cor'-to, tah], *a.* Short-stepped: applied to horses.

Pasiego, ga [pah-se-ay'-go, gah], *m.* & *f.* A highlander of Santander, celebrated for his sturdiness, and the women as the best wet-nurses.

Pasiflora [pah-se-flo'-rah], *f.* The botanical name of the passion-flower.

Pasilargo, ga [pah-se-lar'-go, gah], *a.* Long-stepped: applied to horses.

Pasillo [pah-seel'-lyo], *m.* 1. (Dim.) A short step. 2. A small, narrow passage. 3. Basting-stitch.

Pasión [pah-se-on'], *f.* 1. Passion, any effect caused by external agency; susceptibility of effect from external action; the act of suffering torments. 2. Passion, the last suffering of the Redeemer. 3. Passion, affection or violent emotion of the mind, anger. 4. Passion, ardent inclination, fondness. *Pasión de ánimo,* A passion or emotion of the soul; a broken heart. *Con pasión,* Passionately.

Pasionaria [pah-se-o-nah'-re-ah], *f.* (Bot.) Passion-flower: a climbing-vine, native of Peru, where it is more often called *ñorbo.*

Pasionario [pah-se-o-nah'-re-o], *m. pl.* Passion-book, from which the passion is sung in holy week.

Pasionero [pah-se-o-nay'-ro], *m.* One who sings the passion. *Pasioneros,* Priests who attend patients in the hospital of Saragossa.

Pasionista, *m.* (Prov.) *V.* PASIONERO.

Pasitamente, *adv.* *V.* PASITO.

Pasito [pah-see'-to], *adv.* Gently, softly. *Pasito a pasito,* Very leisurely or gently.

Pasito [pah-see'-to], *m. dim.* A short step.

Pasitrote [pah-se-tro'-tay], *m.* Short trot of horses alone.

Pasiva [pah-see'-vah], *f.* (Gram.) Passive voice of the verb.

Pasivamente, *adv.* Passively.

Pasivo, va [pah-see'-vo, vah], *a.* 1. Passive, receiving impression from some external agent. 2. Passive, unresisting, not acting. 3. (Gram.) Passive. *Voz pasiva,* Passive voice; capable of being elected.

Pasivo, *m.* (Com.) Liabilities.

Pasmar [pas-mar'], *va.* 1. To cause a spasm, or a suspension or loss of the senses. 2. To benumb, to make torpid; to stupefy, to stun. 3. To chill, to deaden.—*vn.* To marvel, to wonder.—*vr.* 1. To wonder, to be astonished. 2. To suffer from lockjaw.

Pasmarota, Pasmarotada [pas-mah-ro'-tah], *f.* 1. A feigned spasm, often used by beggars. 2. Admiration or astonishment without cause or motive.

Pasmazón [pas-mah-thone'], *f.* (Mex.) Swelling upon the loins of horses, caused by the saddle or harness.

Pasmo [pahs'-mo], *m.* 1. Spasm, convulsion; violent and involuntary contraction. 2 (Med.) Lockjaw, tetanus. 3. Astonishment, amazement, admiration. 4. Object of admiration or astonishment. *De pasmo, V.* PASMOSAMENTE.

Pasmosamente, *adv.* Wonderfully, astonishingly.

Pasmoso, sa [pas-mo'-so, sah], *a.* Marvellous, wonderful.

Paso, sa [pah'-so, sah], *a.* & *pp. irr.* of PASAR. Dried: applied to fruit.

Paso [pah'-so], *m.* 1. Pace, step, a measure of space. 2. Passage, the act of passing. 3. Pace, gait, manner of walking. 4. Pace, pacing, a motion of mules and horses. 5. Flight of steps. 6. Passage, lobby, passage for a room; pass, a narrow entrance. 7. Step, measure or diligence in the pursuit of an affair: commonly used in the plural. 8. Step, instance of conduct, mode of life. 9. Footstep. 10. Passport, license, pass. 11. Explanation given by a master or usher. 12. Passage in a book or writing. 13. Progress, advance, improvement. 14. Death, decease. 15. Image carried about during holy week. *Paso de garganta*, (Mus.) Trill, quaver.—*pl.* 1. Running stitches with which clothes are basted. 2. Conduct, proceedings. steps.—*adv.* Softly, gently. *Paso a paso*, Step by step; slowly. *A buen paso*, At a good rate, step, or gait. *A cada paso*, At every step, frequently. *A ese paso*, At that rate. *Al paso*, Without delay, instantly; going along; in the manner of, like. *A ese paso el día es un soplo*, At this rate wealth soon flits. *A paso de buey*, Very slowly. *Andar en malos pasos*, To follow evil paths. *Apretar el paso*, To hasten. *Salir del paso* or *del vado*, To get out of a difficulty. *A pocos pasos*, At a short distance; with little care. *Dar paso*, To clear the way; to promote, to facilitate. *De paso*, Passing by; lightly, briefly, by the way; at the same time, at once. *Vista de paso*, A cursory view. *Más que de paso*, Hastily, in a hurry. *Al paso que*, At the same time that, whilst.

Paspié [pas-pe-ay'], *m.* A kind of dance.

Pasquín [pas-keen'], *m.* Pasquinade, lampoon.

Pasquinada [pas-kee-nah'-dah], *f.* Pasquinade.

Pasquinar [pas-ke-nar'], *va.* To ridicule, to lampoon, to satirize.

Pasta [pahs'-tah], *f.* 1. Paste, any viscous or tenacious mixture. 2. Paste, flour and water boiled; the mass from which are made vermicelli and other things for soup. 3. Pie-crust. 4. Bullion, mass of gold or silver for coining. 5. In bookbinding, pasteboard covered with leather burnished or mottled; roan leather. 6. Pulp from which paper or cardboard is made. 7. *V.* Empaste. 8. *Pasta* or *buena pasta*, Excessive meekness or mildness. *Media pasta*, Half-leather binding.

Pasta de dientes [pahs'-tah day de-ayn'-tess], *f.* Toothpaste.

Pasta dentífrica [pahs'-tah den-tee'-free-cah], *f.* Toothpaste.

Pastar [pas-tar'], *vn.* To pasture, to graze.—*va.* To lead cattle to graze, to feed cattle.

Pasteca [pas-tay'-cah], *f.* (Naut.) Snatch-block.

Pastel [pas-tel'], *m.* 1. Pie, pastry. *Pastel de carne* or *de picadillo*, Mince pie. *Pastel de manzana, etc.*, Apple pie, etc. 2. (Bot.) Woad. Isatis tinctoria. 3. Trick in the dealing of cards. 4. Meeting, assembly for some secret design. 5. (Print.) Mass of types to be recast; words too black, having too much ink. *Pastel de glasto*, Crayon for drawing. 6. (Art) Pastel (drawing).

Pastelada [pas-tay-lah'-dah], *f.* Plot, snare.

Pastelear [pas-tay-lay-ar'], *vn.* To trim politically; to try to secure popularity by time-serving.

Pastelera [pas-tay-lay'-rah], *f.* Pastrycook's wife; she who makes and sells pastry.

Pastelería [pas-tay-lay-ree'-ah], *f.* 1. Pastrycook's shop. 2. Pastry, pies or baked paste.

Pastelero [pas-tay-lay'-ro], *m.* 1. Pastrycook. 2. A political trimmer.

Pastelillo, ito [pas-tay-leel'-lyo], *m. dim.* A little pie, a patty. *Pastelillo*, Tart; a kind of pastry.

Pastelón [pas-tay-lone'], *m. aug.* A large pie.

Pasterización [pas-tay-re-tha-the-on'], *f.* Pasteurization.

Pasterizar [pas-tay-re-thar'], *va.* Pasteurize.

Pastero [pas-tay'-ro], *m.* One who throws the mass of crushed olives into baskets

Pastilla [pas-teel'-lyah], *f.* 1. Tablet, lozenge. 2. Drop, candy. *Pastilla de menta*, Peppermint drop. *Pastilla para la tos*, Cough drop.

Pastinaca [pas-te-nah'-cah], *f.* 1. (Bot.) Parsnip. Pastinaca. 2. (Zool.) Sting-ray. Raia pastinaca.

Pasto [pahs'-to], *m.* 1. Pasture, the act of grazing. 2. Pasture, the grass which serves for the feed of cattle. 3. A pasture-ground. 4. Any pabulum, food, aliment, or nourishment. *Pasto espiritual*, Spiritual nourishment. *A pasto*, Abundantly, plentifully, at meals, as ordinary meat or drink. *A todo pasto*, Said of aliment or drink prescribed as the only one that may be used.

Pastor, ra [pas-tor', rah], *m. & f.* 1. Shepherd, shepherdess, one who tends sheep. 2. Pastor, shepherd, a clergyman. 3. An American fresh-water fish.

Pastoral [pas-to-rahl'], *a.* Pastoral, rural, rustic.—*f.* Pastoral, a poem in which the speakers assume the character of shepherds; an idyll.

Pastoralmente, *adv.* Pastorally, rustically, shepherd-like.

Pastorcico, illo, ito [pas-tor-thee'-co], *m. dim.* A little shepherd.

Pastorear [pas-to-ray-ar'], *va.* 1. To graze, to pasture; to bring cattle to pasture. 2. To feed souls with sound doctrine.

Pastorela [pas-to-ray'-lah], *f.* Pastoral, a simple melody in rustic style.

Pastoreo [pas-to'-ray-o], *m.* Pasturing, act of tending flocks.

Pastoría [pas-to-ree'-ah], *f.* A pastoral or rural life, pastors.

Pastoril [pas-to-reel'], *a.* Pastoral.

Pastorilmente, *adv.* *V.* Pastoralmente.

Pastosidad [pas-to-se-dahd'], *f.* Mellowness, softness.

Pastoso, sa [pas-toh'-so, sah], *a.* 1. Soft, mellow, doughy, clammy. 2. Painted or drawn with a coloured crayon or pencil.

Pastura [pas-too'-rah], *f.* 1. Pasture, the grass on which animals feed. 2. Fodder, dry food for cattle.

Pasturaje [pas-too-rah'-hay], *m.* 1. Pasturage, a common ground on which cattle graze. 2. Duty paid for the right of grazing cattle on a certain ground.

Pasudo, da [pah-soo'-do, dah], *a.* (Amer.) Kinky, woolly, curly, as a Negro's hair.

Pata [pah'-tah], *f.* 1. Foot and leg of beasts. 2. Duck, the female of the drake. 3. A barilla-producing plant of the beaches of the Canary Islands. *Pata de cabra*, (1) A crowbar, a nail-puller. (2) A shoemaker's heel-burnisher. *Pata de gallina*, A radial crack in trees; the beginning of rot. *Pata de gallo*, (1) A ridiculous saying, a bull (used generally with *salir con*). (2) Crow's-foot, a wrinkle near the eye. (3) Stupidity, silliness. *Pata de pobre*, An ulcerated leg. *A la pata coja*, Hopscotch, a game played by hopping on one foot over a diagram upon the ground. *A pata*, On foot. *A pata llana* or *a la pata la llana*, Plainly, without ornament or affectation. *Patas arriba*, Reversed, topsy-turvy, heels-over-head; upside down, in disorder. *Pata es la traviesa*, Tit for tat, the biter bitten. *Quedar, salir*, or *ser, pata* or *patas*, To be a tie.

Pataca [pah-tah'-cah], *f.* 1. (Bot.) Jerusalem artichoke. Helianthus tuberosus. 2. Copper coin worth *two cuartos*.

Pataco, ca [pah-tah'-co, cah], *a.* *V.* Patán.

Patacón [pah-tah-cone'], *m.* Dollar or patacoon, a silver coin weighing an ounce; cut with shears.

Patache [pah-tah'-chay], *m.* (F. Naut.) Tender, a vessel attending a squadron

Patada [pah-tah'-dah], *f.* 1. Kick, a blow with the foot. 2. (Coll.) Step, pace. 3. Track, mark left by the foot of an animal. *No dar pie ni patada*, Not to take the least trouble to obtain some end.

Patagalana [pah-ta-ga-lah'-nah], *f.* (Coll.) Limping; having a short leg.

Patagón [pah-tah-gone'], *m.* 1. A large clumsy foot. 2. A Patagonian.

Patagónico, ca [pah-tah-go'-ne-co, cah], *a.* Patagonian.

Patagorcillo, lla [pah-tah-gor-theel'-lyo], *m. & f.* Fricassee made of the livers and lights of animals.

Patagua [pah-tah'-goo-ah], *f.* 1. Patagua, a stout tree of America, of the linden family, which grows in miry places, and has a white light wood. Tricuspidaria dependens. 2. A nearly cylindrical vessel on which maté is spread.

Patalear [pah-tah-lay-ar'], *vn.* 1. To kick about violently. 2. To stamp the foot. 3. To patter.

Pataleo [pah-tah-lay'-o], *m.* 1. The act of stamping the foot. 2. Noise made by the feet.

Pataleta [pah-tah-lay'-tah], *f.* 1. (Coll.) A fainting-fit. 2. A ridiculous speech or action; an absurd enterprise.

Pataletilla [pah-tah-lay-teel'-lyah], *f.* A kind of dance.

Patán, na [pah-tahn', nah], *a.* Clownish, churlish, rustic.—*m. & f.* Clown, a churl, a countryman or woman.

Patanería [pah-tah-nay-ree'-ah], *f.* Clownishness, churlishness, rusticity, rudeness.

Patarata [pah-ta-rah'-tah], *f.* 1. Fiction, idle story. 2. Affected concern or affectation, kickshaw.

Patarraez [pah-tar-rah-eth'], *m.* (Naut.) Preventer-shroud. *Patarraez de una máquina de arbolar*, (Naut.) The shroud of a sheer-hulk for masting ships.

Patata [pah-tah'-tah], *f.* (Bot.) Potato. Solanum tuberosum.

Patatal [pah-tah-tahl'], *m.* Potato-field.

Patatero, ra [pah-tah-tay'-ro, rah], *m. & f.* 1. A potato-seller. 2. One who is fond of potatoes.

Patatús [pah-tah-toos'], *m.* (Coll.) Swoon, a fainting-fit.

Patax [pah-tahx'], *m.* *V.* Patache.

Pateadura [pah-tay-ah-doo'-rah], *f.* Kicking, stamping.

Patear [pah-tay-ar'], *va. & vn.* 1. To kick. 2. To stamp the foot. 3. To drive about to obtain some end. 4. To be extremely irritated or vexed.

Patena [pah-tay'-nah], *f.* 1. A large medal worn by countrywomen. 2. Paten, a dish for the eucharistic bread.

Patente [pah-ten'-tay], *a.* Patent, manifest, evident, clear, palpable.—*f.* 1. Patent, a writ conferring exclusive right or privilege; warrant, commission. 2. Letters of marque. 3. Letter of obedience expedited by prelates and addressed to their religious subjects. 4. Money paid by new-comers to the members of a company or office. *Patente de sanidad*, Bill of health.

Patentemente, *adv* Openly, clearly, visibly, obviously.

Patentizar [pah-ten-te-thar']. *va.* To make a thing evident.

Patera [pah-tay'-rah], *f.* Goblet, patera.

Paternal [pah-ter-nahl'], *a.* Paternal, fatherly.

Paternalmente, *adv.* Paternally, fatherly.

Paternidad [pah-ter-ne-dahd']. *f.* 1. Paternity, fathership. 2. A title of respect given to religious men.

Paterno, na [pah-terr'-no, nah], *a.* Paternal, fatherly.

Paternóster [pah-ter-nos'-ter], *m.* 1. The Lord's prayer; paternoster. 2. A big tight knot.

Patesca [pah-tes'-cah], *f.* (Naut.) A large block.

Pateta [pah-tay'-tah], *m.* 1. A nick-name given to a lame person. 2. (Coll.) Devil, Old Nick. *¡Que se lo lleve pateta!* The deuce take it! *Ya se lo llevó pateta*, The deuce took it, it is quite lost.

Patéticamente, *adv.* Pathetically.

Patético, ca [pah-tay'-te-co, cah], *a.* 1. Pathetic, passionate, moving. 2. Plaintive.

Patiabierto, ta [pah-te-ah-be-err'-to, tah], *a.* Straddling, club-footed, crooked-legged.

Patialbillo [pah-te-al-beel'-lyo], *m.* Weasel. *V.* PAPIALBILLO.

Patiblanco, ca [pah-te-blahn'-co, cah], *a.* White-footed.

Patibulario, ria [pah-te-boo-lah'-re-o, ah], *a.* Horror-producing.

Patíbulo [pah-tee'-boo-lo], *m.* Gibbet, gallows.

Patico, ito [pah-tee'-co, ee'-to], *m. dim.* A young goose, a gosling.

Paticojo, ja [pah-te-co'-ho, hah], *a.* (Coll.) Lame, crippled.

Patiestevado, da [pah-te-es-tay-vah'-do, dah], *a.* Bow-legged.

Patihendido, da [pah-te-en-dee'-do, dah], *a.* Cloven-footed.

Patilla [pah-teel'-lyah], *f.* 1. (Naut.) Spike nailed to the stern-post, on which the rudder moves. 2. Chape of a buckle. 3. Trigger. —*s. pl.* 1. Whiskers, sideburns. 2. (coll.) Demon.

Patimuleño, ña [pah-te-moo-lay'-nyo, nyah], *a.* Mule-footed: applied to horses with narrow hoofs.

Patín [pah-teen'], *m.* 1. Skate. *Patines de rueda*, Roller skates. *Patines de hielo*, Ice skates. 2. (Orn.) Goosander. 3. Small courtyard.

Pátina [pah'-te-nah], *f.* Patina.

Patinador, ra [pah-te-nah-dor', rah], *m.* & *f.* Skater.

Patinaje [pah-te-nah'-hay], *m.* 1. Skating. 2. Skidding.

Patinar [pah-te-nar'], *vn.* 1. To skate. 2. To skid.

Patineta [pah-te-nay'-tah], *f.* or **patinete** [pah-te-nay'-tay], *m.* Scooter.

Patio [pah'-te-o], *m.* 1. Court, an open space in front of a house or behind it. 2. Pit in play-houses. 3. Hall in universities, academies, or colleges. *Estar a patio*, To live at one's own expense, not to be on the foundation: applied to students in universities and colleges.

Patita [pah-tee'-tah], *f.* A small foot or leg of beasts. *Echar de patitas*, To turn out of the house. *Poner de patitas en la calle*, To put a person in the street, to discharge him.

Patitieso, sa [pah-te-te-ay'-so, sah], *a.* 1. Deprived by sudden accident of sense and feeling. 2. Stiff, stately, starchy: applied to a proud, presumptuous person of an affected gait. 3. Benumbed, stupefied, surprised.

Patituerto, ta [pah-te-too-err'-to, tah], *a.* 1. Crook-legged, having crooked legs or feet. 2. Ill-disposed, perverse.

Patizambo, ba [pah-te-thahm'-bo, bah], *a.* Knock-kneed, bandy-legged.

Pato, ta [pah'-to, tah], *a.* Equal, similar.

Pato [pah'-to], *m.* Drake, duck. *V.* ÁNADE. *El pato, y el lechón, del cuchillo al asador*, Ducks and pigs should be cooked promptly. *Estar hecho un pato*, To get a ducking. *Pagar el pato*, To suffer undeserved punishment. *V.* PAGAR. *Pato, ganso y ansarón, tres cosas suenan y una son*, Little meaning and many words.

Patochada [pah-to-chah'-dah], *f.* Blunder, nonsense, folly.

Patógeno, na [pah-to'-hay-no, nah], *a.* Pathogenic.

Patognómico, ca [pah-tog-no'-me-co, cah], *a.* Pathognomonic: applied to those signs of a disease which are characteristic, or inseparable from it.

Patojear [pah-to-hay-ar'], *vn.* (Cuba) To waddle in walking.

Patojo, ja [pah-to'-ho, hah], *a.* Waddling, like a duck.

Patología [pah-to-lo-hee'-ah], *f.* (Med.) Pathology, the doctrine of diseases.

Patológico, ca [pah-to-lo'-he-co, cah], *a.* Pathologic.

Patologista [pah-to-lo-hees'-tah], or **Patólogo**, *m.* (Med.) Pathologist.

Patón, na [pah-tone', nah], *a.* Large-footed, clumsy-footed.

Patón [pah-tone'], *m.* Clumsy foot.

Patraña [pah-trah'-nyah], *f.* A fabulous story, a fictitious account.

Patrañuela, *f. dim.* An insignificant tale.

Patria [pah'-tre-ah], *f.* 1. Native country, place of birth, home. 2. The native or proper place for any thing. 3. (Met.) Heaven.

Patriarca [pah-tre-ar'-cah], *m.* 1. Patriarch, a father and head of a numerous progeny in primitive ages. 2. Founder of a religious order. 3. Patriarch, a bishop of the highest rank. 4. Patriarch, an honorary title conferred by the Pope. *Vive como un patriarca*, He enjoys all the conveniences of life.

Patriarcado [pah-tre-ar-cah'-do], *m.* Patriarchate, the dignity and jurisdiction of a patriarch.

Patriarcal [pah-tre-ar-cahl'], *a.* Patriarchal.

Patriciado [pah-tre-the-ah'-do], *m.* Dignity of a patrician.

Patricio, cia [pah-tree'-the-o, ah], *a.* Native, national; patrician.

Patricio [pah-tree'-the-o], *m.* Patrician, noble.

Patrimonial [pah-tre-mo-ne-ahl'], *a.* 1. Patrimonial, claimed by right of birth. 2. Patrimonial, relating to a patrimony.

Patrimonialidad [pah-tre-mo-ne-ah-le-dahd'], *f.* Birthright, privilege conferred by birth of obtaining ecclesiastical benefices.

Patrimonio [pah-tre-mo'-ne-o], *m.* 1. Patrimony. 2. Possessions acquired by one's self.

Patrio, tria [pah'-tre-o, ah], *a.* 1. Native, belonging to a native place or country. 2. Paternal.

Patriota [pah-tre-oh'-tah], *m.* Patriot.

Patriótico, ca [pah-tre-oh'-te-co, cah], *a* Patriotic, beneficent.

Patriotismo [pah-tre-o-tees'-mo], *m.* Patriotism.

Patrocinar [pah-tro-the-nar'], *va.* To favour, to patronize, to protect, to countenance.

Patrocinio [pah-tro-thee'-ne-o], *m.* Protection, patronage, favour.

Patrón, ona [pah-trone', nah], *m.* & *f.* 1. Patron, patroness. 2. Master, boss, mistress.—*m.* 1. Standard, model. 2. Pattern (for sewing). *Santo patrón*, Patron saint. *Patrón oro*, Gold standard.

Patrona [pah-tro'-nah], *f.* 1. Patroness, a female patron. 2. Patroness; tutelar saint of a church, protectress of a province, etc. 3. Galley which follows immediately that of the commodore.

Patronado, da [pah-tro-nah'-do, dah], *a.* Having a patron: applied to churches and prebends.—*m.* (Prov.) *V.* PATRONATO.

Patronato, Patronazgo [pah-tro-nah'-to], *m.* 1. Patronage, patronship, the right of presenting to a benefice. 2. Foundation of a charitable or pious establishment.

Patronear [pah-tro-nay-ar'], *va.* To be a commander of a trading vessel.

Patronía [pah-tro-nee'-ah], *f.* Mastership of a vessel.

Patronímico [pah-tro-nee'-me-co], *m.* & *a* 1. Patronymic, family name. 2. A surname formed from the father's name; as from Sancho, Sánchez, from Pedro, Pérez.

Patrono [pah-tro'-no], *m.* 1. Lord of the manor. 2. *V.* PATRÓN.

Patrulla [pah-trool'-lyah], *f.* 1. Patrol, a small detachment of soldiers to secure the safety or peace of a place. 2. A crowd of people going about the streets.

Patrullar [pah-trool-lyar'], *va.* To patrol, to go the rounds in a camp or garrison.

Patudo, da [pah-too'-do, dah], *a.* (Coll.) Having large feet or paws.

Patulea [pah-too-lay'-ah], *f.* (Coll.) Soldiery or disorderly folks.

Patullar [pah-tool-lyar'], *vn.* 1. To trample, to run through thick and thin. 2. To labour hard in the pursuit of any thing.

Paúl [pah-ool'], *m.* A low, damp place, a bog.

Paulatinamente, *adv.* Gently, slowly, by little and little.

Paulatino, na [pah-oo-lah-tee'-no, nah], *a.* Slowly, by degrees.

Paulina [pah-oo-lee'-nah], *f.* 1. Decree of excommunication, interdict. 2. (Coll.) Reproof, chiding, objurgation. 3. An anonymous, offensive letter.

Paulinia [pah-oo-lee'-ne-ah], *f.* Paullinia, or guarana, a shrub of Brazil. The seeds yield a stimulating beverage, and are used medicinally for headache.

Paulonia [pah-oo-lo'-ne-ah], *f.* (Bot.) Paulownia, a tree of Japan with large heart-shaped leaves and pale-violet flowers.

Pauperismo [pah-oo-pay-rees'-mo], *m.* Pauperism, abject poverty.

Paupérrimo, ma [pah-oo-perr'-re-mo mah], *a. sup.* Very poor.

Pausa [pah'-oo-sah], *f.* 1. Pause, stop, intermission. 2. Pause, suspense, delay. 3. Rest, repose. 4. (Mus.) Pause, rest, a stop in music, and the character which marks it. *A pausas*, At leisure, by pauses.

Pausadamente, *adv.* Slowly, deliberately.

Pausado, da [pah-oo-sah'-do, dah], *a.* 1. Slow, deliberate. 2. Calm, quiet, paused.—*pp.* of PAUSAR.

Pausar [pah-oo-sar'], *vn.* To pause, to cease, to hesitate, to forbear from motion or action.
Pauta [pah'-oo-tah], *f.* 1. Ruled paper, and the apparatus by which the lines are ruled upon it. 2. Rule, guide, pattern, example, model.
Pautada [pah-oo-tah'-dah], *f.* The ruled staff on which music is written.
Pautador [pah-oo-tah-dor'], *m.* One who marks lines on paper with a ruling-machine.
Pautar [pah-oo-tar'], *va.* 1. To rule lines on paper. 2. To give rules, to prescribe the manner of performing an action.
Pava [pah'-vah], *f.* 1. Turkey-hen, the female of the turkey. 2. Peahen, the female of the peacock. *Pelar la pava*, To flirt, to have amorous talk between the windows and the street.—*a.* (Coll.) Applied to any woman very inactive or indolent.
Pavada [pah-vah'-dah], *f.* 1. A flock of turkeys. 2. A childish game.
Pavana [pah-vah'-nah], *f.* 1. A Spanish dance. *Pasos de pavana*, A grave, solemn step; a stately gait. 2. Kind of neckcloth, formerly worn by women. *Entrada de pavana*, Unseemly pretension.
Pavería [pah-vay-ree'-ah], *f.* Place for rearing turkeys.
Pavero, ra [pah-vay'-ro, rah], *a.* Rearing or feeding turkeys.—*m.* & *f.* One who feeds or sells turkeys.
Pavés [pah-ves'], *m.* Kind of large, oblong shield.
Pavesa [pah-vay'-sah], *f.* 1. Embers, hot cinders; snuff of the candle. 2. Remains, relic. *Estar hecho una pavesa*, (Coll.) To be very weak or debilitated. *Ser una pavesa*, (Coll.) To be very mild or gentle.
Pavesada [pah-vay-sah'-dah], *f.* *V.* Empavesada.
Pavesear [pah-vay-say-ar'], *vn.* To flicker, to flutter.
Pavía [pah-vee'-ah], *f.* A clingstone peach.
Paviano, na [pah-ve-ah'-no, nah], *a.* Pavian, belonging to Pavia, in Italy.
Pávido, da [pah'-ve-do, dah], *a.* Timid, fearful.
Pavilla, ita [pah-veel'-lyah, ee'-tah], *f. dim.* A little turkey-hen.
Pavillo, ito [pah-veel'-lyo, ee'-to], *m. dim.* A small turkey.
Pavimentación [pah-ve-men-tah-the-on'], *f.* Paving.
Pavimento [pah-ve-men'-to], *m.* Pavement, a floor of stone, tiles, or other materials.
Paviota [pah-ve-o'-tah], *f.* (Orn.) Mew, sea-gull. Larus. *V.* Gaviota.
Pavipollo [pah-ve-pol'-lyo], *m.* A young turkey.
Pavito real [pah-vee'-to ray-ahl'], *m.* Pea-chick or pea-chicken.
Pavo [pah'-vo], *m.* 1. (Orn.) Turkey. Meleagris gallipavo. 2. Peacock-fish. Labrus pavo. *Pavo silvestre*, (Orn.) Wood-grouse. Tetras urogallus. *Pavo real*, (Orn.) Peacock. *V.* Pavón. *Pavo carbonero*, (Orn.) Lapland finch. Fringilla laponica.
Pavo [pah'-vo], *a.* (Coll.) Peacock-like: applied to fops.
Pavón [pah-vone'], *m.* 1. (Orn.) Peacock. Pavo. 2. A piece of wood with which gunpowder is glazed. 3. (Ast.) A northern constellation.
Pavonada [pah-vo-nah'-dah], *f.* 1. Short walk. 2. Strut, an affected stateliness in walking.
Pavonar [pah-vo-nar'], *va.* To give iron or steel a bluish colour.
Pavonazo [pah-vo-nah'-tho], *m.* (Pict.) Crimson or purple colour.
Pavoncillo, ito [pah-von-theel'-lyo], *m dim.* A little peacock.
Pavonear [pah-vo-nay-ar'], *vn.* 1. To strut, to flaunt about the streets, to flutter. 2. (Coll.) To amuse with false hopes.
Pavor [pah-vor'], *m.* Fear, dread, terror.
Pavordear [pah-vor-day-ar'], *va.* To swarm: applied to bees.
Pavorido, da [pah-vo-ree'-do, dah], *a.* Intimidated, struck with terror.
Pavorosamente, *adv.* Awfully, fearfully.
Pavoroso, sa [pah-vo-roh'-so, sah], *a.* Awful, formidable.
Pavura [pah-voo'-rah], *f.* Fear, dread, terror. *V.* Pavor.
Paya [pah'-yah], *f.* Hoiden, a rude, ill-taught country girl.
Payaso [pah-yah'-so], *m.* A clown.
Payo [pah'-yo], *m.* Clown, churl.
Payuelas [pah-yoo-ay'-lahs], *f. pl.* (Med.) Chicken pox.
Paz [path], *f.* 1. Peace, tranquility, ease. 2. Peace, respite from war: truce, armistice, an agreement between belligerents to end a war. 3. Peace, rest from commotions, quiet from disturbances, and reconciliation from differences. 4. Peace, the quiet and good correspondence of one with the others. 5. A pleasant, peaceful disposition. 6. Equality of luck among card-players. 7. Clear or even accounts. 8. A salute or kiss on the meeting of absent friends. 9. A ceremony of the mass. *A la paz de Dios*, God be with you. *Bandera de paz*, A flag of truce. *Paz y pan*, Peace and bread, the source of public tranquility. *En paz*, Quit, clear. *Gente de paz*, A friend: a familiar way of answering to one who asks, Who is there? or, Who knocks at the door?
¡Paz! [path], *int.* Peace! hush! *Paz sea en esta casa*, Peace be in this house, a salute on entering.
Pazán [pah-thahn'], *m.* Egyptian antelope. Antilope oryx.
Pazguato, ta [path-goo-ah'-to, tah], *m.* & *f.* Dolt, a simple, stupid person.
Pazpuerco, ca [path-poo-err'-co, cah], *a.* Dirty, slovenly.
Pe [pay], *f.* Name of the letter P. *De pe a pa*, Entirely, from beginning to end.
Peaje, Pedaje [pay-ah'-hay, pay-dah'-hay], *m.* Bridge-toll, ferriage.
Peajero [pay-ah-hay'-ro], *m.* Toll-gatherer.
Peal [pay-ahl'], *m.* 1. Sock, a covering of the feet, worn between the stocking and the shoe; foot of a stocking. 2. Worthless person.
Peal [pay-ahl'], *a.* Heavy, dull, stupid, sickly.
Peana [pay-ah'-nah], *f.* 1. Pedestal, the basis of a statue. 2. Frame at the foot of an altar to tread upon. *Peana de las muniquetas*, (Naut.) Step of the kevels.
Peatón, ona [pay-ah-ton', nah], *m.* & *f.* Pedestrian.—*m.* Rural postman.
Peazgo [pay-ath'-go], *m.* Bridge-toll. *V.* Peaje.
Pebete [pay-bay'-tay], *m.* 1. An aromatic composition used as a perfume. 2. Stench, an unpleasant smell. 3. Tube filled with gunpowder and other ingredients, and used to convey fire to rockets and other artificial fireworks; fuse.
Pebetero [pay-bay-tay'-ro], *m.* Censer, a vessel in which perfumes are burnt.
Pebrada [pay-brah'-dah], *f.* *V.* Pebre.
Pebre [pay'-bray], *m.* 1. A kind of sauce made of garlic, cloves, and other spice. 2. Pepper. *V.* Pimienta.
Peca [pay'-cah], *f.* Freckle, a speck, a spot.
Pecable [pay-cah'-blay], *a.* Peccable, liable to sin.
Pecadazo [pay-cah-dah'-tho], *m aug.* A heinous or atrocious sin.
Pecadillo [pay-cah-deel'-lyo], *m. dim.* Peccadillo, a slight fault.
Pecado [pay-cah'-do], *m.* 1. Sin. *Pecado mortal*, Deadly sin. 2. Extravagance, excess. 3. (Coll.) Devil, the instigator of sin.—*Pecado, da, pp.* of Pecar.
Pecador [pay-cah-dor'], *m.* 1. Sinner, a person who has committed any sin. 2. Sinner, any individual capable of sinning. 3. (Met.) A sinner, an offender, a delinquent; one who neglects totally that which he ought to do. *¡Pecador de mí!* Poor me, sinner as I am! 4. An ignorant, stupid person.
Pecadora [pay-cah-do'-rah], *f* 1 *V.* Pecador. 2. A prostitute.
Pecadorazo, za [pay-cah-do-rah'-tho, thah], *m.* & *f. aug.* A great sinner.
Pecadorcillo, illa, ito, ita [pay-cah-dor-theel'-lyo], *m.* & *f. dim.* Little sinner.
Pecaminosamente, *adv.* Sinfully, wickedly.
Pecaminoso, sa [pay-cah-me-no'-so, sah], *a.* Sinful.
Pecante [pay-cahn'-tay], *a.* Peccant, vicious, abundant.
Pecar [pay-car'], *vn.* 1. To sin, to violate the laws of God. 2. To sin, to offend against right, to be wanting in what is right and just, or in the rules of art. 3. To commit excesses of any description. 4. To boast, to brag. 5. To predominate: applied to peccant humours of the body. 6. To have a strong propensity. 7. To occasion or to merit punishment. *Darle por donde peca*, To retort or reproach any one with a fault which he cannot deny.
Pecarí [pay-cah-ree'], *m.* (Zool.) Peccary, a wild hog of Mexico and South America.
Pecatriz [pay-cah-treeth'], *a.* (Obs.) *V.* Pecadora.
Peccata minuta [pec-cah'-tah me-noo'-tah]. (Coll.) Slight offence, trivial vice or sin.
Pece [pay'-thay], *m.* 1. Clay wetted for making mud walls. 2. Ridge of land between two furrows. 3. (Obs.) Fish. *V.* Pez.
Pececico, illo, ito [pay-thay-thee'-co], *m. dim.* A small fish.
Peceño, ña [pay-thay'-nyo, nyah], *a.* 1. Of the colour of pitch: applied to the hair of horses. 2. Applied to things which have a pitchy taste.
Pecera [pay-thay'-rah], *f.* Glass globe for gold-fish.
Pecezuela, *f. dim.* A small piece.
Pecezuelo [pay-thay-thoo-ay'-lo], *m. dim.* 1. Small foot. 2. Small fish.
Peciento, ta [pay-the-en'-to, tah], *a.* Of a pitchy colour.
Peciluengo, ga [pay-the-loo-en'-go, gah], *a.* Long-stalked: applied to fruit with stalks on trees.
Pecina [pay-thee'-nah], *f.* 1. Fish-pond. 2. *V.* Lodazal.
Pecinal [pay-the-nahl'], *m.* Pool of standing or muddy water.
Pecio [pay'-the-o], *m.* Fragment of a ship which has been shipwrecked.
Pecíolo [pay-thee'-o-lo], *m.* (Bot.) Petiole, leaf-stalk or flower-stalk.
Pécora [pay'-co-rah], *f.* 1. A sheep, head of sheep. 2. A cunning fellow knave; a gay, merry person.

Pecorea [pay-co-ray'-ah], *f.* 1. Robbery committed by struggling soldiers; marauding. 2. Idle strolling and loitering about the streets.

Pecoso, sa [pay-co'-so, sah], *a.* Freckly, full of freckles, freckled.

Pectina [pec-tee'-nah], *f.* Pectin, vegetable jelly, a substance obtained from pears and used in confectionery.

Pectoral [pec-to-rahl'], *a.* Pectoral, belonging to the breast.—*m.* Cross worn by bishops on the breast; a breast-plate.

Peculado [pay-coo-lah'-do], *m.* Peculation, theft, embezzlement of public money.

Peculiar [pay-coo-le-ar'], *a.* Peculiar, its own, or one's own, special.

Peculiarmente, *adv.* Peculiarly.

Peculio [pay-coo'-le-o], *m.* Stock or capital which the father permits a son to hold for his own use and benefit.

Pecunia [pay-coo'-ne-ah], *f.* (Coll.) Hard cash, specie. *Numerata pecunia,* Ready money.

Pecuniariamente, *adv.* In ready money.

Pecuniario, ria [pay-coo-ne-ah'-re-o, ah], *a.* Pecuniary, relating to money.

Pecha [pay'-chah], *f.* Tax, impost, tribute.

Pechada [pay-chah'-dah], *f.* (Amer.) A blow upon the chest.

Pechar [pay-char'], *vn.* To pay taxes.

Pechera [pay-chay'-rah], *f.* 1. Stomacher. 2. The bosom of a shirt. 3. A breast collar for horses and mules.

Pechería [pay-chay-ree'-ah], *f.* Paying tax, toll, or duty.

Pechero, ra [pay-chay'-ro, rah], *a.* Liable to pay duty or taxes; commoner, in contraposition to nobleman.

Pechero, *m.* Bib, a piece of linen put on the breast of children.

Pechiblanco, ca [pay-che-blahn'-co, cah], *a.* White-breasted.

Pechicatería [pay-che-cah-tay-ree'-ah], *f.* (Cuba) Meanness, parsimony.

Pechico, illo [pay-chee'-co], *m. dim.* A small breast, teat, etc.

Pechicolorado [pay-che-co-lo-rah'-do], *m.* Robin-redbreast, a kind of goldfinch.

Pechigonga [pay-che-gon'-gah], *f.* A game at cards.

Pechina [pay-chee'-nah], *f.* 1. A kind of shell which pilgrims carry on their hats and shoulders. 2. Curvilineal triangle, formed by the arches, where they meet, to receive the annulet of the cupola.

Pechirrojo [pay-cheer-ro'-ho], *m.* (Orn.) *V.* Pechicolorado.

Pechisacado, da [pay-che-sah-cah'-do, dah], *a.* (Met. Coll.) Haughty, arrogant.

Pechito [pay-chee'-to], *m. dim.* *V.* Pechico.

Pecho [pay'-cho], *m.* 1. The breast. *Pecho de carne carnilla,* Brisket. 2. The internal part of the breast, especially in men; chest. 3. Breast, the mammary gland. 4. Bosom, breast, as the seat of the passions, the seat of tenderness, or the receptacle of secrets. 5. Regard, esteem, confidence. 6. Courage, valour, fortitude. 7. Quality and strength of the voice to sing, preach, etc. 8. Breast, heart, conscience. 9. Tax formerly paid to the government by those who did not belong to the nobility. 10. Any contribution paid to any one besides the king. *Criar a los pechos,* To instruct or educate a person. *Dar el pecho,* To suckle. *Hombre de pecho,* A firm, spirited man. *Hombre de pelo en pecho,* A brave, daring man. *Tener pecho,* To have patience, to endure with firmness. *Tomar a pechos,* To take to heart. *A pecho descubierto,* Unarmed, without defence. *Echarse a pechos,* To drink greedily and copiously; to undertake any thing with ardour; to be active in any thing without considering the difficulties. *Echar el pecho al agua,* To undertake a risky thing resolutely.

Pechuelo [pay-choo-ay'-lo], *m. dim.* A small or little breast.

Pechuga [pay-choo'-gah], *f.* 1. Breast of a fowl. 2. Bosom of man or woman.

Pechugón [pay-choo-gone'], *m.* Blow on the breast.

Pechuguera [pay-choo-gay'-rah], *f.* Cough, hoarseness.

Pechuguica, illa [pay-choo-gee'-cah], *f. dim.* A small breast of a fowl.

Pedacico, illo, ito [pay-dah-thee'-co], *m.* A small piece or bit, a gobbet. *A pedacicos,* By piecemeals.

Pedagogía [pay-dah-go-hee'-ah], *f.* Pedagogy, the science and art of teaching.

Pedagógico, ca [pay-dah-go'-he-co, cah], *a.* Pedagogical.

Pedagogo [pay-dah-go'-go], *m.* 1. Pedagogue, schoolmaster, pedant. 2. A prompter, ruler, or director to another.

Pedaje [pay-dah'-hay], *m.* Bridge-toll. *V.* Peaje.

Pedal [pe-dahl'], *m.* 1. The pedal pipes of an organ, and the keys, played by the feet, which control them. 2. The pedal of a pianoforte or harp. 3. The treadle of a sewing-machine, etc. 4. A pedal-base holding-note.

Pedáneo [pay-dah'-nay-o], *a.* Petty, puisne, inferior: applied to the members of inferior courts of justice.

Pedante [pay-dahn'-tay], *m.* Pedant, a schoolmaster; a man vain of low knowledge.

Pedantear [pay-dan-tay-ar'], *vn.* To pedantize, to play the pedant, to use pedantical expressions.

Pedantería [pay-dan-tay-ree'-ah], *f.* Pedantry, awkward ostentation of needless learning.

Pedantesco, ca [pay-dan-tes'-co, cah], *a.* Pedantic, awkwardly ostentatious of learning.

Pedantismo [pay-dan-tees'-mo], *m.* Pedantry.

Pedazo [pay-dah'-tho], *m.* Piece, bit; a part of a whole, a lump. *Pedazo del alma,* My dear, my love. *A pedazos* or *en pedazos,* In bits, in fragments. *Estar hecho pedazos,* 1. To be broken in pieces. 2. (Met.) To be very fatigued. *Morirse por sus pedazos,* To languish with amorous desire; to wish anxiously for one.

Pedazuelo [pay-dah-thoo-ay'-lo], *m. dim.* A small piece or bit.

Pedernal [pay-der-nahl'], *m.* 1. Flint. 2. Silex.

Pedestal [pay-des-tahl'], *m.* 1. Pedestal, the basis of a column or statue. 2. *V.* Peana. 3. Foundation, the fundamental part of a thing.

Pedestre [pay-des'-tray], *a.* Pedestrious, pedaneous, going on foot.

Pediatra [pay-de-ah'-trah], *m.* & *f.* Pediatrician, child specialist.

Pediatría [pay-de-ah-tree'-ah], *f.* Pediatrics.

Pedicoj [pay-de-coh'], *m.* Jump on one foot.

Pedicular [pay-de-coo-lar'], *a.* Pedicular, lousy.

Pedículo [pay-dee'-coo-lo], *m.* 1. (Bot.) Peduncle of a flower. 2. (Med.) The pedicle of a tumour.

Pedicuro [pay-de-coo'-ro], *m.* Chiropodist.

Pedido [pay-dee'-do], *m.* 1. A voluntary contribution, which is called for by government in urgent necessities of the state. 2. *V.* Petición. 3. (Com.) An order of goods or merchandise.—*Pedido, da, pp.* of Pedir.

Pedidor, ra [pay-de-dor', rah], *m.* & *f.* Petitioner, craver.

Pedidura [pay-de-doo'-rah], *f.* Begging, petitioning.

Pedigón [pay-de-gone'], *m.* (Coll.) Craver, an insatiable asker.

Pedigüeño, ña [pay-de-goo-ay'-nyo, nyah], *a.* Craving, demanding frequently and importunately.

Pediluvio [pay-de-loo'-ve-o], *m.* (Med.) Pediluvium, a bath for the feet.

Pedimento [pay-de-men'-to], *m.* Petition. *V.* Petición. *A pedimento,* At the instance, on petition.

Pedir [pay-deer'], *va.* 1. To petition, to beg, to supplicate, to solicit. 2. To ask, to demand or require information. 3. To crave, to manifest a desire of obtaining something from another. 4. To demand and fix a price on goods set for sale. 5. To demand, to inquire after, to wish for. 6. To ask for a woman in marriage. *Pedir limosna,* To beg, to ask alms. *Pedir justicia* or *pedir en juicio,* To claim, to bring an action or claim against a person before a judge. *Pedir cuentas,* To call for the accounts. *Pedir cuenta,* To bring a person to an account. *A pedir de boca,* According to desire; adequately. *Pedírselo a uno el cuerpo,* To long anxiously. *Pedir sobrado por salir con lo mediado,* To ask for much with the hope of obtaining some part.

Pedo [pay'-do], *m.* Wind from the bowels; flatulence. *Pedo de lobo,* (Bot.) Puff-ball. Lycoperdon.

Pedorrear [pay-dor-ray-ar'], *va.* 1. To discharge wind. 2. (Met.) To sing or play badly.

Pedorreras [pay-dor-ray'-ras], *f. pl.* 1. A kind of very tight breeches. 2. Flatulencies.

Pedorrero, ra, Pedorro, rra [pay-dor-ray'-ro, rah], *a.* Discharging much wind, flatulent.

Pedorreta [pay-dor-ray'-tah], *f.* Noise made by children with the mouth.

Pedrada [pay-drah'-dah], *f.* 1. Throw or cast of a stone; lapidation. 2. A blow from a stone or the mark left by it. 3. A smart repartee, taunt, sneer. *Pedrada* or *pedradas,* 1. An exclamation in denouncing a crime, You should be stoned. 2. A sneer at one who shows his teeth. *Como pedrada en ojo de boticario,* Pat, apropos, fitting.

Pedrea [pay-dray'-ah], *f.* 1. Throwing stones. 2. Falling of stones. 3. Conflict of boys fighting with stones; lapidation.

Pedrecita [pay-dray-thee'-tah], *f. dim* A small stone.

Pedregal [pay-dray-gahl'], *m.* Place full of stones.

Pedregoso, sa [pay-dray-go'-so, sah], *a.* 1. Stony, abounding with stones. 2. Afflicted with the gravel.

Pedrejón [pay-dray-hone'], *m.* Large loose stone.

Pedreñal [pay-dray-nyahl'], *m.* Kind of small firelock.

Pedrera [pay-dray'-rah], *f.* Quarry, a stone-pit.

Pedrería [pay-dray-ree'-ah], *f.* A collection of precious stones; jewels.

Pedrero [pay-dray'-ro], *m.* 1. Stonecutter. 2. Pedrero, a swivel-gun. 3. Slinger, one who throws with a sling. 4. Lapidary, one who deals in precious stones. 5. In Toledo, a foundling, a child exposed to chance.

Pedrezuela [pay-dray-thoo-ay'-lah], *f. dim.* A small stone.

Pedriscal, *m. V.* PEDREGAL.

Pedrisco [pay-drees'-co], *m.* Hailstone.

Pedrisquero [pay-dris-kay'-ro], *m.* A stone, hailstone.

Pedriza [pay-dree'-thah], *f.* 1. Quarry *V.* PEDRERA. 2. Heap of loose stones.

Pedrusco [pay-droos'-co], *m.* Rough piece of marble.

Pedunculado, da [pay-doon-coo-lah'-do, dah], *a.* (Bot.) Peduncled.

Pedunculillo [pey-doon-coo-leel'-lyo], *m. dim.* (Bot.) Pedicle or pedicel.

Pedúnculo [pay-doon'-coo-lo], *m.* 1. (Bot.) Peduncle, flower-stalk. 2. Name of certain cerebral appendages.

Peer [pay-err'], *vn.* To break wind.

Pega [pay'-gah], *f.* 1. The art of joining or cementing things. 2. Varnish of pitch put on earthen vessels. 3. Act of firing a blast. 4. (Coll.) A jest, a joke, a trick, a sham. 5. (Orn.) Magpie. Corvus pica. *Ser de la pega,* To belong to the gang. *Le dió una pega de patadas,* He gave him a good kicking. *Saber a la pega,* To adopt bad habits, to keep bad company (literally, to smack of pitch).

Pegadillo [pay-gah-deel'-lyo], *m.* 1. (Dim.) A little patch; a sticking-plaster. 2. Man who is introduced into a house or conversation, and remains, to the general annoyance.

Pegadizo, za [pay-gah-dee'-tho, thah], *a.* 1. Clammy, glutinous, viscous. 2. Catching, contagious. 3. Adhering selfishly: applied to one who sticks to another from base motives.

Pegado [pay-gah'-do], *m.* Patch, sticking-plaster, cataplasm.—*Pegado, da, pp.* of PEGAR.

Pegador [pay-gah-dor'], *m.* Paper-hanger, one who applies wall-paper. *Pegador de carteles,* Bill-poster, bill-sticker.

Pegadura [pay-gah-doo'-rah], *f.* 1. Pitching, daubing with pitch. 2. The sticking of one thing to another.

Pegajoso, sa [pay-gah-ho'-so, sah], *a.* 1. Sticky, viscous, glutinous, dauby, mucous. 2. Catching, contagious. 3. Attractive, alluring; adhesive.

Pegamiento [pay-gah-me-en'-to], *m.* The act and effect of conglutinating or cementing.

Pegante [pay-gahn'-tay], *a.* Viscous, glutinous.

Pegar [pay-gar'], *va.* 1. To join one thing to another with cement or viscous matter. 2. To join, to unite, to sew one thing with another. 3. To close or apply closely two things. 4. To dash things violently together, to clap. 5. To chastise, to punish, to beat. 6. To infect, to communicate a distemper. —*vn.* 1. To root or take root, as plants; to catch: speaking of fire. 2. To make an impression on the mind; to communicate vices, manners, etc. 3. To assault, to attack. 4. To join, to be contiguous, to cleave, to cling. 5. To begin to take effect. 6. To fall asleep. 7. To say or do something disagreeable or displeasing. *Pegarla,* To betray one's confidence. *Pegarla de puño,* To violate the confidence reposed in one. —*vr.* 1. To intrude, to enter without invitation or permission. 2. To stick, to adhere; to unite itself by its tenacity or penetrating power, to cohere, to grow. 3. To insinuate itself, to steal upon the mind. 4. To be taken with, to be strongly affected with a passion. 5. To spend one's fortune on things which belong to others. *Pegar un petardo, un parche* or *un parchazo,* To borrow money and not return it. *Pegar fuego,* (1) To set fire to. (2) To incite, to stir up dissensions. *Pegar la boca a la pared,* To keep one's sorrow to one's self. *No pegar los ojos,* Not to sleep. *Pegar mangas,* To intermeddle in any thing, to intrude, to sponge or act the parasite. *Esa no pega.* (Coll.) That is an absurdity. *Pegársele (a uno),* (1) To stick to one, to derive advantage from something. (2) To be prejudiced in the management of other's interests.

Pega reborda [pay'-gah ray-bor'-dah], *f.* (Zool.) Shrike, butcher-bird.

Pegaseo, sea [pay-gah'-say-o, ah], *a.* (Poet.) Belonging to Pegasus.

Pegásides [pay-gah'-se-days], *f. pl.* The Muses.

Pegaso [pay-gah'-so], *m.* 1. Pegasus, a winged horse. 2. A northern constellation west of Andromeda.

Pegata [pay-gah'-tah], *f.* (Coll.) Trick, fraud, imposition.

Pegatista [pay-gah-tees'-tah], *m.* An indigent wretch, who lives upon the offals of other men's tables; a sponger.

Pegote [pay-go'-tay], *m.* 1. Kind of sticking-plaster. 2. Fricassee with a thick, clammy sauce. 3. A sponger, a toad-eater, a sycophant.

Peguera [pay-gay'-rah], *f.* 1. Pile of pine-wood, burnt for the purpose of making pitch. 2. Place where sheep are marked with pitch.

Peguero [pay-gay'-ro], *m.* One who makes or deals in pitch.

Pegujal, Pegujar [pay-goo-hahl'], *m.* 1. Stock or capital which a son holds by permission of his father, for his own use and benefit. 2. A small dead or live stock on a farm.

Pegujalero, Pegujarero [pay-goo-hah-lay'-ro], *m.* A small farmer, grazier who keeps but a small flock of sheep.

Pegujón [pay-goo-hone'], *m.* Pellet or little ball of wool or hair.

Pegunta [pay-goon'-tah], *f.* Mark of pitch on wool, cattle, etc.

Peguntar [pay-goon-tar'], *va.* To mark cattle, etc., with melted pitch.

Peinada [pay-e-nah'-dah], *f.* Combing, the act of combing and dressing hair.

Peinado [pay-nah'-do], *m.* 1. Hair-dressing, coiffure. 2. Hair style.

Peinado, da [pay-e-nah'-do, dah], *a. & pp.* of PEINAR. 1. Combed, curled, dressed: applied to hair. 2. Applied to a man very effeminate in dress.

Peinador, ra [pay-e-nah-dor', rah], *m. & f.* 1. One who dresses or combs hair. 2. Hair-dresser.—*m.* 3. Cloth put about the neck while the hair is combed.

Peinadura [pay-e-nah-doo'-rah], *f.* 1. The act of combing or dressing the hair. 2. Hair pulled out with a comb.

Peinar [pay-e-nar'], *va.* 1. To comb or dress the hair. 2. To comb wool. 3. To touch or rub slightly. 4. To excavate or eat away part of a rock or earth. 5. (Poet.) To move or divide any thing gently. *Las aves peinan las olas,* The birds skim the waves. *Peinar el estilo,* To correct, to chastise, or to purify the style. *No peinarse para alguno,* To reject a suitor's addresses. *No peinar canas,* (Coll.) To be young.

Peinazo [pay-e-nah'-tho], *m.* Cross-piece of a door or window-frame.

Peine [pay'-ee-nay], *m.* 1. Comb, an instrument for the hair. 2. Card, an instrument to card wool. 3. Rack, an engine of torture. 4. Weaver's reed. 5. Hemp-comb. 6. Instep of the foot; hoof. *A sobre peine,* Lightly, slightly, imperfectly.

Peinería [pay-e-nay-ree'-ah], *f.* Shop where combs are made and sold.

Peinero, ra [pay-e-nay'-ro, rah], *m. & f.* Comb-maker, comb-seller.

Peineta [pay-ee-nay'-tah], *f.* An ornamental convex dressing-comb for the hair which women use.

Peje [pay'-hay], *m.* 1. Fish. 2. Cunning, crafty fellow.

Pejemuller [pay-hay-mool-lyerr'], *f.* Mermaid, a sea-woman.

Pejepalo [pay-hay-pah'-lo], *m.* An inferior kind of codfish, by reason of being tough and dry.

Pejiguera [pay-he-gay'-rah], *f.* Difficulty, embarrassment, disgust.

Pel, *f.* Skin, hide, pelt. *V.* PIEL.

Pela [pay'-lah], *m.* (Prov.) 1. Boy richly dressed, put on the shoulders of a man in processions. 2. (Mex.) A whipping in school. 3. (Met.) A reprimand.

Pelada [pay-lah'-dah], *f.* Pelt, the skin of a sheep stripped of the wool.

Peladera [pay-lah-day'-rah], *f.* Shedding of the hair, alopecia.

Peladero [pay-lah-day'-ro], *m.* Place where birds and hogs are scalded for stripping them.

Peladilla [pay-lah-deel'-lyah], *f.* 1. Sugar-almond. 2. Small pebble; round, whitish stone.

Peladillo [pay-lah-deel'-lyo], *m.* A variety of clingstone peach of smooth purplish skin and firm flesh.

Peladillos [pay-lah-deel'-lyos], *m. pl.* The wool stripped from the skin of a sheep.

Peladiza [pay-lah-dee'-thah], *f.* In tanneries the wool which is removed from sheep-skins.

Pelado, da [pay-lah'-do, dah], *a. & pp.* of PELAR. 1. Plucked; bared; decorticated. 2. Hairless, without hair. 3. Applied to fields or mountains without shrubs or plants; bare, bald. *Letra pelada,* Clear, neat-formed letter. *Muerte pelada,* Baldhead; a nickname. *Estar pelado* or *ser un pelado,* (Coll.) To be penniless; to be nobody.

Pelador [pay-lah-dor'], *m.* Plucker, one who plucks or decorticates.

Peladura [pay-lah-doo'-rah], *f.* Plucking, decortication.

Pelafustán [pay-lah-foos-tahn'], *m.* Ragamuffin, vagabond, vagrant.

Pelagallos [pay-lah-gahl'-lyos], *m.* (Coll.) Nickname applied to persons of the lowest rank who have no known occupation.

Pelagatos [pay-lah-gah'-tos], *m.* 1. Vagrant. 2. Ragamuffin.

Pelagiano, na [pay-lah-he-ah'-no, nah], *a.* Pelagian, denying original sin.

Pelagóscopo [pay-lah-gos'-co-po], *m.* An optical instrument for seeing objects below the water.

Pelagra [pay-lah'-grah], *f.* (Med.) An endemic disease of southern Europe, characterized by scaly inflammation of the skin. It is often fatal.

Pelaire [pay-lah'-e-ray], *m.* Wool-dresser.

Pelairía [pay-lah-e-ree'-ah], *f.* Trade of a wool-comber.

Pelaje [pay-lah'-hay], *m.* 1. Nature and quality of the hair and of wool. 2. Quality and external appearance, especially of clothes.

Pelambrar [pay-lam-brar'], *va.* To steep hides in lime-pits to take off the hair. *V.* APELAMBRAR.

Pelambre [pay-lahm'-bray], *m.* 1. The quantity of hides put into lime-pits. 2. The mixture of lime and water with which tanners strip off hair from hides. 3. Hair of the body in general, particularly that which comes off. 4. Want of hair.

Pelambrera [pay-lam-bray'-rah], *f.* 1. Quantity of hair in one place. 2. Want or shedding of hair. 3. The place where hides are macerated in lime-pits.

Pelambrero [pay-lam-bray'-ro], *m.* The workman who steeps hides in lime-pits.

Pelambrón, na, *a.* (Coll.) *V.* POBRETÓN.

Pelamen [pay-lah'-men], *m.* (Coll.) *V.* PELAMBRE.

Pelamesa [pay-lah-may'-sah], *f.* 1. Scuffle in which the hair is torn off. 2. A bushy head of hair.

Pelámide [pay-lah'-me-day], *f.* Young brood of tunny-fish.

Pelandusca [pay-lan-doos'-cah], *f.* (Coll.) A strumpet.

Pelantrín [pay-lan-treen'], *m.* (Prov.) A petty farmer.

Pelar [pay-lar'], *va.* 1. To cut or pull out the hair; to pluck the feathers. 2. To divest of the bark or husk, to blanch, to shell. 3. To trick, to cheat, to rob. 4. To boil, to scald. *Esta agua está pelando,* This water is boiling.—*vr.* To cast the hair. *Pelárselas,* To execute any thing with vigour and efficiency. *Pelarse de fino,* To be very cunning and astute. *Pelarse alguno las barbas,* To show great indignation by one's actions.

Pelarruecas [pay-lar-roo-ay'-cas], *f.* A poor woman who lives by spinning.

Pelaza [pay-lah'-thah], *f.* 1. Quarrel, affray, scuffle. 2. A caterwauling of cats. *Dejar a uno en la pelaza,* (Coll.) To leave one in the lurch.

Pelaza [pay-lah'-thah], *a.* Applied to chopped or beaten straw of the stalks of barley.

Pelazga [pay-lahth'-gah], *f.* (Coll.) Quarrel, scuffle.

Peldaño [pel-dah'-nyo], *m.* Every step of a flight of stairs.

Pelde, *m.* *V.* APELDE.

Peldefebre [pel-day-fay'-bray], *m.* Camlet, barracan, a stuff made of wool and goat's hair mixed; camel's hair.

Pelea [pay-lay'-ah], *f.* 1. Battle, action, engagement, combat, fight. 2. Quarrel, dispute, conflict. 3. Struggle, toil, fatigue. *Pelea de gallos,* Cock-fight.

Peleador [pay-lay-ah-dor'], *m.* Fighter, combatant.

Peleante [pay-lay-ahn'-tay], *pa.* Combating, fighting.

Pelear [pay-lay-ar'], *va.* 1. To fight, to combat. 2. To quarrel, to contend, to dispute. 3. To toil, to labour hard. *Pelear con todas sus fuerzas,* (Coll.) To fight tooth and nail, might and main.—*vr.* To scuffle, to come to blows. *Pelean los toros, y mal para las ramas,* When the heads of families quarrel it is bad for their dependents.

Pelechar [pay-lay-char'], *va.* 1. To get hair. 2. To change the coat: applied to horses. 3. To fledge, to shed feathers. 4. (Coll.) To improve one's fortune, to recover health.

Pelele [pay-lay'-lay], *m.* A man of straw; insignificant fellow.

Pelendengue [pay-len-den'-gay], *m.* Frivolous foppery, extreme nicety in dress.

Peleón [pay-lay-on'], *a.* & *m.* Very ordinary wine.

Peleona [pay-lay-oh'-nah], *f.* Scuffle, quarrel, dispute.

Pelete [pay-lay'-tay], *m.* 1. One who punts at certain games at cards. 2. (Coll.) A poor man. *En pelete,* Nakedly.

Peletería [pay-lay-tay-ree'-ah], *f.* 1. Trade of a furrier or skinner. 2. Fellmonger's shop, where fine skins and furs are sold.

Peletero [pay-lay-tay'-ro], *m.* Furrier, one who dresses fine skins or deals in furs.

Pelgar [pel-gar'], *m.* A ragamuffin, a blackguard.

Peliagudo, da [pay-le-ah-goo'-do, dah], *a.* 1. Downy, furry, having long fine hair or fur: applied to animals. 2. (Coll.) Arduous, difficult. 3. Ingenious, skilful, dexterous.

Peliblanco, ca [pay-le-blahn'-co, cah], *a.* Having white hair.

Peliblando, da [pay-le-blahn'-do, dah], *a.* Having fine soft hair.

Pelicabra [pay-le-cah'-brah], *f.* Satyr, a fabulous animal.

Pelícano [pay-lee'-cah-no], *m.* (Orn.) Pelican. Pelecanus onocrotalus.

Pelicano, na [pay-le-cah'-no, nah], *a.* Having gray hair; hoary.

Pelicorto, ta [pay-le-cor'-to, tah], *a.* Having short hair.

Película [pay-lee'-coo-lah], *f.* Film, a thin membrane, thin layer. *Película cinematográfica,* Motion-picture film. *Película de largo metraje,* Full-length film. *Película sonora* or *película hablada,* talking picture. *Rollo de películas,* Film roll. *Tira de película,* Filmstrip.

Peliculero [pay-le-coo-lay'-ro], *m.* Scenario writer.

Peligrar [pay-le-grar'], *vn.* To be in danger; to be in peril, to risk, to peril.

Peligro [pay-lee'-gro], *m.* Danger, risk, peril, hazard, jeopardy. *Correr peligro, tener peligro,* or *estar en peligro,* To be in peril or danger.

Peligrosamente, *adv.* Perilously, dangerously, hazardously, jeopardously.

Peligroso, sa [pay-le-groh'-so, sah], *a.* Dangerous, perilous; hazardous.

Pelilargo, ga [pay-le-lar'-go, gah], *a.* Having long hair.

Pelillo [pay-leel'-lyo], *m.* 1. (Dim.) Short, tender hair. 2. Trifle, a slight cause of disgust or displeasure. *Pelillos a la mar,* A phrase of a childish game, meaning "honour bright." *Echar pelillos a la mar,* Not to bear malice; to become reconciled. *No tener pelillos en la lengua,* To speak one's mind openly.

Pelinegro, gra [pay-le-nay'-gro, grah], *a.* Having black hair.

Pelirrojo, ja [pay-leer-ro'-ho, hah], *a.* Red-haired.

Pelirrubio, bia [pay-leer-roo'-be-o, ah], *a.* Having fair, light, or flaxen hair.

Pelitieso, sa [pay-le-te-ay'-so, sah], *a.* Having strong, bushy hair.

Pelito [pay-lee'-to], *m.* Short, tender hair. *Pelitos a la mar,* All animosities done away; the act of friends making up a quarrel.

Pelitre [pay-lee'-tray], *m.* (Bot.) Pellitory of Spain. Anthemis pyrethrum.

Pelitrique [pay-le-tree'-kay], *m.* Fiddle-faddle, trifle.

Pelma [pel'-mah], *f.* *V.* PELMAZO.

Pelmacería [pel-mah-thay-ree'-ah], *f.* Heaviness, slowness.

Pelmazo [pel-mah'-tho], *m.* 1. What is crushed or flattened. 2. Heavy paste or cake: food which lies heavy on the stomach. 3. A slow, heavy person; a procrastinator.

Pelo [pay'-lo], *m.* 1. Hair. 2. Down, the tender feathers of birds. 3. A down or bloom which grows on the skins or husks of fruit. 4. Soft fibres of plants. 5. Any slender thread of wool, silk, etc. 6. Pile, the hair or bur on the right side of cloth. 7. Hair-spring in watches. 8. Flaw in precious stones or crystals; split in metals, horses' hoofs, etc. 9. Abscess in a woman's breast. 10. A hair or splinter; trifle, any thing of little value. 11. (Com.) Raw silk. 12. Colour of animals' skins. *V.* PELAJE. 13. The grain of wood. *Ser de buen pelo,* In an ironical sense, to be ill-disposed. *Venir a pelo,* To come to the purpose. *Pelo arriba* or *a contrapelo,* Against the grain. *A pelo,* For the purpose, to the purpose, timely, apropos. *Al pelo* or *a pelo,* Along the grain. *Gente de pelo,* Rich people. *Tener pelos,* To be intricate: applied to some affair or business. *No tener pelo de tonto,* To be bright, quick, clever. *En pelo,* Bare-backed, naked. *A medios pelos,* Fuddled, flustered, or half-seas over. *Estar con el pelo de la dehesa,* To be a boor, clownish, unpolished. *Tener pelos en el corazón,* To be energetic and courageous in action. *Del lobo un pelo y ese de la frente,* Accept from a miser any thing which he may give you.

Pelón, na [pay-lone', nah], *a.* (Coll.) Hairless, bald.—*m.* & *f.* 1. Poor, indigent man. 2. In Peru, a caressing term applied to children.

Pelona, Pelonía [pay-lo'-nah, pay-lo-nee'-ah], *f.* Baldness.

Pelonería [pay-lo-nay-ree'-ah], *f.* (Coll.) Poverty, want, indigence.

Pelosilla [pay-lo-seel'-lyah], *f.* (Bot.) Mouse-ear, hawkweed. Hieracium pilosella.

Peloso, sa [pay-lo'-so, sah], *a.* Hairy.

Pelota [pay-lo'-tah], *f.* 1. Ball, a round plaything. 2. Ball of soft material. 3. Cannon or musket ball. 4. Ball-game or play performed with balls. *Pelota de viento,* Foot-ball. *Juego de pelota,* Ball-game in general: also tennis and the tennis-court. *Jugar a la pelota con alguno,* (Fig.) To send one back and forth on a fruitless errand, to deceive him. *En pelota,* (1) Entirely naked. (2) Penniless, without a cent. *No tocar pelota,* Not to touch the root of the difficulty. *Sacar pelotas de una alcuza,* To be very clever or ingenious.

Pelotari [pay-lo-tah'-re], *m.* Professional player of jai alai.

Pelota vasca [pay-lo'-tah vahs'-cah], *f.* Jai alai, Basque ball game.

Pelotazo [pay-lo-tah'-tho], *m.* Blow or stroke with a ball.

Pelote [pay-lo'-tay], *m.* Goat's hair.

Pelotear [pay-lo-tay-ar'], *vn.* 1. To play at ball. 2. To argue, to dispute; to contend. 3. To throw from one part to another.—*va.* To examine the items of an account, and compare them with the parcels received.—*vr.* To throw snow-balls at each other; to quarrel, to dispute.

Pelotera [pay-lo-tay'-rah], *f.* Battle, quarrel, dispute, contention: applied in general to women's quarrels.

Pelotería [pay-lo-tay-ree'-ah], *f.* 1. Heap of balls. 2. Heap of goat's hair.

Pelotero [pay-lo-tay'-ro], *m.* Ball-maker.

Pelotilla [pay-lo-teel'-lyah], *f.* 1. (Dim.) A small ball. 2. Small ball of wax, stuck with small pieces of glass, and fastened to a cat-o'-nine-tails, with which penitent persons once lashed themselves. *Hacer pelotillas,* To pick the nose rudely.

Peloto, *a.* (Prov.) *V.* CHAMORRO.

Pelotón [pay-lo-tone'], *m.* 1. (Aug.) A large ball. 2. Bundle or ball of hair closely pressed together. 3. (Mil.) Platoon, a small body of foot-soldiers. 4. A crowd of persons close together without order.

Peltre [pel'-tray], *m.* Pewter, an alloy of tin and lead.

Peltrero [pel-tray'-ro], *m.* Pewterer, pewter-worker.

Peluca [pay-loo'-cah], *f.* 1. Wig; periwig, peruke. 2. The person who wears a wig. 3. A very severe reproof from a superior to an inferior. *Peluca redonda*, Bobwig.

Pelucón [pay-loo-cone'], *m.* One who struts about in a large bushy wig; any fantastical fellow.

Peludo, da [pay-loo'-do, dah], *a.* Hairy, hirsute, covered with hair.

Peludo [pay-loo'-do], *m.* A bass mat of an oval shape.

Peluquera [pay-loo-kay'-rah], *f.* A hair-cutter's or peruke-maker's wife.

Peluquería [pay-loo-kay-ree'-ah], *f.* Shop where wigs are made and sold.

Peluquero [pay-loo-kay'-ro], *m.* Hairdresser, hair-cutter, wig-maker.

Peluquilla, ita [pay-loo-keel'-lyah], *f. dim.* A small wig.

Peluquín [pay-loo-keen'], *m.* A small bag-wig, peruke.

Pelusa [pay-loo'-sah], *f.* 1. Down which covers plants or fruit. 2. Villous substance falling from clothes while wearing. 3. (Joc.) Cash, riches.

Pelusilla [pay-loo-seel'-lyah], *f. dim.* The down of plants or fruit when it is very short.

Pelvímetro [pel-vee'-may-tro], *m.* Pelvimeter.

Pelvis [pel'-vis], *f.* (Anat.) Pelvis, pelvic cavity.

Pella [pel'-lyah], *f.* 1. Ball, any thing in a round form. 2. Mass of metal in its crude state. 3. Lard in the state in which it is taken from hogs. 4. A sum of money borrowed and not paid, or of money taken under false pretences. 5. (Orn.) Heron. Ardea major. 6. Head of cauliflower.

Pellada [pel-lyah'-dah], *f.* 1. Gentle blow, dab. 2. A trowelful of mortar or slaked lime.

Pelleja [pel-lyay'-hah], *f.* 1. Skin or hide stripped from an animal. 2. (Low) A strumpet.

Pellejería [pel-lyay-hay-ree'-ah], *f.* Shop where skins are dressed and sold.

Pellejero [pel-lyay-hay'-ro], *m.* Furrier, he whose trade is to dress and sell skins; leather-dresser, pelt-monger.

Pellejina [pel-lyay-hee'-nah], *f.* A small skin.

Pellejo [pel-lyay'-ho], *m.* 1. Skin, hide, felt, pelt. 2. A skin dressed and pitched, in which liquors are carried. 3. The rind which covers some fruits. 4. (Joc.) Tippler, drunkard. *No caber en el pellejo*, To be very fat. *Pagar con el pellejo*, To pay the forfeit of one's life. *No tener más que el pellejo*, To be destitute (not to have more than one's skin). *Mudar el pellejo*, To change customs and manners. *No quisiera estar en su pellejo*, (Coll.) I would not stand in his shoes.

Pellejudo, da [pel-lyay-hoo'-do, dah], *a.* Having a great quantity of skin.

Pellejuela [pel-lyay-hoo-ay'-lah], *f. dim.* A small skin or hide, stripped from an animal.

Pellejuelo [pel-lyay-hoo-ay'-lo], *m. dim.* A small skin.

Pellica [pel-lyee'-cah], *f.* 1. Coverlet of fine furs. 2. A robe of fine furs. 3. A small dressed skin.

Pellico [pel-lyee'-co], *m.* 1. Dress made of skins or furs. 2. (Prov.) Offensive language.

Pelliquero [pel-lye-kay'-ro], *m.* A maker of coverlets of fine fur.

Pelliza [pel-lyee'-thah], *f.* Pelisse, fur cloak, dress formed of skins.

Pellizcar [pel-lyeeth-car'], *va.* 1. To pinch, to squeeze between the fingers and thumb; to pinch or wound artfully, to gripe. 2. To pilfer. 3. To take but little food; to take only a bit or pinch.—*vr.* (Met.) To long for any thing.

Pellizco [pel-lyeeth'-co], *m.* 1. Pinch, the act of pinching. 2. A nip. 3. A small bit or portion. 4. (Met.) Remorse, disquietude. *Pellizco de monja*, A lozenge or sugar-drop.

Pellón, Pellote [pel-lyone', pel-lyo'-tay], *m.* 1. A long robe made of skins or furs. 2. (Amer.) A skin, checkered in colours, placed on a riding-saddle.

Pelluzgón [pel-lyooth-gone'], *m.* Lock of hair, wool, or tow. *Tener la barba a pelluzgones*, To have an unevenly growing beard.

Pena [pay'-nah], *f.* 1. Punishment, pain, penalty; chastisement, correction. 2. Pain, painfulness, affliction, sorrow, grief, uneasiness of mind, anxiety; a violent emotion of the mind. 3. Pain, labour, hardship, difficulty, toil. 4. Necklace. *Penas de cámara*, Fines forfeited to the royal treasury. *Pena de la mesana*, (Naut.) Peak of the mizzen. *Pena capital, de muerte* or *ordinaria*, Capital punishment or penalty. *A duras penas*, With great difficulty or trouble; scarcely; hardly. *Ni pena ni gloria*, Without pain or pleasure.

Pena, *adv.* *V.* Sopena.

Peñachera, *f.* *V.* Penacho.

Penacho [pay-nah'-cho], *m.* 1. Tuft of feathers on the heads of birds. 2. Plumes, feathers worn as an ornament. 3. Loftiness, haughtiness, presumption. 4. Any thing that rises in the form of a tuft or crest of feathers.

Penachudo, da [pay-nah-choo'-do, dah], *a.* Crested, tufted, plumed.

Penadamente, *adv.* *V.* Penosamente.

Penadilla [pay-nah-deel'-lyah], *f.* A kind of blister or small pustule.

Penado, da [pay-nah'-do, dah], *a.* & *pp.* of Penar. 1. Punished, chastised; suffered. 2. Painful. 3. Narrow-mouthed: applied to vessels.

Penal [pay-nahl'], *a.* Penal, concerning punishment; judicial.

Penalidad [pay-nah-le-dahd'], *f.* 1. Act of suffering punishment. 2. Suffering, calamity, trouble, hardship; penalty.

Pésame [pay'-nah-may], *m.* In Arragon, the same as Pésame.

Penante [pay-nahn'-tay], *pa.* & *a.* 1. Suffering pain or affliction; love lorn, love-sick. 2. Narrow-mouthed: applied to vessels.—*m.* (Prov.) Lover, gallant.

Penar [pay-nar'], *vn.* 1. To suffer pain, to agonize; to be tormented in a future life. 2, To crave, to desire anxiously. 3. To linger.—*va.* To chastise, to inflict punishment.—*vr.* To grieve, to mourn.

Penates [pay-nah'-tes], *m. pl.* Penates, the house-gods of the ancient heathens.

Penatígero [pay-nah-tee'-hay-ro], *m.* (Poet.) He who carried the household gods or penates.

Penca [pen'-cah], *f.* 1. Pricking leaf of a cactus or other similar plant. 2. A leather strap with which convicts are whipped by the hangman. *Hacerse de pencas*, Not to yield what is asked.

Pencazo [pen-cah'-tho], *m.* Lash with the hangman's strap.

Penco [pen'-co], *m.* (Mex. and Cuba) A raw-boned, hard-trotting horse.

Pencudo, da [pen-coo'-do, dah], *a.* Acuminated.

Pendanga [pen-dahn'-gah], *f.* 1. (Coll.) A common prostitute. 2. Knave of diamonds in a game at cards called *Quinolas* or *Reversis*.

Pendejo [pen-day'-ho], *m.* 1. Hair over the pubis and groin. 2. (Vul.) Coward, poltroon.

Pendencia [pen-den'-the-ah], *f.* Quarrel, affray, dispute, feud, jangling contention.

Pendenciar [pen-den-the-ar'], *vn.* To wrangle, to quarrel.

Pendenciero, ra [pen-den-the-ay'-ro, rah], *a.* Quarrelsome.

Pender [pen-derr'], *vn.* 1. To impend, to hang over. 2. To depend. 3. To be irresolute, to leave a thing undecided. *Cuenta pendiente*, An unsettled account. *Deuda pendiente*, A balance unpaid.

Pendiente [pen-de-en'-tay], *a.* Pendent, hanging. *Pendiente de*, Pending, in abeyance.

Pendiente, *f.* Slope, declivity; grade, gradient, of a road or railway; dip or pitch.—*m.* Ear-ring, a pendant.

Pendil [pen-deel'], *m.* A mantle worn by women. *Tomar el pendil*, To elope unexpectedly.

Pendingue (**Tomar el**). To take French leave.

Péndol [pen'-dole], *m.* (Naut.) Boot-topping. *Dar péndoles*, To boot-top a ship, for cleaning the bottom.

Péndola [pen'-do-lah], *f.* 1. A pen. *V.* Pluma. 2. Pendulum.

Pendolaje [pen-do-lah'-hay], *m.* The plunder of a captured vessel.

Pendolario, *m.* *V.* Pendolista.

Pendolero, ra [pen-do-lay'-ro, rah], *a.* Hanging, pendent.

Pendolista [pen-do-lees'-tah], *m.* 1. Penman. 2. (Coll.) Cheat, swindler, impostor.

Pendolita [pen-do-lee'-tah], *f.* The spiral spring of the balance of a watch.

Pendón [pen-done'], *m.* 1. Standard, the colours of a country. 2. Banner carried in processions. 3. Standard, a shoot or principal branch of a stock, preserved at the felling of woods. 4. (Her.) Pennon, a family banner, borne in coats of arms. 5. (Coll.) Nickname of a tall, awkward woman. 6. *pl.* Reins of the leading mule. *A pendón herido*, With all speed and diligence.

Pendoncito [pen-don-thee'-to], *m. dim.* Pennon, a small flag.

Péndulo, la [pen'-doo-lo, lah], *a.* Pendent, hanging, pendulous.—*m.* 1 Pendulum. 2. An instrument for measuring the action of gravity. *Péndulo sideral*, An astronomical clock.

Pene [pay'-nay], *m.* Penis, male organ of generation.

Peneque [pay-nay'-kay], *a.* (Coll.) Intoxicated, drunken.

Penetrabilidad [pay-nay-trah-be-le-dahd'], *f.* Penetrability.

Penetrable [pay-nay-trah'-blay], *a.* 1. Penetrable. 2. That can be understood.

Penetración [pay-nay-trah-the-on'], *f.* 1. Penetration, the act of piercing or penetrating. 2. Penetration, mental discernment, intelligence. 3. Penetration, acuteness, sagacity, clear-sightedness.

Penetrador, ra [pay-nay-trah-dor', rah], *m.* & *f.* Discerner, he who penetrates or distinguishes.

Penetral [pay-nay-trahl'], *m.* (Poet.) The interior or most retired part.

Penetrante [pay-nay-trahn'-tay], *pa.* & *a.* 1. Penetrating, piercing. 2. Heartrending. 3. Clear-sighted, keen. 4. Applied to a deep wound.

Penetrar [pay-nay-trar'], *va.* 1. To penetrate, to pierce; to pass through; to force in. 2. To penetrate, to affect the mind. 3. To penetrate, to fathom, to comprehend. 4. To permeate; to pervade.

Penetrativo, va [pay-nay-trah-tee'-vo, vah], *a.* Penetrative, penetrant.

Penicilina [pay-ne-the-lee'-nah], *f.* (Med.) Penicillin.

Peninsula [pay-neen'-soo-lah], *f.* Peninsula.

Penique [pay-nee'-kay], *m.* Penny, an English copper coin.

Penisla, *f.* *V.* PENÍNSULA.

Penitencia [pay-ne-ten'-the-ah], *f.* 1. Penitence, penance. 2. Repentance. 3. Any act of mortification. 4. Public punishment which the Inquisition inflicted upon some culprits. *Hacer penitencia,* Familiar invitation to a family repast; to take pot-luck.

Penitenciado, da [pay-ne-ten-the-ah'-do, dah], *a.* & *n.* One who was punished by the Inquisition.—*pp.* of PENITENCIAR.

Penitencial [pay-ne-ten-the-ahl'], *a.* Penitential.

Penitenciar [pay-ne-ten-the-ar'], *va.* To impose penance for a fault.

Penitenciaría [pay-ne-ten-the-ah-ree'-ah], *f.* 1. An ecclesiastical court at Rome. 2. Office of a penitentiary canon. 3. Penitentiary, a reformatory prison.

Penitenciario [pay-ne-ten-the-ah'-re-o], *m.* 1. Penitentiary, a dignitary canon who has the power of absolving in certain cases. 2. Penitentiary, the president of an ecclesiatical court at Rome.

Penitente [pay-ne-ten'-tay], *a.* Penitent, repentant, contrite.

Penitente [pay-ne-ten'-tay], *com.* 1. Penitent, one who does penance. 2. Penitent, one who confesses to a confessor. 3. Associate in a party of pleasure or debauchery.

Pennado, da [pen-nah'-do, dah], *a.* (Bot.) Pinnate.

Penol [pay-nol'], *m.* (Naut.) Yard-arm.

Penología [pay-no-lo-hee'-ah], *f.* Penology.

Penosamente, *adv.* Painfully, grievously.

Penoso, sa [pay-no'-so, sah], *a.* Painful, grievous, laborious, distressing, tormenting.

Penoso [pay-no'-so], *m.* An affected fop, a buck or dude.

Pensado, da [pen-sah'-do, dah], *a.* & *pp.* of PENSAR. Deliberate, premeditated. *De caso pensado,* On purpose, designedly.

Pensador, ra [pen-sah-dor', rah], *a.* Thoughtful, meditative, contemplative.—*m.* & *f.* Thinker, profound student.

Pensamiento [pen-sah-me-en'-to], *m.* 1. Thought, idea, meditation, contemplation. 2. Thought, resolution, design. *Ni por pensamiento,* Not even the thought of it. *En un pensamiento,* In a jiffy, in a moment. 3. (Bot.) Pansy.

Pensar [pen-sar'], *vn.* 1. To think, to consider, to reflect, to cogitate, to meditate. 2. To think, to imagine, to fancy, to muse. 3. To think, to intend, to mean. 4. To take into serious consideration; to weigh maturely. 5. To feed cattle. *Sin pensar,* Unexpectedly, thoughtlessly. *Pensar en lo excusado,* To try an impossible thing.

Pensativamente, *adv.* Moodily.

Pensativo, va [pen-sah-tee'-vo, vah], *a.* 1. Pensive, thoughtful, cogitative. 2. (Joc.) Applied to cattle when they stop eating, as if to think.

Penseque [pen-say'-kay], *m.* Error from carelessness or thoughtlessness (fr. *Pensé que*).

Pensil [pen-seel'], *a.* Pensile, hanging supported.—*m.* A beautiful garden.

Pensilvano, na [pen-seel-vah'-no, nah], *a.* Pennsylvanian.

Pensión [pen-se-on'], *f.* 1. Pension, an annual charge laid upon any thing. 2. Pension, a fixed sum paid annually by government. 3. Toil, labour attending an enterprise or office, trouble, encumbrance, painful duty.

Pensionado, da [pen-se-o-nah'-do, dah], *m.* & *f.* Pensioner, pensionary, one who receives a pension.—*pp.* of PENSIONAR.

Pensionar [pen-se-o-nar'], *va.* To impose annual charges, pensions, or other burdens.

Pensionario [pen-se-o-nah'-re-o], *m.* 1. One who pays a pension. 2. Pensionary, the recorder of a city.

Pensionista [pen-se-o-nees'-tah], *com.* 1. Pensioner, pensionary, one who receives a pension. 2. Boarder in a boarding-house.

Penta. A Greek word signifying five.

Pentacórdeo [pen-tah-cor'-day-o], *m.* Pentachord, five-stringed harp.

Pentadáctilo, la [pen-tah-dahc'-te-lo, lah], *a.* Five-fingered or toed; having five finger-like processes or radial arms.

Pentaedro [pen-tah-ay'-dro], *m.* Pentahedron, a solid of five faces.

Pentagloto [pen-tah-glo'-to], *a.* Pentaglottical, written in five languages.

Pentágono [pen-tah'-go-no], *m.* Pentagon.

Pentágrafo [pen-tah'-grah-fo], *m.* Pentagraph.

Pentagrama [pen-tah-grah'-mah], *m.* The musical staff.

Pentámetro [pen-tah'-may-tro], *m.* Petameter.

Pentángulo [pen-tahn'-goo-lo], *m.* Pentangle.

Pentapétalo, la [pen-tah-pay'-tah-lo, lah], *a.* (Bot.) Pentapetalous.

Pentasilabo, ba [pen-tah-see'-lah-bo, bah], *a.* Of five syllables.

Pentástilo [pen-tahs'-te-lo], *m.* (Arch.) Pentastyle.

Pentateuco [pen-tah-tay'-oo-co], *m.* The Pentateuch.

Pentecostés [pen-tay-cos-tays'], *m.* Pentecost, Whitsuntide.

Penúltimo, ma [pay-nool'-te-mo, mah], *a.* Penultimate.

Penumbra [pay-noom'-brah], *f.* Penumbra.

Penuria [pay-noo'-re-ah], *f.* Penury, indigence.

Peña [pay'-nyah], *f.* Rock, large stone. *Por peñas.* A long time.

Peñado [pay-nyah'-do], *m.* *V.* PEÑASCO.

Peñascal [pay-nyas-cahl'], *m.* Rocky hill or mountain.

Peñasco, Peñedo [pay-nyahs'-co], *m.* 1. A large rock. 2. A strong silk stuff.

Peñascoso, sa [pay-nyas-co'-so, sah], *a.* Rocky, mountainous.

Peñol [pay-nyole'], *m.* A large rock.

Péñola [pay'-nyo-lah], *f.* (Poet.) A pen.

Peñón [pay-nyone'], *m.* A large rock, rocky mountain.

Peón [pay-on'], *m.* 1. Pedestrian. *A peón,* (Coll.) A-foot. 2. Day-labourer. *Peón de albañil,* Hodman. 3. Foot-soldier. 4. Top, spinning-top, humming-top. 5. In prosody, a foot of four syllables, three short and one long. 6. Pawn in chess; man, in draughts.

Peonada [pay-o-nah'-dah], *f.* Day-work of a labourer.

Peonaje [pay-o-nah'-hay], *m.* 1. Multitude of people on foot. 2. The body of *peones* who work at once in the same place.

Peonería [pay-o-nay-ree'-ah], *f.* As much land as can be ploughed in a day.

Peonía [pay-o-nee'-ah], *f.* 1. (Bot.) Peony. 2. Quantity of land given to a soldier in a conquered country.

Peonza [pay-on'-thah], *f.* 1. Top, whipping top, gig. 2. A noisy, little fellow. *A peonza,* (Coll.) On foot.

Peor [pay-ore'], *a.* Worse.—*adv.* Worse. *Peor que peor,* Worse and worse.

Peoría [pay-o-ree'-ah], *f.* Deterioration, detriment.

Peormente, *adv.* Worse.

Pepián, *m.* *V.* PIPIÁN.

Pepinar [pay-pe-nar'], *m.* Cucumber-field.

Pepinazo [pay-pe-nah'-tho], *m.* Blow with a cucumber.

Pepinillos [pay-pe-neel'-lyos], *m. pl.* (*dim.*). Gherkins, pickled cucumbers.

Pepino [pay-pee'-no], *m.* (Bot.) Cucumber. Cucumis sativus. *No dársele un pepino,* or *tres pepinos,* Not to give a fig or rush for a thing.

Pepión [pay-pe-on'], *m.* A Spanish gold coin of the reign of Alphonsus the Wise.

Pepita [pay-pee'-tah], *f.* 1. Seed of some fruits, such as melons, apples, etc.; kernel. 2. Pip, a distemper in fowls. *No tener pepita,* To speak out, not to mince matters; to talk all that comes uppermost. 3. Nugget, piece of pure native gold.—*pr. n.* Josie. See JOSEFA in Appendix.

Pepitaña [pay-pe-tah'-nyah], *f.* (Prov.) A pipe made of corn-stalk.

Pepitoria [pay-pe-to'-re-ah], *f.* 1. Fricassee made of giblets, livers, and lights. 2. Medley of things. 3. (Mex.) Peanut or almond candy.

Pepitoso, sa [pay-pe-to'-so, sah], *a.* 1. Abounding in grains or seeds. 2. Applied to fowls with the pip.

Peplo [pay'-plo], *m.* Peplum, a loose gown of the ancient Greek women.

Pepón [pay-pone'], *m.* (Bot.) Water-melon. *V.* SANDÍA.

Pepsina [pep-see'-nah], *f.* Pepsin, the digestive ferment.

Péptico, ca [pep'-te-co, cah], *a.* Peptic.

Peptona [pep-to'-nah], *f.* Peptone.

Pequenamente, *adv.* Little, in a small degree or quantity, not much.

Pequeñez [pay-kay-nyeth'], *f.* 1. Smallness of size; littleness, minuteness. 2. Youth, tender age. 3. Lowness of mind, pusillanimity.

Pequeñito, ta [pay-kay-nyee'-to, tah], *a. dim.* *V.* PEQUEÑUELO.

Pequeño, ña [pay-kay'-nyo, nyah], *a.* 1. Little or small of size, minute. 2. Young, of a tender age. 3. Low-spirited, humble, abject.

Pequín [pay-keen'], *m.* Silk stuff manufactured in Pekin.

Per [per], *prep.* Used in Spanish in composition only, as *perdonable,* pardonable.

Pera [pay'-rah], *f.* 1. Pear, the fruit of the pear-tree. 2. A small tuft of hair left to grow on the chin. 3. (Coll.) A sinecure. *Poner las peras a cuarto* or *a cuatro* or *a ocho,* To compel one to do or concede what he does not wish. *Dar para peras,* To strike or punish. *Partir peras con alguno,* To treat a person familiarly. *Pedir peras al olmo,* To look for pears on elm-trees. *Escoger como entre peras,* To choose very carefully.

Perada [pay-rah'-dah], *f.* Conserve made of the juice of pears.

Peraile [pay-rah'-e-lay], *m.* Wool-comber. *V.* PELAIRE.

Peral [pay-rahl'], *m.* (Bot.) Pear-tree. Pyrus communis.

Peraleda [pay-rah-lay'-dah], *f.* Orchard of pear-trees.

Peraltar [pay-ral-tar'], *va.* To raise the arch of a vault or dome above a semicircle to the figure of a parabola.

Peralte [pay-rahl'-tay], *m.* Height of an arch above a right angle.

Perantón [pay-ran-tone'], *m.* 1. (Bot.) Marvel-plant. Euphorbia cyparissias. 2. A very tall person.

Peraza [pay-rah'-thah], *f.* Fruit of an ingrafted pear-tree.

Perca [perr'-cah], *f.* (Zool.) Perch. Perca fluviatilis.

Percal [per-cahl'], *m.* (Com.) Percale, a dress material. (Per.)

Percalina [per-cah-lee'-nah], *f.* Percaline, a lining material of one colour; book muslin.

Percance [per-cahn'-thay], *m.* 1. Perquisite, something above the settled salary: generally used in the plural. 2. Mischance, misfortune. *Percances del oficio, V.* GAJES DEL OFICIO.

Percarburo [per-car-boo'-ro], *m.* (Chem.) Percarbid(e).

Percatar [per-cah-tar'], *vr.* 1. To think, to consider maturely. 2. To take care, to be on one's guard.

Percebe [per-thay'-bay], *m.* A mollusk having five crusty plates and a fleshy foot. It is common on the coast of Galicia, and eaten cooked without any seasoning.

Percebimiento [per-thay-be-me-en'-to], *m.* Prevention, warning. *V.* APERCIBIMIENTO.

Percepción [per-thep-the-on'], *f.* Perception, notion, idea, feeling.

Perceptibilidad [per-thep-te-be-le-dahd'], *f.* Perceptibility, faculty of perception.

Perceptible [per-thep-tee'-blay], *a.* Perceptible, perceivable.

Perceptiblemente, *adv.* Perceivably, perceptibly.

Perceptivo, va [per-thep-tee'-vo, vah], *a.* Perceptive.

Percibir [per-the-beer'], *va.* 1. To receive, to collect. 2. To perceive, to comprehend.

Percibo [per-thee'-bo], *m.* Act of receiving or perceiving.

Perclórico [per-clo'-re-co], *a.* Perchloric.

Percloruro [per-clo-roo'-ro], *m.* (Chem.) Perchloride.

Percocería [per-co-thay-ree'-ah], *f.* Small work of silver or spangles, filagree, etc.

Percuciente [per-coo-the-en'-tay], *a.* Percutient, striking.

Percudir [per-coo-deer'], *va.* To tarnish the lustre of things.

Percusión [per-coo-se-on'], *f.* Percussion, collision.

Percusor [per-coo-sor'], *m.* One who strikes.

Percutir [per-coo-teer'], *va.* (Med.) To percuss.

Percha [per'-chah], *f.* 1. Perch, a piece of timber to support any thing. 2. Clothes-rack. 3. Snare for catching partridges. 4. String on which fowlers hang their game. 5. (Zool.) Perch. *Perchas,* (Naut.) Floor-timbers. *Estar en percha,* To be safe and secure.

Perchador, ra [per-chah-dor', rah], *m. & f.* Napper, one who raises the nap on cloth.

Perchar [per-char'], *va.* To raise the nap on cloth.

Percheron [per-chay-rone'], *m.* Percheron, Percheron Norman horse.

Perchonar [per-cho-nar'], *vn.* 1. To leave on a vine-stock several long shoots. 2. To lay snares for catching game.

Perdedero [per-day-day'-ro], *m.* Occasion or motive of losing.

Perdedor, ra [per-day-dor', rah], *m. & f.* Loser.

Perder [per-derr'], *va.* 1. To lose, to be deprived of any thing. 2. To lose, to forfeit, to suffer diminution of. 3. To lose, to squander away, to lavish, to misspend. 4. To lose, to miss, not to find. 5. To lose, to ruin, to send to perdition. 6. To lose, to be disappointed, not to obtain what has been wished. 7. To spoil, to mar, to damage. 8. To bet, to lay a wager. *¿Qué quiere Vd. perder?* What will you lay? *La marea pierde,* (Naut.) The tide falls. *Perder la ocasión* or *el lance,* To let an opportunity slip. *Perder terreno,* To lose ground. *Perder tiempo,* (1) To lose time, or not to profit of it. (2) To labour in vain. —*vr.* (1.) To go astray, to miss one's way. 2. To be lost, to be confounded, to be bewildered. 3. To forget or lose the thread of one's subject or discourse. 4. To be spoiled; to be lost or given up to vice. 5. To fall into disuse, to be out of fashion. 6. To cease to be perceived by sight or hearing. 7. To run risk of losing life. 8. To love excessively. 9. (Naut.) To be shipwrecked. 10. To sustain a loss. 11. To conceal itself: applied to rivers which disappear under the earth and rise again. *Perderse de vista,* To excel in an eminent degree. *Tener que perder,* To be a person of credit, to have much to lose. *De la mano a la boca se pierde la sopa,* There's many a slip 'twixt the cup and the lip. *No pierde por delgado sino gordo y mal hilado,* Quality is more important than quantity. *Perder los estribos,* To lose patience.

Perdición [per-de-the-on'], *f.* 1. Losing or the act of losing any thing. 2. Perdition, destruction, ruin, loss. 3. Unbridled, excessive love. 4. Prodigality, extravagance. 5. Perdition, eternal death.

Pérdida [perr'-de-dah], *f.* 1. Loss, privation of what was possessed. 2. Loss, detriment, damage; waste. 3. Quantity or thing lost. *De pérdida,* In a hazardous, perilous manner.

Perdidamente, *adv.* Desperately, furiously; uselessly.

Perdidizo, za [per-de-dee'-tho, thah], *a.* Lost designedly or on purpose. *Hacerse perdidizo,* To lose designedly at cards, as gamesters do at times.

Perdido, da [per-dee'-do, dah], *a. & pp.* of PERDER. Lost, strayed, misguided; profligate, dissolute. *Gente perdida,* Vagrants, vagabonds. *Mujer perdida,* Prostitute. *Pan perdido,* One who becomes a vagrant.

Perdidoso, sa [per-de-do'-so, sah], *a.* Sustaining loss.

Perdigana [per-de-gah'-nah], *f.* (Prov.) A young partridge.

Perdigar [per-de-gar'], *va.* 1. To broil partridges slightly before they are roasted. 2. To stew larded meat in an earthen pan. 3. To dispose, to prepare.

Perdigón [per-de-gone'], *m.* 1. A young partridge. 2. Partridge trained to decoy others. 3. (Prov.) Squanderer, lavisher of money at the gaming-table. *Perdigones,* Hail-shot, small shot, bird-shot.

Perdiguero, ra [per-de-gay'-ro, rah], *a.* Setter, retriever: applied to a dog used by fowlers who pursue partridges.

Perdiguero [per-de-gay'-ro], *m.* Poulterer, dealer in partridges or any other kind of game.

Perdimiento [per-de-me-en'-to], *m. V.* PERDICIÓN and PÉRDIDA.

Perdiz [per-deeth'], *f.* (Orn.) Partridge. Tetrao perdix. *Perdiz real,* Common partridge. *Patas de perdiz,* Nickname to a person who wears red stockings, particularly women. *O perdiz o no comerla,* Neck or nothing. *Perdices en campo raso,* Partridges in an open field (things difficult to obtain).

Perdón [per-done'], *m.* 1. Pardon, forgiveness, absolution; mercy, grace; remission of a debt. 2. Drop of oil, wax, etc., which falls burning. *Con perdón,* Under favour; with your leave.

Perdonable [per-do-nah'-blay], *a.* Pardonable, forgivable.

Perdonador, ra [per-do-nah-dor', rah], *m. & f.* Pardoner, excuser.

Perdonanza [per-do-nahn'-thah], *f. V.* DISIMULO and PERDÓN.

Perdonar [per-do-nar'], *va.* 1. To pardon, to forgive; to remit a debt. 2. To exempt any one from doing what he should execute; to spare, to excuse. 3. To beg leave or permission: an expression of civil denial or light apology. *Perdone,* (Coll.) God help or assist you: used as an excuse for not giving charity.—*vr.* To decline doing any thing; to excuse one's self from doing any thing.

Perdonavidas [per-do-nah-vee'-das], *m.* (Coll.) Bully, hector.

Perdulario, ria [per-doo-lah'-re-o, ah], *a.* Extremely careless of one's own interest or person.

Perdurable [per-doo-rah'-blay], *a.* Perpetual, everlasting, continual.

Perdurablemente, *adv.* Eternally, perpetually.

Perecear [pay-ray-thay-ar'], *va.* To protract, to delay, to put off.

Perecedero, ra [pay-ray-thay-day'-ro, rah], *a.* Perishable, decaying, fading.

Perecedero [pay-ray-thay-day'-ro], *m.* Misery, extreme want.

Perecer [pay-ray-therr'], *vn.* 1. To perish, to die, to be destroyed. 2. To perish, to suffer or undergo damage, toil, or fatigue. 3. To be extremely poor, to perish for want of the necessaries of life.—*vr.* 1. To crave, to desire anxiously. 2. To be violently agitated, to die with love. *Perecer de hambre,* To perish with hunger. *Perecer de risa,* To be convulsed with laughter.

Perecido, da [pay-ray-thee'-do, dah], *a. & pp.* of PERECER. Dying with anxiety, lost, undone.

Pereciente [pay-ray-the-en'-tay], *pa.* Perishing.

Perecimiento [pay-ray-the-me-en'-to], *m.* Loss, decay, decline; wreck of a ship.

Peregrinación [pay-ray-gre-nah-the-on'], *f.* 1. Peregrination, travelling in foreign countries. 2. Pilgrimage. 3. The course of this life.

Peregrinamente, *adv.* Rarely, curiously.

Peregrinante [pay-ray-gre-nahn'-tay], *pa.* Sojourner; travelling; he who peregrinates.

Peregrinar [pay-ray-gre-nar'], *vn.* 1. To peregrinate, to travel in foreign countries. 2. To go on a pilgrimage. 3. To exist in this mortal life.

Peregrinidad [pay-ray-gre-ne-dahd'], *f.* Strangeness, wonderfulness.

Peregrino, na [pay-ray-gree'-no, nah], *a.* 1. Peregrine, foreign. 2. Travelling or sojourning in foreign countries. 3. Going on a pilgrimage; migratory (as used of birds). 4. Strange, wonderful, seldom seen. 5. Very handsome or perfect.

Peregrino [pay-ray-gree'-no], *m.* A pilgrim, a palmer.

Perejil [pay-ray-heel'], *m.* 1. (Bot.) Parsley. Apium petroselinum. 2. Showy dress or apparel.—*pl.* Honorary titles attached to offices.

Perejilón [pay-ray-he-lone'], *m.* (Prov.) Creeping crow-foot. Ranunculus repens.

Perendeca [pay-ren-day'-cah], *f.* (Coll.) Whore, hussy, trull.

Perendengue [pay-ren-den'-gay], *m.* 1. Pendant of the ears, ear-drop. 2. Any cheap or tawdry feminine ornament.

Perene [pay-ray'-nay], *a.* *V.* PERENNE.

Perengano, na [pay-ren-gah'-no, nah], *m.* & *f.* So-and-so: used after other names, as *fulano, mengano, zutano,* y *perengano.* In America the word *parencejo* is commonly used.

Perennal [pay-ren-nahl'], *a.* 1. *V.* PERENNE. 2. Continually mad, without lucid intervals.

Perennalmente, *adv.* *V.* PERENNEMENTE.

Perenne [pay-ren'-nay], *a.* Perennial, perpetual. *Loco perenne,* Madman who has no lucid intervals.

Perennemente, *adv.* Continually, perpetually.

Perennidad [pay-ren-ne-dahd'], *f.* Perennity, continuity.

Perentoriamente, *adv.* Peremptorily.

Perentoriedad [pay-ren-to-re-ay-dahd'], *f.* Peremptoriness, great urgency.

Perentorio, ria [pay-ren-to'-re-o, ah], *a.* Peremptory, absolute, decisive.

Perero [pay-ray'-ro], *m.* Instrument formerly used to pare fruit.

Pereza [pay-ray'-thah], *f.* 1. Laziness, tardiness, negligence, idleness, carelessness, sloth. 2. Slowness in movements. 3. Difficulty in rising from bed or from a seat. *Sacudir la pereza,* To conquer laziness; to learn or set one's self resolutely to a task.

(*Yo perezco, yo perezca,* from *Perecer.* *V.* CONOCER.)

Perezosamente, *adv.* Lazily, slothfully, negligently, idly.

Perezoso, sa [pay-ray-tho'-so, sah], *a.* Lazy, careless, indolent, slothful, negligent, idle; sometimes used as a substantive, for a lazy person or a lubber. —*m.* (Zool.) The sloth.

Perfección [per-fec-the-on'], *f.* Perfection, superior excellence; faultlessness, completeness; beauty, grace; high degree of virtue.—*pl.* Accomplishments.

Perfeccionador [per-fec-the-o-nah-dor'], *m.* (Littl. us.) Perfecter.

Perfeccionamiento [per-fec-the-o-nah-me-en'-to], *m.* The act of perfecting, finishing, completion.

Perfeccionar [per-fec-the-o-nar'], *va.* To perfect, to complete, to finish, to heighten.

Perfectamente, *adv.* Perfectly, completely.

Perfectible [per-fec-tee'-blay], *a.* Perfectible, capable of being made perfect.

Perfectivo, va [per-fec-tee'-vo, vah], *a.* Perfective.

Perfecto, ta [per-fec'-to, tah], *a.* 1. Perfect, complete, accomplished. 2. Faultless, consummate, accurate. 3. Beautiful, fair, handsome. 4. Excellent, of the highest grade. 5. (Gram.) Perfect (tense).

Perfecto, *m.* Improvements made in an inheritance.

Perficiente [per-fe-the-en'-tay], *a.* That which perfects.

Pérfidamente [perr'-fe-dah-men-tay], *adv.* Perfidiously.

Perfidia [per-fee'-de-ah], *f.* Perfidy, treachery.

Pérfido, da [perr'-fe-do, dah], *a.* Perfidious, treacherous, disloyal.

Perfil [per-feel'], *m.* 1. Profile, contour, outline. *Tomar perfiles,* To place oiled paper over a painting, in order to draw its outlines. 2. Light architectural ornament; hair. 3. Stroke of certain letters. 4. Profile, side-view.

Perfilado, da [per-fe-lah'-do, dah], *a.* Applied to a well-formed face, nose, etc.—*pp.* of PERFILAR.

Perfiladura [per-fe-lah-doo'-rah], *f.* Art of drawing profiles; the sketching of outlines.

Perfilar [per-fe-lar'], *va.* To draw profiles, to sketch outlines.—*vr.* To incline, to be bent to one side.

Perfoliada, or **Perfoliata** [per-fo-le-ah'-dah], *f.* (Bot.) Hare's-ear, thorough-wax. Bupleurum rotundifolium. *V.* CORAZONCILLO. St. John's wort. Hypericum.

Perfoliado, da [per-fo-le-ah'-do, dah], *a.* (Bot.) Perfoliate.

Perforación [per-fo-rah-the-on'], *f.* Perforation.

Perforador, ra [per-fo-rah-dor', rah], *a.* Perforating.—*f.* 1. Jackhammer. 2. Punch.

Perforar [per-fo-rar'], *va.* To perforate.

Perfumadero [per-foo-mah-day'-ro], *m.* *V.* PERFUMADOR, 2d def.

Perfumado, da [per-foo-mah'-do, dah], *a.* & *pp.* of PERFUMAR. Odoriferous, perfumated.

Perfumador [per-foo-mah-dor'], *m.* 1. Perfumer. 2. Vessel in which perfumes are kept. 3. Perfuming-pan.

Perfumar [per-foo-mar'], or **Perfumear** [per-foo-may-ar'], *va.* To perfume, to fumigate.

Perfume [per-foo'-may], *m.* Perfume; odour, fragrance; good or bad smell or flavour.

Perfumería [per-foo-may-ree'-ah], *f.* A perfumer's shop.

Perfumero, ra [per-foo-may'-ro, rah], *m.* & *f.* Perfumer.

Perfumista [per-foo-mees'-tah], *m.* Perfumer, dealer in perfumes.

Perfunctoriamente, *adv.* Perfunctorily, superficially.

Perfunctorio, ria [per-foonc-to'-re-o, ah], *a.* Perfunctory.

Perfusión [per-foo-se-on'], *f.* Affusion, sprinkling water on the head.

Pergaminero [per-gah-me-nay'-ro], *m.* Parchment-maker.

Pergamino [per-gah-mee'-no], *m.* 1. Parchment, vellum; skin dressed for writing. 2. Parchment, diploma, a formal writing on parchment.

Pergenio, *m.* *V.* PERGEÑO.

Pergeño [per-hay'-nyo], *m.* (Coll.) Skill, dexterity.

Pérgola [per'-go-lah], *f.* Pergola.

Peri [pay'-re], *f.* 1. A beautiful and beneficent fairy in Persian mythology. 2. (Gram.) An inseparable prefix derived from the Greek, and meaning around.

Periancio, Periantio [pay-re-ahn'-the-o], *m.* (Bot.) Perianth.

Peribolo [pay-ree'-bo-lo], *m.* (Arch.) Peribolos, the inclosed court of an edifice.

Pericardio [pay-re-car'-de-o], *m.* Pericardium.

Pericarpio [pay-re-car'-pe-o], *m.* Pericarp, covering of any fruit.

Pericia [pay-ree'-the-ah], *f.* Skill, knowledge, practical experience.

Perico [pay-ree'-co], *m.* 1. Curls formerly worn by women. 2. A kind of small parrot, parrakeet, indigenous to Cuba and South America. 3. Dim. of PEDRO. *¿ De cuando acá Perico con guantes ?* Surprise at seeing something unusual. *Perico entre ellas,* A cot or cotquean.

Pericón [pay-re-cone'], *m.* 1. Knave of clubs in the game of *Quinolas.* 2. A large fan.

Pericón, na [pay-re-cone', nah], *a.* Fit for all things: generally applied to horses fit for draught or saddle.

Pericona [pay-re-co'-nah], *f.* Shaft mule; a mule fit for the coach as well as the saddle.

Pericráneo [pay-re-crah'-nay-o], *m.* Pericranium.

Peridromo [pay-re-dro'-mo], *m.* (Arch.) Peridrome, a covered gallery around a building.

Periecos [pay-re-ay'-cose], *m. pl.* Periœci, people on the opposite side of the globe, in the same latitude.

Periferia [pay-re-fay'-re-ah], *f.* Periphery. *V.* CIRCUNFERENCIA.

Perifollo [pay-re-fol'-lyo], *m.* (Bot.) Common chervil. Scandix cerefolium. *Perifollos,* Ribbons and other ornaments of women, particularly if excessive or tawdry.

Perifonear [pay-re-fo-nay-ar'], *va.* To broadcast by radio.

Perifrasear [pay-re-frah-say-ar'], *va.* To periphrase, to use circumlocutions.

Perífrasi, Perífrasis [pay-ree'-frah-se], *f.* (Rhet.) Periphrasis, circumlocution.

Perifrástico, ca [pay-re-frahs'-te-co, cah], *a.* Periphrastic, round about, circumlocutory.

Perigallo [pay-re-gahl'-lyo], *m.* 1. Skin hanging from the chin of lean persons. 2. Kind of glossy ribbon worn by women. 3. (Coll.) A tall, lean man. 4. Kind of slender sling. 5. (Naut.) Line, a thin rope; navel-line; topping-lift.

Perigeo [pay-re-hay'-o], *m.* (Astron.) Perigee, perigeum.

Perigonio [pay-re-go'-ne-o], *m.* (Bot.) Perigynium, perianth.

Perihelio [pay-re-ay'-le-o], *m.* (Astron.) Perihelion.

Perilustre [per-e-loos'-tray], *a.* (Ant.) Very illustrious.

Perilla [pay-reel'-lyah], *f.* 1. (Dim.) A small pear. 2. Ornament in form of a pear. 3. Pommel of a saddle-bow, a knob. 4. A small tuft of hair growing on the chin. *V.* PERA, 2d def. *De perilla,* To the purpose, at a proper time.

Perillán, na [pay-reel-lyahn', nah], *a.* (Coll.) Artful, knavish, vagrant.

Perillán, na [pay-reel-lyahn', nah], *m.* & *f.* 1. Huckster, hucksterer, a sly, crafty fellow. 2. (Coll.) A clever fellow.

Perillo [pay-reel'-lyo], *m.* Gingerbread nut.

Perímetro [pay-ree'-may-tro], *m.* Perimeter. *V.* ÁMBITO.

Perinclito, ta [pay-reen'-cle-to, tah], *a.* Famous, renowned, grand.

Perineal [pay-re-nay-ahl'], *a.* Perineal.

Perineo [pay-re-nay'-o], *m.* (Anat.) Perineum.

Perineumonía [pay-re-nay-oo-mo-nee'-ah], *f.* Pneumonia, inflammation of the lungs. *V.* PULMONÍA.

Perinola [pay-re-no'-lah], *f.* 1. A hand-top with four faces; a teetotum. 2. A neat little woman.

Perioca [pay-ree'-o-cah], *f.* Synopsis, argument of a book.

Periódicamente, *adv.* Periodically.

Periódico, ca [pay-re-o'-de-co, cah], *a.* Periodical, periodic.

Periódico [pay-re-o'-de-co], *m.* News

paper, periodical.
Periodismo [pay-re-o-dees'-mo], *m.* Journalism.
Periodista [pay-re-o-dees'-tah], *m.* Author or publisher of a periodical.
Periodístico, ca [pay-re-o-dees'-te-co, cah], *a.* Journalistic. *Informe periodístico,* Newspaper report.
Período [pay-ree'-o-do], *m.* 1. Period, a determinate space of time. 2. Period, clause, a complete sentence. 3. Period, the time of revolution of a planet. 4. (Mus.) Period, phrase.
Periostio [pay-re-os'-te-o], *m.* Periosteum, the nutritive membrane which covers a bone.
Peripatético [pay-re-pah-tay'-te-co], *m.* Peripatetic, a follower of Aristotle.
Peripatético, ca [pay-re-pah-tay'-te-co, cah], *a.* 1. Belonging to the Peripatetics. 2. Applied colloquially to any person of ridiculous or extravagant opinions.
Peripecia [pay-re-pay-the-ah], *f.* (Poet.) Peripetia, sudden change of condition in the persons of a drama, or in fortune.
Periplo [pay-ree'-plo], *m.* Diary of a voyage; voyage around a coast.
Peripuesto, ta [pay-re-poo-es'-to, tah], *a.* Very gay, very fine, very spruce in dress.
Periquete [pay-re-kay'-tay], *m.* (Coll.) Jiffy, instant. *En un periquete,* In a jiffy.
Periquillo [pay-re-keel'-lyo], *m.* A small sweetmeat made of sugar alone.
Periquito [pay-re-kee'-to], *m.* 1. (Orn.) Parrakeet, paroquet, small parrot. 2. (Naut.) Sky-sail, sky-scraper.
Periscios [pay-rees'-the-ose], *m. pl.* Periscii, inhabitants of the polar circles.
Periscopio [pay-ris-co'-pe-o], *m.* Periscope.
Peristáltico, ca [pay-ris-tahl'-te-co, cah], *a.* Peristaltic: applied to the motion of the intestines.
Per istam (Lat.) in phrase, *Quedarse per ístam,* To be ignorant of, to be left in the lurch.
Peristilo [pay-ris-tee'-lo], *m* (Arch.) Peristyle, colonnade.
Perita [pay-ree'-tah], *f. dim.* A small pear.
Perito, ta [pay-ree'-to, tah], *a.* Skilful, able, experienced.—*m.* 1. Connoisseur. 2. Appraiser o goods. 3. A critical person, a skilful workman.
Peritoneo [pay-re-to-nay'-o], *m.* (Anat.) Peritoneum, the serous membrane of the abdomen.
Peritonitis [pay-re-to-nee'-tis], *f.* (Med.) Peritonitis.
Perjudicador, ra [per-hoo-de-cah-dor', rah], *m. & f.* One who prejudices, injures, or causes damage.
Perjudicar [per-hoo-de-car'], *va.* To prejudice, to cause damage to another, to injure, to malign.
Perjudicial [per-hoo-de-the-ahl'], *a.* Prejudicial, hurtful, mischievous, pernicious.
Perjudicialmente, *adv.* Prejudicially, mischievously.
Perjuicio [per-hoo-ee'-the-o], *m.* Prejudice, mischief, injury, detriment, damage, grievance.
Perjurador, ra [per-hoo-rah-dor', rah], *m. & f.* Perjurer, forswearer.
Perjurar [per-hoo-rar'], *vn.* 1. To swear falsely; to commit perjury. 2. To swear, to obtest the great name profanely.—*vr.* To perjure one's self.
Perjurio [per-hoo'-re-o], *m.* Perjury, false oath.
Perjuro, ra [per-hoo'-ro, rah], *a.* Perjured, forsworn.
Perjuro, ra [per-hoo'-ro, rah], *m. & f.* 1. Forswearer, perjurer. 2. *V.* PERJURIO.
Perla [perr'-lah], *f.* Pearl, margarite: any thing precious, clear, or bright. *Perlas,* Fine teeth. *De perlas,* Much to the purpose; excellently, eminently fine.
Perlático, ca [per-lah'-te-co, cah], *a.* Paralytic, palsied.
Perlería [per-lay-ree'-ah], *f.* Collection of pearls.
Perlesía [per-lay-see'-ah], *f.* Paralysis, palsy.
Perlino, na [per-lee'-no, nah] *a.* Pearl-coloured.
Perlita [per-lee'-tah], *f. dim.* A small pearl.
Perlongar [per-lon-gar'], *vn.* (Naut.) To coast, to sail along the coast.
Permanecer [per-mah-nay-therr'], *vn.* To persist, to endure, to last.
Permaneciente [per-mah-nay-the-en'-tay], *pa. & a.* Permanent; persisting.
Permanencia [per-mah-nen'-the-ah], *f.* Duration, permanency, perseverance, constancy, consistency.
Permanente [per-mah-nen'-tay], *a.* Permanent, durable, lasting.—*f.* Permanent, permanent wave.
Permanentemente, *adv.* Permanently.
Permanganato [per-man-gah-nah'-to], *m.* (Chem.) Permanganate.
Permisible [per-me-see'-blay], *a.* Permissible.
Permisión [per-me-se-on'], *f.* 1. Permission, leave. 2. Confession, grant; the thing yielded.
Permisivamente, *adv.* Permissively.
Permisivo, va [per-me-see'-vo, vah], *a.* Permissive.
Permiso [per-mee'-so], *m.* Permission, leave, license, allowance, liberty.
Permisor [per-me-sor'], *m.* Granter. *V.* PERMITIDOR.
Permistión [per-mis-te-on'], *f.* Permission, permixtion, the act of mixing.
Permitente [per-me-ten'-tay], *pa.* He that grants or permits.
Permitidero, ra [per-me-te-day'-ro, rah], *a.* What may be permitted.
Permitidor [per-me-te-dor'], *m.* Permitter, granter.
Permitir [per-me-teer'], *va.* 1. To permit, to consent, to agree to, to give leave. 2. To permit, to suffer without authorizing or approving. 3. To permit, to give time or place to execute a thing. 4. To permit, not to hinder what one could and ought to avoid.—*vr.* To show one's self, to appear benign, generous, and liberal.
Permuta [per-moo'-tah], *f.* Exchange of one thing for another, barter.
Permutable [per-moo-tah'-blay], *a.* Permutable, capable of being permuted.
Permutación [per-moo-tah-the-on'], *f.* 1. *V.* PERMUTA. 2. (Math.) Permutation, alteration of the order of elements or numbers.
Permutante [per-moo-tahn'-tay], *pa. & a.* Permutant; exchanging.
Permutar [per-moo-tar'], *va.* To exchange, to barter, to commute, to permute.
Perna [perr'-nah], *f.* Flat shell-fish.
Pernada [per-nah'-dah], *f.* Blow with the leg; a violent movement of the leg.
Pernaza [per-nah'-thah], *f.* (Aug.) A thick or big leg.
Pernear [per-nay-ar'], *vn.* 1. To kick, to shake the legs. 2. To drive about in pursuit of an affair. 3. To be vexed, to fret.—*va.* To drive pigs to market and sell them by retail.
Perneo [per-nay'-o], *m.* (Prov.) Public sale of hogs.
Pernería [per-nay-ree'-ah], *f.* Collection of pins or bolts.
Pernetas (En) [per-nay'-tas], *adv.* Bare-legged.
Pernete [per-nay'-tay], *m.* (Naut.) Small pin, peg, or bolt.
Perniabierto, ta [per-ne-ah-be-err'-to, tah], *a.* Bandy-legged.
Perniciosamente, *adv.* Perniciously noxiously, hurtfully.
Pernicioso, sa [per-ne-the-oh'-so, sah], *a.* Pernicious, mischievous, destructive.
Pernigón [per-ne-gone'], *m.* Genoese plum.
Pernil [per-neel'], *m.* 1. Ham, shoulder of an animal, especially of pork. 2. Thigh of breeches; pantalets.
Pernio [perr'-ne-o], *m.* A kind of hinges for doors and windows.
Perniquebrar [per-ne-kay-brar'], *va.* To break the legs.
Pernituerto, ta [per-ne-too-err'-to, tah], *a.* Crook-legged.
Perno [perr'-no], *m.* 1. A round-headed pin; a large nail, a spike. 2. Hook of a hinge for doors and windows. 3. (Mech.) Joint pin, crank pin. 4. (Naut.) A bolt. *Perno pinzote,* Main bolt, king bolt. *Perno de gancho,* Hook-bolt. *Perno de ojo,* Eye-bolt. *Perno de argolla,* Ring-bolt. *Perno de cadena,* Chain-bolt.
Pernoctar [per-noc-tar'], *vn.* To pass the night; to be awake, to watch, or to sit up the whole night.
Pero [pay'-ro] *m.* 1. A kind of apple. 2. Apple-tree. Pyrus malus.
Pero, *conj.* But, except, yet.—*m.* Fault, defect.
Perogrullada, or **Verdad de Perogrullo** [pay-ro-grool-lyah'-dah], *f.* (Coll.) Truth of no moment and universally known.
Perojiménez [pay-ro-he-may'-neth], *m.* A variety of grape and the wine made from it.
Perol [pay-role'], *m.* Boiler, kettle, copper.
Perón [pay-rone'], *m.* (Mex. Bot.) *V.* PERO.
Peroné [pay-ro-nay'], *m.* (Anat.) Fibula, perone, the lesser bone of the leg.
Peroración [pay-ro-rah-the-on'], *f.* Peroration, the conclusion of an oration.
Perorar [pay-ro-rar'], *vn.* 1. To conclude a speech or oration. 2. To make an harangue or speech, to declaim. 3. To solicit effectually.
Perorata [pay-ro-rah'-tah], *f.* (Coll.) An harangue, a speech.
Peróxido [pay-rok'-se-do], *m.* Peroxide, highest grade of oxide.
Perpejana [per-pay-hah'-nah], *f.* (Obs.) *V.* PARPALLA.
Perpendicular [per-pen-de-coo-lar'], *a.* Perpendicular.
Perpendicularmente, *adv.* Perpendicularly.
Perpendículo [per-pen-dee'-coo-lo], *m.* 1. Plumb, plummet: an instrument by which perpendicularity is discerned. 2. Pendulum.
Perpetración [per-pay-trah-the-on'], *f.* Perpetration, the act of committing a crime.
Perpetrador, ra [per-pay-trah-dor', rah], *m. & f.* Perpetrator, aggressor.
Perpetrar [per-pay-trar'], *va.* To perpetrate, to commit a crime.
Perpetua [per-pay'-too-ah], *f.* (Bot.) Eternal flower, everlasting, the blossom of goldilocks, the plant Gnaphalium stœchas. *Perpetua encarnada,* (Bot.) Globe amaranth. Gomphrena globosa.

Perpetuación [per-pay-too-ah-the-on'], *f.* Perpetuation.

Perpetual [per-pay-too-ahl'], *a.* (Obs.) *V.* PERPETUO.

Perpetuamente, *adv.* Perpetually, for ever.

Perpetuán [per-pay-too-ahn'], *m.* Everlasting, a kind of woollen stuff.

Perpetuar [per-pay-too-ar'], *va.* 1. To perpetuate. 2. To continue without cessation or intermission.

Perpetuidad [per-pay-too-e-dahd'], *f.* 1. Perpetuity, duration. 2. Perpetuity, exemption from intermission or cessation.

Perpetuo, tua [per-pay'-too-o, ah], *a.* Perpetual.

Perpiaño [per-pe-ah'-nyo], *m.* Perpender, a front binding-stone in a wall.

Perplejamente, *adv.* Perplexedly, confusedly.

Perplejidad [per-play-he-dahd'], *f.* Perplexity, irresolution, embarrassment.

Perplejo, ja [per-play'-ho, hah], *a.* Doubtful, uncertain, perplexed.

Perpunte [per-poon'-tay], *m.* A quilted under-waistcoat to protect the body from cutting weapons.

Perquirir [per-ke-reer'], *va.* To seek diligently.

Perra [perr'-rah], *f.* 1. A female dog; bitch, slut. *Perra salida,* A bitch in heat. *Soltar la perra,* (Prov.) To run through one's fortune; to boast of any thing beforehand. 2. Drunkenness. 3. Slothfulness, laziness.

Perrada [per-rah'-dah], *f.* 1. Pack of dogs. 2. A false compliment. 3. Hasty morning repast of grapes.

Perramente, *adv.* Very ill; badly.

Perrazo [per-rah'-tho], *m. aug.* A large dog.

Perrengue [per-ren'-gay], *m.* (Coll.) 1. One who is peevish; a snarler. 2. Negro.

Perrera [per-ray'-rah], *f.* 1. Kennel, a cot for dogs. 2. Employment attended with much fatigue and little profit. 3. *com.* A bad paymaster. 4. Mule or horse spent with age and cast off.

Perrería [per-ray-ree'-ah], *f.* 1. Pack of dogs. 2. Set or nest of rogues. 3. Expression or demonstration of vexation or wrath.

Perrero [per-ray'-ro], *m.* 1. Beadle who drags dogs out of the church. 2. Boy or servant whose business is to take care of hounds or dogs used in the chase. 3. One who is very fond of hounds and dogs. 4. Impostor, cheat.

Perrezno, na [per-reth'-no, nah], *m.* & *f.* Whelp, puppy.

Perrico [per-ree'-co], *m. dim.* A little dog.

Perrillo [per-reel'-lyo], *m.* 1. (Dim.) A little dog. *Perrillo raposero,* Harrier. *Perrillo de falda,* Lap-dog. 2. Trigger of a gun. 3. A semi-lunar piece of a horse's bridle.

Perrito [per-ree'-to], *m. dim.* A little dog. *Perrito de todas bodas,* A cater-cousin, a busy-body.

Perro [per'-ro], *m.* 1. Dog. Canis. *Perro de aguas,* Water-dog. *Perro de muestra,* Pointer. *Perro de presa,* Bull-dog. *Perro de ayuda,* Newfoundland dog, a large dog kept to defend his master. *Perro de ajeo.* Setter dog used for partridges. 2. One who obstinately asserts an opinion, or perseveres in an undertaking. 3. Damage, loss, deception. 4. (Met.) Name of contempt or ignominy given to a person. *Perro careador,* Shepherd's dog. *Perro chico,* Five centime copper coin, cent (so called from about 1870 because of badly executed figure of the lion in the arms of Spain). *Ponerse como un perro* or *hecho un perro,* To get into a vehement passion. *A perro viejo no hay tus tus,* (prov.) Old birds are not caught with chaff. *¡A otro perro con ese hueso!* Tell that to the marines! *A trágala perro,* Forcibly; with violence. *Como perro con maza,* Like a dog with his tail between his legs. *Dar perro muerto,* To deceive or disappoint a person. *Perro viejo* (an old dog), a clever, experienced man. *Todo junto, como al perro los palos,* The day of reckoning may be long in coming, but it comes at last.

Perroquete [per-ro-kay'-tay], *m.* (Naut.) Top-mast.

Perruna [per-roo'-nah], *f.* Dog-bread, coarse bread for dogs.

Perruno, na [per-roo'-no, nah], *a.* Doggish, canine; currish.

Persa [perr'-sah], *a.* & *n.* Persian.

Persecución [per-say-coo-the-on'], *f.* 1. Persecution. 2. Toils, troubles, fatigue, molestation.

Perseguidor, ra [per-say-gee-dor', rah], *m.* & *f.* Persecutor; one who harasses or molests; a foe.

Perseguimiento [per-say-gee-me-en'-to], *m.* Persecution; hunt.

Perseguir [per-say-geer'], *va.* 1. To pursue a fugitive. 2. To dun, to importune, to beset. 3. To persecute, to pursue with malignity. 4. To persecute, to pursue, to importune much.

Perseo [per-say'-o], *m.* (Ast.) Perseus, a northern constellation.

Persevante [per-say-vahn'-tay], *m.* Pursuivant at arms.

Perseverancia [per-say-vay-rahn'-the-ah], *f.* Perseverance, constancy.

Perseverante [per-say-vay-rahn'-tay], *a.* Perseverant, persistent.

Perseverantemente, *adv.* Constantly, perseverantly.

Perseverar [per-say-vay-rar'], *vn.* To persevere, to persist, to abide.

Persiana [per-se-ah'-nah], *f.* A silk stuff with large flowers. *Persianas,* Venetian blinds.

Persiano, na [per-se-ah'-no, nah], *a.* & *n.* Persian.

Pérsico, ca [perr'-se-co, cah], *a.* Persian.—*m.* Peach-tree and its fruit.

Persignarse [per-sig-nar'-say], *vr.* 1. To make the sign of the cross. 2. To admire, to be surprised at a thing. 3. To handsel, to begin to sell; to make the first act of sale.

Pérsigo [perr'-se-go], *m.* (Bot.) Peach. Amygdalus persica.

(*Yo persigo, persiga; él persiguió, persiguiera;* from *Perseguir.* *V.* PEDIR.

Persistencia [per-sis-ten'-the-ah], *f.* Persistence, steadiness, perseverance, obstinacy.

Persistente [per-sis-ten'-tay], *pa.* & *a.* Permanent, firm, persistent.

Persistir [per-sis-teer'], *vn.* To persist, to continue firm, to persevere.

Persona [per-soh'-nah], *f.* 1. Person, individual, or particular man or woman. 2. Person, the exterior appearance. 3. Personage, a distinguished character; a man of merit or talents. 4. (Gram.) Person, the quality of the noun that modifies the verb. 5. Person, man or woman in a fictitious dialogue. *De persona a persona,* From person to person, from man to man. *En persona* or *por su persona,* Personally, in person. *Hacer de persona,* To boast, to brag, to exalt one's self.

Personado [per-so-nah'-do], *m.* Benefice which confers a prerogative on the incumbent, yet without jurisdiction.

Personaje [per-so-nah'-hay], *m.* 1. Personage, a man or woman of eminence. 2. Personage, character assumed, a disguised person, a stranger. 3. A kind of ecclesiastical benefice.

Personal [per-so-nahl'], *a.* Personal, particular.—*m.* Personnel. *Personal de una oficina,* Office personnel.

Personalidad [per-so-nah-le-dahd'], *f.* 1. Personality, the personal existence of any one. 2. Personality, reflection upon private actions or character. 3. Legal capacity for intervening in some business.

Personalizar [per-so-nah-le-thar'], *va.* To fall into personalities in writing or talking.—*vr.* To show one's self a party at law.

Personalmente, *adv.* Personally, in person; hypostatically.

Personarse [per-so-nar'-say], *vr.* 1. *V.* AVISTARSE. 2. To appear personally.

Personaza [per-so-nah'-thah], *f. aug.* Huge personage.

Personería [per-so-nay-ree'-ah], *f.* Charge or employment of an agent, deputy, or attorney.

Personero, ra [per-so-nay'-ro, rah], *m.* & *f.* Deputy, agent, attorney, trustee, receiver.

Personificación [per-so-ne-fe-cah-the-on'], *f.* Personification.

Personificar [per-so-ne-fe-car'], *va.* To personify, to personalize.

Personilla [per-so-neel'-lyah], *f.* Mannikin, a ridiculous little fellow.

Perspectiva [pers-pec-tee'-vah], *f.* 1. (Art) Perspective, the science of perspective. 2. Work executed according to the rules of perspective. 3. View, vista. 4. A deceitful appearance.

Perspectivo [pers-pec-tee'-vo], *m.* Professor of perspective.

Perspicacia, Perspicacidad [pers-pe-cah'-the-ah], *f.* 1. Perspicaciousness perspicacity, quickness of sight. 2. Perspicacity, clear-sightedness, keenness.

Perspicaz [pers-pe-cath'], *a.* 1. Perspicacious, quick-sighted. 2. Acute, sagacious, clear-sighted.

Perspicuamente [pers-pe-coo-ah-men'-tay], *adv.* Perspicuously.

Perspicuidad [pers-pe-coo-e-dahd'], *f.* 1. Perspicuity, clearness, transparency. 2. Perspicuity, clearness to the mind, neatness of style.

Perspicuo, cua [pers-pee'-coo-o, ah], *a.* 1. Perspicuous, clear, transparent. 2. Perspicuous, clear to the understanding: it is applied to him who writes with clearness and elegance, and to his style.

Perspiración [pers-pe-rah-the-on'], *f.* Perspiration.

Perspirar [pers-pe-rar'], *vn.* To perspire (used of insensible perspiration).

Perspiratorio, ria [pers-pe-rah-to'-re-o, ah], *a.* Perspiratory.

Persuadidor, ra [per-soo-ah-de-dor', rah], *m.* & *f.* Persuader.

Persuadir [per-soo-ah-deer'], *va.* To persuade, to influence by argument or expostulation; to induce.—*vr.* To be persuaded, to form a judgment or opinion; to be convinced.

Persuasible [per-soo-ah-see'-blay], *a.* Persuasible, persuadable.

Persuasión [per-soo-ah-se-on'], *f.* Persuasion, the act or state of being persuaded; opinion, judgment.

Persuasiva [per-soo-ah-see'-vah], *f.* Persuasiveness, persuasive

Persuasivo, va [per-soo-ah-see'-vo, vah] *a.* Persuasive, moving

Persuasor, ra [per-soo-ah-sor', rah], *m.* & *f.* Persuader.

Pertenecer [per-tay-nay-therr'], *vn.* 1. To belong to, to appertain, to concern.

2. To behoove, to become, to pertain; to relate to.
Pertenecido [per-tay-nay-thee'-do], *m.* *V.* PERTENENCIA.—*Pertenecido, da, pp.* of PERTENECER.
Perteneciente [per-tay-nay-the-en'-tay], *pa.* & *a.* 1. Belonging, appertaining. 2. Apt, fit, ready.
Pertenencia [per-tay-nen'-the-ah], *f.* 1. Right of property; place or territory belonging to any one. 2. Appurtenance, dependence; an accessory or appendage.
(*Yo pertenezco, yo pertenezca*, from *Pertenecer. V.* ABORRECER.)
Pértica [perr'-te-cah], *f.* Perch, a measure of 10 geometric feet (9.70 feet).
Pértiga [perr'-te-gah], *f.* 1. A long pole or rod. 2. A tall, slender woman. 3. Hook on which a door or window is hung. 4. *V.* PÉRTICA.
Pertigal, *m.* Pole. *V.* PÉRTIGA.
Pértigo [perr'-te-go], *m.* Pole of a wagon or cart.
Pertiguear [per-te-gay-ar'], *va.* To beat a tree with a pole to gather the fruit.
Pertiguería [per-te-gay-ree'-ah], *f.* Office or employment of a verger.
Pertiguero [per-te-gay'-ro], *m.* Verger, he that carries the mace before the dean.
Pertinacia [per-te-nah'-the-ah], *f.* Pertinancy, obstinacy, stubbornness, doggedness.
Pertinaz [per-te-nath'], *a.* Pertinacious, obstinate, opinionated.
Pertinazmente, *adv.* Pertinaciously, contumaciously.
Pertinente [per-te-nen'-tay], *a.* Pertinent, related to the matter in hand; to the purpose.
Pertinentemente, *adv.* Pertinently, opportunely, congruously.
Pertrechar [per-tray-char'], *va.* 1. To supply a place with ammunition and warlike stores. 2. To dispose, to arrange, to prepare.—*vr.* To be provided with the necessary stores and tools for defence.
Pertrechos [per-tray'-chos], *m. pl.* 1. Ammunition, arms, and other warlike stores. 2. Tools, instruments.
Perturbable [per-toor-bah'-blay], *a.* Capable of being perturbed.
Perturbación [per-toor-bah-the-on'], *f.* Perturbation, disquiet of mind; confusion.
Perturbadamente, *adv.* Confusedly.
Perturbador, ra [per-toor-bah-dor', rah], *m.* & *f.* Perturbator, perturber, disturber; perturbatrix.
Perturbar [per-toor-bar'], *va.* To perturb, to disturb; to interrupt, to harrow.
Peruano, na [pay-roo-ah'-no, nah], *a.* Peruvian, of Peru.
Peruétano [pay-roo-ay'-tah-no], *m.* 1. (Bot.) Wild or choke pear-tree. Pyrus. 2. Any thing that overtops or rises above the rest.
Perulero, ra [pay-roo-lay'-ro, rah], *a.* 1. (Obs.) Made or manufactured in Peru, or native of Peru. 2. One who has come from Peru to Spain. 3. *m.* A wealthy man. (*Cf.* INDIANO.) 4. A narrow-bottomed and strait-mouthed pitcher.
Peruviano [pay-roo-ve-ah'-no], *m.* Peruvian balsam.—*a.* (Obs.) *V.* PERUANO.
Perversamente, *adv.* Perversely, malevolently.
Perversidad [per-ver-se-dahd'], *f.* Perversity, obstinate wickedness, malignity.
Perversión [per-ver-se-on'], *f.* 1. Perversion, the act of perverting. 2. Perversion, perverseness, depravation, corruption.
Perverso, sa [per-verr'-so, sah], *a.* Perverse, extremely wicked, mischievous.
Pervertidor, ra [per-ver-te-dor', rah], *m.* & *f.* Perverter, corrupter.
Pervertimiento [per-ver-te-me-en'-to], *m.* Perversion, act of perverting.
Pervertir [per-ver-teer'], *va.* 1. To pervert, to distort from the true end. 2. To pervert, to corrupt, to turn from the right. 3. To seduce from the true doctrine and faith.—*vr.* To become corrupted or depraved.
(*Yo pervierto, yo pervierta; él pervirtió, pervirtiera*, from *Pervertir. V.* ADHERIR.)
Pervigilio [per-ve-hee'-le-o], *m.* (Med.) Vigilance, pervigilium, watching, want of sleep; restlessness.
Pervulgar [per-vool-gar'], *va.* 1. To divulge, to make public. 2. (Acad.) To promulgate.
Peryodato [per-yo-dah'-to], *m.* (Chem.) Periodate.
Peryoduro [per-yo-doo'-ro], *m.* Periodide, an iodide containing more iodine than a protoiodide.
Pesa [pay'-sah], *f.* 1. Weight, a piece of a determined weight. 2. Piece of metal suspended from clocks. 3. A counter-weight. *Pesa de una romana*, Weight or drop-ball of a steel-yard.
Pesada [pay-sah'-dah], *f.* (Com.) Quantity weighed at once.
Pesadamente, *adv.* 1. Heavily, weightily, ponderously, cumbrously. 2. Sorrowfully, grievously. 3. Slowly, tardily, lazily.
Pesadez [pay-sah-deth'], *f.* 1. Heaviness, the quality of being heavy. 2. Gravity, weight, tendency to the centre. 3. Slowness, sluggishness, drowsiness. 4. Peevishness, fretfulness. 5. Excess, abundance. 6. Trouble, pain, fatigue. 7. Obesity, corpulence.
Pesadilla [pay-sah-deel'-lyah], *f.* Nightmare.
Pesado, da [pay-sah'-do, dah], *a.* 1. Heavy, ponderous, massive. 2. Deep, profound (used of sleep). 3. Peevish, fretful, troublesome, violent; cumbersome, cumbrous. 4. Tedious, wearisome, tiresome, dull, fastidious. 5. Offensive, causing pain, injurious, oppressive. 6. Lazy, clumsy, tardy, sluggish. 7. Fat, gross, corpulent. 8. Hard, insufferable, mischievous. *Día pesado*, A cloudy, gloomy day. —*pp.* of PESAR.—*m.* A bore.
Pesador, ra [pay-sah-dor', rah], *m.* & *f.* Weigher, one who weighs.
Pesadumbre [pay-sah-doom'-bray], *f.* 1. Heaviness, weightiness, gravity. 2. Quarrel, dispute, contest. 3. Grief, trouble, displeasure, affliction, pain, disgust. 4. (Obs.) Mischief, injury.
Pesalicores [pay-sah-le-co'-res], *m.* Hydrometer, areometer.
Pésame [pay'-sah-may], *m.* Compliment of condolence.
Pesamentero, ra [pay-sah-men-tay'-ro, rah], *m.* & *f.* (Mex.) One who under pretext of condolence gets into a house to sponge for meals.
Pesante [pay-sahn'-tay], *m.* A weight of half a drachm.
Pesantez [pay-san-teth'], *f.* Gravity, the force of gravity.
Pesar [pay-sar'], *m.* 1. Sorrow, grief, concern, repentance. 2. The saying or deed which causes sorrow or displeasure.
Pesar (Á) [ah pay-sar'], *adv.* In spite of, notwithstanding.
Pesar [pay-sar'], *vn.* 1. To weigh, to be of weight. 2. To weigh, to be considered as important, to be valuable. 3. To repent, to be sorry for. 4. To prevail, to preponderate.—*va* 1. To weigh, to ascertain the weight of a thing. 2. To weigh, to examine, to consider. 3. (Naut.) To use the lead for establishing the exact position which any piece of the ship should have. *Mal que le pese*, (Coll.) In spite of him.
Pesario [pay-sah'-re-o], *m.* Pessary, an instrument worn in the vagina to correct a displacement of the womb.
Pesaroso, sa [pay-sah-ro'-so, sah], *a.* 1. Sorrowful, full of repentance. 2. Restless, uneasy.
Pesca [pes'-cah], *f.* 1. Fishing, angling. 2. Fish, in the natural state in the water. *Pesca con arpón*, Spear fishing.
Pescadazo [pes-cah-dah'-tho], *m. aug.* Great fish.
Pescadera [pes-cah-day'-rah], *f.* Fish woman.
Pescadería [pes-cah-day-ree'-ah], *f.* Fish-market.
Pescadero [pes-cah-day'-ro], *m.* Fishmonger (by retail).
Pescadillo [pes-cah-deel'-lyo], *m. dim.* A little fish.
Pescado [pes-cah'-do], *m.* 1. Fish, chiefly that which is fit for food. (*Pescado* is a fish when caught; in the water, uncaptured, it is a *pez.*) 2. Codfish when salted. 3. Foodfishes. *Día* or *comida de pescado*, A fish-day, or fasting fare, though not of fish.—*Pescado, da, pp.* of PESCAR.
Pescador [pes-cah-dor'], *m.* 1. Fisherman, fisher, angler. 2. Fish having a pouch under the jaws to catch others. *Pescador, ra*, is used also adjectively.
Pescadora [pes-cah-do'-rah], *f.* Fishwife, fish-woman, a woman that sells fish; the wife of a fisher.
Pescante [pes-cahn'-tay], *m.* 1. Crane, an instrument for raising heavy weights. 2. Coach-box. 3. Machine used in shifting the decorations on the stage. *Pescante de bote.* (Naut.) A davit. *Pescante de ancla*, Fish-davit.
Pescar [pes-car'], *va.* 1. To fish, to angle, to catch fish. 2. To pick up any thing. 3. To take one at his word, to catch in the act. 4. To obtain one's end.
Péscola [pes'-co-lah], *f.* The beginning of a furrow in a ploughed field.
Pescoso, sa [pes-co'-so, sah], *a.* (Obs.) Abounding in fish.
Pescozada [pes-co-thah'-dah], *f.* *V.* PESCOZÓN.
Pescozón [pes-co-thone'], *m.* Blow on the neck or head with the hand.
Pescozudo, da [pes-co-thoo'-do, dah], *a.* Having a thick neck.
Pescuezo [pes-coo-ay'-tho], *m.* 1. The neck. 2. Stiff-necked haughtiness, loftiness, or pride. *Sacar el pescuezo*, To be haughty, to be elated. *Andar al pescuezo*, To take one another by the throat. *Poner a uno el pie sobre el pescuezo*, To humiliate one.
Pescuño [pes-coo'-nyo], *m.* Large wedge for fastening the coulter of a plough.
Pese [pay'-say], *int.* Kind of imprecatory exclamation.
Pesebre [pay-say'-bray], *m.* 1. Crib, rack, or manger in a stable. 2. (Coll.) The place where dinner is got very frequently.
Pesebrejo [pay-say-bray'-ho], *m.* Cavity in which horses' teeth are fixed.
Pesebrera [pay-say-bray'-rah], *f.* Range of mangers in a stable.
Pesebrón [pay-say-brone'], *m.* Boot of a coach.
Peseta [pay-say'-tah], *f.* 1. Piece of two reals *de plata*, equal to four reals

vellón, worth about 10*d.* sterling, equivalent of a franc. *Peseta columnaria*, Piece of two reals and a half *de plata*, or five reals *vellón*, value 12½*d.* sterling, or quarter of a dollar. 2. A fishing-net managed by two men.
Pésete [pay'-say-tay], *m.* A sort of oath, curse, or imprecation; a word of execration.
Pesga [pes'-gah], *f.* Weight. *V.* PESA and PESO.
¡Pesia! ¡pesia tal! [pay'-se-ah, pay-se-ah tahl'], *m.* A kind of curse or imprecation. *¡Pesia á mi!* By my life!
Pesiar [pay-se-ar'], *vn.* To utter curses or execrations.
Pesillo [pay-seel'-lyo], *m.* Small scales for weighing gold or silver coin.
Pésimamente, *adv. super.* Very badly.
Pesimismo [pay-se-mees'-mo], *m.* 1. Pessimism, condition of a pessimist. 2. A system of German philosophy which considers existence as an evil.
Pesimista [pay-se-mees'-tah], *m.* Pessimist, one who looks at the dark side of things.
Pésimo, ma [pay'-se-mo, mah], *a. super.* Very bad.
Pesita [pay-see'-tah], *f. dim.* A small weight.
Peso [pay'-so], *m.* 1. Weight, gravity, heaviness. 2. Weight, importance. 3. Weight or power of reason. 4. Peso, monetary coin of many Sp. Am. countries. 5. Burden. 6. Judgment, good sense. *Caerse de su peso*, To go without saying. (Boxing): *Peso completo*, Heavyweight. *Peso gallo*, Bantamweight. *Peso ligero*, Lightweight. *Peso medio*, Middleweight. *Peso mosca*, Flyweight. *Peso pluma*, Featherweight. *Peso semicompleto*, Light heavyweight.
Pésol [pay'-sole], *m.* French bean. *V.* FRISOL.
Pespuntador, ra [pes-poon-tah-dor', rah], *m.* & *f.* Back-stitcher.
Pespuntar [pes-poon-tar'], *va.* To back-stitch, to sew with a back seam.
Pespunte [pes-poon'-tay], *m.* Back-stitching, back seam.
Pesquera [pes-kay'-rah], *f.* Fishery, a place for catching fish.
Pesquería [pes-kay-ree'-ah], *f.* 1. Trade or calling of a fisherman. 2. Act of fishing. 3. Fishery.
Pesquisa [pes-kee'-sah], *f.* Investigation, inquiry, examination.—*m.* Policeman.
Pesquisante [pes-ke-sahn'-tay], *pa.* Investigating; inquirer.
Pesquisar [pes-ke-sar'], *va.* To inquire, to examine, to investigate.
Pesquisidor, ra [pes-ke-se-dor', rah], *m.* & *f.* Examiner, searcher, inquirer. *Juez pesquisidor*, A magistrate appointed to inquire into the circumstances of a violent death.
Pestaña [pes-tah'-nyah], *f.* 1. Eye-lash. 2. Fag-end of a piece of linen. 3. Fringe, edging.
Pestañear [pes-tah-nyay-ar'], *va.* To wink, to blink. *No pestañear* or *sin pestañear*, To look with the eyes fixed not to wink.
Pestañeo [pes-tah-nyay'-o], *m.* Winking, blinking.
Peste [pes'-tay], *f.* 1. Pest, plague, pestilence. 2. Pest, anything troublesome, vexatious or mischievous. 3. Corruption of manners. 4. Foul smell. 5. (Coll.) Great plenty or abundance.—*pl.* Words of menace.
Pestiferamente, *adv.* Pestiferously, pestilently.
Pestífero, ra [pes-tee'-fay-ro, rah], *a.* 1. Pestiferous, causing much damage. 2. Applied to any thing extremely bad or mischievous. 3. Foul smelling.
Pestilencia [pes-te-len'-the-ah], *f.* Pest, plague, pestilence.
Pestilencial [pes-te-len-the-ahl'], *a.* Pestiferous, pestilential, infectious, contagious, destructive.
Pestilencioso, sa [pes-te-len-the-o'-so, sah], *a.* Pestilential.
Pestilente [pes-te-len'-tay], *a.* Pestilent, pernicious. *V.* PESTÍFERO.
Pestillo [pes-teel'-lyo], *m.* 1. Bolt, for a door. 2. Bolt of a lock.
Pestiño [pes-tee'-nyo], *m.* Fritter or pancake.
Pestorejazo [pes-to-ray-hah'-tho], *m.* *V.* PESCOZÓN.
Pestorejo [pes-to-ray'-ho], *m.* The posterior fleshy part of the neck.
Pestorejón [pes-to-ray-hone'], *m.* Blow on the back of the neck.
Pesuña [pes-soo'-nyah], *f.* Solid hoof of graminivorous animals.
Pesuño [pes-soo'-nyo], *m.* Hoof of cloven-footed animals.
Petaca [pay-tah'-cah], *f.* 1. A trunk or chest covered with hides or leather; a covered hamper. 2. A case for keeping cigars or fine-cut tobacco. *Echarse con las petacas*, (Coll. Mex.) To give up an affair through negligence.
Petaláceo, cea [pay-tah-lah'-thay-o, ah], *a.* (Bot.) Petalaceous, petalous.
Petalismo [pay-tah-lees'-mo], *m.* Petalism, banishment in Syracuse, by writing the name on a leaf.
Pétalo [pay'-tah-lo], *m.* (Bot.) Petal, flower-leaf.
Petaquilla [pay-tah-keel'-lyah], *f.* Hamper covered with hides or leather; a small trunk.
Petar [pay-tar'], *va.* (Coll.) To please, to gratify, to content.
Petardear [pay-tar-day-ar'], *va.* 1. To beat down a gate or door with petards. 2. To cheat, to deceive, to gull, by borrowing and not paying.
Petardero [pay-tar-day'-ro], *m.* 1. Petardeer, a gunner whose duty consists in landing, fixing, and firing petards. 2. Impostor, cheat, swindler.
Petardista [pay-tar-dees'-tah], *com.* 1. Deceiver, defrauder, a cheat, an impostor. 2. Swindler.
Petardo [pay-tar'-do], *m.* 1. Petard, a warlike engine. 2. Cheat, fraud, imposition, gull, hoax, scurvy trick, disappointment.
Petate [pay-tah'-tay], *m.* 1. Fine sort of mat made of palm; used for a sleeping-mat by the natives in South America and the Philippines. 2. Impostor, swindler, extorter. 3. (Prov.) A good-for-nothing fellow, a despicable person. *Liar el petate*, (Coll.) To pack up one's duds, to move away or be dismissed.
Petequia [pay-tay'-ke-ah], *f.* (Med.) Petechia, spot on the skin in malignant fevers.
Petequial [pay-tay-ke-ahl'], *a.* Petechial, pestilentially spotted.
Petición [pay-te-the-on'], *f.* 1. Petition, the act of asking. 2. Petition, single branch or article of a prayer. 3. Demand, claim, request. 4. (Law) Petition, the writing with which one juridically demands before the judge; prayer annexed to a judicial declaration produced in court.
Peticionario, ria [pay-tee-the-on-ah'-re-o, ah], *m.* & *f.* Petitioner. (Used also as an adjective.)
Petillo [pay-teel'-lyo], *m. dim.* A small stomacher; a breast jewel.
Petimetra [pay-te-may'-trah], *f.* A belle, a smart lady.
Petimetre [pay-te-may'-tray], *m.* Fop, coxcomb, beau, dude.
Petirrojo [pay-teer-ro'-ho], *m.* (Orn.) Robin-redbreast.
Petitoria [pay-te-to'-re-ah], *f.* *V.* PETICIÓN.
Petitorio, ria [pay-te-to'-re-o, ah], *a.* Petitory, petitionary.
Petitorio [pay-te-to'-re-o], *m.* Impertinent and repeated petition.
Peto [pay'-to], *m.* 1. Breastplate. 2. Plastron used by fencers. 3. Dickey, false shirt or blouse front.
Petraria [pay-trah'-re-ah], *f.* Ancient machine for throwing stones.
Petrarquista [pay-trar-kees'-tah], *a.* & *m.* Follower of Petrarch.
Pétreo, a [pay-tray'-o, ah], *a.* 1. Rocky. 2. Stony, of stone, hard, inflexible.
Petrera [pay-tray'-rah], *f.* (Prov.) Battle fought with stones.
Petrificación [pay-tre-fe-cah-the-on'], *f.* Petrification.
Petrificante [pay-tre-fe-cahn'-tay], *pa.* Petrifying.
Petrificar [pay-tre-fe-car'], *va.* To petrify, to change to stone.—*vr.* To petrify, to become stone.
Petróleo [pay-tro'-lay-o], *m.* Petroleum, oil.
Petrolero, ra [pay-tro-lay'-ro, rah], *a.* Petroleum.—*m.* 1. Arsonist. 2. Oil tanker.—*m.* & *f.* Dealer in oil.
Petrolífero, ra [pay-tro-lee'-fay-ro, rah], *a.* Oil-bearing.
Petroquímica [pay-tro-kee'-me-cah], *f.* Petrochemistry.
Petroso, sa [pay-tro'-so, sah], *a.* Rocky.
Petrus in cunctis [pay'-troos in coon'-tis]. (Lat.) One who affects to know all things; jack-of all trades.
Petulancia [pay-too-lahn'-the-ah], *f.* Petulance, insolence, flippancy, pertness.
Petulante [pay-too-lahn'-tay], *a.* Petulant, insolent, flippant, pert.
Petunia [pay-too'-ne-ah], *f.* (Bot.) Petunia.
Peucédano [pay-oo-thay'-dah-no], *m.* (Bot.) Sulphur-wort. Peucedanum.
Peyorativo, va [pay-yo-rah-tee'-vo, vah], *a.* Depreciatory, disparaging (mostly as regards morals).
Pez [peth], *f.* Pitch, tar. *Pez blanca*, Refined galipot, Burgundy pitch. *Pez griega*, Rosin, colophony. *Pez naval*, A mixture of pitch, rosin, tallow, etc., melted for applying to ships. *Pez rubia*, Rosin. *Pez con pez*, Quite empty, unoccupied. *Dar la pez*, To be at the last extremity. (Lat. pix, picis.)
Pez [peth], *m.* 1. Fish: a generic term; the zoological class of fishes among vertebrate animals. *Cf.* PESCADO. 2. Fish, a name common to all fresh-water fishes when they are small and eatable. (Lat. piscis.) *Pez colorado*, or *de color*, The gold-fish, golden carp. Carassius auratus. *Pez diablo*, Devil-fish, a huge ray. (Manta, sp.) *Pez espada*, Sword-fish. *Pez jirón*, Pipe-fish, related to the sea-horse. *Pez luna*, Mola, sun-fish. *Pez martillo*, The hammer-headed shark. Sphyrna tudes. *Pez sapo*, The toad-fish. *Pez sierra*, The saw-fish. *Pez volador*, The flying-fish. *Pez de palo*, Stock-fish. 3. (Acad.) Catch, haul; any thing advantageous which has cost toil or solicitude. *Picar el pez*, To be entrapped or deceived. *Salga pez o salga rana*, Hit or miss. *Salga pez o salga rana, a la capacha*, Be it fish or be it frog, into the pouch it goes.
Pezolada [pay-tho-lah'-dah], *f.* Threads at the fag-end of cloth.
Pezón [pay-thone'], *m.* 1. (Bot.) Stem of fruits, leaf-stalk or flower-stalk. 2. Nipple, teat, dug. 3.

Arm of an axletree; end of a vertical beam in paper mills.

Pezonera [pay-tho-nay'-rah], *f.* 1. Nipple-shield. 2. Linch-pin.

Pezpita, *f.* **Pezpitalo,** *m.* [peth-pee'-tah, peth-pee'-tah-lo]. (Orn.) Wagtail. Motacilla.

Pezuelo [pay-thoo-ay'-lo], *m.* The beginning of cloth where the warp is knotted, in order to commence the weaving.

Pezuña [pay-thoo'-nyah], *f.* 1. Nose-worm, a disease incident to sheep. 2. *V.* Pesuña.

Pez vela [peth vay'-lah], *m.* Sailfish.

Ph: all the words formerly beginning with these letters will now be found under F.

Phi [fe], *f.* Phi, twenty-first letter of the Greek alphabet (ϕ).

Piache, or **Tarde piache** [pe-ah'-chay]. Too late, act of coming or being late.

Pïada [pe-ah'-dah], *f.* 1. Chirping of birds, puling of chickens. 2. Mimicking of another's voice.

Pïador, ra [pe-ah-dor', rah], *m.* & *f.* One who pules like a chicken or chirps like a bird.

Piadosamente, *adv.* Piously, holily, clemently, mercifully, faithfully.

Piadoso, sa [pe-ah-do'-so, sah], *a.* 1. Pious, godly, mild, merciful, clement. 2. Reasonable, moderate.

Piafar [pe-ah-far'], *vn.* To paw, to stamp (used of horses).

Piale [pe-ah'-lay], *m.* (Amer.) A cast of the lasso about the legs of the animal to be caught.

Piamáter [pe-ah-mah'-ter], *f.* Pia mater, membrane covering the brain.

Piamente, *adv.* In a mild manner, piously.

Pián, pián [pe-ahn', pe-ahn'], *adv.* One foot after another rising and falling; with precaution.

Pian piano [pe-ahn' pe-ah'-no], *adv.* Gently, softly.

Pianista [pe-ah-nees'-tah], *com.* Pianist, a performer upon the pianoforte. —*m.* 1. A pianoforte-maker. 2. One who sell pianos.

Piano, or **Pianoforte** [pe-ah'-no, pe-ah-no-for'-tay], *m.* Pianoforte. *Piano de cola,* A grand piano.

Pianola [pe-ah-no'-lah], *f.* Pianola, player piano.

Piante [pe-ahn'-tay], *pa.* Peeping. *No dejar piante ni mamante,* To leave neither chick nor child, to root out entirely.

Piar [pe-ar'], *vn.* 1. To peep, to pule, to cry like a chicken, to chirp as a bird. 2. To call, to whine, to cry or wish for any thing with anxiety.

Piara [pe-ah'-rah], *f.* 1. Herd of swine. 2. Drove of mares or mules. 3. (Prov.) Flock of ewes.

Piariego, ga [pe-ah-re-ay'-go, gah], *a.* Applied to a person who has a herd of mares, mules, or swine.

Pica [pee'-cah], *f.* 1. Pike, a long lance. 2. A bull-fighter's javelin. 3. (Med.) Pica, a depraved appetite for things unfit for food, as chalk, etc. *A pica seca,* With great labour and without utility. *Pasar por las picas,* To undergo many trials. *Poner una pica en Flandes,* To beat the Dutch, to do something wonderful, to achieve a triumph. *Saltar por las picas de Flandes,* To stop at nothing, to be deterred by no dangers; against all obstacles.

Picacero, ra [pe-cah-thay'-ro, rah], *a.* Applied to birds of prey that chase magpies.

Picacureba [pe-cah-coo-ray'-bah], *f.* Brazilian pigeon.

Picacho [pe-cah'-cho], *m.* Top, summit; sharp point of any thing.

Picada [pe-cah'-dah], *f.* Puncture, incision made by pricking. *Picadas.* (Her.) Birds whose beak is of a different enamelling.

Picadero [pe-cah-day'-ro], *m.* 1. Riding-house, riding-school. 2. Block, boat skid; (Naut.) stock-block. 3. Stamping-ground of a buck in rutting time.

Picadillo [pe-cah-deel'-lyo], *m.* Minced meat, hash. *Estar* or *venir de picadillo,* To be piqued and desirous of showing it.

Picado, da [pe-cah'-do, dah], *a.* & *pp.* of Picar. Pricked. *Picado* or *picada de viruelas,* Pitted with the small-pox. *Estar picado del alacrán,* (Coll.) To be smitten with love. *Estar picada la piedra,* To eat much and rapidly.

Picado [pe-cah'-do], *m.* Minced meat, hash.

Picador [pe-cah-dor'], *m.* 1. Riding-master; one who tames and breaks in horses. 2. The horseman that expects to be the first attacked by the bull, and is armed with a spear to resist him. 3. Pricker. 4. Block on which meat is chopped. *Picador de limas,* A file-cutter.

Picadura [pe-cah-doo'-rah], *f.* 1. The act of pricking. 2. Puncture, a wound made by pricking. 3. Ornamental gusset in clothes. 4. Bite of an animal or bird.

Picaflor [pe-cah-flor'], *m.* (Orn.) Humming-bird. Trochilus. This beautiful little bird is known also by the names of *Colibrí, Pájaro mosca,* and (in Mexico) *Chupa mirtos. V.* Chupa flores.

Picamaderos [pe-cah-mah-day'-ros], *m.* Wood-pecker.

Picante [pe-cahn'-tay], *pa.* & *a.* Pricking, piercing, stinging; piquant, high-seasoned, acrid, hot.

Picante [pe-cahn'-tay], *m.* 1. Piquancy, pungency, acrimony; keen satire. 2. (Amer.) Dish with red-pepper sauce.

Picantemente, *adv.* Piquantly.

Picapedrero [pe-cah-pay-dray'-ro], *m.* Stone-cutter.

Picapleitos [pe-cah-play'-e-tose], *m.* (Coll.) A litigious person: a pettifogging lawyer.

Picaporte [pe-cah-por'-tay], *m.* A kind of picklock or latch-key.

Picaposte [pe-cah-pos'-tay], *m.* V. Picamaderos.

Picapuerco [pe-cah-poo-err'-co], *m.* (Orn.) Bird of the woodpecker kind.

Picar [pe-car'], *va.* 1. To prick with a pointed instrument. 2. To prick, to pierce with a small puncture. 3. To sting, pierce, or wound with a point darted out, as that of wasps or scorpions. 4. To mince or chop any thing fine, to break into small pieces. 5. To peck like birds. 6. To nibble, to pick up or bite by little at a time; to eat squeamishly. 7. To nibble at the bait, as fish. 8. To begin to get customers and thrive in business. 9. To pursue or harass an enemy. 10. To itch, to smart. 11. To burn or irritate the palate. 12. To prick, to spur, to goad, to incite, to stimulate. 13. To spur a horse. 14. To pique, to vex, to provoke with words or actions. 15. To tame a horse. 16. Joined with *en,* to begin to operate, or have effect. *Picar un dibujo,* To prick out a design. *Picar en poeta,* To be a poet.—*vr.* 1. To be offended or vexed, to be piqued. 2. To be moth-eaten, to be damaged. 3. To begin to rot: applied to fruit. 4. To be elated with pride. 5. (Met.) To be deceived. 6. To be in heat: applied to animals. 7. To fret, to be angry, to be peevish. *Picar el pez,* (Coll.) To insnare. *Picar la carne,* To chop meat. *El sol pica,* The sun scorches. *Quien del alacrán está picado, la sombra le espanta,* A burnt child dreads the fire *Picar muy alto,* To aim too high. *Picar la berza,* To be a beginner, little advanced. *Picar de vara larga,* To seek a mean advantage.

Picaramente [pee'-cah-rah-men-tay], *adv.* Knavishly, roguishly.

Picarazo, za [pe-cah-rah'-tho, thah], *a.* Great rogue.

Picardear [pe-car-day-ar'], *vn.* To play the knave.

Picardía [pe-car-dee'-ah], *f.* 1. Knavery, roguery; deceit, malice, foulness, a wanton trick, wantonness. 2. Lewdness. 3. Meeting of rogues.

Picardihüela [pe-car-de-oo-ay'-lah], *f.* A prank, a roguish trick.

Picaresca [pe-cah-res'-cah], *f.* A nest of rogues, meeting of knaves.

Picaresco, ca, Picaril [pe-cah-res'-co, cah, pe-cah-reel'], *a.* Roguish, knavish.

Picarillo [pe-cah-reel'-lyo], *m. dim.* A little rogue.

Pícaro, ra [pee'-cah-ro, rah], *a.* 1. Knavish, roguish, vile, low. 2. Mischievous, malicious, crafty, sly. 3. Merry, gay.—*m.* & *f.* Rogue, knave, loafer.

Pícaros [pee'-cah-ros], *m. pl.* Scullions, kitchen-boys.

Picarón [pe-cah-rone'], *a.* & *m. aug.* Great rogue, villain. *Picarona,* Jade.

Picaronazo, za [pe-cah-ro-nah'-tho, thah], *a. aug.* Very roguish, villainous.

Picarote [pe-cah-ro'-tay], *a. aug.* Subtle, crafty; notorious villain.

Picarrelincho [pe-car-ray-leen'-cho], *m.* (Orn.) *V.* Aguzanieve.

Picatoste [pe-cah-tos'-tay], *m.* Toast of bread fried with slices of ham.

Picaza [pe-cah'-thah], *f.* 1. (Orn.) Magpie, commonly called *urraca.* Corvus pica. 2. (Prov.) Hoe for clearing the ground of weeds. *Picaza marina,* (Orn.) Flamingo. Phœnicopteros.

Picazo [pe-cah'-tho], *m.* 1. Blow with a pike. 2. Sting of an insect; stroke with the beak of a bird. 3. Young magpie.

Picazón [pe-cah-thone'], *m.* 1. Itching, prurience, itch. 2. Peevishness, fretfulness.

Picea [pee'-thay-ah], *f.* (Bot.) Silver-fir. Pinus picea.

Picnostilo [pic-nos-tee'-lo], *m.* (Arch.) Too little space between columns.

Pico [pee'-co], *m.* 1. Beak of a bird, bill, nib. 2. A sharp point of any kind 3. A pick-axe. 4. Twibill, an iron tool used by paviers. 5. Dock-spade, a spade with a long crooked bill. 6. Spout of a jar or any similar vessel. 7. The beak iron of an anvil. 8. Peak, top, or summit of a hill. 9. Balance of an account, small odds. 10. Mouth. *De pico,* By the mouth, without works or deeds. 11. Loquacity, garrulity. 12. (Orn.) Wood-pecker. Picus. 13. A weight of 137½ pounds used in the Philippine Islands. *Pico verde,* Green wood-pecker. *Pico de oro,* A man of great eloquence. *Pico de un ancla,* (Naut.) Bill of an anchor. *Picos de un sombrero,* Cocks of a hat. *Pico de cigüeña,* Crane's-bill, geranium. (The carpels have long beaks.) *Pico grueso,* The gros-beak. *Callar el pico,* To hold one's tongue. *Tener mucho pico,* To talk too much and divulge secrets. *Perder por el pico,* To lose by too much chattering. *Pico a viento,* With the wind in the face. *Andar a picos pardos,* To loiter, or follow idle pursuits instead of profitable ones. *Lo tengo en el pico de la lengua,* I have it on the tip of my tongue. *Pico delantero y trasero de la silla,* The fore and hind bow of the saddle. *Picos y cabos pendientes,* (Coll.) Odds and ends. *A pico de jarro,* Drinking immoderately. *Pico cruzado,* Crossbill, crossbeak, a bird of the genus loxia. *Pico largo,* A wading bird of California with long curved bill; also (Mex.) a braggart, a scandal-monger.

Picolete [pe-co-lay'-tay], *m.* Staple for the bolt of a lock.

Picón, na [pe-cone', nah], *a.* Applied to animals with the upper teeth projecting over the under ones; or to cattle nipping the grass the contrary way for want of teeth.

Picón [pe-cone'], *m.* 1. Lampoon or nipping jest employed to induce another to do or perform any thing. 2. A sort of very small charcoal used in braziers. 3. Small fresh-water fish. 4. (Prov.) Broken rice.

Piconero [pe-coh-nay'-ro], *m.* Maker of small charcoal for braziers.

Picor [pe-cor'], *m.* 1. The pungent taste left by any thing which is hot or piquant. 2. Itching in any part of the body.

Picoso, sa [pe-co'-so, sah], *a.* Pitted with the small-pox.

Picota [pe-co'-tah], *f.* 1. A kind of pillar or gibbet on which the heads of those who have been hanged are exposed. 2. A kind of pillory. 3. (Naut.) Cheek of a pump. 4. Top or peak of a mountain. 5. Point of a turret or steeple.

Picotada [pe-co-tah'-dah], *f.* *V.* PICOTAZO.

Picotazo [pe-co-tah'-tho], *m.* Stroke with the beak of a bird.

Picote [pe-co'-tay], *m.* 1. Coarse stuff made of goat's hair. 2. A glossy silk stuff.

Picoteado, da [pe-co-tay-ah'-do, dah], *a.* Peaked, having many points or angles.—*pp.* of PICOTEAR.

Picotear [pe-co-tay-ar'], *va.* To strike with the beak.—*vn.* 1. To gossip. 2. To toss the head: applied to a horse. —*vr.* To wrangle or quarrel: applied to women.

Picotería [pe-co-tay-ree'-ah], *f.* Loquacity, volubility, gossip.

Picotero, ra [pe-co-tay'-ro, rah], *a.* Wrangling, chattering, prattling.

Picotillo [pe-co-teel'-lyo], *m.* Inferior cloth of goats' hair.

Picrato [pe-crah'-to], *m.* Picrate, a salt of picric acid.

Pícrico [pee'-cre-co], *a.* Picric, of an exceedingly bitter taste. *Ácido pícrico,* Picric acid, a yellow crystalline body. (Gr. πικρός, bitter.)

Pictografía [pic-to-grah-fee'-ah], *f.* Pictography, picture writing.

Pictórico, ca [pic-to'-re-co, cah], *a.* Pictorial.

Picudilla [pe-coo-deel'-lyah], *f.* 1. Kind of pointed olive. 2. An insectivorous bird.

Picudo, da [pe-coo'-do, dah], *a.* 1. Beaked, pointed. 2. Prattling, babbling, chattering.—*m.* Boll weevil.

Pichel [pe-chel'], *m.* Pewter tankard, a mug. (Mex.) Pitcher.

Pichelería [pe-chay-lay-ree'-ah], *f.* Factory of tankards or tin pots.

Pichelero [pe-chay-lay'-ro], *m.* Maker of pewter pots or tankards.

Pichelete [pe-chay-lay'-tay], *m. dim.* A small tankard or mug.

Pichiciago [pe-che-the-ah'-go], *m.* (Zool.) A burrowing animal of Chile, having the back covered with curious defensive plates, called also CLAMIFORO

Pichón [pe-chone'], *m.* 1. A young pigeon. 2. (coll.) Darling (applied to a man). 3. (Mex. coll.) Push-over. *Tiro de pichón,* Trapshooting.

Pido [pee'-do], *m.* (Coll.) Demand, request, petition.

(*Yo pido, pida; él pidió* or *pidiera. V.* PEDIR.)

Pidón, na [pe-done', nah], *a.* (Coll.) *V.* PEDIGÜEÑO.

Pie [pe-ay'], *m.* 1. The foot. 2. Foot, leg, that by which any thing is supported. 3. Foot, the base. 4. Trunk of trees and plants. 5. Lees, sediment. 6. Last hand or player in a game of cards. 7. The last word pronounced by an actor. 8. Foot, a measure of length: in Castile it is 27.85 centimetres, or about 11 inches. 9. Motive, occasion. 10. Footing, basis, foundation, groundwork. 11. Footing, rule, use, custom. 12. Foot, verse, a certain number of syllables. 13. End or conclusion of a writing. 14. First colour given in dyeing. 15. Foot of a stocking. *Pie con bola,* Exactly, neither too much nor too little. *A pie juntillo,* Tenaciously. *Al pie de la hora,* Instantly, without delay. *Siete pies de tierra,* The grave. *A los pies de Vd.,* At your service (said to a lady only). *Del pie a la mano,* In an instant. *Pie de carnero,* (Naut.) Samson's post. *Pie derecho,* (Naut.) Stanchion. *Pie de roda,* (Naut.) Forefoot, the forepart of the keel. *Pie ante pie,* Step by step. *A pie,* On foot. *Al pie,* Near, close to, at the foot of. *A pie enjuto,* Without labour or pain; dryshod. *A pie firme,* Without stirring, steadfastly. *A pie llano,* On even ground; easily, commodiously. *A pie quedo,* Motionless; without labour or trouble. *En pie,* Constantly, firmly; uprightly, erect. *Estar con un pie en la sepultura,* To have one foot in the grave. *En un pie de tierra,* Shortly, in a little time. *Tener* or *traer debajo de los pies,* To trample under foot. *Tener pies de mar,* (Naut.) To be a swift sailor, to be a good sea-boat. *Pie de amigo,* Prop, shore; iron instrument used to keep up the head of persons when they are publicly whipped. *Pie de león,* (Bot.) *V.* ALQUEMILA VULGAR. *Pie de cabra,* A crowbar. *De pies a cabeza,* From head to foot. *Echar el pie atrás a alguno,* To outdo some one. *Echar el pie atrás,* To flinch, to desist. *Pies de puerco,* Pettitoes or hog's feet. *Soldados de a pie,* Foot, infantry. *Pie geométrico,* The ancient Roman foot; it is to the Castilian foot as 1,000 to 923.

Piecezuela, *f. dim.* Little piece.

Piecezuelo, *m. dim.* A little foot.

Piedad [pe-ay-dahd'], *f* 1. Piety, godliness: mercy, pity, compassion. 2. Charity

Pie de imprenta [pe-ay day im-pren'-tah], *m.* Printer's mark.

Piedra [pe-ay'-drah], *f.* 1. A stone 2. Gravel in the kidneys. 3. Hail. 4. Place where foundlings are exposed. 5. Gun-flint. 6. Hardness of things. *Piedra de amolar* or *afilar,* Whetstone, grinding stone. *Piedra de toque,* Touch-stone. *Piedra imán,* Magnet. *Piedra fundamental,* Headstone. *Piedra pómez,* Pumice-stone. *Piedra infernal,* Caustic. *Piedra lipis,* Copper sulphate. *Piedra sepulcral,* A gravestone, a headstone. *A piedra y a lodo,* Hermetically sealed. *A piedra perdida,* To pile stones loosely. *No dejar piedra por mover,* Not to leave a stone unturned. *Piedras,* Counters to mark the game *Tirar piedras,* To be insane.

Piedrecica, illa, ita, Piedrezuela [pe-ay-dray-thee'-cah], *f. dim.* A little stone.

Piel [pe-el'], *f.* 1. The skin. 2. Hide of an animal cured and dressed; pelt. 3. Peel or skin of fruits. *Piel de gallina,* Goose-flesh, the skin roughened by cold. *Soltó la piel,* He gave up the ghost. *Ser de la piel del diablo,* To be a limb of the devil.

Piélago [pe-ay'-lah-go], *m.* 1. The high sea. 2. Great plenty or abundance. *V.* TARQUÍN.

Pielecita [pe-ay-lay-thee'-tah], *f. dim.* A small hide.

Pienso [pe-en'-so], *m.* The daily allowance of barley, grass, etc., given to horses or mules in Spain. *Dar un pienso,* To bait or give food to an animal. *Ni por pienso,* (Coll.) Not even by a thought.

(*Yo pienso, yo piense,* from *Pensar V.* ACRECENTAR.)

(*Yo pierdo, yo pierda,* from *Perder. V.* ENTENDER.)

Pierna [pe-err'-nah], *f.* 1. The leg. 2. Leg of butcher's meat or of fowls. 3. Down-stroke of letters. 4. Cheek of a printing-press. *A modo de pierna de nuez,* Not done with rectitude, carelessly, obliquely. *En piernas,* Bare-legged. *Pierna de una sábana,* One of the breadths of a sheet. *Las piernas de una nuez,* The lobes of a walnut. *A pierna suelta* or *a pierna tendida,* At one's ease; without care; soundly. *Estirar las piernas,* To take a walk, to stretch one's legs. *Cortar las piernas,* To render a thing impossible. *Echar piernas,* To recover strength after sickness; to boast of beauty or valour. *Meter* or *poner piernas al caballo,* To ride at full speed.

Piernitendido, da [pe-er-ne-ten-dee'-do, dah], *a.* With extended legs.

Pieza [pe-ay'-thah], *f.* 1. Piece, part of a whole; a fragment. 2. Coin, piece of money. *Pieza de a ocho,* A dollar, an ounce of silver, or eight silver reals. 3. Piece of cloth woven at one time. 4. Piece of furniture. 5. Room in a house. 6. Piece of ordnance. 7. Buffoon, wag, jester. 8. Any bird or animal of the chase. 9. Any manufactured article and each of the parts which compose it. 10. Piece or man in the games of draughts, chess, etc. 11. (Her.) Each of the parts into which the coat of arms or shield is divided. *Pieza de autos,* Records or pleadings of a lawsuit stitched together. *¡Buena* or *gentil pieza!* A fine fellow! (sometimes ironical). *Tocar la pieza,* To touch upon a subject. *Quedarse de una pieza* or *hecho una pieza,* (Coll.) To be stunned, to remain astonished. *Jugar una pieza,* To play one a slippery trick *Hacer piezas,* To take any thing to pieces.

Piezgo [pe-eth'-go], *m.* 1. Neck of a leather bottle; the hind or fore foot of an animal. 2. A dressed skin for wine or other liquors.

Pífano, Pífaro [pee'-fah-no, pee'-fah-ro], *m.* 1 Fife, a musical instrument. 2 Fifer

Pifia [pee'-fe-ah], *f.* 1. A failure to properly strike the billiard ball with the cue; a miss. 2. Error, blunder

Pifiar [pe-fe-ar'], *vn.* 1. To suffer the breath to be too audible in playing the flute. 2. To miss the billiard-ball.

Pigargo [pe-gar'-go], *m.* Ring-tail hawk. Falco pygargus.

Pigmento [pig-men'-to], *m.* Pigment, colouring matter of the skin.

Pigmeo, mea [pig-may'-o, ah], *a.* Dwarfish.—*m.* & *f.* A dwarf.

Pignorar [pig-no-rar'], *va.* To pledge, to hypothecate. (F.)

Pigre [pee'-gray], *a.* Slothful, lazy, indolent.

Pigricia [pe-gree'-the-ah], *f.* 1. Laziness, idleness. 2. Place in schools for lazy boys.

Pigro, gra [pee'-gro, grah], *a.* Negligent, careless, lazy.

Pihua, *f.* *V.* Coriza.

Pihuela [pe-oo-ay'-lah], *f.* 1. Leash, a leather strap tied to a hawk's leg. 2. Obstruction, hindrance, impediment. *Pihuelas,* Fetters, shackles.

Piísimo, ma [pe-ee'-se-mo, mah], *a. sup.* Most pious.

Pijama [pe-hah'-mah] or **piyama** [pe-yah-mah], *m.* (Used mostly in the plural.) Pajamas or pyjamas.

Pijota [pe-ho'-tah], *f.* (Zool.) Hake, codling. *V.* Merluza.

Pijote [pe-ho'-tay], *m.* (Naut.) Swivel-gun loaded with small grape-shot.

Pila [pee'-lah], *f.* 1. A large (stone) trough containing water for cattle. 2. Baptismal font. 3. Pile, heap of things thrown together. 4. Pile of shorn wool belonging to one owner. 5. Parish. 6. A holy-water basin. *Nombre de pila,* Christian name. *Sacar de pila,* To stand godfather or godmother. 7. (Arch.) Buttress of an arch of a bridge. 8. Galvanic or voltaic pile.

Pilada [pe-lah'-dah], *f.* Quantity of mortar made at once; pile, heap.

Pilar [pe-lar'], *m.* 1. The large water basin of a fountain. 2. Pillar, a column of stone; post. 3. Pillar, a person who supports any thing. 4. Stone or mound for a landmark on roads. *Pilar de una cama,* Bed-post. *Pilar de una prensa,* The arbour of a press.

Pilarejo, Pilarito [pe-lah-ray'-ho, pe-lah-ree'-to], *m. dim.* A small pillar.

Pila seca [pe'-lah say'-cah], *f.* Dry cell or dry battery.

Pilastra [pe-lahs'-trah], *f.* Pilaster, a square column.

Pilatero [pe-lah-tay'-ro], *m.* In woollen factories, fuller who assists at fulling the cloth.

Pilche [peel'-chay], *m.* (Peru) Cup or bowl of wood. (Acad.)

Píldora [peel'-do-rah], *f.* 1. Pill, a medicine. 2. Affliction, bad news. *Dorar la píldora,* To gild the pill, to smooth over bad news.

Pildorera [peel-do-ray'-rah], *f* Pill box.

Píleo [pee'-lay-o], *m.* 1. A hat or cap worn by the ancient Romans. 2. Red hat worn by cardinals.

Pileta, Pilica [pe-lay'-tah, pe-lee'-cah], *f. dim.* of Pila.

Pilocarpo [pe-lo-car'-po], *m.* Jaborandi, a Brazilian plant, which yields the medicinal alkaloid pilocarpin. Pilocarpus pinnatifolius.

Pilón [pe-lone'], *m.* 1. A large watering trough for cattle, the basin of a fountain. 2. Drop or ball of a steelyard. 3. Great stone or counterpoise in an olive-press. 4. Heap of grapes ready to be pressed. 5. Heap of mortar. *Pilón de azúcar,* A loaf of refined sugar formed in a mould. *Beber del pilón,* To believe current rumours. *Llevar al pilón,* To lead by the nose. *Haber bebido del pilón,* Said of a judge or state official who has relaxed from the vigour with which he began.

Piloncillo [pe-lon-theel'-lyo], *m.* (Amer.) The crust of sugar that remains in the boiler.

Pilonero, ra [pe-lo-nay'-ro, rah], *m.* & *f.* Newsmonger.

Pilongo, ga [pe-lon'-go, gah], *a.* 1. Peeled and dried: applied to a chestnut. 2. Thin, lean, meagre.

Pilórico, ca [pe-lo'-re-co, cah], *a.* Pyloric, relating to the pyloric orifice.

Píloro [pee'-lo-ro], *m.* 1. Musk-rat. Mus pilorides. 2. (Anat.) Pylorus, inferior part of the stomach.

Piloso, sa [pe-loh'-so, sah], *a.* Pilous, hairy.

Pilotaje [pe-lo-tah'-hay], *m.* 1. Piloting. 2. Pilotage, pilot's fee. 3. Pilots. 4. Steering, driving. 5. Piling, piles.

Pilotar, Pilotear [pe-lo-tar, pe-lo-tay-ar'], *va.* 1. To pilot. 2. To steer, to drive.

Pilote [pe-lo'-tay], *m.* Pile.

Pilotín [pe-lo-teen'], *m.* Pilot's apprentice, or second pilot.

Piloto [pe-lo'-to], *m.* 1. Pilot of a ship or aircraft. 2. The pilot fish. 3. (Naut.) First mate. *Piloto automático,* (Aer.) Autopilot. *Piloto de prueba,* Test pilot.

Piltraca, Piltrafa [peel-trah'-fah], *f.* Piece of flesh which is almost nothing but skin.

Pillada [pil-lyah'-dah], *f.* A knavish trick, a sham, an unworthy action.

Pillador [pil-lyah-dor'], *m.* Pillager, plunderer, swindler.

Pillaje [pil-lyah'-hay], *m.* Pillage, plunder, marauding, foray.

Pillar [pil-lyar'], *va.* 1. To pillage, to plunder, to foray. 2. To lay hold of, to chop at. *Quien pilla, pilla,* He who plunders most has most. *No pillar fastidio,* Not to be easily vexed. *Pillar un cernícalo, una mona, un lobo, una zorra, etc.,* To become intoxicated.

Pillastre, Pillastrón [pil-lyahs'-tray, pil-lyas-trone'], *m.* A roguish fellow, an impudent man.

Pillería [pil-lyay-ree'-ah], *f.* 1. A number of vagabonds or rogues going together. 2. A knavish trick or sham.

Pillo, lla [peel'-lyo, lyah], *a.* Applied to a loafer, or blackguard.—*m.* 1. A vagabond, a rascal. 2. A petty thief.

Pilluelo [pe-lyoo-ay'-lo], *m.* Rascal, vagabond, hoodlum.

Pimentada [pe-men-tah'-dah], *f.* Sauce, the principal ingredient of which is Cayenne paper.

Pimental [pe-men-tahl'], *m.* Ground bearing pepper; pepper patch.

Pimentero [pe-men-tay'-ro], *m.* 1. Pepper-box. 2. (Bot.) The plant which produces pepper. Piper nigrum. *Falso pimentero, V.* Molle.

Pimentón [pe-men-tone'], *m.* Ground red pepper, paprika.

Pimienta [pe-me-en'-tah], *f.* (Bot.) Pepper (black pepper). *Pimienta de Tabasco* or *malagueta,* Myrtle. Myrtus pimenta. *Pimienta larga,* Long pepper, the fruit of the long pepper-plant. *Es una pimienta,* He is all life and spirits. *Tener mucha pimienta,* To be very dear.

Pimiento [pe-me-en'-to], *m.* 1 (Bot.) Capsicum; red or Cayenne pepper. Capsicum. 2. The plant of every species of capsicum. 3. The fruit of all the species of capsicum. *Pimiento dulce,* The sweet fruit of the common capsicum. *Pimiento picante,* The fruit of shrubby and bird-pepper capsicum. 4. Mildew, blight in plants, as wheat, barley, etc. 5. Chaste-tree. *V.* Sauzgatillo.

Pímpido [peem'-pe-do], *m.* Kind of dog-fish, resembling the *mielga.*

Pimpín [pim-peen'], *m.* Children's play, like *pizpirigaña.*

Pimpinela [pim-pe-nay'-lah], *f.* (Bot.) Burnet, pimpinel, a rosaceous plant. Poterium sanguisorba.

Pimpleo, a [pim-play'-o, ah], *a.* Belonging to the muses.

Pimplón [pim-plone'], *m.* (Prov. Sant.) Waterfall, cascade.

Pimpollar [pim-pol-lyar'], *m.* Nursery of young plant, and trees.

Pimpollecer [pim-pol-lyay-therr'], *vn.* To sprout, to bud.

Pimpollejo, ico, ito [pim-pol-lyay'-ho], *m. dim.* A small sprout, sucker, or shoot.

Pimpollo [pim-pol'-lyo], *m.* 1. Sucker, sprout, shoot. 2. Rosebud not yet opened. 3. A spruce, lively lad. 4. Any thing perfect in its kind.

Pimpollón [pim-pol-lyone'], *m. aug.* A large sucker, sprout, or shoot.

Pimpolludo, da [pim-pol-lyoo'-do, dah], *a.* Full of buds or sprouts.

Pina [pee'-nah], *f.* 1. A mound of earth in the form of a cone. 2. Jaunt, felloe, any piece of the circumference of a coach or cart wheel.

Pinabete [pe-nah-bay'-tay], *m.* (Bot.) Spruce fir-tree. Pinus abies.

Pinacoteca [pe-nah-co-tay'-cah], *f.* Gallery, or museum, of paintings.

Pináculo [pe-nah'-coo-lo], *m.* Pinnacle, the highest part of a magnificent building.

Pinado, da [pe-nah'-do, dah], *a.* (Bot.) Pinnate, pinnated.

Pinal, Pinar [pe-nahl', pe-nar'], *m.* Grove of pines.

Pinariego, ga [pe-nah-re-ay'-go, gah], *a.* Belonging to pines.

Pinastro [pe-nahs'-tro], *m.* Wild pine.

Pinaza [pe-nah'-thah], *f.* (Naut.) Pinnace, a small vessel. *Pinazas,* A sort of Indian stuffs made of the bark of trees.

Pincel [pin-thel'], *m.* 1. Pencil, a small brush used by painters. 2. Painter. *Es un gran pincel,* He is a great painter. 3. The work painted. 4. Mode of painting. 5 Second feather in a martin's wing.

Pincelada [pin-thay-lah'-dah], *f.* Stroke with a pencil. *Dar la última pincelada,* To give the finishing stroke.

Pincelero [pin-thay-lay'-ro], *m.* Pencil-maker, one who makes and sells hair-pencils or small brushes.

Pincelillo, ito [pin-thay-leel'-lyo], *m. dim* A small pencil.

Pincerna [pin-therr'-nah], *com.* One who serves drinks at feasts.

Pinchadura [pin-chah-doo'-rah], *f* (Coll.) Puncture, act of pricking.

Pinchar [pin-char'], *va.* (Coll.) To prick, to wound.

Pinchazo [pin-chah'-tho], *m.* A prick, a stab

Pinche [peen'-chay], *m.* Scullion, kitchen-boy; any ragged boy.

Pincho [peen'-cho], *m.* Thorn, prickle of plants.

Pindárico, ca [pin-dah'-re-co, cah], *a.* Pindaric, after the style of Pindar.

Pindonga [pin-don'-gah], *f.* A gadabout (woman).

Pindonguear [pin-don-gay-ar'], *vn.* (Coll.) To gad about: applied to women.

Pineda [pe-nay'-dah], *f.* 1. A kind of linen garters. 2. (Prov.) *V.* Pinal.

Pingajo [pin-gah'-ho], *m.* A rag or patch hanging from clothes.

Pinganello, *m.* *V.* Calamoco.

Pinganilla [pin-gah-neel'-lyah], *a.* (Amer. Peru, coll.) Bedecked, fashionably attired. *En pinganillas,* (Mex.) On tiptoe. *V.* De puntillas.

Pinganitos [pin-gah-nee'-tos], *m.* *En pinganitos,* In a prosperous or elevated state.
Pingo [peen'-go], *m.* 1. Rag. 2. *pl.* Worthless clothes, duds, whether ragged or in good repair. 3. (Amer.) A fine saddle horse. *Andar, estar,* or *ir de pingo,* To gad about and neglect home duties: said of a woman.
Pingorote [pin-go-ro'-tay], *m.* *V.* PERUÉTANO, 2d def.
Pingorotudo, da [pin-go-ro-too'-do, dah], *a.* (Prov.) High, lofty, elevated.
Pingüe [peen'-goo-ay], *m.* (Naut.) Pink, a vessel with a very narrow stern; a pink-stern.
Pingüe, *a.* 1. Fat, greasy, oily, pinguid. 2. Rich, plentiful, abundant.
Pingüedinoso, sa [pin-goo-ay-de-noh'-so, sah], *a.* Fatty, oleaginous, pinguid.
Pingüísimo, ma [pin-goo-ee'-se-mo, mah], *a. sup.* Excessively fat.
Pinguosidad [pin-goo-o-se-dahd'], *f.* Fatness.
Pinico [pe-nee'-co], *m. dim.* 1. Small step. 2. Small pine.
Pinífero, ra [pe-nee'-fay-ro, rah], *a.* (Poet.) Piniferous.
Pinillo [pe-neel'-lyo], *m.* (Bot.) Ground-pine, germander. Teucrium chamæpitys.
Pinito [pe-nee'-to], *m. dim.* First step. *Hacer pinitos,* To take the first steps (as of a little child or a convalescent).
Pinjante [pin-hahn'-tay], *m.* (Arch.) Moulding at the eaves of buildings.
Pino, na [pee'-no, nah], *a.* Very perpendicular, as the sides of a mountain.—*m.* (Coll.) The first step of a child or of a convalescent beginning to walk. *A pino,* Erect, upright: applied to bells turned half-round in ringing. (Lat. pennus.)
Pino [pee'-no], *m.* 1. (Bot.) Pine. Pinus. *Pino alerce,* Common white larch. Larix communis or Pinus larix. *Pino carrasco,* Maritime pine. Pinus maritima. *Pino albar,* Scotch pine. Pinus sylvestris. *Pino borde, cortezudo* or *bermejo,* A variety of the Scotch pine. Pinus sylvestris rubra. *Pino cedro, V.* CEDRO DEL LÍBANO. *Pino de comer,* Stone pine. Pinus pinea. *Pino real,* Clustian pine. Pinus clussiana. *Pino rodeno* or *rodezno,* Cluster pine. Pinus pinaster. *Pino uñal,* Siberian pine. Pinus cembra. 2. Ship constructed of pine. *Ser un* or *como un pino de oro,* To be well-disposed, gallant, high-minded.
Pinocha [pe-no'-chah], *f.* Pine leaf.
Pínola [pee'-no-lah], *f.* 1. Detent of a repeating watch. 2. Spindle. *Pínola de cabrestante,* (Naut.) Capstan-spindle. *Pínola de cuadrante,* (Naut.) Vane of a quadrant.
Pinole [pee'-no-lay] (Acad.), or **Pinole** [pe-no'-lay], *m.* 1. An aromatic powder used in making chocolate. 2. (Mex.) Parched corn, ground and mixed with sugar and water, for a drink.
Pinoso, sa [pe-no'-so, sah], *a.* Producing or belonging to pines.
Pinta [peen'-tah], *f.* 1. Spot, blemish, scar. 2. Any mark by which the qualities of a thing are known. 3. Mark on playing cards. 4. Drop. 5. Pint, a liquid measure.—*pl.* 1. Spots on the skin in malignant fevers. 2. Basset, a game at cards. *No quitar pinta,* The greatest similarity in every part of two persons or things.
Pintacilgo, Pintadillo [pin-tah-theel'-go, pin-tah-deel'-lyo], *m.* (Orn.) Goldfinch. Fringilla carduelis.
Pintada [pin-tah'-dah] *f.* The Guinea-fowl.
Pintadera [pin-tah-day'-rah], *f.* Instrument for ornamenting bread.
Pintado, da [pin-tah'-do, dah], *a. & pp.* of PINTAR. Painted, mottled. *Venir pintado,* To fit exactly. *Al más pintado,* To the wisest, to the most able.
Pintamonas [pin-tah-mo'-nas], *m.* (Coll.) Nickname for a bad painter, a dauber.
Pintar [pin-tar'], *va.* 1. To paint, to picture, to represent by delineation and colours. 2. To paint, to describe, to delineate, to represent any thing by writing or words. 3. To fancy, to imagine, to feign according to fancy. 4. To exaggerate, to heighten by representation. 5. To pay, to discharge, to satisfy.—*vn.* 1. To begin to ripen: applied to fruit. 2. To show, to give signs of.—*vr.* To paint one's face.
Pintarrajar, Pintarrajear [pin-tar-rah-har'], *va.* (Coll.) *V.* PINTORREAR.
Pintarrajo [pin-tar-rah'-ho], *m.* (Coll.) A bungling piece of painting.
Pintarrojo [pin-tar-ro'-ho], *m.* (Prov. Gal.) Robin. *V.* PARDILLO.
Pintarroja, *f.* *V.* LIJA.
Pintica, illa, ita [pin-tee'-cah], *f. dim.* A little spot or dot.
Pintiparado, da [pin-te-pah-rah'-do, dah], *a.* Perfectly like, closely resembling; apposite, fit.—*pp.* of PINTIPARAR.
Pintiparar [pin-te-pah-rar'], *va.* In jocular style, to compare, to estimate the relative quality.
Pintojo, ja [pin-toh'-ho, hah], *a.* Spotted, stained, mottled.
Pintor [pin-tor'], *m.* Painter.
Pintora [pin-to'-rah], *f.* Paintress; a painter's wife.
Pintorcillo [pin-tor-theel'-lyo], *m. dim.* Applied to a wretched painter or dauber.
Pintoresco, ca [pin-to-res'-co, cah], *a.* Picturesque.
Pintorreador [pin-tor-ray-ah-dor'], *m.* Dauber, miserable painter.
Pintorrear [pin-tor-ray-ar'], *va.* To daub, to paint without skill.
Pintura [pin-too'-rah], *f.* 1. Painting, the art of representing objects by delineation and colours. 2. Picture, painting, a painted resemblance. *Pintura figulina,* Painting in divers colours on earthenware. *Pintura al temple,* Size painting. 3. Forming letters with the pen. 4. (Met.) Picture, written description of any thing. *Pintura cerífica* or *encáustica,* Encaustic painting, enamelling with coloured wax burnt in. *Pintura embutida,* Painting in mosaic, etc.
Pinturero, ra [pin-too-ray'-ro, rah], *a. & n.* Exaggerating, buffoon-like.
Pinul, Pinullo [pe-nool'-lyo], *m.* An Indian drink made from maize. *Cf.* PINOLE.
Pínula [pee'-noo-lah], *f.* 1. Detent of a repeating watch. 2. Sight of an optical instrument.
Pinzas [peen'-thas], *f.pl.* 1. Pincers. 2. Forceps, tweezers. 3. Clothespin. *Compás de pinzas,* Compass, pair of compasses.
Pinzón [pin-thone'], *m.* (Orn.) Chaffinch. Fringilla cœlebs.
Pinzote [pin-tho'-tay], *m.* (Naut.) Whip-staff, formerly fastened to the rudder.
Piña [pee'-nyah], *f.* 1. Cone or nut of the pine-tree. 2. Pine-apple. Bromelia ananas. 3. Virgin silver treated with mercury. 4. A white, matt, transparent, and very fine fabric, made in the Philippines from the leaves of the pine-apple, and which serves for handkerchiefs, bands, towels, and garments of women and children.
Piñata [pe-nyah'-tah], *f.* 1. Pitcher, pot. 2. Jar or pot ornamented with fancy paper and filled with sweetmeats, which is hung from the ceiling so that the merrymakers, one by one and blindfolded, may break it with a cane. It is very popular at Christmas festivities and at children's parties.
Piñón [pe-nyone'], *m.* 1. The pine-nut seed or kernel. 2. Pinion, the joint of the wing remotest from the body. 3. Pinion, the tooth of a wheel. 4. Spring-nut of a gun. *Comer los piñones,* To celebrate Christmas eve.
Piñonata [pe-nyoh-nah'-tah], *f.* Conserve of pine-nut kernels.
Piñonate [pe-nyoh-nah'-tay], *m.* Paste made of the kernels of pine-nuts and sugar.
Piñoncico, illo, ito [pe-nyon-thee'-co], *m. dim.* 1. A small pine-nut kernel. 2. Pinion, the joint of the wing remotest from the body.
Piñuela [pe-nyoo-ay'-lah], *f.* 1. Figured silk. 2. Nut or fruit of cypress. 3. (Nicaragua) The American agave, from which the *cabuya* is made.
Pío, a [pee'-o, ah], *a.* 1. Pious, devout, religious, holy. 2. Mild, merciful. 3. Pied, piebald: applied to a horse. *Pía máter* or *pía madre,* Pia mater, membrane which covers the brain.
Pío [pee'-o], *m.* 1. Puling of chickens. 2. Anxious desire.
Piocha [pe-o'-chah], *f.* Trinket for women's head-dresses.
Piojento, ta [pe-o-hen'-to, tah], *a.* Lousy.
Piojería [pe-o-hay-ree'-ah], *f.* 1. Lousiness. 2. Misery, poverty.
Piojicida [pe-o-he-thee'-dah], *com.* In jocular style, a louse-killer.
Piojillo [pe-o-heel'-lyo], *m.* 1. (Dim.) A small louse: applied to vermin on plants and birds. 2. A white spot in leather which is not well dressed.
Piojo [pe-o'-ho], *m.* 1. A louse. Pediculus. 2. Disease in hawks and other birds of prey. *Piojo pegadizo,* Crab-louse; a troublesome hanger-on.
Piojoso, sa [pe-o-hoh'-so, sah], *a.* 1. Lousy, mean, contemptible. 2. Miserable, stingy.
Piojuelo [pe-o-hoo-ay'-lo], *m. dim.* A small louse.
Piola [pe-o'-lah], *f.* (Naut.) Housing, house-line; a line of three strands.
Pionía [pe-o-nee'-ah], *f.* A hard, red, bean-shaped seed used in Venezuela among the country people for making collars and bracelets. *V.* BUCARE.
Piorno [pe-or'-no], *m.* (Bot.) Spanish-broom. Spartium scorpius, *L.*
Piorrea [pe-or-ray'-ah], *f.* (Med.) Pyorrhea.
Pipa [pee'-pah], *f.* 1. A cask for wine and other liquors. 2. Pipe, a liquid measure of two hogsheads. 3. *V.* PEPITA. 4. Tobacco-pipe. 5. Pipe which children make of corn-stalks; reed of a clarion. *Tomar pipa,* To go away, to march off.
Pipar [pe-par'], *vn.* To smoke a tobacco-pipe.
Pipería [pe-pay-ree'-ah], *f.* Collection of pipes.
Piperina [pe-pay-ree'-nah], *f.* Piperin, an alkaloidal principle obtained from white pepper.
Pipero [pe-pay'-ro], *m.* Cooper, pipe or butt maker.
Pipí [pe-pee'], *m.* (Orn.) Pitpit, a bird known also as honey-creeper.
Pipián [pe-pe-ahn'], *m.* A kind of Indian fricassee.
Pipiar [pe-pe-ar'], *vn.* To pule, to chirp, to peep.

Pípila [pee'-pe-lah], *f.* (Mex. Amer.) Hen-turkey.
Pipiolo [pe-pe-o'-lo], *m.* (Coll.) Novice, raw hand, beginner; recruit.
Pipirigallo [pe-pe-re-gahl'-lyo], *m.* (Bot.) Sainfoin, a forage plant. Onobrychis sativa.
Pipiripao [pe-pe-re-pah'-o], *m.* (Coll.) A splendid feast.
Pipiritaña [pe-pe-re-tah'-nyah], or **Pipitaña** [pe-pe-tah'-nyah], *f.* Flute made by boys of green cane.
Pipo [pee'-po], *m.* Small bird that eats flies.
Pipote [pe-po'-tay], *m.* A keg.
Pipotillo [pe-po-teel'-lyo], *m. dim.* A small keg.
Pique [pee'-kay] *m.* 1. Pique, offence taken. 2. A beau, gallant, lover. 3. A term in a game. 4. Bottom, ground. *Irse a pique,* (Naut.) To founder. *Echar a pique un bajel,* (Naut.) To sink a ship. *A pique,* In danger, on the point of. *Estar a pique,* To be about or on the point of. *Piques,* (Naut.) Crotches. *V.* Horquillas.
Piqué [pe-kay'], *m.* Piqué, a heavy cotton fabric having a corded or lozenge-shaped pattern.
Piquera [pe-kay'-rah], *f.* 1. A hole in a hive, through which bees fly out and in. 2. Cock-hole in a barrel.
Piquería [pe-kay-ree'-ah], *f.* Body of pikemen.
Piquero [pe-kay'-ro], *m.* (Mil.) Pikeman.
Piqueta [pe-kay'-tah], *f.* Pickaxe, mattock, pitcher.
Piquete [pe-kay'-tay], *m.* 1. Sore or wound of little importance. 2. Small hole made in clothes with a pinking iron. 3. A pointed stake shod with iron. 4. Picket or piquet, a small detachment of soldiers. *Piquete avanzado,* Picket-guard.
Piquetero [pe-kay-tay'-ro], *m.* In mines, the boy who carries the picks or mattocks to the workmen.
Piquetilla [pe-kay-teel'-lyah], *f. dim.* A small pick-axe.
Piquillo [pe-keel'-lyo], *m. dim.* A small beak or bill.
Piquituerto [pe-ke-too-err'-to], *m.* (Orn.) Cross-bill, picarin. Loxia curvirostra.
Pira [pee'-rah], *f.* A funeral pile, on which the dead are burnt.
Piragón, Piral, *m. V.* Pirausta.
Piragua [pe-rah'-goo-ah], *f.* (Naut.) Pirogue, a small vessel.
Piramidal [pe-rah-me-dahl'], *a.* Pyramidal.
Piramidalmente, *adv.* Pyramidally.
Pirámide [pe-rah'-me-day], *f.* Pyramid.
Piramista [pe-rah-mees'-tah], *f.* A kind of butterfly.
Pirata [pe-rah'-tah], *m.* 1. Pirate, corsair. 2. A cruel wretch.
Piratear [pe-rah-tay-ar'], *vn.* To pirate, to rob at sea, to cruise.
Piratería [pe-rah-tay-ree'-ah], *f.* 1. Piracy on the sea. 2. Piracy, any robbery.
Pirático, ca [pe-rah'-te-co, cah], *a.* Piratical, piratic.
Pirausta [pe-rah-oos'-tah], *f.* Large fire-fly; an insect formerly fabled to live in fire, and to die apart from it. Pyra.
Pirenaico, ca [pe-ray-nah'-e-co, cah], *a.* Pyrenean, of the Pyrenees.
Pirexia [pe-rek'-se-ah], *f.* Pyrexia, essential fever.
Pírico, ca [pee'-re-co, cah], *a.* Relating to fire, particularly to fire-works.
Pirita [pe-ree'-tah], *f.* 1. Pyrites, an obsolescent name for the sulphurets of iron, copper, and other metals. 2. Marcasite, a fossil. *V.* Marcasita.
Piritoso, sa [pe-re-to'-so, sah], *a.* Pyritous.
Pirofilacio [pe-ro-fe-lah'-the-o], *m.* Subterraneous fire.
Piróforo [pe-ro'-fo-ro], *m.* 1. Pyrophore, a composition which will ignite in contact with air. 2. A tropical fire-fly.
Piromancia [pe-ro-mahn'-the-ah], *f.* Pyromancy, divination by fire.
Piromanía [pe-ro-mah-nee'-ah], *f.* Pyromania, a morbid desire to start fires.
Piromántico, ca [pe-ro-mahn'-te-co, cah], *a.* Belonging to pyromancy.
Pirómetro [pe-ro'-may-tro], *m.* Pyrometer, an instrument for measuring heat and its effects.
Pironomia [pe-ro-no'-me-ah], *f.* Pyronomy, the art of regulating fire for chemical processes.
Pirópo [pe-ro'-po], *m.* 1. Precious stone. *V.* Carbunclo. 2. Compliment, flattery, endearing expression.
Piróscafo [pe-ros'-cah-fo], *m.* A steamship.
Piróscopo [pe-ros'-co-po], *m.* Pyroscope, an instrument for measuring radiant heat.
Piroseno [pe-ro-say'-no], *m.* Pyroxene, a bisilicate mineral.
Pirosis [pe-ro'-sis], *f.* Pyrosis, a burning sensation in the stomach.
Pirotecnia [pe-ro-tec'-ne-ah], *f.* Pyrotechnics or pyrotechny, the art of making fire-works and of the use of explosive substances.
Pirotécnico, ca [pe-ro-tec'-ne-co, cah], *a.* Pyrotechnical.
Piroxilina [pee-roc-se-lee'-nah], *f.* Gun cotton.
Pirriquio [pir-ree'-ke-o], *m.* Foot of Latin verse.
Pirrónico, ca [pir-ro'-ne-co, cah], *a. V.* Escéptico.
Pirueta [pe-roo-ay'-tah], *f.* Pirouette, circumvolution, twirling round on the toe, dancing, gyration.
Pisa [pee'-sah], *f.* 1. Tread, the act of treading. 2. Kick, a blow with the foot. 3. Portion of olives or grapes pressed at once.
Pisada [pe-sah'-dah], *f.* 1. Footstep, footprint. *Seguir las pisadas,* To follow one's example. 2. Kick with the foot.
Pisador [pe-sah-dor'], *m.* 1. Treader of grapes. 2. Horse that prances in walking.
Pisadura [pe-sah-doo'-rah], *f.* Act of treading.
Pisafalto, Pisasfalto [pe-sah-fahl'-to], *m.* Mixture of bitumen and pitch.
Pisapapeles [pe-sah-pah-pay'-les], *m.* Paper weight.
Pisar [pe-sar'], *va.* 1. To tread, to trample; to stamp on the ground. 2. To beat down stones and earth with a mallet. 3. To touch upon, to be close to. 4. To despise, to abandon. 5. To tread, to copulate: applied to birds. *Pisar el sapo,* (1) To rise late. (2) To have a ridiculous dread of bad success. *Pisar las tablas,* To embark, to go on board a ship. *Pisar buena* or *mala hierba,* To be good or bad tempered.
Pisauvas [pe-sah-oo'-vas], *m.* Treader of grapes.
Pisaverde [pe-sah-verr'-day], *m.* (Coll.) Fop, coxcomb, popinjay.
Piscator [pis-cah-tor'], *m.* A universal almanac.
Piscatorio, ria [pis-cah-to'-re-o, ah], *a.* Piscatory.
Piscicultura [pis-the-cool-too'-rah], *f.* Pisciculture, fish culture.
Pisciforme [pis-the-for'-may], *a.* Fish-shaped.
Piscina [pis-thee'-nah], *f.* 1. Fish pond. 2. Swimming pool. 3. Piscina, basin with a drain for water disposal in connection with sacred rites.
Piscis [pees'-this], *m.* (Ast.) Pisces, a zodiacal sign.
Piso [pee'-so], *m.* 1. Tread, trampling, footing. 2. Floor, pavement, flooring, surface; foundation of a house. 3. Story or floor, as first floor, second floor, etc.; loft. *Piso bajo,* Ground floor. *A un piso,* On the same floor. 4. Money paid for board and lodging in a lodging-house, inn, etc.
Pisón [pe-sone'], *m.* Rammer, an instrument for driving earth, stones, or piles. *A pisón,* By blows of a rammer.
Pisonear [pe-so-nay-ar'], *va.* To ram, to drive down.
Pisotear [pe-so-tay-ar'], *va.* To trample, to tread under foot.
Pisoteo [pe-so-tay'-o], *m.* The act of treading under foot.
Pista [pees'-tah], *f.* 1. Trace, track, spoor of an animal. 2. Footprint. 3. Track for foot or horse racing. 4. (Aer.) Airstrip. *Pista de aterrizaje,* Landing strip, landing field. *Pista de despegue,* Runway.
Pistacho [pis-tah'-cho], *m.* Pistachio, pistachio nut.
Pistadero [pis-tah-day'-ro], *m.* Pestle, for pounding.
Pistar [pis-tar'], *va.* To pound with a pestle; to extract the juice of a thing.
Pistero [pis-tay'-ro], *m.* A round jug with a spout, used to give broth, medicines, etc.
Pistilo [pis-tee'-lo], *m.* (Bot.) Pistil, the central female part of a flower, which contains the ovule.
Pisto [pees'-to], *m.* 1. A kind of thick broth given to the sick. 2. (Prov.) Dish of tomatoes and red pepper fried with oil. *A pistos,* By little and little, by driblets.
Pistola [pis-to'-lah], *f.* Pistol, a small hand-gun. *Un par de pistolas,* A brace of pistols. *Pistolas de arzón,* Horse pistols.
Pistolera [pis-to-lay'-rah], *f.* A leather case in which horse pistols are put.
Pistoletazo [pis-to-lay-tah'-tho], *m.* Pistol-shot; the wound of a pistol; the report of a pistol.
Pistolete [pis-to-lay'-tay], *m.* Pistolet, pocket-pistol.
Pistón [pis-tone'], *m.* 1. Piston, embolus, as the sucker of a pump. 2. A percussion-cap, primer. 3. The piston of a brass wind-instrument.
Pistonera [pis-to-nay'-rah], *f.* A box or case for carrying percussion-caps.
Pistoresa [pis-to-ray'-sah], *f.* Short dagger.
Pistraje, Pistraque [pis-trah'-hay], *m.* Broth or sauce of an unpleasant taste.
Pistura [pis-too'-rah], *f.* Act of pounding.
Pita [pee'-tah], *f.* 1. (Bot.) American agave or century-plant. Agave Americana. 2. Kind of thread made of the agave. 3. Term used to call hens. 4. Play among boys.
Pitaco [pe-tah'-co], *m.* Stem or stalk of the aloe-plant.
Pitagórico, ca [pe-tah-go'-re-co, cah], *a.* & *n.* Pythagorean.
Pitancería [pe-tan-thay-ree'-ah], *f.* 1. Place where allowances of meat and other things are distributed. 2. Distribution or office of distributor of allowances.
Pitancero [pe-tan-thay'-ro], *m.* 1. Per

son appointed to distribute allowances of meat or other things. 2. Friar who is not ordained, but lives upon charity. 3. Steward or purveyor to a convent. 4. Superintendent of a choir in cathedrals.

Pitancica, illa, ita [pe-tan-thee'-cah], *f. dim.* Small pittance.

Pitanza [pe-tahn'-thah], *f.* 1. Pittance, daily allowance; alms. 2. (Coll.) Price of any thing; salary given for any work.

Pitaña [pe-tah'-nyah], *f.* *V.* LEGAÑA.

Pitañoso, sa [pe-tah-nyo'-so, sah], *a.* *V.* LEGAÑOSO.

Pitar [pe-tar'], *vn.* To pipe, to play on a pipe.—*va.* 1. To discharge a debt. 2. To distribute allowances of meat or other things.

Pitarra [pe-tar'-rah], *f.* Distemper of the eyes. *V.* LEGAÑA.

Pitillo [pe-teel'-lyo], *m.* Cigarette.

Pitima [pee'-te-mah], *f.* 1. (Med.) Plaster placed over the heart to quiet it. 2. (Coll.) Drunkenness.

Pitio [pe-tee'-o], *m.* Whistling of a pipe or of birds.

Pitipié [pe-te-pe-ay'], *m.* *V.* ESCALA.

Pito [pee'-to], *m.* 1. Pipe, a small flute; boy's whistle. 2. (Orn.) Magpie. Picus. 3. A species of bug in India. 4. Play among boys. 5. (Prov.) Cocoon of a silk-worm open at one end. *Cuando pitos, flautas; cuando flautas, pitos,* Events are sometimes the reverse of expectations. *No tocar pito,* Not to have a share in a thing. *No vale un pito,* It (he) is not worth a straw.

Pitoflero, ra [pe-to-flay'-ro, rah], *m.* & *f.* Coll.) A musician of little skill.

Pitométrica [pe-to-may'-tre-cah], *f.* Gauge, the art of gauging vessels.

Pitón [pe-tone'], *m.* 1. Tenderling, the top of an animal's horn when it begins to shoot forth. 2. Protuberance, prominence. 3. Sprig or shoot of a tree; sprout of the agave. 4. (Zool.) Python.

Pitonisa [pe-to-nee'-sah], *f.* 1. Pythia, pythoness, the priestess of Apollo. 2. Witch, sorceress, enchantress.

Pitorra [pe-tor'-rah], *f.* (Orn.) Woodcock *V.* CHOCHAPERDIZ.

Pitorreo [pe-tor-ray'-o], *m.* *V.* CHOTEO.

Pitpit [peet'-peet], *m.* Pitpit, guitguit, a small American bird. *Cf.* PIPÍ.

Pituita [pe-too-ee'-tah], *f.* Pituita, mucus.

Pituitario, ria [pe-too-e-tah'-re-o, ah], *a.* (Anat.) Pituitary. *Glándula pituitaria,* Pituitary gland.

Pituitoso, sa [pe-too-e-to'-so, sah], *a.* Pituitous, pituitary, mucous.

Piulco [pe-ool'-co], *m.* Surgical aspirator, syringe-shaped.

Pivotes [pe-vo'-tes], *m. pl.* Pivots, a term used by watchmakers for the axles of wheels.

Pixide [peek'-se-day], *f.* 1. A small box of wood or metal. 2. Pyx, box in which the consecrated host is kept.

Pizarra [pe-thar'-rah], *f.* 1. Slate, a gray mineral. 2. Slate, for writing or figuring; also, a blackboard.

Pizarral [pe-thar-rahl'], *m.* Slate quarry.

Pizarreño, ña [pe-thar-ray'-nyo, nyah], *a.* Slate-coloured, slaty.

Pizarrero [pe-thar-ray'-ro], *m.* Slater, one who polishes slates or slates buildings.

Pizarrin [pe-thar-reen'], *m.* Slate-pencil.

Pizarrón [pe-thar-rone'], *m.* Blackboard.

Pizca [peeth'-cah], *f.* (Coll.) Mite, whit, jot, any thing proverbially small. *Ni pizca,* Nothing at all not an iota.

Pizcar [peeth-car'], *va.* (Coll.) 1. To pinch. *V.* PELLIZCAR. 2. (Mex.) To harvest or glean (maize).

Pizpereta, Pizpireta [pith-pay-ray'-tah], *a.* Sharp, brisk, lively: applied to women.

Pizpirigaña [pith-pe-re-gah'-nyah], *f.* Play among boys, in which they pinch one another's hands.

Pizpita [pith-pee'-tah], *f.* (Orn.) Wagtail. *V.* PEZPITA.

Placa [plah'-cah], *f.* 1. Star, insignia of an order of knighthood. 2. A photographic plate. 3. (Mex.) Check for baggage. Rem. In American usage *placa* denotes a plate, chiefly of other material than metal; thus, *Placas secas ortocromáticas* (*para fotógrafos*), Orthochromatic photographic plates. *Placas de transparencias,* Transparency (or lantern) plates. *Placas de ferrotipia,* Ferrotype plates. *Placa del porta-objetos,* Stage-plate of a microscope. *Placa de cabeza,* Tube plate or sheet (of a steam-engine). *Cf.* PLANCHA.

Placabilidad [plah-cah-be-le-dahd'], *f* Piacability.

Placable [plah-cah'-blay], *a.* Placable.

Placear [plah-thay-ar'], *va.* To publish, to proclaim, to post up.

Placebo [plah-thay'-bo], *m.* (Med.) Placebo.

Placel [plah-thel'], *m.* (Naut.) Banks of sand or rocks in the sea.

Pláceme [plah'-thay-may], *m.* Compliment of congratulation.

Placenta [plah-then'-tah], *f.* 1. (Anat.) Placenta, after-birth. 2. (Bot.) Placenta.

Placenteramente, *adv.* Joyfully.

Placentero, ra [plah-then-tay'-ro, rah], *a.* Joyful, merry, pleasant, mirthful, humorous.

Placer [plah-therr'], *m.* 1. Pleasure, content, rejoicing, amusement, complacence. 2. Will, consent. 3. The place near the bank of a river where gold-dust is found. 4. *V.* PLACEL. *A placer,* (1) With the greatest pleasure. (2)(Prov.) Gently, commodiously. *Por hacer placer,* To oblige or please a person.

Placer, *v. impers.* To please, to gratify, to humour, to content. *Que me place,* It pleases me; I approve of it.

Placero, ra [plah-thay'-ro, rah], *a.* 1. Belonging to a market or other public place. 2. Roving idly about.

Placeta [plah-thay'-tah], *f. dim.* A small square or public place.

Placetilla, Placetuela [plah-thay-teel'-lyah], *f. dim.* *V.* PLACETA.

Placible [plah-thee'-blay], *a.* Placid, agreeable.

Plácido, da [plah'-the-do, dah], *a.* Placid, easy, quiet.

Placiente [plah-the-en'-tay], *a.* Pleasing, mild; acceptable.

Placilla, ita [plah-theel'-lyah], *f. dim.* *V.* PLACETA.

Plafón [plah-fone'], *m.* (Arch.) Soffit of an architrave.

Plaga [plah'-gah], *f.* 1. Plague, any public calamity, as pestilence, scarcity, etc. 2. Plague, state of misery. 3. Plague, any thing vexatious. 4. Plenty, abundance of a harmful thing. 5. Climate, country; zone. 6. (Naut.) Each of the cardinal points of the compass.

Plagar [plah-gar'], *va.* To plague, to torment.—*vr.* To be overrun with.

Plagiar [plah-he-ar'], *va.* 1. To plagiarize, or commit literary thefts. 2. Among the ancient Romans, to buy and enslave a free man.

Plagiario, ria [plah-he-ah'-re-o, ah], *a.* & *m.* & *f.* Plagiary, plagiarist, copier.

Plagiato [plah-he-ah'-to], *m.* 1. Abduction. 2. *V.* PLAGIO.

Plagio [plah'-he-o], *m.* Plagiarism, a literary theft.

Plagoso, sa [plah-goh'-so, sah], *a.* Wounding, making wounds.

Plaguear [plah-gay-ar'], *vn.* To beg alms piteously.

Plan [plahn], *m.* 1. Plan, design, draft of a building, town, etc. 2. Plan, the delineation of the horizontal posture of any thing. 3. Plan, writing in which a thing is described minutely. 4. Slab, (Naut.) floor-timber. *Plan de combate,* (Naut.) Quarter-bill. *Plan de las varengas,* (Naut.) Floor timbers, bottom. *Plan de vuelo,* (Aer.) Flight plan. *Navío de mucho plan,* (Naut.) Flat-bottomed vessel.

Plana [plah'-nah], *f.* 1. Page of a book or writing. 2. A level, fruitful piece of ground. 3. Trowel, a bricklayer's tool. 4. Copy or page written by scholars during school-hours. *A plana renglón,* Copied word for word; arriving or happening at the nick of time. *Plana mayor de un ejército* or *regimiento,* The staff. *Enmendar la plana,* (Met. Coll.) To rectify a mistake; also, to outdo a person.

Planada [plah-nah'-dah], *f.* Plain, level ground.

Planador [plah-nah-dor'], *m.* (Littl. us.) Planisher.

Plancha [plahn'-chah], *f.* 1. Flat-iron. 2. Plate, a thin piece of metal, slab. *Plancha de acero,* Steel plate. *Plancha de cobre,* Copper plate. *Tirarse una plancha,* To be left in the lurch, to be disappointed.

Planchada [plan-chah-dah], *f.* (Naut.) Framing or apron of a gun.

Planchador, ra [plan-chah-dor', rah], *m.* & *f.* Ironer. *Planchadora eléctrica,* Ironer, electric ironer.

Planchar [plan-char'], *va.* To iron linen. *V.* APLANCHAR.

Planchear [plan-chay-ar'], *va.* To plate, to sheath, to cover with metal.

Plancheta [plan-chay'-tah], *f.* Circumferentor, instrument used to measure distances and take heights, plans, etc.

Planchica, illa, ita [plan-chee'-cah], *f. dim.* A small plate.

Planchón [plan-chone'], *m. aug.* A large plate.

Planeador [plah-nay-ah-dor'], *m.* (Aer.) Glider.

Planear [plah-nay-ar'], *va.* 1. To plan. 2. To organize.—*vn.* (Aer.) To glide.

Planeo [plah-nay'-o], *m.* (Aer.) Free flight.

Planeta [plah-nay'-tah], *m.* Planet, a heavenly body.

Planetario [plah-nay-tah'-re-o], *m.* 1 Planetarium, orrery, an astronomical instrument. 2. Astronomer.

Planetario, ria [plah-nay-tah'-re-o, ah], *a.* Planetary.

Planga [plahn'-gah], *f.* Kind of eagle, with black and white feathers.

Planicie [plah-nee'-the-ay], *f.* *V.* LLANO and LLANURA.

Planificación [plah-ne-fe-cah-the-on'], *f.* City planning.

Planilla [plah-neel'-lyah], *f.* 1. List, blank form. 2. List of candidates for office.

Planipedia [plan-ne-pay'-de-ah], *f.* A mean play, acted by strollers.

Planisferio [plah-nis-fay'-re-o], *m.* Planisphere, a sphere projected on a plane.

Plano, na [plah'-no, nah], *a.* Plain, level, smooth, flat.

Plano [plah'-no *m.* 1. Plan, design draft, groundplot, delineation. 2

(Geom.) Plane, a level surface. *De plano*, Openly, clearly. *Caer de plano*, To fall all-fours, or flat-long.

Planocóncavo, va [plah-no-con'-cah-vo, vah], *a.* Plano-concave.

Planocónico, ca [plah-no-co'-ne-co, cah], *a.* Plano-conical.

Planoconvexo, xa [plah-no-con-vec'-so, sah], *a.* Plano-convex.

Planometría [plah-no-may-tree'-ah], *f.* Planometry, the mensuration of plane surfaces.

Planoplano [plah-no-plah'-no], *m.* (Alg.) Biquadrate.

Planta [plahn'-tah], *f.* 1. Sole of the foot. 2. Plant, any vegetable production. 3. Plantation, the act of planting. 4. A plantation or nursery of young plants. 5. Plan of a building. 6. Position of the feet in dancing or fencing. 7. Project: disposition; point of view. 8. Plant or site of a building. *Echar plantas*, To brag, to boast. *De planta*, Anew; from the foundation. *A las plantas*, or *a los pies de Vd.*, Your most obedient (addressing a lady only).

Plantación [plan-tah-the-on'], *f.* Plantation, planting, act of planting.

Plantador, ra [plan-tah-dor', rah], *m.* & *f.* Planter, one who plants; an instrument used for planting.

Plantaje [plan-tah'-hay], *m.* Collection of plants.

Plantaminas [plan-tah-mee'-nas], *m.* Minelayer.

Plántano, *m.* *V.* PLÁTANO.

Plantar [plan-tar'], *va.* 1. To plant, in order to grow. 2. To set up, to fix upright. 3. To strike a blow. 4. To put into any place; to place or introduce somewhere. *Plantar en la cárcel*, To throw into jail. 5. To plant, to found, to establish. 6. (Coll.) To leave in the lurch, to disappoint. 7. To jilt.—*vr.* 1. To stand upright, to stop. 2. To arrive soon. 3. To stop, to halt, to be unwilling to go: said of an animal. 4. In some games not to wish more cards than are held.

Plantaria, *f.* *V.* ESPARGANIO.

Plantario [plan-tah'-re-o], *m.* Plot of ground where young plants are reared.

Plantear [plan-tay-ar'], *va.* To plan, to trace, to try, to attempt.

Plantel [plan-tel'], *m.* 1. Nursery or nursery-garden, a plantation of young trees. 2. Seminary or training-school.

Plantífero, ra [plan-tee'-fay-ro, rah], *a.* Rearing plants.

Plantificar [plan-te-fe-car'], *va.* 1. To plant. *V.* PLANTAR. 2. (Coll.) To beat, to box, or kick.

Plantigrado, da [plan-te-grah'-do, dah], *a.* Plantigrade, walking on the sole of the foot. Also PLANTÍGRADO, DA.

Plantilla [plan-teel'-lyah], *f.* 1. (Dim.) A young plant. 2. The first sole of a shoe. (Coll.) Mustard or other draughts applied to the feet. 3. Vamp, a sole of linen, put to the feet of stockings. 4. Model, pattern, foundry pattern. 5. Plate of a gun-lock. 6. Celestial configuration.

Plantillar [plan-teel-lyar'], *va.* To vamp or sole shoes or stockings.

Plantío, ía [plan-tee'-o, ah], *a.* Planted, ready to be planted: applied to ground.

Plantío [plan-tee'-o], *m.* 1. Plantation, the act of planting. 2. Nursery, a plantation of young trees.

Plantista [plan-tees'-tah], *m.* 1. Bully, hector, bravado. 2. In gardens, royal parks, etc., a planter of trees and shrubbery.

Plantón [plan-tone'], *m.* 1. Scion, a sprout or shoot from a plant; a shoot ingrafted on a stock. 2. (Mil.) Sentry who performs duty as punishment. *Estar de plantón*, To be fixed in a place for a long time. *Llevar un plantón*, To dance attendance.

Planudo, da [plah-noo'-do, dah], *a.* (Naut.) Applied to a vessel which draws little water, as being too flat.

Plañidera [plah-nye-day'-rah], *f.* Mourner, woman paid for weeping at funerals.

Plañido [plah-nye'-do], *m.* Moan, lamentation, crying.—*Plañido, da*, *pp.* of PLAÑIR.

Plañir [plah-nyeer'], *vn.* To lament, to grieve, to bewail, to sob; to whimper and whine.

Plaqué [plah-kay'], *m.* Plaque, an object of metal, covered with a thin layer of gold or silver.

Plaqueta [plah-kay'-tah], *f.* Small plate, tag. *Plaqueta sanguínea*, Blood platelet.

Plasma [plahs'-mah], *f.* Prase, a precious stone.—*m.* Plasma.

Plasmador, ra [plas-mah-dor', rah], *m.* & *f.* Moulder, former.

Plasmante [plas-mahn'-tay], *pa.* Moulding; moulder.

Plasmar [plas-mar'], *va.* To mould, to form of clay; to make moulds.

Plasmo [plahs'-mo], *m.* (Sculpture) Model, type.

Plasta [plahs'-tah], *f.* 1. Paste, soft clay, any thing soft. 2. (Met. Coll.) Any thing done without rule or order.

Plaste [plahs'-tay], *m.* Size, of glue and lime.

Plastecer [plas-tay-therr'], *va.* To size, to besmear with size.

Plastecido [plas-tay-thee'-do], *m.* Act of sizing.—*Plastecido, da*, *pp.* of PLASTECER.

Plástica [plahs'-te-cah], *f.* Art of moulding in clay.

Plástico, ca [plahs'-te-co, cah], *a.* Plastic.

Plastografía [plas-to-grah-fee'-ah], *f.* Plastography.

Plata [plah'-tah], *f.* 1. Silver. 2. Plate, wrought silver. 3. In America, money. 4. (Her.) Plate; white. *Plata quebrada*, Articles of silver that retain the value of their weight, although worn out or disfigured. *Plata piña*, Amalgam of silver from the mine, very light, brittle, and spongy. *Plata virgen* or *bruta*, Crude mass of silver. *Plata labrada*, (1) Wrought-silver. (2) Payment made in articles equivalent to money. *Valer tanto como la plata*, To be worth its weight in gold. *En plata*, Briefly, without turnings or windings. *Como una plata*, Shining like silver, very clean and pretty.

Platabanda [plah-tah-bahn'-dah], *f.* Band or bar of flat iron.

Plataforma [plah-tah-for'-mah], *f.* 1. (Mil.) Platform, an elevation of earth raised on ramparts; temporary platform. 2. A machine for making pieces of watches. 3. The platform of a street-car or tramway. 4. The stage of a microscope. *Plataforma de lanzamiento*, (Aer.) Launching pad. *Plataforma de seguridad*, Safety island. *Plataforma giratoria*, (r.w.) Turntable. *Plataforma subterránea de lanzamiento*, (Aer.) Silo.

Platal [plah'-tahl'], (Coll.) Great wealth. *V.* DINERAL.

Platanal, Platanar [plah-tah-nal', plah-tah-nar'], *m.* Banana grove.

Plátano [plah'-tah-no], *m.* 1. Banana. 2. Plantain. 3. Banana tree. 4. Plane tree.

Platea [plah-tay'-ah], *f.* Parquet, orchestra.

Platear [plah-tay-ar'], *va.* To silver.

Platel, *m.* (Obs.) Dish. *V.* PLATO.

Plateresco, ca [plah-tay-res'-co, cah], *a.* Applied to fanciful ornaments in architecture; over-florid, plateresque.

Platería [plah-tay-ree'-ah], *f.* 1. Silversmith's shop. 2. Trade of a silversmith.

Platero [plah-tay'-ro], *m.* Silversmith, plate-worker. *Platero de oro*, Goldsmith.

Plática [plah'-te-cah], *f.* 1. Discourse, conversation; colloquy, converse. 2. Speech delivered on some public occasion, address, lecture. 3. Pratic or pratique, permission to a ship's crew to come on shore to buy and traffic. 4. *V.* PRÁCTICA. *Tomar plática*, To obtain practice.

Platicar [plah-te-car'], *va.* 1. To converse, to talk, to commune. 2. To practise a profession.

Platija [plah-tee'-hah], *f.* (Zool.) Plaice, flounder. Pleuronectes platessa.

Platilla [plah-teel'-lyah], *f.* Silesian linen.

Platillo [plah-teel'-lyo], *m.* 1. (Dim.) A small dish, saucer. 2. A side dish, as opposed to the entree or main course. 3. (Mus.) Cymbal, a percussion instrument. 4. Valve of a pump. *Platillo volador*, (Aer.) Flying saucer.

Platina [plah-tee'-nah], *f.* 1. An ore of platinum. 2. An exterior metallic ornament of carriages. 3. Platen, bedplate; also imposing-table, in printing. 4. Supports of any machine and lids which inclose the works of watches.

Platino [plah-tee'-no], *m.* Platinum, the heaviest of metals.

Platirrostro, tra [plah-teer-ros'-tro, trah], *a.* Platyrhine, having a broad nose, snout, or beak.—*m.* *V.* TODI.

Plato [plah'-to], *m.* 1. Dish, plate, a vessel to eat on. 2. Dish, mess, food served in a dish. 3. Daily fare. 4. Ornament in the frieze of Doric architecture. 5. Chuck in which are made the teeth of wheels for watches *Platos lisos, llanos* or *trincheros*, Dining-plates. *Poner el plato*, To afford one an opportunity of saying or doing what he did not think of. *Entre dos platos*, Offering a kindness or slight favour with fuss or ostentation. *Es de mi plato*, It is my greatest pleasure. *Plato de segunda mesa*, Makeshift, person or thing which has belonged to another, and whose possession is not flattering.

Platón [plah-tone'], *m.* (Aug.) Platter, a large dish.

Platónicamente, *adv.* Platonically.

Platónico, ca [plah-to'-ne-co, cah], *a.* Platonic, relating to Plato.

Plato tocadiscos [plah'-to to-ca-dees'-cos], *m.* Turntable.

Plato volador [plah'-to voh-lah-dor'], *m.* Flying saucer.

Platuja, *f.* (Prov.) *V.* PLATIJA.

Plausibilidad [plah-oo-se-be-le-dahd'], *f.* Plausibility, speciousness.

Plausible [plah-oo-see'-blay], *a.* Plausible, specious.

Plausiblemente, *adv.* Plausibly, colourably.

Plauso [plah'-oo-so], *m.* Applause by the clapping of hands.

Plaustro [plah'-oos-tro], *m.* (Poet.) Cart, wagon, carriage. *V.* CARRO.

Playa [plah'-yah], *f.* Shore, strand, sea-coast, beach.

Playado, da [plah-yah'-do, dah], *a.* Applied to a river or sea with a shore.

Playazo [plah-yah'-tho], *m.* Wide or extended shore.

Playero [plah-yay'-ro], *m.* Fisherman who brings fish to market.

Playón [plah-yone'], *m. aug.* A large shore or beach.

Playuela [plah-yoo-ay'-lah], *f.* Dim. of PLAYA.

Plaza [plah'-thah], *f.* 1. Square, place, or market-place, where eatables are sold. 2. Place, a fortified town. 3. Room, space; stall. 4. Place, office, public employment. 5. Enlisting or enrolling of soldiers in the king's service. 6. Reputation, character, fame. *Plaza de armas*, Military department, garrison, military parade-ground. (Naut.) The waist. *Plaza fuerte*, A strong place, a fortress. *Plaza viva*, An effective soldier. *Plaza muerta*, False muster. *Hombre de plaza*, One who holds or might occupy an honourable place. *Pasar plaza*, To be reputed something which one is not. *Sacar a plaza*, To publish, to render public. *Plaza, plaza*, Clear the way, make room.

(*Me, te, le plazca.* V. PLACER.)

Plazo [plah'-tho], *m.* 1. Time limit. 2. Installment, payment. 3. Terms. 4. Due date. *A plazo*, On time, on credit. *De largo plazo*, Long-term.

Plazuela [plah-thoo-ay'-lah], *f. dim.* A small square or place.

Ple [play], *m.* (Mex.) *V.* BLE.

Pleamar [play-ah-mar'], *f.* (Naut.) High water, high tide.

Plebe [play'-bay], *f.* Common people, populace.

Plebeyo, ya [play-bay'-yo, yah], *a.* Plebeian.—*m.* & *f.* Commoner.

Plebiscito [play-bis-thee'-to], *m.* 1. Plebiscitum, a Roman law voted by the plebs at the instance of their tribune. 2. Plebiscite, an expression by vote of the will of the people.

Pleca [play'-cah], *f.* (Print.) A straight line, a rule.

Plectro [plec'-tro], *m.* 1. Plectrum, a small staff or tool for plucking the strings of a lyre, etc. 2. (Poet.) Plectrum; poesy.

Plegable [play-gah'-blay], *a.* Pliable, capable of being folded.

Plegadamente, *adv.* Confusedly.

Plegadera [play-gah-day'-rah], *f.* Folder, used by bookbinders.

Plegadizo, za [play-gah-dee'-tho, thah], *a.* Pliable, folding.

Plegador [play-gah-dor'], *m.* 1. An instrument for folding or plaiting. 2. Plaiter, he that plaits. 3. (Coll.) Collector of alms for religious communities. 4. Beam of a silk-loom.

Plegadura [play-gah-doo'-rah], *f.* 1. Fold, double, complication. 2. Plaiting, folding, doubling. 3. Crease, made by doubling.

Plegar [play-gar'], *va.* 1. To fold, to plait, to double. 2. To corrugate, to crimple, to purse up. 3. To turn the warp on the yarn-beam. 4. Among bookbinders, to fold the sheets of a book that is to be bound.

(*Me, te, le, nos, os, les plegue.* V. PLACER.)

Plegaria [play-gah'-re-ah], *f.* 1. Public prayer, supplication. 2. Bell rung at noon for prayer.

Pleguería [plah-gay-ree'-ah], *f.* Fold, crumple.

Pleita [play'-ee-tah], *f.* A plaited strand of bass.

Pleiteador, ra [play-e-tay-ah-dor', rah], *m.* & *f.* Pleader, a litigious person, a wrangler.

Pleiteante [play-e-tay-ahn'-tay], *pa.* & *n.* Litigating; pleader, litigant.

Pleitear [play-e-tay-ar'], *va.* To plead, to litigate, to contend.

Pleitesía [play-tay-see'-ah], *f.* Tribute. *Rendir pleitesía*, To render tribute, to pay homage (to some one).

Pleitista [play-e-tees'-tah], *m.* Pettifogger, an encourager of lawsuits.

Pleito [play'-e-to], *m.* 1. Covenant, contract, bargain. 2. Dispute, contest, controversy. 3. Debate, contention, strife. 4. Litigation, judicial contest, lawsuit. *Pleito de acreedores*, Proceedings under a commission of bankruptcy. *Más vale mala composición que buen pleito*, (prov.) A bad compromise is better than a good verdict.

Plenamar, *f.* *V.* PLEAMAR.

Plenamente, *adv.* Fully, completely.

Plenariamente, *adv.* Completely, fully, plenarily.

Plenario, ria [play-nah'-re-o, ah], *a.* Complete, full, plenary.

Plenilunio [play-ne-loo'-ne-o], *m.* Full moon.

Plenipotencia [play-ne-po-ten'-the-ah], *f.* Plenipotence, fulness of power.

Plenipotenciario [play-ne-po-ten-the-ah'-re-o], *m.* Plenipotentiary.

Plenitud [play-nee-tood'], *f.* Plenitude, fulness, abundance.

Pleno, na [play'-no, nah], *a.* Full. *V.* LLENO.

Pleonasmo [play-o-nahs'-mo], *m.* Pleonasm, a figure of speech.

Pleonástico, ca [play-o-nahs'-te-co, cah], *a.* Pleonastic, involving pleonasm.

Plepa [play'-pah], *f.* A charge; a person who has many defects, physically or morally.

Plétora [play'-to-rah], *f.* Plethora, fulness of blood.

Pletórico, ca [play-to'-re-co, cah], *a.* Plethoric.

Pleural [play-oo-rahl'], *a.* Pleural, relating to the pleura.

Pleuresía [play-oo-ray-see'-ah], *f.* Pleurisy, a disease. *Pleuresía falsa*, Pleurodynia.

Pleurítico, ca [play-oo-ree'-te-co, cah], *a.* Pleuritical, pleuritic.

Pleuritis [play-oo-ree'-tis], *f.* Inflammation of the pleura, pleurisy.

Pleurodinia [play-oo-ro-dee'-ne-ah], *f.* Pleurodynia, stitch in the side; pain in the intercostal muscles.

Pleximetro [plec-see'-may-tro], *m.* Pleximeter, a medical instrument for practising percussion.

Plexo [plec'-so], *m.* (Anat. and Bot.) Plexus; network.

Pléyadas, Pléyades [play'-yah-dahs], *f. pl.* (Ast.) The Pleiades.

Plica [plee'-cah], *f.* 1. Sealed parcel containing a will or document to be published in due time; escrow. 2. (Med.) Matted hair; plica.

Pliego [ple-ay'-go], *m.* 1. Sheet of paper. 2. Parcel of letters inclosed in one cover. 3. A tender or proposal by persons who wish to contract with the government. 4. *V.* PLEGADURA and PLIEGUE.

(*Yo pliego, yo pliegue*, from *Plegar. V.* ACERTAR.)

Pliegue [ple-ay'-gay], *m.* 1. Fold or plait in clothes, crease; gather. 2. Ruff, anciently worn.

Plinto [pleen'-to], *m.* (Arch.) Plinth of a pillar.

Plomada [plo-mah'-dah], *f.* 1. Artificer's lead-pencil. 2. Plumb, plummet. 3. (Naut.) Lead used by mariners for sounding the depth of water. 4. All the weights attached to fishing-nets; sinkers.

Plomar [plo-mar'], *va.* To put a leaden seal, hanging by a thread to some instrument, privilege, etc.

Plomazón [plo-mah-thone'], *f.* Gilding cushion.

Plombagina [plom-bah-hee'-nah], *f.* Plumbago, graphite.

Plomería [plo-may-ree'-ah], *f.* 1. Covering of lead on roofs. 2. Store-house of lead ware.

Plomero [plo-may'-ro], *m.* Plumber, a worker in lead.

Plomizo, za [plo-mee'-tho, thah], *a.* Leaden, made of lead; having the qualities of lead.

Plomo [plo'-mo], *m.* 1. Lead, a very heavy metal. 2. Any piece of lead. *Plomo en galápagos*, Lead in pigs. *Plomo en plancha*, Lead in sheets. 3. Ball of lead. *Andar con pies de plomo*, To proceed with the utmost circumspection. *Arrendador del plomo*, A heavy, unpleasant person, a cunctator. *A plomo*, Perpendicularly, plumb. *Caer a plomo*, To fall flat down. 4. Plumb, a plummet.

Plomoso, sa, *a.* Leaden. *V.* PLOMIZO.

(*Me, te, le, etc., plugo. V.* PLACER.)

Pluma [ploo'-mah], *f.* 1. Feather, the plume of birds. 2. Pen, for writing. 3. Art of writing, penmanship. 4. Writer, author. *Buena pluma*, A good penman, a skilful writer. *Golpe de pluma*, Dash with the pen. 5. (Coll.) Wealth, opulence. 6. (Coll.) Air expelled from the bowels. *Tiene pluma*, He has feathered his nest well.

Plumada [ploo-mah'-dah], *f.* 1. Act of writing something short. 2. Dash with a pen, a line with a crayon. 3. Feathers which falcons have eaten, and have still in the crop.

Plumado, da [ploo-mah'-do, dah], *a.* Feathered, feathery, plumy.

Plumaje [ploo-mah'-hay], *m.* 1. Plumage of a fowl or bird. 2. Plume, an ornament of feathers.

Plumajear [ploo-mah-hay-ar'], *va.* (Obs.) To shove, to move from side to side.

Plumajería [ploo-mah-hay-ree'-ah], *f.* Heap of feathers.

Plumajero [ploo-mah-hay'-ro], *m.* One who dresses feathers and makes plumes.

Plumazo [ploo-mah'-tho], *m.* 1. A mattress or pillow stuffed with feathers. 2. Stroke (of the pen). *Abolir de un plumazo*, To abolish by a stroke of the pen (denoting rapidity of action).

Plumazón [ploo-mah-thone'], *f.* Collection of feathers.

Plúmbeo, bea [ploom'-bay-o, ah], *a.* Leaden, made of lead, having the qualities of lead.

Plumeado [ploo-may-ah'-do], *m.* (Pict.) Series of lines similar to those made with a pen in a miniature.

Plumear [ploo-may-ar'], *va.* (Pict.) To draw lines with a pen or pencil, to shade a drawing.

Plúmeo, mea [ploo'-may-o, ah], *a.* Plumigerous, having feathers, plumous.

Plumería [ploo-may-ree'-ah], *f.* *V* PLUMAJERÍA.

Plumero [ploo-may'-ro], *m.* 1. Bunch of feathers, feather-duster. 2. Box in which feathers or plumes are preserved. 3. Plume. 4. Plumage.

Plumífero, ra [ploo-mee'-fay-ro, rah], *a.* (Poet.) Plumigerous.

Plumilla [ploo-meel' lyah], *f.* Script type.

Plumión, *m.* *V.* PLUMÓN.

Plumista [ploo-mees'-tah], *m.* 1. One who lives by writing, a petty scrivener or notary. 2. A worker in feathers, plume-maker.

Plumita [ploo-mee'-tah], *f. dim.* A small feather or pen.

Plumón [ploo-mone'], *m.* 1. Soft, downy feathers. 2. Feather-bed, flock-bed.

Plumoso, sa [ploo-mo'-so, sah], *a.* Covered with feathers, plumigerous, plumy.

Plúmula [ploo'-moo-lah]. *f.* (Bot.) Plumule.

Plural [ploo-rahl'], *a.* (Gram.) Plural.

Pluralidad [ploo-rah-le-dahd'], *f.* Plurality, multitude; majority. *A pluralidad de votos,* By the majority of voices.

Pluscuamperfecto [ploos-kwam-per-fec'-to], *m.* The pluperfect tense.

Plus minusve [ploos me-noos'-vay]. (Lat.) More or less.

Pluspetición [ploos-pay-te-the-on'], *f.* Asking for more than what is due.

Plus ultra [ploos ool'-trah]. *Ser el non plus ultra,* (Coll.) To be transcendent.

Plúteo [ploo'-tay-o], *m.* Each compartment of book-shelves in a library.

Plutocracia [ploo-to-crah'-the-ah], *f.* Plutocracy.

Plutocrático, ca [ploo-to-crah'-te-co, cah], *a.* Plutocratic.

Plutonio [ploo-to'-ne-o], *m.* Plutonium.

Pluvial [ploo-ve-ahl'], *m.* (Orn.) Golden plover. Charadrius pluvialis.

Pluvial, Pluvioso, sa [ploo-ve-ahl'], *a.* Rainy. *Capa pluvial,* A priest's cope, worn at the celebration of mass.

Pluviátil [ploo-ve-ah'-teel], *a.* Softened or mellowed by rain (temperature or soil).

Pluvímetro (Acad.) [ploo-vee'-may-tro], or **Pluviómetro,** *m.* Rain-gauge.

Pneumático, ca, *a.* *V.* NEUMÁTICO.

Po, *int.* *V.* PU.

Poa [po'-ah], *f.* (Naut.) Bow-line bridle.

Pobeda [po-bay'-dah], *f.* Plantation of poplars.

Población [po-blah-the-on'], *f.* 1. Population, the act of populating. 2. Population, the state of a city, town, or country with regard to the number of its inhabitants. 3. *V.* POBLADO.

Poblacho [po-blah'-cho], *m.* 1. A mean and ugly village. 2. (Obs.) Populace, rabble, mob.

Poblachón [po-blah-chone'], *m. aug.* 1. *V.* POBLACHO, 1st def. 2. A large collection of houses, more than a village and less than a town.

Poblado [po-blah'-do], *m.* Town, village, or place inhabited.—*Poblado, da, pp.* of POBLAR.

Poblador, ra [po-blah-dor', rah], *m. & f.* Populator, founder.

Poblar [po-blar'], *va. & vn.* 1. To found a town, to populate a district, to people. 2. To fill, to occupy. 3. To breed, to procreate fast. 4. To bud, to get leaves.

Poblazo [po-blah'-tho], *m.* *V.* POPULACHO.

Poblezuelo [po-blay-thoo-ay'-lo], *m. dim.* A small village.

Pobo [po'-bo], *m.* (Bot.) White poplar. *V.* ÁLAMO BLANCO.

Pobra [po'-brah], *f.* (Coll. obs.) Female mendicant.

Pobrar, *va.* (Obs.) *V.* POBLAR.

Pobre [po'-bray], *a.* 1. Poor, necessitous, indigent, needy. 2. Poor, barren, dry. 3. Humble, modest. 4. Poor, unhappy, pitiable, wretched. 5. Poor, trifling, paltry, unimportant. *Pobre y soberbio,* Proud pauper. *Ayudado por pobre,* (Law) In forma pauperis.

Pobre [po'-bray], *m.* 1. A poor person, a beggar. 2. A man of very pacific and quiet temper.

Pobrecico, ica, illo, illa, ito, ita [po-bray-thee'-co], *a. dim.* A poor little thing.

Pobremente, *adv.* Poorly, miserably, needily.

Pobrería [po-bray-ree'-ah], *f.* Poor people, beggars.

Pobrero [po-bray'-ro], *m.* One who is appointed by a religious community to distribute charities.

Pobreta [po-bray'-tah], *f.* (Coll.) Strumpet, prostitute.

Pobrete, Pobreto [po-bray'-tay], *m.* 1. A poor, unfortunate man. 2. A useless person, of mean abilities and sentiments.

Pobretería [po-bray-tay-ree'-ah], *f.* 1. Poor people, beggars. 2. Poverty, indigence.

Pobretón, na [po-bray-tone', nah], *a.* Very poor.

Pobreza [po-bray'-thah], *f.* 1. Poverty, indigence, necessity, want, need. 2. Poorness, sterility, barrenness. 3. Heap of worthless trifles. 4. Voluntary vow of poverty. 5. Poorness, lowness or littleness of spirit.

Pobrezuelo [po-bray-thoo-ay'-lo], *m. dim.* A poor man.

Pobrismo [po-brees'-mo], *m.* Poor people, beggars.

Pocero [po-thay'-ro], *m.* 1. One who digs pits and wells. 2. Nightman, one who cleanses wells, pits, or common sewers.

Pocico [po-thee'-co], *m. dim.* A small well.

Pocilga [po-theel'-gah], *f.* 1. Hogsty, a place for swine. 2. Any nasty, dirty place.

Pocillo [po-theel'-lyo], *m.* 1. (Dim.) Small well. 2. Vessel for collecting any liquor or fluid. 3. (Prov.) Chocolate-cup.

Pócima [po'-the-mah], *f.* Potion, a draught of physic.

Poción [po-the-on'], *f.* Drink, liquor; potion. *V.* BEBIDA.

Poco, ca [po'-co, cah], *a.* Little, scanty, limited, small in quantity, small in extent, not much, few, some.

Poco, *adv.* Little, in a small degree or quantity, in a scanty manner, shortly, briefly, in a short time. *Poco antes* or *poco después,* A little before or after. *Poco ha que.* Lately, a short time since, latterly. *Poco a poco,* Gently, softly; stop! by little and little. *De poco tiempo acá,* Latterly. *Hombre para poco,* A cowardly, pusillanimous man. *A poco,* Immediately, in a short time. *Tener en poco,* To set little value on a thing. *A poco, por poco* or *en poco,* To be very near a thing. *Qué poco,* How little: indicating the difficulty or impossibility of any thing. *Dársele poco,* To care nothing for a thing, to despise it entirely.

Poco, *m.* Little, a small part or proportion.

Pocoyán [po-co-yahn'], *m.* A bee of the Philippine Islands, somewhat larger than the European.

Póculo [po'-coo-lo], *m.* 1. Drinking cup or glass. 2. (Obs.) Drink.

Pocho, cha [po'-cho, chah], *a.* (Coll.) Discoloured, that has lost the colour.

Poda [po'-dah], *f.* Pruning of trees, pruning season.

Podadera [po-dah-day'-rah], *f.* Pruning-knife, pruning-hook, hedging-bill.

Podador, ra [po-dah-dor', rah], *m. & f.* Pruner of trees or vines.

Podadura [po-dah-doo'-rah], *f.* (Prov.) *V.* PODA.

Podagra [po-dah'-grah], *f.* Gout in the feet.

Podar [po-dar'], *va.* To prune trees; to head.

Podazón [po-dah-thone'], *f.* The pruning season.

Podenco [po-den'-co], *m.* Hound. Canis familiaris sagax. *Vuelta de podenco,* A severe beating with a stick.

Podenquillo [po-den-keel'-lyo], *m. dim.* A young or small hound.

Poder [po-derr'], *m.* 1. Power, faculty, authority, dominion, command, influence, mastery, force. 2. Military strength of a state. 3. Power or letter of attorney. 4. Power, possession. 5. Power, ability, force, vigour, capacity, possibility. *A poder de,* By force. *Poder de Dios,* Exclamation exaggerating the greatness of any thing as representing the power of God. *Poder esmerado* or *supremo,* Supreme power.

Poder [po-derr'], *va.* 1. To be able, may or can; to possess the power of doing any thing. 2. To be invested with authority or power. 3. To have force or energy to act or resist. 4. In geometry, to value, to produce. *A más no poder,* Able to resist no longer. *No poder más,* Not to be able to do more; to be exhausted; not to help to do a thing.—*v. imp.* To be possible or contingent. *No poder menos,* To be unavoidable, to be necessary.

Poderdante [po-der-dahn'-tay], *com.* The constituent, the person who authorizes another.

Poderhabiente [po-der-ah-be-en'-tay], *m.* Attorney, one authorized or empowered to transact another's business.

Poderío [po-day-ree'-o], *m.* 1. Power, authority, dominion, jurisdiction. 2. Wealth, riches.

Poderosamente, *adv.* Powerfully, mightily.

Poderoso, sa [po-day-ro'-so, sah], *a.* 1. Powerful, mighty, potent. 2. Rich, wealthy. 3. Eminent, excellent. 4. Powerful, efficacious. 5. Powerful, able, forcible.

Podio [po'-de-o], *m.* A long pedestal on which several columns are supported.

Podofilina [po-do-fe-lee'-nah], *f.* Podophyllin, a purgative principle obtained from the may-apple or podophyllum.

Podómetro [po-do'-may-tro], *m.* Pedometer, instrument for measuring a person's steps or the circumvolutions of a wheel.

Podón [po-done'], *m.* Mattock, hoe, an instrument for pulling up weeds.

Podre [po'-dray], *f.* Pus, corrupted blood or humour.

Podrecer [po-dray-therr'], *va. & vn.* *V.* PUDRIR.—*vr.* To be putrid, rotten, or corrupt.

Podrecimiento [po-dray-the-me-en'-to], *m.* 1. Rottenness, putrefaction. 2. Pain, grief.

Podredumbre [po-dray-doom'-bray], *f.* 1. Pus, putrid matter, corruption. 2. Grief, internal pain.

Podredura [po-dray-doo'-rah], *f.* Putrefaction, corruption.

Podrición, *f.* *V.* PODREDURA.

Podridero, *m.* *V.* PUDRIDERO.

Podrimiento, *m.* *V.* PUDRIMIENTO.

Podrir, *va.* *V.* PUDRIR.

Poema [po-ay'-mah], *m.* Poem, a metrical composition.

Poesía [po-ay-see'-ah], *f.* 1. Poetry, poesy. *Poesías,* Poetical works. 2. Poetical composition.

Poeta [po-ay'-tah], *m.* A poet.

Poetastro [po-ay-tahs'-tro], *m.* Poetaster.

Poética [po-ay'-te-cah], *f.* Poetry; poetics, the art or practice of writing poems.

Poéticamente, *adv.* Poetically.

Poético, ca [po-ay'-te-co, cah], *a.* Poetic, poetical.

Poetilla [po-ay-teel'-lyah], *m. dim.* Poetaster.

Poetisa [po-ay-tee'-sah], *f.* Poetess, a female poet.

Poetizar [po-ay-te-thar'], *vn.* To poetize, to write like a poet.

Poetón [po-ay-tone'], *m.* Poetaster, a vile poet.
Pogrom [po-grom'], *m.* Pogrom, organized massacre of helpless people.
Poino [po-ee'-no], *m.* A wooden frame, on which barrels of wine or beer are laid.
Polaca [po-lah'-cah], *f.* 1. Polonaise, a Polish song and dance. 2. (Obs.) Top of the shoe which covers the instep.
Polaco, ca [po-lah'-co, cah], *a.* Polish, relating to Poland.—*m.* The Polish language.—*m. & f.* A native of Poland.
Polacra [po-lah'-crah], *f.* (Naut.) Polacre, a vessel with three pole-masts, used in the Mediterranean.
Polaina [po-lah'-e-nah], *f.* Legging, gaiter, puttee.—*pl.* Spats.
Polar [po-lar'], *a.* Polar.
Polaridad [po-lah-re-dahd'], *f.* Polarity.
Polarización [po-lah-re-thah-the-on'], *f.* Polarization, a modification of light by refraction or by reflection at 35°.
Polarizar [po-lah-re-thar'], *va.* To polarize.
Polca [pol'-kah], *f.* Polka, a well-known dance originally from Poland.
Polcar [pol-car'], *vn.* To dance the polka.
Polea [po-lay'-ah], *f.* 1. Pulley. 2. (Naut.) Tackle-block, or the double block of a tackle.
Poleadas [po-lay-ah'-das], *f. pl.* *V.* Gachas or Puchas.
Poleame [po-lay-ah'-may], *m.* Collection of masts for vessels.
Poleita [po-lay-ee'-tah], *f.* (Naut.) A small block.
Polémica [po-lay'-me-cah], *f.* 1. Polemics, dogmatical divinity. 2. (Mil.) The science of fortification. 3. Literary or political controversy.
Polémico, ca [po-lay'-me-co, cah], *a.* Polemical, polemic.
Polemonio [po-lay-moh'-ne-o], *m.* (Bot.) Jacob's-ladder, Greek valerian. Polemonium cœruleum.
Polemoscopio [po-lay-mos-co'-pe-o], *m.* (Opt.) Polemoscope, telescope used by military commanders.
Polen, *m.* (Bot.) Pollen.
Polenta [po-len'-tah], *f.* Porridge, a kind of batter or hasty pudding.
Poleo [po-lay'-o], *m.* 1. (Bot.) Pennyroyal. Mentha pulegium. 2. A strutting gait; a pompous style. 3. Stiff, cold wind.
Poleví [po-lay-vee'], *m.* A high wooden heel formerly worn by women.
Poliandria [po-le-ahn'-dre-ah], *f.* (Bot.) Polyandria.
Poliantea [po-le-an-tay'-ah], *f.* Polyanthea, a literary collection.
Poliantes tuberosa [po-le-ahn'-tes too-bay-ro'-sah], *f.* (Bot.) Common tuberose. Polyanthes tuberosa.
Poliarquía [po-le-ar-kee'-ah], *f.* Polygarchy, government of many persons.
Poliárquico, ca [po-le-ar'-ke-co, cah], *a.* Relating to polygarchy.
Policán, or **Pelicán** [po-le-cahn'], *m.* Pelican, instrument for drawing teeth.
Policarpo [po-le-car'-po], *a.* (Bot.) Polycarpous.
Pólice [po'-le-thay], *m.* The thumb.
Policía [po-le-thee'-ah], *f.* 1. Police, a branch of the executive government of a country, which watches over the preservation of public order. 2. Politeness, good-breeding. 3. Cleanliness, neatness
Policíaco, ca [po-le-thee'-ah-co, cah], *a.* Police, relating to the police. *Novela policíaca*, Detective novel, mystery, story. *Vigilancia policíaca*, Police watch.
Policromo, ma [po-le-cro'-mo, mah], *a.* Polychrome, vari-colored.
Polietileno [po-le-ay-te-lay'-no], *m.* Polyethylene.
Polifónico, ca [po-le-fo'-ne-co, cah], *a.* Polyphonic.
Polífono, na [po-lee'-fo-no, nah], *a.* V. Polifónico.
Polígala [po-lee'-gah-lah], *f.* (Bot.) Milkwort. Polygala. *Polígala vulgar*, Common milkwort. Polygala vulgaris. *Polígala senega*, Rattlesnake root milkwort. Polygala senega.
Poligamia [po-le-gah'-me-ah], *f.* 1. Polygamy. 2. (Bot.) Polygamia, the name of a class in the Linnæan system.
Polígamo, ma [po-lee'-gah-mo, mah], *m. & f.* 1. Polygamist. 2. One who has had several wives or husbands successively.
Poligarquía, *f.* *V.* Poliarquía.
Poliglota [po-le-glo'-tah], *f.* A polyglot, or a Bible in many languages.
Poligloto, ta [po-le-glo'-to, tah], *a.* Polyglot, written in various languages. —*m. & f.* One who knows many languages.
Polígono [po-lee'-go-no], *m.* 1. Polygon, a multilateral figure. 2. (Bot.) Poly, a small evergreen plant, a species of germander. Tenerium polium. 3. Face of a fortification for instructing pupils how to attack a place. 4. Practical school of artillery.
Polígono, na [po-lee'-go-no, nah], *a.* Polygonal, multangular.
Poligrafía [po-le-grah-fee'-ah], *f.* Polygraphy, the art of writing in ciphers.
Polihedro [po-le-ay'-dro], *m.* (Geom.) Polyhedron.
Polilla [po-leel'-lyah], *f.* 1. Moth, clothes-moth. 2. Consumer, waster. *Comerse de polilla*, (Coll.) To be insensibly wasting property; to be wasting away internally. *No tener polilla en la lengua*, To speak one's mind frankly and openly.
Polimatía [po-le-mah-tee'-ah], *f.* Polymathy, the knowledge of many arts and sciences.
Polimerización [po-le-may-re-tha-the-on'], *f.* Polymerization.
Polímero [po-lee'-may-ro], m. Polymer.
Polimorfismo [po-le-mor-fees'-mo], *m.* Polymorphism.
Polimorfo, fa [po-le-mor'-fo, fah], *a.* Polymorphous, of several forms.
Polín [po-leen'], *m.* (Naut.) Wooden roller, for moving great guns or any other heavy object.
Polinización [po-le-ne-thah-the-on'], *f.* Pollination.
Polinomio [po-le-no'-me-o], *m.* (Math.) Polynomial, an expression of more than two terms.
Poliomielitis [po-le-o-me-ay-lee'-tis], *f.* Infantile paralysis, poliomyelitis, polio.
Polipétalo, la [po-le-pay'-tah-lo, lah], *a.* Polypetalous.
Poliorama [po-le-o-rah'-mah], *m.* Polyorama, an apparatus presenting a view of many objects.
Pólipo [po'-le-po], *m.* 1. Polypus, a genus of zoophytes. 2. Polypus, a fleshy or gelatinous tumour. 3. *V.* Pulpo.
Poliscopio [po-lis-co'-pe-o], *m.* (Opt.) Polyscope.
Polisílabo, ba [po-le-see'-lah-bo, bah], *a.* Polysyllabic, polysyllabical.
Polisílabo [po-le-see'-lah-bo], *m.* Polysyllable.
Polisón [po-le-sone'], *m.* Bustle, pad formerly worn beneath a woman's skirt.
Polispermático, ca [po-lis-per-mah'-te-co, cah], or **Polispermo, ma**, *a.* (Bot.) Polyspermous, many-seeded.
Politécnico, ca [po-le-tek'-ne-co, cah], *a.* Polytechnic, embracing many arts.
Politeísmo [po-le-tay-ees'-mo], *m.* Polytheism.
Politeísta [po-le-tay-ees'-tah], *com. & a.* Polytheist.
Política [po-lee'-te-cah], *f.* 1. Policy, politics; the art or science of government. 2. Politeness, civility.
Políticamente, *adv.* Politically, civilly.
Politicastro [po-le-te-cahs'-tro], *m.* Politicaster: used in contempt.
Político, ca [po-lee'-te-co, cah], *a.* 1. Political, politic. 2. Polite, courteous.
Político [po-lee'-te-co], *m.* Politician.
Politiquear [po-le-te-kay-ar'], *vn.* To affect the politician.
Póliza [po'-le-thah], *f.* 1. Check, cheque, draft, an order for the payment of money. 2. *Póliza de seguro*, Policy of insurance. 3. A permit of the custom-house. 4. Entrance-ticket for some ceremony.
Polizón [po-le-thone'], *m.* 1. Bum. 2. Stowaway.
Polo [po'-lo], *m.* 1. Pole, the extremity of the axis of the earth. 2. Pole of the magnetic needle. 3. Support, foundation. 4. Personal service of forty days in the year by the natives of the Philippine Islands. 5. Popular song of Andalusia. *Polo gnomónico* or *polo del reloj solar*, A gnomonic style, or the cock of a solar dial.
Polo, *m.* Polo, polo game.
Polonés, sa [po-lo-nays', sah], *a.* Polish. *V.* Polaco.
Polonesa [po-lo-nay'-sah], *f.* 1. Polonaise. *V.* Polaca. 2. A fur-trimmed jacket, girded at the waist.
Poltrón, na [pol-trone', nah], *a.* 1. Idle, lazy, lubberly. 2. Commodious, easy. *Silla poltrona*, Elbow-chair.
Poltrón [pol-trone'], *m.* (Coll.) Poltroon.
Poltronería [pol-tro-nay-ree'-ah], *f.* Idleness, laziness, indolence, sluggishness.
Poltronizarse [pol-tro-ne-thar'-say], *vr.* To become lazy.
Polución [po-loo-the-on'], *f.* 1. Pollution, stain; bodily deformity. 2. A voluntary or involuntary emission of semen.
Poluto, ta [po-loo'-to, tah], *a.* Polluted, contaminated, defiled; unclean, filthy.
Polvareda [pol-vah-ray'-dah], *f.* 1. Cloud of dust. 2. Altercation, dispute debate.
Polvera [pol-vay'-rah], *f.* Compact, vanity case.
Polvificar [pol-ve-fe-car'], *va.* (Coll.) To pulverize, to reduce to powder or dust.
Polvillo, ito [pol-veel'-lyo], *m. dim.* Fine dust. *Gente de polvillo*, (Coll.) Day-labourers.
Polvo [pol'-vo], *m.* 1. Dust, earth reduced to dust. 2. Powder, dust, the state of solid bodies comminuted. 3. Powder for the hair: in the two last senses it is commonly used in the plural. 4. A pinch; so much as can be taken between the ends of the fingers. *Polvo de batata* or *batata en polvo*, A confectioned potato. *Polvos de cartas*, Sand for writings. *Polvos de juanes*, Red precipitate, red nitrate of mercury. *Polvos encarnados*, Spanish brown. *Polvos para dientes*, Tooth-powder. *Polvos de la madre Celestina*, (Coll.) Secret and miraculous mode in which any thing is done. *Sacudir el polvo*, To beat out the dust with a stick: to whip severely. *El polvo de la oveja alcohol es para el lobo*, Effort and risk are held lightly when the desired end is gained (literally, the sheep's dust

is a cosmetic for the wolf). *Limpio de polvo y paja*, (1) Without toil or hardship. (2) Free from all charges. *Matar el polvo*, To lay, to settle the dust.

Polvo de hornear [pol'-vo day or-nay-ar'], *m.* Baking powder.

Polvo de talco [pol'-vo day tahl-co], *m.* Talcum powder.

Pólvora [pol'-vo-rah], *f.* 1. Powder, gunpowder. 2. Artificial fire-works. 3. Provocation, cause of anger. 4. Vivacity, liveliness, briskness. 5. Powder, dust. *Es una pólvora*, He is as hot as pepper. *Mojar la pólvora*, To appease, to allay the rage of an angry person. *Gastar la pólvora en salvas*, To work to no purpose. *Ser vivo como la pólvora*, To be as quick as lightning.

Polvorear [pol-vo-ray-ar'], *va.* To powder, to sprinkle as with dust.

Polvoriento, ta [pol-vo-re-en'-to, tah], *a.* Dusty, full of dust; covered with dust.

Polvorín [pol-vo-reen'], *m.* 1. Powder reduced to the finest dust. 2. Powder-flask, priming-horn. 3. Powder-magazine.

Polvorista [pol-vo-rees'-tah], *m.* 1. Manufacturer of gunpowder. 2 Maker of fire-works.

Polvorizable [pol-vo-re-thah'-blay], *a.* Pulverizable.

Polvorización [pol-vo-re-thah-the-on'], *f.* Pulverization.

Polvorizar [pol-vo-re-thar'], *va.* 1. To pulverize. 2. *V.* POLVOREAR.

Polvoroso, sa [pol-vo ro'-so, sah], *a.* Dusty, covered with dust.

Polla [pol'-lyah], *f.* 1. Pullet, young hen, chicken. 2. (Coll.) A comely young lass. 3. Money staked in games at cards by all the players; pool.

Pollada [pol-lyah'-dah], *f.* Flock of young fowls; hatch, covey.

Pollagallina [pol-lyah-gal-lyee'-nah], *f.* Hen-chicken. *Mujer pollagallina que va a Villavieja*, (Coll.) Woman affecting youth, yet thin and old-maidish.

Pollastro, ra [pol-lyahs'-tro, trah], *m.* & *f.* A large chicken.

Pollastro, Pollastrón [pol-lyahs'-tro], *m.* 1. (Coll.) A cunning fellow; a knowing person. 2. A fine stout lad.

Pollazón [pol-lyah-thone'], *m.* Hatching and rearing fowls; hatch.

Pollera [pol-lyay'-rah], *f.* 1. A narrow-mouthed basket or net, in which pullets are kept; a hen-coop. 2. A go-cart, in which children learn to walk. 3. A short, hooped petticoat.

Pollería [pol-lyay-ree'-ah], *f.* Shop or market where poultry is sold.

Pollero [pol-lyay'-ro], *m.* 1. One who keeps or rears fowls. 2. Place or yard where fowls are kept. 3. One who keeps or feeds fowls for sale; a poulterer.

Pollico, ica, illo, illa, ito, ita [pol-lyee'-co], *n.* A small chicken.

Pollina [pol-lyee'-nah], *f.* Young she-ass.

Pollino [pol-lyee -no], *m.* 1. Properly, a young, untamed ass, but now applied to any ass or jument. 2. (Met.) Ass, a stupid fellow.

Pollito, ta [pol-lyee'-to, tah], *m.* & *f.* Chickens: applied to boys and girls of tender age.

Pollo [pol' lyo], *m.* 1. Chicken just hatched, nestling. 2. Young bee. 3. (Coll.) Artful, clever man. 4. A bird which has not yet changed its feathers. *Pollo con espolones*, (Coll.) Man growing oldish.

Polluelo, la [pol-lyoo-ay'-lo, lah], *m.* & *f. dim.* A small chicken

Poma [po' mah], *f.* 1. Apple. *V.* MANZANA. 2. Perfume-box, a bottle containing perfumes. 3. Metallic vessel with different perfumes, having small apertures to admit their escape when set on a fire to perfume rooms.

Pomada [po-mah'-dah], *f.* Pomatum, pomade. *Pomada para los labios*, Lip-salve.

Pomar [po-mar'], *m.* Orchard, a garden of fruit-trees, particularly of apple-trees.

Pómez [po'-meth], *f.* Pumice-stone.

Pomífero, ra [po-mee'-fay-ro, rah], *a.* (Poet.) Pomiferous, having apples.

Pomo [po'-mo], *m.* 1. Fruit in general, but in particular the fruit of the apple-tree. 2. Glass ball in the shape of an apple, used to hold perfumes. 3. Pommel of a sword. 4. (Prov.) Nosegay, a bunch of flowers. 5. A glass bottle. *Pomo del arzón de la silla*, Pommel of a saddle.

Pomología [po-mo-lo-hee'-ah], *f.* Pomology, science and practice of fruitgrowing.

Pompa pom'-pah], *f.* 1. Pomp, ostentation in feasts or funerals, pageantry. 2. Pomp, splendour, parade, grandeur. 3. Pomp, a procession of splendour and ostentation. 4. Bubble. 5. Fold in clothes raised by the wind. 6. The expanded tail of a turkey or peacock. 7. (Naut.) Pump. *V.* BOMBA.

Pompas fúnebres [pom'-pahs foo'-nay-brays], *f. pl.* Funeral, burial, funeral services.

Pompearse, Pomponearse [pom pay-ar'-say], *vr.* To appear with pomp and ostentation.

Pompeyano, na [pom-pay-yah'-no, nah], *a.* Pompeian, of Pompeii.

Pomposamente, *adv.* Pompously, magnificently, loftily, flourishingly.

Pomposo, sa [pom-po'-so, sah], *a.* Pompous, ostentatious, magnificent, splendid, majestic; inflated, swelled.

Pómulo [po'-moo-lo], *m.* Prominence of the cheek-bone.

Ponchada [pon-chah -dah], *f.* The quantity of punch made at one time.

Ponche [pon'-chay], *m.* Punch, a liquor.

Ponchera [pon-chay'-rah], *f.* Punch-bowl.

Poncho [pon'-cho], *m.* Poncho, man's jacket.

Poncho, cha [pon'-cho, chah], *a.* Lazy, indolent, heedless.

Ponchón, na [pon-chone', nah], *a.* Extremely careless, excessively lazy.

Ponderable [pon-day-rah'-blay], *a.* 1. Ponderable, capable of being weighed; measurable by scales. 2. Wonderful, important.

Ponderación [pon-day-rah-the-on'], *f.* 1. Weighing mentally, pondering or considering. 2. Exaggeration, heightening.

Ponderado, da [pon-day-rah'-do, dah], *a.* & *pp.* of PONDERAR. 1. Presumptuous, arrogant, insolent. 2. Exaggerated.

Ponderador, ra [pon-day-rah-dor', rah], *m.* & *f.* 1. Ponderer; he who exaggerates. 2. One who weighs or examines.

Ponderal [pon-day-rahl'], *a.* Ponderal, relating to weight.

Ponderar [pon-day-rar'], *va.* 1. To weigh. 2. To ponder, to consider, to attend. 3. To exaggerate, to heighten; to cry up.

Ponderativo, va [pon-day-rah-tee'-vo, vah], *a.* Exaggerating, hyperbolical.

Ponderosamente, *adv.* Attentively, carefully; with great attention.

Ponderosidad [pon-day-ro-se-dahd'], *f.* Ponderousness, ponderosity, weightiness. *V.* PESADEZ.

Ponderoso, sa [pon-day-ro'-so, sah], *a.* 1. Heavy, ponderous, weighty. 2. Grave, circumspect, cautious.

Ponedero, ra [po-nay-day'-ro, rah], *a.* 1. Laying eggs. 2. Capable of being laid or placed.

Ponedero [po-nay-day'-ro], *m.* 1. Nest, hen's nest. 2. Nest-egg.

Ponedor, ra [po-nay-dor', rah], *m.* & *f.* 1. One who puts, sets, or places. 2. Bettor, wagerer; outbidder. 3. In paper-mills, the maker who delivers the sheet to the coucher.—*a.* Applied to horses trained to rear on their hind legs, and to fowls laying eggs.

Ponencia [po-nen'-the-ah], *f.* Charge, post, or office of a chairman of a committee, or of a final judge or arbiter; and the exercise of such office.

Ponente [po-nen'-tay], *a.* Who has the casting vote; arbitrator, final judge: said of a judge or the chairman of a committee.

Ponentino, na, Ponentisco, ca [po-nen-tee'-no, nah], *a.* Occidental, western, belonging to the west.

Poner [po-nerr'], *va.* 1. To put, to place, to set, to lay a thing in a place. 2. To establish and determine distances. 3. To dispose, to arrange. 4. To suppose, to believe. 5. To impose, to enjoin. 6. To oblige, to compel. 7. To wager, to bet, to stake. 8. To appoint, to invest with office. 9. To bring an example or comparison in confirmation. 10. To leave, to permit without interposition. *Yo lo pongo en Vd.*, I leave it to you. 11. To write, to set down what another dictates. 12. To lay eggs; to bring forth. 13. To employ; to apply one to some employment or office. *Poner toda su fuerza*, To act with all one's might. 14. To labour for an end. 15. To add, to join. 16. To contribute, to bear a part. 17. To enforce; to adduce; to concert; to agree. 18. To treat one badly.—*vr.* 1. To apply one's self to, to set about. 2. To object, to oppose. 3. To undergo a change; to become. *Ponerse pálido*, To grow pale. 4. To set: applied to the luminous heavenly bodies. 5. To arrive in a short time at a determined place. 6. To dress, to deck out, or adorn one's self. 7. Joined with *de, por, cual, como*, to treat as the words express; sometimes in the true sense, sometimes ironically. E. g. *Poner por escrito*, To put in writing. *Ponerse como un trompo*, To eat and drink to satiety. *Al poner del sol*, At sunsetting. *Poner al sol*, To expose to the sun, to sun. *Poner a asar*, To spit, to roast. *Poner colorado*, To flush, to put one to the blush. *Eso no quita ni pone*, That neither adds nor diminishes. *Poner cabeza* or *puño a una cosa*, To head. *Poner en duda*, To question, to doubt. *Poner miedo a uno*, To make one afraid. *Poner pies en polvorosa*, To take to one's heels. *Poner pies en pared*, To maintain one's opinion with obstinacy. *Poner nombre*, To rate or appraise goods. *Poner las velas en facha*, (Naut.) To back the sails. *Poner por tierra un edificio*, To take down a building. *Ponerse bien*, To get on in the world; to obtain full information of an affair. *Ponerse en la calle*, To appear in a splendid manner, to make a showy appearance. *Ponerse en gracia*, To expiate a crime by confession, to put one's self in a state of grace. *Ponerse colorado*, To flush, to blush. *¿ Quién se pone á ello ?* Who dares to do it? *Ponerse en jarras*, To set one's arms akimbo. *Ponerse flaco*, To fall away. *Ponerse bien con Dios*, To make one's peace with God. *Ponerse a razones*, To enter into a dispute.

Ponerse de puntillas, To persist obstinately in one's opinion. *Ponérsele a uno,* To take a whim, a fancy. *Ponerse en ocasión,* To expose one's self to danger. *Ponerse en chapines,* To raise one's self above one's condition. *Ponerse los zapatos, el sombrero,* To put on one's shoes, one's hat. *Ponerse moreno.* To become sunburned. *Póngase Vd. en la razón,* Be moderate in your demands. *Ponerse a gesto,* To endeavour to please. *Ponerse en pies en la dificultad,* To seize upon the point where the difficulty lies. *Ponerse a escribir,* To set about, or devote one's self, to writing. *Poner en relieve.* To carve in relief; to describe graphically. *Poner gesto,* To show anger in one's face. *Poner en seco,* To change one's clothes. *Poner en eso,* To put in practice. *Nada se pone por delante,* Nothing stops him. *Poner en pico,* To speak of what should be kept secret. *Poner las peras a cuatro, a ocho,* To compel a person against his will; to teach a lesson. *Poner en un palo,* To inflict public punishment. *Poner como un Cristo a alguno,* To flog a person severely. *Poner sal a alguno en la mollera,* To punish a person in order to bring him to his senses. *Poner de vuelta y media,* To humiliate a person, by word or action. *Poner a uno como nuevo,* To pick flaws at, to berate soundly. *Poner a uno como un guante,* To render one as pliable as a glove; to insult a person. *Poner en chapines a una hija,* To marry off a daughter. *Poner delante,* To remind, to suggest. *Poner coto,* To stop an abuse; to put a bound. *Poner una pica en Flandes,* To do something wonderful. *V.* sub PICA. *Puesto en el borrico,* Determined to accomplish something. *Ser el mismo que el sol puesto,* To be worth nothing. Other idiomatic expressions containing the verb *poner* will be found under the appropriate nouns.

(*Yo pongo, yo puse, pusiera; ponga. V.* PONER.)

Pongo [pon'-go], *m.* (Peru, Ec.) A narrow and dangerous pass of a river. (Peru and Bol.) An Indian servant. (Zool.) A kind of anthropomorphous ape.

Poniente [po-ne-en'-tay], *m.* 1. The west. 2. (Naut.) West wind.

Ponleví [pon-lay-vee'], *m.* High wooden heel, formerly worn by women.

Pontazgo, Pontaje [pon-tath'-go, pon-tah'-hay], *m.* Bridge-toll, pontage.

Pontear [pon-tay-ar'], *va.* To erect bridges.

Pontezuelo, la [pon-tay-thoo-ay'-lo, lah], *m. & f. dim.* Small bridge.

Pontificado [pon-te-fe-cah'-do], *m.* Pontificate, the government of the Pope; papacy, popedom.

Pontifical [pon-te-fe-cahl'], *a.* Pontifical, papal; belonging to the Pope, or to an archbishop or bishop.

Pontifical [pon-te-fe-cahl'], *m.* 1. A pontifical robe worn by bishops when they officiate at the mass. 2. Pontifical, a book containing the rites and ceremonies of the Roman Catholic church. 3. Parochial tithes.

Pontificalmente, *adv.* Pontifically.

Pontificar [pon-te-fe-car'], *vn.* 1. To govern as high pontiff. 2. To celebrate the solemn mass pontifically.

Pontífice [pon-tee'-fe-thay], *m.* 1. Pope, pontiff. 2. Archbishop or bishop of a diocese.

Pontificio, cia [pon-te-fee'-the-o, ah], *a.* Pontificial.

Pontil [pon-teel'], *m.* 1. Pontil or ponty, an iron rod for handling hot bottles in glass-making. 2. Glass over which emery is spread.

Pontín [pon-teen'], *m.* A vessel for coasting trade in the Philippines.

Ponto [pon'-to], *m.* 1. (Naut.) Starting-pole. 2. (Poet.) The sea.

Pontón [pon-tone'], *m.* 1. Ponton or pontoon, a floating bridge to cross a river. 2. Hulk, an old ship serving as store-ship, hospital, or prison-ship. 3. (Naut.) Mud-scow, a kind of flat-bottomed boat, furnished with pulleys, tackles, etc., to clean harbours. 4. Timber above nineteen feet long. 5. A log bridge.

Ponzoña [pon-tho'-nyah], *f.* 1. Poison, venom, toxine. 2. Any thing infectious or malignant.

Ponzoñar [pon-tho-nyar'], *va.* (Obs.) To poison. *V.* EMPONZOÑAR.

Ponzoñosamente, *adv.* Poisonously.

Ponzoñoso, sa [pon-tho-nyo'-so, sah], *a.* 1. Poisonous, venomous, toxic. 2. Prejudicial to sound morals.

Popa [po'-pah], *f.* (Naut.) Poop, stern. *Navío de popa llana,* (Naut.) A square-sterned vessel. *Bajel de popa de cucharro,* (Naut.) A lute-sterned vessel. *Pasar por la popa,* (Naut.) To pass under a ship's stern. *Quedarse por la popa,* (Naut.) To drop astern. *Velas de popa,* (Naut.) Aftersails. *De popa a proa,* (Naut.) From stem to stern. *A popa, en popa, de popa,* (Naut.) Aft, abaft. *Viento en popa,* (Naut.) Before the wind. (Met.) Prosperity.

Popamiento [po-pah-me-en'-to], *m.* Act of despising or cajoling.

Popar [po-par'], *vn.* 1. To depreciate, to contemn. 2. To cajole, to flatter, to fawn; to caress, to soothe, to wheedle.

Popero [po-pay'-ro], *m.* Helmsman, steersman.

Popeses [po-pay'-ses], *m. pl.* (Naut.) Stays of the mizzen-mast; aftermost, sternmost.

Poplíteo, tea [po-plee'-tay-o, ah], *a.* Popliteal, belonging to the space behind the knees.

Popote [po-po'-tay], *m.* A kind of Indian straw, of which brooms are made.

Populacho [po-poo-lah'-cho], *m.* Populace, mob, rabble, crowd.

Populación [po-poo-lah-the-on'], *f.* Population. *V.* POBLACIÓN.

Popular [po-poo-lar'], *a.* 1. Popular, relating to the people. 2. Popular, pleasing to the people. 3. Popular, plebeian: in this sense it is used as a substantive. 4. Popular, vulgar, current.

Popularidad [po-poo-lah-re-dahd'], *f.* Popularity.

Popularizar [po-poo-lah-re-thar'], *va.* To popularize, to make popular.—*vr* To become popular.

Popularmente, *adv.* Popularly.

Populazo [po-poo-lah'-tho], *m.* Populace, mob, rabble.

Populeón [po-poo-lay-on'], *m.* White poplar ointment.

Populoso, sa [po-poo-lo'-so, sah], *a.* Populous, numerous, full of people.

Poquedad [po-kay-dahd'], *f.* 1. Parvity, paucity, littleness. 2. Cowardice, pusillanimity. 3. Trifle, thing of no value. *Poquedad de ánimo,* Imbecility. 4. Mite, very small portion of a thing.

Poquillo, lla [po-keel'-lyo, lyah], *a. dim.* 1. Small, little. 2. Trifling.

Poquillo, *adv. dim.* Very little time.

Poquísimo, ma [po-kee'-se-mo, mah], *a. sup.* Very little, excessively small.

Poquitico, ica, illo, illa, ito, ita [po-ke-tee'-co], *a. dim.* Almost nothing.

Poquito, ta [po-kee'-to, tah], *a.* 1. (Dim.) Very little. 2. Weak of body and mind, diminutive. *Poquita cosa,* A trifling thing. *A poquitos,* In minute portions. *De poquito,* Pusillanimous. *Poquito a poco,* Gently.

Por [por], *prep.* 1. For, on account of. **Por** refers to source, or to the reason or motive for an action. *Por miedo de las consecuencias,* For fear of consequences. (Note.—This preposition represents the Latin *per* and *pro*; hence the variety of its meanings.) 2. By, through: indicating in passive expressions the agent *by* whom an action is performed. *Esta carta fué escrita por el general para el rey,* This letter was written *by* the general *for* the king. 3. Indicates multiplication or unit of number or measure. *Seis por ocho.* Six (multiplied) by eight. *Por docenas,* By the dozen. *A diez por ciento,* Ten per cent. 4. For the sake of, in behalf of, in favour of. *Hablo por el señor A.,* I speak for Mr. A. *¡Una limosna por Dios!* An alms for God's sake! (*Cf.* PORDIOSERO.) 5. After the verbs, *to go, to send,* and the like, it shows the immediate object of the errand. *Ir por leña,* To go for firewood. *Por ahí, por ahí,* About that, a little more or less. *Por tanto* or *por ende,* For so much, for that. 6. Through; between; to. *¿Por qué calle vino Vd.?* Through what street did you come? 7. As, by, on account of. *Recibir por esposo,* To take as a husband. 8. By means of, indicating the future action of the verb. *Está por venir, por ver, por saber,* That is to come, to be seen, to be known. 9. Indicates exchange or off-set of a thing against another. *Quiere vender su casa por $8,000,* He wants to sell his house for $8,000. "*Ojo por ojo, y diente por diente,*" "An eye for an eye and a tooth for a tooth." 10. It is sometimes redundant, as, *Fernando está por alcalde,* Ferdinand is mayor. *Uno vale por muchos,* One is worth many. *La casa está por acabar,* The house is not yet finished. *Por ahora,* For the present. *Por San Juan,* About Saint John's or midsummer. *Por bien o por mal,* Well or ill. *Por ce o por be,* Some way or other. *Por encima,* Slightly, superficially; over, upon. *Por ende,* For which, for that reason. *Por acá o por allá,* Here or there. *Por más que* or *por mucho que,* However much; in vain. *Por si acaso,* If by chance. *Sin qué ni por qué* or *sin qué ni para qué,* Without rhyme or reason. *¡Sí por cierto!* Yes, indeed; yes, forsooth. *De por sí,* By itself. *Él se fué gritando por toda la casa,* He went crying through the house. *Por más que Vd. diga,* You may say what you will, it is in vain. *Por cuanto,* Whereas. *Por tanto,* Wherefore. *Por entre,* Through. *Por supuesto,* Of course.

Pora [po'-rah], *prep.* (Obs.) *V.* PARA.

Porca [por'-cah], *f.* A ridge of land between two furrows.

Porcal [por-cahl'], *a.* Applied to a kind of large plums.

Porcaso [por-cah'-so], *m.* The hog-tapir.

Porcelana [por-thay-lah'-nah], *f.* 1. Porcelain, chinaware. 2. Enamel, used by goldsmiths and jewellers. 3. Porcelain-colour, a mixture of white and blue. 4. Kind of wide china cup.

Porcentaje [por-then-tah'-hay], *m.* Percentage.

Porcino [por-thee'-no], *m.* 1. A young pig. *Pan porcino,* (Bot.) Sow-bread. *V.* ARTANITA. 2. Bruise, a swelling caused by a blow on the head.

Porcino, na [por-thee'-no, nah], *a.* Hoggish, porcine.
Porción [por-the-on'], *f.* 1. Part, portion. 2. Lot, parcel of goods. 3. Pittance, daily allowance of food. *Porción de círculo,* Among watchmakers, guard-cock or gardecaut. *Porción congrua,* Money paid for the subsistence of a priest.
Porcioncica, illa, ita, *f. dim.* A small portion.
Porcionero, ra [por-the-o-nay'-ro, rah], *a.* Apportioning; participant.
Porcionista [por-the-o-nees'-tah], *com.* 1. Holder of a share or portion. 2. Boarder in a college, or one who pays for his portion and assistance in a college.
Porcipelo [por-the-pay'-lo], *m.* (Coll.) Bristle.
Porco, *m.* (Prov.) *V.* Puerco.
Porcuno, na [por-coo'-no, nah], *a.* Hoggish.
Porchada [por-chah'-dah], *f.* Paper-holder (stretcher) in paper-factories.
Porche [por'-chay], *m.* Porch, portico.
Pordiosear [por-de-o-say-ar'], *va.* To beg, to ask charity.
Pordiosería [por-de-o-say-ree'-ah], *f.* Beggary, asking charity.
Pordiosero, ra [por-de-o-say'-ro, rah], *m.* & *f.* Beggar.
Porfía [por-fee'-ah], *f.* 1. An obstinate dispute or quarrel. 2. Opinionativeness, obstinacy, stubbornness; conceitedness. 3. Repetition; importunity. *A porfía,* In an obstinate manner.
Porfiadamente, *adv.* Obstinately, pertinaciously, contentiously.
Porfiado, da [por-fe-ah'-do, dah], *a.* Obstinate, stubborn, opinionated, conceited.—*pp.* of Porfiar.
Porfiador, ra [por-fe-ah-dor', rah], *m.* & *f.* Contender, wrangler, brawler, pleader.
Porfiar [por-fe-ar'], *va.* 1. To contend. 2. To wrangle. 3. To importune by repetition. 4. To persist in a pursuit.
Porfídico, ca [por-fee'-de-co, cah], *a.* Porphyritic, containing porphyry, or like it.
Pórfido, Pórfiro [por'-fe-do, por'-fe-ro], *m.* Porphyry, jasper.
Poridad, *f.* (Obs.) *V.* Secreto.
Porisma [po-rees'-mah], *f.* (Geom.) Porism.
Pormenor [por-may-nor'], *m.* Detail, minute account.
Pornografía [por-no-grah-fee'-ah], *f.* Pornography, obscenity.
Pornográfico, ca [por-no-grah'-fe-co, cah], *a.* Pornographic, obscene.
Poro [po'-ro], *m.* 1. Pore, as of the skin. 2. Pore, interstice.
Porongo [po-ron'-go], *m.* (Peru, Bol.) An earthenware jug or pitcher.
Pororoca [po-ro-ro'-cah], *f.* Brazilian name for the extraordinary collision of the waters of the river Amazons with the ocean at the great equinoctial tides.
Porosidad [po-ro-se-dahd'], *f.* 1. Porosity. 2. That which is exhaled through the pores.
Poroso, sa [po-ro'-so, sah], *a.* Porous.
Porque [por'-kay], *conj.* 1. Because, for the reason that, on this or that account. 2. Why, for which or what reason: relatively.
Por qué [por-kay'], *conj.* Why? for what reason? interrogatively.
Porqué [por-kay'], *m.* (Coll.) 1. Cause, reason, motive. 2. Allowance, pittance, pension.
Porquecilla, *f. dim.* A small sow.
Porquera [por-kay'-rah], *f.* Lair, the couch of a wild boar.
Porquería [por-kay-ree'-ah], *f.* 1. Nastiness, uncleanliness, filth. 2. Hoggishness, brutishness, rudeness. 3. Trifle, thing of little value. 4. A dirty, ungenteel action. 5. Nuisance, dirty trick. *Porquerías,* (Coll.) Small dishes made of the entrails of swine.
Porqueriza [por-kay-ree'-thah], *f.* Hogsty.
Porquerizo, Porquero [por-kay-ree'-tho], *m.* Swineherd.
Porquerón [por-kay-rone'], *m.* Catchpoll, bumbailiff.
Porqueta, *f.* *V.* Cucaracha.
Porquezuela [por-kay-thoo-ay'-lah], *f. dim.* 1. A small sow. 2. A slut or dirty woman.
Porquezuelo [por-kay-thoo-ay'-lo], *m. dim.* 1. A young pig. 2. A nasty, dirty man.
Porra [por'-rah], *f* 1. Stick with a large head or thick knob at the end; club. 2. The last player in certain games played by boys. 3. (Coll.) Vanity, boast, presumption. 4. (Coll.) A stupid, heavy, ignorant person. *Hacer porra,* To boggle, to stop without being able to proceed.
Porráceo, cea [por-rah'-thay-o, ah], *a.* Of a dark or leek-green colour.
Porrada [por-rah'-dah], *f.* 1. Blow with a club-headed stick. 2. (Coll.) Foolishness, nonsense.
Porrazo [por-rah'-tho], *m.* Blow with any instrument, or that occasioned by a fall.
Porrear [por-ray-ar'], *vn.* (Coll.) To persist importunely, to dwell long upon.
Porrería [por-ray-ree'-ah], *f.* (Coll.) Obstinacy, stupidity, folly, silliness, tediousness.
Porreta [por-ray'-tah], *f.* The green leaf of leeks, garlic, or onions. *En porreta,* (Coll.) Stark naked.
Porrilla [por-reel'-lyah], *f.* 1. A small hammer used by smiths. 2. (Dim.) A small club-headed stick. 3. (Vet.) Osseous tumour in horses' joints.
Porrillo (A) [por-reel'-lyo], *adv.* (Coll.) Copiously, abundantly.
Porrina [por-ree'-nah], *f.* State of crops when small and green.
Porrino [por-ree'-no], *m.* The tender plant of a leek.
Porrizo [por-ree'-tho], *m.* Bed or plot of leeks.
Porro, rra [por'-ro, rah], *a.* (Coll.) Dull, stupid, ignorant.
Porrón [por-rone'], *m.* 1. An earthen pitcher for water. 2. A kind of flask.
Porrón, na [por-rone', nah], *a.* Heavy, sluggish, slow.
Porrudo [por-roo'-do], *m.* (Prov.) Shepherd's crook.
Porta [por'-tah], *f.* 1. (Obs.) Door, gate. *V.* Puerta. 2. (Naut.) Gun-port, embrasure of a battery. *Portas del acastillaje,* (Naut.) Gun-ports of the quarter-deck and forecastle. *Portas de las miras de proa,* (Naut.) Head chase-ports. *Portas de guardatimón,* (Naut.) Stern-ports.
Porta, as a prefix (from *portar,* to carry), is compounded with many other words than those here given of mostly obvious meaning.
Portaaguja [por-tah-ah-goo'-hah], *f.* A surgical needle-holder.
Portaanimálculos [por-tah-ah-ne-mahl'-coo-los], *m.* Live box, animalcule cage. (Microscopy.)
Portaaviones [por-tah-ah-ve-o'-ness], *m.* Aircraft carrier.
Portabandera [por-tah-ban-day'-rah], *f.* Pocket in the girdle which supports the staff of the colours.
Portacaja [por-tah-cah'-hah], *f.* The carrier of a silk loom.
Portacarabina [por-tah-ca-rah-bee'-nah], *f.* Leather bag in which the muzzle of a horseman's carabine rests.
Portacartas [por-tah-car'-tas], *m.* Mail-bag for letters.
Portada [por-tah'-dah], *f.* 1. Portal, porch. 2. Frontispiece, the principal front of a building; façade. 3. Title-page of a book. 4. Division of a certain number of threads to form the warp.
Portadera [por-tah-day'-rah], *f.* A chest in which provisions are carried on a horse or mule: commonly used in the plural.
Portador, ra [por-tah-dor', rah], *m.* & *f.* 1. Bearer, carrier, porter. 2. Tray or board on which bread or meat is carried.
Portaestandarte [por-tah-es-tan-dar'-tay], *m.* (Mil.) Standard-bearer cornet.
Portafolio [por-tah-fo'-le-o], *m.* Briefcase.
Portafusil [por-tah-foo-seel'], *m.* (Mil.) Sling of a musket.
Portaguión [por-tah-gee-on'], *m* Standard-bearer of cavalry.
Portaje [por-tah'-hay], *m.* 1. *V.* Portazgo. 2. (Obs.) *V.* Puerto.
Portal [por-tahl'], *m.* 1. Porch, entry entrance. 2. Portico, piazza. 3. (Prov.) Gate of a town.
Portalazo [por-tah-lah'-tho], *m. aug.* A large door or porch.
Portalejo [por-tah-lay'-ho], *m. dim.* Little porch or portico.
Portaleña [por-tah-lay'-nyah], *f.* 1. Embrasure, for cannon. *V.* Cañonera. 2. Planks of which doors are made.
Portalero [por-tah-lay'-ro], *m.* An officer who has the charge of preventing smuggling, receiving the duties, etc., at the gates of a town.
Portalico, illo, ito [por-tah-lee'-co], *m dim.* A small vestibule or porch.
Portalón [por-tah-lone'], *m.* (Naut.) Gangway.
Portamanteo [por-tah-man-tay'-o], *m.* Portmanteau, cloak-bag.
Portamonedas [por-tah-mo-nay'-das], *m.* A small purse, porte-monnaie.
Portanario' [por-tah-nah'-re-o], *m.* (Anat.) Pylorus.
Portante [por-tahn'-tay], *m.* Quick pace of a horse. *Tomar el portante,* (Coll.) To go away.
Portantillo [por-tan-teel'-lyo], *m. dim.* A gentle amble, an easy pace.
Portanuevas [por-tah-noo-ay'-vas], *com* Newsmonger.
Portanveces [por-tan-vay'-thes], *m.* (Prov.) Coadjutor, assistant.
Portañola [por-tah-nyo'-lah], *f.* (Naut.) Port-hole. *Portañolas de la luz de los camarotes,* (Naut.) Light-ports. *Portañolas de los remos,* (Naut.) Row-ports.
Portañuela [por-tah-nyoo-ay'-lah], *f.* Lining of the fall of breeches.
Portaobjetos [por-tah-ob-hay'-tos], *m.* Object-holder of a microscope, stage; glass slip.
Portaollas [por-tah-ol'-lyas], *m.* Pot-holder.
Portapaz [por-tah-path'], *com.* The plate on which the pax or image is presented to be kissed by the pious at mass.
Portaparaguas [por-tah-pah-rah'-goo-as], *m.* Umbrella-stand.
Portaplacas, Portaplanchas [por-tah-plahn'-chas], *m.* Dark slide, photographic plate-holder.
Portar [por-tar'], *va.* To carry, to bring.—*vr.* To behave, to comport, to act. *Un bajel que se porta bien,* (Naut.) A fine sailer, a good sea-boat.
Porta-rollo [por-tah-rohl'-lyo], *m.* A photographic roll-holder.
Portaronzal [por-tah-ron-thahl'], *m.* A strap fixed at the left holster to which the halter is fastened.

Portátil [por-tah'-teel], *a.* Portable, easily carried.

Portaventanero [por-tah-ven-tah-nay'-ro], *m.* Carpenter who makes windows and doors.

Portaviento [por-tah-ve-en'-to], *m.* Air-blast of a furnace.

Portavoz [por-tah-voth'], *m.* 1. Loudspeaker, megaphone. 2. Spokesman, mouthpiece.

Portax, *m.* (Zool.) The nylghau.

Portazgo [por-tath'-go], *m.* Toll, turnpike-duty.

Portazguero [por-tath-gay'-ro], *m.* Toll-gatherer, collector.

Portazo [por-tah'-tho], *m.* 1. A loud slam with a door. 2. Act of slamming a door in one's face.

Porte [por'-tay], *m.* 1. Cost of carriage; freight, portage, porterage; postage. 2. Deportment, demeanour, conduct. 3. Nobility: illustrious descent. 4. Size or capacity of a thing. 5. (Naut.) Burden or tonnage of a ship. *Porte franco,* Frank, free of postage. *Navío de mil toneladas de porte,* A ship of one thousand tons burden.

Porteador, ra [por-tay-ah-dor', rah], *a.* Carrying, transporting.

Portear [por-tay-ar'], *va.* To carry or convey for a price.—*vr.* To pass from one place to another.

Portento [por-ten'-to], *m.* Prodigy, wonder; portent.

Portentosamente, *adv.* Prodigiously.

Portentoso, sa [por-ten-to'-so, sah], *a.* Prodigious, marvellous, portentous.

Porteo [por-tay'-o], *m.* Transportation, portage. *Gastos de porteo,* Transportation or portage costs.

Portería [por-tay-ree'-ah], *f.* 1. The principal door of a convent or other large building; a porter's lodge. 2. Employment or office of a porter. 3. (Naut.) All the ports in a ship.

Portero, ra [por-tay'-ro, rah], *m.* & *f.* Porter, gate-keeper. *Portero de cadena,* Person appointed to prevent any nuisance near a palace. *Portero de vara,* Petty constable. *Portero de cámara,* Gentleman usher. *Portero de estrados,* Summoner.

Portezuela [por-tay-thoo-ay'-lah], *f.* 1. (Dim.) A little door. 2. Flap, pocket-flap. 3. (Mex.) A pass between hills.

Pórtico [por'-te-co], *m.* Portico, piazza; porch; hall; lobby.

Portillo [por-teel'-lyo], *m.* 1. Aperture in a wall. 2. Opening, passage, gap, breach. 3. Wicket, gate; a small door in another larger. 4. Means to an end. 5. Cavity in any thing broken. 6. Small gate of a town, through which nothing is allowed to pass that is liable to pay duty.

Portón [por-tone'], *m.* The inner or second door of a house.

Portorriqueño, ña [por-tor-re-kay'-nyo, nya], *a.* Puerto Rican. V. PUERTORRIQUEÑO.

Portuario, ria [por-too-ah'-re-o, ah], *a.* Relative to a seaport. *Ciudad portuaria,* Seaport city.

Portugués [por-too-ghes'], *m.* The Portuguese language.

Portugués, sa [por-too-ghes', sah], *a.* Portuguese. *A la Portuguesa,* In the Portuguese fashion.

Portuláceas [por-too-lah'-thay-as], *a.* & *f. pl.* Of the purslane or portulaca family; portulacas.

Porvenir [por-vay-neer'], *m.* Future, time to come.

Porvida [por-vee'-dah], *f.* By the living God, or by the saints: an oath much in use in Spain.

Pos (En), *adv.* After, behind; in pursuit of.

Posa [po'-sah], *f.* 1. Passing bell; the ringing of bells for persons deceased. 2. Stops made by the clergy who conduct a funeral, to sing a response. 3. *pl.* (Coll.) Breech, seat; buttocks.

Posada [po-sah'-dah], *f.* 1. Home, dwelling-house. 2. Lodging or lodging-house. *Posada con asistencia,* Board and lodging, inn, tavern, hotel. 3. Pocket-case, containing a knife, spoon, and fork. *¡ Mas acá hay posada !* How he swells or exaggerates. *Posadas,* Apartments for ladies-in-waiting in the royal palace.

Posadera [po-sah-day'-rah], *f.* Hostess, landlady.

Posaderas [po-sah-day'-ras], *f. pl.* Buttocks. *V.* ASENTADERAS.

Posadería [po-sah-day-ree'-ah], *f.* Inn, tavern, lodging-house.

Posadero [po-sah-day'-ro], *m.* 1. Innkeeper, the keeper of a lodging or boarding-house, or tavern. 2. Seat made of flags or bass-ropes. 3. Breech, seat, buttocks.

Posado, da [po-sah'-do, dah], *a.* & *pp.* of POSAR. 1. Lodged, rested, lined, reclined. 2. (Obs.) Defunct.

Posante [po-sahn'-tay], *pa.* Reposing: used at sea for smooth sailing.

Posar [po-sar'], *vn.* 1. To lodge, to board. 2. To sit down, to repose, to rest. 3. To perch, to light or sit upon.—*va.* To lay down a burden.

Posca [pos'-cah], *f.* Mixture of vinegar and water, formerly given by way of refreshment.

Posdata [pos-dah'-tah], *f.* Postscript.

Pose [po'-say], *m.* A kind of hook for fishing upon sandbanks.

Poseedor, ra [po-say-ay-dor', rah], *m.* & *f.* Possessor, holder, owner.

Poseer [po-say-err'], *va.* 1. To hold, to possess, to have, to own. 2. To be master of a language or other thing.

Poseído, da [po-say-ee'-do, dah], *a.* & *pp.* of POSEER. 1. Possessed. 2. Applied to one who executes desperate actions.

Poseido [po-say-ee'-do], *m.* (Prov.) Arable land belonging to a private person, as distinguished from commons.

Posesión [po-say-se-on'], *f.* 1. Possession, the act of possessing; dominion. 2. Possession, the thing possessed. 3. Possession by evil spirits. 4. (Met.) Reputation, good or bad. *Dar posesión,* To invest or give possession.—*pl.* Lands, real estates.

Posesional [po-say-se-o-nahl'], *a.* Including or relating to possession.

Posesionarse [po-say-se-o-nar'-say], *vr.* To take possession of.

Posesionero [po-say-se-o-nay'-ro], *m.* Cattle-keeper who has acquired possession of pasturage.

Posesivo, va [po-say-see'-vo, vah], *a.* (Gram.) Possessive, denoting possession.

Poseso, sa [po-say'-so, sah], *a.* & *pp. irr.* of POSEER. Possessed; possessed by evil spirits. *Pagar el poseso,* To give an entertainment on entering upon a public office.

Posesor, ra [po-say-sor', rah], *m.* & *f.* *V.* POSEEDOR.

Posesorio, ria [po-say-so'-re-o, ah], *a.* Possessory.

Poseyente [po-say-yen'-tay], *pa.* Possessing, possessive.

Posfecha [pos-fay'-chah], *f.* Post-date.

Posfechar [pos-fay-char'], *va.* To post-date.

Posibilidad [po-se-be-le-dahd'], *f.* 1. Possibility, capability to exist. 2. Possibility, the state of being possible; feasibility; likelihood. 3. Wealth, riches.

Posibilitar [po-se-be-le-tar'], *va.* To render possible, to facilitate.

Posible [po-see'-blay], *a.* Possible. *Posibles,* Wealth, income, capital, means. *Mis posibles no alcanzan a eso,* My means do not extend so far. *Serviré a Vd. con mis posibles,* I will serve you with all my might. *¿ Es posible ?* Is it possible ?

Posiblemente, *adv.* Possibly.

Posición [po-se-the-on'], *f.* 1. Position the art of placing. 2. Position, posture situation. 3. Question and answer of an interrogatory. 4. Position, rule in arithmetic.

Positivamente, *adv.* Positively, absolutely, certainly, by all means.

Positividad [po-se-te-ve-dahd'], *f.* State of positive electricity.

Positivismo [po-se-te-vees'-mo], *m.* 1. Positiveness, holding to what is positive. 2. Positivism, a system of philosophy receiving only proved facts, rejecting a priori notions. 3. Agnosticism, chiefly in England. 4. Utilitarianism.

Positivo, va [po-se-tee'-vo, vah], *a.* 1. Positive, sure, certain, indubitable, true. 2. Positive: applied to laws settled by arbitrary appointment. 3. Positive, absolute, real. 4. (Gram.) Positive, a degree of comparison. *De positivo,* Certainly, without doubt.

Pósito [po'-se-to], *m.* A public granary. *Pósito pío,* Granary which lends grain to widows or poor labourers without charging interest.

Positón, Positrón [po-se-tone', po-se-trone'], *m.* Positron.

Positura [po-se-too'-rah], *f.* 1. Posture, state, disposition. 2. *V.* POSTURA.

Posma [pos'-mah], *f.* (Coll.) Sluggishness, sloth, dulness.—*com.* A dull, sluggish, dronish person. Also *a.*

Poso [po'-so], *m.* 1. Sediment, dregs, lees, feculence. 2. Rest, repose.

Posparto, *m.* *V.* POSTPARTO.

Pospelo (A) [pos-pay'-lo], *adv.* Against the grain; reluctantly.

Pospierna [pos-pe-err'-nah], *f.* The thigh of an animal.

Posponer [pos-po-nerr'], *va.* 1. To place one thing after another. 2. To postpone, to put off, to delay. 3. To postpone, to set in value below something else.

Pospuesto, ta [pos-poo-es'-to, tah], *pp. irr.* of POSPONER.

Posta [pos'-tah], *f.* 1. Post-horses. 2. Post-house, post-office; post stage, where post-horses are stationed. 3. Post, distance from one relay or post-house to another. 4. Chop of meat or fish. 5. Slug of lead, mould-shot. 6. Night-sentry. 7. Stake in cards. —*m.* Person who travels post. *Correr la posta,* or *ir en posta,* To post or travel post. *A posta,* Designedly, on purpose. *Por la posta,* With all speed, in haste.

Postal [pos-tahl'], *a.* Postal. *Giro postal,* Money order. *Paquete postal,* Parcel post. *Tarjeta postal,* Postal card.—*f.* Postcard.

Postdata, *f.* *V.* POSDATA

Poste [pos'-tay], *m.* 1. Post, pillar. 2. Kind of punishment inflicted in colleges upon freshmen, by holding them some hours by the right foot. *Oler el poste,* To smell a rat, to have a presentiment of danger.

Postelero [pos-tay-lay'-ro], *m.* (Naut.) Skid or skeed, knee of the quarter-deck of a ship. *Posteleros de las amuras,* (Naut.) Chess-trees.

Postema [pos-tay'-mah], *f.* 1. An abscess, tumour. 2. Dull, troublesome person.

Postemero [pos-tay-may'-ro], *m.* Large lancet.

Postergación [pos-ter-gah-the-on'], *f.* Act of leaving behind.

Postergar [pos-ter-gar'], *va.* To leave behind.

Posteridad [pos-tay-re-dahd'], *f.* Posterity.

Posterior [pos-tay-re-or'], *a.* Posterior, following.

Posterioridad [pos-tay-re-o-re-dahd'], *f.* Posteriority.

Posteriormente, *adv.* Lastly, afterward, hereafter.

Posteta [pos-tay'-tah], *f.* (Print.) Number of printed sheets stitched together; a quantity of sheets for packing books.

Postigo [pos-tee'-go], *m.* 1. Wicket, small door. 2. Sally-port, postern. 3. A door of one leaf. 4. Any of the divisions of a door or window. 5. *V.* Portillo for a small gate of a town.

Postiguillo [pos-te-geel'-lyo], *m. dim.* A small wicket or back-door.

Postila [pos-tee'-lah], *f.* Postil, marginal note.

Postilación [pos-te-lah-the-on'], *f.* Act of making marginal notes.

Postilador [pos-te-lah-dor'], *m.* Annotator, postiler.

Postilar [pos-te-lar'], *va.* To write marginal notes upon, to gloss, to comment.

Postilla [pos-teel'-lyah], *f.* Scab or crust on wounds.

Postillón [pos-teel-lyone'], *m.* 1. Postilion, driver. 2. Hack.

Postilloso, sa [pos-teel-lyo'-so, sah], *a.* Scabby, pustulous.

Postitis [pos-tee'-tis], *f.* Posthitis, inflammation of the prepuce.

Postiza [pos-tee'-thah], *f.* 1. (Naut.) Dead work on galleys for guiding the oar. 2. *V.* Castañuela.

Postizo, za [pos-tee'-tho, thah], *a.* Artificial, not natural. *Dientes postizos,* False teeth. *Pelo postizo,* False hair.

Postizo [pos-tee'-tho], *m.* With wig-makers, hair to supply the front or back of the head.

Postliminio [post-le-mee'-ne-o], *m.* Postliminy, among the Romans, reinstatement of one taken by the enemy to his possessions.

Postmeridiano, na [post-may-re-de-ah'-no, nah], *a.* Postmeridian, afternoon.

Postor [pos-tor'], *m.* Bidder at a public sale; bettor.

Postparto [post-par'-to], *m.* The latest young of animals in the season: applied chiefly to ewes.

Postración [pos-trah-the-on'], *f.* 1. Prostration, kneeling. 2. Prostration, dejection, depression.

Postrado, da [pos-trah'-do, dah], *a.* & *pp.* of Postrar. Prostrate, prostrated.

Postrador, ra [pos-trah-dor', rah], *m.* & *f.* 1. One who prostrates himself. 2. Foot-stool in the choir, on which the chorister kneels.

Postrar [pos-trar'], *va.* 1. To prostrate, to humble. 2. To debilitate, to exhaust.—*vr.* 1. To prostrate one's self, to kneel to the ground. 2. To be extremely debilitated.

Postre [pos'-tray], *a.* Last in order. *V.* Postrero. *A la postre,* At the long run, at last. *Por fin y postre,* (Coll.) Finally.

Postre [pos'-tray], *m.* Dessert, the last course at table: commonly used in the plural.

Postremas (A) [pos-tray'-mas], *adv.* (Obs.) Ultimately.

Postremo, ma [pos-tray'-mo, mah], *a.* *V.* Postrero and Último.

Postrer, *a.* *V.* Postrero. (Used before a noun.)

Postreramente, *adv.* Ultimately, lastly.

Postrero, ra [pos-tray'-ro, rah], *a.* Last in order, hindermost.

Postrero [pos-tray'-ro], *m.* *V.* Trasero.

Postrimeramente, *adv.* Finally, at last.

Postrimería [pos-tre-may-ree'-ah], *f.* 1. Death. *V.* Novísimo. 2. The last years of life.

Postrimero, ra [pos-tre-may'-ro, rah], *a.* *V.* Postrero and Trasero.

Postula [pos'-too-lah], *f.* Solicitation, petition.

Postulación [pos-too-lah-the-on'], *f.* 1. Postulation; petition. 2. Nomination for prelate of some church, made by the chapter, of a person who requires dispensation.

Postulado [pos-too-lah'-do], *m.* Postulate, position assumed without proof; axiom.

Postulador [pos-too-lah-dor'], *m.* 1. Member of a chapter who votes for an unqualified prelate. 2. One who solicits the canonization of a saint.

Postulanta [pos-too-lahn'-tah], *f.* Postulant, female candidate for admission to a religious order.

Postulante [pos-too-lahn'-tay], *m.* & *f.* Aspirant to a position.

Postular [pos-too-lar'], *va.* 1. To seek for, to solicit, to postulate. 2. To elect a prelate labouring under a canonical impediment.

Póstumo, ma [pos'-too-mo, mah], *a.* Posthumous.

Postura [pos-too'-rah], *f.* 1. Posture, position, situation. 2. Posture, collocation of the parts of the body with respect to each other. 3. Act of planting trees or plants; the tree or plant transplanted. 4. Assize of provisions. 5. Bid, price fixed by a bidder or buyer. 6. Bet, wager. 7. Paint which women put on their faces. 8. Egg of a fowl or bird, and the act of laying it. 9. Agreement, contract.

Potable [po-tah'-blay], *a.* Potable, drinkable.

Potador [po-tah-dor'], *m.* He who examines and marks weights and measures.

Potaje [po-tah'-hay], *m.* 1. Pottage, boiled food. 2. Vegetables dressed for food in days of abstinence. 3. Drink made of several ingredients. 4. Medley of useless things.

Potajería [po-tah-hay-ree'-ah], *f.* 1. Heap of dry pulse. 2. Place where dry pulse or vegetables are preserved for use.

Potajier [po-tah-he-err'], *m.* Officer of the king's palace who has the care of dry pulse and vegetables.

Potala [po-tah'-lah], *f.* 1. Stone which serves to moor boats. 2. A small, slow-going vessel.

Potanza [po-tahn'-thah], *f.* Cock, in clockwork; a bearing for the pallets.

Potar [po-tar'], *va.* To equalize and mark weights and measures.

Potasa [po-tah'-sah], *f.* Potash.

Potásico [po-tah'-se-co], *a.* (Chem.) Potassic, relating to potassium in its higher valence. *Yodo potásico,* Potassic or potassium iodide.

Potasio [po-tah'-se-o], *m.* Potassium, a metallic element lighter than water, upon which it burns with a violet flame.

Pote [po'-tay], *m.* 1. A jug for keeping liquids. 2. Pot, jar; flower-pot. 3. Standard measure or weight. *A pote,* Abundantly.

Potecillo, ito [po-tay-theel'-lyo], *m. dim.* A little pot or jar.

Potencia [po-ten'-the-ah], *f.* 1. Power, the faculty of performing. 2. Power, authority, dominion. 3. Power, ability, potency. 4. Possibility. 5. Power of generation; productive virtue. 6. Power, kingdom, state. 7. (Math.) Power, product of a quantity multiplied by itself. 8. A tool for ironing the brim of a hat. (*Cf.* "potence" in heraldry.)—*pl.* The nine rays of light which encircle the head of the infant Jesus, designed to express his universal power over everything created. *Potencias beligerantes,* Belligerent powers. *Potencias del alma,* The memory, understanding, and will. *Lo último de la potencia,* One's utmost ability or effort.

Potencial [po-ten-the-ahl'], *a.* 1. Potential, possessing a power. 2. Potential, having the effect, without the external properties. 3. (Gram.) Potential mode.

Potencialidad [po-ten-the-ah-le-dahd'], *f.* Potentiality, equivalence.

Potencialmente, *adv.* Potentially: equivalently.

Potentado [po-ten-tah'-do], *m.* Potentate, sovereign, monarch.

Potente [po-ten'-tay], *a.* 1. Potent, powerful, mighty. 2. Potent, strong, vigorous. 3. (Coll.) Great, bulky.

Potentemente, *adv.* Powerfully, potently.

Potentísimo, ma, *a. sup.* Most powerful.

Potenza [po-ten'-thah], *f.* A tau cross.

Poterna [po-terr'-nah], *f.* (Mil.) Postern, sally-port.

Potero, *m.* *V.* Potador.

Potestad [po-tes-tahd'], *f.* 1. Power, dominion, command, jurisdiction. *V.* Potentado. 2. (Arith.) Power, the product of multiplying a number by itself. *Potestades,* Angelic powers.

Potestativo, va [po-tes-tah-tee'-vo, vah], *a.* (For.) That which is in the faculty or power of any one: facultative.

Potista [po-tees'-tah], *com.* (Vul.) Tippler, drunkard.

Potra [po'-trah], *f.* 1. (Coll.) Rupture, scrotal hernia. 2. Filly. *V.* Potro.

Potrada [po-trah'-dah], *f.* Troop of young mares at pasture.

Potranca [po-trahn'-cah], *f.* Filly, young mare (not over three years old).

Potrear [po-tray-ar'], *va.* (Coll.) To vex, to molest, to annoy.

Potrera [po-tray'-rah], *a.* Applied to a hempen head-stall for horses.

Potrero [po-tray'-ro], *m.* 1. Surgeon who cures ruptures. 2. Herder, herdsman of colts. 3. Pasture ground. 4. (Amer.) A farm for rearing horses.

Potrico, illo [po-tree'-co], *m. dim.* A small colt.

Potril [po-treel'], *m.* & *a.* Pasture for young horses.

Potrilla [po-treel'-lyah], *f.* Nickname given to old persons affecting rakish youth.

Potro, tra [po'-tro, trah], *m.* & *f.* 1. Colt, foal; a young horse up to the time when it changes its milk teeth, or about four and a half years of age.—*m.* 2. (Obs.) A wooden horse; rack, a kind of torture. 3. A wooden frame for shoeing unruly horses. 4. Any thing which molests or torments. 5. An earthen chamber-pot. 6. Bubo, a venereal tumour. 7. Pit in the ground in which bee-keepers divide a bee-hive into two portions, giving a queen-bee to each. 8. A kind of stand where they card wool a second time. *Dos potros a un can, bien le morderán,* Two are stronger than one; in union there is strength. *El potro* *primero de otro*, or *El potro dómele otro*, In emergencies we must avail ourselves of the experience of others. *Estar como en un potro*, To be in a peck of trouble. *Manda potros y da pocos*, Large promise, but small performance. *Pacen potros como los otros*, (Colts graze as well as the others) the opinions of young people are not to be despised, for they sometimes hit the mark.

Potroso, sa, *a.* 1. Afflicted with a rupture. 2. (Coll.) Fortunate, lucky.

Poya [po'-yah], *f.* Duty paid for baking bread in a public oven.

Poyal [po-yahl'], *m.* 1. A sort of striped stuff with which benches are covered. 2. *V.* Poyo.

Poyata [po-yah'-tah], *f.* Shelf, cupboard.

Poyatilla [po-yah-teel'-lyah], *f. dim.* A little shelf.

Poyato [po-yah'-to], *m.* Terrace, in landscape gardening.

Poyo [po'-yo], *m.* 1. Bench, a seat made of stone and mortar against a wall. 2. Fee given to judges.

Poza [po'-thah], *f.* 1. Puddle. 2. (Agr.) A pool for macerating hemp. 3. Hole made in children's bread, and filled with must, honey, or treacle. *Lamer la poza*, To lick the honey or butter from bread; to drain one's pocket of money.

Pozal [po-thahl'], *m.* 1. Bucket, pail. 2. Coping of a well. 3. Vessel sunk in the earth to catch any fluid.

Pozanco [po-thahn'-co], *m.* Pond of stagnant water.

Pozero [po-thay'-ro], *m.* Well-digger.

Pozo [po'-tho], *m.* 1. Well. 2. A deep hole in a river; a whirlpool. 3. Any thing complete in its line. *Es un pozo de ciencia*, He is deeply learned. *Navío de pozo*, (Naut.) A deep-waisted ship. *Pozo de cable*, (Naut.) Cable-stage, cable-tier. *Pozo de airón*, (1) A very deep Moorish well. (2) Bottomless well. *Pozo de la hélice*, Well of a screw-propeller. *Pozo de nieve*, Ice-house, snow-pit. *Caer en el pozo airón*, To fall into a bottomless well, to disappear beyond hope of recovery.

Pozol, Pozole [po-thohl'], *m.* Barley and beans boiled. (Aztec.)

Pozuela [po-thoo-ay'-lah], *f. dim.* A small puddle or pond.

Pozuelo [po-thoo-ay'-lo], *m.* 1. (Dim.) A small well or pit. 2. Vessel sunk in the ground to collect oil, etc., in mills.

Práctica [prahc'-te-cah], *f.* 1. Practice, constant habit. 2. Practice, customary use; exercise. 3. Practice, manner, mode, method. 4. Practice of any profession. 5. The act of learning a profession under a master.

Practicable [prac-te-cah'-blay], *a.* Practicable, feasible.

Practicador, ra [prac-te-cah-dor', rah], *m.* & *f.* Practiser, practitioner.

Prácticamente, *adv.* Practically.

Practicante [prac-te-cahn'-tay], *m.* Practitioner in surgery and medicine under a master.—*pa.* Practising.

Practicar [prac-te-car'], *va.* 1. To practise, to perform, to do, to put in execution. 2. To practise, to do habitually. 3. To learn the practice of a profession under a master.

Práctico, ca [prahc'-te-co, cah], *a.* 1. Practical. 2. Skilful, experienced, expert.—*m.* A skilful pilot.

Practicón, na [prac-te-cone', nah], *m.* & *f.* One of great practical knowledge and experience.

Pradal [prah-dahl'], *m.* Extent of country abounding in meadows and pasture-lands.

Pradecillo [prah-day-theel'-lyo], *m.* A small meadow.

Prадeño, ña [prah-day'-nyo, nyah], *a.* Relating to meadows or fields.

Pradera, Pradería [prah-day'-rah, prah-day-ree'-ah], *f.* 1. Country abounding in meadows and pasture-grounds. 2. Mead, meadow, rich pasture-ground.

Praderoso, sa [prah-day-ro'-so, sah], *a.* Relating to meadows.

Pradico, illo [prah-dee'-co], *m. dim.* A small meadow.

Prado [prah'-do], *m.* 1. Lawn, field, meadow; a piece of pasture-ground. 2. Prado, a public walk in Madrid. *Prado de guadaña*, Meadow mowed annually.

Præ mánibus. (Lat.) Between the hands, in hand.

Pragmática [prag-mah'-te-cah], *f.* 1. Royal ordinance. 2. Rescript of a sovereign to an application made to him in a particular case.

Pragmático, ca [prag-mah'-te-co, cah], *a.* Pragmatic, pragmatical.—*m.* Commentator upon national laws.

Prama [prah'-mah], *f.* Praam, a kind of lighter used in northern countries.

Prasio [prah'-se-o], *m.* Prase, quartz of a leek-green colour, usually cryptocrystalline.

Prasma [prahs'-mah], *m.* Dark green agate.

Prática, *f.* *V.* Práctica.

Pravedad [prah-vay-dahd'], *f.* Perversity, iniquity, depravity.

Pravo, va [prah'-vo, vah], *a.* Depraved, perverse, knavish, lewd.

Praxis [prahk'-sis], *f.* Practice. *V.* Práctica.

Pre [pray], *m.* Daily pay allowed to soldiers.

Pre, A preposition used in the composition of nouns and verbs, either to augment the signification or to mark priority of time and rank.

Prea, *f.* (Obs.) *V.* Presa.

Preadamita [pray-ah-dah-mee'-tah], *a.* & *n.* Preadamite, existing before Adam.

Preámbulo [pray-ahm'-boo-lo], *m.* 1. Preamble, exordium, preface. 2. (Coll.) Evasion, circumlocution.

Prebenda [pray-ben'-dah], *f.* 1. Prebend, the right of enjoying any temporal fruits by reason of employment, office, etc. 2. Prebend, ecclesiastical benefice: commonly used to express a canonry. 3. Sinecure. 4. (Acad.) Portion, piously given to a woman, to enable her to marry or to become a nun; or to a student as a foundation scholarship. *Prebenda de oficio*, Any of the four prebends, doctoral, magisterial, lectural, or penitentiary.

Prebendado [pray-ben-dah'-do], *m.* Prebendary, a dignitary who enjoys a prebend in a cathedral or collegiate church.—*Prebendado, da*, *pp.* of Prebendar.

Prebendar [pray-ben-dar'], *va.* To confer an ecclesiastical benefice or prebend.

Prebostal [pray-bos-tahl'], *a.* Provostal.

Prebostazgo [pray-bos-tath'-go], *m.* Provostship.

Preboste [pray-bos'-tay], *m.* 1. Provost, one who governs a college or community. 2. (Mil.) Provost of an army, an officer who secures deserters and superintends the infliction of punishments.

Precariamente, *adv.* (For.) Precariously.

Precario, ria [pray-cah'-re-o, ah], *a.* 1. Precarious, held only as a loan, and at the will of the owner. 2. Precarious, uncertain.

Precaución [pray-cah-oo-the-on'], *f.* Precaution, guard, vigilance.

Precaucionado, da [pray-cah-oo-the-o-nah'-do, dah], *a.* Sagacious, cautious, clear-sighted.

Precaucionarse [pray-cah-oo-the-o-nar'-say], *vr.* To be cautious.

Precautelar [pray-cah-oo-tay-lar'], *va.* To caution, to forewarn.

Precaver [pray-cah-verr'], *va.* To prevent or obviate.—*vr.* To guard against, to be on one's guard.

Precavido, da [pray-cah-vee'-do, dah], *a.* Cautious, far-sighted, on one's guard. —*pp.* of Precaver.

Precedencia [pray-thay-den'-the-ah], *f.* 1. Precedence, priority. 2. Pre-eminence, preference. 3. Superiority, primacy.

Precedente [pray-thay-den'-tay], *a.* Preceding, foregoing.—*n.* Precedent. *Sin precedente*, All-time; without exception.

Preceder [pray-thay-derr'], *va.* To precede, to go before; to be superior in rank or order; to excel.

Precelente, *a.* (Obs.) Very excellent.

Preceptista [pray-thep-tees'-tah], *m.* & *a.* One who gives precepts and injunctions or rules.

Preceptivamente, *adv.* Preceptively.

Preceptivo, va [pray-thep-tee'-vo, vah], *a.* Preceptive, mandatory, directory.

Precepto [pray-thep'-to], *m.* Precept, order, injunction, mandate; rule. *Preceptos*, The ten commandments of the decalogue.

Preceptor [pray-thep-tor'], *m.* Master, teacher, preceptor.

Preces [pray'-thes], *f. pl.* 1. Prayers; public or private devotion. 2. Supplication for a bull or commission from the Vatican.

Precesión [pray-thay-se-on'], *f.* 1. *V.* Reticencia. 2. (Ast.) Precession.

Preciado, da [pray-the-ah'-do, dah], *a.* 1. Valued, appraised; esteemed. 2. Valuable, precious, excellent. 3. Proud, elated, presumptuous.—*pp.* of Preciar.

Preciador, ra [pray-the-ah-dor', rah], *m.* & *f.* Appraiser.

Preciar [pray-the-ar'], *va.* To value, to appraise.—*vr.* To boast, to brag; to take a pride in, to glory.

Precinta [pray-theen'-tah], *f.* 1. Strap of wood, iron, tin, or leather, to secure the corners of boxes. 2. (Naut.) Parcelling, narrow pieces of tarred canvas, with which the seams of ships are covered, and which are also put around cables and ropes.

Precintar [pray-thin-tar'], *va.* 1. To strap the corners of boxes with leather, to prevent their opening. 2. To cross boxes of goods, as a mark that they are not to be opened.

Precinto [pray-theen'-to], *m.* 1. The act of strapping. 2. A sealed strap with which trunks, parcels, etc., are bound lengthwise and crosswise, so that they may be opened only by the proper individuals.

Precio [pray'-the-o], *m.* 1. Price, cost, value. 2. Price, reward; premium. 3. Price, value, estimation, esteem, consideration; character, credit. *Tener en precio*, To esteem.

Preciosa [pray-the-o'-sah], *f.* Allowance in the choir to prebendaries for assisting at prayers for a benefactor.

Preciosamente, *adv.* Preciously, richly.

Preciosidad [pray-the-o-se-dahd'], *f.* Worth, excellence, preciousness.

Precioso, sa [pray-the-o'-so, sah], *a.* 1. Precious, valuable, excellent. 2. Pleasant; gay, merry.

Precipicio [pray-the-pee'-the-o], *m.* 1.

Precipice. 2. A sudden fall. 3. Ruin, destruction.

Precipitación [pre-the-pe-tah-the-on'], *f.* 1. Precipitation, inconsiderate haste, precipitancy. 2. (Chem.) Precipitation, the fall of solid particles to the bottom of a liquid.

Precipitadamente, *adv.* Precipitately, hastily.

Precipitadero [pray-the-pe-tah-day'-ro], *m.* *V.* PRECIPICIO.

Precipitado, da [pray-the-pe-tah'-do, dah], *a.* & *pp.* of PRECIPITAR. Precipitate, hasty, abrupt.

Precipitado, *m.* (Chem.) Precipitate.

Precipitante [pray-the-pe-tahn'-tay], *m.* (Chem.) Precipitater.

Precipitar [pray-the-pe-tar'], *va.* 1. To precipitate, to cast headlong. 2. To expose to ruin. 3. To perform the chemical process of precipitation.—*vr.* To act in a precipitate manner; to run headlong to destruction; to haste, to hurry.

Precipite [pray-thee'-pe-tay], *a.* In danger, on the point of falling.

Precipitosamente, *adv.* *V.* PRECIPITADAMENTE.

Precipitoso, sa [pray-the-pe-to'-so, sah], *a.* 1. Steep, slippery, precipitous. 2. Precipitous, rash, inconsiderate.

Precipuamente, *adv.* Principally.

Precipuo, pua [pray-thee'-poo-o, ah], *a.* Chief, principal.

Precisamente [pray-the-sah-men'-tay], *adv.* 1. Precisely, exactly, nicely. 2. Inevitably, indispensably, necessarily. 3. Just at the moment.

Precisar [pray-the-sar'], *va.* To compel, to oblige, to necessitate.

Precisión [pray-the-se-on'], *f.* 1. Necessity, obligation. 2. Compulsion, the state of being compelled. 3. Preciseness, exactness. 4. Precision, exact limitation. *Tener precisión de hacer alguna cosa,* To be obliged or under the necessity of doing a certain thing.

Precisivo, va [pray-the-see'-vo, vah], *a.* That which prescinds or abstracts, precisive.

Preciso, sa [pray-thee'-so, sah], *a.* 1. Necessary, requisite, needful. 2. Precise, exact, punctual. 3. Distinct, clear. 4. Severed, cut off; abstracted.

Precitado, da [pray-the-tah'-do, dah], *a.* Forecited, quoted before.

Precito, ta [pray-thee'-to, tah], *a.* Damned, condemned to hell.

Preclaramente, *adv.* Illustriously, distinctly.

Preclaro, ra [pray-clah'-ro, rah], *a.* Illustrious, famous, eminent.

Precocidad [pray-co-the-dahd'], *f.* Precocity, untimely ripeness of fruit, forwardness.

Precognición [pray-cog-ne-the-on'], *f.* Precognition.

Preconización [pray-co-ne-thah-the-on'], *f.* Preconization.

Preconizador [pray-co-ne-thah-dor'], *m.* One who proclaims the elected prelates in the Roman consistory.

Preconizar [pray-co-ne-thar'], *va.* To patronize, to proclaim, to publish in the Roman consistory.

Preconocedor, ra [pray-co-no-thay-dor', rah], *m.* & *f.* One who foresees or anticipates a future event.

Preconocer [pray-co-no-therr'], *va.* To foreknow, to foretell.

Precordial [pray-cor-de-ahl'], *a.* Præcordial, relating to the diaphragm.

Precoz [pray-coth'], *a.* Precocious, ripe before the usual time, forward.

Precursor, ra [prah-coor-sor', rah], *a.* Preceding, going before.—*m.* Precursor, harbinger, forerunner, herald.

Predecesor, ra [pray-day-thay-sor', rah], *m.* & *f.* Predecessor, antecessor, forerunner.

Predecir [pray-day-theer'], *va.* To foretell, to anticipate, to predict.

Predefinición [pray-day-fe-ne-the-on'], *f.* Predetermination of the Divine Providence.

Predefinir [pray-day-fe-neer'], *va.* To predetermine.

Predestinación [pray-des-te-nah-the-on'], *f.* Predestination, preordination.

Predestinado [pray-des-te-nah'-do], *m.* Foreordained to eternal glory.—*Predestinado, da, pp.* of PREDESTINAR.

Predestinar [pray-des-te-nar'], *va.* To predestine, to destine beforehand, to foredoom, to predestinate.

Predeterminación [pray-day-ter-me-nah-the-on'], *f.* Predetermination, foreordination.

Predeterminar [pray-day-ter-me-nar'], *va.* To predetermine, to anticipate a resolution, to foredoom.

Predial [pray-de-ahl'], *a.* Predial, consisting of or relating to landed property, or farms.

Prédica [pray'-de-cah], *f.* Preachment, sermon, discourse by a non-Catholic preacher.

Predicable [pray-de-cah'-blay], *a.* 1. Fit to be preached. 2. Commendable, praiseworthy. 3. Predicable.

Predicable [pray-de-cah'-blay], *m.* Predicable, a logical term.

Predicación [pray-de-cah-the-on'], *f.* Preaching, sermon.

Predicadera [pray-de-cah-day'-rah], *f.* (Prov.) Pulpit. *Predicaderas,* (Coll.) Style of the pulpit, facility of preaching or praying.

Predicado [pray-de-cah'-do], *m.* (Log.) Predicate.

Predicador, ra [pray-de-cah-dor', rah], *m.* & *f.* Preacher, orator, homilist, eulogist.

Predicamental [pray-de-cah-men-tahl'], *a.* Predicamental.

Predicamento [pray-de-cah-men'-to], *m.* 1. Predicament, degree of estimation in which a person is held. 2. Category, class or kind described by any definitive marks.

Predicante [pray-de-cahn'-tay], *m.* Sectarian or heretical preacher.

Predicar [pray-de-car'], *va.* 1. To render clear and evident, to publish. 2. To preach. 3. To praise to excess. 4. To reprehend vice.—*vr.* To predicate, to comprise an affirmation. *Subirse a predicar,* (Coll.) To mount to the head: applied to good wine.

Predicatorio [pray-de-cah-to'-re-o], *m.* *V.* PÚLPITO.

Predicción [pray-dic-the-on'], *f.* Prediction.

Predicho, cha [pray-dee'-cho, chah], *pp. irr.* of PREDECIR.

(*Yo predigo, prediga, predije,* from *Predecir.* *V.* DECIR.)

Predilección [pray-de-lec-the-on'], *f.* Predilection.

Predilecto, ta [pray-de-lec'-to, tah], *a.* Beloved in preference to others; darling, favourite.

Predio [pray'-de-o], *m.* Landed property, farm, real property. *Predio rústico,* Piece of arable ground. *Predio urbano,* Dwelling-house in town or country.

Prediolo [pray-de-o'-lo], *m.* A small farm.

Predisponer [pray-dis-po-nerr'], *va.* 1. To predispose, to prearrange. 2. (Not Acad.) To predispose towards, to contract disease readily.

Predisposición [pray-dis-po-se-the-on'], *f.* 1. Predisposition. 2. Inclination, propensity.

Predispuesto, ta [pray-dis-poo-es'-to, tah], *a.* & *pp. irr.* of PREDISPONER. Predisponent, predisposed.

Predominación [pray-do-me-nah-the-on'], *f.* *V.* PREDOMINIO.

Predominante [pray-do-me-nahn'-tay], *pa.* Predominant, prevailing.

Predominar [pray-do-me-nar'], *va.* 1. To predominate, to overrule, to overpower, to control, to compel. 2. To exceed in height, to overlook, to command; to prevail.

Predominio [pray-do-mee'-ne-o], *m.* Predominance, superiority; prevalence of humours.

Preelección [pray-ay-lec-the-on'], *f.* Predestination.

Preeminencia [pray-ay-me-nen'-the-ah], *f.* Pre-eminence, mastery.

Preeminente [pray-ay-me-nen'-tay], *a.* Pre-eminent, superior.

Preestablecer [pray-es-tah-blay-therr'], *va.* (Littl. us.) To pre-establish.

Preexcelso, sa [pray-ex-thel'-so, sah], *a.* Illustrious, great, eminent.

Preexistencia [pray-ek-sis-ten'-the-ah], *f.* Pre-existence.

Preexistente [pray-ek-sis-ten'-tay], *pa.* Pre-existent.

Preexistir [pray-ek-sis-teer'], *vn.* To pre-exist.

Prefabricado, da [pray-fah-bre-cah'-do, dah], *a.* Prefabricated.

Prefacio [pray-fah'-the-o], *m.* 1. Part of the mass which immediately precedes the canon. 2. Preface.

Prefación [pray-fah-the-on'], *f.* Preface, introduction.

Prefacioncilla [pray-fah-the-on-theel'-lyah], *f. dim.* A short preface.

Prefecto [pray-fec'-to], *m.* 1. Prefect, head of a county or municipality. 2. Master or principal of a college. 3. Prefect, a magistrate in ancient Rome.

Prefectura [pray-fec-too'-rah], *f.* Prefecture.

Preferencia [pray-fay-ren'-the-ah], *f.* Preference, choice, pre-eminence.

Preferente [pray-fay-ren'-tay], *pa.* & *a.* Pre-eminent; preferring.

Preferible [pray-fay-ree'-blay], *a.* Preferable.

Preferiblemente, *adv.* Preferably.

Preferir [pray-fay-reer'], *va.* To prefer.—*vr.* To proffer, to offer spontaneously to do any thing.

(*Yo prefiero, prefiera; él prefirió;* from *Preferir.* *V.* ADHERIR.)

Prefiguración [pray-fe-goo-rah-the-on'], *f.* Prefiguration.

Prefigurar [pray-fe-goo-rar'], *va.* To prefigure, to foretoken, to model a statue, to sketch a painting.

Prefijar [pray-fe-har'], *va.* To prefix, to determine.

Prefijo, ja [pray-fee'-ho, hah], *pp. irr.* of PREFIJAR. Prefixed.

Prefijo [pray-fee'-ho], *m.* (Gram.) Prefix.

Prefinición [pray-fe-ne-the-on'], *f.* Act of prefining or fixing a term.

Prefinir [pray-fe-neer'], *va.* To prefine, to determine.

Prefoliacion [pray-fo-le-ah-the-on'], *f.* (Bot.) Vernation, prefoliation, arrangement of leaves within the bud.

Prefulgente [pray-fool-hen'-tay], *a.* Resplendent, lucid, shining.

Pregaria, *f.* *V.* PLEGARIA.

Pregón [pray-gone'], *m.* Publication by the common crier, cry.

Pregonador, ra [pray-go-nah-dor', rah], *m.* & *f.* Hawker, huckster, street-vender.

Pregonar [pray-go-nar'], *va.* 1. To proclaim in public places. 2. To cry goods or provisions about the streets. 3. To render public, to make known; to applaud publicly.

Pregoneo [pray-go-nay'-o], *m.* Hawking, crying goods on the streets.

Pregonería [pray-go-nay-ree'-ah], *f.* 1. Office of common crier. 2. A kind of tax or tribute.

Pregonero [pray-go-nay'-ro], *m.* 1. Common crier, town crier. 2. One who renders public or divulges a secret. 3. One who proclaims the biddings at public sales.

Pregonero, ra [pray-go-nay'-ro, rah], *a.* Publishing, praising, proclaiming.

Preguerra [pray-gayr'-rah], *f.* Prewar.

Pregunta [pray-goon'-tah], *f.* Question, query, inquiry. *Absolver las preguntas*, (For.) To answer under oath. *Estar a la cuarta pregunta*, (Coll.) To be hard up or penniless. (Questions asked by the judges: 1. Your name (*gracia*). 2. Residence (*señas de casa*). 3. Married or single (*estado*). 4. Occupation (*ocupación, oficio*).)

Preguntador, ra [pray-goon-tah-dor', rah], *m.* & *f.* Questioner, examiner, interrogator.

Preguntante [pray-goon-tahn'-tay], *pa.* Inquiring.

Preguntar [pray-goon-tar'], *va.* To question, to demand, to inquire.

Preguntón, na [pray-goon-tone', nah], *m.* & *f.* An inquisitive person, a busy inquirer.

Prehistoria [pray-is-to'-re-ah], *f.* Prehistoric or legendary times.

Prehistórico, ca [pray-is-to'-re-co, cah], *a.* Prehistoric, legendary; previous to the beginning of history.

Preinserto, ta [pray-in-serr'-to, tah], *a.* That which is previously inserted.

Prejudicial [pray-hoo-de-the-ahl'], *a.* 1. (Law) Requiring a previous judicial decision before the final sentence. 2. (Obs.) *V.* PERJUDICIAL.

Prejuicio [pray-hoo-ee'-the-o], *m.* Prejudice, bias, prejudgment.

Prejuzar [pray-hooth-gar'], *va.* To judge or decide things before the right time, to prejudge.

Prelacía [pray-lah-thee'-ah], *f.* Prelacy, prelature.

Prelación [pray-lah-the-on'], *f.* Preference, preferment.

Prelada [pray-lah'-dah], *f.* A female prelate, the abbess or superior of a convent or nunnery.

Prelado [pray-lah'-do], *m.* Prelate, an ecclesiastic of the highest order and dignity; the superior of a convent or religious house.

Prelativo, va [pray-lah-tee'-vo, vah], *a.* Deserving preferment.

Prelatura [pray-lah-too'-rah], *f.* 1. Prelacy, prelature. 2. The whole body of prelates.

Preliminar [pray-le-me-nar'], *a.* Preliminary, proemial, exordial.

Preliminar [pray-le-me-nar'], *m.* A preliminary sketch; protocol.

Prelucir [pray-loo-theer'], *vn.* To sparkle or shine forth.

Preludiar [pray-loo-de-ar'], *vn.* 1. To attempt, to essay. 2. (Mus.) To make a flourish or introduction to the main piece.

Preludio [pray-loo'-de-o], *m.* Prelude; flourish.

Prelusión [pray-loo-se-on'], *f.* Prelude, prologue, preface.

Premática, *f.* (Obs.) *V.* PRAGMÁTICA.

Prematuramente, *adv.* Prematurely.

Prematuro, ra [pray-mah-too'-ro, rah], *a.* 1. Premature, precocious; unseasonable. 2. (For.) Not arrived at the age of consent: said of girls.

Premeditación [pray-may-de-tah-the-on'], *f.* Premeditation, forethought, precogitation.

Premeditado, da [pray-may-de-tah'-do, dah], *a.* & *pp.* of PREMEDITAR. Premeditated, prepense, preconceived.

Premeditar [pray-may-de-tar'], *va.* 1. To consider or meditate carefully, to weigh maturely. 2. To premeditate.

Premiador, ra [pray-me-ah-dor', rah], *m.* & *f.* Rewarder.

Premiar [pray-me-ar'], *va.* To reward, to remunerate, to requite.

Premio [pray'-me-o], *m.* 1. Reward, recompense, remuneration, guerdon, meed. 2. Premium, interest. *Premio de seguro*, Rate or premium of insurance. 3. Premium, increase in value of money or securities.

Premiosamente, *adv.* Tightly, compressedly; by force.

Premiosidad [pray-me-o-se-dahd'], *f.* Want of ease and readiness in the manner of speaking or of writing.

Premioso, sa [pray-me-o'-so, sah], *a.* 1. Tight, close, pinching. 2. Troublesome, tiresome, burdensome. 3. Unready in speech, expressing one's self with difficulty.

Premisa [pray-mee'-sah], *f.* 1. Premise, in logic; an antecedent proposition. 2. Mark, indication.

Premiso, sa [pray-mee'-so, sah], *a.* 1. Premised. *V.* PREVENIDO. 2. (Law) Precedent, former, going before.

Premitir, *va.* (Obs.) *V.* ANTICIPAR.

Premoción [pray-mo-the-on'], *f.* Previous movement or motion.

Premonstratense, Premostratense [pray-mons-trah-ten'-say], *a.* Premonstratensian: applied to an order of regular canons founded by St. Norbert.

Premoriencia [pray-mo-re-en'-the-ah], *f.* (Obs.) Prior death.

Premorir [pray-mo-reer'], *vn.* (Law) To die before another.

Premura [pray-moo'-rah], *f.* (Coll.) Narrowness, pressure, haste, hurry.

Prenda [pren'-dah], *f.* 1. Pledge, security for the fulfilment of an obligation. 2. Pledge, any household ornament or furniture, especially when pawned or sold. *Casa de prendas*, Broker's shop, where old furniture is sold. 3. Pledge, earnest, security. 4. A garment or ornament. 5. Any object dearly loved, as wife or children; jewel, pledge of affection. *Prendas*, Endowments, natural gifts, talents. *Juego de prendas*, Game of forfeits. *Meter prendas*, To take a part in any business.

Prendado [pren-dah'-do], *pp.* of PRENDAR. *Ser muy prendado*, To be very accomplished, very refined.

Prendador, ra [pren-dah-dor', rah], *m.* & *f.* Pledger, pawner; one who redeems a pledge.

Prendamiento [pren-dah-me-en'-to], *m.* Act of pledging or pawning.

Prendar [pren-dar'], *va.* 1. To take pledges, to lend on pledges. 2. To please, to ingratiate one's self.—*vr.* To take a fancy to any thing: used with the preposition *de*.

Prendedero [pren-day-day'-ro], *m.* 1. Hook, fillet, brooch. 2. Fillet, a band tied round the head, which serves to keep up the hair.

Prendedor [pren-day-dor'], *m.* 1. Catcher. 2. Breast-pin.

Prender [pren-derr'], *va.* 1. To seize, to grasp, to catch, to pin. 2. To imprison. 3. (Coll.) To detain for the purpose of entertaining in a friendly manner.—*vn.* 1. To take root: applied to plants. 2. To cover; applied to the act of brutish procreation. 3. To catch or take fire. 4. To adorn, embellish: used of women.

Prendería [pren-day-ree'-ah], *f.* Shop in which old clothes and furniture are sold; pawnbroker's shop; frippery.

Prendero, ra [pren-day'-ro, rah], *m.* & *f.* 1. Broker, one who sells old furniture and clothes; fripper. 2. Pawnbroker.

Prendido [pren-dee'-do], *m.* 1. Dress of women. 2. Pattern for bone-lace.—*Prendido, da, pp.* of PRENDAR.

Prendimiento [pren-de-me-en'-to], *m.* Seizure, capture.

Prenoción [pray-no-the-on'], *f.* Prenotion or first knowledge of things.

Prenombre [pray-nom'-bray], *m.* Prenomen, name prefixed to the family name among the Romans.

Prenosticar, *va.* (Obs.) *V.* PRONOSTICAR.

Prenotar [pray-no-tar'], *va.* To note by anticipation.

Prensa [pren'-sah], *f.* 1. Press, an instrument with which any thing is pressed. 2. Press, a machine for printing. 3. Press. *V.* IMPRENTA. *Prensa recargada*, A hot-press, to give lustre to stuff. *Dar á la prensa*, To publish. *Prensa de lagar*, Wine-press. *Prensa de paños*, Cloth-press.

Prensado [pren-sah'-do], *m.* Lustre, which remains on stuff.—*Prensado, da, pp.* of PRENSAR.

Prensador, ra [pren-sah-dor', rah], *m.* & *f.* Presser, one who presses clothes and stuff.

Prensadura [pren-sah-doo'-rah], *f.* The act of pressing, pressure.

Prensapapeles [pren-sah-pah-pay'-les], *m.* A paper weight.

Prensar [pren-sar'], *va.* To press. *V.* APRENSAR.

Prensista [pren-sees'-tah], *m.* Pressman in a printing-office.

Prenunciar [pray-noon-the-ar'], *va.* To foretell, to prognosticate.

Prenuncio [pray-noon'-the-o], *m.* Prediction, prognostication.

Preñadilla [pray-nyah-deel'-lyah], *f.* A delicate fish of the rivers of Ecuador, olive-green, with black spots and about four inches long; called imba by the Indians. Pimelodes cyclopum.

Preñado, da [pray-nyah'-do, dah], *a.* 1. Full, pregnant. 2. Big with child, pregnant. 3. Inclosing within itself something undiscovered.—*m.* Pregnancy, gestation.

Preñez [pray-nyeth'], *f.* 1. Pregnancy, gestation. *V.* PREÑADO. 2. Conception. 3. The state of a thing that is impending or hanging over. 4. Confusion, difficulty, obscurity.

Preocupación [pray-o-coo-pah-the-on'], *f.* 1. Preoccupation, anticipation in taking possession. 2. Prepossession, bias, prejudice; preconception.

Preocupadamente, *adv.* Prejudicedly.

Preocupar [pray-o-coo-par'], *va.* 1. To preoccupy. 2. To prejudice, to prepossess the mind.

Preordinación [pray-or-de-nah-the-on'], *f.* Preordination.

Preordinadamente, *adv.* In a manner preordained.

Preordinar [pray-or-de-nar'], *va.* To preordain, to foreordain.

Preparación [pray-pah-rah-the-on'], *f.* Preparation.

Preparamento, Preparamiento [pray-pa-rah-men'-to], *m.* Preparation.

Preparar [pray-pah-rar'], *va.* To prepare, to make ready.—*vr.* To be prepared, to be in readiness.

Preparativo, va [pray-pah-rah-tee'-vo, vah], *a.* Preparative, qualifying.

Preparativo [pray-pah-rah-tee'-vo], *m.* Thing prepared, preparative.

Preparatoriamente, *adv.* Preparatorily.

Preparatorio, ria [pray-pah-rah-to'-re-o, ah], *a.* Preparatory, previous, introductory.
Preponderancia [pray-pon-day-rahn'-the-ah], *f.* Preponderance, overbalancing.
Preponderante [pray-pon-day-rahn'-tay], *a.* Preponderant, that which turns the scale.
Preponderar [pray-pon-day-rar'], *vn.* 1. To preponderate, to outweigh, to overbalance. 2. To prevail. 3. To overpower.
Preponer [pray-po-nerr'], *va.* To put before, to prefer.
Preposición [pray-po-se-the-on'], *f.* (Gram.) Preposition, a part of speech.
Prepositivo, va [pray-po-se-tee'-vo, vah], *a.* Prepositive, prefixed.
Prepósito [pray-po'-se-to], *m.* 1. President, chairman. 2. Provost.
Prepositura [pray-po-se-too'-rah], *f.* Dignity of a provost.
Preposteración [pray-pos-tay-rah-the-on'], *f.* Inversion of the regular order of things.
Prepósteramente, *adv.* Preposterously.
Preposterar [pray-pos-tay-rar'], *va.* To render preposterous, to transpose.
Prepóstero, ra [pray-pos'-tay-ro, rah], *a.* Preposterous, absurd.
Prepotencia [pray-po-ten'-the-ah], *f.* Preponderance, superiority, prepotency.
Prepotente [pray-po-ten'-tay], *a.* 1. Very powerful. 2. Abusive of power over one's inferiors.
Prepucial [pray-poo-the-ahl'], *a.* Preputial, relating to the prepuce.
Prepucio [pray-poo'-the-o], *m.* Prepuce, foreskin.
Prepuesto, ta [pray-poo-es'-to, tah], *pp. irr.* of PREPONER. Preferred.
Prerrogativa [pray-ro-gah-tee'-vah], *f.* Prerogative, privilege; liberty.
Presa [pray'-sah], *f.* 1. Capture, seizure. 2. Prize, spoils or booty taken from an enemy. 3. Dike, dam, mole, bank; drain, trench, conduit. 4. Slice of meat; a bit of any other kind of eatables. 5. Tusk, fang. 6. Claw of a bird of prey. 7. Carcass of a fowl or bird killed by a hawk or other bird of prey. 8. Among fishermen, fish weir, stake work. *Presa de caldo,* Pulp, juice. *V.* PISTO. *Hacer presa,* To catch and tie any thing so that it cannot escape.
Presada [pray-sah'-dah], *f.* Colour of a leek; a pale green colour.
Presagiar [pray-sah-he-ar'], *va.* To presage, to forebode, to foretell.
Presagio [pray-sah'-he-o], *m.* Presage, an omen, a token.
Presagioso, sa, Présago, ga [pray-sah-he-oh'-so, sah, pray'-sah-go, gah], *a.* Ominous, presaging, divining, guessing.
Presbicia [pres-bee'-the-ah], *f.* Far-sightedness, presbyopia.
Présbite, ta [pres'-be-tay, tah], *a.* & *m.* & *f.* Presbyopic, seeing objects better at a distance; a presbyope.
Presbiterado, Presbiterato [pres-be-tay-rah'-do, pres-be-tay-rah'-to], *m.* Priesthood, the dignity or order of a priest.
Presbiteral [pres-be-tay-rahl'], *a.* Sacerdotal, relating to a presbyter.
Presbiterianismo [pres-be-tay-re-ah-nees'-mo], *m.* Presbyterianism.
Presbiteriano, na [pres-be-tay-re-ah'-no, nah], *a.* & *m.* & *f.* Presbyterian.
Presbiteriato [pres-be-tay-re-ah'-to], *m.* Dignity of a presbyter or elder among the Presbyterians.
Presbiterio [pres-be-tay'-re-o], *m.* Presbyterium, chancel, the part in a church where the high altar stands.
Presbítero [pres-bee'-tay-ro], *m.* A priest.
Presciencia [pres-the-en'-the-ah], *f.* Prescience, foreknowledge, forethought.
Prescindible [pres-thin-dee'-blay], *a.* Capable of being prescinded or abstracted.
Prescindir [pres-thin-deer'], *va.* 1. To prescind, to cut off; to abstract. *Prescindiendo de eso,* Laying that aside. 2. To cease from doing something.
Prescito, ta [pres-thee'-to, tah], *a.* *V.* PRECITO.
Prescribir [pres-cre-beer'], *va.* 1. To prescribe, to determine. 2. To acquire a right by uninterrupted possession. 3. To despair of success; to stand in need of.—*vn.* To prescribe, to form a custom which has the force of law.
Prescripción [pres-crip-the-on'], *f.* 1. Prescription, the act of prescribing. 2. Introduction, any thing proemial. 3. (Law) Prescription, right or title acquired by peaceful possession.
Prescriptible [pres-crip-tee'-blay], *a.* Prescriptible, that may be prescribed.
Prescripto, ta [pres-creep'-to, tah], *pp. irr.* of PRESCRIBIR. Prescribed, prescript, accurately laid down in a precept.
Presea [pray-say'-ah], *f.* Jewel, any ornament of great value.
Presencia [pray-sen'-the-ah], *f.* 1. Presence, coexistence. 2. Presence, figure, port, air, mien, demeanour. 3. (Met.) Memory or representation of a thing. *Presencia de ánimo,* Serenity, coolness, presence of mind.
Presencial [pray-sen-the-ahl'], *a.* Presential, relating to actual presence.
Presencialmente, *adv.* Presentially.
Presenciar [pray-sen-the-ar'], *vn.* To be present, to witness, to assist at.
Presentable [pray-sen-tah'-blay], *a.* Presentable, producible.
Presentación [pray-sen-tah-the-on'], *f.* 1. Presentation, presentment, exhibition. 2. A church festival in memory of the Virgin's presentation in the temple, celebrated on the 21st of November. 3. The act of offering or presenting an ecclesiastical benefice.
Presentado [pray-sen-tah'-do], *m.* & *a.* 1. Teacher of divinity, who expects soon to be ranked as master. 2. Presentee, person presented.—*Presentado, da, pp.* of PRESENTAR.
Presentador, ra [pray-sen-tah-dor', rah], *m.* & *f.* Presenter, one that presents; one who offers a benefice.
Presentalla [pray-sen-tahl'-lyah], *f.* Gift offered by the faithful to the saints.
Presentáneamente [pray-sen-tah'-nay-ah-men-tay], *adv.* (Obs.) At once, without delay.
Presentar [pray-sen-tar'], *va.* 1. To present, to exhibit to view. 2. To present, to favour with a gift, to offer openly and freely. 3. To present or prefer to ecclesiastical benefices. *Presentar la batalla,* To offer battle. *Presentar la bolina mayor,* (Naut.) To snatch the main bow-line. *Presentar el costado,* (Naut.) To bring the broadside to bear. *Presentar la proa al viento,* (Naut.) To head the wind. *Presentar la proa a las olas,* (Naut.) To head the sea.—*vr.* To appear in a court of justice; to present one's self before any one.
Presente [pray-sen'-tay], *a.* 1. Present, being face to face. 2. (Gram.) Present, one of the tenses of verbs; in this last sense it is also used as a substantive. 3. Present: applied to the time now passing, or what is now in its course.—*m.* Present, gift, keepsake. *Al presente* or *de presente,* At present, now. *Tener presente,* To bear in mind. *Hacer presente,* (1) To state, to set forth, to inform. (2) To consider one as present (for emoluments, etc.). *La presente,* The present writing (these presents). *Ni ausente sin culpa; ni presente sin disculpa,* Those absent are always blamed; those present always have excuses.
Presentemente, *adv.* Presently, at present, now.
Presentero [pray-sen-tay'-ro], *m.* Presenter; one who offers a benefice.
Presentillo [pray-sen-teel'-lyo], *m. dim.* A small gift.
Presentimiento [pray-sen-te-me-en'-to], *m.* Presentiment, foreboding, misgiving.
Presentir [pray-sen-teer'], *va.* To have a presentiment of a future event, to foresee, to forebode.
Presera [pray-say'-rah], *f.* (Bot.) Goose-grass, cleavers. *V.* AMOR DE HORTELANO.
Presero [pray-say'-ro], *m.* The person who has the care of a dam or dike.
Preservación [pray-ser-vah-the-on'], *f.* Preservation, conservation.
Preservador, ra [pray-ser-vah-dor', rah], *m.* & *f.* Preserver.
Preservar [pray-ser-var'], *va.* To preserve, to defend from evil; to save.
Preservativamente, *adv.* Preservatively.
Preservativo [pray-ser-vah-tee'-vo], *m.* Preservative, preventive.
Preservativo, va [pray-ser-vah-tee'-vo, vah], *a.* Preservative, having the power of preserving.
Presidencia [pray-se-den'-the-ah], *f.* 1. Presidency. 2. Chairmanship (of a committee, etc.)
Presidenta [pray-se-den'-tah], *f.* President's wife; moderatrix.
Presidente [pray-se-den'-tay], *m.* 1. President, one placed at the head of others; chairman; speaker; judge. 2. President, the chief executive officer of a republic.
Presidiar [pray-se-de-ar'], *va.* To garrison a place.
Presidiario [pray-se-de-ah'-re-o], *m.* A criminal condemned to hard labour or banishment in a garrison.
Presidio [pray-see'-de-o], *m.* 1. Garrison of soldiers. 2. Fortress garrisoned by soldiers. 3. Assistance, aid, help, protection. 4. Place destined for punishing criminals by hard labour; bridewell, house of correction; penitentiary. 5. Punishment by hard labour.
Presidir [pray-se-deer'], *va.* To preside in an assembly, community, meeting, etc.

(*Yo presiento, yo presienta; él presintió;* from *Presentir. V.* ADHERIR.)

Presilla [pray-seel'-lyah], *f.* 1. A small string with which any thing is tied or fastened. 2. Loop in clothes, which serves as a button-hole. 3. Sort of linen. *Presilla de un sombrero,* Loop for a hat.
Presión [pray-se-on'], *f.* Pressure. *Presión arterial,* Blood pressure. *Hacer presión,* To pressure, to try to influence.
Preso, sa [pray'-so, sah], *m.* & *f.* 1. Prisoner.
Preso, sa [pray'-so, sah], *pp. irr.* of PRENDER. Taken.
Prespiración [pres-pe-rah-the-on'], *f.* Penetration of water into the earth.
Prest, *m.* *V.* PRE.
Presta [pres'-tah], *f.* (Bot. Prov.) *V.* HIERBABUENA or MENTA.

Prestación [pres-tah-the-on'], *f.* (Law) Act of lending or granting.

Prestadizo, za [pres-tah-dee'-tho, thah], *a.* That may be lent or borrowed.

Prestado, da [pres-tah'-do, dah], *a.* & *pp.* of PRESTAR. Lent. *Tomar prestado*, To borrow. *Dar prestado*, To lend. *De prestado*, For a short time; improperly.

Prestador, ra [pres-tah-dor', rah], *m.* & *f.* Lender; one who lends money at usurious interest.

Prestamente, *adv.* Speedily, promptly, quickly.

Prestamera [pres-tah-may'-rah], *f.* A kind of ecclesiastical benefice or sinecure which does not require personal attendance.

Prestamería [pres-tah-may-ree'-ah], *f.* Dignity of an ecclesiastical sinecure.

Prestamero [pres-tah-may'-ro], *m.* Incumbent of a *prestamera*, or ecclesiastical sinecure; he who holds a benefice which does not require personal attendance.

Prestamista [pres-tah-mees'-tah], *com.* Money-lender.

Préstamo [pres'-tah-mo], *m.* Loan. *V.* EMPRÉSTITO.

Prestancia [pres-tahn'-the-ah], *f.* Excellence. *V.* EXCELENCIA.

Prestante [pres-tahn'-tay], *a.* *V.* EXCELENTE.

Prestar [pres-tar'], *va.* 1. To lend, to grant the use of any thing. *Tomar prestado*, or *prestar de N.*, (Coll.) To borrow from such a one. 2. To credit, to give credit. 3. To aid, to assist. 4. To give, to communicate. 5. (Prov.) To extend, to expand. 6. (Law) To pay the interest, duty, etc., which is ordered. *Prestar paciencia*, To bear with patience the frowns of fortune. —*vn.* 1. To be useful, to contribute to the attainment of any object. 2. To guard, to preserve: applied to God, who lends all things.—*vr.* To offer one's self, to agree to any thing.

Preste [pres'-tay], *m.* Priest who celebrates the high mass. *Preste Juan*, Prester John, title of the Abyssinian monarchs, because anciently the king was a priest.

Préster [pres'-ter], *m.* 1. Hurricane. 2. Prester, meteor like lightning.

Presteza [pres-tay'-thah], *f.* Quickness, promptitude, haste, speed, nimbleness.

Prestidigitación [pres-te-de-he-tah-the-on'], *f.* Legerdemain, sleight of hand, jugglery.

Prestidigitador [pres-te-de-he-tah-dor'], *m.* Juggler, prestidigitator.

Prestidigitar [pres-te-de-he-tar'], *va.* To juggle, to perform feats of sleight of hand.

Préstido [pres'-te-do], *m.* (Obs.) *V.* EMPRÉSTITO.

Prestigiador [pres-te-he-ah-dor'], *m.* Cheat, juggler, impostor.

Prestigiar [pres-te-he-ar'], *va.* (Obs.) To cheat, to juggle.

Prestigio [pres-tee'-he-o], *m.* 1. Conjuring, juggling, imposture. 2. Sleight of hand, legerdemain. 3. Prestige, fame, favourable reputation. *Tener buen* or *mal prestigio de una persona*, (Coll.) To be well or ill inclined to a person. *Tener una cosa buen* or *mal prestigio*, To forebode good or evil from an affair.

Prestigioso, sa [pres-te-he-o'-so, sah], *a.* Deceitful, illusory, prestigious.

Prestimonio [pres-te-mo'-ne-o], *m.* Prebend for the maintenance of poor clergymen, on condition of their saying some short prayers; prestimony.

Prestiño [pres-tee'-nyo], *m.* *V.* PESTIÑO.

Prestito [pres-tee'-to], *adv.* Quickly, promptly.

Presto, ta [pres'-to, tah], *a.* 1. Quick, prompt, ready, diligent. 2. Ready, prepared, disposed.

Presto [pres'-to], *adv.* Soon, quickly, speedily. *De presto*, Promptly, swiftly.

Presumible [pray-soo-mee'-blay], *a.* Presumable, supposable.

Presumidico, ica, illo, illa, ito, ita [pray-soo-me-dee'-co], *a. dim.* Confident, a little presumptuous.

Presumido, da [pray-soo-mee'-do, dah], *a.* Presumptuous, arrogant, insolent, forward.—*pp.* of PRESUMIR.

Presumir [pray-soo-meer'], *va.* To presume, to suppose, to suspect, to conjecture.—*vn.* To presume, to boast, to form confident opinions, to make arrogant attempts.

Presunción [pray-soon-the-on'], *f.* 1. Presumption, supposition, conjecture. 2. Presumptuousness, blind and arrogant confidence; vanity, conceitedness. 3. Suspicion.

Presuntamente, *adv.* Presumptively.

Presuntivamente, *adv.* Conjecturally.

Presuntivo, va [pray-soon-tee'-vo, vah], *a.* 1. Presumptive, taken by previous supposition. 2. Presumptive, supposed.

Presunto, ta [pray-soon'-to, tah], *pp. irr.* of PRESUMIR. Presumed.

Presuntuosamente, *adv.* Presumptuously, arrogantly.

Presuntuoso, sa [pray-soon-too-oh'-so, sah], *a.* Presumptuous, vain, arrogant, insolent.

Presuponer [pray-soo-po-nerr'], *va.* To presuppose, to take for granted.

Presuposición [pray-soo-po-se-the-on'], *f.* Presupposition, presupposal, pretext.

Presupuesto [pray-soo-poo-es'-to], *m.* 1. Motive, pretext, pretence. 2. An estimate, calculation; budget of state. 3. Supposition.

Presupuesto, ta [pray-soo-poo-es'-to, tah], *pp. irr.* of PRESUPONER.

Presura [pray-soo'-rah], *f.* 1. Hurry, haste, promptitude. 2. Oppression, pressure, anxiety. 3. Eagerness, importunity.

Presurosamente, *adv.* Hastily, promptly.

Presuroso, sa [pray-soo-ro'-so, sah], *a.* Hasty, prompt, quick; light, nimble.

Pretal [pray-tahl'], *m.* Poitrel, breastplate, or breast-leather of a horse.

Pretender [pray-ten-derr'], *va.* 1. To pretend, to claim, to solicit. 2. To try, to attempt.

Pretendiente, ta [pray-ten-de-en'-tay, tah], *m.* & *f.* Pretender, candidate, office-hunter, solicitor.

Pretensión [pray-ten-se-on'], *f.* 1. Pretension, solicitation for obtaining something. 2. Pretension, claim.

Pretenso, sa [pray-ten'-so, sah], *pp. irr.* of PRETENDER.

Pretensor, ra [pray-ten-sor', rah], *m.* & *f.* Pretender, claimant.

Pretera [pray-tay'-rah], *f.* Backgammon.

Preterición [pray-tay-re-the-on'], *f.* 1. Preterition, the act of going past; the state of being past. 2. (Law) Preterition, the act of omitting lawful children in a last will.

Preterir [pray-tay-reer'], *va.* (Law) To omit lawful children in a last will.

Pretérito, ta [pray-tay'-re-to, tah], *a.* 1. Preterite, past. 2. (Gram.) Preterite: applied to past tenses of verbs.

Pretermisión [pray-ter-me-se-on'], *f.* Preterition, pretermission.

Pretermitir [pray-ter-me-teer'], *va.* To omit, to pretermit, to pass by.

Preternatural [pray-ter-nah-too-rahl'], *a.* Preternatural.

Preternaturalizar [pray-ter-nah-too-rah-le-thar'], *va.* To pervert, to render preternatural.

Preternaturalmente, *adv.* Preternaturally.

Pretexta [pray-tex'-tah], *f.* A long gown worn by magistrates of ancient Rome.

Pretextar [pray-tex-tar'], *va.* To make use of a pretext, to feign an excuse.

Pretexto [pray-tex'-to], *m.* Pretext, pretence, mask, cover.

Pretil [pray-teel'], *m.* Battlement, breastwork.

Pretina [pray-tee'-nah], *f.* 1. Girdle, waistband; belt. 2. Waist; every-thing which girds or surrounds. *Meter en pretina*, (Met.) To crush insolence; to oblige a person to the due performance of his duty.

Pretinazo [pray-te-nah'-tho], *m.* Blow given with a girdle.

Pretinero [pray-te-nay'-ro], *m.* One who makes girdles.

Pretinilla [pray-te-neel -lyah], *f. dim.* A small belt or girdle.

Pretor [pray-tor'], *m.* 1. Pretor, a magistrate in ancient Rome. 2. (fr. *Prieto*) Blackness of the waters where tunny-fish abound.

Pretoría [pray-to-re'-ah], *f.* Dignity of a pretor. *V.* PRETURA.

Pretorial, Pretoriano, na [pray-to-re-ahl'], *a.* Pretorian.

Pretoriense [pray-to-re-en'-say], *a.* Belonging to the pretor's palace.

Pretorio [pray-to'-re-o], *m.* Place in ancient Rome where the pretor resided and administered justice.

Pretorio, ria [pray-to'-re-o, ah], *a.* *V.* PRETORIAL.

Pretura [pray-too'-rah], *f.* Pretorship.

Prevalecer [pray-vah-lay-therr'], *vn.* 1. To prevail, to predominate, to outshine. 2. To take root: applied to plants. 3. To grow and increase (used of things not material).

Prevaleciente [pray-vah-lay-the-en'-tay], *pa.* & *a.* Prevalent; prevailing.

Prevalente [pray-vah-len'-tay], *a.* Prevalent.

Prevalerse [pray-vah-lerr'-say], *vr.* To use any thing, or to avail one's self of it; to prevail.

(*Yo prevalezco, yo prevalezca*, from *Prevalecer.* *V.* CONOCER.)

Prevaricación [pray-vah-re-cah-the-on'], *f.* Prevarication.

Prevaricador, ra [pray-vah-re-cah-dor', rah], *m.* & *f.* 1. Prevaricator. 2. Turn-coat.

Prevaricar [pray-vah-re-car'], *vn.* 1. To fail in one's word, duty, or judgment. 2. (Coll.) To turn the coat, to change sides.

Prevaricato [pray-vah-re-cah'-to], *m.* (Law) Prevarication in a solicitor or advocate.

Prevención [pray-ven-the-on'], *f.* 1. Disposition, preparation. 2. Supply of provisions; sustenance, subsistence. 3. Foresight, forecast, forethought. 4. Advice, intimation, warning, instruction, monition. 5. Prevention, preoccupation. 6. (Mil.) Police guard. *A prevención* or *de prevención*, By way of precaution. (Met.) Prejudice, pro or contra.

(*Yo prevengo, yo prevenga, previne*, from *Prevenir.* *V.* VENIR.)

Prevenidamente, *adv.* Beforehand previously.

Prevenido, da [pray-vay-nee'-do, dah], *a.* & *pp.* of PREVENIR. 1. Prepared, provided; plentiful, abundant. 2 Provident, careful, cautious.

Preveniente [pray-vay-ne-en' tay], *pa* Predisposing, prevenient

Prevenir [pray-vay-neer'], *va.* 1. To

prepare, to arrange beforehand. 2. To foresee, to foreknow. 3. To prevent or anticipate, to forestall. 4. To advise, to caution, to give notice. 5. To prevent, to impede, to hinder. 6. To prevent, to preoccupy. 7. To ingratiate one's self. 8. (Acad.) To come upon, to surprise.—*vr.* To be prepared; to be predisposed; to guard or be in a state of defence.

Preventivamente, *adv.* Preventively.

Preventivo, va [pray-ven-te'-vo, vah], *a.* Preventive; previously prepared or arranged.

(*Yo preveo, yo prevea, él previó,* from *Prever.* *V.* VER.)

Prever [pray-verr'], *va.* To foresee, to foreknow.

Previlejar, *va.* (Obs.) To privilege. *V.* PRIVILEGIAR.

Previo, via [pray'-ve-o, ah], *a.* Previous, antecedent, prior.

Previsión [pray-ve-se-on'], *f.* Foresight, foreknowledge, prescience, forecast.

Previsor, ra [pray-ve-sor', rah], *m.* & *f.* One who foresees.

Previsto, ta [pray-vees'-to, tah], *pp. irr.* of PREVER.

Prez [preth'], *m.* 1. Honour or glory gained by a meritorious act. 2. (Obs.) Notoriety.

Priapismo [pre-ah-pees'-mo], *m.* (Med.) Priapism, a disease.

Priesa [pre-ay'-sah], *f.* *V.* PRISA. *Cuanto más priesa, menos se adelanta,* (prov.) The more haste the less speed.

Prietamente, *adv.* *V.* APRETADAMENTE.

Prieto, ta [pre-ay'-to, tah], *a.* 1. Blackish, of a very dark colour. 2. Narrow-minded, illiberal. 3. Close-fisted, mean. 4. Tight, compressed.

Prima [pree'-mah], *f.* 1. Morning, the first three hours of the day. 2. Prime, one of the seven canonical hours. 3. Tonsure. 4. (Mil.) The first quarter of the night, from eight to eleven o'clock. 5. Treble, the most slender string of stringed instruments. 6. (Com.) Premium given for insurance. 7. Premium, the price in excess beyond the face value of a paper. 8. The obligation of paying the agreed rate per cent. if a paper is not taken up or a purchase completed. 9. Female cousin.

Primacía [pre-mah-thee'-ah], *f.* 1. Priority, precedence in time or place. 2. Primateship, primacy, mastership.

Primacial [pre-mah-the-ahl'], *a.* Relating to primacy.

Primada [pre-mah'-dah], *f.* (Coll.) Trick, of which some one is the object as being slow-witted.

Primado [pre-mah'-do], *m.* 1. Primeness, the state of being first. 2. Primate, the chief ecclesiastic of a country.

Primado, da [pre-mah'-do, dah], *a.* Primary, first in intention; first in dignity. *Iglesia primada,* Primacial church.

Primal, la [pre-mahl', lah], *a.* Yearling: applied to a ewe or a goat.

Primal [pre-mahl'], *m.* Lace, a plaited cord of silk.

Primamente, *adv.* (Obs.) Finely, handsomely.

Primariamente, *adv.* Principally, chiefly, primarily.

Primario, ria [pre-mah'-re-o, ah], *a.* Principal, primary.

Primario [pre-mah'-re-o], *m.* Professor who lectures at the hour of prime.

Primavera [pre-mah-vay'-rah], *f.* 1. The spring season. 2. Kind of flowered silk. 3 (Bot.) Primrose. Primula veris. 4. (Met.) Season of beauty, health and vigour; prime.

Primaveral [pre-mah-vay-rahl'], *a.* Springlike.

Primazgo [pre-math'-go], *m.* Cousinship, relation of consanguinity among cousins.

Primearse [pre-may-ar'-say], *vr.* To treat each other as cousins.

Primer [pre-merr'], *a.* First; used before nouns. *V.* PRIMERO.

Primera [pre-may'-rah], *f.* Kind of game at cards.

Primeramente, *adv.* First; in the first place, mainly, primely.

Primaria, *f.* (Obs.) *V.* PRIMACÍA.

Primerizo, za [pre-may-ree'-tho, thah], *a.* 1. First, that antecedes or is preferred to other persons or things. 2. Firstling, first produced or brought forth; primiparous.

Primeriza [pre-may-ree'-thah], *f.* Woman who has born her first child; primipara.

Primero, ra [pre-may'-ro, rah], *a.* 1. First, the ordinal number of one. 2. Chief, principal, leading. 3. Superior, most excellent. 4. Prior, former. *De buenas a primeras,* All at once, rashly, without reflection.

Primero, *adv.* First, rather, sooner. *Primero pediría limosna que prestado,* He would rather beg than borrow. *De primero,* At the beginning, before.

Primeros auxilios [pre-may'-ros ah-ooc-see'-lee-os], *m. pl.* First aid, assistance.

Primevo, va [pre-may'-vo, vah], *a.* Primeval, original.

Primicia [pre-mee'-the-ah], *f.* 1. First-fruits of any thing. 2. Offering of the first-fruits. *Primicias.* First-fruits; first production of the imagination or mind.

Primicial [pre-me-the-ahl'], *a.* Primitial, relating to first-fruits.

Primichón [pre-me-chone'], *m.* Skein of fine, soft silk, for embroidering.

Primigenio, nia [pre-me-hay'-ne-o, ah], *a.* Primogenial, first-born.

Primilla [pre-meel'-lyah], *f.* 1. (Coll.) Pardon of the first fault committed. 2. (Dim.) A little female cousin.

Primísimo, ma [pre-mee'-se-mo, mah], *a. sup.* Uncommonly neat, extremely spruce.

Primitivamente, *adv.* Originally.

Primitivo, va [pre-me-tee'-vo, vah], *a.* Primitive, original, primeval.

Primo, ma [pree'-mo, mah], *a.* 1. First, the ordinal number of one. 2. Of the first rank, excellent. *Hilo primo,* Fine waxed thread, used by shoemakers.

Primo [pree'-mo], *m.* 1. Cousin. *Primo hermano,* First cousin, cousin german. 2. (Coll.) Simpleton, one easily deceived. *Primos,* Cousins, an appellation given by the kings of Spain to the grandees.—*adv.* First, in the first place.

Primogénito, ta [pre-mo-hay'-ne-to, tah], *a.* Primigenial, first-born, firstling, primogenitive.

Primogenitura [pre-mo-hay-ne-too'-rah], *f.* Primogeniture, seniority, the right of the first-born.

Primoprimus [pre-mo-pree'-moos], *m.* The first impulse or emotion of the mind.

Primor [pre-mor'], *m.* 1. Beauty; dexterity, ability, accuracy, exquisiteness, excellence. 2. Nicety, neatness of workmanship.

Primordial [pre-mor-de-ahl'], *a.* Primordial, original.

Primorear [pre-mo-ray-ar'], *vn.* To perform with elegance and neatness.

Primorosamente, *adv.* Finely, nicely, neatly, handsomely, excellently.

Primoroso, sa [pre-mo-ro'-so, sah], *a.* Neat, elegant, excellent, fine, curious, handsome; graceful, dexterous. *Artesano de manos primorosas,* A neat, able workman.

Primula [pree'-moo-lah], *f.* (Bot.) Primrose, cowslip. Primula vulgaris et veris.

Princesa [prin-thay'-sah], *f.* 1. Princess, the consort or daughter of a prince, or the heiress to a principality. 2. Princess; in Spain, the apparent heiress to the crown.

Principada [prin-the-pah'-dah], *f.* Act of authority or superiority performed by him who has no right to execute it.

Principado [prin-the-pah'-do], *m.* 1. Princedom, the rank, estate, or power of a prince. 2. Principality, the territory of a prince. 3. Pre-eminence, superior excellence.

Principal [prin-the-pahl'], *a.* 1. Principal, chief, capital, essential. 2. Illustrious, renowned, celebrated. 3. Foremost, first, chief. *Casa principal,* Capital house, hotel. *Cuarto principal,* Apartments on the first floor or story.

Principal [prin-the-pahl'], *m.* 1. In a garrison, the main guard. 2. Principal, capital, stock. 3. Principal, head of a commercial establishment.

Principalidad [prin-the-pah-le-dahd'], *f.* Principalness, the state of being principal; nobility.

Principalmente, *adv.* Principally, mainly, chiefly.

Príncipe [preen'-the-pay], *m.* 1. Prince, a sovereign or chief ruler. 2. Prince, a sovereign of rank next to a king. 3. Prince, son of a king, kinsman of a sovereign: popularly, the eldest son of him that reigns under any denomination is called a prince. 4. Prince, the most eminent, chief, or principal of any body of men. 5. Prince, appellation of honour granted by kings. 6. With bee-masters, the young queen bees not yet in a state to breed. *Como un príncipe,* Princely, or in a princelike manner.

Principela [prin-the-pay'-lah], *f.* A sort of light camlet.

Principiador, ra [prin-the-pe-ah-dor', rah], *m.* & *f.* Beginner.

Principiante [prin-the-pe-ahn'-tay], *m.* Beginner, a learner.

Principiar [prin-the-pe-ar'], *va.* To commence, to begin.

Principiera [prin-the-pe-ay'-rah], *f.* (Prov.) A small metal saucepan in which broth is warmed.

Principillo, Principito [prin-the-peel'-lyo], *m. dim.* A petty prince.

Principio [prin-thee'-pe-o], *m.* 1. Beginning, commencement. 2. Principle, element, constituent part. 3. Principle, original cause; ground of action, motive; origin, fountain. 4. Principle, first position, fundamental truth. 5. Principle, tenet on which morality is founded. 6. Any of the courses served up at table besides the boiled meat. 7. (Chem.) An element or body not decomposable by means now at command. *Principios,* The preliminaries to a volume, as license, approbation, dedication, etc. *Al principio* or *a los principios,* At the beginning. *Del principio al fin,* From beginning to end. *Bajo el mismo principio,* On the same ground. *A principios del mes,* Early in the month.

Principote [prin-the-po'-tay], *m.* (Coll.) He who assumes a lofty air and importance; a petty prince.

Pringada [prin-gah'-dah], *f.* Toasted bread steeped in gravy.

Pringar [prin-gar'], *va.* 1. To baste

meat which is roasting. 2. To stain with grease, to scald with boiling fat; to tar a person: this formerly was the punishment of slaves. 3. To wound; to ill-treat. 4. To meddle, to interfere; to take a share in.—*vr.* To draw unlawful advantage from a thing intrusted to one's care.

Pringón, na [prin-gone', nah], *a.* Nasty, dirty, greasy.

Pringón, *m.* 1. The act of begreasing one's self. 2. Stain of grease.

Pringoso, sa [prin-go'-so, sah], *a.* Greasy, fat.

Pringue [preen'-gay], *com.* 1. Grease, lard. 2. Greasiness, oiliness, fatness. 3. The act of begreasing or staining with grease.

Pringuera [prin-gay'-rah], *f.* Dripping-pan.

Prior [pre-or'], *m.* 1. Prior, the superior of convents or religious houses. 2. (Prov.) Rector, curate. 3. Prior in some cathedrals. 4. President of the *Consulado*, in Andalusia, a court appointed to try and decide causes concerning trade and navigation.—*a.* Prior, precedent.

Priora [pre-o'-rah], *f.* Prioress.

Prioral [pre-o-rahl'], *a.* Belonging to a prior or prioress.

Priorato [pre-o-rah'-to], *m.* 1. Priorship, dignity of a prior or prioress. 2. District of the jurisdiction of a prior. 3. Priory of Benedictines.

Priorazgo [pre-o-rath'-go], *m.* Priorship. *V.* PRIORATO.

Prioridad [pre-o-re-dahd'], *f.* Priority; precedence in time or place.

Prioste [pre-os'-tay], *m.* Steward of a brotherhood or confraternity.

Prisa [pree'-sah], *f.* 1. Urgency, celerity, promptness in executing. 2. Skirmish, surprise, confused and hot fight. (Acad.) 3. Press, crowd. (2 and 3 archaic.) *A toda prisa,* With the greatest promptitude. *Darse prisa,* To hurry one's self. *Estar de prisa,* To be in a hurry. *Andar de prisa,* To be much occupied, to be driven for time. *Acabóse con la prisa,* All done. *Vivir de prisa,* To live fast, to abuse bodily and mental vigour. *A más prisa, gran* (or *más*) *vagar,* The more haste, the less speed.

Priscilianismo [pris-the-le-ah-nees'-mo], *m.* The heresy of Priscillian (the first Christian punished with death for heresy).

Prisco [prees'-co], *m.* A kind of peach.

Prisión [pre-se-on'], *f.* 1. Seizure, capture, apprehension. 2. Prison, jail. 3. Any thing which binds or holds physically. 4. Bond, union; cement or cause of union.—*pl.* Chains, shackles, fetters.

Prisioncilla, ita [pre-se-on-theel'-lyah], *f. dim.* A small prison or jail.

Prisionero [pre-se-o-nay'-ro], *m.* 1. Prisoner, a soldier taken by an enemy. 2. Captivated by affection or passion.

Prisma [prees'-mah], *m.* 1. (Geom.) Prism. 2. A triangular prism of glass.

Prismático, ca [pris-mah'-te-co, cah], *a.* Prismatic.

Prismatizar [pris-mah-te-thar'], *va.* To decompose light by a prism.

Priste [prees'-tay], *m.* Saw-fish. Pristis.

Prístino, na [prees'-te-no, nah], *a.* Pristine, first, original.

Prisuelo [pre-soo-ay'-lo], *m.* Muzzle, which serves to keep the mouths of ferrets shut.

Pritaneo [pre-tah-nay'-o], *m.* Prytaneum, senate-house in Athens.

Privación [pre-vah-the-on'], *f.* 1. Privation, want. 2. Privation, the act of degrading from rank or office. 3. (Met.) Deprivation of any thing desired, loss.

Privada [pre-vah'-dah], *f.* 1. Privy, water-closet. 2. Filth thrown into the street.

Privadamente, *adv.* Privately, privily; separately.

Privadero [pre-vah-day'-ro], *m.* One who cleans wells or cesspools.

Privado, da [pre-vah'-do, dah], *a.* & *pp.* of PRIVAR. 1. Privy, private, performed in presence of a few. 2. Private, particular, personal, not relating to the public.

Privado, *m.* Favourite, minion, court minion.

Privanza [pre-vahn'-thah], *f.* Favour, protection; familiar intercourse between a prince or great personage and a person of inferior rank.

Privar [pre-var'], *va.* 1. To deprive, to despoil; to dispossess of a public place or employment. 2. To prohibit, to interdict. 3. To suspend sensation.—*vn.* To enjoy the peculiar protection of a prince or great personage. —*vr.* To deprive one's self.

Privativamente, *adv.* Conclusively, solely, privatively.

Privativo, va [pre-vah-tee'-vo, vah], *a.* 1. Privative, causing privation. 2. Special, singular, particular, peculiar; exclusive.

Privilegiadamente, *adv.* In a privileged manner.

Privilegiar [pre-ve-lay-he-ar'], *va.* To privilege, to grant a privilege.

Privilegiativo, va, *a.* Containing a privilege.

Privilegio [pre-ve-lay'-he-o], *m.* 1. Privilege, immunity; grant, concession, grace; liberty, franchise; faculty. 2. Patent, copyright. *Privilegio del fuero,* Exemption from secular jurisdiction, enjoyed by ecclesiastics.

Pro [pro], *com.* Profit, benefit, advantage. *V.* PROVECHO. *Buena pro,* Much good may it do you. *En pro,* In favour of, for the benefit of. *Hombre de pro,* A worthy man. *Pro,* equivalent to *vice,* one acting in place of another; as, *Procónsul.*

Pro. A Latin prefix signifying forward or in behalf of.

Proa [pro'-ah], *f.* Prow of a ship, foreship, bow. *Por nuestra proa,* (Naut.) Ahead of us. *Llevar la proa hacia la mar,* (Naut.) To stand off, to stand out to sea. *Poner la proa al rumbo,* (Naut.) To stand on the course.

Proal [pro-ahl'], *a.* Relating to the prow; forward.

Probabilidad [pro-bah-be-le-dahd'], *f.* Probability, likelihood, credibility.

Probabilísimo, ma [pro-bah-be-lee'-se-mo, mah], *a. sup.* Most probable.

Probabilismo [pro-bah-be-lees'-mo], *m.* Probability, doctrine of probable opinions.

Probabilista [pro-bah-be-lees'-tah], *m.* Probabilist, one who acts upon probabilities.

Probable [pro-bah'-blay], *a.* Probable, likely, credible, capable of proof.

Probablemente, *adv.* Probably, credibly, likely.

Probación [pro-bah-the-on'], *f.* Proof, probation, trial, examination. *Año de probación,* The year of probation, the novitiate.

Probado, da [pro-bah'-do, dah], *a.* Proved, tried.—*pp.* of PROBAR.

Probador, ra [pro-bah-dor', rah], *m.* & *f.* 1. Taster, one who tries or proves any thing. 2. (Obs.) Defender, advocate.

Probadura [pro-bah-doo'-rah], *f.* Trial, the act of tasting or trying any thing.

Probanza [pro-bahn'-thah], *f.* Proof, evidence.

Probar [pro-bar'], *va.* 1. To try, to examine the quality of a thing. 2. To prove, to give evidence, to justify, to make good. 3. To taste, to try by the mouth. 4. With the preposition *a* and an infinitive mode, it signifies to attempt, to endeavour. *Probó a levantarse y no pudo,* He attempted to rise and could not.—*vn.* To suit, to fit, to agree. *Me probó bien el país,* The country agreed well with me.

Probática [pro-bah'-te-cah], *a.* Applied to a pool near Solomon's temple.

Probativo, va. Probatorio, ria [pro-bah-tee'-vo, vah], *a.* Probatory, probationary.

Probatoria [pro-bah-toh'-re-ah], *f* Legal investigation; preliminary examination.

Probatura [pro-bah-too'-rah], *f.* (Coll.) *V.* PROBADURA.

Probe, *a.* (Obs.) *V.* POBRE.

Probeta [pro-bay'-tah], *f.* 1. A kind of barometer. 2. Powder-prover, a device for testing the explosive force of powder. 3. (Chem.) A test-tube.

Probidad [pro-be-dahd'], *f.* Probity, honesty, sincerity, veracity.

Problema [pro-blay'-mah], *m.* 1. Problem, a doubtful question proposed. 2. (Geom.) Problem, practical proposition.

Problemáticamente, *adv.* Problematically.

Problemático, ca [pro-blay-mah'-te-co, cah], *a.* Problematical, disputable, unsettled.

Probo, ba [pro'-bo, bah], *a.* Upright, honest.

Probóscide [pro-bos'-the-day], *f.* (Non-Acad.) 1. Proboscis, the trunk of an elephant. 2. Proboscis, the projecting sucking mouth-parts of certain insects. *V.* TROMPA.

Procacidad [pro-cah-the-dahd'], *f.* Procacity, petulance, insolence, forwardness.

Procaína [pro-cah-ee'-nah], *f.* Novocaine.

Procaz [pro-cath'], *a.* Procacious, petulant, forward, insolent.

Procedencia [pro-thay-den'-the-ah], *f.* 1. Derivation; the act of proceeding. 2. The place from which persons or articles come.

Procedente [pro-thay-den'-tay], *pa.* 1. Coming from, proceeding from. 2. According to legal rules, according to law.

Proceder [pro-thay-derr'], *m.* Procedure, manner of proceeding, conduct, demeanour, management.

Proceder [pro-thay-derr'], *vn.* 1. To proceed, to go on. 2. To issue, to proceed from. 3. To behave, to conduct one's self. 4. To proceed, to prosecute a design. 5. (Law) To proceed against, to carry on a judicial process. 6. To proceed by generation.

Procedimiento [pro-thay-de-me-en'-to], *m.* 1. Proceeding, procedure, transaction. 2. Proceeding or legal procedure.

Procela [pro-thay'-lah], *a.* (Poet.) Storm, tempest.

Proceloso, sa [pro-thay-lo'-so, sah], *a.* Tempestuous, stormy.

Prócer [pro'-ther], *a.* Tall, lofty, elevated.—*m.* Person who occupies an exalted station or is high in office; the grandees and high-titled nobility of Spain. *Cámara de Próceres,* The House of Lords.

Procerato [pro-thay-rah'-to], *m.* Exalted station.

Proceridad [pro-thay-re-dahd'], *f.* 1. Procerity, tallness, height of stature. 2. Elevation, eminence.

Procero, Prócero, *a.* *V.* PRÓCER.

Procesado [pro-thay-sah'-do], *a.* 1. Applied to the writings in a process. 2. Comprised in a criminal suit.—*pp.* of PROCESAR.

Procesal [pro-thay-sahl'], *a.* Belonging to a process or lawsuit.

Procesar [pro-thay-sar'], *va.* (Law) 1. To indict, to accuse, to inform against, to sue criminally. 2. To institute a suit.

Procesión [pro-thay-se-on'], *f.* 1. Procession, proceeding from another. 2. Procession, train marching in ceremonious solemnity; parade.

Procesional [pro-thay-se-o-nahl'], *a.* Processional or processionary; relating to processions.

Procesionalmente, *adv.* Processionally.

Procesionario [pro-thay-se-o-nah'-re-o], *m.* Book carried about in processions.

Proceso [pro-thay'-so], *m.* 1. Process, lawsuit. 2. Judicial records concerning a lawsuit. *Error de proceso,* (Law. Prov.) One who by ability, although convicted, evades the fine. 3. Progress. *V.* PROGRESO. *Proceso en infinito,* Procession of an endless series.

Procidencia [pro-the-den'-the-ah], *f.* (Med.) Procidence.

Procinto [pro-theen'-to], *m.* Procinct, complete preparation.

Proción [pro-the-on'], *m.* (Ast.) Procyon, a star, the most conspicuous in the constellation Canis minor, famous for its variable proper motion.

Proclama [pro-clah'-mah], *f.* Proclamation, publication, banns of marriage.

Proclamación [pro-clah-mah-the-on'], *f.* 1. Proclamation, the publication of a decree by superior order. 2. Acclamation, public applause.

Proclamar [pro-clah-mar'], *va.* 1. To proclaim, to give public notice. 2. To bestow public praise, to shout.

Proclítico, ca [pro-clee'-te-co, cah], *a.* (Gram.) Proclitic, attached to a following word.

Proclive [pro-clee'-vay], *a.* Proclivous, inclining; disposed.

Proclividad [pro-cle-ve-dahd'], *f.* Proclivity; propensity to evil.

Proco [pro'-co], *m.* (Obs.) Wooer, suitor, lover.

Procomún, Procomunal [pro-co-moon'], *m.* A public utility.

Procónsul [pro-con'-sool], *m.* Proconsul.

Proconsulado [pro-con-soo-lah'-do], *m.* Proconsulship, office of proconsul or vice-consul.

Proconsular [pro-con-soo-lar'], *a.* Proconsular, vice-consular.

Procreación [pro-cray-ah-the-on'], *f.* Procreation, generation.

Procreador, ra [pro-cray-ah-dor', rah], *m.* & *f.* Procreator, generator, getter.

Procreante [pro-cray-ahn'-tay], *pa.* Procreating.

Procrear [pro-cray-ar'], *va.* To procreate, generate, produce.

Procronismo [pro-cro-nees'-mo], *m.* Prochronism, anachronism.

Procumbente [pro-coom-ben'-tay], *a.* (Bot.) Procumbent.

Procura [pro-coo'-rah], *f.* 1. Power of attorney. *V.* PROCURACIÓN. 2. (Prov.) *V.* PROCURADURÍA.

Procuración [pro-coo-rah-the-on'], *f.* 1. Care, diligence, careful management. 2. Power or letter of attorney. 3. Procurement, the act of procuring. 4. Place and office of an attorney or administrator. 5. *V.* PROCURADURÍA.

Procurador, ra [pro-coo-rah-dor', rah], *m.* & *f.* Procurer, obtainer, one that solicits.

Procurador, *m.* 1. Attorney, one who takes upon himself the charge of other people's business. 2. Proctor, attorney at law, solicitor.

Procuradora [pro-coo-rah-do'-rah], *f.* She who manages the affairs of a nunnery.

Procuraduría [pro-coo-rah-doo-ree'-ah], *f.* Attorney's office; the employment of an attorney; procurement; proctorship.

Procurante [pro-coo-rahn'-tay], *pa.* Solicitor, intendant.

Procurar [pro-coo-rar'], *va.* 1. To solicit, to adopt measures for attaining an end, to try. 2. To procure, to manage, to transact for another. 3. To act as an attorney. 4. To get, to obtain.

Procurrente [pro-coor-ren'-tay], *m.* Peninsula, a great mass of earth reaching into the sea: as all Italy.

Prodición [pro-de-the-on'], *f.* Treason, treachery.

Prodigalidad [pro-de-gah-le-dahd'], *f.* 1. Prodigality, profusion, waste, extravagance, lavishness. 2. Plenty, abundance.

Pródigamente [pro'-de-gah-men-tay], *adv.* Prodigally, lavishly, wastefully, profusely.

Prodigar [pro-de-gar'], *va.* To waste, to lavish, to misspend, to fling away.

Prodigiador [pro-de-he-ah-dor'], *m.* Prognosticator, foreteller.

Prodigio [pro-dee'-he-o], *m.* Prodigy, portent, monster; marvel.

Prodigiosamente, *adv.* Prodigiously, miraculously, marvellously, amazingly; monstrously, enormously; beautifully. *Ella cantó prodigiosamente,* She sung charmingly.

Prodigiosidad [pro-de-he-o-se-dahd'], *f.* Prodigiousness, portentousness.

Prodigioso, sa [pro-de-he-oh'-so, sah], *a.* 1. Prodigious, marvellous, extraordinary; monstrous. 2. Fine, exquisite, excellent.

Pródigo, ga [pro'-de-go, gah], *a.* Prodigal, wasteful, lavish; liberal, generous, munificent.

Prodrómico, ca [pro-dro'-me-co, cah], *a.* (Med.) Prodromic, relating to a prodrome.

Pródromo [pro'-dro-mo], *m.* (Med.) Prodrome, a sign of approaching disease.

Producción [pro-dooc-the-on'], *f.* 1. Production, growth, product. 2. Enunciation, mode of expressing one's self, enouncement.

Producibilidad [pro-doo-the-be-le-dahd'], *f.* Producibleness, productiveness.

Producible [pro-doo-thee'-blay], *a.* Producible.

Producidor, ra [pro-doo-the-dor', rah], *m.* & *f.* Producer, procreator.

Producir [pro-doo-theer'], *va.* 1. To produce, to bring forth, to engender, to generate. 2. (Law) To produce, to bring as evidence, to allege, to maintain, to exhibit. 3. To produce, to bear, as a vegetable. 4. To produce, as countries. 5. To produce, to cause, to occasion. 6. To yield revenue. 7. To quote, to cite.—*vr.* 1. To enounce or explain one's self. 2. To become manifest, to be published.

Productible [pro-dooc-tee'-blay], *a.* Capable of yielding some product; productible.

Productivo, va [pro-dooc-tee'-vo, vah], *a.* Productive, constitutive, originary.

Producto [pro-dooc'-to], *m.* 1. Product, something produced, as grain, fruit, metals; production. 2. Proceed, produce, fruit, growth. 3. (Math.) Product, quantity produced by multiplication. 4. Product, the final result of a chemical operation.—*Producto, ta, pp. irr.* of PRODUCIR.

(*Yo produzco, yo produzca; produje;* from PRODUCIR. *V.* CONDUCIR.)

Proejar [pro-ay-har'], *vn.* 1. To row against the wind or current. 2. To resist, to bear up under misfortunes.

Proel [pro-el'], *m.* (Naut.) Seaman stationed at the prow.

Proemial [pro-ay-me-ahl'], *a.* Proemial, preliminary, introductory.

Proemio [pro-ay'-me-o], *m.* Proem, preface, introduction.

Proeza [pro-ay'-thah], *f.* Prowess, valour, bravery.

Profanación [pro-fah-nah-the-on'], *f.* Profanation, profaneness, irreverence.

Profanador, ra [pro-fah-nah-dor', rah], *m.* & *f.* Profaner, polluter, violator.

Profanamente, *adv.* Profanely.

Profanamiento [pro-fah-nah-me-en'-to], *m.* *V.* PROFANACIÓN.

Profanar [pro-fah-nar'], *va.* 1. To profane, to violate. 2. To defile, to disgrace, to dishonour, to abuse.

Profanidad [pro-fah-ne-dahd'], *f.* 1. Indecency, immodesty, or excess in dress and outward show. 2. Want of competence or knowledge for handling a matter. (Note.—Indecency (or lewdness) is the Academy's equivalent; excess, etc., are given by the other authorities.)

Profano, na [pro-fah'-no, nah], *a.* 1. Profane, irreverent. 2. Worldly, irreligious. 3. Extravagant, flashy, loud, immodest or unchaste in dress and outward show. 4. Wanting in knowledge or authority upon a subject.

Profazar [pro-fah-thar'], *va.* (Obs.) To discredit, to speak ill of, to calumniate.

Profecía [pro-fay-thee'-ah], *f.* 1. Prophecy, supernatural knowledge and prediction of future events. 2. Conjecture, surmise.

Profecticio [pro-fec-tee -the-o], *a.* Acquired by a son who lives under his father's direction; derived from one's fathers.

Proferir [pro-fay-reer'], *va.* 1. To pronounce, to utter, to express, to name. 2. (Obs.) To proffer.

Profesante [pro-fay-sahn'-tay], *pa.* & *m.* & *f.* Professor; professing.

Profesar [pro-fay-sar'], *va.* 1. To profess, to declare openly, to teach publicly. 2. To be admitted into a religious order by making the vows. 3. To profess, to exercise, to evince.

Profesion [pro-fay-se-on'], *f.* 1. Profession, calling, vocation, occupation. 2. Declaration, assurance. 3. Custom, habit.

Profesional [pro-fay-se-o-nahl'], *a.* Professional; relating to or in accordance with a profession.

Profeso, sa [pro-fay'-so, sah], *a.* Professed: applied to those who have taken vows.

Profesor, ra [pro-fay-sor', rah], *m.* & *f.* Professor, teacher.

Profesorado [pro-fay-so-rah'-do], *m.* 1. Faculty, body of teachers. 2. Teaching profession.

Profeta [pro-fay'-tah], *m.* 1. Prophet, foreteller. 2. Title given to Mohammed by the Mussulmans.

Profetal [pro-fay-tahl'], *a.* Relating to prophecy.

Profetar [pro-fay-tar'], *va.* (Obs.) To prophesy.

Proféticamente, *adv.* Prophetically.

Profético, ca [pro-fay'-te-co, cah], *a.* Prophetic, prophetical.

Profetisa [pro-fay-tee'-sah], *f.* Prophetess.

Profetizar [pro-fay-te-thar'], *va.* 1. To prophesy; to predict. 2. To conjecture, to surmise.

Proficiente [pro-fe-the-en'-tay], *a.* Proficient, making progress in any business.

Proficuo, cua [pro-fee'-coo-o, ah], *a.* Profitable, useful, advantageous.

(*Yo profiero, yo profiera; él profirió*; from *Proferir.* V. ADHERIR.)

Profiláctica [pro-fe-lahc'-te-cah], *f.* (Med.) Hygiene, prophylactic medicine.

Profiláctico [pro-fe-lahc'-te-co], *a.* Prophylactic, preventive, preservative.

Profilaxis [pro-fe-lahk'-sis], *f.* Prophylaxis, preventive treatment of disease in an individual.

Prófugo, ga [pro'-foo-go, gah], *a.* Fugitive, vagabond.

Profundamente, *adv.* Profoundly, deeply; highly, acutely, high.

Profundar [pro-foon-dar'], *va.* (Obs.) To dig a thing deep. V. PROFUNDIZAR.

Profundidad [pro-foon-de-dahd'], *f.* 1. Profundity, depth, concavity. 2. Height, excellence, grandeur; impenetrability; intensity.

Profundizar [pro-foon-de-thar'], *va.* 1. To make deep, to dig deep, to deepen. 2. To penetrate, to dive into a matter; to fathom, to explore.

Profundo, da [pro-foon'-do, dah], *a.* 1. Profound, deep; descending far below the surface; low with respect to the neighbouring places. 2. Profound, intellectually deep, recondite. 3. Intense, dense; at full extent.

Profundo [pro-foon'-do], *m.* 1. (Poet.) Profound, the sea, the deep. 2. (Poet.) Hell.

Profusamente, *adv.* Profusely, lavishly, prodigally, extravagantly.

Profusión [pro-foo-se-on'], *f.* Profusion, lavishness, profuseness, extravagance, prodigality.

Profuso, sa [pro-foo'-so, sah], *a.* 1. Profuse, plentiful. 2. Lavish, prodigal; extravagant.

Progenie [pro-hay'-ne-ay], *f.* Progeny, race, offspring, issue.

Progenitor [pro-hay-ne-tor'], *m.* Progenitor, ancestor, forefather.

Progenitura [pro-hay-ne-too'-rah], *f.* V. PROGENIE and PRIMOGENITURA.

Progimnasma [pro-him-nahs'-mah], *m.* Essay, attempt; a preparatory exercise.

Progne [prog'-nay], *f.* (Poet.) The swallow.

Programa [pro-grah-mah], *m.* 1. Proclamation, public notice. 2. Theme, subject of a discourse, design, or picture. 3. Prospectus, program or programme, prearranged plan or course of proceedings; scheme of lectures by a professor, or order of exercises. 4. Specification according to which a certain procedure must be carried out, program. *Programa de estudios*, Curriculum.

Programación [pro-grah-mah-the-on'], *f.* Programing, programming.

Progresar [pro-gray-sar'], *vn.* To progress, make progress; to improve, better.

Progresión [pro-gray-se-on'], *f.* Progression, process; progressiveness.

Progresista [pro-gray-sees'-tah], *a.* & *com.* Progressive.

Progresivamente, *adv.* Progressively, onward, forward.

Progresivo, va [pro-gray-see'-vo, vah], *a.* Progressive, advancing.

Progreso [pro-gray'-so], *m.* Progress, advancement, growth; forwardness.

Prohibente [pro-e-ben'-tay], *pa.* Prohibiting.

Prohibición [pro-e-be-the-on'], *f.* Prohibition, interdict.

Prohibicionista [pro-e-be-the-o-nees'-tah], *m.* Prohibitionist.

Prohibir [pro-e-beer'], *va.* To prohibit, to forbid, to restrain.

Prohibitivo, va [pro-e-be-tee'-vo, vah], *a.* Prohibitory, forbidding.

Prohibitorio, ria [pro-e-be-to'-re-o, ah], *a.* Prohibitory.

Prohidiar, *va.* (Obs.) V. PORFIAR.

Prohijación, *f.* V. PROHIJAMIENTO.

Prohijador, ra [pro-e-hah-dor', rah], *m.* & *f.* Adopter, he that adopts a son.

Prohijamiento [pro-e-hah-me-en'-to], *m.* Adoption.

Prohijar [pro-e-har'], *va.* 1. To adopt, to make him a son who is not so by birth. 2. To ascribe, to attribute, to impute.

Prohombre [pro-om'-bray], *m.* 1. In trades-unions the officer who governs the union. 2. One who enjoys especial consideration among those of his class.

Pro indiviso [pro in-de-vee'-so], *adv.* (For.) Undivided, undistributed: said of legacies.

Prois [pro-ees'], *m.* **Proiza** [pro-ee'-thah], *f.* (Naut. Obs.) Breastfast, a rope with which a ship is fastened to the shore.

Prójimo [pro'-he-mo], *m.* Fellow-creature; neighbour. *No tener prójimo*, To be unfeeling or cruel, to be hard-hearted.

Prolabio [pro-lah'-be-o], *m.* (Med.) Prolabium, the red external part of a lip.

Prolapso [pro-lahp'-so], *m.* (Med.) Prolapsus, descent of a viscus.

Prole [pro'-lay], *f.* Issue, offspring, progeny, race; fruit.

Prolegómeno [pro-lay-go'-may-no], *m.* Prolegomena, introductory discourse.

Prolepsis [pro-lep'-sis], *f.* (Rhet.) Prolepsis, anticipation and answering of objections or counter-arguments.

Proletariado [pro-lay-tah-re-ah'-do], *m.* 1. Proletarianism, the condition of the poorest classes. 2. The class of proletarians, the proletariat.

Proletario, ria [pro-lay-tah'-re-o, ah], *a.* Proletarian, without property, very poor; plebeian.

Prolífero, ra [pro-lee'-fay-ro, rah], *a.* (Biol.) Proliferous, reproducing freely; in botany, marked by excessive development of parts.

Prolífico, ca [pro-lee'-fe-co, cah], *a.* Prolific, fruitful, productive.

Prolijamente, *adv.* Prolixly, tediously.

Prolijidad [pro-le-he-dahd'], *f.* 1. Prolixity, tediousness. 2. Minute attention to trifles; trifling nicety.

Prolijo, ja [pro-lee'-ho, hah], *a.* 1. Prolix, tedious, particular. 2. Over-careful, triflingly nice. 3. Troublesome, impertinent, long-winded.

Prólogo [pro'-lo-go], *m.* 1. Prologue, preface; introduction. 2. Prologue to a play.

Prologuista [pro-lo-gees'-tah], *m.* Writer of prologues.

Prolonga [pro-lon'-gah], *f.* (Mil.) Rope which ties the carriage of a cannon when passing difficult places.

Prolongación [pro-lon-gah-the-on'], *f.* Prolongation, lengthening, lingering.

Prolongadamente, *adv.* Tardily.

Prolongado, da [pro-lon-gah'-do, dah], *a.* Prolonged, extended.—*pp.* of PROLONGAR.

Prolongador, ra [pro-lon-gah-dor', rah], *m.* & *f.* One who prolongs or delays any thing.

Prolongamiento [pro-lon-gah-me-en'-to], *m.* Delay. V. PROLONGACIÓN.

Prolongar [pro-lon-gar'], *va.* 1. To prolong, to protract, to lengthen out, to continue. 2. (Com.) To allow to stand over. *Prolongar un plazo*, To grant an extension of time.—*vr.* (Naut.) To go alongside. *Prolongarse a la costa*, (Naut.) To range along the shore.

Proloquio [pro-lo'-ke-o], *m.* Maxim, moral, apothegm.

Prolusión [pro-loo-se-on'], *f.* Prolusion, prelude. V. PRELUSIÓN.

Promediar [pro-may-de-ar'], *va.* To divide into two equal parts, to share equally.—*vn.* To mediate, to form by mediation; to interpose in a friendly manner.

Promedio [pro-may'-de-o], *m.* 1. Middle, the part equally distant from the two extremities. 2. An average.

Promesa [pro-may'-sah], *f.* Promise, offer; pious offering. *Simple promesa*, A promise not confirmed by a vow or oath.

Prometedor, ra [pro-may-tay-dor', rah], *a.* Promising, full of promise.

Prometer [pro-may-terr'], *va.* 1. To promise, to bid fair. 2. To assever, to assure, to insure: often used menacingly.—*vr.* 1. To flatter one's self, to expect with confidence. 2. To devote one's self to the service or worship of God. 3. To give a promise of marriage.—*vn.* To promise, to show signs of forwardness.

Prometido [pro-may-tee'-do], *m.* 1. Promise, offer. 2. Outbidding, over-bidding.—*Prometido, da*, *pp.* of PROMETER.

Prometimiento [pro-may-te-me-en'-to], *m.* Promise, offer.

Prominencia [pro-me-nen'-the-ah], *f.* Prominence, protuberance, process, knob, elevation of a thing above its surroundings.

Prominente [pro-me-nen'-tay], *a.* Prominent, protuberant; jutting out.

Promiscuamente, *adv.* Promiscuously.

Promiscuo, cua [pro-mees'-coo-o, ah], *a.* Promiscuous, confusedly mingled; ambiguous.

Promisión [pro-me-se-on'], *f.* (Obs.) Promise: used only in the phrase, *Tierra de promisión*, Land of promise.

Promisorio, ria [pro-me-so'-re-o, ah], *a.* Promissory.

Promoción [pro-mo-the-on'], *f.* Promotion, advancement, encouragement, preferment.

Promontorio [pro-mon-to'-re-o], *m.* 1. A considerable elevation of ground. 2. Any thing bulky and unwieldy; an impediment, obstruction. 3. Promontory, headland, foreland, cape.

Promotor [pro-mo-tor'], *m.* 1. Promoter, advancer, forwarder, furtherer. 2. *Promotor fiscal*, (Law) A secular or ecclesiastical attorney-general.

Promovedor, ra [pro-mo-vay-dor', rah], *m.* & *f.* Promoter.

Promovendo [pro-mo-ven'-do], *m.* He who aspires to promotion.

Promover [pro-mo-verr'], *va.* 1. To promote, to advance, to further, to forward, to help. 2. To promote, to raise to a higher dignity or employment.

Promulgación [pro-mool-gah-the-on'], *f.* Promulgation.

Promulgador, ra [pro-mool-gah-dor', rah], *m.* & *f.* Publisher, promulgator.

Promulgar [pro-mool-gar'], *va.* To promulgate, to publish.

Pronación [pro-nah-the-on'], *f.* Pronation, the act of turning the hand (or fore limb) downward; also the position of a limb so turned.

Proneidad [pro-nay-e-dahd'], *f.* Proneness, inclination, propensity.

Prono, na [pro'-no, nah], *a.* 1. Prone, bending downward. 2. Prone, inclined, disposed.

Pronombre [pro-nom'-bray], *m.* (Gram.) Pronoun.

Pronominal [pro-no-me-nahl'], *a.* Pronominal.
Pronosticable [pro-nos-te-cah'-blay], *a.* (Littl. us.) Prognosticable.
Pronosticación [pro-nos-te-cah-the-on'], *f.* Prognostication, foreboding, forecasting.
Pronosticador, ra [pro-nos-te-cah dor', rah], *m.* & *f.* Foreteller, prognosticator, foreboder, forecaster.
Pronosticar [pro-nos-te-car'], *va.* To prognosticate, to predict, to foretell, to conjecture, to augur.
Pronóstico, ca [pro-nos'-te-co, cah], *a.* Prognostic, foreshowing.
Pronóstico [pro-nos'-te-co], *m.* 1. Prognostic, prediction, divination, omen, forerunner. 2. Almanac or calendar published by astrologers. *Pronóstico del tiempo*, Weather forecast.
Prontamente, *adv.* Promptly, lightly, nimbly.
Pronteza, *f.* (Obs.) *V.* PRONTITUD.
Prontitud [pron-te-tood'], *f.* 1. Promptitude, promptness. 2. Readiness or liveliness of wit; quickness of fancy; activity.
Pronto, ta [pron'-to, tah], *a.* Prompt, quick, ready, hasty, fast, forward, expedient. *De pronto*, Without premeditation, unintentionally; for the present; to suit the occasion.
Pronto [pron'-to], *adv.* Promptly, quickly, expeditiously.
Pronto [pron'-to], *m.* A sudden emotion of the mind, a quick motion. *Por el pronto*, Provisionally, temporarily. *Primer pronto*, First movement. *Un pronto*, A sally.
Prontuario [pron-too-ah'-re-o], *m.* 1. Memorandum-book. 2. Compendium of rules of some science or art.
Prónuba [pro'-noo-bah], *f.* (Poet.) Bridesmaid; goddess of wedlock.
Pronunciación [pro-noon-the-ah-the-on'], *f.* 1. Pronunciation, utterance; enunciation; articulation. 2. (Law) Publication.
Pronunciador, ra [pro-noon-the-ah-dor', rah], *m.* & *f.* Publisher, pronouncer.
Pronunciamiento [pro-noon-the-ah-me-en'-to], *m.* 1. (Law) Publication. 2. Insurrection, uprising.
Pronunciar [pro-noon-the-ar'], *va.* 1. To pronounce, to utter, to articulate, to enunciate. 2. To pronounce judgment, to issue by authority. 3. To pass upon, or deliberate on, while the principal point is decided. (Acad.) —*vr.* To rise in insurrection.
Propagación [pro-pah-gah-the-on'], *f.* Propagation, successive production, offspring; extension.
Propagador, ra [pro-pah-gah-dor', rah], *m.* & *f.* Propagator.
Propaganda [pro-pah-gahn'-dah], *f.* 1. Propaganda. 2. Advertising.
Propagandista [pro-pah-gahn-dees'-tah], *m.* & *f.* & *a.* Propagandist.
Propagar [pro-pah-gar'], *va.* 1. To propagate, to generate, to multiply the species. 2. To propagate, to diffuse, to extend. 3. To propagate, to enlarge, to increase, to promote.
Propagativo, va [pro-pah-gah-tee'-vo, vah], *a.* That which propagates.
Propaladia [pro-pah-lah'-de-ah], *f.* Title of a play.
Propalar [pro-pah-lar'], *va.* To publish, to divulge.
Propao [pro-pah'-o], *m.* (Naut.) Breastwork, bulkhead.
Propartida [pro-par-tee'-dah], *f.* Time approaching that of departing.
Propasar [pro-pah-sar'], *va.* To go beyond, to transgress, to exceed. *Propasar la estima*, (Naut.) To outrun the reckoning.—*vr.* To be deficient in good-breeding.
Propender [pro-pen-derr'], *vn.* To tend towards, to incline to by nature.
Propensamente, *adv.* In a propense manner, with inclination or propension.
Propensión [pro-pen-se-on'], *f.* Propension, propensity, tendency, inclination, liability.
Propenso, sa [pro-pen'-so, sah], *a.* Inclined, disposed, minded, apt to, prone, open to. *Propenso a accidentes* Accident-prone.
Propiamente, *adv.* Properly, with propriety; fittingly.
Propiciación [pro-pe-the-ah-the-on'], *f.* 1. Propitiation, atonement. 2. Act of making propitious.
Propiciador, ra [pro-pe-the-ah-dor', rah], *m.* & *f.* Propitiator.
Propiciamente, *adv.* Propitiously.
Propiciar [pro-pe-the-ar'], *va.* To propitiate, to conciliate.
Propiciatorio, ria [pro-pe-the-ah-to'-re-o, ah], *a.* Propitiatory.
Propiciatorio, *m.* Propitiatory, mercy-seat; the covering of the ark of the covenant.
Propicio, cia [pro-pee'-the-o, ah], *a.* Propitious, kind, favourable.
Propiedad [pro-pe-ay-dahd'], *f.* 1. (For.) Dominion, possession, eminent domain; exclusive right of possession. *V.* DOMINIO. 2. Landed estate or property. 3. Property, particular quality which is peculiar to a thing. 4. Propriety, fitness, meetness; expedience. 5. (Gram.) Exact signification of a term. 6. Propensity, inclination. 7. Close imitation. 8. (Phil.) *V.* PROPIO. *Elixir de propiedad*, Tincture of aloes, myrrh, and saffron; elixir pro.
Propienda [pro-pe-en'-dah], *f.* Listing nailed to the sides of a quilting or embroidering frame.
Propietaria [pro-pe-ay-tah'-re-ah], *f.* Proprietress, a female possessor in her own right.
Propietariamente, *adv.* With the right of property.
Propietario, ria [pro-pe-ay-tah'-re-o, ah], *a.* Proprietary, invested with the right of property; belonging with full right of property.
Propietario, *m.* 1. Proprietary, proprietor, owner, landlord. 2. *Propietario de una finca*, Freeholder. 3. Proprietary, a religious who sins against the vow of poverty.
Propileo [pro-pee'-lay-o], *m.* Propyleum, vestibule of a temple; a peristyle of columns.
Propina [pro-pee'-nah], *f.* Present, pay beyond the agreed price, gratuity, tip.
Propinación [pro-pe-nah-the-on'], *f.* Treat, invitation to drink.
Propinar [pro-pe-nar'], *va.* 1. To invite to drink, to present a glass of wine or liquor. 2. (Coll.) To prescribe medicines.
Propincuidad [pro-pin-coo-e-dahd'], *f.* Propinquity, proximity, nearness.
Propincuo, cua [pro-peen'-coo-o, ah], *a.* Near, contiguous.
Propio, pia [pro'-pe-o, ah], *a.* 1. Proper, one's own, belonging to any one. 2. Proper, suitable, becoming accommodated, adapted, fit, convenient. 3. Proper, peculiar to any one. 4. Proper, natural, original, genuine. 5. Exact, precise in speaking or writing. 6. *V.* MISMO. 7. Resembling, like, similar. *Propio marte o ingenio*, Of one's own efforts. *Al propio*, Properly.
Propio [pro'-pe-o], *m.* 1. (Phil.) Proper peculiar or distinctive quality; characteristic property of a class, genus, or species. 2. Special delivery for letters of importance; messenger.—*pl.* Lands, estates, etc., belonging to a city or civic corporation. *Junta* or *sesión de propios y arbitrios*, Committee of ways and means.
Propóleos [pro-po'-lay-os], *m.* Propolis, bee-glue. *Cf.* CERA ALEDA. (Gr. πρόπολις.)
Proponedor, ra [pro-po-nay-dor', rah], *m.* & *f.* Proposer, offerer, proponent.
Proponer [pro-po-nerr'], *va.* 1. To propose, to offer for consideration, to hold out, to represent. 2. To resolve, to determine, to mean. 3. To present; to propose the means.
(*Yo propongo, proponga, propuse*, from *Proponer. V.* PONER.)
Proponible [pro-po-nee'-blay], *a.* (Littl. us.) Proposable.
Proporción [pro-por-the-on'], *f.* 1. Proportion, comparative relation of one thing to another. 2. Symmetry, adaptation of one thing to another; aptitude, fitness. 3. Similarity of arguments and reasons. 4. Opportunity, occasion, chance. *A proporción*, Conformably, proportionally; as fast as.
Proporcionable [pro-por-the-o-nah'-blay], *a.* Proportionable. *V.* PROPORCIONADO.
Proporcionablemente, Proporcionadamente, *adv.* Proportionably, proportionally.
Proporcionado, da [pro-por-the-o-nah'-do, dah], *a.* Proportionate, regular, competent, commensurate, conformable, harmonious.—*pp.* of PROPORCIONAR.
Proporcional [pro-por-the-o-nahl'], *a.* Proportional.
Proporcionalidad [pro-por-the-o-nah-le-dahd'], *f.* Proportionableness, proportionality.
Proporcionalmente, *adv.* Proportionally, commensurately.
Proporcionar [pro-por-the-o-nar'], *va.* 1. To proportion, to form symmetrically. 2. To adjust, to adapt. 3. To afford, to furnish.—*vr.* To prepare one's self for any design.
Proposición [pro-po-se-the-on'], *f.* 1. Proposition, the act of proposing. 2. Proposal, scheme, overture. 3. Proposition, assertion of affirmation or denial. 4. (Math.) Proposition, an established truth required to be demonstrated.
Propósito [pro-poh'-se-to], *m.* 1. Purpose, design, intention. 2. Purport of a writing or discourse. *A propósito*, For the purpose; fit for; apropos; by-the-bye. *De propósito*, On purpose, purposely. *Fuera de propósito*, Untimely, not to the purpose, foreign to the subject, out of the question. *Volvamos al propósito*, Let us return to the point in question.
Propretor [pro-pray-tor'], *m.* Roman magistrate.
Proptosis [prop-to'-sis], *f.* (Med.) Ptosis, falling of an organ.
Propuesta [pro-poo-es'-tah], *f.* 1. Proposal, proposition, offer, overture. 2. Representation, declaration. 3. Proposal for employment.
Propuesto, ta [pro-poo-es'-to, tah], *pp. irr.* of PROPONER. Proposed.
Propugnáculo [pro-poog-nah'-coo-lo], *m.* 1. A fortress. 2. (Met.) Bulwark, defence, support.
Propulsión [pro-pool-see-ohn'], *f.* Propulsion. *Propulsión a chorro*, Jet propulsion. *Avión de propulsión a chorro*, Jet plane.
Propulsar [pro-pool-sar'], *va.* To repel. *V.* REPULSAR.
Propulsiva [pro-pool-see'-vah], *f. V.* PROPULSA.
Propulsor [pro-pool-sor'], *m.* Propeller.

propellant: a mechanism driven by a motive power within a vessel, and which acts upon the water, as oars, wheels, screw.

Prora [pro'-rah], *f.* (Poet.) Prow of a ship.

Prorrata [pror-rah'-tah], *f.* 1. Quota, a portion assigned to each contribuent. 2. Apportionment.

Prorratear [pror-rah-tay-ar'], *va.* 1. To divide a quantity into certain shares. —*vn.* 2. To apportion.

Prorrateo [pror-rah-tay'-o], *m.* Division into shares, distribution, average.

Prórroga, Prorrogación [pror'-ro-gah], *f.* 1. Prorogation, lengthening out to a distant time; prolongation. 2. (For.) Amplification of powers to cases and persons which they did not comprise.

Prorrogable [pror-ro-gah'-blay], *a.* Capable of being prorogued.

Prorrogar [pror-ro-gar'], *va.* To prorogue, to put off, to adjourn.

Prorrumpir [pror-room-peer'], *vn.* 1. To break forth, to burst out with violence, to issue. 2. To burst forth, to burst out into cries and lamentations.

Prosa [pro'-sah], *f.* 1. Prose. 2. Tedious conversation; dull, absurd speech. 3. Prose chanted after mass.

Prosador [pro-sah-dor'], *m.* (Coll.) A sarcastic speaker, a malicious babbler.

Prosaico, ca [pro-sah'-e-co, cah], *a.* 1. Prosaic, written in prose; belonging to prose. 2. Prosy, dull, tedious.

Prosaísmo [pro-sah-ees'-mo], *m.* 1. Defect of verses which lack rhythm. 2. Prosiness, dulness.

Prosapia [pro-sah'-pe-ah], *f.* Race, a generation of people.

Proscenio [pros-thay'-ne-o], *m.* Proscenium, place on the stage.

Proscribir [pros-cre-beer'], *va.* To proscribe, to outlaw, to censure capitally; to doom to destruction.

Proscripción [pros-crip-the-on'], *f.* Proscription, banishment, outlawry.

Proscripto [pros-creep'-to], *m.* Outlaw.

Proscripto, ta, Proscrito, ta [pros-creep'-to, pros-cree'-to, tah], *pp. irr.* of Proscribir. Proscribed.

Prosecución [pro-say-coo-the-on'], *f.* 1. Prosecution, pursuit, endeavour to carry on any thing. 2. Pursuit, the act of following another.

Proseguible [pro-say-gee'-blay], *a.* Pursuable.

Proseguimiento [pro-say-gee-me-en'-to], *m.* *V.* Prosecución.

Proseguir [pro-say-geer'], *va.* To pursue, to prosecute, to follow, to continue any thing begun.

Proselitismo [pro-say-le-tees'-mo], *m.* Proselytism, zeal for making proselytes.

Prosélito [pro-say'-le-to], *m.* Proselyte, convert.

Prosevante [pro-say-vahn'-tay], *m.* (Obs.) Pursuivant, king's messenger. *V.* Persevante.

(*Yo prosigo, yo prosiga,* from *Proseguir. V.* Pedir.)

Prosista [pro-sees'-tah], *m.* 1. Author who writes in prose. 2. (Coll.) Prattler, babbler, idle talker, proser.

Prosit. (Lat.) Much good may it do you.

Prosita [pro-see'-tah], *f. dim.* A short discourse in prose.

Prosodia [pro-so'-de-ah], *f.* 1. Orthoepy, the science or art of correct pronunciation. 2. Loquacity, idle talk. 3. Prosody, the science of metrical forms; formerly a division of grammar. 4. Regular mode of pronouncing each syllable of a word when singing.

Prosódico, ca [pro-so'-de-co, cah], *a.* Orthoepic, relating to pronunciation; or prosodic.

Prosopografía [pro-so-po-grah-fee'-ah], *f.* Prosopography, description of the physiognomy of a person or animal.

Prosopopeya [pro-so-po-pay'-yah], *f.* 1. Prosopopœia, personification; a figure of speech. 2. (Coll.) Splendour, pageantry.

Prospecto [pros-pec'-to], *m.* Prospectus.

Prósperamente [pros'-pay-rah-men-tay], *adv.* Prosperously, luckily.

Prosperar [pros-pay-rar'], *va.* To prosper, to make happy; to favour.—*vn.* To prosper, to be prosperous, to thrive.

Prosperidad [pros-pay-re-dahd'], *f.* Prosperity, good fortune, success.

Próspero, ra [pros'-pay-ro, rah], *a.* Prosperous, successful, fortunate, fair.

Prostaféresis [pros-tah-fay'-ray-sis], *f.* (Ast.) Prosthaphæresis, correction to be applied to the mean place of a heavenly body to obtain the true place or movement.

Próstata [pros'-ta-tah], *f.* The prostate gland.

Prostático, ca [pros-tah'-te-co, cah], *a.* Prostatic, pertaining to the prostate.

Prostatitis [pros-ta-tee'-tis], *f.* Prostatitis, inflammation of the prostate.

Prosternación [pros-ter-nah-the-on'], *f.* Profound reverence and humiliation, falling down.

Prosternarse [pros-ter-nar'-say], *vr.* To fall down, to prostrate one's self in adoration, to bend as a suppliant.

Prostíbulo [pros-tee'-boo-lo], *m.* House of prostitution, disorderly place.

Próstilo [pros-tee'-lo], *a.* (Arch.) Prostyle, having only pillars in front.

Prostitución [pros-te-too-the-on'], *f.* 1. Prostitution, the act of setting or being set to sale for vile purposes. 2. Prostitution, the life of a strumpet.

Prostituir [pros-te-too-eer'], *va.* To prostitute, to expose to crimes for a reward; to expose on vile terms.—*vr.* To hack, to turn hackney or prostitute.

Prostituta [pros-te-too'-tah], *f.* Prostitute, woman of the town.

Prostituto, ta [pros-te-too'-to, tah], *pp. irr.* of Prostituir. Prostituted.

Prostrar, *va.* (Obs.) *V.* Postrar.

Protagonista [pro-ta-go-nees'-tah], *m.* Protagonist, principal personage of a dramatic story.

Prótasis [pro'-tah-sis], *f.* 1. Protasis, the first piece of a dramatic poem. 2. (Gram.) Protasis, the first part of a compound period.

Protección [pro-tec-the-on'], *f.* Protection, support, favour, countenance.

Proteccionismo [pro-tec-the-o-nees'-mo], *m.* The economic doctrine of protection or protectionism: opposite of free trade.

Proteccionista [pro-tec-the-o-nees'-tah], *m.* Protectionist, a partisan of protectionism.

Protector [pro-tec-tor'], *m.* 1. Protector, defender, guardian, conservator. 2. Steward of a community, charged with maintaining its interest.

Protectora [pro-tec-to'-rah], *f.* Protectress, a woman who protects.

Protectorado [pro-tec-to-rah'-do], *m.* Protectorate, the dignity of a protector and the time during which it lasts.

Protectoría [pro-tec-to-ree'-ah], *f.* Protectorship, protectorate.

Protectorio, ria [pro-tec-to'-re-o, ah], *a.* Relating to a protector.

Protectriz [pro-tec-treeth'], *f.* Protectress.

Proteger [pro-tay-herr'], *va.* To protect, to defend, to favour, to countenance.

Protegido, da [pro-tay-hee'-do, dah], *m.* & *f.* Protegé, protegée, favorite. —*a.* & *pp.* of Proteger. Protected, sheltered.

Protervamente, *adv.* Frowardly, stubbornly, perversely.

Protervia, Protervidad [pro-terr'-ve ah], *f.* Obstinacy, protervity; peevishness, frowardness, stubbornness.

Protervo, va [pro-terr'-vo, vah], *a.* Stubborn, peevish, obstinate, perverse, froward.

Prótesis [pro'-tay-sis], *f.* (Gram.) Prosthesis or prothesis, addition of letters at the beginning of a word, for the sake of euphony; as *aqueste* for *este.*

Protesta [pro-tes'-tah], *f.* 1. (Law) Protest, a solemn declaration. 2. A solemn promise, asseveration, or assurance.

Protestación [pro-tes-tah-the-on'], *f.* 1. Protestation, profession, á solemn declaration. 2. Threat, menace.

Protestante [pro-tes-tahn'-tay], *com.* A Protestant.

Protestante [pro-tes-tahn'-tay], *a.* Protestant, belonging to Protestants.—*pa.* Protesting.

Protestantismo [pro-tes-tan-tees'-mo], *m.* Protestantism.

Protestar [pro-tes-tar'], *va.* 1. To protest, to give a solemn declaration. 2. To assure, to assever. 3. To threaten, to menace. 4. To make a public declaration of faith and belief. 5. (Law) To make a solemn declaration for the purpose of preserving one's right. *Protestar una letra,* To protest a bill of exchange.

Protestativo, va [pro-tes-tah-tee'-vo, vah], *a.* That which protests.

Protesto [pro-tes'-to], *m.* 1. (Com.) Protest of a bill. 2. *V.* Protesta.

Protético, ca [pro-tay'-te-co, cah], *a.* Prothetic, prefixed.

Proto [pro'-to]. A Greek word used in composition, signifying first; often applied jocularly, as *protopobre, protodiablo,* etc.

Protoalbéitar [pro-to-al-bay'-ee-tar], *m.* First or chief veterinary surgeon, head of the veterinary college, who attends the royal horses and examines students in his art.

Protoalbeiterato [pro-to-al-bay-e-tay-rah'-to], *m.* Tribunal or college for examining veterinary surgeons previously to licensing them to practise.

Protocolar, Protocolizar [pro-to-co-lar'], *va.* To place in the protocol, to record, to register.

Protocolo [pro-to-co'-lo], *m.* Protocol, registry, a judicial record.

Protomedicato [pro-to-may-de-cah'-to], *m.* 1. Tribunal or college of king's physicians, where students of medicine are examined and licensed. 2. Office of a first or royal physician.

Protomédico [pro-to-may'-de-co], *m.* First physician, one of the three physicians to the king.

Protón [pro-tone'], *m.* (Phy.) Proton.

Protonotario [pro-to-no-tah'-re-o], *m.* Prothonotary, chief clerk or chief notary. *Protonotario apostólico,* A papal dignity.

Protoplasma [pro-to-plahs'-mah], *m.* Protoplasm.

Protosulfuro [pro-to-sool-foo'-ro], *m.* Protosulphide.

Prototípico, ca [pro-to-tee'-pe-co, cah], *a.* Prototypal, belonging to a prototype.

Prototipo [pro-to-tee'-po], *m.* Prototype, original.

Protóxido [pro-tok'-se-do], *m.* Protoxide.

Protozoario, ria [pro-to-tho-ah'-re-o, ah], *a.* Protozoic.

Protozoo [pro-to-tho'-o], *m.* Protozoan, protozoon, one-celled organism.

Protuberancia [pro-too-bay-rahn'-the-ah], *f.* Protuberance, prominence, extuberance.

Provecto, ta [pro-vec'-to, tah], *a.* Advanced in years, learning, or experience.

Provecho [pro-vay'-cho], *m.* 1. Profit, benefit, advantage, utility, gain. 2. Profit, improvement, proficiency, progress; advancement. *Hombre de provecho*, A useful man. *Ser de provecho*, To be useful or profitable. *Buen provecho*, Much good may it do you: used at eating or drinking.

Provechosamente, *adv.* Profitably, gainfully, advantageously, usefully.

Provechoso, sa [pro-vay-cho'-so, sah], *a.* Profitable, beneficial, gainful, lucrative, useful, advantageous.

Proveedor, ra [pro-vay-ay-dor', rah], *m.* & *f.* Purveyor, contractor, furnisher.

Proveeduría [pro-vay-ay-doo-ree'-ah], *f.* 1. Store-house for provisions. 2. Employment and office of purveyor.

Proveer [pro-vay-err'], *va.* 1. To provide, to procure beforehand, to get ready, to furnish, to fit, to accommodate. 2. To supply with provisions, to provide provisions for an army. 3. To dispose, to adjust. 4. To confer a dignity or employment. 5. To decree, to doom by a decree, to despatch a suit at law. 6. To minister, to supply with the necessaries of life, to maintain.—*vr.* (Coll.) To ease the body.

Proveído [pro-vay-ee'-do], *m.* Judgment, sentence, decree.—*Proveído, da, pp.* of PROVEER.

Proveimiento [pro-vay-e-me-en'-to], *m.* Supply, the act of providing or supplying with provisions.

Proveniente [pro-vay-ne-en'-tay], *pa.* Proceeding, originating in.

Provenir [pro-vay-neer'], *vn.* To arise, to proceed; to take rise or origin from, to originate in.

Provenzal [pro-ven-thahl'], *a.* Provençal, relating to Provence, and its language; Languedocian.

Proverbiador [pro-ver-be-ah-dor'], *m.* Collection of proverbs.

Proverbial [pro-ver-be-ahl'], *a.* Proverbial.

Proverbialmente, *adv.* Proverbially.

Proverbiar [pro-ver-be-ar'], *vn.* (Coll.) To use proverbs.

Proverbio [pro-vayr'-be-o], *m.* 1. A proverb. 2. Prophecy, prediction from certain words. *Proverbios*, Book of Proverbs, a canonical book of the Old Testament.

Proverbista [pro-ver-bees'-tah], *m.* (Coll.) One attached to the use of proverbs.

Próvidamente [pro'-ve-dah-men-tay], *adv.* Providently, carefully.

Providencia [pro-ve-den'-the-ah], *f.* 1. Providence, foresight, forecast, forethought. 2. Providence, the act of providing; disposition or measures taken to obtain some end. 3. Divine Providence. 4. State or order of things. *Auto de providencia*, Interlocutory decree; provisional judgment.

Providencial [pro-ve-den-the-ahl'], *a.* Providential.

Providencialmente, *adv.* Providentially, provisionally.

Providenciar [pro-ve-den-the-ar'], *va.* To ordain, to command.

Providente [pro-ve-den-tay], *a.* Provident, prudent, careful.

Próvido, da [pro'-ve-do, dah], *a.* Provident, careful, diligent.

Provincia [pro-veen'-the-ah], *f.* 1. Province, one of the divisions of a kingdom. 2. A certain number of convents under the direction of a provincial. 3. Provincial court appointed to try and decide civil causes. 4. Province, an important business which is to be treated upon.

Provincial [pro-vin-the-ahl'], *a.* Provincial.

Provincialismo [pro-vin-the-ah-lees'-mo], *m.* Provincialism.

Provinciano, na [pro-vin-the-ah'-no, nah], *a.* & *n.* Native of Biscay.

Provisión [pro-ve-se-on'], *f.* 1. Store of provisions collected for use; provender. 2. Writ, decree, or sentence issued by Spanish tribunals in the king's name. 3. Title or instrument, by virtue whereof an incumbent holds his benefice. 4. Act of conferring an employment or office. 5. (Com.) A remittance of funds by the drawer of a bill of exchange to the drawee so that he may accept it.

Provisional [pro-ve-se-oh-nahl'], *a.* Provisional.

Provisionalmente, *adv.* Provisionally.

Proviso, or **Al Proviso** [pro-vee'-so], *adv.* Upon the spot, immediately, instantly.

Provisor, ra [pro-ve-sor', rah], *m.* & *f.* 1. Provider. *V.* PROVEEDOR. 2. Vicar-general, an ecclesiastical judge.

Provisoría [pro-ve-so-ree'-ah], *f.* 1. In some convents and colleges, the store-room, where provisions are kept; pantry. 2. Place or office of a *provisor* or vicar-general.

Provisorio, ria [pro-ve-so'-re-o, ah], *a.* Provisional, temporarily established.

Provisto, ta [pro-vees'-to, tah], *a.* Provided with a benefice.—*pp. irr.* of PROVEER.

Provocación [pro-vo-cah-the-on'], *f.* 1. Provocation, displeasure, irritation. 2. Cause or motive of anger.

Provocador, ra [pro-vo-cah-dor', rah], *m.* & *f.* Provoker; causer, promoter.

Provocar [pro-vo-car'], *va.* 1. To provoke, to rouse, to excite, to nettle. 2. To anger, to enrage, to offend. 3. To vomit. 4. To facilitate, to promote. 5. To move, to excite.

Provocativo, va [pro-vo-cah-tee'-vo, vah], *a.* 1. Provocative, exciting, inducing. 2. Quarrelsome, provoking.

Próximamente, *adv.* Nearly, immediately, proximately.

Proximidad [proc-se-me-dahd'], *f.* 1. Proximity, nearness, vicinity. 2. Relation, kindred by birth.

Próximo, ma [proc'-se-mo, mah], *a.* Next, nearest, neighbour, proximate.

Proyección [pro-yec-the-on'], *f.* 1. Projection, shooting forward. 2. (Arch.) Corbel, jetty, projecture. 3. (Math.) Apparent representation of an object upon a plane; graphic representation. 4. Movement impressed upon a projectile.

Proyectar [pro-yec-tar'], *va.* 1. To project, to scheme, to contrive. 2. To throw into the air, to project. 3. To draw a figure in the vertical and horizontal planes of projection.—*vr.* 1. To strike against a bottom. 2. To throw itself forward, as a shadow. 3. (Naut.) To be ranged along the same line.

Proyectil [pro-yec-teel'], *m.* Missile, projectile. *Proyectil balístico*, Ballistic missile. *Proyectil cohete*, Rocket missile; space rocket. *Proyectil de alcance intermedio*, Intermediate range ballistic missile. *Proyectil de sondeo*, Probe rocket. *Proyectil dirigido*, Guided missile. *Proyectil interceptor*, Interceptor missile. *Proyectil antiproyectil*, Anti-missile missile.

Proyectista [pro-yec-tees'-tah], *m.* Projector, schemer.

Proyecto [pro-yec'-to], *m.* Project, scheme, plan, design.

Proyecto, ta [pro-yec'-to, tah], *a.* Projected, expanded, dilated.

Proyector [pro-yec-tor'], *m.* 1. Projector. 2. Searchlight. 3. Spotlight.

Proyectura [pro-yec-too'-rah], *f.* Projecture, part of a building which juts beyond the wall. *V.* VUELO.

Prudencia [proo-den'-the-ah], *f.* 1. Prudence, counsel, management, circumspection. 2. Temperance, moderation.

Prudencial [proo-den-the-ahl'], *a.* Prudential.

Prudencialmente, *adv.* Prudentially.

Prudente [proo-den'-tay], *a.* Prudent, circumspect, judicious, considerate.

Prudentemente, *adv.* Prudently.

Prueba [proo-ay'-bah], *f.* 1. Proof, reason, argument, evidence. 2. Sign, token, indication, mark. 3. Experiment, essay, attempt; a test-portion, a test. 4. (Print.) Proof, proof-sheet. 5. In photography, proof, the first print from a negative. *A prueba de* with a noun is to be rendered by "proof" connected by hyphen with the equivalent of the noun. Thus: *A prueba de luz*, Light-proof. *A prueba de bomba*, Bomb-proof; satisfactorily. *Tomar una cosa a prueba*, To take a thing on trial.

(*Yo pruebo, yo pruebe*, from *Probar*. *V.* ACORDAR.)

Prurito [proo-ree'-to], *m.* 1. Prurience, itching. 2. Great desire or appetite.

Prusiato [proo-se-ah'-to], *m.* (Chem.) Prussiate.

Prúsico [proo'-se-co], *a.* Prussic, hydrocyanic. *Ácido prúsico*, Prussic, hydrocyanic acid.

Psicoanálisis [se-co-ah-nah'-le-sis], *f.* Psychoanalysis.

Psicofísica [se-co-fee'-se-ca], *f.* Psychophysics.

Psicología [se-co-lo-hee'-ah], *f.* Psychology, study of the subconscious. *Psicología industrial*, Industrial psychology.

Psicológico, ca [se-co-lo'-he-co, cah], *a.* Psychological.

Psicologo, ga [se-co'-lo-go, gah], *m.* & *f.* Psychologist.

Psiconeurótico, ca [se-co-nay-oo-roh'-te-co, cah], *a.* Psychoneurotic.

Psicópata [se-co'-pah-tah], *m.* Psychopath.

Psicopatía [se-co-pah-tee'-ah], *f.* Psychopathy.

Psicopático, ca [se-co-pah'-te-co, cah], *a.* Psychopathic.

Psicopatología [se-co-pah-to-lo-hee'-ah], *f.* Psychopathology.

Psicosis [se-co'-sis], *f.* Psychosis.

Psicosomático, ca [se-co-so-mah'-te-co, cah], *a.* Psychosomatic, referring to illnesses not organic in origin.

Psicotecnia [se-co-tec'-ne-ah], *f.* Psychological testing.

Psicotécnico, ca [se-co-tec'-ne-co, cah], *a.* Psychotechnological.

Psicoterapia [se-co-tay-rah'-pe-ah], *f.* Psychotherapy.

Psique [see'-kay], *f.* Psyche.

Psiquiatra [se-ke-ah'-trah], *m.* Psychiatrist.

Psiquiatría [se-ke-ah-tree'-ah], *f.* Psychiatry.

Psíquico, ca [see'-ke-co, cah], *a.* Psychic.

Púa [poo'-ah], *f.* 1. Sharp point, barb. 2. (Bot.) Graft. 3. Tooth (of a comb). 4. Prick. 5. (Zool.) Spine. 6. (Mus.) Plectrum. 7. (Coll.) Sharpie. *Alambre de púas,* Barbed wire.

Púber [poo -ber], *a.* Pubescent.

Púbero, ra [poo'-bay-ro, rah], *a.* Pubescent, arrived at puberty.

Pubertad [poo-ber-tahd'], *f.* Puberty, pubescence. Pubis.

Pubes [poo'-bes], *m.* (Anat.) Pubes, the pubic region.

Pubescencia [poo-bes-then'-the-ah], *f.* Pubescence, puberty.

Pubescer [poo-bes-therr'], *vn.* To attain the age of puberty.

Pública [poo'-ble-cah], *f.* In universities, a lecture before the examination for the degree of licentiate.

Publicación [poo-ble-cah-the-on'], *f.* Publication, proclamation.

Publicador, ra [poo-ble-cah-dor', rah], *m.* & *f.* Publisher, proclaimer.

Públicamente, *adv.* Publicly, openly.

Publicano [poo-ble-cah'-no], *m.* Publican, toll-gatherer.

Publicar [poo-ble-car'], *va.* 1. To publish, to proclaim, to make known. 2. To publish, to print a book.

Publicata [poo-ble-cah'-tah], *f.* 1. Certificate of publication. 2. Each of the three announcements of the banns of marriage.

Publicidad [poo-ble-the-dahd'], *f.* Publicity, notoriety. *En publicidad,* Publicly.

Publicista [poo-ble-thees'-tah], *m.* Publicist, a writer on public law or on topics of public interest.

Público, ca [poo'-ble-co, cah], *a.* 1. Public, notorious, known by all. 2. Vulgar, common, general. *En público,* Publicly.

Público, *m.* Public, the general body of a nation.

Pucuna [poo-coo'-nah], *f.* A blow-gun in Peru. (Indian.)

Pucia [poo'-the-ah], *f.* A closed pharmaceutical vessel, narrow above and broad below.

Pucha [poo'-chah], *f.* (Cuba) A small bouquet of flowers, nosegay.

Puchada [poo-chah'-dah], *f.* 1. A cataplasm, chiefly of flour. 2. Watered mortar, used by stone-masons.

Puchecilla [poo-chay-theel'-lyah], *f.* A thin batter of flour and water.

Pucherito [poo-chay-ree'-to], *m.* (Coll.) Crying grimaces of children.

Puchero [poo-chay'-ro], *m.* 1. A glazed earthen pot. 2. Olla, a dish composed of beef or lamb, ham or bacon, Spanish peas, and vegetables: a standing dish in Spanish countries. 3. Daily food, regular aliment. 4. Grimace or distortion of the face which precedes crying. *Hacer pucheros,* (Coll.) To snivel. *Meter la cabeza en el puchero,* To equivocate and maintain an opinion obstinately.

Puches [poo'-ches], *com. pl.* Sort of pap. *V.* GACHAS.

Pucho [poo'-cho], *m.* (Amer.) 1. Tip or end of a cigar. 2. A small quantity or sum; driblet.

Pudendas, *a.* & *f. pl.* The pudenda.

Pudendo, da [poo-den'-do, dah], *a.* Shameful, obscene, immodest.

Pudendo, *m.* The male organ.

Pudibundo, da [poo-de-boon'-do, dah], *a.* (Joc.) Shamefaced, modest.

Pudicicia [poo-de-thee'-the-ah], *f.* Pudicity, chastity, modesty.

Púdico, ca [poo'-de-co, cah], *a.* Chaste, modest, maidenly.

Pudiente [poo-de-en'-tay], *a.* Powerful, rich, opulent: it is used as a substantive.

Pudín [poo-deen'], *m.* Pudding.

Pudor [poo-dor'], *m.* Bashfulness, modesty, shyness, shamefacedness.

Pudoroso, sa [poo-do-ro'-so, sah], *a.* Modest, shamefaced, bashful, shy.

Pudrición [poo-dre-the-on'], *f.* Rottenness, the act of rotting.

Pudridero [poo-dre-day'-ro], *m.* 1. Rotting-place, where any thing is put to rot; fermenting pit. 2. Royal vault in the monastery at Escurial.

Pudridor [poo-dre-dor'], *m.* Vessel in which rags are steeped for making paper.

Pudrimiento [poo-dre-me-en'-to], *m.* Rottenness, putrefaction. *V.* PUDRICIÓN.

Pudrir [poo-dreer'], *va.* 1. To rot, to make putrid, to bring to corruption. 2. To molest, to consume, to cause extreme impatience.—*vn.* To have died, to be buried, to rot.—*vr.* 1. To corrupt, to become rotten, to decay. 2. To be broken-hearted, to die of grief.

(*Yo pudro, pudra; él se pudrió.* *V.* PODRIR.)

Puebla [poo-ay'-blah], *f.* Seed which a gardener sows.

Pueblecico, ito [poo-ay-blay-thee'-co], *m. dim.* Any small town.

Pueblo [poo-ay'-blo], *m.* 1. Town, village; any inhabited place. 2. Population, inhabitants of a place. 3. Common people, populace. 4. Nation, people.

(*Yo pueblo, pueble,* from *Poblar.* *V.* ACORDAR.)

(*Yo puedo, pude, pueda.* *V.* PODER.)

Puente [poo-en'-tay], *com.* 1. A bridge. *Puente volante,* Flying-bridge. *Puente de cimbria,* (Chili) Suspension rope-bridge: a rope crossing a river, firmly fastened at each end, from which a canoe is suspended to convey passengers. *V.* TARABITA. *Puente levadizo,* Draw-bridge. 2. (Naut.) Deck of a ship. *Puente a la oreja,* (Naut.) Flush-deck. *Puente de enjaretada,* (Naut.) Grating deck. *Puente de redes,* (Naut.) Netting deck. 3. (Mus.) Bridge, in stringed instruments. 4. Transom, lintel, cross-beam. *Hacer la puente de plata,* (Met.) To overcome difficulties by means of a bribe.

Puente aéreo [poo-en'-tay ah-ay'-ray-o], *m.* (Mil.) Airlift.

Puentecico, illo, ito [poo-en-tay-thee'-co], *m. dim.* A small bridge.

Puentecilla [poo-en-tay-theel'-lyah], *f. dim.* A small bridge of a stringed instrument.

Puerca [poo-err'-cah], *f.* 1. A sow. 2. Sow-bug, slater, wood-louse, a crustacean commonly found in damp spots. 3. Scrofulous swelling, glandulous tumour. 4. Slut, slatternly woman.

Puercamente, *adv.* 1. Dirtily, filthily, hoggishly, nastily. 2. Rudely, coarsely, vulgarly, meanly.

Puerco, ca [poo-err'-co, cah], *a.* 1. Nasty, filthy, dirty, foul, abominable. 2. Rude, coarse, mean.

Puerco, *m.* 1. Hog. 2. Wild-boar. *V.* JABALÍ. *Puerco espín,* Porcupine. 3. A brutish, ill-bred man.

Puericia [poo-ay-ree'-the-ah], *f.* Boyhood.

Puericultura [poo-ay-re-cool-too'-rah], *f.* Child care, prenatal and infant welfare.

Pueril [poo-ay-reel'], *a.* 1. Boyish, childish, puerile. 2. Belonging to the first quadrant of the celestial map.

Puerilidad [poo-ay-re-le-dahd'], *f.* Puerility, boyishness, childishness, silliness; trifle.

Puerilmente, *adv.* Puerilely, childishly, boyishly.

Puérpera [poo-err'-pay-rah], *f.* A lying-in woman.

Puerperal [poo-er-pay-rahl'], *a.* Puerperal, relating to childbirth.

Puerperio [poo-er-pay'-re-o], *m.* 1. Childbirth, travail, labour. 2. The puerperal condition; the time immediately following labour.

Puerquezuelo [poo-er-kay-thoo-ay'-lo], *m. dim.* Little pig.

Puerro [poo-err'-ro], *m.* (Bot.) Leek. Allium porrum.

Puerta [poo-err'-tah], *f.* 1. Door or doorway, gateway. 2. Beginning of an undertaking. 3. Door, gate, that which serves to stop any passage. 4. Duty paid at the entrance of the gates in towns. 5. The Turkish government, the Porte. *Puerta de dos hojas,* Folding-door. *Puerta trasera,* Back door, (Joc.) Anus. *Llamar a la puerta,* To knock at the door. *Estar por puertas,* To be reduced to beggary. *A la otra puerta,* That won't do, no objections can persuade me to the contrary. *La Sublime Puerta* or *La Puerta Otomana,* The Ottoman Porte. *A puerta cerrada,* Secretly. *A cada puerta su dueña,* In the care of a household nothing must be neglected. *Dejar a uno por puertas,* To lose another person's fortune. *Dar con la puerta en los hocicos,* To slam the door in one's face.

Puertaventana [poo-er-tah-ven-tah'-nah], *f.* Door with a window in it.

Puertecita [poo-er-tay-thee'-tah], *f. dim.* A small door.

Puertecillo [poo-er-tay-theel'-lyo], *m. dim.* A small port.

Puertezuela [poo-er-tay-thoo-ay'-lah], *f. dim.* *V.* PUERTECITA.

Puertezuelo, *m. dim.* *V.* PUERTECILLO.

Puerto [poo-err'-to], *m.* 1. Port, harbour, haven for ships. *Puerto habilitado,* A port of entry. 2. Pass, through mountains. 3. Asylum, shelter, refuge. 4. (Prov.) Dam in a river.

Puerto aéreo or **aeropuerto** [poo-err'-to ah-ay'-ray-o, ah-ay-ro-poo-err'-to], *m.* Airport.

Puertorriqueño, ña [poo-err-tor-re-kay'-nyo, nyah], *a.* & *m.* & *f.* Puerto Rican, from Puerto Rico.

Pues [poo-es'], *adv., conj.* 1. Then, therefore. 2. Inasmuch as; since. 3. Sure, surely; certainly; ay, yes. 4. (Obs.) *V.* DESPUÉS. At the beginning of a clause it is used to strengthen what has just been said. *¡Pues no faltaba más!* Surely; of course.

Pues, *int.* Well, then; therefore. *¿Y pues?* Well, and what of that? *Pues sí,* (Iron.) Yes, indeed! *¿Pues y qué?* Why not? what else? what then? *Pues no le tenía yo por rico,* Indeed I did not think him rich. *Pues ese es mi rival,* Well, that is my rival.

Puesta [poo-es'-tah], *f.* 1. (Obs.) *V.* POSTA. 2. Resigning a hand of cards. *Puesta del sol,* Sunset. *A puesta* or *puestas de sol,* At sunset.

Puesto [poo-es'-to], *m.* 1. Place or space occupied; particular spot, an assigned post. 2. Shop or place where any thing is sold by retail; stall, booth. 3. Post, employment, dignity, office. 4. House in which stallions are kept and let to mares. 5. (Mil.) Barrack for soldiers. 6. Place covered with bushes to conceal sportsmen.

Puesto, ta [poo-es'-to, tah], *pp. irr.* of PONER. Put.

Puesto [poo-es'-to], *adv.* Because, for this reason that, on this account that. *Puesto que,* Although. *V.* AUNQUE.

¡ **Puf!** [poof], *int.* A word expressive of the unpleasant sensation of a bad smell.

Púgil [poo'-heel], *m.* Prize-fighter, boxer, bruiser, pugilist.

Pugilar [poo-he-lar'], *m.* Hebrew manual of the Scriptures used in synagogues.

Pugilato [poo-he-lah'-to], *m.* Pugilism, boxing or fighting.

Pugna [poog'-nah], *f.* Combat, conflict, battle.

Pugnacidad [poog-nah-the-dahd'], *f.* Pugnacity, quarrelsomeness.

Pugnante [poog-nahn'-tay], *pa.* Fighting, opposing.

Pugnar [poog-nar'], *vn.* To fight, to combat, to contend; to rival; to solicit; to importune.

Pugnaz [poog-nath'], *a.* Pugnacious, quarrelsome.

Puja [poo'-hah], *f.* Outbidding or overbidding at a public sale. *Sacar de la puja,* To outwit, to conquer by stratagem or address.

Pujadero, ra [poo-hah-day'-ro, rah], *a.* That which might be outbid, or enhanced.

Pujador, ra [poo-hah-dor', rah], *m.* & *f.* Outbidder, overbidder, highest bidder.

Pujame, Pujamen [pooh-hah'-may], *m.* (Naut.) Under part of the sails.

Pujamiento [poo-hah-me-en'-to], *m.* Flow or violent agitation of the blood or humours.

Pujante [poo-hahn'-tay], *a.* Powerful, puissant, strong, predominant, forcible.

Pujanza [poo-hahn'-thah], *f.* Power, might, strength, puissance.

Pujar [poo-har'], *va.* 1. To outbid. 2. To labour under an impediment of speech, to falter. 3. To be eager in the pursuit of a thing, to endeavour earnestly. 4. (Coll.) To make a face as if to cry.

Pujavante [poo-hah-vahn'-tay], *m.* Butteris, an instrument for paring a horse's foot.

Pujés [poo-hays'], *m.* (Obs.) Pointing the thumb in contempt. *V.* Higa.

Pujo [poo'-ho], *m.* 1. Tenesmus. 2. Violent desire, eagerness, longing; anxiety. *A pujos,* Slowly, with difficulty.

Pulcritud [pool-cre-tood'], *f.* Pulchritude, beauty, grace, gentility.

Pulcro, cra [pool'-cro, crah], *a.* 1. Beautiful, graceful. 2. Affectedly nice in dress.

Pulga [pool'-gah], *f.* Flea. *Pulgas,* Playing tops for children. *Tener malas pulgas,* To be easily piqued or fretted, to be ill-tempered.

Pulgada [pool-gah'-dah], *f.* Inch, the twelfth part of a foot.

Pulgar [pool-gar'], *m.* 1. The thumb. *Dedo pulgar del pie,* The great toe. 2. Shoots left on vines. *Menear los pulgares,* To hasten the execution of any thing; to turn over a hand of cards.

Pulgarada [pool-gah-rah'-dah], *f.* 1. Fillip, a jerk of the middle finger let go from the thumb. 2. Pinch, quantity taken between the thumb and forefinger. 3. *V.* Pulgada.

Pulgón [pool-gone'], *m.* Vine-fretter, plant louse, aphis.

Pulgoso, sa [pool-goh'-so, sah], *a.* Pulicose, abounding with fleas.

Pulguera [pool-gay'-rah], *f.* 1. Place abounding with fleas. 2. (Bot.) Pulic, flea-wort. Plantago psyllium. *Pulgueras,* Wings of the cross-bow. *V.* Empulgueras.

Pulguita [pool gee'-tah], *f dim.* A little flea.

Pulguilla [pool-geel'-lyah], *f. dim.* A little flea. *Pulguillas, com.,* A restless, fretful person.

Pulicán [poo-le-cahn'], *m.* Pelican, instrument for drawing teeth.

Pulicaria [poo-le-cah'-re-ah], *f.* Fleawort. *V.* Zaragatona.

Pulidamente, *adv.* Neatly, sprucely, cleanly, nicely, compactly.

Pulidero [poo-le-day'-ro], *m.* 1. Polisher, glosser. 2. Polisher, an instrument for polishing or burnishing.

Pulidez, Pulideza [poo-le-deth'], *f.* Neatness, cleanliness.

Pulido, da [poo-lee'-do, dah], *a.* Neat, cleanly, nice.—*pp.* of Pulir.

Pulidor [poo-le-dor'], *m.* 1. Polisher, furbisher. 2. Instrument for polishing and burnishing.

Pulimentable [poo-le-men-tah'-blay], *a.* Susceptible of polish.

Pulimentar [poo-le-men-tar'], *va.* 1. To gloss, to polish very bright. 2. (Coll.) To finish.

Pulimento [poo-le-men'-to], *m.* 1. Polish, glossiness, artificial gloss. 2. (Coll.) Finishing.

Pulir [poo-leer'], *va.* 1. To polish, to burnish, to furbish. 2. To adorn, to beautify.—*vr.* 1. To be polished; to adorn, beautify, embellish, or deck one's self. 2. To become polished or elegant in dress or manners.

Pulmón [pool-mone'], *m.* Lung. *Pulmón acuático,* Aqualung. *Pulmón de hierro,* (Med.) Iron lung.

Pulmonaria [pool-mo-nah'-re-ah], *f.* (Bot.) Lungwort. Pulmonaria. *Pulmonaria oficinal,* Common lungwort. Pulmonaria officinalis.

Pulmonía [pool-mo-nee'-ah], *f.* Pneumonia, lung fever.

Pulmoníaco ca, Pulmonario, ria [pool-mo-nee'-ah-co, cah], *a.* Affected with inflammation of the lungs; pulmonary, pulmonic.

Pulpa [pool'-pah], *f.* 1. Pulp, the most solid part of the flesh. 2. Pulp of fruit.

Pulpejo [pool-pay'-ho], *m.* The fleshy prominence of some organs of the body, especially the ball of the thumb or lobe of the ear.

Pulpería [pool-pay-ree'-ah], *f.* In America, a grocery store, where all sorts of provisions and liquors are retailed. In Cuba, and some parts of South America, it is called *Bodega.*

Pulpero [pool-pay'-ro], *m.* 1. In America, grocer. 2. Catcher of cuttle-fish.

Pulpeta [pool-pay'-tah], *f.* Slice of stuffed meat.

Pulpetón [pool-pay-tone'], *m. aug.* Large slice of stuffed meat.

Púlpito [pool'-pe-to], *m.* 1. Pulpit. 2. The dignity or office of a preacher. *Paño de púlpito,* Pulpit-cloth.

Pulpo [pool'-po], *m.* Cuttle-fish, poulp, octopus. Sepia octopus. *Poner como un pulpo,* To beat severely.

Pulposo, sa [pool-po'-so, sah], *a.* Pulpous, fleshy.

Pulque [pool'-kay], *m.* Liquor prepared in America from the maguey or Agave Americana. *Pulque curado,* (Coll. Mex.) The same liquor, prepared with pine-apple and sugar; a common beverage in that country.

Pulquería [pool-kay-ree'-ah], *f.* The place where the liquor *pulque* is sold.

Pulsación [pool-sah-the-on'], *f.* 1. Pulsation. 2. Pulse, the beating of an artery.

Pulsada [pool-sah'-dah], *f.* Any pulse-beat.

Pulsador, ra [pool-sah-dor', rah], *m.* & *f.* One who examines the pulse.

Pulsar [pool-sar'], *va.* 1. To touch. *V.* Tocar. 2. To feel the pulse. 3. To explore, to try, to sound or examine an affair.—*vn.* To pulsate, to beat as the pulse.

Pulsátil [pool-sah'-teel], *a.* 1. Sounding when struck, as bells. 2. *V.* Pulsativo.

Pulsativo, va [pool-sah-tee'-vo, vah], *a.* Pulsing, beating.

Pulsatorio, ria [pool-sah-to'-re-o, ah], *a.* Relating to the pulse.

Pulsear [pool-say-ar'], *vn.* To test who has most strength in the wrists by grasping hands and resting the elbows on a table.

Pulsera [pool-say'-rah], *f.* 1. Bandage applied to a vein or artery. 2. Bracelet for the wrists.

Pulsímetro [pool-see'-may-tro], *m.* 1. Pulsimeter, an instrument for learning the readiness with which evaporation is effected in a vacuum. 2. Pulsimeter, an instrument for measuring the rapidity of the pulse.

Pulsión [pool-se-on'], *f.* Propulsion, propagation of undulatory motion in an elastic fluid.

Pulsista [pool-sees'-tah], *m.* & *a.* Applied to a medical man well skilled in the doctrine of the pulse.

Pulso [pool'-so], *m.* 1. Pulse, the beating of an artery, perceived by the touch. 2. Part of the wrist where the pulse is felt. 3. Steadiness of the hand. *A pulso,* With the strength of the hand. 4. Attention, care, circumspection. *Obra con gran pulso,* He acts with a deal of circumspection. *Tomar el pulso,* (1) To feel the pulse. (2) To feel one's pulse, to try or know one's mind artfully.

Pultáceo, cea [pool-tah'-thay-o, ah], *a.* Pultaceous, semi-fluid.

Pululante [poo-loo-lahn'-tay], *pa.* Pullulating.

Pulular [poo-loo-lar'], *vn.* 1. To pullulate, to germ, to bud. 2. To multiply with great rapidity, as bacteria or insects. 3. To swarm, to be lively.

Pulverizable [pool-vay-re-thah'-blay], *a.* Reducible to powder; pulverable, pulverizable.

Pulverización [pool-vay-re-thah-the-on'], *f.* Pulverization, comminution.

Pulverizador de átomos [pool-vah-ree-thah-dore' day ah'-to-mos], *m.* Atom smasher.

Pulverizar [pool-vay-re-thar'], *va.* To pulverize, to grind, to comminute.

Pulverulento, ta [pool-vay-roo-len'-to, tah], *a.* Pulverulent, dusty, in the form of powder.

Pulzol, Puzol, Punzó [pool-thole', poon-tho'], *m.* & *a.* A bright scarlet colour.

Pulla [pool'-lyah], *f.* 1. Loose, obscene expression. 2. Repartee, witty saying. 3. Eagle that dwells in the trunks of trees.

Pullista [pool-lyees'-tah], *com.* One fond of witty sayings, or who says loose expressions.

¡ **Pum!** [poom], *int.* Bang! exclamation expressing a noise, explosion, or knock.

Puma [poo'-mah], *m.* (Zool.) Puma, the American panther or cougar. Felis concolor. (Peru.)

Pumarada [poo-ma-rah'-dah], *f.* An Asturian name for an apple-orchard.

Puna [poo'-nah], *f.* (Peru, Bol.) 1. A lofty, bleak region, uninhabitable through cold. 2. Difficulty of breathing from rarefied air. *Cf.* Veta.

Punción [poon-the-on'], *f.* Puncture of a swelling to evacuate it.

Puncha [poon'-chah], *f.* Thorn, prick, any thing that pricks the flesh.

Pundonor [poon-do-nor'], *m.* Point of honour; punctiliousness.

Pundonorcillo [poon-do-nor-theel'-lyo], *m.* Punctilio.

Pundonorosamente, *adv.* Punctiliously.

Pundonoroso, sa [poon-do-no-ro'-so, sah], *a.* Having a nice sense of honour, punctilious.

Punganes [poon-gah'-nes], *m. pl.* Instruments to open cockles, oysters, etc.

Pungente [poon-hen'-tay], *pa.* Pungent.

Pungimiento [poon-he-me-en'-to], *m.* Act of punching or pricking.

Pungir [poon-heer'], *va.* 1. To punch, to prick. 2. To stimulate the passions, the spirit, the heart.

Pungitivo, va [poon-he-tee'-vo, vah], *a.* Punching, pricking.

Punible [poo-nee'-blay], *a.* (Law) Punishable, actionable.

Punición [poo-ne-the-on'], *f.* Punishment, chastisement.

Púnico, ca [poo'-ne-co, cah], *a.* Punic, relating to the Carthaginians.

Punir [poo-neer'], *va.* (Obs.) To punish. *V.* Castigar.

Punta [poon'-tah], *f.* 1. Point, the sharp end of an instrument. 2. Extremity of any thing which terminates in an angle; top, head, summit; point, prong, nib, tip. 3. Point, headland, promontory. 4. Prong or tine of an antler. 5. Tartness, sourish taste. 6. Point-lace. 7. (Typ.) A bodkin for picking type from a form. 8. Somewhat, some good points: implying a high grade of intellectual or moral qualities. (Used with *tener.*) 9. Tracing-point, style, graver. 10. The end of a log, after beams, etc., have been sawed from it. 11. The pointing of game by a dog. *De puntas,* On tiptoe, softly. *Puntas,* On a dress, scallops. *Andar de puntas,* To be on bad terms, to quarrel. *Armar de punta en blanco,* To be armed to the teeth. *Hacer punta,* (1) To take the road, to be the first, to lead; to oppose, to contradict; to excel, to surpass. (2) To knit, to make lace. *Tener algo en la punta de la lengua,* To have something on the tip of one's tongue.

Puntación [poon-tah-the-on'], *f.* Punctuation. *V.* Puntuación.

Puntada [poon-tah'-dah], *f.* 1. Stitch with a needle and thread. 2. Word carelessly dropped in conversation.

Punta de combate [poon'-tah day com-bah'-tay], *f.* (Mil.) Warhead.

Puntal [poon-tahl'], *m.* 1. Prop to support a wall or building; fulcrum. 2. The stay in the bed of a ploughshare. 3. (Naut.) Stanchion. *Puntal de la bodega,* (Naut.) Depth of the hold.

Puntapié [poon-tah-pe-ay'], *m.* A kick. *Mandar (a alguno) a puntapiés,* To have complete ascendency over one.

Puntar [poon-tar'], *va.* To mark with small dots or points.

Punteadura [poon-tay-ah-doo'-rah], *f.* Teeth of a wheel.

Puntear [poon-tay-ar'], *va.* 1. To play upon the guitar. 2. To punctuate, to mark, to point out. 3. To sew, to stitch.—*vn.* (Naut.) To go obliquely, catching the wind when it is slack.

Puntel [poon-tel'], *m.* Pontil or pontee, a glass-blower's iron rod.

Puntera [poon-tay'-rah], *f.* 1. (Bot.) Common houseleek. Sempervivum tectorum. 2. A patch over the tip of a shoe. 3. Tip, a re-enforcing piece put over the toe of a shoe. 4. (Coll.) A kick.

Puntería [poon-tay-ree'-ah], *f.* 1. The act of levelling or pointing fire-arms. 2. Aim, the direction of a weapon. 3. Teeth of a wheel.

Punterico, illo, ito [poon-tay-ree'-co], *m. dim.* A little fescue.

Puntero [poon-tay'-ro], *m.* 1. Fescue, a pointer to point out the letters to children. 2. A pointed instrument for marking any thing. 3. Chisel used by stone-cutters. 4. Graver, style.

Puntero, ra [poon-tay'-ro, rah], *a.* Taking good aim with fire-arms.

Punterola [poon-tay-ro'-lah], *f.* (Min.) Poll-pick, a bar of iron with a steel point.

Puntiagudo, da [poon-te-ah-goo'-do, dah], *a.* Sharp-pointed, mucronated.

Puntica, ita [poon-tee'-cah], *f. dim.* A small point or sharp end of an instrument.

Puntico, ito [poon-tee'-co], *m. dim.* of Punto.

Puntilla [poon-teel'-lyah], *f.* 1. A small point. 2. A narrow lace edging. *De puntillas,* Softly, gently; on tiptoe. *Ponerse de puntillas,* To persist obstinately in one's opinion. 3. (Mech.) Brad, joiner's nail; a carpenter's tracing-point. 4. *V.* Cachete.

Puntillazo [poon-til-lyah'-tho], *m.* Kick.

Puntillo [poon-teel'-lyo], *m.* 1. Punctilio, trifling, despicable thing, in which a punctilious person places honour. 2. (Dim.) A small point.

Puntillón [poon-til-lyone'], *m.* Kick. *V.* Puntillazo.

Puntilloso, sa [poon-til-lyo'-so, sah], *a.* Ticklish, difficult, litigious, punctilious.

Puntiví, or **Pontiví** [poon-te-vee'], *m.* Sort of Silesia linen.

Puntizón [poon-te-thone'], *m.* Holes pricked in the paper sheet by the frisket.

Punto [poon'-to], *m.* 1. Point of time or space. 2. Point, subject under consideration. 3. End or design. 4. Degree, state. 5. Nice point of ceremony: point of honour; punctilio. 6. Opportunity, fit place or time. *A buen punto,* Opportunely. *Al punto,* Instantly. 7. Point, period in writing. 8. Aim, sight. 9. Stitch, in sewing or surgery. 10. Point, gist, substance of a matter. 11. Actual state of any business matter. 12. Turn, finished state of something prepared by the fire. 13. Part or question of a science. 14. The smallest part of a thing. 15. Tumbler of a gun-lock. 16. Hole in stockings; mesh of a net; vacancy in lace. 17. Right sound of musical instruments. 18. Part of the bell where the clapper strikes. 19. Weight used in passementerie to keep the narrow linens stretched. 20. In straps, a hole for receiving the tongue of a buckle. 21. Speckle, dot, the work upon the face of a silk fabric which bears no especial design. 22. Each nib of a pen. 23. A fine cloth of thread, cotton, or silk. 24. In schools, each mistake of a scholar in reciting a lesson from memory. 25. Dot, spot, on dice or cards. 26. End of the course in universities; recess, intermission in business in courts, when the time of vacation arrives. 27. Highest point or pitch. 28. Cab-stand, fixed place for public vehicles for hire. 29. Point, object of destination or action. 30. Twelfth part of a line. *Poner los puntos muy altos,* To soar very high; to make extravagant pretensions. *Por puntos,* From one moment to another. *Punto de malla,* Mesh of a net. *Punto de media,* Stocking-net. *Punto de bobiné,* Bobbinet lace. *Punto de tul,* Tulle. *En su último punto,* In the highest pitch. *Punto en boca,* (A stitch in the lips) silence. *Punto crudo,* The moment in which something happens. *A punto crudo,* Late, inopportunely. *A punto fijo,* Exactly, with certainty. *Punto de apoyo,* Point of support, fulcrum. *Punto menos,* A trifle smaller. *Bajar de punto,* To decay, to decline. *Hacer punto,* To stop reading or talking. *Dar punto,* To give a vacation to classes. *Hombre* or *mujer de punto,* Principal person of distinction. *Punto,* or *punto final,* Period. *Punto y coma,* Semicolon. *Dos puntos,* Colon.

Puntoso, sa [poon-to'-so, sah], *a.* 1. Acuminated, having many points. 2. Spirited, lively, courageous. 3. Too punctilious in etiquette.

Puntuación [poon-too-ah-the-on'], *f.* Punctuation.

Puntual [poon-too-ahl'], *a.* 1. Punctual, exact, accurate. 2. Certain, sure. 3. Convenient, adequate.

Puntualidad [poon-too-ah-le-dahd'], *f.* 1. Punctuality, exactness. 2. Certitude, preciseness.

Puntualizar [poon-too-ah-le-thar'], *va.* 1. To imprint on the mind or memory. 2. To finish, to accomplish, to complete. 3. To give a detailed account.

Puntualmente, *adv.* Punctually, exactly, faithfully, accurately.

Puntuar [poon-too-ar'], *va.* To punctuate, to point.

Puntuoso, sa [poon-too-o'-so, sah], *a.* *V* Puntoso and Pundonoroso.

Puntura [poon-too'-rah], *f.* 1. Puncture. 2. Point which holds the sheet in a printing-press.

Punzada [poon-thah'-dah], *f.* 1. Prick, push. 2. Sting, pain; compunction.

Punzador, ra [poon-thah-dor', rah], *m. & f.* Pricker, wounder.

Punzadura [poon-thah-doo'-rah], *f.* Puncture, prick.

Punzar [poon-thar'], *va.* 1. To punch, to bore or perforate. 2. To prick, to wound. 3. To sting, to cause pain. 4. To sting or afflict the mind.

Punzó, or **Punzón** [poon-tho'], *a.* Deep scarlet red.

Punzón [poon-thone'], *m.* 1. Punch, an instrument used by artists and workmen; puncheon; puncher; type-founder's punch. 2. The ring and shaft of a key worn on the flap of the coat-pocket by gentlemen of the bed-chamber to the King of Spain. 3. Young horn of a deer.

Punzoncico, illo, ito [poon-thon-thee'-co], *m. dim.* A small punch.

Punzonería [poon-tho-nay-ree'-ah], *f.* Collection of moulds for making a fount of types.

Puñada [pooh-nyah'-dah], *f.* Cuff, blow with the fist. *Venir a las puñadas,* (Obs.) To come to blows.—*pl.* Fisticuffs.

Puñado [pooh-nyah'-do], *m.* Handful; a few. *A puñados,* Plentifully, abundantly. *¡ Gran puñado !* or *¡ qué puñado !* (Coll.) Expression of contempt for the quantity or the quality of a thing offered.

Puñal [pooh-nyahl'], *m.* Poniard, dagger.

Puñalada [pooh-nyay-lah'-dah], *f.* 1 Stab with a poniard. 2. A sudden shock of grief or pain. *Dar* or *tirar una puñalada a uno,* To make a pass at a person.

Puñalejo [pooh-nyah-lay'-ho], *m. dim.* Small poniard.

Puñalero [pooh-nyah-lay'-ro], *m.* Maker or seller of poniards.

Puñetazo [pooh-nyay-tah'-tho], *m.* Blow with the shut fist.

Puñete [pooh-nyay'-tay], *m.* Blow with the fist. *Puñetes,* Bracelets for the wrists.

Puño [pooh'-nyo], *m.* 1. The fist. 2. Handful, grasp. 3. Scantiness, narrowness. *Un puño de casa*, A small house. 4. Wristband. 5. Handruffle; cuff, mittens. 6. Hilt, guard of a sword; handle; head of a staff or cane. 7. (Naut.) Each of the lower points of a sail in which the tacks are fastened. *Apretar los puños*, To exert the utmost efforts. *Pegar a puño cerrado*, To strike with might and main. *Creer a puño cerrado*, To believe firmly. *Hombre de puños*, A strong, valiant man. *Ser como un puño*, To be miserable; close-fisted.

Puones [poo-oh'-nes], *m. pl.* The large, uneven teeth of cards.

Pupa [poo'-pah], *f.* 1. Pustule, pimple. 2. The plaintive sound of children to express uneasiness.

Pupila [poo-pee'-lah], *f.* 1. Pupil of the eye. 2. Orphan girl, ward.

Pupilaje [poo-pe-lah'-hay], *m.* 1. Pupilage, wardship. 2. Board, the state of one who boards with another. 3. Boarding-house.

Pupilar [poo-pe-lar'], *a.* Pupillary, belonging to a pupil or ward, or to the pupil of the eye.

Pupilero, ra [poo-pe-lay'-ro, rah], *m.* & *f.* Master or mistress of a boarding-house or boarding-school.

Pupilo [poo-pee'-lo], *m.* 1. Pupil, ward. 2. Pupil, scholar, student.

Pupitre [poo-pee'-tray], *m.* A writing-desk.

Puposo, sa [poo-po'-so, sah], *a.* Pustulous, pustulate.

Puramente [poo-rah-men'-tay], *adv.* Purely, chastely; entirely, merely; genuinely.

Puré [poo-ray'], *m.* Puree, thick soup. *Puré de papas*, Mashed potatoes. *Puré de manzanas*, Apple sauce.

Pureza [poo-ray'-thah], *f.* Purity, innocence, integrity; chastity; purity of diction; fineness, genuineness; cleanness, excellence.

Purga [poor'-gah], *f.* 1. Purge, a cathartic medicine. 2. (Amer.) Refining, especially of sugar.

Purgable [poor-gah'-blay], *a.* That may be purged.

Purgacion [poor-gah-the-on'], *f.* 1. Purgation. 2. Catamenia. 3. Gonorrhœa, gleet: commonly used in the plural. 4. Act of clearing from imputation of guilt.

Purgador, ra [poor-gah-dor', rah], *m.* & *f.* One who purges, purger.

Purgante [poor-gahn'-tay], *a.* & *m.* Purgative, laxative, cleanser.

Purgar [poor-gar'], *va.* 1. To purge, to purify, to cleanse. 2. To atone, to expiate. 3. To purify, to refine. 4. To suffer the penalties of purgatory. 5. To purge, to evacuate the body. 6. To clear from guilt or imputation of guilt.—*vr.* To rid or clear one's self from guilt.

Purgativo, va [poor-gah-tee'-vo, vah], *a.* Purgative, cathartic, purging.

Purgatorio [poor-gah-to'-re-o], *m.* 1. Purgatory. 2. Any place where life is imbittered by painful drudgery and troubles.

Puridad [poo-re-dahd'], *f.* (Obs.) 1. Purity, freedom from foulness or dirt. 2. Integrity, entirety, exact observance. *En puridad*, Clearly, openly, without tergiversation; in secret.

Purificación [poo-re-fe-cah-the-on'], *f.* 1. Purification, making pure; cleansing, expurgation. 2. Purification, a festival of the Christian church, on 2d February. 3. The act of churching women. 4. Cleansing the chalice after the wine is drunk at the mass.

Purificadero, ra [poo-re-fe-cah-day'-ro, rah], *a.* Cleansing, purifying.

Purificador, ra [poo-re-fe-cah-dor', rah], *m.* & *f.* 1. Purifier, purger. 2. Purificator, the cloth with which the priest wipes the chalice.

Purificar [poo-re-fe-car'], *va.* To purify, to clean, to cleanse, to clear, to fine.—*vr.* 1. To be purified, to be cleansed. 2. To be churched.

Purificatorio, ria [poo-re-fe-cah-to'-re-o, ah], *a.* Purificatory, purificative.

Puriforme [poo-re-for'-may], *a.* Puriform, presenting the appearance of pus.

Purísima (La) [lah poo-ree'-se-mah], *f.* Epithet of the Virgin Mary in the mystery of her immaculate conception.

Purismo [poo-rees'-mo], *m.* The act of affecting too much purity of diction, purism.

Purista [poo-rees'-tah], *m.* 1. Purist, one over-particular as to purity of literary style. 2. One who writes or speaks in a pure style.

Puritanismo [poo-re-tah-nees'-mo], *m.* Puritanism.

Puritano, na [poo-re-tah'-no, nah], *a.* Puritan, puritanical, puritanic.

Puritano, na, *m.* & *f.* A Puritan.

Puro, ra [poo'-ro, rah], *a.* 1. Pure, free, unmingled. 2. Pure, clear, clean, neat, genuine, net, fine. 3. Pure, chaste, modest. 4. Pure, guiltless, innocent, just. 5. Pure, incorrupt, not vitiated, exempt from imperfections. *De puro*, Extremely; by dint of.—*m.* Cigar, a little roll of tobacco for smoking, to distinguish it from *cigarro* and *cigarrillo*, a small roll of paper filled with fine-chopped tobacco.

Púrpura [poor'-poo-rah], *f.* 1. Rock-shell, purple-shell, royal purple. Murex. 2. Cloth dyed with purple. 3. Dignity of a king or cardinal. 4. (Poet.) Blood.

Purpurante [poor-poo-rahn'-tay], *pa.* Giving a purple colour.

Purpurar [poor-poo-rar'], *va.* 1. To purple, to make red. 2. To dress in purple.—*vn.* To take or show a purple colour.

Purpúreo, rea [poor-poo'-ray-o, ah], *a.* 1. Purple, puniceous. 2. Belonging to a cardinal or to the cardinalate.

Purpúrico [poor-poo'-re-co], *a.* *Ácido purpúrico*, Purpuric acid, obtained by treating uric acid with nitric acid; murexide.

Purpurina [poor-poo-ree'-nah], *f.* 1. Bronze ground for painting. 2. Purpurin, a colouring matter obtained from madder.

Purpurino, na [poor-poo-re'-no, nah], *a.* Purple.

Purrela [poor-ray'-lah], *f.* Wine of the most inferior quality.

Purriela [poor-re-ay'-lah], *f.* Any thing despicable or of little value.

Purulencia [poo-roo-len'-the-ah], *f.* Purulence, purulency.

Purulento, ta [poo-roo-len'-to, tah], *a.* Purulent.

Pus [poos], *m.* Pus.

Pusilánime [poo-se-lah'-ne-may], *a.* Pusillanimous, mean-spirited, dastardly, timorous, faint-hearted.

Pusilánimemente, *adv.* Heartlessly.

Pusilanimidad [poo-se-lah-ne-me-dahd'], *f.* Pusillanimity, cowardliness, timorousness.

Pústula [poos'-too-lah], *f.* Pustule, pimple.

Pustoloso, sa [poos-to-lo'-so, sah], *a.* Pustulous, pustular.

Puta [poo'-tah], *f.* Whore, prostitute, harlot.

Putaismo, Putanismo [poo-tah-ees'-mo], *m.* Whoredom, harlotry.

Putañear [poo-tah-nyay-ar'], *vn.* (Low) To whore, to go whoring.

Putañero [poo-tah-nyay'-ro], *a.* (Low) Whorish, given to lewdness.—*m.* Whoremaster, whoremonger.

Putativo, va [poo-tah-tee'-vo, vah], *a.* Putative, reputed.

Puteal [poo-tay-ahl'], *m.* Stone used as the cover of a well on which soothsayers prophesied.

Putear [poo-tay-ar'], *vn.* (Coll.) *V.* PUTAÑEAR.

Putería [poo-tay-ree'-ah], *f.* (Low) 1. The manner of living and trade of a prostitute. 2. Brothel. 3. Meretricious arts of lewd women.

Putero [poo-tay'-ro], *m.* (Low) Whoremaster, whoremonger.

Putesco, ca [poo-tes'-co, cah], *a.* (Coll.) Relating to whores.

Putilla, ita [poo-teel'-lyah], *f. dim.* (Coll.) Young prostitute.

Puto [poo'-to], *m.* (Low) Catamite, sodomite. *A puto el postre*, (Coll.) The devil take the hindmost.

Putput [poot'-poot], *m.* (Orn.) Hoopoe. *V.* ABUBILLA.

Putredinal [poo-tray-de-nahl'], *a.* Putrefying, corrupting.

Putrefacción [poo-tray-fac-the-on'], *f.* Putrefaction, corruptness.

Putrefactivo, va [poo-tray-fac-tee'-vo, vah], *a.* Putrefactive.

Putridez [poo-tre-deth'], *f.* Putridity.

Pútrido, da [poo'-tre-do, dah], *a.* Putrid, rotten.

Puya [poo'-yah], *f.* Pointed rod.

Puyar [poo-yar'], *vn.* (Obs.) To mount, to ascend.

Puyero, ra [poo-yay'-ro, rah], *m.* & *f.* (Cuba) 1. *V.* PULLISTA. 2. One who is knock-kneed.

Puzol, *m.* **Puzolana,** *f.* [poo-thole', poo-tho-lah'-nah]. Puzzolana, a porous volcanic production.

Q

Q [koo], twentieth letter of the Castilian alphabet, which is always followed by *u*, sounds as the English *k*. Formerly it had a proper sound, and the following *u* was marked with a diæresis in words beginning with *que*, when the *q* was pronounced, as in *qüestion;* but now all these words, as well as all those beginning with *qua* or *quo*, are to be written with *c*.

Que [kay], *pron. rel.* 1. That. 2. Who, speaking of persons. 3. Which, speaking of things. 4. What, a particle expressive of admiration. *¡Qué desgracia!* What a misfortune! 5. What, as an interrogative. *¿Qué es eso?* or *¿qué cosa es esa?* What is that? *¿Qué es eso?* or *¿qué hay?* What is the matter, or what is the matter there? 6. Than, as, a comparative particle: *más que* or *más de*, more than; *tanto que*, as much as. *Algo que*, more than. 7. Whether. *Que venga o que no venga*, Whether he comes or not. *Tarde que temprano*, Early or late. 8. Because, why. 9. *conj.* Used after a verb it is a particle, which governs and determines another verb. *Le mandó que viniese*, He ordered him to come. 10. Where, in what place? *¿Qué es del libro?* Where is the book? 11. *Lo que*, That which. *Sea lo que fuere*, Let it be what it may. *Hay en eso algo más de lo que se presume*. There is in that affair more than what is imagined. *No hay para qué*, There is no occasion for it. *No hay de qué*, Don't mention it; you are wel come. *¿ Pues y qué?* Why not? what then? *Sin qué ni para qué,* Without cause or motive. Note.—*Que* in interrogatory or exclamatory use receives the accent to distinguish it from the relative and the conjunction. See the examples.

Qué, *m.* Something, somewhat.

Quebrable [kay-brah'-blay], *a.* Breakable.

Quebrada [kay-brah'-dah], *f.* 1. Ravine. 2. A deep pass. 3. A commercial failure.

Quebradero [kay-brah-day'-ro], *m.* Breaker. *Quebradero de cabeza,* 1. That which molests, importunes, or occupies the mind. 2. Object of amorous care.

Quebradillo [kay-brah-deel'-lyo], *m.* 1. Wooden shoe-heel. 2. Flexure of the body in dancing.

Quebradizo, za [kay-brah-dee'-tho, thah], *a.* 1. Brittle, fragile. 2. Infirm, sickly. 3. Flexible: applied to the voice. 4. (Met.) *V.* FRÁGIL.

Quebrado, da [kay-brah'-do, dah], *a.* Broken; debilitated, enervated. *Andar de pie quebrado,* To be on the decline; to be in narrow circumstances. *Azúcar quebrado,* Brown sugar.—*pp.* of QUEBRAR.

Quebrado [kay-brah'-do], *m.* 1. (Arith.) Fraction, broken number. 2. (Poet.) Verse consisting of two, three, or four syllables, left so on purpose after a stanza of verses of eight or more syllables. 3. Bankrupt. 4. (Coll.) A ruptured person.

Quebrador, ra [kay-brah-dor', rah], *m.* & *f.* 1. Breaker. 2. One who violates a law.

Quebradura [kay-brah-doo'-rah], *f.* 1. The act of breaking or splitting. 2. A cleaving or chopping, a gap, a fissure, a slit, a fracture. 3. Rupture, hernia.

Quebraja [kay-brah'-hah], *f.* Crack, flaw, split in wood or iron.

Quebrajar [kay-brah-har'], *va.* *V.* RESQUEBRAJAR.

Quebrajoso, sa [kay-brah-ho'-so, sah], *a.* Brittle, fragile.

Quebramiento [kay-brah-me-en'-to], *m.* *V.* QUEBRANTAMIENTO.

Quebrantable [kay-bran-tah'-blay], *a.* Frangible, brittle.

Quebrantador, ra [kay-bran-tah-dor', rah], *m.* & *f.* 1. Breaker; debilitator. 2. (Met.) Violator, transgressor of any law. 3. *Quebrantador o ladrón de una cosa,* (Law) Burglar.

Quebrantadura [kay-bran-tah-doo'-rah], *f.* Fracture, rupture, a bursting.

Quebrantahuesos [kay-bran-tah-oo-ay'-sos], *m.* 1. (Orn.) Osprey. Falco ossifragus. 2. A troublesome person. 3. Play among boys.

Quebrantamiento [kay-bran-tah-me-en'-to], *m.* 1. Fracture, rupture; breaking a prison. 2. Weariness, fatigue. 3. Violation of the law; e. g. (a) (Law) Act of breaking a will. (b) *Quebrantamiento* or *robo de una casa,* Burglary. (c) *Quebrantamiento de sepultura,* Desecration of a grave.

Quebrantanueces [kay-bran-tah-noo-ay'-thes], *m.* (Orn.) Nutcracker. Corvus caryocatactes.

Quebrantaolas [kay-bran-tah-o'-las], *m.* Breakwater.

Quebrantar [kay-bran-tar'], *va.* 1. To break, to crack, to burst open, to crash. 2. To pound, to grind. 3. To persuade, to induce. 4. To move to pity. 5. To transgress a law, to violate a contract. 6. To vex, to molest, to fatigue. 7. To weaken, to debilitate. 8 To diminish, to temper the excess of any thing. 9. To annul, to revoke; to break a will. *Quebrantar la cabeza,* To humble one's pride.

Quebrantaterrones [kay-brahn-tah-ter-ro'-nes], *m.* (Coll.) Clodhopper, rustic.

Quebranto [kay-brahn'-to], *m.* 1. The act of breaking. 2. Weakness, debility, lassitude. 3. Commiseration, pity, compassion. 4. Object worthy of pity. 5. Great loss, severe damage. 6. (Naut.) Cambering of a ship's deck or keel.

Quebrar [kay-brar'], *va.* 1. To break, to burst open; to cast asunder. 2. To double, to twist. 3. To interrupt, to intercept. 4. To transgress a law, to violate a contract. 5. To temper, to moderate. 6. To spoil the bloom of the countenance. 7. To overcome, to conquer. 8. To diminish friendship, to dissolve a connection, or abandon a correspondence.—*vn.* To fail, to be insolvent, to become bankrupt.—*vr.* 1. To be ruptured, to labour under a rupture. 2. To interrupt the continuity of hills or banks. *Quebrar el ojo al diablo,* (Coll.) To do that which is the best, most just, and reasonable. *Quebrar amistad,* To cut acquaintance. *Quebrar el corazón,* To break one's heart. *A la mala costumbre quebrarle la pierna,* (prov.) An evil habit must be cut short. *La soga quiebra siempre por lo más delgado,* The rope always breaks at its weakest point; when two quarrel, the weaker goes to the wall. *Quebrar la soga por alguno,* Not to perform what one has promised. *No sabe quebrar un plato,* She does not know how to say boo to a goose. *Al quebrar del alba,* At dawn of day. *Quebrarse la cabeza,* To be oversolicitous in the pursuit of any thing.

Queche [kay'-chay], *f.* (Naut.) Smack, a Dutch-built vessel; ketch. (Turk. qâiq.)

Quechemarín [kay-chay-mah-reen'], *m.* Coasting lugger.

Quechua [kay'-choo-ah], *a.* & *m.* Kechuan, the official language of the Peruvian empire at the time of the conquest. It is still preserved in Peru, Bolivia and Ecuador. (Quechúa with accented u, as printed by the Academy, is an erratum.)

Queda [kay'-dah], *f.* The time of retirement marked by the sound of a bell or the beat of a drum; curfew.

Quedada [kay-dah'-dah], *f.* Stay, residence, sojourn.

Quedar [kay-dar'], *vn.* 1. To stay, to stop in a place. 2. To continue, to tarry, to remain. 3. To be wanting. 4. To hold, to last, to subsist. 5. To knock down a thing to the last bidder. 6. To behave, to conduct one's self, to acquire a reputation or to be reputed. *Quedar por andar,* To have to walk farther. *Quedar por cobarde,* To shrink back as a coward. *Quedar por valiente,* To enjoy the reputation of a brave man. *El campo quedó por los americanos,* The Americans were victorious. *Quedar limpio,* (Coll.) To remain with an empty purse, to be square. *Quedar con uno,* To agree, to arrange or compound with any one. *Quedar por uno,* To leave another's business to be executed by himself. *El negocio no quedará por él,* (Met.) The business will not fail on his account. *Quedar por alguno,* To become surety. 7. With a past participle it often is employed in place of *estar,* to be (*V.* any grammar); as, *Quedar armado,* To be armed. *Quedar bien* or *mal,* To behave or come off well or ill in an affair; to fail or succeed in an attempt.—*va.* (Prov.) To leave.—*vr.* 1. To remain, to continue; to retain, to possess, to keep. 2. To falter, to lose the thread of a speech or argument; to stop short. *Quedarse helado,* To be astonished, to be thunderstruck. *Quedarse pío,* To be disappointed; to be surprised. *Quedarse sin pulsos,* To be dispirited, to lose all courage. *Quedarse para tía* or *para vestir imágenes,* (Coll.) To become an old maid. *Quedarse in albis,* (Coll.) Not to receive a share in a distribution. *Quedarse en ayunas de alguna cosa,* Not to understand a word of the matter. *No quedarse a deber nada,* To be up with one, to be even with him. *Quedarse con una afrenta en el cuerpo,* To pocket an insult. *Quedarse fresco,* To be very much disappointed. *Quedarse muerto,* To be surprised and grieved by sudden news. *Quedarse a media miel,* To be deprived of something which one was beginning to enjoy. *Quedarse a obscuras* or *en blanco,* To be left in the dark (literally or figuratively); to be left in the lurch. *Quedársele a uno en el tintero,* To forget a thing entirely.

Quede [kay'-day]. (Typ.) Stet; let it stand: used of matter crossed out by mistake.

Quedito, ta [kay-dee'-to, tah], *a. dim.* Soft, gentle; easy. This diminutive is more energetic than its primitive, *quedo.*

Quedito [kay-dee'-to], *adv.* *V.* QUEDO.

Quedo [kay'-do], *adv.* Softly, gently; in a low voice.

Quedo, da [kay'-do, dah], *a.* Quiet, still, noiseless; easy, gentle. *A pie quedo,* Fair and easy, without trouble or fatigue. *Quedo que quedo,* Obstinate, pertinacious.

Quehacer [kay-ah-therr'], *m.* Occupation, domestic business (chore). *Cada uno tiene sus quehaceres.* Every one has his own affairs.

Queirópteros [kay-e-rop'-tay-ros], *a.* & *m. pl.* Cheiropterous; the cheiroptera, the bats.

Queja [kay'-hah], *f.* 1. Complaint, expostulation, murmur, grumbling, moan. 2. Resentment of an injury or insult. 3. Quarrel, dispute. *Tener una queja de alguno,* (Coll.) To have a bone to pick with one.

Quejarse [kay-har'-say], *vr.* To complain of, to expostulate, to murmur, to grumble. *Quejarse de,* To clamour against; to mention with sorrow, to lament. *Quejarse de vicio,* To complain without cause. *V.* QUERELLARSE.

Quejicoso, sa [kay-he-co'-so, sah], *a.* Plaintful, querulous, always complaining.

Quejidito [kay-he-dee'-to], *m. dim.* Slight complaint, a low moan.

Quejido [kay-hee'-do], *m.* Groan, moan, lament.

Quejigal [kay-he-gahl'], *m.* Plantation of muricated oaks.

Quejigo [kay-hee'-go], *m.* (Bot.) Muricated oak. Quercus muricata.

Quejita [kay-hee'-tah], *f. dim.* Murmur; resenting; slight complaint.

Quejosamente, *adv.* Querulously.

Quejoso, sa [kay-ho'-so, sah], *a.* Plaintful, querulous.

Quejumbre [kay-hoom'-bray], *f.* (Prov.) *V.* QUEJA.

Quejumbroso, sa [kay-hoom-bro'-so, sah], *a.* Complaining, plaintive.

Quelidón [kay-le-done'], *m.* Martin, a bird of the swallow family.

Quelidonia [kay-le-do'-ne-ah], *f.* (Bot.) Celandine, an herb of the poppy family. Chelidonium majus.

Quelónidos [kay-lo'-ne-dos], or **Quelo**

nios, *a.* & *m. pl.* Chelonians: turtles and tortoises.

Quema [kay'-mah], *f.* 1. Burn, the act of burning, combustion, fire, conflagration. *Huir de la quema,* To shun the danger. 2. (Met.) Oven, furnace.

Quemadero [kay-mah-day'-ro], *m.* Place where convicts were burnt.

Quemador, ra [kay-mah-dor', rah], *m.* & *f.* Incendiary; burner.

Quemadura [kay-mah-doo'-rah], *f.* 1. Mark or hurt by fire, burn. 2. (Agr.) Brand, smut upon plants.

Quemajoso, sa [kay-mah-ho'-so, sah], *a.* Smarting, burning.

Quemar [kay-mar'], *va.* 1. To burn, to consume by fire. 2. To fire, to set on fire, to kindle. 3. To burn, to parch, to dry, or scorch. 4. To dispose of a thing at a low price.—*vn.* To be too hot.—*vr.* 1. To be very hot, to be parched with heat; to heat one's self. 2. To fret, to be impatient, to be offended. 3. (Coll.) To be near, to almost attain or touch a thing desired. *Quemarse las cejas,* To study much. *A quema ropa,* (1) Immediate, very near, quite close, contiguous. (2) (Met.) Unawares, unexpectedly: applied to an unanswerable argument, or to an action unobjectionable either from its promptitude or justice. *Tomar algo por donde quema,* To take any thing in the worst sense. *Quemarle a uno la camisa en el cuerpo,* To burn one's shirt off his body. *Quemarse la sangre,* To be subject to constant vexations. *En la puerta del horno se quema el pan,* There is many a slip 'twixt the cup and the lip. *Quien se quemare, que sople,* If one wants a fire, let him blow the bellows; if you think you understand another's business better than he, try to master it. (Lat. cremare.)

Quemazón [kay-mah-thone'], *f.* 1. Burn, hurt by fire; combustion, conflagration. 2. The act of burning. 3. Excessive heat. 4. Eagerness, covetousness. 5. (Coll.) Pert language, smart repartee. 6. (Cuba) Auction where goods are sold very cheap. *Anoche hubo una gran quemazón,* (Vulg.) There was a great fire last night.

Quencho [ken'-cho], *m.* (Orn.) Gull. Larus.

(*Yo quepo, quepa, cupe.* *V.* CABER.)

Quequier, *a.* (Obs.) *V.* CUALQUIERA.

Quequisque [kay-kees'-kay], *m.* (Bot.) An arum. Colocasia esculenta.

Queratitis [kay-rah-tee'-tis], *f.* Keratitis, inflammation of the cornea.

Querella [kay-rayl'-lyah], *f.* 1. Complaint, expression of pain or grief. 2. A complaint before a judge against any one. 3. Petition or libel exhibited to a court of justice by children, praying that the last will of their parents be set aside.

Querellador, ra [kay-rayl-lyah-dor', rah], *m.* & *f.* Lamenter; complainant.

Querellante [kay-rayl-lyahn'-tay], *pa.* Murmuring, complaining.—*m.* & *f.* Complainant.

Querellarse [kay-rayl-lyar'-say], *vr.* 1. To lament, to bewail one's own sorrow; to complain of another, to be querulous. 2. To complain or prefer a complaint in a court of justice.

Querellosamente, *adv.* Plaintively, querulously.

Querelloso, sa [kay-rayl-lyo'-so, sah], *a.* Querulous.

Querencia [kay-ren'-the-ah], *f.* 1. Haunt of wild beasts. 2. Favourite and frequent place of resort.

Querencioso, sa [kay-ren-the-o'-so, sah], *a.* Frequented by wild beasts.

Querer [kay-rerr'], *va.* 1. To wish, to desire, to list. *Quiero comer,* I have an appetite. 2. To love, to cherish, to like. 3. To will, to resolve, to determine. 4. To attempt, to procure; to require. 5. To conform, to agree. 6. To accept a challenge at a game of hazard. 7. To suit, to fit. 8. To cause, to occasion.—*vn.* To be near being, to verify any thing. *Sin querer,* Unwillingly, undesignedly. *Querer más,* To have rather. *Pintar como querer,* To paint or tell a thing according to one's fancy. *¿ Qué quiere decir eso ?* What does that mean ? *¿ Qué quiere ser esto ?* What is all this ? *¿ Qué más quiere ?* What more does he wish ? what more is necessary ? *Como Vd. quiera,* As you will it; let it be so. *Como así me lo quiero,* Conformable to my will and pleasure. *Como quiera,* Any how, in any way. *Quien todo lo quiere, todo lo pierde,* (prov.) All covet, all lose. —*m.* Will, desire, study.

Queresa [kay-ray'-sah], *f.* *V.* CRESA.

Querido, da [kay-ree'-do, dah], *a.* & *pp.* of QUERER. Wished, desired; dear, beloved.—*m.* & *f.* Darling, fondling, lover, sweetheart. *Querido, querida* or *querido mío,* My dear, my love, honey, my pet, my darling.

Quermes [kayr'-mes], *m.* Kermes, an insect used as a scarlet dye. *Quermes mineral,* Kermes mineral, a preparation of antimony.

Querocha, *f.* *V.* CRESA.

Querochar [kay-ro-char'], *vn.* To emit the semen of bees.

Querosina [kay-ro-see'-nah], *f.* Kerosene, coal oil.

Querub, Querube. (Poet.) *V.* QUERUBÍN. (Heb.)

Querúbico, ca [kay-roo'-be-co, cah], *a.* Cherubic, relating to cherubs.

Querubin [kay-roo-been'], *m.* Cherub, a celestial spirit.

Quesadilla [kay-sah-deel'-lyah], *f.* 1. A sort of cheese-cake. 2. A sweetmeat; a fritter.

Quesear [kay-say-ar'], *vn.* To make cheese.

Quesera [kay-say'-rah], *f.* 1. Dairy. 2. Cheese-board, cheese-mould, cheese-vat.

Queseria [kay-say-ree'-ah], *f.* Season for making cheese.

Quesero [kay-say'-ro], *m.* Cheesemonger, cheesemaker.

Quesero, ra [kay-say'-ro, rah], *a.* Caseous, cheesy.

Quesillo, ito [kay-seel'-lyo], *m. dim.* A small cheese.

Queso [kay'-so], *m.* Cheese. *Dos de queso,* (Coll.) A trifle.

Quetzal [ket-thahl'], *m.* 1. (Orn.) Quetzal. 2. Quetzal, Guatemalan monetary unit.

Qui [kee], *pron.* (Obs.) *V.* QUIEN.

¡ Quiá ! [ke-ah']. Interjection denoting incredulity or denial. Come now ! No, indeed ! N ! n ! (sounded with no vowel).

Quiasmo [ke-ahs'-mo], *m.* 1. Chiasm, junction of two things which form a cross. 2. (Anat.) Decussation of the optic nerves.

Quibey [ke-bay'-e], *m.* (Bot.) Dog's-bane, an herb which grows in the island of Puerto Rico, very poisonous to animals which eat it. The flower resembles a violet, but is white.

Quicial, *m.* **Quicialera,** *f.* [ke-the-ahl', ke-the-ah-lay'-rah]. 1. Sidepost, or jamb of a door or window; a jamb. 2. *V.* QUICIO.

Quicio [kee'-the-o], *m.* 1. Hinge of a door; a but-hinge. 2. Prop, support. *Fuera de quicio,* Violently, unnaturally. *Sacar una cosa de quicio,* To unhinge, to overturn, to violate or pervert.

Quichua [kee'-choo-ah], *f.* *V.* QUECHUA (Rem.—*Quichua* is the vulgar term *Quechua* the proper one.)

Quid [kid], *m.* Essence, gist. *El quid del asunto,* The gist of the matter.

Quídam [kee'-dam], *m.* (Coll.) A certain person.

Quididad [ke-de-dahd'], *f.* (Obs.) Quiddity, essence.

Quid pro quo [kid pro kwo]. (Lat.) Quid pro quo, an equivalent.

Quiebra [ke-ay'-brah], *f.* 1. Crack, fracture. 2. Gaping or opening of the ground. 3. Loss, damage. 4. Failure, bankruptcy. 5. *Quiebras del terreno* or *de la tierra,* Undulations of the ground or surface.

Quiebrahacha [ke-ay-brah-ah'-chah], *m.* (Cuba) A tree much esteemed for the solidity and firmness of its wood; a kind of fir.

Quiebro [ke-ay'-bro], *m.* 1. (Mus.) Trill. 2. Movement or inclination of the body.

(*Yo quiebro, quiebre,* from *Quebrar.* *V.* ALENTAR.)

Quien [ke-en'], *pron. rel.* 1. Who, which. 2. One or the other. *V.* CUAL and QUE. When interrogative it is accented; as, *¿ Quién ha venido ?* Who has come ?

Quienquiera [ke-en-ke-ay'-rah], *pron.* Whosoever, whatever.

Quier, *conj.* (Obs.) Or. *V.* YA or YA SEA.

(*Yo quiero, quiera, quise, quisiera.* *V.* QUERER.)

Quietación [ke-ay-tah-the-on'], *f.* (Littl. us.) The act of quieting or appeasing.

Quietador, ra [ke-ay-tah-dor', rah], *m.* & *f.* Quieter.

Quietamente, *adv.* Quietly, calmly.

Quietar [ke-ay-tar'], *va.* To appease. *V.* AQUIETAR.

Quiete [ke-ay'-tay], *f.* Rest, repose, quiet.

Quietismo [ke-ay-tees'-mo], *m.* Quietism, sect of mystics.

Quietista [ke-ay-tees'-tah], *a.* & *m.* Quietist.

Quieto, ta [ke-ay'-to, tah], *a.* 1. Quiet, still; undisturbed. 2. Quiet, peaceable, pacific. 3. Orderly, virtuous, moderate.

Quietud [ke-ay-tood'], *f.* Quietude, quietness, quiet, want of motion, rest, repose; tranquility.

Quijada [ke-hah'-dah], *f.* Jaw or jawbone.

Quijal, Quijar [ke-hahl', ke-har'], *m.* Grinder, a back tooth; jaw.

Quijarudo, da [ke-hah-roo'-do, dah], *a.* Large-jawed.

Quijera [ke-hay'-rah], *f.* 1. Cheeks of a cross-bow. 2. Piece of leather on the headstall of a horse. 3. Among carpenters, a strengthening piece put on each side.

Quijo [kee'-ho], *m.* A hard rock found in several mines as the matrix of ore.

Quijones [ke-ho'-nes], *m. pl.* Dill, an aromatic herb resembling anise.

Quijotada [ke-ho-tah'-dah], *f.* A quixotic enterprise, an action ridiculously extravagant.

Quijote [ke-hoh'-tay], *m.* 1. Armour for the thigh. 2. A man who engages in quixotic enterprises. 3. Fleshy part over the hoofs of horses or asses.

Quijotería [ke-ho-tay-ree'-ah], *f.* Quixotry, quixotism.

Quijotesco, ca [ke-ho-tes'-co, cah], *a.* Quixotic.

Quilatador [ke-lah-tah-dor'], *m.* Assayer of gold and silver.

Quilatar [ke-lah-tar'], *va.* To assay gold and silver.

Quilate [ke-lah'-tay], *m.* 1. Degree of purity of gold or precious stones. 2. A carat, the twenty-fourth part in weight and value of gold. 3. Weight of four grammes. 4. An ancient coin. 5. Decree of perfection.
Quilatera [ke-lah-tay'-rah], *f.* Instrument for ascertaining the carats of pearls.
Quilómetro, *m.* *V.* Kilómetro.
Quiloso, sa [ke-lo'-so, sah], *a.* Chylous, chylaceous.
Quilla [keel'-lyah], *f.* (Naut.) Keel of a ship. *Descubrir la quilla,* To heave down a ship. *Dar de quilla* or *tumbar a la quilla,* To careen, to overhaul a vessel.
Quillaje [keel-lyah'-hay], *m.* Harbour dues which used to be paid in France.
Quillotro, tra [kil-lyo'-tro, trah], *a.* (Coll.) This or that other.
Quimbámbulas [kim-bam'-boo-las], *f. pl.* (Cuba) Rough, craggy spots.
Quimbombó [kim-bom-bo'], *m.* (Bot.) Okra, gumbo. Abelmoschus (or Hibiscus) esculentus.
Quimera [ke-may'-rah], *f.* 1. Dispute, quarrel, scuffle, feud. 2. Chimera, wild fancy.
Quimérico, ca, Quimerino, na [ke-may'-re-co, cah], *a.* Chimerical, fantastic, unreal.
Quimerista [ke-may-rees'-tah], *m.* 1. Wrangler, brawler. 2. One who indulges in chimeras.
Quimerizar [ke-may-re-thar'], *vn.* To fill the head with fantastic ideas.
Química [kee'-me-cah], *f.* Chemistry. *Química de polímeros,* Polymer chemistry.
Químicamente, *adv.* Chemically.
Químico [kee'-me-co], *m.* Chemist.
Químico, ca [kee'-me-co, cah], *a.* Chemical.
Quimificar [ke-me-fe-car'], *va.* To convert into chyme.
Quimista, *m.* *V.* Alquimista.
Quimo [kee'-mo], *m.* (Med.) Chyme.
Quimón [ke-mone'], *m.* Fine printed cotton, chintz. *Quimón para colchas,* Furniture chintz.
Quimono [ke-mo'-no], *m.* Kimono, Japanese garb.
Quimosina [kee-mo-see'-nah], *f.* Rennin.
Quina, Quinaquina [kee'-nah], *f.* Peruvian or Jesuits' bark. Cinchona officinalis.
Quinal [ke-nahl'], *m.* (Peru) The cinchona-tree and a group of such trees.
Quinario, ria [ke-nah'-re-o, ah], *a.* Consisting of five.
Quinario [ke-nah'-re-o], *m.* A Roman coin of five units.
Quinas [kee'-nas], *f. pl.* 1. Arms of Portugal, consisting of five scutcheons, in memory of the five wounds of Christ. 2. Fives, on dice.
Quincalla [kin-cahl'-lyah], *f.* Hardware, notions, trinkets.
Quincallería [kin-cal-lyay-ree'-ah], *f.* 1. Notions store. 2. Hardware store. 3. Trinket manufacturing.
Quince [keen'-thay], *a.* & *m.* 1. Fifteen. 2. Fifteenth. 3. A game at cards.
Quincena [kin-thay'-nah], *f.* 1. Fortnight, two weeks. 2. Semimonthly pay. 3. (Mus.) Interval comprising fifteen successive notes of two octaves. 4. Fifteenth, a register in the pipes of an organ.
Quincenal [kin-thay-nahl'], *a.* Biweekly, fortnightly.
Quincenalmente [kin-thay-nahl-men'-tay], *adv.* Every two weeks, fortnightly.
Quinceno, na [kin-thay'-no, nah], *a.* Fifteenth.
Quincuagenario, ria [kin-coo-ah-hay-nah'-re-o, ah], *a.* Fiftieth.
Quincuagésima [kin-coo-ah-hay'-se-mah], *f.* Quinquagesima Sunday.
Quincuagésimo, ma [kin-coo-ah-hay'-se-mo, mah], *a.* Fiftieth.
Quincuatro [kin-coo-ah'-tro], *m.* Roman festival of five days in honour of Minerva.
Quincunce [kin-coon'-thay], *m.* Quincunx.
Quincurión [kin-coo-re-on'], *m.* A chief or corporal of five soldiers.
Quincha [keen'-chah], *f.* (Peru) A wall of clay and canes.
Quindecágono, na [kin-day-cah'-go-no, nah], *a.* Quindecagon.
Quindécima [kin-day'-the-mah], *f.* The fifteenth part.
Quindejas [kin-day'-has], *f.* (Prov.) Rope of three strands, made of bass or *esparto.*
Quindenio [kin-day'-ne-o], *m.* Space or period of fifteen years.
Quinete [ke-nay'-tay], *m.* Kind of camlet.
Quingentésimo, ma [kin-hen-tay'-se-mo, mah], *a.* The five hundredth.
Quingombó [kin-gom-bo'], *m.* V. Quimbombó
Quinientos, tas [ke-ne-en'-tos, tas], *a.* Five hundred.
Quinina [ke-nee'-nah], *f.* Quinine, the principal alkaloid of cinchona.
Quino [kee'-no], *m.* 1. The cinchona-tree, an evergreen of the madder family. 2. A juice like opium extracted from various African vegetables of the banks of the Gambia.
Quinoidina [ke-noi-dee'-nah], *f.* Quinoidine, a resinous substance of yellow and red cinchona barks.
Quínolas, Quinolillas [kee'-no-las], *f. pl.* Reversis, a game at cards. *Estar en quínolas,* To wear clothes of glaring colours.
Quinolear [ke-no-lay-ar'], *va.* To prepare the cards for the game of reversis.
Quinqué [keen-kay'], *m.* An Argand lamp. The Spanish name is from the French manufacturer Quinquet, who first largely made them.
Quinquefolio [kin-kay-fo'-le-o], *m.* (Bot.) Common cinquefoil. Potentilla reptans.
Quinquenio [kin-kay'-ne-o], *m.* Space or period of five years; lustrum.
Quinquercio [kin-kerr'-the-o], *m.* Five Grecian games of wrestling, jumping, running, quoits, etc.
Quinquenal [kin-kay-nahl'], *a.* Quinquennial.
Quinquillería [kin-keel-lyay-ree'-ah], *f.* Hardware. *V.* Quincallería and Buhonería.
Quinquillero [kin-keel-lyay'-ro], *m.* Hawker, peddler, hardwareman. *V.* Buhonero.
Quinta [keen'-tah], *f.* 1. Country-seat, a country-house. 2. The act of choosing one out of five. 3. The act of drawing lots for men to serve in the army. 4. Quint, the sequence of five cards in the game of piquet. 5. (Mus.) Fifth, an interval of three tones and a semitone major.
Quinta columna [keen'-tah co-loom'-nah], *f.* Fifth column.
Quintacolumnista [kin-tah-co-loom-nees'-tah], *m.* & *f.* Fifth columnist.
Quintador, ra [kin-tah-dor', rah], *m.* & *f.* One who draws lots in fives.
Quintaesencia [kin-tah-ay-sen'-the-ah], *f.* Quintessence.
Quintal [kin-tahl'], *m.* 1. Quintal, a hundred-weight. 2. Fifth part of one hundred. *Quintal métrico,* Weight of one hundred kilogrammes, ton.
Quintalada [kin-tah-lah'-dah], *f.* The sum of 2¼ per cent. on the freights paid to masters of vessels.
Quintaleño, ña, Quintalero, ra [kin-tah-lay'-nyo, nyah], *a.* Capable of containing a quintal.
Quintana [kin-tah'-nah], *f.* A country house.
Quintanar [kin-tah-nar'], *m.* Quintain, ancient tilting-post.
Quintante [kin-tahn'-tay], *m.* An astronomical instrument larger than the sextant.
Quintañón, na [kin-tah-nyone', nah], *a.* A hundred years old; much advanced in years.
Quintar [kin-tar'], *va.* 1. To draw one out of five. 2. To draw lots for soldiers. 3. To come to the number of five. 4. To pay to government the duty of 20 per cent. on gold or silver. 5. To plough ground the fifth time.—*vn.* To attain the fifth: applied to the moon on the fifth day.
Quintería [kin-tay-ree'-ah], *f.* Farm; grange.
Quinterillo [kin-tay-reel'-lyo], *m. dim.* A farmer who rents a small farm.
Quinterno [kin-terr'-no], *m.* 1. Number of five sheets of paper. 2. Lot, or row, of five numbers in the ancient lottery.
Quintero [kin-tay'-ro], *m.* 1. Farmer, one who rents a farm. 2. Overseer of a farm; servant who takes care of a farm.
Quinteto [kin-tay'-to], *m.* Quintet, a musical composition for five performers.
Quintil [kin-teel'], *m.* The month of July, according to the ancient Roman calendar.
Quintilla [kin-teel'-lyah], *f.* A metrical composition of five verses.
Quintillo [kin-teel'-lyo], *m.* 1. The fifth story in the houses of the great square in Madrid. 2. Game of ombre with five persons.
Quintín [kin-teen'], *m.* Sort of fine cloth of a loose texture.
Quinto [keen'-to], *m.* 1. One-fifth. 2. Fifth, a duty of 20 per cent. on prizes, etc., paid to the Spanish government. 3. Share of pasture land. 4. One called up for military service, draft, conscription; draftee.
Quinto, ta [keen'-to, tah], *a.* Fifth, the ordinal number of five.
Quintuplicar [kin-too-ple-car'], *va.* To multiply by five.
Quíntuplo, pla [keen'-too-plo, plah], *a.* Quintuple, five-fold.
Quiñón [ke-nyone'], *m.* Share of profit arising from an enterprise undertaken with another person.
Quiosco [ke-os'-co], *m.* Kiosk, pavilion, stand.
Quipos [kee'-pos], *m. pl.* Ropes of various colours, and with different knots, used by the ancient inhabitants of Peru to record memorable events and keep accounts.
Quiquiriquí [ke-ke-re-kee'], *m.* Imitation of cock-crowing; cock-a-doodle-do.
Quiragra [ke-rah'-grah], *f.* Gout in the hand.
Quirieleisón [ke-re-ay-lay-e-sone'], *m.* Lord, have mercy upon us! the responses chanted in the funeral service. *V.* Kirieleisón.
Quirinal [ke-re-nahl'], *a.* Relating to the feast of Romulus, and to one of the seven hills of Rome.
Quirite [ke-ree'-tay], *m.* Roman citizen or knight.
Quirivel [ke-re-vel'], *m.* (Bot.) *V* Perdiguera.

Quirófano [ke-ro'-fah-no], *m.* Operating room.
Quirografía [ke-ro-grah-fee'-ah], *f.* Chirography, the art of writing.
Quiromancia [ke-ro-mahn'-the-ah], *f.* Chiromancy, palmistry.
Quiromántico [ke-ro-mahn'-te-co], *m.* Palmister, chiromancer.
Quirópteros [ke-rop'-tay-ros], *m. pl.* Bats: the cheiroptera.
Quiroteca [ke-ro-tay'-cah], *f.* (Coll.) Glove.
Quirúrgico, ca [ke-roor'-he-co, cah], *a.* Surgical, chirurgical.
Quirurgo [ke-roor'-go], *m.* (Coll.) Surgeon, chirurgeon.
Quisicosa [ke-se-co'-sah], *f.* (Coll.) Enigma, riddle, obscure question.
Quisling [kees'-lin], *m.* Quisling, traitor of his country.
Quisquilla [kis-keel'-lyah], *f.* A ridiculous nicety; bickering, trifling dispute.
Quisquilloso, sa [kis-kil-lyo'-so, sah], *a.* Fastidious, precise, morose; touchy, irascible.
Quiste [kees'-tay], *m.* (Acad.) Cyst, a tumour with fluid contents.
Quisto, ta [kees'-to, tah], *pp. irr. obs.* of QUERER. It is now only used with the adjectives *bien* and *mal. Bien quisto,* Well received, generally beloved. *Mal quisto,* Ill received, hated.
Quita [kee'-tah], *f.* Acquittance, or discharge from a debt, or a part of it.
¡Quita! *int.* God forbid! *¡Quita de ahí!* Away with you! out of my sight!
Quitación [ke-tah-the-on'], *f.* 1. Salary, wages, pay, income. 2. *V.* QUITA.
Quitador, ra [ke-tah-dor', rah], *m. & f.* One who takes away, remover.
Quitaguas, *m.* *V.* PARAGUAS.
Quitaipón [ke-tah-e-pone'], *m.* *V.* QUITAPÓN. *De quita y pon,* Adjustable, removable: used of mechanical contrivances.
Quitamanchas [ke-tah-mahn'-chas], *m.* A clothes-cleaner.
Quitameriendas [ke-tah-may-re-en'-das], *f.* (Bot.) Common meadow saffron. Colchicum autumnale.
Quitamiento [ke-tah-me-en'-to], *m.* *V.* QUITA.
Quitamotas [ke-tah-mo'-tas], *m. & f.* A servile flatterer.
Quitante [ke-tahn'-tay], *pa.* Taking away, removing.
Quitanza [ke-tahn'-thah], *f.* (Com.) Receipt, discharge.
Quitapelillos [ke-tah-pay-leel'-lyos], *com.* (Coll.) Flatterer, fawner, wheedler.
Quitapesares [ke-tah-pay-sah'-res], *com.* (Coll.) Comfort, consolation.
Quitapón [ke-tah-pone'], *m.* Ornament of the headstall of draught horses and mules.
Quitar [ke-tar'], *va.* 1. To take away, to remove; to separate, to extract. 2. To release or redeem a pledge. 3. To hinder, to disturb. 4. To forbid, to prohibit. 5. To abrogate, to annul. 6. To free from an obligation. 7. To usurp, to rob. 8. To strip or deprive of any thing. 9. To suppress an office. 10. (Fencing) To parry a thrust.—*vr.* 1. To abstain, to refrain. 2. To retire, or withdraw. 3. To get rid of. *A quitar,* Of short duration. *Quitado esto,* (Coll.) Excepting this, besides this. *Quitarse el embozo,* (Coll.) To unmask.
Quitasol [ke-tah-sole'], *m.* Parasol, sunshade.
Quitasueño [ke-tah-soo-ay'-nyo], *m.* (coll.) Anxiety or worry causing sleeplessness.
Quite [kee'-tay], *m.* 1. Obstacle, impediment, hindrance; the act of taking away. 2. Parade, parry, in fencing. *No tiene quite,* It is unavoidable, there is no help for it.
Quiteño, ña [ke-tay'-nyo, nyah], *a.* Native of or belonging to Quito.
Quito, ta [kee'-to, tah], *a. & pp. irr. obs.* of QUITAR. Free from an obligation, clear from a charge, quits.
Quito, *m.* A dye-wood (yielding black) of the Napo region in South America.
Quitrín [ke-treen'], *m.* (Cuba) Gig, a light chaise.
Quiyá [kee-yah'], *f.* Name of an otter of the Argentine Republic.
Quizá, Quizás [ke-thah', ke-thahs'], *adv.* Perhaps. *V.* ACASO.
Quizame [ke-thah'-may], *m.* (Prov. Phil. Is.) Roof, ceiling.
Quorum [kwo'-room], *m.* Quorum, a term from the Latin having the same parliamentary signification as in English.

R

R [er'-ray, er'-ay], *f.* This letter at the beginning of a word, after *l, n, s,* and in compound words, the primitive of which begins with *r,* has a hard and rough sound, as, *rata, malrotar, enriquecer, cariredondo.* When *ab* and *ob* are not prepositions, as in *abrogar, obrepción,* the *r* becomes liquid; as in *abrojo, obrero.*—*R* in the middle of a word, or between two vowels, has a very smooth sound; as in *morosidad, peregrinar.* The harsh and rough sound of *r* between two vowels, in the middle of simple words, is always expressed by double *rr;* thus, *barraca, correcto. R* is used as a contraction of *reprobar,* like *A* for *aprobar,* in voting for degrees in universities; it also is used as a contraction for *real,* royal, and for *reverendo,* reverend, and on wool-packs it means *refina.* In the beginning of a medical prescription, *R* is an abbreviature of *recipe,* take. *Rr,* double in figure, is simple in sound and indivisible.
Raba [rah'-bah], *f.* Bait used in the pilchard-fishery.
Rabada [rah-bah'-dah], *f.* Hind quarter of mutton.
Rabadán [rah-bah-dahn'], *m.* The principal shepherd of a sheep-walk.
Rabadilla [rah-bah-deel'-lyah], *f.* Rump, croup, the extremity of the backbone.
Rabanal [rah-bah-nahl'], *m.* Ground sown with radishes.
Rabanero, ra [rah-bah-nay'-ro, rah], *a.* 1. Very short: applied to the garments of women. 2. *f.* (Coll.) A shameless and insolent woman.—*m. & f.* Seller of radishes.
Rabanete [rah-bah-nay'-tay], *m. dim.* A small radish.
Rabanillo [rah-bah-neel'-lyo], *m.* 1. (Dim.) Small radish. 2. The tart sharp taste of wine which is on the turn. 3. (Coll.) Ardent desire, longing. 4. Acrimony, asperity, rudeness.
Rabaniza [rah-bah-nee'-thah], *f.* Radish seed.
Rábano [rah'-bah-no], *m.* (Bot.) Radish. Raphanus sativus. *Rábano picante* or *rusticano,* Horse-radish. *Cuando pasan rábanos, comprarlos,* (Fig.) Seize the occasion at hand. *Rábanos y queso traen la corte en peso,* (Met.) Pay attention to the little things. *Tomar el rábano por las hojas,* (Coll.) To put the cart before the horse. Cochlearia armoracia. (Lat. raphanus, fr. Gr. ῥάφανος.)
Rabazuz [rah-ba-thooth'], *m.* Inspissated juice of licorice.
Rabear [rah-bay-ar'], *vn.* To wag the tail.
Rabel [rah-bel'], *m.* 1. Rebeck, an ancient musical instrument with three strings, played with a bow. 2. (Coll.) Breech, backside.
Rabelejo, ico, illo, ito [rah-bay-lay'-ho], *m. dim.* of RABEL.
Rabera [rah-bay'-rah], *f.* 1. Tail, the hind or back part of any thing. 2. Handle of a cross-bow. 3. Remains of uncleaned grain or seeds.
Raberón [rah-bay-rone'], *m.* The tops of a felled tree, cut for fire-wood.
Rabí [rah-bee'], *m.* Rabbi, rabbin.
Rabia [rah'-be-ah], *f.* 1. Hydrophobia, rabies. 2. Rage, fury.—*int.* Fury!
Rabiar [rah-be-ar'], *vn.* 1. To labour under hydrophobia. 2. To rage, to be furious. 3. To labour under racking pain. 4. To flush, to be agitated and hurried to excess. *Rabiar por,* To wish or long for a thing with itching desire or anxiety. *Rabiar de hambre,* To be furiously hungry. *Quema que rabia,* It is as hot as hell.
Rabiatar [rah-be-ah-tar'], *va.* To tie by the tail.
Rabiazorras [rah-be-ah-thor'-ras], *m.* (Prov.) Among shepherds, the east wind.
Rabicán, Rabicano [rah-be-cahn'], *a.* White-tailed, having white hairs in the tail: applied to horses.
Rabicorto, ta [rah-be-cor'-to, tah], *a.* Short-tailed.
Rábido, da [rah'-be-do, dah], *a.* (Poet.) *V.* RABIOSO.
Rabieta [rah-be-ay'-tah], *f.* (Coll.) Violent, fretting impatience.
Rabihorcado [rah-be-or-cah'-do], *m.* (Orn.) Frigate bird, or frigate pelican. Fregata aquila.
Rabilargo, ga [rah-be-lar'-go, gah], *a.* Long-tailed; having a long train.
Rabilargo, *m.* (Orn.) Blue crow. Corvus cyanus.
Rabillo [rah-beel'-lyo], *m.* 1. Mildew on the stalk of corn. 2. (Dim.) Little tail.
Rabinegro, gra [rah-be-nay'-gro, grah], *a.* Black-tailed.
Rabínico, ca [rah-bee'-ne-co, cah], *a.* Rabbinical.
Rabinismo [rah-be-nees'-mo], *m.* Rabbinism.
Rabinista [rah-be-nees'-tah], *com.* Rabbinist.
Rabino [rah-bee'-no], *m.* Rabbi, a teacher of the Hebrew law. *Gran rabino,* The chief of a synagogue.
Rabiosamente, *adv.* Furiously, outrageously, madly, ragingly.
Rabioso, sa [rah-be-o'-so, sah], *a.* 1. Rabid, mad: applied to dogs and other brutes. 2. Furious, outrageous, choleric, raging, fierce. *Filo rabioso,* Wire edge.
Rabisalsera [rah-be-sal-say'-rah], *a.* (Coll.) Pert, smart, forward, saucy, impudent: applied to women.
Rabiseco, ca [rah-be-say'-co, cah], *a.* 1. Dry-tailed, poor, lean, starving. 2. (Met.) Snappish, peevish.
Rabito [rah-bee'-to], *m.* (Dim.) A small tail.
Rabiza [rah-bee'-thah], *f.* 1. Point of a fishing-rod, to which the line is fastened. 2. (Naut.) End, tip of any thing, particularly the tapering end of a rope. *Rabiza de cohete,* Rocket-stick. *Rabiza de motón,* Tail of a block.
Rabizar [rah-be-thar'], *va.* To point the end of a rope.
Rable [rah'-blay], *m.* Ferret, an instrument to skim melted glass.

Rabo [rah'-bo], *m.* 1. Tail of animals: applied to certain animals, as pigs, etc., instead of *cola.* 2. Tail, the lower, back, or hind part of any thing; train. 3. An instrument to cut velvet in the loom. 4. In paper-mills, the tail which supports the hammer that beats the pulp. *Ir al rabo,* To be at one's tail continually, to hang at one's elbow. *Rabo de gallo,* (Naut.) Stern-timbers. *Rabo de puerco,* (Bot.) Hog's-fennel, sea-sulphurwort. Peucedanum officinale. *Rabo de junco,* (Orn.) Tropic bird. Phæton. *Rabos,* Tatters, fluttering rags. *Rabo entre piernas,* (Coll.) Crestfallen, dejected. *V.* RABERA. *Asirle por el rabo,* It is difficult to overtake a fugitive; a stern chase is a long chase. *Mirar con el rabo del ojo,* To look askance.

Rabón, na [rah-bohn', nah], *a.* Docked, bob-tailed, short-tailed.

Rabona [rah-bo'-nah], *f.* (Peru) A canteen woman, or wife of a soldier.

Rabosear [rah-bo-say-ar'], *va.* To spatter with dirt.

Raboso, sa [rah-bo'-so, sah], *a.* Ragged, tattered.

Rabotada [rah-bo-tah'-dah], *f.* 1. A gruff and insolent reply with rude gestures. (Acad.) 2. A hit with a tail.

Rabotear [rah-bo-tay-ar'], *va.* To crop the tail.

Rabudo, da [rah-boo'-do, dah], *a.* Long-tailed.

Rábula [rah'-boo-lah], *m.* An ignorant, vociferous lawyer.

Racahut [rah-cah-oot'], *m.* Raccahout, a farinaceous preparation from potatoes, edible acorns, etc., used as an invalid food. (Arab.)

Racimado, da [rah-the-mah'-do, dah], *a.* Clustered, in racemes.

Racimar [rah-the-mar'], *va.* (Prov.) *V.* REBUSCAR.—*vr.* *V.* ARRACIMARSE.

Racimo [rah-thee'-mo], *m.* 1. Bunch of grapes. 2. Cluster of small things disposed in order; raceme. 3. (Coll.) Criminal hanging on the gallows.

Racimoso, sa [rah-the-mo'-so, sah], *a.* Full of grapes, racemose, racemiferous.

Racimudo, da [rah-the-moo'-do, dah], *a.* In large bunches or racemes.

Raciocinación [rah-the-o-the-nah-the-on'], *f.* Ratiocination, the art of reasoning.

Raciocinar [rah-the-o-the-nar'], *vn.* To reason, to argue, to ratiocinate.

Raciocinio [rah-the-o-thee'-ne-o], *m.* Reasoning, argument.

Ración [rah-the-on'], *f.* 1. Ration, food for one meal. 2. Daily allowance for servants, board-wages; allowance for soldiers or sailors, pittance. *Ración de hambre,* Scanty allowance. *Poner a ración,* To keep on short allowance. 3. A prebend in Spanish cathedrals.

Racionabilidad [rah-the-o-nah-be-le-dahd'], *f.* Rationality, the power of reasoning.

Racional [rah-the-o-nahl'], *a.* 1. Rational, reasonable. 2. (Ast.) Rational: applied to the horizon whose plane is conceived to pass through the centre of the earth. 3. Rational, the essential predicate that constitutes the difference between man and beast. 4. (Math.) Rational.—*m.* Rational, pectoral, or breast plate, one of the sacred vestments of the chief priest among the Jews.

Racionalidad [rah-the-o-nah-le-dahd'], *f.* 1. Rationality, reasonableness. 2. Fitness, agreement with right. 3. Faculty of reasoning.

Racionalmente, *adv.* Rationally.

Racionamiento [rah-the-o-nah-me-en'-to], *m.* Rationing.

Racionar [rah-the-o-nar'], *va.* To ration.

Racionista [rah-the-o-nees'-tah], *com.* 1. Person on an allowance. 2. Second-rate actor.

Racismo [rah-thees'-mo], *m.* Racism.

Racista [rah-thees'-tah], *com.* Racist.

Racha [rah'-chah], *f.* 1. Gust of wind. 2. Short period of good luck.

Rada [rah'-dah], *f.* Road, roadstead, anchoring-ground for ships.

Radar [rah-dahr'], *m.* (Radio) Radar.

Radiación [rah-de-ah-the-on'], *f.* Radiation.

Radiado, da [rah-de-ah'-do, dah], *a.* & *pp.* of RADIAR. Radiated.

Radiador [rah-de-ah-dor'], *m.* 1. Radiator. 2. Radiator, steam heater.

Radial [rah-de-ahl'], *a.* Radial.

Radiante [rah-de-ahn'-tay], *a.* Radiant.

Radiar [rah-de-ar'], *va.* 1. To radiate. 2. To broadcast, to radio.

Radicación [rah-de-ca-the-on'], *f.* Taking root.

Radical [rah-de-cahl'], *a.* Radical.—*com.* Radical.—*m.* Radical.

Radicalmente, *adv.* Radically.

Radicar [rah-de-car'], *vn.* 1. To take root. 2. To be located.—*vr.* To establish oneself, to take up residence.

Radícula [rah-dee'-coo-lah], *f.* (Bot.) Radicle, radicule.

Radio [rah'-de-o], *m.* 1. Radius. 2. Spoke. 3. Radium.—*f.* Radio.

Radioactividad [rah-de-o-ac-te-ve-dahd'], *f.* Radioactivity. *Radioactividad atmosférica* (Mil.) Fallout.

Radioactivo, va [rah-de-o-ac-tee'-vo, vah], *a.* Radioactive.

Radioaficionado, da [rah-de-o-ah-fe-the-o-nah'-do, dah], *m.* & *f.* Radio amateur.

Radioastronomía [rah-de-o-as-tro-no-mee'-ah], *f.* Radioastronomy.

Radioaviación [rah-de-o-ah-ve-ah-the-on'], *f.* (Aer.) Radio navigation.

Radiobaliza [rah-de-o-bah-lee'-tha], *f.* Radio beacon.

Radiobiología [rah-de-o-be-o-lo-hee'-ah], *f.* Radiobiology.

Radiocompás [rah-de-o-com-pahs'], *m.* Radio compass, radio direction finder.

Radiocomunicación [rah-de-o-co-moo-ne-cah-the-on'], *f.* Radio communication.

Radiodifundir [rah-de-o-de-foon-deer'], *va.* To broadcast via radio.

Radiodifusora [rah-de-o-de-foo-so'-rah], *f.* Broadcasting station, radio station.

Radioelemento [rah-de-o-ay-lay-men'-to], *m.* Radioelement.

Radioescucha [rah-de-o-es-coo'-chah], *com.* Radio listener.

Radiofaro [rah-de-o-fah'-ro], *m.* Radio beacon.

Radiofoto [rah-de-o-fo'-to], *f.* Radiophoto.

Radiofrecuencia [rah-de-o-fray-coo-en'-the-ah], *f.* Radio frequency.

Radiografía [rah-de-o-grah-fee'-ah], *f.* 1. Radiograph, X-ray film. 2. Radiography.

Radiógrafo [rah-de-o'-grah-fo], *m.* Radiographer, X-ray specialist.

Radiograma [rah-de-o-grah'-ma], *m.* Radiogram.

Radioisótopo [rah-de-o-e-so'-to-po], *m.* Radioisotope.

Radiología [rah-de-o-lo-hee'-ah], *f.* Radiology.

Radiólogo [rah-de-o'-lo-go], *m.* Radiologist.

Radiómetro [rah-de-o'-may-tro], *m.* Radiometer.

Radionavegación [rah-de-o-nah-vay-gah-the-on'], *f.* Radio navigation.

Radionavegante [rah-de-o-nah-vay-gahn'-tay], *m.* Radio navigator.

Radioquímica [rah-de-o-kee'-me-cah], *f.* Radiochemistry.

Radiorreceptor [rah-de-or-ray-thep-tor'], *m.* Radio receiver.

Radioscopia [rah-de-os-co'-pe-ah], *f.* Radioscopy.

Radiosensitivo, va [rah-de-o-sen-se-tee'-vo, vah], *a.* Radiosensitive.

Radioso, sa [rah-de-o'-so, sah], *a.* Radiant.

Radiosonda [rah-de-o-son'-dah], *f.* Radiosonde.

Radiotecnia [rah-de-o-tec'-ne-ah], *f.* Radiotechnology.

Radiotelefonía [rah-de-o-tay-lay-fo-nee'ah], *f.* Wireless.

Radioteléfono [rah-de-o-tay-lay'-fo-no], *m.* Radiotelephone. *Radioteléfono emisor-receptor portátil,* Walkie-talkie.

Radiotelegrafista [rah-de-o-tay-lay-grah-fees'-tah], *com.* Wireless operator.

Radiotelégrafo [rah-de-o-tay-lay'-grah-fo], *m.* Radiotelegraph.

Radiotelegrama [rah-de-o-tay-lay-grah'-mah], *m.* Radiotelegram.

Radiotelescopio [rah-de-o-tay-les-co'-pe-o], *m.* Radio telescope.

Radioterapia [rah-de-o-tay-rah'-pe-ah], *f.* Radiotherapy.

Radiotransmisor [rah-de-o-trans-me-sor'], *m.* Radio transmitter.

Radioyente [rah-de-o-yen'-tay], *m.* & *f.* V. RADIOESCUCHA.

Raedera [rah-ay-day'-rah], *f.* 1. Scraper, raker. 2. Roller or cylinder for reducing lead into sheets.

Raedor, ra [rah-ay-dor', rah], *a.* Scraper, eraser. *V.* RASERO.

Raedura [rah-ay-doo'-rah], *f.* 1. Rasure, erasure. 2. Scrapings, filings, parings.

Raer [rah-err'], *va.* 1. To scrape, to grate; to rub off, to abrade, to fret. 2. To rase or blot out, to erase. 3. To lay aside entirely, to efface, as a vice or bad habit.

Rafa [rah'-fah], *f.* 1. Buttress to sup port mud walls. 2. A small cut or opening in a canal.

Ráfaga [rah'-fah-gah], *f.* 1. A violent gust of wind. 2. Any cloud of small density which appears at a distance. 3. Instantaneous flash or gleam of light.

Raído, da [rah-ee'-do, dah], *a.* & *pp.* of RAER. 1. Scraped. 2. Worn out. 3. Impudent, shameless; free, undisguised.

Raigal [rah-e-gahl'], *a.* Relating to the root.

Raigambre [rah-e-gahm'-bray], *f.* Collection of roots of different trees united.

Raigón [rah-e-gon'], *m.* 1. Large root. 2. Root (of a tooth).

Raimiento [rah-e-me-en'-to], *m.* 1. Scraping. 2. Effrontery.

Raíz [rah-eeth'], *f.* 1. Root. 2. Foundation. *Raíz cuadrada,* Square root. *Raíz cúbica,* Cube root. *A raíz de,* 1. Level with. 2. Right after. 3. As a result of. *De raíz,* Completely, from the ground up.

Raja [rah'-hah], *f.* 1. Splinter, chip. 2. Slice. 3. Crack, fissure.

Rajá [rah-hah'], *m.* Rajah.

Rajable [rah-hah'-blay], **Rajadizo, za** [rah-hah-dee'-tho, tha], *a.* Easily split, easily splintered.

Rajadura [rah-hah-doo'-rah], *f.* Crack, cleft.

Rajar [rah-har'], *va.* 1. To split, as

wood, to break off or break open, to chip, to break into chinks, to cleave. 2. (Coll.) To crack, to boast, to tell falsehoods.

Rajeta [rah-hay'-tah], *f.* Sort of coarse cloth of mixed colours.

Rajica, illa, ita [rah-hee'-cah], *f. dim.* 1. A small chink, crack, or fissure. 2. A small splinter or chip of wood.

Rajuela [rah-hoo-ay'-lah], *f. dim.* *V.* RAJICA.

Ralea [rah-lay'-ah], *f.* 1. Race, breed, stock. 2. Genus, species, quality.

Ralear [rah-lay-ar'], *vn.* 1. To thin, to make thin, or rare. 2. (Prov.) To manifest or discover the bad inclination or breed of any thing. 3. (Agr.) To make thin racemes or bunches of grapes.

Raleón, na [rah-lay-on', nah], *a.* Applied to a bird of prey which takes the game pursued by another.

Raleza [rah-lay'-thah], *f.* Thinness, want of compactness; rarity; liquidity.

Ralillo, illa, ito, ita [rah-leel'-lyo], *a.* Somewhat thin or rare.

Ralo, la [rah'-lo, lah], *a.* 1. Thin, rare, not compact. 2. *V.* RARO.

Ralladera [ral-lyah-day'-rah], *f.* Grater, an instrument for grating.

Ralladura [ral-lyah-doo'-rah], *f.* Mark left by the grater; the small particles taken off by grating.

Rallar [ral-yar'], *va.* 1. To grate, to reduce to powder. 2. To vex, to molest. *Rallar las tripas a alguno,* To importune or vex one.

Rallo [rahl'-lyo], *m.* Grater, an instrument for grating.

Rallón [ral-lyone'], *m.* Arrow or dart.

Rama [rah'-mah], *f.* 1. Shoot or sprig of a plant, bough, limb, of a tree. 2. Branch of a family. 3. Rack used in manufactories, to bring cloth to its proper length and breadth. 4. (Print.) Chase for inclosing types. *En rama,* Raw material, crude stuff. *Tabaco en rama,* Leaf tobacco. *Seda en rama,* Raw silk. *Andarse por las ramas,* To go about the bush, not to come to the point. *Asirse a las ramas,* To seek or make frivolous pretexts.—*pl.* Greens.

Ramada [rah-mah'-dah], *f.* (Prov.) *V.* ENRAMADA.

Ramadán [rah-mah-dahn'], *m.* Ramadan, the Mohammedan month of fasting, their ninth lunar month.

Ramaje [rah-mah'-hay], *m.* 1. Branchage, collection of branches. 2. Flowering branches designed in cloth.

Ramal [rah-mahl'], *m.* 1. A strand of a rope. 2. Any thing springing from another, as a stair-case. 3. Halter, of a horse or mule. 4. Principal passage in mines; branch, division. 5. A thing dependent upon something else; offset, branch, etc.

Ramalazo [rah-mah-lah'-tho], *m.* 1. Lash, a stroke with a cord or rope. 2. Marks left by lashes. 3. A sudden and acute pain or grief. 4. Spot in the face. 5. Result or consequence of injuring another.

Ramalito [rah-mah-lee'-to], *m. dim.* A small halter, small branch, a lash or cord of a cat-o'-nine-tails.

Rambla [rahm'-blah], *f.* 1. A sandy place, ground covered with sand after a flood. 2. A ravine or water-course which carries off the water of heavy rains. (Arab.)

Ramblazo [ram-blah'-tho], *m.* Gravelly bed of a current or rivulet.

Ramblizo [ram-blee'-tho], *m.* (Prov.) *V.* RAMBLAZO.

Ramera [rah-may'-rah], *f.* Whore, prostitute.

Ramería [rah-may-ree'-ah], *f.* Brothel, bawdy-house, formerly the residence of licensed prostitutes in Spanish towns.

Ramerita, Rameruela [rah-may-ree'-tah], *f. dim.* A little whore.

Ramero [rah-may'-ro], *m.* A young hawk hopping from branch to branch.

Ramial [rah-me-ahl'], *m.* Ramie-patch, ground planted in ramie.

Ramificación [rah-me-fe-cah-the-on'], *f.* 1. Ramification, the production of branches. 2. Ramification, division or separation into branches.

Ramificarse [rah-me-fe-car'-say], *vr.* To ramify, to be divided into branches.

Ramilla, ita [rah-meel'-lyah], *f. dim.* 1. Small shoot or sprig, twig. 2. (Met.) Any light trifling thing.

Ramillete [rah-meel-lyay'-tay], *m.* 1. Nosegay, tuft. 2. Cluster of single-pedicelled flowers, umbel. 3. *Ramillete de Constantinopla, V.* MINUTISA. 4. Pyramid of sweetmeats and fruits served at table. 5. Collection of flowers or beauties of literature.

Ramilletero, ra [rah-mil-lyay-tay'-ro, rah], *m.* & *f.* One who makes and sells nosegays.

Ramilletero [rah-mil-lyay-tay'-ro], *m.* Vase with artificial flowers put on altars.

Ramillo, ito [rah-meel'-lyo], *m.* 1. (Dim.) A small branch. 2. (Prov.) *V.* DINERILLO.

Ramina [rah-mee'-nah], *f.* Ramie yarn.

Ramio [rah'-me-o], *m.* Ramie, a plant belonging to the nettle family yielding a fine textile fibre. Boehmeria nivea.

Ramiza [rah-mee'-thah], *f.* Collection of lopped branches.

Rámneo, nea [rahm'-nay-o, ah], *a.* (Bot.) Rhamnaceous, of the buckthorn family.

Ramo [rah'-mo], *m.* 1. Branch of a bough or limb: branchlet; also a limb cut off from a tree. 2. Any part separated from a whole. 3. A string of onions. 4. Branch of trade. 5. Concern, business. 6. Branch or special part of an art or science. 7. Branch, outgrowth of something not material. *Vender al ramo,* To retail wine. *Domingo de Ramos,* Palm Sunday.

Ramojo [rah-mo'-ho], *m.* Small branch lopped from a tree; small wood.

Ramón [rah-mone'], *m.* Top of branches cut off for the feed of sheep in snowy weather.

Ramonear [rah-mo-nay-ar'], *vn.* 1. To cut off the branches of trees. 2. To nibble the tops of branches: applied to cattle.

Ramoneo [rah-mo-nay'-o], *m.* Act of cutting or lopping branches.

Ramoso, sa [rah-mo'-so, sah], *a.* Branchy, ramous.

Rampa [rahm'-pah], *f.* 1. (Prov.) Cramp. 2. (Mil.) Slope of a glacis. 3. Acclivity.

Rampante [ram-pahn'-tay], *a.* (Her.) Rampant.

Rampiñete [ram-pe-nyay'-tay], *m.* Bar of iron with a curved point, used by artillerymen.

Ramplón, na [ram-plone', nah], *a.* Applied to a large coarse shoe; rude, unpolished.—*m.* (Vet.) The calk of a shoe.

Ramplón [ram-plone'], *m.* Calk of horses' shoes. *A ramplón,* Having shoes with calks.

Rampojo [ram-po'-ho], *m.* 1. Rape, the stalk of a cluster of grapes when freed from the fruit. 2. (Mil.) Caltrop, an iron with three spikes, thrown into the road, to annoy the enemy's horse. *V.* ABROJO.

Rampollo [ram-pol'-lyo], *m.* Branch cut from a tree to be planted.

Ramujos [rah-moo'-hose], *m. pl.* Twigs, small wood.

Rana [rah'-nah], *f.* 1. A frog. 2. (Vet.) Ranula. *V.* ALEVOSA. *Rana marina* or *pescadora,* (Zool.) Frog-fish, fishing-frog, or angler. Lophius piscatorius. *No ser rana,* (Coll.) To be able and expert. *Cuando la rana críe,* or *tenga pelos,* (Coll.) Expression of incredulity or remote possibility, about like "When cats and mice agree."

Ranacuajo [rah-nah-coo-ah'-ho], *m.* 1. Spawn of frogs. *V.* RENACUAJO. 2. A little, insignificant man.

Rancajada [ran-cah-hah'-dah], *f.* Wound in plants or sprouts.

Rancajado, da [ran-cah-hah'-do, dah], *a.* Wounded with a splinter of wood.

Rancajo [ran-cah'-ho], *m.* Splinter in the flesh.

Rancanca [ran-cahn'-cah], *m.* South American bird of prey: its plumage is chiefly black, but the cheeks and throat are bare and of a bright carmine colour.

Ranciadura [ran-the-ah-doo'-rah], *f.* *V.* RANCIDEZ.

Ranciarse [ran-the-ar'-say], *vr.* *V.* ENRANCIARSE.

Rancidez [ran-the-deth'], *f.* Rancidity, rancidness, rankness.

Rancio, cia [rahn'-the-o, ah], *a.* Rank, rancid, stale, strong-scented, long kept, old.

Rancio, *m.* Rancidity, rankness, fulsomeness.

Rancioso, sa [ran-the-o'-so, sah], *a.* 1. *V.* RANCIO. 2. Having the taste of oil.

Rancor [ran-cor'], *m.* (Obs.) Rancour. *V.* RENCOR.

Rancheadero [ran-chay-ah-day'-ro], *m.* Place containing huts.

Ranchear [ran-chay-ar'], *va.* To build huts, to form a mess.

Ranchería [ran-chay-ree'-ah], *f.* 1. Hut or cottage where labourers meet to mess together: horde. 2. (Amer.) A collection of huts, like a hamlet. 3. (Cuba) A group of runaway negroes in forests.

Ranchero [ran-chay'-ro], *m.* 1. Steward of a mess. 2. An owner of a small farm. 3. (Mex.) Countryman, farm-dweller, rancher.

Rancho [rahn'-cho], *m.* 1. Food given daily to a set of persons, as soldiers or convicts. 2. Mess, a set of persons who eat and drink together. 3. A free clear passage. *Hacer rancho,* To make room. 4. A friendly meeting of persons to discuss some question. 5. (Naut.) Mess-room; mess. *Rancho de enfermería,* Mess-room for the sick. *Rancho de Santa Bárbara,* (Naut.) Gun-room; chamber of the rudder. 6. Each of the divisions of the crew. 7. Provision of food for a voyage. 8. Hut in which peasants are sheltered over night. 9. (Mex.) A stock-farm; a small farm, a ranch. 10. (Amer.) A place consisting of a few huts, where travellers may find provisions.

Randa [rahn'-dah], *f.* Lace, trimming, netting, network.

Randado, da [ran-dah'-do, dah], *a.* Laced, adorned with lace.

Randaje [ran-dah'-hay], *m.* Network, lace-work.

Randal [ran-dahl'], *m.* Sort of stuff made lace or net fashion.

Randera [ran-day'-rah], *f.* Lace-worker.

Ranear [rah-nay-ar'], *vn.* To croak as frogs.

Raneta [rah-nay'-tah], *f.* Rennet, a kind of apple.

Rangifero [ran-hee'-fay-ro], *m.* Reindeer. Rangifer tarandus. *V.* Reno.

Rango [rahn'-go], *m.* Rank, quality.

Rangua [rahn'-goo-ah], *f.* An iron box in which the spindles of machines move; pivot collar, shaft socket.

Ranilla [rah-neel'-lyah], *f.* 1. (Dim.) A small frog. 2. Frog of the hoof of a horse or mule. 3. Cracks in the hoofs of horses. 4. Disease in the bowels of cattle.

Raninas [rah-nee'-nas], *f. pl.* Ranulary veins, two veins under the tongue.

Raniz [rah-neeth'], *m.* & *f.* A kind of linen.

Ránula [rah'-noo-lah], *f.* Tumour under the tongue of a horse.

Ranunculáceo, cea [rah-noon-coo-lah'-thay-o, ah], *a.* Ranunculaceous, of the crowfoot or buttercup family.

Ranúnculo [rah-noon'-coo-lo], *m.* (Bot.) Crow-foot, buttercup. Ranunculus.

Ranura [rah-noo'-rah], *f.* Groove, rabbet.

Raña [rah'-nyah], *f.* A device which fishermen use for catching cuttle-fishes on rocky bottoms.

Rapa [rah'-pah], *f.* (Prov.) Flower of the olive-tree.

Rapacejo [rah-pah-thay'-ho], *m.* Border, edging.

Rapacería [rah-pah-thay-ree'-ah], *f.* Puerility; a childish, boyish speech or action.

Rapacidad [rah-pah-the-dahd'], *f.* Rapacity, robbery.

Rapacilla [rah-pah-theel'-lyah], *f. dim.* A little girl.

Rapacillo, lla [rah-pah-theel'-lyo, lyah], *m.* & *f. dim.* A little boy or girl.

Rapador, ra [rah-pah-dor', rah], *m.* & *f.* 1. One who scrapes or plunders. 2. (Coll.) Barber.

Rapadura [rah-pah-doo'-rah], *f.* Shaving, the act of shaving; the state of being shaved; rasure; plundering. *V.* Raspadura.

Rapagón [rah-pah-gone'], *m.* A beardless young man.

Rapamiento [rah-pah-me-en'-to], *m.* Act of shaving or erasing.

Rapante [rah-pahn'-tay], *a.* 1. Snatching, robbing, or tearing off. 2. (Her.) Rampant.

Rapapiés [rah-pah-pe-ays'], *m.* Squib that runs along the ground; chaser.

Rapapolvo [rah-pah-pol'-vo], *m.* (Coll.) A sharp reproof.

Rapar [rah-par'], *va.* 1. To shave, as with a razor. 2. (Coll.) *V.* Afeitar. 3. To plunder, to carry off with violence; to skin, to peel. *A rapa terrón*, Entirely, from the root.—*vr.* (Mex.) To pass, bring, or hold.

Rapasa [rah-pah'-sah], *f.* (Min.) A stone very soft and easy to work.

Rapaz [rah-path'], *a.* Rapacious; ferocious.

Rapaz, za [rah-path', thah], *m.* & *f.* A young boy or girl.

Rapazada [rah-pah-thah'-dah], *f.* Childish action or speech.

Rapazuela [rah-pah-thoo-ay'-lah], *f. dim.* *V.* Rapacilla.

Rapazuelo, la, *m.* & *f. dim.* *V.* Rapacillo.

Rapazuelo, ela [rah-pah-thoo-ay'-lo, lah], *a. dim.* Rapacious, greedy.

Rape [rah'-pay], *m.* (Coll.) Shaving, cutting off the hair or beard carelessly. *Al rape.* Very short.

Rapé [rah-pay'], *m.* Rappee, a kind of snuff. *Rapé francés*, French snuff.

Rapeta [rah-pay'-tah], *f.* **Rapetón** [rah-pay-tone'], *m.* (Prov.) A net for sardine-fishing on the Cantabrian coast.

Rápidamente [rah'-pe-dah-men-tay], *adv.* Rapidly.

Rapidez [rah-pe-deth'], *f.* Rapidity, velocity, celerity.

Rápido, da [rah'-pe-do, dah], *a.* Rapid, quick, swift.

Rapidura [rah-pe-doo'-rah], *f.* Crude sugar. *V.* Raspadura, 3d def.

Rapiego, ga [rah-pe-ay'-go, gah], *a.* Ravenous: applied to birds of prey.

Rapiña [rah-pee'-nyah], *f.* Rapine, robbery. *Ave de rapiña*, Bird of prey. *Vivir de rapiña*, To live upon the catch.

Rapiñador, ra [rah-pe-nyah-dor', rah], *m.* & *f.* Plunderer, robber.

Rapiñar [rah-pe-nyar'], *va.* (Coll.) To plunder, to rob.

Rapista [rah-pees'-tah], *m.* (Coll.) Barber, shaver.

Rapo [rah'-po], *m.* A round-rooted turnip.

Rapónchigo [rah-pon'-che-go], *m.* (Bot.) Esculent bellflower, rampion. Campanula rapunculus.

Rapóntico [rah-pon'-te-co], *m.* (Bot.) *V.* Ruibarbo rapóntico.

Raposa [rah-po'-sah], *f.* 1. Female fox. *V.* Zorra. Canis vulpes. 2. (Met.) Cunning, deceitful person.

Raposear [rah-po-say-ar'], *vn.* To use artifices like a fox, to be foxy.

Raposera [rah-po-say'-rah], *f.* Foxhole, fox-den.

Raposería [rah-po-say-ree'-ah], *f.* Cunning of a fox; artful kindness.

Raposilla, ita [rah-po-seel'-lyah], *f. dim.* Artful wench.

Raposino, na [rah-po-see'-no, nah], *a.* Foxy. *V.* Raposuno.

Raposo [rah-po'-so], *m.* Male fox. *Raposo ferrero*, Iron-coloured fox, whose skin is used for furs.

Raposuno, na [rah-po-soo'-no, nah], *a.* Vulpine, foxy.

Rapsoda [rap-so'-dah], *a.* Rhapsodic, rapt.

Rapsodia [rap-so'-de-ah], *f.* Rhapsody, incoherent composition.

Rapta [rahp'-tah], *a.* Applied to a woman who is snatched by a man by force or artifice; abducted.

Rapto [rahp'-to], *m.* 1. Rapine, robbery. 2. Ecstasy, rapture, exultance. 3. Abduction of a woman by force or deceit. 4. Vapours in the head impairing the senses. 5. (Ast.) *V.* Movimiento.

Raptor [rap-tor'], *m.* Abductor.

Raque [rah'-kay], *m.* (Naut.) Salvage, beachcombing.

Raquear [rah-kay-ar'], *vn.* To beachcomb, to salvage shipwrecks.

Raqueta [rah-kay'-tah], *f.* 1. Racket. 2. (Bot.) Wall rocket. 3. Croupier's rake. *Raqueta de nieve*, Snowshoe.

Raquetero [rah-kay-tay'-ro], *m.* Racket-maker, racket-seller.

Raquialgia [rah-ke-ahl'-he-ah], *f.* 1. Rachialgia, pain in the spinal column. 2. Caries of same.

Raquis [rah'-kees], *m.* Backbone. Rachis.

Raquítico, ca [rah-kee'-te-co, cah], *a.* Rickety, diseased with the rickets.

Raquitis [rah-kee'-tis], *f.* Rickets, a disease.

Raramente [rah-rah-men'-tay], *adv.* Rarely, seldom; ridiculously, oddly.

Rara avis [rah'-rah ah'-vis] (Latin). An oddity, a strange creature.

Rarefacción [rah-ray-fac-the-on'], *f.* Rarefaction: applied to the air.

Rarefacer [rah-ray-fah-therr'], *va.* *V.* Rarificar.—*vr.* To rarefy.

Rarefacto, ta [rah-ray-fahc'-to, tah], *pp. irr.* of Rarefacer.

Rareza [rah-ray'-thah], *f.* 1. Rarity, rareness, uncommonness, infrequency. 2. Rarity, a thing valued for its scarcity; a curiosity; oddity.

Raridad [rah-re-dahd'], *f.* 1. Rarity, uncommonness, infrequency. 2. Rarity, thinness, subtilty. 3. Oddity.

Rarificar [rah-re-fe-car'], *va.* To rarefy, to make thin, to dilate.—*vr.* To rarefy, to become thin.

Rarificativo, va [rah-re-fe-cah-tee'-vo, vah], *a.* That which has the power of rarefying.

Raro, ra [rah'-ro, rah], *a.* 1. Rare, porous, having little density. 2. Rare, scarce, uncommon, odd. 3. Renowned, famous, excellent. 4. Extravagant, odd. *Es raro de genio*, He is of a very odd temper. *Rara vez*, Seldom.

Raro, *adv.* Rarely.

Ras [rahs], *m.* Level, an even surface. *Ras en ras* or *ras con ras*, On an equal footing, upon a par.

Rasador [rah-sah-dor'], *m.* 1. (Obs.) One who strikes corn and other dry materials, to level them with the bushel. *Rasador de la sal*, An officer appointed by the king to measure salt with a strickle. 2. Strickle, or strike, the instrument with which dry substances are levelled in the measure.

Rasadura [rah-sah-doo'-rah], *f.* The act of measuring salt, and other dry articles, with a strickle. *Rasaduras*, The grain or salt taken off with a strickle.

Rasamente, *adv.* Publicly, openly, clearly.

Rasar [rah-sar'], *va.* 1. To strike, to level corn with a strickle. 2. To graze, to skim, to touch lightly. *Rasarse los ojos de agua*, To have tears in the eyes.

Rascacielos [ras-cah-the-ay'-los], *m.* Skyscraper.

Rascadera [ras-cah-day'-rah], *f.* *V.* Rascador and Almohaza.

Rascador [ras-cah-dor'], *m.* 1. Scraper, to scrape and clean bones, metal, etc.; scratcher; rasp. 2. Hat-pin, bodkin.

Rascadura [ras-cah-doo'-rah], *f.* 1. The act of scratching, scraping, or rasping. 2. Scratch, made by scraping.

Rascalino, *m.* *V.* Tiñuela.

Rascamiento [ras-cah-me-en'-to], *m.* Act of scraping or scratching.

Rascamoño [ras-cah-mo'-nyo], *m.* Women's hat-pin, bodkin.

Rascar [ras-car'], *va.* To scratch, to scrape. *No descuidarse en el rascar*, Not to miss an opportunity of doing what one likes. *Un asno rasca a otro.* One fool praises another.

Rascazón [ras-cah-thone'], *f.* Pricking, tickling, or itching sensation which induces scratching.

Rasclo [rahs'-clo], *m.* An instrument used in coral-fishing.

Rasco [rahs'-co], *m.* *V.* Rascadura.

Rascón, na [ras-cone', nah], *a.* Sour, sharp, acrid.

Rascón, *m.* (Orn.) Rail, a wading bird; marsh-hen, mud-hen, sora. Rallus.

Rascuñar [ras-coo-nyar'], *va.* *V.* Rasguñar.

Rascuño [ras-coo'-nyo], *m.* *V.* Rasguño.

Rasel [rah-sel'], *m.* (Naut.) Narrow part of a ship towards the head and stern.

Rasero [rah-say'-ro], *m.* Strickle, strike, an instrument for levelling the contents of a dry measure. *Medir por un rasero*, To apply the same measure or standard to everything.

Rasete [rah-say'-tay], *m.* Satinet, a sort of light fabric with a satiny gloss; sateen for lining.

Rasgado, da [ras-gah'-do, dah], *a.* & *pp.* of Rasgar. 1. Rent, open. 2. Applied to a wide balcony or large win-

dow. *Ojos rasgados*, Large or full eyes. *Boca rasgada*, Wide mouth.
Rasgado, *m.* *V.* Rasgón.
Rasgador, ra [ras-gah-dor', rah], *m.* & *f.* Tearer, cleaver, one who scratches, tears, or lacerates.
Rasgadura [ras-gah-doo'-rah], *f.* Rent, tatter, strip torn from a fabric.
Rasgar [ras-gar'], *va.* 1. To tear or cut asunder, to rend, to claw, to lacerate. 2. *V.* Rasguear.
Rasgo [rahs'-go], *m.* 1. Dash, stroke, line elegantly drawn. *Rasgo de pluma*, Dash of a pen. 2. A grand, magnanimous action. *Rasgo de ingenio*, Stroke of wit. *Rasgo de generosidad*, Stroke of generosity. 3. Feature, trait. *Rasgo fisonómico*, Facial feature.
Rasgón [ras-gone'], *m.* Rent, rag, tatter, laceration.
Rasgueado [ras-gay-ah'-do], *m.* Act of making flourishes.—*Rasgueado, da, pp.* of Rasguear.
Rasguear [ras-gay-ar'], *vn.* To flourish, to form figures by lines.—*va.* To play a dash or arpeggio on the guitar.
Rasguillo [ras-geel'-lyo], *m. dim.* A small dash of a pen.
Rasgueo [ras-gay'-o], *m.* 1. The act of forming into fine strokes by a pen. 2. Lines elegantly drawn.
Rasgueta [ras-gay'-tah], *f.* (Mex.) A currycomb.
Rasguñar [ras-goon-nyar'], *va.* 1. To scratch, to scrape. 2. To sketch the outlines of a drawing or picture.
Rasguñito, ñuelo [ras-goon-nyee'-to], *m. dim.* Slight scratch or sketch.
Rasguño [ras-goo'-nyo], *m.* 1. Scratch, scar; nip.. 2. Sketch, the dotted outlines of a drawing or picture.
Rasilla [rah-seel'-lyah], *f.* 1. Serge, a kind of woollen stuff. 2. A fine tile for flooring.
Raso [rah'-so], *m.* Satin. *Rasos franceses dobles lisos*, Double French plain satin. *Rasos franceses labrados*, French figured silk. *Rasos franceses borton*, French ribbed satin.
Raso, sa, *a.* 1. Clear of obstructions or impediments. 2. Clear: applied to the atmosphere. 3. Plain; flat. 4. Having no title or mark of distinction. *Tabla rasa*, (Met.) Applied to the infant mind without ideas; canvas framed for painting. *Tiempo raso*, Fine weather. *Cielo raso*, Clear sky. *Cielo raso de una cama*, The tester or canopy of a bed. *Caballero raso*, A private gentleman. *Soldado raso*, A private, a common soldier. *Al raso*, In the open air.
Raspa [rahs'-pah], *f.* 1. Beard of an ear of corn. 2. Spine, fin-ray of fish. 3. Stalk of grapes. 4. Rasp, a coarse file. 5. Rind of certain fruits. *Ir a la raspa*, (Coll.) To go in search of plunder. *Tender la raspa*, To lay one's self down to rest.
Raspadera [ras-pah-day'-rah], *f.* (Prov.) Raker.
Raspadillo [ras-pah-deel'-lyo], *m.* Fraud or imposition practised by gamblers.
Raspador [ras-pah-dor'], *m.* Rasp, coarse file.
Raspadura [ras-pah-doo'-rah], *f.* 1. The act of filing, rasping, or scraping; rasure. 2. Filings, raspings, scrapings, shavings. 3. (Cuba) Pan sugar, crude sugar. *V.* Chancaca. 4. Certain cakes made with crude sugar.
Raspajo [ras-pah'-ho], *m.* (Prov.) Stalk of a bunch of grapes.
Raspamiento [ras-pah-me-en'-to], *m.* Act of rasping or filing.
Raspante [ras-pahn'-tay], *pa.* & *a.* Rasping, rough: applied to wine which grates the palate.
Raspar [ras-par'], *va.* 1. To scrape, to rasp, to pare off. 2. To prick, to have a sourish taste: applied to wine. 3. To steal, carry off.
Raspear [ras-pay-ar'], *vn.* To have a hair in the pen, which occasions blots.
Raspinegro, gra [ras-pe-nay'-gro, grah], *a.* (Prov.) *V.* Arispprieto.
Raspón (De) [ras-pone', day], *adv.* Scrapingly, thievishly.
Rasqueta [ras-kay'-tah], *f.* (Naut.) Scraper, an instrument for scraping the planks of a ship.
Rastel [ras-tel'], *m.* Bar or lattice of wood or iron.
Rastillador, ra, *m.* & *f.* *V.* Rastrillador.
Rastillar [ras-til-lyar'], *va.* To hackle flax. *V.* Rastrillar.
Rastillero [ras-til-lyay'-ro], *m.* (Low) Shoplifter, robber who steals and flies.
Rastra [rahs'-trah], *f.* 1. Sled or sledge, a carriage without wheels. 2. The act of dragging along. 3. Any thing hanging and dragging about a person. 4. A track or mark left on the ground. *V.* Rastro. 5. String of dried fruit. 6. Train, the result of some action which brings damage or inconveniences.
Rastrallar [ras-tral-lyar'], *vn.* To crack with a whip.
Rastrallido [ras-tral-lyee'-do], *m.* The crack of a whip.
Rastrar [ras-trar'], *va.* (Obs.) To drag. *V.* Arrastrar.
Rastreador, ra [ras-tray-ah-dor', rah], *m.* & *f.* Tracer, smeller, follower.
Rastrear [ras-tray-ar'], *va.* 1. To trace, to follow by the footsteps. 2. To harrow or rake on the farm, or drag in fishing. 3. To inquire into, to investigate, to fathom. 4. *Rastrear por un ancla*, (Naut.) To drag for an anchor. 5. To sell carcasses by wholesale in a slaughter-house.—*vn.* To skim the ground, to fly very low.
Rastreo [ras-tray'-o], *m.* (Prov.) Fringe or small pieces of stuff hanging round.
Rastrero, ra [ras-tray'-ro, rah], *a.* 1. Creeping, dragging. 2. Applied to a dog that runs by a trail. 3. Low, humble, cringing. 4. Applied to things floating in the air or to birds flying near the ground.
Rastrero, *m.* Inspector of a slaughter-house; a workman employed there.
Rastrillada [ras-treel-lyah'-dah], *f.* A rakeful.
Rastrillador, ra [ras-treel-lyah-dor', rah], *m.* & *f.* Hackler; flax-dresser, hatcheller; raker.
Rastrillaje [ras-treel-lyah'-hay], *m.* Raking; hatchelling; handling with a rake or hatchel.
Rastrillar [ras-treel-lyar'], *va.* 1. To hackle, to dress flax, to comb, to hatchel. 2. To separate the straw from the corn with a rake; to rake.
Rastrillazo [ras-treel-lyah'-tho], *m.* Blow from a rake.
Rastrilleo [ras-treel-lyay'-o], *m.* The act of hackling or raking.
Rastrillo [ras-treel'-lyo], *m.* 1. Hackle, an instrument to dress flax and hemp: flax-comb. 2. Portcullis. 3. Hammer of a gun-lock. 4. Ward of a key. 5. Ward of a lock. 6. Gateway of a palisade. *Rastrillo de pesebre*, Rack of a manger.
Rastro [rahs'-tro], *m.* 1. Track on the ground; trail. 2. Rake, harrow. 3 Slaughter-house; place where meat is sold by the carcass. 4. Sign, token, vestige, relic. 5. Grapple for gathering oysters.
Rastrojera [ras-tro-hay'-rah], *f.* Stubble ground and the time which the stubble lasts.
Rastrojo [ras-tro'-ho], *m.* Stubble. *Sacar (a uno) de los rastrojos*, To raise one from a humble position.
Rasura [rah-soo'-rah], *f.* 1. Shaving, as with a razor. 2. Scraping, filing. —*pl.* Boiled lees of wine, which serve to clean plate, etc.
Rasurada [rah-soo-rah'-dah], *f.* Shave.
Rasurar [rah-soo-rar'], *va.* To shave with a razor.
Rata [rah'-tah], *f.* 1. Rat. Mus rattus. 2. She-mouse.
Rata almizclada or **almizclera** [rah'-tah al-mith-clah'-dah, al-mith-clay'-rah], *f.* (Zool.) Muskrat.
Ratafia [ra-tah-fee'-ah], *f.* Ratafia, a spirituous liquor. *V.* Rosoli.
Ratania [ra-tah'-ne-ah], *f.* (Bot.) Ratany or ratanhy, a Peruvian shrub of astringent properties. Krameria triandra.
Ratear [rah-tay-ar'], *va.* 1. To lessen or abate in proportion. 2. To distribute or divide proportionally. 3. To filch, to commit petty thefts.—*vn.* To trail along the ground, to creep.
Rateo [rah-tay'-o], *m.* Distribution made at a certain rate or proportion.
Rateramente, *adv.* Meanly, vilely.
Ratería [rah-tay-ree'-ah], *f.* 1. Larceny, petty theft. 2. Vile conduct in things of little value.
Ratero, ra [rah-tay'-ro, rah], *a.* 1. Creeping on the ground. 2. Skimming on the ground, flying low; spoken of birds. 3. Committing petty thefts; pilfering. 4. Mean, vile.
Rateruelo, ela [rah-tay-roo-ay'-lo, lah], *m.* & *f. dim.* Little pilferer.
Ratificación [rah-te-fe-cah-the-on'], *f.* Ratification, the act of ratifying; confirmation, approbation.
Ratificar [rah-te-fe-car'], *va.* To ratify, to approve.
Ratificatorio, ria [rah-te-fe-cah-to'-re-o, ah], *a.* Ratificatory, confirming.
Ratigar [rah-te-gar'], *va.* (Prov.) To secure any load on carts with a rope.
Rátigo [rah'-te-go], *m.* (Prov.) Articles carried in carts.
Ratihabición [rah-te-ah-be-the-on'], *f.* (Law) Ratification, making valid.
Ratina [rah-tee'-nah], *f.* Petersham, ratteen, woollen cloth woven like serge.
Ratito [rah-tee'-to], *m. dim.* A little while, a short time.
Rato [rah'-to], *m.* 1. (Prov.) He-mouse. *V.* Ratón. 2. Short space of time. *Al cabo de rato*, It turned out ill after thinking so long about it. *Rato ha* or *ya ha rato*, Some time ago. *Buen rato*, A pretty time, a good while; many; a great quantity. *A ratos perdidos*, In leisure hours. *De rato en rato* or *a ratos*, From time to time, occasionally.
Rato, ta [rah'-to, tah], *a.* (For.) Firm, valid, conclusive.
Ratón [rah-tone'], *m.* 1. He-mouse. Mus musculus. 2. (Naut.) Hidden rock which frets cables. 3. (Mil.) Mechanism serving to fire off mines.
Ratona [rah-toh'-nah], *f.* Female mouse or rat.
Ratonar [rah-to-nar'], *va.* To gnaw like mice or rats.—*vr.* 1. To become sick as cats from eating rats. 2. (For hidden rocks) To fret or wear away cables.
Ratoncito, *m. dim.* A little mouse.
Ratonera [rah-to-nay'-rah], *f.* 1. Mouse-trap. *Caer en la ratonera*, To fall into a snare. *Ratonera* or *gato de agua*, Rat-trap, placed on water. 2. Hole where rats breed.
Ratonero, ra [rah-to-nay'-ro, rah], **Ra-**

toneseo, ca [rah-to-nes'-co, cah], *a.* Belonging to mice, mousy.

Raudal [rah-oo-dahl'], *m.* 1. Torrent, rapid stream. 2. Plenty, abundance.

Raudamente, *adv.* Rapidly.

Raudo, da [rah'-oo-do, dah], *a.* Rapid, precipitate.

Rauta [rah'-oo-tah], *f.* (Coll.) Road, way, route. *Coger* or *tomar la rauta,* To take one's course. *V.* RUTA.

Raya [rah'-yah], *f.* 1. Stroke, dash, or line drawn with a pen. 2. A line or limit between two provinces or countries; frontier. 3. The term, line, or boundary put to any thing. 4. Stripe, streak. *Tener a raya,* To keep within bounds. *Tener a uno a raya,* To keep one at bay. 5. Part in the hair. 6. Strip of ground cleared of combustible matter. (Acad.) *Tres en raya,* A boyish play. *A raya,* Correctly, within just limits. 7. *m.* (Zool.) Ray. Raia.

Rayado, da [rah-yah'-do, dah], *a.* 1. Striped. 2. Ruled, lined. 3. Streaked, variegated.

Rayano, na [rah-yah'-no, nah], *a.* Neighbouring, contiguous.

Rayar [rah-yar'], *va.* 1. To form strokes, to draw lines. 2. To mark with lines or strokes, to streak, to variegate in hues. 3. To rifle or striate the interior of fire-arms. 4. To expunge.—*vn.* 1. To excel, to surpass. *Raya muy alto,* He stands very high in his profession. 2. (Met.) To approximate, to touch.

Rayo [rah'-yo], *m.* 1. A right line. 2. Ray of light. 3. Radius of a circle; spoke of a wheel. 4. Thunderbolt; flash of lightning. 5. Fire-arms. 6. (Met.) Sudden havoc, misfortune, or chastisement. 7. A lively, ready genius; great power or efficacy of action. *Rayo directo, incidente, reflejo,* and *refracto,* Direct, incidental, reflected, and refracted light. *Rayo electrónico orientador,* (Aer.) Guidance beam. *Rayo equis,* X ray. *Rayo testorio,* Shuttle for weaving. *Rayo visual,* Field of vision. *Rayos,* Rays representing a crown of glory in religious art. *Echar rayos,* To show great anger or wrath.

Rayón [rah-yone'], *m.* Rayon.

Rayoso, sa [rah-yo'-so, sah], *a.* Full of lines.

Rayuela [rah-yoo-ay'-lah], *f.* 1. (Dim.) A small line. 2. Game of drawing lines.

Rayuelo [rah-yoo-ay'-lo], *m.* (Orn.) Small kind of snipe.

Raza [rah'-thah], *f.* 1. Race, generation, lineage, family, clan; branch of a family: usually taken in a bad sense if applied to mankind. 2. Quality of cloth and other things. 3. Each of the races of mankind. 4. Ray of light. 5. Cleft in a horse's hoof.

Razado [rah-thah'-do], *a.* Applied to coarse woollen cloth of unequal colour.

Rázago [rah'-thah-go], *m.* Coarse cloth made of tow.

Razón [rah-thone'], *f.* 1. Reason, the rational faculty. 2. Ratiocination. 3. Reason, clearness of faculty. 4. Reasonableness, moderation. *Pongase Vd. en la razón,* Be moderate in your demand. 5. Reason, cause, motive, principle. 6. Reason, argument, ground of persuasion; consideration; occasion. 7. Account, calculation. 8. Order, mode, method. 9. Reason, reasonableness, right, justice. 10. Expression or word which explains the idea; term. 11. Ratio, a relation between two mathematical quantities. 12. Firm, partnership, name of a commercial establishment. *Tomar razón,* To register, to take a memorandum or make a record of a thing. *Razón de pie de banco,* (Coll.) Futile, silly allegation; an absurd reason, an unsatisfactory explanation. *A razón de,* At the rate of. *A razón de catorce,* A term denoting want of punctuality in accounts. *En razón,* With regard to. *Hacer la razón,* To pledge in drinking. *Por razón,* Consequently. *Razón adelantada,* A precocious mind. *Tener razón,* To be right. (Lat. ratio.)

Razonable [rah-tho-nah'-blay], *a.* Reasonable; moderate; fair; just.

Razonablejo, ja [rah-tho-nah-blay'-ho, hah], *a.* (Coll.) Moderate, rational.

Razonablemente, *adv.* Reasonably; moderately.

Razonado, da [rah-tho-nah'-do, dah], *a.* Rational, prudent, judicious.—*pp.* of RAZONAR.

Razonador, ra [rah-tho-nah-dor', rah], *m. & f.* 1. Reasoner. 2. (Obs.) Advocate.

Razonamiento [rah-tho-nah-me-en'-to], *m.* Reasoning, argument, discourse, oration.

Razonante [rah-tho-nahn'-tay], *pa.* Reasoning; reasoner.

Razonar [rah-tho-nar'], *vn.* 1. To reason, to discourse. 2. To talk, to converse.—*va.* (Obs.) 1. To name, to call. 2. To advocate, to allege. 3. To take a memorandum of things, to place to account. 4. To compute, to regulate.

Razoncita [rah-thon-thee'-tah], *f. dim.* A short memorandum or account.

Re [ray], *prep.* Always used in composition, signifying repetition. Also as an intensive, signifying *very;* as, *rebueno,* very good.

Re [ray], *m.* (Mus.) Re, the second note of the musical scale.

Rea [ray'-ah], *f.* (Littl. us.) Female criminal.

Reacción [ray-ac-the-on'], *f.* 1. Reaction, revulsion. 2. Rebound. 3. (Met.) Resistance, opposition. 4. An alliance of efforts to overthrow a political power or to replace it by another. 5. (Med.) Reaction, a period of feverishness succeeding a chill.

Reaccionar [ray-ac-the-o-nar'], *va.* To react, to respond.

Reaccionario, ria [ray-ac-the-o-nah'-re-o, ah], *a.* 1. Reactionary; revulsive. 2. Reactionary, revolutionary. 3. Conservative, absolutist.

Reacción en cadena [ray-ac-the-on' en cah-day'-nah], *f.* Chain reaction.

Reacio, cia [ray-ah'-the-o, ah], *a.* Obstinate, intractable, reluctant.

Reactividad [ray-ac-te-ve-dahd'], *f* Quality of being a reagent; reagency.

Reactivo [ray-ac-tee'-vo], *m.* Reagent, an agent employed to determine the composition of other bodies. Used also as adjective.

Reactor [ray-ac-tore'], *m.* Reactor. *Reactor nuclear,* Nuclear reactor.

Readmisión [ray-ad-me-se-on'], *f.* (Obs.) Readmission.

Readmitir [ray-ad-me-teer'], *va.* (Obs.) To readmit.

Readornar [ray-ah-dor-nar'], *va.* (Obs.) To readorn.

Reagradecer [ray-ah-grah-day-therr'], *va.* To estimate highly.

Reagradecimiento [ray-ah-grah-day-the-me-en'-to], *m.* Act of esteeming, estimation.

Reagravación [ray-ah-grah-vah-the-on'], *f.* Reaggravation.

Reagravar [ray-ah-grah-var'], *va.* To aggravate anew.

Reagudo, da [ray-ah-goo'-do, dah], *a.* Very acute.

Real [ray-ahl'], *a.* 1. Real, actual. 2. Royal, kingly, king-like. 3. Grand, magnificent, splendid. 4. Real, true, certain. 5. Open, fair, ingenuous, candid; generous, noble.

Real [ray-ahl'], *m.* 1. Camp, the king's tent. 2. Main body of an army. 3. Real, a Spanish coin containing thirty-four *maravedís* in a real vellón. *Sentar el real,* To settle, to form an establishment. *Real de á ocho,* A dollar, or piece of eight, consisting originally of eight reals of plate, now of twenty reals vellón, and weighing an ounce in silver. *Real de plata,* Real of silver, or two reals vellón. *Real de agua,* The portion of water which can pass an aperture the size of a real. *Real de minas,* In New Spain, town having silver mines in its vicinity. *Tirar como a real de enemigo,* To ruin a person or thing.

Reala [ray-ah'-lah], *f.* Herd which a shepherd forms of his own flock, and of other owners'.

Realce [ray-ahl'-thay], *m.* 1. Raised work, embossment. 2. Brightness of colours, reflection of light; high light. 3. Lustre, splendour.

Realdad [ray-al-dahd'], *f.* Royal power, and its exercise; sovereignty.

Realegrarse [ray-ah-lay-grar'-say], *vr* To be very joyful.

Realeza [ray-ah-lay'-thah], *f.* Royalty, regal dignity.

Realidad [ray-ah-le-dahd'], *f.* Reality, fact; truth and sincerity. *En realidad* or *en realidad de verdad,* Truly, really, effectually.

Realimentación [ray-ah-le-men-tah-the-on'], *f.* (Elec.) Feedback.

Realismo [ray-ah-lees'-mo], *m.* 1. Royalism, adherence to kings. 2. Absolutism in political government. 3. (Neol.) Realism in art, or literature.

Realista [ray-ah-lees'-tah], *m.* 1. Royalist, loyalist, one who adheres to the king: used as an adjective. 2. Realist, a partisan of realism in art or literature.

Realizable [ray-ah-le-thah'-blay], *a.* Realizable.

Realización [ray-ah-le-thah-the-on'], *f.* 1. Realization, accomplishment, fulfillment. 2. Sale, reduction of merchandise for sale.

Realizar [ray-ah-le-thar'], *va.* 1. To realize, to bring into being or action. 2. (Com.) To realize upon, to convert into money.

Realmente, *adv.* Really, effectually; formally, actually; royally.

Realzar [ray-al-thar'], *va.* 1. To raise, to elevate; to emboss. 2. To heighten the colours in a painting, to emboss. 3. To illustrate, to aggrandize.

Reamar [ray-ah-mar'], *va.* To love in return; to love much.

Reanimar [ray-ah-ne-mar'], *va.* To cheer, to reanimate.

Reanudar [ray-ah-noo-dar'], *va.* To renew, to resume. *Reanudar las esperanzas,* To renew one's hopes. *Reanudar el trabajo,* To resume work.

Reañejo, ja [ray-ah-nyay'-ho, hah], *a.* Oldish, growing old.

Reaparecer [ray-ah-pah-ray-therr'], *vn.* To reappear.

Reaparición [ray-ah-pah-re-the-on'], *f.* Reappearing, reappearance.

Reapreciar [ray-ah-pray-the-ar'], *va.* To revalue, to re-estimate.

Reapretar [ray-ah-pray-tar'], *va.* To press again, to squeeze.

Reaquistar, *va.* (Obs.) To reacquire any thing.

Rearar [ray-ah-rar'], *va.* To plough again.

Reasegurar [ray-ah-say-goo-rar'], *va.* (Com.) To reinsure.
Reaseguro [ray-ah-say-goo'-ro], *m.* (Com.) Reinsurance.
Reasignar [ray-ah-sig-nar'], *va.* To as sign anew.
Reasumir [ray-ah-soo-meer'], *va.* To retake, to resume, to reassume.
Reasunción [ray-ah-soon-the-on'], *f.* The act of resuming, reassumption.
Reata [ray-ah'-tah], *f.* 1. Rope which ties one horse or mule to another, to make them go in a straight line. 2. (Met.) Blind submission to the opinion of others. *Reatas,* (Naut.) Woolding, ropes tied round a mast to strengthen it.
Reatadura [ray-ah-tah-doo'-rah], *f.* The act of tying one beast after another with a rope.
Reatar [ray-ah-tar'], *va.* 1. To tie one beast to another with a rope; to retie or tie tightly. 2. (Naut.) To woold, to tie ropes round masts or yards in order to strengthen them.
Reato [ray-ah'-to], *m.* The obligation of atonement for a sin after absolution.
Reaventar [ray-ah-ven-tar'], *va.* To winnow corn a second time.
Rebaba [ray-bah'-bah], *f.* 1. Seam of a casting in plaster or metal; burr or fash. 2. Projecting piece of stone in a wall, etc. 3. Mortar crowded out between stones and bricks. 4. The chipped edge of sawed timbers and planks. (This word is much used in all mechanical trades.)
Rebaja [ray-bah'-hah], *f.* 1. Abatement, deduction, diminution. 2. (Com.) Drawback, a return of duties on exportation; rebate.
Rebajamiento [ray-bah-hah-me-en'-to], *m.* 1. Curtailment, abatement. 2. Abasement.
Rebajar [ray-bah-har'], *va.* 1. To abate, to lessen, to diminish. 2. To lower the price, to dock a bill or account, to allow a discount; to curtail the quantity. 3. To weaken the light and give a deeper shade to the tints of a painting. 4. (Mil.) To dismiss from service, to muster out. *Rebajar un bajel,* (Naut.) To cut down the upper works of a ship. *Un buque rebajado,* A razeed vessel.—*vr.* 1. To humble one's self, to be humbled. 2. To commit low actions.
Rebajo [ray-bah'-ho], *m.* Groove in timber or stone.
Rebalaje [ray-bah-lah'-hay], *m.* Crooks or windings in a river.
Rebalsa [ray-bahl'-sah], *f.* 1 Stagnant water, a pool or puddle. 2. Stagnation of humours in a part of the body.
Rebalsar [ray-bal-sar'], *va.* 1. To dam water to form a pool. 2. To stop, to detain.
Rebanada [ray-bah-nah'-dah], *f.* Slice of bread and other things.
Rebanadilla [ray-bah-nah-deel'-lyah], *f. dim.* A small slice.
Rebanador, ra [ray-bah-nah-dor', rah], *a.* Slicing.—*m.* & *f.* Slicer. —*f.* Slicing machine.
Rebanar [ray-bah-nar'], *va.* 1. To slice, to cut into slices. 2. To slice, to cut, to divide.
Rebanco [ray-bahn'-co], *m.* (Arch.) The second bench or seat.
Rebañadera [ray-bah-nyah-day'-rah], *f.* Drag, a hooked instrument for taking things out of a well.
Rebañadura [ray-bah-nyah-doo'-rah], *f.* *V.* Arrebañadura.
Rebañar [ray-bah-nyar'], *va.* *V.* Arrebañar.
Rebañego, ga [ray-bah-nyay'-go, gah], *a.* Gregarious.
Rebaño [ray-bah'-nyo], *m.* 1. Flock of sheep, herd of cattle. 2. Crowd, heap. 3. Flock, assembly of the faithful.
Rebañuelo [ray-bah-nyoo-ay'-lo], *m. dim.* Small flock or heap.
Rebaptizando, da [ray-bap-te-thahn'-do, dah], *a.* He who is to be rebaptized.
Rebaptizar [ray-bap-te-thar'], *va.* *V.* Rebautizar.
Rebasadero [ray-bah-sah-day'-ro], *m.* (Naut.) Difficult place to pass.
Rebasar [ray-bah-sar'], *va.* 1. (Naut.) To sail past any point or difficult place. 2. (Met.) To exceed, to go beyond, to pass from a line or given point.
Rebastar [ray-bas-tar'], *vn.* To be more than enough.
Rebatar [ray-bah-tar'], *va.* *V.* Arrebatar.
Rebate [ray-bah'-tay], *m.* Dispute, disagreement.
Rebatible [ray-bah-tee'-blay], *a.* That can be refuted or rebutted.
Rebatimiento [ray-bah-te-me-en'-to], *m.* Repulsion, refutation.
Rebatiña [ray-bah-tee'-nyah], *f.* (Obs.) *V.* Arrebatiña. *Andar a la rebatiña,* (Coll.) To run zealously, clapping the hands, to stop any thing.
Rebatir [ray-bah-teer'], *va.* 1. To rebate, to curb, to resist; to repel. 2. To parry, to ward off. 3. To object, to refute; to rebut. 4. (Arith.) To allow from a sum a quantity which ought not to have been comprised in it. 5. To repress the passions of the soul.
Rebato [ray-bah'-to], *m.* 1. An unexpected attack, a surprise; an unexpected event; alarm, a fit, a transport. 2. A sudden fit of passion; rapid change of humours. *De rebato,* Suddenly. 3. Summons of the people by a bell in case of danger.
Rebautizar [ray-bah-oo-te-thar'], *va.* To rebaptize.
Rebeber [ray-bay-berr'], *va.* 1. To drink often. 2. *V.* Embeber.
Rebeco, ca [ray-bay'-co, cah], *a.* Cross-grained, intractable, harsh.
Rebelar [ray-bay-lar'], *va.* To excite rebellion.—*vr.* 1. To revolt; to rebel, to mutiny. 2. To get at variance, to break off friendly intercourse. 3. To resist, to oppose; to excite the passions irrationally.
Rebelde [ray-bel'-day], *m.* Rebel.
Rebelde, *a.* 1. Rebellious. 2. Stubborn, intractable, perverse. 3. (Law) Not attending the summons of a judge, non-appearance in court. 4. Rebellious: applied to the passions or affections.
Rebeldía [ray-bel-dee'-ah], *f.* 1. Rebelliousness, contumacy, disobedience. 2. Obstinacy, stubbornness. 3. (Law) Default, non-appearance in court. *En rebeldía,* By default.
Rebelión [ray-bay-le-on'], *f.* Rebellion, revolt, insurrection.
Rebelón, na [ray-bay-lone', nah], *a.* Restive: applied to a stubborn horse.
Rebellín [ray-bayl-lyeen'], *m.* (Mil.) Ravelin.
Rebencazo [ray-ben-cah'-tho], *m.* Blow with a port-rope.
Rebendecir [ray-ben-day-theer'], *va.* To bless or consecrate anew.
Rebenque [ray-ben'-kay], *m.* 1. Rope for flogging galley slaves. 2. (Naut.) Ratline, or ratlin; a short cross-rope.
Rebeza [ray-bay'-thah], *f.* (Naut.) Change in the course of tides or currents.
Rebién [ray-be-en'], *adv.* (Coll.) Very well.
Rebina [ray-bee'-nah], or **Rebinadura** [ray-be-nah-doo'-rah], *f.* (Agr.) Ploughing a third time.
Rebinar [ray-be-nar'], *va.* (Agr.) *V.* Terciar.
Rebisabuela [ray-be-sah-boo-ay'-lah], *f.* The great-great-grandmother.
Rebisabuelo [ray-be-sah-boo-ay'-lo], *m.* The great-great-grandfather.
Rebisnieta, Rebiznieta [ray-beeth-ne-ay'-tah], *f.* The great-great-granddaughter.
Rebisnieto, Rebiznieto [ray-beeth-ne-ay'-to], *m.* The great-great-grandson.
Reblandecer [ray-blan-day-therr'], *va.* To make bland or tender.
Reblandecimiento [ray-blan-day-the-me-en'-to], *m.* (Med.) Softening of organic tissues. *Reblandecimiento cerebral,* Softening of the brain.
Rebociño [ray-bo-thee'-nyo], *m.* (Prov.) A short cloak or mantle for women.
Rebolisco [ray-bo-lees'-co], *m.* (Cuba) Tumult of people without a real occasion.
Rebolla [ray-bol'-lyah], *f.* Local name of a kind of oak-tree.
Rebollar [ray-bol-lyar'], *m.* Thicket of oak saplings.
Rebollidura [ray-bol-lye-doo'-rah], *f.* (Mil.) Honey-comb; a flaw in the bore of ordnance.
Rebollo [ray-bol'-lyo], *m.* 1. (Bot.) The Turkey oak. Quercus cerris. 2. (Prov.) Boll or trunk of a tree.
Rebolludo, da [ray-bol-lyoo'-do, dah], *a.* 1. *V.* Rehecho and Doble. 2. Applied to a rude, hard diamond.
Reboñar [ray-bo-nyar'], *vn.* (Prov.) To stop on account of too much water: applied to a water-mill.
Reborda [ray-bor'-dah], *f.* A certain mode of fishing along the Levant coasts.
Reborde [ray-bor'-day], *m.* Ledge.
Rebosadero [ray-bo-sah-day'-ro], *m.* Place where any thing overflows.
Rebosadura [ray-bo-sah-doo'-rah], *f.* **Rebosamiento,** *m.* Overflow, as of liquor in a vessel.
Rebosar [ray-bo-sar'], *vn.* 1. To run over, to overflow. 2. To abound, to be plenty. 3. To evince, to display, to be unable to hide an affection or passion of the spirit.
Rebotadera [ray-bo-tah-day'-rah], *f.* Iron plate which raises the nap on cloth to be shorn.
Rebotador, ra [ray-bo-tah-dor', rah], *m.* & *f.* One who rebounds; clincher.
Rebotadura [ray-bo-tah-doo'-rah], *f.* The act of rebounding.
Rebotallero, ra [ray-bo-tal-lyay'-ro, rah], *a.* (Min.) Buscon, searcher, working on a percentage.
Rebotar [ray-bo-tar'], *vn.* 1. To rebound: applied to a ball. 2. To change colour, to turn: applied to wine and other liquors.—*va.* 1. To clinch a spike or nail; to turn the point of something sharp. 2. To raise the nap of cloth to be shorn. 3. To repel.—*vr.* To change one's opinion, to retract.
Rebote [ray-bo'-tay], *m.* Rebound, rebounding, resilience. *De rebote,* On a second mission.
Rebotica [ray-bo-tee'-cah], *f.* Back room behind an apothecary's shop.
Rebotiga [ray-bo-tee'-gah], *f.* (Prov.) *V.* Trastienda.
Rebotín [ray-bo-teen'], *m.* The second growth of mulberry leaves.
Rebozar [ray-bo-thar'], *va.* 1. To overlay or baste meat. 2. *V.* Embozar.—*vr.* To be muffled up in a cloak.
Rebozo [ray-bo'-tho], *m.* 1. The act of muffling one's self up. *V.* Embozo. 2. Muffler for the face. *V.* Rebociño. *Rebozo de calafate,* (Naut.) Drive-bolt, used by calkers to drive out another. *De rebozo,* Secretly, hiddenly.
Rebramar [ray-brah-mar'], *vn.* To low

and bellow repeatedly; to answer one noise by another.

Rebramo [ray-brah'-mo], *m.* Noise with which deer respond to each other.

Rebrotin [ray-bro-teen'], *m.* The second growth of clover which has been cut.

Rebudiar [ray-boo-de-ar'], *vn.* To snuffle and grunt: applied to a wild boar.

Rebueno, na [ray-boo-ay'-no, nah], *a.* (Coll.) Very good, excellent.

Rebufar [ray-boo-far'], *vn.* To blow or snort repeatedly, like animals.

Rebufo [ray-boo'-fo], *m.* The recoil of a fire-arm; expansion of air at the muzzle on firing a shot. (Literally, snorting.)

Rebujal [ray-boo-hahl'], *m.* 1. Number of cattle in a flock below even fifties. (For instance, in a flock of 430 sheep the 30 are *rebujal.)* 2. A small piece of arable land.

Rebujalero [ray-boo-hah-lay'-ro], *m.* A petty farmer.

Rebujar [ray-boo-har'], *va.* To wrap up linen and other cloth in an awkward manner.

Rebujo [ray-boo'-ho], *m.* 1. Muffler, a part of female dress. 2. (Prov.) A portion of tithe paid in money. 3. Wrapper for any common article.

Rebullicio [ray-bool-lyee'-the-o], *m.* Great clamour or tumult.

Rebullir [ray-bool-lyeer'], *vn.* To stir, to begin to move.

Reburujar [ray-boo-roo-har'], *va.* (Coll.) To wrap up, to pack in bundles.

Reburujón [ray-boo-roo-hone'], *m.* Bundle wrapped up carelessly.

Rebusca [ray-boos'-cah], *f.* 1. Research, searching. 2. Gleaning fruit and grain. 3. Refuse, remains, relic. *¡Qué hermosura de rebusca* or *rebusco!* Fine gleaning: applied to those who expect much fruit with little labour.

Rebuscador, ra [ray-boos-cah-dor', rah], *m. & f.* Gleaner; researcher.

Rebuscar [ray-boos-car'], *va.* 1. To glean grapes left by the vintagers. 2. To search, to inquire with great curiosity and attention.

Rebusco [ray-boos'-co], *m.* Research; gleaning. *V.* REBUSCA.

Rebutir [ray-boo-teer'], *va.* (Prov.) To stuff, to fill up.

Rebuznador, ra [ray-booth-nah-dor', rah], *m. & f.* One who brays like an ass.

Rebuznar [ray-booth-nar'], *va.* To bray, as an ass.

Rebuzno [ray-booth'-no], *m.* Braying of an ass.

Recabar [ray-cah-bar'], *va.* To obtain by entreaty.

Recabdar, Recadar, *va.* (Obs.) *V.* RECAUDAR.

Recadero [ray-cah-day'-ro], *m.* (Prov.) Porter, messenger.

Recado [ray-cah'-do], *m.* 1. Message, errand. 2. Present, gift sent to an absent person. 3. Compliments sent to the absent. 4. Provision of things necessary for some purpose. 5. Outfit, all needed implements for doing certain things. 6. Precaution, security. 7. Instrument, record. 8. (Amer.) Saddle and trappings of a horse. *Recado de escribir,* Escritoire, writing-desk. *A recado* or *a buen recado,* With great care and attention. *Llevar recado,* To be reprimanded. *Sacar los recados,* To take out a marriage license. *Ser mozo de buen recado,* (1) To be a youth of good conduct. (2) (Iron.) To mismanage an affair.

Recaer [ray-cah-err'], *vn.* 1. To fall back, to relapse. 2. To devolve. 3. To fall under another's power.

Recaída [ray-cah-ee'-dah], *f.* 1. Relapse, in sickness. 2. A second fall, a second offence.

(*Yo recaigo, yo recaiga,* from *Recaer. V.* CAER.)

Recalada [ray-cah-lah'-dah], *f.* (Naut.) The act of descrying the land; landfall.

Recalar [ray-cah-lar'], *va.* 1. To soak, to impregnate with liquor. 2. (Naut.) To descry a known point, after a cruise. 3. To bring another vessel to port. 4. To penetrate a calm: said of a current of air.

Recalcadamente, *adv.* Closely, contiguously; vehemently.

Recalcar [ray-cal-car'], *va.* 1. To squeeze. 2. To accent words or phrases with marked design.—*vr.* To inculcate, to repeat often. *Recalcarse el pie.* To strain one's foot.

Recalcitrante [ray-cal-the-trahn'-tay], *a.* Recalcitrant, perverse, obstinate.

Recalcitrar [ray-cal-the-trar'], *vn.* 1. To kick or strike with the heel. 2. To wince, to kick as unwilling of the rider: spoken of a horse. 3. To oppose, to make resistance where obedience is due.

Recalentamiento [ray-cah-len-tah-me-en'-to], *m.* Rekindling; heat.

Recalentar [ray-cah-len-tar'], *va.* 1. To heat again, to rekindle. 2. To excite: applied to sexual appetite.—*vr.* To become scorched or injured through heat: applied to farm products.

Recalmón [ray-cal-mohn'], *m.* A sudden decrease in the force of the wind.

Recalvastro, tra [ray-cal-vahs'-tro, trah], *a.* Bald from forehead to crown.

Recalzar [ray-cal-thar'], *va.* 1. To prick the outlines of a design on paper. 2. To mould up plants; to prepare mortar or cement.

Recalzo [ray-cahl'-tho], *m.* 1. The act of repairing a decayed wall. 2. Outside felloe of a cart-wheel.

Recalzón [ray-cal-thone'], *m.* Outer felloe of a wheel.

Recamado [ray-cah-mah'-do], *m.* (Com.) Embroidery of raised work.

Recamador, ra [ray-cah-mah-dor', rah], *m. & f.* Embroiderer.

Recamar [ray-cah-mar'], *va.* To embroider with raised work, to fret.

Recámara [ray-cah'-mah-rah], *f.* 1. Bedroom. 2. Chamber, breech (of a gun).

Recamarera [ray-cah-mah-ray'-rah], *f.* (Mex.) Upstairs maid.

Recamarilla [ray-cah-mah-reel'-lyah], *f. dim.* A small wardrobe; a small chamber of a fire-arm.

Recambiar [ray-cam-be-ar'], *va.* 1. To rechange, to change a second time. 2. To add the re-exchange on a protested bill. 3. (Com.) To draw again upon the drawer or indorser of a bill of exchange not paid when mature.

Recambio [ray-cahm'-be-o], *m.* 1. A new exchange or barter. 2. Re-exchange. 3. Retribution, reward.

Recamo [ray-cah'-mo], *m.* 1. Embroidery of raised work. 2. Button-hole, bordered with lace, and garnished at the end with a tassel.

Recanación [ray-cah-nah-the-on'], *f.* Act of measuring by *canas*, a measure of about two ells.

Recancanilla [ray-can-cah-neel'-lyah], *f.* 1. Affectation of limping, by boys, for amusement. 2. Tergiversation; an affected tone of talking.

Recantación [ray-can-tah-the-on'], *f.* Recantation, public retractation.

Recantón [ray-can-tone'], *m.* Corner-stone, set upright at the corners of houses and streets.

Recapacitar [ray-cah-pah-the-tar'], *vn.* To call to recollection, to recall to mind, to recapacitate.

Recapitulación [ray-cah-pe-too-lah-the-on'], *f.* Recapitulation, summary.

Recapitular [ray-cah-pe-too-lar'], *va.* To recapitulate, to sum up a charge or discourse; to draw to a head.

Recarga [ray-car'-gah], *f.* 1. Additional tax or duty. 2. Second charge of fire-arms.

Recargado, da [ray-car-gah'-do, dah], *a.* Overdone, excessive. *Recargado de adornos,* Overly ornamented.

Recargar [ray-car-gar'], *va.* 1. To reload, to load again. 2. To remand to prison on a new charge. 3. To make a new charge or accusation; to recharge. 4. (For.) To increase the sentence of a culprit.

Recargo [ray-car'-go], *m.* 1. A new charge or accusation. 2. Increase of a fever.

Recata [ray-cah'-tah], *f.* The act of tasting or trying again.

Recatadamente, *adv.* Cautiously; prudently; modestly; cunningly.

Recatado, da [ray-cah-tah'-do, dah], *a.* 1. Prudent, circumspect; shy, coy. 2. Honest, candid, modest.—*pp.* of RECATAR.

Recatamiento [ray-cah-tah-me-en'-to], *m.* (Obs.) *V.* RECATO.

Recatar [ray-cah-tar'], *va.* 1. To secrete. 2. To try or taste again.—*vr.* To take care, to proceed with prudence; to be cautious.

Recatear [ray-cah-tay-ar'], *vn.* 1. To give sparingly, to hold back. 2. *V.* REGATEAR.

Recatería [ray-cah-tay-ree'-ah], *f.* *V.* REGATONERÍA.

Recato [ray-cah'-to], *m.* 1. Prudence, circumspection, caution. 2. Modesty, honour; bashfulness, coyness.

Recatón [ray-cah-tone'], *m.* Metal socket of a lance or pike. *V.* REGATÓN.

Recatonazo [ray-cah-to-nah'-tho], *m.* Stroke with a pike or lance.

Recatonear [ray-cah-to-nay-ar'], *va.* To buy by wholesale, in order to retail again.

Recatonería, Recatonía [ray-cah-to-nay-ree'-ah], *f.* *V.* REGATONERÍA.

Recaudación [ray-cah-oo-dah-the-on'], *f.* 1. The act of collecting rents or taxes; recovery of debts. 2. Collector's office.

Recaudador [ray-cah-oo-dah-dor'], *m.* Tax-gatherer, collector of rents.

Recaudamiento [ray-cah-oo-dah-me-en'-to], *m.* 1. Collection of rents or taxes. 2. Office or district of a collector.

Recaudar [ray-cah-oo-dar'], *va.* 1. To gather, to collect rents or taxes. 2. To put or hold in custody.

Recaudo [ray-cah'-oo-do], *m.* 1. Collection of rents or taxes. 2. Provision, supply. 3. Caution, security for or against. 4. *V.* RECADO.

Recavar [ray-cah-var'], *va.* To dig ground a second time.

Recazar [ray-cah-thar'], *va.* To seize prey in the air or on the ground, like a hawk.

Recazo [ray-cah'-tho], *m.* 1. Guard, part of the hilt of a sword. 2. Back part of the blade of a knife.

Recebar [ray-thay-bar'], *va.* To spread gravel.

Recebo [ray-thay'-bo], *m.* Sand or fine gravel spread over the bed of a highway to even it and make it firm.

Recel [ray-thel'], *m.* A sort of striped tapestry.

Recelar [ray-thay-lar'], *va. & vr.* 1. To fear, to distrust, to suspect. 2. To

excite a mare sexually (towards receiving the jackass: said of a horse).
Recelo [ray-thay'-lo], *m.* Misgiving, imagination of something ill without proof, suspicion.
Receloso, sa [ray-thay-lo'-so, sah], *a.* Distrustful, suspicious.
Recentadura [ray-then-tah-doo'-rah], *f.* Leaven preserved for raising bread.
Recental [ray-then-tahl'], *a.* Applied to a sucking lamb.
Recentar [ray-then-tar'], *va.* To put sufficient leaven into dough to raise it.—*vr.* *V.* RENOVARSE.
Receñir [ray-thay-nyeer'], *va.* To regird, to gird tight.
Recepción [ray-thep-the-on'], *f.* Reception, receiving, acceptation.
Recepta [ray-thep'-tah], *f.* (Obs.) Book in which fines are entered.
Receptación [ray-thep-tah-the-on'], *f.* Reception of stolen goods.
Receptacular [ray-thep-tah-coo-lar'], *a.* (Bot.) Contained in the receptacle.
Receptáculo [ray-thep-tah'-coo-lo], *m.* 1. Receptacle, vessel for liquids. 2. Refuge, asylum. 3. Gutter for the eaves of buildings.
Receptador [ray-thep-tah-dor'], *m.* Receiver of stolen goods; abettor of crimes.
Receptar [ray-thep-tar'], *va.* To receive stolen goods; to abet any crime. —*vr.* To take refuge.
Recepticios, as [ray-thep-tee'-the-os, as], *a.* (For.) Property under the sole control of a married woman.
Receptividad [ray-thep-te-ve-dahd'], *f.* Receptivity, receptiveness.
Receptivo, va [ray-thep-tee'-vo, vah], *a.* Receptive.
Recepto [ray-thep'-to], *m.* Asylum, place of refuge.
Receptor, ra [ray-thep-tor', rah], *a.* Applied to one who receives any thing, especially stolen goods.
Receptor, *m.* 1. Receiver, treasurer. 2. Investigating official. 3. Radio receiver. *Receptor de cabeza,* Headset.
Receptoría [ray-thep-to-ree'-ah], *f.* 1. Receiver's or treasurer's office. 2. Place of a receiver or treasurer. 3. Power of a delegate judge.
Recercador, ra [ray-ther-cah-dor', rah], *a.* Girding, hemming in, investing.
Recésit [ray-thay'-sit], *m.* Vacation. *V.* RECLE.
Receso [ray-thay'-so], *m.* 1. Recess, remote apartment; recession. 2. (Mex.) Recess, the time when the legislature is not in session. *Receso del sol,* The apparent motion of the sun away from the equator.
Receta [ray-thay'-tah], *f.* 1. Prescription, recipe of a physician or surgeon. 2. (Coll.) Memorandum of orders received; order for goods. 3. Account of parcels sent from one office to another.
Recetador [ray-thay-tah-dor'], *m.* Prescriber of medicines.
Recetar [ray-thay-tar'], *va.* 1. To prescribe medicines. 2. (Met.) To make extravagant charges or unreasonable demands. *Recetar en buena botica,* (Coll.) To have rich friends to support extravagance.
Recetario [ray-thay-tah'-re-o], *m.* 1. Memorandum or register of the prescriptions made by a physician. 2. Apothecary's file of prescriptions not paid for by his customers. 3. Pharmacopœia.
Recetor [ray-thay-tor'], *m.* Receiver, treasurer. *V.* RECEPTOR.
Recetoría [ray-thay-to-ree'-ah], *f.* Treasury. place for keeping money.
Recial [ray-the-ahl'], *m.* Rapid, rapids in rivers.
Reciamente, *adv.* Strongly, forcibly, stoutly.
Recibí [ray-the-bee'], *m.* Received payment.
Recibidero, ra [ray-the-be-day'-ro. rah], *a.* Receivable.
Recibidor [ray-the-be-dor'], *m.* 1. Receiver. 2. The knight of Saint John who administers the property of the order.
Recibimiento [ray-the-be-me-en'-to], *m.* 1. Reception, receipt. 2. Entertainment to one from abroad. 3. Antechamber. 4. General reception of company. 5. (Prov.) An altar erected in the streets, for the reception of the sacrament on procession days.
Recibir [ray-the-beer'], *va.* 1. To accept, to receive, to let in. 2. To take charge of. 3. To sustain, to support. 4. To imbibe, to drink in, to draw in. 5. To suffer, to receive, to admit. 6. To receive company or visits as a lady. 7. To receive, to go and meet a person. 8. To fasten, to secure with mortar. 9. To experience an injury; to receive an attack.—*vr.* To be admitted to practise a profession. *Recibir a cuenta,* To receive on account. *Recibir a prueba,* To receive on trial. *A recibir,* (Com.) Receivable.
Recibo [ray-thee'-bo], *m.* 1. Reception. 2. Receipt, discharge, acquittance. *Acusar recibo,* (Com.) To acknowledge receipt. *Estar de recibo,* To be disposed for receiving visits. *Madera de recibo,* (Naut.) Timber fit for service. *Pieza de recibo,* Drawing-room. 3. Visit, entertainment or reception of friends.
Recidiva [ray-the-dee'-vah], *f.* 1. Relapse of a disease when convalescence was progressing. 2. (For.) *V.* REINCIDENCIA.
Recién [ray-the-en'), *adv.* Recently, lately (used before participles instead of *reciente*). *Recién casado,* Newlywed. *Recién muerto,* Recently deceased.
Reciente [ray-the-en'-tay], *adv.* Recent new, fresh; just made, modern.
Recientemente, *adv.* Recently, newly, freshly, just now, latterly, lately.
Recinchar [ray-thin-char'], *va.* To bind round one thing to another with a girdle.
Recinto [ray-theen'-to], *m.* Precinct, district.
Recio, cia [ray'-the-o, ah], *a.* 1. Stout, strong, robust, vigorous. 2. Coarse, thick, clumsy. 3. Rude, uncouth, intractable. 4. Arduous, grievous, hard to bear. 5. Severe, rigorous (weather). 6. Swift, impetuous. *Recio de complexión.* Of a strong constitution.
Recio, *adv.* Strongly, stoutly; rapidly; vehemently, vigorously. *Hablar recio,* To talk loud. *De recio,* Strongly, violently, precipitately, rapidly.
Récipe [ray'-the-pay], *m.* (Coll.) 1. Prescription of a physician. 2. Displeasure, disgust; ungenteel or bad usage.
Recipiente [ray-the-pe-en'-tay], *m.* (Chem.) 1. Recipient, receiver. 2. Receiver, bell-glass, of an air-pump.—*pa.* (Littl. us.) Receiving.
Reciprocación [ray-the-pro-cah-the-on'], *f.* Reciprocation, mutuality.
Recíprocamente, *adv.* Reciprocally, mutually, conversely.
Reciprocar [ray-the-pro-car'], *va.* To reciprocate.—*vr.* To correspond mutually.
Reciprocidad [ray-the-pro-the-dahd'], *f.* (Littl. us.) Reciprocalness, mutual obligation, reciprocity.
Recíproco, ca [ray-thee'-pro-co, cah], *a.* Reciprocal, mutual. *Verbo recíproco,* Reciprocal verb, as *reciprocarse.*
Recisión [ray-the-se-on'], *f.* Recision, abrogation.
Recísimo, ma [ray-thee'-se-mo, mah], *a. sup.* Most vehement.
Recitación [ray-the-tah-the-on'], *f.* Recitation, reciting.
Recitado [ray-the-tah'-do], *m.* (Mus.) Recitative, tuneful pronunciation.—*Recitado, da, pp.* of RECITAR.
Recitador, ra [ray-the-tah-dor', rah], *m. & f.* Reciter.
Recitante, ta [ray-the-tahn'-tay, tah], *m. & f.* (Obs.) *V.* COMEDIANTE and FARSANTE.
Recitar [ray-the-tar'], *va.* To recite, to rehearse.
Recitativo, va [ray-the-tah-tee'-vo, vah], *a.* Recitative.
Recizalla [ray-the-thahl'-lyah], *f.* Second filings or fragments.
Reclamación [ray-clah-mah-the-on'], *f.* 1. Reclamation. 2. Objection, remonstrance. 3. (Com.) Complaint, claim.
Reclamante [ray-clah-mahn'-tay], *m. & f.* Claimant.
Reclamar [ray-clah-mar'], *va.* 1. To decoy birds with a call or whistle. 2. To reclaim, to demand; to cry unto. 3. (Naut.) To hoist or lower a yard by means of a block.—*vn.* To contradict, to oppose.
Reclame [ray-clah'-may], *m.* (Naut.) Sheave-hole in a top-mast-head.
Reclamo [ray-clah'-mo], *m.* 1. Decoy-bird. 2. Call, an instrument to call birds. 3. Allurement, inducement, enticement. 4. (Naut.) Tie-block. 5. Reclamation. 6. (Print.) Catch-word. *Acudir al reclamo,* (Coll.) To answer, to go where there is a thing suitable to one's purpose.
Reclinable [ray-cle-nah'-blay], *a.* Capable of being reclined.
Reclinación [ray-cle-nah-the-on'], *f.* Reclining.
Reclinado, da [ray-cle-nah'-do, dah], *a. pp.* of RECLINAR. Reclined, recumbent.
Reclinar [ray-cle-nar'], *va. & vn.* To recline, to lean back. *Reclinarse en* or *sobre,* To lean on or upon.
Reclinatorio [ray-cle-nah-to'-re-o], *m.* 1. Couch, thing to lean on. 2. A stool for kneeling on at prayers. (Acad.)
Recluir [ray-cloo-eer'], *va.* To shut up, to seclude.
Reclusión [ray-cloo-se-on], *f.* 1. Reclusion, shutting up. 2. Recess, place of retirement; closeness.
Recluso, sa [ray-cloo'-so, sah], *a. & m. & f.* Recluse.—*pp. irr.* of RECLUIR.
Reclusorio [ray-cloo-so'-re-o], *m.* Recess, place of retirement.
Recluta [ray-cloo'-tah], *f.* Recruiting, as for the army; supply.—*m.* Recruit, a new soldier who enlists voluntarily.
Reclutador [ray-cloo-tah-dor'], *m.* Any person employed in recruiting or raising new soldiers.
Reclutamiento [ray-cloo-tah-me-en'-to], *m.* (Littl. us.) Recruiting of soldiers.
Reclutar [ray-cloo-tar'], *va.* 1. To recruit, to supply an army with new men. 2. To repair any thing wasted by new supplies.
Recobrable [ray-co-brah'-blay], *a* (Littl. us.) Recoverable.
Recobrar [ray-co-brar'], *va.* 1. To recover, to get back what was lost. 2. (Naut.) To rouse in, to take up the end of a rope which hangs loose.—*vr.* To recover from sickness, to regain vigour of body or mind; to recollect.
Recobro [ray-co'-bro], *m.* Recovery, restoration of things lost.
Recocer [ray-co-therr'], *va.* To boil again, to boil too much.—*vr.* To con-

sume one's self with rage and indignation.
Recocho, cha [ray-co'-cho, chah], *a.* Boiled too much, over-done.
Recocido, da [ray-co-thee'-do, dah], *a.* 1. Over-boiled. 2. Skilful, clever. 3. Over-ripe, dried up.—*m.* The operation of annealing metals.—*f.* The act of boiling again.—*pp.* of RECOCER.
Recodadero [ray-co-dah-day'-ro], *m.* Place for leaning on one's elbow.
Recodar [ray-co-dar'], *vn. & vr.* To lean with the elbow upon any thing.
Recodir, *vn.* (Obs.) *V.* RECUDIR.
Recodo [ray-co'-do], *m.* 1. A turn in a road or street; the bend of a river. 2. A corner or angle jutting out.
Recogedero [ray-co-hay-day'-ro], *m.* 1. Place where things are gathered or collected. 2. Instrument with which things are gathered.
Recogedor [ray-co-hay-dor'], *m.* 1. One who shelters or harbours. 2. Gatherer, gleaner.
Recoger [ray-co-herr'], *va.* 1. To retake, to take back. 2. To gather, to collect, to hoard; to pick out; to contract. 3. To gather the fruits. 4. To receive, to protect, to shelter. 5. To lock up in a mad-house. 6. To suspend the use, or stop the course of any thing. 7. To extract intelligence from books. *Recoger una proposición,* To retract a proposal. *Recoger un vale,* To take up a note. *Recoger velas,* To conclude a discourse; to become continent or moderate.—*vr.* 1. To take shelter; to withdraw into retirement. 2. To reform, or retrench one's expenses. 3. To go home, to retire to rest. 4. To abstract one's self from worldly thoughts.
Recogida [ray-co-hee'-dah], *f.* 1. The act of taking back any thing which circulates. 2. A woman shut up in a house of correction.
Recogidamente, *adv.* Retiredly.
Recogido, da [ray-co-hee'-do, dah], *a.* Retired, secluded; contracted.—*pp.* of RECOGER.
Recogimiento [ray-co-he-me-en'-to], *m.* 1. Collection, assemblage. 2. Retreat, shelter. *V.* RECLUSIÓN. 3. House where women are confined, or live in retirement. 4. Abstraction from worldly concerns; preparation for spiritual exercises.
Recolar [ray-co-lar'], *va.* To strain a second time.
Recolección [ray-co-lec-the-on'], *f.* 1. Summary, abridgment. 2. Harvest of grain or fruits. 3. Collection of money or taxes. 4. Convent where a strict observance of the rules prevails. 5. Retirement, abstraction from worldly affairs.
Recolectar [ray-co-lec-tar'], *va.* 1. To gather the harvest. 2. To collect many things, to hoard. 3. To collect from different litigants.
Recolegir, *va.* (Obs.) *V.* COLEGIR.
Recoleto, ta [ray-co-lay'-to, tah], *a.* Belonging to a convent where strict order is maintained.—*m. & f.* Devotee who lives retired; a recollect.
Recolorado, da [ray-co-lo-rah'-do, dah], *a.* Copper-nosed, red-faced, red-nosed.
Recombinar [ray-com-be-nar'], *va.* To recombine.
Recomendable [ray-co-men-dah'-blay], *a.* Commendable, laudable.
Recomendablemente, *adv.* Laudably.
Recomendación [ray-co-men-dah-the-on'], *f.* 1. Recommendation. 2. Injunction, application. 3. Praise, eulogy. 4. Dignity, authority. *Carta de recomendación,* Letter of introduction. *Recomendación del alma,* Prayers for the dying.
Recomendar [ray-co-men-dar'], *va.* 1. To charge, to enjoin. 2. To recommend, to commend.
Recomendaticio, cia [ray-co-men-dah-tee'-the-o, ah], *a.* Commendatory.
Recomendatorio, ria [ray-co-men-dah-to'-re-o, ah], *a.* Recommendatory.
(*Yo recomiendo, yo recomiende,* from *Recomendar. V.* ACRECENTAR.)
Recompensa [ray-com-pen'-sah], *f.* 1. Compensation, satisfaction. 2. Recompense, reward, remuneration, fee, gratuity. *En recompensa,* In return.
Recompensable [ray-com-pen-sah'-blay], *a.* Capable of being rewarded.
Recompensación [ray-com-pen-sah-the-on'], *f.* Compensation, reward, recompense.
Recompensar [ray-com-pen-sar'], *va.* To recompense, to reward, to gratify, to fee.
Recomponer [ray-com-po-nerr'], *va.* To recompose, to mend, to repair.
Recomposición [ray-com-po-se-the-on'], *f.* (Chem.) Recomposition.
Recompostura, *f.* *V.* RECOMPOSICIÓN.
Recomprar [ray-com-prar'], *va.* To buy again, to buy back.
Recompuesto, ta [ray-com-poo-es'-to, tah], *pp. irr.* from RECOMPONER.
Reconcentramiento [ray-con-then-trah-me-en'-to], *m.* Act of introducing or establishing in the centre.
Reconcentrar [ray-con-then-trar'], *va.* 1. To introduce, to enter into something else; to concentre. 2. To dissemble.—*vr.* To root, to take root: applied to sentiments and affections.
Reconciliable [ray-con-the-le-ah'-blay], *a.* (Littl. us.) Reconcilable.
Reconciliación [ray-con-the-le-ah-the-on'], *f.* 1. Reconciliation, reconcilement, renewal of friendship; agreement of things seemingly opposite. 2. Short confession detailing things previously omitted.
Reconciliador, ra [ray-con-the-le-ah-dor', rah], *m. & f.* Reconciliator, reconciler.
Reconciliar [ray-con-the-le-ar'], *va.* 1. To reconcile; to make friends with one; to accommodate. 2. To hear a short confession. 3. To consecrate anew any sacred place which has been polluted or defiled.—*vr.* 1. To confess offences. 2. To renew friendship.
Reconciliatorio, ria [ray-con-the-le-ah-to'-re-o, ah], *a.* Conciliatory.
Reconcomerse [ray-con-co-merr'-say], *vr.* To scratch frequently from continual itching.
Reconcomio [ray-con-co'-me-o], *m.* (Coll.) 1. Shrugging the shoulders with satisfaction or resignation, or from itching or stinging. 2. Fear, apprehension. 3. Craving, violent desire.
Recóndito, ta [ray-con'-de-to, tah], *a.* Recondite, secret, hidden, concealed, latent, abstruse.
Reconducción [ray-con-dooc-the-on'], *f.* Renewal of a lease.
Reconducir [ray-con-doo-theer'], *va.* 1. To conduct back. 2. (For.) To renew a lease or contract.
Reconfesar [ray-con-fay-sar'], *va.* To confess again.
Reconocedor, ra [ray-co-no-thay-dor', rah], *m. & f.* Examiner; one who recognizes.
Reconocer [ray-co-no-therr'], *va.* 1. To try, to examine closely, to find out, to ascertain. 2. To submit to the command or jurisdiction of others. 3. To own, to confess. 4. To acknowledge favours received. 5. To consider, to contemplate. 6. To comprehend, to conceive. 7. To acknowledge the right of property of others; to recognize. 8. To reconnoitre, to scout. 9. To recognize the official existence of a country, or to sanction acts done in another land.—*vr.* 1. To repent. 2. To confess one's self culpable. 3. To judge justly of one's own self.
Reconocidamente, *adv.* Gratefully, confessedly.
Reconocido, da [ray-co-no-thee'-do, dah], *a.* 1. Acknowledged, confessed. 2. Grateful, obliged. 3. *n.* Recognizee, one in whose favour a bond is given. —*pp.* of RECONOCER.
Reconociente [ray-co-no-the-en'-tay], *pa.* Recognizing.
Reconocimiento [ray-co-no-the-me-en'-to], *m.* 1. Recognition. 2. Acknowledgment, gratitude; owning, confession. 3. Recognizance; subjection, submission. 4. Examination, inquiry. 5. Recognizance, acknowledgment of a bond or other writing in court. 6. Survey, inspection.
(*Yo reconozco, yo reconozca,* from *Reconocer. V.* CONOCER.)
Reconquista [ray-con-kees'-tah], *f.* Reconquest, a place reconquered.
Reconquistar [ray-con-kis-tar'], *va.* To reconquer.
Reconstituir [ray-cons-te-too-eer'], *va. & vr.* To reconstitute.
Reconstituyente [ray-cons-te-too-yenn'-tay], *m.* (Med.) Tonic.
Reconstrucción, *f.* *V.* REEDIFICACIÓN.
Recontar [ray-con-tar'], *va.* To recount to relate distinctly.
Recontento [ray-con-ten'-to], *m.* Contentment, deep satisfaction.
Recontento, ta [ray-con-ten'-to, tah], *a.* Very content.
Reconvalecer [ray-con-vah-lay-therr'], *vn.* To recover from sickness.
(*Yo reconvalezco, yo reconvalezca,* from *Reconvalecer. V.* CONOCER.)
Reconvención [ray-con-ven-the-on'], *f.* Charge, accusation; recrimination; expostulation; reproach.
Reconvenir [ray-con-vay-neer'], *va.* 1. To charge, to accuse. 2. To retort, to recriminate, to accuse the prosecutor; to convert the plaintiff into the defendant; to expostulate. 3. To call to an account, to reproach, to reprimand, to remonstrate.
Recopilación [ray-co-pe-lah-the-on'], *f.* 1. Summary, abridgment. 2. Collection of things taken from books. *Recopilación de las leyes,* Abridgment or collection of the statutes. *Novísima Recopilación,* Revised code of laws in Spain promulgated July 15th, 1805.
Recopilador [ray-co-pe-lah-dor'], *m.* Compiler, collector, abridger.
Recopilar [ray-co-pe-lar'], *va.* To abridge, to collect.
Recordable [ray-cor-dah'-blay], *a.* Worthy of being recorded.
Recordación [ray-cor-dah-the-on'], *f.* 1. Remembrance, calling to recollection. 2. *V.* RECUERDO.
Recordador, ra [ray-cor-dah-dor', rah], *m. & f.* One who remembers; or that which serves to remind one of something.
Recordar [ray-cor-dar'], *va.* To remind; to call to recollection.—*vn.* To awaken from sleep.—*vr.* To hit upon, to remember.
Recordativo, va [ray-cor-dah-tee'-vo, vah], *a.* That which reminds or may be reminded.
Recordatorio, ria [ray-cor-dah-to'-re-o, ah], *a.* (For.) Said of the official writing or order by which the fulfilment of a requisition or obligation is recalled.
Recorrer [ray-cor-rerr'], *va.* 1. To run over, to examine, to survey. 2. To

read over, to peruse. 3. To mend, to repair.—*vn.* 1. To recur, to have recourse to. 2. To rearrange a paragraph or page in printing. *Recorrer la memoria,* To call to recollection. *Recorrer un buque* or *un barco,* (Naut.) To overhaul or repair a vessel. *Recorrer los cables,* (Naut.) To underrun the cables. *Navío en recorrida,* A ship under repairs. *Recorrer los cañaverales,* To run from house to house asking for something. *Recorrer* or *reconocer el campo,* To scour or scout the field.

Recorrido [ray-cor-ree'-do], *m.* 1. Route (of a streetcar, etc.] 2. Distance travelled. 3. Repair. 4. Scolding.

Recortada [ray-cor-tah'-dah], *f.* In painting, a shadow as strong at the beginning as at the end.

Recortado [ray-cor-tah'-do], *m.* Figure cut out of paper.

Recortado, da, *a.* (Bot.) Notched, incised, cut irregularly.—*pp.* of RECORTAR.

Recortadura, *f.* *V.* RECORTE.

Recortar [ray-cor-tar'], *va.* 1. To cut away, to shorten, to pare off. 2. To cut figures in paper. 3. To delineate a figure in profile.

Recorte [ray-cor'-tay], *m.* Outline, profile.—*pl.* Cuttings, trimmings, projecting pieces trimmed away by a cutting instrument; clippings.

Recorvar [ray-cor-var'], *va.* *V.* ENCORVAR.

Recorvo, va [ray-cor'-vo, vah], *a.* *V.* CORVO.

Recoser [ray-co-serr'], *va.* To sew again a rip or rent.

Recostadero [ray-cos-tah-day'-ro], *m.* Reclining or resting-place.

Recostado, da [ray-cos-tah'-do, dah], *a.* & *pp.* of RECOSTAR. Recumbent, reclined.

Recostar [ray-cos-tar'], *va.* To lean against, to recline.—*vr.* To go to rest; to repose or recline.

Recova [ray-co'-vah], *f.* 1. Purchasing in the country eggs, butter, or poultry, to retail in town. 2. A poultry market. 3. (Peru, Bol. Chili) Marketplace. 4. Pack of hounds.

Recovar [ray-co-var'], *va.* To buy fowls, eggs, etc., to sell again.

Recoveco [ray-co-vay'-co], *m.* 1. Turning, winding. 2. Simulation, artifice.

Recovero [ray-co-vay'-ro], *m.* Huckster, in eggs, butter, or poultry.

Recre [ray'-cray], *m.* Vacation of choristers. *V.* RECLE.

Recreación [ray-cray-ah-the-on'], *f.* Recreation, relief, diversion, amusement.

Recrear [ray-cray-ar'], *va.* To amuse, to delight, to gratify, to glad or gladden, to recreate.—*vr.* To divert one's self.

Recreativo, va [ray-cray-ah-tee'-vo, vah], *a.* Recreative, diverting.

Recrecer [ray-cray-therr'], *va.* & *vn.* 1. To grow again. 2. To augment, to increase. 3. To occur, to happen.—*vr.* 1. To grow big, to be overgrown. 2. To recover one's spirits.

Recrecimiento [ray-cray-the-me-en'-to], *m.* Growth, increase, augmentation.

Recreído, da [ray-cray-ee'-do, dah], *a.* Intractable, returned to liberty: applied to a hawk.

Recremento [ray-cray-men'-to], *m.* Recrement, spume, dregs, dross, scoria, residuum.

Recreo [ray-cray'-o], *m.* 1. Recreation, amusement. 2. Recess. *Hora de recreo,* Recess hour. *Sala de recreo,* Recreation room. *Patio de recreo,* Playground. *Viaje de recreo,* Pleasure trip.

Recría [ray-cree'-ah], *f.* Repasturing of colts.

Recriar [ray-cre-ar'], *va.* To favour, by good feeding and care, the development of colts and mules reared in another region.

Recriminación [ray-cre-me-nah-the-on'], *f.* Recrimination, countercharge.

Recriminar [ray-cre-me-nar'], *va.* To recriminate, to make a countercharge.

Rectamente, *adv.* Rightly, justly, justifiably, honestly, fairly, good.

Rectangular [rec-tan-goo-lar'], *a.* Right-angled.

Rectángulo, la [rec-tahn'-goo-lo, lah], *a.* Rectangular; rectangled.

Rectángulo, *m.* Rectangle.

Rectificable [rec-te-fe-cah'-blay], *a.* Rectifiable, which may be rectified.

Rectificación [rec-te-fe-cah-the on'], *f.* Rectification.

Rectificador, ra [rec-te-fe-cah-dor', rah], *a.* Rectifying, verifying.—*m.* & *f.* Rectifier, verifier.

Rectificar [rec-te-fe-car'], *va.* 1. To rectify, to make right. 2. To verify, to confirm. 3. To rectify, to clarify, to redistil.

Rectificativo, va [rec-te fe-cah-tee'-vo, vah], *a.* That which rectifies or corrects.

Rectilíneo, nea [rec-te-lee'-nay-o, ah], *a.* Rectilinear, rectilineous, rectilineal.

Rectitud [rec-te-tood'], *f.* 1. Straightness, the shortest distance between two points. 2. Rectitude, uprightness, honour, honesty; exactitude.

Recto, ta [rec'-to, tah], *a.* 1. Straight, erect; right. 2. Just, upright, honest, faithful, fair. *En sentido recto y metafórico,* In a literal and metaphorical sense.

Recto [rec'-to], *m.* 1. (Anat.) Rectum. 2. A right angle.

Rector, ra [rec-tor', rah], *m.* & *f.* 1. One who rules or governs. 2. Superior of a community or establishment. *Rector de una universidad,* Rector of a university. 3. Curate, rector.

Rectorado [rec-to-rah'-do], *m.* Rectorship.

Rectoral [rec-to-rahl'], *a.* Rectorial.—*f.* Rectory, a rector's dwelling.

Rectorar [rec-to-rar'], *vn.* To attain the office of rector.

Rectoría [rec-to-ree'-ah], *f.* 1. Rectory, curacy. 2. Office and dignity of a rector.

Recua [ray'-coo-ah], *f.* 1. Drove of beasts of burden. 2. Multitude of things in succession. (Arab.)

Recuadrar, *va.* *V.* CUADRICULAR.

Recuadro [ray-coo-ah'-dro], *m.* (Arch.) Square compartment.

Recuarta [ray-coo-ar'-tah], *f.* One of the chords of a guitar: the second string put in the place of the fourth when the strings are doubled.

Recudimento, Recudimiento [ray-coo-de-men'-to], *m.* Power vested in a person to gather rents or taxes.

Recudir [ray-coo-deer'], *va.* 1. To pay money in part of wages or other dues. 2. (Obs.) *V.* ACUDIR.—*vn.* To rebound, to redound, to set out again, to revert to the original place or state.

Recuelo [ray-coo-ay'-lo], *m.* The lye which is caught in a vat after passing through a strainer.

Recuenco [ray-coo-en'-co], *m.* Ground which forms an inclosed space or corner.

Recuento [ray-coo-en'-to], *m.* 1. (Prov.) Inventory. *V.* INVENTARIO. 2. Recension, muster.

Recuentro [ray-coo-en'-tro], *m.* *V.* REENCUENTRO.

Recuerdo [ray-coo-err'-do], *m.* Remembrance, hint given of what has passed, memento, memory; recognition.

(*Yo recuerdo, yo recuerde,* from *Recordar.* *V.* ACORDAR.)

Recuero [ray-coo-ay'-ro], *m.* Muleteer, mule-driver.

Recuesta [ray-coo-es'-tah], *f.* 1. Request, intimation. *V.* REQUERIMIENTO. 2. Duel. *Á toda recuesta,* At all events.

(*Yo me recuesto, yo me recueste,* from *Recostarse.* *V.* ACORDAR.)

Recuesto [ray-coo-es'-to], *m.* Declivity, a gradual descent.

(*Yo recuezo, yo recueza,* from *Recocer.* *V.* COCER.)

Recula [ray-coo'-lah], *f.* (Prov.) Recoil, retrocession.

Reculada [ray-coo-lah'-dah], *f.* 1. (Naut.) The falling of a ship astern. 2. The action of falling back or retrograding; recoil.

Recular [ray-coo-lar'], *vn.* 1. To fall back, to retrograde, to recoil. 2. (Coll.) To give up, to yield.

Reculo, la [ray-coo'-lo, lah], *a.* Having no tail: applied to hens or pullets.—*m.* *V.* RECULADA.

Reculones (Á) [ray-coo-lo'-nes], *adv.* (Coll.) Retrogradely.

Recuperable [ray-coo-pay-rah'-blay], *a.* Recoverable.

Recuperación [ray-coo-pay-rah-the-on'], *f.* Recovery, the act of recovering or rescuing, recuperative.

Recuperador, ra [ray-coo-pay-rah-dor', rah], *m.* & *f.* Rescuer, redeemer.

Recuperar [ray-coo-pay-rar'], *va.* To recover, to rescue, to regain.—*vr.* To recover from sickness, to gather strength.

Recuperativo, va [ray-coo-pay-rah-tee'-vo, vah], *a.* That which recovers or has the power of recovering.

Recura [ray-coo'-rah], *f.* Comb-saw, used by comb-makers.

Recurar [ray-coo-rar'], *va.* To make or open the teeth of combs.

Recurrente [ray-coor-ren'-tay], *a.* (Anat.) Recurrent: used of certain arteries which turn back towards their origin.—*pa.* of RECURRIR.

Recurrir [ray-coo-reer'], *va.* To recur, to have recourse to.—*vn.* To revert.

Recurso [ray-coor'-so], *m.* 1. Recourse, application for help or protection. 2. Recourse, return to the same place. 3. Appeal, recourse to a higher court of justice. *Sin recurso,* Definitively, without appeal.

Recusable [ray-coo-sah'-blay], *a.* Refusable, exceptionable.

Recusación [ray-coo-sah-the-on'], *f.* Refusal, exception; recusation.

Recusante [ray-coo-sahn'-tay], *pa.* Refusing; recusant.

Recusar [ray-coo-sar'], *va.* 1. To refuse to admit, to decline admission. 2. To recuse or challenge a judge. *Recusar los testigos,* To object to, to challenge, witnesses.

Rechazador, ra [ray-chah-thah-dor', rah], *m.* & *f.* Repeller, contradicter.

Rechazamiento [ray-chah-thah-me-en'-to], *m.* Repulsion.

Rechazar [ray-chah-thar'], *va.* 1. To repel, to repulse, to drive back, to impel in an opposite direction, to force back. 2. To contradict, to impugn.

Rechazo [ray-chah'-tho], *m.* 1. Rejection. 2. Recoil, rebound. *De rechazo,* Incidentally, casually, by rebound.

Rechifla [ray-chee'-flah], *f.* Whistle, whistling of the winds. *Hacer rechifla,* (Coll.) To mock, to laugh at.

Rechiflar [ray-che-flar'], *va.* To mock, to make fun of, to ridicule. To whistle insistently, to make cat-calls.

Rechinador, ra [ray-che-nah-dor', rah], *a.* Creaking, grating.

Rechinamiento [ray-che-nah-me-en'-to], *m.* Creaking of a machine, gnashing of teeth.

Rechinante [ray-che-nahn'-tay], *pa.* Creaking; gnashing.

Rechinar [ray-che-nar'], *vn.* 1. To creak, to clash; to hurtle; to grate. *Rechinar los dientes,* To gnash the teeth. 2. To engage in any thing with reluctance.

Rechinido [ray-che-nee'-do], *m.* *V.* RECHINO.

Rechino [ray-chee'-no], *m.* Creaking, clang, clangour, clash.

Rechoncho, cha [ray-chon'-cho, chah], *a.* (Coll.) Chubby: applied to persons.

Rechupete (De) [ray-choo-pay'-tay]. (Coll.) Exquisite, highly agreeable.

Red [red], *f.* 1. Net, particularly for fishing and fowling. 2. Grate of the parlour in nunneries. 3. Grate through which fish or bread is sold. 4. Prison with a strong grate. 5. Snare, wile, fraud. 6. Silk coif or head-dress. *Red barredera,* Drag-net. *Red de araña,* Cobweb. *Red de combate,* (Naut.) Netting. *Red de pájaros,* A thin, clear stuff. *Caer en la red,* To fall into the snare. *Á red barredera,* In a destructive manner.

Redacción [ray-dac-the-on'], *f.* 1. Compilement: the act of editing a newspaper or other publication. 2. The office where it is published. 3. The editorial staff.

Redactar [ray-dac-tar'], *va.* To compile, to write, to compose, to edit a work or a periodical.

Redactor [ray-dac-tor'], *m.* Compiler, editor. Also used adjectively: *Redactor, ra.*

Redada [ray-dah'-dah], *f.* 1. Casting a net, a netful of fish. 2. Multitude, crowd.

Redamar [ray-dah-mar'], *va.* (Obs.) *V.* REAMAR.

Redaño [ray-dah'-nyo], *m.* (Anat.) Caul, kell, the omentum.

Redar [ray-dar'], *va.* To cast a net.

Redargución [ray-dar-goo-the-on'], *f.* Retort, refutation.

Redargüir [ray-dar-goo-eer'], *va.* 1. To retort, to reply. 2. (For.) To impugn a writing as suffering from some defect.

Redaza [ray-dah'-thah], *f.* A certain fishing-net.

Redazo [ray-dah'-tho], *m.* In artillery, a kind of fire-pillow.

Redear [ray-day-ar'], *va.* *V.* MAJADEAR.

Redecilla [ray-day-theel'-lyah], *f.* 1. A head-dress formerly used in Spain. 2. (Dim.) *V.* REDECICA.

Redecir, *va.* (Obs.) To repeat.

Redecita [ray-day-thee'-tah], *f. dim.* A small net.

Rededor [ray-day-dor'], *m.* Environs. *V.* CONTORNO. *Al rededor,* Round about, thereabout, little more or less. *Andar al rededor,* To go or walk about.

Redel [ray-del'], *m.* (Naut.) Loof-frame.

Redención [ray-den-the-on'], *f.* 1. Redemption, the act of redeeming. 2. Recovery of lost liberty, ransom. 3. Salvation, refuge. *Redención de un censo,* The paying off a mortgage.

Redentor, ra [ray-den-tor', rah], *m.* & *f.* Redeemer, one who rescues, redeems, or ransoms. *Nuestro Redentor,* Our Redeemer, Jesus Christ.

Redero [ray-day'-ro], *m.* Net-maker; one who catches birds or fish with nets.

Redero, ra [ray-day'-ro, rah], *a.* Reticular, retiform; reticulated.

Redhibición [red-e-be-the-on'], *f.* Redhibition, the rescinding of a sale through hiding a defect in the thing sold.

Redhibir [red-e-beer'], *va.* To rescind a sale (by the buyer), on account of the concealment by the seller of some defect or vice in the thing sold.

Redhibitorio, ria [red-e-be-to'-re-o, ah], *a.* Redhibitory, relating to redhibition; giving the right to redhibition.

Redición [ray-de-the-on'], *f.* Repetition of what had been said.

Redicho, cha [ray-dee'-cho, chah], *a.* Speaking with affected precision.

Rediezmar [ray-de-eth-mar'], *va.* To decimate again, to tithe a second time.

Rediezmo [ray-de-eth'-mo], *m.* The ninth part of crops already tithed.

Redil [ray-deel'], *m.* Sheep-fold, sheep cot, fold-coop.

Redimible [ray-de-mee'-blay], *a.* Redeemable.

Redimir [ray-de-meer'], *va.* 1. To redeem, to rescue, to ransom. 2. To redeem a pledge. 3. To succour, to relieve; to extricate or liberate. *Redimirse de algún trabajo,* To extricate one's self from trouble and difficulties. *Redimir un censo,* To pay off a mortgage.

Redina [ray-dee'-nah], *f.* Weigh wheel, a wheel of velvet looms.

Redingote [ray-din-go'-tay], *m.* Riding-coat, a kind of great-coat.

Redistribución [ray-dis-tre-boo-the-on'], *f.* A new or second distribution.

Rédito [ray'-de-to], *m.* Revenue, rent, proceeds.

Redituable, Reditual [ray-de-too-ah'-blay], *a.* Producing rent, benefit, or profit; rentable.

Redituar [ray-de-too-ar'], *va.* To yield or produce any benefit or profit; to rent.

Redivivo, va [ray-de-vee'-vo, vah], *a.* Redivivus, revived, restored.

Redoblado, da [ray-do-blah'-do, dah], *a.* & *pp.* of REDOBLAR. 1. Redoubled. 2. Stout and thick. 3. (Mil.) Quick step.

Redoblamiento [ray-do-blah-me-en'-to], *m.* Reduplication.

Redoblar [ray-do-blar'], *va.* 1. To double, to increase by as much again. 2. To clinch, to rivet. 3. To touch the same chord twice. (Mil.) To play double beats on the drum.

Redoble [ray-do'-blay], *m.* 1. Repeated touching of the same chord; double beat on the drum. 2. Amplification of a discourse by alleging new arguments.

Redoblegar [ray-do-blay-gar'], *va.* *V.* REDOBLAR and DOBLEGAR.

Redoblón [ray-do-blone'], *m.* Rivet, clinch-nail.

Redoler [ray-do-lerr'], *vn.* (Coll.) To suffer pain silently and continually.

Redolino [ray-do-lee'-no], *m.* (Prov.) Wheel for drawing lots.

Redolor [ray-do-lor'], *m.* A dull ache remaining after some acute suffering.

Redoma [ray-do'-mah], *f.* A broad-bottomed bottle; a flask.

Redomadazo, za [ray-do-ma-dah'-tho, thah], *a. aug.* Very artful or sly.

Redomado, da [ray-do-mah'-do, dah], *a.* Artful, sly, crafty, cunning.

Redomazo [ray-do-mah'-tho], *m.* Stroke or blow in the face with a bottle.

Redonda [ray-don'-dah], *a.* Applied to a round ball or capsule of silk.—*f.* 1. Circle, neighbourhood. *V.* COMARCA. 2. Pasture-ground. 3. (Mus.) Semibreve, whole note. *Á la redonda,* Round about.

Redondamente, *adv.* 1. In circumference, in a circle, around. 2. Roundly, clearly, plainly.

Redondeador [ray-don-day-ah-dor'], *m.* Rounding-tool, used for trimming the brims of hats.

Redondeamiento [ray-don-day-ah-me-en'-to], *m.* (Littl. us.) The act of making round.

Redondear [ray-don-day-ar'], *va.* 1. To round, to make round. 2. To give to soles of shoes the same form as the last has on its sole. *Redondear la hacienda,* To manage one's income or property so as to be free from debt.—*vr.* 1. To extricate one's self from difficulties; to clear one's self of debts. 2. To acquire property or revenues so as to live in comfortable circumstances. (Coll.)

Redondel [ray-don-del'], *m.* 1. (Coll.) A circle. 2. A round cloak, a circular.

Redondela [ray-don-day'-lah], *f.* Table stand.

Redondeo [ray-don-day'-o], *m.* (Com.) One free of all indebtedness.

Redondete [ray-don-day'-tay], *a. dim.* Roundish, circular.

Redondez [ray-don-deth'], *f.* Roundness, circular form, globosity.

Redondilla [ray-don-deel'-lyah], *f.* Roundel or roundelay, a stanza of four verses, of eight syllables each.

Redondo, da [ray-don'-do, dah], *a.* 1. Round, circular, spherical; orbed, orbicular. 2. Round or Roman; applied to letters. 3. Free from debts; unencumbered, in easy circumstances. 4. Applied to land turned to pasture. 5. Applied to persons whose grandparents were of equal rank by birth. 6. Clear, manifest, straight. 7. Just, exact, entire. *Á la redonda,* Round about.

Redondo [ray-don'-do], *m.* 1. Specie, hard cash. 2. Globe, orb, any thing round. *De redondo,* In round clothes: applied to children beginning to walk. *En redondo,* All around; in round characters.

Redondón [ray-don-done'], *m.* A large circle or orbicular figure.

Redopelo [ray-do-pay'-lo], *m.* 1. Rubbing cloth against the grain. 2. Scuffle, affray. *Al redopelo,* Against the natural lay of the hair: hence, against all rule and reason. *Traer al redopelo,* To vex, to drag about contemptuously.

Redor [ray-dor'], *m.* 1. A round mat. 2. (Poet.) *V.* REDEDOR. *En redor,* Round about.

Redro [ray'-dro], *adv.* (Coll.) Behind, backwards.—*m.* Each of the rings upon the horns of goats.

Redrojo, Redruejo [ray-dro'-ho], *m.* 1. A small bunch of grapes remaining after the vintage. 2. After-fruit or blossom. 3. A puny child, slow of growth.

Redrojuelo [ray-dro-hoo-ay'-lo], *m.* (Coll.) Languid boy who does not thrive.

Redruña [ray-droo'-nyah], *f.* Left-hand or side in hunting.

Reducción [ray-dooc-the-on'], *f.* 1. Reduction, the act of reducing. 2. Mutation, alteration, exchange for an equivalent. *Reducción de guineas á chelines,* A reduction of guineas into shillings. 3. Reduction of a place or country by force of arms. 4. Conversion of infidels to the true religion; Indian people converted. 5. (Chem.) Resolution of compounds. 6. Reduction, an operation in algebra. 7. Solution, liquefaction.

Reducible [ray-doo-thee'-blay, *a.* Reducible, convertible.

Reducidamente [ray-doo-the-dah-men'-tay], *adv.* Sparingly.

Reducido, da [ray-doo-thee'-do, dah], *a.* & *pp.* of REDUCIR. Reduced, diminished, narrow, close.

Reducimiento [ray-doo-the-me-en'-to], *m.* Reduction, reducement.

Reducir [ray-doo-theer'], *va.* 1. To reduce a thing to its former state. 2. To exchange, to barter; to convert, to commute; to resolve. 3. To diminish, to lessen; to contract, to abridge. 4. To divide into small parts. 5. To convert a solid body into a liquid. 6. To comprehend, to contain, to include, to confine. 7. To reclaim, to bring back to obedience. 8. To persuade, to convert. 9. (Pict.) To reduce a figure or picture to smaller dimensions. 10. (Chem.) To decompose a body.—*vr.* To confine one's self to a moderate way of life; to resolve on punctuality.

Reductillo [ray-dooc-teel'-lyo], *m. dim.* A small redoubt.

Reductivo, va [ray-dooc-tee'-vo, vah], *a.* Reductive.

Reducto [ray-dooc'-to], *m.* (Mil.) Redoubt.

(*Yo reduzco, yo reduzca,* from *Reducir. V.* CONDUCIR.)

Redundancia [ray-doon-dahn'-the-ah], *f.* Superfluity, redundance, overflowing; excess, copiousness.

Redundante [ray-doon-dahn'-tay], *pa.* & *a.* Redundant, superfluous.

Redundantemente, *adv.* Redundantly.

Redundar [ray-doon-dar'], *vn.* 1. To overflow, to be redundant. 2. To redound, to conduce, to contribute.

Reduplicación [ray-doo-ple-cah-the-on'], *f.* Reduplication.

Reduplicado, da, *a.* & *pp.* of REDUPLICAR. Reduplicate, reduplicative.

Reduplicar [ray-doo-ple-car'], *va.* To reduplicate, to double, to redouble; to repeat the same thing.

Reduplicativo, va [ray-doo-ple-cah-tee'-vo, vah], *a.* (Littl. us.) Reduplicative.

Reedificable [ray-ay-de-fe-cah'-blay], *a.* Capable of being rebuilt.

Reedificación [ray-ay-de-fe-cah-the-on'], *f.* Rebuilding.

Reedificador, ra [ray-ay-de-fe-cah-dor', rah], *m.* & *f.* Rebuilder, re-edifier.

Reedificar [ray-ay-de-fe-car'], *va.* To rebuild; to restore, to re-edify.

Reelección [ray-ay-lec-the-on'], *f.* Re-election.

Reelecto, ta [ray-ay-lec'-to, tah], *pp. irr.* of REELEGIR.

Reelegir [ray-ay-lay-heer'], *va.* To re-elect.

Reembarcar [ray-em-bar-car'], *va.* To reship, to re-embark.—*vr.* To re-embark, to take shipping again.

Reembarco [ray-em-bar'-co], *m.* Re-embarkation, reshipment.

Reembargar [ray-em-bar-gar'], *va.* To seize or to embargo a second time.

Reembolsable [ray-em-bol-sah'-blay], *a.* Capable of reimbursing; payable.

Reembolsar [ray-em-bol-sar'], *va.* To recover money advanced; to reimburse.

Reembolso [ray-em-bol'-so], *m.* Recovery of money advanced.

Reempacar [ray-em-pah-car'], *va.* To repack, to pack anew.

Reemplazar [ray-em-pla-thar'], *va.* To substitute, to replace.

Reemplazo [ray-em-plah'-tho], *m.* Replacement, substitution, substitute.

Reemplear [ray-em-play-ar'], *va.* To re-employ; to repurchase.

Reencargar [ray-en-car-gar'], *va.* To recommend again; to recharge.

Reencarnación [ray-en-car-nah-the-on'], *f.* Reincarnation.

Reencarnar [ray-en-car-nar'], *vn.* & *vr.* To reincarnate.

Reencomendar [ray-en-co-men-dar'], *va* To commend again, to recommend eagerly.

Reencuentro [ray-en-coo-en'-tro], *m.* 1. Rencounter, collision; a slight combat, a skirmish. 2. Scufle, affray.

Reenganchar [ray-en-gan-char'], *va.* 1. (Mech.) To couple again. 2. (Mil.) To re-enlist.—*vr.* To enlist one's self again, to be crimped or drafted.

Reenganchamiento, Reenganche [ray-en-gan-chah-me-en'-to], *m.* (Mil.) Act of re-enlisting or being crimped or drafted again into the army: money given to a soldier who enlists again.

Reengendrador [ray-en-hen-drah-dor'], *m.* One who regenerates or restores; regenerator.

Reengendramiento [ray-en-hen-drah-me-en'-to], *m.* Regeneration.

Reengendrante [ray-en-hen-drahn'-tay], *pa.* Regenerating; one who regenerates or restores.

Reengendrar [ray-en-hen-drar'], *va.* 1. To regenerate, to reproduce, to produce anew. 2. To renew, to revive.

Reenrumbar [ray-en-room-bar'], *va.* To reroute, to redirect.

Reensayar [ray-en-sah-yar'], *va.* To re-examine, to prove again.

Reensaye [ray-en-sah'-yay], *m.* Re-examination; second assay.

Reensayo [ray-en-sah'-yo], *m.* Second essay, or rehearsal, of a comedy or other thing.

Reexaminación [ray-ek-sah-me-nah-the-on'], *f.* Re-examination.

Reexaminar [ray-ek-sah-me-nar'], *va.* To re-examine.

Reexportación [ray-ex-por-tah-the-on'], *f.* (Com.) Re-exportation.

Reexportar [ray-ex-por-tar'], *va.* To re-export, to export imported commodities.

Refacción [ray-fac-the-on'], *f.* 1. Refection, refreshment. 2. Restitution, reparation.

Refajo [ray-fah'-ho], *m.* 1. A kind of short petticoat used by mountaineers or highlanders; kilt. 2. An inner petticoat of baize or other strong material.

Refalsado, da [ray-fal-sah'-do, dah], *a.* False, deceitful.

Refección [ray-fec-the-on'], *f.* Refection, refreshment; reparation.

Refectolero, *m. V.* REFITOLERO.

Refectorio [ray-fec-to'-re-o], *m.* Refectory, the eating-room in convents.

Referencia [ray-fay-ren'-the-ah], *f.* Reference, relation to; narration.

Referente [ray-fay-ren'-tay], *pa.* Referring, relating. *Referente a,* Relating to, referring to.

Referible [ray-fay-ree'-blay], *a.* Referrible.

Referir [ray-fay-reer'], *va.* 1. To refer, to relate, to report. 2. To direct, to mark out a certain course. 3. To mark weights and measures.—*vr.* 1. To refer, to have relation to; to respect. 2. To refer to some former remark. *Referirse al parecer de otro,* To refer to another's opinion.

Refez [ray-feth'], *a. De refez,* (Obs.) *V.* FÁCILMENTE.

(*Yo refiero, yo refiera,* from *Referir. V.* ADHERIR.)

Refierta [ray-fe-err'-tah], *f.* (Obs.) Opposition, contradiction.

Refigurar [ray-fe-goo-rar'], *va.* To retrace an image formerly seen or conceived.

Refilón (De) [ray-fe-lone', day], *adv.* Obliquely. *V.* DE SOSLAYO.

Refina [ray-fee'-nah], *f.* A kind of superfine wool.

Refinación [ray-fe-nah-the-on'], *f.* Purification, the act of refining.

Refinadera [ray-fe-nah-day'-rah], *f.* Refiner, a long cylindrical stone used to work chocolate.

Refinado, da [ray-fe-nah'-do, dah], *a.* Refined; subtile, artful; fine, nice.—*pp.* of REFINAR.

Refinador [ray-fe-nah-dor'], *m.* Refiner.

Refinadura [ray-fe-nah-doo'-rah], *f.* Refining, purifying liquors or metals; refinement.

Refinamiento [ray-fe-nah-me-en'-to], *m.* 1. Refining. 2. Nicety, exactness. 3. (Neol.) Exaggeration in drawing distinctions.

Refinar [ray-fe-nar'], *va.* 1. To refine, to purify, to fine. 2. To refine, to make elegant; to bring to perfection; to render more dexterous or useful.

Refino, na [ray-fee'-no, nah], *a.* Double refined. *Lana refina* Very fine white wool.

Refino, *m.* 1. At Seville, a grocer's shop where sugar, cocoa, chocolate, and spices are sold. 2. *V.* REFINACIÓN.

Refirmar [ray-feer-mar'], *va.* To strengthen, to secure, to ratify.

Refitolero, ra [ray-fe-to-lay'-ro, rah], *m.* & *f.* 1. One who has the care of the refectory. 2. (Coll.) Busybody, intermeddler, cotquean. 3. (Cuba) *a.* Obsequious with affectation and fawning.

Refitor [ray-fe-tor'], *m.* In bishoprics, the portion of tithe received by the cathedral chapter.

Refitorio [ray-fe-to'-re-o], *m.* Refectory. *V.* REFECTORIO.

Reflectar [ray-flec-tar'], *vn.* (Opt.) To reflect, to cast back.

Reflector [ray-flec-tor'], *m.* 1. Reflector of light, heat, or sound. 2. Searchlight. 3. Spotlight.

Refleja [ray-flay'-hah], *f.* Reflection, observation, remark.

Reflejar [ray-flay-har'], *vn.* 1. To reflect the rays of light. 2. To reflect, to meditate upon. *V.* REFLEXIONAR.

Reflejo [ray-flay'-ho], *m.* 1. Reflex. 2. Reflection, glare.

Reflejo, ja, *a.* 1. Reflected, reflective reflex. 2. Meditative.

Reflexibilidad [ray-flek-se-be-le-dahd'], *f.* Reflexibility.

Reflexible [ray-flek-see'-blay], *a.* Reflective, reflexible.

Reflexión [ray-flek-se-on'], *f.* 1. Reflection: applied to the reflection of light. 2. (Art.) A reflected or secondary light. 3. Meditation, attentive consideration, reflection, cogitation.

Reflexionar [ray-flek-se-o-nar'], *vn.* To reflect, to meditate, to consider.

Reflexivamente, *adv.* Reflexively.

Reflexivo, va [ray-flek-see'-vo, vah], *a.* Reflexive, reflective; considerate, cogitative. *Verbo reflexivo,* A reflexive verb.

Reflorecer [ray-flo-ray-therr'], *vn.* 1. To reflourish, blossom again. 2. To return to former splendour.

(*Yo reflorezco, yo reflorezca,* from *Reflorecer. V.* CONOCER.)

Refluente [ray-floo-en'-tay], *pa.* & *a.* Refluent; flowing back.

Refluir [ray-floo-eer'], *vn.* To flow back, to reflow.

Reflujo [ray-floo'-ho], *m.* Reflux, ebb. *Reflujo de la marea,* (Naut.) Ebb or ebb-tide.

Refocilación [ray-fo-the-lah-the-on'], *f.* Reinvigoration, restoration of strength by refreshment; refection.

Refocilar [ray-fo-the-lar'], *va.* To strengthen, to revive, to reinvigorate, to refect.—*vr.* To be strengthened or revived.
Refocilo [ray-fo-thee'-lo], *m.* Reinvigoration, pleasure.
Reforestación [ray-fo-res-tah-the-on'], *f.* Reforestation.
Reforjar [ray-for-har'], *va.* To reforge, to execute again.
Reforma [ray-for'-mah], *f.* 1. Reform, correction, amendment. 2. Dismission from an office or employment. 3. Reformation, the act of reforming. 4. Reformation, change from worse to better; reform. 5. Renovated discipline in religious houses.
Reformable [ray-for-mah'-blay], *a.* Reformable.
Reformación [ray-for-mah-the-on'], *f.* Reformation, reform. *V.* Reforma.
Reformado [ray-for-mah'-do], *m.* A reformed officer, an officer on half-pay, a reformado; disbanded.—*pp.* of Reformar.
Reformador, ra [ray-for-mah-dor', rah], *m.* & *f.* Reformer, corrector, mender.
Reformar [ray-for-mar'], *va.* 1. To reform, to restore a thing to its primitive form. 2. To reform, to correct, to mend. 3. To lessen, to reduce, to diminish. 4. To dispossess of a place or employment, to discharge, to dismiss. 5. To clear up, to explain: speaking of the meaning of words or phrases.—*vr.* 1. To reform, to change from worse to better, to mend, to have one's manners reformed. 2. To use prudence and moderation in speech and conduct.
Reformativo, va [ray-for-mah-tee'-vo, vah], *a.* That which reforms.
Reformatorio, ria [ray-for-mah-to'-re-o, ah], *a.* Corrective.
Reformatorio, *m.* House of correction, reformatory.
Reformista [ray-for-mees'-tah], *com.* Reformer, reformist.
Reforzada [ray-for-thah'-dah], *f.* 1. Sort of narrow tape, list, or fillet. 2. A small sausage. 3. The bass string of a stringed instrument.
Reforzado, da [ray-for-thah'-do, dah], *a.* & *pp.* of Reforzar. 1. Strengthened. 2. Applied to a re-enforced gun, which has more metal than usual at the breech, to make it stronger.
Reforzado, *m.* *V.* Reforzada for a kind of tape.
Reforzar [ray-for-thar'], *va.* To strengthen, to fortify; to animate.—*vr.* To be strengthened and recovered.
Refoseto [ray-fo-say'-to], *m.* (Mil.) Cuvette in a fosse.
Refracción [ray-frac-the-on'], *f.* Refraction, as of light.
Refractar [ray-frac-tar'], *va.* To refract, to change the direction of a ray of light.—*vr.* To be refracted.
Refractario, ria [ray-frac-tah'-re-o, ah], *a.* 1. Refractory, disobedient, rebellious, obstinate. 2. Not fulfilling one's promise. 3. Refractory, resisting fusion.
Refracto, ta [ray-frahc'-to, tah], *a.* Refracted: applied to rays of light.
Refrán [ray-frahn'], *m.* Proverb, a short and pithy saying in common use. *Tener refranes,* (Coll.) To be versed in tricks and villainies.
Refrangibilidad [ray-fran-he-be-le-dahd'], *f.* Refrangibility, refrangibleness.
Refrangible [ray-fran-hee'-blay], *a.* Refrangible.
Refregadura, *f.* *V.* Refregón.
Refregamiento [ray-fray-gah-me-en'-to], *m.* Frication, friction.
Refregar [ray-fray-gar'], *va.* 1. To perfricate, to rub one thing against another, to fray. 2. (Coll.) To upbraid, to censure, to reprove.—*vr.* To be stained all over.
Refregón [ray-fray-gone'], *m.* 1. Frication, friction. 2. Mark made or left by rubbing. 3. A brief conversation. *Darse un refregón,* (Coll.) To speak briefly on any subject.
Refreir [ray-fray-eer'], *va.* To fry well or excessively.
Refrenamiento, *m.* **Refrenación,** *f.* [ray-fray-nah-me-en'-to]. Curb, the act of curbing or refraining; refrenation.
Refrenar [ray-fray-nar'], *va.* 1. To curb a horse with a bridle. 2. To refrain, to coerce, to hold back, to rein.
Refrendación [ray-fren-dah-the-on'], *f.* Legalizing by subscription.
Refrendar [ray-fren-dar'], *va.* 1. To legalize a public act, to countersign; to mark weights, etc. 2. To visé passports and countersign them. 3. (Coll.) To repeat what had been done; to return to again.
Refrendario [ray-fren-dah'-re-o], *m.* Officer appointed to countersign edicts, ordinances, or other public acts.
Refrendata [ray-fren-dah'-tah], *f.* Counter-signature, the act of counter-signing; countersign.
Refrescador, ra [ray-fres-cah-dor', rah], *a.* Refreshing, refrigerating.
Refrescadura [ray-fres-cah-doo'-rah], *f.* Refreshing (act and effect).
Refrescamiento, *m.* *V.* Refresco.
Refrescante [ray-fres-cahn'-tay], *pa.* Cooling, refreshing, refreshful.
Refrescar [ray-fres-car'], *va.* 1. To refresh, to moderate the heat of any thing, to cool, to refrigerate. 2. To drink iced drinks. 3. To renew, to refresh; to awaken feeling. 4. To recover strength and vigour. 5. To rest after fatigue. *Refrescar los cables,* (Naut.) To refreshen the hawse. *Refrescar los víveres,* (Naut.) To take in fresh provisions.—*vn.* To cool, to attemperate; to take the air. Used frequently also as a reflexive verb.
Refrescativo, va [ray-fres-cah-tee'-vo, vah], *a.* Refrigerative, refreshing.
Refresco [ray-fres'-co], *m.* 1. Refreshment: moderate food for strengthening one's self and continuing work. 2. A cold beverage. 3. Entertainment of cool beverages, sweetmeats, and chocolate. *De refresco,* Anew, once more.
Refriar, *va.* (Obs.) *V.* Enfriar.
Refriega [ray-fre-ay'-gah], *f.* Affray, skirmish, encounter, scuffle, strife, fray.
Refrigeración [ray-fre-hay-rah-the-on'], *f.* Refrigeration, cooling, refrigerating.
Refrigerador [ray-fre-hay-rah-dor'], Refrigerator.
Refrigerante [ray-fre-hay-rahn'-tay], *a.* Refrigerant, cooling, refrigerative.—*m.* 1. (Chem.) Refrigerator, cooling chamber. 2. (Med.) Cooler.
Refrigerar [ray-fre-hay-rar'], *va.* To cool, to refresh, to comfort, to refrigerate.
Refrigerativo, va [ray-fre-hay-rah-tee'-vo, vah], *a.* Refrigerative, cooling, refrigerant.
Refrigeratorio [ray-fre-hay-rah-to'-re-o], *m.* Refrigerator, part of a still employed to cool the condensing vapours.
Refrigerio [ray-fre-hay'-re-o], *m.* 1. Refrigeration, comfort experienced through coolness. 2. Refreshment, refection, a light repast. 3. Consolation, comfort.
Refringente [ray-frin-hen'-tay], *pa.* & *a.* Refracting; refractive.
Refringir [ray-frin-heer'], *va.* To refract, break, or intercept the rays of light. Also *vr.*
Refrito [ray-free'-to], *pp. irr.* of Refreir.
Refrotar [ray-fro-tar'], *va.* To rub.
Refuelle [ray-foo-ayl'-lyay], *m.* A kind of net for catching fish.
Refuerzo [ray-foo-err'-tho], *m.* 1. Re-enforcement, increase of strength. 2. Backing, bracing, strengthening piece; welt of a shoe. 3. Succour, aid.
(*Yo refuerzo, yo refuerce,* from *Reforzar.* *V.* Acordar.)
Refugiado, da [ray-foo-he-ah'-do, dah], *a.* & *pp.* of Refugiar. Sheltered. It has been used as a substantive for a refugee or emigrant.
Refugiar [ray-foo-he-ar'], *va.* To shelter, to refuge, to afford protection.—*vr.* To take refuge, to fly to for shelter.
Refugio [ray-foo'-he-o], *m.* 1. Refuge, retreat, asylum, safe harbor. 2. In Madrid, a brotherhood formed to alleviate the suffering of the poor. *Refugio antiaéreo,* Bomb shelter.
Refulgencia [ray-fool-hen'-the-ah], *f.* Refulgence, splendour.
Refulgente [ray-fool-hen'-tay], *a.* Refulgent.
Refulgir [ray-fool-heer'], *vn.* To shine with splendour, to be resplendent.
Refundición [ray-foon-de-the-on'], *f.* The act of casting metals anew.
Refundir [ray-foon-deer'], *va.* 1. To melt or cast metals anew. 2. To contain, to include.—*vn.* To redound. *Refundir infamia,* To defame, to dishonour.
Refunfuñador, ra [ray-foon-foo-nyah-dor', rah], *m.* & *f.* Grumbler, growler, snarler.
Refunfuñadura [ray-foon-foo-nyah-doo'-rah], *f.* Growling, grumbling. *V.* Refunfuño.
Refunfuñar [ray-foon-foo-nyar'], *va.* To snarl, to growl, to snort; to grumble, to mutter.
Refunfuño [ray-foon-foo'-nyo], *m.* Grumbling, murmuring, growl, snort.
Refutación [ray-foo-tah-the-on'], *f.* Refutation, confutation.
Refutable [ray-foo-tah'-blay], *a.* Refutable.
Refutador, ra [ray-foo-tah-dor', rah], *m.* & *f.* Refuter.
Refutar [ray-foo-tar'], *va.* To refute, to confute, to convict; to control. *V* Rehusar.
Refutatorio, ria [ray-foo-tah-to'-re-o, ah], *a.* That which refutes.
Regadera [ray-gah-day'-rah], *f.* 1. Shower. *Baño de regadera,* Shower bath. 2. Sprinkling-pot. 3. Canal for irrigation.
Regadío [ray-gah-dee'-o], *m.* Irrigated land.
Regadío, ía, *a.* Irrigated.
Regadizo, za [ray-gah-de'-tho, thah], *a.* That which can be irrigated or watered.
Regador [ray-gah-dor'], *m.* 1. One who waters or irrigates. 2. Instrument used by comb-makers.
Regadura [ray-gah-doo'-rah], *f.* Irrigation.
Regaifa [ray-gah'-e-fah], *f.* A stone in an oil-mill with a grooved channel along which the oil runs into the vat.
Regajal, Regajo [ray-gah-hahl', ray-gah'-ho], *m.* Puddle or pool of stagnant water; rill which makes it.
Regala [ray-gah'-lah], *f.* (Naut.) Gunwale or gunnel.

Regalada [ray-ga-lah'-dah], *f.* 1. King's stables. 2. The number of horses belonging to the king's stables.

Regaladamente, *adv.* Delicately, pleasantly, daintily.

Regalado, da [ray-gah-lah'-do, dah], *a.* Delicate, dainty, suave, lickerish.—*pp.* of REGALAR.

Regalador, ra [ray-gah-lah-dor', rah], *m.* & *f.* 1. One fond of entertaining his friends; a person of a generous disposition. 2. Sort of stick used by wine-bag makers for cleaning the skins.

Regalar [ray-gah-lar'], *va.* 1. To present, to favour with a gift. 2. To regale, to refresh, to entertain. 3. To caress, to cajole, to make much of. 4. To regale, to gratify, to make merry, to delight, to cherish.—*vr.* 1. To regale, to feast; to fare sumptuously. 2. To entertain one's self, to take pleasure.

Regalejo [ray-gah-lay'-ho], *m. dim.* A small gift.

Regalero [ray-gah-lay'-ro], *m.* Purveyor of fruit and flowers for the royal family.

Regalía [ray-gah-lee'-ah], *f.* 1. The rights or prerogatives of the crown. 2. Privilege, exemption.—*pl.* Perquisites.

Regalillo [ray-gah-leel'-lyo], *m.* 1. (Dim.) A small present. 2. Muff, for the hands.

Regaliolo [ray-gah-le-o'-lo], *m.* (Orn.) Golden-crested wren. Motacilla regulus.

Regalito [ray-gah-lee'-to], *m. dim.* A small present.

Regaliz [ray-gah-leeth'], *m.* (Bot.) Licorice. Glycyrrhiza.

Regalo [ray-gah'-lo], *m.* 1. Present, gift, largess. 2. Pleasure, gratification. 3. Dainty, something nice and delicate; regalement. 4. Convenience, repose, comfort, luxury. 5. Affliction dispensed by Providence. *Caballo de regalo*, A fine saddle-horse.

Regalón, na [ray-gah-lone', nah], *a.* 1. Delicate, fond of convenience and ease. 2. Spoiled, pampered: applied to children.

Regantío, ía [ray-gan-tee'-o, ah], *a.* Applied to the land or its fruits, that are usually watered. *V.* REGADÍO.

Regañada [ray-gah-nyah'-dah], *f.* A kind of delicate cake.

Regañado, da [ray-gah-nyah'-do, dah], *a.* 1. Given reluctantly, or with repugnance. 2. Applied to a kind of plum or bread which splits. 3. Frowning.—*pp.* of REGAÑAR.

Regañador, ra [ray-gah-nyah-dor', rah], *m.* & *f.* Grumbler.

Regañamiento [ray-gah-nyah-me-en'-to], *m.* Grumbling, snarling, growl.

Regañar [ray-gah-nyar'], *vn.* 1. To snarl, to growl, to murmur, to grumble, to claw off. 2. To be peevish, to quarrel. 3. To crack or open like ripe fruit. 4. To dispute familiarly at home, to have domestic broils.—*va.* (Coll.) To reprehend, to chide. *A regaña dientes*, Reluctantly, with reluctance.

Regañir [ray-gah-nyeer], *vn.* To yelp, to howl repeatedly.

Regaño [ray-gah'-nyo], *m.* 1. A gesture of annoyance; sternness of look. 2. Threat, warning. 3. Scorched bread. 4. (Coll.) Reprimand.

Regañón, na [ray-gah-nyone', nah], *a.* 1. Snarling, growling; a grumbler, murmurer, snarler. 2. Troublesome: generally applied to the north-east wind.

Regar [ray-gar'], *va.* 1. To water, to irrigate. 2. To sprinkle with water: to rain heavily. 3. To wash or water countries: applied to rivers and to clouds.

Regata [ray-gah'-tah], *f.* 1. A small channel or conduit, through which water is conveyed to gardens. 2. Regatta, a race of boats or light craft (2 fr. Ital.).

Regatar [ray-gah-tar'], *va.* (Naut.) To put a ferrule to a boat-hook.—*vn.* *V.* REGATEAR.

Regate [ray-gah'-tay], *m.* 1. A quick motion of the body to avoid a blow. 2. Escape, evasion.

Regatear [ray-gah-tay-ar'], *va.* 1. To haggle, to higgle, to be tedious in a bargain. 2. To retail provisions bought by wholesale. 3. To refuse or decline the execution of a thing; to avoid.—*vn.* 1. To wriggle, to move sidewise; to use evasions. 2. (Naut.) To rival in sailing.

Regateo [ray-gah-tay'-o], *m.* The act of haggling or bartering, higgling.

Regatería [ray-gah-tay-ree'-ah], *f.* Huckster's shop. *V.* REGATONERÍA.

Regatero, ra [ray-gah-tay'-ro, rah], *a.* & *m.* & *f.* Haggling; hawker. *V.* REGATÓN.

Regato [ray-gah'-to], *m.* A small rivulet.

Regatón, na [ray-gah-tone', nah], *m.* & *f.* 1. Huckster, regrater. 2. Haggler. 3. Socket, ferrule.—*a.* Retailing.

Regatonear [ray-gah-to-nay-ar'], *vn.* To huckster, to buy by wholesale and sell by retail.

Regatonería [ray-gah-to-nay-ree'-ah], *f.* 1. Sale by retail. 2. Huckster's shop.

Regazar [ray-gah-thar'], *va.* To tuck up. *V.* ARREGAZAR.

Regazo [ray-gah'-tho], *m.* 1. Lap of a woman; part of the dress. 2. Lap, part of the body from the waist to the knees. 3. Fond and endearing reception.

Regencia [ray-hen'-the-ah], *f.* 1. Regency, ruling or governing. 2. Regency, administration of a regent; vicarious government. 3. Regency, the district governed by a regent. 4. Regency, those collectively to whom vicarious regality is intrusted. 5. Regentship.

Regeneración [ray-hay-nay-rah-the-on'], *f.* 1. Regeneration. 2. (Surg.) Granulation in a wound.

Regenerado, da [ray-hay-nay-rah'-do, dah], *a.* & *pp.* of REGENERAR. Regenerate, regenerated.

Regenerar [ray-hay-nay-rar'], *va.* To regenerate, to reproduce.

Regenerativo, va [ray-hay-nay-rah-tee'-vo, vah], *a.* That which regenerates.

Regenta [ray-hen'-tah], *f.* Wife of a regent, regentess.

Regentar [ray-hen-tar'], *va.* To rule; to govern; to exercise any business affecting superiority.

Regente [ray-hen'-tay], *m* 1. Regent, one invested with vicarious royalty. 2. Regent, the president of a court of justice. 3. Master of a school in religious orders. 4. In Spanish universities, some supernumerary professors. 5. Manager, director: in printing-offices.—*pa.* Ruling.

Regentear [ray-hen-tay-ar'], *vn.* 1. To domineer, to rule as master. 2. To be a pedant.

Regera [ray-hay'-rah], *f.* (Naut.) Stern-fast, stern-moorings.

Regiamente, *adv.* Royally, in a kingly manner.

Regibado, da [ray-he-bah'-do, dah], *a.* Hump-backed, crook-backed, gibbous.

Regicida [ray-he-thee'-dah], *com.* & *a.* Regicide, murderer of a king.

Regicidio [ray-he-thee'-de-o], *m.* Murder of a king, regicide.

Regidor [ray-he-dor'], *m.* 1. Alderman, a magistrate of a city. 2. Governor, director, prefect.—*a.* *V.* REGITIVO.

Regidora [ray-he-do'-rah], *f.* An alderman's or governor's wife.

Regidoría, Regiduría [ray-he-do-ree'-ah], *f.* Governorship; the place, employment, or office of an alderman.

Regilera [ray-he-lay'-rah], *f.* Windmill of paper, a child's plaything.

Régimen [ray'-he-men], *m.* 1. Regimen, management, rule, conduct, system. 2. (Gram.) Government of parts of speech. 3. (Med.) Regimen, a prescribed manner of living.

Regimentar [ray-he-men-tar'], *va.* To organize a regiment.

Regimiento [ray-he-me-en'-to], *m.* 1. Administration, government. 2. Magistracy of a city; office or employment of an alderman or a city magistrate; municipality. 3. Regiment of soldiers; a corps.

Regio, gia [ray'-he-o, ah], *a.* 1. Royal, regal, kingly. 2. Stately, sumptuous, magnificent. *Agua regia*, Aqua regia, nitro-hydrochloric acid.

Regiomontano, na [ray-he-o-mon-tah'-no, nah], *a.* & *m.* & *f.* Name applied to persons and things from Monterrey, Mexico.

Región [ray-he-on'], *f.* 1. Region, kingdom, tract of land, ground. 2. Space occupied by an element. 3. Region, a cavity of the body.

Regional [ray-he-o-nahl'], *a.* 1. Belonging to a region or district. 2. (Mex.) Peculiar to the country, native.

Regionalismo [ray-he-o-nah-lees'-mo], *m.* 1. Regionalism, localism. 2. Local idiom.

Regir [ray-heer'], *va.* 1. To rule, to govern, to direct. 2. To rule, to conduct, to manage, to lead, to command. 3. To govern as verbs or prepositions. 4. To have the bowels in good order. —*vn.* 1. (Naut.) To obey the helm. 2. To be in force.

Registrado, da [ray-his-trah'-do, dah], *a.* Registered.—*pp.* of REGISTRAR.

Registrador [ray-his-trah-dor'], *m.* 1. Register, registrar, recorder, master or clerk of records. 2. Searcher. 3. Toll-gatherer, who takes the toll at the gates of a town, and enters all imported goods in the toll-register. 4. Controller.

Registrador, ra [ray-his-trah-dor', rah], *a.* Registering, recording. *Registradora* or *Caja registradora*, Cash register.

Registrar [ray-his-trar'], *va.* 1. To inspect, to search. 2. To investigate, to examine, to control. 3. To register, to record. 4. To put slips of paper between the leaves of a book. *No registrar*, (Met. Prov.) To do any thing precipitately.—*vr.* To be registered or matriculated.

Registro [ray-hees'-tro], *m.* 1. The act of searching or examining. 2. Place or spot whence any thing can be surveyed. 3. Entry of goods or merchandise. 4. Enrolling office, where registers or records are kept; census. *V.* PROTOCOLO. 5. Register, in which entries are made; a certificate of entry. 6. Register of a stove or grate. 7. (Print.) Catchword; register or correspondence of the pages. 8. Prier, one who inquires too closely. 9. Regulator of a watch or clock. 10. Mark put in breviaries or missals at certain places. 11. Register in an organ or harpsichord. 12. Direction to bookbinders at the end of a volume. 13. Search.

Regitivo, va [ray-he-tee'-vo, vah], *a.* Ruling, governing.

Regizgar [ray-heeth-gar'], *vn.* (Prov.) To shudder with cold.

Regla [ray'-glah], *f.* 1. Rule, ruler, for drawing a straight line; rule in arithmetic. 2. Rule of religious orders. 3. Rule, maxim, precept; law, statute, precept; canon, fundamental principle. 4. Instrument by which paper is ruled for musical compositions. 5. Manner of making or casting up accounts. 6. Moderation, measure, order, rule, management. 7. Order of nature. 8. Catamenia, courses. *A regla*, Regularly, prudently. *Regla lesbia*, Flexible rule which may be adjusted to any body to be measured. *Regla fija*, Standard.

Regladamente, *adv.* Regularly, orderly.

Reglado, da [ray-glah'-do, dah], *a.* Regulated, temperate.—*pp.* of REGLAR.

Reglamento [ray-glah-men'-to], *m.* Regulation, order, ordinance, by-law.

Reglar [ray-glar'], *a.* Regular. *Puerta reglar*, The regular door for entering nunneries.

Reglar [ray-glar'], *va.* 1. To rule, to draw lines with a rule. 2. To rule, to regulate, to measure.—*vr.* To mend, to reform. *Reglarse a lo justo*, To be right.

Reglero [ray-glay'-ro], *m.* Ruler, for drawing lines.

Regleta [ray-glay'-tah], *f.* (Print.) Lead, piece of metal put between lines of types. Reglet.

Reglón [ray-glone'], *m.* Level, used by masons.

Regnar, *vn.* (Obs.) *V.* REINAR.

Regnícola [reg-nee'-co-lah], *a.* & *m.* & *f.* Native of a kingdom.

Regocijadamente, *adv.* Merrily, joyfully.

Regocijado, da [ray-go-the-hah'-do, dah], *a.* Merry, joyful, rejoicing, festive. —*pp.* of REGOCIJAR.

Regocijador, ra [ray-go-the-hah-dor', rah], *m.* & *f.* Rejoicer, cheerer, gladder.

Regocijar [ray-go-the-har'], *va.* To gladden, to cheer, to delight, to exult, to rejoice, to exhilarate.—*vr.* To rejoice, to be merry.

Regocijo [ray-go-thee'-ho], *m.* 1. Joy, pleasure, satisfaction, mirth, merriment, hilarity, exhilaration. 2. Rejoicing, demonstration of joy. 3. Bull-feast in the morning.

Regodearse [ray-go-day-ar'-say], *vr.* (Coll.) 1. To be merry, to rejoice; to be delighted. 2. To dally, to trifle, to play the fool. 3. To assume an air of reluctance, to cloak some ardent desire. 4. To joke, to jest.

Regodeo [ray-go-day'-o], *m.* 1. Joy, mirth, merriment. 2. A feigned refusal of a thing earnestly desired. 3. Joke, jest, diversion; dalliance.

Regojo [ray-go'-ho], *m.* 1. Crumb or piece of bread left on the table after meals. 2. A puny boy.

Regojuelo [ray-go-hoo-ay'-lo], *m. dim.* A very small morsel of bread.

Regolar [ray-go-lar'], *m.* (Prov.) Scholar, student.

Regoldano, na [ray-gol-dah'-no, nah], *a.* Applied to the wild chestnut.

Regoldar [ray-gol-dar'], *vn.* 1. To belch, to eruct. 2. To boast, to brag.

Regolfar [ray-gol-far'], *va.* & *vr.* To flow back.

Regolfo [ray-gol'-fo], *m.* 1. Reflux, the act of flowing back against the current; whirlpool. 2. Gulf, bay; an arm of the sea.

Regomello [ray-go-mayl'-lyo], *m.* (Prov.) Remorse, compunction.

Regona [ray-go'-nah], *f.* Large canal for irrigating lands.

Regordete, ta [ray-gor-day'-tay, tah], *a.* Chubby, plump, short and stout.

Regordido, da [ray-gor-dee'-do, dah], *a.* (Obs.) Fat, plump.

Regostarse [ray-gos-tar'-say], *vr.* To delight, to take pleasure, to dally.

Regosto [ray-gos'-to], *m.* Delight, pleasure.

Regraciación [ray-grah-the-ah-the-on'], *f.* Act of thanking, gratitude.

Regraciar [ray-grah-the-ar'], *va.* To testify gratitude, to thank.

Regresar [ray-gray-sar'], *vn.* 1. To return to a place, to regress. 2. To retain or recover possession of an ecclesiastical benefice.—*va.* To resign a benefice in favour of another.

Regresión [ray-gray-se-on'], *f.* Regression, return; regress.

Regreso [ray-gray'-so], *m.* 1. Return, regression, regress. 2. Reversion, devolution. 3. The act of resigning a benefice in favour of another. 4. The act of retaking possession of a benefice or property resigned or ceded.

Regruñir [ray-groo-nyeer'], *vn.* To snarl, to growl.

Reguardarse [ray-goo-ar-dar'-say], *vr.* To take care of one's self.

Regüeldo [ray-goo-el'-do], *m.* 1. Eructation, belch. 2. Boast, brag.

(*Yo regüeldo*, *yo regüelde*, from *Regoldar.* *V.* ACORDAR.

Reguera [ray-gay'-rah], *f.* 1. Canal for watering lands or plants. 2. Stern of a ship or tail of a greyhound.

Reguero [ray-gay'-ro], *m.* 1. A small rivulet. 2. Mark, spot left from any liquid being spilt. 3. *V.* REGUERA.

Reguerón [ray-gay-rone'], *m.* The principal canal of irrigation.

Reguilete [ray-gee-lay'-tay], *m.* *V.* REHILETE.

Reguizar [ray-ge-thar'], *va.* (Obs.) To patch a suit of clothes.

Regulación [ray-goo-lah-the-on'], *f.* Regulation, adjustment; comparison, computation.

Regulado, da [ray-goo-lah'-do, dah], *a.* & *pp.* of REGULAR. Regulated; orderly, regular.

Regulador, ra [ray-goo-lah-dor', rah], *m.* & *f.* 1. Regulator, governor, as of a machine, particularly a steam-engine. 2. A standard clock for the regulation of others.

Regulador de humedad [ray-goo-lah-dor' day oo-may-dahd'], *m.* (Mech.) Humidistat.

Regular [ray-goo-lar'], *va.* To regulate, to adjust; to put in order, to methodize, to compare.—*a.* 1. Regular, orderly. 2. Moderate, sober, formal. 3. Common, ordinary, frequent; likely, probable; convenient. 4. Regular: applied to a religious order. *Por lo regular*, Commonly.

Regular [ray-goo-lar'], *m.* Regular, in the Catholic church; person who belongs to a religious order.

Regularidad [ray-goo-lah-re-dahd'], *f.* 1. Regularity, order, orderliness. 2. Common usage, custom. 3. Exact discipline.

Regularizar [ray-goo-lah-re-thar'], *va.* To systemize, to subject to rules.

Regularmente, *adv.* Regularly, orderly in manner: ordinarily, generally, naturally.

Régulo [ray'-goo-lo], *m.* 1. Chief of a petty state. 2. Basilisk. 3. (Chem.) Regulus, the purest part of metals. 4. (Ast.) Regulus, a star of the first magnitude in the constellation Leo. 5. (Orn.) Golden-crested kinglet. Regulus cristatus. *V.* ABADEJO.

Regurgitación, *f.* (Med.) Regurgitation.

Regurgitar [ray-goor-he-tar'], *vn.* To regurgitate, to overflow.

Rehabilitación [ray-ah-be-le-tah-the-on'], *f.* Rehabilitation.

Rehabilitar [ray-ah-be-le-tar'], *va.* 1. To rehabilitate; to reinstate one in his rights and privileges. 2. To refit, to repair, to restore.

Rehabituarse [ray-ah-be-too-ar'-say], *vr.* To return to vicious habits.

Rehacer [ray-ah-therr'], *va.* 1. To mend, to repair, to make again. 2. To add new strength and vigour. 3. To increase the weight or quantity of any thing.—*vr.* 1. To regain strength and vigour. 2. (Mil.) To rally, to form anew; to resume the former position.

Rehacimiento [ray-ah-the-me-en'-to], *m.* Renovation, renewal; recuperation.

Rehacio, cia [ray-ah'-the-o, ah], *a.* Obstinate, stubborn.

(*Yo rehago*, *yo rehaga*, *yo rehice*, from *Rehacer.* *V.* HACER.)

Reharto, ta [ray-ar'-to, tah], *pp. irr.* of REHARTAR. Supersaturated.

Rehartar [ray-ar-tar'], *va.* To satiate again.

Rehecho, cha [ray-ay'-cho, chah], *a.* & *pp. irr.* of REHACER. 1. Renewed, renovated; done over again. 2. Squat, broad-shouldered.

Rehelear [ray-hay-lay-ar'], *vn.* To be bitter. Note.—The h is aspirated in this word. (Acad.)

Reheleo [ray-hay-lay'-o], *m.* Bitterness.

Rehén [ray-en'], *m.* Hostage: generally used in the plural.

Rehenchimiento [ray-en-che-me-en'-to], *m.* Act of stuffing or refilling.

Rehenchir [ray-en-cheer'], *va.* To fill again, to stuff anew.

Rehendija, Rehendrija [ray-en-dee'-hah], *f.* Crevice, cleft.

Reherimiento [ray-ay-re-me-en'-to], *m.* Repulsion.

Reherir [ray-ay-reer'], *va.* To repel, to repulse.

Reherrar [ray-er-rar'], *va.* To reshoe a horse.

Rehervir [ray-er-veer'], *vn.* 1. To boil again. 2. To be inflamed with love, to be blinded by passion.—*vr.* To ferment, to grow sour.

Rehiladillo, *m.* Ribbon. *V.* HILADILLO.

Rehilandera [ray-e-lan-day'-rah], *f.* Wind-mill made of paper. *V.* REGILERA.

Rehilar [ray-e-lar'], *va.* To twist or contract too much.—*vn.* 1. To stagger, to reel. 2. To whiz, to whir, as a missile in flight.

Rehilete, Rehilero [ray-e-lay'-tay], *m.* 1. A kind of shuttlecock played with battledores. 2. A small arrow bearded with paper or feathers. 3. A malicious saying, smart speech.

Rehilo [ray-ee'-lo], *m.* Shaking, shivering.

Rehinchimiento [ray-in-che-me-en'-to], *m.* The act of filling or stuffing again.

Rehirmar, *va.* (Obs.) *V.* REFIRMAR.

Rehogar [ray-o-gar'], *va.* To dress meat with a slow fire, basting it with butter or oil.

Rehollar [ray-ol-lyar'], *va.* To trample under foot, to tread upon. *V.* PISOTEAR.

Rehoya, *f.* *V.* REHOYO.

Rehoyar [ray-o-yar'], *va.* To dig holes again for planting trees.

Rehoyo [ray-o'-yo], *m.* A deep hole or pit.

Rehuida [ray-oo-ee'-dah], *f.* A second flight, running away again; rapid turn of hunted game.

Rehuir [ray-oo-eer'], *vn.* 1. To withdraw, to retire. 2. To return to the place whence it was roused: applied to game. 3. To reject, to condemn. —*va.* To deny or refuse.

Rehumedecer [ray-oo-may-day-therr'], *va.* & *vr.* To dampen well.

Rehundido [ray-oon-dee'-do], *m.* (Arch.) Part which serves as a seat for a projection. *V.* VACIADO.

Rehundir [ray-oon-deer'], *va.* 1. To sink. 2. To melt metals. 3. To waste, to dissipate, to lavish.—*vn.* To increase perceptibly.

Rehurtado, da [ray-oor-tah'-do, dah], *a.* 1. Making windings to make the dogs lose the scent: applied to game. 2. Artfully evasive, delusive, furtive. —*pp.* of REHURTARSE.

Rehurtar [ray-oor-tar'], *va.* To steal or cheat again.—*vr.* To take a different route whence it rose: applied to game.

Rehurto [ray-oor'-to], *m.* A movement of the body to avoid impending danger; a shrug.

Rehusar [ray-oo-sar'], *va.* To refuse. to decline, to deny what is solicited or required, to abnegate.

Reible, *a.* (Obs.) Laughable. *V.* RISIBLE.

Reidero [ray-e-day'-ro], *m.* Immoderate laughter.—*a.* Ready to laugh. *Él tiene buenas reideras,* (Coll.) He laughs at everything.

Reidor, ra [ray-e-dor', rah], *m.* & *f.* Laugher.

Reimpresión [ray-im-pray-se-on'], *f.* 1. Reimpression of a book, etc., reprint. 2. Number of copies reprinted at once.

Reimpreso, sa [ray-im-pray'-so, sah], *pp. irr.* of REIMPRIMIR.

Reimprimir [ray-im-pre-meer'], *va.* To reprint, to print a new edition.

Reina [ray'-e-nah], *f.* 1. Queen. 2. (Coll.) Any woman admired and loved. 3. Queen-bee. 4. Queen at chess. *Reina mora, V.* INFERNÁCULO.

Reinado [ray-e-nah'-do], *m.* Reign, time of a sovereign's rule.

Reinante [ray-e-nahn'-tay], *pa.* Reigning, excelling; prevailing.

Reinar [ray-e nar'], *va.* 1. To reign, to govern, to command. 2. To reign, to prevail, to predominate. 3. To reign, to obtain power or dominion.

Reincidencia [ray-in-the-den'-the-ah], *f.* Backsliding, falling in again, relapse into vice or error.

Reincidente [ray-in-the-den'-tay], *pa.* Relapsing, falling away.

Reincidir [ray-in-the-deer'], *vn.* To relapse back into vice or error; to backslide.

Reincorporación [ray-in-cor-po-rah-the-on'], *f.* Reincorporation, renewing.

Reincorporar [ray-in-cor-po-rar'], *va.* To incorporate a second time.—*vr.* To re-embody.

Reino [ray'-e-no], *m.* 1. Kingdom, reign, dominion of a king. 2. Kingdom, name given to districts which, although only a part of the territories subject to a monarch, had before a king. 3. Kingdom, a class or order of beings, as vegetable or animal kingdom. 4. Kingdom of heaven.

Reintegración [ray-in-tay-grah-the-on'], *f.* Reintegration or redintegration; the act of restoring.

Reintegrar [ray-in-tay-grar'], *va.* To reintegrate, to restore.—*vr.* To be reinstated or restored.

Reintegro [ray-in-tay'-gro], *m.* Redintegration.

Reir [ray-eer'], *vn.* 1. To laugh; to smile. *Reir á carcajadas,* To laugh excessively and loudly. 2. To laugh at or sneer. 3. (Med.) To have convulsions resembling laughter. 4. To smile: applied to agreeable landscapes. arbours, lakes, and meads.—*vr.* 1. To begin to tear or rend: applied to cloth. 2. To scoff, to make jest of. *Reirse por nada,* To giggle or titter idly, to laugh at a feather. *Reirse de,* To laugh at.

Reis [ray'-is], *m.* An imaginary coin of Portugal: a milreis equals 5.60 *pesetas;* about 4s. 5½d., or $1.07½.

Reiteración [ray-e-tay-rah-the-on'], *f.* Repetition, reiteration.

Reiteradamente. *adv.* Repeatedly.

Reiterar [ray-e-tay-rar'], *va.* To reiterate, to repeat, to iterate.

Reiterativo, va [ray-e-tay-rah-tee'-vo, vah], *a.* Reiterative, expressing repeated action.

Reivindicación [ray-e-vin-de-cah-the-on'], *f.* (For.) Recovery.

Reivindicar [ray-e-vin-de-car'], *va.* To recover.

Reja [ray'-hah], *f.* 1. Plough-share; colter or coulter. 2. Ploughing, turning over ground with a plough; tillage. 3. Iron grate of a window or fence.

Rejado [ray-hah'-do], *m.* Grate of a door or window.

Rejalcar [ray-hal-car'], *va.* To plough.

Rejalgar [ray-hal-gar'], *m.* Realgar, red sulphide of arsenic. (Arab.)

Rejazo [ray-hah'-tho], *m.* Stroke or blow with a plough-share.

Rejería [ray-hay-ree'-ah], *f.* Manufactory of the iron-work of grates, doors, or windows.

Rejero [ray-hay'-ro], *m.* Maker of bars, lattices, and grates.

Rejilla [ray-heel'-lyah], *f.* 1. A small lattice in confessionals, to hear women's confessions; or a grating in a door in order to see who knocks. 2. Cane, for the backs and seats of chairs, etc. 3. *V.* REJUELA, 2d def.

Rejo [ray'-ho], *m.* 1. A pointed iron bar or spike. 2. Sting of a bee or other insect. 3. Nail or round iron with which quoits are played. 4. Rim of iron put around the frame of a door to strengthen it. 5. Strength, vigour. 6. In seeds, the radicle, the organ from which the root is formed.

Rejón [ray-hone'], *m.* 1. Dagger, poniard. 2. A kind of lance or spear used by bull-fighters. 3. A short broad knife with a sharp point.

Rejonazo [ray-ho-nah'-tho], *m.* Thrust with a dagger.

Rejoneador [ray-ho-nay-ah-dor'], *m.* Bull-fighter who throws the spear called *rejón.*

Rejonear [ray-ho-nay-ar'], *va.* To wound bulls with the spear used by bull-fighters.

Rejoneo [ray-ho-nay'-o], *m.* The act of fighting bulls with a spear.

Rejuela [ray-hoo-ay'-lah], *f.* 1. (Dim.) A small grate. 2. A small brasier of wood covered with brass used for a stove.

Rejurar [ray-hoo-rar'], *vn.* To swear again.

Rejuvenecer [ray-hoo-vay-nay-therr'], *vn.* To grow young again.

Relación [ray-lah-the-on'], *f.* 1. Relation, report, narration, memoir, account. 2. A brief report to a judge, of the state and merits of a cause. 3. Prologue, a long piece in a dramatic poem which an individual recites. 4. Relation, correspondence, analogy, coherence, concurrence. *Relación jurada,* Deposition upon oath. *Relación de ciego,* Applied to any thing read all in the same tone. *Entrar en relaciones,* (Com.) To connect one's self.

Relacionado, da [ray-lah-the-o-nah'-do, dah], *a.* Relative, related, connected. *Relacionado con,* Related to, in connection with.

Relacionar [ray-lah-the-o-nar'], *va.* To relate, to report, to narrate.

Relacionero [ray-lah-the-o-nay'-ro], *m.* Reporter, narrator; ballad-singer.

Relajación [ray-lah-hah-the-on'], *f.* 1. Relaxation, extension, dilatation; relenting. 2. (For.) Remission or diminution of a penalty imposed upon a delinquent. 3. Commutation of a vow, release from an oath. 4. Delivery of an offender by the ecclesiastical judge to a criminal court of justice, in cases of murder. 5. *V.* QUEBRADURA. 6. Relaxation of discipline or good order, laxity of conduct; relaxation, intermission from a task or work.

Relajadamente, *adv.* Dissolutely, licentiously.

Relajado [ray-lah-hah'-do], *a.* (Coll.) Dissolute, dissipated.—*pp.* of RELAJAR.

Relajador, ra [ray-lah-hah-dor', rah], *a.* Relaxing, remitting.

Relajamiento [ray-lah-hah-me-en'-to], *m.* Relaxation. laxity, slackness.

Relajar [ray-lah-har'], *va.* 1. To relax, to slacken, to make less tense. 2. To relax, to remit, to render less rigorous. 3. To annul a vow, to release from an oath or obligation. 4. To deliver a capital offender from an ecclesiastical to the criminal tribunal. 5. To relax, to ease, to amuse, to divert. 6. (For.) To lighten a penalty.—*vr.* 1. To be relaxed, loosened, or dilated: applied to a member of the animal body. 2. To grow vicious; to be corrupted by evil customs. 3. *V.* QUEBRARSE.

Relamer [ray-lah-merr'], *va.* To relick, to lick again.—*vr.* 1. To lick one's lips; to relish. 2. To be extravagantly fond of dress; to paint. 3. To boast, to brag.

Relamido, da [ray-lah-mee'-do, dah], *a.* Affected, too fine or nice in dress.—*pp.* of RELAMER.

Relámpago [ray-lahm'-pah-go], *m.* 1. Flash of lightning, meteor. 2. Any thing passing as suddenly as a flash of lightning. 3. Thought or idea flashing upon the mind; ingenious witticism. 4. Blemish in the eyes of horses.

Relampagueante [ray-lam-pah-gay-ahn'-tay], *pa.* Lightening.

Relampaguear [ray-lam-pah-gay-ar'], *vn.* 1. To lighten, to emit flashes of lightning. 2. To flash, to sparkle, to gleam.

Relampagueo [ray-lam-pah-gay'-o], *m.* Lightening, flashing or darting light.

Relance [ray-lahn'-thay], *m.* 1. Repeated casting of a net; a second chance or lot. 2. A fortuitous event. 3. A repeated attempt. 4. Series of lucky or unlucky chances. *De relance,* Fortuitously, by chance.

Relanzar [ray-lan-thar'], *va.* 1. To repel, to repulse. 2. To cast in again the tickets or lots to be drawn.

Relapso, sa [ray-lahp'-so, sah], *a.* Relapsed, falling back into criminal conduct.

Relatador, ra [ray-lah-tah-dor', rah], *m.* & *f.* Relater, narrator.

Relatante [ray-lah-tahn'-tay], *pa.* Reporting, narrating.

Relatar [ray-lah-tar'], *va.* 1. To relate, to report, to narrate, to give out. 2. (For.) To make a report of a lawsuit.

Relativamente, *adv.* Relatively, comparatively.

Relatividad [ray-lah-te-ve-dahd'], *f.* Relativity.

Relativo, va [ray-lah-tee'-vo, vah], *a.* 1. Relative, comparative. 2. (Gram.) Relative, relating to an antecedent. 3. (Music.) Relative major or minor key.

Relato [ray-lah'-to], *m.* Statement, narration.

Relator [ray-lah-tor'], *m.* 1. Relater, teller, narrator. 2. Reporter, a counsellor at law appointed by the supreme courts to make the briefs of the causes that are to be tried: he reads them before the court, they having first been examined and approved by both the parties concerned.

Relatora [ray-lah-to'-rah], *f.* The wife of the reporter of a court of justice.

Relatoría [ray-lah-to-ree'-ah], *f.* Office of a reporter of judicial causes in a court of justice.

Relavadura [ray-lah-vah-doo'-rah], *f.* A second washing.

Relavaje [ray-lah-vah'-hay], *m.* Washing-place for stuffs or clothes.

Relavar [ray-lah-var'], *va.* To wash again.

Relave [ray-lah'-vay], *m.* Second washing of metals. *Relaves*, Washings or sweepings in a silversmith's or goldworker's shop.

Relavillo [ray-lah-veel'-lyo], *m. dim.* Slight rewashing.

Releer [ray-lay-err'], *va.* To read over again, to revise.

Relegación [ray-lay-gah-the-on'], *f.* Relegation, judicial banishment; exile.

Relegar [ray-lay-gar'], *va.* To relegate, to banish; to exile.

Relejar [ray-lay-har'], *vn.* To diminish in thickness in proportion to the height: applied to a wall.

Releje [ray-lay'-hay], or **Relej** [ray-lay'], *m.* 1. (Mil.) Raised work in the chamber of a piece of ordnance where the powder is placed, in order to economize it. 2. Tapering of a wall or talus from below upward. 3. A clammy moisture sticking to the lips or mouth.

Relente [ray-len'-tay], *m.* 1. Night dew, softness occasioned by the falling of dew. 2. (Coll. and met.) Slowness, deliberation in speech or action.

Relentecer [ray-len-tay-therr'], *vn.* & *vr.* To be softened, to relent and soften by the falling of dew.

Relevación [ray-lay-vah-the-on'], *f.* 1. Relevation, the act of raising or lifting up; liberation. 2. Alleviation, relief from a burden or obligation. 3. Remission, forgiveness, pardon.

Relevante [ray-lay-vahn'-tay], *a.* Excellent, great, eminent.

Relevar [ray-lay-var'], *va.* 1. To emboss. 2. To exonerate, to disburden; to relieve from a burden or charge. 3. To forgive, to pardon. 4. To exalt, to aggrandize. 5. To relieve or substitute a sentinel or body of troops by another.—*vn.* (Art) To raise an object so as to appear like raised work.

Relevo [ray-lay'-vo], *m.* (Mil.) Relief.

Relicario [ray-le-cah'-re-o], *m.* 1. Shrine, a place where relics are collected and guarded. 2. Reliquary, a casket in which relics are kept.

Relictos [ray-leek'-tos], *m. pl.* (For.) Possessions which one leaves at his death.

Relief [ray-le-ef'], *m.* (Mil.) Warrant for an officer to receive either rank or pay that fell to him during his absence.

Relieve [ray-le-ay'-vay], *m.* 1. Relief, relievo, raised work, embossment. *Alto relieve* or *todo relieve*, Alto-relievo. *Bajo relieve*, Bass-relief. *Medio relieve*, Demi-relief. 2. Offals, scraps, or remnants on the table after meals; leavings; broken victuals. 3. The thread of the arbor of a screw.

Relievo, *m.* (Obs.) *V.* RELIEVE.

Religa [ray-lee'-gah], *f.* The second portion of alloy put to a metal to fit it for working.

Religación [ray-le-gah-the-on'], *f.* Binding, tying.

Religar [ray-le-gar'], *va.* To bind, to solder.

Religión [ray-le-he-on'], *f.* 1. Religion; piety, worship. 2. A community with regulations approved by the Church. 3. Belief in any divinity. *Entrar en religión*, (Coll.) To take the habit of a religious order.

Religionario, Religionista [ray-le-he-o-nah'-re-o], *com.* Religionist; sectary; Protestant.

Religiosamente, *adv.* 1. Religiously, piously. 2. Religiously, exactly, punctually. 3. Moderately.

Religiosidad [ray-le-he-o-se-dahd'], *f.* Religiousness; piety, sanctity; punctuality.

Religioso, sa [ray-le-he-o'-so, sah], *a.* 1. Religious, godly, pious. 2. Religious, teaching or professing religion. 3. Religious, exact, strict in observance of holy duties. 4. Moderate.

Relimar [ray-le-mar'], *va.* To file again.

Relimpiar [ray-lim-pe-ar'], *va.* To clean a second time.

Relimpio, ia [ray-leem'-pe-o, ah], *a.* (Coll.) Very neat, clean.

Relinchador, ra [ray-lin-chah-dor', rah], *a.* Neighing or whinnying often.

Relinchante [ray-lin-chahn'-tay], *pa.* Neighing, whinnying.

Relinchar [ray-lin-char'], *vn.* To whinny, to neigh, as a horse.

Relincho, Relinchido [ray-leen'-cho], *m.* Neigh, neighing, whinny of a horse.

Relindo, da [ray-leen'-do, dah], *a.* Very neat and fine.

Relinga [ray-leen'-gah], *f.* (Naut.) Bolt-rope. *Relinga del gratil*, Head bolt-rope. *Relinga del pujamen*, Foot bolt-rope. *Relinga de las caídas*, Leech bolt-rope.

Relingar [ray-lin-gar'], *va.* (Naut.) To sew bolt-ropes to sails.—*vn.* To rustle: said of bolt-ropes and sails moved by the wind.

Reliquia [ray-lee'-ke-ah], *f.* 1. Relic, residue, remains. 2. Relics of saints. 3. Footstep, tract, vestige. 4. Habitual complaint. *Reliquia insigne*, The head, arm, or leg of a saint.

Reliz [ray-leeth'], *m.* (Mex.) A landslide.

Reloco, ca [ray-lo'-co, cah], *a.* (Coll.) Raving mad, furiously insane.

Reloj [ray-lo'], *m.* Clock, watch. *Reloj de agua*, Clepsydra. *Reloj de arena*, Sand-glass, hour-glass. *Reloj de bolsillo*, Watch. *Reloj de sol* or *reloj solar*, Sun-dial. *Reloj de repetición*, A repeater or repeating-watch. *Reloj lunar*, Lunar dial. *Reloj de longitudes*, Chronometer. *Reloj despertador*, Alarm-clock. *Estar como un reloj*, (Coll.) To be regular and well-disposed. (Lat. horologium.)

Relojera [ray-lo-hay'-rah], *f.* 1. Clock-case. 2. Watchmaker's wife.

Relojería [ray-lo-hay-ree'-ah], *f.* 1. The art of making clocks and watches. 2. Watchmaker's shop.

Relojero [ray-lo-hay'-ro], *m.* Watchmaker, clockmaker.

Reluciente [ray-loo-the-en'-tay], *a.* Resplendent, glittering, brilliant, shining.

Relucir [ray-loo-theer'], *vn.* To shine, to glow, to glisten, to glitter; to excel, to be brilliant.

Reluchar [ray-loo-char'], *vn.* To struggle, to wrestle, to strive, to labour, to debate.

Relumbrante [ray-loom-brahn'-tay], *pa.* Resplendent.

Relumbrar [ray-loom-brar'], *vn.* To sparkle, to shine, to glisten, to glitter, to glare.

Relumbrera [ray-loom-bray'-rah], *f.* *V.* LUMBRERA.

Relumbrón [ray-loom-brone'], *m.* 1. Lustre, dazzling brightness: fleeting idea or sound. 2. Tinsel: any expression or phrase striking but of false showiness.

Rellanar [rayl-lyah-nar'], *va.* To re-level.—*vr.* To stretch one's self at full length.

Rellano [rayl-lyah'-no], *m* Landing-place of a stair.

Rellenar [rayl-lyay-nar'], *va.* 1. To fill again. 2. To stuff with victuals, to feed plentifully. 3. (Coll.) To stuff a fowl or gut with forced meat.—*vr.* To resate one's self.

Relleno [ray-lyay'-no], *m.* 1. Stuffing. 2. Repletion, act of refilling. *Relleno de pavo*, Turkey stuffing.

Relleno, na [rayl-lyay'-no, nah], *a.* & *pp* of RELLENAR. Cropful, crop-sick, satiated.

(*Yo reluzco, yo reluzca*, from *Relucir. V.* DESLUCIR.)

Remachado, da [ray-mah-chah'-do, dah], *a.* 1. Clinched, riveted. 2. Flat-nosed.—*pp.* of REMACHAR.

Remachador [ray-mah-chah-dor'], *m.* Riveter, rivet gun. *Remachador de tipo pistola*, Zipgun.

Remachar [ray-mah-char'], *va.* To flatten; to clinch, to rivet; to secure, to affirm.

Remache [ray-mah'-chay], *m.* Flattening, clinching, securing; rivet.

Remachón [ray-mah-chone'], *m.* Buttress. *V.* MACHÓN.

Remador [ray-mah-dor'], *m.* (Obs.) Rower. *V.* REMERO.

Remadura [ray-mah-doo'-rah], *f.* Rowing.

Remaldecir [ray-mal-day-theer'], *va.* To curse the cursers.

Remallar [ray-mal-lyar'], *va.* To mend the meshes of a net or coat of mail.

Remanadera [ray-mah-nah-day'-rah], *f.* In tanneries, graining-board, on which hides are pounded.

Remandar [ray-man-dar'], *va.* To order several times.

Remanecer [ray-mah-nay-therr'], *vn.* 1. To appear, to occur. 2. To remain, to be left.

Remaneciente [ray-mah-nay-the-en'-tay], *pa.* & *a.* Remaining, remanent, left out.

Remanente [ray-mah-nen'-tay], *m.* Remainder, residue; remanent, remnant.

(*Yo remanezco, yo remanezca*, from *Remanecer. V.* ABORRECER.)

Remangadura [ray-man-gah-doo'-rah], *f.* (Prov.) The act of tucking up.

Remangar [ray-man-gar'], *va.* To tuck up. *V.* ARREMANGAR.

Remango [ray-mahn'-go], *m.* Plaits of the petticoat at the waist.

Remansarse [ray-man-sar'-say], *vr.* To obstruct the course of a fluid.

Remanso [ray-mahn'-so], *m.* 1. Smooth, stagnant water. 2. Tardiness, lentitude.

Remante [ray-mahn'-tay], *m.* Rower.

Remar [ray-mar'], *vn.* 1. To row, to paddle. 2. To toil, to struggle.

Remarcar [ray-mar-car'], *va.* To mark again.

Rematadamente, *adv.* Entirely, totally.

Rematado, da [ray-mah-tah'-do, dah], *a.* 1. Ended, terminated. 2. Totally lost, utterly ruined. *Es loco rematado*, He is stark mad. *Rematado a galeras* or *presidio*, Condemned to the galleys or prison.—*pp.* of REMATAR.

Rematamiento [ray-mah-tah-me-en'-to], *m.* V. REMATE.

Rematar [ray-mah-tar'], *va.* 1. To close, to terminate, to finish, to abut, to end at. 2. To adjudge to the best bidder. 3. To kill game at one shot. 4. To finish a seam.—*vn.* To terminate, to be at an end. *Rematar al mejor postor,* To knock down to the highest bidder. *Rematar un ajuste,* To clap up a bargain.—*vr.* To be utterly ruined or destroyed.

Remate [ray-mah'-tay], *m.* 1. End, conclusion, expiration. *Remate de cuentas,* Closing of accounts. 2. An edge, a border, a limb. 3. The last or best bidding. 4. Artificial flowers put at the corners of altars. 5. Vignette, in a book. 6. (Arch.) Finial, the top or finishing of a pinnacle or gable; also, the entire pinnacle; abutment. *De remate,* Utterly, irremediably, without hope.

Rembalso [rem-bahl'-so], *m.* Rabbeting of a window-shutter, which makes it close with the frame.

Remecedor [ray-may-thay-dor'], *m.* He who beats down olives with a pole or long rod.

Remecer [ray-may-therr'], *va.* To rock; to swing, to move to and fro.

Remedable [ray-may-dah'-blay], *a.* Imitable.

Remedador, ra [ray-may-dah-dor', rah], *m.* & *f.* Imitator, mimic.

Remedar [ray-may-dar'], *va.* 1. To copy, to imitate, to mimic; to gesticulate, to mock. 2. To follow the track and footsteps of others. 3. To adopt the dress and manners of another.

Remediable [ray-may-de-ah'-blay], *a.* Remediable.

Remediador, ra [ray-may-de-ah-dor', rah], *m.* & *f.* Protector, comforter, helper; curer.

Remediar [ray-may-de-ar'], *va.* 1. To remedy, to mend, to repair. 2. To assist, to support, to help. 3. To free from danger, to liberate, to repair mischief. 4. To avoid executing any thing that may cause damage, or to do it contrary to the will of another. *Lo que no se puede remediar, se ha de aguantar,* What cannot be cured must be endured.

Remedición [ray-may-de-the-on'], *f.* Act of measuring a second time.

Remedio [ray-may'-de-o], *m.* 1. Remedy reparation, help. *No tener remedio,* To be irremediable or unavoidable. *No tiene remedio,* There is no help for it. *Sin remedio,* Without fail. 2. Amendment, correction. 3. Remedy, curative medicine. 4. Resource, refuge. 5. Action at law. *No tener un remedio,* To be destitute of aid or assistance.

Remedión [ray-may-de-on'], *m. aug.* A performance at a theatre in place of one previously announced, when the last cannot be presented for some unlooked-for reason.

Remedir [ray-may-deer'], *va.* To remeasure.

Remedo [ray-may'-do], *m.* Imitation, copy; mockery.

Remellado, Remellón [ray-mel-lyah'-do, ray-mel-lyone'], *a.* Unnaturally everted, ectropic.

Remellar [ray-mel-lyar'], *va.* To unhair hides in a tannery.

Remembración, *f.* (Obs.) V. RECORDACIÓN.

Remembrar, *va.* (Obs.) To remember.

Rememorar [ray-may-mo-rar'], *va.* To remember, to recall.

Rememorativo, va [ray-may-mo-rah-tec'-vo, vah], *a.* That which remembers or recalls.

Remendado, da [ray-men-dah'-do, dah], *a.* 1. Patched; mended. 2. Spotted, tabby: applied to horses, dogs, and other animals.—*pp.* of REMENDAR.

Remendar [ray-men-dar'], *va.* 1. To patch, to mend; to correct. 2. To adjust one thing to another.

Remendón [ray-men-done'], *m.* Botcher, patcher; one who mends old clothes; a cobbler, a fripper.

Remense [ray-men'-say], *a.* Belonging to Rheims, a city in France.

Rementir [ray-men-teer'], *vn.* To lie frequently.

Remera [ray-may'-rah], *f.* Flight-feather, each of the large feathers with which the wings of birds terminate.

Remero [ray-may'-ro], *m.* Rower, paddler. V. RIMERO.

Remesa [ray-may'-sah], *f.* Sending of goods; remittance of money.

Remesar [ray-may-sar'], *va.* 1. To pluck out the hair. 2. (Com.) To remit, to send money or goods.

Remesón [ray-may-sone'], *m.* 1. Plucking out of hair; hair plucked out. 2. Stopping a horse in full gallop. 3. A skilful thrust in fencing.

Remeter [ray-may-terr'], *va.* To put back, to put in; to put a clean cloth on children.

Remiche [ray-mee'-chay], *m.* Space in galleys for convicts, between the benches.

Remiel [ray-me-el'], *m.* The second extract of soft sugar taken from the cane.

Remiendo [ray-me-en'-do], *m.* 1. Patch, clout. 2. Amendment, addition. 3. Reparation, repair. 4. Brindle, the state of being spotted or tabby. 5. (Coll.) Badge of military orders worn by the knights. 6. (Print.) Short work of which few copies are printed. *A remiendos,* By patchwork, by piecemeal. *Echar un remiendo a la vida,* To take a light repast between meals. *Es remiendo de otro paño,* (Coll.) That is a horse of another colour. *No hay mejor remiendo que el del mismo paño,* Never trust to another what you can do yourself.

(*Yo remiendo, yo remiende,* from *Remendar.* V. ACERTAR.)

Remilgadamente, *adv.* With affected nicety or gravity; with prudery, squeamishly.

Remilgado, da [ray-meel-gah'-do, dah], *a.* & *pp.* of REMILGARSE. Applied to persons affectedly nice, grave, or prudish: used as a substantive, especially in the feminine.

Remilgarse [ray-meel-gar'-say], *vr* To be affectedly nice or grave.

Remilgo [ray-meel'-go], *m.* Affected nicety or gravity; prudery, squeamishness.

Reminiscencia [ray-me-nis-then'-the-ah], *f.* Reminiscence, recollection, memory.

Remirado, da [ray-me-rah'-do, dah], *a.* Prudent, cautious.—*pp.* of REMIRAR.

Remirar [ray-me-rar'], *va.* To revise; to review.—*vr.* 1. To do or finish a thing with great care. 2. To inspect or consider with pleasure. 3. To reflect on or examine one's self.

Remisamente, *adv.* Remissly, carelessly.

Remisible [ray-me-see'-blay], *a.* Remissible.

Remisión [ray-me-se-on'], *f.* 1. The act of sending. 2. Remission, sending back, remitting, remitment. 3. Remission, forgiveness, grace. 4. Remissness, indolence. 5. Remission, abatement, cessation of intenseness. 6. The act of referring to another book or work.

Remisivamente, *adv.* With remission.

Remisivo, va [ray-me-see'-vo, vah], *a.* Remitting, serving to remit.

Remiso, sa [ray-mee'-so, sah], *a.* 1. Remiss, careless, indolent. 2. Remiss. not rigorous.

Remisoria [ray-me-so'-re-ah], *f.* Order of a superior judge to refer a cause to another tribunal: generally used in the plural.

Remisorio, ria [ray-me-so'-re-o, ah], *a.* Having power to forgive or pardon. *Letras remisorias,* Judge's orders, transferring a cause to another court.

Remitente [ray-me-ten'-tay], *m.* & *f.* Remitter, sender. *Devuélvase al remitente,* Return to sender.

Remitir [ray-me-teer'], *va.* 1. To remit, to transmit. 2. To remit, to pardon, to forgive. 3. To remit, to give up, to suspend, to defer, to put off. 4. To return a cause to an inferior court. 5. To remit, to relax, to make less tense. —*vn.* To remit, to slacken, to grow less tense.—*vr.* 1. To refer or submit to the judgment and opinion of another. 2. To quote, to cite.

Remo [ray'-mo], *m.* 1. (Naut.) An oar. *Pala de un remo,* (Naut.) Blade or wash of an oar. *Manual de un remo,* (Naut.) Handle of an oar. 2. Long and hard labour. *A remo y sin sueldo,* Labouring in vain. *A remo y vela,* Very expeditiously.—*pl.* (Coll.) 1. The arms and legs of a person; the hind and fore legs of a horse. 2. The wings of a bird.

Remoción [ray-mo-the-on'], *f.* Removal, act of removing.

Remojadero [ray-mo-hah-day'-ro], *m.* Steeping-tub.

Remojar [ray-mo-har'], *va.* To steep, to imbrue, to wet much or long, to soak again. *Remojar la palabra,* (Coll.) To go to drink in a dram shop.

Remojo [ray-mo'-ho], *m.* The act of steeping or soaking. *Echar en remojo,* (Coll.) To defer a matter for more successful treatment.

Remolacha [ray-mo-lah'-chah], *f.* (Bot.) Beet-root. The red beet. Beta vulgaris, *L.* var. rubra.

Remolar [ray-mo-lar'], *m.* The master carpenter who makes oars, or the shop where oars are made.

Remolcador [ray-mol-cah-dor'], *m.* 1. Towboat, tug. 2. Towcar.

Remolcar [ray-mol-car'], *va.* To tow, to take in tow (a car, a boat, etc.)

Remoler [ray-mo-lerr'], *va.* To regrind, to grind excessively.

Remolimiento [ray-mo-le-me-en'-to], *m* Act of regrinding.

Remolinante [ray-mo-le-nahn'-tay], *pa* Whirling, making gyrations.

Remolinar [ray-mo-le-nar'], *vn.* To make gyrations.—*vr.* 1. To whirl one's self round. 2. To be surrounded by a multitude; to be confounded with the crowd.

Remolinear [ray-mo-le-nay-ar'], *va.* To whirl any thing about.—*vn.* V. REMOLINAR.

Remolino [ray-mo-lee'-no], *m.* 1. Whirlwind. 2. Whirlpool. 3. Cow-lick, or twisted tuft of hair upon some part of an animal. 4. Crowd, throng. 5. Disturbance, commotion.

Remolón, na [ray-mo-lone', nah], *a.* 1. Soft, indolent, lazy: applied to those who shun labour with art and study. 2. Applied to the upper tusk of a wild boar.

Remolón, *m.* The upper tusk of a wild boar; sharp tooth in horses.

Remolonear [ray-mo-lo-nay-ar'], *vn.* To lag, to loiter in doing what ought to be done.—*vr.* To be idle, to refuse stirring, from sloth and indolence.

Remolque [ray-mol'-kay], *m.* 1. Towing (of a car, a boat, etc.) 2. Towrope. *A remolque,* (fig.) Reluctantly. *Carro de remolque,* Trailer.

Remondar [ray-mon-dar'], *va.* To clean a second time; to take away what is useless.

Remono, na [ray-mo'-no, nah], *a.* Very neat, very pretty.

Remonta [ray-mone'-tah], *f.* 1. Repair of the feet of shoes or boots. 2. The act of supplying the cavalry with fresh horses; collection of cavalry horses; remounting cavalry.

Remontamiento [ray-mon-tah-me-en'-to], *m.* Act of soaring or towering.

Remontar [ray-mon-tar'], *va.* 1. To frighten away, to oblige one to withdraw. 2. To remount the cavalry; to supply them with fresh horses. 3. To repair the saddles of mules and horses. 4. To put new soles or feet to boots.—*vr.* 1. To tower, to soar: applied to birds. 2. To conceive great and sublime ideas; to form sublime conceptions.

Remonte [ray-mon'-tay], *m.* Soar, a towering flight; elevation or sublimity of ideas.

Remontista [ray-mon-tees'-tah], *m.* Commissioner for the purchase of cavalry horses.

Remoquete [ray-mo-kay'-tay], *m.* 1. Thump with the fist. 2. A witty expression. 3. Gallantry, courtship.

Remor, *m.* (Obs.) *V.* RUMOR.

Rémora [ray'-mo-rah], *f.* 1. Sucking-fish, remora. Echineis remora, *L.* 2. Hindrance, obstacle; cause of delay.

Remordedor, ra [ray-mor-day-dor', rah], *a.* Causing remorse.

Remorder [ray-mor-derr'], *va.* 1. To bite repeatedly. 2. To cause remorse, to sting, to make uneasy.—*vr.* To manifest concern, to suffer remorse.

Remordimiento [ray-mor-de-me-en'-to], *m.* Remorse, uneasiness, compunction.

Remosquear [ray-mos-kay-ar'], *va.* & *vr.* To blur: said of ink in printing when it spreads beyond the face of the types.

Remostar [ray-mos-tar'], *va.* To put must into old wine.—*vr.* To grow sweet and assume the flavour of must: applied to wine.

Remostecerse, *vr.* *V.* REMOSTARSE.

Remosto [ray-mos'-to], *m.* The act of putting must into old wine.

Remotamente, *adv.* 1. Remotely, at a distance. 2. Without chance of happening or of succeeding. 3. Confusedly. 4. Unlikely.

Remoto, ta [ray-mo'-to, tah], *a.* Remote, distant, far off; foreign, alien; unlike.

Removedor [ray-mo-vay-dor'], *m.* A mover.

Remover [ray-mo-verr'], *va.* 1. To remove, to shift from place to place. 2. To remove an obstacle. 3. To alter, to change the animal humours. 4. To dismiss.

Removimiento [ray-mo-ve-me-en'-to], *m.* 1. Removal. 2. Revulsion, fermentation of the humours of an animal body.

Remozadura, *f.* **Remozamiento,** *m.* [ray-mo-thah-doo'-rah]. Act of appearing or becoming young.

Remozar [ray-mo-thar'], *va.* To endeavour to appear young; to make one appear younger than he is.

Remplazar [rem-pla-thar'], *va.* V. REEMPLAZAR.

Remplazo [rem-plah'-tho] *m.* V. REEMPLAZO.

Rempujar [rem-poo-har'], *va.* 1. To push a person out of his place. 2. To jostle. 3. To impel, to carry away. 4. To beat up game, so as to drive it to a determined place.

Rempujo [rem-poo'-ho], *m.* 1. Impulse, push, thrust. 2. Pressure of an arch upon its supporters. *Rempujo para coser las velas,* A sail-maker's palm. *V.* EMPUJE.

Rempujón [rem-poo-hone'], *m.* Impulse, push, thrust.

Remuda [ray-moo'-dah], *f.* 1. Exchange, re-exchange. 2. *Remuda de caballos,* Relay of horses.

Remudamiento [ray-moo-dah-me-en'-to], *m.* 1. Removal, exchange. 2. Change of clothing.

Remudar [ray-moo-dar'], *va.* 1. To move or change again. 2. To exchange one thing for another.

(*Yo remuerdo, yo remuerda,* from *Remorder. V.* MOVER.)

(*Yo remuevo, yo remueva,* from *Remover. V.* MOVER.)

Remugar, *va.* (Prov.) *V.* RUMIAR.

Remullir [ray-mool-lyeer'], *va.* To beat up again, to mollify.

Remunerable [ray-moo-nay-rah'-blay], *a.* Remunerable, rewardable.

Remuneración [ray-moo-nay-rah-the-on'], *f.* Remuneration, recompense, reward; gratuity, consideration.

Remunerador, ra [ray-moo-nay-rah-dor', rah], *m.* & *f.* Remunerator.

Remunerar [ray-moo-nay-rar'], *va.* To reward, to remunerate.

Remuneratorio, ria [ray-moo-nay-rah-to'-re-o, ah], *a.* Remunerative.

Remusgo [ray-moos'-go], *m.* Too cool an atmosphere or situation.

Remusguillo [ray-moos-geel'-lyo], *m. dim.* Coolish place, chilly situation.

Ren, *m.* (Obs.) Kidney. *V.* RIÑÓN.

Renacer [ray-nah-therr'], *vn.* 1. To be born again, to spring up again, to grow again. 2. To acquire grace by baptism.

Renaciente [ray-nah-the-en'-tay], *pa.* & *a.* Renascent, springing anew.

Renacimiento [ray-nah-the-me-en'-to], *m.* 1. Regeneration; new birth. 2. The Renaissance in architecture and literature.

Renacuajo [ray-nah-coo-ah'-ho], *m.* 1. Spawn of frogs or young tadpoles. 2. Little, shapeless man.

Renadio [ray-nah-dee'-o], *m.* Crop which, after having been reaped in the blade, sprouts again.

Renal [ray-nahl'], *a.* Renal, belonging to the kidneys.

(*Yo renazco, yo renazca,* from *Renacer. V.* CONOCER.)

Rencilla [ren-theel'-lyah], *f.* A grudge remaining after a quarrel; heart-burning.

Rencilloso, sa [ren-theel-lyo'-so, sah], *a.* Peevish, quarrelsome, touchy.

Rencionar, *va.* (Obs.) To occasion grudges or heart-burnings.

Renco, ca [ren'-co, cah], *a.* Hipshot, having the hip dislocated, lame.

Rencor [ren-cor'], *m.* Rancour, animosity, grudge.

Rencorosamente, *adv.* Rancorously.

Rencoroso, sa [ren-co-ro'-so, sah], *a.* Rancorous, spiteful.

Rencoso [ren-co'-so], *a.* Applied to a ram with one testicle concealed.

Renda [ren'-dah], *f.* (Prov.) The second dressing of vines.

Rendaje [ren-dah'-hay], *m.* Reins of the bridle of horses or mules.

Rendajo [ren-dah'-ho], *m.* Mimic. *V.* ARRENDAJO.

Rendar [ren-dar'], *va.* (Prov.) To dress vines a second time.

Rendición [ren-de-the-on'], *f.* 1. Rendition, surrendering, yielding. 2. Product, profit accruing. 3. (Obs.) The price of redemption.

Rendidamente, *adv.* Humbly, submissively, compliantly.

Rendido, da [ren-dee'-do, dah], *a.* Tired out, fatigued.

Rendija [ren-dee'-hah], *f.* Crevice, crack, cleft.

Rendimiento [ren-de-me-en'-to], *m.* 1. Rendition, delivery into the hands of another. 2. Weariness, faintness. 3. Humiliation, submission; obsequiousness, humbling compliance. 4. Rent, income; yearly produce.

Rendir [ren-deer'], *va.* 1. To subject, to subdue, to conquer, to overcome. 2. To render, to surrender, to yield, to give up, to deliver up. *Rendir el alma a Dios,* To die. *Rendir el puesto,* (Mil.) To give up a post, to commit it to another. *Rendir las armas,* (1) To throw down the arms. (2) To surrender. 3. To render, to give back, to return, to restore; to produce. 4. To vomit, to throw up from the stomach. *Rendir gracias, V.* AGRADECER. *Rendir obsequios, V.* OBSEQUIAR. —*vr.* 1. To be tired, to be worn out with fatigue. 2. To yield, to submit to another, to give way. 3. (Naut.) To spring: applied to a mast. *Rendir la guardia,* To set the watch. *Rendir marea,* To stem the tide.

Rendón (De), *adv.* (Obs.) *V.* DE RONDÓN.

Renegado [ray-nay-gah'-do], *m.* 1. Renegado, apostate. 2. A malicious, wicked person. 3. Ombre, a sort of game at cards.—*Renegado, da, pp.* of RENEGAR.

Renegador, ra [ray-nay-gah-dor', rah], *m.* & *f.* Swearer, blasphemer; apostate.

Renegar [ray-nay-gar'], *va.* 1. To deny, to disown, to abnegate. 2. To detest, to abhor.—*vn.* 1. To apostatize. 2. To blaspheme, to curse.

Rengifero [ren-hee'-fay-ro], *m.* The reindeer.

Renglón [ren-glone'], *m.* 1. Line written or printed from one margin to another. 2. Part of one's revenue or income. *Renglones,* Writings. *Dejarse entre renglones,* or *quedar entre renglones,* To pass over in silence; to forget a thing which one ought to have present.

Renglonadura [ren-glo-nah-doo'-rah], *f* Ruling of paper; ruled lines.

Rengo, ga [ren'-go, gah], *a.* Hurt in the reins, back, or hip. *Dar con la de rengo,* (Coll.) To leave one in the lurch after having excited his hopes. *Hacer la de rengo,* (Coll.) To feign sickness or hurt so as to avoid work.

Rengue [ren'-gay], *m.* (Obs.) A sort of gauze which counsellors formerly wore in Spain on their collars and sleeves.

Reniego [ray-ne-ay'-go], *m.* A kind of execration or blasphemy.

(*Yo reniego, yo reniegue,* from *Renegar. V.* ACRECENTAR.)

Reniforme [ray-ne-for'-may], *a.* Reniform, kidney-shaped.

Renil [ray-neel'], *a.* Barren, a barren ewe.

Renitencia [ray-ne-ten'-the-ah], *f.* Resistance, opposition.

Renitente [ray-ne-ten'-tay], *a.* Renitent, repugnant.

Reno [ray'-no], *m.* Reindeer. Cervus tarandus.

Renombrado, da [ray-nom-brah'-do, dah], *a.* Renowned, celebrated, famous.—*pp.* of RENOMBRAR.

Renombrar [ray-nom-brar'], *va.* (Obs.) To name.

Renombre [ray-nom'-bray], *m.* 1. Surname, family name. 2. Renown, glory, fame.

Renovable [ray-no-vah'-blay], *a.* Renewable, replaceable.

Renovación [ray-no-vah-the-on'], *f.* 1. Renovation, renewal. 2. Change, reform. 3. Act of consuming old bread designed for the host, and of consecrating new.

Renovador, ra [ray-no-vah-dor', rah], *m.* & *f.* Renovator, reformer.

Renovante [ray-no-vahn'-tay], *pa.* Renovating, renewing.

Renovar [ray-no-var'], *va.* 1. To renew, to renovate. 2. To change, to reform. 3. To polish. 4. To barter. 5. To reiterate, to republish. 6. To consume old wafers designed for the host, and consecrate new bread. *Renovar la memoria,* To bring to recollection.—*vr.* To recollect one's self, to reform.

Renquear [ren-kay-ar'], *vn.* To limp, to halt, to claudicate.

Renta [ren'-tah], *f.* 1. Rent, profit, income. 2. Rent, money paid for any thing held of another. 3. Tax, contribution; revenue. *A renta,* Let at a rent.

Rentabilidad [ren-tah-be-le-dahd'], *f.* Return, yield, profitability.

Rentable [ren-tah'-blay], *a.* Profitable, income-yielding.

Rentar [ren-tar'], *va.* To yield.

Rentería [ren-tay-ree'-ah], *f.* Productive land or property.

Rentero [ren-tay'-ro], *m.* 1. Renter, farmer. 2. One who farms out land.

Rentilla [ren-teel'-lyah], *f.* 1. (Dim.) A small rent. 2. A game at cards. 3. A game at dice.

Rentista [ren-tees'-tah], *m.* 1. Financier: a modern word. 2. One who possesses an income whatever be its source. 3. Bondholder, one who lives upon interest paid from the public treasury.

Rentístico, ca [ren-tees'-te-co, cah], *a.* Belonging to public revenues.

Rento [ren'-to], *m.* (Prov.) 1. Country residence with farm-yard. 2. Annual rent paid by a labourer or colonist.

Rentoso, sa [ren-to'-so, sah], *a.* Yielding income, rent-producing.

Renuencia [ray-noo-en'-the-ah], *f.* Contradiction, reluctance.

Renuente [ray-noo-en'-tay], *a.* Indocile, intractable, remiss.

Renuevo [ray-noo-ay'-vo], *m.* 1. Sprout, shoot; a young plant to be transplanted. 2. Nursery of young trees and plants. 3. Renovation, renewal. *V.* REMUDA.

(*Yo renuevo, yo renueve,* from *Renovar. V.* ACORDAR.

Renuncia [ray-noon'-the-ah], *f.* Renunciation, resignation, renouncement, abjurement.

Renunciable [ray-noon-the-ah'-blay], *a.* That can be renounced or resigned: transferable.

Renunciación [ray-noon-the-ah-the-on'], *f.* Renunciation. *V.* RENUNCIA.

Renunciamiento [ray-noon-the-ah-me-en'-to], *m.* Renouncement. *V.* RENUNCIA.

Renunciante [ray-noon-the-ahn'-tay], *pa.* & *m.* & *f.* Renouncer, renouncing, abjurer.

Renunciar [ray-noon-the-ar'], *va.* 1. To renounce, to resign. 2. To renounce, to disown; to abnegate. 3. To renounce, to leave, to forego, to give up; to lay to; to fall from; to refuse, to reject; to depreciate, to abandon.—*vn.* To revoke, to renege at cards. *Renunciarse a sí mismo,* To give up one's own will or taste.

Renunciatario [ray-noon-the-ah-tah'-re-o], *m.* He to whom any thing is resigned.

Renuncio [ray-noon'-the-o], *m.* 1. Revoke, the fault committed in playing at cards, by not furnishing a card of the same suit which was played by another. 2. (Met. Coll.) Error, mistake.

Renvalsar [ren-val-sar'], *va.* To shave off doors or windows so that they may fit well.

Reñidamente [ray-nyee-dah-men'-tay] *adv.* Quarrelsomely, in a wrangling manner.

Reñidero [ray-nyee-day'-ro], *m.* Cockpit; fighting-pit; a place for fighting animals.

Reñido, da [ray-nyee'-do, dah], *a.* At variance with another.—*pp.* of REÑIR.

Reñidor, ra [ray-nye-dor', rah], *m.* & *f.* Quarreler, wrangler.

Reñir [ray-nyeer'], *va.* & *vn.* 1. To wrangle, to quarrel, to dispute, to fight, to fall out. 2. To scold, to reprimand, to chide, to reproach. 3. To argue, to discuss.

Reo [ray'-o]. *com.* 1. Offender, criminal, culprit. 2. Defendant in a suit at law. 3. Series, continuity. 4. Ray trout. Salmo hucho.

Reo, ea [ray'-o, ah], *a.* (Obs.) Criminal, culpable, guilty.

Reoctava, *f. V.* OCTAVILLA.

Reoctavar [ray-oc-tah-var'], *va.* To extract the eighth part of an eighth, as an excise or king's duty.

Reojar [ray-o-har'], *va.* To bleach wax.

Reojo [ray-o'-ho], *m. Mirar de reojo,* To look obliquely, to dissemble the looks by directing the view above a person; to look contemptuously or angrily.

Reopóntico [ray-o-pon'-te-co], *m.* (Bot.) *V.* RUIBARBO REOPÓNTICO.

Reorganización [ray-or-gah-ne-thah-the-on'], *f.* Reorganization.

Reorganizar [ray-or-gah-ne-thar'], *va* To reorganize, organize anew.

Reóstato [ray-os'-tah-to], *m.* Rheostat.

Repacer [ray-pah-therr'], *va.* To consume the entire grass of pasture-ground.

Repadecer [ray-pah-day-therr'], *va.* & *vn.* To suffer extremely.

Repagar [ray-pah-gar'], *va.* To pay a high or excessive price.

Repajo [ray-pah'-ho], *m.* Inclosure for the pasture of cattle.

Repantigarse [ray-pan-te-gar'-say], **Repanchigarse,** *vr.* To lean back in a chair with the legs stretched out.

Repapilarse [ray-pah-pe-lar'-say], *vr.* To eat to excess, to lick one's lips, to smack with relish.

Reparable [ray-pah-rah'-blay], *a.* 1. Reparable, remediable: objectionable. 2. Worthy of attention.

Reparación [ray-pah-rah-the-on'], *f.* 1. Reparation, repair. 2. Repeating a lesson among scholars. 3. Compensation, pay.

Reparada [ray-pah-rah'-dah], *f.* Sudden bound of a horse.

Reparador, ra [ray-pah-rah-dor', rah], *m.* & *f.* 1. Repairer. 2. Observer, one who makes remarks.

Reparamiento [ray-pah-rah-me-en'-to] *m. V.* REPARO and REPARACIÓN.

Reparar [ray-pah-rar'], *va.* 1. To repair, to restore. 2. To observe with careful attention. 3. To consider, to reflect, to give heed. 4. To repair, to amend an injury by an equivalent, to make up, to compensate, to expiate, to make amends, to correct. 5. To suspend, to detain. 6. To guard, to defend, to protect, to help. 7. To give the final touch to moulds. *Reparar en pelillos,* (Coll.) To notice trifles; to take offence at nothing.—*vn.* 1. To regain strength; to recover from illness. 2. To stop or halt in any part. *Reparar el timón,* (Naut.) To right the helm.—*vr.* 1. To refrain to forbear. 2. (Mex.) To rear on the hind feet, as a horse.

Reparativo, va [ray-pah-rah-tee'-vo, vah], *a.* Reparative.

Reparo [ray-pah'-ro], *m.* 1. Repair, reparation, supply of loss, restoration. 2. Restoration, repair of an edifice. 3. Careful inspection and investigation, notice. 4. Inconveniency, difficulty, doubt, objection. 5. Strengthening cataplasm for the stomach. 6. Any thing to support, assist, or defend. 7. Provisional anchorage for repairing damages. 8. Parry or guard, in fencing.

Reparón [ray-pah-ron'], *m.* (Coll.) Great doubt or difficulty.

Reparón, na [ray-pah-ron', nah], *a* Too cautious, too circumspect.

Repartible [ray-par-tee'-blay], *a.* Distributable.

Repartición [ray-par-te-the-on'], *f.* Partition, distribution.

Repartidamente, *adv.* In divers portions or partitions.

Repartidero, ra [ray-par-te-day'-ro, rah], *a.* Distributing, parting.

Repartidor, ra [ray-par-te-dor', rah], *m.* & *f.* 1. Distributer. 2. Assessor of taxes.

Repartimiento [ray-par-te-me-en'-to], *m.* 1. Partition, division, distribution, apportionment. 2. Portion of territory which was given as a fief to the conquerors of Spanish America. 3. Assessment of taxes.

Repartir [ray-par-teer'], *va.* 1. To divide, to distribute, to apportion, to dispart. 2. To scatter, to sow. 3. To assess taxes.

Reparto [ray-par'-to], *m.* 1. (Th.) Cast of characters (in a play, etc.). 2. Distribution.

Repasadera [ray-pah-sah-day'-rah], *f.* Plane, a carpenter's tool.

Repasadora [ray-pah-sah-do'-rah], *f.* Woman occupied in carding wool.

Repasar [ray-pah-sar'], *va.* 1. To repass, to pursue the same course (used also intransitively). 2. To re-examine, to revise, to review and correct or polish work already done. 3. To glance rapidly over something written. 4. To explain again, to run over the results of one's former studies. 5. To clean dyed wool for carding. 6. To sew again, to mend clothes. 7. To air clothes at the fire. 8. To remix mercury with metal to purify it.

Repasata [ray-pah-sah'-tah], *f.* (Coll.) Reprehension, censure, chiding.

Repasión [ray-pah-se-on'], *f.* (Phil.) Reaction of the agent on the patient.

Repaso [ray-pah'-so], *m.* 1. The act and effect of running over a thing that one has already studied. 2. Revision, the act of re-examining and revising; examining a thing after it is finished. 3. The act and effect of repassing or remixing quicksilver with metal. 4. Reprimand, chastisement.—*pl.* A number of flaws or porosities in the body of an organ.

Repastar [ray-pas-tar'], *va.* To feed a second time.
Repasto [ray-pahs'-to], *m.* Increase of food; an additional meal.
Repatriar [ray-pah-tre-ar'], *vn.* (Amer.) To return to one's country, to repatriate. (Not Acad.)
Repechar [ray-pay-char'], *va. & vn.* To mount a declivity or slope.
Repecho [ray-pay'-cho], *m.* Declivity, slope. *A repecho,* Up hill.
Repedir [ray-pay-deer'], *va.* To repeat, to supplicate again.
Repelada [ray-pay-lah'-dah], *f.* Salad of herbs.
Repelado [ray-pay-lah'-do], *m.* Want of cleanness in printed or stamped matter.—*pp.* of REPELAR.
Repeladura [ray-pay-lah-doo'-rah], *f.* 1. A second gathering of bark, or re-stripping. 2. Lack of cleanliness in what is printed or stamped.
Repelar [ray-pay-lar'], *va.* 1. To pull out the hair of the head. 2. To put a horse to his speed. 3. To take by small portions. 4. To nip the top of grass: applied to grazing cattle.—*vn.* To turn out smudged or unclean, as used of matter printed or stamped.
Repeler [ray-pay-lerr'], *va.* To repel; to refute, to reject.
Repeliente [ray-pay-le-en'-tay], *pa.* Repellent.
Repelo [ray-pay'-lo], *m.* 1. A small part or share of any thing that rises against the grain, or has transverse fibres. 2. Any thing which goes against the grain, crooked grain. 3. A slight scuffle or dispute. 4. Repugnance, aversion.
Repelón [ray-pay-lone'], *m.* 1. The action of pulling out the hair. 2. A small part torn from any thing; a thread loose in stockings. 3. A short gallop. *A repelones,* By degrees, by little and little. *De repelón,* By the way; in haste.
Repeloso, sa [ray-pay-lo'-so, sah], *a.* 1. Of a bad grain, having transverse fibres: applied to wood. 2. Touchy, peevish.
Repellar [ray-pel-lyar'], *va.* To run a trowel over the plaster thrown on a wall.
Repensar [ray-pen-sar'], *va.* To consider, to reflect, to contemplate; to think deeply.
Repente [ray-pen'-tay], *m.* A sudden movement, an unexpected event. *De repente,* Suddenly, on a sudden.
Repentinamente, *adv.* Suddenly.
Repentino, na [ray-pen-tee'-no, nah], *a.* Sudden, unforeseen, unexpected, abrupt, extemporaneous, unpremeditated.
Repentirse, *vr.* *V.* ARREPENTIRSE.
Repentista [ray-pen-tees'-tah], *m.* Maker of extemporary verses.
Repentizar [ray-pen-te-thar'], *va.* To improvise, to compose verses off hand.
Repentón [ray-pen-tone'], *m.* 1. An unexpected event or incident. 2. A sudden movement.
Repeor [ray-pay-or'], *a.* Much worse.
Repercudida [ray-per-coo-dee'-dah], *f.* Repercussion, rebound.
Repercudir [ray-per-coo-deer'], *vn.* To rebound. *V.* REPERCUTIR.
Repercusión [ray-per-coo-se-on'], *f.* Repercussion, reverberation.
Repercusivo, va [ray-per-coo-see'-vo, vah], *a.* Repercussive; repellent.
Repercutir [ray-per-coo-teer'], *vn.* To cause repercussion, to repercuss, to drive back, to rebound; to retrograde, to reverberate.—*va.* To repel.
Repertorio [ray-per-to'-re-o], *m.* 1. Repertory, index of noteworthy matters. 2. Repertory, repertoire, a list of pieces, especially such as are presented in a theatre.
Repesar [ray-pay-sar'], *va.* To reweigh, to weigh again.
Repeso [ray-pay'-so], *m.* 1. Weighing a second time. 2. Weight-office, whither articles may be carried to be weighed a second time. 3. Charge of reweighing. *De repeso,* With the whole weight of a body; with the whole force of authority and persuasion.
Repetencia [ray-pay-ten'-the-ah], *f.* (Obs.) Repetition.
Repetición [ray-pay-te-the-on'], *f.* 1. Repetition, reiteration; iteration. 2. Repeater, a repeating clock or watch. 3. Collegial dissertation or discourse; a thesis. 4. (For.) An action for an accounting.
Repetidamente, *adv.* Repeatedly.
Repetidor, ra [ray-pay-te-dor', rah], *m. & f.* Repeater, a teacher or student who repeats with another his lessons, and explains them.
Repetir [ray-pay-teer'], *va.* 1. To demand or claim repeatedly and urgently. 2. To repeat, to reiterate, to use again, to do again, to try again. 3. To repeat, to recite, to rehearse.—*vn.* 1. To have the taste of what was eaten or drunk in the mouth. 2. To deliver a public discourse previous to the examination for the higher degrees in the universities.—*vr.* To repeat one's self: applied to artists.
Repetitivo, va [ray-pay-te-tee'-vo, vah], *a.* That which contains a repetition.
Repicado, da [ray-pe-cah'-do, dah], *a.* 1. Chopped. 2. Starched, stiff; affectedly nice.—*pp.* of REPICAR.
Repicapunto [ray-pe-cah-poon'-to], *adv.* *De repicapunto,* Nicely, delicately, excellently.
Repicar [ray-pe-car'], *va.* 1. To chop. 2. To chime, to ring a merry peal. 3. To reprick. 4. In the game of piquet, to count ninety before the adverse party counts one.—*vr.* To glory, to boast, to pique one's self on.
Repilogar [ray-pe-lo-gar'], *va.* To recapitulate, to epitomize, to repeat the sum of a former discourse.
Repinarse [ray-pe-nar'-say], *va.* To soar, to elevate.
Repintar [ray-pin-tar'], *va.* To repaint, to paint again.—*vr.* 1. To paint one's self. 2. (Print.) To set off, to make a double impression.
Repique [ray-pee'-kay], *m.* 1. Act of chopping or cutting. 2. Chime, a merry peal on festive occasions; the peal of bells. *El último repique* or *llamada,* The last peal. 3. Dispute, altercation; a slight scuffle. 4. In piquet, counting ninety before the other player can count one.
Repiquete [ray-pe-kay'-tay], *m.* 1. A merry peal rung on festive occasions. 2. Chance, opportunity.
Repiquetear [ray-pe-kay-tay-ar'], *va.* To ring a merry peal on festive occasions.—*vr.* To bicker, to wrangle, to quarrel.
Repiqueteo [ray-pe-kay-tay'-o], *m.* A continued peal of bells.
Repisa [ray-pee'-sah], *f.* 1. Pedestal or abutment for a bust or vase. 2. A bracket.
Repiso [ray-pee'-so], *m.* Weak, vapid wine.
Repiso, sa [ray-pee'-so, sah], *a.* Sorrowful, repentant. (Acad.)
Repitiente [ray-pe-te-en'-tay], *pa.* Repeating, he who repeats and defends a thesis.
(*Yo repito, yo repita; él repitió;* from REPETIR. *V.* PEDIR.)
Repizcar [ray-peeth-car'], *va.* To pinch. *V.* PELLIZCAR.
Repizco [ray-peeth'-co], *m.* The act of pinching. *V.* PELLIZCO.
Replantar [ray-plan-tar'], *va.* To replant ground.
Replantear [ray-plan-tay-ar'], *va.* To mark out the ground plan of an edifice again.
Replanteo [ray-plan-tay'-o], *m.* 1. The act of replanting. 2. Second description of the ground plan of a building.
Repleción [ray-play-the-on'], *f.* Repletion arising from abundance of humours in the body.
Replegable [ray-play-gah'-blay], *a.* Capable of being folded back.
Replegar [ray-play-gar'], *va.* 1. To redouble, to fold often. 2. (Mil.) To fall back or to double the wing of an army, regiment, etc., upon its centre or any other part, as the evolution may be necessary.
Repleto, ta [ray-play'-to, tah], *a.* Replete, very full.
Réplica [ray'-ple-cah], *f.* Reply, answer; repartee; objection.
Replicación [ray-ple-cah-the-on'], *f.* 1. (Obs.) Repetition, replication. 2. (Law) *V.* RÉPLICA.
Replicador, ra [ray-ple-cah-dor', rah], *m. & f.* Replier, disputant.
Replicante [ray-ple-cahn'-tay], *pa. & n* Replier, respondent; replying.
Replicar [ray-ple-car'], *vn.* 1. To reply, to make return to an answer. 2. To reply, to impugn the arguments of the adverse party; to contradict.—*va.* (Law) To respond; to repeat.
Replicón, na [ray-ple-cone', nah], *a.* (Coll.) Replier, frequent disputer.
Repliegue [ray-ple-ay'-gay], *m.* 1. The act of doubling or folding often. 2. A fold, crease, convolution.
Repoblación [ray-po-blah-the-on'], *f.* Repopulation, act of repeopling.
Repoblar [ray-po-blar'], *va.* To repeople.
Repoda [ray-poh'-dah], *f.* The act of pruning a second time.
Repodar [ray-po-dar'], *va.* To prune again.
Repodrir [ray-po-dreer'], *va. & vr.* *V.* REPUDRIR.
Repollar [ray-pol-lyar'], *vn.* To form round heads of leaves, like cabbage.
Repollo [ray-pol'-lyo], *m.* 1. (Bot.) White cabbage. 2. Round head formed by the leaves of plants.
Repolludo, da [ray-pol-lyoo'-do, dah], *a.* Cabbage-headed; round-head.
Reponche, *m.* *V.* RUIPONCE.
Reponer [ray-po-nerr'], *va.* 1. To replace; to collocate. 2. To restore a suit at law to its primitive state. 3. To oppose anew, to reply.—*vr.* To recover lost health or property.
(*Yo repongo, yo reponga; yo repuse, repondré;* from *Reponer.* *V.* PONER.)
Reportación [ray-por-tah-the-on'], *f.* Moderation, forbearance.
Reportado, da [ray-por-tah'-do, dah], *a.* Moderate, temperate, forbearing.—*pp.* of REPORTAR.
Reportamiento [ray-por-tah-me-en'-to], *m.* Forbearance.
Reportar [ray-por-tar'], *va.* 1. To moderate or repress one's passions, to refrain, to forbear. 2. To obtain, to reach; to attain. 3. To carry or bring. 4. To return an instrument with the certificate of its execution.—*vr.* To forbear.
Reporteril [ray-por-tay-reel'], *a.* (Neol.) Reportorial, relating to reporters. (Note.—The noun is *Repórter,* taken from the English.)

Reportorio [ray-por-to'-re-o], *m.* 1. (Obs.) Repertory, index, memorandum-book. 2. Almanac, calendar.

Reposadamente, *adv.* Peaceably, quietly.

Reposadero [ray-po-sah-day'-ro], *m.* 1. A vat in which indigo is prepared. 2. A trough for receiving melted metal.

Reposado, da [ray-po-sah'-do, dah], *a.* Quiet, peaceful.—*pp.* of REPOSAR.

Reposar [ray-po-sar'], *vn.* 1. To rest, to repose; to take a sleep, to lie by, to lie to. 2. To rest in the grave; to rest in peace.—*vr.* To settle: applied to liquors.

Reposición [ray-po-se-the-on'], *f.* 1. The act of restoring a suit at law to its primitive state. 2. (Chem.) Preservation of liquids in proper vessels. 3. Reposition.

Repositorio, *m.* (Obs.) Repository.

Reposo [ray-poh'-so], *m.* Rest, repose; tranquility.

Repostar [ray-pos-tar'], *va.* To restock, to resupply with.—*vr.* To lay in a fresh supply. *Repostar combustible,* To refuel.

Repostería [ray-pos-tay-ree'-ah], *f.* 1. Office or shop for preparing confectionery and beverages. 2. All the provisions, instruments, and persons employed in this office.

Repostero [ray-pos-tay'-ro], *m.* 1. The principal officer of the *repostería;* king's butler. 2. Covering ornamented with a coat of arms. *Repostero de camas,* Queen's chamberlain. *Repostero de estrados,* Keeper of the king's drawing-room.

Repregunta [ray-pray-goon'-tah], *f.* 1. A second demand or question on the same subject. 2. (Law) A cross-examination.

Repreguntar [ray-pray-goon-tar'], *va.* To question repeatedly about the same subject.

Reprenda [ray-pren'-dah], *f.* Pledge taken a second time.

Reprender [ray-pren-derr'], *va.* To reprehend, to reprimand, to blame, to censure, to reprove, to chide; to correct.

Reprendiente [ray-pren-de-en'-tay], *pa.* Censuring, reprimanding.

Reprensible [ray-pren-see'-blay], *a.* Reprehensible.

Reprensión [ray-pren-se-on'], *f.* Reprehension, blame, censure, reprimand, reproof, lesson. *Sujeto sin reprensión,* An irreprehensible person.

Reprensor, ra [ray-pren-sor', rah], *m.* & *f.* Reprehender, censurer, reprover.

Represa [ray-pray'-sah], *f.* 1. Water collected for working a mill; dam. 2. The act of stopping or retaining; restriction.

Represalia, Represaria [ray-pray-sah'-le-ah, ray-pray-sah'-re-ah], *f.* Reprisal, reprise.

Represar [ray-pray-sar'], *va.* 1. To recapture or retake from the enemy. 2. To stop, to detain, to retain. 3. To repress, to moderate one's passions.

Representable [ray-pray-sen-tah'-blay], *a.* That which may be represented.

Representación [ray-pray-sen-tah-the-on'], *f.* 1. Representation, the act of representing. 2. Power, authority. 3. Dramatic poem. 4. Figure, image, idea. 5. Remonstrance, memorial, address. 6. Authority, dignity, character of a person. 7. (Law) Right of succession to an inheritance in the person of another.

Representador, ra [ray-pray-sen-tah-dor', rah], *m.* & *f.* 1. Representative. 2. Player, actor.

Representante [ray-pray-sen-tahn'-tay], *pa.* Representing another.

Representante, ta [ray-pray-sen-tahn'-tay, tah], *m.* & *f.* 1. Player, comedian. 2. Representer, representative.

Representar [ray-pray-sen-tar'], *va.* 1. To represent, to make appear, to set forth; to manifest; to refer; to express. 2. To play on the stage, to perform. 3. To represent another, as his agent, deputy, or attorney. 4. To be the symbol or image of any thing.—*vr.* To offer, to occur; to present itself.

Representativamente, *adv.* (Littl. us.) Representatively.

Representativo, va [ray-pray-sen-tah-tee'-vo, vah], *a.* Representative.

Represión [ray-pray-se-on'], *f.* Repression.

Represivo, va [ray-pray-see'-vo, vah], *a.* Repressive, restrictive.

Reprimenda [ray-pre-men'-dah], *f.* Reprimand.

Reprimir [ray-pre-meer'], *va.* To repress, to refrain, to contain, to control, to curb.

Reprobable [ray-pro-bah'-blay], *a.* Reprehensible.

Reprobación [ray-pro-bah-the-on'], *f.* Reprobation, reproof.

Reprobado, da [ray-pro-bah'-do, dah], *a.* 1. Flunked, not passed (in an examination). 2. V. RÉPROBO.

Reprobador, ra [ray-pro-bah-dor', rah], *m.* & *f.* Reprover, condemner.

Reprobar [ray-pro-bar'], *va.* To reject, to condemn, to contradict, to exclude, to upbraid, to reprobate; to damn.

Reprobatorio, ria [ray-pro-bah-to'-re-o, ah], *a.* That which reprobates or reproves; objurgatory.

Réprobo, ba [ray'-pro-bo, bah], *m.* & *f.* & *a.* Reprobate, graceless, wicked.

Reprochar [ray-pro-char'], *va.* 1. To reproach, to impute blame to; to challenge witnesses produced by the adverse party. 2. To reject, to dismiss, to exclude.

Reproche [ray-pro'-chay], *m.* 1. Reproach, reproof. 2. Fault which may be reproved. 3. Repulse, rebuff, displeasure.

Reproducción [ray-pro-dooc-the-on'], *f.* 1. Reproduction. 2. Reproduction of a summons, or any other judicial precept or decree, with the certificate of service.

Reproducir [ray-pro-doo-theer'], *va.* To reproduce.

Reproductible [ray-pro-dooc-tee'-blay], *a.* That can be reproduced or produced anew.

Reproductividad [ray-pro-dooc-te-ve-dahd'], *f.* Reproductiveness.

Reproductivo, va [ray-pro-dooc-tee'-vo, vah], *a.* Reproductive, producing anew.

Reproductor, ra [ray-pro-dooc-tor', rah], *a.* & *n.* Serving for reproduction.

Repromisión [ray-pro-me-se-on'], *f.* Repeated promise.

Repropiarse [ray-pro-pe-ar'-say], *vr.* To be unwilling to obey, to be restive: applied to horses.

Repropio [ray-pro'-pe-o], *a.* Restive: applied to a horse.

Reprueba [ray-proo-ay'-bah], *f.* New proof in addition to a preceding one.

(*Yo repruebo, yo repruebe,* from *Reprobar.* V. ACORDAR.)

Reptar, *va.* (Obs.) V. RETAR.

Reptil [rep-teel'], *a.* & *m.* Reptile; crawler, creeper.

Reptilívoro, ra [rep-te-lee'-vo-ro, rah], *a.* Devouring reptiles, reptilivorous.

República [ray-poo'-ble-cah], *f.* 1. Republic, commonwealth. 2. Republic, public welfare; political government. *República literaria,* The republic of letters.

Republicanismo [ray-poo-ble-cah-nees-mo], *m.* Republicanism.

Republicano, na [ray-poo-ble-cah'-no nah], *a.* 1. Republican, inhabitant of a republic. 2. Republican, approving republican government, democratic.

Republicano, na [ray-poo-ble-cah'-no, nah], *m.* & *f.* Republican, democrat, commonwealthsman. *V.* REPÚBLICO.

Repúblico [ray-poo'-ble-co], *m.* A man greatly attached to the welfare of the public, a patriot; a man capable of holding public offices, a statesman.

Repudiable [ray-poo-de-ah'-blay], *a.* (Littl. us.) Repudiable.

Repudiación [ray-poo-de-ah-the-on'], *f.* Repudiation, divorce.

Repudiar [ray-poo-de-ar'], *va.* 1. To repudiate, to divorce a wife. 2. To renounce, to relinquish.

Repudio [ray-poo'-de-o], *m.* Repudiation, divorce.

Repudrir [ray-poo-dreer'], *va.* To rot greatly.—*vr.* To pine away from dissembling or keeping silent over some affliction.

Repuesta [ray-poo-es'-tah], *f.* Money staked in the game of ombre.

Repuesto [ray-poo-ess'-to], *m.* 1. Refill. 2. Extra, spare. *De repuesto,* As a substitute, extra, as a spare. *Mula de repuesto,* Sumpter mule.

Repuesto, ta [ray-poo-es'-to, tah], *pp. irr.* of REPONER.

Repugnancia [ray-poog-nahn'-the-ah], *f.* 1. Reluctance, repugnance, resistance. 2. Repugnance, aversion, loathing. 3. Opposition, contradiction, contrariety. *Con repugnancia,* In a reluctant manner.

Repugnante [ray-poog-nahn'-tay], *a.* Repugnant, repulsive, loathsome.

Repugnar [ray-poog-nar'], *va.* 1. To oppose, to contradict, to repugn, to withstand. 2. To act with reluctance, to implicate.

Repujado, da [ray-poo-ha'-do, dah], *a.* Repoussé, formed in relief.

Repulgado, *a.* *V.* AFECTADO.—*pp.* of REPULGAR.

Repulgar [ray-pool-gar'], *va.* 1. To hem, to double in the border of cloth with a seam; to border, to double the edge. 2. To put an edging upon pastry.

Repulgo [ray-pool'-go], *m.* 1. Hem, the border of cloth doubled in with a seam. 2. The external ornament of a pie. 3. Vain and ridiculous scruple. *Detenerse en repulgos de empanada* To waste time over trifles.

Repulido, da [ray-poo-lee'-do, dah], *a.* Prim, neat, spruce.—*pp.* of REPULIR.

Repulir [ray-poo-leer'], *va.* 1. To repolish. 2. To dress affectedly. Used also as reflexive.

Repulsa [ray-pool'-sah], *f.* Refusal, counter-check, repulse.

Repulsar [ray-pool-sar'], *va.* To reject, to decline, to refuse.

Repulsión [ray-pool-se-on'], *f.* 1. *V.* REPULSA. 2. Repulsion.

Repulsivo, va [ray-pool-see'-vo, vah], *a.* Repulsive, repulsory.

Repulso, sa [ray-pool'-so, sah], *pp. irr.* of REPELER.

Repulular [ray-poo-loo-lar'], *va.* To repullulate.

Repullo [ray-pool'-lyo], *m.* 1. Jerk, leap; a sudden violent motion of the body. 2. A small arrow or dart. 3. An external mark of pain or grief.

Repunta [ray-poon'-tah], *f.* 1. Point, headland. 2. Sign of displeasure; disagreement, dispute, scuffle. 3. Very short thing, very small portion.

Repuntar [ray-poon-tar'], *vn.* (Naut.) To begin to ebb.—*vr.* 1. To be on the turn: applied to wine. 2. To be soured, to be displeased with one another.

Repurgar [ray-poor-gar'], *va.* 1. To clean or purify again. 2. To administer a second purging draught.

Reputación [ray-poo-tah-the-on'], *f.* Reputation, repute, character, credit, fame, renown.

Reputante [ray-poo-tahn'-tay], *pa.* One who estimates.

Reputar [ray-poo-tar'], *va.* To repute, to estimate, to appreciate.

Requebrado, da [ray-kay-brah'-do, dah], *a.* & *pp.* of REQUEBRAR. Enamored, using tender expressions.—*m.* & *f.* Lover, loving expression.

Requebrador [ray-kay-brah-dor'], *m.* Wooer, suitor.

Requebrar [ray-kay-brar'], *va.* To woo, to court, to make love, to dally.

Requejada, *f.* **Requejal,** *m.* [ray-kay-hah'-dah, ray-kay-hahl']. (Prov.) *V.* REQUEJO.

Requejo [ray-kay'-ho], *m.* (Prov.) Ground ending in a hill before entering upon a plain.

Requemado, da [ray-kay-mah'-do, dah], *a.* 1. Brown-coloured, sun-burnt. 2. Thin silk for veils, black and lustreless.—*pp.* of REQUEMAR.

Requemadura [ray-kay-mah-doo'-rah], *f.* A burn upon a burn.

Requemamiento, *m.* *V.* RESQUEMO.

Requemar [ray-kay-mar'], *va.* 1. To burn a second time. 2. To roast to excess. 3. To extract the juice of plants. 4. To inflame the blood or humours. *V.* RESQUEMAR.—*vr.* To burn with passion, to be deeply in love.

Requemazón [ray-kay-mah-thone'], *f.* *V.* RESQUEMO.

Requerer [ray-kay-rerr'], *vn.* (Littl. us.) To wish again, to desire anxiously.

Requeridor [ray-kay-re-dor'], *m.* He who requests, advises, or intimates; a requirer.

Requerimiento [ray-kay-re-me-en'-to], *m.* 1. Request, requisition. 2. Intimation, injunction, summons.

Requerir [ray-kay-reer'], *va.* 1. To require, to need. 2. To summon. 3. To intimate, to notify. 4. To investigate. 5. To request. 6. To court, to woo a woman. 7. To induce, to persuade.

Requesón [ray-kay-sone'], *m.* Cottage cheese.

Requesonarse [ray-kay-so-nar'-say], *vr.* To become curds a second time: applied to whey or milk.

Requestar [ray-kes-tar'], *va.* (Obs.) To search, to solicit.

Requiebro [ray-ke-ay'-bro], *m.* 1. Endearing expressions, the language of love; love-tale. 2. Quiver, trill of the voice.

(*Yo requiebro, yo requiebre,* from *Requebrar.* *V.* ACRECENTAR.)

(*Yo requiero, yo requiera; él requirió, requiriera;* from *Requerir.* *V.* ASENTIR.)

Requiebro, *m.* Crushed ore.

Requilorio [ray-ke-lo'-re-o], *m.* & *pl.* (Coll.) Useless ceremony, or circumlocution, before doing a simple thing.

Requintador, ra [ray-kin-tah-dor', rah], *m.* & *f.* Outbidder, in the letting of lands or tenements.

Requintar [ray-kin-tar'], *va.* 1. To outbid a fifth part, in tenements, after an agreement is made. 2. To exceed, to surpass, to superadd. 3. (Mus.) To raise or lower the tone five points.

Requinto [ray-keen'-to], *m.* 1. The second fifth taken from a quantity from which one-fifth had before been taken. 2. An advance of a fifth in rent. 3. Extraordinary impost levied on the Peruvians in the time of Philip II. 4. A very small and high-pitched flute, and the one who plays it.

Requirir, *va.* *V.* REQUERIR.

Requisa [ray-kee'-sah], *f.* Night and morning visit of a jailer to his prisoners.

Requisar [ray-ke-sar'], *va.* 1. To inspect, to review. 2. To make a levy of horses for army use.

Requisición [ray-ke-se-the-on'], *f.* A levy of horses for military service.

Requisito [ray-ke-see'-to], *m.* Requisite, necessary condition.

Requisito, ta [ray-ke-see'-to, tah], *pp. irr.* of REQUERIR.

Requisitorio, ria [ray-ke-se-to'-re-o, ah], *a.* Requisitory: applied to a warrant from one judge to another, requiring compliance with his orders: used as a substantive in the feminine termination.

Requive, *m.* *V.* ARREQUIVE.

Res [res], *f.* Head of cattle or sheep; an animal (domestic or wild); a creature. (Arab.)

Resaber [ray-sah-berr'], *va.* To know very well.—*vn.* To affect too much the learned man.

Resabiar [ray-sah-be-ar'], *va.* To cause one to become vicious or contract evil habits.—*vr.* 1. To get vices, to become vicious. 2. To be discontented or dissatisfied, to fall into a pet. 3. *V.* SABOREARSE.

Resabido, da [ray-sah-bee'-do, dah], *a.* Very learned; affecting learning.—*pp.* of RESABER.

Resabio [ray-sah'-be-o], *m.* 1. An unpleasant taste left on the palate. 2. Vicious habit, bad custom.—*a.* (Obs.) Very learned; affecting much knowledge.

Resabioso, sa [ray-sah-be-oh'-so, sah], *a.* (Peru) Crafty, artful.

Resaca [ray-sah'-cah], *f.* 1. (Naut.) Surge, surf, the undertow. 2. (Com.) A redraft, a draft against the indorser of a protested bill.

Resacar [ray-sah-car'], *va.* (Com.) To redraw.

Resalado, da [ray-sah-lah'-do, dah], *a.* Very graceful, charming: commonly said of women only.

Resalir [ray-sah-leer'], *vn.* To jut out, to project.

Resaltar [ray-sal-tar'], *vn.* 1. To rebound, to fly back. 2. To crack, to burst in pieces. 3. To jut out, to project. 4. To appear, to be evident.

Resalte [ray-sahl'-tay], *m.* Prominence, protuberance; any striking point.

Resalto [ray-sahl'-to], *m.* Rebound, resilience; prominence; act of shooting boars when rising from their bed.

Resaludar [ray-sah-loo-dar'], *vn.* To return a salute, to salute again.

Resalutación [ray-sah-loo-tah-the-on'], *f.* Return of a salute, act of resaluting.

Resalvia [ray-sahl'-ve-ah], *f.* (Agr.) A count of the staddles which must be left in felling trees.

Resalvo [ray-sahl'-vo], *m.* Staddle, sapling, or branch of a tree left for new growth in forestry.

Resallar [ray-sal-lyar'], *va.* To weed again.

Resallo [ray-sahl'-lyo], *m.* A re-weeding.

Resanar [ray-sah-nar'], *va.* To regild defective spots.

Resangría [ray-san-gree'-ah], *f.* Bleeding again.

Resarcible [ray-sar-thee'-blay], *a.* Indemnifiable.

Resarcidor, ra [ray-sar-the-dor', rah], *m.* & *f.* Indemnifier.

Resarcimiento [ray-sar-the-me-en'-to], *m.* Compensation, reparation of damage, indemnity.

Resarcir [ray-sar-theer'], *va.* To compensate, to recompense, to reward, to make amends, to repair, to indemnify. *Resarcirse de lo perdido,* To make up one's loss.

Resbaladero [res-bah-lah-day'-ro], *m.* A slippery place or road; any thing dangerous.

Resbaladero, ra [res-bah-lah-day'-ro, rah], *a.* Applied to a slippery place or road.

Resbaladizo, za [res-bah-lah-dee'-tho, thah], *a.* 1. Slippery, glib. 2. *V.* RESBALADERO. 3. Exposed to temptation. *Memoria resbaladiza,* A treacherous memory.

Resbalador, ra [res-bah-lah-dor', rah], *m.* & *f.* Slider; backslider.

Resbaladura [res-bah-lah-doo'-rah], *f.* Slippery track; backsliding.

Resbalante [res-bah-lahn'-tay], *pa.* Slider; slipping.

Resbalar [res-bah-lar'], *vn.* & *vr.* 1. To slip, to slide; not to tread firm. 2. To fail in the performance of engagements.

Resbalo [res-bah'-lo], *m.* (Amer. Ec.) A very precipitous hill.

Resbalón [res-bah-lone'], *m.* 1. Slip, the act of slipping. 2. Slip, fault, error, offence. *De resbalón,* Erroneously; unsteadily.

Resbaloso, sa [res-bah-lo'-so, sah], *a.* Slippery. *V.* RESBALADIZO.

Rescaldar [res-cal-dar'], *va.* To heat, to scorch.

Rescatador, ra [res-cah-tah-dor', rah], *m.* & *f.* Redeemer, ransomer.

Rescatar [res-cah-tar'], *va.* 1. To ransom, to redeem, to extricate. 2. To exchange, to barter, to commute. 3. (Amer.) To buy ore in mines.

Rescate [res-cah'-tay], *m.* 1. Ransom, redemption by purchase. 2. Ransom-money paid for the redemption of slaves. 3. Exchange, permutation, barter.

Rescatín [res-cah-teen'], *m.* (Amer.) One who buys of Indians their small collections of ore.

Rescaza [res-cah'-thah], *f.* *V.* ESCORPINA.

Rescibir, *va.* (Obs.) *V.* RECIBIR.

Rescindente, *pa.* & *a.* Rescinding.

Rescindir [res-thin-deer'], *va.* To rescind, to annul.

Rescisión [res-the-se-on'], *f.* Rescission.

Rescisorio, ria [res-the-so'-re-o, ah], *a.* Rescissory.

Rescoldera [res-col-day'-rah], *f.* Pyrosis, heart-burn.

Rescoldo [res-col'-do], *m.* 1. Embers, hot ashes, cinders. 2. (Met.) Scruple, doubt, apprehension.

Rescontrar [res-con-trar'], *va.* To balance in accounts, to compensate.

Rescribir [res-cre-beer'], *va.* To rescribe, to write an answer to a letter.

Rescripto [res-creep'-to], *m.* Rescript order, mandate.

Rescriptorio, ria [res-crip-to'-re-o, ah], *a.* Belonging to a rescript.

(*Yo rescuentro, yo rescuentre,* from *Rescontrar.* *V.* ACORDAR.)

Rescuentro [res-coo-en'-tro], *m.* Balance of accounts, compensation.

Resecación [ray-say-cah-the-on'], *f.* Exsiccation.

Resecar [ray-say-car'], *va.* To dry again, to dry thoroughly.

Reseco, ca [ray-say'-co, cah], *a.* Too dry: very lean.

Reseco [ray-say'-co], *m.* Exsiccation of trees or shrubs; dry part of a honeycomb.

Reseda [ray-say'-dah], *f.* (Bot.) 1. Mignonette. Reseda. 2. Woad. *V.* GUALDA.

Resegar [ray-say-gar'], *va.* To reap again, to cut or mow a second time.

Resellante [ray-sel-lyahn'-tay], *pa.* Recoining, restamping.

Resellar [ray-sel-lyar'], *va.* 1. To recoin, to coin again. 2. To limp in one's ideas, so as to accept others less advanced.

Resello [ray-sayl'-lyo], *m.* Recoinage.

Resemblar [ray-sem-blar'], *va.* (Obs.) To resemble.

Resembrar [ray-sem-brar'], *va.* To resow.

Resentido, da [ray-sen-tee'-do, dah], *a.* Angry, resentful, displeased.—*pp.* of RESENTIRSE.

Resentimiento [ray-sen-te-me-en'-to], *m.* 1. Flaw, crack, cleft. 2. Resentment, grudge.

Resentirse [ray-sen-teer'-say], *vr.* 1. To begin to give way, to fail, to be out of order. 2. To resent, to express displeasure.

Reseña [ray-say'-nyah], *f.* 1. A distinguishing mark on the human or animal body. 2. Signal. 3. Description, succinct narration, or review of historical events. 4. (Mil.) Review of soldiers; muster.

Reseñar [ray-say-nyar'], *va.* 1. To summarize, to review, to outline 2. To review (troops), etc.

Resequido, da, *a.* *V.* RESECO.

Reserva [ray-serr'-vah], *f.* 1. Reserve, something kept in store. 2. Reserve, secret. 3. Discretion, caution. *A reserva de que,* Provided that. *Andar con reservas,* To proceed cautiously. *Llanta* or *neumático de reserva,* Spare tire.

Reservación [ray-ser-vah-the-on'], *f.* Reservation.

Reservadamente, *adv.* Secretly, reservedly.

Reservado, da [ray-ser-vah'-do, dah], *a.* & *pp.* of RESERVAR. Reserved, cautious, circumspect, close. *Caso reservado,* A great crime, which none but a superior can absolve. (Coll.) Confidential.

Reservado [ray-ser-vah'-do], *m.* The eucharist kept in the ciborium.

Reservar [ray-ser-var'], *va.* 1. To reserve, to keep in store. 2. To defer, to postpone. 3. To privilege, to exempt. 4. To separate, to set aside, to lay aside, to keep back. 5. To restrain, to limit, to confine, 6. To conceal, to hide; to shut up. 7. *V.* JUBILAR.—*vr.* 1. To preserve one's self. 2. To act with circumspection or caution.

Resfriado [res-fre-ah'-do], *m.* Cold, a disease caused by cold; the obstruction of perspiration.—*Resfriado, da, pp.* of RESFRIAR.

Resfriador [res-fre-ah-dor'], *m.* Refrigerator.

Resfriadura [res-fre-ah-doo'-rah], *f.* Cold in horses.

Resfriamiento [res-fre-ah-me-en'-to], *m.* Refrigeration. *V.* ENFRIAMIENTO.

Resfriar [res-fre-ar'], *va.* 1. To cool, to make cold. 2. To moderate ardour or fervour.—*vn.* To begin to be cold. —*vr.* 1. To catch cold. 2. To proceed with coolness, not to pursue a business with the activity it requires.

Resfriecer, *vn.* (Prov.) To begin to grow cold: applied to the weather.

Resfrío [res-free'-o], *m.* Cold. *V.* RESFRIADO.

Resguardar [res-goo-ar-dar'], *va.* To preserve, to defend; to protect, to harbour.—*vr.* To be guarded against, to be on one's guard.

Resguardo [res-goo-ar'-do], *m.* 1. Guard, preservation, security, safety. 2. Defence, shelter, protection. 3. Security for the performance of a contract or agreement. 4. Watchfulness to prevent smuggling. 5. Body of customhouse officers. 6. Preventive-service.

Residencia [ray-se-den'-the-ah], *f.* 1. Residence, mansion, lodging, home. 2. Residence, the time appointed for clergymen to reside at a benefice. 3. Account demanded of a person who holds a public station; instrument or account rendered. 4. Place and function of a resident at foreign courts. 5. Among the Jesuits, a house of residence not yet formed into a college.

Residencial [ray-se-den-the-ahl'], *a.* Residentiary.

Residenciar [ray-se-den-the-ar'], *va.* To call a public officer to account for his administration.

Residenciado, da [ray-se-den-the-ah'-do, dah], *a.* & *pp.* of RESIDENCIAR. Resident, residentiary.

Residente [ray-se-den'-tay], *pa.* & *a.* Residing or resident in a place, residentiary.

Residente [ray-se-den'-tay], *m.* Resident, a minister at foreign courts, of lower rank than a plenipotentiary.

Residentemente, *adv.* Constantly, assiduously.

Residir [ray-se-deer'], *vn.* 1. To reside, to dwell, to lodge. 2. To be present, to assist personally by reason of one's position. 3. To be lodged or inherent in, as a faculty or right.

Residuo [ray-see'-doo-o], *m.* 1. Residue, remainder. *Residuos de una mesa,* Leavings, fragm nts. 2. (Chem.) Residuum.

Resiembra [ray-se-em'-brah], *f.* Seed thrown on ground without letting it remain.

Resigna [ray-seeg'-nah], *f.* Resignation of a benefice.

Resignación [ray-sig-nah-the-on'], *f.* 1. Resignation, submission to the will of another; abnegation. 2. Resignation of a public place or employment.

Resignadamente, *adv.* Resignedly.

Resignante [ray-sig-nahn'-tay], *pa.* & *m.* Resigner; resigning.

Resignar [ray-sig-nar'], *va.* To resign, to give up, to yield up, to abrogate.—*vr.* To resign, to submit to the will of another.

Resignatorio [ray-sig-nah-to'-re-o], *m.* Resignee.

Resina [ray-see'-nah], *f.* Resin, rosin.

Resinero, ra [ray-se-nay'-ro, rah], *a.* Relating to resins. *Industria resinera.*

Resinífero, ra [ray-se-nee'-fay-ro, rah], *a.* Resin-bearing, resiniferous.

Resinita [ray-se-nee'-tah], *f.* Mineral resin, a stone looking like pitch.

Resinócero [ray-se-no'-thay-ro], *m.* A compound of rosin and wax; resin ointment.

Resinoso, sa [ray-se-no'-so, sah], *a.* Resinous.

Resisa [ray-see'-sah], *f.* The eighth part formerly taken as duty on wine, vinegar, or oil.

Resisar [ray-se-sar'], *va.* To diminish any measures or things which have already been taxed.

Resistencia [ray-sis-ten'-the-ah], *f.* Resistance, opposition, defence.

Resistente [ray-sis-ten'-tay], *pa.* Resisting, repelling.

Resistero [ray-sis-tay'-ro], *m.* 1. The hottest part of the day, from twelve to two o'clock in the summer season. 2. Heat produced by the reflection of the sun's rays and the place where it is perceived.

Resistible [ray-sis-tee'-blay], *a.* Resistible, endurable, supportable.

Resistidero [ray-sis-te-day'-ro], *m.* The hottest part of the day. *V.* RESISTERO.

Resistidor, ra [ray-sis-te-dor', rah], *m.* & *f.* Resister, opponent.

Resistir [ray-sis-teer'], *vn.* & *va.* 1. To resist, to oppose. 2. To contradict, to repel. 3. To endure, to tolerate. 4. To reject, to oppugn.—*vr.* To struggle, to contend.

Resma [res'-mah], *f.* Ream of paper; *i. e.* long ream of 500 sheets.

Resmilla [res-meel'-lyah], *f.* Parcel of one hundred sheets of letter-paper.

Resobado, da [ray-so-bah'-do, dah], *a.* Hackneyed, commonplace.

Resobrar [ray-so-brar'], *vn.* To be much over and above.

Resobrino, na [ray-so-bree'-no, nah], *m.* & *f.* Son or daughter of a nephew or niece.

Resol [ray-sole'], *m.* Reverberation of the sun's rays.

Resolana [ray-so-lah'-nah], *f.* (Prov.) *V.* RESOLANO.

Resolano [ray-so-lah'-no], *m.* Place sheltered from the wind for taking the sun.

Resolar [ray-so-lar'], *va.* To repave; to resole, as shoes.

Resoluble [ray-so-loo'-blay], *a.* Resolvable, resoluble.

Resolución [ray-so-loo-the-on'], *f.* 1. Resolution, deliberation; resoluteness. 2. Determination, courage, boldness, firmness. 3. Decision, solution of a doubt; conclusiveness; determination of a difference. 4. Easiness of address, freedom from constraint. *En resolución,* In short, in a word. 5. Dissolution; analysis or resolution. 6. Activity, promptitude; mind. 7. (Med.) Resolution, ordinary termination of an inflammation.

Resolutamente, *adv.* (Obs.) *V.* RESUELTAMENTE.

Resolutivamente, *adv.* Resolutely, determinately.

Resolutivo, va [ray-so-loo-tee'-vo, vah], *a.* 1. (Med.) Resolutive, having the power to dissolve: in this sense it is used as a substantive. 2. Analytical.

Resoluto, ta [ray-so-loo'-to, tah], *a.* & *pp. irr. obs,* of RESOLVER. 1. Resolute, bold, audacious. 2. Compendious, brief 3. Prompt, dexterous.

Resolutoriamente, *adv.* Resolutely.

Resolutorio, ria [ray-so-loo-to'-re-o, ah], *a.* Resolute, prompt.

Resolvente [ray-sol-ven'-tay], *pa.* & *a.* Resolvent, resolving.

Resolver [ray-sol-verr'], *va.* 1. To resolve, to determine, to decide. 2. To sum up, to reduce to a small compass. 3. To decide, to decree. 4. To solve a difficulty, to unriddle; to find out. 5. To dissolve, to analyze; to dissipate. 6. To undo, to destroy. 7. To divide a whole into its parts.—*vr.* 1. To resolve, to determine. 2. To be included or comprised.

Resolladero [ray-so-lyah-day'-ro], *m.* Vent, air-hole; breathing-hole.

Resollar [ray-sol-lyar'], *vn.* 1. To respire, to breathe audibly. 2. To talk; commonly used with a negative. *No resolló.* He did not utter a word. 3. To rest, to take breath. *Resollar por la herida,* (1) To expel air from the body, through a wound. (2) (Met.) To tell anything which shows a latent resentment.

Resonación [ray-so-nah-the-on′], *f.* Resounding, noise of repercussion.
Resonancia [ray-so-nahn′-the-ah], *f.* 1. Resonance, repercussion of sound. 2. (Poet.) Consonance, harmony.
Resonante [ray-so-nahn′-tay], *pa.* & *a.* Resonant, resounding.
Resonar [ray-so-nar′], *vn.* To resound, to be echoed back, to chink, to clatter.
Resoplar [ray-so-plar′], *vn.* 1. To breathe audibly and with force. 2. To snort, as a high-mettled horse or a bull.
Resoplido, Resoplo [ray-so-plee′-do], *m.* 1. A continued audible breathing; a continual blowing through the nose. 2. Snorting as of a horse or bull.
Resorber [ray-sor-berr′], *va.* To sip again, to reabsorb.
Resorte [ray-sor′-tay], *m.* 1. Spring, an elastic body; an elastic piece of tempered steel. 2. Cause, medium, means.
Respailar [res-pah-e-lar′], *va.* (Coll.) To show by gestures vexation over doing something.
Respaldar [res-pal-dar′], *m.* Leaning-stock. *V.* RESPALDO.
Respaldar, *va.* To indorse, as on the back of a writing.—*vr.* 1. To lean, as against a chair or bench. 2. To dislocate the backbone: applied to a horse.
Respaldo [res-pahl′-do], *m.* 1. Back or fore part of anything. 2. Indorsement. 3. Leaning-stock, back of a seat.
Respectivamente, Respective, *adv.* Respectively, proportionally.
Respectivo, va [res-pec-tee′-vo, vah], *a.* Respective, relative, comparative.
Respecto [res-pec′-to], *m.* Relation, proportion; relativeness; respect. *Respecto a* or *respecto de*, In consideration of.—*adv.* With respect to, with regard to. *Al respecto*, Relatively, respectively.
Respetable [res-pay-tah′-blay], *a.* Respectable, considerable.
Respetador, ra [res-pay-tah-dor′, rah], *m.* & *f.* Respector, venerator.
Respetar [res-pay-tar′], *va.* To respect, to venerate, to revere, to honour.
Respeto [res-pay′-to], *m.* Respect, regard, consideration, veneration; attention; observance. *Respeto de*, In respect to. *Respeto a* or *respeto de*, With regard to. *De respeto*, Preventively; for ceremony's sake. *Mastelero de respeto.* (Naut.) A spare top-mast. *Pertrechos de respeto del contramaestre*, (Naut.) The boatswain's spare stores. *Cabos de respeto*, Spare rigging. *Velas de respeto*, Spare sails.
Respetosamente, *adv.* Respectfully.
Respetuoso, sa [res-pay-too-oh′-so, sah], *a.* 1. Respectable. 2. Respectful, ceremonious; obsequious, dutiful.
Réspice [res′-pe-thay], *m.* 1. (Coll.) Short, brusque reply. 2. A short, but sharp reproof.
Respigador, ra [res-pe-gah-dor′, rah], *m.* & *f.* Gleaner.
Respigar [res-pe-gar′], *va.* To glean, as after reapers.
Respigón [res-pe-gone′], *m.* 1. Hang-nail. 2. Sore upon the fleshy part of the foot of horses.
Respingar [res-pin-gar], *vn.* 1. To kick, to wince. 2. To obey reluctantly.
Respingo [res-peen′-go], *m.* 1. Kick, jerk. 2. Reluctance, unwillingness, peevishness.
Respingoso, sa [res-pin-go′-so, sah], *a.* 1. Kicking, wincing; used of beasts. 2. Growing, tetchy.
Respirable [res-pe-rah′-blay], *a.* Respirable, capable of respiration.
Respiración [res-pe-rah-the-on′], *f.* Respiration, breathing; expiration; vent.
Respiradero [res-pe-rah-day′-ro], *m.* 1. Vent, breathing-hole. 2. (Arch.) Air-passage, femerell, louver. 3. Cupping-glass. 4. Rest, repose. 5. An organ of respiration.
Respirante [res-pe-rahn′-tay], *pa.* Respiring, breathing, exhaling.
Respirar [res-pe-rar′], *vn.* 1. To respire, to breathe. (Sometimes used as transitive.) 2. To rest, to respire, to take rest from toil. 3. To exhale scents or odors. 4. To speak: in this sense it is frequently used with a negative. *No respiró*, He did not open his lips. 5. To get breath. 6. To exhale; to animate. *Sin respirar*, Without drawing breath. *No tener por donde respirar*, (Coll.) To have no valid answer to a charge.
Respiratorio, ria [res-pe-rah-to′-re-o, ah], *a.* Respiratory, serving for breathing or related to it.
Respiro [res-pee′-ro], *m.* 1. Act of breathing. 2. Moment of rest. 3. (Met.) Longer time for making payment.
Resplandecencia [res-plan-day-then′-the-ah], *f.* Resplendency, splendor, lustre; fame, glory.
Resplandecer [res-plan-day-therr′], *vn.* 1. To emit rays of light. 2. To glitter, to glisten, to gleam, to glister, to be brilliant, to glow. 3. To shine, to outshine, to be eminent or conspicuous.
Resplandeciente [res-plan-day-the-en′-tay]; *pa.* & *a.* Resplendent, shining, glittering; luminous, light.
Resplandina [res-plan-dee′-nah], F. (Coll.) Sternness of countenance, sharp reproof.
Resplandor [res-plan-dor′], *m.* 1. Splendor, brightness, brilliancy, luminousness. 2. A kind of shining paint for women.
Responder [res-pon-derr′], *va.* & *vn.* 1. To answer; to resolve a doubt, to respond. 2. To re-echo. 3. To acknowledge, to own as a benefit received; to be grateful. 4. To yield, to produce. 5. To answer, to have the desired effect. 6. To correspond; to be situated; to answer to. 7. To show one's self pleased. á. To be, or to make one's self responsible for anything. 9. To reply to a letter.
Respondiente [res-pon-de-en′-tay], *pa.* & *a.* Respondent; answering.
Respondón, na [res-pon-done′, nah], *a.* Giving answers constantly; ever ready to reply.
Responsabilidad [res-pon-sah-be-le-dahd′], *f.* Responsibility, liability, accountableness.
Responsable [res-pon-sah′-blay], *a.* Responsible, liable, accountable, answerable.
Responsar, Responsear [res-pon-sar′], *vn.* To repeat the responses.
Responsión [res-pon-se-on′], *f.* Sum which the members of the Order of St. John, who enjoy an income, contribute to the treasury of the order.
Responsivo, va [res-pon-see′-vo, vah], *a.* (For.) Responsive, pertinent to the question, relevant in reply.
Responso [res-pon′-so], *m.* Responsary separate from the divine office for the dead.
Responsorio [res-pon-so′-re-o], *m.* Response.
Respuesta [res-poo-es′-tah], *f.* 1. Answer, reply; response. 2. Report of fire-arms. 3. Sound echoed back. 4. Refutation. *Respuesta aguda* or *picante*, Repartee.
Resquebradura, Resquebrajadura [res-kay-brah-ha-doo′-rah], *f.* Crack, cleft, flaw, split.
Resquebrajar [res-kay-brah-har′], *vn.* To crack, to split.
Resquebrajo [res-kay-brah′-ho], *m.* Crack, cleft.
Resquebrajoso, sa [res-kay-brah-ho′-so, sah], *a.* Brittle, fragile.
Resquebrar [res-kay-brar′], *vn.* To crack, to split, to begin to open; to burst.
Resquemar [res-kay-mar′], *va.* & *vn.* To burn or sting the tongue: applied to pungent food.
Resquemo [res-kay′-mo], *m.* **Resquemazón** [res-kay-mah-thone′], *f.* 1. Pungency of any food. 2. A disagreeable taste and odor which eatables acquire from being burned by too much fire.
Resquicio [res-kee′-the-o], *m.* 1. Chink between the jamb and leaf of a door; crack, cleft. 2. Subterfuge, evasion. 3. (Met.) Faint hope.
Resta [res′-tah], *f.* Rest, residue, remainder. *V.* RESTO.
Restablecer [res-tah-blay-therr′], *va.* To restore, to re-establish, to reinstate.—*vr.* To recover from a disease, to mend.
Restablecimiento [res-tah-blay-the-me-en′-to], *m.* Re-establishment, restoration, resettlement.
Restador [res-tah-dor′], *m.* (Arith.) Remainder.
Restallar [res-tal-lyar′], *vn.* 1. To crack, as a whip. 2. To crackle, to creak.
Restante [res-tahn′-tay], *pa.* & *m.* Remainder, residue; remaining.
Restañadura [res-tah-nyah-doo′-rah], *f.* The act of recovering with tin; retinning.
Restañar [res-tah-nyar′], *va.* 1. To retin, to cover with tin a second time. 2. To stanch, to stop blood. 3. *V.* RESTALLAR.—*vr.* To restagnate, to stand without flow.
Restaño [res-tah′-nyo], *m.* 1. Kind of glazed silk, interwoven with gold or silver. 2. *V.* ESTANCACIÓN.
Restar [res-tar′], *va.* 1. To subtract, to find the residue of any thing. 2. In tennis, to return a ball, to strike it back.—*vn.* To be left, to remain due.
Restauración [res-tah-oo-rah-the-on′], *f.* 1. Restoration, redintegration, restoring. 2. Restoration, liberty recovered by an oppressed or subjugated people.
Restaurador, ra [res-tah-oo-rah-dor′, rah], *m.* & *f.* Restorer.
Restaurante [res-tah-oo-rahn′-tay], *m.* 1. Restorer, re-establisher. 2. (Gallicism) Restaurant. *V.* FONDA.—*pa.* Restoring.
Restaurar [res-tah-oo-rar′], *va.* To restore, to retrieve; to repair, to renew.
Restaurativo, va [res-tah-oo-rah-tee′-vo, vah], *a.* Restorative.
Restinga [res-teen′-gah], *f.* Ridge of rocks in the sea; sand-bank.
Restingar [res-teen-gar′], *m.* Place containing ridges of rocks or sand banks.

Restitución [res-te-too-the-on'], *f.* Restitution, restoring.
Restituible [res-te-too-ee'-blay], *a.* That which may be restored.
Restituidor, ra [res-te-too-e-dor', rah], *m.* & *f.* Restorer, re-establisher.
Restituir [res-te-too-eer'], *vn.* 1. To restore, to give up, to give back, to lay down. 2. To re-establish. 3. To reanimate.—*vr.* To return to the place of departure.
Restitutivo, va [res-te-too-tee'-vo, vah], **Restitutorio, ria** [res-te-too-to'-re-o, ah], *a.* Relating to restitution.
Resto [res'-to], *m.* 1. Remainder, residue, balance, rest. 2. Sum staked at play. 3. Rebound of the ball in the game of tennis. *A resto abierto,* Un limitedly. 4. Arrest, attachment.
Restregar [res-tray-gar'], *va.* 1. To rub, to scrub. 2. (coll.) To rub it in, to rub sarcastically.
Restregón [res-tray-gone'], *m.* Scrubbing.
Restreñimiento, *m.* (Prov.) *V.* RESTRIÑIMIENTO.
Restreñir, *va.* (Obs.) *V.* RESTRIÑIR.
Restribar [res-tre-bar'], *vn.* To lean upon strongly.
Restricción [res-tric-the-on'], *f.* Restriction, limitation, modification.
Restrictivamente, *adv.* Restrictively.
Restrictivo, va [res-tric-tee -vo, vah], *a.* Restrictive, restringent.
Restricto, ta [res-treec'-to, tah], *a.* Limited, confined; restrictive.
Restringa [res-treen'-gah], *f.* *V.* RESTINGA.
Restringente [res-trin-hen'-tay], *m.* Restrainer; restringent.—*pa.* Restraining.
Restringible [res-trin-hee'-blay], *a.* Restrainable, limitable.
Restringir [res-trin-heer'], *va.* To restrain, to restrict, to restringe, to confine, to control, to constrain, to limit.
Restriñente [res-tre-nyen'-tay], *pa.* & *a.* Restringent; binding.
Restriñidor, ra [res-tre-nye-dor', rah], *m.* & *f.* Restrainer, binder.
Restriñimiento [res-tre-nye-me-en'-to], *m.* Restriction, making costive.
Restriñir [res-tre-nyeer'], *va.* To bind, to make costive, to restrain.
Restrojera [res-tro-hay'-rah], *f.* (Prov.) Female servent taken to attend reapers in harvest-time.
Restrojo [res-tro'-ho], *m.* *V.* RASTROJO.
Resucitado, da [ray-soo-the-tah'-do, dah], *a.* & *pp.* of RESUCITAR. *Pájaro resucitado,* Little humming-bird; it is dormant in winter, hence its name. Trochilus exilis.
Resucitador, ra [ray-soo-the-tah-dor', rah], *m.* & *f.* Restorer, reviver.
Resucitar [ray-soo-the-tar'], *va.* 1. To resuscitate, to revive. 2. To renew, to renovate, to modernize.—*vn.* 1. To revive, to return to life. 2. To recover from a dangerous disease.
Resucha [ray-soo'-chah], *f.* A worthless animal (cow, ox).
Resudación [ray-soo-dah-the-on'], *f.* Perspiration, transudation.
Resudar [ray-soo-dar'], *vn.* To transude, to perspire, to transpire.
Resudor [ray-soo-dor'], *m.* Slight perspiration.
Resuello [ray-soo-ay'-lyo], *m.* 1. Breath, breathing, respiration. 2. Pursiness, shortness of breath.
(*Yo resuello, yo resuelle,* from *Resollar.* *V.* ACORDAR.)
Resueltamente [ray-soo-el-tah-men'-tay], *adv.* Resolutely, resolvedly, confidently, boldly.
Resuelto, ta [ray-soo-el'-to, tah], *a* & *pp. irr.* of RESOLVER. 1. Resolute, audacious, bold, determined, steady, constant, confident. 2. Prompt, quick, diligent.
(*Yo resuelvo, yo resuelva,* from *Resolver.* *V.* MOVER.)
(*Yo resueno, yo resuene,* from *Resonar.* *V.* ACORDAR.)
Resulta [ray-sool'-tah], *f.* 1. Rebound, resilience. 2. Result, effect, consequence. 3. Vacancy, a post or employment unoccupied. 4. Success. *De resultas,* In consequence.
Resultado [ray-sool-tah'-do], *m.* Result, issue, consequence.—*Resultado, da, pp.* of RESULTAR.
Resultancia [ray-sool-tahn'-the-ah], *f.* Result, resultance.
Resultante [ray-sool-tahn'-tay], *pa.* Resulting, following, proceeding from.
Resultar [ray-sool-tar'], *vn.* 1. To rebound. 2. To result, as a consequence or effect, to follow; to proceed from. 3. To remain, to be done or provided for.
Resumbruno, na [ray-soom-broo'-no, nah], *a.* Brown, of the colour of a hawk's feathers, between red and black.
Resumen [ray-soo'-men], *m.* 1. Abridgment, summary, extract, compendium. 2. Recapitulation, detail repeated. 3. (Law) Brief. *En resumen,* Briefly, in short; lastly.
Resumidamente, *adv.* Briefly, compendiously, summarily.
Resumido, da [ray-soo-mee'-do, dah], *a.* & *pp.* of RESUMIR. Abridged. *En resumidas cuentas,* In short, briefly.
Resumir [ray-soo-meer'], *va.* 1. To abridge. 2. To reassume, to resume; to repeat, as the propounder of a thesis, the syllogism of an opponent. *Resumir corona,* (Law) To resume the clerical tonsure and habit. *V.* REASUMIR.—*vr.* To include; to convert.
Resunción [ray-soon-the-on'], *f.* 1. Summary, abridgment. 2. Repetition of several words inserted in a speech.
Resuntivo, va [ray-soon-tee'-vo, vah], *a.* That which restores or resumes.
Resupinado, da [ray-soo-pe-nah'-do, dah], *a.* (Bot.) Resupinate, inverted in position.
Resurgir, *vn.* (Obs.) *V.* RESUCITAR.
Resurrección [ray-soor-rec-the-on'], *f.* Resurrection, revival, resuscitation.
Resurtida [ray-soor-tee'-dah], *f.* Rebound, repercussion.
Resurtir [ray-soor-teer'], *vn.* To rebound, to fly back.
Resuscitar [ray-soos-the-tar'], *va.* (Obs.) *V.* RESUCITAR.
Retablo [ray-tah'-blo], *m.* 1. Picture drawn on a board. 2. Splendid ornament of altars. *Retablo de duelos,* Sight, spectacle of human miseries.
Retacar [ray-tah-car'], *va.* To hit the ball twice on a truck-table.
Retacería [ray-tah-thay-ree'-ah], *f.* Collection of remnants.
Retaco [ray-tah'-co], *m.* 1. A short, light fowling-piece. 2. A short tack or stick of a truck-table. 3. A short, thick person.
Retador [ray-tah-dor'], *m.* Challenger.
Retaguarda [ray-tah-goo-ar'-dah], *f.* (Obs.) *V.* RETAGUARDIA.
Retaguardia [ray-tah-goo-ar'-de-ah], *f.* Rear-guard. *Picar la retaguardia,* To pursue the rear-guard closely.
Retahila [ray-tah-ee'-lah], *f.* File, range, or series of many things following one another.
Retajar [ray-tah-har'], *va.* 1. To cut round. 2. To cut again and again the nib of a pen. 3. To circumcise.
Retal [ray-tahl'], *m.* Remnant of cloth or lace; clipping.
Retallar [ray-tal-lyar'], *vn.* To shoot or sprout anew.—*va.* To regrave, to retouch a graving. *V.* RETALLECER.
Retallecer [ray-tal-lyay-therr'], *vn.* To resprout, to put forth new shoots from the root-stock.
Retallo [ray-tah'-lyo], *m.* A new sprout of a plant sprung from the root-stock.
Retama [ray-tah'-mah], *f.* (Bot.) 1. Broom. Spartium. *Retama de flor blanca,* White single seed broom. Spartium monospermum. *Retama macho, común, de flor* or *de olor,* Spanish broom. Spartium junceum. *Retama blanca,* Spanish genista, furze, green-weed. Genista florida. *Retama de escobas,* Common broom. Spartium scoparium. 2. *Estar mascando* or *mascar retama,* (Met.) To be vexed at not obtaining a thing which is in the hands of another. (Arab.)
Retamal, Retamar [ray-tah-mahl'], *m.* **Retamera,** *f.* Place where furze or broom grows, and is gathered.
Retamilla [ray-tah-meel'-lyah], *f.* (Bot.) Jointed genista or furze. Genista sagittalis.
Retamón [ray-tah-mone'], *m.* (Bot.) 1. Purging broom. Spartium purgans. 2. *V.* RETAMA DE ESCOBAS.
Retapar [ray-tah-par'], *va.* To cover again.
Retar [ray-tar'], *va.* 1. To impeach or charge one with a criminal offence before the king. 2. To challenge to combat; to reprehend.
Retardación [ray-tar-dah-the-on'], *f.* Retardation, delay, detention, loitering.
Retardar [ray-tar-dar'], *va.* To retard, to defer, to delay, to obstruct.
Retardilla [ray-tar-deel'-lyah], *f.* A slight difference or dispute.
Retardo [ray-tar'-do], *m.* Cunctation, delay, procrastination, retardment.
Retasa [ray-tah'-sah], *f.* Second valuation or assessment.
Retasación [ray-tah-sah-the-on'], *f.* (Littl. us.) *V.* RETASA.
Retasar [ray-tah-sar'], *va.* To value or assess a second time.
Retazar [ray-tah-thar'], *va.* To tear in pieces.
Retazo [ray-tah'-tho], *m.* 1. Remaining piece, remnant; cuttings. 2. Fragment or portion of some discourse or reasoning.
Retejador [ray-tay-hah-dor'], *m.* & *a.* Repairer of a tile-roof; mending, reparative.
Retejar [ray-tay-har'], *va.* 1. To repair the roof of a building; to tile anew. 2. To mend, to patch; to risk.
Retejer [ray-tay-herr'], *va.* To weave closely.
Retejo [ray-tay'-ho], *m.* Repairing of a roof, retiling.
Retemblar [ray-tem-blar'], *vn.* To tremble or shake repeatedly: to vibrate.
Retemblor [ray-tem-blor'], *m.* A second vibration, repeated shaking.
Retén [ray-tayn'], *m.* 1. Store, stock, reserve. 2. Military reserve corps. 3. Detent, ratchet, catch.
Retención [ray-ten-the-on'], *f.* 1. Retention, keeping back. 2. Retention of an office which was held before advancing to another. 3. Suspension by the king of the use of any rescript proceeding from ecclesiastical authority. 4. Stagnation, retention within the body of an excretion which ought to be expelled.
Retenedor, ra [ray-tay-nay-dor', rah], *m.* & *f.* Retainer.
Retener [ray-tay-nerr'], *va.* 1. To retain, to withhold; to keep back from its owner. 2. To guard, to preserve. 3. To maintain and enjoy a position

after being advanced to another. 4. To suspend, as by a king, the use of an ecclesiastical rescript.

(*Yo retengo, yo retenga; él retuvo, retuviera;* from *Retener. V.* Tener.)

Retenida [ray-tay-nee'-dah], *f.* (Naut.) Guy. *Retenida de proa*, (Naut.) Headfast, a rope to fasten the head of a ship.

Retenidamente, *adv.* Retentively.

Retentar [ray-ten-tar'], *va.* To threaten with a relapse of a former disorder. *Está retentado de la gota*, He is threatened with another attack of gout.

Retentiva [ray-ten-tee'-vah], *f.* 1. Retentiveness. 2. Memory.

Retentivo, va [ray-ten-tee'-vo, vah], *a.* Retentive, retaining.

Retentriz [ray-ten-treeth'], *a.* (Med.) Retentive.

Reteñir [ray-tay-nyeer'], *va.* To dye over again, to tinge a second time.—*vn.* To tingle, to sound, to resound. *V.* Retiñir. *Reteñir las orejas*, To grate the ear with unpleasant sounds or speeches.

Retesamiento [ray-tay-sah-me-en'-to], *m.* Coagulation, hardness.

Retesarse [ray-tay-sar'-say], *vr.* To become hard, to be stiff, as teats with milk.

Reteso [ray-tay'-so], *m.* 1. Stiffness or distention of teats with milk. 2. *V.* Teso.

Reticencia [ray-te-then'-the-ah], *f.* Reticence, concealment by silence.

Reticulado, da [ray-te-coo-lah'-do, dah], *a.* *V.* Reticular.

Reticular [ray-te-coo-lar'], *a.* Reticular, resembling network.

(*Yo retiemblo, yo retiemble*, from *Retemblar. V.* Acrecentar.)

(*Yo retiento, yo retiente*, from *Retentar. V.* Acrecentar.)

Retículo [ray-tee'-coo-lo], *m.* 1. Network, reticular tissue: used generally of plant structure. 2. Cobweb micrometer of a telescope or microscope.

Retín [ray-teen'], *m.* *V.* Retintín.

Retina [ray-tee'-nah], *f.* Retina of the eye.

(*Yo retiño, yo retiña; él retiñó, retiñera;* from *Reteñir or Retiñir. V.* Pedir.)

Retinte [ray-teen'-tay], *m.* 1. Second dye given to any thing. 2. *V.* Retintín.

Retintín [ray-tin-teen'], *m.* 1. A tinkling sound; jingle; clink. 2. An affected tone of voice, usually satirical.

Retinto [ray-teen'-to], *a.* Dark, obscure, almost black.—*pp. irr.* of Reteñir.

Retiñir [ray-te-nyeer'], *vn.* To tinkle, to resound, to click.

Retiración [ray-te-rah-the-on'], *f.* (Typ.) Second form put in a press in order to print the back of a sheet.

Retirada [ray-te-rah'-dah], *f.* 1. (Mil.) Retreat. *Tocar retirada*, To sound a retreat. 2. Retreat, retirement, place of security. 3. Place of retirement, closet.

Retiradamente, *adv.* Secretly, retiredly.

Retirado, da [ray-te-rah'-do, dah], *a.* & *pp.* of Retirar. Retired, solitary, cloistered; close; remote, distant; retired, pensioned. *Hombre retirado*, A man fond of retirement. *Oficial retirado*, Half-pay officer.

Retiramiento [ray-te-rah-me-en'-to], *m.* Retirement. *V.* Retiro.

Retirar [ray-te-rar'], *va.* 1. To withdraw, to retire, to lay aside, to reserve, to hide away. 2. To repel, to force the enemy to retire or retreat. 3. To print the back of a sheet. 4. To revoke; to retreat.—*vr.* 1. To retire, to retreat, to cease to pursue; to recede, to go back. 2. To retire from intercourse with the world; to retire from trade. 3. To retire from a public station. 4. To retire from company. 5. To take refuge; to retire to one's house or department. 6. (Mil.) To raise a siege or blockade; to abandon a post. 7. To retire or retreat from danger.

Retiro [ray-tee'-ro], *m.* 1. Retreat, the act of retiring; recess; act of declining any business. 2. Retreat, retirement, place of retirement. 3. Concealedness, privacy, obscurity, retirement, private life.

Retirona [ray-te-ro'-nah], *f.* (Coll.) *V.* Retirada.

Reto [ray'-to], *m.* 1. Challenge to combat. 2. Threat, menace.

Retobado, da [ray-to-bah'-do, dah], *a.* (Peru. Met. and coll.) Artful, crafty.

Retobar [ray-to-bar'], *va.* (Amer. Com.) To cover parcels of goods with hides for transportation.

Retobo [ray-to'-bo], *m.* A covering of hides.

Retocamiento [ray-to-cah-me-en'-to], *m.* Action of retouching.

Retocar [ray-to-car'], *va.* 1. To retouch a painting, to mend. 2. To finish any work completely.

Retoñar, Retoñecer [ray-to-nyar', ray-to-nyay-therr'], *vn.* 1. To sprout or shoot again: applied to a plant which has been cut. 2. To appear again: applied to cutaneous distempers.

Retoño [ray-toh'-nyo], *m.* Sprout or shoot from a plant which has been cut above the neck of the root.

Retoque [ray-toh'-kay], *m.* 1. Repeated and frequent pulsation. 2. Finishing stroke, to render a work perfect. 3. Symptom, threatening, of some disease.

Retor, *m.* (Obs.) Rhetorician.

Retorcedura [ray-tor-thay-doo'-rah], *f.* Twisting, wreathing.

Retorcer [ray-tor-therr'], *va.* 1. To twist, to contort, to convolve. 2. To retort, to convince by returning an argument. 3. (Met.) To interpret perversely.

Retorcido [ray-tor-thee'-do], *m.* A kind of twisted sweetmeat.—*Retorcido, da, pp.* of Retorcer.

Retorcijo [ray-tor-thee'-ho], *m.* *V.* Retorcimiento.

Retorcimiento [ray-tor-the-me-en'-to], *m.* Twisting, wreathing, contortion.

Retórica [ray-to'-re-cah], *f.* Rhetoric. —*pl.* (Coll.) Sophistries or reasons not fitted to the case.

Retóricamente, *adv.* Rhetorically.

Retórico, ca [ray-toh'-re-co, cah], *a.* Rhetorical, oratorical.—*m.* Rhetorician, one who speaks with eloquence; one who teaches rhetoric.

Retornamiento [ray-tor-nah-me-en'-to], *m.* Return.

Retornante [ray-tor-nahn'-tay], *pa.* Returning.

Retornar [ray-tor-nar'], *vn.* To return, to come back; to retrocede or retrograde.—*va.* 1. To return, to restore, to give back. 2. To turn, to twist, to contort, to cause to go back.

Retornelo [ray-tor-nay'-lo], *m.* 1. Ritornello, the burden of a song. 2. (Poet.) The final strophe of a song.

Retorno [ray-tor'-no], *m.* 1. Return, coming back; return chaise or horse. 2. Repayment, return of a favour. 3. Barter, exchange, traffic.

Retorsión [ray-tor-se-on'], *f.* 1. Retortion, bending back. 2. Retortion, retorsion, act of replying sharply.

Retorsivo, va [ray-tor-see'-vo, vah], *a.* That which retorts.

Retorta [ray-tor'-tah], *f.* 1. Retort, a chemical vessel. 2. A sort of linen of medium fineness.

Retortero [ray-tor-tay'-ro], *m.* Twirl, rotation. *Andar al retortero*, To hover about. *Traer al retortero*, (1) (Coll.) To bring one from one side almost to the other. (2) (Met. and coll.) To keep one on the go (with peremptory occupations). (3) (Met. and coll.) To twist one around, to deceive with false promises and dissembled flatteries.

Retortijar [ray-tor-te-har'], *va.* To twist, to form into a ring. *V.* Ensortijar.

Retortijón [ray-tor-te-hone'], *m.* The act of twisting, contortion. *Retortijón de tripas*, Griping.

Retostado, da [ray-tos-tah'-do, dah], *a.* & *pp.* of Retostar. Brown-coloured.

Retostar [ray-tos-tar'], *va.* To toast again, to toast brown.

Retozador, ra [ray-to-thah-dor', rah], *m.* & *f.* Frisker, one not constant, a wanton.

Retozadura [ray-to-thah-doo'-rah], *f.* *V.* Retozo.

Retozar [ray-to-thar'], *vn.* 1. To frisk and skip about, to romp, to frolic, to dally with, to sport, to play. 2. To hoiden, to romp immodestly. 3. Of passions, to sport within us.—*va.* To tickle, to invite to laughter and merriment; to titillate amorously. *Retozar con el verde*, To revel, to feast merrily. *Retozar la risa*, To be moved to laughter.

Retozo [ray-to'-tho], *m.* Friskiness romping, wantonness, lascivious gaiety, frisk, a frolic, dalliance. *Retozo de la risa*, Suppressed laugh.

Retozón, na [ray-to-thone', nah], *a.* Wanton, rompish, frolicsome, playful, gamesome, coltish.

Retozona [ray-to-tho'-nah], *f.* Romp, a rude, noisy girl.

Retrabar [ray-trah-bar'], *va.* To revive a quarrel.

Retracción [ray-trac-the-on'], *f.* Retraction, drawing back.

Retractable [ray-trac-tah'-blay], *a.* Retractable, which may be or should be retracted or recanted.

Retractación [ray-trac-tah-the-on'], *f* Retractation, recantation.

Retractar [ray-trac-tar'], *va.* To retract.—*vr.* To go back from one's word.

Retráctil [ray-trahc'-teel], *a.* (Zool.) Retractile, hidden in repose.

Retractilidad [ray-trac-te-le-dahd'], *f.* Retractility.

Retracto [ray-trahc'-to], *m.* (Law) Retrieval, the act or right of retrieving or recovering a thing sold to another.

Retractor [ray-trac-tor'], *m.* Retractor, a surgical instrument for holding apart the edges of an incision.

Retraer [ray-trah-err'], *va.* 1. To reclaim, to dissuade. 2. To retrieve, to recover a thing sold.—*vr.* 1. To take refuge; to flee. 2. To withdraw from, to retire, to live a retired life. 3. In politics, to retire, to abandon all participation in public matters.

Retraído [ray-trah-ee'-do], *m.* 1. Fugitive, one who has taken sanctuary in a sacred place. 2. A lover of solitude.—*Retraído, da, pp.* of Retraer.

(*Yo retraigo, yo retraiga, retraje,* from *Retraer. V.* Traer.)

Retraimiento [ray-trah-e-me-en'-to], *m.* 1. Retreat, refuge, asylum. 2. Inner apartment or room. 3. Retirement from public political life.

Retranca [ray-trahn'-cah], *f.* 1. A kind of large crupper for mules and other beasts of burden. 2. (Amer.) Brake of a wagon or railway car.

Retranquear [ray-tran-kay-ar'], *va.* (Arch.) To model pillars.
Retranqueo [ray-tran-kay'-o], *m.* (Arch.) Position given to bodies outside of their square.
Retrasado, da [ray-trah-sah'-do, dah], *a.* Late, retarded. *Retrasado mental*, Moron, person mentally retarded.
Retrasar [ray-trah-sar'], *va.* To defer, to put off, to dally, to delay.—*vn.* To retrograde, to decline.
Retraso [ray-trah'-so], *m.* Delay, putting off.
Retratable [ray-trah-tah'-blay], *a.* Retractable, retractible.
Ratratación [ray-trah-tah-the-on'], *f.* Retractation, recantation.
Retratador, ra [ray-trah-tah-dor', rah], *m.* & *f.* Limner, portrait-painter.
Retratar [ray-trah-tar'], *va.* 1. To portray, to draw portraits, to limn. 2. To imitate, to copy. 3. To paint, to describe. 4. To photograph. 5. To retract, to gainsay, to disavow. 6. To retrieve, to get back a thing sold.—*vr.* To recant; see 5th def. (With these significations the spelling *retractar* is quite to be preferred.)
Retratillo [ray-trah-teel'-lyo], *m. dim.* A small portrait.
Retratista [ray-trah-tees'-tah], *m.* 1. Portrait-painter, limner. 2. (Amer.) Portrait photographer.
Retrato [ray-trah'-to], *m.* 1. Portrait, effigy. 2. Copy, resemblance, imitation. 3. Metrical description, poetical portrait. 4. (Law) *V.* RETRACTO.
Retrayente [ray-trah-yen'-tay], *pa.* & *m.* & *f.* Retracter, recanter; retrieving.
Retrechería [ray-tray-chay-ree'-ah], *f.* 1. Cunning or craft for eluding the confession of the truth or the fulfilment of what was offered. 2. (Coll.) Flattery, sycophancy.
Retrechero, ra [ray-tray-chay'-ro, rah], *a.* & *n.* (Coll.) 1. Flattering; a flatterer. 2. Dissimulating, concealing the truth; eluding the fulfilment of what was offered.
Retrepado, da [ray-tray-pah'-do, dah], *a.* Leaning backward in a natural or affected manner (implying pride); reclining (chair).
Retreparse [ray-tray-par'-say], *vr.* To lean back; to recline in a chair.
Retreta [ray-tray'-tah], *f.* (Mil.) Retreat or tattoo, the beat of a drum which calls soldiers to withdraw, or to their quarters for the night.
Retrete [ray-tray'-tay], *m.* 1. Closet, a small room for privacy. 2. Water-closet.
Retretico, illo, ito [ray-tray-tee'-co], *m. dim.* Little water-closet, close-stool.
Retribución [ray-tre-boo-the-on'], *f.* Retribution, recompense, reward; damage.
Retribuir [ray-tre-boo-eer'], *va.* (Obs.) To pay back, to recompense.
Retribuyente [ray-tre-boo-yen'-tay], *pa.* & *a.* Retributive, retributory; retributing.
Retroacción [ray-tro-ac-the-on'], *f.* Retroaction.
Retroactivo, va [ray-tro-ac-tee'-vo, vah], *a.* Retroactive: spoken of a law which is applied to past transactions.
Retrocarga [ray-tro-car'-gah], (used in the expression *De retrocarga*), Breech loading.
Retroceder [ray-tro-thay-derr'], *vn.* 1. To retrograde, to go backward, to retrocede, to fall back: to grow worse. 2. To recede from, to draw back from an opinion or judgment.
Retrocesión [ray-tro-thay-se-on'], *f.* Retrocession, returning or receding.
Retroceso [ray-tro-thay'-so], *m.* Retrocession.
Retrocohete [ray-tro-co-ay'-tay], *m.* (Aer.) Retro-rocket.
Retrogradación [ray-tro-grah-dah-the-on'], *f.* Retrogradation, retrogression.
Retrogradar [ray-tro-grah-dar'], *vn.* 1. To retrograde. 2. In politics, to incline to reaction, to oppose progress. *V.* RETROCEDER.
Retrógrado, da [ray-tro'-grah-do, dah], *a.* Retrograde.
Retronar [ray-tro-nar'], *vn.* To thunder again, to continue thundering after a storm is nearly over.
Retropilastra [ray-tro-pe-lahs'-trah], *f.* Pilaster behind a column.
Retropropulsión [ray-tro-pro-pool-se-on'], *f.* Jet propulsion.
Retrotracción [ray-tro-trac-the-on'], *f.* (Law) Antedating any thing.
Retrotraer [ray-tro-trah-err'], *va.* To apply to the present time what happened before.

(*Yo retrotraigo, yo retrotraiga, yo retrotraje*, from *Retrotraer.* *V.* TRAER.)

Retrovender [ray-tro-ven-derr'], *va.* (Law) To sell back to the first vender for the same price.
Retroversión [ray-tro-ver-se-on'], *f.* (Med.) Retroversion, backward displacement.
Retrovisión [ray-tro-ve-se-on'], *f.* Rear view. *Espejo de retrovisión*, Rear-view mirror.
Retrucar [ray-troo-car'], *vn.* To hit again, like a ball rebounding; in billiards, to kiss.
Retruco [ray-troo'-co], *m.* Repercussion of a ball (kiss).
Retruécano [ray-troo-ay'-cah-no], *m.* A pun, a quibble, a play upon words.
Retruque [ray-troo'-kay], *m.* 1. Betting, a higher wager on a card. 2. In billiards, a kiss.
Retuerto, ta [ray-too-err'-to, tah], *pp. irr.* of RETORCER. Retwisted.—*a.* Very bad, very sterile.

(*Yo retuerzo, yo retuerza*, from *Retorcer.* *V.* COCER.)

Retumbante [ray-toom-bahn'-tay], *pa.* & *a.* Resonant, pompous, sonorous, bombastic, ridiculously tumid.
Retumbar [ray-toom-bar'], *vn.* To resound, to make a great noise, to jingle, to clink.
Retumbo [ray-toom'-bo], *m.* Resonance, echo.
Retundir [ray-toon-deer'], *va.* 1. To equal or hew stones in a building. 2. (Met.) To repel, to discuss.
Reuma [ray'-oo-mah]. 1. *f.* Rheum, defluxion. 2. *m.* Rheumatism.
Reumático, ca [ray-oo-mah'-te-co, cah], *a.* Rheumatic.
Reumatismo [ray-oo-mah-tees'-mo], *m.* Rheumatism.
Reunión [ray-oo-ne-on'], *f.* 1. Meeting, conference. 2. Gathering. 3. Joining, reuniting. 4. Bringing together. *Reunión en la cima*, Summit conference.
Reunir [ray-oo-neer'], *va.* 1. To join, to reunite. 2. To bring together, to assemble.—*vr.* 1. To meet. 2. To gather.
Revacunar [ray-vah-coo-nar'], *va.* To revaccinate.
Reválida [ray-vah'-le-dah], *f.* 1. Passing one's final exams. 2. Final exams (for a degree).
Revalidar [ray-vah-le-dar'], *va.* To revalidate.—*vr.* To pass one's final exams (for a degree).
Revalorizar [ray-vah-lo-re-thar], *va.* To reevaluate.
Revancha [ray-vahn'-chah], *f.* 1. Compensation for loss in gaming; return match. (A Gallicism and should not be used.) 2. *V.* DESQUITE.
Revecero, ra [ray-vay-thay'-ro, rah], *a.* Changeable, mutable: applied to labouring cattle.
Reveedor [ray-vay-ay-dor'], *m.* *V.* REVISOR.
Revejecer [ray-vay-hay-therr'], *vn.* To grow prematurely old.
Revejecido, da [ray-vay-hay thee'-do, dah], *a.* & *pp.* of REVEJECER. Prematurely old, antiquated.
Revejido, da [ray-vay-hee'-do, dah], *a.* Become old prematurely.
Revelación [ray-vay-lah-the-on'], *f.* 1. Revelation, the act and effect of revealing. 2. Revelation from heaven; revealed religion.
Revelador, ra [ray-vay-la-dor', rah], *m.* & *f.* 1. Revealer. 2. Developer, in photography.
Revelamiento [ray-vay-lah-me-en'-to], *m.* 1. *V.* REVELACIÓN. 2. Photographic development.
Revelante [ray-vay-lahn'-tay], *pa.* Revealing.
Revelar [ray-vay-lar'], *va.* 1. To reveal, to manifest, to communicate, to disclose. 2. To impart from heaven, to show the future. 3. To develop a photographic plate.
Reveler [ray-vay-lerr'], *va.* (Med.) To make the humours flow in an opposite direction.
Revellín [ray-vel-lyeen'], *m.* (Mil.) Ravelin.
Revendedera, *f.* *V.* REVENDEDORA.
Revendedor [ray-ven-day-dor'], *m.* Retailer, hawker, huckster, peddler.
Revendedora [ray-ven-day-do'-rah], *f.* Huckstress, a female peddler.
Revender [ray-ven-derr'], *va.* To retail, to sell by retail; to peddle.

(*Yo me revengo, yo me revenga; él se revino, revendrá*; from *Revenirse.* *V.* VENIR.)

Revenirse [ray-vay-neer'-say], *vr.* 1. To be consumed by degrees. 2. To be pricked, to grow sour, to ferment: applied to wine and conserves. 3. To relinquish a preconceived opinion, to give up a point obstinately contested. 4. To discharge moisture.
Reventa [ray-ven'-tah], *f.* Retail; second sale.
Reventación [ray-ven-tah-the-on'], *m.* Disruption, rupture; vanishing in spray.
Reventadero [ray-ven-tah-day'-ro], *m.* 1. A rough, uneven ground, of difficult access. 2. Any painful and laborious work.
Reventar [ray-ven-tar'], *vn.* 1. To burst, to break in pieces, to crack; of waves, to break into foam. 2. To toil, to drudge. 3. To burst forth, to break loose; applied to a violent passion. 4. To sprout, to shoot; to grow. 5. To long for, to crave.—*va.* To molest, to harass, to violate. *Reventar de risa*, To burst into laughter, to suppress laughter. *A todo reventar*, At most, at the extreme. *Reventar la mina*, (Met.) To discover any thing hidden.
Reventazón [ray-ven-tah-thone'], *f.* 1. Disruption, rupture. 2. (Naut.) Breaker, the breaking of waves into foam.
Reventon [ray-ven-tone'], *m.* 1. Bursting or cracking. *Reventón de neumático* or *de llanta*, Tire blowout. 2. Great difficulty and distress. 3. Steep declivity. 4. Toil, drudgery, severe labor and fatigue.
Rever [ray-verr'], *va.* To review, to revise, to overlook, to resurvey.

Reverberación [ray-ver-bay-rah-the-on'], *f.* 1. Reverberation, the reflection of light. 2. Calcination in a reverberatory furnace.

Reverberar [ray-ver-bay-rar'], *vn.* To reverberate, to reflect upon a polished surface.

Reverbero [ray-ver-bay'-ro], *m.* 1. *V.* REVERBERACIÓN. 2. Reflector for the light of a light-house. 3. Reflector of polished glass or metal. *Horno de reverbero,* A reverberatory furnace, a smelting furnace.

Reverdecer [ray-ver-day-therr'], *vn.* 1. To grow green again: applied to fields and plants. 2. To sprout again, to acquire new vigour and strength.
(*Yo reverdezco, yo reverdezca,* from *Reverdecer. V.* CONOCER.)

Reverencia [ray-vay-ren'-the-ah], *f.* 1. Reverence, respect, veneration, homage, honour, observance. 2. Bow of reverence; obeisance. 3. Reverence, title given in Spain to members of religious orders.

Reverenciable [ray-vay-ren-the-ah'-blay], *a.* Reverend.

Reverenciador, ra [ray-vay-ren-the-ah-dor', rah], *m.* & *f.* Reverencer.

Reverencial [ray-vay-ren-the-ahl'], *a.* Reverential.

Reverencialmente, *adv.* Reverentially, reverently.

Reverenciar [ray-vay-ren-the-ar'], *va.* to venerate, to revere, to respect; to hallow; to reverence.

Reverendamente [ray-vay-ren-dah-men'-tay], *adv.* Respectfully, reverentially.

Reverendísimo, ma [ray-vay-ren-dee'-se-mo, mah], *a. sup.* Most reverend, right reverend.

Reverendo, da [ray-vay-ren'-do, dah], *a.* 1. Reverend, the honorary epithet of prelates and distinguished members of religious orders; worthy of reverence. 2. Extremely circumspect and cautious. *Reverendas,* Prelate's dimissory letters; qualities and titles worthy of reverence.

Reverente [ray-vay-ren'-tay], *a.* Respectful, reverent; low.

Reversar, *va.* (Obs.) *V.* REVESAR.

Reversible [ray-ver-see'-blay], *a.* (Law) Returnable, revertible.

Reversión [ray-ver-se-on'], *f.* Reversion, return.

Reverso [ray-verr'-so], *m.* 1. Reverse side of coins. 2. Back part of any thing.

Reverter [ray-ver-terr'], *vn.* To overflow. *V.* REBOSAR.

Revés [ray-ves'], *m.* 1. Back part, back side, wrong side. 2. Stroke with the back of the hand. 3. Disappointment, cross, misadventure. 4. Change of temper and disposition. 5. Reverse. *V.* REVERSO. *Revés del tajamar,* (Naut.) Hollow or flaring of the cutwater. *Reveses de la estela,* (Naut.) Eddy of the dead water. *De revés,* Diagonally, from left to right. *Al revés* or *del revés,* On the contrary, contrariwise (in slang, Over the left). *Revés de la medalla,* (Met.) Diametrically opposite in character, genius, and disposition. *Al revés me las calcé,* I understood (or did) the reverse. *Al revés me la vestí, ándese así,* As I began this way, I shall go on so. (Reproof for wrong conduct.)

Revesado, da [ray-vay-sah'-do, dah], *a.* 1. Intractable, stubborn, obstinate. 2. Difficult, entangled, perplexed, obscure.—*pp.* of REVESAR.

Revesar [ray-vay-sar'], *va.* To vomit.

Revesino [ray-vay-see'-no], *m.* Reversis, a game at cards. *Cortar el revesino,* To interrupt, to impede.

Revestimiento [ray-ves-te-me-en'-to], *m.* Revestment, a coating or covering of a surface for strengthening or beautifying it.

Revestir [ray-ves-teer'], *va.* 1. To dress, to put on clerical robes, to revest. 2. To repair or fortify a wall; to lime; to crust.—*vr.* 1. To be swayed or carried along by some power or other; to be invested with. 2. To be haughty, lofty, or elated with pride.

Revezar [ray-vay-thar'], *vn.* To alternate, to come in by turn, to relieve one after another, to work in rotation.

Revezero [ray-vay-thay'-ro], *m.* One who alternates.

Revezo [ray-vay'-tho], *m.* Alternacy, the act of relieving one another; reciprocal succession.

Revidar [ray-ve-dar'], *va.* (Prov.) To reinvite.

Reviejo, ja [ray-ve-ay'-ho, hah], *a.* Very old.—*m.* Withered branch of a tree.
(*Yo reviento, yo reviente,* from *Reventar. V.* ACRECENTAR.)

Reviernes [ray-ve-err'-nes], *m.* Each of the first seven Fridays after Easter.
(*Yo revierto, yo revierta,* from *Reverter. V.* ATENDER.)

Revindicar [ray-vin-de-car'], *va.* To claim.

Revirado, da [ray-ve-rah'-do, dah], *a.* (Bot.) Twisted: applied to fibers of trees.

Revirar [ray-ve-rar'], *va.* (Naut.) To veer again, to tack again.

Reviro [ray-vee'-ro], *m.* (Naut.) Canting or flaring, the curvature given to a timber in a ship.

Revirón [ray-ve-rone'], *m.* Piece of sole leather put between the sole-pieces to make them even.

Revisar [ray-ve-sar'], *va.* To revise, to review, to examine. *Revisar las cuentas,* To audit accounts.

Revisión [ray-ve-se-on'], *f.* Revision, reviewing.

Revisita [ray-ve-see'-tah], *f.* Revision, second examination.

Revisor [ray-ve-sor'], *m.* Reviser, censor, corrector, reviewer.

Revisoria [ray-ve-so-ree'-ah], *f.* Office of censor or reviser.

Revista [ray-vees'-tah], *f.* 1. Review, revision. 2. (Mil.) Review (of troops). 3. Magazine, review, publication. *Revista musical,* Musical comedy, musical review.

Revistar [ray-vis-tar'], *va.* To revise a suit at law, to try a cause a second time; to review troops.
(*Yo revisto, yo revista; él revistió, él revistiera;* from *Revestir. V.* PEDIR.)

Revisto, ta [ray-vees'-to, tah], *pp. irr.* of REVER.

Revite [ray-vee'-tay], *m.* Invitation to play in games.

Revividero [ray-ve-ve-day'-ro], *m.* Place for rearing silk-worms.

Revivificar [ray-ve-ve-fe-car'], *va.* To revivificate, to vivify.

Revivir [ray-ve-veer'], *vn.* To revive, to return to life, to acquire new life; to resuscitate.

Revocable [ray-vo-cah'-blay], *a.* Revocable, reversible.

Revocablemente, *adv.* In a revocable manner.

Revocación [ray-vo-cah-the-on'], *f.* Revocation; abrogation; act of recalling. *Revocación de una sentencia,* (Law) Reversal.

Revocador, ra [ray-vo-cah-dor', rah], *m.* & *f.* 1. One who revokes, abrogates, or recalls. 2. Plasterer, whitewasher.

Revocadura [ray-vo-cah-doo'-rah], *f.* 1. *V.* REVOQUE. 2. (Pict.) Painted borders of canvas.

Revocante [ray-vo-cahn'-tay], *pa.* Revoker, recalling, abrogating.

Revocar [ray-vo-car'], *va.* 1. To revoke, to repeal, to annul, to abrogate, to abolish; to countermand. (Law) To reverse. 2. To dissuade from, to induce one to desist. 3. To plaster, to whitewash, or to freshen paintings. 4. To yield to an impulse, to retrocede. 5. To recall, to call one from one place to another.

Revocatorio, ria [ray-vo-cah-to'-re-o, ah], *a.* That which revokes or annuls; reversal.

Revoco [ray-vo'-co], *m.* 1. Plaster, whitewash. *V.* REVOQUE. 2. Cover of broom or furze laid on charcoal baskets.

Revolar [ray-vo-lar'], *vn.* To fly again, to take a second flight. *V.* REVOLOTEAR.

Revolcadero [ray-vol-cah-day'-ro], *m.* A weltering or wallowing place for wild boars and other beasts.

Revolcadura [ray-vol-cah-doo'-rah], *f.* Action of wallowing.

Revolcar [ray-vol-car'], *va.* 1. To knock down, to tread upon. 2. To overcome, to outshine in a controversy. —*vr.* 1. To wallow in mire or any thing filthy. 2. To be obstinately bent upon an idea or design.

Revolcón [ray-vol-cone'], *m.* (Coll.) *V.* REVUELCO.

Revolear [ray-vo-lay-ar'], *vn.* To flutter, to take short flights; to fly precipitately.

Revolotear [ray-vo-lo-tay-ar'], *vn.* To flutter, to fly round about, to hover.

Revoloteo [ray-vo-lo-tay'-o], *m.* Fluttering; a short flight; a quick motion with the wings.

Revoltijo [ray-vol-tee'-ho], *m.* *V.* REVOLTILLO.

Revoltillo [ray-vol-teel'-lyo], *m.* 1. Parcel of things jumbled together. 2. Tripes of a sheep. 3. Medley, confusion, disorder; mash; jumble. 4. Fricassee.

Revoltón [ray-vol-tone'], *m.* Vine-fretter, vine-grub. (Used also adjectively.)

Revoltoso, sa [ray-vol-toh'-so, sah], *a.* Turbulent, seditious.

Revoltura [ray-vol-too'-rah], *f.* (Mex.), A mixture of fluxes added to silver ore.

Revolución [ray-vo-loo-the-on'], *f.* 1. Revolution, the act of revolving. 2. Revolution of a planet. 3. Revolution, change in the state of a government; disturbance, sedition, commotion.

Revolucionador, ra [ray-vo-loo-the-o-nah-dor', rah], *n.* & *a.* Revolutionist; revolutionary.

Revolucionar [ray-vo-loo-the-o-nar'], *va.* To disturb or agitate a country, to produce a revolution.—*vr.* To rise or break into a commotion: it is a neologism.

Revolucionario, ria [ray-vo-loo-the-o-nah'-re-o, ah], *a.* Revolutionary.—*m.* & *f.* Revolutionist, revolutioner, socialist.

Revolvedero [ray-vol-vay-day'-ro], *m.* Coursing-place.

Revolvedor, ra [ray-vol-vay-dor', rah], *m.* & *f.* Revolter, disturber; a turbulent, seditious, or rebellious person.

Revólver [ray-vol'-ver], *m.* Revolver, a pistol containing five or more revolving chambers. (English.)

Revolver [ray-vol-verr'], *va.* 1. To move a thing up and down; to stir, to shift; to return; to revert; to retrace or go back again. 2. To revolve; to wrap up; to convolve. 3. To stir up disturbances, to excite commotions. *Revolver caldos,* (Coll.) To excite disturbances and disputes anew. 4. To revolve in the mind, to hesitate. 5. To face an enemy in order to attack him. 6. To evolve, to separate. 7. To turn short swiftly: applied to horses.—*vr.* 1. To move to and fro. 2. To change, as the weather.

Revolvimiento [ray-vol-ve-me-en'-to], *m.* Commotion, perturbation, revolution.

Revoque [ray-vo'-kay], *m.* 1. Act of whitewashing. 2. Plaster, whitewash, rough-cast laid on houses or walls.

Revotarse [ray-vo-tar'-say], *vr.* To vote contrary to a previous vote; to reconsider a ballot.

Revuelco [ray-voo-el'-co], *m.* Wallowing, rolling.

(*Yo revuelco, yo revuelque,* from *Revolcar.* V. Acordar.)

Revuelo [ray-voo-ay'-lo], *m.* 1. Flying to and fro of a bird. 2. Irregular motion; disturbance. *De revuelo,* By the way, speedily, promptly.

(*Yo revuelo, yo revuele,* from *Revolar.* V. Acordar.)

Revuelta [ray-voo-el'-tah], *f.* 1. Second turn, return. 2. Revolution, revolt, sedition; contention, dissension. 3. Delay, tardiness. 4. Meditation, reflection. 5. Commutation, change. 6. Point from which a thing commences a tortuous or oblique direction. *A revuelta,* Conjointly.

Revuelto, ta [ray-voo-ell'-to, tah], *a.* & *pp. irr.* of revolver. 1. Mixed up, in a turmoil, in confusion. 2. Perverse, dissatisfied. *Huevos revueltos,* Scrambled eggs.

Revulsión [ray-vool-se-on'], *f.* Revulsion of humours.

Revulsivo, va, Revulsorio, ria [ray-vool-see'-vo, vah], *a.* Revulsory, revulsive.

Rey [ray'-e], *m.* 1. King. 2. Swine-herd. *Rey en el nombre,* Nominal king. *Rey de armas,* (Her.) The king at arms. *Los reyes,* Epiphany; twelfth-night. *Dios guarde al rey,* God save the king. 3. A Spanish dance. 4. Queen-bee; chief among animals. 5. King in cards or chess. *Rey de bastos* or *de copas,* (1) King of clubs or hearts. (2) A wooden king, a king without authority. *Rey de banda,* Partridge which leads the covey. *Rey de codornices,* Large quail which guides others in their flight. *Allá van leyes do quieren reyes,* The laws of kings are their own wills.

Reyecico, illo, ito [ray-yay-thee'-co], *m. dim.* A petty king, the king of a small kingdom.

Reyerta [ray-yerr'-tah], *f.* Dispute, difference, quarrel.

Reyertar [ray-yer-tar'], *va.* (Obs.) To dispute, to contend.

Reyezuelo [ray-yay-thoo-ay'-lo], *m.* 1. A petty king. 2. (Orn.) Kinglet. Motacilla regulus, *L.*

Rezadero, ra [ray-thah-day'-ro, rah], *a.* Praying often.

Rezado [ray-thah'-do], *m.* Prayer, divine service. *V.* Rezo.—*Rezado, da, pp.* of Rezar.

Rezador, ra [ray-thah-dor', rah], *m.* & *f.* One who prays often.

Rezaga [ray-thah'-gah], *f.* (Obs.) Rear-guard. *V.* Retaguardia.

Rezagado [ray-thah-gah'-do], *m.* Straggler, one who is left behind on a march; tramp, one too indolent to work.

Rezagante [ray-thah-gahn'-tay], *pa.* Delayer; leaving behind.

Rezagar [ray-thah-gar'], *va.* 1. To leave behind; to outstrip; more commonly reflexive. 2. To suspend action, to put off, to defer.

Rezago [ray-thah'-go], *m.* Remainder, residue.

Rezar [ray-thar'], *va.* 1. To pray, to say or read prayers. 2. To quote, to recite. 3. (Vulg.) To announce, to say in writing. *El calendario reza agua,* The almanac announces rain. —*vn.* To growl, to mutter. *Bien reza, pero mal ofrece,* Large promise, but small performance. *Rezar con* (*uno*), To belong to, to be incumbent upon, or in the knowledge of (some one).

Rezelar, *va.* **Rezelo,** *m.* (and derivatives). *V.* Recelar, Recelo.

Rezno [reth'-no], *m.* 1. Tick, sheep-tick, dog-tick. 2. *V.* Ricino.

Rezo [ray'-tho], *m.* 1. Prayer, the act of praying. 2. Divine office, formulary of devotion.

Rezón [ray-thone'], *m.* (Naut.) Grappling.

Rezongador, ra [ray-thon-gah-dor', rah], *m.* & *f.* Grumbler, growler, mutterer.

Rezongar [ray-thon-gar'], *vn.* To grumble, to mutter, to murmur, to growl.

Rezonglón, na, Rezongón, na [ray-thon-glohn', nah], *a.* & *n.* Grumbler; grumbling.

Rezumadero [ray-thoo-mah-day'-ro], *m.* Dripping-place; dripping.

Rezumarse [ray-thoo-mar'-say], *vr.* 1. To ooze, to flow by stealth; to run gently, to leak. 2. To transpire, to escape from secrecy to notice.

Rezura [ray-thoo'-rah], *f.* (Obs.) Fastness, stronghold. *V.* Reciura.

Rho [ro], *f.* Rho (ρ), seventeenth letter of the Greek alphabet, corresponding to *r.*

Ría [ree'-ah], *f.* Mouth of a river.

Riachuelo, Riatillo [re-ah-choo-ay'-lo, re-ah-teel'-lyo], *m.* Rivulet, streamlet; small river.

Riada [re-ah'-dah], *f.* Freshet, overflow, flood.

Riba [ree'-bah], *f.* (Prov.) Bank between a higher and lower field.

Ribadoquín [re-bah-do-keen'], *m.* Small gun now disused.

Ribaldería [re-bal-day-ree'-ah], *f.* Ribaldry; wickedness; coarse abuse.

Ribaldo, da [re-bahl'-do, dah], *a.* & *n.* Ribaldous; ribald; wicked, obscene. *V.* Rufián.

Ribazo [re-bah'-tho], *m.* A sloping bank; mound, hillock.

Ribecillo [re-bay-theel'-lyo], *m.* Narrow silk or worsted galloon.

Ribera [re-bay'-rah], *f.* Shore of the sea, bank of a river; strand, verge of any water. *Ser de monte y ribera,* To be fit for everything.

Ribereño, ña [re-bay-ray'-nyo, nyah], *a.* Belonging to the sea-shore or bank of a river.

Riberiego, ga [re-bay-re-ay'-go, gah], *a.* Grazing on the banks of rivers: applied to such flocks as are not removed to other sheep-walks, or are not *trashumantes,* as opposed to *estantes.*—*m.* Grazier of sheep on the banks of rivers.

Ribero [re-bay'-ro], *m.* Bank or parapet of a dam of water.

Ribes [ree'-bes], *f.* (Bot.) Currant-bush. Ribes.

Ribete [re-bay'-tay], *m.* 1. Ribbon or tape sewed to the edge of cloth; seam, border, fringe; binding. 2. Cantle, the small quantity given above the precise measure or weight. 3. Additions to a tale, for embellishment.

Ribetear [re-bay-tay-ar'], *va.* To hem.

Riboflavina [re-bo-flah-vee'-nah], *f.* Riboflavin.

Ricacho, cha [re-cah'-cho, chah, *a.* (Coll.) Very rich.

Ricadueña [re-cah-doo-ay'-nyah], *f.* Lady, daughter or wife of a noble.

Ricafembra, Ricahembra [re-cah-fem'-brah], *f.* Lady, daughter or wife of a noble.

Ricahombría [re-cah-om-bree'-ah], *f.* Dignity of the *ricos hombres,* ancient nobility of Castile.

Ricamente, *adv.* 1. Richly, opulently. 2. Excellently, splendidly.

Ricazo, za [re-cah'-tho, thah], *a. aug.* Very rich, opulent.

Ricial [re-the-ahl'], *a.* Growing again: applied to the after-crop of corn, cut green for the feed of cattle.

Ricino [re-thee'-no], *m.* (Bot.) Palma-Christi, the castor-oil plant. Ricinus communis.

Rico, ca [ree'-co, cah], *a.* 1. Noble, of an ancient and illustrious family. 2. Rich, wealthy, opulent. 3. Pleasing to the taste, delicious. 4. Choice, select; able.

Ricohombre, Ricohome [re-co-om'-bray, re-co-o'-may], *m.* Grandee, a peer of the first rank in Spain; a nobleman of the ancient nobility of Castile.

Rictus [reek'-toos], *m.* Rictus, gaping of the mouth, grimace, grin.

Ridiculamente, *adv.* Ridiculously, contemptibly.

Ridiculez [re-de-coo-leth'], *f.* 1. A ridiculous speech or action. 2. Ridicule, folly, extravagance, oddity, eccentricity. 3. Extreme nicety or sensibility.

Ridiculizar [re-de-coo-le-thar'], *va.* To ridicule, to burlesque, to laugh at.

Ridículo, la [re-dee'-coo-lo, lah], *a.* 1. Ridiculous, odd, eccentric, laughable, ludicrous. 2. Strange, contemptible; despicable; absurd. 3. Excessively nice and sentimental.

Ridículo, *m.* 1. Ridicule, mockery. 2. Hand-bag, reticule.

Ridiculoso, sa [re-de-coo-lo'-so, sah], *a.* Ridiculous, extravagant.

Riego [re-ay'-go], *m.* Irrigation.

(*Yo riego, yo riegue,* from *Regar. V.* Acrecentar.)

Riel [re-el'], *m.* 1. A small ingot of unrefined gold or silver; lingot. 2. Rail of a railway whether for locomotives or for street use. In this sense it is also spelled *rail,* as in English.

Rielado, da [re-ay-lah'-do, dah], *a.* Reduced to ingots: applied to gold or silver.

Rielar [re-ay-lar'], *vn.* (Poet.) 1. To glisten, to be reflected upon the waters: used of moonlight. 2. To shine with a tremulous light.

Rielera [re-ay-lay'-rah], *f.* Mould in which ingots of gold or silver are cast.

Rienda [re-en'-dah], *f.* 1. Rein of a bridle. 2. Moderation, restraint in speech and action.—*pl.* 1. (Met.) Government, direction. 2. Reins of the leading horse. *A rienda suelta,* Loose-reined, violently, swiftly. *Soltar la rienda,* To give way to vices or passions. *Tener las riendas,* To hold the reins, to hold back a horse. *Tirar las riendas,* To draw back, to restrain.

Riente [re-en'-tay], *pa.* Smiling, laughing.

Riesgo [re-es'-go], *m.* Danger, risk, hazard, peril, jeopardy.

Riesgoso, sa [re-es-go'-so, sah], *a.* Risky.

Rieto [re-ay'-to], *m.* (Obs.) *V.* Reto.

Rifa [ree'-fah], *f.* 1. Scuffle, dispute, contest. 2. Raffle, a species of game or lottery.

Rifador [re-fah-dor'], *m.* Raffler; disputer.

Rifadura [re-fah-doo'-rah], *f.* (Naut.) Act of splitting a sail.

Rifar [re-far'], *va.* 1. To raffle, to cast dice for a prize. 2. (Naut.) To split a sail, in a storm.—*vn.* To quarrel, to dispute.

Rifirrafe [re-fir-rah'-fay], *m.* (Coll.) A short quarrel, hasty words.

Rigidamente [ree'-he-dah-men-tay], *adv.* Rigidly.

Rigidez [re-he-deth'], *f.* Rigidity, asperity.

Rigido, da [ree'-he-do, dah], *a.* Rigid, rigorous, severe, inflexible, harsh.

Rigodón [re-go-done'], *m.* Rigadoon, a country dance.

Rigor [re-gor'], *m.* 1. Rigour, a convulsive shuddering with a sense of cold. 2. Rigidity of the nerves. 3. Rigour, sternness, severity, harshness of temper. 4. Rigour, strictness, rigid exactness, precision. 5. Power, intensity, keenness, hardness, vehemence. 6. Cruelty or excess of chastisement. 7. The last push or extremity. *A todo rigor*, If the worst comes to the worst. *En rigor*, At most.

Rigorismo [re-go-rees'-mo], *m.* Rigorousness, severity.

Rigorista [re-go-rees'-tah], *a.* & *com.* Applied to one very rigid, severe, or inflexible in moral opinions.

Rigorosamente, Rigurosamente [re-go-ro-sah-men'-tay], *adv.* Rigorously; severely, scrupulously.

Riguridad [re-goo-re-dahd'], *f.* (Obs.) Rigour, severity. *V.* Rigor.

Riguroso, sa [re-goo-ro'-so, sah], *a.* Rigorous, strict, austere, rigid, severe, harsh; scrupulously nice.

Rija [ree'-hah], *f.* 1. A kind of lachrymal fistula. 2. Quarrel, scuffle, dispute (2 fr. Lat. rixa).

Rijador, ra [re-hah-dor', rah], *a.* Quarrelsome, litigious.

Rijente [re-hen'-tay] *a.* Rough, cruel, horrid.

Rijo [ree'-ho], *m.* Concupiscence, lust, sensuality.

(*Yo rijo, yo rija; él rigió, él rigiera;* from *Regir. V.* Pedir.)

Rijoso, sa [re-ho'-so, sah], *a.* 1. Quarrelsome. 2. Restless at the sight of the female: applied especially to horses.

Rima [ree'-mah], *f.* 1. Rhyme, complete or incomplete, known as assonance. 2. Arrangement of things in a regular series.

Rimado, da [re-mah'-do, dah], *a.* & *pp.* of Rimar. Versified.

Rimar [re-mar'], *va.* & *vn.* 1. To inquire after, to investigate. 2. To rhyme, to make verses.

Rimbombante [rim-bom-bahn'-tay], *pa.* Resounding.

Rimbombar [rim-bom-bar'], *vn.* To resound, to echo.

Rimbombe, Rimbombo [rim-bom'-bay], *m.* Repercussion of sound.

Rimero [re-may'-ro], *m.* Collection of things placed regularly one over another, a pile.

Rincón [rin-cone'], *m.* 1. Inside corner, an angle formed by the meeting of two walls; a coin. 2. Place of privacy, a lurking-place. 3. House, dwelling. 4. Small district or country. *Cf.* Esquina.

Rinconada [rin-co-nah'-dah], *f.* Corner, formed by two houses, streets, or roads.

Rinconcillo [rin-con-theel'-lyo], *m. dim.* A small corner.

Rinconera [rin-co-nay'-rah], *f.* Small triangular table in a corner.

Rinconero, ra [rin-co-nay'-ro, rah], *a.* Transverse, athwart: applied to honey-combs.

(*Yo rindo, yo rinda; él rindió, rindiera:* from *Rendir. V.* Pedir.)

Ringle [reen'-glay], *m.* **Ringla** [reen'-glah], *f. V.* Ringlera.

Ringlera [rin-glay'-rah], *f.* (Coll.) Row, file.

Ringlero [rin-glay'-ro], *m.* Line drawn with a pencil, for writing straight.

Ringorango [rin-go-rahn'-go], *m.* (Coll.) 1. Flourish with a pen. 2. Extravagant nicety in dress.

Rinoceronte [re-no-thay-ron'-tay], *m* Rhinoceros.

Rinoscopia [re-nos-co'-pe-ah], *f.* (Med.) Rhinoscopy, examination of the nasal cavities.

Riña [ree'-nyah], *f.* Quarrel, scuffle, dispute, fray.

(*Yo riño, yo riña; él riñó, riñera;* from *Reñir. V.* Pedir.)

Riñón [ree-nyohn'], *m.* 1. Kidney. *Tener cubierto el riñón*, To be rich. 2. Central point of a country.

Riñonada [ree-nyo-nah'-dah], *f.* 1. Coat of fat about the kidneys. 2. Dish of kidneys.

Rio [ree'-o], *m.* 1. River, stream. 2. Any large quantity of fluids. *A río revuelto*, In confusion or disorder. *Río de lágrimas*, Flood of tears.

(*Yo río, él rió, él riera, yo ría*, from *Reir. V.* Reir.)

Riolada [re-o-lah'-dah], *f.* The assemblage of many things at one time.

Riostra [re-os'-trah], *f.* Post placed obliquely to strengthen an upright post, spur, strut.

Riostrar [re-os-trar'], *va.* To strengthen by means of oblique posts.

Ripia [ree'-pe-ah], *f.* Shingle, for roofing houses.

Ripiar [re-pe-ar'], *va.* To fill up the chinks of a wall with small stones and mortar.

Ripio [ree'-pe-o], *m.* 1. Remainder, residue, rubble. 2. Word used to fill up a verse. *No perder ripio*, Not to miss the least occasion.

Riponce [re-pon'-thay], *m.* (Bot.) *V.* Rapónchigo.

Riqueza [re-kay'-thah], *f.* 1. Riches, wealth, opulence. 2. Fertility, fruitfulness. 3. Ornament, embellishment.

Risa [ree'-sah], *f.* 1. Laugh, laughter. 2. Cause or object of laughter; pleasing emotion. 3. Derisory smile or laugh. *Risa sardónica*, (1) (Med.) Sardonic laugh. (2) (Met.) Sneer. *Caerse de risa*, To shake with laughter. *Comerse de risa*, To suppress a desire to laugh (through respect). *Descalzarse de risa*, To laugh boisterously. *Descoyuntarse* or *desternillarse de risa*, To laugh excessively. *La risa del conejo*, A hysterical laugh. *Tentado a*, or *de, la risa*, (1) Prone to laugh immoderately. (2) Amorous, lascivious.

Risada [re-sah'-dah], *f.* Horse-laugh; immoderate laughter.

Risco [rees'-co], *m.* A steep rock, crag.

Riscoso, sa [ris-co'-so, sah], *a.* Steep and rocky.

Risdala [ris-dah'-lah], *f.* **Risdale** [ris-dah'-lay], *m.* Rixdollar. (Obs.)

Risibilidad [re-se-be-le-dahd'], *f.* Risibility.

Risible [re-see'-blay], *a.* Risible, laughable, ludicrous.

Risica, ita [re-see'-cah, ee'-tah], *f. dim.* 1. Feigned laugh. 2. Smile.

Risotada [re-so-tah'-dah], *f.* Loud laugh, horse-laugh.

Rispido, da [rees'-pe-do, dah], *a. V.* Aspero.

Ristra [rees'-trah], *f.* 1. String of onions or garlic. 2. Row, file, series of things.

Ristre [rees'-tray], *m.* Rest or socket for a lance, used to couch the lance in the posture of attack.

Risueño, ña [re-soo-ay'-nyo, nyah], *a.* Smiling; pleasing, agreeable.

¡Rita! [ree'-tah], *f.* Word used by shepherds in speaking to one creature among their flocks.

Ritmico, ca [reet'-me-co, cah], *a.* Rhythmical.

Ritmo [reet'-mo], *m.* Rhyme, rhythm. *V.* Rima.

Rito [ree'-to], *m.* Rite, ceremony.

Ritual [re-too-ahl'], *m.* Ritual, a book of religious rites and observances; ceremonial.—*a.* Ritual, according to some religious institution.

Rival [re-vahl'], *m.* Rival, competitor.

Rivalidad [re-vah-le-dahd'], *f.* 1. Rivalry. 2. Competition, emulation.

Rivalizar [re-vah-le-thar'], *va.* To corrival, to vie with.

Rivera [re-vay'-rah], *f.* (Prov.) Brook, river, stream.

Riza [ree'-thah], *f.* 1. Green stubble of grain cut for food. 2. Desolation, ravage, destruction.

Rizado [re-thah'-do], *m.* Fluting, crimp, frizzle.

Rizagra [re-thah'-grah], *f.* An instrument for extracting the roots of teeth.

Rizador [re-thah-dor'], *m.* 1. Curling-iron, for the hair. 2. Hair-dresser, frizzler.

Rizal [re-thahl'], *a. V.* Ricial.

Rizar [re-thar'], *va.* 1. To curl hair. 2. To crimple crape with a crimping-iron; to plait.

Rizo, za [ree'-tho, thah], *a.* Naturally curled or frizzled.

Rizo [ree'-tho], *m.* 1. Curling or frizzling the hair; curl, frizzle, ringlet; crimpling of cloth. 2. Cut velvet. *Rizos*, (Naut.) Points, used to reef the courses and top-sails of a ship. *Coger rizos*, (Naut.) To take in reefs.

Ro, *int.* Word used to lull children.

Roa [ro'-ah], *f.* (Naut.) Stem. *V.* Roda.

Roán [ro-ahn'], *m.* A sort of linen manufactured in Rouen.

Roano, na [ro-ah'-no, nah], *a.* Sorrel, roan: applied to a horse.

Rob, *m.* Rob, the inspissated juice of ripe fruit, mixed with honey or sugar to the consistency of a conserve; fruit-jelly.

Roba, *f.* (Prov.) *V.* Arroba.

Robada [ro-bah'-dah], *f.* (Prov.) Space of ground of 400 square yards in extent.

Robado, da [ro-bah'-do, dah], *a.* & *pp.* of Robar. Robbed; naked, without ornament.

Robador, ra [ro-bah-dor', rah], *m.* & *f.* Robber.

Robaliza [ro-bah-lee'-thah], *f.* Kind of fish, perch.

Róbalo [ro'-bah-lo], *m.* Robalo, labrax; a fish like bream. (Gr. λάβραξ.)

Robamiento [ro-bah-me-en'-to], *m. V.* Arrobamiento.

Robar [ro-bar'], *va.* 1. To rob, to plunder, to steal. 2. To abduct, to carry off a woman. 3. To sweep away part of its banks: applied to a river. 4. To overcharge, to overreach in the sale of goods. 5. To gain another's affections, to ingratiate one's self. 6. To diminish the colour, to weaken or lower the colouring. 7. With bee-masters, to take the bees from a divided hive and put them into an empty one, by removing the honey-comb.

Robda [rob'-dah], *f.* Kind of ancient tribute.

Robezo [ro-bay'-tho], *m.* A wild-goat. *V.* Bicerra.

Robín [ro-been'], *m.* Rust of metal.

Robinia [ro-bee'-ne-ah], *f.* The locust tree. Robinia pseudacacia.

Robladero, ra [ro-blah-day'-ro, rah], *a.* Clinched; recurvate, recurvous.
Robladura [ro-blah-doo'-rah], *f.* Riveting, clinching.
Roblar [ro-blar'], *va.* 1. To strengthen, to make strong. 2. To clinch a nail, to rivet.
Roble [ro'-blay], *m.* 1. (Bot.) Oak-tree. Quercus robur. 2. *Roble blanco,* Tecoma pentophylla. *Roble guayo,* Cretia bourreria. (Met.) Any thing very strong and hard.
Roblecillo, ito [ro-blay-theel'-lyo], *m. dim.* A small oak-tree.
Robleda [ro-blay'-dah], *f.* Oak-grove.
Robledal, Robledo [ro-blay-dahl', ro-blay'-do], *m.* Plantation of oak-trees, oak-grove.
Roblizo, za [ro-blee'-tho, thah], *a.* Oaken, strong, hard.
Roblón [ro-blone'], *m.* A rivet.
Robo [ro'-bo], *m.* 1. Robbery, theft; the thing robbed or stolen. 2. (Prov. Navarre) Measure of grain of about half a bushel; 28 litres.
Roboración [ro-bo-rah-the-on'], *f.* Corroboration, strengthening.
Roborante [ro-bo-rahn'-tay], *pa.* & *a.* Corroborant: applied to strengthening medicines; corroborating.
Roborar [ro-bo-rar'], *va.* To confirm, to corroborate, to give strength.
Roborativo, va [ro-bo-rah-tee'-vo, vah], *a.* Corroborative.
Robot [ro'-bot], *m.* Robot.
Robra [ro'-brah], *f.* 1. (Obs.) Cocket, docket, permit. 2. *V.* ALBOROQUE.
Robradura [ro-brah-doo'-rah], *f.* Clinching, riveting.
Robrecillo, ito, *m. dim.* *V.* ROBLECILLO.
Robredo [ro-bray'-do], *m.* *V.* ROBLEDAL.
Robustamente, *adv.* Robustly.
Robustez [ro-boos-teth'], *f.* Robustness, hardiness, lustiness, force.
Robusto, ta [ro-boos'-to, tah], *a.* Strong, robust, vigorous, hale.
Roca [ro'-cah], *f.* 1. Rock, precipice; vein or bed of hard stone. 2. Cliff, rocky height on land or in the sea. 3. (Geol.) Rock, a simple or compound mineral mass, which, by its extent, forms an important part of the earth's crust. 4. Any thing very firm and hard.
Rocada [ro-cah'-dah], *f.* Portion of wool or flax for the distaff.
Rocadero [ro-cah-day'-ro], *m.* 1. Knob or head of a distaff. 2. Piece of paper formed like a cone, and put round the flax or wool on a distaff. 3. Rock of a distaff or spinning-wheel.
Rocador [ro-cah-dor'], *m.* Head of a rock or distaff.
Rocalla [ro-cahl'-lyah], *f.* 1. Drift of pebbles washed together by floods or torrents; talus of rocks. 2. Chippings of stone made in working it. 3. Flint glass, of which beads and rosaries are made.
Roce [ro'-thay], *m.* 1. Friction, frication, rub, attrition. 2. Familiarity, frequent conversation.
Rociada [ro-the-ah'-dah], *f.* 1. The act of sprinkling or irrigating gently; aspersion; a sprinkling. 2. (Naut.) Spray. 3. Drops of dew on plants; herbs with dew on them, given to animals as medicine. 4. Shower of stones or balls; scattering. 5. Slander, aspersion. 6. Roughness, asperity used with a person in discharging him.
Rociadera [ro-the-ah-day'-rah], *f.* *V.* REGADERA.
Rociado, da, *a.* Dewy; bedewed.—*pp.* of ROCIAR.
Rociador [ro-the-ah-dor'], *m.* Sprinkler. *Rociador de aire,* Airbrush.
Rociadura [ro-the-ah-doo'-rah], *f.* (Littl. us.) Aspersion, sprinkling.
Rociamiento [ro-the-ah-me-en'-to], *m.* Sprinkling or bedewing.
Rociar [ro-the-ar'], *vn.* To be bedewed or sprinkled with dew; to fall in dew. —*va.* 1. To sprinkle with wine, water, or other fluids. 2. To strew about. 3. To slander several persons at the same time.
Rocín [ro-theen'], *m.* 1. Hack, jade, working horse; a horse of little value. *Rocín y manzanas,* Resolution of performing any thing even at peril and loss. 2. A heavy, ignorant clown. *Ir de rocín a ruín,* To go from bad to worse. *Allá va Sancho con su rocín,* There go the inseparables.
Rocinal [ro-the-nahl'], *a.* Belonging to a hack horse.
Rocinante [ro-the-nahn'-tay], *m.* *V.* ROCÍN: applied to a miserable hack.
Rocinazo [ro-the-nah'-tho], *m. aug.* 1. A large hack. 2. A very ignorant person.
Rocinillo [ro-the-neel'-lyo], *m. dim.* A very small hack.
Rocío [ro-thee'-o], *m.* 1. Dew. 2. Slight shower of rain; sprinkling. 3. Divine inspiration; holy thoughts. *Rocío de la mar,* (Naut.) Spoon-drift, the foam of the sea in a storm.
Rocoso, sa [ro-co'-so, sah], *a.* Rocky, craggy.
Rocna [ro -chah], *f.* *V.* ROZA, 2d def.
Rochelés, sa [ro-chay-lays', sah], *a.* Of Rochelle.
Rocho [ro'-cho], *m.* Roc, a fabulous bird of extraordinary size and strength. (Arab.)
Roda [ro'-dah], *f.* 1. (Naut.) Stem. 2. Duty or impost on sheep-flocks.
Rodaballo [ro-dah-bahl'-lyo], *m.* Turbot, flounder. Pleuronectes maximus.
Rodada [ro-dah'-dah], *f.* Rut, the track of a wheel.
Rodadero, ra [ro-dah-day'-ro, rah], *a.* Rolling or wheeling easily.
Rodadizo, za [ro-dah-dee'-tho, thah], *a.* Easily rolled round.
Rodado, da [ro-dah'-do, dah], *a.* 1. Dapple, dappled, roan: applied to horses. 2. *V.* PRIVILEGIO. 3. Round, fluent: applied to sentences. *Venir rodado,* To attain an object accidentally.—*pp.* of RODAR.
Rodado [ro-dah'-do], *m.* (Min.) *V.* SUELTO.
Rodador [ro-dah-dor'], *m.* 1. Roller, any thing that rolls or falls rolling down. 2. Vagabond, vagrant. 3. A kind of mosquito.
Rodadura [ro-dah-doo'-rah], *f.* 1. Rolling, the act of rolling. 2. Rut, the track of a wheel.
Rodaja [ro-dah'-hah], *f.* 1. A small wheel. 2. Rowel of a spur. 3. Jagging-iron used by pastry-cooks; bookbinder's tool.
Rodaje [ro-dah'-hay], *m.* Wheel-works, as of a watch.
Rodajilla [ro-dah-heel'-lyah], *f. dim.* A very small wheel or circular body.
Rodal [ro-dahl'], *m.* Place, spot, seat.
Rodante [ro-dahn'-tay], *pa.* Rolling.
Rodapelo [ro-dah-pay'-lo], *m.* Rubbing against the grain. *V.* REDOPELO.
Rodapié [ro-dah-pe-ay'], *m.* 1. Fringe of silk or other stuff round the feet of a bedstead, table, or balcony, to hide the feet. 2. The stained or painted lower part of white-washed walls, about a foot from the ground, a socle. 3. A board or low shutter put on balconies.
Rodaplancha [ro-dah-plahn'-chah], *f.* The main ward of a key.
Rodar [ro-dar'], *vn.* 1. To roll, to revolve on an axis. 2. To roll, to run on wheels. 3. To roll, to move along on the surface; to roll down a hill. 4. *V.* RODEAR. 5. To abound, to be in great plenty. 6. To wander about in vain in quest of business; to be tossed about; to go about, to go up and down. 7. To lose an employ, station, dignity, or esteem. 8. To happen accidentally.—*va.* To drive, to impel, to give an impulse.
Rodeabrazo (A) [ro-day-ah-brah'-tho], *adv.* Drawing the arm to throw any thing with it.
Rodeado, da [ro-day-ah'-do, dah], *a.* & *pp.* of RODEAR. Surrounded. *Rodeado de negocios,* Overwhelmed with business.
Rodeador, ra [ro-day-ah-dor', rah], *m.* & *f.* Roller, wrapper.
Rodear [ro-day-ar'], *vn.* 1. To go round a place or object; to encompass. 2. To go a round-about way, to come about. 3. To make use of circumlocutions; to use circuitous language or indirect expressions.—*va.* 1. To wrap up, to put one thing around another; to circle, to compass, to girdle. 2. To whirl about. 3. To dispose, to arrange.
Rodela [ro-day'-lah], *f.* Shield, a round buckler or target.
Rodelero [ro-day-lay'-ro], *m.* Soldier armed with a shield or target.
Rodenal [ro-day-nahl'], *m.* A clump of rodeno pines.
Rodeno [ro-day'-no], *m.* A kind of pine.
Rodeno, na [ro-day'-no, nah], *a.* Red: applied to earths, rocks, and pines.
Rodeo [ro-day'-o], *m.* 1. Circumition, the act of going round; a circuitous way or road; turn to elude another. 2. Place in a fair or market where horned cattle are exposed to sale. 3. Delay, protraction, tedious method. 4. Evasion, subterfuge. 5. (Coll. Mex.) Inclosing cattle for the purpose of counting and marking them.
Rodeón [ro-day-on'], *m.* A complete rolling or winding round.
Rodera [ro-day'-rah], *f.* Rut, cart track.
Rodero, ra [ro-day'-ro, rah], *a.* Relating to wheels.
Rodero [ro-day'-ro], *m.* Collector of the duty on sheep.
Rodete [ro-day'-tay], *m.* 1. A small wooden wheel for moving a mill-wheel. 2. Bolster, a horizontal circle at the fore axle-tree of a carriage for turning it. 3. A kind of ward in a lock. 4. A rowel of platted hair which women tie on the top of their heads for ornament. 5. A kind of pad or bolster put on the head of women, to carry vessels with greater ease, or for ornament. 6. Border round the sleeves of gowns.
Rodezno [ro-deth'-no], *m.* 1. A large wheel, consisting of many pieces. 2. A toothed wheel in grist-mills.
Ródico, ca [ro'-de-co, cah], *a.* Relating to rhodium.
Rodilla [ro-deel'-lyah], *f.* 1. The knee. 2. Shoulder in a lock to fit the ward of a key. *V.* RODETE, 3d def. 3. Clout, dusting cloth; cloth for cleaning. *De rodillas,* On one's knees. *Doblar las rodillas,* To bend the knees; to kneel down. *Rodillas.* (Naut.) Knees of ship-timber. *Rodilla de bomba,* The pump-box.
Rodillada [ro-dil-lyah'-dah], *f.* Push with the knee; a kneeling position.
Rodillazo [ro-dil-lyah'-tho], *m.* Push with the knee.
Rodillera [ro-dil-lyay'-rah], *f.* 1. Any thing put for comfort or protection over the knees. 2. Patch, or re-enforcing piece, added to the knees of

trousers or drawers; knee-cap. 3. A hurt upon the knees of horses from kneeling. 4. Bulging of pantaloons over the knee.

Rodillero, ra [ro-dil-lyay'-ro, rah], *a.* Belonging to the knees.

Rodillo [ro-deel'-lyo], *m.*. 1. Roller, a cylinder of wood for moving heavy things. 2. Roller or rolling-stone, to level walks or roads. 3. Roller for distributing printing ink; brass roller, used to form plate-glass. *De rodillo* or *a rodillo*, Striking another ball in play. 4. Rolling-pin used by pastry-cooks.

Rodilludo, da [ro-dil-lyoo'-do, dah], *a.* Having large knees.

Rodio [roh'-de-o], *m.* Rhodium, a metal.

Rodio, dia, Rodiota [roh'-de-o, ah, ro-de-o'-tah], *a.* Rhodian, belonging to Rhodes or its inhabitants.

Rododafne [ro-do-dahf'-nay], *f.* (Bot.) Rose-bay, daphne. (Gr.)

Rododendro [ro-do-den'-dro], *m.* Rhododendron, a shrub of the heath family.

Rodomiel [ro-do-me-el'], *m.* The juice of roses mixed with honey.

Rodrigar [ro-dre-gar'], *va.* To prop up vines.

Rodrigazón [ro-dre-gah-thone'], *f.* Time for putting props to vines.

Rodrigón [ro-dre-gone'], *m.* 1. Stay or prop for vines. 2. (Coll.) Page or servant who waits upon women.

Roedero [ro-ay-day'-ro], *m.* Place frequently gnawed.

Roedor, ra [ro-ay-dor', rah], *m.* & *f.* Gnawer; detractor. *Gusano roedor*, A gnawing worm; remorse.

Roedores, *m. pl.* (Zool.) The rodents.

Roedura [ro-ay-doo'-rah], *f.* 1. Gnawing, corroding. 2. The part gnawed off and the mark left behind.

Roel [ro-el'], *m.* (Her.) Bezant, a roundel or upon a shield.

Roela [ro-ay'-lah], *f.* Round piece of crude silver or gold.

Roer [ro-err'], *va.* 1. To gnaw, to corrode; to consume by degrees; to destroy gradually. 2. To molest, to harass. *Roer el anzuelo*, To free one's self from peril. 3. To gnaw bones.

Roete [ro-ay'-tay], *m.* A medicinal wine prepared from pomegranates.

Rofianear, *vn.* (Obs.) *V.* Rufianear.

Roga [ro'-gah], *f.* (Ent.) An ichneumon-fly of the family braconidæ.

Rogación [ro-gah-the-on'], *f.* Request, petition, supplication.—*pl.* Rogation.

Rogador, ra [ro-gah-dor', rah], *m.* & *f.* Supplicant, petitioner.

Rogar [ro-gar'], *va.* 1. To implore, to entreat; to crave, to court; to obtest. 2. To pray, to say prayers.

Rogativa [ro-gah-tee'-vah], *f.* Supplication, prayer.

Rogativo, va [ro-gah-tee'-vo, vah], *a.* Supplicatory.

Rogatorio, ria [ro-gah-toh're-o, re-ah], *a.* Rogatory, pertaining to investigation.

Rogo [ro'-go], *m.* (Poet.) Fire, funeral pyre.

Roido [ro-ee'-do], *a.* & *pp.* of Roer. 1. Gnawed, corroded. 2. Penurious, despicable.—*m.* (Obs.) *V.* Ruido.

Rojeante [ro-hay-an'-tay], *pa.* Rubific, rubifying.

Rojear [ro-hay-ar'], *vn.* To redden, to be ruddy; to blush.

Rojete [ro-hay'-tay], *m.* Rouge for the face.

Rojez, Rojeza [ro-heth'], *f.* Redness.

Rojizo, za [ro-hee'-tho, thah], *a.* Reddish.

Rojo, ja [roh'-ho, hah], *a.* 1. Red, ruby. 2. Ruddy, reddish, of a high gold colour.

Rojura [ro-hoo'-rah], *f.* Redness.

Rol, *m.* 1. List, roll, catalogue. 2. Muster-roll of a merchant ship.

Roldana [rol-dah'-nah], *f.* (Naut.) Sheave, pulley-wheel.

Rolde [rol'-day], *m.* Circle formed by persons or things.

Roleo [ro-lay'-o], *m.* Volute. *V.* Voluta.

Rolla [rol'-lyah], *f.* Collar of a draught-horse.

Rollar [rol-lyar'], *va.* *V.* Arrollar.

Rollete [rol-lyay'-tay], *m. dim.* A small roll.

Rollizo, za [rol-lyee'-tho, thah], *a.* Plump, round, robust, strapping.

Rollo [rol'-lyo], *m.* 1. A roll, any thing of a cylindrical form; roll of cloth; rouleau. 2. *V.* Rolla. 3. A column of stone, an insignia of jurisdiction. 4. Gallows erected in a cylindrical form. 5. Acts or records rolled up, that they may be carried with greater ease. 6. Long round stone. *Enviar* or *irse al rollo*, To pack one off.

Rollón [rol-lyone'], *m.* *V.* Acemite.

Rollona [rol-lyo'-nah], *a.* (Coll.) Fat, plump, and robust: applied to a short, lusty woman.

Romadizarse [ro-mah-de-thar'-say], *vr.* *V.* Arromadizarse.

Romadizo [ro-mah-dee'-tho], *m.* Nasal catarrh; cold in the head.

Romaico, ca [ro-mah'-e-co, cah], *a.* & *n.* Romaic, belonging to modern Greece.

Romana [ro-mah'-nah], *f.* Steelyard, a balance or lever. *La barra de la romana*, Beam of the steelyard. *El pitón de la romana*, Dropball of the steelyard. *Hacer romana*, To balance, to equipoise. *Venir a la romana*, To be of just weight.

Romanador [ro-mah-nah-dor'], *m.* Weighmaster in a slaughter-house.

Romanar [ro-mah-nar'], *va.* To weigh with a steelyard.

Romance [ro-mahn'-thay], *m.* 1. The common or vernacular Spanish language, as derived from the Roman or Latin. 2. Romance, a species of poetry; a tale of wild adventures in war or love, a ballad. *Hablar en romance*, To speak out, to speak plainly. —*pl.* (Coll.) Wiles, stratagems, deceitful tricks.

Romancear [ro-man-thay-ar'], *va.* 1. To translate into Spanish or into the vulgar language. 2. (Gram.) To periphrase, to express by circumlocution.

Romancero, ra [ro-man-thay'-ro, rah], *a.* 1. Singing or composing romances or ballads. 2. Using evasions and subterfuges.

Romancero [ro-man-thay'-ro], *m.* 1. Collection of romances or ballads; legendary tales. 2. Romancer.

Romancesco [ro-man-thes'-co], *a.* Proper to a novel or romance; novelistic, romantic.

Romancista [ro-man-thees'-tah], *m.* Author who writes in the vulgar or native language, on subjects generally discussed in the Latin tongue.—*a.* A surgeon who did not study Latin; (a charlatan).

Romancito [ro-man-thee'-to], *m. dim.* A short romance.

Romanear [ro-mah-nay-ar'], *va.* To weigh with a steelyard.—*vn.* To outweigh, to preponderate.

Romaneo [ro-mah-nay'-o], *m.* Weighing with a steelyard.

Romanero, *m.* *V.* Romanador.

Romanesco [ro-mah-nes'-co], *a.* 1. Roman, belonging to the Roman arts and customs. 2. *V.* Romancesco.

Romania (De), *adv.* Crestfallen.

Románico [ro-mah'-ne-co], *a.* Romanic, Romanesque (in architecture).

Romanilla, ita [ro-mah-neel'-lyah], *f. dim.* A small steelyard.

Romanista [ro-mah-nees'-tah], *a.* & *n.* Romanist, versed in Roman law or Romance philology.

Romanticismo [ro-man-te-thees'-mo], *m.* 1. The spirit of Christian civilization in literature, as contrasted with that of Greco-Roman paganism. 2. Romanticism, romantic literary style as opposed to the classic.

Romántico, ca [ro-mahn'-te-co, cah], *a.* 1. Not bound by the literary rules of classic authors. 2. Romantic, proper to novels. 3. Romantic, sentimental in excess.

Romanizar [ro-mah-ne-thar'], *va.* (Littl. us.) To Romanize, to follow the manners, customs, and fashions of Rome.

Romano, na [ro-mah'-no, nah], *a.* 1. Roman, relating to Rome. 2. Tabby, variegated with gray and black: applied to a cat. 3. (Typ.) A type of about great primer size, 16-point. Bourgeois or 9-point. *A la Romana*, In the Roman fashion.

Romanza [ro-mahn'-thah], *f.* (Music) Romance, romanza, a simple rhythmical melody.

Romanzado, da [ro-man-thah'-do, dah], *a.* Turned or translated into Spanish. —*pp.* of Romanzar.

Romanzar [ro-man-thar'], *va.* *V.* Romancear.

Romanzón [ro-man-thone'], *m.* A long and tedious romance.

Romaza [ro-mah'-thah], *f.* (Bot.) Dock. Rumex. *Romaza aguda*, Sharp-pointed dock. Rumex acutus.

Rombo [rom'-bo], *m.* Rhomb, a quadrangular figure, having its four sides equal, with unequal angles.

Romboidal [rom-boi-dahl'], *a.* Rhomboidal, like a rhomb.

Romboide [rom-bo'-e-day], *m.* (Geom.) Rhomboid.

Romera [ro-may'-rah], *f.* (Bot.) Rosemary-leaved sun-rose. Cistus libanotis.

Romeraje, *m.* *V.* Romería.

Romeral [ro-may-rahl'], *m.* Place abounding with rosemary.

Romería [ro-may-ree'-ah], *f.* Pilgrimage.

Romero [ro-may'-ro], *m.* 1. (Bot.) Rosemary. Rosmarinus, *L.* 2. Pilgrim, palmer.

Romero, ra [ro-may'-ro, rah], *a.* Travelling on religious account.

Romí, Romín [ro-mee', ro-meen'], *m.* Bastard saffron. *V.* Azafrán romín.

Romo, ma [roh'-mo, mah], *a.* 1. Obtuse, blunt. 2. Flat-nosed: in this sense it is used as a substantive.—*n.* Hinny, mule begotten by a horse and a she-ass.

Rompecabezas [rom-pay-cah-bay'-thas], *m.* 1. Puzzle, riddle, jigsaw puzzle. 2. An offensive weapon, a slingshot.

Rompecoches [rom-pay-co'-ches], *m.* Everlasting, a strong cloth.

Rompedera [rom-pay-day'-rah], *f.* Chisel for cutting hot iron.

Rompedero, ra [rom-pay-day'-ro, rah], *a.* Brittle, fit to be broken.

Rompedor, ra [rom-pay-dor', rah], *m.* & *f.* Breaker, destroyer, crusher; one who wears out his clothes very soon

Rompedura [rom-pay-doo'-rah], *f.* *V.* Rotura.

Rompeesquinas [rom-pay-es-kee'-nas], *m.* A hector or braggart who hangs about street corners.

Rompehuelgas [rom-pay-oo-ell'-gahs], *m.* Strikebreaker.

Romper [rom-perr'], *va.* & *vn.* 1. To break, to force asunder; to break in pieces, to dash, to fracture, to crash;

to cut asunder. 2. To wear out clothes soon. 3. To defeat, to rout. 4. To break up land, to plough it for the first time. 5. To pierce, to penetrate. 6. To break off; to fall out, to quarrel. 7. To dawn, to begin. 8. To interrupt a speech or conversation. 9. To deliberate, to resolve. 10. To break out, to spring up; to dissipate clouds. 11. To violate, to infringe; to transgress. 12. To exceed, to go beyond the limits. *De rompe y rasga,* Undaunted; plain, open, free. 13. To prune vine-stalks of their useless green branches. *Romper un palo,* (Naut.) To spend a mast. *Rompe galas,* Ironical nickname for one who goes slovenly dressed.—*vr.* To become free and easy in one's deportment.

Rompesacos [rom-pay-sah'-cos], *m.* (Bot.) Oval-spiked or long-spiked hard-grass. Ægylops.

Rompiente [rom-pe-en'-tay], *m.* Surf, breakers; shore-line or submerged rock on which the sea breaks.

Rompimiento [rom-pe-me-en'-to], *m.* 1. Rupture, the act of breaking. 2. Aperture in a solid body; crack, cleft, fracture. 3. Funeral dues paid by such as have their own tomb. 4. An apparent depth of a piece of painting which seems to break its superficies. 5. First ploughing of land. 6. (Met.) Rupture, dispute among persons.

Rompisacos, *m.* (Bot.) *V.* ROMPESACOS.

Rompope [rom-po'-pay], *m.* (Mex. & C. A.) Kind of eggnog.

Ron, *m.* Rum, spirit made from molasses or cane-juice (fr. Eng.).

Ronca [ron'-cah], *f.* 1. Threat, menace; boast, brag. 2. Cry of a buck in rutting-time. 3. A kind of halberd. *Echar roncas,* (Coll.) (1) To threaten, to menace. (2) To be hoarse.

Roncador, ra [ron-cah-dor', ah], *m.* & *f.* Snorer.—*m.* 1. Snoring-fish. 2. The little bass, roncador, a food-fish of California. Gunyonemus lineatus. 3. *V.* SOBRESTANTE.—*f.* (Peru, Ec.) A large spur which makes noise.

Roncamente, *adv.* Hoarsely, with a harsh voice; in a coarse, vulgar manner.

Roncar [ron-car'], *vn.* 1. To snore, to make a harsh noise; to roar. 2. (Coll.) To threaten, to boast, to brag. 3. To cry like a buck in rutting-time.

Ronce [ron'-thay], *m.* Blandiloquence, flattery.

Roncear [ron-thay-ar'], *vn.* 1. To defer, to protract, to use evasions, to lag. 2. To wheedle. 3. (Naut.) To sail badly or slowly.

Roncería [ron-thay-ree'-ah], *f.* 1. Sloth, laziness, tardiness. 2. Flattery, soothing expressions. 3. (Naut.) Bad sailing.

Roncero, ra [ron-thay'-ro, rah], *a.* 1. Slothful, tardy. 2. Snarling, growling. 3. Flattering, wheedling, melliloquent. 4. Slow, tardy: applied to the sailing of a ship.

Ronco, ca [ron'-co, cah], *a.* Hoarse, husky, having a rough voice.

Ronco [ron'-co], *m.* (Coll.) Snore. *V.* RONQUIDO.

Roncón [ron-cone'], *m.* Drone of a bagpipe.

Roncha [ron'-chah], *f.* 1. Wheal, hives; a bean-like swelling. 2. Bruise, ecchymosis. 3. Loss of money by fraud or imposition. 4. (Prov. Ar.) Slice of any thing cut round.

Ronchar [ron-char'], *va.* To chew any thing crisp or hard. *V.* RONZAR.—*vn.* To make wheals.

Ronchón [ron-chone'], *m. aug.* A large swelling.

Ronda [ron'-dah], *f.* 1. Rounds, the act of going about at night. 2. Night-patrol; rounds performed by a night watch; a beat. *Coger la ronda,* To catch one in the act of committing a crime or offence. 3. Space between the houses and the inside of the wall of a fortress. 4. Three first cards in a hand to play. *Contra ronda,* Counter round.

Rondador [ron-dah-dor'], *m.* 1. Watchman, night guard. 2. One who is going about at night; one who is hovering about one place.

Rondalla [ron-dahl'-lyah], *f.* Fable, story.

Rondar [ron-dar'], *va.* & *vn.* 1. To go round by night in order to prevent disorders. 2. To take walks by night about the streets, to serenade. 3. To go round, to follow any thing continually, to haunt. 4. To hover about one place, to move round a thing. 5. To threaten to relapse, to impend.

Rondel [ron-del'], *m.* Roundelay, kind of poetry little used.

Rondeña [ron-day'-nyah], *f.* Music or song peculiar to Ronda and like that of the fandango.

Rondín [ron-deen'], *m.* 1. Rounds of a corporal on the walls to visit the sentinels. 2. Watchmen in naval arsenals.

Rondí, or **Rondiz** [ron'-dee, ron-deeth], *m.* Base or face of a precious stone.

Rondó [ron-doh'], *m.* (Mus.) Rondeau, a kind of jig or lively tune, which ends with the first strain repeated.

Rondón [ron-done']. A word merely used adverbially. *De rondón,* Rashly, abruptly; intrepidly.

Ronfeo [ron-fay'-o], *f.* A long, broad sword.

Rongigata, *f.* *V.* REHILANDERA.

Ronquear [ron-kay-ar'], *vn.* To be hoarse with cold.

Ronquedad [ron-kay-dahd'], *f.* Hoarseness, roughness of voice.

Ronquera [ron-kay'-rah], *f.* Hoarseness, occasioned by catching cold.

Ronquido [ron-kee'-do], *m.* 1. Snore. 2. Any rough, harsh sound.

Ronquillo, illa, ito, ita [ron-keel'-lyo], *a. dim.* of RONCO. Slightly hoarse.

Ronronear [ron-ro-nay-ar'], *vn.* To purr.

Ronza [ron'-thah], *f.* (Naut.) The state of a vessel adrift.

Ronzal [ron-thahl'], *m.* 1. Halter, a fastening for a beast. 2. (Naut.) *V.* PALANCA.

Ronzar [ron-thar'], *va.* 1. (Naut.) To rouse, to haul without the aid of a tackle. 2. To chew hard things.

Roña [ro'-nyah], *f.* 1. Scab, mange in sheep, manginess. 2. (Coll.) Craft, fraud, cunning. 3. (Met.) Nastiness, dirt, filth. 4. (Met.) Moral infection, or hurt.

Roñada [ro-nyah'-dah], *f.* (Naut.) Garland. *Roñada de rancho,* (Naut.) Mess-garland; a bag or hanging locker for sailors' provisions. *Roñada de la guirnalda de un palo,* (Naut.) Dolphin of a mast.

Roñería [ro-nyay-ree'-ah], *f.* 1. Craft, cunning, deceitfulness. 2. Niggardliness, sordid parsimony.

Roñoso, sa [ro-nyo'-so, sah], *a.* 1. Scabby, diseased with a scab, leprous. 2. Dirty, nasty, filthy. 3. Wily, sly, crafty. 4. Mean, niggardly, sordidly parsimonious.

Ropa [ro'-pah], *f.* 1. Cloth; all kinds of silk, woollen, or linen, used for domestic purposes. 2. Wearing apparel, clothes. 3. Robe, loose garment worn over the clothes; gown. *Ropa blanca,* Linen. *Ropa de cámara* or *de levantar,* Morning gown. *Poca ropa,* Ill-clothed; poor. 4. Dress of particular authority for the bar, senate, etc. 5. Any thing put between or under others for a seat. *Ropa vieja,* Boiled meat, afterwards fried in a pan. *Ropa buena,* Person or thing of good quality. *Ropa usada* or *ropa vieja,* Cast-off wearing apparel. *Ropa talar,* Long clothing, roomy and loose-fitting. *A quema ropa,* (1) Point-blank. (2) Off one's guard. *Guardar la ropa,* To ward off bodily harm. *No tocar a la ropa,* To do no injury at all. *Palpar la ropa,* (1) To be near death. (2) To be confused, irresolute, perplexed. *Tentar la ropa,* To be at a loss, to hesitate. *Tentarse la ropa,* To hesitate before saying or doing a thing.

Ropaje [ro-pah'-hay], *m.* 1. Wearing apparel. 2. Drapery in pictures and statues. 3. Apparel, generally elegant, proper to some authority.

Ropálico, ca [ro-pah'-le-co, cah], *a.* Applied to verses with the first word a monosyllable, and all the others increasing progressively.

Ropavejería [ro-pah-vay-hay-ree'-ah], *f.* Frippery, old-clothes shop.

Ropavejero [ro-pah-vay-hay'-ro], *m.* Fripper, old-clothes man.

Ropería [ro-pay-ree'-ah], *f.* 1. Trade of dealers in old clothes. 2. Store for ready-made clothing. 3. Wardrobe of a community or clothes-room of a hospital. 4. Office or keeper of a wardrobe. *Ropería de viejo,* *V.* ROPAVEJERÍA.

Ropero [ro-pay'-ro], *m.* 1. Salesman who deals in clothes. 2. Keeper of the wardrobe or vestiary in a religious community. 3. Head shepherd, who superintends the making of cheeses, and has the care of them. 4. Boy who guards the clothes of herdsmen.

Ropeta [ro-pay'-tah], *f. dim.* A short garment.

Ropetilla [ro-pay-teel'-lyah], *f.* 1. A wretched, short garment. 2. Jacket with loose hanging sleeves.

Ropilla [ro-peel'-lyah], *f.* 1. Kind of short jacket with double sleeves, the outer ones hanging loose. 2. (Dim.) A short garment. *Dar una ropilla,* To give a friendly reproof.

Ropita [ro-pee'-tah], *f. dim.* *V.* ROPETA.

Ropón [ro-pone'], *m.* A wide, loose gown, worn over the clothes.

Roque [ro'-kay], *m.* Rook, castle, a man at chess. *V.* TORRE. *Ni rey ni roque,* No living soul.

Roqueda [ro-kay'-dah], *f.* Rocky place.

Roquedo [ro-kay'-do], *m.* Rock, stony precipice.

Roqueño, ña [ro-kay'-nyo, nyah], *a.* Rocky, full of rocks. *Montañas Roqueñas,* The Rocky Mountains.

Roquero, ra [ro-kay'-ro, rah], *a.* Rocky, abounding with rocks; situated on rocks.

Roqués [ro-kes'], *a.* Applied to a kind of falcon.

Roqueta [ro-kay'-tah], *f.* Ancient kind of tower in a fortress.

Roquete [ro-kay'-tay], *m.* 1. A garment worn by bishops and abbots. 2 Rocket. *V.* ATACADOR.

Rorro [ror'-ro], *m.* A sucking child.

Rosa [ro'-sah], *f.* 1. (Bot.) Rose. Rosa. 2. Red spot in any part of the body. 3. Rose diamond. 4. Bunch of ribbons or like things in the form of a rose; rosette. 5. Rosy or florid aspect; rose-colour. 6. Flower of saffron; artificial rose. *Rosas.* Flowers, delights, pleasures; amenity. *Rosa naútica* or *Rosa de los vientos*, (Naut.) The traverse board, card of a mariner's compass. *Rosa de oro*, A golden rose which the Pope blesses in Lent and sends as a present to some sovereign. *Rosa de Jericó*, Rose of Jericho. *Rosa seca*, Pale red or flesh-colour, dried rose-colour. *Agua de rosas*, Rose-water. *Palo de rosa*, Rosewood.

Rosáceo, cea [ro-sah'-thay-o, ah], *a.* Rosaceous, rose-coloured.—*f. pl.* The rose family of plants.

Rosacruz [ro-sah-crooth'], *m.* Rosicrucian, a name given to a sect of philosophers.

Rosada [ro-sah'-dah], *f.* *V.* ESCARCHA.

Rosado, da [ro-sah'-do, dah], *a.* & *pp.* of ROSARSE. 1. Rose, crimsoned, flushed. 2. Rosy, relating to roses. 3. Made up with roses. *Agua rosada*, Rose-water. *Miel rosada*, Honey of roses.

Rosal [ro-sahl'], *m.* (Bot.) Rose-bush. *Rosal amarillo*, Single yellow rose. Rosa lutea, *Mill.* *Rosal blanco*, Single white rose. Rosa alba. *Rosal castellano* or *de rosa rubia*, Red rose. Rosa gallica. *Rosal damasceno*, Damask rose. Rosa damascena. *Rosal de cien hojas*, Cabbage-rose. Rosa centifolia. *Rosal perruno, silvestre, escaramujo* or *cinorbato*, Dog or hip-rose. Rosa canina. *Rosal rubiginoso*, Sweet-brier rose. Rosa rubiginosa. *Rosal siempreverde* or *mosqueta*, Evergreen rose. Rosa sempervirens. *Rosal siempre en flor* or *de la China*, Ever-blooming rose. Rosa semperflorens.

Rosariero [ro-sah-re-ay'-ro], *m.* Maker and seller of rosaries.

Rosario [ro-sah'-re-o], *m.* 1. Rosary, a string of beads for praying. 2. The collection of *avemarías* and *padrenuestros* said at once, and counted by the beads of a rosary. 3. An assemblage of people who sing the prayers of the rosary in procession. *Parte de rosario*, The third part of the rosary, or five tens. 4. Chain-pump. 5. (Coll.) Back-bone. 6. Feminine proper name. *Acabar como el rosario de la aurora*, To break up in disorder. *El rosario al cuello, y el diablo en el cuerpo*, Proverb reproving hypocrites.

Rosarse, *vr.* *V.* SONROSEARSE.

Rosbif [ros-beef'], *m.* Roast beef. (Eng.)

Rosca [ros'-cah], *f.* 1. Screw, a mechanical power. 2. Any thing round and spiral; spiral motion. 3. A distinctive badge of the scholars in some colleges in Spain. *Rosca de pan*, A round twisted loaf of bread. *Rosca de cable*, (Naut.) Flake of a cable. *Rosca de mar*, (Naut.) Sea-rusks, a kind of biscuit.

Roscón [ros-cone'], *m. aug.* 1. A large screw. 2. A twisted loaf of bread.

Rosega [ro-say'-gah], *f.* (Naut.) Creeper, grapnel, to recover things fallen into the water.

Róseo, sea [ro'-say-o, ah], *a.* Rosy, roseate.

Roséola [ro-say'-o-lah], *f.* Roseola, an exanthem commonly without fever, of small rosy spots; false measles, rötheln.

Rosero, ra [ro-say'-ro, rah], *m.* & *f.* Collector of saffron flowers.

Roseta [ro-say'-tah], *f.* 1. *V.* COROLA. 2. Tassel worn instead of shoe-buckles. 3. Rosette, rosette copper.

Rosetón [ro-say-tone'], *m.* 1. A large rose on pieces of architecture and sculpture. 2. (Aug.) A large rose.

Rosita [ro-see'-tah], *f. dim.* A small rose.

Rosicler [ro-se-clerr'], *m.* 1. Roset, a bright rose colour. 2. Rich silver ore, ruby silver.

Rosillo, illa [ro-seel'-lyo], *a.* Clear red.

Rosmarino [ros-mah-ree'-no], *m.* (Bot. Obs.) *V.* ROMERO.

Rosmaro [ros-mah'-ro], *m.* Walrus, morse, rosmarine. Trichechus rosmarus.

Roso, sa [ro'-so, sah], *a.* Red, rosy. *V.* ROJO. *A roso y velloso*, Without distinction, totally.

Rosoli [ro-so'-le], *m.* Rossolis, sundew, a pleasant, sweet spirituous liquor, composed of brandy, sugar, cinnamon, anise, etc.

Rosquete [ros-kay'-tay], *m.* (Prov.) A small cake made in a spiral shape.

Rosquilla [ros-keel'-lyah], *f.* 1. A kind of very sweet cakes made in a spiral shape. 2. Vine fretter.

Rostral [ros-trahl'], *a.* 1. *V.* ROSTRATA. 2. (Arch.) Rostral column.

Rostrado, da [ros-trah'-do, dah], *a.* Rostral, resembling the beak of a ship.

Rostrico, Rostrillo [ros-tree'-co, ros-treel'-lyo], *m.* 1. Veil or head-dress on images. 2. Small seed pearl.

Rostrituerto, ta [ros-tre-too-err'-to, tah], *a.* Showing anger or displeasure in the countenance.

Rostro [ros'-tro], *m.* 1. Rostrum, the beak of a ship, and the bill or beak of a bird. 2. Countenance, human face. 3. Aspect of affairs. *A rostro firme*, Resolutely, in front of. *Hacer rostro*, To bear up under adversities. *Rostro a rostro*, Face to face.

Rota [ro'-tah], *f.* 1. Rout, defeat. 2. (Naut.) Course. 3. Rota, an ecclesiastical court in Catholic countries. 4. *V.* NUNCIATURA. 5. Rattan, a kind of Indian cane. Calamus rotan. *De rota* or *de rota batida*, On a sudden, in a careless manner; with total ruin.

Rotación [ro-tah-the-on'], *f.* 1. Rotation, circular motion; circumrotation. 2. Revolution of planets.

Rotador, ra [ro-tah-dor', rah], *a.* Serving for rotation.—*m. pl.* The rotifera or so-called wheel-animalcules.

Rotamente, *adv.* Impudently, barefacedly.

Rotante [ro-tahn'-tay], *pa.* Rolling, vagrant.

Rotar [ro-tar'], *vn.* *V.* RODAR.

Rotativo, va [ro-tah-tee'-vo, vah], *a.* Rotating.

Roto, ta [ro'-to, tah], *a.* & *pp. irr.* of ROMPER. 1. Broken, destroyed. 2. Leaky, battered, or pierced. 3. Debauched, lewd, intemperate; ragged.

Rotograbado [ro-to-grah-bah'-do], *m.* Rotogravure.

Rotonda [ro-ton'-dah], *f.* 1. The hindmost of the three parts of a diligence. 2. Rotunda, a circular temple or meeting-room.

Rotor [ro-tor'], *m.* Rotor.

Rótula [ro'-too-lah], *f.* 1. Kneecap. 2. Lozenge. 3. (Mech.) Swivel.

Rotulación [ro-too-lah-the-on'], *f.* Labeling.

Rotulado [ro-too-lah'-do], *m.* 1. Label. 2. Poster, sign.

Rotulador, ra [ro-too-lah-dor', rah], *a.* Labeling, lettering.—*m.* & *f.* Labeler, letterer.

Rotular [ro-too-lar'], *va.* 1. To label. 2. To self-address.

Rotulista [ro-too-lees'-tah], *m.* 1. Poster artist. 2. Sign painter.

Rótulo [ro'-too-lo], *m.* 1. Inscription on books and papers, title. 2. Printed bill posted up; show-bill, poster. 3. Certificate of the virtues of one for beatification. 4. List, manifest, of the contents of a chest, of a boat, etc.

Rotunda [ro-toon'-dah], *f.* 1. Rotunda, a round building. 2. Round-house for locomotives.

Rotundamente [ro-toon-dah-men'-tay], *adv.* 1. Spherically. 2. Explicitly.

Rotundidad [ro-toon-de-dahd'], *f.* Roundness, rotundity, sphericity.

Rotundo, da [ro-toon'-do, dah], *a.* Round, circular, rotund, spherical.

Rotura [ro-too'-rah], *f.* 1. Rupture, fracture, crack, breakage. 2. (Agr.) Breaking up of ground which has never been tilled. 3. Hernia in beasts. 4. Dissoluteness, libertinism.

Roturación [ro-too-rah-the-on'], *f.* Plowing of new ground, breaking up ground for tilling.

Roya [ro'-yah], *f.* Rust, a disease of corn; mildew, red blight.

Royal [ro-yahl'], *m.* Kind of French linen.

Royo, ya [ro'-yo, yah], *a.* (Prov.) Red. *V.* ROJO.

Roza [ro'-thah], *f.* 1. Stubbing, clearing the ground of brambles and bushes. 2. Ground cleared of brambles and bushes.

Rozadero [ro-thah-day'-ro], *m.* Stubbing-place; ground cleared of trees.

Rozado, da [ro-thah'-do, dah], *a.* & *pp.* of ROZAR. 1. Stubbed, cleared of brambles and bushes. 2. (Naut.) Fretted, galled.

Rozador, ra [ro-thah-dor', rah], *m.* & *f.* Stubber, weeder.

Rozadura [ro-thah-doo'-rah], *f.* 1. Friction; frication. 2. Gall, a slight hurt by fretting off the skin. 3. Clashing, clash.

Rozagante [ro-thah-gahn'-tay], *a.* 1. Pompous, showy, trailing on the ground: applied to robes and gowns. 2. Haughty, lofty, arrogant.

Rozamiento [ro-thah-me-en'-to], *m.* Friction; frication.

Rozar [ro-thar'], *va.* 1. To stub up, to clear the ground of brambles and bushes. 2. To nibble the grass: applied to cattle. 3. To scrape or pare off. 4. To graze, to touch slightly. 5. To remove the bulging or curvature of a wall. 6. To gall, to hurt by fretting the skin.—*vn.* To touch slightly against each other.—*vr.* 1. To strike or cut each other: applied to the feet. 2. To treat or discourse familiarly. 3. To falter, to stammer. 4. (Naut.) To fret, to gall: applied to cables or things which rub against one another. 5. To have a resemblance or connection with something else.

Roznar [roth-nar'], *vn.* 1. To grind hard things with the teeth: said of animals. 2. To bray, as an ass.

Roznido [roth-nee'-do], *m.* 1. Noise made by the teeth in eating hard things. 2. Braying of an ass.

Rozno [roth'-no], *m.* A little ass.

Rozo [ro'-tho], *m.* 1. Chip of wood. 2. Stubbing, weeding; rubbing; fretting.

Rua [roo'-ah], *f.* 1. Village street. 2. High road.

Ruán [roo-ahn'], *m.* 1. *V.* RUANO. 2. Sort of linen manufactured at Rouen.

Ruana [roo-ah'-nah], *f.* (Amer. Colombia) *V.* PONCHO.

Ruanete [roo-ah-nay'-tay], *m.* Kind of foreign linen.

Ruano, na [roo-ah'-no, nah], *a.* 1. Prancing about the streets; applied to horses. 2. Sorrel-coloured, roan: spoken of horses. 3. Round, of a circular form.

Ruante [roo-ahn'-tay], *a.* 1. Prancing or strutting through the streets; rider. 2. (Her.) Spreading the tail: applied to peacocks.

Ruar [roo-ar'], *vn.* 1. To roll through the streets: applied to carriages. 2.

To strut about the streets, to court the ladies. 3. To ride.
Rúbeo, ea [roo'-bay-o, ah], *a.* Ruby, reddish.
Rubéola [roo-bay'-o-lah], *f.* Measles.
Rubeta [roo-bay'-tah], *f.* Toad. Rana bufo.
Rubí [roo-bee'], *m.* 1. Ruby, a precious stone of a red colour. 2. Red colour, redness of the lips. *Rubí de Bohemia,* Rosy quartz. *Rubí del Brasil,* Red topaz. *Rubí espinela,* Spinel ruby, tinged with chromium oxide.
Rubia [roo'-be-ah], *f.* 1. (Bot.) Madder, a root used by dyers and in medicine. Rubia tinctorium. 2. Small red-coloured river fish.
Rubiáceas [roo-be-ah'-thay-as], *f. pl.* The madder family of plants; rubiaceæ.
Rubial [roo-be-ahl'], *m.* 1. Field planted with madder. 2. District or soil having a red colour.
Rubicán [roo-be-cahn'], *a.* Rubican, of a bay or sorrel colour with white hairs: applied to a horse.
Rubicela [roo-be-thay'-lah], *f.* A reddish-yellow topaz.
Rubicundez [roo-be-coon-deth'], *f.* 1. Flush, red colour. 2. Ruby colour.
Rubicundo, da [roo-be-coon'-do, dah], *a.* 1. Golden-red; blonde. 2. Rosy with health. 3. Reddish, rubicund.
Rubificar [roo-be-fe-car'], *va.* To rubify, to make red.
Rubín [roo-been'], *m.* Ruby. *V.* Rubí.
Rubio, bia [roo'-be-o, ah], *a.* Golden, fair, ruddy.
Rubio, *m.* Red gurnard. Trigla cuculus.
Rubión [roo-be-on'], *a.* Of a bright reddish colour: applied to a kind of wheat.
Rublo [roo'-blo], *m.* Ruble, a Russian silver coin, their monetary unit: 2s. 0½d., or 49 cents; also a gold standard, worth about 3s. 2d., or 77 cents.
Rubor [roo-bor'], *m.* 1. Blush, red colour of the cheeks, flush. 2. Shame, bashfulness.
Ruborizarse [roo-bo-re-thar'-say], *vr.* To blush, to flush with embarrassment.
Ruboroso, sa [roo-bo-ro'-so, sah], *a.* Shameful. *V.* Vergonzoso.
Rúbrica [roo'-bre-cah], *f.* 1. Red mark. 2. Rubric, a peculiar mark or flourish added to one's signature among Spaniards. 3. Rubric, in law and prayer-books. 4. (Met.) Blood used to attest a truth. *Rúbrica sinópica, V.* Minio. *Rúbrica* or *rúbrica fabril,* Ruddle, red earth or red ochre, which carpenters use for drawing lines.
Rubricante [roo-bre-cahn'-tay], *pa. & a.* Rubifying; rubific.
Rubricante, *m.* Junior counsel appointed to sign the divisions of the acts or proceedings of the council.
Rubricar [roo-bre-car'], *va.* 1. To mark with a red colour. 2. To sign with one's peculiar mark or flourish without writing the name. 3. To subscribe, sign, and seal a writing. 4. (Met.) To sign any thing with one's blood.
Rubriquista [roo-bre-kees'-tah], *m.* A person versed in the ceremonies of the church.
Rubro, bra [roo'-bro, brah], *a.* Red, reddish; rubric.
Ruc [rooc], *m.* Very large fabulous bird. *V.* Rocho.
Rucio, cia [roo'-the-o, ah], *a.* 1. Bright silver gray: applied to horses and asses. 2. (Coll.) Light gray: applied to the hair; gray-haired.
Ruda [roo'-dah], *f.* (Bot.) Rue. Ruta. *Ruda cabruna. V.* Galega oficinal.
Rudamente, *adv.* Rudely, roughly, churlishly, loutishly, abruptly, ruggedly.
Rudera [roo-day'-rah], *f.* Rubbish, ruins of demolished buildings.
Rudeza [roo-day'-thah], *f.* 1. Roughness, asperity or unevenness of surface. 2. Roughness of temper, rudeness, coarseness of behaviour and address, churlishness, grossness. 3. Stupidity, dulness.
Rudimentario, ria [roo-de-men-tah'-re-o, ah], *a.* (Biology) Rudimentary, undeveloped.
Rudimento [roo-de-men'-to], *m.* 1. *V.* Principio. 2. Rudiment, first trace of an organ.—*pl.* Rudiments of a science or art.
Rudo, da [roo'-do, dah], *a.* 1. Rude, rough, unpolished, coarse, churlish, clownish. 2. Hard, rigorous, severe. 3. Stupid, dull.
Rueca [roo-ay'-cah], *f.* 1. Distaff for flax. 2. Winding, twisting. 3. (Naut.) Fish of a mast or yard. *Armar una rueca,* (Naut.) To fish a mast or yard; to strengthen it with pieces of timber.
Rueda [roo-ay'-dah], *f.* 1. A wheel. 2. Circle formed by a number of persons; crown. 3. A round slice of eatables. 4. Short sun-fish. Tetrodon mola. 5. (For.) The placing of one prisoner among others in order to obtain recognition. 6. Breaking on the wheel, a torture anciently used. 7. A kind of hoops for feminine attire. 8. The semicircular spread of a peacock's tail. 9. Turn, time, succession. *Rueda del timón,* (Naut.) Steering-wheel. *Hacer la rueda,* To cajole, to flatter, to coax.
Ruedecica [roo-ay-day-thee'-cah], **cilla, zuela,** *f. dim.* A small wheel.
Ruedo [roo-ay'-do], *m.* 1. Rotation, turning or going around; circuit. 2. Border, selvage, fringe. *A todo ruedo,* At all events. 3. Plat, mat, or rug made of bass, and formed into round or square mats. *Ruedo de cama,* Valance. 4. A plush mat. 5. Circumference of any thing.
(*Yo ruedo, yo ruede,* from *Rodar. V.* Acordar.)
Ruego [roo-ay'-go], *m.* Request, prayer, petition, entreaty, supplication. *A ruego* or *a su ruego,* At the petition or request of any one.
(*Yo ruego, yo ruegue,* from *Rogar. V.* Acordar.)
Ruejo de Molina [roo-ay'-ho], *m.* (Prov.) Mill-wheel.
Ruequecilla [roo-ay-kay-theel'-lyah], *f.* A small distaff.
Rufalandaina [roo-fah-lan-dah'-e-nah], *f.* Noisy mirth.
Rufalandario, ria [roo-fah-lan-dah'-re-o, ah], *a.* Slovenly, negligent in dress; not cleanly.
Rufián [roo-fe-ahn'], *m.* Ruffian, pimp, pander, the bully of a brothel.
Rufiana [roo-fe-ah'-nah], *f.* Bawd, procuress.
Rufianar [roo-fe-ah-nar'], *va.* To pimp, to pander.
Rufiancete, cillo [roo-fe-an-thay'-tay], *m. dim.* Little ruffian or pimp.
Rufianejo [roo-fe-ah-nay'-ho], *m. dim. V.* Rufiancete.
Rufianería [roo-fe-ah-nay-ree'-ah], *f.* Pimping. *V.* Alcahuetería.
Rufianesco, ca [roo-fe-ah-nes'-co, cah], *a.* Pimp-like, relating to bawds and pimps.
Rufo, fa [roo'-fo, fah], *a.* 1. Carroty, red-haired. 2. Frizzed, curled.
Ruga [roo'-gah], *f.* 1. Wrinkle, corrugation. *V.* Arruga. 2. A slight fault.
Rugar [roo-gar'], *va.* To wrinkle, to corrugate. *V.* Arrugar.
Rugible [roo-hee'-blay], *a.* Capable of bellowing or roaring.
Rugido [roo-hee'-do], *m.* 1. Roaring of a lion. 2. Rumbling in the bowels.
Rugiente [roo-he-en'-tay], *a.* Bellowing, roaring.
Rugimiento, *m. V.* Rugido.
Ruginoso, sa [roo-he-no'-so, sah], *a.* Covered with rust, rusty.
Rugir [roo-heer'], *vn.* 1. To roar, to bellow; to halloo. 2. To make a noise, to crack, to rustle.—*vr.* To be whispered about.
Rugosidad [roo-go-se-dahd'], *f.* The state of being wrinkled or corrugated, rugosity.
Rugoso, sa [roo-go'-so, sah], *a.* Rugose, full of wrinkles.
Ruibarbo [roo-e-bar'-bo], *m.* (Bot.) Rhubarb. Rheum. *Ruibarbo palmeado* or *oficinal,* Officinal rhubarb. Rheum palmatum. *Ruibarbo rapóntico* or *reopóntico,* Common rhubarb. Rheum rhaponticum. *Ruibarbo compacto,* Thick-leaved rhubarb. Rheum compactum, *L. Ruibarbo tartárico,* Tartarian rhubarb. Rheum tartaricum. *Ruibarbo rebes,* Warted-leaved rhubarb. Rheum rebes. *Ruibarbo híbrido* or *bastardo,* Bastard rhubarb. Rheum hybridum. *Ruibarbo mutante,* Nodding rhubarb. Rheum mutans. *Ruibarbo ondeado* or *rabárbaro,* Buck's rhubarb. Rheum undulatum.
Ruido [roo-ee'-do], *m.* 1. Noise, clamour, din, clatter; murmur, outcry. 2. Dispute, difference, lawsuit. 3. Rumour, report, empty sound or show. 4. Sound made purposely and for some individual end. *Ser más el ruido que las nueces,* Great cry and little wool (more noise than nuts).
Ruidosamente, *adv.* Noisily, loudly.
Ruidoso, sa [roo-e-do'-so, sah], *a.* Noisy, clamorous, obstreperous.
Ruin [roo-een'], *a.* 1. Mean, vile, low, despicable, churlish, forlorn; little. 2. Humble; decayed; wicked, malicious. 3. Covetous, avaricious; insidious, treacherous, infamous. 4. Applied to a vicious animal.—*m.* A wicked, infamous person.—*f.* Small nerve in the tail of cats.—*pl.* (Coll.) Beard. *Un ruin ido, otro venido,* When one evil is gone another comes. *En nombrando al ruin de Roma, luego asoma,* Talk of the devil, and he will appear.
Ruina [roo-ee'-nah], *f.* 1. Ruin, decline, downfall, destruction, confusion, overthrow, fall.—*pl.* Ruins of an edifice. *Ir en ruina,* To be destroyed, to go to ruin. 2. Cause of ruin, decadence. *Batir en ruina,* (Mil.) To batter in breach.
Ruinar [roo-e-nar'], *va.* To ruin, to destroy. *V.* Arruinar.
Ruindad [roo-in-dahd'], *f.* 1. Meanness, baseness, malice. 2. Humility, poverty. 3. Covetousness, avariciousness.
Ruinmente, *adv.* Basely, meanly.
Ruinosamente, *adv.* (Littl. us.) Ruinously.
Ruinoso, sa [roo-e-no'-so, sah], *a.* Worthless, ruinous, baneful, destructive.
Ruiponce [roo-e-pon'-thay], *m.* (Bot.) *V.* Rapónchigo.
Ruipóntico [roo-e-pon'-te-co], *m.* (Bot.) Rhubarb, pie-plant, an herb the leaf-stalks of which are used in cookery. Rheum rhaponticum.
Ruiseñor [roo-e-say-nyor'], *m.* (Orn.) Nightingale. Motacilla luscinia.
Rujada [roo-hah'-dah], *f.* (Prov. Ar.) Heavy shower of rain.
Rujar [roo-har'], *va.* (Prov.) To irrigate, to bathe.

Rular [roo-lar'], *vn.* (Vulg.) To roll. *V.* Rodar.

Ruleta [roo-lay'-tah], *f.* Roulette, a game of chance.

Rulo [roo'-lo], *m.* 1. Ball, bowl. 2. A conical stone which turns in oil-mills.

Ruló [roo-lo'], *m.* A printer's ink-roller.

Rumano, na [roo-mah'-no, nah], *a.* Rumanian, belonging to Rumania.—*m.* Rumanian, the Romance tongue of this country.

Rumba [room'-bah], *f.* Rumba or rhumba.

Rumbadas, *f. pl.* *V.* Arrumbadas.

Rumbo [room'-bo], *m.* 1. Rhumb, a point of the compass. 2. Road, route, way. 3. Course of a ship. *Rumbo compuesto,* (Naut.) Traverse, a compound course. *Hurtar el rumbo,* (Naut.) To alter the course. *Rumbo estimado,* The dead reckoning. 4. Pomp, ostentation, pageantry. *Rumbos,* Tassels of coarse silk, fastened to the headstalls of mules.

Rumbosamente, *adv.* Pompously, magnificently, liberally.

Rumboso, sa [room-bo'-so, sah], *a.* Pompous, magnificent, splendid, liberal.

Rumia [roo'-me-ah], *f.* Rumination, chewing the cud.

Rumiador, ra [roo-me-ah-dor', rah], *m.* & *f.* & *a.* Ruminator; mediator; ruminant.

Rumiadura [roo-me-ah-doo'-rah], *f.* Rumination.

Rumiante [roo-me-ahn'-tay], *pa.* & *a.* Ruminant; musing.

Rumiar [roo-me-ar'], *va.* 1. To ruminate, to chew the cud. 2. To brood upon a subject; to muse, to meditate.

Rumión, na [roo-me-on', nah], *a.* Ruminating much.

Rumo [roo'-mo], *m.* The first hoop of the head of a cask.

Rumor [roo-mor'], *m.* 1. Rumour, report, hearsay. 2. A gentle sound, murmur.

Rumorcico, illo, ito [roo-mor-thee'-co], *m. dim.* A flying report.

Rumoroso, sa [roo-mo-ro'-so, sah], *a.* Causing rumour.

Runas [roo'-nas], *f. pl.* (Acad.) Runes, alphabetical characters employed by the ancient Scandinavians.

Runcho [roon'-cho], *m.* (Ec. Colom.) Opossum.

Runfla [roon'-flah], *f.* Series, multitude, number of things.

Rúnico, ca [roo'-ne-co, cah], *a.* Runic, relating to the Goths, Scandinavians, and other nations of ancient Europe, or their language.

Runrún [roon-roon'], *m.* (Coll.) Rumour, report. *V.* Rumor.

Ruñar [roo-nyar'], *va.* To groove the ends of staves for the heads and bottoms of barrels, to fit.

Rupia [roo'-pe-ah], *f.* 1. Rupee, an East Indian silver coin. 2. A skin disease characterized by the formation of large crusts, rupia. (1 fr. Sanscrit; 2 fr. Greek.)

Rupicabra [roo-pe-cah'-brah], *f.* Chamois-goat.

Ruptil [roop-teel'], *a.* (Bot.) Ruptile, dehiscing irregularly: said of seed-vessels.

Ruptura [roop-too'-rah], *f.* Rupture. *V.* Rotura.

Ruqueta [roo-kay'-tah], *f.* (Bot.) *V.* Jaramago.

Rural [roo-rahl'], *a.* Rural, country.

Ruralmente, *adv.* Rurally.

Rus [roos], *m.* *V.* Zumaque.

Rusco, ca [roos'-co, cah], *a.* Rude, peevish, froward. *V.* Brusco.

Rusiente [roo-se-en'-tay], *a.* Turning red by the action of fire.

Ruso, sa [roo'-so, sah], *a.* Russian.—*m.* The Slavic tongue spoken in Russia.

Rustical [roos-te-cahl'], *a.* Rustical, rural, wild.

Rústicamente [roos'-te-cah-men-tay], *adv.* Rustically, rudely, boisterously.

Rusticano, na [roos-te-cah'-no, nah], *a.* 1. Wild: said of the radish and other plants. 2. (Obs.) Rural.

Rusticar [roos-te-car'], *vn.* To go to the country, to pass time there; to rusticate.

Rusticidad [roos-te-the-dahd'], *f.* Rusticity, simplicity; rudeness, clownishness, clumsiness.

Rústico, ca [roos'-te-co, cah], *a.* 1. Rustic, belonging to the country. 2. Rustic, unmannerly, clownish. *A la* or *en rústica,* In paper covers, unbound.

Rústico [roos'-te-co], *m.* Rustic, peasant, country clown.

Rustiquez, Rustiqueza [roos-te-keth'], *f.* Rusticity. *V.* Rusticidad.

Rustro [roos'-tro], *m.* *V.* Rumbo.

Ruta [roo'-tah], *f.* Route, itinerary.

Ruteno, na [roo-tay'-no, nah], *a.* (Obs.) Russian. Now used only of the Russian liturgy.

Rutilante [roo-te-lahn'-tay], *a.* Brilliant, flashing.

Rutilar [roo-te-lar'], *vn.* (Poet.) To radiate, to shine, to be splendid.

Rútilo, la [roo'-te-lo, lah], *a.* Of a bright yellow or orange colour.

Rutina [roo-tee'-nah], *f.* Routine, custom, habit.

Rutinario, ria [roo-te-nah'-re-o, ah], *a.* Done by routine, routinary.

Rutinero, ra [roo-te-nay'-ro, rah], *a.* Fond of routine, routinist.

Ruzafa [roo-thah'-fah], *f.* Garden, park. (Arab. rusāfa.)

S

S [ay'-say] is the twenty-second letter in the order of the Spanish alphabet. It has always a harsh, hissing sound, like *ss* in English; as in *desaposesionar* (to dispossess). No Spanish word begins with *s* followed by a consonant: in all words derived from other languages, the *s* is either omitted or preceded by *e*; as, *ciencia,* science; *espíritu,* spirit; *Cipión* or *Escipión,* Scipio. *S* is never doubled.—*S.* is a contraction for *Señor,* Mr. or Sir; *Santo,* Saint; *Su, sus,* His, her, their, or your; *Sud* or *Sur,* South; *S. O.,* South-west; *S. E.,* South-east; *S. M., Su Majestad, SS. AA., Sus Altezas; S. S. S., Su seguro servidor,* His, her, their, or your faithful servant.—*Ssmo.* stands for *santísimo,* very holy; *Ssno.* for *escribano,* a notary public. In commerce *s/c* stands for *Su cuenta* (his or their account).

Sa [sah], *f.* (Coll. Obs.) Contraction of *Señora.*

Sábado [sah'-bah-do], *m.* 1. Saturday. 2. Sabbath, among the Jews. *Ni sábado sin sol, ni moza sin amor,* or *ni vieja sin arrebol,* No Sabbath without sun, nor lass without a lover (nor old lady without rouge); *i. e.* everything in its determined course.

Sabalar [sah-bah-lar'], *m.* Net for catching shad in the Guadalquivir.

Sabalera [sah-bah-lay'-rah], *f.* Kind of fire-grate in furnaces.

Sabalero [sah-bah-lay'-ro], *m.* Shad-fisher.

Sábalo [sah'-bah-lo], *m.* Shad. Clupea alosa.

Sábana [sah'-bah-nah], *f.* 1. Sheet for a bed. 2. Altar-cloth. *Pegársele a uno las sábanas,* To rise late (to lie abed) from laziness.

Sabana [sah-bah'-nah], *f.* (Amer. Cuba) Savannah, an extended plain.

Sabandija [sah-ban-dee'-hah], *f.* Any disgusting insect or reptile.

Sabandijilla, juela, *f. dim.* A very small insect.

Sabanear [sah-bah-nay-ar'], *va.* (Amer.) To scour the savannah, in order to find an animal or to collect the herd.

Sabanero, ra [sah-bah-nay'-ro, rah], *a.* 1. Dwelling in a savannah. 2. Relative to a savannah.

Sabanero [sah-bah-nay'-ro], *m.* The man on horseback who takes care of the cattle grazing on the plains.

Sabanilla [sah-bah-neel'-lyah], *f.* 1. (Dim.) A small sheet. 2. A short piece of linen. 3. Altar-cloth; napkin. 4. (Prov.) Handkerchief worn by married women round the head-dress.

Sabañón [sah-bah-nyone'], *m.* Chilblain. *Comer como un sabañón,* To eat greedily, to devour.

Sabatario [sah-bah-tah'-re-o], *a.* Applied to the Jews who keep Saturday for their Sabbath; Sabbatarian.

Sabático, ca [sah-bah'-te-co, cah], *a.* 1. Sabbatical, belonging to Saturday, or the Jewish Sabbath. 2. Every seventh year among the Jews.

Sabatina [sah-bah-tee'-nah], *f.* 1. Divine service performed on Saturday. 2. A literary exercise performed by students on Saturday evening.

Sabatino, na [sah-bah-tee'-no, nah], *a.* Performed on Saturday or belonging to it.

Sabedor, ra [sah-bay-dor', rah], *m.* & *f.* One who knows or is informed of any thing.

Sabeísmo [sah-bay-ees'-mo], *m.* Ancient fire-worship.

Sabeliano, na [sah-bay-le-ah'-no, nah], *a.* & *n.* Sabellian, relating to Sabellius or Sabellianism.

Sabeo, bea [sah-bay'-o, ah], *a.* Sabæan, Arabian, of Sheba.

Saber [sah-berr'], *va.* 1. To know, to have knowledge of. 2. To experience, to know by experience. 3. To be able, to be possessed of talents or abilities; to be learned or knowing. *Saber mucho latín,* To be very sagacious and prudent. 4. To subject, to submit. 5. To fit, to suit. 6. To relish, to savour, to taste. 7. To use, to practise customarily; to be in the habit. *No saber lo que se pesca,* Not to know what one is about. 8. To resemble, to appear like. 9. *V.* Poder. *Él dice que no sabe escribir,* He says that he cannot write.—*v. imp.* To have a taste of. *Saber a pez,* To taste of pitch. *Es a saber* or *conviene a saber,* Viz., to wit, that is. *Hacer saber,* To make known, to communicate. *Sabérselo todo,* In an ironical sense, to know everything: applied to assuming, intolerant persons. *No se sabe,* It is not known. *Quien las sabe, las tañe,* One should speak only of what one understands. *Saber cuántas son cinco,* To be well-informed. *No sabe en dónde tiene la cara,* He does not know his duty. *No saber de sí,* To be overwhelmed with occupation. *No sé qué,* I know not what; an indefinable something. *Sabe que rabia,* It has a sharp taste. *Sépase quién es Calleja,* They will soon know with whom they have to deal.

Saber [sah-berr'], *m.* 1. Learning, knowledge, lore. *V.* Sabiduría. 2. (Obs.) Science, faculty.

Sabiamente, *adv.* Wisely, knowingly, learnedly, sagely.
Sabicú [sah-be-coo'], *m.* (Amer. Cuba) A handsome tree of Cuba, belonging to the pulse family, having white fragrant flowers and a hard wood.
Sabidillo, lla [sah-be-deel'-lyo, lyah], *a. dim.* of SABIDO. Commonly applied to persons who have pretensions to learning and wisdom. *Marisabidilla,* A blue-stocking woman.
Sabido, da [sah-bee'-do, dah], *a. & pp.* of SABER. Learned, well-informed.
Sabidor, ra [sah-be-dor', rah], *m. & f.* (Obs.) 1. Literato, sage; a wise man. 2. *V.* SABEDOR.
Sabiduría [sah-be-doo-ree'-ah], *f.* 1. Learning, knowledge, wisdom, sapience. 2. *V.* NOTICIA.
Sabiendas (A) [ah sah-be-en'-das], *adv.* Knowingly and prudently, consciously.
Sabiente [sah-be-en'-tay], *pa.* Sapient, knowing.
Sabieza, *f.* (Obs.) *V.* SABIDURÍA.
Sabihondez [sah-be-on-deth'], *f.* Assumption of being wise, without being really so.
Sabihondo, da [sah-be-on'-do, dah], *a.* Presuming to decide difficult questions without sufficient knowledge.
Sabina [sah-bee'-nah], *f.* (Bot.) Savin or sabine. Juniperus sabina.
Sabinar [sa-be-nar'], *m.* A clump of sabines.
Sabino, na [sah-bee'-no, nah], *a.* 1. Applied to horses or mules of a mixed white and chestnut colour. 2. Sabine, of the Sabines, neighbours of the ancient Romans.
Sabio, bia [sah'-be-o, ah], *a.* Sage, wise, learned, sapient, knowing; cunning.
Sabio, bia, *m. & f.* A sage, a wise person.
Sablazo [sah-blah'-tho], *m.* Stroke with a sabre.
Sable [sah'-blay], *m.* 1. Sabre, cutlass. 2. (Her.) Sable, black. 3. (Obs.) Sand. *Esgrimir* or *manejar el sable,* To ask for a loan of small change without purposing to return it.
Sablón [sah-blone'], *m.* Coarse sand, gravel.
Saboca, *f.* (Prov.) *V.* SABOGA.
Saboga [sah-bo'-gah], *f.* A species of shad. Clupea alosa.
Sabogal [sah-bo-gahl'], *a.* Applied to the net for catching shad.
Saboneta [sah-bo-nay'-tah], *f.* A hunting-case watch.
Sabor [sah-bor'], *m.* 1. Relish, taste, savour. 2. Pleasure; desire. *A sabor,* At pleasure; to the taste; according to one's wish. *Sabores,* Pieces attached to the bits of a bridle to guard the horse's mouth.
Saborear [sah-bo-ray-ar'], *va.* 1. To give a relish; to give a zest. 2. To engage one's affections; to make one embrace our opinion.—*vr.* 1. To enjoy eating and drinking with peculiar pleasure. 2. To be pleased or delighted.
Saboreo, *m.* *V.* PALADEO.
Sabotaje [sah-bo-tah'-hay], *m.* Sabotage.
Sabotear [sah-bo-tay-ar'], *va.* To sabotage.
Saboyana [sah-bo-yah'-nah], *f.* 1. A kind of wide petticoat. 2. A delicious paste of a particular composition.
Saboyano, na [sah-bo-yah'-no, nah], *a.* Of Savoy, Savoyard.
Sabre, *m.* (Obs.) *V.* ARENA.
Sabrosamente [sah-bro-sah-men'-tay], *adv.* Pleasantly, tastefully.
Sabrosico, ica, illo, illa, ito, ita [sah-bro-see'-co], *a. dim.* A little savoury.
Sabroso, sa [sah-bro'-so, sah], *a.* 1. Savoury, palatable, salted, saltish. 2. Delightful, pleasurable to the mind.
Sabucal [sah-boo-cahl'], *m.* Clump of willows.
Sabuco [sah-boo'-co], *m.* *V.* SAÚCO.
Sabuesa [sah-boo-ay'-sah], *f.* Bitch of a hound or beagle.
Sabueso [sah-boo-ay'-so], *m.* Hound, bloodhound, beagle, harehound, foxhound.
Sábulo [sah'-boo-lo], *m.* Gravel, coarse sand.
Sabuloso, sa [sah-boo-lo'-so, sah], *a.* Sabulous, gritty, sandy, gravelly.
Saburra [sah-boor'-rah], *f.* Accumulation of matters in the stomach, in consequence of bad digestion, saburra.
Saburral [sah-boor-rahl'], *a.* Saburral, relating to foulness of the stomach.
Saca [sah'-cah], *f.* 1. Exportation, extraction; the act of extracting or exporting. 2. Sack, a large bag made of coarse stuff. 3. First authorized register of a sale. 4. (Prov.) Valuation, computation; agreement. *No parecer saca de paja,* To have a genteel appearance. *Renta de sacas,* Duty on exports. *Estar de saca,* (1) To be on sale. (2) To be marriageable: spoken of women.
Sacabala [sah-ca-bah'-lah], *f.* (Surg.) A kind of bullet-drawer used by surgeons to extract balls; crow's-bill.
Sacabalas [sah-cah-bah'-las], *m.* A kind of forceps for drawing a ball from a great gun.
Sacabocado, Sacabocados [sah-ca-bo-cah'-do], *m.* 1. A hollow punch. 2. Any thing that cuts out a round piece. 3. Any thing that effects one's purpose.
Sacabotas [sah-cah-bo'-tas], *m.* Boot-jack.
Sacabrocas [sah-cah-bro'-cas], *m.* Pincers used by shoemakers.
Sacabuche [sah-cah-boo'-chay], *m.* 1. (Naut.) A tube or pipe which serves as a pump. 2. Sackbut, a musical wind-instrument. 3. Player on the sackbut. 4. Nickname of a despicable person.
Sacacorchos [sah-cah-cor'-chos], *m.* Corkscrew.
Sacacuartos, *m.* *V.* SACADINERO.
Sacada [sah-cah'-dah], *f.* District separated from a province.
Sacadilla [sah-cah-deel'-lyah], *f.* Noise made to rouse game.
Sacadinero, Sacadineros [sah-cah-de-nay'-ro], *m.* (Coll.) Catchpenny; expensive toys or baubles.
Sacador, ra [sah-cah-dor', rah], *m. & f.* Extracter, exporter.
Sacadura [sah-cah-doo'-rah], *f.* A sloping cut, by which tailors make clothes fit better.
Sacafilásticas [sah-cah-fe-lahs'-te-cas], *f.* A kind of iron used by artillerymen to take the spikes out of guns.
Sacafondo [sah-cah-fon'-do], *m.* A cooper's auger.
Sacaliña [sah-cah-lee'-nyah], *f.* 1. An ancient kind of dart. 2. A knack of tricking a person out of something; a wheedle to get one's money. *V.* SOCALIÑA.
Sacamanchas [sah-cah-mahn'-chas], *m.* 1. He who takes out spots or stains from clothes. 2. (Coll.) He who publishes another's faults. *Tierra de sacamanchas,* Fuller's-earth.
Sacamiento [sah-cah-me-en'-to], *m.* Taking a thing from the place where it is; taking or drawing out.
Sacamolero, *m.* *V.* SACAMUELAS.
Sacamuelas [sah-cah-moo-ay'-las], *m.* 1. Tooth-drawer, dentist. 2. Any thing which causes a shedding of teeth.
Sacanabo [sah-cah-nah'-bo], *m.* (Naut.) Pump-hook.
Sacanete [sah-cah-nay'-tay], *m.* Lansquenet, a game at cards.
Sacapelotas [sah-cah-pay-lo'-tas], *m.* 1. Nickname given to common people. 2. Ancient instrument for extracting balls.
Sacapotras [sah-cah-po'-tras], *m.* Nickname of a bad surgeon.
Sacar [sah-car'], *va.* 1. To extract, to draw out, to remove, to put out of place. 2. To dispossess of an employment or office; to except or exclude. 3. To manufacture, to produce. 4. To imitate, to copy. 5. To clear, to free; to place in safety. 6. To find out, to resolve, to know; to dissolve; to discover, to invent. 7. To pull out, to eradicate, to take, to extort, to sack. 8. To brood, to hatch eggs. 9. To compel to bring forth what was hidden; to show, to manifest. 10. To excite passion or anger; to lose the judgment. *Esa pasión lo saca de sí,* This passion carries him beside himself. 11. To deduce, to infer; to deride. 12. To ballot, to draw lots. 13. To procure, to obtain; to gain at play. 14. To throw a ball, making it bounce on the ground. 15. To produce, to create, to invent. 16. To extend, to enlarge. 17. To buy in a shop. 18. To transcribe, to copy. 19. To appear or go out with any thing new. 20. To carry corn to be thrashed. 21. To draw a sword, bayonet, etc. 22. It is used instead of *salir con;* as, *Hemos sacado buen tiempo,* We set out with fine weather. *V.* TRAER. 23. To cite, to name, to quote. *Sacar a bailar,* (Coll.) To name or cite unnecessarily any person or thing not alluded to in conversation. 24. To injure, to impair: applied to things which affect the beauty, health, etc. 25. To obtain by cunning and craft. *Sacar agua,* To draw water. *Sacar a bailar a una señora,* To invite a lady to dance. *Sacar al campo,* To challenge, to call out. *Sacar de pila,* To become sponsor at baptism. *Sacar el bajel a tierra,* (Naut.) To haul a vessel on shore. *Sacar en claro* or *en limpio,* To clear up all doubts, to come to a conclusion. *Sacar fruto,* To reap the fruit of one's labour. *Sacar raja,* To obtain part of a demand. *Sacar a luz,* To print, to publish; to develop, to exhibit. *Sacar a la vergüenza,* To put a criminal in the pillory; also, to pass him through certain public streets, mounted on an ass, in order to make him known as a criminal. *Sacar apodos,* To call nicknames. *Sacar una letra,* To draw a bill of exchange. *Sacar el pecho,* To come up to the breast. (Met.) To stand up in defence of a person. *Sacar astilla,* To profit by a thing. *Sacar de madre,* To make one lose patience. *Sacar el ascua con mano ajena,* To make a cat's-paw of any one. *Sacar el buche a alguno,* To pump a person, to draw out his secrets. *Sacar a volar a alguno,* To bring one forward in public. *Sacar bien su capa* or *su caballo,* To extricate one's self from difficulty. *Sacar la cara,* To present one's self by proxy. *Sacar los recados,* To take out a marriage license. *Sacar los piés al niño,* To put a child into short clothes. *Sacar la espina,* To eradicate an evil. *Sacar un fuego con otro fuego,* To fight fire with flame: to turn the tables. *Sacar mal la cuenta,* To turn out unfavourably. *Sacar las uñas,* To avail one's self of every means in an emergency. *Sacar de*

pañales, To relieve from distress. *Sacar con los pies adelante a alguno*, To carry one out feet foremost: to bury him. *Sacar el alma de pecado a alguno*, To wring an unwilling admission from one.

Saca sillas y mete muertos. (Coll.) A phrase used to designate persons employed for the menial works of the stage; servants, or persons holding mean offices.

Sacarífero, ra [sah-cah-ree'-fay-ro, rah], *a.* Sugar-producing.

Sacarificación [sah-cah-re-fe-cah-the-on'], *f.* Conversion into sugar.

Sacarina [sah-cah-ree'-nah], *f.* Saccharin, artificial sweetener.

Sacarino, na [sah-cah-ree'-no, nah], *a.* Saccharine.

Sacaroideo, ea [sah-cah-roi-day'-o, ah], *a.* Like sugar.

Sacarol [sah-cah-rohl'], *m.* Sugar as an excipient.

Sacarimetro, Sacarómetro, *m.* Saccharimeter.

Sacatapón [sah-cah-tah-pone'], *m.* Corkscrew; bung-drawer.

Sacate [sah-cah'-tay], *m.* (Mex.) Grass, herb; hay.

Sacatrapos [sah-cah-trah'-pos], *m.* 1. Worm for drawing the wad of a firelock. 2. One who obtains what he wants by artifice.

Sacelación [sah-thay-lah-the-on'], *f.* (Med.) Application of small bags of heating materials to a diseased part.

Sacelo [sah-thay'-lo], *m.* Chapel or hermitage among the Romans.

Sacerdocio [sah-ther-do'-the-o], *m.* Priesthood, ministry.

Sacerdotal [sah-ther-do-tahl'], *a.* Sacerdotal, ministerial.

Sacerdote [sah-ther-do'-tay], *m.* Priest, clergyman, minister.

Sacerdotisa [sah-ther-do-tee'-sah], *f.* Priestess.

Saciable [sah-the-ah'-blay], *a.* Satiable, that may be satiated.

Saciar [sah-the-ar'], *va.* 1. To satiate, to cloy. 2. To gratify desire.

Saciedad [sah-the-ay-dahd'], *f.* Satiety.

Saciña [sah-thee'-nyah], *f.* (Bot.) A kind of willow.

Saco [sah'-co], *m.* 1. Sack, bag. *Sacos vacíos*, Ready-made bags. 2. A coarse stuff worn by country people. 3. Coarse cloth worn as penance. 4. Any thing which includes within itself many other things. 5. Pillage, sack, plunder; heap. *V.* SAQUEO. *A saco*, Sacking, plundering. *Saco del mar*, (Naut.) Bay, port, harbour. *Saco de una vela*, (Naut.) Drop of a sail. *Tres* (or *siete*) *al saco, y el saco en tierra*, Between two stools one falls to the ground. *Meter a saco*, To put to sack, to plunder. *No le fiara un saco de alacranes*, I would not trust him with so much as a bag of scorpions. *No echar una cosa en saco roto*, Not to be heedless of advice, not to waste an opportunity. 6. Sagum, short, round jacket worn by Roman soldiers. (Note.—The fourth acceptation is commonly taken in an unfavourable sense.)

Sacra [sah'-crah], *f.* Each of the three tablets on the altar, which the priest, in saying mass, may read without opening the missal.

Sacramental [sah-crah-men-tahl'], *a.* Sacramental.—*m.* & *f.* Individual or confraternity destined to the worship of the sacrament of the altar.

Sacramentalmente, *adv.* Sacramentally; in confession.

Sacramentar [sah-crah-men-tar'], *va.* To administer the sacraments.—*vn.* *V.* JURAMENTAR.—*vr.* To transubstantiate Christ into the eucharist.

Sacramentario [sah-crah-men-tah'-re-o], *a.* Applied to heretics who deny the real presence in the eucharist.

Sacramente, *adv.* *V.* SAGRADAMENTE.

Sacramento [sah-crah-men'-to], *m.* 1. Sacrament. 2. *V.* MISTERIO. 3. Sacrament, Christ transubstantiated in the host. 4. (Obs.) Sacrament, an oath or any ceremony producing an obligation. *Sacramento del altar*, The eucharist.

Sacratisimo, ma [sah-crah-tee'-se-mo, mah], *a. sup.* of SAGRADO.

Sacre [sah'-cray], *m.* 1. (Orn.) Saker, a large lanner falcon. Falco sacer. 2. Small cannon.

Sacrificable [sah-cre-fe-cah'-blay], *a.* (Littl. us.) Sacrificable.

Sacrificadero [sah-cre-fe-cah-day'-ro], *m.* Place where a sacrifice is performed.

Sacrificador [sah-cre-fe-cah-dor'], *m.* Sacrificer, sacrificator.

Sacrificante [sah-cre-fe-cahn'-tay], *pa.* & *a.* Sacrificing, hazarding, sacrifical, sacrificatory.

Sacrificar [sah-cre-fe-car'], *va.* 1. To sacrifice, to offer or perform a sacrifice. 2. To pay homage. 3. To sacrifice, to destroy or give up for the sake of something else. 4. To sacrifice, to devote with loss, to expose to hazard and danger.—*vr.* 1. To devote one's self to God. 2. To submit, to conform one's self to.

Sacrificio [sah-cre-fee'-the-o], *m.* 1. Sacrifice, the act of offering to heaven; offering. 2. Sacrifice, submission, obsequiousness; obedience, compliance. 3. Sacrifice, any thing destroyed or quitted for the sake of something else. *Sacrificio del altar*, Sacrifice of the mass. *Sacrificio propiciatorio*, Peace-offering, propitiatory sacrifice. 4. Any dangerous surgical operation.

Sacrílegamente [sah-cree'-lay-gah-men-tay], *m.* Sacrilegiously.

Sacrilegio [sah-cre-lay'-he-o], *m.* Sacrilege; church-robbing pecuniary punishment for sacrilege.

Sacrílego, ga [sah-cree'-lay-go, gah], *a.* Sacrilegious.

Sacrismoche, cho [sah-cris-mo'-chay, cho], *m.* In jocular style, a man in a ragged black coat.

Sacristán [sah-cris-tahn'], *m.* 1. Sacristan, sexton, clerk. 2. Hoop formerly worn by women.

Sacristana [sah-cris-tah'-nah], *f.* 1. Sacristan or sexton's wife. 2. Nun, or lay woman who provides things necessary for church service.

Sacristancillo, ito, *m. dim.* A little sexton or clerk.

Sacristania [sah-cris-tah-nee'-ah], *f.* Office of a sexton.

Sacristía [sah-cris-tee'-ah], *f.* 1. Sacristy, vestry. 2. Office and employment of a sacristan or sexton. 3. (Coll.) Stomach. *Llenar la sacristía*, To guzzle, to gormandize.

Sacro, cra [sah'-cro, crah], *a.* Holy, sacred. *V.* SAGRADO. *Fuego sacro*, St. Anthony's fire, erysipelas. *Hueso sacro*, The sacrum. Os sacrum.

Sacrosanto, ta [sah-cro-sahn'-to, tah], *a.* Sacred, consecrated, very holy.

Sacudida [sah-coo-dee'-dah], *f.* The act of shaking off or rejecting any thing, jerk. *De sacudida*, Resulting from.

Sacudidamente. *adv.* Rejectingly.

Sacudido, da [sah-coo-dee'-do, dah], *a.* & *pp.* of SACUDIR. 1. Harsh, indocile, intractable. 2. Unembarrassed, resolved.

Sacudido [sah-coo-dee'-do], *m.* Spanish step in dancing.

Sacudidor [sah-coo-de-dor'], *m.* 1. Shaker, one who shakes off. 2. Instrument for beating or cleansing.

Sacudidura [sah-coo-de-doo'-rah], *f.* Dusting, cleansing.

Sacudimiento [sah-coo-de-me-en'-to], *m.* Act of shaking off or rejecting.

Sacudir [sah-coo-deer'], *va.* 1. To shake, to jerk, to hustle. 2. To dart, to throw, to discharge; to beat, to chastise with blows. 3. To remove, to separate. 4. (Naut.) To flap in the wind: applied to sails. *Sacudir el polvo*, To strike, to beat, to chastise severely; to reprehend; to refute. *Sacudir el yugo*, To shake off the yoke.—*vr.* To reject with disdain, to turn away in a harsh and violent manner.

Sacha [sah'-chah], *f.* A garden hoe.

Sachadura [sah-chah-doo'-rah], *f.* Hoeing or turning up the ground with a hoe or dibble.

Sachar [sah-char'], *va.* To turn the ground with a hoe or dibble.

Sacho [sah'-cho], *m.* A hoe.

Sadismo [sah-dees'-mo], *m.* Sadism.

Saduceismo [sah-doo-thay-ees'-mo], *m.* Sadduceeism, Sadducism.

Saduceo, ea [sah-doo-thay'-o, ah], *a.* Sadducean.

Saeta [sah-ay'-tah], *f.* 1. Arrow, dart. 2. Cock of a sun-dial, gnomon; hand of a watch or clock. 3. Magnetic needle. 4. Bud of a vine. 5. (Ast.) A northern constellation. 6. *pl.* Moral sentence or couplet of missionaries; pious ejaculations. *Echar saetas*, To evince agitation by words or gestures.

Saetada [sah-ay-tah'-dah], *f.* **Saetazo** [sah-ay-tah'-tho], *m.* Arrow-wound.

Saetear, *va.* *V.* ASAETEAR.

Saetera [sah-ay-tay'-rah], *f.* 1. Loophole in turrets and old walls, through which fire-arms are discharged. 2. A small grated window in prisons.

Saetero, ra [sah-ay-tay'-ro, rah], *a.* 1. Relating to arrows. 2. Applied to a honey-comb made in a right line.

Saetero, *m.* Archer, bowman.

Saetia [sah-ay-tee'-ah], *f.* 1. (Naut.) Settee, a vessel with lateen sails, used in the Mediterranean. 2. Loophole. *V.* SAETERA.

Saetilla [sah-ay-teel'-lyah], *f. dim.* 1. Small arrow or dart. 2. Small magnetic needle. 3. Hand of a watch. 4. Moral sentence.

Saetin [sah-ay-teen'], *m.* 1. Mill-race through which water runs from the dam to the wheel of a mill. 2. Peg, pin, tack. 3. (Com.) Sateen, a variety of plain satin.

Saetón [sah-ay-tone'], *m.* Dart, a sharp-pointed weapon from a cross-bow.

Sáfico, ca [sah'-fe-co, cah], *a.* Sapphic: applied to a kind of verse of five feet.

Safio [sah'-fe-o], *m.* (Prov.) *V.* CONGRIO.

Safra [sah'-frah], *f.* (Cuba) The season for cutting the sugar-cane, and boiling its juice for sugar. *V.* ZAFRA.

Safre [sah'-fray], *m.* Saffre, cobalt blue. *V.* ZAFRE.

Safumar, *va.* (Obs.) *V.* SAHUMAR.

Saga [sah'-gah], *f.* 1. Witch. 2. Saga, a primitive mythological tradition or legend of Scandinavia.

Sagacidad [sah-gah-the-dahd'], *f.* 1. Sagacity, quickness of scent in dogs. 2. Sagaciousness, penetration.

Sagapeno [sah-gah-pay'-no], *m.* Sagapenum or gum sagapen, a resinous juice.

Sagati [sah-gah-tee'], **Saeti,** *m.* Sagathee, a kind of woollen cloth like serge.

Sagaz [sah-gath'], *a.* 1. Sagacious, quick of scent: applied to dogs. 2

Sagacious, discerning, far-sighted, farseeing, prescient, keen-witted.
Sagazmente, *adv.* Sagaciously.
Sagita [sah-hee'-tah], *f.* 1. The versed sine of an arc, sagitta. 2. The height of an arch.
Sagital [sah-he-tahl'], *a.* 1. Sagittal, belonging to an arrow, sagittated. 2. (Anat.) Sagittal: applied to a suture of the skull.
Sagitario [sah-he-tah'-re-o], *m.* 1. Archer. 2. Sagittarius, sign in the zodiac.
Sagma [sahg'-mah] *f.* (Arch.) Measure taken of many members, as of a cornice.
Sago [sah'-go], *m.* A loose, wide great-coat. *V.* Sayo.
Sagradamente, *adv.* Sacredly, inviolably, religiously.
Sagrado, da [sah-grah'-do, dah], *a.* 1. Sacred, consecrated; venerable, holy. 2. Cursed, execrable.
Sagrado, *m.* 1. Asylum, a sacred place where debtors or malefactors take refuge. 2. Asylum, haven of refuge, even though not sacred.
Sagrariero [sah-grah-re-ay'-ro], *m.* Keeper of relics.
Sagrario [sah-grah'-re-o], *m.* 1. Place in a church wherein consecrated things are deposited. 2. Cibary, the place where the consecrated host is kept.
Sagú, or Sagui [sah-goo', sah'-gee], *m.* Sago, a farinaceous food obtained from various Asiatic palms and cycads. Cycas. (Malay.)
Ságula [sah'-goo-lah], *f.* (Prov.) A small frock. *V.* Sayuelo.
Saguntino, na [sah-goon-tee'-no, nah], *a.* Native of or belonging to Saguntum.
Sahina [sah-ee'-nah], *f.* *V.* Zahina.
Sahornarse [sah-or-nar'-say], *vr.* To be excoriated.
Sahorno [sah-or'-no], *m.* Excoriation.
Sahumado, da [sah-oo-mah'-do, dah], *a.* & *pp.* of Sahumar. Fumigated; select, apposite, proper.
Sahumador [sah-oo-mah-dor'], *m.* 1. Perfumer. 2. A perfuming-pot, used to impregnate any thing with a sweet scent.
Sahumadura [sah-oo-mah-doo'-rah], *f.* 1. The act of perfuming with a sweet scent. 2. (Naut.) Fumigation in ships.
Sahumar [sah-oo-mar'], *va.* 1. To perfume. 2. To fumigate, to smoke, to fume.
Sahumerio [sah-oo-may'-re-o], *m.* 1. Smoke, vapour, steam, fumigation. 2. The medical application of fumes to parts of the body. 3. Aromatics burnt for perfumes.
Sahumo [sah-oo'-mo], *m.* Smoke, steam, vapour. *V.* Sahumerio.
Saica [sah-ee'-cah], *f.* Saick, a kind of Turkish vessel.
Sain [sah-een'], *m.* Grease or fat of an animal; dirt on clothes.
Saina [sah-ee'-nah], *f.* *V.* Alcandía.
Sainar [sah-e-nar'], *va.* To fatten animals.
Sainete [sah-e-nay'-tay], *m.* 1. A kind of farce or short dramatic composition. 2. Flavour, sauce, relish, zest. 3. A high-flavoured sauce. 4. Any delicate bit of a fine taste. 5. Any thing pleasing or engaging. 6. Taste or elegance in dress.
Sainetear [sah-e-nay-tay-ar'], *vn.* To act farces.
Sainetillo [sah-e-nay-teel'-lyo], *m. dim.* A slight relish or flavour.
Saino [sah-ee'-no], *m.* A kind of West Indian hog.
Saja, Sajadura [sah'-hah, sah-hah-doo'-rah], *f.* Scarification.
Sajar [sah-har'], *va.* To scarify.
Sajelar [sah-hay-lar'], *va.* Among potters, to sift and to clean the clay.
Sajón, na [sah-hone', nah], *a.* Saxon.
Sal [sahl], *f.* 1. Salt, common salt. 2. (Chem.) Salt, a compound of a base and an acid. 3. Wit, facetiousness. 4. Grace, charm, pep. *Sal gema*, Rock salt. *Sal y pimienta*, Salt and pepper. *Ser un terrón de sal*, To be witty and charming. *Sal de Higuera*, Epsom salts.
Sala [sah'-lah], *f.* 1. Hall, the first large room in a house. 2. Hall where judges meet to try and decide causes. 3. Board of commissioners. 4. A public meeting, a public entertainment. *Sala de muestras*, Show-room. *Sala de estrados*, Hall or court of justice. *Sala de estado*, Chamber of presence. *Sala de galibos*, (Naut.) The mould-loft of a ship. *Sala de mil y quinientas*, A former court of appeals in Spain. *Sala de secretos*, A whispering-gallery. *Hacer sala*, (1) To form a court or quorum. (Coll.) To dance attendance. (2) (Obs.) To give splendid entertainments.
Salacidad [sah-lah-the-dahd'], *f.* Salacity, lechery.
Salacot [sah-lah-cot'], *m.* A Philippine hat in the shape of a parasol, and with many trimmings.
Saladamente, *adv.* Wittily, facetiously; saltly.
Saladar [sah-lah-dar'], *m.* Salt-marsh.
Saladero [sah-lah-day'-ro], *m.* Salting-place, salting-tub.
Saladillo [sah-lah-deel'-lyo], *m. dim.* of Salado. Fresh bacon half-salted.
Salado, da [sah-lah'-do, dah], *a.* & *pp.* of Salar. 1. Salted, salty. 2. Witty, facetious. 3. (Bot.) Applied to plants growing on the sea-shore from which soda is obtained by burning.
Salado, *m.* 1. Sea. 2. Land rendered barren by too large a portion of saline particles.
Salador, ra [sah-lah-dor', rah], *m.* & *f.* Salter; salting-place for meat.
Saladura [sah-lah-doo'-rah], *f.* Salting, seasoning with salt.
Salamandra [sah-lah-mahn'-drah], *f.* 1. Salamander, a kind of lizard. Lacerta salamandra. 2. (Met.) That which exists in the ardour of love or affection.
Salamandria, *f.* *V.* Salamanquesa.
Salamanqués, sa [sah-lah-man-kays', kay'-sah], *a.* *V.* Salmantino.
Salamanquesa [sah-lah-man-kay'-sah], *f.* Star-lizard. Lacerta stellio.
Salángana [sah-lahn'-gah-nah], *f.* An Asiatic swift which makes the edible nests of which the Chinese are fond. Cocallia.
Salar [sah-lar'], *va.* To salt, to season with salt; to preserve with salt, to cure, to corn.
Salariar [sah-lah-re-ar'], *va.* To give a salary or wages.
Salario [sah-lah'-re-o], *m.* Wages, salary, hire; a temporary stipend; military pay.
Salaz [sah-lath'], *a.* 1. Salty. 2. Salacious, lustful.
Salazón [sah-lah-thon'], *f.* Seasoning, salting.
Salce [sahl'-thay], *m.* (Bot.) Willow. Salix. *V.* Sauce.
Salceda [sal-thay'-dah], *f.* Plantation of willows.
Salcedo [sal-thay'-do], *m.* A damp spot naturally overgrown with trees.
Salcereta [sal-thay-ray'-tah], *f.* Dice-box.
Salcochar [sal-co-char'], *va.* To dress meat, leaving it half raw and without salt. *Lonja de carne salcochada*, Beefsteak. *V.* Sancochar.
Salchicha [sal-chee'-chah], *f.* 1. Kind of small sausage. 2. (Mil.) Saucisse, a long narrow bag of pitched cloth, filled with powder, serving to set fire to mines.
Salchichería [sal-che-chay-ree'-ah], *f* Shop in which sausages are sold.
Salchichero, ra [sal-che-chay'-ro, rah], *m.* & *f.* Maker or seller of sausages.
Salchichón [sal-che-chone'], *m. aug.* 1. A large sausage. 2. (Obs.) A large saucisse filled with powder.
Saldar [sal-dar'], *va.* To liquidate a debt, to settle an account.
Saldo [sahl'-do], *m.* 1. Balance (of an account). 2. Amount left (of merchandise). *Saldo acreedor*, Credit balance. *Saldo deudor*, Debit balance.
Salebrosidad [sah-lay-bro-se-dahd'], *f.* Saltness.
Saledizo [sah-lay-dee'-tho], *m.* Jutting; corbel; jetty, coving.
Saledizo, za, *a.* Salient.
Salegar [sah-lay-gar'], *m.* Salt-lick, a spot where salt is fed to cattle.
Salep [sah-lep'], *m.* Salep or salop-root.
Salera [sah-lay'-rah], *f.* One of the stones of which the salt-lick (*salegar*) is composed.
Salero [sah-lay'-ro], *m.* 1. Salt-cellar, for the table. 2. Salt-pan; magazine of salt. 3. (Coll.) Witty saying; gracefulness.
Saleroso, sa [sah-lay-ro'-so, sah], *a.* Facetious, witty, humorous; graceful.
Saleta [sah-lay'-tah], *f. dim.* A small hall.
Sálgada, Salgadera [sal-gah'-dah, sal-gah-day'-rah], *f.* (Bot.) *V.* Orzaga.
(*Yo salgo, yo salga, yo saldré, saldría. V.* Salir.)
Salguera [sal-gay'-rah], *f.* *V.* Mimbrera.
Salguero [sal-gay'-ro], *m.* Osier, willow.
Salicilato [sah-le-the-lah'-to], *m.* (Chem.) Salicylate.
Sálico, ca [sah'-le-co, cah], *a.* Salic, of the Salian Franks. *Ley sálica*, The Salic law (excluding women from the throne).
Salicor [sah-le-cor'], *f.* (Bot.) Long, fleshy-leaved salwart. Salsola soda.
Salicornia [sah-le-cor'-ne-ah], *f.* Glasswort. Salicornia.
Salida [sah-lee'-dah], *f.* 1. Start, setting or going out, departure, exit. 2. Outlet, outgate. 3. Environs of a town. 4. Issue, result, conclusion. 5. Projection, prominence. 6. Salableness. 7. Expenditure, outlay. 8. (Mil.) Sally, sortie. *Puerta de salida*, Sally-port. 9. Subterfuge, pretext. 10. Means or reasons by which an argument, difficulty, or peril is overcome. 11. (Naut.) Headway. *Estar de salida*, To be ready for sailing. *Llevar salida*, To be under weigh. *Llevar buena salida*, To have fresh headway.
Salidizo, za [sah-le-dee'-tho, thah], *m.* & *f.* & *a.* *V.* Saledizo.
Salido, da [sah-lee'-do, dah], *a.* & *pp.* of Salir. Gone out, departed. *Salido*, Projecting, prominent. *Salida*, In heat, eager for the male.
Saliente [sah-le-en'-tay], *a.* & *pa.* Outjutting, salient, projecting.
Salifero, ra [sah-lee'-fay-ro, rah], *a.* Salt-bearing.
Salificable [sah-le-fe-cah'-blay], *a.* Salifiable.
Salin [sah leen'], *m.* Salt magazine. *V.* Salero.
Salina [sah-lee'-nah], *f.* Salt-pit, salt-pan, salt-work, salt-mine.

Salinero [sah-le-nay'-ro], *m.* Salter, dealer in salt; salt-man, salt-maker.
Salino, na [sah-lee'-no, nah], *a.* Saline.
Salir [sah-leer'], *vn. irr.* 1. To go out of a place. 2. To depart, to set out, to march out, to come out, to go forth, to go away or to go abroad, to come forth. 3. To get out of a narrow place or crowd. 4. To appear, to show itself. *Salió entonces una nueva moda.* At that time a new fashion appeared. 5. To shoot, to spring; to grow. 6. To proceed, to issue from. 7. To get over difficulties, to escape from danger; to extricate one's self from errors or doubts. 8. (Naut.) To exceed, to excel, to pass another vessel in sailing. 9. To happen, to occur. *Salga lo que saliere,* (Coll.) Happen what will, it does not concern me. 10. To cost. *El caballo me salió en sesenta guineas,* The horse stood me in sixty guineas. *Salen caros en Madrid los géneros ingleses,* English goods are dear in Madrid. 11. To finish well or ill; to correspond or imply; to complete a calculation. 12. (Mil.) To sally, to issue out. 13. To acquire; to become; to grow common or vulgar. 14. To dismiss, to dispose of. 15. To say or do a thing unexpectedly or unseasonably. 16. To resemble, to appear like. 17. To separate, to retire, to desist; to be chosen or elected. *Salir al cabo* or *salir con,* To go through. *Salir a luz,* To leave the press, to be published or printed; to be produced; to be developed. *Salir con algo,* To obtain any thing. *Salir de sí,* To be enraptured. *Salir de sus casillas,* To step out of one's line or usual way of acting; to be off the hinges; to be out of one's self; to lose one's temper. *Salir de militar,* (Coll.) To personate a soldier: to wear a full court-dress. *Salir de alguno,* To get rid of a person. *El salió herido,* He came out wounded. *Salir de la dificultad,* To extricate one's self from a difficulty. *Salir de mantillas,* To get beyond leading-strings. *Salir los colores al rostro,* To blush. *Salir por la ventana,* To be turned out.—*vr.* 1. To violate a contract; not to fulfil one's engagements. 2. To drop, to leak. *Ese barril se sale,* That barrel leaks. 3. To support or maintain an opinion. *Salirse de la religión,* To quit a religious order. *Salirse con la suya,* To accomplish one's end, to have one's way. *Salir a nado,* To save one's self by swimming; to do something very difficult. *Salir a su padre,* To resemble one's father. *Salir de su padre,* To be released from paternal guardianship. *Salir con una empresa,* To carry out an enterprise. *Salir de una empresa,* To relinquish an enterprise. *Salir del vado* or *del paso,* To get out of a difficulty. *Salir calabazas,* To be plucked; to fail in an examination. *Salir con un domingo siete,* To say or to pretend something utterly irrational. *Salir a volar,* To make public, to expose. *Del monte sale con que se arde,* One always causes his own misfortunes. *Salir tres pies a la francesa,* At once, immediately. *Salir pitando,* (1) To run away hastily and in confusion. (2) (Coll.) To get hot quickly in debate. *Salirse allá,* To amount to nearly the same thing.
Salisipán [sah-le-se-pahn'], *m.* A Philippine boat much like the fishing-boat called *panca.*
Salitrado, da [sah-le-trah'-do, dah], *a.* Impregnated with or composed of saltpetre.
Salitral [sah-le-trahl'], *a.* Nitrous.—*m.* Saltpetre bed or works.
Salitre [sah-lee'-tray], *m.* Saltpetre, nitre.
Salitrería [sah-le-tray-ree'-ah], *f.* Saltpetre-work.
Salitrero, ra [sah-le-tray'-ro, rah], *a.* Saltpetre-refiner, dealer in saltpetre.
Salitroso, sa [sah-le-tro'-so, sah], *a.* Nitrous, salinitrous.
Saliva [sah-lee'-vah], *f.* Saliva.
Salivación [sah-le-vah-the-on'], *f.* Salivation, spitting out.
Salival [sah-le-vahl'], *a.* Salivous, salivary.
Salivar [sah-le-var'], *vn.* To spit, to salivate.—*a.* Salivary.
Salivera [sah-le-vay'-rah], *f.* Round knob on the bits of a bridle.
Salivoso, sa [sah-le-vo'-so, sah], *a.* Salivous. *V.* SALIVAL.
Salma [sahl'-mah], *f.* Ton, twenty hundred-weight.
Salmantino, na [sal-man-tee'-no, nah], *a.* Salamancan, relating to Salamanca.
Salmear, Salmodiar [sal-may-ar'], *va.* To sing psalms.
Salmer [sal-merr'], *m.* (Arch.) Plane or impost from which an arch springs.
Salmerón [sal-may-rone'], *a* Fanfarron wheat.
Salmista [sal-mees'-tah], *m* Psalmist; chanter of psalms.
Salmo [sahl'-mo], *m.* Psalm.
Salmodia [sal-mo'-de-ah], *f.* 1 Psalmody. 2. The Psalter.
Salmógrafo [sal-mo'-grah-fo], *m.* Writer of psalms.
Salmón [sal-mone'], *m.* (Zool.) Salmon. Salmo salar. *Salmón pequeño,* Samlet, salmonet, parr.
Salmonado, da [sal-mo-nah'-do, dah], *a.* Tasting like salmon.
Salmoncillo, ito [sal-mon-theel'-lyo], *m. dim.* A small salmon.
Salmonera [sal-mo-nay'-rah], *f.* A net for fishing for salmon.
Salmonete [sal-mo-nay'-tay], *m.* Red-mullet, or surmullet. Mullus barbatus.
Salmorejo [sal-mo-ray'-ho], *m.* Sauce for rabbits.
Salmuera [sal-moo-ay'-rah], *f.* 1. Brine. 2. Pickle made of salt and water.
Salmuerarse [sal-moo-ay-rar'-say], *vr.* To be diseased by eating too much salt: applied to cattle.
Salobral [sah-lo-brahl'], *a.* Salty, briny.—*m.* Brine.
Salobre [sah-lo'-bray], *a.* Brackish, saltish.
Salobreño, ña [sah-lo-bray'-nyo, nyah], *a.* Saltish, containing salt: applied to earth.
Saloma [sah-lo'-mah], *f.* (Naut.) Singing out of sailors, chantey.
Salomar [sah-lo-mar'], *vn.* (Naut.) To sing out.
Salón [sah-lone'], *m.* 1. (Aug.) Saloon, a large hall. 2. Meat salted and smoked.
Salpa [sahl'-pah], *f.* (Zool.) Gilt-head, salpa, bighead. Sparus salpa.
Salpicadera [sahl-pe-cah-day'-rah], *f.* Fender (of an auto, etc.).
Salpicadura [sal-pe-cah-doo'-rah], *f.* The act of spattering, and the stain made by it; dab, dash of dirt.
Salpicar [sal-pe-car'], *va.* 1. To bespatter with dirt, to dab, to dash. 2. To work without continuity or order to fly from one subject to another.
Salpicón [sal-pe-cone'], *m.* 1. Salmagundi, a mixed dish. 2. Any thing else in small pieces. 3. Bespattering.
Salpimentar [sal-pe-men-tar'], *va.* To season with pepper and salt.
Salpimentón [sal-pe-men-tone'], *m.* Salmagundi. *V.* SALPICÓN.
Salpimienta [sal-pe-me-en'-tah], *f.* Mixture of salt and pepper.
Salpinga [sal-peen'-gah], *f.* African serpent.
Salpresar [sal-pray-sar'], *va.* To season with salt.
Salpreso, sa, *pp. irr.* of SALPRESAR.
Salpuga [sal-poo'-gah], *f.* A poisonous kind of ant.
Salpullido or **Sarpullido** [sal-pool-lyee'-do, sar-pool-lyee'-do], *m.* Prickly heat, skin rash.
Salpullir [sal-pool-lyeer']. *va.* To break out in pustules or pimples.
Salsa [sahl'-sah], *f.* 1. Sauce, condiment. 2. Ornaments, decorations. *Salsa de San Bernardo,* (Coll.) Hunger.
Salsedumbre [sal-say-doom'-bray], *f.* Salineness, saltness.
Salsera [sal-say'-rah], *f.* 1. Saucer, a pan for sauce. 2. *V.* SALSERILLA.
Salsereta [sal-say-ray'-tah], *f. dim.* A small saucer; a dice-box.
Salserilla [sal-say-reel'-lyah], *f. dim.* A small saucer, in which colours are mixed.
Salsero [sal-say'-ro], *m.* (Bot.) Spanish thyme. Thymus zygis, *L.*
Salserón [sal-say-rone'], *m.* (Prov.) Measure of grain, containing about a peck.
Salseruelo [sal-say-roo-ay'-lo], *m. V.* SALSERILLA.
Salsifí [sal-se-fee'], *m.* Salsify, oyster-plant.
Salsilla, ita [sal-seel'-lyah], *f. dim.* Sauce of little flavour or taste.
Saltabanco, Saltabancos, Saltaembanco or **Saltaembancos** [sal-tah-bahn'-co], *m.* Saltinbanco, mountebank, quack.
Saltabardales [sal-tah-bar-dah'-les], *m* Romp, a wild youth.
Saltabarrancos [sal-tah-bar-rahn'-cos], *m.* (Coll.) A noisy, turbulent fellow.
Saltacabras [sal-tah-cah'-bras], *f.* Kind of Spanish serpent which attracts the eyes of goats.
Saltación [sal-tah-the-on'], *f.* 1. Saltation, leaping or hopping. 2. Dancing, dance.
Saltacharquillos [sal-tah-char-keel'lyos], *m.* Boy who walks on tiptoes.
Saltadero [sal-tah-day'-ro], *m.* 1. Leaping-place, high ground from which leaps can be taken. 2. An artificial fountain, a jet. *Estar al saltadero,* (Coll.) To be near promotion.
Saltado, da [sal-tah'-do, dah], *a.* Prominent, jutting over.—*pp.* of SALTAR.
Saltador, ra [sal-tah-dor', rah], *m. & f.* Jumper, leaper; hopper.
Saltadura [sal-tah-doo'-rah], *f.* Hollow made in the surface of a stone when hewing it.
Saltambarca [sal-tam-bar'-cah], *f.* A rustic dress, open behind.
Saltamontes [sal-tah-mon'-tes], *m.* Locust, grasshopper.
Saltante [sal-tahn'-tay], *pa.* Salient, leaping, jumping.
Saltaojos [sal-tah-oh'-hos], *m.* Kind of peony.
Saltaparedes, *m. V.* SALTABARDALES.
Saltaperico [sal-tah-pay-ree'-co], *m.* (Prov.) *V.* SALTAMONTES.
Saltar [sal-tar']. *vn.* 1. To leap, to jump, to hop; to frisk, to skip; to rebound, to dash. *Saltar en tierra.* To land, to disembark. 2. To burst, to break in pieces; to fly asunder, to crack, to flash. 3. To be clear and obvious, to occur to the memory; to excel, to surpass. 4. To be irritated, to be agitated, to betray emotion. 5.

To speak incoherently and irrelevantly. 6. (Naut.) To chop about, to change suddenly: applied to the wind. *El viento saltó al este*, The wind veered round to the east; the wind shifted. *Salte gente a la banda*, (Naut.) Man the ship's side: a word of command. *Saltar de gozo*, To be highly delighted. *Andar a la que salta*, To give one's self up to a vagabond life.—*va.* 1. To leap, to pass over or into by leaping. 2. To cover the female: applied to male animals. *Salta tú y dámela tú*, A children's game very like hunt-the-slipper.

Saltarelo [sal-tah-ray'-lo], *m.* Ancient Spanish dance.

Saltarén [sal-tah-ren'], *m.* 1. Certain tune on the guitar. 2. Grasshopper.

Saltarín, na [sal-tah-reen', nah], *m.* & *f.* 1. Dancer, dancing-master. 2. A restless young rake.

Saltarregla [sal-tar-ray'-glah], *f.* Bevel-square, sliding-rule.

Saltaterandate [sal-tah-tay-ran-dah'-tay], *m.* A kind of embroidery.

Saltatriz [sal-tah-treeth'], *f.* A female rope-dancer; ballet-girl; danseuse, a professional dancing woman.

Salteador [sal-tay-ah-dor'], *m.* Highwayman, footpad.

Salteamiento [sal-tay-ah-me-en'-to], *m.* Assault, highway robbery.

Saltear [sal-tay-ar'], *va.* 1. To assault, to attack, to invade; to rob on the highway; to hold up. 2. To fly from one work to another without continuity. 3. To anticipate maliciously in the purchase of any thing; to surprise, to take by surprise. 4. To circumvent or gain ascendency over another's feelings.

Salteo [sal-tay'-o], *m.* Assault on the high road; highway robbery.

Salterio [sal-tay'-re-o], *m.* 1. Psalter, psalm-book. 2. Psaltery, a kind of harp. 3. Rosary, as composed of 150 Ave Marias. 4. A kind of flute.

Saltero, ra [sal-tay'-ro, rah], *a.* Living on mountains, highlander.

Saltico, ito [sal-tee'-co, ee'-to], *m. dim.* A little hop or leap.

Saltillo [sal-teel'-lyo], *m.* 1. A little hop or leap. *A saltillos*, Leaping, hopping. 2. (Naut.) Beak, bulk-head. *Saltillos de los pasamanos*, (Naut.) Steps of the gangway.

Saltimbanco, Saltimbanqui [sal-tim-bahn'-co], *m.* *V.* SALTABANCO.

Salto [sahl'-to], *m.* 1. Leap, bound; distance leaped; leaping, jerk, jump. 2. Leaping-place, ground from which leaps can be taken. 3. Irregular transition from one thing to another. 4. Assault, plunder, robbery. 5. Skip, omission of clauses, lines, or leaves in reading or writing. 6. Ascent to a higher post without passing through the intervening. 7. (Amer. Colom. Argen.) Cataract, falls. *Salto de corazón*, Palpitation. (Met.) A foreboding. *A salto de mata*, By flight for fear of punishment. *Salto de trucha*, Tumbling; tricks played by various vibrations of the body. *Salto mortal.* Somerset. *Salto de viento*, (Naut.) The sudden shifting of the wind. *Dar un salto a bolina*, (Naut.) To check the bowline. *A saltos*, Leaping by hops. *De salto*, On a sudden. *De un salto*, At one jump. *Por salto*, Irregularly, by turns. *A saltos y corcovos*, (Coll.) By fits and starts.

Saltón [sal-tohn], *m.* Grasshopper.

Saltón, na [sal-tohn', nah], *a.* Hopping or leaping much. *Ojos saltones*, Goggle-eyes.

Salubérrimo, ma [sah-loo-ber'-re-mo, mah], *a. sup.* Most salubrious (fr. *Salubre*).

Salubre [sah-loo'-bray], *a.* Healthful. *V.* SALUDABLE.

Salubridad [sah-loo-bre-dahd'], *f.* Healthfulness, salubrity, salutariness, wholesomeness.

Salud [sah-lood'], *f.* 1. Health. 2. Welfare, prosperity. 3. Salvation. *En sana salud*, In good health. *Saludes*, Compliments, greetings.

Saludable [sah-loo-dah'-blay], *a.* Salutary, healthful, salubrious, wholesome for soul or body.

Saludablemente, *adv.* Salubriously, healthfully, healthily.

Saludación, *f.* *V.* SALUTACIÓN.

Saludador [sah-loo-dah-dor'], *m.* 1. Greeter, saluter. 2. Quack, who pretends to cure distempers by the breath, the saliva, etc.

Saludar [sah-loo-dar'], *va.* 1. To greet, to salute, to hail, to accost. 2. To express content or joy by words or actions. 3. To proclaim a king or emperor. 4. To fire a salute. 5. To apply delusive remedies to cure diseases, like quacks. *Saludar a la voz*, (Naut.) To give cheers, to huzza.

Saludo [sah-loo'-do], *m.* 1. Salute with a volley of fire-arms. 2. Salute, salutation, greeting. *Volver el saludo*, To return the salute or bow.

Salumbre [sah-loom'-bray], *f.* Flower of salt, red spume which forms on salt.

Salutación [sah-loo-tah-the-on'], *f.* 1. Salutation, greeting, salute. 2. Exordium of a sermon.

Salute [sah-loo'-tay], *m.* Ancient Castilian gold coin.

Salutiferamente, *adv.* Salubriously.

Salutífero, ra [sah-loo-tee'-fay-ro, rah], *a.* Salutiferous, healthful, salubrious.

Salva [sahl'-vah], *f.* 1. Pregustation, the tasting of viands before they are served up to royalty. 2. Salute of fire-arms, salvo. 3. (Obs.) *V.* SALVILLA. Salver. *Hacer la salva*, To drink to one's health, to beg leave to speak. 4. Rash proof of innocence, given by running a great risk. 5. Oath, solemn promise, assurance. *Señor de salva*, Person of great distinction.

Salvación [sal-vah-the-on'], *f.* 1. Salvation. 2. Preservation from great danger. *Ejército de Salvación*, The Salvation Army.

Salvachia [sal-vah-chee'-ah], *f.* (Naut.) Salvage, a strap formed by braided cords, used to fasten shrouds and stays.

Salvadera [sal-vah-day'-rah], *f.* Sand-box for writing.

Salvado [sal-vah'-do], *m.* Bran. *Salvado, da, pp.* of SALVAR.

Salvador, ra [sal-vah-dor', rah], *m.* & *f.* Saviour, rescuer, redeemer. *El Salvador* or *el Salvador del mundo*, Our Saviour, our Redeemer.

Salvaguardia [sal-vah-goo-ar'-de-ah], *m.* 1. Safeguard, security, protection, shield of friendship, palladium. 2. Guard, watchman.—*f.* Safe-conduct, a kind of passport.

Salvajada [sal-va-hah'-dah], *f.* Rude, unmannerly behaviour.

Salvaje [sal-vah'-hay], *a.* 1. Savage, wild, barbarous, ferocious, ignorant, foolish, undomesticated. 2. Wild, rough, mountainous.

Salvaje [sal-vah'-hay], *m.* A savage, born and brought up in wildernesses.

Salvajemente, *adv.* Savagely, wildly.

Salvajería [sal-vah-hay-ree'-ah], *f.* Rusticity; clownish, uncouth conduct, savageness.

Salvajez [sal-vah-heth'], *f.* Savageness, rustic indocility.

Salvajina [sal-vah-hee'-nah], *f.* 1. A wild beast. 2. A multitude of wild animals. 3. Collection of skins of wild beasts.

Salvajino, na [sal-vah-hee'-no, nah], *a.* 1. Savage, wild, untamed. 2. Having the taste of game: applied to meat.

Salvajismo [sal-vah-hees'-mo], *m.* Barbarism, savagery.

Salvamente, *adv.* Securely, safely.

Salvamento, Salvamiento [sal-vah-men'-to], *m.* Safety, the act of saving; place of safety; salvation. *Derechos de salvamento*, Salvage-money.

Salvante [sal-vahn'-tay], *pa.* Saving, excepting.—*adv.* (Coll.) Save.

Salvar [sal-var'], *va.* 1. To save, to free from danger; to receive into eternal happiness. 2. To salve, to help or save by an excuse or reservation. 3. To remove impediments or difficulties. 4. To mention and correct errors of the pen in a notarial instrument, at the foot thereof. 5. To pass over or near a thing. 6. To taste, to prove the food or drink of nobles. 7. To prove judicially the innocence of a person.—*vr.* To escape from danger, to get over difficulties, to attain salvation.

Salvavidas [sal-vah-vee'-das], *m.* 1. Life-preserver. 2. Life-boat made unsinkable by the help of cork.

¡Salve! [sahl'-vay], *v. defective.* God bless you!—*f.* Salutation or prayer to the Virgin Mary.

Salvedad [sal-vay-dahd'], *f.* License, security, safe-conduct; excuse.

Salvia [sahl'-ve-ah], *f.* (Bot.) Sage. Salvia. *Salvia oficinal*, Garden sage. Salvia officinalis. *Salvia hojiesplegada* or *del Moncayo*, Lavender-leaved sage. Salvia lavandulæfolia. *Salvia de españoles* or *de la Alcarria*, Narrow-leaved sage. Salvia hispanorum.

Salviado, da [sal-ve-ah'-do, dah], *a.* Containing sage.

Salvilla [sal-veel'-lyah], *f.* 1. Salver, a glass stand. 2. A tray, a waiter, a plate on which any thing is presented.

Salvo, va [sahl'-vo, vah], *pp. irr.* of SALVAR. Saved, proved, corrected.

Salvo [sahl'-vo], *adv.* Saving, excepting. *Salvo el guante*, Excuse the glove: used in shaking hands with a glove on. *A salvo*, Without injury or diminution. *A su salvo*, To one's satisfaction, safely, leisurely, easily. *En salvo*, In security, at liberty. *Dejar a salvo su derecho*, (Law) To reserve one's right safe and in full force; to save harmless.

Salvoconducto [sal-vo-con-dooc'-to], *m.* Pass, safe-conduct or letters of safe-conduct; passport; license or permission.

Salvohonor [sal-vo-o-nor'], *m.* (Coll.) Breech, posteriors.

Salz [salth'], *m.* *V.* SAUCE.

Salza [sahl'-thah], *f.* A mud-volcano.

Sallador [sal-lyah-dor'], *m.* Weeder, weeding-hook, hoe.

Sallar [sal-lyar'], *va.* To weed.

Sallo [sah'lyo], *m.* (Prov.) Hoe.

Sama [sah'-mah], *f.* A kind of sea-bream.

Sámago [sah'-mah-go], *m.* A defective useless piece of building wood.

Samaritano, na [sah-mah-re-tah'-no, nah], *a.* Samaritan.

Samba [sam'-ba], *f.* Samba, popular dance and musical rhythm of Brazil.

Sambenitar [sam-bay-ne tar], *va.* To make infamous, to dishonour publicly.

Sambenito [sam-bay-nee'-to], *m.* 1. Garment worn by penitent convicts of the Inquisition. 2. An inscription in churches, containing the name, punishment, and signs of the chastisement of those doing penance; note of infamy. 3. Evil report due to an act.

Sambeque [sam-bay'-kay], *m.* (Cuba) *V.* ZAMBRA.

Samblaje [sam-blah'-hay], *m.* Joinery. *V.* ENSAMBLADURA.

Sambuca [sam-boo'-cah], *f.* 1. Ancient triangular musical stringed instrument. 2. Ancient warlike machine, a sort of huge bridge for storming walls.

Sambumbia [sam-boom'-be-ah], *f.* 1. (Cuba) A fermented drink made from cane-juice, water, and peppers. 2. (Peru) Hubbub, confusion.

Samio, mia [sah'-me-o, ah], *a.* Of Samos, an Ægean island; Samian.

Samnitico, ca [sam-nee'-te-co, cah], *a.* Belonging to the Samnites or to the ancient gladiators.

Samotracio, cia [sah-mo-trah'-the-o, ah], *a.* Samothracian, of Samothrace, an island in the Ægean Sea.

Sampaguita [sam-pah-gee'-tah], *f.* A flower of the Philippine Islands resembling the jasmine.

Sampsuco [samp-soo'-co], *m.* (Bot.) Marjoram. *V.* ALMORADUX.

San [sahn], *a.* Saint: used always in the masculine gender, and before the name. *V.* SANTO.

Sanable [sah-nah'-blay], *a.* Curable, healable, sanable.

Sanador, ra [sah-nah-dor', rah], *m.* & *f.* Curer, healer.

Sanalotodo [sah-nah-lo-to'-do], *m.* Panacea, remedy or plaster for all distempers and sores; a general remedy.

Sanamente, *adv.* Naturally, agreeably.

Sanar [sah-nar'], *va.* 1. To heal, to cure, to restore to health. 2. To reclaim from vice.—*vn.* To heal, to recover from sickness.

Sanate [sa-nah'-tay], *m.* A Nicaragua bird like the magpie. Quiscalus.

Sanativo, va [sah-nah-tee'-vo, vah], *a.* Sanative, curative.

Sanatorio [sah-nah-to'-re-o], *m.* Sanatorium, sanitarium.

Sanción [san-the-on'], *f.* 1. Sanction, law. 2. Solemn authorization.

Sancionar [san-the-o-nar'], *va.* To sanction, to authorize.

Sancochar [san-co-char'], *va.* To parboil.

Sancocho [san-co'-cho], *m.* (Amer. Ec.) A dish composed of yucca, meat, plantains, cocoa, the chief breakfast dish through all South America.

Sanctasanctórum [sanc-tah-sanc-to'-room], *m.* Sanctuary.

Sanctórum [sanc-to'-room], *m.* A tribute which all the natives of the Philippines, from the age of sixteen years, pay to the church.

Sanctus [sahnc'-toos], *m.* A part of the mass. *Tocan a sanctus* or *santus*, They ring the bell at mass before the canon.

Sanchete [san-chay'-tay], *m.* Ancient silver coin.

Sancho [sahn'-cho], *m.* (Prov.) Word used to call tame rabbits.

Sandalia [san-dah'-le-ah], *f.* Sandal, a kind of slippers.

Sandalina [san-dah-lee'-nah], *f.* A stuff manufactured in Venice.

Sandalino, na [san-dah-lee'-no, nah], *a.* Tinctured with sanders.

Sándalo [sahn'-dah-lo], *m.* (Bot.) 1. Bergamot mint. Mentha odorata. 2. True sandal-wood or sanders. Santalum album. 3. (Bot.) Sanders, sandal-wood. Santalum.

Sandáraca [san-dah'-ra-cah], *f.* 1. Sandarach, a red sulphuret of arsenic. 2. Sandarac, a white resin exuded by the juniper-tree.

Sandez [san-deth'], *f.* Folly, simplicity: want of understanding.

Sandía [san-dee'-ah], *f.* (Bot.) Watermelon. Cucurbita citrullus. (Arab.)

Sandiar [san-de-ar'], *m.* Watermelon-patch.

Sandio, dia [sahn'-de-o, ah], *a.* Foolish, nonsensical.

Sandix [san-dix'], *m.* Minium, red lead.

Sandunga [san-doon'-gah], *f.* (Coll.) Gracefulness, elegance; cajoling, wheedling; flattering, allurement, fascination. *Tener* or *usar, mucha sandunga*, To be very graceful, cajoling, fascinating; to delude by flattery, to wheedle.

Sandunguero, ra [san-doon-gay'-ro, rah], *a.* Alluring, wheedling, fascinating; elegant.

Saneable [sah-nay-ah'-blay], *a.* Reparable, savable.

Saneado, da [sah-nay-ah'-do, dah], *a.* 1. Drained. 2. Best of its kind.

Saneamiento [sah-nay-ah-me-en'-to], *m.* 1. Surety, bail, guarantee; indemnification, reparation. 2. Drainage.

Sanear [sah-nay-ar'], *va.* 1. To give security, to give bail. 2. To indemnify, to repair. 3. To save harmless. 4. To drain.

Sanedrín [sah-nay-dreen'], *m.* Sanhedrim, the supreme council of the Jewish nation.

Sanes [sah'-nes]. *Por vida de sanes*, A minced oath.

Sangley [san-glay'-e], *m.* Chinese trader in the Philippine Islands.

Sangradera [san-grah-day'-rah], *f.* 1. Lancet for blood-letting. 2. An earthen basin. 3. Lock, sluice, drain.

Sangrador [san-grah-dor'], *m.* 1. Phlebotomist, blood-letter. *Es grān sangrador*, He is a great blood-letter. 2. Fissure, opening.

Sangradura [san-grah-doo'-rah], *f.* 1. (Surg.) Bleeding; part of the arm usually bled. 2. Draining of a canal or river.

Sangrante [san-grahn'-tay], *a.* Bleeding.

Sangrar [san-grar'], *va.* 1. To bleed, to let blood; to open a vein. 2. To drain, to draw water from a canal or river. 3. (Print.) To indent the first line of a paragraph. *Me sangró bien la bolsa*, He drained my purse well.—*vn.* To bleed.—*vr.* To be bled.

Sangraza [san-grah'-thah], *f.* Corrupt or filthy blood.

Sangre [sahn'-gray], *f.* 1. Blood; gore. 2. Blood, race, family, kindred. *Ser de la sangre azul*, (Coll.) To belong to the nobility. 3. Substance, fortune. 4. Wound from which blood issues. *A sangre fría*, In cold blood. *A sangre y fuego*, By violent means, with the utmost rigour, without mercy; by fire and sword. *Sangre de espaldas, V.* ALMORRANAS. *Bajarse* or *irse la sangre a los talones* or *a los zancajos*, To be struck with terror or fear. *La sangre se me hiela en las venas*, My blood curdles in my veins. *Sangre de drago*, Dragon's-blood, a gum. *Bullir la sangre*, To be vigorous and healthy as in youth. *Escupir sangre*, To boast of nobility. *Escupir sangre en bacín de oro*, To enjoy little happiness in the midst of luxury. *Pudrirse* or *quemarse la sangre*, To be subject to constant vexations. *Querer beber la sangre a otro*, To hate a person mortally. *Tener sangre en el ojo*, To be prompt and honourable in filling engagements.

Sangría [san-gree'-ah], *f.* 1. (Surg.) Bleeding, blood-letting. 2. Any incision which emits blood. 3. Present made to a person who bleeds. 4. An extraction or stealing of any thing in small parcels. 5. (Print.) Indenting a line. 6. Inside of the arm, where a vein is usually opened. 7. *V.* SANGRADURA. 8. A beverage of red wine, lemon, and water; sangaree.

Sangrientamente [san-gre-en-tah-men'-tay], *adv.* Bloodily, cruelly.

Sangriento, ta [san-gre-en'-to, tah], *a.* 1. Bloody, blood-stained, gory. 2. Bloody, cruel, sanguinary, blood-thirsty.

Sangual [san-goo-ahl'], *m.* (Orn.) Osprey. Falco ossifragus.

Sanguaza [san-goo-ah'-thah], *f.* 1. Serous blood. 2. Reddish fluid of vegetables.

Sangüeño [san-goo-ay'-nyo], *m.* (Bot.) Dogberry-tree, cornelian cherry-tree. Cornus sanguinea.

Sangüeso [san-goo-ay'-so], *m.* (Bot.) Raspberry-bush. Rubus idæus.

Sanguífero, ra [san-gee'-fay-ro, rah], *a.* Sanguiferous.

Sanguificación [san-gee-fe-cah-the-on'], *f.* (Med.) Sanguification.

Sanguificar [san-gee-fe-car'], *va.* To sanguify, to make blood.

Sanguificativo, va [san-gee-fe-cah-tee'-vo, vah], *a.* Producing blood.

Sanguijuela [san-gee-hoo-ay'-lah], *f.* 1. Leech. Hirudo. 2. Sharper, a cheat. *Sanguijuelas del Estado*, Sinecure offices (drawing pay, but doing nothing for it).

Sanguinaria [san-gee-nah'-re-ah], *f.* 1. (Bot.) Blood-root, a medicinal herb. 2. Bloodstone, of a dark green colour, variegated by red spots; hematite; an amulet to prevent bleeding at the nose.

Sanguinariamente, *adv.* Sanguinarily.

Sanguinario, ria [san-gee-nah'-re-o, ah], *a.* Sanguinary, cruel, bloody.

Sanguíneo, nea, Sanguino, na [san-gee'-nay-o, ah], *a.* 1. Sanguine, red, the colour of blood. 2. Sanguineous.

Sanguinolencia [san-gee-no-len'-the-ah], *f.* Bloodiness, bloodthirstiness.

Sanguinolento, ta, *a. V.* SANGRIENTO.

Sanguinoso, sa [san-gee-no'-so, sah], *a.* 1. Sanguine, sanguinous. 2. Bloody, sanguinary, cruel.

Sanguiñol [san-gee-nyol'], *m.* (Bot.) *V.* SANGUEÑO.

Sángüis [sahn'-goo-is], *m.* (Lat.) Blood of Christ; consecrated wine.

Sanguisorba [san-gee-sor'-bah], *f.* (Bot.) Great burnet. Sanguisorva.

Sanguisuela, Sanguja [san-goo'-hah], *f.* (Prov. Coll.) Leech. *V.* SANGUIJUELA.

Sanícula [sah-nee'-coo-lah], *f.* (Bot.) Sanicle. Sanicula. *Sanicula europea*, Wood sanicle. Sanicula europea.

Sanidad [sah-ne-dahd'], *f.* 1. Soundness, health, vigour, sanity. *En sanidad*, In health. *Carta de sanidad*, Bill of health. *Casa de sanidad*, Health-office. *Juez de sanidad*, Commissioner of the board of health. 2. Candour, ingenuousness.

Sanie, Sanies [sah'-ne-ay, sah'-ne-es], *f.* (Med.) Sanies.

Sanioso, sa [sah-ne-o'-so, sah], *a.* (Med.) Sanious.

Sanitario, ria [sah-ne-tah'-re-o, ah], *a.* Sanitary, promotive of health.

Sanjacado, Sanjacato [san-hah-cah'-do], *m.* Government of a Turkish province.

Sanjaco [san-hah'-co], *m.* Turkish governor of a province.

Sanjuanada [san-hoo-ah-nah'-dah], *f.* (Prov.) Vigil of St. John.

Sanjuanero, ra [san-hoo-ah-nay'-ro, rah], *a.* Applied to fruits ripe at St John's day.

Sanjuanista [san-hoo-ah-nees'-tah], *a.* & *m.* A knight of St. John of Jerusalem.
Sanmiguelada [san-me-gay-lah'-dah], *f.* (Prov.) Michaelmas.
Sanmigueleño, ña, *a.* Applied to fruits ripe at Michaelmas.
Sano, na [sah'-no, nah], *a.* 1. Sound, healthy, wholesome, hale, hearty; salutary; sane; secure. 2. Sincere, well-disposed; discreet, wise, steady. 3. Safe, free from fault, harmless. 4. Entire, complete. *Sano y salvo,* Safe and sound.
Sánscrito [sahns'-cre-to], *m.* Sanskrit, the sacred language of Hindustan.
Sant, *a.* (Obs.) *V.* San.
Santa [sahn'-tah], *f.* Female saint.—*m. V.* Santuario.
Santa Bárbara [san'-tah bar'-ba-rah], *f.* 1. (Naut.) Magazine, powder-room. 2. St. Barbara.
Santamente, *adv.* 1. Reverently, piously, religiously; simply. 2. Briskly, freely. *Me entré santamente en la casa,* I stepped into the house without ceremony.
Santasantórum [san-tah-san-to'-room], *m.* 1. Sanctuary, sanctum-sanctorum, holy of holies. 2. Sanctum; something especially valued by any one. 3. The mysterious or occult.
Santazo, za [san-tah'-tho, thah], *a. aug.* A great saint.
Santelmo [san-tel'-mo], *m.* (Naut.) St. Elmo's light, a fiery meteor on the masts of ships in stormy weather.
Santero, ra [san-tay'-ro, rah], *m.* & *f.* Caretaker of a sanctuary.
Santiago [san-te-ah'-go], *m.* 1. St. James, the war-whoop of the Spaniards on engaging with Moors and other infidels. 2. A middling sort of linen manufactured in Santiago.
Santigueño, ña [san-te-gay'-nyo, nyah], *a.* Applied to fruits ripe at St. James's day, towards the end of July.
Santiagués, sa [san-te-ah-ghes', sah], *a.* Belonging to Santiago de Galicia.
Santiaguino, na [san-te-ah-gee'-no, nah], *a.* Belonging to Santiago de Chile.
Santiaguista [san-te-ah-gees'-tah], *a.* Belonging to the order of Santiago.—*m.* A knight of Santiago or St. James.
Santiamén [san-te-ah-men'], *m.* (Coll.) Moment, twinkling of an eye.
Santico, ca [san-tee'-co, cah], *m.* & *f.* 1. (Dim.) Little image of a saint. 2. In familiar language, a good child.
Santidad [san-te-dahd'], *f.* 1. Sanctity, sanctitude, piety, holiness, godliness. 2. Holiness, a title given to the Pope.
Santificable [san-te-fe-cah'-blay], *a.* Sanctifiable.
Santificación [san-te-fe-cah-the-on'], *f.* Sanctification, making holy. *Santificación de las fiestas,* Feriation, or keeping holidays.
Santificador [san-te-fe-cah-dor'], *m.* Sanctifier.
Santificante [san-te-fe-cahn'-tay], *pa.* Blessing, sanctifying.
Santificar [san-te-fe-car'], *va.* 1. To sanctify, to hallow. 2. To dedicate to God. 3. To bless, to praise. 4. To honour and serve as a saint. 5. (Met.) To justify, to exculpate.—*vr.* 1. To employ one's self in pious works. 2. To justify, to clear from guilt.
Santiguada [san-te-goo-ah'-dah], *f.* Blessing, the act of making the sign of the cross. *Para mi santiguada,* Faith, in truth, by this cross.
Santiguadera [san-te-goo-ah-day'-rah], *f.* Act of superstitiously making the sign of the cross over a sick person. *V.* Santiguadora.
Santiguadero [san-te-goo-ah-day'-ro], *m.* He who makes the sign of the cross over sick persons, using superstitious acts and prayers.
Santiguador, ra [san-te-goo-ah-dor', rah], *m.* & *f.* One who cures by the sign of the cross.
Santiguamiento [san-te-goo-ah-me-en'-to], *m.* Act of crossing or curing with the sign of the cross.
Santiguar [san-te-goo-ar'], *va.* 1. To bless, to make the sign of the cross over a sick person. 2. To chastise, to punish.—*vr.* To make the sign of the cross over one's self; to cross one's self.
Santiguo [san-tee'-goo-o], *m.* The act of making the cross over one's self.
Santimonia [san-te-mo'-ne-ah], *f.* 1. Sanctity, sanctimony, holiness. 2. (Bot.) Corn marigold, garden chrysanthemum. Chrysanthemum coronarium.
Santiscario [san-tis-cah'-re-o], *m.* (Coll.) Caprice, whim: used only in the colloquial and rather uncommon phrase, *De mi santiscario.*
Santísimo, ma [san-tee'-se-mo, mah], *a. sup.* Most holy. *El Santísimo,* The holy sacrament.
Santo, ta [sahn'-to, tah], *a.* & *n.* 1. Saintly, holy, virtuous, ghostly. 2. Saint, a person eminent for piety. 3. (Coll.) Simple, plain, artless. 4. Sacred, dedicated to God; inviolable. 5. Grateful, delightful, pleasant. 6. Just, upright, pious. 7. Holy: applied to the Roman Catholic and apostolic church. *Santo y bueno,* Well and good. *Santo día,* The whole day. *Pasó el santo día en la ociosidad,* He spent the whole day in idleness. *Santo de pajares,* Hypocrite. *Todos Santos,* All Saints' day. *Santo varón,* A holy man; a harmless idiot or simpleton; a great hypocrite. *A santo tapado,* Clandestinely, cautiously, and secretly. *Santo mocarro,* A vulgar play.
Santo [sahn'-to], *m.* 1. Saint, the image of a saint. 2. (Mil.) Watchword. *Anda con mil santos,* Leave me; away with you.
Santolina [san-to-lee'-nah], *f.* (Bot.) Lavender-cotton. Santolina.
Santón [san-tone'], *m.* 1. (Aug.) A pretended saint, a hypocrite. 2. A kind of recluse among the Moors.
Santoral [san-to-rahl'], *m.* A collection of sermons or lives of the saints; church-choir book.
Santuario [san-too-ah'-re-o], *m.* Sanctuary; temples and sacred things.
Santucho, cha [san-too'-cho, chah], *m.* & *f.* (Coll.) Hypocrite.
Santurrón, na [san-toor-rohn', nah], *m.* & *f.* & *a.* (Coll.) Hypocrite, canter, zealot.
Santurronería [san-toor-ro-nay-ree'-ah], *f.* Hypocrisy. *V.* Beatería.
Santus, *m.* *V.* Sanctus.
Saña [sah'-nyah], *f.* Anger, passion, rage and its effects.
Sañosamente, *adv.* Furiously.
Sañoso, sa [sah-nyo'-so, sah], *a.* Furious.
Sañudo, da [sah-nyoo'-do, dah], *a.* Furious, enraged.
Sapa [sah'-pah], *f.* Woody residue left after chewing *buyo,* a compound of areca and betel-nuts with lime. *Cf.* Buyo, 3d def.
Sapajú [sah-pa-hoo'], *m.* Sapajou, capuchin, a South American monkey, often seen in captivity.
Sapán [sah-pahn'], *m.* (Bot.) Sapan wood, a brownish-red dye-wood; sapan-tree. Cæsalpinia sapan. *V.* Sibucao.
Sapera [sah-pay'-rah], *f.* (Bot.) Sea-heath. Frankenia lævis.
Sápido, da [sah'-pe-do, dah], *a.* High-flavoured, of an exquisite taste.
Sapiencia [sah-pe-en'-the-ah], *f.* Wisdom.
Sapienciales [sah-pe-en-the-ah'-les], *m. pl.* Books of wisdom, works on morals: used in the singular as an adjective.
Sapiente [sah-pe-en'-tay], *a.* Wise. *V.* Sabio.
Sapientísimamente [sah-pe-en-tee'-se-mah-men-tay], *adv.* Most wisely.
Sapillo [sah-peel'-lyo], *m.* 1. (Dim.) A little toad. 2. A small tumour under the tongue.
Sapina [sah-pee'-nah], *f.* A glasswort, or plant yielding barilla, which grows in the Levant and in southern Spain.
Sapino [sah-pee'-no], *m.* (Bot.) Savin, sabin, a small tree of the pine family.
Sapo [sah'-po], *m.* A large toad. *V.* Escuerzo. *Pisar el sapo, V.* Pisar. *Echar sapos y culebras,* (Coll.) To be beside one's self; to be extremely angry.
Saponáceo, cea [sah-po-nah'-thay-o, ah], *a.* Saponaceous, soapy.
Saponaria [sah-po-nah'-re-ah], *f.* (Bot.) Common soapwort. Saponaria officinalis.
Saponificable [sah-po-ne-fe-cah'-blay], *a.* Saponifiable.
Saponificación [sah-po-ne-fe-cah-the-on'], *f.* Saponification, the process or result of making soap.
Saponificar [sah-po-ne-fe-car'], *va.* To saponify, to convert a fat or oil into soap by the action of an alkali.—*vr.* To become saponified.
Saporífero, ra [sah-po-ree-fay-ro, rah], *a.* Imparting savor.
Saprino [sah-pree'-no], *m.* (Ent.) A diminutive beetle of the silpha family, about one-tenth of an inch in length; of most brilliant colouring, punctated with black. Found all over the world.
Saque [sah'-kay], *m.* 1. The act of tossing a ball. 2. He that tosses the ball. 3. A line or base from which a ball is tossed.
Saqueador, ra [sah-kay-ah-dor', rah], *m.* & *f.* Depopulator, ransacker, free-booter.
Saquear [sah-kay-ar'], *va.* 1. To ransack, to plunder, to foray, to pillage. 2. To take away unlawfully.
Saqueamiento, *m.* (Littl. us.) *V.* Saqueo, Saco.
Saqueo [sah-kay'-o], *m.* Pillage, plunder, foray.
Saquera [sah-kay'-rah], *f.* (Prov.) Needle for sewing sacks, a packing-needle.
Saquería [sah-kay-ree'-ah], *f.* Place for or collection of sacks.
Saquete, Saqueto [sah-kay'-tay], *m. dim.* Little sack.
Saquilada [sah-ke-lah'-dah], *f.* A small quantity of grain put into a sack to be ground.
Saquillo, ito [sah-keel'-lyo, ee'-to], *m. dim.* A small bag.
Saraguete [sah-rah-gay'-tay], *m.* Hop, a family dance.
Sarampión [sa-ram-pe-on'], *m.* Measles, an eruptive disease.
Sarangosti [sa-ran-gos'-te], *m.* (Naut.) Saragosti, a gum used in the East Indies, instead of pitch and tar, to caulk ships.
Sarao [sah-rah'-o], *m.* Ball, an entertainment of dancing.
Sarape [sa-rah'-pay], *m.* Serape, Mexican blanket.
Sarcasmo [sar-cahs'-mo], *m.* Sarcasm, keen and bitter irony.
Sarcástico, ca [sar-cahs'-te-co, cah], *a.* Sarcastic, taunting.

Sarcia [sar-the-ah], *f.* Load, burden. *V.* CARGA.
Sarcillo [sar-theel'-lyo], *m.* (Prov.) Hoe.
Sarcócola [sar-co'-co-lah], *f.* Sarcocolla, a resinous gum from Ethiopia.
Sarcófago [sar-co'-fah-go], *m.* 1. Tomb, grave. 2. Sarcophagus.
Sarcologia [sar-co-lo'-he-ah], *f.* (Anat.) Sarcology, that part of anatomy which treats of the fleshy parts of the body.
Sarcótico, ca [sar-co'-te-co, cah], *a.* Sarcotic, promotive of healing wounds by generating new flesh.
Sarda [sar'-dah], *f.* A kind of mackerel. Scomber colias. *V.* CABALLA.
Sardesco, ca [sar-des'-co, cah], *a.* 1. Belonging to a small ass or horse. 2. (Coll.) Rude; stubborn.
Sardesco, *m.* A small ass.
Sardina [sar-dee'-nah], *f.* Sardine; anchovy. Clupea encrasicolus. *La última sardina de la banasta,* The last shift. *Echar otra sardina,* (Coll.) To squeeze in, to make one's way in where it causes inconvenience.
Sardinel [sar-de-nel'], *m.* Work of bricks placed on edge.
Sardinero, ra [sar-de-nay'-ro, rah], *a.* Belonging to anchovies.—*m.* & *f.* Dealer in anchovies or pilchards.—*m.* Name of a beautiful public walk near Santander, close to the beach.
Sardineta [sar-de-nay'-tah], *f.* 1. A small anchovy or pilchard. 2. Part of cheese which overtops the cheese-vat. 3. (Naut.) Knittle, a small line for various purposes on shipboard. 4. *pl.* Loops of galloon ending in a point placed on certain military uniforms. *Sardinetes,* Fillips with wet fingers.
Sardio, Sardo [sar'-de-o], *m.* Sard, sardine, a precious stone.
Sardo, da [sar'-do, dah], *a.* Sardinian.
Sardonia [sar-do'-ne-ah], *f.* (Bot.) Crow-foot, spearwort.
Sardónice [sar-do'-ne-thay], *f.* Sardonyx, a precious stone.
Sardónico, ca [sar-do'-ne-co, cah], *a.* 1. Sardonic, relating to the herb sardonia. 2. Insincere, affected (laughter).
Sardonio, Sardónique, Sardónix, *m.* *V.* SARDÓNICE.
Sarga [sar'-gah], *f.* 1. Serge, a silk stuff; also, a kind of woollens. 2. (Art) Fabric painted in distemper or oil, like tapestry, used for decorating rooms. 3. A kind of osier or willow.
Sargadilla [sar-gah-deel'-lyah], *f.* A soda-ash plant common in Spain and in the south of France.
Sargado, da [sar-gah'-do, dah], *a.* Serge-like. *V.* ASARGADO.
Sargal [sar-gahl'], *m.* A clump of osiers.
Sargatillo [sar-gah-teel'-lyo], *m.* A kind of willow of Spain.
Sargazo [sar-gah'-tho], *m.* (Bot.) Sea-lentils, gulf-weed, sargasso. Sargassum.
Sargenta [sar-hen'-tah], *f.* 1. Sergeant's halberd. 2. Sergeant's wife.
Sargentear [sar-hen-tay-ar'], *va.* 1. To perform the duty of a sergeant. 2. To take the command. 3. To act in an overbearing manner.
Sargentería [sar-hen-tay-ree'-ah], *f.* Place or duty of a sergeant.
Sargentía [sar-hen-tee'-ah], *f.* Office of a sergeant.
Sargento [sar-hen'-to], *m.* Sergeant. *Sargento primero.* Sergeant-major. *Sargento mayor de un regimiento,* (Mil.) A major.
Sargentón [sar-hen-tone'], *m.* 1. (Aug.) A tall sergeant. 2. (Coll.) A strong, masculine woman.
Sargo [sar'-go], *m.* (Zool.) A kind of sea-roach or sea-bream. Sparus sargus.
Sarguero [sar-gay'-ro], *m.* Painter of sarga (2d def.).
Sargueta [sar-gay'-tah], *f.* A thin, light serge.
Sarilla [sah-reel'-lyah], *f.* (Bot.) Marjoram. Thymbra.
Sarjia [sar-hee'-ah], *f.* Scarification. *V.* SAJA.
Sármata [sar'-ma-tah], *a.* *V.* SARMÁTICO.
Sarmático, ca [sar-mah'-te-co, cah], *a.* Sarmatian.
Sarmentador, ra [sar-men-tah-dor', rah], *m.* & *f.* One, who gathers pruned vine-shoots.
Sarmentar [sar-men-tar'], *va.* To gather pruned vine-shoots.
Sarmenticio, cia [sar-men-tee'-the-o, ah], *a.* Applied to Christians in derision, because they suffered themselves to be burned with the slow fire of vine-shoots.
Sarmentillo [sar-men-teel'-lyo], *m. dim.* of SARMIENTO.
Sarmentoso, sa [sar-men-to'-so, sah], *a.* 1. Full of vine-shoots. 2. Creeping, twining, leaning on other bodies for support: used of plants.
Sarmiento [sar-me-en'-to], *m.* Vine-shoot, the branch on which grapes grow.
Sarna [sar'-nah], *f.* 1. Itch, a cutaneous disease. *No le falta sino sarna que rascar,* (Coll.) He has everything which his heart can wish for. 2. Mange, the itch or scab in cattle.
Sarnazo [sar-nah'-tho], *m.* A malignant itch.
Sarnoso, sa [sar-no'-so, sah], *a.* Itchy, affected with itch, scabbed, scaly; mangy.—*m.* Scab, a nickname for a paltry fellow.
Sarpullido or **Salpullido** [sar-pool-lyee'-do, sal-pool-lyee'-do], *m.* Prickly heat, skin rash.
Sarpullir, *vn.* To be flea-bitten.—*vr.* To be full of flea-bites.
Sarracénico, ca [sar-rah-thay'-ne-co, cah], *a.* Saracenic, belonging to the Saracens.
Sarraceno, na [sar-rah-thay'-no, nah], *m.* & *f.* Saracen, Moor; a name of the middle ages for the Arabs and their descendants.
Sarracín, na, *a.* *V.* SARRACENO.
Sarracina [sar-rah-thee'-nah], *f.* A tumultuous contest between a number of persons.
Sarria [sar'-re-ah], *f.* 1. A wide net made of ropes, in which straw is carried: in Toledo it is called *sarrieta.* 2. (Prov.) Large basket.
Sarrillo [sar-reel'-lyo], *m.* 1. A rattling in the throat of a dying person. 2. (Bot.) *V.* YARO.
Sarrio [sar'-re-o], *a.* A kind of wild goat, with the horns bent forward.
Sarro [sar'-ro], *m.* 1. A hard, strong bitumen. 2. Sediment which adheres to vessels. 3. Incrustation of the tongue in fevers; sordes: tartar of the teeth. 4. A tumour which grows in the tongue and roughens it.
Sarroso, sa [sar-ro'-so, sah], *a.* Incrusted, covered with sediment.
Sarta [sar'-tah], *f.* String of beads or pearls; any set of things filed on a line; series.
Sartal [sar-tahl'], *a.* Stringed.—*m.* String of beads, etc.
Sartalejo [sar-tah-lay'-ho], *m. dim.* A small string of pearls or precious stones.
Sartén [sar-tayn'], *f.* Frying-pan. *Fruta de sartén,* Fritter, pancake. *Tener la sartén por el mango,* To have the command or advantage in a situation. *Dijo la sartén a la caldera: ¡quítate allá, culinegra!* The pot called the kettle black. *Saltar de la sartén y dar* (or *caer*) *en las brasas,* To jump out of the frying-pan into the fire.
Sartenada [sar-tay-nah'-dah], *f.* As much meat or fish as a frying-pan can hold.
Sartenazo [sar-tay-nah'-tho], *m.* 1. Blow with a frying-pan. 2. (Coll.) A weighty blow with any thing. 3. (Met. Coll.) Trick played off; jest, joke.
Sarteneja [sar-tay-nay'-hah], *f. dim.* A small frying-pan.
Sartenica, illa, ita [sar-tay-nee'-cah], *f. dim.* A small frying-pan.
Sartorio [sar-to'-re-o], *m.* Sartorius, the tailor's muscle.
Sarzo, *m.* *V.* ZARZO.
Sasafrás [sah-sa-frahs'], *m.* (Bot.) Sassafras. Sassafras officinale.
Sastra [sahs'-trah], *f.* Wife of a tailor, tailoress.
Sastre [sahs'-tray], *m.* Tailor. *Sastre remendón,* Botching tailor, mender of old clothes. *Es un cajón de sastre,* He is a superficial scribbler. *Es un corto sastre,* (Coll.) He is not skilled in his profession, or he does not know his own business. *Es un buen sastre,* (Coll.) He is a cunning blade.
Sastrecillo [sas-tray-theel'-lyo], *m. dim.* A petty tailor.
Sastrería [sas-tray-ree'-ah], *f.* 1. Tailor's trade; tailoring. 2. A tailor's shop.
Satán, Satanás [sah-tahn', sah-tah-nahs'], *m.* Satan. (Heb.)
Satánicamente, *adv.* Satanically.
Satánico, ca [sah-tah'-ne-co, cah], *a.* Satanic, devilish.
Satélite [sah-tay'-le-tay], *m.* 1. (Ast.) Satellite. *Satélite artificial,* Artificial satellite, man-made satellite. 2. Satellite, obsequious follower, subordinate associate. 3. (coll.) Bailiff, constable.
Saterión [sah-tay-re-on'], *m.* (Bot.) *V.* SATIRIÓN.
Satín [sah-teen'], *m.* (Neol.) Satin. *V.* RASO.
Satinador, ra [sah-te-nah-dor', rah], *m.* & *f.* Glazing apparatus, rolling-press; one who calenders.
Satinar [sah-te-nar'], *va.* To calender, to glaze.
Sátira [sah'-te-rah], *f.* 1. Satire, a poem, in which wickedness or folly is censured. 2. A lively, bitter, and witty woman. 3. A biting joke.
Satíricamente, *adv.* Satirically.
Satírico [sah-tee'-re-co], *m.* Satirist, one who writes satires.
Satírico, ca [sah-tee'-re-co, cah], *a.* Satirical, censorious.
Satirilla [sah-te-reel'-lyah], *f. dim.* A sharp, sneering insinuation.
Satirillo [sah-te-reel'-lyo], *m. dim.* A little satyr.
Satirio [sah-tee'-re-o], *m.* Kind of water-rat.
Satirión [sah-te-re-on'], *m.* (Bot.) The orchis which yields salep. Orchis.
Satirizante [sah-te-re-thahn'-tay], *pa.* Satirizing, writing satires.
Satirizar [sah-te-re-thar'], *va.* To satirize, to write satires, to lampoon, to libel.
Sátiro [sah'-te-ro], *m.* Satyr, a sylvan god.
Satisdación [sah-tis-dah-the-on'], *f.* (Law) *V.* FIANZA.
Satisfacción [sah-tis-fac-the-on'], *f.* 1. Satisfaction, amends, atonement, recompense, apology, excuse. 2. Gratification, the act of pleasing, content, complacence, satisfaction, the state of

being pleased. 3. Presumption; confidence, security. 4. Satisfaction, one of the three parts of the sacrament of penance. *A satisfacción*, Fully, according to one's wishes. *Con satisfacción*, (Coll.) Without ceremony, in a friendly manner. *Tomar satisfacción*, To satisfy one's self, to vindicate one's self, to revenge.

Satisfacer [sah-tis-fah-therr'], *va.* 1. To satisfy, to pay fully what is due. 2. To satisfy, to content, to gratify, to humour. 3. To satisfy, to expiate, to atone; to reward. 4. To satisfy, to give a solution. 5. To allay the passions; to indulge; to sate or satiate. 6. To free from debt, perplexity, or suspense.—*vr.* 1. To satisfy one's self; to take satisfaction; to be revenged. 2. To be satisfied, to vindicate one's self. 3. To be convinced, to be undeceived or disabused. *Satisfacer una letra*, To honour a draft.

Satisfactoriamente, *adv.* Satisfactorily.

Satisfactorio, ria [sah-tis-fac-to'-re-o, ah], *a.* Satisfactory.

(*Yo satisfago, yo satisfice, yo satisfaga*, from *Satisfacer.* *V.* HACER.)

Satisfecho, cha [sah-tis-fay'-cho, chah], *a.* & *pp. irr.* of SATISFACER. Satisfied, confident, content; arrogant.

Sativo, va [sah-tee'-vo, vah], *a.* Sown, that which is cultivated, as opposed to what grows wild.

Sato [sah'-to], *m.* (Obs.) Corn-field. *V.* SEMBRADO.

Sátrapa [sah'-trah-pah], *m.* 1. Satrap, a Persian governor. 2. (Met. Coll.) A sly, crafty fellow.

Satrapía [sah-trah-pee'-ah], *f.* Dignity of a Persian satrap.

Saturable [sah-too-rah'-blay], *a.* Saturable.

Saturación [sah-too-rah-the-on'], *f.* 1. Saturity, filling one thing with another. 2. Saturation; the solution in a liquid of all the solid which it can hold; the impregnation of an acid with alkali.

Saturar [sah-too-rar'], *va.* 1. To saturate, to imbibe, to impregnate. 2. To fill, to glut.

Saturativo, va [sah-too-rah-tee'-vo, vah], *a.* Possessing the power of saturating, saturant.

Saturnal [sah-toor-nahl'], *a.* Saturnalian. *Saturnales*, Saturnalia.

Saturnino, na [sah-toor-nee'-no, nah], *a.* Saturnine, melancholy, grave, gloomy.

Saturno [sah-toor'-no], *m.* 1. (Ast.) Saturn. 2. Lead.

Sauce [sah'-oo-thay], *m.* (Bot.) Willow. Salix.

Saucedal, *m.* **Saucera**, *f.* [sah-oo-thay-dahl', sah-oo-thay'-rah]. Plantation of willows. *V.* SALCEDA.

Saucegatillo, *m.* (Bot.) *V.* SAUZGATILLO.

Saucillo, *m.* (Bot.) *V.* SANGUINARIA.

Saúco [sah-oo'-co], *f.* 1. (Bot.) Elder or alder-tree. Sambucus. 2. Second hoof of horses.

Sauquillo [sah-oo-keel'-lyo], *m.* (Bot.) Dwarf elder. Sambucus ebulus.

Saurios [sah'-oo-re-os], *m. pl.* Saurians, a division of reptiles; lizards.

Sausería [sah-oo-say-ree'-ah], *f.* Larder in a palace.

Sausier [sah-oo-se-err'], *m.* Chief of the larder in a palace.

Sauz [sah'-ooth], *m.* (Bot.) *V.* SAUCE.

Sauzal [sah-oo-thahl'], *m.* *V.* SAUCEDAL and SALCEDA.

Sauzgatillo [sah-ooth-gah-teel'-lyo], *m.* (Bot.) Agnus castus tree, chaste tree. Vitex agnus castus.

Savia [sah'-ve-ah], *f.* The sap of plants, the nutrient fluid.

Saxafrax [sak-sah-frahx'], *f.* (Bot.) *V.* SAXIFRAGA.

Saxátil [sak-sah'-teel], *a.* Growing among or adhering to rocks: said of animals and plants; saxicolous.

Sáxeo, ea [sak'-say-o, ah], *a.* Stony.

Saxícola [sak-see'-co-lah], *f.* (Zool.) A genus of birds of the family Turdidæ; the chats.

Saxífraga, Saxifragua [sak-see'-frah-gah, sak-se-frah'-goo-ah], *f.* (Bot.) The saxifrage plant; mountain saxifrage. Saxifraga.

Saxofón, saxófono [sax-o-fone', sax-o'-fo-no], *m.* Saxophone.

Saya [sah'-yah], *f.* 1. Dress skirt, outer skirt, of a woman, with pleats at the upper part, and which descends to the feet. 2. A certain sum of money which the Queen of Spain gives her maids when they marry. 3. Ancient tunic or gown worn by men. *Saya saya*, Chinese silk. *Saya entera*, A gown with a train.

Sayal [sah-yahl'], *m.* A coarse woollen stuff, sackcloth.

Sayalería [sah-yah-lay-ree'-ah], *f.* Shop for weaving coarse cloth.

Sayalero [sah-yah-lay'-ro], *m.* Weaver of coarse stuff.

Sayalesco, ca [sah-yah-les'-co, cah], *a.* Made of sackcloth or other coarse stuff.

Sayalete [sah-yah-lay'-tay], *m. dim.* A thin or light stuff used for under-garments.

Sayaza [sah-yah'-thah], *f. aug.* An outward coarse petticoat.

Sayete, Sayito [sah-yay'-tay], *m. dim.* A small frock, a short dress.

Sayo [sah'-yo], *m.* A large wide coat without buttons; any loose coat or dress; small frock. *Sayo bobo*, Tight dress worn by clowns in plays. *Sayo vaquero*, A loose jacket worn by cowherds. *A su sayo*, Of one's own accord, in one's own mind. *Cortar (a uno) un sayo*, To blame or censure any one in his absence. *Decir a* (or *para*) *su sayo*, To say in one's sleeve, to one's self.

Sayón [sa-yon'], *m.* 1. (Obs.) Bailiff; executioner. 2. A corpulent, ill-looking fellow. 3. Aug. of SAYO.

Sayonazo [sah-yo-nah'-tho], *m. aug.* of SAYÓN.

Sayuela [sah-yoo-ay'-lah], *f.* 1. Woollen shift worn by some religious. 2. Kind of fig-tree.

Sayuelo [sah-yoo-ay'-lo], *m. dim.* Little frock, small kind of jacket.

Saz [sahth], *m.* (Obs.) *V.* SAUCE.

Sazgatillo, *m.* (Bot.) SAUZGATILLO.

Sazón [sah-thone'], *f.* 1. Maturity, state of perfection. 2. Season, taste, relish, flavour, seasoning. 3. Occasion, opportunity, season, conjunction. *A la sazón*, Then, at that time. *En sazón*, Seasonably, opportunely.

Sazonadamente, *adv.* Maturely, seasonably.

Sazonado, da [sah-tho-nah'-do, dah], *a.* & *pp.* of SAZONAR. 1. Seasoned, mature, mellow. 2. Applied to a witty saying, or to a word to the purpose.

Sazonador, ra [sah-tho-nah-dor', rah], *m.* & *f.* Seasoner.

Sazonar [sah-tho-nar'], *va.* 1. To season, to give a relish. 2. To mature, to bring to maturity.—*vr.* To ripen, to mature.

Se [say]. The reflexive pronoun, possessive to the person or thing that governs the verb; used before the pronouns *me, te, le,* it reflects the action of the verb on the object which they represent. *Se* is used instead of the other cases of the pronouns of the third person, as *¿Le entregó V. la carta?* Did you deliver him or her the letter? *Sí, se la entregué*, Yes, I delivered it *to him*, or *to her*. *Se* represents frequently the passive form of a verb, as *Se dice*, It is said.

(*Yo sé, yo supe, yo sepa, yo supiera.* *V.* SABER.)

Sea que [say'-ah kay], *adv.* Whether.

Sebáceo, cea [say-bah'-thay-o, ah], *a.* Sebaceous, tallowy.

Sebastiano [say-bas-te-ah'-no], *m.* *V.* SEBESTÉN.

Sebato [say-bah'-to], *m.* (Chem.) Sebate.

Sebe [say'-bay], *f.* Stockade, wattle of high pales interwoven with long branches.

Sebesta [say-bes'-tah], *f.* Sebesten-fruit, sebestine.

Sebestén [say-bes-ten'], *m.* (Bot.) Sebesten-tree, a tree of India and western Asia resembling the sloe. Cordia sebestena.

Sebillo [say-beel'-lyo], *m.* Paste made with suet, to soften the hands; kind of soap.

Sebo [say'-bo], *m.* 1. Tallow, candle-grease, suet; any kind of grease or fat. *Sebo en rama* or *en bruto*, Rough tallow. *Sebo colado* or *derretido*, Melted tallow. *Dar sebo a un barco*, (Naut.) To pay a vessel's bottom. 2. (Met. Coll.) A large capital, a great fortune. 3. (Naut.) Animal grease, with which the bottoms of ships, the masts, etc., are besmeared.

Seboso, sa [say bo'-so, sah], *a.* Tallowy, fat, greasy, unctuous; greased.

Seca [say'-cah], *f.* 1. Drought, dry weather. 2. Inflammation and swelling in the glands. 3. *V.* SECANO, 3d def. *A secas*, Alone, singly. *A gran seca, gran mojada*, (1) After a drought, a heavy wetting. (2) Excessive activity after a period of inaction or a piece of unexpected good fortune, windfall. (3) Law of compensation.

Secacul [say-cah-cool'], *m.* (Bot.) A plant like a parsnip, and having a very aromatic root.

Secadal [say-cah-dahl'], *m.* A dry, barren ground.

Secadero [say-cah-day'-ro], *m.* Place where any thing is dried; drying shed, room, or floor; drier; fruit-drier.

Secadero, ra, *a.* Capable of being dried: applied to fruit.

Secadillo [say-cah-deel'-lyo], *m.* A sort of dry, round biscuit: commonly used in the plural.

Secamente, *adv.* 1. Dryly, morosely; crabbedly, peevishly. 2. Coldly, frigidly.

Secano [say-cah'-no], *m.* 1. Dry, unirrigated, arable land. 2. Dryness. 3. Sandbank uncovered by water.

Secansa [say-cahn'-sah], *f.* A game at cards ending in one-and-thirty.

Secante [say-cahn'-tay], *m.* Drier, a drying oil used for painting.—*f.* (Geom.) Secant.

Secar [say-car'], *va.* To dry out, to exsiccate, to dry.—*vr.* 1. To dry, to be dried up, to grow dry. 2. To become lank, lean, or meagre, to decay. 3. To grow cool in intercourse with a friend. 4. To be extremely thirsty. 5. To feel repugnance to do any thing, however necessary.

Secaral [say-cah-rahl'], *m.* Dryness, drought. *V.* SEQUERAL.

Secatura [say-cah-too'-rah], *f.* 1. Insipidity; want of spirit or life, flatness, want of understanding. 2. Coolness, indifference.

Sección [sec-the-on'], *f.* 1. Act of cutting. 2. Section, a division of a book. 3. (Geom.) Section, the cutting of lines, figures, and solid bodies. 4. (Arch.) Section of a building; delineation of its height and depth. 5. Topographical division, section: in hydraulics, section, capacity of the bed of a river, its width and depth.

Seccionar [sec-the-o-nar'], *va.* To section, to divide into sections.

Seccionario, ria [sec-the-o-nah'-re-o, ah], *a.* Sectional, relating to a section.

Seceno, na [say-thay'-no, nah], *a.* Sixteenth. (Obs.) *V.* DIECISEISENO.

Secesión [say-thay-se-on'], *f.* Secession.

Seceso [say-thay'-so], *m.* Excrement, stool.

Secluso, sa [say-cloo'-so, sah], *a.* (Obs.) Secluded, separated.

Seco, ca [say'-co, cah], *a.* 1. Dry, not wet, not moist. 2. Dry, not rainy. 3. Dry, not succulent. 4. Barren, arid, sapless, withered. 5. Lean, lank, meagre. 6. Bare, only, mere. *A secas*, Solely. 7. Barren, without ornament or embellishment. 8. Rude, dry, ill-mannered. *Es un hombre seco*, He is a man of few words, he is not sociable. 9. Lukewarm, cold, without affection. *Pan seco*, Dry bread. *A secas y sin llover*, Without preparation or advice, unexpectedly. *En seco*, (1) Without cause or motive. (2) In a dry place. *Navío a palo seco*, (Naut.) Ship under bare poles. *Correr a palo seco*, (Naut.) To scud under bare poles. *Dar en seco*, To run aground.

Secor [say-cor'], *m.* (Obs.) *V.* SEQUEDAD.

Secreción [say-cray-the-on'], *f.* 1. (Med.) Secretion, act of separating the fluids of the body. 2. *V.* APARTAMIENTO.

Secreta [say-cray'-tah], *f.* 1. The private examen which, in Spanish universities, precedes the graduation of licentiates. 2. Privy, water-closet. 3. Certain orisons at the beginning of the mass. 4. Secret inquiry or verbal investigation.

Secretamente, *adv.* Secretly, clandestinely.

Secretar [say-cray-tar'], *va.* 1. (Med.) To secrete, to secern, to separate. 2. To prepare skins, the hair of which is to be taken off and prepared for making felt hats.

Secretaria [say-cray-tah'-re-ah], *f.* 1. The wife of a secretary. 2. Woman who writes a lady's letters; secretary of a nunnery.

Secretaría [say-cray-tah-ree'-ah], *f.* 1. Secretary's office. 2. Secretaryship.

Secretariar [say-cray-tah-re-ar'], *vn.* (Littl. us.) To fill the office of secretary.

Secretario [say-cray-tah'-re-o], *m.* 1. Secretary, an officer employed in writing the letters, despatches, etc., of a council, a court of justice, or of a person constituted in high authority. 2. One intrusted with the management of the business of a society, institution, or company. 3. A scribe, a notary. 4. Clerk, amanuensis, one who writes for another. *Secretario de Estado*, etc., *V.* MINISTRO.

Secretear [say-cray-tay-ar'], *vn.* (Coll.) To speak in private, to whisper.

Secretico, illo, ito [say-cray-tee'-co], *m. dim.* A trifling secret. *Secretillos*, Private conversation between friends.

Secretista [say-cray-tees'-tah], *m.* 1. Author who writes on the secrets of nature: naturalist. 2. Secretist, a dealer in secrets.

Secreto, ta [say-cray'-to, tah], *a.* 1. Secret; hidden, obscure, occult; dark; clandestine. 2. (Coll.) Confidential.

Secreto [say-cray'-to], *m.* 1. Secrecy, careful silence. 2. Secret, the thing hidden or concealed; arcanum; nostrum. 3. Caution, silence, dissimulation, concealment; darkness. 4. Scrutoire, a case or hidden drawer for papers; a secret drawer in a desk or trunk. *Secreto a voces*, Open secret. *Observar el secreto*, To maintain secrecy. *Secreto de Estado*, State secret. *Secreto profesional*, Professional confidence. *De secreto*, Secretly. *De secreto inviolable*, Top-secret. *En secreto*, In secret, in private; informally. *Tener una cosa secreta*, To keep something to oneself.

Secretón [say-cray-tone'], *m.* Fine dimity.

Secretorio, ria [say-cray-to'-re-o, ah], *a.* (Med.) Secretory.

Secta [sec'-tah], *f.* 1. A sect. 2. Doctrine or opinion of a sect.

Sectador, ra [sec-tah-dor', rah], *m.* & *f.* Sectarist.

Sectario, ria [sec-tah'-re-o, ah], *a.* & *n.* Sectarian; sectary.

Sector [sec-tor'], *m.* (Geom.) Sector.

Secuaz [say-coo-ath'], *a.* & *m.* & *f.* Following the opinions of others, sectary of the school of; sequacious; attendant.

Secuela [say-coo-ay'-lah], *f.* 1. Sequel, continuation. 2. (Obs.) Sequence, the act of following a party or doctrine. 3. (Obs.) Consequence, induction.

Secuencia [say-coo-en'-the-ah], *f.* A sequence said in mass after the epistles.

Secuestrable [say-coo-es-trah'-blay], *a.* Sequestrable, legally forfeitable.

Secuestración [say-coo-es-trah-the-on'], *f.* Sequestration, the setting aside of property from the possession and control of persons, pending judicial proceedings. *V.* SECUESTRO.

Secuestrador [say-coo-es-trah-dor'], *m.* Sequestrator.

Secuestrar [say-coo-es-trar'], *va.* To sequestrate, to sequester, to distress.

Secuestrario, ria [say-coo-es-trah'-re-o, ah], *a.* Belonging to sequestration.

Secuestro [say-coo-es'-tro], *m.* 1. Sequestration. 2. The person in whose hands sequestered property is trusted as a deposit. 3. Seizure of a person by robbers, demanding money for ransom. 4. Sequestrum, a piece of dead bone separated from the living. *Depositario de un secuestro*, Garnishee, he in whose hands money is attached.

Secular [say-coo-lar'], *a.* 1. Secular, happening or coming once in a century. 2. Secular, not spiritual or ecclesiastical. 3. Not bound by monastic rules. 4. Lay, laical.

Secularidad [say-coo-lah-re-dahd'], *f.* Secularity.

Secularizable [say-coo-la-re-thah'-blay], *a.* Secularizable, capable of being secularized.

Secularización [say-coo-lah-re-thah-the-on'], *f.* Secularization.

Secularizar [say-coo-lah-re-thar'], *va.* To secularize.

Secundar [say-coon-dar'], *va.* 1. To aid another in some toil. 2. To favour the purposes of another, to second. 3. To repeat a second time.

Secundariamente, *adv.* Secondarily.

Secundario, ria [say-coon-dah'-re-o, ah], *a.* 1. Secondary, second in order; subordinate. 2. Accessory.

Secundinas [say-coon-dee'-nas], *f. pl.* After-birth and secundines.

Secura [say-coo'-rah], *f.* 1. Dryness, droughtiness. 2. Coolness, indifference.

Secutar, *va.* (Obs.) *V.* EJECUTAR.

Sed [sayd], *f.* 1. Thirst. 2. Drought. 3. Eagerness, anxiety; violent desire. *No dar una sed de agua*, Not to give as much as a draught of water. (The d in this word is almost inaudible in pronunciation.)

Seda [say'-dah], *f.* 1. Silk, the thread of the silk-worm. 2. Stuff formed of silken threads. 3. Sewing-silk. *Seda en rama* or *cruda*, Raw silk. *Seda floja*, Floss silk. *Seda torcida*, Twisted silk. *Seda de coser*, Sewing-silk. *Seda joyante*, Very glossy silk. 4. Wild-boar's bristles. *Ser una seda* or *como una seda*, To be of a sweet temper. *Tejedor de seda*, Silk-weaver. *Seda de candongo*, The finest silk reeled into small skeins. *Seda de todo capullo*, Coarse, thick silk.

Sedadera [say-dah-day'-rah], *f.* Hackle for dressing flax.

Sedal [say-dahl'], *m.* 1. Angling-line fixed to a fishing-hook. 2. Seton, an artificial ulcer; by farriers it is called a rowel. 3. *Sedal de zapatero*, Shoemaker's thread.

Sedán [say-dahn'], *m.* A cloth manufactured in the city of the same name.

Sedar [say-dar'], *va.* To allay, to quiet.

Sedativo, va [say-dah-tee'-vo, vah], *a.* (Med.) Sedative.

Sede [say'-day], *f.* See, the seat of episcopal power. *La Santa Sede*, The holy see, or the papal dignity. *Sede plena*, Actual occupation of a chair or dignity. *Sede vacante*, Vacant bishopric.

Sedear [say-day-ar'], *va.* To clean jewels, gold, or silver with a brush.

Sedentario, ria [say-den-tah'-re-o, ah], *a.* Sedentary, wanting motion or action.

Sedeña [say-day'-nyah], *f.* Fine tow of flax, produced by the second hackling; cloth made of such tow.

Sedeño, ña [say-day'-nyo, nyah], *a.* 1. Silky, silken; silk-like. 2. Made or consisting of hair.

Sedera [say-day'-rah], *f.* 1. A brush made of bristles. 2. (Prov.) Weaver's seat.

Sedería [say-day-ree'-ah], *f.* 1. Silks, silk stuff. 2. Shop of a silk-mercer.

Sedero [say-day'-ro], *m.* Silk-mercer.

Sedición [say-de-the-on'], *f.* Sedition, popular commotion; an insurrection, mutiny.

Sediciosamente, *adv.* Seditiously, factiously, mutinously.

Sedicioso, sa [say-de-the-o'-so, sah], *a.* Seditious, factious, mutinous.

Sediento, ta [say-de-en'-to, tah], *a.* 1. Thirsty, dry. 2. Eagerly desirous, anxious.

Sedimentación [say-de-men-tah-the-on'], *f.* Sedimentation.

Sedimentar [say-de-men-tar'], *va.* & *vr.* To settle, deposit.

Sedimento [say-de-men'-to], *m.* Sediment, feculence, lees.

Sedoso, sa [say-do'-so, sah], *a.* Silky, like silk, silk-like, silken.

Seducción [say-dooc-the-on'], *f.* Seduction, deceiving; abuse.

Seducir [say-doo-theer'], *va.* To seduce, to corrupt, to abuse.

Seductivo, va [say-dooc-tee'-vo, vah], *a.* Seductive, apt to mislead; corruptful.

Seductor, ra [say-dooc-tor', rah], *a.* Seductive, fascinating.—*m.* & *f.* 1. Seducer, corrupter, deceiver. 2. Seducer, charmer.

Segable [say-gah'-blay], *a.* Fit to be reaped.

Segada [say-gah'-dah], *f.* (Obs.) *V.* SIEGA.

Segadera [say-gah-day'-rah], *f.* Reaping-hook, sickle.

Segadero, ra [say-gah-day'-ro, rah], *a.* Fit to be reaped.

Segador, ra [say-gah-dor', rah], *m.* & *f.* Reaper, harvester; sickle man.—*f.* A reaping or harvesting-machine.

Segar [say-gar'], *va.* 1. To reap, to cut down with a reaping-hook, to crop; to mow. 2. To cut off, to abscind any thing grown higher than the rest.

Segazón [say-gah-thone'], *f.* Harvest season, reaping.

Seglar [say-glar'], *a.* 1. Worldly. 2. Secular, laical, lay: in this last sense it is used as a substantive.

Seglarmente, *adv.* Secularly.

Segmento [seg-men'-to], *m.* 1. Segment, part cut off. 2. (Geom.) Segment, the part of a circle comprised between an arc and its chord. 3. Segment, each ring or articulation of articulated animals.

Segoviano, na, Segoviense [say-go-ve-ah'-no, nah, say-go-ve-en'-say], *a.* Segovian, belonging to Segovia.

Segregación [say-gray-gah-the-on'], *f.* Segregation, separation.

Segregar [say-gray-gar'], *va.* 1. To segregate, to set apart. 2. To disunite, to unfasten. 3. (Med.) To secrete. 4. To excommunicate.

Segregativo, va [say-gray-gah-tee'-vo, vah], *a.* That which separates.

Segrí [say-gree'], *m.* A silk stuff resembling double taffety.

Segudar [say-goo-dar'], *va.* (Obs.) To persecute, to pursue or persevere.

Segueta [say-gay'-tah], *f.* A very slender fine saw for jewellers or marquetry.

Seguetear [say-gay-tay-ar'], *vn.* To use the *segueta.*

Seguida [say-gee'-dah], *f.* The act of following or state of being followed; succession; continuation. *De seguida,* Successively, without interruption. *En seguida,* Forthwith, immediately.

Seguidero [say-gee-day'-ro], *m.* Guide rule, ruled lines to follow in writing.

Seguidilla [say-gee-deel'-lyah], *f.* A merry Spanish tune and dance. *Seguidillas,* (Coll.) Diarrhœa.

Seguidillera [say-gee-deel-lyay'-rah], *f.* Person fond of singing and dancing *seguidillas.*

Seguido, da [say-gee'-do, dah], *a.* Continued, successive, straight, directed. —*pp.* of SEGUIR.

Seguido, *m.* Narrowing a stocking at the foot.

Seguidor, ra [say-gee-dor', rah], *m.* & *f.* 1. Follower. 2. A leaf of ruled paper to guide boys in writing straight.

Seguimiento [say-gee-me-en'-to], *m.* Pursuit, the act of following another, hunt; continuation of a lawsuit.

Seguir [say-geer'], *va.* 1. To follow, to pursue. 2. To follow, to prosecute, to be in pursuit of one. 3. To follow, to accompany; to attend; to come after; to make at; to march in. 4. To follow, profess, or exercise any science or art. 5. To manage a suit at law or any other business. 6. To agree or conform to. 7. To copy, to imitate. 8. To direct to the proper road or method. *Seguir en compañía,* (Naut.) To sail in company with other ships.—*vr.* 1. To ensue, to follow as a consequence. 2. To succeed, to follow in order. 3. To issue, to spring from. 4. To go on.

Segullo [say-gool'-lyo], *m.* The first stratum of a gold-mine.

Según [say-goon'], *prep.* According to. *Según Vd. me dice,* According to what you tell me. *Según y como,* Just as. *Vuelvo la caja según y como la recibí,* I return the box just as I received it.

Segunda [say-goon'-dah], *f.* 1. Second in music. 2. Double wards of a lock or key. 3. *V.* INTENCIÓN. *V.* SEGUNDO, DA.

Segundamente, *adv.* (Obs.) *V.* SEGUNDARIAMENTE.

Segundar [say-goon-dar'], *vn.* 1. To repeat over again. 2. To be second, to follow next to the first.

Segundero, ra [say-goon-day'-ro, rah], *a.* (Agr.) Second crop from some plants in the same year.—*m.* (Naut.) Second hand upon a chronometer and other time-pieces.

Segundilla [say-goon-deel'-lyah], *f.* 1. (Coll.) Snow-water again frozen after congealing other water. 2. Small bell used for certain acts of devotion. 3. (Peru) The end of some ceremony which may be seen without paying.

Segundillo [say-goon-deel'-lyo], *m.* 1. The second portion of bread distributed at table in convents. 2. (Mus.) Semitone, one of those which are called accidentals.

Segundo, da [say-goon'-do, dah], *a.* Second, immediately following the first; favourable. *De segunda mano* or *por segunda mano,* At second hand. *Segunda cubierta,* (Naut.) The middle deck. *Segunda guardia,* The dog-watch. *En segundo lugar,* Secondly. *Segunda intención,* Duplicity, falsity.

Segundo [say-goon'-do], *m.* Second of time or of a degree.

Segundogénito, ta [say-goon-do-hay'-ne-to, tah], *a.* Second-born: applied to children.

Segundón [say-goon-don'], *m.* The second son of a family or any of the brothers after the eldest.

Segur [say-goor'], *f.* 1. Axe. 2. Axe or emblem of the law. 3. Sickle, a reaping-hook.

Segurador [say-goo-rah-dor'], *m.* Securer, asserter, security, bondsman.

Seguramente, *adv.* Securely, certainly; fastly; safely.

Seguramiento, *m.* **Seguranza,** *f.* (Obs.) *V.* SEGURIDAD.

Segurar, *va.* *V.* ASEGURAR.

Segureja [say-goo-ray'-hah], *f. dim.* A small hatchet, a hollow drawing-knife for cleaning the inside of staves.

Seguridad [say-goo-re-dahd'], *f.* 1. Security, surety, certainty, safety, confidence. 2. Fastness; custody; corroboration. 3. Pledge-bail.

Seguro, ra [say-goo'-ro, rah], *a.* 1. Secure, free from danger; easy, assured, confident, confiding. 2. Secure, sure, certain. 3. Firm, constant. *Estar seguro de una cosa,* (Coll.) To depend upon a thing. *A Segura le llevan preso,* That which is most secure is not beyond danger.

Seguro, *m.* 1. Permission, leave, license. 2. Insurance of goods on sea or land. 3. (Mech.) Click, stop, detent, pawl, ratchet; tumbler of a lock. *Compañía de seguros,* Insurance company. *Cámara u oficina de seguros,* Insurance-office. *Póliza de seguro,* Policy of insurance. *Premio de seguro,* Premium of insurance. *A buen seguro,* Certainly, indubitably. *Al seguro,* Securely. *De seguro,* Assuredly. *En seguro,* In security or safety. *Sobre seguro,* Confidently. *Hacer el seguro,* To insure.

Seguro colectivo [say-goo'-ro co-lec-tee'-vo], *m.* Group insurance.

Seguro de enfermedad [say-goo'-ro day en-fer-may-dahd'], *m.* Health insurance.

Seguro sobre la vida [say-goo'-ro so'-bray lah vee'-dah], *m.* Life insurance.

Seguro social [say-goo'-ro so-the-ahl'], *m.* Social security.

Seis [say'-ees], *a.* Six, sixth. *V.* SEXTO. —*m.* 1. The figure 6. 2. Six, upon cards or dice. *Seis por ocho,* (Mus.) 6/8, six-eight measure; six eighth notes to a measure.

Seisavado, da [say-e-sah-vah'-do, dah], *a.* That which has six sides and six angles.

Seisavo [say-e-sah'-vo], *m.* 1. *V.* HEXÁGONO. 2. The sixth part of a number.

Seiscientos, tas [say-ees-the-en'-tos, tas], *a.* Six hundred.

Seise [say'-e-say], *m.* One of the boys, in some cathedrals, who sing in the choir and serve as acolytes.

Seisén [say-e-sen'], *m.* Silver coin worth half a real, or six *dineros* of Arragon.

Seiseno, na [say-e-say'-no, nah], *a.* Sixth. *V.* SEXTO.

Seisillo [say-e-seel'-lyo], *m.* (Mus.) Union of six equal notes.

Seismógrafo [say-ees-mo'-grah-fo], *m.* Seismograph, an instrument for recording the direction and force of earthquakes.

Seismología [say-ees-mo-lo-hee'-ah], *f.* Seismology, the study of earthquakes.

Seismológico, ca [say-ees-mo-lo'-he-co, cah], *a.* Seismological.

Seismómetro [say-ees-mo'-may-tro], *m.* Seismometer. *V.* SEISMÓGRAFO.

Selección [say-lec-the-on'], *f.* Selection, choice, exception.

Selectividad [say-lec-te-ve-dahd'], *f.* Selectivity, selectiveness.

Selecto, ta [say-lec'-to, tah], *a.* Select, choice, excellent.

Selene [say-lay'-nay], *f.* The moon. (Gr. σελήνη.)

Selenio [say-lay'-ne-o], *m.* Selenium, a chemical element, related to sulphur.

Selenita [say-lay-nee'-tah], *com.* Inhabitant of the moon.

Selenites [say-lay-nee'-tes], *f.* Selenite, crystallized gypsum.

Selenografía [say-lay-no-grah-fee'-ah], *f.* Selenography, description of the moon.

Seleúcide [say-lay-oo'-the-day], *f.* (Orn.) A bird which devours locusts.

Selva [sel'-vah], *f.* Forest. *Selva espesa,* Thicket.

Selvático, ca [sel-vah'-te-co, cah], *a.* Forest-born, reared in a forest, belonging to a forest.

Selvatiquez [sel-vah-te-keth'], *f.* Rusticity, savageness, wildness.

Selvicultura [sel-ve-cool-too'-rah], *f.* Forest culture, forestry.

Selvoso, sa [sel-vo'-so, sah], *a.* 1. Belonging to forests. 2. Well-wooded.

Sellador [sel-lyah-dor'], *m.* Sealer.

Selladura [sel-lyah-doo'-rah], *f.* Sealing.

Sellar [sel-lyar'], *va.* 1. To seal, to put on a seal. 2. To seal, to stamp. 3. To conclude, to finish a thing. 4. To cover, to close up. 5. To obligate as by benefits. *Sellar los labios,* To silence.

Sello [sel'-lyo], *m.* 1. Stamp. 2. Signet. 3. Seal. 4. (Fig.) Seal, stamp, impression. *Sello fiscal,* Revenue stamp. *Sello postal, Sello de correo,* Postage stamp. *Sellos de premio,* Trading stamps.

Semafórico, ca [say-ma-fo'-re-co, cah] *a.* Semaphoric, telegraphic.

Semáforo [say-mah'-fo-ro], *m.* 1. Traffic light, stoplight. 2. Semaphore, marine signal telegraph, railroad traffic sign.

Semana [say-mah'-nah], *f.* 1. A week. *Mala semana,* Menstruation. *Semana santa,* Passion-week; book containing the offices of this week. *Día entre semana,* Working-day. 2. Any septenary period of time; hebdomad. *La semana que no tenga viernes,* (Coll.) Never; impossible (lit. the week which has no Friday).

Semanal [say-mah-nahl'], *a.* Hebdomadal, weekly.
Semanalmente, *adv.* Weekly.
Semanario, ria [say-mah-nah'-re-o, ah] *a. & m. & f.* Weekly publication.
Semanería [say-mah-nay-ree'-ah], *f.* Functions performed, or work done in the course of a week.
Semanero [say-mah-nay'-ro], *m.* One who enters upon weekly functions in his turn.
Semanero, ra [say-mah-nay'-ro, rah], *a.* Applied to persons engaged by the week.
Semántica [say-man'-te-cah], *f.* Semantics.
Semblante [sem-blahn'-tay], *m.* 1. Expression in the face of some emotion; look, mien, feature. 2. Face, countenance. 3. Aspect, looks, phase of things, on which we base a concept of them; feature. *Las cosas han tomado otro semblante* or *cambiado de semblante,* (Coll.) Things have taken a different aspect. *Beber el semblante,* (1) To listen intently. (2) To serve another carefully.
Semblanza [sem-blahn'-thah], *f.* 1. (Obs.) *V.* SEMEJANZA. 2. In literature, biographical sketch.
Semblar, *vn.* (Obs.) *V.* SEMEJAR.
Semble, En sembra, *adv.* (Obs.) Similarly; jointly.
Sembradera [sem-brah-day'-rah], *f.* Any thing used for sowing seed; seeder.
Sembradío, día [sem-brah-dee'-o, ah], *a.* Fit or prepared for sowing of seed: applied to land.
Sembrado [sem-brah'-do], *m.* Corn-field; ground sown with grain.
Sembrador, ra [sem-brah-dor', rah], *a.* Sowing seed.—*m. & f.* Sower.—*f.* (Amer.) Seeder, a machine for sowing seeds.
Sembradura [sem-brah-doo'-rah], *f.* Insemination, sowing or scattering seed.
Sembrar [sem-brar'], *va.* 1. To sow, to scatter seed. 2. To scatter, to spread, to propagate, to divulge. 3. To give a cause or beginning. 4. To perform a useful undertaking. 5. To collect without order. *Sembrar de sal,* To sow the land with salt (a punishment for treason). *Como sembráredes, cogéredes,* As you sow, so shall you reap.
Semeja say-may'-hah], *f.* 1. Resemblance, likeness. 2. Mark, sign. *No es él, ni su semeja,* It is not he, nor any thing like him.
Semejable [say-may-hah'-blay], *a.* Like, resembling, similar.
Semejablemente, *adv.* Likely.
Semejado, da [say-may-hah'-do, dah], *a.* Like. *V.* PARECIDO.—*pp.* of SEMEJAR.
Semejante [say-may-hahn'-tay], *a.* Similar, like, conformable.—*m. V.* SEMEJANZA. *Nuestros semejantes,* Our fellow-creatures.
Semejantemente, *adv.* Likewise, in the same manner, similarly.
Semejanza [say-may-hahn'-thah], *f.* Resemblance, conformity, semblance, similitude; likeness, likelihood.
Semejar [say-may-har'], *vn.* To be like, to resemble; to liken.—*vr.* To resemble.
Semen [say'-men], *m.* 1. Semen, sperm, the fertilizing fluid of animals. 2. (Bot.) Seed.
Semencera [say-men-thay'-rah], *f.* Sowing, scattering seed for growth. *V.* SEMENTERA.
Semental [say-men-tahl'], *a.* Seminal.
Sementar [say-men-tar'], *va.* To sow, to scatter seed.
Sementera [say-men-tay'-rah], *f.* 1. Sowing seed. 2. Land sown with seed. 3. The seed sown. 4. Seed-time. 5. Origin, [illegible]e, beginning.
Sementero [say-men-tay'-ro], *m.* 1. Seedlip or seedlop, a vessel in which the sower carries his seed; hopper. 2. Sowing, scattering seed.
Sementilla [say-men-teel'-lyah], *f. dim.* of SIMIENTE.
Sementino, na [say-men-tee'-no, nah], *a.* Belonging to seed or seed-time.
Semestral [say-mes-trahl'], *a.* Semi-yearly, semiannually. *Informe semestral,* Semiannual report. *Cuota semestral,* Semiannual fee.
Semestre [say-mes'-tray], *a.* Lasting six months.—*m.* Space of six months, semester; leave of absence for six months.
Semi [say'-me], *prefix.* Semi, a word which, in composition, signifies *half;* sometimes it is equivalent to *casi,* almost.
Semianual [say-me-ah-noo-ahl'], *a.* Semi-annual, half-yearly.
Semibreve [say-me-bray'-vay], *f.* (Mus.) Semibreve, whole note (𝅝).
Semicabrón, Semicapro [say-me-cah-brone'], *m.* Satyr.
Semicircular [say-me-theer-coo-lar'], *a.* Semicircular, semiangular.
Semicírculo [say-me-theer'-coo-lo], *m.* Semicircle.
Semicorchea [say-me-cor-chay'-ah], *f.* (Mus.) Semiquaver; sixteenth note.
Semicircunferencia [say-me-theer-coon-fay-ren'-the-ah], *f.* Semicircumference.
Semicopado [say-me-co-pah'-do], *m.* A note which joins the second part of a measure with the first of that which follows it; a syncopated note.
Semicromático, ca [say-me-cro-mah'-te-co, cah], *a.* (Mus.) Semichromatic.
Semidea [say-me-day'-ah], *f.* (Poet.) Demigoddess.
Semidiáfano, na [say-me-de-ah'-fah-no, nah], *a.* Semidiaphanous.
Semidiámetro [say-me-de-ah'-may-tro], *m.* Semidiameter, radius.
Semidiapasón [say-me-de-ah-pah-sone'], *m.* (Mus.) Semidiapason, defective octave.
Semidiapente [say-me-de-ah-pen'-tay], *m.* (Mus.) Semidiapente, defective fifth.
Semidiatesarón [say-me-de-ah-tay-sah-rone'], *m.* (Mus.) Semidiatessaron, defective fourth.
Semidifunto, ta [say-me-de-foon'-to, tah], *a.* Half-dead, almost dead.
Semidiós [say-me-de-os'], *m.* **Semidiosa** [say-me-de-oh'-sah], *f.* Demi-god; demi-goddess.
Semidítono [say-me-dee'-to-no], *m.* (Mus.) Semiditone, minor third.
Semidoble [say-me-do'-blay], *a.* Semi-double: applied in the Catholic church to feasts.
Semidocto [say-me-doc'-to], *m.* Sciolist, a half-learned man, half scholar.
Semidocto, ta [say-me-doc'-to, tah], *a.* Half-learned.
Semidormido, da [say-me-dor-mee'-do, dah], *a.* Half asleep, sleepy.
Semidragón [say-me-drah-gone'], *m.* Semidragon.
Semiesfera [say-me-es-fay'-rah], *f.* Hemisphere.
Semiesférico, ca [say-me-es-fay'-re-co, cah], *a.* Semiglobular, hemispherical.
Semifinal [say-me-fee-nahl'], *a.* Semifinal. *Semifinales,* Semifinals.
Semiflósculo [say-me-flos'-coo-lo], *m.* (Bot.) Semifloret.
Semiflosculoso, sa [say-me-flos-coo-lo'-so, sah], *a.* (Bot.) Semifloscular, semiflosculous.
Semifluido, da [say-me-floo'-e-do, dah], *a.* Semi-fluid.
Semifusa [say-me-foo'-sah], *f.* (Mus.) Double demisemiquaver, a sixty-fourth note.
Semigola [say-me-go'-lah], *f.* (Mil.) Demigorge, half the entrance into a bastion.
Semihombre [say-me-om'-bray], *m.* Half-man.
Semilunar [say-me-loo-nar'], *a.* Semilunar, semilunary.
Semilunio [say-me-loo'-ne-o], *m.* Half the time in which the moon performs her course; half-moon.
Semilla [say-meel'-lyah], *f.* 1. Seed, from which plants are produced. 2. Origin, cause. *Semillas,* All sorts of seed and grain, wheat and barley excepted; quantity of seed sown.
Semilladero [say-meel-lyah-day'-ro], *m.* (Prov.) *V.* SEMILLERO.
Semillero [say-meel-lyay'-ro], *m.* Seed-plot, ground on which plants are sown to be afterwards transplanted; nursery.
Semimetal [say-me-may-tahl'], *m.* Semimetal, imperfect metal.
Seminal [say-me-nahl'], *a.* 1. Seminal; radical. 2. Spermatic.
Seminario [say-me-nah'-re-o], *m.* 1. Seed-plot, nursery, ground in which plants are sown to be afterwards transplanted. 2. Seminary, a school. 3. Musical school for children. 4. Beginning, root, origin, source.
Seminarista [say-me-nah-rees'-tah], *m.* A scholar who boards and is instructed in a seminary.
Semínima [say-mee'-ne-mah], *f.* 1. (Mus.) Crotchet, quarter note. 2. Trifle, thing of no moment.
Semioctava [say-me-oc-tah'-vah], *f.* Poetical composition of four verses in alternate rhymes.
Semiordenada [say-me-or-day-nah'-dah], *f.* (Math.) Semiordinate.
Semipedal [say-me-pay-dahl'], *a.* Measuring half a foot in length.
Semipelagiano, na [say-me-pay-lah-he-ah'-no, nah], *m. & f.* Semi-Pelagian, one who adopts part of the errors of Pelagius.
Semiplena [say-me-play'-nah], *f.* (For.) Imperfect proof, half proof.
Semiplenamente, *adv.* Half proved.
Simpleno, na [say-me-play'-no, nah], *a.* (Littl. us.) Half full, half finished.
Semipoeta [say-me-po-ay'-tah], *m.* Poetaster.
Semiprobanza [say-me-pro-bahn'-thah], *f.* A half proof, imperfect evidence.
Semiprueba [say-me-proo-ay'-bah], *f.* (Law) Semiproof.
Semipútrido, da [say-me-poo'-tre do, dah], *a.* Half putrid.
Semiracional [say-me-rah-the-o-nahl'], *a.* Stupid, ignorant.
Semirrecto [say-mir-rec'-to], *a.* Of forty-five degrees: half a right angle.
Semirrubio, bia [say-mir-roo'-be-o, ah], *a.* Nearly blonde.
Semis [say-mees'], *m.* Half a Roman pound.
Semisabio, bia [say-me-sah'-be-o, ah], *a. & m. & f. V.* SEMIDOCTO.
Semisalvaje [say-me-sal-vah'-hay], *m.* Semisavage, half savage.
Semisestil [say-me-ses-teel'], *m.* (Ast.) Semisextile.
Semita [say-mee'-tah], *m.* Semite, a descendant of Shem.
Semiterciana [say-me-ter-the-ah'-nah], *f.* Semitertian.
Semítico, ca [say-mee'-te-co, cah], *a.* Semitic, relating to Shem. *Lengua semítica,* Semitic tongue, one of a great family of languages, of which Hebrew, Arabic, Ethiopic, and Assyrian are types.
Semitono [say-me-toh'-no], *m.* (Mus.) Semitone.

Semitransparente [say-me-trans-pah-ren'-tay], *a.* Almost transparent.
Semivibración [say-me-ve-brah-the-on'], *f.* Vibration of the pendulum that ascends or descends.
Semivivo, va [say-me-vee'-vo, vah], *a.* Half alive.
Semivocal [say-me-vo-cahl'], *a.* Semi-vowel, as *f, l, m, n, r, s.*
Semivulpa [say-me-vool'-pah], *f.* Animal like a wolf.
Sémola [say'-mo-lah], *f.* 1. Groats or grits, made of decorticated wheat; wheat ground coarse. 2. An Italian paste of the quality of vermicelli, in the form of very small grain, for the use of the sick.
Semoviente [say-mo-ve-en'-tay], *a.* Moving of itself.
Sempiterna [sem-pe-terr'-nah], *f.* Sort of serge, everlasting.
Sempiternamente, *adv.* Eternally.
Sempiterno, na [sem-pe-terr'-no, nah], *a.* Eternal, everlasting, sempiternal.
Sen, *m.* **Sena** *f.* [sen, say'-nah]. 1. (Bot.) Senna, a purgative shrub. Cassia senna. 2. *f.* Six marks on dice.—*pl. Senas,* Double sixes.
Sena, *m.* The river Seine. See Appendix.
Senado [say-nah'-do], *m.* 1. Senate, a council of senators. 2. Any meeting of grave persons. 3. Senate-house, town-hall.
Senadoconsulto [say-nah-do-con-sool'-to], *m.* Senatus-consultum, decree of a senate.
Senador [say-nah-dor'], *m.* Senator.
Senaduría [say-nah-doo-ree'-ah], *f.* Senatorship, a senator's dignity.
Senara [say-nah'-rah], *f.* A piece of sown ground, assigned to servants as part of their wages.
Senarero [say-nah-ray'-ro], *m.* Servant who enjoys a piece of sown ground as part of his wages.
Senario [say-nah'-re-o], *m.* A senary number; a verse consisting of six iambic feet.
Senatorio, ria [say-nah-to'-re-o, ah], *a.* Senatorial.
Senciente [sen-the-en'-tay], *pa.* & *a.* Sentient, perceiving.
Sencillamente, *adv.* Ingenuously, plainly: abstractedly.
Sencillez [sen-theel-lyeth'], *f.* 1. Slightness, slenderness. 2. Simplicity, plainness, artlessness, harmlessness. 3. Silliness, weakness, ignorance.
Sencillo, lla [sen-theel'-lyo, lyah], *a.* 1. Simple, unmixed, uncompounded. 2. Light, slight, thin, of light body (fabrics). 3. Silly, weak, easily imposed upon. 4. Ingenuous, plain, artless, harmless. 5. Simple, not ornate in style, expressing ideas naturally. 6. Single: applied to coin of less value than another of the same name.
Senda [sen'-dah], *f.* 1. Path, foot-path. 2. Means for attaining an end.
Senderar [sen-day-rar'], *va.* To make a path.—*vn.* To walk on a path or foot path.
Senderear [sen-day-ray-ar'], *va.* 1. To guide or conduct on a foot-path. 2. To adopt extraordinary means to obtain an end. 3. To make a path.
Sendero [sen-day'-ro], *m.* Path, foot-path. *V.* SENDA.
Sendica, illa, ita [sen-dee'-cah], *f. dim.* Little pathway.
Sendos, das [sen'-dos, das], *a.* 1. Each of two, either. 2. (Not Acad.) Great; abundant.
Sene [say'-nay], *m.* (Obs.) An old man. *V.* VIEJO.
Senectud [say-nec-tood'], *f.* (Littl. us.) Old age, senescence.
Senescal [say-nes-cahl'], *m.* 1. Seneschal, lord high chamberlain or high steward. 2. Chief commander of a town, especially in time of war. 3. Lord chief justice. It is used only in speaking of foreign countries.
Senescalía [say-nes-cah-lee'-ah], *f.* Place, dignity, or employment of a seneschal.
Senil [say-neel'], *a.* 1. Senile. 2. (Ast.) Fourth quadrant of the celestial map.
Senior, ra, *m.* & *f.* & *a.* (Obs.) *V.* SEÑOR and SEÑORA.
Seno [say'-no], *m.* 1. Chest, thoracic cavity; bosom. 2. Womb. 3. Lap of a woman. 4. Circular space formed by moving round. 5. Hole, cavity, sinus. 6. Gulf, bay. 7. Any cavity in the interior of the human body. 8. Security, support; asylum, refuge. 9. (Geom.) The sine of an arc. 10. Sinus, cavity of a wound. 11. Centre, middle part. 12. (Naut.) Curvature of a sail. *Seno recto,* Sine. *Seno segundo,* Cosine. *Seno todo* or *total,* Total sine or radius. *Seno verso,* Versed sine.
Senojil, *m.* (Bot.) *V.* CENOJIL.
Sensación [sen-sah-the-on'], *f.* Sensation, feeling.
Sensatez [sen-sah-teth'], *f.* Judiciousness, reasonableness, prudence, good sense.
Sensato, ta [sen-sah'-to, tah], *a.* Sensible, judicious, prudent, reasonable, wise.
Sensibilidad [sen-se-be-le-dahd'], *f.* Sensibility, quickness of perception, sensitiveness.
Sensible [sen-see'-blay], *a.* 1. Sensible, perceptible by the senses. 2. Sensible, having the power of perceiving by the senses. 3. Sensitive, having sense or perception, but not reason. 4. Perceived by the mind. 5. Causing grief or pain. 6. Sensible, having quick intellectual feeling, easily moved or affected.
Sensiblemente, *adv.* Sensibly, with grief or pain.
Sensitiva [sen-se-tee'-vah], *f.* (Bot.) Sensitive plant. Mimosa sensitiva.
Sensitivo, va [sen-se-tee'-vo, vah], *a.* Sensitive; sensual; sensible.
Sensorio [sen-so'-re-o], *m.* Sensorium or sensory, the seat of sensation.
Sensorio, ria [sen-so'-re-o, ah], *a.* Belonging to the sensorium.
Sensual [sen-soo-ahl'], *a.* 1. Sensitive, having sense or perception. 2. Sensual, lewd, lustful. 3. Belonging to the carnal appetites.
Sensualidad [sen-soo-ah-le-dahd'], *f.* Sensuality, lust, lewdness.
Sensualismo [sen-soo-ah-lees'-mo], *m.* 1. Sensationalism, a doctrine opposed to idealism, which places the origin of ideas in the senses. 2. Sensuality.
Sensualista [sen-soo-ah-lees'-tah], *a.* Sensualistic.
Sensualmente, *adv.* Sensually, carnally.
Sentada [sen-tah'-dah], *f.* Stone put in its proper place. *V.* ASENTADA.
Sentadillas (A) [sen-tah-deel'-lyas], *adv.* With the legs both on one side; side-saddlewise; as women ride horseback.
Sentado, da [sen-tah'-do, dah], *a.* Sedate, judicious, grave, prudent. *Pulso sentado,* A steady pulse.—*pp.* of SENTAR.
Sentamiento, *m.* (Arch.) *V.* ASIENTO.
Sentar [sen-tar'], *vn.* 1. To fit, to become, to suit. *Esta casaca no me sienta bien,* This coat does not fit me well. *Ese color sienta bien al de su cara,* That colour suits well her complexion—*va.* 2. To set up, to establish. *Sentar los reales,* To establish one's self in a place. 3. To seat. *V.* ASENTAR. 4. To press down the seams of clothes, as tailors, with a goose. *Sentar la costuras,* (Met.) To chastise with blows, to reprehend or accuse. 5. To please, to be agreeable. *No le sentó bien la conversación,* The conversation did not please him.—*vr.* 1. To sink, to subside. *V.* ASENTARSE. 2. To sit down, to squat, to seat one's self. 3. (Coll.) To fall plump upon one's breech. 4. To occupy the seat which belongs to one's place or employment; to seat one's self in an office or dignity. *Sentarse los pájaros sobre una rama,* To perch upon a branch: applied to birds.
Sentencia [sen-ten'-the-ah], *f.* 1. Sentence, the judicial decision of a suit at law, judgment; the penalty in a criminal case. 2. Opinion, persuasion of the mind. 3. Sentence, a maxim. 4. Sentence, a period in writing. *Decir sentencias a alguno,* To scold, to abuse one. *Fulminar la sentencia,* To pass judgment.
Sentenciar [sen-ten-the-ar'], *va.* 1. To sentence, to pass judgment; to condemn. 2. To express one's opinion. 3. To determine, to decide. *Estar a juzgado y sentenciado,* (Law) To be obliged to hear and submit to the sentence pronounced.
Sentenciario [sen-ten-the-ah'-re-o], *m.* Collection of sentences.
Sentención [sen-ten-the-on'], *f.* A severe, rigorous sentence.
Sentenciosamente, *adv.* Sententiously.
Sentencioso, sa [sen-ten-the-o'-so, sah], *a.* Sententious, pithy, axiomatic.
Sentenzuela, *f. dim.* Slight sentence.
Senticar, *m.* (Obs.) A place full of briers and brambles.
Sentidamente, *adv.* Feelingly, painfully.
Sentido, da [sen-tee'-do, dah], *a.* 1. Sensible, feeling, expressive of sensibility. 2. Split, cloven, relaxed. 3. Putrefying. *Darse por sentido,* To show resentment.—*pp.* of SENTIR.
Sentido [sen-tee'-do], *m.* 1. Sense, the faculty of perceiving objects; any one of the five senses. 2. Sense, understanding, reason. 3. Acceptation, signification, import, sense, meaning, construction. 4. Mode of understanding something, or the judgment made of it. 5. Intelligence or knowledge by which certain things are executed. *Sentido común,* Common sense. *Estar sentido,* (Coll.) To be miffed, to be a little offended.
Sentimental [sen-te-men-tahl'], *a.* 1. Sentimental, affecting, pathetic. 2. Emotional, easily affected. 3. Sentimental, ridiculously affected.
Sentimentalismo [sen-te-men-tah-lees'-mo], *m.* Sentimentalism, exaggeration of sentiment.
Sentimiento [sen-te-me-en'-to], *m.* 1. Sentiment, the sense considered distinctly from the language. 2. Perception, perceiving objects by the senses. 3. Feeling, sensation. 4. Grief, pain, concern. 5. Chink in a wall. 6. Resentment, deep sense of injury, grudge. 7. Judgment, opinion, sentiment.
Sentina [sen-tee'-nah], *f.* 1. (Naut.) Well, which incloses a ship's pumps. 2. Sink, drain; place of iniquity.
Sentir [sen-teer'], *va.* 1. To feel, to perceive by the senses. 2. To hear. *Sin sentir,* Without being seen, felt, or known. 3. To endure, to suffer. 4. To grieve, to regret, to mourn, to be sorry for.—*vn.* 1. To judge, to form an opinion. 2. To foresee, to foreknow. 3. To accommodate the

action to the expression, to exhibit a suitable feeling.—*vr.* 1. To be moved, to be affected, to complain. 2. To get a crack or flaw: applied to a glass, bell, or other thing. 3. To be in a ruinous state. 4. To be sensible of, to feel pain in any part of the body; to acknowledge the obligation or necessity. 5. To resent. 6. (Naut.) To spring: applied to a yard or mast. *Nuestro palo mayor se sintió,* (Naut.) Our main-mast sprang.

Sentir [sen-teer'], *m.* 1. Feeling, opinion, judgment. 2. *V.* SENTIMIENTO.

Seña [say'-nyah], *f.* 1. Sign, mark, token or note given without words, nod, dumb motion. 2. Signal, notice given by a sign. 3. Sign, a token of any thing. 4. (Mil.) Password, watchword. 5. (Obs.) Standard, banner, colours. *Por señas* or *por más señas,* As a stronger proof of it.

Señal [say-nyahl'], *f.* 1. Sign, mark, signature, token; mark or note of distinction. 2. Landmark to mark a boundary. 3. Sign, indication, symptom. *Señales claras* or *evidentes,* Open marks. 4. Vestige, stamp, impression, footstep; scar. 5. Representation, image. 6. Earnest, handsel, pledge; earnest money, given in token that a bargain is ratified. 7. (Mil.) Standard, banner. 8. Sign, wonder, prodigy, prognostic. 9. Signal, a sign to give notice. 10. A diagnostic or prognostic symptom.—*pl.* (Naut.) Signals. *Señales de hacerse a la vela,* Sailing signals. *Señales de bruma,* Fog-signals. *Señales de peligro,* Signals of distress. *En señal,* In proof of. *Señal de borrica frontina,* Indication of double dealing. *Ni señal,* Not a trace.

Señaladamente, *adv.* Especially, remarkably, namely; signally.

Señaladamiente, Señaladamientre, *adv.* (Obs.) *V.* SEÑALADAMENTE.

Señalado, da [say-nyah-lah'-do, dah], *a.* & *pp.* of SEÑALAR. Famous, celebrated, noble.

Señalamiento [say-nyah-lah-me-en'-to], *m.* Assignation, determining or appointing a certain time or place.

Señalar [say-nyah-lar'], *va.* 1. To stamp, to mark out. 2. To sign decrees or despatches. 3. To signalize, to point out, to make known. 4. To speak positively, to say expressly. 5. To name, to nominate, to constitute; to fix; to determine. 6. To mark with a wound, especially in the face. 7. To make signals, to indicate. *Señalar con el dedo,* To point with the finger.—*vr.* 1. To distinguish one's self, to excel. 2. To mark the game at piquet. *Señalar los motivos de,* To account for.

Señaleja [say-nyah-lay'-hah], *f. dim.* A little sign or mark.

Señalero [say-nayh-lay'-ro], *m.* He who formerly bore the royal ensign; king's ensign.

Señas [say'-nyahs], *f. pl.* Address, residence of someone.

Señero, ra [say-nyay'-ro, rah], *a.* (Obs.) Making signs or signals; solitary.

Señolear [say-nyo-lay-ar'], *vn.* To catch birds with a lure.

Señor [say-nyor'], *m.* 1. Lord, master, or owner of a thing. 2. Sir, a title given to an equal or inferior; mister. 3. God, the lord and master of all things. 4. The sacrament of the eucharist. 5. Master; governor; father-in-law. *Señor mayor,* An old man or aged man.

Señora [say-nyo'-rah], *f.* 1. Lady, a word of complaisance used of women. 2. Lady, mistress or owner of a thing. 3. Madam: used in address to ladies of every degree. 4. Dame, gentlewoman. 5. Mother-in-law. 6. Mistress of a house or school. *Nuestra Señora,* The Virgin Mary. *Una señora mayor,* An old or aged woman. *Señora,* In jocular style, Dame; as, *La Señora Fortuna,* Dame Fortune.

Señoraje, *m.* Seigniorage. *V.* SEÑOREAJE.

Señorazo, za [say-nyo-rah'-tho, thah], *m.* & *f. aug.* One of feigned nobility: used ironically.

Señoreador, ra [say-nyo-ray-ah-dor', rah], *m.* & *f.* Domineerer.

Señoreaje [say-nyo-ray-ah'-hay], *m.* 1. Seigniorage, acknowledgment of power. 2. Duty belonging to the king for the coining of money.

Señoreante [say-nyo-ray-ahn'-tay], *pa.* Domineering.

Señorear [say-nyo-ray-ar'], *va.* 1. To master, to domineer, to lord, to rule despotically. 2. To excel, to occupy a higher station. 3. To treat another repeatedly with the title of lord. 4. To govern one's passions.—*vr.* To affect peculiar gravity in one's deportment; to assume an air of importance.

Señoría [say-nyo-ree'-ah], *f.* 1. Lordship, a title given to persons of a certain rank and distinction. 2. Person to whom this title is given. 3. Government of a particular state; senate; prince. 4. Seigniory, a lordship.

Señorial [say-nyo-re-ahl'], *a.* Manorial, manerial.

Señoril [say-nyo-reel'], *a.* Lordly, belonging to a lord, genteel.

Señorilmente, *adv.* Nobly, grandly, majestically, lordly.

Señorío [say-nyo-ree'-o], *m.* 1. Seigniory, dominion, command. 2. Imperiousness, arrogance of command. 3. Lordship, manor or territory belonging to a lord. 4. Gravity or stateliness of deportment. 5. Freedom and self-control in action.

Señorita [say-nyo-ree'-tah], *f. dim.* 1. Miss: a title of honour given to young ladies; a little, pretty, or amiable young lady. 2. Madam, a term of compliment used in addressing young ladies.

Señorito [say-nyo-ree'-to], *m. dim.* 1. Master: a title of honour given to young gentlemen; a little, pretty, or amiable young lord. 2. Lordling, one who assumes an air of dignity and importance.

Señorón, na [say-nyo-rone', nah], *m.* & *f. aug.* Great seignior or lady.

Señuelo [say-nyoo-ay'-lo], *m.* Lure, enticement, attachment.

Seor, ra [say-or', rah], *m.* & *f.* (Obs. Coll.) Lord, sir; madam, lady. *V.* SEÑOR.

Sépalo [say'-pah-lo], *m.* (Bot.) Sepal, each division of the calyx.

Sepancuantos [say-pan-coo-ahn'-tos], *m.* (Coll.) Box on the ear, slap on the face.

Separable [say-pah-rah'-blay], *a.* Separable.

Separación [say-pah-rah-the-on'], *f.* 1. Separation. 2. Resignation, withdrawal. 3. Parting. *Separación de poderes,* Separation of powers. *Separación racial,* Racial segregation.

Separadamente, *adv.* Separately, severally.

Separado, da [say-pah-rah'-do, dah], *a.* & *pp.* of SEPARAR. Separate, separated.

Separador, ra [say-pah-rah-dor', rah], *m.* & *f.* Separator, divider.

Separar [say-pah-rar'], *va.* 1. To separate, to part, to divide, to cut, to chop, to hackle. 2. To separate, to set apart, to lay aside; to repose; to divorce. 3. To anatomize; to dissect in order to show or study the structure of animal bodies.—*vr.* To separate, to part, to be disunited; to come off, to go from, to fly off; to withdraw, to drop all communication and intercourse to retire, to sequester.

Separatista [say-pah-rah-tees'-tah], *a.* & *n.* Separatist, labouring to part a territory or colony from the capital.

Separativo, va, Separatorio, ria [say-pa-rah-tee'-vo, vah], *a.* That which separates, separatory.

Sepedón [say-pay-done'], *m.* Seps, a kind of serpent.

Sepelio [say-pay'-le-o], *m.* Burial by the church of the faithful.

Sepelir [say-pay-leer'], *va.* (Obs.) To bury, to inter. *V.* SEPULTAR.

Sepia [say'-pe-ah], *f.* 1. (Zool.) Cuttle-fish. *V.* JIBIA. 2. Sepia, a colouring matter obtained from the cuttle-fish, and used in water-colours.

Sepsis [sep'-sis], *f.* (Med.) Sepsis.

Septenario [sep-tay-nah'-re-o], *m.* 1. Septenary, septenarious, of seven figures. 2. Of seven elements.—*m.* Space of seven days, seven years, etc.

Septenio [sep-tay'-ne-o], *m.* Space of seven years.

Septentrión [sep-ten-tre-on'], *m.* 1. Septentrion, the north; that part of the sphere which extends from the equator to the arctic pole. 2. (Naut.) North wind. 3. (Ast.) The Great Bear.

Septentrional [sep-ten-tre-o-nahl'], *a.* Septentrional, northern, north, northerly.

Septicemia [sep-te-thay'-me-ah], *f.* (Med.) Septicemia, blood poisoning.

Séptico, ca [sep'-te-co, cah], *a.* Septic, septical, productive of putrefaction.

Septiembre [sep-te-em'-bray], *m.* September. *Por Septiembre calabazas,* (Coll.) Over the left, or in a horn (that is, you will not get the opportunity).

Séptima [sep'-te-mah], *f.* 1. Sequence of seven cards, in the game of piquet. 2. (Mus.) The interval of a seventh.

Séptimo, ma [sep'-te-mo, mah], *a.* Seventh, the ordinal number of seven; one of the seven parts into which a whole is divided.

Septo [sep'-to], *m.* (Anat.) Septum.

Septuagenario, ria [sep-too-ah-hay-nah'-re-o, ah], *a.* Septuagenary, seventy years old.

Septuagésima [sep-too-ah-hay'-se-mah], *f.* The third Sunday before the first Sunday in Lent.

Septuagésimo, ma [sep-too-ah-hay'-se-mo, mah], *a.* 1. Seventieth, the ordinal number of seventy. 2. Septuagesimal, consisting of seventy.

Septuplicación [sep-too-ple-cah-the-on'], *f.* Multiplying by seven.

Septuplicar [sep-too-ple-car'], *va.* To make seven-fold; to multiply by seven.

Séptuplo, pla [sep'-too-plo, plah], *a.* Septuple, seven-fold.

Sepulcral [say-pool-crahl'], *a.* Sepulchral, monumental.

Sepulcro [say-pool'-cro], *m.* 1. Sepulchre, grave, tomb, 2. A small chest in which the sacred host is preserved in Roman Catholic churches. 3. (Met.) An unhealthy country.

Sepultación [say-pool-tah-the-on'], *f.* (Obs.) Sepulture; interment.

Sepultador [say-pool-tah-dor'], *m.* Burier, grave-digger.

Sepultar [say-pool-tar'], *va.* 1. To bury, to inter, to entomb. 2. To hide, to conceal.

Sepultura [say-pool-too'-rah], *f.* 1. Sepulture, interment. 2. Tomb, grave.
Sepulturero [say-pool-too-ray'-ro], *m.* Grave-digger, sexton.
Sequedad [say-kay-dahd'], *f.* 1. Aridity, dryness. 2. Barrenness, sterility, scarcity of provisions in a country. 3. Defect in nutrition of a member. 4. Asperity of intercourse, sourness of temper, abruptness: dryness of style. 5. Want of devotion and fervour in spiritual matters.
Sequedal, Sequeral [say-kay-dahl', say-kay-rahl'], *m.* A dry, barren soil.
Sequero [say-kay'-ro], *m.* 1. Dry, unirrigated arable ground. *De sequero*, Adry, arid, not irrigated. 2. *V.* SECADERO.
Sequeroso, sa [say-kay-ro'-so, sah], *a.* Dry, wanting moisture.
Sequete [say-kay'-tay], *m.* 1. Piece of hard, dry bread. 2. Harshness and asperity of address or intercourse. 3. A violent shock.
Sequía [say-kee'-ah], *f.* Dryness; thirst; drought. *V.* SEQUEDAD.
Sequillo [say-keel'-lyo], *m.* Biscuit made of flour and sugar.
Sequío [say-kee'-o], *m.* Dry, unirrigated arable ground.
Séquito [say'-ke-to], *m.* 1. Retinue, suite. 2. Popularity, public applause.
Sequizo, za [say-kee'-tho, thah], *a.* Dry: applied to fruits and other eatables that are not juicy.
Ser [serr], *vn.* 1. To be: an auxiliary verb, by which the passive is formed. 2. To be in some place or situation. 3. To be or to exist really. 4. To be, to happen, to occur, to fall out. *¿Cómo fué eso?* How did that happen? 5. To be worth. *¿A cómo es eso?* What is the price of that? 6. To be born in a place; to originate in. *Soy de Sevilla*, I am a native of Seville. 7. To affirm or deny. 8. To be the property of one, to belong to, to pertain. 9. To be useful, to serve, to contribute to any thing. 10. Joined to nouns which signify employment or occupation, it means to be occupied in them. *Ya sea de este modo o de otro*, Whether it be this way or the other. *Sea lo que fuere*, Be that as it may. *Soy con Vd.*, I will attend you presently. *Ser de alguno*, To belong to a person's party. *Ser de bulto*, To be as clear as possible. *En ser*, In being, in existence. *Ser uno de tantos*, To be one of the number. *Es quien es*, or *se porta como quien es*, He is what he ought to be, or he behaves as he should. *Ser cómplice de*, To have a hand in. *Ser para todo*, To be fit for everything; to be up to everything. *Si yo fuera que Vd.*, Were I in your place; had I your means. *Ser un juicio*, To be a multitude, a great quantity. *Ahí será ello*, or *ahí fuera ello*, Then we shall see. *No ser rana*, To be able and expert. *Eso es de N.*, That is right, to a T, just as it should be. *Ser el dado malo*, To get all the blame. *Érase que*, or *se era*, Once upon a time. *Es otro tanto oro*, So much the better. *¿Qué es del libro?* Where is the book? *Ciertos son los toros*, So then, it is true. *Un si es no es*, Something, somewhat; even a little. *Ser de sobre sí mismo*, To proceed with great caution. *Ser de la cáscara amarga*, To be ill-tempered, disaffected, or factious. *Mañana será otro día*, To-morrow may bring better luck. *Soy muy de Vd.*, I am entirely yours; yours very truly. *Ser uña y carne*, To be hand and glove, to be close friends. *Otra cosa es con guitarra*, You will sing a different song when the time comes. *Eso no es de la incumbencia de Vd.*, That does not concern you; it is none of your business. *Ser cuchillo de alguno*, To be a thorn in one's side. Idioms containing the verb *ser* are numerous.
Ser [serr], *m.* Being, the entity, essence, or nature of things; value; point or burden of a piece.
Sera [say'-rah], *f.* A large pannier or basket.
Serado [say-rah'-do], *m.* A parcel of panniers or baskets.
Seráfico, ca [say-rah'-fe-co, cah], *a.* Seraphic, angelic: applied especially to St. Francis and his religionists. *Hacer la seráfica*, (Coll.) To play the angel in order to effect some purpose.
Serafín [say-rah-feen'], *m.* 1. Seraph, seraphim, angel. 2. An extreme beauty.
Serafina [say-rah-fee'-nah], *f.* A sort of swan-skin, resembling fine baize.
Seraje [say-rah'-hay], *m.* Panniers or baskets, especially of charcoal.
Serancolín [say-ran-co-leen'], *m.* A sort of marble, found in the Pyrenees.
Serao, *m.* (Obs.) *V.* SARAO.
Serape [say-rah'-pay], *m.* (Mex.) A narrow blanket, worn by men, or thrown over the saddle. *V.* MANGA.
Serapino [say-rah-pee'-no], *m.* A sort of gum, obtained by incision from the fennel-giant.
Serasa [say-rah'-sah], *f.* Chintz. *V.* ZARAZA.
Serasquier [say-ras-ke-err'], *m.* Seraskier, a Turkish generalissimo.
Serba [serr'-bah], *f.* Service, a kind of wild pear, the fruit of the service-tree.
Serbal, Serbo [ser-bahl', serr'-bo], *m.* (Bot.) Service-tree. Sorbus. *Serbal cultivado*, True service-tree. Sorbus domestica. *Serbal de cazadores*, Mountain-ash service-tree. Sorbus aucuparia. *Serbal mestizo*, Hybrid service-tree. Sorbus hybrida.
Serbrar [ser-brar'], *va.* (Obs.) 1. To put water into the night air to cool. 2. To quiet, to pacify, to quell disturbances.
Serena [say-ray'-nah], *f.* Evening dew. *A la serena*, *V.* AL SERENO.
Serenamente, *adv.* Serenely, composedly, coolly, quietly.
Serenar [say-ray-nar'], *va.* & *vn.* 1. To clear up, to grow fair, to become serene: applied to the weather. 2. To settle, to grow clear: applied to liquors. 3. To pacify, to tranquillize, to moderate, to compose; to be serene.
Serenata [say-ray-nah'-tah], *f.* Serenade, concert, night-music.
Serenero [say-ray-nay'-ro], *m.* Night-wrap, a loose cover which ladies used to throw over the head at night.
Sereni [say-ray-nee'], *m.* 1. A light boat on board large vessels, used for greater despatch. 2. A yawl.
Serenidad [say-ray-ne-dahd'], *f.* 1. Serenity, the clearness of mild and temperate weather. 2. Serene highness, a title given to princes. 3. Serenity, meekness, mildness, sereneness, serenitude. 4. *V.* DESVERGÜENZA.
Serenísimo, ma [say-ray-nee'-se-mo, mah], *a. sup.* 1. Most serene, honorary title of princes, or kings' children. 2. Extremely serene, calm, or quiet.
Sereno [say-ray'-no], *m.* 1. Evening dew, night dew. 2. Night-watch, watchman.
Sereno, na, *a.* 1. Serene, clear, fair, cloudless. 2. Calm, quiet, unruffled, cold. *Al sereno*, In the night air, in the open air, exposed to the evening dew.
Sergas [serr'-gas], *f. pl.* (Obs.) Exploits, achievements, adventures.
Seriamente, *adv.* Seriously, gravely, solemnly, in earnest, for good and all.
Sericícola [say-re-thee'-co-lah], *a.* Sericultural, relating to silk-culture.
Sericicultura [say-re-the-cool-too'-rah], *f.* Silk-culture, sericulture. (Lat. sericum, silk.)
Sérico, ca [say'-re-co, cah], *a.* Silken.
Serie [say'-re-ay], *f.* Series, order, gradation, sequence, suite.
Seriedad [say-re-ay-dahd'], *f.* 1. Seriousness, gravity. 2. Sternness of mien, rudeness of address. 3. Simplicity, plainness, sincerity.
Serigrafía [say-re-grah-fee'-ah], *f.* Silk-screen process.
Serijo, Serillo [say-ree'-ho, say-reel'-lyo], *m.* A small basket made of palm-leaves.
Serio, ria [say'-re-o, ah], *a.* 1. Serious, grave, dignified. 2. Serious, important, weighty. 3. Grand, majestic, solemn. 4. Uncouth, rude, severe, cold. 5. Plain, true, sincere.
Sermocinal [ser-mo-the-nahl'], *a.* Oratorical, relating to a public speech.
Sermón [ser-mohn'], *m.* 1. Sermon, homily. 2. Censure, reprehension.
Sermonario, ria [ser-mo-nah'-re-o, ah], *a.* Relating to a sermon.
Sermonario, *m.* 1. Collection of sermons. 2. (Obs.) Author who has published sermons, or a divine who preaches sermons.
Sermonear [ser-mo-nay-ar'], *va.* (Coll.) To lecture, to censure, to reprimand; to sermonize.
Sermonización [ser-mo-ne-thah-the-on'], *f.* Speaking in public; colloquy, conversation.
Serna [serr'-nah], *f.* (Obs.) Cultivated field.
Seroja, *f.* **Serojo**, *m.* [say-ro'-hah, ho]. A withered leaf, fallen from a tree. *Serojas*, Small trees left on a piece of woodland, after the large trees have been cut down.
Serón [say-rone'], *m.* 1. A large frail or pannier used to carry figs, raisins, etc.; seroon. 2. Hamper, crate. *Serón caminero*, Horse-pannier.
Serondo [say-ron'-do], *a.* Late: used of produce. (Acad.)
Seronero [say-ro-nay'-ro], *m.* The maker of frails or panniers called *serones.*
Serosidad [say-ro-se-dahd'], *f.* Serosity, serousness, thin or watery blood.
Seroso, sa [say-ro'-so, sah], *a.* Serous, thin, watery.
Serotino, na [say-ro-tee'-no, nah], *a.* Serotinous, produced late in the season.
Serpa [serr'-pah], *f.* Layer, a long twig or spray of vine planted in the ground, without being separated from the mother plant, in order to raise another stock.
Serpear [ser-pay-ar'], *vn.* To wind like a serpent, to move in undulations, to crawl, to creep; to meander, to serpentize.
Serpentaria [ser-pen-tah'-re-ah], *f.* (Bot.) Snake-root, a medicinal root. Aristolochia serpentaria.
Serpentario [ser-pen-tah'-re-o], *m.* A northern constellation: the constellation Ophiuchus.
Serpentear [ser-pen-tay-ar'], *vn.* To move like a serpent, to serpentine.
Serpenticida [ser-pen-te-thee'-dah], *com.* Serpent-killer.
Serpentígero, ra [ser-pen-tee'-hay-ro, rah], *a.* (Poet.) Serpentigerous, bearing serpents.
Serpentín [ser-pen-teen'], *m.* 1. (Min.) Serpentine, a speckled green stone resembling the serpent's skin. 2.

Cock. hammer of a gun or musket-lock. 3. (Chem.) Worm for distilling liquors. 4. Serpent, a musical instrument; a wind-instrument of low pitch, now disused. 5. Ancient piece of ordnance.

Serpentina [ser-pen-tee'-nah], *f.* 1. Cock, hammer of a gun-lock. 2. Culverin; missile weapon. 3. (Chem.) Serpentine, or worm for distilling liquors.

Serpentinamente, *adv.* In a serpentine manner.

Serpentino, na [ser-pen-tee'-no, nah], *a.* 1. Serpentine, winding like a serpent; resembling a serpent; belonging to the oil of serpents. 2. Applied to a slanderous tongue. 3. Serpentine: applied to a kind of marble.

Serpentón [ser-pen-tohn'], *m.* 1. (Aug.) A large serpent. 2. A musical instrument. *V.* SERPENTÍN.

Serpezuela [ser-pay-thoo-ay'-lah], *f. dim.* of SIERPE. Applied to any little, spiteful; ugly woman.

Serpia [serr'-pe-ah], *f.* (Prov.) Gummy or viscous matter of a vine-stock.

Serpiente [ser-pe-en'-tay], *f.* 1. Serpent. *Serpiente de cascabel,* Rattlesnake. 2. Serpent, devil, Satan.

Serpiginoso, sa [ser-pe-he-no'-so, sah], *a.* (Med.) Serpiginous.

Serpigo [ser-pee'-go], *m.* (Med.) Tetter, ring-worm, serpigo.

Serpol [ser-pole'], *m.* (Bot.) Wild thyme. Thymus serpyllum.

Serpollo [ser-pol'-lyo], *m.* Shoot, sprout, especially of a tree which has been pruned.

Serradizo, za [ser-rah-dee'-tho, thah], *a.* Fit to be sawed: applied to timber.

Serrado, da [ser-rah'-do, dah], *a.* Serrate, toothed like a saw, laciniate.—*pp.* of SERRAR.

Serrador [ser-rah-dor'], *m.* Sawer or sawyer. *V.* ASERRADOR.

Serraduras [ser-rah-doo'-ras], *f. pl.* Sawdust. *V.* SERRÍN.

Serrallo [ser-rahl'-lyo], *m.* 1. Seraglio, the palace of the grand signior. 2. Place of obscenity. (Per.)

Serranía [ser-rah-nee'-ah], *f.* Ridge of mountains, a mountainous country.

Serraniego, ga [ser-rah-ne-ay'-go, gah], *a.* *V.* SERRANO.

Serranil [ser-rah-neel'], *m.* Kind of knife.

Serrano, na [ser-rah'-no, nah], *a.* & *m.* & *f.* Mountaineer, highlander, inhabiting mountains.

Serrar [ser-rar'], *va.* To saw. *V.* ASERRAR.

Serreta [ser-ray'-tah], *f.* 1. Dim. of SIERRA. 2. Piece of a cavesson or nose-band, used in breaking a horse.

Serrato, ta [ser-rah'-to, tah], *a.* (Anat.) Denticulated, serrated.

Serrezuela [ser-ray-thoo-ay'-lah], *f. dim.* A small saw.

Serrijón [ser-re-hone'], *m.* Short chain of mountains.

Serrín [ser-reen'], *m.* Sawdust. *V.* ASERRADURAS.

Serrino, na [ser-ree'-no, nah], *a.* 1. Belonging to chains of mountains. 2. Applied to a quick, irregular pulse.

Serrones [ser-ro'-nes], *m.* (Bot.) Good King Harry; a goose-foot. Chenopodium bonus henricus.

Serrucho [ser-roo'-cho], *m.* Hand-saw with a small handle. *Serrucho braguero,* Pit-saw.

Servador [ser-vah-dor'], *m.* Preserver: applied by poets to Jupiter.

Serval, *m.* (Bot.) *V.* SERBAL.

Servato [ser-vah'-to], *m.* (Bot.) *V.* ERVATO.

Serventesio [ser-ven-tay'-se-o], *m.* (Poet.) Quartetto, like the first four verses of an octave.

Servible [ser-vee'-blay], *a.* Fit for service, serviceable, adaptable.

Serviciador [ser-ve-the-ah-dor'], *m.* (Obs.) Collector of the sheep-walk dues.

Servicial [ser-ve-the-ahl'], *a.* Obsequious, diligent, obliging, compliant, friendly, accommodating, serviceable. —*m.* (Coll.) Clyster.

Servicialmente, *adv.* Obsequiously, serviceably.

Serviciar [ser-ve-the-ar'], *va.* To collect the sheep-walk dues, donations to the state, etc.

Servicio [ser-vee'-the-o], *m.* 1. Service, the act of serving; the state of a servant. 2. Service, favour, kind office; good turn. 3. Divine service. 4. Sum of money voluntarily offered to the king. 5. Utility, benefit, advantage. 6. Close-stool, privy-chair. 7. Service, cover, course. *Servicio de mesa,* Service for the table. 8. Personal service or residence of beneficed clergy. 9. Service to kings in war.

Servidero, ra [ser-ve-day'-ro, rah], *a.* 1. Fit for service, utilizable. 2. Requiring personal attendance.

Servido, da [ser-vee'-do, dah], *a.* & *pp.* of SERVIR. 1. Served, pleased. *Donde Dios es servido,* Wherever God pleases. *Ser servido,* To please, to deign, to grant. *Siendo Dios servido,* Please God. 2. Second-hand, used.

Servidor [ser-ve-dor'], *m.* 1. Servant, waiter. 2. One who pays court to a lady. 3. One who politely tenders his services to another. *Servidor de Vd.,* Your servant; at your service. 4. Pan of a close-stool.

Servidora [ser-ve-do'-rah], *f.* 1. Maid, female servant. 2. A term of courtesy used by women.

Servidumbre [ser-ve-doom'-bray], *f.* 1. Attendance, servitude; whole establishment of servants. 2. Slavery, mancipation, state of a slave. 3. Mighty or inevitable obligation to do any thing. 4. Servitude, service, the act of serving or attending at command. 5. (Law) Right which one has over another person or thing, as the liberty of passing through a house or garden; right of way. 6. Subjection of the passions.

Servil [ser-veel'], *a.* & *m.* 1. Servile, slavish, fawning; sneaking. 2. Servile, peculiar to servants, dependent, menial. 3. Servile, low, mean, abject; mechanical.

Servilidad [ser-ve-le-dahd'], *f.* (Prov.) Servility, meanness, baseness, submission from fear.

Servilismo [ser-ve-lees'-mo], *m.* Servilism, blind adhesion to authority.

Servilmente, *adv.* Servilely, slavishly; basely; indecently.

Servilla [ser-veel'-lyah], *f.* A kind of thin-soled shoe.

Servilleta [ser-veel-lyay'-tah], *f.* Napkin, used at table. *Doblar la servilleta,* (Met. Coll.) To die.

Servilletero, ra [ser-veel-lyay-tay'-ro, rah], *a.* Relating to table-linen.

Servio, via [serr'-ve-o, ah], *a.* Servian, native of or relating to Servia.

Serviola [ser-ve-o'-lah], *f.* (Naut.) Cathead, anchor beam.

Servir [ser-veer'], *va.* 1. To serve, to perform menial services. *Servir de mayordomo,* To serve as steward. 2. To serve, to do a favour or kind office. 3. To serve, to hold an employment, to occupy a public station. 4. To court a lady. 5. To serve, to worship the Supreme Being. 6. To perform another's functions; to act as a substitute. 7. To pay money voluntarily to the king or government. 8. To serve, to wait at table. 9. To heat the oven. 10. To dress victuals for the table. 11. To administer. *Para servir a Vd.,* At your service. *Servir de,* To serve for.—*vn.* 1. To serve, to be in the service of another, to be subject to another. 2. To correspond, to agree. 3. To serve, to answer the purpose; to conduce; to be useful or convenient. 4. To serve, to be a soldier. 5. To be employed at any thing by another's orders.—*vr.* 1. To deign, to vouchsafe, to condescend, to please. *Sírvase Vd. venir,* Please to come. *Sírvase Vd. decirme,* Pray tell me. *Sirva de aviso,* Let this be a warning. 2. To make use of; to employ for some purpose.

Servitas, Siervos de María [ser-vee'-tas], *n.* Religious order dedicated to the service of the blessed Virgin after the rule of St. Augustine.

Servofreno [ser-vo-fray'-no], *m.* Power brake.

Servomotor [ser-vo-mo-tor'], *m.* Servo-motor.

Sesada [say-sah'-dah], *f.* Fried brains.

Sésamo [say'-sah-mo], *m.* Sesame, gingili, an annual herb the seeds of which yield a bland oil.

Sesear [say-say-ar'], *vn.* To pronounce the *c* before *e* and *i* as *ss*, which is a great fault in Spanish pronunciation.

Seseli [say-say'-le], *m.* (Bot.) Wild spicknel, meadow saxifrage. Seseli, *L.*

Sesén [say-sen'], *m.* A copper coin in Arragon, of six maravedis.

Sesenta [say-sen'-tah], *m.* Sixty, figures of 60.—*a.* Sixty; sixtieth.

Sesentavo, va [say-sen-tah'-vo, vah], *a.* & *n.* One-sixtieth; a sixtieth part.

Sesentón, na [say-sen-tone', nah], *m.* & *f.* & *a.* One turned of sixty, sexagenarian, sixty years old.

Sesera [say-say'-rah], *f.* 1. Brain-pan. 2. The entire brain.

Sesga [ses'-gah], *f.* Gore or goring.

Sesgadamente, *adv.* Slantwise, slopewise, slopingly. *V.* SESGAMENTE.

Sesgado, da [ses-gah'-do, dah], *a.* & *pp.* of SESGAR. Sloped, oblique, slanting.

Sesgadura [ses-gah-doo'-rah], *f.* Slope, the act of sloping.

Sesgamente, *adv.* Obliquely, slopingly; mildly.

Sesgar [ses-gar'], *va.* To slope, to cut slantwise, to take or give an oblique direction.

Sesgo, ga [ses'-go, gah], *a.* 1. Sloped, oblique, turned or twisted obliquely. 2. Serene, tranquil, unruffled. 3. Severe of aspect, grave, uncouth. *Al sesgo,* Slopingly; obliquely.

Sesgo, *m.* 1. Slope, obliqueness, oblique direction. 2. Mean, medium.

Sesil [say-seel'], *a.* (Bot.) Sessile, joined to the stem without any stalk.

Sesión [say-se-on'], *f.* 1. Session, sitting, meeting of a council or congress. 2. Conference, consultation.

Sesma [ses'-mah], *f.* 1. The sixth part of a yard or any other thing. 2. A division of territory. 3. *V.* SEXMA.

Sesmero [ses-may'-ro], *m.* A person appointed to manage the public affairs, belonging to the district called *sesma* or *sesmo.* *V.* SEXMERO.

Sesmo [ses'-mo], *m.* 1. A division of territory in some Spanish provinces. 2. *V.* LINDE. 3. (Obs.) Six.

Seso [say'-so], *m.* 1. The brain: generally used in the plural. 2. Brain, understanding, prudence, wisdom. 3. Stone put under a pot to keep it steady on the fire. *No tener seso,* Not to have common sense. *Tener los sesos* or *los cascos á la jineta,* (Coll.) To have little judgment; to be a giddy-brained, wild, harem-skarem person. *Tener los sesos de un mosquito* or *de un chorlito*, Not to have the brains of a sparrow.

Sesqui [ses'-ke]. (Lat.) Used in composition, and implying one and a half, as *sesquihora*, an hour and a half.

Sesquiáltero, ra [ses-ke-ahl'-tay-ro, rah], *a.* Sesquialter, one and a half.

Sesquidoble [ses-ke-do'-blay], *a.* Two and a half times.

Sesquimodio [ses-ke-mo'-de-o], *m.* A bucket and a half.

Sesquióxido [ses-ke-ok'-se-do], *m.* Sesquioxide.

Sesquipedal [ses-ke-pay-dahl'], *a.* Sesquipedal, sesquipedalian, a foot and a half in length.

Sesquiplicado, da [ses-ke-ple-cah'-do, dah], *a.* Sesquiplicate.

Sesteadero [ses-tay-ah-day'-ro], *m.* A proper place for taking a nap after dinner; resting-place for cattle.

Sestear [ses-tay-ar'], *vn.* To take a nap or rest after dinner; to sleep from 1 to 3 o'clock P. M.

Sestero [ses-tay'-ro], *m.* *V.* SESTEADERO.

Sesudamente, *adv.* Maturely, wisely, prudently.

Sesudo, da [say-soo'-do, dah], *a.* Judicious, discreet, prudent, wise.

Seta [say'-tah], *f.* 1. Bristle, the stiff hair of swine. 2. (Bot.) A general name for all the species of mushroom: it is given particularly to the field agaric, Agaricus campestris: called also in Spanish *seta de cardo.* 3. Blobber-lip. *V.* JETA. 4. Snuff of a candle.

Sete [say'-tay], *m.* Mint, or office where money is struck with a die.

Setecientos, tas [say-tay-the-en'-tos, tas], *a.* & *n.* Seven hundred.

Setena [say-tay'-nah], *f.* Seven things of a kind.—*pl.* A punishment by which, anciently, seven-fold payment was obligated.

Setenta [say-ten'-tah], *a.* Seventy.

Setentavo, va [say-ten-tah'-vo, vah], *a.* & *n.* One-seventieth; a seventieth part.

Setentón, na [say-ten-tone', nah], *a.* & *n.* Seventy years old; turned of seventy.

Setentrión [say-ten-tre-on'], *m.* Septentrion, the north; the north wind.

Setentrional [say-ten-tre-o-nahl'], *a.* Septentrional, northern, northerly.

Setero, ra [say-tay'-ro, rah], *a.* Bristly, hairy.

Setiembre [say-te-em'-bray], *m.* *V.* SEPTIEMBRE.

Sétima, *f.* *V.* SÉPTIMA.

Sétimo, ma [say'-te-mo, mah], *a.* Seventh. *V.* SÉPTIMO, MA.

Seto [say'-to], *m.* Fence, defence, inclosure. *Seto vivo*, Hedge, quickset.

Setuagenario, ria. *V.* SEPTUAGENARIO.

Setuagésima, *f.* *V.* SEPTUAGÉSIMA.

Setuagésimo, ma, *a.* *V.* SEPTUAGÉSIMO.

Setuní [say-too-nee'], *m.* *V.* ACEITUNÍ.

Setuplicar [say-too-ple-car'], *va.* *V.* SEPTUPLICAR.

Sétuplo, pla, *a.* *V.* SÉPTUPLO.

Seudo [say-oo'-do], *a.* Pseudo, false.

Seudomédico [say-oo-do-may'-de-co], *m.* Charlatan, quack.

Seudomorfo, fa [say-oo-do-mor'-fo, fah], *a.* Pseudomorphous, crystallizing in a manner foreign to its class.

Seudónimo, ma [say-oo-do'-ne-mo, mah], *a.* Pseudonymous, fictitious. —*m.* Pseudonym, pen name.

Severamente, *adv.* Severely.

Severidad [say-vay-re-dahd'], *f.* 1. Severity, rigour, harshness, austerity, acerbity. 2. Severity, strictness, punctuality, exactness. 3. Gravity, seriousness.

Severizarse [say-vay-re-thar'-say], *vr.* To become serious or grave.

Severo, ra [say-vay'-ro, rah], *a.* 1. Severe, rigorous, rigid, harsh. 2. Grave, serious. 3. Severe, punctual, exact, strict.

Sevicia [say-vee'-the-ah], *f.* (Obs.) Fierceness, cruelty.

Sevillano, na [say-veel-lyah'-no, nah], *a.* Of Seville, Sevillan.

Sexagenario, ria [sek-sah-hay-nah'-re-o, ah], *a.* Sexagenary, sixty years old.

Sexagésima [sek-sah-hay'-se-mah], *f.* Sexagesima, second Sunday before Lent.

Sexagésimo, ma [sek-sah-hay'-se-mo, mah], *a.* Sexagesimal, sixtieth.

Sexagonal [sek-sah-go-nahl'], *a.* Hexagonal.

Sexángulo, la [sek-sahn'-goo-lo, lah], *a.* Sexangular.—*m.* Sexangle.

Sexenio [sek-say'-ne-o], *m.* Space of six years.

Sexo [sek'-so], *m.* 1. Sex, the organic difference between male and female. 2. Womankind, by way of emphasis.

Sexta [sex'-tah], *f.* 1. One of the hours into which the Hebrews and Romans divided the artificial day, and including three of the hours now used. 2. A sequence of six cards at the game of piquet. 3. Sixth, one of the minor canonical hours after tierce.

Sextante [sex-tahn'-tay], *m.* 1. Coin weighing two ounces. 2. Sextant, an astronomical instrument.

Sextario [sex-tah'-re-o], *m.* Ancient measure.

Sextercio, *m.* *V.* SESTERCIO.

Sextil [sex-teel'], *a.* (Astro.) Sextile. —*m.* (Obs.) August.

Sextilla [sex-teel'-lyah], *f.* Sextain, a Spanish metrical composition of six feet.

Sextina [sex-tee'-nah], *f.* A kind of Spanish metrical composition.

Sexto, ta [sex'-to, tah], *a.* Sixth, the ordinal number of six.

Sexto, *m.* Book containing canonical decrees.

Sexual [sek-soo-ahl'], *a.* Sexual.

Si [see], *conj.* If, although; in case that, provided that, unless, when. *Si bien*, Although. *V.* AUNQUE. *Si acaso* or *por si acaso*, If by chance. *Un si es no es*, Somewhat, a trifle. *Si no*, If not, otherwise. (Lat. si.)

Sí [see], *adv.* Yes, yea; without doubt indeed. Often used ironically, and is then a negation. (Lat. sic.)—*m.* 1. Assent, consent, permission. 2. (Mus.) Si, the seventh note of the scale. *Dar el sí*, To say yes; to promise to marry.

Sí, *pronoun.* Reflexive form of the personal pronoun of the third person, in both genders and numbers; employed in oblique cases and always with a preposition. Himself, herself, themselves. *De por sí*, Apart, separately. *De sí*, Of itself, spontaneously.

Siampán [se-am-pahn'], *m.* Dye-stuff produced in the province of this name.

Sibarita [se-bah-ree'-tah], *com.* Sybarite, a native of Sybaris.—*a.* Given to pleasures, luxurious, sensuous.

Sibarítico, ca [se-ba-ree'-te-co, cah], *a.* 1. Sybaritical, luxurious. 2. Sensual.

Sibil [se-beel'], *m.* A small cellar under ground, where wine, water, or other things are kept fresh.

Sibila [se-bee'-lah], *f.* Prophetess; sibyl. *Sibila doctora* or *sibila jamona*, Old maid who pretends to be very learned and discreet.

Sibilante [se-be-lahn'-tay], *a.* (Poet.) Sibilant, hissing.

Sibilino, na [se-be-lee'-no, nah], *a.* Sibylline.

Sibucao [se-boo-cah'-o], *m.* Sapan-tree which furnishes a dye-wood; it belongs to the leguminosæ. *Cf.* SAPÁN.

Sic [seek]. A Latin word employed in manuscripts or printed matter to indicate that the word or idea is literally exact. Used in a parenthesis (*sic*).

Sicamor [se-cah-mor'], *m.* (Bot.) European Judas-tree. Cercis siliquastrum. *V.* CICLAMOR.

Sicario [se-cah'-re-o], *m.* A paid assassin. *Cf.* SEIDE.

Siciliano, na [se-the-le-ah'-no, nah], *a.* Sicilian, relating to Sicily.

Siclo [see'-clo], *m.* Shekel, an ancient Jewish coin.

Sicoanálisis [se-co-ah-nah'-le-sis], *f.* V. PSICOANÁLISIS

Sicofante [se-co-fahn'-tay], *m.* Sycophant, flatterer, parasite.

Sicología [se-co-lo-hee'-ah], *f.* V. PSICOLOGÍA.

Sicológico, ca [se-co-lo'-he-co, cah], *a.* V. PSICOLÓGICO.

Sicólogo, ga [se-co'-lo-go, gah], *m.* & *f.* V. PSICÓLOGO.

Sicomoro [se-co-mo'-ro], *m.* (Bot.) Sycamore, the mulberry-leaved fig-tree. Ficus sycomorus.

Siconeurótico, ca [se-coh-nay-oo-roh'-te-co, cah], *a.* V. PSICONEURÓTICO.

Sicópata [se-co'-pah-tah], *m.* V. PSICÓPATA.

Sicopático, ca [se-co-pah'-te-co, cah], *a.* V. PSICOPÁTICO.

Sicosis [se-co'-sis], *f.* V. PSICOSIS.

Sicoterapia [se-co-tay-rah'-pe-ah], *f.* V. PSICOTERAPIA.

Sideral [see-day-rahl'], *a.* Sidereal, astral, space. *Viajes siderales*, Space travel.

Sidéreo, rea [se-day'-ray-o, ah], *a.* Sidereal, starry.

Siderismo [se-day-rees'-mo], *m.* (Neol.) Worship of the stars. *V.* SABEÍSMO.

Sideritis [se-day-ree'-tis], *f.* Siderites, a mineral. *Sideritis* or *Sideritide*, (Bot.) Iron-wort. Sideritis, *L.*

Siderografía [se-day-ro-grah-fee'-ah], *f.* The art of engraving on steel.

Siderotecnia [se-day-ro-tek'-ne-ah], *f.* Siderotechny, the art of working iron.

Siderurgia [se-day-roor'-he-ah], *f.* Siderurgy.

Siderúrgico, ca [se-day-roor'-he-co, cah], *a.* Pertaining to iron and steel. *Industria siderúrgica*, Iron and steel industry.

Sidra [see'-drah], *f.* Cider.

Siega [se-ay'-gah], *f.* Harvest, reaping time, mowing, fruits gathered.

(*Yo siego, yo siegue*, from *Segar. V.* ACRECENTAR.)

Siembra [se-em'-brah], *f.* 1. Seed-time. 2. Corn-field.

(*Yo siembro, yo siembre*, from *Sembrar. V.* ACERTAR.)

Siempre [se-em'-pray], *adv.* Always, at all times. *Siempre jamás*, For ever and ever. *Siempre enjuta*, Blue daisy. Globularia vulgaris.

Siempreviva [se-em-pray-vee'-vah], *f.* (Bot.) House-leek. Sempervivum.

Sien [se-ayn'], *f.* Temple, the upper part of the side of the head.

(*Yo siento, yo siente*, from *Sentar. V.* ACERTAR.)

(*Yo siento, yo sienta; él sintió, sintiera;* from *Sentir. V.* ADHERIR.)

Sierpe [se-err'-pay], *f.* 1. Serpent. *V.* SERPIENTE. 2. A shrew, a peevish, clamorous, spiteful woman. 3. Any thing which moves by undulation in a serpentine shape. 4. A peevish, fretful person. 5. (Bot.) Sucker.

Sierra [se-er'-rah], *f.* 1. Saw. *Sierra de mano*, A panel-saw or hand-saw.

Sierra de ingletes, A tenon-saw. *Sierra bracera*, A kind of bow or frame-saw. 2. Ridge of mountains and craggy rocks. 3. Waves rising mountain-high in a storm. 4. (Zool.) Saw-fish. Pristis. *Sierra de agua*, Saw-mill. *Cuando la sierra está tocada, en la mano viene el agua*, Cloud-caps on the mountains portend early rain.

Sierrecilla [se-er-ray-theel'-lyah], *f. dim.* Small saw.

(*Yo sierro, yo sierre*, from *Serrar. V.* Acertar.)

Siervo, va [se-err'-vo, vah], *m.* & *f.* 1. Serf, slave, servant. 2. Servant by courtesy.

Sieso [se-ay'-so], *m.* Fundament, anus.

Siesta [se-es'-tah], *f.* 1. The hottest part of the day; the time for a nap after dinner: generally from 1 to 3 o'clock. 2. Sleep taken after dinner. 3. Afternoon music in churches.

Siete [se-ay'-tay], *a.* & *m.* 1. Seven. 2. Seventh. 3. Seven, the figure 7. 4. Card with seven figures. *De siete en siete*, By seven and seven. *Más que siete*, (Coll.) Very much, in excess, too much. *Hablar más que siete*, To talk too much.

Sieteañal [se-ay-tay-ah-nyahl'], *a.* Septennial.

Sietedurmientes [se-ay-tay-door-me-en'-tes], *m. pl.* Seven sleepers, great sleepers.

Sieteenrama [se-ay'-tay-en-rah'-mah], *f.* (Bot.) *V.* Tormentila.

Sietelevar [se-ay-tay-lay-var'], *m.* In the game of bank, the third chance, by which seven times the stake is won.

Sietemesino, na [se-ay-tay-may-see'-no, nah], *a.* Born seven months after conception.

Sieteñal [se-ay-tay-nyahl'], *a.* Seven years old, septennial.

Sífilis [see'-fe-lis], *f.* Syphilis, a specific venereal disease; vulgarly, the pox.

Sifilítico, ca [se-fe-lee'-te-co, cah], *a.* Syphilitic, relating to syphilis or affected by it.

Sifón [se-fone'], *m.* Siphon, a bent tube with unequal arms, for drawing liquids over the side of a cask or other vessel.

Sigilación [se-he-lah-the-on'], *f.* Impression, mark.

Sigilado, da [se-he-lah'-do, dah], *a.* Marked with some defect or affected by some disease.—*pp.* of Sigilar.

Sigilar [se-he-lar'], *va.* 1. To keep a thing secret. 2. To seal.

Sigilo [se-hee'-lo], *m.* 1. Seal. *V.* Sello. 2. Secret. *Sigilo sacramental*, Inviolable secrecy of the confessional.

Sigilosamente, *adv.* Silently, secretly.

Sigiloso, sa [se-he-lo'-so, sah], *a.* Silent, reserved; keeping a secret.

Sigla [see'-glah], *f.* Initial letter, employed as an abbreviation (in inscriptions, etc.).

Siglo [see'-glo], *m.* 1. Century, a hundred years. 2. Age, duration of any thing. 3. A very long time. *Un siglo ha que no te veo*, I have not seen you this age. 4. Worldly intercourse, the concerns of this life; the world. *Buen siglo*, Eternal bliss, eternal life. *Por el siglo de mi madre* or *por el siglo de todos mis pasados*, By the life of my fathers; a familiar oath generally accompanied by a menace. *Por* or *en los siglos de los siglos*, For ever and ever. *Siglo de cobre*, The brazen age. *Siglo de hierro*, The iron age. *Siglo de oro*, The golden age. *Siglo de plata*, The silver age.

Sigma [seeg'-mah], *f.* Sigma, eighteenth letter of the Greek alphabet, corresponding to *s*.

Signáculo [sig-nah'-coo-lo], *m.* Seal, signet.

Signar [sig-nar'], *va.* To sign, to mark with a signet.—*vr.* To make the sign of the cross.

Signatario, ria [sig-nah-tah'-re-o, ah], *a.* Signatory, signing. *Poderes signatarios*, Authority to sign. —*m.* & *f.* Signatory, signer.

Signatura [sig-nah-too'-rah], *f.* Sign, mark; signature in printing; a Roman tribunal.

Significación [sig-ne-fe-cah-the-on'], *f.* 1. Signification, meaning expressed by a sign or word, 2. Signification, the act of making known by signs; significance. 3. *V.* Significado.

Significado [sig-ne-fe-cah'-do], *m.* Signification, object signified by means of words.—*Significado, da, pp.* of Significar.

Significador, ra [sig-ne-fe-cah-dor', rah], *m.* & *f.* One who signifies.

Significante [sig-ne-fe-cahn'-tay], *a.* Significant, expressive.

Significantemente, *adv.* *V.* Significativamente.

Significar [sig-ne-fe-car'], *va.* 1. To signify, to denote, to mean. 2. To declare, to make known. 3. To import, to be worth.

Significativamente, *adv.* Significatively.

Significativo, va [sig-ne-fe-cah-tee'-vo, vah], *a.* Significative, expressive.

Signo [seeg'-no], *m.* 1. Sign, mark. 2. (Coll.) Fate, destiny. 3. Benediction with the sign of the cross. 4. Notarial signet or flourish, which notaries in Spain add to their signatures. 5. (Ast.) Sign of the zodiac. 6. Type, emblem. *Signo por costumbre*, Sign established by usage, as a branch, at the door of a liquor-seller. 7. Any of the characters in which music is written.

(*Yo sigo, yo siga*, from *Seguir. V.* Pedir.)

Siguiente [se-gee-en'-tay], *a.* Following, successive, sequent.

Sílaba [see'-la-bah], *f.* 1. Syllable. 2. (Mus.) Two or three sounds which correspond with every letter of the gamut.

Silabar [se-la-bar'], *vn.* *V.* Silabear.

Silabario [se-la-bah'-re-o], *m.* A book which contains and explains syllables; syllabary.

Silabear [se-lah-bay-ar'], *vn.* To pronounce by syllables.

Silabeo [se-la-bay'-o], *m.* Syllabication, the act of forming syllables.

Silábico, ca [se-lah'-be-co, cah], *a.* Syllabical, syllabic.

Silba [seel'-bah], *f.* Whistling, catcall, hissing (in public derision).

Silabus, or **Silabo**, *m.* Syllabus, a brief statement by the Pope of errors condemned (in 1864).

Silbador, ra [sil-bah-dor', rah], *m.* & *f.* Whistler; exploder, a hisser.

Silbar [sil-bar'], *vn.* 1. To whistle. 2. To whiz, as a musket-ball—*va.* To hiss, to express disapprobation (in public), to catcall.

Silbatico, illo, ito [sil-bah-tee'-co], *m. dim.* A small whistle.

Silbato [sil-bah'-to], *m.* 1. Whistle, a wind instrument. *Silbato de cazador*, A call. *V.* Reclamo. 2. A small chink or crack, through which passes any liquid or air that whizzes.

Silbido [sil-bee'-do], *m.* Whistle, whistling; hiss; sibilation. *Silbido de oídos*, Whizzing or humming in the ear

Silbo [seel'-bo], *m.* Whistle, hiss, whistling.

Silboso, sa [sil-bo'-so, sah], *a.* (Poet.) Whistling, hissing.

Silenciario, ria [se-len-the-ah'-re-o, ah], *a.* Observing profound silence.

Silenciario, *m.* Silentiary, officer appointed to preserve silence in a place or assembly; silent place.

Silenciero, ra [se-len-the-ay'-ro, rah], *a.* Charged with preserving silence; which preserves peace.

Silencio [se-len'-the-o], *m.* 1. Silence; habitual taciturnity; secrecy. 2. State of holding the peace. 3. Reservedness, prudence. 4. Stillness, repose.—*int.* Silence! hush.

Silenciosamente, *adv.* Silently, softly, gently.

Silencioso, sa [se-len-the-oh'-so, sah], *a.* Silent; solitary, mute.

Sileno [se-lay'-no], *m.* Silenus, a demi-god.

Siler montano [se-lerr' mon-tah'-no], *m.* (Bot.) Mountain lasserwort. Laserpitium siler.

Silería [se-lay-ree'-ah], *f.* Place where subterraneous granaries are made.

Silero [se-lay'-ro], *m.* A subterraneous granary for wheat; a silo.

Sílex [se'-lex], *m.* Silex.

Sílfide [seel'-fe-day], *f.* **Silfo**, *m.* Sylph.

Silguero [sil-gay'-ro], *m.* (Orn. Prov.) Linnet. *V.* Jilguero.

Silibo [se-lee'-bo], *m.* (Bot.) Silybum, a genus of plants.

Silicato [se-le-cah'-to], *m.* Silicate, a compound of silicic acid.

Sílice [see'-le-thay], *m.* Silica, silicon dioxide (occurring as quartz or as opal).

Silíceo, ea [se-lee-thay-o, ah], *a.* Siliceous, flinty.

Silicio [se-lee'-the-o], *m.* 1. Silicon, a non-metallic element, next in abundance to oxygen. 2. *V.* Cilicio.

Silicua [se-lee'-coo-ah], *f.* 1. Siliqua, carat, a former weight of four grains. 2. Silique, a seed-vessel, husk, pod, or shell of leguminous plants.

Silícula [se-lee'-coo-lah], *f.* (Bot.) Silicle, a short silique.

Silicuoso, sa, *a.* Siliquose, having a pod or capsule.

Siligo [se-lee'-go], *m.* *V.* Neguilla.

Silo [see'-lo], *m.* 1. A subterraneous granary for wheat, a silo. 2. Any cavern or dark place.

Silogismo [se-lo-hees'-mo], *m.* Syllogism.

Silogístico, ca [se-lo-hees'-te-co, cah], *a.* Syllogistic, syllogistical.

Silogizar [se-lo-he-thar'], *vn.* To syllogize, to reason, to argue.

Silueta [se-loo-ay'-tah], *f.* Silhouette, a profile in shadow.

Siluro [se-loo'-ro], *m.* Catfish, sheatfish, silurus. Silurus glanis.

Silva [seel'-vah], *f.* 1. A miscellany. 2. A kind of Spanish metrical composition. 3. (Obs.) Forest, wood.

Silvamar [sil-vah-mar'], *m.* Sarsaparilla.

Silvano [sil-vah'-no], *m.* 1. Sylvan, a wood-god or satyr. 2. Tellurium.

Silvático, ca [sil-vah'-te-co, cah], *a.* *V.* Selvático.

Silvestre [sil-ves'-tray], *a.* Wild, uncultivated; rustic, savage.

Silvoso, sa [sil-vo'-so, sah], *a.* *V.* Selvoso.

Silla [seel'-lyah], *f.* 1. Chair, movable seat. 2. See, the seat of episcopal power; the diocese of a bishop. 3. *Silla* or *silla de montar*, Saddle. 4. Seat. 5. Seat, anus. *Silla de manos*, Sedan-chair. *Silla poltrona*, Arm or elbow-chair; a lazy chair. *Silla de posta*, Post-chaise. *Silla volante*, A light gig. *Silla de rejilla* or *de junco*, Cane or bamboo-bottomed chair. *Silla* *de palo*, Wooden-bottomed chair. *Silla de columpio*, Rocking-chair. *Silla giratoria*, Pivot chair. *Silla plegadiza*, Folding-chair, camp-stool. *De silla a silla*, Face to face. *Hombre de ambas sillas* or *de todas sillas*, A man of general information; a clever fellow. *Pegársele (a uno) la silla*, To make a very long call, to be a stayer. *Tópaste en la silla; por acá, tía*, Either avoid peril or meet it bravely.

Silla de cubierta [seel'-lyah day coo-be-err-tah], *f.* (Naut.) Deck chair.

Sillar [sil-lyar], *m.* 1. A square hewn stone. 2. Back of a horse where the saddle is placed.

Sillarejo [sil-lyah-ray'-ho], *m.* A small hewn stone.

Sillera [sil-lyay'-rah], *f.* Place where sedan-chairs are shut up.

Sillería [sil-lyay-ree'-ah], *f.* 1. Seat, set or parcel of chairs. 2. Shop where chairs are made or sold. 3. Stalls about the choir of a church. 4. Building of hewn stone.

Sillero [sil-lyay'-ro], *m.* Saddler, chair-maker.

Silleta [sil-lyay'-tah], *f.* 1. (Dim.) A small chair. 2. Hollow stone on which chocolate is ground. 3. Close stool, privy-chair. 4. Side-saddle.

Silletero [sil-lyay-tay'-ro], *m.* 1. Chair-man, one employed in carrying sedan-chairs. 2. Chair-maker, one who makes or sells chairs.

Sillico [sil-lyee'-co], *m.* Basin of a close-stool.

Sillín [sil-lyeen'], *m.* 1. A small, light riding-saddle. 2. A small saddle for a driving-horse.

Sillita [sil-lyee'-tah], *f. dim.* A small chair.

Sillón [sil-lyone'], *m.* 1. A large arm or elbow-chair. 2. Side-saddle for ladies.

Sima [see'-mah], *f.* 1. Deep and dark cavern; abyss, gulf. 2. Whirlwind, hurricane.

Simado, da [se-mah'-do, dah], *a.* (Prov.) Deep: applied to land.

Simarruba [se-mar-roo'-bah], *f.* (Bot.) Bitter-wood, quassia. Quassia simaruba.

Simbólicamente, *adv.* Symbolically, typically, hieroglyphically.

Simbólico, ca [sim-bo'-le-co, cah], *a.* 1. Symbolical, representative, expressing by signs. 2. Analogous, resembling.

Simbolización [sim-bo-le-thah-the-on'], *f.* Symbolization.

Simbolizar [sim-bo-le-thar'], *vn.* To symbolize, to resemble, to figure.

Símbolo [seem'-bo-lo], *m.* 1. Symbol. mark, sign, device. 2. (Mil.) Watchword. 3. Symbol, a badge to know one by. 4. Symbol, type, representation, figure. 5. Creed, belief, articles of faith.

Símbolo, la, *a.* *V.* Simbólico.

Simetría [se-may-tree'-ah], *f.* Symmetry, proportion, shapeliness, harmony.

Simétricamente, *adv.* Symmetrically.

Simétrico, ca [se-may'-tre-co, cah], *a.* Symmetrical, proportionate.

Simia [see'-me-ah], *f.* A female ape. *V.* Mona.

Simiente [se-me-en'-tay], *f.* 1. Seed. *V.* Semilla. 2. *V.* Semen. 3. Source, origin. *Guardar para simiente de rábanos*, (Met. and coll.) To wait for the sky to fall (or anything which will not happen; a reproof).

Simienza [se-me-en'-thah], *f.* (Prov.) Seed-time. *V.* Sementera.

Símil [see'-mil], *m.* 1. Resemblance, similarity. *V.* Semejanza. 2. Simile, comparison, similitude.—*a.* Similar, like. *V.* Semejante.

Similar [se-me-lar'], *a.* 1. Similar, homogeneous. 2. Resembling.

Similitud [se-me-le-tood'], *f.* Similitude, resemblance.

Similitudinariamente, *adv.* Similarly.

Similitudinario, ria [se-me-le-too-de-nah'-re-o, ah], *a.* Similar, similitudinary.

Simio [see'-me-o], *m.* Male ape. *V.* Mono.

Simón [se-mone'], *a.* & *n.* Applied to hackney coaches or coachmen in Madrid. *Alquilé un simón para ir al paseo*, I let or hired a hackney coach to go to the public walk.

Simonía [se-mo-nee'-ah], *f.* Simony.

Simoníaco, ca, Simoniático, ca [se-mo-nee'-ah-co, cah], *a.* Simoniac or simoniacal.

Simpatía [sim-pah-tee'-ah], *f.* 1. Sympathy, fellow-feeling, congeniality. 2. Charm, personality. *Tener simpatía por alguien*, To find someone charming and congenial.

Simpáticamente, *adv.* Sympathetically. *V.* Conformemente.

Simpático, ca [sim-pah'-te-co, cah], *a.* Sympathetic, sympathetical, analogous.

Simpatizar [sim-pah-te-thar'], *vn.* (used with the prep. *con*). To be congenial, to have a liking for someone. *Simpatizo mucho con él*, I like him, he and I get along well.

Simplazo, za [sim-plah'-tho, thah], *aug* A great simpleton; a stupid person.

Simple [seem'-play], *a.* 1. Single, simple, pure, mere, naked; unsigned; unconditional. 2. Silly, foolish, simple, crazy, idiotical. 3. Simple, undesigning, artless. 4. Simple, plain, mild, gentle; ingenuous. 5. Insipid, tasteless. 6. Single, brief: applied to the church services in which there is no repetition. 7. Informal, extra-judicial. *Beneficio simple*, An ecclesiastical living without duty; a sinecure. *Simple sacerdote*, Clergyman without dignity, degree, benefice, or ecclesiastical jurisdiction.—*m.* Simple, an herb or plant which alone serves for medicine.

Simplecillo, illa, ito, ita [sim-play-theel'-lyo], *m.* & *f.* A little simpleton.

Simplemente, *adv.* Simply, with simplicity and plainness, sillily; absolutely, merely.

Simpleza [sim-play'-thah], *f.* 1. Simpleness, silliness, fatuity. 2. Rusticity, rudeness. 3. (Obs.) Simplicity, sincerity.

Simplicidad [sim-ple-the-dahd'], *f.* 1. Simplicity, plainness, artlessness, homeliness. 2. Simpleness, silliness, fatuity.

Simplicista [sim-ple-thees'-tah], *m.* Simplist, simpler, herbalist.

Simplificar [sim-ple-fe-car'], *va.* To simplify, to make simple.

Simplísimo, ma [sim-plee'-se-mo, mah], *a. sup.* Extremely silly or foolish.

Simplista [sim-plees'-tah], *m.* Simplist, herbalist.

Simplón, na [sim-plone', nah], *m.* & *f. aug.* of Simple. Great simpleton.

Simplonazo, za [sim-plo-nah'-tho, thah], *a. aug.* of Simplón. Extremely simple or silly.

Simulación [se-moo-lah-the-on'], *f.* 1. Simulation, feigning, hollowness. 2. Subterfuge, evasion.

Simulacro [se-moo-lah'-cro], *m.* 1. Simulachre, image, idol. 2. Ghost, phantom.

Simuladamente, *adv.* In a dissembling or hypocritical manner.

Simulador, ra [se-moo-lah-dor', rah], *m.* & *f.* Simulator, dissembler.

Simular [se-moo-lar'], *va.* To simulate, to practise simulation.

Simulcadencia [se-mool-cah-den'-the-ah], *f.* (Rhet.) Figure of rhetoric repeating a consonant in a word forming a cadence.

Simulcadente [se-mool-cah-den'-tay], *a.* Applied to words or sentences having a cadence.

Simultad, *f.* (Obs.) *V.* Simultaneidad.

Simultáneamente, *adv.* Simultaneously.

Simultaneidad [se-mool-tah-nay-e-dahd'], *f.* Simultaneity.

Simultáneo, nea [se-mool-tah'-nay-o, ah], *a.* Simultaneous.

Simún [se-moon'], *m.* Simoom, a hot wind of the desert in Africa and Arabia. (Arab. "poisoned.")

Sin [seen], *prep.* Without, besides. Joined to a verb it is a negative or privative. *Sin embargo*, Notwithstanding, nevertheless, however. *Sin pies ni cabeza*, Without head or tail, without order. *Almendras sin cáscara*, Shelled almonds. *Pavo sin huesos*, Boned turkey. *Sin un cuarto*, Penniless. *Sin qué ni por* or *para qué*, Without cause or motive.

Sinabafa [se-nah-bah'-fah], *f.* Cloth or stuff of the natural colour of wool.

Sinagoga [se-nah-go'-gah], *f.* Synagogue, a Jewish congregation, and the place where they meet for worship and religious instruction.

Sinalefa [se-nah-lay'-fah], *f.* (Gram.) Synalepha, the union or blending into a single syllable of two successive vowels of different syllables.

Sinamay [se-nah-mah'-e], *m.* A very light fabric made in the Philippines from the filaments of *abacá*.

Sinamayera [se-nah-mah-yay'-rah], *f.* A woman who sells **sinamay** and other fabrics.

Sinantéreas [se-nan-tay'-ray-ahs], *a.* & *f. pl.* (Bot.) Synantherœ, a former order of plants now called *Compositæ*.

Sinapismo [se-nah-pees'-mo], *m.* Sinapism, mustard-poultice.

Sincategoremático, ca [sin-cah-tay-go ray-mah'-te-co, cah], *a.* Syncategorematic.

Sincerador, ra [sin-thay-rah-dor', rah], *m.* & *f.* Exculpator, excuser.

Sinceramente, *adv.* Sincerely, frankly, heartily, cordially.

Sincerar [sin-thay-rar'], *va.* To exculpate.—*vr.* To excuse, justify, or vindicate one's self.

Sinceridad [sin-thay-re-dahd'], *f.* Sincerity, purity of mind, frankness, cordiality, good-will.

Sincero, ra [sin-thay'-ro, rah], *a.* Sincere, ingenuous, honest; pure.

Sincipucio [sin-the-poo'-the-o], *m.* Sinciput.

Sincondrosis, *f.* (Anat.) Synchondrosis, union of two bones by means of a cartilage.

Síncopa [seen'-coo-pah], *f.* 1. Syncope, a contraction of words, by cutting off a part. 2. (Mus.) Syncopation, the beginning of a tone upon an unaccented beat, and its continuation through the following accented beat.

Sincopado, da [sin-co-pah'-do, dah], *a.* Syncopated.

Sincopal, *m.* *V.* Síncope.

Sincopal [sin-co-pahl'], *a.* Applied to malignant fevers.

Sincopar [sin-co-par'], *va.* 1. To syncopate, to contract words. 2. To abridge.

Síncope [seen'-co-pay], *f.* (Med.) Syncope, a fainting-fit.
Sincopizar [sin-co-pe-thar'], *va.* & *vr.* To swoon, to faint.
Sincresis [sin-cray'-sis], *f.* Fusion, mixture.
Sincretismo [sin-cray-tees'-mo], *m.* 1. Syncretism, a philosophical system allied to electicism. 2. Conciliation of different religious doctrines.
Sincronismo [sin-cro-nees'-mo], *m.* Synchronism, coincidence in time of different events; simultaneousness.
Sincrónico, ca [sin-cro'-ne-co, cah], *a.* Synchronous, synchronistic, occurring at the same time; simultaneous.
Sincronizar [sin-cro-ne-thar'], *va.* To synchronize.
Sindéresis [sin day'-ray-sis], *f.* Discretion, natural capacity for judging rightly.
Sindicación [sin-de-cah-the-on'], *f.* The act of informing against.
Sindicado [sin-de-cah'-do], *m.* 1. A body of trustees; a syndicate. 2. (Obs.) Tribunal appointed to try and punish such crimes as were denounced. 3. (Obs.) Judgment or sentence of the court. 4. (Obs.) The assemblage of the members of the Cortes.—*Sindicado, da, pp.* of SINDICAR.
Sindicador, ra [sin-de-cah-dor', rah], *m.* & *f.* Informer, prosecutor.
Sindicadura [sin-de-cah-doo'-rah], *f.* Office and dignity of a syndic.
Sindical [sin-de-cahl'], *a.* Syndical, relating to a syndic or syndicate.
Sindicalismo [sin-de-cah-lees'-mo], *m.* Unionism.
Sindicar [sin-de-car'], *va.* To inform, to lodge an information; to accuse.
Sindicatura [sin-de-ca-too'-rah], *f.* Trusteeship.
Síndico [seen'-de-co], *m.* 1. Syndic; recorder. 2. One whose office is to collect the fines imposed by a court. 3. Treasurer of the alms of religious houses. *Síndico de un concurso de acreedores,* (Amer.) An assignee, a trustee. *Síndico* or ***procurador general*** or ***del común,*** The attorney-general of a town or corporation.
Sinécdoque, Sinédoque [se-nec'-do-kay], *f.* (Rhet.) Synecdoche, a trope which puts a part for the whole, or the whole for a part.
Sinecura [se-nay-coo'-rah], *f.* Sinecure, an office having emoluments with few or no duties.
Sinedra [se-nay'-drah], *f.* Seats for the audience in a public hall.
Sinedrio [se-nay'-dre-o], *m.* *V.* SANEDRÍN.
Sinéresis [se-nay'-ray sis], *f.* Syneresis, a figure whereby two syllables are united into one.
Sínfisis [seen'-fe-sis], *f.* (Anat.) Symphysis, union of bones by means of an intervening body.
Sínfito [seen'-fe-to], *m.* (Bot.) Comfrey. Symphytum.
Sinfonía [sin-fo-nee'-ah], *f.* 1. Symphony, concert of concordant sounds; composition of instrumental music. 2. Symphony, a concerted instrumental piece for many instruments. 3. *V.* GAITA.
Sinfonista [sin-fo-nees'-tah], *com.* 1. Symphonist, one who composes a symphony. 2. A player in an orchestra.
Sinfonola [sin-fo-no'-lah], *f.* Jukebox.
Singladura [sin-glah-doo'-rah], *f.* (Naut.) A day's run; the distance traversed by a ship in 24 hours.
Singlar [sin-glar'], *vn.* (Naut.) To sail daily with a favourable wind on a direct course.
Singlón [sin-glone'], *m.* (Naut.) Any of the timbers placed over the keel.
Singular [sin-goo-lar'], *a.* 1. Singular, single. not common to others; unique. 2. Singular, individual, particular. 3. Singular, extraordinary, extravagant, strange. 4. Singular, excellent. 5. (Gram.) Singular.
Singularidad [sin-goo-lah-re-dahd'], *f.* Singularity, notability, oddity.
Singularizar [sin-goo-lah-re-thar'], *va.* To distinguish, to particularize, to singularize.—*vr.* To distinguish one's self; to be singular.
Singularmente. *adv.* Singularly.
Singulto [sin-gool'-to], *m.* Hiccough, singultus.
Siniestra [se-ne-es'-trah], *f.* The left hand. *V.* IZQUIERDA.
Siniestramente, *adv.* Sinistrously, perversely.
Siniestro, tra [se-ne-es'-tro, trah], *a.* 1. Sinister, left, on the left side. 2. Sinistrous, vicious, froward. 3. Sinister, unhappy, unlucky, inauspicious.
Siniestro, *m.* 1. Perverseness, depravity, evil habit. 2. (Com.) Shipwreck, or great damage.
Sinnúmero [sin-noo'-may-ro], *m.* A numberless quantity. *Un sinnúmero de personas,* An endless number of persons.
Sino [see'-no], *conj.* 1. But: used in contrasting an affirmative idea with a negative. *No es blanco, sino negro,* It is not white, but black. 2. Except, besides. *Nadie lo sabe sino Juan,* Nobody knows it except John. 3. Solely, only; always preceded by a negative proposition. *No sino,* Not only so. *No sino no,* It cannot be otherwise.
Sino, *m.* 1. Fate, destiny. 2. (Obs.) *V.* SIGNO.
Sinoble, *a.* (Her.) *V.* SINOPLE.
Sinoca [se-no'-cah], *f.* (Med.) Synocha, inflammatory continued fever.
Sinocal [se-no-cahl'], *a.* Synochal, pertaining to the synocha fever.
Sinodal [se-no-dahl'], *a.* Synodic, synodal.—*m.* Examiner of curates and confessors.
Sinodático [se-no-dah'-te-co], *m.* Pecuniary contribution paid by the clergy to the bishops.
Sinódico, ca [se-no'-de-co, cah], *a.* 1. Synodal, synodical. 2. Synodic, reckoned from one conjunction of the moon with the sun until another.
Sínodo [see'-no-do], *m.* 1. Synod, an ecclesiastical assembly. 2. Conjunction of the heavenly bodies. 3. Stipend allowed to missionaries in America.
Sinólogo, ga [se-no'-lo-go, gah], *m.* & *f.* Sinologue, versed in the Chinese language and literature.
Sinón, *conj. cond.* (Obs.) *V.* SINO.
Sinónimo, ma [se-no'-ne-mo, mah], *a.* Synonymous.—*pl.* Synonima.
Sinónimo, *m.* Synonym.
Sinónomo, ma [se-no'-no-mo, mah], *a.* *V.* SINÓNIMO.
Sinople [se-no'-play], *a.* (Her.) Sinople, green.
Sinopsis [se-nop'-sis], *f.* Synopsis, compendium, epitome.
Sinóptico, ca [se-nop'-te-co, cah], *a.* Synoptic, synoptical, compendious.
Sinovia [se-no'-ve-ah], *f.* Synovia, the fluid of the joints.
Sinovial [se-no-ve-ahl'], *a.* Synovial, secreting synovia.
Sinrazón [sin-rah-thone'], *f.* Wrong, injury, injustice.
Sinsabor [sin-sah-bor'], *m.* Displeasure, disgust, pain, uneasiness, offensiveness.
Sinsonte [sin-son'-tay], *m.* The mocking-bird. **Mimus polyglottus.** (Aztec, Censontli.)
Sintáctico, ca [sin-tahc'-te-co, cah], *a.* (Gram.) Syntactic, belonging to syntax.
Sintagma [sin-tahg'-mah], *m.* Orderly method, system.
Sintaxis [sin-tahk'-sis], *f.* 1. (Gram.) Syntax. 2. Co-ordination of things among themselves.
Síntesis [seen'-tay-sis], *f.* Synthesis opposed to analysis.
Sintético, ca [sin-tay'-te-co, cah], *a.* Synthetical.
Sintetizar [sin-tay-te-thar'], *va.* To synthesize or synthetize; to unite by synthesis.
Síntoma [seen'-to-mah], *m.* 1. (Med. Symptom. 2. Sign, token.
Sintomáticamente, *adv.* Symptomatically.
Sintomático, ca [sin-to-mah'-te-co, cah], *a.* Symptomatic, symptomatical.
Sintomatología [sin-to-mah-to-lo-hee'-ah], *f.* (Med.) Symptomatology, a part of pathology.
Sintonizar [sin-to-ne-thar'], *va.* (Radio) To syntonize.
Sinuosidad [se-noo-o-se-dahd'], *f.* Sinuosity, sinuousness.
Sinuoso, sa [se-noo-oh'-so, sah], *a.* Sinuous, wavy.
Siño, *m.* (Obs.) *V.* SIGNO and SEÑAL.
Sipia [see'-pe-ah], *f.* Refuse of olives, which remains in oil-mills.
Siquiatra [se-ke-ah'-trah], *m.* & *f.* V. PSIQUIATRA.
Siquiatría [se-ke-ah-tree'-ah], *f.* V. PSIQUIATRÍA.
Síquico, ca [see'-ke-co, cah], *a.* V. PSÍQUICO.
Siquier, Siquiera [se-ke-err', se-ke-ay'-rah], *conj.* At least; though, although; or; scarcely; otherwise. ***Dame siquiera un poquito,*** Give me ever so little of it. ***Ni siquiera quiso escucharle,*** He would not even listen to him
Sirena [se-ray'-nah], *f.* 1. Syren, a sea-nymph. 2. A woman who sings charmingly. 3. (Zool.) Siren, a batrachian.
Sirga [seer' gah], *f.* 1 (Naut.) Tow-rope, tow-line. 2. Line used in dragging nets. *A la sirga,* Sailing with a dragging line.
Sirgadura [seer-gah-doo'-rah], *f.* (Naut.) Towing or hauling a barge or vessel along a canal, or by the banks of a river.
Sirgar [seer-gar'], *va.* (Naut.) To tow a vessel with a line.
Sirgo [seer'-go], *m.* Twisted silk; stuff made of silk.
Siriaco, ca [se-re-ah'-co, cah], *a.* Syrian, of Syria.—*m.* Syriac, the language of ancient Syria.
Sirio [see'-re-o], *m.* (Ast.) Sirius or dog-star.
Sirle [seer'-lay], *m.* Sheep-dung or goat's dung.
Siro, ra [see'-ro, rah], *a.* *V.* SIRIACO.
Siroco [se-ro'-co], *m.* Sirocco, a south-east wind on the Mediterranean.
Sirte [seer'-tay], *f.* 1. Syrtes, hidden rock, quicksand, moving sandbank. 2. Peril, danger.
Sirvienta [seer-ve-en'-tah], *f.* Female servant, serving-maid.
Sirviente [seer-ve-en'-tay], *pa.* & *com.* Serving, being a servant, menial, serving-man. *V.* SIRVIENTA.

(*Yo sirvo, yo sirva; él sirvió, sirviera;* from *Servir.* *V.* PEDIR.)

Sisa [see'-sah], *f.* 1. Petty theft. 2 Any pilfering trifle clipped from the whole. 3. Clippings, tailors' cabbage. 4. Size, linseed-oil boiled with ochre used by gilders. 5. Assize. ***Sisa de pan,*** Assize of bread. 6. Excise on eatables or liquors.

Sisador, ra [se-sah-dor', rah], *m.* & *f.* Filcher, petty thief; one that exacts more than is due; sizer; cutter.

Sisar [se-sar'], *va.* 1. To pilfer, to filch; to steal small quantities of a thing; to curtail, to lessen. 2. To cut clothes. 3. To size, to prepare with size, for gilding.

Sisca [sees'-cah], *f.* (Bot. Prov.) Cylindrical sugar-cane. Saccharum cilindricum.

Sisear [se-say-ar'], *vn.* To hiss, to sound *s* inarticulately, in order to express disapproval.

Siseo [se-say'-o], *m.* Hissing.

Sisero [se-say'-ro], *m.* Excise collector.

Sisimbrio [se-seem'-bre-o], *m.* (Bot.) Water-radish, radish water-cress. Sisymbrium amphibium.

Sísmico, ca [sees'-me-co, cah], *a.* *a.* Seismic. *Movimiento sísmico,* Earthquake.

Sismógrafo [sis-mo'-grah-fo], *m.* Seismograph, apparatus to register the motions of an earthquake.

Sisón [se-sone'], *m.* 1. Filcher, pilferer, petty thief. 2. (Orn.) Godart or moor-cock.

Sistema [sis-tay'-mah], *m.* 1. System, a combination of things acting together. 2. System, a scheme which reduces many things to a regular dependence or corporation. 3. Hypothesis, supposition. 4. Gold or silver-lace of one pattern.

Sistemar [sis-tay-mar'], *va.* (Amer.) To systematize, to order.

Sistemáticamente, *adv.* Systematically.

Sistemático, ca [sis-tay-mah'-te-co, cah], *a.* Systematic.

Sistematizar [sis-tay-mah-te-thar'], *va.* To reduce to system, to systematize. (Acad.)

Sistilo [sis-tee'-lo], *m.* (Arch.) Systyle.

Sistole [sees'-to-lay], *f.* 1. (Anat.) Systole, contraction of the heart. 2. (Rhet.) Shortening of a long syllable.

Sistro [sees'-tro], *m.* Sistrum, an ancient musical stringed instrument; a curved metal band crossed by many wires or rods.

Sitácidos [se-tah'-the-dos], *m. pl.* The psittacid birds, the gray parrots.

Sitiador [se-te-ah-dor'], *m.* Besieger.

Sitial [se-te-ahl'], *m.* 1. Seat of honour for princes and prelates in a public assembly. 2. Stool, form, seat without a back.

Sitiar [se-te-ar'], *va.* 1. To besiege, to lay siege to a place. 2. To surround, to hem in, to compass. 3. To deprive of the means of effecting any thing. *Sitiar por hambre,* (Met.) To compel one by necessity to submit.

Sitibundo, da [se-te-boon'-do, dah], *a.* (Poet.) *V.* SEDIENTO.

Sitio [see'-te-o], *m.* 1. Room, place, space taken up by a body or object. 2. Situation, location of a town, city, or building. 3. (Mil.) Siege, blockade. 4. Country house, country residence. *Real sitio,* The country residence of one of the kings of Spain. *Sitio de inspección,* Checkpoint.

Sito, ta [see'-to, tah], *a.* Situated, lying, assigned. *V.* SITUADO.

Sitófago, ga [se-toh'-fah-go, gah], *a.* Living upon wheat.

Situación [se-too-ah-the-on'], *f.* 1. Situation, position. 2. Situation, condition of affairs. 3. Assignation, appointment, assignment. *Muerta situación,* (Com.) Standstill, stagnation, slackness.

Situado [se-too-ah'-do], *m.* 1. Allowance, pay, or salary assigned upon certain goods or effects. 2. Post, position.

Situado, da, *a.* & *pp.* of SITUAR. Situate, situated, placed.

Situar [se-too-ar'], *va.* 1. To put a thing in a certain place, to situate. 2. To assign a fund, out of which a salary, rent, or interest is to be paid.—*vr.* To be established in any place or business: to station one's self.

Smoking [es-mo'-kin], *m.* Tuxedo.

Snob or **Esnob** [es-nob'], *m.* Snob.

Snobismo [es-no-bees'-mo], *m.* V. ESNOBISMO.

So, *prep.* Under; below. Used in composition, it occasionally diminishes the import of the verb, as in *soasar,* to underdo meat; in other cases it augments it, as *sojuzgar,* to subjugate; and it sometimes retains its signification, as in *soterrar,* to put underground, to inter. *So color,* Under colour; on pretence. *De so uno,* (Obs.) Conjointly, at one time.—*pron. pos.* (Obs.) *V.* SU.—*int.* Used as *cho* and *jo,* to stop horses or cattle.

Soasar [so-ah-sar'], *va.* To half roast, to parboil, to underdo meat.

Soata [so-ah'-tah], *f.* (Amer. Ven.) Dish composed of maize and uyama, a kind of squash, serving for breakfast use in Guayana, Venezuela.

Soba [so'-bah], *f.* The act and effect of making any thing soft and limber; rumpling, contusion; beating.

Sobacal [so-bah-cahl'], *a.* Axillary, relating to the armpit or to an axil.

Sobaco [so-bah'-co], *m.* 1. Armpit, arm-hole, axilla. 2. (Bot.) Axil.

Sobadero, ra [so-bah-day'-ro, rah], *a.* That may be handled.

Sobado [so-bah'-do], *m.* 1. The repeated and violent working and handling of any thing. 2. *V.* SOBADURA. *Sobados,* Loaves of bread made in La Mancha.—*Sobado, da. pp.* of SOBAR.

Sobadura [so-bah-doo'-rah], *f.* Kneading, rubbing.

Sobajadura [so-bah-hah-doo'-rah], *f.* Scrubbing, frication.

Sobajamiento [so-bah-hah-me-en'-to], *m.* Friction, rubbing, scrubbing.

Sobajanero [so-bah-hah-nay'-ro], *m.* (Coll.) Errand-boy.

Sobajar [so-bah-har'], *va.* To scrub, to rub hard.

Sobanda [so-bahn'-dah], *f.* Bottom or end of a cask.

Sobaquera [so-bah-kay'-rah], *f.* Opening left in clothes under the armpit; arm-hole, arm-scye. *Coger (a uno) las sobaqueras,* To gain ascendency over a person.

Sobaquina [so-bah-kee'-nah], *f.* Smell of the armpit.

Sobar [so-bar'], *va.* 1. To handle, to soften. 2. To pummel, to chastise with blows. 3. To handle with too much familiarity and frequency.

Sobarba [so-bar'-bah], *f.* Nose-band of a bridle.

Sobarbada [so-bar-bah'-dah], *f.* 1. A check given a horse by pulling the reins with violence. 2. Chuck under the chin; jerk. 3. (Met.) Reprimand, scolding.

Sobarbo [so-bar'-bo], *m.* Lever or pallet for raising the pestles in a fulling-mill.

Sobarcar [so-bar-car'], *va.* 1. To carry any thing heavy under the arm. 2. To draw the clothes up to the arm-holes.

Sobeo [so-bay'-o], *m.* (Prov.) Leather draughts or traces.

Soberanamente, *adv.* Sovereignly, supremely.

Soberanear [so-bay-rah-nay-ar'], *vn.* To lord it, to domineer like a sovereign.

Soberanía [so-bay-rah-nee'-ah], *f.* 1. Sovereignty, supreme power over others, majesty. 2. Pride, haughtiness, arrogance, loftiness.

Soberano, na [so-bay-rah'-no, nah], *a.* 1. Sovereign, supreme, kingly. 2 Sovereign, superior, predominant.

Soberano [so-bay-rah'-no], *m.* Sovereign; lord paramount; king; liege.

Soberbia [so-berr'-be-ah], *f.* 1. Pride, haughtiness; an inordinate desire of being preferred to others; presumption; arrogance; loftiness. 2. Pomp, pageantry. 3. Anger, passion. 4. Insulting word or action.

Soberbiamente, *adv.* Haughtily, arrogantly, proudly, superbly.

Soberbio, bia [so-berr'-be-o, ah], *a.* 1. Proud, arrogant, elated, haughty, passionate. 2. Lofty, sublime, eminent, superb. 3. Fiery, mettlesome: applied to horses.

Sobina [so-bee'-nah], *f.* A wooden pin or peg.

Sobo [so'-bo], *m.* Frequent working of a thing to make it soft and limber.

Sobón, na [so-bone', nah], *a.* 1. One who makes himself offensive by excessive familiarity and caresses. 2. A sly, lazy fellow.

Sobordo [so-bor'-do], *m.* Manifest, freight-list; the statement of a cargo taken on board of a vessel; a memorandum of the articles daily received while a vessel is lading.

Sobornación [so-bor-nah-the-on'], *f.* *V.* SOBORNO.

Sobornado [so-bor-nah'-do], *m.* Misshaped loaf of bread in the oven.—*Sobornado, da, pp.* of SOBORNAR.

Sobornador, ra [so-bor-na-dor', rah], *m.* & *f.* Suborner, corrupter; one who is guilty of subornation.

Sobornal [so-bor-nahl'], *a.* Added to the load which a beast carries.—*m.* A small bale; a seroon.

Sobornar [so-bor-nar'], *va.* To suborn, to bribe, to procure by secret collusion, to corrupt.

Soborno [so-bor'-no], *m.* 1. Subornation. 2. Bribe, gift or money offered for doing a bad action. 3. Incitement, inducement. 4. In Peru, used for *Sobornal.*

Sobra [so'-brah], *f.* 1. Overplus, surplus, excess. *Sobras de la comida.* Offals, leavings, broken victuals. 2. Grievous offence, injury. *De sobra,* Over and above; superfluously. *Estar de sobra,* (Coll.) To be one too many.

Sobradamente, *adv.* Abundantly; superabundantly; excessively.

Sobradar [so-brah-dar'], *va.* To erect edifices with lofts or granaries.

Sobradillo [so-brah-deel'-lyo], *m.* 1. (Dim.) A cock-loft. 2. Pent-house; a shelter over a balcony or window.

Sobrado [so-brah'-do], *m.* 1. *V.* DESVÁN and GUARDILLA. 2. (Prov.) Granary.

Sobrado, da [so-brah'-do, dah], *a.* 1. Bold, audacious, licentious. 2. Rich, wealthy.—*adv.* *V.* SOBRADAMENTE.

Sobraja [so-brah'-hah], *f.* **Sobramiento,** *m.* (Obs.) *V.* SOBRA.

Sobrancero, ra [so-bran-thay'-ro, rah], *a.* 1. Disengaged, unemployed. 2. A supernumerary ploughman, who supplies the place of another.

Sobrante [so-brahn'-tay], *m.* 1. Residue, superfluity, overplus. 2. Rich, wealthy.—*pa.* of SOBRAR.

Sobrar [so-brar'], *vn.* 1. To have more than is necessary or required. 2. To be over and above; to be intrusive. 3. To remain, to be left. ***Más vale que sobre***

que no que falte, (prov.) It is better to have too much of a thing than to be in want of it.

Sobrasada, *f.* *V.* SOBREASADA.

Sobrasar [so-brah-sar'], *va.* (Prov.) To add fire under a pot to make 't boil sooner or better; to surround with coals.

Sobre [so'-bray], *prep.* 1. Above, over. *V.* ENCIMA. 2. Super, over; used in composition, as *sobrecargar*, to overcharge or overload. *Tiene mucha ventaja sobre todos los demás*, He possesses great advantages over the rest. 3. Moreover, besides. 4. A little more; a few more. *Tendré sobre cien reales*, I shall have about or a little more than a hundred reals. 5. Above, higher; with power or superiority. 6. (Naut.) Off. *El bajel está sobre el cabo de San Vicente*, The vessel is off Cape St. Vincent. *Sobre sí*, Selfishly; carefully, separately; elated by real or supposed acquirements; very cool. 7. To, towards, near. 8. On, upon. 9. After, since. *Sobre comida*, After dinner. *Sobre manera*, Excessively, irregularly. *Ir sobre alguno*, To go in pursuit of a person. 10. Before or around. *Estar sobre una plaza*, To besiege a place. *Ser de sobre sí mismo*, To proceed with caution (slang, to be on to one's self).

Sobre, *m.* 1. Envelope (cover) of a letter. 2. Address, superscription.

Sobreabundancia [so-bray-ah-boon-dahn'-the-ah], *f.* Superabundance.

Sobreabundante [so-bray-ah-boon-dahn'-tay], *a.* Superabundant, more than enough; luxuriant.

Sobreabundantemente, *adv.* Superabundantly.

Sobreabundar [so-bray-ah-boon-dar'], *vn.* To superabound; to be exuberant.

Sobreaguar [so-bray-ah-goo-ar'], *vn.* To be on the surface of water, to float on water.

Sobreaguda [so-bray-ah-goo'-dah], *f.* One of the seven small letters in music.

Sobreagudo [so-bray-ah-goo'-do], *m.* (Mus.) Highest treble in music.

Sobrealiento [so-bray-ah-le-en'-to], *m.* Difficult respiration.

Sobrealimentar [so-bray-ah-le-men-tar'], *va.* 1. Supercharge. 2. To give extra nourishment.

Sobrealzar [so-bray-al-thar'], *va.* To praise, to extol.

Sobreañadidura [so-bray-ah-nyah-de-doo'-rah], *f.* (Littl. us.) Superaddition.

Sobreañadir [so-bray-ah-nyah-deer'], *va.* To superadd, to superinduce.

Sobreañal [so-bray-ah-nyahl'], *a.* Applied to animals more than a year old.

Sobreasada [so-bray-ah-sah'-dah], *f.* In Mallorca, a kind of sausage half roasted, and done over again when it is to be eaten.

Sobreasar [so-bray-ah-sar'], *va.* To roast again what was half roasted before.

Sobrebásico, ca [so-bray-bah'-se-co, cah], *a.* (Chem.) Having an excess of base; a basic salt.

Sobreboya [so-bray-bo'-yah], *f.* (Naut.) Marking buoy, a small buoy fastened to a large one in the water, to show its position.

Sobrebrazal [so-bray-brah-thahl'], *m.* (Naut.) False rail.

Sobrecaja [so-bray-cah'-hah], *f.* Outer case.

Sobrecalza [so-bray-cahl'-thah], *f.* *V.* POLAINA.

Sobrecama [so-bray-cah'-mah], *f.* Coverlet, quilt.

Sobrecaña [so-bray-cah'-nyah], *f.* (Vet.) Tumour on a horse's leg.

Sobrecarga [so-bray-car'-gah], *f.* 1. An additional bundle thrown over a load. 2. Additional trouble or vexation. 3. Surcharge, overburden. 4. Rope thrown over a load to make it fast.

Sobrecargado, da [so-bray-car-gah'-do, dah], *a.* & *pp.* of SOBRECARGAR. Overloaded. (Bot.; rare) Pinnate.

Sobrecargar [so-bray-car-gar'], *va.* 1. To overload, to surcharge, to overburden. 2. To make one seam over another.

Sobrecargo [so-bray-car'-go], *m.* 1. Ship's purser. 2. Plane stewardess.

Sobrecarta [so-bray-car'-tah], *f.* 1. Cover, envelope, of a letter. 2. The second injunction; decree or warrant, repeating a former order.

Sobrecartar [so-bray-car-tar'], *va.* To repeat a former injunction.

Sobrecebadera [so-bray-thay-bah-day'-rah], *f.* (Naut.) Sprit top-sail.

Sobrecédula [so-bray-thay'-doo-lah], *f.* Second royal order or despatch.

Sobreceja [so-bray-thay'-hah], *f.* The part of the forehead over the eyebrows.

Sobrecejo [so-bray-thay'-ho], *m.* Frown; supercilious aspect, cloudiness of look.

Sobrecelestial [so-bray-thay-les-te-ahl'], *a.* Supercelestial.

Sobreceño [so-bray-thay'-nyo], *m.* Frown. *V.* SOBRECEJO.

Sobrecerco [so-bray-therr'-co], *m.* Ornament or fringe placed round another to strengthen it.

Sobrecincha [so-bray-theen'-chah], *f.* One of the girths of a saddle; a surcingle.

Sobrecincho [so-bray-theen'-cho], *m.* Surcingle, an additional girth, put over the common girth.

Sobreclaustro [so-bray-clah'-oos-tro], *m.* Apartment over a cloister.

Sobrecoger [so-bray-co-herr'], *va.* To surprise, to overtake.—*vr.* To become apprehensive.

Sobrecogimiento [so-bray-co-he-me-en'-to], *m.* Fearfulness, apprehension.

Sobrecomida [so-bray-co-mee'-dah], *f.* Dessert. *V.* POSTRE.

Sobrecomprimir [so-bray-com-pre-meer'], *va.* (Aer.) To pressurize.

Sobrecopa [so-bray-co'-pah], *f.* Cover or lid of a cup.

Sobrecrecer [so-bray-cray-therr'], *vn.* To out-grow, to over-grow.

Sobrecreciente [so-bray-cray-the-en'-tay], *pa.* Out-growing, over-growing.

Sobrecruces [so-bray-croo'-thes], *m. pl.* Cross-joints to strengthen a wheel.

Sobrecubierta [so-bray-coo-be-err'-tah], *f.* 1. Double cover. 2. Coverlet, quilt. 3. (Naut.) Upper deck.

Sobredezmero [so-bray-deth-may'-ro], *m.* Assistant in collecting duties.

Sobredicho, cha [so-bray-dee'-cho, chah], *a.* Above-mentioned.

Sobrediente [so-bray-de-en'-tay], *m.* Gag-tooth which grows over another.

Sobredorar [so-bray-do-rar'], *va.* 1. To gild anew, to over-gild. 2. To palliate, to extenuate, to exculpate.

Sobreedificar [so-bray-ay-de-fe-car'], *va.* To build over any thing.

Sobreempeine [so-bray-em-pay'-e-nay], *m.* That part of spatterdashes or gaiters which covers the instep.

Sobreentender [so-bray-en-ten-derr'], *va.* & *vr.* *V.* SOBRENTENDER.

Sobreescrito [so-bray-es-cree'-to], *m.* 1. Superscription, inscription, direction, address. 2. Mien, aspect; pretext.

Sobreesdrújulo, la [so-bray-es-droo'-hoo-lo, lah], *a.* *V.* SOBRESDRÚJULO.

Sobreestadía [so-bray-es-tah-dee'-ah], *f.* (Com.) One of the extra lay days; an allowance of time made in loading or unloading a vessel, and the sum paid. (More used in plural.)

Sobreexceder [so-bray-ex-thay-derr'], *va.* *V.* SOBREXCEDER.

Sobreexcelente [so-bray-ex-thay-len'-tay], *a.* Superexcellent.

Sobrefaz [so-bray-fath'], *f.* 1. Superficies, surface, outside. 2. (Mil.) Face prolonged, the distance between the angle of the shoulder of a bastion and the curtain.

Sobrefino, na [so-bray-fee'-no, nah], *a.* Superfine, overfine.

Sobreguarda [so-bray-goo-ar'-dah], *m.* Second guard placed for greater security.

Sobreguardilla [so-bray-goo-ar-deel'-lyah], *f.* Penthouse, shelter, shed.

Sobrehaz [so-bray-ath'], *f.* 1. Surface, outside. 2. Outside cover of any thing.

Sobrehueso [so-bray-oo-ay'-so], *m.* 1. Morbid swelling on the bones or joints. 2. Trouble, encumbrance, burden.

Sobrehumano, na [so-bray-oo-mah'-no, nah], *a.* Superhuman.

Sobrehusa [so-bray-oo'-sah], *f.* A stew made in Andalusia from fried fish.

Sobrejalma [so-bray-hahl'-mah], *f* Woollen cover for a pack-saddle.

Sobrejuez [so-bray-hoo-eth'], *m.* (Obs.) Superior judge.

Sobrelecho [so-bray-lay'-cho], *m.* That side of a stone which lies on a bed of mortar.

Sobrellave [so-brel-lyah'-vay], *f.* Double key; a large key.—*m.* In royal palaces, an officer who keeps a second key of every door.

Sobrellenar [so-brel-lyay-nar'], *va.* To overfill, to overflow, to glut.

Sobrelleno, na [so-brel-lyay'-no, nah], *a.* Overfull, superabundant.

Sobrellevar [so-brel-lyay-var'], *va.* 1. To ease another's burden; to carry. 2. To inure to hardships by degrees, to undergo. 3. To overlook the failings of inferiors or subjects.

Sobremallero [so-bray-mal-lyay'-ro], *m.* One of the four kinds of net used in the sardine-fishery off the Cantabrian coast.

Sobremanera [so-bray-mah-nay'-rah], *adv.* Beyond measure; excessively.

Sobremano [so-bray-mah'-no], *f.* (Vet.) Osseous tumour on the hoofs of horses' fore feet.

Sobremesa [so-bray-may'-sah], *f.* 1. Table-carpet, table-cloth. 2. Dessert. *V.* POSTRE. *De sobremesa*, Immediately after dinner.

Sobremesana [so-bray-may-sah'-nah], *f.* (Naut.) Mizzen top-sail.

Sobremuñonera [so-bray-moo-nyo-nay'-rah], *f.* (Naut.) Clamp or cap-square, a piece of iron which covers the trunnions of a cannon.

Sobrenadar [so-bray-nah-dar'], *vn.* To swim on the surface of any fluid, to overfloat.

Sobrenatural [so-bray-nah-too-rahl'], *a.* Supernatural, preternatural, metaphysical.

Sobrenaturalmente, *adv.* Supernaturally.

Sobrenombre [so-bray-nom'-bray], *m.* 1. Surname, the family name. 2. Nickname; a name given in contempt.

Sobrentender [so-bren-ten-derr'], *va.* & *vr.* To understand something not expressed, but which must be supposed from what has gone before; to be understood.

Sobreojo [so-bray-o'-ho], *m.* A supercilious aspect; a look of envy, hatred,

or contempt. *Llevar de sobrecejo a uno,* (Prov.) To keep a watchful eye over one.
Sobrepaga [so-bray-pah'-gah], *f.* Increase of pay; extra pay.
Sobrepaño [so-bray-pah'-nyo], *m.* Upper cloth, put over others; wrapper.
Sobreparto [so-bray-par'-to], *m.* 1. Time of lying-in, which follows the delivery. 2. Delicate state of health which follows confinement.
Sobrepasar [so-bray-pah-sar'], *va.* 1. To excel, to surpass. 2. To exceed.
Sobrepeine [so-bray-pay'-e-nay], *m.* The act of cutting the hair but slightly.—*adv.* (Coll.) Slightly, briefly.
Sobrepelliz [so-bray-pel-lyeeth'], *f.* Surplice.
Sobrepeso [so-bray-pay'-so], *m.* Overweight.
Sobrepié [so-bray-pee-ay'], *m.* (Vet.) Osseous tumour at the top of horses' hoofs.
Sobreplán [so-bray-plahn'], *m.* (Naut.) Rider.
Sobreponer [so-bray-po-nerr'], *va.* To add one thing to another; to put one over another.—*vr.* To exalt one's self above other things; to raise one's self, to overcome, to overpower.
(*Yo sobrepongo, yo sobreponga; yo sobrepuse;* from *Sobreponer. V.* PONER.)
Sobreprecio [so-bray-pray'-the-o], *m.* 1. Surcharge. 2. Markup.
Sobreprima [so-bray-pree'-ma], *f.* Increased premium (on insurance).
Sobreproducción [so-bray-pro-dooc-the-on'], *f.* Overproduction.
Sobrepuerta [so-bray-poo-err'-tah], *f.* 1. Cornice, a kind of louver-board put over interior doors, from which curtains are hung. 2. In a general sense, any painting, woven stuff, carved work, etc., put over doors for ornament.
Sobrepuesto, ta [so-bray-poo-es'-to, tah], *a.* & *pp. irr.* of SOBREPONER. Counterfeit, fictitious.
Sobrepuesto [so-bray-poo-es'-to], *m.* 1. Honeycomb formed by bees after the hive is full. 2. Earthen vessel added to bee-hives when they are too full.
Sobrepuja [so-bray-poo'-hah], *f.* Outbidding, bidding more than another.
Sobrepujamiento [so-bray-poo-hah-me-en'-to], *m.* The act and effect of surpassing, excelling.
Sobrepujante [so-bray-poo-hahn'-tay], *pa.* Surpassing, excelling.
Sobrepujanza [so-bray-poo-hahn'-thah], *f.* Great strength and vigour.
Sobrepujar [so-bray-poo-har'], *va.* To exceed, to surpass, to excel, to foil, to overturn.
Sobrequilla [so-bray-keel'-lyah], *f.* (Naut.) Keelson.
Sobrerronda [so-brer-ron'-dah], *f.* (Mil.) Counter-round.
Sobrerropa [so-brer-ro'-pah], *f.* A sort of long robe worn over other clothes.
Sobresal [so-bray-sahl'], *f.* (Chem.) An acid salt.
Sobresalario [so-bray-sah-lah'-re-o], *m.* Perquisites: what is added to a salary.
Sobresalido, da [so-bray-sah-lee'-do, dah], *a.* & *pp.* of SOBRESALIR. Elated, inflated, haughty.
Sobresaliente [so-bray-sah-le-en'-tay], *a.* Excelling, surpassing, excellent.
Sobresaliente [so-bray-sah-le-en'-tay], *m.* 1. (Mil.) Officer who commands a piquet, or small body of troops, always ready for any emergency. 2. Substitute. 3. An actor or actress (*sobresalienta*), ready to perform the part of one absent or sick.
Sobresalir [so-bray-sah-leer'], *va.* To exceed in height, to overtop, to overreach, to surpass, to outvie.
(*Yo sobresalgo, yo sobresalga,* from *Sobresalir. V.* SALIR.)
Sobresaltadamente, *adv.* Suddenly, unexpectedly.
Sobresaltado, da [so-bray-sal-tah'-do, dah], *a.* Startled, frightened.
Sobresaltar [so-bray-sal-tar'], *va.* 1. To rush violently upon, to assail, to surprise or to fall upon unexpectedly. 2. To frighten, to terrify, to startle.—*vn.* To fly in one's face; to be striking: applied especially to paintings.—*vr.* To be startled at, to be surprised, confused, or perplexed.
Sobresalto [so-bray-sahl'-to], *m.* A sudden assault, a surprise; a sudden dread or fear. *De sobresalto,* Unexpectedly, unawares.
Sobresanar [so-bray-sah-nar'], *va.* 1. To heal superficially. 2. To screen, to palliate.
Sobresanos [so-bray-sah'-nos], *m. pl.* (Naut.) Tabling, a broad hem on sails, to strengthen that part which is fastened to the bolt-rope.
Sobrescribir [so-bres-cre-berr'], *va.* To superscribe, to inscribe, to address or direct a letter.
Sobrescrito [so-bres-cree'-to], *m.* Superscription, address or direction of a letter.—*Sobrescrito, ta, pp.* of SOBRESCRIBIR.
Sobresdrújulo, la [so-bres-droo'-hoo-lo, lah], *a.* Accented upon the syllable preceding the antepenult; as, *devuélvemelo.*
Sobreseer [so-bray-say-err'], *vn.* 1. To desist from a design; to supersede; to relinquish a claim or pretension; to overrule. 2. (Law) To discontinue an action.
Sobreseguro [so-bray-say-goo'-ro], *adv.* In a safe manner; without risk.
Sobreseimiento [so-bray-say-e-me-en'-to], *m.* Omission, suspension; discontinuance.
Sobresello [so-bray-sel'-lyo], *m.* A double seal.
Sobresembrar [so-bray-sem-brar'], *va.* 1. To sow over again. 2. To diffuse erroneous doctrines; to sow discord.
Sobreseñal [so-bray-say-nyahl'], *f.* Ensign or standard arbitrarily adopted by the ancient knights.
Sobresolar [so-bray-so-lar'], *va.* 1. To pave anew. 2. To new-sole boots or shoes.
Sobrestadías, *f.* *V.* SOBREESTADÍA.
Sobrestante [so-bres-tahn'-tay], *m.* Overseer; foreman; comptroller; overlooker.
Sobrestante [so-bres-tahn'-tay], *a.* Immediate, near.
Sobresueldo [so-bray-soo el'-do], *m.* Addition to one's pay or allowance.
Sobresuelo [so-bray-soo-ay'-lo], *m.* A second floor or pavement laid over another.
Sobretarde [so-bray-tar'-day], *f.* Close of the evening.
Sobretejer [so-bray-tay-herr'], *va.* To work a stuff on both sides.
Sobretercero [so-bray-ter-thay'-ro], *m.* (Prov.) One more than three to collect duties.
Sobretodo [so-bray-to'-do], *m.* Overcoat, surtout, a great-coat.
Sobretodo [so-bray-to'-do], *adv.* Above all; before all things.
Sobretrancaniles [so-bray-tran-cah-nee'-les], *m. pl.* (Naut.) Spirketing, the range of planks which lies between the water-ways and the lower edge of a ship's gun-ports.
Sobreveedor [so-bray-vay-ay-dor'], *m.* Supervisor, overseer.
Sobrevela [so-bray-vay'-lah], *f.* (Obs.) Second sentinel.
Sobrevenda [so-bray-ven'-dah], *f.* (Med.) Surband, bandage placed over others.
(*Yo sobrevengo, yo sobrevenga, ello sobrevendrá,* from *Sobrevenir. V.* VENIR.)
Sobrevenida [so-bray-vay-nee'-dah], *f.* Supervention.
Sobrevenir [so-bray-vay-neer'], *vn.* To happen; to fall out; to come unexpectedly; to come between; to come in the way; to supervene.
Sobreventar [so-bray-ven-tar'], *va.* (Naut.) To gain the weather-gauge of another ship.
Sobreverterse [so-bray-ver-terr'-say], *vr.* To run over, to overflow.
Sobrevesta, Sobreveste [so-bray-ves'-tah], *f.* (Obs.) Surtout, great-coat.
Sobrevestir [so-bray-ves-teer'], *va.* To put on a great-coat.
Sobrevidriera [so-bray-ve-dre-ay'-rah], *f.* Wire net before a glass window.
Sobreviento [so-bray-ve-en'-to], *m.* Gust of wind; impetuous fury, surprise.
Sobreviniente [so-bray-ve-ne-en'-tay], *pa.* Happening, falling out, coming in the way.
Sobreviviente [so-bray-ve-ve-en'-tay], *pa.* & *m.* & *f.* Survivor; surviving.
Sobrevivir [so-bray-ve-veer'], *vn.* To survive, to outlive. *Sobrevivir a alguno,* To outlive or survive a person.
Sobrexceder [so-brex-thay-derr'], *va.* To surpass, to excel another, to exceed.
Sobrexcitación [so-brex-the-tah-the-on'], *f.* Over-stimulation of vital organs.
Sobriamente, *adv.* Soberly, frugally, abstemiously.
Sobriedad [so-bre-ay-dahd'], *f.* Sobriety, abstemiousness, abstinence.
Sobrina [so-bree'-nah], *f.* Niece.
Sobrinazgo [so-bre-nath'-go]. 1. The relationship of a nephew or niece. 2. Nepotism.
Sobrino [so-bree'-no], *m.* Nephew.
Sobrio, ria [so'-bre-o, ah], *a.* Sober, temperate, frugal, abstemious.
Soca, or **Soca de planta** [so'-cah], *f.* (Amer.) The sugar-cane which is cut down to be planted for the new crop.
Socaire [so-cah'-e-ray], *m.* 1. (Naut.) Slatch, slack of a rope or cable. 2. Shelter, lee, lee-gauge.
Socairero, *m.* Skulker, lurker, one who hides himself from his business or duty.
Socaliña [so-cah-lee'-nyah], *f.* Cunning or artifice to gain a thing from one who is not obliged to give it.
Socaliñar [so-cah-lee-nyar'], *va.* To extort by cunning or stratagem.
Socaliñero, ra [so-cah-le-nyay'-ro, rah], *m.* & *f.* Artful exacter, a cheat.
Socalzar [so-cal-thar'], *va.* To strengthen the lower part of a building or wall which threatens ruin.
Socamarero [so-cah-ma-ray'-ro], *m.* 1. The second steward, or man-servant of a great house. 2. The second lord chamberlain.
Socapa [so-cah'-pah], *f.* Pretext, pretence. *A socapa,* On pretence, under colour.
Socapiscol [so-cah-pis-cole'], *m.* *V.* SOCHANTRE.
Socar [so-car'], *va.* (Naut.) To set taut a rope, shroud, or stay.
Socarra [so-car'-rah], *f.* 1. The act of half roasting meat, or leaving it half rare. 2. Craft, cunning.
Socarrar [so-car-rar'], *va.* To half roast or dress meat.
Socarrén [so-car-rayn'], *m.* Eave, the edge of the roof, gable end.

Socarrena [so-car-ray'-nah], *f.* Hollow, cavity, interval.

Socarrina [so-car-ree'-nah], *f.* (Coll.) Scorching, singeing.

Socarrón, na [so-car-rone', nah], *a.* Cunning, sly, crafty.

Socarronería [so-car-ro-nay-ree'-ah], *f.* Craft, cunning, artfulness.

Socava [so-cah'-vah], *f.* 1. The act of mining or undermining. 2. The act of opening the ground around trees.

Socavar [so-cah-var'], *va.* To excavate, to undermine. *Socavar la tierra,* To turn up the ground: applied to wild boars.

Socavón [so-cah-vone'], *m.* 1. Cave, cavern; a passage under ground. 2. Adit, the entrance to a mine. *Socavones,* Pits or shafts in mines.

Sociabilidad [so-the-ah-be-le-dahd'], *f.* Sociableness, sociability, civility.

Sociable [so-the-ah'-blay], *a.* 1. Sociable, ready to unite in a general interest. 2. Sociable, inclined to company, companionable. 3. Sociable, familiar, friendly, courteous.

Sociablemente, *adv.* Sociably, companionably.

Social [so-the-ahl'], *a.* 1. Social, relating to society, or to a general or public interest. 2. Social, companionable, relating to company or friendly intercourse.

Socialismo [so-the-ah-lees'-mo], *m.* Socialism, a political doctrine proposing a reconstruction of society.

Socialista [so-the-ah-lees'-tah], *com.* Socialist, one professing socialism.

Sociedad [so-the-ay-dahd'], *f.* 1. Society, the company and converse of persons of sense and information. 2. Friendship, familiar intercourse. 3. Society, union of many in one general interest; corporation, consociation, fraternity, fellowship. 4. Society, partnership.

Sociedad anónima [ah-no'-ne-mah], *f.* (Abbreviated S.A.) Incorporated company (Inc.)

Socio [so'-the-o], *m.* 1. Partner, associate. 2. Member (of a club, etc.)

Sociología [so-the-o-lo-hee'-ah], *f.* Sociology, the study of the evolution and organization of society.

Sociológico, ca [so-the-o-lo'-he-co, cah], *a.* Sociological.

Sociólogo, ga [so-the-o'-lo-go, gah], *m. & f.* Sociologist.

Socolor [so-co-lor'], *m.* Pretext, pretence, colour. *So color* (adverbial phrase), Under pretence.

Socollada [so-col-lyah'-dah], *f.* (Naut.) Jerk, the violent straining of the ropes, cables, and shrouds, caused by the rolling and pitching of a ship.

Soconusco [so-co-noos'-co], *m.* The cocoa from the province of that name in Chiapas (Mexico) and in N. W. Guatemala, considered to be of the best quality.

Socorredor, ra [so-cor-ray-dor', rah], *m. & f.* Succourer, assister; administering relief, helper.

Socorrer [so-cor-rerr'], *va.* 1. To succour, to aid, to help, to favour. 2. To pay a part of what is due.

Socorrido, da [so-cor-ree'-do, dah], *a. & pp.* of SOCORRER. Furnished, well supplied. *La plaza de Madrid es muy socorrida,* The market of Madrid is well supplied. (Coll.) Handy, useful.

Socorro [so-cor'-ro], *m.* 1. Succour, support, assistance, help. 2. Part of a salary or allowance paid beforehand. 3. Succour, a fresh supply of men or provisions thrown into a besieged place.

Socrático, ca [so-crah'-te-co, cah], *a.* Socratic, relating to the doctrines of Socrates.

Socrocio [so-cro'-the-o], *m.* 1. Poultice or cataplasm of a saffron colour. 2. Pleasure, delight, satisfaction.

Socucho [so-coo'-cho], *m.* (Mex.) 1. A large and narrow room in the lower story of a house. 2. Hiding-place, cave.

Sochantre [so-chahn'-tray], *m.* Subchanter, the deputy of the precentor in a cathedral.

Soda [so'-dah], *f.* (Bot.) *V.* SOSA.

Sodio [so'-de-o], *m.* (Chem.) Sodium, a silver-white, alkaline, metallic element.

Sodomía [so-do-mee'-ah], *f.* Sodomy, an unnatural crime.

Sodomita [so-do-mee'-tah], *m. & a.* Sodomite, one who commits sodomy.

Sodomítico, ca [so-do-mee'-te-co, cah], *a.* Belonging to sodomy.

Soez [so-eth'], *a.* Mean, vile, base, worthless, shameful.

Soezmente, *adv.* Meanly, basely, vilely, shamefuly.

Sofá [so-fah'], *m.* Sofa. (Arab.)

Sofá cama [so-fah' cah'-mah], *m.* Studio couch.

Sofaldar [so-fal-dar'], *va.* To truss up; to raise up; to tuck up; to lift up any thing in order to discover it.

Sofaldo [so-fahl'-do], *m.* The act of trussing or tucking up clothes.

Sofi [so-fee'], *m.* 1. Sufi, sofi, the Emperor or Shah of Persia. 2. A sect of mystics of that country. *V.* SUFÍ.

Sofión [so-fe-one'], *m.* Hoot, shout in scorn or contempt; reprimand, censure.

Sofisma [so-fees'-mah], *m.* Sophism, a fallacious argument.

Sofismo, *m.* *V.* SUFISMO.

Sofista [so-fees'-tah], *m.* Sophister, a disputant; an artful but insidious logician; a caviller, anciently a sophist.

Sofistería [so-fis-tay-ree'-ah], *f.* Sophistry, fallacy.

Sofisticación [so-fis-te-cah-the-on'], *f.* Sophistication, adulteration.

Sofisticamente, *adv.* Sophistically, fallaciously.

Sofisticar [so-fis-te-car'], *va.* To cavil, to falsify; to sophisticate.

Sofístico, ca [so-fees'-te-co, cah], *a.* Sophistical, fallacious.

Sófito [so'-fee-to], *m.* (Arch.) Soffit, under side of the cornice ornamented with panels, etc.

Soflama [so-flah'-mah], *f.* 1. A subtile flame; the reverberation of fire. 2. Glow, blush. 3. Deceitful language.

Soflamar [so-flah-mar'], *va.* 1. To use deceitful language, to impose upon, to deceive. 2. To raise a blush.

Soflamero [so-flah-may'-ro], *m.* Sophister, one that makes use of captious or deceitful language.

Sofocación [so-fo-cah-the-on'], *f.* 1. Suffocation, strangling. 2. (Med.) Suffocation, apnea, loss of breath.

Sofocante [so-fo-cahn'-tay], *m.* Ribbon with a tassel, worn by ladies round the neck.—*pa.* of SOFOCAR.

Sofocar [so-fo-car'], *va.* 1. To choke, to impede respiration, to suffocate. 2. To quench, to smother. 3. To oppress, to harass. 4. To importune, to molest. 5. To provoke by abusive language.

Sofoco [so-fo'-co], *m.* 1. Suffocation. 2. Great aversion given or received, loathing.

Sofocón [so-fo-cone'], *m.* Displeasure, provocation.

Sófora [so'-fo-rah], *f.* (Bot.) A tree of Japan cultivated for ornament in European gardens.

Sofreír [so-fray-eer'], *va.* To fry slightly.

Sofrenada [so-fray-nah'-dah], *f.* 1. A sudden check given to a horse with the bridle. 2. A rude reprehension; a severe reprimand. 3. A fit of sickness, or any other accident that forewarns us of our frailties.

Sofrenar [so-fray-nar'], *va.* 1. To check a horse by a violent pull of the bridle. 2. To reprehend rudely; to reprimand severely.

Sofrenazo [so-fray-nah'-tho], *m.* A violent pull of the bridle.

Sofrito, ta [so-free'-to, tah], *pp. irr* of SOFREIR.

Soga [so'-gah], *f.* 1. Rope of bassweed or any other matter; halter, cord. 2. (Coll.) A sly, cunning fellow. 3. Measure of land which varies in different provinces; measure of rope. *Soga de un pozo,* Bucket-rope for a well. *Hacer soga,* To make a rope; to remain behind one's company; to introduce improper things in conversation.—*int.* A term expressive of astonishment and aversion. *Dar soga,* To make fun of some one. *Siempre se rompe la soga por lo más delgado,* The rope always breaks at the thinnest part. *Traer la soga arrastrando,* To be in danger of arrest for a crime committed. *Estar* or *verse con la soga a la garganta,* (Met.) To be in imminent danger. *Echar la soga tras el caldero,* (prov.) To throw the helve after the hatchet. *Cortar sogas,* Among miners, it means to abandon a mine and its hoists. *No hay que* or *no se ha de mentar la soga en casa del ahorcado,* Do not talk of ropes in the house of a man who was hanged; avoid painful subjects of conversation.

Soguear [so-gay-ar'], *va.* (Prov. Arragon) To measure with a rope.

Soguería [so-gay-ree'-ah], *f.* Rope-walk, rope-yard; collection of ropes.

Soguero [so-gay'-ro], *m.* A rope-maker, a cord-maker.

Soguica, illa, ita [so-gee'-cah], *f. dim.* A small rope.

Soguilla [so-geel'-lyah], *f.* (Prov.) A small band of braid or plaited hair.

Sojuzgador [so-hooth-gah-dor'], *m.* Conqueror, subduer.

Sojuzgar [so-hooth-gar'], *va.* To conquer, to subjugate.

Sol [sole], *m.* 1. The sun, and hence the day. 2. (Met.) The light, warmth, or influence of the sun. 3. A kind of lace of ancient make. 4. (Mus.) Sol, the fifth note of the scale. 5. Sol, a Peruvian dollar; a "peso fuerte." *Rayo de sol,* Sunbeam. *Quemadura del sol,* Sunburning. *Reloj de sol,* Sun-dial. *La luz del sol,* Sunlight. *El sol sale,* The sun rises. *El sol se pone,* The sun sets. *Al sol puesto,* At nightfall. *Al poner del sol,* At sunset. *Al salir del sol,* At sunrise. *Aun hay sol en las bardas,* There is a little hope; all is not lost. *Jugar el sol antes que salga,* To gamble away to-morrow's salary. *El sol pica* or *abrasa,* The sun scorches. *No dejar ni a sol ni a sombra,* To molest or pursue a person constantly. *Tomar el sol,* To bask in the sun. *Soles,* Sparkling, dazzling eyes.—*adv.* (Obs.) *V.* SOLAMENTE. *Al sol que nace,* (Met.) To pay a cringing court to a rising power. *De sol a sol,* From sunrise to sunset. *Ser lo mismo que el sol puesto,* (Coll.) To be worth nothing.

Solacear [so-lah-thay-ar'], *va.* To solace, to administer consolation. *V.* SOLAZAR.

Solacio [so-lah'-the-o], *m.* (Obs.) *V.* CONSUELO.

Solada [so-lah'-dah], *f.* Floor, site; seat.
Solado [so-lah'-do], *m.* Floor, covered with tiles or flags: pavement.—*Solado, da, pp.* of Solar.
Solador [so-lah-dor'], *m.* Tiler, pavier.
Soladura [so-lah-doo'-rah], *f.* Act of paving; materials used for paving or flooring.
Solamente, *adv.* Only, solely.
Solana [so-lah'-nah], *f.* Sunparlor, sunporch, a place warmed by the sun, open gallery for taking the sun, solarium, sunroom.
Solanáceas [so-lah-nah'-thay-as], *f. pl.* The solanaceæ, the nightshade family.
Solanar [so-lah-nar'], *m.* (Prov.) *V.* Solana for a gallery.
Solanazo [so-lah-nah'-tho], *m. aug.* A violent, hot, and troublesome easterly wind.
Solano [so-lah'-no], *m.* 1. Easterly wind. 2. (Bot.) Night-shade. Solanum nigrum.
Solapa [so-lah'-pah], *f.* 1. Lappel, a double breast on clothes. 2. Colour, pretence, pretext. 3. (Vet.) Cavity of a small wound in animals.
Solapadamente, *adv.* In a dissembling manner; deceitfully.
Solapado, da [so-lah-pah'-do, dah], *a.* Cunning, crafty, artful.—*pp.* of Solapar.
Solapadura (Obra de) [so-lah-pah-doo'-rah], *f.* (Naut.) Clincher-work, clinching.
Solapamiento [so-lah-pah-me-en'-to], *m.* (Vet.) Cavity of a wound in animals.
Solapar [so-lah-par'], *va.* 1. To button one breast-part of clothes over another. 2. To cloak, to hide under a false pretence.
Solape, Solapo [so-lah'-pay], *m.* Lappel; pretence. *V.* Solapa. *A solapo,* In a hidden or furtive manner.
Solar [so-lar'], *m.* 1. Ground on which a house is built, ground-plot. 2. Spot on which stands the original mansion of a noble family.—*a.* Solar, solary, belonging to the sun.
Solar, *va.* 1. To floor a room; to pave a stable or coach-yard. 2. To sole shoes or boots.
Solariego, ga [so-lah-re-ay'-go, gah], *a.* 1. Belonging to the ancient mansion of a noble family. 2. Relating to freehold and other estates, which appertain with full and unlimited right of property to the owner. 3. Descending from an ancient noble family.
Solas (A mis, tus, sus), *adv.* All alone by myself, thyself, him- or herself, themselves. *V.* Solo.
Solaz [so-lath'], *m.* Solace, consolation, relaxation, comfort. *A solaz,* Pleasantly, agreeably.
Solazar [so-lah-thar'], *va.* To solace, to comfort, to cheer, to amuse.—*vr.* To be comforted, to be joyful, to relax.
Solazo [so-lah'-tho], *m. aug.* (Coll.) A scorching sun.
Solazoso, sa [so-lah-tho'-so, sah], *a.* Comfortable, delectable.
Soldada [sol-dah'-dah], *f.* Wages, pay given for service.
Soldadazo [sol-dah-dah'-tho], *m. aug.* A great soldier; a very tall soldier.
Soldadero, ra [sol-dah-day'-ro, rah], *a.* Stipendiary, receiving wages or hire.
Soldadesca [sol-dah-des'-cah], *f.* 1. Soldiery, the profession of a soldier; military art or science, soldiership (used in a depreciative sense). 2. Sham-fight. *A la soldadesca,* In a soldierly manner, for the use of soldiers.
Soldadesco, ca [sol-dah-des'-co, cah], *a.* Soldierly, soldier-like, military.
Soldado [sol-dah'-do], *m.* 1. Soldier. *Soldado* or *soldado raso,* A common soldier, a private. *Soldado de infantería* or *de a pie,* A foot-soldier. *Soldado de a caballo,* Trooper, horse-soldier, cavalryman. 2. A Christian. —*Soldado, da, pp.* of Soldar.
Soldador [sol-dah-dor'], *m.* 1. Solderer. 2. Soldering-iron.
Soldadura [sol-dah-doo'-rah], *f.* 1. The act of soldering by means of a metallic cement. 2. Solder. 3. Correction or mending of any thing. *Este desacierto no tiene soldadura,* That error cannot be redressed.
Soldán [sol-dahn'], *m.* Sultan, Mohammedan title. *V.* Sultán.
Soldar [sol-dar'], *va.* To solder, to mend, to correct.
Solear, *va.* *V.* Asolear.
Solecismo [so-lay-thees'-mo], *m.* Solecism; violation of purity of style. (From Soles, a maritime city in Cilicia, founded by Athenians, who lost the purity of their native tongue.) *V.* Soles in Appendix.
Solecito [so-lay-thee'-to], *m.* (Coll.) A scorching sun.
Soledad [so-lay-dahd'], *f.* 1. Solitude, loneliness, solitariness. 2. Solitude, a lonely place, a desert. 3. The state of an orphan, orphanage.
Soledoso, sa [so-lay'-do-so, sah], *a.* Solitary.
Solejar [so-lay-har'], *m.* A place exposed to the sun.
Solemne [so-lem'-nay], *a.* 1. Yearly, anniversary, performed once a year at the revolution of the sun. 2. Celebrated, famous. 3. Grand, solemn, high. 4. Festive, joyous, gay, cheerful. *Es un solemne bobo,* (Coll.) He is a downright booby.
Solemnemente, *adv.* Solemnly, in a festive manner.
Solemnidad [so-lem-ne-dahd'], *f.* 1. Solemnity, solemnness. 2. Solemnity, a religious festival, and the pomp or magnificence of a feast or festival. 3. *pl.* Formalities prescribed by law. *Pobre de solemnidad,* A poor man in real distress.
Solemnizador, ra [so-lem-ne-thah-dor', rah], *m. & f.* One who solemnizes; a panegyrist.
Solemnizar [so-lem-ne-thar'], *va.* 1. To solemnize, to praise, to applaud. 2. To solemnize, to perform in a festive manner; to keep or celebrate joyously.
Sóleo [so'-lay-o], *m.* Soleus, a muscle of the calf of the leg.
Soler [so-lerr'], *vn. irr. & defect.* To accustom or be accustomed; to be used to; to be apt to, to be wont; to keep.
Soler, *m.* (Naut.) Under-flooring of a ship.
Solera [so-lay'-rah], *f.* 1. Entablature, the uppermost row of stones of a wall, on which the beams rest; string-piece, cross-beam, rib. 2. A flat stone, which serves as a foundation to the base of a pillar; a plinth. 3. The nether millstone. 4. (Prov.) Lees or mother-liquor of wine. *Solera de balaustres de balcones,* (Naut.) Foot-rails of the gallery of a ship. *Solera de cureña,* Sole of a gun-carriage.
Solercia [so-lerr'-the-ah], *f.* Industry; abilities, talents; artfulness.
Solería [so-lay-ree'-ah], *f.* 1. Floor or pavement of a room. 2. Parcel of skins used for soles. *V.* Solado.
Solero [so-lay'-ro], *m.* (Prov.) Lower millstone.
Solerte [so-lerr'-tay], *a.* 1. Cunning, sagacious. 2. (Obs.) Able, industrious.
Soleta [so-lay'-tah], *f.* 1. A linen sole put into stockings. 2. (Mex.) A biscuit covered with sugar icing. 3 Ladies' fingers; a cake. *Apretar* or *picar de soleta,* To run away; to sheer off. *Tomar soleta,* To run off.
Soletar, Soletear [so-lay-tar', so-lay-tay-ar'], *va.* To vamp a pair of stockings with a linen sole.
Soletero, ra [so-lay-tay'-ro, rah], *m. & f.* Vamper, one who soles and pieces old things with something new.
Solevantado, da [so-lay-van-tah'-do, dah], *a. & pp.* of Solevantar. Inquiet, agitated, perturbed.
Solevantamiento [so-lay-van-tah-me-en'-to], *m.* The act of rising in rebellion. *V.* Sublevación.
Solevantar [so-lay-van-tar'], *va.* 1. To raise any thing and put another under it. 2. To induce one to leave his habitation, home, or employment. 3. To agitate, to excite commotion.
Solevar [so-lay-var'], *va.* To raise, to lift up. *V.* Solevantar.
Solfa [sol'-fah], *f.* 1. The art of uniting the various sounds of music, sol-fa. 2. Accordance, harmony; concord. 3. (Coll.) A sound beating or flogging. *Estar* or *poner en solfa,* To be arranged (or to arrange) with art and judgment. *Tocar la solfa a alguno,* (Coll.) To cudgel, to flog.
Solfatara [sol-fa-tah'-rah], *f.* (Geol.) Solfatara, a volcanic area emitting vapours and sublimates. (Italian.)
Solfeador [sol-fay-ah-dor'], *m.* 1. Songster, one who sings according to the rules of melody and measure. 2. Music-master. 3. (Coll.) One who deals out blows.
Solfear [sol-fay-ar'], *vn.* 1. To sing according to the rules of melody and measure. 2. (Coll.) To cudgel, to flog.
Solfeo [sol-fay'-o], *m.* 1. Melodious song. 2. (Coll.) Beating, flogging, drubbing.
Solfista [sol-fees'-tah], *com.* Musician.
Solicitación [so-le-the-tah-the-on'], *f.* Solicitation, importunity, temptation, inducement.
Solicitado, da [so-le-the-tah'-do, dah], *a.* (Com.) In good request or demand.
Solicitador, ra [so-le-the-tah-dor', rah], *m. & f.* Solicitor, agent; one who solicits for another.
Solicitamente, *adv.* Solicitously, diligently.
Solicitante [so-le-the-tahn'-tay], *pa.* *V.* Solicitador.
Solicitar [so-le-the-tar'], *va.* To solicit, to importune, to entreat; to urge; to court.
Solícito, ta [so-lee'-the-to, tah], *a.* Solicitous, anxious, careful, nice.
Solicitud [so-le-the-tood'], *f.* Solicitude, anxiety, importunity.
Sólidamente, *adv.* Solidly, firmly, with true reasons.
Solidar [so-le-dar'], *va.* 1. To harden, to render firm and solid. 2. To consolidate, to establish.
Solidaridad [so-le-dah-re-dahd'], *f.* Solidarity, community, equal participation.
Solidario, ria [so-le-dah'-re-o, ah], *a.* 1. Solidary, equal in participation, one in interests. 2. Individually and collectively responsible.
Solideo [so-le-day'-o], *m.* Calotte, a small cap worn by clergymen under the hat.
Solidez [so-le-deth'], *f.* 1. Solidity, firmness, strength. 2. Integrity, firmness of mind.
Sólido, da [so'-le-do, dah], *a.* 1. Solid, firm, compact, consistent. 2. Built on sound reasons.
Sólido [so'-le-do], *m.* 1. A solid, compact body. 2. (Med.) Solid, the part

containing the fluids of the animal body.

Soliloquiar [so-le-lo-ke-ar'], *vn.* To discourse or reason with one's self; to talk to one's self, to soliloquize.

Soliloquio [so-le-lo'-ke-o], *m.* Soliloquy, monologue.

Solimán [so-le-mahn'], *m.* (Chem.) Corrosive sublimate.

Solio [so'-le-o], *m.* Throne with a canopy.

Solípedo, da [so-lee'-pay-do, dah], *a.* Solipede, solidungulous, whole-hoofed.

Solitaria, *f.* Tapeworm. *V.* Tenia.

Solitariamente, *adv.* Solitarily, lonesomely.

Solitario, ria [so-le-tah'-re-o, ah], *a.* 1. Solitary, lonely, lonesome, isolated. 2. Cloistered, retired.

Solitario, *m.* 1. Solitary, recluse, a hermit. 2. Solitaire, a sort of game played by one person alone. 3. Post-chaise, with one seat only; a sulky. 4. (Prov.) Solitaire, a single rich diamond. *Pájaro solitario,* (Orn.) Solitary thrush, erroneously called the solitary sparrow. Turdus solitarius.

Sólito, ta [so'-le-to, tah], *a.* Wont, accustomed.

Soliviadura [so-le-ve-ah-doo'-rah], *f.* The act of raising a little.

Soliviantar [so-le-ve-an-tar'], *va.* To induce to novelties or changes.

Soliviar [so-le-ve-ar'], *va.* 1. To raise or lift up in order to take any thing from underneath. 2. To rob, to steal. —*vr.* To rise, to get up a little.

Solivio [so-lee'-ve-o], *m.* The act of rising or raising a little.

Solivión [so-le-ve-on'], *m. aug.* A sudden and violent lifting up.

Solo, *m.* 1. Solo, musical composition for one voice; a tune played by a single instrument. 2. A game at cards. 3. A play in certain games of cards, a lone hand.

Solo, la, *a.* 1. Alone, single, solitary. 2. Alone, only, lonely, without company; bereft of favour and protection. ***A solas,*** Alone, unaided. ***A solas*** or ***a sus solas,*** Quite alone, in solitude.

Sólo, *adv.* Only. *V.* Solamente.

Solomillo, Solomo [so-lo-meel'-lyo, so-lo'-mo], *m.* Loin, the fleshy and boneless part on the spine; chine.

Solsticial [sols-te-the-ahl'], *a.* Solstitial.

Solsticio [sols-tee'-the-o], *m.* Solstice, the tropical point.

Soltadizo, za [sol-tah-dee'-tho, thah], *a.* Easily untied, cleverly loosened.

Soltador, ra [sol-tah-dor', rah], *m. & f.* One that unites, loosens, lets go, or dismisses.

Soltar [sol-tar'], *va.* 1. To untie, to loosen. 2. To set at liberty, to discharge. 3. To burst out into laughter or crying. 4. To explain, to decipher, to solve. 5. (Obs.) To pardon, remit, absolve, or annul. *Soltar la capa,* (1) To pull off the cloak. (2) (Met.) To make a slight sacrifice to avoid danger. *Soltar la carga,* To throw down a burden. *Soltar la deuda,* To forgive a debt. *Soltar la taravilla,* To give a loose to one's tongue. *Soltar la palabra,* To absolve one from an obligation or promise; to pledge one's word for any thing. *Soltar una especie,* To throw out a suggestion by way of sounding the opinions of others. *Soltar el trapo* or *la rienda,* (Met.) To give one's self entirely up to vices, passions, or bad habits. *Soltar el preso,* (Joc.) To break wind. *Soltar el reloj,* To raise the spring that a clock may run down, in token of public rejoicing. *El tablón ha soltado su cabeza,* (Naut.) The butt-end of the plank has started. *El ancla ha soltado el fondo,* (Naut.) The anchor is a-weigh.—*vr.* 1. To get loose. 2. To grow expeditious and handy in the performance of a thing. 3. To forego all decency and modesty.

Soltera [sol-tay'-rah], *f.* A spinster, an unmarried woman. *V.* Soltero, ra.

Soltería [sol-tay-ree'-ah], *f.* Celibacy.

Soltero [sol-tay'-ro], *m.* Bachelor, a man unmarried.

Soltero, ra [sol-tay'-ro, rah], *a.* Single: applied to a person who has never been married.

Solterón [sol-tay-rone'], *m.* An old bachelor.

Solterona [sol-tay-ro'-nah], *f.* An old maid.

Soltura [sol-too'-rah], *f.* 1. The act of discharging or setting at liberty. 2. Release, dismission from confinement. 3. Agility, activity. 4. Laxity, looseness, licentiousness.

Solubilidad [so-loo-be-le-dahd'], *f.* Solubility, solubleness.

Soluble [so-loo'-blay], *a.* 1. Soluble, that can be loosened or untied. 2. Resoluble, that may be resolved. 3. Solvable.

Solución [so-loo-the-on'], *f.* 1. Solution, the act of loosening or untying. 2. Resolution of a doubt, removal of an intellectual difficulty. 3. Solution, the reduction of a solid body into a fluid state. 4. The climax or catastrophe in a drama or epic poem. 5. Pay, satisfaction. *Dar solución a una duda,* To solve or explain a doubt.

Solutivo, va [so-loo-tee'-vo, vah], *a.* Solutive, having the power of loosening, untying, or dissolving.

Solvabilidad [sol-vah-be-le-dahd'], *f.* (Com.) Solvency, ability to pay one's debts.

Solvencia [sol-ven'-the-ah], *f.* Solvency, ability to pay debts contracted.

Solventar [sol-ven-tar'], *va.* To pay debts.

Solvente [sol-ven'-tay], *pa. & a.* 1. Solvent, unbinding, dissolvent, having power to cause dissolution. 2. Solvent, able to pay debts contracted.

Solver [sol-verr'], *va.* To loosen, to untie; to solve, to find out.

Solviente [sol-ve-en'-tay], *pa.* Solving, loosening, having power to cause solution.

Solla, *f.* (Prov.) *V.* Suela.

Sollado [sol-lyah'-do], *m.* (Naut.) Orlop. *Sollado de los pañoles de la despensa,* (Naut.) Cock-pit.—*Sollado, da, pp.* of Sollar.

Sollador [sol-lyah-dor'], *m.* (Obs.) Blower, one who blows.

Sollamar [sol-lyah-mar'], *va.* To scorch, to singe; to burn slightly.

Sollar [sol-lyar'], *va.* (Met.) To blow, to blow with bellows.

Sollastre [sol-lyahs'-tray], *m.* 1. Scullion, kitchen-boy. 2. (Coll.) A skilful rogue.

Sollastría [sol-lyas-tree'-ah], *f.* Scullery; the business of a scullion.

Sollastrón [sol-lyas-trone'], *m. aug.* 1. A very crafty, subtle, sly fellow. 2. A loafer. 3. A designing, low fellow.

Sollo [sol'-lyo], *m.* Common pike. Esox lucius.

Sollozar [sol-lyo-thar'], *vn.* To sob.

Sollozo [sol-lyo'-tho], *m.* 1. Sob. 2. (Cal. and Mex.) Huckleberry.

Soma [so'-mah], *f.* 1. The coarse sort of flour, which by farmers, especially in Spain, is generally destined for servants' bread. 2. (Prov.) Load, burdensomeness. *Bestia de soma,* A beast of burden.

Somanta [so-mahn'-tah], *f.* (Coll.) Beating, severe chastisement.

Somatén [so-mah-ten'], *m.* 1. Armed corps for the defence of a city or province. 2. One who serves in such a corps. 3. Mob, an unexpected attack.

Somatología [so-mah-to-lo-hee'-ah], *f.* Somatology, the doctrine of organic bodies, especially of the human body; embracing anatomy and physiology.

Sombra [som'-brah], *f.* 1. Shade, interception of light. 2. Shadow, shade, the representation of a body by which the light is intercepted. 3. Shade, shadow, spirit, ghost, manes. 4. (Met.) Shade, shadow, shelter, favour, protection. 5. Resemblance, appearance. 6. Sign, vestige. 7. Shadow, dark part of a picture. 8. Shade, parts of a picture not brightly coloured. 9. Umber, a brown colour. *Andar a sombra de tejado,* To abscond. *Andar sin sombra,* To crave, to desire anxiously. *Ni por sombra,* By no means. *Sombras chinescas* or *invisibles,* Dance behind a curtain where the shadows only are seen. *Hacer sombra,* To protect; to impede; to obscure, to outshine. *No ser ni su sombra,* To be but the shadow of one's former self. *Tener buena sombra,* To be pleasing, popular, agreeable. *Tener mala sombra,* (1) To exert an evil influence over others: said of a person. (2) (Coll. Met.) To be disagreeable, to excite antipathy. *Poner a la sombra,* (Coll.) To imprison.

Sombraje [som-brah'-hay], *m.* Hut covered with branches.

Sombrajo [som-brah'-ho], *m.* 1. Shadow or figure corresponding to the body by which the light is intercepted. 2. A shed or hut in vineyards.

Sombrar [som-brar'], *va.* To frighten, to astonish. *V.* Asombrar.

Sombreado [som-bray-ah'-do], *m.* Shading, the act of marking with different gradations of colours.—*Sombreado, da, pp.* of Sombrear.

Sombrear [som-bray-ar'], *va.* To shade, to mark with different gradations of colour; to paint in obscure colours.

Sombrerazo [som-bray-rah'-tho], *m.* 1. (Aug.) A large hat. 2. A flap or blow with a hat.

Sombrerera [som-bray-ray'-rah], *f.* 1. Hat-box, hat-case. 2. Hatter's wife.

Sombrerería [som-bray-ray-ree'-ah], *f.* 1. Manufactory of hats. 2. Shop where hats are sold.

Sombrerero [som-bray-ray'-ro], *m.* Hatter, hat-maker.

Sombrerete [som-bray-ray'-tay], *m. dim.* 1. A small hat. 2. (Mech.) Bonnet, cap. 3. Spark-arrester, spark-catcher of a locomotive.

Sombrerillo, ito [som-bray-reel'-lyo, ee'-to], *m.* 1. (Dim.) A small or little hat. *Sombrerillo de señora,* Lady's hat. 2. (Bot.) Navel-wort. Cotyledon umbilicus.

Sombrerito [som-bray-ree'-to], *m. dim.* *V.* Sombrerete, 1st def.

Sombrero [som-bray'-ro], *m.* 1. A hat. *Sombrero apuntado* or *de tres picos,* A cocked hat. 2. Sounding-board; canopy of a pulpit. 3. Rights and privileges of a Spanish grandee. *Sombrero de cabrestante,* (Naut.) Drum of the capstan. *Sombrero del patrón,* (Naut.) Hat-money, allowance per ton to captains on their cargo. *Sombrero acantilado,* Hat cocked in sharp points, worn in the almshouses in Spain. *Sombrero calañés,* A hat with a brim turned upward, and low crown narrower above than below. *Sombrero de tres candiles,* A three-cornered hat. *Sombrero jarano,* A stiff felt hat

much used in America, white, broad-brimmed and of low crown, with cord ending in two tassels. *Sombrero jíbaro*, A very ordinary straw hat used by rustics in Cuba and Puerto-Rico.
Sombría [som-bree'-ah], *f.* Shady place.
Sombrilla [som-breel'-lyah], *f.* 1. Parasol. 2. Slight shade.
Sombrita [som-bree'-tah], *f. dim.* A slight shade.
Sombrío, bría [som-bree'-o, ah], *a.* 1. Shady, gloomy, sombre. 2. Hazy, murky, thick (of weather). 3. Taciturn.
Sombrío [som-bree'-o], *m.* 1. Part of a piece of painting, which is to be shaded or painted in darker colours than the rest. 2. A dull, heavy colour. 3. A shady place.
Sombroso, sa [som-bro'-so, sah], *a* Shady.
Someramente, *adv.* Superficially.
Somero, ra [so-may'-ro, rah], *a.* Superficial, shallow; making but a slight impression on the mind.—*f.* Sleeper of a printing press; a thick, square timber.
Someter [so-may-terr'], *va.* To subject, to submit, to subdue, to reduce to submission.—*vr.* To humble one's self; to submit, to acquiesce, to comply.
Sometimiento [so-may-te-me-en'-to], *m.* Submission, subjection, subduing.
Somnambulismo [som-nam-boo-lees'-mo], *m.* Somnambulism, walking in sleep. *Somnambulismo artificial*, Hypnotism.
Somnámbulo, la [som-nahm'-boo-lo, lah], *m.* & *f.* & *a.* 1. Somnambule, somnambulist. 2. Medium, a person habitually submitted to the influence of hypnotism.
Somnífero, ra [som-nee'-fay-ro, rah], *a.* Somniferous, soporiferous.
Somnílocuo, cua [som-nee'-lo-cwo, cwah], *a.* Somniloquous, given to talking in sleep.
Somnolencia [som-no-len'-the-ah], *f.* Sleepiness, drowsiness, somnolency.
Somo, *m.* (Obs.) Top, summit.
Somonte [so-mon'-tay], *a.* Coarse, rough, shaggy.
Somorgujador [so-mor-goo-hah-dor'], *m.* Diver, one that goes under water to search for any thing.
Somorgujar [so-mor-goo-har'], *va.* To dive, to duck. Also *vr.*
Somorgujo, Somorgujón, Somormujo [so-mor-goo'-ho], *m.* (Orn.) Dun-diver, diver, merganser. Mergus castor. *A lo somorgujo* or *a lo somormujo*, Under water. *A lo somorgujo*, Privately, secretly.
Sompesar [som-pay-sar'], *va.* To take up a thing in order to guess its weight; to heft.
Son [sohn], *m.* Sound, noise, report, tale, reason, mode. *En son*, In such a manner; apparently. *Sin ton ni son*, Without rhyme or reason. *A qué son* or *a son de qué*, With what motive, for what reason. *A son*, At or to the sound of. *Bailar a cualquier son*, To be easily moved by affection or passion. *Bailar uno al son que le tocan*, To adapt one's self to circumstances. *Bailar sin son*, To be exceedingly eager. *¿A qué son?* or *¿a son de qué?* With what motive?
Sonable [so-nah'-blay], *a.* 1. Sonorous, loud, sounding. 2. Celebrated, famous.
Sonada [so-nah'-dah], *f.* *V.* SONATA.
Sonadera [so-nah-day'-rah], *f.* The act of blowing the nose.
Sonado, da [so-nah'-do, dah], *a.* 1. Celebrated, famous. 2. Generally reported.—*pp.* of SONAR.
Sonador, ra [so-nah-dor', rah], *m.* & *f.* 1. One who makes a noise. 2. Handkerchief.
Sonajá [so-nah'-hah], *f.* Timbrel, a musical instrument.
Sonajero [so-nah-hay'-ro], *m.* 1. A small timbrel. 2. A rattle.
Sonajica, illa, ita, uela [so-nah-hee'-cah], *f. dim.* Small tabor or timbrel.
Sonambulismo, *m.* *V.* SOMNAMBULISMO. (Acad.)
Sonámbulo, la [so-nahm'-boo-lo, lah], *m.* & *f.* & *a.* Somnambule, somnambulist.
Sonante [so-nahn'-tay], *a.* Sounding, sonorous. *Dinero contante y sonante*, Ready cash.
Sonar [so-nar'], *va.* 1. To sound, to play upon a musical instrument. 2. To like or dislike. *Mal me suena la cantada*, I do not like the song. *Bien me sonó lo que dijo*, I was much pleased with what he said. 3. To sound, to pronounce. 4. To allude, to refer to a thing without any direct mention.—*vn.* To sound or make a noise, to chink.—*v. imp.* To raise or propagate rumours, to be reported, to be whispered.—*vr.* To blow one's nose.
Sonata [so-nah'-tah], *f.* Sonata, a musical composition in three or four movements.
Sonda [son'-dah], *f.* 1. (Naut.) Sounding, heaving the lead. 2. Sound, lead, a cord with a heavy weight attached for sounding. 3. Borer, an instrument for examining the strata of the earth. 4. (Med.) Sound; probe. 5. In artillery, searcher, proof stick. *Sonda del escandallo*, (Naut.) Lead soundings. *Navegar en sonda por la sondalesa*, To sail by the log.
Sondable [son-dah'-blay], *a.* That may be sounded.
Sondalesa [son-dah-lay'-sah], *f.* (Naut.) Lead-line, the log sounding-line. *Sondalesa de mano*, (Naut.) Hand-lead. *Sondalesa de la bomba*, (Naut.) Gauge-rod of the pump.
Sondar, Sondear [son-dar', son-day-ar'], *va.* 1. (Naut.) To sound, to heave the lead. *Sondar la bomba*, (Naut.) To sound the pump. 2. To try, to sift, to sound another's intentions; to explore, to fathom.
Sondeo [son-day'-o], *m.* The act and effect of sounding; exploring, fathoming.
Sonecillo [so-nay-theel'-lyo], *m. dim.* 1. A sound scarcely perceptible. 2. A short little tune.
Sonetazo [so-nay tah'-tho], *m. aug.* of SONETO: generally used in an ironical sense.
Sonetico [so-nay-tee'-co], *m.* 1. (Dim.) *V.* SONETÍN. 2. A merry little song.
Sonetín [so-nay-teen'], *m.* An insignificant sonnet.
Sonetista [so-nay-tees'-tah], *m.* One who writes sonnets.
Soneto [so-nay'-to], *m.* Sonnet.
Songuita [son-gee'-tah], *f.* (Cuba) Jest, irony.
Sónico, ca [soh'-ne-co, cah], *a.* Sonic. *Barrera sónica*, Sonic barrier.
Sonido [so-nee'-do], *m.* 1. Sound, noise. 2. Fame, report, rumour. 3. Sound, pronunciation. 4. Literal signification. *Sonido agudo*. Acute sound.
Sonlocado, da, *a.* *V.* ALOCADO.
Sonochada [so-no-chah'-dah], *f.* 1. The beginning of night. 2. Watching in the early hours of night.
Sonochar [so-no-char'], *vn.* To watch the first hours of the night.
Sonómetro [so-no'-may-tro], *m.* Sonometer, an instrument for testing the vibration of strings.
Sonora [so-no'-rah], *f.* Cithern, a musical instrument.
Sonoramente, *adv.* Sonorously; harmoniously.
Sonoridad [so-no-re-dahd'], *f.* Sonorousness.
Sonoro, ra, Sonoroso, sa [so-no'-ro, rah], *a.* 1. Sonorous, soniferous. 2. Pleasing, agreeable, harmonious.
Sonreír, Sonreírse [son-ray-eer', eer'-say], *vn.* & *vr.* To smile.
(*Yo sonrío, yo sonría; él sonrió or sonriyó, sonriyera*; from *Sonreír.* *V.* REÍR.)
Sonrisa [son-ree'-sah], *f.* **Sonriso,** *m* Smile.
Sonrodadura [son-ro-dah-doo'-rah], *f.* The act of sticking in the mud.
Sonrodarse [son-ro-dar'-say], *vr.* To stick in the mud: applied to a carriage.
Sonrojar, Sonrojear [son-ro-har'], *va.* To make one blush with shame, to flush. Also *vr.*
Sonrojo [son-ro'-ho], *m.* 1. Blush. 2. Offensive word which causes a blush.
Sonrosado, da [son-ro-sah'-do, dah], *a.* Pink, blushing pink.
Sonrosar, Sonrosear [son-ro-sar'], *va.* To dye a rose colour. *Sonrosearse*, *vr.* To blush.
Sonroseo [son-ro-say'-o], *m.* Blush.
Sonsaca [son-sah'-cah], *f.* Wheedling; petty theft.
Sonsacador, ra [son-sah-cah-dor', rah], *m.* & *f.* 1. Wheedler, prier, shooter, coaxer. 2. A petty thief.
Sonsacamiento [son-sah-cah-me-en'-to], *m.* Wheedling, extortion, petty theft.
Sonsacar [son-sah-car'], *va.* 1. To steal privately out of a bag. 2. To obtain by cunning and craft. (Met.) To entice, to allure. 3. To pump a secret out of a person.
Sonsaque [son-sah'-kay], *m.* Wheedling; petty theft.
Sonsonete [son-so-nay'-tay], *m.* 1. Noise arising from repeated gentle beats imitating some musical sound. 2. Sing-song voice.
Soñador, ra [so-nyah-dor', rah], *m.* & *f.* Dreamer; one who relates dreams and idle stories.
Soñante [so-nyahn'-tay], *pa.* Dreaming.
Soñar [so-nyar'], *va.* 1. To dream, to be troubled with dreams. 2. To dream, to think idly, to entertain fantastical ideas. *Ni soñarlo*, Not even dreamed of.
Soñarrera [so-nyar-ray'-rah], *f.* 1. (Prov.) Dreaming, heavy sleep. 2. Drowsiness, propensity to sleep long.
Soñera [so-nyay'-rah], *f.* Sleepiness, wish to sleep.
Soñolencia [so-nyo-len'-the-ah], *f.* Sleepiness, drowsiness, somnolence.
Soñolientamente, *adv.* Sleepily heavily.
Soñoliento, ta [so-nyo-le-en'-to, tah], *a.* 1. Heavy, sleepy, drowsy. 2. Sleepy, soporiferous, causing sleep. 3. Sleepy, dull, lazy.
Sopa [so'-pah], *f.* 1. Sop, a piece of bread steeped in any liquid. 2. Soup. 3. Bread cut or broken to be thrown into soup; generally in plural. 4. Broken victual given to the poor *Sopa de ajo* or *de gato*, Meagre soup, made of bread, oil, salt, garlic, and water. *Sopa de leche*, Milk porridge or milk soup. *Sopa de guisantes*, Pea-soup. *Sopa borracha*, Soup made with wine, biscuit, sugar, and cinnamon. *Andar a la sopa*, To go begging from door to door. *Hecho una sopa de agua*, Wet through to the skin. *Sopa de vino*, (Bot.) Flower of the small caltrops. Flos tribuli terrestris. *¿Por*

quería son sopas? Familiar retort to one who depreciates any thing worthy of respect.

Sopaipa [so-pah'-ee-pah], *f.* A sort of fritter steeped in honey.

Sopalancar [so-pah-lan-car'], *va.* To put a lever under any thing to lift it.

Sopalanda [so-pah-lahn'-dah], *f.* Ragged clothes worn by poor students.

Sopanda [so-pahn'-dah], *f.* 1. Brace, any of the leather thongs which support the body of a coach. 2. Joist, cross-beam, a stout timber placed horizontally.

Sopapeadura [so-pah-pay-ah-doo'-rah], *f.* 1. Buffet or slap with the hand under the chin; a chuck. 2. (Coll.) A number of slaps or chucks.

Sopapear [so-pah-pay-ar'], *va.* 1. (Coll.) To chuck under the chin, to slap. 2. (Coll. Met.) To vilify, to abuse.

Sopapo [so-pah'-po], *m.* 1. Box, blow, or slap with the hand. 2. Sucker, a movable valve in hydraulic vessels or pumps.

Sopar [so-par'], *va.* To sop bread. *V.* ENSOPAR.

Sopear [so-pay-ar'], *va.* 1. To sop, to steep bread. *V.* ENSOPAR. 2. To tread, to trample, to domineer. 3. To maltreat.

Sopeña [so-pay'-nyah], *f.* Cavity formed by a rock at its foot.

Sopera [so-pay'-rah], *f.* Tureen.

Sopero [so-pay'-ro], *m.* Soup-plate; lover of soups.

Sopesar [so-pay-sar'], *va.* To try the weight. *V.* SOMPESAR.

Sopetear [so-pay-tay-ar'], *va.* 1. To sop; to steep bread in sauce, broth, or other liquors. 2. To abuse with foul language.

Sopeteo [so-pay-tay'-o], *m.* The act of dipping bread in broth, etc.

Sopetón [so-pay-tone'], *m.* 1. Plentiful soup. *Sopetón de molino*, Bread toasted and steeped in oil. 2. A heavy box or slap with the hand. *De sopetón*, Suddenly.

Sopica, illa, ita [so-pee'-cah], *f. dim.* Sippet, a light soup.

Sopilote [so-pe-lo'-tay], *m.* (Mex.) A vulture.

Sopista [so-pees'-tah], *m.* Person living upon charity.

¡ Sopla ! [so'-plah], *int.* O strange! expressing admiration.

Sopladero [so-plah-day'-ro], *m.* Draught or air-hole to subterraneous passages.

Soplado, da [so-plah'-do, dah], *a.* & *pp.* of SOPLAR. Blown; overnice and spruce.

Soplador, ra [so-plah-dor', rah], *m.* & *f.* 1. Blower, that which blows. 2. That which excites or inflames.

Soplamocos [so-plah-mo'-cos], *m.* (Coll.) Box or slap on the nose.

Soplar [so-plar'], *vn.* & *va.* 1. To blow, to emit wind at the mouth. 2. To blow with bellows. 3. To blow, to make a current of air. 4. To be blown away by the wind. 5. To blow, to drive by the wind, to separate with wind. 6. To rob or steal in an artful manner. 7. To suggest notions or ideas, to inspire. *Soplar la musa*, To get a strain or vein of poetry, to inspire: said of the muse. 8. In the game of draughts to huff a man. 9. To tipple, to drink much. *Soplar la dama*, (Met.) To marry a woman supposed to be engaged or offered to another.—*vr.* To eat or drink a great deal. *Soplarse las manos* or *las uñas*, (Met.) To be disappointed and burlesqued. *Soplársela a alguno*, To deceive a person.

Soplete [so-play'-tay], *m.* In glass-houses, a blow pipe; a soldering pipe.

Soplico [so-plee'-co], *m. dim.* A slight puff or blast.

Soplido [so-plee'-do], *m.* *V.* SOPLO.

Soplillo [so-pleel'-lyo], *m.* 1. Crape, a thin stuff. 2. Any thing extremely thin and light. 3. (Dim.) *V.* SOPLICO.

Soplo [so'-plo], *m.* 1. Blowing, act of blowing. 2. Instant, moment, short space of time. 3. Blast, a gust or puff of wind. 4. Advice given secretly, and with caution; generally malicious advice or information.

Soplón, na [so-plone', nah], *a.* & *n.* Tale-bearer, informer.

Soploncillo, illa [so-plon-theel'-lyo, lyah], *m.* & *f.*, & *a. dim.* Little tattler.

Sopón [so-pone'], *m.* Person living upon charity soup. Aug. of SOPA.

Soponcio [so-pon'-the-o], *m.* Grief or fit arising from disappointment.

Sopor [so-por'], *m.* Heaviness, drowsiness, sleepiness.

Soporifero, ra [so-po-ree'-fay-ro, rah], *a.* Soporific, soporiferous. *V.* SOPORÍFICO.

Soporífico, ca [so-po-ree'-fe-co, cah], *a.* Opiate, narcotical, soporific, somniferous.

Soporoso, sa [so-po-ro'-so, sah], *a.* Soporiferous.

Soportable [so-por-tah'-blay], *a.* Tolerable, supportable.

Soportador, ra [so-por-tah-dor', rah], *m.* & *f.* Supporter.

Soportal [so-por-tahl'], *m.* Portico.

Soportar [so-por-tar'], *va.* To suffer, to tolerate. to support, to abide.

Soprano [so-prah'-no], *m.* *V.* TIPLE. (Ital.)

Soprior, *m.* (Obs.) *V.* SUBPRIOR.

So protesta [so pro-tes'-tah], *adv.* (Com.) Under protest.

Sopuntar [so-poon-tar'], *va.* To place marks under a superfluous or erroneous word.

Sor [sore], *f.* Sister. *V.* HERMANA. *Sor María*, Sister Mary: used only to or between nuns.

Sora [so'-rah], *f.* Peruvian drink made of a decoction of maize.

Sorba [sor'-bah], *f.* Sorb-apple. *V.* SERBA.

Sorbedor [sor-bay-dor'], *m.* Sipper, one who sips.

Sorber [sor-berr'], *va.* 1. To sip, to suck; to sup. 2. To imbibe, to soak as a sponge, to absorb. *Sorbérsele a alguno*, To conquer or surpass any one.

Sorbete [sor-bay'-tay], *m.* Sherbet, a beverage of fruit-juice, sugar, etc., chilled; water ice. (Arab.)

Sorbetón [sor-bay-tone'], *m. aug.* A large draught of liquor.

Sorbible [sor-bee'-blay], *a.* Sorbible, that may be sipped.

Sorbición [sor-be-the-on'], *f.* (Med.) Absorption.

Sorbillo, ito [sor-beel'-lyo], *m. dim.* Sup, a small draught.

Sorbo [sor'-bo], *m.* 1. Imbibition, drinking or sipping; absorption. 2. Sup, draught. 3. Any thing comparatively small.

Sorce [sor'-thay], *m.* Field-mouse.

Sorda [sor'-dah], *f.* 1. Woodcock. *V.* CHOCHA. 2. (Naut.) Stream-cable employed in launching a ship.

Sordamente, *adv.* Secretly, silently.

Sordastro, tra [sor-dahs'-tro, trah], *a.* Deaf.

Sordera, Sordez [sor-day'-rah, sor-deth'], *f.* Deafness.

Sórdidamente, *adv.* Sordidly, dirtily.

Sordidez [sor-de-deth'], *f.* 1. Sordidness, nastiness. 2. Covetousness, avarice.

Sórdido, da [sor'-de-do, dah], *a.* 1. Sordid, dirty, filthy. 2. Licentious, impure, indecent, scandalous.

Sordina [sor-dee'-nah], *f.* 1. Kit, a small fiddle. 2. Mute, a piece put on the bridge of a fiddle, to weaken the sound. 3. Sordono, a mute for a trumpet. *A la sordina*, Secretly, privately, without noise.

Sordo, da [sor'-do, dah], *a.* 1. Deaf, insensible to reason. 2. Silent, still, quiet. 3. Deafening. 4. Surd; incapable of hearing; insensible. *A la sorda, a lo sordo* or *a sordas*, Silently, quietly. *Dar música a un sordo*, To labour in vain.

Sorgo [sor'-go], *m.* *V.* ZAHINA.

Soriasis [so-re-ah'-sis], *f.* Psoriasis, a squamous disease of the skin, of remarkable chronicity.

Sórico [so'-re-co], *a.* Belonging to psoriasis.

Sorites [so-ree'-tes], *m.* (Log.) Sorites, proposition or argument accumulated on another.

Sormigrar, *va.* (Obs.) *V.* SUMERGIR.

Sorna [sor'-nah], *f.* 1. Sluggishness, laziness, slowness. 2. A feigned sloth in doing or saying any thing.

Sornavirón [sor-nah-ve-rone'], *m.* (Coll.) Sudden stroke with the back of the open hand.

Soro [so'-ro], *m.* Year-old hawk.

Soroche [so-ro'-chay], *m.* (Peru and Ec.) 1. Disease caused by rarefaction of the air at great altitudes in men and beasts. 2. A friable, shining silver ore.

Soroque [so-ro'-kay], *f.* (Min.) Matrix of ores.

Sóror, *f.* Sister. *V.* SOR. (Lat. idem.)

Sororicidio [so-ro-re-thee'-de-o], *m.* (Littl. us.) Sororicide.

Sorprendente [sor-pren-den'-tay], *a.* 1. Surprising. 2. Rare, extraordinary, strange.—*pa.* of SORPRENDER.

Sorprender [sor-pren-derr'], *va.* 1. To surprise, to fall upon unexpectedly, to take by surprise; to come upon; to overtake. 2. To execute any thing silently and with caution. 3. To surprise, to astonish by something wonderful or sudden.

Sorpresa [sor-pray'-sah], *f.* 1. Surprise; taking by surprise; deceit, imposition. 2. Surprise, sudden confusion or perplexity. 3. Amazement, astonishment, consternation. *Sorpresa de una carta*, The act of intercepting a letter. *Tomar por sorpresa*, To surprise, to take unawares.

Sorra [sor'-rah], *f.* 1. (Naut.) Ballast of stones or coarse gravel. 2. Side of a tunny-fish.

Sorregar [sor-ray-gar'], *va.* To water in another course: applied to rivulets which casually change their channels.

Sorrero, ra [sor-ray'-ro, rah], *a.* (Prov.) *V.* ZORRERO.

Sorriego [sor-re-ay'-go], *m.* Water which passes occasionally from one channel to another.

Sorrostrada [sor-ros-trah'-dah], *f.* Great face or beak.

Sorteador [sor-tay-ah-dor'], *m.* 1. One who casts lots. 2. Skilful bull-fighter.

Sorteamiento [sor-tay-ah-me-en'-to], *m.* *V.* SORTEO.

Sortear [sor-tay-ar'], *va.* 1. To draw or cast lots. 2. To fight bulls with skill and dexterity. 3. To cleverly elude or shun a conflict, risk, or difficulty.

Sorteo [sor-tay'-o], *m.* Act of casting or drawing lots.

Sortero [sor-tay'-ro], *m.* Fortune-teller. *V.* AGORERO.

Sortiaria [sor-te-ah'-re-ah], *f.* Superstitious divination by letters, schedules, or playing-cards. (Acad.)

Sortija [sor-tee'-hah], *f.* 1. Ring, finger-ring. 2. Ring, a circle of metal, used for a variety of purposes; hoop. 3. A curl of hair, naturally or artificially made. *Sortijas,* (Prov.) Hoops of vessels.

Sortijita, Sortijuela [sor-te-hee'-tah], *f. dim.* Little ring, ringlet.

Sortijón [sor-te-hone'], *m. aug.* A large ring.

Sortilegio [sor-te-lay'-he-o], *m.* Sortilege, sorcery.

Sortílego, ga [sor-tee'-lay-go, gah], *m. & f. & a.* Sorcerer, conjurer, fortune-teller.

Sos. Used in composition for sub, as an inseparable preposition; as, *Sostituto,* Substitute.

Sosa [so'-sah], *f.* 1. (Bot.) A name given to various marine plants which, on being burned, afford soda or mineral alkali; glasswort, kelp. 2. Soda-ash, barilla; sal soda. 3. Soda, sodium oxide, a strong alkali.

Sosacar, *va.* *V.* SONSACAR.

Sosamente [so-sah-men'-tay], *adv.* Insipidly, tastelessly.

Sosaño [so-sah'-nyo], *m.* Derision, mockery.

Sosegadamente, *adv.* Quietly, calmly.

Sosegado, da [so-say-gah'-do, dah], *a.* Quiet, peaceful, pacific, calm.—*pp.* of SOSEGAR.

Sosegador, ra [so-say-gah-dor', rah], *m. & f.* Pacifier, appeaser.

Sosegar [so-say-gar'], *va.* 1. To appease, to calm, to pacify, to silence, to quiet. 2. To lull, to put to sleep.—*vn.* 1. To rest, to repose. 2. To be calm or composed. *Sosegarse el aire,* To grow calm. *Sosiéguese Vd.,* Compose yourself.

Sosería [so-say-ree'-ah], *f.* Insipidity, tastelessness; insipid expression.

Sosez [so-seth'], *f.* (Prov.) Insipidness, silliness. *Decir soseces,* To use silly jokes.

Sosiego [so-se-ay'-go], *m.* Tranquillity, calmness.

Sosio [so'-se-o], *m.* (Chem.) *V.* SODIO.

(*Yo sosiego, yo sosiegue, yo sosegué,* from *Sosegar.* *V.* ACRECENTAR.)

Soslayar [sos-lah-yar'], *va.* To do or place a thing obliquely.

Soslayo [sos-lah'-yo], *m.* Slant, obliquity. *Al soslayo* or *de soslayo,* Askew, sidewise.

Soso, sa [soh'-so, sah], *a.* 1. Insipid, unsalted, tasteless. 2. Cold, coy, silly, senseless.

Sospecha [sos-pay'-chah], *f.* Suspicion, mistrust, jealousy.

Sospechar [sos-pay-char'], *va.* To suspect; to mistrust; to conjecture.

Sospechilla [sos-pay-cheel'-lyah], *f. dim.* Slight suspicion.

Sospechosamente, *adv.* Suspiciously, doubtfully, jealously.

Sospechoso, sa [sos-pay-cho'-so, sah], *a.* Suspicious, liable to suspicion; inclined to suspect; suspected; mistrustful.

Sospesar [sos-pay-sar'], *va.* To suspend, to raise above the ground.

Sospiro, *m.* (Obs.) *V.* SUSPIRO.

Sosquin [sos-keen'], *m.* Slap or blow treacherously given.

Sostén [sos-ten'], *m.* 1. Support, the act of sustaining or supporting. 2. (Naut.) Firmness or steadiness of a ship in pursuing her course.

Sostenedor, ra [sos-tay-nay-dor', rah], *m. & f.* Supporter.

Sostener [sos-tay-nerr'], *va.* 1. To sustain, to support, to maintain, to hold out, to countenance. 2. To sustain, to bear, to endure, to suffer, to tolerate. 3. To sustain, to maintain, to supply with the necessaries of life. *Sostener la caza,* (Naut.) To pursue the chase.—*vr.* 1. To support or maintain one's self. 2. (Naut.) To bear up.

(*Yo sostengo, sostenga, sostuve, sostendré,* from *Sostener.* *V.* TENER.)

Sostenido, da [sos-tay-nee'-do, dah], *a. & pp.* of SOSTENER. Supported, supportful, sustained.—*m.* (Music) Sharp, a note raised a semitone; also the character which denotes it, namely ♯.

Sostenimiento [sos-tay-ne-me-en'-to], *m.* Sustenance, the act of sustaining; supporter.

Sostituir [sos-te-too-eer'], *va.* To substitute. *V.* SUBSTITUIR.

Sostituto [sos-te-too'-to], *m.* Substitute. *V.* SUBSTITUTO.

Sota [so'-tah], *f.* 1. Knave, at cards. 2. Deputy, substitute: used in composition to express the last meaning. 3. Helper.

Sota [so'-tah], *prep.* (Obs.) Under, below. *V.* DEBAJO.

Sotabanco [so-tah-bahn'-co], *m.* (Arch.) Pediment of an arch over a cornice.

Sotabraga [so-tah-brah'-gah], *f.* (Mil.) Axletree band, yoke hoop.

Sotacaballerizo [so-tah-cah-bal-lyay-ree'-tho], *m.* Deputy equerry.

Sotacochero [so-tah-co-chay'-ro], *m.* Postilion.

Sotacola [so-tah-co'-lah], *f.* Crupper. *V.* ATAHARRE.

Sotacómitre [so-tah-co'-me-tray], *m.* (Naut.) Boatswain's mate.

Sotacoro [so-tah-co'-ro], *m.* Place under the upper choir.

Sotalcaide [so-tal-cah'-e-day], *m.* Sub-warden.

Sotamaestro [so-tah-mah-es'-tro], *m.* Usher at a school.

Sotaministro [so-tah-me-nees'-tro], *m.* *V.* SOTOMINISTRO.

Sotamontero [so-tah-mon-tay'-ro], *m.* Under-huntsman, deputy forester.

Sotana [so-tah'-nah], *f.* 1 Cassock, of a priest or scholar. 2. (Coll.) Flogging, drubbing.

Sotanado, da [so-tah-nah'-do, dah], *a.* Vaulted, arched, groined.

Sotanear [so-tah-nay-ar'], *va.* (Coll.) To beat, to chastise or reprehend severely.

Sotaní [so-tah-nee'], *m.* Short round under petticoat without plaits.

Sotanilla [so-tah-neel'-lyah], *f.* 1. (Dim.) A small cassock. 2. The dress of collegians.

Sótano [so'-tah-no], *m.* Cellar under ground.

Sotaventado, da [so-tah-ven-tah'-do, dah], *a.* (Naut.) Driven to leeward, lee.—*pp.* of SOTAVENTAR.

Sotaventar, *va.* (Naut.) To fall to leeward, to lose the weather-gauge.

Sotavento [so-tah-ven'-to], *m.* Leeward, lee. *Tener buen sotavento,* (Naut.) To have sea-room. *Banda de sotavento,* (Naut.) Lee-side of a ship. *Costa de sotavento,* (Naut.) Lee-shore. *A sotavento,* Under the lee.

Sotayuda [so-tah-yoo'-dah], *m.* Under-assistant to officers at court.

Sotechado [so-tay-chah'-do], *m.* A roofed or covered place.

Soteño, ña [so-tay'-nyo, nyah], *a.* Produced in groves or forests.

Soterráneo, nea [so-ter-rah'-nay-o, ah], *a.* (Obs.) Subterraneous.

Soterraño [so-ter-rahn'-nyo], *m. & a.* (Obs.) *V.* SUBTERRÁNEO.

Soterrar [so-ter-rar'], *va.* 1. To bury, to put under ground. 2. To hide, to conceal; to overwhelm.

(*Yo sotierro, yo sotierre,* from *Soterrar.* *V.* ACRECENTAR.)

Sotil [so-teel'], *a.* (Obs.) Subtle, subtile. *V.* SUTIL.

Sotillo [so-teel'-lyo], *m. dim.* Little grove.

Soto [so'-to], *m.* Grove, thicket, forest.

Sotrozo [so-tro'-tho], *m.* Linch-pin, axle-pin. (Mech.) Key.

(*Yo soy, yo era, yo fuí, yo sea.* *V.* SER.)

Soviet [so-ve-et'], *m.* Soviet.

Soviético, ca [so-ve-ay'-te-co, cah], *a.* Soviet.

Soya [so'-yah], *f.* Soy bean.

Sputnik [ess-poot'-nik], *m.* Sputnik, Russian satellite.

Standard [es-tand'-ard], *m.* Standard. *Standard de vida,* Standard of living.

Su [soo], *pron. poss.* His, her, its, their, one's. *Se alaba a un soldado por su valor, a una mujer por su hermosura, a una casa por su situación y a los libros por su mérito,* A soldier is praised by *his* courage, a woman by *her* beauty, a house by *its* situation and books by *their* merit. *Fuí en su busca,* I went in search of him, of her, or of them.

Suarda [soo-ar'-dah], *f.* 1. Grease which clings to the clothes. 2. The greasy matter which sweat brings on the skin of animals.

Suasivo, va [soo-ah-see'-vo, vah], *a.* *V.* PERSUASIVO.

Suasorio, ria [soo-ah-so'-re-o, ah], *a.* Suasory, suasive.

Suave [soo-ah'-vay], *a.* 1. Smooth, soft, delicate, mellow. 2. Easy, tranquil, quiet. 3. Gentle, tractable, docile, mild, meek. *Tabaco suave,* Mild tobacco.

Suavecico, illo, ito [soo-ah-vay-thee'-co], *a. dim.* of SUAVE.

Suavemente, *adv.* Gently, sweetly, softly, mildly, kindly.

Suavidad [soo-ah-ve-dahd'], *f.* 1. Softness, delicacy, sweetness. 2. Suavity, meekness; tranquillity; gentleness, lenity, forbearance.

Suavización [soo-ah-ve-thah-the-on'], *f.* (Littl. us.) Mollification.

Suavizador [soo-ah-ve-thah-dor'], *m.* Razor-strop.

Suavizar [soo-ah-ve-thar'], *va.* 1. To soften. 2. To mollify, to mitigate. 3. To render metals pliable or ductile.

Sub [soob]. A Latin preposition signifying *under, below.*—It is used only in composition, and then it means under, less, or in a subordinate degree; also a deputy; as, *Sublunar,* Under the moon. *Sub-inspector,* The deputy inspector.

Subacetato [soob-ah-thay-tah'-to], *m.* (Chem.) Subacetate.

Subácido, da [soob-ah'-the-do, dah], *a.* Subacid.

Subalcaide [soob-al-cah'-e-day], *m.* Deputy or sub-governor or jailer.

Subalternante [soob-al-ter-nahn'-tay], *pa.* That to which another thing is subject.

Subalternar [soob-al-ter-nar'], *va.* To subject, to subdue.

Subalterno, na [soob-al-terr'-no, nah], *a.* Subaltern, inferior, subject.

Subalterno, *m.* Subaltern, a subaltern officer.

Subarrendador, ra [soob-ar-ren-dah-dor', rah], *m. & f.* Undertenant, subrenter.

Subarrendamiento [soob-ar-ren-dah-me-en'-to], *m.* Farming or renting under another renter.

Subarrendar [soob-ar-ren-dar'], *va.* To sublet, to sublease.

Subarrendatario, ria [soob-ar-ren-dah-tah'-re-o, ah], *m. & f.* One who takes a sub-lease: a sub-renter.

(*Yo subarriendo, yo subarriende,* from *Subarrendar.* *V.* ACRECENTAR.)

Subasta, Subastación [soo-bahs'-tah], *f.* Juridical sale of goods by public auction.
Subastar [soo-bas-tar'], *va.* To sell by auction.
Subcarbonato [soob-car-bo-nah'-to], *m.* (Chem.) Subcarbonate, a salt in which the base is in excess of the carbonic acid.
Subcolector [soob-co-lec-tor'], *m.* Subcollector.
Subcomendador [soob-co-men-dah-dor'], *m.* Deputy-commander of a military order.
Subconsciencia [soob-cons-the-en'-the-ah], *f.* Subconsciousness.
Subconsciente [soob-cons-the-en'-tay], *a.* Subconscious.
Subcutáneo, nea [soob-coo-tah'-nay-o, ah], *a.* Subcutaneous; below the skin.
Subdecano [soob-day-cah'-no], *m.* Subdean.
Subdécuplo, pla [soob-day'-coo-plo, plah], *a.* Subdecuple, containing one part of ten.
Subdelegable [soob-day-lay-gah'-blay], *a.* That which may de subdelegated.
Subdelegación [soob-day-lay-gah-the-on'], *f.* Subdelegation, substitution.
Subdelegado [soob-day-lay-gah'-do], *m.* Subdelegate.
Subdelegante [soob-day-lay-gahn'-tay], *pa.* He who subdelegates.
Subdelegar [soob-day-lay-gar'], *va.* To subdelegate, to commit to another one's jurisdiction or power.
Subdesarrollado, da [soob-day-sah-rol-lyah'-do, dah], *a.* Underdeveloped.
Subdesarrollo [soob-day-sah-rol'-lyo], *m.* Underdevelopment.
Subdiaconado, Subdiaconato [soob-de-ah-co-nah'-do], *m.* Subdeaconship.
Subdiácono [soob-de-ah'-co-no], *m.* Subdeacon.
Subdistinción [soob-dis-tin-the-on'], *f.* Subdistinction.
Subdistinguir [soob-dis-tin-geer'], *va.* To distinguish that which has already been distinguished.
Súbdito, ta [soob'-de-to, tah], *a.* Subject, inferior.
Subdividir [soob-de-ve-deer'], *va.* To subdivide.
Subdivisible [soob-de-ve-see'-blay], *a.* Subdivisible.
Subdivisión [soob-de-ve-se-on'], *f.* Subdivision, subsection.
Subduplo, pla [soob-doo'-plo, plah], *a.* Subduple, containing one part of two.
Subejecutor [soob-ay-hay-coo-tor'], *m.* Deputy executor.
Subentender [soob-en-ten-derr'], *va.* To understand what is tacitly meant.
Subérico [soo-bay'-re-co], *a.* Suberic, extracted from cork.
Suberina [soo-bay-ree'-nah], *f.* Suberine, a modification of cellulose found in cork.
Suberoso, sa [soo-bay-ro'-so, sah], *a.* Suberose, corky.
Subfletar [soob-flay-tar'], *va.* (Naut.) To hire a ship of another freighter.
Subgerente [soob-hay-ren'-tay], *m.* Assistant manager.
Subida [soo-bee'-dah], *f.* 1. Ascension, going up; mounting. 2. Ascent, acclivity, rise. 3. Accession of a disease. 4. Enhancement, rise, augmentation of value or price; melioration of things.
Subidero, ra [soo-be-day'-ro, rah], *a.* Mounting, rising.
Subidero, *m.* Ladder, mounting-block.
Subido, da [soo-bee'-do, dah], *a.* & *pp.* of SUBIR. 1. Raised on high, mounted. 2. Strong, having a deep tinge of colour; strong-scented. 3. Finest, most excellent.
Subidor [soo-be-dor'], *m.* Porter, one who carries things from lower to higher places.
Subiente [soo-be-en'-tay], *m.* (Arch.) Ornaments of foliage ascending on columns or pilasters.
Subilla [soo-beel'-lyah], *f.* Awl. *V.* ALESNA.
Subinquilino [soob-in-ke-lee'-no], *m.* Undertenant, one who rents a house of another tenant.
Subintración [soob-in-trah-the-on'], *f.* 1. Immediate succession of things. 2. (Med.) Subingression.
Subintrante [soob-in-trahn'-tay], *a.* Applied to fevers, one paroxysm of which has not subsided when another begins.
Subintrar [soob-in-trar'], *va.* To enter successively one after another.
Subir [soo-beer'], *vn.* 1. To mount, to ascend, to come up, to go up, to climb. 2. To increase, to swell, as rivers, etc. 3. Of numbers, to amount to. 4. To enter leaves, as silk-worms on commencing their cocoons. 5. To rise in dignity, fortune, etc. 6. (Mus.) To raise the voice gradually.—*va.* 1. To enhance, to increase the value. *Subir el color*, To raise a colour, to render it brighter. 2. To raise, to lift up; to build up, to erect. 3. To set up, to straighten from an inclined position. *Subir a caballo*, To mount a horse. *Subir la consulta al rey*, To lay an affair before the king. *Subirse de talones*, To grow proud and haughty. *Subirse a las bovedillas*, (Coll.) To be violently irritated. *Subirse a mayores*, (Coll.) To become supercilious, to act the lord. *Subirse el vino* or *licor a la cabeza*, To become tipsy, to be half-seas over. *Subirse a predicar*, To mount to the head (wine).
Súbitamente, Subitáneamente [soo'-be-tah-men-tay], *adv.* Suddenly, on a sudden.
Subitáneo, nea [soo-be-tah'-nay-o, ah], **Subitaño, ña**, *a.* Sudden, unexpected.
Súbito, ta [soo'-be-to, tah], *a.* Sudden, hasty, unforeseen, unexpected. *Súbito* or *de súbito*, *adv.* Suddenly, unexpectedly.
Subjectar, Subjetar, *va.* (Obs.) *V.* SUJETAR.
Subjeción [soob-hay-the-on'], *f.* (Rhet.) A figure used in debating and answering within ourselves.
Subjecto, *m.* (Obs.) *V.* SUJETO.
Subjetivo, va [soob-hay-tee'-vo, vah], *a.* Subjective.
Subjuntivo [soob-hoon-tee'-vo], *m.* (Gram.) Subjunctive.
Sublevación [soo-blay-vah-the-on'], *f.* **Sublevamiento**, *m.* Insurrection, sedition, revolt.
Sublevar [soo-blay-var'], *va.* To excite a rebellion.—*vr.* To rise in rebellion.
Sublimación [soo-ble-mah-the-on'], *f.* Sublimation, act of sublimating.
Sublimado [soo-ble-mah'-do], **Sublimado corrosivo**, *m.* (Chem.) Corrosive sublimate.—*Sublimado, da, pp.* of SUBLIMAR.
Sublimar [soo-ble-mar'], *va.* 1. To heighten, to elevate, to sublime, to exalt. 2. (Chem.) To sublimate.
Sublimatorio, ria [soo-ble-mah-to'-re-o, ah], *a.* Sublimatory.
Sublime [soo-blee'-may], *a.* Sublime, exalted, eminent, heroic, majestic.
Sublimemente, *adv.* Sublimely, loftily.
Sublimidad [soo-ble-me-dahd'], *f.* Sublimity, loftiness, grandeur.
Sublujación [soo-bloo-hah-the-on'], *f.* An imperfect luxation of a joint.
Sublunar [soob-loo-nar'], *a.* Sublunar, sublunary; terrestrial, earthly.
Submarino, na [soob-mah-ree'-no, nah], *a.* Submarine.—*m.* Submarine, submarine torpedo boat.
Subministrar, *va.* (Obs.) *V.* SUMINISTRAR.
Subordinación [soob-or-de-nah-the-on'], *f.* Subordination, subjection, subordinacy.
Subordinadamente, *adv.* Subordinately, subserviently.
Subordinado, da [soob-or-de-nah'-do, dah], *a.* & *pp.* of SUBORDINAR. Subordinate, subservient; subordinated.
Subordinar [soob-or-de-nar'], *va.* To subordinate, to subject.
Subpolar [soob-po-lar'], *a.* Under the pole.
Subprecio [soob-pray'-the-o], *m.* (Com.) Markdown.
Subprefecto [soob-pray-fec'-to], *m.* Subprefect, deputy prefect.
Subprefectura [soob-pray-fec-too'-rah], *f.* 1. In France and America, subprefecture, a division of a prefecture. 2. The office of subprefect, and time of its duration. 3. Town in which the subprefect lives and the place where he has his offices.
Subproducto [soob-pro-dooc'-to], *m.* By-product.
Subrayar [soob-rah-yar'], *va.* To underscore, to underline.
Subrepción [soob-rep-the-on'], *f.* 1. A hidden action, an underhand business. 2. Subreption, obtaining a favour by false representation; surreption.
Subrepticiamente, *adv.* Surreptitiously.
Subrepticio, cia [soob-rep-tee'-the-o, ah], *a.* 1. Surreptitious, fraudulently obtained. 2. Surreptitious, done in a clandestine manner.
Subrigadier [soob-bre-gah-de-err'], *m.* Sub-brigadier, an officer who discharged the duties of second sergeant in the Royal Guards.
Subrogación [soob-ro-gah-the-on'], *f.* Surrogation or subrogation, the act of putting in another's place.
Subrogar [soob-ro-gar'], *va.* To surrogate or to subrogate, to substitute.
Subsacristán [soob-sah-cris-tahn'], *m.* Deputy sacristan or sexton.
Subsacristanía [soob-sah-cris-tah-nee'-ah], *f.* Office of deputy sacristan.
Subsanar [soob-sah-nar'], *va.* 1. To exculpate, to excuse. 2. To mend, to repair.
Subscribir [soobs-cre-beer'], *va.* 1. To subscribe, to put a signature at the end of a writing. 2. To subscribe to, to accede, to agree to.—*vr.* To subscribe, to promise to pay a stipulated sum for the aid of some undertaking.
Subscripción, *f.* 1. Subscription, signature. 2. Subscription, contribution to an enterprise.
Subscripto, ta, Subscrito, ta [soobs-creep'-to, tah], *pp. irr.* of SUBSCRIBIR.
Subscriptor, ra, *m.* & *f.* Subscriber.
Subsecretario [soob-say-cray-tah'-re-o], *m.* The assistant secretary.
Subsecuencia [soob-say-coo-en'-the-ah], *f.* Subsequence.
Subsecuente [soob-say-coo-en'-tay], *a.* Subsequent. *V.* SUBSIGUIENTE.
Subsecuentemente, *adv.* *V.* SUBSIGUIENTEMENTE.
Subseguirse [soob-say-geer'-say], *vr.* To follow next.
Subséxtuplo, pla [soob-sex'-too-plo, plah], *a.* Subsextuple, containing one part of six.
Subsidiariamente, *adv.* In a subsidiary manner.
Subsidiario, ria [soob-se-de-ah'-re-o, ah], *a.* Subsidiary, auxiliary.

Subsidio [soob-see'-de-o], *m.* 1. Subsidy, aid: commonly of money. 2. Subsidy, war-tax.

Subsiguiente [soob-se-gee-en'-tay], *a.* Subsequent, succeeding.

Subsiguientemente, *adv.* Subsequently.

Subsistencia [soob-sis-ten'-the-ah], *f.* 1. Subsistence, permanence, stability. 2. Subsistence, competence, livelihood, living.

Subsistente [soob-sis-ten'-tay], *pa.* & *a.* Subsistent, subsisting.

Subsistir [soob-sis-teer'], *vn.* 1. To subsist, to last. 2. To subsist, to have the means of living.

Subsolano [soob-so-lah'-no], *m.* North-east wind.

Substancia [soobs-tahn'-the-ah], *f.* 1. Nutriment, sustenance, aliment, pabulum; whatever nourishes. 2. Sap which nourishes. 3. Substance, essence, being, nature of things. 4. Substance, property, wealth. *En substancia,* (1) (Med.) In substance. (2) *V.* SUSTANCIA.

Substancial [soobs-tan-the-ahl'], *a.* 1. Substantial, real, material. 2. Nutritive, nutritious. 3. Essential, of prime importance.

Substancialmente, *adv.* Substantially.

Substanciar [soobs-tan-the-ar'], *va.* 1. To extract the substance, to abridge. 2. To substantiate, to prove fully. 3. To pursue the proceedings in a cause until its final determination.

Substancioso, sa, *a.* 1. Nutritive, nutritious. 2. Substantial.

Substantivar [soobs-tan-te-var'], *va.* To use adjectives as substantives. *V.* SUSTANTIVAR.

Substantivo [soobs-tan-tee'-vo], *m.* (Gram.) *V.* SUSTANTIVO.

Substitución [soobs-te-too-the-on'], *f.* Substitution. *V.* SUSTITUCIÓN.

Substituir [soobs-te-too-eer'], *va.* To substitute. *V.* SUSTITUIR.

Substituyente [soobs-te-too-yen'-tay], *pa.* Substituting. *V.* SUSTITUYENTE.

Substituto [soobs-te-too'-to], *m.* Substitute. *V.* SUSTITUTO.

Substracción [soobs-trac-the-on'], *f.* 1. Subtraction, taking part from a whole. 2. Privation, concealment.

Substraendo [soobs-trah-en'-do], *m.* The subtrahend.

Substraer [soobs-trah-err'], *va.* To subtract, to remove.—*vr.* To withdraw one's self, to elude.

Subtangente [soob-tan-hen'-tay], *f.* (Geom.) Subtangent.

Subtender [soob-ten-derr'], *va.* 1. To sustain, to bear up. 2. (Geom.) To subtend.

Subteniente [soob-tay-ne-en'-tay], *m.* *V.* ALFÉREZ.

Subtensa [soob-ten'-sah], *f.* (Geom.) Subtense; chord.

Subtenso, sa [soob-ten'-so, sah], *pp. irr.* of SUBTENDER.

Subterfugio [soob-ter-foo'-he-o], *m.* Subterfuge, evasion, trick.

Subterráneamente, *adv.* Subterraneously.

Subterráneo, nea [soob-ter-rah'-nay-o, ah], *a.* Subterraneous, subterranean.

Subterráneo, *m.* 1. Subway. 2. Subterraneous structure. 3. Underground cave or vault.

Subtileza [soob-te-lay'-thah], *f.* (Obs.) *V.* SUTILEZA.

Subtilmente, *adv.* *V.* SUTILMENTE.

Subtilización, *f.* *V.* SUTILIZACIÓN.

Suburbano, na [soob-oor-bah'-no, nah], *a.* Suburban, relating to a suburb.—*n.* Suburban resident.

Suburbio [soob-oor'-be-o], *m.* Suburb, outskirt.

Subvención [soob-ven-the-on'], *f.* Help, assistance, aid, subvention.

Subvencionar [soob-ven-the-o-nar'], *va.* To subvention, to aid for an end.

Subvenir [soob-vay-neer'], *va.* 1. To aid, to assist, to succour. 2. To provide, to supply, to furnish, to defray.

Subversión, *f.* Subversion.

Subversivo, va [soob-ver-see'-vo, vah], *a.* Subversive, destructive.

Subversor [soob-ver-sor'], *m.* Subverter, overturner.

Subvertir [soob-ver-teer'], *va.* To subvert, to destroy, to ruin.

Subyugar [soob-yoo-gar'], *va.* To subdue, to subjugate, to overcome.

Succeder [sooc-thay-derr'], *vn.* *V.* SUCEDER. (Acad.)

Succesión [sooc-thay-se-on'], *f.* SUCESIÓN.

Succesor, ra [sooc-thay-sor', rah], *m.* & *f.* *V.* SUCESOR.

Succino [sooc-thee'-no], *m.* Succinite, amber.

Succión [sooc-the-on'], *f.* 1. Suction drawing in with the breath. 2. Suck.

Suceder [soo-thay-derr'], *vn.* 1. To succeed, to come after one, to follow in order. 2. To inherit, to succeed by inheritance, to come to an estate. 3. (For.) To come into the place of one who has quitted or died.—*v. impers.* To happen, to come to pass, to come about, to fall out. *Sucedió así,* It happened so. *Suceda lo que sucediere,* Happen what may.

Sucesible [soo-thay-see'-blay], *a.* Capable of success.

Sucesión [soo-thay-se-on'], *f.* 1. Succession, series, concatenation. 2. Issue, offspring, children.

Sucesivamente, *adv.* Successively.

Sucesivo, va [soo-thay-see'-vo, vah], *a.* Successive, following in order, consecutive. *En lo sucesivo,* In time, in process of time; hereafter.

Suceso [soo-thay'-so], *m.* 1. Event, incident. 2. Issue, result, outcome; success. 3. *V.* TRANSCURSO.

Sucesor, ra [soo-thay-sor', rah], *m.* & *f.* Successor, succeeder.

Suciamente, *adv.* Nastily, filthily, foully.

Suciedad [soo-the-ay-dahd'], *f.* Nastiness, filthiness, obscenity.

Sucino [soo-thee'-no], *m.* Amber. *V.* SUCCINO.

Sucintamente, *adv.* Succinctly, briefly.

Sucintarse, *vr.* *V.* CEÑIRSE.

Sucinto, ta [soo-theen'-to, tah], *a.* 1. Girded, tucked up. 2. Brief, succinct, compendious, concise.

Sucio, cia [soo'-the-o, ah], *a.* 1. Dirty, nasty, filthy. 2. Stained with sin, tainted with guilt and imperfections. 3. Obscene, unchaste, smutty. 4. Uncivil, unpolished. 5. (Naut.) Foul: applied to a ship's bottom, to the sky or weather; to rowing out of rhythm; and to a rocky shore, or a bottom where there are reefs.

Suco [soo'-co], *m.* Juice; sap.—*a.* (Amer.) Orange-coloured.

Sucoso, sa [soo-co'-so, sah], *a.* Juicy, succulent. *V.* JUGOSO.

Sucotrino [soo-co-tree'-no], *a.* Socotrine: applied to a kind of aloes from the island of Socotra, hence its name.

Súcubo [soo'-coo-bo], *m.* Succubus, a pretended demon, which, in intercourse with men, took the form of a woman.

Sucucho [soo-coo'-cho], *m.* Store-room of a ship. *Sucucho del condestable,* (Naut.) Gunner's room. *Sucucho del contramaestre,* Boatswain's store-room.

Súcula [soo'-coo-lah], *f.* Cylinder. *V.* CABRIA.

Suculencia [soo-coo-len'-the-ah], *f.* Juiciness, succulence.

Suculento, ta [soo-coo-len'-to, tah], *a.* Succulent, juicy. *V.* JUGOSO.

Sucumbir [soo-coom-beer'], *vn.* 1. (Law) To lose a suit at law. 2. To succumb, to yield, to sink under a difficulty. 3. (Met.) To die.

Sucursal [soo-coor-sahl'], *a.* & *f.* Ancillary, subsidiary, succursal: used primarily of a minor church, thence of other establishments; branch of a commercial house.

Suche [soo'-chay], *m.* 1. A fragrant yellow flower esteemed in Peru. 2. A fish of Lake Titicaca, held in high esteem.

Suchicopal [soo-che-co-pahl'], *m.* A kind of copal or styrax.

Sud [sood], *m.* 1. The south. 2. South, the south wind.

Sudadero [soo-dah-day'-ro], *m.* 1. Handkerchief, for wiping off the sweat. 2. Bath, sweating-room, sudatory. 3. Moist ground, a place where water oozes out by drops. 4. Sweating-place for sheep previous to their being shorn.

Sudamericano, na [soo-dah-may-re-cah'-no, nah], *a.* South American.

Sudador, ra [soo-dah-dor', rah], *a.* & *n.* That which sweats or exudes.

Sudante [soo-dahn'-tay], *pa.* Sweating.

Sudar [soo-dar'], *vn.* 1. To sweat, to perspire, to exude. Sometimes used transitively. 2. To give with repugnance. 3. To toil, to labour. 4. To ooze, to distil. *Hacer sudar la prensa,* To print much.

Sudario [soo-dah'-re-o], *m.* 1. Handkerchief or cloth for wiping off the sweat. 2. Cloth put on the face of the dead.

Sudatorio, ria [soo-dah-to'-re-o, ah], *a.* Sudorific, causing sweat.

Sudeste [soo-des'-tay], *m.* South-east.

Sudoeste [soo-do-es'-tay], *m.* 1. South-west. *Sudoeste cuarto al oeste,* South-west by west. *Sudoeste cuarto al sur,* South-west by south. 2. South-west wind; (naut.) sou'-wester.

Sudor [soo-dor'], *m.* 1. Sweat, perspiration. 2. Sweat, labour, toil, drudgery. 3. Viscous matter or gum that distils from trees. *Cubrirse de sudor,* To sweat profusely.

Sudoriento, ta [soo-do-re-en'-to, tah], *a.* Sweated, moistened with sweat.

Sudorífero, ra [soo-do-ree'-fay-ro, rah], *a.* Sudorific, causing sweat.

Sudorífico, ca [soo-do-ree'-fe-co, cah], *a.* (Med.) Sudorific, promoting sweat.

Sudorífico [soo-do-ree'-fe-co], *m.* Sudorific, a medicine promoting sweat.

Sudoso, sa [soo-do'-so, sah], *a.* Sweaty, moist with sweat.

Sudsudeste [sood-soo-des'-tay], *m.* South-south-east.

Sudsudoeste [sood-soo-do-es'-tay], *m.* South-south-west.

Sudueste [soo-doo-es'-tay], *m.* South west. *V.* ÁFRICO and SUDOESTE.

Sueco, ca [soo-ay'-co-cah], *a.* Swedish *Hacerse uno el sueco,* (Coll.) To wink at a thing, to pretend not to have taken notice.

Suegra [soo-ay'-grah], *f.* 1. Mother in-law. 2. A hard crust of bread.

Suegrecita [soo-ay-gray-thee'-tah], *f. dim.* (Coll.) Little mother-in-law.

Suegro [soo-ay'-gro], *m.* Father-in-law.

Suela [soo-ay'-lah], *f.* 1. Sole of the shoe. 2. Sole-leather. 3. (Zool.) Sole. Pleuronectes solea. 4. A horizontal rafter, laid as the foundation for partition-walls. 5. Leather tip of a billiard cue. *Suelas*, A kind of sandals, worn by some religious orders. *De tres* or *cuatro suelas*, Firm, solid. *Tonto de cuatro suelas*, A downright fool.

Suelda, or **Suelda consuelda** [soo-el'-dah], *f.* (Bot.) *V.* SÍNFITO OFICINAL.

Sueldacostilla [soo-el-dah-cos-teel'-lyah], *f.* (Bot.) A bulbous plant.

Sueldo [soo-el'-do], *m.* 1. In Arragon, coin or money worth half a real of plate. 2. An ancient Roman coin. 3. Sou or sol, a French penny. 4. Sold, pay given to soldiers. 5. Wages, salary, stipend. *Sueldo menos los descuentos*, Take-home pay, net amount due an employee after deductions have been made.

(*Yo sueldo, yo suelde*, from *Soldar. V.* ACORDAR.)

Suelo [soo-ay'-lo], *m.* 1. Ground, soil, surface of the earth. 2. Earth, terra firma, the principal part of the world; hence the earth. 3. Pavement, ground-floor. 4. Floor, flooring, story. 5. The bottom or lower part of various things, as of a well, a vase, of a jar of wine; sole of any thing that touches the ground. 6. Dregs, lees, settlings of any liquid. 7. Ground-plot, ground on which a building stands. 8. End; bottom.—*pl.* 1. (Vulg. Vet.) Sole, plantar face of a horse's hoof. 2. Scatterings or leavings of grain. *Suelo del estribo*, Rest of a stirrup. *Dar en el suelo con una cosa*, To bring any thing to the ground. *Echarse por los suelos*, (1) To stretch one's self on the ground. (2) To humble one's self too much. *Llevar de suelo y propiedad*, To be peculiar to a person or thing from its source or origin. *Venirse al suelo*, To fall to the ground. *Sin suelo*, To excess; without bounds. *Dar consigo en el suelo*, To fall down. *Medir el suelo*, To stretch one's self on the ground at full length. *No salir del suelo*, To be short of stature; not to grow, not to thrive. *Por los suelos*, Cast down, in a state of depreciation; prostrate.

(*Yo suelo, yo suela*, from *Soler V.* SOLER.)

Suelta [soo-el'-tah], *f.* 1. Act of loosening or letting loose; solution. 2. Fetters, with which the feet of a beast are tied when grazing. *Dar suelta*, To give permission to a scholar or inferior to go out and amuse himself.

Sueltamente, *adv.* Loosely, lightly, expeditiously; licentiously; spontaneously; laxly.

Suelto, ta [soo-el'-to, tah], *a.* & *pp. irr.* of SOLTAR. 1. Loose, light, expeditious, swift, able. 2. Free, bold, daring. 3. Easy, disengaged. 4. Voluble, fluent. 5. Blank: applied to verse without rhyme. 6. (Coll.) *V.* SOLTERO. 7. (Scil. dinero) Small change. *Suelto de lengua*, Audacious, shameless, ill-tongued, free to speak. *Arena suelta*, Loose sand. *Comprar cosas sueltas* or *al suelto*, To buy things by the lump or bulk.

Suelto [soo-el'-to], *m.* Loose piece of metal or mineral found near mines.

(*Yo suelto, yo suelte*, from *Soltar. V.* ACORDAR.)

(*Yo suelvo, yo suelva*, from *Solver. V.* ABSOLVER.)

(*Yo sueno, yo suene*, from *Sonar. V.* ACORDAR.)

Sueño [soo-ay'-nyo], *m.* 1. Sleep, the act of sleeping. 2. Vision, dream, phantasm, the fancies of a sleeping person. 3. Drowsiness, heaviness inclination to sleep. *Tengo sueño*, I am sleepy. 4. Any fantastical idea without foundation. 5. Shortness, lightness, or swiftness with which any thing appears or passes. *A sueño suelto*, Without care. *Caerse de sueño*, To be overcome with drowsiness. *Conciliar el sueño*, To woo sleep. *Descabezar el sueño*, To take a nap. *El sueño de la liebre*, A hare's sleep (that is, feigned). *Espantar el sueño*, To scare away sleep, to prevent sleeping. *En sueños* or *entre sueños*, Dreaming, sleeping. *A sueño pesado*, In a profound sleep; deep sleep; difficult to dispel. *Ni por sueño*, By no means; it was never dreamed of. *No dormir sueño*, To be watchful, to be unable to sleep.

(*Yo sueño, yo sueñe*. from *Soñar. V.* ACORDAR.)

Suero [soo-ay'-ro, *m.* 1. Whey. 2. Serum, aqueous humour of the blood.

Sueroso, sa [soo-ay-ro'-so, sah], *a. V.* SEROSO.

Suerte [soo-err'-tay], *f.* 1. Chance, fortuitous event; lot, fortune, luck, fate, doom, good-luck, haphazard. 2. Kind, sort; species. 3. Manner, mode, way. *De la misma suerte*, The same way. 4. Skilful movements of a bull-fighter. 5. Piece of ground separated from the rest by bounds or landmarks. 6. Original, stock, lineage. *La suerte está echada*, The die is cast. *Suerte y verdad*, Appeal from players to the spectators for the justness of their case. *Suerte* or *suerte de caña*, (Amer.) Each patch or lot into which a large sugar-cane field is divided. *De suerte*, So as, so that, thus. *De suerte que no debe nada*, So that he owes nothing. *Caerle a uno la suerte*, To fall to one's lot. *Entrar en suerte*, To take part in a raffle. *Echar suertes*, To cast or draw lots. *Este me cupo en suerte*, It fell to my lot.—*pl. Suertes*, Feats, tricks; legerdemain.

Suestar [soo-es-tar'], *vn.* (Naut.) To veer towards the south-east.

Sueste [soo-es'-tay], *m.* South-east. *Sueste cuarto al este*, (Naut.) South-east by east. *Sueste cuarto al sur*, (Naut.) South-east by south.

Sufi [soo-fee'], *m.* Sufi. a Mohammedan mystic in Persia. *V.* SUFISMO.

Suficiencia [soo-fe-the-en'-the-ah], *f.* Sufficiency. *A suficiencia*, Sufficiently, enough.

Suficiente [soo-fe-the-en'-tay], *a.* 1. Sufficient, enough. 2. Qualified, apt, fit, capable, competent.

Suficientemente, *adv.* Sufficiently, competently.

Sufijo, ja [soo-fee'-ho, hah], *a.* Suffixed, affixed.—*m.* Suffix, affix.

Sufismo [soo-fees'-mo], *m.* A pantheistic mystical doctrine among Mohammedans, chiefly in Persia.

Sufocación [soo-fo-cah-the-on'], *f.* Suffocation. *V.* SOFOCACIÓN.

Sufocador, ra [soo-fo-cah-dor', rah], *m.* & *f.* Suffocator, choker.

Sufocante [soo-fo-cahn'-tay], *pa.* & *a.* Suffocating, suffocative.

Sufocar [soo-fo-car'], *va.* 1. To suffocate, to choke, to smother. 2. To quench or put out fire. 3. To molest, to harass, to oppress. *V.* SOFOCAR.

Sufoco [soo-fo'-co], *m.* (Prov.) Suffocation, fumigation.

Sufra [soo'-frah], *f.* A stout strap which receives the shafts of a carriage; ridge-band.

Sufragáneo, Sufragano [soo-frah-gah'-nay-o], *m.* Suffragan, a bishop subject to a metropolitan.

Sufragáneo, ea, *a.* Belonging to a suffragan.

Sufragar [soo-frah'-gar], *va.* 1. To favour, to aid, to assist. 2. To suffice, to be sufficient. 3. To defray; to make up.

Sufragio [soo-frah'-he-o], *m.* 1. Vote, suffrage, voice. 2. Favour, support, aid, assistance. 3. Suffrage, any work appropriated to the souls of the deceased in purgatory.

Sufragista [soo-frah-hees'-tah], *f.* Suffragist.

Sufrible [soo-free'-blay], *a.* Sufferable, tolerable, bearable.

Sufridera [soo-fre-day'-rah], *f.* Smith's tool for punching holes on an anvil.

Sufridero, ra [soo-fre-day'-ro, rah], *a.* Supportable, tolerable.

Sufrido, da [soo-free'-do, dah], *a.* & *pp.* of SUFRIR. 1. Bearing up under adversities, long-suffering. 2. Consenting, accommodating: spoken of a contented cuckold. *Mal sufrido*, Impatient, rude, severe.

Sufridor, ra [soo-fre-dor', rah], *m.* & *f.* Sufferer, one who suffers patiently.

Sufriente [soo-fre-en'-tay], *pa.* Tolerating, bearing.

Sufrimiento [soo-fre-me-en'-to], *m.* Sufferance, patience, tolerance.

Sufrir [soo-freer'], *va.* 1. To suffer, to bear with patience, to undergo. 2. To bear or carry a load; to sustain an attack. 3. To clinch a nail. 4. To permit, to tolerate. 5. To pay and suffer. 6. To abide; to comport; to go under. *No sufrir cosquillas* or *morisquetas*, Not to suffer jokes or tricks; to be easily displeased or angry. *No sufrir pulgas*, To be ill-tempered. *Es menester sufrir y consufrir*, (prov.) We must bear and forbear. *Sufre por saber, y trabaja por tener*, Bear inconveniences to acquire knowledge, and labour to get wealth.

Sufumigación [soo-foo-me-gah-the-on'], *f.* Suffumigation, operation of fumes, administered as a remedy or cure.

Sufusión [soo-foo-se-on'], *f.* Suffusion, kind of cataract in the eyes.

Sugerente [soo-hay-ren'-tay], *pa.* Suggesting.

Sugerir [soo-hay-reer'], *va.* 1. To hint, to suggest, to intimate. 2. To suggest, to prompt, to instigate to an evil action.

Sugestión [soo-hes-te-on'], *f.* 1. Suggestion, intimation, hint. 2. Temptation by the devil. 3. *Sugestión magnética* or *hipnótica*, Hypnotic suggestion, control of the will of the person hypnotized.

Sugestionar [soo-hes-te-o-nar'], *va.* & *vr.* To influence by suggestion.

Sugo [soo'-go], *m.* (Prov.) *V.* JUGO.

Suicida [soo-e-thee'-dah], *com.* Suicide, a self-murderer.

Suicidarse [soo-e-the-dar'-say], *vr.* To commit suicide.

Suicidio [soo-e-thee'-de-o], *m.* Suicide, self-murder.

Suite [soo-ee'-tay], *m.* A Central American dwarf palm used for thatching. Geonoma (species).

Suiza [soo-ee'-thah], *f.* Company of persons dressed in the Swiss fashion at a public festival.

Suizo, za [soo-ee'-tho, thah], *a.* Swiss.

Sujeción [soo-hay-the-on'], *f.* 1. Subjection, the act of subduing; coercion, control, obedience; the act of submitting or surrendering; connection. 2. Objection, argument.

Sujetar [soo-hay-tar'], *va.* 1. To subdue, to reduce to submission. 2. To subject, to put under, to keep down, to overcome, to conquer, to make liable.—*vr.* To be inherent, to adhere.

Sujeto, ta [soo-hay'-to, tah], *a.* & *pp. irr.* of SUJETAR. 1. Subject, liable, exposed, chargeable. 2. Amenable before a court of justice.

Sujeto [soo-hay'-to], *m.* 1. Subject, topic, theme, matter in discussion. 2. (Gram.) Subject, that of which something is affirmed (or denied). 3. A person: commonly used to express any undefined person or individual. *Es un buen sujeto,* (Coll.) He is a clever fellow; also, he is an honest man.

Sulfanilamida [sool-fah-ne-lah-mee'-dah], *f.* Sulfanilamide, sulfa.

Sulfapiridina [sool-fah-pe-re-dee'-nah], *f.* Sulfapyridine.

Sulfatiazol [sool-fah-te-ah-thole'], *m.* Sulfathiazole.

Sulfato [sool-fah'-to], *m.* Sulphate. *Sulfato de cobre,* Copper sulphate.

Sulfido [sool-fee'-do], *m.* Sulphid, sulfid, or sulphide

Sulfhídrico [soolf-ee'-dre-co], *a.* Sulphydric, hydrosulphuric (acid).

Sulfito [sool-fee'-to], *m.* Sulphite, a salt of sulphurous acid.

Sulfonamida [sool-fo-nah-mee'-dah], *f.* Sulfonamide.

Sulfonamidas [sool-fo-nah-mee'-dahs], *f. pl.* Sulfa drugs.

Súlfur [sool'-foor], *m.* Brimstone, sulphur. *V.* AZUFRE.

Sulfurar [sool-foo-rar'], *va.* To irritate, to anger, to enrage.

Sulfúreo, rea [sool-foo'-ray-o, ah], *a.* Sulphureous, sulphurous.

Sulfúrico [sool-foo'-re-co], *a.* 1. Sulphuric: applied to an acid. 2. Sulphuric, consisting of sulphur.

Sulfuro [sool-foo'-ro], *m.* Sulphid, sulphide, sulfid: a combination of sulphur with a metal.

Sulfuroso, sa [sool-foo-ro' so, sah], *a.* 1. Sulphurous, containing sulphur. 2. Sulphurous acid, containing one molecule of sulphur to two of oxygen. SO_2.

Sultán [sool-tahn'], *m.* 1. Sultan, an appellation which the Turks give to their emperor. 2. Mohammedan prince or governor.

Sultana [sool-tah'-nah], *f.* Sultana or sultaness, the queen of a Turkish emperor.

Suma [soo'-mah], *f.* 1. Sum, the whole of any thing. 2. Sum, many particulars aggregated to a total; a sum of money. 3. Substance, heads of any thing. 4. Sum, amount or result of reasoning or computation; act of summing up, conclusion. 5. Sum, compendium, abridgment. *Suma del frente* or *suma de la vuelta,* Brought forward. *En suma,* In short; finally.

Sumaca [soo-mah'-cah], *f.* A small schooner used in the coasting trade along the Atlantic coast of South America.

Sumadora mecánica [soo-mah-do'-rah may-cah'-ne-cah], *f.* Adding machine.

Sumamente, *adv.* Chiefly; extremely, mightily, highly.

Sumando [soo-mahn'-do], *m.* (Math.) Each of the quantities which are added together.

Sumar [soo-mar'], *va.* 1. To sum, to collect particulars into a total; to add. 2. To collect into a narrow compass; to sum up, to recapitulate.—*vn.* To cast up accounts; to result.

Sumaria [soo-mah'-re-ah], *f.* The preparatory proceeding in a suit at law; verbal process.

Sumariamente, *adv.* Summarily; in a plain manner.

Sumario, ria [soo-mah'-re-o, ah], *a.* Summary, compendious; plain, without formalities.

Sumario, *m.* Compendium, abridgment, summary, abstract, compend; result of computation.

Sumergible [soo-mer-hee'-blay], *a.* Submergible, submersible, sinkable.—*m.* Submersible, submarine.

Sumergimiento [soo-mer-he-me-en'-to], *m.* *V.* SUMERSIÓN.

Sumergir [soo-mer-heer'], *va.* 1. To submerge, to drown, to immerse. 2. To embarrass, to involve in difficulties.

Sumersión [soo-mer-se-on'], *f.* Submersion, immersion.

Sumidad [soo-me-dahd'], *f.* Top, summit.

Sumidero [soo-me-day'-ro], *m.* Sewer, drain, sink.

Sumido, da [soo-mee'-do, dah], *a.* & *pp.* of SUMIR. Drowned; overflowed; plunged into vice.

Sumiller [soo-mil-lyerr'], *m.* Chief of several offices in the king's household. *Sumiller de corps,* Lord chamberlain. *Sumiller de cortina,* Vice-groom of the king's bedchamber: a title of honour given to dignified clergymen. *Sumiller de la cava,* Yeoman butler of the king's cellar. *Sumiller de la panetería,* Yeoman baker of the king.

Sumillería [soo-mil-lyay-ree'-ah], *f.* Lord chamberlain's office.

Suministración [soo-me-nis-trah-the-on'], *f.* Supply, the act of furnishing or supplying, subministration.

Suministrador, ra [soo-me-nis-trah-dor', rah], *m.* & *f.* Provider, one who subministers.

Suministrar [soo-mee-nis-trar'], *va.* To subminister, to supply, to furnish, to minister.

Sumir [soo-meer'], *va.* To take; to receive: in this sense it is confined to the receiving of the chalice in the celebration of the mass.—*vr.* 1. To sink under ground, to be swallowed up. 2. To be sunk: applied to features of the face. *Sumir un barco,* (Naut.) To stave a vessel.

Sumisamente, *adv.* Submissively, low.

Sumisa voce [soo-mee'-sah vo'-thay]. (Lat.) In a low voice.

Sumisión [soo-me-se-on'], *f.* 1. Submission, obsequiousness, compliance, acquiescence, obedience. 2. (Law) Renunciation.

Sumiso, sa [soo-mee'-so, sah], *a.* Submissive, humble, resigned, compliant, meek.

Sumista [soo-mees'-tah], *m.* Abridger, writer of compendiums or summaries; computer; young student in morality.

Sumo, ma [soo'-mo, mah], *a.* Highest, loftiest, greatest; most elevated; excessive. *A lo sumo,* At most; to the highest pitch.

Sunción [soon-the-on'], *f.* Receiving the chalice at mass.

Suncho [soon'-cho], *m.* (Naut.) Clamp. *Sunchos de la bomba,* Pump-clamps. *Sunchos de botalones de las alas,* Studding-sail-boom irons. *Sunchos de cabrestante,* Capstan-hooks. *Sunchos del cepo del ancla,* Anchor-stock-hoops. *Sunchos de fogonaduras,* Partners. *Sunchos de los palos,* Mast-hoops.

Sunsún [soon-soon'], *m.* (Cuban) A humming-bird.

Suntuario, ria [soon-too-ah'-re-o, ah], *a.* Sumptuary: applied to laws relating to expense or regulating the cost of living.

Suntuosamente, *adv.* Sumptuously.

Suntuosidad [soon-too-o-se-dahd'], *f.* Sumptuosity, costliness, sumptuousness.

Suntuoso, sa [soon-too-oh'-so, sah], *a.* Sumptuous, expensive; new-fangled.

Supedáneo [soo-pay-dah'-nay-o], *m.* Species of pedestal to a crucifix.

Supeditación [soo-pay-de-tah-the-on'], *f.* The act of subduing or trampling under foot.

Supeditado, da [soo-pay-de-tah'-do, dah], *pp.* of SUPEDITAR. Trampled under foot. *Supeditado de los contrarios,* Suppressed by enemies.

Supeditar [soo-pay-de-tar'], *va.* To subdue, to trample under foot, to overpower.

Súper. A Latin preposition, used in composition, denoting (a) over, above; (b) pre-eminence.

Superable [soo-pay-rah'-blay], *a.* Superable, conquerable.

Superabundancia [soo-per-ah-boon-dahn'-the-ah], *f.* Superabundance, overflow.

Superabundante [soo-per-ah-boon-dahn'-tay], *pa.* & *a.* Superabundant, luxuriant.

Superabundantemente, *adv.* Superabundantly, overflowingly.

Superabundar [soo-per-ah-boon-dar'], *vn.* To superabound.

Superano [soo-pay-rah'-no], *m.* (Mus.) *V.* TIPLE.

Superante [soo-pay-rahn'-tay], *pa.* Surpassing, surmounting.

Superar [soo-pay-rar'], *va.* To overcome, to conquer, to surpass, to excel, to overpower.

Superávit [soo-pay-rah'-vit], *m.* (Lat.) Overplus, residue.

Superciliar [soo-per-the-le-ar'], *a.* Superciliary, above the eye-brows.

Supercheria [soo-per-chay-ree'-ah], *f.* Artful fallacy, fraud, deceit, or cozenage; foul dealing.

Superchero, ra [soo-per-chay'-ro, rah], *a.* Wily, deceitful, insidious.

Supereminencia [soo-per-ay-me-nen'-the-ah], *f.* Supereminence.

Supereminente [soo-per-ay-me-nen'-tay], *a.* Supereminent.

Supererogación [soo-per-ay-ro-gah-the-on'], *f.* Supererogation.

Supererogatorio, ria [soo-per-ay-ro-gah-to'-re-o, ah], *a.* Supererogatory.

Superestructura [soo-per-es-trooc-too'-rah], *f.* Superstructure.

Superfetación [soo-per-fay-tah-the-on'], *f.* Superfetation, superimpregnation.

Superficial [soo-per-fe-the-ahl'], *a.* 1. Superficial, on the surface. 2. Superficial, shallow, smattering.

Superficialidad [soo-per-fe-the-ah-le-dahd'], *f.* Superficiality.

Superficialmente, *adv.* Superficially, flashily; on the surface.

Superficiario, ria [soo-per-fe-the-ah'-re-o, ah], *a.* *V.* SUPERFICIONARIO.

Superficie [soo-per-fee'-the-ay], *f.* Superficies, surface, area.

Superficionario, ria [soo-per-fe-the-o-nah'-re-o, rah], *a.* (Law) Applied to those who occupy the property of others by paying rent.

Superfino, na [soo-per-fee'-no, nah], *a.* Superfine.

Superfluamente [soo-per-floo-ah-men'-tay], *adv.* Superfluously.

Superfluidad [soo-per-floo-e-dahd'], *f.* Superfluity.

Superfluo, ua [soo-per'-floo-o, ah], *a.* Superfluous, exuberant.

Superfosfato [soo-per-fos-fah'-to], *m.* Superphosphate.

Superhombre [soo-per-om'-bray], *m.* Superman.

Superhumeral [soo-per-oo-may-rahl'], *m.* Ephod, scapulary; band for the cover of a reliquary.

Superintendencia [soo-per-in-ten-den'-the-ah], *f.* 1. Superintendence, supervision. 2. Charge and jurisdiction of a superintendent; superintendency.

Superintendente [soo-per-in-ten-den'-tay], *com.* 1. Superintendent, intendant; an officer of high rank, who oversees any allotment of public business. *Superintendente de la casa de moneda,* Warden of the mint. 2. Comptroller, overseer, supervisor.

Superior [soo-pay-re-or'], *a.* Superior, paramount, higher, greater. *Alemania superior,* Upper Germany.

Superior, ra [soo-pay-re-or', rah], *m.* & *f.* Superior.

Superiorato [soo-pay-re-o-rah'-to], *m.* Office of a superior and the term of such office.

Superioridad [soo-pay-re-o-re-dahd'], *f.* Superiority, pre-eminence.

Superiormente [soo-pay-re-or-men'-tay], *adv.* Masterly, in a superior manner.

Superlativar [soo-per-lah-te-var'], *va.* To make a term superlative.

Superlativo, va [soo-per-lah-tee'-vo, vah], *a.* Superlative. *En grado superlativo,* Superlatively.

Supermercado [soo-per-mer-cah'-do], *m.* Supermarket.

Superno, na [soo-per'-no, nah], *a.* Supreme, highest, supernal.

Supernumerario, ria [soo-per-noo-may-rah'-re-o, ah], *a.* Supernumerary.

Superpoblado, da [soo-per-po-blah'-do, dah], *a.* Overpopulated.

Superposición [soo-per-po-se-the-on'], *f.* 1. Addition. 2. Placing above. 3. Superposition.

Superpotencia [soo-per-po-ten'-the-ah], *f.* (Pol.) Superpower.

Superproducción [soo-per-pro-dooc-the-on'], *f.* Overproduction.

Supersaturar [soo-per-sah-too-rar'], *va.* To supersaturate.

Supersónico, ca [soo-per-so'-ne-co, cah], *a.* Supersonic.

Superstición [soo-pers-te-the-on'], *f.* Superstition.

Supersticiosamente, *adv.* Superstitiously.

Supersticioso, sa [soo-pers-te-the-o'-so, sah], *a.* Superstitious; scrupulous beyond need.

Supersubstancial [soo-per-soobs-tahn-the-ahl'], *a.* Supersubstantial: applied to the eucharistical bread.

Supervalente [soo-per-vah-len'-tay], *a.* Prevalent, exceeding in value.

Supervaler [soo-per-vah-lerr'], *vn.* (Obs.) To exceed in value, to be worth more.

Supervención [soo-per-ven-the-on'], *f.* (For.) The taking effect of a new law.

Superveniencia [soo-per-vay-ne-en'-the-ah], *f.* Supervention, the act of supervening.

Superveniente [soo-per-vay-ne-en'-tay], *pa.* & *a.* Supervenient, supervening.

Supervenir [soo-per-vay-neer'], *vn.* To supervene; to come as an extraneous addition. *V.* SOBREVENIR.

Supervivencia [soo-per-ve-ven'-the-ah], *f.* 1. Survivorship. 2. Money or annuity, stipulated in marriage settlements in favour of the surviving consort.

Supinación [soo-pe-nah-the-on'], *f.* Supination, lying with the face upward.

Supinador [soo-pe-nah-dor'], *a.* Supinator, a muscle turning the hand palm upward.

Supino, na [soo-pee'-no, nah], *a.* 1. Supine, indolent, lying with the face upward. 2. Ignorant from negligence.

Supino, *m.* (Gram.) Supine.

(*Yo supongo, suponga, supuse, supondré,* from *Suponer. V.* PONER.)

Supir, *va.* (Obs.) *V.* SABER.

Súpito, ta [soo'-pe-to, tah], *a.* (Obs. Coll.) *V.* SÚBITO.

Suplantación [soo-plan-tah-the-on'], *f.* Supplanting, the act of supplanting.

Suplantador, ra [soo-plan-tah-dor', rah], *m.* & *f.* Supplanter.

Suplantar [soo-plan-tar'], *va.* 1. To falsify a writing by blotting out words, and putting others in their place. 2. (Coll.) To supplant, to displace by stratagem.

Supleción [soo-play-the-on'], *f.* (Obs.) Act and effect of supplying.

Suplefaltas [soo-play-fahl'-tas], *m.* (Coll.) Substitute.

Suplemento [soo-play-men'-to], *m.* 1. Supply, the act of supplying. 2. Supplement.

Supletorio, ria [soo-play-to'-re-o, ah], *a.* Suppletory, supplemental, that which fills up deficiencies.

Súplica [soo'-ple-cah], *f.* Petition, request, supplication, memorial. (Coll.) A favour asked.

Suplicación [soo-ple-cah-the-on'], *f.* 1. Request, petition, supplication. 2. (For.) Appeal from the decision of a court. 3. Conical tube of thin and light paste; a kind of pastry. *V.* BARQUILLO. *A suplicación,* By petition, memorializing.

Suplicante [soo-ple-cahn'-tay], *pa.* & *m.* & *f.* Supplicant, petitioning; memorialist, petitioner, suitor; suitress.

Suplicar [soo-ple-car'], *va.* 1. To entreat, to implore, to supplicate, to crave. 2. To make a humble reply to a superior. *Suplicar en revista,* To apply for a new trial. *Suplicar de la sentencia,* To petition against the sentence; to appeal to a higher court.

Suplicatoria [soo-ple-cah-to'-re-ah], *f.* (Law) Letters rogatory, or a writ or any legal instrument sent in the king's name by a tribunal or judge to another of equal authority, that they may attend to what is solicited.

Suplicio [soo-plee'-the-o], *m.* 1. Punishment, torture. *Último suplicio,* Capital punishment, pain of death. 2. Place of execution. 3. (Met.) Bodily or mental suffering, anguish.

Suplidor, ra [soo-ple-dor', rah], *m.* & *f.* Substitute, deputy.

Supliente [soo-ple-en'-tay], *pa.* & *a.* Substitute, supplying.

Suplimiento [soo-ple-me-en'-to], *m. V.* SUPLEMENTO.

Suplir [soo-pleer'], *va.* 1. To supply, to fill up as deficiencies happen, to furnish. 2. To supply, to serve instead of. 3. To excuse, to overlook, to disguise.

Suponedor, ra [soo-po-nay-dor', rah], *m.* & *f.* Supposer.

Suponer [soo-po-nerr'], *va.* 1. To suppose, to surmise. *Supongamos* or *supóngase,* Let us suppose. 2. To suppose, to fancy, to imagine.—*vn.* To possess weight or authority.

Suportar [soo-por-tar'], *va. V.* SOBRELLEVAR.

Suposición [soo-po-se-the-on'], *f.* 1. Supposition, surmise. 2. Authority, distinction, eminence in point of talents. 3. Imposition, falsehood. 4. (Logic) Acceptance of one term in place of another.

Supositar [soo-po-se-tar'], *va.* (Divin.) To exist under both divine and human nature in one person.

Supositicio, cia [soo-po-se-tee'-the-o, ah], *a.* Supposititious. *V.* FINGIDO.

Supositivo, va [soo-po-se-tee'-vo, vah], *a.* Suppositive, implying supposition.

Supósito [soo-po'-se-to], *m.* (Obs.) *V.* SUPUESTO.

Supositorio [soo-po-se-to'-re-o], *m.* (Med.) Suppository. *V.* CALA.

Suprarrenal [soo-prar-ray-nahl'], *a.* Suprarenal. *Glándula suprarrenal,* Suprarenal gland.

Supraspina [soo-pras-pee'-nah], *f.* (Anat.) Cavity at the top of the shoulder, the supra-spinal fossa of the scapula.

Supraspinato [soo-pras-pe-nah'-to], *m.* (Anat.) Supra-spinatus, muscle which raises the arm.

Suprema [soo-pray'-mah], *f.* The supreme council of the Inquisition.

Supremacía [soo-pray-mah-thee'-ah], *f.* Supremacy.

Supremamente, *adv.* Ultimately, supremely.

Supremidad, *f.* (Obs.) *V.* SUPREMACÍA.

Supremo, ma [soo-pray'-mo, mah], *a.* Supreme; highest, most excellent, paramount; excessive.

Supresión [soo-pray-se-on'], *f.* Suppression; obstruction; extinction.

Supresivo, va [soo-pray-see'-vo, vah], *a.* Suppressive, tending to suppress.

Supreso, sa [soo-pray'-so, sah], *pp. irr.* of SUPRIMIR. Suppressed.

Suprimir [soo-pre-meer'], *va.* 1. To suppress, to impede, to obstruct. 2. To abolish a place or employment, to extinguish. 3. To suppress, to keep in, to omit, to conceal.

Suprior, ra [soo-pre-or', rah], *m.* & *f.* Sub-prior, sub-prioress.

Supriorato [soo-pre-o-rah'-to], *m.* Office of sub-prior or prioress.

Supuesto [soo-poo-es'-to], *m.* 1. Supposition. 2. (Phil.) Individuality of a complete and incommunicable substance.

Supuesto, ta, *a.* & *pp. irr.* of SUPONER. Supposititious, suppositive, supposed. *Por supuesto,* Of course. *Supuesto que,* Allowing that; granting that; since.

Supuración [soo-poo-rah-the-on'], *f.* Suppuration

Supurante [soo-poo-rahn'-tay], *pa.* Suppurating, generating pus.

Supurar [soo-poo-rar'], *va.* To waste or consume moisture by heat.—*vn.* (Med.) To suppurate, to form pus.

Supurativo, va [soo-poo-rah-tee'-vo, vah], *a.* Suppurative.

Supuratorio, ria [soo-poo-rah-to'-re-o, ah], *a.* That which suppurates.

Suputación [soo-poo-tah-the-on'], *f.* Computation, calculation, supputation.

Suputar [soo-poo-tar'], *va.* To compute, to calculate, to suppute.

Sur [soor], *m.* South; south wind. *Navegar al sur,* (Naut.) To steer a southerly course; to stand to the southward.

Sura [soo'-rah], **Surata** [soo-rah'-tah], *f.* A chapter or section of the Koran. (Arabic, from Hebrew.)

Sura, *f.* (Obs.) 1. Fibula. 2. The calf of the leg.

Surada [soo-rah'-dah], *f.* (Naut.) A strong south wind.

Sural [soo-rahl'], *a.* Sural: applied to the veins that run down the calf of the leg.

Surcador, ra [soor-cah-dor', rah], *m.* & *f.* Ploughman, plowman, plougher.

Surcar [soor-car'], *va.* 1. To furrow, to make furrows with a plough. 2. (Met.) To furrow, to flute. 3. To pass through a liquid. *Surcar los mares,* (Naut.) To plough the seas.

Surco [soor'-co], *m.* 1. Furrow, hollow track. 2. Line, wrinkle. *A surco,* Applied to pieces of ground furrowed in the middle.

Surculado, da [soor-coo-lah'-do, dah], *a.* Applied to plants of one stem without branches.
Súrculo [soor'-coo-lo], *m.* Single stem of a tree or plant without branches.
Surculoso, sa [soor-coo-lo'-so, sah], *a.* Applied to a plant which has only one stem.
Sureste [soo-rays'-tay], *m.* South-east.
Surgente [soor-hen'-tay], *pa.* Surging, salient.
Surgidero [soor-he-day'-ro], *m.* Road, port, anchoring-place.
Surgidor [soor-he-dor'], *m.* He who anchors.
Surgir [soor-heer'], *vn.* 1. To spout, to spurt (said of water). *V.* SURTIR. 2. To appear, to present itself, to sprout. 3. (Naut.) To anchor.
Surirela [soo-re-ray'-lah], *f.* Surirella, a genus of diatoms, mostly fresh-water.
Suroeste [soo-ro-ess'-tay], *m.* South-west.
Sursueste [soor-soo-es'-tay], *m.* (Naut.) South-south-east.
Surtida [soor-tee'-dah], *f.* 1. (Mil.) Sallyport. 2. Sally, sortie. 3. Back-door.
Surtidero [soor-te-day'-ro], *m.* Conduit. *V.* BUZÓN. *Surtidero de agua*, Reservoir, basin.
Surtido [soor-tee'-do], *m.* Assortment, supply. *De surtido*, In common use.—*Surtido, da, pp.* of SURTIR.
Surtidor, ra [soor-te-dor', rah], *m.* & *f.* Purveyor, caterer. *Surtidor*, Jet, spout, or shoot of water.
Surtimiento [soor-te-me-en'-to], *m.* Supply, the act of supplying; assortment.
Surtir [soor-teer'], *vn.* To spout, to spurt with violence: used of water.—*va.* To supply, to furnish, to provide, to accommodate, to fit out. *Surtir efecto*, To have the desired effect.
Surto, ta [soor'-to, tah], *pp.* Anchored: it is the old irregular participle of *Surgir*.
Sus [soos], *prep.* (Obs.) *V.* ARRIBA. *Sus de gaita*, (Coll.) Blast, whiff; any light, airy thing; wind of a syringe.—*int.* Cheer up! Forward!
Susamiel [soo-sah-me-el'], *f.* Paste, made of almonds, sugar, and spice.
Susano, na [soo-sah'-no, nah], *a.* (Obs.) Superior, above.
Susecpción [soos-thep-the-on'], *f.* The act of receiving sacred orders.
Susceptibilidad [soos-thep-te-be-le-dahd'], *f.* 1. Susceptibility to influences, aptitude for receiving an action. 2. Delicacy, susceptibility of emotions; sensibility.
Susceptible [soos-thep-tee'-blay], *a.* Susceptible.
Susceptivo, va [soos-thep-tee'-vo, vah], *a.* Susceptible, susceptive.
Suscitación [soos-the-tah-the-on'], *f.* Excitation; an excited state.
Suscitar [soos-the-tar'], *va.* 1. To excite, to stir up. *Suscitar una pendencia*, To stir up a quarrel. 2. To rouse, to promote vigour, to suscitate.
Suscribir [soos-cre-beer'], *va.* *V.* SUBSCRIBIR. Still a popular spelling.
Suscripción [soos-crip-the-on], *f.* *V.* SUBSCRIPCIÓN.
Suscriptor, ra [soos-creep-tor', rah], *m.* & *f.* Subscriber. *V.* SUBSCRIPTOR.
Suscrito, ta [soos-cree'-to, tah], *a.* & *pp. irr.* of SUSCRIBIR.
Suscritor, ra [soos-cre-tor', rah], *m.* & *f.* *V.* SUSCRIPTOR.
Susero, ra, *a.* (Obs.) Superior, above.
Susidio [soo-see'-de-o], *m.* (Amer.) Inquietude, restlessness, sudden dread.
Suso [soo'-so], *adv.* (Obs.) Above.
Susodicho, cha [soo-so-dee'-cho, chah], *a.* Forementioned, aforesaid.
Suspendedor, ra [soos-pen-day-dor', rah], *m.* & *f.* Suspender.
Suspender [soos-pen-derr'], *va.* 1. To suspend, to keep suspended; to hang. 2. To suspend, to stop, to delay, to dally. *Suspender el fuego*, To hang fire. 3. To surprise, to amaze. *Suspenderse el caballo*, To rear, as a horse. *Suspender los pagos*, To stop payment.
Suspensión [soos-pen-se-on'], *f.* 1. Suspension, detention, pause. 2. Hesitation, suspense, uncertainty, indetermination. 3. Admiration, amazement. 4. Suspension, privation, an ecclesiastical censure. *Suspensión de armas*, Cessation of hostilities.
Suspensivo, va [soos-pen-see'-vo, vah], *a.* That which has the power of suspending.—*pl.* (Gram.) Dotted lines showing that something has been omitted; thus . . .
Suspenso, sa [soos-pen'-so, sah], *pp. irr.* of SUSPENDER. Hung; suspended, suspense.
Suspensorio, ria [soos-pen-so'-re-o, ah], *a.* Suspensory.
Suspensorio, *m.* Suspensory bandage.
Suspicacia [soos-pe-cah'-the-ah], *f.* Suspiciousness, jealousy.
Suspicaz [soos-pe-cath'], *a.* Suspicious, jealous.
Suspicazmente, *adv.* Suspiciously.
Suspición, *f.* (Obs.) *V.* SOSPECHA.
Suspirador, ra [soos-pee-rah-dor', rah], *m.* & *f.* One who continually sighs or suspires; one who breathes with difficulty.
Suspirar [soos-pe-rar'], *vn.* 1. To sigh, to suspire, to groan. 2. To crave, to desire anxiously. *Suspirar por el favor de la corte*, To gape for court favour. *Suspirar por el mando*, To aspire after command.
Suspiro [soos-pee'-ro], *m.* 1. Sigh, suspiration; breath. 2. Hissing of the wind; sharp sound of a piece of glass. 3. *pl.* Lady's-fingers, a variety of cake. 4. (Bot.) *V.* TRINITARIA. *El último suspiro*, The end of a thing; the last gasp or breath.
Sustancia [soos-tahn'-the-ah], *f.* *V.* SUBSTANCIA. *Sustancia* is the more conversational form; *substancia* the Academical and strictly etymological form. *En sustancia*, Briefly, summarily.
Sustancial [soos-tan-the-ahl'], *a.* *V.* SUBSTANCIAL.
Sustancialmente, *adv.* *V.* SUBSTANCIALMENTE.
Sustanciar, *va.* *V.* SUBSTANCIAR.
Sustancioso, sa [soos-tan-the-oh'-so, sah], *a.* *V.* SUBSTANCIOSO.
Sustantivadamente, *adv.* Substantively, as a substantive.
Sustantivar [soos-tan-te-var'], *va.* To use adjectives or any other part of speech as substantives.
Sustantivo [soos-tan-tee'-vo], *m.* (Gram.) Substantive, noun.
Sustantivo, va, *a.* Substantive, betokening existence.
Sustener [soos-tay-nerr'], *va.* (Obs.) To support. *V.* SOSTENER.
Sustenido [soos-tay-nee'-do], *m.* 1. Spanish step in dancing. 2. (Mus.) Sharp. *V.* SOSTENIDO.
Sustenido, da, *a.* (Mus.) Sharp, a semitone higher.
Sustentable [soos-ten-tah'-blay], *a.* Defensible, sustainable.
Sustentación [soos-ten-tah-the-on'], *f.* Sustentation, support.
Sustentáculo [soos-ten-tah'-coo-lo], *m.* Prop, stay, support.
Sustentador, ra [soos-ten-tah-dor', rah], *m.* & *f.* Sustainer.
Sustentamiento [soos-ten-tah-me-en'-to], *m.* Sustenance, necessaries of life.
Sustentante [soos-ten-tahn'-tay], *pa.* Sustaining.
Sustentante, *m.* Defender, supporter; he who sustains conclusions in a faculty.
Sustentar [soos-ten-tar'], *va.* 1. To sustain, to bear up; to feed or support, to nourish. 2. To sustain, to assert, to maintain. *Sustentarse del aire*, To live on vain hopes; to live upon the air; to be extravagant.
Sustento [sus-ten'-to], *m.* 1. Food, sustenance, maintenance. 2. Support, the act of supporting, sustaining, or maintaining.
Sustillo [soos-teel'-lyo], *m. dim.* A slight fright.
Sustitución [soos-te-too-the-on'], *f.* Substitution, surrogation.
Sustituidor, ra [soos-te-too-e-dor', rah], *m.* & *f.* One that substitutes.
Sustituir [soos-te-too-eer'], *va.* 1. To substitute, to surrogate. 2. To substitute, to put one thing instead of another.
Sustituto [soos-te-too'-to], *m.* Substitute, one acting with delegated power.
Sustituto, ta, *a.* & *pp. irr.* of SUSTITUIR. Substitute, surrogate, delegate.
Sustituyente [soos-te-too-yen'-tay], *pa.* Substituting.
Susto [soos'-to], *m.* Fright, sudden terror.
Sustracción [soos-trac-the-on'], *f.* *V.* SUBSTRACCIÓN.
Sustraendo [soos-trah-en'-do], *m.* Subtrahend. *V.* SUBSTRAENDO.
Sustraer [soos-trah-err'], *va.* *V.* SUBSTRAER.
(*Yo sustraigo, sustraiga, sustraje,* from *Sustraer*. *V.* TRAER.)
Susurración [soo-soor-rah-the-on'], *f.* Susurration, a whisper.
Susurrador, ra [soo-soor-rah-dor', rah], *m.* & *f.* Whisperer.
Susurrante [soo-soor-rahn'-tay], *pa.* Whispering, murmuring.
Susurrar [soo-soor-rar'], *vn.* 1. To whisper; to divulge a secret. 2. To purl, as a stream; to hum gently, as the air, to murmur.—*vr.* To be whispered about, to begin to be divulged.
Susurro [soo-soor'-ro], *m.* Whisper, humming, murmur.
Susurrón, na [soo-soor-rone', nah], *a.* Murmuring or whispering secretly.—*m.* Grumbler, malcontent.
Sutil [soo-teel'], *a.* 1. Subtile, thin, slender. 2. Subtle, acute, cunning, keen. 3. Light, volatile.
Sutileza [soo-te-lay'-thah], *f.* 1. Subtilty, thinness, slenderness, fineness. 2. Subtlety, cunning, artifice, sagacity; acumen, perspicacity; nicety. 3. One of the four qualities of the glorified body. *Sutileza de manos*, Address in handling or operating; sleight of hand; light-fingeredness or nimbleness of a thief.
Sutilidad [soo-te-le-dahd'], *f.* *V.* SUTILEZA.
Sutilización [soo-te-le-thah-the-on'], *f.* Subtilization, the act of subtilizing; subtilation.
Sutilizador, ra [soo-te-le-thah-dor', rah], *m.* & *f.* One who subtilizes or attenuates.
Sutilizar [soo-te-le-thar'], *va.* 1. To subtilize, to make thin and subtile. 2. To subtilize, to file, to polish. 3. To subtilize, to discuss in a profound and ingenious manner.

Sutilmente, *adv.* Subtilely, pointedly; nicely, finely, delicately.

Sutorio, ria [soo-to'-re-o, ah], *a.* Belonging to the shoemaker's trade; sutorial.

Sutura [soo-too -rah], *f.* 1. Seam, suture. *V.* COSTURA. 2. (Anat.) Suture, the close connection of two bones.

Suversión [soo-ver-se-on'], *f.* Subversion, ruin, destruction. *V.* SUBVERSIÓN.

Suversivo, va [soo-ver-see'-vo, vah], *a.* Subversive. *V.* SUBVERSIVO.

Suvertir [soo-ver-teer'], *va.* *V.* SUBVERTIR.

Suyo, ya [soo'-yo, yah], *pron. poss.* His, hers, theirs, one's; his, her, or its own, one's own or their own. *De suyo,* Spontaneously, of one's own accord.

Suya [soo'-yah], *f.* View, intention, design. *Llevar la suya adelante,* To carry one's point. *Salirse con la suya,* To put one's wished-for end in execution. *Él hizo una de las suyas,* He played one of his pranks.

Suyos [soo'-yos], *m. pl.* Their own, near friends, relations, acquaintances, servants.

Svástica [es-vahs'-te-cah], *f.* Swastika or swastica.

T

T [tay], twenty-third letter of the alphabet, is pronounced in Spanish as in the English words *tap, true.* It never undergoes the variations it does in English, in *creature, nation,* etc.; consequently, *criatura, patio, tia,* etc., must be pronounced *cre-ah-too'-rah, pah'-te-o, tee'-ah.* *T* is never written double. Formerly it was sometimes used instead of *d.*

Ta! [tah], *int.* Take care, beware; stay, I recollect. *Ta, ta,* Tut, tut.

Taba [tah'-bah], *f.* 1. Ankle-bone, astragalus. 2. Vulgar game with sheep's shanks. *Menear las tabas,* To stir about nimbly. *Tomar la taba,* To give a loose rein to one's tongue. (Arab.)

Tabacal [tah-bah-cahl'], *m.* Tobacco-field.

Tabacalero, ra [tah-bah-ca-lay'-ro, rah], *a.* (Phil. Islands) Relating to the culture, manufacture, or sale of tobacco; tobacco, as adjective.—*n.* Tobacconist.

Tabaco [tah-bah'-co], *m.* 1. (Bot.) Tobacco. Nicotiana, *L.* *Tabaco de* or *en polvo,* Snuff. *Tabaco en rama* or *de hoja,* Leaf-tobacco. *Tabaco de Virginia,* Virginian tobacco. Nicotiana tabacum, *L.* *Tabaco fruticoso,* Shrubby tobacco. Nicotiana fruticosa, *L.* *Tabaco somonte, sumonte,* or *habano,* Tobacco in a natural state. *Tabaco de palillos,* Snuff made of the stalks of tobacco-plants. *Tabaco rapé,* Rappee. *Tabaco cura seca,* Dry cured tobacco. *Tabaco picado,* Cut or chipped tobacco. 2. Mildew on plants, as wheat, barley, etc. *V.* ROYA. 3. Cigar. (Acad.) *A mal dar tomar tabaco,* What cannot be cured must be endured. *Tomar tabaco,* To take snuff.

Tabacoso, sa [tah-bah-co'-so, sah], *a.* (Coll.) Using much tobacco, snuffy.

Tabalada [tah-bah-lah'-dah], *f.* 1. A heavy fall upon the breech. 2. (Coll.) *V.* TABANAZO.

Tabalario [tah-bah-lah'-re-o], *m.* (Coll.) The breech, posteriors.

Tabalear [tah-bah-lay-ar'], *va.* To rock to and fro.—*vn.* To drum with the finger on a table.

Tabaleo [tah-bah-lay'-o], *m.* 1. Drumming with the fingers on the table. 2. (Coll.) A spanking.

Tabalete [tah-bah-lay'-tay], *m.* A kind of woollen stuff finer than drugget.

Tabanazo [tah-bah-nah'-tho], *m.* (Coll.) Blow with the hand.

Tabanco [tah-bahn'-co], *m.* 1. Stall for selling eatables to the poor. 2. (Mex.) A floor dividing a room into upper and lower apartments. *V.* TAPANCO.

Tabanera [tah-bah-nay'-rah], *f.* A place where there are many horse-flies.

Tábano [tah'-bah-no], *m.* (Ent.) Gadfly, horse-fly, breeze-fly. Tabanus.

Tabanque [tah-bahn'-kay], *m.* Treadle, which serves for putting a potter's wheel in motion.

Tabaola [tah-bah-o'-lah], *f.* Confused noise of a crowd. *V.* BATAHOLA.

Tabaque [tah-bah'-kay], *m.* 1. A small work-basket. 2. A kind of nails somewhat larger than tacks. *Como pera en tabaque,* Carefully kept. (Arab. ṭabaq.)

Tabaquera [tah-bah-kay'-rah], *f.* 1. A kind of round snuff-box used by common people. 2. Case for a tobacco-pipe. *Tabaquera de humo,* Tobacco-pipe for smoking. 3. Bowl of a tobacco-pipe.

Tabaquería [tah-bah-kay-ree'-ah], *f.* Tobacco and snuff shop.

Tabaquero [tah-bah-kay'-ro], *m.* Tobacconist.

Tabaquillo [tah-bah-keel'-lyo], *m.* (Dim.) 1. A weak sort of tobacco. 2. A small work-basket.

Tabaquista [tah-bah-kees'-tah], *com.* One who takes much snuff, or professes to be a judge of tobacco.

Tabardete, *m.* *V.* TABARDILLO.

Tabardillo [tah-bar-deel'-lyo], *m.* A burning fever. *Tabardillo pintado,* A spotted fever.

Tabardina [tah-bar-dee'-nah], *f.* A coarse coat like the *tabardo,* but shorter.

Tabardo [tah-bar'-do], *m.* Wide, loose coat of coarse cloth with hanging sleeves, worn by labourers in bad weather; tabard.

Tabasco [tah-bahs'-co], *m.* Tabasco pepper or sauce.

Tabaxir [tah-bak-seer'], *m.* (Bot.) Tabasheer, a silicious concretion formed in the joints of the bamboo, opal-like, and used in the East Indies as a medicine. (Arab. tabāshir.)

Tábega [tah'-bay-gah], *f.* A small kind of sailing craft.

Tabelario, ria [tah-bay-lah'-re-o, ah], *a.* Tabellary, relating to secret balloting by tablets, among the ancient Romans.

Tabelión [tah-bay-le-on'], *m.* (Roman history.) *V.* ESCRIBANO.

Tabellar [tah-bel-lyar'], *va.* 1. To fold cloth in woollen manufactories, leaving the ends free so that the purchaser may easily mark them. 2. To mark with the maker's name or seal.

Taberna [tah-berr'-nah], *f.* 1. A tavern: always applied to a house where wine is retailed. 2. (Cuba) Trading on the highways. *Ya que no bebo en la taberna, huélgome en ella,* He who cannot drink at the tavern may at least smell the fumes.

Tabernáculo [tah-ber-nah'-coo-lo], *m.* 1. Tabernacle; a movable chapel, where the Jews kept the ark of the Testament. 2. Tabernacle, the place where the host is kept. *Fiesta de los tabernáculos,* Feast of tabernacles: kept by the Jews.

Tabernario, ria [tah-ber-nah'-re-o, ah], *a.* (Coll.) Relating to a tavern.

Tabernera [tah-ber-nay'-rah], *f* Tavern-keeper's wife: woman who keeps a tavern.

Tabernería [tah-ber-nay-ree'-ah], *f.* Business of a tavern-keeper.

Tabernero [tah-ber-nay'-ro], *m.* 1. Tavern-keeper, one who keeps a liquor shop. 2. (Obs.) A frequenter of dram shops.

Tabernil [tah-ber-neel'], *a.* (Coll.) *V* TABERNARIO.

Tabernilla [tah-ber-neel'-lyah], *f. dim.* A small tavern: very often applied to the house where the best wine is retailed.

Tabes [tah'-bes], *f* (Med.) Consumption, tabes.

Tabí [tah-bee'], *m.* Tabby, an ancient kind of silken stuff like a heavy taffetan. (Arab. 'atābi.)

Tabica [tah-bee'-cah], *f.* (Arch.) Lintel or cross-board put over a vacancy in a wall.

Tabicar [tah-be-car'], *va.* 1. To shut up with a wall; to wall up. 2. To close, to shut up something which ought to be open or free.

Tabicón [tah-be-cone'], *m.* A thick wall. *V.* TABIQUE MAESTRO

Tábido, da [tah'-be-do, dah], *a.* (Med.) 1. Tabid, wasted by disease, consumptive. 2. Putrid, corrupted.

Tabífico, ca [tah-bee'-fe-co, cah], *a.* Wasting, causing consumption.

Tabillas [tah-beel'-lyas], *f. pl.* Husks of clover-seed; husks of radish-seed.

Tabinete [tah-be-nay'-tay], *m.* A silk and cotton stuff much used for making women's footwear.

Tabique [tah-bee'-kay], *m.* A thin wall, a partition-wall made of bricks or tiles placed on edge. *Tabique colgado,* A partition raised on a beam. *Tabique maestro,* The chief partition-wall. *Tabique de panderete,* Brick on edge partition. *Tabique sordo,* A brick partition. (Arab. tashbik.)

Tabiteña [tah-be-tay'-nyah], *f.* (Prov.) A kind of pipe or small flute, made of a stalk of wheat.

Tabla [tah'-blah], *f.* 1. A board. 2. A similar piece of other material, as of marble or copper. 3. Plain space on clothes. 4. Table, for eating and other purposes. 5. *V.* ARANCEL. 6. *V.* TABLILLA, 4th def. 7. Table of contents prefixed to a book. 8. List, catalogue. 9. A piece of painting on boards or stones. 10. The broadest and most fleshy part of any of the members of the body. 11. Bed or plot of earth in a garden. 12. House where merchandise is registered as sold at market, in order to collect the duty. 13. Plank or board of a ship to escape drowning in shipwreck. 14. Place where meat is weighed and sold; butcher's block.—*pl.* 1. Stages on which actors perform. 2. An equal or drawn game at chess or drafts. 3. Astronomical tables. 4. Tables containing the decalogue. *Tabla de sembrado,* A fine field of corn. *Tabla de juego,* Gambling-house. *Tabla de chilla,* Thin board of slit deal. *Tabla de río,* Bed of a river. *Dinero en tabla,* Ready money. *Tabla de manteles,* Table-cloth. *A la tabla del mundo,* In public, before the world. *Tablas reales,* Backgammon-board or tables.

Tablachina [tah-blah-chee'-nah], *f* Kind of wooden shield or buckler.

Tablacho [tah-blah'-cho], *m.* Sluice or flood-gate. *Echar* or *hacer el tablacho,* To interrupt one that is speaking with some reason.

Tabladillo [tah-blah-deel'-lyo], *m. dim.* A small stage.

Tablado [tah-blah'-do], *m.* 1. Stage, flooring. 2. Stage of a theatre. 3. Boards or bottom of a bedstead. 4. (Met.) Scaffold. *Tablado de la cirugía*, (Naut.) Cockpit. *Tablado de la cosa*, (Naut.) Flooring of the cap.

Tablaje [tah-blah'-hay], *m.* 1. Pile of boards. 2. Gambling or gaming-house; perquisites of the keeper of a gaming-table.

Tablajear [tah-blah-hay-ar'], *vn.* To gamble; to be a gambler by profession.

Tablajería [tah-blah-hay-ree'-ah], *f.* Gaming, gambling; hire of the gaming-table.

Tablajero [tah-blah-hay'-ro], *m.* 1. Scaffold-maker; a carpenter, who builds scaffolds and stages. 2. Collector of the king's taxes. 3. Keeper of a gaming-house; gambler. 4. Butcher. *V.* Cortador. 5. (Prov.) Young surgeon walking the hospital.

Tablar [tah-blar'], *m.* Division of gardens into plots or beds.

Tablazo [tah-blah'-tho], *m.* 1. Blow or stroke with a board. 2. Arm of the sea or of a river.

Tablazón [tah-blah-thone'], *f.* 1. Boards or planks put together, so as to form a platform or other piece of construction; lumber. 2. Decks and sheathing of a ship. *Tablazón de la cubierta*, (Naut.) Deck planks. *Tablazón exterior*, (Naut.) Outside planks or planking. *Tablazón de los fondos*, (Naut.) Floor-planking. *Tablazón inferior* or *forro*, (Naut.) Inside planking; ceiling, foot-railing.

Tablear [tah-blay-ar'], *va.* 1. To divide a garden into beds or plots. 2. To make the ground even with a thick board. 3. To hammer bars of iron into plates.

Tablera [tah-blay'-rah], *f.* She who begs for the hospitals of St. Lazarus.

Tablero [tah-blay'-ro], *m.* 1. Board planed and fashioned for some purpose. 2. Timber fit for sawing into boards. 3. Dog-nail, a sort of nails used in flooring houses. 4. Stock of a cross-bow. 5. *Tablero de ajedrez* or *de damas*, Chess or checker-board, draft-board. *Tablero de chaquete* or *tablas reales* or *pretera*, (Mex.) Backgammon-board, tables. 6. Gambling-house, gaming-table. 7. (Arch.) Any plane level part of a building surrounded with a moulding. *V.* Abaco. 8. Shop-counter; money-table. *Estar en el tablero*, To be exposed to public view. *Poner* or *traer al tablero alguna cosa*, To hazard, to risk or endanger any thing. *Tablero de cocina*, Dresser; kitchen-table. *Tablero de conmutadores*, A switch-board, among telegraphers.

Tableta [tah-blay'-tah], *f.* 1. (Dim.) Tablet, a small piece of board. 2. A tablet or memorandum. 3. Cracknel, a kind of paste hard baked, a sweet mass. *Estar en tabletas*, To be in suspense. *Quedarse tocando tabletas*, (Coll.) To be disappointed. *Tableta para escribir*, Tablet, writing-pad.

Tableteado [tah-blay-tay-ah'-do], *m.* The crackling sound of boards trod upon.—*Tableteado, da, pp.* of Tabletear.

Tabletear [tah-blay-tay-ar'], *vn.* To move tables or boards, making a noise with them.

Tabletera [tah-blay-tay'-rah], *f.* & *a.* *V.* Tablera.

Tabletica, illa [tah-blay-tee'-cah], *f. dim.* 1. A small tablet. 2. Kind of hard pastry cakes. *Trueno de tabletilla*, Thundering or hollow sound made on a table

Tablica, ita [tah-blee'-cah, ee'-tah], *f. dim.* A small board or table.

Tablilla [tah-bleel'-lyah], *f.* 1. (Dim.) *V.* Tablica. 2. Kind of sweet cakes; in pharmacy, a tablet or troche. 3. Table or lists of persons excommunicated, exhibited in churches. 4. Bands on a billiard or truck table. *Tablilla de mesón*, Sign of an inn. *Tablilla de santero*, Poor-box of a hermit. *Tablillas de San Lázaro*, Three pieces of wood united with a cord and made to sound together: used in begging for the hospitals of St. Lazarus. *Por tablilla*, Indirectly.

Tablón [tah-blone'], *m. aug.* Plank, a thick board; beam; strake. *Tablón de aparadura*, Garboard strake.

Tabloncillo [tah-blon-theel'-lyo], *m.* Flooring-board; in some bull-rings, a row of seats at the foot of the guard-rail.

Tabloza [tah-blo'-thah], *f.* Painter's palette. *V.* Paleta.

Tabuco [tah-boo'-co], *m.* Hut, small apartment.

Tabuquillo, Tabuquito [tah-boo-keel'-lyo], *m. dim.* A small, miserable hut or cottage.

Taburacura [tah-boo-rah-coo'-rah], *f.* A kind of yellow rosin.

Taburete [tah-boo-ray'-tay], *m.* Chair without arms. *Taburetes*, Forms with backs in the pit of a play-house.

Taburetillo [tah-boo-ray-teel'-lyo], *m. dim.* Drawing-room chair for ladies.

Taca, *f.* 1. Cupboard, small closet. 2. Each plate of the crucible of a forge.

Tacada [tah-cah'-dah], *f.* 1. Act of striking the ball with the cue. 2. (Prov.) *V.* Mancha.

Tacamaca, Tacamahaca [tah-cah-mah'-cah], *f.* 1. Tacamahac, kind of medicinal gum resin from various tropical trees. 2. The balsam-poplar of the United States. Populus balsamifera.

Tacañamente [tah-cah-nyah-men'-tay], *a.* Sordidly, meanly, niggardly.

Tacañear [tah-cah-nyay-ar'], *vn.* To act the miser; to behave in a wicked or malicious manner.

Tacañería [tah-cah-nyay-ree'-ah], *f.* 1. Malicious cunning; low craft. 2. Narrowness of mind; sordid parsimony, niggardness, closeness, meanness.

Tacaño, ña [tah-cah'-nyo, nyah], *a.* 1. Malicious, artful, knavish. 2. Stingy, sordid, close, mean.

Tacar [tah-car'], *va.* (Obs.) To mark; to stain.

Tacazo [tah-cah'-tho], *m.* A smart stroke with a cue.

Taceta [ta-thay'-tah], *f.* A copper basin or bowl, used in oil-mills.

Tacica, illa, ita, *f. dim.* A small cup.

Tácitamente, *adv.* Silently, secretly; tacitly, informally.

Tácito, ta [tah'-the-to, tah], *a.* 1. Tacit, silent. 2. Implied, inferred.

Taciturnidad [tah-the-toor-ne-dahd'], *f.* 1. Taciturnity, silence. 2. Melancholy, deep sadness.

Taciturno, na [tah-the-toor'-no, nah], *a.* Tacit, silent, reserved; melancholy.

Taco [tah'-co], *m.* 1. Stopper, stopple. 2. Wad, wadding. 3. Rammer. 4. Pop-gun. 5. (Coll.) Volley of oaths. 6. Mace of a billiard-table. *Tacos de los escobenes*, (Naut.) Hawse-plugs. *Aire de taco*, (Coll.) Gracefulness, genteel, lively motion: applied to women. *Echar tacos*, (Coll.) To swear or speak in a great rage.

Tacón [tah-cone'], *m.* Heel-piece of a shoe.

Taconazo [tah-co-nah'-tho], *m.* Blow with a shoe-heel.

Taconear [tah-co-nay-ar'], *vn.* (Coll.) To make a noise with the heel-piece, to heel; to walk or strut loftily on the heels.

Taconeo [tah-co-nay'-o], *m.* Noise made with the heels in dancing steps or in walking.

Taconero [tah-co-nay'-ro], *m.* Heel-maker, one who makes wooden heels.

Táctica [tahc'-te-cah], *f.* 1. The art of orderly array. 2. (Mil.) Tactics. *Táctica naval*, Naval tactics.

Táctico [tahc'-te-co], *m.* Tactician.

Táctil [tak'-till], *a.* Tactual.

Tacto [tahc'-to], *m.* 1. Touch, the sense of feeling. 2. The act of touching or feeling. 3. Handiness, dexterity, certainty, tact.

Tacuacha [tah-coo-ah'-chah], *f.* (Cuba) A trick skilfully done. *Jugar una tacuacha*, To play a very pretty trick.

Tacha [tah'-chah], *f.* 1. Fault, defect, imperfection, macula. 2. Crack, fissure, flaw. 3. A sort of small nails, somewhat larger than tacks. *¡ Miren qué tacha !* (Coll.) An exclamation indicating the particular quality of a thing which enhances its merit. *Sano y sin tacha*, Sound and without blemish. *V.* Tacho. *Poner tacha*, To make objections.

Tachable [tah-chah'-blay], *a.* (Littl. us.) Exceptionable, liable to objection, censurable.

Tachar [tah-char'], *va.* 1. To censure, to tax, to find fault with; to charge with a fault; to reprehend. *Tachar a alguno de ligero*, To accuse one of levity. 2. To blot, to efface, to scratch out, to dash. 3. To blame, to reprehend. (Law) To impeach. *Tachar testigos*, To object to, refuse, or challenge a witness.

Tachero [tah-chay'-ro], *m.* (Cuba) One who works at molasses boilers.

Tacho [tah'-cho], *m.* 1. (Cuba) A boiler in which molasses is brought to the consistency necessary to convert it into sugar. 2. (Peru, Bol.) A narrow-mouthed earthen jar used for heating water.

Tachón [tah-chone'], *m.* 1. Stroke or line drawn through a writing, to blot it out. 2. Tacks used as an ornament for chairs; lace trimming. 3. A sort of large tacks with gilt or plated heads.

Tachonar [tah-cho-nar'], *va.* 1. To adorn with lace trimming. 2. To garnish with tacks or nails with gilt heads. 3. To spot, to sprinkle.

Tachonería [tah-cho-nay-ree'-ah], *f.* Ornamental work with gilt-headed tacks.

Tachoso, sa [tah-cho'-so, sah], *a.* Faulty, defective, blemished.

Tachuela [tah-choo-ay'-lah], *f.* Tack, a small nail.

Tadorno [tah-dor'-no], *m.* (Orn.) Shell-drake. Anas tadorna.

Tael [tah'-el], *m.* 1. A silver coin used in the Philippine Islands, equivalent to 6.25 pesetas, or $1.25; in China, $1.40. 2. A weight in these islands of 39 grammes; in China, 30.

Tafallo [ta-fahl'-lyo], *m.* (Prov.) *V.* Chafallo.

Tafanario [tah-fa-nah'-re-o], *m.* (Coll.) Breech, nates.

Tafetán [tah-fay-tahn'], *m.* Taffeta, a thin silk. *Tafetanes*, Flags, colours, standard, ensign. *Tafetán inglés*, Court-plaster; sticking-plaster.

Tafetanillo [tah-fay-ta-neel'-lyo], *m. dim.* A very thin taffeta.

Tafia [tah'-fe-ah], *f.* (Ven.) Rum.

Tafilete [tah-fe-lay'-tay], *m.* Morocco leather. *Tafiletes para sombreros*, Morocco linings for hats.

Tafiletear [tah-fe-lay-tay-ar'], *va.* To adorn with morocco leather.

Tafiletería [tah-fe-lay-tay-ree'-ah], *f.* Art of dressing morocco leather, and the place where it is dressed.

Tafurea [tah-foo-ray'-ah], *f.* (Naut.) A flat-bottomed boat for carrying horses.

Tagalo, la [tah-gah'-lo, lah], *a.* Tagal, belonging to the Tagala, the aboriginal Malay race of the Philippine Islands.—*m.* Their language, which has a written form.—*pl.* The Tagala.

Tagarino [tay-ga-ree'-no], *m.* Moor who lived among the Christians, and by speaking their language well could scarcely be known.

Tagarnillera [tah-gar-neel-lyay'-rah], *f.* An artful, deceitful person.

Tagarnina [tah-gar-nee'-nah], *f.* 1. *V.* CARDILLO. 2. (Coll.) A bad cigar.

Tagarote [tah-ga-ro'-tay], *m.* 1. (Orn.) Hobby. Falco subbuteo. 2. Quill-driver, a writer in an office. 3. A decayed gentleman, who earns a dinner by flattery and adulation. 4. A tall, ill-shaped person.

Tagarotear [tah-ga-ro-tay-ar'], *va.* (Coll.) To write a bold, free, and running hand.

Taha [tah'-ah], *f.* (Littl. us.) District, region. (Arab.)

Tahalí [tah-ah-lee'], *m.* Shoulder-belt.

Taharal [tah-ah-rahl'], *m.* Plantation of tamarisk-trees.

Taheño [tah-ay'-nyo], *a.* Having a red beard.

Tahona [tah-oh'-nah], *f.* 1. Horse-mill; a corn-mill, worked by mules or horses; crushing-mill. 2. Bake-house or baker's shop, where bread is baked and sold: generally applied to places where fine bread is baked. (Arab. tahona.)

Tahonero [tah-o-nay'-ro], *m.* Miller, who directs or manages a horse-mill.

Tahulla [tah-ool'-lyah], *f.* (Prov.) A piece of ground, near forty square yards, sown with about two pecks of grain.

Tahur [tah-oor'], *m.* Gambler, gamester, cogger.

Tahur, ra [tah-oor', rah], *a.* Belonging to gambling or to gamblers.

Tahurería [tah-oo-ray-ree'-ah], *f.* Gambling; gaming-house; fraudulent gambling.

Taifa [tah'-e-fah], *f.* 1. Faction, party. 2. (Coll.) Assemblage of evil life or little sense. (Arab. taifa)

Taimado, da [tah-e-mah'-do, dah], *a.* Sly, cunning, crafty. (Gr. δαήμων.)

Taimería [tah-e-may-ree'-ah], *f* Rascality, viciousness, shameless craftiness.

Taimonía [tah-e-mo-nee'-ah], *f.* (Obs.) Malicious cunning or slyness, impudent craft.

Taita [tah'-e-tah], *f.* A fondling name with which a child calls its father. *¡ Ajó, taita !* (Coll.) Said to one who acts like a child.

Taja [tah'-hah], *f.* 1. (Prov.) A kind of saddle-tree put over pack-saddles for carrying burdens. 2. Cut, incision; dissection; operation of cutting for the stone. 3. Tally, a stick notched in conformity with another stick.

Tajada [tah-hah'-dah], *f.* 1. Slice, a cut, a fritter. 2. (Coll.) Hoarseness.

Tajadera [tah-hah-day'-rah], *f.* 1. Chopping-knife, chopping-block. 2. (Prov.) Sluice of a mill-dam. 3. *V.* CORTAFRÍO. 4. (Mech.) Round chisel, gouge.

Tajadero [tah-hah-day'-ro], *m.* Chopping-block for meat; trencher.

Tajadilla [tah-hah-deel'-lyah], *f.* 1. A small slice of any thing. 2. A small slice of liver, etc., in low chop-houses. 3. (Prov.) Bit of confected orange or lemon, sold as a relish by retailers of brandy.

Tajado, da [tah-hah'-do, dah], *pp.* of TAJAR. 1. Cut, notched. 2. (Her.) Applied to a diagonal bar of a shield.

Tajador, ra [tah-hah-dor', rah], *m.* & *f.* One who cuts or chops. *V.* TAJADERO.

Tajadura [tah-hah-doo'-rah], *f.* 1. Cut, notch; section. 2. Act and effect of cutting.

Tajalápices [tah-ha-lah'-pe-thess], *m.* Pencil sharpener.

Tajamanil, *m.* & *f.* *V.* TEJAMANIL.

Tajamar [tah-hah-mar'], *m.* 1. (Naut.) Cutwater, stem. 2. Cutwater, edge on the up-stream side of a bridge-pier. *Escoras del tajamar*, Props of the cutwater.

Tajamiento [ta-hah-me-en'-to], *m.* *V.* TAJADURA.

Tajamoco [tah-hah-mo'-co], *m.* (Ent.) Goatchafer. Cerambyx.

Tajante [tah-hahn'-tay], *m.* (Prov.) Butcher.—*pa.* Cutting.

Tajaplumas [tah-hah-ploo'-mas], *m.* Penknife. *V.* CORTAPLUMAS.

Tajar [tah-har'], *va.* 1. To cut, to chop, to cut off, to cut out, to hew. 2. To cut a pen.

Tajea [tah-hay'-ah], *f.* 1. Furrow or small channel for the irrigation of lands. *V.* ATARJEA. 2. Culvert, drain under a road.

Tajero [tah-hay'-ro], *m.* *V.* TARJERO.

Tajo [tah'-ho], *m.* 1. Cut, incision. 2. Cutting of a quill with a penknife. 3. Chopping-block or board. 4. Cutting, reaping, or digging of labourers in a line; cut or opening in a mountain. 5. Cutting edge. 6. As name of a river, see Appendix.

Tajón [tah-hone'], *m.* 1. (Aug.) A large block. 2. Chopping-block. 3. A vein of earth or soft stone in a lime-stone quarry.

Tajoncillo [tah-hon-theel'-lyo], *m. dim.* A small block.

Tajuela, *f.* **Tajuelo,** *m.* [tah-hoo-ay'-lah] A low stool with four feet.

Tal [tahl'], *a.* 1. Such, so, as. 2. Equal, similar, of the same form or figure. 3. As much, so great. 4. Used before the names of persons not known, and to determine what is not specified. *Estaba allí un tal Ramírez*, One Ramirez was there. *Tal cual*, Middling, so-so; so as it is. *El tal* or *la tal*, That person, such a one: generally used contemptuously. *Tal cual vez*, Sometimes, from time to time. *Tal cual carga de pan*, A few loads of bread. *Tal para cual*, Every one with his like; also, tit for tat; a Roland for an Oliver. *Tal por cual*, Worthless, of no importance; good and bad. *No hay tal*, There is no such thing. *A tal*, With such a condition, under the circumstances. *Con tal que*, Provided that. *Otro que tal*, Similar, very like, equally worthless. *¿ Qué tal ?* How's that? how goes it? what do you say? what do you think?

Tala [tah'-lah], *f.* 1. Felling of trees. 2. Destruction, ruin, desolation, havoc.

Talabarte [tah-lah-bar'-tay], *m.* Sword-belt.

Talabartero [tah-lah-bar-tay'-ro], *m.* Belt-maker.

Talabricense [tah-lah-bre-then'-say], *a.* Of Talavera.—*n.* A Talaveran.

Talador, ra [tah-lah-dor', rah], *m.* & *f.* Destroyer, one who lays waste.

Taladrador, ra [tah-lah-drah-dor', rah], *m.* & *f.* Borer, piercer, penetrater.

Taladrar [tah-lah-drar'], *va.* 1. To bore, to perforate. 2. To pierce, to penetrate the ear. 3. To penetrate into or comprehend a difficult point.

Taladrillo [tah-lah-dreel'-lyo], *m. dim.* A small borer, little bore.

Taladro [tah-lah'-dro], *m.* 1. Drill. 2. Auger. 3. Drill hole.

Talaje [tah-lah'-hay], *m.* (Sp. Am.) 1. Pasturage. 2. Grazing.

Talamera [tah-lah-may'-rah], *f.* Tree used for insnaring birds.

Talamite [tah-lah-mee'-tay], *m.* A galley rower.

Tálamo [tah'-lah-mo], *m.* 1. Pre-eminent place where brides celebrated their weddings and received congratulations. 2. Bride-chamber, bridal bed.

Talanquera [tah-lan-kay'-rah], *f.* 1. Parapet, breast-work of pales. 2. Defence, a spot which defends from danger. *Hablar de*, or *desde la talanquera*, To find fault with the absent.

Talante [tah-lahn'-tay], *m.* 1. Mode or manner of performing any thing. 2. Appearance, aspect. 3. Will, pleasure, disposition. *Estar de buen talante*, To be ready or in a good disposition to do any thing.

Talantoso, sa [tah-lan-to'-so, sah], *a.* (Obs.) Good-humoured, of a pleasant disposition.

Talar [tah-lar'], *va.* 1. To fell trees. 2. To desolate, to lay waste a country. 3. To steal flour out of meal-bags.

Talar [tah-lar'], *a.* Applied to long robes reaching to the heels.

Talares, *m. pl.* The wings on the heels of Mercury; talaria.

Talavera [tah-lah-vay'-rah], *f.* Earthenware manufactured in Talavera.

Talaverano, na [tah-lah-vay-rah'-no, nah], *a.* Of Talavera.

Talco [tahl'-co], *m.* 1. Mica, a laminated translucent mineral. 2. A class of silicates. 3. Talcum powder.

Talcualillo, lla [tal-coo-ah-leel'-lyo, lyah], *a.* (Coll.) 1. Somewhat beyond mediocrity. 2. Somewhat improved in health: said of the sick. (Acad.)

Tálea [tah'-lay-ah], *f.* Stockade or palisade which the Romans made use of in their camps.

Taled [tah-led'], *m.* A kind of woollen amice with which the Jews covered the head and neck in their religious ceremonies.

Talega [tah-lay'-gah], *f.* 1. Bag, a wide, short sack. 2. Sack of hard dollars, containing 20,000 reals vellón, or 1,000 dollars in silver. *Una* or *dos talegas*, (Met.) One or two thousand dollars. 3. A bagful. 4. (Coll.) Sins which a penitent sinner is going to confess. 5. Bag for the hair. 6. (Coll.) Knowledge which one has acquired previous to attending a public school. 7. (Obs.) Store of provisions; ration.

Talegazo [tah-lay-gah'-tho], *m.* Stroke or blow with a full bag.

Talego [tah-lay'-go], *m.* 1. Bag or sack made of coarse sackcloth. *Tener talego*, To have money. 2. A clumsy, awkward fellow.

Talegón [tah-lay-gone'] *m. aug.* of TALEGA or TALEGO.

Taleguilla [tah-lay-geel'-lyah], *f.* 1. A small bag. *Taleguilla de la sal*, (Coll.) Daily expenditure, money spent each day. 2. The breeches that bull-fighters wear.

Taleguito [tah-lay-gee'-to], *m. dim.* of TALEGO.

Talentada [tah-len-tah'-dah], *f.* (Prov.) Will, propensity, inclination.

Talento [tah-len'-to], *m.* 1. Talent, ancient weight or money of different value. 2. Talent, abilities, endowments, or gifts of nature; ingenuity, genius, accomplishments: in the sense of abilities it is commonly used in the plural.

Talentoso, sa [tah-len-to'-so, sah], *a.* Able, ingenious, talented.

Táler [tah'-lerr], *m.* Thaler, a German coin prior to 1871, equal to three marks.

Talictro, *m.* (Bot.) Meadow-rue. Thalictrum.

Talidad [tah-le-dahd'], *f.* That which determines a thing to be included generically or specifically in another.

Talión [tah-le-on'], *m.* Retaliation, requital.

Talionar [tah-le-o-nar'], *va.* To retaliate, to requite.

Talismán [tah-lis-mahn'], *m.* 1. Talisman, a magical character. 2. Doctor of the Mohammedan law.

Talmente, *adv.* (Coll.) In the same manner.

Talmud [tal-mood'], *m.* Talmud, a book which contains the doctrines and ceremonies of the law of Moses.

Talmúdico, ca [tal-moo'-de-co, cah], *a.* Talmudic, relating to the Talmud.

Talmudista [tal-moo-dees'-tah], *m.* Professor or interpreter of the Talmud.

Talo [tah'-lo], *m.* A kind of cake of maize flour.

Talón [tah-lone'], *m.* 1. The heel. 2. Heel-piece of a shoe. 3. (Arch.) Cymatium, ogee fluting. 4. (Com.) Sight draft, cut from a book which serves as a voucher. 5. The stub of such a draft; hence, (6) a coupon or check for baggage. *Ir a talón*, (Coll.) To go on foot. *Apretar* or *levantar los talones*, To take to one's heels. *Dar con el talón en el fondo*, (Naut.) To touch ground with the stern-post. This word is used in Spain for luggage-receipt or baggage check; in America the more common word is *contraseña*.

Talonario [tah-lo-nah'-re-o], *m.* Stubs, coupons. *Talonario de cheques*, Check book.

Talonear [tah-lo-nay-ar'], *vn.* To be nimble, to walk fast.

Talonesco [tah-lo-nes'-co], *a.* (Coll.) Relating to the heels.

Talpa, Talparia [tahl'-pah], *f.* (Coll.) Abscess in the pericranium, tumour in the head.

Talque [tahl'-kay], *m.* A kind of argillaceous earth, of which crucibles are made.

Talus, Talud [tah'-loos, tah-lood'], *m.* Talus, a slope on the outside part of a wall or rampart.

Talvina [tal-vee'-nah], *f.* A kind of milk, extracted from several seeds, of which porridge and dumplings are made.

Talla [tahl'-lyah], *f.* 1. Raised work, cut in wood or stone, sculpture. *Obra de talla*, Carved work. 2. Dues paid by vassals to the lord of the manor. 3. Ransom, or reward for the capture of some noted criminal. 4. (Prov.) Jug with water put into the air to cool, or suspended in a draught. 5. Stature, size. *A media talla*, Carelessly, perfunctorily. *Media talla*, Half-relief, in sculpture. 6. Operation of cutting for the stone. 7. (Mil.) A wooden instrument for measuring a man's height. *Poner talla*, To offer a reward for the apprehension of a criminal.

Tallado, da [tal-lyah'-do, dah], *a.* & *pp.* of TALLAR. Cut, chopped, carved, engraved. *Bien* or *mal tallado*, Of a good or bad figure.

Tallador [tal-lyah-dor'], *m.* 1. Engraver. 2. Carver. 3. Die-sinker.

Talladura [tal-lyah-doo'-rah], *f.* Engraving.

Tallar [tal-lyar'], *m.* Grove or forest of fire-wood fit for cutting.

Tallar [tal-lyar'], *a.* Applied to wood fit for cutting or for fuel.

Tallar [tal-lyar'], *va.* 1. To cut, to chop. 2. To carve in wood, to engrave on copper-plate. 3. To charge with dues or imposts. 4. To show all the cards in one's hand at basset.

Tallarín [tal-lyah-reen'], *m.* A kind of thin paste.

Tallarola [tal-lyah-ro'-lah], *f.* Iron plate used for cutting the silk in velvet looms.

Tallazo [tal-lyah'-tho], *m. aug.* of TALLE and TALLO.

Talle [tahl'-lyay], *m.* 1. Shape, form, figure, proportion of the human body. 2. Waist, the middle of the body. 3. Mode or manner of performing a thing. 4. Fit of clothes. 5. Genus, species, class. *Largo de talle*, (Coll.) Long drawn out.

Tallecer [tal-lyay-therr'], *vn.* To shoot, to sprout.

Tallecillo [tal-lyay-theel'-lyo], *m. dim.* of TALLE: generally used in an ironical sense.

Taller [tal-lyerr'], *m.* 1. Workshop, office, laboratory. 2. School, academy, a seminary of arts and sciences. 3. Ancient coin. *Taller de mesa*, Casters.

Talleta [tal-lyay'-tah], *f.* (Amer.) A paste of almonds, nuts, and honey. *V.* ALFAJOR.

Tallista [tal-lyees'-tah], *m.* Carver in wood, engraver.

Tallo [tahl'-lyo], *m.* Shoot, sprout, stem which bears leaves, etc. (Lat. thallus.)

Talludo, da [tal-lyoo'-do, dah], *a.* 1. Grown into long stalks. 2. Tall, slender. 3. Callous, hardened in vicious habits. 4. Overgrown, grown to seed.

Talluelo [tal-lyoo-ay'-lo], *m. dim.* of TALLO.

Tamal [tah-mahl'], *m.* 1. (Amer.) A kind of small dumpling, made of Indian meal, stuffed with minced meat or other eatables, and boiled in the husk of the Indian corn. 2. (Honduras) A bundle of sarsaparilla.

Tamalero, ra [tah-mah-lay'-ro, rah], *m.* & *f.* (Mex.) Tamal-seller.

Tamándoa [tah-mahn'-do-ah], *f.* Anteater of Peru. Myrmecophaga.

Tamañamente [ta-mah-nyah-men'-tay], *adv.* As great as, tantamount.

Tamañico, ica, illo, illa, ito, ita [tah-mah-nyee'-co], *a.* Very small.

Tamañito, ta [tah-mah-nyee'-to, tah], *a.* 1. Fearful, intimidated. 2. Abashed, ashamed.

Tamaño [tah-mah'-nyo], *m.* Size, shape, bulk, stature, magnitude. *Hombre de tamaño*, A man of great respectability and endowments; one who holds a high employment.

Tamaño, ña [tah-mah'-nyo, nyah], *a.* 1. Showing the size, shape, or bulk of any thing. 2. Very little.

Tamañuelo, la [tah-mah-nyoo-ay'-lo, lah], *a. dim.* Small, slender, little.

Támaras [tah'-ma-ras], *f. pl.* 1. Clusters of dates. 2. Chips, faggots of brush-wood.

Tamarindo [tah-ma-reen'-do], *m.* (Bot.) Tamarind-tree and fruit. Tamarindus indica.

Tamarisco, Tamariz [tah-ma-rees'-co, tah-mah-reeth'], *m.* (Bot.) Tamarisk-shrub. Tamarix.

Tamarizquito, Tamarrusquito, ta [tah-ma-rith-kee'-to, tah-mar-roos-kee'-to, tah], *a.* (Coll.) Very small.

Tamba [tahm'-bah], *f.* (Low) Blanket of a bed.

Tambalear, Tambalearse [tam-bah-lay-ar'], *vn.* & *vr.* To stagger, to waver.

Tambaleo [tam-bah-lay'-o], *m.* Reeling, staggering.

Tambanillo [tam-bah-neel'-lyo], *m.* A raised ornament on the angles of buildings.

Tambarillo [tam-bah-reel'-lyo], *m.* Chest or trunk with an arched cover.

Tambero, ra [tam-bay'-ro, rah], *m.* & *f.* (Peru) Innkeeper.

También [tam-be-en'], *conj.* & *adv.* Also, too, likewise; as well, moreover.

Tambo [tahm'-bo], *m.* (Peru, Amer.) Inn.

Tambor [tam-bor'], *m.* 1. A drum. 2. Drummer. *Baquetas del tambor*, Drum-sticks. *Tambor mayor*, Drum-major. 3. (Mil.) Small inclosure as a screen to the gates of a fortress. 4. A small room, made in another room by partition-walls; tambour or wooden screen at the doors of churches. 5. (Arch.) Tambour, tholus, keystone of a vaulted roof or cupola. 6. Barrel, arbor, of a watch or clock; any cylindrical part of machinery. Hence further: rolling-pin, band-pulley, tumbler, wheel-house, paddle-box. 7. Tambour-frame for embroidering silk, muslin, or linen. *A tambor* or *con tambor batiente*, Beating the drum. *Tambor del oído*, Drum of the ear.

Tambora [tam-bo'-rah], *f.* Bass drum.

Tamborete [tam-bo-ray'-tay], *m. dim.* 1. Timbrel. 2. (Naut.) Cap of the mast-head, moorshead.

Tamboril [tam-bo-reel'], *m.* 1. Tambourine, tabour, tabouret, a kind of drum beaten in villages on festive occasions. 2. (Obs. Coll.) Breech.

Tamborilada [tam-bo-re-lah'-dah], *f.* (Coll.) Fall on the breech; a slap on the face or shoulders.

Tamborilazo [tam-bo-re-lah'-tho], *m.* Blow or fall on the breech.

Tamborilear [tam-bo-re-lay-ar'], *vn.* 1. To tabour, to beat the tabour with one stick, accompanied by a pipe. 2. To cry up, to be loud in one's praise. 3. (Print.) To plane or level types.

Tamborilero [tam-bo-re-lay'-ro], *m.* Tabourer, one that beats the tabour, tabouret, or tambourine.

Tamborilete [tam-bo-re-lay'-tay], *m.* (Typ.) Planer, a smooth wooden block used for levelling a form of type.

Tamborilillo [tam-bo-re-leel'-lyo], *m.* A small tambourine.

Tamborinero [tam-bo-re-nay'-ro], *m. V.* TAMBORILERO.

Tamboritear [tam-bo-re-tay-ar'], *va. V.* TAMBORILEAR.

Tamboritero [tam-bo-re-tay'-ro], *m. V.* TAMBORILERO.

Tamborito [tam-bo-ree'-to], *m.* National dance and musical rhythm of Panama.

Tamboron [tam-bo-rone'], *m.* A large drum.

Tamén, Tamene [tah-mayn', tah-may'-nay], *m.* (Mex.) Indian porter or carrier.

Tamerlán [tah-mer-lahn'], *m.* Emperor of the Tartars.

Tamiz [tah-meeth'], *m.* A fine sieve, made of silk or hair. *Pasar por tamiz*, To sift.

Tamo [tah'-mo], *m.* 1. Down which falls from woollen or linen in weaving. 2. Dust in corn. 3. Mould under beds on dusty floors.

Tamojo [tah-mo'-ho], *m.* (Bot.) *V.* BARRILLA TAMOJO.

Tampoco [tam-po'-co], *adv.* Neither, not either.

Tamujo [tah-moo'-ho], *m.* (Bot.) Buckthorn, box-thorn. Rhamnus lycioides.

Tan [tahn'], *m.* Sound of the tabour or tambourine, or of any thing like them.

Tan, *adv.* So, so much, as well, as much. *Tan grande*, So great, very much. *V.* TANTO.

Tanate [tah-nah'-tay], *m.* (Mex.) A seroon made of hide, to transport articles; in some parts a basket of particular form, and also a *pita* bag.

Tanatero [tah-nah-tay'-ro], *m.* (Mex.) The miner who takes out the ore, and carries it in the *tanate.*

Tanato [tah-nah'-to], *m.* (Chem.) Tannate, a salt of tannic acid.

Tanca [tahn'-cah], *f.* A viscous matter with which bees daub their hives before they begin to work at the honey-comb; bee-glue.

Tanda [tahn'-dah], *f.* 1. Turn, rotation. 2. Task, something to be done imposed by another. 3. Certain number of persons or cattle employed in a work. 4. Any undetermined number or quantity: generally applied to a number of stripes and lashes.

Tanganillas (En) [tan-gah-neel'-lyas], *adv.* Waveringly, in danger of falling.

Tanganillo [tan-gah-neel'-lyo], *m. dim.* A small prop or stay.

Tángano [tahn'-gah-no], *m.* Hob, a play among boys; bone or stone used in this play.

Tangencia [tan-hen'-the-ah], *f.* Tangency, the state of touching.

Tangente [tan-hen'-tay], *a.* (Geom.) Tangent.

Tangerina [tan-hay-ree'-nah], *f.* Tangerine.

Tangibilidad [tan-he-be-le-dahd'], *f.* (Littl. us.) Tangibility.

Tangible [tan-hee'-blay], *a.* Tactile, susceptible of touch.

Tangidera [tan-he-day'-rah], *f.* (Naut.) Cable.

Tango [tahn'-go], *m.* Tango, Argentine musical rhythm and dance.

Tanino [tah-nee' no], *m.* (Chem.) Tannin, tannic acid, gallotannic acid.

Tanor, ra [tah-nor', rah], *a.* A Philippine Malay who served as domestic to the Spaniards.

Tanoría [tah-no-ree'-ah], *f.* Domestic service by the Philippines to the Spaniards.

Tanque [tahn'-kay], *m.* 1. Vat, large trough, tank. 2. A small pool, a pond. 3. (Mil.) Tank. 4. Beeswax.

Tanquía (tan-kee'-ah], *f.* An ointment for making hair fall off.

Tantalato [tan-ta-lah'-to], *m.* (Chem.) Tantalate, a salt of tantalic acid.

Tantálico [tan-tah'-le-co], *a.* Tantalic, an acid from tantalium.

Tantalita, *f.* **Tantalito**, *m.* [tan-ta-lee'-tah, to]. Tantalite, a mineral composed chiefly of ferrous tantalate.

Tántalo [tahn'-tah-lo], *m.* (Min.) Tantalum, a metal.

Tantarantán, *m.* 1. Rub-a-dub-dub, redoubled beat of a drum.

Tanteador [tan-tay-ah-dor'], *m.* Measurer, calculator, marker.

Tantear [tan-tay-ar'], *va.* 1. To measure, to proportion. 2. To mark the game with counters. 3. To consider carefully, to scrutinize. 4. (Art) To sketch the outlines of a design.

Tanteo [tan-tay'-o], *m.* 1. Computation, calculation, average. 2. Number of counters for marking a game. 3. Prudent judgment of an affair. 4. Outlines of a picture.

Tantico, Tantillo [tan-tee'-co, tan-teel'-lyo], *m.* Small sum or quantity.

Tanto [tahn'-to], *m.* 1. A certain sum or quantity. 2. Copy of a writing. 3. Counter, mark of a game.

Tanto, ta, *a.* 1. So much, as much; very great. 2. Odd, something over a determined number. *Veinte y tantos*, Twenty and upwards.

Tanto, *adv.* 1. So, in such a manner. 2. A long time. *Tanto más o menos*, So much more or less. *Tanto que*, As much as. *Tanto mejor*, So much the better. *Tanto peor*, So much the worse. *Tanto monta*, It is as good as the other; it is all the same. *Tanto más cuanto*, Thereabouts, more or less. *En tanto* or *entre tanto*, In the mean time. *Tanto por tanto*, At the same price; upon a par. *Tantos a tantos*, Equal numbers. *Al tanto*, For the same price: used to express one's desire of an article at the same price paid by others. *Por el tanto* or *por lo tanto*, (1) For that same reason; on that ground. (2) For the same price. *Por tanto* or *por lo tanto*, Therefore, for the reasons expressed. *Tanto de ello*, Enough, abundantly. *En su tanto*, Proportionably. *Algún tanto*, A trifle, a little, a few. *La mitad y otro tanto*, The half and as much more. *Tanto uno como otro*, Both one and the other; both of them.

Tañedor, ra [tah-nyay-dor', rah], *m.* & *f.* Player on a musical instrument.

Tañer [tah-nyerr'], *va.* To play an instrument harmoniously. *Quien las sabe las tañe*, Every man to his own trade.—*vn.* (Obs.) *V.* ATAÑER.

Tañido, da [tah-nyee'-do, dah], *pp.* of TAÑER. Played; touched.

Tañido, *m.* Tune; sound; clink.

Tao [tah'-o], *m.* Badge worn by officers of the orders of St. Anthony and St. John.

Tapa [tah'-pah], *f.* 1. Lid, cover, cap. 2. Horny part of a hoof. 3. Heel-piece of a shoe. *Tapa de los sesos*, Top of the skull. *Tapa de bomba*, (Naut.) The hood of the pump.

Tapaagujeros [tah-pa-ah-goo-hay'-ros], *m.* (Coll.) 1. A clumsy mason. 2. One who supplants another in any matter; a makeshift.

Tapabalazo [tah-pah-bah-lah'-tho], *m.* (Naut.) Shot-plug.

Tapaboca [tah-pah-bo'-cah], *m.* (Coll.) 1. Slap on the mouth. 2. Any action or observation which interrupts the conversation, and cuts one short. 3. Choke-pear; any sarcasm by which another is put to silence. 4. (Mil.) Tampion, tamkin.

Tapacubos [tah-pah-coo'-bos], *m.* Hubcap (of an automobile, etc.)

Tapaculo [tah-pah-coo'-lo], *m.* Fruit of the dog-rose.

Tapada [tah-pah'-dah], *f.* A woman concealing her face under a thick veil or Spanish mantilla to avoid being known. *De tapaditas*, (1) Behind the curtain. (2) Underhandedly.

Tapadera [tah-pah-day'-rah], *f.* 1. A loose lid or movable cover of a pot or other vessel; covercle. 2. The leather cover of the stirrup of a Mexican saddle.

Tapadero [tah-pah-day'-ro], *m.* A large stopper or stopple.

Tapadijo [tah-pah-dee'-ho], *m.* Evasion, subterfuge, blind term. (Neol.)

Tapadillo [tah-pah-deel'-lyo], *m.* 1. The act of a woman's covering herself with her veil or mantle, that she may not be seen. 2. (Prov.) *V.* COBERTIZO. 3. A certain flute-stop of an organ. *De tapadillo*, Without ceremony or show, secretly.

Tapadizo [tah-pah-dee'-tho], *m.* 1. Action of women hiding the face with a mantle. 2. (Prov.) *V.* COBERTIZO.

Tapado [tah-pah'-do], *m.* (Arg., Ch.) 1. Spotless horse or mare. 2. (Col. & Hond.) Indian barbecue. 3. Ladies' wrap or cape.

Tapador, ra [tah-pah-dor', rah], *m.* & *f.* 1. One who stops or shuts up, coverer. 2. Plug, stopper, stopple.

Tapadura [tah-pah-doo'-rah], *f.* Act of stopping, covering, or hiding.

Tapafogón [tah-pah-fo-gone'], *m.* Cap of a gun, which covers the vent-hole.

Tapafunda [tah-pah-foon'-dah], *f.* Holster-cover of pistols.

Tapajuntas [tah-pah-hoon'-tahs], *m.* 1. Flashing joint (in construction). 2. Molding on window or doorframe.

Tápalo [tah'-pah-lo], *m.* (Mex.) Shawl. *V.* CHAL.

Tapamiento [tah-pah-me-en'-to], *m.* Act of stopping or covering.

Tapaojos [tah-pah-o'-hos], *m.* (Amer.) A bandage for the eyes of horses or mules.

Tapar [tah-par'], *va.* 1. To stop up, to cover, to put under cover, to choke up, to obstruct, to occlude. 2. To conceal, to hide, to cover up, to mantle, to hoodwink, to dissemble. *Tapar la boca*, To stop one's mouth. *Tapar una abertura de agua*, (Naut.) To stop or fother a leak. *Taparse de medio ojo*, To cover the face to the eyes with a mantle, as women do to conceal themselves. *Taparse el caballo*, To cover the track of the fore feet with those of the hind ones.

Tapara [tah-pah'-rah], *f.* (Sp. Am.) Calabash.

Tápara [tah'-pah-rah], *f.* Caper.

Taparo [tah-pah'-ro], *m.* (Sp. Am.) Calabash tree.

Taparrabo [tah-par-rah'-bo], *m.* 1. Breechclout, loincloth. 2. Swim trunks.

Tapatío, tía [tah-pah-tee'-o, ah], *a.* & *m.* & *f.* Name applied to persons and things from Guadalajara, Mexico.

Tapetado, da [tah-pay-tah'-do, dah], *a.* Of a dark-brown or blackish colour.

Tapete [tah-pay'-tay], *m.* 1. A small floor-carpet or rug. 2. A cover for a table or chest. *Estar sobre el tapete*, To be on the tapis (under discussion).

Tapia [tah'-pe-ah], *f.* 1. Mud-wall. 2. Massive wall. *Sordo como una tapia*, Stone-deaf.

Tapiador [tah-pe-ah-dor'], *m.* Builder of mud-walls.

Tapial [tah-pe-ahl'], *m.* Mould for making mud-walls. *Tener el tapial*, (Coll.) To have patience, to rest.

Tapiar [tah-pe-ar'], *va.* 1. To stop up with a mud-wall. 2. To stop a passage, to obstruct a view.

Tapicería [tah-pe-thay-ree'-ah], *f.* 1. Tapestry. 2. Office in the royal palace where the tapestry and carpets are kept. 3. Shop where tapestries are sold.

Tapicero [tah-pe-thay'-ro], *m.* One who makes tapestry. *Tapicero mayor*, Tapestry-keeper in a palace.

Tapiería [tah-pe-ay-ree'-ah], *f.* Series of mud-walls.

Tapines, Tapinos [tah-pee'-nes, tah-pee'-nos], *m. pl.* (Naut.) Stoppers for vent-holes.

Tapinosis [tah-pe-no'-sis], *f.* (Rhet.) Figure where, with words and low phrases, any great thing is explained

Tapioca [tah-pe-o'-cah], *f.* Tapioca, the prepared starch of the cassava.

Tapir [tah-peer'], *m.* Tapir, a pachydermatous mammal, having a sort of proboscis. It lives in forests and by rivers. Found in Malay and in South America. Syn. DANTA, ANTA, GRAN BESTIA.

Tapirujarse, *vr.* *V.* TAPERUJARSE.

Tapisote [tah-pe-so'-tay], *m.* (Bot.) Yellow-flowered pea. Pisum ochrus.

Tapiz [tah-peeth'], *m.* 1. Tapestry. 2. Grass-plot adorned with flowers. *Arrancado de un tapiz*, Nickname for a ridiculous-looking, ill-dressed person.

Tapizar [tah-pe-thar'], *va.* To hang with tapestry.

Tapón [tah-pone'], *m.* Cork, plug, bung. *Tapón de cuba*, (Coll.) A short, fat person. *Al primer tapón, zurrapas*, (Coll.) Unlucky from the start.

Tapsia [tap'-se-ah], *f.* (Bot.) Deadly carrot. Thapsia. *Tapsia vellosa*, Villous deadly carrot. Thapsia villosa.

Tapujarse [tah-poo-har-say'], *vr.* To muffle one's self in a cloak or veil.

Tapujo [tah-poo'-ho], *m.* 1. Muffle, a cover for the face. 2. False pretext, subterfuge, feigned excuse.

Taque [tah'-kay], *m.* 1. Noise made by a door on being locked. 2. Bang or rap given to it in order to call some one.

Taquera [tah-kay'-rah], *f.* Rack or stand for billiard-cues.

Taquigrafía [tah-ke-grah-fee'-ah], *f.* Tachigraphy, the art of quick writing. Syn. ESTENOGRAFÍA.

Taquigráfico, ca [tah-ke-grah'-fe-co, cah], *a.* Tachygraphic, short-hand.

Taquígrafo [tah-kee'-grah-fo], *m.* Short-hand writer.

Taquilla [tah-keel'-lyah], *f.* 1. Ticket office, box office. *Éxito de taquilla*, Box-office hit, dramatic success. 2. Letter file or cabinet for documents in offices.

Taquillero, ra [tah-keel-lyay'-ro, rah], *a.* (Th.) Relating to box office. *Éxito taquillero*, Box-office hit. —*m.* & *f.* Ticket seller.

Taquímetro [tah-kee'-may-tro], *m.* Tachymeter, kind of theodolite for surveying.

Taquín, *m.* *V.* CARNICOL.

Taquinero [tah-ke-nay'-ro], *m.* (Prov.) Player with a bone.

Tara [tah'-rah], *f.* 1. (Com.) Tare, an allowance made to a purchaser of the weight of the box, cask, sack, etc., in which goods are packed. 2. Tally, a stick on which the weight is marked. *Menos de tara*, Making an allowance for. (Arab. tarha, deduction, fr. tarah, to throw away.)

Tarabita [tah-rah-bee'-tah], *f.* (S. A.) Rope bridge. *V.* PUENTE DE CIMBRIA. Called *oroya* in Peru.

Taracea [tah-rah-thay'-ah], *f.* 1. Marquetry, checkered work, inlaid work. 2. (Coll.) Patchwork of cloth or linen.

Taracear [tah-rah-thay-ar'], *va.* To inlay, to make inlaid work. (Arab.)

Tarafes [tah-rah'-fes], *m. pl.* (Cant.) Dice.

Taragallo [tah-rah-gahl'-lyo], *m.* Clog, suspended from the necks of beasts, to prevent them from running away.

Taraja [tah-rah'-hah], *f.* (S. A.) Screw-plate. *Mochuelos de taraja*, Screw-taps for the same.

Tarambana [tah-ram-bah'-nah], *com.* Giddy, unstable person; madcap.

Tarando [tah-rahn'-do], *m.* Reindeer. Cervus tarandus.

Tarángana [tah-rahn'-gah-nah], *f.* *V.* MORCILLA.

Tarantela [tah-ran-tay'-lah], *f.* A powerful, impressive tune, such as is played for the bite of the tarantula. *Dar la tarantela*, (Coll.) To excite or agitate one inordinately.

Tarántula (ta-rahn'-too-lah], *f.* Tarantula, a kind of venomous spider, most frequent in the city and neighborhood of Tarento, in Apulia. Aranea tarantula. *Picado de la tarántula*, (Met.) Infected with some malady.

Tarantulado, da [tah-ran-too-lah'-do, dah], *a.* *V.* ATARANTADO.

Tarará [tah-ra-rah'], *f.* Sound of a trumpet, as a signal for action.

Tararear [tah-rah-ray-ar'], *va.* & *vn.* 1. To sound the trumpet. 2. To chuck under the chin. 3. (Coll.) To sing a song using the word *tarara* instead of the proper words.

Tararira [tah-rah-ree'-rah], *f.* (Coll.) Noisy mirth.—*com.* Noisy person.

Tarasca [tah-rahs'-cah], *f.* 1. Figure of a serpent formerly borne in the procession of Corpus Christi day, indicating the triumph of Christ over the devil. 2. Crooked, ugly, ill-natured, licentious, and impudent woman.

Tarascada [tah-ras-cah'-dah], *f.* 1. Bite, a wound with the teeth. 2. (Coll.) A pert, harsh answer.

Tarascar [tah-ras-car'], *va.* To bite.

Tarascón [tah-ras-cone'], *m. aug.* of TARASCA.

Taratántara [tah-ra-tahn'-tah-rah], *f.* A word imitative of the sound of a trumpet. (Latin.)

Taravilla [tah-ra-veel'-lyah], *f.* 1. A mill-clack. 2. A kind of wooden latch for doors or windows; sneck. 3. A person who prattles much and fast. *Soltar la taravilla*, To talk too much and little to the purpose.

Taray [tah-rah'-e], *m.* (Bot.) Tamarisk, an evergreen shrub.

Tarazar [tah-ra-thar'], *va.* 1. To bite. 2. To molest, to harass, to mortify.

Tarazón [tah-ra-thone'], *m.* A large slice, especially of fish.

Tarazoncillo [tah-ra-thon-theel'-lyo], *m. dim.* A small slice.

Tarbea [tar-bay'-ah], *f.* A large hall.

Tardador, ra [tar-dah-dor', rah], *m.* & *f.* Delayer, deferrer, tarrier.

Tardamente, *adv.* (Littl. us.) Slowly, softly.

Tardanaos, *m.* *V.* RÉMORA.

Tardanza [tar-dahn'-thah], *f.* Slowness, delay, tardiness, detention; dalliance, lingering.

Tardar [tar-dar'], *vn.* & *vr.* To delay, to put off, to dally. *A más tardar*, At the latest, no later than.

Tarde [tar'-day], *f.* 1. Afternoon; the time from noon till night. 2. Evening, the close of the day.—*adv.* Late; past the time. *De tarde en tarde*, Now and then, occasionally; seldom. *Tarde, mal y nunca*, Slow and unpunctual. *Hacerse tarde*, To grow late. *Más vale tarde que nunca*, Better late than never. *Para luego es tarde*, By-and-bye is too late; don't put off. *Algo tarde*, Backward, latish. *Tarde o temprano*, Sooner or later.

Tardecer [tar-day-therr'], *vn.* To verge upon evening; to grow late.

Tardecica, ita [tar-day-thee'-cah], *f. dim.* The close of the evening.

Tardecillo [tar-day-theel'-lyo], *adv.* A little late; slowly.

Tarde piache [-pe-ah'-chay], *a.* (Coll.) Very late; the opportune time past.

Tardíamente, *adv.* Too late, out of time.

Tardío, día [tar-dee'-o, ah], *a.* 1. Late, too late. 2. Slow, tardy, dilatory.

Tardo, da [tar'-do, dah], *a.* 1. Slow, sluggish, tardy. 2. Dull, inactive, lazy.

Tardón, na [tar-don', nah], *a. aug.* Very tardy, phlegmatic.

Tarea [ta-ray'-ah], *f.* 1. Task, work imposed by another; shift. 2. Care, toil, drudgery; exercise. 3. The number of pounds of chocolate which the maker can prepare in a day; commonly thirty-two. *Ahora disfruta sus tareas*, He now enjoys the fruit of his labour. (Arab. tariha.)

Tarentino, na [tah-ren-tee'-no, nah], *a.* Native of, or belonging to Tarentum

Targum [tar-goom'], *m.* Targum, Chaldaic version of the Bible.

Tarida [tah-ree'-dah], *f.* Ancient vessel used in the Mediterranean for carrying implements of war.

Tarifa [tah-ree'-fah], *f.* Tariff, a list of the prices of goods or merchandise book of rates or duties. (Arab. ta'rif.)

Tarima [tah-ree'-mah], *f.* 1. A movable platform on a floor or pavement; low bench, table, foot-stool. 2. Bedstead. (Arab.)

Tarimilla [tah-re-meel'-lyah], *f. dim.* A small bedstead.

Tarimón [tah-re-mone'], *m. aug.* A large bedstead; a foot-stool.

Tarín [tah-reen'], *m.* (Prov.) Silver real of 8½ *cuartos.*

Tarín barín [tah-reen' bah-reen']. (Coll. adverbial phrase) Barely, pretty closely, just about.

Tarina [tah-ree'-nah], *f.* Middle-sized dish for meat.

Tarja [tar'-hah], *f.* 1. An ancient Spanish copper coin worth about one-fourth of a real. 2. Tally. 3. Target, shield, buckler. 4. Sign-board. *Beber sobre tarja*, (Coll.) To get drink on tick.

Tarjador, ra [tar-hah-dor', rah], *m.* & *f.* One who keeps a tally.

Tarjar [tar-har'], *va.* To tally, to mark on a tally what has been sold on credit.

Tarjea [tar-hay'-ah], *f.* 1. A canal for watering lands or plants. 2. Sewer.

Tarjero [tar-hay'-ro], *m.* Tally-keeper. *V.* TARJADOR.

Tarjeta [tar-hay'-tah], *f. dim.* of TARJA. 1. Sign-board, sign. 2. Card, used in messages of civility or business. *Tarjeta de visita*, A visiting card. *Tarjeta de correos* or *postal*, Postal card. *Tarjeta de negocios*, Business card. *Tarjeta de despedida*, A farewell card: these last are marked thus, *N. N. se despide para Cádiz;* equivalent to NN.—T. T. L.

Tarjeta de crédito [tar-hay'-tah day cray'-de-to], *f.* Credit card.

Tarjeteo [tar-hay-tay'-o], *m.* Exchange of cards.

Tarjetero [tar-hay-tay'-ro], *m.* 1. Cardcase. 2. Card index.

Tarjetón [tar-hay-tone'], *m. aug.* A large buckler or target.

Tarlatana [tar-lah-tah'-nah], *f.* A sort of thin linen or thread crape.

Tarpón [tar-pon'], *m.* Tarpon.

Tarquín [tar-keen'], *m.* Mire, mud.

Tarquinada [tar-kee'-nah-dah], *f.* (Coll.) Rape.

Tarraja [tar-rah'-hah], *f.* (Arch.) Metal instrument for cutting ornamental mouldings in gypsum.

Tarro [tar'-ro], *m.* Earthenware or glass vessel. *Cabeza de tarro*, (coll.) Big-headed fool.

Tarso [tar'-so], *m.* (Anat.) Tarsus, the ankle.

Tarta [tar'-tah], *f.* 1. Tart, a delicate pastry. 2. Pan for baking tarts.

Tártago [tar'-tah-go], *m.* 1. (Bot.) Spurge. Euphorbia lathyris. 2. Mis-

fortune, unfortunate event. 3. A severe test, galling satire or lash.
Tartajear [tar-tah-hay-ar'], *vn.* To stutter, to stammer.
Tartajoso, sa [tar-tah-ho'-so, sah], *a.* Stammering, stuttering.
Tartalear [tar-tah-lay-ar'], *vn.* (Coll.) 1. To reel, to stagger. 2. To be perplexed; not to be able to talk.
Tartaleta [tar-tah-lay'-tah], *f.* A kind of light paste for covering tarts. *Tartaletas.* Fruit-pies.
Tartamudear [tar-tah-moo-day-ar'], *vn.* To stutter, to stammer, to falter, to lisp, to fumble, to halt.
Tartamudeo, *m.* **Tartamudez,** *f.* [tar-tah-moo-day'-o, tar-tah-moo-deth']. Lisp, stuttering, stammering.
Tartamudo, da [tar-tah-moo'-do, dah], *a.* & *n.* Stuttering, stammering; stutterer.
Tartán [tar-tahn'], *m.* (Com.) Tartan, a Scotch plaid.
Tartana [tar-tah'-nah], *f.* 1. (Naut.) Tartan, a small coasting vessel in the Mediterranean. 2. Long covered wagon for passengers, with two wheels.
Tartanero [tar-tah-nay'-ro], *m.* The driver of a *tartana.*
Tartáreo, rea [tar-tah'-ray-o, ah], *a.* (Poet.) Tartarean, hellish.
Tartárico [tar-tah'-re-co], *a.* Tartaric, relating to tartar of wine. *V.* Tártrico.
Tartarizar [tar-tah-re-thar'], *va.* To tartarize, to impregnate with tartar, to refine with the salt of tartar.
Tártaro [tar'-tah-ro], *m.* 1. Argol, tartar, the lees of wine. 2. Dental tartar. *Crémor tártaro,* Cream of tartar.
Tártaro, ra [tar'-tah-ro, rah], *a.* Tartarian, of Tartary.
Tartera [tar-tay'-rah], *f.* 1. Baking-pan for tarts and other pastry. 2. Dripping-pan.
Tartrato [tar-trah'-to], *m.* (Chem.) Tartrate, a salt of tartaric acid.
Tártrico [tar'-tre-co], *a.* Tartaric. *Ácido tártrico,* Tartaric acid.
Taruga [tah-roo'-gah], *f.* (Amer. Obs.) A deer.
Tarugo [tah-roo'-go], *m.* A wooden peg or pin; stopper, plug, bung.
Taruguillo [tah-roo-geel'-lyo], *m. dim.* of Tarugo.
Tarumba [tah-room'-bah]. *Volver a uno tarumba,* (Coll. phrase) To confuse one, to get him mixed. *Volverse tarumba,* To become rattled. (Amer. syn. *Turumba.*)
Tas [tahs], *m.* Kind of anvil used by silversmiths.
Tasa [tah'-sah], *f.* 1. Rate, price of provisions fixed by magistrates, assize. 2. Measure, rule. 3. Valuation or appraisement of valuables.
Tasación [tah-sah-the-on'], *f.* Valuation, appraisement. *V.* Tasa.
Tasadamente [tah-sah-dah-men'-tay], *adv.* Barely, scantily, scarcely.
Tasado, da [tah-sah'-do, dah], *a.* Limited, restricted. *Tiempo tasado,* Limited amount of time.
Tasador [tah-sah-dor'], *m.* 1. Appraiser, valuator, valuer. 2. (Law) Taxing judge.
Tasajear [tah-sah-hay-ar'], *va.* (Amer.) 1. To cut meat for making jerked beef. 2. (Met.) To slash one with knife-cuts.
Tasajo [tah-sah'-ho], *m.* Jerked beef, hung-beef.
Tasar [tah-sar'], *va.* 1. To appraise, to value, to estimate. 2. To observe method and rule; to fix a regimen. 3. *Tasar judicialmente,* To tax, to rate at. 4. To give scantily of what one is obliged to give.
Tascador [tas-cah-dor'], *m.* Brake, for dressing flax or hemp.
Tascar [tas-car'], *va.* 1. To brake, to scutch or dress flax or hemp. 2. To nibble the grass: applied to beasts. *Tascar el freno,* To bite the bridle; to resist; to do a thing unwillingly.
Tascina [tas-thee'-nah], *f.* (Min.) Silver selenide.
Tasco [tahs'-co], *m.* 1. Refuse of flax or hemp. 2. (Naut.) Toppings of hemp.
Tasconio [tas-co'-ne-o], *m.* *V.* Talque.
Tasquera [tas-kay'-rah], *f.* Dispute, scuffle, contest.
Tasquil [tas-keel'], *m.* Chip which flies from a stone on working it.
Tástara [tas'-ta-rah], *f.* (Prov.) Coarse bran.
Tastaz [tas-tath], *m.* Polishing powder made of old crucibles.
Tata [tah'-tah], *m.* Word by which little children begin to call their parents. Used in Mexico vulgarly at all ages.
Tatarabuela [tah-tah-ra-boo-ay'-lah], *f.* The great-great-grandmother.
Tatarabuelo [tah-tah-ra-boo-ay'-lo], *m.* The great-great-grandfather.
Tataradeudo, da [tah-tah-rah-day'-oo-do, dah], *m.* & *f.* Very old and distant relation.
Tataranieta [tah-tah-rah-ne-ay'-tah], *f.* A great-great-granddaughter.
Tataranieto [tah-tah-rah-ne-ay'-to], *m.* A great-great-grandson.
Tatas [tah'-tas], *adv.* (Prov.) *Andar a tatas,* To walk timidly; to go on all-fours.
¡Tate! [tah'-tay], *int.* Take care, beware; stay, so it is. *Tate, tate,* Little by little.
Tato [tah'-to], *m.* 1. (Coll. Prov.) A younger brother. 2. Hog-headed armadillo.
Tato, ta [tah'-to, tah], *a.* & *n.* Stammering; stutterer who converts *c* and *s* into *t.*
Tatuaje [tah-too-ah'-hay], *m.* Tattooing, tattoo.
Tatuar [tah-too-ar'], *va.* To tattoo.
Tau [tah'-oo], *m.* *V.* Tao.—*f.* The Greek τ, nineteenth letter of the Greek alphabet.
Taumaturgo [tah-oo-mah-toor'-go], *m.* The author of great and stupendous things, miracle-worker; thaumaturgus.
Taurina [tah-oo-ree'-nah], *f.* Taurin, a crystallizable substance found in the bile of various animals, first of the ox.
Taurino, na [tah-oo-ree'-no, nah], *a.* Relating to a bull; taurine.
Tauro [tah'-oo-ro], *m.* (Ast.) Taurus, a sign of the zodiac.
Taurómaco [tah-oo-ro'-mah-co], *m.* One fond of bull-fighting.
Tauromaquia [tah-oo-ro-mah'-ke-ah], *f.* The art of bull-fighting.
Tautología [tah-oo-to-lo-hee'-ah], *f.* Tautology.
Tautológico, ca [tah-oo-to-lo'-he-co cah], *a.* Tautological.
Tautologista [tah-oo-to-lo-hees'-tah], *com.* Tautologist.
Tautometría [tah-oo-to-may-tree'-ah], *f.* Repetition of the same measure.
Tauxia [tah'-ooc-se-ah], *f.* *V.* Atauxia.
Taxativamente, *adv.* Limitedly.
Taxativo, va [tak-sah-tee'-vo, vah], *a.* (Law) Limited to circumstances.
Taxi [tak'-se], *m.* Taxi, taxicab.
Taxidermia [tak-se-derr'-me-ah], *f.* Taxidermy, the art of preserving dead animals so as to present a life-like appearance.
Taxímetro [tak-see'-may-tro], *m.* 1. Taximeter. 2. Taxi, taxicab.
Taz a taz, or **Taz por taz** [tath ah tath], *adv.* (Coll.) This for that; tit for tat. *Cambiar* or *feriar una cosa taz por taz,* To barter or swap even hands, or without odds. *Salir una cosa taz con taz,* To be brim full, complete, exact.
Taza [tah'-thah], *f.* 1. Cup. 2. Cup, the liquor contained in a cup. 3. Basin of a fountain. 4. A large wooden bowl. 5. (Coll.) Buttocks, breech. 6. (Mil.) Bucket, a pouch in which a dragoon rests the muzzle of his carbine, while he is on horseback. *Amigo de taza de vino,* A selfish friend, a sponger.
Tazaña [tah-thah'-nyah], *f.* Serpent. *V.* Tarasca.
Tazmía [tath-mee'-ah], *f.* Share of tithes.
Tazón [tah-thone'], *m. aug.* A large bowl or basin; pitcher: commonly applied to basins of fountains.
Té [tay], *m.* 1. (Bot.) Tea; a plant. Thea. 2. Tea, decoction of tea-leaves. —*f.* Name of the letter T.—*pron.* Thee, the oblique case of Thou.
Tea [tay'-ah], *f.* Candlewood, a piece of resinous wood, which burns like a torch.
Teame, Teamide [tay-ah'-may, tay-ah-mee'-day], *f.* A stone repelling iron.
Teatino [tay-ah-tee'-no], *m.* 1. A delicate sort of paste. 2. Theatin, one of a religious order founded by Pope Paul IV.
Teatral [tay-ah-trahl'], *a.* Theatrical, belonging to a theatre.
Teatralmente [tay-ah-tral-men'-tay], *adv.* Theatrically.
Teatro [tay-ah'-tro], *m.* 1. Stage, on which any show is exhibited. 2. Theatre, stage, play-house. 3. The people attending at a play-house. 4. Theatre, collection of plays belonging to a nation. 5. The profession or practice of dramatic art. 6. Stage, place where any thing is exposed to the applause or censure of the world.
Tebaico, ca [tay-bah'-e-co, cah], *a.* Thebaic, belonging to Egyptian Thebes.
Tebano, na [tay-bah'-no, nah], *a.* Theban, of Thebes.
Teca [tay'-cah], *f.* Teak, a large East-Indian tree, and its hard, elastic wood valued for ship-building. (Tagal, ticla.)
Tecale, Tecali [tay-cah'-lay], *m.* (Mex.) A very white, transparent marble: in many of the windows of convents it is used instead of glass.
Tecla [tay'-clah], *f.* 1. Key. 2. (Fig.) Touchy subject. *Dar en la tecla,* (Coll.) 1. To catch on, to get the knack. 2. To get into the habit.
Teclado [tay-clah'-do], *m.* Keyboard.
Teclear [tay-clay-ar'], *vn.* 1. To finger. 2. (Fig.) To drum, to rap one's fingers.—*vt.* To feel out, to try out, to experiment with.
Tecleo [tay-clay'-o], *m.* Fingering.
Tecnecio [tec-nay'-the-o], *m.* Technetium.
Técnicamente, *adv.* Technically.
Tecnicidad [tec-ne-the-dahd'], *f.* Technicality.
Tecnicismo [tec-ne-thees'-mo], *m.* 1. Technical vocabulary. 2. Technical term.
Técnico, ca [tec'-ne-co, cah], *a.* Technical.—*m.* Technician.—*f.* Technique.
Tecnicolor [tec-ne-co-lor'], *m.* Technicolor.
Tecnocracia [tec-no-crah'-the-ah], *f.* Technocracy.
Tecnología [tec-no-lo-hee'-ah], *f.* Tech-

nology, language proper and exclusive to the arts and sciences.

Tecnológico, ca [tec-no-lo'-he-co, cah], *a.* Technological, technical.

Tecomate [tay-co-mah'-tay], *m.* 1. (Mex.) A cup made of a gourd. 2. (Ant.) A word of contempt given by European Spaniards to the white natives of Mexico.

Techado [tay-chah'-do], *m.* *V.* TECHO. *Techado, da, pp.* of TECHAR.

Techar [tay-char'], *va.* To roof; to cover with a roof.

Techo [tay'-cho], *m.* 1. Roof, ceiling, the inner roof of a building 2. (Met.) Dwelling-house, habitation, place of abode; native soil; cover.

Techumbre [tay-choom'-bray], *f.* Upper roof, ceiling; a lofty roof, as of a church.

Tedero [tay-day'-ro], *m.* Iron candlestick for holding burning fir or torch.

Tedéum [tay-day'-oom], *m.* Te Deum, a hymn of the church.

Tediar [tay-de-ar'], *va.* To loathe, to hate, to abhor.

Tedio [tay'-de-o], *m.* Disgust, dislike, abhorrence, tediousness.

Tedioso, sa [tay-de-oh'-so, sah], *a.* Tedious, loathful, fastidious, tiresome, disgusting, nauseous to the taste or mind.

Tegual [tay-goo-ahl'], *m.* Tax or duty paid to the king.

Tegumento [tay-goo-men'-to], *m.* Tegument, covering.

Teína [tay-ee'-nah], *f.* (Chem.) Thein, the alkaloid of the tea-plant.

Teinada, *f.* *V.* TINADA.

Teísmo [tay-ees'-mo], *m.* Theism, deism.

Teísta [tay-ees'-tah], *com.* Theist, deist.

Teja [tay'-hah], *f.* Roof-tile, for covering buildings. *Teja cóncava*, Gutter or pan-tile. *A teja vana*, With a shed cover. *Caerse las tejas.* (Coll.) To be growing dark. *De tejas abajo*, In a natural order, without supernatural interference; in this world. *Teja de la silla*, (Mex.) The hind bow of a saddle: the fore bow of a saddle. *la cabeza de la silla.*

Tejadillo [tay-hah-deel'-lyo], *m.* Roof of a coach.

Tejado [tay-hah'-do], *m.* Roof covered with tiles; shed. *Andar a sombra de tejado*, To lurk, to skulk, to lie hid. *Tejado de un rato, labor para todo el año*, Hasty work calls for long repairs. *Quien tiene tejado de vidrio, no tire piedras al de su vecino*, He who lives in a glass house should not throw stones.—*Tejado, da, pp.* of TEJAR.

Tejamanil [tay-hah-mah-neel'], *m.* (Mex.) Shingles. *V.* TAJAMANIL.

Tejano, na [tay-hah'-no, nah], *m.* & *f.* & *a.* Texan.

Tejar [tay-har'], *m.* Tile-works, tile-kiln.

Tejar [tay-har'], *va.* To tile, to cover with tiles.

Tejaroz [tay-hah-roth'], *m.* Penthouse, a shed covered with tiles.

Tejazo [tay-hah'-tho], *m.* Blow with a tile.

Tejedera [tay-hay-day'-rah], *f.* 1. *V.* TEJEDORA. 2. Water-spider.

Tejedor [tay-hay-dor'], *m.* 1. Weaver. 2. Cloth manufacturer. 3. (Orn.) Weaver-bird.

Tejedora [tay-hay-do'-rah], *f.* Female weaver.

Tejedura [tay-hay-doo'-rah], *f.* 1. Texture, weaving, the act of weaving. 2. Any thing woven.

Tejeduría [tay-hay-doo-ree'-ah], *f.* 1. The art of weaving. 2. Mill, a factory for weaving.

Teje maneje [tay'-hay mah-nay'-hay], *m.* (Coll.) Doing things in an artful way.

Tejer [tay-herr'], *va.* 1. To weave cloth. 2. To regulate, to adjust. 3. To discuss, to devise; to entangle. 4. To cross and mix according to rule, as in dancing.

Tejera, Tejería [tay-nay'-rah, tay-hay-ree'-ah], *f.* Tile-kiln. *V.* TEJAR.

Tejero [tay-hay'-ro], *m.* Tile-maker.

Tejido [tay-hee'-do], *m.* 1. Texture, weaving, the act of weaving. 2. Texture, fabric, web, a thing woven. *V.* TELA. 3. Tissue of an organized body. *Tejido adiposo*, Adipose tissue. *Tejido celular*, Cellular tissue (bot.), connective tissue (anat.).—*Tejido, da, pp. of* TEJER.

Tejillo [tay-heel'-lyo], *m.* 1. A band used by women as a girdle. 2. (Dim.) A small quoit.

Tejo [tay'-ho], *m.* 1. Quoit, round tile with which boys play; also the game. 2. (Bot.) Yew-tree. Taxus baccata. 3. A round metal plate.

Tejocote [tay-ho-co'-tay], *m.* (Bot. Mex.) A fruit resembling a sloe.

Tejoleta [tay-ho-lay'-tah], *f.* 1. Piece of burnt clay; tile. 2. A shuffle-board.

Tejolote [tay-ho-lo'-tay], *m.* (Mex.) Stone pestle for a culinary mortar.

Tejón [tay-hone'], *m.* 1. A wedge or plate of gold. 2. (Zool.) Badger.

Tejuelo [tay-hoo-ay'-lo], *m.* 1. Space between the bands on the back of a book for the title. 2. (Mech.) Bush, pillow block, socket, sole-plate.

Tela [tay'-lah], *f.* 1. Cloth, fabric, any stuff woven in a loom. 2. Gold or silver lace. 3. Chain or warp of cloth; that which is put at one time in a loom. 4. Pellicle, the thin interior skin of the animal body or of fruits; membrane. 5. Film or pellicle on the surface of liquors. 6. Quibble, quirk. 7. Cobweb of a spider; web of some other insects. 8. Argument; matter; thread of a discourse. 9. Membrane or opacity in the eye. *Tela encerada* or *engomada*, Buckram.

Telabrejo [tay-lah-bray'-ho], *m.* (Mex.) 1. A thing of small account. 2. A person of small account.

Telamón [tay-lah-mon'], *m.* (Arch.) *V.* ATLANTE.

Telar [tay-lar'], *m.* 1. Loom, in which cloth is woven; a frame in which other things are made. 2. Upper part of the scene-work in a theatre, out of sight of the public, where the curtains are raised and lowered.

Telaraña [tay-lah-rah'-nyah], *f.* 1. Cobweb. 2. A small cloud. 3. Any thing trifling and of little weight. *Mirar las telarañas*, (Coll.) To be in a brown study, or to be absent-minded.

Telecomunicación [tay-lay-co-moo-ne-cah-the-on'], *f.* Telecommunication.

Teledirección [tay-lay-de-rec-the-on'], *f.* Remote control.

Teledirigido, da [tay-lay-de-re-hee'-do, dah], *a.* Remote-control.

Teledirigir [tay-lay-de-re-heer'], *vt.* To operate by remote control.

Teleférico [tay-lay-fay'-re-co], *m.* Cable car.

Telefio [tay-lay'-fe-o], *m.* Orpine.

Telefonazo [tay-lay-fo-nah'-tho], *m.* (Coll.) Phone call.

Telefonear [tay-lay-fo-nay-ar'], *va.* To telephone, to phone.

Telefonema [tay-lay-fo-nay'-mah], *m.* Telephone message.

Telefonía [tay-lay-fo-nee'-ah], *f.* Telephony.

Telefónico, ca [tay-lay-fo'-ne-co, cah], *a.* Telephonic, telephone.

Telefonista [tay-lay-fo-nees'-tah], *f.* Telephone operator.—*m.* Telephone service man.

Teléfono [tay-lay'-fo-no], *m.* Telephone, phone. *Teléfono automático*, Dial phone.

Telefoto, *m.* **Telefotografía,** *f.* [tay-lay-fo'-to, tay-lay-fo-to-grah-fee'-ah]. Telephotography.

Telegrafía [tay-lay-grah-fee'-ah], *f.* Telegraphy.

Telegrafiar [tay-lay-grah-fe-ar'], *va.* To telegraph.

Telegráficamente, *adv.* Telegraphically.

Telegráfico, ca [tay-lay-grah'-fe-co, cah], *a.* Telegraphic, telegraph.

Telegrafista [tay-lay-grah-fees'-tah], *com.* Telegrapher, telegraphist.

Telégrafo [tay-lay'-grah-fo], *m.* Telegraph.

Telegrama [tay-lay-grah'-mah], *m.* Telegram.

Teleguiar [tay-lay-gee-ar'], *va.* To operate by remote control.

Teleimpresor [tay-lay-im-pray-sor'], *m.* Teleprinter.

Telemando [tay-lay-mahn'-do], *m.* Remote control.

Telemecánico, ca [tay-lay-may-cah'-ne-co, cah], *a.* Telemechanic.—*f.* Telemechanics.

Telemedición [tay-lay-may-de-the-on'], *f.* Telemetering.

Telemetría [tay-lay-may-tree'-ah], *f.* Telemetry.

Telemétrico, ca [tay-lay-may'-tre-co, cah], *a.* Telemetric.

Telémetro [tay-lay'-may-tro], *m.* 1. Range finder. 2. Telemeter.

Teleobjetivo [tay-lay-ob-hay-tee'-vo], *m.* Telephoto lens.

Teleología [tay-lay-o-lo-hee'-áh], *f.* Teleology.

Telepatía [tay-lay-pah-tee'-ah], *f.* Telepathy.

Telepático, ca [tay-lay-pah'-te-co, cah], *a.* Telepathic.

Telera [tay-lay'-rah], *f.* 1. Plough pin. 2. Pen (for sheep or cattle). 3. Jaw (of a vise).

Telerán [tay-lay-ran'], *m.* Teleran.

Telerreceptor [tay-ler-ray-thep-tor'], *m.* Television set.

Telescópico, ca [tay-les-co'-pe-co, cah], *a.* Telescopic.

Telescopio [tay-les-co'-pe-o], *m.* Telescope.

Telesilla [tay-lay-seel'-lya], *m.* Chair lift.

Telespectador, ra [tay-les-pec-tah-dor', rah], *m.* & *f.* Televiewer.

Telesquí [tay-les-kee'], *m.* Ski lift.

Telestesia [tay-les-tay'-se-ah], *f.* Telesthesia.

Telestudio [tay-les-too'-de-o], *m.* Television studio.

Teleta [tay-lay'-tah], *f.* Blotting paper.

Teletipo [tay-lay-tee'-po], *m.* Teletype.

Teletubo [tay-lay-too'-bo], *m.* Television picture tube.

Televidente [tay-lay-ve-den'-tay], *m.* Television viewer, televiewer.

Televisar [tay-lay-ve-sar'], *va.* To televise.

Televisión [tay-lay-ve-se-on'], *f.* Television.

Televisor [tay-lay-ve-sor'], *m.* Television set.

Telón [tay-lon'], *m.* (Th.) Drop curtain. *Telón de boca*, Front curtain. *Telón de hierro*, Iron curtain.

Telúrico, ca [tay-loo'-re-co, cah], *a.* Telluric.

Telurio [tay-loo'-re-o], **Teluro**, *m.* (Min.) Tellurium, a metallic element.

Tellina [tel-lyee'-nah], *f.* Bivalve shell-fish; mussel.

Telliz [tel-lyeeth'], *m.* Cloth thrown over the saddle of a horse for ornament.

Telliza [tel-lyee'-thah], *f.* Coverlet of a bed.

Tema [tay'-mah], *m.* Text, proposition, theme, subject, composition.—*f.* 1. Topic of madmen's discourses. 2. Dispute, contention; obstinacy in asserting a controverted point. 3. Animosity, passionate malignity; capricious opposition. *A tema*, Emulously, obstinately. *Tema celeste*. (Ast.) Map or delineation of the heavens. *Tener tema a alguna persona*, To have a grudge against some person. *Cada uno tiene su tema*, (Coll.) Every man has his hobby.

Temario [tay-mah'-re-o], *m.* 1. Schedule. 2. List of topics.

Temático, ca [tay-mah'-te-co, cah], *a.* 1. Relating to a theme or subject, thematic. 2. *V.* TEMOSO.

Tembladal, *m.* *V.* TREMEDAL.

Tembladera [tem-blah-day'-rah], *f.* 1. Tankard, a wide-mouthed vessel with two handles. 2. Diamond-pin, or other similar ornament of the head-dress of ladies. 3. (Zool.) Torpedo, electric ray. Torpedo marmorata or occidentalis.

Tembladero [tem-blah-day'-ro], *m.* *V.* TREMEDAL.

Temblador, ra [tem-blah-dor', rah], *m.* & *f.* Quaker, shaker, trembler.

Temblante [tem-blahn'-tay], *m.* Kind of loose bracelet worn by women.—*pa.* Trembling, quavering.

Temblar [tem-blar'], *vn.* To tremble, to shake with fear, to move with violent agitation; to quake. *Temblar la barba*, To enter with caution and dread on an arduous undertaking. *Temblar la contera*, (Met. Coll.) To be greatly afraid of any thing. *Temblar las carnes*, (Coll.) To have a horror of a thing.

Tembleque [tem-blay'-kay], *m.* 1. Diamond-pin or plume, or other similar ornament of the head-dress of ladies. 2. *V.* LENTEJUELA.

Temblequear, Tembletear [tem-blay-kay-ar'], *vn.* To tremble, to shake with fear; to move with violent agitation.

Temblón, na [tem-blone', nah], *a.* Tremulous. *Hacer la temblona*, To affect timidity.

Temblón [tem-blone'], *m.* (Bot.) Aspen or asp tree. Populus tremula.

Temblor [tem-blor'], *m.* Trembling, involuntary motion proceeding from fear or weakness. *Temblor de tierra*, Earthquake.

Temblorcillo [tem-blor-theel'-lyo], *m. dim.* A slight shivering.

Tembloroso, sa [tem-blo-ro'-so, sah], *a.* Trembling, trembly, tremulous, quivering, shaking.

Tembloso, sa [tem-blo'-so, sah], *a.* Tremulous.

Temedero, ra [tay-may-day'-ro, rah], *a.* Awful, dreadful.

Temedor, ra [tay-may-dor', rah], *a.* 1. Applied to a trembler. 2. Awful, dreadful.

Temedor, ra, *m.* & *f.* Trembler.

Temer [tay-merr'], *va.* 1. To apprehend, to fear, to dread; to reverence, to respect. 2. To suspect, to misdoubt.

Temerariamente, *adv.* Rashly, hastily, inconsiderately.

Temerario, ria [tay-may-rah'-re-o, ah], *a.* Rash, inconsiderate, imprudent, daring, overbold, hasty, headlong.

Temeridad [tay-may-re-dahd'], *f.* Temerity, rashness, imprudence; foolhardiness. *Ser una temeridad*, (1) Said of imprudence or rashness. (2) (Coll.) To be excessive.

Temerón, na [tay-may-rone', nah], *a.* Affecting noise, authority, or bullying.

Temerosamente, *adv.* Timorously.

Temeroso, sa [tay-may-ro'-so, sah], *a.* 1. Awe-inspiring; exciting fear or suspicion, dreadful. 2. Timid, timorous; fearful; cowardly.

Temesquitato [tay-mes-ke-tah'-to], *m.* (Mex.) Dross from the surface of lead into which pulverized silver ore is introduced.

Temible [tay-mee'-blay], *a.* Dreadful terrible, awful.

Temiente [tay-me-en'-tay], *pa.* One who dreads or apprehends.

Temor [tay-mor'], *m.* Dread, fear, apprehension, suspicion.

Temorizar [tay-mo-re-thar'], *va.* (Obs.) *V.* ATEMORIZAR.

Temoso, sa [tay-mo'-so, sah], *a.* Obstinate, stubborn.

Tempanador [tem-pa-nah-dor'], *m.* Instrument for cutting off the tops of bee-hives.

Tempanar [tem-pa-nar'], *va.* To furnish staves; to cover the tops of bee-hives.

Témpano [tem'-pah-no], *m.* 1. Flitch of bacon. 2. *V.* TÍMPANO. 3. Tympan, stretched skin or other thing; open, plain space. 4. Large cork put in the top of bee-hives. 5. (Arch.) Tympan of an arch. *Témpano de cuba*, Heading or head-staves of a barrel or cask. *Témpano de hielo*, A piece of ice.

Temperación [tem-pay-rah-the-on'], *f.* *V.* TEMPERAMENTO.

Temperadamente [tem-pay-ra-dah-men'-tay], *adv.* *V.* TEMPLADAMENTE.

Temperamento [tem-pay-rah-men'-to], *m.* 1. Temperature, climate. 2. Arbitration, compromise, means for ending disputes or dissensions. 3. Temperament, constitution; as nervous, lymphatic, etc.

Temperancia, Temperanza [tem-pay-rahn'-the-ah], *f.* *V.* TEMPLANZA.

Temperante [tem-pay-rahn'-tay], *pa.* (Med.) That which tempers.

Temperar [tem-pay-rar'], *va.* 1. *V.* ATEMPERAR. 2. (Amer.) *V.* VERANEAR.

Temperatura [tem-pay-rah-too'-rah], *f.* Temperature, the degree of cold or warmth, measured by the thermometer.

Temperie [tem-pay'-re-ay], *f.* Temperature of the air; its constitution as produced by different degrees of heat and cold, dryness and dampness.

Tempero [tem-pay'-ro], *m.* Seasonableness, fitness of the soil for the growth of seeds.

Tempestad [tem-pes-tahd'], *f.* 1. Tempest, storm. 2. Violent perturbation of the mind. *Tempestades*, Violent, abusive language.

Tempestar [tem-pes-tar'], *vn.* To be a tempest, to screech out.

Tempestivamente, *adv.* Seasonably, opportunely.

Tempestivo, va [tem-pes-tee'-vo, vah], *a.* Seasonable, opportune.

Tempestuosamente, *adv.* Tempestuously, turbulently.

Tempestuoso, sa [tem-pes-too-oh'-so, sah], *a.* Tempestuous, stormy, turbulent.

Templa [tem'-plah], *f.* (Art.) Distemper, size for painting.

Templación [tem-plah-the-on'], *f.* (Obs.) *V.* TEMPLANZA and TEMPLE.

Templadamente [tem-plah-dah-men-tay], *adv.* Temperately, moderately, abstemiously, freshly; calmly.

Templadera [tem-plah-day'-rah], *f.* (Prov.) Sluice put into a channel to let a certain quantity of water pass.

Templadico, ca [tem-plah-dee'-co, cah], *a. dim.* Somewhat temperate.

Templado, da [tem-plah'-do, dah], *a.* Temperate, tempered, moderate, abstemious, frugal, lukewarm.—*pp.* of TEMPLAR.

Templador, ra [tem-plah-dor', rah], *m.* & *f.* Tuner; one who tempers.—*m.* 1. Tuning key for musical instruments. 2. (Peru) Circular stockade in the midst of the arena for refuge of bull-fighters.

Templadura [tem-plah-doo'-rah], *f.* Temper, the act of tempering.

Templanza [tem-plahn'-thah], *f.* 1. Temperance, moderation, abstinence, abstemiousness. 2. Sobriety. 3. Disposition of the air or climate of a country; degree of heat or cold. 4. (Art.) Due proportion and good disposition of colours.

Templar [tem-plar'], *va.* 1. To temper, to soften, to moderate, to cool. 2. To temper steel; to anneal glass. 3. To tune musical instruments. 4. To observe a due proportion of parts in a painting. 5. (Naut.) To trim the sails to the wind. 6. To mix, to assuage, to soften. 7. To prepare, to dispose. 8. To train a hawk.—*vr.* To be moderate; to refrain from excess. *Templar la gaita*, (Coll.) To pacify, to please.

Templario [tem-plah'-re-o], *m.* Templar, one of the order of Templars.

Temple [tem'-play], *m.* 1. Temperature of the season or climate. 2. Temper given to metals. 3. Temperament, medium, due mixture of opposites. 4. Frame or disposition of the mind. 5. The concordance of musical instruments. 6. Religion of the Templars; a temple or church. *Al temple*, Painted in distemper.

Templecillo [tem-play-theel'-lyo], *m. dim.* A small temple.

Templete [tem-play'-tay], *m. dim.* *V.* TEMPLECILLO. Applied to architectural ornaments in form of a temple.

Templista [tem-plees'-tah], *m.* Painter in distemper.

Templo [tem'-plo], *m.* 1. Temple, church for the worship of God. 2. Blessed soul. 3. Temple dedicated to the false gods of the Gentiles.

Témpora [tem'-po-rah], *f.* Ember week, days of fast prescribed by the Roman Catholic church, in the four seasons of the year: generally used in the plural.

Temporada [tem-po-rah'-dah], *f.* A certain space of time. *La temporada de la ópera* or *del teatro*, The opera or play season.

Temporal [tem-po-rahl'], *a.* 1. Temporary, temporal. 2. Secular, temporal, pertaining to the civil power. 3. Temporal, belonging to the temples of the head.—*m.* 1. Season, whether good or bad. 2. Tempest, storm. 3. (Prov.) Temporary labourer.

Temporalidad [tem-po-rah-le-dahd'], *f.* 1. Temporality, the secular revenues of the clergy. 2. Temporal concerns, affairs of this life.

Temporalizar [tem-po-rah-le-thar'], *va.* To make temporary what might or should be everlasting.

Temporalmente [tem-po-ral-men'-tay], *adv.* Temporally, with respect to this life; for some time, or for a certain time.

Temporáneo, nea [tem-po-rah'-nay-o, ah], *a.* Temporary, unstable.
Temporario, ria [tem-po-rah'-re-o, ah], *a.* Temporary, not lasting.
Temporero, Temporil [tem-po-ray'-ro], *m.* Temporary labourer, one who works only for a season.
Temporizador, ra [tem-po-re-thah-dor', rah], *m.* & *f.* Temporizer, trimmer.
Temporizar [tem-po-re-thar'], *vn.* 1. To pass the time in any place or thing. 2. To comply with the times, to temporize. *V.* CONTEMPORIZAR.
Tempranal [tem-prah-nahl'], *a.* Producing early fruits: applied to land.
Tempranamente [tem-prah-nah-men'-tay], *adv.* Early, prematurely.
Tempranero, ra [tem-prah-nay'-ro, rah], *a.* *V.* TEMPRANO.
Tempranilla [tem-prah-neel'-lyah], *f.* (Prov.) Sort of early grape.
Temprano, na [tem-prah'-no, nah], *a.* Early, soon, anticipated, forehanded.
Temprano [tem-prah'-no], *adv.* Very early, prematurely, soon.
Temulento, ta [tay-moo-len'-to, tah], *a.* Intoxicated, inebriated.
Tena [tay'-nah], *f.* (Agr.) A flock of sheep or goats, not over sixty head.
Tenacear [tay-nah-thay-ar'], *va.* To tear with pincers.—*vn.* To insist obstinately and pertinaciously.
Tenacero [tay-nah-thay'-ro], *m.* He who makes or uses pincers.
Tenacicas [tay-nah-thee'-cas], *f. pl.* 1. (Dim.) Small tongs. 2. Pincers; snuffers.
Tenacillas [tay-nah-theel'-lyas], *f. pl. dim.* Small tongs. *Tenacillas de boca,* Flat-pointed pliers. *Tenacillas de punta,* Sharp-pointed pliers.
Tenacidad [tay-nah-the-dahd'], *f.* 1. Tenacity, viscosity, glutinousness. 2. Tenacity, tenaciousness, pertinacity, contumacy.
Tenáculo [tay-nah'-coo-lo], *m.* (Med.) Tenaculum, a curved sharp hook for holding an artery which is to be tied.
Tenada [tay-nah'-dah], *f.* (Prov.) Sheep-fold, sheep-cot.
Tenallón [tay-nal-lyone'], *m.* (Mil.) Tenaillon, outwork on the flanks of a fortification: commonly used in the plural in both languages.
Tenante [tay-nahn'-tay], *m.* (Her.) Supporter; figure of a man, angel, etc., supporting a shield.
Tenate [tay-nah'-tay], *m.* (Mex.) *V.* TANATE.
Tenaz [tay-nath'], *a.* 1. Tenacious, sticking. 2. Firm, stubborn, obstinate, contumacious. 3. Avaricious, niggardly, covetous.
Tenaza [tay-nah'-thah], *f.* 1. Tenaille, a kind of outwork of a fortress. 2. Claws or talons of animals.—*pl.* 3. Tongs. 4. Pincers, forceps.
Tenazada [tay-nah-thah'-dah], *f.* 1. The act of griping with pincers or tongs. 2. The act of biting strongly.
Tenazmente [tay-nath-men'-tay], *adv.* Tenaciously.
Tenazón [tay-nah-thone'], *f.* *A tenazón,* Point-blank, without taking aim. *Parar de tenazón,* To stop a horse short in his course.
Tenazuelas [tay-nah-thoo-ay'-las], *f. pl. dim.* Tweezers.
Tenca [ten'-cah], *f.* (Zool.) Tench. Cyprinus tinca.
Tención [ten-the-on'], *f.* Holding, retaining.
Tencón [ten-cone'], *f.* (Zool.) A large tench.
Ten con ten [ten con ten'], *m.* Moderation, temperance. *Ten con ten,* Equally, making both ends meet. *Andar con un ten con ten,* To act guardedly, to proceed with moderation and equity.
Tendajo [ten-dah'-ho], *m.* *V.* TENDEJÓN.
Tendal [ten-dahl'], *m.* 1. Tilt, canvas cover. 2. A long and broad piece of canvas placed under olive-trees when picking the fruit. 3. *V.* TENDEDERO.
Tendalera [ten-dah-lay'-rah], *f.* (Coll.) Confusion and disorder of things lying about on the floor.
Tendalero [ten-dah-lay'-ro], *m.* Place where washed wool is dried.
Tendedero [tan-day-day'-ro], *m.* 1. Clothesline. 2. Place for hanging clothes.
Tendedura [ten-day-doo'-rah], *f.* Tension, stretching or extending.
Tendejón [ten-day-hone'], *m.* Sutler's tent in a camp.
Tendel [ten-del'], *m.* Line by which masons raise a wall; plumb-line.
Tendencia [ten-den'-the-ah], *f.* Tendency, inclination, direction towards a place; inference or result.
Tendencioso, sa [ten-den-the-o'-so, sah], *a.* Tendentious. *Literatura tendenciosa,* Propaganda literature.
Tendente [ten-den'-tay], *a.* Tending, leading, directing.
Tender [ten-derr'], *va.* To stretch or stretch out, to unfold, to expand, to spread out; to distend.—*vn.* To direct, to tend, to refer a thing to some end or object.—*vr.* 1. To stretch one's self at full length. 2. In card-playing, to throw all the cards upon the table. *Tenderla,* To challenge, to provoke a dispute. *Tender el paño de púlpito,* (Coll.) To speak largely and diffusely. *Tender la raspa,* (Coll.) To lay one's self down to sleep or rest. *Tender las redes,* (1) To cast the nets. (2) (Met.) To use proper names for attaining an object.
Tenderete [ten-day-ray'-tay], *m.* 1. Kind of game at cards. 2. *V.* TENDALERA. 3. (Mex.) A second-hand clothing shop.
Tendería [ten-day-ree'-ah], *f.* Place full of shops.
Tendero, ra [ten-day'-ro, rah], *m.* & *f.* Shopkeeper; haberdasher; tent-maker.
Tendezuela [ten-day-thoo-ay'-lah], *f. dim.* of TIENDA.
Tendidamente, *adv.* Diffusely, diffusively.
Tendido [ten-dee'-do], *m.* 1. A row of seats for spectators at a bull-feast. 2. Quantity of clothes dried by a laundress at once. 3. Roof of a house from the ridge to the eaves. 4. (Amer.) Riffle, among miners.—*Tendido, da, pp.* of TENDER.
Tendiente [ten-de-en'-tay], *pa.* Tending, expanding.
Tendón [ten-done'], *m.* Tendon. *Tendón de Aquiles,* (Anat.) Achilles' tendon.
Tenducha, Tenducho [ten-doo-chah, cho], *f.* & *m.* A wretched shop.
Tenebrario [tay-nay-brah'-re-o], *m.* A large candlestick or girandole, used in Roman Catholic churches in Holy week.
Tenebrosidad [tay-nay-bro-se-dahd'], *f.* Darkness, obscurity, gloom.
Tenebroso, sa [tay-nay-bro'-so, sah], *a.* Tenebrous, dark, gloomy; obscure in style; horrid.
Tenedero [tay-nay-day'-ro], *m.* (Naut.) Bottom of the sea where the anchor catches. Gripe of an anchor. *Fondo de buen tenedero,* Good anchoring ground.
Tenedor [tay-nay-dor'], *m.* 1. Holder, keeper, tenant; guardian. *Tenedor del gran sello,* Keeper of the great seal. *Tenedor de libros,* Book-keeper. *Tenedor de póliza,* Policy-holder. *Tenedor de bastimentos,* (Naut.) Store-keeper of the navy. 2. Fork to eat with. *Tenedor de caldero,* Flesh-hook. 3. He who detains balls at play.
Teneduría [tay-nay-doo-ree'-ah], *f.* 1. The position of book-keeper. 2. The art of book-keeping.
Tenencia [tay-nen'-the-ah], *f.* 1. Possession, holding, the act of holding or possessing. 2. Lieutenancy, lieutenantship.
Tener [tay-nerr'], *va.* 1. To contain, to comprise, to comprehend, to have within. 2. To take, to gripe, to hold fast. 3. To hold, to possess, to enjoy, to have. 4. To be rich and opulent in ready money. 5. To hold, to maintain, to support. 6. To subject, to domineer, to hold in subjection. 7. To hold an opinion, to keep, to retain. 8. To hold, to estimate, to judge, to take, to set a value upon. In this sense it is followed by the preposition *en* and the adjectives *poco, mucho,* etc. 9. To lodge, to receive in one's house. 10. To be obliged, to have to do; to be at the expense of any thing. 11. To be adorned or favoured with any thing. 12. To detain, to stop. 13. To keep or fulfil. 14. With nouns of time, it signifies duration or age; when united with *que* and followed by an infinitive verb, it implies necessity or obligation. *Tener que hacer,* To have something to do. *Tener que ir,* To be obliged to go. 15. To have: used as an auxiliary verb. 16. With some nouns it means to suffer what the noun signifies. *Tener hambre,* To be hungry. *Tener sueño,* To be sleepy. *Tener miedo,* To be afraid. *Tener vergüenza,* To be ashamed. *Tener celos de uno,* To be jealous of one. *Tener brazos,* To have interest or powerful friends. *Tener mucho de miserable,* To have much of the miser. *Tener para sí,* To maintain a particular or singular opinion, liable to objections. *Tener de ahí,* Hold! stop! to be clever in something.—*vr.* 1. To take care not to fall. 2. To stop, to halt. 3. To resist, to oppose. 4. To adhere, to stand to. *Tenerse en pie,* To keep on foot; to stand. *Tenga Vd. la bondad de decirme,* Pray tell me. *Tener gana,* To have a mind, an inclination. *Tener razón,* To be right. *Tener consigo,* To have with or about one. *No tenerlas todas consigo,* To be not easy in mind, to be suspicious. *V. No llevarlas todas consigo. Tenerlas tiesas,* To resist stoutly. *No tener hiel,* To be meek and gentle. *Tener correa,* To bear raillery calmly. *Tener malos dedos para organista,* To be incompetent. *Tener cataratas,* Not to understand clearly. *Tener refranes,* To be versed in tricks and villainies. *Tener soga de ahorcado,* To have the rope with which a man was hanged; that is, to have good luck. *¿Tenemos hijo o hija?* Have we a son or a daughter? has this affair succeeded or failed? *Tened y tengamos,* Give and take; stand by me and I'll stand by you. *La semana que no tenga viernes,* Never (the week in which there is no Friday). *Tiene pluma,* He has feathered his nest well. *Tener sangre en el ojo,* To be prompt and honourable in fulfilling engagements. *Tener* forms numerous other phrases, many of which will be found under the respective nouns or adjectives with which it is associated.

Tenería [tay-nay-ree'-ah], *f.* Tan-yard, tannery.

Tenesmo [tay-nes'-mo], *m.* Tenesmus. (*Yo tengo, tuve, tenga, tendré.* *V.* TENER.)

Tengua [ten'-goo-ah], *a.* & *n.* (Amer. Mex.) Hare-lipped.

Tenia [tay'-ne-ah], *f.* Tape-worm.

Teniente [tay-ne-en'-tay], *a.* 1. Immature, unripe. 2. Deaf. *Es teniente* or *teniente de oídos,* Said of a person hard of hearing. 3. Miserly, mean.

Teniente, *m.* 1. Deputy, substitute. 2. Lieutenant. *Teniente de una compañía,* Lieutenant of a company. *Teniente general,* Lieutenant-general. 3. Miser.

Tenis [tay'-nis], *m.* Tennis. *Cancha de tenis,* Tennis court.

Tenista [tay-nees'-tah], *m.* & *f.* Tennis player.

Tenor [tay-nor'], *m.* 1. Permanent establishment or order of any thing; continuity of state. 2. Tenor, contents, sense contained. 3. Tenor, one of the four voices in music; tenorist, who sings tenor. 4. Tenor, a musical instrument of this pitch. *A tenor de,* (Com.) Pursuant to, in compliance with.

Tensión [ten-se-on'], *f.* 1. Tension, the act of stretching. 2. Tension, the state of being extended.

Tenso, sa [ten'-so, sah], *a.* Tense, tight, extended, stiff.

Tentación [ten-tah-the-on'], *f.* 1. Temptation, enticement. 2. That which is offered to the mind.

Tentacioncilla [ten-tah-the-on-theel'-lyah], *f. dim.* A slight temptation.

Tentaculado, da [ten-tah-coo-lah'-do, dah], *a.* (Zool.) Tentaculate, having tentacles.

Tentáculo [ten-tah'-coo-lo], *m.* Tentacle, a flexible process generally about the head.

Tentadero [ten-tah-day'-ro], *m.* Corral or inclosed place for taming calves.

Tentador, ra [ten-tah-dor', rah], *m.* & *f.* Tempter.

Tentadura [ten-tah-doo'-rah], *f.* (Min.) Test for finding out the metal incorporated with mercury.

Tentalear [ten-tah-lay-ar'], *va.* (Prov.) To try, to feel, to examine.

Tentar [ten-tar'], *va.* 1. To touch; to try, to examine or prove by touch, to feel. 2. To grope. 3. To tempt, to instigate, to incite, to stimulate. 4. To attempt, to procure. 5. To hesitate. 6. To probe a wound; to tent. 7. To experiment; to try; to prove. *Andar tentando,* To make essays or trials; to grope or feel where one cannot see. *Tentar el vado,* To sound one's abilities or sentiments; to try the depth, either physical or moral. *Tentar la ropa,* (Met.) To tergiversate, to use evasions.

Tentativa [ten-tah-tee'-vah], *f.* Attempt, trial; first examination.

Tentativo, va [ten-tah-tee'-vo, vah], *a.* Tentative.

Tente bonete [ten'-tay bo-nay'-tay], *adv.* Abundantly, excessively. *A tente bonete* or *hasta tente bonete,* Excessively, extremely. *Tente en el aire,* (*com.*) The child of a quadroon and a mulatto, on either side. *Tente en pie, m.* (Coll.) A light repast taken between meals.

Tentemozo [ten-tay-mo'-tho], *m.* Prop to a house, to prevent its falling.

Tentempié [ten-tem-pe-ay'], *m.* Snack, hasty repast.

Tentón [ten-tone'], *m.* (Coll.) Touch, act of touching: especially applied to touching any thing suddenly.

Tenudo, da [tay-noo'-do, dah], *pp. irr. obs.* of TENER. Held. It was generally joined with the verb *ser,* when it signified, To be obliged, to be necessitated.

Tenue [tay'-noo-ay], *a.* 1. Thin, tenuous, slender, delicate. 2. Worthless, of little value or importance. 3. Applied to soft consonants.

Tenuemente [tay-noo-ay-men'-tay], *adv.* Slightly.

Tenuidad [tay-noo-e-dahd'], *f.* 1. Tenuity, weakness. 2. Trifle, thing of little value or importance.

Tenuta [tay-noo'-tah], *f.* Provisional possession of an estate during a lawsuit.

Tenutario, ria [tay-noo-tah'-re-o, ah], *a.* Provisional tenant.

Teñidura [tay-nye-doo'-rah], *f.* Art of dyeing or tingeing.

Teñir [tay-nyeer'], *va.* 1. To tinge, to dye; to stain; to paint the face. *Teñir en rama,* To dye in grain, to ingrain. 2. (Met.) To give another colour to things, to dissemble or misrepresent. 3. (Pict.) To darken, to sadden a colour.

Teocalli [tay-o-cahl'-lyee], *m.* (Mex.) Teocalli, a pyramidal mound on which the Aztecs celebrated their sacrifices.

Teocracia [tay-o-crah'-the-ah], *f.* Theocracy, government by priests.

Teocrático, ca [tay-o-crah'-te-co, cah], *a.* Theocratic, theocratical.

Teodolito [tay-o-do-lee'-to], *m.* Theodolite.

Teologal [tay-o-lo-gahl'], *a.* Theological. *Virtud teologal,* Theological virtue, faith, hope, or charity.—Theological prebendary. *V.* LECTORAL.

Teología [tay-o-lo-hee'-ah], *f.* Theology, divinity. *Teología moral,* Casuistry. *No meterse en teologías,* (Coll.) Not to involve one's self in subtleties.

Teológicamente, *adv.* Theologically.

Teológico, ca [tay-o-lo'-he-co, cah], *a.* *V.* TEOLOGAL.

Teologizar [tay-o-lo-he-thar'], *vn.* To treat or discourse upon the principles of theology, to theologize.

Teólogo [tay-o'-lo-go], *m.* 1. A divine, a clergyman. 2. A professor or student of theology.

Teólogo, ga, *a.* Theological.

Teorema [tay-o-ray'-mah], *m.* Theorem.

Teorético, ca [tay-o-ray'-te-co, cah], *a.* Theoretic.

Teoría, Teórica [tay-o-ree'-ah, tay-o'-re-cah], *f.* Theory, speculation.

Teóricamente, *adv.* Theoretically.

Teórico, ca [tay-o'-re-co, cah], *a.* Theoretical, speculative.

Teoso, sa [tay-oh'-so, sah], *a.* Resinous.

Teosofía [tay-o-so-fee'-ah], *f.* Theosophy, a philosophy of the universe, universal religion, a mystical speculation.

Teosófico, ca [tay-o-so'-fe-co, cah], *a.* Theosophical, pertaining to theosophy.

Teósofo [tay-oh'-so-fo], *m.* Theosophist.

Teotl, Teutl [tay-otl'], *m.* The supreme being among the Aztecs.

Tepalcate [tay-pal-cah'-tay], *m.* (Mex.) Small pieces of broken earthenware; potsherd: generally used in the plural.

Tepe [tay'-pay], *m.* Green sod.

Tepeguaje [tay-pay-goo-ah'-hay], *m.* A very hard and compact Mexican wood. —*a.* (Met. Mex.) Set, obstinate.

Tepeizquinte [tay-pay-eeth-keen'-tay], *m.* South American animal, resembling a sucking pig.

Tepetate [tay-pay-tah'-tay], *m.* 1. A layer of soil which answers for building houses in Mexico. 2. All mining ground which holds no ore.

Tepexilote [tay-pek-se-lo'-tay, properly tay-pay-she-lo'-tay], *m.* (Bot.) A nut like a filbert, very hard, from which counters and rosaries with various figures are made.

Tequila [tay-kee'-lah], *m.* Tequila, Mexican liquor distilled from the century plant.

Tequío [tay-kee'-o], *m.* In Mexico, charge, tax. *V.* CARGA CONCEJIL.

Terapéutica [tay-rah-pay'-oo-te-cah], *f.* Therapeutics, the branch of medicine, which treats of remedies.

Terapéutico, ca [tay-rah-pay'-oo-te-co, cah], *a.* Therapeutic, remedial, curative.

Tercamente [ter-cah-men'-tay], *adv.* Opinionately, opinionatively, obstinately.

Tercena [ter-thay'-nah], *f.* Wholesale tobacco warehouse.

Tercenal [ter-thay-nahl'], *m.* (Prov.) Heap containing thirty sheaves of corn.

Tercenista [ter-thay-nees'-tah], *m.* Keeper of a wholesale tobacco warehouse.

Tercer [ter-therr'], *m.* Third.—*a.* Third: used before a substantive.

Tercera [ter-thay'-rah], *f.* 1. (Mus.) Third, a consonance comprehending an interval of two tones. 2. One of the strings of a guitar. 3. Series of three cards in order at play. 4. Procuress, bawd.

Terceramente, *adv.* Thirdly.

Tercería [ter-thay-ree'-ah], *f.* 1. Mediation, arbitration. 2. Arbitration dues or fees. 3. Depositary. 4. Temporary occupation of a castle, fortress, etc.

Tercerilla [ter-thay-reel'-lyah], *f.* Triplet, metrical composition.

Tercero, ra [ter-thay'-ro, rah], *a.* Third.

Tercero, *m.* 1. A third person. 2. Mediator, arbitrator. 3. Collector of tithes. 4. Religious of the third order of St. Francis. 5. Pimp, procurer, bawd. *Tercero en discordia,* Umpire between two disputants.

Tercerol [ter-thay-role'], *m.* (Naut.) Main-sail; third pair of oars.

Tercerola [ter-thay-ro'-lah], *f.* 1. A short kind of carbine. 2. Tierce, small cask.

Tercerón, na [ter-thay-rone', nah], *m.* & *f.* (Amer.) A yellow man or woman, the offspring of a white and a mulatto woman.

Terceto [ter-thay'-to], *m.* 1. A kind of metrical composition; a tiercet, terzet, or terza-rima. 2. (Mus.) Terzetto, trio, a composition for three voices. 3. *V.* TERCERILLA.

Tercia [terr'-the-ah], *f.* 1. Third, the third part. 2. Store-house or barn, where tithes are deposited. 3. One of the hours into which the Romans divided the day. 4. Canonical hour which follows immediately the first, so called from falling at three o'clock.

Terciación [ter-the-ah-the-on'], *f.* Act of ploughing a third time.

Terciado [ter-the-ah'-do], *m.* 1. Cutlass, a short and broad sword. 2. Kind of ribbon somewhat broader than tape. —*a. Azúcar terciado,* Brown sugar. *Pan terciado,* Rent of ground paid in grain, two-thirds wheat and one-third barley.—*Terciado, da, pp.* of TERCIAR.

Terciana [ter-the-ah'-nah], *f.* Tertian, an ague intermitting but one day.

Tercianario, ria [ter-the-ah-nah'-re-o, ah], *m.* & *f.* 1. A person affected with a tertian. 2. A country obnoxious to tertian fevers.

Tercianela [ter-the-ah-nay'-lah], *f.* A sort of silk, resembling taffeta.
Tercianiento, ta [ter-the-ah-ne-en'-to, tah], *a.* (Amer. Peru) *V.* TERCIANARIO.
Terciano, na [ter-the-ah'-no, nah], *a.* Tertian, occurring with a regular intermission between two or more things.
Terciar [ter-the-ar'], *va.* 1. To sling any thing diagonally. 2. To divide a thing into three parts. 3. To tertiate, to plough the third time.—*vn.* 1. To make up the number of three. 2. To mediate, to arbitrate, to go between. 3. To join, to share, to make one of a party. *Terciar el bastón* or *el palo,* To strike one directly with a stick. *Terciar la cara,* To cut one's face across. *Terciar la carga,* To divide a burden into three equal parts. *Terciar una pieza,* (Mil.) To prove a gun.
Terciario, ria [ter-the-ah'-re-o, ah], *a.* 1. Third in order or degree. 2. Tertiary, belonging to a geological period following the Mesozoic.—*m.* (Arch.) Rib in the vaulting of Gothic arches.
Terciazón [ter-the-ah-thone'], *m.* Third ploughing.
Tercio, cia [terr'-the-o, ah], *a.* Third.
Tercio [terr'-the-o], *m.* 1. The third part. 2. Half a load. 3. Regiment of infantry in ancient Spanish warfare. 4. Third part of a horse-course. 5. Third part of the rosary; third part of a sword. *En tercio y quinto,* Great advantage which one does to another. *Hacer buen tercio,* To do good to a person. *Hacer tercio,* To join an association. *Hacer mal tercio.* To do a bad turn, to serve ill.—*pl.* 1. Height of horses, measured by hands. 2. Robust or strong limbs of a man.
Terciodécuplo, pla [ter-the-o-day'-coo-plo, plah], *a.* Product of any quantity multiplied by thirteen.
Terciopelado [ter-the-o-pay-lah'-do], *m.* Stuff resembling velvet.
Terciopelado, da [ter-the-o-pay-lah'-do, dah], *a.* Velvet-like.
Terciopelero [ter-the-o-pay-lay'-ro], *m.* Velvet-weaver.
Terciopelo [ter-the-o-pay'-lo], *m.* Velvet.
Terco, ca [terr'-co, cah], *a.* 1. Pertinacious, obstinate, opinionative, contumacious. 2. Firm or hard as marble.
Terebinto [tay-ray-been'-to], *m.* (Bot.) Turpentine or mastich-tree. Pistacia terebinthinus.
Terebrante [tay-ray-brahn'-tay], *a.* (Med.) Boring, piercing: applied to pain.
Tereniabín [tay-ray-ne-ah-been'], *m.* White, sweetish, purgative matter, resembling mastich, which adheres to the leaves of plants; liquid manna.
Térete [tay'-ray-tay], *a.* Round, plump, robust. Pronounced colloquially tay-ray'-tay in America.
Tergiversación [ter-he-ver-sah-the-on'], *f.* Tergiversation, evasion, subterfuge.
Tergiversar [ter-he-ver-sar'], *va.* To distort (the meaning or the intentions), to boggle, to shift.
Terliz [ter-leeth'], *m.* Tick, ticking, bed-ticking; tent-cloth.
Termal [ter-mahl'], *a.* Thermal.
Termas [terr'-mas], *f. pl.* Hot baths.
Terminable [ter-me-nah'-blay], *a.* Terminable.
Terminación [ter-me-nah-the-on'] *f.* 1. Termination, conclusion. 2. (Gram.) Termination, or last syllable of a word.
Terminacho [ter-me-nah'-cho], *m.* (Coll.) Rude word or phrase.
Terminado [ter-me-nah'-do], *m.* Story, floor, or flight of rooms.—*Terminado, da, pp.* of TERMINAR.
Terminador, ra [ter-me-nah-dor', rah], *m.* & *f.* One who terminates.
Terminal [ter-me-nahl'], *a.* Final, ultimate.
Terminante [ter-me-nahn'-tay], *pa.* Ending, closing, terminating.—*a.* Conclusive or decisive with regard to a point in question; definite. *En términos terminantes,* In definite terms, with propriety or punctuality, in point.
Terminantemente [ter-me-nan-tay-men'-tay], *adv.* Absolutely, conclusively, by all means.
Terminar [ter-me-nar'], *va.* & *vn.* 1. To end, to close, to terminate. 2. To finish, to consummate; to end at, to abut. 3. (Med.) To come to a crisis. 4. (Gram.) To end a word.
Terminativo, va [ter-me-nah-tee'-vo, vah], *a.* Terminative, respective, relative to a term.
Término [terr'-me-no], *m.* 1. The end of any thing. 2. Term, boundary, land-mark; limit, goal. 3. Manner, behaviour, conduct. 4. District of a town or city. 5. Aim, object. 6. Term, the word by which a thing is expressed. 7. Term, the appointed time or determined place. 8. Crisis of a disease. 9. Determinate object of an operation. 10. Period including the beginning and end of any thing. 11. The precise moment to do any thing. 12. Term or word of any language, a technical word, diction; conception. 13. Condition, constitution, state. 14. (Arch.) Stay, resembling the support which the ancients gave the head of their god Terminus. 15. Compartment in a painting. 16. (Mus.) Tone, pitch. *Primer término,* Foreground of a picture. *En buenos términos,* (Coll.) In plain English. *En términos hábiles,* On reasonable terms, so as not to prejudice another. *Términos,* Terms of an argument, syllogism, or arithmetical question. *Medio término,* Any prudent step or medium taken for settling an affair. *¿ En qué términos ?* Upon what terms? *Medios términos,* Evasions by which any one avoids a disagreeable subject.
Terminología [ter-me-no-lo-hee'-ah], *f.* (Neol.) Terminology, the technical terms of a science or an art.
Terminote [ter-me-no'-tay], *m. aug.* of TÉRMINO. A vulgar or affected expression.
Termite [ter-mee'-tay], *m.* Termite, a white ant.
Termodinámica [ter-mo-de-nah'-me-cah], *f.* Thermodynamics. *Termodinámica aérea,* Aerothermodynamics.
Termoeléctrico, ca [ter-mo-ay-lec'-tre-co, cah], *a.* Thermoelectric.
Termófilo, la [ter-mo'-fe-lo, lah], *a.* Fond of living in warm countries.
Termología [ter-mo-lo-hee'-ah], *f.* A treatise on heat.
Termómetro [ter-mo'-may-tro], *m.* Thermometer,
Termos [ter'-mos], *m.* Thermos or vacuum bottle.
Termostato [ter-mos-tah'-to], *m.* Thermostat.
Terna [terr'-nah], *f.* 1. A ternary number. 2. A kind of stuff of a fine appearance after the fur or pile is fallen off. 3. Game at dice.
Ternario, ria [ter-nah'-re-o, ah], *a.* Ternary, ternarious, containing three unities.
Ternario, *m.* 1. Three days' devotion or religious offices. 2. (Mus.) A measure of three equal parts.
Terne [terr'-nay], *a.* (Coll.) *V.* VALENTÓN.
Ternecico, ica, ito, ita [ter-nay-thee-co], *a.* Very tender.
Ternejal [ter-nay-hahl'], *a.* *V.* TERNE.
Ternejón, na [ter-nay-hone', nah], *a.* *V.* TERNERÓN.
Ternerico, ica, illo, illa, ito, ita [ter-nay-ree'-co, cah, eel'-lyo, eel'-lyah, ee'to, ee'-tah], *m.* & *f.* A young calf.
Ternero, ra [ter-nay'-ro, rah], *m.* & *f.* Calf; veal; heifer.
Ternerón, na [ter-nay-rone', nah], *a.* Easily moved, weeping at will.
Terneruela [ter-nay-roo-ay'-lah], *f. dim.* A sucking calf.
Terneza [ter-nay'-thah], *f.* 1. Softness, delicacy, pliantness. 2. Tenderness, affection, endearment, fondness. 3. Suavity. 4. Readiness to shed tears.
Ternilla [ter-neel'-lyah], *f.* Gristle, the cartilaginous part of the body.
Ternilloso, sa [ter-neel-lyo'-so, sah], *a.* Gristly, cartilaginous, webbed, finfooted.
Ternísimo, ma [ter-nee'-se-mo, mah], *a. super.* of TIERNO.
Terno [terr'-no], *m.* 1. Ternary number. 2. (Coll.) Wearing apparel, dress; rich clothes. *Un terno de diamantes,* A set of diamonds. 3. Ornaments for celebrating high-mass. 4. Oath. *V.* VOTO. *Echar ternos* or *tacos,* To swear excessively, to speak in a great rage. 5. (Print.) Union of three sheets one within another. 6. In the game lotto, the lot of obtaining three numbers in the row of five. *Terno seco,* Happy and unexpected fortune.
Ternura [ter-noo'-rah], *f.* Tenderness, delicacy, humanity, fondness. *V.* TERNEZA.
Terquedad [ter-kay-dahd'], *f.* Stubbornness, obstinacy, pertinacity, contumacy, inflexibility.
Terquería, Terqueza [ter-kay-ree'-ah, ter-kay'-thah], *f.* (Obs.) *V.* TERQUEDAD.
Terracota [ter-rah-co'-tah], *f.* Terra cotta.
Terrácueo, cuea [ter-rah'-coo-ay-o, ah], *a.* Terraqueous.
Terrada [ter-rah'-dah], *f.* Kind of bitumen made with ochre and glue.
Terradgo. *m.* (Obs.) *V.* TERRAZGO.
Terradillo [ter-rah-deel'-lyo], *m. dim.* A small terrace.
Terrado [ter-rah'-do], *m.* Terrace, flat roof of a house. *V.* AZOTEA.
Terraja [ter-rah'-hah], *f.* 1. A screw-plate, screw-stock, or die-stock. 2. *V.* TARRAJA.
Terraje [ter-rah'-hay], *m.* Rent paid to the owner of land.
Terrajero [ter-rah-hay'-ro], *m.* *V.* TERRAZGUERO.
Terral [ter-rahl'], *m.* & *a.* Applied to a land breeze.
Terrapene [ter-rah-pay'-nay], *m.* (Zool.) Terrapin.
Terraplén, Terrapleno [ter-rah-playn'], *m.* (Mil.) The horizontal surface of a rampart, terrace, mound; hence the graded road-bed of a railway.
Terraplenar [ter-rah-play-nar'], *va.* To raise a rampart; to make a platform or terrace.
Terraplenador [ter-rah-play-nah-dor'], *m.* One who makes a terrace or platform.
Terráqueo, quea [ter-rah'-kay-o, ah], *a.* Terraqueous, containing both land and water.
Terrateniente [ter-rah-tay-ne-en'-tay], *m.* Master or possessor of land or property.

Terraza [ter-rah'-thah], *f.* 1. A glazed jar with two handles. 2. Terrace, a space somewhat raised and separated from the surface which is prolonged along the wall of a garden or court-yard.

Terrazgo [ter-rath'-go], *m.* 1. Arable land. 2. Land-tax or rent of arable land paid to the landlord.

Terrazguero [ter-rath-gay'-ro], *m.* Labourer who pays rent to the lord of the manor for the land which he occupies.

Terrazo [ter-rah'-tho], *m.* (Art) Ground of a painting.

Terrazuela [ter-rah-thoo-ay'-lah], *f. dim.* of TERRAZA.

Terrear [ter-ray-ar'], *vn.* To show the ground: speaking of crops which stand very thin.

Terrecer [ter-ray-therr'], *va.* (Obs.) To terrify.

Terregoso, sa [ter-ray-go'-so, sah], *a.* Cloddy, full of clods.

Terremoto [ter-ray-mo'-to], *m.* Earthquake.

Terrenal [ter-ray-nahl'], *a.* Terrestrial, earthly, mundane.

Terrenidad [ter-ray-ne-dahd'], *f.* Quality of the soil or ground.

Terreno, na [ter-ray'-no, nah], *a.* 1. Terrene, earthly, terrestrial. 2. Worldly, terrestrial, perishable.

Terreno, *m.* 1. Land, ground, a field. 2. Field, sphere of action. 3. (Geol.) A group of several formations which have a certain analogy by their antiquity, form, or composition. *Terreno abierto,* (Mil.) Open ground: that is, free of rocks, mountains, or other formidable obstacles and of fortified posts.

Térreo, rea [ter'-ray-o, ah], *a.* Terreous, earthy.

Terrera [ter-ray'-rah], *f.* 1. A steep piece of ground. 2. (Orn.) Kind of lark.

Terrero [ter-ray'-ro], *m.* 1. Terrace, platform. 2. Heap of earth. 3. Mark, to shoot at. 4. Terrace, or other part of the palace, where court is paid to the ladies. *Hacer terrero,* To court a lady. 5. In the Canary Islands, an open, clear spot where the athletic contest common in the country takes place. 6. (Mil.) An artificial wall of earth.

Terrero, ra [ter-ray'-ro, rah], *a.* 1. Earthly, terreous. 2. Abject, humble. 3. Skimming the ground: used of the flight of birds.

Terrestre [ter-res'-tray], *a.* Terrestrial.

Terrestridad [ter-res-tre-dahd'], *f.* Earthiness.

Terrezuela [ter-ray-thoo-ay'-lah], *f.* 1. (Dim.) A small piece of ground. 2. Light and poor soil.

Terribilidad [ter-re-be-le-dahd'], *f.* Terribleness, roughness, asperity, ferocity.

Terrible [ter-ree'-blay], *a.* 1. Terrible, dreadful, ferocious, horrible. 2. Rude, unmannerly. 3. Immense, very large.

Terriblemente, *adv.* Terribly, frightfully.

Terrícola [ter-ree'-co-lah], *com.* Inhabitant of the earth.

Terrífico, ca [ter-ree'-fe-co, cah], *a.* Terrific, frightful.

Terrígeno, na [ter-ree'-hay-no, nah], *a.* Terrigenous, earth-born.

Terrino, na [ter-ree'-no, nah], *a.* Terrene, earthy.

Territorial [ter-re-to-re-ahl'], *a.* Territorial.

Territorio [ter-re-to'-re-o], *m.* 1. Territory; district; ground; land. 2. Territory, a district still under provisional or colonial government.

Terrizo, za [ter-ree'-tho, thah], *a.* 1. Earthy, earthen. 2. Unglazed.

Terrojo [ter-ro'-ho], *m.* 1. Red earth. 2. *V.* TERRAZGO.

Terromontero [ter-ro-mon-tay'-ro], *m.* Hill, hillock.

Terrón [ter-rone'], *m.* 1. A flat clod of earth, glebe. 2. Lump of any thing. 3. Heap, collection of things. 4. Dregs of olives which remain in the mill.—*pl.* Landed property. *Terrón de sal,* (Met.) A great wit. *A rapa terrón,* Entirely, completely, from the root.

Terronazo [ter-ro-nah'-tho], *m.* 1. (Aug.) A large clod of earth. 2. Blow with a clod.

Terroncillo [ter-ron-theel'-lyo], *m. dim.* A small clod.

Terrontera [ter-ron-tay'-rah], *f.* Break in a mountain.

Terror [ter-ror'], *m.* Terror, dread, consternation.

Terrorífico, ca [ter-ro-ree'-fe-co, cah], *a.* *V.* TERRÍFICO.

Terrorismo [ter-ro-rees'-mo], *m.* The act of terrifying: applied to unlawful violence.

Terrorista [ter-ro-rees'-tah], *m.* A person who employs authority to commit unlawful violence.

Terrosidad [ter-ro-se-dahd'], *f.* Earthiness.

Terroso, sa [ter-ro'-so, sah], *a.* Terreous, earthy.

Terruca [ter-roo'-cah], *f.* 1. (Dim.) *V.* TERREZUELA. 2. (Neol. Coll.) Native country.

Terruño [ter-roo'-nyo], *m.* 1. A piece of land. 2. One's native soil.

Tersar [ter-sar'], *va.* To smooth, to polish, to clean, to make smooth and clean.

Tersícore [ter-see'-co-ray], *f.* Terpsichore, the muse of the dance.

Tersidad [ter-se-dahd'], *f.* Smoothness, terseness.

Terso, sa [terr'-so, sah], *a.* 1. Smooth, polished, glossy. 2. Pure, elegant, correct, terse: applied to style.

Tersura [ter-soo'-rah], *f.* Smoothness, cleanliness, purity; elegance, terseness.

Tertil [ter-teel'], *m.* Tax on silk in the ancient kingdom of Granada.

Tertulia [ter-too'-le-ah], *f.* 1. Club, assembly, circle, coterie, conversazione, evening party. 2. Part of the boxes in a play-house reserved for women only.

Tertuliano, na [ter-too-le-ah'-no, nah], *a.* Member of a club, assembly, or circle of friends.

Tertulio, a [ter-too'-le-o, ah], *a.* Relating to a meeting of friends or a party.

Teruelo [tay-roo-ay'-lo], *m.* (Prov.) Bowl or box in which lots are put to be cast.

Teruncio [tay-roon'-the-o], *m.* A Roman coin, the fourth part of an as.

Terutero [tay-roo-tay'-ro], *m.* A bird which lives by the banks of rivers and whose note resembles the sound of its name.

Terzón, na [ter-thone', nah], *a.* & *n.* Heifer or ox three years old.

Terzuela [ter-thoo-ay'-lah], *f.* Distribution gained for attending mass at the hour of tierce.

Terzuelo, la [ter-thoo-ay'-lo, lah], *a.* Applied to the third bird which leaves the nest.

Terzuelo [ter-thoo-ay'-lo], *m.* Third part of any thing.

Tesaliense, Tesalio, lia, Tésalo, la [tay-sah-le-en'-say, tay-sah'-le-o, ah, tay'-sah-lo, lah], *a.* Thessalian, of Thessaly.

Tesalónico, ca [tay-sah-lo'-ne-co, cah], *a.* Thessalonian, of Thessalonica.

Tesar [tay-sar'], *va.* 1. (Naut.) To haul (a rope) taut, to tauten. *Tesar las jarcias,* To set up the shrouds. 2. (Prov.) As applied to yoked oxen, to back, to pull back.

Tesauro [tay-sah'-oo-ro], *m.* Dictionary, vocabulary, index.

Tesela [tay-say'-lah], *f.* Tessella, or tessera, each of the small cubes or squares for making mosaic pavements.

Teselato, ta [tay-say-lah'-to, tah], *a.* Tessellate, tessellated, inlaid, mosaic.

Tésera [tay'-say-rah], *f.* Sign or countersign; a cubical piece of wood or bone used by the Romans as a pledge of hospitality, etc.

Tesis [tay'-sis], *f.* 1. Thesis. 2. *V.* CONCLUSIÓN.

Teso, sa [tay'-so, sah], *a.* *V.* TIESO.

Teso [tay'-so], *m.* Brow of a hill.

Tesón [tay-sone'], *m.* Tenacity, firmness, inflexibility.

Tesorar [tay-so-rar'], *va.* (Obs.) To treasure, to hoard up.

Tesorería [tay-so-ray-ree'-ah], *f.* Treasury, treasurer's office, exchequer: treasurership, office or dignity of a treasurer.

Tesorero, ra [tay-so-ray'-ro, rah], *m.* & *f.* 1. Treasurer. 2. Canon who keeps the relics.

Tesoro [tay-so'-ro], *m.* 1. Treasure, wealth, riches. 2. Treasury, exchequer. 3. Any thing valuable and precious. 4. Treasure, a complete abridgment of useful knowledge.

Testa [tes'-tah], *f.* 1. Forehead, front, face. 2. Front, face, of material things.

Testáceo, cea [tes-tah'-thay-o, ah], *a.* Testaceous, provided with a hard continuous shell, as a mollusk.—*m.* Testacean, a shell-bearing invertebrate especially a mollusk.

Testación [tes-tah-the-on'], *f.* 1. Leaving by will. 2. Obliteration.

Testada, *f.* *V.* TESTARADA.

Testado, da [tes-tah'-do, dah], *a.* & *pp.* of TESTAR. Dying testate.

Testador [tes-tah-dor'], *m.* Testator.

Testadora [tes-tah-do'-rah], *f.* Testatrix.

Testadura [tes-tah-doo'-rah], *f.* Obliteration, lineal erasure of written letters.

Testaférrea, *m.* *V.* TESTAFERRO.

Testaferro [tes-tah-fer'-ro], *m.* One who lends his name on a contract or business belonging to another: used in a depreciative sense.

Testamentaría [tes-tah-men-tah-ree'-ah], *f.* Testamentary execution.

Testamentaria [tes-tah-men-tah'-re-ah], *f.* Executrix.

Testamentario [tes-tah-men-tah'-re-o], *m.* Executor.

Testamentario, ria [tes-tah-men-tah'-re-o, ah], *a.* Testamentary.

Testamento [tes-tah-men'-to], *m.* 1. Last will, testament. *Testamento cerrado,* A sealed testament. *Testamento ológrafo,* Holographic will, one written by the testator's own hand. *Testamento abierto,* A will made viva voce before three witnesses and a notary, before five witnesses, citizens of the place in which it is executed, or before seven, even though non-resident, and without a notary. 2. Part of the Holy Scriptures. *Testamento nuncupativo,* *V.* TESTAMENTO ABIERTO.

Testar [tes-tar'], *va.* & *n.* 1. To will, to make a last will or testament, to leave, to bequeath. 2. To blot, to scratch out.

Testarada [tes-tah-rah'-dah], *f.* 1. A stroke or blow with the head. 2. Stubbornness, obstinacy.

Testarrón, na [tes-tar-rone', nah], *a.* *V.* Testarudo.

Testarronería [tes-tar-ro-nay-ree'-ah], *f.* Stubbornness, obstinacy, tenacity.

Testarudo, da [tes-tah-roo'-do, dah], *a.* Obstinate, stubborn.

Teste [tes'-tay], *m.* 1. Testis, testicle. 2. (Obs.) *V.* Testigo.

Testera [tes-tay'-rah], *f.* 1. Front or fore part of any thing; forehead of an animal. 2. Head-stall of the bridle of a horse, or head-piece of a bridle. *Testera de un coche,* Back seat of a coach.

Testerada [tes-tay-rah'-dah], *f.* *V.* Testarada.

Testero [tes-tay'-ro], *m.* *V.* Testera.

Testicular [tes-te-coo-lar'], *a.* Testicular, pertaining to the testicles.

Testículo [tes-tee'-coo-lo], *m.* A testicle.

Testificación [tes-te-fe-cah-the-on'], *f.* Attestation, testification.

Testificante [tes-te-fe-cahn'-tay], *pa.* Witnessing, attesting.

Testificar [tes-te-fe-car'], *va.* To attest, to witness, to certify, to testify.

Testificata [tes-te-fe-cah'-tah], *f.* (Law) Legal testimony.

Testificativo, va [tes-te-fe-cah-tee'-vo, vah], *a.* That which testifies.

Testigo [tes-tee'-go], *m.* 1. Witness, one who gives testimony. 2. Inanimate witness, evidence. *Testigo de oídos,* Auricular witness. *Testigo de vista* or *ocular,* An eye-witness.

Testimonial [tes-te-mo-ne-ahl'], *a.* That which bears a true testimony: applied to a testimonial or writing produced as an evidence.

Testimoniales [tes-te-mo-ne-ah'-les], *f. pl.* Testimonials, an authentic writing verifying what is contained in it; a certificate: in particular, a certificate of good character given by a bishop to a parishioner who removes to another diocese.

Testimoniar [tes-te-mo-ne-ar'], *va.* To testify, to attest, to bear witness, to aver, to avouch.

Testimoniero, ra [tes-te-mo-ne-ay'-ro, rah], *a.* 1. Bearing false witness. 2. Dissembling, hypocritical.

Testimonio [tes-te-mo'-ne-o], *m.* 1. Testimony, deposition of a witness, proof by witness. 2. Testimony, open attestation, attestation. 3. An instrument legalized by a notary. *Testimonio* or *falso testimonio,* False accusation or testimony; imposture.

Testimoñero, ra [tes-te-mo-nyay'-ro, rah], *a.* Hypocritical. *V.* Testimoniero.

Testón [tes-tone'], *m.* A coin having a head.

Testudo [tes-too'-do], *m.* Machine for covering soldiers in an attack on a fortification.

Testuz, Testuzo [tes-tooth', tes-too'-tho], *m.* (Vet.) Hind part of the head, nucha; in some animals, crown of the head. (Acad.)

Tesú [tay-soo'], *m.* (Obs.) Tissue of gold and silver. *V.* Tisú.

Tesura [tay-soo'-rah], *f.* 1. Stiffness, firmness. 2. Starched and affected gravity.

Teta [tay'-tah], *f.* 1. Mammary gland, breast. 2. Nipple, teat; dug of animals. *Teta de vaca,* Teat or dug of a cow; kind of large grapes. *Dar la teta al asno,* (Coll.) To waste one's effort; to throw pearls before swine. *Mamar una teta,* (Coll.) To be tied to his mother's apron-string. *Niño de teta,* A child at the breast; a suckling.

Tetánico, ca [tay-tah'-ne-co, cah], *a.* Tetanic, tetanical.

Tétano [tay'-tah-no], **Tétanos,** *m.* (Med.) Tetanus, lockjaw; tonic spasm. (Gr.)

Tetar [tay-tar'], *va.* To suckle, to give suck. *V.* Atetar.

Tetaza [tay-tah'-thah], *f. aug.* Flabby, ugly dugs. *Tetazas,* (Coll.) A good-tempered person.

Tetera [tay-tay'-rah], *f.* Tea-pot, tea-kettle, with strainer.

Tetero [tay-tay'-ro], *m.* (Amer.) Nursing bottle. (Acad.) *V.* Biberón.

Tetica, ita [tay-tee'-cah], *f. dim.* A small dug or teat.

Tetilla [tay-teel'-lyah], *f.* 1. (Dim.) A small nipple or teat: applied chiefly to those of the man. 2. Kind of paste in the figure of a teat. *Dar por la tetilla,* (Coll.) To touch a person to the quick.

Tetona [tay-to'-nah], *a.* Having large teats.

Tetracordio [tay-trah-cor'-de-o], *m.* (Mus.) Tetrachord, fourth.

Tetraédrico, ca [tay-trah-ay'-dre-co, cah], *a.* Tetrahedral.

Tetraedro [tay-trah-ay'-dro], *m.* (Geom.) Tetrahedron.

Tetragínico, ca [tay-trah-hee'-ne-co, cah], *a.* (Bot.) Having four pistils.

Tetrágono [tay-trah'-go-no], *m.* (Geom.) Tetragon.

Tetrágono, na, *a.* (Geom.) Tetragonal.

Tetragrámaton [tay-trah-grah'-mah-tone], *m.* Word composed of four letters, particularly the name of *Dios.*

Tetrámetro [tay-trah'-may-tro], *m.* Iambic verse of eight feet or four measures.—*pl.* (Zool.) A section of coleoptera, having four joints upon the tarsi.

Tetrapétalo, la. (Bot.) Tetrapetalous: four-petalled.

Tetrarca [tay-trar'-cah], *m.* Tetrarch.

Tetrarquía [tay-trar-kee'-ah], *f.* Tetrarchate, tetrarchy. (Gr.)

Tetrástilo [tay-trahs'-te-lo], *m.* Building sustained by four columns or pilasters.

Tetrasílabo, ba [tay-trah-see'-lah-bo, bah], *a.* *V.* Cuatrisílabo.

Tétricamente, *adv.* Gloomily.

Tétrico, ca [tay'-tre-co, cah], *a.* Crabbed, grave, gloomy, sullen.

Tetro, tra [tay'-tro, trah], *a.* (Obs.) Black, spotted.

Tetuda [tay-too'-dah], *a.* 1. Having large nipples. 2. (Prov.) Applied to a kind of oblong olives.

Teucali [tay-oo-cah-lee'], *m.* (Acad.) *V.* Teocalli.

Teucrio [tay'-oo-cre-o], *m.* (Bot.) Germander. Teucrium.

Teucro, cra [tay'-oo-cro, crah], *a.* & *n.* Trojan.

Teurgia [tay-oor'-he-ah], *f.* Theurgy, black magic, superstitious art of calling on beneficent genii.

Teutón [tay-oo-tone'], *m.* (& *pl.*). Teuton, especially the ancient Germanic tribes or language.

Teutónico, ca [tay-oo-toh'-ne-co, cah], *a.* 1. Teutonic, of a German military order. 2. German, Teutonic.

Textil [tex-teel'], *a.* Textile, capable of being made into threads and woven.

Texto [tex'-to], *m.* 1. Text, the original words of an author. 2. Text of Scripture. 3. (Print.) Name of a size of types: great primer.

Textorio, ria [tex-to'-re-o, ah], *a.* Textrine, textorial, belonging to weaving.

Textual [tex-too-ahl'], *a.* Textual, agreeing with the text.

Textualista [tex-too-ah-lees'-tah], *m.* 1. Textualist, he who adheres to the text. 2. Texturist, one ready in quotation of texts.

Textualmente, *adv.* According to the text; textually.

Textura [tex-too'-rah], *f.* 1. Texture, as of stuff or cloth. 2. Succession and order of things.

Tez [teth], *f.* 1. Grain; shining surface. 2. Bloom of the complexion, hue.

Tezado, da [tay-thah'-do, dah], *a.* Very black. *V.* Atezado.

Tezcucano, na [teth-coo-cah'-no, nah], *a.* Tezcucan, belonging to Tezcuco, a city of Mexico.

Tezontle [tay-thon'-tlay], *m.* (Mex.) A porous stone esteemed for building in Mexico.

Theta [thay'-tah], *f.* Eighth letter of the Greek alphabet; represented in Latin by *th,* in modern Spanish by *t* alone.

Ti [tee]. The oblique case of *tú,* thou. When preceded by the preposition *con,* it takes the termination *go,* as *contigo,* With *thee.* *Tí mismo,* Thyself.

Tía [tee'-ah], *f.* 1. Aunt. 2. (Coll.) A good old woman. 3. (Coll.) Used in Spain to express colloquially a common woman. *A tu tía que te dé para libros,* I am neither willing nor obliged to give you any thing. *Cuéntaselo a tu tía,* (Coll.) Tell it to your grandmother. *Tía,* A name given to decent old persons in low condition, instead of *Doña*; as, *Da esto a la tía Isabel,* Give this to dame Elizabeth. *Una vieja tía,* An old crone.

Tialismo [te-ah-lees'-mo], *m.* Ptyalism, abnormal discharge of saliva.

Tiangui [te-ahn'-gee], **Tiangue** [te-ahn'-gay] (in the Philippine Islands), *m.* The market, and market-days, in the small towns of the Mexican republic and in the Philippine Islands.

Tiara [te-ah'-rah], *f.* 1. Tiara, mitre worn by the Pope. 2. Pontificate, papal dignity. 3. Diadem of the ancient kings of Persia.

Tibia [tee'-be-ah] *f.* 1. Shin-bone. 2. A flute.

Tibial [te-be-ahl'], *a.* (Anat.) Tibial, relating to the tibia.

Tibiamente, *adv.* Tepidly, carelessly, lukewarmly.

Tibieza [te-be-ay'-thah], *f.* 1. Tepidity, lukewarmness, coldness. 2. Coolness, frigidity, jejuneness. 3. Carelessness negligence.

Tibio, bia [tee'-be-o, ah], *a.* Tepid, lukewarm, careless, remiss.

Tibir [te-beer'], *m.* Name of gold-dust on the African coast.

Tibor [te-bor'], *m.* 1. A large china jar. 2. (Amer. Cuba) A chamber pot.

Tiburón [te-boo-ron'], *m.* Shark. Squalus carcharias.

(*Yo tiemblo, yo tiemble,* from *Temblar.* *V.* Acertar.)

Tictac [tic-tac'], *m.* Tick tock.

Tiempecillo, Tiempecito [te-em-pay-theel'-lyo, thee'-to], *m. dim.* A little time.

Tiempo [te-em'-po], *m.* 1. Time. 2. Term, a limited space of time. 3. Any of the four seasons. 4. Time, opportunity, occasion; tide, season; leisure. 5. Weather, temperature, climate. 6. State, condition. 7. Draft. portion. 8. (Gram.) Time, tense. 9. Age. 10. Time, space, duration of an action. 11. Time, musical measure. *Tiempo cargado,* (Naut.) Thick, hazy weather. *Tiempo borrascoso,* Stormy weather. *Tiempo grueso,* Hazy weather. *El tiempo va a meterse en agua,* The weather sets in for rain. *Tiempo variable,* Unsettled weather. *Tiempo hecho,* Settled weather. *Tiempo contrario,*

Foul weather. *Tiempo apacible*, Moderate weather. *Haga buen o mal tiempo*, Rain or shine. *Tiempo de juanetes*, (Naut.) Top-gallant gale. *A tiempo*, Timely, in time. *A un tiempo*, At once; at the same time. *Con tiempo*, Timely, beforehand. *De tiempo en tiempo*, From time to time. *En tiempo*, Occasionally. *Por tiempo*, For some time, undetermined time. *Un tiempo*, Formerly, in other times. *La carta llegó a su tiempo*, The letter was duly received. *A tiempo que*, Just as. *Abrir el tiempo*, The weather clears up. *Acordarse del tiempo del rey que rabió* or *rabió por gachas*, That is a very old story, from "away back." *Alzarse el tiempo*, The weather clears off. *Cargarse el tiempo* or *la atmósfera*, To cloud over. *Dar tiempo al tiempo*, To await occasion for doing something. *Engañar el tiempo*. To kill time, to while away tedium. *Tomarse tiempo*, To take time, to defer. *Del tiempo de Maricastaña*, A very old thing or story; a "chestnut." *En tiempo hábil*, Within the appointed time. *Tiempo tras tiempo viene*, Better times ahead. (Said in consolation.)

Tienda [te-en'-dah], *f.* 1. (Mil.) Tent. 2. (Naut.) Awning over vessels. 3. Tilt for carts or wagons. 4. Shop or stall. *La tienda de los cojos*, The next shop. *Poner* or *abrir tienda*, To open a shop. *Alzar tienda*, To shut up shop, to quit. *A quien está en su tienda, no le achacan que se halló en la contienda*, Crimes are not ascribed to those who have regular occupations, but to vagrants.

(*Yo tiendo, yo tienda*, from *Tender*. *V.* Entender.)

Tienta [te-en'-tah], *f.* 1. (Med.) Probe. 2. Craft, cunning, artful industry. *A tientas*, Doubtfully, uncertainly, in the dark, at random. *Andar a tientas*, To grope in the dark, to fumble.

Tientaaguja [te-en-tah-ah-goo'-hah], *f.* An auger for testing the ground on which it is proposed to build.

Tiento [te-en'-to], *m.* 1. Touch, the act of feeling. 2. A blind man's stick. 3. Circumspection, prudent consideration. 4. Poy, a rope-dancer's pole. 5. Sureness of the hand, a steady hand. 6. Stroke. *V.* Golpe. 7. Mahlstick, maulstick, a painter's staff. 8. (Mus.) Prelude, flourish. 9. (Zool.) Tentacle. *Dar un tiento*, To make a trial. *Por el tiento*, By the touch. *A tiento*, Obscurely, doubtfully. *Cual el tiempo, tal el tiento*, Act according to circumstances, with judgment.

(*Yo tiento, yo tiente*, from *Tentar*. *V.* Acrecentar.)

Tiernamente [te-er-nah-men'-tay], *adv.* Tenderly, compassionately.

Tiernecico, ica, illo, illa, ito, ita [te-er-nay-thee'-co], *a. dim.* of Tierno.

Tierno, na [te-err'-no, nah], *a.* 1. Tender, soft, docile; delicate; lady-like. 2. Affectionate, fond, amiable, mild, easily moved to tears. 3. Recent, modern, young; tender: applied to age. *Tierno de ojos*, Tender-eyed.

Tierra [te-er'-rah], *f.* 1. Earth, the solid part of our globe; land, soil, ground, mould. 2. Native country. 3. Earth, the terraqueous globe. 4. Arable land. 5. Land, country, region, a distinct part of the globe: as *Tierra Santa*, The Holy Land. *Tierra de los duendes*, Fairy-land. *Tierra de batán* or *de manchas*, Fuller's-earth. *Sin sentirlo la tierra*, Without any one's knowledge. *Tierra a tierra*, (Naut.) Coasting: cautiously, securely. *Tierra adentro*, (Naut.) Inland. *Correr hacia la tierra*, (Naut.) To stand inshore. *Buscar tierra*, (Naut.) To make for the land. *Tomar tierra*, (Naut.) To anchor in a port. *Tierra de Sevilla*, *V.* Aceche. *Tierra firme*, Continent. *Besar la tierra*, (Coll.) To fall with one's mouth against the ground. *Besar la tierra que otro pisa*, To kiss the ground another treads on (excessive respect). *Coserse con la tierra*, To creep along the ground. *Dar con una persona en tierra*, To throw a person down, as in wrestling. *Echar tierra a alguna cosa*, To bury an affair in oblivion. *Echarse por tierra*, To be humiliated. *Irse* or *venirse una cosa a tierra*, To fall down, to be destroyed. *Poner tierra en*, or *por medio*, To absent one's self.

Tiesamente, *adv* Firmly, stiffly, strongly.

Tieso, sa [te-ay'-so, sah], *a.* 1. Stiff, hard, firm, solid. 2. Robust, strong; valiant, animated. 3. Stubborn, obstinate, inflexible. 4. Tight, rigid; too grave or circumspect. *Tieso de cogote*, (Coll.) Stiff-necked, vain, obstinate. *Tenerse tieso* or *tenérselas tiesas*. (Coll.) To be firm in one's opinion or resolution; to oppose another firmly.

Tieso [te-ay'-so], *adv.* *V.* Tiesamente.

Tieso [te-ay'-so], *m.* Firmness, inflexibility; hardness. *Tieso que tieso*, (Coll.) Pertinacity, obstinacy.

Tiesta [te-es'-tah], *f.* Edge of the staves which serve for the ends of casks.

Tiesto [te-es'-to], *m.* 1. Potsherd. 2. A large earthen pot.

Tiesura [te-ay-soo'-rah], *f.* 1. Stiffness, rigidity. 2. Stiffness, harshness in behaviour.

Tifo [tee'-fo], *m.* (Med.) Typhus, a malignant fever. *Tifo de América*, Yellow fever. *Tifo asiático*, Asiatic cholera. *Tifo de Oriente*, The plague.

Tifoideo, dea [te-foi-day'-o, ah], *a.* Typhoid, typhus-like.—*f.* (scil. fiebre) Typhoid fever.

Tifón [te-fone'], *m.* 1. Whirlwind. *V.* Torbellino. 2. Typhoon.

Tifus [tee'-foos], *m.* Typhus fever. *Tifus icterodes*, Yellow fever.

Tignaria [tig-nah'-re-ah], *f.* Knowledge of the fittest timber for building.

Tigre [tee'-gray], *m.* Tiger. Felis tigris.

Tigridia [te-gree'-de-ah], *f.* (Bot.) Tigridia, tiger-flower, a plant of the iris family, native of Mexico, cultivated for the beauty of its flowers.

Tija [tee'-hah], *f.* The shaft of a key.

Tijera, or **Tijeras** [te-hay'-rah], *f.* 1. Scissors. 2. Carpenter's horse, cooper's mare, for holding the wood while dressing; any instrument in the form of an X. 3. Sheep-shearer. 4. A small channel or drain. *Buena tijera*, A great eater; good cutter. 5. Detracter, murmurer. *Tijeras*, Beams across a river to stop floating timber. *Hacer tijera*, To twist the mouth: applied to horses.

Tijerada [te-hay-rah'-dah], *f.* *V.* Tijeretada.

Tijereta [te-hay-ray'-tah], *f.* 1. (Dim.) Small scissors. 2. Small tendril of vines. 3. A common insect, the earwig. 4. A South American bird.

Tijeretada [te-hay-ray-tah'-dah], *f.* A cut with scissors, a clip.

Tijeretazo [te-hay-ray-tah'-tho], *m.* A cut with scissors.

Tijeretear [te-hay-ray-tay-ar'], *va.* 1. To cut with scissors. 2. To dispose of other people's affairs at one's pleasure.

Tijerica, ita [te-hay-ree'-cah], *f. dim.* A small pair of scissors.

Tijerilla, *f. dim.* *V.* Tijereta.

Tijeruela [te-hay-roo-ay'-lah], *f.* Small tendril of vines.

Tila [tee'-lah], *f.* (Bot.) 1. Lime-tree, linden-tree. 2. The flower of this tree. Tilia, *L.* 3. Infusion, tea, of linden flowers.

Tilar [te-lar'], *m.* Grove or plantation of lime or linden trees.

Tildar [til-dar'], *va.* 1. To blot, to scratch out. 2. To brand, to stigmatize. 3. To mark letters with a dash, as the ñ.

Tilde [teel'-day], *f.* Dot or dash over a letter; iota, a tittle; point, very small thing.

Tildón [til-done'], *m.* (Aug.) A long dash or stroke.

Tilia, *f.* (Bot.) *V.* Tilo.

Tilichero [te-le-chay'-ro], *m.* (Amer.) Peddler, a vender of small articles.

Tiliches [te-lee'-ches], *m. pl.* (Amer.) Small fancy articles.

Tilín [te-leen'], *m.* A word imitating the sound of a bell. *Hacer tilín*, To please, to become a favourite. *Tener tilín*, To be a favourite or attractive.

Tilma [teel'-mah], *f.* (Mex.) A cloak fastened at the shoulder by a knot.

Tilo [tee'-lo], *m.* (Bot.) Linden-tree, lime-tree. Tilia.

Tilosis [te-lo'-sis], *f.* Falling out of the eyelashes.

Tilla [teel'-lyah], *f.* (Naut.) Midship, gangway.

Tillado [teel-lyah'-do], *m.* A wooden floor.

Tillar [teel-lyar'], *va.* To floor. *V.* Entarimar.

Timalo [tee'-mah-lo], *m.* Grayling. Salmo thymallus. (Gr. θύμαλλος.)

Timba [teem'-bah], *f.* 1. (Coll.) Hand in a game of chance; also a low gambling-house. 2. (Phil. Is.) A bucket for water.

Timbal [tim-bahl'], *m.* Kettle-drum. *V.* Atabal.

Timbalear [tim-bah-lay-ar'], *vn.* To beat the kettle-drum.

Timbaleo [tim-bah-lay'-o], *m.* Beat of the kettle-drum.

Timbalero [tim-bah-lay'-ro], *m.* Kettle-drummer.

Timbirimba [tim-be-reem'-bah], *f.* (Coll.) *V.* Timba.

Timbra [teem'-brah], *f.* (Bot.) Mountain hyssop. Thymbra, *L.*

Timbrar [tim-brar'], *va.* 1. To put the crest to the shield in a coat of arms. 2. To stamp a seal or device upon paper.

Timbre [teem'-bray], *m.* 1. (Her.) Timbre or timmer, crest of a coat of arms. 2. Seal, device, stamped upon paper, indicating a person's name, etc. 3. A bell provided with a spring. 4. Tone colour, clang-tint, peculiar harmonious sound of the voice or instruments. 5. Any glorious deed or achievement. *Es el mejor timbre de su escudo*, That is the best gem in his crown.

Timiama [te-me-ah'-mah], *f.* Sweet perfume. *V.* Almea.

Timidamente, *adv.* Timidly, fearfully, timorously.

Timidez [te-me-deth'], *f.* Timidity, fear, cowardice.

Timido, da [tee'-me-do, dah], *a.* Timid, cowardly, dastardly.

Timo [tee'-mo], *m.* *V.* Tímalo.

Timón [te-mone'], *m.* 1. Beam of a plough; pole of a coach. 2. (Naut.) Helm, rudder. 3. Part which governs the movement of various machines. *La madre del timón*, The main piece of the rudder. *El aza-*

frán del timón, The afterpiece of the rudder. *La cabeza del timón*, The rudder-head. *La mortaja del timón*, The mortise of the rudder. *Forro* or *espalda del timón*, The back of the rudder. *Sacar* or *apear el timón*, To unship the rudder. *Calar el timón*, To hang the rudder. 4. (Met.) Person or office in which the chief power exists.

Timonear [te-mo-nay-ar'], *va.* (Naut.) To govern the helm; to steer.

Timonel [te-mo-nel'], *m.* (Naut.) Timoneer, helmsman.

Timonera [te-mo-nay'-rah], *f.* 1. (Naut.) The helmsman's post before the bittacle. 2. Each of the large tail-feathers of a bird.

Timonero [te-mo-nay'-ro], *m.* Timoneer, helmsman.

Timorato, ta [te-mo-rah'-to, tah], *a.* Full of the fear of God.

Timpa [teem'-pah], *f.* Bar of iron in a furnace hearth.

Timpánico, ca [tim-pah'-ne-co, cah], *a.* (Anat.) Tympanic, relating to the ear-drum.

Timpanillo [tim-pah-neel'-lyo], *m. dim.* 1. A small kettle-drum; a small tympanum or tympan. 2. (Print.) Inner tympan of a printing-press. 3. (Arch.) Gablet, a small onamental gable or gabled canopy.

Timpanitico, ca [tim-pah-nee'-te-co, cah], *a.* Affected with tympanites or wind-dropsy.

Timpanitis [tim-pah-nee'-tis], *f.* (Med.) 1. Tympanites, distension of the abdomen by gases. 2. Myringitis, inflammation of the ear-drum.

Timpano [teem'-pah-no], *m.* 1. Kettle-drum. 2. (Anat.) Tympanum, the drum of the ear. 3. Tympan of a printing-press. 4. Cylinder. 5. (Arch.) Tympan, pediment.

Tina [tee'-nah], *f.* 1. A large earthen jar. 2. Vat, dyer's copper. 3. Bathing-tub.

Tinaco [te-nah'-co], *m.* Wooden trough, tub, or vat.

Tinada [te-nah'-dah], *f.* 1. Pile of wood or timber. 2. Shed for cattle.

Tinado, Tinador [te-nah'-do, te-nah-dor'], *m.* Shed for sheltering cattle.

Tinaja [te-nah'-hah], *f.* A large earthen jar.

Tinajería [te-nah-hay-ree'-ah], *f.* (Prov.) The place where large earthen jars are kept.

Tinajero [te-nah-hay'-ro], *m.* 1. One who makes or sells water-jars. 2. (Mex.) Kitchen dresser. 3. *V.* Tinajería.

Tinajica, illa, ita [te-nah-hee'-cah], *f. dim.* A small earthen wide-mouthed jar.

Tinajón [te-nah-hone'], *m.* 1. A large wide-mouthed jar for catching rain. 2. A fat and lusty person.

Tindado [tin-dah'-do], *m.* A tree of the Philippine Islands, the wood of which, as lasting well in water, is much used in boat-building.

Tinea [tee'-nay-ah], *f.* (Obs.) Worm in wood rotten in the earth.

Tinelero, ra [te-nay-lay'-ro, rah], *m.* & *f.* Keeper of the servants' room.

Tinelo [te-nay'-lo], *m.* Dining-room of servants in great houses.

Tinero [te-nay'-ro], *m.* Dyer who takes care of the copper in woollen manufactories.

Tineta [te-nay'-tah], *f. dim.* of Tina. Kit, small tub.

Tinge [teen'-hay] *m.* (Orn.) Kind of black owl.

Tingitano, na [tin-he-tah'-no, nah], *a.* Of ancient Tingitania, now Tangiers.

Tingladillo [tin-glah-deel'-lyo], *m.* (Naut.) Clinker-work, lap-jointed work having the edges overlapping and riveted together.

Tinglado [tin-glah'-do], *m.* 1. A small roof jutting out from the wall, to shelter people from the rain. 2. A hovel, a covered passage. 3. Workshop, shed. *Tinglado de la tonelería*, Cooper's shed, cooperage.

Tinglar [tin-glar'], *vn.* (Naut.) To make lap-jointed work.

Tingle [teen'-glay], *f.* Instrument used by glaziers for opening the lead and flatting it on the glass.

Tinica, illa, ita [te-nee'-cah], *m. dim.* A small vat.

Tiniola [te-nee'-olah], *f.* (Mil. Antiq.) Large coat of arms.

Tiniebla [te-ne-ay'-blah], *f.* Darkness, obscurity, privation of light.—*pl.* Utter darkness, hell; the night; gross ignorance; matins sung the last three days of Holy week.

Tinillo [te-neel'-lyo], *m.* A tank for collecting must as it flows from the wine-press.

Tino [tee'-no], *m.* 1. Skill in discovering things by the act of feeling. 2. A steady hand to hit the mark. 3. Judgment, prudence, circumspection. 4. Knack, dexterity. 5. (Zool.) A wood-boring beetle. *Salir de tino*, To be out of one's senses. *Sacar de tino*, (1) To astound, to confound. (2) To make one angry; to act inconsiderately.

Tinta [teen'-tah], *f.* 1. Tint, hue, colour. 2. Ink. *Tinta encarnada* or *roja*, Red ink. 3. Act, process of dyeing. 4. *pl.* Colours prepared for painting. *De buena tinta*, (Coll.) Efficaciously, ably. *Saber algo de buena tinta*, To know from good authority. *Tinta de imprenta*, Printing-ink. *Tinta simpática*, Sympathetic or invisible ink.

Tintar [tin-tar'], *va.* To tinge, to dye. *V.* Teñir.

Tinte [teen'-tay], *m.* 1. Act and effect of dyeing or staining. 2. Tint, paint, colour, stain; dye. 3. A dyer's shop. 4. Palliation, cloak, colour.

Tintero [tin-tay'-ro], *m.* 1. Ink-well, inkstand. 2. A printer's ink-fountain or ink-table. *Dejar* or *dejarse en el tintero*, (Coll.) To forget or omit designedly. *Quedársele a uno en el tintero*, (Coll.) To forget a thing entirely.

Tintillo [tin-teel'-lyo], *m.* (Dim.) A light-coloured wine.

Tintin [tin-teen'], *m.* Clink, a sharp sound of metals, or of glasses striking together.

Tintinear [tin-te-nay-ar'], *vn.* To tinkle, to jingle.

Tintineo [tin-te-nay'-o], *m.* Tinkling (of a bell, etc.)

Tintirintin [tin-te-rin-teen'], *m.* Echo or sound of a trumpet, or other sharp-sounding instrument.

Tinto, ta [teen'-to, tah], *a.* Deep-coloured: applied to wine. *V.* Teñido. *Vino tinto*, Red wine.

Tintóreo, rea [tin-toh'-ray-o, ah], *a.* Tinctoreal, affording colour, or pertaining to hues.

Tintorera [tin-to-ray'-rah], *f.* (Zool. Amer.) The female of the shark.

Tintorería [tin-to-ray-ree'-ah], *f.* 1. Dry cleaning and dyeing. 2. Dry-cleaning shop.

Tintorero, ra [tin-to-ray'-ro, rah], *m.* & *f.* Dyer.

Tintura [tin-too'-rah], *f.* 1. Dyeing or staining. 2. Tincture, colour or taste superadded by something. 3. Tint, colour, stain, spot. 4. Paint for ladies. 5. Superficial knowledge, smattering. 6. Tincture, extract of drugs.

Tinturar [tin-too-rar'], *va.* 1. To tinge, to dye, to imbue or impregnate with colour or taste. 2. To tincture, to imbue the mind, to teach superficially.

Tiña [tee'-nyah], *f.* 1. Scalled-head, ring-worm of the scalp, favus. It forms yellow crusts. Tinea favosa. 2. (Coll.) Want, indigence, wretchedness. 3. Niggardliness, meanness, close-fistedness. 4. Small spider which injures bee-hives.

Tiñería [te-nyay-ree'-ah], *f.* Poverty, indigence, misery. (Vulg.) Meanness.

Tiñoso, sa [te-nyo'-so, sah], *a.* 1. Scabby, scurvy. 2. Penurious, niggardly, miserable; sordid, mean.

(*Yo tiño, él tiñó, yo tiña*, from *Teñir. V.* Pedir.)

Tiñuela [te-nyoo-ay'-lah], *f. V.* Cuscuta.

Tio [tee'-o], *m.* 1. Uncle. 2. (Coll.) Good old man: used colloquially for a peasant. *V.* Tía.

Tiorba [te-or'-bah], *f.* Theorbo, a large lute.

Tiovivo [tee-oh-vee'-vo], *m.* Merry-go-round, carrousel.

Tipa [tee'-pah], *f.* (Amer.) 1. A basket made of hide. 2. A great tree of Peru the wood of which is prized for the cabins of ships.

Típico, ca [tee'-pe-co, cah], *a.* Typical, characteristic.

Tiple [tee'-play], *m.* 1. Treble, the highest musical register of instruments or voices; soprano. 2. (*com.*) One who sings treble. 3. A small guitar. 4. *m.* (Slang.) Tipple, wine. 5. (Naut.) Mast of a single piece.

Tiplisonante [te-ple-so-nahn'-tay], *a.* (Coll.) Treble-toned.

Tipo [tee'-po], *m.* 1. Type, pattern, model, figure. 2. Printing type. 3. Rate. *Tipo de cambio*, Rate of exchange. *Tipo de interés*, Rate of interest.

Tipografía [te-po-grah-fee'-ah], *f.* 1. Printing. *V.* Imprenta. 2. Typography, type-setting.

Tipográfico, ca [te-po-grah'-fe-co, cah], *a.* Typographical.

Tipógrafo [te-po'-grah-fo], *m.* Printer.

Tipolita [te-po-lee'-tah], *f.* Typolite, a stone or fossil which preserves the impression of an animal or plant.

Tipula [tee'-poo-lah], *f.* Tipula, crane-fly, daddy-long-legs; an insect looking like a huge mosquito.

Tiquin [te-keen'], *m.* A long cane used in place of oars by Philippine Indians.

Tiquistiquis [te-kees-tee'-kees], *m.* A tree common in the Philippine Islands from which "quassia-cups" are made.

Tira [tee'-rah], *f.* 1. A long narrow stripe; list. 2. A light dart or arrow. 3. (Naut.) Fall. *Tira de un aparejo*, Fall of a tackle. *Tira de un aparejo real*, A winding tackle-fall. *Tira del aparejo de la gata*, The cat-tackle-fall. *Tira de las aparejuelas de portas*, Port-tackle-fall. *Tiras*, Fees at the clerks' office in appeal causes.

Tirabala [te-rah-bah'-lah], *m.* Pop-gun.

Tirabeque [te-rah-bay'-kah], *m.* (Agr.) Tender peas.

Tirabotas [te-rah-bo'-tas], *f.* Boot-hook for pulling on boots.

Tirabraguero [te-rah-brah-gay'-ro], *m.* (Surg.) Truss.

Tirabuzón [te-rah-boo-thone'], *m.* 1. Cork-screw. 2. (Met.) Curl, ringlet of hair.

Tiracabeza [te-rah-cah-bay'-thah], *f.* Obstetric forceps.

Tiracol [te-rah-cole'], *m. V.* Tiracuello.

Tiracuello [te-rah-coo-ay'-lyo], *m.* A sword-belt worn by officers.
Tirada [te-rah'-dah], *f.* 1. Cast, throw; the act of throwing. 2. Distance of one place from another. 3. Process or space of time. *De una tirada* or *en una tirada*, At one stretch. *Caminó seis leguas de una tirada*, He travelled six leagues at one stretch. 4. Act of printing or stamping. 5. Edition, total number of copies printed.
Tiradera [te-rah-day'-rah], *f.* 1. Strap. 2. Indian arrow.
Tiradero [te-rah-day'-ro], *m.* Post where a hunter stations himself to shoot game.
Tirado, da [te-rah'-do, dah], *a.* As applied to a ship, long and low.—*m.* 1. Wire-drawing. 2. Act of printing; press-work.
Tirador, ra [te-rah-dor', rah], *m.* & *f.* 1. Thrower; drawer. 2. Sharp-shooter, a good marksman. 3. An iron button fixed to a door, window, etc., whereby it is opened or shut. 4. (Print.) Pressman. *Tirador de oro*, Gold-wire drawer. (Prov.) Rifleman.
Tirafondo [te-rah-fon'-do], *m.* (Med.) A ball extractor; extractor for foreign bodies in a wound.
Tiralíneas [te-rah-lee'-nay-as], *m.* Instrument for drawing lines; ruling-pen, ruler.
Tiramiento [te-rah-me-en'-to], *m.* Tension, act of stretching or making tense.
Tiramira [te-rah-mee'-rah], *f.* A long, narrow path; a long ridge of mountains.
Tiramollar [te-rah-mol-lyar'], *va.* (Naut.) To ease off, to slacken. *Tiramollar un aparejo*, To overhaul a tackle. *Tiramollar las amuras y escotas*, To overhaul the sheets and tacks.
Tirana [te-rah'-nah], *f.* 1. A certain Spanish song, accompanied by dancing. 2. *V.* TIRANO.
Tiranamente [te-rah-nah-men'-tay], *adv.* Tyrannically. *V.* TIRÁNICAMENTE.
Tiranía [te-rah-nee'-ah], *f.* 1. Tyranny, despotic government. 2. Tyranny, severity, inclemency, rigorous command. 3. Exorbitant price of merchandise. 4. Ascendency of some passion.
Tiránicamente, *adv.* Tyrannically, violently, imperiously.
Tiranicida [te-rah-ne-thee'-dah], *a.* & *m.* Tyrannicide, one who kills a tyrant.
Tiranicidio [te-rah-ne-thee'-de-o], *m.* Tyrannicide, the killing of a tyrant.
Tiránico, ca [te-rah'-ne-co, cah], *a.* Tyrannical, despotic, imperious.
Tiranización [te-rah-ne-thah-the-on'], *f.* Tyranny, despotism.
Tiranizadamente [te-rah-ne-thah-dah-men'-tay], *adv.* Tyrannically.
Tiranizar [te-rah-ne-thar'], *va.* 1. To tyrannize, to domineer, to oppress. 2. To usurp. 3. To extort high prices.
Tirano, na [te-rah'-no, nah], *a.* & *n.* 1. Tyrannical, despotic, arbitrary. 2. Applied to a merchant who sells goods at an exorbitant price. 3. Tyrannical; applied to passions.
Tirano, *m.* 1. Tyrant, a despotic ruler; severe master. 2. Merchant who sells goods at an exorbitant price. 3. Ruling passion. 4. (Zool.) Tyrant fly-catcher.
Tirante [te-rahn'-tay], *m.* 1. Joist which runs across a beam. 2. Trace, part of a harness; gear. *A tirantes largos*, With long traces. 3. (Mech.) Brace, collar-piece, beam; stay rod, tie rod. 4. Suspenders, braces. 5. (Arch.) Anchor, truss-rod, an especial apparatus employed in certain constructions.—*a.* Tight, extended, drawn; tightly bound. *Traer* or *tener la cuerda tirante*, To use too much rigour.
Tirantez [te-ran-teth'], *f.* 1. Length of a thing which runs in a straight line. 2. Tenseness, tightness.
Tirapié [te-rah-pe-ay'], *m.* Stirrups or strap, with which shoemakers make their work fast.
Tirar [te-rar'], *va.* & *vn.* 1. To throw, to cast, to dart, to fling; to toss. 2. To imitate, to resemble. 3. To attract, to draw towards one. 4. To incline to, to tend. 5. To hurt, to injure, to thwart. 6. To tug, to pull; to draw. 7. To discharge fire-arms, to fire, to let off. 8. To persuade, induce, or lead by compulsion. 9. To earn, to acquire, to gain, or become entitled to. 10. To continue in the same state without declining from it. *El enfermo va tirando*, The invalid is pulling through. 11. To enlarge, to extend. 12. To lavish. 13. (Print.) To print sheets. 14. To draw metal into slender threads. 15. *V.* QUITAR. 16. To receive or take an allotted part. 17. To direct one's course, to take the road. *Tire Vd. por este camino*, Take this way. *Tire Vd. a la derecha*, Turn to the right. 18. To tend, to aim at; to make use of means and direct them to some end. *Tirar a la mar*, (Naut.) To throw overboard; to stand out to sea. *Tirar las riendas*, To subject. *Andar alguna cosa muy tirada*, (Met.) To be difficult to find, to be sold dear. *A todo tirar*, To the utmost, to the greatest extent. *Tirar largo* or *por lo largo*, (1) To exceed in what one says or does. (2) (Coll.) To build castles in the air. *Tirar coces*, To kick, to rebel. *Tirar alguno la barra*, (Coll.) To sell things as dear as possible. *Tira y afloja*, (1) A boyish play. (2) (Met.) Fast and loose, blowing hot and cold, ordering and counter-ordering. *A más tirar*, At most, at the utmost. *Tirar un cañonazo*, To fire a gun. *Tirarlas de guapo* or *de rico*, To claim (presume on being) to be pretty, or rich.
Tirela [te-ray'-lah], *f.* A striped stuff.
Tireta [te-ray'-tah], *f.* (Prov.) Ribbon or thong of leather.
Tirica, ita [te-ree'-cah], *f. dim.* A small stripe of linen.
Tiricia [te-ree'-the-ah], *f.* Jaundice. *V.* ICTERICIA.
Tirilla [te-reel'-lyah], *f.* A piece of backstitched linen used for a neck-band of a shirt.
Tirio, ria [tee'-re-o, ah], *a.* Tyrian, of Tyre.
Tiritaña [te-re-tah'-nyah], *f.* 1. A sort of thin silk; thin woollen cloth. 2. A thing of little value.
Tiritar [te-re-tar'], *vn.* To shiver, to shake with cold. *Tiritar de risa*, To titter.
Tiritón [te-re-tone'], *m.* (Coll.) Shivering, shaking with cold.
Tiritona [te-re-to'-nah], *f.* (Coll.) Shivering, especially affected.
Tiro [tee'-ro], *m.* 1. Cast, throw, shot, fling. 2. Shot, range, the distance traversed by a projectile. 3. Mark made by a throw. 4. Charge, shot; gun which is discharged. 5. Theft. *Le hicieron un tiro de cien guineas*, They robbed him of one hundred guineas. 6. Prank, imposition. 7. Serious physical or moral injury. 8. Set of coach-horses or mules. 9. Trace of coach-harness. 10. Rope which pulls up the materials used in building. 11. Landing-place of a stairway. 12. The report of fire-arms. 13. *Tiro de una mina*, The shaft of a mine. *Tiros*, Sword-belts. *A tiro de piedra*, Within a stone's throw. *Casi a tiro de flecha*, About an arrow's flight. *Una pistola de tres o cuatro tiros*, A three or four barrelled pistol or revolver. *Hacer tiro*, To incommode, to prejudice. *Errar el tiro*, To miss one's shot; to be deceived or mistaken.
Tirocinio [te-ro-thee'-ne-o], *m.* 1. First attempt, essay, or trial. 2. Novitiate, in the religious sense.
Tiroideo, dea [te-ro'-e-day-o, ah], *a.* Thyroid.
Tiroides [te-ro'-e-des], *f.* Thyroid, thyroid gland.
Tirolés, sa [te-ro-les', sah], *a.* Tyrolian, of the Tyrol.—*m.* Peddler, trader in toys and tinware.
Tirón [te-ron'], *m.* 1. Tyro, beginner, novice, apprentice. 2. Pull, haul, tug. 3. *V.* ESTIRÓN. 4. Time. *V.* VEZ. *De un tirón*, At once, at a stroke. *Ni a dos tirones*, Not easily obtained or carried out.
Tiroriro [te-ro-ree'-ro], *m.* (Coll.) Sound of a musical wind-instrument; the instrument itself.
Tirotear [te-ro-tay-ar'], *vn.* To shoot at random.
Tiroteo [te-ro-tay'-o], *m.* Shooting at random, sharp-shooting; irregular discharge of musketry.
Tirreno, na [tir-ray'-no, nah], *a.* Tyrrhene, relating to ancient Tuscany.
Tirria [teer'-re-ah], *f.* (Coll.) Aversion, antipathy, dislike.
Tirso [teer'-so], *m.* Wand, used in sacrifices to Bacchus. *V.* TALLO.
Tisana [te-sah'-nah], *f.* Ptisan, a medical drink.
Tisanuro, ra [te-sah-noo'-ro, rah], *a.* Thysanuran: applied to a division of wingless insects; spring-tails, bristle-tails.
Tísica [tee'-se-cah], *f.* Phthisis. *V.* TISIS.
Tísico, ca [tee'-se-co, cah], *a.* & *n.* 1. Phthisical. 2. Applied to a person troubled with phthisis or consumption. *Estar tísico*, To be phthisical, consumptive.
Tisis [tee'-sis], *f.* Phthisis, phthisic, pulmonary consumption.
Tisú [te-soo'], *m.* Tissue, a silk stuff interwoven with gold and silver.
Titanato [te-tah-nah'-to], *m.* (Chem.) Titanate, a salt of titanic acid.
Titánico, ca [te-tah'-ne-co, cah], *a.* 1. Titanic, relating to the Titans. 2. Huge, colossal. 3. (Chem.) Pertaining to the metal titanium.
Titano [te-tah'-no], *m.* (Chem.) Titanium, a dark-gray metallic element.
Títere [tee'-tay-ray], *m.* 1. Puppet, marionette. 2. Dwarf, a ridiculous little fellow.
Titerero, ra [te-tay-ray'-ro, rah], *a.* *V.* TITIRITERO.
Tití [te-tee'], *m.* A very small monkey.
Titicana [te-te-cah'-nah], *f.* (Bot.) A sour cane of America.
Titilación [te-te-lah-the-on'], *f.* Titillation, tickling, slight pleasure.
Titilar [te-te-lar'], *va.* 1. To titillate, to tickle. 2. To please by slight gratification.
Titimalo [te-tee'-mah-lo], *m.* (Bot.) Spurge, a plant with a milky acrid juice. Euphorbia. *V.* LECHETREZNA.
Titiritaina [te-te-re-tah'-e-nah], *f.* (Coll.) Confused noise of flutes or festive amusements.
Titiritero [te-te-re-tay'-ro], *m.* Puppet player, a puppet-show man.
Tito [tee'-to], *m.* (Bot.) A kind of chick-pea. Lathyrus cicera.

Titubear [te-too-bay-ar'], *vn.* 1. To totter, to stagger. 2. To stutter, to stammer. 3. To waver, to hesitate. *Titubear en,* To hesitate to.

Titubeo [te-too-bay'-o], *m.* Vacillation, wavering; making trials or essays.

Titulado [te-too-lah'-do], *m.* Person having a title of nobility.—*Titulado, da, pp.* of TITULAR.

Titular [te-too-lar'], *a.* Titular, distinguished by a title; titulary.

Titular, *va.* To title, to give a title or name.—*vn.* To obtain a title from a sovereign.—*vr.* 1. To be given some title. 2. To hold such and such a title, to be entitled.

Titulillo [te-too-leel'-lyo], *m. dim.* 1. A petty title. 2. In typography, the caption or motto put at the top of the page above the text. *Andar en titulillos.* To stick at trifles.

Titulizado, da [te-too-le-thah'-do, dah], *a.* Titled, distinguished.

Título [tee'-too-lo], *m.* 1. Title, an inscription on the exterior of any thing. 2. Title, heading, a division of the contents of a literary work. 3. Title, an appellation of honour: in Spain it designates the dignity of duke, marquis, count, viscount, or baron. 4. Title, foundation of a claim or right; legal title to property. 5. A diploma, a patent, a title, given to empower any one to exercise a profession. 6. Cause, reason, pretext. 7. (Com.) Claim, a name given to divers documents which represent public debt. *A título,* On pretence, under pretext. *Títulos al portador,* Claims payable to bearer.

Tiza [tee'-thah], *f.* 1. Calcined stag's horn. 2. Whiting, a kind of chalk or pipeclay, used by silversmiths. 3. Chalk for blackboards or for billiard cues.

Tizna [teeth'-nah], *f.* Matter for staining or blackening.

Tiznajo [teeth-nah'-ho], *m.* (Coll.) *V.* TIZNÓN.

Tiznar [teeth-nar'], *va.* 1. To smut, to stain. 2. To tarnish, to blot.

Tizne [teeth'-nay], *com.* Soot which sticks to frying-pans or kettles; the smut of coal.

Tiznón [teeth-none'], *m.* A large spot, soil, or stain.

Tizo [tee'-tho], *m.* Half-burnt charcoal.

Tizón [tee-thon'], *m.* 1. Half-burnt wood. 2. Smut in wheat and other grains. 3. (Met.) Spot, stain, disgrace. 4. That part of a hewn stone which is concealed in the wall. *Apagóse el tizón, y pareció quien lo encendió,* When the quarrel is over, the instigator appears.

Tizona [tee-tho'-nah], *f.* (Coll.) Sword; from the name of the famous sword of El Cid.

Tizonada [te-tho-nah'-dah], *f.* Stroke with a half-burnt stick.

Tizonazo [te-tho-nah'-tho], *m.* 1. Stroke with burning charred wood. 2. In jocular style, hell fire.

Tizoncillo [te-thon-theel'-lyo], *m.* 1. (Dim.) A small burning coal. 2. Mildew, a little smut in corn.

Tizonear [te-tho-nay-ar'], *vn.* To stir up a fire; to arrange wood or coals for lighting a fire.

Tizonera [te-tho-nay'-rah], *f.* Heap of ill-burnt charcoal.

Tizonero [te-tho-nay'-ro], *m.* Poker, for stirring the fire.

Tlaco [tlah'-co], *m.* (Mex.) The eighth part of a Spanish silver shilling.

Tlascalteca [tlas-cal-tay'-cah], *a.* Of Tlascala, a state in Mexico.

Tlazole [tlah-tho'-lay], *m.* (Mex.) Maize tops serving as forage to beasts.

Tmesis [may'-sis], *f.* (Gram.) Figure in poetry which divides a compound word into two.

TNT, Abbreviation of *Trinitrotolueno, m.* TNT, Trinitrotoluene.

To! [toh], *int.* 1. A word used to call a dog: little used. 2. Oh, expressing knowledge of any thing.

Toa [to'-ah], *f.* In some parts of America, rope, hawser.

Toalla [to-ahl'-lyah], *f.* 1. Towel. 2. Pillow-sham. *Toalla afelpada,* Turkish towel.

Toalleta [to-al-lyay'-tah], *f. dim.* Napkin; small towel.

Toba [to'-bah], *f.* 1. (Bot.) Cotton thistle. Onopordon acanthium. 2. (Prov.) Stalk of a thistle given to asses. 3. Calcareous matter on the teeth. 4. Tophus, a spongy stone; a calcareous tufa; sinter.

Tobera [to-bay'-rah], *f.* Tewel, tuyère, an iron pipe, through which the nozzle of bellows is thrust in a forge.

Tobillera [to-be-lyay'-rah], *f.* 1. Anklet. 2. (coll.) Bobby-soxer, adolescent girl.

Tobillo [to-beel'-lyo], *m.* The ankle.

Tobogán [to-bo-gahn'], *m.* Toboggan.

Toca [to'-cah], *f.* A hood; a thin stuff; toque, a kind of head-dress.

Tocadiscos [to-cah-dees'-cos], *m.* (coll.) Phonograph, record player.

Tocado [to-cah'-do], *m.* Ornament, dress; coiffure, head-dress, head-gear; a set of ribbons for garnishing a dress. *Tocado de monja,* A nun's hood or head-dress. *Tocado de mujer,* Commode, the head-dress.

Tocado, da, *a.* & *pp.* of TOCAR. Touched, felt; contaminated; infected. *Estar tocada alguna cosa,* To have begun to rot or putrefy.

Tocador, ra [to-cah-dor', rah], *m.* & *f.* 1. One who beats or touches.—*m.* 2. Handkerchief round the head. 3. Toilet, a lady's dressing-case or table. 4. Dressing-room. 5. (Prov.) Key for tuning musical instruments.

Tocadorcito [to-cah-dor-thee'-to], *m. dim.* of TOCADOR.

Tocamiento [to-cah-me-en'-to], *m.* 1. Touch, contact. 2. Supernatural inspiration.

Tocante [to-cahn'-tay], *a.* Respecting, relative.

Tocante, or **Tocante a,** *prep.* Concerning, relating to; in order to.

Tocar [to-car'], *va.* 1. To touch. 2. touch a thing lightly; to reach with the hand. 3. To play on a musical instrument. 4. To toll or ring a bell. 5. To try metals on a touch-stone; to touch, to magnetize; to examine, to prove. 6. To touch, to treat of, to discuss a matter lightly. 7. To know a thing certainly. 8. To touch, to inspire, to move, to persuade. 9. To strike slightly, to sound any thing. *No tocar pelota,* (Coll.) Not to hit the mark, to err totally. 10. To touch, to communicate or infect; to chastise. 11. To comb and dress the hair with ribbons.—*vn.* 1. To appertain, to belong. 2. To interest, to concern; to be a duty or obligation; to import. 3. To fall to one's share or lot. 4. To touch, to be contiguous to; to arrive in passing. 5. To be allied or related. *Tocar de cerca,* (Met.) To be nearly related. *Tocar de cerca alguna cosa,* To have an interest, to be concerned. *Tocar de cerca algún asunto,* To have complete knowledge of a subject or matter. *Tocar a la puerta,* To rap at the door. *Tocar a la bomba,* (Naut.) To ring for pumping ship. *Tocar a mudar la guardia,* (Naut.) To ring for relieving the watch. *Tocar en un puerto,* (Naut.) To touch at a port. *El barco ha tocado,* The ship has struck aground. *Las velas tocan,* The sails are filling. *Tocar la diana,* (Mil.) To beat the reveille. *Tocar la generala,* (Mil.) To beat the general. *A toca tejá,* (Coll.) Ready money. *Tocar a alguno,* (Met.) To tempt or stimulate any one.—*vr.* 1. (Coll.) To be covered, to put on the hat. 2. To comb and arrange the hair.

Tocasalva [to-cah-sahl'-vah], *f.* *V.* SALVILLA.

Tocata [to-cah'-tah], *f.* A musical composition of brief extent for some instrument: toccata. (Ital.)

Tocayo, ya [to-cah'-yo, yah], *a.* Having the same name, namesake.

Tocinero, ra [to-the-nay'-ro, rah], *m.* & *f.* Porkman, one who sells pork or bacon.

Tocino [to-thee'-no], *m.* 1. Bacon, salt pork. 2. Hog's lard. *Témpano de tocino,* Flitch of bacon. *Tocino rancio,* Rank pork.

Tocología [to-co-lo-hee'-ah], *f.* Tocology, the art of obstetrics.

Tocólogo [to-co'-lo-go], *m.* Tocologist, obstetrician.

Tocón [to-cone'], *m.* Stump of a tree; stump of an arm or leg.

Toconal [to-co-nahl'], *m.* An olive-yard planted with stumps.

Tocororo [to-co-ro'-ro], *m.* (Zool.) A Cuban trogon, with lively colours (green and gray, with a red breast).

Tocuyo [to-coo'-yo], *m.* (Ven. Peru, etc.) A plain home-spun cotton stuff.

Tochedad [to-chay-dahd'], *f.* Clownishness, rusticity, ignorance.

Tocho [toh'-cho], *m.* 1. (Prov.) Pole. 2. Bar of iron.

Tocho, cha [toh'-cho, chah], *a.* Clownish, unpolished, homespun.

Tochura [to-choo'-rah], *f.* (Prov.) Waggishness, sarcastic gaiety.

Todabuena, Todasana [to-dah-boo-ay'-nah, to-dah-sah'-nah], *f.* (Bot.) A medicinal species of St. John's-wort.

Todavía [to-dah-vee'-ah], *adv.* 1. Notwithstanding, nevertheless. 2. Yet, still. 3. (Obs.) *V.* SIEMPRE.

Todí [to'-de], *m.* (Zool.) Tody, a West Indian insectivorous bird, having the head and neck of brilliant green.

Todo, da [toh'-do, dah], *a.* All, entire. *Todo un Dios,* The whole power of God, used to indicate great difficulty. *Todos la matamos,* We are guilty of the same fault. *Con todo eso,* Notwithstanding, nevertheless, however. *Todo a la banda,* (Naut.) Hard over. *Todo el mundo abajo,* (Naut.) Down all hands. *Me es todo uno,* It is all one to me. *A todo,* At most. *Del todo,* Entirely, quite. *En todo y por todo,* Wholly, absolutely. *En un todo.* Together, in all its parts. *Ser el todo.* To be the principal or chief. *Hacer a todo,* To be fit for any thing. *Quien todo lo niega, todo lo confiesa,* Too much denial amounts to confession. —*adv.* Entirely, totally.

Todo [toh'-do], *m.* 1. Whole composition of integral parts. 2. (Geom.) A greater quantity compared with a less.

Todopoderoso, sa [to-do-po-day-ro'-so, sah], *a.* All-powerful, almighty; properly applied to God only.—*m.* The Almighty.

Toesa [to-ay'-sah], *f.* Toise, fathom; a French measure.

Tofana [to-fah'-nah], *f.* & *a.* A very active poison, transparent as water, once used in Italy, and said to have been invented by a woman of this name. Probably a strong arsenical solution.

Tofo [to'-fo], *m.* Tumour in the belly of cattle.

Toga [to'-gah], *f.* 1. Toga, loose cloak (worn by professors, judges, graduates, etc.). 2. Dignity of a superior judge. *Toga y birrete*, Cap and gown.

Togado, da [to-gah'-do, dah], *a.* Togated, gowned: applied to those who have a right to wear a toga.

Tohalla, *f.* (Obs.) Towel. *V.* TOALLA.

Toisón [to-e-sone'], *m.* The name of the highest order of Spanish knighthood; the Golden Fleece. *V.* TUSÓN.

Tojal [to-nahl'], *m.* Clump of furze or whin.

Tojines [to-hee'-nes], *m. pl.* (Naut.) Belaying cleats. *Tojines de los peñoles de las vergas*, (Naut.) Cleats of the yard-arms.

Tojino [to-hee'-no], *m.* (Naut.) Notch or knob to secure any thing from moving in a ship; pieces of wood on the sides of a vessel used as steps.

Tojo [to'-ho], *m.* (Bot.) Whin, furze. Ulex europeus, *L.*

Tola [to'-lah], *f.* An Indian mound (S. America.)

Tolano [to-lah'-no], *m.* Tumour in horses' gums —*pl.* (Coll.) Short hair on the neck.

Tolda [tol'-dah], *f.* (Naut.) Awning.

Toldadura [tol-dah-doo'-rah], *f.* Hanging of stuff to moderate the light or heat.

Toldar [tol-dar'], *va.* *V.* ENTOLDAR.

Toldero [tol-day'-ro], *m.* (Prov.) Retailer of salt.

Toldilla [tol-deel'-lyah], *f.* (Naut.) Round-house.

Toldillo [tol-deel'-lyo], *m.* 1. Covered sedan-chair. 2. (Dim.) Small awning.

Toldo [tol'-do], *m.* 1. Awning. 2. (Prov.) Shop where salt is retailed. 3. Ostentation, pomp. *Toldo del alcázar*, (Naut.) Quarter deck awning. *Toldo del combés*, Main-deck awning. *Candeleros de los toldos*, (Naut.) Stanchions of the awnings.

Tole tole [to'-lay to'-lay], *m.* (Lat. tolle) Confused noise of the populace. (Coll.) *Tomar el tole*, To run off, to flee.

Toledano, na [to-lay-dah'-no, nah], *a.* Toledan, of Toledo.

Toledo [to-lay'-do], *m.* A song-bird of Central America. Chiroscíphia lineata. (As proper name, see Appendix.)

Tolerable [to-lay-rah'-blay], *a.* Tolerable, supportable.

Tolerablemente, *adv.* Tolerably, middlingly.

Toleración, *f.* (Obs.) *V.* TOLERANCIA.

Tolerancia [to-lay-rahn'-the-ah], *f.* Toleration, permission; tolerance, indulgence.

Tolerante [to-lay-rahn'-tay], *a.* Tolerant: applied to a government which tolerates freedom of worship, and to persons who tolerate what they cannot approve.

Tolerantismo [to-lay-ran-tees'-mo], *m.* Free exercise of all worship and religious opinions.

Tolerar [to-lay-rar'], *va.* To tolerate, to suffer, to permit; to indulge, to overlook, to comport.

Tolete [to-lay'-tay], *m.* 1. (Naut.) Thole, thole-pin. 2. (Amer.) A small club for catching alligators. 3. (Cuba) A stick.

Tolondro, Tolondrón [to-lon'-dro], *m.* 1. Contusion on the head arising from a blow. *A topa tolondro*, Inconsiderately, rashly. 2. A giddy, hare-brained fellow.

Tolondrón, na [to-lon-drone', nah], *a.* Giddy, hare-brained; foolish. *A tolondrones*, Precipitately, giddily, inconsiderately, interruptedly; with contusions or bruises.

Tolú [to-loo'], *m.* A balsam which owes its name to a town in Colombia.

Tolva [tol'-vah], *f.* Hopper, in a mill.

Tolvanera [tol-vah-nay'-rah], *f.* Cloud of dust raised by whirlwinds.

Tolla [tol'-lyah], *f.* 1. Bog, commonly covered with moss. *V.* TOLLADAR. 2. (Cuba) A canoe-shaped trough for watering horses.

Tolladar [tol-lyah-dar'], *m.* *V.* ATOLLADERO.

Tollecer [tol-lyay-therr'], *va.* (Obs.) *V.* TULLIR.

Toller [tol-lyerr'], *va.* (Obs.) *V.* QUITAR.

Tollina [tol-lyee'-nah], *f.* (Coll.) Cudgelling, cowhiding.

Tollo [tol'-lyo], *m.* 1. (Zool.) Spotted dog-fish. Squalus catulus. 2. Cave or hollow for concealing sportsmen in wait for game. 3. Bog. *V.* ATOLLADERO.

Toma [to'-mah], *f.* 1. Taking, receiving, hold, gripe, grasp. 2. Capture, conquest, seizure. 3. Portion of any thing taken at once. *Toma de razón*, Entry of receipts, bills of sale, etc., in books of accounts; counting-house journal, account or memorandum book. *Una toma de quina*, A dose of bark. 4. Opening into a canal or drain.—*int.* There, well, what.

Tomada [to-mah'-dah], *f.* 1. (Obs.) Conquest, capture, seizure. 2. Take, the quantity of copy taken at one time by a compositor for setting up; the same in type.

Tomadero [to-mah-day'-ro], *m.* 1. Handle, haft. 2. Opening into a drain.

Tomado [to-mah'-do], *m.* Ornamental plait in cloths.—*Tomado, da, pp.* of TOMAR.

Tomador, ra [to-mah-dor', rah], *m.* & *f.* 1. Taker, receiver. 2. Retriever, a dog that finds or fetches the game. 3. (Coll.) Pickpocket, pilferer. *Tomadores*, (Naut.) Ropebands, gaskets.

Tomadura [to-mah-doo'-rah], *f.* Catch, seizure, gripe, hold, grasp, capture: commonly, the portion of a thing taken at once.

Tomajón, na [to-mah-hone', nah], *a.* Taking or accepting easily or frequently.

Tomar [to-mar'], *va.* 1. To take, to catch, to seize, to grasp, to recover. 2. To receive in any mode; to get. 3. To occupy, capture, to take possession of. 4. To eat or drink. 5. To understand, to apprehend; to interpret, to perceive. 6. To contract, to acquire. 7. To take into service, to employ. 8. To intercept or block roads or paths. 9. To take by stealth, to rob. 10. To buy, to purchase. 11. To undertake, to apply one's self to a business. 12. To imitate, to copy. 13. To take, to choose, to select. 14. To surprise, to overtake. *Tomarle a uno el sueño*, To be overtaken by sleep. 15. To surprise, to overwhelm. 16. To cover the female. 17. To take a trick in cards. 18. (Naut.) To arrive in port or at an anchoring-place. 19. To take into one's company. 20. With names of instruments, to set about, or execute the action implied. *Tomar la pluma*, To write. *Tomar la aguja*, To sew. 21. In playing ball, to call a halt, because the players are not in their proper places, or some other reason.—*vr.* To get covered with rust: used of metals.—It forms numerous phrases. *Más vale un "toma" que dos "te daré,"* A bird in the hand is worth two in the bush. *Tomar calor*, To get warm, to push an affair warmly. *Tomar frío*, To catch cold. *Tomar cuentas*, To audit accounts, or to take and examine accounts. *Tomar el fresco*, To take the air. *Tomar el sol*, To take the sun, or expose one's self to the sun. *Tomar lengua* or *lenguas*, To take tidings or signs of any thing. *Tomar viento*, (Naut.) To trim the sails to the wind. *Tomar fuerzas*, To gather strength. *Tomar a cuestas*, To carry on one's back; to take upon one's self, or to take charge of the management of an affair. *Tomar resolución*, To resolve. *Tomar estado*, To change condition; to marry; to become a clergyman; to take the black veil. *Tomar por su cuenta*, To take upon one's account. *Tomar puerto*, (Naut.) To get into a port. *Tomar rizos*, To reef, to take in reefs. *Tomar rizos en la mesana*, To balance the mizzen. *Tomar por avante*, To work to windward. *Tomarse con alguno* or *tomarla con alguno*, To pick a quarrel with one. *Tomarse con Dios*, To contend with God, to persevere obstinately in evil. *Tomarse del vino*, To get in liquor. *Tomarse de cólera*, To fly into a passion. *Tomar la mañana*, (1) To rise early. (2) (Coll.) To take a morning drink. *Tomar las aguas*, To cover a building during its construction. *Tomar la muerte a alguno*, To die a natural death. *Tomar a alguno las medidas*, To form an opinion of one. *Tomar la voz*, To continue a subject. *Tomar el chorrillo*, To fall into a habit. *Tomar el cielo con las manos*, To be transported with joy, grief, or anger. *Tomar pipa*, To take one's hat and go away. *Tomar la puerta*, To go out of the house, to be off. *Tomar las de Villadiego*, To run off in haste. *Tomar a pechos*, To take to heart; to undertake a thing with too much zeal. *Tomar plática*, To obtain practice. *Tomar razón*, To register, to take a memorandum. *Tomar mosca*, To take offence. *Tomar a uno entre cejas* or *entre dientes*, To take a dislike to a person. *Tomar el trabajo* (or *tanto trabajo*), To take trouble for the sake of helping another. *Tomar la delantera*, To excel another. *Tomar el rábano por las hojas*, To put the cart before the horse.

Tomate [to-mah'-tay], *m.* (Bot.) Tomato, a nutritious vegetable, the fruit of the tomato-plant. (Mex. tomatl.) Solanum lycopersicum.

Tomatera [to-mah-tay'-rah], *f.* Tomato-plant.

Tomavistas [to-mah-vees'-tas], *m.* 1. Motion picture camera. 2. Television camera.

Tómbola [tom'-bo-lah], *f.* Raffle.

Tomento, Tomiento [to-men'-to], *m.* Coarse tow.

Tomentoso, sa [to-men-to'-so, sah], *a.* (Bot.) Tomentose, tomentous; coated with downy wool-like hairs.

Tomillar [to-mil-lyar'], *m.* Bed of thyme.

Tomillo [to-meel'-lyo], *m.* (Bot.) Thyme.

Tomín [to-meen'], *m.* 1. Tomin, third part of a drachm, Spanish weight. 2. In some parts of America, a real.

Tominejo, ja [to-me-nay'-ho, hah], *m.* & *f.* Genus of small bright-plumaged birds, of which the humming-bird is the smallest.

Tomiza [to-mee'-thah], *f.* Bass rope.

Tomo [to'-mo], *m.* 1. Bulk or body of a thing. 2. Importance, value, consequence. *Es cosa de mucho tomo*, It is a matter of great consequence. 3. Tome, volume. *De tomo y lomo*, Of weight and bulk; of importance.

Tomón, na, *a.* Accepting. *V.* TOMAJÓN.

Ton, *m.* *V.* TONO. Used only in the phrase, *Sin ton ni son*, Without motive or cause, without rhyme or reason; unreasonably, inordinately.

Tona [to'-nah], *f.* (Prov.) Surface of a liquid.

Tonada [to-nah'-dah], *f.* Tune, a metrical composition suited for singing and the music set to it.

Tonadica [to-nah-dee'-cah], *f. dim.* A short tune or song.

Tonadilla [to-nah-deel'-lyah], *f.* 1. (Dim.) *V.* TONADICA. 2. An interlude of music formerly used in comedies; now seldom employed, and then only at the end.

Tonante [to-nahn'-tay], *pa.* (Poet.) Thundering: applied to Jupiter.

Tonar [to-nar'], *vn.* (Poet.) To thunder, to emit a thundering noise.

Tonca, Tonga [ton'-cah], *f.* (Bot.) The tonka bean, employed in flavouring tobacco (adulterating vanilla, etc.). In Peru called *Pucheri.*

Tondino [ton-dee'-no], *m.* (Arch.) Moulding on the astragal of a column.

Tondir [ton-deer'], *va.* (Obs.) *V.* TUNDIR.

Tonel [to-nel'], *m.* 1. Cask, barrel. 2. (Naut.) An ancient measure of ships; ten *toneles* make twelve *toneladas.*

Tonelada [to-nay-lah'-dah], *f.* 1. Tun, ton, a measure or weight of twenty hundred-weight. 2. Tonnage, carrying capacity of a ship. 3. Collection of casks in a ship. *Bajel de quinientas toneladas*, (Naut.) A ship of five hundred tons burden. 4. Tonnage-duty. *Tonelada de arqueo*, The volume of twenty hundred-weight of water; a trifle over nine hundred and twenty cubic decimetres.

Tonelaje [to-nay-lah'-hay], *m.* Tonnage.

Toneleria [to-nay-lay-ree'-ah], *f.* 1. Trade of a cooper; workshop of a cooper. 2. Quantity of water-casks for a ship.

Tonelero [to-nay-lay'-ro], *m.* Cooper, hooper.

Tonelete [to-nay-lay'-tay], *m.* 1. Ancient armour passing from the waist to the knees. 2. (Dim.) Little butt or barrel.

Tonga, Tongada [ton'-gah], *f.* Couch; a layer or stratum; lay, row, ledge, flake.

Tónica [toh'-ne-cah], *f.* (Mus.) Key-note, tonic.

Tónico, ca [toh'-ne-co, cah], *a.* Tonic, strengthening.

Tónico, *m.* (Med.) Tonic, a medicine.

Tonillo [to-neel'-lyo], *m.* Disagreeable, monotonous tone in reading or speaking.

Tonina [to-nee'-nah], *f.* (Com.) Fresh tunny.

Tonismo [to-nees'-mo], *m.* Tetanus, according to some writers.

Tono [toh'-no], *m.* 1. Tone, modulation of the voice. 2. The manner of doing a thing. 3. Tune. 4. (Med.) Tone. 5. A small spiral of metal, which, placed in horns or trumpets, modifies their tone. 6. Tuning-fork. 7. Deportment, manner, social address.

Tonsila [ton-see'-lah], *f.* Tonsil.

Tonsilar [ton-se-lar'], *a.* Tonsillar, belonging to the tonsils.

Tonsilitis [ton-se-lee'-tis], *f.* (Med.) Tonsilitis.

Tonsura [ton-soo'-rah], *f.* 1. Tonsure, the first clerical degree of the Roman Catholic church. 2. The act of cutting hair or wool.

Tonsurar [ton-soo-rar'], *va.* 1. To give the first clerical degree. 2. To cut the hair, to cut off wool.

Tontada [ton-tah'-dah], *f.* Nonsense; a foolish speech or action.

Tontaina [ton-tah'-e-nah], *com.* & *a.* Stupid, fool; foolish.

Tontamente, *adv.* Foolishly, stupidly.

Tontazo, za [ton-tah'-tho, thah], *a. aug.* Doltish, very stupid.

Tontear [ton-tay-ar'], *vn.* To talk nonsense, to act foolishly; to fool.

Tontedad, Tontera [ton-tay-dahd', ton-tay'-rah], *f.* *V.* TONTERÍA.

Tonteria [ton-tay-ree'-ah], *f.* Foolishness, foolery, folly, foppery, ignorance; nonsense.

Tontico [ton-tee'-co], *m. dim.* A little dolt.

Tontillo [ton-teel'-lyo], *m.* 1. (Dim.) *V.* TONTICO. 2. Hoop-skirt, a part of a lady's dress.

Tontina [ton-tee'-nah], *f.* Tontine, a division of a sum of money among various persons, to be divided at a fixed epoch, with the interest, among the survivors.

Tonto, ta [ton'-to, tah], *a.* Stupid, foolish, ignorant, fatuous. *Hacerse el tonto*, To play the fool. *Tonto de capirote*, Great fool, idiot. *A tontas y a locas*, Sillily and madly. without rhyme or reason, inordinately.

¡Top! (Naut.) Hold! stop! a word of command (fr. Eng. stop).

Topacio [to-pah'-the-o], *m.* Topaz, a precious stone.

Topada [to-pah'-dah], *f.* *V.* TOPETADA.

Topadizo, za [to-pah-dee'-tho, thah], *a.* (Coll.) *V.* ENCONTRADIZO.

Topador [to-pah-dor'], *m.* Encounterer, one who butts or strikes against another. Said properly of rams and other horned animals.

Topar [to-par'], *va.* 1. To run or strike against. 2. To meet with by chance. 3. To depend upon, to consist in. *La dificultad topa en esto*, (Coll.) The difficulty consists in this. 4. To accept a bet at cards.—*vn.* 1. To butt or strike with the head. 2. (Met.) To abut or lean against. *Tope donde tope*, (Coll.) Strike where it will.

Toparca [to-par'-cah], *m.* Toparch, a ruler of a small state, composed of very few places. (Gr. τοπάρχης.)

Toparquia [toh'-par-kee'-ah], *f.* Toparchy, seigniory, jurisdiction or lordship. (Gr. τοπαρχία.)

Tope [toh'-pay], *m.* 1. Top, the highest point or part. 2. Butt, the striking of one thing against another. 3. Rub, the point of difficulty. 4. Obstacle, impediment. 5. Scuffle, quarrel. 6. The highest point of a mast. *Tope de un tablón*, (Naut.) Butt-end of a plank. *Tope de la arboladura*, Mast-head. *A tope o al tope*, Juncture, union, or incorporation of the extremities of things. *Al tope*, Conjointly, contiguously. *Hasta el tope*, Up to the top, or the brim.

Topera [to-pay'-rah], *f.* Mole-hole.

Topetada [to-pay-tah'-dah], *f.* Butt, by a horned animal.

Topetar [to-pay-tar'], *va.* To butt; to offend, to encounter.

Topetón [to-pay-tone'], *m.* Collision, encounter, blow.

Topetudo, da [to-pay-too'-do, dah], *a.* Applied to animals accustomed to butt.

Tópico, ca [toh'-pe-co, cah], *a.* Topical, belonging to a particular place.—*m.* (Med.) Topical application.

Topil [to-peel'], *m.* (Mex.) *V.* ALGUACIL.

Topinaria [to-pe-nah' re-ah], *f.* *V.* TALPARIA.

Topinera [to-pe-nay'-rah], *f.* *V.* TOPERA.

Topo [toh'-po], *m.* 1. (Zool.) Mole. Talpa. 2. Stumbler. 3. (Coll.) A numbskull, a dolt. 4. A league and a half among the Indians.

Topografía [to-po-grah-fee'-ah], *f.* Topography.

Topográficamente, *adv.* Topographically.

Topográfico, ca [to-po-grah'-fe-co, cah], *a.* Topographical.

Topógrafo [to-po'-grah-fo], *m.* Topographer.

Toque [toh'-kay], *m.* 1. Touch, the act of touching. 2. Ringing of bells. *Toque a muerto*, Passing-bell. 3. A military call by drum or bugle. 4. Essay, trial, test. 5. Touch-stone. 6. Experience, proof. 7. Aid, assistance, or inspiration by God. 8. (Coll.) Blow given to any thing. *Toque de luz*, Light in a picture. *Dar un toque*, To give one a trial in any business. *El primero* or *el segundo toque* (*de un tambor*), The first or second beat of a drum. *El último toque* (*de una campana*), The last peal of a bell. *Ahí está el toque*, (Met.) There the difficulty lies.

Toqueado [to-kay-ah'-do], *m.* Sound of a stroke with the hands or feet.

Toqueria [to-kay-ree'-ah], *f.* 1. Collection of women's head-dresses. 2. Business of making women's veils.

Toquero [to-kay'-ro], *m.* Veil-maker for nuns; head-dress maker.

Toquilla [to-keel'-lyah], *f.* 1. (Dim.) Small head-dress of gauze, small veil. 2. Ribbon or lace round the crown of a hat. 3. A small triangular kerchief used by women to put at the neck or on the head. 4. The plant from which Panama hats are made. Carludovica palmata.

Tora [toh'-rah], *f.* 1. Tribute paid by Jewish families. 2. Book of the Jewish law; Pentateuch, torah (or thorah). (Heb.) 3. A herb.

Tora, *f.* Frame or figure of a bull in artificial fire-works (fr. *Toro*).

Torácico, ca [to-rah'-the-co, cah], *a.* (Anat.) Thoracic.

Torada [to-rah'-dah], *f.* Drove of bulls.

Toral [to-rahl'], *a.* Main, principal.

Toral, *m.* (Prov.) Yellow wax in cakes unbleached. *Torales*, Boxes filled with pitch.

Tórax [to'-rax], *m.* Chest, breast, thorax.

Torazo [to-rah'-tho], *m. aug.* Large bull.

Torbellino [tor-bel-lyee'-no], *m.* 1. Whirlwind, cyclone. 2. A lively, boisterous, restless person. 3. A concurrence or multitude of things that present themselves at the same time.

Torca [tor'-cah], *f.* Cavern in mountains.

Torcal [tor-cahl'], *m.* Place where there are caves.

Torcaz [tor-cath'], *a.* Applied to gray wild pigeons with white necks.

Torce [tor'-thay], *f.* Link of a chain or collar.

Torcecuello [tor-thay-coo-ayl'-lyo], *m.* (Orn.) Wry-neck. Yunx torquilla.

Torcedero [tor-thay-day'-ro], *m.* Twisting-mill, an engine for twisting.

Torcedero, ra [tor-thay-day'-ro, rah], *a.* *V.* TORCIDO.

Torcedor, ra [tor-thay-dor', rah], *m.* & *f.* 1. Twister, a spindle for twisting thread. 2. Any thing which causes displeasure or grief.

Torcedura [tor-thay-doo'-rah], *f.* 1. Twisting. *Quitar la torcedura de un* *cable*, (Naut.) To untwist a cable. 2. A light, paltry wine.

Torcer [tor-therr'], *va.* 1. To twist, to double, to curve, to distort, to warp. 2. To turn, to deviate from the right road, to deflect, to turn aside. 3. To crook, to pervert from rectitude; to leave the paths of virtue. (Used intransitively in this sense.) 4. To put a wrong construction on any thing. 5. To pervert, as judges do justice. 6. To dissuade, to induce to change an opinion. 7. To impugn, to retort, to refute an argument. *Torcer las narices*, To turn up the nose in disgust. *Torcer la llave*, To turn the key, to lock.—*vr.* 1. To be dislocated; to be sprained; to go crooked. 2. To turn sour: applied to wine. 3. To deceive at gaming. *Torcer la cabeza*, (Met.) *V.* ENFERMAR.

Torcida [tor-thee'-dah], *f.* Wick for lamps and candles.

Torcidamente, *adv.* Obliquely, tortuously, crookedly.

Torcidillo [tor-the-deel'-lyo], *m.* A kind of twisted silk.

Torcido, da [tor-thee'-do, dah], *a.* & *pp.* of TORCER. Oblique, tortuous, crooked.

Torcido, *m.* 1. A kind of twisted sweetmeat. 2. (Prov.) Light, bad wine.

Torcijón [tor-the-hone'], *m.* 1. Gripes, pains in the bowels. 2. *V.* TOROZÓN.

Torcimiento [tor-the-me-en'-to], *m.* 1. Turning or bending of what was straight. 2. Deflection, deviation from the paths of virtue. 3. Circumlocution or periphrasis.

Torculado [tor-coo-lah'-do], *m.* Female screw.

Tórculo [tor'-coo-lo], *m.* A small press; a rolling press for prints.

Torcho [tor'-cho], *a.* Said of iron forged into very thin bars.

Tordella [tor-day'-lyah], *f.* Large kind of thrush.

Tórdiga [tor'-de-gah], *f.* Neat's leather for coarse shoes.

Tordillo, lla [tor-deel'-lyo, lyah], *a.* Of a thrush-colour, grayish, grizzled.

Tordo [tor'-do], *m.* (Orn.) Thrush, throstle. Turdus musicus. *Tordo de agua*, (Orn.) Reed thrush. Turdus arundinaceus. *Tordo loco*, (Orn.) Solitary thrush. Turdus solitarius.

Tordo, da [tor'-do, dah], *a.* Speckled black and white: commonly applied to horses.

Toreador [to-ray-ah-dor'], *m.* Bull-fighter: commonly applied to bull-fighters on foot.

Torear [to-ray-ar'], *vn.* 1. To fight in the ring: said of bulls. 2. To let a bull to cows.—*va.* (Coll.) To burlesque, to mock; to make bulls.

Toreo [to-ray'-o], *m.* Art or practice of fighting bulls.

Torería [to-ray-ree'-ah], *f.* (Cuba, Peru, etc.) 1. Pranks of young folks. 2. The office of bull-fighter.

Torero [to-ray'-ro], *m.* Bull-fighter.

Torés [to-res'], *m.* (Arch.) Torus, large ring or round moulding at the base of a column.

Torete [to-ray'-tay], *m.* 1. (Dim.) A small bull. 2. (Coll.) A difficult point, an intricate business. 3. (Obs.) A popular rumour.

Torga [tor'-gah], *f.* Yoke put on the necks of hogs.

Toril [to-reel'], *m.* Place where bulls are shut up until they are brought out.

Torillo [to-reel'-lyo], *m.* 1. (Dim.) Little bull. 2. Dowel, a pin for fastening timber. 3. (Obs.) Frequent subject of conversation. 4. (Anat.) Peritoneum.

Torio [to'-ree-o], *m.* (Chem.) Thorium.

Toriondez [to-re-on-deth'], *f.* (Prov.) The cow's desire for the bull.

Toriondo, da [to-re-on'-do, dah], *a.* Applied to cattle rutting.

Torloroto [tor-lo-ro'-to], *m.* A shepherd's pipe or flute.

Tormellera [tor-may-lyay'-rah], *f* Craggy, covered with high rocks.

Tormenta [tor-men'-tah], *f.* 1. Perturbation of the waters of the ocean through the violence of winds. 2. Storm, tempest; hurricane. *Correr tormenta*, (Naut.) To run before the wind in a storm. 3. Storm, adversity, misfortune.

Tormentador, ra [tor-men-tah-dor', rah], *m.* & *f.* *V.* ATORMENTADOR.

Tormentar [tor-men-tar'], *vn.* To be violently agitated; to suffer a storm.

Tormentario, ria [tor-men-tah'-re-o, ah], *a.* Projectile: applied to gunnery.

Tormentila [tor-men-tee'-lah], *f.* (Bot.) Tormentil, septfoil, a slender trailing Old World herb with yellow flowers; its root is a powerful astringent, and has been used in diarrhœa. Potentilla tormentilla.

Tormentín [tor-men-teen'], *m.* (Naut.) A small mast on the bowsprit.

Tormento [tor-men'-to], *m.* 1. Torment, pain, anguish, torture, pang, affliction. 2. Rack, torture. 3. (Mil.) Battering ordnance. *Dar tormento*, To torture, to put to the rack. *Tormento de toca*, Ancient mode of torturing, by making the victim drink strips of thin gauze and water; tedious affliction.

Tormentoso, sa [tor-men-to'-so, sah], *a.* 1. Stormy, boisterous, turbulent. 2. (Naut.) Easily dismasted: applied to a ship.

Tormo [tor'-mo], *m.* Tor, a high, pointed, isolated rock.

Torna [tor'-nah], *f.* 1. Restitution. 2. Return. *V.* TORNADA. 3. Drain of water for irrigation.—*pl.* 1. Return, recompense, restitution.

Tornaboda [tor-nah-bo'-dah], *f.* Day after a wedding.

Tornachile [tor-nah-chee'-lay], *m.* (Mex.) A thick pepper.

Tornada [tor-nah'-dah], *f.* Return from a journey.

Tornadera [tor-nah-day'-rah], *f.* A two-pronged winnowing fork used in Castile.

Tornadizo, za [tor-nah-dee'-tho, thah], *a.* & *m.* & *f.* Turncoat, deserter.

Tornado [tor-nah'-do], *m.* Hurricane in the Gulf of Guinea off western Africa; tornado.

Tornadura [tor-nah-doo'-rah], *f.* 1. Return: recompense. 2. Land measure of ten feet.

Tornaguía [tor-nah-gee'-ah], *f.* Return of a receipt issued by the custom-house, showing that the goods have arrived at their destination.

Tornajo [tor-nah'-ho], *m.* Trough.

Tornapunta [tor-nah-poon'-tah], *f.* (Arch.) Stay, prop. *V.* PUNTAL.

Tornar [tor-nar'], *va.* & *vn.* 1. To return, to restore, to make restitution. 2. To return, to come back again. 3. To repeat, to do again. *Tornar por*, To defend, to protect. *Tornar cabeza a alguna cosa*, (Coll.) To attend to any thing, to consider, to be attentive. *A tornapeón* or *a tornayunta*, (Coll.) Mutually and reciprocally. *Tornar las espaldas*, To turn a cold shoulder. *Tornarse el sueño del perro*, To fail of success after much endeavour.

Tornasol [tor-nah-sole'], *m.* 1. (Bot.) Turnsole, sunflower. *V.* GIRASOL. 2. Changeable colour of stuff. 3. Litmus. (Improperly so-called.)

Tornasolar [tor-nah-so-lar'], *va.* To cause changes in colour.

Tornátil [tor-nah'-teel], *a.* Turned, made by a turner or with a wheel.

Tornaviaje [tor-nah-ve-ah'-hay], *m.* Return-trip.

Tornavirada [tor-nah-ve-rah'-dah], *f.* A roundabout way; a round trip.

Tornavoz [tor-nah-voth'], *m.* Sound-board, or sounding-board.

Torneador [tor-nay-ah-dor'], *m.* 1. Turner, one who works on a lathe. *V.* TORNERO, 1st def. 2. Tilter at tournaments.

Torneante [tor-nay-ahn'-tay], *pa.* Tilting at tournaments, turning, revolving.

Tornear [tor-nay-ar'], *va.* & *vn.* 1. To shape by turning on a lathe. 2. To turn, to wind round about, to put into a circular motion. 3. To tilt at tournaments. 4. To meditate.

Torneo [tor-nay'-o], *m.* 1. Tournament; public festival of knights. 2. Dance in imitation of tournaments.

Tornera [tor-nay'-rah], *f.* Doorkeeper of a nunnery.

Tornería [tor-nay-ree'-ah], *f.* Turning, the act of forming on a lathe.

Tornero [tor-nay'-ro], *m.* 1. Turner, one who turns on a lathe. 2. The maker of lathes. 3. (Prov.) Messenger or servant of a nunnery.

Tornés, sa [tor-nes', sah], *a.* Applied to money made at Tours. *Libra tornesa*, Livre Tournois.

Tornillero [tor-nil-lyay'-ro], *m.* (Coll.) Deserter.

Tornillo [tor-neel'-lyo], *m.* 1. Bolt. 2. Screw. 3. (Mil.) Desertion. 4. Small vise. *Tornillo sin fin*, Worm gear. *Faltar un tornillo a*, (Coll.) To have a screw loose. *Apretar los tornillos a*, (Coll.) To put the screws on.

Torniquete [tor-ne-kay'-tay], *m.* 1. Turnstile. 2. Tourniquet.

Torniscón [tor-nis-con'], *m.* (Coll.) 1. Crack on the head. 2. Slap in the face. 3. (Sp. Am.) Sharp pinch.

Torno [tor'-no], *m.* 1. Winch. 2. Lathe. 3. Potter's wheel. 4. Vise. 5. Revolution, turn. 6. Turn, bend (in a river). *Torno de hilar*, Spinning wheel. *Torno de mano*, Clamp. *En torno a*, Around.

Toro [toh'-ro], *m.* 1. Bull. Bos taurus. *Toro mejicano*, Bison. *V.* BISONTE. *Correr toros*, To fight bulls. 2. (Arch.) Ogee moulding. 3. Moulding of the breech of a cannon.

Torondo, Torondón [to-ron'-do, done'], *m.* *V.* TOLONDRO.

Toronja [to-ron'-hah], *f.* (Bot.) Grape-fruit, shaddock.

Toronjil, *m.* **Toronjina**, *f.* [to-ron-heel']. (Bot.) Balm-gentle. Melissa officinalis.

Toronjo [to-ron'-ho], *m.* (Bot.) Shaddock-tree.

Toroso, sa [to-ro'-so, sah], *a.* Strong, robust.

Torozón [to-ro-thone'], *m.* Gripes, pains in the bowels: said only of animals.

Torpe [tor'-pay], *a.* 1. Slow, dull, heavy; torpid, having a slow motion. 2. Dull, stupid, rude. 3. Lascivious, unchaste, obscene. 4. Indecorous, disgraceful, infamous. 5. Dull, slow of comprehension.

Torpedad [tor-pay-dahd'], *f.* (Obs.) Dulness, rudeness. *V.* TORPEZA.

Torpedero [tor-pay-day'-ro], *m.* Torpedo-boat, a small fighting craft, very swift, designed for discharging torpedoes.

Torpedo [tor-pay'-do], *m.* 1. (Zool.) Torpedo, electric ray, cramp-fish, numbfish. 2. Torpedo, an explosive weapon of naval warfare.
Torpemente, *adv.* Obscenely, basely; slowly.
Torpeza [tor-pay'-thah], *f.* 1. Heaviness, dulness, rudeness. 2. Torpidness, torpor; slowness. 3. Impurity, unchastity, lewdness, obscenity. 4. Want of ornament or culture. 5. Rudeness, ugliness.
Torpor [tor-por'], *m.* Torpor, numbness, want of motion.
Torrar [tor-rar'], *va.* *V.* TOSTAR.
Torre [tor'-ray], *f.* 1. A tower; turret, embattled tower. 2. Steeple of a church, in which bells are hung. 3. (Prov.) Country-house with a garden. 4. Castle, rook (in chess). 5. (Naut.) Turret. *Torre de albarrana,* Watchtower. *Torre de control, Torre de mando,* (Aer.) Control tower. *Torre del homenaje,* Keep. *Torre de perforación,* Derrick. *Torre de viento,* (Fig.) Castles in Spain.
Torrear [tor-ray-ar'], *va.* To fortify with towers or turrets.
Torrecilla [tor-ray-theel'-lyah], *f.* Turret.
Torrefacción [tor-ray-fac-the-on'], *f.* Torrefaction, roasting.
Torreja [tor-ray'-hah], *f.* (Mex.) Fritter.
Torrejón [tor-ray-hone'], *m.* Ill-shaped turret.
Torrencial [tor-ren-the-ahl'], *a.* Torrential; overpowering.
Torrentada [tor-ren-tah'-dah], *f.* Sweep of a torrent, impetuous current.
Torrente [tor-ren'-tay], *m.* 1. Torrent, a rapid stream; an impetuous current. 2. Abundance, plenty. 3. Strong, coarse voice.
Torrentera [tor-ren-tay'-rah], *f.* Gully washed out by a freshet.
Torreón [tor-ray-one'], *m.* A great tower in fortresses for defence.
Torrero [tor-ray'-ro], *m.* 1. Bailiff or steward of a country-house and garden. 2. A lighthouse-keeper.
Torreznada [tor-reth-nah'-dah], *f.* Plentiful dish of rashers.
Torreznero [tor-reth-nay'-ro], *m.* (Coll.) A lazy fellow, who sits over the fire.
Torrezno [tor-reth'-no], *m.* 1. Rasher of bacon. 2. A voluminous book.
Tórrido, da [tor'-re-do, dah], *a.* Torrid, parched, hot.
Torrija [tor-ree'-hah], *f.* Slice of bread, fried in white wine, eggs, and butter or oil.
Torrontés [tor-ron-tes'], *a.* Applied to a kind of white grapes.
Torsión [tor-se-on'], *f.* 1. Torsion, act and effect of twisting. 2. State of being twisted.
Torso [tor'-so], *m.* Trunk or body of a statue.
Torta [tor'-tah], *f.* 1. A round cake made of various ingredients. 2. (Coll.) *Torta* or *torta de pan,* A loaf of bread. 3. Font, or portion of type fresh from the casting. *Tortas y pan pintado,* These are trifles to the fatigues yet to come: said to persons who complain of trifles. *Costar la torta un pan,* To pay dear for one's whistle; also to be in for it.
Tortada [tor-tah'-dah], *f.* A kind of large pie.
Tortedad [tor-tay-dahd'], *f.* Condition of twist. (Acad.)
Tortera [tor-tay'-rah], *f.* 1. Pan for baking tarts or pies. 2. Knob at the end of a twisting spindle.
Tortero [tor-tay'-ro], *m.* Knob of a spindle for twisting.
Torticoli [tor-te-co'-le], *m.* (Med.) Torticollis, the wry neck.
Tortilla [tor-teel'-lyah], *f.* 1. Omelet, beaten eggs cooked in a frying pan. 2. (Mex.) A pancake made of Indian corn mashed. 3. *Tortilla de huevos,* Omelet. *Hacerse tortilla,* To break into small pieces, to cake. *Volverse la tortilla,* (Met.) To turn the scale, to take a course contrary to that expected.
Tortis [tor'-tis]. Used only in the phrase *Letra de tortis,* A kind of Gothic printing letter.
Tortita [tor-tee'-tah], *f. dim.* Small loaf or cake.
Tórtola [tor'-to-lah], *f.* (Orn.) Turtle dove. Columba turtur.
Tortolico [tor-to-lee'-co], *a.* 1. Innocent, candid, inexperienced. 2. *V.* TORTOLILLO.
Tortolillo, ito [tor-to-leel'-lyo], *m. dim.* A small cock turtle-dove.
Tórtolo [tor'-to-lo], *m.* (Orn.) Male turtle-dove.
Tortor, *m. pl.* (Naut.) Fraps. *Dar tortores a un navío,* (Naut.) To frap a ship.
Tortozón [tor-to-thone'], *m.* Kind of large grapes.
Tortuga [tor-too'-gah], *f.* Tortoise. Testudo. *Paso de tortuga,* Snail-gallop. *Concha de tortuga,* Tortoise-shell.
Tortuosamente, *adv.* Tortuously, circuitously.
Tortuosidad [tor-too-o-se-dahd'], *f.* Tortuosity, flexure, tortuousness.
Tortuoso, sa [tor-too-o' so, sah], *a.* Tortuous, winding.
Tortura [tor-too'-rah], *f.* 1. Tortuosity, flexure. 2. Rack, torture.
Torvo, va, *a.* Fierce, stern, severe, grim.
Tory, *m.* 1. Tory, name of a party in English history opposed to Whig, at present called Conservative. 2. (In American history) One who, in the time of the Revolution, supported the English government. (*Realista.*)
Torzadillo [tor-thah-deel'-lyo], *m.* A kind of twisted cord, less thick than common.
Torzal [tor-thahl'], *m.* Cord, twist, twisted or plaited lace, torsel, intertexture.
Torzón [tor-thone'], *m.* (Vet.) *V.* TOROZÓN.
Torzonado, da [tor-tho-nah'-do, dah], *a.* Contracted or twisted: applied to animals diseased in the bowels.
Torzuelo [tor-thoo-ay'-lo], *a.* *Halcón torzuelo,* The third hawk which leaves the nest.
Tos, *f.* Cough. *Tos ferina* or *sofocante,* Hooping-cough.
Tosa, *f.* *V.* TOZA.
Toscamente, *adv.* Coarsely, rudely, grossly, clownishly, lubberly, fatly.
Toscano, na [tos-cah'-no, nah], *a.* 1. Tuscan: applied to an architectural order. 2. Native of Tuscany.—*m.* The purest of the Italian dialects, which has prevailed as the literary and official language.
Tosco, ca [tos'-co, cah], *a.* 1. Coarse, rough, unpolished. 2. Ill-bred, uninstructed, clownish, clumsy, crabbed.
Tosecilla [to-say-theel'-lyah], *f. dim.* Slight cough.
Toser [to-serr'], *vn.* To cough; to feign a cough.
Tosidura [to-se-doo'-rah], *f.* The act of coughing.
Tosigar [to-se-gar'], *va.* *V.* ATOSIGAR.
Tósigo [toh'-se-go], *m.* 1. Poison, especially that from the yew-tree. 2. Grief, pain, anguish, vexation.
Tosigoso, sa [to-se-go'-so, sah], *a.* 1. Poisonous, venomous. 2. Coughing, having a cough.
Tosquedad [tos-kay-dahd'], *f.* Roughness, coarseness; rudeness; clumsiness.
Tostada [tos-tah'-dah], *f.* 1. Toast, slice of toasted bread. 2. Disappointment. *Pegar una tostada a alguno,* (Coll.) (1) To play a serious trick up[illegible] disappoint him. (2) To put on[illegible] blush.
Tostadera [tos-tah-day'-rah], *f.* Toaster, an instrument for toasting.
Tostado, da [tos-tah'-do, dah], *a.* & *pp.* of TOSTAR. 1. Torrid, parched, dried with heat; toasted. 2. Applied to a lively light-brown colour.
Tostador, ra [tos-tah-dor', rah], *m.* & *f.* 1. Toaster, one who toasts. 2. Toaster, a toasting instrument.
Tostadura [tos-tah-doo'-rah], *f.* Act and effect of toasting.
Tostar [tos-tar'], *va.* To toast, to torrefy, to roast. *Tostar café,* To roast coffee.
Tostón [tos-tone'], *m.* 1. Sop, made of toasted bread and new oil; roasted Spanish pea. 2. Any thing too much toasted. 3. Testoon, Portuguese silver coin containing 100 reis, and equal to 6¾*d.* sterling. 4. In South America, a *real de a cuatro,* or four silver reals, four bits; i. e., half a dollar or half an ounce.
Total [to-tahl], *m.* Whole, total, complement.—*a.* General, universal, total; entire, all-out.
Totalitario, ria [to-tah-le-tah'-re-o, ah], *a.* & *m.* & *f.* Totalitarian.
Totalidad [to-tah-le-dahd'], *f.* Totality, whole quantity.
Totalmente [to-tal-men'-tay], *adv.* Totally.
Totem [to-tem'], *m.* Totem.
Totémico, ca [to-tay'-me-co, cah], *a.* Totem. *Poste totémico,* Totem pole.
Totemismo [to-tay-mees'-mo], *m.* Totemism.
Totilimundi [to-te-le-moon'-de], *m.* Raree-show, carried about in a box. *V.* MUNDINOVI.
Totoloque [to-to-lo'-kay], *m.* A game of the ancient Mexicans.
Totoposte [to-to-pos'-tay], *m.* (Amer.) Corn-bread of Indian meal.
Totora [to-toh'-rah], *f.* (Amer.) A cattail or reed-mace of Peru and Bolivia.
Totovía [to-to-vee'-ah], *f.* (Orn.) Woodlark. Alauda arborea.
Totuma, *f.* **Totumo,** *m.* [to-too'-mah, mo]. (Amer.) 1. A large dish made from a gourd. 2. Chocolate-cup, in some parts of America. 3. (Amer. and Canary Islands.) A massive head.
Toucán [to-oo-cahn'], *m.* (Orn.) Toucan. Rhamphastos.
Toxemia [tok-say'-me-ah], *f.* Toxemia, blood poisoning.
Toxicar [toc-se-car'], *va.* To poison. *V.* ATOSIGAR.
Tóxico, ca [toc'-se-co, cah], *a.* Toxic, poisonous.—*m.* (Obs.) *V.* TÓSIGO.
Toxicohemia [toc-se-co-ay'-me-ah], *f.* (Med.) Toxicohæmia, toxæmia, a poisoned condition of the blood.
Toxicología [toc-se-co-lo-hee'-ah], *f.* Toxicology.
Toxicológico, ca [toc-se-co-lo'-he-co, cah], *a.* Toxicological, relating to poisons and their effects.
Toxina [tok-see'-nah], *f.* (Med.) Toxin.
Toza [to'-thah], *f.* 1. (Prov.) Piece of the bark of a tree. 2. (Amer.) Log, a bulky piece of wood.
Tozo, za [to'-tho, thah], *a.* (Art) Low in stature, dwarf.

Tozolada [to-tho-lah'-dah], *f.* **Tozolón,** *m.* Stroke or blow on the neck.

Tozudo, da [to-thoo'-do, dah], *a.* Stubborn. *V.* OBSTINADO and TERCO.

Tozuelo [to-thoo-ay'-lo], *m.* Fat part of the neck.

Traba [trah'-bah], *f.* 1. Ligament, ligature. 2. Hobble, cord with which the feet of cattle are tied. 3. Obstacle, impediment, hindrance; trammel, fetter, shackle; any thing which hinders the easy execution of something else. 4. Piece of cloth uniting the two parts of the scapulary of certain monastic habits.

Trabacuenta [trah-bah-coo-en'-tah], *f.* 1. Error, mistake. 2. Difference, dispute, controversy.

Trabadero [trah-bah-day'-ro], *m.* The small part of animals' feet.

Trabado, da [trah-bah'-do, dah], *a.* & *pp.* of TRABAR. 1. Connected, joined; thickened, inspissated. 2. Robust, strong. 3. Having two white fore feet, or two white feet on one side: applied to a horse.

Trabador [trah-bah-dor'], *m.* A carpenter's saw-set.

Trabadura [trah-bah-doo'-rah], *f.* Union, junction.

Trabajadamente, *adv.* *V.* TRABAJOSAMENTE.

Trabajado, da [trah-bah-hah'-do, dah], *a.* & *pp.* of TRABAJAR. 1. Laboured. 2. Tired, weary; exhausted with fatigue. 3. Wrought: applied to metals.

Trabajador, ra [trah-bah-hah-dor', rah], *m.* & *f.* 1. Labourer, an assiduous or industrious person, painstaker. 2. A day-labourer.

Trabajar [trah-bah-har'], *va.* & *vn.* 1. To work, to labour, to manufacture, to form by labour. 2. To work, to travail, to toil. 3. To work, to be in action, to be diligent. 4. To work, to act, to execute. 5. To work, to endeavour, to contend for. 6. To solicit, to procure. 7. To support, to sustain: applied to building or machinery. 8. To nourish and produce: applied to the earth. 9. To work the ground, to till the soil. 10. To molest, to vex, to harass. *Trabajar atrozmente,* To work to excess. *Trabajar por la arboladura,* (Naut.) To strain the rigging in a storm.

Trabajillo [trah-bah-heel'-lyo], *m. dim.* Slight work, toil, labour, trouble, or hardship.

Trabajo [trah-bah'-ho], *m.* 1. Work, labour, toil, occupation. 2. Obstacle, impediment, hindrance, difficulty. 3. Trouble, hardship, ill-success. 4. Work, a writing on any subject; thing wrought.—*pl.* Poverty, indigence, need, want. *Trabajo de manós,* Manual or handiwork. *Trabajo de punto,* Knitting, knitting-work. *Día de trabajo,* Working-day. *Sacar á uno de trabajos,* To extricate one from troubles and difficulties. *Mucho trabajo para nada,* Much ado about nothing. *No hay atajo sin trabajo,* (prov.) No gains without pains.

Trabajosamente, *adv.* Laboriously, difficultly, painfully.

Trabajoso, sa [trah-bah-ho'-so, sah], *a.* 1. Laborious, elaborate. 2. Imperfect, defective. 3. Painful, hard.

Trabal [trah-bahl'], *a.* Applied to clasp-nails.

Trabamiento [trah-bah-me-en'-to], *m.* Act of joining or uniting.

Trabanco [trah-bahn' co], *m.* Piece of wood attached to a dog's collar, to prevent him from putting down his head.

Trabar [trah-bar'], *va.* 1. To join, to unite; to connect. 2. To join, to bring into harmony or concord. 3. To fetter, to shackle. 4. To thicken, to inspissate. 5. To dispute, to quarrel, to scuffle. *Trabarse de palabras,* To become angry in a dispute. 6. To set the teeth of a saw. 7. To seize, to take hold of. *Trabar plática,* To chatter together. *Trabar batalla,* To combat, to fight. *Trabarse la lengua,* To stammer, to speak with unnatural hesitation. *Trabar conversación,* To enter upon or keep up a long conversation. *Trabar conocimiento,* To scrape acquaintance. *Trabar amistad,* To become friends. *Trabar ejecución,* (Law) To distrain, to seize judicially.

Trabazón [trah-bah-thone'], *f.* Juncture, union; connection; coalescence.

Trabe [trah'-bay], *f.* Beam.

Trábea [trah'-bay-ah], *f.* A long gown.

Trabilla [trah-beel'-lyah], *f.* 1. (Dim.) A small clasp or tie. 2. In knitting, a dropped stitch.

Trabón [trah-bone'], *m.* 1. Fetter for a horse's foot. 2. Cross-planks in oil-mills.

Trabuca [trah-boo'-cah], *f.* Cracker, a fire-work.

Trabucación [trah-boo-cah-the-on'], *f.* Confusion, mistake.

Trabucador, ra [trah-boo-cah-dor', rah], *m.* & *f.* Disturber.

Trabucante [trah-boo-cahn'-tay], *pa.* Preponderating; causing mistakes.

Trabucar [trah-boo-car'], *va.* 1. To derange, to throw into confusion, to perturbate. 2. To interrupt a conversation, to cut the thread of a discourse.—*vn.* To stumble, to tumble.—*vr.* To equivocate, to mistake.

Trabucazo [trah-boo-cah'-tho], *m.* 1. Shot with a blunderbuss. 2. The report of a blunderbuss. 3. (Coll.) A sudden fright.

Trabuco [trah-boo'-co], *m.* 1. Catapult, ancient battering engine. 2. Blunderbuss.

Trabuquete [trah-boo-kay'-tay], *m.* Machine used by the ancients to throw large stones.

Traca [trah'-cah], *f.* (Naut.) Strake, the uniform range of the planks of a ship. *Traca de palmejares,* (Naut.) Strake of the ceiling or foot wale.

Trácala [trah'-cah-lah], *f.* (Mex.) Artifice, scheme, trick.

Tracalero, ra [trah-cah-lay'-ro, rah], *a.* (Mex.) Tricky, artful.

Tracamundana [trah-cah-moon-dah'-nah], *f.* (Coll.) A ridiculous change of trifles.

Tracción [trac-the-on'], *f.* 1. Act and effect of drawing. 2. Traction, pulling a load, as on railways.

Tracias [trah'-the-as], *m.* North-northwest wind.

Tracio, cia [trah'-the-o, ah], *a.* Thracian, of Thrace.

Tracista [trah-thees'-tah], *m.* Projector, schemer; intriguer.

Tracoma [trah-co'-mah], *f.* (Med.) Trachoma.

Tractor [trac-tor'], *m.* Tractor. *Tractor blindado,* Armored tractor. *Tractor de oruga,* Caterpillar tractor.

Tradición [trah-de-the-on'], *f.* 1. Tradition. 2. (Law) *V.* ENTREGA.

Tradicional [trah-de-the-o-nahl'], *a.* Traditional.

Traducción [trah-dooc-the-on'], *f.* 1. Translation, version, interpretation. 2. A rhetorical figure, by which a word is used in different senses.

Traducir [trah-doo-theer'], *va.* 1. To translate, to interpret in another language. 2. To change, to truck.

(*Yo traduzco, traduzca; traduje, tradujera;* from *Traducir.* *V.* CONDUCIR.)

Traductor, ra [trah-dooc-tor', rah], *m* & *f.* Translator.

Traedizo, za [trah-ay-dee'-tho, thah], *a.* That which may be drawn; tractable.

Traedor, ra [trah-ay-dor', rah], *m.* & *f.* Carrier.

Traedura [trah-ay-doo'-rah], *f.* The act of carrying, bringing, or conducting.

Traer [trah-err'], *va.* 1. To fetch, to bring, to carry, to conduct any way. 2. To bring, to carry, to attract, to draw towards one's self. 3. To bring about, to cause, to occasion. 4. To come, to handle, to manage. *Traer bien la espada,* To handle the sword dexterously. 5. To assign reasons or authorities to prove a thing. 6. To bring to, to oblige, to compel to do something. 7. To bring over, to reduce, to bind, to prevail upon, to persuade. 8. To be engaged in, to carry on, to have. 9. To use, to wear. *Traer medias de seda,* To wear silk stockings. *Traer y llevar cuentos,* To carry tales backwards and forwards. *Traer a mal traer,* To go hard with one, to disturb, to trouble, to vex. *Traer en bocas* or *lenguas,* To traduce one's reputation, to censure or speak ill of one's actions. *Traer perdido a alguno,* To be deeply in love: to be the ruin of a person. *Traer a consecuencia,* To place a thing in a situation which enhances or diminishes its value; to say something pertinent. *Traer un pleito con alguno,* To be engaged in a lawsuit against some one. *Traer una comisión delicada,* To be commissioned in a very delicate affair. *Traer a uno al retortero,* To trouble one by overwork, or to lead him from place to place. *Traer a uno entre ojos,* (Met.) To be suspicious of a person. *Traer consigo,* To carry along. *Traer a la mano,* To fetch or carry. *Traer al ojo alguna cosa,* To keep a thing carefully in sight; to impress a thing upon one's mind. *Traer la barba sobre el hombro,* To be alert, watchful, careful. *Traer delante,* To have on one's mind. *Traer a cuento,* To turn the conversation to a desired point. *Traer malas cartas,* To be without documents needful to assert a claim. *Traer a la melena,* To compel one to act against his will. *¿Qué aires le traen a Vd. por acá?* What good wind brings you here? *Traer la cuerda tirante,* To use too much rigour. *Traer al redopelo,* To vex; to treat with scant ceremony. *Buena vida, arrugas trae,* Those who live comfortably live long.—*vr.* 1. To be dressed well or poorly. 2. To have a graceful or ungainly deportment. As a reflexive verb used always with the adverbs *bien* or *mal.*

Trafagador [trah-fah-gah-dor'], *m.* Trafficker, dealer.

Trafagante [trah-fah-gahn'-tay], *pa.* Trafficking, trading.

Trafagar [trah-fah-gar'], *vn.* 1. To traffic, to carry on trade. *V.* TRAFICAR. 2. (Prov.) To travel, to journey.

Tráfago [trah'-fah-go], *m.* 1. Traffic, commerce, trade. 2. A careful management of affairs.

Trafagón, na [trah-fah-gone', nah], *a.* Active, industrious, deeply engaged in trade and commerce.

Trafalmejo, ja [trah-fal-may'-ho, hah], *a.* Bold, intrepid, audacious.

Traficación [trah-fe-cah-the-on'], *f.* Traffic, trade, commerce; shopping *V.* TRÁFICO.

Traficante [trah-fe-cahn'-tay], *pa.* & *m.* Merchant, trader; trading.

Traficar [trah-fe-car'], *vn.* 1. To traffic, to carry on trade and commerce, to trade. 2. To travel, to journey.

Tráfico [trah'-fe-co], *m.* Commerce, traffic, trade, negotiation.

Trafulla [trah-fool'-lyah], *f.* (Coll.) Cheating, defrauding, swindling in gaming.

Tragacanta [trah-gah-cahn'-tah], *f.* 1. (Bot.) Goat's-thorn, milk-vetch. Astragalus verus. 2. Tragacanth, a gum.

Tragacanto [trah-gah-cahn'-to], *a.* Tragacanth: applied to the gum obtained from various species of astragalus.

Tragacete [trah-gah-thay'-tay], *m.* Javelin, a Moorish missive weapon.

Tragadero [trah-gah-day'-ro], *m.* 1. Œsophagus, gullet. 2. Pit, gulf, abyss. *Tragadero de un puerto*, (Naut.) Mouth of a harbour. *Estar en el tragadero del mar*, (Naut.) To be in the trough of the sea. *Tener buenos tragaderos* or *buenas tragaderas*, To be very credulous.

Tragadieces [trah-gah-de-eth'-ess], **tragaveintes** [trah-gah-vayn'-tess], *m.* (Mex.) Jukebox.

Tragador, ra [trah-gah-dor', rah], *m.* & *f.* Glutton, gobbler. *Tragador de leguas*, *V.* TRAGALEGUAS.

Tragahombres [trah-gah-om'-bres], *m.* (Coll.) Bully, hector.

Trágala [trah'-gah-lah], *m.* A song of the liberals against the absolutists which began with this word. *Cantarle a uno el trágala*, To crow over one who has to accept what he detested.

Tragaldabas [trah-gal-dah'-bas], *m.* (Coll.) Glutton.

Tragaleguas [trah-gah-lay'-goo-as], *m.* (Coll.) A brisk walker.

Tragaluz [trah-gah-looth'], *f.* Skylight.

Tragamallas [trah-gah-mahl'-lyas], *m.* (Coll.) 1. Impostor, cheat, swindler. 2. Glutton, gormandizer.

Tragantada [trah-gan-tah'-dah], *f.* A large draught of liquor.

Tragantón, na [trah-gan-tone', nah], *m.* & *f.* (Coll.) A glutton.—*a.* Gluttonous, voracious.

Tragantona [trah-gan-to'-nah], *f.* 1. A plentiful repast. 2. The act of swallowing or forcing down the throat. 3. (Met.) Difficulty of believing an extraordinary thing.

Tragar [trah-gar'], *va.* 1. To swallow. 2. To devour, to eat voraciously, to glut. 3. To swallow up, to ingulf. 4. To swallow, to receive or believe without examination.—*vr.* To dissemble, to play the hypocrite; to pocket an affront. *Tragar el anzuelo*, (Met.) To allow one's self to be deceived. *No poder tragar a alguno*, To abhor or dislike one.

Tragavirotes [trah-gah-ve-ro'-tes], *m.* (Coll.) A man who without cause is rude and puffed with pride.

Tragazo [trah-gah'-tho], *m. aug.* A large draught.

Tragazón [trah-ga-thone'], *f.* Voracity, gluttony.

Tragedia [trah-hay'-de-ah], *f.* 1. Tragedy, a dramatic representation which has a mournful end. 2. Tragedy, any mournful event. *Parar en tragedia*, To have a disastrous issue. 3. Among the pagans a song in praise of Bacchus.

Tragélafo [trah-hay'-lah-fo], *m.* A fabulous animal between a goat and deer.

Trágicamente, *adv.* Tragically.

Trágico, ca [trah'-he-co, cah], *a.* 1. Tragic, relating to tragedy. 2. Tragic, calamitous, disastrous.

Tragicomedia [trah-he-co-may'-de-ah], *f.* Tragi-comedy.

Tragicómico, ca [trah-he-co'-me-co, cah], *a.* Tragi-comical.

Trago [trah'-go], *m.* 1. Draught of liquid, swallowed at one time; swallow. 2. Calamity, adversity, misfortune. *A tragos*, By degrees, slowly, gently. *Echar un trago*, To take a dram. *Un trago de agua*, A drink of water.

Tragón, na [trah-gone', nah], *a.* Gluttonous, voracious, ravenous.

Tragón, *m.* Glutton. Ursus gulo. *L.*

Tragonazo, za [trah-go-nah'-tho, thah], *a. aug.* Applied to a great glutton.

Tragonería, Tragonía [trah-go-nay-ree'-ah], *f.* Gluttony.

Traguillo, ito [trah-geel'-lyo], *m. dim.* of TRAGO.

Traición [trah-e-the-on'], *f.* Treason, disloyalty; faithlessness; falsehood. *Alta traición*, High treason. *A traición*, Treacherously, treasonably. *La traición aplace, mas no el que la hace*, Men love the treason, but hate the traitor.

Traicionar [trah-e-the-o-nar'], *va.* To do treason.

Traicionero, ra [trah-e-the-o-nay'-ro, rah], *a.* (Littl. us.) Treasonous, treasonable. *V.* TRAIDOR.

Traida [trah-ee'-dah], *f.* Carriage, the act of fetching or carrying from place to place.

Traido, da [trah-ee'-do, dah], *a.* & *pp.* of TRAER. 1. Brought, fetched, carried. 2. Used, worn, second-hand.

Traidor, ra [trah-e-dor', rah], *a.* 1. Treacherous, faithless, disloyal, perfidious, false, traitorous. 2. Insidious, deceitful: applied to animals.—*m.* Traitor, betrayer.

Traidora [trah-e-do'-rah], *f.* Traitress.

Traidoramente, *adv.* Treacherously, treasonably, traitorously, perfidiously.

(*Yo traigo, traiga, traje, trajera.* *V.* TRAER.)

Traílla [trah-eel'-lyah], *f.* 1. Leash, lash, a cord or leather thong, by which a dog is led. 2. Pack-thread. 3. Instrument for levelling ground; a road-scraper.

Traillar [trah-eel-lyar'], *va.* To level ground.

Traiña [trah-ee'-nyah], *f.* 1. Net for deep-sea fishing. 2. Jack, a small bowl. *V.* BOLICHE.

Traja [trah'-hah], *f.* (Amer.) A load which vessels carry on deck.

Trajano, na [trah-hah'-no, nah], *a.* Trajan; relating to the Emperor Trajan. *Columna trajana*, Trajan's column.

Traje [trah'-hay], *m.* 1. Garb, the usual dress in a province or country, habit, guise, apparel, clothes. 2. A complete dress of a woman, wardrobe, attire. 3. Mask, a dress used for disguise. *Trajes de merino bordados de realce*, Merino dresses embroidered with silk. *Traje de a caballo*, Riding habit. *Traje de etiqueta*, Dress suit. *Traje de teatro*, Theatrical costume. *Traje para la nieve*, Snowsuit. *Traje para vuelos espaciales*, Space suit. *Traje sastre*, Tailored suit.

Trajear [trah-hay-ar'], *va.* (Obs.) To dress a person in a manner suited to his or her rank or condition.

Traje de etiqueta [trah'-hay day ay-te-kay'-tah], *m.* Dress suit.

Trajilla [trah-heel'-lyah], *f.* A harrow without teeth for levelling ground.

Trajín [trah-heen'], *m.* Carriage. *V.* TRAJINO and TRÁFAGO.

Trajinante [trah-he-nahn'-tay], *m.* Carrier.

Trajinar [trah-he-nar'], *va.* 1. To transport goods from place to place. 2. To travel. 3. (Coll.) To fidget about.

Trajinería [trah-he-nay-ree'-ah], *f.* Carrying trade.

Trajinero [trah-he-nay'-ro], *m.* Carrier.

Trajino [trah-hee'-no], *m.* Carriage, the act of transporting merchandise.

Tralla [trahl'-lyah], *f.* 1. Cord, bass-weed rope. 2. Lash, snapper of a whip. 3. (Mil.) Pontoons for forming bridges.

Trama [trah'-mah], *f.* 1. Weft or woof of cloth. 2. Kind of weaving silk. 3. Deceit, imposition, fraud, plot, machination.

Tramador, ra [trah-mah-dor', rah], *m.* & *f.* 1. Weaver. 2. Plotter; artful contriver, hatcher.

Tramar [trah-mar'], *va.* 1. To weave. 2. To plot, to form crafty designs, to hatch, to scheme.

Tramilla [trah-meel'-lyah], *f.* (Amer.) Twine.

Tramitación [trah-me-tah-the-on'], *f.* (For.) Progressive forwarding of a judicial proceeding according to prescribed procedure.

Trámite [trah'-me-tay], *m.* 1. Step, requirement, each step in a transaction. 2. (for.) Procedure or course of a judicial process.

Tramo [trah'-mo], *m.* 1. Piece, morsel. 2. Piece of ground separated from another. 3. Flight of stairs.

Tramojo [trah-mo'-ho], *m.* 1. Part of grain, which the reaper holds in his hand. 2. Band for tying the sheaf. 3. Trouble, affliction. *Pasó* or *mamó el tramojo*, He experienced a dreadful alarm; he met a severe misfortune, or swallowed a bitter draught.

Tramón [trah-mone'], *m.* The shortest wool which remains in the comb during the combing.

Tramontana [trah-mon-tah'-nah], *f.* 1. The north wind. 2. Vanity, pride, haughtiness. *Perder la tramontana*, (Met.) To become mad with passion.

Tramontano, na [trah-mon-tah'-no, nah], *a.* Transmontane, beyond the mountains.

Tramontar [trah-mon-tar'] *vn.* To pass to the other side of the mountains.—*va.* To assist, to relieve.—*vr.* To flee, to escape.

Tramoya [trah-mo'-yah], *f.* 1. Machinery used in theatres to represent sudden disappearances, wonderful feats, etc. 2. Craft, wile, artifice.

Tramoyista [trah-mo-yees'-tah], *m.* 1. The machinist of a theatre. 2. The scene-shifter. 3. Impostor, swindler, deceiver.

Trampa [trahm'-pah], *f.* 1. Trap, snare. 2. Trap-door. 3. Movable part of a counter fitted with hinges for raising and lowering. *Caer en la trampa*, To fall into the snare, to be deceived by artifice. 4. Fraud, deceit, stratagem, malpractice. 5. Debt fraudulently contracted. *Trampa adelante*, Deceitful procrastination: applied to persons who go borrowing with one hand to pay with another. *Si hiciera la trampa*, If fate would decree. *Parece que lo quiso la trampa*, It appears that the deuse wished it.

Trampal [tram-pahl'], *m.* Quagmire; a dirty or muddy place.

Trampantojo [tram-pan-to'-ho], *m.* Trick played before one's eyes in order to deceive.

Trampazo [tram-pah'-tho], *m.* The last twist of the cord employed to torture an offender.

Trampeador, ra [tram-pay-ah-dor', rah], *m.* & *f.* Borrower, swindler, cheat, sharper.

Trampear [tram-pay-ar'], *vn.* & *va.* 1. To obtain money on false pretences, to swindle one out of his money, to lurch, to shift, to play tricks, to cog. 2. To impose upon, to deceive.

Trampilla [tram-peel'-lyah], *f.* 1. Floor peephole. 2. Coal bin door. 3. Trouser fly.

Trampista [tram-pees'-tah], *a.* Cheating, deceitful.—*com.* Cheat, swindler.

Trampolín [tram-po-leen'], *m.* 1. Springboard. 2. Diving board. 3. Trampoline. 4. (Fig.) Stepping stone, springboard.

Tramposo, sa [tram-po'-so, sah], *a.* Deceitful, swindling.—*m.* Cheater, swindler.

Tranca [trahn'-cah], *f.* 1. Bar across a door or window, to prevent entrance. 2. (Naut.) Cross-bar.

Trancada [tran-cah'-dah], *f.* *V.* TRANCO and TRANCAZO.

Trancado [tran-cah'-do], *m.* A small harpoon for catching eels.—*pp.* of TRANCAR.

Trancahilo [tran-cah-ee'-lo], *m.* Knot in thread or ropes.

Trancanil [tran-cah-neel'], *m.* (Naut.) Water-way, for carrying off the water from the deck through the scupper-holes; stringer plate. *Trancaniles reservados* or *interiores*, Under water-ways.

Trancar [tran-car'], *va.* To barricade. *V.* ATRANCAR.

Trancazo [tran-cah'-tho], *m.* Blow with a bar; influenza, grippe.

Trance [trahn'-thay], *m.* 1. Peril, danger. 2. A critical moment. 3. The last stage of life. 4. Sale of a debtor's property to satisfy his creditors. *A todo trance*, Resolutely, at any risk. *Trance apretado*, Imminent danger or peril.

Trancenil [tran-thay-neel'], *m.* A gold or silver hat-band, garnished with jewels.

Tranco [trahn'-co], *m.* 1. A long step or stride. 2. Threshold of a door. *En dos trancos*, Briefly, swiftly. *A trancos*, In haste, in a trice.

Tranchete [trahn-chay'-tay], *m.* A broad, curvated knife, used for pruning, etc.; shoemaker's heel-knife.

Trancho [trahn'-cho], *m.* (Prov.) *V.* ALACHA.

Trangallo [tran-gahl'-lyo], *m.* Yoke fixed on shepherds' dogs' necks, during the brooding-time of game.

Tranquera [tran-kay'-rah], *f.* Palisade, palisado.

Tranquero [tran-kay'-ro], *m.* Jamb or lintel of a door or window, made of stone.

Tranquilamente, *adv.* Quietly, peacefully, tranquilly, composedly.

Tranquilar [tran-kee-lar'], *va.* 1. (Obs.) To quiet, to appease, to tranquillize. 2. To balance accounts; to mark each entry with two dashes; to check off.

Tranquilidad [tran-ke-le-dahd'], *f.* Tranquility, tranquilness, rest, peace, repose, composure.

Tranquilizante [tran-ke-le-thahn'-tay], *m.* Tranquilizer.

Tranquilizar [tran-ke-le-thar'], *va.* To calm, to appease, to tranquillize, to pacify.

Tranquilo, la [tran-kee'-lo, lah], *a.* Tranquil, calm, quiet, pacific, gentle, contented.

Tranquilla [tran-keel'-lyah], *f.* 1. (Dim.) A small bar. 2. Trap, snare, stratagem.

Tranquillón [tran-keel-lyone'], *m.* Mashlin, meslin, mixed grain.

Trans. *prep.* (Lat.) Used in composition, and signifying over, beyond or across.

Transacción [tran-sac-the-on'], *f.* Composition of a difference, accommodation, adjustment.

Transalpino, na [trans-al-pee'-no, nah], *a.* Transalpine.

Transatlántico or **trasatlántico** [tran-sah-tlan'-te-co, trah-sah-tlan'-te-co], *m.* Transatlantic, ocean liner.

Transar, *va.* (Canary Islands and Amer.) *V.* TRANSIGIR. Much used reflexively.

Transbordar [trans-bor-dar'], *va.* (Naut.) To transship.

Transbordo [trans-bor'-do], *m.* Transshipment.

Transcendencia [trans-then-den'-the-ah], *f.* *V.* TRASCENDENCIA.

Transcendental [trans-then-den'-tahl], *a.* *V.* TRASCENDENTAL.

Transcendente [trans-then-den'-tay], *pa.* *V.* TRASCENDENTE.

Transcender [trans-then-derr'], *va.* & *vn.* *V.* TRASCENDER.

Transcontinental [trans-con-te-nen-tahl'], *a.* Transcontinental, crossing the continent.

Transcribir [trans-cre-beer'], *va.* To transcribe.

Transcripción [trans-crip-the-on'], *f.* Transcription, the process and result of transcribing.

Transcripto, ta, Transcrito, ta [trans-creep'-to, tah, cree'-to, tah], *pp. irreg.* of TRANSCRIBIR.

Transcurrir [trans-coor-reer'], *vn.* To pass away, to elapse.

Transcurso [trans-coor'-so], *m.* Course or process of time.

Tránseat [trahn'-say-at]. A Latin word, signifying, Let it pass.

Transeunte [tran-say-oon'-tay], *a.* Transient; transitory.—*com.* 1. Sojourner. 2. Passer-by.

Transferencia [trans-fay-ren'-the-ah], *f.* Transfer, transference.

Transferible [trans-fay-ree'-blay], *a.* Transferable, capable of being transferred.

Transferidor, ra [trans-fay-re-dor', rah], *m.* & *f.* *V.* TRASFERIDOR.

Transferir [trans-fay-reer'], *va.* 1. To move, to remove, to transport. 2. (Law) To transfer, to convey, to make over. 3. To employ a word figuratively.

Transfigurable [trans-fe-goo-rah'-blay], *a.* Changeable, that can be transformed.

Transfiguración [trans-fe-goo-rah-the-on'], *f.* Transformation, transfiguration.

Transfigurar [trans-fe-goo-rar'], *va.* To transfigure, to transform.—*vr.* To be transfigured; to lose form or figure. (Used particularly as a reflexive verb.)

Transfijo, ja [trans-fee'-ho, hah], *a.* Transfixed.

Tranfixión [trans-fik-se-on'], *f.* Transfixion, piercing through.

Transflorar [trans-flo-rar'], *va.* To copy a picture or drawing at a side light.

Transflorear [trans-flo-ray-ar'], *va.* To enamel, to inlay, to variegate with colours.

Transfojar [trans-fo-har'], *va.* *V.* TRASHOJAR.

Transfollado, da [trans-fol-lyah'-do, dah], *a.* (Vet.) Applied to tumours round a horse's legs.

Transformación [trâns-for-ma-the-on'], *f.* Transformation, metamorphosis.

Transformador, ra [trans-for-mah-dor', rah], *a.* Transforming.—*m.* & *f.* Transformer, one who transforms.—*m.* (Phy. & elec.) Transformer.

Transformamiento [trans-for-mah-me-en'-to], *m.* Transformation.

Transformar [trans-for-mar'], *va.* 1. To transform, to transmute; to transfigure, to metamorphose. 2. To gain such an ascendency in another's affections, that it almost changes his or her character.—*vr.* To assume different sentiments or manners.

Transformativo, va [trans-for-mah-tee'-vo, vah], *a.* That possesses power to transform.

Transfregar [trans-fray-gar'], *va.* To rub.

Transfretar [trans-fray-tar'], *va.* To cross an arm of the sea.

Tránsfuga, Tránsfugo [trans'-foo-gah], *m.* Deserter, fugitive.

Transfundición [trans-foon-de-the-on'], *f.* *V.* TRANSFUSIÓN.

Transfundir [trans-foon-deer'], *va.* 1. To transfuse. 2. To communicate.

Transfusión [trans-foo-se-on'], *f.* Transfusion; communication.

Transgangético, ca [trans-gan-hay'-te-co, cah], *a.* Beyond the Ganges.

Transgredir [trans-gray-deer'], *va.* (Obs.) To transgress.

Transgresión [trans-gray-se-on'], *f.* Transgression, crime, fault, sin.

Transgresor, ra [trans-gray-sor', rah], *m.* & *f.* Transgressor, offender.

Transición [tran-se-the-on'], *f.* Transition, change, removal.

Transido, da [tran-see'-do, dah], *a.* 1. Worn out with anguish or grief. 2. Avaricious.

Transigir [tran-se-heer'], *va.* To accommodate differences; to settle disputes; to compound.

Transistor [tran-ses-tor'], *m.* Transistor.

Transitable [tran-se-tah'-blay], *a.* That may be passed through; passable, practicable.

Transitar [tran-se-tar'], *vn.* To travel, to go on a journey; to pass by a place.

Transitivo, va [tran-se-tee'-vo, vah], *a.* Transitive.

Tránsito [trahn'-se-to], *m.* 1. Passage, transition. 2. Inn, for travellers. 3. Road, way. 4. Change, removal. 5. Death of holy persons. 6. (Ast.) Transit.

Transitoriamente, *adv.* Transitorily.

Transitorio, ria [tran-se-to'-re-o, ah], *a.* Transitory, perishable.

Translación [trans-lah-the-on'], *f.* Translation. *V.* TRASLACIÓN.

Translaticiamente, *adv.* Metaphorically. *V.* TRASLATICIAMENTE.

Translaticio, cia [trans-lah-tee'-the-o, ah]. *V.* TRASLATICIO.

Translativo, va [trans-lah-tee'-vo, vah], *a.* *V.* TRASLATIVO.

Translimitación [trans-le-me-tah-the-on'], *f.* Sending of troops to the territory of a neigbouring state with the purpose of intervening in favour of one of two contending parties.

Translimitar [trans-le-me-tar'], *va.* To pass unexpectedly, or by previous authorization, beyond the boundary of a state, for a military operation, without the purpose of violating the territory.

Translucidez [trans-loo-the-deth'], *f.* Translucence.

Translúcido, da [trans-loo'-the-do, dah], *a.* Translucent, semi-transparent.

Transmarino, na [trans-ma-ree'-no, nah], *a.* Transmarine.

Transmigración [trans-me-grah-the-on'], *f.* Transmigration, the removal of families from one country to another. *Transmigración pitagórica*, Pythagorean transmigration of souls.

Transmigrar [trans-me-grar'], *vn.* To transmigrate, to pass from one country to another.
Transminar [trans-me-nar'], *va.* To undermine.
Transmisibilidad [trans-me-se-be-le-dahd'], *f.* Transmissibility.
Transmisible [trans-me-see' blay], *a.* Transmissible, capable of transmission.
Transmisión [trans-me-se-on'], *f.* Transmission, transmittal.
Transmisor, ra [trans-me-sor', rah], *a.* Transmitting.—*m.* (Elec.) Transmitter.
Transmitir [trans-me-teer'], *va.* To transfer, to transmit, to make over, to convey.
Transmontar [trans-mon-tar'], *va.* *V.* TRAMONTAR.
Transmutable [trans-moo-tah'-blay], *a.* Transmutable, convertible.
Transmutación [trans-moo-tah-the-on'], *f.* Transmutation.
Transmutar [trans-moo-tar'], *va.* To transmute.
Transmutativo, va [trans-moo-tah-tee'-vo, vah], **Transmutatorio, ria** [trans-moo-tah-to'-re-o, ah], *a.* Transmutative, that which transmutes.
Transpadano, na [trans-pa-dah'-no, nah], *a.* Beyond the Po.
Transparencia [trans-pa-ren'-the-ah], *f.* Transparency, clearness, diaphaneity.
Transparentarse [trans-pa-ren-tar'-say], *vr.* 1. To be transparent. 2. To shine through: used sometimes as an active verb.
Transparente [trans-pa-ren'-tay], *a.* Transparent, lucid, fine, clear, limpid.
Transparente, *m.* 1. Window-shade. 2. A glass window in churches behind the altar.
Transpirable [trans-pe-rah'-blay], *a.* Perspirable, transpirable.
Transpiración [trans-pe-rah-the-on'], *f.* Transpiration, insensible perspiration.
Transpirar [trans-pe-rar'], *vn.* To transpire, to perspire insensibly.
Transpirenaico, ca [trans-pe-ray-nah'-e-co, cah], *a.* Beyond the Pyrenees.
Transplantación [trans-plan-tah-the-on'], *f.* (Prov.) *V.* TRASPLANTE.
Transplante [trans-plahn'-tay], *m.* *V.* TRASPLANTE.
Transponedor, ra [trans-po-nay-dor', rah], *m.* & *f.* Transposer, transplanter.
Transponer [trans-po-nerr'], *va.* 1. To remove, to transport, to transpose. 2. To hide, to conceal craftily. 3. To transplant.—*vr.* 1. To be rather drowsy. 2. To set below the horizon.
Transportación [trans-por-tah-the-on'], *f.* Transportation, conveyance, carriage.
Transportador, ra [trans-por-tah-dor', rah], *a.* Transporting, conveying. —*m.* Transporter, conveyor, carrier.
Transportamiento [trans-por-tah-me-en'-to], *m.* 1. Transportation, carriage. 2. Transport, ecstasy, perturbation which impedes freedom of action.
Transportar [trans-por-tar'], *va.* 1. To transport, to convey, to remove. 2. (Mus.) To change the key. *Estar transportado con alguna persona,* (Met. Coll.) To be wrapt up in a person.—*vr.* To be in a transport, to be out of one's senses.
Transporte [trans-por'-tay], *m.* 1. Transport, transportation, conveyance. *Bajel de transporte,* (Naut.) Transport or transport-ship, to carry stores and soldiers. 2. Transport, fury, fit of passion. *Un transporte de cólera,* A fit of anger.
Transportín [trans-por-teen'], *m.* *V.* TRASPORTÍN.
Transposición [trans-po-se-the-on'], *f.* Transposition, transposal.
Transpositivo, va [trans-po-se-tee'-vo, vah], *a.* Transpositional, transpositive, consisting in transposition.
Transterminante [trans-ter-me-nahn'-tay], *pa.* Transgressing the limits.—*m.* (Littl. us.) Travelling flock of sheep.
Transterminar [trans-ter-me-nar'], *va.* To pass from the limits of one jurisdiction to another; to trespass.
Transtiberino, na [trans-te-bay-ree'-no, nah], *a.* Across the Tiber.
Transubstanciación [tran-soobs-tan-the-ah-the-on'], *f.* Transubstantiation.
Transubstancial [tran-soobs-tan-the-ahl'], *a.* Converted into another substance.
Transubstanciar [tran-soobs-tan-the-ar'], *va.* To transubstantiate.
Transversal [trans-verr-sahl'], *a.* Transversal.
Transversalmente, *adv.* Transversally, collaterally.
Transverso, sa [trans-verr'-so, sah], *a.* Transverse.
Tranvía [tran-vee'-ah], *m.* Tramway, a line of horse-cars. (Eng. tramway).
Tranza [trahn'-thah], *f.* (Prov.) Sale of a debtor's property to satisfy his creditors.
Tranzadera [tran-thah-day'-rah], *f.* Knot of plaited cords or ribbons.
Tranzar [tran-thar'], *va.* 1. To plait or weave cords or ribbons; to braid. 2. To cut, to truncate. 3. *V.* REMATAR.
Tranzón [tran-thone'], *m.* Part of a forest which has been cut or cleared for fuel.
Trapa [trah'-pah], *f.* Noise made by stamping with the feet, or bawling. *Trapas,* (Naut.) Relieving-tackle: used for heaving down a vessel which is to be careened. *Trapas de las velas,* Spilling-lines, ropes fastened to the mainsail and foresail.
Trapacear [trah-pa-thay-ar'], *vn.* To deceive by falsehoods and artful contrivances.
Trapacería [trah-pa-thay-ree'-ah], *f.* Fraud, deceit, counterfeit. *V.* TRAPAZA.
Trapacero, ra [trah-pa-thay'-ro, rah], *a.* & *m.* & *f.* Cheating, deceitful. *V.* TRAPACISTA.
Trapacete [trah-pa-thay'-tay], *m.* (Com.) Waste-book.
Trapacista [trah-pa-thees'-tah], *m.* & *a.* Impostor, cheat, sharper, swindler; deceiver; fraudulent, false.
Trapajo [trah-pah'-ho], *m.* Rag, tatter.
Trapajoso, sa [trah-pah-ho'-so, sah], *a.* Ragged, tattered.
Trápala [trah'-pah-lah], *f.* 1. A violent noise by stamping with the feet, or bawling. 2. Deceit, cheat by false representations.—*com.* Garrulous, loquacious babbler.—*m.* Garrulity, loquacity, talkativeness.
Trapalear [trah-pah-lay-ar'], *vn.* To be loquacious or garrulous; to babble.
Trapalón, na [trah-pah-lone', nah], *a.* & *m.* & *f.* Loquacious; babbler, prater. Deceitful, bombastic fellow.
Trapaza [trah-pah'-thah], *f.* Fraud, a deceitful trick upon a buyer.
Trapazar [trah-pa-thar'], *vn.* *V.* TRAPALEAR.
Trapazo [trah-pah'-tho], *m.* A large rag.
Trape [trah'-pay], *m.* Buckram.
Trapeado [trah-pay-ah'-do], *m.* (Art term) The drapery of a figure.
Trapear [trah-pay-ar'], *va.* (Art) To drape the figure.
Trapecio [trah-pay'-the-o], *m.* 1. (Geom.) Trapezium. 2. Trapeze for gymnastic exercises.
Trapería [trah-pay-ree'-ah], *f.* 1. Street inhabited by woollen-drapers. 2. Frippery, rag-fair. 3. Woollen-draper's shop.
Trapero, ra [trah-pay'-ro, rah], *m.* & *f.* & *a.* Dealing in rags or frippery.
Trapezoide [trah-pay-tho'-e-day], *m.* 1. Trapezoid, a geometrical figure of unequal sides, none parallel. 2. Trapezoid, a bone of the wrist.
Trapico [trah-pee'-co], *m. dim.* Little rag.
Trapiche [trah-pee'-chay], *m.* 1. A sugar-mill, or engine for preparing the sugar-cane. *Trapiche de vapor.* Steam sugar-mill. 2. (Cuba) A small sugar plantation. 3. (Mex.) Both the machinery and plantation.
Trapichear [trah-pe-chay-ar'], *vn.* (Coll.) 1. To trade in a small way. 2. (Coll.) To contrive, to seek artifices not always permissible for the attainment of some object.
Trapicheo [trah-pe-chay'-o], *m.* Small trading; a dodge.
Trapichero [trah-pe-chay'-ro], *m.* A worker in a sugar-mill.
Trapiento, ta [trah-pe-en'-to, tah], *a.* Ragged, tattered.
Trapillo [trah-peel'-lyo], *m.* 1. Courtier of a vulgar woman. 2. Little rag. *Estar, andar* or *salir de trapillo,* To be in an undress, to be in dishabille, to have a loose or negligent dress.
Trapío [trah-pee'-o], *m.* 1. Sprightly manner, graceful gestures, whether respectable or vulgar and loose, which some women have. 2. Liveliness and smartness in a fighting bull.
Trapisonda [trah-pe-son'-dah], *f.* (Coll.) Bustle, noise, confusion, clatter; snare, deception. (Vul.) Carousing.
Trapito [trah-pee'-to], *m. dim.* *V.* TRAPICO.
Trapo [trah'-po], *m.* 1. Cloth. 2. Rag, tatter. 3. Sails of a ship. *A todo trapo,* (1) With all the might. (2) (Naut.) All sails set. *Poner como un trapo,* To reprimand severely.
Traque [trah'-kay], *m.* Crack, the noise made by a bursting rocket, or the priming of a gun. *Traque barraque,* (Coll.) At all times, with whatever motive.
Tráquea [trah'-kay-ah], *f.* 1. Windpipe, trachea. 2. Tracheæ of insects.
Traqueal [trah-kay-ahl'], *a.* 1. Tracheal, of or pertaining to a trachea. 2. Breathing by means of tracheæ.
Traquear [trah-kay-ar'], *vn.* To crack, to make a loud noise.—*va.* 1. To frequent; to handle a thing much. 2. To shake, to agitate, to move to and fro.
Traquearteria [trah-kay-ar-tay'-re-ah], *f.* Trachea, windpipe.
Traqueo [trah-kay'-o], *m.* 1. Noise of artificial fire-works. 2. The act of shaking or moving to and fro.
Traqueotomía [trah-kay-o-to-mee'-ah], *f.* Tracheotomy.
Traquescote [trah-kes-co'-tay], *m.* (Naut.) Trackscout.
Traquetear [trah-kay-tay-ar'], *va.* To shake, to agitate, to move to and fro, to handle too much.
Traqueteo [trah-kay-tay'-o], *m.* Shaking. shake, concussion.
Traquiarteria [trah-ke-ar-tay'-re-ah], *f.* *V.* TRAQUEARTERIA.
Traquido [trah-kee'-do], *m.* Report of fire-arms.
Traquítico, ca [trah-kee'-te-co, cah], *a.* Trachytic, like trachyte.
Traquito [trah-kee'-to], *m.* Trachyte, a dull grayish volcanic rock of granite-like aspect.

Tras [trahs], *prep.* After, behind, besides. *Tras una puerta*, Behind a door. *Tras de venir tarde*, Besides coming late. In composition it is equivalent to *trans*, as *traspasar*. Usage authorizes its employment in nearly all cases in place of *trans*. (Acad.) *Ir* or *andar tras alguno*, To go in pursuit of one, to seek diligently; to follow after one. *No tener tras qué parar*, To be extremely poor.

Tras [trahs], *m.* (Coll.) 1. Breech, bottom. *V.* TRASERO. 2. Blow or stroke attended with noise; crash, dash. (Onomatopoetic.) *Tras, tras*, Repeated strokes or noise. *Trastrás*, The last but one, in boys' plays.

Trasabuelo, la [trahs-ah-boo-ay'-lo, lah], **Trasagüelo, la,** *m.* & *f.* (Obs.) *V.* TATARABUELO.

Trasalcoba [trahs-al-co'-bah], *f.* Alcove behind the principal recess.

Trasalpino, na [trahs-al-pee'-no, nah], *a. V.* TRANSALPINO.

Trasanteayer [trahs-an-tay-ah-yerr'], *adv. V.* ANTEANTEAYER.

Trasañejo, ja [trahs-ah-nyay'-ho, hah], *a.* Three years old: applied to wine.

Trasatlántico, ca [trahs-at-lahn'-te-co, cah], *a. V.* TRANSATLÁNTICO.

Trasbisnieto, ta [trahs-bis-ne-ay'-to, tah], *m.* & *f. V.* TATARANIETO.

Trasbordar and **Trasbordo.** *V.* sub TRANS-.

Trasca [trahs'-cah], *f.* (Prov.) Leather thong.

Trascabo [trahs-cah'-bo], *m.* Trip, a trick by which a wrestler throws his antagonist.

Trascantón [trahs-can-tone'], *m.* 1. Stone placed at the corner of a street; curb-stone. 2. Porter who stands at the corner of a street and waits for employment. *Dar trascantón* or *trascantonada*, To hide one's self behind a corner.

Trascantonada [trahs-can-to-nah'-dah], *f.* 1. *V.* TRASCANTÓN. 2. Action of waiting beside a corner.

Trascartarse [trahs-car-tar'-say], *vr.* To remain behind: applied to a card which, had it come sooner, would have won the game.

Trascartón [trahs-car-tone'], *m.* Drawing of a winning card after the game is lost.

Trascendencia [trahs-then-den'-the-ah], *f.* 1. Transcendency, perspicacity of things. 2. Result, consequence.

Trascendental [trahs-then-den-tahl'], *a.* 1. Transcendental, far-reaching, extending to other things, transcendent. 2. Transcendental, of very high degree, of great importance by reason of its probable consequences. 3. (Philosophy) Investigating the nature of our faculties, the value of ideas, etc. 4. (Math.) Transcendental (curve), into whose calculation the infinite enters.

Trascendentalismo [trahs-then-den-tah-lees'-mo], *m.* Transcendentalism, every philosophical system transcending observation and experience, and rising into abstract investigations.

Trascendentalista [trahs-then-den-tah-lees'-tah], *m,* & *a.* Transcendentalist, one who holds the doctrine of transcendentalism.

Trascendente, *pa.* & *a.* Transcendent.

Trascender [trahs-then-derr'], *vn.* 1. To be transcendent, to extend itself. 2. To emit a strong, good odour; to be pervasive, to penetrate. 3. To penetrate, to perceive quickly and clearly. 4. To transcend, to go beyond (not recognised by the Academy in this sense).

Trascendido, da [trahs-then-dee'-do, dah], *a.* & *pp.* of TRASCENDER. Acute, endowed with great penetration.

(*Yo trasciendo, trascienda*, from *Trascender. V.* ENTENDER.)

Trascocina [trahs-co-thee'-nah], *f.* Back-kitchen.

Trascol [trahs-cole'], *m.* (Obs.) Woman's train.

Trascolar [trahs-co-lar'], *va.* (Med.) 1. To strain, to percolate. 2. (Coll.) To pass over a mountain.

Trasconejarse [trahs-co-nay-har'-say], *vr.* 1. To squat: applied to game pursued by dogs. 2. To sheer off, to escape. 3. (Coll.) To be missing or mislaid: said of papers, documents, or small articles.

Trascordarse [trahs-cor-dar'-say], *vr.* To forget.

Trascoro [trahs-co'-ro], *m.* Space in a church at the back of the choir.

Trascorral [trahs-cor-rahl'], *m.* 1. Back court or back yard. 2. (Coll.) Breech, buttocks.

Trascribir [trahs-cre-beer'], *va. V.* TRANSCRIBIR.

Trascripción, *f. V.* TRANSCRIPCIÓN.

Trascuarto [trahs-coo-ar'-to], *m.* Back room.

(*Yo trascuelo, trascuele*, from *Trascolar. V.* ACORDAR.)

(*Yo me trascuerdo, trascuerde*, from *Trascordarse. V.* ACORDAR.)

Trascurso [trahs-coor'-so], *m.* Course or process of time. *V.* TRANSCURSO.

Trasdobladura [trahs-do-blah-doo'-rah], *f.* Treble, triple.

Trasdoblar [trahs-do-blar'], *va.* To treble, to multiply by three.

Trasdoblo [trahs-do'-blo], *m.* Treble, triple. *V.* TRIPLE.

Trasdós [trahs-dose'], *m.* (Arch.) Extrados, the back or outer surface of an arch: opposed to soffit.

Trasdosear [trahs-do-say-ar'], *va.* To strengthen upon the back.

Trasechador [trahs-ay-chah-dor'], *m.* Fighter, contestant.

Trasegador [trah-say-gah-dor'], *m.* One who racks wine.

Trasegar [trah-say-gar'], *va.* 1. To overset, to turn topsy-turvy. 2. To decant, to rack wine.

Traseñalador, ra [trah-say-nyah-lah-dor', rah], *m.* & *f.* One who alters marks.

Traseñalar [trah-say-nyah-lar'], *va.* To alter or blot out a mark and make a new one.

Trasera [trah-say'-rah], *f.* Back or posterior part; croup.

Trasero, ra [trah-say'-ro, rah], *a.* Remaining behind, coming after, hinder.

Trasero, *m.* Buttock, rump of animals. *Traseros*, In jocular style, our ancestors, or predecessors.

Trasferencia, *f. V.* TRANSFERENCIA.

Trasferible, *a. V.* TRANSFERIBLE.

Trasferidor [trahs-fay-re-dor'], *m.* Transferrer. *V.* TRANSFERIDOR.

Trasferir [trahs-fay-reer'], *va. V.* TRANSFERIR.

Trasfigurable, *a.* **Trasfiguración,** *f.* and **Trasfigurar,** *va. V.* TRANSFIGURABLE, TRANSFIGURACIÓN, and TRANSFIGURAR.

Trasfijo, ja, *a.* and **Trasfixión,** *f. V.* TRANSFIJO and TRANSFIXIÓN.

Trasflorar and **Trasflorear,** *va. V.* TRANSFLORAR and TRANSFLOREAR.

Trasfojar [trahs-fo-har'], *va.* To run over the leaves of a book. *V.* TRASHOJAR.

Trasfollado, da [trahs-fol-lyah'-do, dah], *a. V.* TRANSFOLLADO.

Trasformación [trahs-for-mah-the-on'], *f.* Transformation. *V.* TRANSFORMACIÓN.

Trasformador, *m. V.* TRANSFORMADOR.

Trasformamiento, *m. V.* TRASFORMACIÓN.

Trasformar, *va. V.* TRANSFORMAR.

Trasformativo, va, *a. V.* TRANSFORMATIVO.

Trasfregar [trahs-fray-gar'], *va.* To rub.

Trasfretación, *f. V.* TRANSFRETACIÓN.

Trasfretano, na [trahs-fray-tah'-no, nah], *a.* Transmarine.

Trásfuga, Trásfugo [trahs'-foo-gah, trahs'-foo-go], *m.* Deserter, fugitive. *V.* TRÁNSFUGA.

Trasfundición, *f.* Transfusion. *V.* TRANSFUSIÓN.

Trasfusión or **transfusión** [trahs-foo-see-on'], *f.* Transfusion. *Trasfusión de sangre*, Blood transfusion.

Trasgo [trahs'-go], *m.* 1. Goblin, hobgoblin, sprite. *V.* DUENDE. 2. A lively, restless, noisy boy.

Trasgredir [trahs-gray'-deer], *va.* (Obs. and Amer.) To transgress.

Trasgresión [trahs-gray-se-on'], *f. V.* TRANSGRESIÓN.

Trasgresor, ra [trahs-gray-sor', rah], *m.* & *f.* Transgressor. *V.* TRANSGRESOR.

Trasguear [trahs-gay-ar'], *vn.* To play the hobgoblin.

Trasguero [trahs-gay'-ro], *m.* One who imitates the tricks of hobgoblins.

Trashogar [trahs-o-gar'], *m.* 1. Front of a chimney. 2. *V.* TRASHOGUERO, 1st def.

Trashoguero [trahs-o-gay'-ro], *m.* 1. Iron plate, placed at the back part of a fire-place. 2. Block of wood placed against the wall to keep in the fire.

Trashoguero, ra [trahs-o-gay'-ro, rah], *a.* Idling, loitering the whole day near the fire-place.

Trashojar [trahs-o-har'], *va.* To run over the leaves of a book.

Trashumante [trahs-oo-mahn'-tay], *pa.* & *a.* Applied to flocks of sheep which pasture in the north of Spain in summer and in the south in winter. *Trashumantes*, Travelling or merino sheep.

Trashumar [trahs-oo-mar'], *va.* To drive sheep to or from the common pasture-grounds in spring and autumn.

Trasiego [trah-se-ay'-go], *m.* 1. Removal, the act of moving things. 2. The act of decanting liquors.

(*Yo trasiego, yo trasiegue, trasegué*, from *Trasegar. V.* ACERTAR.)

Trasijado, da [trah-se-hah'-do, dah], *a.* Lank, meagre; thin-flanked.

Trasijar [trah-se-har'], *vn.* & *vr.* To grow thin or meagre.

Traslación, Trasladación [trahs-lah-the-on'], *f.* 1. Translation, removal. 2. Translation, version, rendering into another language, and the subject-matter so translated.

Trasladador, ra [trahs-lah-dah-dor', rah], *m.* & *f.* (Obs.) Translator.

Trasladante [trahs-lah-dahn'-tay], *pa.* Translating, transcribing.

Trasladar [trahs-lah-dar'], *va.* 1. To move, to remove, to transport. 2. To translate. 3. To transcribe.

Traslado [trahs-lah'-do], *m.* 1. A copy. 2. Imitation, resemblance, likeness, counterpart. 3. (Law) The reference or act of delivering written judicial proceedings to the other party, in order that on examination of them he may prepare the answer.

Traslapar [trahs-lah-par'], *va. V.* SOLAPAR.

Traslaticiamente [trahs-lah-te-the-ah-men'-tay], *adv.* Metaphorically, figuratively.

Traslaticio, cia, Traslato, ta [trahs-lah-tee'-the-o, ah], *a.* Metaphorical, figurative.

Traslativo, va [trahs-lah-tee'-vo, vah], *a.* Metaphorical, figurative.

Trasloar [trahs-lo-ar'], *va.* (Obs.) To bestow fulsome praise.

Traslúcido, da [trahs-loo'-the-do, dah], *a.* Transparent, clear, pellucid.

Traslucido, da [trahs-loo-thee'-do, dah], *pp.* of TRASLUCIRSE.

Trasluciente [trahs-loo-the-en'-tay], *a.* Translucent, transparent, translucid.

Traslucirse [trahs-loo-theer'-say], *vr.* 1. To be transparent; to shine through. 2. To conjecture, to infer.

Traslumbramiento [trahs-loom-brah-me-en'-to], *m.* The state of being dazzled by excessive light.

Traslumbrarse [trahs-loom-brar'-say], *vr.* 1. To be dazzled with excessive light. 2. To vanish, to disappear.

Trasluz [trahs-looth'], *m.* 1. Light which passes through a transparent body. 2. (Art) Transverse light.

Trasmallo [trahs-mahl'-lyo], *m.* 1. Trammel-net, drag-net; a coarse-meshed net, having a smaller one behind it. 2. Iron handle of a hammer.

Trasmano [trahs-mah'-no], *m.* Second player at a game of cards. *A trasmano*, Out of the right way; not within the common intercourse of life.

Trasmañana [trahs-mah-nyah'-nah], *f.* The day after to-morrow.

Trasmarino, na [trahs-mah-ree'-no, nah], *a.* *V.* TRANSMARINO.

Trasmatar [trahs-mah-tar'], *va.* (Coll.) To persuade one's self of having longer to enjoy life than another; to outlive.

Trasmigración [trahs-me-grah-the-on'], *f.* *V.* TRANSMIGRACIÓN.

Trasmigrar [trahs-me-grar'], *va.* *V.* TRANSMIGRAR.

Trasminar [trahs-me-nar'], *va.* To undermine, to excavate, to dig under ground.—*vn.* To emit a strong scent. —*vr.* To pierce, to penetrate.

Trasmisible [trahs-me-see'-blay], *a.* *V.* TRANSMISIBLE.

Trasmisión [trahs-me-se-on'], *f.* *V.* TRANSMISIÓN.

Trasmisor, ra [trahs-me-sor', rah], *a.* V. TRANSMISOR.

Trasmitido, da [trahs-me-tee'-do, dah], *a.* & *pp.* of TRASMITIR. Transmitted, traditive.

Trasmitir [trahs-me-teer'], *va.* (Law) *V.* TRANSMITIR.

Trasmochadero [trahs-mo-chah-day'-ro], *m.* A thicket of fire-wood.—*a.* Serving for fuel.

Trasmochar [trahs-mo-char'], *va.* To cut branches of trees for fuel.

Trasmontar [trahs-mon-tar'], *va.* To pass to the other side of the mountain. *V.* TRAMONTAR.

Trasmota [trahs-mo'-tah], *f.* (Prov.) After wine, made by water poured on the pressed grapes.

Trasmudar [trahs-moo-dar'], *va.* *V.* TRANSMUDAR.

Trasmutable [trahs-moo-tah'-blay], *a.* *V.* TRANSMUTABLE.

Trasmutación [trahs-moo-tah-the-on'], *f.* *V.* TRANSMUTACIÓN.

Trasmutar [trahs-moo-tar'], *va.* To alter, to transmute, to convert. *V.* TRANSMUTAR.

Trasmutativo, va [trahs-moo-tah-tee'-vo, vah], **Trasmutatorio, ria,** *a.* *V.* TRANSMUTATIVO.

Trasnochada [trahs-no-chah'-dah], *f.* 1. Last night. 2. Watch, the act of watching a whole night. 3. (Obs.) Military surprise or nocturnal attack.

Trasnochado, da [trahs-no-chah'-do, dah], *a.* & *pp.* of TRASNOCHAR. Having watched the whole night; fatigued from night-watching.

Trasnochador, ra [trahs-no-chah-dor', rah], *m.* & *f.* Night-watcher.

Trasnochar [trahs-no-char'], *vn.* To watch, to sit up a whole night.

Trasnombrar [trahs-nom-brar'], *va.* To change or confound names.

Trasnominación [trahs-no-me-nah-the-on'], *f.* *V.* METONIMIA.

Trasoir [trahs-o-eer'], *va.* To mistake, to misunderstand.

Trasojado, da [trahs-o-hah'-do, dah], *a.* Having sunken eyes, emaciated, worn out.

Trasoñar [trah-so-nyar'], *vn.* To dream, to fancy erroneously.

Trasordinario, ria [trahs-or-de-nah'-re-o, ah], *a.* (Obs.) Extraordinary.

Traspadano, na [trahs-pah-dah'-no, nah], *a.* Beyond the Po. *V.* TRANSPADANO.

Traspágina [trahs-pah'-he-nah], *f.* Back page.

Traspalar [trahs-pah-lar'], *va.* 1. To shovel, to remove with a shovel. 2. To move, to remove. 3. (Prov.) To dig under a vine; to clear the ground of grass.

Traspapelarse [trahs-pah-pay-lar'-say], *vr.* To be mislaid among other papers: applied to a writing.

Trasparencia [trahs-pa-ren'-the-ah], *f.* Transparency. *V.* TRANSPARENCIA.

Trasparentarse, *vr.* *V.* TRANSPARENTARSE.

Trasparente, *a.* *V.* TRANSPARENTE.

Traspasación [trahs-pah-sah-the-on'], *f.* (Law) Conveyance, transfer. *V.* TRASPASO.

Traspasamiento [trahs-pah-sah-me-en'-to], *m.* 1. Transgression; trespass. 2. Transfer, the act of conveying. 3. Grief, anguish.

Traspasar [trahs-pah-sar'], *va.* 1. To pass over, to go beyond; to cross. 2. To remove, to transport. 3. To transfix, to transpierce; to introduce with great force. 4. To cross a river. 5. To return, to repass. 6. To transgress, to violate a law. 7. To exceed proper bounds; to trespass. 8. To transfer, to make over.—*vn.* To be touched with compassion, to be afflicted.

Traspaso [trahs-pah'-so], *m.* 1. Conveyance, transfer. 2. Grief, anguish. 3. Trespass, violation of a law; treachery. *Por el traspaso,* (Coll.) For the goodwill. *Ayunar al traspaso,* To neither eat nor drink from noon of Maundy-Thursday until daybreak of the following Saturday.

Traspecho [trahs-pay'-cho], *m.* Bone on the back of a cross-bow, as an ornamental guard on the stock.

Traspeinar [trahs-pay-e-nar'], *va.* To comb again.

Traspellar [trahs-pel-lyar'], *va.* *V.* CERRAR.

Traspié [trahs-pe-ay'], *m.* 1. Slip, stumble. *Dar traspiés,* (1) To stumble without falling. (2) (Met.) To stumble, to slip, to commit errors or faults. 2. Trip, a wrestler's trick with his antagonist.

Traspilastra [trahs-pe-lahs'-trah], *f.* (Arch.) *V.* CONTRAPILASTRA.

Traspillarse [trahs-peel-lyar'-say], *vr.* To grow thin, to be emaciated.

Traspintar [trahs-pin-tar'], *va.* To know from the cards drawn those that are to follow.—*vr.* To be disappointed; to turn out contrary to one's expectation.

Traspirable [trahs-pe-rah'-blay], *a.* Transpirable. *V.* TRANSPIRABLE.

Traspiración [trahs-pe-rah-the-on'], *f.* *V.* TRANSPIRACIÓN.

Traspirar [trahs-pe-rar'], *va.* *V.* TRANSPIRAR.

Trasplantación [trahs-plan-tah-the-on'], *f.* (Prov.) *V.* TRASPLANTE.

Trasplantar [trahs-plan-tar'], *va.* 1. To transplant, to remove plants. 2. To migrate.

Trasplante [trahs-plahn'-tay], *m.* Transplantation.

Trasponedor, ra [trahs-po-nay-dor', rah], *m.* & *f.* *V.* TRANSPONEDOR.

Trasponer [trahs-po-nerr'], *va.* *V.* TRANSPONER.

(*Yo traspongo, trasponga; traspuse, traspondré, traspusiera;* from *Trasponer.* *V.* PONER.)

Traspontin [trahs-pon-teen'], *m.* (Coll.) *V.* TRASERO.

Trasporarse [trahs-po-rar'-say], *vr.* *V.* TRANSPORARSE.

Trasportación [trahs-por-tah-the-on'], *f.* Transportation. *V.* TRANSPORTACIÓN.

Trasportador, ra [trahs-por-tah-dor', rah], V. TRANSPORTADOR.

Trasportamiento [trahs-por-tah-me-en'-to], *m.* *V.* TRANSPORTAMIENTO.

Trasportar [trahs-por-tar'], *va.* *V.* TRANSPORTAR.

Trasporte [trahs-por'-tay], *m.* *V.* TRANSPORTE.

Trasportín [trahs-por-teen'], *m.* A thin and small mattress, put between other mattresses.

Trasposición [trahs-po-se-the-on'], *f.* Transposition, transposal. *V.* TRANSPOSICIÓN.

Traspositivo, va [trahs-po-se-tee'-vo, vah], *a.* *V.* TRANSPOSITIVO.

Traspuesta [trahs-poo-es'-tah], *f.* 1. Transport, removal. 2. Corner or turning of a mountain, which serves for a lurking-place. 3. Flight, disappearance. 4. Back yard or court; back door; out-offices of a dwelling-house.

Traspuesto, ta [trahs-poo-es'-to, tah], *pp. irr.* of TRASPONER. Transported.

Traspunte [trahs-poon'-tay], *m.* A prompter in a theatre. *V.* APUNTADOR.

Trasquero [trahs-kay'-ro], *m.* Leather-cutter, one who cuts out leather thongs.

Trasquiladero [trahs-ke-lah-day'-ro], *m* Place where sheep are shorn.

Trasquilador [trahs-ke-lah-dor'], *m.* Shearer.

Trasquiladura [trahs-ke-lah-doo'-rah], *f.* The act of shearing.

Trasquilar [trahs-ke-lar'], *va.* 1. To shear sheep; to cut the hair in an irregular manner. 2. To clip, to cur tail, to diminish.

Trasquilimocho, cha [trahs-ke-le-mo'-cho, chah], *a.* (Coll.) Close shorn or cropped.

Trasquilón [trahs-ke-lone'], *m.* 1. Cut of the shears; as much wool or hair as is cut off by one snip of the shears. *A trasquilones,* Irregularly, rudely. 2. (Coll.) Part of one's fortune, which has been clipped or lost through the fraud of others.

Trastada [trahs-tah'-dah], *f.* (Coll.) A bad act, or one ill-judged and ill-advised.

Trastano [trahs-tah'-no], *m.* (Obs.) *V.* ZANCADILLA.

Trastazo [trahs-tah'-tho], *m.* (Coll.) A whack, thump, blow.

Traste [trahs'-tay], *m.* 1. Fret, a cord or slender strip of metal fastened at intervals in the neck of a guitar, or like instrument, to determine the intervals of the scale. 2. (Prov.) A small glass or cup, kept in wine-cellars for the use of wine-tasters. 3.

(Prov.) *V.* Trasto. *Sin trastes,* Without head or tail; in a disorderly manner. *Dar al traste con los negocios,* (Coll.) To fail, to be unfortunate in business. *Dar al traste con el caudal,* To come to ruin, having misspent one's wealth. *Dar al traste un barco,* (Naut.) To sink, to founder. *Ir fuera de trastes,* To proceed without good order, to conduct one's self badly.

Trasteado [trahs-tay-ah'-do], *m.* Number of frets upon the neck of a lute or guitar.—*Trasteado, da, pp.* of Trastear.

Trasteador, ra [trahs-tay-ah-dor', rah], *m.* & *f.* A noisy fellow, who throws everything into disorder and confusion.

Trasteante [trahs-tay-ahn'-tay], *pa.* & *a.* Applied to a dexterous performer on the guitar.

Trastear [trahs-tay-ar'], *va.* 1. To put frets upon the neck of a guitar. 2. To remove furniture from one part of a house to another. 3. To play well on the guitar. 4. To talk upon a subject in a lively manner.

Trastejadura [trahs-tay-hah-doo'-rah], *f.* *V.* Trastejo.

Trastejar [trahs-tay-har'], *va.* 1. To tile; to cover with tiles. 2. To go over, to examine any thing in order to repair it. *Por aquí trastejan,* Thither they repair; applied to debtors who avoid their creditors.

Trastejo [trahs-tay'-ho], *m.* 1. Tiling, covering houses with tiles. 2. Any uninterrupted and disorderly motion.

Trastera [tras-tay'-rah], *f.* Lumber-room.

Trastería [trahs-tay-ree'-ah], *f.* 1. Heap of lumber. 2. A ridiculous or foolish action.

Trasterminante [trahs-ter-me-nahn'-tay], *pa.* & *m.* *V.* Transterminante.

Trasterminar [trahs-ter-me-nar'], *va.* *V.* Transterminar.

Trastesado, da [trahs-tay-sah'-do, dah], *a.* (Obs.) Hardened, solid, tight.

Trastiberino, na, *a.* *V.* Transtiberino.

Trastienda [trahs-te-en'-dah], *f.* 1. Back-room behind a shop. 2. Prudence, precaution, forecast.

Trasto [trahs'-to], *m.* 1. Furniture movables or goods put in a house for use or ornament; luggage. *Trastos de cocina,* Kitchen utensils. 2. Useless person, puppy. *Trastos excusados,* Useless lumber. *Trastos,* Useful arms, as sword, dagger, etc.

Trastornable [trahs-tor-nah'-blay], *a.* 1. Movable; easily turned topsy-turvy. 2. Fickle, restless.

Trastornadamente [trahs-tor-nah-dah men'-tay], *adv.* Upside down, in confusion.

Trastornado, da [trahs-tor-nah'-do, dah], *a.* 1. Mentally unbalanced. 2. Overthrown, in disorder, in confusion.

Trastornador, ra [trahs-tor-nah-dor', rah], *m.* & *f.* Disturber, a turbulen person; subverter.

Trastornadura [trahs-tor-nah-doo'-rah], *f.* Overturning, inversion, perversion.

Trastornamiento [trahs-tor-nah-me-en'-to], *m.* Overturning, inverting.

Trastornar [trahs-tor-nar'], *va.* 1. To overthrow, to reverse, to overturn. 2. To confuse, to perplex the mind.—*vr.* To go crazy, to become mentally unbalanced.

Trastorno [trahs-tor'-no], *m.* 1. Overthrow, overturn, confusion. 2. Calamity, misfortune. 3. Mental disorder.

Trastrabado, da [trahs-trah-bah'-do, dah], *a.* Applied to a horse with the far hind foot and the near fore foot white.

Trastrás [trahs-trahs'], *m.* The last in some children's games.

Trastrigo [trahs-tree'-go], *m.* (Prov.) Wheat of the best quality.

Trastrocamiento [trahs-tro-cah-me-en'-to], *m.* Transposition, inversion.

Trastrocar [trahs-tro-car'], *va.* To invert or change the order of things.

Trastrueco, Trastrueque [trahs-troo-ay'-co], *m.* Inversion, transposition.

Trastuelo [trahs-too-ay'-lo], *m. dim.* Little, useless person.

Trastumbar [trahs-toom-bar'], *va.* To throw down, to overturn, to overset.

Trasudadamente [trah-soo-dah-dah-men'-tay], *adv.* With sweat and fatigue.

Trasudar [trah-soo-dar'], *va.* & *vn.* 1. To sweat, to perspire. 2. To apply one's self to a business with assiduity and care.

Trasudor [trah-soo-dor'], *m.* A gentle sweat; transudation.

(*Yo trasueño, trasueñe,* from *Trasoñar. V.* Acordar.)

Trasuntar [trah-soon-tar'], *va.* 1. To copy, to transcribe. 2. To abridge.

Trasuntivamente [trah-soon-te-vah-men'-tay], *adv.* Compendiously.

Trasunto [trah-soon'-to], *m.* 1. Copy, transcript. 2. Likeness, close resemblance. *El es un trasunto de su padre,* He is the picture of his father.

Trasvenarse [trahs-vay-nar'-say], *vr.* 1. To be forced out of the arteries or veins: applied to blood. 2. To be spilled.

Trasverberación, *f.* *V.* Transfixión.

Trasversal, *a.* Transversal. *V.* Transversal.

Trasversalmente, *adv.* *V.* Transversalmente.

Trasverso, sa, *a.* Transverse.

Trasverter, *vn.* To overflow, to run over.

Trasvinarse [trahs-ve-nar'-say], *vr.* 1. To leak out: applied to wine. 2. To be guessed, surmised, or supposed.

Trasvolar [trahs-vo-lar'], *va.* To fly across.

Trata [trah'-tah], *f.* The African slave-trade formerly carried on. (Acad.)

Tratable [trah-tah'-blay], *a.* 1. Tractable, ductile, flexible. 2. Tractable, compliant, kindly.

Tratadico, illo, ito [trah-tah-dee'-co], *m. dim.* A brief tract or treatise.

Tratadista [trah-tah-dees'-tah], *com.* Author of treatises.

Tratado [trah-tah'-do], *m.* 1. Treaty, convention, compact, relating to public affairs. 2. Treatise, tractate.—*Tratado, da, pp.* of Tratar.

Tratador, ra [trah-tah-dor', rah], *m.* & *f.* Mediator, arbitrator, umpire.

Tratamiento [trah-tah-me-en'-to], *m.* 1. Treatment, usage. 2. Compellation, style of address, title of courtesy.

Tratante [trah-tahn'-tay], *m.* Dealer, merchant. *Tratante en víveres,* Dealer in provisions, who buys by wholesale and sells by retail. *Tratante en caballos,* Dealer in horses, horse-jockey.—*pa.* Treating, handling.

Tratar [trah-tar'], *va.* 1. To treat on a subject, to discuss; to confer, to consult. 2. To touch, to handle, to manage. 3. To traffic, to trade. 4. To manage, to conduct. 5. To use, to to treat; (and Med.) to treat, to employ curative measures. 6. (Met.) To study or be careful to attain an object. 7. To have illicit relations with a person. 8. To give a person the title of courtesy to which he is entitled.—*vr.* 1. To entertain a friendly intercourse. 2. To be on terms of intimacy. 3. To live well or ill. *Tratar con Dios,* To meditate, to pray. *Tratar verdad,* To profess or love the truth. *Tratar de hacer alguna cosa,* (Coll.) To be resolved upon doing a thing. *Tener tratada alguna cosa,* To have spoken for or engaged a thing. *Tratar en grueso,* To deal by wholesale. *Tratarse como unas verduleras,* To use billingsgate. *Tratarse como cuerpo de rey,* To indulge in selfish luxuries.

Tratillo [trah-teel'-lyo], *m. dim.* A peddling trade.

Trato [trah'-to], *m.* 1. Treatment, manner of using; behaviour, conduct. 2. Manner, address. 3. Concernment; pact, agreement. 4. Treat. 5. Trade, traffic, commerce. 6. Friendly intercourse, conversation, communication. 7. Gallantry; criminal conversation between man and woman. 8. Treachery, infidelity. 9. Religious meditation, prayer. 10. Compellation, title of courtesy. *Trato de cuerda,* Punishment by suspending the criminal by the hands tied behind his back. *Mal trato,* (Met.) Bad conduct with any one, ill usage. *Tener buen trato,* (Coll.) To be affable and polite. *Tener trato de gentes,* To be accustomed to good society. *Ese no es el trato,* That was not the agreement, or, You flinch.

Trauma [trah'-oo-mah], *f.* (Med.) Trauma.

Traumático, ca [trah-oo-mah'-te-co cah], *a.* Traumatic, relating to wounds.

Traumatismo [trah-oo-ma-tees'-mo], *m.* 1. Traumatism, wound. 2. State in which a grave wound puts the system.

Travata [trah-vah'-tah], *f.* Tornado, hurricane in the Gulf of Guinea.

Traversa [trah-verr'-sah], *f.* 1. (Naut.) Back-stay. 2. (Mil.) Traverse, a ditch with one or two parapets of planks loaded with earth.

Traverso [trah-verr'-so], *m.* A certain net of esparto used in the tunny-fisheries.

Travertino [trah-ver-tee'-no], *m.* Travertine, a calcareous tufa, which, on exposure, acquires a reddish colour.

Través [trah-ves'], *m.* 1. Inclination to one side, bias. 2. Misfortune, calamity, adversity. 3. *V.* Flanco. *De través* or *al través,* Across, athwart. *Por el través,* (Naut.) On the beam. *Por la proa del través,* (Naut.) Before the beam. *Por la popa del través,* (Naut.) Abaft the beam. *Por el través de las barbas,* (Naut.) Athwart hawse. *Viento por el través,* (Naut.) Wind on the beam. *Por el través de Margate,* (Naut.) Abreast of Margate. *Ir al través,* (Naut.) To go to any place not to return: applied to old ships. *Dar al través con,* To throw away, to misspend, to destroy.

Travesaño [trah-vay-sah'-nyo], *m.* 1. Cross-timber; transom. 2. Long bolster of a bed.

Travesear [trah-vay-say'-ar], *vn.* 1. To be uneasy; to run to and fro in a restless manner; to be flighty. 2. To jest, to joke. 3. To lead a debauched life; to behave improperly.

Travesero [trah-vay-say'-ro], *m.* Bolster of a bed; transom.

Travesero, ra [trah-vay-say'-ro, rah], *a.* Transverse, across. *Flauta travesera,* A German flute.

Travesía [trah-vay-see'-ah], *f.* 1. Oblique or transverse position or manner. 2. Distance, road, passage; traject, cross-road. *Hacer buena travesía,* (Naut.) To have a fine passage. 3. Fortification with traverses. 4. Money won or lost at gambling. 5. (Naut.) Side wind.

Travesío, ía [trah-vay-see -o, ah], *a.* 1. Traversing: applied to cattle that traverse the limits of their pasture. 2. Transverse, oblique, or lateral wind.

Travesío [trah-vay-see'-o], *m.* Crossing, place where persons or things cross.

Travestido, da [trah-ves-tee'-do, dah], *a.* (Antiq.) Disguised.

Travesura [trah-vay-soo'-rah], *f.* 1. Prank, ludicrous or jocose trick to amuse. 2. Penetration, lively fancy; sprightly conversation. 3. Mischief, trick, a culpable action, and worthy of reproof or punishment.

Traviesa [trah-ve-ay'-sah], *f.* 1. Oblique position, passage. *V.* TRAVESÍA. 2. Wager laid by bystanders at card-tables.

Travieso, sa [trah-ve-ay'-so, sah], *a.* 1. Transverse, oblique. 2. Restless, uneasy, flighty, knavish, turbulent, noisy; mischievous: commonly applied to children. 3. Subtle, shrewd. 4. (Obs.) Dissolute, lewd, debauched. *Ser de mesa traviesa,* To be an old member of a corps or society.

Tráxito, ta [trak'-se-to, tah], *a.* (Biol.) Rough.

Traxitofito [trak-se-to-fee'-to], *m.* (Bot.) A plant with leaves rough to the touch.

Trayecto [trah-yec'-to], *m.* 1. Trajection, space cast across. 2. Trajecting, act of casting over it.

Trayectoria [trah-yec-toh'-re-ah], *f.* Trajectory, the curved path described by a projectile.

Trayente [trah-yen'-tay], *pa.* Bringing, carrying, conducting.

Traza [trah'-thah], *f.* 1. First sketch or draught, trace, outline. 2. Plan, scheme, project, contrivance, a plot, an artifice; manner, means. 3. Appearance, aspect, prospect. *Tiene trazas de ser un pícaro,* He has the looks of a rogue. *Esa no tiene traza de verdad,* (Met.) That has not a shadow of truth.

Trazado, da [trah-thah'-do, dah], *a.* & *pp.* of TRAZAR. Traced, outlined. *Bien* or *mal trazado,* Person of a good or bad disposition or figure.

Trazador, ra [trah-thah-dor', rah], *m.* & *f.* 1. Planner, sketcher, contriver, inventor, schemer. 2. Tracer.

Trazar [trah-thar'], *va.* 1. To contrive, to devise, to plan out, to scheme, to project. 2. To trace, to mark out. 3. To draw the first sketch or plan.

Trazo [trah'-tho], *m.* 1. Sketch, plan, design, project. 2. Moulding. *V.* LÍNEA. 3. (Painting) Fold of the drapery.

Trazumarse [trah-thoo-mar'-say], *vr.* To leak, to ooze. *V.* REZUMARSE.

Treballa [tray-bahl'-lyah], *f.* Sauce for goose, consisting of almonds, garlic, bread, eggs, spices, sugar, etc.

Trébedes [tray'-bay-des], *f. pl.* Trivet, trevet, a tripod used in kitchens.

Trebejar [tray-bay-har'], *vn.* (Obs.) To play merry tricks, to jest, to sneer, to scoff.

Trebejo [tray-bay'-ho], *m.* 1. Top, plaything. 2. Fun, jest, joke.—*pl.* 1. The pieces of a chess-board. 2. Implements of an art or trade.

Trebeliánica, or Cuarta Trebeliánica [tray-bay-le-ah'-ne-cah], *f.* The fourth part of an estate, to be deducted by the fiduciary heir, who holds it in trust for another.

Trébol [tray'-bol], *m.* (Bot.) Trefoil, clover. Trifolium. *Trébol real,* (Bot.) Melilot. Trifolium melilotus. *Trébol silvestre,* Shamrock.

Trece [tray'-thay], *a.* 1. Thirteen. *Estarse en sus trece,* To persist, to execute with perseverance. 2. Thirteenth. *V.* DECIMOTERCIO.—*m.* The figures 13.

Trecemesino, na [tray-thay-may-see'-no, nah], *a.* Of thirteen months.

Trecenario [tray-thay-nah'-re-o], *m.* Space of thirteen days.

Trecenato, Trecenazgo [tray-thay-nah'-to], *m.* Office in the order of Santiago for which thirteen knights are chosen.

Treceno, na [tray-thay'-no, nah], *a.* Thirteenth, completing thirteen.

Trecésimo, ma [tray-thay'-se-mo, mah], *a.* Thirtieth, completing thirty.

Trecientos, tas [tray-the-en'-tos, tas], *a.* Three hundred.

Trechel [tray-chel'], *m.* (Bot.) A somewhat brown variety of wheat.

Trecheo [tray-chay'-o], *m.* Passing of ores and soil in baskets, which the workmen in a row pass from one to another.

Trecho [tray'-cho], *m.* Space, distance of time or place. *A trechos,* By intervals. *De trecho en trecho,* At certain distances.

Tredécimo, ma [tray-day'-the-mo, mah], *a.* Thirteenth.

Trefe [tray'-fay], *a.* 1. Lean, thin, meagre. 2. Spurious, adulterated.

Trefedad [tray-fay-dahd'], *f.* (Obs.) Consumption, hectic fever.

Tregua [tray'-goo-ah], *f.* 1. Truce, cessation of hostilities. 2. Rest, repose.

Treilla [tray-eel'-lyah], *f.* *V.* TRAÍLLA.

Treinta [tray'-in-tah], *a.* & *n.* Thirty. *Treinta y una,* A game at cards.

Treintaidoseno, na [tray-in-tah-e-do-say'-no, nah], *a.* 1. Thirty-second. 2. Applied to the cloth the warp of which consists of thirty-two hundreds of threads.

Treintanario, Treintenario [tray-in-tah-nah'-re-o], *m.* Space of thirty days; thirty masses said for a person deceased; a trental.

Treintañal [tray-in-tah-nyahl'], *a.* Containing thirty years.

Treintena [tray-in-tay'-nah], *f.* 1. Thirty. 2. The thirtieth part.

Treinteno, na [tray-in-tay'-no, nah], *a.* Thirtieth.

Treja [tray'-hah], *f.* Mode of playing at billiards.

Tremadal [tray-mah-dahl'], *m.* *V.* TREMEDAL.

Tremebundo, da [tray-may-boon'-do, dah], *a.* Dreadful, frightful, fearful.

Tremedal [tray-may-dahl'], *m.* Quagmire, marsh, morass.

Tremendo, da [tray-men'-do, dah], *a.* 1. Tremendous, dreadful, terrible. 2. Awful, grand; worthy of respect. 3. Huge or excessive in its line.

Tremente [tray-men'-tay], *pa.* Trembling.

Trementina [tray-men-tee'-nah], *f.* Turpentine.

Tremer [tray-merr'], *vn.* To tremble.

Tremés, Tremesino, na [tray-mes'], *a.* Three months old.

Tremielga [tray-me-el'-gah], *f.* (Zool.) Electric-ray, cramp-fish, torpedo.

Tremís [tray-mees'], *m.* Ancient gold coin.

Tremó [tray-mo'], *m.* A pier-glass.

Tremolante [tray-mo-lahn'-tay], *pa.* Waving in the air.

Tremolar [tray-mo-lar'], *va.* & *vn.* 1. (Naut.) To hoist the colours, jacks, or pendants. 2. To wave, to move or scatter through the air.

Tremolina [tray-mo-lee'-nah], *f.* 1. Rustling of the wind. 2. Bustle, noise. *Levantar una tremolina,* (Coll.) (1) To raise a rumpus. (2) To excite a quarrel.

Tremor [tray-mor'], *m.* Trembling; tremor.

Trémulamente [tray'-moo-lah-men-tay], *adv.* Tremblingly, tremulously.

Tremulante, Tremulento, ta [tray-moo-lahn'-tay], *a.* *V.* TRÉMULO.

Trémulo, la [tray'-moo-lo, lah], *a.* Tremulous, quivering, shaking.

Tren [trayn], *m.* 1. Travelling equipage, train, retinue. 2. Show, pomp, ostentation. 3. Railroad train. *Tren de aterrizaje,* (Aer.) Landing gear. *Tren de correo,* Mail train. *Tren de recreo,* Excursion train. *Tren de ruedas,* Running gear. *Tren elevado,* Elevated train. *Tren ascendente,* Train from the coast to Madrid. *Tren descendente,* Train from Madrid to the coast.

Trena [tray'-nah], *f.* 1. Scarf, sash. 2. Garland of flowers. 3. (Coll.) Prison, jail. 4. Burnt silver.

Trenado, da [tray-nah'-do, dah], *a.* Reticulated, formed of network.

Trenca [tren'-cah], *f.* Each of two pieces of wood put across in a beehive. *Meterse hasta las trencas en algún negocio,* To be deeply implicated or involved in an affair.

Trencellín [tren-thel-lyeen'], *m.* *V.* TRENCILLO.

Trencica, ita [tren-thee'-cah], *f. dim.* of TRENZA.

Trencilla [tren-theel'-lyah], *f.* Braid. *Trencilla de oro, de plata, de seda, de algodón,* Gold, silver, silk, or cotton braid.

Trencillar [tren-theel-lyar'], *va.* To garnish with a band of gold or silver lace and jewels.

Trencillo [tren-theel'-lyo], *m.* 1. (Com.) *V.* TRENCILLA. 2. Hat-band of gold or silver, garnished with jewels.

Trencha [tren'-chah], *f.* (Naut.) A ripping chisel.

Treneo [tray-nay'-o], *m.* (Obs.) Sledge. *V.* TRINEO.

Treno [tray'-no], *m.* 1. A kind of sledge. 2. *pl.* Lamentations.

Trenque [tren'-kay], *m.* (Prov.) Mole or bank to turn off the current of a river.

Trenteno, na, *a.* (Obs.) *V.* TREINTENO.

Trenza [tren'-thah], *f.* 1. Braid of three strands. 2. All a woman's hair though not braided; tresses.

Trenzadera [tren-thah-day'-rah], *f.* Tape. *V.* TRANZADERA.

Trenzado [tren-thah'-do], *m.* 1. Braided hair. 2. A step in dancing.—*Trenzado, da, pp.* of TRENZAR.

Trenzar [tren-thar'], *va.* To braid the hair.

Treo [tray'-o], *m.* (Naut.) Square-sail, cross-jack sail.

Trepa [tray'-pah], *f.* 1. Climbing. 2. Edging sewed to clothes for ornament. 3. (Coll.) Flogging, lashing, beating. 4. Artful trick; malice; subtlety.

Trepado, da [tray-pah'-do, dah], *a.* Strong, robust: applied to animals.—*pp.* of TREPAR.

Trepado, *m.* Edging sewed on clothes.

Trepador, ra [tray-pah-dor', rah], *a.* Climber, climbing.—*m.* 1. A climbing-place. 2. (Zool.) A sea-wolf, wolf-fish.—*f.* 1. (Bot.) Climber, a climbing-plant. 2. *pl.* (Zool.) Climbers.

Trepanar [tray-pa-nar'], *va.* To trepan, to trephine.

Trépano [tray'-pa-no], *m.* (Surg.) Trepan, trephine, an instrument for perforating the skull.

Trepante [tray-pahn'-tay], *pa.* Wily, artful, crafty.

Trepar [tray-par'], *vn.* 1. To climb, to clamber, to crawl. 2. To creep upon supports: applied to ivy and other plants.—*va.* To ornament with edging.

Trepe [tray'-pay], *m.* (Coll.) Scolding: in the phrase *Echar un trepe.*

Trepidación [tray-pe-dah-the-on'], *f.* 1. (Obs.) Dread, fear, trepidation. 2. Tremor, quaking of the earth. 3. An apparent vibration which ancient astronomers attributed to the firmament.

Trepidante [tray-pe-dahn'-tay], *a.* *V.* TEMEROSO and TRÉMULO.

Trepidar [tray-pe-dar'], *vn.* 1. To quiver, to tremble. 2. (Met. Amer.) To waver, to vacillate.

Trépido, da [tray'-pe-do, dah], *a.* Tremulous.

Tres [trays], *a.* & *n.* 1. Three. 2. Third. *V.* TERCERO. 3. The figure 3. *Con dos treses,* With two threes. *Un tres,* A card with three spots. 4. (Obs.) Magistrate of a city governed by three magistrates. *Capítulo tres,* Third chapter. *Tres veces,* Three times, very.

Tresalbo, ba [tray-sahl'-bo, bah], *a.* (A horse) having three white feet.

Tresañal [tray-sah-nyahl'], *a.* *V.* TRESAÑEJO.

Tresañejo, ja [tray-sah-nyay'-ho, hah], *a.* Three years old; done three years ago.

Tresbolillo (Al), *adv. exp.* Quincunx, a mode of planting trees and grapevines, so that each four form a square with a fifth in the middle, like the five-spot on a die.

Trescientos, tas [trays-the-en'-tose, tas], *a.* & *n.* Three hundred.

Tresdoblar [tres-do-blar'], *va.* To triple. *V.* TRIPLICAR.

Tresdoble [tres-do'-blay], *m.* The state or quality of being three-fold.

Tresillo [tray-seel'-lyo], *m.* Ombre, a game played by three.

Tresmesino, na [tres-may-see'-no, nah], *a.* *V.* TREMESINO.

Tresnal [tres-nahl'], *m.* (Prov.) Collection of triangular plots of ground disposed for irrigation.

Trespasar [tres-pah-sar'], *va.* (Obs.) *V.* TRASPASAR.

Trestanto [tres-tahn'-to], *m.* *V.* TRIPLO.—*adv.* Three times as much.

Trestiga, *f.* (Obs.) *V.* CLOACA.

Treta [tray'-tah], *f.* 1. Thrust in fencing. 2. Trick, wile, artifice, craft, finesse.

Treudo [tray'-oo-do], *m.* (Prov.) *V.* CATASTRO.

Trezavo, va [tray-thah'-vo, vah], *a.* Thirteenth, any of thirteen equal parts.

Treznar [treth-nar'], *va.* (Prov.) *V.* ATRESNALAR.

Tria [tree'-ah], *f.* Frequent entering and going out of bees in a strong hive.

Triaca [tre-ah'-cah], *f.* 1. Theriaca, treacle. 2. An antidote, preservative, or preventive.

Triacal [tre-ah-cahl'], *a.* Made of treacle, theriacal.

Triache [tre-ah'-chay], *m.* (Amer. Cuba) Coffee of inferior quality.

Triangulación [tre-an-goo-lah-the-on'], *f.* Triangulation, laying out triangles on the earth; trigonometrical survey.

Triangulado, da [tre-an-goo-lah'-do, dah], *a.* In the shape of a triangle.

Triangular [tre-an-goo-lar'], *a.* Triangular.

Triangularmente, *adv.* Triangularly.

Triángulo [tre-ahn'-goo-lo], *m.* Triangle. *Triángulo cuadrantal,* Spheric triangle having one or more sides quadrants. *Triángulo ambligonio, escaleno, esférico, isósceles, ortogonio* or *oxigonio,* An obtuse-angled, scalene, spheric, isosceles, rectangled, or acute-angled triangle. *Triángulo austral y boreal,* (Ast.) Southern and northern triangle, constellations so called.

Trianular [tre-ah-noo-lar'], *a.* (Zool.) Presenting three rings; three-ringed.

Triaquera [tre-ah-kay'-rah], *f.* Vessel for theriaca or other medicine.

Triar [tre-ar'], *vn.* To go out and in frequently, as bees in a bee-hive; to work, as bees.

Triario [tre-ah'-re-o], *m.* Veteran Roman soldier forming a reserve corps in rear.

Tribón, *m.* *V.* TRIGÓN.

Tribraquio [tre-brah'-ke-o], *m.* Foot of Latin verse consisting of three short syllables; tribrach (◡ ◡ ◡).

Tribu [tree'-boo], *f.* Tribe.

Tribuir [tre-boo-eer'], *va.* To attribute. *V.* ATRIBUIR.

Tribulación [tre-boo-lah-the-on'], *f.* Tribulation, affliction.

Tribulante [tre-boo-lahn'-tay], *pa.* Afflicting.

Tribular [tre-boo-lar'], *va.* (Obs.) To afflict. *V.* ATRIBULAR.

Tribulo [tree'-boo-lo], *m.* (Bot.) Caltrop thistle: generic name of several prickly plants. *V.* ABROJO.

Tribuna [tre-boo'-nah], *f.* 1. Rostrum or pulpit among the ancients; tribune. 2. A raised stand from which to address an assembly. 3. Tribunal, a gallery or raised place in a church where persons of distinction assist at the divine offices. 4. Gallery for spectators in assemblies.

Tribunado [tre-boo-nah'-do], *m.* Tribuneship, the office and dignity of tribune.

Tribunal [tre-boo-nahl'], *m.* 1. Hall, where judges meet to administer justice. 2. Tribunal, court of justice; judicature.

Tribunali (Pro) [tre-boo-nah'-le], *adv.* *Pro tribunali,* 1. Applied to the sentence or decision of a judge, sitting in a court of justice, with the solemnities required by the laws. 2. (Met.) In a decisive tone, decisively.

Tribunicio, cia [tre-boo-nee'-the-o, ah], *a.* *V.* TRIBÚNICO.

Tribúnico, ca [tre-boo'-ne-co, cah], *a.* Tribunitial.

Tribuno [tre-boo'-no], *m.* 1. Tribune, a magistrate of ancient Rome. 2. Tribune, one who defends the rights of the people. 3. An agitator, public haranguer.

Tributación [tre-boo-tah-the-on'], *f.* Tribute, contribution. *V.* TRIBUTO.

Tributar [tre-boo-tar'], *va.* 1. To pay taxes or contributions. 2. To pay homage and respect.

Tributario, ria [tre-boo-tah'-re-o, ah], *a.* Liable to pay taxes or contributions, tributary.

Tributo [tre-boo'-to], *m.* 1. Tax, contribution; tribute. 2. Toil, trouble, difficulty.

Trica, Tricas [tree'-cah], *f.* (Prov.) Quibbles, sophisms.

Tricenal [tre-thay-nahl'], *a.* Continuing thirty years.

Tricentésimo, ma [tre-then-tay'-se-mo, mah], *a.* Containing three hundred: three hundredth.

Tricésimo, ma [tre-thay'-se-mo, mah], *a.* Thirtieth.

Triciclo [tre-thee'-clo], *m.* 1. A three-wheeled carriage among the ancients. 2. A tricycle.

Tricípete [tre-thee'-pay-tay], *a.* Three headed.

Triclinio [tre-clee'-ne-o], *m.* 1. A table with three benches about it. 2. Couch, commonly for three persons, on which the ancient Greeks and Romans reclined to eat. 3. Dining-room of the ancient Romans.

Tricolor [tre-co-lor'], *a.* Tri-coloured.

Tricoma [tre-co'-mah], *f.* (Med.) Plica Polonica, a Polish disease of the hair.

Tricordiano, na [tre-cor-de-ah'-no, nah], *a.* Three-stringed, consisting of three cords.

Tricorne [tre-cor'-nay], *a.* Three-horned.

Tricornio [tre-cor'-ne-o], *a.* & *n.* 1. Three-horned. 2. A three-cornered hat.

Tridente [tre-den'-tay], *a.* Trident, having three teeth.—*m.* Trident, Neptune's three-pointed scepter.

Tridentífero, ra [tre-den-tee'-fay-ro, rah], *a.* Tridentiferous, bearing a trident.

Tridentino, na [tre-den-tee'-no, nah], *a.* Of Trent, in the Tyrol: especially of the church council held there.

Tridimensional [tre-de-men-se-o-nahl'], *a.* Tridimensional.

Triduano, na [tre-doo-ah'-no, nah], *a.* Tertian.

Triduo [tree'-doo-o], *m.* Space of three days.

Triedro [tre-ay'-dro], **Ángulo triedro.** The meeting of three plane angles at one point.

Trienal [tre-ay-nahl'], *a.* Triennial.

Trienio [tre-ay'-ne-o], *m.* Space of three years.

Trieñal [tre-ay-nyahl'], *a.* Triennial.

Trífido, da [tree'-fe-do, dah], *a.* (Poet.) Trifid, three-cleft.

Trifillo, lla [tre-feel'-lyo, lyah], *a.* (Bot.) 1. Three-leaved. 2. Three-lobed, or disposed in three leaflets. 3. (Zool.) A beetle.

Trifolio [tre-fo'-le-o], *m.* Trefoil. *V.* TRÉBOL. *Trifolio fibrino.* *V.* MENIANTES.

Triforme [tre-for'-may], *a.* Triform.

Trifulca [tre-fool'-cah], *f.* 1. (Coll.) Quarrel and confusion among various persons. 2. (Min.) A combination of levers for moving the bellows.

Trifurcar [tre-foor-car'], *va.* & *vr.* To trifurcate, to divide into three parts, or branches.

Trigal [tre-gahl'], *m.* Wheat-field.

Trigamia [tre-gah'-mee-ah], *f.* 1. Trigamy, the state of having been married three times. 2. The state of having three husbands or three wives at one time.

Trígamo, ma [tree'-gah-mo, mah], *m.* & *f.* 1. Trigamous, thrice married. 2. (Bot.) Applied to plants containing three sorts of flowers on the same flower-head.

Trigaza [tre-gah'-thah], *f.* Short straw of wheat.

Trigésimo, ma [tre-hay'-se-mo, mah], *a.* Thirtieth.

Trigla [tree'-glah], *f.* (Zool.) Red surmullet, gurnet. Mullus barbatus.

Triglifo [tre-glee'-fo], *m.* (Arch.) Triglyph.

Trigo [tree'-go], *m.* (Bot.) Wheat. Triticum.—*pl.* Crops; grain-fields. *Trigo candeal, valenciano, tremes, tremesino, piche, teja, blanquillo,* or *hembrilla,* Summer wheat. Triticum æstivum, *L.* *Trigo mocho, pelón sinarista, sin raspa, chamorro,* or *toseta,* Lammas wheat. Triticum hybernum. *Trigo fanfarrón,* Bearded wheat originating from Barbary, with long heads, yielding much bran and little flour, but that of good quality. *Echar por esos trigos,* To go astray. *Ni mío*

es el trigo, ni mía es la cibera, y muela quien quiera, It is not my corn or my hopper, let him grind who will; none of my business.
Trigón [tre-gone'], *m.* A triangular musical instrument, having wire strings.
Trigono [tree'-go-no], *m.* 1. (Ast.) Three celestial signs. 2. (Geom.) Triangle.
Trigonometría [tre-go-no-may-tree'-ah], *f.* Trigonometry.
Trigonométrico, ca [tre-go-no-may'-tre-co, cah], *a.* Trigonometrical.
Trigrama [tre-grah'-mah], *m.* A word of three letters: trigram.
Trigueño, ña [tre-gay'-nyo, nyah], *a.* Swarthy, brownish.
Triguera [tre-gay'-rah], *f.* 1. (Bot.) Common wheat-grass. Triticum repens. 2. Canary-seed.
Triguero, ra [tre-gay'-ro, rah], *a.* Growing among wheat.
Triguero [tre-gay'-ro], *m.* 1. Sieve for corn. 2. Corn-merchant, grain-dealer.
Trilátero, ra [tre-lah'-tay-ro, rah], *a.* Trilateral, having three sides.
Trilingüe [tre-leen'-goo-ay], *a.* 1. Trilingual, talking or relating to three languages. 2. Trilingual, recorded in three languages.
Trilio [tree'-le-o], *m.* (Bot.) Trillium.
Trilítero, ra [tre-lee'-tay-ro, rah], *a.* Triliteral, employing or consisting of three letters. A characteristic of Semitic languages.
Trilogía [tre-lo-hee'-ah], *f.* Trilogy.
Trilla [treel'-lyah], *f.* 1. (Zool.) Red surmullet, gurnard. Mullus barbatus. 2. A sort of harrow for separating corn from chaff. 3. The act and time of thrashing.
Trilladera [treel-lyah-day'-rah], *f.* A harrow used to separate corn from chaff.
Trillado, da [treel-lyah'-do, dah], *a.* & *pp.* of TRILLAR. 1. Thrashed, beaten. 2. Trite, stale, hackneyed. *Camino trillado,* Beaten track, common routine.
Trillador, ra [treel-lyah-dor', rah], *a.* Thrashing, threshing. *Máquina trilladora,* Threshing machine. —*m.* & *f.* Thresher.
Trilladura [treel-lyah-doo'-rah], *f.* Act of thrashing.
Trillar [treel-lyar'], *va.* 1. To thrash, to separate corn from the chaff; to tread out corn. 2. To beat, to abuse. 3. To frequent, to visit often; to repeat.
Trillis [tril-lyees'], *m.* A song-bird of Chili, a species of thrush.
Trillo [treel'-lyo], *m.* 1. A harrow, used in Spain for thrashing, or separating corn from the chaff. 2. (Amer.) Foot-path, pathway, trail little used.
Trillón [tril-lyone'], *m.* Trillion, a million billions.
Trimembre [tre-mem'-bray], *a.* Consisting of three members or parts.
Trimestral [tre-mes-trahl'], *a.* 1. Trimestrial, belonging to a trimester or period of three months. 2. Lasting three months.
Trimestre [tre-mes'-tray], *m.* Space of three months.
Trimielga, *f.* *V.* TORPEDO, 1st def.
Trinacrio, ia [tre-nah'-cre-o, ah], *a.* (Poet.) Sicilian, Trinacrian.
Trinado [tre-nah'-do], *m.* 1. Trill, shake, quaver, tremulous sound. 2. Twittering of birds.
Trinar [tre-nar'], *vn.* 1. To trill, to quaver, to shake the voice; to speak in a tremulous voice. 2. (Met. Coll.) To get vexed or furious.
Trinca [treen'-cah], *f.* 1. Assemblage of three things or persons of the same class or description. 2. (Naut.) Any cord used for making fast. *A la trinca.* (Naut.) Close-hauled. *Trincas,* (Naut.) Seizings. *Trincas del bauprés,* (Naut.) Gammoning of the bowsprit.
Trincadura [trin-cah-doo'-rah], *f.* A barge of very large size with two masts and leg-of-mutton sails.
Trincafía [trin-cah-fee'-ah], *f.* (Naut.) Clove-hitch, a kind of turn or knot.
Trincafiar [trin-cah-fe-ar'], *va.* (Naut.) To marl.
Trincar [trin-car'], *va.* 1. To break, to chop, to divide into small pieces. 2. (Naut.) To fasten the rope-ends. *Trincar las puertas,* (Naut.) To bar in the port-lids. 3. (Peru. Coll.) To tie strongly, to secure. 4. *vn.* (Coll.) To drink wine or liquor in company with others. (Acad.) (4 comes from German trinken.)
Trincos [treen'-cose], *m.* (Orn.) Kind of stork like a swan.
Trincha [treen'-chah], *f.* 1. A belt for securing the outer clothes to the body. 2. (Amer.) Socket chisel, cutting gouge.
Trinchante [trin-chahn'-tay], *m.* 1. Carver at table. 2. Carving-knife.
Trinchar [trin-char'], *va.* 1. To carve, to divide meat. 2. To dispose or decide with an air of authority.
Trinchera [trin-chay'-rah], *f.* 1. (Mil.) Trench, intrenchment, ditch to cover the troops from the enemy's fire. 2. Trench coat. 3. (Naut.) Parapet upon the gunwales of the quarter-deck.
Trinchero [trin-chay'-ro], *m.* Any plate on which meat is eaten at table: trencher.
Trincherón [trin-chay-rone'], *m. aug.* A large plate or platter.
Trinchete [trin-chay'-tay], *m.* Shoemaker's paring-knife; stone-cutter's chisel. *V.* TRANCHETE.
Trineo [tre-nay'-o], *m.* Sledge, sled.
Trinidad [tre-ne-dahd'], *f.* The Trinity. *Meterse en trinidades,* To endeavour to find out what is impossible to be known.
Trinitaria [tre-ne-tah'-re-ah], *f.* (Bot.) Three-coloured violet, pansy, heart's-ease, forget-me-not. Viola tricolor.
Trinitario, ria [tre-ne-tah'-re-o, ah], *a.* & *n.* 1. Trinitarian. 2. (Mex.) A member of a society hired to carry the corpse and accompany the funeral procession.
Trinitrotolueno [tre-ne-tro-to-loo-ay'-no], *m.* (Chem.) Trinitrotoluene, high explosive. It is used more in the abbreviation TNT.
Trino, na [tree'-no, nah], *a.* Containing three distinct things; ternary.
Trino, *m.* (Ast.) 1. Trine, the aspect of two planets when 120° apart. 2. Trill. *V.* TRINADO.
Trinomio [tre-no'-me-o], *m.* (Alg.) Trinomial, an algebraic quantity of three terms.
Trinquetada [trin-kay-tah'-dah], *f.* (Naut.) Sailing under the foresail.
Trinquete [trin-kay'-tay], *m.* 1. (Naut.) Foremast, foresail. 2. Tennis, a game. *A cada trinquete,* At every step.
Trinquetilla [trin-kay-teel'-lyah], *f.* (Naut.) Fore stay-sail.
Trinquis [treen'-kis], *m.* (Coll.) A draught of wine or liquor. (Acad.)
Trio [tree'-o], *m.* 1. Working of bees in a hive. 2. (Mus.) Trio.
Triones [tre-o'-nes], *m.* (Ast.) Stars, called Charles's Wain, the Great Dipper.
Triorque [tre-or'-kay], *m.* (Orn.) Triorchis, a kind of falcon.
Tripa [tree'-pah], *f.* 1. Gut, intestine, bowel. *Tripas para longanizas,* Hogs' casings for sausages. 2. Belly, especially of the pregnant woman. 3. Belly or wide part of vessels.—*pl.* 1. Core, the inner part of fruit. 2. The interior of something. *Tripas de tabaco,* Fillers. *Tripas del jarro,* (Joc.) The wine contained in a jar. *Tripa del cagalar,* Cæcum or blind gut. *Hacer de tripas corazón,* To hide one's dissatisfaction or disappointment; also to pluck up heart.
Tripartido, da [tre-par-tee'-do, dah], *a.* & *pp.* of TRIPARTIR. Tripartite, divided into three parts.
Tripartir [tre-par-teer'], *va.* To divide into three parts.
Tripartito, ta [tre-par-tee'-to, tah], *a.* Tripartite.
Tripastos [tre-pahs'-tos], *m.* Pulley with three sheaves.
Tripe [tree'-pay], *m.* Shag, a kind of woollen cloth. *Tripe para alfombras,* (Amer.) Brussels carpeting.
Tripería [tre-pay-ree'-ah], *f.* Shop where tripe is sold; a heap of tripe.
Tripero, ra [tre-pay'-ro, rah], *m.* & *f.* One who sells tripe.
Tripero, *m.* Woollen belt to keep the belly warm; cummerbund.
Tripétalo, la [tre-pay'-tah-lo, lah], *a.* (Bot.) Tripetalous.
Tripilla [tre-peel'-lyah], *f. dim.* A small gut.
Tripitrape [tre-pe-trah'-pay], *m.* 1. (Coll.) Heap of old furniture and lumber. 2. Confusion of thoughts or ideas.
Triple [tree'-play], *a.* Triple, treble.
Tríplica [tree'-ple-cah], *f.* (Law) Rejoinder.
Triplicación [tre-ple-cah-the-on'], *f.* Multiplication by three.
Triplicadamente, *adv.* (Littl. us.) Trebly.
Triplicado, da [tre-ple-cah'-do, dah], *a.* & *pp.* of TRIPLICAR. Triplicate.
Triplicar [tre-ple-car'], *va.* 1. To treble, to triple. 2. (Law. Prov.) To rejoin.
Tríplice [tree'-ple-thay], *a.* Treble, triple.
Triplicidad [tre-ple-the-dahd'], *f.* Triplicity, trebleness.
Triplito [tre-plee'-to], *m.* (Min.) Triplite, a ferrous manganese phosphate.
Triplo, pla [tree'-plo, plah], *a.* Treble, triplicate, triple: used as a substantive.
Trípode [tree'-po-day], *com.* Tripod, trevet, trivet.
Trípol, Trípoli [tree'-pol, tree'-po-le], *m.* Tripoli, rottenstone, tripolite, a polishing powder.
Tripolio [tre-po'-le-o], *m.* (Bot.) Sea starwort. Aster tripolium.
Tripón, na [tre-pone', nah], *a.* Pot-bellied, big-bellied.
Triptongo [trip-ton'-go], *m.* Triphthong.
Tripudiar [tre-poo-de-ar'], *vn.* (Obs.) To dance.
Tripudio [tre-poo'-de-o], *m.* Dance, ball.
Tripudo, da [tre-poo'-do, dah], *a.* Pot-bellied, big-bellied.
Tripulación [tre-poo-lah-the-on'], *f.* (Naut.) Crew of a ship.
Tripular [tre-poo-lar'], *va.* (Naut.) To man ships; to fit out, to equip.
Triquete [tre-kay'-tay], *m.* (Obs.) *V.* TRINQUETE. *A cada triquete,* At every stir or step.
Triquina [tre-kee'-nah], *f.* Trichina, a worm, parasitic in muscles in the larval stage and in the intestines when mature. The cause of the disease trichinosis.

Triquinosis [tre-ke-no'-sis], *f.* Trichinosis, a serious disease produced by trichinæ in the muscles and intestines of the body.
Triquiñuela [tre-ke-nyoo-ay'-lah], *f.* (Coll.) Cheat, fraud: applied either to dealing or gaming.
Triquitraque [tre-ke-trah'-kay], *m.* 1. Crack, clack, clattering, clashing. 2. Fire-cracker, pulling-cracker. 3. Rocket, serpent.
Trirreme [trir-ray'-may], *m.* (Naut.) Trireme.
Tris [trees], *m.* 1. Noise made by the breaking of glass. 2. Trice, an instant. *Venir en un tris,* To come in an instant. *Estar en un tris,* To be on the verge of; to be on the point of; to be within an ace. *Tris tras* (or coll. *tras tras*), Tedious repetition; "the same old story."
Trisa [tree'-sah], *f.* (Zool.) Shad. *V.* SÁBALO.
Trisagio [tre-sah'-he-o], *m.* Trisagion, angelic chorus of Holy, holy, holy; any festivity repeated three days.
Trisarquía [tre-sar-kee'-ah], *f.* Triumvirate.
Trisca [trees'-cah], *f.* Noise made by treading on any thing which breaks under the feet; any noise.
Triscador, ra [tris-cah-dor', rah], *m.* & *f.* 1. A noisy, rattling person. 2. *m.* (Mech.) Saw-set, an instrument for setting the teeth of a saw.
Triscar [tris-car'], *vn.* 1. To stamp, to make a noise with the feet. 2. To caper, to frisk about, to frolic.—*va.* Among carpenters to set the teeth of a saw; to bend these alternately to the one side or the other. *V.* also TRABAR.
Trisecar [tre-say-car'], *va.* To divide into three equal parts, to trisect.
Trisección [tre-sec-the-on'], *f.* Trisection, division into three parts.
Trisílabo, ba [tre-see'-lah-bo, bah], *a.* Trisyllabic, containing three syllables.
Tristacho, cha [tris-tah'-cho, chah], *a.* (Prov.) Sorrowful, melancholy.
Triste [trees'-tay], *a.* 1. Sorrowful, sad, mournful. 2. Gloomy, dismal, heavy, morose. 3. Abject, mean, low. 4. Dull, gloomy, sombre, murky.
Tristecico, ica, illo, illa, ito, ita, *a. dim.* of TRISTE.
Tristemente [trees-tay-men'-tay], *adv.* Mournfully, heavily, grievously.
Tristeza [tris-tay'-thah], *f.* 1. Grief, sorrow, affliction, melancholy, gloom. 2. Lowness or depression of spirits. *Morirse de tristeza,* (Met.) To be broken-hearted; also, to die broken-hearted.
Tristicia, Tristura, Tristor [tris-tee'-the-ah], *f.* (Obs.) See TRISTEZA.
Trisulco, ca [tre-sool'-co, cah], *a.* 1. Three-pronged, having three points. 2. Of three furrows, or channels.
Trisulo [tree'-soo-lo], *m.* (Chem.) A salt produced by two neutral salts, both with the same acid, but with different bases.
Triticeo, ea [tre-tee'-thay-o, ah], *a.* Triticean, belonging to wheat, wheaten.
Tritón [tre-tone'], *m.* 1. (Myth.) Triton. 2. (Zool.) Triton, newt.
Tritono [tree'-to-no], *m.* (Mus.) Tritone, an interval of three tones: the ratio of 45 to 32.
Triturable [tre-too-rah'-blay], *a.* (Littl. us.) Triturable.
Trituración [tre-too-rah-the-on'], *f.* Trituration, pulverization.
Triturador, ra [tre-too-rah-dor', rah], *a.* Crushing.—*f.* Crusher, crushing machine.
Triturar [tre-too-rar'], *va.* To triturate, to comminute.
Triunfada [tre-oon-fah'-dah], *f.* Trumping at cards.
Triunfador, ra [tre-oon-fah-dor', rah], *m.* & *f.* Conqueror, victor, triumpher.
Triunfal [tre-oon-fahl'], *a.* Triumphal.
Triunfalmente, *adv.* Triumphally.
Triunfante [tre-oon-fahn'-tay], *a.* & *pa.* Triumphant, magnificent, conquering.
Triunfantemente, *adv.* Triumphantly.
Triunfar [tre-oon-far'], *vn.* 1. To conquer. 2. To triumph, to celebrate a victory, to exult; to conquer the passions. 3. To make an idle show of grandeur and wealth. 4. To trump at cards.
Triunfo [tre-oon'-fo], *m.* 1. Triumph, victory; conquest; exultation. 2. Slap with the back of the hand. 3. Trump card.
Triunviral [tre-oon-ve-rahl'], *a.* Triumviral, pertaining to the triumvirs.
Triunvirato [tre-oon-ve-rah'-to], *m.* Triumvirate.
Triunviro [tre-oon-vee'-ro], *m.* Triumvir.
Trivial [tre-ve-ahl'], *a.* 1. Frequented, beaten: applied to a road or path. 2. Trivial, vulgar, common, known by all.
Trivialidad [tre-ve-ah-le-dahd'], *f.* Trivialness, triteness; vulgarity; idleness.
Trivialmente, *adv.* Trivially.
Trivio [tree'-ve-o], *m.* Cross-road, point where three roads meet.
Triza [tree'-thah], *f.* 1. Mite, a small particle. 2. (Naut.) Cord, rope.
Tro, *m.* A musical instrument, after the fashion of a violin, used in Siam.
Troa, *f.* (Obs.) *V.* HALLAZGO.
Trocable [tro-cah'-blay], *a.* Changeable.
Trocada (A la), A la trocadilla. *V.* TROCADO, *a.* ad fin.
Trocadamente, *adv.* Contrarily, falsely.
Trocado [tro-cah'-do], *m.* Change, small coin.
Trocado, da [tro-cah'-do, dah], *a.* & *pp.* of TROCAR. Changed, permuted. *A la trocada* or *a la trocadilla,* In the contrary sense; in exchange.
Trocador, ra [tro-cah-dor', rah], *m.* & *f.* One who exchanges or permutes.
Trocaico [tro-cah'-e-co], *a.* Trochaic, of trochees.
Trocamiento [tro-cah-me-en'-to], *m.* (Obs.) *V.* TRUEQUE.
Trocar [tro-car'], *va.* 1. To exchange, to barter; to change, to commute; to equivocate. 2. To vomit.—*vr.* 1. To be changed or reformed. 2. To exchange seats with another.
Trocar [tro-car'], *m.* (Surg.) Trocar.
Trocatinta [tro-cah-teen'-tah], *f.* (Coll.) 1. A sad or unintentional mistake, in taking one thing for another 2. A ridiculous barter or exchange.
Trocatinte [tro-cah-teen'-tay], *m.* Mixed colour, changing colour.
Trocear [tro-thay-ar'], *va.* (Obs.) To divide into pieces.
Troceo [tro-thay'-o], *m.* (Naut.) Parrel, a thick rope for securing the yards.
Trociscar [tro-thees-car'], *va.* To make troches or lozenges.
Trocisco [tro-thees'-co], *m.* Troche, lozenge, a medicine prepared as a cake.
Trocla [tro'-clah], *f.* *V.* POLEA.
Troco [tro'-co], *m.* (Zool.) *V.* RUEDA.
Trocha [tro'-chah], *f.* A narrow path across a high road.
Trochemoche (A) [tro-chay-mo'-chay], *adv.* Helter-skelter, pell-mell, in confusion and hurry. *Hacer las cosas a trochemoche,* (Coll.) To do things at random.
Trochuela [tro-choo-ay'-lah], *f. dim.* A little path.
Trofeo [tro-fay'-o], *m.* Trophy, colours, things taken from an enemy; emblem of triumph; victory; pageant. Trophies, military insignia.
Trófico, ca [tro'-fe-co, cah], *a.* Trophic, relating to nutrition.
Trofología [tro-fo-lo-hee'-ah], *f.* Dietetic regimen, or a treatise concerning it.
Trofológico, ca [tro-fo-lo'-he-co, cah], *a.* Dietetic.
Troglodita [tro-glo-dee'-tah], *com.* & *a.* 1. Troglodyte, a cave-dweller. 2. Name given by the Greeks to certain barbarous peoples of Africa who lived in caverns. 3. A barbarous, cruel man. 4. A great eater. 5. A chimpanzee. 6. A wren.
Troglodítico, ca [tro-glo-dee'-te-co, cah], *a* Troglodytic.
Trogón [tro-gone'], *m.* Trogon. *V.* TROGÓNIDOS.
Trogónidos [tro-go'-ne-dose], *m. pl.* Trogons, a family of climbing birds, of warm climates, having brilliant plumage.
Troj [troh], *f.* *V.* TROJE.
Trojado, da [tro-hah'-do, dah], *a.* Contained in a knapsack.
Troje, Troj [tro'-hay], *f.* 1. Granary, mow. 2. (Met. Obs.) The church; the congregation of the faithful.
Trojero [tro-hay'-ro], *m.* Store-keeper, guard of a granary.
Trolebus [tro-lay-boos'], *m.* Trolley bus.
Tromba [trom'-bah], *f.* A water-spout.
Trombón [trom-bone'], *m.* Trombone, a brass wind-instrument. *V.* SACABUCHE.
Trombosis [trom-bo'-sis], *f.* (Med.) Thrombosis.
Trompa [trom'-pah], *f.* 1. Trumpet, horn. 2. Proboscis or trunk of an elephant. 3. A large top. *Trompa de caza con círculos,* A French horn or hunting horn. *Trompa marina,* (1) A marine trumpet; a musical instrument with one cord, played with a bow. (2) *V.* TROMBA.—*m.* Trumpeter. *A trompa tañida,* At the sound of the trumpet, inconsiderately, rashly. *A trompa y talega,* Helter-skelter. *Trompa de Eustaquio,* Eustachian tube connecting the middle ear with the pharynx.
Trompada [trom-pah'-dah], *f.* 1. (Coll.) Blow with a top. 2. Encounter of two persons face to face. 3. (Andal. and Amer.) A blow with a fist.
Trompar [trom-par'], *vn.* To whip a top.
Trompazo [trom-pah'-tho], *m.* 1. Blow with a top, trumpet, or fist. 2. Misfortune, accident.
Trompear [trom-pay-ar'], *vn.* To whip a top, to play at chess.
Trompero [trom-pay'-ro], *m.* 1. Top maker. 2. Cheat, impostor.
Trompero, ra [trom-pay'-ro, rah], *a.* Deceptive, false, deceiving.
Trompeta [trom-pay'-tah], *f.* 1. Trumpet. 2. Trumpet-shell. Buccinum. *Pobre trompeta,* An idle prattler.—*m.* Trumpeter.
Trompetada [trom-pay-tah'-dah], *f.* (Coll.) *V.* CLARINADA.
Trompetazo [trom-pay-tah'-tho], *m.* 1. (Littl. us.) Stroke with a trumpet. 2. Trumpet-blast.
Trompetear [trom-pay-tay-ar'], *vn.* (Coll.) To sound the trumpet.
Trompetería [trom-pay-tay-ree'-ah], *f.* Pipes of an organ.

Trompetero [trom-pay-tay'-ro], *m.* Trumpeter, horn-blower; trumpet-maker.
Trompetilla [trom-pay-teel'-lyah], *f.* 1. (Dim.) A small trumpet. 2. Hearing-trumpet. 3. Proboscis, lancet, of gnats and other insects. 4. A Philippine cigar of conical shape.
Trompicar [trom-pe-car'], *vn.* To stumble frequently; to falter.—*va.* 1. (Coll.) To appoint one irregularly to an employment which belonged to another. 2. To trip, to occasion stumbling.
Trompicón [trom-pe-cone'], *m.* Stumbling. *V.* TROPEZÓN.
Trompilla [trom-peel'-lyah], *f. dim.* A small trumpet or horn.
Trompillar [trom-pil-lyar'], *vn.* To stumble; to falter. *V.* TROMPICAR.
Trompis [trom'-pis]. In colloquial phrase, *Andar a trompis,* To come to fisticuffs.
Trompo [trom'-po], *m.* 1. Man at chess. 2. Whipping-top. *Ponerse como un trompo,* (Met.) To be as full as a top; to eat or drink to satiety.
Trompón [trom pone'], *m.* A big whipping-top. *A trompón* or *de trompón,* In a disorderly manner.
Tron, *m.* (Coll.) Report of fire-arms.
Tronada [tro-nah'-dah], *f.* Thunder-storm.
Tronador, ra [tro-nah-dor', rah], *m.* & *f.* 1. Thunderer, thundering. 2. Squib, cracker, rocket.
Tronar [tro-nar'], *v. imper.* To thunder.—*vn.* 1. To thunder, to make a noise like thunder or the discharge of guns, to fulminate. 2. To break relations with any one. 3. Among gamblers, to lose all one's money. *Por lo que pueda* or *por lo que pudiere tronar,* For what may happen.
Troncal [tron-cahl'], *a.* Relating to the trunk or stock.
Troncar [tron-car'], *va.* 1. To truncate, to mutilate, to cut off. 2. To interrupt a conversation, to cut the thread of a discourse.
Tronco [tron'-co], *m.* 1. Trunk of a tree; a log of wood. 2. Stock, the origin of a family. 3. Trunk of an animal without the head and limbs. 4. An illiterate, despicable, useless person. 5. Hind pair of horses in a coach. *Estar hecho un tronco,* To be bereft of feeling and sensation: literally, to be like a log of wood.
Tronco, ca [tron'-co, cah], *a.* (Obs.) Truncated, cut, mutilated. *V.* TRUNCADO.
Troncón [tron-cone'], *m. aug.* A large stalk or trunk; a large log of wood.
Tronchado [tron-chah'-do], *a.* (Her.) Applied to a shield having a diagonal bar. *Tronchado, da, pp.* of TRONCHAR.
Tronchar [tron-char'], *va.* To cut by the trunk or root, to chop off; to break with violence.
Tronchazo [tron-chah'-tho], *m.* 1. (Aug.) A large stalk. 2. A blow with a stalk or stem.
Troncho [tron'-cho], *m.* Sprig, stem, or stalk of garden plants. *Bravo troncho de mozo,* (Coll.) Stout, well-disposed youth.
Tronchudo, da [tron-choo'-do, dah], *a.* Having a long stem or stalk.
Tronera [tro-nay'-rah], *f.* 1. (Mil.) Embrasure of a battery. 2. (Naut.) Loophole. 3. Louver. 4. Dormer, a small sky-light. 5. A harum-scarum fellow, a hare-brained, foolish person. 6. Paper cracker; squib.—*pl.* 1. Holes and pockets of truck and billiard-tables. 2. Openings.
Tronerar [tro-nay-rar'], *va.* *V.* ATRONERAR.
Tronerilla [tro-nay-reel'-lyah], *f. dim.* of TRONERA.
Tronga [tron'-gah], *f.* (Slang or low) Kept mistress, concubine.
Tronido [tro-nee'-do], *m.* Thunder. *V.* TRUENO.
Tronitoso, sa [tro-ne-to'-so, sah], *a.* (Coll.) Resounding, thundering.
Trono [tro'-no], *m.* Throne; royal dignity; seat of the image of a saint. —*pl.* Thrones, seventh choir of angels.
Tronquillo [tron-keel'-lyo], *m.* Ornamental metal-work for applying to the covers of books.
Tronquista [tron-kees'-tah], *m.* Coachman that drives a pair of horses.
Tronquito [tron-kee'-to], *m. dim.* of TRONCO.
Tronzar [tron-thar'], *va.* 1. To shatter, to break in pieces. 2. To plait, to fold.
Tronzo, za [tron'-tho, thah], *a.* Having one or both ears cut off: applied to horses.
Tropa [tro'-pah], *f.* 1. Troop, a body of soldiers. 2. Troop, a small body of cavalry. 3. A number of people collected together; crowd, multitude; troop, herd. 4. Beat to arms. *Tropa de marina,* Marines. *En tropa,* In crowds, without order.
Tropel [tro-pel'], *m.* 1. Noise made by a quick movement of the feet. 2. Hurry, bustle, confusion, huddle. 3. Heap of things, confusedly tumbled together; crowd. *De tropel,* Tumultuously, in a throng.
Tropelía [tro-pay-lee'-ah], *f.* 1. Precipitation, hurry, confusion. 2. Vexation, oppression, injustice, outrage.
Tropellar [tro-pel-lyar'], *va.* (Prov.) To trample.
Tropezadero [tro-pay-thah-day'-ro], *m.* Any stumbling or slippery place; a bad, uneven road or path.
Tropezado, da [tro-pay-thah'-do, dah], *a.* & *pp.* of TROPEZAR. Stumbled, obstructed. *Conserva tropezada,* Conserve made of very small pieces.
Tropezador, ra [tro-pay-thah-dor', rah], *m.* & *f.* Tripper, stumbler.
Tropezadura [tro-pay-thah-doo'-rah], *f.* Stumbling, obstructing, entangling.
Tropezar [tro-pay-thar'], *vn.* 1. To stumble in walking. 2. To be detained or obstructed. 3. To slip into crimes or blunders. 4. To wrangle, to dispute. 5. To discover a fault or defect. 6. To meet accidentally. 7. To light on, to happen to find.—*vr.* To stumble, to cut the feet in walking: applied to horses. *Sin tropezar en barras,* Inconsiderately.
Tropezón, na [tro-pay-thone', nah], *a.* Stumbling, tripping frequently. *A tropezones,* With a variety of obstructions.
Tropezón, *m.* 1. *V.* TROPIEZO. 2. Act of tripping.
Tropezoncico, illo, ito [tro-pay-thon-thee'-co], *m. dim.* of TROPEZÓN.
Tropezoso, sa [tro-pay-tho'-so, sah], *a.* Apt to stumble or trip.
Tropical [tro-pe-cahl'], *a.* Tropical, belonging to the tropics.
Trópico [tro'-pe-co], *m.* (Ast.) Tropic, either of two parallels at a distance from the equator N. and S. of 23° 28′ and corresponding to the solstitial points.
Trópico, ca [tro'-pe-co, cah], *a.* 1. (Ast.) Tropical. 2. (Rhet.) Tropical, containing tropes.
Tropiezo [tro-pe-ay'-tho], *m.* 1. Stumble, trip. 2. Obstacle, obstruction, impediment. 3. Slip, fault, error. 4. Difficulty, embarrassment. 5. Quarrel, dispute.
(*Yo tropiezo, tropiece,* from *Tropezar. V.* ACRECENTAR.)
Tropilla [tro-peel'-lyah], *f. dim.* A small body or detachment of troops.
Tropo [tro'-po], *m.* (Rhet.) Trope, figurative sense.
Tropología [tro-po-lo-hee'-ah], *f.* 1. Figurative language, allegorical sense, tropology. 2. Mingling of morality and doctrine in a discourse; tropology.
Tropológico, ca [tro-po-lo'-he-co, cah], *a.* 1. Tropological, expressed by tropes. 2. Doctrinal, moral, relative to reform in customs.
Trotamundos [tro-tah-moon'-dos], *m.* & *f.* Globetrotter.
Troque [tro'-kay], *m.* A kind of bunch formed in cloths when dyeing them.
Troquel [tro-kel'], *m.* Die, in which a hollow figure is engraved.
Troqueo [tro-kay'-o], *m.* Trochee, a foot in Greek and Latin poetry, consisting of a long and a short syllable: — ⏑.
Troquillo [tro-keel'-lyo], *m.* (Arch.) Trochilus, concave moulding next the torus.
Trotaconventos [tro-tah-con-ven'-tose], *f.* (Vulg.) Procuress. *V.* ALCAHUETA.
Trotada [tro-tah'-dah], *f.* (Obs.) Stretch, route, way.
Trotador, ra [tro-tah-dor', rah], *m.* & *f.* Trotter.
Troposfera [tro-pos-fay'-rah], *f.* Troposphere.
Trotar [tro-tar'], *vn.* To trot; to move swiftly, to be in haste.—*va.* To make a horse trot.
Trote [tro'-tay], *m.* Trot. *Al trote,* In a trot; in haste or hastily. *Tomar el trote,* To run away.
Trotero [tro-tay'-ro], *m.* (Obs.) *V.* CORREO.
Trotillo [tro-teel'-lyo], *m. dim.* A light trot.
Trotón, na [tro-tone', nah], *a.* Trotting, whose ordinary pace is a trot: spoken of a horse.
Trotón, *m.* A trotter.
Trotonería [tro-to-nay-ree'-ah], *f.* A continual trot.
Trova [tro'-vah], *f.* (Obs.) 1. Metrical composition. *V.* VERSO. 2. Parody.
Trovador, ra [tro-vah-dor', rah], *m.* & *f.* 1. Troubadour, versifier, poet. 2. (Obs.) Finder.—*a.* Versifying; parodic.
Trovar [tro-var'], *va.* 1. To versify. 2. To imitate a metrical composition by turning it to another subject, to parody. 3. To invert or pervert the sense of a thing.
Trovero [tro-vay'-ro], *m.* Poet of the northern langue d'oil in the middle ages, corresponding to the troubadour of the south.
Trovista [tro-vees'-tah], *m.* Finder; versifier.
Trox, *f.* (Obs.) *V.* TROJ.
Troya [tro'-yah], *f.* Troy. *Aquí fué Troya,* Here was Troy: applied to the site of a memorable place. *¡Arda Troya!* Let happen what will: proceed with the disorder! (ironical).
Troyano, na [tro-yah'-no, nah], *a.* Trojan.
Troza [tro'-thah], *f.* Trunk of a tree to be sawn into boards.
Trozo [tro'-tho], *m.* 1. Piece or part of a thing cut off. 2. (Naut.) Junk for making oakum. 3. (Mil.) Division of a column, forming the van or rear guard. 4. Throstle, a species of spindle. *Trozo de madera,* A log. *Trozo de abordaje,* A division of the crew appointed to board an enemy's ship while in action.

Trucar [troo-car'], *vn.* To play the first card.
Trucidar [troo-the-dar'], *va.* (Obs.) To kill, to destroy.
Truco [troo'-co], *m.* A skilful push at trucks. *Trucos,* Trucks, a game resembling billiards.
Truculencia [troo-coo-len'-the-ah], *f.* (Littl. us.) Truculence, ferocity.
Truculento, ta [troo-coo-len'-to, tah], *a.* Truculent, fierce.
Trucha [troo'-chah], *f.* 1 Trout. Salmo trutta. 2. Crane. *V.* CABRIA. *Ayunar, o comer trucha,* Either to fast or eat trout; the best or nothing. *No se cogen truchas a bragas enjutas,* (prov.) No gains without pains.
Truchero [troo-chay'-ro], *m.* A fisher who catches and sells trout.
Truchimán, na [troo-che-mahn', nah], *a.* (Coll.) Fond of business, or of making agreements.—*m.* & *f.* A go-between. *V.* TRUJAMÁN.
Truchimanear [troo-che-mah-nay-ar'], *vn.* To act as a go-between.
Truchuela [troo-choo-ay'-lah], *f.* Small codfish. *V.* ABADEJO.
Trué [troo-ay'], *m.* A sort of fine linen, manufactured at Troyes. The Madrid traders call it *Troé.*
Trueco [troo-ay'-co], *m.* Exchange, barter. *V.* TRUEQUE. *A trueco,* So that, provided that, on condition that. *A trueco* or *en trueco,* In exchange.
(*Yo trueco, trueque, troqué,* from *Trocar. V.* ACORDAR.)
Trueno [troo-ay'-no], *m.* 1. Thunder-clap. 2. Report of fire-arms; a noise like thunder.
(*Yo trueno, truene,* from *Tronar. V.* ACORDAR.)
Trueque [troo-ay'-kay], *m.* Exchange, truck, barter, commutation. *A trueque* or *en trueque, V.* A TRUECO or EN TRUECO.
Trufa [troo'-fah], *f.* 1. Imposition, fraud, deceit. 2. (Bot.) Truffle. Tuber cibarium.
Trufador, ra [troo-fah-dor', rah], *m.* & *f.* Fabulist, story-teller, liar.
Trufar [troo-far'], *va.* To stuff or cook with truffles.—*vn.* (Obs.) To tell stories, to deceive. *V.* MENTIR.
Trufeta [troo-fay'-tah], *f.* A sort of linen.
Truhán, na [troo-ahn', nah], *m.* & *f.* 1. A scoundrel, a knave. 2. Buffoon, jester, juggler, mountebank.
Truhanada [troo-ah-nah'-dah], *f. V.* TRUHANERÍA.
Truhanamente [troo-ah-nah-men'-tay], *adv.* Jestingly, buffoon-like.
Truhanear [troo-ah-nay-ar'], *vn.* 1. To deceive, to swindle. 2. To banter, to jest, to play the buffoon.
Truhanería [troo-ah-nay-ree'-ah], *f.* 1. Imposture, swindle. 2. Buffoonery, low jest.
Truhanesco, ca [troo-ah-nes'-co, cah], *a.* Belonging to a buffoon.
Truhanillo, illa [troo-ah-neel'-lyo], *m.* & *f. dim.* A mean, petty buffoon.
Truja [troo'-hah], *f.* (Prov.) Place where olives are kept before being pressed in the mill.
Trujal [troo-hahl'], *m.* 1. (Prov.) Oil-mill. 2. Copper, in which the materials for manufacturing soap are prepared. 3. (Prov.) *V.* LAGAR.
Trujaleta [troo-hah-lay'-tah], *f.* (Prov.) Vessel in which the juice of olives falls from the mill.
Trujamán [troo-hah-mahn'], *m.* 1. Dragoman, interpreter. 2. Broker, factor. (Arab.)
Trujamanear [troo-hah-mah-nay-ar'], *vn.* 1. To act as an interpreter. 2. To exchange, barter, buy, or sell goods for others; to act as a broker or factor. 3. To play the buffoon.
Trujamanía [troo-hah-mah-nee'-ah], *f.* Brokering, brokerage.
Trujillano, na [troo-heel-lyah'-no, nah], *a.* Of Trujillo.
Trujimán, na [troo-he-mahn', nah], *a. V.* TRUJAMÁN.
Trulla [trool'-lyah], *f.* 1. Noise, bustle; multitude. 2. Trowel, mason's level.
Trullo [trool'-lyo], *m.* 1. (Orn.) Teal. Anas coccea. 2. (Prov.) Kind of vat for pressed grapes.
Truncadamente, *adv.* In a truncated manner.
Truncado, da [troon-cah'-do, dah], *a.* & *pp.* of TRUNCAR. Truncate.
Truncar [troon-car'], *va.* To truncate, to maim; to mutilate a discourse.
Trunco, ca [troon'-co, cah], *a. V.* TRONCHADO, TRUNCADO.
Trupial [troo-pe-ahl'], *m.* (Orn.) Troupial. *V.* TURUPIAL.
Truque [troo'-kay], *m.* A game at cards.
Truquero [troo-kay'-ro], *m.* Keeper or owner of a truck-table.
Truquiflor [troo-ke-flor'], *m.* A game at cards.
Trusas [troo'-sas], *f. pl.* Trunk-hose, wide slashed breeches, in Greek fashion, which reached to the middle of the thigh.
Truyada [troo-yah'-dah, troo-jah'-dah in Cuba], *f.* (Amer.) Crowd, multitude.
Tsar, *m.* (Russian spelling) Czar, tsar. *V.* ZAR.
Tsetsé [tset-say'], *f.* Tsetse fly, a blood-sucking fly of southern Africa; its bite is deadly to cattle and horses, but not harmful to man, to the ass, and the goat. Glossina morsitans.
Tú [too], *pron. pers.* Thou: used in the familiar style of friendship. *A tú por tú,* Thee for thee; disrespectful or vulgar language. *Salta tú y dámela tú,* Juvenile play of thread-needle. *Hoy por ti, y mañana por mí,* (Coll.) Turn about is fair play.
Tu [too]. Possessive pronoun. Thy, thine. Plural *tus.* Apocopated from *tuyo, tuya.*
Tuáutem [too-ah'-oo-tem], *m.* (Coll.) Principal person, leader, mover, author; essential point.
Tuba [too'-bah], *f.* 1. (Mus.) Tuba. 2. Liquor obtained from the Nipa and other palms of the Philippine Islands.
Tuberculífero, ra [too-ber-coo-lee'-fay-ro, rah], *a.* Tuberculous, affected by tuberculosis; tubercular, characterized by the presence of tubercles.
Tuberculiforme [too-ber-coo-le-for'-may], *a.* Tubercular, tuberculiform.
Tuberculina [too-ber-coo-lee'-nah], *f.* (Med.) Tuberculin (used in the diagnosis and treatment of tuberculosis).
Tuberculización [too-ber-coo-le-thah-the-on'], *f.* Tuberculosis, tuberculization.
Tubérculo [too-berr'-coo-lo], *m.* 1. (Bot.) Tuber, a thick underground stem like the potato. 2. (Med.) Tubercle in the lungs, etc.
Tuberculoso, sa [too-ber-coo-lo'-so, sah], *a.* Tuberculous, affected with tuberculosis.
Tuberculosis [too-ber-coo-lo'-sis], *f.* (Med.) Tuberculosis, infection with tubercles; consumption.
Tubería [too-bay-ree'-ah], *f.* Tubing; a series of tubes or pipes.
Tuberosa [too-bay-ro'-sah], *f.* (Bot.) Tuberose, oriental hyacinth. Hyacinthus orientalis.
Tuberosidad [too-bay-ro-se-dahd'], *f.* Tuberosity; swelling.
Tuberoso, sa [too-bay-ro'-so, sah], *a.* Tuberous.
Tubífero, ra [too-bee'-fay-ro, rah], *a.* (Biol.) Provided with tubes.
Tubiforme [too-be-for'-may], *a.* Tubiform, tubular, tube-shaped.
Tubo [too'-bo], *m.* Tube. *V.* CAÑÓN. *Tubo de radio,* Radio tube. *Tubo lanzatorpedos,* Torpedo tube. *Tubo snorkel,* Snorkel.
Tubular [too-boo-lar'], *a.* 1. Tubular; tube-shaped. 2. Fitted to receive a tube.
Tubuliforme [too-boo-le-for'-may], *a.* Tubuliform, like a tubule.
Tubuloso, sa [too-boo-lo'-so, sah], *a.* Tubulose, tubulous; tubular.—*f.* (Chem.) A special arrangement of vessels to which a tube may be adapted, crossing through a cork or plug.
Tucán [too-cahn'], *m.* 1. Toucan, a climbing bird of South America, noted for its great and long beak. 2. Constellation near the Antarctic pole.
Tucia [too-thee'-ah], *f.* Tutty. *V.* ATUTÍA.
Tuciorista [too-the-o-rees'-tah], *com.* One who follows the safest doctrine.
Tudel [too-del'], *m.* A metal pipe with a reed put into a bassoon.
Tudesco [too-des'-co], *m.* 1. A kind of wide cloak. *V.* CAPOTE. 2. German, native of Germany.
Tueca, Tueco [too-ay'-cah], *f.* & *m.* Cavity made by wood-lice in timber.
Tuera [too-ay'-rah], *f.* (Bot.) Colocynth, bitter apple. Cucumis colocynthis.
Tuerca [too-err'-cah], *f.* Nut or female screw.
Tuerce [too-err'-thay], *m. V.* TORCEDURA.
Tuero [too-ay'-ro], *m.* 1. Dry wood cut for fuel. 2. (Bot.) Spicknel, a European aromatic perennial. Meum athamanticum.
Tuertamente, *adv.* (Obs.) *V.* TORCIDAMENTE.
Tuerto, ta [too-err'-to, tah], *a.* & *pp. irr.* of TORCER. One-eyed, blind of one eye; squint-eyed. *A tuertos,* On the contrary, on the wrong side; obliquely. *A tuertas,* Contrariwise, on the contrary. *A tuertas o a derechas,* or *a tuerto o a derecho,* Right or wrong; inconsiderately.
Tuerto, *m.* (Obs.) Wrong, injury. *Tuertos,* Pains after child-birth; more commonly called *entuertos.*
(*Yo tuesto, tueste,* from *Tostar. V.* ACORDAR.)
Tuétano [too-ay'-tah-no], *m.* Marrow; pith of trees. *Hasta los tuétanos,* With all vigour and activity; to the quick.
(*Yo tuerzo, tuerza,* from *Torcer. V.* COCER.)
Tufarada [too-fah-rah'-dah], *f.* A strong scent or smell.
Tufo [too'-fo], *m.* 1. A warm exhalation from the earth or from chimneys or lamps which do not burn well. 2. A strong and offensive smell. 3. Locks of hair which fall over the ear. 4. High notion, lofty idea, vanity. 5. *V.* TOBA.
Tugurio [too-goo'-re-o], *m.* (Coll.) Hut, cottage.
Tuición [too-e-the-on'], *f.* (Law) Tuition; protection.
Tuina [too-ee'-nah], *f.* A long, full jacket. (In Peru, *Tuín,* masculine.)
Tuitivo, va [too-e-tee'-vo, vah], *a.* (Law) Defensive, that which shelters or protects.
Tul [tool], *m.* Tulle, an open-meshed fabric of silk or cotton used for veils, mantillas, etc.

Tulipán [too-le-pahn'], *m.* (Bot.) Tulip. Tulipa. (Turk. dulband, turban.)
Tulipero [too-le-pay'-ro], *m.* (Bot.) Tulip-tree. Liliodendron tulipifera.
Tullidura [tool-lye-doo'-rah], *f.* Dung of birds of prey.
Tullimiento [tool-lye-me-en'-to], *m.* Contraction of the tendons.
Tullir [tool-lyeer'], *vn.* 1. To void, to emit dung: applied to birds. 2. (Obs.) To ill-treat.—*vr.* To be crippled.
Tumba [toom'-bah], *f.* 1. Tomb, sepulchral monument, vault. 2. Roof of a coach. 3. Tumble. *V.* TUMBO.
Tumbacuartillos [toom-bah-coo-ar-teel'-lyose], *m.* Sot, a vicious frequenter of taverns.
Tumbadero, ra [toom-bah-day'-ro, rah], *a.* Tumbler; falling. *Redes tumbaderas,* Drop-nets for catching wild animals.
Tumbado, da [toom-bah'-do, dah], *a.* & *pp.* of TUMBAR. 1. Tumbled. 2. Vaulted, arched.
Tumbaga [toom-bah'-gah], *f.* Pinchbeck; ring or toy of pinchbeck.
Tumbagón [toom-bah-gone'], *m. aug.* Any large piece made of pinchbeck; bracelet set with stones.
Tumbar [toom-bar'], *va.* 1. To tumble, to throw down. 2. To overwhelm (as a powerful odour), to deprive of sensation. *Tumbar un navío,* (Naut.) To heave a ship down.—*vn.* 1. To tumble. 2. (Naut.) To heel, to lie along, to have a false list: applied to a ship.—*vr.* (Coll.) To lie down to sleep.
Tumbilla [toom-beel'-lyah], *f.* Horse for airing bed-linen.
Tumbo [toom'-bo], *m.* 1. Tumble, fall. 2. A matter of consequence. 3. Book containing the privileges and title-deeds of monasteries, etc. *Tumbo de olla,* What remains in the pot after the meat is taken out. *Tumbo de dado,* (1) Imminent peril. (2) Within the cast of a die, near happening. (3) By mere chance.
Tumbón [toom-bone'], *m.* 1. Coach; trunk with an arched roof or lid. 2. (Coll.) *V.* TUNO.
Tumbonear [toom-bo-nay-ar'], *vn.* 1. To vault, to make arches. 2. *V.* TUNAR.
Tumefacción [too-may-fac-the-on'], *f.* Tumefaction, swelling.
Tumefacerse [too-may-fah-therr'-say], *vr.* To tumefy, to swell.
Tumefacto, ta [too-may-fac'-to, tah], *a.* Tumescent.
Tumescencia [too-mes-then'-the-ah], *f.* Tumescence, swelling from a tumor.
Tumescente [too-mes-then'-tay], *a.* Tumescent, slightly swollen.
Túmido, da [too'-me-do, dah], *a.* 1. Swollen, tumid, inflated. 2. Pompous, tumid, elevated: applied to style.
Tumor [too-more'], *m.* 1. Tumour, extuberance. 2. Tumour, affected pomp.
Tumorcico, illo, ito [too-mor-thee'-co], *m. dim.* A small tumour.
Túmulo [too'-moo-lo], *m.* Tomb, sepulchral monument; funeral pile.
Tumulto [too-mool'-to], *m.* 1. Tumult, uproar, commotion. 2. Faction, mob.
Tumultuar [too-mool-too-ar'], *vn.* To raise a tumult, to stir up disturbances, to mob.—*vr.* To rise, to make a tumult.
Tumultuariamente, *adv.* Tumultuously, outrageously.
Tumultuario, ria [too-mool-too-ah'-re-o, ah], *a.* Tumultuary, tumultuous.
Tumultuosamente, *adv.* Tumultuously. *V.* TUMULTUARIAMENTE.
Tumultuoso, sa [too-mool-too-oh'-so, sah], *a.* Tumultuous, clamorous, mobbish.
Tuna [too'-nah], *f.* 1. (Bot.) The prickly pear or Indian fig, the fig of the *Cactus opuntia.* 2. An idle and licentious life; truantship. *Andar a la tuna,* (Coll.) To play the truant; to wander idly about; to loiter.
Tunal [too-nahl'], *m.* (Bot.) The prickly pear cactus. Cactus opuntia. *V.* NOPAL.
Tunantada [too-nan-tah'-dah], *f.* Rascality, wickedness, debauchery.
Tunante [too-nahn'-tay], *pa.* Leading a licentious life.—*m.* Truant, idler, rake, a lazy loiterer.—*a.* Truant, lazy, loitering; sly, cunning, crafty.
Tunantería [too-nan-tay-ree'-ah], *f.* (Coll.) 1. Debauchery, idleness, vagrancy, libertinism. 2. Truantship.
Tunar [too-nar'], *vn.* To lead a licentious, vagrant life, to loiter.
Tunda [toon'-dah], *f.* 1. The act of shearing cloth. 2. A severe chastisement.
Tundente [toon-den'-tay], *a.* Doing injury to a part of the body without drawing blood; raising a tumour.
Tundición [toon-de-the-on'], *f.* Shearing of cloth.
Tundidor [toon-de-dor'], *m.* Shearer of cloth. *Banco del tundidor,* Shearing-board.
Tundidura [toon-de-doo'-rah], *f.* The act of shearing.
Tundir [toon-deer'], *va.* 1. To shear cloth. 2. (Coll.) To cudgel, to flog.
Tundizno [toon-deeth'-no], *m.* Shearings cut from cloth.
Tundra [toon'-drah], *f.* Tundra, treeless plain of Arctic regions.
Túnel [too'-nel], *m.* Tunnel (fr. English).
Tungstato [toongs-tah'-to], *m.* (Chem.) Tungstate, a salt of tungstic acid.
Tungsteno [toongs-tay'-no], *m.* Tungsten, wolfram, a steel-gray, heavy metallic element.
Túngstico, ca [toongs'-te-co, cah], *a.* Tungstic, an oxide and an acid derived from tungsten; tungstenic.
Túnica [too'-ne-cah], *f.* 1. Tunic, a garment worn by the ancients. 2. Tunic, a woollen shirt worn by religious persons. 3. Tunicle, pellicle, or integument which covers the shell of fruit. 4. Tunic, tunicle, integument of parts of the body. 5. A long, wide gown.
Tunicela [too-ne-thay'-lah], *f.* 1. Tunic. 2. Garment worn by bishops; wide gown.
Tuno [too'-no], *m.* Truant, rake, cunning rogue, a lazy loiterer.—*a.* Truant, lazy, loitering; sly, cunning.
Tun tun (Al), *phrase.* (Coll.) At random, heedlessly, come what will, impulsively.
Tupa [too'-pah], *f.* 1. (Coll.) Satiety, repletion. 2. The act of pressing close.
Tupé [too-pay'], *m.* 1. Toupee, foretop. 2. (Met.) Effrontery, insolence.
Tupí [too-pee'], *a.* & *m.* Name of the principal race of Indians in Brazil and their language which is in general use in the Amazonian regions.
Tupido, da [too-pee'-do, dah], *a.* & *pp.* of TUPIR. 1. Dense, thick, close-woven. 2. (Met.) Dense, overgrown, rank.
Tupir [too-peer'], *va.* To press close, to squeeze, closing the pores or interstices.—*vr.* To stuff or glut one's self; to overeat.
Turaní [too-rah-nee'], **Turaniense** [too-rah-ne-en'-say], *a.* Turanian, a family of agglutinative languages.
Turba [toor'-bah], *f.* 1. Crowd, confused multitude, heap. 2. Turf, sod, peat, used for fuel.
Turbación [toor-bah-the-on'], *f.* Perturbation, confusion, disorder; lightheadedness; the act of exciting disturbances.
Turbadamente [toor-bah-dah-men'-tay], *adv.* In a disorderly manner.
Turbador, ra [toor-bah-dor', rah], *m.* & *f.* Disturber, perturbator.
Turbal [toor-bahl'], *m.* Turf-bog, peat-moss; collection of peat or fuel.
Turbamulta [toor-bah-mool'-tah], *f.* Crowd, multitude.
Turbante [toor-bahn'-tay], *m.* 1. Turban worn by the Turks. 2. Disturber.
Turbar [toor-bar'], *va.* To disturb, to alarm; to surprise.—*vr.* To be uneasy, alarmed, discomposed.
Turbativo, va [toor-bah-tee'-vo, vah], *a.* Troublesome, alarming.
Turbiamente [toor-be-ah-men'-tay], *adv.* Obscurely, confusedly.
Turbiedad [too-be-ay-dahd'], *f.* Muddiness, turbidness; obscurity.
Turbina [toor-bee'-nah], *f.* A turbine water-wheel placed horizontally.
Turbinado, da [toor-be-nah'-do, dah], *a.* Turbinated, twisted, spiral-formed: applied to shells.
Turbinita [toor-be-nee'-tah], *f.* (Conch.) Wreath shell, spiral shell. Turbo.
Turbino [toor-bee'-no], *m.* Powder made of the root of turbith.
Turbio, bia [toor'-be-o, ah], *a.* 1. Muddy, turbid, disturbed, troubled. 2. Unhappy, unfortunate. 3. Dark, obscure: applied to language. *A turbio correr* or *cuando todo turbio corra,* (Coll.) However bad or unfortunate it may be or happen.
Turbión [toor-be-on'], *m.* 1. A heavy shower of rain. 2. Hurricane; violent concussion of things.
Turbit [toor-beet'], *m.* (Bot.) Turpeth, turbith, the root of an East Indian plant allied to jalap. Ipomœa turpethum. *Turbit mineral,* (Pharm.) Turpeth mineral, yellow oxide of mercury.
Turbohélice [toor-bo-ay'-le-thay], *m* Turbo-propeller engine.
Turbopropulsor [toor-bo-pro-pool-sor'], *m.* Turboprop.
Turborreactor [toor-bor-ray-ac-tor'], *m.* (Aer.) Turbojet.
Turborretropropulsión [toor-bor-ray-tro-pro-pool-se-on'], *f.* Turbo-jet propulsion.
Turbulencia [toor-boo-len'-the-ah], *f.* 1. Turbidness, muddiness. 2. Turbulence, confusion, disorder.
Turbulentamente, *adv.* Turbulently.
Turbulento, ta [toor-boo-len'-to, tah], *a.* 1. Turbid, thick, muddy. 2. Turbulent, disorderly, tumultuous.
Turca [toor'-cah], *f.* (Coll.) Tipsiness. *Vestirse una turca* or *coger una turca,* To get drunk.
Turco, ca [toor'-co, cah], *adj.* Turkish.—*m.* & *f.* A Turk; a Turkish woman.—*m.* (Slang) Wine. *El gran turco,* The Sultan of Turkey.
Turcomano, na [toor-co-mah'-no, nah], *a.* Turkoman, a Tartar inhabitant of Turkestan, of Turkish origin.
Túrdiga [toor'-de-gah], *f.* 1. Piece of new leather, of which the poor in Spain make coarse shoes, called *abarcas.* 2. Strip of hide.
Turdión [toor-de-on'], *m.* Ancient Spanish dance.
Turgencia [toor-hen'-the-ah], *f.* 1. Swelling, turgescence. 2. Ostentation, vanity, pride.

Turgente [toor-hen'-tay], *a.* 1. Turgescent, tumid, protuberant. 2. (Poet.) Massive, lofty.

Túrgido, da [toor'-he-do, dah], *a.* (Poet.) Lofty, bulky.

Turíbulo [too-ree'-boo-lo], *m.* (Littl. us.) Incensory, a vessel in which incense is burnt.

Turicha [too-ree'-chah], *f.* *V.* TURUPIAL.

Turiferario, Turibulario [too-re-fay-rah'-re-o, too-re-boo-lah'-re-o], *m.* (Littl. us.) The acolothist, who carries the incensory.

Turífero, ra [too-ree'-fay-ro, rah], *a.* Incense-producing or bearing.

Turificación [too-re-fe-cah-the-on'], *f.* (Obs.) Perfuming with incense.

Turismo [too-rees'-mo], *m.* Tourism, touring, travelling.

Turista [too-rees'-tah], *m.* & *f.* Tourist, traveller.

Turma [toor'-mah], *f.* Testicle. *Turma de tierra,* (Bot.) Truffle. Tuber cibarium.

Turmalina [toor-mah-lee'-nah], *f.* (Miner.) Tourmaline, a translucent mineral of various colours, generally blackish: schorl. It is a complex aluminum-boron silicate: used in polariscopes.

Turmera [toor-may'-rah], *f.* (Bot.) Ledum-leaved rock-rose. Cistus ledifolius.

Turmeruela [toor-may-roo-ay'-lah], *f.* (Bot.) Umbel-flowered rock-rose. Cistus umbellatus.

Turnar [toor-nar'], *vn.* To alternate, to go or work by turns.

Turnio, nia [toor'-ne-o, ah], *a.* 1. Squint-eyed: in this sense it is used as a substantive. 2. Torvous, of a stern countenance.

Turno [toor'-no], *m.* 1. Turn, successive or alternate order; change, vicissitude. 2. (Naut.) Time in which sailors are employed in some particular business. *Relevar el turno a la bomba* or *a sondalesa,* To spell the pump or the lead. *Al turno,* By turns. *Por su turno,* In one's turn.

Turón [too-rone'], *m.* A kind of field-mouse. Mus silvaticus.

Turpe. *a.* (Obs.) *V.* TORPE.

Turpial [toor-pe-ahl'], *m.* Troopial. *V.* TURUPIAL.

Turquesa [toor-kay'-sah], *f.* 1. Turquoise or turkois, a precious stone. 2. Mould for making pellets or balls to be thrown from a cross-bow.

Turquesado, da [toor-kay-sah'-do, dah], *a.* Of the turquoise colour.

Turquesco, ca [toor-kes'-co, cah], *a.* Turkish. *A la turquesca,* In the Turkish manner.

Turquí, Turquino, na [toor-kee'], *a.* Of a deep blue colour.

Turrar [toor-rar'], *va.* To toast, to roast.

Turrón [toor-rone'], *m.* Nougat, paste made of almonds, pine-kernals, nuts, and honey.

Turronero [toor-ro-nay'-ro], *m.* One who makes or retails the sweatmeat called *turrón.*

Tursión [toor-se-on'], *m.* Fish resembling a dolphin.

Turulato, ta [too-roo-lah'-to, tah], *a.* (Coll.) Silly, stupefied, confounded, startled (fr. *Atortolado*).

Turulés [too-roo-lays'], *a.* Said of a kind of strong grapes.

Turumbón [too-room-bone'], *m.* Contusion on the head.

Turupial [too-roo-pe-ahl'], *m.* Troopial, a bird of Venezuela, of the size of a thrush, with black and gold plumage, a great songster and easy to tame. (Acad.) *V.* TURICHA.

Tus [toos], *int.* A word used in calling dogs. *A perro viejo no hay tus tus,* (prov.) There is no catching old birds with chaff. *Sin decir tus ni mus.* (Coll.) Without saying a word.

Tusa [too'-sah], *f.* (Amer.) 1. The corn-cob. 2. (Cuba) Cigarette covered with the finest husk of the corn.

Tusco, ca [toos'-co, cah], *a.* Tuscan, Etruscan.

Tusílago [too-see'-lah-go], *m.* (Bot.) Coltsfoot. Tussilago farfara.

Tuso, sa [too'-so, sah], *m.* & *f.* (Coll.) Name given to dogs.

Tusón [too-sone'], *m.* 1. Fleece of a sheep. 2. (Prov.) Colt not two years old. *Orden del tusón* (*toisón*) *de oro,* Order of the Golden Fleece.

Tusona [too-so'-nah], *f.* 1. Strumpet, having her head and eye-brows either shaved, as a punishment, or lost by disease. 2. (Andal.) Filly not two years old.

Tute [too'-tay], *m.* A special card game.

Tuteamiento [too-tay-ah-me-en'-to], *m.* *V.* TUTEO.

Tutear [too-tay-ar'], *va.* To thou, to treat with familiarity.

Tutela [too-tay'-lah], *f.* Guardianship, tutelage, tutorage, protection. *Tutela dativa,* (Law) Guardianship appointed by a court.

Tutelar [too-tay-lar'], *a.* Tutelar, tutelary.

Tuteo [too-tay'-o], *m.* Thouing, addressing persons by the pronoun *Tú* (thou).

Tutia [too-tee'-ah], *f.* Tutty. *V.* ATUTÍA.

Tutilimundi [too-te-le-moon'-de], *m.* *V.* MUNDINOVI.

Tutiplén [too-te-plen']. Only used in the colloquial phrase, *a tutiplén,* abundantly, to satiety.

Tuto, ta [too'-to, tah], *a.* (Obs.) Safe. *V.* SEGURO.

Tutor [too-tor'], *m.* 1. Tutor, instructor. 2. Guardian of the person and estate of a minor. 3. Defender, protector.

Tutora [too-to'-rah], *f.* Tutoress, guardian; governess.

Tutoría [too-to-ree'-ah], *f.* Tutelage, guardianship. *V.* TUTELA.

Tutriz [too-treeth'], *f.* Tutoress, governess. *V.* TUTORA.

Tuya [too'-yah], *f.* Thuya, white cedar or red cedar. One species yields sandarac.

Tuyo, ya [too'-yo, yah], *pron. poss.* Thine. *Ese sombrero es tuyo.* That hat is thine. *Los tuyos,* The friends and relatives of the party addressed.

U

U [oo] is the twenty-fourth letter in the Castilian alphabet and fifth of the vowels; it loses its sound after *q* and *g,* and becomes a liquid, except where it is followed by an *a,* as in *guarismo,* or when marked with a diaresis, as in *agüero,* when it retains its proper sound. The letters *b, v,* and *u* were formerly used as equivalent to each other in writing or printing. Example: *Las cosas de Perpiñán* estauan *en mucha quiebra, por* auer *quitado* vn gouernador, *que* tratáua *bien la ciudad.* (*Comentarios de Herrera,* Madrid, 1624.) This observation will prevent many mistakes in reading. Each of these letters is at present restricted to its own proper sound, and particular care should be taken not to confound them, as they differ both in sound and in import; as, *él desuela,* he unpaves; *él desvela,* he keeps others awake. *U* in chemical formulas stands for uranium. *U valona,* Double u, w.

U [oo]. A disjunctive conjunction used in the place of *o,* to avoid cacophony (before *o* or *ho*); as, *plata u oro,* Silver or gold; *víctima u holocausto,* A victim or a holocaust.

Ualita [oo-ah-lee'-tah], *f.* A mineral substance occurring in the aspect of raw cotton.

Ubérrimo, ma [oo-berr'-re-mo, mah], *a.* Very fruitful; extremely abundant.

Ubicación [oo-be-cah-the-on'], *f.* Situation in a determined place, position.

Ubicar [oo-be-car'], *vn.* & *vr.* To locate or situate, to be located.

Ubicuidad [oo-be-coo-e-dahd'], *f.* Ubiquity, presence everywhere at once.

Ubicuo, cua [oo-bee'-kwo, kwah], *a.* Ubiquitous, omnipresent.

Ubiquidad [oo-be-ke-dahd'], *f.* *V.* UBICUIDAD.

Ubiquitario, ria [oo-be-ke-tah'-re-o, ah], *a.* & *n.* Ubiquitarian, one of a sect which denies transubstantiation, affirming that the body of Jesus Christ in virtue of his divinity is present in the eucharist.

Ubio [oo'-be-o], *m.* (Prov.) *V.* YUGO.

Ubre [oo'-bray], *f.* Dug or teat of female animals, udder.

Ubrera [oo-bray'-rah], *f.* Thrush, ulcerations in the mouth of sucking children.

Ucencia [oo-then -the-ah], *com.* Your excellency. *V.* VUECELENCIA.

Udómetro [oo-doh'-may-tro], *m.* Udometer, a rain-gauge.

Uesnorueste [oo-es-no-roo-es'-tay], *m.* *V.* OESNORUESTE.

Uessudueste [oo-es-soo-doo-es'-tay], *a.* *V.* OESSUDUESTE.

Ueste [oo-es'-tay], *m.* 1. West. 2. Zephyr, west wind.

¡Uf! *int.* Exclamation denoting weariness or annoyance.

Ufanamente, *adv.* Ostentatiously, boastfully.

Ufanarse [oo-fah-nar'-say], *vr.* To boast, to be haughty, or elated.

Ufanía [oo-fah-nee'-ah], *f.* 1. Pride, haughtiness. 2. Joy, gaiety, pleasure, satisfaction.

Ufano, na [oo-fah'-no, nah], *a.* 1. Proud, haughty, arrogant. 2. Gay, cheerful, content; masterly.

Ufo (A) [oo'-fo], *adv.* In a sponging manner; parasitically.

Ujier [oo-he-err'], *m.* Usher, an employee in the king's palace, corresponding to a porter. *Ujier de cámara del rey,* A gentleman usher of the king's privy chamber.

Ulcera [ool'-thay-rah], *f.* Ulcer. *Ulcera duodenal,* (Med.) Duodenal ulcer.

Ulceración [ool-thay-rah-the-on'], *f.* Ulceration.

Ulcerado, da [ool-thay-rah'-do, dah], *a.* & *pp.* of ULCERAR. Ulcered, ulcerated.

Ulcerar [ool-thay-rar'], *va.* To ulcerate. —*vr.* To exulcerate.

Ulcerativo, va [ool-thay-rah-tee'-vo, vah], *a.* Causing ulcers.

Ulceroso, sa [ool-thay-ro'-so, sah], *a.* Ulcerous.

Ule [oo'-lay], *m.* The caoutchouc-, or rubber-tree. *V.* HULE.

Ulema [oo-lay'-mah], *m.* Doctor of the law among the Turks.

Ulmáceas [ool-mah'-thay-as], *f. pl.* Ulmaceæ, the elm family.

Ulmaria [ool-mah'-re-ah], *f.* Meadow-sweet, meadow-wort, queen of the meadows. Spiræa ulmaria.

Ulterior [ool-tay-re-or'], *a.* Ulterior, posterior, farther.
Ulteriormente, *adv.* Farther, beyond, any more or longer.
Ultimado, da [ool-te-mah'-do, dah], *a.* & *pp.* of Ultimar. Ended, finished, ultimate.
Últimamente [ool'-te-mah-men-tay], *adv.* Lastly, finally, just now, ultimately.
Ultimar [ool-te-mar'], *va.* To end, to finish.
Ultimátum [ool-te-mah'-toom], *m.* 1. Ultimatum: used in diplomacy. 2. (Coll.) A final resolution.
Ultimidad [ool-te-me-dahd'], *f.* Ultimity, the last stage.
Ultimo, ma [ool'-te-mo, mah], *a.* 1. Last, latest, hindmost; late, latter. 2. Highly finished, most valuable. 3. Remote; extreme. 4. Final, conclusive, ultimate. *Estar a lo último,* To understand completely. *Estar a lo último* or *en las últimas,* To be expiring. *Por último,* Lastly, finally. *Último entre todos,* Last of all, last among them all. *A últimos de mes, semana, etc.,* At the latter end of the month, week, etc.
Últimas [ool'-te-mas], *f. pl.* Last or end syllables.
Ultra [ool'-trah], *adv.* Besides, moreover: beyond.
Ultracatólico, ca [ool-trah-cah-to'-le-co, cah], *a.* Ultramontane.
Ultrajador, ra [ool-trah-hah-dor', rah], *m.* & *f.* One who outrages or insults.
Ultrajamiento [ool-trah-hah-me-en'-to], *m.* Outrage, affront, injury.
Ultrajar [ool-trah-har'], *va.* 1. To outrage, to offend, to treat injuriously. 2. To despise, to depreciate; to abuse.
Ultraje [ool-trah'-hay], *m.* Outrage, contempt, injurious language, abuse.
Ultrajosamente, *adv.* Outrageously.
Ultrajoso, sa [ool-trah-ho'-so, sah], *a.* Outrageous, overbearing.
Ultramar [ool-trah-mar'], *a.* Ultramarine, foreign.—*m.* (Art) *V.* Ultramarino.
Ultramarino, na [ool-trah-mah-ree'-no, nah], *a.* Ultramarine, from overseas.—*m. pl.* Fancy, imported groceries.
Ultramarino [ool-trah-mah-ree'-no], *m.* Ultramarine, the finest blue, from the lapis lazuli.
Ultramaro [ool-trah-mah'-ro], *m.* Ultramarine blue.
Ultramicroscopio [ool-trah-me-cros-co'-pe-o], *m.* Dark-field microscope.
Ultramoderno, na [ool-trah-mo-der'-no, nah], *a.* Ultramodern.
Ultramontanismo [ool-trah-mon-tah-nees'-mo], *m.* Ultramontanism, the policy of the authority of the Pope over any national church.
Ultramontano, na [ool-trah-mon-tah'-no, nah], *a.* Ultramontane, supporting the policy of the widest power of the Pope over all ecclesiastical matters.
Ultrasónico, ca [ool-trah-so'-ne-co, cah], *a.* Ultrasonic.
Ultrasonido [ool-trah-so-nee'-do], *m.* Ultrasonic, ultrasound.
Ultratumba [ool-trah-toom'-bah], *f.* Beyond the grave, other world.
Ultravioleta [ool-trah-ve-o-lay'-tah], *a.* Ultraviolet.
Ulula [oo'-loo-lah], *f.* (Orn.) Owl. *V.* Autillo.
Ulular [oo-loo-lar'], *vn.* (Prov.) To howl; to cry aloud, to ululate.
Ululato [oo-loo-lah'-to], *m.* Howl, screech, hue and cry.
Umbela [oom-bay'-lah], *f.* Umbel, inflorescence resembling a parasol.
Umbelífero, ra [oom-bay-lee'-fay-ro, rah], *a.* Umbelliferous, in the form of a parasol.—*f. pl.* The parsley family.
Umbilicado, da [oom-be-le-cah'-do, dah], *a.* Navel-shaped; umbilicated.
Umbilical [oom-be-le-cahl'], *a.* Umbilical.
Umbla [oom'-blah], *f.* Umber, fish of the salmon family. Salmo umbla.
Umbra [oom'-brah], *f.* 1. (Obs.) *V.* Sombra. 2. *V.* Umbla.
Umbral [oom-brahl'], *m.* 1. Threshold: lintel, architrave. 2. Beginning, commencement, rudiment. 3. *Umbrales,* (S. Am.) Timber for thresholds.
Umbralar [oom-brah-lar'], *va.* To lay down the ground-timber of a door or gate; to place an architrave.
Umbrático, ca [oom-brah'-te-co, cah], *a.* (Obs.) Umbrageous, shady.
Umbrátil [oom-brah'-teel], *a.* Umbratile; resembling.
Umbría [oom-bree'-ah], *f.* Umbrosity, umbrageousness; a shady place.
Umbrío, bría [oom-bree'-o, ah], *a.* Umbrageous.
Umbroso, sa [oom-bro'-so, sah], *a.* Shady.
Un [oon], *a.* One, a; used for *uno,* but always before words: it is also used occasionally before verbs, to give force to an expression. *Un hombre,* A man.
Una [oo'-nah], *a.* *V.* Uno. *A una,* With one accord.
Unánime [oo-nah'-ne-may], *a.* Unanimous.
Unánimemente, *adv.* Unanimously.
Unanimidad [oo-nah-ne-me-dahd'], *f.* Unanimity.
Unanufa [oo-nah-noo'-fah], *f.* A febrifuge plant which the Indians employ with good result.
Uncia [oon'-the-ah], *f.* 1. An ancient coin. 2. (Obs.) Ounce. *V.* Onza.
Uncial [oon-the-ahl'], *a.* Uncial, said of a form of (capital) letters used in manuscripts from the fourth to the eighth century.
Unciforme [oon-the-for'-may], *a.* Unciform, shaped like a hook.—*n.* Unciform, a bone of the wrist.
Unción [oon-the-on'], *f.* 1. Unction, anointing. 2. Extreme unction. 3. Unction, any thing that excites piety and devotion.—*pl.* Course of salivation, practised in venereal cases.
Uncionario, ria [oon-the-o-nah'-re-o, ah], *a.* Being under salivation.—*m.* Place of salivating.
Uncir [oon-theer'], *va.* To yoke oxen or mules for labour.
Undante [oon-dahn'-tay], *a.* (Poet.) *V.* Undoso.
Undecágono [oon-day-cah'-go-no], *m.* (Math.) Undecagon, a figure having eleven angles and eleven sides.
Undécimo, ma [oon-day'-the-mo, mah], *a.* Eleventh.
Undécuplo, pla [oon-day'-coo-plo, plah], *a.* Eleven times as much.
Undísono, na [oon-dee'-so-no, nah], *a.* Billowy, sounding like waves.
Undívago, ga [oon-dee'-vah-go, gah], *a.* Wavy, moving like the waves.
Undoso, sa [oon-do'-so, sah], *a.* Wavy, undulary, undulatory.
Undulación [oon-doo-lah-the-on'], *f.* Undulation.
Undular [oon-doo-lar'], *vn.* To rise or play in waves, to undulate.
Undulatorio, ria [oon-doo-lah-to'-re-o, ah], *a.* Undulatory.
Ungarina [oon-gah-ree'-nah], *f.* *V.* Anguarina.
Ungido [oon-hee'-do], *m.* Anointed of the Lord, king, sovereign.—*Ungido, da, pp.* of Ungir.
Ungimiento [oon-he-me-en'-to], *m.* Unction, the act of anointing.
Ungir [oon-heer'], *va.* To anoint, to consecrate.
Ungüentario, ria [oon-goo-en-tah'-re-o, ah], *a.* Preparing sweet-scented ointment or perfumes.
Ungüentario, *m.* Perfume-box, in which sweet-scented ointments are kept; anointer.
Ungüento [oon-goo-en'-to], *m.* 1. Unguent, ointment, liniment. 2. Perfume, balsam. *Ungüento de Méjico,* (Coll.) Money, cash. *Ungüento cetrino,* Ointment made of ceruse, camphor, and oil, mixed with citron-juice, used to remove freckles or cicatrices.
Unguiculado, da [oon-ge-coo-lah'-do, dah], *a.* (Zool.) Unguiculate, having claws.
Unguífero, ra [oon-gee'-fay-ro, rah], *a.* Unguiferous, bearing a nail or a claw.
Ungüis [oon'-goo-ees], *m.* The lachrymal bone of the nose, thin like a nail.
Ungulado, da [un-goo-lah'-do, dah], *a.* Ungulate, having hoofs.
Uniarticulado, da [oo-ne-ar-te-coo-lah'-do, dah], *a.* (Biol.) Uniarticulate, single-jointed.
Unible [oo-nee'-blay], *a.* That which may be united.
Únicamente [oo'-ne-cah-men-tay], *adv.* Only, simply.
Unicario [oo-ne-cah'-re-o], *m.* A tree of India, the leaves of which the Malays boil and mix with the betel, which they constantly chew.
Unicaule [oo-ne-cah'-oo-lay], *a.* Having but one stalk: applied to plants.
Unicidad [oo-ne-the-dahd'], *f.* (Phil.) Singularity, distinctive quality.
Único, ca [oo'-ne-co, cah], *a.* Singular, alone, that of which there is but one; single, unique, sole; only; rare, unmatched, unparalleled.
Unicoloro, ra [oo-ne-co-lo'-ro, rah], *a.* Unicolour, of one colour.
Unicornio [oo-ne-cor'-ne-o], *m.* 1. Unicorn. 2. A northern constellation, Monoceros. 3. (Zool.) Narwhal. 4. A mineral rock, yellow, ashy, or gray.
Unidad [oo-ne-dahd'], *f.* 1. Unity. 2. Unit, the root of numbers. 3. (Arith.) A number less than ten. 4. Principle of dramatic unity. 5. Conformity, union. *Unidad termal británica,* (Phy.) BTU. British thermal unit.
Unidamente [oo-ne-dah-men'-tay], *adv.* Jointly, unanimously, conjunctively, compactly, unitedly.
Unificar [oo-ne-fe-car'], *va.* To unite into one.
Uniflorígero, ra [oo-ne-flo-ree'-hay-ro, rah], **Unifloro, ra** [oo-ne-flo'-ro, rah], *a.* One-flowered, uniflorous.
Unifoliado, da [oo-ne-fo-le-ah'-do, dah], *a.* Unifoliate, unifoliar, one-leaved.
Uniformar [oo-ne-for-mar'], *va.* 1. To make uniform. 2. To put into uniform.
Uniforme [oo-ne-for'-may], *a.* Uniform.
Uniforme, *m.* (Mil.) Uniform, regimentals. *Petiuniforme,* (Coll.) The undress of an officer (the military coat only).
Uniformemente, *adv.* Uniformly.
Uniformidad [oo-ne-for-me-dahd'], *f.* Uniformity, resemblance, harmony.
Unigénito [oo-ne-hay'-ne-to], *a.* Only-begotten.
Unilateral [oo-ne-lah-tay-rahl'], *a.* (For.) Unilateral, binding on one party only.
Unión [oo-ne-on'], *f.* 1. Union, conjunction. 2. Conformity, resemblance. 3. Concord, unity. 4. Union, marriage. 5. Composition of ingredients. 6. Combination, physical or chemical union. 7. Consolidation of the lips of a wound. 8. Alliance, confederacy

coalition, consociation. 9. Contiguity; continuity. 10. Incorporation, coherence; sameness, similarity. 11. Hoop, ring. 12. Among jewellers, match, likeness in form and size of one pearl with another. *Unión hipostática*, Hypostatic union of the divine Word and human nature.

Unipara [oo-nee'-pa-rah], *a.* Uniparous, bringing one at a birth.

Unípede [oo-nee'-pay-day], *a.* Uniped, having only one foot.

Unipersonal [oo-ne-per-so-nahl'], *a.* Unipersonal, consisting of one person only.

Unipolar [oo-ne-po-lar'], *a.* Unipolar, having one pole only.

Unipolaridad [oo-ne-po-lah-re-dahd'], *f.* State of a unipolar body; unipolarity.

Unir [oo-neer'], *va.* 1. To join, to unite, to conjoin, to couple, to knit. 2. To join, to mix, to incorporate, to combine, to coalesce. 3. To bind, to tie, to consociate; to confederate. 4. To approach, to bring near; to close. 5. To collect, to aggregate. 6. To conform. 7. To consolidate.—*vr.* 1. To join, to unite, to associate, to be united; to adhere, to concur. 2. To be contiguous. 3. To be united, to be married.

Unisexual [oo-ne-sek-soo-ahl'], *a.* (Bot.) Unisexual, having flowers of one sex only.

Unisón [oo-nee'-son], *m.* Unison, musical consonance.

Unisonancia [oo-ne-so-nahn'-the-ah], *f.* Uniformity of sound, unison; monotony.

Unísono, na [oo-nee'-so-no, nah], *a.* 1. Unison, sounding alone. 2. Having the same sound.

Unísono, *m.* Unison, a single unvaried note.

Unitario [oo-ne-tah'-re-o], *m.* Unitarian, one who rejects the doctrine of the Trinity.—*a.* Advocating political centralization.

Unitarismo [oo-ne-tah-rees'-mo], *m.* 1. The doctrine of those who deny the Trinity. 2. Political centralization.

Unitivo, va [oo-ne-tee'-vo, vah], *a.* Unitive.

Univalvo, va [oo-ne-vahl'-vo, vah], *a.* Univalve: applied to shells.

Universal [oo-ne-ver-sahl'], *a.* Universal, general, œcumenical; learned, well-informed.

Universalidad [oo-ne-ver-sah-le-dahd'], *f.* 1. Universality. 2. Generality of information.

Universalismo [oo-ne-ver-sah-lees'-mo], *m.* Opinion founded on the authority of universal consent.

Universalista [oo-ne-ver-sah-lees'-tah], *com.* One who holds the foregoing opinion.

Universalmente [oo-ne-ver-sal-men'-tay], *adv.* Universally, generally.

Universidad [oo-ne-ver-se-dahd'], *f.* 1. Universality, generality. 2. University. 3. Corporation, community. 4. The whole circle of nature; the vegetable, animal, or mineral kingdom. *Universidades*, (Obs.) Cities, towns, or other corporations.

Universo [oo-ne-verr'-so], *m.* The universe.

Universo, sa [oo-ne-verr'-so, sah], *a.* Universal.

Univocación [oo-ne-vo-cah-the-on'], *f.* Univocation.

Unívocamente [oo-nee'-vo-cah-men-tay], *adv.* Univocally, unanimously.

Univocarse [oo-ne-vo-car'-say], *vr.* To have the same meaning.

Unívoco, ca [oo-nee'-vo-co, cah], *a.* 1. Univocal: used as a substantive. 2. Unanimous; resembling.

Uno [oo'-no], *m.* 1. One. 2. One, any individual; intimate friend, another self. 3. (Math.) Radical, or root of a number.

Uno, na [oo'-no, nah], *a.* 1. One; closely resembling the same; sole, only. 2. It is used relatively or to supply a name, as *Uno dijo*, It was said, or one said. *Uno a otro*, One another, reciprocally. *Todo es uno*, It is all the same; it is foreign to the point. *Uno a uno*, One by one. *Uno por uno*, One and then another: used to mark the distinction more forcibly. *Ya uno, ya otro*, By turns; now one, now another. *Váyase uno por otro*, Let one go for the other. *Una cosa*, A thing undetermined. *Una por una*, At all events, at any rate, certainly. *Una y no más*, Never, no more. *A una*, Jointly, together. *Ser para en una*, To be well matched: applied to a married couple. *Ir a una*, To act of the same accord, or to the same end.

Untador, ra [oon-tah-dor', rah], *m.* & *f.* Anointer, surgeon who administers or performs mercurial frictions.

Untadura [oon-tah-doo'-rah], *f.* 1. Unction, the act of anointing. 2. Unction, ointment.

Untamiento [oon-tah-me-en'-to], *m.* Unction, the act of anointing.

Untar [oon-tar'], *va.* 1. To rub, to anoint, to grease, to oint. 2. To suborn, to bribe. *Untar las manos*, To grease the hands, *i. e.* To bribe. 3. To varnish a piece of painting. *Untar el carro*, (Coll.) To bribe. *Untar el casco, los cascos* or *la cara*, To flatter, to wheedle, to cajole.—*vr.* 1. To be greased with unctuous matter. 2. To embezzle.

Untaza [oon-tah'-thah], *f.* Grease. *V.* Enjundia.

Unto [oon'-to], *m.* 1. Grease, fat of animals. 2. Unguent, ointment. *Unto amarillo, de rana* or *de Méjico*, (Coll.) Bribe, money given to suborn. *Unto de oso*, Bear's grease. *Unto de puerco*, Hog's lard.

Untoso, sa [oon-to'-so, sah], *a.* (Prov.) *V.* Untuoso.

Untuosidad [oon-too-o-se-dahd'], *f.* Unctuosity, greasiness.

Untuoso, sa [oon-too-o'-so, sah], *a.* Unctuous, greasy.

Untura [oon-too'-rah], *f.* 1. Unction, act of anointing. 2. Unction, ointment, matter used in anointing.

Uña [oo'-nyah], *f.* 1. Nail of the fingers and toes. 2. Hoof, claw, or talon of beasts; fang. 3. Pointed hook of instruments. 4. Part of the trunk of a felled tree, which sticks to the root. 5. Crust on sores or wounds. 6. Excrescence or hard tumour on the eyelids. 7. Dexterity in stealing or filching. 8. Curved beak of a scorpion. *Uñas de la gran bestia*, Elk's hoofs. *Uñas de cangrejo*, Crab's claws. *Cara de beato y uñas de gato*, (prov.) The face of a devotee, and the deeds of a rogue. *De uñas a uñas*, From head to foot. *Hincar* or *meter la uña*, To overcharge, to sell at an exorbitant price. *Mostrar las uñas*, To be inexorable. *Mostrar la uña*, To show one's teeth, to discover one's foibles. *Quedarse soplando las uñas*. To bite one's thumbs, to be disappointed. *Tener uñas algún negocio*, (Coll.) To be arduous or extremely difficult: applied to a task or business. *Uña olorosa*, Shell used in pharmacy. *Sacar las uñas*, (Coll.) To avail one's self of every means in a difficulty. *Uña de caballo*, (Bot.) Coltsfoot. Tussilago farfara. *Uña de la caña*, (Naut.) The gooseneck of the tiller. *Uñas del ancla*, The flukes of the anchor. *Ser uña y carne*, To be fast friends.

Uñada [oo-nyah'-dah], *f.* Impression made with the nail, scratch, nip.

Uñarada [oo-nyah-rah'-dah], *f.* Scratch with the nail.

Uñate [oo-nyah'-tay], *m.* 1. (Coll.) Pinching with the nail. 2. *V.* Uñeta.

Uñaza [oo-nyah'-thah], *f. aug.* Large nail.

Uñero [oo-nyay'-ro], *m.* 1. A callous excrescence at the root of a nail. 2. An in-growing nail.

Uñeta [oon-nyay'-tah], *f. dim.* Chuck-farthing, a play among boys.

Uñidura [oo-nye-doo'-rah], *f.* The act of yoking oxen or mules for labour.

Uñir [oo-nyeer'], *va.* (Prov.) To yoke. *V.* Uncir.

Uñita [oo-nyee'-tah], *f. dim.* Little nail.

Uñoso, sa [oo-nyo'-so, sah], *a.* Having long nails or claws.

¡Upa! [oo-pah], *int.* Up, up: a term used to make children get up from the ground. *V.* Aupa.

Upar [oo-par'], *vn.* (Coll.) To endeavour to get up.

Uracho [oo-rah'-cho], *m.* 1. (Anat.) Urachus, a ligamentous cord that terminates in the naval-string. 2. (Obs.) Urethra.

Urania [oo-rah'-ne-ah], *f.* (Myth.) Urania, the muse of astronomy.

Uranio [oo-rah'-ne-o], *m.* (Chem.) Uranium, a rare, heavy metallic element.

Uranita [oo-rah-nee'-tah], *f.* (Chem.) Uranite, autunite; phosphate of uranium and calcium.

Uranografía [oo-rah-no-grah-fee'-ah], *f.* Uranography, ouranography, description of the heavens.

Uranometría [oo-rah-no-may-tree'-ah], *f.* Uranometry, the measurement of the heavens.

Uranómetro [oo-rah-no'-may-tro], *m.* An instrument for measuring heavenly bodies and their movements.

Uranoscopio [oo-rah-nos-co'-pe-o], *m.* Star-gazer, a fish with eyes on the top of the head. Uranoscopus scaber.

Uraño, ña [oo-rah'-nyo, nyah], *a.* Coy, reserved, timid; wild, untamed. *V.* Huraño.

Urari [oo-rah'-re], *m.* Woorare, curare, arrow-poison of South America.

Urato [oo-rah'-to], *m.* 1. (Chem.) Urate, a salt of uric acid. 2. (Agr.) A manure of urine and plaster or earth.

Urbanamente [oor-bah-nah-men'-tay], *adv.* Courteously, politely, complacently.

Urbanidad [oor-bah-ne-dahd'], *f.* Urbanity, civility, politeness, courteousness; gentleness, complaisance.

Urbanización [oor-bah-ne-thah-the-on'], *f.* City planning.

Urbanizar [oor-bah-ne-thar'], *va.* To urbanize.

Urbano, na [oor-bah'-no, nah], *a.* 1. Urban, peculiar to towns or cities. 2. Urbane, courteous, polite, well-bred.

Urca [oor'-cah], *f.* 1. (Naut.) Hooker, dogger; a pink-built and sloop-rigged vessel. 2. (Naut.) Storeship. 3. (Zool.) Species of whale. *V.* Orca.

Urce [oor'-thay], *m.* (Bot.) Heath. *V.* Brezo.

Urceiforme [oor-thay-e-for'-may], *a.* (Bot.) Urceolate, swollen below and contracted at the orifice.

Urchilla [oor-cheel'-lyah], *f.* Archil or orchil, a violet colour, used by dyers.

Urdidera [oor-de-day'-rah]. *f.* 1. Woman who warps. 2. A warping frame.

Urdidor, ra [oor-de-dor', rah], *m.* & *f.* 1. Warper. 2. *m.* Warping-frame, warping-mill.

Urdidura [oor-de-doo'-rah], *f.* The act of warping.

Urdiembre, *f.* (Obs.) *V.* URDIMBRE.

Urdimbre [oor-deem'-bray], *f.* Chain, warp, as opposed to woof.

Urdir [oor-deer'], *va.* 1. To warp, to dispose threads for the loom. 2. To contrive, to scheme.

Urea [oo-ray'-ah], *f.* Urea, a crystallizable substance excreted in the urine.

Urente [oo-ren'-tay], *a.* Hot, burning, parching. (Acad.)

Uremia [oo-ray'-me-ah], *f.* (Med.) Uræmia, a morbid state occasioned by presence of urea in the blood.

Urémico, ca [oo-ray'-me-co, cah], *a.* Uræmic, relating to or affected by uræmia.

Urétera [oo-ray'-tay-rah], *f.* (Anat.) *V.* URETRA.

Urétere [oo-ray'-tay-ray], *m.* (Anat.) Ureter, the duct by which the urine passes from the kidney to the bladder or cloaca.

Urético, ca [oo-ray'-te-co, cah], *a.* Belonging to the urethra.

Uretra [oo-ray'-trah], *f.* (Anat.) Urethra, the canal by which urine is expelled from the bladder.

Uretritis [oo-ray-tree'-tis], *f.* 1. Urethritis, inflammation of the urethra. 2. Gonorrhœa.

Uretrorrea [oo-ray-tror-ray'-ah], *f.* (Med.) Gleet; flux from the urethra.

Uretrótomo [oo-ray-tro'-to-mo], *m.* Urethrotome.

Urgencia [oor-hen'-the-ah], *f.* Urgency, exigence; obligation.

Urgente [oor-hen'-tay], *a.* Urgent, pressing, cogent.

Urgentemente, *adv.* Urgently.

Urgir [oor-heer'], *vn.* To be urgent, to require speedy cure or immediate execution; to be actually obliged; to urge, to press forward.

Úrico, ca [oo'-re-co, cah], *a.* Uric, relating to urine. *Ácido úrico,* Uric acid.

Urinálisis [oo-re-nah'-le-sis], *m.* Urinalysis, urine analysis.

Urinario, ria [oo-re-nah'-re-o, ah], *a.* Urinary.

Urna [oor'-nah], *f.* 1. Urn, in which the ashes of the dead were formerly put. 2. Glass case, in which small statues or images are kept. 3. Urn used by painters and sculptors to represent rivers.

Urnición [oor-ne-the-on'], *f.* (Naut.) Top-timbers. *V.* BARRAGANETE.

Uro [oo'-ro], *m.* A kind of wild ox. Bos urus.

Urogallo [oo-ro-gahl'-lyo], *m.* (Orn.) Bird like a cock.

Uromancia [oo-ro-mahn'-the-ah], *f.* Uromancy, pretended divination by the examination of urine.

Uroscopia [oo-ros-co'-pe-ah], *f.* Uroscopy, methodical inspection of urine for medical diagnosis.

Urraca [oor-rah'-cah], *f.* (Orn.) Magpie. Corvus pica.

Ursa [oor'-sah], *f.* She-bear. *V.* OSA.

Ursulina [oor-soo-lee'-nah], *f.* Nun of the order of St. Ursula.

Urticáceas [oor-te-cah'-thay-as], *f. pl.* & *a.* Urticaceæ, the nettle family, including elms, mulberries, hops, etc.; urticaceous.

Urticaria [oor-te-cah'-re-ah], *f.* Urticaria, nettle-rash, hives; an eruptive skin disease provoking great itching.

Uruca [oo-roo'-cah], *f.* (Bot.) Arnotto. *V.* ACHIOTE.

Uruguayo, ya [oo-roo-goo-ah'-yo, yah], *a.* & *n.* Belonging to, or native of Uruguay.

Usación [oo-sah-the-on'], *f.* Use, the act of using.

Usadamente, *adv.* According to custom.

Usado, da [oo-sah'-do, dah], *a.* & *pp.* of USAR. 1. Used, employed. 2. Used, worn out. 3. Experienced, skilful; fashionable, frequent. 4. Second-hand articles. *Libros usados,* Second-hand books. *Ropa usadá,* Second-hand wearing apparel; cast-off clothing. *Al usado,* (Com. Law) At usance, the time fixed for the payment of bills of exchange.

Usagre [oo-sah'-gray], *m.* A breaking out in the faces of teething children; scald-head, infantile eczema.

Usaje [oo-sah'-hay], *m.* Usage, custom. *V.* USO.

Usanza [oo-sahn'-thah], *f.* Usage, custom.

Usar [oo-sar'], *va.* 1. To use, to make use of; to wear. 2. To use, to accustom, to habituate, to practise. 3. To exercise an employment or office. 4. To enjoy a thing. 5. To communicate, to treat or use familiarly.—*vr.* To use, to be in use or fashion, to be wont.

Usencia [oo-sen'-the-ah], *com.* Your reverence, a contraction of *vuestra reverencia:* an appellation of honour among friars.

Usía [oo-see'-ah], *com.* Your lordship or your ladyship, a contraction of *vuestra señoría.*

Usier [oo-se-err'], *m.* Usher, porter. *V.* UJIER.

Usiría [oo-se-ree'-ah], *com.* *V.* USÍA.

Usitado, da [oo-se-tah'-do, dah], *a.* (Prov.) Frequently used.

Uso [oo'-so], *m.* 1. Use, employment, service. 2. Usufruct; enjoyment. 3. Use, custom, style, fashion, mode. 4. (Com. Law) Usance, a time fixed for the payment of bills of exchange. 5. Office, exercise; wearing, wear. 6. Frequent continuation, constant use, experience; assiduousness. 7. Wear; wear and tear. *Andar al uso,* To conform to the times, to temporize. *A uso* or *al uso,* According to custom. *Al mal uso, quebrarle la pierna,* or *la hueca,* Habit is no excuse for evil practices.

Ustaga [oos-tah'-gah], *f.* (Naut.) Tie.

Usted, [oos-ted'], *com.* You (your worship, your honour), a contraction of *vuestra merced* (*vuesarced, vusted*). a pronoun used in polite style to address all persons of respectability, either orally or by letter. *Usted* and *ustedes* have always been written in abbreviation, thus: *Vm., Vms., Vmd., Vmds.* At present *usted* is represented by *V.* or *Vd.*, and *ustedes* (*pl.*) by *VV.* or *Vds.*, and often printed in full. The loose articulation of the *d* frequently causes it to become inaudible, particularly in Spanish America; so that *usted* sounds as if *usté.*

Ustión [oos-te-on'], *f.* Ustion, the act of making medical preparations by burning; exustion.

Ustorio [oos-to'-re-o], *a.* Burning. *V.* ESPEJO USTORIO.

Usual [oo-soo-ahl'], *a.* 1. Usual, customary, ordinary, general. 2. Tractable, social. *Año usual,* Current year.

Usualmente, *adv.* Usually.

Usuario, ria [oo-soo-ah'-re-o, ah], *a.* (Law) Having the sole use of a thing.

Usucapión [oo-soo-cah-pe-on'], *f.* (Law) Usucapion or usucaption.

Usucapir [oo-soo-cah-peer'], *va.* (Law) To acquire a right of property in any thing, by possession for a specified time.

Usufructo [oo-soo-frooc'-to], *m.* Usufruct, profit, advantage; enjoyment.

Usufructuar [oo-soo-frooc-too-ar'], *va.* 1. To enjoy the usufruct of any thing. 2. To render productive or fruitful.

Usufructuario, ria [oo-soo-frooc-too-ah'-re-o, ah], *a.* Possessing the usufruct of a thing.

Usura [oo-soo'-rah], *f.* 1. Interest, payment for the use of money lent. 2. Gain, profit. 3. Usury.

Usurar [oo-soo-rar'], *vn.* *V.* USUREAR.

Usurariamente, *adv.* Usuriously, interestedly.

Usurario, ria [oo-soo-rah'-re-o, ah], *a.* Usurious, practising usury.

Usurear [oo-soo-ray-ar'], *vn.* 1. To practise usury, to lend or to borrow money on interest. 2. To reap great benefit or advantage.

Usurero, ra [oo-soo-ray'-ro, rah], *m.* & *f.* Usurer, money-lender, griper.

Usurero, ra, *a.* (Obs.) Usurious.

Usurpación [oo-soor-pah-the-on'], *f.* Usurpation.

Usurpador, ra [oo-soor-pah-dor', rah], *m.* & *f.* Usurper.

Usurpar [oo-soor-par'], *va.* 1. To usurp; to assume another's office, dignity, or employment; to grasp. 2. To make use of a word instead of another, or in another sense.

Ut [oot], *m.* (Obs.) Ut, now called do, the first note of the musical scale.

Utensilio [oo-ten-see'-le-o], *m.* Utensil; tool, device, contrivance. *Utensilios,* (1) (Mil.) Articles which the tenant of a house is to furnish the soldier quartered with him. (2) Implements.

Uteral, *a.* (Obs.) *V.* UTERINO.

Uterino, na [oo-tay-ree'-no, nah], *a.* 1. Uterine, belonging to the womb. 2. Uterine, born of the same mother.

Útero [oo'-tay-ro], *m.* Uterus, womb.

Uteromania [oo-tay-ro-mah-nee'-ah], *f.* Nymphomania.

Útil [oo'-teel], *a.* Useful, profitable; commodious.

Útil, *m.* *V.* UTILIDAD.—*pl.* Utensils.

Utilidad [oo-te-le-dahd'], *f.* 1. Usefulness, utility. 2. Profit. *Utilidad neta,* Net profit.

Utilitario, ria [oo-te-le-tah'-re-o, ah], *a.* Utilitarian.

Utilitarismo [oo-te-le-tah-rees'-mo], *m.* Utilitarianism.

Utilizable [oo-te-le-thah'-blay], *a.* Usable, practicable for use.

Utilizar [oo-te-le-thar'], *vn.* To be useful.—*va.* To reap benefit or profit; to take advantage of or profit by.—*vr.* To interest one's self in a business.

Útilmente, *adv.* Usefully.

Utopia [oo-to'-pe-ah], *f.* *V.* UTOPÍA.

Utopía [oo-to-pee'-ah], *f.* 1. Utopia, an imaginary island having a perfect social and political system. 2. Plan or system which is charming in theory, but unrealizable in practice.

Utópico, ca [oo-to'-pe-co, cah], *a.* Utopian, chimerically good, ideal.

Utopista [oo-to-pees'-tah], *m.* 1. A dreamer. 2. Utopian schemer.

Utrero, ra [oo-tray'-ro, rah], *m.* & *f.* Bull or heifer between two and three years old.

Ut retro [oot ray'-tro], *adv.* As above.

Ut supra [oot soo'-prah], *adv.* (Lat.) As above.

Uva [oo'-vah], *f.* 1. Grape. 2. Tippler. *Hecho una uva,* Very drunk. 3. Wart on the eyelid. 4. Fruit of the barberry-bush. 5. Tumour on the epiglottis. *Uva de Corinto,* (Bot.) Currants. *Uva pasa,* Raisins. *Uva de gato* or *canella,* White stone-crop, Sedum album. *Uva espín, espina* or *crespa,* Goose-berry *Uva de mar,* Shrubby horsetail. Ephedria distachia. *Uva lupina* or *vérga*, Wolf-bane. Aconitum Lycoctonum. *Uva de raposa*, Night-shade. Solanum nigrum. *Uva tamínea* or *taminia*, Lousewort.—*pl.* Bunch of grapes. *Conocer las uvas de su majuelo*, To understand his own business.

Uvada [oo-vah'-dah], *f.* 1. Abundance of grapes. 2. (Prov.) Kind of land-measure.

Uvaguemaestre [oo-vah-gay-mah-es'-tray], *m.* (Mil. Obs.) Officer who commanded the train of baggage-wagons.

Uval [oo-vahl'], *a.* Belonging to grapes.

Uvate [oo-vah'-tay], *m.* Conserve of grapes.

Uvayema [oo-vah-yay'-mah], *f.* Species of wild vine.

Úvea [oo'-vay-ah], *f.* Uvea, the outermost coat of the eye.

Uvero, ra [oo-vay'-ro, rah], *m. & f.* Retailer of grapes.

Uviforme [oo-ve-for'-may], *a.* Shaped like a bunch of grapes.

Uvula [oo'-voo-lah], *f.* (Anat.) Uvula.

Uxoricida [ook-so-re-thee'-dah], *m.* Uxoricide, wife-murderer.

Uzas [oo'-thas], *f.* Kind of Brazilian crab.

Uyama [oo-yah'-mah], *f.* A species of calabash of Guayana, a province of Venezuela.

V

V [vay], *f.* In the Castilian alphabet *V* is the twenty-fifth letter in order, and should be pronounced as in English. As the Spaniards press very lightly their lower lips against the upper teeth in pronouncing this letter, it frequently sounds like *b*; especially at the start of words. *V.* was very often used in manuscript instead of the capital *U;* as, *Vn día* for *Un día. V.*, or *Vd.*, stands as a contraction for *Usted*, (*sing.*) You, and *VV.*, or *Vds.*, for *Ustedes*, (*pl.*) You (formerly *Vm. Vmd.*, *Vms. Vmds.*); also, for *vuestra, vuestras*; as, V. M., *vuestra majestad*, Your majesty; V. S., *Usía* (*vuestra señoría*), Your lordship or ladyship, etc. *V* in Roman numerals stands for five, for verb in grammar, for wind (*viento*) in meteorology, and volume in mathematical calculations. *V doble*, W: used only in words of foreign extraction.

Vaca [vah'-cah], *f.* 1. Cow. *Vaca de leche*, Milch-cow. 2. Beef. *Solomo de vaca*, Sirloin of beef. 3. (Prov.) Joint stock of two partners in gambling. 4. A leather case for luggage on top of coaches. 5. Tanned leather. *Vaca de la boda*, He to whom every one applies in distress; laughing-stock. *Vaca de San Antón*, (Ent.) Lady-bird, lady-cow. Coccinella. *Vaca marina*, Sea-cow. *V.* MANATÍ. *Más vale vaca en paz, que pollos con agraz*, Simple fare in peace is better than wealth with care and anxiety. *Quien come la vaca del rey, a cien años paga los huesos*, He who steals from a powerful man will suffer in the end, though a hundred years pass first.

Vacación [vah-cah-the-on'], *f.* Vacation, intermission; recess of courts of law and public boards.—*pl.* Holidays.

Vacada [vah-cah'-dah], *f.* Drove of cows.

Vacancia [vah-cahn'-the-ah], *f.* Vacancy.

Vacante [vah-cahn'-tay], *a.* Vacant, disengaged.—*f.* 1. Vacancy of a post or employment. 2. Vacation, time unengaged. 3. Rent fallen due during the vacancy of a benefice.

Vacar [vah-car'], *vn.* 1. To cease, to stop; to be vacant. 2. To devote one's self to a particular thing; to follow a business.—*va.* To vacate an office.

Vacarí [vah-cah-ree'], *a.* Leathern: said of a leather shield, etc.

Vacatura, *f.* (Obs.) Vacancy.

Vácceo, cea [vahc'-thay-o, ah], *a.* Belonging to a region of ancient Spain, along the banks of the Douro.

Vaciadero [vah-the-ah-day'-ro], *m.* Drain, sink.

Vaciadizo, za [vah-the-ah-dee'-tho, thah], *a.* Cast, moulded.

Vaciado [vah-the-ah'-do], *m.* 1. Form or image, moulded or cast in plaster of Paris or wax; excavation. 2. (Arch.) Cavity in a pedestal below its ornamental mouldings.—*Vaciado, da, pp.* of VACIAR.

Vaciador [vah-the-ah-dor'], *m.* Moulder, one who casts or moulds; one who evacuates, hollows, or makes empty.

Vaciamiento [vah-the-ah-me-en'-to], *m.* 1. Casting, moulding; evacuating, hollowing. 2. *V.* VACÍO.

Vaciar [vah-the-ar'], *va.* 1. To empty, to evacuate, to exhaust, to clear. *Vaciar el costal*, To give vent to one's feelings; to divulge the whole secret. 2. To mould, to form, to model. 3. To fall into, to discharge itself: applied to rivers. 4. (Arch.) To excavate. 5. To explain at large.—*vn.* 1. To fall, to decrease: applied to waters. 2. Not to make a good use of one's time. 3. To fade, to lose colour or lustre.—*vr.* 1. To be spilt: applied to liquors. 2. To divulge what should be kept secret. 3. To be empty or vacant. *Vaciarse como costal*, To talk too much.

Vaciedad [va-the-ay-dahd'], *f.* 1. (Obs.) Emptiness, vacuity. 2. Emptiness, frothiness. 3. An inconsiderate or arrogant speech; obscene language.

Vaciero [vah-the-ay'-ro], *m.* Shepherd whose sheep are all dry or barren.

Vacilación [vah-the-lah-the-on'], *f.* 1. Vacillation, reeling, staggering. 2. Perplexity, irresolution.

Vacilante [vah-the-lahn'-tay], *pa. & a.* Vacillating; irresolute; unstable.

Vacilar [vah-the-lar'], *vn.* To vacillate, to waver, to fluctuate; to be perplexed; to wander or be confused; to reel, to stagger.

Vacío, cía [vah-thee'-o, ah], *a.* 1. Void, empty; vacuous. 2. Unoccupied, disengaged; idle; fruitless. 3. Concave, hollow. 4. Defective, deficient. 5. Vain, arrogant, presumptuous. 6. Not with young: applied to cattle. 7. Unloaded or empty: applied to horses, mules, carts, etc. 8. Uninhabited. 9. Unoccupied by people. *Tacho al vacío*, Vacuum-pan. *Freno al vacío*, Vacuum-brake. *Filtro al vacío*, Vacuum-filter. *Bomba atmosférica de vacío*, Vacuum-pump.

Vacío, *m.* 1. Void, empty space, vacuum, aperture. 2. Mould for casting metal. 3. Vacancy, place or employment unfilled. 4. Concavity, hollowness. 5. Blank space in a book or writing. 6. (Com.) Ullage of a cask or other vessel; wantage. 7. Spanish step in dancing. 8. Animal not with young. 9. Vacuity, cavity. 10. Flank of animals. *De vacío*, Empty; unemployed. *En vacío*, In vacuo; (Mus.) vibrating when not touched.

Vacisco [vah-thees'-co], *m.* Fragment in quicksilver mines.

Vaco, ca [vah'-co, cah], *a.* Vacant.

Vacuidad [vah-coo-e-dahd'], *f.* Vacuity, emptiness.

Vacuista [vah-coo-ees'-tah], *m.* Vacuist, a philosopher that holds a vacuum.

Vacuna [vah-coo'-nah], *f.* 1. Vaccine. 2. Vaccination, shot. *Vacuna antidiftérica*, Diphtheria shot. *Vacuna contra la viruela*, Smallpox shot. *Vacuna Salk*, Salk vaccine.

Vacunación [vah-coo-nah-the-on'], *f.* Vaccination.

Vacunador [vah-coo-nah-dor'], *m.* Vaccinator.

Vacunar [vah-coo-nar'], *va.* To vaccinate.

Vacuno, na [vah-coo'-no, nah], *a.* Belonging to cattle, vaccine, bovine.

Vacuo, a [vah'-coo-o, ah], *a.* (Obs.) Unoccupied. *V.* VACÍO and VACANTE.

Vacuo, *m.* Vacuum.

Vade [vah'-day], *m.* *V.* VADEMÉCUM.

Vadeable [vah-day-ah'-blay], *a.* 1. Fordable. 2. (Met.) Conquerable, superable.

Vadeador, ra [vah-day-ah-dor', rah], *a.* Wading.

Vadeamiento [vah-day-ah-me-en'-to], *m.* Act of fording.

Vadear [vah-day-ar'], *va.* 1. To wade, to ford. 2. To conquer, to surmount. 3. To sound, to try, to examine.—*vr.* To conduct one's self.

Vademécum [vah'-day-may'-coom], *m.* 1. A book, a case, or other portable and useful thing, which is habitually carried on the person. 2. Portfolio in which school children keep their papers.

Vadera [vah-day'-rah], *f.* Ford, a shallow part of a river.

¡Vade retro! [vah'-day ray'-tro], *adv. expres.* Get you gone! away!

Vadiano, na [vah-de-ah'-no, nah], *a.* Anthropomorphite, ascribing human attributes to a deity.

Vado [vah'-do], *m.* 1. Ford, a broad, shallow, level part of a river. 2. Expedient; resource. *No hallar vado*, To be at a loss how to act. *Al vado o a la puente*, Choose one way or the other; either this or that.

Vadoso, sa [vah-do'-so, sah], *a.* Shoaly, shallow.

Vafe [vah'-fay], *m.* (Prov.) Bold stroke or undertaking.

Vagabundo, da [vah-gah-boon'-do, dah], *a. & m. & f.* Vagabond, idle vagrant, loitering about; having no fixed abode.

Vagabundear [vah-gah-boon-day-ar'], *vn.* (Coll.) To rove or loiter about, to act the vagrant.

Vagamente, *adv.* In a vague, unsettled manner.

Vagamundear, *vn.* *V.* VAGABUNDEAR.

Vagamundo, da, *a.* *V.* VAGABUNDO.

Vagancia [vah-gahn'-the-ah], *f.* Vagrancy.

Vagante [vah-gahn'-tay], *pa.* Vagrant.

Vagar [vah-gar'], *vn.* 1. To rove or loiter about; to wander, to range. 2. To be at leisure, to be idle. 3. To revolve in the mind. 4. To be loose and irregular.

Vagar [vah-gar'], *m.* 1. Leisure. 2 Slowness, indolence. *De vagar*, Slowly.

Vagarosamente, *adv.* Vagrantly.

Vagaroso, sa [vah-gah-ro'-so, sah], *a.* 1. Errant, vagrant. 2. (Obs.) Slothful.

Vagido [vah-hee'-do], *m.* Cry of a child; a convulsive sob.

Vagina [vah-hee'-nah], *f.* (Anat.) Vagina.

Vaginal [vah-he-nahl'], *a.* Vaginal, relating to the vagina.

Vaginante [vah-he-nahn'-tay], *a.* (Zool.) Sheathing, used of the upper wings of coleoptera and orthoptera.

Vaginitis [vah-he-nee'-tis], *f.* Vaginitis, inflammation of the vagina.
Vago, ga [vah'-go, gah], *a.* 1. Errant, vagrant. 2. Restless, uneasy. 3. Vague, wavering, fluctuating, unsettled; lax, loose. 4. *V.* VACO. *Voz vaga,* A vague report. *En vago,* Unsteadily, unfirmly; unsuccessfully, in vain, vaguely.
Vago [vah'-go], *m.* 1. (Prov.) Uncultivated plot of ground. 2. Vagabond.
Vagón [vah-gone'], *m.* A railway coach or car for passengers or merchandise. (Eng. wagon.) *Vagón-cama,* Sleeping-car. *Vagón-cuadra,* Cattle-van. *Vagón-jaula,* Latticed van or wagon. *Vagón de borde alto o bajo,* A truck.
Vagón-comedor [vah-gone'-co-may-dor'], *m.* (r.w.) Dining car.
Vagón-dormitorio [vah-gone'-dor-me-toh'-re-o], *m.* (r.w.) Pullman, sleeping car.
Vagoneta [vah-go-nay'-tah], *f.* A small open car for transportation.
Vagón-salón [vah-gone'-sah-lone'], *m.* (r.w.) Parlor car.
Vaguada [vah-goo-ah'-dah], *f.* 1. Waterway. 2. Line of the channel; a line which marks the course of the water in rivers.
Vagueación [vah-gay-ah-the-on'], *f.* Restlessness, levity, unsteadiness; flight of fancy.
Vaguedad [vah-gay-dahd'], *f.* Levity, inconstancy.
Vaguido [vah-gee'-do], *m.* Giddiness, the state of being giddy.
Vahar [vah-ar'], *vn.* To exhale, to emit steam or vapour.
Vaharada [vah-ah-rah'-dah], *f.* The act of emitting steam, vapour, or breath.
Vaharera [vah-ah-ray'-rah], *f.* 1. (Med.) Thrush, a disease of sucking children. 2. (Prov.) An unripe melon.
Vaharina [vah-ah-ree'-nah], *f.* (Coll.) Steam, vapour, mist.
Vahear [vah-ay-ar'], *vn.* To exhale, to emit steam or vapour.
Vahido [vah-ee'-do], *m.* Vertigo, giddiness.
Vaho [vah'-o], *m.* Steam, vapour.
Vaida [vah-ee'-dah], *f.* (Arch.) Vault or arch cut into four vertical planes.
Vaina [vah'-e-nah], *f.* 1. Scabbard of a sword. 2. Knife or scissors case. 3. Pod, capsule, husk, hull, cod. 4. (Naut.) Bolt-rope tabling, to which the bolt-rope is fastened. *Vaina abierta,* Scabbard of a large sword formerly used, which covered only one-third of it, in order to be easily drawn. *De vaina abierta,* Hastily, boldly.
Vainazas [vah-e-nah'-thas], *m.* (Coll.) A humdrum, dull, or dronish person.
Vainero [vah-e-nay'-ro], *m.* Scabbard-maker.
Vainica [vah-e-nee'-cah], *f.* 1. (Dim.) A small pod or husk. 2. Hemstitch.
Vainilla [vah-e-neel'-lyah], *f.* 1. (Dim.) A small pod or husk. 2. (Bot.) Vanilla; vanilloes. Vanilla aromatica et al. 3. Fruit of this plant. 4. A heliotrope which grows in America.
Vaivén [vah-e-ven'], *m.* 1. Fluctuation, vibration. (Mech.) Alternating movement. 2. Unsteadiness, inconstancy, vacillation. 3. Giddiness. 4. Risk, danger. 5. (Naut.) Line, cord, or rope, of different thickness.
Vajilla [vah-heel'-lyah], *f.* Table-service of dishes, plates, etc.
Val [vahl], *m.* 1. Vale, dale, valley: a contraction of *valle.* 2. (Prov.) Sewer, drain, sink. 3. Ancient contraction of *vale,* from *valer.*
Valaco, ca [vah-lah'-co, cah], *a.* 1. Wallachian. 2. The language spoken in Wallachia, a Romance tongue.
Valais [vah-lah'-ees], *m.* Lumber. (Acad.)
Valar [vah-lar'], *a.* Relating to a rampart, inclosure, or hedge.
Vale [vah'-lay], *m.* 1. Farewell, adieu; valediction. 2. Bond or promissory note. *Vale real* or *vales reales,* Government bonds, exchequer bills. 3. Note of pardon given to school-boys by the master. 4. First or single hand at cards. *El último vale,* The last farewell; the point of death.
Valedero, ra [vah-lay-day'-ro, rah], *a.* Valid, efficacious, binding.
Valedor, ra [vah-lay-dor', rah], *m. & f.* Protector, defender.
Valencia [vah-len'-the-ah], *f.* (Chem.) Valence.
Valenciano, na [vah-len-the-ah'-no, nah], *a.* Valencian, of Valencia.
Valentacho [vah-len-tah'-cho], *m.* Hector, bully, braggadocio.
Valentía [vah-len-tee'-ah], *f.* 1. Valour, courage, gallantry, bravery, manliness. 2. Feat, heroic exploit. 3. Brag, boast. 4. Fire of imagination. 5. (Art) Uncommon dexterity in imitating nature. 6. An extraordinary or vigorous effort. 7. A public place where mended shoes were anciently sold in Madrid. *Hambre y valentía,* Misery and ostentation, or pride and poverty. *Pisar de valentía,* To strut.
Valentísimo, ma [vah-len-tee'-se-mo, mah], *a. sup.* Most valiant; perfect in an art or science.
Valentón [vah-len-tone'], *m.* Braggadocio, hector.
Valentón, na [vah-len-tone', nah], *a.* Arrogant, vainglorious.
Valentonada, Valentona [vah-len-to-nah'-dah], *f.* Brag, boast.
Valentonazo [vah-len-to-nah'-tho], *m. aug.* Bully, boaster. *V.* VALENTÓN.
Valentoncillo, lla [vah-len-ton-theel'-lyo, lyah], *a. dim.* A little vain or presumptuous.
Valeo [vah-lay'-o], *m.* 1. Round mat; shaggy mat. 2. Rug or plat of bass.
Valer [vah-lerr'], *va.* 1. To protect, to defend, to favour, to patronize. 2. To yield, to produce fruits or rent. 3. To equal, to be equivalent to. 4. To amount to (in numbers and accounts). 5. To bear a certain price, to be worth. —*vn.* 1. To be valuable, meritorious, deserving. 2. To prevail, to avail. 3. To serve as an asylum or refuge. 4. To be valid or binding; to be a head or have authority; to have power, to be able; to hold. 5. To have course, to be current; also to be worth: applied to coins. 6. To be in favour, to have influence or interest.—*vr.* 1. To employ, to make use of. 2. To avail one's self of, to have recourse to. *¡Válgate Dios!* Heaven bless or pardon you! exclamation of surprise or disapprobation, according to circumstances. *¡Válgame Dios!* Good God! bless me! expression of surprise or disgust. *Más vale* or *más valiera,* It is better, it would be better. *No valer un diablo,* (Coll.) To be very despicable and worth nothing. *Más vale algo que nada,* Something is better than nothing. *Más vale tarde que nunca,* Better late than never. *Vale lo que pesa,* He is worth his weight in gold. *Valga la que valiere,* Happen what may. *Más vale maña que fuerza,* (prov.) Wiles often do what force cannot. *No poderse valer con alguno,* Not to be able to manage a person. *Vale la pena de,* It is worth while, worth the trouble of. *Eso vale tanto como decir,* That is as much as to say. *Más vale vergüenza en cara que mancilla en corazón,* Better the shame of confession than remorse in concealing. *Hacer valer,* To give authority or support. *No poderse valer,* To be incapable; not to know how to help one's self.
Valer [vah-lerr'], *m.* Value. *Menos valer,* 1. Loss of the privileges of nobility or other rights. 2. (Met.) Mark of infamy, disgrace, or disrespect.
Valeriana [vah-lay-re-ah'-nah], *f.* (Bot.) Valerian. Valeriana. *Valeriana griega,* Jacob's-ladder or Greek valerian. Polemenium cæluleum.
Valerosamente [vah-lay-ro-sah-men'-tay], *adv.* Valiantly, courageously.
Valeroso, sa [vah-lay-ro'-so, sah], *a.* 1. Valiant, brave, courageous, gallant, heroic. 2. Strong, active; powerful.
Valetudinario, ria [vah-lay-too-de-nah'-re-o, ah], *a.* Valetudinarian, valetudinary, infirm of health.
(*Yo valgo, yo valga, valdré. V.* VALER.)
Valhala [val-hah'-lah], *f.* Walhalla, the paradise of Odin, in Scandinavian mythology. (In this word the h is aspirated. Acad.)
Vali [vah-lee'], *m.* Governor of a Mussulman province or territory.
Valía [vah-lee'-ah], *f.* Appraisement, valuation. 2. Credit, favour, use. 3. Party, faction. *A las valías,* At the highest price which a commodity fetches in the course of a year.
Validable [vah-le-dah'-blay], *a.* Justifiable, ratifiable.
Validación [vah-le-dah-the-on'], *f.* Validity of an act.
Válidamente [vah'-le-dah-men-tay], *adv.* In a solid or binding manner.
Validar [vah-le-dar'], *va.* To give validity, to render firm or binding.
Validez [vah-le-deth'], *f.* Validity, stability.
Válido, da [vah'-le-do, dah], *a.* 1. Valid, firm, prevalent, weighty, conclusive. 2. Binding, obligatory.
Valido, da [vah-lee'-do, dah], *a. & pp.* of VALER. 1. Availing of, relying upon, confident of. *Valido del favor,* Confident of favour. 2. Favoured, regarded with peculiar kindness; accepted, esteemed. 3. Universally respected. 4. Strong, powerful.
Valido [vah-lee'-do], *m.* A favourite of a sovereign; a court minion.
Valiente [vah-le-en'-tay], *a.* 1. Strong, robust, vigorous, powerful. 2. Valiant, spirited, brave, courageous, active, strenuous; efficacious, valid. 3. Eminent, excellent. 4. (Coll.) Great, excessive. *Hace un valiente frío,* It is excessively cold. 5. *V.* VALENTÓN.
Valiente [vah-le-en'-tay], *m.* 1. Bully, hector, braggadocio. 2. Gallant.
Valientemente, *adv.* 1. Vigorously, strongly. 2. Valiantly, courageously, strenuously, manfully. 3. Superabundantly, excessively. 4. Elegantly, with propriety.
Valija [vah-lee'-hah], *f.* 1. Valise, grip sack. 2. Mail-bag. 3. The post, mail.
Valijero [vah-le-hay'-ro], *m.* Postal clerk who distributes mail to towns along a route.
Valimiento [vah-le-me-en'-to], *m.* 1. Use, the act of using or employing. 2. Utility, benefit, advantage. 3. A temporary or gratuitous contribution. 4. Interest, favour, protection, support; good graces.
Valioso, sa [vah-le-o'-so, sah], *a.* 1. Very valuable, highly esteemed, of great influence. 2. Rich, wealthy.
Valisoletano, na [vah-le-so-lay-tah'-no, nah], *a.* Native of or belonging to Valladolid.
Valiza [vah-lee'-thah], *f.* (Naut.) Beacon, buoy, pointing out sandbanks

or shoals. *Valiza terrestre*, Landmark (fr. Anglo-Sax. *balye*, cask).

Valizaje [vah-le-thah'-hay], *m.* Duties paid by the shipping in some ports, towards keeping in repair the beacons and buoys.

Valón, na [vah-lone', nah], *a.* Walloon, belonging to southern provinces of Belgium. *A la valona*, In the Walloon style.

Valones [vah-lo'-nes], *m. pl.* A sort of trousers or wide breeches, formerly worn in Spain.

Valor [vah-lor'], *m.* 1. Value, price; equivalency. 2. Validity, force. 3. Activity, power. 4. Valour, fortitude, courage, manliness. 5. Income, revenue. 6. Surety, firmness of an act. *Este contrato será entonces de ningún valor ni efecto*, (Law) This agreement will then be void and null. *Relaciones de valores*, Account of rates.

Valoración, *f.* *V.* VALUACIÓN.

Valorar [vah-lo-rar'], *v.* To value, to evaluate, to appraise.

Valoría [vah-lo-ree'-ah], *f.* Value, price, worth.

Valorizar [vah-lo-re-thar'], *va.* (Mex.) *V.* VALORAR.

Valquiria [val-kee'-re-ah], *f.* Valkyr, valkyrie, one of the maidens who serve in Walhalla, whence they are sent by Odin to point out those to be slain in battle and bear their souls to Walhalla.

Vals [vahls], *m.* Waltz.

Valsar [val-sar'], *vn.* To waltz.

Valúa, *f.* (Prov. Murcia) *V.* VALÍA.

Valuación [vah-loo-ah-the-on'], *f.* Appraisement, valuation.

Valuador, ra [vah-loo-ah-dor', rah], *m. & f.* Valuer, appraiser.

Valva [vahl'-vah], *f.* 1. (Zool.) Valve, shell of mollusks. 2. (Bot.) Valve, a portion of the pericarp of plants.

Valuar [vah-loo-ar'], *va.* To rate, to value, to appraise.

Valvasor [val-vah-sor'], *m.* Gentleman, nobleman, hidalgo.

Válvula [vahl'-voo-lah], *f.* 1. Valve, as in the piston of a pump. 2. An aperture, opening. *Válvula de radio*, Radio tube. *Válvula de rayos catódicos*, Cathode-ray tube.

Valvulado, da [val-voo-lah'-do, dah], *a.* (Bot.) Valvate, provided with a valve.

Valvular [val-voo-lar'], *a.* Valvular, having many valves.

Valvulilla [val-voo-leel'-lyah], *f. dim.* Valvule.

Valla [vahl'-lyah], *f.* 1. Intrenchment; ground surrounded with palisadoes. 2. Barrier, barricade. *Romper* or *saltar la valla*, To be foremost in undertaking a difficult affair.

Valladar [val-lyah-dar'], *m.* 1. (Prov.) *V.* VALLADO. 2. Obstacle.

Valladear [val-lyah-day-ar'], *va.* To inclose with stakes, pales, or palisadoes. *V.* VALLAR.

Vallado [val-lyah'-do], *m.* Inclosure with stakes or palisadoes, paling, fence, lock.—*Vallado, da, pp.* of VALLAR.

Vallar [val-lyar'], *va.* To fence, to hedge, to inclose with pales or stakes.

Valle [vah'-lyay], *m.* 1. Vale, dale valley. 2. The whole number of villages, places, and cottages situated within a district or jurisdiction. *Hasta el valle de Josafat*, Unto the valley of Jehoshaphat, or until the day of judgment.

Vallejo [val-lyay'-ho], *m. dim.* A small valley. *Quien no aprieta en vallejo, no aprieta en concejo*, A poor man wields small influence.

Vallejuelo [val-lyay-hoo-ay'-lo], *m. dim.* of VALLEJO.

Vallico [val-lyee'-co], *m.* (Bot.) Ray-grass. Lolium perenne. *V.* JOYO.

¡**Vamos**! [vah'-mose], *int.* (Coll.) Well, come! Well, go on! come.

Vampiro [vam-pee'-ro], *m.* 1. Ghoul. 2. Vampire bat. 3. Usurer, miser, skinflint.

Vanadiato [vah-nah-de-ah'-to], *m.* (Chem.) Vanadate, a salt of vanadic acid.

Vanádico, ca [vah-nah'-de-co, cah], *a.* Vanadic, of or derived from vanadium.

Vanadio [vah-nah'-de-o], *m.* Vanadium, a white metal, not ductile, soluble in nitric acid, but resisting sulphuric and hydrochloric acids.

Vanagloria [vah-nah-glo'-re-ah], *f.* Vaingloriousness, ostentatiousness, boast.

Vanagloriarse [vah-nah-glo-re-ar'-say], *vr.* To be vainglorious, to boast of, to flourish.

Vanagloriosamente, *adv.* Vaingloriously.

Vanaglorioso, sa [vah-nah-glo-re-o'-so, sah], *a.* Vainglorious, conceited, ostentatious.

Vanamente [vah-nah-men'-tay], *adv.* 1. Vainly, uselessly. 2. Superstitiously. 3. Without foundation. 4. Arrogantly, presumptuously, proudly; frivolously, idly.

Vandalismo [van-dah-lees'-mo], *m.* Vandalism.

Vándalo, la [vahn'-dah-lo, lah], *m. & f.* Vandal.

Vandálico, ca [van-dah'-le-co, cah], *a.* Vandalic.

Vandola [van-do'-lah], *f.* (Naut.) Jury-mast. *En vandolas*, Under jury-masts.

Vanear [vah-nay-ar'], *vn.* To talk nonsense.

Vanesa [vah-nay'-sah], *f.* Vanessa, a genus of butterflies.

Vaneta [vah-nay'-tah], *f.* (Her.) Scallop.

Vanguardia [van-goo-ar'-de-ah], *f.* Vanguard, van.

Vanidad [vah-ne-dahd'], *f.* 1. Vanity. 2. Ostentation, vain parade. 3. Nonsense, unmeaning speech. 4. Inanity, levity, conceit; foppishness; flirtation. 5. Illusion, phantom. *Hacer vanidad*, To boast of any thing.

Vanidoso, sa [vah-ne-do'-so, sah], *a.* Vain, showy, foppish, haughty.

Vanilocuencia [vah-ne-lo-coo-en'-the-ah], *f.* Verbosity, pomposity.

Vanilocuo, cua [vah-nee'-lo-coo-o, ah], *a.* Talking foolishly.

Vaniloquio [vah-ne-lo'-ke-o], *m.* Useless talk.

Vanistorio [vah-nis-to'-re-o], *m.* (Coll.) Ridiculous or affected vanity.

Vano, na [vah'-no, nah], *a.* 1. Vain, wanting solidity. 2. Inane, empty, fallacious. 3. Useless, frivolous. 4. Arrogant, haughty, presumptuous, conceited, foppish. 5. Insubstantial, groundless, futile. *En vano*, In vain, unnecessarily, uselessly, wantonly.

Vano [vah'-no], *m.* (Arch.) Vacuum in a wall, as the windows, doors, etc.

Vapor [vah-pore'], *m.* 1. Vapour, steam, breath. 2. Exhalation, mist. 3. Vertigo, faintness. 4. A steamboat, steamer.—*pl.* Vapours, a hysterical attack.

Vaporable [vah-po-rah'-blay], *a.* Vaporous, fumy, exhalable.

Vaporación [va-po-rah-the-on'], *f.* Evaporation.

Vaporar, Vaporear, Vaporizar [vah-po-rar', ray-ar', vah-po-re-thar'], *va.* *V.* EVAPORAR.

Vaporizador [vah-po-re-thah-dor'], *m.* Vaporizer, sprayer.

Vaporoso, sa [vah-po-ro'-so, sah], *a.* Vaporous, fumy, vapourish.

Vapulación [vah-poo-lah-the-on'], *f.* (Coll.) Whipping, flogging.

Vapulamiento [vah-poo-lah-me-en'-to], *m.* *V.* VAPULACIÓN.

Vapular [vah-poo-lar'], *va.* (Coll.) To whip, to flog.

Vapuleo [vah-poo-lay'-o], *m.* (Coll.) Whipping, flogging.

Vaquear [vah-kay-ar'], *va.* To cover cows with the bull.

Vaquería [vah-kay-ree'-ah], *f.* 1. Herd or drove of black cattle. 2. A farm for grazing cattle; milk-dairy.

Vaqueriles [vah-kay-ree'-les], *m. pl.* Winter pasture for cows.

Vaquerillo [vah-kay-reel'-lyo], *m. dim.* Boy who attends cows.

Vaqueriza [vah-kay-ree'-thah], *f.* Stable for cattle in winter.

Vaquerizo, za [vah-kay-ree'-tho, thah], *a.* Relating to cows.

Vaquerizo, *m.* *V.* VAQUERO.

Vaquero [vah-kay'-ro], *m.* 1. Cowherd, cow-keeper. 2. Jacket or loose dress worn by women and children.

Vaquero, ra [vah-kay'-ro, rah], *a.* Belonging to cowherds.

Vaqueta [vah-kay'-tah], *f.* Sole-leather, tanned cow-hide.

Vaquetear [vah-kay-tay-ar'], *va.* To flog with leather thongs.

Vaqueteo [vah-kay-tay'-o], *m.* Flogging with leather thongs.

Vaquilla, Vaquita [vah-keel'-lyah], *f. dim.* A small cow, a young cow, a heifer.

Vara [vah'-rah], *f.* 1. Rod, slender twig. 2. Pole, staff. 3. Verge, a rod, a wand, an emblem of authority: to its upper end is fixed a cross, on which oaths are administered. *Vara de alguacil*, The appointment, commission, or office of a constable. 4. Verge: it is commonly taken for the very jurisdiction of which it is an emblem. 5. Yard-stick, for measuring. 6. Yard, a measure of three feet, 33 British inches, or 8.36 decimetres; a yard of cloth, of this length. 7. Herd of forty or fifty head of swine. 8. Chastisement, rigour. 9. Shaft of a carriage. *Vara alta*, Sway, high hand. *Vara de pescar*, Fishing-rod. *Vara* or *varilla de cortina*, A curtain-rod. *Vara de Jesé*, (Bot.) Tuberose. Polyanthes tuberosa, *L.* *Vara de luz*, Shaft of light through clouds; the phenomenon familiarly called the sun drawing water. *Nadie le dió la vara; él se hizo alcalde, y manda*, Nobody has put you in authority or made you magistrate (i. e. do not interfere).

Varada [vah-rah'-dah], *f.* (Naut.) The act of a vessel running aground or stranding.

Varadera [vah-rah-day'-rah], *f.* Skid, or skeed.

Varadero [vah-rah-day'-ro], *m.* A shipyard; a place for repairing vessels.

Varador [vah-rah-dor'], *m.* (Obs.) *V.* VARADERO.

Varadura [vah-rah-doo'-rah], *f.* (Naut.) The grounding of a vessel.

Varal [vah-rahl'], *m.* 1. A long pole or perch. 2. (Coll.) A tall, slender person.

Varapalo [vah-rah-pah'-lo], *m.* 1. A long pole or perch; switch. 2. Blow with a stick or pole. 3. (Coll.) Grief, trouble, vexation.

Varar [vah-rar'], *va.* (Naut.) 1. To run aground. 2. To launch a new-built ship.—*vn.* 1. (Naut.) To ground, to be stranded. 2. To be stopped.

Varaseto [vah-rah-say'-to], *m.* Treillage, a contexture of poles used in gardens.
Varazo [vah-rah'-tho], *m.* Stroke with a pole or stick.
Varbasco [var-bahs'-co], *m.* *V.* VERBASCO.
Varchilla [var-cheel'-lyah], *f.* Measure of grain, which contains the third part of a *fanega.*
Vardasca [var-dahs'-cah], *f.* A thin twig.
Vardascazo [var-das-cah'-tho], *m.* Stroke with a twig or switch.
Vareador [vah-ray-ah-dor'], *m.* One who beats down with a pole or staff.
Vareaje [vah-ray-ah'-hay], *m.* 1. Retail trade, selling by the yard; measuring by the yard. 2. The act of beating down the fruit of trees.
Varear [vah-ray-ar'], *va.* 1. To beat down the fruit of trees with a pole or rod. 2. To cudgel, to beat. 3. To wound bulls or oxen with a goad. 4. To measure or sell by the yard.—*vr.* To grow thin or lean.
Varejón [vah-ray-hone'], *m.* A thick pole or staff.
Varendaje [vah-ren-dah'-hay], *m.* (Naut.) Collection of floor-timbers.
Varenga [vah-ren'-gah], *f.* (Naut.) Floor-timber. *Varenga de plan,* (Naut.) Midship floor-timber. *Varenga de sobreplanos,* (Naut.) Floor-rider.
Vareo [vah-ray'-o], *m.* 1. Measurement, measuring. 2. The act of beating down the fruit of trees.
Vareta [vah-ray'-tah], *f.* 1. (Dim.) A small rod or twig. 2. Lime-twig for catching birds. 3. Stripe in a stuff different in colour from the ground. 4. A piquant expression. 5. A circuitous manner of speech. *Irse de vareta,* (Coll.) To have a diarrhœa. *Gorrión con vareta,* (Joc.) A little man with a long sword.
Varetazo [vah-ray-tah'-tho], *m.* A stroke with a twig.
Varetear [vah-ray-tay-ar'], *va.* To variegate stuffs with stripes of different colours.
Varga [var'-gah], *f.* The steepest part of an eminence.
Várgano [var'-gah-no], *m.* (Prov.) Fence of a rural farm.
Variable [vah-re-ah'-blay], *a.* Variable, changeable; fickle.
Variablemente, *adv.* Variably, fast and loose.
Variación [vah-re-ah-the-on'], *f.* 1. Variation, varying. 2. Change, mutation. *Variación de la aguja,* (Naut.) Variation of the compass.
Variado, da [vah-re-ah'-do, dah], *a.* Variegated, coloured.—*pp.* of VARIAR.
Variamente [vah-re-ah-men'-tay], *adv.* Variously, differently.
Variante [vah-re-ahn'-tay], *pa.* Varying, deviating.—*f.* Difference or discrepancy, deviation.
Variar [vah-re-ar'], *va.* To change, to alter; to shift; to variegate, to diversify.—*vn.* 1. To vary, to differ from. 2. (Naut.) To cause a deviation of the magnetic needle.
Várice [vah'-re-thay], *f.* (Med.) Varix, a dilated vein.
Varicela [vah-re-thay'-lah], *f.* (Med.) Varicella, chicken-pox, an eruptive disease.
Varicocele [vah-re-co-thay'-lay], *m.* (Med.) Varicocele, a swelling formed by dilated veins of the scrotum.
Varicoso, sa [vah-re-co'-so, sah], *a.* (Surg.) Varicose.
Variedad [vah-re-ay-dahd'], *f.* Variety, particular distinction; change, variation.
Variegado, da [vah-re-ay-gah'-do, dah], *a.* (Obs.) Variegated.
Varilarguero [vah-re-lar-gay'-ro], *m.* In bull-fighting, the horseman or *picador* armed with a spear to resist the attack of the bull.
Varilla [vah-reel'-lyah], *f.* 1. (Dim.) A small rod. 2. A curtain-rod. 3. Spindle, pivot. 4. Switch. *Varillas,* Jaw-bones; frame of a sieve or strainer. 5. Rib or stick of a fan. *Un abanico con varillas de marfil,* A fan with ivory ribs. *Varilla de virtudes,* A magician's or conjurer's wand.
Varillaje [vah-ril-lyah'-hay], *m.* Collection of ribs of a fan, umbrella, or parasol.
Vario, ria [vah'-re-o, ah], *a.* 1. Various, divers, different. 2. Inconstant, variable, unsteady. 3. Vague, undetermined. 4. Variegated.—*pl.* Some, several.
Vario [vah-ree'-o], *m.* Pink, minnow. Cyprinus phoxinus.
Varioloide [vah-re-o-lo'-e-day], *f.* (Med.) Varioloid, modified small-pox.
Varioloso, sa [vah-re-o-lo'-so, sah], *a.* Variolous, variolar, relating to small-pox.
Variz [vah-reeth'], *m.* (Surg.) *V.* VÁRICE.
Varón [vah-ron'], *m.* 1. Man, a human being of the male sex. 2. A male human being, grown to manhood, which is considered from 30 to 45 years. 3. Man of respectability. *Varón de Dios,* A holy, virtuous man. *Santo varón,* (Coll.) A good but not clever man. *Buen varón,* (1) A wise and learned man. (2) (Iron.) A plain, artless being. *Varón del timón,* (Naut.) Rudder-pendant.
Varona, *f.* (Obs.) Masculine woman.
Varoncico, illo, ito, *m. dim.* of VARÓN.
Varonesa [vah-ro-nay'-sah], *f.* A woman. (Acad.)
Varonía [vah-ro-nee'-ah], *f.* Male issue; male descendants.
Varonil [vah-ro-neel'], *a.* Male, manly, of the male kind; masculine; vigorous, spirited.
Varonilmente, *adv.* Manfully, valiantly, courageously.
Varraco [var-rah'-co], *m.* *V.* VERRACO.
Vasallaje [vah-sal-lyah'-hay], *m.* 1. Vassalage, dependence, servitude. 2. Liege-money, a tax paid by vassals to their lord. 3. Surrender, yielding to another, or of one thing to another.
Vasallo, lla [vas-sahl'-lyo, lyah], *m.* & *f.* 1. Vassal, subject; one who acknowledges a superior lord. 2. Feudatory.
Vasallo, lla [vas-sahl'-lyo, lyah], *a.* Subject, relating to a vassal. *Mal vasallo,* Disobedient, unsubjected.
Vasar [vah-sar'], *m.* Buffet on which glasses or vessels are put.
Vasco, ca [vahs'-co, cah], *a.* *V.* VASCONGADO.
Vascongado, da [vas-con-gah'-do, dah], *a.* & *m.* & *f.* The native of the provinces of Álava, Guipúzcoa, and Biscay, and the things belonging to them.
Vascuence [vas-coo-en'-thay], *m.* 1. Biscay dialect, which is considered the primitive language of Spain, called also *Lengua Éuscara.* 2. (Coll.) Jargon, gibberish. *Hablar en vascuence,* To speak Spanish so brokenly as not to be understood.
Vascular [vas-coo-lar'], *a.* Vascular.
Vasculoso, sa [vas-coo-lo'-so, sah], *a.* Vascular, vasculiferous.
Vase [vah'-say], *vr.* Third person singular of the present indicative of *Ir,* To go. In plays, *Exit.*
Vaselina [vah-say-lee'-nah], *f.* Vaseline, trademark for petroleum jelly.
Vasera [vah-say'-rah], *f.* Buffet, a kind of cupboard.
Vasico [vah-see'-co], *m. dim.* A small glass, cup, or vessel.
Vasija [vah-see'-hah], *f.* 1. Vessel in which liquors or food-stuffs are kept; any butt, pipe, or cask. 2. Collection of vessels in a cellar for keeping liquors. *Vasija que rezuma,* A leaky cask.
Vasillo, ito [vah-seel'-lyo], *m. dim.* A small glass or cup. *Vasillo,* Cell or comb of bees.
Vaso [vah'-so], *m.* 1. Vessel in which any thing, but particularly liquids, is put; vase. 2. Tumbler, glass, drinking vessel of any kind; the quantity of liquid contained in it. 3. Vessel, any vehicle in which men or goods are carried on the water; and the burden or capacity of a vessel. 4. The capacity, room, or extent of any thing. 5. (Ast.) Crater, a southern constellation. 6. Horse's hoof. 7. Vessel, vein, or artery. 8. Receptacle, capacity of one vessel to contain another. *Vaso de barro,* The human body; an earthen vessel. *Vasos,* Close-stools, chamber-pots.
Vasos sanguíneos [vah'-sos san-gee'-nay-os], *m. pl.* Blood vessels.
Vástago [vahs'-tah-go], *m.* 1. Stem, bud, shoot. 2. (Met.) Descendant, the offspring of an ancestor.
Vastamente [vas-tah-men'-tay], *adv.* Vastly, extensively.
Vastedad [vas-tay-dahd'], *f.* Vastness, immensity.
Vasto, ta [vahs'-to, tah], *a.* Vast, huge, immense.
Vate [vah'-tay], *m.* (Poet.) Bard, Druid.
Vaticano [vah-te-cah'-no], *m.* 1. Vatican, a hill of Rome, west of the Tiber, containing the basilica of St. Peter and the Pope's palace. 2. (Met.) Papal authority, or the pontifical court.
Vaticinador, ra [vah-te-the-nah-dor', rah], *m.* & *f.* Prophet, diviner.
Vaticinar [vah-te-the-nar'], *va.* To divine, to foretell.
Vaticinio [vah-te-thee'-ne-o], *m.* Divination, vaticination.
Vatídico, ca [vah-tee'-de-co, cah], *a.* (Poet.) Prophetical.
Vatio [vah'-te-o], *m.* Watt, an electrical unit of the rate of work, being the rate when the electro-motive force is one volt and the volume of current one ampere; equal to ten ergs per second (fr. Watt, Acad.).
Vaya [vah'-yah], *f.* Scoff, jest.—*int.* Go; go to; come! indeed! certainly!
Ve [vay], *f.* Name of the letter V.
Véase [vay'-ah-say]. See; a direction of reference.
Vecera [vay-thay'-rah], *f.* (Prov.) Drove of swine and other animals.
Vecería [vay-thay-ree'-ah], *f.* Herd of swine, or animals belonging to a neighbourhood.
Vecero, ra [vay-thay'-ro, rah], *a.* & *m.* & *f.* 1. One who performs alternately, or by turns. 2. Applied to trees which yield fruit one year and none another.
Vecinal [vay-the-nahl'], *a.* Belonging to the neighbourhood.
Vecinamente [vay-the-nah-men'-tay], *adv.* Near, contiguously.
Vecindad [vay-theen-dahd'], *f.* 1. Population, inhabitants of a place. 2. Vicinity, contiguity, vicinage. 3. Right of an inhabitant, acquired by residence

in a town for a time determined by law. 4. Affinity, similarity, proximity. *Hacer mala vecindad,* To be a troublesome neighbour.

Vecindario [vay-theen-dah'-re-o], *m.* 1. Number of inhabitants of a place. 2. Roll or list of the inhabitants of a place. 3. Neighbourhood, vicinity; right acquired by residence.

Vecino, na [vay-thee'-no, nah], *a.* 1. Neighbouring, living in the neighbourhood. 2. Neighbour, near to another, adjoining, next, near. 3. Like, resembling, coincident.

Vecino [vay-thee'-no], *m.* 1. Neighbour, inhabitant, housekeeper. 2. Denizen, citizen, freeman. *Medio vecino,* (Prov.) He who, in a parish distinct from his residence, paying half the contributions, enjoys the right of depasturing his cattle on the commons.

Vectación [vec-tah-the-on'], *f.* Action of carrying in a vehicle; passive exercise.

Vector [vec-tor'], *m.* 1. (Aer.) Vector. 2. (Geom.) Radius vector.

Vectorizar [vec-to-re-thar'], *va.* To vector.

Veda [vay'-dah], *f.* Prohibition, interdiction by law.

Vedado [vay-dah'-do], *m.* Warren, park, inclosure for game.—*Vedado, da, pp.* of VEDAR.

Vedamiento [vay-dah-me-en'-to], *m.* Prohibition.

Vedar [vay-dar'], *va.* 1. To prohibit, to forbid. 2. To obstruct, to impede; to suspend or deprive.

Vedas [vay'-das], *m. pl.* The Vedas, four sacred books, collections of hymns, the most ancient Sanscrit literature.

Vedegambre [vay-day-gahm'-bray], *m.* (Bot.) Hellebore. *Vedegambre* or *verdegambre blanco,* White hellebore or white veratrum. Veratrum album. *Vedegambre negro,* Christmas rose hellebore. Helleborus niger. *V.* ELÉBORO.

Vedeja [vay-day'-hah], *f.* *V.* GUEDEJA.

Vedejudo, da [vay-day-hoo'-do, dah], *a.* (Prov.) *V.* VEDIJUDO.

Védico, ca [vay'-de-co, cah], *a.* (Neol.) Vedaic, derived from or pertaining to the Vedas.

Vedija [vay-dee'-hah], *f.* 1. Entangled lock of wool; flake. 2. Tuft of entangled hair; matted hair.

Vedijero, ra [vay-de-hay'-ro, rah], *m.* & *f.* Collector of loose locks of wool at shearing.

Vedijudo, da [vay-de-hoo'-do, dah], **Vedijoso, sa** [vay-de-ho'-so, sah], *a.* Having entangled or matted hair.

Vedijuela [vay-de-hoo-ay'-lah], *f. dim.* Small lock of wool.

Véduño [vay-doo'-nyo], *m.* 1. Quality, variety, strain of vines or grapes. 2. *V.* VIÑEDO.

Veedor, ra [vay-ay-dor', rah], *m.* & *f.* 1. Spy, watcher, busybody. 2. Overseer, inspector. 3. Caterer, provider of provisions. 4. (Obs.) *V.* VISITADOR.

Veeduría [vay-ay-doo-ree'-ah], *f.* Place or employment of an overseer or inspector; the inspector's office; controllership.

Vega [vay'-gah], *f.* 1. An open plain; a tract of level and fruitful ground; a mead or a meadow. 2. (Cuba) A tobacco field generally by the bank of a river. (Arab. betha, a pleasant valley.)

Vegada [vay-gah'-dah], *f.* (Obs.) Time, turn. *A las vegadas,* At times; by turns.

Vegetabilidad [vay-hay-tah-be-le-dahd'], *f.* Vegetability.

Vegetable [vay-hay-tah'-blay], *a.* & *m.* *V.* VEGETAL.

Vegetación [vay-hay-tah-the-on'], *f.* Vegetation, growing or growth of plants.

Vegetal [vay-hay-tahl'], *a.* & *m.* Vegetable, vegetal, plant.

Vegetante [vay-hay-tahn'-tay], *pa.* Vegetating.

Vegetar [vay-hay-tar'], *vn.* To vegetate, to shoot out.

Vegetariano, na [vay-hay-tah-re-ah'-no, nah], *m.* & *f.* & *a.* Vegetarian.

Vegetativo, va [vay-hay-tah-tee'-vo, vah], *a.* Vegetative.

Veguer [vay-gayr'], *m.* 1. In Arragon, the magistrate of a certain district. 2. The chief magistrate of the republic of *Andorra,* a valley in Catalonia bordering on France.

Veguería [vay-gay-ree'-ah], *f.* In Arragon, the jurisdiction of the magistrate called *Veguer.*

Veguerío [vay-gay-ree'-o], *m.* *V.* VEGUERÍA.

Veguero, ra [vay-gay'-ro, rah], *a.* Belonging to an open plain.—*m.* 1. (Cuba) The steward who takes care of a *vega.* 2. A cigar rudely made of a single leaf.

Vehemencia [vay-ay-men'-the-ah], *f.* 1. Vehemence, violence, impetuosity. 2. Efficacy, force. 3. Fervour, heat.

Vehemente [vay-ay-men'-tay], *a.* Vehement, impetuous; persuasive, vivid; fervent, fiery; keen.

Vehementemente, *adv.* Vehemently, fervently, forcibly, urgently, hotly.

Vehículo [vay-ee'-coo-lo], *m.* 1. Vehicle, carriage, means of transporting. 2. Vehicle, conductor, as of sound or of electricity.

Vehme (La Santa) [vay'-may], *f.* Name of a kind of German Inquisition during the middle ages. Charles V. abolished it.

Veigelia [vay-e-hay'-le-ah], *f.* (Bot.) Weigelia, an ornamental plant from China. Diervilla, formerly Weigelia rosea.

Veintavo [vay-in-tah'-vo], *m.* The twentieth part of a thing.

Veinte [vay'-in-tay], *a.* & *m.* 1. Twenty. 2. *V.* VIGÉSIMO. *A las veinte,* Unseasonably. 3. Number or figure 20.

Veintén [vay-in-ten'], *m.* A gold dollar of the size of half a dime, equal to 20 reals *vellón,* or one dollar.

Veintena [vay-in-tay'-nah], *f.* 1. A score. 2. The twentieth part.

Veintenar [vay-in-tay-nar'], *m.* *V.* VEINTENA.

Veintenario, ria [vay-in-tay-nah'-re-o, ah], *a.* Containing twenty years.

Veinteno, na [vay-in-tay'-no, nah], **Veintésimo, ma,** *a.* (Ant.) Twentieth. *Veinteno,* Applied to cloth containing two thousand threads in the warp.

Veinteñal [vay-in-tay-nyahl'], *a.* Lasting twenty years.

Veinticinco [vay-in-te-theen'-co], *a.* & *m.* Twenty-five.

Veinticuatreno, na [vay-in-te-coo-ah-tray'-no, nah], *a.* Twenty-fourth.

Veinticuatría [vay-in-te-coo-ah-tree'-ah], *f.* Aldermanry, the office and dignity of a *veinticuatro* (alderman) in some towns of Andalusia, such as Seville.

Veinticuatro [vay-in-te-coo-ah'-tro], *a.* Twenty-four.—*m.* 1. Alderman of Seville and other towns of Andalusia, the corporation of which consists of twenty-four members. 2. Twenty-fourmo (24mo), a book or pamphlet containing twenty-four leaves to the sheet. 3. The twenty-second day of a month. 4. The figure 24.

Veintidós [vay-in-te-dose'], *a.* & *m.* Twenty-two.

Veintidoseno, na [vay-in-te-do-say'-no, nah], **Veintedoseno, na,** *a.* 1. Applied to cloth the warp of which contains 2,200 threads. 2. Twenty-second.

Veintinueve [vay-in-te-noo-ay'-vay], *a.* & *m.* Twenty-nine.

Veintiocheno, na [vay-in-te-o-chay'-no, nah], *a.* *V.* VEINTEOCHENO.

Veintiocheno, na [vay-in-te-o-chay'-no, nah], *a.* Applied to a warp of 2,800 threads.

Veintiocho [vay-in-te-o'-cho], *a.* & *m.* Twenty-eight.

Veintiséis [vay-in-te-say'-ees], *a.* & *m.* Twenty-six.

Veintiseiseno, na [vay-in-tay-say-e-say'-no, nah], *a.* Twenty-sixth.

Veintiseiseno, na [vay-in-te-say-e-say'-no, nah], *a.* Applied to the warp of cloth having 2,600 threads.

Veintisiete [vay-in-te-se-ay'-tay], *a.* & *m.* Twenty-seven.

Veintitantos, tas [vayn-te-tahn'-tos, tahs], *a. pl.* Twenty-odd, over twenty.

Veintitrés [vay-in-te-trays'], *a.* & *m.* Twenty-three.

Veintiún [vay-in-te-oon'], *a.* Abbrev. of *Veintiuno.* Only before nouns.

Veintiuna [vay-in-te-oo'-nah], *f.* The game of twenty-one.

Veintiuno, na [vay-in-te-oo'-no, nah], *a.* & *n.* Twenty-one.

Vejación [vay-hah-the-on'], *f.* Vexation, molestation, oppression.

Vejador, ra [vay-hah-dor', rah], *m.* & *f.* Scoffer, molester, teaser.

Vejamen [vay-hah'-men], *m.* Taunt, scurrilous criticism.

Vejaminista [vay-hah-me-nees'-tah], *m.* Censor, critic.

Vejancón, na [vay-han-cone', nah], *a.* & *n. aug.* (Coll.) Decrepit; peevish from old age.

Vejar [vay-har'], *va.* 1. To vex, to molest, to harass. 2. To scoff, to censure. 3. To tease.

Vejarrón, na [vay-har-rone', nah], *a.* & *n. aug.* (Coll.) Very old.

Vejecito, ta [vay-hay-thee'-to, tah], *a.* & *m.* & *f. dim.* *V.* VIEJECITO.

Vejestorio [vay-hes-to'-re-o], *m.* (Coll.) Old trumpery; a petulant old man.

Vejazo, za [vay-hah'-tho, thah], *a. aug.* of VIEJO. (Also noun.)

Vejeta [vay-hay'-tah], *f.* The crested lark. *V.* COGUJADA.

Vejete [vay-hay'-tay], *m.* (Coll.) 1. A ridiculous old man. 2. Actor who personates an old man.

Vejez [vay-heth'], *f.* 1. Old age. 2. Decay, the state of being worn out. 3. Imbecility and peevishness of old age. 4. A trite story.

Vejezuela [vay-hay-thoo-ay'-lah], *f. dim.* An old hag.

Vejezuelo [vay-hay-thoo-ay'-lo], *m. dim.* A little old man.

Vejiga [vay-hee'-gah], *f.* 1. Bladder; urinary bladder, gall-bladder. 2. Blister; any slight elevation on a plain surface.—*pl.* 1. Pustules of small-pox. 2. Wind-galls in horses. *Vejiga de perro,* (Bot.) Common winter-cherry. Physalis alkekengi. *Vejiga natatoria de los peces,* The swimming bladder of a fish.

Vejigación [vay-he-gah-the-on'], *f.* Vesication, blistering.

Vejigatorio, ria [vay-he-gah-to'-re-o, ah], *a.* Blistering, raising blisters.—*m.* A blistering plaster, vesicatory.

Vejigazo [vay-he-gah'-tho], *m.* Blow with a bladder full of wind. *Dar un vejigazo,* To trick, to cheat.

Vejigón [vay-he-gone'], *m. aug.* Large bladder or blister.

Vejigüela, or Vejiguica, illa, ita [vay-he-goo-ay'-lah, vay-he-gee'-cah], *f. dim.* Small bladder.

Vejiguero [vay-he-gay'-ro], *m.* (Coll. Littl. us.) Spectator, bystander, looker-on at a gaming-table.

Vejilo [vay-hee'-lo], *m.* (Obs.) Standard, banner.

Vejón, na [vay-hone', nah], *m.* & *f.* Very old person.

Vejote [vay-ho'-tay], *m. aug.* (Obs.) An old man.

Vela [vay'-lah], *f.* 1. Watch, attendance without sleep, vigil. 2. Watchfulness, vigilance. 3. Watchman, night-guard. 4. Pilgrimage. *V.* ROMERÍA. 5. Candle. *Velas de molde*, Mould candles. *Velas de cera*, Wax candles. *Velas de sebo*, Tallow candles. *Velas de esperma*, Spermaceti candles. 6. Night-work in offices. 7. Awning. 8. Sail, ship. 9. Erect ear of a horse or other animal. 10. (Naut.) Sail, sheet. 11. Wing or arm of a wind-mill. 12. Devout waiting by order, hours, or turn before the most sacred sacrament. *Vela romana*, Roman candle. *Vela mayor*, Main-sail. *Vela de trinquete*, Fore-sail. *Vela de mesana*, Mizzen. *Vela de gavia*, Main-top-sail. *Vela de velacho*, Fore-top-sail. *Vela de sobremesana*, Mizzen-top-sail. *Vela de juanete mayor*, Main-top-gallant-sail. *Vela de juanete de proa*, Fore-top-gallant-sail. *Vela de periquito de sobremesana*, Mizzen-top-gallant-sail. *Vela de cebadera*, Sprit-sail. *Vela de sobre-cebadera*, Sprit-sail-top-sail. *Vela seca*, Cross-jack-sail. *Vela de estay*, Stay-sail. *Vela de maricangallo*, Driver. *Vela de senda*, Try-sail. *Vela de cangreja*, Boom-sail. *Velas de proa*, Head-sails. *Velas de popa*, After-sails. *Vela bastarda*, The largest sail of lateen boats; bastard. *Vela latina*, Lateen sail. *Velas mayores*, Courses. *Vela baradera*, Drabbler. *Vela de cruz*, A square-sail. *Vela de lustrar*, Port-sail. *Vela de abanico*, Convergent sail, sprit-sail. *Caída de una vela*, Drop or depth of a sail. *Gratil de una vela*, Head of a sail. *Vela encapillada*, Sail blown over the yard. *Vela aferrada*, Furled sail. *Vela cazada*, Trimmed sail. *Vela larga* or *desaferrada*, Unfurled sail. *Vela cargada arriba* or *sobre las candelizas*, A sail hauled up in the brails. *Vela tendida*, Taut or full sail. *Vela desrelingada*, Sail blown from the bolt-rope. *Vela en facha*, Backed sail. *Vela que flamea*, Sail which shivers in the wind. *Vela cuadrada*, Square-sail. *Marear una vela*, To set a sail. *Hacerse a la vela*, To set sail. *Llevar poca vela*, To carry an easy sail. *Hacer fuerza de vela*, To crowd sail. *En vela*, Vigilantly, without sleep. *A la vela*, Prepared, equipped, ready. *A vela y pregón*, Auction by inch of candle. *Juego de velas*, A set of sails. *Acortar la vela* or *acortar vela*, To reef a sail, to shorten sail. *Alzar velas*, (1) To raise sail, to make ready to sail. (2) (Met.) To disappear carrying off one's effects. *Apocar las velas*, (Obs.) To take in sail, to shorten sail. *Cambiar la vela*, To shift the sail (towards the wind). *Levantar velas*, To abandon one's residence. *Recoger velas*, To contain one's self, to be moderate. *Correrse la vela*, To run in drops, to gutter: used of a candle. *Tender las velas* or *velas*, (Met.) To take proper steps or to pave the way for obtaining an object; to seize an opportunity for obtaining one's desires; to dilate a subject, to embellish a discourse with figurative language.

Velación [vay-lah-the-on'], *f.* Watch, act of watching. *Velaciones*, Nuptial benedictions. *Cerrarse las velaciones*, Time in which the church prohibits the solemnization of marriage.

Velacho [vay-lah'-cho], *m.* (Naut.) Fore-top-sail.

Velada [vay-lah'-dah], *f.* 1. Watch. V. VELACIÓN. 2. Evening party, evening gathering. *Velada musical*, Musicale.

Velado [vay-lah'-do], *m.* (Coll.) Husband, married man.

Velador, ra [vay-lah-dor', rah], *m.* & *f.* 1. Watchman, night-guard. 2. Careful observer, vigilant keeper, spy. 3. A large wooden candlestick, used by tradesmen to work at night; table or bench on which a night-light is placed.

Veladura [vay-lah-doo'-rah], *f.* (Art) A mellow and transparent tint employed to alter the tone of what has been painted.

Velaje [vay-lah'-hay], *m.* (Naut.) Sails in general. *V.* VELAMEN.

Velamen [vay-lah'-men], *m.* (Naut.) Sails in general; set of sails; trim of sails. *Arreglar el velamen*, (Naut.) To trim the sails. *Estar con un mismo velamen*, (Naut.) To be under the same sails.

Velar [vay-lar'], *vn.* 1. To watch, to be watchful, to wake. 2. To watch, to keep guard by night. 3. To watch, to be attentive, to be vigilant. 4. (Naut.) To appear above the water, as rocks. 5. To assist by turns before the holy sacrament when it is manifested. *Velar las escotas*, (Naut.) To stand by the sheets.—*va.* 1. To guard to watch, to keep. 2. To throw a piece of white gauze, over a married couple, after the nuptial benediction has been given. 3. To observe attentively. 4. (Poet.) To cover, to hide. 5. To watch with the sick or deceased at night.

Velarte [vay-lar'-tay], *m.* Sort of fine broadcloth.

Veleidad [vay-lay-e-dahd'], *f.* 1. Velleity, the lowest degree of desire; feeble will. 2. Levity, inconstancy, fickleness, versatility.

Veleidoso, sa [vay-lay-e-do'-so, sah], *a.* Fickle, inconstant, feeble-willed, giddy, fast and loose.

Velejar [vay-lay-har'], *vn.* (Naut.) To make use of sails.

Velería [vay-lay-ree'-ah], *f.* A tallow-chandler's shop.

Velero [vay-lay'-ro], *m.* 1. Tallow-chandler. 2. Pilgrim.

Velero, ra [vay-lay'-ro, rah], *a.* Swift-sailing: applied to a ship.

Velesa [vay-lay'-sah], *f.* (Bot.) Lead-wort. Plumbago europea.

Veleta [vay-lay'-tah], *f.* 1. Weather-cock. 2. The float or cork of a fishing-line. 3. (Met.) A fickle person.

Velete [vay-lay'-tay], *m.* A light, thin veil.

Velfalla [vel-fahl'-lyah], *f.* A sort of linen.

Velicación [vay-le-cah-the-on'], *f.* (Med.) Vellication, stimulation.

Velicar [vay-le-car'], *va.* To vellicate, to twitch.

Velico, illo, ito [vay-lee'-co, eel'-lyo, ee'-to], *m.* 1. (Dim.) A small veil. 2. Embroidered gauze.

Velilla, ita [vay-leel'-lyah], *f. dim.* A small candle.

Velis nolis. (Latin phrase), Willy-nilly, whether or no.

Velo [vay'-lo], *m.* 1. Veil, curtain. 2. Veil, a part of female dress. 3. Veil, a part of the dress of nuns. 4. Piece of white gauze thrown over a couple at marriage. 5. Feast at the profession of a nun or at taking the veil. 6. Veil, cover, disguise. 7. Pretence, pretext, cover, mask. 8. Confusion, obscurity, perplexity, of the sight or intellect. *Correr el velo*, To pull off the mask; to disclose something before unknown. *Tomar el velo*, To become a nun.

Velocidad [vay-lo-the-dahd'], *f.* Speed, velocity, rapidity. *Velocidad aérea*, Air speed. *Velocidad de crucero*, Cruising speed.

Velocímetro [vay-lo-thee'-may-tro], *m.* Speedometer.

Velocípedo [vay-lo-thee'-pay-do], *m.* Velocipede; bicycle or tricycle.

Velódromo [vay-lo'-dro-mo], *m.* Velodrome.

Velon [vay-lone'], *m.* Lamp in which oil is burnt.

Velonera [vay-lo-nay'-rah], *f.* Wooden lamp-stand or bracket.

Velonero [vay-lo-nay'-ro], *m.* Lamp-maker.

Veloz [vay-loth'], *a.* Swift, nimble, active, fleet.

Velozmente, *adv.* Swiftly, fleetly, nimbly.

Vellecillo [vel-lyay-theel'-lyo], *m. dim.* Very short, soft hair.

Vellido, da [vel-lyee'-do, dah], *a.* Downy, villous.

Vello [vayl'-lyo], *m.* 1. Down, soft hair on parts of the skin; nap. 2. The downy matter which envelopes seeds or fruit, gossamer. 3. Short, downy hair of brutes.

Vellocino [vel-lyo-thee'-no], *m.* (Obs.) Applied to the golden fleece of fable.

Vellón [vel-lyone'], *m.* 1. Fleece, wool of one sheep; lock of wool. 2. Copper coin of Castile, one-fourth of a *peseta*, five cents: it is also used like the English word *sterling*.

Vellonero [vel-lyo-nay'-ro], *m.* Collector of fleeces at shearing.

Vellora [vel-lyo'-rah], *f.* (Prov.) Knot taken from woollen cloth.

Vellorita [vel-lyo-ree'-tah], *f.* (Bot.) Cowslip. Primula veris.

Vellosa [vel-lyo'-sah], *f.* (Prov.) Coarse cloth or rug worn by mariners.

Vellosidad [vel-lyo-se-dahd'], *f.* Downiness, hirsuteness.

Vellosilla [vel-lyo seel'-lyah], *f.* (Bot.) Creeping mouse-ear, mouse-ear hawk-weed. Hieracium pilosella.

Velloso, sa [vel-lyo'-so, sah], *a.* Downy, villous, hairy, cottony.

Velludillo [vel-lyoo-deel'-lyo], *m.* Velveteen.

Velludo, da [vel-lyoo'-do, dah], *a.* Downy, hairy, shaggy, woolly.

Velludo [vel-lyoo'-do], *m.* Shag, velvet.

Vellutero [vel-lyoo-tay'-ro], *m.* (Prov.) Velvet-worker.

Vena [vay'-nah], *f.* 1. Vein, a blood-vessel. 2. Fibre of plants. 3. Hollow, cavity. 4. Vein of metal in a mine. 5. Tendency of mind or genius. *Vena poética*, A poetical vein. 6. Diverse quality or colour of earth or stones. 7. Vein or stripe in stones; mineral water found under ground. *Coger* or *hallar a alguno de vena*, To find one in a favourable disposition. *Dar en la vena* or *hallar la vena*, To hit upon the right means. *Acostarse la vena*, Used of a vein of ore when it dips in some new direction. *Descabezarse una vena*, To break a blood-vessel. *Estar en vena*, To be inspired to write verses. *Estar de vena*, To be in the mood or vein. *Picarle la vena*, (Coll.) *V. Estar en vena.*

Venablo [vay-nah'-blo], *m.* Javelin, formerly used in hunting wild boars. *Echar venablos*, To break out into violent expressions of anger.

Venadero [vay-nah-day'-ro], *m.* Place much frequented by deer.
Venadico, illo, ito [vay-nah-dee'-co], *m. dim.* A small deer.
Venado [vay-nah'-do], *m.* Deer, venison. *Pintar venados,* (coll.) To play hooky.
Venaje [vay-nah'-hay], *m.* Current of a stream.
Venal [vay-nahl'], *a.* 1. Venal, relating to the veins. 2. Marketable, salable. 3. Venal, mercenary.
Venalidad [vay-nah-le-dahd'], *f.* Venality, mercenariness.
Venalogía [ven-nah-lo-hee'-ah], *f.* Treatise on the veins.
Venate [vay-nah'-tay], *m.* A small bird.
Venático, ca [vay-nah'-te-co, cah], *a.* Having a vein of madness.
Venatorio, ria [vay-nah-to'-re-o, ah], *a.* Venatic, used in hunting.
Vencedor, ra [ven-thay-dor', rah], *m. & f.* Conqueror, victor.
Vencejo [ven-thay'-ho], *m.* 1. String, band. 2. (Orn.) Swift, black-martin, martlet, martinet. Hirundo apus.
Vencer [ven-therr'], *va.* 1. To conquer, to subdue, to defeat, to vanquish, to overpower, to master, to foil. 2. To conquer, to surpass, to excel. 3. To surmount, to overcome, to clear. 4. To gain a lawsuit. 5. To bend, to turn down. 6. To prevail upon, to persuade. 7. To suffer, to tolerate or bear with patience. 8. To incline, to twist a thing.—*vn.* 1. To fall due. 2. To conquer, to gain, to succeed.—*vr.* To govern one's passions or desires.
Vencible [ven-thee'-blay], *a.* Vincible, conquerable; superable.
Vencida [ven-thee'-dah], *f.* Action of conquering or being conquered.
Vencido, da [ven-thee'-do, dah], *a. & pp.* of VENCER. 1. Conquered, subdued. 2. Due; payable. *Llevar de vencida,* To prove victorious. *Ir alguno de vencida,* To begin or be about to be conquered. *Llevar a alguno de vencida,* To begin to conquer one.
Vencimiento [ven-the-me-en'-to], *m.* 1. Victory, conquest. 2. Bent, the act of bending or turning down. 3. *Vencimiento de plazo,* (Com.) Maturity of a bill of exchange, period of falling due. *Al vencimiento del plazo,* At the expiration of the time that a bill comes due.
Venda [ven'-dah], *f.* 1. Bandage, roller. 2. (Ant.) Fillet, a band tied round the head or other part; a diadem.
Vendaje [ven-dah'-hay], *m.* 1. Commission or the sale of goods by a factor or agent. 2. Ligature with a fillet, bandage, or roller.
Vendar [ven-dar], *va.* 1. To tie with a band, fillet, bandage, or roller; to fillet. 2. To hoodwink, to darken the understanding. *Vendar los ojos,* To hoodwink.
Vendaval [ven-dah-vahl'], *m.* A strong wind south by west.
Vendavalada [ven-dah-vah-lah'-dah], *f.* A storm of southerly wind.
Vendedero, ra [ven-day-day'-ro, rah], *m. & f.* (Obs.) One employed in selling.
Vendedor, ra [ven-day-dor', rah], *m. & f.* Seller, trader, retailer, huckster, vender.
Vendehumos [ven-day-oo'-mos], *m.* He who boasts his influence with persons in power, in order to sell it to expectants; literally, a smoke-seller.
Vendeja [ven-day'-hah], *f.* A public sale.
Vender [ven-derr'], *va.* 1. To sell, to vend. 2. To expose for sale. 3. To sell, to betray for money, to prostitute, to devote to crimes for a reward. 4. To render dear or difficult. 5. To persuade, to delude with false pretences. 6. (Met.) To betray faith, confidence, or friendship. *Vender salud,* (Coll.) To be or appear very robust. *Vender juncias,* (Coll.) To boast of what one ought not, or of what he has not. *Vender humos,* (Met.) To boast of influence with men in power, in order to swindle expectants. *Vender por mayor,* To sell in the lump, or by wholesale. *Vender al pormenor* or *a destajo,* To sell at retail. *Vender palabras,* To deceive by fair words.—*vr.* 1. To boast of talents or merits one does not possess. 2. To devote one's self to the service of another. *Venderse caro,* To be of difficult access. *Venderse barato,* To make one's self cheap. *Vender cara la vida,* To fight desperately. *A mí que las vendo,* (Coll.) No deceiving those who are thoroughly acquainted with the business or thing. *Vender al contado,* To sell for cash. *Vender a plazo,* To sell on credit. *El que nos vendió el galgo,* He who sold us the dog (the very man of whom we spoke). *Vender gato por liebre,* To sell a cat for a hare (to deceive in the quality of things sold). *Vender al quitar,* To sell with the privilege of buying back.
Vendible [ven-dee'-blay], *a.* Salable, marketable.
Vendica, illa, ita [ven-dee'-cah], *f. dim.* Small fillet or bandage; a small diadem.
Vendicativo, va [ven-de-cah-tee'-vo, vah], *a.* (Obs.) *V.* VENGATIVO.
Vendición [ven-de-the-on'], *f.* Sale, selling, vendition.
Vendido, da [ven-dee'-do, dah], *a. & pp.* of VENDER. Sold. *Estar vendido,* To be duped, to be exposed to great risks. *Estar como vendido,* To be disgusted in the company of those holding opposite sentiments, or of strangers.
Vendimia [ven-dee'-me-ah], *f.* 1. Vintage. 2. Large gain or profit. *Después de vendimias, cuévanos,* The day after the fair; too late.
Vendimiado, da [ven-de-me-ah'-do, dah], *a. & pp.* of VENDIMIAR. Gathered vintage. *Como por viña vendimiada,* Easily, freely.
Vendimiador, ra [ven-de-me-ah-dor', rah], *m. & f.* Vintager.
Vendimiar [ven-de-me-ar'], *va.* 1. To gather the vintage. 2. To enjoy unlawful perquisites; to reap benefits or profit unjustly. 3. (Coll.) To kill, to murder.
Vendimiario [ven-de-me-ah'-re-o], *m.* First month of the calendar of the French Republic (22d September to 22d October).
Venduta [ven-doo'-tah], *f.* (Amer.) Auction, vendue.
Vendutero [ven-doo-tay'-ro], *m.* Auctioneer.
Veneciano, na [vay-nay-the-ah'-no, nah], *a.* Venetian, relating to Venice.
Veneficiar [vay-nay-fe-the-ar'], *va.* (Obs.) To bewitch, to injure by witchcraft.
Veneficio [vay-nay-fee'-the-o], *m.* (Obs.) Charm, witchcraft: the act of bewitching; poisoning.
Venéfico, ca [vay-nay'-fe-co, cah], *a.* (Obs.) Poisonous, using witchcraft.
Venenar [vay-nay-nar'], *va.* (Obs.) To poison. *V.* ENVENENAR.
Venenario [vay-nay-nah'-re-o], *m.* (Obs.) *V.* BOTICARIO.
Venencia [vay-nen'-the-ah], *f.* A small vessel, like a piece of reed, at the end of a long rod, which is used in Xerez for testing wines.
Venenífero, ra [vay-nay-nee'-fay-ro, rah], *a.* (Poet.) *V.* VENENOSO.
Veneno [vay-nay'-no], *m.* 1. Poison, venom, any thing injurious to health: venenation. 2. (Obs.) Medicine, medicament. 3. Poisonous mineral ingredients in paints or dye-stuffs. 4. Wrath, fury, passion. 5. Bad, insipid taste. 6. (Met.) Poison, any thing pernicious to morals and religion.
Venenosamente [vay-nay-no-sah-men'-tay], *adv.* Venomously.
Venenosidad [vay-nay-no-se-dahd'], *f.* Poisonousness; venomousness.
Venenoso, sa [vay-nay-no'-so, sah], *a.* Venomous, poisonous.
Venera [vay-nay'-rah], *f.* 1. Porcelain shell, or Mediterranean scallop, worn by pilgrims who return from St. Jago or Santiago in Galicia. Ostrea jacobæa. 2. Badge, jewel, or star worn by the knights of military orders. 3. Vein of metal in a mine; spring of water. *No se le caerá la venera,* Said of a person too vain or too proud to do a certain thing.
Venerable [vay-nay-rah'-blay], *a.* 1. Venerable. 2. Epithet of respect to ancient ecclesiastics and prelates.
Venerablemente, *adv.* Venerably; with respect or veneration.
Veneración [vay-nay-rah-the-on'], *f.* 1. Veneration. 2. Worship; honour.
Venerador, ra [vay-nay-rah-dor', rah], *m. & f.* Venerator, worshipper.
Venerando, da [vay-nay-rahn'-do, dah], *a.* Venerable.
Venerante [vay-nay-rahn'-tay], *pa.* Venerating, worshipping.
Venerar [vay-nay-rar'], *va.* To venerate, to respect, to worship, to honour.
Venéreo, rea [vay-nay'-ray-o, ah], *a.* Venereous, venereal, sensual.
Venero [vay-nay'-ro], *m.* 1. A vein of metal in a mine. 2. A spring of water. 3. Radius or horary line of sun-dials. 4. Origin, root, source.
Veneruela [vay-ne-roo-ay'-lah], *f.* 1. A small porcelain shell. 2. Dim. of VENERA.
Venezolano, na [vay-nay-tho-lah'-no, nah], *a.* Venezuelan, of Venezuela.
Vengable [ven-gah'-blay], *a.* Worthy of revenge, that may be revenged.
Vengador, ra [ven-gah-dor', rah], *m. & f.* Avenger, revenger.
Venganciila [ven-gan-theel'-lyah], *f dim.* A slight revenge.
Venganza [ven-gahn'-thah], *f.* Revenge, vengeance.
Vengar [ven-gar'], *va.* To revenge, avenge.—*vr.* To be revenged.
Vengativamente, *adv.* Revengefully.
Vengativo, va [ven-gah-tee'-vo, vah], *a.* Revengeful, vindictive.
(*Yo vengo, yo venga,* from *Venir. V.* VENIR.)
Venia [vay'-ne-ah], *f.* 1. Pardon, forgiveness. 2. Leave, permission. 3. Royal license to minors to manage their own estates. 4. Bow with the head.
Venial [vay-ne-ahl'], *a.* Venial, pardonable; excusable.
Venialidad [vay-ne-ah-le-dahd'], *f.* Venialness.
Venialmente [vay-ne-al-men'-tay], *adv.* Venially.
Venida [vay-nee'-dah], *f.* 1. Arrival; return, regress, coming. 2. Overflow of a river. 3. Attack in fencing. 4. Impetuosity, rashness.
Venidero, ra [vay-ne-day'-ro, rah], *a.* Future, coming. *En lo venidero*

Henceforth.—*m. pl.* Posterity, successors.

Venido, da [vay-nee'-do, dah], *a.* & *pp.* of Venir. Come, arrived. *Venido del cielo,* Come from heaven; expressing the excellence of a thing. *Bien venido* or *venida,* Welcome.

Veniméocum [vay-ne-may'-coom], *m.* Vademecum.

Venino, na [vay-nee'-no, nah], *a.* (Obs.) Venomous, poisonous.—*m.* (Obs.) Boil, furuncle.

Venir [vay-neer'], *vn.* 1. To come, to draw near, to advance towards. 2. To come, to move towards another. *Ven acá,* (Coll.) Come hither: used to call the attention and to advise any one. 3. To come, to happen, to come to pass. 4. To follow, to succeed. 5. To come, to proceed from, to originate in, to be occasioned by; to be inferred, to be deduced. 6. To appear before a judge; to come into court. 7. To assent, to submit, to yield. 8. To answer, to fit, to suit. *Esta chaqueta no me viene,* That jacket does not fit me. *Me viene de molde,* It fits me like a glove. 9. To grow, to shoot up. 10. To make an application, to ask. 11. To occur, to be presented to the memory or attention. 12. To resolve, to determine. 13. To attack, to assault. 14. (Arith.) To result. 15. To be of one's party or opinion; to accompany. 16. To fall, to be overset. 17. Used impersonally, Come here, take this. 18. To succeed finally. *Vino a conseguir la plaza,* He obtained the place. *Vino a morir,* He has just died. Here it is an auxiliary with the preposition *a* after it; in this case it sometimes signifies either the action of the following verb, or the state of readiness for action, as *venir bailando,* To dance; *venir a cuentas,* To calculate, to count. 19. To change the state or quality. 20. To be transferred, to pass from one to another. 21. To adduce; to produce. 22. To excite, to effect; to attain a degree of excellence or perfection. 23. Used to express politely satisfaction or pleasure at the arrival of any one; to welcome. *Vengamos al caso,* Let us come to the point. *Venir a menos,* To decay, to decline. *Venir de perilla,* To come at the nick of time: to fit or to answer perfectly well. *Venir pie con bola,* Just enough, exactly, as much as is wanted, neither too much nor too little. *Cosas que van y vienen,* Things which wax and wane. *No hay mal que por bien no venga,* (prov.) There is no evil which may not be turned to good. *¿A qué viene eso?* To what purpose is that? What does it amount to? *Él se mete en lo que no le va, ni le viene,* He meddles in business that does not concern him. *Con quien vengo, vengo,* (Coll.) I am constant to my friends. *Venga lo que viniere,* Come what will; happen what may. *Venir a la romana,* To be of just weight. *Venir a pelo,* To come just at the right time. *Venir a deshora,* To arrive at an awkward time. *Fulano vino de antuvión,* So and So came unexpectedly. *Venir como pedrada en ojo de boticario,* To come in opportunely; apropos, fitting. *Venir angosto,* To fall short of one's expectations. *Venir el cuervo,* To receive repeated relief. *Venirle a la mano alguna cosa,* To get something without exertion. *Venir muy ancho,* To be in abundance; to be beyond the desert of the receiver. *Venir rodado,* To attain an object accidentally. *Venir a las manos,* To come to blows. *Vengo en ello,* I agree to that. *Si a mano viene,* Perhaps. *Bien vengas mal, si vienes solo,* Misfortunes seldom come singly. *De mis viñas vengo,* I come from my vineyards (that is, I had no hand in the affair). *Tras los años viene el seso,* Experience brings wisdom. *No viene el son con la castañeta,* The castanets do not click (said of persons or things not agreeing). *A quien le venga el guante, que se lo plante,* If the shoe fits, put it on. *El mal viene con malos aparatos,* The patient shows bad symptoms. *Tiempo tras tiempo viene,* Do not despair; times will change. *De Dios viene el bien, y de las abejas la miel,* The blessing is from God, through whatever means it may come.—*vr.* To ferment, to attain perfection by fermentation, as bread or wine. It is often used the same as the neuter verb *venir. Venirse a buenas,* To yield, to submit, to comply with things required or enforced. *Venirse a casa,* To come home. *Venirse durmiendo,* To be falling asleep. *Venirse cayendo,* To be falling down. *Venirse abajo,* To fall, to collapse. *Venirse a los ojos,* To show in one's eyes; to betray by one's glances. *Venirse al suelo,* To fall to the ground. *Venirse a la boca,* To taste unpleasantly. *Venirse el cielo abajo,* To rain very heavily. *Venirse con buena música,* To make an impertinent request. *Venirse la caza a las manos,* To obtain unexpected advantages. *Como se viene, se va,* Easy come, easy go. So too, *Hoy venida, cras garrida. Venir sobre,* To fall (on).

Venora [vay-no'-rah], *f.* (Prov.) Range of stones or bricks in a drain or trench.

Venoso, sa [vay-no'-so, sah], *a.* 1. Venous, belonging to veins. 2. Veiny, veined, full of veins.

Venta [ven'-tah], *f.* 1. Sale, act of selling, market; custom. *Venta confidencial,* A trust sale. 2. A poor inn on roads far from towns or villages. *Hacer venta,* To stop at a poor inn; to invite a passenger or traveller to dinner. *Ser una venta,* To be a dear place; to be an open and uncomfortable place. *Estar de venta* or *estar en venta,* To be on sale. (Coll.) Applied to a woman who stands much at a window, to see and be seen. 3. (Met.) Open place exposed to the weather.

Ventada [ven-tah'-dah], *f.* A gust of wind.

Ventador [ven-tah-dor'], *m.* (Obs.) *V.* Aventador.

Ventaja [ven tah'-hah], *f.* 1. Advantage, preference; gain, good; commodity, commodiousness; hand; additional pay. 2. Odds given at play.

Ventajosamente, *adv.* Advantageously, gainfully.

Ventajoso, sa [ven-tah-ho'-so, sah], *a.* Advantageous, comparatively superior; profitable, lucrative, fruitful, good.

Ventalla [ven-tahl'-lyah], *f.* Valve. *V.* Válvula.

Ventalle [ven-tahl'-lyay], *m.* Fan. *V.* Abanico.

Ventana [ven-tah'-nah], *f.* 1. Window. 2. Window-shutter. 3. Nostril. 4. Either of the senses of seeing or hearing. *Hacer la ventana,* To be constantly at the window: applied to women who show themselves at the window. *Tener ventana al cierzo,* (Coll.) To be elated with pride.

Ventanaje [ven-tah-nah'-hay], *m.* Number or series of windows in a building.

Ventanazo [ven-tah-nah'-tho], *m.* Slap of a window.

Ventanear [ven-tah-nay-ar'], *vn.* To frequent the window, to gaze repeatedly from the window.

Ventanera [ven-tah-nay'-rah], *a.* Window-gazer: applied to women who are constantly at the window.

Ventanero [ven-tah-nay'-ro], *m.* Window-maker.

Ventanica, illa [ven-tah-nee'-cah], *f. dim.* A small window.

Ventanico, illo [ven-tah-nee'-co, neel'-lyo], *m. dim.* A small window-shutter.

Ventar [ven-tar'], *va.* & *vn.* *V.* Ventear.

Ventarrón [ven-tar-rone'], *m.* Violent wind.

Venteadura [ven-tay-ah-doo'-rah], *f.* Split made in timber by the wind.

Ventear [ven-tay-ar'], *vn.* & *a.* 1. To blow. *Ventea muy fresco del N. O.,* It blows very fresh from the N. W. 2. To smell, to scent. 3. To investigate, to examine. 4. To dry, to expose to the air.—*vr.* 1. To be filled with wind or air. 2. To break wind.

Venteo [ven-tay'-o], *m.* Vent-hole in a cask.

Venteril [ven-tay-reel'], *a.* (Depreciatory) Suited to a poor inn.

Ventero, ra [ven-tay'-ro, rah], *m.* & *f.* Keeper of a small inn on roads.

Ventiera [ven-te-ay'-rah], *f.* (Obs.) A sort of leather case or purse fastened to a belt.

Ventilación [ven-te-lah-the-on'], *f.* Ventilation; discussion.

Ventilador [ven-te-lah-dor'], *m.* Ventilator.

Ventilar [ven-te-lar'], *va.* 1. To ventilate; to winnow, to fan. 2. To examine, to discuss.—*vn.* To move with a current of air, to circulate: applied to the air.

Ventilla [ven-teel'-lyah], *f.* Pallet, valve-pallet of an organ.

Ventisca [ven-tees'-cah], *f.* Storm, attended with a heavy fall of snow.

Ventiscar [ven-tis-car'], *vn.* To blow hard, attended with snow; to drift, to be drifted by the wind, as snow.

Ventisco [ven-tees'-co], *m.* *V.* Ventisca.

Ventiscoso, sa [ven-tis-co'-so, sah], *a.* Windy, stormy, tempestuous.

Ventisquear [ven-tis-kay-ar'], *v. imp.* To snow hard.

Ventisquero [ven-tis-kay'-ro], *m.* 1. Snow-drift; glacier. 2. Mountain height most exposed to snow-storms. 3. Snow-storm.

Ventola [ven-to'-lah], *f.* (Naut.) Top-hamper, resistance of the upper works to the wind.

Ventolera [ven-to-lay'-rah], *f.* 1. Gust, a sudden blast of wind. 2. Vanity, pride, loftiness; fancy. 3. *V.* Rehilandera. 4. Whim, unexpected and extravagant thought or resolution.

Ventolina [ven-to-lee'-nah], *f.* (Naut.) Light, variable wind; cat's-paw.

Ventor [ven-tor'], *m.* Pointer, pointer dog; fox-hound.

Ventorrillo, Ventorro [ven-tor-reel'-lyo, ven-tor'-ro], *m.* A petty inn or tavern near a town.

Ventosa [ven-to'-sah], *f.* 1. (Med.) Cupping-glass. 2. Vent, air-hole, spiracle. 3. (Zool.) Sucker, a muscular organ of certain aquatic creatures for sucking, catching prey, or clinging to rocks. *Pegar una ventosa,* To swindle one out of his money.

Ventosear, Ventosearse [ven-to-say-ar', ar'-say], *vn.* & *vr.* To break wind.

Ventosero, ra [ven-to-say'-ro, rah], *a.* Fond of cupping.

Ventosidad [ven-to-se-dahd'], *f.* Flatulency, windiness.

Ventoso, sa [ven-to'-so, sah], *a.* 1. Windy; flatulent. 2. Pointing: applied to a pointer-dog. 3. Vain, inflated. 4. Windy, tempestuous.

Ventrada [ven-trah'-dah], *f.* (Obs.) Brood of young brought forth at once.

Ventral [ven-trahl'], *a.* Ventral: applied to any thing used to encircle the belly.

Ventrecha [ven-tray'-chah], *f.* Belly of fishes.

Ventregada [ven-tray-gah'-dah], *f.* 1. Brood, litter. 2. Abundance.

Ventrera [ven-tray'-rah], *f.* Roller or girdle for the belly; sash, cummerbund.

Ventricular [ven-tre-coo-lar'], *a.* Ventricular; belonging to the ventricles of the heart.

Ventrículo [ven-tree'-coo-lo], *m.* 1. Ventricle, the stomach. 2. Any of the cavities of the heart or brain.

Ventril [ven-treel'], *m.* 1. A piece of wood which serves to counterpoise the movement of the beam in oil-mills. 2. Belly-band of a harness.

Ventrílocuo [ven-tree'-lo-coo-o], *m.* Ventriloquist.

Ventriloquia [ven-tre-lo'-ke-ah], *f.* Ventriloquism, the art or practice of the ventriloquist.

Ventrón [ven-trone'], *m. aug.* of VIENTRE.

Ventrosidad [ven-tro-se-dahd'], *f.* (Med.) Excessive development of the belly; ventrosity.

Ventroso, sa, Ventrudo, da [ven-tro'-so, sah, ven-troo'-do, dah], *a.* Big-bellied.

Ventura [ven-too'-rah], *f.* 1. Luck, fortune. 2. Contingency, casualty, hazard, hap, venture. *Buena ventura*, Good fortune told by gipsies and vagrants. *Por ventura*, By chance. *Probar ventura*, To try one's fortune, to venture at, on, or upon. 3. Risk, danger. *A ventura* or *a la ventura*, At a venture, at hazard. *La ventura de García*, (Iron.) Misfortune.

Venturero, ra [ven-too-ray'-ro, rah], *a.* 1. Casual, incidental. 2. Lucky, fortunate. 3. Vagrant, idle, adventurous.

Venturero [ven-too-ray'-ro], *m.* Fortune-hunter, adventurer, land-loper.

Venturilla [ven-too-reel'-lyah], *f.* Good luck.

Venturina [ven-too-ree'-nah], *f.* Goldstone, a precious stone of a brown colour spotted with gold. *Venturina artificial*, Aventurin, a brown glass flecked with brass filings.

Venturo, ra [ven-too'-ro, rah], *a.* Future; that which is to come.

Venturón [ven-too-rone'], *m. aug.* Great luck.

Venturosamente, *adv.* Luckily, fortunately.

Venturoso, sa [ven-too-ro'-so, sah], *a.* Lucky, fortunate, successful, happy, prosperous.

Venus [vay'-noos], *f.* 1. Venus, the goddess of beauty and love. 2. A beautiful woman. 3. Venery, sensual pleasure. 4. (Chem.) Copper.—*m.* (Acad.) Venus; Hesper; the evening star, the planet nearest the earth.

Venusio [vay-noo'-se-o], *m.* Copper in the highest grade of perfection, inalterable in the free air, and hence highly useful in the industrial arts.

Venustidad [vay-noos-te-dahd'], *f.* Beauty, gracefulness.

Venusto, ta [vay-noos'-to, tah], *a.* Beautiful, graceful.

Venza [ven'-thah], *f.* Scarfskin, used by gold-beaters.

(*Yo veo, yo ví, yo vea. V.* VER.)

Ver [verr], *va.* 1. To see, to look into. 2. To see, to observe, to consider, to reflect. 3. To see, to visit. 4. To foresee, to forecast. 5. To fancy, to imagine; to judge. 6. To see, to find out, to discover; to explore. 7. To be present at the report of a law-suit. 8. To experience. 9. To examine. 10. To see at a future time. 11. Used with the particle *ya*, it is generally a menace; as, *ya verá*, he shall see. *Ver venir*, To see what one is driving at; to await the resolution or determination of another person. *Es de ver, es para ver* or *es digno de ser visto*, It is worth notice, it is worthy of being observed. *Estar de ver*, To be worth seeing. *Estar por ver*, To be yet to come to pass; to be doubtful. *No poder ver a alguno*, To abhor or detest one, not to suffer or endure him. *Al ver*, On seeing a thing. *A mi ver*, In my opinion, as far as I can see. *Dar a ver*, To show any thing. *¿A ver?* Is it not so? let us see (for "*vamos a ver*"). *A ver* or *veámoslo*. Let us see it. *A más ver* or *hasta más ver*, (Coll.) Farewell, until we see you again. (*Cf.* German, *auf wiedersehen*, and French, *au revoir*.) *Hacer ver*, To show or to make appear. *Si te ví (ya) no me acuerdo*, Out of sight, out of mind. *Ver tierras* or *mundo*, To travel. *Tener que ver una persona con otra*, To have relation or connection; to have carnal communication. *Eso nada tiene que ver con esto*, That has nothing to do with this. *Ver a hurtadillas*, To look over the shoulders. *Ojos que no ven, corazón que no siente*, (prov.) Out of sight, out of mind. *Ver el pleito mal parado*, To see a thing in great danger; to see the weak points of a case. *Ver por vista de ojos*, To see with one's own eyes. *Ver las orejas del lobo*, To see the ears of the wolf, to be in great danger. *¡A Dios y veámonos!* Farewell! we shall meet again. *No ver gota*, To lack sufficient light for seeing. *No ver siete sobre un asno*, To be short-sighted. *Por atún, y ver al duque*, To kill two birds with one stone. *Ver visiones*, To build castles in the air. *Ver el cielo abierto*, To see a great opportunity. *Ojos que le vieron ir, no le verán venir*, An opportunity lost never returns. *Ver con muchos ojos*, To observe very carefully.—*vr.* 1. To be seen; to be in a place proper to be seen; to be conspicuous. 2. To find one's self in a state or situation. *Verse pobre*, To be reduced to poverty. *Verse negro*, To be in great want or affliction; to be greatly embarrassed. 3. To be obvious or evident. 4. To concur, to agree. 5. To represent the image or likeness, to see one's self in a glass. 6. To know the cards, at play. *Ver si*, To try to, to attempt. *Verse en ello*, To consider, to weigh in the mind. *Verse con alguno*, To have a crow to pluck with one. *Ya se ve*, (1) It is undeniable; it is evident; it is as you say; it is easily to be seen; certainly; to be sure. (2) (Iron.) Likely indeed that such a thing should happen. *Verse* or *irse viendo*, To discover, to view what should be concealed. *Verse y desearse*, To have very great care, anxiety, and fatigue in executing a thing. *No te verás en ese espejo*, You will not succeed. *No verse de polvo*, To have been grossly insulted. *Verse las caras*, (lit. To see each other face to face) "There'll be the mischief to pay." *Verse entre* or *en las astas del toro*, To be in the greatest danger. *Hacer ver a uno las estrellas*, To make one feel a quick, lively pain; to make him see stars.

Ver, *m.* 1. Sense of sight, seeing. 2. Light, view, aspect, appearance.

Vera [vay'-rah], *f.* 1. (Prov.) Edge, border. *V.* ORILLA. 2. An American tree of very hard wood. *Vera efigies*, A faithful portrait.

Veracidad [vay-rah-the-dahd'], *f.* Veracity, fidelity.

Veramente [vay-rah-men'-tay], *adv.* (Obs.) Truly.

Veranada [vay-rah-nah'-dah], *f.* Summer season.

Veranadero [vay-rah-nah-day'-ro], *m.* Place where cattle pasture in summer.

Veranal [vay-rah-nahl'], *a.* Summer, relating to summer.

Veranar, Veranear [vay-rah-nar', vay-rah-nay-ar'], *vn.* To spend or pass the summer.

Veraneo [vay-rah-nay'-o], *m.* 1. The act of passing the summer, or part of it, in some particular way or place. 2. *V.* VERANERO.

Veranero [vay-rah-nay'-ro], *m.* Place where cattle graze in summer.

Veranico, illo, ito [vay-rah-nee'-co], *m. dim.* of VERANO. *El veranico* or *veranillo de San Martín*, (Coll.) The Indian summer.

Veraniego, ga [vay-rah-ne-ay'-go, gah], *a.* 1. Relating to the summer season. 2. Thin or sickly in summer. 3. Imperfect, defective.

Verano [vay-rah'-no], *m.* 1. Summer season. 2. In Ecuador, the dry season.

Veras [vay'-ras], *f. pl.* 1. Reality, truth. 2. Earnestness, fervour, and activity with which things are done or desired. *De veras*, In truth, really; joking apart. *Con muchas veras*, Very earnestly. (Lat. verus, true.)

Veratrina [vay-ra-tree'-nah], *f.* Veratrine, alkaloid of hellebore.

Veratro, *m. V.* ELÉBORO.

Veraz [vay-rath'], *a.* Veracious.

Verbal [ver-bahl'], *a.* Verbal; oral; nuncupatory. nuncupative. *Copia verbal*, A literal copy.

Verbalmente, *adv.* Verbally, orally.

Verbasco [ver-bahs'-co], *m.* (Bot.) Great mullein. Verbascum thapsus.

Verbásculo [ver-bahs'-coo-lo], *m.* (Bot.) Mullein. Verbascum lichnitis.

Verbena [ver-bay'-nah], *f.* 1. (Bot.) Vervain, verbena. Verbena officinalis. *Coger la verbena*, (Met.) To rise early to take a walk. 2. In Madrid, the evening, given to diversions, before some celebrated saint's day.

Verbenáceas [ver-bay-nah'-thay-as], *f. pl.* The verbena or vervain family of plants.

Verberación [ver-bay-rah-the-on'], *f.* Verberation; the act of the wind or water striking against any thing.

Verberar [ver-bay-rar'], *va.* To verberate, to beat, to strike; to dart against: applied to wind and water.

Verbigracia [ver-be-grah'-the-ah], *adv.* For example, for instance: in abbreviation, *v. g.* or *v. gr.*, corresponding to *e. g.* in English books.

Verbo [verr'-bo], *m.* (Gram.) Verb. 2. Word, second person of the holy Trinity. *Verbos*, Swearing, angry expressions; abusive language. *Echar verbos*, To curse, to swear. *De verbo ad verbum*, Word for word, literally. *Verbo activo*, Transitive or active verb. *Verbo neutro*, Intransitive or

neuter verb. *Verbo substantivo*, The verb *ser*, as indicating essence or substance. *En un verbo*, At once, without delay. *Verbo unipersonal*, An impersonal verb, one used only in the third person.
Verbosidad [ver-bo-se-dahd'], *f.* Verbosity, wordiness.
Verboso, sa [ver-bo'-so, sah], *a.* Verbose, prolix.
Verdacho [ver-dah'-cho], *m.* A kind of gritty green earth, used by painters.
Verdad [ver-dahd'], *f.* 1. Truth, veracity, reality. 2. Truth, verity, clear expression; certain existence of things. 3. A sort of delicate paste. 4. Axiom, maxim, truism. 5. Virtue of veracity or truth. *Verdad de Perogrullo*, A notorious truth. *Verdad es que* or *es verdad que*, True it is that. *Tratar verdad*, To love truth. *A la verdad* or *de verdad*, Truly, in fact, in truth. *Es verdad*, It is true. *En verdad*, *V.* VERDADERAMENTE.
Verdaderamente, *adv.* Truly, in fact, verily, indeed, legitimately.
Verdadero, ra [ver dah-day'-ro, rah], *a.* True, real, sincere, ingenuous, good, veritable; truthful.
Verdal [ver-dahl'], *a.* 1. *Ciruela verdal*, green gage, a plum. 2. (Calif.) *Uva verdal, o verdeja*, an early white grape of sweet flavour.
Verdasca [ver-dahs'-cah], *f.* *V.* VARDASCA.
Verde [verr'-day], *m.* 1. Green, verdure. 2. Verdigris. 3. Youth. 4. Person in the bloom of age. 5. Green barley or grass, given to horses or mules as a purge. *Darse un verde*, To amuse one's self for a short time. *Verde forzado*, Green made by mixing blue and yellow. *Verde limón*, Bright green. *Verde botella*, Bottle green. *Verde pardo*, Brown green. —*a.* 1. Green, of the colour of plants. 2. Unripe, immature, not perfect; fresh. 3. Young, blooming; verdant. *Viejo verde*, A boyish old man. 4. Loose, immodest, smutty, savouring of obscenity.
Verdea [ver-day'-ah], *f.* A sort of Florence white wine.
Verdear [ver-day-ar'], *vn.* To grow green, to get a greenish colour.—*va.* To collect grapes and olives to sell.
Verdeceledón [ver-day-thay-lay-done'], *m.* Sea-green, a colour made of light blue and straw colour.
Verdecer [ver-day-therr'], *vn.* To grow green.
Verdecico, ica, ito, ita [ver-day-thee'-co], *a. dim.* of VERDE.
Verdecillo [ver-day-theel'-lyo], *m.* (Orn.) Greenfinch. Loxia chloris.
Verdecillo, illa [ver-day-theel'-lyo], *a. dim.* Greenish.
Verdeesmeralda [ver-day-es-may-rahl'-dah], *a.* Emerald green.
Verdegay [ver-day-gah'-e], *m.* & *a.* Verditer: applied to a light bright green.
Verdeguear [ver-day-gay-ar'], *vn.* To grow green.
Verdeja [ver-day'-hah], *a.* *V.* VERDAL, 2d def.
Verdemar [ver-day-mar'], *m.* & *a.* Sea-green, used by painters.
Verdemontaña [ver-day-mon-tah'-nyah], *f.* Mountain-green, a mineral imported from Hungary, and a green paint prepared from it.
Verdeoscuro, ra [ver-day-os-coo'-ro, rah], *a.* & *m.* (Prov.) Dark green, greenish.
Verderol [ver-day-role'], *m.* 1. (Orn.) The yellow-hammer. 2. Kind of green shell-fish.
Verderón [ver-day-ron'], *m.* 1. (Zool.) A shell-fish about two inches long with deep grooves. 2. (Prov.) *V.* VERDEROL, the bird.
Verdete [ver-day'-tay], *m.* Verditer, copper acetate. *V.* CARDENILLO.
Verdevejiga [ver-day-vay-hee'-gah], *f.* Sap-green, deep-coloured green.
Verdezuelo [ver-day-thoo-ay'-lo], *m.* *V.* VERDEROL.
Verdín [ver-deen'], *m.* 1. *V.* VERDINA. 2. Green scum on still water or damp walls. 3. Oxide of copper.
Verdina [ver-dee'-nah], *f.* The green colour of fruits when not ripe.
Verdinegro, gra [ver-de-nay'-gro, grah], *a.* Of a deep green colour.
Verdino, na [ver-dee'-no, nah], *a.* Of a bright green colour.
Verdiseco, ca [ver-de-say'-co, cah], *a.* Pale green.
Verdolaga [ver-do-lah'-gah], *f.* (Bot.) Purslane. Portulaca oleracea.
Verdón [ver-done'], *m.* (Orn.) Greenfinch. Loxia chloris.
Verdor [ver-dor'], *m.* 1. Verdure, herbage, green colour of plants. 2. Acerbity or unpleasant taste of unripe fruit. 3. Vigour and strength of the animal body. *Verdores*, Youth, age of vigour.
Verdoso, sa [ver-do'-so, sah], *a.* Greenish.
Verdoyo [ver-do'-yo], *m.* A green mould growing on walls.
Verdugado [ver-doo-gah'-do], *m.* Under petticoat formerly worn.
Verdugal [ver-doo-gahl'], *m.* Young shoots growing in a wood after cutting.
Verdugo [ver-doo'-go], *m.* 1. The young shoot of a tree. 2. Rapier, a long, narrow sword. 3. Welt, mark of a lash on the skin. 4. Hangman, executioner, headsman. *Pagar los azotes al verdugo*, To return good for evil. 5. Things which afflict the mind. 6. Very cruel person. 7. (Arch.) Row of bricks in a stone or mud wall. 8. Small rings for the ears, hoop. 9. (Mil.) Leathern whip.
Verdugón [ver-doo-gone'], *m.* 1. A long shoot of a tree. 2. (Aug.) A large mark of a lash.
Verduguillo [ver-doo-geel'-lyo], *m.* 1. (Dim.) A small shoot of a tree. 2. A small, narrow razor. 3. A long, narrow sword.
Verdulera [ver-doo-lay'-rah], *f.* 1. Market-woman, who sells vegetables and herbs. 2. A mean, low woman; a word of contempt.
Verdulería [ver-doo-lay-ree'-ah], *f.* Vegetable stand, vegetable shop.
Verdulero [ver-doo-lay'-ro], *m.* Greengrocer.
Verdura [ver-doo'-rah], *f.* 1. Verdure. 2. Greens, culinary vegetables, garden stuff. 3. Foliage in landscape and tapestry. 4. Vigour, luxuriance.
Verdurita [ver-doo-ree'-tah], *f.* Slight herbage or vegetation.
Verdusco, ca [ver-doos'-co, cah], *a.* Greenish, verging upon green.
Verecundo, da [vay-ray-coon'-do, dah], *a.* Bashful, diffident. *V.* VERGONZOSO.
Vereda [vay-ray'-dah], *f.* 1. Path, footpath. 2. Circular order or notice sent to several towns or places. 3. Route of travelling preachers. 4. (Peru) Sidewalk.
Veredario, ria [vay-ray-dah'-re-o, ah], *a.* Hired, on hire: applied to horses, carriages, etc.
Veredero [vay-ray-day'-ro], *m.* Messenger sent with orders or despatches.
Veredicto [vay-ray-deec'-to], *m.* 1. (For.) Verdict, the decision of a trial jury. 2. Sentence, decree, opinion.
Veretilo [vay-ray-tee'-lo], *m.* Sea-pen, veretillum, a pennatulid polipary common in the Mediterranean.
Verga [ver'-gah], *f.* 1. (Naut.) Yard. *Verga seca*, Cross-jack yard. *Poner las vergas en cruz*, To square the yards. 2. The organ of generation in male animals, penis. 3. Nerve or cord of the cross-bow.
Vergajo [ver-gah'-ho], *m.* Cord of the penis of the bull and other quadrupeds, especially when separated from them (pizzle).
Vergajón [ver-gah-hone'], *a.* *Hierro vergajón*, Round iron.
Vergarzoso [ver-gar-tho'-so], *m.* (Zool.) A species of American armadillo.
Vergel [ver-hel'], *m.* 1. Fruit and flower garden. 2. Luxuriant vegetation.
Vergeta [ver-hay'-tah], *f.* A small twig.
Vergeteado, da [ver-hay-tay-ah'-do, dah], *a.* (Her.) Vergette, paley, having the field divided by several small pales.
Vergonzante [ver-gon-thahn'-tay], *a.* Bashful, shamefaced.—*com.* An honest, decent, needy person.
Vergonzosamente, *adv.* Shamefully, bashfully; confoundedly.
Vergonzoso, sa [ver-gon-tho'-so, sah], *a.* 1. Bashful, modest, shamefaced; diffident. 2. Shameful; contumelious. *Partes vergonzosas*, Privy parts.
Verguear [ver-gay-ar'], *va.* To beat with a rod.
Vergüenza [ver-goo-en'-thah], *f.* 1. Shame. 2. Bashfulness, confusion; modesty; diffidence, honour. 3. A base action. 4. Regard of one's own character; dignity, honour. 5. (Obs.) Curtain before windows or doors. *Perder la vergüenza*, To become abandoned. *Tener vergüenza*, To be ashamed. *Es una vergüenza*, It is a shameful thing. *Vergüenzas*, Privy parts.
Vergueta [ver-gay'-tah], *f.* A small switch or rod.
Verguilla [ver-geel'-lyah], *f.* Gold or silver wire without silk.
Vericueto [vay-re-coo-ay'-to], *m.* A rough and pathless place. *Vericuetos*, Strange or ridiculous ideas.
Verídico, ca [vay-ree'-de-co, cah], *a.* Veridical, telling truth.
Verificación [vay-re-fe-cah-the-on'], *f.* Inquiry, examen, verification, by argument or evidence.
Verificador, ra [vay-re-fe-cah-dor', rah], *a.* Verifying, checking.—*m.* & *f.* Checker, tester, verifier.
Verificar [vay-re-fe-car'], *va.* 1. To verify, to prove what was doubted. 2. To verify, to confirm, to prove by evidence; to examine the truth of a thing.—*vr.* To be verified, to prove true.
Verificativo, va [vay-re-fe-cah-tee'-vo, vah], *a.* Tending to prove; verificative.
Verija [vay-ree'-hah], *f.* Region of the genitals.
Veril [vay-reel'], *m.* (Naut.) The shore of a bay, of a sound, etc.
Verilear [vay-re-lay-ar'], *vn.* (Naut.) To sail along the shore.
Verino [vay-ree'-no], *m.* 1. A fine sort of South American tobacco, grown in a locality of the same name. 2. (Prov.) Pimple, small pustule.
Verisímil [vay-re-see'-meel], *a.* Probable, likely, credible.
Verisimilitud [vay-re-se-me-le-tood'], *f.* Verisimilitude, probability, likelihood.
Verisímilmente [vay-re-see'-meel-men-tay], *adv.* Probably, likely.

Verja [ver'-hah], *f.* Grate of a door or window; a grate with cross-bars.
Verjel [ver-hel'], *m.* 1 Flower-garden; a beautiful orchard. 2. Any thing pleasing to the sight.
Vermes [verr'-mes], *m. pl.* Intestinal worms.
Vermiculación [ver-me-coo-lah-the-on'], *f.* (Littl. us.) Vermiculation.
Vermicular [ver-me-coo-lar'], *a.* Vermiculous, full of grubs; vermicular.
Vermicular [ver-me-coo-lar'], *va.* (Arch.) To vermiculate, to ornament an edifice with worm-like figures.
Vermiforme [ver-me-for'-may], *a.* Vermiform, worm-like.
Vermífugo [ver-mee'-foo-go], *a.* & *m.* (Med.) Vermifuge, anthelmintic.
Verminoso, sa [ver-me-no'-so, sah], *a.* Full of grubs, verminous.
Vermíparo, ra [ver-mee'-pa-ro, rah], *a.* Vermiparous, producing worms.
Vermívoro, ra [ver-mee'-vo-ro, rah], *a.* Vermivorous, eating worms or grubs.
Vernáculo, la [ver-nah'-coo-lo, lah], *a.* Vernacular, native, of one's own country. *Lengua vernácula*, Vernacular language.
Vernal [ver-nahl'], *a.* Vernal, belonging to spring.
Vernerita [ver-nay-ree'-tah], *f.* (Min.) Wernerite, a translucent sodium-calcium silicate.
Vernier [ver-ne-err'], *m.* (Opt.) Vernier.
Veronense, Veronés, sa [vay-ro-nen'-say, vay-ro-nes', sah], *a.* Veronese, of Verona, in Italy.
Vero, ra [vay'-ro, rah], *a.* (Obs.) True, real. *De veras*, In truth.
Vero [vay'-ro], *m.* (Her.) Cup or bell-formed vase on a shield.
Verónica [vay-ro'-ne-cah], *f.* 1. Image of the face of our Lord Jesus Christ. 2. (Bot.) Speedwell. Veronica officinalis.
Verosímil [vay-ro-see'-meel], *a.* Verisimilar. *V.* VERISÍMIL.
Verosimilitud [vay-ro-se-me-le-tood'], *f.* Verisimility. *V.* VERISIMILITUD.
Verraca [ver-rah'-cah], *f.* (Naut.) A tent pitched on shore by sailors for sheltering stores or utensils.
Verraco [ver-rah'-co], *m.* Boar, male swine.
Verraquear [ver-rah-kay-ar'], *vn.* 1. To grunt like a boar. 2. (Met. Coll.) To cry angrily and long: used of little children.
Verriondez [ver-re-on-deth'], *f.* 1. Rutting-time of boars and other animals. 2. Withering state of herbs.
Verriondo, da [ver-re-on'-do, dah], *a.* 1. Foaming like a boar at rutting-time. 2. Withering, flaccid.
Verrón [ver-rone'], *m.* *V.* VERRACO. (Acad.)
Verrucaria [ver-roo-cah'-re-ah], *f.* (Bot.) Wartwort. Euphorbia helioscopia.
Verruga [ver-roo'-gah], *f.* Wart, pimple.
Verrugoso, sa [ver-roo-go'-so, sah], *a.* Warty.
Verruguera [ver-roo-gay'-rah], *f.* (Bot.) European turnsole. Heliotropium europæum.
Verruguica, illa, ita, *f. dim.* A small wart or pimple.
Verruguiento, ta [ver-roo-gee-en'-to, tah], *a.* Full of warts, warty.
Versado, da [ver-sah'-do, dah], *a.* & *pp.* of VERSAR. Versed, conversant. *Versado en diferentes lenguas*, Conversant in different languages.
Versal [ver-sahl'], *a.* (Print.) *V.* MAYÚSCULA.
Versalilla, Versalita [ver-sah-leel'-lyah, ee'-tah], *f.* & *a.* (Print.) Small capital letter.
Versar [ver-sar'], *vn.* & *vr.* To be versed or conversant; to grow skilful in the management of a business. With the preposition *sobre*, to treat of, to write upon, to discuss.
Versátil [ver-sah'-teel], *a.* 1. Versatile, which may be turned readily. 2. Changeable, variable.
Versatilidad [ver-sah-te-le-dahd'], *f.* Variability, inconstancy.
Versecillo [ver-say-theel'-lyo], *m. dim.* *V.* VERSILLO.
Versería [ver-say-ree'-ah], *f.* A collection of verses; poetry.
Versico [ver-see'-co], *m. dim.* *V.* VERSILLO.
Versícula [ver-see'-coo-lah], *f.* Place where the choir-books are placed.
Versiculario [ver-se-coo-lah'-re-o], *m.* One who takes care of the choir-books.
Versículo [ver-see'-coo-lo], *m.* 1. Versicle, a small part of the responsory which is said in the canonical hours. 2. Verse of a chapter.
Versificación [ver-se-fe-cah-the-on'], *f.* Versification.
Versificador, ra [ver-se-fe-cah-dor', rah], *m.* & *f.* Versifier, versificator.
Versificar [ver-se-fe-car'], *va.* To versify, to make verses.
Versiforme [ver-se-for'-may], *a.* Subject to change of form.
Versillo [ver-seel'-lyo], *m. dim.* A little verse.
Versión [ver-se-on'], *f.* 1. Translation, version. 2. Version, manner of relation. 3. (Med.) Version, turning of a child for facilitating delivery.
Versista [ver-sees'-tah], *m.* (Coll.) Versifier, verseman, versificator, one who writes blank verse.
Verso [verr'-so], *m.* 1. Verse, a line consisting of a certain succession of sounds and number of syllables; metre. 2. Culverin of a small bore, now disused. *Verso de arte mayor*, Verse of twelve syllables.—*pl.* Lines.
Vértebra [verr'-tay-brah], *f.* Vertebra, a joint in the back-bone.
Vertebrado, da [ver-tay-brah'-do, dah], *a.* Vertebrate, having vertebræ.—*m. pl.* (Zool.) Vertebrate animals.
Vertebral [ver-tay-brahl'], *a.* Vertebral.
Vertedera [ver-tay-day'-rah], *f.* (Agr.) The mould-board of a plough.
Vertedero [ver-tay-day'-ro], *m.* Sewer, drain.
Vertedor, ra [ver-tay-dor', rah], *m.* & *f.* 1. Nightman, who empties the common sewer. 2. Conduit, sewer. 3. (Naut.) Scoop, made of wood, for throwing out water: used in boats.
Vertello [ver-tayl'-lyo], *m.* (Naut.) Truck to form the parrels.
Verter [ver-terr'], *va.* 1. To spill, to shed. 2. To empty vessels. 3. To translate writings. 4. To divulge, to publish, to reveal a secret. 5. To exceed, to abound.
Vertibilidad [ver-te-be-le-dahd'], *f.* Versatility, versatileness.
Vertible [ver-tee'-blay], *a.* Movable, changeable, variable.
Vertical [ver-te-cahl'], *a.* Vertical, perpendicular to the horizon. *Primer vertical*, (Ast.) *m.* The plane which intersects the horizon in the points of the true east and west.
Verticalmente, *adv.* Vertically.
Vértice [ver'-te-thay], *m.* Vertex, zenith; crown of the head.
Verticidad [ver-te-the-dahd'], *f.* The power of turning, verticity; rotation.
Verticilado, da [ver-te-the-lah'-do, dah], *a.* (Bot.) Verticillate.
Verticilo [ver-te-thee'-lo], *m.* (Bot.) Verticil, a whorl.
Vertiente [ver-te-en'-tay], *com.* 1. Waterfall, cascade. 2. Spring, source. —*pa.* Flowing.
Vertiginoso, sa [ver-te-he-no'-so, sah], *a.* Giddy, vertiginous.
Vértigo [verr'-te-go], *m.* 1. Giddiness, vertigo. 2. Transient disturbance of the judgment.
Vertimiento, *m.* Effusion, shedding.
Vesana [vay-sah'-nah], *f.* (Agr.) A straight furrow.
Vesania [vay-sah'-ne-ah], *f.* Incipient insanity, craziness.
Vesical [vay-se-cahl'], *a.* 1. (Zool.) Vesical, relating to the bladder. 2. Forming bubbles on escaping from an orifice.
Vesícula [vay-see'-coo-lah], *f.* 1. (Anat.) Vesicle, a membranous sac like a bladder. 2. (Bot.) Vesicle, a little air-sac of some aquatic plants. *Vesícula biliar*, The gall-bladder. *Vesícula elemental* or *orgánica*, Elementary mass of bioplasm, cell.
Vesicular [vay-se-coo-lar'], *a.* Vesicular, like a little bladder or vesicle.
Vesiculoso, sa [vay-se-coo-lo'-so, sah], *a.* Vesiculate, full of vesicles.
Veso [vay'-so], *m.* (Zool.) Weasel, a carnivorous animal. *Veso fétido*, Pole-cat.
Véspero [ves'-pay-ro], *m.* Vesper, the evening star.
Vespertillo [ves-per-teel'-lyo], *m.* Bat. *V.* MURCIÉLAGO.
Vespertina [ves-per-tee'-nah], *f.* Evening discourse in universities.
Vespertino, na [ves-per-tee'-no, nah], *a.* Vespertine, happening in the evening.
Vespertino [ves-per-tee'-no], *m.* Doctrinal sermon preached in the evening.
Vesquir [ves-keer'], *vn.* (Obs.) *V.* VIVIR.
Vesta [ves'-tah], *f.* 1. Vesta, goddess of the domestic hearth. 2. One of the asteroids.
Vestal [ves-tahl'], *f.* & *a.* Vestal virgin, a priestess of the temple of Vesta.
Veste [ves'-tay], *f.* (Poet.) Clothes, garments. *V.* VESTIDO.
Vestfaliano, na [vest-fah-le-ah'-no, nah], *a.* (Acad.) Westphalian, of Westphalia.
Vestíbulo [ves-tee'-boo-lo], *m.* 1. Vestibule, portal, hall, lobby. 2. Vestibule, a cavity of the internal ear.
Vestido [ves-tee'-do], *m.* 1. Dress, wearing apparel, clothes, garments, clothing, garb, habiliments. 2. Ornament, embellishment. *Vestidos usados*, Second-hand clothes. *Vestido de corte*, Court-dress. *Vestido y calzado*, Without labour. *Vestido de mujer*, Gown. —*Vestido, da, pp.* of VESTIR.
Vestidura [ves-te-doo'-rah], *f.* 1. Vesture, robe of distinction. 2. Vestment for divine worship.
Vestidurilla, ita [ves-te-doo-reel'-lyah], *f. dim.* of VESTIDURA.
Vestigio [ves-tee'-he-o], *m.* 1. Vestige, footstep; ruins, remains of buildings. 2. Memorial, mark, sign, index. *Vestigio horizontal* or *vertical*, In stone cutting, the horizontal or vertical figure of the shadows formed by the sun's perpendicular rays.
Vestiglo [ves-tee'-glo], *m.* Horrid and formidable monster.
Vestimenta [ves-te-men'-tah], *f.* Clothes, garments.—*pl.* Ecclesiastical robes.
Vestimento [ves-te-men'-to], *m.* (Obs.) *V.* VESTIDO and VESTIDURA.
Vestir [ves-teer'], *va.* 1. To clothe, to dress, to accoutre. 2. To deck, to adorn. 3. To make clothes for others. 4. To cloak, to disguise, to palliate. 5. To instruct, to inform, to advise. 6. To rough-cast the walls of a building.

7. To affect a passion or emotion. 8. To give liberally, to make liberal presents. 9. (Met.) To embellish a discourse. 10. Used of animals and plants in respect to their coverings. *Vestir el proceso*, To carry on a suit according to law.—*vn.* To dress in an especial colour or fashion. *Vestir de uniforme*, To dress in uniform.—*vr.* 1. To be covered; to be clothed. *El cielo se vistió de nubes*, The sky was overcast with clouds. *La primavera viste los campos*, Spring clothes the fields. 2. To dress one's self on rising after sickness. *Al que de ajeno se viste, en la calle lo desnudan*, He who wears borrowed plumes risks public exposure. *Vestirse una turca*, (Coll.) To get drunk. *Al revés me la vestí, ándese así*, As I began this way, I shall go on so; to be in for it.

Vestuario [ves-too-ah'-re-o], *m.* 1. Vesture, all the necessaries of dress; clothes; uniform; equipment, habiliment for the troop. 2. Tax for the equipment of the troop. 3. Vestry, place where clergymen dress. 4. Money given to ecclesiastics for dress, and stipends to assistants. 5. Greenroom, dressing-room in a theatre; vestiary. *Vestuarios*, Deacon and subdeacon who attend the priest at the altar.

Vestugo [ves-too'-go], *m.* Stem or bud of an olive.

Veta [vay'-tah], *f.* 1. Vein of ore, metal, or coal in mines. 2. Vein in wood or marble, grain. 3. Stripe of a different colour in cloth or stuff. *Descubrir la veta*, To discover one's sentiments or designs. 4. (Ecuador) Sickness, nausea, and headache from great elevations in the Andes. *Cf.* ZAROCHE.

Vetado, da [vay-tah'-do, dah], *a.* & *pp.* of VETEAR. *V.* VETEADO.

Vetar [vay-tar'], *va.* To veto.

Veteado, da [vay-tay-ah'-do, dah], *a.* Striped, veined, streaky, crossgrained.

Vetear [vay-tay-ar'], *va.* To variegate, to form veins of different colours, to grain.

Veterano, na [vay-tay-rah'-no, nah], *a.* Experienced, veteran, long practised: particularly applied to soldiers.

Veterano, *m.* Veteran, an old soldier.

Veterinaria [vay-tay-re-nah'-re-ah], *f.* Veterinary medicine or surgery.

Veterinario [vay-tay-re-nah'-re-o], *m.* Veterinary surgeon.

Vetica, illa [vay-tee'-cah, eel'-lyah], *f. dim.* A small vein; a narrow stripe.

Veto [vay'-to], *m.* Veto, official disapproval of a law.

Vetustamente [vay-toos-tah-men'-tay], *adv.* Anciently.

Vetustez [vay-toos-teth'], *f.* Antiquity, notable old age.

Vetusto, ta [vay-toos'-to, tah], *a.* Very ancient.

Vez [veth], *f.* 1. Turn, the alternative of things in successive progression. 2. Time, or the determinate time or occasion on which any thing is performed. 3. Epoch. 4. Return, the act or performance of any thing that bears a successive progression. 5. Draught, the quantity of liquor drunk at once. 6. Herd of swine belonging to the inhabitants of a place. 7. United with *cada*, it intimates repetition. *Cada vez*, Each time.—*pl.* Power or authority committed to a substitute. ***A la vez*** or ***por vez***, Successively, by turns, by order or series. *Una vez*, Once. *Dos veces*, Twice. *Tres veces*, Thrice or three times. *De una vez*, At once. *Más de una vez*, More than once. *En vez*, Instead of. *Tal vez*, Perhaps; seldom, once in a way. *Tal cual vez*, On a singular occasion or time, seldom, rarely, once in a way. *Llegará mi vez*, My turn will come. *Hacer las veces de otro*, To supply one's place. *A veces*, Sometimes, by turns, on some occasions. *Todas las vecés que*, Whenever, as often as. *A las veces, do cazar pensamos, cazados quedamos*, Sometimes the biter is bitten, one falls into one's own trap. *Al que yerra, perdónale una vez, mas no después*, Pardon the first fault, but punish subsequent ones.

Veza [vay'-thah], *f.* (Bot.) Vetch. Vicia. *Veza cultivada*, Winter and summer tares, vetch. Vicia sativa. *V.* ARVEJA.

Vezar [vay-thar'], *va.* To accustom, to habituate. *V.* AVEZAR.

Vía [vee'-ah], *f.* 1. Way, road, route. *V.* CAMINO. 2. Carriage track, mark of wheels. 3. Grade, track, permanent way, line, of a railway; also rail. 4. Way, mode, manner, method, procedure, gait. 5. Profession, calling, trade. 6. Post-road. 7. Passage, gut in the animal body. 8. Spiritual life. *Por vía*, In a manner or form. *Vía ejecutiva*, (Law) Levy, a legal writ of execution; attachment. *Vía férrea*, Railroad, railway. *Vía láctea*, (Ast.) The Milky Way. *Vía pública*, The streets of a town. *Vía recta*, Straight along, straight forward. *Vía reservada*, Office of a secretary of state and foreign affairs, for a private correspondence on secret affairs. *Vía Crucis* or *vía sacra*, Calvary, a place having paths, stations for crosses, altars, etc., in imitation of Christ's journey on Mount Calvary. *Vía purgativa*, (Theol.) First stage of a soul to perfection, by washing away its sins with tears.

Viabilidad [ve-ah-be-le-dahd'], *f.* (Med.) Viability, probability of life of the fœtus.

Viable [ve-ah'-blay], *a.* Viable, capable of living.

Viadera [ve-ah-day'-rah], *f.* Part of a loom near the treadles.

Viador [ve-ah-dor'], *m.* Passenger, traveller: generally used in a mystical sense.

Viaducto [ve-ah-dooc'-to], *m.* 1. Viaduct. 2. (Mex.) Expressway for rapid transit.

Viajador, ra [ve-ah-hah-dor', rah], *m.* & *f.* *V.* VIAJERO.

Viajante [ve-ah-hahn'-tay], *com.* & *pa.* 1. Traveller, voyager; travelling. 2. Commercial traveller.

Viajar [ve-ah-har'], *vn.* To travel, to perform a journey or voyage, to itinerate.

Viajata [ve-ah-hah'-tah], *f.* A short journey, especially one for a few days of diversion.

Viaje [ve-ah'-hay], *m.* 1. Journey, tour, voyage, travel. 2. Way, road. 3. (Arch.) Deviation from a right line. 4. Gait. 5. Excursion; errand. 6. Load carried at once. 7. Quantity of water from the general reservoir, to be divided into particular channels or conduits. *Buen viaje*, (1) Good journey or voyage. (2) Used to express indifference whether a thing is lost or not. Used also on throwing dead bodies into the sea, and signifies, Rest in peace. *Viaje redondo*, Voyage out and home, round trip.

Viajero, ra [ve-ah-hay'-ro, rah], *m.* & *f.* Traveller, passenger.

Viajes astronáuticos [ve-ah'-hays as-tro-nah'-oo-te-cos], *m. pl.* Space travel.

Vial [ve-ahl'], *a.* Wayfaring; belonging to a journey: used in a mystical sense.—*m.* Avenue, a road formed by two parallel rows of trees or shrubbery. (Acad.)

Vianda [ve-ahn'-dah], *f.* 1. Food, viands, meat, victuals, fare. 2. A meal served at table.

Viandante [ve-an-dahn'-tay], *m.* Traveller, passenger, especially a tramp.

Viandista [ve-an-dees'-tah], *m.* Waiter, who serves viands or puts them on the table.

Viaraza [ve-ah-rah'-thah], *f.* Looseness, diarrhœa: used only of animals.

Viático [ve-ah'-te-co], *m.* 1. Viaticum, provision for a journey. 2. Viaticum, the sacrament administered to the sick.

Vibdo, da [veeb'-do, dah], *a.* (Obs.) *V.* VIUDO.

Víbora [vee'-bo-rah], *f.* 1. Viper. Pelias berus. 2. (Met.) Viper, a malicious and perfidious person.

Viborera [ve-bo-ray'-rah], *f.* (Bot.) Viper's bugloss. Echium. *Viborera común*, Common viper's bugloss. Echium vulgare.

Viborezno, na [ve-bo-reth'-no, nah], *a.* Viperine, viperous.—*m.* Young, small viper.

Viborillo, illa [ve-bo-reel'-lyo, lyah], *m.* & *f. dim.* *V.* VIBOREZNO.

Vibración [ve-brah-the-on'], *f.* Vibration, oscillation, fluttering.

Vibrante [ve-brahn'-tay], *pa.* 1. Vibrating, undulating. 2. Bounding: used of the pulse.

Vibrar [ve-brar'], *va.* 1. To vibrate, to oscillate, to brandish. 2. To throw, to dart.—*vn.* To vibrate, to play up and down or to and fro.

Vibrátil [ve-brah'-teel], *a.* 1. Vibratile, capable of vibration. 2. (Med.) Vibratory, used of a pain in which the nerves of the patient vibrate like drawing cords.

Vibratilidad [ve-brah-te-le-dahd'], *f.* Faculty of producing vibrations.

Vibratorio, ria [ve-brah-to'-re-o, ah], *a.* Vibratory.

Vibrión [ve-bre-on'], *m.* (Biol.) Vibrio, a microbe endowed with an oscillating movement.

Viburno [ve-boor'-no], *m.* (Bot.) Viburnum. Viburnum. *Viburno común* or *lantana*, Wayfaring-tree, mealy guelder-rose. Viburnum lantana.

Vicaría [ve-cah-ree'-ah], *f.* Vicarship; vicarage. *Vicaría perpetua*, Perpetual curacy.

Vicaria [ve-cah'-re-ah], *f.* Vicar, the second superior in a convent of nuns. *Vicaria de coro*, *V.* VICARIO DE CORO.

Vicarial [ve-cah-re-ahl'], *a.* Vicarial, relating to a vicar, held by a vicar.

Vicariato [ve-cah-re-ah'-to], *m.* Vicarage; the dignity of a vicar; the district subjected to a vicar; vicarship.

Vicario [ve-cah'-re-o], *m.* 1. Vicar, deputy in ecclesiastical affairs. 2 Vicar, he who exercises the authority of the superior of a convent in his absence; one who transacts all ecclesiastical affairs as substitute for a bishop or archbishop. *Sacar por el vicario*, To convey a woman into a place of safety, by ecclesiastical authority, against the will of her parents or guardians, where she may freely declare her consent to a marriage. *Vicario apostólico*, Missionary bishop in non-Catholic countries. *Vicario de coro*, Choral-vicar, superintendent of the choir. *Vicario general*, Vicar-general, an ecclesiastical judge appointed to exercise jurisdiction over a whole territory, in opposition to a

vicario pedáneo, who has authority over a district only.
Vicario, ria [ve-cah'-re-o, ah], *a.* Vicarial, vicarious; vicariate.
Vice [vee'-thay]. Vice, used in composition to signify deputy, or one of the second rank.
Vicealmiranta [ve-thay-al-me-rahn'-tah], *f.* The galley next in order to the admiral's.
Vicealmirantazgo [ve-thay-al-me-ran-tath'-go], *m.* 1. Office or rank of vice-admiral. 2. Vice-admiralty.
Vicealmirante [ve-thay-al-me-rahn'-tay], *m.* Vice-admiral.
Vicecamarero [ve-thay-cah-ma-ray'-ro], *m.* Vice-chamberlain.
Vicecancelario [ve-thay-can-thay-lah'-re-o], *m.* *V.* VICECANCILLER.
Vicecanciller [ve-thay-can-theel-lyerr'], *m.* Vice-chancellor.
Viceconsiliario [ve-thay-con-se-le-ah'-re-o], *m.* Vice-counsellor.
Vicecónsul [ve-thay-con'-sool], *m.* Vice-consul.
Viceconsulado [ve-thay-con-soo-lah'-do], *m.* Vice-consulate.
Vicediós [ve-thay-de-os'], *m.* Sovereign pontiff.
Vicegerente [ve-thay-hay-ren'-tay], *a.* Vicegerent.
Vicelegado [ve-thay-lay-gah'-do], *m.* Vice-legate.
Vicelegatura [ve-thay-lay-gah-too'-rah], *f.* Office and jurisdiction of a vice-legate.
Vicemaestro [ve-thay-mah-es'-tro], *m.* Vice-principal.
Vicenal [ve-thay-nahl'], *a.* Arrived at the age of twenty years.
Vicepatrono [ve-thay-pah-tro'-no], *m.* Vice-patron.
Vicepresidencia [ve-thay-pray-se-den'-the-ah], *f.* Vice-presidency.
Vicepresidente [ve-thay-pray-se-den'-tay], *m.* Vice-president.
Viceprovincia [ve-thay-pro-veen'-the-ah], *f.* Collection of religious houses which are not erected into a province, but occasionally enjoy that rank.
Viceprovincial [ve-thay-pro-vin-the-ahl'], *m.* & *a.* Vice-provincial.
Vicerrector, ra [ve-ther-rec'-tor, rah], *m.* & *f.* Vice-rector.
Vicerrectorado, *m.* **Vicerrectoría**, *f.* [ve-ther-rec-to-rah'-do]. Vicerectorship.
Vicesenescal [ve-thay-say-nes-cahl'], *m.* Vice-seneschal or steward.
Vicesimario, ria [ve-thay-se-mah'-re-o, ah], *a.* Vicenary, belonging to the number twenty: twentieth.
Vicésimo, ma [ve-thay'-se-mo, mah], *a.* Twentieth. *V.* VIGÉSIMO.
Viceversa [vee-thay-ver'-sah], *adv.* On the contrary; to the contrary; vice versa.
Viciar [ve-the-ar'], *va.* 1. To vitiate, to mar, to spoil or corrupt. 2. To counterfeit, to adulterate. 3. To forge, to falsify. 4. To annul, to make void. 5. To deprave, to pervert. 6. To put a false construction on a passage or expression.—*vr.* To deliver one's self up to vices; to become too much attached or addicted to any thing.
Vicicilín [ve-the-the-leen'], *m.* (Orn.) A small American bird which seldom perches or sits. *V.* RESUCITADO.
Vicio [vee'-the-o], *m.* 1. Defect, imperfection of body, of soul, or of things; viciousness, faultiness, depravation, folly. 2. Vice, moral corruption, depravity. 3. Artifice, fraud. 4. Excessive appetite, extravagant desire. 5. Deviation from rectitude, defect or excess. 6. Luxuriant growth. *Los sembrados llevan mucho vicio*, The cornfields are luxuriant. 7. Forwardness or caprice of children. *De vicio*. By habit or custom. 8. Vices of horses or mules. *Echar de vicio*, To talk impudently. *Hablar de vicio*, To be an empty chatterer. *Quejarse de vicio*, To complain without cause, or make ado about trifles. *Tras el vicio viene el fornicio*, Idleness leads to debauchery.
Viciosamente [ve-the-o-sah-men'-tay], *adv.* Viciously; falsely; corruptly.
Vicioso, sa [ve-the-o'-so, sah], *a.* 1. Vicious. 2. Luxuriant, overgrown, vigorous. 3. Abundant; provided; delightful. 4. (Prov.) Spoiled: speaking of children.
Vicisitud [ve-the-se-tood'], *f.* Vicissitude.
Vicisitudinario, ria [ve-the-se-too-de-nah'-re-o, ah], *a.* Changeable, variable.
Víctima [veec'-te-mah], *f.* Victim; sacrifice.
Victimario [vic-te-mah'-re-o], *m.* Servant who attends the sacrificing priest.
Víctor, Vítor [veec'-tor, vee'-tor], *m.* 1. Shout, cry of acclamation. Long live! 2. Public rejoicing in honour of the achiever of some glorious deed. 3. Tablet containing a eulogy of the hero of a festival.
Victorear [vic-to-ray-ar'], *va.* To shout, to huzza. *V.* VITOREAR.
Victoria [vic-to'-re-ah], *f.* Victory, triumph, conquest, palm.—*int.* Victory. *Cantar victoria*, or *la victoria*, To triumph, to obtain victory or to rejoice for victory.
Victorial [vic-to-re-ahl'], *a.* Relating to victory.
Victoriosamente, *adv.* Victoriously.
Victorioso, sa [vic-to-re-oh'-so, sah], *a.* 1. Victorious, conquering. 2. Title given to warriors.
Vicuña [ve-coo'-nyah], *f.* Vicuña or vicugna, a South American wool-bearing quadruped, allied to the *Alpaca*, celebrated for its wool. Auchenia vicugna.
Vid [veed], *f.* 1. (Bot.) Vine, grapevine. Vitis. 2. (Obs.) Navel-string. *De mala vid, mal sarmiento*, Evil things cannot produce good results.
Vida [vee'-dah], *f.* 1. Life. 2. Living, continuance in life. 3. Life, the duration of it. 4. Livelihood. 5. Life, conduct, behaviour, deportment; state, condition. 6. Life, history of one's actions during life. 7. Aliment necessary to preserve life. 8. (Met.) Life, any thing animating and agreeable, liveliness. *Vida mía* or *mi vida*, My life: expression of endearment. *A vida*, With life. *No dejar hombre a vida*, Not to leave a living soul. 9. State of grace, eternal life. 10. Principle of nutrition, vital motions or functions. 11. (Law) The determined number of ten years. *Agua de vida*, (Obs.) Brandy. *Buscar la vida*, To earn an honest livelihood; to scrutinize the life of another. *Dar mala vida*, To treat very ill. *Darse buena vida*, To give one's self up to the pleasures of life; to conform one's self to reason and law. *De por vida*, For life, during life. *En mi vida* or *en la vida*, Never. *Hacer vida*, To live together as husband and wife. *Ser de vida*, To give hopes of life. *Personas de mala vida*, Profligate libertines. *Artículos de media vida*, Half-worn articles. *Artículos de dos tercios de vida*, Articles one-third worn out. *Pasar la vida*, To live very frugally, on necessaries only. *¡ Por vida!* By Jove! Interjection used for urging a concession or for asseveration and mild oath. *Saber las vidas ajenas*, To spy into other people's affairs. *Tener siete vidas*, To have escaped many perils.
Vidalita [ve-da-lee'-tah], *f.* A special form of Argentine folk poem.
Vida media [vee'-dah may'-de-ah], *f.* (Chem.) Half life.
Vide [vee'-day] (*imp.* of Lat. videre). See: a direction, in books, to the reader. Commonly abbreviated to V. *V.* VÉASE.
¡ Vidita ! [ve-dee'-tah], *f.* My life. Used in South America as an expression of tenderness.
Vidente [ve-den'-tay], *pa.* 1. He who sees, seeing. 2. (Obs.) A seer.
Vidriado [ve-dre-ah'-do], *m.* Glazed earthenware, crockery.
Vidriado, da [ve-dre-ah'-do, dah], *a.* Fretful, peevish, cross.—*pp.* of VIDRIAR.
Vidriar [ve-dre-ar'], *va.* To varnish, to glaze earthenware.
Vidriera [ve-dre-ay'-rah], *f.* 1. A glass window. 2. A glass case or cover. *Licenciado Vidriera*, Nickname for a person too delicate or fastidious.
Vidriería [ve-dre-ay-ree'-ah], *f.* Glazier's shop, a shop where glasswares are sold: glass-house, glass-shop, glassware.
Vidriero [ve-dre-ay'-ro], *m.* Glazier, a dealer in glass, glass-maker.
Vidrio [vee'-dre-o], *m.* 1. Glass. *Vidrio colorado* or *teñido de color*, Stained glass. *Vidrios planos* or *de vidriera*, Window glass. *Un vidrio de agua*, (Coll.) A tumbler of water. *Quien tiene tejado de vidrio, no tire piedras al de su vecino*, (prov.) He who lives in house of glass, should not throw stones at those who pass. 2. Vessel or other thing made of glass. 3. Any thing very nice and brittle. 4. A very touchy person. 5. (Poet.) Water. *Ir al vidrio*, To ride backward in a coach. *Pagar los vidrios rotos*, To receive undeserved punishment. *Vidrio cascado*, A singer who has lost his voice.
Vidrioso, sa [ve-dre-o'-so, sah], *a.* 1. Vitreous, brittle, glassy. 2. Slippery, as from ice or sleet. 3. Peevish, touchy, irascible. 4. Very delicate.
Vidual [ve-doo-ahl'], *a.* Belonging to widowhood.
Viduño, Vidueño [ve-doo'-nyo], *m.* Peculiar quality of grapes or vines. *V.* VEDUÑO.
Viejarrón, na [ve-ay-har-rone', nah], *m.* (Coll.) An old codger: it implies contempt.
Viejazo [ve-ay-hah'-tho], *m.* (Coll.) An old man worn out with age.
Viejecito, ita, Viejezuelo, ela [ve-ay-hay-thee'-to], *a.* Somewhat old.
Viejo, ja [ve-ay'-ho, hah], *a.* 1. Old, stricken in years. 2. Ancient, antiquated. 3. Applied to a youth of judgment and knowledge beyond his years. *Cuentos de viejas*, Old woman's stories. *Perro viejo*, (Coll.) A keen, clever, experienced person; old dog. *El viejo desvergonzado hace al niño osado*, If old people would have respect from the young, they must deserve it. *¿ Por qué va la vieja a la casa de moneda? Por lo que se le pega*, Why does the old woman go to the mint? For what she can get. (Imputation of mercenary motives.)
Vienense [ve-ay-nen'-say], *a.* Relating to Vienne in France.
Vienés, sa [ve-ay-nes', sah], *a.* Viennese, of Vienna (Austria).
Vientecillo [ve-en-tay-theel'-lyo], *m. dim.* A light wind.
Viento [ve-en'-to], *m.* 1. Wind. 2. The air, and the space it occupies. 3. Wind, its direction from a particular point. 4. Wind, any thing insignifi-

cant or light as wind; vanity, petty pride. 5. Windage of a gun. 6. Scent of dogs. 7. Nape-bone of a dog, between the ears. 8. Rope or cord, by which a thing is suspended. 9. Any thing that violently agitates the mind. 10. That which contributes to an end. *Viento de bolina*, (Naut.) A scant wind. *Viento contrario*, Foul wind. *Viento galerno*, A fresh gale. *Vientos generales*, Trade-winds. *Viento en popa*, Wind right aft. *Viento derrotero*, Wind on the beam. *Viento a la cuadra*, Quartering wind. *Viento escaso*, Slack wind. *Viento terral* or *de tierra*, A land breeze. *Quitar el viento a un bajel*, To becalm a ship. *Dar con la proa al viento*, To throw a ship up in the wind. *El viento refresca*, (Naut.) The wind freshens. *Cosas de viento*, Vain, empty trifles. *Moverse a todos vientos*, To be fickle, changeable, or wavering. *Dar el viento*, (Met.) To presume, to conjecture truly.

Vientre [ve-en'-tray], *m.* 1. Belly, abdomen. 2. Fœtus in the womb; pregnancy. 3. The belly or widest part of vessels. 4. The body, or essential part of an instrument or act. 5. Stomach, when speaking of a great eater. *El parto sigue al vientre*, The offspring follows the womb, respecting slavery or freedom. *Reses de vientre*, Breeding cattle. *Descargar el vientre*, To exonerate the belly. *Desde el vientre de su madre*, From his birth. *Regir el vientre*, To be set in order without disturbing the natural functions. *Sacar el vientre de mal año*, To dine better than usual, particularly in another's house.

Vientrecillo [ve-en-tray-theel'-lyo], *m. dim.* Ventricle.

Viernes [ve-err'-nes], *m.* 1. Friday. 2. Fast-day, when meat is not to be eaten. *Cara de viernes*, A wan, thin face. *Viernes Santo*, Good Friday.

(*Yo vierto, yo vierta*, from *Verter.* *V.* Entender.)

Viga [vee'-gah], *f.* Beam. *Viga de lagar*, Beam with which grapes or olives are pressed.

Vigente [ve-hen'-tay], *a.* In force: applied to laws, regulations, etc.

Vigésimo, ma [ve-hay'-se-mo, mah], *a.* Twentieth.

Vigía [ve-hee'-ah], *f.* 1. (Naut.) Rock which projects but slightly from the sea. 2. *V.* Atalaya. 3. Act of watching.—*m.* Lookout, watch.

Vigiar [ve-he-ar'], *vn.* (Naut.) To look out, to watch.

Vigilancia [ve-he-lahn'-the-ah], *f.* Vigilance, watchfulness, heedfulness.

Vigilante [ve-he-lahn'-tay], *a.* Watchful, vigilant, careful.—*m.* Watchman, guard.

Vigilantemente, *adv.* Vigilantly, heedfully.

Vigilar [ve-he-lar'], *vn.* To watch over, to keep guard.

Vigilativo, va [ve-he-lah-tee'-vo, vah], *a.* That which makes watchful.

Vigilia [ve-hee'-le-ah], *f.* 1. The act of being awake, or on the watch. 2. Lucubration, nocturnal study. 3. Vigil, a fast kept before a holiday; service used on the night before a holiday. 4. Watchfulness, want of sleep. 5. Watch, limited time for keeping guard. 6. Office of the dead, to be sung in churches.

Vigor [ve-gor'], *m.* Vigour, strength, force, energy.

Vigorar [ve-go-rar'], *va.* To strengthen, to invigorate.

Vigorizar [ve-go-re-thar'], *va.* 1. To invigorate. 2. (Met.) To animate, to inspirit.

Vigorosamente, *adv.* Vigorously, lustily.

Vigorosidad [ve-go-ro-se-dahd'], *f.* Vigour, strength.

Vigoroso, sa [ve-go-ro'-so, sah], *a.* Vigorous, strong, active; generous.

Vigota [ve-go'-tah], *f.* (Naut.) Dead-eye, chain plate.

Viguería [ve-gay-ree'-ah], *f.* (Naut.) The timber-work of a vessel.

Vigués, sa [ve-gays', sah], *a.* & *n.* Native of Vigo.

Vigueta [ve-gay'-tah], *f. dim.* A small beam.

Vihuela [ve-oo-ay'-lah], *f.* Guitar (fr. Viola).

Vihuelista [ve-oo-ay-lees'-tah], *com.* Guitar-player.

Vil [veel'], *a.* 1. Mean, despicable, sordid, servile. 2. Worthless, infamous, ungrateful, vile. 3. Contemptible, abject, paltry.

Vilano [ve-lah'-no], *m.* 1. Burr or down of the thistle. 2. (Obs.) *V.* Milano.

Vileza [ve-lay'-thah], *f.* 1. Meanness, vileness, depravity. 2. Contemptibleness, abjectness. 3. A disgraceful action, an infamous deed; turpitude, paltriness. 4. Rabble, mob.

Vilipendiador, ra [ve-le-pen-de-ah-dor', rah], *a.* & *n.* Reviling; reviler.

Vilipendiar [ve-le-pen-de-ar'], *va.* To contemn, to revile.

Vilipendio [ve-le-pen'-de-o], *m.* Contempt, disdain.

Vilipendioso, sa [ve-le-pen-de-oh'-so, sah], *a.* Contemptible, causing contempt.

Vilmente [veel-men'-tay], *adv.* Vilely; abjectly, contemptibly, villainously.

Vilo [vee'-lo]. A word only used adverbially; as, *En vilo*, (1) In the air. (2. Met.) Insecurely.

Vilordo, da [ve-lor'-do, dah], *a.* Slothful, lazy, heavy.

Vilorta [ve-lor'-tah], *f.* 1. Ring of twisted willow. 2. A kind of cricket, played in Old Castile.

Vilorto [ve-lor'-to], *m.* 1. A certain reed which grows in the north of Spain. 2. Snare of this reed.

Vilos [vee'-los], *m.* A two-masted vessel of the Philippine Islands, much like the *panco.*

Viltoso, sa, *a.* (Obs.) *V.* Vil.

Villa [veel'-lyah], *f.* 1. Town which enjoys by charter peculiar privileges. 2. Corporation of magistrates of a *villa.* 3. (Obs.) Country house.

Villadiego [vil-lyah-de-ay'-go], *m.* *Coger* or *tomar las de Villadiego*, To run away, to pack off bag and baggage.

Villaje [vil-lyah'-hay], *m.* Village; hamlet.

Villanaje [vil-lyah-nah'-hay], *m.* Villanage, the middling class in villages; peasantry.

Villanamente, *adv.* Rudely, boorishly.

Villancejo, Villancete [vil-lyan-thay'-ho], *m.* *V.* Villancico.

Villancico [vil-lyan-thee'-co], *m.* Christmas carol: a metric composition sung in churches on certain festivals. *Villancicos*, (Coll.) Hackneyed answers, frivolous excuses.

Villanciquero [vil-lyan-the-kay'-ro], *m.* One who composes small metric compositions, to be sung in churches.

Villanchón, na [vil-lyan-chone', nah], *a.* Clownish, rustic, rude.

Villanería [vil-lyah-nay-ree'-ah], *f.* 1. Lowness of birth, meanness. *V.* Villanía. 2. Middling classes of society. *V.* Villanaje.

Villanesco, ca [vil-lyah-nes'-co, cah], *a.* Rustic, rude, boorish.

Villanía [vil-lyah-nee'-ah], *f.* 1. Lowness of birth, meanness. 2. Villainy, villainousness, rusticity: indecorous word or act.

Villano, na [vil-lyah'-no, nah], *a.* 1. Belonging to the lowest class of country people. 2. Rustic, clownish. 3. Worthless, unworthy. 4. Villainous, wicked.

Villano [vil-lyah'-no], *m.* 1. A kind of Spanish dance. 2. A vicious horse. 3. Villain, a rustic; an unsociable villager. *Villano harto de ajos*, (Coll.) Rude, ill-bred, forward bumpkin. *Cuando el villano está en el mulo, ni conoce a Dios ni al mundo*, (prov.) Set a beggar on horseback and he will ride to the devil. *Al villano dale el pie, y se tomará la mano*, Give an inch, and he will take an ell. *Cuando el villano está rico, ni tiene parientes ni amigos*, When a mean person becomes rich, he recognises neither relatives nor friends.

Villanote [vil-lyah-no'-tay], *a. aug.* of Villano. Highly rude.

Villazgo [vil-lyath'-go], *m.* 1. Charter of a town. 2. Tax laid upon towns.

Villeta [vil-lyay'-tah], *f. dim.* A small town or borough.

Villica, ita [vil-lyee'-cah], *f. dim.* Small town.

Villivina [vil-lye-vee'-nah], *f.* A kind of linen.

Villoría [vil-lyo-ree'-ah], *f.* Farm-house.

Villorín [vil-lyo-reen'], *m.* A sort of coarse cloth.

Villorrio [vil-lyor'-re-o], *m.* A small village; a miserable little place or hamlet.

Vimbre [veem'-bray], *m.* (Bot.) Osier. *V.* Mimbre.

Vimbrera [veem-bray'-rah], *f.* *V.* Mimbrera.

Vinagre [ve-nah'-gray], *m.* 1. Vinegar. 2. Acidity, sourness. 3. (Met. Coll.) A person of a peevish temper.

Vinagrera [ve-nah-gray'-rah], *f.* 1. Vinegar-cruet. 2. Caster, with both vinegar- and oil-cruets. 3. (Peru and Colombia) *V.* Acedía.

Vinagrero [ve-nah-gray'-ro], *m.* Vinegar-merchant.

Vinagrillo [ve-nah-greel'-lyo], *m.* 1. (Dim.) Weak vinegar. 2. A cosmetic lotion, used by women. 3. Rose-vinegar; snuff prepared with rose-vinegar.

Vinagroso, sa [ve-nah-gro'-so, sah], *a.* 1. Sourish; peevish, fretful. 2. (Coll.) In bad condition.

Vinajera [ve-nah-hay'-rah], *f.* Vessel in which wine and water are served at the altar for the mass.

Vinariego [ve-nah-re-ay'-go], *m.* Vintager, one who possesses and cultivates a vineyard.

Vinario, ria [ve-nah'-re-o, ah], *a.* Belonging to wine.

Vinatería [ve-nah-tay-ree'-ah], *f.* 1. Wine-trade. 2. Wine-shop.

Vinatero [ve-nah-tay'-ro], *m.* Vintner, wine-merchant.

Vinático, ca [ve-nah'-te-co, cah], *a.* (Obs.) Belonging to wine.

Vinaza [ve-nah'-thah], *f.* Last wine drawn from the lees.

Vinazo [ve-nah'-tho], *m.* Very strong wine.

Vinculable [vin-coo-lah'-blay], *a.* That may be entailed.

Vinculación [vin-coo-lah-the-on'], *f.* Entail, act of entailing.

Vincular [vin-coo-lar'], *va.* 1. To entail an estate. 2. To ground or found upon; to assure. 3. To continue, to perpetuate. 4. To secure with chains.

Vínculo [veen'-coo-lo], *m.* 1. Tie, link, chain. 2. Entail, an estate entailed. 3. Charge or encumbrance laid upon a foundation.

Vindicación [vin-de-cah-the-on'], *f.* 1.

Vindication, just vengeance or satisfaction for a grievance. 2. The act of giving every one his due.

Vindicar [vin-de-car'], *va.* 1. To vindicate, to revenge, to avenge. 2. To vindicate, to claim, to reclaim, to assert. 3. To vindicate, to justify, to defend, to support.

Vindicativo, va [vin-de-cah-tee'-vo, vah], *a.* 1. Vindictive, revengeful. 2. Defensive, vindicatory.

Vindicta [vin-deec'-tah], *f.* Vengeance, revenge.

Vínico, ca [vee'-ne-co, cah], *a.* Vinic, belonging to wine.

Vinícola [ve-nee'-co-lah], *a.* Relating to production of wine, wine-growing.—*m. V.* VINARIEGO.

Viniebla [ve-ne-ay'-blah], *f.* (Bot.) Hound's-tongue. Cynoglossum officicinale.

Viniente [ve-ne-en'-tay], *pa.* Coming.

Vinificación [ve-ne-fe-cah-the-on'], *f.* Vinification, fermentation of must and its conversion into wine.

Vinílico, ca [ve-nee'-le-co, cah], *a.* Vinyl.

Vinilo [ve-nee'-lo], *m.* (Chem.) Vinyl.

Vino [vee'-no], *m.* 1. Wine. *Vino arropado,* Ropy wine. *Vino por trasegar,* Unracked wine. *Vino clarete,* Claret or pale red wine. *Vino de agujas,* Sharp, rough wine. *Vino de cuerpo,* A strong-bodied wine. *Vino de lágrima,* Mother-drop or virgin wine, which flows spontaneously from the grape. *Vino doncel,* Sweet, clear wine. *Vino tinto,* Red wine. *Una buena cosecha de vino,* A good vintage. 2. Preparation of fruit or vegetables by fermentation, called by the general name of *wine.* 3. Any thing which intoxicates. *Vino de pasto,* Wine for daily use. *Vino de Jerez,* Sherry wine. *Vino carlón,* Benicarlo wine. *Vino de Borgoña,* Burgundy wine. *Vino de Champaña,* Champagne wine. *Vino de Oporto,* Port wine. *Vino del Rhin,* Hock. *Vino de Malvasía,* Malmsey wine. *Vino de frambuesa,* Raspberry wine. *Vino de grosella,* Currant wine. —N. B. There are delicious wines in Spain, known by the name of the province from which they come, such as sweet and dry *Málaga; Peralta, Montilla, Tudela, Pedro Jiménez, Rivadavia, Torrente, Moscatel, Valdepeñas,* etc. *Vino de dos orejas,* Good, strong wine. *Vino de dos, tres o más hojas,* Wine two, three, or more years old. *El vino, como rey, y el agua, como buey,* Water may be drunk freely, but wine sparingly.

Vinolencia [ve-no-len'-the-ah], *f.* Intoxication, inebriation, excess in drinking wine.

Vinolento, ta [ve-no-len'-to, tah], *a.* Intoxicated, inebriated.

Vinosidad [ve-no-se-dahd'], *f.* Quality of being vinous, vinosity.

Vinoso, sa [ve-no'-so, sah], *a.* 1. Vinous, vinose. 2. Intoxicated, inebriated.

Vinote [ve-no'-tay], *m.* The liquid remaining in the boiler after the wine is distilled and the brandy made. (Aug. fr. *vino.*)

Vinterana [vin-tay-rah'-nah], *f.* (Bot.) A tree of South America, the bark of which is known by the name of "white cinnamon" in Ecuador, and used as a substitute for cinnamon.

Viña [vee'-nyah], *f.* Vineyard. *La viña del Señor,* The church. *Como hay viñas,* As sure as fate. *Viñas,* (Low) Escape, flight. *De mis viñas vengo,* I come from my vineyards, i. e. I have no hand in the affair.

Viñadero [ve-nyah-day'-ro], *m.* Keeper of a vineyard.

Viñador [ve-nyah-dor'], *m.* Cultivator of vines; husbandman.

Viñedo [ve-nyay'-do], *m.* Country or district abounding in vineyards.

Viñero [ve-nyay'-ro], *m.* Vintager who owns and cultivates vineyards.

Viñeta [ve-nyay'-tah], *f.* 1. Vignette, an ornament at the beginning or end of chapters in books. 2. (Not Acad.) Vignette, a photograph, engraving, etc., having a border gradually shaded off.

Viñetero [ve-nyay-tay'-ro], *m.* (Typ.) A font-case for ornamental letters and vignettes.

Viola [ve-o'-lah], *f.* 1. Viola, a tenor violin or alto. *Viola de amor,* A twelve-stringed viol. 2. (Bot.) Violet. Viola. *V.* ALHELÍ.

Violáceo, ea [ve-o-lah'-thay-o, ah], *a.* Violaceous, violet-coloured.

Violación [ve-o-lah-the-on'], *f.* Violation.

Violado, da [ve-o-lah'-do, dah], *a.* & *pp.* of VIOLAR. 1. Having the colour of violets; made or confectioned with violets. 2. Violated.

Violador, ra [ve-o-lah-dor', rah], *m.* & *f.* Violator; profaner.

Violar [ve-o-lar'], *va.* 1. To violate a law, to offend. 2. To ravish, to violate a woman. 3. To spoil, to tarnish. 4. To profane or pollute the church.

Violencia [ve-o-len'-the-ah], *f.* 1. Violence, impetuousness, compulsion, force. 2. Wrong construction, erroneous interpretation. 3. Rape. 4. Excessiveness, intenseness of cold, etc.

Violentamente, *adv.* Violently, forcibly.

Violentar [ve-o-len-tar'], *va.* 1. To enforce by violent means, to violate. 2. To put a wrong construction on a passage or writing. 3. (Met.) To open or break a thing by force, to enter a place against the will of its proprietor. —*vr.* To be violent.

Violento, ta [ve-o-len'-to, tah], *a.* 1. Violent, impetuous, boisterous, furious. 2. Violent, forced, unnatural. 3. Strained, absurd, erroneous: applied to construction or interpretation. *Poner manos violentas,* To lay violent hands on a clergyman or ecclesiastic.

Violero [ve-o-lay'-ro], *m.* A player upon the viola.

Violeta [ve-o-lay'-tah], *f.* (Bot.) Violet. Viola.

Violeto [ve-o-lay'-to], *m.* A clingstone peach. *V.* PELADILLO.

Violín [ve-o-leen'], *m.* 1. Violin, fiddle. 2. Fiddler, violinist.

Violinete [ve-o-le-nay'-tay], *m.* Kit, a pocket-violin, used by dancing-masters.

Violinista [ve-o-le-nees'-tah], *m.* Violinist.

Violón [ve-o-lone'], *m.* 1. Bass-viol, double bass. 2. Player on the bass-viol. *Tocar el violón,* To be absent-minded; to talk or do not to the purpose.

Violoncelo [ve-o-lon-thay'-lo], *m.* Violoncello.

Violoncillo [ve-o-lon-theel'-lyo], *m.* Small bass-viol or player on it.

Violonchelo [ve-o-lon-chay'-lo], *m. V.* VIOLONCELO.

Vipéreo, rea [ve-pay'-ray-o, ah], *a. V.* VIPERINO.

Viperino, na [ve-pay-ree'-no, nah], *a.* Viperine, viperous.

Viquitortes [ve-ke-tor'-tes], *m. pl.* (Naut.) Quarter-gallery knees.

Vira [vee'-rah], *f.* 1. A kind of light dart or arrow of ancient warfare. 2. Stuffing between the upper leather and inner sole. 3. Welt of a shoe.

Viracocha [ve-rah-co'-chah], *m.* (Peru) Name of the Creator among the Incas, and which the Indians later applied to their white conquerors.

Virada [ve-rah'-dah], *f.* (Naut.) Tacking, tack. *Virada de bordo,* Tack putting the ship about.

Virador [ve-rah-dor'], *m.* (Naut.) Top rope; viol. *Virador de mastelero sencillo* or *doble,* A single or double top-rope. *Virador de cubierta,* Voyol, voyal.

Virar [ve-rar'], *vn.* (Naut.) To tack, to put about.—*va.* To wind, to twist. *Virar el cabrestante,* To heave at the capstan. *Virar para proa,* To heave ahead. *Virar el cable,* To heave taut. *Virar de bordo,* To tack or go about. *Virar de bordo tomando por avante,* To put the ship to windward. *Virar de bordo en redondo,* To put the ship to leeward. *Virar por las aguas de otro bajel,* To tack in the wake of another ship. *¡Vira, vira!* Heave cheerily!

Viratón [ve-rah-tone'], *m.* A kind of large dart or arrow.

Virazón [ve-rah-thone'], *f.* (Naut.) Sea-breeze.

Virreina [vir-ray'-e-nah], *f.* Lady of a viceroy.

Virreinato, Virreino [vir-ray-e-nah'-to], *m.* Viceroyship; duration of this office; the district governed by a viceroy.

Víreo [vee'-ray-o], *m. V.* VIRIO.

Virrey [vir-ray'-e], *m* Viceroy.

Virgen [veer'-hen], *com.* Virgin, maid. Man who has not had carnal connection with a woman.—*a.* Any thing in its pure and primitive state. *Cera virgen,* Virgin wax. *Plata virgen,* Native silver.—*f.* 1. One of the upright posts, between which the beam of an oil-mill moves. 2. The Holy Virgin Mary; image of the Virgin. 3. A nun. *Vírgenes,* Nuns vowed to chastity.

Virgiliano, na [veer-he-le-ah'-no, nah], *a.* Virgilian, characteristic of Virgil.

Virginal [veer-he-nahl'], *a.* Virginal, maiden, virgin.

Virgíneo, nea [veer-hee'-nay-o, ah], *a. V.* VIRGINAL.

Virginia, [veer-hee'-ne-ah], *f.* (Bot.) Virginia tobacco. Nicotiana tabacum.

Virginidad [veer-he-ne-dahd'], *f.* Virginity, maidenhood.

Virgo [veer'-go], *m.* 1. (Ast.) Virgin, a sign of the zodiac. 2. Virginity. 3. (Anat.) Hymen.

Vírgula [veer'-goo-lah], *f.* 1. A small rod. 2. Slight line. 3. (Med.) *Bacilo vírgula,* The bacillus of tuberculosis.

Virgulilla [veer-goo-leel'-lyah], *f.* 1. Comma: it is called *coma* in printing and *tilde* in writing. 2. Any fine stroke or light line.

Virgulto [veer-gool'-to], *m.* Shrub, bush, small tree.

Viril [ve-reel'], *m.* 1. A clear and transparent glass. 2. A small locket or round case in the centre of the monstrance, with two plates of glass, between which the host is placed, to expose it to the congregation in Catholic churches.

Viril [ve-reel'], *a.* Virile, manly.

Virilidad [ve-re-le-dahd'], *f.* 1. Virility, manhood. 2. Vigour, strength.

Virilla, ita [ve-reel'-lyah], *f. dim.* of VIRA. *Virilla,* Ornament of gold or silver formerly worn in shoes.

Virilmente, *adv.* In a manly manner.

Virio [vee'-re-o], *m.* (Orn.) Vireo, a green and yellow bird of the United

States.

Viripotente [ve-re-po-ten'-tay], *a.* Marriageable, nubile: applied to women.

Virol [ve-role'], *m.* (Her.) *V.* PERFIL.

Virola [ve-ro'-lah], *f.* Collar, hoop, ferrule, ring put upon canes, pocket-knives, etc.

Virolento, ta [ve-ro-len'-to, tah], *a.* Diseased with small-pox, pock-marked.

Virología [ve-ro-lo-hee'-ah], *f.* Virology.

Virotazo [ve-ro-tah'-tho], *m.* 1. (Aug.) *V.* VIROTÓN. 2. Wound with a dart or arrow.

Virote [ve-ro'-tay], *m.* 1. Shaft, dart, arrow. 2. Dude, fop, a showy, vain young man; inflated person. 3. A long iron rod fastened to a collar on the neck of a slave, who shows an intention of running away. 4. (Prov.) Vine three years old. 5. A puffed-up man, too serious and erratic. 6. A carnival trick. *Mirar por el virote,* (Met.) To be attentive to one's own concerns or convenience. *Traga virotes,* A starched coxcomb.

Virotón [ve-ro-tone'], *m. aug.* Large dart or arrow.

Virtual [veer-too-ahl'], *a.* Virtual.

Virtualidad [veer-too-ah-le-dahd'], *f.* Virtuality, efficacy.

Virtualmente, *adv.* Virtually, in effect.

Virtud [veer-tood'], *f.* 1. Virtue, efficacy, power, force. 2. Virtue, acting power. 3. Virtue, efficacy without visible action. 4. Virtue, medicinal efficacy. 5. Virtue, moral goodness, integrity, rectitude. 6. Habit, disposition, virtuous life. 7. Vigour, courage. 8. In mechanics, the moving power. 9. In the sacraments, their efficacy and value. *En virtud de,* In virtue of. *Virtudes,* The fifth of the nine choirs into which the celestial spirits are divided. *Hacer virtud,* To do well. *Varita de virtudes,* Juggler's wand.

Virtuosamente, *adv.* Virtuously.

Virtuoso, sa [veer-too-oh'-so, sah], *a.* 1. Virtuous, just. 2. Powerful, vigorous.

Viruela [ve-roo-ay'-lah], *f.* 1. Pock, a pustule on the skin. 2. Small-pox. *Viruelas locas,* Good or favourable small-pox. *Viruelas bastardas,* Chicken-pox.

Virulencia [ve-roo-len'-the-ah], *f.* 1. Virulence, virus. 2. Virulence, acrimony, malignance.

Virulento, ta [ve-roo-len'-to, tah], *a.* 1. Virulent, malignant. 2. Purulent, sanious.

Virus [vee'-roos], *m.* (Med.) Virus, poison, contagion.

Viruta [ve-roo'-tah], *f.* Shaving, a thin slice of wood; chip.—*pl.* Cuttings.

Visa [vee'-sah], *f.* Visa.

Visaje [ve-sah'-hay], *m.* Grimace. *Hacer visajes,* To make wry faces.

Visar [ve-sar'], *va.* To examine a document, to visé (a passport).

Víscera [vees'-thay-rah], *f.* Viscus, any organ of the body which has an appropriate use.—*pl.* Viscera.

Visceral [vis-thay-rahl'], *a.* Visceral, belonging to the viscera.

Viscina [vis-thee'-nah], *f.* (Chem.) Viscin, a principle peculiar to bird-lime.

Viscosa [vis-co'-sah], *f.* (Chem.) Viscose (for making rayon and other synthetic fabrics].

Viscosidad [vis-co-se-dahd'], *f.* Viscosity, glutinousness, glutinous or viscous matter.

Viscoso, sa [vis-co'-so, sah], *a.* Viscous, viscid, glutinous, mucilaginous.

Visera [ve-say'-rah], *f.* 1. Eye protector, eye shade; visor, that part of the head-piece which covers the face. 2. Box with a spy-hole, through which a pigeon-keeper observes the pigeons. 3. (Cuba) Blind of a horse's bridle. *Visera para poner en foco,* Focusing-screen, in photography.

Visibilidad [ve-se-be-le-dahd'], *f.* Visibility.

Visible [ve-see'-blay], *a.* 1. Visible, perceptible to the eye. 2. Visible, apparent, open, conspicuous.

Visiblemente, *adv.* Visibly, clearly; evidently.

Visillo [ve-seel'-lyo], *m.* Type of window blind or curtain.

Visión [ve-se-on'], *f.* 1. Sight, vision; object of sight. 2. Vision, the act of seeing. 3. (Coll.) A frightful, ugly, or ridiculous person. 4. Phantom, apparition, freak. 5. Spiritual vision, revelation, prophecy; beatifical vision. *Ver visiones,* To be led by fancy, to build castles in the air. *Vision beatífica,* Celestial bliss.

Visionario, ria [ve-se-o-nah'-re-o, ah], *a.* & *n.* Visionary; not real; fanatical.

Visir [ve-seer'], *m.* Vizier, the Turkish prime minister. (Turk. vezir, fr. Arab. wazir.)

Visita [ve-see'-tah], *f.* 1. Visit. 2. Visitor, visitant. 3. Visit to a temple to pray. 4. Visit of a medical man to a patient. 5. Visitation, inquisition. 6. Recognition, register, examination. 7. House in which the tribunal of ecclesiastical visitors is held. 8. Body of ministers who form a tribunal to inspect the prisons; visit to prisons. *Visita de cárcel,* Brief view of the charges against prisoners drawn up by a judge at certain periods.—*pl.* (Coll.) Frequent visits; haunts, places of resort.

Visitación [ve-se-tah-the-on'], *f.* Visitation, visiting, visit.

Visitador, ra [ve-se-tah-dor', rah], *m.* & *f.* 1. Visitor, visitant. 2. Visitor, an occasional judge, searcher, surveyor. *Visitador de registro,* (Naut.) Searcher of goods on board of ships; tide-waiter.

Visitante [ve-se-tahn'-tay], *m.* & *f.* Visitor, guest.

Visitar [ve-se-tar'], *va.* 1. To visit, to pay a visit; to visit a temple or church; to visit a patient as physician. 2. To make a judicial visit, search, or survey; to try weights and measures. 3. To search ships; to examine prisons. 4. To travel, to traverse many countries. 5. To inform one's self personally of any thing. 6. To appear, as a celestial spirit. 7. To frequent a place. 8. To visit religious persons and establishments as an ecclesiastical judge. 9. (Theol.) To send a special counsel from heaven. 10. (Law) To make an abstract of the charge against a prisoner at visitation.—*vr.* 1. To visit, to keep up the intercourse of ceremonial salutations at the houses of each other. 2. To absent one's self from the choir. *Visitar los altares,* To pray before each altar for some pious purpose.

Visiteo [ve-se-tay'-o], *m.* Making or receiving of many visits.

Visitero, ra [ve-se-tay'-ro, rah], *a.* (Coll.) Visitor, frequent caller.

Visitón [ve-se-tone'], *m.* (Aug. of VISITA) (Coll.) A long and tedious visit.

Visivo, va [ve-see'-vo, vah], *a.* Visive, having the power of seeing.

Vislumbrar [vis-loom-brar'], *va.* 1. To have a glimmering sight of a thing; not to perceive it distinctly. 2. (Met.) To know imperfectly, to conjecture by indications.—*vr.* To glimmer, to appear faintly.

Vislumbre [vis-loom'-bray], *f.* 1. A glimmering light. 2. Glimmer, glimmering, faint or imperfect view. 3 Conjecture, surmise. 4. Imperfect knowledge, confused perception. 5. Appearance, slight resemblance. 6. Projecting part of a thing which is scarcely discovered.

Viso [vee'-so], *m.* 1. Prospect, an elevated spot, affording an extensive view. 2. Lustre, the shining surface of things; brilliant reflection of light. 3. Colour, cloak, pretence, pretext. 4. Apparent likeness; aspect, appearance. 5. (Obs.) Sight, act of seeing, view. *A dos visos,* With a double view or design. *Al viso de,* At the sight of. *Viso de altar,* Small square embroidered cloth placed before the eucharist.

Visor [ve-sor'], *m.* Viewfinder (in a camera).

Visorio, ria [ve-so'-re-o, ah], *a.* Belonging to the sight, visual.

Víspera [vees'-pay-rah], *f.* 1. Evening before the day in question; the last evening before a festival. 2. Forerunner, prelude. 3. Immediate nearness or succession.—*pl.* 1. Vesper, one of the parts into which the Romans divided the day. 2. Vespers, the evening service. *En vísperas de,* At the eve of. *Vísperas Sicilianas,* Sicilian vespers: a threat of general punishment. *Estar como tonto en vísperas,* (Coll.) To be present at a discussion, conversation, or business, without understanding it; not to be able to take part in it, through ignorance or want of information.

Vista [vees'-tah], *f.* 1. Sight, vision, the sense of seeing. 2. Sight, the act of seeing, vision, view. 3. Sight, eye eyesight, organ of sight. 4. Aspect appearance. 5. Prospect, view, landscape, vista. 6. Apparition, appearance. 7. Meeting, interview. 8. Clear knowledge or perception. 9. Relation, respective connection, comparison. 10. Intent, view, purpose. 11. First stage of a suit at law. 12. Opinion, judgment.—*m.* A surveyor in a custom-house.—*f. pl.* 1. Meeting, conference, interview. 2. Presents to a bride by a bridegroom, the day preceding the nuptials. 3. Lights, windows in a building, balconies, verandas. 4. Prospect, an extensive view. *Vista de un pleito,* or *día de la vista de un proceso,* or *una causa,* (Law) The trial, or the day of trial of a civil lawsuit, or a criminal prosecution. *A vista de,* In presence of; in consideration of. *A vista de ojos,* At a glance. *A la vista,* On sight, immediately; before, near, or in view; carefully observing, seeing, or following. *A primera vista,* At first view *Aguzar la vista,* To sharpen the sigh or perception. *Dar una vista,* To give a passing glance. *Echar la vista,* To choose mentally. *¡ Hasta la vista!* Good-bye! *Perderse de vista,* (Coll. and met.) To have great superiority in its line (slang, to be "Out of sight"). *Conocer de vista,* To know by sight. *Echar una vista,* To look after. *Tener vista,* To be showy; to be beautiful. *Hacer la vista gorda,* To wink, to connive. *En vista de,* In consequence of; in consideration of. *Comer y tragar con la vista,* (Met.) To have a fierce and terrible aspect.

Vistazo [vees-tah'-tho], *m.* Glance *Dar un vistazo,* To glance, to play the eye.

Vistillas [vees-teel'-lyas], *f. pl.* Eminence, affording an extensive prospect, views.

(*Yo visto, él vistió; yo vista, vistiera;* from *Vestir.* *V.* PEDIR.)

Visto, ta [vees'-to, tah], *a.* Obvious to the sight, clear.—*pp. irr.* of VER. *El está bien visto* or *mal visto*, He is respected, or not respected. *Eso es bien* or *mal visto*, That is proper, or approved; improper, or disapproved. *Visto bueno* (in manuscript, *V°. B°.*), set after a draft, order, permit, license, account, etc., in public offices, means, The preceding document has been examined and found to be correct; consequently it may signify, Pay the bearer; Let him or the merchandise pass, etc. *Visto es* or *visto está*, It is evident. *No visto*, Extraordinary, prodigious. *A escala vista*, Openly, without defence. *Visto que*, Considering that.

Vistosamente, *adv.* Beautifully, delightfully.

Vistoso, sa [vees-to'-so, sah], *a.* Beautiful, delightful.

Visual [ve-soo-ahl'], *a.* Visual.

Visualidad [ve-soo-ah-le-dahd'], *f.* Visuality, the agreeable effect which beautiful objects as a whole produce.

Visura [ve-soo'-rah], *f.* Minute inspection of any thing.

Vita [vee'-tah], *f.* (Naut.) Cross-beam on the forecastle, to which cables are fastened.

Vital [ve-tahl'], *a.* Vital.

Vitalicio, cia [ve-tah-lee'-the-o, ah], *a.* Lasting for life; during life. *Pensión vitalicia*, Annuity, life pension. *Empleo vitalicio*, Employment or place for life.

Vitalicista [ve-tah-le-thees'-tah], *com.* One who enjoys an annuity or income for life.

Vitalidad [ve-tah-le-dahd'], *f.* Vitality.

Vitalismo [ve-tah-lees'-mo], *m.* Vitalism, a doctrine that the phenomena of the organism are due to so-called vital forces, distinct from the general laws of matter.

Vitalista [ve-tah-lees'-tah], *a.* & *n.* Vitalist, relating to vitalism; one who holds that doctrine.

Vitalmente, *adv.* Vitally.

Vitamina [ve-tah-mee'-nah], *f.* Vitamin.

Vitando, da [ve-tahn'-do, dah], *a.* 1. That ought to be shunned or avoided. 2. Odious, execrable.

Vitela [ve-tay'-lah], *f.* 1. Calf. 2. Vellum. calf-skin.

Vitelina [ve-tay-lee'-nah], *a.* Of a dark yellow colour: applied to the bile.

Vitícola [ve-tee'-co-lah], *a.* Viticultural, relating to cultivation of the grape.—*m.* Viticulturist, vine-grower.

Viticultura [ve-te-cool-too'-rah], *f.* Viticulture, culture of the vine.

Vitiligo [ve-te-lee'-go], *m.* Vitiligo, a skin disease, characterized by spots showing loss of pigment.

Vito [vee'-to], *m.* 1. A lively dance in ⅜ time proper to Andalusia. 2. (Med.) Chorea.

Vitola [ve-to'-lah], *f.* 1. (Mil.) Ball calibre, gauge for musket and cannon balls. 2. Measure, size for cigars. 3. (Amer. Met.) Appearance, mien, of a person.

Vitor ! [vee'-tor], *int.* Shout of joy: Huzza! long live!

Vitor [vee'-tor], *m.* 1. Triumphal exclamation; public rejoicing. 2. Tablet containing panegyrical epithets to a hero.

Vitorear [ve-to-ray-ar'], *va.* To shout, to huzza, to address with acclamations of joy and praise, to clap.

Vitoria [ve-to'-re-ah], *f.* *V.* VICTORIA.

Vitorioso, sa [ve-to-re-oh'-so, sah], *a.* *V.* VICTORIOSO.

Vitre [vee'-tray], *m.* Thin canvas.

Vítreo, trea [vee'-tray-o, ah], *a.* Vitreous, glassy, resembling glass.

Vitrificable [ve-tre-fe-cah'-blay], *a.* Vitrificable.

Vitrificación [ve-tre-fe-cah-the-on'], *f.* Vitrification, vitrifaction.

Vitrificar [ve-tre-fe-car'], *va.* To vitrify.

Vitrina [ve-tree'-nah], *f.* Glass case, show case, display-window.

Vitriolado, da [ve-tre-o-lah'-do, dah], *a.* Vitriolate, vitriolated.

Vitriólico, ca [ve-tre-o'-le-co, cah], *a.* Vitriolic.

Vitriolo [ve-tre-o'-lo], *m.* Vitriol. *Vitriolo azul*, Blue vitriol, copper sulphate. *Vitriolo verde*, Green vitriol, ferrous sulphate. *Vitriolo blanco*, White vitriol, zinc sulphate. *Vitriolo amoniacal*, Ammonium sulphate.

Vitualla [ve-too-ahl'-lyah], *f.* Victuals, viands, food, provisions: generally used in the plural.

Vituallado, da [ve-too-al-lyah'-do, dah], *a.* Victualled, provided with victuals.

Vitulino, na [ve-too-lee'-no, nah], *a.* Belonging to a calf.

Vítulo marino, *m.* *V.* BECERRO MARINO.

Vituperable [ve-too-pay-rah'-blay], *a.* Vituperable, blameworthy, condemnable.

Vituperación [ve-too-pay-rah-the-on'], *f.* Vituperation.

Vituperador, ra [ve-too-pay-rah-dor', rah], *m.* & *f.* A blamer, censurer.

Vituperante [ve-too-pay-rahn'-tay], *pa.* Vituperating, censuring, decrying.

Vituperar [ve-too-pay-rar'], *va.* To vituperate, to censure, to reproach, to decry, to condemn.

Vituperio [ve-too-pay'-re-o], *m.* 1. Vituperation, reproach, blame, censure. 2. Infamy, disgrace.

Vituperiosamente [ve-too-pay-re-o-sah-men'-tay], *adv.* Opprobriously, reproachfully.

Vituperosamente [ve-too-pay-ro-sah-men'-tay], *adv.* Reproachfully.

Vituperoso, sa [ve-too-pay-ro'-so, sah], *a.* Opprobrious, reproachful.

Viuda [ve-oo'-dah], *f.* 1. Widow. *Condesa viuda de*, Countess dowager of. 2. (Zool.) Viuda, a noteworthy bird of South America and Africa; a tyrant fly-catcher. Tænioptera trupero. 3. (Bot.) Mourning widow or mourning bride; scabious.

Viudal [ve-oo-dahl'], *a.* Belonging to a widow or widower.

Viudedad [ve-oo-day-dahd'], *f.* 1. Widowhood, viduity. 2. Dowry. 3. Usufruct enjoyed during widowhood of the property of a deceased person.

Viudez [ve-oo-deth'], *f.* Widowhood.

Viudita [ve-oo-dee'-tah], *f.* *dim.* 1. A spruce little widow. 2. (Bot.) Scabious, mourning bride.

Viudo [ve-oo'-do], *m.* Widower.—*a.* Applied to birds that pair.

¡ Viva ! [vee'-vah], *int.* Long live, hurrah, huzza, a shout of joy, triumph, applause, or encouragement.

Viva, *m.* Huzza, a shout, a cry of acclamation.

Vivac [ve-vahc'], *m.* Town-guard to keep order at night; bivouac, night-guard, a small guard-house.

Vivacidad [ve-vah-the-dahd'], *f.* Vivacity, liveliness, briskness, vigour; brilliancy.

Vivamente [ve-vah-men'-tay], *adv.* Vividly, to the life, with a strong resemblance.

Vivandero, ra [ve-van-day'-ro, rah], *m.* & *f.* (Mil.) Sutler.

Vivaque [ve-vah'-kay], *m.* Bivouac, a small guard-house.

Vivaquear [ve-vah-kay-ar'], *vn.* To bivouac.

Vivar [ve-var'], *m.* 1. Warren for breeding rabbits or other animals; vivary. 2. Burrow of a rabbit.

Vivar [ve-var'], *va.* (Peru, etc.) *V.* VITOREAR.

Vivaracho, cha [ve-vah-rah'-cho, chah], *a.* Lively, smart, sprightly, frisky.

Vivario [ve-vah'-re-o], *m.* Fish-pond.

Vivaz [ve-vath'], *a.* 1. Lively, active, vigorous. 2. Ingenious, acute, witty. 3. As used of plants, perennial, evergreen.

Víveres [vee'-vay-res], *m. pl.* Provisions for an army or fortress.

Vivero [ve-vay'-ro], *m.* 1. (Bot.) The mastic-tree. 2. Warren; fish-pond; vivary.

Viveza [ve-vay'-thah], *f.* 1. Liveliness, vigour, activity, gaiety. 2. Celerity, briskness. 3. Ardour, energy, vehemence. 4. Acuteness, perspicacity, penetration. 5. Witticism. 6. Strong resemblance. 7. Lustre, splendour. 8. Grace and brilliancy in the eyes. 9. Inconsiderate word or act.

Vividero, ra [ve-ve-day'-ro, rah], *a.* Habitable.

Vividor, ra [ve-ve-dor', rah], *m.* & *f.* A long liver.

Vividor, ra [ve-ve-dor', rah], *a.* Frugal, economical, careful, in mode of life.

Vivienda [ve-ve-en'-dah], *f.* 1. Dwelling-house, apartments, lodgings. 2. (Obs.) Mode of life.

Viviente [ve-ve-en'-tay], *a.* Living. *Todo ser viviente*, Every living thing.

Vivificación [ve-ve-fe-cah-the-on'], *f.* Vivification, enlivening.

Vivificador, ra [ve-ve-fe-cah-dor', rah], *m.* & *f.* One who vivifies, animates, or enlivens.

Vivificante [ve-ve-fe-cahn'-tay], *pa.* Vivifying, lifegiving.

Vivificar [ve-ve-fe-car'], *va.* 1. To vivify, to vivificate, to animate, to enliven. 2. To comfort, to refresh.

Vivificativo, va [ve-ve-fe-cah-tee'-vo, vah], *a.* Vivificative, lifegiving, animating, comforting.

Vivífico, ca [ve-vee'-fe-co, cah], *a.* Vivific, springing from life.

Vivíparo, ra [ve-vee'-pah-ro, rah], *a.* Viviparous; opposed to oviparous.

Vivir [ve-veer'], *vn.* 1. To have life, to live; to enjoy life. 2. To live, to continue, to last, to keep. 3. To have the means of supporting life. 4. To live; emphatically, to enjoy happiness. 5. To live, to pass life in a certain manner. 6. To be remembered, to enjoy fame. 7. To be, to exist; to be present in memory. 8. To live, to inhabit, to reside, to lodge. 9. To temporize. 10. To guard the life. 11. To have eternal life *Viva Vd. mil años* or *muchos años*, Live many years; thank you, or I return you many thanks: expression of courtesy. *¡ Viva !* Hurrah! exclamation of joy and applause. *¿ Quién vive?* (Mil.) Who is there? *Vive*, An exclamatory oath, generally accompanied with another word. *Recogerse* (*retirarse*) *a buen vivir*, To amend a disorderly life. *Vivir para ver*, Live and learn (or strange enough). *Como se vive, se muere*, As the twig is bent, the tree is inclined: habit is second nature. *Vivir bien, que Dios es Dios*, Live righteously; God will guard you.

Vivisección [ve-ve-sec-the-on'], *f.* Vivisection, dissection of a living animal for purposes of scientific inquiry.

Vivo, va [vee'-vo, vah], *a.* 1. Living, enjoying life, active. 2. Lively, efficacious, intense. 3. Disencumbered, disengaged. 4. Alive, kindled: applied to things burning. 5. Acute, ingenious; vivid, bright, smart. 6. Hasty, inconsiderate. 7. Diligent, nimble. 8. Pure, clean. 9. Constant, enduring. 10. Vivid, florid, excellent. 11. Very expressive or persuasive. 12. Blessed. *Al vivo,* To the life; very like the original. *Copia al vivo de la firma de Cervantes,* A facsimile of Cervantes' signature. *Tocar en lo vivo,* (Met.) To hurt one's feelings; to touch to the quick. *En vivo,* Living. *Viva voz,* By word of mouth. *Cal viva,* Quicklime. *Carne viva,* Quick flesh in a wound. *Ojos vivos,* Very bright, lively eyes.

Vivo [vee'-vo], *m.* 1. Edging, border of clothing, stone, wood, etc., after dressing and trimming, or polishing. 2. (Arch.) Jut, any prominent part of a building which juts out. 3. Mange, the itch or scab in dogs.

Vizcacha [veeth-cah'-chah], *f.* A large kind of hare, Peruvian hare. Lepus viscacia.

Vizcaino, na [veeth-cah-ee'-no, nah], *a.* Biscayan, of Biscay.

Vizcondado [veeth-con-dah'-do], *m.* Viscountship.

Vizconde [veeth-con'-day], *m.* Viscount.

Vizcondesa [veeth-con-day'-sah], *f.* Viscountess.

Viznaga [veeth-nah'-gah], *f.* (Bot.) Carrot-like ammi. Ammi visnaga.

Vizvirindo, da [vith-ve-reen'-do, dah], *a.* (Mex.) *V.* VIVARACHO.

Voacé [vo-ah-thay'], *m.* (Obs.) A contraction of VUESAMERCED or USTED.

Vocablo [vo-cah'-blo], *m.* Word, term, diction, vocable.

Vocabulario [vo-cah-boo-lah'-re-o], *m.* 1. Vocabulary, dictionary, lexicon. 2. (Coll.) Person who announces or interprets the will of another.

Vocabulista, *m.* (Obs.) *V.* VOCABULARIO.

Vocación [vo-cah-the-on'], *f.* 1. Vocation, calling by the will of God. 2. Trade, employment, calling. 3. *V.* ADVOCACIÓN and CONVOCACIÓN.

Vocal [vo-cahl'], *a.* Vocal, oral.—*f.* Vowel.—*m.* Voter, in a congregation or assembly.

Vocalización [vo-cah-le-thah-the-on'], *f.* Vocalization.

Vocalizar [vo-cah-le-thar'], *vn.* To vocalize, to articulate.

Vocalmente, *adv.* Vocally, articulately.

Vocativo [vo-cah-tee'-vo], *m.* (Gram.) Vocative, the fifth case of nouns.

Voceador, ra [vo-thay-ah-dor', rah], *m.* & *f.* Vociferator.

Vocear [vo-thay-ar'], *va.* & *vn.* 1. To cry, to cry out, to clamour, to scream, to bawl, to halloo. 2. To cry, to publish, to proclaim; to call to: applied occasionally to inanimate things. 3. To shout, to huzza; to applaud by acclamation; to boast publicly. *Vocear a un bajel,* (Naut.) To hail a ship.

Vocería [vo-thay-ree'-ah], *f.* Clamour, outcry, hallooing.

Vocero [vo-thay'-ro], *m.* (Obs.) Advocate.

Vociferación [vo-the-fay-rah-the-on'], *f.* Vociferation, clamour, outcry, boast.

Vociferador, ra [vo-the-fay-rah-dor', rah], *m.* & *f.* Boaster, bragger.

Vociferante [vo-the-fay-rahn'-tay], *pa.* & *n.* Vociferating: caller.

Vociferar [vo-the-fay-rar'], *vn.* To vociferate, to bawl, to proclaim, to clamour.—*va.* (Obs.) To boast, to brag loudly or publicly.

Vocinglear [vo-thin-glay-ar'], *va.* (Littl. us.) To shout, to cry out.

Vocinglería [vo-thin-glay-ree'-ah], *f.* 1. Clamour, outcry, a confused noise of many voices. 2. Loquacity.

Vocinglero, ra [vo-thin-glay'-ro, rah], *a.* Brawling, prattling, chattering, vociferous.—*m.* & *f.* Loud babbler.

Voila [vo'-e-lah], *f.* A term in the game of dibs (jackstones) in order that the cast may not count.

Volada [vo-lah'-dah], *f.* (Obs.) *V.* VUELO.

Voladera [vo-lah-day'-rah], *f.* One of the floats or pallets of a water-wheel.

Voladero, ra [vo-lah-day'-ro, rah], *a.* Volatile, flying, fleeting.—*m.* Precipice, abyss.

Voladizo, za [vo-lah-dee'-tho, ah], *a.* Projecting from a wall, jutting out.

Voladizo, *m.* Any short cover projecting from a wall; corbel.

Volado [vo-lah'-do], *m.* *V.* AZUCARILLO.

Volado, da [vo-lah'-do, dah], *a.* (Typ.) Superior, set above the level of the line of type: as n[4].

Volador, ra [vo-lah-dor', rah], *a.* 1. Flying, running fast. 2. Hanging in the air. 3. Blowing up with gunpowder: applied to artificial fireworks.—*m.* 1. Rocket. 2. Flying-fish. —*f.* Fly-wheel of a steam-engine.

Volandas, or En volandas [vo-lahn'-das], *adv.* 1. In the air, through the air, as if flying. 2. (Coll.) Rapidly, in an instant.

Volandera [vo-lan-day'-rah], *f.* 1. (In oil-mills) Runner, the stone which runs edgewise upon another stone. 2. (Coll.) A vague or flying report, lie. 3. Wash of an axle-tree, nave-box of a wheel. 4. (Print.) Ledge on a type galley.

Volandero, ra [vo-lan-day'-ro, rah], *a.* 1. Suspended in the air, volatile. 2. Fortuitous, casual. 3. Unsettled, fleeting, variable, volatile.

Volandillas (En) [en vo-lan-deel'-lyas], *adv.* *V.* VOLANDAS (EN).

Volanta [vo-lahn'-tah], *f.* (Cuba) A two-wheel covered vehicle with very long shafts.

Volante [vo-lahn'-tay], *pa.* & *a.* 1. Flying, volant, fluttering, unsettled. 2. Applied to the pulsation of the arteries. 3. Applied to a kind of meteors. *Papel volante,* Short writing or manuscript easily disseminated: it generally contains some satire or libel. *Sello volante,* Open seal on a letter, that those to whose care it is directed may read it.

Volante [vo-lahn'-tay], *m.* 1. An ornament of light gauze hanging from a woman's head-dress. 2. Shuttle-cock. 3. Coining-mill, or that part of it which strikes the die. 4. Balance of a watch. 5. (Mech.) Fly-wheel, a heavy governing wheel. 6. Livery servant or foot-boy who runs before his master, or rides behind. 7. Lawn tennis. 8. Flier, a long narrow sheet of paper. 9. (Cuba) (1) *V.* VOLANTA. (2) A linen coat. (Mex.) A dress-coat.

Volantín [vo-lan-teen'], *m.* A certain apparatus for fishing.

Volantón [vo-lan-tone'], *m.* A fledged bird able to fly.

Volapié [vo-lah-pe-ay'], *m.* A lot in bull-baiting which consists in wounding the beast while running, the latter standing. *A volapié, adv.* Half running, half flying.

Volapuk [vo-lah-pook'], *m.* A commercial universal language invented by the Swiss professor J. M. Schleyer.

Volar [vo-lar'], *vn.* 1. To fly, as with wings. 2. To fly, to pass through the air. 3. To fly, to move swiftly. 4. To vanish, to disappear on a sudden. 5. To rise in the air like a steeple or pile. 6. To make rapid progress in studies; to subtilize, to refine sentiments; to move with rapidity or violence. 7. To project, to hang over. 8. To execute with great promptitude and facility; to extend, to publish any thing rapidly.—*va.* 1. To rouse the game. 2. To fly, to attack by a bird of prey. 3. To blow up, to spring a mine; to blast rocks or mines. 4. (Met.) To irritate, to exasperate. 5. To ascend high. *Volar la mina* (1) To blow up a mine. (2) (Met.) To discover any secret business. *Como volar,* As impossible as it is to fly. *Echar a volar,* (Met.) To disseminate, to give to the public. *Sacar* or *salir a volar,* To publish, to expose. *Voló el pollo* or *golondrino,* (Coll.) It escaped from between the hands. *Volar las escotinas de juanetes,* (Naut.) To let fly the top-gallant sheets.

Volatería [vo-lah-tay-ree'-ah], *f.* 1. Fowling; sporting with hawks. 2. Fowls, a flock of birds. 3. A vague or desultory speech; idle or groundless ideas.—*adv.* Fortuitously, adventitiously.

Volátil [vo-lah'-teel], *a.* 1. Volatile, flying through the air, or capable of flying; wafting. 2. Changeable, inconstant, fugitive. 3. (Chem.) Volatile, vaporizing slowly at ordinary temperatures.

Volatilla [vo-lah-teel'-lyah], *f.* (Obs.) Flying bird.

Volatilidad [vo-lah-te-le-dahd], *f.* Volatility, quality of flying away by evaporation.

Volatilización [vo-lah-te-le-thah-the-on'], *f.* Volatilization.

Volatilizar [vo-lah-te-le-thar'], *va.* To volatilize, to vaporize, to transform into the gaseous state.—*vr.* To be dissipated in vapour, to be exhaled or vapourized.

Volatín [vo-lah-teen'], *m.* Rope-dancer, and each of his exercises.

Volatinero [vo-lah-te-nay'-ro], *m.* Rope-walker; acrobat.

Volatizar [vo-lah-te-thar'], *va.* (Chem.) To volatilize.

Volavérunt [vo-lah-vay'-roont]. A Latin word, used colloquially in Spanish, to express that something has disappeared.

Volcán [vol-cahn'], *m.* 1. Volcano. 2. Excessive ardour; violent passion.

Volcánico, ca [vol-cah'-ne-co, cah], *a.* Volcanic, relating to a volcano.

Volcar [vol-car'], *va.* 1. To overset, to capsize, to turn one side upwards. 2. To make dizzy or giddy. 3. To make one change his opinion. 4. To tire one's patience with buffoonery or scurrilous mirth.—*vn.* To overturn, to upset.

Volear [vo-lay-ar'], *va.* To throw any thing up in the air so as to make it fly; particularly to bat a ball or serve it in tennis.

Voleas [vo-lay'-as], *f. pl.* Snaffle-trees, whipple-trees.

Voleo [vo-lay'-o], *m.* 1. Blow given to a ball in the air. 2. Step in a Spanish dance. 3. (Coll.) Scolding, harsh reproof. *De un voleo* or *del primer voleo,* At one blow; at the first blow; in an instant.

Volframio [vol-frah'-me-o], *m.* Wolfram, tungsten.

Volibol [vo-le-bol'], *m.* Volleyball.

Volición [vo-le-the-on'], *f.* Volition, power of willing, act of will.

Volitivo, va [vo-le-tee'-vo, vah], *a.* Having power to will.
Volquearse [vol-kay-ar'-say], *vr.* To tumble, to wallow. *V.* Revolcarse.
Volquete [vol-kay'-tay], *m.* Dumping truck.
Voltaismo [vol-tah-ees'-mo], *m.* Voltaism, electricity produced by the contact of dissimilar substances.
Voltaje [vol-tah'-hay], *m.* (Elec.) Voltage.
Voltamperio [vol-tam-pay'-re-o], *m.* (Elec.) Volt-ampere.
Voltariedad [vol-tah-re-ay-dahd'], *f.* Fickleness, inconstancy, volatility.
Voltario, ria [vol-tah'-re-o, ah], *a.* Fickle, inconstant, giddy.
Volteador [vol-tay-ah-dor'], *m.* Tumbler, one who shows or teaches postures and feats of activity.
Voltear [vol-tay-ar'], *va.* 1. To whirl, to revolve. 2. To overturn, to overset. 3. To change the order or state of things. 4. To knock down, to throw down violently, to fell. 5. To throw an arch across, to construct it. —*vn.* To roll over (used of persons or things); to tumble, to exhibit feats of agility.
Volteo [vol-tay'-o], *m.* 1. Whirl, whirling. 2. Overturning. 3. Tumbling. 4. Dumping.
Voltereta [vol-tay-ray'-tah], *f.* Somersault.
Volterianismo [vol-tay-re-ah-nees'-mo], *m.* Voltairianism, cynicism, scepticism.
Volteriano, na [vol-tay-re-ah'-no, nah], *a.* Voltairian, of Voltaire; following Voltaire, particularly in scoffing at the Catholic religion.
Voltímetro [vol-tee'-may-tro], *m.* (Elec.) Voltmeter.
Voltio [vol'-te-o], *m.* Volt.
Voltizo, za [vol-tee'-tho, thah], *a.* Inconstant, fickle.
Voltura, *f.* (Obs.) *V.* Mezcla.
Volubilidad [vo-loo-be-le-dahd'], *f.* Volubility; inconstancy, fickleness, glibness, fluency.
Voluble [vo-loo'-blay], *a.* 1. Easily moved about. 2. Voluble, inconstant, fickle. 3. (Bot.) Twining, said of a stem which climbs in spirals.
Volublemente, *adv.* Volubly.
Volumen [vo-loo'-men], *m.* 1. Volume, size, bulkiness; corpulence. 2. Volume, bound book. 3. (Geom.) Volume, space occupied by a body.
Volúmine, *m.* (Obs.) Volume, book.
Voluminoso, sa [vo-loo-me-no'-so, sah,] *a.* Voluminous; of large bulk.
Voluntad [vo-loon-tahd'], *f.* 1. Will, choice, determination. 2. Divine determination. 3. Goodwill, benevolence, kindness. 4. Desire, pleasure; free-will, volition, election, choice. 5. Disposition, precept; intention, resolution. *De voluntad* or *de buena voluntad,* With pleasure, gratefully. *Voluntad es vida,* Pleasure in doing contributes to repose of life. *Última voluntad,* One's last will. *Zurcir voluntades, V.* Alcahuetear.
Voluntariamente, *adv.* Spontaneously, voluntarily, fain.
Voluntariedad [vo-loon-tah-re-ay-dahd'], *f.* Free-will, spontaneousness.
Voluntario, ria [vo-loon-tah'-re-o, ah], *a.* Voluntary, spontaneous, willing, gratuitous, free.
Voluntario [vo-loon-tah'-re-o], *m.* Volunteer; a soldier who serves of his own accord.
Voluntariosamente, *adv.* Spontaneously, selfishly.
Voluntarioso, sa [vo-loon-tah-re-oh'-so, sah], *a.* Selfish, humorous, one who merely follows the dictates of his own will; desirous.
Voluptuosamente [vo-loop-too-o-sah-men'-tay], *adv.* Voluptuously, sensuously; licentiously.
Voluptuosidad [vo-loop-too-o-se-dahd'], *f.* Voluptuousness, licentiousness.
Voluptuoso, sa [vo-loop-too-oh'-so, sah], *a.* Voluptuous, sensuous; licentious, sensual, lustful.
Voluta [vo-loo'-tah], *f.* 1. (Arch.) Volute, an ornament of the capitals of columns. 2. A mollusk having an oval shell of a short spiral.
Volvedor [vol-vay-dor'], *m.* Screw-driver, turn-screw.
Volver [vol-verr'], *va.* & *vn.* 1. To turn, to give turns. 2. To return, to restore, to repay, to give back, to give up. 3. To come back, to return, to come again to the same place. 4. To return to the same state. 5. To turn from a straight line: applied to roads. 6. To direct, to aim; to remit; to send back a present. 7. To translate languages. 8. To change the outward appearance; to invert, to change from one place to another. 9. To vomit, to throw up victuals. 10. To make one change his opinion; to convert, to incline. 11. To return a ball. 12. To reflect a sound. 13. To turn away, to discharge. 14. To regain, to recover. 15. To repeat, to reiterate: in this sense it is accompanied by *á.* 16. To stand out for a person, or to undertake his defence; to defend: here it is used with *por.* 17. To re-establish, to replace in a former situation. 18. To plough land a second time. 19. To resume the thread of a discourse interrupted. 20. To reiterate, to repeat. 21. (Obs.) To mix. *Volver la puerta,* To shut the door. *Hacer volver* or *mandar volver,* To recall. *Volver atrás,* To come back. *Volver por sí,* To defend one's self; to redeem one's credit. *Volver a uno loco,* To confound one with arguments, so that he appears stupid. *Volver sobre sí,* To reflect on one's self with purpose of amendment; to make up one's losses; to recover serenity of mind. *Volver en sí,* To recover one's senses. *Volver el rostro,* (1) To flee, to evade. (2) To pay attention by turning to look at one. (3) To show contempt by turning away. *Volver la cara,* To face about.—*vr.* 1. To turn, to grow sour. 2. To turn towards one. 3. To retract an opinion, to change. *Volverse blanco,* To become white. *Volverse el cuajo,* To let the milk run from the mouth: applied to a child when its head is too low. *Volverse loco,* To be deranged, to become a fool. *Volverse atrás,* To flinch, to retract. *La burla se volvió contra él,* The jest rebounded on him. *Volverse la tortilla,* To turn the tables or scales. —**N. B. Volver,** followed by a verb in the infinitive preceded by the preposition *a,* is generally omitted in English, and the verb in the infinitive mood is translated in the corresponding tense and person, with the addition of the adverb *again;* as *El volvió a hablar,* He spoke again. *Ellos lo volverán a negar,* They will deny it over again. *Volver a la carga,* To return to the charge, to insist. *Volver lo de arriba abajo,* To turn upside down; to invert the order of things. *Volver pies atrás,* To withdraw from an enterprise; to run away.
Volvible [vol-vee'-blay], *a.* That may be turned.
Volvimiento [vol-ve-me-en'-to], *m.* Act of turning.
Volvo, Vólvulo [vol'-vo, vol'-voo-lo], *m.* Volvulus, iliac passion.
Vólvoce [vol'-vo-thay], *m.* Volvox, the so-called globe-animalcule, a minute green globe, of microscopic life, now referred to the vegetable kingdom.
Vómer [vo'-mer], *m.* Vomer, a thin plate of bone dividing the nostrils vertically.
Vómica [vo'-me-cah], *f.* (Med.) Vomica, a sac of pus in the lungs or other viscus.
Vómico, ca [vo'-me-co, cah], *a.* Causing vomiting: applied to the nut called vomic, or *nux vomica;* it is not, however, *emetic,* as its name implies.
Vomipurgante [vo-me-poor-gahn'-tay], *a.* Purgative and emetic at once.
Vomitado, da [vo-me-tah'-do, dah], *a.* & *pp.* of Vomitar. (Coll.) Meagre; pale-faced.
Vomitador, ra [vo-me-tah-dor', rah], *m.* & *f.* One who vomits.
Vomitar [vo-me-tar'], *va.* 1. To vomit. 2. To foam, to break out into injurious expressions. 3. (Coll.) To reveal a secret, to discover what was concealed. 4. (Coll.) To pay what was unduly retained. *Vomitar sangre,* (Met.) To boast of nobility and parentage.
Vomitivo, va [vo-me-tee'-vo, vah], *a.* Emetic, vomitive.—*m.* (Med.) Emetic.
Vómito [vo'-me-to], *m.* 1. The act of vomiting. *Volver al vómito,* To relapse into vice. 2. Vomit, matter thrown from the stomach. *Provocar a vómito,* To nauseate, to loathe: used in censuring indecent expressions, or to contemn any thing. *Vómito negro,* A bilious disease; yellow fever.
Vomitón, na [vo-me-tone', nah], *a.* Often throwing milk from the stomach: applied by nurses to a sucking child.
Vomitona [vo-me-to'-nah], *f.* (Coll.) Violent vomiting after eating heartily.
Vomitorio, ria [vo-me-to'-re-o, ah], *a.* Vomitive, emetic.—*m.* Passage or entrance in Roman theatres.
Voracidad [vo-rah-the-dahd'], *f.* 1. Voracity, greediness. 2. (Met.) Destructiveness of fire, etc.
Vorágine [vo-rah'-he-nay], *f.* Vortex, whirlpool.
Voraginoso, sa [vo-rah-he-no'-so, sah], *a.* Engulfing; full of whirlpools.
Voraz [vo-rath'], *a.* 1. Voracious, greedy to eat, ravenous. 2. Extremely irregular; excessively destructive, fierce.
Vorazmente, *adv.* Voraciously, greedily, gluttonously.
Vormela [vor-may'-lah], *f.* Kind of spotted weasel.
Vortanqui [vor-tan-kee'], *m.* Sapanwood. (Obs.)
Vórtice [vor'-te-thay], *m.* Whirlpool, whirlwind, hurricane. *Vórtice aéreo,* Whirlwind, water-spout.
Vorticela [vor-te-thay'-lah], *f.* Vorticella, a typical genus of infusorians; the "bell-animalcule."
Vortiginoso, sa [vor-te-he-no'-so, sah], *a.* Vortical.
Vos [vose], *pron.* You, ye. *V.* Vosotros. Used as respectful to persons of dignity.
Vosco. (Obs.) *Con vos,* With you.
Vosearse [vo-say-ar'-say], *vr.* (Prov.) To treat each other with you or ye.
Voso, sa, *a.* (Obs.) *V.* Vuestro.
Vosotros, tras [vo-so'-tros, trahs], *pron. pers. pl.* You, ye.
Votación [vo-tah-the-on'], *f.* Voting.
Votado, da [vo-tah'-do, dah], *a.* & *pp.* of Votar. Devoted.

Votador, ra [vo-tah-dor', rah], *m.* & *f.* 1. One who vows or swears. 2. Voter.

Votante [vo-tahn'-tay], *a.* Voter in a corporation or assembly.

Votar [vo-tar'], *vn.* 1. To vow. 2. To vote. 3. To give an opinion. 4. To curse, to utter oaths.

Votivo, va [vo-tee'-vo, vah], *a.* Votive, offered by a vow.

Voto [vo'-to], *m.* 1. Vow. 2. Vote, suffrage. 3. Opinion, advice, voice: hence, also, voter. *Voto de calidad* or *decisivo*, Casting vote. *A pluralidad de votos*, By a majority of votes. 4. A gift offered to saints by the faithful. 5. Supplication to God. 6. Angry oath or execration. 7. Wish, desire. *Ciudad de voto en cortes*, Town that sends deputies to the cortes. *Voto en cortes*, Deputy of a town in the cortes. *Voto a Dios*, (Low) A menacing oath. *Voto a tal*, (Coll.) A mixed oath indicating disgust and vengeance. *Voto de amén*, A vote blindly given in obedience to the will of another. *Voto pasivo*, Qualification to be voted for, or elected by a corporation. *Voto de reata*, An inconsiderate vote, given just to follow another's will. *Ser* or *tener voto*, (1) To come to a vote. (2) To understand clearly the matter under consideration, or to be free from bias. *¡ Voto al chápiro!* Good gracious! *¡ Voto va!* Confound it! *Meterse a dar su voto*, To meddle in other people's affairs.

Voz [voth], *f.* 1. The voice. 2. Any sound made by breath. 3. Clamour, outcry. *Dar voces*, To cry, to call aloud. 4. Vocable, expression, word, term. 5. Power or authority to speak in the name of another. 6. Voice, vote, suffrage; right of suffrage; opinion expressed. 7. Rumour, public opinion. 8. Motive, pretext. 9. Word, divine inspiration. 10. (Gram.) Voice, active or passive. 11. (Mus.) Vocal music; treble, tenor; tune corresponding to the voice of a singer. 12. Order, mandate of a superior. 13. (Law) Life. *Voz activa*, Right or power of voting. *Voz pasiva*, Right or qualification to be elected. *Tomar voz*, To acquire knowledge, to reason: to confirm or support any thing by the opinions of others. *A media voz*, With a slight hint; with a low voice; in a submissive tone. *A una voz*, Unanimously. *A voces*, Clamorous cry, loud voice. *Es voz común*, It is generally reported. *En voz*, (1) Verbally. (2) (Mus.) In voice. *A voz en cuello* or *á voz en grito*, In a loud voice; shouting. *Voz argentada* or *argentina*, A clear and sonorous voice. *A voz de apellido*, (Obs.) By summons from church or assembly. *Voz de cabeza*, Falsetto voice. *Mala voz*, A blot upon one's credit, or a lack of clear title to land. *Anudarse la voz*, To be unable to speak because of violent excitement. *Dar una voz*, To hail one from a distance. *Dar voces al viento*, To toil in vain. *Dar voces al lobo* (to give words to the wolf), To preach in the desert. *Meter a voces*, To bewilder by bluster; to make much ado about nothing.

Vozarrón [vo-thar-rone'], *m.* A strong, heavy voice.

Voznar [voth-nar'], *vn.* To cry like swans, to cackle like geese.

Vuecelencia, Vuecencia [voo-ay-thay-len'-the-ah], *com.* A contraction of *vuestra excelencia*, Your excellency.

Vuelco [voo-el'-co], *m.* Eversion, overturning, upset.

(*Yo vuelco, yo vuelque*, from *Volcar. V.* Acordar.)

Vuelo [voo-ay'-lo], *m.* 1. Flight, the act of flying. 2. Wing of a bird. 3. Part of a building which projects beyond the wall. 4. Width or fulness of clothes. 5. Ruffle, flounce, ornament set to the wristband of a shirt; frill. 6. Space flown through at once. 7. Elevation or loftiness in discoursing or working. 8. Leap or bound in pantomimes. *Coger al vuelo*, To catch in flight. *Vuelo a ciegas* or *con instrumentos*, (Aer.) Instrument flying. *Vuelo en formación*, Formation flying. *Vuelo libre*, Free flight. *Vuelo sin motor*, Gliding, glide. *Vuelo sin parar*, Nonstop flight. *Vuelo tripulado*, Manned flight.

(*Yo vuelo, yo vuele*, from *Volar. V.* Acordar.)

Vuelta [voo-el'-tah], *f.* 1. Turn, the act of turning, gyration, twirl; turn of an arch; circumvolution; circuit. 2. Requital, recompense; regress. 3. Iteration, rehearsal. 4. Back side, wrong side. 5. Whipping, flogging, lashing on the back-side. 6. Turn-out, deviation from a line or straight road. 7. Return from a spot. 8. Turn, time of execution. 9. Turn, inclination, bent. 10. Ruffle. *V.* Vuelo. 11. (Naut.) Turn, hitch, lashing. 12. Turn, change of things. 13. Trip, excursion, short voyage. 14. Reconsideration, recollection. 15. Land once, twice, or thrice laboured. 16. Wards in a lock or key. 17. Order of stitches in stockings. 18. Roll, envelope. 19. Unexpected sally or witticism. 20. Change, surplus money to be returned in dealing. 21. (Mus.) Number of verses repeated. 22. (Mech.) Rotation, stroke; potter's wheel. *Vueltas de coral*, String or necklace of coral. *Á la vuelta* or *pasa a la vuelta*, Carried (an amount) over, carried forward (in accounts) on the next page. *Á vuelta de*, In the course of, within. *A la vuelta*, At your return; that laid aside; about the time; upon. *La vuelta de*, Towards this or that way. *Vuelta dada con los cables*, (Naut.) Turn in the hawse. *Media vuelta en los cables*, (Naut.) Elbow in the hawse. *Dar una vuelta*, To make a short excursion; to clean any thing; to examine a thing properly. *Darse una vuelta*, To reflect on one's conduct or actions. *Dar vuelta con un cabo de labor*, (Naut.) To belay a running rope. *Andar a vueltas*, (1) To shuffle, to make use of subterfuges. (2) To dog a person. (3) To be at variance. *Dar vueltas*, To walk to and fro on a public walk; to seek any thing; to discuss repeatedly the same topic. *A vuelta* or *a vueltas*, Very near, almost; also, with another thing otherwise. *Á vuelta de cabeza*, In the twinkling of an eye. *Andar en vueltas*, To make difficulties, to avoid doing something. *Coger las vueltas*, To seek evasive measures or artifices to attain an end. *Darse una vuelta a la redonda*, (to take a turn about) To examine one's self before reproving another. *No tener vuelta de hoja*, To be unanswerable. *Tener vueltas alguno*, To be inconstant or fickle. *Tener vuelta*, (Coll.) An admonition to return a thing lent.—*int.* Return; let him return or go back the same way. *No hay que darle vueltas*, (Met.) No quibbling about it, it will prove to be the very thing. *Poner de vuelta y media*, To abuse a person by word or action. *La vuelta del humo*, Unwelcome return.

Vuelto, ta [voo-el'-to, tah], *pp. irr.* of Volver.

(*Yo vuelvo, yo vuelva*, from *Volver. V.* Absolver.)

Vuesa [voo-ay'-sah], *a.* Contracted from *vuestra*, and used before *merced*, *eminencia*, etc.

Vuesamerced [voo-ay-sah-mer-thed'], *f.* You, sir; you, madam; your worship, your honour; a contraction of *vuestra merced*, a title of courtesy to a person who is not entitled to that of *vueseñoría* or *vuestra señoría*, your lordship.

Vuesarced [voo-ay-sar-thed'], *f.* Contraction of *vuesamerced*.

Vueseñoría [voo-ay-say-nyo-ree'-ah], *f.* Contraction of *vuestra señoría*.

Vuestro, tra [voo-es'-tro, trah], *a. pron.* Your, yours. It is used absolutely by subjects to a sovereign, or by a sovereign to a subject. *Muy vuestro*, Entirely yours. *Vuestra señoría*, Your lordship or ladyship.

Vulcanita [vool-cah-nee'-tah], *f.* Vulcanite.

Vulcanizar [vool-cah-ne-thar'], *va.* To vulcanize, to mix sulphur with rubber at a high temperature.

Vulgacho [vool-gah'-cho], *m.* Mob, populace, dregs of the people.

Vulgado, da [vool-gah'-do, dah], *a.* (Obs.) Vulgar.

Vulgar [vool-gar'], *a.* Vulgar, common, ordinary; vulgar or vernacular dialect, as opposed to the learned languages; without specific peculiarity.

Vulgar [vool-gar'], *m.* The vulgar.

Vulgaridad [vool-gah-re-dahd'], *f.* Vulgarity; vulgarism, manners or speech of the lowest people; vulgar effusion.

Vulgarismo [vool-gah-rees'-mo], *m.* Colloquialism, colloquial expression.

Vulgarizar [vool-gah-re-thar'], *va.* 1. To make vulgar or common. 2. To translate from another idiom into the common language of the country.—*vr.* To become vulgar.

Vulgarmente, *adv.* Vulgarly, commonly; among the common people.

Vulgata [vool-gah'-tah], *f.* Vulgate, the Latin version of the Bible, approved by the Roman Church.

Vulgo [vool'-go], *m.* 1. Multitude, populace, mob. 2. Way of thinking of the populace. 3. Universality or generality of people.—*adv. V.* Vulgarmente.

Vulnerable [vool-nay-rah'-blay], *a.* Vulnerable.

Vulneración [vool-nay-rah-the-on'], *f.* The act of wounding.

Vulnerar [vool-nay-rar'], *va.* 1. (Obs.) To wound. *V.* Herir. 2. To injure the reputation.

Vulneraria [vool-nay-rah'-re-ah], *f.* (Bot.) Kidney vetch.

Vulnerario, ria [vool-nay-rah'-re-o, ah], *a.* 1. Vulnerary, useful in healing wounds. 2. (Law) Applied to an ecclesiastic who has wounded or killed any one.

Vulnerario, *m.* Clergyman guilty of killing or wounding.

Vulpécula [vool-pay'-coo-lah], *f.* *V.* Vulpeja.

Vulpeja [vool-pay'-hah], *f.* A bitch-fox.

Vulpinita [vool-pe-nee'-tah], *f.* Vulpinite, a variety of anhydrite from Vulpino in Italy: used in Milan for tables, chimneys, etc.

Vulpino, na [vool-pee'-no, nah], *a.* 1. Proper to a fox, foxy, vulpine. 2. (Met.) Foxy, crafty, deceitful.

Vultúridos [vool-too'-re-dos], *m. pl.* A division of the birds of prey; the vultures.

Vulva [vool'-vah], *f.* (Anat.) Vulva, the external orifice of the female genitals.

Vulvaria [vool-vah'-re-ah], *f.* Vulvaria, the fetid orach, a common European plant.

Vulvario, ria, [vool-vah'-re-o, ah], *a.* (Anat.) Vulvar, pertaining to the vulva.

W

This letter does not belong to the Spanish alphabet and is only used in terms, chiefly proper names, taken from languages of northern Europe. It is named *V doble* (double v). In chemistry W stands for Wolfram (tungsten).

X

X [ay'-kis], *f.* The twenty-sixth letter of the alphabet. This letter is pronounced like *cs* or *gs* in English; the Castilians give it constantly only the sound of *cs;* in the other Spanish provinces both sounds are indifferently used. When it is the last letter of a word it has a guttural sound, like that of the Spanish *j* (the German *ch* in *Ich*), as in *carcax* (quiver); but such words are no longer written with *x*, but with *j;* thus *reloj* (watch), formerly *relox.* As this sound is rather difficult to utter, words ending with *j* are pronounced either by dropping that letter, or sounding it like *cs;* thus, *reló* or *relocs.* To give this letter its true guttural sound is considered by many as an affectation.—X had formerly two distinct sounds; one like *cs,* which was indicated by a circumflex accent over the vowel that followed the *x*, and the other guttural, like an English *h* very strongly aspirated, in which case the vowel was unaccented; thus, *prôximo* (*adj.* proximate, next), and *próximo* (*n.* a fellow-being): the first was pronounced *proc'-se-mo,* and the second *pro'-he-mo.* At present, all those words in which the *x* has a guttural sound are written with *j*, which the scholar is requested to consult. It is becoming a very censurable fashion, particularly in America, for want of proper instruction, to pronounce and write *s* instead of *x* in a great number of words beginning with *ex;* thus, *esámen, esperiencia, etc.:* but this use is not supported by the old Castilians and educated persons. X (and j) often represent the Arabic letter shin. Thus *carcax* (now carcaj); *xábeca* (net, now jábeca); *Xerez* (now Jerez, whence "sherry").

Xa, Xe, Xi, Xo, Xu. Words formerly beginning with either of these syllables, will be found in JA, JE, JI, JO, JU.

Xantóxilo [csan-tok'-se-lo], *m.* (Bot.) Xanthoxlum, prickly ash. *V.* ZANTÓXILO.

Xapurcar [csah-poor-car'], *va.* (Prov.) To stir up dirty water.

Xara [csah'-rah, properly shah'-rah], *f.* The law of the Moors.

Xerofagia [csay-ro-fah'-he-ah], *f.* Xerophagy.

Xerófila [csay-ro'-fe-lah], *m.* (Bot.) Xerophyte.

Xerqueria [cser-kay-ree'-ah], *f.* (Obs.) Slaughter-house.

Xi [csee], *f.* Fourteenth letter of the Greek alphabet, corresponding to X.

Xifoideo, ea [cse-foi-day'-o, ah], *a.* Xiphoid, relating to the xiphoid cartilage.

Xifoides [cse-foi'-days], *a.* & *m.* (Zool.) Xiphoid, sword-shaped; the cartilage ending the sternum below.

Xilófago, ga [cse-lo'-fah-go, gah], *a.* Xylophagous, feeding on or boring in wood.—*m.* A dipterous insect living in elms.

Xilofón, xilófono [se-lo-fone', se-lo'-fo-no], *m.* (Mus.) Xilophone.

Xilografía [cse-lo-grah-fee'-ah], *f.* Xylography, wood-engraving.

Xilográfico, ca [cse-lo-grah'-fe-co, cah], *a.* Xylographic, relating to engraving upon wood.

Xo [cso], *int.* Whoa! *V.* JO and CHO.

Y

Y [yay, ee gre-ay'-gah], *f.* The twenty-seventh letter of the Castilian alphabet, stands as a vowel and a consonant. Y, when alone, or after a vowel, or followed by a consonant, or at the end of a word, is a vowel, and sounds as *e* or *ee* in English: *Hoy y mañana* (To-day and to-morrow), *o'-e ee mah-nyah'-nah.*—Y, before a vowel in the same syllable, or between two vowels in the same word, is a consonant, and sounds like the English *y* in the words yard, yell, you. Of late attempts have been wrongly made to revive the old fashion of writing *i* instead of *y* at the end of words, and when it is a conjunction; thus, *estoi, doi, i, etc.,* in place of *estoy, doy, y.* Words formerly written with *y* before a consonant, as *reyna, peyne,* have changed it into *i;* thus, *reina, peine.*

Y [ee], *conj.* And. It is frequently used in interrogatives, or by way of a reply; as *¿ Y tú, no haces lo mismo?* And you, do you not do the same? *¿ Y tú, dónde has estado?* And thou, where hast thou been? *¿ Y bien?* And well then? *¿ Y qué tenemos con eso?* And what is that to us? or, And what of all that? Generally it is a copulative conjunction; as, *Alfonso, Fernando y Manuel,* Alphonsus, Ferdinand, and Emmanuel. When the conjunction *y* is followed by a word beginning with *i* or *hi*, the conjunction *e* is used in its stead; as, *Sabiduría e ignorancia,* Wisdom and ignorance. *Padre e hijo,* Father and son.

Y, *adv.* (Obs.) There. *V.* ALLÍ.

Ya [yah], *adv.* 1. Already. 2. Presently, immediately, now. 3. Finally, ultimately. 4. At another time, on another occasion. *Ya no es lo que ha sido,* It is not now what it has been. *Ya estamos en ello,* We are about it, we understand it. *Ya se hará eso,* That will be done. *Ya voy,* I am going, or I am going presently.—*part.* Now. *Ya esto, ya aquello,* Now this, now that. *Ya que,* Since that, seeing that. *Ya que has venido,* Since you are coming, or since you are here. *Ya si,* (Prov.) When, while, if.—*int.* Used on being brought to recollect any thing. *¿ No se acuerda Vd. de tal cosa? Ya, ya,* Do not you remember such a thing? Yes, yes: *Ya se ve,* Yes, forsooth! it is clear, it is so. *Ya estaba yo en eso,* I was already of that mind. *Él busca la muerte, ya que no el triunfo,* He seeks for death, since he cannot triumph.

Yaacabó [yah-ah-cah-bo'], *m.* A hawk or falcon of Venezuela, whose note sounds like *ya acabó.* (Imitative.)

Yaca [yah'-cah], *f.* (Bot.) A large-leaved Indian tree.

Yacaré [yah-cah-ray'], *m.* (Zool. Amer.) Crocodile.

Yacedor [yah-thay-dor'], *m.* A lad who takes horses to graze by night.

Yacente [yah-then'-tay], *pa.* & *a.* Jacent, vacant; lying. *Herencia yacente,* Inheritance not yet occupied.

Yacer [yah-therr'], *vn.* 1. To lie, to lie down. 2. To lie down in the grave. 3. To be fixed or situated in a place; to exist. 4. To graze by night in the field.

Yaciente [yah-the-en'-tay], *a.* Extended, stretched: applied to honey-combs.

Yacija [yah-thee'-hah], *f.* 1. Bed, couch. 2. Tomb, grave. *Ser de mala yacija,* To be a vagrant; to be restless; to have a bad bed.

Yactura [yac-too'-rah], *f.* Loss, damage.

Yáculo [yah'-coo-lo], *m.* 1. A serpent which darts from trees in order to attack. 2. (Zool.) Dace.

Yacumana [yah-coo-mah'-nah], *f.* Name given to the boa in the Amazonian provinces.

Yagre [yah'-gray], *m.* Sugar, extracted from the palm or cocoa-tree. *V.* JACRA.

Yagua [yah'-goo-ah], *f.* Bark of the royal palm.

Yak [yahk], *m.* Yak, a bovine quadruped of central Asia.

Yalotecnia [yah-lo-tec'-ne-ah], *f.* The art of working glass.

Yámbico, ca [yahm'-be-co, cah], *a.* Iambic: applied to a Latin verse.

Yambo [yahm'-bo], *m.* An iambic foot (⏑ —).

Yanacona [yah-nah-co'-nah], **Yanacuna** [yah-nah-coo'-nah], *com.* (Peru) The Indian bound to personal service.

Yankee [yahn'-kee], *com.* & *a.* 1. A person born or living in New England. 2. A native of the United States.

Yanqui [yahn'-kee], *a.* (fr. English, Yankee). A native of the United States.

Yanta [yahn'-tah], *f.* 1. (Obs.) Dinner, midday meal. 2. *V.* LLANTA.

Yantar [yan-tar'], *va.* (Obs.) To dine. *V.* COMER.

Yantar, *m.* 1. (Prov.) Viands, food. 2. A kind of king's taxes.

Yapa [yah'-pah], *f.* A thing or quantity which the seller presents to the buyer. *V.* ÑAPA and CONTRA.

Yarda [yar'-dah], *f.* An English yard, equal to 91 centimetres; a *vara,* the Spanish measure of 3 feet, is equivalent to 8.36 decimetres.

Yarey [yah-ray'-e], *m.* (Cuba) A species of *guano* (palm-tree). *Sombrero de yarey,* A coarse kind of hat made with the leaves of this palm.

Yaro [yah'-ro], *m.* (Bot.) Arum, an aquatic plant.

Yareta [yah-ray'-tah], *f.* A kind of combustible; peat.

Yatagán [yah-tah-gahn'], *m.* A kind of a sabre-dagger used by the orientals.

Yate [yah'-tay], *m.* Yacht, a pleasure craft, sailing or propelled by steam.

Yayero, ra [yah-yay'-ro, rah], *a.* (Cuba) Intermeddling, busybody.

(*Yo yazgo* or *yago, yazga* or *yaga.* *V.* YACER.)

Yedra, or **Yedra arborácea** [yay'-drah], *f.* (Bot.) Ivy. Hedera felix, *L.* *Yedra terrestre,* Ground ivy. **Glechoma hederacea.** *V.* HIEDRA.

Yegua [yay'-goo-ah], *f.* Mare. *Yegua paridera,* A breeding mare. *Yegua de vientre,* Mare fit to breed. *Yegua madre,* A dam. *Donde hay yeguas, potros nacen,* Where there is smoke there is some fire; known causes produce known results. *El que desecha la yegua, ese la lleva.* The depreciating that which one is at the same time trying to obtain. *Yegua parada prado halla,* The difficulty suggests the way out; necessity is the mother of invention.

Yeguada, Yegüería [yay-goo-ah'-dah, yay-goo-ay-ree'-ah], *f.* Stud, a herd of breeding mares and stallions.

Yeguar [yay-goo-ar'], *a.* Belonging to mares.

Yegüero, Yegüerizo [yay-goo-ay'-ro, yay-goo-ay-ree'-tho], *m.* Keeper of breeding mares.

Yegüezuela [yay-goo-ay-thoo-ay'-lah], *f. dim.* Little mare.

Yelmo [yel'-mo], *m.* Helmet, helm, a part of ancient armour.

Yelo [yay'-lo], *m.* Frost, ice. (Obs.) *V.* Hielo.

Yema [yay'-mah], *f.* 1. Bud, first shoot of trees. 2. Yelk of an egg. 3. Centre, middle. *En la yema del invierno,* In the dead of winter. *Dar en la yema,* (Met.) To hit the nail on the head. 4. The best or best placed in its line. 5. Fleshy tip of the finger. 6. (Coll.) Ace of diamonds in cards. *Yemas de faltriquera,* (Coll.) Candied yelks.

Yente [yen'-tay], *pa. irr.* of Ir. Going, one that goes.

Yerba [yerr'-bah], *f. V.* Hierba, which is the modern spelling of this word. 1. Herb, a generic name for all the smaller plants. 2. Flaw in the emerald which tarnishes its lustre. 3. Grass (see plural). 4. *Yerba, yerba mate* or *mate,* The leaves of a tree of that name in South America, of which, when finely chopped and boiled in water, a decoction is made, which is drunk instead of tea. It is a very important article of commerce. *Pisar buena* or *mala yerba,* To be of a good or bad temper. *Yerba cana* (named from its hoary pappus), Groundsel, ragwort. Senecio vulgaris. *Yerba carmín,* Virginian poke. Phytolacca decandra. *Yerba de cuajo, V.* Alcachofa. *Yerba de la princesa,* Lemon-scented verbena. Aloysia citriodora, *Pallau. Yerba de los lazarosos. V.* Angélica arcangélica. *Yerba del ballestero,* White hellebore. Veratrum album. *Yerba de pordioseros, V.* Flámula. *Yerba de San Juan,* or *yerbas del Señor San Juan,* Odoriferous herbs ripe for sale on St. John's day. *Yerba doncella,* Periwinkle. Vinca major. *Yerba lombriguera, V.* Abrótano. *Yerba mora,* Nightshade. Solanum nigrum. *Yerba pastel,* Woad. Isatis. *Yerba piojera,* Stavesacre. Delphinium staphysagria. *Yerba puntera, V.* Siempreviva arbórea. *Yerba tora,* Strangle-weed, broom-rape. Orobanche major. *Yerba de mar* or *marina,* Sea-weed. *Yerba del Paraguay,* Yerba mate Paraguay. *Barro de yerbas,* Mug or jug made of perfumed clay, with the figures of herbs upon it. *En yerba,* Greenly, tenderly: applied to fruits or seeds. *Queso de yerba,* Cheese made of vegetable rennet. *Sentir nacer la yerba,* Used to indicate one's vivacity or quickness; to be sensible.—*pl.* 1. Greens, vegetables; all kinds of garden stuff. 2. Grass of pasture land for cattle. 3. Poison given in food; poisonous plant. 4. Time when colts are born. *Otras yerbas,* (Hum.) Et cetera: used after several epithets.

Yerbabuena [yer-bah-boo-ay'-nah], *f.* Mint, peppermint. *V.* Hierbabuena. Mentha.

Yerbatear [yer-bah-tay-ar'], *vn.* (Amer. Argen.) To take *maté,* Paraguay tea.

Yerbatero, ra [yer-bah-tay'-ro, rah], *a.* & *n.* 1. Using arrow-poison. 2. (Peru) One who sells or carries grass or fodder for horses.

Yerbazal [yer-bah-thahl'], *m. V.* Herbazal.

(*Yo yergo, él irguió, yo yerga. V.* Erguir.)

Yermar [yer-mar'], *va.* To dispeople, to lay waste.

Yermo [yerr'-mo], *m.* Desert, wilderness, waste country. *Padre del yermo,* Ancient hermit.

Yermo, ma [yerr'-mo, mah], *a.* Waste, desert, uninhabited; herbless. *Tierra yerma,* Uncultivated ground.

Yernalmente, *adv.* In jocular style, in the manner of a son-in-law.

Yernar [yer-nar'], *va.* (Coll. Prov.) To make one a son-in-law by force.

Yerno [yerr'-no], *m.* Son-in-law. *Engaña yernos,* Baubles, gee-gaws, trifles. *Ciega yernos,* Showy trifles.

Yero [yay'-ro], *m.* (Bot.) *V.* Yervo.

Yerro [yer'-ro], *m.* Error, mistake, inadvertency, fault. *Yerros,* Faults, defects, errors. *Yerro de imprenta,* Erratum, literal error. *El yerro del entendido,* (Coll.) Learned men commit the greatest faults.

(*Yo yerro, yo yerre. V.* Errar.)

Yerto [yerr'-to, tah], *a.* Stiff, motionless, inflexible; rigid, tight. *Quedarse yerto,* (Met.) To be petrified with fear or astonishment.

Yervo [yerr'-vo], *m.* (Bot.) Tare, true bitter vetch. Ervum tetrapernum.

Yesal, Yesar [yay-sahl'], *m.* Gypsum-pit, where gypsum is dug.

Yesca [yes'-cah], *f.* 1. Spunk, tinder. 2. Fuel, incentive or aliment of passion. 3. Flint and tinder for making a light.—*pl. Yescas,* Any thing excessively dry or combustible.

Yesera [yay-say'-rah], *f.* Kiln, where gypsum is calcined and prepared for use.

Yesería [yay-say-ree'-ah], *f.* 1. *V.* Yesera. 2. Building constructed with gypsum.

Yesero, ra [yay-say'-ro, rah], *a.* Belonging to gypsum.

Yesero, *m.* One that prepares or sells gypsum.

Yesgo [yes'-go], *m.* (Bot. Prov.) Dwarf elder. Sambucus ebulus.

Yeso [yay'-so], *m.* Gypsum, gypse, sulphate of lime. *Yeso mate,* Plaster of Paris. *Yeso blanco,* Whiting.

Yesón [yay-sone'], *m.* Piece of rubbish or fragment of gypsum already used in building.

Yesoso, sa [yay-so'-so, sah], *a.* Gypseous.

Yesquero [yes-kay'-ro], *m.* Tinder-box.

Yeyuno [yay-yoo'-no], *m.* Jejunum, the second portion of the small intestines between the duodenum and the ileum.

Yezgo [yeth'-go], *m.* (Bot.) Dwarf elder. Sambucus ebulus.

Y griega [ee gre-ay'-gah], *f.* Name of the letter y. (Greek y, as contrasted to the Latin I.)

Yo [yo], *pron. pers.* I. *Yo mismo,* I myself. Pronounced with emphasis, *yo* is an exclamation of contempt, of surprise, and negation; of commanding and threatening; it is also a sign of majesty, as, *Yo el rey,* I the king.

Yodado (or **ato**) [yo-dah'-do, to], *a.* Iodic, containing iodine.

Yodo [yo'-do], *m.* Iodine, a bluish black haloid element used in medicine and in photography.

Yoduro [yo-doo'-ro], *m.* Iodid, iodide, a compound of iodine.

Ypsilon [eep'-se-lon], *f.* Twentieth letter of the Greek alphabet, corresponding to y.

Yole [yo'-lay], *m.* (Naut.) Yawl.

Yuca [yoo'-cah], *f.* (Bot.) Adam's needle; the root of this plant is farinaceous, and eaten like potatoes. Yucca. *Yuca de cazave* or *casave,* Cassava, Barbadoes nut, physic nut. Jatropha manioth.

Yucateco, ca [yoo-cah-tay'-co, cah], *a.* Of Yucatan.

Yugada [yoo-gah'-dah], *f.* Extent of ground which a yoke of oxen can plough in a day; a yoke of land.

Yuge [yoo'-hay], *m.* (Obs.) *V.* Juez.

Yugo [yoo'-go], *m.* 1. Yoke, for draught-oxen. 2. Nuptial tie, with which a new-married couple is veiled; marriage ceremony. 3. Oppressive authority, absolute power. 4. Confinement, prison, yoke. 5. Kind of gallows under which the Romans passed their prisoners of war. 6. (Naut.) Transom, a beam across the sternpost. *Yugo de la caña,* (Naut.) Counter-transom. *Yugo de la cubierta,* (Naut.) Deck-transom. *Yugo principal,* (Naut.) Wing-transom. *Sacudir el yugo,* To throw off the yoke.

Yuguero [yoo-gay'-ro], *m.* Ploughman, ploughboy.

Yugular [yoo-goo-lar'], *a.* (Anat.) Jugular.

Yumbo, ba [yoom'-bo, bah], *m.* & *f.* & *a.* A savage Indian of eastern Ecuador.

Yunga [yoon'-gah], *f.* (Peru, Bol.) *a.* & *m. pl.* Name given in Bolivia to the hot region of the north-east where famous coffee is raised.

Yungir [yoon-heer'], *va.* (Obs.) *V.* Uncir.

Yunque [yoon'-kay], *m.* 1. Anvil. 2. Constancy, fortitude. 3. (Anat.) Incus, a bone of the ear. 4. One of the blades of a cloth-shearer's shears. *Estar al yunque,* To bear up under the frowns of fortune; to bear impertinent or abusive language.

Yunta [yoon'-tah], *f.* 1. Couple, pair, yoke. 2. (Prov.) *V.* Yugada.

Yuntar [yoon-tar'], *va.* (Obs.) *V.* Juntar.

Yuntería [yoon-tay-ree'-ah], *f.* Place where draught-oxen are fed.

Yuntero [yoon-tay'-ro], *m.* *V.* Yuguero.

Yunto, ta [yoon to, tah], *a.* Joined, united, close. *V.* Junto. *Arar yunto,* To plough together.

Yuruma [yoo-roo'-mah], *f.* Starch obtained from a species of palm along the Orinoco.

Yusano, na [yoo-sah'-no, nah], *a.* (Obs.) Inferior, lower.

Yusera [yoo-say'-rah], *f.* The horizontal stone in oil-mills which lies under the roller.

Yusión [yoo-se-on'], *f.* Precept, command.

Yuso [yoo'-so], *adv.* (Obs.) *V.* Debajo and Ayuso.

Yute [yoo'-tay], *m.* 1. Jute, a textile fibre, obtained from an Asiatic herb of the linden family. 2. Jute fabric.

Yuxtaponer [yoox-tah-po-nerr'], *va.* To juxtapose, to put side by side.

Yuxtaposición [yoox-tah-po-se-the-on'], *f.* Juxtaposition.

Yuyuba [yoo-yoo'-bah], *f.* *V* Azufaifa.

Z

Z [thay'-dah, thay'-tah], *f.* The twenty-eighth letter of the Spanish alphabet. Whether at the beginning, middle, or end of words, it sounds in Spanish like the English *th* in *thank, cathedral, tenth.* Latin words terminating in *x* take *z* in Spanish, as *lux, luz; velox, veloz.* In the plural and in compound words it is superseded by *c*, as *paz* makes *paces, pacífico, apaciguar.*

¡Za! [thah], *int.* A word used to frighten dogs or other animals.

Zábida, Zábila [thah'-be-dah, thah'-be-lah], *f.* (Bot.) Common or yellow-flowered aloe. Aloe vulgaris.

Zaborda, *f.* **Zabordamiento,** *m.* [thah-bor'-dah, thah-bor-dah-me-en'-to]. (Naut.) Stranding; the act of getting on shore.

Zabordar [thah-bor-dar'], *vn.* (Naut.) To touch ground, to get on shore, to be stranded.

Zabordo [thah-bor'-do], *m.* (Naut.) Stranding.

Zaboyar [thah-bo-yar'], *va.* (Prov.) To join bricks with mortar.

Zabra [thah'-brah], *f.* (Naut.) A small vessel, used on the coast of Biscay.

Zabucar [thah-boo-car'], *va.* 1. To re volve something. 2. To shake, to agitate. *V.* BAZUCAR.

Zabullida [thah-bool-lyee'-dah], *f.* Dipping, ducking.

Zabullidor, ra [thah-bool-lyee-dor', rah], *m.* & *f.* One who ducks or puts under water.

Zabullidura [thah-bool-lye-doo'-rah], *f.* Submersion, ducking.

Zabullimiento [thah-bool-lyee-me-en'-to], *m.* *V.* ZAMBULLIDA.

Zabullir [thah-bool-lyeer'], *va.* To plunge, to immerse, to put under water, to immerge.—*vr.* 1. To plunge suddenly under water, to sink. 2. To lurk, to lie concealed.

Zabuqueo [thah-boo-kay'-o], *m.* *V.* BAZUQUEO.

Zacapela, Zacapella [thah-cah-pay'-lah, pay'-lyah], *f.* Uproar, yell, noisy bustle. *Cf.* GAZAPELA.

Zacate [thah-cah'-tay], *m.* (Mex. and Philip. Islands) 1. Grass, herbage. 2. Hay, forage.

Zacateca [thah-cah-tay'-cah], *m.* (Cuba) Undertaker, funeral director, sexton.

Zacatin [thah-cah-teen'], *m.* A place where garments are sold.

Zacear [thah-thay-ar'], *va.* To frighten dogs away by crying *za.*

Zádiva [thah'-de-vah], *f.* (Bot.) A plant the leaves of which soften corns.

Zadorija [thah-do-ree'-hah], *f.* (Bot.) An annual herbaceous plant with four unequal yellow petals, in pairs, four stamens, and a jointed many-seeded pod. It serves as food for canaries. *V.* PAMPLINA. 3d def.

Zafa [thah'-fah], *f.* (Prov.) *V.* ALJOFAINA.

Zafacoca [thah-fah-co'-cah], *com.* (Amer. Coll.) Noisy confusion, squabbling, rioting.

Zafada [thah-fah'-dah], *f.* 1. Flight, escape. 2. (Naut.) The act of lightening the ship.

Zafar [thah-far'], *va.* 1. To adorn, to embellish. 2. To disembarrass. 3. (Naut.) To lighten a ship.—*vr.* 1. To escape, to avoid risk, to run away. 2. To avoid, to decline; to excuse; to free one's self from trouble, to get clear off. 3. To slip off the border of a wheel: applied to the belt of machinery. *Zafarse de los bajos,* (Naut.) To get clear of the shoals.

Zafareche [thah fah-ray'-chay], *m.* (Prov.) *V.* ESTANQUE.

Zafarí [thah-fah-ree'], *m.* A sort of pomegranate, with quadrangular seeds.

Zafariche [thah-fah-ree'-chay], *m.* (Prov.) Shelf for holding water vessels or jars.

Zafarrancho [thah-far-rahn'-cho], *m.* 1. (Naut.) The state of being clear for action. *Hacer zafarrancho,* (Naut.) To make ready for action. 2. (Coll.) Ravage, destruction. 3. Scuffle, wrangle, squabble.

Zafería [thah-fay-ree'-ah], *f.* A small village, a farm-house.

Zafiamente [thah-fe-ah-men'-tay], *adv.* Clownishly, lubberly, clumsily.

Zafiedad [thah-fe-ay-dahd'], *f.* Clownishness, rusticity, clumsiness.

Zafio, fia [thah'-fe-o, ah], *a.* Clownish, coarse, uncivil, ignorant.

Zafío [thah-fee'-o], *m.* (Zool.) *V.* SAFÍO or CONGRIO.

Zafir, Zafiro [thah-feer', thah-fee'-ro], *m.* Sapphire, a precious stone.

Zafíreo, ea [thah-fee'-ray-o, ah], *a.* Sapphire-coloured.

Zafirino, na [thah-fe-ree'-no, nah], *a.* Of the colour of sapphire.

Zafo, fa [thah'-fo, fah], *a.* 1. Free, disentangled, empty. 2. (Naut.) Clear. 3. Free, exempt from danger or risk.

Zafón [thah-fone'], *m.* *V.* ZAHÓN.

Zafra [thah'-frah], *f.* 1. Drip-jar, a large metal bowl, pierced at the bottom, placed over a jar for draining oil; or a dish in which oil is kept. 2. Crop of sugar-cane and the making of sugar. 3. A broad strap which holds the thills of a cart. 4. (Min.) Poor ore mingled with rubbish.

Zafrán [thah-frahn'], *m.* (Obs.) *V.* AZAFRÁN.

Zafre [thah'-fray], *m.* (Min.) Zaffre or saffre, cobalt oxyd roasted with silica, and employed chiefly for giving a blue colour to porcelain.

Zafreño, ña [thah-fray'-nyo, nyah], *a.* Belonging to the town of Zafra.

Zaga [thah'-gah], *f.* 1. Load packed on the back part of a carriage. 2. The extremity behind. 3. (Mil.) *V.* RETAGUARDIA.—*m.* The last player at a game of cards.—*adv.* *V.* DETRÁS. *A zaga* or *en zaga,* Behind. *No ir* or *no quedarse en zaga,* (Coll.) Not to be less than any other, or inferior to any man.

Zagal [thah-gahl'], *m.* 1. A stout, spirited young man. 2. Swain, a young shepherd subordinate to the chief herd; subordinate coachman. 3. Under petticoat.

Zagala [thah-gah'-lah], *f.* A shepherdess, lass, girl.

Zagalejo, ja [thah-gah-lay'-ho, hah], *m.* & *f. dim.* A young shepherd or shepherdess.

Zagalejo [thah-gah-lay'-ho], *m.* An under petticoat of close woven stuff worn over the white petticoat. *Zagalejo picado,* (Mex.) A fine red cloth petticoat, embroidered with spangles.

Zagalico, illo, ito [thah-gah-lee'-co], *m. dim.* A little shepherd.

Zagalón, na, [thah-gah-lone', nah], *m.* & *f.* An overgrown lad or girl.

Zagú [thah-goo'], *m.* The sago-plant. *V.* SAGÚ.

Zagua [thah'-goo-ah], *f.* A shrub yielding barilla which grows in southern Europe and northern Africa.

Zaguán [thah-goo-ahn'], *m.* Porch, entrance, hall.

Zaguanete [thah-goo-ah-nay'-tay], *m.* 1. (Dim.) Small entrance of a house. 2. A small party of the king's life-guards.

Zaguera [thah-gay'-rah], *f.* (Obs.) *V.* RETAGUARDIA.

Zaguero, ra [thah-gay'-ro, rah], *a.* Going or remaining behind.

Zahareño, ña [thah-ah-ray'-nyo, nyah], *a.* 1. Intractable, wild, haggard: applied to birds. 2. (Met.) Sour, haughty, indocile.

Zaharí [thah-ah-ree'], *a.* *V.* ZAFARÍ.

Zaharrón [thah-ar-rone'], *m.* (Obs.) *V.* MOHARRACHE.

Zahén [thah-ayn'], *a.* *Dobla zahén* or *zahena,* A Moorish gold coin.

Zaherible [thah-ay-ree'-blay], *a.* Blamable, censurable, blameworthy.

Zaheridor, ra [thah-ay-re-dor', rah], *m.* & *f.* Censurer, one who blames.

Zaherimiento [thah-ay-re-me-en'-to], *m.* Censure, blame.

Zaherir [thah-ay-reer'], *va.* 1. To censure, to blame, to reproach; to upbraid. 2. To mortify one by criticising him with a bad intention.

(*Yo zahiero, yo zahiera, él zahirió,* from *Zaherir.* *V.* ADHERIR.)

Zahina [thah-ee'-nah], *f.* Sorghum, a graminaceous plant resembling broom-corn, cultivated in Spain for fodder. Andropogon sorghum.

Zahinar [thah-e-nar'], *m.* Land sown with sorghum, sorghum-field.

Zahinas, *f. pl.* (Prov. Andal. fr. Arabic) Light and soft fritters, puff-cakes. *Zahinas de levadura,* Froth of barm.

Zahón [thah-on'], *m.* 1. A leather apron divided at the lower part and tied behind the thighs and at the waist; worn to protect the clothes. 2. *pl.* A kind of wide breeches, overalls.

Zahonado, da [thah-oh-nah'-do, dah], *a.* Of a dark colour, brownish.

Zahondar [thah-on-dar'], *va.* To dig the ground, to penetrate. *V.* AHONDAR.—*vn.* To sink into the ground: used of the feet.

Zahora [thah-o'-rah], *f.* (Prov.) Luncheon among friends, with music.

Zahorar [thah-o-rar'], *vn.* To have a repast with music.

Zahorí [thah-o-ree'], *m.* Vulgar impostor pretending to see hidden things, although in the bowels of the earth, if not covered with blue cloth.

Zahorra [thah-or'-rah], *f.* (Naut.) Ballast. *V.* LASTRE (fr. Lat. saburra).

Zahumador [thah-oo-mah-dor'], *m.* (Obs.) 1. (Prov.) A kind of perfuming pot. 2. Clothes-horse, drying-horse for clothes.

Zahumar [thah-oo-mar'], *va.* (Obs.) To fumigate, to smoke. *V.* SAHUMAR.

Zahumerio [thah-oo-may'-re-o], *m.* (Obs.) *V.* SAHUMERIO.

Zahurda [thah-oor'-dah], *f.* 1. Pigsty, hogsty. 2. A small, dirty, miserable house. 3. A dipterous insect of Europe (fr. German).

Zaida [thah'-e-dah], *f.* (Orn.) A variety of the African heron. Ardea caspica.

Zaino, na [thah'-e-no, nah], *a.* 1. Of a chestnut colour: applied to horses. 2. Vicious: applied to animals. 3. Treacherous, wicked, vicious. *Mirar de zaino* or *a lo zaino,* To look sidewise, to cast an insidious glance.

Zalá [thah-lah'], *f.* Religious adoration paid by the Moors to God; prayer with various ceremonies. *Hacer la zalá,* (Coll.) To flatter in order to obtain something.

Zalagarda [thah-lah-gar'-dah], *f.* 1. Ambuscade, ambush. 2. Gin, trap, snare. 3. Sudden attack, surprise. 4. Mock-fight: vulgar noise. 5. (Coll.) Malicious cunning.

Zalama, Zalamería [thah-lah'-mah, thah-lah-may-ree'-ah], *f.* Flattery, adulation, wheedling. (Arab. salam.)
Zalamelé [thah-lah-may-lay'], *m.* *V.* ZALAMA.
Zalameramente, *adv.* Fawningly.
Zalamero, ra [thah-lah-may'-ro, rah], *m.* & *f.* Wheedler, flatterer, fawner.
Zalea [thah-lay'-ah], *f.* 1. An undressed sheep-skin. 2. Sheep-skin mats. *Estacar la zalea,* (Mex. Vulg.) To die. (Arab. saleha, 'hide.')
Zalear [thah-lay-ar'], *va.* 1. To move a thing with care. 2. To frighten dogs. *V.* ZACEAR.
Zalema [thah-lay'-mah], *f.* Bow, courtesy. (Arab.)
Zaleo [thah-lay'-o], *m.* 1. Skin of a beast lacerated by the wolf, which the herd carries to his master as an excuse; undressed sheep-skin. 2. The act of shaking or moving to and fro.
Zalmedina [thal-may-dee'-nah], *m.* Ancient magistrate with civil and criminal powers, in Arragon.
Zaloma [thah-lo'-mah], *f.* (Naut.) Singing out of seamen when they haul with a rope; chantey.
Zalomar [thah-lo-mar'], *vn.* (Naut.) To sing out. *V.* SALOMAR.
Zalona [thah-lo'-nah], *f.* (Prov. Andal.) A large earthen jar.
Zallar [thal-lyar'], *va.* (Obs.) 1. To direct and level warlike arms. 2. (Naut.) To outrig, to train. (Ger. zeile.)
Zamacuco [thah-mah-coo'-co], *m.* (Coll.) 1. Dunce, dolt. 2. Intoxication, inebriation.
Zamanca [thah-mahn'-cah], *f.* (Coll.) Drubbing, flogging, castigation.
Zamarra [thah-mar'-rah], *f.* 1. Dress worn by shepherds, made of undressed sheep-skins. 2. The skin so used. *La zamarra y la vileza al que se la aveza,* Habit becomes a second nature (endurance of repugnant things.)
Zamarrear [thah-mar-ray-ar'], *va.* 1. To shake, to drag or pull to and fro. 2. To pin up close in a dispute. 3. (Met.) To drag, to ill-treat.
Zamarreo [thah-mar-ray'-o], *m.* Action of dragging or shaking from side to side.
Zamarrico [thah-mar-ree'-co], *m. dim.* of ZAMARRO. A portmanteau or bag of sheep-skin, having the wool inside.
Zamarrilla [thah-mar-reel'-lyah], *f.* 1. (Dim.) A short loose coat of sheep-skins. 2. (Bot.) Poly, mountain germander, a medicinal plant with yellow flowers which are very bitter. Teucrium polium.
Zamarro [thah-mar'-ro], *m.* 1. A shepherd's coat of sheep-skins. 2. Sheep or lamb-skin. 3. Dolt, stupid person. *Barbas de zamarro,* Nickname for persons having large irregular beards.—*m. pl.* (Amer. Colom.) Leather leggings.
Zamarrón [thah-mar-rone'], *m. aug.* of ZAMARRA and ZAMARRO. A large sheep-skin.
Zamarruco [thah-mar-roo'-co], *m.* (Orn.) Titmouse. Parus pendulinus.
Zambaigo, ga [tham-bah'-e-go, gah], *a.* & *m.* & *f.* Son or daughter of an Indian by a Chinese woman, or of a Chinaman and Indian woman.
Zambapalo [tham-bah-pah'-lo], *m.* Ancient dance.
Zambarco [tham-bar'-co], *m.* A broad breast-harness for coach-horses and mules.
Zámbigo, ga [thahm'-be-go, gah], *a.* Bandy-legged.
Zambo, ba [thahm'-bo, bah], *a.* 1. Bandy-legged. 2. Applied to the son of an Indian by a Chinese woman, or of a Chinaman by an Indian woman.—*m.* An American wild monkey, resembling a dog, with the head of a horse.
Zamboa [tham-bo'-ah], *f.* 1. (Bot.) A sweet kind of quince-tree. Pyrus cydonia. 2. Citron-tree. *V.* AZAMBOA.
Zambomba [tham-bom'-bah], *f.* A kind of rustic drum, consisting of a skin stretched over the mouth of a jar, with a reed fastened at the centre. This rubbed up and down with the moistened hand produces a strong, hoarse, monotonous sound.—*int.* Whew! interjection denoting surprise.
Zambombo [tham-bom'-bo], *m.* Clown, rustic, ill-bred person.
Zamborondón, na, Zamborotudo, da [tham-bo-ron-done', nah, tham-bo-ro-too'-do, dah], *a.* Clownish, clumsy, ill-shaped.
Zambra [thahm'-brah], *f.* 1. A Moorish festival or feast, attended with dancing and music. 2. Shout, noisy mirth. 3. Kind of Moorish boat. (Arab. zamra, flute.)
Zambucar, Zambucarse [tham-boo-car'], *vn.* & *vr.* To be hidden, to be concealed; to hide one's self.
Zambuco [tham-boo'-co], *m.* Squatting, lying close to the ground, withdrawn from sight; hiding, concealing.
Zambullida [tham-bool-lyee'-dah], *f.* 1. Dipping, ducking, submersion. 2. In fencing, thrust on the breast.
Zambullidura [tham-bool-lyee-doo'-rah], *f.* **Zambullimiento** [tham-bool-lyee-me-en'-to], *m.* *V.* ZABULLIDURA.
Zambullir [tham-bool-lyeer'], *va.* & *vr.* To plunge into water, to dip, to dive.
Zambullo [tham-bool'-lyo], *m.* (Naut.) A large bucket for the use of the sick.
Zamorano, na [thah-mo-rah'-no, nah], *a.* Belonging to Zamora. *Gaita Zamorana,* Kind of bagpipe.
Zampabodigos, Zampabollos [tham-pah-bo-dee'-gos, tham-pah-bol'-lyos], *m.* (Coll.) Glutton. *V.* ZAMPATORTAS.
Zampada [tham-pah'-dah], *f.* (Prov.) Act of concealing or putting one thing within another.
Zampadura [tham-pah-doo'-rah], *f.* *V.* ZAMPAMIENTO.
Zampalimosnas [tham-pah-le-mos'-nas], *m.* A sturdy beggar.
Zampamiento [tham-pah-me-en'-to], *m.* The act of concealing or covering over a thing.
Zampapalo [tham-pah-pah'-lo], *m.* (Coll.) *V.* ZAMPATORTAS.
Zampar [tham-par'], *va.* 1. To conceal in a clever manner; to thrust one thing into another, so as to be covered by it and withdrawn from light. 2. To devour eagerly.—*vr.* To thrust one's self suddenly into a place.
Zampatortas [tham-pah-tor'-tas], *m.* (Coll.) 1. A glutton. 2. Clown, rustic.
Zampear [tham-pay-ar'], *vn.* To drive stakes in a ground to make it solid.
Zampeado [tham-pay-ah'-do], *m.* (Arch.) Wood-work and masonry in marshy foundations.
Zampoña [tham-po'-nyah], *f.* 1. A rustic instrument, a kind of bagpipe. *V.* PIPITAÑA. 2. A poetical vein; genius or talent for poetry. 3. At Madrid, a poor person belonging to a work-house; a term of derision. 4. (Coll.) Frivolous saying.
Zampoñear [tham-po-nyay-ar'], *vn.* 1. To play the bagpipe. 2. (Met.) To be prolix and frivolous in conversation, to prose. *Marear* or *zampoñear la gata,* (Coll.) To be tiresome and prolix in gossiping.
Zampuzar [tham-poo-thar'], *va.* 1. To plunge, to dip, to dive. 2. To hide to conceal.
Zampuzo [tham-poo'-tho], *m.* Immersion, submersion, concealment.
Zamuro [thah-moo'-ro], *m.* (Orn.) Carrion-vulture, Vultur aura.
Zanahoria [thah-nah-o'-re-ah], *f.* (Bot.) Carrot. Daucus carota. *Zanahorias,* Deceitful caresses.
Zanahoriate [thah-nah-o-re-ah'-tay], *m.* *V.* AZANORIATE.
Zanca [thahn'-cah], *f.* 1. Shank, part of the leg of a fowl or bird which extends from the claws to the thigh. 2. A long shank or leg. 3. Large pin. *Zancas de araña,* Shifts, evasions, subterfuges. *Zancas largas, m.* (Long shanks) woodcock, a European bird of the snipe family. *Por zancas o por barrancas,* By extraordinary means (fr. Ger. schenkel).
Zancada [than-cah'-dah], *f.* Long stride. *En dos zancadas,* (Coll.) Expeditiously, speedily.
Zancadilla [than-cah-deel'-lyah], *f.* 1. Trip, a stroke or catch by which a wrestler supplants his antagonist. 2. Trick, deceit, craft; act of supplanting. 3. (Naut.) Elbow in the hawse. *Armar zancadilla,* To lay a snare.
Zancado, da [than-cah'-do, dah], *a.* Insipid: applied only to salmon.
Zancajear [than-cah-hay-ar'], *va.* To run about the streets bespattering the legs with dirt and mud.
Zancajera [than-cah-hay'-rah], *f.* Coach-step.
Zancajiento, ta [than-cah-he-en'-to, tah], *a.* Bandy-legged. *V.* ZANCAJOSO.
Zancajo [than-cah'-ho], *m.* 1. Heel-bone of the foot. 2. The part of a shoe or stocking which covers the heel. 3. A short, ill-shaped person. 4. An ignorant, stupid person. *No llegar al zancajo* or *a los zancajos,* Not to come up or near one in any line. *Roer los zancajos (a uno),* To backbite; to gossip about the faults of an absent person.
Zancajoso, sa [than-cah-ho'-so, sah], *a.* 1. Bandy-legged. 2. Wearing dirty stockings with holes at the heels. 3. Clumsy, awkward, unhandy.
Zancarrón [than-car-rone'], *m.* 1. The bare heel-bone. 2. Any large bone without flesh. 3. A withered, old, ugly person. 4. An ignorant pretender at any art or science. *Zancarrón de Mahoma,* (Coll.) Mohammed's bones, which are at Mecca.
Zanco [thahn'-co], *m.* 1. Stilt. 2. Dancer or walker on stilts. 3. (Naut.) Flag-staff. *Poner a alguno en zancos,* (Met.) To favour one in obtaining fortune. *Subirse en zancos,* To be haughty and elated with good fortune.
Zancudo, da [than-coo'-do, dah], *a.* Long-shanked, having long, thin legs.—*m.* A long-beaked mosquito.—*f. pl.* (Zool.) Wading birds, such as the heron, the flamingo, the jacana, etc.
Zandalia [than-dah'-le-ah], *f.* Sandal. *V.* SANDALIA.
Zándalo [thahn'-dah-lo], *m.* (Obs.) *V.* SÁNDALO.
Zandía [than-dee'-ah], *f.* (Obs. Bot. Water-melon. *V.* SANDÍA.
Zandial [than-de-ahl'], *m.* (Obs.) Patch of water-melons; place where water-melons are cultivated.
Zandunga [than-doon'-gah], *f.* *V.* SANDUNGA. (Coll.) Gracefulness, elegance; cajoling, wheedling; flattering, allurement, fascination. *Tener* or *usar mucha zandunga,* (1) To delude by flattery, to allure, to cajole,

to wheedle. (2) To be very graceful, elegant, cajoling, fascinating.

Zandunguero, ra [than-doon-gay'-ro, rah], *m.* & *f.* *V.* SANDUNGUERO.

Zanefa [thah-nay'-fah], *f.* A printed border. *V.* CENEFA.

Zanga [thahn'-gah], *f.* Ombre played by four.

Zangada [than-gah'-dah], *f.* Raft or float made of cork.

Zangala [than-gah'-lah], *f.* Buckram.

Zangamanga [than-gah-mahn'-gah], *f.* Falsehood, tending to deceive or defraud a person.

Zanganada [than-gah-nah'-dah], *f.* 1. Dronish or sluggardly act. 2. (Coll.) An impertinent saying or act.

Zangandongo [than-gan-don'-go], *m.* 1. (Coll.) Idler, a lazy person, who affects ignorance and want of abilities. 2. Dolt, an ignorant, stupid, awkward person.

Zangandullo, Zangandungo [than-gan-dool'-lyo], *m.* (Coll.) *V.* ZANGANDONGO.

Zanganear [than-gah-nay-ar'], *vn.* To drone, to live in idleness.

Zángano [thahn'-gah-no], *m.* 1. Drone, a bee which makes no honey; the male bee. 2. Sluggard, idler, sponger. 3. (Coll.) Sly, cunning, or playful cunning person, taking it either in a good or bad meaning, according to the sense of the phrase.

Zangarilla [than-gah-reel'-lyah], *f.* A small watermill for grinding wheat, on the banks of rivers in Estremadura.

Zangarilleja [than-gah-re-lyay'-hah], *f.* Trollop, a dirty, lazy girl.

Zangarrear [than-gar-ray-ar'], *vn.* To scrape a guitar.

Zangarriana [than-gar-re-ah'-nah], *f.* 1. An infirmity of the head, incident to sheep. 2. (Coll.) Sadness, melancholy. 3. (Coll.) Any periodical disease.

Zangarullón [than-gah-rool-lyone'], *m.* A tall, sluggish, lazy lad.

Zangolotear [than-go-lo-tay-ar'], *vn.* 1. To move in a violent yet ridiculous manner. 2. To slam, to move because the screws or nails which hold certain things are loose.

Zangoloteo [than-go-lo-tay'-o], *m.* A violent yet ridiculous waddling; a wagging motion or movement.

Zangolotino, na [than-go-lo-tee'-no, nah], *a.* Said of the boy whom it is desired to pass for a child.

Zangón [than-gone'], *m.* (Coll.) *V.* ZANGARULLÓN.

Zangotear [than-go-tay-ar'], *va.* *V.* ZANGOLOTEAR.

Zangoteo [zan-go-tay'-o], *m.* *V.* ZANGOLOTEO.

Zanguanga [than-goo-ahn'-gah], *f.* (Coll.) A feigned disease; a fictitious disorder.

Zanguango [than-goo-ahn'-go], *m.* (Coll.) 1. Lazy fellow who always finds pretexts to avoid work. 2. A fool, a booby.

Zanguayo [than-goo-ah'-yo], *m.* (Coll.) Tall idler, that pretends to be ill, silly, or unable to work.

Zanja [thahn'-hah], *f.* Ditch, trench, drain; a pit dug in the ground. *Abrir las zanjas,* To lay the foundation of a building; to begin any thing.

Zanjar [than-har'], *va.* 1. To open ditches or drains, to excavate. 2. To lay a foundation, to ground; to establish. 3. To terminate or settle a business amicably.

Zanjica, illa, ita [than-hee'-cah], *f. dim.* Small drain; slender foundation.

Zanjón [than-hone'], *m. aug.* A deep ditch; a large drain.

Zanjoncillo [than-hon-theel'-lyo], *m. dim.* A small drain or trench.

Zanqueador, ra [than-kay-ah-dor', rah]. *m.* & *f.* 1. One who waddles in walking. 2. A great walker.

Zanqueamiento [than-kay-ah-me-en'-to], *m.* The act of waddling in walking.

Zanquear [than-kay-ar'], *vn.* To waddle, to trot or run about; to walk much and fast.

Zanquilargo, ga [than-ke-lar'-go, gah], *a.* Long-shanked, long-legged.

Zanquilla, Zanquita [than-keel'-lyah, kee'-tah], *f. dim.* Thin, long shank or leg.

Zanquituerto, ta [than-ke-too-err'-to, tah], *a.* Bandy-legged.

Zanquivano, na [than-ke-vah'-no, nah] *a.* Spindle-shanked.

Zantoxileo, ea [than-tok-see'-lay-o, ah], *a.* Like prickly ash, xanthoxylaceous.

Zantóxilo [than-tok'-se-lo], *m.* Xanthoxylum, prickly ash (fr. Greek).

Zapa [thah'-pah], *f.* 1. Spade. 2. A trench for military purposes. 3. Shagreen, a skin made rough in imitation of sealskin. 4. Kind of carving in silver. *Caminar a la zapa,* (Mil.) To advance by sap or mine.

Zapador [thah-pah-dor'], *m.* (Mil.) Sapper.

Zapapico [thah-pah-pee'-co], *m.* Pickaxe.

Zapar [thah-par'], *vn.* To sap, to mine.

Zaparrada [thah-par-rah'-dah], *f.* A violent fall.

Zaparrastrar [thah-par-ras-trar'], *vn.* To trail: applied to gowns or clothes.

Zaparrastroso, sa [thah-par-ras-tro'-so, sah], *a.* 1. Dirty from trailing on the ground. 2. Ill-made, badly done.

Zaparrazo [thah-par-rah'-tho], *m.* 1. A violent fall, attended with great noise. 2. (Coll.) Sudden calamity, misfortune.

Zapata [thah-pah'-tah], *f.* 1. A piece of sole leather put on the hinge of a door to prevent its creaking. 2. A kind of coloured half-boots. 3. Bracket of a beam. 4. (Naut.) Shoe. *Zapata de un ancla,* (Naut.) Shoe of an anchor. *Zapata de la quilla,* (Naut.) The false keel.

Zapatazo [thah-pah-tah'-tho], *m.* 1. (Aug.) Large shoe. 2. Blow with a shoe. 3. Fall; the noise attending a fall. 4. Clapping noise of a horse's foot. *Mandar (a uno) a zapatazos,* To lead one by the nose, to have complete control over one. *Tratar (a uno) a zapatazos,* To treat one badly and with scorn.

Zapateado [thah-pah-tay-ah'-do], *m.* A dance consisting of keeping time by beating the feet on the floor.—*Zapateado, da, pp.* of ZAPATEAR.

Zapateador, ra [thah-pah-tay-ah-dor', rah], *m.* & *f.* Dancer, who beats time with the sole of his shoe.

Zapatear [thah-pah-tay-ar'], *va.* 1. To kick or strike with the shoe. 2. To lead by the nose. 3. To beat time with the sole of the shoe. 4. To hit frequently with the button of the foil. 5. To strike the ground with the feet: used of rabbits when chased.—*vr.* To oppose with spirit; not to give up a contested point; to resist in debating.

Zapateo [thah-pah-tay'-o], *m.* Act of keeping time by beating the foot on the floor.

Zapatera [thah-pah-tay'-rah], *f.* 1. A shoemaker's wife. 2. Olive spoiled in the pickle.

Zapatería [thah-pah-tay-ree'-ah], *f.* 1. Trade of a shoemaker; a shoemaker's shop. 2. Place or street which contains a number of shoemakers' shops. 3. Shoemaking business. *Zapatería de viejo,* A cobbler's stall.

Zapateril [thah-pah-tay-reel'], *a.* Belonging to a shoemaker.

Zapaterillo, illa [thah-pah-tay-reel'-lyo], *m.* & *f. dim.* A petty shoemaker.

Zapatero [thah-pah-tay'-ro], *m.* Shoemaker. *Zapatero de viejo,* Cobbler.

Zapateta [thah-pah-tay'-tah], *f.* 1. Slap on the sole of a shoe. 2. Caper, leap, jump.—*int.* Oh! an exclamation of admiration.

Zapatico, illo, ito [thah-pah-tee'-co], *m. dim.* A nice little shoe.

Zapatilla [thah-pah-teel'-lyah], *f.* 1. Slipper. 2. (Dim.) A little shoe. 3. Pump, any shoe with a thin sole neatly finished. 4. Piece of chamois or buckskin put behind the lock of a gun or pistol. 5. Button at the end of a foil. 6. Exterior hoof of animals.

Zapatillero [thah-pah-teel-lyay'-ro], *m.* Shoemaker who makes slippers, pumps, and children's shoes.

Zapato [thah-pah'-to], *m.* Shoe. *Zapato botín,* A half-boot. *Zapato ramplón,* Thick-soled coarse shoe. *Zapatos abotinados,* Laced shoes. *Zapatos abotinados para señoras,* Ladies' gaiters. *Zapatos de tafilete para señoras,* Ladies' morocco shoes. *Zapatos de cabritilla,* Kid shoes. *Zapato de madera,* A wooden shoe. *Zapato de tierra,* Earth or clay which sticks to the shoes. *Andar con zapatos de fieltro,* To proceed with great caution and silence. *Zapatos papales,* Overshoes. *Meter a uno en un zapato,* (Coll.) To cow one, to put him to his trumps. *Como tres en un zapato,* Squeezed into insufficient space; in great poverty.

Zapatón [thah-pah-tone'], *m.* 1. (Aug.) A large, clumsy shoe. 2. A wooden shoe.

Zapatudo, da [thah-pah-too'-do, dah], *a.* 1. Wearing large or strong shoes. 2. Large hoofed or clawed: applied to beasts.

¡Zape! [thah'-pay], *int.* 1. A word used to frighten cats away. 2. An exclamation of aversion, or of negation at cards. 3. God forbid! far be it from me!

Zapear [thah-pay-ar'], *va.* To frighten cats away by crying *zape.*

Zapito [thah-pee'-to], *m.* (Prov.) Milk-pail.

Zapote [thah-po'-tay], *m.* (Bot.) Sapota-tree, sapodilla, and its luscious apple-shaped fruit. Achras sapota. *Zapote mamey,* Sweet sapota. Achras mammosa.

Zapuzar [thah-poo-thar'], *va.* To duck. *V.* CHAPUZAR.

Zaque [thah'-kay], *m.* 1. Bottle or wine-bag made of leather. 2. (Coll.) Tippler, drunkard. *Es un zaque,* He is a walking tun.

Zaquear [thah-kay-ar'], *va.* To rack, to defecate; to draw off liquor from one vessel into another.

Zaquizamí [thah-ke-thah-mee'], *m.* 1. Garret, cockloft. 2. A small, dirty house (fr. Arabic).

Zar [thar], *m.* Czar, the Emperor of all the Russias (fr. Lat. Cæsar).

Zara [thah'-rah], *f.* (Bot.) Indian corn, maize. *V.* MAÍZ.

Zarabanda [thah-rah-bahn'-dah], *f.* 1. Saraband, a lively dance and tune. 2. Bustle, noise.

Zarabandista [thah-rah-ban-dees'-tah], *com.* Dancer.

Zarabutero, ra [thah-rah-boo-tay'-ro, rah], *a.* (Prov.) *V.* EMBUSTERO.

Zaradión, Zaradique [thah-rah-de-on'], *m.* Medicine for dogs, especially for curing the mange.

Zaragata [thah-rah-gah'-tah], *f.* Turmoil, scuffle, quarrel.
Zaragatada [thah-rah-gah-tah'-dah], *f.* A roguish or cunning trick.
Zaragate, Zarayate, or **Saragate** [thah-rah-gah'-tay], *m.* (Mex.) Loafer, vagabond, rogue. This word, as well as *zángano*, is often used in an affectionate, jocular style, and answers to the English, little rogue, in the same sense.
Zaragatona [thah-rah-gah-toh'-nah], *f.* (Bot.) Flea-wort. Plantago psyllium.
Zaragocí [thah-rah-go-thee'], *m.* Kind of plum.
Zaragozano, na [thah-rah-go-thah'-no, nah], *a.* Saragossan, of Saragossa.
Zaragüelles [thah-rah-goo-el'-lyes], *m. pl.* 1. A sort of drawers or wide breeches; a large pair of breeches ill made. 2. Overalls, or overall pantaloons.
Zaramago [thah-rah-mah'-go], *m.* (Prov.) *V.* JARAMAGO.
Zaramagullón [thah-rah-mah-gool-lyone'], *m.* (Orn.) Didapper, minute merganser. Mergus minutus.
Zarambeque [thah-ram-bay'-kay], *m.* A kind of merry tune and noisy dance.
Zaramullo [thah-rah-mool'-lyo], *m.* Busybody; a vain, meddling person.
Zaranda [thah-rahn'-dah], *f.* 1. Screen or frame for sifting earth or sand. 2. Riddle of esparto in oblong shape for screening stems of grapes, etc. *Harto soy ciego, si por zaranda no veo*, I must be blind indeed not to see through such flimsy pretexts (fr. Per. sarand).
Zarandador [thah-ran-dah-dor'], *m.* Sifter of wheat.
Zarandajas [thah-ran-dah'-has], *f. pl.* 1. Trifles, worthless scraps or remnants. 2. Odds given at the game of trucks.
Zarandajillas [thah-ran-dah-heel'-lyas], *f. pl. dim.* Little trifles.
Zarandalí [thah-ran-dah-lee'], *adv.* (Prov.) Applied to a black-spotted dove.
Zarandar, Zarandear [thah-ran-dar, thah-ran-day-ar'], *va.* 1. To winnow corn with a sieve. 2. To stir and move nimbly. 3. To separate the precious from the common. 4. To sift and toss about pins in a vessel.—*vr.* To be in motion, to move to and fro.
Zarandeo [thah-ran-day'-o], *m.* Act of sifting or winnowing.
Zarandero [thah-ran-day'-ro], *m.* *V.* ZARANDADOR.
Zarandija [thah-ran-dee'-hah], *f.* (Zool.) An insect which burrows in the ground and devastates gardens: the mole-cricket. (*Cf.* SABANDIJA.) *V.* GRILLOTALPA.
Zarandillo [thah-ran-deel'-lyo], *m.* 1. (Dim.) A small sieve or riddle. 2. (Coll.) One who frisks nimbly about.
Zarapallón [thah-rah-pal-lyone'], *m.* A shabby, dirty fellow.
Zarapatel [thah-rah-pah-tel'], *m.* & *f.* A kind of salmagundi.
Zarapeto [thah-rah-pay'-to], *m.* (Coll.) Intriguer, crafty person.
Zarapito [thah-rah-pee'-to], *m.* (Orn.) Whimbrel, curlew-jack. Scolopax phæopus.
Zaratán [thah-rah-tahn'], *m.* Cancer in the breast. (Arab.)
Zaraza [thah-rah'-thah], *f.* Chintz, a delicate cotton stuff. *Zarazas*, Paste made of pounded glass and poison for killing dogs, rats, etc.
Zarcear [thar-thay-ar'], *va.* To clean pipes or conduits with briers.—*vn.* To move to and fro.
Zarcero, ra [thar-thay'-ro, rah], *a.* Fit to pursue the game among briers: applied to pointers.
Zarceto, ta [thar-thay'-to, tah], *m.* & *f.* (Orn.) Widgeon. *V.* CERCETA.
Zarcillo [thar-theel'-lyo], *m.* 1. Ear-ring. 2. Tendril of a vine or other climbing plant. 3. (Prov.) Hoop of a butt or barrel.
Zarco, ca [thar'-co, cah], *a.* 1. Wall-eyed, of a light blue colour: applied to the eyes. 2. Clear and pure: applied to water.
Zarevitz [thah-ray-veeth'], *m.* Czarowitz, the first-born son of the Emperor of Russia, and heir-apparent to the throne. His wife is called *Zarevna.*
Zargatona [thar-gah-to'-nah], *f.* *V.* ZARAGATONA.
Zariano, na [thah-re-ah'-no, nah], *a.* Belonging to the Czar.
Zarina [thah-ree'-nah], *f.* Czarina, empress, the wife of the Emperor of Russia.
Zarja [thar'-hah], *f.* Reel, for winding silk. *V.* AZARJA.
Zaroche [thah-ro'-chay], *m.* (Ecuador) Mountain sickness from too rapid advance into rarefied air. *V.* VETA.
Zarpa [thar'-pah], *f.* 1. Weighing anchor. 2. Dirt or mud sticking to the skirts of clothes. 3. Superior thickness of foundation walls. 4. Claw of a beast or bird. *Echar la zarpa*, To gripe, to claw. *Hacerse una zarpa*, To wet one's self extremely.
Zarpada [thar-pah'-dah], *f.* Clawing, a strike or dig with claws.
Zarpanel [thar-pah-nel'], *a.* (Arch.) *V.* CARPANEL.
Zarpar [thar-par'], *va.* (Naut.) To weigh anchor. *El ancla está zarpada*, (Naut.) The anchor is atrip.
Zarpazo [thar-pah'-tho], *m.* Sound of a body falling on the ground.
Zarposo, sa [thar-po'-so, sah], *a.* Bespattered with mire or dirt.
Zarracatería [thar-rah-cah-tay-ree'-ah], *f.* Deceitful flattery.
Zarracatín [thar-rah-cah-teen'], *m.* Haggler, miser.
Zarrampla [thar-rahm'-plah], *com.* (Coll.) Blockhead; awkward.
Zarramplín [thar-ram-pleen'], *m.* Bungler, botcher; an insignificant fellow.
Zarramplinada [thar-ram-ple-nah'-dah], *f.* Work clumsily performed; thing of little moment.
Zarrapastra [thar-rah-pahs-trah], *f.* Dirt or mire sticking to the skirts of clothes.
Zarrapastrón, na [thar-rah-pas-trone', nah], *a.* & *n.* Tatterdemalion, ragged fellow.
Zarrapastrosamente, *adv.* Raggedly.
Zarrapastroso, sa [thar-rah-pas-tro'-so, sah], *a.* Ragged, dirty, uncleanly.
Zarria [thar'-re-ah], *f.* 1. Dirt or mire sticking to clothes. 2. Leather thongs for tying on *abarcas.*
Zarriento, ta [thar-re-en'-to, tah], *a.* Bespattered with mud or mire.
Zarrio [thar'-re-o], *m.* *V.* CHARRO.
Zarza [thar'-thah], *f.* (Bot.) Common bramble, the European blackberry-bush. Rubus fruticosus. *Zarzas*, (Met.) Thorns, difficulties. *La zarza da el fruto espinando, y el ruín, llorando*, The bramble yields fruit with prickles, and the churl with weeping. (Rebuke to ill-natured bestowal of favours.) (fr. Basque.)
Zarzagán [thar-thah-gahn'], *m.* A cold north-east wind.
Zarzaganete [thar-thah-gah-nay'-tay], *m. dim.* A light north-east wind.
Zarzaganillo [thar-thah-gah-neel'-lyo], *m.* A violent storm at north-east.
Zarzahán [thar-thah-ahn'], *m.* A kind of striped silk. (Arab.)
Zarzaidea [thar-thah-e-day'-ah], *f.* (Bot.) Raspberry-bush. Rubus idæus.
Zarzal [thar-thahl'], *m.* Briery, a place where briers grow; place full of briers or brambles.
Zarzamora [thar-thah-mo'-rah], *f.* (Bot.) Blackberry, berry of the bramble.
Zarzaparrilla [thar-thah-par-reel'-lyah], *f.* (Bot.) Sarsaparilla. Smilax sarsaparilla.
Zarzaparrillar [thar-thah-par-reel-lyar'], *m.* Plantation of sarsaparilla.
Zarzaperruna [thar-thah-per-roo'-nah], *f.* (Bot.) Dog-rose. Rosa canina.
Zarzarrosa [thar-thar-ro'-sah], *f.* (Bot.) Dog-rose. *V.* ZARZAPERRUNA.
Zarzo [thar'-tho], *m.* Hurdle, a texture of canes, sticks, or twigs. *Menear el zarzo*, (Coll.) To threaten to beat or chastise.
Zarzoso, sa [thar-tho'-so, sah], *a.* Briery, full of brambles or briers.
Zarzuela [thar-thoo-ay'-lah], *f.* Spanish operetta or musical comedy.
¡Zas! [thahs]. Word used to express the sound of repeated blows: raps at a door.
Zascandil [thas-can-deel'], *m.* 1. (Coll.) A crafty impostor or swindler. 2. An upstart.
Zata, Zatara [thah'-tah, thah-tah'-rah], *f.* Raft made by laying pieces of timber across each other (fr. Arab. shatora, bark).
Zatico, illo [thah-tee'-co], *m.* A small bit of bread.
Zatiquero [thah-te-kay'-ro], *m.* (Obs.) Pantler, a former officer of the king's household who kept the bread.
Zato [thah'-to], *m.* (Prov.) Morsel of bread (fr. Basque, zati).
Zayar [thah-yar'], *va.* (Naut.) To bowse, to haul a tackle.
Zazahán [thah-thah-ahn'], *m.* Sort of flowered silk.
Zazosito, ita [thah-tho-see'-to, tah], *a. dim.* of ZAZOSO.
Zazoso, sa [tha-tho'-so, sah], *a.* Pronouncing a *c* or *z* instead of an *s.* *V.* CECEOSO.
Zea [thay'-ah], *f.* 1. Hip-bone. *V.* CEA. 2. (Bot.) Spelt-corn. Triticum spelta.
Zebra [thay'-brah], *f.* Zebra. *V.* CEBRA.
Zebú [thay-boo'], *m.* Zebu, the Indian ox, having a hump on the shoulders. (Geog.) *V.* Appendix.
Zeda [thay'-dah], *f.* Name of the letter *z* in Spanish.
Zedilla [thay-deel'-lyah], *f.* Cedilla, the ancient letter which was formed of a *c* and a comma under it, thus, *ç*: and the mark , itself.
Zedoaria [thay-do-ah'-re-ah], *f.* (Bot.) Zedoary. Curcuma zedoaria.
Zeé [thay-ay'], *a.* *V.* ZAHÉN.
Zelandés, sa [thay-lan-days', sah], *a.* Zealandian, of Zealand.
Zelo [thay'-lo], *m.* (Obs.) *V.* CELO.
Zeloso, sa [thay-lo'-so, sah], *a.* (Obs.) *V.* CELOSO.
Zend [thend], *m.* Zend, the ancient Persian language.
Zendavesta [then-dah-ves'-tah], *m.* The sacred books of the Persians, attributed to Zoroaster.
Zenit [thay-neet'], *m.* *V.* CENIT.
Zenzalino, na [then-thah-lee'-no, nah], *a.* Belonging to gnats.
Zénzalo [then'-thah-lo], *m.* Gnat, mosquito. *V.* CÉNZALO.
Zeppelín [thay-pay-leen'], *m.* Zeppelin.
Zequí [thay'-kee], *m.* Zechin; an Arabic gold coin formerly used in

Spain, worth about two dollars. *V.* Cequí.

Zequia [thay'-ke-ah], *f.* Canal for irrigating lands. *V.* Acequia.

Zero [thay'-ro], *m.* (Obs.) *V.* Cero.

Zeta [thay'-tah], *f.* 1. Name of the letter *z.* *V.* Zeda. 2. Sixth letter of Greek alphabet.

Zeugma [thay-oog'-mah], *f.* (Rhetoric) Zeugma, a kind of ellipsis.

Zigena [the-hay'-nah], *f.* (Zool.) 1. The hammer-headed shark. 2. Zygæna, a genus of moths typical of the zygenidæ, stout-bodied moths.

Zigofilo [the-go-fee'-lo], *m.* (Bot.) Bean-caper. Zigophillum.

Zigzag [theeg-thahg'], *m.* *V.* Ziszás. (Acad.)

Zilórgano [the-lor'-gah-no], *m.* A kind of musical instrument. *V.* Xilórgano.

Zimología [the-mo-lo-hee'-ah], *f.* Zymology, the knowledge or study of the principles of fermentation, or a treatise on this subject.

Zimosímetro [the-mo-see'-may-tro], *m.* Kind of thermometer.

Zimotecnia [the-mo-tec'-ne-ah], *f.* (Chem.) Treatise on fermentation.

Zinc [thinc], *m.* Zinc, a metal. *V.* Cinc.

Zincografía [theen-co-grah-fee'-ah], *f.* Zincography, the art of preparing relief-plates for printing upon zinc instead of stone.

Zinga [theen'-gah], *f.* (Naut.) *V.* Singladura.

Zinnia [thee'-ne-ah], *f.* (Bot.) Zinnia.

Zipizape [the-pe-thah'-pay], *m.* (Coll.) A noisy scuffle with blows.

Zirigaña [the-re-gah'-nyah], *f.* (Prov.) Adulation. *V.* Chasco and Friolera.

¡Zis, Zas! [this, thas]. (Coll.) Words expressing the sound of repeated blows or strokes.

Ziszás [this-thahs'], *m.* Zigzag.

Zizaña [the-thah'-nyah], *f.* 1. (Bot.) Darnel. Lolium temulentum. 2. Discord, disagreement; any thing injurious. 3. Vice mixed with good actions. *Sembrar zizaña,* To sow discord. This word is now written Cizaña.

Zizañador, ra [the-thah-nyah-dor', rah], *m.* & *f.* (Obs.) *V.* Zizañero.

Zizañar [the-thah-nyar'], *va.* (Obs.) To sow discord or vice.

Zizañero [the-thah-nyay'-ro], *m.* (Obs.) Makebate, a breeder of quarrels, firebrand.

Zizigia [the-thee'-he-ah], *f.* Syzygy, a point of opposition or conjunction of the moon. (Also spelt **Cicigia.**)

Zoantropía [tho-an-tro-pee'-ah], *f.* Insanity in which the patient believes himself transformed into an animal.

Zoca [tho'-cah], *f.* Square. *V.* Plaza. *Andar de zoca en colodra, V.* Andar de Ceca en Meca.

Zócalo [tho'-cah-lo], *m.* (Arch.) Socle or zocle, a flat, square member under the base of a pedestal.

Zocato, ta [tho-cah'-to, tah], *a.* 1. Over-ripe: applied to cucumbers or egg-plants which grow yellow. 2. *V.* Zurdo.

Zoclo [tho'-clo], *m.* *V.* Zueco.

Zoco, ca [tho'-co, cah], *a.* (Coll.) *V.* Zurdo.—*m.* 1. A wooden shoe. 2. Plinth.

Zocoba [tho-co'-bah], *f.* 1. (Bot.) Herb in South America used as an antidote to poisons. 2. Tree in New Spain yielding fine yellow wood.

Zodiacal [tho-de-ah-cahl'], *a.* Zodiacal, relating to the zodiac.

Zodiaco [tho-dee'-ah-co], *m.* (Ast.) The zodiac, an imaginary belt or zone about 8° each side of the ecliptic and parallel to it (fr. Greek).

Zofra [tho'-frah], *f.* A Moorish carpet.

Zoilo, *m.* Zoilus, a malicious critic or censurer.

Zolocho, cha [tho-lo'-cho, chah], *a.* (Coll.) Stupid, silly.

Zollipar [thol-lye-par'], *vn.* To sob.

Zollipo [thol-lyee'-po], *m.* Sob, sigh.

Zoma [tho'-mah], *f.* A coarse sort of flour. *V.* Soma.

Zompo, pa [thom'-po, pah], *a.* Clumsy, awkward. *V.* Zopo.

Zona [tho'-nah], *f.* Zone. *Zona de radiación Van Allen,* Van Allen radiation belt.

Zoncería [thon-thay-ree'-ah], *f.* Insipidity, tastelessness.

Zonote [tho-no'-tay], *m.* Deep deposit of water. *V.* Cenote. (Acad.)

Zonzamente, *adv.* Insipidly.

Zonzo, za [thon'-tho, thah], *a.* 1. Insipid, tasteless. 2. Stupid, thoughtless. *Ave zonza,* (Coll.) Careless, inert simpleton.

Zonzorrión, na [thon-thor-re-on', nah], *m.* & *f.* A very dull and stupid person.

Zoófago, ga [tho-o'-fah-go, gah], *a.* Zoophagous, feeding upon animal substances.

Zoófito [tho-o'-fe-to], *m.* (Zool.) Zoophyte, an animal which resembles a plant in form or growth, especially which grows in branching colonies.

Zoofórica [tho-o-fo'-re-cah], *a.* (Arch.) Zoophoric: applied to a column bearing the figure of an animal.

Zoogloea [tho-o-glo-ay'-ah], *f.* (Biol.) Zooglœa, muciform masses of vibrios or other bacteria.

Zoografía [tho-o-grah-fee'-ah], *f.* Zoography, descriptive zoology.

Zooide [tho-oi'-day], *a.* (Miner.) Resembling an animal or a part of one.

Zoolatría [tho-o-lah-tree'-ah], *f.* Zoolatry, worship of animals.

Zoología [tho-o-lo-hee'-ah], *f.* Zoology, the science or branch of biology which treats of animals.

Zoológico, ca [tho-o-lo'-he-co, cah], *a.* Zoological, zoologic, pertaining to zoology.

Zoólogo [tho-oh'-lo-go], *m.* Zoologist, a professor of zoology.

Zoonomía [tho-o-no-mee'-ah], *f.* Zoonomia, laws of animal life.

Zoonosis [tho-o-no'sis], *m.* Zoonosis.

Zoósporo [tho-os'-po-ro], *m.* (Biol.) Zoospore, name given to the spores of certain algæ provided with cilia or vibratile filaments.

Zootecnia [tho-o-tec'-ne-ah], *f.* Zootechnics, the science relating to the breeding and domestication of animals.

Zootomía [tho-o-to-mee'-ah], *f.* Zootomy, dissection of animals; comparative anatomy.

Zootómico [tho-o-to'-me-co], *m.* Zootomist.

Zoótropo [tho-oh'-tro-po], *m.* Zootrope, zoetrope, the wheel of life, a philosophical toy.

Zopas, Zopitas [tho'-pas, tho-pee'-tas], *m.* (Coll.) Nickname given to a person pronouncing *z* for *s.*

Zopenco, ca [tho-pen'-co, cah], *a.* (Coll.) Doltish, very dull.

Zopenco [tho-pen'-co], *m.* (Coll.) (Coll.) Block, dolt, blockhead.

Zopilote [tho-pe-lo'-tay], *m.* (Orn. Mex.) Buzzard, a species of hawk. N. B. In Mexico this word is generally written and pronounced *sopilote.* Vultur aura.

Zopisa [tho-pee'-sah], *f.* Pitch scraped from the bottom of ships; pitch mixed with wax. (Gr. ζώπισσα.)

Zopo, pa [tho'-po, pah], *a.* 1. Lame, maimed, injured in hands or feet. 2. Clumsy, awkward, unhandy.

Zopo [tho'-po], *m.* A clumsy, stupid fellow. (Ital. zoppo.)

Zoquete [tho-kay'-tay], *m.* 1. Block, a short piece of timber. 2. Bit or morsel of bread. 3. A rude, thick, sluggish, ugly little person. 4. A dolt, a blockhead. 5. Belfry. 6. A short, thick stick, used in bending or twisting ropes. *Zoquete de cuchara,* (Naut.) Scoop-handle. (Arab. soquet.)

Zoquetería [tho-kay-tay-ree'-ah], *f.* Heap of blocks, plank-ends, or short pieces of timber.

Zoquetero, ra [tho-kay-tay'-ro, rah], *a.* Beggarly, poor, indigent, asking charity.

Zoquetico, Zoquetillo [tho-kay-tee'-co], *m. dim.* A small morsel of bread.

Zoquetudo, da [tho-kay-too'-do, dah], *a.* Rough, ill-finished.

Zorcico [thor-thee'-co], *m.* 1. A musical composition in five-eight ($\frac{5}{8}$) time, popular in the Basque provinces. 2. Words or dance set to this music.

Zorita [tho-ree'-tah], *f.* (Orn.) Stock-dove, wood-pigeon. Columba œnas.

Zorollo [tho-rol'-lyo], *a.* Reaped while unripe: applied to wheat.

Zorongo [tho-ron'-go], *m.* 1. A handkerchief folded like a bandage which the Arragonese wear upon the head. 2. A broad flattened chignon which some women of the people wear. 3. A lively Andalusian dance and its music.

Zorra [thor'-rah], *f.* 1. Fox. Canis vulpes. 2. Low, strong cart for heavy goods. 3. (Coll.) Prostitute, strumpet. *Zorra corrida,* Artful street-walker. 4. Drunkenness, inebriation. 5. A sly, crafty person. *Caldo de zorra,* A false appearance. 6. *V.* Sorra. *Tener zorra,* (Met.) To have the headache; to be melancholy. *Á la zorra candilazo,* Address with which one cunning person deceives another knowing one: diamond cut diamond. *Tomar una zorra,* To grow drunk, to overdrink one's self. *Zorra mochilera,* The opossum. *La zorra mudará los dientes mas no las mientes,* A fox may change its teeth, but not its nature. *El que toma la zorra y la desuella ha de saber* (or *ser*) *más que ella,* A sharper sometimes finds his match. *No hace tanto la zorra en un año como paga en una hora,* Craft and crime may succeed temporarily, but the day of retribution is sure to come. (*Zorra,* 3d acceptation, is from the Arabic zo'ar, same meaning; the other equivalents are from the Basque azari.)

Zorrastrón, na [thor-ras-trone', nah], *m.* & *f.* (Coll.) Crafty, cunning, roguish person.

Zorrazo [thor-rah'-tho], *m. aug.* 1. A big fox. 2. A very artful fellow; a great knave.

Zorrera [thor-ray'-rah], *f.* 1. Fox-hole; kennel. 2. A smoking chimney, a smoky kitchen or room. 3. Heaviness of the head, drowsiness.

Zorrería [thor-ray-ree'-ah], *f.* 1. Artfulness of a fox. 2. Cunning, craft knavery.

Zorrero, ra [thor-ray'-ro, rah], *a.* 1. Slow, tardy, inactive; lagging. 2. (Naut.) Sailing heavily: applied to a ship. 3. Applied to large shot. 4. Cunning, capricious.

Zorrero [thor-ray'-ro], *m.* 1. Terrier, a hunting dog. Canis Gallicus. 2. Keeper of a royal forest.

Zorrillo [thor-reel'-lyo], *m.* (Zool.) Skunk.

Zorrita [thor-ree'-tah], *f. dim.* Little bitch fox.

Zorro [thor'-ro], *m.* 1. A male fox. 2. Fox, a knave or cunning fellow. 3. *V.* ZORROCLOCO, 2d def. *Estar hecho un zorro*, To be extremely drowsy or heavy with sleep.—*pl.* Fox-skins; fox-tails used in dusting furniture.

Zorro, ra [thor'-ro, rah], *a.* *V.* ZORRERO.

Zorrocloco [thor-ro-clo'-co], *m.* 1. (Prov.) A thin paste rolled up in a cylindric shape. 2. A dronish, humdrum heavy fellow; one who feigns weakness to avoid work. 3. (Coll.) Caress, demonstration of love or friendship. *V.* ARRUMACO.

Zorronglón, na [thor-ron-glone', nah], *a.* Slow, heavy, lazy.

Zorruela [thor-roo-ay'-lah], *f. dim.* A little bitch fox.

Zorrullo [thor-rool'-lyo], *m.* A cylindrical piece of timber.

Zorruno, na [thor-roo'-no, nah], *a.* Vulpine, foxy, fox-like.

Zorzal [thor-thahl'], *m.* 1. (Orn.) Thrush. Turdus musicus. 2. Artful, cunning man. (Arab.)

Zorzaleña [thor-thah-lay'-nyah], *f.* Applied to a small, round kind of olives.

Zorzalico, illo, ito [thor-thah-lee'-co], *m. dim.* of ZORZAL.

Zoster [thos-terr'], *f.* (Med.) Shingles, an eruptive disease.

Zote [tho'-tay], *m.* Ignorant, stupid, lazy person.

Zozobra [tho-tho'-brah], *f.* 1. Uneasiness, anguish, anxiety. 2. (Naut.) A foul or contrary wind. 3. An unlucky cast of the die.

Zozobrante [tho-tho-brahn'-tay], *pa.* & *a.* That which is in great danger; sinking.

Zozobrar [tho-tho-brar'], *vn.* 1. (Naut.) To be weather-beaten; to sink, to founder; to upset, to capsize. 2. To be in great danger. 3. To grieve, to be in pain; to be afflicted.

Zua, Zuda [thoo'-ah, thoo'-dah], *f.* Persian wheel. *V.* AZUDA.

Zuavo [thoo-ah'-vo], *m.* Zouave, a French Algerian soldier, or one who wears the same uniform.

Zubia [thoo'-be-ah], *f.* Drain, channel for water. (Arab. zub.)

Zucarino, na [thoo-cah-ree'-no, nah], *a.* Sugary. *V.* SACARINO.

Zúchil [thoo'-cheel], *m.* (Mex.) 1. A bouquet. 2. A marigold. N. B. In the U. S. of Mexico this word is pronounced and written *Súchil.*

Zudería [thoo-day-ree'-ah], *f.* (Obs.) *V.* CONFITERÍA.

Zueca pella [thoo-ay'-cah payl'-lah]. (*Jugar con alguno a la*) (Coll.) To tease, to bore, to vex.

Zueco [thoo-ay'-co], *m.* 1. A wooden shoe. 2. A sort of shoe with a wooden or cork sole. 3. Clog, galosh or galoche. 4. (Bot.) Lady's slipper. Cypripedium calceatus. 5. (Poet.) A plain, simple style.

Zuiza [thoo-ee'-thah], *f.* 1. A tournament. 2. A party of young men at a feast. 3. Quarrel, dispute.

Zuizón [thoo-e-thone'], *m.* (Naut.) A half pike, used in boarding.

Zulacar [thoo-lah-car'], *va.* To anoint or cover with bitumen.

Zulaque [thoo-lah'-kay], *m.* 1. Bitumen. *V.* BETÚN. 2. (Naut.) Stuff, a composition of quicklime, fish-oil, tar, and other ingredients, with which the bottom of a ship is paid.

Zulú [thoo-loo'], *com.* & *a.* Zulu, a warlike tribe of southern Africa.

Zulla [thool'-lyah], *f.* 1. (Bot.) French honey-suckle. Hedysarum coronarium. 2. (Coll.) Human excrements.

Zullarse [thool-lyar'-say], *vr.* (Coll.) To go to stool, to break wind.

Zullenco, ca [thool-lyen'-co, cah], **Zullón, na** (Coll.), *a.* Breaking wind behind; flatulent.

Zullón [thool-lyone'], *m.* The act of breaking wind, flatulence.

Zullonear [thool-lyo-nay-ar'], *va.* To expel wind.

Zumacal, Zumacar [thoo-mah-cahl'], *m.* Plantation of sumach.

Zumacar [thoo-mah-car'], *va.* To dress or tan with sumach.

Zumacaya [thoo-mah-cah'-yah], *f.* *V.* ZUMAYA.

Zumaque [thoo-mah'-kay], *m.* 1. (Bot.) Sumach-tree. Rhus. 2. (Coll.) Wine. *Ser aficionado al zumaque*, To be fond of wine, to be addicted to drinking. (Arab. sumāq.)

Zumaya [thoo-mah'-yah], *f.* (Orn.) The common owl, barn-owl. Strix flammea.

Zumba [thoom'-bah], *f.* 1. A large bell, used by carriers. 2. Joke, jest; facetious raillery.

Zumbador, ra [thoom-bah-dor', rah], *a.* Humming, buzzing.—*m.* Buzzer.

Zumbar [thoom-bar'], *vn.* 1. To resound, to emit a harsh sound; to buzz, to hum. 2. To be near a certain time or place. *Él no tiene aún cincuenta años, pero le zumban*, He is not yet fifty years old, but very near that age.—*va.* & *vr.* To jest, to joke. *Hacer zumbar las orejas*, (Coll.) To make one feel by a smart reprehension. *Ir zumbando*, To go with great violence and celerity.

Zumbel [thoom-bel'], *m.* 1. (Coll.) Frown, an angry mien or aspect. 2. (Prov.) Cord with which boys spin tops.

Zumbido, Zumbo [thoom-bee'-do, thoom'-bo], *m.* 1. Humming, a continued buzzing sound. 2. (Coll.) A blow.

Zumbilin [thoom-be-leen'], *m.* A dart, or javelin, used in the Philippine Islands.

Zumbón, na [thoom-bone', nah], *a.* 1. Waggish, casting jokes. *Cencerro zumbón*, Bell placed on the head of the leading horse or mule in carts. 2. (Prov. Andal.) Applied to a kind of pigeon with a small maw: in this sense it is also used as a substantive.

Zumiento, ta [thoo-me-en'-to, tah], *a.* Juicy, succulent.

Zumillo [thoo-meel'-lyo], *m.* 1. (Bot.) Dragon arum, "Aaron's beard." 2. Deadly carrot. Thapsia villosa.

Zumo [thoo'-mo], *m.* 1. Sap, juice, liquor, moisture; properly, any expressed juice, in contradistinction to that obtained by boiling, which is called *jugo.* 2. (Met.) Profit, utility. *Zumo de cepas o parras*, (Coll.) Juice of the grape, wine. (Gr. ζωμός.)

Zumoso, sa [thoo-mo'-so, sah], *a.* Juicy, succulent.

Zuncho [thoon'-cho], *m.* Band, hoop, collar, ferrule.

Zuño [thoo'-nyo], *m.* Frown, angry mien or countenance. *V.* CEÑO.

Zupia [thoo'-pe-ah], *f.* 1. Wine which is turned, and has a bad taste and colour; any liquor of a bad taste and looks. 2. Refuse, useless remains, lees.

Zura, Zurana [thoo'-rah, thoo-rah'-nah], *f.* Stock-dove. *V.* ZORITA.

Zurcidera [thoor-the day'-rah], *f.* Bawd, pimp.

Zurcido [thoor-thee'-do], *m.* Stitching, uniting, finedrawing.

Zurcidor, ra [thoor-the-dor', rah], *m.* & *f.* 1. Finedrawer, one whose business is to sew up rents. 2. Pimp, procuress.

Zurcidura [thoor-the-doo'-rah], *f.* Finedrawing, sewing up rents, darning.

Zurcir [thoor-theer'], *va.* 1. To darn to sew up rents, to finedraw. 2. To join, to unite. 3. To hatch lies. *Zurcir voluntades*, To unite, to agree, to join issue; to pander.

Zurdear [thoor-day-ar'], *vn.* To be left-handed.

Zurdillo, illa [thoor-deel'-lyo], *a. dim.* Applied to one who is somewhat left-handed.

Zurdo, da [thoor'-do, dah], *a.* 1. Left: applied to one of the hands. 2. Belonging to the left hand. 3. Left-handed. *No ser zurdo*, To be very clever. *Á zurdas*, The wrong way. *Ahí la juega un zurdo*, (Coll.) He's a smart player (seriously or ironically).

Zurear [thoo-ray-ar'], *vn.* To bill and coo: spoken of doves.

Zureo [thoo-ray'-o], *m.* Billing and cooing.

Zurita [thoo-ree'-tah], *f.* (Orn.) Stock-dove. *V.* ZORITA.

Zuriza [thoo-ree'-thah], *f.* Quarrel, dispute. *V.* ZUIZA.

Zuro, ra [thoo'-ro, rah], *a.* Belonging to a stock-dove.

Zurra [thoor'-rah], *f.* 1. The act of tanning or currying leather. 2. Flogging, drubbing, castigation. 3. Quarrel, dispute. 4. A severe reprimand. *Zurra al cáñamo*, (Coll.) An expression used to stimulate the punishment of any one, or to indicate obstinate perseverance in a thing (fr. Arab. zo'ar, scanty-haired).

Zurra, *int.* A term expressive of displeasure or anger.

Zurraco [thoor-rah'-co], *m.* (Coll.) Cash.

Zurrado, da [thoor-rah'-do, dah], *a.* & *pp.* of ZURRAR. Curried, dressed.—*m.* (Coll.) Glove. *Salvo el zurrado*, (Coll.) *V.* SALVO EL GUANTE.

Zurrador [thoor-rah-dor'], *m.* 1. Leather-dresser, currier, tanner. 2. One who flogs or chastises.

Zurrapa [thoor-rah'-pah], *f.* 1. Lees, sediment, dregs. 2. Any thing vile or despicable. *Con zurrapas*, In an uncleanly manner.

Zurrapiento, ta [thoor-rah-pe-en'-to, tah], *a.* *V.* ZURRAPOSO.

Zurrapilla [thoor-rah-peel'-lyah], *f.* Small lees in liquor.

Zurraposo, sa [thoor-rah-po'-so, sah], *a.* Full of lees and dregs.

Zurrar [thoor-rar'], *va.* 1. To curry, to dress leather. 2. To flog, to chastise with a whip. 3. To contest, to urge with vehemence.—*vr.* 1. To have a sudden call of nature; to dirty one's self. 2. To be possessed by a great dread or fear. *Zurrar el bálago*, (Coll.) To beat, to strike, to bruise, to cudgel. *Zurrar la badana*, To beat, to flog. *¡Zurra, que es tarde!* Reproof for impertinent persistence.

Zurriaga [thoor-re-ah'-gah], *f.* 1. Thong, a long leather strap; a whip for tops. 2. (Orn. Prov.) Lark. *V.* CALANDRIA.

Zurriagar [thoor-re-ah-gar'], *va.* To flog, to chastise with a whip.

Zurriagazo [thoor-re-ah-gah'-tho], *m.* 1. A severe lash or stroke with a whip. 2. Unexpected ill-treatment; unfortunate calamity.

Zurriago [thoor-re-ah'-go], *m.* 1. Whip for inflicting punishment. 2. (Mex. Vulg.) A mean, despicable fellow.

Zurriar [thoor-re-ar'], *vn.* 1. (Prov.) To hum, to buzz. 2. To speak in a harsh and violent tone.

Zurribanda [thoor-re-bahn'-dah], *f.* 1. Repeated flogging or chastisement with a whip. 2. A noisy quarrel.

Zurriburri [thoor-re-boor'-re], *m.* (Coll.) Ragamuffin, despicable person, low fellow.

Zurrido, Zurrio [thoor-ree'-do, thoor-ree'-o], *m.* 1. Humming, buzzing. 2. Confused noise or bustle.

Zurrir [thoor-reer'], *vn.* To hum, to buzz, to sound gratingly or confusedly.

Zurrón [thoor-rone'], *m.* 1. Bag or pouch in which shepherds carry their provisions; game-bag. 2. Rind of fruits; chaff, husks of grain. 3. Bag, sack, of cow-hide in which Peruvian bark and other merchandise is brought from America; seroon. *Un zurrón de añil*, A seroon of indigo. 4. (Anat.) Placenta.

Zurrona [thoor-ro'-nah], *f.* Prostitute who ruins her gallants.

Zurroncillo [thoor-ron-theel'-lyo], *m. dim.* A small bag.

Zurronero [thoor-ro-nay'-ro], *m.* One who makes bags or sacks.

Zurruscarse [thoor-roos-car'-say], *vr.* (Coll.) To experience a sudden call of nature; to dirty one's self.

Zurrusco [thoor-roos'-co], *m.* (Coll.) A slice of bread which is overtoasted. *V.* CHURRUSCO.

Zurugía, *f.* (Obs.) *V.* CIRUGÍA.

Zurullo [thoo-rool'-lyo], *m.* 1. (Coll.) A piece of something long and round, as of dough. 2. Rolling-pin. 3. Human excrement.

Zurumbet [thoo-room-bet'], *m.* (Bot.) A large East Indian tree.

Zurupeto [thoo-roo-pay'-to], *m.* An intrusive money-broker. (Acad.)

Zutanico, illo [thoo-tah-nee'-co], *m. dim.* of ZUTANO.

Zutano, na [thoo-tah'-no, nah], *m.* & *f.* A word invented to supply the name of some one, when the latter is not known or not desired to be expressed. Such a one. It is used with ***fulano*** or ***mengano***, or with both; but neither ***mengano*** nor ***zutano*** car be used alone. When these three words are combined, the phrase always begins with ***fulano***. Thus: ***Fulano, zutano y mengano***, Such and such a one.

Zuzar [thoo-thar'], *va.* To set on dogs *V.* AZUZAR.

¡Zuzo! [thoo'-tho], *int.* A word used to call or set on a dog. *V.* ¡CHUCHO!

¡Zuzón [thoo-thone'], *m.* (Bot.) Groundsel, ragwort. Senecio; so-called from the hoary pappus. (Lat. senecio.) *V.* HIERBA CANA.

APPENDIX.

A Vocabulary of Geographical Terms

WHICH ARE NOT IDENTICAL IN THE ENGLISH AND SPANISH LANGUAGES.

NOTE.—Adjectives derived from proper names, geographical and other, are entered in the body of the dictionary and therefore not repeated here. Thus: Abisinio, a, Abyssinian; Cesariano, na, Cæsarian, belonging to Julius Cæsar.

A

Abisinia [ah-be-see'-ne-ah], Abyssinia, V. ETIOPÍA.
Acaya [ah-cah'-yah], Achaea (district of ancient Greece).
Addis Abeba [ah'-dees ah-bay'-bah], Addis Ababa (Ethiopia).
Adrianópolis [ah-dre-ah-no'-po-lees] or **Andrinópolis** [ahn-dre-no'-po-lees], Adrianople or Edirne (Turkey).
Adriático, Mar [mar ah-dre-ah'-te-co], Adriatic Sea.
África Ecuatorial Francesa [ah'-free-cah ay-coo-ah-to-re-ahl' frahn-thay'-sah], French Equatorial Africa.
Alasca [ah-lahs'-cah], Alaska.
Alejandría [ah-lay-han-dree'-ah], Alexandria (Egypt).
Alemania [ah-lay-mah'-ne-ah], Germany.
Aleutianas, Islas [ees'-lahs ah-lay-oo-te-ah'-nas], Aleutian Islands.
Almirantazgo, Islas del [ees'-lahs del al-me-rahn-tath'-go], Admiralty Islands.
Alpes [ahl'-pays], Alps (mountains in S. Central Europe).
Alsacia-Lorena [al-sah'-the-ah lo-ray'-nah], Alsace-Lorraine.
Amarillo, Mar [mar ah-mah-ree'-lyo], Yellow Sea or Hwang Hai.
Amarillo, Río [ree'-o ah-mah-ree'-lyo] or **Hoang Ho** [ho-ang'-ho], Yellow River or Hwang Ho.
Amazonas, Río [ree'-o ah-mah-tho'-nas], Amazon River.
Amberes [am-bay'-rays], Antwerp (Belgium).
América Central, V. CENTRO AMÉRICA.
América Ibera [ah-may'-ree-cah e-bay'-rah], Latin America.
Amigos, Islas de los, V. TONGA.
Amistad, Islas de la, V. TONGA.
Andalucía [an-dah-loo-thee'-ah], Andalusia (Spain).
Antártico, Océano [o-thay'-ah-no ahn-tar'-tee-co], Antarctic Ocean.
Antillas, Mar de las, V. MAR CARIBE.
Antillas Mayores [ahn-tee'-lyas mah-yo'-rays], Greater Antilles.
Antillas Menores [ahn-tee'-lyas may-no'-rays], Lesser Antilles.
Antioquía [an-te-o-kee'-ah], Antioch (Turkey).
Apalaches, Montes [mon'-tess ah-pah-lah'-chays], Appalachian Mountains.
Apeninos [ah-pay-nee'-nos], Apennines (mountains of Italy).
Aquisgrán [ah-kees-grahn'], Aachen or Aix-la-Chapelle (Germany).
Arabia Saudita [ah-rah'-bee-ah sah-oo-dee'-tah], Saudi Arabia.
Arábigo, Mar [mar ah-rah'-bee-go], Arabian Sea.
Ardenas, Sierra [see-ay'-rrah ar-day'-nahs], Ardennes Mountains.
Argel [ar-hel'], Algiers (Algeria).
Argelia [ar-hay'-lee-ah], Algeria.
Ártico, Océano [o-thay'-ah-no ar'-tee-co], Arctic Ocean.
Asiria [ah-see'-re-ah], Assyria.
Asís [ah-sees'], Assisi (Italy).
Atenas [ah-tay'-nas], Athens (Greece).
Ática [ah'-tee-cah], Attica (Greece).
Atlántico, Océano [o-thay'-ah-no ah-tlahn'-tee-co], Atlantic Ocean.
Austria-Hungría [ah'-oos-tree-ah oon-gree'-ah], Austria-Hungary.
Aviñón [ah-ve-nyone'], Avignon (France).
Azincourt [ah-theen-coor'], Agincourt (France).
Azules, Montañas [mon-tah'-nyahs ah-thoo'-lays], Blue Mountains.

B

Babilonia [bah-be-lo'-ne-ah], Babylon.
Baja California [bah'-hah cah-lee-for'-nee-ah], Lower California (Mexico)
Balcanes [bahl-cah'-nays], Balkans.
Baleares, Islas [ees'-lahs bah-lay-ah'-rays], Balearic Islands.
Báltico, Mar [mar bahl'-te-co], Baltic Sea.
Barlovento, Islas de [ees'-lahs day bar-lo-vayn'-to], Windward Islands.
Basilea [bah-se-lay'-ah], Basle or Basel (Switzerland).
Baviera [bah-ve-ay'-rah], Bavaria (Germany).
Bayona [bah-yo'-nah], Bayonne (France).
Beirut [bay-root'], Beirut or Beyrouth (Lebanon).
Belén [bay-layn'], Bethlehem (Jordan).
Bélgica [bel'-he-cah], Belgium.
Belgrado [bel-grah'-do], Belgrade or Beograd (Yugoslavia).
Belice [bay-lee'-thay] or **Honduras Británica** [ohn-doo'-rahs bree-tah'-nee-cah], British Honduras.
Bengala (ben-gah'-lah], Bengal.
Berbería [ber-bay-ree'-ah], Barbary Coast (Africa).
Berna [behr'-nah], Berne or Bern (Switzerland).
Birmania [beer-mah'-nee-ah], Burma.
Bizancio [be-than'-the-o], Byzantium. V. ISTAMBUL or CONSTANTINOPLA.
Bolonia [bo-lo'-ne-ah), Bologna (Italy).
Borgoña [bor-go'-nyah], Burgundy.
Bósforo, Estrecho del [es-tray'-cho del bos'-fo-ro], Strait of Bosporus or Bosphorus.
Brasil [brah-seel'], Brazil.

Bretaña, Gran [grahn bray-tah'-nyah], Great Britain.
Británicas, Islas [ees'-lahs bree-tah'-nee-cahs], British Isles.
Brujas [broo'-has], Bruges (Belgium).
Bruselas [broo-say'-lahs], Brussels (Belgium).
Bucarest [boo-cah-rest'], Bucharest (Rumania).
Buena Esperanza, Cabo de [cah'-bo day boo-ay'-nah es-pay-rahn'-thah], Cape of Good Hope.
Burdeos [boor-day'-ose], Bordeaux (France).

C

Cabo Bretón, Isla [ees'-lah cah'-bo bray-tone'], Cape Breton Island (Nova Scotia, Canada).
Cabo, Ciudad del [thee-oo-dahd' del cah'-bo], Capetown (Union of South Africa).
Cabo de Hornos [cah'-bo day or'-nos], Cape Horn.
Cachemira [cah-chay-mee' rah], Cashmere or Kashmir (state of the Himalayas).
Calcuta [cahl-coo'-tah], Calcutta (India).
Camboja [cahm-bo'-hah], Cambodia (Indochina).
Canal de la Mancha [cah-nahl' day lah mahn'-chah], English Channel.
Canal de Panamá, Zona del, V. ZONA DEL CANAL DE PANAMÁ.
Canarias, Islas [ees'-lahs cah-nah'-re-ahs], Canary Islands.
Cantábrica, Cordillera [cor-dee-lyay'-rah cahn-tah'-bree-cah], Cantabrian Mountains.
Caribe, Mar [mar cah-ree'-bay], or **Mar de las Antillas** [mar day lahs ahn-tee'-lyahs], Caribbean Sea.
Cárpatos, Montes [mon'-tess car'-pah-tose], Carpathian Mountains.
Cartago [car-tah'-go], Carthage (ancient clty of N. Africa. Also a city in Costa Rica, C.A.).
Caspio, Mar [mar cahs'-pe-o], Caspian Sea.
Castilla la Nueva [cas-teel'-lyah lah noo-ay'-vah], New Castile (Spain).
Castilla la Vieja [cas-teel'-lyah lah ve-ay'-hah], Old Castile (Spain).
Cataluña [cah-tah-loo' nyah], Catalonia (Spain).
Cáucaso [cow'-cah-so], Caucasus.
Cayena [cah-yay'-nah], Cayenne (French Guiana).
Cayo Hueso [cah'-yo oo-ay'-so], Key West (Florida, U.S.A.).
Ceilán [thay-e-lahn'], Ceylon.
Centro América [then'-tro ah-may'-ree-cah] or **América Central** [then-trahl'], Central América.
Cercano Oriente, V. ORIENTE, CERCANO.
Cerdeña [ther-day'-nyah], Sardinia or Sardegna (Italian island in the Mediterranean).
Ciudad del Vaticano [the-oo-dahd' del vah-tee-cah'-no], Vatican City.
Colombia Británica [co-lom'-bee-ah bre-tah'-nee-cah], British Columbia.
Colonia [co-lo'-ne-ah], Cologne (Germany).
Congo Belga [cohn'-go bel'-gah], Belgian Congo.
Constantinopla [cons-tan-te-no'-plah], Constantinople, V. ISTAMBUL.
Copenhague [co pen-ah'-gay], Copenhagen (Denmark).
Córcega [cor'-thay-gah], Corsica (island in the Mediterranean).
Corea [coh-ray'-ah], Korea.
Corinto [co-reen'-to], Corinth (Greece).
Costa de Oro [cos'-tah day o' ro], Gold Coast (W. Africa).
Cracovia [crah-co'-ve-ah], Cracow (Poland).
Creta [cray'-tah], Crete or Krete (island in the Mediterranean).

Ch

Champaña [cham-pah'-nyah], Champagne (France).
Checoslovaquia [chay-cohs-lo-vah'-kee-ah], Czechoslovakia.
Chipre [chee'-pray], Cyprus (island in the Mediterranean).

D

Dalmacia [dal-mah'-the-ah], Dalmatia.
Damasco [dah-mahs'-co], Damascus (Syria).
Danubio [dah-noo'-be-o], Danube (river of Europe).
Dardanelos [dar-dah-nay'-los], Dardanelles (formerly Hellespont).
Dinamarca [de-nah-mar'-cah], Denmark.
Dordoña [dor-do'-nyah], Dordogne (a river of France).
Dresde [dres'-day], Dresden (Germany).
Duero [doo-ay'-ro], Douro or Duero (river of the Iberian Peninsula).
Dunquerque [doon-kerr'-kay], Dunkirk (France).

E

Edimburgo [ay-deem-boor'-go], Edinburgh (Scotland).
Efeso [ay-fay'-so], Ephesus (ancient Greek city in Asia Minor).
Egeo, Mar [mar ay-hay'-o], Aegean Sea.
Egipto [ay-heep'-to], Egypt.
Elba [el'-bah], Elbe (river in Europe).
Epiro [ay-pee'-ro], Epirus (ancient Greece).
Escalda [es-cahl'-dah], Scheldt (river in Belgium).
Escocia [es-co'-thee-ah], Scotland.
Esmirna [es-meer'-nah], Smyrna (Turkey).
España [es-pah'-nyah], Spain.
Española, Isla [ees'-lah es-pah-nyo'-lah], V. HAITÍ or SANTO DOMINGO.
Esparta [es-par'-tah], Sparta (ancient city of Greece).
Estados Pontificios [es-tah'-dos pon-tee-fee'-the-os], Papal States or States of the Church.
Estados Unidos de América [es-tah'-dos oo-nee'-dos day ah-may'-re-cah], United States of America.
Estocolmo [es-to-col'-mo], Stockholm (Sweden).
Estrómboli [es-trom'-bo-lee], Stromboli (volcano N. of Sicily).
Etiopía [ay-tee-o-pee'-ah], Ethiopia (formerly Abyssinia).
Eufrates [ay-oo-frah'-tays], Euphrates (river in Asia).

F

Falkland or **Malvinas, Islas**, V. MALVINAS, ISLAS.
Fenicia [fay-nee'-the-ah], Phoenicia.
Filadelfia [fe-lah-del'-fe-ah], Philadelphia (U.S.A.)
Filipinas [fe-le-pee'-nas], Philippines.
Finlandia [fin-lahn'-de-ah], Finland.
Flandes [flahn'-des], Flanders.
Florencia [flo-ren'-the-ah], Florence (Italy).
Francia [fran'-the-ah], France.
Frisias, Islas [ees'-lahs free'-see-ahs], Frisian Islands.

G

Gales [gah'-less], Wales.
Galia [gah'-le-ah], Gaul.
Galilea [gah-le-lay'-ah], Galilee.
Gante [gahn'-tay], Ghent (Belgium).
Garona [gah-ro'-nah], Garonne (river of France).
Gascuña [gas-coo'-nyah], Gascony (France).
Génova [hay'-no-vah], Genoa (Italy).
Ginebra [he-nay'-brah], Geneva (Switzerland).
Gran Bretaña [grahn bray-tah'-nyah], Great Britain.
Grecia [gray'-thee-ah], Greece.
Groenlandia [gro-enn-lahn'-de-ah], Greenland.
Groninga [gro-neen'-gah], Groningen (Netherlands).
Guayana Británica [goo-ah-yah'-nah bree-tah'-nee-cah], British Guiana.
Guayana Francesa [goo-ah-yah'-nah fran-thay'-sah], French Guiana.
Guayana Holandesa [goo-ah-yah'-nah oh-lahn-day'-sah] or **Surinam** [soo'-ree-nam], Dutch Guiana or Surinam.

H

Habana [ah-bah'-nah], Havana (Cuba).
Haitiano, Cabo [cah'-bo ah-e-te-ah'-no], Cap Haitien.
Haití [ah-ee-tee'] or **Santo Domingo** [sahn'-to do-meen'-go] or **Isla Española** [ees'-lah es-pa-nyo'-lah], Haiti Island or Hispaniola.
Haití, República de [ray-poo'-blee-cah day ah-ee-tee'], Rep. of Haiti.
Hamburgo [am-boor'-go], Hamburg (Germany)
Hangcheú [ahn-chay-oo'], Hangchow (Chinese seaport).
Hankeú [ahn-kay-oo'], Hankow (Chinese city).
Havre, El [el ah'-vr], Le Havre (port of France).
Hawaii, Islas [ees'-lahs ha-wa'-ee], Hawaiian Islands.
Haya, La [lah ah'-yah], The Hague (Netherlands).
Hébridas, Islas [ees'-lahs ay'-bree-dahs], Hebrides Islands.
Helesponto [ay-les-pone'-to], V. DARDANELOS.
Holanda [o-lahn'-dah] or **Países Bajos** [pah-ee'-ses bah'-hos], Holland or The Netherlands.
Honduras Británica, V. BELICE.
Hungría [oon-gree'-ah], Hungary.

I

Ibérica, Península [pay-neen'-soo-lah e-bay'-re-cah], Iberian Peninsula.
Indias Occidentales [in'-dee-ahs ok-thee-den-tah'-less], West Indies.
Indias Orientales [in'-dee-ahs o-ree-en-tah'-less], East Indies.
Indico, Océano [oh-thay'-ah-no in'-dee-co], Indian Ocean.
Indo [in'-do], Indus (river of India and Pakistan).
Inglaterra [in-glah-tay'-rrah], England.
Irak [e-rak'], Iraq.
Irlanda [eer-lahn'-dah], Ireland.
Islandia [ees-lahn'-de-ah], Iceland.

Istambul [ees-tam-bool'], Istanbul (formerly Constantinople).
Italia [e-tah'-le-ah], Italy.

J

Japón [hah-pone'], Japan.
Jerusalén [hay-roo-sah-layn'], Jerusalem.
Jónico, Mar [mar ho'-ne-co], Ionian Sea.
Jordania [hor-dah'-ne-ah], Jordan.
Jutlandia [hoot-lahn'-de-ah], Jutland.

K

Kioto [kee-o'-to], Kyoto (Japan).

L

Lagos, Grandes [grahn'-days lah'-gos], Great Lakes (U.S.A.)
Laponia [lah-po'-ne-ah], Lapland.
Lausana [lah-oo-sah'-nah], Lausanne (Switzerland).
Lejano Oriente, V. ORIENTE, LEJANO.
Leningrado [lay-neen-grah'-do], Leningrad (formerly San Petersburgo and Petrogrado, U.S.S.R.).
Líbano [lee'-bah-no], Lebanon.
Libia [lee'-bee-ah], Libya.
Lieja [le-ay'-hah], Liege (Belgium).
Lila [lee'-lah], Lille (France).
Liorna [lee-or'-nah], Leghorn (Italy).
Lisboa [lis-bo'-ah], Lisbon (Portugal).
Lituania [lee-too-ah'-nee-ah], Lithuania.
Londres [lon'-dress], London (England).
Lorena [lo-ray'-nah], Lorraine. V. ALSACIA-LORENA.
Lovaina [lo-vah'-e-nah], Louvain (Belgium).
Lucerna [loo-ther'-nah], Lucerne or Luzern (Switzerland).
Luisiana [loo-e-see-ah'-nah], Louisiana (U.S.A.).

M

Magallanes, Estrecho de [es-tray'-cho day mah-gal-lyah'-ness], Strait of Magellan.
Maguncia [mah-goon'-the-ah], Mainz (Germany).
Malaca, Península de [pay-neen'-soo-lah day mah-lah'-cah], Malay Peninsula.
Maldivas, Islas [ees'-lahs mal-dee'-vahs], Maldive Islands.
Malvinas or **Falkland, Islas** [ees'-lahs mal-vee'-nahs, fok'-land], Falkland Islands.
Mallorca [mal-lyor'-cah], Majorca or Mallorca (island in the Mediterranean).
Mancha, Canal de la [cah-nahl' day lah mahn'-chah], English Channel.
Marfil, Costa de [cos'-tah day mar-feel], Ivory Coast.
Mármara, Mar de [mar day mar'-mah-rah], Sea of Marmora or Marmara.
Marruecos [mah-roo-ay'-cos], Morocco.
Marsella [mar-say'-lyah], Marseille or Marseilles (France).
Martinica [mar-te-nee'-cah], Martinique.
Mauricio [mah-oo-ree'-the-o], Mauritius or Ile de France (British island in Indian Ocean).
Mediterráneo, Mar [mar may-de-tay-rah'-nay-o], Mediterranean Sea.
Menfis [men'-fees], Memphis (cap. of ancient Egypt).
Menorca [may-nor'-cah], Minorca or Menorca (island in the Mediterranean).
México or **Méjico** [may'-he-co], Mexico.
Misisipi, Río [ree'-o me-see-see'-pee], Mississippi River (U.S.A.).
Misuri [me-soo'-re], Missouri (river and state of U.S.A.).
Molucas, Islas [ees'-lahs mo-loo'-cahs] or **Islas de las Especias** [day lahs es-pay'-thee-ahs], Moluccas or Spice Islands.
Mosa [mo'-sah], Meuse (river of France and Belgium).
Moscú [mos-coo'], Moscow (U.S.S.R.).
Mosela [mo-say'-lah], Moselle (river of France and Germany).
Muerto, Mar [mar moo-err'-to], Dead Sea.

N

Nápoles [nah'-po-less], Naples (Italy).
Negro, Mar [mar nay'-gro], Black Sea.
Niágara, Cataratas del [cah-tah-rah'-tahs del nee-ah'-gah-rah], Niagara Falls.
Nilo [nee'-lo], Nile (river of Africa).
Nínive [nee'-nee-vay], Nineveh (ancient city of Assyrian Empire].
Nipón [nee-pone'], Nippon. V. JAPÓN.
Niza [nee'-thah], Nice (France).
Normandía [nor-man-dee'-ah], Normandy (France).
Norte América [nor'-tay ah-may'-ree-cah] or **América del Norte** [del nor'-tay], North America.
Noruega [no-roo-ay'-gah], Norway.
Nueva Escocia [noo-ay'-vah es-co'-thee-ah], Nova Scotia (Canada).
Nueva Gales del Sur [noo-ay'-vah gah'-less del soor], New South Wales.
Nueva Orleans [noo-ay'-vah or-lay-ahns'], New Orleans (U.S.A.).
Nueva York [noo-ay'-vah york], New York (U.S.A.).
Nueva Zelanda [noo-ay'-vah thay-lahn'-dah], New Zealand.

O

Odesa [o-day'-sah], Odessa (U.S.S.R. seaport on Black Sea).
Olimpo, Monte [mon'-tay o-leem'-po], Mount Olympus.
Oriente, Cercano [ther-cah'-no o-ree-en'-tay], Near East.
Oriente, Lejano [lay-hah'-no o-ree-en'-tay], Far East.
Ostende [os-ten'-day], Ostend (Belgium).

P

Pacífico, Océano [o-thay'-ah-no pah-thee'-fee-co], Pacific Ocean.
Países Bajos, V. HOLANDA.
Palestina [pah-les-tee'-nah], Palestine.
Parnaso [par-nah'-so], Parnassus.
Peloponeso [pay-lo-po-nay'-so], Peloponnesus (Greece).
Pensilvania [pen-sil-vah'-ne-ah], Pennsylvania (U.S.A.).
Perusa [pay-roo'-sah], Perugia (Italy).
Pirineos [pe-re-nay'-ose], Pyrenees (range of mountains separating Spain and France].
Polaco, Corredor [cor-ray-dor' po-lah'-co], Polish Corridor.
Polonia [po-lo'-ne-ah], Poland.
Polo Norte [po'-lo nor'-tay], North Pole.
Polo Sur [po'-lo soor], South Pole.
Pompeya [pom-pay'-yah], Pompeii (Italy).
Praga [prah'-gah], Prague (Czechoslovakia).
Puerto España [poo-err'-to es-pah'-nyah], Port of Spain (Trinidad).
Puerto Príncipe [poo-err'-to preen'-thee-pay], Port-au-Prince (Haiti).
Puerto Said [poo-err'-to sah-eed'], Port Said (Egypt).

R

Rangún [rahn-goon'], Rangoon (Burma).
Reino Unido [ray'-no oo-nee'-do], United Kingdom (Great Britain and N. Ireland).
Rin or **Rhin** [rin], Rhine (river in Europe].
Rocosas, Montañas [mon-tah'-nyahs ro-co'-sahs], Rocky Mountains.
Ródano [ro'-dah-no], Rhone (river of Europe).
Rodas [ro'-dahs], Rhodes (island in the Aegean Sea).
Rojo, Mar [mar ro'-ho], Red Sea.
Ruan [roo-ahn'], Rouen (France).
Rusia [roo'-see-ah], Russia. V. UNIÓN DE LAS REPÚBLICAS SOCIALISTAS SOVIÉTICAS (U.R.S.S.).

S

Sajonia [sah-ho'-nee-ah], Saxony (old German kingdom).
Salónica [sah-loh'-nee-kah], Salonika or Thessalonike (Greece).
Selva Negra [sell'-vah nay'-grah], Black Forest.
Sena [say'-nah], Seine (river of France).
Siam [see-am'], V. THAILANDIA.
Sicilia [see-thee'-le-ah], Sicily (island of the Mediterranean).
Siracusa [see-rah-coo'-sah], Syracuse (Italy).
Siria [see'-re-ah], Syria.
Somalia Británica [so-mah'-lee-ah bre-tah'-nee-cah], British Somaliland.
Somalia Francesa [so-mah'-lee-ah fran-thay'-sah], French Somaliland.
Somalia Italiana [so-mah'-lee-ah e-tah-lee-ah'-nah], Italian Somaliland.
Sud América [sood ah-may'-ree-cah] or **América del Sur** [del soor], South America.
Suecia [soo-ay'-thee-ah], Sweden.
Suiza [soo-ee'-thah], Switzerland.
Surinam, V. GUAYANA HOLANDESA.

T

Tajo [tah'-ho], Tagus, Tajo or Tejo (river of Spain and Portugal).
Támesis [tah'-may-sis], Thames (river of England).
Tánger [tahn'-her], Tangier (Morocco).
Tauro, Montañas [mon-tah'-nyahs tah'-oo-ro], Taurus Mountains (Turkey).
Tebas [tay'-bas], Thebes (ancient cities of Greece and Egypt).
Teherán [tay-rahn'], Tehran or Teheran (Iran).
Tejas [tay'-has], Texas (U.S.A.)
Termópilas [ter-mo'-pee-lahs], Thermopylae (Greek pass).

Terranova [ter-rah-no'-vah], Newfoundland.
Tesalia [tay-sah'-le-ah], Thessaly (Greece).
Thailandia [tah-ee-lahn'-dee-ah] or **Siam** [see-am'], Thailand or Siam.
Tierra Santa [tee-ay'-rrah sahn'-tah], Holy Land.
Tiro [tee'-ro], Tyre (ancient Phoenician port, now a port of Lebanon).
Tirreno, Mar [mar te-rray'-no], Tyrrhenian Sea.
Tokio [to'-kyo], Tokyo (Japan).
Tolón [to-lone'], Toulon (France).
Tolosa [to-lo'-sah], Toulouse (France).
Tonga [tohn'-gah] or **Islas de los Amigos** [ees'-lahs day los ah-mee'-gos] or **Islas de la Amistad** [day lah ah-mees-tahd'], Tonga or Friendly Islands.
Toscana [tos-cah'-nah], Tuscany (Italy).
Tracia [trah'-thee-ah], Thrace
Trento [tren'-to], Trent or Trento (Italy).
Troya [tro'-yah], Troy.
Túnez [too'-neth], Tunis.
Turquía [toor-kee'-ah], Turkey.

U

Unión Sudafricana [oo-ne-on' sood-ah-free-cah'-nah], Union of South Africa.
Urales, Montes [mon'-tess oo-rah'-less], Ural Mountains.

V

Varsovia [var-so'-ve-ah], Warsaw (Poland).
Vaticano, Ciudad del [thee-oo-dahd' del vah-tee-cah'-no], Vatican City.
Venecia [vay-nah'-the-ah], Venice (Italy).
Versalles [ver-sahl'-lyes], Versailles (France).
Vesubio [vay-soo'-be-o], Vesuvius (mountain and volcano of Italy).
Viena [ve-ay'-nah], Vienna (Austria).
Vírgenes, Islas [ees'-lahs veer'-hay-nays], Virgin Islands.
Vizcaya [veeth-cah'-yah], Biscay (Spain).

Z

Zona del Canal de Panamá [tho'-nah del cah-nahl' day pah-nah-mah'] Panama Canal Zone.

Alphabetical List

of the Most Usual Proper Names in Spanish,

INCLUDING BIBLICAL AND HISTORICAL NAMES,

WHICH ARE WRITTEN DIFFERENTLY IN ENGLISH.

Abrahán [ah-brah-ahn′], Abraham.
Adán [ah-dahn′], Adam.
Adela [ah-day′-lah], Adele.
Adelaida [ah-day-lah′-e-dah], Adelaide.
Adolfo [ah-dol′-fo], Adolphus.
Adrián, Adriano [ah-dre-ahn′, ah-dre-ah′-no], Adrian, Hadrian.
Ágata [ah′-gah-tah], Agatha.
Agripina [ah-gre-pee′-nah], Agrippina.
Agustín [ah-goos-teen′], Augustin, Austin.
Alarico [ah-la-ree′-co], Alaric.
Alberto [al-berr′-to], Albert.
Alejandra or **Alejandrina** [ah-lay-hahn′-drah, ah-lay-hahn-dree′-nah], Alexandra, Alexandrina.
Alejandro [ah-lay-hahn′-dro], Alexander; *coll.* Aleck.
Alejo [ah-lay′-ho], Alexis.
Alfonso [al-fon′-so], Alphonsus.
Alfredo [al-fray′-do], Alfred.
Alicia [ah-lee′-the-ah], Alice.
Alonso [ah-lon′-so], Alphonsus.
Aluino [ah-loo-ee′-no], Alwin.
Amadeo [ah-mah-day′-o], Amadeus.
Ambrosio [am-bro′-se-o], Ambrose, Ambrosius.
Amelia [ah-may′-le-ah], Amelie.
Ana [ah′-nah], Ann, Anne, Hannah; *coll,* Nan or Nancy.
Anacreón, Anacreonte [ah-nah-cray-on′, ah-nah-cray-on′-tay], Anacreon.
Andrés [an-drays′], Andrew.
Aníbal [ah-nee′-bal], Hannibal.
Anselmo [an-sel′-mo], Anselm.
Antígono [an-tee′-go-no], Antigonus.
Antioco [ahn-tee-o′-co], Antiochus.
Antonino [an-to-nee′-no], Antonine.
Antonio [an-to′-ne-o], Anthony; *coll.* Tony.
Apuleyo [ah-poo-lay′-o], Apuleius.
Aquiles [ah-kee′-less], Achilles.
Arabela [ah-ra-bay′-lah], Arabella; *coll.* Bel.
Archibaldo [ar-che-bahl′-do], Archibald.
Aristófanes [ah-rees-to′-fah-ness], Aristophanes.
Aristóteles [ah-ris-to′-tay-less], Aristotle.
Arnaldo [ar-nahl′-do], Arnold.
Arquímedes [ahr-kee′-may-days], Archimedes.
Arturo [ar-too′-ro], Arthur.
Atanasio [ah-tah-nah′-se-o], Athanasius.
Atila [ah-tee′-lah], Attila.
Augusto [ah-oo-goos′-to], Augustus.
Aureliano, Aurelio [ah-oo-ray-le-ah′-no, ah-oo-ray′-le-o], Aurelius.

Baco [bah′-co], Bacchus.
Balduino [bahl-doo-ee′-no], Baldwin.
Bárbara [bar′-bah-rah], Barbara; *coll.* Bab.
Bartolo [bar-toh′-lo], Bartholomew; *coll.* Bart.
Bartolomé [bar-to-lo-may′], Bartholomew.
Basilio [bah-see′-le-o], Basil.
Beatriz [bay-ah-treeth′], Beatrix, Beatrice.
Belisario [bay-lee-sah′-ree-o], Belisarius.
Beltrán [bel-trahn′], Bertram.
Benita [bay-nee′-tah], Benedicta.
Benito [bay-nee′-to], Benedict.
Bernabé [ber-nah-bay′], Barnabas, Barnaby.
Bernardo [ber-nar′-do], Bernard.
Bernardino [ber-nar-dee′-no], Bernardinus.
Berta [berr′-tah], Bertha.
Blas [blahs], Blase.
Bonifacic [bo-ne-fah′-the-o], Boniface.
Brígida [bree′-he-dah], Bridget.
Buenaventura [boo-ay′-nah-ven-too′-rah], Bonaventure. V. VENTURA.

Camila [cah-mee′-lah], Camilla.
Camilo [cah-mee′-lo], Camillus.
Carlos [car′-los], Charles; *coll.* Charley.
Carlota [car-lo′-tah], Charlotte.
Carolina [cah-ro-lee′-nah], Caroline.
Casandra [cah-sahn′-drah], Cassandra.
Casimiro [cah-se-mee′-ro], Casimir.
Catalina or **Catarina** [cah-tah-lee′-nah, ree′-nah], Catharine; *coll.* Kate, Kitty.
Catón [cah-tone′], Cato.
Cayetano [cah-yay-tah′-no], Cajetan.
Cecilia [thay-thee′-le-ah], Cecile; *coll.* Cis.
Cecilio [thay-thee′-le-o], Cecil.
César [thay′-sar], Cæsar.
Cipriano [the-pre-ah′-no], Cyprian.
Ciriaco [the-re-ah′-co], Cyriacus.
Cirilo [the-ree′-lo], Cyrilus.
Ciro [thee′-ro], Cyrus.
Claudia, Claudina [clah′-oo-de-ah, clah-oo-dee′-nah], Claudia.
Claudio [clah′-oo-de-o], Claude, Claudius.
Clemente [clay-men′-tay], Clement.
Clodoveo [clo-do-vay′-o], Clovis.
Clotilde [clo-teel′-day], Clotilda.
Conrado [con-rah′-do], Conrad.
Constancia, Constancio [cons-tahn′-the-ah, cons-tahn′-the-o], Constance.
Constantino [cons-tan-tee′-no], Constantine.
Constanza [cons-tahn′-thah], Constance.
Cornelio [cor-nay′-le-o], Cornelius.
Cosme [cos′-may], Cosmas.
Crisóstomo [cre-sos′-to-mo], Chrysostom.
Cristián [cris-te-ahn′], Christian.
Cristina [cris-tee′-nah], Christina.
Cristóbal [cris-to′-bal], Christopher.

Darío [dah-ree′-o], Darius.
Diego [de-ay′-go], James.
Dionisia [de-o-nee′-se-ah], Dionysia.
Dionisio [de-o-nee′-se-o], Dennis.
Domingo [do-meen′-go], Dominic.
Dorotea [do-ro-tay′-ah], Dorothy.

Edmundo [ed-moon′-do], Edmund.
Eduardo [ay-doo-ar′-do], Edward; *coll.* Eddy, Ned, Neddy.
Eduvigis [ay-doo-vee′-hees], Hedwig.
Elena [ay-lay′-nah], Ellen.
Elisa [ay-lee′-sah], Eliza.
Eliseo [ay-le-say′-o], Elisha, Ellis.
Ema [ay′-mah], Emma.
Emilia [ay-mee′-le-ah], Emily.
Emilio [ay-mee′-le-o], Emil, Emile.
Eneas [ay-nay′-as], Æneas.
Engracia [en-grah′-the-ah], Grace.
Enrique [en-ree′-kay], Henry.
Enriqueta [en-re-kay′-tah], Henrietta, Harriet.
Erasmo [ay-rahs′-mo], Erasmus.
Ernesto [err-nays′-to], Ernest.
Escipión [ess-thee-pe-one′], Scipio.
Esopo [ay-so′-po], Æsop.
Esquilo [es-kee′-lo], Æschylus.
Esteban [es-tay′-ban], Stephen.
Ester [es-terr′], Esther, Hester.
Euclides [ay-oo-clee′-dess], Euclid.
Eufemia [ay-oo-fay′-me-ah], Euphemia.

Eufrosina [ay-oo-fro-see'-nah], Euphrosyne.
Eugenio [ay-oo-hay'-ne-o], Eugene.
Eusebio [ay-oo-say'-be-o], Eusebius.
Eustaquio [ay-oos-tah'-ke-o], Eustace.
Eva [ay'-vah], Eve.
Ezequías [ay-thay-kee'-as], Hezekiah.
Ezequiel [ay-thay-ke-el'], Ezekiel.

Federico [fay-day-ree'-co], Frederic; *coll.* Fred.
Felipa [fay-lee'-pah], Philippa.
Felipe, Filipo [fay-lee'-pay, fe-lee'-po], Philip; *coll.* Phil.
Felisa, Felicia [fay-lee'-sah, fay-lee'-the-ah], Felicia.
Fernando [fer-nahn'-do], Ferdinand.
Filemón [fee-lay-mone'], Philemon.
Florencia, Florencio [flo-ren'-the-ah, flo-ren'-the-o], Florence.
Francisca [fran-thees'-cah], Frances; *coll.* Fan, Fanny.
Francisco [fran-thees'-co], Francis.

Gaspar [gas-par'], Jasper.
Gedeón [hay-day-on'], Gideon.
Gerardo [hay-rar'-do], Gerard.
Gertrudis [herr-troo'-dees], Gertrude.
Gervasio [herr-vah'-se-o], Gervas.
Gil [heel], Giles.
Gilberto [heel-berr'-to], Gilbert.
Godofredo [go-do-fray'-do], Godfrey.
Gregorio [gray-go'-re-o], Gregory.
Gualterio [gwal-tay'-re-o], Walter.
Guillermina [gheel-lyer-mee'-nah], Wilhelmina.
Guillermo [gheel-lyerr'-mo], William.
Gustavo [goos-tah'-vo], Gustavus.

Herberto, Heriberto [er-ber'-to, ay-ree-ber'-to], Herbert
Herón [ay-rone'], Hiero or Hieron.
Hilario [e-lah'-re-o], Hilary.
Homero [o-may'-ro], Homer.
Horacio [o-rah'-the-o], Horace, Horatio.
Hugo [oo'-go], Hugh.
Humberto [oom-berr'-to], Humbert.

Ignacio [ig-nah'-the-o], Ignatius.
Ildefonso [il-day-fon'-so], Alphonsus.
Inés [ee-nes'], Agnes, Inez.
Isabel [e-sah-bel'], Elizabeth; *coll.* Bess, Bet, Betsy, Betty.
Isidoro, Isidro [e-se-do'-ro, e-see'-dro], Isidor.

Jacobo, Jaime [hah-co'-bo, hah'-e-may], James; *coll.* Jim or Jimmy.
Javier [ha-vee-er'], Xavier.
Jenofonte [hay-no-fon'-tay], Xenophon.
Jeremías [hay-ray-mee'-as], Jeremy.
Jerjes [her'-hays], Xerxes.
Jerónimo [hay-ro'-ne-mo], Jerome; *coll.* Jerry.
Jesucristo [hay-soo-crees'-to], Jesus Christ.
Jesús [hay-soos'], Jesus.
Joaquín [ho-ah-keen'], Joachim.
Jonás [ho-nahs'], Jonah.
Jorge [hor'-hay], George.
José [ho-say'], Joseph.
Josefa [ho-say'-fah], Josephine.
Josías [ho-see'-as], Josiah.
Josué [ho-soo-ay'], Joshua.
Juan [hoo-ahn'], John; *coll.* Jack or Johnny.
Juana [hoo-ah'-nah], Jane, Jennie; Joan, Joanna; *coll.* Jinny.
Judit [hoo-deet'], Judith.
Julio [hoo'-le-o], Julius.
Justiniano [hoos-tee-nee-ah'-no], Justinian.

Ladislao [lah-dees-lah'-o], Ladislas.
Lamberto [lam-berr'-to], Lambert.
Lázaro [lah'-thah-ro], Lazarus.
Leandro [lay-ahn'-dro], Leander.
León [lay-on'], Leo, Leon.
Leonardo [lay-o-nar'-do], Leonard.
Leonor [lay-o-nor'], Eleanor.
Leopoldo [lay-o-pole'-do], Leopold.
Leticia [lay-tee'-the-ah], Lætitia, Lettice.
Licurgo [le-coor'-go], Lycurgus.
Lisandro [lee-sahn'-dro], Lysander.
Livio [lee'-ve-o], Livy.
Lorenzo [lo-renn'-tho], Lawrence.
Lucas [loo'-cas], Luke.
Lucía [loo-thee'-ah], Lucy.
Lucio [loo'-the-o], Lucius.
Lucrecia [loo-cray'-the-ah], Lucretia.
Luis [loo-ees'], Lewis, Louis.
Luisa [loo-ee'-sah], Louisa.
Lutero [loo-tay'-ro], Luther.

Magdalena [mag-dah-lay'-nah], Magdalen.
Mahoma [mah-o'-mah], Mahomet or Mohammed.
Malaquías [mah-lah-kee'-as], Malachy.
Manuel [mah-noo-el'], Emanuel.
Manuela [mah-noo-ay'-lah], Emma.
Marcelo [mar-thay'-lo], Marcel.
Marcos [mar'-cos], Mark.
Margarita [mar-gah-ree'-tah], Margaret, Margery; *coll.* Madge, Meg.
María [mah-ree'-ah], Mary, Maria; *coll.* Mol, Molly.
Mariana [mah-re-ah'-nah], Marian.
Marta [mar'-tah], Martha.
Mateo [mah-tay'-o], Matthew; *coll.* Mat.
Matías [mah-tee'-as], Mattias.
Matilde [mah-teel'-day], Matilda.
Mauricio [mah-oo-ree'-the-o], Maurice, Morice.
Maximiliano [mak-se-me-le-ah'-no], Maximilian.
Miguel [mee-ghel'], Michael; *coll.* Mike.
Moisés [moi-says'], Moses.

Nabucodonosor [nah-boo-co-do-no-sore'], Nebuchadnezzar.
Nataniel [nah-tah-ne-el'], Nathaniel.
Nerón [nay-rone'], Nero.
Néstor [ness'-tore], Nestorius.
Nicolás [ne-co-lahs'], Nicholas; *coll.* Nick.
Noé [no-ay'], Noah.

Octavio [oc-tah'-ve-o], Octavius.
Oliverio [o-le-vay'-reo], Oliver; *coll.* Noll.
Otón [o-tone'], Otho.
Ovidio [o-vee'-de-o], Ovid.

Pablo [pah'-blo], Paul.
Patricio [pah-tree'-the-o], Patrick.
Pedro [pay'-dro], Peter.
Pelayo [pay-lah'-yo], Pelajo.
Pío [pee'-o], Pius.
Pirro [pe'-rro], Pyrrhus.
Platón [plah-tone'], Plato.
Plinio [plee'-ne-o], Pliny.
Plutarco [ploo-tar'-co], Plutarch.
Policarpo [po-lee-car'-po], Polycarp.
Pompeyo [pom-pay'-yo], Pompey.
Prudencia [proo-den'-the-ah], Prudence.

Quintiliano [keen-te-le-ah'-no], Quintilian.
Quintín [keen-teen'], Quentin.

Rafael [rah-fah-el'], Raphael.
Raimundo, Ramón [rah-e-moon'-do, rah-mone'], Raymond.
Raquel [rah-kel'], Rachel.
Rebeca [ray-bay'-cah], Rebecca.
Régulo [ray'-goo-lo], Regulus.
Reinaldo [ray-e-nahl'-do], Reynold, Reginald.
Renato [ray-nah'-to], René.
Ricardo [re-car'-do], Richard; *coll.* Dick, Dicky.
Roberto [ro-berr'-to], Robert; *coll.* Bob, Rob.
Rodolfo [ro-dole'-fo], Rodolphus, Ralph, Rolph.
Rodrigo [ro-dree'-go], Roderic.
Roger, Rogerio [ro-herr', ro-hay'-re-o], Roger.
Rolando [ro-lahn'-do], Rowland.
Rómulo [ro'-moo-lo], Romulus.
Rosa [ro'-sah], Rose.
Rosario [ro-sah'-ree-o], Rosary.
Rubén [roo-bayn'], Reuben.
Ruperto [roo-perr'-to], Rupert.

Salomón [sah-lo-mon'], Solomon.
Salustio [sah-loos'-tee-o], Sallust.
Samuel [sah-moo-el'], Samuel; *coll.* Sam.
Sansón [sahn-son'], Samson.
Santiago [sahn-te-ah'-go], V. JACOBO.
Sara [sah'-rah], Sarah; *coll.* Sal, Sally.
Severo [say-vay'-ro], Severus.
Sigismundo [se-his-moon'-do], Sigismund.
Silvano [sil-vah'-no], Silvan.
Silvestre [sil-ves'-tray], Silvester.
Sofía [so-fee'-ah], Sophia.
Susana [soo-sah'-nah], Susan, Susanna.

Tadeo [tah-day'-o], Thaddeus.
Teobaldo [tay-o-bahl'-do], Theobald.
Teodora, Teodoro [tay-o-do'-rah, do'-ro], Thodora, Theodore.
Teodorico [tay-o-do-ree'-co], Theodorick, Dorick.
Teodosio [tay-o-do'-se-o], Theodosius.
Teófilo [tay-o'-fe-lo], Theophilus.
Terencio [tay-ren'-the-o], Terence.
Teresa [tay-ray'-sah], Theresa; *coll.* Tracy.
Timoteo [te-mo-tay'-o], Timothy.
Tito [tee'-to], Titus.
Tobías [to-bee'-as], Toby.
Tolomeo [to-lo-may'-o], Ptolemy.
Tomás [to-mahs'], Thomas.

Urbano [oor-bah'-no], Urban.

Valentín [vah-len-teen'], Valentine.
Ventura [ven-too'-rah], Bonaventure.
Veremundo [vay-ray-moon'-do], Veremond.
Vicente [ve-then'-tay], Vincent.
Virgilio [veer-hee'-le-o], Virgil.

Zacarías [thah-cah-ree'-as], Zachary.
Zenón [thay-non'], Zeno.
Zoroastro [tho-ro-ahs'-tro], Zoroaster.

An Alphabetical List of the Abbreviations

MOST COMMONLY USED IN SPANISH.

á. área.
(a) alias.
A. Alteza; aprobado (en examen); amperio.
ACTH. Hormona adrenocorticotropa.
a. de J. C. antes de Jesucristo.
admón. administración.
admor. administrador.
adv. adverbio.
afmo. afectísimo.
agr. agricultura.
a la v/. a la vista (bank draft).
alg. álgebra.
alt. altitud.
a.m. antemeridiano.
amb. ambiguo.
anat. anatomía.
ant. antiguo, anticuado.
arit. aritmética.
arq. arquitecto, arquitectura.
art. artículo.
arz. or **arzbpo.** arzobispo.
astr. astronomía.
atto. atento.

B. Beato; Bueno (en examen).
BCG Bacilo Calmette-Guérin, vacuna antituberculosa.
bot. botánica.
bto. bulto; bruto.
Br. or **br.** bachiller.

C. centígrado.
c. or **cap.** capítulo.
C. A. corriente alterna (elec.).
C/a. cuenta abierta.
Cap. capitán.
C. C. corriente continua (elec.).
C. D. corriente directa (elec.).
cénts. céntimos or centavos.
CEPAL Comisión Económica para América Latina (Naciones Unidas).
C. F. caballos de fuerza.
cg. centigramo, centigramos.
Cía. compañía.
cir. cirugía.
cl. centilitro, centilitros.
cm. centímetro, centímetros.
Cnel. coronel.
col. columna.
Com. comercio.
Const. Constitución.
C. P. T. Contador Público Titulado.
cs. centavos or céntimos.
cta. cuenta.
c/u. cada uno.

D. Don.
D. D. T. dicloro-difenil-tricloro-metil-metano.
der. derecha o derecho.
des. desusado.
dg. decigramo.
dic. diciembre.
dim. diminutivo.
div. división.
dl. decalitro.
Dls. or **$** dólares.
dm. decímetro.
D. M. Dios mediante.
dom. domingo.
d/p. días plazo.
Dr. doctor.
Dres. doctores.

E. este, oriente.
econ. economía.
elec. or **elect.** electricidad.
E. M. Edad Media.
ENE. estenordeste.
E. P. D. En paz descanse.
esc. escudo; escultura, escultor.
ESE. estesudeste
etc. or **&.** etcétera.
etim. etimología.
E. U. A. Estados Unidos de América.
f. femenino, femenina.
F. Fahrenheit.
FAB. franco a bordo.
fam. familia; familiar.
FAO. Organización de las Naciones Unidas para la Agricultura y la Alimentación.
farm. farmacia.
f. c. or **F. C.** ferrocarril.
Fco. Francisco.
feb. febrero.
fig. figurado.
fil. filosofía.
fís. física.
For. forense.
fotog. fotografía.
fr. francés.
fut. futuro.

g. or **gm.** or **gr.** gramo.
gal. galicismo; galón.
geog. geografía.
geom. geometría.
ger. gerundio.
gob. gobernador, gobierno.
Gral. general.

h. hijo.
hect. or **ha.** hectárea.
Hg. or **hg.** hectogramo, hectogramos.
Hl. or **hl.** hectolitro, hectolitros.
Hm. or **hm.** hectómetro, hectómetros.
hna., **hno.** hermana, hermano.
hol. holandés.
hosp. hospital.
ib. *ibidem.*
Ilmo., **Ilma.** Ilustrísimo, Ilustrísima.
Impr. imprenta.
Ing. ingeniero, ingeniería.
ingl. inglés.
izq. izquierda.

J. C. Jesucristo.
jue. jueves.

kg. kilogramo.
Kgm. kilográmetro.
kl. kilolitro.
km. kilómetro.
km.² kilómetro cuadrado.
kms./h. kilómetros por hora.
kv. kilovatio.

l. litro, litros.
LAB. libre a bordo.
lb., **lbs.** libra, libras.
Lic. Licenciado, abogado.
lín. línea.
lit. literatura.
lits./seg. litros por segundo.
lun. lunes.

m. metro; masculino; murió; meridiano; mediodía; minuto.
m³/seg. metros cúbicos por segundo.
mar. martes.
mat. matemáticas.
mec. mecánica.
med. medicina.
meng. menguante.
m/f. mi favor.
mg. miligramo, miligramos.
mierc. miércoles.
Min. minería.
mit. mitología.
m/L. mi letra (bank draft).
MM. miriámetro, miriámetros.
mm. milímetro, milímetros.
Mons. Monseñor.
m.p.h. millas por hora.
m.s.n.m. metros sobre el nivel del mar.
mús. música.

n. noche.
n/. nuestro.
N. Norte.
nac. nacional.
N. B. *Nota Bene.*
NE. nordeste.
neol. neologismo.
NNE. nornordeste.
NO. Noroeste.
No. or **núm.** número. (**1o.**, primero; **2o.**, segundo; **3o.**, tercero, etc.).
nov. noviembre.

N.U. Naciones Unidas.
núm., **núms.** número, números.
N. S. Nuestro Señor
N. S. J. C. Nuestro Señor Jesucristo.

O. Oeste.
OACI. Organización de Aviación Civil International (N.U.).
ob. obpo. obispo.
oct. octubre.
OIT. Organización Internacional del Trabajo (N.U.).
OMS. Organización Mundial de la Salud (N.U.).
ONO. oestenoroeste.
onz. onza.
OSO. oestesuroeste.
OTAN or **OTAS.** Organización del Atlántico del Norte o Septentrional (NATO).

P. Papa.
p. participio.
p. a. participio activo.
p. A. Por ausencia.
PBAI. Proyectil balístico de alcance intermedio.
PBI. Proyectil balístico intercontinental.
pág., **págs.** página, páginas.
P. D. or **P. S.** Posdata.
p. ej. por ejemplo.
p. esp. peso específico.
pl. plural.
p. m. pasado meridiano.
P. O. Por orden.
P. P. or **p. p.** porte pagado; por poder.
p. pdo. or **ppdo.** próximo pasado.
P. R. Puerto Rico.
prep. preposición; preparatorio.
pres. presente; presidente.
pret. pretérito.
prof. profesor; profeta.
pron. pronombre.
prov. provincia.
P. S. *post scriptum*, posdata.
ps. or **$** pesos.

S. San or Santo; sur.
S. A. sociedad anónima; Sud América.
sáb. sábado.
S. A. de C. V. sociedad anónima de capital variable.
S. A. R. Su Alteza Real.
s/c. su cuenta.
S. C. or **s. c.** su casa.
S. C. de R. L. sociedad cooperativa de responsabilidad limitada.
s/cta. su cuenta.
S. en C. sociedad en comandita.
SE. sudeste, sureste.
sept. septentrional; septiembre.
s. e. u. o. salvo error u omisión.
s/f. su favor; sin fecha.
sing. singular.
S. M. Su Majestad.
SO. sudoeste, suroeste.
spre. siempre.
Sr. señor.
Sra., **Sras.** señora, señoras.
Sres. señores.
Sria. secretaria.
Sría. secretaría.
ptas. pesetas.
pza. pieza.

q. que; quintal.
Q. B. S. M. or **q. b. s. m.** que besa su mano.
Q. D. G. que Dios guarde.
q. e g. e. que en gloria esté
q. e. p. d. que en paz descanse.
qm. quintal métrico.
qq. quintales.
quím. química.

Rep. República.
ret. retórica.
R. P. Reverendo Padre.
r. p. m. revoluciones por minuto.
rs. reales (moneda).
Srio. secretario
Srta. señorita.
S. S. Su Santidad; seguro servidor.
s. s. or **ss.** seguro servidor.
SSE. sudsudeste, sursureste.
SSO. sudsudoeste, sursuroeste.
S. S. S. Su seguro servidor.
Sta. Santa.
Sto. Santo.
subj. subjuntivo.

t. tonelada.
TNT. trinitrotolueno.
Tte. teniente.
Tte. Cnel. teniente coronel.

U. or **Ud.** usted.
UIT. Unión Internacional de Telecomunicaciones (N.U.).
UNESCO. Organización de las Naciones Unidas para la Educación, la Ciencia y la Cultura.
UNICEF. Fondo de las Naciones Unidas para la Infancia.
UPU. Unión Postal Universal.
U. R. S. S. Unión de Repúblicas Socialistas Soviéticas.

V. usted; venerable; véase.
v. verbo.
va. verbo activo.
Vd., **Vds.** Usted, Ustedes.
V. E. Vuestra Excelencia.
vg. or **v. gr.** verbigracia.
vier. viernes.
V. M. Vuestra Majestad.
vn. verbo neutro.
Vo. Bo. visto bueno.
vol. volumen; voluntad.
vulg. vulgarismo.
VV. Ustedes.

zool. zoología.

Weights and Measures

(Pesas y Medidas)

LINEAR
(Lineales)

Metric Measures (Medidas métricas)		**U. S. Measures** (Medidas de E.U.A.)	
Kilómetro	0.62137 millas.	Milla	1.6093 kms.
Metro	39.37 pulgadas.	Milla marina	1.853 "
Decímetro	3.937 "	Yarda	0.9144 ms.
Centímetro	0.3937 "	Pie	0.3048 ms.
Milímetro	0.03937 "	Pulgada	2.54 cms.

SURFACE
(Superficie)

Kilómetro cuadrado	247.104 acres.	Acre	0.4453 hectáreas.
Hectárea	2.471 acres.	Milla cuadrada	259 "
Metro cuadrado	1550 pulg.^{2}	Yarda cuadrada	0.8361 m.^{2}
Decímetro cuadrado	15.50 " "	Pie cuadrado	929.03 cms.^{2}
Centímetro	0.155 " "	Pulgada cuadrada	6.4516 " "

CUBIC
(Volumen)

Metro cúbico	1.308 yardas^3	Pulgada cúbica	16.387 cm.^{3}
Decímetro cúbico	61.023 pulgadas^3	Pie cúbico	0.0283 m^3
Centímetro cúbico	0.0610 " "	Yarda cúbica	0.7646 m^3

CAPACITY
(Capacidad)

Hectolitro	2.838 bushels ó 26.418 galones.	Cuarto de gal. (líq.)	0.9463 litros.
		Cuarto de gal. (áridos)	1.101 "
Litro	0.9081 cuarto de galón (áridos) ó 1.0567 cuarto de galón (líq.).	Galón	3.785 "
		Bushel	35.24 "

WEIGHTS
(Pesas)

Tonelada	2204.6 lb.	Onza (avoirdupois)	28.35 gms.
Kilogramo	2.2046 lb.	Libra "	0.4536 kgs.
Gramo	15.432 granos.	Tonelada larga	1.0161 ton. met.
Centigramo	0.1543 "	Tonelada corta	0.9072 " "
		Grano	0.0648 gms.

Monetary Units

of America and the Iberian Peninsula

(Monedas de América y de la Península Ibérica)

País	**Moneda**
ARGENTINA	— Peso
BOLIVIA	— Boliviano
BRASIL	— Cruzeiro
CANADÁ	— Dólar
COLOMBIA	— Peso
COSTA RICA	— Colón
CUBA	— Peso
CHILE	— Escudo
ECUADOR	— Sucre
EL SALVADOR	— Colón
ESPAÑA	— Peseta
ESTADOS UNIDOS DE AMÉRICA	— Dólar
GUATEMALA	— Quetzal
HAITÍ	— Gourde
HONDURAS	— Lempira
MÉXICO	— Peso
NICARAGUA	— Córdoba
PANAMÁ	— Balboa
PARAGUAY	— Guaraní
PERÚ	— Sol
PORTUGAL	— Escudo
REP. DOMINICANA	— Peso
URUGUAY	— Peso
VENEZUELA	— Bolívar

1985
SUPPLEMENT

Contemporary additions of scientific, technological, commercial, and colloquial terms to maintain the authority of this work for accurate modern Spanish as used in Latin America and Spain.

Velázquez
SPANISH AND ENGLISH
Dictionary

ESPAÑOL E INGLÉS – SPANISH AND ENGLISH

A [ah], p. 19. Add, *prep*. 1. *A costillas de*, At the expense of (fig.). *No me gustan las bromas a mis costillas*. I don't like jokes at my expense. 2. *A decir verdad*, To tell the truth. 3. *A deshora*, At the wrong time (on the clock). 4. *A destiempo*, At the wrong time (not on the clock). 5. *A diferencia de*, Unlike. *A diferencia de su esposa, él habla inglés*. Unlike his wife, he speaks English. 6. *A esa hora más o menos*, About that time. 7. *A flor de*, Right at the surface of. *Una neblina subía a flor del agua*. Right at the surface of the water a mist was rising. 8. *A grandes rasgos*, In broad outline. 9. *A la hora*, At the right time. 10. *A la vista*, From appearances. *A la vista da esa impresión*. From appearances he gives that impression. 11. *A las anchas de uno*, To one's heart's content. *En aquel balneario podrás divertirte a tus anchas*. At that bathing resort you'll be able to enjoy yourself to your heart's content. 12. *A las ocho de la noche*, At eight o'clock at night. 13. *A lo largo de*, a. Through. *Trazamos el tema a lo largo de cinco novelas*. We traced the theme through five novels. b. Along. *Íbamos a lo largo del malecón*. We walked along the embankment. 14. *A más no poder*, To beat the band (coll.), for all one is worth. *Cantaba a más no poder*. He was singing for all he was worth. 15. *A medias*, Half-baked (fig.). *¡Basta de esas ideas tuyas a medias!* Enough of those half-baked ideas of yours! 16. *A no habérnoslo dicho él, nunca nos habríamos enterado de ello*. If he hadn't told us, we never would have found out about it. 17. *A no ser por*, But [Except] for. *A no ser por su amabilidad, me habría sentido muy solo*. Except for her kindness, I would have felt very lonely. 18. *A pedir de boca*, As many [much] + noun + as one's heart desires. *Puedes apetecer los mariscos a pedir de boca*. You can enjoy as much seafood as your heart desires. 19. *A raíz de*, As a result of. *Las cosechas eran flacas a raíz de la sequía*. The harvests were meager [meagre] as a result of the drought. 20. *A tarea completa*, Full-time. *Buscan un empleo a tarea completa*. They are looking for full-time jobs. 21. *A tiempo*, On time, at the right time. 22. *A todas horas*, At all times. *Deberías desempeñarte bien a todas horas*. You should conduct yourself well at all times. 23. *Al* + noun, Done in + noun, e.g.: *Pintura al óleo*, Painting done in oils, oil painting. 24. *Al calce*, (Mex.) At the bottom of the page. 25. *Al decir de*, According to. *Al decir de él, ya se fueron*. According to him, they already left. 26. *Al hilo de*, Right up against. *Un musgo crecía al hilo de la muralla*. Moss was growing right up against the wall. 27. *Al par que*, As well as. *Le proporcionaron dos tratados al par que citaciones nombrosas*. They provided her with two studies as well as numerous references. 28. *Al precio de*, At the cost of (fig.). *El bienestar económico al precio de la libertad es sospechoso*. Economic wellbeing at the cost of freedom is suspect. 29. *Al subsiguiente*, Two days later. *Miento. No fue al otro día sino al subsiguiente que se celebró la primera piedra*. I'm wrong. It wasn't the following day but two days later that the corner-stone was laid. 30. *Esta noche a las ocho*, At eight o'clock tonight, tonight at eight o'clock. (EN INGLÉS LAS DOS FORMAS SE USAN INDIFERENTEMENTE.)

Abrir [ah-breer'], p. 22. Add, *va*. 1. (EL TIEMPO) To clear up. *A ver si abre el tiempo mañana*. Let's see if the weather clears up tomorrow. 2. (EL TERRENO) To clear. 3. (UN POZO) To dig. 4. *Abrir el apetito*, To whet one's appetite, to give an appetite. 5. *Abrir la marcha*, To lead the way. *Abrió la marcha la directora del departamento*. The manager of the department led the way. 6. *Abrirle a uno las carnes*, To make one's flesh creep [crawl]. 7. *Abrir paso*, To make way. *Abrieron paso a la reina*. They made way for the Queen. —*vr*. *Abrírsele a uno las carnes*, To get goose pimples [goose flesh, G.B.]. *El mero pensar en ello y se me abren las carnes*. I get goose flesh just thinking about it.

Abultar [ah-bool-tar'], p. 23, Add, *va*. 1. To make too large [long]. *El sastre abultó las mangas*. The tailor made the sleeves too long. 2. To increase the volume [number, intensity] of. *El trámite abulta sin necesidad el trabajo*. The procedure increases the volume of work unnecessarily. *Así se abultan los errores*. That way the number of mistakes is increased. 3. (fig.) To exaggerate. *El chico abultaba con mucho la gravedad del caso*. The boy really exaggerated the seriousness of the matter.

Acabar [ah-cah-bar'], p. 23. Add, *vn*. 1. (ant.) To come to an end. *Acabó el torneo*. The tournament came to an end. 2. *Acabar con*, To put an end to. *Acabemos con tanta hilaridad negra*. Let's put an end to so much black humor [humour, G.B.]. 3. *Acabar de*, a. To have just. *Acababa de decírselo yo mismo*. I had just told them so myself. *Acaban de agradecer a los simpatizantes*. They have just thanked the well-wishers. b. Completely, e.g.: *Su ademán acabó de convencerme*. I was completely convinced by his manner. *Su manera de hablar acabó de engañarme*. Her way of speaking fooled me completely. *Tal acto acabaría de deshonrar su buen nombre*. Such an action would completely ruin his good name. c. (TONO IRÓNICO) To do a good job of. *Ella acabó de lisonjearme*. She did a good job of flattering me. *Acabaron de malograr mis posibilidades*. They did a good job of ruining my chances. 4. *Acabar por*, To end by. *Acabó por decirnos todo lo contrario*. He ended by telling us the exact opposite. 5. *No acabar de*, Not to be able to, e.g.: *No acababa de consolarse por la pérdida de tan fina persona*. He couldn't get over the loss of such a fine person. —*vr*. 1. *Acabársele*, To run out of. *Se nos ha acabado la leche*. We've run out of milk. 2. *El acabóse*, The last straw (Amer.), the capstone (G.B.). *El acabóse era la falta de una cineteca*. The capstone was the lack of a film library.

Acartonado, da [ah-car-to-nah'-dō, dah], p. 24. Add, *a*. 1. (ASPECTO) Withered and wrinkled, wizened. 2. (fig.) Stiff. *El ademán acartonado que usaba sorprendía a sus huéspedes*. His stiff manner surprised his guests.

Acartonamiento [ah-car-to-nah-me-en'-to], m. 1. Wrinkled and withered look, wizened look. *A pesar de su acartonamiento, la viejecita se desplazaba con soltura*. Despite her wizened look, the little old lady got around gracefully. 2. (fig.) Stiffness. *El acartonamiento de su actuación le quitó vida a la pieza*. The stiffness of her performance hurt the play.

Acartonarse [ah-car-to-nar'-say], *vr*. 1. (UNA CARA) To become withered and wrinkled [wizened]. 2. (fig.) To grow stiff. *Se acartonaba su actuación en el segundo acto*. His acting grew stiff in the second act.

Acceso [ac-thay'-so], p. 24. Add, *m*. 1. *Acceso de ira*, Outburst of anger. 2. *Acceso de melancolía*, Fit of depression. 3. *Acceso prohibido*, Keep out, no admittance. 4. *De fácil acceso*, Accessible, easy to reach. *Este* *gerente es de fácil acceso, el otro no*. This manager is easy to reach; the other one isn't. 5. *Período [Tiempo] de acceso*, (Information Science) Access time. *El tiempo de acceso varía de acuerdo con el ordenador del cual usted se vale*. Access time will vary according to the data processor you are using.

Aceptar [ah-thep-tar'], p. 25. Add, *va*. 1. (UN RETO) To take on, to accept. 2. (A UNA PERSONA) To take up with. *En aquella familia aceptan a la gente un poco estrafalaria*. In that family they take up with rather strange people. 3. (Com.) To honor [honour, G.B.], to accept. *Lo siento pero no podemos aceptar este giro bancario*. I'm sorry, but we can't honor this bank draft.

Acervo [ah-ther'-vo], p. 26. Add, *m*. 1. (for.) Joint property. *La casa es acervo de ambos cónyuges*. The house is joint property of both spouses. 2. (fig.) Birthright. *El lenguaje pintoresco es un acervo de todo el mundo*. Picturesque language is a birthright of us all. *La libertad de culto es un acervo que encarecemos*. Freedom of worship is a birthright we hold dear [cherish].

Acertar [ah-ther-tar'], p. 26. Add, *vn*. 1. By chance, e.g.: *Acerté a encontrar las gafas cerca del pantano*. I found the spectacles by chance near the swamp. *Acertó a conocerla en la tertulia*. He met her by chance at the literary gathering. 2. To happen, to chance (ant.), e.g.: *Acerté a saberlo ayer*. I happened to find out yesterday. *Acertamos a partir muy de mañana*. We happened to go very early. 3. *Acertar alto*, To make one's mark. *Acertó alto como periodista*. He made his mark as a journalist.

Acomodadizo, za [ah-co-mo-dah-dee-tho, thah], *a*. 1. Accommodating. *Su ademán acomodadizo encontraba ambiente por todas partes*. His accommodating manner found a warm reception everywhere. 2. Adaptable. *Es muy acomodadizo para las situaciones nuevas*. He is quite adaptable to new situations.

Acomodar [ah-co-mo-dar'], p. 27. Add, *va*. (P.R.) To bring around to one's point of view. *Si esperamos un poco, podremos acomodarlo*. If we wait a while, we can bring him around to our point of view.

Acompañar [ah-com-pah-nyar'], p. 27. Add, *va*. 1. To go along with, to walk. *La acompañaron a la guagua* (P.R.). They walked her to the bus. 2. *Acompañar en*, To share (with). *Te acompañamos en la tristeza que sientes*. We share your feeling of sorrow.

Actuación [ac-too-ah-the-on'], p. 28. Add, *f*. 1. Action. *La actuación del oleaje en la playa cambia continuamente el litoral*. The action of the waves on the beach changes the shoreline continually. 2. Performance. *Su actuación agradó sobremanera al público*. His performance pleased the audience enormously. 3. *Actuaciones*, (for.) Proceedings.

Actualizar [ac-too-ah-le-thar'], p. 28. Add, *va*. 1. To bring up to date. *Actualizó todos su ficheros*. She brought all her files up to date. 2. (UN ACONTECIMIENTO) To give an air of immediate reality. *Actualizaba en sus cuentos la época colonial*. In his short stories he gave an air of immediate reality to the colonial period. 3. To put into effect. *Actualizaron el nuevo sistema*. They put the new system into effect.

Acudir [ah-coo-deer'], p. 29. Add, *vn*. *Acudir a*, 1. To consult, to consult with. *Acudieron al mejor arquitecto disponible*. They consulted the best architect available. 2. (EN UN APURO) To turn to. 3. (VALERSE DE) To resort to. 4. *Acudir al reclamo*, To go where the work is. *Partían a regañadientes, pero tenían que acudir al reclamo*. They hated to leave, but they had to go where the work was.

Adán [ah-dahn'], p. 29. Add, *m*. 1. (fig.) Father, founder. *Era el adán del movimiento*. He was the founder of the movement. 2. (PERSONA DESALIÑADA) Fright, scarecrow.

Aeróbica [ah-ay-ro'-be-cah], f. (Neol.) Aerobics. *La aeróbica trata de cómo el ejercicio reacciona con el mecanismo de la respiración*. Aerobics deals with how exercise affects the respiratory system.

Aerodeslizador [ah-ay-ro-des-le-thah-dor'], *m*. (Neol.) Hovercraft. *El aerodeslizador hace innecesario el aterrizaje complicado*. A hovercraft makes difficult landings unnecessary.

Aflorar [ah-flo-rar'], *vn*. 1. (Min.) To crop out. 2. (Neol., DESTACAR) To make one's presence felt. *Ella afloraba en todas las reuniones*. She made her presence felt at all the meetings. —*va*. To sift. *El cateador afloraba la tierra con cuidado*. The prospector sifted the earth carefully.

Ahi [ah-ee'], p. 38, Add, *adv*. 1. *De ahí*, As a result. *Machacaba siempre el mismo tema*. *De ahí la evitación de ella por parte de sus colegas*. She continually harped on the same thing. As a result, her associates avoided her. 2. *De ahí que*, a. As a result. *Se peraió el guión. De ahí que trabajara mal*. The script was lost. As a result he acted badly. *El libro quedó agotado. De ahí que el librero no se lo suministrara*. The book was out of print. As a result, the dealer could not supply it to them. b. That's the reason why. *De ahí que fracasara*. That's the reason why he failed. 3. *Por ahí*, a. In that direction, that way. b. (fig.) More or less, about.

Alberca [al-ber'-cah], p. 41, Add, *f*. (Mex.) 1. Swimming pool. 2. *Alberca olímpica*, Olympic-size swimming pool.

Alcanzar [al-can-thar'], p. 43. Add, *va*. 1. To catch up (G.B.). *La alcanzó en la esquina*. He caught her up at the corner. 2. To catch up with (Amer.). *Trató de alcanzarla*. He tried to catch up with her. 3. (UNA ÉPOCA) To know [see] first hand. *Mi abuelo alcanzó aquella guerra*. My grandfather knew that war first hand. 4. (A UNA PERSONA) To be a contemporary of. *Yo la alcanzo*. I'm a contemporary of hers. —*vn*. *Alcanzar a*, To manage to. *Alcancé a introducir la moneda en la ranura*. I managed to put the coin into the slot.

Aldeanismo [al-day-ah-nees'-mo], *m*. 1. Excessive regionalism, chauvinism toward one's home town or region. 2. (BARBARISMO) Substandard usage. *Muchas veces los aldeanismos llegan a ser moneda corriente*. Substandard usages often become coin of the realm.

Alentar [ah-len-tar'], p. 45. Add, *vr*. 1. To cheer up. 2. To take courage. 3. (P.R.) To be up and around. *Guardó cama por dos días, pero ya se alienta*. She stayed in bed for two days, but now she's up and around.

Alternar [al-ter-nar'], p. 50, Add, *va*. 1. Both, e.g.: *Alternabas las dos palabras en tu ensayo*. You used both words in your theme. *Alternaba las dos voces en el estribillo*. He sang both words in the refrain. 2. To give by turns [in turn]. *El maestro alternaba el libro entre los alumnos*. The teacher gave the book to each student in turn.

Alzar [al-thar'], p. 51, Add, *va*. 1. *Alzar cabeza*, (fig.) To get back on one's feet. 2. *Alzar el vuelo*, To take flight. 3. *Alzar la mirada*, To look up. *Alzó la mirada y lo vio acercarse*. She looked up and saw him approaching [approach]. —*vr*. 1. (UN ANIMAL DOMÉSTICO) To revert to the wild. 2. *Alzarse con*, To abscond with (for.).

Ambientalista [am-be-en-tah-lees'-tah], *m*. & *f*. (Neol.) Environmentalist. *Los ambientalistas deben poner en la misma balanza fines de largo y corto plazo antes de dar sus recomendaciones*. Environmentalists should weigh long-range goals against short-range ones before they make their recommendations.

Anciano, na [an-the-ah'-no, nah], p. 56. Add, *a*. (Neol., DE ANTES) Former. *La anciana reina, es decir la reina madre, realizó un recorrido de la galería*. The former queen, that is, the Queen Mother, made a tour of the gallery.

Andada [an-dah'-dah], p. 56. Add, *f*. 1. (Amer.) Walk. *La andada de una hora al menos es muy saludable*. A walk of at least an hour is quite healthful. 2. *Volver a las andadas*, To go back to the way things used to be [were before]. *Hartos del nuevo estilo, volvimos a las andadas*. Sick of the new style, we went back to the way things were before.

Andar [an-dar'], p. 56. Add, *vn*. 1. *A todo andar*, a. At top speed. *A todo andar hace ciento veinte millas la hora*. At top speed it will make one hundred twenty miles an hour. b. As quickly as one can. *Regresamos a todo andar*. We returned as quickly as we could. 2. *Andar a caballo*, To ride horseback. 3. *Andar a derechas*, To do the right thing. *Hay que andar a derechas en este asunto*. We must do the right thing in this matter. 4. *Andar a lar par con*, To keep up with. *Es imposible andar a la par con su habi-*

lidad. It's impossible to keep up with his ability. 5. *Andar a la que salta*, To seize [be on the lookout for] every opportunity that comes one's way. *Si deseas tener éxito en la vida, tienes que andar a la que salta*. If you wish to succeed in life, you must seize every opportunity that comes your way. 6. *Andar con*, (coll.) To proceed with. *Andaremos con esto mañana*. We'll proceed with this tomorrow. 7. *Andar con pies de plomo*, To proceed with great caution [extreme care]. 8. *Andar de* + noun, To follow the life of, to frequent. *Andaba de tertulia*. He followed the life of literary society. *Andan de teatro*. They frequent the theatre world. 9. *Andar en buen buque*, (fig.) To be in good company. 10. *Andar estaciones*, (fig.) To go through channels. *Andando estaciones, mi solicitud tardó dos años*. My application took two years going through channels. 11. *Andar por*, (coll.) To be trying to. *Andaban por terminar ese mismo día*. They were trying to finish the same day. 12. *Andar tras*, (coll.) To be after, to be looking for. *Ando tras su nombre y su dirección*. I'm after his name and address. 13. *No andar con miramientos*, To be curt, to be rude.

Antideportivo, va [an-te-day-por-tee'-vo, vah], *a*. (Acad., Neol.) *Es acto muy antideportivo el de quejarse cuando has perdido en juego limpio*. It's very unsportsmanlike behavior [behaviour, G.B.] to complain when you've lost fair and square.

Antipatizar [an-te-pah-te-thar'], *va*. (Acad., Neol.) To dislike. *Antipatiza tales derroches de afecto*. He dislikes such displays of affection.

Antropocósmico, ca [an-tro-po-cos'-me-co], *a*. (Neol.) Related to Man's place in the Universe.

Apreciar [ah-pray-the-ar'], p. 66. Add, *va*. 1. (UN OBJETO) To appraise. 2. *Apreciar mucho*, To look up to. *Aprecia mucho a su padre*. He looks up to his father.

Arrastrar [ar-ras-trar'], p. 73. Add, *va*. 1. (UNA EMOCIÓN) To carry away. 2. (LOS PIES) To shuffle. 3. (EMPUJAR) To drive. 4. (LLEVAR, EN SENTIDO NEGATIVO) To bring with oneself [along]. *Los chismes siempre arrastran las desazones*. Gossip always brings unpleasantness with it. *Siempre arrastra esa actitud suya de criticón*. He always brings that critical attitude of his along. —*vr*. To touch the floor. *Su vestido se arrastra*. Her dress touches the floor.

Arrinconado, da [ar-rin-co-nah'-do, dah], p. 75. Add, *a*. (fig.) Out-of-the-way. *Les gustaban los monumentos arrinconados*. They liked out-of-the-way tourist attractions.

Arrinconar [ar-rin-co-nar'], p. 75. Add, *va*. 1. To put in its place [away]. *Arrinconó sus juguetes*. She put away her toys. 2. (fig.) To put on the shelf. *No es menester que la vejez nos arrincone*. Old age doesn't have to put us on the shelf.

Arrojar [ar-ro-har'], p. 76. Add, *va*. 1. (Math.) To amount to, to add up to. *Arroja cien libras*. It adds up to one hundred pounds. 2. (fig.) To lead to, to produce. *Hay que arrojar resultados concretos*. We must produce definite results.

Asomar [ah-so-mar'], p. 80. Add, *va*. (LA CABEZA) To stick in, to lean over. *Asomé la cabeza a la tapia*. I leaned my head over the garden wall. —*vn*. *Asomar a la superficie*, To come to the surface. *Asomó a la superficie del agua casi en seguida*. He came to the surface of the water almost at once. —*vr*. *Asomarse a*, 1. To look down over. *La montaña se asoma a la aldea*. The mountain looks down over the village. 2. To look in at [into], to take a look into. *De repente un forastero se asomó a la ventana*. Suddenly a stranger looked in at the window. *Se asomó a la puerta*. He looked into the room.

Aspaviento [as-pah-ve-en'-to], p. 80. Add, *m*. Histrionics (fig.). *Su aspaviento no ayudaba en nada la causa que apoyaba*. His histrionics didn't help his cause at all.

Astillero [as-teel-lyay'-ro], p. 81. Add, *m*. (Neol., Mex.) Think tank. *El astillero es la fuente de muchas mejoras que alumbran la vida que menamos*. The think tank is the source of many improvements that enlighten our lifestyle.

Atadero [ah-tah-day'-ro], p. 82. Add, *m*. 1. Way to pin someone [someone, G.B.] down (to the truth or a decision). *No hay atadero en él*. There's no way to pin him down. 2. (fig.) Limitation, restriction. *Los ataderos que nos impone la sociedad van por costumbres*. The restrictions that society puts on us are called conventions.

Atar [ah-tar'], p. 82. Add, *va*. 1. (fig.) To bring together, to combine. *El escritor ataba bien los dos temas*. The writer brought the two themes together well. 2. *Atar cabos*, To put two and two together. *Él ató cabos y se dio cuenta de ser ella la madre*. He put two and two together and realized she was the mother. 3. *Atar corto a uno*, (fig.) Not to give much room to maneuver. 4. *Atar la lengua a*, (fig.) To shut up. *El gerente le ató la lengua*. The manager shut him up. —*vr*. (fig.) To go out on a limb. *Con la promesa se ató*. She went out on a limb by promising.

Atracada [ah-trah-cah'-dah], *f*. 1. (DE DOS NAVES ESPACIALES) Docking. 2. (DE UN BUQUE) Coming alongside. 3. (Mex., Cuba) Stuffing, gorging oneself with food.

Atrechar [ah-tray-char'], *vn*. (P.R.) To take a shortcut. *Atrechamos por San Germán*. We took a shortcut through San Germán.

Atrecho [ah-tray'-cho], m. (P.R.) Shortcut. *El regente de la ciudad ofreció varios atrechos*. The city manager offered several shortcuts.

Autoayuda [ah-oo-to-ah-yoo'-dah], *f*. Self-help. *La autoayuda tiende a mejorar la opinión que uno tiene de sí mismo*. Self-help tends to improve the opinion that one has of himself.

Autocar [ah-oo-to-car'], *m*. Tour bus. *El autocar nos llevó desde Ávila hasta Segovia*. The tour bus took us from Ávila to Segovia.

Autodefinirse [ah-oo-to-day-fe-neer'-say], *vr*. (Neol.) To be one's own person. *En nuestro complicado mundo moderno el autodefinirse llega a ser cada vez más difícil*. In our complicated modern world, being one's own person is becoming increasingly difficult.

Autodeterminación [ah-oo-to-day-ter-me-nah-the-on'], *f*. Self-determination. *El principio de la autodeterminación es muy importante para las naciones en desarrollo*. The principle of self-determination is very important to developing nations.

Autoenclaustramiento [ah-oo-to-en-clah-oos-trah-me-en'-to], *m*. (Neol.) 1. Shutting oneself off from others. *El autoenclaustramiento puede provocar gran daño a la personalidad*. Shutting oneself off from others can cause great harm to one's personality. 2. (Med.) Alienation.

Autoformación [ah-oo-to-for-mah-the-on'], *f*. (Neol.) Self-actualization.

Autoimagen [ah-oo-to-e-mah'-hen], *f*. (Neol.) Self-image.

Automarginación [ah-oo-to-mar-he-nah-the-on'], *f*. (Neol.) 1. Relegating oneself to the sidelines. 2. (Med.) Alienation. *La automarginación puede provocar un sentido de inutilidad*. Alienation can cause a sense of worthlessness.

Automatecnia [ah-oo-to-mah-tec'-ne-ah], *f*. (Neol.) Robotics. *La automatecnia fácilmente provoca desempleo de gran envergadura*. Robotics can easily lead to widespread unemployment.

Avasallar [ah-vah-sal-lyar'], p. 88. Add, *va*. To subjugate. —*vr*. *Avasallarse ante*, To take lying down. *No se avasallaba ante la injusticia*. He didn't take the injustice lying down.

Ayudantía [ah-yoo-dan-tee'-ah], *f*. 1. (Mil.) Adjutancy. 2. Assistantship. 3. *Ayudantía docente*, Teaching assistantship.

Azacán, na [ah-thah-cahn', nah], *m*. & *f*. (fig.) Drudge, toiler. *El lexicógrafo, según el escritor inglés Samuel Johnson, es un azacán sin pretensiones*. The lexicographer, according to the English writer Samuel Johnson, is a harmless drudge. —*a*. Menial, toilsome.

Azacaneado, da [ah-thah-cah-nay-ah'-do, dah], *a*. Fast-paced. *La vida azacaneada de la ciudad le era antipática*. Fast-paced city life was too much for him.

Azacanear [ah-thah-cah-nay-ar'], *vn*., **Azacanearse** [ah-thah-cah-nay-ar'-say], *vr*. To work furiously [at a rapid rate], to drudge.

Bache [bah'-chay], p. 93. Add, *m*. 1. (Aer.) Air pocket. 2. (ECONÓMICO) Slump. 3. (EN LA CALLE) Pothole (coll.).

Bajar [bah-har'], p. 93. Add, *va*. 1. (LA ESCALERA) To go down. 2. (UNA LÍNEA) To drop. *Baje un perpendicular* *hasta la base del triángulo*. Drop a perpendicular to the base of the triangle. 3. (LA MANO) To put down. 4. (UNA CIFRA) To carry. *Dos más nueve son once, baje uno*. Two plus nine make eleven, carry one. 5. *Bajar los humos a,* To put in one's place, to take down a peg or two (coll.). *La crítica que le asestaron le bajó los humos de verdad*. The criticism that they leveled at him really put him in his place. —*vn*. (LA NOCHE) To fall. *Bajaba la noche por encima de la aldea*. Night was falling over the village.

Bañar [bah-nyar'], p. 96. Add, *va*. 1. (LOS DULCES) To sugar-coat. 2. (CON PINTURA) To coat. 3. *Bañar en,* (fig.) To cover with. *Su hazaña lo bañó en fama*. His exploit covered him with fame. —*vr*. 1. To take a bath. 2. *Bañarse en agua rosada con,* (fig.) To be tickled pink by. *Ella se baña en agua rosada con la idea*. She's tickled pink by the idea.

Batey [bah'-tay], p. 101. Add, *m*. (P.R.) Front porch. *Vamos a gozar de la sobremesa en el batey*. Let's enjoy our after-dinner conversation on the front porch.

Batiburrillo [bah-te-boor-reel'-lyo], *m*. Hodge-podge, jumble. *Contestó a la pregunta con un batiburrillo de idiomas*. He answered the question with a hodge-podge of languages.

Beber [bay-berr'], p. 102. Add, *va*. 1. (Acad., SOPORTAR) To take, to put up with, to tolerate. *No puedo beber esa actitud suya de criticón*. I can't take his overly critical attitude. 2. *Beber en buenas fuentes,* (fig.) To have reliable sources of information. 3. *Beber los vientos por,* To long for. *El poeta bebía los vientos por los días de Maricastaña*. The poet longed for days of yore.

Bibliotecología [be-ble-o-tay-co-lo-hee'-ah], *f*. (Mex.) Library science.

Biotecnología [be-o-tec-no-lo-hee'-ah], *f*. (Neol.) Biotechnology. *La biotecnología procura encuadrar mejor la biología y la ingeniería*. Biotechnology attempts to relate biology and engineering more clearly.

Boca [bo'-cah], p. 108. Add, *f*. 1. *Andar en boca de todos,* To be the talk of the town. *Su bondad anda en boca de todos*. His kindness is the talk of the town. 2. *Boca con boca,* Cheek by jowl. *Los dos contrincantes estaban boca con boca*. The two opponents stood cheek by jowl. 3. *Boca de agua,* Fire hydrant. 4. *Boca de verdades,* Straight shooter. 5. *Buscar a uno la boca,* To draw someone out. *Ella sabe la verdad del caso. Tratemos de buscarle la boca*. She knows the truth of the matter. Let's try to draw her out. 6. *Callar la boca,* To hold one's tongue. 7. *Dejar con la palabra en la boca,* Not to give a chance to finish (what one was saying). *Salió dejándome con la palabra en la boca*. He left without giving me a chance to finish. 8. *Hablar por boca de ganso,* To put up to say something. *El señor Jones hablaba por boca de ganso*. They put Mr. Jones up to say that. 9. *Hacer boca,* To work up an appetite. *Hago boca con el ejercicio*. I exercise to work up an appetite. 10. *Meterse en la boca del lobo,* To put one's head in the lion's mouth. 11. *Poner en boca de,* To attribute to. *Pusieron injustamente en boca de él una enorme cantidad de mentiras*. They falsely attributed an enormous number of lies to him. 12. *Propaganda de boca,* Word of mouth. *La propaganda de boca modeló el oído de los aficionados*. Word of mouth built up the interest of the fans. 13. *Respirar por la boca de,* To hang on every word of. *Ella respira por la boca de él*. She hangs on his every word. 14. *Torcer la boca,* To make a wry face.

Borne [bor'-nay], p. 112. Add, *m*. (DEL ACUMULADOR) Terminal.

Buque [boo'-kay], p. 119. Add, *m*. 1. *Buque de ruedas,* Paddle wheeler. *En el siglo diez y nueve el buque de ruedas era un atractivo muy común de los ríos Misisipí y Ohio*. In the nineteenth century the paddle wheeler was a common sight on the Mississippi and the Ohio rivers. 2. *Buque de vapor,* Steamship. 3. *Buque escuela,* Training ship. 4. *Buque tanque [cisterna],* Tanker. 5. *Buque transbordador,* Train [Car] ferry.

Bucear [boo-thay-ar'], p. 118. Add, *vn*. 1. (COMO EMPLEO) To work as a diver. 2. *Bucear en,* To throw oneself into, to delve into. *Buceaba en el estudio del francés*. He threw himself into the study of French.

Buscar [boos-car'], p. 120. Add, *va*. 1. To get. *Búscame un lápiz, por favor*. Get me a pencil, please. 2. To look up. *Buscamos nuevos matices en el diccionario*. We looked up new shades of meaning in the dictionary. 3. (Mex.) To provoke. *Más vale no buscarlos*. It's better not to provoke them. 4. *Buscar con la mirada,* To look [watch] for. *Hacía media hora que estaba allí buscando el buque con lo mirada*. She stood there looking for the ship for half an hour. 5. *Buscarle más pies al gato,* To look for more trouble. *Lo único que hice escribiendo la carta era buscarle más pies al gato*. All that I did by writing the letter was to look for more trouble.

Caber [cah-berr'], p. 122. Add, *vn*. 1. To be right. *Cabe pensar de tal manera*. It's right to think that way. 2. To have (enough) room. *Quepo aquí*. I have enough room here. *No caben en esa sala de clase*. They don't have enough room in that classroom. 3. *Caber en los sentimientos de,* To be like. *Tal actitud no cabe en los sentimientos de él*. Such an attitude isn't like him. 4. *Caberle a uno el honor de,* To have the honor [honour, G.B.] to. *Me cabe el honor de presentarles a un antiguo alumno mío*. I have the honor to introduce to you a former student of mine. 5. *Caberle a uno la suerte de,* To fall to the lot of. *Le cabía siempre la suerte de ir a la zaga*. It always fell to his lot to be last. 6. *No caber de pies,* (fig.) To be packed tighter than sardines. 7. *No caber duda,* To be no doubt. *No cabe duda de ello*. There is no doubt of [about] it. 8. *No caber en,* (fig.) To be too good for. *Él no cabe en tal empleo*. He's too good for such a job. 9. *No caber en el mismo saco,* To make strange bedfellows, to be entirely different. *Jorge y Felipe no caben en el mismo saco*. George and Philip make strange bedfellows. 10. *No caberle en la cabeza a uno,* Not to be able to believe, not to be able to get into one's head. *No me cabe en la cabeza el que ella haya hecho tal cosa*. I can't believe she did such a thing [that she did such a thing]. (EN TALES CASOS EL USO DE THAT ES FACULTATIVO.) 11. *No caber en sí de gozo*. To be beside oneself with happiness [joy].

Cabeza [cah-bay'-thah], p. 123. Add, *f*. 1. *Cabeza clara,* Clear thinker. 2. *Cabeza de grabación,* Recording head. 3. *Cabeza de hierro,* a. Brain, intellectual. b. (IRÓNICO) Dunce. 4. *Cabeza de playa,* Beachhead. 5. *Cerrado de cabeza,* Narrow-minded. 6. *Con cabeza de cartón,* (fig.) With one's head in the sand [sky]. *Estaban allí con cabeza de cartón mientras que el perro se fugaba*. They stood there with their heads in the sky while [whilst, G.B.] the dog ran away. 7. *Flaco de cabeza,* Weak-minded. 8. *Llenar de humo la cabeza,* To give a big head. *Las reseñas le llenaban de humo la cabeza*. The reviews gave him a big head. 9. *No tener donde [a quien] volver la cabeza*. Not to know where [to whom] to turn. 10. *Sacar de su cabeza,* To make up. *Sacó de su cabeza aquella patraña*. He made up that fish story. 11. *Tornar la cabeza a,* To turn one's attention to.

Caer [cah-err'], p. 126. Add, *vn*. 1. *Caer bien,* To make a good impression. 2. *Caer de,* To fall on. *Cayó de brazo*. He fell on his arm. 3. *Caer del burro,* (fig.) To get down from one's high horse. 4. *Caer en la cuenta,* To see one's point, to get it (coll.) *Caí en la cuenta casi en el acto*. I saw his point almost immediately. 5. *Caer mal,* To make a bad impression. 6. *Caer por de fuera* (fig., coll.) Not to feel too much, to do little damage. *El golpe le cayó por de fuera*. He didn't feel the blow too much. 7. *Cayó que hacer*. (fig., coll.) An opportunity arose unexpectedly.

Calar [cah-lar'], p. 128. Add, *va*. 1. (A UNA PERSONA) To see through. *La caló en seguida*. He saw through her at once. 2. (UN FARDO, Mex., P.R.) To plug, to tap. —*vn*. 1. (PENETRAR) To take hold. *Finalmente llegó a calar la idea de su pérdida*. Finally the idea of her loss began to take hold. 2. *Calar en,* To reach, to touch, to capture. *Cala en el sentimiento nacional*. He touches the feeling of nationhood. 3. (IR A FONDO) To sink to the bottom. —*vr*. 1. (LAS GAFAS) To put on. 2. To slip into. *Se caló en la casa*. He slipped into the house. 3. *Calarse hasta los huesos,* To get soaked.

Calidad [cah-le-dahd'], p. 129. Add,

f. 1. *A calidad de que,* On condition that. *Te ayudaré a calidad de que me des razón de lo ocurrido.* I'll help you on condition that you give me an account of what happened. 2. *Calidad cívica,* Civic pride. *La calidad cívica jalona el desarrollo de una ciudad.* Civic pride is the mark of a city's growth. 3. *En calidad de,* With one's authority as.

Calle [cahl'-lyay], p. 131. Add, *f.* 1. (DE PISCINA) Lane. 2. (MEDIO) Gateway (fig.) *El estudio es una calle al porvenir.* Study is a gateway to the future. 3. (DE OTRA POBLACIÓN) Extension. *Río Bravo es una calle de Santiago.* Río Bravo is an extension of Santiago. 4. *Calle hita,* An entirely built-up street. 5. *Un pedido para la calle,* An order to take out.

Caminata [cah-me-nah'-tah], p. 133. Add, *f.* 1. (PASEO FATIGOSO) Trek. 2. *Caminata espacial,* (Aer.) Space walk. *Las caminatas espaciales nos están enseñando a sacudir el polvo a nuestro conocimiento del aerospacio.* Space walks are teaching us to brush up on our knowledge of aerospace.

Capacitación [cah-pah-the-tah-the-on'], *f.* (Neol.) Preparation, qualification. *Capacitación del magisterio,* Teacher preparation.

Capacitar [cah-pah-the-tar'], *va.* (Neol.) (A UNA PERSONA) To prepare, to qualify. —*vr.* To qualify oneself. *El capacitarse para la abogacía cuesta muchos años.* Qualifying oneself for the bar takes many years.

Cara [cah'-rah], p. 141. Add, *f.* 1. Look, appearance, e.g.: *Cara de ahorcado,* Hang-dog look. *Cara de susto,* Frightened look. *Se puso una cara de susto.* A frightened look came over his face. *Cara de aleluya,* Cheerful appearance. *Su cara de aleluya llegó a convencerlo.* Her cheerful appearance finally convinced him. 2. *Lavar la cara a,* (fig.) To lick the boots of.

Cargo [car'-go], p. 144. Add, *m.* 1. (Com.) Debit, charge. 2. (fig.) Duty. 3. *Cargo docente,* Teaching position [appointment]. 4. *Librar a cargo de,* To draw on (the account of). 5. *Ser en cargo a,* To be in the debt of (fig.). *Le éramos en cargo por lo mucho que hizo.* We were in his debt for the great deal that he did. 6. *Vestir el cargo,* To look the part.

Carril [car-reel'], *m.* 1. (DE CARRETERA) Lane. 2. *Carril único,* Monorail.

Cartelera [car-tay-lay'-rah], p. 148. Add, *f.* 1. (Neol.) Amusement section (of the newspaper). *Cuando busco la cartelera, jamás la puedo encontrar.* I can never find the amusement section of the newspaper when I want it. 2. (AL AIRE LIBRE) Hoarding (G.B.)

Catapulta [cah-tah-pool'-tah], p. 151. Add, *f.* Catapulta de lanzamiento, (Aer.) Launch vehicle. *La catapulta de lanzamiento lleva la nave espacial por encima de la gravedad de la Tierra.* The launch vehicle carries the spacecraft above earth's gravity.

Celar [thay-lar'], p. 155. Add, *va.* 1. To keep an eye on. *Celaban el despliegue de las tropas extranjeras.* They kept an eye on the deployment of foreign troops. 2. To watch (suspiciously). *Le celaba mientras contaba la vuelta.* She watched him suspiciously while he counted the change. *Celeban cada paso suyo.* They watched his every move.

Celo [tha'y-lo], p. 155. Add, *m.* 1. (HACIA UNA COSA) Regard, concern, care. 2. (ENTUSIASMO) Zeal. 3. *Celos,* Jealousy. 4. *Dar celos,* To make jealous. 5. *Sin celos de,* Without regard to. *La colocación se ofrece a todos los aspirantes, sin celos de raza, religión o nacionalidad.* The position is open to all candidates, without regard to race, religion or nationality.

Célula [thay'-loo-lah], p. 156. Add, *f.* 1. Cell. 2. *Célula de combustible,* (Aer.) Fuel cell.

Central [then-trahl'], p. 157. Add, *f.* 1. Headquarters. *Esta oficina es la central para el territorio sureño.* This office is the headquarters for the southern territory. 2. *Central de abastos,* Supply center [centre, G.B.]. 3. *Central solar.* (Neol.) Solar energy plant.

Centro [then'-tro], p. 157. Add, *m.* 1. (DE LA CIUDAD) Downtown. 2. *Centro de diversiones,* Amusement park. *El centro de diversiones tiene una montaña rusa.* The amusement park has a roller coaster. 3. *Centro de mesa,* Centerpiece. 4. *Centro docente,* Learning center [centre, G.B.]. 5. *Estar en su centro,* To be in one's element. *Mirándole trabajar, se notaba que estaba en su centro.* Watching him work, you could tell [see] he was in his element.

Cibernación [the-ber-nah-the-on'], *f.* (Neol.) Cybernation. *La cibernación permite que las computadoras dirijan la automatización.* Cybernation lets computers direct the automation process.

Ciclo [thee'-clo], p. 161. Add, *m.* 1. Series. *Hubo un ciclo de conferencias que resultó ser un enorme éxito de taquilla.* There was a series of lectures that turned out to be an enormous success at the box office [box office success]. 2. *Ciclo escolar,* (Mex.) School year. *El ciclo escolar y el año no corresponden.* The school year and the calendar year do not correspond.

Ciencia [the-en'-the-ah], p. 161. Add, *f.* 1. *A [de] ciencia cierta,* For a certainty. 2. *A ciencia y paciencia,* (Lit.) By your leave. 3. *A ciencia y paciencia de,* With the tacit approval of. 4. *Ciencia de información,* Information science. 5. *Ciencia estelar,* Space science.

Ciudad [the-oo-dahd'], p. 165. Add, *f.* 1. *Ciudad satélite,* (Neol.) Bedroom community. *De costumbre las ciudades satélites se despueblan de día para proporcionar la mano de obra en una urbe vecina.* Bedroom communities usually empty by day to provide the work force for a nearby large city. 2. *Ciudad universitaria,* Campus.

Cobrar [co-brar'], p. 168. Add, *va.* 1. (IMPORTANCIA) To take on, to assume. 2. (UN CHEQUE) To cash. 3. (PERCIBIR EL SUELDO) To get paid. *¿Cuándo cobramos?* When do we get paid? 4. (UN PRECIO) To charge. *¿Qué precio te cobró?* What price did he charge you? 5. *Cobrarle cariño a uno,* To take a liking to someone.

Coche [co'-chay], p. 169. Add, *m.* 1. *Caminar [ir] en el coche de San Fernando,* To go by shanks' mare. 2. *Coche cuna,* Baby carriage. 3. *Coche de línea,* Intercity bus. 4. *No pararse los coches de,* (Lit., fig.) To be ships that pass in the night. *Gozaron de la plática, pero no se pararon sus coches.* They enjoyed the chat, but they were ships that pass in the night.

Coincidir [co-in-the-deer'], p. 170, Add, *vn. Coincidir en,* 1. Both, e.g.: *Coinciden en presentar el punto de vista europeo.* They both present the European point of view. 2. To be at the same time. *Coincidimos en el Prado.* We were at the Prado at the same time.

Colector [co-lec-tor'], p. 171. Add, *m.* 1. *Colector de aguas,* Main sewage system. 2. *Colector de radiación,* (Neol.) Solar collector. 3. *Colector pantógrafo,* (r. w.) Pantograph trolley. 4. *Colector de pértiga,* (r. w.) Pole trolley.

Coletilla [co-lay-teel'-lyah], p. 172. Add, *f.* 1. Small queue, pigtail. 2. *La coletilla,* The last word. *Le gusta decir la coletilla.* He likes to have the last word.

Componenda [com-po-nen'-dah], p. 177. Add, *f.* 1. (EN SENTIDO NEGATIVO) Shady deal. 2. (Neol.) Compromise. *La componenda llegó a complacer a contados socios.* The compromise ended up pleasing a few members. (NOTE: THIS NEW USAGE AVOIDS THE CONFUSION OF **Compromiso** WITH ITS MORE COMMON MEANING.)

Comportamiento [com-por-tah-me-en'-to], p. 178. Add, *m.* 1. (DE UNA PERSONA) Behavior [Behaviour, G.B.]. 2. (DEL TIEMPO, LA BOLSA) Activity.

Computadora [com-poo-tah-do'-rah], *f.* (Neol.) Data processor. *La palabra "data processor" tiene dos significados en inglés, el ordenador de datos y la computadora que los elabora.* The word "data processor" has two meanings in English, the person who organizes the data and the computer that processes them.

Comunicólogo [co-moo-ne-co'-lo-go], *m.* (Neol.) Communications specialist.

Con [cone], p. 197. Add, *prep.* 1. *Con conocimiento de causa,* With one's eyes wide open. 2. *Con desparpajo,* In an uninhibited way. 3. *Con ello,* In this way. *Con ello se llenaron los requisitos.* The requirements were met in this way. 4. *Con lujo de detalles,* In great detail. 5. *Con miras de,* With the aim of. 6. *Con muy equiparados esfuerzos,* On the same footing. *Las dos editoriales rivalizaban con muy equiparados esfuerzos.* The two publishing houses were competing on the same footing. 7. *Con pinta de,* (coll.) With the look of. *Se fue con* *pinta del hombre que ha perdido a su último amigo*. He left with the look of a man who has lost his last friend. 8. *Con que*, a. So. *Con que fuiste tú quien lo hizo*. So it was you who did it. b. If only. *Con que me lo hubieras dicho antes*. If only you had told me before. c. As long as. *Con que me digas antes acerca de tus planes no habrá problema*. As long as you tell me about your plans in advance, there won't be any problem. d. Whereupon. *Regresó, con que la dificultad surgió de nuevo*. She returned, whereupon the difficulty arose once more. 9. *Con razón* + verb, To be right in + verb. *Con razón piensa eso*. He's right in thinking that.

Concatenarse [con-cah-tay-nar'-say], *vr.* 1. To lead to another. *Los libros se concatenan*. One book leads to another. 2. *Concatenarse con*, To lead to. *El estudio de la Antropología se concatena naturalmente con el estudio del Lenguaje*. The study of anthropology leads naturally to the study of language.

Concientización [con-the-en-te-thah-the-on'], *f.* (Neol.) Awareness. (NOTE: THIS NEW USAGE AVOIDS THE CONFUSION OF **Conciencia** WITH ITS MORE COMMON MEANING.).

Conforme [con-for'-may], p. 183, Add, *adv.* 1. Just as. *Conforme yo lo indiqué arriba, su encumbramiento varió la convivencia nacional*. Just as I indicated above, his rise to power changed the national life. 2. To the same degree that. *Conforme el bochorno azotaba la población, el fuero interior de sus habitantes mejoraba*. The inner strength of the town's inhabitants improved to the same degree that the heat wave devastated it.

Conllevar, [con-lyay-var'], p. 184. Add, *va.* 1. To bring with oneself [along]. *Este paso conllevará muchos retos nuevos*. This step will bring many new challenges with it. 2. (SOPORTAR) To put up with. *Cada cual conllevaba como mejor podía la desazón*. Each one put up with the unpleasant situation as best he could.

Constructor [cons-trooc-tor'], *m.* (Neol.) Construct. *Es indudable que la motivación no sea un constructor hipotético en lo que al aprendizaje de los idiomas atañe*. Motivation is certainly not a hypothetical construct where language learning is concerned.

Consulta [con-sool'-tah], p. 188. Add, *f.* 1. Advice, opinion. *La consulta que recibí era desastrosa*. The advice I got was terrible. 2. *Consulta popular*, (Neol.) Public opinion. *Hacer la consulta popular*, To consult public opinion. *Hicieron la consulta popular antes de construir el puente*. They consulted public opinion before they built the bridge. 3. *Horas de consulta*, Office hours (of a professional).

Contrasentido [con-trah-sen-tee'-do], p. 192. Add, *m.* 1. Contradiction in terms. *La mentira en unión de la honradez es un contrasentido*. Falsehood in the company of honesty is a contradiction in terms. 2. Inconsistency. *El informe trae un gran número de contrasentidos*. The report contains numerous inconsistencies.

Contratapa [con-trah-tah'-pah], *f.* (Neol.) Back cover (of a book). *En la contratapa figuraban varias reseñas del libro*. Several reviews of the book appeared on the back cover.

Correr [cor-rerr'], p. 199. Add, *va.* 1. (EL TORO) To fight. 2. (UN TRANCE) To go through. 3. (LA LLAVE, EL CERROJO) To turn. 4. (UN MUEBLE) To push [pull] out of the way. *¿Por que no corremos la silla?* Why don't we push the chair out of the way? 5. (UN ARTÍCULO) To take orders for. *El corría una batería de cocina*. He was taking orders for a set of kitchen utensils. 6. *Correr albures de*, To take a chance on. *Es cierto que corríamos albures del éxito de la nueva tienda*. We certainly were taking a chance on the success of the new store. 7. *Correr con*, a. (UNA COSA) To take care of. *Yo corro con los gastos*. I'll take care of the expenses. b. (UNA PERSONA) To be on friendly terms with. 8. *Correr la plaza de*, To be the [a] sales representative in. *Yo corro la plaza de Bayamón*. I'm the sales representative in Bayamón. 9. *Correr pareja con*, To keep up [pace] with. *Le cuesta trabajo correr pareja con su madre*. It's hard for her to keep up with her mother. 10. *Correr por cuenta de*, To be the concern of. *Esto corre por cuenta de los padres*. That is the parents' concern. 11. *Correrla*, To be a night owl. 12. *¡Corriendo!* Get going! (fam.) —*vr.* a. To get away from. *Se les corrió*. He got away from them. b. (coll.) To be too outgoing, to overdo it.

Cruzar [croo-thar'], p. 207. Add, *va.* 1. (TOPAR) To meet, to come upon. 2. (Chile, Perú, P.R.) To quarrel with. 3. *Cruzarse de brazos*, (fig.) To stand idly by, not to lift a finger (to help). 4. *Cruzarse en el camino de*, (Acad.) To get in the way of. *Su egolatría se cruzaba en el camino de su éxito*. His inflated ego got in the way of his success.

Cuenta [coo-en'-tah], p. 211. Add, *f.* 1. (DE LA CONSUMICIÓN) Check. 2. (Com.) Bill. 3. *Dar buena cuenta de su persona*, To turn in a good account of oneself. 4. *Darse cuenta de*, To be aware of, to realize. 5. *Hacer(se) (la) cuenta que*, To assume. Me hago la cuenta que se fueron ya. I assume they already left. 6. *No ser cuenta de*, To have no business, to be none of the business of. *No es cuenta de él decirles cuántos son cinco*. He has no business telling them what to do. *No es cuenta de él*. It's none of his business. 7. *Pedir cuentas*, To take to account. *El maestro le pidió cuentas al niño*. The teacher took the child to account. 8. *Vivir a cuenta de*, To live at the expense of.

Cumplir [coom-pleer'], p. 213. Add, *va.* 1. To keep. *Siempre cumple su palabra*. He always keeps his word. 2. *Cumplir bien*, To do a good job of [on]. *El pintor cumplió bien el fondo*. The painter did a good job on the background. 3. *Cumplir de palabra*, To make an idle promise [idle promises]. *Siempre cumplía de palabra, nunca de hecho*. He always made idle promises he never kept. 4. *Cumplir una condena*, To serve a sentence in prison, to do one's time. 5. *No cumplir*, To go back on, not to keep. *No cumplió su palabra*. He went back on his word. —*vn*. To do one's national service. —*vr.* To come true. *Se cumplió su anhelo*. Her longing came true.

Cuna [coo'-nah], p. 213. Add, *f.* 1. Place of birth. *Su cuna era Barcelona*. Her place of birth was Barcelona. 2. (DEL ASTILLERO) Stocks. 3. *Cuna y reducto*, (fig.) Stronghold. *En aquel entonces París era cuna y reducto de la llamada generación perdida*. At that time Paris was a stronghold of the so-called lost generation.

Cundir [coon-deer'], p. 213. Add, *vn.* 1. To catch on, to take hold. *Es que no cundió la nueva moda*. The new style just didn't catch on. *La nueva voz cundió rápidamente*. The new word took hold rapidly. 2. To go a long way, to last a long time. *La mantequilla cunde bien si la usas con cuidado*. The butter will really go a long way if you use it carefully.

Cupo [coo'-po], *m.* (Neol.) 1. (DE UN LOCAL) Seating capacity. 2. (CABIDA) Space, room. *Hay cupo para dos*. There's room for two. 3. (NÚMERO DETERMINADO) Quota. *¿Cuál es el cupo para aquel centro docente?* What's the quota for that teaching center [centre, G.B.]?

Chapuza [chah-poo'-thah], *f.* 1. (Neol.) Odd job. *Vive de las chapuzas que le caen en suerte*. He lives on the odd jobs that come his way. 2. (ARTESANÍA INFERIOR) Botched-up job, mess.

Dar [dar], p. 223. Add, *va.* 1. (UNA CONFERENCIA) To deliver. 2. (UNA CLASE) To teach. 3. *Dar a conocer*, To make known. *Me dio a conocer los nombres de los ganadores*. He made the names of the winners known to me. 4. *Dar a lo dicho significado suyo*, To put words in the mouth of. *¡Él siempre da significado suyo a lo que digo!* He always puts words in my mouth! 5. *Dar barro a la mano de*, To be grist for the mill of. *Los sucesos son barro a la mano del estudioso de la Historia*. Events are grist for the mill of the student of history. 6. *Dar con*, a. (DESPUÉS DE MUCHA FATIGA) To come up with. *Finalmente dio con la respuesta*. At long last he came up with the answer. b. To run across [into], to come upon, to bump into (coll.). *Di con él en la esquina*. I ran across him at the corner. 7. *Dar con su testa en el yunque*, To hit a stone wall (fig.). 8. *Dar de barato*, To concede, to grant. *Le doy de barato ese punto*. I'll grant you that point. 9. *Dar en comitiva*, To team-teach. *Muchas veces los maestros se desempeñan con más eficacia cuando las clases se dan en comitiva*. Teachers can often function more effectively when classes are team-taught. 10. *Dar en rostro a*, To fly in the face of. 11. *Dar fe*, To give testimony. 12. *Dar grima,* To irritate, to vex. 13. *Dar hambre,* To make hungry. *Las tapas me dan hambre.* The hors d'oeuvre make me hungry. 14. *Dar hospedaje,* To put up. *Pudimos dar hospedaje a cuatro alumnos, nada más.* We could only put up four of the students. 15. *Dar la tecla a,* To put on to. *Su comento le dio la tecla a la liquidación.* Her comment put him on to the sale. 16. *Dar la vuelta,* To turn back. *Dieron la vuelta en un apeadero llamado Dos Cruces.* They turned back at a whistle-stop called Dos Cruces. 17. *Dar marcha atrás,* To back up. *Lentamente daba marcha atrás al coche por la entrada del garaje.* She slowly backed the car up the driveway. 18. *Dar paso atrás,* To back up. *Mientras hablaba daba paso atrás.* As he spoke he backed up. 19. *Dar pena,* To make sad. *El mero pensar en ello me da pena.* Just to think of it makes me sad. 20. *Dar pie a,* To back up, to support. *Hay que dar pie a las declaraciones con los hechos.* You must back up your statements with facts. 21. *Dar pon a,* (Acad., P.R.) To give a ride. *Nos dieron pon a la playa.* They gave us a ride to the beach. 22. *Dar por* + pp. [a.], To consider + pp. [a.]. *Ella da por bien empleada la tarde.* She considers the afternoon well spent. *Lo dábamos por inocente.* We considered him innocent. *Doy por concluido el asunto.* I consider the matter closed. 23. *Dar por sentado [supuesto],* To take for granted. *Damos por sentada aquella ley.* We take that law for granted. 24. *Dar sombra,* a. To shade. b. (fig.) To make look bad. *En el tenis él siempre me da sombra.* He always makes me look bad at tennis. 25. *Dar un día de muchas campanillas,* To make one's day. *Su carta me dio un día de muchas campanillas.* Her letter made my day. 26. *Dar un dolor,* To feel a pain. *De repente me dio un dolor.* Suddenly I felt a pain. 27. *Dar un portazo,* To slam the door. 28. *Dar un portazo a,* To slam the door on [in the face of]. 29. *Dar un repasón,* To take a backward glance. 30. *Dar una ojeada* [Mex., *un vistazo*], To take a look at. 31. *Dar vista a,* To catch sight of. *Dio vista al hombre, quien corría calle abajo.* He caught sight of the man running down the street. 32. *Dar vueltas a,* a. To turn over. *Daba vueltas al libro en las manos.* He was turning the book over in his hands. b. To go around. *La Tierra da vueltas al Sol.* The earth goes around the sun. 33. *No dar pie con bola,* To do everything wrong, to have two left feet (fig.).

Darse [dar′-say], p. 224. Add, *vr.* 1. *Darse cuenta de,* a. (UNA COSA) To (take) notice (of). *No se daba cuenta de la silla nueva.* She didn't notice the new chair. b. (UN HECHO) To realize. *No me di cuenta de lo difícil que era.* I didn't realize how difficult it was. 2. *Darse maña para,* To manage to. *El domador se dio maña para volver la culebra a la jaula.* The trainer managed to return the snake to the cage. 3. *Darse tono,* To put on airs. 4. *Dársele disgusto por,* To take a disliking for. *Se le ha dado un disgusto por el té.* He has taken a disliking for tea. 5. *Dársele una aversión por,* To take a dislike to. *Se le daba una aversión por Juan.* She took a dislike to John. 6. *Se da el caso que,* It so happens that, as it happens. *Se da el caso que la edición que usted requiere está agotada.* It so happens that the edition that you require is out of print.

De [day], p. 224. Add, *prep.* 1. If, e.g.: *De haber ido antes, los habría encontrado.* If I had gone earlier, I would have met them. *De haberlas cantado todas, la cantante habría lucido más.* If she had sung them all, the singer would have shown herself to greater advantage. 2. With, e.g.: a. (ROPA) *El hombre de la bata azul,* The man with the blue robe. *La mujer del sombrero parisiense,* The lady with the Paris hat. b. (ESTADO) *Enfermo de preocupaciones,* Sick with worry. *Loco de celos,* Insane with jealousy. 3. *De común acuerdo,* With one accord. *Decidieron de común acuerdo.* They decided with one accord. 4. *De día,* By day. *De día se ven claramente.* By day they can be seen clearly. 5. *De enorme arrastre,* With us for a long time. *Es un problema de enorme arrastre.* The problem has been with us for a long time. 6. *De gran aliento,* Of great strength and vigor [vigour, G.B.]. *Es un actor de gran aliento.* He is an actor of great strength and vigour. 7. *De la vida fácil,* Of easy virtue. *Era una dama de la vida fácil.* She was a lady of easy virtue. 8. *De mañana,* In the morning. 9. *De noche,* At night, by night (Lit.). 10. *De pie,* On foot, standing. 11. *De un momento a otro,* At any time. *Llegará de un momento a otro.* He'll arrive at any time. 12. *De un tirón,* All at one time. *Leyó la novela de un tirón.* She read the novel all at one time.

Degradar [day-grah-dar′], p. 228, Add, *va.* (A UN ALUMNO) To demote, put back. *Muchas veces a la larga es mejor degradar al alumno que fracasa.* In the long run, it is often better to demote the failing student.

Dejar [day-har′], p. 228. Add, *va.* 1. (DINERO) To lend, to loan. 2. *Dejar caer,* To hint. *Dejó caer que le hacía falta más pañuelos.* He hinted that he needed more handkerchiefs. 3. *Dejar de,* a. (OMITIR) To fail to. b. (CESAR) To stop. 4. *Dejar de existir,* To pass out of existence, to exist no longer. *La plaza ha dejado de existir.* The job no longer exits. 5. *Dejar molido,* (fig.) To wear out. *La prueba lo dejó molido.* The match wore him out. 6. *Dejar paso,* To stand aside. 7. *Dejar por hacer,* To put off doing. —*vr.* 1. *Dejarse de composturas,* To drop all formality. 2. *Dejarse ver,* To show up. *Se dejó ver en todas las tertulias más elegantes.* He showed up at all the most elegant literary gatherings.

Delfin [del-feen′], p. 229. Add, *m.* (Neol.) Chosen successor. *Era el delfín del líder comunista.* He was the chosen successor to the Communist leader.

Deportividad [day-por-te-ve-dahd′], *f.* (Acad., Neol.) Good sportsmanship. *En estos días la deportividad se encuentra difícilmente.* Good sportsmanship is hard to find nowadays.

Depotenciar [day-po-ten-the-ar′], *va.* (Neol.) To weaken. *Tal jugada depotenciaría la eficacia de la nueva campaña de ventas.* Such a move would weaken the effectiveness of the new sales campaign.

Deprender [day-pren-der′], *va.* (Neol, Mex.) To derive. *Deprende muchas ideas suyas de sus propios antecedentes.* He derives many of his ideas from his own life.

Derrochar [der-ro-char′], p. 233. Add, *va.* 1. (EN LA LUCHA) To take down [to the mat]. 2. *Derrochar cariño con,* To lavish kindness on.

Desaforado, da [des-ah-fo-rah′-do, dah], p. 234. Add, *a.* 1. *A voz desaforada,* At the top of one's lungs. 2. *Felicidad desaforada,* Boundless joy. 3. *Imaginación desaforada,* Unbridled imagination.

Desdecir [des-day-theer′], p. 244. Add, *va.* To take back. *Desdijo todas las cosas bonitas que le había contado.* He took back all the nice things he had told her. —*vn. Desdecir de,* To be out of keeping with. *El cuento desdice de su estilo.* The short story is out of keeping with his style. —*vr.* To take back what one has said. *La muchacha se desdijo en seguida.* The girl immediately took back what she had said.

Desdoblar [des-do-blar′], p. 244. Add, *vn.* (Neol.) To play two roles. *Aquel actor agraciado desdobló en la comedia.* That gifted actor played two roles in the play.

Desechable [des-ay-chah′-blay], *a.* (Neol.) Disposable. *Los platos desechables de cartón son el sostén principal de cualquier merienda.* Disposable paper plates are the mainstay of any picnic.

Desempeñar [des-em-pay-nyar′], *va.* 1. (UNA OBLIGACIÓN) To satisfy. 2. (DE UN APURO) To get out of a tight spot (coll.). —*vr.* 1. To acquit oneself, to handle oneself, to function. 2. (LAS MODALES ESPECÍFICAMENTE) To conduct oneself. 3. *Desempeñarse bien,* To do a good job. *Me gusta la pintura. El artista se desempeñó muy bien.* I like the painting. The artist did a very good job. 4. *Desempeñarse libremente,* To be oneself.

Desentrañar [des-en-tra-nyar′], p. 247. Add, *va.* To get to the bottom of. *Dentro de poco desentrañarán quién robó el lienzo.* They will soon get to the bottom of who stole the canvas.

Desertor, ra [day-ser-tor′, rah], *m. & f. Desertor de la enseñanza,* Dropout (Amer.), school leaver (G.B.). *Muchas veces el desertor de la enseñanza permite que una suerte enorme entre las colocaciones perjudique su porvenir.* The school leaver often lets one stroke of good luck in the job market hurt his future.

Deshacer [des-ah-therr'], p. 249. Add, *vr.* 1. (EN EL TRABAJO) To work one's fingers to the bone. 2. (CON EL USO) To wear out. 3. (DESCOMPONERSE) To fall apart. 4. *Deshacerse en cumplidos,* To go out of one's way (fig.). *Ella se deshizo en cumplidos para que nuestra estancia* [Amer., *estadía*] *fuera más agradable.* She went out of her way to make our stay more enjoyable.

Deslindar [des-lin-dar'], p. 251. Add, *va.* (Neol.) 1. To outline, to define. *Hay que deslindar las responsabilidades.* We must outline responsibilities. 2. To show where one leaves off and another begins. *Ella deslindó nuestros deberes.* She showed us where my duties left off and his began.

Deslinde [des-leen'-day], p. 251. Add, *m.* (Neol.) Outline. *Escriba un deslinde del proyecto.* Write up an outline of the project.

Deslizar [des-le-thar'], p. 251. Add, *va.* *1. To let slip. Deslizó su nombre.* She let his name slip. 2. To slip, to slide. *Deslizó el libro entre los papeles.* He slipped the book among the papers. 3. *Deslizarle al oído,* To whisper into one's ear. —*vn.* (UNA DEVISA) To fall. *El peso deslizó contra la peseta.* The peso fell against the peseta. —*vr.* 1. To slink about, to slither. 2. *Deslizarse al vicio,* To get into bad habits. 3. *Deslizarse por el pendiente,* To slide down the hill.

Desmandar [des-man-dar'], p. 252. Add, *vr.* 1. To talk back, to be insolent. 2. (P.R.) To get a head start. 3. (fig.) To stray from the group, to get off the beaten track.

Desnutrición [des-noo-tre-the-on'], p. 253. Add, *f.* (Neol.) Poor nutrition. *La desnutrición provoca un marcado arrastre en sus víctimas.* Poor nutrition brings about a definite lack of vitality in its victims.

Desnutrido, da [des-noo-tree'-do, dah], *a.* Undernourished. —*m.* & *f.* 1. Undernourished person. 2. Victim of malnutrition.

Desplazar [des-plah-thar'], p. 256. Add, *va.* 1. (Naut.) To displace. 2. (Neol.) To keep out of sight. *Desplazaban al viejo cuando llegaron los soldados.* They kept the old man out of sight when the soldiers arrived. 3. (AL ENEMIGO) To force out of their position. —*vr.* 1. To keep [stay] out of sight. *Él siempre se desplazaba cuando ella les hacía una visita.* He always kept out of sight when she paid them a visit. 2. To move about. *El tenista se desplazaba bien en la cancha y tenía el arrojo que exige el éxito.* The tennis player moved about the court well and had the drive that success demands.

Destacar [des-tah-car'], p. 257. Add, *va.* 1. To bring out. *Destacó varios detalles importantes que jalaban su maqueta.* He brought out several important details that advanced his model. 2. (SUBRAYAR) To play up. *Deseamos destacar su idoneidad para la vacante.* We want to play up how ideal he is for the vacancy. —*vr.* To stand out. *Las diferencias se destacaban acusadamente.* The differences stood out clearly.

Destrozón, na [des-tro-thone', nah], p. 258. Add, *a.* 1. Wearing out one's clothing in a short time [hurry]. *Es una gran destrozona de zapatos.* She certainly wears out her shoes in a hurry. 2. *Ser destrozón,* To be hard on one's clothing.

Detención [day-ten-the-on'], p. 260. Add, *f,* (Mech.) 1. Shutoff. 2. *Detención automática,* Automatic shutoff. 3. *Válvula de detención,* Shutoff valve.

Deterioro [day-tay-re-o'-ro], p. 260. Add, *m.* 1. (Mech.) Wear and tear. 2. *Deterioro ambiental,* Environmental pollution. *El deterioro ambiental puede sanearse.* Environmental pollution can be corrected. 3. (DE MERCANCÍAS) Spoilage, waste.

Dibujo [de-boo'-ho], p. 262. Add, *m.* 1. *Dibujo animado,* Animated cartooning. 2. *Dibujo del natural,* Life class.

Dictar [dic-tar'], p. 262. Add, *va.* 1. (Arg., Chile) To teach. *Dicta cuatro clases todos los días.* He teaches four classes every day. 2. (LEY, FALLO) To promulgate. 3. *Dictar en comitiva,* To team-teach.

Directorial [de-rec-to-re-ahl'], p. 266. Add, *a.* (Neol.) Managerial. *El acuerdo directorial puede conjurar problemas graves para una empresa.* Managerial agreement can ward off serious problems for a company.

Dirigir [de-re-heer'], p. 266. Add, *vr.* *Dirigirse hacia,* To make toward. *Se dirigieron hacia la casa.* They made toward the house.

Disculpar [dis-cool-par'], p. 266. Add, *va.* *Disculpar con pretextos,* To make excuses for. *Ella siempre disculpa con pretextos su mal caracter.* She always makes excuses for his bad temper.

Dispositivos [dis-po-se-tee'-vos], *m.pl.* (Neol). Equipment. *Los dispositivos que hacen falta para la botadura naval llegarán al astillero mañana.* The equipment needed for the launching will arrive at the shipyard tomorrow. (NOTE: THIS NEW USAGE AVOIDS THE CONFUSION OF) **Equipo,** WITH ITS MORE COMMON MEANING.)

Disyuntiva [dis-yoon-tee'-vah], *f.* (Neol.) New course of action. *Esta disyuntiva ha de mejorar el cuadro económico.* This new course of action is to improve the economic picture.

Doblar [do-blar'], p. 270. Add, *va.* 1. (LAS SÁBANAS) To turn down. 2. (UN ÁNGULO) To turn. 3. (UN CABO) To round. 4. (fig.) To change the mind of. *Es terco. Es imposible doblarlo.* He's stubborn. It's impossible to change his mind.

Echar [ay-char'], p. 275. Add, *va.* 1. (LA LLAVE, EL CERROJO) To turn. 2. (UN BOCADO) To have. 3. (AL BUZÓN) To drop. 4. *Echar a,* To start, to begin. *Echó a cantar.* He began to sing. 5. *Echar a un lado,* To shove aside, to push to one side. 6. *Echar a volar,* (fig.) To put in the public eye, to launch the career of. *Él ha echado a volar a varios escritores.* He has launched the career of several writers. 7. *Echar de menos,* To miss. *Echa de menos a su hermana.* He misses his sister. 8. *Echar el resto,* To do a bang-up job (coll.). *Echó el resto con la casa.* She did a bang-up job on the house. 9. *Echar la culpa a,* To put the blame on. 10. *Echar mano de,* To make use of. 11. *Echar por,* To rush down. *Echó por la calle por,* To rush down. *Echó por la calle al lado de la casa.* He rushed down the street next to the house. 12. *Echar por tierra,* (fig.) To dash. *Echó por tierra todas mis ilusiones.* She dashed all my dreams. 13. *Echar una indirecta,* To drop a hint. 14. *Echar raíces,* To take root. 15. *Echar sapos y culebras,* To be in a towering rage. 16. *Echar sobre los hombros,* To take upon oneself. *Ella echó sobre los hombros la responsabilidad de la seguridad de los niños.* She took upon herself the responsibility for the safety of the children. 17. *Echar tras,* To rush after. 18. *Echarle en cara,* To throw up to. *Siempre le echa en cara lo mucho que renunció.* She always throws up to him how much she gave up. 19. *Echarlo todo a rodar,* a. (ENFADARSE) To lose one's head completely. b. (Com.) To mismanage a business deal completely. —*vr.* 1. To lie down. 2. (EN LA CAMA) To go to bed. 3. *Echarse a perder,* a. (LA CARNE) To spoil. b. (UNA PERSONA) To go to rack and ruin. 4. *Echarse al surco,* To lie down on the job. *A nadie le gustan los empleados que se echan al surco.* No one [No-one, G.B.] likes employees who lie down on the job. 5. *Echarse de recio,* To get tough with (coll.). 6. *Echárselas de presuntuoso,* To put on airs, to get on one's high horse.

Edad [ay-dahd'], p. 276. Add, *f.* 1. Time of one's life. *Es una edad que debería vivirse holgadamente.* It's a time of one's life that should be spent comfortably. 2. *Edad adulta,* Adulthood. 3. *Edad antigua,* Antiquity. 4. *Edad de hierro,* Iron Age. 5. *Edad de oro,* Golden Age. 6. *Edad madura,* Middle age.

Egresar [ay-gray-sar'], *va. (Neol., Arg., Mex.) To graduate. De los principiantes, ¿cuántos egresan?* How many graduate of those who begin? (NOTE: THIS NEW USAGE AVOIDS THE CONFUSION OF **Graduarse** WITH THE QUITE DIFFERENT MEANING OF **Graduar.**)

Elaboración [ay-lah-bo-rah-the-on'], p. 277. Add, *f.* (Neol.) 1. Thought process. *Trató de trazar la elaboración que le había llevado a tal determinación.* He tried to trace the thought process that had brought him to such a decision. 2. *Elaboración de datos,* Data processing. 3. *Elaboración de palabras,* Word processing.

Elaborador, ra [ay-lah-bo-rah-dor', rah], p. 277. Add, *m.* & *f.* *Elaborador de datos,* (Neol.) Word processor.

Electrónica [ay-lec-tro'-ne-cah], p. 278. Add, *f.* *Electrónica de las micro-*

lascas, Microchip electronics.

Elemental [ay-lay-men-tahl'], p. 278. Add, *a.* 1. Elementary. 2. (COLOR) Primary.

Empleadismo [em-play-ah-dees'-mo], *m.* (Neol.) Poor government hiring procedures.

Empresa [em-pray'-sah], p. 284. Add, *f.* 1. (Com.) Business concern, company. 2. (Th.) Management. 3. *Fracasar en la empresa,* To fail in the attempt. 4. *Ser empresa llana,* To be an easy matter. *Apagar el sistema es empresa llana.* It's an easy matter to turn off the system.

En [en], p. 285. Add, *prep.* 1. *En alguna forma,* One way or another. *En alguna forma le buscó la boca a su amiga.* One way or another she drew her friend out. 2. *En aquel entonces,* At that time. *En aquel entonces escaseaban los contratos.* At that time contracts were scarce. 3. *En carne viva,* (fig.) Deeply. *Sentía en carne viva su desinterés.* He felt their lack of interest deeply. 4. *En ciernes,* Budding (fig.). Es un dramaturgo en ciernes. He's a budding dramatist. 5. *En cuerpo y alma,* With all one's might, with might and main. 6. *En dos palabras,* In a word. *En dos palabras, vale la pena.* In a word, it's worth the effort. 7. *En el momento que,* Just as. *En el momento que yo doblaba la esquina, lo vi entrar en la tienda.* Just as I turned the corner, I saw him go into the store. 8. *En el peor de los casos,* No matter what. *Yo voy en el peor de los casos.* I'm going no matter what. 9. *En ese entonces,* At that moment. *En ese entonces sonó el timbre.* At that moment the bell rang. 10. *En esto,* a. At that moment. b. Having done [finished, said] that. *Nos regañó. En esto salió.* He scolded us. Having done that, he left the room. 11. *En estos días,* Nowadays. 12. *En las barbas de,* Right under the nose of. 13. *En lo que va del mes,* So far this month. 14. *En peligro de extinción,* Endangered. *Una especie en peligro de extinción,* An endangered species. 15. *En pie,* Under way. *Hay planes en pie para quitarlo.* There are plans under way to remove it. 16. *En primer término,* First of all. 17. *En procura de,* In search of, looking for. 18. *En resumidas palabras,* In so many words. 19. *En su fuero interno,* In one's heart. *En su fuero interno sabía que no era justo.* In his heart he knew it wasn't right. 20. *En su lugar descanso,* (Mil.) Parade rest. 21. *En todo momento,* At all times. 22. *En un abrir y cerrar de ojos,* In no time, in the twinkling of an eye (Lit.). 23. *En un principio,* At first. 24. *En vista de,* What with, in view of (Lit.). *En vista de la neblina, atardaron el vuelo.* What with the fog, they put off the flight.

Encaje [en-cah'-hay], p. 286. Add, *m.* 1. Insertion. 2. (Mech.) Housing. 3. *Encaje de la cara,* Look of one's face, set of one's features.

Encargar, [en-car-gar'], p. 287. Add, *vr.* 1. *Encargarse de,* a. To take care [charge] of. *Los maestros nos encargamos de la campaña.* We teachers are taking care of the campaign. b. To take it upon oneself to. *Se encargó de servir de nuestro guía.* He took it upon himself to act as our guide. 2. *Encargarse de que,* To see to it that. *Se encargó de que llegaran a tiempo.* He saw to it that they arrived on time.

Encasillado, da [en-cah-se-lyah-do, dah], *a.* 1. (fig.) Stereotyped. *Es una versión encasillada de lo que somos muy dueños de pensar de aquel país.* It's a stereotyped version of what we're apt to think of that country. 2. (P.R., Chile, Perú) In a checker-board pattern.

Encasillar [en-cah-se-lyar'], p. 288. Add, *va.* (fig.) To stereotype. *Es un vicio encasillar a la gente antes de llegar a conocerla.* It's a bad habit to stereotype people before getting to know them.

Encuadernación [en-coo-ah-der-nah-the-on'], p. 290. Add, *f.* 1. Book bindery. 2. *Encuadernación endurecida,* Library binding. 3. *Encuadernación en pasta,* Paper-back binding.

Encuesta [en-coo-es'-tah], p. 290. Add, *f.* 1. Investigation, inquiry. 2. (Neol.) Opinion poll. *La encuesta acarreó la revocación de una ley bizantina.* The opinion poll led to the repeal of an archaic law.

Energético [ay-ner-hay'-te-co], *m.* (Neol.) Source of energy. *Infelizmente, muchos energéticos no son renovables.* Sadly, many sources of energy are not renewable.

Enfrascar [en-fras-car'], p. 292. Add, *va.* To bottle. —*vr.* 1. *Enfrascarse en,* To throw oneself into. *Se enfrascó en el proyecto con su arrojo acostumbrado.* He threw himself into the project with his customary drive. 2. *Enfrascarse en hasta las manitas* [Mex., *hasta las chanclas*], To throw oneself wholeheartedly into.

Enfrentamiento [en-fren-tah-me-en'-to], *m.* (Neol.) Confrontation. *El enfrentamiento predisponía a muchos otros países en su contra [contra ellos].* The confrontation turned many other countries against them.

Engreir [en-gray-eer'], p. 294. Add, *va.* 1. (P.R.) To spoil. *Trate de no engreír al muchacho.* Try not to spoil the boy. 2. To turn one's head. *Tantas alabanzas te engreirán.* So much praise will turn your head.

Enlace [en-lah'-thay], p. 295. Add, *m.* 1. (r. w.) Junction. 2. *Enlace de los acontecimientos,* Timing. *En cuanto al éxito, el enlace de los acontecimientos lo dice todo.* Timing is everything where success is concerned.

Entablar [en-tah-blar'], p. 298. Add, *va.* 1. (UN ASUNTO) To take up, to introduce. 2. (LAS PIEZAS) To set on the board. 3. *Entablar discusiones,* To look for arguments. *Entabla discusiones por puro gusto.* He looks for arguments for the fun of it. —*vr.* To die down. *Se entabló el viento.* The wind died down.

Entrar [en-trar'], p. 300. Add, *vn.* 1. *Entrar de rondón en,* To burst into. *Su hermano entró de rondón en la alcoba.* Her brother burst into the bedroom. 2. *Entrar dentro de sí,* To do some soul-searching. 3. *Entrar en,* a. To come [go] into, to enter. b. (UNA CONVERSACIÓN) To engage in. 4. *Entrar en a empujones,* To press into. *La muchedumbre entró en el salón a empujones.* The crowd pressed into the room. 5. *Entrar en vigor,* To take effect. *Durante años la ley no entraba en vigor.* For years the law didn't take effect. 6. *No entrar una persona,* Not to be able to stand a person. *Ricardo no me entra.* I can't stand Richard.

Entretela [en-tray-tay'-lah], p. 301. Add, *f. Entretelas,* (fig.) Inner workings. *Es difícil identificar las entretelas del espíritu humano.* The inner workings of the human spirit are hard to identify.

Errar [er-rar'], p. 305. Add, *vn.* 1. (EL TIRO, EL GOLPE) To miss. 2. (LA ATENCIÓN) To wander. —*va.* 1. (MALOGRAR) To ruin. 2. *Errar la vocación,* To miss one's calling. —*vr.* 1. To be mistaken. 2. (DOS PERSONAS EN EL CAMINO) To miss each other. *Hubieron debido encontrarse, pero de alguna manera se erraron.* They should have met, but somehow they missed each other.

Escamotear [es-cah-mo-tay-ar'], p. 306. Add, *va.* 1. To make vanish, to spirit away. 2. (fig.) To make short shrift of, to rush through, to hurry. *Escamotearon mi solicitud.* They made short shrift of my application.

Escaño [es-cah'-nyo], p. 306. Add, *m.* Seat (in an assembly or legislature).

Escatimar [es-cah-te-mar'], p. 308. Add, *va.* 1. To skimp on, to stint on. 2. *Escatimar cortesías,* To treat coldly. *El mesonero escatimaba cortesías a sus huéspedes.* The innkeeper treated his guests coldly. 3. *Escatimar esfuerzos,* To hold back one's efforts, to do less than one's best.

Esgrimir [es-gre-meer'], p. 312. Add, *va.* (fig.) To bandy about. *Por dos horas corridas esgrimían posibles motivos por el escamoteo del ídolo.* For two whole hours, they bandied about possible reasons for the sudden disappearance of the idol.

Estación [es-tah-the-on'], p. 318. Add, *f. Estación espacial [orbital],* (Aer.) Space station. *El empleo de la estación orbital permite que el Hombre aprenda más sobre los astros sin la barrera atmosférica que le cohibe desde la Tierra.* The use of the space station allows Man to learn more about the atmospheric interference that gets in his way on earth.

Estancamiento [es-tan-cah-me-en'-to], *m.* 1. Stalemate. *El enfrentamiento provocó un estancamiento en las negociaciones.* The confrontation caused a stalemate in the negotiations. 2. (ESTATAL) State monopoly.

Estar [es-tar'], p. 319. Add, *vn.* 1. *¿A cuántos estamos?* What's today's date [the date today]? *Hoy estamos a veinte de abril.* It's the twentieth of April. 2. *Estar a,* a. To sell for. b. To abide by. *Tienes que estar a lo que él dice*. You must abide by what he says. 3. *Estar a dos velas,* To be down at the heel. 4. *Estar a la disposición de,* To be available to. *El uso de la biblioteca no está a la disposición de todos*. Use of the library is not available to everyone. 5. *Estar a la mira de,* To watch for. *Ella está a la mira de su marido*. She is watching for her husband. 6. *Estar a todo,* To take care of everything. 7. *Estar alerta,* To take care. 8. *Estar bien empleado,* To serve right. *Le está bien empleada la pérdida del libro*. It serves him right that he lost the book. 9. *Estar de común acuerdo,* To see eye to eye. 10. *Estar de más,* To be out of place. *Está de más en aquella tienda*. He is out of place in that store. 11. *Estar de muda,* To be changing one's voice. *Su hijo está de muda*. Her son's voice is changing. 12. *Estar de paseo,* To be taking a walk [stroll]. 13. *Estar de vacaciones,* To be taking a vacation [on a vacation]. 14. *Estar dentro de,* (fig.) To be part of. *Este libro está dentro de una tradición que hemos llegado a admirar.* This book is part of a tradition that we have grown to admire. 15. *Estar desocupado,* To be out of a job. 16. *Estar en la Luna [en Babia],* To be in a dream world. 17. *Estar mal,* a. (UNA PERSONA) To be sick. b. (UNA COSA) To be unbecoming, to be improper. 18. *Estar para,* To be about to. *Estoy para irme*. I'm about to go. 19. *Estar por,* To be in favor [favour, G.B.] of. *¿Estarán por la idea?* Will they be in favour of the idea? 20. *Estar volado,* To be at one's wits' end. 21. *No estar para fiestas,* To be out of sorts, to be in a bad mood.

Etapa [ay-tah'-pah], p. 324. Add, *f.* 1. Stage, level. 2. (Mil.) Staging area. 3. *Etapa de tanteos,* Beginning stages, period of trial and error. *En aquel entonces la ciencia museográfica se encontraba todavía en una etapa de tanteos*. At that time museum science was still in the beginning stages.

Excursionismo [ex-coor-se-o-nees'-mo], *m.* Touring, travel. *El excursionismo deja un recuerdo más duradero si uno tiene al menos una salpicadura del idioma del país*. Travel leaves a more lasting impression if one has at the very least a smattering of the language of the country.

Excursionista [ex-coor-se-o-nees'-tah], p. 326. Add, *m. & f.* Tripper (G.B.). *El excursionista británico tiene a la mano todos los encantos de la Europa continental*. The tripper has near at hand all the charms of Continental Europe.

Expectativa [ex-pec-tah-tee'-vah], p. 328. Add, *f.* Anticipation. *La expectativa es más que la tertulia*. Anticipation is greater than the realization. *La expectativa de un niño es la clave de las Navidades*. The anticipation of a child is the key to Christmas.

Faltar [fal-tar'], p. 332. Add, *vn.* 1. *To be short of [on], to be wanting in*. *Le falta experiencia*. He's wanting in experience. *Nos faltan libros de lectura*. We're short of [on] readers. 2. Not to measure up to expectations. *Faltaba con mucho la comedia*. The play didn't measure up to expectations at all. 3. *Faltar a,* a. To be absent from, not to go to. *Faltó a la reunión*. She didn't go to the meeting. b. To be untrue to. *El escritor faltaba a sus principios*. The writer was untrue to his principles. c. Not to keep. *Faltó a su promesa*. He didn't keep his promise. d. To be disrespectful toward. *Faltaban mucho al profesor.* They were very disrespectful toward the teacher. 4. *Faltar a la transmisión,* To miss one's connection. *Faltó a la transmisión y tuvo que trasnochar allí*. He missed his connection and had to spend the night there. 5. *Faltar poco para que,* Almost, e.g.: *Faltó poco para que muriera del frío*. She almost died of cold. 6. *Faltar un rato para que,* In a short time, e.g.: *Faltaba un rato para que el otoño los deslumbrara de nuevo*. In a short time autumn would dazzle them once more. 7. *Faltarle al respeto,* To show a lack of respect (for). *A su padre le faltaba al respeto*. He showed his father a lack of respect. *A la bandera le faltaba al respeto*. He showed a lack of respect for the flag. 8. *¡No faltaba más!* That would be the last straw! 9. *No faltaba más, sino que publicaran tal mentira*. If they published such a lie, that would be the last straw.

Falto, ta [fahl'-to; tah], p. 332. Add, *a.* 1. *Falto de,* Lacking in, short of. 2. *Falto de cohibiciones,* Uninhibited. *Me queda ver dos personas más faltas de cohibiciones. Es natural que sean paga excelente*. Two more uninhibited persons I've yet to see. Naturally they're on the best of terms.

Faltón, na [fal-tone', nah], *a.* Unreliable, undependable. *El recuento de los campos disponibles quedó bastante faltón*. The listing of the available fields turned out quite unreliable.

Fantasia [fan-tah-see'-ah], p. 333. Add, *f.* 1. The creative process. 2. *Con fantasía,* a. (Venez.) By ear. *Toca con fantasía*. He plays by ear. b. (Arg.) Really hard. *Trabajó con fantasía en el proyecto*. He worked hard on the project. 3. *De fantasía,* Fancy, elegant. 4. *Fantasía científica,* (Neol.) Science fiction. *Se acusan las diferencias entre la fantasía científica y la literatura clsíca*. The differences between science fiction and classical literature are clear-cut. 5. *Joyas de fantasía,* Costume jewelry.

Farándula [fah-rahn'-doo-lah], p. 333. Add, *f.* 1. (Neol.) Show business. 2. (fig.) Hogwash, bunkum, hooey (coll.). 3. Traveling minstrel show.

Farfullar [far-fool-lyar'], p. 334. Add, *va.* 1. (ALGO CONSTRUIDO) To throw together (fig.). *Farfullaron la casa*. They threw the house together. 2. (UN TRABAJO) To stumble through, to bungle. *Su arrastre hizo que farfullara la encomienda*. His lack of vitality made him stumble through the job.

Fetichizar [fay-te-che-thar'], *va.* (Neol.) To make a fetish of. *Algunas personas fetichizan a la juventud*. Some persons make a fetish of youth.

Ficha [fee'-chah], p. 337. Add, *f.* 1. Index [File] card. 2. Domino. 3. (COLECCIÓN DE DATOS) File. 4. *Ficha catalográfica,* Catalogue [Catalog] card. 5. *Ficha de inscripción,* Registration form. 6. *Fichas,* Credits for a film, credits for a television presentation.

Fichar [fe-char'], *va.* 1. To file. 2. (A UN JUGADOR) To sign on. 3. (EVALUAR) To size up. 4. (fig.) To put on one's list. *La fichó de atolondrada*. He put her on his list of scatterbrains. —*vn.* To punch in. *Él siempre ficha temprano*. He always punches in early.

Fichaje [fe-chah'-hay], *m.* (Neol.) Signing on. *El fichaje de los nuevos jugadores se efectuó esta mañana*. The signing on of the new players took place this morning.

Formación [for-mah-the-on'], p. 343. Add, *f.* Development, training. *La formación que él y los demás artistas recibieron sí que separó el tamo del grano*. The training that he and the other artists received really separated the wheat from the chaff.

Formalizar [for-mah-le-thar'], p. 344. Add, *va.* 1. To formalize. 2. (ENUNCIAR) To formulate. —*vr.* To take offense [offence, G.B.]. *Se formalizaron ante una supuesta descortesía por parte de los extranjeros*. They took offence at what they thought was rudeness on the part of the foreigners.

Furgoneta [foor-go-nay'-tah], *f.* (Neol.) 1. Delivery truck [van]. 2. Van. *En nuestra sociedad corrediza la furgoneta por poco llega a ser hogar*. In our mobile society the van has almost become a home.

Galardón [gah-lar-done'], p. 352. Add, *m.* Honor [Honour, G.B.], award, feather in one's cap. *El artículo era un galardón más y bien merecido*. The article was another well-deserved feather in her cap.

Ganar [gah-nar'], p. 354. Add, *va.* 1. To reach. *Ganaron la meseta*. They reached the plateau. 2. (DINERO) To earn. 3. (UNA CIUDAD) To take. 4. (A UNA PERSONA) To win over. 5. *Ganarle el campeonato a,* To put to shame. *Su regalo le ganaba el campeonato a los demás*. His gift put the others to shame. —*vn.* To improve, to get better. *El barrio está ganando*. The neighborhood is improving.

Ganga [gahn'-gah], p. 354. Add, *f.* 1. Bargain. *Íbamos de tiendas, buscando gangas*. We went from store to store looking for bargains. 2. (fig.) Cake-walk.

Geotérmico, ca [hay-o-ter'-me-co, cah], *a.* (Neol.) Geothermal. *La calefacción geotérmica es una ventaja de la vivienda subterránea*. Geothermal heating is an advantage of the underground housing unit.

Germen [herr'-men], p. 359. Add, *m.*

(fig.) Source. *Ese libro será el germen de un roce continuo entre los dos*. That book will be a source of continual friction between the two of them.

Guardar [goo-ar-dar'], p. 369. Add, *va*. 1. *Guardar cama*, To stay in bed. 2. *Guardar el secreto de algo*, To keep something a secret. 3. *Guardar miramientos*, To stand on ceremony. 4. *Guardar rencor*, To hold a grudge. 5. *Guardar silencio*, To keep quiet, to be silent.

Guardián, na [goo-ar-de-ahn',nah], p. 369. Add, *m. & f.* Lifeguard (Amer.), lifesaver (G.B.).

Hablista [ah-blees'-tah], p. 372. Add, *m. & f.* Stylist. *En sus ensayos y en sus ponencias siempre se ha considerado una hablista*. In her essays and in her addresses she has always been considered a stylist.

Hablante [ah-blahn'-tay], *m. & f.* (Neol.) Speaker. *Al hablante de español le llamaría la atención en seguida*. A Spanish speaker could tell the difference at once.

Hacer [ah-therr'], p. 373. Add, *va*. 1. To play the role of. *Siempre le fascinaba hacer el correvedile [soplón]*. He was always fascinated by (playing) the role of tattle-tale [tale-bearer]. 2. To make out to be, to think to be. *Yo le hacía de Salamanca*. I thought he was from Salamanca. Yo le hacía de Salamanca. I thought he was from Salamanca. *Yo Yo hacía a Ana*. I thought it was Ann. 3. *Hacer a un lado*, (UN PROYECTO) To set aside. *Al recibir la noticia, hicieron los dibujos a un lado en seguida*. When they got the news, they set the sketches aside at once. 4. *Hacer acto de presencia*, To put in an appearance. *Hizo acto de presencia en la fiesta*. He put in an appearance at the party. 5. *Hacer con*, To provide with. *Le hizo a su hija con un juego completo*. He provided his daughter with a complete set. 6. *Hacer cuentas*, To keep accounts [an account]. *Hace cuentas de todas sus ganancias y pérdidas*. He keeps an account of all his earnings and losses. 7. *Hacer disparar*, To set off. *Harán disparar la dinamita a la una*. They'll set off the dynamite at one o'clock. 8. *Hacer donaire de*, To make light of. *Hacíamos donaire de nuestros apuros*. We would make light of our troubles. 9. *Hacer el oso*, (coll.) To make out (coll.). *La pareja estaba sentada en el parque, haciendo el oso*. The couple sat making out in the park. 10. *Hacer gala de*, To demonstrate. *Su conversación hace gala de amplios conocimientos*. His conversation demonstrates wide knowledge. 11. *Hacer la vista gorda*, To look the other way (fig.). *Hicieron la vista gorda en vez de ayudarle*. They looked the other way instead of helping him. 12. *Hacer las amistades*, To make up, to become reconciled. 13. *Hacer las delicias de*, To delight. *Hacía las delicias de sus amigos con dichos salados en todas sus tarjetas*. She delighted her friends with clever sayings on all her cards. 14. *Hacer mella*, To make a strong impression. *Sus maestros siempre le hacían mella*. His teachers always made a strong impression on him. 15. *Hacer mutis*, (fig.) To drop out of the conversation. *Hizo mutis casi inmediatamente*. He dropped out of the conversation almost at once. 16. *Hacer presente*, To put in mind of. *Eso me hace presente la fiesta*. That puts me in mind of the party. 17. *Hacer proa a*, To head into. *Hicieron proa directa a la tormenta*. They headed right into the storm. 18. *Hacer un nuevo aparte en*, To approach in a new way. *Es preciso que hagamos un nuevo aparte en el estudio de los idiomas extranjeros*. We must approach the study of foreign languages in a new way. 19. *Hacer una maleta*, To pack a suitcase. 20. *Hacer una pregunta*, To ask a question. 21. *Hacer vida de*, To lead the life of. 22. *Hacerle tilín en la mente*, (coll.) To ring a bell in one's mind. *Su nombre me hizo tilín en la mente*. Her name rang a bell in my mind. 23. *No hacer remilgos a*, To make no bones about. *No hace remilgos a los años que tiene*. She makes no bones about her age.

Hacerse [ah-therr'-say], p. 374. Add, *vr*. 1. To turn into. *Se ha hecho un aguafiestas acabado*. He's turned into a real spoilsport. 2. To take. *Se hacen dos horas para desmontarlo*. It takes two hours to take it down. 3. *Hacerse a la mar*, To put out to sea. 4. *Hacerse al camino*, To set off. *Se hicieron al camino muy de mañana*. They set off early in the morning. 5. *Hacerse cargo de*, To take charge of, to see to it that. *El maestro se encargó de que su sueño se volviera realidad*. The teacher saw to it that her dream became a reality.

Halo [ah'-lo], p. 374. Add, *m*. 1. (fig.) Atmosphere, air. *Trae consigo cierto halo de encanto*. She brings a certain air of enchantment with her. 2. (Arch.) Nimbus.

Heliopila [ay-le-o-pee'-lah], *f*. (Aer.) Solar cell. *Se supone que las heliopilas provean la electricidad necesaria para ciertos dispositivos a bordo de la unidad*. Solar cells are supposed to provide the electricity needed for certain equipment on board the craft.

Hidrospacio [e-dros-pah'-the-o], *m*. (Neol.) Hydrospace. *El hidrospacio y el aerospacio son las dos nuevas fronteras del mañana*. Hydrospace and aerospace are the two new frontiers of tomorrow.

Hilar [e-lar'], p. 381. Add, *va*. 1. *Hilar muy delgado en*, To be too choosy about. *En lo de un empleo él hilaba muy delgado*. He was too choosy about a job. 2. *Hilar muy fino en*, To be a past master at. *Hila muy fino en engañar el tiempo*. She's a past master at wasting time.

¡**Hola**! [oh'-lah], p. 383. Add, *int*. 1. Hello! 2. (ADMIRACIÓN) What have we here!

Hontanar [on-tah-nar'], p. 385. Add, *m. (fig.) Source*. *Tal nombramiento será hontanar de roce continuo*. Such an appointment will be a source of continual friction.

Horario [o-rah'-re-o], p. 385. Add, *m*. 1. Timetable. 2. *Con horario completo*, Full time. *Está buscando un destino con horario completo*. He is looking for a full-time position. 3. *Horario escolar*, School day. *El horario escolar es de seis horas*. The school day is six hours long.

Humanista [oo-mah-nees'-tah], p. 388. Add, *m. & f.* Humanitarian. *El humanista se dedica al desarrollo del prójimo*. The humanitarian devotes himself to the development of his fellow man.

Huso [oo'-so], p. 389. Add, *m*. *Huso horario*, Time zone. *Los husos horarios no pueden más que aproximar la hora del Sol*. Time zones can only approximate sun time.

Ilustración [e-loos-trah-the-on'], p. 391. Add, *f*. (Lit.) Enlightenment. *Los cimientos de la Ilustración se fincaron en el Renacimiento*. The foundations of the Enlightenment were established in the Renaissance.

Ilustrativo, va [e-loos-trah-tee'-vo, vah], *a*. (Neol.) Graphic. *Nos dio una relación ilustrativa de los acontecimientos que acarrearon la huelga*. He gave us a graphic account of the events that led up to the strike.

Imán [e-mahn'], p. 391. Add, *m*. (calidad llamativa) *Quality, i.e.*: *Imán de compra*, Quality that attracts buyers. *Imán de estudio*, Quality that attracts students. *Esa universidad es un imán de estudio*. That university has a certain quality that attracts students.

Impartir [im-par-teer'], p. 392. Add, *va*. (Mex.) 1. To teach. *Imparte cuatro clases todos los días*. He teaches four classes every day. 2. *Impartir en comitiva*, To team-teach. 3. *Impartir una conferencia*, To deliver a lecture.

Implantar [im-plan-tar'], p. 393. Add, *va*. *(UNA COSTUMBRE) To introduce*. 2. *Implantar acciones*, To take steps. *Deberíamos implantar acciones para que nunca acaiga otra desgracia tal*. We should take steps so that such a misfortune will never take place again.

Impulsar [im-pool-sar'], p. 394. Add, *va*. (Neol.) To make go [run]. *¿Qué impulsa el aeromodelo*? What makes the model plane go?

Indicado, da [in-de-cah'-do, dah], *a*. Right. *Es la persona indicada para el empleo*. He's the right person for the job.

Indocumentado, da [in-do-coo-mentah'-do, dah], *m. & f.* (Neol.) Illegal alien. *El indocumentado da en rostro a las leyes del país donde reside*. The illegal alien flies in the face of the laws of the country where he resides.

Informática [in-for-mah'-te-cah], *f*. (Neol.) 1. Data processing. 2. Information science. *Muchas investigadores se hacen lenguas de la informática; otros tantos titubean en apoyarla rotundamente*. Many researchers are praising information science to the sky; an equal number hesitate to support it fully.

Infraestructura [in-frah-es-trooc-too′-rah], p. 401. Add, *f.* (Neol.) Economic base. *La infraestructura de la productividad industrial del país tiene que ser sólida para aguantar reveses temporáneos*. The economic base of a country's industrial productivity must be strong in order for it to weather temporary setbacks [reversals].

Inoperante [in-o-pay-rahn′-tay], *a.* Inoperative. *Se afanaban por lograr éxito con la empresa a pesar de las células de combustible inoperantes*. They struggled to make the mission a success despite the inoperative fuel cells.

Insalubridad [in-sah-loo-bre-dahd′], p. 404. Add, *f.* Poor sanitary conditions, lack of sanitary conditions. *Su cara se descompuso al ver la insalubridad*. His face fell when he saw the poor sanitary conditions.

Instrumentar [ins-troo-men-tar′], *va.* (Neol.) To put into effect. *Instrumentaron la nueva ley*. They put the new law into effect.

Interfaz [in-ter-fath′], *f.* (Neol.) Interface. *La interfaz entre los trabajadores y los dirigentes no debe ser una comarca de murallas y enajenamiento*. The interface between workers and management should not be a region of walls and estrangement.

Intervalo [in-ter-vah′-lo], p. 408. Add, *m. Intervalo de lanzamiento,* (Aer.) Launch window. *Sabían de sobra lo cerrado que era el intervalo de lanzamiento*. They knew only too well how narrow the launch window was.

Involucrar [in-vo-loo-crar′], p. 410. Add, *va.* To involve. —*vr.* To get involved. *Se involucró en el mundo de la vida galante*. He got involved with the demi-monde.

Ir [eer], p. 410. Add, *vn.* 1. To suit. *El libro no le va*. The book doesn't suit him. 2. To fare, to be. *¿Cómo va usted?* How are you (faring)? 3. To be. *De hoy a la boda van dos meses*. The wedding is two months from today. 4. To be there. *Entre la estación y el museo van dos calles*. There are two streets between the station and the museum. 5. (Arith.) To leave. *Ocho a doce van cuatro*. Eight from twelve leaves four. 6. *A eso voy*. That's what I'm driving at. 7. *¡Allá va (eso)!* Look out below! 8. *Ir a más,* To increase. *Los quehaceres disponibles van a más rápidamente*. The activities available are increasing rapidly. 9. *Ir al grano,* To get down to brass tacks, to get [come] to the point. 10. *Ir con,* (fig.) To go along with. *En eso voy contigo*. I go along with you on that. 11. *Ir con cuidado,* To proceed with caution. 12. *Ir de vacaciones,* To take a vacation, to go on a vacation. 13. *Ir en,* To be at stake in, to depend on. *En el resultado va su carrera*. His career depends on the outcome. 14. *Ir por partes,* To go into detail. 15. *Ya irás viendo*. You'll see what I mean.

Jalonar [hah-lo-nar′], *va.* 1. To stake out. *El señor Washington jalonó el solar*. Mr. Washington staked out the property. 2. (fig.) To mark. *Hoy jalona dos años de mejora sostenida*. Today marks two years of continued improvement.

Jornada [hor-nah′-dah], p. 415. Add, *f.* 1. (PERÍODO DE LUZ) Day. 2. Workday. 3. *En jornadas parciales,* Part time. *A su mujer le sería muy valioso un empleo [trabajo] en jornadas parciales*. A part-time job for his wife would be very helpful.

Juego [hoo-ay′-go], p. 416. Add, *m.* 1. *Juegos de manos,* Horseplay. *Los juegos de manos dentro de o cerca de la piscina son enteramente prohibidos*. Horseplay in or near the pool is strictly forbidden. 2. *Juegos malabares,* Contortions. *Sus juegos malabares al tratar de servirse de los palillos chinos eran cómicos*. Her contortions were comical when she tried to use the chopsticks.

Libertad [le-ber-tahd′], p. 428. Add, *f.* 1. *Libertad de culto,* Freedom of worship. 2. *Libertad de imprenta,* Freedom of the press. 3. *Libertad de reunión,* Freedom of assembly. 4. *Libertad del espíritu,* Mind over matter.

Librar [le-brar′], p. 428. Add, *va.* (UN ATAQUE) To launch. *Libraron una campaña de odio contra ellos*. They launched a hate campaign against them.

Licenciatura [le-then-the-ah-too′-rah], p. 428, Add, *f.* 1. Undergraduate degree. 2. Studies for the undergraduate degree. 3. *Años de licenciatura,* Undergraduate years. 4. *Estudios de licenciatura,* Undergraduate studies. (NOTE: THE **Licenciatura** IS APPROXIMATELY THE EQUIVALENT OF AN AMERICAN BACHELOR'S DEGREE IN YEARS OF STUDY.)

Lineamiento [le-nay-ah-me-en′-to], p. 430. Add, *f.* 1. Outline. *En el trasfondo se vislumbraba el lineamiento de una montaña*. In the distance the outline of a mountain was barely visible. 2. (Neol.) Guideline. *¿Cuáles son los lineamientos que se han establecido para el presupuesto?* What guidelines have been set for the budget? (NOTE: THIS NEW USAGE AVOIDS THE CONFUSION OF **norma** WITH ITS MORE COMMON MEANING.)

Lo [lo], p. 432. Add, *indef. pron.* 1. *Lo mismo* + verb + *que,* Both, e.g.: *Lo mismo se reían que se lloraban de la noticia*. They both laughed and cried at the news. 2. How, e.g.: *Me sorprende lo mucho que sabe*. I am surprised at how much he knows. 3. The part, e.g.: *Lo mejor,* The best part. *Lo difícil,* The hard part.

Locución [lo-coo-the-on′], p. 432. Add, *f. Locución verbal,* Phrasal verb. *En inglés la locución verbal puede ser un traspié acusado para la persona de habla española*. The phrasal verb in English can be a real pitfall for the Spanish speaker.

Lucimiento [loo-the-me-en′-to], p. 433. Add, *m.* 1. Display, showing to advantage. 2. *Poco lucimiento,* Poor showing. *Su poco lucimiento en el festejo de arte le costó muchas ventas*. His poor showing at the art fair cost him many sales.

Luminotecnia [loo-me-no-tec′-ne-ah], *f.* (Theat.) Lighting. *La alharaca respecto de la luminotecnia era colosal*. The hue and cry about the lighting was enormous.

Luminotécnico, ca [loo-me-no-tec′-ne-co, cah], *a.* (Theat.) Lighting. *Las inovaciones luminotécnicas han robustecido el teatro*. Lighting innovations have strengthened the theatre.

Llegar [lyay-gar′], p. 435. Add, *vn.* 1. (VERBO AUXILIAR PARA INDICAR EL TIEMPO) To begin, e.g.: *Llegar a creer,* To begin to think. *Después de tantos años, sus amigos llegaron a creer que se había olvidado de ellos*. After so many years her friends began to think she had forgotten them. *Al fin y al cabo llegué a sentirme mejor*. At long last I began to feel better. *Llegó a desempeñarse cuerdamente*. He began to come to grips with himself. 2. *No llegar a,* Not to measure up to. *La secuela no llega a la obra original*. The sequel doesn't measure up to the original work.

Llevar [lyay-var′], p. 435. Add, *va.* 1. To be + quantity + comp. a. [adv.], e.g.: *Me lleva dos años*. He is two years older than I (am). *Este velero le lleva dos nudos al otro*. This sailboat is two knots ahead of the other. 2. To have been, e.g.: *Llevan dos meses en San Juan*. They have been in San Juan for two months. 3. To have on, to wear. *¿Qué traje llevaba?* What suit did he have on? 4. (UNA CUENTA) To keep. *Él lleva los libros de la casa*. He keeps the books for the firm. 5. To take. *¿Me puedes llevar allá?* Can you take me there? 6. (UNA VIDA) To lead. 7. To put up with, to tolerate. *Ella no le lleva*. She can't put up with him. (NÓTESE QUE SE AÑADE EL VERBO AUXILIAR **can** EN INGLÉS.) 8. *Llevar a cabo,* To go through with, to carry to completion [out]. *Nunca lleva a cabo nada*. He never goes through with anything. 9. *Llevar a la casa de uno,* To bring by. *¿Por qué no la llevas a mi casa mañana?* Why don't you bring her by tomorrow? 10. *Llevar adelante,* To carry on with. *Yo solo puedo llevar adelante el proyecto*. I can carry on with the project alone. 11. *Llevar de la mano,* To take by the hand. 12. *Llevar la contraria,* To take the opposite point of view. 13. *Llevar vida solitaria,* To keep to oneself. 14. *Llevarse los ojos,* To attract attention. *Nos llevaremos menos los ojos si echamos de esta parte*. We will attract less attention if we go this way.

Maletín [mah-le-teen′], p. 440. Add, *m.* 1. Attaché case. 2. *Maletín de grupa,* (Mil.) Saddlebag.

Malinchismo [mah-len-chees′-mo], *m.* Cult of things foreign. *Un complejo de inferioridad conduce al malinchismo*. An inferiority complex leads to a cult of things foreign.

Malinchista [mah-len-chees'-tah], *m.* & *f.* Follower of a cult of things foreign. *El malinchista nunca echa mano de la voz indígena si puede servirse de un término extranjero*. The follower of a cult of things foreign never makes use of an indigenous term if he can avail himself of a foreign one.

Mantener [man-tay-nerr'], p. 444. Add, *va*. 1. (CONTINUAR) To keep up. 2. (PARA QUE NO SE CAIGA) To hold up, to support. 3. *Mantener algo en secreto*, To keep something a secret. *Mantenían en secreto su paradero*. They kept his whereabouts a secret. 4. *Mantener el secreto para*, To keep a secret from. *Es difícil mantener el secreto para ella*. It's hard to keep a secret from her.

Maqueta [mah-kay'-tah], *f.* 1. Model, reproduction in miniature. *Una maqueta en el Zócalo presenta el esplendor de la antigua Tenochtitlan*. A model in the Zocalo shows the magnificence of ancient Tenochtitlan. 2. (typ.) Dummy. *La maqueta exhibe el ordenamiento del libro*. The dummy shows the arrangement of the book. (NOTE: **Maqueta** IS A BORROWING FROM ITALIAN **machietta.**)

Marcador, ra [mar-cah-dor', rah], *m.* & *f.* 1. Title holder. 2. *Marcador [Marcadora] global*, World title holder. —*m*. Scoreboard. —*a*. Designating, indicating.

Marcar [mar-car'], p. 446. Add, *va*. 1.(DEPORTE) To score. 2. (EL NÚMERO) To dial. 3. *Marcar su acento sobre*, To stress. *Favor de marcar su acento sobre la segunda sílaba*. Please stress the second syllable.

Marchamo [mar-chah'-mo], p. 446. Add, *m.* (fig.) Hallmark. *El éxito que ella ha logrado es un marchamo de la mujer en gira*. The success that she has attained is a hallmark of a woman on the go.

Marginado, da [mar-he-nah'-do, dah], p. 446. Add, *m.* & *f. Marginado [Marginada] (social)*, Second-class citizen. *Muchas veces el marginado social no existe sino en el concepto del observador.* The second-class citizen often exists only in the eye of the beholder.

Mascota [mas-co'-tah], p. 448. Add, *f.* 1. Good-luck charm. 2. (Neol.) Pet. *Tenía dos mascotas, una tortuga y una lagartija*. He had two pets, a turtle and a small lizard.

Matizado, da [mah-te-thah'-do, dah], p. 449. Add, *a*. 1. Blended, shaded. 2. *No matizado*, (fig.) Unvarnished. *Una relación no matizada de los hechos le devolvería la sangre fría*. An unvarnished report of the facts would restore her composure.

Medio, dia [may'-de-o, ah], p. 451. Add, *a*. 1. Mean, average. 2. (central) Middle. 3. *Media naranja*, (coll.) Second self. *En la calle topé con mi media naranja*. In the street I ran into my second self. 4. *Medio perfil*, Half profile. 5. *Término medio*, Average.

Medio [may'-de-o], p. 452. Add, *m*. 1. (ENTRE EXTREMOS) Mean. 2. *Medio ambiente*, (Neol.) Environment. *Gozar del medio ambiente es un acervo de todo ciudadano*. To enjoy the environment is a birthright of every citizen. 3. *Medio embrague*, (Mech.) Riding the clutch. 4. *Medios informativos*, (Neol.) a. Communications. b. Information media. *Dentro de poco los medios informativos le buscaron la boca*. The information media soon drew him out.

Memoria [may-mo'-re-ah], p. 453. Add, *f*. 1. *Aprender de memoria*, To learn by heart. 2. *Memoria lasérica*, (Neol.) Laser memory. *La memoria lasérica recupera los datos mediante un rayo lasérico*. Laser memory collects data by means of a laser beam. 3. *Memorias*, Regards. 4. *Ser flaco de memoria*, To have a poor [weak] memory.

Mentir [men-teer'], p. 454. Add, *va*. (AL DECIR ALGO) To make a mistake. *Perdóneme. Mentí. Sale a la una*. I'm sorry. I made a mistake. It departs at one.

Meter [may-terr'], p. 456. Add, *va*. 1. To insert, to thrust. *Metí la moneda en la ranura*. I inserted the coin into the slot. 2. *Meter enredos*, To sow discord. 3. *Meter la cuchara [la pata]*, To put one's foot in it. 4. *Meter miedo*, To spread fear. 5. *Meter raya a*, To bring to an end. *Hay que meter raya a esta barahúnda*. We must bring this hurlyburly to an end. 6. *Meter ruido*, To raise a ruckus (coll.), to make a fuss (coll.). —*vr*. 1. To go. *Se metieron en la selva*. They went into the jungle. 2. *Meterse de*, To become. *Se metió de hazmerreír*. He became a clown.

Microcomputadora [me-cro-com-poo-tah-do'-rah], *f*. (Neol.) Microcomputer. *La microcomputadora ha mejorado la manera de proyectar el presupuesto familiar de muchos hogares*. The microcomputer has improved the way many households plan the family budget.

Microelectrónica [me-cro-ay-lec-tro'-ne-cah], *f*. (Neol.) Microelectronics. *La miniaturización del dispositivo es producto de la microelectrónica*. Miniaturized elements are a result of microelectronics.

Microlasca [me-cro-lahs'-cah], *f*. (Neol.) Microchip. *En cada microlasca se estampa gran número de circuitos*. A large number of circuits are imprinted on each microchip.

Minusvalido, da [me-noos-vah-lee'-do, dah], *m.* & *f.* (Neol.) Handicapped person. *Actualmente muchos autobuses son provistos de asientos especiales para los minusvalidos*. Many buses now provide special seats for handicapped persons. —*a*. Handicapped.

Mirar [me-rar'], p. 460. Add, *va*. 1. *Bien mirado*, All things considered. 2. *Mirar bien*, To think well of. *Miraba bien a su prima*. He thought well of his cousin. 3. *Mirar con buenos ojos*, To look favorably [kindly] upon. *Miraban su petición con buenos ojos*. They looked favorably upon his request. 4. *Mirar de hito en hito*, To gaze [stare] at. 5. *Mirar de reojo*, a. To look out of the corner of one's eye at. b. (fig.) To look askance at. 6. *Mirar hacia el otro lado*, To look the other way. *Miré hacia el otro lado y vi el pueblo*. I looked the other way toward the town. 7. *Mirar por*, To watch out for. *Miraba por su abuela con mucha atención*. He watched out carefully for his grandmother. 8. *Mirar por encima*, To glance at [over]. *Miraban mis notas por encima*. They were glancing at my notes. 9. *Mirarle a los ojos*, a. (CON TERNURA) To look into someone's eyes. b. (FIJADAMENTE) To look someone in the eye. ¡*Mírame a los ojos al decir eso*! Look me in the eye when you say that! 10. *Mirarse en*, To think over [reflect on] carefully. *Hay que mirarse mucho en la decisión*. We must think the decision over very carefully. 11. *Quien más mira, menos ve*. He who looks too closely at the trees misses the forest.

Mostrenco, ca [mos-tren'-co, cah], p. 467. Add, *a*. (fig.) Heavy-handed. *Su ensayo quedó deformado por un estillo mostrenco*. His essay was flawed by a heavy-handed style.

Muda [moo'-dah], p. 468. Add, *f*. (*DE UNA CASA EN OTRA*) *Move*. *Se hizo un mes para la muda*. The move took a month.

Mudar [moo-dar'], p. 468. Add, *vr*. 1. To turn over a new leaf. *Después de su jubilación, se mudó*. After his retirement he turned over a new leaf. 2. *Mudarse a*, To move to. *Se mudaron a San Antonio el año pasado*. They moved to San Antonio last year. 3. *Mudarse de casa*, To move. *Se mudaron de casa el mes pasado*. They moved last month. 4. *Mudarse de ropa*, To change clothes [clothing].

Multiplicar [mool-te-ple-car'], p. 470. Add, *va*. (fig.) To expand. *Un esfuerzo tenaz les ayudó a multiplicar rápidamente su mercado*. Serious effort helped them expand their market rapidly.

Muralismo [moo-rah-lees'-mo], *m*. (Neol.) Mural art. *El muralismo embellece muchos monumentos públicos*. Mural art beautifies many public buildings.

Museografía [moo-say-o-grah-fee'-ah], *f*. Museum science. Últimamente la museografía ha mejorado enormemente. Lately museum science has improved a great deal.

Muy [moo'-e], p. 471. Add, *adv*. 1. Too. *Él es muy inexperto para tal responsabilidad*. He's too inexperienced for such a responsibility. 2. *Muy de mañana*, Early in the morning. 3. *Muy de noche*, Late at night.

Nadar [nah-dar'], p. 472. Add, *vn*. *Nadar entre dos aguas*, To walk a dangerous line.

Norma [nor'-mah], p. 477. Add, *f*. 1. Norm, control. 2. *Normas de calidad*, Quality controls. *Las normas de calidad aseguran que el cliente esté satisfecho*. Quality controls assure satisfied customers.

Nutrido, da [noo-tree'-do, dah], *a*. 1. Well-stocked. *Tiene una biblioteca* *nutrida*. He has a well-stocked library. 2. Copious. *Tomó apuntes nutridos*. She took copious notes. 3. Substantial, solid. *Tiene un fundamento nutrido en ello*. (NOTE: A LITERARY BORROWING FROM RENAISSANCE ITALIAN **nutrito.**)

Obedecer [o-bay-day-therr′], p. 480. Add, *vn*. *Obedecer a*, To arise from, to be the result of. *La situación actual obedece a una cadena de enfrentamientos*. The present situation is the result of a series of confrontations.

Obrar [o-brar′], p. 481. Add, *va*. *Obrar en serio*, To get down to business. *Después del recreo tuvieron que obrar en serio*. After recess they had to get down to business.

Oído [o-ee′-do], p. 483. Add, *m*. 1. Attention, interest. *Era difícil captar el oído del público*. It was hard to get the attention of the audience. 2. *Abrir tanto oído*, To be all ears. 3. *Aguzar los oídos*, To prick up one's ears. 4. *Al oído de*, To come to the attention of, e.g.: *Las noticias se publicaron al oído de unos cuantos*. The publication of the news came to the attention of only a few. *El buque se perdió al oído de casi todo el mundo*. The loss of the ship came to the attention of almost everyone. 5. *Dar oídos*, To listen favorably [favourably, G.B.]. *Los alumnos deban oídos al ponente*. The students listened favourably to the speaker. 6. *Hacer oídos de mercader*, To turn a deaf ear to. 7. *Llegar al oído de*, To come to the attention of. *Llegar al oído del pueblo entero*. The injustice came to the attention of the whole town. 8. *Negar los oídos a*, To refuse to listen to. *¿Así que negaste los oídos a otras mentiras más?* So you refused to listen to more lies? 9. *Pegarse al oído*, To stick in one's memory. *La canción se le pegó al oído*. The song stuck in her memory.

¡Ojalá! [o-hah-lah′], p. 484. Add, *int*. Amen to that!

Oportunamente [o-por-too-nah-men′-tay], p. 486. Add, *adv*. At the right time. *Veo que he llegado oportunamente*. I see that I arrived at the right time.

Órbita [or′-be-tah], p. 486. Add, *f*. 1. (DEL OJO) Socket. 2. *Órbita temporal*, (Aer.) Parking orbit.

Ordenador, ra [or-day-nah-dor′, rah], p. 487. 1. Arranger. 2. (Com.) Comptroller, auditor. 3. *Ordenador de datos*, (Neol.) Data processor.

Orientador, ra [o-re-en-tah-dor′, rah], *m. & f.* (Neol.) Guidance counselor. *Muchas veces los orientadores pueden ayudar a los alumnos a escoger la carrera indicada para ellos*. Guidance counselors can often help students choose the right career. —*a*. Guiding, giving one's bearings.

Palabra [pah-lah′-brah], p. 491. Add, *f*. *Palabras blancas*, Empty [idle] words. *Todo lo que dijo eran palabras blancas*. Everything that he said was idle words.

Parecido [pah-ray-thee′-do], *m*. 1. Likeness, resemblance. 2. *Escaso parecido*, Poor likeness. *En el lienzo se veía un escaso parecido del modelo*. The canvas showed a poor likeness of the model.

Pagar [pah-gar′], p. 490. Add, *va*. 1. *Pagarla con*, To take it out on. *Se la pagaba con una actitud resentida*. He took it out on her with a hurt attitude. 2. *Pagarle en su propia moneda*, To get back at. *Él procuró pagarle en su propia moneda por lo que ella le había hecho*. He tried to get back at her for what she had done to him.

Parque [par′-kay], p. 498. Add, *m*. 1. (DE UNA CASA) Gardens. 2. *Parque de diversiones*, Amusement park. 3. *Parque industrial*, Industrial park. *El parque industrial es el recinto de gran número de los adelantos técnicos que jalonan el desarrollo de la nación moderna*. The industrial park is the scene of a great number of the technical advances that mark the growth of a modern nation. 4. *Parque zoológico*, Zoo.

Parquear [par-kay-ar′], *va*. (Amer.) To park.

Parquímetro [par-kee′-may-tro], *m*. (Neol.) Parking meter. *El parquímetro parece tragaperras al automovilista que no trae moneda*. The parking meter looks like a one-armed bandit to the motorist who doesn't have any change.

Parteaguas [par-tay-ah′-goo-ahs], *m*. Turning point, watershed. *El parteaguas para el gobierno era una reordenación en orden descendiente*. The turning point for the government was a restructuring from top to bottom.

Pasada [pah-sah′-dah], p. 499. Add, *f*. 1. (DE NAIPES) Game. 2. (DE PÁJAROS) Flight. 3. *Mala pasada*, (coll.) Dirty trick, underhanded thing to do. 4. *Pasada en vuelo*, (Aer.) Flyby. *La pasada en vuelo de un planeta permite la observación detenida de las características de su superficie*. The flyby of a planet permits a close inspection of the features of its surface.

Pasar [pah-sar′], p. 500. Add, *vn*. *Pasar por las horcas caudinas de*, To put up with the nightmare of. *Todos tuvieron que pasar por las horcas caudinas de unos chismes apabullantes*. They all had to put up with the nightmare of devastating gossip. —*va*. 1. To take [carry] across. *Los pasaron en dos balsas*. They took them across on two rafts. 2. (UN RÍO) To go across. *Pasaron la Magdalena cerca de aquí*. They went across the Magdalena near here. 3. (UNA LECCIÓN) To review, to study. 4. To transmit, to send. *Le pasé la copia ayer*. I sent him a copy yesterday. 5. To swallow. *No puede pasar la carne*. He can't swallow the meat. 6. To leave behind, to pass up [by]. *Hemos pasado a toda la concurrencia*. We've passed by all the competition. 7. *Pasar a máquina*, To type (up). *¿Pasaste a máquina el borrador?* Did you type up the rough copy? 8. *Pasar a nado*, To swim across. 9. *Pasar a vuelo*, To fly across. 10. *Pasar de largo*, To pass by. *Todas las parejas la pasaron de largo*. All the partners passed her by. 11. *Pasar sudores*, To have a bad time of it [a terrible time]. *Pasé sudores tratando de abrir la ventana*. I had a terrible time trying to open the window [get the window open]. 12. *Pasarle por las mientes*, To cross one's mind. *Nunca le pasó por las mientes desatar el paquete*. It never crossed her mind to untie the parcel. 13. *Pasarse sin*, To get along without. *Se pasa sin la ayuda de ellos*. She's getting along without their help. 14. *Pasárselas*, To get along, to made do. *Me las paso bastante bien*. I'm getting along pretty well.

Patriotería [pah-tre-o-tay-ree′-ah], *f*. Jingoism, chauvinism toward one's country.

Pensar [pen-sar′], p. 508. Add, *va*. 1. To think about [of]. *Piensa un número de uno a diez*. Think of a number from one to ten. 2. *Pensar bien*, To think over. *Piensa bien lo que vas a decir*. Think over what you are going to say. 3. *Pensar de nuevo*, To think better of. *Lo pensó de nuevo y durmió hasta tarde*. He thought better of it and slept late. —*vn*. 1. *Pensar con acierto*, To think straight. *Hay tanto bullicio que no pienso con acierto*. There's so much noise that I can't think straight. 2. *Pensar en*, To think of. *Siempre piensa en el tiempo venidero*. He always thinks of times to come.

Pesar [pay-sar′], p. 513. Add, *vn*. 1. To regret. *Tu decisión te pesará*. You'll regret your decision. 2. To be brought to bear. *Si no pesan sus ideas, el plan fracasará por completo*. If his ideas aren't brought to bear, the plan will fail utterly. 3. To weigh heavily on. *Mi decisión me pesa mucho*. My decision really weighs heavily on me. 4. *Hacer pesar*, To bring to bear. *Hay que hacer pesar el sentido común*. We must bring some common sense to bear. 5. *Pese a quien pese*, Regardless of what anyone says about it, come what may.

Picado, da [pe-cah′-do, dah], p. 515. Add, *a*. (MAR) Choppy. *El pronóstico indica mar ligeramente picado para la tarde*. The forecast is for slightly choppy seas by this afternoon.

Picar [pe-car′], p. 515. Add, *va*. 1. (UNA CULEBRA) To bite. 2. (UNA ABEJA) To sting. 3. (UN LIBRO) To open at random. 4. *Picar en*, a. To dabble in. b. To border on (fig.). *Su actitud pica en insubordinación*. His attitude borders on insubordination. 5. *Picar en historia*, To be legendary. *Su ademán poroso pica en historia*. His open manner is legendary.

Pila [pee′-lah], p. 517. Add, *f*. 1. (DE UN PUENTE) Pier. 2. *Pila atómica*, Atomic pile. 3. *Pila solar*, (Aer.) Solar cell.

Pintar [pin-tar′], p. 518. Add, *vn*. *Pintar en*, (fam.) To have to do with. *Y tú, ¿qué pintas en eso?* And what do you have to do with that?

Pista [pees′-tah], p. 519. Add, *f*. 1.

(DE UN CIRCO) Ring. 2. *Pista de carreras*, Running track. 3. *Pista de descenso*, Ski slope [run]. 4. *Pista de patinaje*, Skating rink. 5. *Pista de salto*, Jumping course.

Planificación [plah-ne-fe-cah-the-on′], p. 520. Add, *f.* 1. *Planificación familiar*, Family planning. *El motivo de la planificación familiar protagonizaba el congreso*. The theme of family planning dominated the convention. 2. *Planificación urbana*, City planning.

Plano [plah′-no], p. 520. Add, *m.* 1. (DE UNA CIUDAD) Map. 2. *Plano hidrodinámico*, (Neol.) Hydrofoil. *El plano hidrodinmico facilita movimiento rápido sobre la superficie del agua*. A hydrofoil allows rapid movement over the water's surface. 3. *Plano muy corto*, (Phot.) Closeup. 4. *Primer plano*, Foreground.

Planteamiento [plan-tay-ah-me-en′-to], *m.* Stance. *El planteamiento que usó era inderrocable*. The stance he took was unshakable.

Plantear [plan-tay-ar′], *va.* 1. To outline, to state. 2. To take up, to consider. *Luego planteamos esa cuestión*. We took up that question next.

Plantel [plan-tel′], p. 521. Add, *m.* 1. (Mex.) Learning center [centre, G.B.]. 2. (DE ARTISTAS) Proving ground. *San Miguel de Allende es un plantel para el pintor*. San Miguel de Allende is a proving ground for painters. 3. Workshop.

Plasmar [plas-mar′], p. 521. Add, *va.* (UNA IMAGEN) To capture. *El artista plasmaba con mucho tino el colorido de las montañas*. The artist captured the coloring [colouring, G.B.] of the mountains very skillfully [skilfully, G.B.].

Polución [po-loo-the-on′], p. 524. Add, *f. Polución ambiental*, Environmental pollution. *La polución ambiental le quita belleza al paisaje*. Environmental pollution detracts from the beauty of the landscape.

Ponencia [po-nen′-the-ah], p. 525. Add, *f. (Neol.)* Speech, report. *Se hizo toda la tarde para las ponencias*. The reports took the whole afternoon. (NOTE: THIS NEW USAGE AVOIDS THE CONFUSION OF **discurso** AND **charla** WITH THEIR OTHER MEANINGS.)

Ponente [po-nen′-tay], *m. & f.* (Neol.) Speaker. *En el congreso participaron cien ponentes*. One hundred speakers took part in the convention.

Poner [po-nerr′], p. 525. Add, *va.* 1. (LA LUZ) To turn on. 2. To make. *Él me puso furioso*. He made me furious. 3. To spend. *Puso dos días en ello*. He spent two days on it. 4. *Poner a prueba*, To put to the test. *La crisis puso a prueba su encumbramiento*. The crisis put his rise to power to the test. 5. *Poner al corriente*, To inform. *Me pusieron al corriente de la pérdida*. They informed me of the loss. 6. *Poner bien a*, To rehabilitate, to restore to one's good graces. 7. *Poner de manifiesto*, (Lit.) To make known. 8. *Poner el grito en el cielo*, To bay at the moon. 9. *Poner en las nubes*, To praise to the skies. 10. *Poner en la picota del pasquín*, (fig.) To pillory. *Los periódicos pusieron en la picota del pasquín su actuación de Sempronio*. The newspapers pilloried his performance of Sempronio. 11. *Poner freno a*, To keep in check [under control]. *La mejor manera de poner freno a los gastos es el presupuesto*. A budget is the best way to keep expenses under control. 12. *Poner la mesa*, To set the table. 13. *Poner sitio a*, To lay siege to. 14. *Poner una pica en Flandes*, To make one's [a] point. *¡Pusiste tu pica en Flandes! ¡No insistas más!* You made your point! Don't overdo it! 15. *Ponerle a uno la batola*, (P.R.) To wear the pants (coll.). *Ella le pone la batola a su marido*. She wears the pants in the family. 16. *Ponerse al día*, To catch up. *Por fin me puse al día*. I finally caught up.

Por [por], p. 526. Add, *prep.* 1. (DISTRIBUCIÓN) The, per, a. *Diez pesetas por libra*, Ten pesetas per pound. 2. (COMPARACIÓN) For. *Libro por libro, él prefiere el más viejo*. Book for book, he prefers the older one. 3. (OPINIÓN) To be, as. *Lo considero por honrado y honesto*. I consider him to be honest and fair. 4. (DEBIDO A) From, out of. *Lo hizo por misericordia*. He did it out of pity. 5. Still [Yet] to be + pp., e.g.: *El libro está por leer*. The book is still to be read. *La habitación está por leer*. The room is yet to be swept. 6. *Por de pronto*, For the time being. 7. *Por demás*, In his [her, their] own right. *Por demás son pintores*. They're painters in their own right. 8. *Por entonces*, About that time. 9. *Por esas fechas*, About that time. 10. *Por más señas*, From all appearances. 11. *Por si esto fuera poco*, As if that weren't enough. *Por si esto fuera poco, ascendieron el alquiler*. As if that weren't enough, they raised the rent. 12. *Por tanto*, As a result. 13. *Por todos lados*, At every turn, on every side.

Presentir [pray-sen-teer′], p. 533. Add, *va.* To take for granted. *Es fácil que presintamos a los demás*. It's easy for us to take others for granted.

Prestación [pres-tah-the-on′], p. 534. Add, *f.* (Neol., Mech.) Performance. *La prestación del nuevo electrodoméstico dista mucho de ser cumplida*. The performance of the new appliance leaves a lot to be desired.

Procomún [pro-co-moon′], p. 537. Add, *m.* (Neol.) Public good. *Se debe ejercer mucho cuidado para que los impuestos se utilicen en el procomún*. Great care should be taken to insure that taxes are used for the public good.

Prodigar [pro-de-gar′], p. 537. Add, *va.* (fig.) To exude. *Sus modales prodigaban embeleso*. Her manner exuded charm.

Programación [pro-grah-mah-the-on′], p. 538. Add, *f. Elementos de programación*, (Information Science) Software.

Protagonizar [pro-tah-go-ne-thar′], *va.* (Neol.) 1. To take the leading part in. *Él patronizaba la campaña*. He took the leading part in the campaign. 2. To dominate. *Los tintes transparentes patronizan su lienzo*. Transparent shades dominate his canvas.

Puesta [poo-es′-tah], p. 542. Add, *f.* 1. (Ast.) Setting. 2. *Primera puesta*, (Mil.) First issue. 3. *Puesta a punto*, Final [Finishing] touches. *El novelista se dedicaba a la puesta a punto de su obra*. The novelist was putting the final touches on his novel. 4. *Puesta en escena*, Staging. *La puesta en escena de "Las paredes oyen" representaba un ambiente típicamente español*. The staging of *The Walls Have Ears* showed a typically Spanish setting.

Quitar [ke-tar′], p. 549. Add, *va.* 1. To make give up. *Su hijo le quitó el fumar*. His son made him give up smoking. 2. To free from. *Me has quitado mis preocupaciones*. You've freed me from my worries. 3. *Quitar de en medio*, To get rid of. *Quitaron el árbol muerto de en medio*. They got rid of the dead tree. 4. *Quitar el sueño*, To keep from sleeping. *Muchas veces el mismo pensar en ello le quitaba el sueño*. The very thought of it would often keep him from sleeping. 5. *Quitar la luz*, To cut off [stand in] one's light. *Me quitas la luz*. You're standing in my light. 6. *Quitar la mesa*, To clear the table. —*vr. Quitarse de en medio*, To get out of the way.

Quedar [kay-dar′], p. 546. Add, *vn.* 1. To have left. *Me quedan dos copias*. I have two copies left. 2. *No quedar por corta ni mal echada*, (coll.) To leave no stone unturned. 3. *Quedar en*, To decide [agree] on. *¿En qué quedaron?* What did they decide? *Quedemos en que la fiesta sea mañana*. Let's agree that the party will be tomorro. 4. *Quedar por*, To remain, to be left. *Nos quedan dos canciones por cantar*. We have two songs left to sing. *Quedan dos libros por leer*. Two books remain to be read. —*vr.* 1. To be. *Me quedé atónito*. I was astonished. 2. To be left. *Se quedó huérfano*. He was left an orphan. *Yo me quedé en Madrid*. I was left in Madrid. 3. *Quedarse con*, To take, to choose, to select. 4. *Quedarse tamañito con*, Not to be able to hold a candle to. *Se queda tamañito con nuestro campeón de nado libre*. He can't hold a candle to our free-style swimming champion.

Rastrear [ras-tray-ar′], p. 553. Add, *va.* 1. To track, to trail. *Rastrearon el carcayú por el bosque*. They tracked the wolverine through the forest. 2. To look through thoroughly, to go through. *Rastreó dos veces todos y cada uno de los libros*. He looked through each and every one of the books twice. *He rastreado todos mis bolsillos, pero no puedo hallarlo*. I've gone through all my pockets, but I can't find it. 3. (UN ASUNTO) To investigate thoroughly, to probe. 4.(UN

RÍO) To dredge.

Rastreo [ras-tray'-o], p. 553. Add, *m.* *1.* Tracking, trailing. 2. Searching through. 3. Investigation, probe. 4. (Neol., Aer.) Tracking. *El rastreo del satélite en la pantalla resultaba difícil*. Tracking the satellite on the screen proved to be difficult. 5. Dredging.

Rayo [rah'-yo], p. 554. Add, *m.* 1. (fig.) Lively intelligence, intellectual powerhouse. *Ese hombre es un rayo*. That man is an intellectual powerhouse. 2. *Rayo lasérico,* (Neol.) Laser beam. 3. *Rayo textorio,* Weaver's shuttle. *El rayo se lanzaba a través del telar cuan colibrí alegre*. The shuttle darted across the loom like a happy hummingbird.

Reacción [ray-ac-the-on'], p. 554. Add, *f.* 1. *Reacción acústica,* Acoustic feedback. *La reacción acústica establece la calidad del tocadiscos*. Acoustic feedback determines the quality of a record player. 2. *Reacción de cadena,* Chain reaction. 3. *Reacciones acústicas,* Acoustics. *Las reacciones acústicas del salón de actos eran pésimas*. The acoustics of the assembly hall were terrible [wretched, G.B.].

Reajustar [ray-ah-hoos-tar'], *va.* (Neol.) To readjust. *Su hija lo cortejaba para que reajustara el sonido*. His daughter pestered him to readjust the sound.

Reajuste [ray-ah-hoos'-tay], *m.* 1. Readjustment. 2. *Reajuste semántico,* (Neol.) Semantic shift.

Rebasar [ray-bah-sar'], p. 555. Add, *va.* 1. (OTRO COCHE) To pass. 2. (Naut.) To clear. *Rebasamos el escollo*. We cleared the reef.

Receso [ray-thay'-so], p. 557. Add, *m.* 1. (Neol.) Break. *El receso de las labores patrocina su eficacia*. A break from one's labors [labours, G.B.] promotes their effectiveness. 2. Withdrawal. *Su receso de la vida de la gran metrópoli le curaba en salud*. His withdrawal from the life of the great metropolis restored his health.

Recinto [ray-theen'-to], p. 557. Add, *m.* 1. Scene. *Visitaron el recinto de tanta historia*. They visited the scene of so much history. 2. (DEL ALCÁZAR) Enceinte. 3. *Recinto central,* Main campus. 4. *Recinto cerrado del alma,* Innermost reaches of the soul. 5. *Recinto suplente,* Branch campus.

Recorrido [ray-cor-ree'-do], p. 559. Add, *m.* 1. Ride. *El recorrido le dio la ocasión de enseñarnos la isla*. The ride gave him the chance to show us the island. 2. (VISTA GLOBAL) Survey. *Se realizó un recorrido de la literatura quinientista*. A survey of the literature of the sixteenth century was undertaken. 3. (OFICIAL) Tour. *Realizar un recorrido de,* To make a tour of. 4. (Mech.) Stroke. 5. (DEL EBANISTA) Finishing.

Recortable [ray-cor-tah'-blay], *m.* (Neol.) Cutout. *Con los recortables impresos en estas hojas se arma un castillo medioeval*. A Medieval castle can be put together with the cutouts printed on these sheets.

Recrear [ray-cray-ar'], p. 559. Add, *va.* 1. To please. 2. To recreate. *Era imposible recrear el recinto de tanta alegría*. It was impossible to recreate the scene of so much happiness. 3. *Recrear los oídos a,* To say delightful things to. —*vr.* 1. To enjoy recreation. 2. *Recrearse en,* To delight in. *Se recreaban en paseos frecuentes por el parque*. They delighted in frequent walks through the park.

Recuento [ray-coo-en'-to], p. 559. Add, *m.* 1. Account, telling. 2. (Math.) Recount.

Recuperación [ray-coo-pay-ra-the-on'], p. 559. Add, *f. Recuperación de información*. (Information Science) Information retrieval.

Redactar [ray-dac-tar'], p. 560. Add, *va.* 1. (UN DOCUMENTO) To make out. 2. (LOS PENSAMIENTOS) To word, to put into words. *Es difícil a veces redactar los pensamientos de uno*. Sometimes it's hard to put one's thoughts into words.

Regate [ray-gah'-tay], p. 563. Add, *m.* 1. Sudden turn. *Un regate del río les ofrecía una vista encantadora de la aldea*. A sudden turn in the river offered them an enchanting view of the village. 2. (fig.) Clever maneuver.

Regatear [ray-gah-tay-ar'], p. 563. Add, *va.* 1. To be nip and tuck in. *Los dos nadadores regatean la última carera del nado libre*. The two swimmers are nip and tuck in the final heat of the free style. 2. To fight or. *Regatean la pelota*. They're fighting over the ball. 3. *Regatear el elogio a,* To damn with faint praise. *Los críticos le regatearon el elogio a la comedia y a las dos semanas fracasó*. The critics damned the play with faint praise and it closed two weeks later. 4. *Regatearle,* (fig.) To take away from. *Nadie puede regatearte tu educacón*. No one can take your education away from you. —*vn.* To be evasive. *Sigue regateando*. He's still evasive.

Remarcar [ray-mar-car'], p. 566. Add, *va.* To turn into new channels. *Podemos remarcar nuestra manera de pensar si es nuestro deseo verdadero hacerlo*. We can turn our thinking into new channels if we really wish to do so.

Remozamiento [ray-mo-thah-me-en'-to], *m.* (Neol.) Renovation. *El remozamiento del ámbito de la universidad produjo resultados asombrosos*. The renovation of the university area produced surprising results.

Reparón, na [ray-pah-ron', nah], p. 569. Add, *a.* (Neol.) That takes the trouble to look. *Ella es de veras reparona*. She really takes the trouble to look.

Repasar [ray-pah-sar'], p. 569. Add, *va.* 1. To go back on (G.B.). *El gerente repasó el primer renglón*. The manager went back on the first item. 2. To review (Amer.). *Desea repasar los verbos*. He wants to review the verbs.

República [ray-poo'-ble-cah], p. 571. Add, *f. República ciudadana,* City state. *La república ciudadana de Florencia se hizo la cuna del Renacimiento*. The city state of Florence became the cradle of the Renaissance.

Rescoldo [res-col'-do], p. 572. Add, *m.* (fig.) Leftover. *El problema era un rescoldo de la administración anterior*. The problem was a leftover from the previous administration.

Resistir [ray-sis-teer'], p. 573. Add, *va.* 1. To withstand. 2. (TOLERAR) To put up with. 3. *Resistir la comparación con,* To measure up well with. *Su plan de estudios es muy socorrido y resiste la comparación con el nuestro*. Their curriculum is quite helpful and measures up well with ours. —*vr.* 1. To resist. 2. *Resistirse a,* To refuse to. *Él se resiste a ayudarnos*. He refuses to help us.

Resorte [ray-sor'-tay], p. 574. Add, *m.* *Resorte íntimo,* Inner resources. *Él que se llama así mismo contento de verdad vive de su resorte íntimo*. He who calls himself truly happy lives on his inner resources.

Retazo [ray-tah'-tho], p. 575. Add, *m.* (fig.) Touch, reminder. *Su carta me trajo un retazo del hogar*. Her letter brought me a touch of home.

Retomar [ray-to-mar'], *va.* (Neol.) 1. To bring back. *El escritor retomaba el ambiente que les hacía falta*. The writer brought back the atmosphere they missed. 2. To look at again [once more]. *Deberíamos retomar el problema*. We should look at the problem once more.

Retrato [ray-trah'-to], p. 577. Add, *m.* 1. Likeness. *Me dio un retrato de su madre*. She gave me a likeness of her mother. 2. *Retrato hablado,* Verbal description, description in words. *Les dio un retrato hablado de su huésped*. She gave them a verbal description of her guest. 3. *Retrato hablante,* Speaking likeness (G.B.), spitting image (coll., Amer.). *La chica era el retrato hablante de Alicia*. The girl was a speaking likeness of Alice.

Revolver [ray-vol-verr'], p. 578. Add, *va.* 1. To rummage through. *Revolvía los documentos buscándolo*. He was rummaging through the papers looking for it. 2. To shake. *Revolvió la botella*. She shook the bottle. 3. (EN LA MENTE) To turn over. 4. *Revolver contra,* To turn against. *Te han revuelto contra tu padre*. They've turned you against your father. —*vr.* 1. *Revolverse,* To turn around. 2. *Revolverse contra,* To turn against.

Rúbrica [roo'-bre-cah], p. 585. Add, *f.* 1. Headline. *Las rúbricas de todos los periódicos lo gritaban*. The headlines of all the newspapers shouted it out. 2. *Ser de rúbrica,* (coll.) To be customary. *Es de rúbrica anotar el informe*. It is customary to footnote a paper.

Rubro [roo'-bro], *m.* (Neol., Amer.) Heading, rubric. *En tu ensayo deberás encabezar cada tópico con un nuevo rubro*. In your essay you should lead into each topic with a new heading.

Rueda [roo-ay'-dah], p. 585. Add, *f.* 1. *Hacer la rueda a,* To swarm around, to pay court to. *Sus aficionados le hacían la rueda al actor.* The actor's fans swarmed around him. 2. *Rueda de paletas,* Paddle wheel. 3. *Rueda de prensa,* (Neol.) Press conference. 4. *Rueda de presos,* Lineup of suspects. 5. *Rueda del timón,* (Naut.) Wheel. 6. *Traer en rueda,* To bring swarming around one. *Traía en rueda a toda su clase.* He brought his whole class swarming around him.

Rumiar [roo-me-ar'], p. 586. Add, *va.* 1. To ponder. *Rumiaba la suerte de ellos.* She pondered their fate. 2. To fret about, to fume over. 3. *Rumiar la derrota,* To lick one's wounds.

Sacar [sah-car'], p. 587. Add, *va.* 1. (DE LA ESCUELA) To withdraw. *Sacaron a su hija en seguida.* They withdrew their daughter at once. 2. (UNA BOLA) To put into play. 3. To bring out. *Sacó varias lámparas.* He brought out several lamps. 4. (LA VERDAD DE UNO) To get out of. *No pude sacarle la hora de la partida de ellos.* I couldn't get the time of their departure out of him. 5. (DEL ESTUDIO) To find out, to learn. *¿Qué has sacado del libro?* What did you learn from the book? 6. To get, to deriv. *No saco nada de lo que has dicho.* I don't get anything from what yu've said. 7. (UNA COPIA) To make. 8. (UNA FOTO) To take. 9. *Sacar a bailar,* To choose as one's partner. 10. *Sacar a colación,* To bring up (by way of comparison). *Sacó a colación el primer sondeo.* He brought up the first survey by way of comparison. 11. *Sacar a pública plaza,* To parade through the streets (fig.). *Sacaba a pública plaza las faltas de él.* She paraded his faults through the streets. 12. *Sacar a relucir,* To bring up (at the wrong time). *Sacó a relucir la riña sin pensar.* He brought up the argument without meaning to do so. 13. *Sacar a volar,* a. (LA PERSONALIDAD DE UNO) To bring out. *La maestra logró sacar a volar a la chica.* The teacher succeeded in bringing out the child. b. (EN EL GRAN MUNDO) To teach social graces. *Su madre la sacó a volar.* Her mother taught her social graces. 14. *Sacar avante de,* To take advantage of. *Hay que sacar avante de lo que le cae en suerte.* One should take advantage of what comes his way. 15. *Sacar de encima,* To get off one's back. *Por fin sacó de encima la responsabilidad.* Finally he got the responsibility off his back. 16. *Sacar de la nada,* To take from nothing. *De la nada no se saca nada.* Nothing is taken from nothing. 17. *Sacar de pobre,* To lift out of poverty. 18. *Sacar de sí,* To drive mad (fig.). *Su desenfado la sacaba de sí.* His nonchalance was driving her mad. 19. *Sacar en claro,* To get out of. *¿Qué sacaste en claro de lo que dijo?* What did you get out of what he said? 20. *Sacar partido dem* To get an advantage from. *¿Qué partido sacas tú del arreglo?* What advantage do you get from the arrangement? 21. *Sacar provecho de,* To turn to advantage. *Siempre sabía sacar provecho de sus conocimientos.* He always knew how to turn his knowledge to advantage.

Saltar [sal-tar'], p. 590. Add, *va.* 1. To skip. *Vamos a saltar la primera poesía.* Let's skip the first poem. 2. (FARFULLAR) To do with a lick and a promise. 3. To jump over. *Saltó el arroyo.* He jumped over the stream. —*vn.* 1. To stick out, to jut out. *Saltan sus orejas.* His ears stick out. 2. To jump down. *Saltaron de la roca.* They jumped down from the rock. 3. (UN BOTÓN) To come off. 4. (EL AGUA) To spurt up. 5. (LAS CHISPAS) To fly up. 6. *Saltando de limpio,* Sparkling clean. *Dejó los vasos saltando de limpio.* It left the glasses sparkling clean. 7. *Saltar a la vista,* To be as plain as the nose on one's face. 8. *Saltar con,* To come out with. *De repente saltó con la verdad del caso.* Suddenly he came out with the truth of the matter. 9. *Si el sapo salta y se ensarta, la culpa no es de la estaca.* (P.R.) Look before you leap.

Satélite [sah-tay'-le-tay], p. 594. Add, *m. Satélite de telecomunicación,* (Neol.) Communications satellite.

Sede [say'-day], p. 596. Add, *f.* 1. Headquarters, main office(s). 2. *Sede del poder,* Seat of power. 3. *Sede social,* Headquarters. *La sede social del club está en el centro.* The headquarters of the club is downtown.

Semblanza [sem-blahn'-thah], p. 598. Add, *f.* (Lit.) Outline. *El florilegio proporciona una semblanza para cada movimiento literario.* The anthology provides an outline for each literary movement.

Sentimentalismo [sen-te-men-tah-lees'-mo], p. 599. Add, *m.* (Neol.) Expressing one's feelings. *El sentimentalismo puede procurar gran daño o gran beneficio de acuerdo con la forma que toma.* Expressing one's feelings can cause great damage or a great deal of benefit according to the form it takes.

Ser [serr], p. 601. Add, *vn.* 1. *¿Cómo ha de ser?* What else did you expect? 2. *Era que,* What happened was (that). *Era que se le perdieron los guantes.* What happened was she lost her gloves. 3. *Más eres tú.* That's the pot calling the kettle black. 4. *No es para tanto.* It isn't that bad [important]. 5. *Ser como la hoja del yagrumo,* (P.R.) To be unreliable [fickle]. 6. *Ser de,* a. To belong to. *El libro es de ella.* The book belongs to her. b. To be from. *Soy de Bogotá.* I'm from Bogotá. c. To become of. *¿Qué será de él?* What will become of him? d. To be made of. *Es de cristal.* It's made of glass. 7. *Ser de ver,* To be worth seeing. *El palacio es de ver.* The palace is worth seeing. 8. *Ser despedido (de un empleo),* To get one's walking papers [the sack, G.B.]. 9. *Ser mérito de,* To show off to advantage. *El hermoso jardín era mérito de la casa.* The beautiful garden showed the house off to advantage. 10. *Ser mucha casualidad,* To be hard to believe. *Es mucha casualidad para que se hayan olvidado todos del mismo libro.* It's hard to believe they all forgot the same book. 11. *Ser mucha palabra para,* To be too strong a word for. *"Ciudad" es mucha palabra para eso.* 'City' is too strong a word for that. 12. *Ser muy dueño de,* To be apt. to. *Es muy dueña de entregarse a todo el mundo.* She is apt to tell her life story to everyone she meets. *Éramos muy dueños de hacer las cosas bajo el impulso del momento.* We were apt to do things on the spur of the moment. 13. *Ser oro molido para,* To be music to the ears of. *La noticia era oro molido para mí.* The news was music to my ears. 14. *Ser paga excelente,* To be on the best of terms, to get along very well. 15. *Ser querido,* Loved one. *Abandonaba a regañadientes a sus seres queridos.* He hated to leave his loved ones behind. 16. *Ser un retraso [una rémora] para,* To hold back. *Le era un atraso su ortografía.* His handwriting held him back.

Sigla [see'-glah], p. 604. Add, *f.* Acronym. *Las siglas OTAN, OEA y NNUU casi siempre hacen las veces de las palabras que representan.* The acronyms NATO, OAS and UN have almost completely taken the place of the words they represent.

Sindéresis [sin-day'-ray-sis], p. 606. Add, *f.* Careful thought. *Mucha sindéresis entró en planear la nueva galería.* Much careful thought went into the plan for the new gallery.

Singapur [sin-gah-poor'], Singapore.

Sintonizar [sin-to-ne-thar'], p. 606. Add, *va.* 1. To tune. 2. (UNA ESTACIÓN, UN CANAL) To switch [turn] on. 3. *Sintonizar con,* To tune in. —*vr. Sintonizarse con,* To keep [be] in tune with. *Por poco no se sintoniza con el piano.* He barely keeps in tune with the piano.

Sobra [so'-brah], p. 607. Add, *f.* 1. *De sobra,* More than enough. *Tengo libros de sobra.* I have more than enough books. 2. *Saber de sobra,* To know only too well. 3. *Sobras,* Leftovers. *Las sobras le parecían manjares.* The leftovers looked like delicacies to her.

Sobrar [so-brar'], p. 607. Add, *vn.* 1. To have more than enough. *Me sobran las etiquetas.* I have more than enough labels. 2. To be left over. *Sobra un libro.* One book is left over. 3. To be out of place. *Sobra en aquel ambiente.* She's out of place in that atmosphere. 4. *Sobrar decir,* To go without saying. *Sobra decir que prodigaba su reconocimiento.* It goes without saying that her gratitude knew no bounds.

Sobrecubierta [so-bray-coo-be-err'-tah], p. 608. Add, *f.* (Neol.) Dustjacket. *La sobrecubierta cita las opiniones de diversos científicos.* The dustjacket quotes the opinions of various scientists.

Sobrevolar [so-bray-vo-lar'], *va.* (Aer.) To fly over. *Sobrevolar de cerca,* To make a pass over. *El avión sobrevoló la aldea de cerca y dejó caer los pertrechos.* The plane made a pass over the village and dropped the supplies.

Sociolingüística [so-the-o-lin-goo-ees'-

te-cah], *f.* (Neol.) Sociolinguistics. *La sociolingüística estudia de cerca los dechados en el habla de distintos gremios.* Sociolinguistics studies the speech patterns of different groups.

Sondear [son-day-ar'], p. 613. Add, *va.* 1. (A UNA PERSONA) To sound out. *El enunciado deberá sondear los sentimientos del comité.* The notice ought to sound out the feelings of the committee.

Soslayar [sos-lah-yar'], p. 615. Add, *va.* (fig.) 1. To evade. *Estás soslayando el tema.* You're evading the issue. 2. To treat superficially. *El artículo soslayaba con mucho el saneamiento del ambiente.* The article treated restoration of the environment very superficially.

Subcampeón [soob-cam-pay-on'], *m.* (Neol.) Runner-up. *De repente alumbró en su cabeza la sospecha de que, todos sus esfuerzos no obstante, sería siempre el subcampeón.* It suddenly dawned on him that, despite all his efforts, he would always be a runner-up.

Subsuelo [soob-soo-ay'-lo], *m.* 1. Substratum. 2. (Agr.) Subsoil.

Suspender [soos-pen-derr'], p. 621. Add, *va.* 1. To call off. *Suspendieron la gala al último momento.* They called off the event at the last minute. 2. (A UN ALUMNO) To give an incomplete to.

Taller [tal-lyerr'], p. 625. Add, *m.* 1. (DEL ARTISTA) Studio. 2. *Maestro de taller y obras,* Shop teacher. 3. *Taller y obras,* Shop class. 4. *Talleres gráficos,* Print shop (coll.), printing establishment. 5. *Taller de maestros,* Teachers' workshop.

También [tam-be-en'], p. 625. Add, *adv.* Fellow. *Se casó con una también maestra.* He married a fellow teacher. *Buscó en vano una también Chicagoense.* She looked for a fellow Chicagoan without success. *Los también oficinistas le brindaron una fiesta de despedida.* His fellow office workers gave him a farewell party.

Tapón [tah-pone'], p. 627. Add, *m.* 1. (DE BOTELLA) Cap. 2. (P.R.) Traffic jam. *Durante las horas de aglomeración siempre hay tapones allí.* During rush hours there are always traffic jams there.

Teatro [tay-ah'-tro], p. 628. Add, *m.* *Teatro de conciertos.* Concert hall.

Teclear [tay-clay-ar'], p. 628. Add, *va.* To type (up). *Él me teclea los apuntes ahora mismo.* He is typing up the notes for me now.

Tener [tay-nerr'], p. 631. Add, *va.* 1. To be wrong with. *¿Qué tiene él?* What's wrong with him? 2. To keep, to hold. *Le tendrán allí hasta el lunes.* They're keeping him there until Monday. 3. To have got (coll.). *¿Tienes un fósforo?* Have you got a match? 4. *No tener alma de,* Not to have the heart to. *No tengo alma de decírselo.* I haven't the heart to tell him. 5. *No tener ánimo para.* (One's heart) not to be in something. *Ya no tengo ánimo para ello.* My heart just isn't in it any longer. 6. *Tened y tengamos,* Share and share alike. 7. *Tener a bien,* To be pleased, to deem it an honor [honour, G.B.]. *Tengo a bien avisarles que saldrá mañana.* I am pleased to advise you that it will depart tomorrow. 8. *Tener a la vista,* To keep in mind. *Tendré la idea a la vista.* I'll keep the idea in mind. *Tener a menos,* To be beneath one's dignity. *Tienen a menos el estudiar.* Studying is beneath their difnity. 10. *Tener algún propósito solapado,* To be up to something. 11. *Tener el alma en un hilo,* To be on pins and needles. 12. *Tener años,* To be so many years old. *Tiene dos años.* He is two years old. 13. *Tener calor,* To be warm [hot]. 14. *Tener carta de ciudadanía,* To be accepted. *La palabra tiene carta de ciudadanía desde hace muchos años.* The word has been accepted for many years. 15. *Tener contrariedades,* To have mixed feelings. *Tengo contrariedades en cuanto a la propiedad de tal acto.* I have mixed feelings about the propriety of such an action. 16. *Tener cuidado,* To take care. 17. *Tener cuidado con,* To watch out for. 18. *Tener de largo [ancho, grueso],* To be long [wide, thick]. *La tabla tiene un metro de largo, diez centímetros de ancho y tres de alto.* The board is a meter [metre, G.B.] long, ten centimeters wide and three high. 19. *Tener en contra de,* To have against. *¿Qué tienes en su contra?* What do you have against him [her, them]? 20. *Tener en gracia,* To be thankful (for). *Tengo en gracia las noticias.* I am thankful for the news. 21. *Tener frío,* To be cold. 22. *Tener gran arraigo,* To be firmly entrenched. *La costumbre tiene gran arraigo.* The custom is firmly entrenched. 23. *Tener hambre,* To be hungry. 24. *Tener madera de,* To have the makings [potential] of. *Su hija tiene madera de artista.* His daughter has the makings of an artist. 25. *Tener la mancha del plátano,* (P.R.) To be Puerto Rican through and through. 26. *Tener lugar,* To take place. 27. *Tener mal ambiente entre,* (Acad.) To turn a cold shoulder to. *Sus sugerencias siempre tienen mal ambiente entre ellos.* They always turn a cold shoulder to his suggestions. 28. *Tener malas entrañas,* To have a mean disposition. 29. *Tener mucho ojo a,* To keep an eye out for. *Tenía mucho ojo a su regreso todo el santo día.* He kept an eye out for her return the entire day. 30. *Tener presente,* To take into consideration. 31. *Tener prisa,* To be in a hurry. 32. *Tener que,* a. To have to. b. To have got (coll.). *Tiene que irse.* He's got to go. 32. *Tener salida para,* To have a market [an outlet] for. *No tenemos salida para los florilegios literarios.* We have no market for literary anthologies. 33. *Tener sed,* To be thirsty. 34. *Tener sentido,* (fig.) To make sense. *La crítica no tiene sentido.* The criticism doesn't make sense. 35. *Tener sin cuidado,* Not to bother a [one] bit. *Sus apuros le tienen sin cuidado.* His troubles don't bother him one bit. 36. *Tener sobradas razones para,* To have all the reason in the world to. 37. *Tener sólida vocación de,* To be very apt at. *Tenían sólida vocación de pintor.* They were very apt at painting. 38. *Tener sueño,* To be sleepy. 39. *Tener tesón para,* To be serious about. *Tiene tesón para la pintura.* He is serious about painting. 40. *Tener una deuda de gratitud con,* To owe a debt of gratitude. *Tenía una deuda de gratitud con su madre.* He owed his mother a debt of gratitude. 41. *Tener voz y voto,* To have one's voice, to have one's role to play (fig.). *Cada uno de nosotros tiene voz y voto en la decisión.* Each one of us has his role to play in the decision. 42. *Tenérselas tiesas,* To hold one's own. *A pesar de la contrariedad, se las tenía tiesas.* Despite the inconvenience, she held her own.

Terciar [ter-the-ar'], p. 633. Add, *vn.* To chime in. *Mientras lo discutíamos, él terció con nombre completamente otro.* While we were arguing about it, he chimed in with an entirely different name. —*vr.* To arise, to present itself. *Cuando se tercia la ocasión, acude donde él.* When need arises, call on him.

Teledifundir [tay-lay-de-foon-deer'], *va.* (Neol.) To telecast.

Tiempo [te-em'-po], p. 635. Add, *m.* 1. (DE UN PARTIDO DE FÚTBOL) Period. 2. *A su tiempo,* In due course. 3. *A tiempo,* a. On time. b. (ANTES DE QUE SE VENCIERA EL PLAZO) In time. 4. *Agarrarse el tiempo,* (The weather) To close in. 5. *Ajustar los tiempos,* To put the events in proper order. 6. *Al mismo tiempo,* At the same time. 7. *Darse buen tiempo,* To have a good time. 8. *Dejar el tiempo,* To let things take their course. 9. *Hacer buen tiempo,* To be good weather. 10. *Hacer mal tiempo,* To be bad weather. 11. *La mayor parte del tiempo,* Most of the time. 12. *Largo tiempo,* A long time. *Largo tiempo se pasó tratando de convencerla.* A long time was spent trying to convince her. 13. *Medio tiempo,* Time of transition. *Era el medio tiempo entre la primavera y el verano.* It was the time of transition between spring and summer. 14. *Medir el tiempo,* To use one's time well. 15. *Mucho tiempo,* A great deal of time, much time. 16. *Tiempo de fortuna,* Stormy weather, season of hard weather. 17. *Todo el tiempo,* All the time. *Todo lo que pasé en ello fue tiempo perdido.* All the time that I spent on it was wasted. 18. *Vendrá un tiempo en que,* The time will come when.

Titular [te-too-lar'], *m.* 1. (Neol.) Head. *No está el titular del departamento.* The head of the department isn't here. 2. Capital letter (for a headline).

Tocacintas [to-cah-theen'-tas], *m.* Tape player.

Tomar [to-mar'], p. 640. Add, *va.* 1. *Tomar a broma,* To take as a joke. *Los padres tomaban a broma los planes de su hijo.* The parents took their son's plans as a joke. 2. *Tomar a mal,* To resent, to take offense [offence, G.B.] at. *Tomó a mal la lindeza*. He took offence at the insult. 3. *Tomar a pechos,* To take seriously. 4. *Tomar acta de,* To make a record of. *La historia tomará acta de un materialista a rajatablas*. History will make a record of an out-and-out materialist. 5. *Tomar bajo palabra (la verdad de lo dicho),* To take someone's [some-one's, G.B.] word for (it). *Tomé bajo palabra la condición del río*. I took his word for the condition of the river. 6. *Tomar bajo palabra que cumplirá uno lo prometido,* To take some-one at his word. *Tomé bajo palabra que haría el trabajo*. I took him at his word that he would do the work. 7. *Tomar cuerpo,* To take shape. 8. *Tomar el pelo,* To put on (coll.), to pull one's leg. *¡Me estás tomando el pelo!* You're putting me on! 9. *Tomar en cuenta,* To take into account. *Hay que tomar en cuenta la desnivelación entre los barrios*. One must take the difference between the neighborhoods into account. 10. *Tomar parte,* To take part. 11. *Tomar por,* To take for. *Lo tomaban por un mentecato*. They took him for a dolt. 12. *Tomar por su cuenta,* To take upon oneself, to take charge of. 13. *Tomar un nuevo cariz,* To take on a new look. *Su porvenir ha tomado un nuevo cariz*. Her future has taken on a new look. 14. *Tomar un recurso,* To take a measure. *Se tomaron recursos para socavar el proyecto*. Harsh measures were taken to undermine the plan. 15. *Tomar una determinación,* To make up one's mind.

Tornadizo, za [tor-nah-dee'-tho, thah], p. 642. Add, *a*. Shifty

Traer [trah-err'], p. 644. Add, *va*. 1. To get. *¿Me has traído el periódico?* Have you gotten [got, G.B.] me the newspaper? 2. To make. *El informe los trae inquietos*. The report is making them nervous. 3. *¡Hasta aquí me trajo el río!* (P.R.) That's the last straw! 4. *Traer entre ceja y ceja,* To have on one's mind. *Trae mucho entre ceja y ceja*. He has a lot on his mind. 5. *Traer entre manos,* To deal with at the moment. *El problema que traemos entre manos es de fácil resolución*. The problem that we are dealing with at the moment is easy to resolve.

Trampolín [tram-po-leen'], p. 646. Add, *m*. *Trampolín de saltos,* Ski jump.

Transbordador espacial [trans-bor-dah-dor' es-pah-the-ahl'], *m*. (Neol.) Space shuttle.

Transbordo [trans-bor'-do], p. 646. Add. *m*. (Aer.) Transfer. *El transbordo de una nave en órbita a otra se efectuó sin fallo*. The transfer from one orbiter to the other went off without a hitch.

Trasfondo [trahs'-fon-do], *m*. 1. Subconscious. 2. (PINTURA) Distance. 3. *Trasfondo histórico,* Substratum. *El latín arromanzado variaba en cada provincia según el trasfondo histórico de los hablantes de él*. Proto-Romance varied in each province according to the substratum of its speakers.

Trasnacional [trahs-nah-the-o-nahl'], *a*. (Neol.) Multinational. *Las compañías trasnacionales aprenden forzosamente varios códigos legales*. Multinational companies are required to learn several legal codes.

Trasnochado, da [trahs-no-chah'-do, dah], p. 649. Add, *a*. 1. Trite. *El comentario trasnochado dañó la edición*. The trite commentary hurt the edition. 2. (RENDIDO) Haggard.

Turno [toor'-no], p. 658. Add, *m*. 1. Shift. 2. *De turno,* On duty. *¿Quién está de turno?* Who is on duty? 3. *Turno de día,* Day shift. 4. *Turno nocturno,* Night shift.

Urbanización [oor-bah-ne-thah-the-on'], p. 660. Add. *f*. Housing development (Amer.), housing estate (G.B.). *La nueva urbanización se vale de los más modernos adelantos técnicos*. The new housing estate makes use of the most modern technical advances.

Veda [vay'-dah], p. 666. Add, *f*. Ban. *Veda total,* Total ban. *Hay una veda total de los vehículos automotores en el recinto céntrico*. There is a total ban on fuel-driven vehicles in the downtown area.

Velero [vay-lay'-ro], *m*. 1. Sailmaker. 2. (BARCO) Sailboat.

Velocidad [vay-lo-the-dahd'], p. 667. Add, *f*. *Velocidad de liberación,* (Aer.) Escape velocity. *La velocidad de liberación desencadena la nave de la gravedad de la Tierra*. Escape velocity frees the spaceship from the earth's gravity.

Ver [verr], p. 670. Add, *va*. 1. To look at. *Vea este libro*. Look at this book. 2. *A más ver,* (coll.) See you later. 3. *No poder ver,* Not to be able to stand. *A ese tipo no le puedo ver*. I can't stand that guy. 4. *No ver la hora [las santas horas] de,* a. Not to be able to + inf. + fast enough. *No veo la hora de irme de aquí*. I can't get out of here fast enough. b. To look forward to impatiently. 5. *Ver con buenos ojos,* To look favorably upon. 6. *Ver venir a,* (fig.) To be on to (coll.).

Vez [veth], p. 673. Add, *f*. 1. *A la vez,* At the same time. *Llegaron a la vez,* They arrived at the same time. 2. *Alguna vez,* a. Now and then, sometimes. b. (EN UNA PREGUNTA) Ever. *¿Has visto tal alguna vez?* Have you ever seen the like? 3. *Cada vez más,* Gradually, more and more. 4. *De vez en cuando,* From time to time. 5. *Las más de las veces,* Most of the time. 6. *Las veces que* + verb, (Just) As often as + verb. *Venga las veces que usted quiera*. Come as often as you like. 7. *Muchas veces,* Often. 8. *Otras tantas veces,* Just as often. *Pero otras tantas veces marchábamos viento en popa*. But just as often we breezed right along. 9. *Un sinnúmero de veces,* Time after time (Amer.), times out of number (G.B.).

Vigencia [ve-hen'-the-ah], *f*. Enjoyment, use, exercise. *Plena vigencia de los derechos humanos,* Full exercise of human rights.

Vivienda [ve-ve-en'-dah], p. 678. Add, *f*. Housing. *Nos vemos obligados a proveer vivienda para muchos gremios diferentes*. We must provide housing for many different groups.

Volver [vol-verr'], p. 680. Add, *va*. 1. (CON DESABRIMIENTO) To send back. *Volvió su regalo*. She sent back his gift. 2. (UN SONIDO) To deflect, to throw back. 3. *Volver del revés,* a. To turn around, to turn the other way. *Volví el televisor del revés*. I turned the television set around. b. (UNA PRENDA DE VESTIR) To turn inside out. 4. *Volver la espalda,* To turn one's back on. *Le volvieron la espalda a su amiga*. They turned their backs on their friend. 5. *Volver tandas,* To turn into a spectacle. *Volvieron tandas el baile*. They turned the dance into a spectacle. —*vn*. 1. To go back. 2. *En un volver de ojos,* In the twinkling of an eye. 3. *Volver en la mente,* To think back. *Le gustaba volver en la mente a los días de Maricastaña*. He liked to think back to days of yore. 4. *Volver en sí,* To come to. 5. *Volver sobre los pasos de uno,* (Lit.) To retrace one's steps. *Traslucimos de su respuesta que no sabía nada de ello, de manera que volvimos sobre nuestros pasos*. We gathered from his answer that he knew nothing about it, so we retraced our steps. —*vr*. 1. To turn around. 2. *Volverse atrás,* To back out.

Zafacón [that-fah-cone'], *m*. (Acad., P.R.) Garbage can.

ENGLISH AND SPANISH – INGLÉS Y ESPAÑOL

Abstract [ab-stract'], p. 18. Add, *va.* Trasuntar. *The writer abstracted her memoirs.* El escritor trasuntó las memorias de ella.

Access time [ac'-ses taim], *s.* (Information science) Período de espera, tiempo de acceso. *Access time will vary according to the data processor.* El tiempo de acceso varía de acuerdo con el ordenador del cual usted se vale.

Accommodating [ạc-com'-o-dê-ting], p. 19. Add, *a.* Acomodadizo. *His accommodating manner found a warm reception everywhere.* Su ademán acomodadizo encontraba ambiente por todas partes.

Acronym [ac'-ro-nim], *s.* Sigla. *The acronyms NATO, OAS and UN have almost completely taken the place of the words they represent.* Las siglas OTAN, OEA y NNUU casi siempre hacen las veces de las palabras que representan.

Acoustic feedback [a-cūs'-tic fid'-bac], *s.* Reacción acústica. *Acoustic feedback determines the quality of a record player.* La reacción acústica establece la calidad del tocadiscos.

Acoustics [a-cūs'-tics], p. 21. Add, *s.* Reacciones acústicas de un recinto. *The acoustics of the assembly hall were terrible* [G.B., *wretched*]. Las reacciones acústicas del salón de actos eran pésimas.

Activity [ac-tiv'-i-ti], p. 22. Add, *s.* 1. (OF THE WEATHER, THE MARKET) Comportamiento. 2. (SOMETHING TO DO) Quehacer. *What are the activites for the morning class?* ¿Cuáles son los quehaceres para la clase de la mañana?

Address [ạd-dres'], p. 22. Add, *va.* 1. (PUT NAME, ADDRESS ON) Rotular. *Did you address all the letters?* ¿Rotulaste todas las cartas? 2. (Information science) Ubicar en un sistema de informática. *They addressed the name of the book in the computer.* Ubicaron el nombre del libro en el computador. 3. (A PROBLEM) Abordar. *We can address that problem tomorrow.* Podremos abordar ese problema mañana.

Adulthood [a-dult'-hud], *s.* Edad adulta.

Advertiser [ad-vẹr-taiz'-ẹr], p. 25. Add, *s.* Anunciante. *Which advertiser placed this ad?* ¿Qué anunciante pidió este anuncio?

Aerobics [ẹr-o'-bics], *s.* (Neol.) Aeróbica. *Aerobics deals with how exercise affects the respiratory system.* La aeróbica trata de cómo el ejercicio reacciona con el mecanismo de la respiración.

Aftermath [af'-tẹr-math], p. 27. Add, *s.* Resaca, secuelas. *The aftermath of the war was grinding poverty.* La resaca de la guerra era una pobreza abrumadora.

Age-date [êj'-dêt], *va.* (Neol.) Datar con pruebas científicas los años de. *They age-dated the artifacts from the river basin with astonishing accuracy.* Dataron con pruebas científicas y tino sorprendente los años que tenían los artefactos de la cuenca.

Air bridge [ār' brij], *s.* (Neol.) 1. (BETWEEN BUILDINGS) Pasarela encerrada que reúne dos rascacielos por encima del plan terreno, conexión andadera. 2. (BETWEEN CITIES) Puente aéreo de transporte.

Alienation [êl-yen-ê'-shun], p. 31. Add, *s.* (Med.) Automarginación, autoenclaustramiento. *Alienation can cause a sense of worthlessness and despair.* La automarginación puede provocar un sentido de inutilidad y desesperanza.

All [ōl], p. 32. Add, *a.* 1. *All in,* (fam.) Cansadísimo, enteramente agotado. 2. *All over,* Terminado de una vez para siempre. *The celebration is all over.* Ya se acabó la fiesta. —*s.* 1. *All about,* Todo lo de. *He told us all about turtles* [G.B., *tortoises.*] Nos contó todo lo de las tortugas. 2. *All in all,* En resumidas cuentas. 3. *It's all the same.* Tanto monta. *Do what you like. It's all the same to her.* Haz lo que guste. Tanto monta para ella.

Amen [ê-men'], p. 36. Add, *adv. Amen to that!* ¡Ojalá!

Amusement [a-miūz'-ment], p. 38. Add, *s.* 1. *Amusement section (of the newspaper),* Cartelera. *I can never find the amusement section of the newspaper when I want it.* Cuando busco la cartelera, jamás la puedo encontrar. 2. *Amusement park,* Centro de diversión, parque de diversiones. *The amusement park has a roller coaster.* El centro de diversión tiene una montaña rusa.

Anticipation [an-tis-i-pê'-shun], p. 42. Add, *s.* Expectativa. *Anticipation is greater than the realization.* La expectativa es más que la tertulia. *The anticipation of a child is the key to Christmas.* La expectativa de un niño es la clave de las Navidades.

Appearances [ap-pîr'-ans-ez], *s. pl.* 1. La faz que toman las cosas. *All they worry about is appearances.* No se preocupan por más que la faz que toman las cosas. 2. *Appearances are deceiving.* Las apariencias engañan. 3. *From all appearances,* Por más señas. 4. *From appearances,* A la vista.

Apt [apt], p. 48. Add, *a.* 1. Competente. *He is an apt pupil.* Es un alumno competente. 2. Dueño, e.g.: *To be apt to do,* Ser muy dueño de hacer. *She was apt to do whatever she wanted.* Era muy dueña de hacer lo que le daba la gana. *I am apt to do things on the spur of the moment.* Soy muy dueño de hacer las cosas bajo el impulso del momento.

As [az], p. 53. Add, *conj.* 1. Y todo, e.g.: *Unhappy as she was,* Triste y todo. *Unhappy as she was, she went to the party.* Pero triste y todo, asistió a la tertulia. *Lazy as he was,* Haragán y todo. *Lazy as he was, they gave him the chance to improve.* Pero haragán y todo, le dieron la oportunidad de mejorarse. 2. al, amén, e.g.: *As well as,* Al par que, Amén de. *They provided her with two studies as well as numerous references.* Le proporcionaron dos tratados al par que citaciones nombrosas. 3. De, e.g.: *The book was out of print. As a result, the dealer could not supply it to them.* El libro quedó agotado. De ahí que el mercader no se lo suministrara. 4. Por, e.g.: *As if this weren't enough,* Por si esto fuera poco. *As if this weren't enough, they raised the rent.* Por si esto fuera poco, ascendieron el alquiler. 5. Siempre, e.g. *As long as it really is theatre. I enjoy it.* Siempre y cuando sea teatro, me gusta.

Ask [ạsk], p. 54. Add, *vn. To ask for the impossible,* Pedir peras al olmo. *I hated to dampen his enthusiasm, but he was asking for the impossible.* Le ponía sordina a su entusiasmo a regañadientes, pero él pedía peras al olmo.

Assistant [as-sist'-ant], p. 55. Add, *s. Assistant manager,* Subdirector, subgerente. *Of course you know the assistant manager!* ¿Cómo no has de conocer al subdirector?

Attaché [a-ta-shê'], *s.* Agregado diplomático. *Attaché case,* Maletín.

Avoid [a-void'], p. 60. Add. *va.* Dar de lado a. *Whenever she saw him at the store she avoided him.* Siempre que lo veía en la tienda, le daba de lado.

Aware [a-wār'], p. 61. Add, *a.* 1. Consciente. *To be aware of,* Darse cuenta de. 2. Enterado. *To make aware of,* Enterar. *They made him aware of his mistake.* Le enteraron de su error.

Awareness [a-wār'-nes], *s.* 1. (KNOWLEDGE) Conocimiento. 2. (PERCEPTION) Concientización. *Man can improve his awareness with practice.* El hombre puede adiestrar su concientización.

Back [bac], p. 62. Add, *adv*. 1. *To bring back*, (fig.) Retomar, captar de nuevo. *The writer brought back the atmosphere they missed*. El escritor retomaba el ambiente que les hacía falta. 2. *To draw back*, a. (A CURTAIN) Descorrer. b. (WITH FRIGHT) Encogerse. c. (ONE'S FORCES) Retirar. 3. *To get back*, a. (A POSSESSION) Recobrar. *They got their books back*. Recobraron sus libros. b. (TO A PLACE) Llegar. *When did you get back*? ¿Cuándo llegaste? 4. *To give back*, Devolver, reintegrar. 5. *To go back*, Volver, regresar. *He went back, but everything was different*. Regresó, pero todo era distinto. 6. *To go back to (IN TIME)*, *Remontar hasta*. *The custom goes back to the turn of the century*. La costumbre remonta hasta la época finesecular. 7. *To help* [G.B., *hand] back*, Ayudar a volver. *They helped her back to her seat*. La ayudaron a volver a su asiento. 8. *To hold back*, a. (CONTAIN) Suprimir. *She held back her laughter*. Suprimió la risa. b. (RETARD) Ser un atraso [una rémora] para. *His handwriting held him back*. Le era un atraso su ortografía. *Her stubbornness held him back*. Su terquedad era una rémora para él. c. (DELAY) Prorrogar. *They held back the payment*. Prorrogaron el pago. 9. *To put back*, a. (REPLACE) Reponer, poner de nuevo. b. (A STUDENT) Degradar. 10. *To smile back*, Devolver la sonrisa. *She smiled back at the young man*. Le devolvió la sonrisa al jóven. 11. *To take back (what one has said)*, Desdecir, desdecirse. *He took back all the nice things he had told her*. Desdijo todas las cosas bonitas que le había contado. *She took back what she had said*. Se desdijo. 12. *To talk back*, (fig.) Desmandarse. 13. *To think back*, Volver en la mente. *He thought back to his youth*. Volvió en la mente a sus mocedades. —*va*. 1. *To back down*, (fig.) Recular (fam.), dar paso atrás. 2. *To back up*, a. (SUPPORT) Dar pie a. *You must back up your statements with facts*. Hay que dar pie a las declaraciones con los hechos. b. (MOVE BACK) Dar paso atrás, retroceder. c. (A CAR) Dar marcha atrás a. *She slowly backed the car up the driveway*. Lentamente daba marcha atrás al coche por la entrada del garaje.

Ban [ban], p. 65. Add, *s*. Veda. *Total ban*, Veda total. *There is a total ban on fuel-driven vehicles in the downtown area*. Hay una veda total de los vehículos automotores en el recinto céntrico. —*va*. Proscribir. *They ended up by banning the book*. Llegaron a proscribir el libro.

Bandy [ban′-di], p. 65. Add, *va*. Esgrimir. *To bandy words about*, Esgrimir las palabras. *For two whole hours, they bandied about possible reasons for the sudden disappearance of the idol*. Por dos horas corridas esgrimían posibles motivos por el escamoteo del ídolo.

Be [bî], p. 70. Add, *vn*. 1. *Let it be said*, Huelga decir. *Let it be said that truth was never given a back seat*. Huelga decir que la verdad nunca fue a la zaga. 2. *Not to be able to* + verb + *fast enough*, No ver la hora [las santas horas] de. *I can't get out of here fast enough*. No veo la hora de irme de aquí. 3. *To be a past master at*, Hilar muy fino en. *She's a past master at wasting time*. Hila muy fino en engañar el tiempo. 4. *To be accepted* (IN A NEW PLACE), Tener carta de ciudadanía. *The word has been accepted here for many years*. La palabra tiene carta de ciudadanía desde hace muchos años. 5. *To be an easy matter*, Ser empresa llana. *It's an easy matter to turn off the system*. Apagar el sistema es empresa llana. 6. *To be as plain as the nose on one's face*, Saltar a la vista. 7. *To be at one's wits' end*, Estar volado. 8. *To be available to*, Estar a la disposición de. *Use of the library is not available to everyone*. El uso de la biblioteca no está a la disposición de todos. 9. *To be beneath one's dignity*, Tener a menos. *Studying is beneath their dignity*. Tienen a menos el estudiar. 10. *To be changing one's voice*, Estar de muda. *Her son's voice is changing*. Su hijo está de muda. 11. *To be firmly entrenched*, Tener gran arraigo. *The custom is firmly entrenched*. La costumbre tiene gran arraigo. 12. *To be in a dream world*, Estar en la Luna [en Babia]. 13. *To be in good company*, Andar en buen buque. 14. *To be in tune with*, Sintonizarse con. 15. *To be like*, Caber en los sentimientos de. *Such an attitude isn't like him*. Tal actitud no cabe en sus sentimientos. 16. *To be much better than*, Superar con mucho. *He is much better at that than I am*. En eso él me supera con mucho. 17. *To be music to the ears of*, Ser oro molido para. *The news was music to my ears*. La noticia era oro molido para mí. 18. *To be neither here nor there*, No entrar en la cuestión bajo discusión. *Her age is neither here nor there*. Los años que tiene no entra en eso. 19. *To be nip and tuck in*, Regatear. *The two swimmers are nip and tuck in the final heat of the free style*. Los dos nadadores regatean la última carrera del nado libre. 20. *To be on pins and needles*, Tener el alma en un hilo. 21. *To be one's own person*, Autodefinirse, desempeñarse sin influencias ajenas. 22. *To be one's own worst enemy*, Deslustrarse. 23. *To be oneself*, Desempeñarse libremente. 24. *To be out of place*, Estar de más. *He is out of place in that store*. Está de más en aquella tienda. 25. *To be out of sorts*, No estar para fiestas. 26. *To be part of*, (fig.) Estar dentro de. *This book is part of a tradition that we have grown to admire*. Este libro está dentro de una tradición que hemos llegado a admirar. *She is part of his life*. Ella está dentro de la vida de él. 27. *To be Puerto Rican through and through*, Tener la mancha del plátano (P.R.). 28. *To be seen as*, Perfilarse como. *The change was seen as an enormous improvement*. El cambio se perfilaba como una mejora descomunal. 29. *To be serious at*, Tener tesón para. *He is a serious student*. Tiene tesón para el estudio. 30. *To be still standing*, Permanecer en pie, mantenerse en pie. *The Greek theatre is still standing*. El teatro griego permanece en pie. 31. *To be tickled pink by*, (fam.) Bañarse en agua rosada con. *She's tickled pink by the idea*. Ella se baña en agua rosada con la idea. 32. *To be too choosy about*, (fam.) Hilar muy delgado en. *He was too choosy about a job*. En lo de un empleo él hilaba muy delgado. 33. *To be unreliable*, Ser como la hoja del yagrumo (P.R.). 34. *To be up and around (after having been sick)*, Alentarse (P.R.). 35. *To be up to something*, (fam.) Tener algún propósito solapado.

Bedroom community [bed′-rūm com-miū′-ni-ti], *s*. Ciudad satélite. *Bedroom communities usually empty by day to provide the work force for a nearby large city*. De costumbre, las ciudades satélites se despueblan de día para proporcionar la mano de obra en una urbe vecina.

Begin [be-gin′], p. 73. Add, *va*. (AFTER A LONG TIME) Llegar, e.g.: *To begin to think*, Llegar a creer. *After so many years her friends began to think that she had forgotten [forgot] them*. Después de tantos años sus amigos llegaron a creer que se había olvidado de ellos. *I began to feel better at long last*. Al fin y al cabo llegué a sentirme mejor.

Beginning stages [be-gin′-ing stêj′-ez], *s*. Etapa de tanteos. *At that time museum science was still in the beginning stages*. En aquel entonces la ciencia museográfica se encontraba todavía en una etapa de tanteos.

Birthright [berth′-rait], p. 80. Add, *s*. (fig.) Acervo. *Picturesque language is a birthright of us all*. El lenguaje pintoresco es un acervo de todo el mundo. *Freedom of worship is a birthright we hold dear [cherish]*. La libertad de culto es un acervo que encarecemos.

Both [bōth], p. 89. Add, *a*. 1. Coincidir en, e.g.: *They both present the European viewpoint*. Coinciden en presentar el punto de vista europeo. 2. Alternar, e.g.: *You used both words in your theme*. Alternabas las dos palabras en tu ensayo. —*pron*. *Both of them*, Uno y otro. *Both of them said so*. Uno y otro lo dijeron. —*adv*. Lo mismo + verb + que + verb, e.g.: *They both laughed and cried at the news*. Lo mismo se reían que se lloraban de la noticia.

Bother [bodh′-er], p. 89, Add, *va*. 1. (WORRY) Preocupar. *Not to bother a [one] bit*, Tener sin cuidado. *His troubles don't bother him one bit*. Sus apuros le tienen sin cuidado. 2. (INCONVENIENCE) Molestar. *His unexpected visits don't bother us*. Sus visitas inesperadas no nos molestan.

Break [brêk], p. 93. Add, *s*. 1. (PAUSE)

Receso. *A break from one's labors [labours] promotes their effectiveness*. El receso de las labores patrocina su eficacia. *The break gives you time for a cup of tea or coffee*. El receso le da tiempo para tomar una taza de té o una taza de café. 2. (GOOD FORTUNE) Suerte. *The opening of the new factory was the break the workers had been waiting for*. La inauguración de la nueva fábrica era la suerte que los obreros esperaban.

Bring [bring], p. 95. Add, *va*. 1. *To bring around to one's point of view*, Acomodar (P.R.). *If we wait a while, we can bring him around to our point of view*. Si esperamos un poco, podremos acomodarlo. 2. *To bring by*, Llevar a la casa de uno. *Why don't you bring her by tomorrow?* ¿Por qué no la llevas a mi casa mañana? 3. *To bring oneself to*, Inducirse a. *I couldn't bring myself to tell them*. No pude inducirme a decírselo. 4. *To bring out*, a. (A THEME) Destacar. *He brought out several important details*. Destacó varios detalles importantes. b. (AN OBJECT) Sacar. *He brought out several lamps*. Sacó varias lámparas. c. (ONE'S PERSONALITY) Sacar a volar. *With much hard work, the teacher brought the shy girl out*. Con mucho trabajo la maestra sacó a volar a la chica difidente. d. (UNCOVER) Desnidar. *His efforts brought out the truth*. Sus esfuerzos desnidaron la verdad. 5. *To bring to an end*, Meter raya a. *We must bring this hurlyburly to an end*. Hay que meter raya a esta barahúnda. 6. *To bring to bear*, Hacer pesar. *We must bring some common sense to bear*. Hay que hacer pesar el sentido común. *If his ideas aren't brought to bear, the plan will fail utterly*. Si no pesan sus ideas, el plan fracasará por completo. 7. *To bring up*, a. (BY WAY OF COMPARISON) Sacar a colación. *He brought up the first survey by way of comparison*. Sacó a colación el primer sondeo. b. (AT THE WRONG TIME) Sacar a relucir. *He brought up the argument without meaning to do so*. Sacó a relucir la riña sin pensar. 8. *To bring up to date*, Actualizar. She brought all her files up to date. Actualizó todos sus ficheros. 9. *To bring with oneself [along]*, a. Conllevar. *This step will bring many new challenges with it*. Este paso conllevará muchos nuevos retos. b. (ALWAYS USED IN A NEGATIVE SENSE) Arrastrar. *Gossip always brings unpleasantness with it*. Los chismes siempre arrastran las desazones. *He always brings that critical attitude of his along*. Siempre arrastra esa actitud suya de criticón.

Bus [bus], p. 101. Add, *s*. 1. *City bus*, Autobús. 2. *Intercity bus*, Coche de línea. 3. *Tour bus*, Autocar.

Calm [cām], p. 105. Add, *va*. *To calm down*, Desenojar. *They tried to calm down the angry customer*. Procuraron desenojar al cliente amostazado.

Camlet [cam'-let], p. 106. Add, *s*. (G.B.) 1. Tejido de lana y pelo de cabra. 2. *Camlet-cloak*, (obs.) Capa de lana y pelo de cabra. *He sat there in his camlet-cloak dwelling on the past*. Estaba allí arropado de su capa de lana y pelo de cabra y se explayaba sobre el pasado.

Campus [cam'pus], p. 106. Add, *s*. 1. Ciudad universitaria. 2. *Branch campus*, Recinto suplente. 3. *Main campus*, Recinto central.

Capture [cap'-chur], p. 109. Add, *va*. 1. (AN IMAGE) Plasmar. 2. (INTEREST, ATTENTION) Captar.

Care [cār], p. 110. Add, *s*. *To take care of*, 1. (RESOLVE) Solucionar. *Their father took care of the problem*. Su padre solucionó el problema. 2. (TEND) Cuidar. *She is taking care of the child*. Ella cuida al niño. 3. (TAKE CHARGE OF) Encargarse de. *We teachers are taking care of the campaign*. Los maestros nos encargamos de la campaña. —*vn*. 1. *To care for*, a. (TEND) Cuidar. *She is caring for the child*. Ella cuida al niño. b. (LIKE) Gustarle. *I don't care for candy* (G.B., *sweets*). No me gustan los dulces. 2. *Not to care if*, No importar. *I don't care if he goes with us or not*. No me importa si nos acompaña o no. 3. *Not to care to*, No gustar. *I don't care to tell my troubles to the whole world*. No me gusta contar mis penas a todo bicho viviente.

Careful thought [cār'-ful thōt], *s*. Sindéresis. *Much careful thought went into the plan for the new gallery*. Mucha sindéresis entró en planear la nueva galería.

Catch [cach], p. 114. Add, *va*. 1. *To catch fire*, Encenderse. 2. *To catch on*, Cundir. *The new style just didn't catch on*. Es que no cundió la nueva moda. 3. *To catch sight of*, Dar vista a. *He caught sight of the man running down the street*. Dio vista al hombre quien corría calle abajo. 4. *To catch up*, a. (G.B., REACH) Alcanzar. *He caught her up at the corner*. La alcanzó en la esquina. b. (Amer., FINISH ONE'S WORK) Ponerse al día. *I finally caught up*. Al fin me puse al día. 5. *To catch up with*, (Amer., REACH) Alcanzar. *He tried to catch up with her*. Trató de alcanzarla.

Cause [cōz], p. 115. Add, *s*. Bandería. *Just as she had warned us, the cause came to nothing*. Al igual que ella nos lo profetizara, la bandería acabó en la nada.

Chance [chans], p. 119. Add, *s*. 1. Encontradizo, e.g.: *Chance acquaintance*, Conocimiento encontradizo. 2. Por casualidad. *Chance meeting*, Encuentro por casualidad. 3. *By chance*, Acertar, i.e.: *I found it by chance near the swamp*. Acerté a encontrarlo cerca del pantano. *I met her by chance at the party*. Acerté a conocerla en la fiesta. —*va*. 1. Arriesgar. 2. *To chance it*. Correr el riesgo, correr albures [el abur].

Chauvinism [shō'vin-izm], p. 121. Add, *s*. 1. (TOWARD ONE'S COUNTRY) Patriotería. 2. (TOWARD ONE'S HOME TOWN) Aldeanismo. 3. (TOWARD THE MALE GENDER) Machismo.

Chime [chaim], p. 123. Add, *vn*. *To chime in*, Terciar. *He chimed in with his usual words of encouragement*. Terció con sus acostumbradas dos palabras de aliento.

Choppy [chop'-i], p. 124. Add, *a*. (WATER) Picado. *The forecast is for slightly choppy seas by this afternoon*. El pronóstico indica mar ligeramente picado para la tarde.

City [sit'-i], p. 128. Add, *s*. *City manager*, Regente de la ciudad.

Civic pride [siv'-ic praid], *s*. Calidad cívica. *Civic pride is the mark of a city's growth*. La calidad cívica jalona el desarrollo de una ciudad.

Clone [clōn], s. (Neol.) Retrato idéntico de algún organismo que crece de una célula de éste. *Some parents look upon their children as clones of themselves*. Algunos padres consideran a sus hijos como retratos idénticos de ellos mismos.

Come [cum], p. 138. Add, *vn*. 1. *To come to*, Volver en sí. *When he came to, the cockpit was empty*. Cuando volvió en sí, la carlinga estaba desierta. 2. *To come to grips with*, a. Agarrarse a. *He came to grips with his opponent*. Se agarró a su contrincante. b. (fig.) Afrontar. *She couldn't come to grips with her loss*. Ella no pudo afrontar su pérdida. 3. *To come to grips with oneself*, Llegar a desempeñarse cuerdamente. 4. *To come to the attention of*, a. Llegar al oído de. *The injustice came to the attention of the whole town*. La injusticia llegó al oído del pueblo entero. b. Al oído de, e.g.: *The publication of the news came to the attention of only a few*. Las noticias se publicaron al oído de unos cuantos. 5. *To come up with* a. (A SUM OF MONEY) Juntar. b. (FOB OFF) Tratar de pasar. *He came up with some silly story or other*. Trató de pasar cualquier patraña. c. (AFTER MUCH DILIGENCE) Dar con. *At long last he came up with the answer*. Finalmente dio con la respuesta.

Communications [com-miū-ni-kê'-shunz], *s. pl*. (Neol.) 1. Medios informativos. 2. *Communications specialist*, Comunicólogo. 3. *Communications satellite*, Satélite de telecomunicación.

Completely [com-plīt'-li], p. 143. Add, *adv*. Acabar de, e.g.: 1. *To convince completely*, Acabar de convencer. *I was completely convinced by his manner*. Su ademán acabó de convencerme. 2. *To fool completely*, Acabar de engañar. *Her way of speaking fooled me completely*. Su manera de hablar acabó de engañarme. 3. *To dishonor [G.B. dis-honour] completely*, Acabar de deshonrar. *Such an action would completely dishonor his good name*. Tal acto acabaría de deshonrar su buen nombre.

Compromise [com'-pro-maiz], p. 144. Add, *s*. 1. Componenda. *The compromise ended up pleasing a few members*. La componenda llegó a complacer a contados socios. 2. (For.) Compromiso.

Confrontation [con-frun-tê'-shun], p. 148. Add, *s*. 1. (WITH DISCORD) Enfrentamiento. 2. (COMPARISON) Confrontación.

Construct [con'-struct], *s*. (Neol.) Constructor. *Motivation is certainly not a hypothetical construct where language learning is concerned*. Es indudable que la motivación no sea un constructor hipotético en lo que al aprendizaje de los idiomas atañe.

Consult [con-sult'], p. 153. Add, *va*. 1. (SPECIFICALLY FOR HELP) Acudir a. 2. *To consult public opinion*, Hacer la consulta popular. *They consulted public opinion before they built the bridge*. Hicieron la consulta popular antes de construir el puente. —*vn*. 1. Conferenciar. 2. *To consult together*, Conferenciar. 3. *To consult with*, Aconsejarse con, acudir a.

Contortion [con-ter'-shun], p. 154. Add, *s*. *Contortions*, (fig.) Juegos malabares. *Her contortions were comical when she tried to use the chopsticks*. Sus juegos malabares al tratar de servirse de los palillos chinos eran cómicos.

Contradiction in terms [con-tra-dic'-shun in termz], *s*. Contrasentido. *Falsehood in the company of honesty is a contradiction in terms*. La mentira en unión a la honradez es un contrasentido.

Cross [cros], p. 169. Add, *va*. *To cross one's mind*, Pasarle por las mientes. *It never crossed her mind to untie the parcel*. Nunca le pasó por las mientes desatar el paquete. —*a*. *To be cross with*, Enojarse con, enfadarse con.

Cult [cult], p. 171. Add, *s*. 1. *Cult of personality*, Interés exagerado por la aréola personal. 2. *Cult of things foreign*, Malinchismo. 3. *Follower of such a cult*, Malinchista.

Cutout [cut'-out], p. 174. Add, *s*. Recortable. *A Medieval castle can be put together with the cutouts printed on these sheets*. Con los recortables impresos en estas hojas se arma un castillo medioeval.

Cybernation [sci-bẹr-nê'-shun], *s*. (Information science) Cibernación.

Damn [dam], p. 175. Add, *va*. *To damn with faint praise*, Regatear el elogio a. *The critics damned the play with faint praise and it closed two weeks later*. Los críticos le regatearon el elogio a la comedia y a las dos semanas fracasó.

Data [dê'-ta], p. 176. Add, *s. pl*. (Information science) 1. *Data processing*, a. (GENERAL TERM) Informática. b. (ACTIVITY ITSELF) Elaboración de datos. 2. *Data processor*, a. (PERSON) Ordenador de datos, ordenadora de datos. b. (MACHINE) Elaborador de datos, computadora.

Day [dê], p. 177. Add, *s*. 1. (OPPOSED TO NIGHT) Jornada. 2. *Day shift*, Turno de día. 3. *Two days later*, Al subsiguiente. *I'm wrong. It wasn't the following day, but two days later that the corner-stone was laid*. Miento. No fue al otro día sino al subsiguiente que se clebró la primera piedra.

Delight [dẹ-lait'], p. 183. Add, *va*. Hacer las delicias de. *She delighted her friends with clever sayings on all her cards*. Hacía las delicias de sus amigos con dichos salados en todas sus tarjetas. —*vn*. *To delight in*, Recrearse en. *They delighted in frequent walks through the park*. So recreaban en paseos frecuentes por el parque.

Demonstrate [dem'-on-strêt], p. 185. Add, *va*. Hacer gala de. *His conversation demonstrates wide reading*. Su conversación hace gala de unas lecturas de gran envergadura.

Demote [dî-mōt'], *va*. 1. (A STUDENT) Degradar. 2. Rebajar. *They demoted five colonels*. Rebajaron a cinco coroneles.

Derive [dẹ-raiv'], p. 187. Add, *va*. Deprender (Mex.). *He derives many of his ideas from his own life*. Deprende muchas ideas suyas de sus propios antecedentes.

Development [dẹ-vel'-op-m̦ent], p. 190. Add, *s*. Formación. *The development that he and the other artists showed really separated the wheat from the chaff*. La formación que él y los demás artistas mostraron sí que separó el tamo del grano.

Dislike [dis-laik'], p. 199. Add, *va*. Antipatizar. *He dislikes such displays of affection*. Antipatiza tales derroches de afecto.

Disposable [dis-pōz'-a-bl], p. 201. Add, *a*. Desechable. *Disposable paper plates are the mainstay of any picnic*. Los platos desechables de cartón son el sostén principal de cualquier merienda.

Docking [dok'-ing], s. 1. (Mar.) Entrada al dique. *The docking of an ocean liner is no mean feat*. La entrada al dique de un transatlántico no es empresa llana. 2. (Aer., OF SPACE VEHICLES) Atracada, conexión. 3. *Docking adapter*, (Aer.) Pasillo que se forma al atracar dos cápsulas en órbita.

Drop [drop], p. 211. Add, *va*. 1. *To drop a hint*, Echar una indirecta. 2. *To drop all formality*, Dejarse de composturas, no andar con miramentos. 3. *To drop off*, a. (A PERSON) Dejar en determinado sitio. *The bus driver dropped her off right across from her house*. El conductor la dejó en la acera frente por frente a su casa. b. (A THING) Entregar. *We dropped off the books on the way home*. De vuelta a casa, entregamos los libros. 4. *To drop out of the conversation*, Hacer mutis (fig.). *He dropped out of the conversation almost immediately*. Casi inmediatamente hizo mutis.

Dustjacket [dust'-jak-et], *s*. Sobrecubierta, *The dustjacket quotes the opinions of various scientists*. La sobrecubierta cita las opiniones de diversos científicos.

Ecod! [î'-cod], *interj*. (G.B., obs.) ¡Cáspita! *He let out an 'ecod' and slammed the door in the stranger's face*. Soltó su cáspita y le dio un portazo al forastero.

Economic [î-co-nom'-ic], p. 217. Add, *a*. *Economic slump*, Bache. *The economic slump worsened the rate of unemployment*. El bache empeoró el índice de desempleo.

Economic base [ec-o-nom'ic bês], *s*. Infraestructura. *The economic base of a country's industrial productivity must be strong in order for it to weather temporary setbacks [reversals]*. La infraestructura de la productividad industrial del país tiene que ser sólida para aguantar reveses temporáneos.

Embedding [em-bed'-ing], *s*. (Linguistics) Incrustación. *Embedding combines two sentences in one*. La incrustación reúne dos oraciones en una.

Endorsement [en-dōrs'-mẹnt], p. 225. Add, *s*. (fig.) Aval. *He sought the endorsement of a real intellectual powerhouse*. Buscaba el aval de un rayo acabado.

Engagement [en-gêj'-mẹnt], p. 225. Add, *s*. (to marry) Compromiso. *The engagement lasted two months longer than their friends thought it would*. El compromiso duró dos meses más de lo que sus amigos habían ideado [pensado].

Engineering [en-ji-nîr'-ing], *s*. Ingeniería.

Enjoy [en-joi'], p. 226. Add, *va*. Degustar. *All the guests at the national inn enjoyed the Valencian rice table*. Todos los huéspedes del parador nacional degustaron la paella a la valenciana.

Environmental [en-vai-run-men'-tal], p. 228. Add, *a*. 1. *Environmental protection*, Protección al medio ambiente. *Environmental protection is a legacy for future generations*. La protección al medio ambiente es un patrimonio para las generaciones venideras. 2. *Environmental pollution*. a. (ACT) Polución ambiental. b. (RESULT) Deteriorio ambiental. *Environmental pollution can be corrected*. El deteriorio ambiental puede sanearse.

Environmentalist [en-vai-run-men'-ta-list], *s*. (Neol.) Ambientalista. *Environmentalists should weigh long-range goals against short-range ones before they make their recommendations*. Los ambientalistas deben poner en la misma balanza fines de largo y corto plazo antes de dar sus recomendaciones.

Equipment [e-cwip'-mẹnt], p. 230. Add, *s*. Dispositivos. *The equipment needed for the launching will arrive at the shipyard tomorrow*. Los dispositivos que hacen falta para la botadura naval llegarán al astillero mañana.

Ergonomics [ẹr-go-nom'-ics], *s*. (Neol., G.B.) Ingeniería del factor humano, biotecnología.

Escape velocity [es-kêp' vẹ-los'-i-ti], *s*. (Aer.) Velocidad de liberación. *Escape velocity frees the spaceship from the earth's gravity*. La velocidad de liberación desencadena la nave de la gravedad de la Tierra.

Expand [ex-pand'], p. 238. Add,

va. 1. (Mec.) Desplegar. *He expanded the telescope*. Desplegó el telescopio. 2. (fig.) Multiplicar. *Serious effort helped them expand their market rapidly*. Un esfuerzo tenaz les ayudó a multiplicar rápidamente su mercado.
Exude [ex-yūd′], p. 242. Add, *va*. (fig.) Prodigar. *Her manner exuded charm*. Sus modales prodigaban embeleso.

Family planning [fam′-i-li plan′-ing], *s*. Planificación familiar.
Fashion [fash′-un], p. 248. Add, *s*. *Fashion show*, Desfile de modas. *The fashion show was history-making*. El desfile de modas hizo historia.
Fast-paced [fast′-pêst], *a*. 1. (BUSY) Azacaneado. *Fast-paced city life was too much for him*. La vida azacaneada de la ciudad le era antipática. 2. (ACTION-PACKED) Accidentado. *He liked fast-paced Picaresque novels best of all*. Más que nada le gustaban las accidentadas novelas picarescas.
Father [fā′-dher], p. 248. Add, *s*. (fig.) Abuelo, adán. *The father of modern botany was Swedish*. El abuelo de la botánica moderna era sueco.
Feelings [fīl′-ingz], *s*. 1. *Expressing one's feelings*. Sentimentalismo. 2. *To have mixed feelings*. Tener contrariedades. *I have mixed feelings about the propriety of such an action*. Tengo contrariedades en cuanto a la propiedad de tal acto.
Fellow [fel′-ō], p. 251. Add, *a*. También. *He married a fellow teacher*. Se casó con una también maestra. *She looked for a fellow Chicagoan without success*. Buscó en vano una también Chicagoense. *His fellow office workers gave him a good-bye party*. Los también oficinistas le brindaron una fiesta de despedida.
Fire [fair], p. 257. Add, *s*. *Fire hydrant*, Boca de agua.
Flap [flap], p. 260. Add, *s*. (OF A DUSTJACKET) Solapa. *It's better not to compromise with untruths on the flap copy*. Es mejor no transigir con la falsedad en la solapa.
Forge [fōrj], p. 270. Add, *va*. *To forge together*, (fig.) Lañar. *They forged together a nation*. Lañaron a una nación.
Freedom [frī′-dum], p. 273. Add, *s*. 1. (fig.) Desenvoltura. *There's a certain freedom in his style that's much to my liking*. Su estilo tiene cierta desenvoltura que es muy de mi agrado. 2. *Freedom of information*, (Neol.) Alcance desenfadado por parte de los ciudadanos de todo documento gubernamental que no perjudique ni los derechos de ninguno de ellos ni la seguridad de la nación. 3. *Freedom of worship*, Libertad de culto.
Flyby [flai′-bai], *s*. (Aer.) Pasada en vuelo. *The flyby of a planet permits a close inspection of the features of its surface*. La pasada en vuelo de un planeta permite la observación detenida de las características de su superficie.
Front [frunt], p. 276. Add, *a*. *Front porch*, Batey (P.R.). *Let's enjoy our after-dinner conversation on the front porch*. Vamos a gozar de la sobremesa en el batey.
Fuel [fiū′-el], p. 277. Add, *s*. 1. (fig.) Esca. 2. *To add fuel to the fire*, (fig.) Encrudecer un apuro con más trámites. *Sending him to New York was only adding fuel to the fire*. El enviarle a Nueva York no hizo sino encrudecer el apuro. 3. *Fuel cell* (Aer.) Célula de combustible.
Fulminate [ful′-mi-nêt], p. 278. Add, *vn*. *To fulminate against*, Despotricar contra, fulminar críticas contra. *He continued to fulminate against the plan*. Seguía despotricando contra el propósito. *She grumbled and fulminated against the idea the whole day through*. Refunfuñaba y fulminaba críticas contra la idea todo el santo día.

Garbage can [garb′-ij can], *s*. 1. Zafacón (P.R.). 2. Cubo de desperdicios.
Geothermal [je̜-o-the̜r′-mal], *a*. (Neol.) Geotérmico.
Get [get], p. 285. Add, *va*. (G.B., pret. y pp. GOT; Amer. pret. GOT, pp. GOT y GOTTEN). 1. Captar. *He didn't get what you said*. No captó lo que dijiste. *After many attempts he got the attention of the crowd*. Después de muchas tentativas, captó la atención de la muchedumbre. 2. (fam.) Tener. *Have you got a match?* ¿Tienes un fósforo? 3. Traer, buscar. *Have you gotten [G.B., got] me the newspaper?* ¿Me has traído el periódico? *Get me a pencil, please*. Búscame un lápiz, por favor. 4. Ponerse. *He's gotten [G.B., got] extremely gloomy lately*. Recientemente se ha puesto muy melancólico. 5. (fam.) Tener que. *He's got to go*. Tiene que irse. 6. *Get going!* (fam.) ¡Corriendo! 7. *Get ready for a surprise!* ¡Pásmese usted! 8. *To get a move on [get going]*, (fam.) Espabilarse, despabilarse. 9. *To get an advantage from*, Sacar partido de. *What advantage do you get from the arrangement?* ¿Qué partido sacas tú del arreglo? 10. *To get along*, a. (MAKE DO) Pasárselas. *I'm getting along pretty well*. Me las paso bastante bien. b. (AGREE) Llevarse bien, entenderse. 11. *To get along without*, Pasarse sin. *She's getting along without their help*. Se pasa sin la ayuda de ellos. 12. *To get back at*, Pagarle en su propia moneda. 13. *To get down to brass tacks*, Ir al grano. 14. *To get down to business*, Obrar en serio. 15. *To get goose pimples* [G.B., *goose flesh*], (fam.) Abrírsele a uno las carnes. *I get goose flesh just thinking about it*. El mero pensar en ello y se me abren las carnes. 16. *To get in the way of*, Cruzarse en el camino de. *His inflated ego got in the way of his success*. Su egolatría se cruzaba en el camino de su éxito. 17. *To get involved*, Involucrarse, comprometerse. 18. *To get one's walking papers* [G.B., *the sack*], a. (A JOB) Ser despedido. b. (AN AFFAIR OF THE HEART) Recibir calabazas. 19. *To get out of*, (fig.) Sacar en claro. *What did you get out of what he said?* ¿Qué sacaste en claro de lo que dijo? 20. *To get the worst of it*, Tocarle la peor parte. *She got the worst of it*. Le tocó la peor parte. 21. *To get to the bottom of* (A COMPLICATED MATTER), Desentrañar. *They will soon get to the bottom of who stole the canvas*. Dentro de poco desentrañarán quién robó el lienzo.
Give [giv], p. 287. Add, *va*. 1. *Not to give a chance to finish*, Dejar con la palabra en la boca. *He ran out without giving me a chance to finish*. Salió corriendo, dejándome con la palabra en la boca. 2. *Not to give a damn*, No dársele un bledo. *Frankly I don't give a damn*. Francamente no se me da un bledo.
Go [go], p. 290. Add, *vn*. 1. *To go across*, (Amer.) Atravesar. *Go across the street at the bridge*. Atraviesa la calle al puente. 2. *To go ahead with* (DESPITE OPPOSITION), Porfiar. *When the rain ended, they went ahead with the party*. Cuando escampó, porfiaban con la fiesta. *It doesn't matter what they say. Go ahead with it!* No importa lo que digan. ¡Porfíe en ello! 3. *To go along with*, a. (HUMOR) Consentirle a uno los caprichos que tiene. *You had to go along with him or he grew quite angry*. Había que consentirle los caprichos que tenía o se enojaba bastante. b. (AGREE) Aprobar. *I can't go along with such foolishness*. No puedo aprobar tal tontería. c. (ACCOMPANY) Acompañar. *He'll go along with you to the store*. Él te acompañará a la tienda. 4. *To go back on*, a. (G.B., REVIEW) Repasar, tratar de nuevo. *The manager went back on the first item*. El gerente repasó el primer renglón. b. (A PROMISE) No cumplir. *He went back on his word*. No cumplió su palabra. 5. *To go beyond*, Superar. *She goes far beyond what her job requires*. Supera con mucho los requisitos de su empleo. 6. *To go it alone*, Desempeñarse sin ayuda ajena. 7. *To go over*, a. (Amer., REVIEW) Repasar, tratar de nuevo. b. (G.B., CROSS) Atravesar. *Cross over the road at the bridge*. Atraviesa la calle al puente. 7. *To go through*, a. (EXPERIENCE) Vivir. *He's gone through many interesting experiences*. Ha vivido muchas experiencias interesantes. b. (SEARCH) Rastrear. *I've gone through all my pockets but I can't find it*. He rastreado todos mis bolsillos, pero no puedo hallarlo. 8. *To go through with*, Llevar a cabo. *He never goes through with anything*. Nunca lleva nada a cabo. 9. *To go where the work is*, Acudir al reclamo. *They hated to leave, but they had to go where the work was*. Partían a regañadientes, pero tenían que acudir al reclamo. 10. *It goes without saying that her gratitude knew no bounds*. Sobra decir que prodigaba su reconocimiento.
Good sportsmanship [gud spōrts′-man-ship], *s*. Deportividad. *Good sportsmanship is hard to come by nowadays*. Hoy en día la deportividad

es de difícil alcance.

Graduate [grad'-yu-êt], p. 294. Add, *vn*. Egresar. *How many graduate of those who begin?* De los principiantes, ¿Cuántos egresan?

Graphic [graf'-ic], p. 295. Add, *a*. (fig.) Ilustrativo. *He gave us a graphic account of the events that led up to the strike*. Nos dio una relación ilustrativa de los acontecimientos que acarrearon la huelga.

Group [grūp], p. 299. Add, *s*. 1. (WITH COMMON INTEREST) Gremio. 2. *Member of a group*, Agremiado, agremiada. — *a*. Gremial. *Group pressure brought about the change*. La presión gremial acarreó el cambio.

Guard [gārd], p. 300, Add, *s*. *To stay on one's guard*, Permanecer en atalaya.

Guidance counselor, counsellor [gaid'-ans caun'-sel-ọr], *s*. Orientador, Orientadora. *Guidance counsellors can often help students choose the right career*. Muchas veces los orientadores pueden ayudar a los alumnos a escoger la carrera indicada para ellos.

Guideline [gaid'-lain], s. Lineamiento. *What guidelines have been set for the budget?* ¿Cuáles son los lineamientos que se han establecido para el presupuesto?

Handicapped person [hand'-i-capt pęr'-sn], *s*. Minusvalido, minusvalida. *Many buses now provide special seats for handicapped persons*. Actualmente muchos autobuses son provistos de asientos especiales para los minusvalidos.

Handwriting [hand-rait'-ing], p. 305. Add, *s*. *In one's own handwriting*, En el propio puño y letra de uno. *She liked to receive letters in his own handwriting*. Le gustaba recibir cartas en su propio puño y letra.

Hard [hārd], p. 306. Add, *a*. 1. Casualidad, e.g.: *To be hard to believe*, Ser mucha casualidad. *It's hard to believe they all forgot the same book*. Es mucha casualidad para que se hayan olvidado todos del mismo libro. 2. Difícilmente, e.g.: *Hard to come by*, Difícilmente asequible. *The report is hard to come by from all accounts*. A decir de todos el informe es difícilmente asequible. 3. Difícil, e.g.: *Hard to reach*, De difícil alcance. *The meadow is hard to reach*. El prado es de difícil alcance.

Hardly [hārd'-li], p. 306. Add, *adv*. Apenas si. *It hardly seems possible that Tuesday morning is already here*. Apenas si parece posible que haya llegado la mañana del martes.

Haste [hêst], p. 308. Add, *s*. *Haste makes [is] waste*. La prisa no hace migas con la artesanía.

Hate [hêt], p. 308. Add, *va*. De muy mal agrado, a regañadientes, e.g.: *I hate to turn him down*. Le estoy comunicando una negativa a regañadientes.

Have [hav], p. 309. Add, *va*. 1. *To have a bad time of it [a terrible time]*, Pasar sudores. *I had a terrible time trying to get the window open*. Pasé sudores tratando de abrir la ventana. *I had a bad time of it, that I did*. Pasé sudores. Eso sí. 2. *To have a market [outlet] for*, Tener salida para. *We have no market for literary anthologies*. No tenemos salida para los florilegios literarios. 3. *To have a mean disposition*, Tener malas entrañas. *Be careful with him! He has a really mean disposition*. ¡Cúidese con él! Tiene muy malas entrañas. 4. *To have against*, Tener en contra de. *What do you have against him [her, them]?* ¿Qué tienes en su contra? 5. *To have all the reason in the world [good reason] to*, Tener sobradas razones para. *They had good reason to refuse*. Tenían sobradas razones para rehusar. 6. *To have half a mind to*, Estar casi decidido a. *I have half a mind to tell him to forget it*. Estoy casi decidido a decirle que se lo olvide. 7. *To have no business*, No ser cuenta de, no tocarle. *He has no business telling them what to do*. No es cuenta de él decirles cuántos son cinco. *We have no business being there*. No nos toca estar allí. 8. *To have the makings [potential] of*, Tener madera de. Her daughter has the makings of an artist. Su hija tiene madera de artista. 9. *To have to do with*, Pintar en (fam.). *And what do you have to do with that?* Y tú, ¿qué pintas en eso?

Head [hed], p. 310. Add, *s*. 1. *To give a big head*, (fam.) Llenar de humo la cabeza. *The reviews gave him a big head*. Las reseñas le llenaban de humo la cabeza. 2. *To turn one's head*, Engreírle a uno. *All that praise will turn your head*. Tantas alabanzas te engreirán. 3. *With one's head in the sky [in the sand]*, Con cabeza de cartón. *They stood there with their heads in the sky while* [G.B., *whilst*] *the dog ran away*. Estaban allí con cabezas de cartón mientras que el perro se fugaba. —*vn*. *To head into*, Hacer proa a. *They headed right into the storm*. Hicieron proa directa a la tormenta.

Headquarters [hed'-cwēr-tęrz], p. 310. Add, *s*. Sede, central.

Heart [hart], p. 311. Add, *s*. 1. *As many* + noun + *as one's heart desires*, A pedir de boca. *You may have as many books as your heart desires*. Puedes tener libros a pedir de boca. 2. *After one's own heart*, Enteramente del agrado de uno. *It's a play after my own heart*. Es una comedia enteramente de mi agrado. 3. *In the heart of*, En el seno de. *They came upon the museum in the heart of the city*. Dieron con el museo en el seno de la ciudad. 4. *Loyal heart*, Pecho leal. *Every loyal heart thrilled with pride to the music*. Todo pecho leal temblaba de orgullo al oír la música. 5. *(One's heart) not to be in something*, No tener ánimo para algo. *My heart just isn't in it any longer*. Ya no tengo ánimo para ello. 6. *To one's heart content*, A las anchas de uno. *You may sing to your heart's content*. Puedes cantar a tus anchas. 7. *To open one's heart to*, Desahogarse con. *She opened her heart to her mother*. Se desahogó con su madre.

Heated [hît'-id], *a*. 1. Con calefacción. *I want a heated room*. Deseo una habitación con calefacción. 2. (fig.) Enconado. *The argument was long, heated and long-winded*. La discusión fue larga, enconada y kilométrica.

Heavy-handed [hev-i-hand'-ed], *a*. Mostrenco. *His essay was flawed by a heavy-handed style*. Su ensayo quedó deformado por un estilo mostrenco.

Height [hait], p. 313. Add, *s*. *Heights*, (fig.) Cotos. *The Mayans achieved great heights of civilization* [G.B., *civilisation]*. Los mayas alcanzaron grandes cotos de civilización.

Helpful [help'-ful], p. 314. Add, *a*. Socorrido. *His method is quite helpful*. Su método es bastante socorrido.

Hold [hōld], p. 320. Add, *va*. 1. *Not to be able to hold a candle to*, Quedarse tamañito con. *He can't hold a candle to our free-style champion*. Se queda tamañito con nuestro campeón de nado libre. 2. *To hold dear*, Encarecer. *She holds those memories dearer every year*. Cada año encarece más aquellos recuerdos. 3. *To hold one's tongue*, Callarse la boca. *Hold your tongue!* (fam.) ¡Cállate la boca! 4. *To hold up*, a. (DELAY) Demorar. *The rain held up our departure*. La lluvia demoró nuestra partida. b. (DELAY A PERSON) Detener. *I hate to hold you up like this, but the letter must go out today*. No me gusta detenerla así, pero la carta tiene que salir hoy. c. (ROB) Atracar. *The bandits held up the train*. Los bandidos atracaron el tren. —*s*. 1. (IN WRESTLING) a. Toma. b. (PINNING COMBINATION) Llave. 2. *No holds barred*, (fig.) A brazo partido. *The argument was a no-holds-barred affair*. La riña era a brazo partido.

Household [haus'-hōld], p. 326. Add, *s*. *Household appliance*, Electrodoméstico. *Household chores*, Tareas de casa. *Household goods*, Enseres domésticos.

Housing [hauz'-ing], p. 326. Add, *s*. 1. (Mec.) Encaje. 2. (DWELLINGS IN GENERAL) Vivienda. *We must provide housing for many different kinds of people*. Nos vemos obligados a proveer vivienda para muchos gremios diferentes. 3. *Housing development* [G.B., *estate*], Urbanización. *The new housing estate makes use of the most modern technical advances*. La nueva urbanización se vale de los más modernos adelantos técnicos.

Hovercraft [hov'ęr-craft], *s*. (Neol.) Aerodeslizador. *A hovercraft makes difficult landings unnecessary*. El aerodeslizador hace innecesario el aterrizaje complicado.

Human [hiū'-man], p. 327. Add, *a*. *Human engineering*, (Neol., Amer.) Ingeniería del factor humano, biotecnología.

Hydrofoil [hai'-dro-foil], *s*. (Neol.) Plano hidrodinámico. *A hydrofoil allows rapid movement over the water's surface*. El plano hidrodinámico facilita movimiento rápido sobre la superficie del agua.

Hydrospace [hai′-dro-spês], *s.* (Neol.) Hidrospacio, espacio submarino. *Hydrospace and aerospace are the two new frontiers of tomorrow.* El hidrospacio y el aerospacio son las dos nuevas fronteras del mañana.

If [if], p. 331. Add, *conj. If only,* Con que. *If only we knew the right answer, we could ward off further trouble.* Con que supiéramos la respuesta indicada, podríamos conjurar más apuros.

Illegal alien [il-lî′-gal êl′-yen], *s.* Indocumentada, indocumentada. *The illegal alien flies in the face of the laws of the country where he resides.* El indocumentado da en rostro a las leyes del país donde reside.

Inconsistency [in-con-sist′-en-si], p. 342. Add, *s.* Contrasentido.

Increase [in-crîs′], p. 342. Add, *va.* 1. Multiplicar. *If you want to increase your chances of success, you must send out more applications.* Si deseas multiplicar tus posibilidades de éxito, tendrás que enviar más solicitudes. 2.(A QUANTITY) Aumentar. *It would be preferable to increase the cash amount.* Sería preferible aumentar el efectivo. *—vn.* Ir a más. *The activities available are increasing rapidly.* Los quehaceres disponibles van a más rápidamente.

Industrial park [in-dus′-tri-al pārc], s. (Neol.) Parque industrial. *The industrial park is the scene of a great number of the technical advances that mark the growth of a modern nation.* El parque industrial es el recinto de gran número de los adelantos técnicos que jalonan el desarrollo de la nación moderna.

Information [in-fōr-mê′-shun], p. 348. Add, *s.* 1. *Information media,* Medios informativos. *The information media soon drew him out.* Dentro de poco los medios informativos le buscaban la boca. 2. *Information retrieval,* Recuperación de información. 3. *Information science,* Informática, ciencia de información. *Many researchers are praising information science to the sky; an equal number hesitate to offer it their complete approval.* Muchos investigadores se hacen lenguas de la informática; otros tantos titubean en aprobarla rotundamente. 4. *Information system,* Sistema de información.

Inoperative [in-op-′er-ê-tiv], p. 351. Add, *a.* Inoperante. *They struggled to make the mission a success despite the inoperative fuel cells.* Se afanaban por lograr éxito con la empresa a pesar de las células de combustible inoperantes.

Interface [in′-ter-fês], *s.* (Neol.) Interfaz. *The interface between workers and management should not be a region of walls and estrangement.* La interfaz entre los trabajadores y los dirigentes no debe ser una comarca de murallas y enajenamiento.

Invoicing [in′-vois-ing], *s.* (Com.) Facturación.

Job [job], p. 366. Add, *s.* 1. (POSITION) Destino. 2. *To be out of a job,* Estar desocupado. *He's almost always out of a job.* Está casi siempre desocupado. 3. *To do a bang-up job,* (fam.) Echar el resto. *She did a bang-up job on the house.* Echó el resto con la casa. 4. *To do a good job,* Desempeñarse bien. *I like the painting. The artist did a very good job.* Me gusta la pintura. El artista se desempeñó muy bien. 5. *To do a good job of,* (Fest.) Acabar de. *She did a good job of flattering me.* Ella acabó de lisonjearme. *They did a good job of spoiling my chances.* Acabaron de malograr mis posibilidades. 6. *To do a good job on,* Cumplir bien. *The painter did a good job on the background.* El pintor cumplió bien el fondo. 7. *To lie down on the job,* (fam.) Echarse al surco. *No one likes employees who lie down on the job.* A nadie le gustan los empleados que se echan al surco. 8. *Odd job,* Chapuza. *He lives on the odd jobs that come his way.* Vive de las chapuzas que le caen en suerte.

Just [just], p.369. Add, *adv.* 1. No más, e.g.: *I have just enough paper.* Tengo bastante papel, no más. *She is just a child.* No es más que una criatura. 2. *Just as,* (PROPORTION) Conforme, al igual que. *Just as I indicated above, his rise to power changed the national life.* Conforme yo lo indiqué arriba, su encumbramiento varió la convivencia nacional. *Just as she had warned us, the cause came to nothing.* Al igual que ella nos lo profetizara, la bandería acabó en la nada. b. (TIME) En el momento que. *Just as I turned the corner, I saw him go into the store.* En el momento que yo doblaba [transponía] la esquina [calle], lo ví entrar en la tienda. 3. *Just as often,* Otras tantas veces. *But just as often we breezed right along.* Pero otras tantas veces marchábamos viento en popa. 4. *Just as often as* + verb, Las veces que + verb, e.g.: *Come just as often as you like.* Venga las veces que usted quiera. 5. *To just finish,* Acabar de, e.g.: *He just finished his lunch.* Acaba de almorzar. 6. *Just in case,* Por si acaso. *Bring an umbrella, just in case it rains.* Trae un paraguas, por si acaso llueve. 7. *Just like,* Muy proprio de, muy suyo, e.g.: *That joke is just like him.* Esa chanza es muy suya [propia de él].

Keep [kîp], p. 370. Add, *va.* 1. (A PROMISE) Cumplir. *He always keeps his word.* Siempre cumple su palabra. 2. *To keep a secret from,* Mantener el secreto para. *It's hard to keep a secret from her.* Es difícil mantener el secreto para ella. 3. *To keep accounts,* Hacer cuentas. 4. *To keep a close eye on,* Vigilar de cerca. 5. *To keep an eye on,* Celar. *They kept an eye on the deployment of foreign troops.* Celaban el despliegue de las tropas extranjeras. 6. *To keep an eye out for,* Tener mucho ojo a. *He kept an eye out for her return the entire day.* Tenía mucho ojo a su regreso todo el santo día. 7. *To keep from sleeping,* Quitar el sueño. *The very thought of it would often keep him from sleeping.* Muchas veces el mismo pensar en ello le quitaba el sueño. 8. *To keep in check [under control],* Poner freno a. 9. *To keep in mind,* Tener a la vista, tener presente. *I'll keep your offer in mind.* Tendré a la vista el ofrecimiento que usted me ha hecho. 10. *To keep in tune with,* Sintonizarse con. *He barely kept in tune with the piano.* Por poco no se sintoniza con el piano. 11. *To keep pace [up] with,* a. (A PERSON) Correr pareja con. *It's hard for her to keep up with her mother.* Le cuesta trabajo correr pareja con su madre. b. (A SUBJECT) Traer entre ceja y ceja. *No one keeps up with the subject better than he.* Nadie trae la materia entre ceja y ceja más que él. 12. *To keep out of sight,* Desplazar, desplazarse. *They kept the old man out of sight when the soldiers arrived.* Desplazaban al viejo cuando llegaron los soldados. *He always kept out of sight when she paid them a visit.* Él siempre se desplazaba cuando ella les hacía una visita. 13. *To keep something a secret,* Mantener algo en secreto, guardar el secreto de algo. *They kept his whereabouts a secret.* Guardaron el secreto de su paradero. 14. *To keep to oneself,* a. (HUSH UP) Callar. *He kept their names to himself.* Calló sus nombres. b. (AVOID OTHERS) Llevar vida solitaria. *He kept to himself.* Llevaba vida solitaria. 15. *To keep watch (over),* a. Velar. *She kept watch all night.* Veló toda la noche. b. (SUSPICIOUSLY) Celar.

Lane [lên], p. 377. Add, *s.* 1. (HIGHWAY) Carril. 2. (SWIMMING POOL) Calle. 3. (Aer.) Ruta. *Traffic control assigns each flight a lane all its own.* La regulación [ordenación] del tráfico le señala a cada vuelo una ruta toda a él.

Lanky [lank′-i], p. 377. Add, *a.* Talludo. *As lanky as he was, it was hard for him to get into the car.* Talludo que era, le era difícil subir al coche.

Laser [lê′-zer], p. 378. Add, *s.* 1. *Laser beam,* Rayo lasérico. 2. *Laser memory,* (Neol.) Memoria de computadora que recupera los datos mediante un rayo lasérico, memoria lasérica.

Launch [lānch], p. 380. Add, *s.* 1. *Launch vehicle,* (Aer.) Catapulta de lanzamiento. 2. *Launch window,* (Aer.) Intervalo de lanzamiento. *They knew only too well how narrow the launch window was.* Sabían de sobra lo cerrado que era el intervalo de lanzamiento. *—va.* 1. (A CAMPAIGN) Emprender. 2. (AN ATTACK) Librar. 3. *To launch into,* a. Lanzarse a. b. Acometer. *He launched into a devastating* *criticism of the plan*. Acometió una crítica apabullante del proyecto.

Learning [lẹrn'-ing], p. 382. Add, *s*. 1. Aprendizaje. *Learning foreign languages was very difficult for him*. El aprendizaje de los idiomas extranjeros le era muy difícil. 2. *Learning center [centre,* G.B.], Plantel (Mex.). *The learning center should serve all groups*. Es menester que el plantel sirva a todos los gremios.

Leftover [left'-ō-vẹr], *s*. 1. Vestigio. *Lizards are a leftover from the Age of the Dinosaurs*. Los lagartos son vestigios de la Edad de los Dinosauros. 2. (fig.) Rescoldo. *The problem was a leftover from the previous administration*. El problema era un rescoldo de la administración anterior.

Legendary [lej'-end-ẹ-ri], p. 383. Add, *a*. *To be legendary*, Picar en historia. *His open manner is legendary*. Su ademán poroso pica en historia.

Library [lai'-bra-ri], p. 386. Add, *s*. 1. (IN A PRIVATE HOME) Gabinete. 2. *Library binding*, Encuadernación endurecida. 3. *Library school*, Facultad de biblioteconomía. 4. *Library science*, Biblioteconomía, bibliotecología (Mex.) 5. *Library steps*, Escalereja (corrediza) de biblioteca. 6. *Library van*, Biblioteca ambulante, furgoneta que contiene una biblioteca. [Se llama también *Bookmobile*.]

Lead [lîd], p. 381. Add, *vn*. 1. *To lead to*, a. (ANOTHER ROOM) Corresponder con. *The kitchen leads to the hall*. La cocina corresponde con el pasillo. b. (ANOTHER TOPIC) Concatenarse con. *The study of anthropology leads naturally to the study of language*. El estudio de la antropología se concatena naturalmente con el estudio del lenguaje. 2. *To lead to another*, Concatenarse. *One book leads to another*. Los libros se concatenan.

Look [luk], p. 394. Add, *vn*. 1. *To look a gift horse in the mouth*. Considerar la dádiva con ojos de mercader. 2. *To look at again [once more]*, Retomar. *We should look at the problem once more*. Deberíamos retomar el problema. 3. *Look before you leap*. Si el sapo salta y se ensarta, la culpa no es de la estaca (P.R.). 4. *To look down over*, Asomar a. *The mountain looks down over the village*. La montaña se asoma a la aldea. 5. *To look for*, (WITHOUT MOVING) Buscar con la mirada. *She stood looking for the ship for half an hour*. Hacía media hora que estaba allí buscando el buque con la mirada. 6. *To look for more trouble*, Buscarle más pies al gato. *All that I did by writing the letter was to look for more trouble*. Lo único que hice escribiendo la carta era buscarle más pies al gato. 7. *To look favorably [kindly] on*, Mirar con buenos ojos. *They looked favorably on his request*. Miraban su petición con buenos ojos. 8. *To look forward to*, a. Anticipar, esperar con placer. b. (IMPATIENTLY) No ver la hora de. *I'm really looking forward to the party*. No veo la hora de la fiesta. 9. *To look in at [into]*, Asomar a. *Suddenly a stranger looked in at the window*. De repente un forastero se asomó a la ventana. *He looked into the room*. Se asomó a la puerta. 10. *To look into someone's eyes [someone in the eye]*, Mirarle a los ojos. *Look me in the eyes when you say that*! ¡Mírame a los ojos al decir eso! 11. *To look the other way*, a. Mirar hacia el otro lado. b. (fig.) Hacer la vista gorda. *They looked the other way instead of helping him*. Hicieron la vista gorda en vez de ayudarle. 12. *To look through*, a. Registrar. b. (THOROUGHLY) Rastrear. *He looked through each and every one of the books twice*. Rastreó dos veces todos y cada uno de los libros. 13. *To look up*, a. Alzar la mirada. *He looked up to find that she had gone for a dip*. Alzó la mirada para hallar que se había dado un chapuzón. b. Buscar. *We looked up new shades of meaning in the dictionary*. Buscamos nuevos matices en el diccionario. 14. *To look up to*, Apreciar mucho. *He looks up to his father*. Aprecia mucho a su padre. —*s*. 1. Pinta, e.g.: *With the look of*, Con pinta de. *He left with the look of a man who had lost his last friend*. Salió con pinta del hombre que ha perdido a su último amigo. 2. Cara, e.g.: *Frightened look*, Cara de susto. *A frightened look came over his face*. Se puso una cara de susto.

Make [mêk], p. 401. Add, *va*. 1. (INDUCE) Decidir a. *Trying to make him take a vacation is next to impossible*. El tratar de decidirlo a ir de vacaciones es casi imposible. 2. *To make a fetish of*, Fetichizar. *Some persons [people] make a fetish of youth*. Algunas personas fetichizan a la juventud. 3. *To make a hole*, Practicar un agujero. *First you make a hole in the cardboard*. Primero se practica un agujero en el cartón. 4. *To make a mistake*, (WHILE SPEAKING) Mentir. *I'm sorry, I made a mistake. It leaves at one*. Perdóneme. Mentí. Sale a la una. 5. *To make a point of*, Siempre acostumbrar. *He makes a point of chiming in whether he knows or not*. Él siempre acostumbra terciar, que sepa que no sepa. 6. *To make a record of*, Tomar acta de. *History will make a record of an out-and-out materialist*. La historia tomará acta de un materialista a rajatablas. 7. *To make a strong impression on*, Hacer mella. *His teachers always made a strong impression on him*. Sus maestros siempre le hacían mella. 8. *To make an appeal on behalf of*, Presentar apelación en favor de. *The librarian made an appeal on behalf of incunabula everywhere*. El bibliotecario presentó apelación en favor de incunables por todas partes. 9. *To make an idle promise [idle promises]*, Cumplir de palabra. *He always made idle promises that he never kept*. Siempre cumplía de palabra, nunca de hecho. 10. *To make excuses for*, Disculpar con pretextos. *She always makes excuses for his bad temper*. Ella siempre disculpa con pretextos su mal carácter. 11. *To make go [run]*, Impulsar. *What makes the model plane go*? ¿Qué impulsa el aeromodelo? 12. *To make hungry*, Dar hambre. *The hors d'oeuvre make me hungry*. Las tapas me dan hambre. 13. *To make known*, a. Dar a conocer. b. (Lit.) Poner de manifiesto. 14. *To make light of*, Hacer donaire de. *We would [used to] make light of our troubles*. Hacíamos donaire de nuestros apuros. 15. *To make look bad*, Dar sombra. *He always makes me look bad at tennis*. En el tenis él siempre me da sombra. 16. *To make no bones about*, No hacer remilgos a. *She makes no bones about her age*. No hace remilgos a los años que tiene. 17. *To make one's day*, Darle un día de muchas campanillas. *Her letter made my day*. Su carta me dio un día de muchas campanillas. 18. *To make one's mark*, Acertar alto. *He made his mark as a journalist*. Acertó alto como periodista. 19. *To make one's [a] point*, Poner una pica en Flandes. 20. *To make one's presence felt*, Aflorar. *She made her presence felt at all the meetings*. Ella afloraba en todas las reuniones. 21. *To make out*, a. (A DOCUMENT) Redactar. b. (SIGHT) Divisar. c. (BARELY) Vislumbrar. *From here I can just make out the name of the inn*. Desde aquí vislumbro el nombre de la fonda, nada más. d. (Amer., KISS) Hacer el oso. 22. *To make peace*, Hacer las paces. 23. *To make sad*, Dar pena, afligir. 24. *To make short shrift of*, Escamotear. *They made short shrift of her application*. Escamotearon su solicitud. 25. *To make strange bedfellows*, No caber en el mismo saco. 26. *To make too large [long]*, Abultar. *The tailor made the sleeves too long*. El sastre abultó las mangas. 27. *To make toward*, Dirigirse hacia. *They made toward the house*. Se dirigieron hacia la casa. 28. *To make up*, a. Constituir, integrar. *These states make up what is commonly called the Eastern Seaboard*. Estos estados constituyen lo que comúnmente se llama el Litoral Oriental. b. (RECONCILE) Hacer las amistades. *They made up yesterday*. Se hicieron las amistades ayer. c. (INVENT) Falsificar. d. (ONE'S FACE) Afeitar. 29. *To make use of*, a. Echar mano de. b. (Lit.) Comprometer. c. (MORE THAN ONE) Conjugar. *His paintings make use of several styles*. Sus pinturas conjugan varios estilos.

Measure [mezh'-ur], p. 411. Add, *vn*. 1. *To measure up well with*, Resistir la comparación con. *Their curriculum is quite helpful and measures up well with ours*. Su plan de estudios es bastante socorrido y resiste la comparación con el nuestro. 2. *To take the measure of*, (fig.) Ponderar.

Median [mî-di-an], p. 412. Add, *a*. (Auto.) *Median strip*, Faja central.

Microchip [mai'-crō-chip], *s*. (Neol.) Microlasca. *Microchip electronics*, Electrónica de las microlascas.

Microcomputer [mai-cro-com-piū'-t er], *s*. (Neol.) Microcomputadora.

Microelectronics [mai-crō-ẹ-lec-tron'-

ics], *s*. (Neol.) Microelectrónica.

Mind [maind], p. 419. Add, *s*. 1. *To have on one's mind,* Traer entre ceja y ceja. *He has a lot on his mind*. Trae mucho entre ceja y ceja. 2. *To make up one's mind,* Tomar [Llegar a] una determinación. 3. *To ring a bell in one's mind,* Hacerle tilín en la mente. *What she said about the enclosure rang a bell in my mind*. Lo que dijo sobre el palenque me hizo tilín en la mente. —*va*. *Mind your own business*! ¡No arregle mundo!

Miss [mis], p. 423. Add, *va*. 1. *To miss one's calling,* Errar la vocación. *You missed your calling. You should have become a teacher.* Erraste la vocación. Hubieras debido hacerte maestra. 2. *To miss one's connection,* Faltar a la transmisión. *He missed his connection and had to spend the night there*. Faltó a la transmisión y tuvo que trasnochar allí. 3. *To miss one's [the] train,* Perder el tren. —*vn*. (WHEN FIRING) Fallar el tiro. *Did he hit the target? No, he missed*. ¿Dio en el blanco? No, falló el tiro.

Model [mod'-el], p. 425. Add, *a*. El modelo de + s.pl., e.g.: *She was a model wife*. Ella era el modelo de mujeres [esposas]. *He was a model student*. Él era el modelo de alumnos. (NOTE: **Mujer** MAY BE USED ONLY WHEN SPEAKING OF ONE'S OWN WIFE.)

Monorail [mon'-o-rêl], *s*. Carril único.

Move [mūv], p. 432. Add, *s*. 1. (IN WRESTLING) Toma. 2. (TO A NEW HOME) Muda. *The move took a month*. Se hizo un mes para la muda. 3. *On the move,* (fam.), En gira. —*vn*. 1. Mudarse de casa. *They moved last month*. Se mudaron de casa el mes pasado. 2. (TO A NEW CITY) Mudarse a. *They moved to San Antonio last year.* Se mudaron a San Antono el año pasado. 3. *To move about,* Desplazarse. *The tennis player moves about the court well and has the drive success demands*. El tenista se desplaza bien en la cancha y tiene el arrojo que exige el éxito.

Moving [mūv'-ing], p. 432. Add, *a*. Arrebatador. *He was truly a moving speaker.* Él era de verdad un orador arrebatador.

Multinational [mul-ti-nash'-un-al], *a*. Transnacional.

Mural [miū'-ral], p. 434. Add, *s*. 1. Pintura mural. 2. *Mural art,* Muralismo.

Museum [miū-zī'-um], p. 435. Add, *s*. *Museum science,* Museografía.

Nook [nuc], p. 446. Add, *s*. (fig.) Remanso. *He had his favorite [favourite,* G.B.] *nook for reading near the river.* Tenía su remanso predilecto para la lectura cerca del río.

Nowadays [nau'-a-dêz], p. 448. Add, *adv*. En estos días.

Opinion poll [o-pin'-yun pōl], *s*. Encuesta, sondeo. *The opinion poll led to the repeal of an archaic law*. La encuesta acarreó la revocación de una ley bizantina.

Organization [ōr-gan-i-zê'-shun], p. 461. Add, *s*. 1. (ACT) Organización. 2. (RESULT) Organismo, sociedad. *The organization struggled to dispel such rumors*. El organismo se afanaba por desvanecer tales rumores.

Outage [out'-ij], *s*. (Neol.) Apagón.

Outline [out'-lain], p. 465. Add, *s*. 1. (Lit.) Semblanza. *The anthology provides an outline for each literary movement*. El florilegio proporciona una semblanza para cada movimiento literario. 2. (DISTINGUISHING FEATURES) Deslinde. *Write up an outline of the project*. Escriba un deslinde del proyecto. 3. *In broad outline,* A grandes rasgos. —*va*. Deslindar. *We must outline responsibilities*. Hay que deslindar las responsabilidades.

Out-of-the-way [aut'-ov-dhe-wê'], p. 465. Add, *a*. Arrinconado (fig.). *They were looking for an out-of-the-way inn*. Buscaban una fonda arrinconada.

Overnight [ō'-ver-nait], p. 467. Add, *adv*. (des.) La noche pasada [anterior], anoche. *It rained overnight*. Llovía anoche.

Pack [pac], p. 470. Add, *va*. (fam.) Abarrotar (fig.) *The team always packed the stadium*. El equipo siempre abarrotaba el estadio.

Parade [pa-rêd'], p. 475. Add, *s*. (MARCHING PAST) Desfile. *Parade rest,* (Mil.) En su lugar descanso. —*va*. Desfilar. *To parade through the streets,* (fig.) Sacar a pública plaza. *She paraded his faults through the streets*. Sacaba a pública plaza sus faltas.

Parking [pārk'-ing], p. 476. Add, *s*. 1. *Parking meter,* Parquímetro. 2. *Parking orbit,* (Aer.) Órbita temporal.

Pass [pas], p.478. Add, *va*. 1. (ANOTHER CAR) Rebasar. 2. *To pass by,* a. (AVOID) Pasar de largo. *All the partners passed her by*. Todas las parejas la pasaron de largo. b. (DO BETTER THAN) Adelantarse a. *All the students passed him by.* Todos los alumnos se adelantaron a él. 3. *To pass judgment [judgement],* (fig.) Formar juicio. *It's impossible to pass judgment without making use of all the facts in the case*. Es imposible formar juicio sin conjugar todos los hechos del caso. —*vn*. 1. (TO A HIGHER GRADE) Salir aprobado. 2. *To pass out of existence,* Dejar de existir. —*s*. 1. (THROUGH THE MOUNTAINS) a. Cortadura. b. (NARROW) Garganta. 2. *To make a pass at,* Insinuarse con. *He made a pass at the young lady.* Se insinuó con la señorita. 3. *To make a pass over,* Sobrevolar de cerca. *The plane made a pass over the village and dropped the supplies*. El avión sobrevoló de cerca la aldea y dejó caer los pertrechos.

Performance [per-form'-ans], p. 487. Add, s. 1. Actuación. *His performance pleased the audience enormously*. Su actuación agradó sobremanera al público. 2. (OF A MACHINE) Prestación. *The performance of the new appliance leaves a lot to be desired*. La prestación del nuevo electrodoméstico dista mucho de ser cumplida.

Pester [pes'-ter], p. 490. Add, *va*. Cortejar. *She pestered him to let her go with him*. Lo cortejaba para que la permitiera acompañarlo.

Pet [pet], p. 490. Add, s. Mascota. *He had two pets, a turtle and a small lizard*. Tenía dos mascotas, una tortuga y una legartija. —*vn*. (FONDLE ONE ANOTHER) Sobarse.

Phrasal verb [frêz'-il verb], s. (Neol.) Locución verbal. *The phrasal verb in English can be a real pitfall for the Spanish-speaking person*. En inglés la locución verbal puede ser un traspié para la persona de habla española.

Pillory [pil'-o-ri], p. 495. Add, *va*. (fig.) Poner en la picota del pasquín. *The newspapers pilloried his performance of Macbeth*. Los periódicos pusieron en la picota del pasquín su actuación de Macbeth.

Play [plê], p. 500. Add, *vn*. 1. *To play fast and loose with,* (fig.) Jugar grueso con. *He played fast and loose with her savings*. Jugó grueso con los ahorros de ella. 2. *To play with,* (A BABY) *Juguetear con*. 3. *To play up to,* Congraciarse con. —*va*. 1. (A CHARACTER) Jugar el papel de. *He played Sempronio in "La Celestina."* Jugó el papel de Sempronio en *La Celestina*. 2. *To have one's role to play,* (fig.) Tener voz y voto. *Each of us has his role to play in the decision*. Cada uno de nosotros tiene voz y voto en la decisión. 3. *To play the bully,* Baldronear. 4. *To play two roles,* Desdoblar. *That gifted actor played two roles in the play.* Aquel actor agraciado desdobló en la comedia. 5. *To play up,* (fig.) Destacar, perfilar. —*s*. *Playing two roles,* Desdoblamiento.

Poor [pūr], p. 507. Add, *a*. 1. (YIELD) Magro. 2. *Poor government hiring procedures,* Empleadismo. 3. *Poor likeness,* Escaso parecido. *The canvas showed a poor likeness of the model*. En el lienzo se veía un escaso parecido del modelo. 4. *Poor nutrition,* Desnutrición. *Poor nutrition brings on many diseases*. La desnutrición acarrea muchas enfermedades. 5. *Poor sanitary conditions,* Insalubridad. 6. *Poor showing,* Poco lucimiento, poco éxito. 7. *Poor wine,* Aguachirle.

Poorly [pūr'-li], p. 507. Add, *adv*. *Poorly defined,* (fig.) Desdibujado. *Their future plans were poorly defined*. Sus planes para el futuro eran desdibujados.

Prerequisite [prî-rec'-wi-zit], p. 515. Add, *s*. (fig.) Premisa. *The reading of Dante is a necessary prerequisite to full enjoyment of Eliot*. La lectura de Dante es premisa necesaria al pleno disfrute de Eliot.

Press [pres], p. 516. Add, *va*. (fig.) Presionar. *Don't try to press him into going if he doesn't want to*. No trates de presionarlo a que vaya si no es su deseo. —*vn*. *To press into,* Entrar en a empujones. *The crowd pressed into the room*. La muchedumbre entró en el salón a empujones. —*s*. *Press conference,* Rueda de prensa.

Prey [prê], p. 518. Add, *s. Easy prey*, Bocado propio. *She was easy prey for such an inposter.* Era bocado propio para tal embustero.

Print [print], p. 520. Add, *va.* Escribir en letra de imprenta [molde]. *Please print your name.* Favor de escribir su nombre en letra de molde.

Property [prop'-ẹr-ti], p. 525. Add, *s.* Inmueble. *The tenant improved the property.* El inquilino mejoró el inmueble.

Proto-Romance [prō-to-rō'-mans], *s.* (Linguistics) Latín arromanzado. *Proto-Romance and Latin developed together.* El latin arromanzado y el latín se desarrollaron juntos.

Public [pub'-lic], p. 529. Add, *a. Public good*, Procomún. *Great care should be taken to insure that taxes are used for the public good.* Se debe ejercer mucho cuidado para que los impuestos se utilicen en el procomún.

Put [put], p. 533. Add, *va.* 1. *To put around one's waist*, Ceñir. *She put a sash around his waist.* Le ciñó una faja. 2. *To put down*, a. (ONE'S HAND) Bajar. b. (A RIOT) Contener. c. (fam., RIDICULE) Aplastar. *His friends were always putting him down.* Sus amigos siempre le aplastaban. 3. *To put forward*, Adelantar. *Several extremely interesting but totally erroneous solutions were put forward.* Se adelantaron varias resoluciones que eran interesantísimas pero a la vez enteramente equivocadas. 4. *To put forth*, Ejercer. *He put forth his best efforts*, Ejerció sus mejores esfuerzos. 5. *To put in an appearance*, Hacer acto de presencia. 6. *To put in its place [away]*, Arrinconar. *She put away her toys.* Arrinconó sus juguetes. 7. *To put in mind of*, Hacer presente, recordar. *That puts me in mind of the party.* Eso me hace presente la fiesta. 8. *To put in one's place*, Bajar los humos a. 9. *To put into effect*, Instrumentar. *They put the new law into effect.* Instrumentaron la nueva ley. 10. *To put into play*, (A BALL) Sacar. 11. *To put one's foot in it*, Meter la cuchara [la pata]. 12. *To put on*, a. (ONE'S GLASSES) Calarse. b. (fam., FOOL) Tomar el pelo. c. (STAGE) Representar. 13. *To put on airs*, Echárselas de presuntuoso, darse tono. 14. *To put on to*, Darle la tecla a. *Her comment put him on to the sale.* Su comentario le dio la tecla a la liquidación. 15. *To put out to sea*, Hacerse a la mar. 16. *To put the best light [construction] on*, Interpretar de la mejor forma [manera] posible. *She put the best possible construction on the criticism.* Ella interpretó la crítica de la mejor forma posible. 17. *To put the fear of God into*, Enseñarle a uno la cara del castigo. *His bad grades put the fear of God into him.* Sus malas notas le enseñaban la cara del castigo. 18. *To put to rights*, (fig.) Sanear. 19. *To put to shame*, Ganarle el campeonato a uno. *His gift put the others to shame.* Su regalo le ganaba el campeonato a los demás. 20. *To put to the test*, Poner a prueba. *The crisis put his rise to power to the test*, La crisis puso a prueba su encumbramiento. 21. *To put two and two together*, Atar cabos. *He put two and two together and realized she was the mother.* Él ató cabos y se dio cuenta de ser ella la madre. 22. *To put up*, a. (ASSEMBLE) Armar. b. (LODGE) Dar hospedaje. 23. *To put up with*, Conllevar. *Each one put up with the unpleasant situation as best he could.* Cada cual conllevaba como mejor podía la desazón. 24. *To put up with the nightmare of*, Pasar por las horcas caudinas de. *They all had to put up with the nightmare of devastating gossip.* Todos tuvieron que pasar por las horcas caudinas de unos chismes apabullantes. 25. *To put words in the mouth of*, Dar a lo dicho significado suyo. *He always puts words in my mouth!* ¡Él siempre da significado suyo a lo que digo! 26. *To put zest in*, Sazonar. *To put zest in her life she tried dancing.* Para sazonar su vida escogió el bailar.

Quality [cwol'-i-ti], p. 536. Add, *s.* *(MAGNETIC APPEAL) Imán, e.g.: Quality that attracts buyers.* Imán de compra. *Quality that attracts students*, Imán de estudio. *That university has a certain quality that attracts students.* Esa universidad es un imán de estudio.

Rail [rêl], p. 542. Add, *s. Rail center*, Entronque de ferrocarriles.

Readable [rîd'-a-bl], p. 546. Add, *a.* Inteligible. *It was the most readable of all the texts that were given to me to consider.* Era el más inteligible de todos los textos que se me dieron para considerar.

Recording [rẹ-cōrd'-ing], *s.* (Mús.) 1. Grabación 2. *Recording head*, Cabeza de grabación. 3. *Recording secretary*, Secretario de actas.

Reduced [rẹ-diūst'], *a.* (des.) Empobrecido. *They had to live in reduced circumstances.* Tenían que vivir en circumstancias empobrecidas.

Regard [rẹ-gārd'], p. 554. Add, *s.* 1. (CARE) Celo. 2. (DEVOTION) Estima. 3. *In regard to*, Respecto de. 4. *Without regard to*, Sin celos de. *The position is open to all without regard to race, religion or nationality.* La colocación se ofrece a todos los aspirantes, sin celos de raza, religión o nacionalidad.

Registration form [rej-is-trê'-shun fōrm], *s.* Ficha de inscripción.

Relaxation [rî-lax- o rel-ax-ê'-shun], p. 556. Add, *s.* Esparcimiento. *Relaxation puts a hectic day right.* El esparcimiento sanea el día perseguido.

Reliable [rẹ-lai'-a-bl], p. 557. Add, *a.* *(DATA, INFORMATION)* Solvente. *The text provides reliable information on the Renaissance.* El texto proporciona datos solventes sobre el Renacimiento.

Renovate [ren'-o-vêt], p. 559. Add, *va.* Remozar.

Renovation [ren-o-vê'-shun], p. 559. Add, *s.* Remozamiento. *The renovation of the subway system took three years.* Se llevaron tres años para el remozamiento de la red del metropolitano.

Restore [rẹ-stōr'], p. 564. Add, *va.* 1. *To restore one's composure*, Devolverle la sangre fría a uno. *His good-natured attitude helped restore her composure.* Su actitud bonachona ayudó a devolverle la sangre fría. 2. *To restore the environment*, Sanear el ambiente. *Such an environment can't be restored overnight.* Tal ambiente no puede sanearse de la noche a la mañana.

Restructure [rî-struc'-chur], *va.* Reordenar. *He restructured the seniority scale.* Reordenó el escalafón. —*s.* Reordenación.

Result [rẹ-zult'], p. 564. Add, *s.* 1. *As a result*, a. Como resultado, por tanto, por consecuencia. b. (INTRODUCING A SENTENCE) De ahí que. *The script was lost. As a result, he acted badly.* Se perdió el guión. De ahí que trabajara mal. c. (INTRODUCING A MINOR SENTENCE) De ahí. *She continually harped on the same thing. As a result, her associates avoided her.* Machacaba siempre el mismo tópico. De ahí la evitación de ella por parte de sus colegas. [Nótese: "De ahí" se traduce también *That's the reason why. That's the reason why he failed.* De ahí que fracasara.] 2. *As a result of*, A raíz de. *The crops were bad as a result of the drought.* Las cosechas eran malas a raíz de la sequía. 3. *Indirect results*, Salpicaduras. —*vn. To result in*, Venir a. *Her drive resulted in their forging together a whole new system.* Su arrojo vino a que lañaran todo un sistema flamante.

Retrace [rẹ-três'], p. 565. Add, *va. To retrace one's steps*, 1. Desandar camino. *After we located the spring, we retraced our steps.* Ubicado el manantial, desandamos camino. 2. (Lit.) Volver sobre los pasos de uno. *We gathered from his answer that he knew nothing about it, so we retraced our steps.* Traslucimos de su respuesta que no sabía nada de ello, de manera que volvimos sobre nuestros pasos.

Retrofit [ret'-ro-fit], *s.* (Neol.) Modificación retroactiva.

Rickety [rik'-et-i], p. 569. Add, *a.* Paticojo. *All the furniture was rickety.* Todos los muebles eran paticojos.

Ride [raid], p. 569. Add, *s.* 1. Pon (P.R.). 2. *To give someone a ride*, Darle pon a uno. *They gave us a ride to the beach.* Nos dieron pon a la playa. 3. (DISTANCE TRAVERSED) Recorrido. *The ride gave him the chance to show us the island.* El recorrido le dio la ocasión de enseñarnos la isla. 4. (ON HORSEBACK) Cabalgata.

Right [rait], p. 570. Add, *a.* 1. (PROPER) Propicio. 2. (FOR SOMETHING) Indicado. *He's the right person for the job.* Es la persona indicada para el empleo. 3. *To be right in* + verb, Con razón + verb. *He's right in thinking that.* Con razón piensa eso. 4. *To be right to*, Caber. *It is right to think that way.* Cabe pensar de tal forma. 5. *Right you are!* ¡Efectivamente! ¡A punto! —*adv.* 1. *Right along*, Viento en popa, e.g.: *Their studies were coming right along.* Sus estudios iban viento en popa. 2.

Right at the surface of, (A LIQUID) A flor de. *Right at the surface of the water a mist was rising*. Una neblina subía a flor del agua. 3. *Right now,* a. (THIS MOMENT) Ahora mismo. b. (THESE DAYS) Hoy por hoy. *Right now it's hard to tell*. Hoy por hoy es difícil cerciorarlo. 4. *Right under the nose of,* En las barbas de, ante las narices de. 5. *Right up against,* a. (AN OBJECT) Al hilo de. *Right up against the wall moss was growing*. Un musgo crecía al hilo de la muralla. b. (A PERSON) Pegado a. *Her daughter stood right up against her mother's skirt*. Su hija estaba pegada a la falda de su madre. —*s*. *In his [her, their] own right,* Por demás. *They're painters in their own right*. Por demás son pintores.

Robotics [rō-bọt'-ics], *s*. (Neol.) Automatecnia, ciencia del empleo de los autómatas. *Robotics can easily lead to wide-spread unemployment*. La automatecnia fácilmente provoca desempleo de gran envergadura.

Root [rūt], p. 574. Add, *s*. 1. *Root causes,* Causas de fondo. 2. *To trace one's roots,* Rescatar las raíces de uno.

Rule [rūl], p. 577. Add, *vn*. (A COURT) Dictaminar. *The judge ruled differently*. El juez dictaminó de otra forma.

Ruling [rūl'-ing], p. 578. Add, *s*. (OF A COURT) Juicio. *The ruling established guidelines for the project*. El juicio determinó lineamientos para el proyecto.

Runner-up [run'-ẹr-up], p. 579. Add, *s*. Subcampeón. *It suddenly dawned on him that, despite all his efforts, he would always be a runner-up*. De repente alumbró en su cabeza la sospecha de que, todos sus esfuerzos no obstante, sería siempre el subcampeón.

Say [sê], p. 586. Add, *va*. *To say at the same time,* Sobredecir. *The girls (both) said the word at the same time*. Las chicas sobredijeron la palabra.

Scene [sîn], p. 588. Add, *s*. 1. (fig.) Recinto. *They visited the scene of so much history*. Visitaron el recinto de tanta historia. 2. *Behind the scenes,* Tras bambalinas.

School [scūl], p. 589. Add, *a*. 1. *School leaver,* (G.B.) Desertor [Desertora] de la enseñanza. *The school leaver* [Amer., *dropout*] *often lets one stroke of good luck in the job market hurt his future*. Muchas veces el desertor de la enseñanza permite que una suerte enorme entre las colocaciones perjudique su porvenir. 2. *School year,* Ciclo escolar. *The school year and the calendar year do not correspond*. El ciclo escolar y el año no corresponden.

Science fiction [sai'-ens fic'-shun], p. 589. Add, *s*. (Neol.) Fantasía científica. *The differences between science fiction and classical literature are clear cut*. Se acusan las diferencias entre la fantasía científica y la literatura clásica.

Script [script], p. 592. Add, *s*. (OF A PLAY) Guión. *Script writer,* Guionista.

Second-class citizen [sec-und-clạs' sit'-i-zn], *s*. Marginado [Marginada] social. *The second-class citizen often exists only in the eye of the beholder*. Muchas veces el marginado social no existe sino en el concepto del observador.

See [sî], p. 596. Add, *va*. 1. *To see eye to eye,* Estar de común acuerdo. 2. *To see one's point,* Caer en la cuenta. *I saw his point almost immediately*. Caí en la cuenta casi en el acto. 3. *To see one's way clear to,* Ajustárselas para. *I can't see my way clear to make the trip*. No me las ajusto para hacer el viaje. 4. *You'll see what I mean*. Ya irás viendo. —*vn*. 1. *To see through,* (A PERSON) Calar. *He saw through her at once*. La caló en seguida. 2. *To see to it that,* Encargarse de que. *He saw to it that they arrived on time*. Se encargó de que llegaran a tiempo.

Self-actualization [self-ac-chu-al-i-zê'-shun], *s*. Autoformación.

Self-determination [self-dẹ-tẹr-mi-nê'-shun], *s*. Autodeterminación.

Self-help [self-help'], *s*. Autoayuda.

Self-image [self-im'-ẹj], *s*. Autoimagen.

Semantic [sem-an'-tic], a. Semántico. 1. *Semantic diffusion,* (Linguistics) Varillaje semántico. *The migration of a word from one area to another is an example of semantic diffusion*. La emigración de un vocablo de una comarca en otra es ejemplo del varillaje semántico. 2. *Semantic net,* (Information Science) Disposición cibernética de los datos en la memoria de una computadora. 3. *Semantic shift,* (Linguistics) Reajuste semántico.

Serve [sẹrv], p. 601. Add, *va*. *To serve one right,* Estarle bien empleado a uno. *It served him right to lose his place in line*. Le estaba bien empleado perder su turno en la cola.

Set [set], p. 602. Add, *va*. 1. *To set apart,* Apartar. 2. *To set into motion,* Desencadenar. *His envy set a whole series of misfortunes into motion*. Sus celos desencadenaron toda una serie de infortunios. 3. *To set off,* (EXPLODE) Hacer estellar, disparar. 4. *To set sail,* a. Darse a la vela. b. (A LINER) Zarpar. —*vn*. *To set off,* Hacerse al camino. *They set off early in the morning*. Se hicieron al camino muy de mañana.

Shallow [shal'-ō], p. 605. Add, *a*. (Acad.) Pando. *The stream was so shallow that the pebbles at the bottom could be seen clearly*. El riachuelo era tan pando que los guijarros al fondo se veían claramente.

Shop [shop], s. p. 610. Add, *s*. 1. *Shop class,* Taller y obras. 2. *Shop teacher,* Maestro de taller y obras.

Shortcut [shōrt'-cut], *s*. 1. Atajo. 2. Atrecho (P.R.) *To take a shortcut,* Atrechar (P.R.)

Show [shō], p. 611. Add, *va*. 1. *To show a lack of respect for,* Faltarle al respeto. *He showed his father a lack of respect*. A su padre le faltaba al respeto. 2. *To show off to advantage,* Ser mérito de. *The beautiful garden showed the house off to advantage*. El hermoso jardín era mérito de la casa. 3. *To show where one leaves off and another begins,* Deslindar. *She showed me where my duties left off and his began*. Ella deslindó nuestros deberes. —*s*. 1. *Given to show,* Contrastante. 2. *Show business,* Farándula.

Shutoff [shut'-of], *s*. Detención. 1. *Automatic shutoff,* Detención automática. 2. *Shutoff valve,* Válvula de detención.

Singapore [sin-ga'-pōr], Singapur.

Sociolinguistics [so-shi-o-lin-gwis'-tics], *s*. (Neol.) Sociolingüística.

Ski [skí], p. 617. Add, *s*. *Ski slope,* Pista de descenso.

Skid [skid], p. 617. Add, *vn*. Patinar. *The car skidded into a tree during the blizzard*. Durante la nevasca el coche patinó hasta chocar con un árbol.

Software [soft'-wār], *s*. (Information Science) Elementos de programación.

Solar [sō'-lar], p. 627. Add, *a*. 1. *Solar cell,* (Aer.) Pila solar, heliopila. 2. *Solar collector,* Colector de radiación solar. 3. *Solar energy plant,* Central solar. 4. *Solar power,* Energía solar.

Sound [sound], p. 630. Add, *va*. *To sound out,* Sondear. *The notice ought to sound out the feelings of the committee*. El enunciado deberá sondear los sentimientos del comité.

Source [sōrs], p. 630. Add, *s*. 1. Manantial, fuente. 2. (fig.) Hontanar. 3. *Source of supply,* Fuente de abastecimiento. 4. *Source of energy,* Energético. *Sadly, many sources of energy are not renewable*. Infelizmente, muchos energéticos no son renovables.

Space [spês], p. 631. Add, *s*. 1. Cupo (fam.). *There's space for two*. Hay cupo para dos (fam.). 2. *Manned space laboratory,* Laboratorio orbital tripulado. 3. *Space probe,* Sonda espacial. 4. *Space science,* Ciencia estelar. 5. *Space shuttle,* (Neol.) Transbordador. 6. *Space station,* Estación espacial [orbital]. 7. *Space walk,* Caminata espacial.

Speaker [spîk'-ẹr], p. 633. Add, *s*. 1. Hablante. *A Spanish speaker could tell the difference at once*. Al hablante de español le llamaría la atención en seguida. 2. (AT A MEETING) Ponente. *One hundred speakers took part in the convention*. En el congreso participaron cien ponentes.

Staging [stê'-jing], p. 642. Add, *s*. Puesta en escena. *The staging of "The Walls Have Ears" showed typically Spanish surroundings*. La puesta en escena de *Las paredes oyen* representaba un ambiente típicamente español.

Stalemate [stêl'-mêt], p. 643. Add, *s*. (fig.) Estancamiento.

Startling [stārt'-ling], *a*. Sobrecogedor. *The results of the survey were startling*. Los resultados del sondeo eran sobrecogedores.

Stereotype [ster'-ẹ-o-taip], p. 648. Add, *va*. (fig.) Encasillar. *It's a bad habit to stereotype people [persons] before getting to know them*. Es un vicio encasillar a la gente antes de llegar a conocerla.

Stereotyped [ster'-ẹ-o-taipd], p. 648. Add, *a*. (fig.) Encasillando. *It was a stereotyped version of what we are* *apt to think of that country*. Era una versión encasillada de lo que somos muy dueños de pensar de aquel país.

Stiff [stif], p. 649. Add, *a*. Acartonado. *His stiff manner surprised his guests*. El ademán acartonado que usaba sorprendía a sus huéspedes.

Stiffness [stif'-nes], p. 649. Add, *s*. (fig.) Acartonamiento. *The stiffness of her performance hurt the play*. El acartonamiento de su actuación le quitó vida a la pieza.

Straw [strō], p. 654. Add, *a*. 1. *That's the last straw*! ¡Hasta aquí me trajo el rio! (P.R.) 2. *The straw that broke the camel's back*, La gota que derramó el vaso. 3. *The last straw*, El acabóse. *The last straw was when he wrote the letter with my pen*. El acabóse era cuando él redactó la carta con mi pluma.

Stress [stres], p. 654. Add, *va*. Marcar su acento sobre. *You should stress the last syllable*. Hay que marcar su acento sobre la última sílaba.

Stronghold [strong'-hōld], p. 656. Add, *s*. (fig.) Cuna y reducto, *At that time Paris was a stronghold of the so-called lost generation*. En aquel entonces París era cuna y reducto de la llamada generación perdida.

Student [stiū'-dent], p. 657. Add, *s*. *Student enrollment* [G.B., *enrolment*], Asistencia escolar.

Substratum [sub-strê'-tum], p. 660. Add, *s*. 1. Subsuelo. 2. (Linguistics) Trasfondo histórico.

Successor [suc-ses'-ęr], p. 661. Add, *s*. *Chosen successor*, Delfín. *She was the chosen successor of the best-known poet*. Ella era el delfín del poeta mejor conocido.

Sway [swê], p. 668. Add, *va*. Doblar. *They attempted to sway him to their point of view*. Procuraron doblarle a su punto de vista.

Take [têk], p. 673. Add, *va*. 1. (INVOLVE) Costar. *It took a lot of work for me to put it up*. Me costó mucho trabajo armarlo. 2. (PUT UP WITH) Beber. *I can't take his overly critical attitude*. No puedo beber esa actitud suya de criticón. 3. (TIME) Hacerse. *It takes two hours to take it down*. Se hacen dos horas para desmontarlo. 4. *Don't take all day*! (fam.) ¡Apúrate! ¡Volando! 5. *That takes the trouble to look*, Reparón. *She really takes the trouble to look*. Ella es de veras reparona. 6. *To take a backward glance*, (fig.) Dar un repasón. 7. *To take a census of*, Censar. 8. *To take a chance on*, Correr albures de. *We certainly were taking a chance on the success of the new store*. Es cierto que corríamos albures del éxito de la nueva tienda. 9. *To take a dislike to*, (A PERSON) Dársele una aversión por. *She took a dislike to John*. Se le daba una aversión por Juan. 10. *To take a disliking for*, (A THING) Dársele disgusto por. *He has taken a disliking for tea*. Se le ha dado disgusto por el té. 11. *To take a liking for*, (A THING) Empezar a gustarle. *He took a liking for long walks*. Empezaban a gustarle las caminatas de larga duración. 12. *To take a liking to*, (A PERSON) Amistarse con. *She took a liking to her teacher*. Se amistó con su maestra. 13. *To take a look*, a. (INTO) Asomarse. *He took a look into the room*. Se asomó a la puerta. b. (GLANCE) Atisbar, dar una ojeada [(Mex.), un vistazo]. *He took a quick look at the score*. Atisbó los tantos. 14. *To take a lot of attention [care]*, Necesitar mucho ojo. *Babies always take a lot of care*. Los nenes siempre necesitan mucho ojo. 15. *To take a measure*, Tomar un recurso. *Harsh measures were taken to undermine the plan*. Se tomaron recursos desabridos para socavar el proyecto. 16. *To take a vacation*, Ir de vacaciones. 17. *To take advantage of*, a. (BENEFIT FROM) Sacar avante de. b. (IN A NEGATIVE SENSE) Abusar de. *She takes advantage of his kindness*. Ella abusa de su bondad. 18. *To take advantage of circumstances*, Aprovechar las coyunturas. 19. *To take after*, a. (RESEMBLE) Salir a. *He takes after his father*. Sale a su padre. b. (PURSUE) Perseguir corriendo. 20. *To take amiss*, Entender de mala parte. 21. *To take away from*, (fig.) Regatearle. *No one* [G.B., *No-one*] *can take your education away from you*. Nadie puede regatearte tu educación. 22. *To take by the hand*, Llevar de la mano. 23. *To take care*, Tener cuidado, estar alerta. 24. *To take care of*, a. Cuidar. b. (Ven.) Manejar. c. (A CUSTOMER) Despachar. 25. *To take care of oneself*, a. (PERSONAL GROOMING) Asearse. *She takes good care of herself*. Se asea mucho. b. Cuidarse. 26. *To take charge of*, Hacerse cargo de, encargarse de. 27. *To take down*, a. (IN WRESTLING) Derribar al colchoncillo. b. (APART) Desarmar. 28. *To take down a peg or two*, (fam.) Bajar los humos a. 29. *To take effect*, a. Surtir efecto. b. (ACCORDING TO LAW) Entrar en vigor. *For years the law did not take effect*. Durante años la ley no entraba en vigor. 30. *To take for granted*, a. (A THING) Dar por sentado, dar por supuesto. *We take that law for granted*. Damos por sentada aquella ley. b. (A PERSON) Presentir. *It's easy for us to take others for granted*. Es fácil que presintamos a los demás. 31. *To take flight*, Alzar el vuelo. 32. *To take from nothing*, Sacar de la nada. *Nothing is taken from nothing*. De la nada no se saca nada. 33. *To take great pride in*, a. Enorgullecerse de. b. (BOASTFULLY) Vanagloriarse de. 34. *To take heart*, Animarse. 35. *To take hold*, a. (PENETRATE) Calar. *At last the idea of his loss began to take hold*. Finalmente llegó a calar la idea de su pérdida. b. (SPREAD) Cundir. *The new word took hold quickly*. La nueva voz cundió rápidamente. c. (ESTABLISH ITSELF) Asentarse. *With time the new point of view took hold*. Con el tiempo el nuevo enfoque se asentó. 36. *To take hold of*, Apoderarse de. *He took hold of the screaming child*. Se apoderó del niño chillón. 37. *To take into account*, Tomar en cuenta. *One must take the difference of the neighborhoods into account*. Hay que tomar en cuenta la desnivelación entre los barrios. 38. *To take into consideration*, Tener presente. *You must take all the facts into consideration*. Tienes que tener presentes todos los hechos. 39. *To take issue with*, Desacordarse con. *He took issue with her*. Él se desacordaba con ella. 40. *To take it into one's head that*, Antojarle que. *He took it into his head that his feet were too small*. Le antojaba que tenía muy pequeños los pies. 41. *To take it out on*, a. (WITH AN ACTION) Pagarla con, ensañarse contra. *He took it out on her with a hurt attitude*. Se la pagaba con una actitud resentida. b. (WITH AN ATTITUDE) Ensañarse contra. 42. *To take it upon oneself to*, Encargarse de. *He took it upon himself to act as our guide*. Se encargó de servir de nuestro guía. 43. *To take lying down*, Avasallarse ante. *He didn't take the injustice lying down*. No se avasallaba ante la injusticia. 44. *To take notice of*, Darse cuenta de. *She didn't take notice of the new chair*. No se daba cuenta de la silla nueva. 45. *To take offense* [G.B., *offence*], Formalizarse. *They took offense at what they thought was rudeness on the part of the foreigners*. Se formalizaron ante una supuesta descortesía por parte de los extranjeros. 46. *To take on*, a. (A CHARACTERISTIC) Revestir. b. (A CHALLENGE) Aceptar. c. (A RESPONSIBILITY) Asumir. d. (IMPORTANCE) Cobrar. 47. *To take on a new look*, Tomar un nuevo cariz. *Her future has taken on a new look*. Su porvenir ha tomado un nuevo cariz. 48. *To take one's mind off of*, Desviar el interés de. 49. *To take orders*, Ordenarse. *He took orders to become a priest in the Anglican Church*. Se ordenó para llegar a ser sacerdote de la Iglesia anglicana. 50. *To take out one's revenge on*, Encarnizarse en. 51. *To take over*, Enseñorearse de. *He took over the village*. Se enseñoreó de la aldea. 52. *To take part*, a. (SHARE) Tomar parte. b. (APPEAR) Figurar, intervenir. *He took part in the meeting*. Intervino en la reunión. c. (NEGATIVE) *His refusal to take part*, La ninguna parte que tomó. d. (LEND ONE'S AUTHORITY) Prestarse. *I can't take part in such a thing*. No me puedo prestar a tal cosa. 53. *To take place*, a. (OCCUR) Tener lugar. b. (A PAYMENT) Tramitarse. 54. *To take revenge for*, Reparar. 55. *To take root*, Arraigar. 56. *To take seriously*, Tomar a pechos. 57. *To take shape*, Tomar cuerpo. 58. *To take sides*, Alistarse. 59. *To take someone* [G.B., *some-one*] *at his word*, Tomar bajo palabra que cumplirá lo prometido. *I took him at his word that he would do the work*. Tomé bajo palabra que haría el trabajo. 60. *To take someone's word for*, Tomar bajo palabra la verdad de lo dicho. *I took his word for the condition of the river*. Tomé bajo palabra la condición del río. 61. *To take steps*, Implantar acciones. 62. *To take the bull by the horns*, (fig.) Embestir de una vez. 63. *To take the leading part in*, Protagonizar. *He took the leading part in the campaign*. Él protagonizaba la campaña. 64. *To take the opposite point of view,* Llevar la contraria. 65. *To take to account,* Pedir cuentas. *The teacher took the child to account.* El maestro le pidió cuentas al niño. 66. *To take too many liberties with,* Insinuarse con. *The young man took too many liberties with his date and she slapped his face.* El joven se insinuó con la chica y ella le dio una bofetada. 67. *To take up,* Plantear, entablar. *We took up that question next.* Luego planteamos esa cuestión. 68. *To take upon oneself,* Echar sobre los hombros. *She took upon herself the responsibility for the safety of the children.* Ella echó sobre los hombros la responsabilidad de la seguridad de los niños.

Tape [têp], p. 675. Add, *s. Tape player,* Tocacintas.

Teach [tîch], p. 677. Add, *va. 1.* (A CLASS) *a.* Dar. *He teaches four classes every day.* Da cuatro clases todos los días. b. (Mex.) Impartir. c. (Arg., Chile) Dictar. 2. *To teach how to read and write,* Alfabetizar. 3. *To teach social graces,* Sacar a volar.

Teacher [tîch'-ȩr], p. 677. Add, *s. Teacher preparation,* Capacitación del magisterio.

Teaching [tîch'-ing], p. 677. Add, *s.* 1. Docencia, enseñanza. 2. (ACT ITSELF) Instrucción. 3. (PROFESSION IN GENERAL) Magisterio. 4. *Teaching assistantship,* Ayudantía docente. 5. *Teaching methods,* Pedagogía. 6. *Teaching position,* Cargo docente. 7. *Teaching profession,* Magisterio.

Team-teach [tîm'-tîch], *va.* Dar [(Mex.) Impartir, (Arg., Chile) Dictar] en comitiva. —*vi.* Dar clases en comitiva.

Telecast [tel'-ȩ-ca̧st], *va.* Teledifundir.

Television [tel-ȩ-vizh'-un], p. 678. Add, *s. Closed-circuit television,* Televisión en circuito interior.

Terminal [tȩr'-mi-nal], p. 681. Add, *s.* 1. (OF A BATTERY) Borne. 2. (AIRLINE) Terminal aéreo. 3. (Elec.) Terminal.

Think [think], p. 684. Add, *vn.* 1. *To think about,* (DOING SOMETHING) Proponerse. *We're thinking about going early.* Nos proponemos ir temprano. 2. *To think better of,* Pensar de nuevo. *He thought better of it and slept late.* Lo pensó de nuevo y durmió hasta tarde. 3. *To think over,* Pensar bien. 4. *To think straight,* Pensar con acierto. 5. *To think up,* Idear, tramar. *How could Mr. Franklin think up so many inventions?* ¿Cómo pudo el Sr. Franklin idear tantas invenciones? 6. *Think tank,* (fam.) Astillero (Mex.) *The think tank is the source of many improvements that enlighten our lifestyle.* El astillero es la fuente de muchas mejoras que alumbran la vida que menamos.

Throw [thrō], p. 686. Add, *va.* 1. *To throw off,* (fig.) Despedir. *We must throw off such negative thoughts.* Tenemos que despedir tales pensamientos negativos. 2. *To throw oneself into,* (fig.) Enfrascarse en, bucearen, ahondaren. *He threw himself into the project with his customary zeal.* Se enfrascó en el proyecto con su arrojo acostumbrado. 3. *To throw oneself wholeheartedly into,* Enfrascarse en hasta las manitas [(Mex.) hasta las chanclas]. 4. *To throw out of balance,* Trastrocar. 5. *To throw out the baby with the bathwater,* Olvidar lo principal de una empresa, atascado en pormenores. 6. *To throw the book at,* (fam.) Multar con severidad exagerada. 7. *To throw together,* (fig.) Farfullar. *They threw the house together.* Farfullaron la casa. 8. *To throw up to,* Echarle a uno en cara. *He always throws up to her how much he gave up.* Siempre le echa en cara lo mucho que renunció.

Time [taim], p. 689. Add, *s.* 1. (ON THE CLOCK) Hora. *It's time to go.* Es hora de irse. 2. (ALLOTTED FOR SOMETHING) Plazo. *The time is up.* Se venció el plazo. 3. *A great deal of time,* Mucho tiempo. 4. *A long time,* Largo tiempo. *A long time was spent trying to convince her.* Largo tiempo se pasó tratando de convencerla. 5. *About that time,* a. Por entonces. b. (COUNTING HOURS) A esa hora más o menos. c. (COUNTING DAYS) Por esas fechas. 6. *All at one time,* De un tirón. *She read the book all at one time.* Leyó el libro de un tirón. 7. *All the time,* Todo el tiempo. *All the time that I spent on it was wasted.* Todo lo que pasé en ello fue tiempo perdido. 8. *At all times.* En todo momento, a todas horas. 9. *At any time,* Cuando menos se espera, de un momento a otro. *He'll arrive at any time.* Llegará de un momento a otro. 10. *At that time,* a. (MOMENT) En ese entonces. b. (TIME FRAME) En aquel entonces. 11. *At the present time,* En estos días, actualmente. 12. *At the right time,* a. Oportunamente. b. (ON THE CLOCK) A la hora. 13. *At the same time,* a. Al mismo tiempo. b. (ON THE CLOCK) A la vez. 14. *At the wrong time,* a. Inoportunamente, a destiempo. b. (ON THE CLOCK) A deshora. 15. *For the time being,* Por de pronto. *For the time being, these books ought not to be overlooked.* Por de pronto estos libros no son desdeñables. 16. *From time to time,* De vez en cuando. 17. *Full time,* Con horario completo. *He is looking for a full-time position.* Está buscando un destino con horario completo. 18. *In a short time,* Faltar un rato para que, e.g.: *In a short time autumn would dazzle them once more.* Faltaba un rato para que el otoño los desalumbrara de nuevo. 19. *In no time,* En un abrir y cerrar de ojos. 20. *To mention at the wrong time,* Sacar a relucir. *She mentioned his name at the wrong time.* Sacó a relucir su nombre. 21. *Most of the time,* a. (AS A UNIT) La mayor parte del tiempo. b. Las más de las veces. 22. *Part time,* En jornadas parciales. 23. *To spend time on,* Dedicarse a. 24. *The time will come when,* Vendrá un tiempo en que. 25. *Time after time,* [G.B., *Times out of number*], Un sinnúmero de veces. 26. *Time of one's life,* Edad. *It's a time of one's life that should be spent comfortably.* Es una edad que debería vivirse holgadamente. 27. *Time payment,* Abono. 28. *Time span,* Plazo. 29. *Time zone,* Huso horario. 30. *Up to the present time,* Hasta la actualidad. 31. *Waste of time,* Letra muerta. *Theory without practice is a waste of time.* La teoría sin práctica es letra muerta.

Timing [taim'-ing], *s.* 1. (Mús.) Seguimiento del compás. 2. (Mec.) Regulación. 3. (OF EVENTS) Enlace de los acontecimientos. *Timing is everything where success is concerned.* En cuanto al éxito, el enlace de los acontecimientos lo dice todo.

Title-holder [tai'-tl hōld'-ȩr], s. Marcador, marcadora. *World title-holder,* Marcador global.

Toddle [tod'-l], p. 691. Add, *vn.* (fam., G.B.) Descampar.

Tour [tūr], p. 694. Add, *s.* Recorrido. *The tour of the house begins at four o'clock.* El recorrido de la casa empieza a las cuatro. —*va.* Recorrer. *We toured the old sections of the city.* Recorrimos los barrios antiguos de la ciudad.

Tracking [trac'-ing], *s.* (Aer.) Rastreo, seguimiento. *Tracking the satellite on the screen proved to be difficult.* El rastreo del satélite en la pantalla resultaba difícil.

Transfer [trans'-fȩr], p. 697. Add, *s.* (FROM ONE VEHICLE TO ANOTHER) Transbordo. *The transfer from one orbiter to the other went off without a hitch.* El transbordo de una nave en órbita a otra se efectuó sin falla.

Treat [trît], p. 699. *Add, va. To treat superficially,* Soslayar. *The article treated restoration of the environment very superficially.* El artículo soslayaba con mucho el saneamiento del ambiente.

Tripper [trip'-ȩr], p. 702. Add, *s.* (G.B.) Excursionista.

Turn [tūrn], p. 706. Add, *va.* 1. (A CORNER) Transponer, doblar. 2. (ONE'S EYES) Tornar. 3. (A PAGE) Doblar. 4. *To turn a cold shoulder to,* Tener mal ambiente entre. *They always turn a cold shoulder to his suggestions.* Sus sugerencias siempre tienen mal ambiente entre ellos. 5. *To turn a deaf ear to,* Desoir. 6. *To turn down,* a. (THE COVERS) Doblar. b. (A PERSON) Comunicarle una negativa, decirle que no. 7. *To turn into a spectacle,* Volver tandas. *They turned the dance into a spectacle.* Volvieron tandas el baile. 8. *To turn into new channels,* Remarcar. *We can turn our thinking into new channels if we really want to.* Podemos remarcar nuestra manera de pensar si es verdaderamente nuestro deseo hacerlo. 9. *To turn one's back on,* Volver la espalda. *They turned their backs on their friend.* Le volvieron la espalda a su amiga. 10. To turn over, (AN OBJECT) Dar vueltas a. 11. *To turn to advantage,* Sacar provecho de. 12. *To turn up one's nose at,* Arrugar la nariz ante. —*vn.* 1. *To turn around,* Revolverse, volverse. 2. *To turn against,* Revolverse contra. 3. *To turn away from,* Abandonar. 4. *To turn back,* Dar la vuelta. *They turned back at a whistle stop*. Dieron la vuelta en un apeadero. 5. *To turn in,* Acostarse. 6. *To turn into,* a. (fig.) Resultar. *It turned into a shouting match*. Resultó una contienda a gritos. b. Hacerse. *He's turned into a real spoilsport*. Se ha hecho un aguafiestas de verdad. 7. *To turn on,* a. (IN RAGE) Ensañarse en. b. (THE LIGHTS) Encender, poner. 8. *To turn off, (THE LIGHTS) Apagar.* 9. *To turn to,* Acudir a. —*s*. 1. (TO DO SOMETHING) Tanda. 2. (OF EVENTS) Sesgo, giro. *The turn that the case had taken interested him*. El giro que había tomado el asunto le interesaba. 3. *At every turn,* Por todos lados. 4. *Sudden turn,* Regate. *A sudden turn in the river offered them an enchanting view of the town*. Un regate del río les ofrecía una vista encantadora del pueblo. 5. *To talk out of turn,* Terciar a deshora.

Turning point [tũrn′-ing point], *s*. Parteaguas, eje.

Type [taip], p. 708. Add, *va*. Teclear. *He typed (up) my notes*. Él tecleó mis notas.

Undergraduate [un-der-grad′-yu-êt], p. 714. Add, *s*. 1. *Undergraduate degree,* Licenciatura. 2. *Undergraduate studies,* Estudios de licenciatura. 3. *Undergraduate years,* Años de licenciatura.

Underwater [un-der-wō′-tęr], *a*. Subacuático. 1. *Underwater photography,* Fotografía subacuática. 2. *Underwater vehicle,* Submersible. —*adv*. Bajo agua.

Unemployment [un-em-ploi′-męnt], *s*. Desempleo. *Unemployment compensation,* Seguro de desempleo.

Uninhibited [un-in-hib′-i-ted], *a*. 1. (LACKING RESTRAINT) Falto de cohibiciones. *Two more uninhibited persons I've yet to see. Naturally they're on the best of terms*. Me queda ver dos personas más faltas de cohibiciones. Es natural que sean paga excelente. 2. (FREE) Desenfadado, desenvuelto. 3. *In an uninhibited way,* Con desparpajo.

Unlike [un-laic′], p. 720. Add, *prep*. A diferencia de. *Unlike his wife, he speaks Spanish*. A diferencia de su esposa; él habla español.

Unsportsmanlike [un-spōrts′-man-laik], *a*. Antideportivo. *It's very unsportsmanlike behavior* [G.B., *behaviour*] *to complain when you've lost fair and square*. Es acto muy antideportivo el de quejarse cuando has perdido en juego limpio.

Unvarnished [un-vār′-nisht], *a*. (FACTS, TRUTH) No matizado. *An unvarnished report of the facts would be welcome*. Una relación no matizada de los hechos sería valiosa.

Utterance [ut′-ęr-ans], p. 730. Add, *s*. (Linguistics) Manifestación. *An utterance is an example of language activity*. La manifestación es un ejemplo de actividad lingüística.

Van [van], p. 731. Add, *s*. Furgoneta. *In our mobile society the van has almost become a home*. En nuestra sociedad corrediza la furgoneta por poco llega a ser hogar.

Walk [wōk], p. 742. Add, *va*. *To walk a dangerous line,* Nadar entre dos aguas.

Ward [wōrd], p. 743. Add, *va*. *To ward off,* 1. (A BLOW) Parar, detener. 2. (fig.) Conjurar. *They tried to ward off fatigue with exercise*. Procuraban conjurar la fatiga con el ejercicio.

Watch [woch], p. 745. Add, *va*. 1. (WITH SUSPICION OR JEALOUSY) Celar. *They watched his every move*. Celaban cada paso suyo. 2. *To watch for,* Buscar con la mirada, estar a la mira de. 3. *To watch one's step,* Proceder con pies de plomo. 4. *To watch out for,* Tener cuidado con.

Way [wê], p. 747. Add, *s*. 1. *To approach in a new way,* Hacer un nuevo aparte en. *We must approach the study of foreign languages in a new way*. Es preciso que hagamos un nuevo aparte en el estudio de los idiomas extranjeros. 2. *To go out of one's way,* a. Desviarse. b. (DO ONE'S BEST) Deshacerse en cumplidos. *She went out of her way to make our stay more enjoyable*. Ella se deshizo en cumplidos para que nuestra estancia [estadía, Amer.] fuera más agradable. 3. *In this way,* Con ello. The requirements were met in this way. Con ello se llenaron los requisitos. 4. *One way or the other,* En alguna forma. *One way or another, she drew her friend out*. En alguna forma le buscó la boca a su amiga. 5. *To push [pull] out of the way,* (AN OBJECT) Correr. *Why don't we push the chair out of the way*? ¿Por qué no corremos la silla? 6. *The way things were before [used to be]* Las andadas. *We went back to the way things used to be,* Volvimos a las andadas. 7. *The way one's luck is going,* Las suertes que tiene. *She lived according to the way her luck was going*. Vivía de acuerdo con las suertes que tenía. 8. *Under way,* En pie. *Plans are under way to remove it*. Hay planes en pie para quitarlo. 9. *Way to pin someone* [G.B., *some-one*], *down,* (TO A DECISION, THE TRUTH) Atadero. *There's no way to pin him down*. No hay atadero en él.

Weaken [wī′-cn], p. 747. Add, *va*. (fig.) Depotenciar. *Such a move will weaken the effectiveness of the new sales campaign*. Tal jugada depotenciará la eficacia de la nueva campaña de ventas.

Wear [wār], p. 747. Add, *va*. 1. *To wear gracefully,* Valerse de sin afectación. *He wears his knowledge gracefully*. Se vale de sus conocimientos sin afectación. 2. *To wear the pants,* (fam.) Ponerle a uno la batola (P.R.). 3. *To wear thin,* Cansársele a uno. *My patience is wearing thin*. Se me cansa la paciencia. 4. *Wearing out one's clothing in a hurry,* Destrozón. *She certainly wears out her shoes in a hurry*. Es una gran destrozona de zapatos.

Well-wisher [wel-wish′-ęr], *s*. Simpatizante. *Her well-wishers walked her to the train*. Sus simpatizantes la acompañaron al tren.

What [hwot], p. 750. Add, *pron*. 1. *No matter what,* En el peor de los casos. *I'm going no matter what*. Yo voy en el peor de los casos. 2. *That's what I'm driving at*. A eso voy. 3. *That's what you say*! ¡Eso dices tú! 4. *What about me*? ¿Y yo? 5. *What do you think of that*? ¿Si te parece poco? *She already finished. What do you think of that*? Terminó ya. ¿Si te parece poro? 6. *What happened was (that),* Era que. *What happened was she lost her gloves*. Era que se le perdieron los guantes. 7. *What it takes,* Lo necesario. *We'll do what it takes*. Haremos lo necesario. 8. *What's happening now* (ANAPHORIC), Esto de ahora. *What's happening now could have been prevented*. Esto de ahora hubiera podido evitarse. 9. *What money do you have with you*? (G.B.) ¿Cuánto dinero traes encima? 10. *What will they [he, she, you] think of next*! ¡Buena me espera! *A talking clock*! *What will they think of next*! ¡Un reloj que habla! ¡Buena me espera! 11. *What with,* En vista de. *What with the fog, they put off the flight*. En vista de la neblina, atardaron el vuelo.

With [widh], p. 757. Add, *prep*. 1. *With all one's might,* En cuerpo y alma. 2. *With one accord,* De común acuerdo. 3. *With one's eyes wide open,* Con conocimiento de causa. 4. *With respect to,* Respecto a. *Nothing has been decided with respect to the art fair*. Respecto al festejo de arte no se ha decidido nada. 5. *With the aim of,* Con miras de. 6. *With us for a long time,* De enorme arrastre. *The problem has been with us for a long time*. Es un problema de enorme arrastre.

Word [wũrd], p. 759. Add, *s*. 1. *To be too strong a word for,* Ser mucha palabra para. *City is too strong a word for that*. Ciudad es mucha palabra para eso. 2. *In a word,* En dos palabras. 3. *In so many words,* En resumidas palabras. *It's hard to relate in so many words*. Es difícil referirlo en resumidas palabras. 4. *My word*! ¡Válgame On my word! ¡Palabra! 6. *The last word,* La coletilla. 5. *He likes to have the last word*. Le gusta decir la coletilla. 7. *Word description [Description in words],* Retrato hablado. *She gave them a word description of her guest*. Les dio un retrato hablado de su huésped. 8. *Word for word,* a. Al pie de la letra. *He copied the entire article word for word*. Copió el artículo entero al pie de la letra. b. Palabra por palabra. *I'm quoting him word for word*. Le cito palabra por palabra. 9. *Word of mouth,* Propaganda de boca. *Word of mouth built up the interest of the fans*. La propaganda de boca modeló el oído de los aficionados. 10. *Word processing,* (Information Science) Elaboración de palabras.

NUEVO DICCIONARIO

VELÁZQUEZ

REVISADO

Español e Inglés

SEGUNDA PARTE: INGLÉS–ESPAÑOL

Prólogo

La humanidad avanza con ritmo cada vez más acelerado, y las obras de consulta destinadas a servirla, como este diccionario, deben mantenerse a tono con tal progreso si han de suministrar satisfactoriamente la información que en ellas se busca. Por eso el *Diccionario Velázquez*, reconocido mundialmente como el diccionario bilingüe español-inglés más autorizado, necesita estar al dia con relación a todas las voces nuevas que va imponiendo el prodigioso progreso de nuestra época en el campo de las ciencias, de los inventos y los descubrimientos; así como en las voces que las costumbres, en constante evolución, y los acontecimientos, van introduciendo en ambos idiomas.

De este modo el NUEVO DICCIONARIO VELÁZQUEZ REVISADO, cuidadosamente revisado, sin sacrificar ninguna de las tradicionales características que han hecho de sus anteriores ediciones el prototipo de los diccionarios de su género, viene a ser, sin lugar a duda, la más moderna y completa de las ediciones de dicha obra publicadas hasta hoy.

Se han incluido en esta novísima edición miles de voces nuevas, y también modismos y locuciones de uso general, que remplazan expresiones que han dejado de ser de uso común y que, en consecuencia, ya no tienen razón de ocupar lugar en una obra eminentemente práctica como ésta.

Esta última revisión del diccionario ha sido exhaustiva. Se ha tratado de conseguir que el *Diccionario Velázquez* responda cada día más eficazmente a las necesidades de quienes recurren a él como medio práctico para resolver sus problemas de traducción en el campo de los negocios, de la cotidiana información, de la tecnología, de las ciencias en general, de la literatura, etc., y se ha prestado particular atención a las voces y locuciones de uso común en la América Hispana y en los Estado Unidos, ya que diariamente crecen y se intensifican las relaciones comerciales y amistosas entre estas dos grandes e importantes regiones del mundo moderno.

La revisión de las listas de equivalentes de los nombres geográficos que se escriben de manera diferente en español y en inglés se ha realizado con cuidado meticuloso. Las listas que forman parte de la presente edición incluyen todos los cambios que en tales nombres han determinado los acontecimientos históricos recientes.

De similar estudio han sido objeto las listas de nombres propios y de gentilicios que forman parte de los apéndices de la obra, así como las tablas de pesas y medidas. La de abreviaturas ha sido puesta al día para que responda, asimismo, al carácter fundamentalmente práctico de la obra.

Con tales innovaciones se ha acrecentado poderosamente la utilidad de este diccionario, y sus directores y editores se atreven a esperar que resultará un instrumento más valioso aún que las anteriores ediciones para quienes lo consulten, ora se trate de estudiantes de un nuevo idioma, de doctos que realicen estudios literarios en cualquiera de las dos lenguas, o en ambas, o de traductores profesionales, de hecho, para todos y cada uno de cuantos necesiten un guía autorizado que los ayude a recorrer el siempre escabroso camino que entraña la traducción de ideas del inglés al español, y viceversa.

Para mejor servir las necesidades contemporáneas, la edición 1985 nuevamente corregida incorpora un apédice de 700 anotaciones adicionales con clarificaciones múltiples de los vocablos más modernos, científicos, técnicos, mercantiles, culturales, y políticos y provee variedades regionales de modismos y expresiones familiares de Lationamérica y el castellano también.

Sinopsis
de la Lengua Inglesa.

ALFABETO.

Las letras que componen el alfabeto inglés son veintiseis, a saber:—

a, b, c, d, e, f, g, h, i, j, k, l, m, n, o, p, q, r, s, t, u, v, w, x, y, z.

Las vocales son *a, e, i, o, u*, y algunas veces *w, y*. Las consonantes son todas las demás.

[Para los sonidos de las letras inglesas, véase la "Introducción" que sigue a esta Sinopsis.]

PARTES DE LA ORACIÓN.

Las partes de la oración son diez, a saber: *The Article* (el Artículo), *the Noun* o *Substantive* (el Nombre ó Sustantivo), *the Adjective* (el Adjetivo), *the Pronoun* (el Pronombre), *the Verb* (el Verbo), *the Participle* (el Participio), *the Adverb* (el Adverbio), *the Preposition* (la Preposición), *the Conjunction* (la Conjunción), y *the Interjection* (la Interjección).

DE LOS ARTÍCULOS.

Los Artículos son dos, *a* o *an* (un, una), y *the* (el, los; la, las; lo).

A se usa delante de consonante: como, *a* man (*un* hombre); y *an* delante de vocal o *h* muda: como, *an* age (*un* siglo), *an* hour (*una* hora).

The se usa delante de nombres en ambos números: como, *The* man (*el* hombre), *the* men (*los* hombres).

A se llama artículo *indefinido*, porque no se refiere á ninguna persona o cosa en particular: como, *a* president (*un* presidente). *The* se llama artículo *definido*, porque se refiere siempre a una persona o cosa en particular: como, "*The* President of *the* United States" (*El* Presidente de *los* Estados Unidos).

El artículo *a* se pone delante de los nombres de peso, medida, número; los de oficios, empleos, dignidades, y en las admiraciones, aunque no se usa en español: como, "Tea is sold at *a* dollar *a* pound" (El te se vende a peso *la* libra). "He has *a* sister who is *a* widow, and *a* brother who is *a* captain" (Él tiene una hermana viuda, y un hermano que es capitán). "He is *an* American" (Él es americano). "What *a* beautiful woman!" (¡Qué hermosa mujer!)

El artículo definido castellano, delante de un nombre común tomado en toda la extensión de su significado, no se traduce en inglés: v. g., "Man is mortal" (*El* hombre es mortal); pero si el sustantivo sólo designa una especie, aunque tomado en un sentido general, se expresa: v. g., "*The* negro is our brother" (*El* negro es nuestro hermano).

Cuando un nombre propio va precedido del de la dignidad, cargo, etc., no admite el artículo en inglés: v. g., "General Washington" (*El* general Washington), "Judge Field" (*El* juez Field). El artículo se omite también a menudo en inglés cuando se repite delante de varios sustantivos seguidos: v. g.. "The father, mother, and children are sick" (El padre, *la* madre y *los* niños están enfermos). Tampoco se traduce cuando precede a los nombres *Señor* o *Señora* (*Mr.* o *Mrs.*), seguidos de un nombre propio: v. g., "Have you seen Mr. or Mrs. N.?" (¿Ha visto V. *al* Señor o *a la* Señora N.?).

DEL NOMBRE O SUSTANTIVO.

El Nombre se divide en *común* y *propio*.

Nombre *común* es el que conviene a muchas personas o cosas: como, *city* (ciudad), *man* (hombre).

Nombre *propio* es el que conviene a una sola cosa o persona: como, *London* (Londres), *Peter* (Pedro).

Del Género.

Los géneros son tres: *masculino, femenino* y *neutro*.

Todo nombre de varón, o animal macho, es masculino; todo nombre de mujer, o animal hembra, es femenino; todos los nombres de cosas inanimadas son del género neutro.

Hay nombres que distinguen el género por una palabra diferente: v. g., *brother* (hermano), *sister* (hermana); otros lo expresan por medio de la terminación: v. g., *lion* (león), *lioness* (leona); y otros que lo distinguen por medio de las palabras *male* o *female*: como, "A *male* child" (un niño), "A *female* child" (una niña); *man* o *maid*: como, "A *man*-servant" (un criado), "a *maid*-servant" (una criada); *cock* o *hen*: como, "A *cock* sparrow" (un gorrión) "a *hen* sparrow" (la hembra del gorrión); *he* o *she*: como, "A *he*-bear" (un oso), "a *she*-bear" (una osa).

Del Número.

Los Números de los nombres son dos, *singular* y *plural*.

El *plural* se forma generalmente añadiendo una *s* al singular: v. g., *guide* (guía), *guides* (guías); *book* (libro), *books* (libros).

Los nombres acabados en *ch* (cuando suena como en castellano), o en *ss, x* u *o*, precedida de consonante, forman el plural añadiendo *es* al singular: v. g., *church* (iglesia), *churches* (iglesias); *kiss* (beso), *kisses* (besos); *fox* (zorra), *foxes* (zorras); *hero* (héroe), *heroes* (héroes); pero si la *ch* suena como *k*, añaden solamente *s*: v. g., *monarch* (monarca), *monarchs* (monarcas).

Los terminados en *y*, precedida de una vocal, siguen la regla general: v. g., *day* (día), *days* (días); pero si la precede una consonante, la mudan en *i* y añaden *es*: v. g., *fly* (mosca), *flies* (moscas); *lady* (señora), *ladies* (señoras).

Los nombres que acaban en *f* o *fe* mudan estas letras en *v* y añaden *es*: v. g., *leaf* (hoja), *leaves* (hojas); *life* (vida), *lives* (vidas). Se exceptúan *chief* (jefe), *dwarf* (enano), *handkerchief* (pañuelo de mano), etc., y también *muff* (manguito), que forman el plural añadiendo *s*.

Hay algunos nombres cuyos plurales son irregulares: v. g., *man* (hombre), *men* (hombres); *foot* (pie), *feet* (pies), etc.; *child* (hijo), *children* (hijos). Estos nombres corresponden generalmente a palabras semejantes del alemán.

De los Casos de los Nombres.

Los casos son tres: *The Nominative* (el Nominativo), *the Possessive* o *Genitive* (el Posesivo o Genitivo), y *the Objective* o *Accusative* (el Objetivo o Acusativo).

El *Nominativo* y el *Objetivo* se distinguen sólo por su colocación en la frase: v. g., "The *father* loves *the son*" (El *padre* ama *al hijo*); "The *son* loves *the father*" (El *hijo* ama *al padre*).

El *Posesivo* denota *posesión*, y se forma invirtiendo el orden y poniendo primero en inglés el nombre que es último en español, después del cual se pone un apóstrofo y la letra *s*: v. g., "My *father's* house" (La casa de mi *padre*); "The *boy's* hat" (El sombrero del *muchacho*). Cuando los plurales terminan en *s*, el Posesivo se forma añadiendo solamente el apóstrofo: como, "My *brothers'* horse" (El caballo de mis *hermanos*). Viniendo más de dos sustantivos seguidos, el apóstrofo y la *s* se ponen a cada uno de ellos: v. g., "The captain's son's servant's horse" (El caballo del criado del hijo del capitán). En tal caso sería mejor cambiar la construcción. Con el apóstrofo y la *s* (*'s*) se indica también el lugar, sitio o casa en donde se ha hecho alguna cosa: v. g., "He supped last night at your sister's" (*house*, sobreentendido), (Él cenó anoche en casa de la hermana de Vd.).

DE LOS ADJETIVOS.

Los Adjetivos en inglés no admiten variación de género ni número: v. g., "A *prudent* man" (un hombre *prudente*), "*prudent* men" (hombres *prudentes*); "a *prudent* woman" (una mujer *prudente*), "*prudent* women" (mujeres *prudentes*); y se colocan generalmente antes del sustantivo: v. g., "He wishes *warm* water" (Él quiere agua *caliente*).

La sola variación que admiten es la de los grados de comparación. Estos son *Positivo, Comparativo* y *Superlativo*.

El *comparativo de aumento* se forma por medio del adverbio *more* (más), seguido de *than* (que): v. g., *wise* (sabio); "*more* wise *than* he" (*más* sabio *que* él). También se forma añadiendo una *r* à los monosílabos que acaban en *e*, o *er* a los que terminan en otra letra: v. g., *wiser* (más sabio); *black* (negro), *blacker* o *more black* (más negro).

El *comparativo de inferioridad* o *diminucion* se forma por medio del adverbio *less* (menos), o *less than* (menos de o que): v. g., "He is *less* rich *than* she" (Él es *menos* rico *que* ella).

El *comparativo de igualdad* con los adjetivos se expresa con los adverbios *as* . . . . (tan . . . .), *as* (como); o *not less* . . . . (no menos . . . .) *than* (que): v. g., "He is *as* generous *as* she" (Él es *tan* generoso *como* ella); "She is *not less* generous *than* he" (Ella *no es menos* generosa *que* él).

El *comparativo de igualdad* con los sustantivos se expresa por *as* o *so much* (tanto, tanta), en singular; y por *as many* (tantos, tantas), en plural, y el como siguiente por *as*: v. g., "She has *as much* gold *as* silver" (Ella tiene *tanto* oro *como* plata); "He has *as many* dogs *as* horses" (Él tiene *tantos* perros *como* caballos).

El *Superlativo* se forma con los adverbios *very* (muy), *most* o *least*, y también añadiendo *st* a los acabados en *e*, o *est* a los terminados en otras letras.

Cuando el positivo acaba en *y* la muda en *i*, y a esta añade las letras *er* para el comparativo, y *est* para el superlativo: v. g., *dry* (seco), *drier* o *more dry* (más seco), *driest* (sequísimo), *very dry* (muy seco).

COMPARATIVOS Y SUPERLATIVOS IRREGULARES.

Pos.	Comp.	Superl.	
Good,	*better*,	*best*,	*very good.*
Bueno,	mejor,	óptimo,	bonísimo.
Bad,	*worse*,	*worst*,	*very bad.*
Malo,	peor,	pésimo,	malísimo.
Little,	*less o lesser*,	*least*,	*very little.*
Pequeño,	menor,	mínimo,	pequeñísimo.

DEL PRONOMBRE.

Los Pronombres son de cuatro especies, a saber: *Personales, Relativos, Interrogativos* y *Adjetivos*.

PRONOMBRES PERSONALES.

PRIMERA PERSONA.

Gênero Masculino o Femenino.

Singular.

Nom.	I	yo.
Pos.	Mine	de mí, el mío, la mía, etc.
Obj.	Me	me, a mí.

Plural.

Nom.	We	nosotros, nosotras.
Pos.	Ours	el nuestro, la nuestra, etc.
Obj.	Us	nos, a nosotros, a nosotras.

SEGUNDA PERSONA.

Gênero Masculino o Femenino.

Singular.

Nom.	You	tú.
Pos.	Yours	de tí, el tuyo, la tuya, etc.
Obj.	You	te, a ti.

Plural.

Nom.	You	vosotros, etc.; Vd., VV., Vds., etc.
Pos.	Yours	el de Vd., el de VV., Vds., etc.
Obj.	You	os, a vosotros, a Vd., VV., Vds., etc.

TERCERA PERSONA.

Gênero Masculino.

Singular.

Nom.	He	él.
Pos.	His	de él, el suyo, la suya, etc.
Obj.	Him	le, a él.

Plural.

Nom.	They	ellos.
Pos.	Theirs	el de ellos, etc.
Obj.	Them	los, les, a ellos.

Gênero Femenino.

Singular.

Nom.	She	ella.
Pos.	Hers	de ella, el suyo, la suya, etc.
Obj.	Her	la, a ella.

Plural.

Nom.	They	ellas.
Pos.	Theirs	el de ellas, etc.
Obj.	Them	las, les, a ellas.

Gênero Neutro.

Singular.

Nom.	It	ello, etc.
Pos.	Its	el suyo, la suya, etc.
Obj.	It	lo, la.

Plural.

El plural del pronombre neutro *It*, es lo mismo que el del género masculino o femenino.

PRONOMBRES RELATIVOS.

Los Pronombres Relativos son *who* (que, quien), *which* (que, cual), *that* (que), y *what* (lo que); los cuales son invariables en ambos números.

Nom.	*Who*	Que, quien.
Pos.	*Whose*	De quien, cuyo
Obj.	*Whom*	A quien, etc.

Who se aplica a personas: como, "The boy *who*" (el muchacho *que*).

Which se aplica a animales irracionales y a cosas: como, "A dog *which* barks" (un perro *que* ladra); "the book *which* was lost" (el libro *que* se perdió).

That se emplea frecuentemente en vez de *who* o *which*, por preferencia, antes de una cláusula o frase: como, "The boy *that* reads constantly" (el muchacho *que* lee asiduamente); "the book *that* was lost" (el libro *que* se perdió).

What es un relativo compuesto, que comprende tanto el relativo simple como el antecedente: como, "This is *what* I wanted; es decir, *the thing which* I wanted" (esto es *lo que* yo quería).

PRONOMBRES INTERROGATIVOS.

Los Pronombres Interrogativos son *who* (quién), *whose* (de quién), *whom* (a quién); *which* (qué), y *what* (qué). Se usan en las interrogaciones: como, "*Who* said that?" (*¿quién* dijo eso?) "*Whose* is this book?" (¿de quién es este libro?) "*Whom* did you see?" (¿a quién vió Vd.?) "*Which* book do you wish?" (*¿qué* libro quiere Vd.?) "*What* did he do?" (*¿qué* hizo él?)

PRONOMBRES ADJETIVOS.

Hay cuatro clases de Pronombres Adjetivos:

1ª. *Los posesivos.—My* (mi, mis); *your* (tu, tus); *his* (su, sus, de él); *her* (su, sus, de ella); *our* (nuestro, nuestra; nuestros, nuestras); *your* (su, sus; de Vd., de VV.); *their* (su, sus; de ellos, de ellas); *its* (su, sus); *own* (propio).

2ª. *Los distributivos.—Each* (cada); *every* (todo, toda); *either* (uno u otro); *neither* (ni uno ni otro).

3ª. *Los demostrativos.—This* (este, esta, esto); *that* (ese, esa, eso; aquel, aquella, aquello); con sus plurales—*these* (estos, estas); *those* (esos, esas, etc.).

4ª. *Los indefinidos.—None* (ninguno, etc.); *any* (alguno, etc.); *all* (todos, etc.); *such* (tal, etc.); *whole* (todo, etc.); *some* (alguno, etc.); *both* (ambos); *one* (uno); *other* (otro, etc.); *another* (otro, etc.). Los tres últimos se declinan como nombres.

OBSERVACIÓN.—*His* y *her* son pronombres posesivos cuando preceden inmediatamente al nombre; pero cuando vienen solos, *his* es el caso posesivo del pronombre personal *he*, y *her* el objetivo de *she*.

DEL VERBO.

Los *Verbos* son de tres clases: *Transitivos ó Activos, Pasivos*, e *Intransitivos* o *Neutros*.

Verbo activo o *transitivo* es aquel cuya acción recae sobre algún objeto: v. gr., "James *strikes* the table" (Jaime *golpea* la mesa).

Verbo pasivo es el que representa una acción como sufrida o recibida por el sujeto: v. gr., "The table *was struck*" (la mesa *fue golpeada*).

Verbo neutro o *intransitivo* es el que expresa la existencia o el estado de los seres, o una acción que no pasa del sujeto: v. gr., "I *am* here" (yo *estoy* aquí); "he *sleeps*" (él *duerme*); "I *run*" (yo *corro*).

Divídese el verbo, por razón de su forma, en *Regular, Irregular* y *Defectivo*.

Verbo regular es el que forma su imperfecto y pretérito de indicativo (*Indicative Imperfect*) y su participio pasivo (*Past Participle*) agregando *d* o *ed* al presente (*Present*); como, *love* (amo); *loved* (amaba, amé); *loved* (amado); *hoist* (alzar), *hoist*ed (alzaba, alcé; alzado).

Verbo irregular es el que se separa de la regla establecida en el párrafo anterior; como, *write* (escribo); *wrote* (escribía, escribí); *written* (escrito).

Llámase *verbo defectivo* el que carece de alguno de sus tiempos y personas; a esta clase pertenecen la mayor parte de los auxiliares y todos los impersonales.

De los Modos y Tiempos del Verbo.

Los verbos tienen cuatro *modos:* a saber, *Infinitivo, Indicativo, Imperativo* y *Subjuntivo* o *Potencial*.

Los *tiempos* del verbo son seis: á saber, the present (*el Presente*); the past (*el Imperfecto y Pretérito*); the perfect (*el Perfecto Próximo*); the pluperfect (*el Pluscuamperfecto*); the future (*el Futuro*); y the future perfect (*el Futuro Anterior*).

Formación de los Tiempos del Verbo.

El Presente de Infinitivo es como la raíz de que nacen y se forman los demás tiempos y personas, y se distingue por la preposición *to:* v. g., *to* admire (admirar); *to* abandon (abandonar). Cuando el presente de infinitivo se usa solo, debe estar precedido siempre de dicha preposición.

El Gerundio, que en inglés es *Participio Presente*, se forma añadiendo la terminación *ing* al presente del infinitivo, el cual, en este caso, omite la preposición *to*, y también la *e*, si acaba en esta letra: v. g., *to* admire (admirar), admir*ing* (admirando); *to* abandon (abandonar), abandon*ing* (abandonando).

El Participio Pasivo de los verbos regulares se forma añadiendo una *d* al infinitivo de los que terminan en *e*, y *ed* a los que acaban en otra letra: v. g., *to* admire (admirar), admire*d* (admirado); *to* abandon (abandonar), abandon*ed* (abandonado). Si el infinitivo acaba en *y* precedida de una vocal, añade *ed:* v. g., *to* pray (suplicar), pray*ed* (suplicado); pero si es una consonante la que precede a la *y*, la convierte en *i* y añade *ed:* v. g., *to* satisf*y* (satisfacer), satisf*ied* (satisfecho).

Presente de Indicativo.—La primera persona singular, y la primera, segunda y tercera persona plural del *Presente de Indicativo* son lo mismo que el presente de infinitivo, sin la preposición *to;* pero en su lugar deben expresar el pronombre correspondiente: v. g., *to* admire (admirar); *I* admire, *we* admire, *you* admire, *they* admire (yo admiro, nosotros admiramos, etc.). Se exceptúa de esta regla el verbo *to be* (ser).

La segunda persona singular del *Presente de Indicativo* se forma añadiendo *st* al presente de infinitivo de los acabados en *e*, o *est* a los que no terminan en esta letra: v. g., *to* admire (admirar), *thou* admir*est* (tú admiras); *to* abandon (abandonar), *thou* abandon*est* (tú abandonas). Si el infinitivo acaba en *y*, precedida de vocal, se añade *est;* y si de consonante, muda la *y* en *i*, y añade *est:* v. g., *to* pray (suplicar), *thou* pray*est* (suplicas); *to* cry (gritar), thou cr*iest* (gritas).

La tercera persona singular del *Presente de Indicativo* se forma añadiendo una *s* (antiguamente *eth*) al presente de infinitivo: v. g., *to* love (amar), *he* love*s* (él ama); *to* abandon (abandonar), *he* abandon*s* (él abandona). *Excepciones.*—Cuando el infinitivo acaba en *o, ch, sh, ss, th, x* o *z*, se añade *es:* v. g., *to* go (ir), *he* go*es* (él va); *to* beseech (suplicar), *he* beseech*es* (él suplica), etc. Si el verbo acaba en *y* precedida de una consonante, la convierte en *i* y añade *es;* pero si viene después de vocal, añade *s* solamente: v. g., *to* reply (replicar), *he* repl*ies* (él replica); *to* pay (pagar), *he* pay*s* (él paga).

El Imperfecto y *Pretérito* (past tense) de indicativo de los verbos regulares es lo mismo que su participio pasivo: v. g., *to* promise (prometer), promise*d* (prometido), *I* promise*d* (yo prometía o prometí): excepto la segunda persona singular, que añade *st:* v. g., *thou* promised*st* (tú prometiste). Si el infinitivo acaba en *y* precedida de consonante, la muda en *i* y añade *ed;* pero si no, la retiene y añade *ed:* v. g., *to* reply (replicar), I repl*ied* (yo replicaba o repliqué); *to* delay (dilatar), *I* delay*ed* (yo dilataba o dilaté).

El Futuro, cuando significa simplemente una accion por venir, se forma por medio del auxiliar *shall* prefijado al infinitivo, sin la partícula *to*, en las primeras personas, y *will* en las demás. Pero cuando indica promesa, deseo vehemente, mando o amenaza, se expresa por medio de *will* en las primeras personas, y de *shall* en las demás, exceptuando las segundas singulares, que se expresan por *wilt* y *shalt:* v. g., "Thou *shalt* not *bear* false witness against thy neighbour" (No *levantarás* falso testimonio contra tu prójimo).

El Presente del Modo Subjuntivo o *Potencial* se forma por medio de los auxiliares *may* o *can*, o de las conjunciones, *if, though* o *whether*, prefijados al infinitivo sin la partícula *to:* "I *may* write" (puede ser que yo escriba, o yo escriba). "*Whether* it prove true or not" (Sea que el caso resulte verdadero o no). "*Though* he slay me, yet will I trust in him" (Aun cuando me matare, en él esperaré).

El Imperfecto del Subjuntivo o *Potencial* se forma por medio de los auxiliares *might, could, would* o *should*, según su respectiva significación, prefijados al infinitivo sin la partícula *to:* v. g., *to* sell (vender), "I *would* sell" (yo querría vender *o* yo vendería).

Los Tiempos Compuestos se forman, como en castellano, por medio del auxiliar to *have* (haber), seguido del participio pasivo del verbo principal: v. g., I *have* armed (he armado); I *had* armed (yo había *o* hube armado); I *shall have* armed (yo habré armado); I *may have* armed (yo haya armado); I *might, could, would,* o *should have* armed (yo hubiera, habría, *o* hubiese armado).

CONJUGACIÓN DE UN VERBO REGULAR.

INFINITIVO.

To love,	*amar.*

Participio Presente.

Loving,	*amando.*

Participio Pasivo.

Loved,	*amado.*

INDICATIVO.

Presente.

I love,	*yo amo.*
You love,	*tú amas.*
He loves,	*él ama.*
We love,	*nos. amamos.*
You love,	*vos. amáis.*
They love,	*ellos aman.*

Imperfecto y Pretérito. (Past.)

I loved,	*yo amaba, amé.*
You loved,	*tú amabas, amaste.*
He loved,	*él amaba, amó.*
We loved,	*nos. amábamos, amamos.*
You loved,	*vos. amabais, amasteis.*
They loved,	*ellos amaban, amaron.*

Perfecto.

I have loved,	*yo he amado.*
You have loved,	*tú has amado.*
He has loved,	*él ha amado.*
We have loved,	*nos. hemos amado.*
You have loved,	*vos. habéis amado.*
They have loved,	*ellos han amado.*

Pluscuamperfecto.

I had loved,	*yo había amado.*
You had loved,	*tú habías amado.*
He had loved,	*él había amado.*
We had loved,	*nos. habíamos amado.*
You had loved,	*vos. habíais amado.*
They had loved,	*ellos habían amado.*

Futuro.

I shall *o* will love,	*yo amaré.*
You shall *o* will love,	*tú amarás.*
He shall *o* will love,	*él amará.*
We shall *o* will love,	*nos. amaremos.*
You shall *o* will love,	*vos. amaréis.*
They shall *o* will love,	*ellos amarán.*

Futuro Anterior. (*Future Perfect.*)

I shall *o* will have loved,	*yo habré amado.*
You shall *o* will have loved,	*tú habrás amado.*
He shall *o* will have loved,	*él habrá amado.*
We shall *o* will have loved,	*nos. habremos amado.*
You shall *o* will have loved,	*vos. habréis amado.*
They shall *o* will have loved,	*ellos habrán amado.*

IMPERATIVO.

Love (you),	*ama tú.*
Let him love,	*ame él.*
Let us love,	*amemos nosotros.*
Love (you),	*amad vosotros.*
Let them love,	*amen ellos.*

SUBJUNTIVO.

Presente.

That I may love,	*que yo ame.*
That you may love,	*que tú ames.*
That he may love,	*que él ame.*
That we may love,	*que nos. amemos.*
That you may love,	*que vos. améis.*
That they may love,	*que ellos amen.*

Imperfecto.

I might, could, would, should love,	*yo amara, amaría, amase.*
You might, could, would, should love,	*tú amaras, amarías, amases.*
He might, could, would, should love,	*él amara, amaría, amase.*
We might, could, would, should love,	*nos. amáramos, amaríamos, amásemos.*
You might, could, would, should love,	*vos. amarais, amaríais, amaseis.*
They might, could, would, should love,	*ellos amaran, amarían, amasen.*

Perfecto.

That I may have loved,	*que yo haya amado.*
That you may have loved,	*que tú hayas amado.*
That he may have loved,	*que él haya amado.*
That we may have loved,	*que nos. hayamos amado.*
That you may have loved,	*que vos. hayáis amado.*
That they may have loved,	*que ellos hayan amado.*

Pluscuamperfecto.

I might, could, would, should have loved,	*yo hubiera, habría, hubiese amado.*
You might, could, would, should have loved,	*tú hubieras,* etc., *amado.*
He might, etc., have loved,	*él hubiera,* etc., *amado.*
We might, etc., have loved,	*nos. hubiéramos,* etc., *amado.*
You might, etc., have loved,	*vos. hubierais,* etc. *amado.*
They might, etc., have loved,	*ellos hubieran,* etc. *amado.*

Futuro.

If I shall *o* will love,	*si yo amare.*
If you shall *o* will love,	*si tú amares.*
If he shall *o* will love,	*si él amare.*
If we shall *o* will love,	*si nos. amáremos.*
If you shall *o* will love,	*si vos. amareis.*
If they shall *o* will love,	*si ellos amaren.*

Futuro Anterior. (*Future Perfect.*)

If I shall *o* will have loved,	*si yo hubiere amado.*
If you shall *o* will have loved,	*si tú hubieres amado.*
If he shall *o* will have loved,	*si él hubiere amado.*
If we shall *o* will have loved,	*si nos. hubiéremos amado.*
If you shall *o* will have loved,	*si vos. hubiereis amado.*
If they shall *o* will have loved,	*si ellos hubieren amado.*

CONJUGACIÓN DE LOS VERBOS AUXILIARES —*To Have* y *To Be.*

To Have.

INFINITIVO.

To have,	*haber tener.*

Participio Presente.

Having,	*habiendo, teniendo.*

Participio Pasivo.

Had,	*habido tenido.*

INDICATIVO.

Presente.

I have,	*yo he o tengo.*
You have,	*tú has o tienes.*
He has,	*él ha o tiene.*
We have,	*nos. hemos o tenemos.*
You have,	*vos. habéis o tenéis.*
They have,	*ellos han o tienen.*

Imperfecto y Pretérito.

I had	*yo había, hube; tenía, tuve.*
You had	*tú habías, hubiste; tenías, tuviste.*
He had,	*él había, hubo; tenía, tuvo.*
We had,	*nos. habíamos, hubimos; teníamos, tuvimos.*
You had,	*vos. habíais, hubisteis; teníais, tuvisteis.*
They had,	*ellos habían, hubieron; tenían, tuvieron.*

Los demás tiempos de este verbo son regulares, y se conjugan por consiguiente como los de *To Love.*

Como ya se ha visto, por medio de este auxiliar se forman los tiempos compuestos de los verbos.

To Be.

INFINITIVO

To be,	*ser, estar*

Participio Presente.

Being,	*siendo, estando.*

Participio Pasivo.

Been,	*sido, estado*

INDICATIVO.

Presente.

I am,	*yo soy o estoy.*
You are,	*tú eres o estás.*
He is,	*él es o está.*
We are,	*nos. somos o estamos.*
You are,	*vos. sois o estáis.*
They are,	*ellos son o están.*

Imperfecto y Pretérito.

I was,	*yo era, fui; estaba, estuve.*
You were,	*tú eras, fuiste; estabas, estuviste.*
He was,	*él era, fue; estaba, estuvo.*
We were,	*nos. éramos, fuimos; estábamos, estuvimos.*
You were,	*vos. erais, fuisteis; estabais, estuvisteis.*
They were,	*ellos eran, fueron; estaban, estuvieron.*

SUBJUNTIVO.

Presente.

That I may be,	*que yo sea o esté.*
That you may be,	*que tú seas o estés.*
That he may be,	*que él sea o esté.*
That we may be,	*que nos. seamos o estemos.*
That you may be,	*que vos. seáis o estéis.*
That they may be,	*que ellos sean o estén.*

Imperfecto.

I were,	*yo fuera, sería, fuese; estuviera, estaría, estuviese.*
You were,	*tú fueras, serías, fueses; estuvieras, estarías estuvieses.*
He were,	*él fuera, sería, fuese; estuviera, estaría, estuviese.*
We were,	*nos. fuéramos,* etc.; *estuviéramos,* etc.
You were,	*vos. fuerais,* etc.; *estuvierais,* etc.
They were,	*ellos fueran,* etc.; *estuvieran,* etc.

Lo restante del verbo es regular, y se conjuga como *To Love.*

La Voz Pasiva se forma agregando el Participio Pasivo del verbo que se quiere conjugar, al tiempo correspondiente del auxiliar *To Be:* v. g., "I *am loved*" (yo soy amado); "I *was loved*" (yo era amado); "I *have been loved*" (yo he sido amado), etc.

El Verbo To Do.

Frases interrogativas, negativas y enérgicas se forman generalmente por medio del auxiliar *To Do,* en el presente de indicativo y en el imperfecto y pretérito del mismo. *Ejemplos:* He buys (él compra); he *does not* buy (él no compra); *does* he buy? (¿compra él?); *does* he *not* buy? (¿no compra él?); he bought (él compró); he *did not* buy (él no compró); *did* he buy? (¿compró él?); *did* he *not* buy? (¿no compró él?) Cuando *To Do* se usa enérgicamente, equivale a una afirmación.

VERBOS IRREGULARES

Son *Verbos Irregulares* en inglés los que no forman su participio pasivo ni su imperfecto o pretérito con la adición de las letras *d* o *ed:* v. g., to *see* (ver), I *saw* (yo veía o vi), I have *seen* (he visto). Todas estas irregularidades están incluídas en este Diccionario, en sus respectivos lugares; pero para facilitar a los principiantes el hallarlas, se pone la siguiente lista de todas ellas en inglés solamente, para no hacer muy difusa esta Sinopsis. Los que están marcados con una R indican que pueden formarse de la manera regular: v. g., *to work* (trabajar); he *worked* o *wrought* (él trabajó); he has *worked* o *wrought* (él ha trabajado); y en tales casos se prefiere la forma regular, por regla general.

Presente.	*Imperf.*	*Part. pas.*
Abide	abode	abode
Am	was	been
Arise	arose	arisen
Awake	awoke, R	awoke, R
Bear, *producir*	bore	born
Bear, *llevar*	bore	borne
Beat	beat	beaten, beat
Begin	began	begun
Bend	bent	bent
Bereave	bereft, R	bereft, R
Beseech	besought	besought
Bid	bid, bade	bidden, bid
Bind	bound	bound
Bite	bit	bitten, bit
Bleed	bled	bled
Blow	blew	blown
Break	broke	broken
Breed	bred	bred
Bring	brought	brought
Build	built, R	built, R
Burst	burst	burst
Buy	bought	bought
Cast	cast	cast
Catch	caught	caught
Chide	chid, R	chidden, chid
Choose	chose	chosen
Cleave, *hender*	clove, cleft, R	cleft, cloven, R
Cling	clung	clung
Clothe	clothed, clad	clad, R
Come	came	come
Creep	crept	crept
Crow	crew (Ant.), R	crowed
Cut	cut	cut
Dare, *atreverse*	durst, R	dared
Deal	dealt, R	dealt, R
Dig	dug, R	dug, R
Do	did	done
Draw	drew	drawn
Drink	drank	drunk
Drive	drove	driven
Dwell	dwelt	dwelt
Eat	ate, eat (Ant.)	eaten
Fall	fell	fallen
Feed	fed	fed
Feel	felt	felt
Fight	fought	fought
Find	found	found
Flee	fled	fled
Fling	flung	flung
Fly	flew	flown
Forget	forgot	forgotten
Forsake	forsook	forsaken
Freeze	froze	frozen
Get	got	got, gotten
Gild	gilt, R	gilt, R
Gird	girt, R	girt, R
Give	gave	given
Go	went	gone
Grave	graved	graven, R
Grind	ground	ground
Grow	grew	grown
Have	had	had
Hang	hung, R	hung, R
Hear	heard	heard
Hew	hewed	hewn, R
Hide	hid	hidden *o* hid
Hit	hit	hit
Hold	held	held
Hurt	hurt	hurt
Keep	kept	kept
Knit	knit, R	knit, R
Know	knew	known
Lade	laded	laden, R
Lay	laid	laid
Leave	left	left
Lend	lent	lent
Let	let	let
Lie, *yacer*	lay	lain
Lose	lost	lost
Make	made	made
Meet	met	met
Mow	mowed	mown, R
Pay	paid	paid
Read (rid), *leer*	read (red)	read (red)
Rend	rent	rent
Rid	rid, R	rid
Ride	rode	ridden *y* (Ant.) rid
Ring	rang, rung	rung
Rise	rose	risen
Rive	rived	riven, R
Run	ran	run
Saw	sawed	sawn, R
Say	said	said
See	saw	seen
Seek	sought	sought
Sell	sold	sold
Send	sent	sent
Set	set	set
Shake	shook	shaken
Shape	shaped	shaped, shapen (Ant.)
Shave	shaved	shaven, R
Shear	sheared	shorn, R
Shed	shed	shed
Shine	shone, R	shone, R
Shoe	shod	shod
Shoot	shot	shot
Show	showed	shown
Shrink	shrank, shrunk	shrunk, shrunken
Shut	shut	shut
Sing	sang, sung	sung
Sink	sank, sunk	sunk
Sit	sat	sat
Slay	slew	slain
Sleep	slept	slept
Slit	slit *o* slitted	slit *o* slitted
Smite	smote	smitten
Sow	sowed	sown, R
Speak	spoke	spoken
Speed	sped	sped
Spend	spent	spent
Spill	spilt, R	spilt, R
Spin	spun, span (Ant.)	spun
Spit	spit, spat	spit, spat
Split	split, R	split, R
Spread	spread	spread
Spring	sprang, sprung	sprung
Stand	stood	stood
Steal	stole	stolen
Stick	stuck	stuck
Sting	stung	stung
Stride	strode	stridden (Ant. strid)
Strike	struck	struck *o* stricken
String	strung	strung
Strive	strove	striven, R
Strew	strewed	strewn, R
Strow (Ant.)	strowed	strown
Swear	swore, sware (Ant.)	sworn
Sweat	sweat, R	sweat, R
Sweep	swept	swept
Swell	swelled	swollen, R
Swim	swam, swum	swum
Swing	swung (swang Ant.)	swung
Take	took	taken
Teach	taught	taught
Tear	tore	torn
Tell	told	told
Think	thought	thought
Thrive	throve, R	thriven, R
Throw	threw	thrown
Thrust	thrust	thrust
Tread	trod	trodden, trod
Wax	waxed	waxen, R
Wear	wore	worn
Weave	wove	woven
Weep	wept	wept
Wet	wet, R	wet, R
Win	won	won
Wind	wound	wound
Work	wrought (Ant.), R	wrought (Ant.), R
Wring	wrung, R	wrung
Write	wrote	written

DEL ADVERBIO

Los *Adverbios* de *modo* o *calidad*, que en castellano se forman añadiendo la terminación *mente* al adjetivo, se expresan en inglés por medio de la sílaba *ly* añadida al mismo: v. g., *wise* (sabio), wise*ly* (sabia*mente*); *dear* (caro); dear*ly* (cara*mente*).

Los *Adverbios* admiten los grados de comparación, y los expresan con las mismas letras que los adjetivos: v. g., *near* (cerca), *near*er (más cerca), the *near*est (lo más cerca).

En inglés no se puede usar más de una negación; y así, *No quiero nada* se traduce, "I want nothing."

DE LA PREPOSICIÓN

Hay gran número de verbos en inglés que van acompañados de ciertas preposiciones, las cuales son como parte de ellos, entran en su significación y la hacen variar, a manera de los verbos separables en alemán: v. g., *To bring*, Traer, llevar. *To bring about*, Poner por obra, efectuar. *To bring forth*, Dar de sí, producir parir; dar a luz; exhibir. *To bring in*, Introducir, hacer entrar; alegar, declarar; producir dejar utilidad o ganancia. *To bring over*, Transportar, hacer atravesar; atraer, ganar a alguno a su partido. *To bring out*, Sacar, extraer, hacer salir; poner en evidencia; mostrar; descubrir; publicar. *To bring up*, Subir, hacer subir; presentar; servir a la mesa; educar, enseñar. Estas modificaciones van indicadas con mucho cuidado en el texto de este diccionario.

DE LA CONJUNCIÓN.

Las *Conjunciones* se dividen en inglés, como en español, en *copulativas* y *disyuntivas*.

Copulativas son las que enlazan simplemente unas palabras con otras, y las oraciones entre sí; v. g., "Peter *and* John will speak" (Pedro *y* Juan hablarán); "Wisdom *and* ignorance are opposites" (Sabiduría *e* ignorancia son cosas opuestas).

Disyuntivas son las que significan división o alternativa entre las cosas: v. g., "I speak *neither* English *nor* German" (Yo no hablo *ni* inglés *ni* alemán).

DE LA INTERJECCIÓN O EXCLAMACIÓN.

La *Interjección* es una palabra que sirve para expresar los varios afectos del ánimo, o para llamar la atención: como, "*Oh*, what a beautiful creature!" (¡Oh, qué hermosa criatura!) "*See!*" (¡Mira!)

OBSERVACIONES SOBRE ALGUNAS REGLAS DE LA SINTAXIS.

Cuando los poseedores de una misma cosa son dos o más, el apóstrofo y la *s* se ponen sólo después del último: v. g., "The father and son'*s* house" (La casa del padre y del hijo); "John and Henry'*s* book" (El libro de Juan y de Enrique).

Dos o más sustantivos singulares, regidos por las conjunciones *either—or, neither—nor*, rigen al verbo, al adjetivo y al pronombre en singular: v. g., "*Either* Peter *or* John *is* guilty" (*o* Pedro *o* Juan *son* culpados); "*Neither* time *nor* distance *is* able to diminish our friendship" (*ni* el tiempo *ni* la distancia *son* capaces de disminuir nuestra amistad).

La preposición *to*, que designa el infinitivo, se omite frecuentemente después de los verbos *to bid, dare, need, make, see, hear, let*, y los auxiliares *may, can, will, shall, must*, y sus pretéritos: v. g., "I dare *say*" (Me atrevo *a decir*).

Los verbos que significan *esperar, mandar, desear*, etc., rigen al otro verbo en presente de infinitivo con preferencia al perfecto del mismo: v. g., "I found him better than I expected *to find him*," y no "*to have found him*," (Le hallé mejor de lo que yo esperaba *hallarle*, y no *haberle hallado*).

El participio presente inglés (gerundio español) se traduce en el presente de infinitivo con la misma preposición, excepto cuando esta es *by*, pues en tal caso se omite, y el participio se traduce por el gerundio: v. g., "The *taking* from another what is his, without his permission, is called *stealing*" (El *tomar* de otro lo que es suyo, sin su permiso, se llama *robar*). En este caso el participio es un nombre. "John was sent to prepare the way *by preaching* repentance" (Juan fue enviado para preparar el camino *predicando* la penitencia).

Algunas conjunciones requieren el indicativo y otras el subjuntivo; en general, cuando el sentido es contingente o dudoso se debe usar el último: v. g., "If I *were* to write, he *would* not *do* it" (Si yo le *escribiera*, él no lo *haría*); "He will not be pardoned unless he *repent*" (El no será perdonado, a menos que se *arrepienta*).

Introducción Sobre la Pronunciación de la Lengua Inglesa.

Para hablar el inglés no basta saber pronunciar las letras del alfabeto, pues no hay quizás lengua alguna que presente sonidos tan varios y excepciones tan numerosas a la regla general; de modo que sólo por medio de una lectura asidua y constante, bajo la dirección de un maestro ó practicando con ingleses ó norteamericanos inteligentes, se puede conseguir una pronunciación más o menos perfecta.

Hay también otra irregularidad importante en la ortografía del inglés, la de que una misma letra se pronuncia de diferentes maneras, con sonidos enteramente distintos: v. g., *a* suena a veces como *e*, *e* como *i*, *o* como *u*, etc. Así en inglés, *lo!* (he aquí), se pronuncia precisamente como el pronombre *lo* en español; pero *do* (hacer), se pronuncia *du; to* (a), *tu*, etc. Esta irregularidad se extiende a numerosísimas palabras, al paso que en español sólo sucede lo mismo con la *y*, que cuando es conjunción se pronuncia como *i*, v. g., *Europa* y *América*, y se pronuncia como consonante cuando hiere a una vocal, como en *y*erro, *y*ugo.

Estas excepciones o irregularidades son tan abundantes en inglés que casi puede decirse que las letras de ese idioma de ninguna manera representan los sonidos del lenguaje. Una cosa es aprender a escribir una palabra, y otra enteramente diferente el saber pronunciarla después de escrita. Tan grande es esta dificultad que así los americanos como los ingleses están obligados a emplear Diccionarios de Pronunciación con su clave correspondiente; esto es, diccionarios en que las palabras están impresas tal cual deben escribirse, y a continuación las mismas palabras con ciertos signos, que muestran cómo deben pronunciarse. Estos Diccionarios de Pronunciación no los hay en castellano, porque no se necesitan.

La diferencia entre la manera de escribir y la de pronunciar las palabras en inglés se debe en parte a que la lengua inglesa se ha formado de la mezcla de gran número de diferentes lenguas; y en parte a los grandes cambios que han ocurrido en la manera de pronunciar muchas palabras durante muchos siglos, mientras que el modo de escribirlas no ha cambiado en proporción; pero principalmente a causa de haber adoptado el alfabeto romano para representar el inglés, que tiene muchos más sonidos que aquél o el latino, y aun más que el castellano, y por lo tanto no puede representarlos el alfabeto romano.

Una vez adoptado el método de escribir una lengua hablada por muchos millones de personas, queda tan completamente establecido que, por más absurdos que contenga, es sumamente difícil reformarlo enteramente o hacer en él algunas de las más necesarias correcciones. Pero la lengua inglesa continúa escribiéndose de una manera tan poco conforme con su pronunciación, que la explicación de ésta se hace necesaria aun para aquellos que la hablan como lengua materna; de aquí provienen, como queda dicho, los Diccionarios de Pronunciación para uso de los ingleses.

Recientemente se ha compuesto un alfabeto para servir de clave a la pronunciación de la lengua inglesa, tan superior a todos los sistemas precedentes, que el autor se ha visto obligado a adoptarlo en esta parte de su Diccionario. Por su medio y el de las explicaciones que le acompañan se obvian en gran manera las dificultades que ofrece la pronunciación inglesa. Llámase el *Alfabeto Científico* (preparado y difundido por La Asociación Filológica Americana y empleado en el "Standard Dictionary"). Contiene treinta y dos letras en vez de veintiseis, que es el número del alfabeto común inglés; porque realmente hay treinta y dos distintos sonidos en dicha lengua. Seis de estas letras son dobles o dígrafas, a saber: ch, dh, ng, sh, th, zh; y tres de los sonidos están provistos de nuevas letras, ɑ, ɐ, ʋ. En el Alfabeto Científico hay siempre *un solo sonido* para un *solo signo o letra*, y un *solo signo* para *un solo sonido*. El que quiera aprender a hablar por él deberá principiar procurando entender perfectamente dicho Alfabeto Científico, estudiándolo bien, a fin de hablar el idioma inglés de manera que pueda distinguir el sonido que cada una de sus letras representa, desentendiéndose enteramente al principio del abecedario común. Conseguido esto, se hallará en estado de aprender la pronunciación de cada palabra, por cuanto cada una está impresa a continuación *fonotípicamente* en la segunda columna, esto es, precisamente como debe pronunciarse. Á medida que el lector se acostumbre a ver las palabras de la primera columna, ora estén impresas o escritas, sabrá cómo hacer uso de ellas según el alfabeto antiguo, generalmente usado, y es como sigue:

El alfabeto inglés consta de veintiseis letras cuyas formas y nombres son:

A a	*se pronuncia*	e	N n	*se pronuncia*	en
B b	"	bi	O o	"	o
C c	"	si	P p	"	pi
D d	"	di	Q q	"	quiú
E e	"	i	R r	"	ar
F f	"	ef	S s	"	es
G g	"	yi	T t	"	ti
H h	"	etch	U u	"	iú
I i	"	ai	V v	"	vi
J j	"	yé	W w	"	doble iú
K k	"	qué	X x	"	ecs
L l	"	el	Y y	"	uai
M m	"	em	Z z	"	dsi *o* dsed

Como estas letras no pueden representar propiamente todos los sonidos de la lengua inglesa, se ha adoptado el siguiente:—

ALFABETO CIENTÍFICO (FONÉTICO).*

CLAVE PARA LA VERDADERA PRONUNCIACIÓN DE LA LENGUA INGLESA.

☞ Las letras fonéticas tienen el sonido correspondiente al que se expresa por las voces en letra cursiva.

Letras.	*Nombres.*	*Castellano.*	*Inglés.*
A ɑ ɑ̄	ah	c*a*ro	f*a*t
A a ā	*a* en caro	*a*i (*e* fran.)	*a*sk, f*ā*r, f*a*t, f*ā*re, o *e* francés (m*é*re)
B b	bi	*b*anco	
C c (=k, q)	ki, qui	*c*omo	
Ch ch.	chi	*ch*ico	*ch*ur*ch*
D d	di	*d*ía	*d*o
Dh dh	dhî	se*d*, uste*d*	*th*en
E ê	e (ay)	*e*n, f*e*	m*e*t, th*ey*
F f	ef	*f*e	*f*it
G g	gui (ghi)	*g*oce	*g*o
H h	ji	*j*o	*h*e
I i î	i	*i*gnaro, *i*da	*i*t, capr*í*ce
J j	dche	y en *y*ugo, ج arábiga o gi it liana	*j*et

* *Fonético*, adjetivo con que se califica la escritura en que cada signo o letra representa un sonido distinto.

Letras.	*Nombres.*	*Castellano.*	*Inglés.*
K k	ke	*k*a	*k*iu
L l	el	*l*a	*l*o
M m	em	*m*i	*m*e
N n	en	*n*o	*n*o
Ng ng	ing	(ñ) no tiene equivalente	ki*ng*
O o ō	oh	l*o*	*o*bey, nō
O ɵ ɵ	(awe)	no existe; por	n*o*t, wh*a*t, n*o*r, f*a*ll
P p	pi	*p*acer	*p*et
[Q q]	kiu, quiú	véase C.	quit (cwit)
R r	ar	*r*aso	*r*at
S s	es	a*s*í, *s*illa	*s*o
Sh sh	ish	no existe; *ch* francesa, ش arábiga, *sch* alemana	*sh*e
T t	ti	*t*al	*t*ell
Th th	ith	*z* en *z*apato	*th*in
U u ū	u (ŏŏ inglés)	n*u*do	f*u*ll, r*u*le
U ʋ ʋ̄	u(r)	no existe; casi *o* en opa; *eu* francesa o *ö* alemana	b*u*t, b*u*rn
V v	vi	*v*ida	*v*at
W w	wu	como *u* en g*u*apo	*w*o
[X x]	ex	(=cs) ne*x*o	wa*x*
Y y	yı	*y*acer	*y*e
Z z	(dsi)	no existe; como *z* francesa, *z*èle	*z*one
Zh zh	(zhi)	*J* francesa (Jean)	a*z*ure

Notas.

ɑ. Este carácter representa el sonido de la *a* en español, particularmente cuando lleva el acento tónico: v. g., papɑ̄. Es el sonido correcto de la *a* antes de la *l* muda, seguida de *f*, *m*, o *v:* v. g., cɑlf, bɑlm, cɑlve. Tiene también el mismo sonido antes de *gh* (cuando estas dos letras equivalen a una *f*), y antes de *nch*, *nd*, *nt*, pero en estos casos se escribe *au:* v. g., ɑunt, lɑugh, lɑunch.

ɑ̣ o ɑ *variant;* semejante a la *a* castellana, pero pronunciada breve y de golpe.

A, a. Este sonido ocurre comúnmente en una sílaba acentuada que termina en consonante; es breve, y se asemeja al sonido de la *i* francesa en crin: v. g., h*a*t, f*a*t. Cuando es larga, ā, va delante de una *r*, como en fāre; también se halla en lugar de *ea*, en b*ea*r, de *ai* en b*ai*r, *e* en th*e*re, *ei* en th*ei*r, y es equivalente a la *e* francesa. ạ, representa el mismo sonido, pero algo confuso, con cierta tendencia hacia la *eu* francesa o ʋ de este alfabeto.

B, b. Esta letra se pronuncia como en castellano; pero cuidando de comprimir fuertemente los labios, a fin de no confundirla con la *v*, y abrirlos sin extenderlos, para que no resulte una *p*. Los que no tengan oportunidad de oirla de un natural del país, podrán aprovechar mucho haciendo que un natural de Burgos, Toledo o Madrid pronuncie despacio en su presencia, *b*a*b*ador, *b*e*b*er, *b*iri*b*ís, *b*o*b*o, *b*ur*b*uja, procurando después imitarlos, teniendo siempre un poco comprimidos los labios antes de pronunciar la vocal.

Por este medio se percibirá fácilmente que la diferencia entre los sonidos de la *b* y de la *p* consiste en que salga de la garganta el aliento al pronunciar la primera, deteniéndole entre los labios, y en la segunda se despide sólo de los labios con alguna más fuerza, extendiéndolo muy ligeramente: v. g., en *p*a*p*á, *p*e*p*ena, *p*i*p*í, *p*o*p*ote, *p*u*p*ila.

C, c, como la *c* castellana antes de la *a* o la *o*.

Ch, ch, como en castellano.

D, d. Esta letra representa en ambas lenguas el sonido *parlante* correspondiente al susurrante que representa la *t*, el cual se forma colocando la punta de la lengua contra el cielo de la boca cerca de los dientes superiores y apartándola de ellos de golpe; pero al pronunciar la *d* es necesario hacerlo con suavidad, porque si se esfuerza mucho, se convierte en el sonido de la *t*. El sonido de que aquí se habla es el que tiene la *d* en *d*ama, *d*eja, *d*ime, *d*ote, *d*uro, teniendo mucho cuidado de evitar el provincialismo de pronunciarla como *z*, como *t*, o como *th*, en inglés: v. g., verda*t*, verda*z*, en vez de verda*d*.

Dh, dh, como *d* en Madri*d*, se*d*, to*d*o, uste*d*, o de*d*o en algunas provincias, la *dh*al (ذ) arábiga o la delta griega moderna: v. g., *th*y (*dh*ɑi), *th*at (*dh*at); está siempre escrita con *th* en la ortografía común.

E, e. Esta vocal es breve como en p*e*n (inglés), piel (castellano); larga (ê), como en fe o p*ai*n y f*a*te (inglés). La *e* obscura (ẹ), tiene una pronunciación familiar que se aproxima á la *u* en r*u*n. ẹr acentuada, como en h*er*, o *ir* en st*ir*, se pronuncia comúnmente como *ur* en b*ur*n (ó el diptongo francés *eu*); sin embargo, tiene una pronunciación formal más cerrada y más hacia adelante en la boca, parecida a la *e* en m*e*rry. *ê* larga se representa en la ortografía común por:

1. *ea* en br*ea*k, *ei* en v*ei*n, *eigh* en *eigh*t [êt], *ey* en th*ey*.

2. *a* antes de una vocal, como en *a*orist*;* antes de consonantes y de la *e* muda: v. g., f*a*te, str*a*nge; antes de *mb*, *nci*, *ss*: v. g., c*a*mbric [kêm], *a*ncient [ên], b*a*ss [bês].

3. *ai* en l*ai*d, *aigh* en str*aigh*t, *ao* en g*ao*l [jêl], *au* en g*au*ge [gêj], *ay* en d*ay*. ệ, variante, es un sonido intermedio entre *ê* y *e*, o como *ê* pronunciada breve y de golpe.

G, g. Esta letra en el sistema fonético se pronuncia siempre como la *g* en *g*ato, *g*ota, *g*ula.

H, h. El sonido de esta letra es gutural, y semejante al de la *j* española, aunque no tan fuerte como ésta. H, versalita, es el sonido fuerte de la *j* española, o de la *ch* alemana, como en *ach!*

I, i. Esta vocal breve se parece a la *i* española, pero pronunciada breve y de golpe.

I larga (î), suena como en español, cuando está acentuada: v. g., v*i*da, (o inglés), mach*i*ne [mɑ-shîn']. Se representa en la ortografía común por: 1. *i* (capr*i*ce). 2. *ie:* v. g., f*ie*ld, gr*ie*f. 3. *ei:* v. g., conc*ei*ve, c*ei*l, *ei*ther [î'-dhẹr]. 4. *e*, en b*e*, h*e*; *ee*, en b*ee*, f*ee*t, etc.; *ea*, en b*ea*st [bîst], s*ea*, etc.; *æ*, *ay*, *œ:* v. g., C*æ*sar, qu*ay*, Ph*œ*bus. 5. Antes de la *r:* v. g., h*e*re, b*ie*r, car*ee*r. ị, variante, se pronuncia breve y de golpe.

J, j. Equivalente a *dch*, *dy;* tiene el mismo sonido que la *jîm* arábiga or la *gi* italiana en *gi*orno. Los que entiendan francés podrán obtener este sonido prefijando una *d* a la *j* en las voces *j*e, *j*amais, pronunciando los dos sonidos muy juntos.

K, L, M, N, no requieren observación.

ṅ, sin embargo, es un sonido nasal tomado del francés, y retiene su sonido en dicha lengua: v. g., boṅ mot.

Ng, ng, letra dígrafa, representa un sonido común a las lenguas inglesa y alemana; se oye, casi perfecto, en el castellano bla*n*co, te*n*go; en inglés, si*ng*, wro*ng*, si*ng*i*ng*, wro*ng*i*ng*. La letra *n*, acentuada, tiene el mismo sonido cuando va antes de la *g*, como en a*n*ger [ang'-gẹr], E*n*glish [ing'-glish]; o antes de los sonidos de *k:* v. g., si*n*k [singk o siŋk], a*n*xious [angk'-shus], ha*n*dkerchief [hang'-kẹr-chif]. Se expresa generalmente en este volumen por medio de ng y por el signo ŋ.

O, o, como en castellano. ō larga se halla además de su propio carácter en *au* y *eau* (tomadas del francés): v. g., m*au*ve, b*eau*; *ew*, en s*ew* [sō], etc.; *oa*, como en f*oa*l [fōl]; *oe*, en t*oe* [tō]; *ou*, en s*ou*l [sōl]; *ow*, en r*ow* [rō]; *ough* en th*ough*, etc.

Ɵ, ɵ. No hay en castellano sonido que corresponda exactamente al de esta vocal, por cuanto participa de *a* y *o;* pero de una manera tan confusa que no puede distinguirse cuál de ellas predomina. Este sonido se forma manteniendo el aliento dentro de la boca, y arrojándolo contra el cielo de ella. Para aprenderlo bien, es necesario oir pronunciar por un americano o un inglés la voz *all* (todo), cual fonéticamente se escribe, ɵ̄l. La *o* en p*o*r se pronuncia de un modo muy parecido al sonido de esta vocal. La ɵ breve, como en *o*bstante (inglés n*o*t), se halla representada por ɑ, en *wa*, *wha*, *qua*, antes de un sonido consonante final: v. g., w*a*s, wh*a*t [wɵz, hwɵt]; por *ou*, en h*ou*gh [hɵk]; por *ow*, en kn*ow*ledge [nɵl'-ej]; por *oh*, en J*oh*n; por *ach*, en y*ach*t [yɵt]. La ɵ̄ larga, como en act*o*r (*o*rb, s*o*rt), se halla además de o (su forma propia).

impresa *ou*, como en c*ou*gh, *ou*ght.

impresa *oa*, como en br*oa*d.

impresa *au*, como en g*au*dy; *aw*, en l*aw*.

impresa *a* antes de *l*, *ll*, *lc*, *ld*, *lm*, *ls:* v. g., app*a*ll, *a*ll, *a*lmost, f*a*lcon, b*a*ld, *a*lmanac, b*a*lsam, etc.

impresa *a*, en *wa*, *wha*, como en w*a*r, wh*a*rf, etc.; así como en qu*a*rt [cwɵ̄rt], etc. ɵi, como en h*oy*.

P, Q, R, S, no requieren observación.

Sh, sh, letra dígrafa, que tiene el sonido de la *ch* francesa o la *shín* arábiga, se representa en la ortografía común, además de su propia forma, por:

1. *Si, ssi, s(e), sc(i)*, antes de una vocal no acentuada: v. g., sugar, pension, passion, nauseate, conscience.
2. *ti*, antes de una vocal no acentuada, como en partial [pär'-shal], etc.
3. *c(i), ce, che*, antes de una vocal no acentuada, como en ancient, ocean, luncheon, etc.
4. *ch*, después de *l* y *n* finales (en la Gran Bretaña), y en muchas palabras extranjeras, principalmente tomadas del francés: v. g., champagne, charade; capuchin, machine, etc.

T, t. Además de su propia forma, la representa *th*, como en thyme, *Thomas*, etc.; y *d, ed*, finales en los tiempos pretéritos y los participios después de una letra sorda: v. g., faced [fēst], asked [ɑskt].

Th, th, letra dígrafa, corresponde a la *z* castellana, como en zapa.

U, u, ū. La *u* bréve tiene casi el mismo sonido que el de la *u* en tumba, pronunciada breve y de golpe. Se halla (1) en full, bulrush, etc.; (2) en la sílaba *-ful:* v. g., cupful; (3) después de la *s*, cuando equivale a *sh:* v. g., censure, sugar; (4) antes de *sh:* bush, cushion, etc.; (5) en *wo:* v. g., woman, wolf; *oul*, en would, could; en *oo*, como en book, good, etc.; (6) en sílabas breves tomadas del latín y otros idiomas extranjeros.

La *ū* larga suena como la *u* castellana acentuada, como en tubo. Se halla: 1, comúnmente después de *r, l*, o *j:* v. g., rude [rūd], etc.; 2, impresa *ew*, como en crew, lewd, rheum; 3, impresa *ui*, como en cruise, fruit, etc.; 4, impresa *ou*, como en you, through, tour, etc.; 5, impresa *oo*, como en food, wooing [wū'-ing], etc.; 6, en sílabas acentuadas de palabras procedentes de idiomas extranjeros. Hay también la *u* de diptongo, que se llama ordinariamente la *u larga:* v. g., music [miū'-zic].

U, ʋ, ʋ̄. La ʋ breve, como en but (pero) tiene un sonido que debería oirse de labios de un hijo del país; es análogo al de la *eu* francesa, pronunciada breve y de golpe. Se usa en vez de la *o* antes de *n, ne, ng, m, mb, mp, me, ve, th, dh*, y *z:* v. g., son, done, tongue, among, comfort; compass, come, above, etc.; brother, etc., dozen, etc. También, en vez de *oo*, en blood; de *oe* en does; *ou*, en double, pious; *io*, en -sion, -tion [shʋn]; v. g., nation, etc. La ʋ̄ larga, como en burn, se oye en *ur:* v. g., hurl, etc.; y en la *o* en work [wʋ̄rk], etc. Corresponde al diptongo alemán *oe* y al francés *eu:* v. g., douceur, böse, oel.

V, v. Los españoles deben cuidar mucho de la pronunciación de esta letra para no confundirla, como frecuentemente sucede, con la *b*. Esta se pronuncia comprimiendo los labios, y aquella tocando con el labio inferior los dientes superiores, como si se fuera a expresar *fe*, y forma un par con la *f*, siendo la *v* la *parlante* y la *f* la *susurrante* de un par.

W, w. Esta letra se pronuncia precisamente como en castellano la *u* antes de *a:* v. g., guardia, o como la *o* en Joaquin, *Oajaca*; pero pronunciando ambos sonidos con tal rapidez que no formen más que una sílaba, es decir, que la *o* se junte de tal manera con la vocal siguiente que no se distinga. Este sonido es realmente el de una consonante brevísima, y se forma comprimiendo un poco los labios para impedir que el aliento salga libremente. Los españoles no observan esto, que, no obstante, es muy perceptible para un inglés; es decir, que aunque los españoles pronuncian sin dificultad y correctamente esta letra en su lengua, de conformidad con lo que se dice arriba, y que esto lo hacen diariamente, piensan que solamente pronuncian una *u* o una *o*, mientras que el inglés percibe una ligera distinción entre el sonido de estos elementos, cuando se hallan delante de otra vocal, v. g., en guapo, *Oajaca*, y el sonido de los mismos elementos estando solos o antes de una consonante, como *u*, v. g., en Cuba, e indica esa distinción escribiendo *w* en lugar de *u* en el primer caso.

X, x, equivale a *cs*, como en español.

Y, y, en este alfabeto es siempre consonante.

Z, z. Este carácter representa también el sonido *parlante* correspondiente a la *s* consonante, *susurrante* o semi-muda, por cuanto las dos forman un par. No hay en castellano sonido que le cuadre, pero puede aplicársele el de la *z* francesa en zèle, o el de la zai arábiga.

Zh, zh, letra dígrafa o doble; tiene el sonido de la *j* francesa, como en jamais. Es el sonido de *si* en la desinencia *-sion* después de una vocal acentuada: v. g., occasion, vision; de la *s* en *su*, como en composure [cʋm-pō'-zhur], pleasure [plezh'-yur], etc.

La división de las sílabas en este diccionario se ha efectuado con el objeto de representar las divisiones de la pronunciación.

Este sistema de pronunciación, sancionado por autoridades de tanto peso como las Asociaciones Filológicas Americana e Inglesa, merece plena aprobación y la mejor acogida por su exactitud y claridad.

Al principio parece extraño, como lo son en general todas las cosas nuevas; pero estas aparentes dificultades desaparecen luego que se experimentan los excelentes efectos que produce, dando un signo a cada sonido y distinguiendo claramente las diferencias de éstos, medio por el cual se hacen más fáciles y correctas la pronunciación y la escritura.

El alfabeto fonético no ofrece dificultad que no sea fácilmente superable, con un poco de estudio y aplicación, como se verá por la recapitulación del mismo contenida en la siguiente Guía.

Guía Para el Uso de la Clave Que Va al Pie de las Páginas.

ī *ida*; ȩ cerca; ê *hé*; ā *ala*; ɵ *por*; ō *oro*; u *uno*.—i *idea*; e *esté*; ɑ *así*; o *osó*; ʋ *opa*; ʋ̄ como en *leur* (Fr.).—ɑi *aire*; ei *voy*; ɑu *aula*;

iu *viuda*; y *yunta*; w *guapo*; h *jaco*; ch *chico*; j *yema*; th *zapa*; dh *dedo*; z *zèle* (Fr.); sh *chez* (Fr.); zh *Jean*; ng *sangre*.

1. El lector que quiera aprovecharse de la ventaja y facilidad que proporciona el alfabeto fonético, y por su medio adquirir la verdadera pronunciación de la lengua inglesa, deberá advertir que la clave que se halla al pie de cada página indica los sonidos que las vocales y diptongos tienen en inglés, correspondientes exactamente a las vocales y diptongos que en las voces españolas están impresos en letra cursiva, a saber:—

ī, *ida*; ê, *hé*; ā, *ala*; ō, *oro*; u, *uno*; y, *yunta*; w, *guapo*;—ɑi, *aire*; ɑu, *aula*; ei, *voy*.

2. Las siguientes consonantes de la clave corresponden también exactamente a las mismas letras en español y francés, indicadas con caracteres cursivos en las voces siguientes:—

h, *jaco*; ch, *chico*; th, *zapa*; n, ng, *sangre*; z, *zèle* (Fr.); sh, *chez* (Fr.); zh, *Jean* (Fr.).

3. Las letras cursivas en las voces siguientes de la misma clave no dan exactamente el mismo sonido que sus correspondientes tienen en inglés (véanse las Notas precedentes en sus lugares respectivos); pero son las que en castellano se aproximan más a los sonidos ingleses: y si el lector se aplica con atención a compararlos, adquirirá una pronunciación muy poco diferente de la de un inglés o americano de nacimiento, y bastante exacta para ser entendido:—

ɵ, *por*; i, *idea*; e, *esté*; ɑ, *así*; o, *osó*; ʋ, *opa*; u, *fumó*; oi, *voy*; iu, *viuda*.

4. Las observaciones hechas en el número 3 deben aplicarse también a las consonantes *j* y *d;* v. g., en *yema*, *dedo*. Véanse las notas precedentes.

5. Las demás letras consonantes que no se hallen en la clave al pie de cada página (v. g., p, b, t, d, c, g, f, v, s, r, l, m, n), corresponden exactamente en su sonido a las castellanas.

Explicación de las Abreviaturas Usadas en Esta Obra.

a.	adjetivo.
acep.	acepción.
adv.	adverbio.
Aer.	Aeronáutica.
Agr.	Agricultura.
Al.	Alemán.
Álg.	Álgebra
Amer.	América, o americanismo.
Anat.	Anatomía.
Ant.	antiguo, anticuado
Arit.	Aritmética.
Arq.	Arquitectura.
Art. y Of.	Artes y oficios.
A.-S.	Anglosajón.
Astr.	Astronomía.
Auto.	Automovilismo.
Biol.	Biología.
Bot.	Botánica.
Carp.	Carpintería.
Cir.	Cirugía.
Com.	Comercio.
comp.	comparativo.
conj.	conjunción.
des. o †	desusado.
Dial.	dialecto.
dim.	diminutivo.
Elec.	Electricidad.
Ento.	Entomología.
Esco.	Escocia, escocés.
Esc.	Escultura.
etim.	etimología.
E. U.	Estados Unidos.
f.	femenino.
fam.	familiar.
F. C.	Ferrocarril.
Fest.	festivo.
fig.	figurado.
Fil.	Filosofía.
Fís.	Física.
For.	Foro, o forense.
Fr.	francés.
fr.	frase.
gal.	Galicismo.
Geogr.	Geografía.
Geol.	Geología.
Geom.	Geometría.
Ger.	Germanía.
ger.	gerundio.
Gram.	Gramática.
Gr.	Griego.
gr. o *gms.*	gramos.
Heb.	Hebreo.
Her.	Heráldica.
Hort.	Horticultura.
íd.	ídem, del mismo nombre.
Impr.	Imprenta.
imper.	impersonal.
Ingl.	Inglaterra.
inter.	interjección.
irr.	irregular.
Lat.	latín.
Lit.	Literatura.
loc.	locución.
m.	masculino.
Mar.	Marina.
Mat.	Matemática.
Mec.	Mecánica.
Med.	Medicina.
Met.	Metafórico.
Mil.	Milicia.
Min.	Mineralogía, minería.
Mús.	Música.
N.	Nombre; substantivo.
Neol.	Neologismo.
Orn.	Ornitología.
pa.	participio activo.
p. ej.	por ejemplo.
Pint.	Pintura.
pl.	plural.
pert.	perteneciente.
poét.	poético.
pp.	participio pasivo.
prep.	preposición.
pret.	pretérito.
pron.	pronombre.
prov.	proverbio.
Prov.	Provincial.
Quím.	Química.
Ret.	Retórica.
s.	substantivo.
sing.	singular.
sup.	superlativo.
Teat.	Teatro.
V.	Véase.
va.	verbo activo.
Var.	Variedad.
Vet.	Veterinaria.
vn.	verbo neutro.
vul.	vulgar.
Zool.	Zoología.
<	derivado de.
†	desusado.
=	igualdad; significado, equivalente.
§	poco usado, raro.

New Revised Velázquez DICTIONARY

English and Spanish — Inglés y Español

A

A [ê], primera letra del alfabeto y una de las cinco vocales, tiene cuatro sonidos distintos en inglés; el primero como la *e* en castellano, aunque prolongada de modo que se parece algo al diptongo *ei*, como en *fate*, *face*, *waste*, etc.; el segundo como la *a* larga en castellano, en *far*; el tercero participa del sonido de *o* y *a* indistinto, cual se oye en *fall*, *wall*; y el cuarto es como una *a* breve en *fat*. Tiene también dos sonidos indistintos, como queda explicado en la introducción, donde se indican los respectivos signos para todos estos sonidos.

A [ê, y cuando no tiene acento, ɑ], artículo indefinido singular, significa *un* o *una* en castellano, v. g. *A man*, un hombre; pero cuando precede a una palabra que empieza con vocal o *h* no aspirada, se convierte en *an*; v. g. *An ox*, un buey; *an hour*, una hora. Muchas veces se pospone a palabras que en castellano la preceden; v. g. *Such a man*, Un tal hombre.

A es algunas veces nombre substantivo, como, *A capital A*, Una *A* mayúscula.

A [ɑ], *prep.*, se halla a veces delante del participio activo, para denotar la acción de un verbo; v. g. *A hunting Chloe went*, Cloe fué á cazar. *A* muchas veces denota proporción, como, *Six thousand a year*, Seis mil libras esterlinas, o seis mil pesos, al año o cada año. *A* se usa también en lugar de *in*; v. g. *To be abed*, estar en cama.

A se emplea en las abreviaturas: v. g. *A. B.*, *Bachelor of Arts*, Bachiller en Artes. *A. M.*, *Master of Artes*, Maestro en Artes. *A. D.*, *Anno Domini*, El año del Señor. *A. M.*, *Ante Meridian*, (Antes del mediodía) En o por la mañana.

A' [e], *a. s.* y *adv.* (Escocés) Todo.

Aaron's-beard [ār'-unz-bīrd], *s.* (Bot.) 1. Barba de Aarón, arbusto perenne de unos dos pies de altura, con flores amarillas, que crece en terrenos elevados; es una especie de hipérico. 2. Hiedra de Kenilworth, planta de las escrofulariáceas. Linaria Cymbalaria. 3. Hierba china de flores blancas, especie de saxífraga. Saxifraga sarmentosa. Hay también otras plantas que se llaman Aaron's-beard.

Aaronic [ɑ-ren'-ic], **Aaronical** [ɑ-ren'-i-cal], *a.* Aarónico; lo perteneciente al sacerdocio de Aarón.

Ab [ab], *prefijo.* Significa lo mismo que en castellano: lejos, á distancia; desde; separación.

Abaca [ab'-ɑ-ca], *s.* Abacá, plátano de las Islas Filipinas.

Abacist [ab'-ɑ-sist], *s.* El que calcula con el ábaco.

Aback [ɑ-bac'], *adv.* Detrás, atrás. (Mar.) En facha. *To lay flat aback*, Poner las velas en facha. *To lay the top-sails aback*, Poner las gavias en facha.—*s.* (Des.) Una superficie plana cuadrada. *V.* ABACUS, 3a acep.

§**Abaction** [ab-ac'-shun], *s.* (For.) Abigeato, hurto de ganado o bestias.

Abactor [ab-ac'-tẹr], *s.* (For.) Abigeo, cuatrero, ladrón de ganado o bestias.

Abacus [ab'-ɑ-cus], *s.* 1. Ábaco, tabla aritmética, aparato para contar y calcular. 2. Ábaco, el tablero que corona el capitel de una columna. 3. Cualquier loseta o tablilla de forma rectangular. 4. Aparader. 5. Báculo.

Abaft [ɑ-bɑft'], *adv.* (Mar.) A popa o en popa; atrás, hacia la popa.

Abaisance [ɑ-bé'-sạns], *s.* *V.* OBEISANCE.

Abalienate [ab-él'-yen-êt], *va.* Enajenar.

Abalienation [ab-êl-yen-é'-shun], *s.* Enajenación, traspaso.

Abalone [ab''-ɑ-lō'-nẹ], *s.* Oreja marina, molusco gasterópodo, común en la costa de California. La concha se emplea para taracear y para hacer abalorios, etc.; y la carne se seca para alimento y para la exportación. (< aulón.) Haliotis tuberculata.

Abandon [ɑ-bañ-deñ'], *s.* 1. Abandono, entrega. 2. Cesión. 3. Desamparo. (Francés.)

Abandon [ɑ-ban'-dun], *va.* Abandonar, dejar, desamparar, entregar; desertar.

Abandoned [ɑ-ban'-dund], *pp.* Abandonado, dejado, desamparado, entregado a los vicios.

Abandoner [ɑ-ban'-dun-ẹr], *s.* Abandonador, desamparador.

Abandoning [ɑ-ban'-dun-ing], *s.* Abandono, desamparo, cesión.

Abandonment [ɑ-ban'-dun-mẹnt], *s.* Abandono, abandonamiento.

Abarticulation [ab-ɑr-tic-yu-lé'-shun], *s.* Articulación de huesos con movimiento. *V.* DIARTHROSIS.

Abase [ɑ-bês'], *va.* Abatir, humillar, envilecer, degradar. Rebajar, reducir.

Abasement [ɑ-bês'-mẹnt], *s.* Abatimiento, envilecimiento, humillación, degradación.

Abash [ɑ-bash'], *va.* 1. Avergonzar, sonrojar, correr. 2. Consternar.

Abashment [ɑ-bash'-mẹnt], *s.* 1. Confusión, vergüenza, rubor. 2. Consternación.

Abasing [ɑ-bês'-ing], *pa.* y *a.* Humillante, vergonzoso.

Abassi [ɑ-bas'-i], *s.* Moneda de Rusia; vale cerca de quince centavos, o 7½ peniques (tres reales vellón).

Abatable [ɑ-bêt'-ɑ-bl], *a.* Abolible.

Abate [ɑ-bêt'], *va.* 1. Minorar, disminuir, bajar, rebajar. 2. Abatir, contristar. 3. Abolir, hacer cesar (un abuso).—*vn.* Menguar, disminuirse o minorarse alguna cosa, ir a menos, ceder, anular, derribar, apoderarse de, irse disminuyendo. 4. (For.) Anular, revocar. 5. (Met.) Humillar. *The fever begins to abate*, La calentura va a menos.

Abatement [ɑ-bêt'-mẹnt], *s.* Rebaja, descuento que se hace del todo de alguna cosa; extenuación, diminución. (Her.) Brisadas.

Abater [ɑ-bé'-tẹr], *s.* Lo que disminuye una cosa, o hace o causa una rebaja. Regatero. Demeritorio.

Abatis, Abattis [ab'-ɑ-tis], *s.* (Mil.) Estacas, árboles cortados para formar con ellos una obra defensiva.

Abattoir [ɑ-bɑ-twār'], *s.* Matadero, particularmente uno de mucha extensión. (Fr.)

Abb [ab], *s.* 1. Urdiembre o urdimbre. 2. Lana en borra.

Abba [ab'-ɑ], *s.* 1. Voz hebrea que significa padre. 2. Superior (de un convento).

Abbacy [ab'-ɑ-si], *s.* Abadía, la dignidad, jurisdicción, rentas y privilegios pertenecientes a un abad.

Abbatial [ɑ-bé'-shal], *a.* Abacial, abadengo.

Abbé [ɑ-bé'], *s.* Voz francesa, lo mismo que *abbot.*

Abbess [ab'-es], *s.* Abadesa.

Abbey [ab'-ẹ], *s.* Abadía, monasterio, convento de monjes o monjas; también, refugio, santuario. *Abbey-lubber*, Monje gordo y holgazán; bigardo; santurrón.

Abbot [ab'-ẹt], *s.* Abad.

Abbotship [ab'-ęt-ship], *s.* La dignidad y oficio de abad; abadía.
Abbreviate [ąb-brī'-vi-ēt], *va.* Abreviar, reducir, compendiar.
Abbreviation [ąb-brī-vi-ē'-shun], *s.* Abreviación; abreviatura.
Abbreviator [a-brī-vi-ē'-tęr], *s.* Abreviador, compendiador.
Abbreviatory [a-brī'-vi-a-to-ri], *a.* Abreviatorio.
Abbreviature [a-brī'-vi-a-chūr o tiur], *s.* Abreviatura, compendio, epítome.
Abdicant [ab'-di-cant], *a.* Abdicante, renunciante.
Abdicate [ab'-di-kēt], *va.* Abdicar, renunciar, dejar, desprenderse; hacer dimisión.
Abdication [ab-di-kē'-shun], *s.* Abdicación, renuncia. Dimisión.
Abdicative [ab'-di-kē-tiv], *a.* Abdicativo, renunciativo.
Abditory [ab'-di-to-ri], *s.* Escondrijo, lugar o sitio para esconder y guardar joyas, plata o dinero.
Abdomen [ab-dō'-men], *s.* Abdomen.
Abdominal, Abdominus [ab-dem'-i-nal], *a.* Abdominal.
Abduce [ab-diūs'], *va.* 1. Desviar, apartar, separar una cosa de otra. 2. (Anat.) Mover de un lado a otro.
Abducent [ab-diū'-sent], *a.* *V.* ABDUCTOR.
Abduct [ab-duct'], *va.* 1. Arrebatar, tomar, llevarse por fuerza. 2. Cometer un rapto (hablando de una mujer, de un menor, etc.).
Abduction [ab-duc'-shun], *s.* 1. (Anat.) Abducción, acción por la cual una parte del cuerpo se separa de la línea que se supone dividirlo en dos segmentos iguales. 2. Abducción, forma particular de argumento. 3. Abducción, la acción de sacar hacia fuera. 4. (For.) El acto de sacar por fuerza o engaño á alguna persona; rapto.
Abductor [ab-duc'-tęr], *s.* 1. Abductor, nombre que dan los anatómicos a varios músculos que sirven para la abducción. 2. (For.) El que saca por fuerza o engaño a una mujer u otra persona; raptor.
Abeam [a-bīm'], *adv.* (Mar.) Por el través.
Abear [a-bār'], *va.* (Prov.) Sufrir; soportar.
Abearance [a-bār'-ens], *s.* (For.) Conducta, porte. *V.* BEHAVIOUR.
Abecedarian [ē-bī-sī-dē'-ri-an], *s.* El que enseña o aprende el abecé o la cartilla. Niño de escuela.
Abecedary [ē-bī-sī'-dē-ri], *s.* Abecedario, alfabeto.
Abed [a-bed'], *adv.* En cama o en la cama. Acostado.
Aberr [ab-ęr'], *vn.* Errar, extraviarse; apartarse.
Aberrance, Aberrancy [ab-ęr'-ans], *s.* Error, descamino, extravío, equivocación.
Aberrant [ab-er'-ant], *a.* Errado, descaminado, equivocado, extraviado. (Anal.) Anómalo.
Aberration [ab-er-ē'-shun], *s.* 1. Error. 2. Aberración, desvío de los rayos de la luz. 3. Aberración, movimiento aparente de las estrellas fijas.
Aberring [ab-er'-ing], *part.* Errante, descaminado, extraviado.
Aberuncate [ab-i-run'-kēt], *va.* 1. Desarraigar, arrancar de raíz. 2. Extirpar.
Abet [a-bet'], *va.* Apoyar, favorecer, patrocinar, sostener, excitar, animar, inducir.
Abetment [a-bet'-męnt], *s.* Apoyo, protección, auxilio o favor.
Abetter o **Abettor** [a-bet'-ęr], *s.* 1. Fautor, promovedor, fomentador, ayudador. 2. Cómplice, partidario, instigador.
Abeyance [a-bē'-ans], *s.* (For.) Expectación, espera, expectativa de una reversión. *To have in abeyance,* Tener en expectativa, en reserva. *Lands in abeyance,* Bienes mostrencos, sin dueño conocido.
Abeyant [a-bē'-ant], *a.* En reposo, durmiente.
Abgregation [ab-grī-gē'-shun], *s.* Separación de la manada.
Abhor [ab-hor'], *va.* Aborrecer, detestar, odiar; desdeñar.
Abhorrence [ab-hor'-ens], *s.* Aborrecimiento, odio, detestación, horror, aversión, execración.
Abhorrent [ab-hor'-ent], *a.* 1. Horroroso. 2. Ajeno, lo que es impropio o no correspondiente, contrario, extraño.
Abhorrently [ab-hor'-ent-li], *adv.* Aborreciblemente.
Abhorrer [ab-hor'-ęr], *s.* Aborrecedor, enemigo jurado.
Abhorring [ab-hor'-ing], *s.* Hastío, náusea; objeto de aversión.
Abidance [a-baid'-ans], *s.* Residencia, morada.
Abide [a-baid'], *vn.* 1. Habitar, morar, vivir o estar de asiento en algún paraje—(*to abide,* pa. *abiding;* pp., pret. imp. y pret. perf. *abode*). 2. Quedar, continuar.—*va.* 1. Soportar, sufrir, aguantar. 2. Defender, sostener. 3. Atenerse a alguna cosa. 4. Perseverar. *To abide by* o *in,* Sostenerse en su opinión, mantenerse en lo dicho. Pasar por, consentir.
Abider [a-baid'-ęr], *s.* Habitador, habitante, vecino, inquilino.
Abiding [a-baid'-ing], *s.* Continuación, perseverancia, estabilidad, permanencia.—*a.* Permanente.
Abigail [ab'-i-gēl], *s.* Criada confidente al servicio de una señora. (Heb.)
Ability [a-bil'-i-ti], *s.* 1. Potencia, habilidad, capacidad, aptitud. En el plural, talento, ingenio; v. g. *A man of abilities,* Hombre de talento. 2. Haber o bienes, medios.
Abintestate [ab-in-tes'-tēt], *a.* Abintestato, el que muere sin hacer testamento. *Heir abintestate,* Heredero abintestato.
Abiogenesis [ab-i-o-jen'-e-sis], *s.* Abiogénesis, generación espontánea; la de los organismos vivos cuyo supuesto origen es la materia inanimada.
Abiological [ab''-i-o-lej'-ical], *a.* Perteneciente a substancia inanimada; abiológico. (Gr.)
Abject [ab'-ject], *s.* Hombre vil, bajo, abyecto; abatido, humillado, desesperanzado.
Abject, *a.* Vil, despreciable, bajo, indecente, abatido, abyecto; desalmado.
Abjectedness [ab-jec'-ted-nes], *s.* Abyección, desesperación, pérdida de la esperanza, humillación, envilecimiento.
Abjection, Abjectness [ab-jec'-shun], *s.* Abyección, bajeza, vileza, abatimiento de alma; servilismo, cobardía. *Abjection,* Envilecimiento, abyección.
Abjectly [ab'-ject-li], *adv.* Vilmente, bajamente, abyectamente.
Abjudicated [ab-jiu'-di-kē-ted], *a.* Abjudicado.
Abjudication [ab-jiu-di-kē'-shun], *s.* Abjudicación.
Abjuration [ab-jiu-rē'-shun], *s.* Abjuración, el acto de abjurar.
Abjure [ab-jiūr'], *va.* 1. Jurar, hacer o prestar juramento de no hacer alguna cosa. 2. Abjurar, desdecirse o retractarse con juramento de algún error. 3. Desterrar.
Abjurement [ab-jiūr'-męnt], *s.* Renuncia, adjuración.
Abjurer [ab-jiūr'-ęr], *s.* El que abjura o renuncia; renunciante.
Ablactate [ab-lac'-tēt], *va.* Destetar. Quitar el pecho a un niño.
Ablactation [ab-lac-tē'-shun], *s.* 1. Destete. 2. Manera de injertar los árboles.
†**Ablaqueation** [ab-lē-cwę-ē'-shun], *s.* Excava de árboles.
Ablation [ab-lē'-shun], *s.* Quite, la acción de quitar. Extirpación; separación.
Ablative [ab'-la-tiv], *a.* Lo que quita. *The ablative case,* Ablativo, el sexto caso de la declinación del nombre en algunas lenguas.
Ablaze [a-blēz'], *a.* En llamas.
-able. Terminación, o sufijo, muy común en adjectivos ingleses, equivalente a apto, a propósito, conveniente.
Able [ē'-bl], *a.* Fuerte, poderoso, capaz, hábil, rico, opulento, experto, experimentado. *To be able* o *to be able for,* Poder; tener poder.
Able-bodied [ē-bl-bed'-ed], *a.* Forzudo, robusto, fornido.
†**Ablegate** [ab'-lę-gēt], *va.* Enviar o dar empleo a alguno en país extranjero; diputar.
Ablegate, *s.* Representante del Papa, enviado con determinada comisión a un país extranjero.
Ableness [ē'-bl-nes], *s.* Fuerza, vigor; habilidad, poder.
Ablepsy [ab'-lep-si], *s.* Ceguera, ceguedad; ablepsia.
Ablest [ē'-blest], *a.* Superlativo de able. Poderosísimo, riquísimo. Muy hábil, may capaz.
Abloom [a-blūm'], *a.* En flor; floreciente.
Abluent [ab'-lu-ent], *a.* Detersivo, detergente, limpiante.
Ablush [a-blush'], *a.* y *adv.* Sonrojante, abochornado.
Ablution [ab-lū'-shun], *s.* Ablución; acción de lavar, limpiar.
Ably [ē'-bli], *adv.* Hábilmente, con habilidad, con maña.
-ably. Sufijo que convierte en adverbios los adjectivos terminados en -able.
Abnegate [ab'-ne-gēt], *va.* Negar, rehusar, resignar, renunciar, renegar.
Abnegation [ab-nę-gē'-shun], *s.* Abnegación. Renuncia, repudiación.
Abnegator [ab-nę-gē'-ter], *s.* Negador; impugnador.
§**Abnodation** [ab-no-dē'-shun], *s.* (Jardin.) El acto de cortar los nudos de un árbol.
Abnormal [ab-nōr'-mal], *a.* Irregular, mal formado, disforme.
Abnormality [ab-ner-mal'-i-ti] o **Abnormity** [ab-nōr'-mi-ti], *s.* Irregularidad, deformidad; monstruo; producción contraria al orden de la naturaleza.
Aboard [a-bōrd'], *adv.* (Mar.) A bordo. *To fall aboard of a ship,* Abordar un navío. *To keep the land on board,* Mantenerse inmediato a la tierra. *To go aboard,* Ir a bordo, embarcarse.
Abode [a-bōd'], *s.* 1. Domicilio, residencia, habitación. 2. Mansión, mo-

ī *ida*; ē *hé*; ā *ala*; e *por*; ō *oro*; u *uno*.—i *idea*; e *esté*; a *así*; o *osó*; u *opa*; ū como en *leur* (Fr.).—ai *aire*; ei *voy*; au *aula*;

rada o estancia de asiento en algún paraje.
Abode, *pret.* y *pp.* de ABIDE.
Abolish [a-bel'-ish], *va.* Abolir, anular; revocar.
Abolishable [a-bel'-ish-a-bl], *a.* Abolible.
Abolisher [a-bel'-ish-ɐr], *s.* Abolidor, anulador, revocador.
Abolition, Abolishment [ab-o-li'-shun], *s.* Abolición.
Abolitionist [ab-o-lish'-un-ist], *s.* Abolicionista, el partidario de la abolición de alguna cosa, especialmente de la esclavitud.
Abomasum [ab-o-mā'-sum], *s.* Abomaso, el cuarto estómago de un animal rumiante.
A-bomb [ê-bem], *s.* Bomba atómica.
Abominable [a-bem'-i-na-bl], *a.* Abominable, execrable, detestable; inmundo.
Abominableness [a-bem'-i-na-bl-nes], *s.* La propiedad o calidad que hace a alguna cosa abominable.
Abominably [a-bem'-i-na-bli], *adv.* Abominablemente.
Abominate [a-bem'-i-nêt], *va.* Abominar, detestar, aborrecer.
Abomination [a-bem-i-nê'-shun], *s.* 1. Abominación, odio, detestación. 2. Polución, maldad, corrupción.
Aboral [ab-ō'-ral], *a.* Opuesto a la boca, situado fuera de ella.
Aboriginal [ab-o-rij'-i-nal], *a.* Primitivo; originario, aborigen.
Aborigines [ab-o-rij'-i-niz], *s. pl.* Los primeros habitantes de algún país; aborígenes, indígenas.
Abort [ɐ-bōrt'], *vn.* Abortar, malparir.—*s.* (Aer.) Fracaso en el lanzamiento de un cohete.
Abortion [ɐ-bōr'-shun], *s.* Aborto, malparto. 2. Aborto, lo nacido antes de tiempo. (Fig.) Aborto, proyecto detenido en su desarollo.
Abortive [a-bōr'-tiv], *a.* 1. Abortivo. 2. Infructuoso, inútil, intempestivo, malogrado, frustrado.—*s.* Aborto, engendro.
Abortively [a-bōr'-tiv-li], *adv.* 1. Abortivamente. 2. Intempestivamente. 3. Prematuramente.
Abortiveness [a-bōr'-tiv-nes], *s.* Aborto; mal éxito de algo.
Abound [a-baund'], *vn.* Abundar. *To abound with,* Abundar en.
Abounding [a-baund'-ing], *a.* y *part.* (*in, with,* en). Abundante (en).
About [a-baut'], *prep.* 1. Al rededor, cerca de, por ahí, hacia. 2. Acerca, tocante a. 3. Pendiente, colgante. *I know nothing about that matter,* Nada sé de aquel asunto. *He is about coming,* Está para venir. *I carry no money about me,* No traigo dinero. *To beat about the bush,* Andarse por las ramas.—*adv.* En contorno, por rodeos; aquí y allá. *To go about,* Rodear. *To bring about,* Efectuar alguna cosa. *To go about a thing,* (Mar.) Virar. *Within about 60 yards,* Cerca de o poco menos de 60 varas.—IDIOTISMOS. *Look about you,* Tenga Vd. cuidado. *What are you about?* ¿Qué va Vd. a hacer? *Send him about his business,* Envíele Vd. a paseo; despídale Vd.
Above [a-buv'], *prep.* Encima, sobre, superior, más alto en cuanto a situación, dignidad, poder, etc.—*adv.* Arriba, la parte alta o lugar en alto. *Above all,* Sobre todo, principalmente. *Above-board,* Abiertamente, públicamente, a vista de todos. *Above cited* o *above mentioned,* Ya citado o ya mencionado, supracitado, susodicho. *Above ground,* Vivo; expresión que denota que aun no ha muerto alguno. *From above,* De arriba, de lo alto, del cielo. *To be above a thing,* (1) Ser incapaz de una cosa, ser superior á, no usar de. (2) Más que, ó de; v. g. *He was not above three hours in doing it,* No empleó más de tres horas en hacerlo. *I value honour above life,* Precio mi honra más que la vida.
Abradant [ab-rê'-dant], *a.* Que desgasta ó raspa.—*s.* Substancia raspante.
Abrade [ab-rêd'], *va.* Raer ó gastar, quitar estregando.
Abrasion [ab-rê'-zhun], *s.* 1. Raspadura, la acción de raspar. 2. Lo que se quita de la superficie raspando.
Abrasive [ab-rê'-siv], *a.* Rayente, raspante; que produce la acción de raspar ó raer.—*s.* Substancia raspante.
Abreast [a-brest'], *adv.* De frente. *Four abreast,* Cuatro de frente, ó en fila. De costado. *Abreast,* (Mar.) Por el través. *Abreast the port,* Por el través del puerto.
Abrenunciation [ab-re-nun-si-ê'-shun], *s.* Renuncia, renunciación.
Abreption [ab-rep'-shun], *s.* Abstracción; arrebatiña. Rapto.
Abreuvoir [a-brū-vwār'], *s.* 1. Abrevadero, bebedero. 2. Degolladura, hueco entre los ladrillos ó piedras para llenarlo de argamasa. (Fr.)
Abridge [a-brij'], *va.* 1. Abreviar, compendiar. 2. Cercenar, acortar, disminuir. 3. Privar, despojar ó quitar. (Alg.) Reducir.
Abridged [a-brijd'], *pp.* Privado; acortado.
Abridger [a-brij'-ɐr], *s.* 1. Abreviador. 2. Compendiador.
Abridgment [a-brij'-mɐnt], *s.* 1. Compendio, epítome, recopilación. 2. Contracción, limitación.
Abroach [a-brōch'], *adv.* (Ant.) Para derramarse; en estado de difundirse o propagarse. *To set abroach,* Horadar, barrenar.
Abroad [a-brōd'], *adv.* Fuera de casa o del país; en países extranjeros, en todas partes o direcciones. *To walk abroad,* Salir, ir a dar una vuelta. *The schoolmaster is abroad,* Educación difundida. *To set abroad,* Divulgar, publicar. *Report abroad,* Rumor común o público.
Abrogable [ab'-ro-ga-bl], **Abrogative** [ab'-ro-gê-tiv], *a.* Abrogable; que tiende a revocar o abrogar, o tiene tal propósito.
Abrogate [ab'-rō-gêt], *va.* Abrogar, anular, revocar.
Abrogation [ab-ro-gê'-shun], *s.* Abrogación, anulación, revocación, abolición.
Abrotanum [ab-ret'-a-num], *s.* (Bot.) Abrótano, artemisa.
Abrupt [ab-rupt'], *a.* 1. Quebrado, desigual. 2. Precipitado, repentino; desunido, bronco, rudo, fogoso.
Abruption [ab-rup'-shun], *s.* Rotura o separación repentina y violenta de una cosa.
Abruptly [ab-rupt'-li], *adv.* Precipitadamente; rudamente, ásperamente, bruscamente, ex-abrupto.
Abruptness [ab-rupt'-nes], *s.* Precipitación, inconsideración; prontitud; sequedad, claridad.
Abscess [ab'-ses], *s.* Absceso, apostema.
Abscind [ab-sind'], *va.* Cortar, tajar.
Abscissa [ab-sis'-a], *s.* Abscisa, la línea coordenada de la cual se hacen depender los valores de las demás
Abscission [ab-sizh'-un], *s.* Cortadura; anulación.
Abscond [ab-scend'], *vn.* Esconderse.—*va.* Ocultar, tapar.
Absconder [ab-scend'-ɐr], *s.* 1. Fugitivo, que toma las de Villadiego. 2. (For.) Contumaz, prófugo, que se oculta.
Absence [ab'-sɐns], *s.* 1. Ausencia. 2. Abstracción de ánimo, distracción. 3. Descuido, negligencia. *Leave of absence,* (Mil.) Permiso para ausentarse, licencia temporal.
Absent [ab'-sent], *a.* 1. Ausente. 2. Enajenado o fuera de sí; descuidado, negligente. 3. Divertido, distraído, abstraído.
Absent-minded [ab'-sɐnt-maind'-ɐd], *a.* Fuera de sí; absorto, abstraído en meditación.
Absent [ab-sent'], *vr.* Ausentarse, retirarse de.
Absentaneous [ab-sen-tê'-nɐ-us], *a.* Ausente, lo que se ausenta.
Absentee [ab-sen-tī'], *s.* Ausente, el que lo está de su empleo, país o hacienda.
Absenteeism [ab'-sen-tī'-izm], *s.* Ausentismo
†**Absenter** [ab-sen'-tɐr], *s.* El que abandona su obligación u oficio.
Absinthe [ab'-sinth o ab-sañt'], *s.* (Fr.) Licor francés popular, compuesto con ajenjo y otras hierbas.
Absinthian [ab-sin'-thi-an], *a.* Lo perteneciente al ajenjo; amargo.
Absinthiated [ab-sin'-thi-êt-ed], *a.* Tinturado o mezclado con ajenjo.
Absinthium [ab'-sin-thi-um], *s.* (Bot.) Ajenjo. Artemisia absinthium.
Absolute [ab'-so-lūt], *a.* 1. Absoluto, libre, irresponsable. 2. Amplio, completo. 3. Perentorio. 4. Positivo, arbitrario. *Absolute altitude,* (Aer.) Altitud absoluta. *Absolute zero,* (Quím.) Cero absoluto.
Absolutely [ab'-so-lūt-li], *adv.* 1. Absolutamente, enteramente. 2. Positivamente, sin reserva.
Absoluteness [ab'-so-lūt-nes], *s.* 1. Amplitud, independencia. 2. Despotismo, poder absoluto.
Absolution [ab-so-lū'-shun], *s.* Absolución; perdón.
Absolutism [ab'-so-lū-tizm], *s.* 1. Absolutismo, despotismo. 2. La doctrina de la predestinación.
Absolutist [ab'-so-lūt''-ist], *s.* Absolutista, partidario del absolutismo.
Absolutory [ab-sel'-yu-to-ri], **Absolvatory** [ab-sel'-va-to-ri], *a.* Absolutorio.
Absolve [ab-selv'], *va.* 1. Absolver, dar por libre de una acusación. 2. Absolver de un convenio o promesa. 3. Absolver de un pecado. 4. Dispensar, exentar.
Absolver [ab-sel'-vɐr], *s.* Absolvedor, dispensador.
Absonant, Absonous [ab'-so-nant], *a.* 1. Absurdo, repugnante a la razón. 2. Disonante, ridículo.
Absorb [ab-sōrb'], *va.* 1. Absorber. 2. Empapar, embeber. 3. Amortiguar. 4. Asumir.
Absorbable [ab-sōrb'-a-bl], *a.* Que puede ser absorbido o chupado.
Absorbability [ab-sōrb-a-bil'-iti], *s.* Propiedad de ser absorbido.
Absorbent [ab-sōr'-bent], *a.* Absorbente, una clase de medicina; dase el nombre de absorbentes a los vasos y glándulas que sirven en el cuerpo humano para efectuar la absorción. Úsase también como substantivo. Capaz de absorber.
Absorbed o **Absorpt** (Ant.) [ab-

sŏrbd'], *pp.* Absorbido, chupado. desecado; hablando de los humores del cuerpo. (Met.) Absorto, arrebatado, enajenado.

Absorption [ab-sŏrp'-shun], *s.* 1. Absorción, el acto de absorber. 2. Preocupación.

Absorptive [ab-sŏrp'-tiv], *a.* Absorbente, capaz de absorber.

Abstain [ab-stên'], *vn.* Abstenerse, privarse de algún gusto o placer.

Abstainer [ab-stên'-ęr], *s.* Abstinente, sobrio.

Abstaining [ab-stên'-ing], *s.* Abstinencia.

Abstemious [ab-stî'-mi-us], *a.* Abstemio, sobrio, templado, moderado.

Abstemiously [ab-stî'-mi-us-li], *adv.* Sobriamente, moderadamente, templadamente.

Abstemiousness [ab-stî'-mi-us-nes], *s.* Sobriedad, moderación, templanza.

Abstention [ab-sten'-shun], *s.* 1. Detención, el acto de detener o impedir. 2. Abstinencia; privación.

Absterge [ab-stęrj'], *va.* Absterger, limpiar, enjugar.

Abstergent [ab-stęr'-jent], *a.* Abstergente, lo que sirve para purificar o limpiar.

Abstersion [ab-stęr'-shun], *s.* Abstersión.

Abstersive [ab-stęr'-siv], *a.* Abstergente.—*s.* Limpiador.

Abstinence, Abstinency [ab'-sti-nens], *s.* 1. Abstinencia. 2. Sobriedad, templanza. *Day of abstinence,* Día de ayuno.

Abstinent [ab'-sti-nent], *a.* Abstinente, mortificado, sobrio, moderado.

Abstinently [ab'-sti-nent-li], *adv.* Abstinentemente.

Abstract [ab-stract'], *va.* 1. Abstraer, substraer. 2. Extractar, extraer o hacer un extracto. 3. Considerar separadamente. *Abstracting from,* Separado de, sin contar con.

Abstract [ab'-stract], *a.* Abstracto, separado; refinado. Ideal, puro. Opuesto a concreto.

Abstract [ab'-stract], *s.* 1. Extracto, cantidad pequeña de alguna cosa. 2. Extracto, resumen, compendio, sumario. 3. Abstracción. 4. Preparación particular de una droga en polvos.

Abstracted [ab-strac'-ted], *pp.* 1. Separado. 2. Abstraído, distraído. 3. Abstruso, metafísico. 4. Extraído, puro, sin mezcla.

Abstractedly [ab-strac'-ted-li], *adv.* Abstractivamente; sencillamente.

Abstractedness [ab-strac'-ted-nes], *s.* Abstracción.

Abstracter [ab-strac'-tęr], *s.* 1. Extractador, abreviador, el que extracta, abrevia o compendia. 2. Ratero, ladrón.

Abstraction [ab-strac'-shun], *s.* 1. Abstracción, la acción y efecto de abstraer o abstraerse. 2. Abstracción, el retiro de la comunicación o trato con las gentes. 3. Concepto, idea; noción. 4. Concepción no real; alguna cosa imaginaria. 5. Desatención, descuido. 6. Ratería, hurto.

Abstractionism [ab-strac'-shun-izm], *s.* Abstraccionismo.

Abstractive [ab-strac'-tiv], *a.* Abstractivo.

Abstractly, Abstractively [ab-stract'-li], *adv.* En abstracto, abstractivamente.

Abstractness [ab-stract'-nes], *s.* Separación; abstracción, sin relación con ningún objeto.

Abstruse [ab-strūs'], *a.* Abstruso, recóndito de difícil inteligencia. Oculto, obscuro.

Abstrusely [ab-strūs'-li], *adv.* Obscuramente, difícilmente.

Abstruseness, Abstrusity [ab-strūs'-nes], *s.* Obscuridad, dificultad; arcano, misterio.

Absurd [ab-sŭrd'], *a.* Absurdo, repugnante a la razón, irracional, ridículo, inconsistente, disparatado.

Absurdity [ab-sŭr'-di-ti], *s.* Absurdo, dicho o hecho repugnante a la razón. *The height of absurdity,* El colmo de lo absurdo.

Absurdly [ab-sŭrd'-li], *adv.* Absurdamente, irracionalmente.

Absurdness [ab-sŭrd'-nes], *s.* Absurdo, irracionalidad, disparate.

Abundance [a-bun'-dans], *s.* Abundancia, copia o gran cantidad de alguna cosa; exuberancia.

Abundant [a bun'-dant], *a.* Abundante, copioso, rico; lleno.

Abundantly [a-bun'-dant-li], *adv.* Abundantemente.

Abuse [a-biūz'], *va.* 1. Abusar. 2. Engañar, seducir; profanar, ultrajar, violar. 3. Maltratar de palabra, burlarse con desprecio; denostar.

Abuse [a-biūs'], *s.* 1. Abuso. 2. Abuso, corruptela. 3. Seducción, engaño. 4. Contumelia, injuria u ofensa de palabra, afrenta, burla, ultraje.

Abuser [a-biūz'-ęr], *s.* 1. Abusador. 2. Seductor. 3. Denostador. 4. Embaucador, embaidor, engañador.

Abusive [a-biū'-siv], *a.* 1. Abusivo, insultante, injurioso, vil. *Abusive language,* Palabras injuriosas. 2. Corrompido; mal empleado o usado.

Abusively [a-biū'-siv-li], *adv.* 1. Abusivamente. 2. Impropiamente. Insolentemente.

Abusiveness [a-biū'-siv-nes], *s.* Vituperación; palabras injuriosas, vituperio, propensión a injuriar a otro, insulto; abuso, calidad de abusivo.

Abut [a-but'], *vn.* Terminar, confinar, lindar, parar, rematar. *To abut upon,* Salir a, terminar en, confinar con, empalmarse con, sobre.

Abutilon [a-biū'-ti-len], *s.* Abutilón, malvavisco de Indias.

Abutment [a-but'-męnt], *s.* 1. Linde, confín. 2. Refuerzo, estribo. Lindero; mojón. 3. (Carp.) Empalme; remate.

Abuttal [a-but'-al], *s.* Límite, linde.

Aby [a-bai'], *va.* 1. (Ant.) Sufrir la pena, expiar. 2. (Des.) Comprar.—*vn.* (Des.) Hacer restitución; equivaler.

Abysmal [a-biz'-mal], *a.* Abismal; insondable.

Abyss [a-bis'], **Abysm** [a-bizm'], *s.* 1. Abismo, profundidad a que no se halla fondo. 2. El infierno. 3. Sima. (Her.) Abismo, el centro del escudo.

Abyssal [a-bis'-al], *a.* 1. Perteneciente a grandes profundidas del océano. 2. Abismal, insondable.

Abyssinian [ab-is-in'-i-an], *a.* Abisinio, de Abisinia.

Ac [ac], *prefijo.* Forma de AD cuando se halla delante de *c* y *q*: como en *accept.*

-ac, *sufijo.* Con relación a, que tiene, o es afectado por: como *cardiac,* lo que tiene relación al corazón, o lo afecta.

Acacia [a-kê'-shia o a-ca'-si-a], *s.* 1. Acacia, nombre de un árbol de Egipto, que da la goma arábiga. 2. Acacia, arbolillo espinoso con flores en racimos colgantes. 3. Acacia, el zumo de las endrinas silvestres.

Academial [ac-a-dí'-mi-al], *a.* Académico.

Academian, Academic [ac-a-dí'-mi-an, a-ca-dem'-ic], *s.* Académico; cursante en alguna universidad, estudiante. Colegial.

Academic, Academical [ac-a-dem'-ic], *a.* Académico, lo que pertenece a las universidades. *Academic freedom,* Libertad académica.

Academically [ac-a-dem'-i-ca-li], *adv.* En estilo o en forma académica.

Academician, Academist [ac-ad-ę-mi'-shun], *s.* Académico, el individuo de alguna academia.

Academy [a-cad'-ę-mi], *s.* 1. Academia, sitio o lugar ameno, cerca de Atenas, donde Platón y sus discípulos tenían sus conferencias filosóficas. 2. Academia, sociedad establecida para el cultivo y adelantamiento de las ciencias y artes. 3. Academia, la casa o paraje en que se enseñan las ciencias o se tienen academias; universidad. 4. Figura académica, figura diseñada por el modelo vivo.

Acaleph [ac'-a-lef], *s.* Uno de los acalefos.

Acalephæ [ac-a-lî'-fî], *s. pl.* Acalefos, grupo de zoófitos que comprende las medusas y los hidróides.

Acanaceous [a-ca-nê'-shus], *a.* (Bot.) Espinoso.

Acanthine [a-can'-thin], *a.* Acantino, na; concerniente, relativo o análogo al acanto.

Acanthus [a-can'-thus], *s.* (Bot.) Acanto o branca ursina.

Acarus [ac'-ar-us], *s.* ACARI, *pl.* Ácaro.

Acatalectic [a-cat-a-lec'-tic], *s.* Acataléctico.

Acaulescent, Acauline, Acaulous [a-cō-les'-ent, a-cō'-lin], *a.* (Bot.) Acaule, sin renuevo o vástago; de tallo muy poco visible.

Accede [ac-síd'], *vn.* 1. Acceder, venir o convenir en alguna cosa; asentir, consentir. 2. Subir, llegar a, obtener posesión de, alcanzar.

Accelerando [ac-sel-ęr-an'-do], *a.* (Mús.) Acelerando gradualmente el tiempo.

Accelerate [ac-sel'-ęr-êt], *va.* Acelerar.—*vn.* Despacharse, apresurarse, darse prisa.

Acceleration [ac-sel-ęr-ê'-shun], *s.* Aceleración; prisa; despacho.

Accelerative [ac-sel'-ęr-a-tiv], *a.* Lo que aumenta la velocidad. Impulsivo, acelerador.

Accelerator [ac-sel'-ęr-ê-tęr], *s.* Acelerador.

Accelerometer [ac-sel-er-om'-e-tęr], *s.* (Aer.) Acelerómetro.

Accent [ac'-sent], *s.* 1. Acento, la señal o virgulilla que se pone sobre una vocal, para denotar su pronunciación. 2. Acento, la modulación de la voz, y el tono que se pronuncia una palabra. 3. El modo peculiar de pronunciar de las diferentes provincias en una misma nación. 4. (Poét.) Lenguaje, palabras.

Accent [ac-sent'], *va.* 1. Acentuar, pronunciar con el respectivo acento prosódico. 2. Acentuar, colocar la nota o signo que indica el acento.

Accentual [ac-sen'-chu-al o tiu-al], *a.* Rítmico, que pertenece al acento o ritmo.

Accentuate [ac-sen'-chu-êt o tiu-êt], *va.* Acentuar, colocar los acentos según regla.

Accentuation [ac-sen-chu-é'-shun], *s.* Acentuación.

Accept [ac-sept'], *va.* Aceptar, admitir lo que se da, ofrece o encarga; recibir cariñosamente. *To accept a bill of exchange,* Aceptar una letra de cambio. *To accept of,* Aceptar.

Acceptability [ac-sep-ta-bil'-i-ti], *s.* Aceptabilidad; agrado, gracia.

Acceptable [ac-sep'-ta-bl], *a.* 1. Aceptable, grato, digno de aceptación. 2. Admisible. 3. Bien recibido.

Acceptableness [ac-sep'-ta-bl-nes], *s.* *V.* ACCEPTABILITY.

Acceptably [ac-sep'-ta-bli], *adv.* Gustosamente, agradablemente.

Acceptance [ac-sep'-tans], *s.* Aceptación; buena acogida. *Acceptance of a bill of exchange,* Aceptación de una letra de cambio.

Acceptation [ac-sep-té'-shun], *s.* 1. Aceptación, recepción, recibimiento o recibo bueno o malo. 2. Acepción, sentido o significado en que se toma una palabra. 3. Aprobación, aplauso.

Accepter [ac-sep'-ter], *s.* Aceptador. *Accepter of persons,* Aceptador de personas.

Acception [ac-sep'-shun], *s.* Acepción, el sentido o significado en que se toma alguna cosa.

Acceptive [ac-sep'-tiv], *a.* Pronto a aceptar.

Acceptor [ac-sep'-ter], *s.* (Com.) Aceptante, el que acepta una letra de cambio.

Access [ac'-ses], *s.* 1. Acceso, entrada, camino. 2. Acceso, modo de llegar a las personas o cosas. 3. Aumento, acrecentamiento, añadidura. 4. Accesión o acceso periódico de alguna enfermedad.

Access road [ac'-ses rōd], *s.* Camino de acceso.

Accessarily [ac-ses'-e-ri-li], *adv.* Accesoriamente.

Accessariness [ac-ses'-a-ri-nes], *s.* Complicidad, la calidad de cómplice.

Accessary [ac-ses'-a-ri], *s.* Cómplice, persona o cosa que se une a otra con alguna dependencia. *V.* ACCESSORY.

Accessary, *a.* Accesorio, lo que se une a otra cosa o se agrega a ella con alguna dependencia.

Accessible [ac-ses'-i-bl], *a.* Accesible. lo que es de fácil acceso, aquello a que se puede llegar.

Accession [ac-sesh'-un], *s.* 1. Aumento, acrecentamiento. 2. Advenimiento, accesión. *Since the king's accession to the throne,* Desde el advenimiento del rey al trono. 3. Acceso.

Accessory [ac-ses'-o-ri], *a.* Accesorio, contribuyente, secundario; que depende de lo principal.—*s.* 1. Persona o cosa que ayuda con alguna dependencia. 2. (For.) Cómplice.

Accidence[1] [ac'-si-dens], *s.* Libro de rudimentos de la gramática.

Accidence[2] [ac'-si-dens], *s.* Accidente, lance, contratiempo.

Accident [ac'-si-dent], *s.* 1. Accidente. 2. Accidente o propiedad de una voz. 3. Accidente, casualidad, suceso imprevisto, incidente, lance. *A sad accident,* Lance funesto. *By accident,* Accidentalmente, casualmente. (Gram.) Desinencia, modo, caso, etc.

Accidental [ac-si-den'-tal], *s.* 1. Accidente, propiedad no esencial. 2. (Mús.) Bemol o sostenido accidental.

Accidental, *a.* 1. Accidental, lo que no es esencial. 2. Casual, contingente.

Accidentally [ac-si-den'-tal-i], *adv.* Accidentalmente, por casualidad.

Accident-prone [ac'-si-dent-prōn], *a.* Propenso a accidentes.

Accipient [ac-sip'-i-ent], *s.* Recibidor o recipiente; receptor.

Accite [ac-sait'], *va.* Llamar, citar. Convocar, reunir.

Acclaim [ac-clêm'], *va.* y *vn.* Aclamar, aplaudir.

Acclamation, Acclaim [ac-la-mé'-shun], *s.* Aclamación, gritería o voces de la multitud en honor y aplauso de alguna persona.

Acclamatory [ac-clam'-a-to-ri], *a.* Laudatorio.

Acclimate [ac-clai'-mêt], *va.* Aclimatar, connaturalizar, dícese de las personas.

Acclimated [ac-clai'-ma-ted], *pp.* y *a.* Aclimatado.

Acclimation, Acclimatization [ac-cli-mé-shun, ac-clai''-ma-ti-zé'-shun], *s.* Aclimatación.

Acclimatize [ac-clai'-ma-taiz], *va.* Aclimatar, acostumbrar a otro clima; dícese de animales y plantas con motivo de la agencia humana.—*vn.* Aclimatarse los animales y plantas.

Acclivity [ac-cliv'-i-ti], *s.* Cuesta, rampa, subida, ladera.

Acclivous, Acclive [ac-claiv'-us], *a.* Pendiente, que sube formando cuesta.

Accloy [ac-cloi'], *va.* 1. (Ant.) Impedir. 2. (Des.) *V.* CLOY.

Accolade [ac-o-lêd'], *s.* 1. (Mús.) Corchete. Abrazadera vertical o barra gruesa. 2. (Arq.) Moldura curva de adorno. 3. Acolada, parte del antiguo rito para armar a uno caballero.

Accommodable [ac-cem'-o-da-bl], *a.* Acomodable, lo que se puede acomodar; componible, concordable.

Accommodableness [ac-cem'-o-da-bl-nes], *s.* Capacidad de acomodarse.

Accommodate [ac-cem'-o-dêt], *va.* 1. Surtir, proveer o hacer alguna cosa como gracia o favor; socorrer, amparar. 2. Hospedar, alejar. 3. Acomodar, ajustar. 4. Reconciliar, componer. 5. (Com.) Prestar dinero.—*vn.* Conformarse. *To accommodate one's self with,* Componerse con, conformarse a.

§**Accommodate,** *a.* Acomodado, apto.

Accommodateness [ac-cem'-o-det-nes], *s.* Aptitud, acomodo.

Accommodating [ac-cem'-o-dê-ting], *a.* Obsequioso, oficioso, servicial, galante.

Accommodation [ac-cem''-o-dé'-shun], *s.* 1. Comodidad, conveniencia. 2. Ajuste, compostura o concierto de alguna disputa. 3. Adaptación, idoneidad, reconciliación. *Accommodation bill* o *note,* Letra de cambio, aceptada sin recibir su valor para ayudar a algún amigo y sostener su crédito mercantil. Letra pro forma. *Accommodation train,* (E. U.) Tren de escala. Puede ser también tren ómnibus.

Accommodator [ac-cem-o-dé''-ter], *s.* El que maneja, ajusta o acomoda.

†**Accompanable** [ac-cum'-pa-na-bl], *a.* Sociable.

Accompanier [ac-cum'-pa-ni-er], *s.* Acompañador o compañero.

Accompaniment [ac-cum'-pa-ni-ment], *s.* Acompañamiento.

Accompanist [ac-cum'-pa-nist], *s.* (Mús.) Acompañador, acompañante.

Accompany [ac-cum'-pa-ni], *va.* Acompañar, estar o ir en compañía de otro.—*vn.* Asociarse; cohabitar.

Accomplice [ac-cem'-plis], *s.* Cómplice, compañero en el delito.

Accomplish [ac-cem'-plish], *va.* 1. Efectuar, completar. 2. Concluir, llevar a cabo. Satisfacer, saciar. 3. Cumplir, verificar. 4. Adornar, hermosear física o moralmente. *An accomplished mathematician,* Un matemático consumado.

Accomplishable [ac-cem'-plish-a-bl], *a.* Capaz de ser cumplido, cumplidero; realizable.

Accomplished [ac-cem'-plisht], *a.* Perfecto, cabal, acabado, completo, elegante, consumado, lleno de perfecciones.

Accomplisher [ac-cem'-plish-er], *s.* Perfeccionador, el que completa alguna cosa. Ejecutor.

Accomplishment [ac-cem'-plish-ment], *s.* 1. Consumación o cumplimiento entero de alguna cosa. 2. Complemento, perfección, adquisición. En plural, talentos, conocimientos, prendas.

Accompt [ac-caunt'], *s.* (Ant.) Cuenta. *V.* ACCOUNT.

Accomptant [ac-caun'-tant], *s.* (Ant.) Contador. *V.* ACCOUNTANT.

Accord [ac-cērd'], *va.* Ajustar, igualar una cosa con otra, acomodar, otorgar, conciliar, poner de acuerdo.—*vn.* Acordar, concordar, convenir una cosa con otra; conciliar, acomodarse.

Accord, *s.* 1. Acuerdo, convenio. 2. Acuerdo, unión de ánimos. 3. Buena inteligencia o armonía. *Of one's own accord,* Espontáneamente. 4. Simetría. *With one accord,* Unánimemente.

Accordable [ac-cērd'-a-bl], *a.* Agradable, conforme.

Accordance, Accordancy [ac-cērd'-ans], *s.* Conformidad, correspondencia de una cosa con otra; acuerdo, convenio, buena inteligencia.

Accordant [ac-cērd'-ant], *a.* Acorde, conforme, propio, conveniente.

Accordantly [ac-cērd'-ant-li], *adv.* Acordemente.

Accorder [ac-cērd'-er], *s.* Ayudador, favorecedor.

According [ac-cēr'-ding], *part.* Según. conforme. *According to,* Según, conforme a, en cumplimiento de. *According as, conj.* Según que, como.

Accordingly [ac-cer'-ding-li], *adv.* En conformidad, en efecto, de consiguiente.

Accordion [ac-cēr'-di-on], *s.* Acordeón, instrumento músico de viento, con fuelle y llaves.

Accost [ac-cest'], *va.* Saludar a uno yendo hacia él; trabar conversación, acercarse.

Accostable [ac-cest'-a-bl], *a.* Accesible, familiar, de fácil acceso, tratable, sociable.

Accosted [ac-ces'-ted], *a.* (Her.) Acostado, lado a lado.

Accouchement [a-cūsh'-māñ], *s.* Parto. (Fr.)

Accoucheur [a-cu-shūr'], *s.* Comadrón, partero. *V.* MAN-MIDWIFE u OBSTETRICIAN. (Fr.)

Accoucheuse [a-cu-shūz'], *s.* Partera.

Account [ac-caunt'], *s.* 1. Cuenta, cálculo. *To settle accounts,* Ajustar cuentas. *To keep an account,* Tener cuenta abierta. 2. Caso, estimación o aprecio; dignidad, rango, consideración, respeto. 3. Informe, declaración, información; relación o narrativa de alguna cosa; motivo, modo. 4. Cómputo, manera de contar el tiempo; período. *The Julian account*, El período Juliano. *On no account*, De ninguna manera, por ningún concepto. *On account of*, Por motivo de, por cuenta de. *Upon your account* o *for your sake*, Por amor de Vd. *To turn to account*, Sacar provecho. *On your account*, A cargo de Vd. *Account current*, Cuenta corriente. *To pay an account*, Saldar una cuenta. *To pay on account*, Pagar a cuenta, a buena cuenta. *Profit and loss account*, Cuenta de ganancias y pérdidas. *People of no account*, Gente de poca importancia.

Account, *va.* 1. Tener, reputar, estimar, juzgar. 2. Contar, numerar, computar. 3. Dar cuenta o señalar los motivos de alguna cosa, explicar el porqué.—*vn.* Responder; hacer patente, explicar alguna cosa. *To account for*, Dar razón de, responder de.

Accountability, Accountableness [ac-caunt-a-bil'-i-ti, a-bl-nes], *s.* Responsabilidad, obligación de dar cuenta.

Accountable [ac-caunt'-a-bl], *a.* 1. Responsable, que está obligado a responder o satisfacer algún cargo. 2. Aquello de que se ha de dar o se puede dar cuenta o razón.

Accountant [ac-caunt'-ant], *s.* 1. Tenedor de libros. 2. Contador; aritmético.

Account-book [ac-caunt'-buc], *s.* Libro de cuentas.

Accounted [ac-caunt'-ed], *pp.* Estimado, considerado, reputado, tenido por. *Accounted for*, De que ya se ha dado cuenta, o razón; que ya se ha tenido presente.

Accounting [ac-caunt'-ing], *s.* 1. Contabilidad, el acto de contar o hacer cuentas. 2. Arreglo de cuentas.

Accounting-day [ac-caunt'-ing-dê], *s.* El día de ajuste de cuentas.

Accouple [ac-cup'-l], *va.* Unir, juntar, encadenar, acoplar, aparear.

Accouplement [ac-cup'-l-ment], *s.* Unión, ayuntamiento, pareja.

Accourt [ac-cōrt'], *va.* Cortejar, hacer la corte, galantear; recibir con cortesía, tratar bien.

Accoutre [ac-cū'-ter], *va.* Aviar, equipar, vestir, ataviar.

Accoutrement [ac-cū'-ter-ment], *s.* Avío, prevención, apresto, atavío, vestido, vestidura, ornamento, equipaje.

Accredit [ac-cred'-it], *va.* Dar crédito, favorecer, patrocinar, fomentar, acreditar, abonar una cantidad.

Accreditation [ac-cred-i-tê'-shun], *s.* Credencial, crédito.

Accredited [ac-cred'-it-ed], *pp.* Acreditado, abonado de confianza, confidente. (Dipl.) Autorizado.

Accrescent [ac-cres'-ent], *a.* Creciente, lo que va en aumento.

Accretion [ac-crī'-shun], *s.* Acrecentamiento, aumento. (For.) Acrecencia (derecho de).

Accretive [ac-crī'-tiv], *a.* Aumentativo, lo que aumenta o acrecienta; acrecentado, aumentado.

Accroach [ac-crōch'], *va.* 1. Usurpar, v. g. tratándose de prerrogativas regias. 2. (Des.) Enganchar, traer a sí alguna cosa con gancho, agarrar, atraer a uno con maña.

Accrue [ac-crū'], *vn.* 1. Acrecentar, tomar incremento. 2. Resultar, provenir. *What profits do thence accrue?* ¿Qué ganancias resultan de eso? *Accrued interest*, Interés acumulado.

Accrument [ac-crū'-ment], *s.* Reclinación, acrecencia, aumento, acrecentamiento.

Accubation [ac-yu-bê'-shun], *s.* Reclinación. Postura que usaban y usan algunas naciones recostándose para comer.

†**Accumb** [ac-cumb'], *vn.* Reclinarse o echarse para comer.

Accumbent [ac-cum'-bent], *s.* El que está reclinado.—*a.* Reclinado para comer; apoyado sobre el codo.

Accumulate [ac-kiū'-miu-lêt], *va.* Acumular, amontonar, atesorar.—*vn.* Crecer, aumentarse.

Accumulate, *a.* Juntado, acumulado, amontonado.

Accumulation [ac-kiū-miu-lê'-shun], *s.* Acumulación ó amontonamiento.—*pl.* Ahorros.

Accumulative [ac-kiū-miu-lê'-tiv], *a.* 1. Acumulativo. 2. Acumulado, amontonado, añadido.

Accumulatively [ac-kiū-miu-lê'-tiv-li], *adv.* Acumulativamente.

Accumulator [ac-kiū'-miu-lê''-ter], *s.* Acumulador, amontonador, especialmente la batería o celda de acumulación; condensador.

Accuracy [ac'-yu-re-si], *s.* Cuidado, exactitud, diligencia, primor, esmero.

Accurate [ac'-yu-ret], *a.* 1. Exacto, puntual. 2. Cabal, perfecto, primoroso. 3. Limado, pulido, acabado. *Accurate sciences*, Las ciencias exactas.

Accurately [ac'-yu-ret-li], *adv.* Exactamente, primorosamente, puntualmente, correctamente.

Accurateness [ac'-yu-ret-nes], *s.* Exactitud, primor, puntualidad, precisión.

Accurse [ac-cūrs'], *va.* Maldecir, anatematizar, excomulgar.

Accursed [ac-cūrst'], *pp.* Maldito, maldecido.—*a.* Detestable, execrable, excomulgado, desventurado, perverso, infausto, fatal. *Accursed be*, Mal haya.

Accusable [ac-kiūz'-a-bl], *a.* Culpable, que puede ser acusado.

Accusant [ac-kiūz'-ant], *s.* Acusador.

Accusation [ac-yu-zê'shun], *s.* 1. Acusación. 2. Cargo.

Accusative [ac-kiūz'-a-tiv], *s.* Acusativo, el cuarto caso en la declinación de los nombres latinos.

Accusatory [ac-kiūz'-a-to-ri], *a.* Acusatorio, lo que contiene algún cargo o acusación.

Accuse [ac-kiūz'], *va.* 1. Acusar, delatar, denunciar o manifestar el delito de otro. 2. Culpar, notar, tachar. 3. Censurar.

Accuser [ac-kiūz'-er], *s.* Acusador; denunciador, delator.

Accustom [ac-cus'-tum], *va.* Acostumbrar, habituar.—*vn.* Soler.

Accustomable [ac-cus'-tum-a-bl], *a.* Acostumbrado; común, ordinario, habitual.

Accustomably [ac-cus'-tum-a-bli], *adv.* Acostumbradamente, según costumbre, habitualmente, frecuentemente, a menudo.

Accustomarily [ac-cus'-tum-ê-ri-li], *adv.* Acostumbradamente, como de costumbre, comunmente, ordinariamente, según el uso.

Accustomary [ac-cus'-tum-e-ri], *a.* Acostumbrado, usual, ordinario.

Accustomed [ac-cus'-tumd], *a.* Frecuente, usual, acostumbrado.

Ace [ês], *s.* 1. Unidad; as, un punto solo de naipe o dado. 2. Migaja, parte pequeña de alguna cosa, partícula, átomo.

Acentric [a-sen'-tric], *a.* Sin centro; no situado en el centro; no dirigido desde un centro.

Acephala [a-sef'-a-la], *s. pl.* Acéfalos, clase de moluscos, como la ostra.

Acephalous [a-sef'-a-lus], *a.* 1. Acéfalo, lo que no tiene cabeza. 2. Deficiente al principio, como una línea de poesía.

Acer [ê'-ser], *s.* Arce, árbol. *V* MAPLE.

Acerate, Acerated [as'-e-ret o rêt, as-e-rê'-ted], *a.* Puntiagudo, como una aguja.

Acerb [a-serb'], *a.* Acerbo, ácido, agrio, áspero.

Acerbate [as'-er-bêt], *va.* Agriar, exasperar.

Acerbity [a-ser'-bi-ti], *s.* 1. Acerbidad. 2. Amargura, rigor, severidad, aspereza, crueldad, dureza, agrura, desabrimiento.

Acerose [as'-e-rōs], *a.* 1. (Bot.) Aciculado. 2. (Poco us.) Lleno de zurrón; aristado.

Acerous [as'-e-rus], *a.* 1. Que no tiene antenas, o las tiene rudimentarias. 2. Sin astas.

Acervose [as'-er-vōs], *a.* (Poco us.) Lleno de montones.

Acescency [a-ses'-en-si], *s.* Agrura, acedía.

Acescent [a-ses'-ent], *a.* Repuntado, lo que empieza a tener punta de agrio.

Acetabulum [as-e-tab'-yu-lum], *s.* (Anat.) 1. Acetábulo, cavidad cotiloidea (de la cadera). 2. Medida antigua de quince dracmas.

Acetanilid [as-et-an'-i-lid], *s.* Acetanilida, medicamento usado para aliviar la fiebre.

Acetate [as'-e-têt], *s.* Acetato, sal formada con alguna base y ácido acético. *Acetate of copper*, Cardenillo, verdegris.

Acetic [a-set'-ic ó a-sī'-tic], *a.* Acético. *Acetic acid*, Ácido acético.

Acetification [a-set-i-fi-kê'-shun], *s.* Acetificación.

Acetify [a-set'-i-fai], *va.* Acetificar; convertir en ácido acético,

Acetimeter [as-e-tim'-e-ter], *s.* Acetímetro, instrumento usado para reconocer la calidad del vinagre.

Acetone [as'-e-tōn], *s.* Acetona; C_3H_6O: espíritu privacético; líquido incoloro, límpido y muy inflamable, que se obtiene por la destilación de algunos acetatos.

Acetosity [as-e-tos'-i-ti], *s.* (Poco us.) *V.* ACIDITY.

Acetous, Acetose [a-sī'-tus], *a.* Agrio, acedo, acetoso.—*Acetous acid*, (Quím.) Vinagre; nombre antiguo y erróneo.

Acetylene [a-set'-i-lin], *s.* Acetileno, compuesto gaseoso de carbono e hidrógeno, C_2H_2. Es gas incoloro con olor peculiar y desagradable.

Ache [êk], *s.* Dolor continuo, mal. *Headache*, Dolor de cabeza. *Toothache*, Dolor de muelas. *Earache*, Dolor de oído.

Ache, Ake [êk], *vn.* Doler. *My head aches*, Me duele la cabeza.

Achievable [a-chīv'-a-bl], *a.* Ejecutable, hacedero, factible.

Achievance [a-chīv'-ans], *s.* Ejecución; hazaña, hecho.

Achieve [a-chīv'], *va.* 1. Ejecutar, acabar o perfeccionar alguna cosa. 2. Ganar, obtener.

Achievement [a-chīv'-mẹnt], *s.* 1. Ejecución, el acto de ejecutar alguna cosa; hazaña o acción heroica. 2. Timbre o insignia de un escudo de armas, que denota alguna proeza o acción heroica.
Achiever [a-chīv'-ẹr], *s.* Ejecutor, hacedor. (Met.) Vencedor.
Achilles' tendon [a-kil'-es ten'-dẹn], *s.* (Anat.) Tendón de Aquiles.
Aching [ēk'-ing], *s.* Dolor, desasosiego, incomodidad.
Achlamydeous [a-cla-mid'-e-us], *a.* (Bot.) Desnudo; sin cáliz ni corola.
Achor [é'-cor], *s.* Acores, especie de herpe. Tiña mucosa.
Achromatic [ac-ro-mat'-ic], *a.* (Opt.) Acromático; dícese del lente preparado de manera que no deja ver los colores del iris.
Achromatize [a-crō'-ma-taiz], *va.* Acromatizar; hacer acromático,
Acicular [a-sic'-yu-lar], *a.* Aciculado, acicular, alesnado, en forma de pequeñas agujas.
Acid [as'-id], *a.* Ácido, agrio, acedo.
Acidifiable [a-sid-i-fai'-a-bl], *a.* Acidificable.
Acidification [a-sid-i-fi-kē'-shun], *s.* Acidificación.
Acidify [ẹ-sid'-i-fai] *va.* 1. Acedar, hacer ácido, agriar. 2. (Quím.) Acidular.
Acidimeter [as-i-dim-ẹ-tẹr], *s.* Acidímetro, aparato para determinar la fuerza de los ácidos.
Acidity, Acidness [a-sid'-i-ti, as'-id-nes], *s.* Agrura, agrio, acedía, acidez.
Acidosis [a-si-dō'-sis] *s.* (Med.) Asecencia, acidez, acidismo.
Acidulae [ẹ-sid'-yu-lī], *s. pl.* Aguas minerales que contienen una gran cantidad de gas ácido carbónico, llamadas aguas aciduladas.
Acidulate [a-sid'-yu-lēt], *va.* 1. Acidular poner ligeramente ácido. 2. Amargar, causar penas, poner de mal humor.
Acidulous [a-sid'-yu-lus], *a.* Agrio, de la naturaleza de los ácidos, acídulo.
Ack ack [ac ac], *s.* V. ANTIAIRCRAFT.
Acknowledge [ac-nel'-ej], *va.* 1. Reconocer o confesar la verdad de alguna cosa. 2. Confesar algún delito. 3. Confesar con agradecimiento algún beneficio recibido, ser agradecido. 4. Declarar confesando plenamente. 5. Acusar recibo. *Please acknowledge receipt of this letter,* Sírvase Vd. acusar recibo de esta carta.
Acknowledging [ac-nel'-ej-ing], *a.* Reconocido, agradecido al beneficio que se ha recibido.
Acknowledgment [ac-nel'-ej-mẹnt], *s.* 1. Reconocimiento, el acto de reconocer o conceder la verdad de alguna cosa. 2. Confesión de alguna culpa. 3. Gratitud, reconocimiento, agradecimiento. 4. Concesión, consentimiento.
Aclinic [a-clin'-ic], *a.* Aclínico, magnético.
Acme [ac'-mẹ], *s.* Cima, colmo. (Met.) Cenit, complemento, último punto de una cosa.
Acne [ac'-ne], *s.* Acne, enfermedad cutánea, frecuente en la cara durante la adolescencia.
Acolothist, Acolyte [a-col'-o-thist], *s.* Acólito; monacillo.
Aconite [ac'-o-nait], *s.* (Bot.) Acónito, hierba venenosa; planta medicinal.
Acorn [ē'-cōrn], *s.* Bellota.
Acorned [ē'-cōrnd], *a.* 1. Que tiene bellotas, cargada de su fruto (la encina). 2. Alimentado con bellotas.
Acotyledon [a-co-ti-lī'-don], *s.* Acotilédone; vegetal desprovisto de cotilédones u hojas seminales.
Acoustic [a-cūs'-tic ó a-caus'-tic], *a.* Acústico, lo perteneciente al oído.
Acoustics [a-cūs'-tics ó a-caus'-tics], *s.* 1. Acústica, ciencia que trata del oído y de los sonidos en general. 2. Acústicos, los medicamentos que se aplican al oído.
Acquaint [ạc-cwēnt'], *va.* 1. Imponer, instruir de raíz, familiarizar. 2. Informar, dar parte o aviso. 3. Advertir, comunicar, hacer saber, avisar. 4. Dar a conocer, instruir. *I shall acquaint you,* Yo le informaré a Vd.
Acquaintance [ạc-cwênt'-ans], *s.* 1. Conocimiento, familiaridad. *I have no acquaintance with him,* Yo no le trato. 2. Conocido, la persona que tiene trato con otra, sin que llegue a verdadera amistad. *He is an old acquaintance of mine,* Es antiguo conocido mío. 3. Inteligencia.
Acquaintanceship [ạc-cwênt'-ans-ship], *s.* Conocimiento; trato de una persona con otra.
Acquainted [ạc-cwênt'-ed], *a.* Conocido; impuesto, instruído, informado. *I am not acquainted with the circumstances of that affair,* Yo no estoy impuesto de las circunstancias de ese asunto. *To make acquainted,* Cerciorar, hacer saber, informar.
Acquest [ạc-cwest'], *s.* (Des.) 1. Adquisición, el acto de adquirir y la misma cosa adquirida. 2. (Ant.) Conquista.
Acquiesce [ạc-wi-es'], *vn.* Allanarse o asentir a alguna cosa; someterse, consentir.
Acquiescence [ạc-wi-es'-ens], *s.* Aquiescencia, asenso, consentimiento, conformidad; sumisión.
Acquiescent [ạc-wi-es'-ent], *a.* Condescendiente, cómodo, conforme, sumiso.
Acquirable [ạc-cwair'-a-bl], *a.* Adquirible; ganable.
Acquire [ạc-cwair'], *va.* Adquirir, ganar, alcanzar; aprender; obtener algo, ya buscándolo, ya comprándolo, o por medio de la práctica o del propio esfuerzo.
Acquired [ạc-cwaird'], *pp.* Adquirido. *An acquired fortune,* Bienes adquiridos o no heredados.
Acquirement [ạc-cwair'-mẹnt], *s.* Adquisición.—*pl.* Conocimientos, saber.
Acquirer [ạc-cwair'-ẹr], *s.* Adquiridor.
Acquiring [ạc-cwair'-ing], *s.* Adquisición, la acción y efecto de adquirir.
Acquisition [ạc-cwi-zish'-un], *s.* Adquisición, la cosa adquirida.
Acquisitive [ạc-cwiz'-i-tiv], *a.* Adquirido, logrado, ganado.
Acquisitively [ạc-cwiz'-i-tiv-li], *adv.* Por adquisición.
Acquisitiveness [ạc-cwiz'-i-tiv-nes], *s.* Adquisividad, disposición a adquirir.
Acquit [ạc-cwit'], *va.* 1. Libertar, poner en libertad. 2. Descargar, absolver, dar por libre al reo demandado civil o criminalmente. 3. Desempeñar, cumplir, exentar, pagar. *To acquit one's self well,* Desempeñar bien su obligación o cometido. *To acquit a debt,* Pagar una deuda.
Acquitment [ạc-cwit'-mẹnt], *s.* Absolución, descargo, pago.
Acquittal [ạc-cwit'-al], *s.* Absolución, la acción de absolver de los cargos hechos a un acusado; descargo.
Acquittance [ạc-cwit'-ans], *s.* 1. Descargo de una deuda. 2. Carta de pago. Finiquito o instrumento en que el acreedor confiesa haber recibido del deudor la cantidad que le debía.
Acre [ē'-kẹr], *s.* 1. Acre, medida de tierra que tiene 4,840 varas cuadradas. 2. Campo; en plural, terrenos, finca. *God's acre,* Campo santo, cementerio.
Acreage [ē'-kẹr-ẹj], *s.* Acres (o acras) colectivamente.
Acred [ē'-kẹrd], *a.* Hacendado.
Acrid [ac'-rid], *a.* Acre, mordaz, picante o aspero al paladar, irritante corrosivo.
Acridity, Acridness [ac-rid'-i-ti, ac'-rid-nes], *s.* Acritud, acrimonia.
Acrimonious [ac-ri-mō'-ni-us], *a.* Acre, corrosivo; sarcástico, sañudo; mordaz.
Acrimoniously [ac-ri-mō'-ni-us-li], *adv.* Con acrimonia, con aspereza.
Acrimoniousness [ac-ri-mō'-ni-us-nes], *s.* Aspereza de genio, acritud.
Acrimony [ac'-ri-mo-ni], *s.* 1. Acrimonia, acritud. 2. Aspereza de genio.
Acritical [ẹ-crit'-i-cal], *a.* Acrítico, sin crisis.
Acritude [ac'-ri-tiūd], *s.* Acrimonia, amargura; aspereza degenio, mordacidad de palabras.
‡**Acroatic** [a-cro-at'-ic], *a.* Acroático, recóndito; de difícil inteligencia.
Acrobat [ac'-ro-bat], *s.* Acróbata, volatín.
Acrobatic [ac-ro-bat'-ic], *a.* Acrobático.
Acrogen [ac'-ro-jen], *s.* Planta del orden superior de las criptógamas, como el helecho.
Acrogenous [ac-roj'-ẹ-nus], *a.* Que crece por el vértice o extremidad superior; dícese de ciertas plantas criptógamas y algunos zoófitos.
Acromion [ac-rō'-ni-en], *s.* Acromio, apófisis que forma la parte más elevada del omoplato.
Acronycal [ac-ren'-i-cal], *a.* (Astr.) Acrónico, acronicto.
Acronycally [ac-ren'-i-cal-i], *adv.* Acrónicamente.
Acropolis [ac-rep'-o-lis], *s.* Acrópolis, la ciudadela de un pueblo griego, especialmente la de Atenas.
Acrospired [ac'-ro-spaird], *pp.* y *a.* Espigado, germinado, brotado.
Across [a-cros'], *adv.* De través o en postura atravesada, al través, de una parte a otra.—*prep.* De medio a medio, por medio de.
Across-the-board [a-cros-dhe-bōrd], *a* 1. perteneciente a todas las clases y categorías, sin excepción. 2. (apuestas de carreras) puesto en combinación para ganar segundo puesto.
Acrostic [a-cres'-tic], *s.* Poema acróstico.—*a.* Acróstico.
Acroter [ac'-ro-tẹr], *s.* Acrotera, uno de los pedestales pequeños, que se ponen en medio o a los lados de un frontispicio, y sobre los cuales se colocan las figuras.
Acrylic [ẹ-cril'-ic], *a.* Acrílico.
Act [act], *vn.* 1. Obrar, ejercer fuerza mecánica, producir movimiento o efecto. 2. Hacer, estar ocupado en alguna cosa; ponerse en acción. 3. Conducirse, portarse. 4. Fingir, simular.—*va* 1. Hacer un papel, remedar, representar. *To act the buffoon,* Hacer el bufón o gracioso.

2. Obrar, causar algún efecto, mover, ejecutar. *To act upon,* (1) Obrar a impulso de. (2) Influir. (3) Ejercer, desempeñar. *To act the part of a judge,* Ejercer las funciones de juez.

Act, *s.* 1. Hecho, acción bien o mal ejecutada, efecto. 2. Acto o jornada de una comedia. *Act of oblivion,* Amnistía. *Act of faith,* Acto de fe.

Acting [act'-ing], *s.* Acción; representación, obra.

Actin [ac'-tin], *s.* Actina.

Actinia [ac-tin'-i-g], *s.* Clase de pólipos cuyos tentáculos se abren como los de las flores.

Actinic [ac-tin'-ic], *a.* Actínico, capaz de producir cambios químicos: se dice de los rayos de luz. También se escribe *actinical.*

Actinism [ac'-tin-izm], *s.* Actinismo, calidad de actínico.

Action [ac'-shun], *s.* 1. Acción, operación, ocupación. *Always in action,* Siempre en movimiento, activo. 2. Hecho, acción. 3. Acción, la serie de sucesos relacionados entre sí que forman el argumento de un poema o drama. 4. Acción, batalla. 5. Acción, gesticulación. 6. Proceso. 7. Influencia.

Actionable [ac'-shun-a-bl], *a.* Punible, criminal, procesable.

Actionably [ac'-shun-a-bli], *adv.* De un modo procesorio.

Actionary, Actionist [ac'-shun-a-ri, ac'-shun-ist], *s.* Accionista.

Action-taking [ac'-shun-têk'-ing], *a.* Litigioso.

Actitation [ac-ti-tê-shun], *s.* Acción rápida y frecuente.

Activate [ac'-ti-vêt], *va.* Activar, hacer activo. (Quím.) Activar.

Activator [ac'-ti-vêt-gr], *s.* (Quím.) Activador.

Active [ac'-tiv], *a.* 1. Activo, lo que tiene actividad para obrar. 2. Activo, lo que obra. 3. Diligente, eficaz, ocupado. 4. Ágil, pronto, ligero.

Actively [ac'-tiv-li], *adv.* Activamente, ágilmente, vivamente; eficazmente.

Activeness [ac'-tiv-nes], *s.* Agilidad, soltura, actividad, prontitud.

Activity [ac-tiv'-i-ti], *s.* Actividad; agilidad, vivacidad, vigor.

Actor [ac'-tgr], *sm.* 1. Agente, la persona que obra. 2. Cómico; actor, el que representa o hace papel en los teatros. 3. Actor, demandante en juicio.

Actress [ac'-tres], *sf.* Comedianta, actriz, cómica.

Actual [ac'-chu-al], *a.* 1. Actual, práctico. 2. Actual, lo que realmente existe o es efectivo; lo que no es meramente potencial. 3. Efectivo.

Actuality [ac-chu-al'-i-ti], *s.* Actualidad, el estado actual de alguna cosa.

Actually [ac'-chu-al-i], *adv.* De hecho, en efecto, realmente.

Actualness [ac'-chu-al-nes], *s.* Actualidad.

Actuary [ac'-chu-g-ri ó ac'-tiu-a-ri], *s.* 1. El empleado que tiene a su cargo los cómputos y las tarifas en las compañías de seguros. 2. Actuario, escribano. Secretario, registrador.

Actuate [ac'-chu-êt], *va.* Mover, excitar, animar, poner en acción.

Actuation [ac-chu-ê'-shun], *s.* Operación.

Acuity [a-kiū'-i-ti], *s.* Agudeza, sutileza en el corte o punta de armas, instrumentos, etc.

Aculeate [a-kiū'-le-êt], *a.* 1. Punzante, puntiagudo. 2. Erizado, espinoso.

Acumen [a-kiū'mgn], *s.* 1. Punta aguzada. 2. Agudeza, penetración, ingenio, vivacidad, chispa.

Acuminate [a-kiū'-mi-nêt], *vn.* Rematar en punta, terminar en cono. —*va.* Aguzar, afilar.

Acuminate, *a.* (Biol.) Aguzado, que va disminuyendo en forma de punta; terminado en punta.

Acuminated [a-kiū'-mi-nê-ted], *a.* Punzante, puntiagudo.

Acumination [a-kiū'mi-nê-shun], *s.* Punta aguda.

Acupuncture [ac'iu-punc'-tiūr ó chur], *s.* Acupuntura; inserción de agujas en carne viva como medio curativo. Se emplea mucho y desde muy antiguo por los chinos y japoneses.

Acute [a-kiūt'], *a.* 1. Agudo, delgado, sutil, penetrante. 2. Agudo, ingenioso, perspicaz, de vivo ingenio. 3. (Med.) Agudo, sutil.

Acute, *s.* (Gram.) Acento agudo.

Acute, *va.* Pronunciar algo con acento agudo. (Poco usado.)

Acutely [a-kiūt'-li], *adv.* Agudamente, con agudeza.

Acuteness [a-kiut'-nes], *s.* 1. Agudeza, sutileza o delicadeza en los filos, cortes o puntas de las armas o instrumentos. 2. Perspicacia o viveza de ingenio, talento, penetración. 3. Violencia de una enfermedad.

-ad, *sufijo.* Hacia, en la dirección de. *Centrad,* hacia el centro.

Adage [ad'-ēj], *s.* Adagio o refrán.

§**Adagial** [ad-ê'-ji-al], *a.* Proverbial.

Adagio [ā-dā'-jō], *s.* Adagio, término usado en la música para denotar lentitud. También composición música en este tiempo. Es voz italiana y quiere decir lentamente.

Adam [ad'-am], *s.* 1. Adán, el primer hombre; el género humano. 2. La naturaleza humana depravada, no regenerada. *Adam's ale,* (fam.) Agua. *Adam's apple,* (fam.) Nuez de la garganta.

Adamant [ad'-a-mant], *s.* 1. Mineral o metal muy duro, real o imaginario. 2. (Des.) Diamante. 3. (Des.) Piedra imán. 4. (Poét.) Dureza.

Adamantine [ad-a-man'-tin], **Adamantean** [ad-a-man-tī'-an], *a.* 1. Diamantino, duro como el diamante. 2. (Poét.) Impenetrable, adamantino.

Adam's apple [ad'-amz-ap'-l], *s.* 1. Nuez de la garganta. 2. (Bot.) Especie de limón. 3. Especie de banana grande.

Adapt [a-dapt'], *va.* Adaptar, acomodar o aplicar una cosa a otra; ajustar, cuadrar.

Adaptable [a-dap'-ta-bl], *a.* Adaptable, acomodable.

Adaptability [a-dap-ta-bil'-i-ti], *s.* Adaptabilidad.

Adaptation [ad-ap-tê'-shun], **Adaption** [a-dap'-shun], *s.* Adaptación; aplicación de una cosa a otra.

Adaptive [a-dapt'-iv], *a.* Capaz de adaptación; perteneciente o a propósito a ella.

Adays [a-dêz'], *adv.* Actualmente, ahora, al presente.

Add [ad], *va.* Añadir, aumentar, acrecentar, juntar, contribuir. *To add up,* Sumar.

Addendum [ad-den'-dum], *s.* Apéndice, adición o suplemento. *Addenda.* Adiciones, añadiduras.

Adder [ad'-gr], *s.* Sierpe, serpiente culebra.

Adder's grass [ad'-grz gras], **Adder's wort** [ad'-grz wūrt], *s.* (Bot.) Escorzonera.

Adder's tongue [ad'-grz tung], *s.* (Bot.) Lengua de sierpe. Ofioglosa.

Addible [ad'-i-bl], *a.* Lo que se puede añadir o sumar.

Addibility [ad-i-bil'-i-ti], *s.* La propiedad o posibilidad de ser añadido o sumado.

Addict [a'-dict], *s.* 1. Adicto, enviciado. 2. Adepto, partidario.

Addict [gd-dict'], *va.* Dedicar, destinar, aplicar. *To addict one's self to vice,* Entregarse a los vicios.

Addicted [gd-dic'-ted], *a.* y *pp.* Dado, entregado, afecto a, apasionado por, adicto.

Addictedness [gd-dic'-ted-nes], *s.* Inclinación, propensión.

Addiction [gd-dic'-shun], *s.* Dedicación, entrega, rendimiento, sacrificio. Disposición, gusto.

Adding machine [ad'-ing ma-shin'], *s.* Calculadora, máquina de calcular, sumadora.

Addition [a-di'-shun], *s.* 1. Adición, agregación. 2. Añadidura, aditamento. 3. (Arit.) Suma, adición. *In addition to,* Además de. *In addition,* Además. *In addition to which,* Por lo demás.

Additional [gd-dish'-un-al], *a.* Adicional.—*s.* Aditamento.

Additionally [gd-dish'-un-al-i], *adv.* Adicionalmente.

Additive [ad'-i-tiv], *a.* Que ha de ser añadido; que sirve para aumentar. Casi lo mismo que *additory.*

Additory [ad'-i-to-ri], *a.* Aumentativo.

Addle [ad'l], *a.* Huero, vacío, vano, sin substancia, infecundo, estéril; podrido.

Addle, *va.* Hacer huero o vacío; podrir; esterilizar, hacer estéril.

Addle-pated [ad'l-pêt'-ed], **Addle-headed** [ad'l-hed'-ed], *a.* Negado, totalmente inepto para alguna cosa; cabeza hueca o vacía.

Address [gd-dres'], *va.* 1. Prepararse o disponerse para alguna cosa. 2. Hablar, interceder o rogar; recurrir, hacer presente alguna cosa de palabra; dirigir la palabra, dirigirse a uno, arengar. 3. Obsequiar. 4. *vn.* Encararse, engestarse. *To address the king,* Hablar al rey o suplicarle. *To address a letter,* Dirigir una carta, poner el sobrescrito.

Address, *s.* 1. Dirección, señas de una casa. 2. Discurso, plática. *Cable address,* Dirección cablegráfica. *Change of address,* Cambio de dirección.

Addressee [gd-dres-sī'], *s.* Destinatario (de una carta, mercancías, etc.).

Addresser [gd-dres'-gr], *s.* Suplicante, exponente.

Addressing machine [g-dres'-ing ma-shin'], *s.* Máquina para dirigir sobres, tarjetas, etc.

Adduce [gd-diūs'], *va.* Traer, llevar o asignar alguna cosa para juntarla a otra; alegar, aducir.

Adducent [ad-diū'-sgnt], *a.* (Anat.) Aductores, músculos que sirven para recoger o conducir hacia dentro algunas partes del cuerpo.

Adducible [ad-diū'-si-bl], *a.* Aducible, que se puede aducir o alegar.

Adduction [ad-duc'-shun], *s.* 1. (Anat.) Aducción. 2. Alegación.

Adductive [ad-duc'-tiv], *a.* Aductivo.

Adductor [ad-duct'-er], *s.* Aductor (músculo). *V.* ADDUCENT.

Addulce [ad-duls'], *va.* (Des.) Dulcificar, endulzar.
Adelphous [a-del'-fus], *a.* Adelfo; dícese de los estambres cuando están pegados por sus filamentos formando uno o varios grupos. Usase comunmente como sufijo, v. g. *diadelphous*, es decir, en dos grupos.
Ademption [a-demp'-shun], *s.* Privación, revocación, diminución.
Adenitis [ad-en-ai'-tis o i'-tis], *s.* Inflamación de una glándula.
Adenography [ad-e-nog'-ra-fi], *s.* Adenografía, la parte de la anatomía que trata de las glándulas.
Adenoid [ad'-en-oid], *a.* y *s.* Glandiforme. Como sustantivo, se usa en plural.
Adept [a-dept'], *s.* Adepto, el que está iniciado y el que es consumado en un arte.—*a.* Versado, cursado; profundo, consumado; iniciado.
Adequate [ad'-e-cwêt], *va.* Adecuar, asemejar, igualar.
Adequate, *a.* Adecuado, proporcionado.
Adequately [ad'-e-cwet-li], *adv.* Adecuadamente, proporcionadamente.
Adequateness [ad'-e-cwêt-nes], **Adequation** [ad-e-cwê'-shun], *s.* Adecuación o proporción exacta, igualdad.
Adhere [ad-hîr'], *vn.* 1. Adherirse, unirse, avenirse o allegarse al partido o dictamen de otro. 2. Pegarse. 3. Aficionarse.
Adherence [ad-hîr'-ens], **Adherency** [ad-hîr'-en-si], *s.* 1. Adhesión, tenacidad, viscosidad; calidad de ahesivo o pegajoso. 2. Adhesión, adherencia.
Adherent [ad-hîr'-ent], *a.* 1. Adherente, pegajoso, lo que se pega. 2. Adherente, el que adhiere.
Adherent, *s.* Adherente, secuaz, partidario, parcial.
Adherently [ad-hîr'-ent-li], *adv.* Con adhesión, parcialmente.
Adherer [ad-hîr'-er], *s.* El que adhiere, partidario, parcial.
Adhesion [ad-hî'-zhun], *s.* Adhesión. (Med.) Adherencia.
Adhesive [ad-hî'-siv], *a.* Adhesivo, adherente, pegajoso. *Adhesive plaster*, Esparadrapo, tela adhesiva.
Adhesively [ad-hî'-siv-li], *adv.* Tenazmente, en unión estrecha.
Adhesiveness [ad-hî'-siv-nes], *s.* Tenacidad, viscosidad.
Adieu [a-diû'], *int.* A Dios.—*s.* Despedida; adiós. *To bid adieu*, Despedirse.
Adipocere [ad-i-po-sîr'], *s.* Adipocira; grasa de los cadáveres; jabón amoniacal producido por la descomposición de las materias animales enterradas o sumergidas.
Adipose [ad'-i-pōs], *a.* Adiposo, seboso.
Adit [ad'-it], *s.* Mina, conducto subterráneo; entrada casi horizontal de una mina. (Mex.) Socavón.
Adjacency [ad-jê'-sen-si], *s.* Adyacencia, proximidad, contigüidad, vecindad.
Adjacent [ad-jê'-sent], *a.* Adyacente, contiguo, vecino.—*s.* Alguna cosa contigua o adyacente.
Adjection [ad-jec'-shun], *s.* Adición, añadidura.
Adjectival [aj'-ec-tiv-al], *a.* Del adjetivo, como adjetivo.
Adjective [aj'-ec-tiv], *s.* Adjetivo.
Adjectively [aj'-ec-tiv-li], *adv.* Adjetivado.
Adjoin [ad-join], *va.* Juntar, asociar, unir.—*vn.* Lindar, estar contiguo o cercano.
Adjoining [ad-join'-ing], *a.* Contiguo, inmediato.
Adjourn [ad-jūrn'], *va.* Diferir, alargar, retardar; citar, emplazar; remitir; levantar una sesión.—*vn.* Separarse para volverse a reunir en un día señalado, retirarse.
Adjournment [ad-jūrn'-ment], *s.* Citación, llamamiento, emplazamiento, emplazo, comparendo; suspensión de una deliberación diferida hasta un día señalado.
Adjudge [ad-juj'], *va.* 1. Adjudicar; dar una recompensa; decidir, juzgar. 2. Sentenciar a una pena, condenar. 3. Juzgar, decretar.—*vn.* Pronunciar la sentencia.
Adjudgment [ad-juj'-ment], *s.* Adjudicación.
Adjudicate [ad-jū'-di-kêt], *va.* Determinar judicialmente; adjudicar, declarar a favor de alguno la pertenencia de alguna cosa. *V.* ADJUDGE.—*vn.* Ejercer las funciones de juez; llegar a una decisión judicial.
Adjudication [ad-jū-di-kê'-shun], *s.* Adjudicación.
Adjunct [ad'-junct], *s.* Adjunto, lo que está unido con otra cosa; compañero, colega, asociado.
Adjunct, *a.* Adjunto, unido o arrimado, junto, contiguo.
Adjunction [ad-junc'-shun], *s.* 1. Unión. 2. Unión, la misma cosa unida. 3. Adición.
Adjunctive [ad-junc'-tiv], *s.* 1. El que junta o une. 2. Adjunto o agregado.—*a.* Lo que junta.
Adjunctively [ad-junc'-tiv-li], *adv.* Juntamente.
Adjunctly [ad-junct'-li], *adv.* Consiguientemente.
Adjuration [ad-jū-rê'-shun], *s.* El acto y modo de juramentar, la forma del juramento: conjuro.
Adjure [ad-jūr'], *va.* Juramentar, tomar juramento a otro, proponiendole la fórmula o términos en que ha de jurar; conjurar.
Adjurer [ad-jūr'-er], *s.* El que toma el juramento.
Adjust [ad-just'], *va.* Ajustar, arreglar, acomodar, acordar, terminar, componer.
Adjuster [ad-just'-er], *s.* El que arregla o ajusta; mediador; tasador.
Adjustment [ad-just'-ment], *s.* Ajuste, ajustamiento, aliño, arreglo.
Adjustor [ad-just'-er], *s.* Músculo que une ciertas partes; por ejemplo, el de los braquiópodos.
Adjutancy [aj'-ū-tan-si], *s.* 1. Ayudantía, el oficio o empleo de ayudante. 2. Hábil manejo, dirección acertada de algún cargo o negocio.
Adjutant [aj'-ū-tant], *s.* Ayudante.
Adjuvant [aj'-ū-vant], *a.* Lo que ayuda, es útil o provechoso.—*s.* Ayudante.
Ad-lib [ad-lib'], *a.* *Ad libitum*, a voluntad, improvisado. —va. Improvisar, decir a voluntad, sin atenerse a lo escrito. (Aplícase a actores, oradores, etc.)
Adman [ad'-man], *s.* (Com.) Agente publicitario, agente de publicidad.
Admeasurement [ad-mezh'-iūr-ment], *s.* La medida, arte o práctica de medir según reglas.
Admensuration [ad-men-shu-rê'-shun], *s.* Mensura o medida, medición.
Administer [ad-min'-is-ter], *va.* 1. Administrar, suministrar, dar, surtir o proveer de lo que se necesita. 2. Administrar, servir o ejercer algún ministerio o empleo. 3. Regir, manejar, gobernar, contribuir. *To administer an oath*, Tomar juramento.
Administerial [ad-min-is-tî'-ri-al], *a.* Administrativo, perteneciente a la administración.
Administrable [ad-min'-is-tra-bl], *a.* Lo que se puede administrar.
Administrant [ad-min'-is-trant], *a.* y *s.* Manejador, director de un negocio, jefe ejecutivo; administrador, ra.
Administrate [ad-min'-is-trêt], *va.* Dar o administrar remedios.
Administration [ad-min-is-trê'-shun], *s.* 1. Administración, la acción de administrar o ejercer algún ministerio o empleo. 2. Ministerio, gobierno, administración de negocios públicos. 3. Manejo, distribución.
Administrative [ad-min-is-trê'-tiv], *a.* Administrativo.
Administrator [ad-min-is-trê'-ter], *s.* 1. (For.) Tenedor de bienes, fideicomisario abintestato. 2. Administrador, el que administra. 3. El que administra los sacramentos. 4. El que oficia en el rito divino. 5. Gobernante.
Administratorship [ad-min-is-trê'-ter-ship], *s.* Administración, el empleo de administrador.
Administratrix [ad-min-is-trê-trics], *sf.* 1. Administradora, la que administra. 2. La que gobierna. 3. Tenedora de bienes, fidei-comisaria abintestato.
Admirable [ad'-mi-ra-bl], *a.* Admirable, digno de admiración.
Admirableness [ad'-mi-ra-bl-nes], **Admirability** [ad-mi-ra-bil'-i-ti], *n.* Excelencia de alguna cosa.
Admirably [ad'-mi-ra-bli], *adv.* Admirablemente.
Admiral [ad'-mi-ral], *s.* 1. Almirante, el que manda una armada o escuadra. *Admiral of the red*, Almirante de la escuadra roja; *Admiral of the white*, Almirante de la blanca; *Admiral of the blue*, Almirante de la azul: tres grados que antes existían en la escuadra inglesa, así llamados por los colores de sus banderas respectivas. *Vice-Admiral* Vicealmirante. *Rear-Admiral*, Contraalmirante o jefe de escuadra. 2. Almiranta, la nave que monta el almirante.
Admiralship [ad'-mi-ral-ship], *s.* Almirantía.
Admiralty [ad'-mi-ral-ti], *s.* Almirantazgo, tribunal en que se determinan los asuntos de la marina. *The Lords Commissioners of the Admiralty*, El consejo o junta del almirantazgo.
Admiration [ad-mi-rê-shun], *s.* Admiración.
Admire [ad-mair'], *va.* 1. Admirar. 2. Amar, tener amor y afición a alguna persona o cosa.—*vn.* Admirarse de alguna cosa.
Admirer [ad-mair'-er], *s.* 1. Admirador. 2. Amante, apasionado. *He is a great admirer of painting*, Es muy aficionado a la pintura.
Admiringly [ad-mair'-ing-li], *adv.* Estupendamente, admirablemente.
Admissibility [ad-mis-i-bil'-i-ti], *s.* Admisibilidad.
Admissible [ad-mis'-i-bl], *a.* Admisible, aceptable; permitido, lícito.
Admission [ad-mish'-un], *s.* Admisión, entrada, ingreso. *Admission fee*, Cuota de inscripción, matrícula.
Admissive [ad-mis'-iv], **Admissory** [ad-mis'-or-i], *a.* Lo que implica o concede admisión.
Admit [ad-mit'], *va.* 1. Admitir, recibir o dar entrada. 2. Admitir o recibir para algún empleo. 3. Con-

ceder o asentir a alguna proposición. 4. Admitir, conceder o permitir.

Admittance [ad-mit'-ans], *s.* 1. Entrada, permisión. 2. Entrada, el derecho de entrar en alguna parte. 3. Derechos de entrada. 4. Concesión de una proposición. 5. Admisión.

Admitter [ad-mit'-ẹr], *s.* Admitidor, el que admite, o concede alguna proposición.

Admittible [ad-mit'-i-bl], *a.* Admisible.

Admix [ad-mix'], *va.* Mezclar, juntar, unir o incorporar una cosa con otra.

Admixtion [ad-mix'-chun], *s.* Mezcla, la mixtura o incorporación de una cosa con otra.

Admixture [ad-mix'-chur ó tiūr], *s.* Mixtura o mezcla, el ingrediente mezclado con otro o incorporado a él.

Admonish [ad-men'-ish], *va.* Amonestar, prevenir, advertir, reprender, exhortar.

Admonisher [ad-men'-ish-ẹr], *s.* Amonestador.

Admonishment [ad-men'-ish-mẹnt], *s.* Advertencia, prevención, amonestación, reprensión.

Admonition [ad-mo-nish'-un], *s.* 1. Consejo, aviso. 2. Represión, amonestación, admonición.

Admonitioner [ad-mo-nish'-un-ẹr], *s.* Admonitor o monitor. Es voz irónica con que se moteja al que todo lo censura.

Admonitor [ad-men'-i-tor], *n.* Admonitor, censor.

Admonitory, Admonitive [ad-men'-i-to-ri], *a.* Admonitorio.

†**Admove** [ad-mūv], *va.* Arrimar o acercar una cosa a otra.

Adnascence [ad-nas'-ens], *s.* Adhesión de partes entre sí por toda su superficie.

Adnascent [ad-nas'-ent], **Adnate** [ad'-nêt], *a.* 1. (Bot.) Adnato, íntimamente adherido. 2. Entenado.

Adnoun [ad'-naun], *s.* (Gram.) Adjetivo.

Ado [a-dū'], *n.* 1. Trabajo, dificultad. 2. Bullicio, baraúnda, tumulto, ruido. 3. Pena, fatiga. *Much ado about nothing,* Nada entre dos platos, o, más es el ruido que las nueces; poco mal y bien quejado. *I had much ado to do it,* Lo hice a duras penas. *Without more ado,* Sin más ni menos; sin más acá, ni más allá.

Adobe [a-dō'-bê], *s.* Adobe, ladrillo sin cocer.

Adolescence [ad-o-les'-ẹns] o **Adolescency** [ad-o-les'-en-si], *s.* Adolescencia.

Adolescent [ad-ol-es'-ent], *a* y *s.* Adolescente.

Adonic [a-den'-ic], *a.* Verso adónico que consta de un dáctilo y un espondeo: (— ⏑ ⏑ | — —).

†**Adoors** [a-dōrz'], *adv.* A la puerta o a las puertas.

Adopt [a-dept'], *va.* Adoptar, prohijar, ahijar.

Adopter [a-dep'-tẹr], *s.* Prohijador, padre adoptivo, o madre adoptiva.

Adoption [a-dep'-shun], *s.* Adopción.

Adoptive [a-dep'-tiv], *a.* 1 Adoptivo. El que adopta o prohija. *He was her adopter,* o *adoptive father,* Él era su padre adoptivo. *She was his adoptive daughter,* Ella era su hija adoptiva. 2. Adoptante, el que adopta.

Adorable [a-dōr'-a-bl], *a.* Adorable.

Adorableness [a-dōr'-a-bl-nes], *s.* Adoración, mérito.

Adorably [a-dōr'-a-bli], *adv.* Adorablemente.

Adoral [ad-ō'-ral], *a.* Perteneciente á la boca o situado cerca de ella. *Cf.* ABORAL.

Adoration [ad-o-rê'-shun], *s.* 1. Adoración. 2. Incienso, adoración política o séquito por adulación o interés. 3. Respeto.

Adore [a-dōr'], *va.* 1. Adorar, honrar y reverenciar con culto externo religioso. 2. Adorar, amar con extremo, idolatrar.

Adorer [a-dōr'-ẹr], *s.* 1. Adorador. 2. (Coll.) Amante.

Adorn [a-dērn'], *va.* Adornar, ornar, embellecer, ataviar.

†**Adorn,** *s.* Adorno, atavío, ornamento, ornato.—*a.* Adornado, ataviado.

Adorning [a-dērn'-ing], *s.* Adorno, decoración.

Adornment [a-dērn'-mẹnt], *s.* Adorno, atavío, gala.

Adown [a-daun'], *adv.* Bajo, abajo, en el suelo, en tierra.

Adown, *prep.* Abajo, hacia abajo.

Adragant [ad'-ra-gant], *s.* Adraganto, tragacanto.

Adrenal [a-drin'-al], *a.* (Med.) Suprarrenal.

Adrenalin, Adrenaline [a-dren'-a-lin], *s.* (Med.) Adrenalina.

Adrift [a-drift'], *adv.* Flotando, a merced de las olas; a la ventura.

Adrip [a-drip'], *a.* Que está goteando.

Adroit [a-dreit'], *a.* Diestro, hábil. (<Fr. *à+droit,* derecho.)

Adroitly [a-dreit'-li], *adv.* Hábilmente, diestramente.

Adroitness [a-dreit'-nes], *s.* Destreza, habilidad, prontitud.

Adry [a-drai'], *adv.* Sediento.

Adscititious [ad-si-tish'-us], *a.* Completivo, lo que sirve para completar otra cosa; aumentado, añadido, interpuesto.

Adstriction [ad-stric'-shun], *s.* Astricción. *V.* ASTRICTION.

Adulate [ad'-yu-lêt], *va.* Adular, lisonjear, servilmente.

Adulation [ad-yu-lê'-shun], *s.* Adulación, lisonja, servil; alabanza exagerada y no sincera.

Adulator [ad'-yu-lê-tor], *s.* Adulador; parásito, lisonjero.

Adulatory [ad'-yu-la-to-ri], *a.* Adulatorio, lisonjero, cumplimentero, adulador.

§**Adulatress** [ad'-yu-la-tres], *s.* Aduladora, lisonjera.

Adult [a-dult'], *a.* 1. Adulto, el que ha llegado al término de la adolescencia. 2. Llegado a su mayor crecimiento o desarrollo. También es substantivo.

Adultness [a-dult'-nes], *s.* Edad adulta.

Adulterant [a-dul'-tẹr-ant], *s.* 1. Adulterador, la persona que adultera; falsificador. 2. Lo que se usa para falsificar.

Adulterate [a-dul'-tẹr-êt], *vn.* Adulterar, cometer adulterio.—*va.* Adulterar, corromper o mezclar con alguna cosa heterogénea, falsificar, viciar; sofisticar.

Adulterate, *a.* 1. Adulterado. 2. Adulterado, corrompido o mezclado con alguna cosa extraña; falsificado.

Adulterately [a-dul'-tẹr-êt-li], *adv.* 1. Adulterinamente. 2. Adulteradamente.

Adulterateness [a-dul'-tẹr-êt-nes], *s.* Corrupción, contaminación.

Adulteration [a-dul-tẹr-ê'-shun], *s.* Adulteración, corrupción, falsificación.

Adulterer [a-dul'-tẹr-ẹr], *sm.* Adúltero.

Adulteress [a-dul'-tẹr-es], *sf.* Adúltera.

Adulterine [a-dul'-tẹr-in], *s.* Hijo adulterino.—*a.* Espurio.

Adulterous [a-dul'-tẹr-us], *a.* Adulterino, espurio.

Adultery [a-dul'-tẹr-i], *s.* 1. Adulterio. 2. Corrupción.

Adumbrant [ad-um'-brant], *a.* 1. Bosquejado, trazado; lo que representa o da una idea, aunque imperfecta, de la semejanza de una cosa con otra. 2. Sombreado ligeramente.

Adumbrate [ad-um'-brêt], *va.* Esquiciar, formar un esquicio o diseño de alguna cosa; bosquejar, sombrear, delinear.

Adumbration [ad-um-brê'-shun], *s.* Esquicio, esbozo, trazo, diseño, rasgo; bosquejo o borrón de un trabajo en la pintura o escritura.

Aduncate [ad-un'-kêt], *vn.* Encorvarse como un garfio.—*a.* Encorvado, torcido a manera gancho o pico de halcón.

Aduncity [a-dun'-si-ti], *s.* Corvadura, curvatura, la propiedad de ser o estar corvo o encorvado; sinuosidad.

Aduncous [a-dun'-cus], **Adunque** [a-dunc'], *a.* Corvo, encorvado, torcido, ganchoso; sinuoso, adunco.

Adusk [a-dusk'], *adv.* (Poco us.) A la hora del crepúsculo, o en la obscuridad.

Adust [a-dust'], *a.* 1. Adusto; tostado o requemado, consumido. 2. Moreno, como tostado por el sol; curtido.—*adv.* En el polvo; polvoriento.

Adusted [a-dus'-ted], *a.* Quemado o tostado al fuego; caliente.

Adustion [a-dus'-chun], *s.* Adustión, quemadura, inflamación.

Ad valorem [ad-va-lō'-rem]. (Com.) Por avalúo.

Advance [ad-vạns'], *va.* 1. Avanzar. 2. Adelantar, promover. 3. Adelantar, mejorar; elevar, poner a mayor altura, o en más alto rango. 4. Acelerar, apresurar. 5. Adelantar o anticipar dinero, pagar adelantado. 6. Proponer, ofrecer, insinuar. 7. Encarecer, hacer subir el precio de una cosa.—*vn.* 1. Adelantar, hacer progresos; ir adelante. 2. Subir de valor o precio.

Advance, *s.* 1. Avance, 2. Adelanto, paga adelantada. 3. Adelantamiento, mejora, adelanto, aprovechamiento, progreso. 4. Suplemento, préstamo. 5. Requerimiento de amores; insinuación.

Advancement [ad-vạns'-mẹnt], *s.* 1. Adelantamiento, progresión. 2. Adelantamiento, progreso; promoción. 3. Subida, prosperidad. 4. Elevación, promoción, ascenso.

Advancer [ad-vạns'-ẹr], *s.* 1. Promotor, impulsor. 2. Protector; adelantador; el que avanza.

Advantage [ad-vạn'-têj], *s.* 1. Ventaja, superioridad, preponderancia. 2. Ganancia, provecho, aprovechamiento, beneficio, lucro. 3. Ocasión favorable. 4. Sobrepaga, provecho excesivo. 5. Prerrogativa, comodidad.

Advantage, *va.* 1. Adelantar, ganar. 2. Remunerar. 3. Promover. *To take advantage of,* Aprovecharse de, valerse de; engañar.

Advantageable [ad-vgn'-têj-a-bl], *a.* Provechoso, ganancioso.
Advantage-ground [ad-vgn'-têj-graund], *s.* Puesto ventajoso; situación favorable.
Advantaged [ad-vgn'-tejd], *a.* Adelantado, ventajoso.
Advantageous [ad-van-tê'-jus], *a.* Ventajoso, útil, provechoso.
Advantageously [ad-van-tê'-jus-li], *adv.* Ventajosamente, con ventaja o utilidad.
Advantageousness [ad-van-tê'-jus-nes], *s.* Ventaja, utilidad, conveniencia.
‡**Advene** [ad-vín'], *vn.* Venir, arrimarse o añadirse una cosa a otra; acceder.
†**Advenient** [ad-ví'-ni-ent], *a.* Sobreañadido, accesorio, adviniente. *V.* ADVENTITIOUS.
Advent [ad'-vent], *s.* 1. Adviento, las cuatro semanas que preceden a la festividad del Nacimiento de nuestro Redentor. 2. Venida o llegada.
Adventitious [ad-ven-tish'-us], *a.* 1. Adventicio, lo que sobreviene por casualidad; extraño, exterior. 2. (Med.) Adventicio, no hereditario. 3. (Bot.) Formado sin orden, o en lugar insólito (espontáneo). 4. (Biol.) Accidental, que se presenta fuera de la habitación o el terreno natural. *V.* ADVENTIVE.
Adventitiously [ad-ven'-tish-us-li], *adv.* Accidentalmente.
Adventive [ad-ven'-tiv], *a.* 1. (Biol.) Advenedizo, es decir, sólo parcialmente naturalizado o aclimatado. 2. Accidental, casual.
Adventual [ad-ven'-tiu-al ó chu-al], *a.* 1. Relativo al Adviento. 2. Casual.
Adventure [ad-ven'-chur ó tiūr], *s.* 1. Aventura, casualidad, contingencia; lance. 2. Expedición ó empresa rodeada de peligros y contingencias, riesgo; designio. 3. Ancheta, pacotilla, porción corta de mercaderías que se lleva o envía de un lugar a otro para su venta o despacho. *At all adventures,* Al acaso, casualmente. Sea lo que fuere.
Adventure, *va.* Osar, atreverse, emprender, arriesgar.—*va.* Aventurar.
Adventurer [ad-ven'-chur-gr], *s.* 1. Aventurero, el que busca aventuras. 2. Pacotillero, anchetero.
Adventuresome [ad-ven'-chur-sum], *a.* *V.* ADVENTUROUS.
Adventurous [ad-ven'-chur-us], *a.* 1. Animoso, valeroso, esforzado, intrépido, arriesgado. 2. Aventurado, peligroso. 3. Osado, atrevido.
Adventurously [ad-ven'-chur-us-li], *adv.* Arriesgadamente, arrojadamente.
Adventurousness [ad-ven'-chur-us-nes], **Adventuresomeness** [ad-ven'-chur-sum-nes], *s.* Intrepidez, arrojo, temeridad, osadía.
Adverb [ad'-vgrb], *s.* Adverbio, una de las partes de la oración.
Adverbial [ad-vgr'-bi-al], *a.* Adverbial, lo perteneciente al adverbio.
Adverbially [ad-vgr-bi-al-i], *adv.* Adverbialmente.
Adversary [ad'-vgr-sê-ri], *s.* Adversario, contrario, enemigo, antagonista. *The Adversary,* Satanás, el diablo.
Adversative [ad-vgr'-sa-tiv], *a.* Adversativo.
Adverse [ad'-vgrs], *a.* 1. Adverso, contrario, opuesto. 2. Adverso, desgraciado.
Adversely [ad'-vgrs-li], *adv.* Adversamente, desgraciadamente; al contrario.
Adverseness [ad'-vgrs-nes], *s.* Oposición, resistencia.
Adversity [ad-vgr'-si-ti], *s.* Adversidad, suceso adverso, desgracia, miseria, calamidad, infortunio.
Advert [ad-vgrt'], *vn.* Atender, cuidar o tener cuidado, hacer referencia. *I advert to his discourse,* Me estoy refiriendo a su discurso.—*va.* Cuidar, aconsejar, considerar atentamente, advertir, notar.
Advertence [ad-vgr'-tens], **Advertency** [ad-vgr'-ten-si], *s.* Atención, cuidado, consideración.
Advertent [ad-vgr'-tent], *a.* Atento, vigilante.
Advertise [ad'-vgr-taiz], *va.* 1. Avisar, informar, advertir. 2. Dar aviso al público, noticiar, poner o publicar anuncios.
Advertisement [ad-vgr-taiz'-mgnt ó ad-vgr'-tiz-mgnt], *s.* 1. Noticia, aviso, anuncio. 2. Aviso al público; advertencia o aviso en los periódicos.
Advertiser [ad-vgr-taiz'-gr], *s.* 1. Avisador. 2. Cartel, anuncio, papel o periódico por cuyo medio se da algún aviso al público.
Advertising [ad-vgr-taiz'-ing], *s.* 1. Publicidad. 2. Propaganda. *Advertising media,* Medios de publicidad.
Advice [ad-vais'], *s.* 1. Consejo, el dictamen que se da o toma; consultación, deliberación. 2. Aviso, noticia. 3. Consulta. 4. Conocimiento, reflexión. 5. Advertencia.
Advisability [ad-vaiz''-a-bil'-i-ti], *s.* Prudencia, cordura; conveniencia.
Advisable [ad-vaiz'-a-bl], *a.* Prudente, conveniente, propio.
Advisableness [ad-vaiz'-a-bl-nes], *s.* Prudencia, cordura, conveniencia, propiedad.
Advise [ad-vaiz'], *va.* 1. Aconsejar, dar consejo. 2. Avisar, informar, advertir, enterar, dar noticia.—*vn.* 1. Aconsejarse, pedir o tomar consejo. 2. Considerar, deliberar, examinar. *To advise with,* Aconsejarse con o de.
Advised [ad-vaizd'], *a.* 1. Avisado, advertido, prudente. 2. Premeditado, deliberado, discurrido, considerado.
Advisedly [ad-vaiz'-ed-li], *adv.* Deliberadamente, prudentement.
Advisedness [ad-vaiz'-ed-nes], *s.* Cordura, juicio, reflexión, prudencia, deliberación.
Advisement [ad-vaiz'-mgnt], *s.* 1. Consejo, parecer, dictamen. 2. Prudencia, circunspección. 3. Deliberación, consideración.
Adviser [ad-vaiz'-gr], *s* Consejero, aconsejador.
Advising [ad-vaiz'-ing], *s.* Consejo, aviso.
Advisory [ad-vais'-o-ri], *a.* Consultor, autorizado para dar su parecer, que tiene consejo.
Advocacy [ad'-vo-ca-si], *s* Vindicación, defensa, apología.
Advocate [ad'-vo-kêt], *va.* Abogar, defender, sostener, interceder, mediar.
Advocate [ad'-vo-kêt], *s.* 1. Abogado, letrado. 2. Intercesor, medianero, favorecedor, defensor, protector.
†**Advocation** [ad-vo-kê'-shun], *s.* Vindicación; patronato; apelación.
Advolution [ad-vo-lū'-shun], *s.* Desarrollo o crecimiento hacia alguna cosa o algún estado.
Advowee [ad-vau-í'], *s.* Patrón, el que tiene el derecho de patronato de algún beneficio; colador.
Advowson [ad-vau'-zn], *s.* Patronato, derecho de presentar ó nombrar para algún beneficio eclesiástico; colación; patronazgo.
Adynamia [ad-i-nê'-mi-a], *s.* Adinamia, debilidad de las fuerzas vitales.
Adynamic [ad-i-nam'-ic], *a.* Débil, adinámico.
Adytum [ad'-i-tum], *s.* Adiote ó ádito, santuario de los antiguos.
Adz ó **Adze** [adz], *s.* Azuela, herramienta de carpintería.
Æ [í o ê]. Diftongo de origen latino, equivalente al griego ai. En muchas palabras se reemplaza æ por la e sola. Véase E, y en los nombres griegos propios Aĭ.
Ædile [í'-dail], *s.* Edil, magistrado romano; oficial municipal.
Ædileship [í'-dail-ship], *s.* Edilidad.
Ægilops [í'-ji-lops], *s.* 1. Egílope, tumor o hinchazón en el ángulo mayor o interno del ojo. 2. (Bot.) Egílope, rompesacos o rompisacos, una especie de grama.
Ægis [í'-jis], *s.* Escudo, broquel, égide o égida.
Ægyptiacum [í-jip-tai'-a-cum], *s.* Egipciaco, especie de ungüento compuesto de cardenillo, miel y vinagre.
Æolian [í-ō'-li-an], *a.* *V.* EOLIAN.
Æquinoctial [í'-cwi-noc'-shal], *a.* Equinoccial. *V.* EQUINOCTIAL.
Aerate [ê'-gr-êt], *va.* 1. Airear, ventilar, exponer a la acción del aire, proveer de aire, dar aire. 2. Impregnar, saturar un líquido de aire o de ácido carbónico. 3. Arterializar la sangre. 4. Hacer etéreo, espiritualizar. *Aerated waters,* Aguas cargadas de ácido carbónico natural o artificialmente; aguas gaseosas.
Aeration [ê-gr-ê'-shun], *s.* Renovación del aire, acción y efecto de darlo; ventilación.
Aerator [ê-gr-ê'-tgr], *s.* Aparato para airear o para saturar un líquido de aire o de gas; aireador.
Aerial [ê-í'-ri-al], *a.* 1. Aéreo. 2. Puesto en el aire; elevado. 3. Etéreo.
Aerial, *s.* Antena (de radio o de televisión).
Aerial photography [êí-ri-al fō-tog'-ra-fi], *s.* Fotografía aérea.
Aerie [ê'-gr-i], *s.* Nido de ave de rapiña. *V.* EYRY.
Aerify [ê'-gr-i-fai], *va.* 1. Aerificar, reducir al estado de aire. 2. Aerificar, llenar de aire.
Aerodynamics [ê-gr-o-dai-nam'-ics], *s.* Aerodinámica.
Aeroembolism [ê-gr-o-em'-bo-lizm], *s.* (Med.) Aeroembolismo.
Aerography [ê-gr-og'-ra-fi], *s.* Aerografía, descripción o teoría del aire
Aerolite [ê'-gr-o-lait], *s.* Aerolito; meteorito. *V.* METEORITE.
Aerology [ê-er-ol'-o-ji], *s.* Aerología, ciencia que trata de las leyes y fenómenos de la atmósfera.
Aeromechanics [ê-gr-ō-me-can'-ics], *s.* Aeromecánica.
Aeromedicine [ê-gr-o-me'-di-sin], *s.* Aeromedicina.
Aerometer [ê-er-om'-e-tgr], *s.* Aerómetro.
Aerometric [ê-gr-o-met'-ric], *a.* Aerométrico, relativo a la aerometría.
Aerometry [ê-gr-om'-e-tri], *s.* Aerometría, medición de la fuerza, condensación o rarefacción del aire.
Aeronaut [ê'-gr-o-nōt], *s.* Aeronauta, el que se remonta por los aires en un globo.
Aeronautics [ê-gr-o-nōt'-ics] o **Aerostation** [ê-gr-o-stê'-shun], *s.* Aerostación.

el arte de viajar por el aire en globos llenos de gas. *Aerostation* se usa algunas veces para denotar la ciencia de pesar el aire.

Aerophyte [ē'-ẹr-o-fait], *s.* Aerofita; planta que crece totalmente en el aire y se alimenta de él.

Aeroplane [ē'-ẹr-o-plên], *s.* Aeroplano, avión.

Aeroscopy [ē-ẹr-es'-co-pi], *s.* Aeroscopia, observación del aire.

Aerosol [ē'-ẹr-o-sōl], *s.* 1. Aerosol, suspensión de partículas sólidas o líquidas en medio gaseoso. 2. Pulverizador, vaporizador.

Aerospace [ē'-ẹr-o-spēs], *s.* Aerospacio, espacio aéreo.

Aerostat [ē'-ẹr-o-stat], *s.* 1. Globo aerostático. 2. ‡. Aeronauta.

Aerostatic [ē-ẹr-os-tat'-ic], *a.* Aerostático.

Aerostatics, *s.* Aerostática, aeronáutica.

Aerothermodynamics [ē-ẹr-o-therm-o-dai-nam'-ics], *s.* Aerotermodinámica, termodinámica de gases o aérea.

Æsthete [es'-thīt], *s.* Esteta, admirador de la belleza natural o artística.

Æsthetic [es-thet'-ic], *a.* Estético. *V.* Esthetic.

Æsthetics [es-thet'-ics], *s.* Estética.

Æstival [es'-ti-val o es-tai'-val], *a.* 1. Estival, lo que pertenece al estío o verano. 2. Estivo, lo que dura todo el estío. *V.* Estival.

Ætites [i-tai'-tīz], *s.* Etites, piedra del águila.

Afar [a-fār'], *adv.* Lejos, distante, a gran distancia. *From afar,* De lejos, desde lejos, a distancia. *Afar off,* Distante, muy distante, remoto.

Afeard [a-fird'], *part. a.* (Vulg.) Espantado, atemorizado, aterrado, temeroso.

Afebrile [a-feb'-ril], *a.* Exento de fiebre.

Afer [ē'-fẹr], *s.* Ábrico, ábrego, el viento sudoeste.

Aff [af], *adv.* y *prep.* (Esco.) A distancia. *V.* Off.

Affability [af-a-bil'-i-ti], *s.* Afabilidad, suavidad, dulzura, agrado, cortesanía, urbanidad, atención.

Affable [af'-a-bl], *a.* Afable, cortés, benigno, favorable; comedido; cariñoso.

Affableness [af'-a-bl-nes], *s.* Afabilidad, dulzura, cariñó.

Affably [af'-a-bli], *adv.* Afablemente, cariñosamente.

Affair [af-fār'], *s.* 1. Asunto o negocio. 2. (Mil.) Acción, encuentro entre dos tropas. *Affair of honour,* Lance de honor, duelo.

Affect [af-fect'], *s.* 1. Afecto, cualquiera de las pasiones del ánimo. 2. Calidad, circunstancia. 3. Pasión, sensación, afición.

Affect, *va.* 1. Obrar, causar efecto en el ánimo; afectar, enternecer. 2. Conmover, mover o excitar las pasiones del ánimo. 3. Aspirar, anhelar. 4. Amar, tener afición a alguna persona o cosa. 5. Afectar, aparentar, fingir, hacer ostentación de cualidades o vicios; poner demasiado estudio en las palabras, movimiento o adornos.

Affectation [af-ec-tē'-shun], *s.* 1. Afectación, la acción y efecto de afectar. 2. Afectación, pretensión mal fundada.

Affected [af-fec'-ted], *part. a.* 1. Movido, impresionado, conmovido. 2. Afectado, lleno de afectación. 3. Inclinado. 4. Sujeto a algún mal o enfermedad. 5. Enternecido, conmovido.

Affectedly [af-fec'-ted-li], *adv.* Afectadamente.

Affectedness [af-fec'-ted-nes], *s.* Afectación, la acción y efecto de afectar; fingimiento.

Affecter [af-fec'-tẹr], *s.* Afectador, fingidor, el que afecta o finge alguna cosa.

Affecting [af-fec'-ting], *a.* Sensible, tierno, interesante, lastimero, lastimoso.

Affectingly [af-fec'-ting-li], *adv.* Con afecto.

Affection [af-fec'-shun], *s.* 1. Impresión, el efecto que causan las cosas en el ánimo. 2. Afecto, amor, benevolencia, afición, cariño, inclinación. 3. Estado del cuerpo o alma, cualidad, propiedad, afección. 4. (Med.) Enfermedad, dolencia.

Affectionate [af-fec'-shun-et], *a.* Cariñoso, benévolo, afectuoso, prendado, aficionado.

Affectionately [af-fec'-shun-et-li], *adv.* Cariñosamente, afectuosamente. *Affectionately yours,* Suyo afectuosamente (despedida en una carta).

Affectionateness [af-fec'-shun-ēt-nes], *s.* Afecto, amor, benevolencia.

Affectioned [af-fec'-shund], *a.* 1. (Ant.) Inclinado, dispuesto. 2. (Des.) Afectado, lleno de afectación.

Affective [af-fec'-tiv], *a.* Afectivo, tierno, afectuoso, persuasivo.

Affectively [af-fec'-tiv-li], *adv.* Apasionadamente.

Affector [af-fec'-tẹr], *s.* Fingidor, imitador.

Affeer [af-fīr'], *va.* (Der. ing. ant.) 1. *V.* Assess. 2. Confirmar.

Affeerers [af-fīr'-ẹrz], *s.* (Derecho inglés) Jueces que tienen facultad de imponer multas por ciertos delitos leves.

Afferent [af'-ẹr-ẹnt], *a.* Aferente, que trae, que conduce hacia dentro; opuesto a *efferent.*

Affiance [af-fai'-ans], *s.* 1. Esponsales o contrato matrimonial. 2. Confianza.

Affiance, *va.* 1. Tomar los dichos, contraer esponsales. 2. Inspirar confianza.

Affianced [af-fai'-anst], *a.* El que ha hecho un contrato matrimonial. *Affianced bride,* Novia desposada, prometida.

Affiancer [af-fai'-an-sẹr], *s.* 1. El o la que ha contraído o celebrado esponsales. (Coll.) El o la que ha dado la palabra. 2. El que toma los dichos a los que se van a casar.

Affiant [af-fai'-ant], *s.* El que hace declaración jurada; deponente, declarante.

Affidavit [af-i-dē'-vit], *s.* Declaración jurada.

Affied [af-faid'], *a.* Desposado.—*pp.* El o la que ha contraído esponsales.

Affiliate [af-fil'-i-ēt], *va.* 1. Prohijar, ahijar, adoptar. 2. Venir o quedar en íntimas relaciones: asociar (v. g. en una universidad o corporación).

Affiliated [af-fil'-i-ē-ted], *a.* 1. Prohijado, afiliado. 2. Asociado.

Affiliation [af-fil-i-ē'-shun], *s.* 1. Adopción. 2. Asociación, conexión, relación amistosa.

†**Affinage** [af-fai'-nēj], *s.* Ensaye de los metales.

Affined [af-faind'], *a.* Emparentado por afinidad.

Affinity [af-fin'-i-ti], *s.* 1. Afinidad, parentesco contraído por matrimonio. 2. Afinidad, relación o conexión.

Affirm [af-fẹrm], *vn.* 1. Afirmarse en alguna cosa. 2. Declarar formalmente, en especial ante un juez o con su sanción.—*va.* Confirmar, ratificar o aprobar alguna ley o fallo anterior; afirmar, declarar.

Affirmable [af-fẹrm'-a-bl], *a.* Lo que se puede afirmar.

Affirmably [af-fẹrm'-a-bli], *adv.* Afirmativamente.

Affirmance [af-fẹrm'-ans], *s.* Confirmación de alguna cosa.

Affirmant [af-fẹrm'-ant], *s.* Afirmante.

Affirmation [af-fer-mē'-shun], *s.* 1. Afirmación, la acción de afirmar. 2. Afirmación, aserto. 3. Confirmación, ratificación.

Affirmative [af-fẹrm'-a-tiv], *a.* Afirmativo.—*s.* Aserción, lo que contiene una afirmación.

Affirmatively [af-fẹrm'-a-tiv-li], *adv.* Afirmativamente, con aseveración.

Affirmed [af-fẹrmd'], *a.* Afirmado, ratificado.

Affirmer [af-fẹrm'-ẹr], *s.* Afirmante, el que afirma.

Affix [af-fix'], *va.* Anexar, unir al fin de otra cosa; añadir, fijar, pegar, atar, unir.

Affix [af'-ix], *s.* (Gram.) Afijo, partícula unida a una voz, particularmente un prefijo o sufijo.

Affixion [af-fic'-shun], *s.* Anexión, la unión de alguna partícula al fin de una voz; el acto de añadir.

Afflation [af-flē'-shun], *s.* Resuello, inspiración.

Afflatus [af-flē'-tus], *s.* 1. Inspiración divina. 2. (Med.) Exhalación, emanación.

Afflict [af-flict'], *va.* Afligir, causar dolor, pena o sentimiento, oprimir, inquietar, enfadar, desazonar, atormentar.—*vr.* Afligirse desconsolarse, amohinarse. *To be afflicted with,* Estar afligido, oprimido por o a causa de.

Afflictedness [af-flic'-ted-nes], *s.* Aflicción, pena, sentimiento.

Afflicting [af-flic'-ting], *a.* Penoso, devorador, atormentador.

Afflictingly [af-flic'-ting-li], *adv.* Opresivamente, afligidamente.

Affliction [af-flic'-shun], *s.* Aflicción, calamidad, miseria, dolor.

Afflictive [af-flic'-tiv], *a.* Aflictivo, lastimoso, penoso, molesto.

Afflictively [af-flic'-tiv-li], *adv.* Penosamente, afligidamente.

Affluence [af'-lū-ens], **Affluency** [af'-lū-en-si], *s.* 1. Concurrencia, concurso o junta de muchas personas. 2. Copia o abundancia, opulencia.

Affluent [af'-lū-ent], *a.* Opulento, afluente, abundante, copioso. *To be in affluent circumstances,* Estar en la opulencia.—*s.* Afluente, río que se echa en otro.

Affluently [af'-lū-ent-li], *adv.* Abundantemente, copiosamente.

Affluentness [af-lū-ent-nes], *s.* Opulencia, abundancia de riquezas.

Afflux [af'-flux], **Affluxion** [af-fluc'-shun], *s.* Concurrencia o confluencia; montón. Flujo.

Afford [af-fōrd'], *va.* 1. Dar, producir. 2. Dar o conceder alguna cosa. 3. Abastecer, proveer, proporcionar, franquear. *I cannot afford to sell it for less,* No puedo venderlo menos *or* por menos. *I cannot afford such expenses,* No puedo soportar semejantes gastos.

Afforest [af-fer'-est], *va.* Plantar un bosque.

Afforestation [af-fer-es-té'-shun], *s.* La plantación de un bosque.
Affranchise [af-fran'-chiz o af-fran'-chaiz], *va.* Manumitir, dar libertad al esclavo. *V.* ENFRANCHISE.
Affranchisement, *s.* *V.* ENFRANCHISEMENT.
Affray [af-fré'], *s.* Asalto o sorpresa tumultuaria, riña, pendencia, combate, tumulto.
Affreight [af-frét'], *va.* Fletar, alquilar un buque.
Affreightment [af-frét'-ment], *s.* Acción y efecto de fletar un buque.
Affriction [af-fric'-shun], *s.* Fricción, el acto de estregar una cosa con otra; frotación.
Affright [af-frait'], *va.* Aterrar, espantar, causar terror o espanto, atemorizar, asustar.
Affright, *s.* Terror, espanto; lo que causa miedo.
Affrightedly [af-frait'-ed-li], *adv.* Con espanto; espantosamente.
Affrighter [af-frait'-er], *s.* Asombrador, espantador, el que mete miedo o asombra.
Affront [af-frunt'], *vn.* Encararse, ponerse cara á cara con otro, engestarse.—*va.* 1. Afrentar, insultar, provocar, ultrajar, ajar. 2. Arrostrar, hacer frente.
Affront, *s.* Afrenta, sonrojo, bochorno, provocación, insulto, ultraje, injuria.
Affronter [af-frun'-ter], *s.* Agresor, provocador.
Affronting [af-frun'-ting], *part. a.* Injurioso, provocativo.
Affrontive [af-frun'-tiv], *a.* Afrentoso, injurioso.
Affuse [af-fiūz'], *va.* Echar alguna cosa líquida sobre otra; verter o derramar; difundir.
Affusion [af-fiū'-zhun], *s.* El acto de echar alguna cosa líquida sobre otra.
Afghan [af'-gan], *a.* 1. Afghan, ana, de Afganistán. 2. *s.* Género de cobertura de estambre trabajado a punto de aguja, o de crochet.
Afield [a-fīld'], *adv.* A campo travieso, fuera de camino, por el campo.
Afire [a-fair'], *adv.* Encendidamente, inflamado. En fuego.
Aflame [a-flēm'], *a.* En llamas. (Fig.) Inflamado.
Aflat [a-flat'], *adv.* Al ras con la tierra, a nivel del suelo.
Afloat [a-flōt'], *adv.* (Mar.) Flotante sobre el agua.
Afoot [a-fut'], *adv.* 1. Á pie. 2. En acción o movimiento. En preparación.
Afore [a-fōr'], *prep.* 1. Antes, más cerca, hablando de lugar. 2. Antes, con anterioridad de tiempo. 3. Delante.—*adv.* 1. Antes, anticipadamente, en tiempo pasado. 2. Primero; en frente. 3. (Mar.) A proa.
Aforegoing [a-fōr'-gō-ing], *a.* Antecedente, precedente.
Aforehand [a-fōr'-hand], *adv.* De antemano; con preparación.
Aforementioned [a-fōr'-men-shund], **Aforenamed** [a-fōr'-nēmd], **Aforesaid** [a-fōr'-sed], *a.* Susodicho, ya dicho, ya mencionado, sobredicho, antedicho, supracitado.
Aforethought [a-fōr'-thōt], *a.* Premeditado. *With malice aforethought,* Con premeditación.
Aforetime [a-fōr'-taim], *adv.* En otro tiempo, en tiempo pasado, antiguamente.
Afoul [a-faul'], *adv.* y *a.* En colisión; enredado.
Afraid [a-fréd'], *part. a.* Amedrentado, atemorizado, intimidado, espantado, temeroso, tímido. *I am afraid,* Temo, tengo miedo.
Afresh [a-fresh'], *adv.* De nuevo, otra vez.
African [af'-ri-can], **Afric** [af'-ric], *a.* y *s.* Africano.
Africander [af-ri-can'-der], *s.* El que ha nacido en Africa, pero es de raza europea.
Afront [a-frunt'], *adv.* Enfrente, al frente, de cara.
Aft [aft], *adv.* (Mar.) A popa o en popa. *To haul down the mizzen sheet aft,* Cazar del todo la escota de mesana.
After [af'-ter], *prep.* 1. Después. 2. Detrás, en seguimiento de. 3. Según. *After the manner,* Según, a la manera de.—*adv.* Después, en seguida de. *Soon after,* Poco después. *Day after to-morrow,* Pasado mañana. *Day after day,* Día tras día, cada día. *The day after.* El día siguiente.—*a.* Posterior, ulterior, subsiguiente. *After* se usa en muchas voces compuestas, pero casi siempre en el sentido de después. *After the example of,* Á ejemplo de.
After-acceptation [af'-ter-ac-sep-té'-shun], *s.* Aceptación tardía.
After-account [af'-ter-ac-caunt'], *s.* Cuenta nueva o venidera.
After-act [af'-ter-act], *s.* Acto subsiguiente.
After-age [af'-ter-êj], *s.* Posteridad, tiempo venidero. *After-ages,* Tiempos o siglos venideros.
After all [af'-ter ōl], *adv.* Después de todo, bien pensado todo.
After-attack [af'-ter-at-tac'], *s.* Ataque o choque subsiguiente.
After-birth [af'-ter-berth], *s.* Secundinas o parias. Placenta.
Afterburner [af'-ter-bur-ner], *s.* (Aer.) 1. Quemador auxiliar para motores de turborreacción. 2. Inyector del combustible.
After-clap [af'-ter-clap], *s.* Accidente o lance repentino que sucede después de acabarse al parecer alguna cosa; repetición de una acción. Golpe inesperado, revés.
After-comer [af'-ter-cum'-er], *s.* Sucesor, el que viene después.
After-conduct [af'-ter-con'-duct], *s.* Conducta subsiguiente.
After-conviction [af'-ter-con-vic'-shun], *s.* Convencimiento subsiguiente.
After-cost [af'-ter-cost], *s.* Gasto extraordinario.
After-course [af'-ter-cōrs], *s.* Viaje futuro. Proceder o conducta subsiguiente.
After-crop [af'-ter-crop], *s.* Segunda cosecha.
After-damp [aft'-er-damp], *s.* La mofeta que queda en las minas después de una explosión de fuego grisú.
After-days [af'-ter-dêz], *s.* Posteridad, tiempos venideros.
After-dinner [af'-ter-din'-er], *a.* Hecho u ocurrido después de la comida y antes de dejar mesa.—*s.* El tiempo que sigue a la comida. *At table after dinner,* De sobremesa.
After-endeavour [af'-ter-en-dev'-er], *s.* Nuevo esfuerzo.
After-game [af'-ter-gêm], *s.* Juego de desquite; medio ó recurso de que se vale uno después de haberle salido mal lo que intentó.
After-gathering [af'-ter-gadh'-er-ing], *s.* Rebusco, la acción de recoger después de otro; espigadura.
Afterglow [aft'-er-glō''], *s.* Brillo, viveza de color hacia el ocaso, despúes de la puesta del sol.
After-help [af'-ter-help], *s.* Socorro o auxilio subsiguiente.
After-hope [af-ter-hōp], *s.* Esperanza renovada.
After-hours [af'-ter-aurz], *s.* A horas extraordinarias; tarde.
After-inquiry [af'-ter-in-cwai'-ri], *s.* Exámen o investigación subsiguiente.
After-law [af'-ter-lō], *s.* Ley posterior.
After-life [af'-ter-laif], *s.* 1. El resto de la vida. 2. Vida venidera.
After-liver [af'-ter-liv'-er], *s.* Sobreviviente, venidero, descendiente; posteridad.
After-living [af'-ter-liv'-ing], *s.* *V.* AFTER-DAYS.
After-love [af'-ter-luv], *s.* Segunda pasión, nuevos amores.
Aftermath [af'-ter-math], *s.* 1. Segunda siega; la hierba que crece después de la primera cosecha de heno en la misma estación. 2. (Fig.) Las consecuencias de una acción o un acontecimiento.
After-meeting [af'-ter-mīt'-ing], *s.* Reunión o junta que sigue a otra.
Aftermost [af'-ter-mōst], *s.* (Mar.) El postrero, el último.
Afternoon [af'-ter-nūn], *s.* Tarde, el tiempo que media desde el mediodía hasta el anochecer.
After-pains [af'-ter-pênz], *s.* Dolores de sobreparto.
After-part [af-ter-part], *s.* Parte posterior.
Afterpiece [af'-ter-pīs], *s.* Sainete, entremés.
After-proof [af'-ter-prūf], *s.* Prueba o evidencia posterior.
After-reckoning [af'-ter-rec'-un-ing], *s.* Cuenta futura; nueva cuenta.
After-repentance [af'-ter-re-pent'-ans], *s.* Arrepentimiento tardío.
After-report [af'-ter-re-pōrt'], *s.* Noticia o conocimiento posterior.
After-state [af'-ter-stét], *s.* El estado o vida futura.
After-sting [af'-ter-sting], *s.* Picadura subsiguiente a otra.
After-supper [af'-ter-sup'-er], *s.* El tiempo entre cenar y acostarse.
After-taste [af'-ter-tést], *s.* Resabio, el sabor que deja alguna cosa; dejo, gustillo.
After-thought [af'-ter-thōt], *s.* Nuevo pensamiento, reflexión o reparo. (Fig.) Expediente tardío.—*adv.* Con madura reflexión.
After-times [af'-ter-taimz], *s.* Tiempos venideros, porvenir.
After-tossing [af'-ter-tes'-ing], *s.* Marejada, movimiento de las olas después de una borrasca.
After-touch [aft'-er-tuch], *s.* (Pint.) Retoque.
Afterward [af'-ter-ward] o **Afterwards** [wardz], *adv.* Después. *Long afterwards,* Mucho tiempo después. En prosa, *afterwards* es el más usado.
Afterwise [af'-ter-waiz], *a.* Discreto o prudente pasada la ocasión.
After-wit [af'ter-wit], *s.* Discurso o expediente fuera de sazón; entendimiento tardío.
Afterwitness [af'-ter-wit-nes], *s.* Testigo subsiguiente al acto o suceso de que se trata.
After-wrath [af'-ter-rath], *s.* Resentimiento, rencor.
Afterwriters [af'-ter-rai'-terz], *s.* Escritores sucesivos.

Aftward [qft'ward], *adv.* *V.* AFTERMOST.

Aga [ē'-ga], *s.* Agá, título de honor en Turquía.

Again [a-gen'], *adv.* 1. Otra vez, secunda vez, aun, de nuevo. 2. Por otra parte, además. 3. En recompensa. 4. Dos veces tanto. *Again and again,* Muchas veces. *As much again,* Otra tanto más. *To do again,* Volver a hacer. *He wrote again,* Él volvió a escribir. *I will not do so again,* No lo haré más. *Give it to me again,* Devuélvamelo Vd. *Come again to-morrow,* Vuelva Vd. mañana.

Against [a-genst'], *prep.* 1. Contra. 2. Enfrente. *Over against my house,* Enfrente de mi casa. 3. Para cuando. *Against we arrive,* Para cuando lleguemos. *Against Christmas,* Para Navidad. 4. Junto, cerca. *To be against,* Oponerse a, reprobar.

Agamic [a-gam'-ic], *a.* 1. Agámico, no provisto de órganos visibles de reproducción; asexual. 2. Producido sin unión, v. g. huevos agámicos.

Agamous [ag'-a-mus], *a.* Asexual, criptógamo.

Agapæ [ag'-a-pī], *s.* Ágape, comida de los primeros cristianos en las iglesias.

Agape [a-gāp' o a-gēp'], *adv.* Con la boca abierta.

Agapetæ [ag'-a-pet-ī], *s.* Agapetas, doncellas que en la primitiva iglesia vivian en comunidad, pero sin hacer voto alguno.

Agaric [ag'-a-ric], *s.* Agárico, género de hongos; droga medicinal que usan también los tintoreros.

Agasp [a-gasp'], *adv.* y *a.* En el último suspiro; con viva aspiración, anhelante, deseando ardientemente.

Agate [ag'-ēt], *s.* 1. Ágata, piedra preciosa. 2. Agata, carácter de letra de 5½ puntos: se llama *ruby* en Inglaterra.

☞ Esta línea está impresa en ágata.

Agaty [ag'-a-ti], *a.* Lo que participa de la naturaleza del ágata.

Agave [a-gē'-vī ó a-gā'-vē], *s.* Pita, maguey; erróneamente llamada áloe.

Agaze [a-gēz'], *a.* y *adv.* En el acto de mirar.

Age [ēj], *s.* 1. Edad. *Seventy years of age,* Setenta años de edad. 2. Edad o siglo, sucesión o generación de hombres. *The golden age,* El siglo de oro. 3. Siglo, centuria, el espacio de cien años. 4. Senectud, vejez. *Full age,* Mayoría o mayor edad. *Under age,* Minoridad. *He is under age,* Aun es menor, está en su minoridad. (Fam.) Es hijo de familia. *Of age,* En mayor edad. *Tender age,* Primera edad, la infancia. *Age of discretion,* La edad de la razón. *What is your age?* ¿Qué edad tiene Vd.?

Aged [ē'-jed], *a.* 1. Viejo, cargado de años, anciano. 2. De la edad de.

Agedly [ē-jed-li], *adv.* A manera de viejo.

Agency [ē'-jen-si], *s.* 1. Acción, operación. 2. Agencia, diligencia hecha por agente; intervención. *In the human agency,* En lo humano. 3. Agencia, empleo ó cargo de agente, de factor, etc. *Agency office,* Oficina de negocios. *Agency house,* Casa de comisión. 4. Influencia. *The agency of climate,* La influencia del clima.

Agend [a'-jend], *§* **Agendum** [a-jen'-dum], *s.* Agenda, libro de memoria.

Agent [ē'-jent], *a.* Operativo, lo que obra o causa efecto en otra cosa.—*s.* 1. Agente, el que solicita o gestiona en pro de negocios de otro. 2. Agente, lo que obra y tiene facultad de producir o causar algún efecto. 3. Factor, diputado, delegado. 4. Asistente, auxiliar.

Agentship [ē'-jent-ship], *s.* Agencia, factoría, el oficio de agente o factor.

Agglomerate [ag-glom'-er-ēt], *va.* Aglomerar, hacer ovillos; juntar o reunir en pelotón.

Agglutinant [ag-glū'-ti-nant], *a.* Conglutinativo, que sirve para unir y pegar.

Agglutinants [ag-glū'-ti-nants], *s. pl.* Aglutinantes, medicamentos que tienen virtud de adherir las partes desunidas.

Agglutinate [ag-glū'-ti-nēt], *va.* Conglutinar, trabar, unir, pegar.

Agglutination [ag-glū'-ti-nē'-shun], *s.* Conglutinación o trabazón de una cosa con otra, unión, ligazón.

Agglutinative [ag-glū'-ti-na-tiv], *a.* Conglutinativo, adhesivo.

Aggrandize [ag'-ran-daiz], *va.* 1. Engrandecer, hacer grande una cosa o mayor de lo que era. 2. Elevar, exaltar.—*vn.* Acrecentarse, aumentarse.

Aggrandizement [ag'-ran-daiz-ment ó ag-gran'-diz-ment], *s.* Engrandecimiento, elevación, exaltación.

Aggrandizer [ag'-ran-daiz-er], *s.* Ensalzador, el que engrandece a otro.

Aggravate [ag'-ra-vēt], *va.* 1. Agravar, hacer alguna cosa más pesada o dolorosa. 2. Hacer alguna cosa más enorme, exagerar. 3. Irritar.

Aggravating [ag'-ra-vēt-ing], *a.* Agravante; irritante, que molesta.

Aggravatingly [ag'-ra-vēt-ing-li], *adv.* Con agravación; de un modo irritante, que veja o impacienta.

Aggravation [ag-ra-vē'-shun], *s.* 1. Agravación. 2. Circunstancia agravante, lo que agrava algún delito. 3. Provocación, enormidad, exageración. 4. Vejación, molestia.

Aggregate [ag'-re-gēt], *a.* Agregado, juntado, unido.—*s.* Colección, agregado, el conjunto de muchas o varias cosas.

Aggregate, *va.* Agregar, añadir uniendo o juntando unas personas o cosas con otras, reunir, incorporar; admitir.

Aggregately [ag'-re-gēt-li], *adv.* Colectivamente.

Aggregation [ag-re-gē'-shun], *s.* 1. Agregación; agregado, colección. 2. Masa, conjunto, total. 3. Coherencia, agregado de cuerpos de distinta naturaleza.

Aggregative [ag'-re-gē-tiv], *a.* Colectivo, junto.

Aggregator [ag'-re-gē-ter], *s.* Colector, recaudador.

Aggress [ag-gres'], *vn.* Acometer, embestir, ofender, atacar.

Aggression [ag-gresh'-un], *s.* Agresión, acometimiento, ataque, asalto, ofensa sin motivo.

Aggressive [ag-gres'-iv], *a.* Agresivo; que tiene el carácter de agresión.

Aggressiveness [ag-gres'-iv-nes], *s.* Carácter agresivo; agresión.

Aggressor [ag-gres'-er], *s.* Agresor, el que acomete, ofende o provoca a otro.

Aggrievance [ag-grīv'-ans], *s.* Agravio, injuria, daño, perjuicio, pérdida.

Aggrieve [ag-grīv'], *va.* Apesadumbrar, dar pesadumbre, vejar, oprimir, gravar, dañar.—*vn.* Lamentar.

Aggroup [ag-grūp'], *va.* Agrupar.

Aghast [a-gqst'], *a.* Espantado, horrorizado, estupefacto, despavorido; fuera de sí; atolondrado de horror; azorado, alborotado. (Fam.) Con la boca abierta.

Agile aj'-il], *a.* Ágil, ligero, pronto, expedito, vivo.

Agility [a-jil'-i-ti], **Agileness** [aj'-il-nes], *s.* Agilidad, ligereza, expedición para hacer alguna cosa, prontitud.

Agillochum [a-jil'-o-cum], *s.* (Bot.) Áloe, madera del árbol así llamado.

Agio [aj'-i-o], *s.* (Com.) Agio, agiotaje, el lucro o interés que deja la negociación de billetes, cédulas de banco, letras, vales reales o cualquier papel-moneda.

Agist [a-jist'], *va.* (For. *§*) Apacentar ganado por un precio convenido.

Agistment [a-jist'-ment], *s.* (For.) 1. Modificación del diezmo. 2. Pasto, pasturaje. 3. Montón, terrón, gavilla. 4. Ajuste, composición.

Agistor [a-jis'-ter], *s.* (For.) Guardabosque.

Agitable [aj'-i-ta-bl], *a.* Agitable.

Agitate [aj'-i-tēt], *va.* 1. Agitar, mover, afectar. 2. Inquietar el ánimo. 3. Agitar una cuestión. 4. Maquinar, imaginar. 5. Debatir, disputar, discutir. *The narration greatly agitated her,* La narración la conmovió mucho.

Agitation [aj-i-tē'-shun], *s.* 1. Agitación, la acción y efecto de agitar. 2. Discusión, ventilación; deliberación; perturbación. *The project now in agitation,* El proyecto que actualmente se controvierte.

Agitator [aj'-i-tē-ter], *s.* Agitador, el que o lo que agita; incitador, instigador político.

Agleam [a-glīm'], *a.* (Poét.) Centelleante.

Aglet [ag'-let], *s.* 1. Herrete de agujeta o cordón. 2. Lámina u hoja de metal. *Aglets,* (Bot.) Borlillas, las puntas o remates de los estambres de las flores.

Agley [a-glē'], *adv.* (Escocés) Aparte, a un lado, al través o de través.

Aglow [a-glō'], *adv.* y *a.* En llamas, en incandescencia; ardiente, brillante.

Agnail [ag'-nēl], *s.* Panadizo, uñero.

Agnate, Agnatic [ag-nēt', ag-nat'-ic], *a.* Agnaticio. (For.) Agnado.

Agnathous [ag-nē'-thus], *a.* Que no tiene quijadas, o que las tiene rudimentarias. (Gr.)

Agnation [ag-nē'-shun], *s.* Agnación, descendencia de un mismo padre por línea masculina no interrumpida; alianza, conexión.

Agnomen [ag-nō'-men], *s.* Sobrenombre debido a algún acto o suceso determinado.

Agnominate [ag-nom'-i-nēt], *va.* Nombrar.

Agnomination [ag-nom-i-nē'-shun], *s.* 1. (Ret.) Agnominación o paronomasia. 2. *§*. Agnomento, cognomento, sobrenombre.

Agnostic [ag-nos'-tic], *a.* Agnóstico, relativo al agnosticismo o caracterizado por él; que aparenta ignorar. —*s.* Partidario de la teoría del agnosticismo.

Agnosticism [ag-nos'-tis-izm], *s.* Agnosticismo; doctrina que consiste en suponer que se ignora sistemáticamente todo lo que no cae bajo el dominio de los sentidos, Dios y el alma

humana inclusive. (Palabra propuesta por Huxley en 1869.)
Agnus castus [ag'-nus cas'-tus], *s.* (Bot.) Agnocasto o sauzgatillo.
Ago [a-gō'], *adv.* Largo tiempo, pasado, después. *Some time ago*, Hace algún tiempo. *Long ago*, Tiempo ha o mucho tiempo ha. *How long ago?* ¿Cuánto ha? *A good while ago*, Hace ya algún tiempo.
Agog [a-gog'], *adv.* Con deseo o antojo, con apresuramiento o ansia. *To be agog*, Tener gana, desear. *To set agog*, Dar gana, hacer desear.
Agoing [a-gō'-ing], *adv.* A punto de, dispuesto a, en acción, en movimiento.
Agometer [a-gom'-e-ter], *s.* Instrumento para medir o regular la resistencia eléctrica.
Agone [a-gōn'], *adv.* *V.* AGO.
Agonic [a-gon'-ic], *a.* Agono, lo que no tiene ángulos. (Gr.)
Agonism [ag'-o-nizm], *s.* Combate de atletas.
Agonistes, Agonist [ag-o-nis'-tīz], *s.* Atleta o combatiente; rival.
Agonistic, Agonistical [ag-o-nis'-tic, ag-o-nis'-ti-cal], *a.* Atlético.
Agonistically [ag-o-nis'-ti-cal-i], *adv.* Atléticamente.
Agonize [ag'-o-naiz], *vn.* 1. Estar agonizando o en las agonías de la muerte, en las últimas. 2. Luchar desesperadamente.
Agonizingly [ag-o-nai'-zing-li], *adv.* En agonías.
Agonothete [a-gō'-no-thīt], *s.* El que dirigía los juegos en la antigua Grecia.
Agonothetic [ag-o''-no-thet'-ic], *a.* Gímnico, lo que pertenece a los juegos o ejercicios públicos.
Agony [ag'-o-ni], *s.* 1. Agonía. 2. Agonía, angustia o aflicción extrema; paroxismo.
Agouti [a-gū'-ti], *s.* Agutí, roedor de la América tropical, del tamaño de un conejo.
Agraffe [a-graf'], *s.* 1. Broche o gancho, que a veces sirve de adorno. 2. Grapa sobre una cuerda del pianoforte para evitar la vibración entre ciertas piezas (el perno y el puente). (Fr. agrafe.)
Agraphia [a-graf'-i-a], *s.* Incapacidad de escribir por enfermedad del cerebro.
Agrarian [a-grē'-ri-an], *a.* 1. Agrario, lo que pertenece a los campos o tierras. *Agrarian law*, Ley agraria. Ley para la distribución de las tierras públicas entre los soldados y el pueblo. 2. Agreste, selvático. 3. Comunista.
Agrarianism [a-grē'-ri-an-izm], *s.* Agrarianismo. División igual de la propiedad raíz. Los principios o la práctica de los que favorecen la redistribución de las tierras.
Agree [a-grī'], *vn.* 1. Concordar, convenir, acordar. 2. Ceder, entenderse, ponerse de acuerdo. *I will never agree to it*, Jamás cederé o jamás convendré en ello. 3. Estipular. 4. Ajustar el precio. 5. Convenir. *The authors do not agree in this*, Los autores no convienen o no son del mismo parecer en esto. *To agree in opinion*, Ser de la misma opinión. 6. Acomodar o acomodarse, venir bien una cosa con otra. *That climate does not agree with me*, Aquel clima no me prueba. 7. Sentar bien. *Chocolate does not agree with me*, El chocolate no me sienta bien.—*va.* Adaptar, acomodar, reconciliar.
Agreeability [a-grī-a-bil'-i-ti], *s.* Afabilidad, agrado.
Agreeable [a-grī'-a-bl], *a.* 1. Conveniente, proporcionado. 2. Agradable, lo que agrada, conforme, amable.
Agreeableness [a-grī'-a-bl-nes], *s.* 1. Conformidad, proporción. 2. Agrado, afabilidad. 3. Semejanza. 4. Amabilidad, gracia.
Agreeably [a-grī'-a-bli], *adv.* Según; agradablemente.
Agreed [a-grīd'], *part. a.* 1. Convenido, establecido, ajustado, determinado, aprobado. 2. De acuerdo.
Agreeingly [a-grī'-ing-li], *adv.* Conforme.
Agreeingness [a-grī'-ing-nes], *s.* Conformidad, conveniencia, proporción, aptitud.
Agreement [a-grī'-ment], *s.* 1. Concordia, conformidad, unión, correlación, conveniencia. 2. Semejanza de una cosa con otra. 3. Ajuste, convenio. *To come to an agreement*, Convenirse, ajustarse. 4. Contrato transacción, tratado, acomodamiento.
Agrestial, Agrestic, Agrestical [a-gres'-tial, a-gres'-tic, a-gres'-ti-cal], *a.* Agreste, rústico, tosco, campestre, grosero, descortés.
Agricole [ag'-ri-cōl], *s.* (Poco us.) **Agricultor** [ag-ri-cul'-tor], *s.* Agricultor. *V.* AGRICULTURIST.
Agricultural [ag-ri-cul'-chur-al], *a.* Agricultural.
Agriculture [ag'-ri-cul-chur], *s.* Agricultura, el arte de cultivar la tierra.
Agriculturist [ag-ri-cul'-chur-ist], *s.* Labrador, agricultor, agrícola.
Agriculturism [ag-ri-cul'-chur-izm], *s.* La ciencia de la agricultura.
Agrimony [ag'-ri-mo-ni], *s.* (Bot.) Agrimonia.
Agrin [a-grin'], *adv.* En el acto de hacer visajes, o de rechinar los dientes.
Agronomics [ag-ro-nom'-ics], *s.* Agrografía, descripción de las cosas del campo relacionadas con la agricultura; ciencia que trata de la distribución y la administración de la tierra, especialmente considerada como fuente de riqueza.
Agronomist [a-gron'-o-mist], *s.* Agrónomo.
Agronomy [a-gron'-o-mi], *s.* Agronomía, arte y teoría de la agricultura.
Agrope [a-grōp'], *adv.* En el acto de tentar; a tientas, a ciegas.
Aground [a-graund'], *adv.* 1. (Mar.) Barado, encallado. *The ship ran aground*, La embarcación baró o dió en un bajío, o en un banco. 2. Empantanado, embarazado, impedido en el progreso de algún asunto.
Ague [ē'-giū], *s.* Fiebre o calentura intermitente; calofrío, escalofrío. *Dumb ague*, Una forma de fiebre intermitente en la que los síntomas no se manifiestan, o aparecen de una manera vaga e indefinida.
§**Ague**, *va.* Acometer una calentura intermitente.
Agued [ē'-giūd], *a.* Febricitante, tercianario, calenturiento.
Ague-cake [ē-giū-kēk], *s.* Hinchazón del bazo resultante de la fiebre intermitente.
Ague-fit [ē'-giū-fit], *s.* Accesión o paroxismo de una calentura intermitente.
Ague-proof [ē'-giū-prūf], *a.* Capaz de resistir las calenturas, a prueba de calentura.
Ague-spell [ē'-giū-spel], *s.* Encanto o hechizo para curar la calentura intermitente.
Ague-struck [ē'-giū-struc], *a.* Acometido de calentura.
Ague-tree [ē'-giu-trī], *s.* Sasafrás, árbol medicinal de la Virginia.
Aguish [ē'-giu-ish], *a.* Febricitante ó calenturiento; que se calofría, friolente; atacado de paludismo.
Aguishness [ē'-giu-ish-nes], *s.* Calofrío o síntoma de fiebre intermitente.
Ah! [ā], *inter.* ¡Ah! ¡ay!
Aha! Aha! [a-hā'], *inter.* ¡Ha, ha!
Ahead [a-hed'], *adv.* 1. Más allá, delante de otro. 2. (Mar.) Por la proa, avante. 3. Temerariamente. *To be ahead*, Ir a la cabeza, ir delante. *To get ahead*, Adelantar o ganar la delantera; también, tener el riñón bien cubierto. *Go ahead!* ¡Adelante! ¡avancen! *To forge ahead*, Avanzar rápidamente como cuando un buque da fondo inmediatamente después de aferrar velas; también, avanzar lentamente. *To run ahead*, Obrar sin reflexión. *To run ahead of one's reckoning*, Perder la cuenta.
Aheap [a-hīp'], *adv.* En montón, en medio de un montón.
Aheight, Ahigh [a-hait'], *adv.* (Ant.) Arriba, en lo alto.
Ahold [a-hōld'], *adv.* (Mar.) Al viento.
Ahoy [a-hoi'], *inter.* ¡Ah del barco! ¡Ha! Voz para llamar a los de un buque o bote.
Ahungry [a-hung'-gri], *a.* Hambriento.
Aid [ēd], *va.* Ayudar, auxiliar, socorrer, coadyuvar, apoyar.
Aid, *s.* 1. Ayuda, auxilio. 2. Subsidio, socorro que se da al gobierno como tributo extraordinario. 3. Ayudante, la persona que ayuda o asiste.
Aide-de-camp [ēd-'de-cañ'], *s.* Edecán, ayudante de campo.
Aider [ēd'-er], *s.* Auxiliador, auxiliante.
Aidless [ēd'-les], *a.* Desvalido, desamparado, dejado.
Aigre [ē'-ger], *s.* Flujo impetuoso del mar.
Aigret [ē'-gret], *s.* *V.* EGRET. Cresta, penacho; plumero.
Aigulet [ē'-giu-let], *s.* Herrete de agujeta o franja.
Ail [ēl], *va.* Afligir, molestar, causar alguna pena o dolor. *What ails you?* ¿Qué le duele á Vd.? ¿qué tiene Vd.? ¿qué hay? *Nothing ails me*, Nada me duele, nada tengo. Este verbo se usa siempre de un modo indefinido y para inquirir acerca de algún dolor o pena.—*vn.* Sufrir, estar indispuesto.
Ailanthus ó **Ailantus** [ē-lan'-thus, tus], *s.* Ailanto, árbol del cielo, de China.
Aileron [ē'-le-ren], *s.* (Aer.) Alerón.
Ailing [ēl'-ing], *a.* Doliente, achacoso, enfermizo, valetudinario.
Ailment [ēl'-ment], *s.* Dolencia, indisposición, dolor, incomodidad.
Aim [ēm], *vn.* 1. Apuntar, asestar el tiro de alguna arma de fuego o arrojadiza. 2. Tirar, poner los medios dirigiéndolos a algún fin, poner la mira en alguna cosa. 3. Adivinar.—*va.* Apuntar o dirigir el tiro con el ojo, aspirar a, pretender, intentar, maquinar.
Aim, *s.* 1. Puntería. 2. Blanco, la señal fija á que se tira con alguna arma arrojadiza ó de fuego. *To miss one's aim*, Errar el tiro. *To*

take one's aim well, Tomar bien sus medidas. 3. Designio, mira, fin u objeto.

Aimless [ēm'-les], *a.* Sin objeto, sin designio, á la ventura.

Ain't [ēnt], *v.* (Vulg.) *V.* A'N'T.

Air [ār], *s.* 1. Aire, la atmósfera, el fluido que respiramos. *To take the air*, Tomar el aire. 2. Zéfiro, viento ligero. 3. Tono, tonada, aire de música. 4. Cara, semblante, aire o disposición personal de alguno. Ademán, exterior, modo, porte de una persona. 5. Olor; vapor. *Factitious airs* o *gases*, Aire facticio. *Open air*, Al raso. *Foul air*, Aire viciado.

Air, *va.* Airear, estar o poner al aire; secar. *To air a room*, Orear o ventilar un cuarto. *To air a shirt*, Secar una camisa a la lumbre o al fuego.

Air age [ār' ēj], *s.* Edad o era de la aviación.

Air-balloon [ār'-bal-ūn], *s.* Globo aerostático.

Air base [ār'-bēs], *s.* Base aérea.

Air-bladder [ār'-blad-ęr], *s.* Vejiga llena de aire.

Air blast [ār'-blast], *s.* Chorro de aire.

Air-borne [ār'-bōrn], *a.* (Mil.) Aéreo, transportado por el aire.

Air-brake [ār'-brēc], *s.* Freno neumático, o de aire.

Air brush [ār' brush], *s.* Aerógrafo.

Air-chamber [ār'-chēm-br], *s.* Cámara de aire.

Air-cock [ār'-coc], *s.* Espita para permitir la salida del aire.

Air-condition [ār-con-dish'-un], *va.* Acondicionar el aire.

Air-conditioned [ār-con-dish'-und], *a.* Con aire acondicionado, con clima artificial.

Air-conditioner [ar-con-dish'-un-ęr], *s.* Acondicionador del aire, aparato para acondicionar el aire.

Air-conditioning [ār-con-dish'-un-ing], *s.* Acondicionamiento del aire, clima artificial.

Air-cooled [ār'-cūld], *a.* Enfriado por aire.

Air-cooling [ār-cūl'-ing], *s.* Enfriamiento por aire.

Aircraft [ār'-craft], *s.* Aeronave. *Aircraft carrier*, Portaaviones.

Air-drill [ār'-dril], *s.* Taladro neumático.

Airdrome [ār'-drōm], *s.* Aeródromo.

Air-engine [ār-en'-jin], *s.* Máquina de aire. El aire caliente reemplaza en ella al vapor.

Airfoil [ār'-foil], *s.* (Aer.) Cualquier superficie, como las de las alas o el timón, que al cambiar de posición modifica la dirección del vuelo.

Air force [ār' fors], *s.* Fuerza aérea.

Airfreight [ār' frēt], *s.* Flete aéreo.

Air gun [ār'gun], *s.* Escopeta de viento.

Air-hole [ār'-hōl], *s.* 1. Respiradero, lumbrera, la abertura por donde entra y sale el aire. 2. Paja (en el hierro, etc.).

Airily [ār'-i-li], *adv.* Ligeramente; vivamente, alegremente.

Airiness [ār'-i-nes], *s.* 1. Ventilación, oreo. 2. Vivacidad, viveza. 3. Ligereza, actividad.

Airing [ār'-ing], *s.* 1. Caminata, viaje corto que se hace por diversión; paseo para tomar el aire. 2. Ventilación.

Airless [ār'-les], *a.* Falto de ventilación, sofocado.

Airletter [ār'-let-ęr], *s.* Carta aérea o por avión.

Air lift [ār'-lift], *s.* Puente aéreo de transporte.

Air line [ār' lain], *s.* 1. Línea aérea. 2. Compañía de aviación.

Air liner [ār lain'-ęr], *s.* Gran avión de pasajeros.

Air lock [ār'-loc], *s.* (Mec.) Cámara de presión intermedia.

Air mail [ār' mēl], *s.* Vía aérea, correo aéreo.

Air mail [ār' mēl], *a.* Aeropostal, por avión.

Airman [ār'-man], *s.* Aviador.

Air-mattress [ār'-mat'-res], *s.* Colchón de aire.

Air meet [ār' mīt], *s.* Concurso aéreo; congreso de aeronáutica.

Air-minded [ār' maind-ed], *a.* Interesado en la aviación.

Air-pipe [ār'-paip], *s.* Cañería para extraer el aire viciado; tubo de goma para dar aire a los buzos.

Airplane [ār'-plēn], *s.* Avión, aeroplano. *Airplane carrier*, Portaaviones.

Air-plant [ār'-plant], *s.* Epifito.

Air pocket [ār pok'-et], *s.* (Aer.) Bolsa de aire.

Airport [ār'-pōrt], *s.* Puerto aéreo, aeropuerto, aeródromo.

Airproof [ār'-prūf], *a.* Hermético.

Air-pump [ār'-pump], *s.* Bomba de aire; bomba neumática.

Air raid [ār' rēd], *s.* Incursión aérea, ataque o bombardeo aéreo.

Air-raid shelter [ār'-rēd shel-tęr], *s.* Refugio contra aeroplanos.

Air-sac [ār'-sac], *s.* Celda para aire, en las aves.

Air-shaft [ār'-shaft], *s.* Respiradero de mina.

Airship [ār'-ship], *s.* Aeronave.

Air sickness [ār sic'-nes], *s.* Mareo en el aire.

Air speed [ār' spīd], *s.* Velocidad aérea.

Airstrip [ār'-strip], *s.* Pista de despegue, pista de aterrizaje.

Air-tight [ār'-tait], *a.* Herméticamente cerrado o tapado.

Airway [ār'-wē], *s.* Aerovía, vía aérea.

Airy [ār'-i], *a.* 1. Aéreo, lo que es del aire o pertenece a él. 2. Aéreo, ligero, trivial, lo que no tiene solidez ni fundamento. 3. Vivaz, vivo, alegre. 4. Abierto, vano, sin substancia. 5. Vano, orgulloso, altanero.

Aisle [ail], *s.* Nave de una iglesia. Ala, costado.

Ajar [a-jār'], *adv.* y *a.* 1. Semiabierto, entreabierto. Entornado. 2. En desacuerdo.

Akimbo [a-kim'-bo], *a.* En jarras, o en asas.

Akin [a-kin'], *a.* 1. Consanguíneo, emparentado. 2. Del mismo género, de cualidades conformes.

Alabaster [al-a-bas'-tęr], *s.* Alabastro, especie de mármol blanco lechoso, y a veces con tintas de color.

Alabaster, *a.* Alabastrino, de alabastro.

Alacrity [a-lac'-ri-ti], *s.* Alegría, buen humor; ardor, celo.

Aland [a-land'], *adv.* A tierra.

Alarm [a-lārm'], *s.* 1. Alarma, toque para tomar las armas. 2. Sobresalto, alarma, grito o señal para advertir un peligro. 3. Reloj con despertador.

Alarm, *va.* 1. Tocar al arma. 2. Alarmar, asustar, sorprender: perturbar, inquietar.

Alarm-bell [a-lārm'-bel], *s.* Campana de rebato.

Alarm-clock [a-lārm'-cloc], *s.* Despertador; reloj despertador.

Alarming [a-lārm'-ing], *a.* Alarmante, sorprendente.

Alarmingly [a-lārm'-ing-li], *adv.* Espantosamente; de modo alarmente.

Alarmist [a-lārm'-ist], *s.* Alarmista, el que alarma o asusta.

Alarm-post [a-lārm'-pōst], *s.* Atalaya, puesto de aviso.

Alarm-watch [a-lārm'-wēch], *s.* Reloj con despertador.

Alarum [a-lār'-um], *s.* *V.* ALARM.

Alas [a-las'], *inter.* ¡Ay! *V.* ALACK!

Alate [ē'-lēt], **Alated** [ē'-lē-ted], *a.* Alado, con alas.

Alb [alb], *s.* Alba, vestidura de lienzo blanco que se ponen los sacerdotes para celebrar la misa y otros oficios divinos.

Albanian [al-bē'-ni-an], *a.* Albanés.

Albatross [al'-ba-tros], *s.* Albatros.

Albeit [āl-bī'-it], *adv.* Aunque, bien que, no obstante, sin embargo, con todo.

Albescent [al-bes'-ent], *a.* Blanquecino.

Albigenses [al-bi-jen'-sez], *s.* Albigenses, nombre de unos sectarios franceses.

Albino [al-bī'-no], *s.* Albino.

Albion [al'-bi-an], *s.* Albión, nombre antiguo de Inglaterra.

Albugineous [al-biu-jin'-ę-us], *a.* Albuginoso, lo que tiene apariencia de clara de huevo.

Album [al'-bum], *s.* 1. Librito de memoria. 2. Album, libro en que los amigos o conocidos del dueño de él, escriben alguna máxima suya o de otros, o alguna composición original, para que se conserve como autógrafa. 3. Libro para conservar fotografías, sellos de correo, etc.

Albumen o **Albumin** [al-biū'-men], *s.* 1. (Quím.) Albúmina, clara de huevo. 2. (Bot.) Albumen, materia nutritiva que rodea la semilla en muchas plantas.

Albumenize [al-biū'-men-aiz], *va.* Impregnar con albumen, como se hace con el papel para la fotografía.

Albuminoid [al-biū'-min-oid], *a.* Albuminiforme.—*s.* Albuminoide, principio albuminoso que forma gran parte de los tejidos animales.

Albuminous [al-biū'-min-us], *a.* Albuminoso: que contiene albumen.

Albuminuria [al-biu-min-ū'-ri-a], *s.* Albuminuria; albúmina en la orina.

Alburnum [al-būr'-num], *s.* (Bot.) Alburno o albura, la materia blanca que se halla entre la corteza y la madera del árbol. *V.* SAPWOOD.

Alcaic [al-kē'-ic], *s.* Verso alcaico.—*a.* Alcaico.

Alcaid [al-kēd'], *s.* Alcaide de un castillo.

Alchemist [al'-kę-mist], *s.* Alquimista, el que profesa el arte de la alquimia.

Alchemy [al'-kę-mi], *s.* 1. Alquimia, el arte quimérica de purificar y trasmutar los metales. 2. Metal trabajado con el arte de la alquimia.

Alcohol [al'-co-hol], *s.* Alcohol. *Denatured alcohol*, Alcohol desnaturalizado. *Grain alcohol*, Alcohol de granos. *Wood alcohol*, Alcohol metílico

Alcoholic [al-co-hol'-ic], *a.* Alcohólico, que tiene alcohol, o las cualidades de él; producido por alcohol; conservado en alcohol.—*s. pl.* Líquidos alcohólicos.

Alcoholimeter [al-co-hol-im'-ę-tęr], **Al-**

coholmeter [al-co-hol-mī'-tẹr], **Alcoholometer** [al-co-hol-om'-ẹ-tẹr], *s.* Alcoholímetro, alcohómetro, especie de areómetro para medir la fuerza del alcohol.
Alcoholism [al'-co-hol-izm], *s.* Alcoholismo, enfermedad causada por el uso desarreglado o prolongado de bebidas alcohólicas.
Alcoholization [al-co-hol-i-zé'-shun], *s.* Alcoholización, el acto de alcoholar o alcoholizar.
Alcoholize [al'-co-hol-aiz], *va.* Alcoholar o alcoholizar, extraer y rectificar el espíritu de cualquier licor.
Alcoran [al-co-rān'], *s.* Alcorán, libro que contiene la ley de Mahoma con sus ritos y creencia. *V.* KORAN.
Alcoranish [al-co-ran'-ish], *a.* Lo que pertenece al alcorán.
Alcove [al'-cōv], *s.* 1. Alcoba, pieza o aposento destinado para dormir. 2. Cenador, glorieta o emparrado de jardín.
Alcyon [al'-si-on], *a.* y *s.* Lo mismo que HALCYON.
Aldebaran [al-deb'-ar-an], *s.* (Astr.) Aldebarán, estrella principal de la constelación Tauro.
Aldehyde [al'-de-haid], *s.* (Quím.) Aldehido; líquido incoloro y muy volátil, obtenido por la oxidación del alcohol. (Abreviado de *al*cohol *dehyd*ratum.)
Alder [ōl'-dẹr], *s.* (Bot.) Aliso, árbol que tiene las hojas algo parecidas a las del avellano.
Alderman [ōl'-dẹr-man], *s.* Regidor.
Alderman-like [ōl'-dẹr-man-laic], *a.* Magisterial; a manera de regidor.
Aldermanly [ōl'-dẹr-man-li], *a.* Como un regidor, con gravedad.
Aldern [ōl'-dẹrn], *a.* Hecho de aliso.
Ale [ēl], *s.* Cerveza fuerte.
Aleak [a-līk'], *adv.* y *a.* En el acto de verterse y estado de perderse un líquido, en avería; derramándose.
Aleatory [ē'- (ó ą'-) lẹ-a-to-ri], *a.* 1. Aleatorio, dependiente de un suceso fortuito. 2. Relativo o perteneciente a tahures y fulleros.
Ale-bench [ēl-bench], *s.* Mostrador que suele ponerse en frente de las tabernas o casas en que se vende cerveza.
Aleberry [ēl'-ber-i], *s.* Bebida hecha de cerveza hervida con especias, azúcar y tostadas de pan.
Ale-brewer [ēl-brū-ẹr], *s.* Cervecero, el que por oficio hace la cerveza llamada *ale.*
Ale-conner [al'-con-ẹr], *s.* Oficial o inspector de las cervecerías de Londres.
Alecost [ēl'-cost], *s.* (Bot.) *V.* TANZY.
A-lee [a-lī'], *adv.* (Mar.) A sotavento.
Ale-fed [ēl'-fed], *a.* Alimentado con cerveza.
Alegar [ēl'-e-gār], *s.* (Prov. Ingla.) Cerveza agria, vinagre de cerveza.
Alehoof [ēl'-hūf], *s.* Hiedra terrestre.
Alehouse [ēl'-haus], *s.* Cervecería.
Alehouse-keeper [ēl'-haus-kīp-ẹr], *s.* Cervecero.
Alembic [a-lem'-bic], *s.* Alambique.
Alert [a-lẹrt'], *a.* 1. Alerta, cuidadoso, vigilante. 2. Vivo, activo, dispuesto. *To be on the alert,* Estar alerta.
Alertness [a-lẹrt'-nes], *s.* Cuidado, vigilancia, viveza, actividad, diligencia, agilidad; alegría.
Ale-stake [ēl'-stēc], *s.* Ramo o palo que se pone en las cervecerías, al modo que en España se cuelga un ramo a la puerta de las tabernas.
Ale-taster [ēl'-tēs-tẹr], *s.* Inspector oficial encargado de examinar la calidad de la cerveza.
Aleutian [a-lū'-shan ó al-ẹ-ū'-shi-an], *a.* Aleuta, aleutino.
Ale-vat [ēl'-vat], *s.* Cuba o tina en que fermenta la cerveza.
Ale-washed [ēl-wesht], *a.* (Ant.) Mojado en cerveza.
Alewife [ēl'-waif], *s.* 1. Cervecera, la mujer del cervecero. 2. Pez norteamericano, parecido a un sábalo pequeño; empléase generalmente como abono. Clupea pseudoharengus. Propiamente, *aloof,* nombre indígena de este pez.
Alexanders [al'-eg-zan-dẹrz], *s.* (Bot.) Esmirnio, o apio caballar.
Alexandrine [al-eg-zan'-drin], *s.* Verso alejandrino.
Alexipharmic, Alexiteric, ó **Alexiterical** [a-lec-si-fār'-mic, a-lec-si-ter'-ic, a-lec-si-ter'-i-cal], *a.* Alexifármaco o alexitérico, medicamento que tiene virtud preservativa o correctiva de los malos efectos del veneno.
Alfalfa [al-fal'-fa], *s.* Alfalfa.
Alfilaria [al-fil-ē'-ri-a], *s.* Hierba de California que se emplea como forraje. Erodium cicutarium. *Cf.* ALFILERERA.
Al fresco [āl-fres'-co]. Al raso. (Ital.)
Alga [al'-ga], *pl.* **Algæ** [al'-jī], *s.* (Bot.) Alga, planta que se cría en las aguas, particularmente en el mar.
Algal [al'-gal], *a.* Algáceo, perteneciente a las algas.
Algaroth [al'-ga-roth], *s.* Régulo de antimonio.
Algebra [al'-je-bra], *s.* Álgebra, parte de las matemáticas.
Algebraic, Algebraical [al-je-brē'-ic, al-je-brē'-i-cal], *a.* Algebraico, lo que pertenece al álgebra.
Algebraist [al-je-brē'-ist], *s.* Algebrista.
Algerian [al-jī'-ri-an], *a.* Argelino: de Argel.
Algerine [al-jẹ-rīn'], *a.* y *s.* 1. Argelino, natural de Argel. 2. *s.* Tejido blando de lana o chal con franjas de color claro.
Algid [al'-jid], *a.* Álgido; que hiela, o causa frío.
Algoid [al'-goid], *a.* Algáceo, algoide, que se parece a las algas.
Algology [al-gol'-o-ji], *s.* Estudio o ciencia que trata de las algas.
Algous [al'-gus], *a.* Algoso; que pertenece a las algas: o lleno de algas.
Algorithm [al'-go-ridhm], *s.* Algoritmo, ciencia del cálculo aritmético y algebraico; teoría de los números.
Alguazil [al-gwa-zil], *s.* Alguacil, corchete, esbirro.
Alias [ē'-li-as], *adv.* Alias, voz latina que significa *de otro modo, de otra manera,* o *por otro nombre.*
Alibi [al'-i-bai], *s.* (For.) Voz latina que significa ausencia, esto es, no haber estado en un lugar al tiempo de que se trata; coartada. *To prove an alibi,* Probar la coartada.
Alible [al'-i-bl], *a.* Nutritivo.
Alidade [al'-i-dēd], *s.* Alidada, regla movediza que gira alrededor del centro de un instrumento y sirve para medir los ángulos.
Alien [ēl' yen], *a.* Ajeno, extraño; forastero, extranjero; discorde, contrario.
Alien, *s.* Extranjero, forastero.
Alien, *va.* *V.* ALIENATE.
Alienable [ēl'-yen-a-bl], *a.* Enajenable, traspasable.
Alienate [ēl'-yen-ēt], *va.* 1. Enajenar, transferir, ceder. 2. Enajenar, desviar o apartar el afecto o cariño que se tenía hacia alguna persona; indisponer.
Alienate, *a.* Ajeno, enajenado.—*s.* Extranjero.
Alienation [ēl-yen-ē'-shun], *s.* 1. Enajenamiento o enajenación, la acción y efecto de enajenar o traspasar el dominio. 2. Enajenamiento, el acto de entibiarse la amistad y correspondencia entre dos o más personas; desunión, frialdad, desavenencia, desvío. 3. Enajenación del ánimo, locura, desbarro, devaneo.
Alienator [ēl-yen-ē'-tẹr], *s.* Enajenador, cesionista. El que enajena a otro.
Alienee [ēl-yen-ī'], *s.* Aquel a quien pasa la propiedad de una cosa.
Alienism [ēl'-yen-izm], *s.* 1. El estado legal de un extranjero. 2. El tratamiento de las enfermedades mentales.
Alienist [ēl'-yen-ist], *s.* (Med.) Alienista, especialista en enfermedades mentales.
Alienor [ēl'-yen-or], *s.* Enajenante: el o la que enajena.
†**Aliferous, Aligerous** [a-lif'-ẹr-us, a-lij'-ẹr-us], *a.* Alado, lo que tiene alas. (Poét.) Alígero.
Aliform [al'-i-fōrm], *a.* Aliforme, en forma de alas.
Alight [a-lait'], *vn.* 1. Descender, bajar de un coche, etc. *To alight from a horse,* Apearse de un caballo. 2. Echarse sobre alguna cosa, caer, posarse. 3. Caer en cuenta de alguna cosa por casualidad.—*a.* y *adv.* Encendido, inflamado; en llamas.
Align [a-lain'], *va.* Alinear, poner en línea. Lo mismo que ALINE.
Alignment [a-lain'-mẹnt], *s.* Alineamiento, acción y efecto de alinear.
Alike [a-laic'], *adv.* 1. Igualmente, del mismo modo. 2. A la vez.—*a.* Semejante, igual.
Alike-minded [a-laic'-maind-ed], *a.* Del mismo ánimo, o modo de pensar.
Alimental [al-i-men'-tal], *a.* Nutritivo, lo que nutre o alimenta, alimenticio, alimentoso.
Alimentally [al-i-men'-tal-i], *adv.* Nutritivamente.
Alimentariness [al-i-men'-ta-ri-nes], *s.* Alimentación, nutrición.
Alimentary [al-i-men'-ta-ri], *a.* 1. Alimenticio, lo que toca al alimento. 2. Alimentoso, lo que tiene virtud de alimentar, jugoso.
Alimentation [al-i-men-tē'-shun], *s.* Alimentación.
Alimentiveness [al-i-men'-tiv-nes], *s.* Apetito o deseo de tomar alimento.
Alimonious [al-i-mō'-ni-us], *a.* Alimenticio, alimentoso.
Alimony [al'-i-mo-ni], *s.* Alimentos, asistencias, la parte de los bienes del marido, que por sentencia judicial se señala a la mujer por causa de divorcio o separación.
Aline [a-lain'], *va.* Poner en línea, alinear.—*vn.* Ponerse en línea.
Aliped [al'-i-ped], *a.* Alípede, quiróptero.
Aliquant [al'-i-cwant], *a.* Alicuanta, la parte que no mide cabalmente a su todo; así, tres es alicuanta de diez.
Aliquot [al'-i-cwot], *a.* Alícuota, la parte que mide cabalmente a su todo; p. ej. tres es parte alícuota de doce.
Alish [ēl'-ish], *a.* Acervezado, parecido o semejante a la cerveza llamada *ale.*

Alive [a-laiv'], *a.* 1. Vivo o viviente. 2. Vivo, no apagado, ni destruido. 3. Activo, vivo, alegre. 4. Se usa muchas veces enfáticamente para ponderar: v. g. *The best man alive,* El mejor hombre que existe, o que hay entre los vivientes.

Alkahest, *s. V.* ALCAHEST.

Alkalescent [al-ca-les'-ent], *a.* Alcalescente, lo que tiene tendencia o propiedades alcalinas.

Alkalescence [al-ca-les'-cns], *s.* Alcalescencia.

Alkali [al'-ca-lai], *s.* Álcali, cualquiera substancia que mezclada con los ácidos produce sales: base.

Alkalify [al-cal'-i-fai o al'-ca-li-fai]], *va.* Convertir en álcali.

Alkaligenous [al-ca-lij'-en-us], *a.* Alcalígeno, generador de álcalis.

Alkalimeter [al-ca-lim'-e-ter], *s.* Alcalímetro, instrumento para medir la cantidad de álcali que contiene una substancia.

Alkaline [al'-ca-lain], *a.* Alcalino, lo que tiene propiedades de álcali.

Alkalinity [al-ca-lin'-i-ti], *s.* Alcalinidad, estado alcalino, efecto de los álcalis.

Alkalization [al-ca-li-zé'-shun], *s.* Alcalización.

Alkalize [al'-ca-laiz], *va.* Alcalizar, hacer alcalino.

Alkaloid [al'-ca-leid], *s.* Alcaloide, álcali orgánico o vegetal; base orgánica.

Alkanet [al'-ca-net], *s.* (Bot.) Búgula o melera; ancusa.

Alkermes [al-ker'-miz], *s.* Alquermes, confección cuyo principal ingrediente es el quermes.

All [ōl], *a.* 1. Todo, lo que se comprende entera y cabalmente en el número. *All hands aloft,* (Mar.) Todo el mundo arriba. *All hands below,* (Mar.) Todo el mundo abajo. 2. Todo, lo que se comprende entera y cabalmente en la cantidad. *All his money is spent,* Todo su dinero se ha gastado.

All, *s.* Todo, el compuesto de partes integrantes. *All in the wind,* (Mar.) En facha. *When all comes to all,* Con todo eso, en fin. *It is all the same,* Es absolutamente lo mismo. *For good and all,* Enteramente, para siempre. *To be all in all with one,* Ser el favorito de alguna persona. *Not at all,* No por cierto, nada de eso, de ninguna manera. *All along,* Por todo el tiempo, siempre. *By all means,* Sin duda, absolutamente, sea como fuere. *He is undone to all intents and purposes,* Está enteramente arruinado o perdido. *For all, loc. prep.* A pesar de.

All, *adv.* Del todo, enteramente. *All on a sudden,* De golpe y porrazo, de repente, repentinamente. *All the better,* Tanto mejor. *All the worse,* Tanto peor. *All at once* De repente, de golpe.

ALL, muchas veces se une con adjetivos y participios, como se ve por los siguientes. En las voces *Almighty, Already,* etc., suprímese una *l.* (*V.* estas palabras en su lugar alfabético.) Comúnmente se une *all-*, por medio de un guión, con la palabra siguiente, como se verá a continuación.

All-abandoned [ōl-a-ban'-dund], *a.* Desamparado por todos.

All-abhorred [ōl-ab-hōrd'], *a.* Aborrecido de todos.

All-admiring [ōl-ad-mair'-ing], *a.* Admirador de todo.

All-advised [ōl-ad-vaizd'], *a.* Aconsejado de todos.

All-approved [ōl-ap-prūvd'], *a.* Aprobado por todos.

All-atoning [ōl-a-tōn'-ing], *a.* Lo que compensa o lo expía todo.

All-bearing [ōl-bār'-ing], *a.* Lo que produce o cría todas las cosas.

All-beauteous [ōl-biū'-te-us], *a.* Enteramente hermoso.

All-beholding [ōl-be-hōld'-ing], *a.* Lo que ve todas las cosas.

All-blasting [ōl-blast'-ing], *a.* Lo que difama o arruina a todas las personas o cosas.

All-changing [ōl-chênj'-ing], *a.* Lo que está cambiando perpetuamente.

All-cheering [ōl-chîr'-ing], *a.* Lo que todo lo alegra.

All-commanding [ōl-com-and'-ing'], *a.* Lo que manda en todas partes.

All-complying [ōl-com-plai'-ing], *a.* Lo que se acomoda a todo.

All-composing [ōl-com-pōz'-ing], *a.* El que sosiega y lo compone todo.

All-comprehensive [ōl-com-pre-hen'-siv], *a.* Lo que lo comprende todo.

All-concealing [ōl-con-sîl'-ing], *a.* Lo que todo lo oculta.

All-conquering [ōl-ceng' ker-ing], *a.* Lo que todo lo vence.

All-constraining [ōl-con-strên'-ing], *a.* Lo que todo lo refrena, reprime o retiene.

All-consuming [ōl-con-siūm'-ing], *a.* Lo que todo lo consume o gasta.

All-daring [ōl-dār'-ing], *a.* Lo que osa o se atreve a todo.

All-destroying [ōl-des-troi'-ing], *a.* Lo que todo lo arruina.

All-devastating [ōl-dev'-as-tê-ting], *a.* Lo que todo lo devasta.

All-devouring [ōl-de-vaur'-ing], *a.* Lo que todo lo consume o devora.

All-dimming [ōl-dim'-ing], *a.* Lo que obscurece todas las cosas.

All-discovering [ōl-dis-cuv'-er-ing], *a.* Lo que todo lo descubre.

All-disgraced [ōl-dis-grêst'], *a.* Enteramente deshonrado.

All-dispensing [ōl-dis-pen'-sing], *a.* El que dispensa de todo, o el que tiene facultad de permitirlo todo por sí mismo.

All-divine [ōl-di-vain'], *a.* Divinísimo, divino en sumo grado.

All-divining [ōl-di-vain'-ing], *a.* El que lo adivina o pronostica todo.

All-dreaded [ōl-dred'-ed], *a.* Temido de todos.

All-drowsy [ōl-drauz'-i], *a.* Muy soñoliento.

All-eloquent [ōl-el'-o-cwent], *a.* Elocuentísimo, muy elocuente.

All-embracing [ōl-em-brês'-ing], *a.* Lo que lo comprende o abraza todo.

All-ending [ōl-end'-ing], *a.* Lo que acaba todas las cosas.

All-enlightening [ōl-en-lait'-en-ing], *a.* Lo que ilumina por todas partes.

All-enraged [ōl-en-rêjd'], *a.* Muy enojado o enfurecido.

All-flaming [ōl-flêm'-ing], *a.* Lo que echa llamas por todos lados.

All-fools' Day [ōl-fūls' dê'], *s.* El día primero de Abril; dásele el nombre de día de los bobos o simples, por la costumbre que hay en Inglaterra de chasquearse mutuamente en ese día, como en España el día de Inocentes.

All-forgiving [ōl-fōr-giv'-ing], *a.* Que todo lo perdona.

All fours [ōl-fōrz'], *s.* Los cuatro palos, juego de naipes. *To go on all-fours,* Gatear, andar á gatas.

All-giver [ōl-giv'-er], *s.* Dios, el dador de todas las cosas.

All-good [ōl-gud'], *s.* Dios, el ser infinitamente bueno.—*a.* Dios, la suprema bondad.

All-guiding [ōl-gaid'-ing], *a.* Lo que guía o conduce todas las cosas.

All-hail [ōl-hêl'], *s.* Salud completa.

All-hail, *va.* Saludar, desear cabal salud. *All hail,* en los documentos públicos, significa *salud,* esto es, os deseo salud o felicidad.

All-hallow, All-hallows [ōl-hal'-o, ōl-hal'-ōz], *s.* El día de Todos los Santos.

All-hallowe'en [el-hal'-o-în], *s.* La noche del 31 de Octubre; víspera del día de Todos los Santos.

All-heal [ōl-hîl], *s.* (Bot.) Panacea, planta.

All-healing [ōl-hîl'-ing], *a.* Que lo cura o sana todo.

All-helping [ōl-help'-ing], *a.* Lo que a todos ayuda.

All-hiding [ōl-haid'-ing], *a.* Lo que todo lo oculta.

All-honoured [ōl-en'-erd], *a.* Honrado por todos.

All-hurting [ōl-hūrt'-ing], *a.* Lo que a todo hiere o lastima.

All-idolizing [ōl-ai'-del-aiz-ing], *a.* El que lo adora, venera o idolatra todo.

All-imitating [ōl-im'-i-têt-ing], *a.* Lo que lo imita todo.

All-informing [ōl-in-fōrm'-ing], *a.* Lo que lo mueve ó anima todo.

All-interpreting [ōl-in-ter'-pret-ing], *a.* El que todo lo explica.

All-judging [ōl-juj'-ing], *a.* El que tiene el derecho soberano de juzgar.

All-knowing [ōl-nō'-ing], *a.* Omnisciente, que todo lo sabe.

All-licensed [ōl-lai'-senst], *a.* Con libertad para todo.

All-loving [ōl-luv'-ing], *a.* Amantísimo.

All-making [ōl-mêk'-ing], *a.* El que lo crea o cría todo, el que todo lo hace.

All-murdering [ōl-mūr'-der-ing], *a.* Sangrientísimo, aniquilador, destructor.

All-obedient [ōl-o-bî'-di-ent], *a.* Obediente en absoluto.

All-oblivious [ōl-eb-liv'-i-us], *a.* Lo que causa olvido total.

All-obscuring [ōl-eb-skiūr'-ing], *a.* Lo que esconde u obscurece todas las cosas.

All-out [el'-aut], *a.* Total, completo.—*adv.* Totalmente, resueltamente.

Allover [ōl-ō'-ver], *a.* De diseño repetido.

All-penetrating [ōl-pen'-e-trêt-ing], *a.* Que todo lo penetra.

All-perfect [ōl-per'-fect], *a.* Perfectísimo.

All-perfectness [ōl-per'-fect-nes], *s.* Perfección completa, conjunto de perfecciones.

All-piercing [ōl-pîrs'-ing], *a.* Lo que penetra por todo.

All-powerful [ōl-pau'-er-ful] o **All-potent** [ol-pō'-tent], *a.* Omnipotente, todopoderoso.

All-praised [ōl-prêzd'], *a.* Alabado por todos.

All right [el rait], *adv.* Bien, bueno, perfectamente, está bien.

All-round [el'-raund], *a.* Completo, en todas formas. *All-round athlete,* Deportista o atleta completo o en todos los campos.

All-ruling [ōl-rūl'-ing], *a.* El que todo lo gobierna.

All-saints' Day [ōl-sênts' dê], *s.* El día o fiesta de Todos los Santos, Nov. 1.

All-sanctifying [ōl-sanc'-ti-fai-ing], *a.* Que todo lo santifica.

All-saving [ōl-sêv'-ing], *a.* Salvador o conservador de todo.

All-searching [ōl-sẹrch'-ing], *a.* Lo que lo examina o penetra todo.

All-seeing [ōl-sī'-ing], *a.* Que todo lo ve.

All-seer [ōl-sī'-ẹr], *s.* Veedor u observador de todo, el que ve todas las cosas.

All-shunned [ōl-shund'], *a.* Evitado o huído por todos.

All-souls' Day [ōl-sōlz' dê], *s.* El día de las Ánimas, o día de Difuntos. (Mex.) El día de los muertos, Nov. 2.

All-sufficiency [ōl-su-fi'-shen-si], *s.* Habilidad infinita.

All-sufficient [ōl-su-fi'-shent], *a.* Bastante o suficiente para todo.—*s.* Dios.

All-surveying [ōl-sūr-vê'-ing], *a.* Que todo lo mira.

All-sustaining [ōl-sus-tên'-ing], *a.* Sostenedor y mantenedor de todas las cosas.

All-telling [ōl-tel'-ing], *a.* Hablador, el que todo lo dice o divulga.

All-time [ōl-taim], *a.* Sin precedente, absoluto; de todos los tiempos. *All-time high,* Lo mas álto hasta ahora.

All-triumphant [ōl-trai-um'-fant], *a.* Triunfante en todas partes.

All-watched [ōl-wōcht'], *a.* Vigilado por todos.

All-wise [ōl-waiz'], *a.* Infinitamente sabio, sapientísimo.

All-witted [ōl-wit'-ed], *a.* Ingeniosísimo.

All-worshipped [ōl-wūr'-shipt], *a.* Adorado de todos.

Allah [al'-la], *s.* Alá, voz árabe que significa Dios.

Allantois [al-lan'-tois], *s.* Alantóides, saco membranoso situado entre el corion y el amnios en el feto.

Allay [al-lé'], *va.* Aliviar, aquietar, apaciguar, reprimir, suavizar, mitigar, endulzar.

Allayment [al-lé'-mẹnt], *s.* Alivio, descanso o desahogo.

Allegation [al-ẹ-gé'-shun], *s.* 1. Alegación o alegato. 2. Alegación, excusa o disculpa ; razón. 3. Alegato, cita.

Allege [al-lej'], *va.* 1. Alegar, afirmar, declarar, sostener. 2. Alegar, sacar a su favor algún dicho u otra cosa que sirva de disculpa ; citar, exponer.

Allegeable [al-lej'-a-bl], *a.* Lo que se puede alegar.

Allegement [al-lej'-mẹnt], *s.* *V.* ALLEGATION.

Alleger [al-lej'-ẹr], *s.* Alegador, afirmante, declarante.

Allegiance [al-lī'-jans], *s.* Lealtad, fidelidad, la obligación que debe todo vasallo a su soberano ; sumisión, fidelidad, obediencia, homenaje. *To swear allegiance,* Jurar fidelidad ; hacer pleito homenaje.

†**Allegiant** [al-lī'-ji-ant], *a.* Leal, obediente, sumiso.

Allegoric [al-ẹ-gor'-ic], **Allegorical** [al-ẹ-gor'-i-cal], *a.* Alegórico.

Allegorically [al-ẹ-gor'-i-cal-i], *adv.* Alegóricamente, en sentido alegórico.

Allegoricalness [al-e-gor'-i-cal-nes], *s.* La calidad de ser alegórico.

Allegorist [al'-ẹ-go-rist], *s.* El que alegoriza, el autor u orador que explica el sentido de las cosas por alegorías.

Allegorize [al'-e-go-raiz], *va.* Alegorizar, interpretar alegóricamente.—*vn.* Tratar o discurrir alegóricamente.

Allegory [al'-e-go-ri], *s.* Alegoría, metáfora continuada, discurso figurado.

Allegretto [al-le-gret'-o] (Ital.), *a.* Más vivo que el andante, pero no tanto como el alegro.—*s.* Movimiento en este tiempo.

Allegro [al-lé'-gro], *s.* (Mús.) Alegro, voz tomada de la lengua italiana, que significa un movimiento moderadamente vivo en la música.

Allelujah [al-ẹ-lū'-ya], *s.* Aleluya, voz hebrea que expresa júbilo espiritual y significa "Alabad a Dios, o al Señor." *V.* HALLELUJAH.

Allemande [al-ẹ-mānd'], *s.* Alemana o alemanda, especie de baile o aire de música de carácter majestuoso.

Allergen [al'-ẹr-jen], *s.* Alergeno.

Allergic [a-lẹr'-jic], *a.* (Med.) Alérgico.

Allergy [al'-ẹr-ji], *s.* (Med.) Alergia.

Alleviate [al-lī'-vi-ét], *va.* Aligerar, aliviar, mitigar, aplacar.

Alleviation [al-lī-vi-é'-shun], *s.* 1. Aligeramiento, la acción de aligerar. 2. Alivio, diminución de algún dolor, o circunstancia atenuante de algún delito ; mitigación.

Alleviative [al-lī'-vi-a-tiv], *s.* Paliativo.

Alley [al'-ẹ], *s.* 1. Calle o paseo de jardín. 2. Callejuela, calle más angosta que las comunes en las ciudades y pueblos grandes. 3. Espacio largo y angosto para el juego de bolos. *Blind-alley,* Callejón sin salida. *Alleyway,* Callejuela, calle estrecha.

Alliable [al-lai'-a-bl], *a.* Capaz de aliarse.

Alliaceous [al-i-é'-shus], *a.* Aliáceo.

Alliance [al-lai'-ans], *s.* 1. Alianza, unión, liga o confederación que forman entre sí los estados para defenderse mutuamente de sus enemigos o para ofenderlos. 2. Alianza, conexión o parentesco, contraído por casamiento. 3. Parentesco, sea por afinidad o por consanguinidad. 4. Parentela, el conjunto de todo género de parientes.

Allied [al-laid'], *a.* Aliado, unido, confederado. *Allied to,* Pariente de.

Allies [al-laiz'], *s. pl.* Aliados, confederados. *V.* ALLY.

Alligate [al'-i-gét], *va.* Ligar, atar o afianzar una cosa a otra.

Alligation [al-i-gé'-shun], *s.* 1. Aligación, la acción de ligar o atar. 2. (Arit.) Aligación, la regla por la cual se computa y averigua el precio común de la mezcla de especies de diferente valor. 3. Ligazón, atadura, unión.

Alligator [al'-i-gé-tẹr], *s.* Caimán o aligador, especie de cocodrilo de América. Lacerta alligator. (Mex.) Lagarto. *Alligator-pear,* Avocado, aguacate (Cuba) o agualate (en Perú, palta). *Alligator-tree,* Liquidámbar común de América. Liquidámbar styraciflua. *Alligator-apple,* Anona de los pantanos. Este árbol de las Antillas da un fruto que es manjar predilecto de los cocodrilos.

†**Allision** [al-lizh'-un], *s.* Choque, la acción de golpear o dar una cosa contra otra.

Alliteration [al-lit-ẹr-é'-shun], *s.* Aliteración, paronomasia.

Alliterative [al-lit'-ẹr-a-tiv], *a.* Lo que pertenece a las voces que empiezan con la misma letra.

¿**Allocate** [al'-o-két], *va.* Colocar, señalar puesto. Distribuir.

Allocation [al-o-ké'-shun], *s.* 1. Distribución, colocación. 2. Asignación, fijación.

Allocatur [al-o-ké'-tur ó cạ'-tur], *s.* Voz forense que significa permiso : se refiere a un mandato o una orden.

Allocution [al-ō-kiū'-shun], *s.* Alocución, arenga, discurso.

Allodial [al-lō'-di-al], *a.* Alodial, libre de toda carga, independiente.

Allodium [al-lō'-di-um], *s.* Alodio, posesión absoluta e independiente de tierras o bienes, sin reconocimiento de ningún dominio soberano.

Allonge [al-lunj'], *s.* 1. Bote, botonazo, estocada, el golpe que se tira de punta con la espada o estoque. 2. El ramal largo con que se enseña a los caballos en el picadero.

Allopath [al'-o-path] ó **Allopathist** [al-lop'-a-thist], *s.* Alópata, médico que profesa los principios de la alopatía.

Allopathic [al-o-path'-ic], *a.* Alopático relativo a la alopatía, o que la favorece y prefiere.

Allopathy [al-lop'-a-thi], *s.* Alopatía, sistema de medicina por el cual se trata de curar una enfermedad produciendo un estado y fenómenos incompatibles con la misma ; la práctica ordinaria de la medicina como opuesta a la homeopatía.

Allot [al-let'], *va.* 1. Distribuir por suerte. 2. Conceder. 3. Repartir, asignar, adjudicar, destinar, dar a cada uno su parte o lo que le toca.

Allotment [al-let'-mẹnt], *s.* Lote, parte o porción de cualquier cosa que se da a alguno en el reparto de ella ; asignación, repartimiento.

Allotropic [al-o-trep'-ic], *a.* Alotrópico ; lo que pertenece al alotropismo.

Allotropism [al-et'-rep-izm], **Allotropy** [al-et'-ro-pi], *s.* (Quím.) Alotropía, la diferencia o el cambio en las propiedades físicas de ciertas sustancias o sus compuestos, sin cambio correspondiente en su composición química.

Allotted [al-let'-ed], *pp.* y *a.* 1. Repartido, dividido, distribuido en lotes o porciones. 2. Asignado, señalado.

Allow [al-lau'], *va.* 1. Admitir. 2. Conceder o ceder, consentir, confesar, aprobar. 3. Permitir. 4. Dar, pagar. 5. Abonar en cuenta. 6. Descontar, desfalcar. 7. Señalar, adjudicar. *I allow of that,* Concedo eso.

Allowable [al-lau'-a-bl], *a.* 1. Admisible, lo que se puede admitir sin contradicción. 2. Lícito, permitido, legítimo, justo.

Allowableness [al-lau'-a-bl-nes], *s.* Legitimidad, legalidad ; propiedad ; exención ; permiso.

Allowably [al-lau'-a-bli], *adv.* Con permiso, legítimamente.

Allowance [al-lau'-ans], *s.* 1. Permiso, concesión. 2. Indulgencia o diminución de rigor. 3. Ración, gajes, salario. 4. Señalamiento, pensión, abono, alimentos, mesada. 5. Licencia, excusa, connivencia. 6. Carácter establecido. *To keep on allowance,* Poner a ración ; poner a dieta. *To make allowance for,* Hacerse cargo de, ser indulgente. *To give allowance to one's inclinations,* Ceder a las propias inclinaciones.

Alloy [al-loi'], *va.* 1. Ligar, mezclar un metal con otro para poderlo acuñar con más facilidad , alear los metales. 2. Ligar, juntar una cosa con otra, o mezclarla para rebajar sus calidades.

Alloy, *s.* 1. Liga, el metal de baja ley que se mezcla con el oro o la plata en la acuñación de la moneda. 2. Liga, la cosa que, añadida o mezclada con otra, rebaja sus calidades predominantes; mezcla.

Alloyage [al-loi'-êj], *s.* Liga, mezcla de metales; acción de ligar los metales.

Allspice [ōl'-spais], *s.* *V.* PIMENTO.

Allude [al-lūd'], *va.* Aludir, hacer relación a alguna cosa sin mencionarla directamente.

Alluminate [al-lū'-min-êt], *va.* Iluminar dibujos.

Alluminor [al-lū'-min-er], *s.* Iluminador. (Poco us.)

Allure [al-lūr'], *va.* 1. Halagar, atraer con halagos, alucinar, cebar. 2. Atraer, seducir. *That can allure none but fools,* Eso no puede seducir más que a los necios.

Allurement [al-lūr'-ment], *s.* Halago, engañifa; atractivo, cebo, lisonja, aliciente, seducción.

Allurer [al-lūr'-er], *s.* Halagador, seductor, engañador.

Alluring [al-lūr'-ing], *a.* Halagüeño, seductivo, atractivo.

Alluringly [al-lūr'-ing-li], *adv.* Halagüeñamente, seductoramente.

Alluringness [al-lūr'-ing-nes], *s.* Aliciente, atractivo, incentivo, agrado.

Allusion [al-lū'-zhun], *s.* 1. Alusión. 2. Indirecta.

Allusive [al-lū'-siv], *a.* Alusivo.

Allusively [al-lū'-siv-li], *adv.* Alusivamente.

Allusiveness [al-lū'-siv-nes], *s.* La calidad de ser alusivo.

Alluvial [al-lū'-vi-al], *a.* Aluvial; lo que pertenece al aluvión, está contenido en él, o es producido por él.

Alluvion [al-lū'-vi-en], *s.* 1. Aluvión, aumento de tierras causado por las avenidas o corrientes de los ríos; terrero. 2. Avenida, inundación.

Alluvious [al-lū'-vi-us], *a.* (Poco us.) *V.* ALLUVIAL.

Alluvium [al-lū'-vi-um], *s.* Terreno de origen reciente formado por la acumulación de cieno, arenas, etc., debida a la acción de las aguas; aluvión, 1ª acep.

Ally [al-lai'], *va.* 1. Hacer alianza o unión por afinidad o confederación. 2. Concordar o poner en relación una cosa con otra.—*vn.* Confederarse, aliarse.

Ally, *s.* Aliado, confederado, el que tiene alianza con otro por afinidad, amistad o confederación.

Almagra [al-mā'-gra], *s.* Almagre.

Alma-mater [al'-ma-mê'-ter], *s.* La universidad en donde se ha estudiado y se han recibido los grados escolásticos.

Almanac [ōl'-ma-nac], *s.* Almanaque, calendario. *Almanac-maker,* Almanaquista, calendarista, el que hace los calendarios.

Almandine [al'-man-dain] o **Almandite** [al'-man-dait], *s.* Almandina, especie de rubí más basto y ligero que el oriental. (*Almandite* es la forma preferida.)

Almightiness [el-mait'-i-nes], *s.* Omnipotencia, poder supremo para todas las cosas; atributo sólo de Dios.

Almighty [el-mait'-i], *a.* Omnipotente, todopoderoso.

Almond [ā'-mund o al'-mund], *s.* Almendra. *Almonds of the throat,* (Anat.) Las amígdalas, dos glándulas de la garganta. *Almond-oil,* Aceite de almendras. *Almond-paste,* Pasta de almendras. *Bitter almonds,* Almendras amargas. *Burnt almonds,* Almendras bañadas o garapiñadas. *Unshelled almonds,* Almendras con cáscara.

Almond-tree [ā'-mund-trī], *s.* (Bot.) Almendro, árbol que da por fruto las almendras.

Almond-willow [ā'-mund-wil'-ō], *s.* (Bot.) Una especie de sauce.

Almoner [al'-mun-er], *s.* Limosnero, el que está encargado de distribuir las limosnas.

Almonry [al'-mun-ri], *s.* El sitio o paraje en que se distribuyen las limosnas.

Almost [ōl'-mōst], *adv.* Casi, cerca de. *It is almost night,* Es casi de noche, es casi noche.

Alms [āmz], *s.* Limosna, caridad.

Alms-basket [āmz'-bas-ket], *s.* Canasto o cesto en que se echa limosna para los pobres.

Alms-box [āmz'-bex] o **Chest** [chest], *s.* Cepillo o caja de limosna; alcancía.

Almsdeed [āmz'-dīd], *s.* Caridad, limosna, obra de caridad.

Alms-folk [āmz'-fōc], *s.* Personas caritativas.

Almsgiver [āmz'-giv-er], *s.* Limosnero, el que da limosna.

Almsgiving [āmz'-giv-ing], *s.* El acto de dar limosna. Caridad.

Almshouse [āmz'-haus], *s.* 1. Hospicio de pobres o casa de misericordia. 2. Asilo.

Almsman [āmz'-man], *s.* 1. Pobre, mendigo, pordiosero. 2. Limosnero, el que da limosna.

Alms-people [āmz'-pī-pl], *s.* Hospicianos, los asilados de la casa de misericordia.

Almug-tree [al'-mug-trī], *s.* Árbol que produce la goma arábiga. Escríbese también y preferentemente, ALGUM.

Alnagar [al'-na-gār], **Alnager** [al'-nê-ger], *s.* El que mide por anas.

Alnage [al'-nêj], *s.* La medición por anas.

Aloe [al'-o], *s.* 1. (Des.) Aloe o lináloe, madera preciosa que se usa para perfumes. 2. (Bot.) Áloe, árbol que se cría en los países cálidos. 3. *pl.* [al'-ōz], aunque en sintaxis singular: Áloe o acíbar, zumo o jugo medicinal que se saca del árbol llamado áloe común. 4. Zábida o zábila, planta parecida a la pita, de la que se saca también el acíbar.

Aloetic [al-o-et'-ic], **Aloetical** [al-o-et'-i-cal], *a.* Aloético, cosa perteneciente al acíbar.

Aloft [a-lōft'], *prep.* Arriba, sobre. *All hands aloft,* (Mar.) Todo el mundo arriba. *To set aloft,* Elevar, subir.—*adv.* En alto.

Aloin [al'-o-in], *s.* Principio amargo, purgante, que se extrae del áloe.

Alone [a-lōn'], *a.* Solo, solitario, sin compañía. *To let* (*o leave*) *alone,* No desarreglar, no tocar las cosas; no mezclarse en algo; no molestar, dejar en paz a las personas.—*adv.* Solamente. *Let me alone,* Déjeme Vd. en paz.

Aloneness [a-lōn'-nes], *s.* El estado de ser solo y sin igual; se aplica a Dios.

Along [a-leng'], *adv.* 1. A lo largo o por lo largo, por medio de cualquier espacio medido a lo largo. 2. Adelante. 3. Con, en compañía de, junto con. *Come along with me,* Venga Vd. conmigo. 4. En consecuencia, en virtud de. *All along,* a lo largo, de un cabo a otro, desde el principio al fin. *He lies all along,* Está echado a la larga.

Alongside [a-leng'-said], *adv.* A lo largo de, al lado, al costado. (Mar.) Al costado, o costado con costado. *To lie alongside a ship,* Atracar al costado de un buque.

Aloof [a-lūf'], *adv.* 1. Lejos. De lejos, a lo largo. *To keep aloof from a rock,* (Mar.) Mantenerse lejos de un escollo. 2. Prudentemente; cautelosamente. *To stand aloof from politics,* No mezclarse en la política.

Alopecia [al-o-pī'-si-a], *s.* (Med.) Alopecia, especie de tiña, que hace caer el cabello. (Vulg.) Pelona.

Aloud [a-laud'], *adv.* Alto, con voz fuerte, recio.

Alow [a-lō'], *adv.* Abajo o bajo: lo opuesto a *aloft.* (Ant. o Mar.)

Alow, Alowe [a-lau'], *adv.* (Esco.) En llamas.

Alpaca [al-pac'-a], *s.* 1. Alpaca, una especie de llama; el camello del Perú. 2. Tela que se fabrica con el pelo de este animal.

Alpenstock [al'-pen-stoc], *s.* (Alem.) Palo con punta de hierro que se emplea en la ascensión de los Alpes.

Alps [alps], *s.* Alpes; montes o montañas en general; lo que es durable como los Alpes.

Alpha [al'-fa], *s.* 1. Alfa, nombre de la primera letra del alfabeto griego. 2. Sinónimo de principio. *Alpha and omega,* El primero y el último, el principio y el fin.

Alpha ray [al'-fa rê], *s.* Rayo alfa.

Alphabet [al'-fa-bet], *s.* Alfabeto, abecedario.

Alphabet, *va.* Colocar por orden alfabético.

Alphabetarian [al-fa-be-tê'-ri-an], *s.* Alfabetista, el que sabe el *a, b, c.*

Alphabetic [al-fa-bet'-ic], **Alphabetical** [al-fa-bet'-i-cal], *a.* Alfabético.

Alphabetically [al-fa-bet'-i-cal-i], *adv.* Alfabéticamente.

Alphabetize [al'-fa-bet-aiz], *va.* 1. Colocar alfabéticamente. 2. Proveer de un alfabeto.

Alphenic [al-fen'-ic], *s.* Alfeñique: azúcar candi.

Alphonsin [al-fen'-sin], *s.* Sacabalas, instrumento quirúrgico para extraer las balas de las heridas.

Alpine [al'-pin], *a.* 1. Alpino, perteneciente a los Alpes. 2. Alto, elevado.

Alpist [al'-pist], *s.* Alpiste, semilla menuda que se da a los pájaros.

Alquifou [al'-ki-fū], *s.* Alquifol, mineral de plomo que se usa en las alfarerías. Sulfuro de plomo.

Already [ōl-red'-i], *adv.* Ya, a la hora de esta, antes de ahora.

Alsike [al'-sic], *s.* Especie de trébol sueco, planta valiosa empleada como forraje, de flores rojizas o blancas. Trifolium hybridum.

Also [ōl'-so], *adv.* También, igualmente, del mismo modo, aun, además.

Alt [alt], *s.* La parte más alta de la gama musical. (Abrev. de alto.)

Altar [ōl'-tar], *s.* Altar; ara.

Altarage [ōl'-tar-ej], *s.* Pie de altar, los emolumentos que se dan a los sacerdotes por el ejercicio de su ministerio; ofrenda hecha sobre el altar.

Altar-cloth [ōl'-tar-clōth], *s.* Sabanilla, la cubierta exterior del altar. (Mex.) Mantel o manteles.

Altar-piece [ōl'-tar-pīs], *s.* Retablo, el cuadro o pintura del altar. Retablo, el altar en conjunto.

Altar-screen [ōl'-tar-scrīn], *s.* Contra-retablo.
Altar-table [ōl'-tar-tê'-bl], *s.* Mesa del altar.
Altarwise [ōl'-tar-waiz], *adv.* En forma de altar.
Alter [ōl'-tẹr], *va.* Alterar, mudar. *To alter one's condition,* Tomar estado, casarse.—*vn.* Mudarse o cambiarse, alterarse.
Alterability [ōl-tẹr-a-bil'-i-ti], *s.* Alterabilidad.
Alterable [ōl'-tẹr-a-bl], *a.* Alterable; mudable.
Alterableness [ōl'-tẹr-a-bl-nes], *s.* Alterabilidad.
Alterably [ōl'-tẹr-a-bli], *adv.* De una manera mudable.
Alterant [ōl'-tẹr-ant], *a.* Alterante, lo que altera.
Alteration [ōl-tẹr-ê'-shun], *s.* Alteración; mudanza, innovación, cambio.
Alterative [ōl'-tẹr-ê-tiv], *a.* Alterativo.—*s.* Remedio alterativo, alterante.
Altercate [al'-tẹr-kêt], *vn.* Altercar, controvertir.
Altercation [al-tẹr-kê'-shun], *s.* Altercación, debate, disputa, controversia.
Alterer [ōl'-tẹr-ẹr], *s.* Alterador, cambiador.
Altern [al'-tẹrn], *a.* Alterno o alternativo, lo que obra por turno.
Alternant [al-tẹr'-nant], *a.* (Geol.) Compuesto de capas alternadas, como algunas rocas.
Alternate [al-tẹr'-net], *a.* Alternativo, recíproco, lo que se hace o ejecuta con alternación.—*s.* Vicisitud.
Alternate [al'-tẹr-nêt], *va.* 1. Alternar, hacer alguna cosa alternativamente. 2. Alternar, variar.—*vn.* Turnar.
Alternately [al-tẹr'-net-li], *adv.* Alternativamente, recíprocamente, por turno.
Alternateness [al-tẹr'-net-nes], *s.* Alternación, sucesión, recíproca.
Alternating [al'-tẹr-nê'-ting], *pa.* y *a.* Alternante, alterno. *Alternating current,* (Elec.) Corriente alterna.
Alternation [al-tẹr-nê'-shun], *s.* Alternación, vez, turno, vicisitud.
Alternative [al-tẹr'-nẹ-tiv], *s.* Alternativa.—*a.* Alternativo.
Alternatively [al-tẹr'-nê-tiv-li], *adv.* Alternativamente, recíprocamente, por turno, en sucesión recíproca.
Alternativeness [al-tẹr'-na-tiv-nes], **Alternity** [al-tẹr'-ni-ti], *s.* El estado recíproco o alternativo de alguna cosa: vicisitud, reciprocidad; turno.
Alternator [al'-tẹr-nê'-tor], *s.* (Elec.) Alternador.
Althea [al-thī'-a], *s.* (Bot.) Malvavisco. Altea.
Although [ōl-dhō'], *conj.* Aunque, no obstante, bien que, aun cuando, sin embargo. Escríbese algunas veces *altho,* especialmente hoy en día.
Altiloquent [al-til'-o-cwent], *a.* Altilocuente, pomposo.
Altimeter [al-tim'-e-tẹr], *s.* Altímetro, instrumento para medir las alturas.
Altimetry [al-tim'-e-tri], *s.* Altimetría, parte de la geometría práctica, que enseña a medir las alturas.
Altisonant [al-tis'-o-nant], **Altisonous** [al-tis'-o-nus], *a.* Altisonante; pomposo y retumbante. (Poét.) Altísono.
Altitude [al'-ti-tiūd], *s.* 1. Altura o altitud. 2. Elevación, cumbre, cima.
Alto [al'tō], *s.* 1. Contralto (de la voz). 2. Violón. 3. Alto de las cornetas.
Altogether [ōl-to-gedh'-ẹr], *adv.* Enteramente, del todo, para siempre.
Alto-relievo [āl'-to-rī-lyê-vo], *s.* (Escul.) Alto relieve.
Altruism [al'-trū-izm], *s.* Altruísmo, consideración por los intereses de los demás; benevolencia; lo contrario de egoísmo.
Altruist [al'-trū-ist], *s.* Partidario del altruísmo o el que lo profesa.
Altruistic [al-trū-is'-tic], *a.* Altruístico, perteneciente al altruísmo.
Aludel [al'-u-del], *s.* Aludel, vasija para sublimar.
Alum [al'-um], *s.* Alumbre, piedra mineral salina de sabor ácido.
Alum, *va.* Alumbrar, dar a los paños un baño de agua de alumbre.
Alumed [al'-umd], *a.* Aluminado, mezclado con alumbre.
Alumina [a-lū'-mi-na] o **Alumine** [al'-yu-min], *s.* (Quím.) Alúmina, arcilla pura y blanca.
Aluminium [al-u-min'-i-um] o **Aluminum** [a-lū'-mi-num], *s.* Aluminio.
Aluminous [a-lū'-mi-nus], *a.* 1. Aluminoso, lo que tiene calidad o mezcla de alúmina; arcilloso. 2. Alumbroso.
Alumna, Alumnus [a-lum'-nus], *s.* Alumna, alumno; el discípulo de un colegio o universidad.
Alumniate [a-lum'-ni-êt], *s.* El tiempo que dura la instrucción; en un establecimiento de enseñanza.
Alum-stone [al'-um-stōn], *s.* Piedra alumbre; alumbre calcinado.
Alum-water [al-um-wō'-tẹr], *s.* Agua de alumbre.
Alum-works [al-um-wūrcs], *s.* Alumbrera, la mina de donde se saca, o la factoría en que se hace el alumbre.
Alutation [al-iu-tê'-shun], *s.* Curtimiento, la acción de curtir la piel o el cuero.
Alveary [al'-ve-ê-ri], *s.* Colmena.
Alveolar [al-vī'-o-lar], *a.* Lo perteneciente a los alvéolos.
Alveolate [al'-vẹ-o-lêt], *a.* Alveolado, excavado profundamente, como el panal.
Alveolus [al-vī'-o-lus], *s.* ALVEOLI, *pl.* 1. Alvéolo, la cavidad que ocupan los dientes en la encía. 2. Celdilla que hacen las abejas en los panales. 3. Alvéolo de las plantas.
Alvine [al'-vin ó al'-vain], *a.* Alvino, lo que pertenece al vientre.
Alway [ōl'-wê], **Always** [ōl'-wêz], *adv.* 1. Siempre, en todo o cualquier tiempo. 2. Constantemente, invariablemente.
Alyssum [a-lis'-um], *s.* (Bot.) Alisón, planta de la familia de las crucíferas que produce racimos de flores amarillas o blancas. *Sweet alyssum,* Alisón fragante, con pequeñas flores blancas. Alyssum maritimum.
A. M. (Lat.) 1. *Artium magister,* Maestro en Artes; este es el segundo grado en las universidades de Inglaterra y de los Estados Unidos de América; en Alemania y otros países es Doctor en Filosofía. 2. *Ante meridiem,* Antes del mediodía. 3. *Anno mundi,* Año del mundo.
Am [am], *1a per. pers. de indicat. del verbo* TO BE. *I am,* Yo soy o estoy.
Amability [am-a-bil'-i-ti], *s.* Amabilidad, agrado. *V.* AMIABILITY.
Amadetto [am-a-det'-o], **Amadot** [am'-a-det], *s.* Especie de pera.
Amadou [am'-a-dū], *s.* Yesca para encender.
Amain [a-mên'], *adv.* 1. Con vehemencia, fuerza o vigor, vigorosamente. 2. (Mar.) En banda.
Amalgam [a-mal'-gam], **Amalgama** [a-mal'-ga-ma], *s.* 1. Amalgama, mezcla de diferentes metales incorporados unos con otros. 2. (Met.) Toda mezcla o combinación de diversas substancias, castas o cosas.
Amalgamate [a-mal'-ga-mêt], *va.* y *vn.* Amalgamar, unir o mezclar el azogue con los metales.
Amalgamation [a-mal-ga-mê'-shun], *s.* Amalgamación, la acción de amalgamar los metales.
Amalgamator [am-al'-gam-ê-tẹr], *s.* Máquina de amalgamar.
Amanuensis [a-man-yu-en'-sis], *s.* Amanuense, el que escribe lo que otro le dicta.
Amaranth [am'-a-ranth], *s.* 1. (Bot.) Amaranto. 2. Planta del género Gomphrena de las misma familia. 3. (Poét.) Una flor imaginaria que nunca se marchita.
Amaranthine [am-a-ran'-thin], *a.* 1. Compuesto de amaranto. 2. De color de amaranto. 3. Inmarcesible.
Amaryllis [am-a-ril'-is], *n.* Amarilis, planta bulbosa originaria del África del Sur, y su flor. Entre las especies de la familia de las plantas amarilídeas se cuentan los narcisos, el junquillo y la pita.
Amass [a-mgs'], *va.* Acumular, amontonar. *To amass a fortune,* Acumular riquezas.
Amassment [a-mgs'-ment], *s.* Cúmulo, montón, conjunto, agregado.
Amateur [am-a-tūr'], *s.* Aficionado.
Amateurish [am-a-tūr'-ish], *a.* A modo de aficionado; superficial.
Amative [am'-a-tiv], *a.* Lleno de amor; amatorio; que se refiere al amor entre los sexos.
Amativeness [am'-a-tiv-nes], *s.* Amorosidad, principio amatorio o propensión o tendencia a amar.
Amatorial [am-a-tō'-ri-al], **Amatorious** [am-a-tō'-ri-us], *a.* Amatorio, lo que pertenece al amor.
Amatory [am'-a-to-ri], *a.* Amatorio, lo que trata de amor o lo inspira.
Amaurosis [am-ō-rō'-sis], *s.* Pérdida de la vista por enfermedad del nervio óptico; amaurosis.
Amaurotic [am-ō-ret'-ic], *a.* 1. Amaurótico, que está relacionado con la amaurosis. 2. Que la padece.
Amaze [a-mêz'], *va.* 1. Aterrar, espantar, aturdir. 2. Confundir, dejar perplejo o parado, sorprender, asombrar; usado con la preposición *at;* menos frecuentemente con *by* o *with.*
Amaze, *s.* Espanto, pasmo, confusión causada por miedo o admiración; asombro, sorpresa. (Poét.)
Amazedly [a-mêz'-ed-li], *adv.* Atolondradamente, con atolondramiento o pasmo.
Amazedness [a-mêz'-ed-nes], **Amazement** [a-mêz'-mẹnt], *s.* Espanto, pasmo, confusión. *With amazement,* Con mucha admiración.
Amazing [a-mêz'-ing], *a.* Pasmoso, asombroso, extraño.
Amazingly [a-mêz'-ing-li], *adv.* Pasmosamente, asombrosamente.
Amazon [am'-a-zon], *s.* 1. Amazona, mujer guerrera. 2. Marimacho. 3. Papagayo de la América del Sur.
Amazonian [am-a-zō'-ni-an], *a.* 1. Guerrera. 2. Lo perteneciente a las amazonas.

Amazon-like [am'-a-zen-laic], *a.* Semejante a una amazona o a un marimacho.
Ambages [am-bé'-jez], *s.* Ambages, circunloquios o rodeos de palabras; subterfugios.
Ambassador [am-bas'-a-der], *s.* Embajador.
Ambassadress [am-bas'-a-dres], *sf.* Embajadora, la esposa del embajador.
Ambassage [am'-ba-séj], **Ambassy** [am'-ba-si], *s.* (Ant.) Embajada, la comisión ó encargo que lleva el embajador al estado a que va enviado. *V.* EMBASSY.
Amber [am'-bęr], *s.* 1. Ambar, resina fósil de color amarillo claro u obscuro. 2. Especie de cerveza pálida.—*a.* Ambarino, lo que contiene o está hecho de ámbar. *Amber beads,* Rosario ambarino o de ámbar. *Yellow amber,* Succino.
Amber, *va.* Perfumar con ámbar, que antiguamente se decía ambarar.
Amber-coloured [am'-bęr-cul'-ęrd], *a.* Lo que es de color de ámbar. *Amber-coloured hair,* Pelo castaño.
Amber-drink [am'-bęr-drinc], *s.* Bebida de color de ámbar.
Amber-dropping [am'-bęr-drep'-ing], *a.* Lo que destila ámbar; dícese de los rizos o bucles del cabello.
Ambergris [am'-bęr-gris], *s.* Ámbar gris, especie de droga que se derrite como la cera y se usa como perfume y cordial.
Amber-seed [am'-bęr-sîd], *s.* Ambarilla, la semilla del abelmosco o algalia, de olor almizcleño.
Amber-tree [am'-bęr-trî], *s.* (Bot.) Árbol de ámbar.
Amber-varnish [am'-bęr-vār'-nish], *s.* Barniz de succino.
Amber-weeping [am'-bęr-wîp'-ing], *a.* Lo que echa lágrimas como ámbar.
Ambidexter [am-bi-dex'-tęr], *s.* 1. Hombre ambidextro. 2. Hombre falso, engañoso. 3. (Fam.) El que come a dos carrillos. 4. Prevaricador.
Ambidexterity [am-bi-dex-ter'-i-ti], *s.* 1. Igual manejo de ambas manos. 2. Doblez, simulación.
Ambidextrous [am-bi-dex'-trus], *a.* 1. Ambidextro, el que usa igualmente de la mano izquierda que de la derecha. 2. El que procede con doblez.
Ambidextrousness [am-bi-dex'-trus-nes], *s.* *V.* AMBIDEXTERITY.
Ambient [am'-bi-ent], *a.* Ambiente, lo que rodea, lo que está o anda al rededor. *The ambient air,* El ambiente, el aire que nos rodea.
Ambigu [am'-bi-giū], *s.* Ambigú, comida, por lo común nocturna, compuesta de manjares calientes y fiambres. (Fig.) Baturrillo; mezcolanza de cosas opuestas.
Ambiguity [am-bi-giū'-i-ti], *s.* Ambigüedad, duda, confusión, incertidumbre.
Ambiguous [am-big'-yu-us], *s.* 1. Ambiguo, lo que tiene ambigüedad. 2. Ambiguo, el que usa de equívocos.
Ambiguously [am-big'-yu-us-li], *adv.* Ambiguamente, de un modo ambiguo, confusamente.
Ambiguousness [am-big'-yu-us-nes], *s.* Ambigüedad, la calidad de ser ambiguo.
Ambit [am'-bit], *s.* Ámbito, circuito o circunferencia de algún espacio o lugar; contorno.
Ambition [am-bish'-un], *s.* Ambición, deseo de conseguir fama, honras o dignidades.
Ambitious [am-bish'-us], *a.* Ambicioso, poseído de la ambición.
Ambitiously [am-bish'-us-li], *adv.* Ambiciosamente, con ambición.
Ambitiousness [am-bish'-us-nes], *s.* Ambición, deseo ardiente de posición, de gloria, de renombre.
Ambivert [am'-bi-vęrt], *s.* Ambivertido, tipo psicológico intermedio entre el extravertido y el introvertido.
Amble [am'-bl], *vn.* Amblar, andar a paso de andadura.
Amble, *s.* Paso de andadura del caballo, llamado también paso castellano.
Ambler [am'-blęr], *s.* Caballo que marcha a paso de andadura.
Amblingly [am'-bling-li], *adv.* A paso de andadura.
Amblygon [am'-bli-gęn], *s.* Ambligonio, obtusángulo.
Amblyopia [am-bli-ō'-pi-a], *s.* Ambliopía, obscurecimiento y debilidad de la vista, sin defecto apreciable del ojo.
Ambo [am'-bo], *s.* Púlpito antiguo, tribuna que había antes en las iglesias, adonde se subía a leer o predicar. (Méx.) Ambón, dos púlpitos, al lado del altar mayor, en que se cantan en el uno la epístola, y en el otro el evangelio del día.
Ambrosia [am-brō'-zi-a], *s.* 1. Ambrosía, manjar o alimento de los dioses. 2. (Bot.) Ambrosía, un género de plantas de la familia de las compuestas.
Ambrosial [am-brō'-zi-al], *a.* Delicioso, deleitable, celestial.
Ambry [am'-bri], **Almery** [al'-me-ri], *s.* 1. Casa de beneficencia, limosnería. 2. Armario, despensa. 3. Sausería, oficina en que se guarda la plata y demás servicio la mesa. *V.* ALMONRY.
Ambs-ace [amz-ês'], *s.* (Ant.) Ases: parejas de ases en algunos juegos.
Ambulance [am'-biu-lans], *s.* 1. Hospital de campaña, o de sangre. 2. Ambulancia, vagón cubierto para retirar los heridos del campo, o transportar los enfermos a un hospital.
Ambulant [am'-biu-lant], *a.* Ambulante.
Ambulate [am'-biu-lêt], *vn.* Andar.
Ambulation [am-biu-lé'-shun], *s.* Paseo, la acción de pasearse.
Ambulative [am'-biu-lê-tiv], *a.* Ambulativo.
Ambulatory [am'-biu-la-to-ri], *a.* Lo que anda o puede andar; ambulante, ambulativo, mudable, inconstante, ambulatorio.—*s.* Galería cubierta o descubierta, sitio para pasearse.
Ambury [am'-bur-i], *s.* Verruga o tumor en el cuerpo de caballo. Lo mismo que ANBURY.
Ambuscade, Ambuscado [am-bus-kêd', o], *s.* Emboscada, celada.
†**Ambuscadoed** [am-bus-kê'-dōd], **Ambushed** [am'-busht], *a.* Emboscado.
Ambush [am'-bush], **Ambushment** [am'-bush-ment], *s.* 1. Emboscada, celada. 2. Sorpresa, acometimiento repentino del que está emboscado. *To lie in ambush,* Estar emboscado.
Ambustion [am-bus'-chun], *s.* Quemadura.
Ameba [a-mî'-ba], *s.* *V.* AMŒBA.
Ameboid [a-mî'-beid], *a.* *V.* AMŒBOID.
Ameer [a-mîr'], **Amir.** *V.* EMIR. Gobernador del Afghanistán.
†**Amel** [am'-el], *s.* Esmalte, la materia con que se esmalta alguna cosa. *V.* ENAMEL. *Amel corn,* Centeno blanco.
Ameliorate [a-mî'-lio-rêt], *va.* *V.* MELIORATE.
Amelioration [a-mî-lio-ré'-shun], *s.* Mejoramiento, mejora; medro; adelanto; perfeccionamiento.
Ameliorator [a-mî-lio-ré'-tęr], *s.* Mejorador, aumentador, perfeccionador.
Amen [ê-men' o (Mús.) ā-men'], *adv.* Amén, voz por la cual al fin de cada oración o petición se entiende, *así sea;* y al fin del credo, *así es.*
Amenability [a-mî-na-bil'-i-ti] ó **Amenableness,** *s.* Responsabilidad, obligación de reparar un daño.
Amenable [a-mî'-na-bl], *a.* 1. Responsable, obligado a satisfacer por algún cargo. 2. Tratable, dócil.
Amend [a-mend'], *va.* Enmendar, corregir el error, reparar.—*vn.* Enmendarse, reformarse, restablecerse.
Amendable [a-men'-da-bl], *a.* Reparable, reformable, corregible, componible.
Amende [ā-mānd' o a-mend'], *s.* Enmienda, recompensa, castigo penal, multa. *Amende honorable,* Reparación, satisfacción pública. (For.) Castigo con nota de infamia, que se imponía por ciertos crímenes contra la decencia o moral pública.
Amender [a-men'-dęr], *s.* Reformador, corrector.
Amending [a-men'-ding], *s.* La acción de enmendar.
Amendment [a-mend'-męnt], *s.* Enmienda, mudanza de malo a mejor; reformación, reforma; restauración, corrección.
Amends [a-mendz'], *s.* Recompensa, compensación, satisfacción, reparación. *He will never be able to make amends for the favours he has received,* Jamás podrá él corresponder a los favores que ha recibido.
Amenity [a-men'-i-ti], *s.* Amenidad, lo agradable de una situación o paraje. Afabilidad, dulzura.
Amenorrhea [ā-men-or-rî'-a], *s.* Amenorrea, detención del flujo menstrual.
A mensa et thoro [a-men'-sa-et-thō'-ro]. (Lat. For.) De mesa y tálamo. Separación o divorcio, que no disuelve en absoluto el matrimonio. La frase equivale a *judicial separation.*
Ament [am'-ent], **Amentum** [a-men'-tum], *s.* (Bot.) Amento, espiga articulada por su base y compuesta de flores de un mismo sexo. *V.* CATKIN.
Amentaceous [a-men-tê'-shus], *a.* Amentáceo, lo que tiene amentos o se refiere o pertenece a ellos.
Amentia [a-men'-shi-a], *s.* Demencia, locura.
Amerce [a-męrs'], *va.* Multar, imponer pena pecuniaria por algún delito.
Amerceable [a-męrs'-a-bl], *a.* Digno de ser multado.
Amercement [a-męrs'-męnt], **Amerciament** [a-męr'-shi-a-męnt], *s.* Multa, pena pecuniaria que se impone por algún delito.
Amercer [a-męr'-sęr], *s.* Multador, el que multa.
American [a-mer'-i-can], *s.* y *a.* Americano.
Americanism [a-mer'-i-can-izm], *s.* 1. Americanismo, palabra, frase o idioma peculiar de la América en general, o en particular de los Esta-

dos Unidos. 2. Ciudadanía americana; afición a las instituciones y costumbres americanas.
Americanize [a-mer'-i-can-aiz], *va.* Americanizar; asemejar a los americanos en costumbres o ideas.
†**Amethodical** [a-meth-ed'-i-cal], *a.* Irregular, sin método.
Amethyst [am'-e-thist], *s.* Amatista, piedra preciosa de color violado que tira a purpúreo.
Amiability [ê-mi-a-bil'-i-ti], *s.* Amabilidad. *V.* AMABILITY.
Amiable [ê-mi-a-bl], *a.* Amable, digno de ser amado, amigable, amistoso, agradable.
Amiableness [ê'-mi-a-bl-nes], *s.* Amabilidad.
Amiably [ê'-mi-a-bli], *adv.* Amablemente, cariñosamente.
Amianth [am'-i-anth], **Amianthus** [am-i-an'-thus], *s.* (Min.) Amianto, mineral parecido al asbesto que se deshace en hebras y astillas, y del cual se obtiene una tela incombustible.
Amicable [am'-i-ca-bl], *a.* Amigable, amistoso.
Amicability [am'-i-ca-bil'-i-ti] o **Amicableness** [am'-i-ca-bl-nes], *s.* Afecto cariño, amistad.
Amicably [am'-i-ca-bli], *adv.* Amigablemente, amistosamente.
Amice [am'-is], *s.* Amito, el primero de los ornamentos sagrados que se pone el sacerdote cuando se reviste.
Amicus curiæ [a-mai'-cus kiū'-ri-i], *s. m.* (Lat. For.) Literalmente, *El amigo del tribunal.* Es el letrado que estando presente durante la vista de un proceso, suplica al juez se sirva oir su opinión cuando él juzgue que hay motivo de duda, o confusión en la aplicación de la ley.
Amid [a-mid'], **Amidst** [a-midst'], *prep.* 1. Entre, en medio de. *Amidships,* (Mar.) En medio del navío. 2. Mezclado con, rodeado por.
Amino acid [am'-i-nō as'-id], *s.* Aminoácido.
Amiss [a-mis'], *adv.* Culpablemente, erradamente, mal, impropiamente, fuera del caso. *It would not be amiss if you went thither,* No sería malo que Vd. fuese allá. *It would not be amiss to do it,* No estaría de más el hacerlo. *Do not take it amiss,* No lo lleve Vd. a mal. *Nothing comes amiss to a hungry stomach,* A buen hambre no hay pan duro.
Amiss [a-mis'], *a.* Vicioso. impuro, criminal; impropio; decaído de salud.
Amity [am'-i-ti], *s.* Amistad, afecto recíproco entre dos o más personas.
Ammeter [am'-mi-tẹr], *s.* (Elec.) Amperímetro.
Ammonia [am-mō'-ni-a], *s.* (Quím.) Álcali volátil, amoniaco.
Ammoniac [am-mō'-ni-ac], *s.* Amoniaco o sal amoniaca. *Gum ammoniac,* Goma amoniaca.
Ammoniacal [am-mo-nai'-a-cal], *a.* Amoniacal, lo que pertenece al amoniaco.
Ammonite [am'-en-ait], *s.* (Geol.) Amonita, caracol fósil perteneciente a un molusco extinguido.
Ammonium [am-mō'-ni-um], *s.* Amonio.
Ammunition [am-miu-nish'-un], *s.* Munición, los pertrechos y bastimentos necesarios para la manutención de un ejército, una plaza, etc.
Amnesia [am-nī'-si-a ó nê'-si-a], *s.* Amnesia, pérdida de la memoria.
Amnesty [am'-nes-ti], *s.* Amnistía, olvido general.
Amnion [am'-ni-en], **Amnios** [am'-ni-es], *s.* Amnios, la segunda membrana que envuelve al feto en el útero.
Amœba [a-mī'-ba], *s.* Amibea (amiba o ameba), una de las formas más simples de la vida animal: rizópodo común de agua dulce, que puede cambiar de forma.
Amœboid [a-mī'-beid], *a.* Semejante a la amibea; dícese especialmente del movimiento.
Amomum [a-mō'-mum], *s.* Amomo, fruta de cierta planta en las Indias orientales.
Among [a-mung'], **Amongst** [a-mungst'], *prep.* y *adv.* Entre, mezclado con, o en medio de.
Amoral [ê-mer'-al], *a.* Amoral, sin responsabilidad moral.
Amoret [am'-o-ret], *s.* Amante.
Amorette [am-o-ret'], **Amourette** [am-u-ret'], *s.* 1. Amorío, intriga amorosa. 2. Cupido, amorcillo.
Amorist [am'-o-rist], **Amoroso** [am-o-rō'-so], *s.* Galanteador, amante, galán.
†**Amornings** [a-mērn'-ingz], *adv.* De mañana.
Amorous [am'-o-rus], *a.* 1. Enamorado, amoroso, tierno, apasionado, cariñoso. 2. Amatorio, lo que pertenece al amor.
Amorously [am'-o-rus-li], *adv.* Amorosamente, cariñosamente.
Amorousness [am'-o-rus-nes], *s.* Amor, cariño; la calidad de ser amoroso; galantería, terneza.
Amorphism [a-mēr'-fizm], *s.* Amorfia, carencia de forma, deformidad orgánica.
Amorphous [a-mēr'-fus], *a.* Amorfo, informe, imperfecto, lo que no tiene la forma que le corresponde.
§**Amort** [a-mert'], *a.* Deprimido, abatido, amortiguado, mohino, triste, taciturno.
Amortization [a-mer-ti-zê'-shun], **Amortizement** [a-mēr'-tiz-mẹnt], *s.* (For.) Amortización.
Amortize [a-mēr'-taiz], *va.* Amortizar, pasar los bienes a manos muertas.
Amotion [a-mō'-shun], *s.* Remoción.
Amount [a-maunt'], *s.* Importe, la suma total del valor de una o muchas cosas. *Gross amount,* Importe total. *Net amount,* Importe neto. *To the amount of . . . .* Hasta la cantidad de . . . , por la suma de. *Whole amount,* Importe total. *The amount of what he said was this,* He aquí en substancia lo que dijo.
Amount, *vn.* Montar, importar, subir, ascender.
Amour [a-mūr'], *s.* Amores, amoríos, intriga de amor.
Amove [a-mūv'], *va.* 1. Deponer, retirar o quitar a alguno del empleo que tiene. 2. Remover, mover, alterar, mudar.
Amperage [am'-pẹr-ẹj], *s.* (Elec.) Amperaje, la fuerza de una corriente eléctrica en amperios.
Ampere [am'-pīr], *s.* (Elec.) Amperio, unidad de medida de corriente eléctrica.
Ampersand [am'-pẹr-sand], *s.* El signo & que significa *y.*
Amphibia [am-fib'-i-a], *s. pl.* Anfibios, los animales que habitan así en el agua como en la tierra.
Amphibious [am-fib'-i-us], *a.* Anfibio, lo que puede vivir en dos elementos.
Amphibiousness [am-fib'-i-us-nes], *s.* La calidad de ser anfibio.
Amphibole [am'-fi-bōl], *s.* (Min.) Anfíbol, género de substancias minerales llamadas metasilicatos, el cual comprende la hornblenda, el amianto o asbesto, etc.
Amphibological [am-fi-bo-lej'-i-cal], *a.* Anfibológico, dudoso.
Amphibologically [am-fi-bo-lej'-i-cal-i], *adv.* Anfibológicamente.
Amphibology [am-fi-bel'-o-ji], *s.* Anfibología, palabra o sentencia que se puede entender de dos modos.
Amphibolous [am-fib'-o-lus], *a.* Impelido de una a otra parte.
Amphisbæna [am-fis-bī'-na], *s.* Anfisbena, especie de serpiente fabuloso, con una cabeza a cada extremo del cuerpo y capaz de moverse en una u otra dirección.
Amphibrach [am'-fi-brac], *s.* Anfíbraco, pie de verso latino, de tres sílabas, la primera y la tercera breves y la segunda larga (⏑ — ⏑).
Amphictyons [am-fic'-ti-onz], *s.* Anficciones, diputados de las ciudades de Grecia, que se reunían dos veces al año para resolver sobre los asuntos de la república.
Amphipod [am'-fi-ped], *s.* Orden numeroso de los crustáceos, con catorce pies.
Amphiscii [am-fish'-i-ai], *s. pl.* Anfiscios, los habitantes de la zona tórrida, porque su sombra se dirige ya al norte ya al mediodía, según las estaciones.
Amphitheater, Amphitheatre [am-fi-thī'-a-tẹr], *s.* Anfiteatro, edificio de figura redonda u oval con gradas al rededor.
Amphitheatrical [am-fi-thī-at'-ri-cal], *a.* Anfiteatral.
Amphora [am'-fe-ra], *s.* Ánfora, vaso antiguo de dos asas.
Amphoric [am-fer'-ic], *a.* Anfóreo: dícese de una cavidad en los pulmones que da sonido semejante al que se produce soplando en una garrafa vacía; como *amphoric resonance.*
Ample [am'-pl], *a.* 1. Amplio, extendido, dilatado, extenso, ancho. 2. Liberal, largo, dadivoso; magnífico, ilimitado. *Ample room,* Lugar amplio, espacio dilatado. *Ample resources,* Abundantes recursos.
Ampleness [am'-pl-nes], *s.* 1. Amplitud, anchura. 2. Abundancia, pro fusión, magnificencia.
Amplexicaul [am-plex'-i-cel], *a.* Amplexicaule; dícese de las hojas que rodean el tallo por su base.
Ampliate [am'-pli-êt], *va.* Ampliar, extender, dilatar, aumentar, exagerar.
Ampliation [am-pli-ê'-shun], *s.* 1. Ampliación. 2. (For.) Plazo, término, prorrogación; respiro, plazo.
Amplification [am-pli-fi-kê'-shun], *s.* 1. Amplificación, razonamiento en que se explican ampliamente las causas que influyen en lo que se quiere demostrar. 2. Extensión, ampliación; ampliación del microscopio. 3. Descripción prolija.
Amplificative [am'-plif-i-ca-tiv], **Amplificatory** [am'-plif-i-ca-to-ri], *a.* Ampliativo, amplificador.
Amplifier [am'-pli-fai-ẹr], *s.* Amplificador, ampliador.
Amplify [am'-pli-fai], *va.* 1. (Ret.) Amplificar algún asunto o discurso con expresiones o imágenes. 2. Ampliar, extender, dilatar.
Amplitude [am'-pli-tiūd], *s.* 1. Amplitud, extensión, dilatación. 2. Abundancia. 3. (Astr.) Amplitud. *Amplitude modulation,* (Radio) Modulación de amplitud.

Amply [am'-pli], *adv.* Ampliamente, liberalmente, copiosamente.
Ampulla [am-pul'-a], *s.* Ampolla: vaso de cuello angosto, y de cuerpo ancho y redondo.
Ampullaceous [am-pul-é'-shus], *a.* Ampolláceo; semejante a una botella.
Amputate [am'-piu-têt], *va.* Amputar o cortar algun miembro del cuerpo humano.
Amputation [am-piu-tê'-shun], *s.* Amputación.
Amuck [a-muc'], *adv.* Furiosamente, de una manera frenética. *To run amuck,* Correr de acá para allá con propósito de matar a quien se encuentre al paso; atacar a ciegas, a troche y moche. También se escribe *amok.* (< Malayo amoq.)
Amulet [am'-yu-let], *s.* Amuleto, objeto portátil al que supersticiosamente se atribuye virtud para preservar de enfermedad o peligro.
Amuse [a-miūz'], *va.* 1. Entretener, divertir. 2. Embobar, entretener, engañar, adormecer, engaitar.—*vn.* Meditar.
Amusement [a-miūz'-ment], *s.* Diversión, entretenimiento, recreo, pasatiempo.
Amuser [a-miūz'-ęr], *s.* Entretenedor, engañador, embaucador, engaitador.
Amusingly [a-miūz'-ing-li], *adv.* Divertidamente.
Amusive [a-miū'-siv], *a.* Divertido, lo que divierte, entretenido.
Amusively [a-miū-siv-li], *adv.* Entretenidamente.
Amygdalate [a-mig'-da-lêt], *a.* Hecho de almendras.
Amygdaline [a-mig'-da-lin], *a.* Almendrado, lo que se parece a la almendra en la figura.
Amygdaloids [a-mig'-da-loidz], *s. pl.* (Min.) Piedras compuestas de varios pedazos como almendras.
Amyl [am'-il], *s.* (Quím.) Amilo: radical hidrocarbono, C_5H_{11}, de la serie parafina, y que se encuentra en el alcohol amílico.
An [an], *art.* Un, uno, una; es el mismo artículo indefinido, *A,* al cual se añade la *n* cuando la voz que le sigue empieza por una vocal o *h* muda. *An eel,* Una anguila. *An hour,* Una hora. *A horse,* Un caballo.
Ana [an'-a], *s.* (Med.) Ana, parte o porción igual de cada ingrediente: comunmente en la abreviatura āā. (Gr.)
Ana [an'-a], *s. pl.* Apuntes curiosos respecto á alguna persona, lugar o asunto.
-ana. Sufijo (muchas veces con i eufónica); perteneciente a: relacionado con alguna persona o lugar notable.
Anabaptism [an-a-bap'-tizm], *s.* Herejía de los anabaptistas.
Anabaptist [an-a-bap'-tist], *s.* Anabaptista o anabatista, nombre de unos sectarios.
Anabaptistic [an-a-bap-tis'-tic], **Anabaptistical** [an-a-bap-tis'-ti-cal], *a.* Anabaptístico, lo que pertenece a los anabaptistas.
Anabas [an'-a-bas], *s.* Género de peces que pueden andar por tierra y trepar árboles. *V.* CLIMBING-FISH. (Gr.)
Anabolism [an-ab'-o-lizm], *s.* El procedimiento de la asimilación de los alimentos.
Anacamptic [an-a-camp'-tic], *a.* Reverberado, reflejado. *An anacamptic hill,* Monte o roca que produce un eco reflejando los sonidos.
Anacardium [an-a-cār'-di-um], *s.* (Bot.) Anacardo, árbol que se cria en la India oriental.
Anacathartic [an-a-ca-thār'-tic], *s.* Anacatártico, medicamento que opera por arriba.
Anachoret [an-ac'-o-ret], **Anachorite** [an-ac'-o-rait], *s.* Anacoreta, el que vive en un lugar solitario, retirado del comercio humano.
Anachorism [an-ac'-o-rizm], *s.* Lo que no se aviene con las condiciones locales de un país.
Anachronism [an-ac'-ro-nizm], *s.* Anacronismo, error de cronología.
Anachronistic [an-ac-ro-nis'-tic], *a.* Anacronístico.
Anaclastics, *s.* *V.* DIOPTRICS.
Anaconda [an-a-con'-da], *s.* Anaconda, serpiente sudamericana.
Anacreontic [an-ac-re-on'-tic], *a.* Anacreóntico.
Anadromous [an-ad'-ro-mus], *a.* Anadromo; dícese de los peces que saliendo del mar suben por los ríos en ciertas estaciones, para procrear.
Anæmia [a-nī'-mi-a], *s.* Anemia, diminución de los glóbulos de la sangre.
Anæmic [a-nī'-mic], *a.* Anémico, en estado de anemia.
Anæsthesia [an-es-thī'-si-a], *s.* Anestesia; pérdida del sentido; estado producido por enfermedad o por la inspiración o aplicación de un anestésico.
Anæsthetic [an-es-thet'-ic], *a.* Anestésico, anestético; capaz de producir insensibilidad o pérdida completa del sentido.—*s.* Anestésico, lo que produce insensibilidad al dolor, como el cloroformo, la cocaína, etc.
An(a)esthetist [an-es'-thet-ist], *s.* Anestesista, médico anestesista.
An(a)esthetize [an-es'-the-taiz], *va.* Anestesiar.
Anaglyph [an'-a-glif], *s.* Anaglifo; ornamento de escultura de talla.
Anagogical [an-a-gej'-i-cal], **Anagogetical** [an-a-go-jet'-i-cal], *a.* Anagógico, místico.
Anagogics [an-a-gej'-ics], *s.* Anagogía, sentido místico.
Anagram [an'-a-gram], *s.* Anagrama, transposición de las letras de una palabra o sentencia, de la cual resulta otra palabra o sentencia distinta; v. g. *amor,* ramo, mora.
Anagrammatical [an-a-gram-at'-i-cal], *a.* Anagramático.
Anagrammatist [an-a-gram'-a-tist], *a.* Anagramatizador.
Anagrammatize [an-a-gram'-a-taiz], *vn.* Anagramatizar.
Anal [ê'-nal], *a.* Anal; que tiene relación con el ano.
Analect [an'-a-lect], *s.* Fragmento escogido de un autor; se usa más en plural.
Analepsis [an-a-lep'-sis], *s.* Analepsia, restauración de las fuerzas extenuadas.
Analeptic [an-a-lep'-tic], *a.* (Med.) Analéptico, restaurativo.
Analgesic [an-al-jī'-zic], *s.* y *a.* (Med.) Analgésico.
Analog computer [an'-a-leg com-piū'-tęr], *s.* Computadora analógica.
Analogical [an-a-lej'-i-cal], *a.* Analógico.
Analogically [an-a-lej'-i-cal-i], *adv.* La calidad de ser anfibio.
Analogism [a-nal'-o-jizm], *s.* Analogismo, argumento de la causa al efecto.
Analogize [a-nal'-o-jaiz], *va.* Analogizar, explicar por analogía.
Analogous [a-nal'-o-gus], *a.* Análogo; proporcional.
Analogously [a-nal'-o-gus-li], *adv.* Analógicamente.
Analogue [an'-a-leg], *s.* Lo análogo, lo que guarda relación de semejanza con otra cosa o idea. *Analogue computer,* Máquina calculadora de términos semejantes.
Analogy [a-nal'-o-ji], *s.* Analogía, proporción o semejanza de una cosa con otra, relación, conformidad.
Analysis [a-nal'-i-sis], *s.* Análisis, *s. com.* separación de algún compuesto en las varias partes de que se compone.
Analyst [an'-a-list], **Analyzer** [an'-a-lai-zęr], *s.* Analizador.
Analytic [an-a-lit'-ic], *s.* Método analítico.
Analytical [an-a-lit'-i-cal], *a.* Analítico.
Analytically [an-a-lit'-i-cal-i], *adv.* Analíticamente.
Analyze [an'-a-laiz], *va.* Analizar, hacer análisis.
Anamorphosis [an-a-mōr'-fo-sis], *s.* Anamorfosis; la pintura que representa separadas, y al parecer informes, las varias partes de un objeto; pero que se hallan perfectas y en su propio lugar, cuando se mira desde cierto punto de vista.
Ananas [a-nā'-nas o a-nê'-nas], *s.* Ananas, nombre dado en Europa a la piña de América.
Anapest [an'-a-pest], *s.* Anapesto, ⏑ ⏑ —. Se llama así por ser opuesto al dáctilo.
Anapestic [an-a-pes'-tic], *a.* Anapéstico.
Anaphora [an-af'-o-ra], *s.* Anáfora, figura que consiste en la repetición de una misma palabra al principio de dos o más frases.
Anaphrodisia [an-af-ro-dis'-i-a], *s.* Ausencia del apetito venéreo.
Anaphrodisiac [an-af-ro-dis'-i-ac], *a.* Anafrodisiaco; calmante del deseo venéreo.
Anaplasty [an'-a-plas-ti], *s.* (Med.) Anaplastia, autoplastia, cirugía plástica.
Anarchist [an'-ār-kist], **Anarch** [an'-ārc], *s.* Anarquista.
Anarchic [an-ār'-kic], **Anarchical** [an-ār'-kic-al], *a.* Anárquico, confuso, desordenado.
Anarchism [an'-ār-kizm], **Anarchy** [an'-ār-ki], *s.* Anarquía, confusión, desorden.
Anasarca [an-a-sār'-ca], *s.* (Med.) Anasarca, especie de hidropesía.
Anasarcous [an-a-sār'-cus], *a.* Hidrópico.
Anastasis [an-as'-ta-sis], *s.* Resurrección.
Anastatic [an-as-tat'-ic], *a.* Anastático, en relieve. *Anastatic printing,* Impresión anastática; manera de obtener copia en relieve de una página impresa, etc., sobre una plancha de zinc que sirve para la reimpresión.
Anastomose [an-as'-to-mōz], *vn.* Unirse por sus extremos las ramificaciones salientes de las arterias y venas; anastomarse.
Anastomosis [a-nas-to-mō'-sis], *s.* (Med.) Anastomosis, unión de dos vasos sanguíneos o linfáticos.
Anastomotic [an-as-tem-et'-ic], *a.* Anastomótico; que forma anastomosis o se refiere a ella.
Anastrophe [a-nas'-tro-fę], *s.* Anás-

trofe; inversión del orden usual de las palabras.
Anathema [a-nath'-e-ma], *a.* Anatema, excomunión, execración.
Anathematical [a-nath-e-mat'-i-cal], *a.* Lo perteneciente al anatema.
Anathematically [a-nath-e-mat'-i-cal-i], *adv.* A modo de anatema.
Anathematization [a-nath-e-mat-i-zé'-shun], *s.* La acción de excomulgar.
Anathematize [a-nath'-e-ma-taiz], *va.* Anatematizar, excomulgar.
Anathematizer [a-nath'-e-ma-taiz-er], *s.* Excomulgador, anatematizador.
‡**Anatocism** [a-nat'-o-sizm], *s.* Contrato usurario, usura de la misma usura o interés del interés.
Anatomical [an-a-tem'-i-cal], *a.* Anatómico.
Anatomically [an-a-tem'-i-cal-i], *adv.* Anatómicamente.
Anatomist [a-nat'-o-mist], *s.* Anatomista o anatómico, el profesor de anatomía.
Anatomize [a-nat'-o-maiz], *va.* Anatomizar, hacer disección o anatomía de un cuerpo; disecar.
Anatomy [a-nat'-o-mi], *s.* 1. Anatomía, parte de la medicina que trata de la descripción del cuerpo humano: llámase también así la disección de un cuerpo humano. 2. División de alguna cosa. 3. Esqueleto.
Anbury [an'-bur-i], *s.* Tumor blando y grumoso que se presenta en el cuerpo de las caballerías y los ganados.
Ancestor [an'-ses-ter], *s.* Uno de los mayores, abuelos o antepasados de alguno, predecesor.
Ancestral [an-ses'-tral] o **Ancestrel** [an-ses'-trel], *a.* Hereditario.
Ancestry [an'-ses-tri], *s.* Linaje o serie de antepasados, extracción, raza, alcurnia.
Ancientry [ên'-shent-ri], *s.* Antigüedad de una familia; dignidad antigua.
Anchor [ang'-cer], *s.* 1. Ancla o áncora de una embarcación. *Best bower anchor,* Ancla de ayuste. *Small bower anchor,* Ancla sencilla. *Sheet anchor,* Anclote o ancla de esperanza. *Anchor arms,* Uñas del ancla. *Anchor back,* Galga del ancla. *Anchor bill,* Pico del ancla. *Anchor cross,* Cruz del ancla. *Anchor flukes,* Orejas del ancla. *Anchor shank,* Caña del ancla. *Anchor stock,* Cepo del ancla. *To stock the anchor,* Encepar el ancla. *At anchor,* Al ancla. *Foul anchor,* Ancla enredada con su cable. *Anchor beam,* Serviola. *Anchor chocks,* Calzos de ancla. *Anchor escapement,* Escape de áncora. *Anchor ground,* Fondeadero. *Anchor stopper,* Capón. *Drag anchor,* Ancla flotante o de arrastre. *Foul anchor,* Ancla encepada. *Kedge anchor,* Anclote. *To ride at anchor,* Estar al ancla. 2. (Ant.) *V.* ANACHORITE.
Anchor, *vn.* Anclar, ancorar, echar las anclas. *To drop or let go anchor,* Dar fondo. *To weigh anchor,* Levar el ancla. *To drag the anchor,* Garrar o arrastrar el ancla. *Anchored,* Anclado; formado como ancla.—*va.* Ancorar; fijar. *Anchoring,* Anclaje. *Anchoring of a bridge,* Amarras de un puente. *Anchoring ground,* Agarradero; fondeadero.
Anchorable [ang'-cer-a-bl], *a.* Propio para anclaje.
Anchorage [ang'-cer-êj], *s.* 1. Anclaje, el sitio o lugar para anclar: llámase también ancoraje o surgidero. 2. Anclaje, las áncoras de una embarcación. 3. Anclaje, el tributo o derecho que se paga en los puertos de mar por dar fondo en ellos.
Anchoress [ang'-cur-es], *s.* Ermitaña, la mujer que vive en una ermita.
Anchoret [ang'-cor-et], **Anchorite** [ang'-cor-ait], *s.* Ermitaño, anacoreta. *V.* ANACHORITE.
Anchor-hold [ang'-cer-hōld], *s.* 1. Agarro de ancla. 2. (Fig.) Seguridad.
Anchorsmith [ang'-cer-smith], *s.* Forjador de anclas.
Anchovy [an-chō'-vi], *s.* Anchova o anchoa, pez pequeño, menor que la sardina.
Anchylose, Anchylosis. *V.* ANKYLOSE y ANKYLOSIS.
Ancient [ên'-shent], *a.* Antiguo.—*s.* 1. (Ant.) Bandera; insignia. El porta-estandarte, porta-guión, o abanderado. 2. En plural, antepasados, mayores.
Anciently [ên'-shent-li], *adv.* Antiguamente.
Ancientness [ên'-shent-nes], *s.* Antigüedad.
Ancientry [ên'-shent-ri], *s.* Antigüedad de linaje.
Ancillary [an'-sil-a-ri], *a.* El que sirve bajo otro sirviente. Ancilario; subordinado.
Ancipital, Ancipitous [an-sip'-i-tal], *a.* 1. Con dos caras o formas. 2. De dos cortes.
Ancoral [an'-ce-ral], *a.* 1. Perteneciente o semejante a un áncora. 2. (Zool.) En forma de gancho, encorvado.
And [and], *conj.* Y, e, conjunción copulativa; aun, si, que, a.—*s.* Nombre del signo &. *V.* AMPERSAND. *Now and then,* De cuando en cuando, o de vez en cuando. *And therefore,* Por esta razón, por tanto. *By and by,* Luego, al instante. *By little and little,* Poco a poco. *Better and better,* Cada vez mejor; o mejor que mejor, o más que más. *Here and there,* Tan pronto aquí como allí, o acá y allá; de aquí para allí. *To go and see,* Ir a ver. *And yet,* Sin embargo. *With ifs and ands,* Con o en dimes y diretes; con si y no. *And so forth,* Y así de los demás; etcétera.
Andalusian [an-da-lū'-si-an], *a.* Andaluz, andaluza; de Andalucía.
Andante [ān-dān'-te], *a.* (Mús.) Andante, que significa distinto, primoroso, más vivo que larghetto y menos que allegretto.
Andantino [ān-dān-tí'-no], *a.* Algo más lento que andante. Se usa algunas veces para denotar movimiento entre andante y allegretto.
Andean [an-dí'-an], *a.* Andino, de los Andes.
Andirons [and'-ai-urnz], *s. pl.* Morillos, caballetes de hierro.
Androgen [an'-dro-jen], *s.* (Biol.) Andrógeno.
Androginal [an-drej'-i-nal], **Androgynous** [an-drej'-i-nus], *a.* Andrógino, lo que pertenece a los hermafroditas.
Androgynus [an-drej'-i-nus], **Androgyne** [an-drej'-i-ne], *s.* Hermafrodita, andrógino.
Android [an'-dreid], *a.* Que tiene forma humana.—*s.* Autómata, que tiene la figura y los movimientos del hombre.
Androtomy [an-dret'-o-mi], *s.* Androtomía, la disección del cadáver de un hombre.
Anecdote [an'-ec-dōt], *s.* Anécdota, relación breve de un suceso curioso más o menos importante.
Anemography [an-e-meg'-ra-fi], *s.* Anemografía, descripción de los vientos.
Anemometer [an-e-mem'-e-ter], *s.* Anemómetro, instrumento para medir el viento y sus grados.
Anemometry [an-e-mem'-e-tri], *s.* Anemometría, el arte de medir la fuerza del viento.
Anemone [a-nem'-o-ne], *s.* (Bot.) Anémone, anémona, especie de flor; planta ranunculácea que contiene numerosas especies. *Sea-anemone,* Actinia, anémona marina.
Anemoscope [a-nem'-o-scōp], *s.* Anemoscopio, instrumento para indicar los cambios de dirección del aire.
Anent [a-nent'], *prep.* 1. Tocante, por lo concerniente. 2. Contra, opuesto.
Aneroid [an'-er-eid], *a.* Aneroide: sin líquido. *Aneroid barometer,* Barómetro aneroide.
Aneurism [an'-yu-rizm], *s.* Aneurisma, dilatación de las arterias.
Aneurismal [an-yu-riz'-mal], *a.* Aneurismal.
Anew [a-niū'], *adv.* 1. De nuevo, otra vez. 2. Nuevamente, de un modo nuevo, de refresco.—N. B. *Anew* se traduce elegantemente por el verbo *Volver,* (irreg.) v. g. *He writes anew,* Él vuelve a escribir.
Anfractuous [an-frac'-tiu-us], **Anfractuose** [an-frac'-tiu-ōs], *a.* Tortuoso, sinuoso, anfractuoso, desigual.
Anfractuosity [an-frac-tiu-es'-i-ti], *s.* Desigualdad, sinuosidad, anfractuosidad.
Angel [ên'-jel], *s.* 1. Ángel. *Guardian angel,* Ángel de la guarda. 2. Ángel, expresión de cariño para ponderar la hermosura de alguna persona. 3. Mensajero. 4. Moneda antigua del valor de cincuenta reales.—*a.* Angélico, angelical.
Angel-age [ên'-jel-êj], *s.* Estado o existencia de los ángeles.
Angelic [an-jel'-ic], **Angelical** [an-jel'-ic-al], *a.* Angelical, angélico.
Angelica [an-jel'-i-ca], *s.* 1. (Bot.) Angélica, planta. 2. Cierto vino dulce de California.
Angelically [an-jel'-i-cal-i], *va.* Angélicamente, angelicalmente.
Angelicalness [an-jel-i-cal-nes], *s.* Excelencia sobrehumana, hermosura angelical.
Angel-like [ên'-jel-laic], *a.* Angelical.
Angelot [an'-je-let], *s.* 1. Instrumento músico, semejante al laúd. 2. Moneda acuñada por los ingleses, cuando los reyes de Inglaterra lo eran también de Francia, y que tenía la mitad del valor del ángel. 3. Especie de queso muy estimado, que se hace en Normandía.
Angel-shot [ên'-jel-shet], *s.* Balas enramadas o encadenadas, palanquetas.
Angelus [an'-jel-us], *s.* El Ave María, la oración de este nombre y el toque de campanas que indica esta oración.
Angel-winged [ên'-jel-wingd], *a.* Alado como los ángeles.
Angel-worship [ên'-jel-wūr'-ship], *s.* Culto de los ángeles.
Anger [ang'-ger], *s.* 1. Ira, cólera. 2. Inflamación de un órgano o tejido del cuerpo. 3. Enojo, enfado, disgusto. *A fit of anger,* Un acceso de cólera. *To provoke to anger,* Encolerizar, causar ira.
Anger, *va.* Provocar, enfurecer; enojar, irritar, encolerizar.
Angina [an'-ji-na o an-jai'-na], *s.* An-

gina, afección inflamatoria de la faringe, la laringe, etc. *Angina pectoris*, Angina de pecho, o esternalgia.

Angiocarpous [an-ji-o-cār'-pus], *a.* Angiocarpio o angiocarpo; dícese de la planta cuyo fruto está contenido en una cubierta distinta y separada del fruto mismo.

Angiography [an-ji-eg'-ra-fi], *s.* Angiografía, descripción de los vasos del cuerpo humano.

Angiology [an-ji-el'-o-ji], *s.* (Anat.) Angiología, parte de la anatomía que trata de los vasos.

Angiomonospermous [an-ji-o-men-o-sper'-mus], *a.* Dícese de las plantas que tienen una semilla en su pericarpio.

Angiosperm [an'-ji-o-sperm], *s.* (Bot.) Angiosperma, orden de plantas cuya semilla está envuelta en vaina diferente del cáliz.

Angiospermous [an-ji-o-spēr'-mus], *a.* Angiospermo; dícese de un fruto cuyos granos están encerrados en un pericarpio distinto o de diversa naturaleza.

Angiosporous [an-ji-o-spō'-rus], *a.* Angiospóreo; se dice de la planta cuyos esporos están contenidos en un receptáculo hueco, como ciertos hongos.

Angle [ang'-gl], *s.* 1. Ángulo, la inclinación de dos líneas que se cortan en un punto. 2. (Geom.) Angulo, espacio comprendido entre dos líneas —curvas o rectas—que se reunen en un punto. 3. Esquina. 4. Caña de pescar. 5. Anzuelo. *Visual angle*, Ángulo óptico. *Angle-bevel*, Falsa escuadra. *Angle-brace*, Cuadral. *Angle-brackets*, Modillones angulares. *Angle-rafter*, Lima. *Angle* (roofing), Caballete.

Angle, *va.* 1. Pescar con caña. 2. (Met.) Insinuarse, introducirse con maña para lograr de otro lo que se pretende.—*va.* Atraer, halagar.

Angled [ang'-gld], *a.* Anguloso.

Angler [ang'-gler], *s.* Pescador de caña.

Angle-rod [ang'-gl-red], *s.* Trozo de la caña de pescar, al cual se afianzan el sedal y anzuelo del pescador.

Angle-worm [ang'-gl-wūrm], *s.* Lombriz de tierra.

Anglican [ang'-gli-can], *a.* Anglicano.—*s.* Individuo de la iglesia anglicana.

Anglicize [ang'-gli-saiz], *va.* Traducir o convertir en inglés; dar a otra lengua los giros y el carácter del idioma inglés.

Anglicism [ang'-gli-sizm], *s.* Anglicismo, modo de hablar particular y privativo de la lengua inglesa.

Angling [ang'-gling], *s.* El arte o práctica de pescar con caña.

Anglo-American [ang'-glō-a-mer'-i-can], *a.* y *s.* Angloamericano.

Anglo-Indian [an-glō-in'-di-an], *a.* y *s.* Angloindiano, relacionado con los ingleses y las Indias orientales.

Anglomania [an-glō-mē'-ni-a], *s.* Anglomanía, admiración exagerada de los ingleses y de lo perteneciente a ellos.

Anglomaniac [an-glō'-mē'-ni-ac], *a.* y *s.* Anglómano, el que imita servilmente a los ingleses o lo hace con extravagancia.

Anglo-Norman [ang'-glō-nōr'-man], *s.* y *a.* Anglonormando.

Anglo-Saxon [ang'-glō-sax-en], *s.* y *a.* Anglosajón.

Angora [an-gō'-ra], *s.* Angora, ciudad de Anatolia. *Angora cat, goat*, Gato, cabra de Angora o Angola.

Angrily [ang'-gri-li], *adv.* Coléricamente, airadamente.

Angry [ang'-gri], *a.* 1. Colérico, irritado, enfadado, enojado, encolerizado, airado. 2. (Med.) Irritado, inflamado, que presenta inflamación. *They never spoke an angry word to each other*, Jamás se han hablado con cólera. *To angry waves*, A las olas irritadas.

Anguilliform [an-gwil'-i-fōrm], *a.* En forma de anguila.

Anguish [ang'-gwish], *s.* Ansia, pena, angustia, congoja, aflicción, dolor.

Anguished [ang'-gwisht], *a.* Atormentado, angustiado.

Angular [ang'-giu-lar], *a.* Angular, anguloso, lo que pertenece al ángulo, o los tiene.

Angularity [ang-giu-lar'-i-ti], **Angularness** [ang'-giu-lar-nes], **Angulosity** [ang-giu-les'-i-ti]. *s.* La propiedad de tener ángulos o esquinas.

Angulate, Angulated [ang'-giu-lēt-ed], *a.* (Bot.) Anguloso, angular.

Anhelation [an-he-lē'-shun], *s.* Jadeo, anhélito vehemente, anhelación.

Anhydride [an-hai'-drid o draid], *s.* Óxido que se convierte en ácido cuando se le añade agua; o ácido del cual se ha extraído el agua, y que forma sales.

Anhydrous [an-hai'-drus], *a.* Anhidro, que no contiene agua.

Anil [an'-il], *s.* (Bot.) Añil, la planta de cuyas hojas y tallos se hace el índigo o añil.

Anile [an'il], *a.* Semejante a una vieja; falto de juicio, que chochea; chocha. (< Lat. *anus*, mujer vieja.)

Anilin o **Aniline** [an'-i-lin], *s.* Anilina, base de la cual se obtienen muchos tintes brillantes. Líquido incoloro oleoso, obtenido hoy del alquitrán de carbón, pero originalmente del añil. (< Anil.) *Anilin colours*, Colores de anilina.

Animadversion [an-i-mad-ver'-shun], *s.* 1. Animadversión, nota crítica o reparo. 2. Animadvertencia, advertencia u observación. 3. Reflexión, reprensión, castigo, apercibimiento.

Animadversive [an-i-mad-ver'-siv], *a.* Judicativo, lo que juzga o puede hacer juicio de algo.

Animadversiveness [an-i-mad-ver'-siv-nes], *s.* Poder o facultad de considerar o formar juicio. Censura, reproche.

Animadvert [an-i-mad-vert'], *vn.* 1. Advertir, considerar, observar. 2. Censurar, formar juicio, dar dictamen, juzgar. 3. Reprochar, castigar.

Animadverter [an-i-mad-vert'-er], *s.* Censurador, crítico.

Animal [an'-i-mal], *s.* 1. Animal, cuerpo animado. 2. Animal, por injuria o desprecio se llama así al hombre incapaz o ignorante. *A stupid animal*, Hombre estúpido; dícese por desprecio.

Animal, *a.* Animal, que pertenece a cualquiera criatura viviente y corpórea. *Animal kingdom*, Reino animal. *Animal spirits*, Vivacidad, ardor, fuego. *His advanced age does not subdue his animal spirits*, Su avanzada edad no subyuga su ardor.

Animalcular [an-i-mal'-kiu-lar], *a.* Animalcular, referente a los animálculos.

Animalcule [an-i-mal'-kiūl], *s.* Animalillo microscópico: animálculo, como un infusorio o rotador. *Animalcule-cage*, El porta animálculos para un microscopio.

Animalism [an'-i-mal-izm], *s.* 1. Animalismo, estado animal. 2. Sensualidad.

Animality [an-i-mal'-i-ti], *s.* El estado de la existencia animal, vida animal.

Animalization [an-i-mal-i-zē'-shun], *s.* Animalización.

Animalize [an'-i-mal-aiz], *va.* 1. Animalizar, dotar de propiedades animales. 2. Asimilar los alimentos, convertirlos en materia animal.

Animate [an'-i-mēt], *va.* 1. Animar, infundir alma. 2. Animar, infundir ánimo o valor, excitar.

Animate [an'-i-mēt], *a.* Viviente, animado.

Animated [an-i-mē'-ted], *a.* Animado, vivo, vigoroso. *Animated cartoon*, Caricatura animada.

Animating [an'-i-mēt-ing], *a.* 1. Animante, vivificante, excitante. 2. Alegre, divertido.

Animation [an-i-mē'-shun], *s.* Animación. (Fig.) Viveza, espíritu.

Animative [an'-i-mē-tiv], *a.* Animante, lo que anima.

Animator [an'-i-mē-ter], *s.* Animador.

Anime [an'-i-mē], **Gum anime** [gum an'-i-mē], *a.* 1. Anime, goma o resina del curbaril, árbol de Cayena y de las Indias. 2. Goma copal.

Animism [an'-i-mizm], *s.* 1. Animismo, creencia en el ser del espíritu, o alma, con independencia de la materia orgánica. 2. Sistema médico-fisiológico que considera el alma como principio de acción y causa primera.

Animosity [a-ni-mes'-i-ti], *s.* Animosidad, mala voluntad, ojeriza, rencor, odio, encono, aversión, aborrecimiento, rencilla.

Animus [an'-i-mus], *s.* Ánimo, intención, designio.

Anise [an-is'], *s.* (Bot.) Anís o matalahuva, planta anual umbelífera y su semilla. *Anise-seed*, Anís o simiente de anís. *Indian aniseed*, Badiana o anís de la China.

Anisette [an-is-et'], *s.* (Fr.) Anisete, licor compuesto de aguardiente, azúcar y anís.

Anker [ang'-ker], *s.* Anker, medida de líquidos que es la cuarta parte del *aam* o *ham* de Holanda.

Ankle [ang'-cl], *s.* Maléolo o tobillo del pie. *Ankle-bone*, Hueso del tobillo.

Ankled [ang'-cld], *a.* Lo que pertenece al tobillo.

Anklet [ang'-clet], *s.* 1. Aro de adorno para el tobillo. 2. Vendaje para mantener el tobillo en debida posición. 3. Media tobillera.

Ankylose [ang'-ki-lōz], *va.* y *vn.* Anquilosar, fijar una articulación.

Ankylosis [ang-ki-lō'-sis], *s.* Anquilosis, inflexibilidad de una articulación.

Annalist [an'-nal-ist], *s.* Analista, el que escribe anales, cronista.

Annalize [an'-nal-aiz], *va.* Escribir anales.

Annals [an'-nalz], *s. pl.* 1. Anales, historia o relación de sucesos por años, de año en año. 2. Misas celebradas de tiempo en tiempo durante el año; y también las misas de aniversario, o cabo de año.

Annats [an'-nats], *s.* Anata, la renta, frutos o emolumentos que produce en un año cualquier beneficio o empleo.

Annatto [an-nat'-o], *s.* Orellana, achiote; dícese del árbol y de la tintura.
Anneal [an-nîl'], *va.* Templar el cristal o vidrio para que se penetren los colores; atemperar, frotar con aceite.
Annealing [an-nîl'-ing], *s.* 1. El acto o arte de templar el vidrio. 2. Recocción, destemple. *Annealing furnace* u *oven*, Horno de recocido. *Annealing-pot*, Crisol de templar.
Annex [an-nex'], *va.* Anexar, unir o agregar una cosa a otra con dependencia de ella; juntar, reunir.
Annex [an-nex'], *s.* Aditamento, anexo.
Annexation [an-nex-ê'-shun], **Annexment** [an-nex'-mẹnt], *s.* Anexión, la acción y efecto de anexar, o la misma cosa anexa; conjunción, adición, unión.
Annexed [an-ext'], *pp.* y *a.* Adjunto.
Annexive [an-nex'-iv], *a.* Anexorio, que une o anexa, o que tiende a anexar.
Annihilable [an-nai'-hi-la-bl], *a.* Destructible, lo que se puede destruir o aniquilar.
Annihilate [an-nai'-hi-lêt], *va.* Aniquilar, reducir a la nada.
Annihilation [an-nai-hi-lê'-shun], *s.* Aniquilación, la acción y efecto de aniquilar.
Annihilator [an-nai'-hi-lê-tor], *s.* Aniquilador.
Anniversary [an-ni-vẹr'-sa-ri], *s.* 1. Aniversario, día en que se cumplen años de algún suceso. 2. Aniversario, la fiesta o ceremonia que se celebra en cierto día señalado de cada año.
Anniversary, *a.* Anual.
Anno domini [an'-no dem'-i-nai], *s.* (Lat.) En el año de Nuestro Señor.
Annomination [an-nem-i-nê'-shun], *s.* Agnominación o paronomasia.
Anno mundi [an'-no mun'-dai], *s.* (Lat.) En el año del mundo.
Annotate [an'-no-têt], *va.* Anotar, comentar.
Annotation [an-no-tê'-shun], *s.* Anotación o nota que se pone a algún escrito.
Annotator [an-no-tê'-tor], **Annotationist** [an-no-tê'-shun-ist], *s.* Anotador, comentador, ilustrador.
Annotto [an-net'-o], *s.* (Bot.) Orellana, achiote. Lo mismo que **Annatto.**
Announce [an-nauns'], *va.* Anunciar, publicar, proclamar; declarar, jurídicamente.
Announcement [an-nauns'-mẹnt], *s.* Aviso, advertencia, declaración.
Announcer [a-naun'-sẹr], *s.* Anunciador. *Radio announcer*, Locutor o anunciador de radio.
Annoy [an-noi'], *va.* Molestar, incomodar, hacer mal, vejar, fastidiar. *The least sound annoys him*, El menor ruido le incomoda.
Annoyance [an-noi'-ans], *s.* Molestia, injuria, pena, incomodidad; disgusto, fastidio.
Annoyer [an-noi'-ẹr], *s.* Molestador, persona enojosa.
Annoying [an-noi'-ing], *pa.* Fastidioso, molesto, incómodo, importuno.
Annual [an'-yu-al], †**Annuary** [an'-yu-e-ri], *a.* Anual, lo que se hace o sucede cada año; lo que dura sólo por un año.
Annually [an'-yu-al-li], *adv.* Anualmente, de año en año, cada año.
Annuitant [an-niû'-i-tant], *s.* El que tiene una renta vitalicia.
Annuity [an-niû'-i-ti], *s.* Anualidad, renta vitalicia.
Annul [an-nul'], *va.* 1. Anular, invalidar, revocar, dar por nulo. 2. Aniquilar, reducir a la nada alguna cosa.
Annular [an'-yu-lar], *a.* Anular; que se parece al anillo en la figura.
Annulary [an'-yu-lẹ-ri], *a.* Adornado con anillo; dícese del dedo anular.
Annulate, Annulated [an'-yu-lẹt, lê''-ted], *a.* Anuloso, anillado; que se compone de anillos o lo parece.
Annulet [an'-yiu-let], *s.* Anillejo, sortijilla.
Annulment [an-nul'-mẹnt], *s.* Anulación, la acción de anular.
Annulose [an'-yu-lōs], *a.* 1. Anuloso, rodeado de anillos o rayas circulares. 2. Guarnecido de sortijas o anillos.
Annum [an'-um], *s.* Año; se emplea sólo en la locución, *Per annum*, Al año, o por año.
†**Annumerate** [an-niû'-me-rêt], *va.* Anumerar, añadir al número anterior, poner en el número, contar entre, comprender.
Annunciate [an-nun'-shi-êt], *va.* Anunciar, llevar o traer noticia o aviso.
Annunciation [an-nun-shi-ê'-shun], *s.* 1. Anunciación, día celebrado por la Iglesia en memoria de la embajada que el ángel trajo a la Virgen santísima; es el día veinte y cinco de Marzo. 2. Proclamación, promulgación.
Annunciator [an-nun'-shi-ê-tor], *s.* 1. Proclamador. 2. Indicador (como en los hoteles); aparato para señalar un número, nombre, etc., cuando llaman.
Anodal [an'-o-dal], *a.* Que se refiere al anodo.
Anode [an'-ōd], *s.* Anodo, polo positivo de una batería eléctrica. (Gr.)
Anodic [ạ-nod'-ic], *a.* Perteneciente al anodo; que procede hacia arriba.
Anodize [an'-o-daiz], *va.* Anodizar.
Anodyne [an'-o-dain], *a.* Anodino, lo que tiene virtud de suavizar y mitigar los dolores.
Anoint [a-neint'], *va.* 1. Untar, pringar, aplicar a alguna cosa aceite u otra materia pingüe. 2. Ungir, signar con óleo sagrado. *To anoint a dying person*, Administrar la extremaunción, u olear a un moribundo.
Anointer [a-nein'-tẹr], *s.* Untador, el que unta; también se puede entender del que unge.
Anointing [a-neint'-ing], **Anointment** [a-neint'-mẹnt], *s.* Unción, el acto y efecto de untar, o de ungir.
Anomalism [a-nem'-a-lizm], *s.* Irregularidad, anomalía.
Anomalistic, Anomalistical [a-nem''-a-lis'-tic, al], *a.* Anomalístico, perteneciente a la anomalía. *Anomalistic year*, Año anomalístico, el tiempo que emplea la tierra en volver a un punto dado de su órbita.
Anomalous [a-nem'-a-lus], *a.* Anómalo, irregular, que se separa de la regla común.
Anomalously [a-nem'-a-lus-li], *adv.* Irregularmente.
Anomalousness [a-nem'-a-lus-nes], **Anomaly** [a-nem'-a-li], *s.* Anomalía, irregularidad.
Anon [a-nen'], *adv.* 1. Pronto, a poco. 2. De cuando en cuando. 3. A cada instante. 4. En seguida, inmediatamente. *Ever and anon*, Una y otra vez, a menudo.
Anonym [an'-o-nim], *s.* 1. Persona o escritor anónimo. 2. Seudónimo.
Anonymous [a-nen'-i-mus], *a.* Anónimo, que no tiene nombre.
Anonymously [a-nen'-i-mus-li], *adv.* Anónimamente.
Anorexia [an-or-ex'-i-a], *s.* Anorexia, inapetencia.
Anosmia [an-es'-mi-a], *s.* Anosmia, anosfresia, pérdida total o parcial del olfato.
Another [an-udh'-ẹr], *a.* 1. Otro, diferente, distinto. *It is one thing to promise and another to perform*, Una cosa es prometer y otra cumplir; del dicho al hecho hay gran trecho. 2. Uno más; otro. *He owns already four houses and now has bought another*, Ya posee cuatro casas y ahora ha comprado una más.—*pron.* Otro, otra. *That painting was mine, but is now another's*, Esa pintura era mía, pero ahora es de otro. *One another*, Uno a otro.
Anoxia [a-nex'-i-a], *s.* (Med.) Anoxia, falta de oxígeno en los tejidos.
Ansated [an'-sê-ted], *a.* Con asas, ansato, que tiene asas.
Anserine [an'-sẹr-in], *a.* 1. Anserino, que se refiere al ánsar o la oca. 2. Semejante al ánsar, como el cutis cuando está frío. 3. Tonto, necio, mentecato.
Answer [an'-sẹr], *vn.* 1. Responder, dar satisfacción a la pregunta, duda o dificultad que se propone. 2. Replicar. 3. Responder, ser responsable. 4. Corresponder o venir bien una cosa con otra. *This year's crop does not answer our expectations*, La cosecha de este año no corresponde a nuestras esperanzas. 5. (For.) Comparecer. 6. Equivaler. 7. Salir bien, tener o dar buen resultado. *No, that will never answer*, No, eso no saldrá bien, no dará buen resultado. —*va.* 1. Responder, dar respuesta, contestar. 2. Satisfacer a, cumplir, obedecer. 3. Disputar, refutar. 4. Resolver (un problema, etc.). 5. Ser suficiente para; convenir a. *This answers my purpose*, Esto conviene a mi designio. 6. Expiar. 7. Ser correlativo a, responder recíprocamente. 8. Otorgar, conceder una petición. 9. Talionar, pagar en la misma moneda. *To answer for*, (1) Fiar a, responder de. (2) Expiar (una falta).
Answer, *s.* 1. Respuesta, contestación. 2. Refutación, réplica. 3. Solución correcta.
Answerable [an'-sẹr-a-bl], *a.* 1. Aquello a que se puede responder. 2. Responsable, obligado a satisfacer por algún cargo. 3. Correspondiente; equivalente; conforme. 4. Refutable. *He is answerable to no one for what he does*, El no debe a nadie cuenta de su conducta.
Answerably [an'-sẹr-a-bli], *adv.* Correspondientemente, proporcionadamente.
Answerableness [an'-sẹr-a-bl-nes], *s.* Responsabilidad; también significa correspondencia o relación de una cosa con otra.
Answerer [an'-sẹr-ẹr], *s.* Fiador, el que da caución.
Ant [ant], *s.* Hormiga, insecto himenóptero, notable por su inteligencia; en este respecto tal vez el mejor dotado de todos los insectos. *White ant*, Hormiga blanca, termita; insecto neuróptero. *Ant-eater, antlion*, V. más adelante.
†**An't** [ant]. Contracción de *and if it.*

Ain't o a'n't [ênt], *v.* Contracción defectuosa de *am not, is not, are not.* (Vulg.)
Anta [an'-tá], *s.* (Arq.) Anta, pilastra saliente en los ángulos de un edificio. (Plural ANTÆ o ANTES.)
Anta [an'-ta], *s.* (Zool.) Danta, tapir.
Antacid [ant-as'-id], *a.* y *s.* Antiácido, álcali. Remedio para la acidez del estómago.
Antagonism [an-tag'-o-nizm], *s.* Contienda, oposición.
Antagonist [an-tag'-o-nist], *s.* Antagonista, el que es opuesto o contrario a otro.
Antagonistic [an-tag-o-nis'-tic], *a.* Antagónico, perteneciente a los antagonistas; que implica o denota antagonismo.
Antagonize [an-tag'-o-naiz], *vn.* Competir con otro.
Antalgic [ant-al'-jic], *a.* Anodino, opuesto al dolor; antálgico. Equivalente, ANTALGESIC.
Antaphrodisiac [ant-af-ro-diz'-i-ac], *s.* y *a.* Antiafrodisíaco, que calma el apetito venéreo.
Antaphroditic [ant-a-fro-dit'-ic], *a.* Antiafrodisíaco; dícese de los remedios para calmar el apetito venéreo.
Antarctic [ant-ārc'-tic], *a.* Antártico, lo que pertenece al polo meridional.
Antarthritic [ant-ār-thrit'-ic], *a.* (Med.) Antiartrítico; dícese de los remedios para la gota.
Antasthmatic [ant-as-mat'-ic], *a.* Antiasmático.
Ant-bear [ant'-bār], *s.* Tamándoa o tamanuar, mamífero desdentado de la América tropical que se mantiene de hormigas. Oso hormiguero. Myrmecophaga.
Ante [an'-tẹ]. Preposición latina que se halla antes de varios nombres compuestos y que significa: ante, antes, que precede en tiempo o posición.
Anteater [ant'-it-ẹr], *s.* (Zool.) Oso hormiguero.
Ante bellum [an'-tẹ bel'-um], *a.* Antes de la guerra. En los Estados Unidos de Norte América, antes de la guerra civil.
Antecede [an-tẹ-síd'], *vn.* Anteceder, preceder.
Antecedence [an-tẹ-sí'-dens], **Antecedency** [an-tẹ-sí'-den-si], *s.* Precedencia, la acción y efecto de preceder o anteceder.
Antecedent [an-tẹ-sí'-dent], *a.* y *s.* Antecedente, precedente.
Antecedently [an-tẹ-sí'-dent-li], *adv.* Anteriormente.
Antecessor [an-tẹ-ses'-er], *s.* Antecesor, el que precede a otro.
Antechamber [an'-tẹ-chêm"-bẹr], *s.* Antecámara, la pieza que está inmediata a la sala principal de alguna casa.
Antedate [an'-tẹ-dêt], *va.* Antedatar, poner la fecha anticipada en alguna escritura o carta.
Antedate, *s.* Anticipación; antedata.
Antediluvian [an-tẹ-di-lū'-vi-an], *a.* y *s.* Antediluviano, lo que pertenece al tiempo anterior al diluvio.
Antelope [an'-tẹ-lōp], *s.* Antílope, cuadrúpedo rumiante parecido al ciervo; hay varias especies.
Antelucem [an-tẹ-lū'-sem], *a.* Temprano; antes del amanecer.
Antemeridian [an-tẹ-mẹ-rid'-i-an], *a.* Antes de mediodía, por la mañana.
Ante meridiem [an'-tẹ mẹ-rid'-i-em], *loc. lat.* Antes del mediodía. Úsase comunmente en la abreviatura A.M.; 9 A.M., las nueve de la mañana.
Antemetic [ant-ẹ-met'-ic], *a.* Antiemético, remedio que hace cesar el vómito.
Antemundane [an-tẹ-mun'-dên], *a.* Que antecedió a la creación del mundo.
Antenna [an-ten'-a], *pl.* ANTENNÆ [an-ten'-ni], *s.* Antena, apéndice articulado de la cabeza, uno de los cuernecillos de algunos insectos y otros animales artrópodos.
Antenumber [an-tẹ-num'-bẹr], *s.* Número anterior.
Antenuptial [an-tẹ-nup'-shal], *a.* Antenupcial, antes de la boda.
Antepaschal [an-tẹ-pas'-cal], *a.* Antepascual.
Antepast [an'-tẹ-pqst], *s.* (Ant. o poét.) Anticipación; gusto anticipado.
Antepenult [an-tẹ-pẹ-nult'] o **Antepenultimate** [an-tẹ-pẹ-nult'-i-met], *a.* y *s.* Antepenúltima, la sílaba que está antes de la penúltima.
Antepileptic [ant-ep-i-lep'-tic], *a.* (Med.) Antepiléptico; dícese de los remedios contra la epilepsia.
Anteport [an'-tẹ-pōrt] o **Antiport**, *a.* Antepuerta, puerta exterior.
Anterior [an-tí'-ri-er], *a.* Anterior, precedente.
Anteriority [an-tẹ-ri-er'-i-ti], *s.* Anterioridad, precedencia.
Anteroom [an'-tẹ-rūm], *s.* Antecámara.
Antes [an'-tiz], *s. pl.* (Arq.) Antas, pilastras.
Anteversion [an-tẹ-vẹr'-shun], *s.* Anteroversión, posición anormal del útero, que consiste en dirigirse el fondo hacia el pubis y el cuello hacia el sacro.
Antevert [an'-tẹ-vẹrt], *va.* Volver hacia adelante.
Anteverted, *pp.* Vuelto hacia adelante; en posición de anteroversión.
Anthelmintic [an-thel-min'-tic], *a.* Antielmíntico, lo que mata las lombrices.
Anthem [an'-them], *s.* Antífona, motete.
Anthemis [an'-the-mis], *s.* (Bot.) Género de plantas que comprende, entre otras numerosas especies, la manzanilla o camomila.
Anthem-wise [an'-them-waiz], *adv.* A modo de antífona.
Anther [an'-thẹr], *s.* (Bot.) Antera, el ápice del estambre que contiene el polen; es el órgano masculino de las plantas.
Ant-hill [ant'-hil], *s.* Hormiguero. *V.* FORMICARIUM.
Anthological [an-tho-lej'-i-cal], *a.* Antológico, lo perteneciente a la antología.
Anthology [an-thel'-o-ji], *s.* 1. Antología, florilegio; colección de trozos literarios selectos. 2. (Poco us.) Colección de flores.
Anthony's fire [an'-to-niz fair], *s.* Fuego de S. Antón; erisipela.
Anthozoa [an-tho-zō'-a], *s.* Antozoarios, los pólipos, una clase de los zoófitos o coelenterados.
Anthracic [an-thras'-ic], *a.* Que pertenece al ántrax, o que lo padece.
Anthracite [an'-thra-sait], *s.* Antracita, hulla lustrosa, carbón de piedra no bituminoso que arde sin humo y casi sin llama.
Anthrax [an'-thrax], *s.* 1. Ántrax, carbunclo, avispero. 2. Fiebre contagiosa y maligna; llámase también fiebre esplénica.
Anthropography [an-thro-po'-gra-fi], *s.* Antropografía, la descripción del hombre.
Anthropoid [an'-thro-paid], *s.* Antropoide, mono antropoideo.—*a.* Antropoide, antropoideo.
Anthropology [an-thro-pel'-o-ji], *s.* Antropología, la ciencia que trata del hombre física y moralmente considerado.
Anthropomorphism [an-thro-po-mōr'-fizm], *s.* Antropomorfismo, doctrina u opinión de los que atribuyen a Dios cuerpo humano, o cualidades y sentimientos humanos.
Anthropophagi [an-thro-pef'-a-jai], *s.* Antropófagos, los que comen carne humana.
Anthroposophy [an-thro-pes'-o-fi], *s.* Antroposofía, ciencia de la naturaleza del hombre.
Anti [an'-ti]. Partícula muy usada, compuesta con voces de derivación griega, y significa *contra* o *contrario a.*
Antiacid, *a.* *V.* ALKALI.
Antiaircraft [an-ti-ār'-crqft], *s.* Fuego o artillería antiaérea.—*a.* Antiaéreo.
Antiapostle [an-ti-a-pes'-tl], *s.* Antiapóstol.
Antiarthritic [an-ti-ār-thrit'-ic], *a.* Antiartrítico, remedio contra la gota.
Antibilious [an-ti-bil'-yus], *a.* Antibilioso.
Antibiotic [an-ti-bai-e'-tic], *s.* y *a.* Antibiótico.
Antibody [an'-ti-bed-i], *s.* (Med.) Anticuerpo.
Antic [an'-tic], *a.* Extraño, raro, ridículo, grotesco.—*s.* 1. Acción, fantástica o extravagante, cabriola, travesura. 2. Antigualla, figura o grupo grotesco. 3. Bufón, truhán, saltimbanco.
Antichamber, *s.* *V.* ANTECHAMBER.
Antichrist [an'-ti-craist], *s.* Antecristo.
Antichristian [an-ti-cris'-chan], *s.* y *a.* Anticristiano.
Anticipate [an-tis'-i-pêt], *va.* 1. Mirar a lo venidero, esperar, prever. 2. Anticipar, tomar alguna cosa antes que otro; adelantarse, prevenir. 3. Estar al frente de, en adelante.
Anticipation [an-tis-i-pê'-shun], *s.* Anticipación, la acción y efecto de anticipar o anticiparse.
Anticipator [an-tis'-i-pê-ter], *s.* Anticipador.
Anticipatory [an-tis'-i-pa-tō-ri], *a.* Lo que anticipa.
Anticlerical [an-ti-cler'-ic-al], *a.* Anticlerical.
Anticlinal [an-ti-clai'-nal], *a.* Anticlinal, que señala en la estratificación de los terrenos una inclinación en direcciones opuestas.
Anticly [an'-tic-li], *adv.* Ridículamente, por vía de travesura, grotescamente.
Anti-climax [an-ti-clai'-max], *s.* (Ret.) Anticlímax, gradación descendente.
Anticoagulant [an-ti-co-ag'-yu-lant], *s.* y *a.* Anticoagulante.
Anticolonialism [an-ti-co-lō'-ni-al-izm], *s.* Anticolonialismo.
Anticommunism [an-ti-cem'-yu-nizm], *s.* Anticomunismo.
Anticommunist [an-ti-cem'-yu-nist], *s.* Anticomunista.
Anticonstitutional [an-ti-con-sti-tū'-shun-al], *a.* Anticonstitucional, lo que es contra la constitución o sistema de gobierno establecido.
Anticorrosive [an-ti-cẹr-rō'-siv], *a.* Anticorrosivo, que obra contra la corrosión o la impide.

Anticosmetic [an-ti-cez-met'-ic], *a.* Anticosmético.
Anticourt [an'-ti-cōrt], *a.* Lo que es opuesto a la corte.
Anticyclone [an-ti-sai'-clōn], *s.* Movimiento de la atmósfera, que por la dirección del viento y la distribución de la presión barométrica, se opone al de un ciclón.
Antidotal [an'-ti-do-tal], *a.* Perteneciente al antídoto.
Antidotary [an-ti-dō'-ta-ri], *a.* (Ant.) Antidotario; antídoto.
Antidote [an'-ti-dōt], *s.* Antídoto, contraveneno, preservativo.
Antidysenteric [an-ti-dis-en-ter'-ic], *a.* Antidisentérico, que tiene virtud contra la disentería.
Antiepiscopal [an-ti-e-pis'-co-pal], *a.* El que se opone al episcopado.
Antiface [an'-ti-fés], *s.* Antifaz.
Antifanatic [an-ti-fa-nat'-ic], *s.* Antifanático.
Antifebrile [an-ti-fi'-bril], *a.* (Med.) Antifebril, lo que sirve para corregir y curar las calenturas.
Antifebrin [an-ti-fi'-brin]. *V.* ACETANILID.
Antifreeze [an-ti-friz'], *s.* y *a.* Anticongelante.
Antifriction [an-ti-fric'-shun], *a.* Que disminuye el rozamiento. *Antifriction alloy*, *Antifriction metal*, Antifricción.
Antigen [an'-ti-jen], *s.* Antígeno.
Antihistamine [an-ti-his'-tam-in], *s.* (Med.) Antihistamina.
Antihypnotic [ant-ip-not'-ic], *a.* Antipnótico, lo que impide el sueño, sopor o letargo.
Antihysteric [an-ti-his-ter'-ic], *s.* Antihistérico, medicamento para las afecciones histéricas y espasmódicas.
Antiknock [an'-ti-nok], *s.* & *a.* Antidetonante.
Antilogy [an-til'-o-ji], *s.* Antilogía, contradicción de palabras o de algunas sentencias o pasages de un autor.
Antimacassar [an-ti-ma-cas'-ar], *s.* Cubierta, adornada por lo común, del respaldo de un sofá o sillón, o de una mecedora.
Antimalarial [an-ti-ma-lé'-ri-al], *a.* Antipalúdico, eficaz contra la dañina influencia de aires malsanos.
Antimatter [an'-ti-mat-er], *s.* Antimateria.
Antimilitarism [an-ti-mil'-i-ta-rizm], *s.* Antimilitarismo.
Antimilitarist [an-ti-mil'-i-ta-rist], *s.* Antimilitarista.
Antimissile [an-ti-mis'-il], *a.* Antiproyectil. *Antimissile missile*, Proyectil antiproyectil.
Antimonarchic [an-ti-mo-nār'-kic], **Antimonarchical** [an-ti-mo-nār'-ki-cal], *a.* Antimonárquico, opuesto al gobierno monárquico.
Antimonarchist [an-ti-men'-ark-ist], *s.* Antimonárquico, el que es contrario al gobierno monárquico.
Antimonial [an-ti-mō'-ni-al], *a.* Antimonial, hecho de antimonio o perteneciente a él.
Antimonic [an-ti-mō'-nic], *a.* Antimónico; que se refiere al antimonio.
Antimony [an'-ti-mo-ni], *s.* Antimonio, metal duro, blanco argentino, cristalizable, brillante, que se usa mucho en la química, en la medicina y en las artes en forma de aleaciones. *Tartarized antimony* o *tartar emetic*, Tártaro emético.
Antimoralist [an-ti-mer'-al-ist], *s.* Enemigo de la moralidad.
Antineutron [an-ti-niū'-tren], *s.* Antineutrón.
Antinomian [an-ti-nō'-mi-an], **Antinomist** [an-tin'-o-mist], *s.* Herejes que negaban la obligación de la ley moral.
Antinomianism [an-ti-nō'-mi-an-izm], *s.* Herejía por la cual se niega la virtud u obligación de la ley moral y la necesidad de las buenas obras.
Antinomy [an-tin'-o-mi], *s.* 1. Antinomia, oposición o contrariedad de las leyes entre sí. 2. Incompatibilidad entre dos o más conclusiones que sin embargo parecen ser igualmente inevitables; paradoja.
Antinucleon [an-ti-niū'-cle-en], *s.* Antinucleón.
Antiparticle [an-ti-pār'-ti-cl], *s.* Antipartícula.
Antipasto [an-ti-pas'-to], *s.* Aperitivo.
Antipathetic [an-ti-pa-thet'-ic], **Antipathetical** [an-ti-pa-thet'-i cal], *a.* Antipático, que causa antipatía.
Antipathetically [an-ti-pa-thet'-i-ca-li], *adv.* De un modo contrario.
Antipathic [an-ti-path'-ic], *a.* Antipático, contrario, opuesto; adverso, naturalmente contrario.
Antipathy [an-tip'-a-thi], *s.* Antipatía, oposición natural, repugnancia instintiva entre personas, o de una persona hacia una cosa.
Antipendium [an-ti-pen'-di-um], *s.* Frontal de altar.
Antiperiodic [an-ti-pi-ri-od'-ic], *a.* Antiperiódico; se dice de los medicamentos que sirven para evitar el acceso de una enfermedad intermitente.
Antipersonnel [an-ti-per-se-nel'], *a.* Contrapersonal.
Antiperspirant [an-ti-per'-spi-rant], *s.* Desodorante.
Antipestilential [an-ti-pes-ti-len'-shal], *a.* Antipestilencial.
Antiphlogistic [an-ti-flo-jis'-tic], *s.* y *a.* Antiflogístico, el medicamento propio para calmar la inflamación.
Antiphon [an'-ti-fen], **Antiphony** [an-tif'-o-ni], *s.* Antífona; eco.
Antiphonal [an-tif'-o-nal], **Antiphonical** [an-ti-fen'-i-cal], *a.* Antifonal, perteneciente a las antífonas.
Antiphonal [an-tif'-o-nal], **Antiphonar** [an-tif'-o-nar], *s.* Antifonal o antifonario.
Antiphrasis [an-tif'-ra-sis], *s.* Antífrasis o antífrase, figura irónica por la que diciendo una cosa se entiende la contraria.
Antipodal [an-tip'-o-dal], *a.* 1. Lo que es antípoda, que se halla al lado opuesto del globo. 2. Contrario; diametralmente opuesto.
Antipode [an'-ti-pōd], *s.* 1. Lo directamente contrario u opuesto; la cosa opuesta a otra. 2. Uno de los antípodas.
Antipodean [an-ti-pō'-de-an], *a.* Antipodal, lo que se refiere o pertenece a los antípodas.
Antipodes [an-tip'-o-dīz], *s. pl.* 1. Antípodas, los que habitan en el otro lado del globo y tienen sus pies opuestos a los nuestros. 2. (Fig.) Antípoda, contrario, opuesto.
Antipoison [an'-ti-pei"-zn], *s.* Antídoto, contraveneno.
Antipope [an'-ti-pōp], *s.* Antipapa, el que usurpa el papado.
Antiprelatic [an-ti-pre-lat'-ic], **Antiprelatical** [an-ti-pre-lat'-i-cal], *a.* Hostil o contrario a la prelacía.
Antipriest [an'-ti-prīst], *s.* Hostilidad a los sacerdotes.
Antiprinciple [an-ti-prin'-si-pl], *s.* Principio opuesto.
Antiproton [an-ti-prō'-ten], *s.* Antiprotón.
Antipyretic [an-ti-pai-ret'-ic], *a.* y *s.* Antipirético, febrífugo.
Antipyrin [an-ti-pai'-rin], *s.* Antipirina, medicamento nuevo, compuesto blanco cristalizable ($C_{11}H_{12}N_2O$), usado para calmar la fiebre.
Antiquarian [an-ti-cwé'-ri-an], *a.* Anticuario, el que es aficionado al estudio de las antigüedades: relativo a lo antiguo.
Antiquarianism [an-ti-cwé'-ri-an-izm], *s.* La afición a las antigüedades.
Antiquary [an'-ti-cwē-ri], *s.* Anticuario, el que se dedica al estudio especial de las cosas antiguas.
Antiquate [an'-ti-cwēt], *va.* Anticuar, abolir el uso de alguna cosa; anular.
Antiquated [an'-ti-cwē-ted], *a.* 1. Anticuado, fuera de uso, propio de tiempos pasados. 2. Añejo, viejo, fuera de servicio; imposibilitado.
Antique [an-tīc'], *a.* Antiguo, lo que tiene antigüedad.—*s.* Antigüedad, monumento de tiempos antiguos o remotos; antigualla.
Antiqueness [an-tīc'-nes], *s.* Antigüedad, la calidad de ser antiguo.
Antiquity [an-tic'-wi-ti], *s.* 1. Antigüedad, los tiempos antiguos. 2. Vestigios de los tiempos antiguos. 3. Ancianidad, vejez, vetustez.
Antirevolutionary [an-ti-rev-o-lū'-shun-e-ri], *a.* Antirrevolucionario.
Antirevolutionist [an-ti-rev-o-lū'-shun-ist], *s.* Antirrevolucionario.
Antirheumatic [an-ti-rū-mat'-ic], *a.* Antirreumático, eficaz contra el reumatismo.
Antisacerdotal [an-ti-sas-er-dō'-tal], *a.* Hostil a los sacerdotes.
Antiscians [an-tish'-ianz] o **Antiscii** [an-tish'-i-ai], *s. pl.* Antiscios, los pueblos que habitan en el hemisferio opuesto de la tierra.
Antiscorbutic [an-ti-scēr-biū'-tic], **Antiscorbutical** [an-ti-scēr-biū'-ti-cal], *a.* Antiescorbútico, eficaz para curar el escorbuto.
Antiscripturist [an-ti-scrip'-chur-ist], *s.* Antiescriturista, el que niega la revelación o impugna la sagrada escritura.
Antisemitic [an-ti-se-mit'-ic], *s.* y *a.* Antisemítico, antisemita.
Antisemitism [an-ti-sem'-i-tizm], *s.* Antisemitismo.
Antiseptic [an-ti-sep'-tic], *a.* Antiséptico, antipútrido, lo que impide la putrefacción o fermentación. Úsase también como nombre.
Antiseptical [an-ti-sep'-tic-al], *a.* *V.* ANTISEPTIC.
Antiseptically [an-ti-sep'-tic-al-i], *adv.* De un modo antiséptico.
Antislavery [an-ti-slē'-ver-i], *a.* Partidario de la manumisión, opuesto a la esclavitud.
Antisocial [an-ti-sō'-shal], *a.* 1. Antisocial. 2. Antisociable.
Antispasmodic [an-ti-spaz-med'-ic], *a.* Antiespasmódico, eficaz contra los espasmos.
Antispastic [an-ti-spas'-tic], *a.* Antispástico; dícese de los medicamentos que causan una revulsión de los humores.
Antisplenetic [an-ti-sple-net'-ic o splen'-e-tic], *a.* Antiesplénico, lo que es eficaz contra las enfermedades del bazo.
Antistrophe [an-tis'-tro-fe], *s.* 1. Antistrofa, la segunda parte del canto lírico en la poesía griega. 2. (Ret.)

Inversión de voces en cláusulas sucesivas; de aquí, toda inversión de relación.

Antistrumatic [an-ti-strū-mat'-ic], *a.* Antiescrofuloso; se aplica a los medicamentos usados para curar lamparones.

Antisyphilitic [an-ti-sif-i-lit'-ic], *a.* y *n.* Antisifilítico, remedio contra la sífilis.

Antitank [an'-ti-tank], *a.* (Mil.) Antitanque.

Antithesis [an-tith'-e-sis], *s.* 1. (Ret.) Antítesis, figura que consiste en contraponer una frase o una palabra a otra de contraria significación. 2. Antítesis, oposición, contrariedad, contraste.

Antithetical [an-ti-thet'-i-cal], *a.* Antitético, lo que contiene antítesis.

Antitoxin [an-ti-tex'-in], *s.* (Med.) Antitoxina.

Antitrinitarian [an-ti-trin-i-tē'-ri-an], *s.* Antitrinitario; dícese de los herejes que niegan la santísima Trinidad.

Antitrust [an'-ti-trust], *a.* Contra los monopolios o los *trusts.*

Antitype [an'-ti-taip], *s.* Antitipo, figura, imagen.

Antitypical [an-ti-tip'-i-cal], *a.* Antitípico.

Antivirus [an-ti-vai'-rus], *s.* Antivirus.

Antler [ant'-ler], *s.* 1. Cuerna, asta. 2. Mogote. 3. Candil.—*pl.* Cornamenta.

Antlered [ant'-lerd], *a.* Lo que tiene cercetas o astas ramosas.

Ant-lion [ant'-lai-en], *s.* Hormigaleón, insecto neuróptero, el mirmeleón; y particularmente su larva que se alimenta de hormigas. Myrmeleon formicarius.

Antœci [an-ti'-sai], *s.* (Geog.) Antecos, los pueblos que habitan en lugares de una misma latitud y longitud, pero en lados opuestos del ecuador.

Antonomasia [ant-en-o-mē'-zhi-a ó ma'-si-a], *s.* (Ret.) Figura retórica que consiste en usar el nombre apelativo por el propio o éste en lugar del apelativo.

Antonym [an'-to-nim], *s.* Antónimo.

Antrum [an'-trum], *s.* Antro, cueva, caverna; con particularidad la cavidad o "antro de Highmore" en la cara.

Anus [ē'-nus o g'-nus], *s.* Ano, orificio por el cual se expele del cuerpo el excremento.

Anvil [an'-vil], *s.* Yunque, ayunque, bigornia. *The stock of an anvil,* Cepo de yunque.

Anvilled [an'-vild], *a.* Formado a modo de yunque.

Anxiety [an-zai'-e-ti], *s.* 1. Ansia, solicitud acerca de alguna cosa venidera. 2. Aflicción o abatimiento de ánimo. 3. Perplejidad, desasosiego, afan, anhelo, cavilación, inquietud, dificultad, ansiedad.

Anxious [anc'-shus], *a.* Inquieto, perturbado, ansioso, anheloso, impaciente, penoso, roedor. *To be* (o *feel*) *anxious about,* Estar inquieto á causa de, respecto a. *Anxious forebodings,* Presentimientos alarmantes.

Anxiously [anc'-shus-li], *adv.* Ansiosamente, impacientemente.

Anxiousness [anc'-shus-nes], *s.* Ansia, ansiedad, solicitud, anhelo.

Any [en'-i], *a.* Cualquier o cualquiera, algún, alguno, alguna, todo. *Any further,* Más lejos. *Any more,* Más aún. *Any longer,* Más allá, todavía, mucho más tiempo. *Any thing,* Algo. *Anywise, adv.* En o de algún modo.—*Any,* después de negación o preposición privativa, Ninguno, na. *I have not seen any of your friends,* No he visto a ninguno de sus amigos. *Without any difficulty,* Sin ninguna dificultad, sin la menor dificultad. —*Any,* en sentido partitivo, no suele traducirse en castellano. *Have you any money?* ¿Tiene Vd. dinero? o ¿Tiene Vd. algún dinero encima?

Anybody [en'-i-bed-i], *pro.* 1. Alguno, alguien, cualquiera; si con negación, nadie. 2. Todo el mundo, toda persona. *Is anybody at home?* ¿Hay alguien en casa? *Not anybody,* Nadie. *Anybody can do that,* Cualquiera, todo el mundo, puede hacer eso. *Hardly anybody thinks so,* Nadie lo piensa apenas.

Anyhow [en'-i-hau], *adv.* 1. De cualquier modo que sea; bien que, sin embargo; en cualquier caso. 2. Con indiferencia, no importa como.

Anything [en'-i-thing], *pro.* 1. Algo, alguna cosa, cualquier cosa; si con negación, nada. 2. Todo, todo lo que. *Have you anything to do just now?* ¿Tiene Vd. algo que hacer ahora mismo? *Not anything,* Nada. *Anything you choose,* Todo lo que Vd. quiera.

Anyway, Anyways [en'-i-wê, wêz], *adv.* 1. Salga lo que saliere; sin embargo, con todo eso, sea lo que se fuere. 2. De cualquier modo que sea; en este sentido debería ser escrito en dos palabras.

Anywhere [en'-i-hwār], *adv.* Dondequiera, en cualquier parte, en todas partes. *Not anywhere,* En ninguna parte.

Aorist [ē'-o-rist], *s.* (Gram.) Aoristo.

Aorist, Aoristic, *a.* Parecido al aoristo; sin limitación de tiempo.

Aorta [ē-ōr'-ta], *s.* Aorta, la arteria mayor del cuerpo.

Aortic [ē-ōr'-tic], *a.* Aórtico, que pertenece a la aorta, o tiene relación con ella.

Apace [a-pês'], *adv.* Aprisa, con presteza ó prontitud.

Apagoge [ap-a-gō'-je], *s.* 1. (Mat.) El empleo de una proposición ya demostrada para probar otra. 2. Apagojía, razonamiento que sirve para probar la verdad de una proposición, demostrando lo absurdo de la contraria.

Apagogical [ap-a-gej'-i-cal], *a.* Apagógico, lo que pertenece a la demostración de una proposición por lo absurdo de la contraria.

Apart [a-pārt'], *adv.* Aparte, a un lado, separadamente.

Apartment [a-part'-ment], *s.* Departamento, apartamiento, vivienda.

Apathetic [ap-a-thet'-ic], **Apathistical** [ap-a-this'-ti-cal], *a.* Apático, indolente, sin pasión por nada, indiferente, insensible.

Apathist [ap'-a-thist], *s.* Hombre apático o insensible.

Apathy [ap'-a-thi], *s.* Apatía, insensibilidad a toda pasión.

Apatite [ap'-a-tait], *s.* Apatito, fosfato de cal nativo, cristalizado.

Ape [êp], *s.* 1. Mono. 2. (Met.) Mono, el que imita o remeda.

Ape, *va.* Hacer muecas o monadas, imitar, remedar.

Apeak [a-pîc'], *adv.* 1. En postura o ademán de penetrar la tierra. 2. (Mar.) A pique.

Apepsia, Apepsy [a-pep'-si], *s.* (Med.) Apepsia, mala digestión.

Aper [ē'-per], *s.* Imitador o mimo ridículo, bufón.

Aperient [a-pî'-ri-ent], **Aperitive** [a-per'-i-tiv], *a.* Aperitivo.

Aperture [ap'-er-tiūr o chur], *s.* Abertura, paso, rendija.

Apetalous [a-pet'-a-lus], *a.* (Bot.) Apétalo, sin pétalos.

Apex [ē'-pecs], *s.* APEXES o APICES, *pl.* Ápice, el extremo superior o la punta de alguna cosa, cima. *Apices of a flower,* (Bot.) Ápices de los estambres de la flor.

Aphæresis [a-fer'-e-sis], *s.* Aféresis, supresión de lo superfluo.

Aphaniptera [a-fa-nip'-te-ra], *s.* Afanípteros, orden de insectos sin alas, de que la pulga es tipo.

Aphasia [a-fē'-zi-a], *s.* Afasia, pérdida de la facultad de hablar, quedando intactos los órganos vocales y sin alteración de la inteligencia. Resulta de enfermedad del cerebro.

Aphasic [a-fē'-zic], *a.* Afásico.

Aphelion [a-fē'-li-un], *s.* (Astr.) Afelio, el punto de la órbita de un planeta en que éste se halla más distante del sol.

Aphid [āf'-id], *s.* (Ento.) Áfido.

Aphilanthropy [a-fi-lan'-thro-pi], *s.* Falta de filantropía.

Aphis [ē'-fis], *s.* APHIDES [af'-i-dîz], *pl.* Áfido, el pulgón; el género de los Áfidos; insecto del género Aphis.

Aphonia [a-fō'-ni-a], **Aphony** [af'-o-ni], *s.* Afonía, pérdida de la voz a consecuencia de una afección de la laringe; ronquera crónica.

Aphonic [a-fen'-ic], *a.* 1. Sin sonido; afónico, afono. 2. Mudo, que no representa un sonido. *Aphonic letter,* Letra muda.

Aphorism [af'-o-rizm], *s.* Aforismo, sentencia breve, máxima o regla general.

†**Aphorismer** [af'-o-riz-mer], **Aphorist** [af'-o-rist], *s.* Escritor de aforismos.

Aphoristical [af-o-ris'-ti-cal], *a.* Sentencioso, lo que contiene uno o muchos aforismos; aforístico.

Aphoristically [af-o-ris'-ti-cal-i], *adv.* Sentenciosamente.

Aphrodisiac [a-fro-diz'-i-ac], **Aphrodisiacal** [a-fro-di-zai'-a-cal], *a.* 1. Afrodisíaco, lo que conduce al apetito venéreo o lo excita. 2. Lascivo, lujurioso.

Aphrodite [af'-ro-dai'-ti o di'-tē], *s.* 1. La diosa griega del amor; corresponde a la Venus latina. 2. Mariposa de hermosos colores de los Estados Unidos de América.

Aphtha [af'-tha], *pl.* APHTHÆ [af'-thî], *s.* Aftas, úlceras pequeñas y superficiales en la boca.

§**Aphthong** [af'-theng], *s.* Letra muda, o combinación de las mismas; como p en pseudo.

Aphthous [af'-thus], *a.* Aftoso, perteneciente a las aftas o afectado con ellas.

Aphyllous [a-fil'-us], *a.* (Bot.) Afilo, que no tiene hojas.

Apiary [ē'-pi-e-ri], *s.* Colmenar, abejar, lugar en que se crían las abejas; colección de abejas, colmenas, utensilios, etc.

Apiculture [ê-pi-cul'-chur], *s.* Apicultura, cuidado de las abejas.

Apiculturist [ê-pi-cul'-chur-ist], *s.* Apicultor, el que cuida de las abejas.

Apiece [a-pîs'], *adv.* Por barba, por cabeza, por persona o cada uno.

Apis [ē'-pis], *s.* 1. Apis, nombre del buey que adoraban como dios los antiguos egipcios. 2. Nombre científico de la abeja; género de insec-

tos himenópteros interesantes por el gran desarrollo de su inteligencia.
Apish [ê'-pish], *a.* Gestero, bufón, monero, acostumbrado a hacer gestos y remedar como el mono; afectado, frívolo.
Apishly [ê'-pish-li], *adv.* Afectadamente, frívolamente.
Apishness [ê'-pish-nes], *s.* Monada, gesto o figura afectada y enfadosa.
Apitpat [a-pit'-pat], *adv.* Con palpitación acelerada: es voz vulgar. *V.* PIT-A-PAT.
Apivorous [ę-piv-o-rus], *a.* Apívoro, que come abejas.
Aplanatic [a-pla-nat'-ic], *a.* Aplanático, exento de aberración esférica y cromática.
Aplomb [a'-plōñ], *s.* 1. Confianza en sí mismo; aplomo. 2. Posición recta; postura vertical. (Gal.)
Apocalypse [a-pec'-a-lips], *s.* Apocalipsis, revelación, el último libro del Nuevo Testamento.
Apocalyptic [a-pec-a-lip'-tic], **Apocalyptical** [a-poc-a-lip'-ti-cal], *a.* Apocalíptico, lo que contiene revelaciones.
Apochromatic [ap-o-cro-mat'-ic], *a.* Apocromático, corrector del espectro secundario.
Apocopate [a-pec'-o-pêt], *va.* (Gram.) Apocopar, cometer apócope.
Apocope [a-pec'-o-pę], *s.* (Ret.) Apócope, figura por la cual se quita la última letra o sílaba de una dicción.
Apocrypha [a-pec'-ri-fa], *s. pl.* Libros apócrifos o no canónicos.
Apocryphal [a-pec'-ri-fal], *a.* Apócrifo, no canónico, dudoso o falso.
Apod, Apodal [ap'-od-al], *a.* Ápodo, sin pies; sin aletas ventrales.
Apodictic [ap-o-dic'-tic], **Apodictical** [ap-o-dic'-tic-al], *a.* Apodíctico, demostrativo o convincente. Sinónimo, APODEICTIC [ap-o-daic'-tic]. (Gr. apodeiktikós.)
Apodosis [a-ped'-o-sis], *s.* Apódosis, segunda parte del período, en la que se completa el sentido que queda pendiente en la primera, llamada prótasis.
Apodous [ap'-o-dus], *a.* Ápodo, sin pies. *V.* APODAL.
Apogee [ap'-o-ji], *s.* Apogeo, el punto en que el sol o cualquier otro planeta se halla a la mayor distancia de la tierra en toda su revolución.
Apoggiatura (a-pej-i-a-tū'-ra], *s.* (Mús.) Apoyatura.
Apograph [ap'-o-graf], *s.* Apógrafo, copia de algún libro o escrito.
Apollinarian [a-pel-i-nê'-ri-an], **Apollinarist** [a-pel-i-nê'-rist], *s.* Apolinarista, hereje que negaba que Jesucristo hubiese tomado carne en un cuerpo como el nuestro.
Apollinaris-water [a-pel-in-ar'-is], *s.* Agua efervescente, mineral y alcalina, que se usa en la mesa. Viene de un manantial en Apollinarisburg cerca de Bonn.
Apologetic, Apologetical [a-pel-o-jet'-ic-al], *a.* Apologético.
Apologetically [a-pel-o-jet'-ic-al-i], *adv.* Apologéticamente.
Apologetics [a-pel-o-jet'-ics], *s.* 1. Apologética, ramo de la teología consagrado a la defensa de la religión cristiana. 2. Apologética, nombre dado a la defensa de los cristianos por Tertuliano.
Apologist [a-pel'-o-jist], *s.* Apologista.
Apologize [a-pel'-o-jaiz], *va.* Apologizar, defender; excusar, disculpar o sacar la cara por, o en defensa de. —*vn.* Disculparse, excusarse.
Apologizer [a-pel'-o-jaiz-ęr], *s.* Defensor, defendedor, apologista.
Apologue [ap'-o-leg], *s.* Apólogo, fábula moral e instructiva.
Apology [a-pel'-o-ji], *s.* Apología, defensa; excusa, justificación.
Apomorphia [ap-o-mōr'-fi-a], *s.* Apomorfina, alcaloide que se extrae del opio; emético enérgico.
Aponeurosis [ap-o-niu-rō'-sis], *s.* Aponeurosis, membrana fibrosa y resistente, destinada a mantener en su lugar los músculos que envuelve o a servirles de punto de inserción.
Aponeurotic [ap-o-niu-ret'-ic], *a.* Aponeurótico.
Apophasis [a-pef'-a-sis], *s.* Apófasis, refutación. Figura retórica en la cual el orador, negando un punto favorable, produce, no obstante, el efecto deseado.
Apophlegmatic [ap-o-fleg-mat'-ic], *a.* Apoflemático, expectorante.
Apophthegm, *s.* *V.* APOTHEGM.
Apophysis [a-pef'-i-sis], *s.* (Anat.) Apófisis, eminencia o parte saliente de un órgano y particularmente de un hueso.
Apoplectic [ap-o-plec'-tic], **Apoplectical** [ap-o-plec'-tic-al], *a.* Apoplético.
Apoplexy [ap'-o-plec-si], *s.* Apoplejía, privación súbita del sentido.
Aport [a-pōrt'], *adv.* (Mar.) Ababor (el timón).
Aposiopesis [ap-o-sai''-o-pī'-sis], *s.* Aposiópesis, reticencia; figura retórica que se comete cuando empezando a decir una cosa se interrumpe la frase y se deja el razonamiento por concluir.
Apostasy [a-pes'-ta-si], *s.* Apostasía, deserción o abandono de la religión que uno profesaba.
Apostate [a-pes'-têt], *s.* Apóstata, el que comete apostasía.—*a.* Falso, pérfido, rebelde.
Apostatical [ap-es-tat'-i-cal], *a.* Apostático.
Apostatize [a-pes'-ta-taiz], *vn.* Apostatar, abandonar la religión que uno profesaba.
Apostem [ap'-es-tem], **Aposteme** [a-pes'-tîm], *s.* Apostema, absceso.
Apostemate [a-pes'-ti-mêt], *vn.* (Des.) Apostemarse.
Apostemation [a-pes-ti-mê'-shun], *s.* (Med.) Apostemación, apostema, absceso.
Apostle [a-pes'-l], *s.* Apóstol, enviado.
Apostleship [a-pes'-l-ship], **Apostolate** [a-pes'-to-lêt], *s.* Apostolado.
Apostolic [ap-es-tel'-ic], **Apostolical** [ap-es-tel'-ic-al], *a.* Apostólico.
Apostolically [ap-es-tel'-i-cal-i], *adv.* Apostólicamente.
Apostolicalness [ap-es-tel'-i-cal-nes], *s.* La calidad de ser apostólico; autoridad apostólica.
Apostrophe [a-pes'-tro-fę], *s.* 1. Apóstrofe, figura por la cual el orador suspende el discurso y dirige la palabra a una persona. 2. Apóstrofo, virgulilla que se pone para señalar alguna contracción, como *lov'd* por *loved, tho'* por *though;* también es la señal del caso genitivo, como *man's duty*, la obligación del hombre.
Apostrophic [ap-es-tref'-ic], **Apostrophical** [ap-es-tref'-ic-al], *a.* Lo perteneciente al apóstrofe.
Apostrophize [a-pes'-tro-faiz], *va.* Apostrofar, dirigir o convertir el discurso con vehemencia á alguna persona o cosa.—*vn.* 1. Abreviar una palabra, suprimiendo una letra o letras. 2. Designar esta elisión por medio del apóstrofo.
†**Apostume**, *s.* *V.* APOSTEME.
Apothecary [a-peth'-ę-kê-ri], *s.* Boticario. *An apothecary's shop*, Botica.
Apothegm [ap'-o-them], *s.* Apotegma, sentencia breve, dicha con agudeza.
Apothegmatical [ap''-o-theg-mat'-i-cal], *a.* Apotegmático.
Apothegmatist [ap-o-theg'-ma-tist], *s.* Apotegmatista, colector de apotegmas.
Apothegmatize [ap-o-theg'-ma-taiz], *vn.* Emplear o decir apotegmas.
Apotheosis [ap-o-thī'-o-sis o a-peth''-ę-ō'-sis], *s.* Apoteosis, deificación.
Apotheosize [ap-o-thī'-o-saiz], *va.* Deificar, poner entre los dioses.
Apozem [ap'-o-zem], *s.* Pócima, bebida medicinal.
Appal, Appall [ap-pōl'], *va.* Espantar, aterrar; desmayar, desanimar.—*vn.* (Des.) Desmayar, debilitarse.
Appall [ap-pel'], *s.* Espanto, aterramiento.
Appalling [ap-pōl'-ing], *a.* Espantoso, aterrador.
Appanage [ap'-a-nęj], *s.* 1. Propiedad o territorio dependiente de otro, o de alguien. 2. Alimentos, la porción de rentas que corresponden a un hermano menor; heredamiento; infantazgo.
Apparatus [ap-a-rê'-tus o ra'-tus], *s.* 1. Aparato, aparejo, apresto, prevención. 2. Tren, pompa, ostentación. 3. Aparato, conjunto de piezas de una máquina; útiles empleados para la obtención de una cosa.
Apparel [ap-par'-el], *s.* Traje, vestido. *Wearing apparel*, Vestidos, ropaje.
Apparel, *va.* 1. Vestir, trajear. 2. Adornar, componer.
Apparency [ąp-pār'-en-si], *s.* Calidad de evidente o claro.
Apparent [ap-pār'-ęnt], *a.* 1. Claro, patente, indubitable, evidente, manifiesto. 2. Aparente, lo que parece y no es. 3. Cierto. *The heir-apparent to the crown*, El heredero presuntivo de la corona.
Apparently [ap-pār'-ent-li], *adv.* Evidentemente, claramente, al parecer.
Apparentness [ap-pār'-ent-nes], *s.* Claridad.
Apparition [ąp-pa-rish'-un], *s.* 1. Aparición o aparecimiento. 2. Aparición, visión, fantasma, espectro.
Apparitor [ap-par'-i-ter], *s.* 1. Alguacil de corona o de la curia eclesiástica. 2. Macero o bedel de universidad.
Appeach [ap-pīch'], *va.* (Des.) *V.* IMPEACH.
Appeal [ap-pīl'], *vn.* 1. Apelar, recurrir de un tribunal o juez inferior a otro superior; hacer a uno árbitro. 2. Llamar por testigo. *I appeal to God*, Pongo a Dios por testigo.
Appeal, *s.* 1. Apelación; recurso a un tribunal superior. 2. Rogación, súplica, petición, instancia.
Appealable [ap-pīl'-a-bl], *a.* Apelable.
Appealer [ap-pīl'-ęr], *s.* 1. Apelante. 2. Acusador.
Appear [ąp-pīr'], *vn.* 1. Aparecer o aparecerse, manifestarse, estar a la vista. 2. Comparecer, presentarse ante el juez; responder en persona o por procurador o abogado. 3. Parecer, dar alguna cosa muestras o señales de lo que es. *I will make it appear*, Yo lo haré constar. (Fam.)

As it appears, A la cuenta; por lo que parece. 4. Evidenciarse, ser evidente, manifiesto, obvio.

Appearance [ap-pīr'-ans], *s.* 1. Vista, la acción de dejarse ver alguna cosa; aparición, llegada, presentación al público. 2. Apariencia, semejanza. 3. Apariencia, exterioridad. 4. Comparecencia, el acto de comparecer ante el juez o tribunal. 5. Porte, la disposición, decencia o lucimiento de alguna persona. 6. Probabilidad, verisimilitud. 7. Aparición, fenómeno.

§**Appearer** [ap-pīr'-er], *s.* 1. El que parece. 2. (For.) Compareciente, la persona que comparece ante un juez.

Appearing [ap-pīr'-ing], *s.* 1. Aparición, la acción de aparecer. 2. (For.) Comparecencia, el acto de presentarse en juicio.

Appeasable [ap-pīz'-a-bl], *a.* Aplacable, reconciliable.

Appeasableness [ap-pīz'-a-bl-nes], *s.* Aplacabilidad.

Appease [ap-pīz'], *va.* 1. Aliviar, aquietar el hambre o la sed, o el dolor. 2. Aplacar, apaciguar, pacificar, calmar, endulzar, aquietar.

Appeasement [ap-pīz'-ment], *s.* Apaciguamiento, el acto y efecto de apaciguar o de aliviar; alivio, pacificación.

Appeaser [ap-pīz'-er], *s.* Aplacador, apaciguador, reconciliador, pacificador.

Appeasive [ap-pīz'-iv], *a.* El que o lo que aplaca, calma o pacifica; apaciguador, sosegador, pacificador.

Appellancy [ap-pel'-an-si], *s.* Apelación.

Appellant [ap-pel'-ant], *s.* Apelante; demandador, demandante.—*a.* Lo perteneciente al apelante o a la apelación.

Appellate [ap-pel'-ĕt], *a.* De apelación; que tiene jurisdicción en las apelaciones; a que se puede recurrir.

Appellation [ap-pel-ē'-shun], *s.* Apelación, denominación, nombre.

Appellative [ap-pel'-a-tiv], *s.* Apelativo, nombre común que conviene a todos los individuos de una especie. (Fam.) Apellido.—*a.* Apelativo, común, usual, opuesto a propio ó peculiar.

Appellatively [ap-pel'-a-tiv-li], *adv.* Apelativamente.

Appellee [ap-el-ī'], *s.* Persona contra la cual se procede en apelación; demandado, acusado, apelado.

Append [ap-pend'], *va.* 1. Colgar, poner alguna cosa pendiente de otra. 2. Añadir o anexar; fijar, atar o ligar, p. ej. ponerle un sello a un documento.

Appendage [ap-pen'-dĕj], *s.* 1. Pertenencia, dependencia, cosa accesoria o dependiente de la principal y de ningún modo necesaria a su esencia. 2. (Bot. y Zool.) Apéndice.

Appendant [ap-pen'-dant], *a.* Pendiente, colgante, que cuelga de otra cosa; dependiente, anexo, accesorio, unido, pegado.—*s.* Pertenencia, dependencia.

Appendectomy [a-pen-dec'-to-mi], *s.* (Med.) Apendicectomía, extirpación del apéndice.

Appendices [ap-pen-di-sīz], *s.* Un plural de APPENDIX.

Appendicitis [ap-pen-di-sai'-tis o sī'-tis], *s.* Apendicitis, inflamación del apéndice vermiforme.

Appendix [ap-pen'-dix], *s.* (*pl.* APPENDIXES o APPENDICES). 1. Apéndice, adición o suplemento que se hace a alguna obra. 2. Accesoria, dependencia, parte suplementaria. *V.* APPENDAGE.

Apperception [ap-er-sep'-shun], *s.* (Fil.) Percepción del conocimiento interior.

Appertain [ap-er-tên'], *vn.* Pertenecer, tocar a alguno por derecho o por naturaleza.

Appertaining [ap-er-tên'-ing], **Appertinent** (Des.) [ap-er'-ti-nent], *a.* Perteneciente.

Appertenance [ap-per'-ti-nans], *s.* (Ant.) Pertenencia. *V.* APPURTENANCE.

Appetence [ap'-e-tens], **Appetency** [ap'-e-ten-si], *s.* 1. Deseo ardiente; viva apetencia o apetito; inclinación. 2. Apetencia, instinto, tendencia natural. *The appetence of ducks for water,* La afición instintiva de los patos al agua.

Appetent [ap'-e-tent], *a.* Apetecedor, muy deseoso, ávido.

Appetible [ap'-et-i-bl], *a.* Apetecible, deseable.

Appetite [ap'-e-tait], *s.* 1. Apetito, deseo natural de algún bien. 2. Sensualidad, concupiscencia. 3. Antojo. 4. Apetito, hambre o gana de comer. *To whet the appetite,* Estimular, abrir el apetito. *A good appetite is the best sauce,* A buen hambre no hay pan duro.

Appetitive [ap'-e-tai-tiv], *a.* 1. Perteneciente o semejante al apetito; que tiene apetito. 2. Que estimula el apetito; atrayente, atractivo.

Appetizer [ap'-e-taiz-er], *s.* Lo que excita el apetito; aperitivo.

Appetizing [ap-e-tai'-zing], *p. adj.* 1. Grato, gustoso; tentador. 2. Que estimula un deseo cualquiera.

Applaud [ap-plōd'], *va.* 1. Palmear, palmotear, aplaudir con palmoteos. 2. Aplaudir, alabar.—*vn.* Expresar aplauso o alabanza; dar palmadas.

Applauder [ap-plōd'-er], *s.* El que aplaude o alaba.

Applause [ap-plōz'], *s.* Aplauso, aprobación o alabanza pública con demostraciones de alegría. *Loud applause,* Aplausos estrepitosos. *Applause* no se usa en plural.

Applausive [ap-plō'-siv], *a.* Laudatorio.

Apple [ap'-l], *s.* Manzana, fruta; manzano, el árbol que da esta fruta. *Apple of discord,* Manzana de la discordia. *Apple-harvest,* Cosecha de manzanas. *Apple-tart,* Pastelillo de manzanas. *Apple-yard,* Huerto. *Apple-tree,* (Bot.) Manzano. *Apple-woman,* La mujer que vende manzanas. *The apple of the eye,* La pupila o niña del ojo y también el globo del ojo: y de aquí, cualquier cosa muy apreciada. *Apple-core,* Corazón de manzana. *Apple-corer,* Despepitador de manzanas. *Apple-fritter,* Frituras de manzanas; fruta de sartén. *Apple-jack,* Aguardiente de manzanas. *Apple-orchard,* Manzanal. *Apple-pie,* Pastel de manzanas. *In apple-pie order,* (Coll.) En orden perfecto. *Apple-parer,* Mondador de manzanas. *Apple-sauce,* Compota de manzanas. *Crab-apple,* Manzana silvestre. *Oak-apple,* Agalla de roble. *Thorn-apple,* Estramonio; se llama también *Jamestown weed.* Datura stramonium. *Adam's apple,* Nuez de la garganta.

†**Appliable** [ap-plai'-a-bl] o **Applicable** [ap'-li-ca-bl], *a.* Aplicable, conforme.

Appliance [ap-plai'-ans], *s.* 1. Herramienta, instrumento, utensilio, medios; una cosa cualquiera por medio de la cual se efectúa algo instrumentalmente. 2. Aplicación: recurso.

Applicability [ap-li-ca-bil'-i-ti], *s.* Aplicabilidad.

Applicable [ap'-li-ca-bl], *a.* A propósito de, aplicable, pertinente; propio para.

Applicableness [ap'-li-ca-bl-nes], *s.* La propiedad de ser aplicable.

Applicably [ap'-li-ca-bli], *adv.* De un modo aplicable.

Applicant [ap'-li-cant], *s.* El suplicante; pretendiente, candidato, aspirante.

§**Applicate** [ap'-li-kêt], *s.* Línea coordenada de una sección cónica.

Application [ap-li-kē'-shun], *s.* 1. Aplicación, la acción de aplicar una cosa a otra, y la cosa aplicada. 2. Súplica o petición. 3. Aplicación, la dedicación a un uso, demanda, o propósito particular; la aplicación de un principio o ley general al caso particular o a los negocios prácticos; empleo, uso, y la capacidad de ser empleado de esta manera. 4. Aplicación, estudio intenso o atención a alguna cosa particular. *To make application to,* Recurrir a; dirigirse a. *A written application,* Un memorial, una solicitud por escrito.

Applicative [ap'-li-ke-tiv], **Applicatory** [ap'-li-ca-to-ri], *a.* Aplicable.

Applied [ap-plaid'], *pp.* y *a.* Aplicado; adaptado, utilizado. *Applied for,* Pedido, encargado. *Applied science,* Ciencia aplicada.

Applier [ap-plai'-er], *s.* El que aplica o adapta.

Appliqué [ap-pli-ké'], *a.* Aplicado, pegado encima; dícese de los bordados. (Fr.)

Apply [a-plai'], *va.* 1. Aplicar, poner o juntar una cosa con otra. 2. Aplicar, apropiar, acomodar. 3. Aplicar, destinar a algún fin o para un uso particular; traer en relación con una persona o cosa; introducir en la práctica los principios de una ciencia, o valerse de una verdad general en el caso particular; utilizar. 4. Aplicarse, estudiar o dedicarse a algún estudio. 5. Recurrir, acudir a alguno como suplicante. *To apply colours,* Dar color, aplicar colores sobre. *To apply a sum of money to,* Destinar una suma de dinero a o para. *To apply one's attention to,* Fijar su atención en. *Apply to me in case of need,* Recurra Vd. a mí en caso de necesidad. *Apply to Mr. D.,* Diríjase Vd. al Sr. D.—*vn.* 1. Pedir, dirigir una petición, hacer solicitud formal. 2. Dirigirse a, recurrir. 3. Convenir, acudir. *To apply one's self to,* Aplicarse a, dirigirse a, recurrir a.

Appoint [ap-point'], *va.* 1. Señalar, determinar. 2. Decretar, establecer por decreto. 3. Surtir, equipar. 4. Nombrar, designar, elegir. *At the appointed time,* Al tiempo prescrito o señalado, a la hora acordada. *Well appointed,* Bien equipado, en buen estado.—*vn.* Ordenar.

Appointee [ap-point-ī'], *s.* Funcionario, nombrado, designado.

Appointer [ap-point'-er], *s.* Ordenador, director, el que fija o determina alguna cosa o lugar.

Appointment [ap-point'-ment], *s.* 1. Estipulación, acuerdo o convenio. 2. Decreto, establecimiento. 3. Dirección, orden o mandato. 4. Equipaje, aparato; equipo (de tropas). 5. Ración, sueldo, gajes, honorario, la cantidad de dinero que se paga a alguna persona por su servicio. 6. Cita. 7. Nombramiento.

Apportion [ap-pōr'-shun], *va.* Proporcionar o dividir igualmente, prorratear.

Apportioner [ap-pōr'-shun-ẹr], *s.* Limitador.

Apportionment [ap-pōr'-shun-mẹnt], *s.* División en dos partes o porciones, prorrateo.

Appose [ap-pōz'], *va.* 1. Poner, fijar junto a, cerca de, aplicar. 2. Yuxtaponer. 3. (Des.) Cuestionar, examinar, considerar.

Apposite [ap'-o-zit], *a.* 1. Adaptado, propio, proporcionado. 2. Justo, conforme : oportuno, a propósito.

Appositely [ap'-o-zit-li], *adv.* Convenientemente, á propósito.

Appositeness [ap'-o-zit-nes], *s.* Adaptación ; propiedad.

Apposition [ap-o-zi'-shun], *s.* 1. Añadidura, lo que se añade de nuevo a alguna cosa. 2. (Gram.) Aposición, figura por la cual se ponen dos substantivos en el mismo caso sin conjunción. 3. Crecimiento o aumento por yuxtaposición. *Minerals grow by apposition,* Los minerales crecen por aposición.

Appositive [ap-poz'-i-tiv], *a.* 1. (Gram.) Que se forma o construye por aposición. 2. Aplicable, propio.

Appraisable [ap-prēz'-a-bl], *a.* Apreciable, estimable, ponderable, tasable.

Appraise [ap-prēz'], *va.* Apreciar, valuar, poner precio o tasar alguna cosa ; estimar, ponderar, dar valor.

Appraisal [ap-prē'-zl] o **Appraisement** [ap-prēz'-mẹnt], *s.* Aprecio, avalúo, estimación, valuación, tasación.

Appraiser [ap-prēz'-ẹr], *s.* Apreciador, tasador, avaluador.

Appreciable [ap-prī'-shi-a-bl], *a.* Apreciable, estimable, que admite estimación ; perceptible, sensible.

Appreciate [ap-prī'-shi-ēt], *va.* Apreciar, estimar, valuar, tasar alguna cosa.—*vn.* Subir en valor.

Appreciater [ap-prī'-shi-ē-tẹr], *s.* Apreciador, valuador, estimador, tasador.

Appreciation [ap-prī-shi-ē'-shun], *s.* 1. Valuación, estimación, tasa, aprecio, avalúo. 2. Alza, aumento de precio. 3. Susceptibilidad o sensibilidad que permite apreciar ligeros cambios o diferencias ; percepción perspicaz de un punto o cosa no manifiestos.

Appreciative, Appreciatory [ap-prī'-shi-a-tiv, a-tō'-ri], *a.* Que manifiesta aprecio, estimación.

Apprehend [ap-rẹ-hend'], *va.* 1. Aprehender, asir. 2. Aprehender, prender, asegurar alguna persona delincuente. 3. Aprender, comprender, concebir alguna cosa. 4. Recelar, temer, desconfiar, sospechar. *I had reason to apprehend,* Tenía motivos para recelar. 5. Notar. *As I apprehend,* Según creo. *To apprehend one's meaning,* Comprender lo que otro se propone o quiere decir.

Apprehender [ap-rẹ-hen'-dẹr], *s.* El que aprehende.

Apprehensible [ap-rẹ-hen'-si-bl], *a.* Comprensible, que puede comprenderse.

Apprehension [ap-rẹ-hen'-shun], *s.* 1. Aprehensión, comprensión, el acto de entender o concebir las cosas. 2. Aprehensión, primera operación del entendimiento que no llega a formar juicio ni discurso. 3. Aprehensión, recelo, sospecha o temor. 4. Aprehensión, presa o captura ; embargo. *To be dull of apprehension,* Tener la cabeza dura, ser rudo de inteligencia. *Be under no apprehension on that account,* No tenga Vd. aprehensión a ese respecto.

Apprehensive [ap-rẹ-hen'-siv], *a.* 1. Aprehensivo, agudo, penetrante, capaz o perspicaz. 2. Aprehensivo, receloso, tímido. 3. Sensible, que responde a las impresiones sobre los sentidos.

Apprehensively [ap-rẹ-hen'-siv-li], *adv.* Aprehensivamente.

Apprehensiveness [ap-rẹ-hen'-siv-nes], *s.* Estado de ansiedad o temor.

Apprentice [ap-pren'-tis], *s.* 1. Aprendiz, el que aprende un arte u oficio. 2. Tirón, novicio, principiante.

Apprentice, *va.* Poner a alguno de aprendiz.

†**Apprenticeage** [ap-pren'-tis-êj], *s.* Aprendizaje.

Apprenticeship [ap-pren'-tis-ship], *s.* Aprendizaje, el tiempo fijado para estar de aprendiz. *To serve one's apprenticeship,* Hacer o pasar su aprendizaje.

Apprise [ap-praiz'], *va.* Informar, avisar, instruir, dar parte.

Apprize, *va.* 1. Informar o dar parte, instruir. 2. Valuar, apreciar, tasar. *V.* APPRAISE.

Apprizement [ap-praiz'-mẹnt], *s.* Avalúo, tasa, valuación, aprecio.

Apprizer [ap-praiz'-ẹr], *s.* Valuador, tasador.

Approach [ap-prōch'], *vn.* Acercarse, aproximarse física o moralmente ; parecerse a, ser parecido a.—*va.* Acercar, poner una cosa o persona cerca de otra.

Approach, *s.* 1. Acceso, la acción de llegar o acercarse. 2. Proximidad, condición de propincuidad. 3. Acceso, entradas, facilidad al trato y comunicación con alguno. 4. Entrada, paso a una habitación ; medios, camino o modo de acercarse. 5. *Approaches, pl.* (Fort.) Aproches, ataques, los trabajos que hacen los que sitian una plaza.

Approachable [ap-prōch'-a-bl], *a.* Accesible, de fácil acceso.

Approacher [ap-prōch'-ẹr], *s.* El que se acerca o aproxima.

Approaching [ap-prōch'-ing], *a.* Próximo, cercano. *The approaching convention,* La próxima convención.

Approbate [ap'-ro-bêt], *va.* 1. Aprobar (en este sentido se usa en los Estados Unidos y no en Inglaterra). 2. Licenciar, autorizar.

Approbation [ap-ro-bê'-shun], *s.* Aprobación.

Approbative [ap'-ro-bê''-tiv], **Approbatory** [ap'-ro-bê''-to-ri], *a.* Aprobatorio, que denota aprobación.

Appropinquate [ap-ro-pin'-cwêt], *vn.* (Des.) Apropincuarse, aproximarse, acercarse.

Appropriable [ap-prō'-pri-a-bl], *a.* Apropiable.

Appropriate [ap-prō'-pri-êt], *va.* 1. Apropiar, destinar para algún objeto o uso particular. 2. Apropiar o apropiarse, alegar o ejercer dominio haciéndose dueño de alguna cosa. 3. Enajenar un beneficio. 4. Aplicar, acomodar, adaptar.

Appropriate, *a.* Apropiado, apto, destinado para algún uso, particular, peculiar.

Appropriately [ap-prō'-pri-êt-li], *adv.* Propiamente, aptamente.

Appropriateness [ap-prō'-pri-êt-nes], *s.* Aptitud ; propiedad de aplicación.

Appropriation [ap-pro-pri-ê'-shun], *s.* 1. Apropiación ; alguna cosa puesta aparte formal u oficialmente para uso particular ; la acción y efecto de apropiar. 2. Enajenación de un beneficio.

Appropriator [ap-pro-pri-ê'-tẹr], *s* Apropiador.

Approprietary [ap-pro-prai'-ẹ-tê-ri], *s.* Apropiador secular.

Approvable [ap-prūv'-a-bl], *a.* Digno de aprobación, que merece aprobación.

Approval [ap-prū'-val], **Approvance** (Ant.) [ap-prū'-vans], **Approvement** [ap-prūv'-mẹnt], *s.* Aprobación. *Approvement,* (For.) 1. El testimonio de un reo que confiesa su delito y acusa a sus cómplices. 2. Mejoramiento o cercamiento y cultivo de tierras incultas.

Approve [ap-prūv'], *va.* 1. Gustar, aprobar, calificar o dar por bueno ; consentir, dar el beneplácito. 2. Probar, hacer patente y manifiesta alguna cosa. *To approve one's self to one,* Hacerse agradable a alguno. 3. Probar, ensayar. 4. Mejorar (las tierras). *V.* IMPROVE.—*vn.* Dar por bueno ; estimar con favor, gracia ; se emplea a menudo con *of. I approve of it,* Lo doy por bueno.

Approver [ap-prūv'-ẹr], *s.* 1. Aprobador, aprobante. 2. (For. Ant.) El reo que acusa a sus cómplices.

†**Approximant** [ap-prec'-si-mant], **Approximate** [ap-prec'-si-mẹt], *a.* 1. Casi perfecto o completo. 2. Próximo, inmediato, aproximativo.

Approximate, *va.* Aproximar.—*vn.* Acercarse.

Approximation [ap-prec-si-mê'-shun], *s.* 1. Aproximación, el acto y efecto de aproximarse. 2. Aproximación, estimación aproximada de una cosa. 3. (Mat.) Aproximación, cálculo que se acerca en lo posible al valor real de una cantidad.

Approximative [ap-prex'-i-ma-tiv], *a.* Aproximativo, que aproxima, perteneciente a la aproximación ; poco más o menos.

Approximatively [ap-prex'-i-ma-tiv-li], *adv.* Aproximativamente, por aproximación.

Appulse [ap'-uls], *s.* Choque, el encuentro de una cosa con otra.

Appurtenance [ap-pŏr'-te-nans], *s.* (For.) Adjunto ; pertenencia, cualquier cosa menor anexa a otra mayor ; dependencia.

Appurtenant [ap-pŏr'-te-nant], *a.* (For.) Perteneciente, lo que pertenece por derecho.

Apricot [ê'-pri-cot o ap'-ri-cot], *s.* Albaricoque, fruta de hueso ; damasco, *Apricot-tree, and its fruit also,* Albarcoque o albaricoque. (Mex.) Chabacano.

April [ê'-pril], *s.* Abril, el cuarto mes del año. *April-fool-day,* El primer día de Abril. *April-fool,* El que es burlado el primero de Abril. *V.* ALL-FOOLS'-DAY.

Apron [ê'-prun o ê'-pŏrn], *s.* 1. Devantal, delantal, pieza de vestir que usan las mujeres para cubrir la parte delantera de la falda, y que se ata por la cintura. 2. Mandil, delantal tosco de que usan ciertos artesanos. 3. Batiente de un dique ; plataforma a la entrada de un dique ; cuero de coche para proteger las piernas. 4. (Art.) Planchada o plomada de cañón, pieza delgada de plomo que se pone sobre el fogón para que no entre la humedad. *Apron of the stem,*

(Mar.) Albitana o contraroda. *Apron-man*, El tendero o artesano que lleva delantal. *Apron-strings*, Cintas del delantal. *To be tied to the apron-strings*, Estar dominado por una mujer.

Aproned [ê'-prund], *a.* Vestido con delantal.

Apropos [a-prō-pō'], *adv.* A propósito, oportunamente.

Apse, Apsis [aps, ap'-sis], *s.* 1. (Arq.) Ábside, bóveda, nicho. 2. (Astr.) *V.* APSIS.

Apsidal [ap'-si-dal], *a.* Del ábside.

Apsis [ap'-sis], *s.* APSIDES [ap'-si-dīz], *pl.* 1. (Astr.) Ápside, cada uno de los dos puntos de la órbita de un planeta, que se llaman apogeo y perigeo. 2. *V.* APSE.

Apt [apt], *a.* 1. Apto, idóneo, propio. 2. Inclinado, dado a alguna cosa u ocasionado a ella. 3. Pronto, vivo. *Too apt to forgive*, Muy indulgente. *Apt to break*, Frágil. *An apt scholar*, Un estudiante capaz.

Apterous [ap'-tę-rus], *a.* 1. (Ent.) Áptero, sin alas; dícese de los insectos. 2. (Bot.) Desprovisto de alas o prolongaciones parecidas a alas.

Apteryx [ap'-tę-rix], *s.* Apterix, kivi, género de aves de la Nueva Zelandia que sólo tienen rudimentos de alas y carecen de cola.

Aptitude [ap'-ti-tiūd], *s.* 1. Aptitud, idoneidad. 2. Tendencia o disposición natural para alguna cosa; facilidad.

Aptly [apt'-li], *adv.* 1. Aptamente. 2. Prontamente, perspicazmente.

Aptness [apt'-nes], *s.* *V.* APTITUDE.

Aptote [ap'tōt], *s.* Nombre que no se declina. (Gr.)

Apyrexia [ap-i-rex'-ia], *s.* Apirexia, ausencia de fiebre.

Apyrous [a-pai'-rus], *a.* No alterado por el calor extremo, como la mica; se diferencia de refractario.

Aqua [ê'-cwa o ą'-cwa], *s.* Agua: voz muy empleada en la farmacia y la química antigua. (Lat.) *Aqua ammoniæ*, Agua de amoníaco.

Aquacade [ak'-wa-kêd], *s.* Ballet acuático.

Aqua-fortis [ê'-cwa-fōr'-tis], *s.* Agua fuerte, el licor que se saca por destilación al fuego del nitro purificado y el ácido vitriólico. *Aqua vitæ*, Aguardiente. *Aqua regia*, Agua regia, el ácido nitro-muriático.

Aqualung [a'-cwa-lung], *s.* Escafandra autónoma.

Aquamarine [a-cwa-ma-rīn'], *s.* Aguamarina.—*a.* De color de aguamarina.

Aquanaut [a'cwa-net], *s.* Acuanauta.

Aquaplane [ak'-wa-plên], *s.* Acuaplano, hidropatín.

Aquarium [a-cwê'-ri-um], *s.* Acuario, receptáculo o depósito para conservar peces y plantas acuáticas.

Aquarius [a-cwê'-ri-us], *s.* (Astr.) Acuario, el undécimo signo del zodíaco.

Aquatint [ê'-cwa-tint], *s.* Acuatinta, especie de grabado o estampado, semejante al dibujo de tinta de china.

Aquatic [a-cwat'-ic], †**Aquatile** [ac'-wa-til], *a.* Acuático o acuátil, lo que vive o se cría en el agua.

Aqueduct [ac'-we-duct], *s.* Acueducto, conducto de agua. (Mex.) Cañería.

Aqueous [ê'- [o ą'-] cwę-us], **Aquose** [ê'- [o ą'-] cwōs], *a.* Ácueo, acuoso.

Aqueousness [ê'- [o ą'-] cwę-us-nes], **Aquiferous** [a-cwif'-ęr-us], *a.* Que conduce o surte agua o fluido acuoso.

Aquiform [ê'-cwi-fōrm], *a.* Semejante al agua; líquido.

Aquiline [ac'-wi-lin], *a.* Aguileño, parecido al águila.

-**ar**, *sufijo*. Perteneciente a: semejante; también la persona a quien pertenece algo.

Aquosity [ê-cwes'-i-ti], *s.* Acuosidad.

Arab [ar'-ab], **Arabian** [a-rê'-bi-an], *s.* 1. Árabe, el natural de Arabia. 2. Caballo árabe. 3. Sin hogar, vagamundo por las calles, especialmente un niño. *Street arab*, Pillete de calle.

Arabesque [ar-a-besc'], *a.* Arabesco, al estilo de los árabes.—*s.* 1. Arabescos, adornos primorosos usados en la pintura y la escultura, hechos con figuras geométricas, caracteres cúficos u hojas y flores entrelazadas. 2. Adornos fantásticos en formas de animales y plantas, como se emplean en los estilos romano y del renacimiento.

Arabian [a-rê'-bi-an], **Arabic** [ar'-a-bic], **Arabical** [a-rab'-i-cal], *a.* Arábigo, arábico.

Arabic [ar'-a-bic], *s.* Lengua arábiga. El árabe.

Arabically [a-rab'-i-cal-i], *adv.* A manera de los árabes.

Arabism [ar'-a-bizm], *s.* Arabismo, giro propio de la lengua árabe, adoptado en otra.

Arabist [ar'-a-bist], *s.* Persona versada en la lengua arábiga.

Arable [ar'-a-bl], *a.* Labrantío, dispuesto o apto para la labranza. *Arable ground*, Tierra labrantía o de pan llevar.

Arachnida [a-rac'-ni-da], *s. pl.* (Ento.) Arácnidos o aracnéidos, una de las clases de los artrópodos. Comprende las arañas y otros artrópodos de ocho patas.

Arachnoid [a-rac'-noid], *a.* y *s.* (Anat.) Aracnoides, una de las tres membranas que envuelven el encéfalo.

Arack [ar'-ac], *s.* (Des.) Aguardiente de azúcar. *V.* ARRACK.

Aragonese [ar-ag-o-nīs'], *a.* y *s.* Aragonés, de Aragón.

Aragonite [ar'-ag-o-nait], *s.* Aragonito, cal carbonatada cristalina. Se llama vulgarmente, "piedra de Santa Casilda."

Aramaic [ar-a-mê'-ic], *a.* Arameo, aramea, que se refiere al país de Aram. —*s.* Lengua aramea, nombre dado al asirio y al caldeo; la clase septentrional de las lenguas semíticas.

Aramean [ar-a-mī'-an], *a.* *V.* ARAMAIC.—*s.* 1. Habitante de la Aramea (Siria y Mesopotamia). 2. Lengua aramea.

Araneous [a-rê'-nę-us], *a.* Semejante a la telaraña.

Aration [a-rê'-shun], *s.* (Ant.) Aradura, la acción o ejercicio de arar.

Aratory [ar'-a-to-ri], *a.* Aratorio, lo que pertenece al oficio de arar.

Araucanian [ar-ō-kê'-ni-an], *a.* y *s.* Araucano, relativo a los indígenas de la Araucania, en Chile, y a su lengua.

Arbalest, Arbalist [ār'-ba-lest, list], *s.* Ballesta, arma para disparar flechas o saetas.

Arbiter [ār'-bi-tęr], *s.* 1. Arbitrador, compromisario, el juez árbitro con quien las partes se avienen para que ajuste sus controversias. 2. Arbitro, el que puede hacer una cosa por sí solo, sin dependencia de otro.

Arbitrable [ār'-bi-tra-bl], *a.* Arbitrable, que pende del arbitraje; que se puede arbitrar.

Arbitrably [ār'-bi-tra-bli], *adv.* A discreción.

Arbitrament [ar-bit'-ra-męnt], *s.* Arbitraje. *V.* ARBITRATION.

Arbitrarily [ār'-bi-trê-ri-li], *adv.* Arbitrariamente.

Arbitrariness [ār'-bi-trê-ri-nes], *s.* Arbitrariedad, despotismo, poder absoluto.

Arbitrarious [ār-bi-trê'-ri-us], *a.* (Des.) *V.* ARBITRARY.

Arbitrary [ār'-bi-trê-ri], *a.* Arbitrario, despótico, absoluto.

Arbitrate [ār'-bi-trêt], *va.* Arbitrar, juzgar o determinar como árbitro. —*vn.* Dar juicio, decidir como árbitro.

Arbitration [ār-bi-trê'-shun], *s.* Arbitramento, arbitraje, arbitración, la sentencia dada por un juez árbitro; la audiencia y determinación de una controversia ante una persona o personas mutuamente aceptadas por los interesados. *By arbitration*, Por arbitraje, arbitralmente. *Arbitration bond*, Compromiso. *Arbitration of exchange*, Arbitraje de cambio; operación de cambio de valores mercantiles, buscando la utilidad en los precios comparados de diferentes plazas.

Arbitrator [ār'-bi-tre-ter], *sm.* Arbitrador, árbitro.

Arbitratrix [ār-bi-trê'-trix], **Arbitress** [ār'-bi-tres], *sf.* Arbitradora.

Arbitrement [ār-bit'-rę-męnt], *s.* Arbitrio, elección, determinación, compromiso.

Arbor [ār'-ber], *s.* 1. Árbol, eje de una rueda, de una máquina. 2. Árbol, en ciertos nombres botánicos, v. g. *Arbor-vitæ*, q. v. *Arbor Dianæ*, Árbol de Diana; árbol de plata.

Arbor, Arbour [ār'-ber], *s.* Emparrado, enramada; glorieta. *Arbour* es la forma usual en Inglaterra.

Arbor-vitæ [ār'-ber-vai'-ti], *s.* 1. Tuya, árbol conífero. 2. (Anat.) Aspecto ramoso en una sección radial del cerebelo.

Arboreal, Arboreous [ār-bō'-rę-us], **Arborous** [ār'-bo-rus], *a.* Arbóreo.

Arborescence [ār-bo-res'-ens], *s.* 1. Arborescencia. 2. (Miner.) Arborización, ramaje dibujado naturalmente en algunos minerales y cristalizaciones.

Arborescent [ār-bo-res'-ent], *a.* Arborescente, que crece como un árbol; que va pareciendo árbol.

Arboret [ār'-bo-ret], *s.* 1. Arbolillo, arbusto. 2. Soto, arboleda.

Arboretum [ār-bo-rī'-tum], *s.* Plantel, almáciga, criadero de árboles.

Arboriculture [ār-bor-i-cul'-chur], *s.* Arboricultura, arte de cultivar los árboles y arbustos.

Arborist [ār'-bo-rist], *s.* Arbolista, el que se dedica por oficio al cultivo de los árboles.

Arbuscle [ār'-busl], *s.* Arbustillo o arbusto pequeño.

Arbute [ār'-biūt], *s.* (Bot.) Fresal. *V.* ARBUTUS.

Arbutean [ār-biū'-tę-an], *a.* Lo perteneciente al fresal.

Arbutus [ār-biū'-tus], *s.* 1. Madroño, reducido género de árboles y arbustos de la familia de las ericáceas. 2. *Trailing arbutus*, Gayuba, planta rastrera de la primavera; la Epigæa repens. *V.* MAYFLOWER.

Arc [ărc], *s.* Arco de círculo.
Arc-light [ărc-lait'], *s.* Alumbrado eléctrico en que se usa el arco galvánico.
Arcade [ăr-kêd'], *s.* 1. Arcadá, bóveda continuada o una continuación de arcos. 2. Pasaje, galería cubierta llena de tiendas.
Arcadian [ăr-kê'-di-an], *a.* Arcadio, árcade; idealmente rural o sencillo; pastoral.—*s.* Arcadio, habitante de Arcadia.
Arcane [ăr-ken'], *a.* Arcano, misterioso.
Arcanum [ăr-ke'-num], *s.* Arcano, voz latina. *Arcana*, Misterios, arcanos.
Arch [ărch], *s.* Arco. 1. Arco de círculo. 2. Arco de puente. 3. Bóveda, obra de mampostería, etc., en forma de arco. 4. Arco del cielo. *The arch of heaven*, La bóveda celeste. *Arch of the aorta*, (Anat.) La curvatura de la aorta. *Segmental arch*, Arco abocinado. *Gothic arch, pointed arch*, Arco ojival, arco gótico. *Horse-shoe arch*, Arco de herradura. *Semicircular arch*, Arco de medio punto.
Arch, *va.* 1. Arquear, formar en figura de arco; encorvar. 2. Abovedar, cubrir con bóvedas o arcos. —*vn.* Formar bóveda o bóvedas. *The trees arch overhead*, Los árboles forman bóveda en lo alto.
Arch, *a.* 1. Travieso, inquieto; picaresco, socarrón, astuto. 2. Principal, insigne, de primer orden, grande. *An arch wag*, Un gran perillán, un martagón. Se usa en composición como aumentativo. *An arch look*, Una mirada picaresca.
Archæan, Archaian [ăr-kí'-an, ăr-kê'-an], *a.* Arqueano, perteneciente a los estratos o al período más viejos de la historia geológica.
Archæology [ăr-kẹ-el'-o-ji], *s.* Arqueología, discurso o tratado de cosas antiguas.
Archaic [ăr-kê'-ic], *a.* 1. Arcáico, anticuado, que va cayendo en desuso. 2. De un período anterior al desarrollo cumplido de un arte.
Archaism [ăr'-ke-izm], *s.* Arcaísmo, uso afectado de voces o frases anticuadas.
Archangel [ărk-ên'-jel], *s.* 1. Arcángel. 2. (Bot.) Ortiga muerta.
Archangelical [ărk-an-jel'-i-cal], *a.* Arcangelical, arcangélico.
Archapostle [ărch-a-pes'-l], *s.* Apóstol principal.
Archarchitect [ărch-ărk'-i-tect], *s.* Arquitecto supremo.
Archbishop [ărch-bish'-up], *s.* Arzobispo.
Archbishopric [ărch-bish'-up-ric], *s.* Arzobispado.
Archbuilder [ărch-bil'-dẹr], *s.* Arquitecto o fabricador principal.
Archchanter [ărch-chgn'-tẹr], *s.* Cantor principal.
Archchemic [ărch-kem'-ic], *a.* Químico principal.
Archconspirator [ărch-cen-spir'-a-ter], *s.* Conspirador principal.
Archcritic [ărch-crit'-ic], *s.* Criticón.
Archdeacon [ărch-dí'-cn], *s.* Arcediano, antes el primero de los diáconos. Hoy es alta dignidad eclesiástica y tiene el primer rango después del obispo; auxiliar de un obispo.
Archdeaconry [ărch-dí'-cn-ri], **Archdeaconship** [ărch-dí'-cn-ship], *s.* Arcedianato, la dignidad o jurisdicción del arcediano.
Archdivine [ărch-di-vain'], *s.* Teólogo principal.
Archducal [ărch-diū'-cal], *a.* Archiducal.
Archduchess [ărch-duch'-es], *sf.* Archiduquesa, princesa de Austria; la hija del emperador y la hija o mujer de un archiduque.
Archduchy [ărch-duch'-i], *s.* Archiducado; distrito o dignidad de archiduque.
Archduke [ărch-diūc'], *s.* Archiduque, título que se da a los príncipes de la casa de Austria.
Archdukedom [ărch-diūc'-dem], *s.* Archiducado.
Arched [ărcht], *a.* Arqueado, hecho en forma de arco.
Archenemy [ărch-en'-e-mi], *s.* El mayor enemigo; el demonio.
Archeologian [ăr-kẹ-o-lō'-jan], *s.* *V.* ARCHEOLOGIST.
Archeologic, Archeological [ăr-kẹ-o-lej'-ic, lej'-ic-al], *a.* Arqueológico, relativo o la arqueología, o versado en ella.
Archeologist [ăr-kẹ-el'-o-jist], *s.* Arqueólogo, el versado en la arqueología.
Archeology [ăr-kẹ-el'-o-ji], *s.* Arqueología, estudio de monumentos, medallas, inscripciones, etc., de la antigüedad.
Archer [ărch'-ẹr], *s.* Arquero, el que tira con arco o ballesta.
Archeress [ărch'-ẹr-es], *sf.* Arquera, ballestera.
Archery [ărch'-ẹr-i], *s.* El arte de tirar con arco y flecha.
Arches-court [ărch'-ez-cōrt], *s.* Un tribunal eclesiástico de Londres.
Archetypal [ărk-ẹ-tai'-pal], *a.* Lo perteneciente al arquetipo.
Archetype [ărk'-e-taip], *s.* Arquetipo, patrón o modelo.
Archfelon [ărch-fel'-un], *s.* Reo principal.
Archfiend [ărch-fínd'], *s.* El demonio, el diablo, el enemigo mortal.
Archflatterer [ărch-flat'-ẹr-ẹr], *s.* Gran adulador.
Archfounder [ărch-faun'-dẹr], *s.* Fundador principal.
Archgovernor [ărch-guv'-ẹrn-ẹr], *s.* Gobernador en jefe.
Archheresy [ărch-her'-e-si], *s.* Herejía enorme.
Archheretic [ărch-her'-e-tic], *s.* Gran heresiarca.
Archhypocrite [ărch-hip'-o-crit], *s.* Hipocritón, santurrón.
Archiater [ăr-ki-é'-tẹr], *s.* Protomédico.
Archical [ăr'-ki-cal], *a.* Principal, primario.
Archidiaconal [ăr-ki-di-ac'-o-nal], *a.* Perteneciente al arcediano.
Archiepiscopacy [ăr-ki-ẹ-pis'-co-pa-si], *s.* Rango, dignidad de arzobispo.
Archiepiscopal [ăr-ki-ẹ-pis'-co-pal], *a.* Arquiepiscopal o arzobispal.
Archiepiscopate [ăr-ki-ẹ-pis'-co-pêt], *s.* Arzobispado, dignidad, jurisdicción de un arzobispo.
Archil [ăr'-chil], *s.* 1. (Bot.) Archilla, especie de liquen del género Roccella. R. tinctoria. 2. Materia de tinte que se obtiene de esta planta. *V.* ORCHIL.
Archimandrite [ăr-ki-man'-drait], *s.* Archimandrita, superior de un monasterio en la iglesia griega.
Arching [ărch'-ing], *a.* Arqueado, en forma de arco.
Archipelago [ăr-ki-pel'-a-go], *s.* Archipiélago, parte del mar poblada de islas; por antonomasia (con mayúscula), las islas de Grecia en el Mar Egeo.
Architect [ăr'-ki-tect], *s.* 1. Arquitecto, alarife. 2. (Fig.) Artífice.
Architectonic [ăr-ki-tec-ten'-ic], †**Architectonical** [ăr-ki-tec-ten'-i-cal], *a.* Arquitectónico, versado en la arquitectura, o perteneciente a ella.
Architectonics [ăr-ki-tec-ten'-ics], *s.* Arquitectura, arte arquitectónico.
Architectural [ăr-ki-tec'-chu-ral], *a.* Arquitectural, perteneciente a la arquitectura; constructor, que construye.
Architecture [ăr'-ki-tec-chur], *s.* 1. Arquitectura, el arte de construir y hacer edificios. 2. Arquitectura, la obra ejecutada según las reglas del arte.
Architrave [ăr'-ki-trêv], *s.* Arquitrabe, la parte inferior del cornisamento que decansa inmediatamente sobre el capitel de la columna.
Archive [ăr'-kaiv], *s.* 1. Archivo, el paraje en que se guardan papeles, escrituras, instrumentos o documentos importantes. Más usado en plural. 2. Archivo, documento o escritura que se guarda en el lugar de ese nombre.
Archivist [ăr'-ki-vist], *s.* Archivero.
Archlike [ărch'-laik], *a.* Fabricado como arco.
Archly [ărch'-li], *adv.* Jocosamente, sutilmente.
Archmagician [ărch-ma-jish'-an], *s.* Mágico principal.
Archness [ărch'-nes], *s.* Travesura, astucia, sutileza de ingenio.
Archon [ăr'-cen], *s.* Arconte, magistrado supremo de la antigua Atenas.
Archpastor [ărch-pgs'-ter], *s.* El Pastor de almas, Jesucristo.
Archphilosopher [ărch-fi-les'-o-fẹr], *s.* Arquifilósofo, filósofo principal.
Archpillar [ărch-pil'-ar], *s.* Columna principal.
Archpoet, *s.* *V.* POET LAUREATE.
Archpolitician [ărch-pel-i-tish'-an], *s.* Político profundo.
Archprelate [ărch-prel'-êt], *s.* Arcipreste, el primero o principal de los presbíteros.
Archpriest [ărch-príst'], *s.* Gran sacerdote.
Archprimate [ărch-prai'-mêt], *s.* Primado principal.
Archprophet [ărch-pref'-et], *s.* Profeta principal.
Archrebel [ărch-reb'-el], *s.* Rebelde principal; Satanás.
Archtraitor [ărch-trê'-ter], *s.* Gran traidor; el demonio.
Archtreasurer [ărch-trezh'-ur-ẹr], *s.* Tesorero mayor.
Archtyrant [ărch-tai'-rant], *s.* El tirano o déspota por excelencia.
Archvillain [ărch-vil'-en], *s.* Bellaconazo, picarón.
Archvillainy [ărch-vil'-e-ni], *s.* Bellaquería grande.
Archwise [ărch'-waiz], *a.* En figura de arco.
Arcograph [ăr'-co-graf], *s.* Arcógrafo, instrumento con que se traza un arco circular sin punto céntrico.
Arctation [ărc-tê'-shun], *s.* Angostura, estrechez.
Arctic [ărc'-tic], *a.* Ártico, septentrional; que designa el polo septentrional o las regiones cercanas a él; frígido.
Arcturus [ărc-tū'-rus], *s.* Arturo, estrella fija de primera magnitud, situada en la constelación Bootes.

Arcuate [ār'-kiu-ēt], *a.* Arqueado, formado en figura de arco.
Arcuation [ār-kiu-ē'-shun], *s.* 1. Encorvamiento, curvatura, calidad de corvo. 2. Obras encorvadas. 3. (Hort.) Acodadura. *V.* LAYERING.
Arc weld [ārc weld], *s.* Soldadura de arco.
Ardash [ār'-dash], *s.* Ardaza, seda basta de Persia.
Ardassine [ār-dq-sīn'], *s.* Ardasina, seda finísima de Persia.
Ardency [ār-den-si], **Ardentness** [ār'-dent-nes], *s.* Ardor, vehemencia, ansia, anhelo, calor.
Ardent [ār'-dent], *a.* 1. Ardiente, lo que arde. 2. Ardiente, vehemente. 3. Apasionado, vivo, ansioso.
Ardently [ār'-dent-li], *adv.* Apasionadamente, ardientemente.
Ardor, Ardour [ār'-der], *s.* 1. Ardor, calor. 2. (Fig.) Ardor, pasión.
Ardour, *s.* *V.* ARDOR. (Forma usual en Inglaterra.)
Arduous [ār'-ju-us], *a.* 1. Arduo, alto, inaccesible o difícil de subir. 2. Arduo, difícil.
Arduously [ār'-ju-us-li], *adv.* Arduamente, difícilmente.
Are [ār]. Plural del presente de indicativo del verbo *To Be. We are, you are, they are,* Somos, sois, son, o estamos, estais, están.
Âre [ār], *s.* Medida de superficie, cuadrado que tiene diez metros de lado.
Area [ē'-rę-a], *s.* 1. Área, la superficie comprendida entre ciertas líneas o límites. 2. Espacio o extensión superficial. *Area of a building,* Área de un edificio, todo el espacio que ocupa. 3. Patio, corral; cualquier espacio cercado y no cubierto. 4. Un pequeño patio a nivel más bajo que el de la calle, delante de las puertas o ventanas del sótano.
Areca [a-rī'-ca], *s.* 1. Árbol de Malabar, especie de palma altísima. 2. Su fruta, que se masca como el betel.
Arefaction [ar-e-fāc'-shun], *s.* (Des.) La acción y efecto de secar o secarse.
Arefy [ar'-ę-fai], *va.* (Des.) Secar, extraer la humedad de algún cuerpo.
Arena [a-rī'-na], *s.* Arena, sitio destinado a las luchas entre los antiguos. Campo de combate, círculo de acción.
Arenaceous [ar-ę-nē'-shus], **Arenose** [ar'-ę-nōs], *a.* Arenisco, arenoso, lleno de arena o de arenillas.
Areola [a-rī'-o-la], *s.* 1. (Anat.) Aréola, círculo mamario. 2. Círculo que rodea una pústula, un punto inflamado.
Areolar [a-rī'-o-lar], *a.* Areolar. *V.* CONNECTIVE.
Areometer [a-rę-em'-ę-tęr], *s.* Areómetro, instrumento para pesar los licores espirituosos.
Areopagite [ar-e-ep'-a-gait], *s.* Areopagita, juez del Areópago.
Areopagus [ar-e-ep'-a-gus], *s.* Areópago, tribunal supremo de Atenas.
Argal [ār'-gal], **Argol** [ār'-gel], *s.* Tártaro.
Argand [ār'-gand], *a.* Perteneciente al alumbrado inventado por Aimé Argand, de Ginebra; se llama en España quinqué, del nombre del fabricante francés de dichas lámparas, Mr. Quinquet.
Argent [ār'-jent], *a.* (Her.) Blanco; plata, en los escudos de armas.
Argentation [ār-jen-tē'-shun], *s.* La acción de platear.
Argentiferous [ār-jen-tif'-ęr-us], *a.* Argentífero, que contiene plata.
Argentine [ār'-jen-tin], *a.* 1. Argentino, sonoro como la plata, de color de plata. 2. Argentino, perteneciente a la República Argentina, o Río de la Plata.—*s.* 1. Metal blanco plateado. 2. Un precipitado de estaño y cinc. 3. La materia plateada del color de las escamas de los peces. 4. Argentino, natural de la República Argentina, o residente en ella.
Argil [ār'-jil], *s.* Arcilla, tierra o barro que usan los alfareros. *V.* ALUMINA.
Argillaceous [ār-ji-lē'-shus], **Argillous** [ār-jil'-us], *a.* Arcilloso, lo que tiene arcilla o alúmina.
Argonaut [ār'-go-nēt], *s.* 1. Argonauta, uno de los compañeros de Jasón. 2. (Zool.) Argonauta, nautilo papiráceo: especie de molusco cefalópodo. Es una jibia octópoda con concha papirácea. Argonauta argo.
Argosy [ār'-go-si], *s.* Bajel o buque grande mercante.
Argot [ār'-gōt], *s.* Jerga, jerigonza.
Argue [ār'-giu], *vn.* Razonar, disputar, discurrir. *To argue with,* Argüir, discutir con.—*va.* 1. Probar, hacer ver, persuadir con razones. 2. Argüir, disputar; probar con argumentos.
Arguer [ār'-giu-ęr], *s.* Argumentador, el que arguye.
Arguing [ār'-giu-ing], *s.* Razonamiento, argumento.
Argument [ār'-giu-męnt], *s.* 1. Argumento, tema o materia de algún discurso o escrito, asunto. 2. Argumento, la razón que se alega a favor o en contra de alguna cosa. (For.) Alegato. 3. Razonamiento, silogismo, prueba. 4. Argumento, el contenido de una obra en compendio o extracto. 5. (Des.) Argumento, controversia.
Argumental [ār-giu-men'-tal], *a.* Argumentista, que pertenece a los argumentos.
Argumentation [ār-giu-men-tē'-shun], *s.* Argumentación, raciocinio.
Argumentative [ār-giu-men'-ta-tiv], *a.* Argumentativo, demostrativo, aficionado a la argumentación; fundado en el raciocinio, que tiende a probar.
Argumentatively [ār-giu-men'-tē-tiv-li], *adv.* Argumentativamente.
Argus [ār'-gus], *s.* 1. Argos, personaje fabuloso que tenía cien ojos. 2. Argos, faisán de China.
Argute [ār-giūt'], *a.* 1. Agudo, sutil; astuto, perspicaz. 2. Agudo, penetrante (hablando de sonidos). 3. (Bot.) Provisto de dientes agudos como una hoja aserrada.
Arguteness [ār-giūt'-nes], *s.* Argucia, agudeza, sutileza, perspicacia.
Arhizal, Arhizous [a-rai'-zal, a-rai'-zus], *a.* (Bot.) *V.* ARRHIZOUS.
Aria [g'-ri-a], *s.* (Mús.) Aria, composición lírica para una sola voz.
Arian [ē'-ri-an], *s.* Arriano, el que sigue la herejía de Arrio.
Arianism [ē'-ri-an-izm], *s.* Arrianismo, la herejía de Arrio.
Arid [ar'-id], *a.* Árido, seco, sequizo, enjugado, enjuto.
Aridity [a-rid'-i-ti] o **Aridness** [ar'-id-nes], *s.* 1. Aridez, gran sequedad de la tierra. 2. Sequedad; falta de devoción y fervor.
Aries [ē'-ri-iz], *s.* (Astr.) Aries, el primer signo del zodíaco, cuyo símbolo es ♈: también, constelación del zodíaco.
Arietta [a-ri-et'-a], *s.* (Mús.) Arieta, aria corta.
Aright [a-rait'], *adv.* 1. Acertadamente. 2. Rectamente, puramente, bien. *To set aright,* Rectificar, enderezar o poner una cosa o negocio en el estado que debe tener.
Aril [ar'-il], **Arillus** [a-ril'-us], *s.* 1. Arila, cubierta o zurrón del grano. 2. Arila, parte carnosa de un fruto.
Arillated [ar-il-ē'-ted], *a.* Arilado, que tiene arila.
Ariolation [a-ri-o-lē'-shun], *s.* Adivinación.
Arise [a-raiz'], *vn.* (*Pret.* AROSE, *pp.* ARISEN.) 1. Subir, elevarse. 2. Surgir, aparecer. 3. Levantarse, ponerse en pie. 4. Proceder (de); provenir (de). 5. Presentarse, ofrecerse; suscitarse, originarse. 6. Sublevarse, levantarse. *When the sun arose,* Cuando salió el sol. *Another difficulty then arose,* Entonces surgió otra dificultad. *The people arose against the tyrant,* El pueblo se sublevó contra el tirano.
Arisen [a-riz'-en], *pp.* de ARISE.
Arista [a-ris'-ta], *s.* (Bot.) Arista. *V.* AWN.
Aristarchus [a-ris-tār'-cus], *s.* Aristarco, nombre que se da a los críticos severos.
Aristocracy [ar-is-tec'-ra-si], *s.* 1. Aristocracia, la clase noble; la nobleza hereditaria. 2. Aristocracia, gobierno en que sólo intervienen los nobles.
Aristocrat [ar-is'-to-crat], *s.* Aristócrata, de familia noble; aficionado a la aristocracia y sostenedor de ella.
Aristocratic [ar-is-to-crat'-ic], **Aristocratical** [a-ris-to-crat'-ic-al], *a.* Aristocrático, lo perteneciente a la aristocracia.
Aristocratically [ar-is-to-crat'-i-cal-i], *adv.* Aristocráticamente.
Aristotelic [ar-is-to-tel'-ic], *a.* y *s.* Aristotélico, lo que pertenece al sistema filosófico de Aristóteles, y el que lo sigue.
Arithmancy [a-rith'-man-si], *s.* Aritmancia, el arte de adivinar por los números.
Arithmetic [a-rith'-me-tic], *s.* Aritmética, la ciencia de los números o el arte de contar.
Arithmetical [a-rith-met'-i-cal], *a.* Aritmético, perteneciente a la aritmética, o según las reglas de la misma.
Arithmetician [a-rith-me-tish'-an], *s.* Aritmético, el que sabe o enseña la aritmética.
Ark [ārc], *s.* 1. Arca, la embarcación en que se salvaron Noé y su familia del diluvio. 2. Arca del Testamento. *Ark of the covenant,* El arca de la alianza. 3. Barco de trasporte con fondo chato; lanchón.
Arles [ārlz], *s.* (Inglaterra del norte y Escocia) 1. Arras, parte del precio que se anticipa como prenda y señal de un contrato. 2. Prenda segura. *V.* EARNEST.
Arlet [ār'-let], *s.* (Bot.) Especie de comino.
Arm [ārm], *s.* 1. Brazo. 2. Miembro delantero de un vertebrado. 3. Vara o rama del árbol. 4. Brazo de mar. 5. Brazo, poder, fuerza. *Arm's reach,* Alcance. *An arm or elbow chair,* Una silla de brazos. *Arm in arm,* (Fam.) De bracete, del brazo. 6. Brazo (de un sillón). 7. Radio de una rueda. 8. Brazo, ramo, parte distinta. 9. (Mar.) Cabo de una verga. *At arm's length,* A

una brazada. (Fig.) A distancia. *Forearm*, Antebrazo.

Arm, *s.* (Mil.) 1. Arma, instrumento de ataque o de defensa. *V.* ARMS. 2. Cada uno de los diferentes institutos o ramos del servicio militar.

Arm, *va.* 1. Armar. 2. Armar o reforzar. 3. Armar, aprestar.—*vn.* Tomar las armas, levantarse las tropas ; armarse.

Armada [ār-mē'-da o ar-mā'da], *s.* Armada, conjunto de las fuerzas marítimas ; flota.

Armadillo [ār-ma-dil'-o], *s.* Armadillo o tatuay, mamífero del orden de los desdentados, peculiar de América ; tato. Para defenderse se enrolla como el erizo.

Armament [ār'-ma-mẹnt], *s.* 1. Fuerza militar o naval. 2. Armamento de navíos ; equipo y pertrechos de guerra de una fortificación o de un navío.

Armamentary [ār-ma-men'-ta-ri], *s.* Armería. *V.* ARMORY.

Armature [ār'-ma-chur o tiūr], *s.* 1. (Elec.) (1) Armadura, trozo de hierro que une los polos de un imán. (2) Centro de metal rodeado por un rollo de alambre, que gira cerca de los polos de un imán en una máquina dinamo-eléctrica. 2. Armadura, arma defensiva, instrumento o medio de defensa u ofensa.

Armed [ārmd], *a.* 1. Armado, provisto de armas ; en botánica, espinoso. 2. Eficaz. 3. (Fís.) Provisto de una armadura. *Long-armed, short-armed*, De brazos largos, de brazos cortos.

Armenian [ār-mī'-ni-an], *a.* y *s.* Armenio.

Armenian bole [ār-mī'-ni-an bōl], *s.* *V.* BOLE.

Armental [ār-men'-tal], **Armentine** [ār'-men-tain], **Armentose** [ār-men-tōs'], *a.* (Des.) Pecuario, lo perteneciente al ganado.

Armful [ārm'-ful], *s.* Brazado, medida de lo que se puede abarcar con los brazos, o lo que se tiene en los brazos.

Armhole [ārm'-hōl], *s.* Sobaco, abertura en los vestidos para el brazo. Escote (de camisa).

Armiger [ār'-mi-jẹr], *s.* 1. Armígero, caballero. 2. Escudero.

Armigerous [ār-mij'-ẹr-us], *a.* Armígero, el que lleva armas.

Armillary [ār'-mil-ẹ-ri], *a.* Armilar, lo que se parece a brazalete ; que consta de un anillo o de anillos. *Armillary sphere*, Esfera armilar, la que representa los círculos de los movimientos de los astros.

Armings [ārm'-ingz], *s. pl.* (Mar.) Empavesadas.

Arminian [ār-min'-i-an], *s.* y *a.* Arminiano, el que pertenece a la secta de Arminio.

Arminianism [ār-min'-i-an-izm], *s.* Arminianismo, doctrina calvinista de Arminio.

Armipotence [ār-mip'-o-tens], *s.* Armipotencia.

‡**Armipotent** [ār-mip'-o-tent], *a.* Armipotente.

‡**Armisonous** [ār-mis'-o-nus], *a.* Sonoro como las armas o la armadura.

Armistice [ār'-mis-tis], *s.* Armisticio, suspensión de las hostilidades.

Armless [ārm'-les], *a.* Desarmado, desbrazado ; sin armas ; sin brazos.

Armlet [ārm'-let], *s.* 1. Brazuelo o brazo pequeño. 2. Brazal o brazalete, armadura de hierro que cubre y defiende el brazo.

Armor, armour, [ār'-mur], *s.* Armadura. *Armor plate*, Plancha de coraza o blindaje.

Armor, *va.* Acorazar, blindar con planchas de hierro o acero.

Armor-bearer [ār'-mẹr-bār-ẹr], *s.* Escudero, el que lleva la armadura.

Armorer [ār'-mẹr-ẹr], *s.* 1. Armero, el artífice que fabrica armas. 2. Armador, el que arma, viste y pone a otro las armas.

Armorial [ār-mō'-ri-al], *a.* Heráldico, que pertenece al escudo de armas de alguna familia.

Armoric [ār-mer'-ic], **Armorican** [ār-mer'-i-can], *a.* Armórico, lo que pertenece a la Armórica antigua, o la Baja Bretaña en Francia.

Armory [ār'-mo-ri], *s.* 1. Armería, el sitio en que se guardan las armas. 2. (E. U.) Arsenal en que se fabrican armas. 3. Armadura, armazón colectivamente. 4. Heráldica. 5. Escudo de armas.

Armour, Armoured, Armoury, etc. Modo usual de escribir *armor*, etc., en Inglaterra.

Armpit [ārm'-pit], *s.* Sobaco, la parte hueca que está debajo del hombro.

Arms [ārmz], *s. pl.* 1. Armas, instrumentos ofensivos o defensivos. *To arms !* ¡ A las armas ! 2. Hostilidad, guerra, como profesión, ciencia o arte. 3. Armas, partes u órganos defensivos, como púas, espinas, etc. 4. Armas, las insignias de que usan las familias nobles en sus escudos, para distinguirse unas de otras. *Fire-arms*, Armas de fuego. *Side-arms*, Armas blancas, o armas que se llevan al costado, como espada y bayoneta. *Under arms*, Con las armas listas para usarlas. *Man at arms*, Hombre armado. *Present arms!* ¡ Presenten armas ! *To lay down arms*, Rendir las armas.

Arm-scye [ārm'-sai], *s.* Escote. *V.* ARM-HOLE.

Army [ār'-mi], *s.* 1. Ejército. 2. Multitud, muchedumbre.

Army corps [ār'-mi cōr], *s.* Cuerpo de ejército.

Army register [ār'-mi rej'-is-tẹr], *s.* Escalafón del ejército.

Army-worm [ār'-mi-wūrm], *s.* 1. Oruga de una falena (mariposa nocturna) que a menudo pasa de un lugar a otro en grandísimo número, devorando la hierba, el grano y otras cosechas. La del norte de los Estados Unidos es la Leucania unipuncta. 2. La oruga llamada "de las tiendas" (tent-caterpillar) que se cría en los bosques. Clisiocampa sylvática, de los bombícidos.

Arnatto [ār-nat'-o], **Arnotto** [ār-net'-o]. *V.* ANNATTO.

Arnica [ār'-ni-ca], *s.* 1. Árnica, planta medicinal de flores amarillas, que así como la raíz, tienen sabor acre y aromático y olor fuerte. Pertenece á la familia de las sinantéreas. Arnica montana, *Linn.* 2. Tintura que se obtiene de la raíz, hojas o flores de dicha planta.

Aroint [a-reint'], *vr.* Irse, apartarse ; más usado en el imperativo y entonces equivale a fuera, afuera.

Aroma [a-rō'-ma], *s.* (Quím.) Aroma, principio odorífero agradable ; fragrancia de las plantas.

Aromatic [ar-o-mat'-ic], **Aromatical** [ar-o-mat'-i-cal], *a.* Aromático, lo que tiene fragrancia o aroma ; odorífero.

Aromatics [ar-o-mat'-ics], *s. pl.* Aromas, especias.

Aromatize [a-rō'-ma-taiz], *va.* Aromatizar, comunicar olor aromático a alguna cosa.

Aromatizer [a-rō'-ma-taiz-ẹr], *s.* Aromatizador.

Arose [a-rōz'], *pret.* del verbo *To Arise.*

Around [a-raund'], *prep.* En, cerca. —*adv.* Al rededor o al derredor.

Arousal [a-rauz'-al], *s.* Despertamiento, acción de despertar.

Arouse [a-rauz'], *va.* 1. Despertar, quitar el sueño al que está durmiendo. 2. Despertar, excitar.

Arow [a-rō'], *adv.* (Poét.) En fila, en línea.

Arpeggio [ar-pej'-ō], *s.* Arpegio, la rápida sucesión de los sonidos de un acorde.

Arquebuse [ār'-cwe-bus], *s.* Arcabuz, arma de fuego.

Arrack [ar'-ac], *s.* Arak, especie de licor fuerte y espirituoso. *Arrack-punch*, Bebida o ponche hecho de arak. (< Árabe, 'araq.)

Arragonese [ar-a-go-nīs'], *a.* Aragonés. *V.* ARAGONESE.

Arraign [ar-rên'], *va.* 1. (For.) Citar, emplazar, delatar en justicia. 2. Acusar, hacer cargo de alguna cosa.

Arraignment [ar-rên'-mẹnt], *s.* 1. (For.) Emplazo, emplazamiento. 2. Acusación. 3. Proceso, autos. 4. Presentación al tribunal.

Arrange [ar-rênj'], *va.* 1. Colocar, arreglar, poner en orden. 2. Preparar, disponer, aprestar ; ajustar, convenir por lo que toca a los detalles de una cosa. 3 (Mús.) Cambiar, adaptar.—*vn.* 1. Prevenir, hacer preparaciones. 2. Concordar.

Arrangement [ar-rênj' mẹnt], *s.* 1. Colocación, orden, arreglo. 2. (Fig.) Medida, providencia, disposición, cálculo.

Arranger [ar-rên'-jẹr], *s.* Trazador, arreglador, ordenador.

Arrant [ar'-ant], *a.* Notorio, famoso; consumado, insigne. *An arrant thief*, Ladrón famoso. *An arrant whore*, Ramera infame. *An arrant fool*, (Fam.) Tonto de marca.

Arrantly [ar'-ant-li], *adv.* Corruptamente, vergonzosamente.

Arras [ar'-as], *s.* Tapicería de Arras en Flandes. Tela rica figurada para cubrir las paredes.

Array [ar-rê'], *s.* 1. Orden regular o propio ; arreglo en líneas o filas ; orden de batalla, pompa, aparato. 2. Formación, el cuerpo colectivo de personas, o cosas así colocadas ; de aquí, una fuerza militar, una colocación de los jurados. 3. Adorno, vestido, atavío, particularmente si es rico. *In rich array*, Con sus más ricos atavíos.

Array, *va.* 1. Colocar, poner en orden de batalla ; formar las tropas. 2. Vestir, adornar. 3. (For.) Colocar los jurados.

Arrear [ar-rīr'], *s.* 1. Caídos, lo que se debe por no haberlo pagado a su tiempo ; se emplea generalmente en plural. 2. Atraso, calidad de atrasado o tardío.

Arrearage [ar-rīr'-ẹj], *s.* Atrasos, caídos : se entiende de rentas o sueldos devengados y no pagados, o pagados en parte.

Arrect [ar-rect'], **Arrected** [ar-rec'-ted], *a.* (Ant.) Elevado, erguido. *Cf.* ERECT y PORRECT.

Arrentation [ar-ren-tê'-shun], *s.* (Ant. der. ingl.) Licencia que concede el dueño de un bosque o monte para cercar las tierras que están sembradas en él.

Arrest [ar-rest'], *s.* Embargo de bienes; prisión o arresto de una persona; parada, interrupción; aprehensión, embargo.

Arrest, *va.* 1. Impedir, detener, hacer cesar, atajar, reprimir. 2. Arrestar o prender a las personas; embargar las cosas. 3. Atraer y fijar la atención. 4. Suspender la ejecución de una sentencia, auto, etc.

Arrester [ar-rest'ẹr], *s.* 1. Lo que, o la persona que, arresta o detiene. 2. (Art. y Of.) *Spark arrester,* Chispero, sombrerete.

Arrhizous, Arrhizal [ar-rai'-zus, zal], *a.* Sin raíces; como ciertas plantas parásitas.

Arris [ar'-ris], *s.* (Arq.) Esquina, ángulo externo; canto o lomo, especialmente el canto agudo entre dos estrías de una columna dórica.

Arrival [ar-rai'-val], *s.* 1. Arribo o llegada. 2. Logro, consecución de lo que se intenta; el fin de un viaje acabado o el principio de uno nuevo. 3. El que o lo que llega o arriba. *A new arrival,* Un recien venido.

Arrive [ar-raiv'], *vn.* 1. Arribar, llegar a algún paraje por mar o por tierra. 2. Llevar a cabo, lograr, conseguir. 3. Suceder, acontecer. *To arrive at,* Llegar a, lograr, alcanzar, conseguir.—*va.* (Ant.) Alcanzar, obtener: llegar a.

Arrogance [ar'-o-gans], **Arrogancy** [ar'-o-gan-si], **Arrogantness** [ar'-o-gant-nes], *s.* Arrogancia, orgullo, altivez, presunción, fiereza, insolencia.

Arrogant [ar'-o-gant], *a.* Arrogante, orgulloso, altivo, fiero, presuntuoso, insolente, soberbio, altanero.

Arrogantly [ar'-o-gant-li], *adv.* Arrogantemente.

Arrogate [ar'-o-gêt], *va.* Arrogarse, usurpar o alegar algún derecho infundado; atribuirse, hacerse mérito de, presumir de sí, tener pretensiones.

Arrogation [ar-o-gê'shun], *s.* Arrogación.

Arrogative [ar'-o-ga-tiv], *a.* Arrogativo, lo que arroga o usurpa.

Arrow [ar'-ō], *s.* Flecha, saeta. *Arrow-root* o *Indian arrow-root,* Polvo nutritivo de la raíz de varias especies de la Maranta de los botánicos; también la planta que produce este almidón. *Arrow-grass,* Trigloquín, planta acuática. Recibe su nombre de la forma de su cápsula después de hendida. *Arrow-head,* 1. Punta de flecha. 2. Flecha de agua, planta. *Arrow-headed, arrow-shaped,* Aflechado, sagital. *Arrow-headed characters,* Caracteres cuneiformes.

Arrowy [ar'-o-i], *a.* 1. Lo que consta de flechas o saetas. 2. Semejante a una flecha o saeta. 3. Rápido como la flecha.

Arroyo [ar-roi'-o], *s.* Arroyo, el caudal corto de agua y el lecho seco por donde corre. (Esp.)

Arse [ārs], *s.* Culo, trasera, nalgas, la parte posterior del cuerpo. (Vulg.)

Arsenal [ār'-se-nal], *s.* Arsenal, depósito en que se guardan armas, pertrechos y municiones de guerra.

Arsenate, Arseniate [ār'-sẹ-nêt, ār-sī'-ni-êt], *s.* Arseniato, sal formada de ácido arsénico con alguna base de tierra, álcali o metal.

Arsenic [ār'-sen-ic], *s.* Arsénico, mineral corrosivo y veneno violento.

Arsenic, Arsenical [ār-sen'-ic, al], *a.* Arsenical, perteneciente al arsénico o que le contiene. *Arsenic oxide,* Óxido de arsénico (As_2O_5).

Arsenid, Arsenide [ār'-sen-id, aid], *s.* Compuesto de arsénico, en que el arsénico es el elemento negativo.

Arsenious [ār-sī'-ni-us], *a.* Arsenioso, perteneciente al arsénico, o que lo contiene en su equivalencia de tres. *Arsenious oxide,* Óxido arsenioso (As_2O_3).

Arsenite [ār'-se-nait], *s.* Arsenito, sal compuesta de ácido arsenioso y de una base.

Arsis [ār'-sis], *s.* 1. Arsis, la sílaba sobre la cual recae la fuerza del acento, en oposición al resto del verso, que se llama *thesis.* 2. (Mús.) La parte no acentuada de un compás.

Arson [ār'-sẹn], *s.* Incendio premeditado; el delito de incendiar.

Art. Segunda persona del presente de indicativo del verbo *To Be. Thou art,* Tú eres, o tú estás.

Art [ārt], *s.* 1. Arte, la facultad de ejecutar alguna cosa por industria. 2. Arte, la aplicación práctica del conocimiento o del talento natural; habilidad, maña, destreza; poder. 3. Arte, conjunto de reglas para hacer bien alguna cosa. 4. Los principios de la construcción artística y de la crítica estética. 5. Arte, la incorporación del pensamiento bello en formas que afectan los sentidos, como en mármol o en lenguaje; también, obras de las bellas artes. 6. Arte, oficio. 7. Arte, cautela, maña, astucia, artificio. *The fine arts,* Las bellas artes. *The liberal arts,* Las artes liberales. *The black art,* La magia negra.

Arterial [ār-tī'-ri-al], *a.* Arterial, lo perteneciente a las arterias o lo contenido en ellas.

Arterialize [ār-tī'-ri-al-aiz], *va.* Arterializar, convertir la sangre venosa en arterial.

Arterialization [ār-tī-ri-al-ai-zê'-shun], *s.* Arterialización: acto y efecto de arterializar.

Arteriosclerosis [ār-ti-ri-o-scle-rō'-sis], *s.* (Med.) Arteriosclerosis, endurecimiento de las arterias.

Arteriotomy [ār-tī-ri-et'-o-mi], *s.* Arteriotomía, la acción de abrir una arteria para sacar sangre.

Arteritis [ār-tẹr-ai'-tis o rī'-tis], *s.* Inflamación de una arteria.

Artery [ār'-tẹr-i], *s.* Arteria, canal destinado a recibir la sangre del corazón y distribuirla por todo el cuerpo.

Artesian [ār-tī'-zhan], *a.* Artesiano, de Artois en Francia. *Artesian well,* Pozo artesiano.

Artful [ārt'-ful], *a.* 1. Artificioso, hecho con arte o según arte. 2. Artificial, no natural. 3. Artificioso, astuto, cauteloso. 4. Diestro, ingenioso, industrioso.

Artfully [ārt'-ful-i], *adv.* Artificiosamente, diestramente; con arte; insidiosamente, con astucia y artificio.

Artfulness [ārt'-ful-nes], *s.* Arte, astucia, habilidad, industria.

Arthritic [ār-thrit'-ic], **Arthritical** [ār-thrit'-ic-al], *a.* Artrítico, lo que pertenece a la gota, artritis o articulaciones; artético.

Arthritis [ar-thrai'-tis], *s.* Artritis. *Rheumatoid arthritis,* Artritis reumática.

Arthropod [ār'-thro-ped], *s.* Uno de los artrópodos. *V.* ARTHROPODA.

Arthropoda [ār-threp'-o-da], *s.* (Zool.) Artrópodos, un subreino de los animales; los articulados propiamente dichos (en oposición a los gusanos); presentan órganos de locomoción articulados, esto es, formados de varias piezas o artejos, y se dividen en cuatro clases: insectos, miriápodos, arácnidos y crustáceos.

Arthropodal [ār-threp'-od-al], **Arthropodous** [ār-threp'-o-dus], *a.* Relativo a los artrópodos o articulados propiamente dichos.

Arthrosis [ār-thrō'-sis], *s.* Artrosis, articulación.

Artichoke [ār'-ti-chōk], *s.* (Bot.) Alcachofa, planta muy parecida al cardo que arroja una cabeza a manera de piña, la que también se llama alcachofa. *Jerusalem artichoke,* (Bot.) Especie de girasol; cotufa, chufa.

Article [ār'-ti-cl], *s.* 1. Artículo, parte de la oración, como *el, la,* etc. 2. Artículo, una composición corta. 3. Artículo, parte o división de cualquier conjunto. 4. Artículo, término, o estipulación. 5. Articulación, coyuntura; parte entre dos nudos de una planta; segmento de un apéndice articulado. 6. (Ant.) Artículo, punto exacto de tiempo. *To surrender upon articles,* Capitular. *Articles of merchandise,* Mercaderías, mercancías, efectos, renglones. *Small articles,* Menudencias. *Trifling articles,* Bagatelas. *To be under articles,* Estar escriturado. *To sign articles,* Escriturarse. *Articles of war,* El código penal militar. *The most necessary articles,* Los objetos de primera necesidad.

Article, *vn.* Capitular, pactar o contratar mutuamente, convenir.—*va.* Colocar en artículos distintos. *To article one for treason,* Acusar y procesar a alguno por delito de lesa majestad o por alta traición. Contratar, poner a uno a trabajar en un oficio por contrata. *To article an apprentice to,* Poner en aprendizaje.

Articular [ār-tic'-yu-lar], *a.* Articular, lo que pertenece a las junturas o articulaciones del cuerpo.

Articularly [ār-tic'-yu-lar-li], *adv.* Articuladamente.

Articulate [ār-tic'-yu-lêt], *a.* 1. Articulado, dividido en sílabas consecutivas; unido para formar el lenguaje. 2. Claro, distinto (palabras, sonidos). 3. Articulado, que tiene articulaciones. 4. (Zool.) Articulado, perteneciente a los animales articulados.—*s.* Uno de los animales articulados.—*pl. s.* Articulados o entomozoos, una de las cuatro grandes divisiones (tipos) del reino animal, que comprende los animales cuyo cuerpo está compuesto de segmentos unidos o articulados.

Articulate, *va.* 1. Articular, pronunciar las palabras clara y distintamente. 2. Articular, formar algún convenio por artículos. 3. Formar nudos.—*vn.* Hablar distintamente.

Articulately [ār-tic'-yu-lêt-li], *adv.* Articuladamente.

Articulateness [ār-tic'-yu-lêt-nes], *s.* La calidad de ser articulado.

Articulation [ār-tic-yu-lê'-shun], *s.* 1. Articulación, juego de las coyunturas de los huesos; nudo en las plantas. 2. Articulación, la acción de articular las palabras.

Artifact [ār'-ti-fact], *s.* Artefacto.

Artifice [ār'-ti-fis], *s.* 1. Artificio, engaño, fraude, estratagema, treta, destreza, habilidad, maña, artería. 2. (Des.) Arte, empleo u oficio mecánico, industria.

Artificer [ār-tif'-i-sẹr], *s.* Artífice, el que hace algún artefacto; el que construye o diseña; artesano hábil; también, inventor, autor.

Artificial [ār-ti-fish'-al], †**Artificious** [ār-ti-fish'-us], *a.* 1. Artificial, hecho por arte. 2. Artificial, fingido. 3. Artificioso.

Artificiality [ār-ti-fish-i-al'-i-ti], *s.* Carácter artificial, apariencia, arte, conducta artificiosa.

Artificially [ār-ti-fish'-al-i], *adv.* Artificialmente, artificiosamente.

Artificialness [ār-ti-fish'-al-nes], *s.* Arte, astucia.

Artillerist [ār-til'-ẹr-ist], *s.* Artillero.

Artillery [ār-til'-ẹ-ri], *s.* 1. Arte de construir y usar las armas, máquinas y municiones de guerra. 2. Artillería, el tren de cañones, morteros y otras máquinas militares. *Artillery park*, Parque de artillería. *Train of artillery*, Tren de artillería. *Artillery-wagon*, Carro de artillería, furgón. *Field, siege artillery*, Artillería de campaña, de sitio. *Artilleryman*, Artillero. *Artillery practice*, Ejercicio de cañón.

Artisan [ār'-ti-zan], *s.* Artesano, el que ejerce algún arte mecánica.

Artist [ār'-tist], *s.* 1. Artista, el que profesa algún arte liberal o bella. 2. Maestro, el que es inteligente en su oficio o profesión.

Artistic [ār-tis'-tic], *a.* Artístico, de las artes.

Artistry [ār'-tis-tri], *s.* Arte, habilidad artística.

Artless [ārt'-les], *a.* 1. Natural, sin arte, sencillo, simple; sin dolo. 2. (Fam.) Chabacano, hecho sin arte.

Artlessly [ārt'-les-li], *adv.* 1. Sencillamente, simplemente, naturalmente, sin arte; chabacanamente. 2. (Fam.) A la buena de Dios.

Artlessness [ārt'-les-nes], *s.* Sencillez, candidez, naturalidad.

Arum [ē'-rum o ḁ'-rum], *a.* Arum, yaro, planta común parecida a la serpentaria.

Arundinaceous [a-run-di-nē'-shus], **Arundineous** [a-run-din'-i-us], *a.* Arundináceo, hecho de cañas, lo que abunda de cañas.

Aruspice [a-rus'-pis], **Aruspex** [a-rus'-pex], *s.* Arúspice: entre los Romanos, el ministro de la religión que examinaba las entrañas de las víctimas para adivinar por ellas algún suceso.

Aruspicy [a-rus'-pi-si], *s.* Aruspicina, arte supersticiosa de adivinar los sucesos por la inspección de las entrañas de las víctimas.

Arytenoid [ā-rit'-en-oid], *a.* Aritenal, aritenóideo. *Arytenoid cartilages*, Dos cartílagos situados en la parte posterior y superior de la laringe.

As [az], *conj.* 1. Como, del mismo modo que otra cosa. *As you please*, Como Vd. quiera. *As good as*, Tan bueno como. *As sure as can be*, Seguramente, sin duda alguna. *As I am informed*, Por lo que he oído decir. 2. Mientras. 3. Como, igualmente. 4. Se usa en sentido recíproco y corresponde con *so*. *As so*, Así como, así también. 5. *As for, as to*, En cuanto a, por lo que toca a. 6. Según, como, a medida que. *I find it easier as I advance*, Lo encuentro más fácil a medida que adelanto. *As* indica el tiempo, y también el lugar, y entonces se traduce *como*, o *al*, y las más veces no se expresa; v. g. *As he was at the door*, Estando él a la puerta. *As they were walking*, Al ir ellos andando. *As I was there*, Estando yo allá. *As far as*, Hasta. *As soon as*, Luego que. *As yet*, Aun, todavía. *As if* o *as though*, Como si. *As well as*, Tan bien o tan bueno como. *As it is*, Así como así. *As is the beginning, so is the end*, Según es el principio, así es el fin. *As for me*, Por lo que a mí toca; en cuanto a mí. *As big again*, Dos veces tan grande. *As* después de *such* hace veces de los pronombres relativos *who* y *which*. *All such as went there*, Todos los que fueron allí.

Asafœtida [as-a-fet'-i-da], *s.* Asafétida, goma-resinosa empleada en medicina, que se trae de las Indias orientales.

Asbestine [as-bes'-tin], *a.* Asbestino, incombustible.

Asbestos [as-bes'-tọs], *s.* Asbesto o amianto, mineral fibroso y flexible, que tiene la propiedad singular de ser incombustible.

Ascarides [as-car'-i-dīz], *s.* Ascárides, lombricillas que se hallan en los intestinos, pero sobre todo en el recto. Se llaman también *thread-worms* o *pin-worms*. En el singular se escribe *ascaris* y *ascarid*.

Ascend [ạs-send'], *vn.* 1. Ascender, subir. 2. Adelantar, o subir de un grado de conocimiento a otro mayor. 3. Estar en grado ascendiente de parentesco.—*va.* Ascender o subir. *To ascend a hill*, Subir una colina o cuesta.

Ascendable [ạs-sen'-da-bl], *a.* Accesible, que se puede subir.

Ascendant [ạs-sen'-dant], **Ascendent**, *s.* 1. Altura, elevación. 2. Ascendiente, influjo, poder; el que tiene influencia. 3. Ascendiente, la persona de quien se desciende.

Ascendant, Ascendent, *a.* 1. Ascendiente. 2. Superior, predominante.

Ascendancy, Ascendency [ạs-sen'-den-si], *s.* Ascendiente, influjo, poder.

Ascension [as-sen'-shun], *s.* 1. Ascensión, la acción de ascender. 2. Ascensión, la subida de nuestro Redentor a los cielos. 3. Ascensión, la cosa que asciende o sube.

Ascensional [ạs-sen'-shun-al], *a.* (Astr.) Ascensional.

Ascent [ạs-sent'], *s.* 1. Subida, la acción de subir. 2. Eminencia, paraje elevado, altura.

Ascertain [as-ẹr-tēn'], *va.* 1. Indagar, averiguar, hallar, descubrir por experimento o investigación. 2. (Ant.) Asegurar, fijar, establecer, confirmar, afirmar. *To ascertain the price*, (Ant.) Reglar o determinar el precio.

Ascertainable [as-ẹr-tēn'-a-bl], *a.* Averiguable, descubrible.

Ascertainer [as-er-tēn'-ẹr], *s.* Averiguador, indagador.

Ascertainment [as-er-tēn'-mẹnt], *s.* 1. Averiguación, indagación. 2. (Ant.) Regla fija y determinada.

Ascetic [as-set'-ic], *a.* Ascético, dedicado a la práctica de la devoción y mortificación.—*s.* Asceta.

Asceticism [as-set'-i-sism], *s.* Ascetismo, profesión de la vida ascética.

Ascians [as'-ki-ans], **Ascii** [as'-ki-ai], *s.* (Geo.) Ascios, ascianos, habitantes de la zona tórrida que dos veces el año no hacen sombra al mediodía.

Ascites [as-sai'-tīz], *s.* Ascitis o hidropesía del abdomen.

Ascitic [as-sit'-ic], **Ascitical** [as-sit'-ic-al], *a.* Ascítico, hidrópico, el que padece ascitis.

Ascititious [as-si-tish'-us], *a.* Adicional, lo que se añade o suple. *V.* ADSCITITIOUS.

Ascribable [as-craib'-a-bl], *a.* Aplicable, imputable, que se puede atribuir, imputar o aplicar.

Ascribe [as-craib'], *va.* 1. Adscribir. 2. Atribuir, achacar. 3. Aplicar, adjudicar.

Ascription [as-crip'-shun], *s.* Atribución; imputación.

Asea [a-sī'], *adv.* Sobre el mar; hacia el mar.

Asepsis [a-sep'-sis], *s.* Asepsia, no emponzoñamiento de la sangre; exención de la putrefacción y sus consecuencias.

Aseptic [a-sep'-tic], *a.* Aséptico; preventivo de la putrefacción, y en particular del emponzoñamiento de la sangre.

Asepticism [a-sep'-ti-sizm] o **Asepsis**. Estado o calidad de aséptico.

Asexual [a-sex'-yu-al], *a.* Asexual, sin reproducción sexual.

Ash [ash], *s.* Singular de *ashes*: úsase principalmente en la formación de palabras compuestas. *Ash-pit, ash-pan*, Cenicero, cenizal. *Ash-pail*, Cubo para la ceniza. *Ash-tub*, Coladero, cubeta de lejía. *That coal burns to a white ash*, Ese carbón da ceniza blanca.

Ash [ash], *s.* (Bot.) Fresno, cualquier árbol del género Fraxinus. *Ash-grove*, Fresneda. *Mountain-ash* o *rowan-tree*, Serbal.

¿**Ashame** [a-shēm'], *va.* *V.* SHAME.

Ashamed [a-shēmd'], *a.* Avergonzado, vergonzoso. *To be ashamed*, Tener vergüenza, avergonzarse de, correrse de, sonrojarse.

Ashamedly [a-shēm'-ed-li], *adv.* Vergonzosamente.

Ash-coloured [ash'-cul-ẹrd], *a.* Ceniciento.

Ashelf [a-shelf'], *adv.* (Mar.) Arrimado sobre un peñasco o bajío.

Ashen [ash'-n], *a.* 1. Hecho de fresno. 2. Semejante a la ceniza; ceniciento, pálido.

Ashes [ash'-ez], *s. pl.* 1. Ceniza. 2. Ceniza o cenizas, los restos de un cadáver.

Ashlar, Ashler [ash'-lar, lẹr], *s.* Las piedras en el estado que tienen cuando salen de la cantera.

Ashlaring, Ashlering [ash'-lar-ing, ash'-lẹr-ing], *s.* Ligazones que suben a los cabríos del techo en las guardillas.

Ashore [a-shōr'], *adv.* En tierra, a tierra. *To get ashore*, Desembarcar. *To run ashore*, Encallar, echarse a la costa, hablando de un buque.

Ash-tub [ash'-tub], *s.* Cenicero.

Ash Wednesday [ash-wenz'-dē], *s.* Miércoles de ceniza.

Ash-weed [ash'-wīd], *s.* (Bot.) Angélica, planta.

Ashy [ash'-i], *a.* Cenizoso, ceniciento.

Ashy-pale [ash-i-pēl'], *a.* Pálido como ceniza.

Asian [ē'-shian], **Asiatic** [ē-shi-at'-ic], *a.* Asiático. *Asiatic flu*, Gripe asiática.

Asiaticism [a-shi-at'-i-sizm], *s.* Imitación de las costumbres asiáticas.

Aside [a-said'], *adv.* 1. Al lado, a un lado. 2. A parte. *To lay aside*, Despreciar, no hacer caso, desechar, no admitir. (Fam.) Arrinconar. *To lay a project aside*, Abandonar un proyecto. (For.) *To set aside a judgment*, Anular una sentencia.

Asinine [as'-i-nain o as'-i-nin], *a.* Asinino, asnal, lo perteneciente al asno.

Ask [ɑsk], *va.* 1. Pedir, rogar. 2. Preguntar, interrogar. *I must ask you one question,* Tengo que hacer a Vd. una pregunta, o tengo que preguntar a Vd.—*vn.* Buscar, inquirir, rogar. *To ask for* o *after one,* Preguntar por alguno. *To ask in, up, down,* Rogar (a una persona) que entre, suba, o baje.
Askance [ɑ-skɑns'], *adv.* 1. Al sesgo, de soslayo, oblicuamente. 2. Con desdén.
Asker [ɑsk'-ɛr], *s.* Inquiridor; suplicante. *Asker* o *ask,* Especie de lagartija.
Askew [ɑ-skiū'], *adv.* Al lado; con desdén o desprecio; oblicuamente.
Asking [ɑsk'-ing], *s.* 1. Súplica, acción de pedir, demanda. 2. Publicación (de amonestaciones). *This is the third time of asking,* Esta es la tercera amonestación.
Aslant [ɑ-slɑnt'], *adv.* Oblicuamente.
Asleep [ɑ-slīp'], *adv.* Dormido. *To fall asleep,* Dormirse, quedarse dormido. *My foot is asleep,* Se me ha entumecido o dormido un pie.
Aslope [ɑ-slōp'], *adv.* En declive, en pendiente.
Asp [ɑsp], **Aspic** [ɑs'-pic], *s.* Áspid, serpiente venenosa, cuya mordedura es mortal.
Aspalathus [ɑs-pal'-ɑ-thus], *s.* (Bot.) Aspalato, palo de rosa o del águila.
Asparagus [ɑs-par'-ɑ-gus], *s.* Espárrago, planta; y sus tallos tiernos que se comen antes de endurecerse.
Aspect [as'-pect], *s.* 1. Aspecto, semblante, cara. 2. Mirada, vista, ojeada. 3. Aspecto, postura o situación, disposición, dirección, traza, aire, ademán. 4. (Astr.) Aspecto, posición relativa de los planetas. *The house has a northern aspect,* La casa da o mira al norte.
Aspen [asp'-en], *s.* Álamo temblón, árbol cuyas hojas siempre se están moviendo.
Aspen, *a.* Perteneciente al álamo temblón o hecho de él.
Asper [as'-pɛr], *s.* (Gram. griega) El signo (ʻ) que indica la pronunciación gutural de una letra, equivalente a la h aspirada: como en ὅτι.
Asper [as'-pɛr], *s.* Aspro o áspero, moneda de Turquía.
Asperate [as'-pɛr-ēt], *va.* Hacer áspera alguna cosa.
Asperation [as-pɛr-ē'-shun], *s.* El acto de hacer áspera alguna cosa.
Asperifolious [as-per-i-fō'-li-us], *a.* (Bot.) Dícese de las plantas que tienen ásperas las hojas.
Asperity [as-per'-i-ti], *s.* Aspereza, desigualdad, rigidez, rudeza.
Aspermous [as-per'-mus], **Aspermatous,** *a.* (Bot.) Aspermo, sin semilla.
Asperse [as-pɛrs'], *va.* Difamar, calumniar, denigrar, infamar.
Asperser [as-pɛrs'-ɛr], *s.* Infamador.
Aspersion [as-pɛr'-shun], *s.* Difamación, la acción de difamar o calumniar; mancha, mácula, tacha, deshonra, calumnia; aspersión, rociadura. (Fam.) Rociada, reprensión. *To cast aspersion on one,* Difamar a alguno, calumniarle.
Aspersive [as-pɛrs'-iv], *a.* Calumnioso, difamatorio.
Asphalt [as'-falt] o **Asphaltum** [as-fal'-tum], *s.* Asfalto, especie de betún sólido.
Asphaltic [as-fal'-tic], *a.* Asfáltico, bituminoso.
Asphodel [as'-fo-del], *s.* (Bot.) Asfodelo o gamón.

Asphyxia [as-fic'-si-ɑ], *s.* (Med.) Asfixia, privación de los sentidos por falta de respiración.
Asphyxiate [as-fix'-i-ēt], *va.* Asfixiar, sofocar.
Asphyxiated [as-fix'-i-ēt-ed], *pp.* Sofocado.
Asphyxiation [as-fix-i-ē'-shun], *s.* Asfixia, sofocación.
Aspic [as'-pic] (Oil of), *s.* Aceite de espliego. *V.* Lavender.
Aspic. *s.* Jalea gustosa que contiene picadillo de carne, pescado, huevos, etc.
Aspirant [as-pai'-rɑnt], *s.* Aspirante, el que aspira, pretendiente, candidato.
Aspirate [as'-pi-rēt], *va.* 1. Aspirar, pronunciar con aspiración, como en las voces, *horse, hog* y otras. 2. (Med.) Extraer fluido, por ejemplo de la cavidad torácica, sin permitir la entrada al aire.
Aspirate, *a.* Aspirado.—*s.* Acento señal, virgulilla. El signo (ʻ) en la lengua griega para indicar el sonido gutural de una letra.
Aspiration [as-pi-rē'-shun], *s.* 1. Anhelo, deseo vehemente. 2. Ambición, la pasión de aspirar a cosas elevadas, como dignidades, etc. 3. Aspiración, la acción de aspirar una vocal o darle más fuerza con el aliento. 4. Aspiración, acto de extraer fluido sin permitir la entrada al aire.
Aspirator [as-pi-rē'-ter], *s.* Aspirador, instrumento para la aspiración quirúrgica.
Aspiratory [as-pair'-ɑ-to-ri], *a.* Propio de la aspiración, lo que la produce; aspiratorio.
Aspire [as-pair'], *vn.* Aspirar, pretender, desear con ansia algún empleo o dignidad.—*va.* 1. Aspirar. 2. Soplar.
Aspirer [as-pair'-ɛr], *s.* Aspirante, el que aspira.
Aspirin [as'-pi-rin], *s.* Aspirina.
Aspiring [as-pair'-ing], *s.* Pretensión, deseo de algún empleo o dignidad.
Asplanchnic [as-planc'-nic], *a.* Sin canal alimenticio.
Asplenium [as-plī'-ni-um], *s.* (Bot.) Asplenia, género de helechos que comprende muy numerosas especies; entre ellas, la doradilla, el culantrillo, etc.
Asportation [as-por-tē'-shun], *s.* Extracción.
Asquint [ɑ-scwint'], *adv.* De o al soslayo, de través.
Ass [ɑs], *s.* 1. Burro, borrico, asno, jumento. *A she-ass,* Burra, borrica. *A young ass,* Pollino. 2. (Fig.) Tonto, ignorante, bestia, asno, jumento, hablando de personas.
Assagai o **Assegai** [as'-ɑ-gai, ɛ-gai], *s.* Azagaya, especie de dardo ligero y arrojadizo, usado entre los cafres, zulúes, etc. (< Arab. az-zagāya.)
Assail [as-sēl'], *va.* Acometer, invadir, asaltar, atacar, embestir.
Assailable [as-sēl'-ɑ-bl], *a.* Lo que puede ser asaltado.
Assailant [as-sēl'-ɑnt], *a.* El que acomete, acometedor, acometiente.
Assailant, Assailer [as-sēl'-ɛr], *s.* Acometedor, asaltador, agresor, embestidor, chocador en una lid o contienda.
Assailment [as-sēl'-mɛnt], *s.* Asalto, acometimiento, acometida.
Assart [ɑs-sɑrt'], *va.* (Ingla.) Rozar, desmontar y desbrotar la tierra.
Assart, *s.* Rozo de la tierra; roza, tierra nuevamente rozada, para sembrar; árbol o planta arrancados.
Assassin [as-sas'-in], **Assassinator** [as-sas'-i-nē-tɛr], *s.* Asesino, el que mata alevosamente.
Assassinate [as-sas'-i-nēt], *va.* Asesinar, matar alevosamente.—*vn.* Ser asesino, cometer asesinato.
Assassination [as-sas-i-nē'-shun], *s.* Asesinato, la acción y el delito de asesinar.
Assault [as-sōlt'], *s.* 1. Asalto o acometimiento de alguna plaza. 2. Asalto, invasión u hostilidad. 3. Acometimiento, la acción de acometer a otro con violencia, ataque, asalto, insulto.
Assault, *va.* Acometer, invadir, asaltar.
Assaulter [as-sōlt'-ɛr], *s.* Agresor o injusto invasor.
Assay [as-sē'], *s.* 1. Ensayo, reconocimiento o examen. 2. Prueba o reconocimiento de pesos y medidas por el fiel. 3. Ensayo, estreno, experimento, tentativa, el primer acto de ejercer y poner por obra alguna cosa. 4. Valor. 5. Ensaye, hablando de metales, aquilatación. *Assay-furnace,* Horno de copelación. *Assay-office,* Oficina de ensayador.
Assay, *va.* 1. Ensayar, hacer prueba de alguna cosa, experimentar. 2. Tentar o hacer tentativa, intentar. 3. Gustar, probar.
Assayer [as-sē'-ɛr], *s.* Ensayador, el que ensaya; en especial, oficial de la casa de moneda, cuyo deber es reconocer la ley de la plata u oro.
Assaying [as-sē'-ing], *s.* Ensaye, ensay (de metales). *Art of assaying,* Docimástica, el arte de ensayar los metales y minerales.
Assemblage [as-sem'-blēj], *s.* 1. Colección, agregado, compuesto o conjunto de muchas cosas. 2. Asamblea, multitud.
Assemble [as-sem'-bl], *va.* Congregar, convocar.—*vn.* Juntarse o unirse en junta o congreso.
Assembler [as-sem'-blɛr], *s.* El que se junta con otros.
Assembling [as-sem'-bling], *s.* La acción de juntarse o congregarse, y también la acción de convocar.
Assembly [as-sem'-bli], *s.* 1. Asamblea, junta, congreso. 2. (Mil.) Asamblea, toque de la caja, para que la tropa se recoja a sus cuerpos respectivos o al lugar designado. *General Assembly,* (1) El más alto tribunal de justicia entre los presbiterianos, o los de alguna otra denominación. (2) Legislatura, cuerpo legislativo. *Place of assembly,* Lugar de reunión.
Assembly line [as-sem'-bli lɑin], *s.* Línea de montaje.
Assemblyman [as-sem'-bli-man], *s.* Individuo de un congreso o asamblea, y en especial de la cámara baja de la legislatura de un Estado.
Assembly-room [as-sem'-bli-rūm], *s.* Sala de juntas.
Assent [as-sent'], *s.* Asenso, la acción y efecto de asentir, consentimiento; confesión, reconocimiento, declaración; aprobación, beneplácito.
Assent, *vn.* Asentir, convenir en el juicio con otro, ser de un mismo dictamen; aprobar.
Assentation [as-sen-tē'-shun], *s.* Condescendencia a la opinión de otro por adulación o disimulo; lisonja, complacencia servil.
Assenter [as-sen'-tɛr], *s.* Consentidor, favorecedor.

Assentient [as-sen'-shient], *a.* 1. Que conviene o asiente. 2. *s.* Consentidor, el que aprueba.
Assentingly [as-sent'-ing-li], *adv.* 1. Con asenso, aprobación o consentimiento. 2. En signo de asentimiento.
Assert [as-sert'], *va.* 1. Sostener, mantener, defender, hacer bueno. 2. Afirmar, asegurar. 3. Alegar derecho o título á alguna cosa.
Assertion [as-ser'-shun], *s.* Aserción, afirmación.
Assertive [as-ser'-tiv], *a.* Afirmativo, que afirma o envuelve aserción.
Asserter, Assertor [as-ser'-ter], *s.* Afirmador, defensor, protector, libertador.
Assertory [as-ser'-to-ri], *a.* Afirmativo: declaratorio.
†**Assess** [as-ses'], **Assessment** [as-ses'-ment], *s.* Amillaramiento, o tasa de los impuestos, cargas o gabelas, que se deben pagar por el importe de los bienes que se poseen, o por otros títulos.
Assess, *vd.* Amillarar, declarar, señalar la cantidad que cada individuo debe pagar por el importe de los bienes que posee, o por otros títulos. *To assess damages,* Fijar los daños y perjuicios.
Assessable [as-ses'-a-bl], *a.* Imponible, que puede ser amillarado.
Assessionary [as-sesh'-un-é-ri], *a.* Lo perteneciente al asesor.
Assessor [as-ses'-er], *s.* 1. Asesor, el letrado que acompaña al juez lego. 2. Tasador de impuestos o gabelas.
Asset [as'-set], *s.* Cada una de las partidas que componen el caudal de una persona o corporación.
Assets [as'-sets], *s. pl.* 1. Capital, o caudal en caja, o existente; fondos, créditos activos, cantidad o cantidades para pagar. 2. (Com.) Activo, fondos de una quiebra, o de una sucesión. *Real assets,* Bienes raíces. *Personal assets,* Bienes muebles.
Asseverate [as-sev'-er-ét], *va.* Aseverar, afirmar, asegurar solemnemente.
Asseveration [as-sev-er-é'-shun], *s.* Aseveración, afirmación; protesta.
Ass-head [as'-hed], *s.* (Ant.) Tonto, estúpido.
Assibilate [as-sib'-i-lét], *va.* Pronunciar con sonido sibilante; convertir en sibilante.
Assiduity [as-si-diú'-i-ti], *s.* Asiduidad, aplicación y constancia, laboriosidad.
Assiduous [as-sid'-yu-us], *a.* Asiduo, constante, aplicado, continuo, laborioso.
Assiduously [as-sid'-yu-us-li], *adv.* Constantemente, de continuo, sin cesar, perennemente, diligentemente.
Assiduousness [as-sid'-yu-us-nes], *s.* Diligencia, asiduidad.
Assign [as-sain'], *va.* 1. Asignar, señalar, destinar. 2. Dar la razón o motivo de alguna cosa; indicar, señalar, atribuir. 3. Probar, hacer ver. 4. (For.) Asignar, diputar; transferir, ceder, traspasar algún derecho a otro.
Assign, *s.* (For.) Cesionario, la persona a cuyo favor se traspasa algún bien o derecho.
Assignable [as-sain'-a-bl], *a.* Asignable, lo que se puede asignar.
Assignat [as-in-yá' o as'-ig-nat], *s.* Asignado, cierto papel moneda que corrió en Francia, 1790--1796.
Assignation [as-sig-né'-shun], *s.* 1. Asignación, cita o señalamiento de día, hora o lugar para verse o hablarse dos o más personas. 2. Renuncia, cesión o traslación de dominio. *House of assignation,* Casa de asignación, lugar de mala fama donde se dan cita personas de opuesto sexo para entregarse a tratos ilícitos.
Assignee [as-sai-ní'], *s.* 1. Poderhabiente, apoderado. 2. (Der. com.) Síndico. Cesionario. *V.* ASSIGN.
Assigner [as-sain'-er], *s.* Asignante, transferidor, el que asigna o transfiere.
Assignment [as-sain'-ment], *s.* 1. Asignación, señalamiento, cesión. 2. (For.) Escritura de cesión de bienes, traspaso, renuncia, o traslación de dominio.
Assignor [as-in-ōr'], *s.* Cedente, el que asigna o transfiere.
Assimilable [as-sim'-i-la-bl], *a.* Semejable; asimilable, lo que puede asimilarse.
Assimilate [as-sim'-i-lét], *va.* 1. Asemejar, asimilar, hacer alguna cosa semejante a otra. 2. Convertir una cosa en la sustancia de otra.—*vn.* Conventir el alimento en quilo.
Assimilation [as-sim-i-lé'-shun], *s.* 1. Asimilación, la conversión de una cosa en la sustancia de otra. 2. Asimilación, semejanza.
Assimilative [as-sim'-i-le-tiv], *a.* Asimilativo.
Assimulation [as-sim-yiú-lé'-shun]. *V.* DISSIMULATION.
Assist [as-sist'], *va.* Asistir, ayudar, socorrer, auxiliar.—*vn.* Asistir, hallarse presente, presenciar.
Assistance [as-sist'-ans], *s.* Asistencia, auxilio, socorro, apoyo.
Assistant [as-sist'-ant], *s.* Asistente o ayudante, el que está empleado en alguna cosa no como principal, sino como dependiente de otro.—*a.* Ayudador, que ayuda; auxiliar. *Assistant bishop,* Obispo auxiliar. *Assistant teacher,* (1) Pasante, ayo. (2) Maestro segundo. *Assistant engineer,* Segundo maquinista, segundo ingeniero.
Assister [as-sis'-ter], *s.* Asistente, ayudador.
Assistless [as-sist'-les], *a.* Sin ayuda o auxilio; sin apoyo, desamparado.
Assize [as-saiz'], *s.* 1. Tribunal de justicia que se reune dos veces al año en cada condado de Inglaterra para decidir las causas civiles y criminales; la sesión de un tribunal. Úsase en plural, por lo general. 2. Ley o decreto para arreglar y fijar el peso y precio del pan. 3. Tipo normal de peso, medida o precio.
Assizer [as-saiz'-er], *s.* Fiel almotacén, la persona diputada para el reconocimiento de pesos y medidas.
Ass-like [as'-laic], *a.* Semejante al asno; asinino, asnal; borricote.
Associable [as-sō'-shi-a-bl], *a.* Sociable.
Associate [as-sō'-shi-ét], *va.* 1. Asociar, tomar por compañero o confederado a otro. 2. Asociar, acompañar.—*vn.* Asociarse.
Associate, *a.* Asociado, confederado. —*s.* Socio o compañero.
Association [as-so-shi-é'-shun], *s.* Asociación, unión, sociedad, confederación, alianza, compañía, asamblea; cábala.
Associator [as-sō'-shi-é-ter], *s.* Confederado.
Assoil [as-soil'], *va.* 1. Resolver, responder. 2. Absolver, perdonar.
Assonance [as'-o-nans], *s.* Asonancia, similitud de sonidos. Asonancia, semejanza de sonido entre las últimas vocales de dos palabras, siendo las consonantes de sonido diferente. Esta clase de rima es exclusiva de la poesía española.
Assonant [as'-o-nant], *a.* Asonante, lo que hace asonancia.
Assort [as-sērt'], *va.* Colocar, ordenar, poner en orden; adecuar, proporcionar; clasificar.
Assortment [as-sērt'-ment], *s.* 1. Colección ordenada; surtido. 2. El acto de arreglar ó coordinar.
Assuage [as-swéj'], *va.* Mitigar, apaciguar, calmar, suavizar, ablandar. —*vn.* Minorar, disminuir, deshincharse.
Assuagement [as-swéj'-ment], *s.* Mitigación, calma.
Assuager [as-swéj'-er], *s.* Apaciguador.
Assuasive [as-swé'-siv], *a.* Mitigativo, calmante.
Assume [as-siūm'], *va.* 1. Tomar. 2. Arrogar, apropiar, usurpar. 3. Presumir, suponer alguna cosa sin prueba o fundamento.—*vn.* Arrogarse, atribuirse, apropiarse.
Assumed [as-siūmd'], *a.* Afectado, fingido. *Assumed modesty,* Modestia fingida.
Assumer [as-siūm'-er], *s.* Persona arrogante.
Assuming [as-siūm'-ing], *a.* Arrogante, altivo, presumido.
Assumpsit [as-sump'-sit], *s.* (For.) Promesa voluntaria y verbal; pacto, contrato.
Assumption [as-sump'-shun], *s.* 1. Apropiación, la acción de apropiarse alguna cosa. 2. Asunción de la bienaventurada Vírgen María, su tránsito y subida al cielo. 3. Asunción, proposición tomada sin prueba.
Assumptive [as-sump'-tiv], *a.* Apropiado; lo que puede ser supuesto.
Assurance [a-shūr'-ans], *s.* 1. Seguridad, certeza. 2. Seguridad, firmeza. 3. Descaro, llaneza, demasiada confianza o falta de modestia. 4. Seguridad, fianza, garantía; convicción. 5. Intrepidez, arrojo, valor, ánimo, resolución. 6. Seguro, de vida, contra incendios, etc. *V.* INSURANCE.
Assure [a-shūr'], *va.* 1. Asegurar, afirmar o dar seguridades de la certeza de lo que se refiere o promete. *Assure yourself that,* Esté Vd. seguro. 2. Contratar un seguro contra pérdidas, perjuicios, etc.
Assured [a-shūrd'], *a.* 1. Seguro, cierto, indubitable. 2. Seguro, cierto, persuadido, libre de duda. 3. Descarado, atrevido, la persona que se toma demasiada confianza o llaneza. 4. Protegido por un contrato de seguro.
Assuredly [a-shūr'-ed-li], *adv.* Ciertamente, indubitablemente, sin duda.
Assuredness [a-shūr'-ed-nes], *s.* Certeza, seguridad.
Assurer [a-shūr'-er], *s.* Asegurador, el que asegura.
Assyrian [as-sir'-i-an], *a.* Asirio, de Asiria.
Astatic [a-stat'-ic], *a.* Astático, que no es estable, que no tiende a tomar dirección definida o fija. *Astatic needle,* Aguja astática imantada.
Aster [as'-ter], *s.* Aster, género de plantas radiadas (compuestas) con flores azuladas o blancas.

Asterias [as-tí'-ri-as], *s.* (Zool.) Asteria, género de zoófitos, estrella de mar.

Asterisk [as'-tẹr-isc], *s.* Asterisco, una estrellita que usan los impresores en los libros (*).

Asterism [as'-tẹr-izm], *s.* 1. (Astr.) Constelación, pequeño grupo de estrellas. 2. Grupo de asteriscos (*** ****).

Astern [a-stẹrn'], *adv.* (Mar.) Por la popa, a popa.

Asteroid [as'-tẹr-oid], *s.* Asteroide, planeta telescópico perteneciente a un grupo de 340 entre las órbitas de Marte y Júpiter.

Asthenic [as-then'-ic], *a.* Asténico, flaco, débil.

Asthma [as'-ma], *s.* Asma, enfermedad espasmódica del pecho, a menudo catarral.

Asthmatic, Asthmatical [as-mat'-ic, al], *a.* Asmático.

Asthmatic, *s.* Asmático.

Astigmatic [as-tig-mat'-ic], *a.* Astigmático, que tiene astigmatismo.

Astigmatism [a-stig'-ma-tizm], *s.* Astigmatismo, defecto de visión causado por falta de simetría en la córnea.

Astir [a-stẹr'], *adv.* En estado de movimiento o actividad; fuera de la cama.

Astomatous [a-stō'-ma-tus], *a.* (Biol.) Sin boca, ni poros para respirar; ástomo, que carece de boca.

Astonied [a-ston'-id], *a.* (Ant.) Pasmado, turulato, enajenado.

Astony [as-ton'-i], *va.* (Ant.) Pasmar.

Astonish [as-ton'-ish], *va.* Asombrar, pasmar, sorprender, enajenar.

Astonishingly [as-ton'-ish-ing-li], *adv.* Pasmosamente, asombrosamente.

Astonishingness [as-ton'-ish-ing-nes], *s.* La calidad o propiedad pasmosa de alguna cosa.

Astonishment [as-ton'-ish-mẹnt], *s.* Pasmo, asombro, espanto, enajenamiento, sorpresa.

Astound [as-taund'], *va.* 1. Consternar, aturdir. 2. Asombrar, aterrar, sorprender.—*vn.* Temblar, enajenarse.

Astounding [as-taund'-ing], *a.* Asombroso, consternado.

Astraddle [a-strad'-l], *adv.* A horcajadas o a horcajadillas. *To ride astraddle,* Montar a horcajadas.

Astragal [as'-tra-gal], *s.* 1. (Arq.) Astrágalo, cordón en forma de anillo, con que se adorna la parte superior e inferior de las columnas. 2. Astrágalo, empeine del pie. 3. *pl.* Dados: porque originalmente fueron tabas.

Astragalus [as-trag'-a-lus], *s.* 1. (Anat.) Astrágalo, talón, empeine del pie, chita. 2. (Bot.) Astrágalo, alquitira, género de plantas papilionáceas.

Astrakhan [as'-tra-can], *a.* De Astracán en Rusia.—*s.* Piel de astracán. Escríbese también **Astrachan.**

Astral [as'-tral], *a.* Astral, que pertenece a los astros, o que viene de ellos.

Astrand [a-strand'], *adv.* (Mar.) Encallado, varado; echado sobre la costa.

Astray [as-tré'], *adv.* Desviado, errado, fuera del camino recto. *To go astray,* Errar el camino; perderse, extraviarse. *To lead astray,* (Fig.) Desviar, apartar, descaminar, descarriar, extraviar.

‡**Astrict** [as-trict'], *va.* Astringir, apretar, estreñir.

Astriction [as-tric'-shun], *s.* Astricción, calidad o propiedad de una cosa astringente.

Astride [a-straid'], *adv.* A horcajadas, montado con una pierna a cada lado del caballo.

Astringe [as-trinj'], *va.* Astringir, apretar, estreñir.

Astringency [as-trin'-jen-si], *s.* 1. Astricción, el poder de astringir. 2. Aspereza de carácter.

Astringent [as-trin'-jent], *a.* 1. Astringente, que aprieta o astringe los tejidos blandos; estíptico; que detiene el vientre. 2. Aspero, agrio de genio, duro. *Astringent principle,* (Quím.) Principio astringente, uno de los principios vegetales.

Astrobiology [as-tro-bai-el'-o-ji], *s.* Astrobiología.

Astrography [as-treg'-ra-fi], *s.* Astrografía, descripción de los astros.

Astrolabe [as'-trō-lêb], *s.* Astrolabio, instrumento matemático que servía principalmente para observar en el mar la altura, lugar y movimientos de los astros.

Astrologer [as-trel'-o-jẹr], *s.* Astrólogo, el que profesa la astrología.

Astrologic [as-trō-lej'-ic], **Astrological** [as-trō-lej'-i-cal], *a.* Astrológico.

Astrologically [as-tro-lej'-i-cal-i], *adv.* Astrológicamente.

Astrology [as-trel'-o-ji], *s.* Astrología, el arte de pronosticar los sucesos por la situación de los planetas.

Astronaut [as'-tro-net], *s.* Astronauta.

Astronautics [as-tro-nē'-tics] *s.* Astronáutica, viajes astronáuticos, viajes interestelares.

Astronavigation [as-tro-nav-i-gê'-shun], *s.* Astronavegación.

Astronomer [as-tren'-o-mẹr], *s.* Astrónomo, el que profesa la astronomía.

Astronomic [as-tro-nem'-ic], **Astronomical** [as-tro-nem'-i-cal], *a.* Astronómico.

Astronomically [as-tro-nem'-i-cal-i], *adv.* Astronómicamente.

Astronomize [as-tren'-o-maiz], *vn.* Estudiar la astronomía.

Astronomy [as-tren'-o-mi], *s.* Astronomía, la ciencia que trata de la naturaleza, magnitud y movimiento de los cuerpos celestes.

Astrophysics [as-tro-fiz'-ics], *s.* Astrofísica.

Astro-theology [as'-tro-thẹ-el'-o-ji], *s.* Astroteología. Ciencia que demuestra por los astros el infinito poder, sabiduría y bondad de Dios.

Astrut [a-strut'], *adv.* Hinchadamente, pomposamente.

Astucious [as-tiū'-shus], *a.* *V.* ASTUTE.

Astute [as-tiūt'], *a.* Astuto, agudo; aleve.

Astuteness [as-tiūt'-nes], *s.* Astucia, penetración, sutileza.

Asunder [a-sun'-dẹr], *adv.* Separadamente, desunidamente, a parte. *To cut a thing asunder,* Cortar alguna cosa en dos partes.

Aswim [a-swim'], *adv.* Flotante, nadando.

Asylum [a-sai'-lum], *s.* Asilo, refugio.

Asymmetral [a-sim'-e-tral], **Asymmetrical** [a-sim-et'-ri-cal], *a.* Irregular, desproporcionado.

Asymmetry [a-sim'-e-tri], *s.* Asimetría, desproporción.

Asymptote [as'-im-tōt], *s.* (Mat.) Asíntota, línea recta que se acerca a una curva sin jamás encontrarse con ella.

Asynchronism [a-sin'-cro-nizm], *s.* Asincronismo, divergencia o no coincidencia en tiempo o fechas.

Asynchronous [a-sin'-cro-nus], *a.* Asincrónico, que no ocurre en la misma fecha.

Asyndeton [a-sin'-de-ten], *s.* (Ret.) Asíndeton, figura de locución que omite la conjunción copulativa.

At [at], *prep.* 1. A, en; preposición que antepuesta a lugar, denota el mismo lugar o su proximidad. *At Rome,* En Roma. *I arrived at London,* Llegué a Londres. *A man is at the house,* Hay un hombre arrimado a la casa. 2. Antepuesta a una voz que signifique tiempo, denota la coexistencia de este con lo que ha sucedido. *At nine o'clock this morning a man fell down dead in the street,* A las nueve de esta mañana cayó un hombre muerto en la calle. *At first,* Al principio, desde luego. *At last,* Por último. *At that,* (Fam.) También; en adición. *At once,* De un golpe, a la vez, de una vez, al instante. *At no time,* Nunca, jamás. *At last* o *at length,* Por fin, al fin. 3. Delante de un superlativo significa el estado de la cosa. *At most,* A lo más, cuando más, a lo sumo. *At least,* A lo menos. *At best,* Cuando mejor, a mejor andar. *At the worst,* A peor andar. 4. Significa la condición o estado particular del sujeto. *They are at peace,* Ellos están en paz. *He is at work,* Está al trabajo o está trabajando. *He is at home,* Está en casa. *He is at my command,* Está a mi disposición. *At all,* En modo alguno; hasta cualquier grado; en todo caso; por cierto. *Is it at all likely?* ¿Es probable en modo alguno? *At all events,* A todo trance, sea lo que fuere, en todo caso. *At large,* En general; sin limitación. *At sea,* (1) En el mar. (2) Perplejo, turbado. *At hand,* A la mano. *At leisure,* Despacio. *At ease,* Descansadamente. *At play,* Jugando. *At a push,* En una urgencia. *At a pinch,* En un apuro. *At a venture,* A lo que salga, a la buena ventura. *At a loss,* Indeciso, perplejo, dudoso. *All at once,* De repente. *At a distance,* A lo lejos. *At the hazard of,* Con peligro de. *At a mouthful,* De un bocado. *To be at,* Es un modo de hablar muy común que se usa para expresar toda suerte de ocupación.

Atabal [at'-a-bal], *s.* Atabal, especie de timbal usado por los moros.

Ataghan [at'-a-gan], *s.* Lo mismo que YATAGHAN.

Atamasco [at-a-mas'-cō], *s.* (Bot.) Lirio atamasco, planta norte-americana, de la familia de las amarilídeas, que produce una gran flor blanca y rojiza. (Nombre indio.)

Atavism [at'-a-vizm], *s.* Atavismo, semejar de un animal o una planta con sus progenitores.

Ataxia [a-tax'-i-a], *s.* Ataxia, irregularidad en las funciones del sistema muscular o en la marcha de una enfermedad.

Ate [et]. Pretérito del verbo *To eat.*

-ate. Sufijo que corresponde por lo general al español -ado.

Atelier [ā-tẹ-lyé'], *s.* Taller, estudio de un artista. (Fr.)

Atellan [a-tel'-an], *s.* y *a.* (Ant.) Representación dramática o satírica.

Athanasian [ath-a-nê'-shi-an], *s.* y *a.* Atanasiano, el que sigue la doctrina de San Atanasio, o lo que pertenece a su credo.

Atheism [ê'-thẹ-izm], *s.* Ateismo, opi-

nión impía que niega la existencia de Dios.
Atheist [é'-thę-ist], *s.* Ateista o ateo, el que niega la existencia de Dios.
Atheistic [é-thę-is'-tic], **Atheistical** [é-thę-is'-ti-cal], *a.* Impío, ateista.
Atheistically [é-thę-is'-ti-cal-i], *adv.* Impíamente.
Atheneum [ath-ę-ní'-um], *s.* 1. Ateneo, lugar público de Atenas donde los escritores daban lectura a sus obras. 2. Ateneo, nombre que se da hoy a diversos establecimientos científicos y literarios, y a varias bibliotecas.
Athenian [a-thí'-ni-an], *a.* Ateniense.
Atheroma [ath-ę-rō'-ma], *s.* Ateroma, enfermedad de la túnica interior de una arteria que se caracteriza por espesamiento y degeneración crasa.
Athirst [a-thęrst'], *adv.* Sediento.
Athlete [ath'-līt], *s.* Atleta, deportista. *All-round athlete,* Atleta completo, deportista en todos los campos.
Athletic [ath-let'-ic], *a.* 1. Atlético, que pertenece a la atlética o arte de luchar. 2. Fuerte, robusto, vigoroso.
Athwart [a-thwērt'], *prep.* Al o a través, de través, por el través, de un modo atravesado. *Athwart the fore-foot,* (Mar.) Por el través de la gorja. *Athwart hawse,* (Mar.) Por el través de las barbas. *Athwart ship,* (Mar.) De babor a estribor.—*adv.* Contrariamente, a tuertas.
-atic. Sufijo: de, de la suerte de: usado en adjetivos de origen griego o latino, como *erratic,* errático; *grammatic,* gramático.
Atilt [a-tilt'], *adv.* 1. En postura de dar una lanzada; en ristre. 2. En la posición de un barril inclinado.
-ation [é'-shun]. Sufijo que forma nombres de acción: muchas veces equivale al nombre verbal o gerundio en *ing.*
Atlantean [at-lan-tí'-an], *a.* Lo perteneciente al Atlante.
Atlantic [at-lan'-tic], *a.* Atlántico.—*s.* El mar Atlántico.
Atlas [at'-las], *s.* 1. Atlas, el libro u obra geográfica que contiene todos los mapas del mundo. 2. (Arq.) Atlante o telamón. 3. Atlas, tela de seda. 4. Primera vértebra del cuello. 5. Atlas, cadena de montañas en África.
Atmology [at-mel'-o-ji], *s.* Atmología, ciencia que trata de las leyes de los vapores acuosos.
Atmosphere [at'-mgs-fír], *s.* 1. Atmósfera, el aire que rodea la tierra por todos lados. 2. Alcance, o espacio a que se extienden las influencias ejercidas por una persona, cosa o idea. 3. Unidad de fuerza o tensión fundada en la presión atmosférica.
Atmospheric, Atmospherical [at-mes-fer'-ic, al], *a.* Atmosférico.
Atoll [a-tel'], †**Atollon,** *s.* Atol, atolón, isla madrepórica sumergida en su centro, de modo que aparece como un banco circular de coral que rodea una laguna central. Curiosa formación abundante en el Océano Pacífico.
Atom [at'-em], *s.* 1. Atomo, un cuerpo tan pequeño que es físicamente indivisible. 2. Átomo, cualquier cosa sumamente pequeña.
Atomic [a-tem'-ic], **Atomical** [a-tem'-i-cal], *a.* Atómico. *Atomic age,* Era atómica. *Atomic bomb,* Bomba atómica. *Atomic energy,* Energía atómica.
Atomism [at'-o-mizm], *s.* La doctrina de los átomos.
Atomist [at'-o-mist], *s.* Atomista, el que sigue o defiende el sistema de los átomos.
Atomization [at-ęm-ai-zé'-shun], *s.* Pulverización. Reducción a átomos o rocío (hablando de líquidos).
Atomize [at'-ęm-aiz], *va.* Pulverizar, reducir a átomos o niebla (vapor visible), rociar.
Atomizer [at'-em-aiz-ęr], *s.* Pulverizador, aparato para reducir un líquido o partículas muy tenues, a manera de polvo, formando un rocío o vapor visible, con objeto de desinfectar, inhalar, perfumar, etc.
Atom-like [at'-um-laic], *a.* Semejante al átomo.
Atom smasher [at'-em smash'-ęr], *s.* Pulverizador de átomos.
Atomy [at'-ęm-i], *s.* Atomo; motita. (Fam.) Enano.
Atone [a-tōn'], *va.* Expiar, pagar las penas debidas por las culpas; apaciguar, aplacar.—*vn.* 1. Equivaler, corresponder una cosa con otra en la estimación, precio o valor. 2. (Ant.) Acordar, convenir una cosa con otra.
Atonement [a-tōn'-męnt], *s.* 1. Expiación, pago de las penas debidas por las culpas; propiciación, sacrificio. 2. (Ant.) Concordia o asonancia, correspondencia de una cosa con otra.
Atoner [a-tōn'-ęr], *s.* Reconciliador, apaciguador.
Atonic [a-ten'-ic], *a.* Atónico, que padece atonía, que está falto de vigor o elasticidad.
Atony [at'-o-ni], *s.* Atonía, debilidad de las fibras.
Atop [a-tep'], *adv.* Encima, en la punta o parte superior de alguna cosa.
-ator. Sufijo que denota agente, actor, como *arbitrator.*
-atory. Sufijo que denota perteneciente a; producente o producido por.
Atrabilarian [at-ra-bi-lé'-ri-an], **Atrabilarious** [at-ra-bi-lé'-ri-us], *a.* Atrabiliario, atrabilioso, melancólico, hipocondriaco.
Atramental [at-ra-men'-tal], **Atramentous** [at-ra-men'-tus], *a.* Negro; perteneciente a la tinta.
Atrocious [a-trō'-shus], *a.* Atroz, enorme, extremamente malo o cruel.
Atrociously [a-trō'-shus-li], *adv.* Atrozmente.
Atrociousness [a-trō'-shus-nes], **Atrocity** [a-tres'-i-ti], *s.* Atrocidad, enormidad de algún delito; maldad horrible.
Atrophic [a-tref'-ic], *a.* Atrófico, concerniente a la atrofia, o afectado por ella; descaecido.
Atrophous [at'-ro-fus], *a.* *V.* ATROPHIC.
Atrophy [at'-ro-fi], *s.* (Med.) Atrofia, enflaquecimiento.—*vn.* Atrofiarse, ir a menos, descaecer, decaer.
Atropia [a-trō'-pi-a], **Atropine** [at'-ro-pin], *s.* Atropina, alcaloide venenoso que se extrae de la belladona.
Attach [at-tach'], *va.* 1. Pegar, juntar, atar, ligar; enganchar; conectar. 2. Prender, agarrar, pillar, asir, coger. 3. (For.) Embargar, secuestrar. 4. Ganar, lograr, adquirir, atraer a sí. 5. *vr.* Apegarse, adherirse.
Attachment [at-tach'-męnt], *s.* 1. Amistad, enlace, adherencia, afecto, apego, adhesión, afición; fidelidad; presa, aprehensión. 2. (For.) Embargo, secuestro.
Attack [at-tac'], *va.* Atacar, acometer, embestir; impugnar, combatir.
Attack, *s.* Ataque, la acción de atacar, acometimiento, embestida.
Attacker [at-tak'-ęr], *s.* Atacador, acometedor.
Attain [at-tén'], *va.* Ganar, procurar, conseguir, lograr, alcanzar.—*vn.* Llegar a, obtener, alcanzar.
Attainable [at-tén'-a-bl], *a.* Asequible, lo que se puede conseguir o alcanzar.
Attainableness [at-tén'-a-bl-nes], *s.* Probabilidad o posibilidad de alcanzar alguna cosa.
Attainder [at-tén'-dęr], *s.* 1. (For.) Imputación de algún delito, deshonra; proscripción, muerte civil. *Bill of attainder,* Decreto de proscripción. 2. (Ant.) Mancha, mácula, tacha.
Attainment [at-tén'-męnt], *s.* Logro, consecución de lo que se pretende. Adquisición.
Attaint [at-ténť'], *va.* 1. Convencer de algún delito, especialmente del de traición. 2. Corromper, viciar, manchar.
Attaint, *a.* Convencido.—*s.* 1. Mancha, mácula. 2. (For.) Auto jurídico.
Attaintment [at-tént'-męnt], *s.* El estado de haber sido convicto de algún delito.
Attainture [at-tént'-yūr], *s.* (Des.) Deshonra. *V.* ATTAINDER.
Attar [at'-ar], *s.* Aceite esencial fragrante, en especial el de rosas. *V.* OTTAR.
Attemper [at-tem'-pęr], *va.* Atemperar, diluir, molificar, mezclar; acomodar.
Attempt [at-tempt'], *va.* 1. Intentar, atentar; aventurar, arriesgar; atacar, embestir; tentar. 2. Probar, experimentar, ensayar.—*vn.* Procurar; hacer esfuerzos para conseguir algo, tirar a, pretender.
Attempt, *s.* 1. Ataque, acometimiento. 2. Empresa, atentado, prueba, experimento peligroso, esfuerzo.
Attemptable [at-tempt'-a-bl], *a.* Sujeto o expuesto a ser atacado.
Attempter [at-tempt'-ęr], *s.* Emprendedor, el que se esfuerza por hacer o conseguir alguna cosa.
Attend [at-tend'], *va.* 1. Atender, estar con cuidado y aplicación a lo que se mira, oye, hace o dice; escuchar atentamente. *Attend to what I say,* Atienda Vd. a lo que digo. 2. Servir, asistir, cuidar. *He attended the meeting,* Asistió a la reunión. *To attend the sick,* Cuidar al enfermo. 3. Acompañar. *His physician attended him through the whole journey,* Su médico le acompañó durante todo el viaje. 4. Presentarse, acudir, comparecer. 5. Acompañar o seguir como efecto necesario. 6. Esperar. 7. Traer tras de sí.—*vn.* 1. Atender, prestar atención. 2. Esperar; tardar. 3. Considerar. *To attend to a business,* Tener a su cargo un negocio. *To be attended with,* Causar, ocasionar, acarrear.
Attendance [at-tend'-ans], *s.* 1. Presencia, asistencia; (For.) comparecencia. *Your attendance is necessary,* La presencia de V. es necesaria. 2. Corte, obsequio. 3. Tren, séquito, comitiva, boato, acompañamiento. 4. Servidumbre, asistencia, servicio. (Fam.) *To dance attendance,* Estar de plantón, o de poste, hacer antesala. *Lady in attendance,* Camarera mayor.
Attendant [at-tend'-ant], *s.* 1. Sirviente, servidor. 2. Cortesano. 3.

Acompañante. 4. Concomitante, lo que acompaña a otra cosa u obra con ella. 5. Criado, sirviente, asistente. 6. Cortejo, galán, galanteador, obsequiante. *Attendants*, Subalternos (que acompañan a un ministro, u oficial superior). Tren, séquito. Servidumbre, criados, gentes de servicio.—*a.* Concomitante, acompañante.

Attender [at-ten'-dẹr], *s.* Compañero, socio, el que atiende.

Attent [at-tent'], *a.* Atento, cuidadoso.

Attentates [at-ten'-têts], *s. pl.* Atentado, procedimiento ilegal de algún tribunal o juez.

Attention [at-ten'-shun], *s.* 1. Atención, miramiento, cuidado, aplicación, reflexión. 2. Cortejo; galanteo, obsequio a una mujer. Más usado en el plural. 3. (Mil.) Voz de mando con que se advierte que va a empezar cierta maniobra; la postura o actitud misma que toman los soldados al oir dicha voz.

Attentive [at-ten'-tiv], *a.* Atento, el que tiene o fija la atención en alguna cosa.

Attentively [at-ten'-tiv-li], *adv.* Atentamente, con atención y cuidado.

Attentiveness, *s.* 1. Calidad de atento; miramiento, circunspección, cuidado. 2. Cortesía, finura, afabilidad en los modales.

Attenuant [at-ten'-yu-ant], *a.* Atenuante, lo que atenúa o adelgaza.

Attenuate [at-ten'-yu-êt], *va.* Atenuar, adelgazar, disminuir; hacer más tenue, como se hace, por ejemplo, con un alambre.

Attenuate, *a.* Atenuado, delgado, diminuto.

Attenuation [at-ten-yu-ê'-shun], *s.* Atenuación, la acción de atenuar o adelgazar.

Attest [at-test'], *va.* 1. Atestiguar, deponer, declarar, afirmar como testigo alguna cosa. 2. Citar o llamar por testigo. 3. Confirmar. (For.) *I attest*, Doy fe.

Attest, Attestation [at-tes-tê'-shun], *s.* Atestación, evidencia o deposición de testigo; prueba, testimonio, confirmación.

Attestor [at-tes'-tẹr], *s.* 1. Testigo, el que da testimonio. 2. Certificador, el que certifica.

Attic [at'-ic], *s.* 1. Desván, guardilla; también piso de poca elevación construido sobre una cornisa o un entablamento. *Attic story*, El último piso o alto de la casa; ático. 2. Ático, el natural de Ática.

Attic, Attical [at'-i-cal], *a.* Ático, agudo, juicioso, picante; aplícase al estilo.

Atticism [at'-i-sizm], *s.* Aticismo, la pulidez, brevedad y elegancia de lenguaje que usaban los atenienses, así como la de los romanos se llamó urbanidad.

Attire [at-tair'], *va.* Ataviar, componer, ascar, adornar, vestir.

Attire, *s.* 1. Atavío, el adorno y compostura de la persona; cofia, escofieta; traje, vestido en general. 2. Astas de ciervo. 3. (Ant.) El pistilo y los estambres de las flores; sus partes interiores.

Attiring [at-tair'-ing], *s.* Cofia, escofieta; vestido en general.

Attitude [at'-i-tiūd], *s.* Actitud, la disposición del objeto atendida su postura.

Attitudinal [at-i-tiū'-di-nal], *a.* De la actitud o referente a ella.

Attitudinarian [at-i-tiū-di-nê'-ri-an], *s.* Pintor o escultor que sobresale en el estudio y reproducción de las actitudes.

Attitudinize [at-i-tiū'-di-naiz], *vn.* Pavonearse, tomar posturas afectadas o académicas.

Attollent [at-tel'-ent], *a.* Elevador, que levanta o eleva, por ejemplo un músculo.

Attorn [at-tūrn], *vn.* (For. Ant.) Transferir los bienes o derechos a otro.—*va.* Reconocer a un nuevo poseedor de los bienes, y aceptar sus poderes.

Attorney [at-tūr'-ni], *s.* 1. Procurador, agente, apoderado; poderhabiente, el que en virtud de poder o facultad de otro ejecuta en su nombre alguna cosa. *Letter of attorney*, Poder, procuración. 2. Procurador de la curia eclesiástica. *V.* PROCTOR y SOLICITOR.

Attorney-General [at-tūr'-ni-jen'-ẹr-al], *s.* Fiscal, en los tribunales superiores; en los ayuntamientos, procurador, o síndico general.

Attorneyship [at-tūr'-ni-ship], *s.* Procuraduría, el oficio de procurador, agencia.

Attract [at-tract'], *va.* 1. Atraer, traer hacia sí alguna cosa. 2. Atraer, inclinar o reducir a otro a su voluntad; granjear.

Attractable [at-trac'-ta-bl], *a.* Atraíble, capaz de ser atraído, susceptible de atracción.

Attracter, Attractor [at-trac'-tẹr], *s.* El agente que atrae.

Attractile [at-trac'-til], *a.* Atractivo, con fuerza material de tracción o atracción; atráctil.

Attractingly [at-trac'-ting-li], **Attractively** [at-trac'-tiv-li], *adv.* Atractivamente.

Attraction [at-trac'-shun], *s.* 1. Atracción, la acción o virtud de atraer a sí alguna cosa. 2. Atractivo, la fuerza con que se atrae la voluntad. 3. Perturbación, desviación de las agujas imantadas. *Attraction of cohesion*, Atracción molecular. *Capillary attraction*, Atracción capilar.

Attractive [at-trac'-tiv], *a.* 1. Atractivo, atrayente, lo que tiene la fuerza y virtud de traer. 2. Atractivo, halagüeño, lo que se atrae o inclina a sí la voluntad.

†**Attractive**, *s.* Atractivo, incentivo, aliciente; encanto, embeleso.

Attractiveness [at-trac'-tiv-nes], *s.* Fuerza atractiva; gracia.

Attrahent [at'-ra-hent], *s.* Atrayente, lo que atrae o lleva hacia sí.

Attributable [at-trib'-yu-ta-bl], *a.* Imputable, lo que se puede imputar; lo que se puede aplicar o atribuir.

Attribute [at-trib'-yut], *va.* 1. Atribuir, dar o aplicar. 2. Atribuir, achacar, imputar.

Attribute [at'-ri-biūt], *s.* 1. Atributo, la cosa atribuida a otro. 2. Calidad o propiedad inherente. 3. Honra, reputación.

Attribution [at-ri-biū'-shun], *s.* Calidades atribuidas, atributo; recomendación.

Attributive [at-trib'-yu-tiv], *a.* Atributivo, que atribuye.—*s.* La cosa atribuida.

Attrite [at-trait'], *a.* 1. Estregado, frotado. 2. (Teol.) Pesaroso, atrito.

Attrition [at-trish'-un], *s.* 1. Rozadura, colisión, trituración, o molimiento de una cosa contra otra. 2. Atrición, arrepentimiento por temor al castigo.

Attune [at-tiūn'], *va.* Armonizar, acordar. V. TUNE.

Atwain [a-twên'], *adv.* Separadamente, en dos.

Atwirl [a-twẹrl'], *a.* y *adv.* En rotación, girando, dando vueltas.

Atwist [a-twist'], *adv.* y *a.* Torcidamente, al través, sesgado.

Atypic, Atypical [a-tip'-ic, al], *a.* Atipo, atípico, irregular.

Auburn [ē'-būrn], *a.* 1. Castaño; moreno rojizo; castaño es algo más obscuro que *auburn*. 2. Rojizo (del pelo).

Auction [ēc'-shun], *s.* 1. Almoneda, venta pública en que uno puja el precio después de otro hasta rematarse en el que más ofrece. 2. Pública subasta. 3. Vendeja. (Amer.) Venduta. 4. La alhaja o cosa vendida en almoneda. *To put up at auction*, Poner a pública subasta.

Auction, *va.* Subastar, vender a pública subasta. Almonedear, vender en almoneda.

Auctionary [ēc'-shun-ẹ-ri], *a.* Lo que pertenece a una almoneda.

Auctioneer [ēc-shun-īr'], *s.* Subastador, vendutero.—*va.* Vender a pública subasta.

Audacious [ē-dê'-shus], *a.* 1. Audaz, osado, atrevido, temerario. 2. Descarado, impudente.

Audaciously [ē-dê'-shus-li], *adv.* Atrevidamente.

Audaciousness [ē-dê'-shus-nes], *s.* Impudencia, descaro, temeridad, atrevimiento, audacia, desuello, desvergüenza, avilantez.

Audacity [ē-das'-i-ti], *s.* Audacia, osadía, atrevimiento.

Audible [ē'-di-bl], *a.* Oíble, lo que se puede oir. Inteligible; perceptible al oído.

Audibility [ē-di-bil'-i-ti], **Audibleness** [ē'-di-bl-nes], *s.* Capacidad de ser oído.

Audibly [ē'-di-bli], *adv.* De modo que se puede oir; alto.

Audience [ē'-di-ens], *s.* 1. Audiencia, la acción de oir a otro que habla, o la libertad que se concede a alguno para que diga lo que tiene que decir. 2. Auditorio, concurso de oyentes. 3. Audiencia, el recibimiento que tiene el que lleva una embajada.

Audience-chamber [ē'-di-ens-chêm'-bẹr], *s.* Sala o cámara de recepción. (For.) Audiencia.

Audio-frequency [ē-di-o-frī'-cwen-si], *s.* (Radio) Audiofrecuencia.

Audiology [ē-di-el'-o-ji], *s.* Audiología.

Audiometer [ē-di-em'-e-tẹr], *s.* Audiómetro, instrumento para medir la agudeza del oído.

Audion [e'-di-on], *s.* Audión (usado en transmisiones telefónicas y de radio a larga distancia).

Audiophile [ē'-di-o-fail], *s.* El entusiasta de la música fonográfica, particularmente de la alta fidelidad. Audiófilo.

Audio-visual [ē-di-o-vizh'-yu-al], *a.* Audiovisual.

Audiphone [ē'-di-fōn], *s.* Instrumento que, colocado contra los dientes, transmite el sonido a los oídos. Úsanlo con ventaja las personas algo sordas.

Audit [ē'-dit], *s.* Remate de una cuenta.

Audit, *va.* Rematar; examinar; pelotear.

Audition [ē-dish'-un], *s.* La acción de oir. La facultad de oir, el sentido del oído.

Auditive [ō'-di-tiv], *a.* Auditivo. *V.* AUDITORY.
Auditor [ō'-di-tẹr], *s.* 1. Oyente, el que oye; oidor, auditor. 2. Contador, revisor de cuentas.
Auditorium [ō-di-tō'-ri-um], *s.* Auditorio, la parte de una iglesia, de un teatro, etc., destinada al auditorio.
Auditorship [e'-di-ter-ship], *s.* Oficio de oidor o auditor.
Auditory [ō'-di-to-ri], *s.* Auditorio, concurso de oyentes.—*a.* Auditivo, auditorio, que oye y lo que sirve para oir. *Auditory canal, nerve,* Conducto, nervio auditivo.
Auditress [ō'-di-tres], *sf.* Oidora, la que oye.
Augean [ō-jī'-an], *a.* 1. Referente a Augeas, rey de Elida, cuyo establo contenía 3,000 bueyes, y no había sido limpiado en 30 años. Hércules lo limpió en un solo día. 2. Sucísimo.
Auger [ō'-gẹr], *s.* Barrena, taladro, instrumento de carpintero para taladrar. *Bolting auger,* (Mar.) Barrena de empernar. *Auger* o *auger-hole,* Agujero; barreno. *Auger-bit,* Gusanillo de rosca o de taladro. *Auger-handle,* Mango, ástil de barrena. *Auger-shank,* Vástago de barrena. *Expanding auger,* Barrena de extensión. *Ground-auger,* Barrena terrera. *Well-auger,* Barrena de pocero.
Aught [ōt], *pron.* Algo, alguna cosa: (con negación) nada. *For aught that I know, it was not so,* En cuanto yo sé, no fué así.
Augment [ōg-mẹnt'], *va.* Aumentar, acrecentar.—*vn.* Crecer, tomar aumento.
Augment [ōg'-mẹnt], *s.* Añadidura, aumento, acrecentamiento.
Augmentation [ōg-men-tē'-shun], *s.* 1. Aumentación, la acción de aumentar. 2. Aumento, el efecto de ser aumentado. 3. Aumento, añadidura por la cual se hace una cosa mayor de lo que era.
Augmentative [ōg-men'-ta-tiv], *a.* Aumentativo, que aumenta.
Augur [ō'-gur], **Augurer** [ō'-gur-ẹr], *s.* Augur, agorero, adivino.
Augur, Augurate [ō'-gur, ēt], *va.* Augurar, pronosticar, predecir.—*vn.* Augurar, agorar, pronosticar, adivinar por conjeturas.
Augural [ō'-giu-ral], **Augurial** [ō-giū'-ri-al], *a.* Augural, perteneciente a los agüeros o a los augures.
Augury [ō'-giu-ri], *s.* Agüero, adivinación o pronóstico ya sea favorable o contrario; presagio, auspicio, adivinación.
August [ō-gust'], *a.* Augusto, grande, real, majestuoso.
August [ō'-gust], *s.* Agosto, el octavo mes del año.
Augustan [ō-gus'-tan], *a.* Augusto, perteneciente al emperador Augusto o a su tiempo.
Augustinian [ō-gus-tin'-i-an], *a.* Agustiniano, Agustino; que se refiere o pertenece a San Agustín, a su doctrina o a la orden religiosa de su nombre.
Augustness [ō-gust'-nes], *s.* Majestuosidad, elevación de aire o porte, grandeza, majestad.
Auk [ōk] *s.* (Orn.) Alca; una ave marítima. *V.* Puffin.
Auld [ōld], *a.* (Esco.) Viejo, antiguo. *Auld Reekie,* "Vieja humeante"; apodo de la ciudad de Edimburgo.
Auld lang syne [ōld lang sain]. (Expresión escocesa) Frase que se usa para expresar los días pasados mucho ha, antaño, tiempos que fueron.
Aulic [ō'-lic], *a.* Áulico, lo que pertenece a la corte o palacio.
Aunt [ānt], *sf.* Tía, la hermana del padre o de la madre.
Aunty [ānt'-i], *sf.* 1. Tía, comadre; mujer vieja. 2. (E. U. del Sur) Negra vieja. También se escribe AUNTIE.
Aura [ō'-ra], *s.* 1. Aura, fluido, sutil exhalación o emanación de fuerza; influencia psíquica. 2. Sensación especial como de un vaho que procedente del tronco o de los miembros sube a la cabeza, síntoma monitorio de la epilepsia y de la histeria. 3. Céfiro, viento apacible y suave.
Aural [ō'-ral], *a.* Auditivo, auricular, que se refiere al oído.
Aurated [ō'-rē-ted], *a.* 1. Auriculado, que tiene apéndices como orejas. 2. Dorado, áureo.
Aureola [ō-rī'-o-la], **Aureole** [ō'-re-ōl], *s.* Aureola, círculo de luz con que se representan las cabezas de los santos.
Aureomycin [ō-ri-o-mai'-sin], *s.* (Trademark) Aureomicina.
Auricle [ō'-ri-cl], *s.* Oreja, el órgano exterior del oído. *Auricles, pl.* 1. Aurículas, las alas del corazón. 2. Las orejas o crestas que tienen algunas aves encima de los ojos, como el buho.
Auricula [ō-ric'-yu-la], *s.* 1. (Bot.) Oreja de oso, una planta. 2. (Biol.) Pequeño apéndice en forma de oreja.
Auricular [ō-ric'-yu-lār], *a.* 1. Auricular, lo que pertenece al oído; se aplica a la confesión de los católicos. 2. Secreto, dicho al oído. 3. Tradicional, lo que se sabe por tradición.
Auricularly [ō-ric'-yu-lār-li], *adv.* Al oído, secretamente.
Auriculate, Auriculated [ō-ric'-yu-lẹt], *a.* 1. Auriculífero, que tiene aurícula. 2. Auriculado, en forma de oreja; dícese de ciertos bivalvos y hojas.
Auriferous [ō-rif'-ẹr-us], *a.* (Poét.) Aurífero, lo que produce oro, o contiene oro.
Auriform [ō'-ri-fōrm], *a.* Auriforme, en forma de oreja.
Auriga [ō-rai'-ga], *s.* Auriga, cochero; constelación boreal entre Perseo y Géminis.
Aurigation [ō-ri-gē'-shun], *s.* El acto o la práctica de conducir carruajes.
Aurist [ō'-rist], *s.* Aurista, el que tiene por profesión curar las enfermedades de los oídos.
Aurochs [ō'-rocs], *s.* Aurochs, toro bravío de la antigua Galia y Alemania. Hoy sólo quedan ejemplares en los bosques de Lituania y el Cáucaso. Bisonte europeo.
Aurora [ō-rō'-ra], *s.* 1. Aurora, la primera luz que se descubre antes de salir el sol. 2. Crepúsculo de la mañana. 3. Aurora boreal.
Aurora Borealis [ō-rō'-ra-bō-ri-ā'-lis o ē'-lis], *s.* Aurora boreal. *V.* NORTHERN LIGHTS.
Auroral [ō-rō'-ral], *a.* Producido por el alba o crepúsculo matutino, o semejante a la aurora; rosáceo.
Auscultate [ōs'-cul-tēt], *va.* Auscultar, examinar por medio de la auscultación.—*vn.* Practicar la auscultación.
Auscultation [ōs-cul-tē'-shun], *s.* 1. Auscultación, acción y efecto de auscultar; aplicación del oído ó el estetoscopio á ciertos puntos del cuerpo para explorar los sonidos y ruidos de los órganos del pecho, vientre, etc. 2. Atención, la acción de atender o escuchar lo que se dice.
Auspice [ōs'-pis], *s.* 1. Auspicio, presagio de algún suceso por el vuelo de las aves. 2. Auspicio, protección, amparo, apoyo, autoridad.
Auspicial [ōs-pish'-al], *a.* Lo perteneciente a los pronósticos.
Auspicious [ōs-pish'-us], *a.* Próspero, feliz, favorable; benigno, propicio.
Auspiciously [ōs-pish'-us-li], *adv.* Prósperamente, felizmente.
Auspiciousness [ōs-pish'-us-nes], *s.* Prosperidad, esperanza de felicidad.
Austere [ōs-tīr'], *a.* 1. Austero, severo, rígido; rudo. 2. Agrio, ácido, acerbo al gusto.
Austerely [ōs-tīr'-li], *adv.* Austeramente.
Austereness [es-tīr'-nes], *s.* Austeridad, crueldad, severidad.
Austerity [es-ter'-i-ti], *s.* Austeridad. *Austerity program,* Programa de austeridad.
Austral [ōs'-tral], *a.* Austral, lo que pertenece al austro o mediodía.
Australian [ōs-trē'-lyan], *a.* Australiano, perteneciente a Australia.
Austrian [ōs'-tri-an], *a.* Austriaco, de Austria.
Autarchy [ō'-tār-ki], *s.* Autarquía, soberanía absoluta.
Autarky [ō'-tār-ki], *s.* Autarquía, suficiencia económica nacional.
Authentic [ō-then'-tic], **Authentical** [ō-then'-tic-al], *a.* Auténtico, lo autorizado o legalizado públicamente; solemne, cierto, original.
Authentically [ō-then'-tic-al-i], **Authenticly** [ō-then'-tic-li], *adv.* Auténticamente.
Authenticalness [ō-then'-tic-al-nes], **Authenticity** [ō-then-tis'-i-ti], **Authenticness** [ō-then'-tic-nes], *s.* Autenticidad.
Authenticate [ō-then'-ti-kēt], *va.* Autenticar, autorizar, hacer auténtico.
Author [ō'-ther], *s.* 1. Autor, el que es causa primera de alguna cosa. 2. Autor, el que es causa eficiente de alguna cosa. 3. Autor, el que ha compuesto alguna obra literaria, artística o científica, con respecto a la misma obra compuesta; escritor. 4. Conjunto de las obras o los escritos de un autor.
Author [ō'-thẹr], *va.* Ser autor de, hacer, escribir, inventar, crear.
Authoress [ō'-thẹr-es], *sf.* Autora, escritora.
Authoritarian [ō-ther-i-tē'-ri-an], *s.* y *a.* Autoritario.
Authoritative [ō-ther'-i-tē-tiv], *a.* 1. Autorizado, que tiene la autoridad necesaria. 2. Que ejerce autoridad; positivo, perentorio, terminante.
Authoritatively [ō-ther'-i-tē-tiv-li], *adv.* 1. Autoritativamente. 2. Autorizadamente.
Authoritativeness [ō-ther'-i-tē-tiv-nes], *s.* Autoridad debidamente sancionada; calidad de lo autorizado; apariencia autoritativa.
Authority [ō-ther'-i-ti], *s.* 1. Autoridad, potestad, facultad, poder legal. 2. Crédito y fe que se da a alguna cosa. 3. Autoridad, el texto o palabras con que se apoya lo que se dice. *I have it from the best authority,* Lo sé de muy buen original o de buena tinta; lo tengo de buena mano. *Printed by authority,* Impreso con licencia.
Authorization [ō-ther-i-zē'-shun], *s.*

Autorización, la acción y efecto de autorizar.
Authorize [ō'-ther-aiz], *va.* 1. Autorizar, dar autoridad o facultad para hacer alguna cosa. 2. Autorizar, legalizar algún instrumento de forma que haga fe pública. 3. Autorizar, sancionar, comprobar alguna cosa con autoridad. *Authorized Version,* Traducción inglesa de la Biblia hecha en 1611, sancionada por el rey Jaime I, y que se dispuso fuera leída en las iglesias. *Cf.* REVISED VERSION.
Authorized [ō'-ther-aizd], *a.* Autorizado, facultado.
Authorless [ō'-ther-les], *a.* Desautorizado; sin autor.
Authorship [ō'ther-ship], *s.* 1. El estado, la calidad o profesión de autor. 2. Manantial, origen.
Autobiography [ō-to-bai-eg'-ra-fi], *s.* Autobiografía.
Autobus [ō'-to-bus], *s.* Autobús, ómnibus, camioneta.
Autocade [ō'-to-kêd], *s.* Caravana de automóviles.
Autoclave [ō'-to clêv], *s.* Autoclave, aparato de esterilización por vapor y presión.
Autocrasy [ō-tec'-ra-si], *s.* Autocracia, poder absoluto o independiente.
Autocrat [ō'-to-crat], *s.* Autócrata.
Autocratical [ō-to-crat'-i-cal], *a.* Autocrático.
Autogiro, Autogyro [ō-to-jai'-rō], *s.* (Aer.) Autogiro.
Autograph [ō'-to-graf], **Autography** [ō-teg'-ra-fi], *s.* Autógrafo.
Autographical [ō-to-graf'-i-cal], *a.* Autográfico, escrito de propio puño.
Automat [ō'-to-mat], *s.* Restaurante automático.
Automate [ō'-to-mêt], *va.* Automatizar.
Automatic [ō-to-mat'-ic] o **Automatical** [ō-to-mat'-i-cal], *a.* Automático, lo que se mueve por sí mismo. *Automatic brake,* Freno automático. *Automatic tracking,* Sistema de localización automática.
Automation [e-to-mê'-shun], *s.* Automatización.
Automaton [ō-tem'-a-ten], *s.* Autómata, la máquina que se mueve por sí misma.
Automobile [ō-to-mō'-bil], *a.* Automóvil, que se mueve por sí mismo. —*s.* Carruaje de paseo, carretón o vehículo para el transporte de mercancías, que tiene un mecanismo que lo pone en movimiento.
Automotive [ō-to-mō'-tiv], *a.* Automotor, automotriz.
Autonomous [ō-ten'-o-mus], *a.* Autónomo.
Autonomy [ō-ten'-o-mi], *s.* Autonomía, derecho de gobernarse por sí mismo.
Autopilot [ō'-to-pai-lot], *s.* (Aer.) Piloto automático.
Autopsy [ō'-tep-si], *s.* Autopsia, examen anatómico de un cadáver para descubrir la causa de la muerte.
Autosuggestion [ō-to-su-jes'-chun], *s.* Autosugestión.
Autotruck [ō'-to-truc], *s.* Autocamión.
Autotype [ō'-to-taip], *s.* 1. Autotipo, facsímil, copia exacta.
Autumn [ō'-tum], *s.* Otoño, la estación del año que media entre el verano y el invierno.
Autumnal [ō-tum'-nal], *a.* Otoñal, autumnal, lo perteneciente al otoño.
Auxiliar [ōg-zil'-i-ar], *a.* Auxiliar, auxiliatorio.
Auxiliary, *s.* Auxiliador.
Avail, [a-vêl'], *va.* 1. Aprovechar, emplear útilmente alguna cosa. 2. Promover, adelantar. *To avail one's self of an opportunity,* Valerse de la ocasión.—*vn.* Servir, importar, ser útil, ser ventajoso; ayudar. *It avails nothing,* Nada importa; de nada sirve.
Avail, *s.* Provecho, ventaja, utilidad.—*pl.* Beneficios, producto (de una venta).
Availability [a-vêl"-a-bil'-i-ti], *s.* Eficacia, utilidad, actividad.
Available [a-vêl'-a-bl], *a.* 1. Útil, ventajoso, provechoso: (Com.) disponible. 2. Eficaz, activo y poderoso en el obrar. *Available assets,* Activo disponible.
Availableness [a-vêl'-a-bl-nes], *s.* Eficacia, virtud, actividad, fuerza y poder para obrar; utilidad, ventaja.
Availably [a-vêl'-a-bli], *adv.* Eficazmente, provechosamente, útilmente.
Avalanche [av'-a-lansh], *s.* Lurte o alud, masas grandes de nieve que se desprenden de las cumbres de las montañas, y cayendo en los valles o en el mar causan muchos daños.
Avant-guard [a-vant'-gārd], *s.* Vanguardia. *V.* VAN-GUARD.
Avarice [av'-a-ris], *s.* Avaricia, codicia.
Avaricious [av-a-rish'-us], *s.* Avaro, avariento, miserable.
Avariciously [av-a-rish'-us-li], *adv.* Avaramente, avarientamente.
Avariciousness [av-a-rish-'us-nes], *s.* Codicia, avaricia, la calidad de ser avaro.
Avast [a-vāst'], *adv.* (Mar.) Forte. *Avast heaving,* (Mar.) Forte al virar. También suele usarse en el sentido de ¡basta! ¡bueno está! ¡no más!
Avaunt [a-vānt'], *inter.* ¡Fuera! ¡fuera de aquí! ¡Quita! ¡quita allá! ¡Lejos de aquí! ¡Quítateme de delante!
Ave Mary o **Ave Maria** [ê'-vi mê' ri o ā'-vê ma-ri'-a], *s.* Ave María, la salutación angélica.
Avenaceous [av-en-ê'-shus], *a.* Avenáceo, perteneciente a la avena; avenáceo, de la naturaleza de la avena.
Avenge [a-venj'], *va.* Vengarse, tomar satisfacción de un agravio o injuria; castigar algún delito.
Avengement [a-venj'-ment], *s.* Venganza, satisfacción que se toma del agravio recibido.
Avenger [a-ven'-jer], *s.* 1. Castigador, el que castiga. 2. Vengador, el que venga o se venga.
Avens [av'-enz], *s.* (Bot.) Gariofilea, una planta cualquiera del género Geum, familia de las rosáceas.
Aventurine, Aventurin [a-ven'-chu-rin], *s.* 1. Venturina, cuarzo con laminitas de mica amarilla. 2. Venturina artificial, cristal fundido con limaduras de cobre. 3. Un lacre moreno claro lleno de puntos brillantes.
Avenue [av'-e-niū], *s.* 1. Avenida, calle ancha o calle principal; calzada. 2. Calle de árboles, alameda, carrera. 3. Entrada, pasadizo.
Aver [a-ver'], *va.* Asegurar, afirmar, verificar, certificarse.
Average [av'-er-ej] *s.* 1. Promedio, tanteo, precio medio de una cosa o lo que ella vale o renta por un cómputo o cálculo prudencial o aproximado, ya relativamente a los diversos puntos donde se vende a un mismo tiempo, ya respecto de un quinquenio, lo que en castellano suele expresarse por ***una cosa con otra, un precio con otro, un año con otro.*** 2. Avería, daño que sufren las embarcaciones y sus cargamentos. 3. Capa o sombrero del capitán, el plus que se asigna al capitán de un buque en las pólizas de embarque por su cuidado de los efectos que se le entregan. 4. Parte igual o proporcional. 5. Servicio o servidumbre, obligación que contrae el vasallo de servir al rey personalmente, franqueándole el uso de sus bestias y carruajes. —*a.* 1. Medio, uno con otro, entre uno y otro. 2. Típico, ordinario. 3. Hecho o computado por un método de averías. *Average amount,* Valor medio. *Average duties,* Derechos de avería. *Average price,* Precio medio. *Average weight,* Peso aproximado.
Average, *va.* 1. Comparar o cotejar y fijar un precio o término medio; proporcionar. 2. Costar, dar, tomar, tener, ocurrir, etc., como término medio.
Averment [a-ver'-ment], *s.* Afirmación o seguridad de alguna cosa de suerte que sea evidente; testimonio.
†**Averruncate** [a-ve-run'-kêt], *va.* Desarraigar, arrancar de raíz.
Averse [a-vers'], *a.* 1. Adverso, contrario. 2. Repugnante, opuesto; enemigo.
Aversely [a-vers'-li], *adv.* Repugnantemente.
Averseness [a-vers'-nes], *s.* Repugnancia, mala gana.
Aversion [a-ver'-shun], *s.* Aversión, aborrecimiento, disgusto, odio.
Avert [a-vert'], *va.* Desviar, apartar, separar, alejar; prevenir. *To avert the danger,* Prevenir, desviar el peligro. *To avert the eyes,* Apartar los ojos o la mirada.
Averter [a-vert'-er], *s.* Apartador, el que desvía.
Avian [ê'-vi-an], *a.* Perteneciente a las aves.
Aviary [ê'-vi-e-ri], *s.* Pajarera, jaula grande o aposento para criar o tener pájaros.
Aviation [ê-vi-ê'-shun], *s.* Aviación.
Aviculture [ê-vi-cul'-chur], *s.* Avicultura, cría de las aves.
Avid [av'-id], *a.* Avido, ansioso, codicioso.
Avidity [a-vid'-i-ti], *s.* Voracidad, ansia, codicia, avidez.
Avocado [av-o-cā'-do], *s.* Aguacate, palta. (Mex.) Pagua.
Avocation [av-o-kê'-shun], *s.* 1. Evocación. 2. La acción de llamar o separar a uno de lo que está haciendo. 3. Estorbo, el asunto que llama o quita a uno de lo que está haciendo. 4. Obstáculo, impedimento, distracción. 5. Empleo, ocupación; uso familiar y común, pero impropio en lugar de *vocation.*
Avocet, Avoset [av'-o-set], *s.* (Orn.) Avoceta, ave del orden de las zancudas; tiene pies palmeados y pico encorvado hacia arriba.
Avoid [a-veid'], *va.* 1. Evitar, escapar, huir, esquivar, dejar. 2. Evacuar, desalojar; anular.—*vn.* 1. Retirarse. 2. Zafarse, escaparse.
Avoidable [a-veid'-a-bl], *a.* Evitable, que se puede evitar o huir. (For.) Revocable.
Avoidance [a-veid'-ans], *s.* 1. El acto y efecto de evitar alguna cosa. (For.) Vacación. Evasión, efugio. 2. Anulación (de un acto), invalidación.

Avoidless [a-void'-les], *a.* Inevitable.
Avoirdupois [av-or-du-poiz'], *s.* La clase de peso cuya libra tiene diez y seis onzas. Peso común, donde no se usa el sistema métrico.
Avouch [a-vauch'], *va.* Afirmar, justificar, sostener; alegar en favor de otro; protestar.
Avouchable [a-vauch'-a-bl], *a.* Justificable, afirmable.
Avoucher [a-vauch'-er], *s.* El que afirma, justifica, sostiene o alega a favor de otro.
Avow [a-vau'], *va.* Declarar, manifestar abiertamente, protestar, confesar.
Avowable [a-vau'-a-bl], *a.* Lo que se puede declarar abiertamente.
Avowal [a-vau'-al], *s.* Declaración justificativa, aprobación, confesión, reconocimiento.
Avowedly [a-vau'-ed-li], *adv.* Declaradamente, manifiestamente, abiertamente.
†**Avowee** [a-vau-i'], *s.* Patrono, el que tiene el patronato de alguna iglesia o beneficio.
Avower [a-vau'-er], *s.* Declarante, el que declara o justifica.
Avowry [a-vau'-ri], *s.* (For.) Justificación de algún secuestro ya ejecutado, o el motivo que se alega para haberlo hecho.
Avulsion [a-vul'-shun], *s.* La acción de separar una cosa de otra.
Avuncular [a-vun'-kiu-lar], *a.* De un tío, o parecido a un tío. (Lat. avunculus.)
Awa [a-wā'], *adv.* (Esco.) Fuera, afuera, ausente.
Awaft [a-waft'], *adv.* (Mar.) Bandera amorronada, pabellón izado en lo alto del asta pero anudado de trecho en trecho.
Await [a-wêt'], *va.* 1. Aguardar, esperar. 2. Esperar, estar aguardando alguna cosa.
Awake [a-wêc'], *va.* Despertar, quitar el sueño al que está dormido.—*vn.* Despertar, dejar de dormir.
Awake, *a.* Despierto. *To keep awake,* Impedir el sueño; tener alerta. *Wide-awake,* Bien despierto, alerta.
Awaken [a-wê'-kn], *vn.* *V.* AWAKE.
Awakener [a-wê'-kn-er], *s.* Despertador.
Awakening [a-wê'-kn-ing], *s.* Despertamiento, el acto de despertar.
Awanting [a-wānt'-ing], *pa.* (Esco. y poét.) Falto, necesitado, escaso.
Award [a-wērd'], *va.* Juzgar, sentenciar. (For.) Adjudicar, declarar a favor de alguno.—*vn.* Determinar.
Award, *s.* Sentencia, determinación, decisión, adjudicación.
Awardable [a-wērd'-a-bl], *a.* Adjudicable.
Awarder [a-wērd'-er], *s.* Juez árbitro.
Aware [a-wār'], *a.* Cauto, vigilante, que prevé; sabedor. *He is not aware of such a thing,* No sabe tal cosa. *You are not aware what man you are speaking to,* Vd. no sabe con quién habla.
Awash [a-wesh'], *a.* y *adv.* (Mar.) A flor de agua.
Away [a-wê'], *adv.* Ausente, afuera, fuera. *Away he went,* Se marchó. *Away* se emplea con gran número de verbos y denota en general la idea de alejamiento, aunque también expresa a veces continuación, persistencia. Por ejemplo: *To get away,* Huir, evadirse. *To go away,* Irse, marcharse. *To send away,* Despedir. *To run away,* Tomar las de Villadiego, escaparse. *To make away with one's self,* Darse la muerte, suicidarse. *Work away,* Persista Vd. en el trabajo. *Write away,* Escriba Vd. sin cesar.
Away, *inter.* Fuera, fuera de aquí, quita, o quítate de aquí o de ahí. *Away with you,* ¡Márchate! ¡Quítateme de delante! ¡Que no te vean mis ojos! *Away with it,* ¡Quitádmelo de delante! ¡Basta, no más!
Awe [ē], *s.* 1. Miedo o temor reverencial. 2. Pavor. *To keep one in awe,* Tener enfrenado o sujeto a alguno.
Awe, *va.* Amedrentar, asombrar, despavorir, atemorizar; infundir miedo, temor reverencial, o pavor.
Aweary [a-wī'-ri], *a.* (Poét.) Cansado, fatigado.
Aweather [a-wedh'-er], *adv.* (Mar.) A barlovento, por el lado del viento (en oposición a *alee,* sotavento).
Awe-commanding [ē'-com-and''-ing], *a.* Lo que infunde respeto.
Awe-inspiring [ē'-in-spair''-ing], *a.* Impresionante, imponente.
Awesome [ē'-sum], *a.* 1. Terrible, temible, que infunde miedo; aterrador, pavoroso. 2. Reverencial, respetuoso.
Awe-struck [ē'-struc], *a.* Espantado, despavorido, dominado por el terror, o el respeto.
Aweigh [a-wê'], *adv.* (Mar.) Pendiente, a plomo.
Awful [ē'-ful], *a.* 1. Tremendo; digno de respeto y reverencia. 2. Amedrentado, atemorizado. 3. Temible, funesto, horroroso, espantoso. 4. (Fam.) Muy malo, muy grande, enorme; horrendo.
Awfully [ē'-ful-i], *adv.* 1. Respetuosamente, con respeto y veneración; solemnemente, terriblemente. 2. (Fam.) Muy; excesivamente.
Awful-eyed [ē'-ful-aid], *a.* El que tiene ojos espantosos.
Awfulness [ē'-ful-nes], *s.* Veneración, respeto o temor reverencial que infunde alguna cosa por ser grande y majestuosa.
Awhile [a-hwail'], *adv.* Un rato, algun tiempo. *Wait awhile,* Espérese un rato. *Not for awhile,* Todavía no, por ahora no.
Awhirl [a-hwerl'], *adv.* En rotación; en giro, en torbellino.
Awkward [ēk'-ward], *a.* 1. Zafio, tosco, inculto, rudo, zopenco, agreste. 2. Desmañado, falto de maña, torpe, poco diestro. 3. Indócil, indómito. 4. Embarazoso, difícil, delicado; también, desgraciado, peligroso. *An awkward situation,* Una situación embarazosa. *An awkward question,* Una cuestión delicada. *An awkward customer,* Un sujeto peligroso.
Awkwardly [ēk'-ward-li], *adv.* 1. Groseramente, toscamente. 2. Torpemente, desmañadamente. 3. Embarazosamente, en una posición difícil, delicada. *Awkwardly placed,* En una posición embarazosa.
Awkwardness [ēk'-ward-nes], *s.* Tosquedad, grosería, torpeza, poca habilidad o maña.
Awl [ēl], *s.* Lesna, instrumento de hierro puntiagudo de que usan los zapateros y los carpinteros. *Bradawl,* Lesna para puntillas. *Scratch-awl,* Punzón de marcar. *Pegging-awl,* Estaquillador. *Sailmaker's-awl,* Aguja de veleros. *Sewing-awl,* Lesna de coser.
Awless [ē'-les], *a.* 1. Irreverente, el que falta a la reverencia y respeto que debe. 2. Lo que no causa ni infunde respeto o reverencia.
Awl-shaped [el'-shêpt], *a.* Alesnado. (Bot.) Subulado.
Awme [ēm], *s.* Medida líquida de Holanda.
Awmous [ē'-mus], *s.* (Esco.) Limosna, caridad.
Awn [ēn], *s.* Arista, la barba de la espiga.
Awning [ēn'-ing], *s.* 1. (Mar.) Toldo, cubierta de lienzo u otra tela que se pone en la embarcación para guardarse del sol. 2. Toldo (de almacén o puesto de mercado; o de carro). 3. (Hort.) Abrigaña; estera para abrigar las plantas. *Awning stanchions,* (Mar.) Candeleros de los toldos.
Awoke [a-wōc']. Pretérito del verbo *To Awake.*
Aworking [a-wūrk'-ing], *adv.* Trabajando, al trabajo.
Awry [a-rai'], *adv.* 1. Oblicuamente, torcidamente, al través. 2. Con la vista atravesada, de lado, de soslayo.
Ax o **Axe** [ax], *s.* Segur o hacha. *A battle-axe,* Hacha de armas. *A pole-axe,* Hacha de mano. *A pick-axe,* Zapapico, azadón, piqueta. *Axe-head,* La cabeza o la parte cortante del hacha, destral. *Broad-axe, Cooper's axe,* Doladera.
Axial [ac'-si-al], *a.* Axil, perteneciente al eje o semejante a un eje: dispuesto alrededor de un eje común.
Axil [ac'-sil], *s.* (Bot.) Axila, ángulo formado por el lado superior de una hoja o de un ramo y el tallo o la rama de que nace.
Axil, *a.* *V.* AXIAL.
Axilla [ac-sil'-a], *s.* 1. (Anat.) Sobaco. 2. Axila de las aves.
Axillar [ac'-si-lar], **Axillary** [ac'-si-le-ri], *a.* 1. Axilar, lo que pertenece al sobaco. 2. (Bot.) Axilar, que crece en los ángulos de los ramos de las plantas.
Axiom [ac'-si-um], *s.* Axioma, proposición, sentencia o principio sentado. Verdad evidente.
Axiomatic, Axiomatical [ac-si-o-mat'ic-al], *a.* Axiomático; evidente, irrefutable.
Axis [ac'-sis], *s.* 1. Eje. 2. Pivote, centro de oscilación. 3. Áxis, la segunda vértebra del cuello. 4. Alianza. *The Axis Nations,* Las Naciones del Eje (Alemania, Italia y el Japón).
Axle [ac'-sl], **Axle-tree** [ac'-sl-trī], *s.* Eje de una rueda. Árbol de una máquina.
Axle-clip, *s.* Abrazadera que sujeta el cibicón al eje.
Axolotl [ax'-o-letl], *s.* Axolote, reptil anfibio del lago de Méjico.
Ay, Aye [ai], *adv.* Sí; adverbio, por el cual se responde afirmativamente. *V.* YES.
Aye [ê], *adv.* Siempre, para siempre jamás.
Aye-aye [ai'-ai], *s.* Ay-ay, mamífero nocturno de Madagascar, del orden de los cuadrumanos, familia de los lemúridos.
†**Ayry** [ê'-ri], *s.* El nido del halcón. *V.* EYRY.
Azalea [a-zê'-le-a], *s.* Azalea, arbusto de la familia de las ericáceas, género Azalea, notable por la belleza de sus flores.
Azerole [az'-er-ōl], *s.* (Bot.) Acerola.
Azimuth [az'-i-muth], *s.* Azimut del sol o de una estrella; al arco del horizonte que hay entre el círculo vertical en que está el astro, y el

meridiano del observador. *Azimuth-compass*, Brújula de azimut.
Azoic [a-zō'-ic], *a.* Azóico.
Azon bomb [é'-zōn bem], *s.* Bomba aérea que puede ser guiada hacia la derecha o izquierda por radiocontrol.
Azonic [a-zen'-ic], *a.* Azónico, no propio y peculiar de una zona o región; no local.
Aztec [az'-tec], *a.* y *s.* Azteca, nombre que se da a los antiguos indígenas de Méjico, notables por su civilización; y también, a su lengua, etc.
Azure [azh'-yūr], **Azured** [azh'-yūrd], *a.* Azulado claro, azul celeste.
Azure, *va.* Azular.
Azurine [azh'-yur-in], *a.* Azulado.

B

B [bī]. Se pronuncia lo mismo que en castellano, pero cuidando de apretar los labios con doble fuerza. Cuando al fin de las voces la precede la *m*, como en *dumb*, y cuando está puesta delante de la letra *t*, como en *debt*, no suena la *b*.
La B se usa como abreviatura; así *B. A.* quiere decir, Bachiller en Artes; *B. D.*, Bachiller en Teología; *LL. B.*, Bachiller en Leyes; o en ambos Derechos; *B. Sc.*, Bachiller en Ciencias.
Baa [bā], *s.* Balido, la voz que forma la oveja, el carnero o cordero.
Baa, *vn.* Balar, dar balidos la oveja, carnero o cordero.
Babbit [bab'-it], *s.* Nombre despectivo que se da a personas demasiado apegadas a las normas sociales y morales de su grupo.
Babbitt, Babbitt metal [bab'-it met'-al], *s.* Metal de Babbitt, metal antifricción para cojinetes.
Babble [bab'-l], *vn.* 1. Balbucear, hablar como un niño. 2. Charlar, hablar mucho y sin sustancia. 3. Parlar, revelar lo que se debe callar. 4. Murmurar un arroyo.—*va.* Charlar.
Babble, *s.* 1. Charla, conversación sin sustancia, cháchara, parla, charlatanería. 2. El susurro o murmullo de una corriente.
Babbler [bab'-lẹr], *s.* 1. Charlador, charlante, chacharero, charlatán, parlador, hablador, el que charla o habla mucho y sin sustancia. 2. Parlero, el que habla de lo que se debe callar.
Babbling [bab'-ling], *s.* Habla vana y sin provecho, cháchara, flujo de hablar.
Babe [bêb], *s.* Criatura, criaturita, infante, el niño pequeño que aun no está en edad de hablar. (Fam.) Nene.
Babel [bé'-bel], *s.* Muchedumbre y confusión de pareceres; desorden, alboroto
Baboon [bab-ūn'], *s.* Cinocéfalo, mono grande.
Baby [bê'-bi], *s.* 1. Criatura, infante, niño pequeño, nene. 2. Muñeca.
Baby, *va.* Hacer o tratar como niño.
Baby buggy [bê'-bi bʊg'-i], *s.* Cochecito para niños.
Baby carriage [bê'-bi car'-ij], *s.* Cochecito para niños.
Babyish [bê'-bi-ish], *a.* Niñero; pueril.
Babyishness [bê'-bi-ish-nes], *s.* Puerilidad, niñada.
Babyhood [bê'-bi-hud], *s.* Niñez, el primer período de la infancia; también, los nenes colectivamente.
Babylonian [bab-i-lō'-ni-an], *a.* Babilónico, de Babilonia.
Babysit [bê'-bi-sit], *va.* Servir de niñera por horas.
Baby-sitter [bé'-bi-sit-ẹr], *s.* Cuidaniños, niñera por horas.
Baccalaureate [bac-a-lō'-ri-et], *a.* Bachillerato, el grado de bachiller. *Baccalaureate sermon*, Sermón que se predica como discurso de despedida a los graduandos de una clase. (Amer.)
Baccate [bak'-ẹt], *a.* (Bot.) 1. Parecido a una baya. 2. Que produce bayas.
Bacchanal [bac'-a-nal], **Bacchanalian** [bac-a-nê'-li-an], *s.* Un borracho, un alborotador.—*a.* Borracho, alborotado, relajado, licencioso, disoluto.
Bacchanals [bac'-a-nalz], *s. pl.* Bacanales, fiestas en honor de Baco.
Bacchic, Bacchical [bak'-ic, al], *a.* Báquico.
Bacchus [bac'-us], *s.* (Mit.) Baco, hijo de Júpiter y de Semele.
Baccivorous [bac-siv'-o-rus], *a.* Bacívoro, que come con mucha ansia las bayas de las plantas.
Bachelor [bach'-el-er], *s.* 1. Soltero, célibe. 2. Bachiller, el que ha recibido el primer grado en alguna facultad. 3. Caballero de la última clase en tiempos antiguos.
Bachelor's-button [bach'-el-erz-but'-n], *s.* (Bot.) Botón de oro. Azulejo, planta. Centaurea cyanea.
Bachelorship [bach'-el-er-ship], *s.* 1. Celibato, soltería. 2. Bachillerato, el grado de bachiller.
Bacillus [ba-sil'-us], *s.* BACILLI [ba-sil'-ai o li], *pl.* Bacilos, variedad de las bacterias, organismo microscópico vegetal, en forma cilíndrica, virguliforme o filiforme.
Bacitracin [bas-i-trê'-sin], *s.* Bacitracina.
Back [bac], *s.* 1. Espalda, espaldar, espinazo, hablando de personas; y lomo, cerro, espinazo, hablando de animales. 2. Metacarpo, dorso. *Back of the hand*, El envés, o el revés de la mano. 3. Recazo, lomo, canto, la parte opuesta al filo de algún instrumento cortante. 4. Tras, dorso. *Back of a house*, Espalda de una casa. *Back of a chair*, Respaldo de silla. *Back of a coach*, Trasera de coche. *Back of a book*, Lomo de un libro. *A back blow* or *a back stroke*, Un revés. *Back yard*, Patio interior. 5. Tina o enfriadera de cerveza. 6. (Mar.) Galga de ancla. 7. (Mar.) Espalda de un bote. *On one's back*, A cuestas. *Back to back*, Espalda con espalda. *To break one's back*, Deslomar a alguno. *To have a pain in the back*, Tener dolor de espaldas, de cintura, de riñones. *To cast behind the back*, (1) Perdonar y olvidar. (2) Desechar con desdén. *To see the back of*, Desembarazarse o librarse de. *To turn the back*, Huir. *To turn the back on*, Abandonar, desertar.—*a.* 1. Trasero, interior, de atrás o detrás, del interior. 2. Separado, apartado, lejano, extraviado. 3. Publicado en tiempo anterior al presente. 4. Que ha pasado del tiempo debido. *Back room*, Cuarto interior, pieza apartada. *Back pension*, Pensión debida, y no pagada todavía. *Back number*, Entrega o ejemplar no muy reciente. *V.* NUMBER.
Back, *adv.* 1. Atrás o detrás. 2. De vuelta, de retorno. *Give me back my money*, Vuélvame Vd. mi dinero. *When will you come back?* ¿Cuando volverá Vd.? 3. Otra vez o segunda vez. Este adverbio, colocado después de un verbo, tiene en general el sentido de retrocesión o del prefijo español re. *To beat back*, Rechazar (al enemigo). *To hold* o *keep back*, Retener. *To come back*, Volver otra vez, volver atrás o de nuevo.
Back, *va.* 1. Montar a caballo; montar un caballo por primera vez. 2. Sostener, apoyar; justificar, favorecer. 3. Mantener, soportar.
Back, *inter.* (abrev. de *go back*). ¡Atrás! ¡Vuélvanse Vds.!
Backbite [bac'-bait], *va.* Murmurar, hablar mal del que está ausente; difamar, desacreditar.
Backbiting [bac'-bait-ing], *s.* Detracción, difamación.
Back-board [bac'-bōrd], *s.* 1. (Mar.) Respaldo o escudo de bote. 2. Respaldo, forro, materia delgada empleada en los espaldares de los espejos, cuadros, etc.
Backbone [bac-bōn'], *s.* 1. Hueso dorsal, espinazo. 2. Firmeza, decisión, principio moral. (Fam.)
Backdoor [bac'-dōr], *s.* Puerta trasera.
Backdown [bac'-daun], *s.* (Fam.) Cesión; rendición; palinodia.
Backed [bact], *a.* 1. Lo que tiene dorso o espalda. 2. Apoyado, sostenido, autorizado.
Backer [bak'-ẹr], *s.* 1. Sostenedor, el que secunda o apoya a otro en una contienda. 2. Apostador (en las carreras de caballos).
Backfire [bac'-fair], *s.* 1. Incendio provocado para contener el avance de otro. 2. Explosión prematura, o en el escape, de motores de explosión. 3. Explosión hacia atrás de una arma de fuego.—*va.* Explotar prematuramente. (fig.) Resultar contraproducente.
Backgammon [bac-gam'-un], *s.* Juego de chaquete. *Backgammon-board*, Tablas reales. (Mex.) Pretera.
Background [bac'-graund], *s.* 1. Fondo. 2. Historial, antecedentes. 3. Cualidades, requisitos, calificaciones.
Backhanded [bac-hand'-ed], *a.* 1. Referente al revés de la mano. 2. Falto de sinceridad, irónico. *A backhanded compliment*, Un cumplimiento poco sincero. 3. Inclinado a la izquierda; v. g. *Backhanded letters*, hablando de la letra de una persona. 4. De revés. *A backhanded blow*, Golpe de revés.
Backhouse [bac'-haus], *s.* 1. Trascuarto. 2. El común, la necesaria.
Backing [bak'-ing], *s.* 1. Apoyo dado a una persona o causa. 2. Retroceso. 3. Refuerzo (encuadernación). 4. Respaldo, forro, materia que forma el espaldar de alguna cosa.
Backlog [bac'-leg], *s.* 1. Leño trasero en una hoguera. 2. (Com.) Pedidos pendientes por llenar.
Backpiece [bac'-pīs], *s.* Espaldar, armadura para cubrir la espalda.
Backset [bac'-set], *s.* Contratiempo, revés, infortunio; recaída.
Backshop [bac'-shep], *s.* 1. Trastienda, el cuarto o pieza que está más adentro de la tienda. 2. Trasero (de animal).
Backside [bac-said'], *s.* 1. Espalda, la parte de atrás de cualquier cosa. 2. Trascorral o trasero. 3. Trascorral, sitio cercado que hay después del corral en las casas.

Backslide [bac-slaid'], *vn.* 1. Resbalar o caer hacia atrás; torcerse; apostatar; tergiversar. 2. Recaer, hablando moralmente.
Backslider [bac-slaid'-ẹr], *s.* 1. Apóstata. 2. Reincidente.
Backsliding [bac-slaid'-ing], *s.* Apostasía; reincidencia.
Backstaff [bac'-staf], *s.* Instrumento para medir la altura del sol en el mar.
Backstage [bac'-stêj], *s.* (Teat.) Parte del escenario oculta a la vista del público.—*adv.* Entre bastidores.
Backstairs [bac'-stārz], *s. pl.* Escalera excusada, secreta.
Backstays [bac'-stêz], *s. pl.* (Mar.) Brandales, ramales que mantienen los masteleros fijos, para que no caigan hacia proa. *Shifting backstays,* (Mar.) Brandales volantes. *Backstay-stools,* (Mar.) Mesetas de los brandales.
Backstitch [bak'-stich], *s.* Pespunte, punto-atrás, puntada hecha clavando la aguja la mitad del largo de la puntada precedente. *To backstitch, va.* y *vn.* Pespuntear, coser al pespunte.
Backstop [bac'-stop], *s.* 1. (Beisbol) Mampara colocada detrás del *home* para detener la pelota. 2. Cualquier cosa a que se recurra con propósitos similares.
Backstroke [bac'-strōc], *s.* En natación, brazada de dorso.
Backsword [bac'-sōrd], *s.* Sable, alfanje.
Backtrack [bac'-trac], *va.* y *vn.* Seguir un rastro o huella en sentido inverso.
Back-up light [bac'-up lait], *s.* Luz blanca para marcha atrás.
Backward, Backwards [bac'-ward, wardz], *adv.* 1. Prepósteramente, con lo de atrás delante; de espaldas, atrás. *To walk backwards,* Andar de espaldas, o caminar hacia atrás. 2. Hacia atrás, hablando de lugar o tiempo. 3. Atrasadamente. *To go backward and forward,* Ir y venir, adelantar y retroceder.
Backward, *a.* 1. Opuesto, enemigo; el que hace alguna cosa de mala gana. 2. Lerdo, pesado, tardo, lento, negligente, perezoso.
Backwardly [bac'-ward-li], *adv.* Con repugnancia, de mala gana.
Backwardness [bac'-ward-nes], *s.* Torpeza, pesadez, tardanza, negligencia. Atraso.
Backwash [bac'-wash], *s.* 1. Estela, agua removida por hélices o remos. 2. Agitación resultante de algún acontecimiento.
Backwater [bac'-wē''-tẹr], *s.* 1. Agua que repele una rueda hidráulica. 2. Remanso, agua estancada (de un río).
Backwoods [bac'-wuds], *s.* Región apartada de los centros de población o situada en fronteras lejanas, por lo general cubierta total o parcialmente de bosques.
Backwound, *va.* *V.* BACKBITE.
Bacon [bê'-cun], *s.* Tocino; la carne salada del puerco. *Flitch of bacon,* Hoja de tocino. *Gammon of bacon,* Jamón, pernil. *Rusty bacon,* Tocino rancio.
Bacteria [bac-tí'-ria], *s. pl.* Bacterias.
Bacterial [bac-tí'-ri-al], *a.* Bacterial, bactérico, perteneciente a las bacterias.
Bactericidal [bac-tí-ri-sai'-dal], *a.* Destructor de las bacterias.
Bactericide [bac-tí'-ri-said], *s.* *V.* GERMICIDE.
Bacteriological [bac-tí-ri-o-loj'-i-cal], *a.* Perteneciente a la bacteriología.
Bacteriologist [bac-ti-ri-ol'-o-jist], *n.* Bacteriólogo, el que se dedica al estudio de la bacteriología.
Bacteriology [bac-ti-ri-ol'-o-ji], *s.* Bacteriología, la ciencia que trata de las bacterias.
Bacterium [bac-tí'-ri-um], *s.* Singular de BACTERIA.
Bad [bad], *a.* 1. Mal, malo. 2. Perverso. 3. Infeliz, desgraciado. 4. Nocivo, dañoso. 5. Indispuesto, malo. *To be bad of a fever,* Estar con calentura. *From bad to worse,* De mal en peor.
Bad, Bade [bad]. Pretérito del verbo *To bid.*
Badge [baj], *s.* Divisa, señal, distintivo, símbolo. *Badge of honour,* Divisa de honor. *Badges of the stern and quarters,* (Mar.) Escudos de popa.
Badge, *va.* Divisar, señalar con divisa.
Badgeless [baj'-les], *a.* Sin divisa o señal.
Badger [baj'-ẹr], *s.* 1. Tejón, animal cuadrúpedo. 2. (Prov. Ingl.) Vivandero, regatón de víveres.
Badger, *va.* Molestar, cansar, fatigar, fastidiar.
Badger-legged [baj'-ẹr-legd], *a.* Patituerto o estevado.
Badinage [bad'-i-nêj, ba-di-nazh'], *s.* Gracejo, jocosidad, burla, chanza, chacota; cháchara.
Badly [bad'-li], *adv.* Mal o malamente.
Badminton [bad'-min-tẹn], *s.* *Badminton,* juego parecido al tenis.
Badness [bad'-nes], *s.* Maldad, falta de bondad, sea en lo físico o en lo moral; mala calidad de una cosa.
Baffle [baf'-l], *va.* Frustrar, interponiendo obstáculos, hacer inútil; eludir, huir de la dificultad.—*vn.* Engañar, burlarse.
Baffler [baf'-lẹr], *s.* Engañador, el que elude.
Bag [bag], *s.* 1. Saco, talega. 2. Bolsita o vejiguilla en la que algunos animales tienen jugos particulares, como la víbora el veneno, y la algalia el licor así llamado; ubre, teta (de vaca, de cabra, de oveja). 3. (Ant.) Bolsa que solían llevar los hombres para contener la coleta de la peluca. 4. Saco, talego o talega, término que se usa para significar la cantidad determinada de alguna cosa, como cuando con el nombre de una *talega* designamos la cantidad de mil duros. *Game-bag,* Morral, zurrón. *Cinnamon-bag,* Churla de canela. *Cigar-bag,* Petaquilla, cigarrera. *To pack up bag and baggage,* Liar el hato, liar el petate, tomar el tole.
Bag, *va.* 1. Ensacar, meter alguna cosa en sacos. 2. Entalegar, meter alguna cosa en talego o talega.—*vn.* 1. Abotagarse, hincharse. 2. Hacer bolsa o pliegue (una prenda de vestir).
Bagatelle [bag-a-tel'], *s.* Bagatela, cosa de poca sustancia y valor, futesa, fruslería.
Baggage [1] [bag'-êj], *s.* 1. (E. U.) Equipaje (de un viajero); se llama *luggage,* en la Gran Bretaña. 2. Bagaje, equipaje de tropa. 3. †Armatoste, desecho. *Baggage check,* Contraseña de equipaje. *Baggage car,* Carro furgón, de equipaje. *Baggage wagon,* Furgón.
Baggage, [2] *s.* Zorra, pelleja, (Fam.) coqueta; maula, buena alhaja.
Bagging [bag'-ing], *s.* Tela basta; arpillera.
Bagnio [ban'-yō], *s.* 1. Lupanar, burdel. 2. Casa de baños; baño. 3. Mazmorra de los esclavos en Turquía.
Bagpipe [bag'-paip], *s.* Gaita.
Bagpiper [bag'-paip-ẹr], *s.* Gaitero.
Bah [bā], *inter.* ¡Bah! exclamación de desprecio o enfado.
Bail [1] [bêl], *s.* 1. Caución, fianza; caución juratoria; fianza carcelera. 2. El fiador o abonador de otro. *On bail,* Bajo fianza. *To give bail,* Sanear.
Bail, [2] *s.* 1. Asa (de un cubo, de una caldera, etc.). 2. División entre los compartimentos de un establo. 3. (Ingla.) Mojón, mojonera. 4. Achicador; cubo o vertedor para achicar.
Bail *va.* 1. Dar fianza o salir fiador por otro. 2. Poner en libertad bajo fianza. 3. Desaguar, vaciar un estanque, achicar un bote. *To bail out,* Vaciar; (Aer.) Lanzarse en paracaídas.
Bailable [bêl'-a-bl], *a.* El que puede ser puesto en libertad bajo fianza; caucionable.
Bail-bond [bêl'-bond], *s.* Fianza de excarcelación; escritura de fianza.
Bailee [bêl-í'], *s.* (For.) Depositario, el que recibe cierta propiedad mueble en depósito.
Bailer [bêl'-ẹr], *s.* (For.) El que es fiador de otro.
Bailey [bê'-li], *s.* Patio exterior de un castillo o cualquier patio de una fortaleza. *Old Bailey,* El tribunal central de lo criminal en Londres.
Bailie o **Baillie** [bê'-li], *s.* Alcalde, baile, magistrado municipal en Escocia.
Bailiff [bê'-lif], *s.* 1. Alguacil, corchete, ministro inferior de justicia cuya obligación es prender o ejecutar prisiones. 2. Mayordomo.
Bailment [bêl'-ment], *s.* (For.) 1. Depósito, entrega de alguna cosa a tercera persona. 2. Acción de procurar la libertad de un preso bajo fianza.
Bailiwick [bêl'-i-wik], *s.* Alguacilazgo; mayordomía.
Bailor [bêl'-er], *s.* (For.) Fiador; el que da fianza por otro.
Bairn [bārn], *s.* Niño; hijo o hija de cualquier edad, descendiente: es voz escocesa.
Bait [bêt], *va.* 1. Cebar, dar cebo a los animales, para engordarlos, o atraerlos. 2. Azuzar, incitar á los perros para que ataquen; molestar, hostigar, acosar, fatigar.—*vn.* 1. Hacer parada o alto para tomar un refrigerio. Dar un pienso a los animales en el camino. 2. Aletear, mover las alas con violencia. 3. Atraer, incitar.
Bait, *s.* 1. Cebo, la comida que se echa a los animales para atraerlos; anzuelo, añagaza, señuelo. 2. Cebo, el formento de algún afecto o pasión; añagaza. 3. Refrigerio o refresco que se toma en los descansos que se hacen en una jornada. 4. Pienso, el alimento que se da a los animales. *To take the bait,* Tragar el anzuelo, caer en un lazo.
Baize [bêz], *s.* Bayeta, tela basta de lana. *Scarlet baize,* Bayeta de grana. *Long-napped baize,* Bayeta de pellón. *Green baize,* Tapete verde.

Bake [bêk], *va.* 1. Cocer en horno. 2. Desecar, endurecer, calcinar. *The earth is baked by the heat,* La tierra está desecada por el calor.—*vn.* Hornear, ejercer el oficio de hornero. *Baked meat,* Guisado, carne guisada o cocida al horno.
Bakehouse [bêk'-haus], *s.* Horno, panadería.
Bakelite [bê'-ke-lait], *s.* Bakelita, resina sintética.
Baker [bê'-kẹr], *s.* Hornero, panadero. *A baker's dozen,* Trece por doce, docena de fraile.
Bakery [bê'-kẹr-i], *s.* Panadería, tahona.
Baking [bêk'-ing], *s.* Hornada; cocimiento.
Baking-pan [bêk'-ing-pan], *s.* Tortera o tartera.
Baking powder [bêk'-ing pau'-dẹr], *s.* Polvo de hornear, levadura en polvo.
Baking soda [bêk'-ing sō'-da], *s.* Bicarbonato de sosa o de soda.
Bakshish [bak'-shish], *s.* Propina en los países orientales. Se escribe también **Backsheesh.** (Per.)
Balance [bal'-ans], *s.* 1. Balanza, el peso compuesto de fiel, brazos y platillos. 2. Cotejo de una cosa con otra. 3. Equilibrio; balance. 4. Volante de reloj. 5. (Astr.) Libra, el séptimo signo del zodíaco. *The balance of an account,* Saldo de una cuenta, o el bilance, balance o ajuste final de ella. *Balance sheet,* Balance. *Balance weight,* Contrapeso. *Balance wheel,* Rueda catalina, volante, péndulo de reloj. *To strike a balance,* Hacer o pasar balance.
Balance, *va.* 1. Equilibrar, tener en equilibrio; igualar en peso, en poder, etc. 2. Balancear, contrapesar. 3. Dar finiquito, saldar, satisfacer el alcance que resulta de una cuenta. 4. Pesar en balanza; pesar, considerar, examinar.—*vn.* 1. Estar en equilibrio; ser iguales en peso. 2. Balancear, dudar, estar perplejo en la resolución de alguna cosa. 3. Balancearse, agitarse, menearse de acá para allá.
Balancing [bal'-an-sing], *s.* Equilibrio; la acción de pesar. *Balancing-pole,* Balancín, contrapeso de los volatines y funámbulos.
Balas ruby [bal'-as rū-bi], *s.* Balaje, rubí espinela de color vinoso.
Balausta [ba-lēs'-ta ó ba-laus'-ta], *s.* Balaustra, fruto con el cáliz adnato, y que contiene numerosas semillas; p. ej. el del granado silvestre.
Balbriggan [bal-brig'-an], *s.* Especie de tejido de punto para ropa interior.
Balcony [bal'-co-ni], *s.* 1. Balcón, plataforma rodeada de un antepecho de madera, piedra o hierro, que proyecta de una pared y suele ponerse delante de una puerta o ventana grande. 2. Galería de los teatros.
Bald [bōld], *a.* 1. Calvo, falto de pelo. 2. Escueto, pelado; desnudo, pelón, raído. 3. Soso, desabrido, grosero, sin elegancia ni dignidad. *A bald translation,* Una traducción grosera, sin elegancia.
Baldachin [bōl'-da-kin], *s.* (Arq.) Dosel, baldaquín.
Balderdash [bōl'-dẹr-dash], *s.* (Fam.) 1. Disparate, jerga, jerigonza. 2. Menjurje, mezcolanza, especialmente de licores.
Baldhead [bōld'-hed], *s.* Calvo, sin pelo en la cabeza.
Baldly [bōld'-li], *adv.* Chabacanamente, groseramente.
Baldness [bōld'-nes], *s.* Calvez, calvicie, falta de pelo en la cabeza.
Bald-pate, Bald-pated [bōld'-pêt, ed], *a.* Tonsurado; calvo. *Baldpate,* Cabeza pelada; dícese de los frailes.
Baldric [bōl'-dric], *s.* 1. Zona, banda o faja. 2. (Astr.) Zodíaco.
Bale [bêl], *s.* 1. Bala o fardo de mercaderías. 2. Bala de papel que contiene diez resmas. 3. (Ant.) Calamidad, miseria. *Bale of fire,* Lumbrada, luminaria, fuego.
Bale, *vn.* Embalar, empaquetar, enfardar.—*va.* (Mar.) Achicar, sacar el agua del bote.
Baleen [ba-līn'], *s.* (Ant.) Ballena.
Balefully [bêl'-ful-i], *adv.* Desgraciadamente, tristemente.
Balize [ba-līz'], *s.* Valiza, boya o señal que se pone en algunos puntos del mar o de los ríos para indicar a las embarcaciones que hay peligro.
Balk [bōk], *s.* 1. Viga, madera larga y gruesa. 2. Lomo entre surcos. 3. Chasco, contratiempo, suceso contrario a lo que se esperaba. 4. Deshonor; desgracia. 5. Agravio, perjuicio.
Balk, Baulk, *va.* 1. Frustrar o dar chasco, faltar a la palabra. 2. Amontonar en un bulto o lomo. 3. (Ant.) Pasar, omitir, desaparroquiar una tienda.—*vn.* Pararse obstinadamente; quedarse detenido; dícese de las caballerías.
Balky [bōk'-i], *a.* Obstinado, porfiado, dispuesto a plantarse; aplícase más a las caballerías que se detienen de pronto y se niegan a seguir andando.
Ball [bōl], *s.* 1. Bola, cuerpo redondo de cualquiera materia, globo. *Eye-ball,* Globo del ojo. 2. Pelota. 3. Bala. *Snow-ball,* Bola de nieve. *Wash-ball,* Bola de jabón. *Printer's ball,* Bala de impresor. *The ball of the thumb,* Eminencia en la base del dedo pulgar. *Ball of the foot,* Eminencia carnosa en la base del dedo grueso del pie. 4. Baile, festejo en que se juntan varias personas para bailar. *Fancy ball,* Baile de trajes, en el que los concurrentes se presentan disfrazados. *Dress ball,* Sarao; baile serio, o de etiqueta. *Masquerade ball,* Baile de máscaras. *Ball-bearings,* Cojinete de bolas (de acero).
Ballad [bal'-ad], *s.* Balada o balata, canción; jácara, romance.
Ballad-maker, Ballad-writer [bal'-ad-mê'-kẹr, rai'-tẹr], *s.* Coplero, coplista, jacarista, escritor de canciones.
Ballad-monger [bal'-ad-mung-gẹr], *s.* Coplero, el que trafica en baladas, coplas o canciones.
Ballad-singer [bal'-ad-sing-ẹr], *s.* Jacarero, cantor de jácaras o baladas.
Ballad-tune [bal'-ad-tiūn], *s.* Entonación o aire de balada.
Ballast [bal'-ast], *s.* 1. Lastre, el peso que se echa en el fondo del navío para que navegue. 2. (F. C.) Cascajo, balaste, arena y pedrisco para terraplenar. *To go in ballast,* Ir en lastre. *Washed ballast,* Lastre lavado o guijarro. *Ballast lighter,* Lanchón de deslastrar. *Ballast ports,* Portas de lastrar.
Ballast, *va.* 1. Lastrar, echar lastre al navío. 2. Hacer o tener alguna cosa firme. (F. C.) Balastar, afirmar.
Ballasting [bal'-ast-ing], *s.* 1. El acto de lastrar o de balastar. 2. Material para terraplenes; balaste; afirmación. (Mar.) Lastre.
Ballerina [bū-lê-rī'-nā], *s.* Bailarina de ballet. *Ballerina-length dress,* Vestido de noche que llega un poco más arriba del tobillo.
Ballet [bal-é'], *s.* Ballet, baile clásico.
Ballistic missile [bą-lis'-tic mis'-il] *s.* (Mil.) Proyectil balístico.
Ballistics [ba-lis'-tics], *s.* Balística.
Balloon [bal-lūn'], *s.* Globo. *Balloon tire,* Llanta o neumático balón.
Balloonist [bal-lūn'-ist], *s.* Aeronauta.
Ballot [bal'-et], *s.* 1. Balota, bolilla o haba para votar. 2. Papeleta impresa o manuscrita que sirve para votar. 3. La acción de votar. *Ballot-box,* Urna electoral; urna de escrutinio.
Ballot, *vn.* 1. Balotar, votar con balotas. 2. Votar, en general; ejercer el derecho de sufragio.
Ballplayer [bōl'-plê-ẹr], *s.* Jugador de pelota.
Ball-point pen [bōl'-point pen], *s.* Pluma de bola, pluma esferográfica, pluma atómica.
Ballroom [bōl'-rūm], *s.* Salón de baile.
Ballyhoo [bal'-i-hū], *s.* Bombo, exagerada publicidad.—*va.* Dar bombo, anunciar algo exageradamente.
Balm [bām], *s.* 1. Bálsamo, el jugo o licor que se saca de un arbusto que se llama también *bálsamo.* 2. Bálsamo, cualquier ungüento precioso y fragrante. 3. Bálsamo, lo que mitiga y suaviza. *Balm of Gilead,* Bálsamo de Canarias. 4. (Bot.) Balsamita mayor, toronjil. *Balm-gentle,* Melisa.
Balm, *va.* 1. Embalsamar. 2. Mitigar, suavizar, calmar.
Balmy [bām'-i], *a.* 1. Balsámico, lo que tiene las cualidades del bálsamo y lo que produce bálsamo. 2. Balsámico; untuoso; lo que mitiga y suaviza. 3. Fragrante. 4. (Fig.) Calmante, dulce, suave, reparador. *Balmy sleep,* Sueño reparador.
Balneal [bal'-nẹ-al], **Balneary** [bal'-nẹ-ẹ-ri], *a.* Balneario, perteneciente a los baños públicos, o al baño.
Balsam [bōl'-sam], *s.* 1. Bálsamo, substancia oleosa, resinosa y aromática que se extrae de ciertas plantas y árboles. *Balsam of Copaiba,* Bálsamo de Copaiba. *Balsam of Peru,* Bálsamo del Perú, o del Salvador. *Balsam of Tolu,* Bálsamo de Tolú, ó de María. *Copal balsam,* Bálsamo de copal. Liquidámbar Styraciflua. *Canada balsam* (*balsam of fir*), Bálsamo (o terebentina) del Canadá. 2. Planta anual de jardín, con hermosas flores; balsamina. Impatiens balsamina.
Balsam-apple [bōl'-sam-ap-l], *s.* (Bot.) Balsamina.
Balsamic, Balsamical [bōl-sam'-ic, al], *a.* Balsámico; untuoso; lo que mitiga y suaviza.
Balsamine [bōl'-sa-min], *s.* Balsamina, planta anua de dos o tres pies de altura, tallos sarmentosos, hojas hendidas en tiras, flores pequeñas y fruto oval, carnoso y de color naranjado. En inglés tiene la balsamina de jardín los nombres de *Lady's-slipper* y *Touch-me-not.* En español se la llama también, según las diferentes localidades, Madamas, Adornos, Miramelindos, etc.
Baluster [bal'-us-tẹr], *s.* Balaustre, columna pequeña. *Balusters of a*

ship, (Mar.) Balaustres, pilares de madera colocados en el balcón de popa.
Balustrade [bal-us-trêd'], *s.* Balaustrada.
Bamboo [bam-bū'], *s.* Bambú. (Bot.) Bamboa, especie de caña o junco. Bambusa arundinacea.
Bamboozle [bam-bū'-zl], *va.* (Vulg.) Engañar; burlar, cansar.
Bamboozler [bam-bū'-zlẹr], *s.* (Vulg.) Engañador, el que engaña.
Ban [ban], *s.* 1. Bando, el acto de publicar algún edicto, ley o mandato; noticia pública dada a voz de pregonero; anuncio. 2. Excomunión. 3. Entredicho. 4. *Ban of the empire*, Bando del imperio, censura pública por la cual se suspenden los privilegios de algún príncipe del imperio. *Bans of marriage*, Amonestaciones, monición, proclama de casamiento que se hace antes de contraer matrimonio. En este sentido la manera de escribirlo más común y preferida es *banns*.
Ban, *va.* y *vn.* Maldecir, execrar.
Banal [ban'-al], *a.* 1. Trivial, vulgar, banal, insignificante. 2. Que pertenece al servicio feudal.
Banality [ba-nal'-i-ti], *s.* 1. Trivialidad, banalidad. 2. En tiempos pasados, derecho del señor feudal a obligar a sus vasallos a que usaran su molino, lagar, etc.
Banana [ba-nan'-a], *s.* (Bot.) Plátano, planta arbórea de gran tamaño que se cría en los países cálidos, cuya fruta se come. Banana, fruta del banano. *Banana-tree*, Banano, plátano.
Banc [banc], *s.* Banco de la justicia. *Court in banc*, Reunión completa de un tribunal cuando todos los jueces, o casi todos, están presentes.
Band [band], *s.* 1. Venda, tira o faja, que sirve para atar o ligar alguna cosa cubriéndola. 2. Cadena o ramal, con que se sujeta algun animal. 3. Enlace, unión o conexión de unas cosas con otras. 4. Cuadrilla, gavilla, junta de muchas personas para algún fin o intento. *Band of music*, Orquesta. *Band in a church*, Capilla. 5. Alzacuello, especie de cuello o corbata que usan los clérigos, abogados, legistas y estudiantes. 6. Filete o listón. *Bands*, Fajas del arzón de una silla. 7. Banda de soldados. *Band-saw*, Sierra de hoja sin fin, sierra continua.
Band, *va.* 1. Congregar, unir o juntar. 2. Vendar, atar o ligar con venda.—*vn.* Asociarse.
Bandage [ban'-dêj], *s.* 1. Venda, tira o faja, que sirve para atar o ligar alguna cosa cubriéndola. 2. Vendaje, venda o faja, que se pone a algún miembro herido, roto o dislocado.
Bandanna [ban-dan'-a], *s.* (Com.) Bandana, pañuelo grande de colores vivos con manchas o figuras.
Bandbox [band'-box], *s.* Caja de cartón, para sombreros, encajes, cintas y cosas de poco peso.
Bandelet [ban'-de-let], *s.* (Arq.) Fajita.
Bander [ban'-dẹr], *s.* El que se une con otros.
Banderole [ban'-dẹ-rōl], *s.* Banderola, bandera pequeña.
Bandit [ban'-dit], *s.* Un bandido o salteador de caminos. *Banditti*, Bandidos, bandoleros.
Bandmaster [band'-mas-tẹr], *s.* Músico mayor (de banda militar).
Bandog [ban'-deg], *s.* Mastín, perro grande y fornido.
Bandoleers, *s. pl.* *V.* CARTRIDGE.
Bandoline [ban'-do-lin], *s.* Bandolina, líquido espeso, adherente y perfumado, para fijar y asentar el pelo.
Bandore [ban-dōr'], *s.* Bandurria, instrumento de música semejante al laúd.
Bandrol [band'-rol], *s.* *V.* BANDEROLE.
Bandstand [band'-stand], *s.* Plataforma para banda de música.
Bandwagon [band'-wag-un], *s.* Vehículo para banda de música. *To get on the bandwagon*, Adherirse a una candidatura probablemente triunfante.
Bandy [ban'-di], *s.* Palocorvo, especie de palo para botar una pelota.
Bandy, *va.* 1. Botar la pelota con palocorvo. 2. Pelotear, arrojar una cosa de una parte a otra.—*vn.* Contender, discutir, examinar atentamente; ligarse; cambiar. *To bandy compliments*, Cumplimentarse mutuamente.
Bandyleg [ban'-di-leg], *s.* Pierna zamba.
Bandylegged [ban'-di-legd], *a.* Patizambo, el que es zambo de piernas.
Bane [bên], *s.* 1. Veneno, tósigo. *Rat's bane*, Arsénico. *Wolf's bane*, Acónito. 2. Ruina, destrucción, peste, muerte. *Henbane*, Beleño (Hyoscyamus).
Baneful [bên'-ful], *a.* Venenoso, destructivo, mortal, funesto, mortífero.
Banefulness [bên'-ful-nes], *s.* Calidad venenosa o perniciosa.
Banewort [bên'-wūrt], *s.* (Bot.) Cualquier planta venenosa, especialmente la belladona, la hierbamora, y la francesilla (Ranunculus flammula), a la cual se supone venenosa para el ganado lanar.
Bang [bang], *va.* 1. Lanzar, arrojar, golpear, con ruido. 2. Cascar, dar a uno con la mano, dar de puñadas, sacudir, zurrar.—*vn.* 1. Hacer estrépito; dar con ruido una cosa contra otra. 2. Saltar.
Bang, *va.* Cortar el cabello de la frente al través, casi en línea recta.
Bang, *s.* 1. Puñada, golpe que se da con el puño. 2. Ruido de un golpe. 3. El cabello corto que se peina sobre la frente y la cubre en parte. (Se llama *fringe* en Inglaterra.)
Bang, *adv.* Con un golpe violento; estrepitosamente, estruendosamente.
Bangle [bang'-gl], *s.* Brazalete delgado de la India oriental, y de África.
Banian [ban'-yan], *s.* Se escribe también *banyan.* 1. (Bot.) Baniano, árbol de la India y de la Persia, cuyas ramas se inclinan hasta llegar al suelo, donde se reproducen, echando raíces. Un solo árbol puede cubrir así algunos acres de terreno. Es la higuera india. Ficus indica. 2. El natural de la India oriental de la clase comerciante. 3. (Anglo-Ind.) Bata, ropa talar, prenda de vestir holgada y cómoda.
Banish [ban'-ish], *va.* Desterrar, echar a alguno de su propio país o territorio; expeler, echar fuera, despedir; deportar.
Banisher [ban'-ish-ẹr], *s.* El que destierra.
Banishment [ban'-ish-mẹnt], *s.* Destierro, la acción y efecto de desterrar.
Banister, *s.* *V.* BALUSTER.
Banjo [ban'-jo], *s.* Banjo, instrumento músico de cinco cuerdas, algo parecido a la bandurria y la guitarra. (Corrupción de *bandore*). Es instrumento predilecto de los negros norteamericanos.
Bank [bank], *s.* 1. Orilla, ribera, márgen, o banda de río. 2. Banco o montón de tierra. 3. Banco de remeros en una galera. 4. Banco, el sitio, paraje o casa donde se deposita el dinero con interés o sin él. 5. Banco, la compañía de los individuos que gobiernan el banco; directores del banco. *Bank-note*, Cédula o billete de banco, papel moneda del banco. 6. Dique. 7. Eminencia. *Bank of the sea*, Escollo, banco de arena. 8. (Mús.) Teclado; hilera de teclas (piano y órgano). *Savings-bank*, Caja de ahorros.
Bank, *va.* 1. Poner dinero en un banco. 2. Aislar o detener el agua con diques, o construirlos. 3. *To bank up a fire*, Cubrir el fuego (como con cenizas o tierra).—*vn.* Tener por banquero. *We bank with D. & Co.*, D. y Cía. son nuestros banqueros.
Bankable [bank'-a-bl], *a.* Recibidero por un banco.
Bankbill [bank-bil'], *s.* Billete, vale o cédula de banco.
Banker [bank'-ẹr], *s.* Banquero, cambista.
Banking-house [bank'-ing-haus], *s.* Casa de banquero, banco particular.
Bankrupt [bank'-rupt], *a.* Insolvente.—*s.* Quebrado, fallido, el que hizo bancarrota o quiebra.
Bankrupt, *va.* Quebrar, declararse insolvente.
Bankruptcy [bank'-rupt-si], *s.* Bancarrota, quiebra de un comerciante u hombre de negocios.
Bank-stock [bank'-stec], *s.* Acción de banco.
Banner [ban'-ẹr], *s.* Bandera, insignia, estandarte.
Banner [ban'-ẹr], *va.* Asignar una bandera o estandarte a; proveer de una bandera.—*a.* Digno de llevar la bandera; primero en dignidad.
Banneret [ban'-ẹr-et], *s.* 1. Caballero con derecho a enarbolar bandera en vez de pendón. 2. Bandera pequeña.
Bannerol [ban'-ẹr-ōl], *s.* Bandera pequeña. *V.* BANDEROL.
Banns, *s.* Amonestaciones. *V.* BAN.
Banquet [ban'-cwet], *s.* Banquete, comida espléndida a que concurren muchos convidados; festín.
Banquet, *va.* Banquetear, dar banquetes o concurrir a ellos.
Banquet-house [ban'-cwet-haus], **Banqueting-house** [ban'-cwet-ing-haus], *s.* Casa de banquetes o convites.
Banqueting [ban'-cwet'-ing], *s.* El acto de banquetear.
Banquette [bań-ket'], *s.* 1. (Fort.) Banqueta, banco corrido de tierra o mampostería, desde el cual pueden los soldados disparar a cubierto, detrás de muralla o parapeto. 2. (E. U. del Sur) Acera. 3. Andén de un puente; tongada en una trinchera (trabajos de ingeniería).
Banshee [ban'-shi], **Benshie** [ben'-shi], *s.* Una especie de duende cuyos lamentos son precursores de la muerte. (Irlanda y Escocia.)
Bantam [ban'-tam], *s.* Gallina pequeña de Bantam, distrito de Java.
Bantamweight [ban'-tam-wêt], *s.* (Boxeo) Peso gallo.
Banter [ban'-tẹr], *va.* Zumbar o zumbarse, dar chasco o vaya a alguno; divertirse a costa de alguno.
Banter, *s.* Zumba, vaya, burla chasco, petardo.

Banterer [ban'-tẹr-ẹr], *s.* Zumbón, el que se zumba, da vaya o chasco; burlón.

Bantling [bant'-ling], *s.* Chicuelo o chicuela, criatura racional pequeña y de poca edad. (Es corrupción de *bandling*, criatura envuelta en pañales.)

Banyan, *s.* Baniano. *V.* BANIAN.

Baobab [bé'-o-bab], *s.* Baobal, árbol corpulento del África central.

Baptism [bap'-tizm], *s.* Bautismo, el primero de los sacramentos de la Iglesia; bautizo, acción de bautizar.

Baptismal [bap-tiz'-mal], **Baptistical** [bap-tis'-ti-cal], *a.* Bautismal, lo perteneciente al sacramento del bautismo.

Baptist [bap'-tist], *s.* 1. El que administra al bautismo. *Saint John the Baptist,* San Juan Bautista. 2. Anabaptista, el sectario que sostiene que no debe bautizarse a los niños hasta que lleguen a la edad de la razón.

Baptistery [bap'-tis-tẹ-ri], *s.* Bautisterio, baptisterio, sitio donde está la pila bautismal.

Baptize [bap-taiz'], *va.* Bautizar.

Bar [bār], *s.* 1. Palenque, barra, pedazo de madera u otra cosa atravesada para impedir la entrada en alguna parte. 2. Barra de metal, lingote. 3. Reja de una ventana, de una cárcel. 4. Tranca de puerta o ventana; barrote. 5. Impedimento, obstáculo. 6. Barra o banco de arena en un río o a su embocadura, o en la entrada de algún puerto. 7. (Mús.) Barra, raya perpendicular a las del pentagrama. La música que queda entre dos barras también se llama *bar.* 8. Estrados, foro, tribunal, el lugar en que se sientan los jueces para examinar y decidir las causas. 9. Conjunto de abogados en el tribunal; por extensión, la profesión del foro. 10. (For.) Excepción perentoria a alguna alegación. 11. Mostrador o banco de las tabernas, botillerías o cafés en donde se recibe el dinero. *Bar-maid,* Criada de taberna o café. 12. Venda, varilla ancha, o raya: como *bar of colour,* faja de color; *bar of light,* raya de luz. 13. Barandilla que separa al público de los vocales de una asamblea. *Bar iron,* Hierro en barras. *Bar of gold,* Lingote de oro. *Bar loom,* Telar de barras. *In bar of,* Como excepción perentoria. *To be admitted to the bar* (E. U.), *to be called to the bar* (Ingla.), Recibirse de abogado.

Bar, *va.* 1. Atrancar, cerrar con barras. 2. Impedir, obstar, estorbar, prohibir; exceptuar, excluir. *To bar in a harbour,* (Mar.) Encadenar la boca de un puerto. *To bar out,* Excluir, cerrar la puerta a.

Barb [bārb], *s.* 1. Púa que en los anzuelos y dardos proyecta en dirección opuesta a la punta, para impedir que ésta salga fácilmente de la herida; lengüeta de saeta o flecha. 2. (Bot.) Barba, arista de espiga. 3. Caballo berberisco o de Berbería. 4. (Des.) Barda, arnés o armadura de caballo.

Barb, *va.* 1. Armar flechas con lengüetas; hacer incisivo, mordaz, picante. 2. (Des.) Guarnecer a un caballo con barda.

Barbadoes [bār-bé'-dōz], *s.* Barbada, una de las Antillas. *Barbadoes leg,* Mal de la Barbada, elefantiasis.

Barbadoes cherry [bār-bé'-dōz cher'-i], *s.* (Bot.) Guinda de Indias.

Barbadoes tar [bār-bé'-dōz tār], *s.* Especie de petróleo o betún.

Barbarian [bār-bé'-ri-an], *s.* 1. Hombre bárbaro o salvaje. 2. Extranjero. 3. Hombre cruel o inhumano. —*a.* Bárbaro; en griego, no helénico; inculto.

Barbaric [bār-bar'-ic], *a.* Extranjero, exótico, lo que viene de lejos; bárbaro, inculto.

Barbarism [bār'-ba-rizm], *s.* 1. Barbarismo, vicio contra las reglas y pureza del lenguaje. 2. Barbaridad o barbarie, falta de cultura o política. 3. Crueldad, inhumanidad. 4. Ignorancia.

Barbarity [bār-bar'-i-ti], *s.* 1. Barbaridad, falta de cultura. 2. Ferocidad, inhumanidad, crueldad. 3. Barbarismo.

Barbarize [bār'-ba-raiz], *va.* Barbarizar.—*vn.* Cometer barbarismos, viciar el lenguaje.

Barbarous [bār'-ba-rus], *a.* 1. Bárbaro, salvaje, inculto. 2. Bárbaro, que emplea barbarismos en el lenguaje; no purista; no idiomático. 3. Cruel, inhumano. 4. Extranjero. 5. De sonido áspero y bronco.

Barbarously [bār'-ba-rus-li], *adv.* 1. Bárbaramente, ignorantemente. 2. Bárbaramente, con barbarismo. 3. Inhumanamente, cruelmente.

Barbarousness, *s.* *V.* BARBARISM.

Barbary [bār'-ba-ri], *s.* 1. Caballo berberisco. 2. Berbería.

Barbate [bār'-bét], *a.* 1. Barbado, que tiene púas, lengüetas, pelos o plumas. 2. (Bot.) Barbado, aristado.

Barbecue [bār'-be-kiū], *va.* Aderezar, guisar o cocer un animal entero, sin despedazarle. (Mex.) Hacer barbacoa.

Barbecue, *s.* Animal guisado sin despedazarle; barbacoa, (Amer.) carne asada en un hoyo que se abre en tierra y se calienta como los hornos. *A barbecue-pig,* Un cochinillo en barbacoa.

Barbed [bārbd], *a.* 1. Barbado, armado con lengüetas, como las saetas, flechas, etc. 2. Bardado, armado con barda. *V.* BARD, *va.* *Barbed wire,* Alambre de púas (para cercas).

Barbel [bār'-bel], *s.* 1. Uno de los apéndices blandos y filiformes, o barbillas, que crecen en las mandíbulas de ciertos peces. 2. Barbo, pez de río.

Barbell [bār'-bel], *s.* Haltera.

Barber [bār'-bẹr], *s.* Barbero, el que tiene por oficio afeitar o hacer la barba.

Barber, *va.* Afeitar y cortar el pelo.

Barberess [bār'-bẹr-es], *sf.* Barbera.

Barber-surgeon [bār'-bẹr-sūr'-jun], *s.* (Ant.) Barbero cirujano, flebotomiano.

Barberry [bār'-bẹr-i], *s.* (Bot.) Bérbero, berberís, agracejo, cualquiera planta del género Berberis; arbusto.

Barbet [bār'-bet]. 1. Ave tropical de brillantes colores; barbudo, ave trepadora. 2. Variedad del perro de lanas. 3. Larva de un insecto que se alimenta de pulgones.

Barbital [bār'-bi-tal], *s.* (Quím.) Barbital.

Barbiturate [bār-bit'-tiu-rét] (Quím.) Barbitúrico.

Barbican [bār'-bi-can], *s.* 1. Barbacana, fortificación, que en lo antiguo se colocaba delante de las murallas y después se llamó falsabraga. 2. Tronera, abertura que se hace en un parapeto para apuntar y disparar la artillería.

Barcarolle [bār'-ca-rōl], *s.* 1. Barcarola, canción popular de los gondoleros italianos. 2. Composición musical del mismo carácter y puramente instrumental.

Bard [bārd], *s.* 1. Poeta, bardo. 2. Barda, antigua armadura con que cubrían a los caballos. 3. *Bards,* Las lonjas de tocino con que cubren las aves para asarlas. 4. Pez, mustela de río.

Bard, *va.* 1. Guarnecer a un caballo con barda. 2. Guarnecer con lonjas delgadas de tocino.

Bardic, Bardish [bārd'-ic, ish], *a.* Lo pertenece a los bardos o poetas, o lo que ellos dicen o escriben.

Bare [bār], *a.* 1. Desnudo, falto de vestido o abrigo. 2. Descubierto, raso, pelado. 3. Liso, llano; sencillo, simple. 4. Descubierto, público. 5. Desnudo, pobre. 6. Mero, puro. 7. Raído, gastado, usado. 8. Puro, solo, no mezclado ni unido con otra cosa. *Bare of money,* Sin un cuarto, sin blanca, sin dinero. *To lay bare,* Desnudar, poner a descubierto. *To be bare of,* Estar desprovisto de. *A bare account,* Un relato pobre, sin interés, sin adorno.

Bare, *va.* Desnudar, descubrir, privar, despojar.

†**Bare** o **Bore,** pretérito del verbo *To bear.*

Barebacked [bār'-bact], *a.* Sin silla, p. ej. un caballo. *Bareback, a.* Montado en pelo, sobre un caballo desensillado.—*adv.* Sin silla o albarda, quitado el aparejo.

Barebone [bār'-bōn], *s.* Esqueleto, la persona muy flaca.

Bareboned [bār'-bōnd], *a.* Muy flaco, descarnado, amojamado, acecinado.

Barefaced [bār'-fést], *a.* Descarado, desvergonzado, impudente, insolente, atrevido, cara de vaqueta.

Barefacedly [bār-fést'-li], *adv.* Descaradamente, con descaro; con la cara descubierta, sin empacho ni miedo, al descubierto.

Barefacedness [bār-fést'-nes], *s.* Descaro, desvergüenza, atrevimiento, insolencia, impudencia.

Barefoot, Barefooted [bār'-fut, ed], *a.* Descalzo.

Barege (Fr.) [ba-rézh'], *s.* 1. Barés, tela de lana muy fina. 2. Agua mineral de los manantiales de Barèges, pueblo de Francia.

Bareheaded [bār'-hed-ed], *a.* Descubierto, con la cabeza al aire, sin sombrero ni gorra.

Barelegged [bār'-legd], *a.* Descalzo.

Barely [bār'-li], *adv.* Meramente, simplemente, puramente, solamente, únicamente; pobremente.

Barenecked [bār'-nect], *a.* El que tiene el cuello desnudo.

Bareness [bār'-nes], *s.* 1. Desnudez, falta de vestido, desabrigo. 2. Flaqueza, falta de gordura. 3. Laceria, desnudez andrajosa.

Bareribbed [bār'-ribd], *a.* Muy flaco.

Bargain [bār'-gen], *s.* 1. Ajuste, contrato, convenio, pacto, trato o concierto de compra ó venta. 2. Compra o venta. 3. Ganga, chiripa. *A bargain,* Sea, convengo, queda hecho. *At a bargain,* Baratísimo, por una bicoca, por casi nada. *To give into the bargain,* Dar de más, de contra, de ñapa. (Mex.) Dar de pilón o de ganancia. *To strike a bargain, make a bargain,* Cerrar un trato, efectuar una compra.

Bargain, *vn.* Pactar, ajustar, hacer contrato o convenio sobre la venta

de alguna cosa; negociar, contratar; regatear, concertar.
Bargainee [bār-gen-ī'], *s.* El que admite o acepta algún ajuste, pacto o convenio.
Bargainer [bār'-gen-ęr], *s.* La persona que propone algún ajuste, pacto o convenio.
Barge [bārj], *s.* 1. Alijador, lanchón de descarga, bote de fondo chato para la navegación en los puertos. 2. Falúa o faluca, bote muy adornado. 3. Gabarra, barco de transporte.
Bargeman [bārj'-man], **Barger** [bār'-jęr], *s.* Barquero, el que gobierna o dirige un barco.
Baric [bar'-ic], *a.* 1. De bario, o que lo contiene. 2. Perteneciente al peso, especialmente del aire; barométrico.
Barilla [ba-rīl'-a], *s.* 1. Barrilla, un carbonato impuro de sosa, obtenido quemando varias especies de plantas que crecen en los terrenos salitrosos. 2. Barrilla, cualquier planta cuyas cenizas dan la sosa.
Barite [bé'-rait], *s.* Baritina, sulfato de bario. *V.* Barytes.
Baritone [bar'-i-tōn], *a.* *V.* Barytone.
Barium [bé'-ri-um], *s.* (Quím.) Bario, el metal de barita.
Bark [bārk], *s.* 1. Corteza, la parte exterior del árbol. *Peruvian bark,* Quina. *Angustura bark,* Corteza de Angustura. 2. Barco, barca, embarcación pequeña. *Bark-louse,* Insecto de escama que infesta los árboles. *Oyster-shell bark-louse,* Mytilaspis; se llama así por la forma de su escama, semejante a la concha de la ostra. *Tanner's oak-bark,* Casca, corteza del roble para el curtido de las pieles.
Bark [bārk], *s.* Ladrido del perro; latido de la zorra; aullido del lobo.
Bark, *va.* 1. Descortezar, quitar la corteza al árbol. 2. Raer, raspar, quitar raspando la piel u otra cubierta exterior. 3. Cubrir, dar una capa de corteza. Curtir o teñir en un infusión de corteza. 4. Aturdir o matar la caza menuda tirando a la corteza a la cual se agarra.—*vn.* 1. Ladrar, el perro. 2. Ladrar, vocear; latir, gañir como perro o zorra.
Barkeeper [bār-kīp'-ęr], *s.* (E. U.) El que sirve bebidas a los parroquianos sobre el mostrador de un café, tienda de vinos o taberna; tabernero.
Barker [bārk'-ęr], *s.* 1. Ladrador. 2. Descortezador.
Barking [bārk'-ing], *s.* Ladrido.
Barky [bārk'-i], *a.* Cortezudo, lo que tiene mucha corteza.
Barley [bār'-li], *s.* Cebada, planta de las gramíneas y su grano. (Hordeum.) *Barley bread,* Pan de cebada. *Barley broth,* Caldo hecho con cebada; calducho. *Barley water,* Agua de cebada. *Barley mow,* Montón de cebada. *Pearl barley,* Cebada perlada.
Barleycorn [bār'-li-cērn], *s.* 1. Grano de cebada. 2. Una medida que es la tercera parte de la pulgada.
Barley-sugar [bār'-li-shug'-ar], *s.* 1. Azúcar clarificado con cebada. 2. Alfeñique, azúcar preparado con cáscara de limón.
Barm [bārm], *s.* Jiste, el fermento de la cerveza; levadura, el fermento del pan.
Barmecide [bār'-mę-said], *a.* Semejante al festín imaginario que dió el príncipe Barmecida al mendigo en "*Las Mil y Una Noches*"; ilusorio, fantástico.
Barmy [bārm'-i], *a.* Que tiene jiste o levadura.
Barn [bārn], *s.* Granero, henil, pajar. (Mex.) Troje.
Barn-door [bārn'-dōr], *s.* La puerta del granero.
Barn-floor [bārn'-flōr], *s.* Era, pajar.
Barn-owl [bārn'-aul], *s.* Lechuza, zumaya (Strix flammea). *Barn-swallow,* Golondrina que hace su nido entre las vigas de los graneros.
Barn-yard [bārn'-yārd], *s.* Patio de granja.
Barnacle [bār'-na-cl], *s.* 1. Broma, escaramujo, especie de caracolillo marino que se adhiere al casco de las embarcaciones; cualquier crústaceo cirrípedo, especialmente el *Goose-barnacle,* Anatifa o Lepas Balanus. 2. Bernicla, branta o ánsar de Escocia, ave semejante al ganso. 3. Acial, instrumento con el cual los herradores sujetan a los caballos para herrarlos. *Barnacles,* (Vulg.) Antecojos, antiparras.
Barograph, Barometrograph [bar'-o-grqf, bar''-o-met'-ro-grqf], *s.* Barógrafo, barometrógrafo, instrumento que registra y deja anotadas las variaciones de la presión atmosférica, de modo que puedan conocerse sin que sea necesaria la presencia de un operador u observador.
Barometer [ba-rem'-ę-tęr], *s.* Barómetro, instrumento para pesar la presión de la atmósfera. *Aneroid barometer,* Barómetro aneroide. *Barometer reading,* Indicación del barómetro.
Barometrical [bar-o-met'-ri-cal], *a.* Barométrico.
Baron [bar'-un], *s.* 1. Barón, nombre de dignidad inferior a la de vizconde. 2. (For. Ant.) Varón, el marido en contraposición a la mujer. *A baron of the Exchequer,* Un juez de la tesorería. *The lord chief baron,* El primer juez de la tesorería. *Baron of beef,* Solomo, filete.
Baronage [bar'-un-ẹj], *s.* Baronía, la dignidad de barón.
Baroness [bar'-un-es], *sf.* Baronesa, la mujer del barón.
Baronet [bar'un-et], *s.* Título de honor inferior al de barón y superior al de caballero; es el último grado de los hereditarios en Inglaterra.
Baronetage [bar'-un-et-ẹj], *s.* La dignidad de *Baronet.*
Baronetcy, Baronetship [bar'-un-et-si, ship], *s.* La dignidad o patente de barón; dominio o territorio de un barón, baronía.
Baronial [ba-rō'-ni-al], *a.* Baronial, perteneciente a barón o baronía.
Barony [bar'-o-ni], *s.* Baronía, señorío de barón.
Baroscope [bar'-o-scōp], *s.* Especie de barómetro; higrómetro.
Barouche [ba-rūsh'], *s.* Birlocho, carruaje de cuatro asientos.
Barracan [bar'-a-can], *s.* Barragán, especie de camelote basto.
Barrack [bar'-ac], *s.* Cuartel, edificio en que se alojan los soldados. *Barrack-master,* Superintendente o jefe de cuartel.
Barracoon [bar-a-cūn'], *s.* Barracón, cobertizo para negros apresados en la costa africana.
Barracuda [bar-a-cū'-da], *s.* Barracuda o esfirena, pez de cuerpo prolongado, parecido al sollo; becuna. Sphyræna picuda.
Barrage [ba-rāzh'], *s.* 1. Dique de contención. (Mil.) 2. Barrera de fuego. 3. Andanada. *Barrage balloon,* Globo cautivo para formar barreras.
Barrator [bar'-a-tęr], *s.* Pleitista, camorrista, el que con ligero motivo mueve y ocasiona contiendas y pleitos; trapacero, altercador. (For. mar.) Empleado de a bordo culpable de baratería.
Barratry [bar'-a-tri], *s.* 1. (For.) Pleito, o demanda fraudulenta. 2. Engaño, trapacería. 3. (Com.) Baratería, la pérdida causada a los dueños de un barco, o sus aseguradores, por dolo o malicia del capitán o tripulación.
Barrel [bar'-el], *s.* 1. Barril o barrica, vasija de madera que sirve para conservar licores y otros géneros. 2. Cañón de escopeta. 3. Cañón de pluma. 4. Cañón de bomba. 5. Tímpano del oído. 6. (Mar.) Cuerpo o eje de cabrestante o molinete. 7. Huso. *V.* Fusee. 8. Caja de tambor. *Barrel-organ,* Organillo de cilindro.
Barrel, *va.* Embarrilar, poner alguna cosa dentro de un barril. *To barrel up,* Envasar.
Barrelled [bar'-reld], *pp.* Embarrilado, entonelado. *Double-barrelled gun,* Escopeta de dos cañones.
Barren [bar'-en], *a.* Estéril, infructuoso, erial, infecundo, infructífero.
Barrenly [bar'-en-li], *adv.* Infructuosamente, estérilmente.
Barrenness [bar'-en-nes], *s.* Esterilidad, infructuosidad, infecundidad; falta de ingenio o de invención; tibieza.
Barrenwort [bar'-en-wūrt], *s.* (Bot.) Epimedio, planta cuyas hojas se parecen a las de la hiedra.
Barrette [bā-ret'], *s.* Pasador o broche para el cabello.
Barricade, Barricado [bar-i-kéd', o], *s.* Barrera, empalizada, barricada, estacada, parapeto para defenderse de los enemigos.
Barricade, *va.* Barrear, empalizar, atrancar, cerrar con barricadas.
Barrier [bar'-i-ęr], *s.* 1. Barrera. 2. Fortaleza. 3. Impedimento, obstáculo, estacada, embarazo; término.
Barring [bār'-ing], *pa.* de *To Bar.* (*Expresión adverbial*) Amén de, aparte de, excepto.
Barrister [bar'-is-tęr], *s.* 1. Abogado, el que con título legítimo defiende en juicio por escrito o de palabra. (Amer.) Licenciado. 2. Curial.
Bar-room [bar'-rūm], *s.* Sala con mostrador donde se sirven licores y refrescos; taberna.
Barrow [bar'-o], *s.* 1. Angarillas. 2. Marrano o puerco. 3. Montón de tierra levantado en memoria de los que perecieron en una batalla; cementerio. *Barrow hog,* Berraco. *Barrow grease,* Pringue de cerdo. *Wheel-barrow,* Carretón o carretilla de una rueda. *Hand-barrow,* Angarillas de mano, litera.
Barshot [bār'-shet], *s.* (Mar.) Palanqueta, barreta de hierro con dos cabezas que suele servir como carga de cañón para destrozar los aparejos y palos del enemigo.
Bartender [bār-ten'-dęr], *s.* Cantinero.
Barter [bār'-tęr], *vn.* Baratar, trafagar o traficar permutando géneros. —*va.* Trocar, cambiar.
Barter, *s.* 1. Cambio, trueque. 2. Tráfico, el acto de traficar.
Barterer [bār'-tęr-ęr], *s.* Traficante.

Bartholomew-tide [bār-tel'-o-miū-taid], *s.* Temporada o días inmediatos al de San Bartolomé.
Bartlett [bārt'-let], *s.* Pera de Bartlett, variedad de pera muy estimada, oriunda de Inglaterra en 1770, de donde la llevó a América Enoch Bartlett, de Massachusetts.
Baryta [ba-rai'-ta], *s.* (Quím.) Barita u óxido de bario.
Barytes o **Barite** [ba-rai'-tīz, bé'-rait], *s.* Espato pesado, sulfato de bario.
Barytic [ba-rit'-ic], *a.* Barítico, lo perteneciente a la barita.
Barytone [bar'-i-tōn], *s.* 1. Barítono, voz media entre las de tenor y bajo. 2. Barítono, el que posee esta voz.
Barzah [bār'-zā], *s.* El portal de una casa árabe-africana que sirve como sala de recepción.
Basal [bé'-sal], *a.* Fundamental: lo que pertenece a la base o está situada en ella; básico.
Basal metabolism [bê-sal me-tab'-o-lizm], *s.* Metabolismo basal.
Basalt [ba-sōlt'], **Basaltes** [ba-sōl'-tīz], *s.* Basalto.
Basaltic [ba-sōl'-tic], *a.* Basáltico, que pertenece al basalto.
Base [bês], *a.* 1. Bajo, humilde, despreciable, vil, villano, ruin. 2. Bajo de ley, hablando del oro y plata. 3. Bajo, grave; hablando de instrumentos y voces. 4. Ilegítimo. 5. Vergonzoso, infame, indigno. 6. Poltrón, mandria, cobarde.
Base, *s.* 1. Fondo o suelo; base. 2. Basa, pedestal o basamento de columna o estatua. 3. Bajo, la cuerda que lleva este punto. 4. (Quím.) Base, substancia que puede unirse con un ácido, formando una sal; en la farmacia, ingrediente principal. 5. (Geom.) Base, parte inferior de una figura, de un sólido. 6. (Mús.) Bajo, grave. *V.* BASS. Voz de bajo. 7. Barrera o *base* en el juego de base-ball.
Base, *va.* 1. Envilecer, deteriorar. 2. Apoyar, fijar sobre alguna cosa, fundamentar, establecer.
Baseball [bês'-bōl], *s.* 1. Beisbol, juego de pelota con cuatro bases que indican la distancia que cada jugador debe procurar recorrer después de golpeada la pelota. Se considera el juego nacional de los E. U. 2. La pelota que se usa en este juego.
Base-born [bês'-bērn], *a.* 1. Bastardo, espurio, hijo natural. 2. Vil, bajo. *Base-burner, base-burning stove,* Estufa de alimentación automática.
Base-court [bês'-cōrt], *s.* Patio, el espacio que en algunas casas se deja al descubierto, empedrado o enlosado, y cerrado por paredes, columnas, galerías o corredores, detrás del patio principal.
Base hit [bês'-hit], *s.* En el beisbol, golpe del bateador a la pelota que le permite llegar a primera base.
Base-minded [bês'-main-ded], *a.* Ruin, vil, el que tiene bajos pensamientos.
Base-mindedness [bês'-main-ded-nes], *s.* Bajeza de ánimo, abyección.
Base o **Bass-viol** [bês'-vai'-el], *s.* Violón o violoncelo.
Baseless [bês'-les], *a.* Desfondado: sin apoyo, sin fondo; sin fundamento.
Basely [bês'-li], *adv.* Bajamente, con bajeza o vileza. *Basely born,* De vil cuna u origen.
Baseman [bês'-man], *s.* En el beisbol, cada uno de los jugadores que protegen las bases.
Basement [bês'-ment], *s.* (Arq.) Basamento. El cuarto bajo de una casa. En Madrid y algunas otras partes de España lo llaman *sótano vividero.*
Baseness [bês'-nes], *s.* 1. Bajeza, vileza, infamia, bastardía. 2. Ilegitimidad de nacimiento. 3. Avaricia, mezquinería, tacañería.
Base string [bês'-string], *s.* (Mús.) Bajo segundo.
Bashful [bash'-ful], *a.* Vergonzoso, modesto, tímido, corto, encogido; esquivo.
Bashfully [bash'-ful-i], *adv.* Vergonzosamente, modestamente.
Bashfulness [bash'-ful-nes], *s.* Vergüenza, modestia, timidez, cortedad; esquivez.
Basic [bê'-sic], *a.* Básico, relativo a una base química, u otra.
Basic English [bê'-sic in'-glish], *s.* Inglés básico.
Basify [bê'-si-fai], *va.* Convertir en base por medios químicos.
Basil [baz'-il], *s.* 1. (Bot.) Albahaca. 2. (Carp.) Filo achaflanado de escoplo o cepillo. 3. Badana, la piel curtida del carnero u oveja.
Basilic [ba-sil'-ic], *s.* (Anat.) Basílica, la vena media o central del brazo.
Basilic, Basilical [ba-sil'-ic, al], *a.* 1. (Anat.) Lo que pertenece a la vena basílica. 2. Real, regio.
Basilica [ba-sil'-i-ca], *s.* 1. (Arq.) Originalmente en Atenas, un pórtico que servía como tribunal de justicia. 2. Basílica, iglesia o templo magnífico; iglesia principal.
Basilicon [ba-sil'-i-con], *s.* Basilicón, ungüento amarillo de resina.
Basilisk [bas'-i-lisc], *s.* 1. Basilisco, animal fabuloso. 2. Basilisco, pieza antigua de artillería.
Basin [bê'-sn], *s.* 1. Jofaina o aljofaina, bacía, palangana, lebrillo, vasija en que se echa agua para varios usos. 2. Reserva de un dique, reserva o concha de un puerto; arca de agua o depósito, estanque. 3. Cavidad de la pelvis. 4. Tazón de una fuente. 5. Platillo de balanza. 6. Vasija redonda de que usan como molde los ópticos y sombrereros. 7. Cuenca de un río. 8. Hoya, valle extenso, cuyo fondo comunmente contiene agua. Formación geológica cuyas capas se inclinan interiormente hacia el centro. 9. Pilón de fuente o surtidor. 10. Represa de un molino. 11. Taza más grande que las usuales; tazón.
Basined [bê'-snd], *a.* Situado o encerrado en una hoya u hondonada.
Basinet [bas'-i-net], *s.* Bacinete, capacete, pieza de la armadura antigua que cubría la cabeza.
Basis [bê'-sis], *s.* 1. Basa, el fundamento de cualquier cosa. 2. Basa de columna, pedestal. 3. Base, fundamento.
Bask [basc], *va.* Asolear, calentar alguna cosa al sol.—*vn.* Ponerse a tomar el sol.
Basket [bas'-ket], *s.* Cesta, canasta; cesto, cestón; espuerta, cuévano, capacha, capacho. *Wicker basket,* Cuévano, cesta o canasta de mimbres. *A basket coach,* Carrito de junco. *Basket-ball,* Juego parecido al de la pelota de viento, pero lo juegan también las jóvenes. Sus metas son cestos de hierro y red. *Basket-work,* (1) Trabajos o tejido hechos con mimbres, o una imitación de cestería en metal. (2) (Mil.) Cestón, cestonada, tejido de mimbres o ramas lleno de tierra que sirve como defensa. *Basket-hilt,* La guarnición de la espada o florete que cubre toda la mano. (Prov.) La taza de la espada. *Basket-maker,* Cestero. *Basket-making,* Cestería. *Basket-salt,* Sal gema filtrada en cestas.—*sf. Basket-woman,* Cestera, la mujer del cestero o la que vende cestas.
Basketball [bas'-ket-bōl], *s. Basketball,* baloncesto.
Basketful [bas'-ket-ful], *s.* Cestada.
Bason [bê-sn], *s. V.* BASIN.
Basque [basc], *a.* 1. Vascongado, da. 2. La lengua del país vascongado, vascuence, éuscaro. 3. Jubón, ajustador, prenda de vestir que usan las mujeres, semejante a una chaqueta. Su nombre viene probablemente del traje de las vascongadas.
Bass [bas] o **Striped bass** [straipt-bas], *s.* Lobina, pez delicioso.
Bass [bês], *a.* (Mús.) Bajo, grave. *Bass* o *bass-viol,* Violoncelo. *Double-bass,* Contrabajo; bordón.
Bass [bas], †**Bassock** [bas'-ec], *s.* 1. Esparto. 2. Estera de iglesia.
Bass [bas], *s.* 1. *V.* BASSWOOD. 2. *V.* BAST.
Bass-relief [bas-re-līf'], **Basso-relievo** [bas'-o-re-lī'-vo], *s.* Bajo relieve, especie de escultura: llámase también algunas veces *low relief.*
Basset [bas'-et], *s.* Baceta, en el juego de naipes. *Basset-horn,* Clarinete de tenor.
Basset, *vn.* (Min.) Apoyarse; dícese de los ramos de metales o lechos de piedras que estriban sobre otros.
Bassinet [bas'-i-net], *s.* 1. Cuna de mecer niños. 2. (Mil.) Bacinete, almete.
Basso [bas-sō], *s.* 1. Bajo, el que canta con voz de bajo. 2. La parte baja, bajo. (It.)
Bassoon [bas-sūn'], *s.* (Mús.) Bajón, instrumento de viento; fagot.
Basswood [bas'-wud], *s.* Tilo americano, llamado también *whitewood-tree* (árbol de madera blanca).
Bast [bast], *s.* 1. Corteza interior textil del tilo y otros árboles. 2. Estera, cuerda, etc., hecha con esta corteza.
Bastard [bas'-tard], *s.* 1. Bastardo, espurio, la persona procreada fuera de legítimo matrimonio. 2. (Mar.) Vela grande de galera para navegar con poco viento.
Bastard, *a.* 1. Bastardo, ilegítimo. 2. Bastardo, degenerado. lo que degenera de su origen y naturaleza.
Bastardize [bas'-tard-aiz], *va.* 1. Probar que alguno es bastardo. 2. Procrear hijos bastardos. 3. Depravar, alterar, bastardear.
Bastardly [bas'-tard-li], *adv.* Como bastardo.
Baste [bêst], *va.* 1. Apalear, cascar, dar golpes con palo o bastón en las plantas de los pies. 2. Pringar o untar la carne en el asador. 3. Hilvanar, asegurar con hilo lo que se ha de coser después. 4. Bastear.
Bastile [bas-tīl'], *s.* Castillo, fortaleza, prisión.
Bastinade, Bastinado [bas-ti-nêd' o nā'-do], *s.* Paliza, zurra de palos en las plantas de los pies; bastonazo, bastonada.
Bastinade, Bastinado, *va. V.* BASTE.
Basting [bês'-ting], *s.* 1. Hilván. 2. (Fam.) Apaleamiento, paliza.
Bastion [bas'-ti-un o bas'-chun], *s.* (Fort.) Bastión o baluarte.
Bat [bat], *s.* 1. Garrote o maza. 2. Murciélago. 3. (Beisbol) Bate.

Bat, *va.* Golpear o impeler con una maza o porra.—*vn.* Usar de una maza en cierto juego de pelota.

Bat, *va.* (E. U. y prov. en Inglaterra) Pestañear; moverse, agitarse.

Batable [bé'-ta-bl], *a.* Disputable, lo que se puede controvertir, disputar o defender por ambas partes.

Batavian [ba-té'-vi-an], *a.* Bátavo, va.

Bat-fowling [bat'-faul-ing], *s.* Caza de pájaros por la noche.

Batch [bach], *s.* 1. Cochura, hornada, la cantidad de pan que de una vez se cuece en el horno. 2. Número o cantidad de cosas que se reciben, se despachan o se coleccionan de una vez.

Bate [bét], *s.* Contienda, altercación, debate, disputa. *Make-bate*, Cizañero, soplón, cuentero; bufón.

Bate, *va.* 1. Minorar, disminuir. 2. Rebajar o bajar el precio de alguna cosa.—*vn.* Minorarse, mermar.

Bate, *va.* Remojar, como un cuero o piel; separar y ablandar, como henequén, jute.

Bateful [bét'-ful], *a.* Contencioso, controvertible.

Batement [bét'-mẹnt], *s.* Diminución, merma o menoscabo.

Bath [bạth], *s.* 1. Baño, cantidad suficiente de agua puesta en un receptáculo conveniente para lavarse, sea por gusto o por remedio. 2. Cuarto de baño; bañadera. *Hot baths*, Baños calientes o termas. *Cold baths*, Baños fríos. *Dry bath*, Estufa. *Water bath* o *balneum mariæ*, (Quím.) Baño de María, calentamiento del líquido contenido en una vasija poniendo esta dentro de otra que contiene agua caliente. *Sand bath*, Baño de arena, vasija con arena caliente en que se ponen retortas para la destilación de algún líquido. *Knight of the Bath*, o en abreviatura después de los nombres, K. B., Caballero de la orden del Baño, orden de caballería de Inglaterra.

Bath-brick [bạth-bric], *s.* Piedra para limpiar cuchillos. Toma su nombre de la ciudad de Bath en Inglaterra.

Bathe [bédh], *va.* Bañar, lavar en baño.—*vn.* Bañarse, estar en el baño.

Bathing [bé'-dhing], *s.* Baño, la acción de bañar o bañarse.—*a.* De baño. *Bathing beach*, Balneario, playa para bañarse. *Bathing resort*, Balneario. *Bathing suit*, Traje de baño.

Bathrobe [bạth'-rōb], *s.* Bata de baño.

Bathroom [bạth'-rūm], *s.* Cuarto de baño.

Bath-tub [bạth'-tub] (más usado) o **Bathing-tub** [bé'-dhing-tub], *s.* Baño, bañera, pieza grande de madera, metal o mármol para bañarse. (Mex.) Tina.

Bathos [bé'-thes], *s.* El estilo bajo en la poesía.

Bathymetry [ba-thim'-ẹ-tri], *s.* Batimetría.

Bathyscaphe [ba'-this-caf], *s.* Batíscafo.

Batik [bā-tīk'], *s.* Batik, arte malayo para teñir telas con cera.

Bating [bét'-ing], *prep.* Excepto, exceptuando, menos, fuera de, amen de.

Batiste [ba-tīst'], *s.* Batista, lino fino; olán. (Fr.)

Batlet [bat'-let], *s.* Paleta de lavandera.

Baton [bat'-un], *s.* 1. Bastón. 2. (Mus.) Batuta.

Baton [bat'-un], *va.* Bastonear, golpear con un bastón.

Batoon [ba-tūn'], *s.* 1. Clava o palo grande. 2. Bastón o insignia de mando. 3. (Her.) Señal de nacimiento ilegítimo en el escudo de armas. (Des.)

Batrachia [ba-tré'-ki-a], *s. pl.* Los batracios o anfibios, una de las clases de los vertebrados.

Batrachian [ba-tré'-ki-an], *a.* Batracio, relativo o perteneciente a las ranas.—*s.* Uno de los batracios.

Battalia [ba-tal'-ya], *s.* (Ant.) Orden de batalla, parte principal de un ejército.

Battalion [ba-tal'-yun], *s.* Batallón, un cuerpo de infantería.

Batten [bat'-n], *s.* Lata, tabla de chilla, listón de madera; alfajia, tablilla.

Batten, *va.* Construir con lata, tablillas, o tablas de chilla. *To batten down the hatches*, (Mar.) Cerrar las escotillas y asegurarlas con listones de madera.

Batten, *va.* 1. Cebar, dar cebo para engordar. 2. Reparar, rehacer, restablecer las fuerzas o el vigor perdido.—*vn.* Engordar, ponerse gordo; revolcarse.

Batter [bat'-ẹr], *va.* 1. Apalear, dar de palos, cascar, golpear. 2. Batir, cañonear; romper, desmenuzar; destruir, demoler, derribar.—*vn.* (Mec.) Hacer barriga o comba.

Batter, *s.* Batido, mezcla de varios ingredientes batidos y trabados; pasta culinaria.

Batter, *s.* El que da con la maza, o *bat*, en el juego de pelota llamado *base-ball* y otros.

Batter, *s.* 1. Golpazo; golpes repetidos. 2. Batidor de yeso. 3. (Tip.) Rotura o mutilación de los tipos o de una plancha. 4. Declive de un parapeto.

Batterer [bat'-ẹr-ẹr], *s.* Apaleador.

Battering-piece [bat'-ẹr-ing-pīs], *s.* (Art.) Pieza de batir. *Battering-ram*, Ariete, máquina usada en lo antiguo para demoler las murallas.

Battering-train [bat'-ẹr-ing-trén], *s.* Tren de batir, cureña de sitio.

Battery [bat'-ẹr-i], *s.* 1. (Elec.) Batería, acumulador. 2. (Mil.) Batería. 3. Violencia, asalto. *Battery cell*, Pila eléctrica.

Batting [bat'-ing], *s.* 1. Agramaje, espadillaje; (Cer.) moldeaje. 2. Algodón o lana en hojas o capas. 3. El acto de apalear, y la manera de usar un garrote o cachiporra. *Cotton batting*, Algodón en rama.

Battle [bat'-l], *s.* 1. Batalla, pelea general entre dos ejércitos, armadas o cuerpos numerosos de hombres, combate. 2. (Des.) El centro o la parte principal del ejército.

Battle, *vn.* Batallar, pelear en batalla, combatir.

Battle-array [bat'-l-a-ré'], *s.* Orden de batalla.

Battle-axe [bat'-l-ax], *s.* Hacha de armas.

Battledoor [bat'-l-dōr], *s.* Pala o raqueta, el instrumento que impele la pelota o volante. *Battledoor and shuttlecock*, La raqueta y el volante.

Battlefield [bat'-l-fīld], *s.* Campo de batalla.

Battlement [bat'-l-mẹnt], *s.* Muralla almenada o con almenas y boquillas.

Battle-piece [bat'-l-pīs], *s.* Cuadro que representa una batalla.

Battleship [bat'-l-ship], *s.* Acorazado.

Battling [bat'-l-ing], *s.* Conflicto, combate.

Battologize [bat-tel'-o-jaiz], *vn.* Repetir palabras inútil y enojosamente. (< Gr.)

Battology [ba-tel'-o-ji], *s.* Batología, repetición inútil de palabras.

Battue [bạ-tū'], *s.* 1. Batida, montería de caza mayor. 2. Matanza inexcusable. (Fr.)

Bauble, Bawble [bō'-bl], *s.* Chuchería, miriñaque, cosa de poca importancia, pero pulida y delicada; bujería.

Baulk, *vn.* *V.* Balk.

Bauxite [bok'-sait], *s.* Bauxita, compuesto de aluminio y óxido férrico.

Bavarian [ba-vé'-ri-an], *a.* y *s.* Bávaro, perteneciente a Baviera; natural de este reino.

Bavaroy [bav-a-rei'], *s.* Tudesco, especie de capote.

Bavin [bav'-in], *s.* Fagina, hacecillo de leña menuda.

Bawbee [bō-bī'], *s.* (Esco.) Medio penique (cinco céntimos).

Bawd [bōd], *s.* Alcahuete o alcahueta.

Bawd, *vn.* Alcahuetear, servir de alcahuete o alcahueta.—*va.* Ensuciar.

Bawdily [bō'-di-li], *adv.* Obscenamente.

Bawdiness [bō'-di-nes], *s.* Obscenidad; alcahuetería; suciedad.

†**Bawdrick** [bō'-dric], *s.* Cinturón; cuerda; tahalí. *V.* Baldric.

Bawdry [bō'-dri], *s.* Alcahuetería, el acto de alcahuetear.

Bawdy [bō'-di], *a.* Obsceno, impuro, torpe; sucio, impúdico, deshonesto, infame.

Bawdy-house [bō'-di-haus], *s.* Lupanar, burdel.

Bawl [bōl], *vn.* Gritar, vocear; úsase por desprecio; ladrar, chillar.—*va.* Pregonar; publicar a voces.

Bawler [bōl'-ẹr], *s.* Voceador, vocinglero, alborotador.

Bawsin, Bauson [bō'-sn], *s.* Tejón, animal cuadrúpedo. (Poco us.) *Bauson* es la forma preferida.

Bay [bé], *a.* Bayo, de color rojizo parecido al castaño; aplícase a los caballos.

Bay [bé], *s.* 1. Bahía, rada, puerto abierto donde se abrigan las embarcaciones. 2. Bahía, brazo de mar. 3. (Bot.) Laurel, planta. 4. La situación del que se halla rodeado de enemigos. *To be at bay*, Estar rodeado de enemigos; hallarse en el último aprieto; estar en el mayor peligro. *To keep at bay*, Tener a raya; contener; tener a distancia. 5. División de un edificio. Parte saliente de una ventana o un balcón en forma de mirador 6. Laurel, lauro, el premio de la victoria. 7. Compuerta.

Bay, *vn.* 1. Dar ladridos ahogados, como los del perro sobre la pista. 2. Balar.—*va.* 1. Encerrar. 2. Ladrar.

Bayard [bé'-ard], *s.* 1. Caballo bayo. 2. Bausán, boquiabierto.

Bayardly [bé'-ard-li], *a.* Estúpido, ciego.

Bayberry [bé'-bẹr-i], *s.* (Bot.) 1. Árbol de la cera, arbusto de las miriáceas. Mirica cerifera. 2. El laurel. (Laurus nobilis.)

Bayberry tallow [tal'-ō], *s.* Substancia que se obtiene del árbol de la cera.

Baying [bé'-ing], *s.* Ladrido; balido.

Bayonet [bé'-o-net], *s.* Bayoneta.

Bayou [bai'-ū], *s.* Canalizo: brazo de

río de escasa corriente, o volumen de agua casi estancada proviniente de una bahía o un lago, o que pone en comunicación dos masas de agua. (E. U. del Sur.)

Bay rum [bé' rum], *s.* Ron con aceite escencial de laurel o de malagueta.

Bay-salt [bé'-sōlt], *s.* Sal morena o sal marina.

Bay-window [bé'-win'-do], *s.* Ventana salidiza, mirador.

Bazaar, Bazar [ba-zār'], *s.* 1. Bazar, nombre que se da en Oriente a los mercados públicos. 2. Baño, lugar donde se encierra a los esclavos.

Bazooka [ba-sū'-ka], *s.* Lanzador portátil de proyectiles-cohete.

Bdellium [del'-i-um], *s.* 1. Bedelio, el árbol y la resina que éste produce. 2. Joya, tal vez perla, pero con más probabilidad el ámbar.

Be [bī], *vn.* 1. Ser, tener algún estado, condición o calidad. 2. Estar. 3. Tener, en algunas significaciones, v. g., *To be hungry*, Tener hambre. *To be* es el verbo auxiliar que sirve para formar la voz pasiva. *To be for*, Inclinarse a. *To be out*, Cortarse o perderse en alguna recitación, confundirse. *To be a great way off*, Estar muy distante. *To be off*, (Fam.) Tomar soleta, picar de soleta, irse a la francesa; echarse fuera; tomar las de Villadiego. *He is on and off*, Tan pronto quiere como no quiere. *To be up to everything*, Ser para todo, no asustarse por nada. *To be gone*, Irse, haberse ido. *To be being*, Estarse haciendo. *Secret meetings were being held*, Se estaban celebrando juntas secretas. *To let, a house that is being finished in Third Street*, Se alquila una casa que se está acabando, o está para acabarse, en la Calle Tercera.

Be-, *prefijo.* Por; cerca de; sobre; en rededor. Sirve para hacer verbos activos de los neutros; para hacer más intenso el sentido del verbo: para formar verbos de adjetivos o sustantivos, etc.

Beach [bīch], *s.* Costa, ribera, playa, orilla; cabo.

Beach, *va.* Impelir a la playa, o arrastrar sobre ella.—*vn.* Desembarcar en una playa o costa.

Beachhead [bīch'-hed], *s.* Cabeza de playa.

Beachy [bīch'-i], *a.* Que tiene riberas o playas.

Beacon [bī'-cn], *s.* (Mar.) Faro, fanal, valiza, almenara, señal que se pone o que se hace para dirigir a los navegantes u otros.

Beaconage [bī'-cn-ēj], *s.* Valizaje, derecho que se paga para mantener los fanales, valizas o almenaras.

Beaconed [bī'-cund], *a.* Lo que tiene valizas o almenaras.

Bead [bīd], *s.* 1. Cuenta, cada una de las bolitas ensartadas, que componen el rosario. 2. Cuenta o cuentas, bolitas ensartadas que llevan las mujeres como collar para adorno. 3. Cualquier cuerpo globoso. 4. Ornamento formado de una hilera de cuentas. *Glass bead*, Mostacilla, chaquira, abalorio. *Steel beads*, Abalorios de acero. 5. (Carp.) Filete, nervio, astrágalo. 6. (Arq.) Perla. 7. (Joy.) Grano, perla, cuenta. 8. Burbuja, espuma sobre un líquido. *To draw a bead on*, Apuntar cuidadosamente con un arma de fuego. *To tell*, o *say, one's beads*, Rezar el rosario.

Bead, *va.* 1. Adornar con abalorios. 2. Ensartar cuentas. 3. En tornería, hacer rizos o filetes en la madera.

Beading [bīd'-ing], *s.* 1. Guarnición o adorno de abalorios. (Arq.) Listón, pestaña, borde. 2. Preparación para formar espuma sobre licores. 3. Conjunto de cuentas o abalorios.

Bead-tree [bīd'-trī], *s.* (Bot.) Coco de Indias, el árbol con cuyas semillas se hacen los rosarios.

Beadle [bī'-dl], *s.* Pertiguero o macero en las catedrales; muñidor en las parroquias o cofradías; bedel en las universidades; y alguacil, ministro o ministril en los tribunales.

Beadleship [bī'-dl-ship], *s.* Bedelía.

Beadroll [bīd'-rōl], *s.* Catálogo o lista de los cofrades del rosario.

Beadsman [bīdz'-man], *s.* Hombre empleado en rezar por otros.

Beadwork [bīd'-wurk], *s.* 1. Abalorio. 2. (Arq.) Listón, reborde.

Beady [bīd'-i], *a.* 1. Parecido a cuentas. 2. Cubierto de cuentas. 3. Lo que tiene espuma o está cubierto de burbujas.

Beagle [bī'g'-l], *s.* 1. Sabueso, perro con el cual se cazan las liebres. 2. Alguacil. 3. Tiburón pequeño de ciertas especies.

Beak [bīc], *s.* 1. Pico, el extremo de la cabeza del ave que le sirve como de boca. 2. Pico o cañón de alambique. 3. (Mar.) Saltillo de proa; espolón de navío. 4. Pico, hocico, cualquiera cosa que remata en punta. 5. Cabo, promontorio.

Beaked [bīct], *a.* Picudo, lo que tiene pico; encorvado.

Beaker [bīk'-er], *s.* 1. Taza con pico. 2. (Quím.) Bocal con pico; vaso cilíndrico con fondo llano, de vidrio delgado; se usa en los análisis.

Beam [bīm], *s.* 1. (Arq.) Viga maestra de un edificio. 2. Astil, brazo del peso de cruz, de cuyos extremos penden las balanzas. 3. Madero cilíndrico, en el cual los tejedores arrollan la tela al paso que la van tejiendo; enjullo o vara de empaño. 4. Rayo de luz. 5. Lanza de coche. 6. ‖Rama de venado. 7. Brazos de balanza. *Beams*, (Mar.) Baos, vigas gruesas que mantienen firmes los costados del navío y sobre las cuales asientan las cubiertas. *Beams of the upper decks*, Baos de las cubiertas altas. *Aftermost beam*, Bao popero. *Foremost beam*, Bao proel. *Midship beam*, Bao maestro. *On the beam*, Por el través. *Before the beam*, Por la proa del través. *Abaft the beam*, Por la popa del través.

Beam, *vn.* Emitir o arrojar rayos.

Beaming [bīm'-ing], *a.* Radiante, que despide rayos de luz; luciente, luminoso; alegre, vivo.

Beamless [bīm'-les], *a.* Sin rayos.

Beamy [bīm'-i], *a.* 1. Radiante, lo que despide y arroja de sí rayos de luz. 2. Alegre, vivo. 3. Parecido a una viga; pesado como una lanza. 4. (Mar.) Que tiene baos anchos.

Bean [bīn], *s.* 1. Haba. 2. Judía, habichuela, fréjol, alubia. (Mex., Cuba) Frijol. *String beans*, (Mex.) Ejotes; habichuelas o judías tiernas o verdes.

Bean-fed [bīn'-fed], *a.* Alimentado con habas.

Bear [bār], *va.* (*pret.* BORE, *pp.* BORNE, o BORN). 1. Llevar alguna cosa como carga. 2. Llevar o mudar alguna cosa de una parte a otra. 3. Usar alguna insignia de autoridad o distinción. *To bear a crown*, Ceñirse una corona. 4. Cargar, llevar alguna cosa como carga; cargar con, imponerse una carga u obligación. *You shall bear the guilt*, Vd. cargará con la responsabilidad. 5. Sostener, apoyar, mantener alguna cosa para que no caiga. 6. Tener amor u odio a uno. 7. Padecer, sufrir, aguantar, soportar, tolerar. 8. Llevar, producir. 9. Parir, dar a luz. En este sentido, el part. pasado de *bear* es *born.* 10. Entretener, engañar. 11. Poseer poder u honra. 12. Animar, impeler. 13. (Com.) Hacer bajar el valor, jugar a la baja. *Bear a hand!* (Mar.) Vamos! pronto! *To bear a hand*, (Mar.) Socorrer pronto; coger, agarrar. *To bear back*, Retirarse, hacerse atrás. *To bear company*, Acompañar. *To bear date*, Llevar fecha, estar fechado. *To bear in mind*, Acordarse.—*vn.* 1. Padecer o sufrir algún dolor. 2. Aguantar, tolerar. 3. Tener virtud generativa, criar; llevar fruto. 4. Dirigirse o encaminarse a algún paraje determinado. *To bear and forbear*, Llevar y conllevar. *To bear away*, Vencer, sobrepujar. *To bear down*, Arrastrar; ahondar; tropezar, derribar, derrocar, echar por tierra. Hacer bajar por fuerza: dícese de la mujer que está de parto. *To bear off*, (1) Desviar el golpe o evitarle. (2) (Mar.) Hacerse mar adentro. *To bear in*, Ir a, dirigirse a. *To bear out*, Mantener, sostener, apoyar; sacar de paso; justificar, afirmar; avanzar. *To bear up*, Llevar, transportar, conducir, sostener; resistir; subir, crecer, elevarse, alzarse, sostenerse. *To bear up against*, Resistir, oponerse fuertemente, hacer esfuerzos contra alguna cosa, arrostrar, mantenerse tieso o firme. *To bear up to a ship*, Transportar a un navío. *To bear upon*, Estribar. *To bring to bear upon*, Apuntar los cañones contra. *To bear a good price*, Tener buen precio. *To bear a part*, Participar, tener parte. *To bear faith*, Ser fiel. *To bear likeness*, Parecerse. *To bear resemblance to*, Tener semejanza con, parecerse a. *To bear one a grudge, spite* o *ill-will*, Querer mal a alguno, tenerle ojeriza. *To bear one good-will*, Tener buena voluntad a alguno. *To bear sway* o *rule*, Gobernar, dominar, mandar, tener el poder en su mano. *To bear the charges*, Pagar los gastos, llevar las cargas. *To bear too hard upon one*, Tratar a alguno con sobrada dureza. *To bear with one*, Sufrir a alguno, perdonarle, ser indulgente para con él. *To bear witness*, Atestiguar, testificar, dar testimonio, ser testigo. *To bear away*, (Mar.) Arribar. *To bear away before the wind*, (Mar.) Arribar todo o amollar viento en popa. *To bear away large*, (Mar.) Arribar a escota larga. *To bear down on a ship*, (Mar.) Arribar sobre un bajel. *Past bearing*, Improductivo (hablando de árboles frutales y de animales); infecunda, la mujer que ha pasado la edad crítica.

Bear, *s.* 1. Oso, animal fiero. 2. Bajista, el jugador de bolsa que juega a la baja de los fondos públicos u otros valores. *Great and Little Bear*, (Astr.) Osa mayor y menor. 3. (Ento.) Oruga lanuda del *tiger-moth* (Deiopæa bella). *Brown bear*, Oso pardo. *White* o *polar bear*, Oso blanco. *Grizzly bear*, Oso gris de América. *The Bear*, Rusia.

Bearable [bār'-a-bl], *a.* Sufrible, soportable.

Bear-berry [bār'-ber-i], *s.* 1. (Bot.) Gayuba, hierba medicinal. Uva-ursi. 2. La "cáscara sagrada" de California y el arbusto que la produce. Se llama también *bearwood.*

Bear-binder [bēr'-bain-dęr], *s.* (Bot.) Correhüela.

Beard [bīrd], *s.* 1. Barba, el pelo que nace en la parte inferior de la cara. 2. Cara, rostro. 3. (Bot.) Arista de espiga. 4. Barba de flecha.

Beard, *va.* 1. Desbarbar, agarrar a uno por la barba, arrancarle las barbas. 2. Hacer frente, subirse á las barbas; oponerse fuertemente.

Bearded [bīrd'-ed], *a.* 1. Barbado, el que tiene barbas. 2. Barbado, lo que tiene barbas o aristas, como el maíz y otras espigas de grano. 3. Armado con lengüetas, como la saeta, etc.

Beardless [bīrd'-les], *a.* 1. Imberbe, joven; barbilampiño. 2. Derraspado: se dice del trigo.

Bearer [bār'-ęr], *s.* 1. Portador, el que lleva o trae alguna cosa. 2. Faquín, el que sirve para llevar cargas. 3. Sepulturero. 4. Árbol frutífero. 5. Apoyo, lo que sostiene alguna cosa, sostén, gancho, soporte. *A cross-bearer,* Crucífero o crucero. *An ensign-bearer,* Portaestandarte.

Bear-garden [bār'-gār-dn], *s.* Corral, foso o patio donde se tienen osos para diversión del público.—*a.* Rústico, rudo.

Bear-herd [bār'-hęrd], *s.* Guarda de osos, el que los cuida.

Bearing [bār'-ing], *s.* 1. Situación, colocación de una cosa respecto de otra. 2. Saledizo. 3. Porte exterior, maneras, presencia. 4. Donaire, aire; gracia. 5. Relación, conexión, fuerza, valor de una expresión. *I do not see the bearing of that remark,* No veo la fuerza de esa observación. 6. (Mec.) Manga de eje, cojinete, soporte. 7. (Arq.) Apoyo, apuntalamiento. 8. (Top.) Ángulo formado en el punto de observación entre el meridiano magnético y el objeto; orientación. 9. (Agr.) Fruto. *Armorial bearing,* (Her.) Escudo de armas. *Past bearing,* Insufrible, inaguantable, insoportable, demasiado.

Bearish [bār'-ish], *a.* Rudo, áspero, feroz como un oso.

Bearlike [bār'-laic], *a.* Semejante o parecido al oso.

Bear's-breech [bārz'-brich], *s.* (Bot.) Branca ursina, acanto.

Bear's-ear [bārz'-īr], *s.* (Bot.) Oreja de oso. Primula auricula.

Bear's-foot [bārz'-fut], *s.* (Bot.) Eléboro negro. Helleborus fœtidus.

Bearskin [bār'-skin], *s.* Piel de oso, especie de peletería.

Bearwood [bār'-wud], *s.* Nombre común del arbusto cuya corteza es la "cáscara sagrada" de California.

Bearwort [bār'-wūrt], *s.* (Bot.) *V.* BALDMONEY.

Beast [bīst], *s.* 1. Bestia, animal cuadrúpedo. 2. Animal irracional, a distinción del hombre. *Beast of burden,* Bestia de carga, acémila. 3. Bestia, hombre brutal. *Wild beast,* Bestia feroz, fiera.

Beastlike [bīst'-laic], *a.* Bestial, abrutado.

Beastliness [bīst'-li-nes], *s.* Bestialidad, brutalidad, suciedad.

Beastly [bīst'-li], *a.* Bestial, brutal, irracional; sucio.—*adv.* Brutalmente, bestialmente.

Beat [bīt], *va.* 1. Apalear, golpear, sacudir, dar de palos. 2. (Mús.) Llevar el compás. 3. Batir el soto o el monte. 4. Batir, mezclar unas cosas con otras, agitándolas y golpeándolas con frecuencia. 5. (Mil.) Batir una muralla o plaza. 6. Ganar, vencer o exceder a otro en alguna cosa. 7. Batir las alas. 8. Tocar un tambor. 9. Rebajar el precio que se pide por alguna cosa. 10. Pisar la senda. 11. Deprimir, abatir. 12. Empujar con violencia. —*vn.* 1. Moverse con pulsación o con movimiento pulsativo, como un reloj, las arterias, etc.; latir, palpitar. 2. Ludir o rozar una cosa con otra. 3. Batir, golpear; batir, hablando del sol, del aire, del mar, etc.; dar o herir en alguna parte sin impedimento alguno. 4. Fluctuar, estar en movimiento. 5. Tentar el vado, buscar todos los medios para la consecución de alguna cosa. 6. Dar con violencia con alguna cosa. *To beat up for* o *to raise soldiers,* (Mil.) Reclutar tropas. *To beat against,* Estrellarse, echarse contra o sobre. *To beat away,* Ahuyentar a alguno a fuerza de golpes. *To beat back,* Reverberar, rechazar. *To beat down,* Abatir, derribar, demoler, destruir. Rebajar (una costura). Rebajar, disminuir (el precio pedido). (Art. y Of.) Apilar, amontonar. *To beat in,* Cascar, machacar, moler; echar dentro. Hundir, echar hacia abajo o hacia dentro; desfondar, quitar el fondo. *To beat into,* Inculcar, hacer entrar. *To beat off,* Echar, arrojar, despedir, rechazar. *To beat out,* Arrancar; lanzar. *To beat to powder,* Reducir a polvo. *To beat black and blue,* Acardenalar. *To beat one's brains,* Romper a alguno los cascos, hacerle saltar la tapa de los sesos. *To beat up,* Batir (huevos), sorprender (al enemigo).—*vn.* Dar una batida, levantar tropas. *To beat upon,* Echarse contra, estrellarse; batir (del sol). (Fam.) *He beats all,* Él los gana a todos. *That beats all,* Eso es más que todo.

Beat, *a.* Fatigado, agotado.

Beat, *s.* 1. Golpe o modo de golpear. 2. Pulsación, latido. 3. Oscilación del péndulo de un reloj. 4. Toque de tambor, sonido. 5. Quiebro de la voz. 6. Ronda, el distrito o cuartel al cuidado de un alguacil, o sereno.

Beatchick [bīt'-chik], *s.* Tipo femino que corresponde al de *Beatnik,* bohemio estrafalario de los E.U.A.

Beaten [bīt'-n], *part. adj.* Trillado, pisado.—*pp.* Batido, golpeado, apaleado; derrotado, vencido, etc.

Beater [bīt'-ęr], *s.* 1. Martillo, maza, pisón, golpeador, batidor, el instrumento con que se bate, pisa o golpea. 2. Apaleador, el que apalea. *Egg-beater,* Batidor de huevos.

Beatific, Beatifical [bī-a-tif'-ic, al], *a.* Beatífico, lo que constituye la última felicidad.

Beatifically [bī-a-tif'-i-cal-i], *adv.* Beatíficamente.

Beatification [bī-at''-i-fi-kē'-shun], *s.* Beatificación, declaración del Papa de que alguna persona goza de la eterna bienaventuranza después de su muerte.

Beatify [bī-at'-i-fai], *va.* Beatificar, declarar bienaventurado.

Beating [bīt'-ing], *s.* Paliza, zurra de palos o golpes. Corrección; pulsación. Golpeo, batidura.

Beatitude [bī-at'-i-tiūd], *s.* Beatitud, felicidad.

Beatnik [bīt'-nik], *s.* Bohemio estrafalario de los E.U.A.

Beau [bō], *s.* (en pl. BEAUX y BEAUS). 1. Petimetre, pisaverde, currutaco. (Fr.) *Beau-monde,* Gente de moda. 2. Galán, chichisveador, cortejo, pretendiente.

Beau-ideal [bō-ai-dī'-al], *s.* Bello ideal, concepción de la belleza perfecta tal como sólo existe en la imaginación. (Gal.)

Beauish [bo'-ish], *a.* Guapo, galán, lucido; lo que es propio de un petimetre o pisaverde.

Beauteous [biū'-ti-us], *a.* Bello, hermoso, lo perfecto en su línea.

Beauteously [biū'-tę-us-li], *adv.* *V* BEAUTIFULLY.

Beauteousness [biū'-tę-us-nes], *s.* Belleza, encantos; gracia, elegancia.

Beautification [biū-ti-fi-kē'-shun], *s.* Acción y efecto de hermosear o adornar.

Beautifier [biū'-ti-fai-ęr], *s.* Hermoseador.

Beautiful [biū'-ti-ful], *a.* Hermoso, bello.—*s.* Lo bello.

Beautifully [biū'-ti-ful-i], *adv.* Hermosamente, con belleza, con perfección.

Beautifulness [biū'-ti-ful-nes], *s.* Hermosura, belleza.

Beautify [biū'-ti-fai], *va.* Hermosear, acicalar, componer, adornar.

Beautifying [biū'-ti-fai-ing], *s.* La acción de adornar o hermosear una cosa; afeite, compostura, adorno, aderezo.

Beautiless [biū'-ti-les], *a.* Feo, falto de belleza.

Beauty [biū'-ti], *s.* 1. Belleza, hermosura. 2. Hermosura, persona hermosa o bella. 3. Encanto, embeleso. 4. (fam.) Lo mejor, lo gracioso, lo singular. *The beauty of the story was,* Lo mejor del cuento fue. *Beauty contest,* Concurso de belleza. *Beauty salon, Beauty parlor,* Salón de belleza.

Beautydom [biū'-ti-dęm], *s.* Conjunto de hermosuras (mujeres bellas).

Beauty-spot [biū'-ti-spot], *s.* Parche o lunar postizo.

Beaver [bī'-vęr], *s.* 1. Castor, animal cuadrúpedo anfibio. 2. Sombrero de castor, sombrero hecho de pelo de castor. 3. Visera, la parte de la armadura que cubre la cara.

Beaverteen [bī-vęr-tīn'], *s.* Piel de tusa, especie de fustán.

Bebop [bī'-bop], *s.* Variedad de *jazz.*

Becalm [bę-cām'], *va.* 1. Serenar o calmar alguna tempestad o borrasca. 2. Serenar el ánimo, sosegar. (Mar.) Calmar, quedarse en calma.

Becalming [bę-cām'-ing], *s.* Calma.

Became [bę-kēm']. Pretérito del verbo *To* BECOME.

Because [bę-cēz'], *conj.* Porque, por esta razón, a causa de.

Bechance [bę-chgns'], *va.* y *vn.* Acaecer, suceder, acontecer.

Becharm [bę-chārm'], *va.* Encantar, captar, cautivar.

Beck [bec], *va.* y *vn.* Hacer seña con la cabeza.

Beck, *s.* 1. *V.* NOD. 2. Riachuelo. 3. Tanque para lejía, tinte o jabón.

Becket [bek'-et], *n.* (Mar.) Vinatera, arraigado o manzanillo de aparejo.

Beckon [bec'-n], *vn.* Hacer seña con

la cabeza.—*va.* Hacer seña a. *To beckon with the hand,* Hacer una seña con la mano.
Beckon, *s.* Seña con la cabeza.
Becloud [bẹ-claud'], *va.* Obscurecer, cubrir como con una nube, anublar. También se usa en sentido figurado. *Beclouded intellect,* Una inteligencia obscurecida.
Become [bẹ-cum'], *va.* Convenir, parecer, sentar, caer bien, ser propio, estar bien.—*vn.* 1. Hacerse, volverse, pasar de un estado o condición a otro, convertirse, venir a parar; ser lo que no era; ponerse a, meterse a. 2. *To become of,* Parar en algo. *What will become of me?* ¿Qué será de mí? *What has become of my hat?* ¿Qué se ha hecho de mi sombrero? *To become warm in,* Acalorarse en. *To become forfeited,* Incurrir en alguna pena, confiscación o multa. *To become crazy,* Perder el juicio, volverse loco; perder la chabeta. *Become* o *come to be,* Llegar a ser. El verbo inglés *become* con un adjetivo se expresa a veces en español por medio de los prefijos *a* o *en*; p. ej. *To become warm,* Enardecerse, acalorarse.
Becoming [bẹ-cum'-ing], *pa.* 1. Gracioso, primoroso, decoroso, propio; decente, conveniente, acomodado, justo. 2. Lo que adorna, que sienta bien, que va bien. *A becoming dress,* Un vestido que sienta bien.
Becomingly [bẹ-cum'-ing-li], *adv.* Decorosamente, decentemente, con garbo y elegancia, a propósito.
Becomingness [bẹ-cum'-ing-nes], *s.* Decencia, elegancia, en los modales; propiedad, garbo, compostura.
Becurl [bẹ-cūrl'], *va.* Formar rizos.
Bed [bed], *s.* 1. Cama, lecho; la armazón de madera o hierro, ya por sí sola ya con ropa y colchones. *Bed of state,* Cama de respeto. *Feather-bed,* Colchón de plumas, plumón. *Flock-bed,* Colchón de borra. *Straw-bed,* Jergón de paja. *Folding-bed,* Cama plegadiza. *Death-bed,* Lecho mortuorio. 2. Cuadro de jardín; era, tablar, de una huerta. 3. Lecho, tongada, la capa o cama con que por su orden se ponen unas cosas sobre otras. 4. Madre de río, cauce, lecho. 5. Afuste de mortero. 6. Almohadilla de cureña. 7. Capa mineral horizontal. 8. (Carp.) Asiento, armadura. 9. Mesa (de billar). *To lay to bed,* Partear, ayudar la partera o comadrón al parto. *To be brought to bed,* (Fam.) Parir. *To make the bed,* Hacer la cama. *A crazy bed,* Una cama desvencijada, una mala cama. *To go to bed,* Ir a acostarse. *To jump out of bed,* Saltar de la cama. *To lie late in bed,* Levantarse tarde. *To make one's (own) bed,* Quien mala cama hace, en ella se yace.
Bed, *va.* 1. Meter en la cama, acostar. 2. Acostarse, o irse a la cama con otra persona. 3. Sembrar o plantar. 4. Poner una cosa en tongadas o capas sobrepuestas.—*vn.* Cohabitar, hacer vida maridable.
Bedabble [bẹ-dab'-l], *va.* Rociar, mojar.
†**Bedaggle** [bẹ-dag'-l], *va.* Enlodar, embarrar, ensuciar la parte inferior de un vestido.
†**Bedash** [bẹ-dash'], **Bedaub** [bẹ-dōb'], *va.* Salpicar, esparcir en gotas pequeñas alguna cosa líquida; ensuciar.
Bedawi [bed'-a-wi], *s.* (*pl.* BEDAWIN). *V.* BEDOUIN.
Bedazzle [bẹ-daz'-l], *va.* Deslumbrar, desvistar, quitar la vista o confundirla con el resplandor.
Bedbug [bed'-bug], *s.* La chinche, insecto muy fétido, que pica y chupa la sangre. Cimex lectularius.
Bedchamber [bed'-chêm"-bẹr], *s.* Dormitorio, la alcoba o el aposento donde se duerme. (Mex.) Recámara. *A gentleman of the king's bedchamber,* Gentilhombre de cámara.
Bedclothes [bed'-clodhz], *s. pl.* Coberturas de cama, ropa de cama, mantas y sábanas.
Bedded [bed'-ẹd], *pp.* 1. Con una o varias camas. *A single-bedded, a double-bedded room,* Alcoba de una cama, de dos camas. 2. (Geol.) Estratificado, dividido en capas. 3. Que crece en tongadas, lechos o tablares; reunido o recogido en un tablar, lecho, o tongada (ostras, plantas, etc.).
Bedder [bed'-ẹr], **Bedetter** [bẹ-det'-ẹr], *s.* Piedra de los molinos sobre la cual se mueve la muela.
Bedding [bed'-ing], *s.* Ajuar o ropa de cama.
Bedeck [bẹ-dec'], *va.* Adornar, asear.
†**Bedehouse** [bīd'-haus], *s.* Casa de misericordia.
Bedel, *s.* (Ant.) *V.* BEADLE.
Bedelry [bī'-dl-ri], *s.* Jurisdicción del bedel.
Bedevil [bẹ-dev'-l], *va.* 1. Endemoniar, endiablar, maleficiar; hechizar; enloquecer, volver loco o demente. 2. Endiablar, dañar, hacer sufrir abuso o tratamiento diabólico.
Bedew [bẹ-diū'], *va.* Rociar, esparcir alguna cosa sobre la tierra con la misma suavidad con que cae el rocío; regar.
Bedfellow [bed'-fel-o], *s.* Compañero o compañera de cama.
Bedhangings [bed'-hang-ingz], *s.* Cortinas de cama.
Bedhead [bed'-hed], *s.* Cabecera de cama.
†**Bedight** [bẹ-dait], *va.* (*pret.* y *pp.* BEDIGHT o BEDIGHTED). Adornar, hermosear.
Bedim [bẹ-dim'], *va.* Obscurecer, ofuscar; desvistar, deslumbrar.
Bedizen [bẹ-diz'-n], *va.* (Vulg.) Adornar, aderezar, acicalar.
Bedlam [bed'-lam], *s.* 1. Casa de orates, aquella en que hay mucho bullicio y poco gobierno; un gran tropel o bullicio, desbarajuste. 2. Casa de locos. Bedlam es corrupción de Bethlehem, o Belén, nombre de un convento que fué después destinado a hospital de dementes, en Londres.
Bedlamite [bed'-lam-ait], *s.* Loco.
Bedmaker [bed'-mêk'-ẹr], *s.* Criada o persona que hace las camas.
Bedmate [bed'-mêt], *s.* Compañero o compañera de cama.
Bedmoulding [bed'-mōld-ing], *s.* Moldura de cornisa.
Bedouin [bed'-ū-in], *s.* 1. Beduíno, árabe del desierto. 2. Vagabundo callejero.
Bed-pan [bed'-pan], *s.* 1. Vasija de loza para uso de los enfermos en el lecho. 2. Calentador de cama.
Bedplate [bed'-plêt], *s.* Bancaza o cama de una máquina.
Bedpost [bed'-pōst], *s.* Pilar o columna que sostiene el cielo de la cama.
Bedpresser [bed'-pres-ẹr], *s.* Dormilón, el que duerme mucho.
Bed-quilt [bed'-cwilt], *s.* Cobertor de cama.
Bedraggle [bẹ-drag'-l], *va.* Ensuciar o manchar la ropa.
Bedrench [bẹ-drench'], *va.* Empapar, embeber.
Bedrid o **Bedridden** [bed'-rid], *a.* Postrado en cama, por vejez o enfermedad.
†**Bed-right,** †**Bed-rite** [bed'-rait], *s* Derecho conyugal.
Bed-rock [bed'-rec"], *s.* La roca sólida que está debajo de minerales, etc., en la superficie de la tierra. Es voz muy usada entre los mineros.
Bedroom [bed'-rūm], *s.* Recámara, dormitorio, alcoba.
Bedrop [bẹ-drep'], *va.* Rociar, salpicar.
Bedside [bed'-said], *s.* Lado de cama, el espacio entre la cama y la pared.
Bedsore [bed'-sōr], *s.* Llaga causada por la prolongada permanencia en el lecho.
Bedspread [bed'-spred], *s.* Colcha de cama; cobertor.
Bedspring [bed'-spring], *s.* Colchón de muelles o de resortes.
Bedstead [bed'-sted], *s.* Armazón de cama, el catre o tablas con sus pies.
Bed-straw [bed'-strē], *s.* 1. Paja de o para jergón. 2. (Bot.) Cuajaleche, galio, hierba del género Galium.
Bedswerver [bed'-swẹr-vẹr], *s.* (Des.) Adúltero o adúltera.
Bedtick, Bedticking [bed'-tic, tik-ing], *s.* Cutí, tela para colchones.
Bedtime [bed'-taim], *s.* La hora de irse a la cama o de recogerse, de acostarse.
Beduck [bẹ-duc'], *va.* Sumergir debajo del agua.
Bedung [bẹ-dung'], *va.* Estercolar, cubrir con estiércol, engrasar y beneficiar la tierra con estiércol.
Bedust [bẹ-dust'], *va.* Empolvar, polvorear, esparcir polvo o llenar de polvo.
Bedward [bed'-ward], *adv.* Hacia la cama.
Bedwarf [bẹ-dwērf'], *va.* Achicar, reducir a menos el tamaño de alguna cosa.
§**Bedwork** [bed'-wūrc], *s.* Obra hecha en la cama; obra hecha sin trabajo, o la que no cuesta pena ni fatiga.
Bee [bī], *s.* 1. Abeja, insecto social himenóptero que fabrica la cera y la miel; en especial, la Apis mellifica. 2. (Fam.) Reunión de vecinos o amigos para hacer algún trabajo o para divertirse. *Queen-bee,* Abeja madre o reina. *Worker-bee,* Abeja obrera. *Bee-bread,* Polen almacenado. *Bee-fly,* Mosca-abeja, díptero del género Bombylius. También, pero incorrectamente, la Eristalis, o *drone-fly. Swarm of bees,* Enjambre de abejas. *Bee-culture,* Cultivo o cuidado de las abejas, apicultura.
Beech [bīch], *s.* (Bot.) Haya, árbol alto, grueso y copudo, de corteza blanca y madera tenaz y flexible.
Beechen [bīch'-n], *a.* De haya, compuesto o hecho de haya.
Beech-mast o **Beech-nut** [bīch'-mast], *s.* Fabuco, el fruto que produce la haya.
Beech-oil [bīch'-oil], *s.* Aceite de fabuco, que se saca del fruto de la haya.
Bee-eater [bī'-īt-ẹr], *s.* (Orn.) Abejaruco, pájaro que se come las abejas y destruye los colmenares.
Beef [bīf], *s.* Carne de res. *Beef broth,* Consommé, caldo de carne. *Beef steak,* Bistec, lomo de carne. *Roast beef,* Carne de res para asar.
Beef-eater [bīf'-īt-ẹr], *s.* 1. Alabar-

dero, especie de guardia del rey de Inglaterra. Corrupción de "buffeteer," el que sirve en el "buffet" o aparador; criado rollizo. 2. Un inglés, apodo que les dan los franceses.
Beef-witted [bīf'-wit-ed], *a.* Lerdo, estúpido.
Bee-garden [bī'-gār-dn], *s.* Abejar, colmenar.
Bee-glue [bī'-glū], *s.* Cera aleda. *V.* PROPOLIS.
Bee-hive [bī'-haiv], *s.* Colmena, especie de caja en que se crían las abejas y donde labran la miel y la cera.
Bee-line [bī'-lain], *s.* Línea recta.
Bee-master [bī'-mas-ter], *s.* Colmenero o abejero, el que tiene abejas y colmenas, o el que las cuida.
Bee-moth [bī'-mēth], *s.* Mariposa cuyas larvas se crían en los colmenares y destruyen los panales. Gallerea cereana.
Been [bin o bīn], *pp.* del verbo *To* BE.
Beer [bīr], *s.* Cerveza, bebida fermentada que se hace de cebada y hombrecillo o lúpulo. *Small beer,* Cerveza floja. *Strong beer,* Cerveza fuerte. *Stale beer,* Cerveza agriada. *Lager beer,* Cerveza que contiene poco lúpulo. *V.* LAGER. *Pale beer,* Cerveza blanca.
Beer-house, *s. V.* ALE-HOUSE.
Beestings, Biestings [bīst'-ingz], *s.* Calostro, la primera leche que se ordeña de la vaca después que pare.
Bees-wax [bīz'-wax], *s.* Cera de abejas.
Beet [bīt], *s.* (Bot.) Acelga, remolacha. (Mex.) Betabel. *Sugar-beet,* Remolacha. *Beet-sugar,* Azúcar de remolacha.
Beetle [bī'-tl], *s.* 1. Escarabajo, o cualquier insecto coleóptero. 2. Pisón, maza, instrumento que sirve para apretar la tierra, piedras, etc. *Colorado beetle,* Dorífera, "insecto del Colorado," coleóptero que causa grandes destrozos en la patata. Llamado también *potato-bug.* (Doryphora decemlineata.)
Beetle, *vn.* 1. Hacer barriga; colgar sobre. 2. Sobresalir.
Beetle-browed [bī'-tl-braud], *a.* Cejudo, el que tiene las cejas muy salidas.
Beetle-headed [bī'-tl-hed-ed], *a.* Lerdo, pesado.
Beetle-stock, [bī'-tl-stec], *s.* Mango de pisón.
Beetling [bīt'-ling], *a.* Saliente, pendiente, colgante.
Beetling-machine [bī'-tling-ma-shīn"], *s.* Sacabocados mecánico, estampador mecánico.
Beet-radish [bīt'-rad-ish], **Beet-rave** [bīt'-rêv], *s.* Betarraga o remolacha.
Beet-sugar [bīt'-shug-ar], *s.* Azúcar de remolacha.
Beeves [bīvz], *s. pl.* Ganado mayor.
Befall [be-fel'], *vn.* (*pret.* BEFELL, *pp.* BEFALLEN). Suceder, acontecer, sobrevenir. Usase generalmente para significar un acontecimiento desgraciado. *Whatever befalls,* Suceda lo que quiera. *The worst that can befall,* Lo peor que puede acontecer.
Befit [be-fit'], *va.* Venir bien, convenir, acomodarse a.
Befitting, *pa.* y *a.* Conveniente, propio, digno, que se aviene con.
Befoamed [be-fōmd'], *a.* Cubierto de espuma.
Befog [be-feg'], *va.* Envolver en niebla; confundir, obscurecer.
Befool [be-fūl'], *va.* Infatuar, entontecer.
Before [be-fōr'], *prep.* 1. Más adelante, hablando de lugar. 2. Delante, enfrente. 3. Delante, ante, en presencia de alguna persona. 4. Antes de. *Before nightfall,* Antes de anochecer. 5. Antes o delante. *Look before you leap,* Antes que te cases, mira lo que haces. 6. Anterior a; superior a.—*adv.* 1. Antes, primero, hablando de tiempo. *I was there before him,* Yo estuve allí antes que él. 2. Antes, en tiempo pasado. *I have never seen him before,* Nunca le he visto antes de ahora. 3. Antes, en algún tiempo recien pasado. *A little before,* Poco antes. 4. Antes, hasta ahora. *Before it was not so,* Antes no era así. 5. Ya. *To get before one,* Adelantarse a alguno. *I told you so before,* Ya se lo he dicho a Vd. *Before cited,* Ya citado. *Before mentioned,* Mencionado más arriba, de que queda hecha mención.
Beforehand [be-fōr'-hand], *adv.* 1. De antemano, a prevención, anticipadamente. *To be beforehand with one,* Llevar la delantera a uno. 2. Primeramente, ya. 3. Con muchos ahorros. *I know beforehand that,* Ya sé que.
Beforetime [be-fōr'-taim], *adv.* En tiempo pasado, en otro tiempo, tiempo atrás.
Befoul [be-faul'], *va.* Ensuciar, emporcar, embadurnar.
Befriend [be-frend'], *va.* Favorecer, patrocinar, amparar, ayudar, proteger. *To befriend one's self,* Mirar por sí.
Befringe [be-frinj'], *va.* Guarnecer con franjas.
Beg [beg], *vn.* Mendigar, pordiosear, vivir de limosna; hacer la cuestación o colecta.—*va.* 1. Rogar, pedir con sumisión, suplicar. *I beg it as a favour of you,* Se lo suplico a Vd., se lo pido a Vd. por favor. 2. Suponer, dar por supuesto. (Lógica) *To beg the question,* Dar por admitido el punto que se discute, dar por supuesto.
Began [be-gan'], *pret.* del verbo *To* BEGIN.
Beget [be-get'], *va.* (*pret.* BEGOT—ant. BEGAT—*pp.* BEGOTTEN). 1. Engendrar. 2. Producir, causar. *To beget strifes,* Suscitar contiendas.
Begetter [be-get'-er], *s.* Engendrador, el que engendra.
Begetting [be-get'-ing], *s.* Generación; producción.
Beggar [beg'-ar], *s.* 1. Mendigo, el pobre que pide limosna y vive de ella. 2. Suplicante. 3. Miserable; gorrón. (Prov.) *It is better to be a king among beggars than a beggar among kings,* Más vale ser cabeza de ratón que cola de león.
Beggar, *va.* 1. Empobrecer, arruinar, reducir a pobreza o mendicidad. 2. Apurar, agotar. *To beggar description,* Ser indescriptible, no haber palabras para describir.
Beggarliness [beg'-ar-li-nes], *s.* Mezquindad, pobreza, miseria, mendicidad.
Beggarly [beg'-ar-li], *a.* Pobre, miserable. *Beggarly action,* Bajeza.—*adv.* Mezquinamente, pobremente.
Beggary [beg'-ar-i], *s.* Mendicidad o mendiguez.
Begging [beg'-ing], *a.* Mendicante. *To go begging,* Pedir limosna. (Met.) Carecer de valor; no hallar comprador.
Begilt [be-gilt'], *pa.* Dorado.
Begin [be-gin'], *va.* Empezar, comenzar, principiar, dar principio a alguna cosa. *To begin the world,* Empezar a vivir. *To begin one's march,* Ponerse en camino. *To begin afresh* o *again,* Volver a empezar o empezar de nuevo; proseguir lo que se había empezado y dejado.—*vn.* Nacer, principiar a existir.
Beginner [be-gin'-er], *s.* 1. Autor, inventor, el que da principio a alguna cosa. 2. Principiante, el sujeto que empieza a aprender o ejercer algún arte o facultad.
Beginning [be-gin'-ing], *s.* 1. Principio, origen o causa. 2. Principios o rudimentos de alguna facultad.
Begird [be-gerd'] **Begirt** [be-gert'], *va.* (*pret.* y *pp.* BEGIRT). 1. Ceñir, atar. 2. Ceñir, rodear, abrazar al rededor. 3. Sitiar o poner sitio a alguna plaza.
Begnaw [be-nō'], *va.* Roer.
Begone! [be-gōn'], *inter.* ¡Fuera, apártate de ahí, quita allá!
Begonia [be-gō'-ni-a], *s.* Begonia, género de plantas exóticas, de flores irregulares, que crecen en países cálidos. Sus especies son muy numerosas.
Begored [be-gōrd'], *a.* Manchado con sangre.
Begot, *pret.* **Begotten,** *pp.* del verbo *To* BEGET.
Begrime [be-graim'], *va.* Encenagar, ensuciar con cieno; ennegrecer.
Begrudge [be-gruj'], *va.* Envidiar la posesión de; repugnar.
Beguile [be-gail'], *va.* Engañar, seducir; entretener con falsas esperanzas. *To beguile the time,* Hacer pasar el tiempo.
Beguiler [be-gail'-er], *s.* Engañador, seductor, impostor.
Begum [bī'-gum], *s.* Princesa mahometana, o dama de calidad en India.
Begum [be-gum'], *va.* Engomar, empapar o cubrir de goma.
Begun, *pp.* y *pret.* del verbo *To* BEGIN.
Behalf [be-hāf'], *s.* 1. Favor, patrocinio, consideración, beneficio. *In behalf of,* A favor o en nombre de. 2. Defensa, amparo. *In his behalf,* En su defensa.
Behave [be-hêv'], *va.* y *s.* Proceder, obrar, conducirse, comportarse o portarse bien o mal. *He behaves very ill,* Él se porta muy mal. (Fam.) *Behave!* ¡Estése Vd. quieto! ¡No moleste Vd.! (Fam.) ¡No sea Vd. majadero! ¡No muela Vd.! *Well-behaved,* De buena conducta, de buenas maneras. *Ill-behaved,* De mala conducta.
Behavior, Behaviour [be-hê'-vier], *s.* 1. Proceder, conducta, el modo de portarse o de gobernarse uno en sus acciones. 2. Continente, gesto. 3. Modal, la acción particular y propia de algún sujeto con que se hace reparar. 4. Crianza; porte, maneras, aire. *What extraordinary behavior!* ¡Qué proceder tan extraordinario! *Behaviour,* es como se escribe en Inglaterra.
Behead [be-hed'], *va.* Degollar, decapitar.
Beheader [be-hed'-er], *s.* Degollador.
Beheading [be-hed'-ing], *s.* Decapitación, degollación, acto y efecto de decapitar.
Beheld [be-held'], *pret.* y *pp.* del verbo *To* BEHOLD.
Behemoth [bī-hī'-meth], *s.* En la Biblia, bestia colosal, probablemente el hipopótamo. (Heb. b'hemōth.)
Behest [be-hest'], *s.* Mandato, precepto, requirimiento.

Behind [bẹ-haind'], *prep.* 1. Detrás, **tras.** *Behind the curtain,* Detrás del **telón,** en la escena o entre bastidores. *Behind one's back,* En ausencia o a espaldas de una persona. 2. Atrás. 3. Inferior. *To ride behind one,* Montar a las ancas o en ancas. —*adv.* 1. Atrás, detrás. *To follow behind,* Ir o seguir atrás de otro. 2. Atrasadamente. 3. No a la vista ; sin tocar, de reserva.

Behindhand [bẹ-haind'-hand], *adv.* Atrasadamente, con atraso.

Behold [bẹ-hōld'], *va.* Ver, mirar, contemplar, considerar, notar.

Behold! *inter.* ¡ He ! he aquí ! aquí está ! vele ahí !

Beholden [bẹ-hōld'-n], *a.* Deudor, obligado por gratitud.

Beholder [bẹ-hōld'-er], *s.* Espectador, mirón.

Beholding [bẹ-hōld'-ing], *a.* Obligado, deudor.

Behoney [bẹ-hun'-i], *va.* Dulcificar, endulzar (con miel).

Behoof [bẹ-hūf'], *s.* Provecho, utilidad, ventaja.

Behoove, Behove [bẹ-hūv'], *vn.* Este verbo sólo se usa impersonalmente, y significa convenir, importar, ser útil, ser necesario. *It behoves us to be prepared for death,* Nos importa estar preparados para la muerte.

Behooveful, Behoveful [bẹ-hūv'-ful], *a.* Provechoso, útil ; idóneo, necesario, expediente.

Behovable [bẹ-hūv'-a-bl], *a.* Ganancioso, útil.

Beige [bêzh], *s.* Beige, color natural de la lana. Color arena, entre gris y pardo.

Beild [bīld], *v.* y *s.* *V.* BIELD.

Being [bī'-ing], *s.* 1. Existencia, el ser o esencia actual de alguna cosa. 2. Estado o condición particular. 3. Ente, ser. 4. Vivienda, morada, habitación. *A man's first being,* El primer momento de la vida. *The well-being,* La felicidad, el bien estar. —*conj.* Ya que, puesto que, supuesto.—*Part.* del verbo *To* BE. *I do no good by being here,* Mi presencia no sirve de nada aquí, yo no hago aquí nada. *To keep a thing from being done,* Impedir que una cosa se haga ; no dejar hacer una cosa. *Such being the case,* Ya que tal es el caso. *For the time being,* Por el momento.

Bejade [bẹ-jêd'], *va.* Cansar.

Bel [bel], *s.* El dios supremo, o uno de los dioses principales de los Babilonios: forma caldaica de *Baal,* y aun el mismo Baal según algunos escritores.

Belabor, Belabour [bẹ-lê'-ber], *va.* Apalear, dar de puñadas, cascar. (La forma *belabour,* es la común en Inglaterra.)

Belaced [be-lêst'], *a.* Adornado con encaje, galoneado.

Belate [bẹ-lêt'], *va.* 1. Tardar, retardar hasta pasada la hora debida, o de costumbre. 2. Cogerle , uno la noche.

Belated [bẹ-lê'-ted], *a.* El que anda de noche, el que llega tarde ; retardado.

Belatedness [bẹ-lê'-ted-nes], *s.* Tardanza ; frialdad.

Belay [bẹ-lê'], *va.* 1. Bloquear. 2. Asechar, poner asechanzas, armar emboscadas. 3. (Mar.) Amarrar o dar vuelta. *To belay a running rope,* Amarrar un cabo de labor. *Belaying-pins,* Cavillas.

Belch [belch], *vn.* 1. Regoldar, eructar ; vomitar. 2. Salir o aparecer violentamente de dentro a fuera, como salen, por ejemplo, las llamas de un horno.—*va.* Arrojar, echar de sí, v. g. llamas, o disparos.

Belch, Belching [belch'-ing], *s.* Regüeldo, eructo, eructación, la acción de regoldar.

Beldam, Beldame [bel'-dam, dêm], *f.* 1. Vejezuela, la mujer vieja, fea o maliciosa. 2. Bruja.

Beleaguer [bẹ-lī'-ger], *va.* Sitiar, bloquear, oprimir.

Belee [be-lī'], *va.* (Mar.) Sotaventar.

Belemnite [bel-em'-nait], *s.* (Min.) Belemnita, molusco fósil, puntiagudo, en forma de dedo ; cefalópodo.

Belfry [bel'-fri], *s.* Campanario, la torre o paraje en que están las campanas.

Belgian [bel'-ji-an], *a.* Bélgico, de Bélgica.—*s.* Belga.

Belial [bī'-lial], *s.* Belial, Satanás, el espíritu del mal.

Belibel [bẹ-lai'-bel], *va.* Calumniar.

Belie [bẹ-lai'], *va.* 1. Contrahacer, fingir, remedar. 2. Desmentir, decirle a uno que miente. 3. Calumniar, acusar falsamente. 4. Representar alguna cosa falsamente. *To belie one's self,* Contradecirse ; cortarse. *His looks belie his words,* Sus miradas desmienten sus palabras.

Belief [bẹ-līf'], *s.* 1. Fe, creencia que se da respecto de las cosas que no vemos. 2. Creencia, lo que cada uno cree en su religión. 3. Credo. 4. Opinión, parecer, sentimiento. *Past all belief,* Increible. *Light of belief,* Crédulo. *Hard of belief,* Incrédulo. *In the firm belief that,* En la firme creencia (o convicción) de que.

Believable [bẹ-līv'-a-bl], *a.* Creíble, que se puede creer.

Believe [bẹ-līv'], *va.* Creer, dar asenso o crédito a alguna cosa.—*vn.* 1. Creer, estar firmemente persuadido de la verdad de alguna cosa. 2. Creer, ejercer la virtud teologal de la fe. 3. Pensar, imaginar. 4. Fiarse.

Believer [bẹ-līv'-ẹr], *s.* 1. Creyente, el que cree o da crédito a lo que se le dice. 2. Creyente, fiel, cristiano, el que profesa la ley de Cristo.

Believing [bẹ-līv'-ing], *s.* Fe, creencia.

Believingly [bẹ-līv'-ing-ly], *adv.* Con fe o creencia.

Belike [bẹ-laik'], *adv.* Probablemente, quizá, acaso ; aparentemente.

Belime [bẹ-laim'], *va.* Enligar, enviscar, untar con liga.

Belittle [bẹ-lit'-l], *va.* Deprimir, hacer poco caso, dar escasa importancia.

Bell [bel], *s.* 1. Campana. *Clapper of a bell,* Badajo de campana. *Ring of bells,* Son o toque de campanas. *Passing-bell,* Campana que toca a muerto. 2. Campana, cualquiera cosa que tiene semejanza de campana. *Diving* o *diver's bell,* Campana de buzo, aparato para bucear. 3. Cascabel. *To bear away the bell,* Llevar el cencerro, ser el primero, ganar el premio. *To lose the bell,* Ser vencido ; rendirse. 4. Pabellón de un instrumento de viento. *Chime of bells,* Repique de campanas, juego de campanas. *To set the bells going,* Echar las campanas a vuelo. *To ring the bell,* (1) Tocar la campana, tocar a rebato. (2) Tirar de la campanilla.

Bell, *vn.* (Bot.) Crecer una planta o una parte de la planta en figura de campana.

Belladonna [bel-a-den'-a], *s.* (Bot.) Belladama o belladona; hierba mora.

Bellboy [bel'-bei], *s.* Botones, mozo de hotel.

Bell-buoy [bel], *s.* Boya de campana.

Belle [bel], *sf.* Señorita ; una mujer joven y hermosa.

Belles-lettres [bel-let'-r], *s.* Bellas letras, literatura.

Bell-fashioned [bel'-fash-und], *a.* Campaniforme, lo que tiene la forma o figura de campana.

Bell-flower [bel'-flaur], *s.* (Bot.) 1. Ruiponce o repónchigo ; campanilla. 2. Variedad de manzana.

Bell-founder [bel'-faund-ẹr], *s.* Campanero, el artífice que vacía y funde las campanas.

Bell-glass [bel'-glas], *s.* Campana de cristal.

Bell-hanger [bel'-hang-er], *s.* Campanillero, instalador de campanillas.

Bell-hanging [hang-ing], s. Instalación de campanillas.

Bell-horse [bel'-hērs], *s.* *Cf.* BELL-WETHER.

Bellicose [bel'i-cōs], *a.* Belicoso, bélico, guerrero.

Bellied [bel'-id], *a.* 1. Ventrudo. 2. (Arq.) Combado, acombado, con barriga, convexo.

Belligerent [bel-lij'-ẹr-ent], *a.* Beligerante, belígero, belicoso, marcial, guerrero.

Bellipotent [bel-lip'-o-tent], *a.* Poderoso en la guerra.

Bell-man [bel'-man], *s.* Pregonero de campana, el que pregona alguna cosa al son de una campana, avisador, despertador al toque de campana.

Bell-metal [bel'-met-l], *s.* Metal campanil, el metal de que se hacen las campanas.

Bell-mouthed [bel'-maudhd], *a.* 1. Abocinado, de boca de campana. 2. De voz sonora y profunda.

Bellow [bel'-ō], *vn.* 1. Bramar. 2. Vociferar, gritar. 3. Bramar, embravecerse o estar agitado el mar o el viento.

Bellower [bel'-o-ẹr], *s.* Bramador, gritador.

Bellow, Bellowing [bel'-o-ing], *s.* Bramido, rugido ; grito.

Bellows [bel'-ez], *s.* Fuelle, instrumento para soplar y encender el fuego ; fuelle del órgano.

Bell-pull [bel'-pul], *s.* Botón, tirador de campanilla. *V.* BELL-ROPE.

Bell-punch [bel'-punch], *s.* Sacabocados con timbre ; sirve para marcar y anunciar los billetes de pasaje pagados en los tranvías, etc.

Bell-ringer [bel'-ring-ẹr], *s.* Campanero, tocador de campana.

Bell-rope [bel'-rōp], *s.* Cuerda o soga de campana.

Bell-shaped [bel'-shêpt], *a.* Campaniforme.

Belluine [bel'-yu-in], *a.* (Ant.) Bestial, brutal.

Bell-wether [bel'-wedh-ẹr], *s.* Manso, el carnero que lleva el cencerro, y va delante, guiando a los demás.

Belly [bel'-i], *s.* 1. Vientre, barriga, panza, la parte del cuerpo humano desde el pecho al empeine. 2. Seno, entrañas. 3. Barriga, la parte de alguna cosa que sobresale a lo demás de ella. *Belly-ache,* Cólico o dolor de vientre. *Belly-band,* Cincha, ventrera, cinto. *Bellyful,* Panzada, hartazgo de comida, hartura. *Belly-god,* Glotón, el que come mu-

cho y desordenadamente. *Belly-slave*, Esclavo de su apetito. *Belly-worm*, Lombriz del vientre.—*a. Belly-bound*, Estreñido de vientre. *Belly-pinched*, Hambriento.
Belly, *vn.* Hacer barriga; hartarse. —*va.* Llenar, inflar, hinchar.
Belong [bẹ-leng'], *vn.* 1. Pertenecer, tocar a alguno o ser propia de él alguna cosa. 2. Tocar a alguno por oficio u obligación. 3. Concernir, mirar a, tocar a. 4. Residir, estar domiciliado en, ser natural de; tener lugar o esfera particular. *He belongs in Quito*, Reside en Quito.
Belongings [bẹ-leng'-ings], *s. pl.* Efectos, enseres, posesiones. *You and all your belongings*, Vd. y todo lo que le pertenece.
Belove [bẹ-luv'], *va.* Amar; usado solamente en la voz pasiva.
Beloved [bẹ-luv'-ed], *a.* Querido, amado. [be-luvd'], *pp.* de BELOVE.
Below [bẹ-lō'], *prep.* 1. Debajo, en paraje más bajo. 2. Debajo, inferior en dignidad o excelencia.—*adv.* Abajo, bajo, debajo, por bajo. *He is there below*, Él está allá abajo. *The regions below*, Las regiones infernales. *Below par*, Desigual; a descuento; pierde o está más bajo que el valor figurado, hablando de letras de cambio o del papel moneda.
Belt [belt], *s.* 1. Cinto o cinturón, faja. 2. Correa de transmisión. 3. Zona, región ancha sobre un globo o esfera; extensión considerable de terreno que tiene forma de banda. 4. Toda fuerza o influencia que restriñe. *Sword-belt*, Biricú, o cinturón. *Shoulder-belt*, Tahalí.
Belt, *va.* 1. Cercar, rodear como una correa. 2. Azotar con una correa, dar latigazos.
Belt-saw [belt'-sō], *s.* Sierra sin fin, sierra de cinta. *V.* BAND-SAW.
Belting [belt'-ing], *s.* 1. Correaje, correas motoras o de transmisión. 2. Material de que se hacen las correas.
Beluga [bel-ū'-ga], *s.* 1. La ballena blanca de los mares árticos. 2. El gran esturión blanco.
Belus [bī'-lus o bē'-lus], *s.* Lo mismo que Bel. (Latín.)
Belvedere [bel'-ve-dīr], *s.* Belvedere, glorieta.
‡**Bemangle** [bẹ-man'-gl], *va.* Lacerar. *V.* MANGLE.
Bemask [bẹ-masc'], *va.* Esconder, tapar, ocultar.
Bemaze [bẹ-mêz'], *va.* Confundir, enredar; descaminar.
Bemire [bẹ-mair'], *va.* Enlodar, encenagar, emporcar.
Bemoan [bẹ-mōn'], *va.* Lamentar, deplorar, plañir.
Bemoanable [bẹ-mōn'-a-bl], *a.* Lamentable.
Bemoaner [bẹ-mōn'-ẹr], *s.* Lamentador, plañidor.
Bemoaning [bẹ-mōn'-ing], *s.* Lamentación.
†**Bemock** [bẹ-mec'], *va.* Mofarse, reirse de.
Bemuse [bẹ-miūz'], *va.* Embriagar ligeramente, dejar algo atontado, como con los efectos del licor.
Bench [bench], *s.* 1. Banco, asiento largo con respaldo o sin él. 2. Tribunal de justicia en Inglaterra. 3. Las personas sentadas en un banco. *King's o Queen's Bench*, Un tribunal principal de justicia, y una prisión de Londres. *Bench show*, Exposición de perros, bajo cubierto, en casetas colocadas sobre bancos. *Bench warrant*, Auto de prisión expedido por uno de los tribunales superiores. *To play to empty benches*, Representar para las butacas, es decir, ante muy reducido público.
Bench, *va.* 1. Hacer bancos o asientos. 2. Asentar sobre un banco.
Bencher [bench'-ẹr], *s.* 1. Nombre de los decanos de los colegios de abogados. 2. Individuo de algún ayuntamiento. 3. Asesor.
Bend [bend], *va.* (*pret.* y *pp.* BENT). 1. Encorvar, doblar, plegar o torcer alguna cosa poniéndola corva. 2. Dirigir, inclinar o encaminar a cierto o determinado paraje. 3. Sujetar, vencer. 4. Tender, estirar. 5. (Fig.) Dirigir, aplicar; dícese del ánimo. 6. (Mar.) Entalingar, amarrar, un cable, envergar una vela.—*vn.* 1. Encorvarse, doblarse. 2. Inclinarse, bajar o encorvar el cuerpo para significar rendimiento, sumisión o cortesía. 3. Ceder, doblarse. *The beam bent under the weight*, La viga cedió bajo el peso. *Bent on mischief*, Determinado a hacer mal. *To bend back*, Encorvar o doblar hacia atrás. *To bend one's brows*, Fruncir o arrugar las cejas. *To bend the head*, Inclinarse, bajar la cabeza. *To bend the knee*, Doblar la rodilla. *To bend one's efforts* o *endeavours*, Dirigir o encaminar sus esfuerzos. *To bend down*, Inclinarse, torcerse, pandearse, ladearse.
Bend, *s.* 1. Comba, encorvadura. 2. Venda. *Bends*, (Mar.) Las ligazones de cada una de las cuadernas de una embarcación, desde la quilla hasta el remate del costado. (Her.) Bandas. *Bend sinister*, (Her.) Barra, figura ordinaria del escudo que coge desde el ángulo siniestro superior al diestro inferior.
Bendable [bend'-a-bl], *a.* Flexible, que se puede doblar; plegable.
Bender [bend'-ẹr], *s.* El que encorva o tuerce alguna cosa.
Bending [bend'-ing], *s.* Pliegue, doblez, encorvadura, comba; pendiente, declive; rodeo, vuelta.
Bendlet [bend'-let], *s.* (Her.) Banda pequeña, de media anchura.
Bendwith [bend'-with], *s.* (Bot.) Viburno, especie de arbusto.
Beneaped [bẹ-nīpt'], *a.* (Mar.) Barado, encallado.
Beneath [bẹ-nīdh' o bẹ-nīth'], *adv.* y *prep.* Bajo o en paraje más bajo, debajo, abajo; del centro, de lo más hondo.
Benedicite [ben-e-dis'-i-tẹ], *s.* Cántico que empieza con esta palabra (en latín); de una adición apócrifa al tercer capítulo del libro de Daniel.
Benedick, Benedict (de un personaje de la comedia de Shakspeare, *Much Ado About Nothing*), *s.* Un hombre casado, o recién casado.
Benedictine [ben-e-dic'-tin], *s.* y *a.* Benedictino, benito.
Benediction [ben-e-dic'-shun] *s.* Bendición.
Benedictus [ben-e-dic'-tus], *s.* El cántico de Zacarías relativo al nacimiento de San Juan Bautista; es la primera palabra de la traducción latina.
Benefactor [ben-e-fac'-tẹr], *s.* Bienhechor; fundador; patrón.
Benefaction [ben-e-fac'-shun], *s.* Beneficio, favor, gracia.
Benefactress [ben-e-fac'-tres], *sf.* Bienhechora; fundadora, patrona.
Benefice [ben'-e-fis], *s.* 1. Beneficio, el bien que se hace a otro. 2. Beneficio eclesiástico.
Beneficed [ben'-e-fist], *a.* Beneficiado, el que goza algún beneficio eclesiástico.
Beneficence [bẹ-nef'-i-sens], *s.* Beneficencia; liberalidad, largueza.
Beneficent [bẹ-nef'-i-sent], *a.* Benéfico, el que o lo que hace bien.
Beneficently [bẹ-nef'-i-sent-li], *adv.* Benéficamente.
Beneficial [ben-e-fish'-al], *a.* Beneficioso, provechoso, útil, ventajoso.
Beneficially [ben-e-fish'-al-i], *adv.* Benéficamente, provechosamente.
Beneficialness [ben-e-fish'-al-nes], *s.* Utilidad, provecho.
Beneficiary [ben-e-fish'-ia-ri], *s.* 1. Beneficiario, el que goza de los rendimientos de algún predio o usufructo; la persona que recibe un beneficio, a manera de privilegio o concesión caritativa. 2. Beneficiado, el que está en posesión de algún beneficio eclesiástico. 3. Persona que tiene derecho a los productos de un caudal o hacienda cuyo título de propiedad está en nombre de otro; por ejemplo, un síndico o un fideicomisario. 4. Portador de una libranza postal.—*a.* Beneficiario.
Benefit [ben'-e-fit], *s.* 1. Beneficio, el bien que se hace o recibe; bondad, favor, gracia, servicio. 2. Utilidad, provecho, ventaja. *Benefit of clergy*, Inmunidad del clérigo. (For.) Privilegio antiguo en Inglaterra, por el cual la persona convicta de algún delito capital, si sabía leer un libro en latín, sólo sufría el castigo de señalársele la mano con un hierro ardiendo. 3. Representación dramática en beneficio de un actor o de una actriz.
Benefit, *va.* Beneficiar, hacer bien. —*vn.* Aprovecharse o utilizarse; prevalerse.
Benet [bẹ-net'], *va.* Asechar, hacer caer en el lazo; poner asechanzas, lazos.
Benevolence [bẹ-nev'-o-lens], *s.* 1. Benevolencia, amor, buena voluntad, afecto, amistad. 2. Benevolencia, el bien hecho o recibido; donativo gratuito, servicio.
Benevolent [bẹ-nev'-o-lent], *a.* Benévolo, el que tiene buena voluntad o afecto a otro; dulce, clemente.
Benevolently [bẹ-nev'-o-lent-li], *adv.* Benignamente.
Bengal [ben-gōl'], *s.* Bengala, especie de tela delgada de Bengala. *Bengal light*, Luz de Bengala.
Bengalee [ben-ga-lī'], *s.* Bengalí, lengua que se habla en Bengala.—*a.* Bengalí, de Bengala.
Benight [be-nait'], *va.* Cogerle a uno la noche, anochecerse a uno; obscurecer.
Benighted [bẹ-nait'-ed], *pp.* Anochecido. *We were benighted about four miles from town*, Nos anocheció a unas cuatro millas de la ciudad. (Fig.) *To be benighted*, (1) Estar ciego o sin luz, descarriado, extraviado, errante. (2) Estar sin saber, ignorante.
Benign [bẹ-nain'], *a.* 1. Benigno, afable, generoso, liberal, dulce, humano, obsequioso, servicial. 2. Benigno, saludable.
Benignant [bẹ-nig'-nant], *a.* Benéfico, propicio.
Benignity [bẹ-nig'-ni-ti], *s.* 1. Benignidad, bondad, dulzura. 2. Benignidad, salubridad.
Benignly [bẹ-nain'-li], *adv.* Benignamente.
Benison [ben'-i-sun], *s.* *V.* BENEDICTION.

Benjamin [ben'-ja-min], *s.* Corrupción de BENZOIN.
Bennet, Herb bennet [ǫrb ben'-et], *s.* (Bot.) Gariofilata o gariofilea.
Ben-nut [ben'-nut], *s.* Nuez de ben o behén de que se saca un aceite fragante.
Benorth [bę-nōrth'], *prep.* (Esco.) Al norte de.
Bent [bent], *s.* 1. Encorvadura, la acción de poner o estar una cosa en figura corva y torcida. 2. Último esfuerzo. 3. Disposición, inclinación, propensión, determinación, dirección, tendencia. 4. Pendiente, declive, cuesta. 5. (Carp.) Una sección del maderamen de un edificio que se arma y concierta en tierra, y luego se alza y coloca en posición de una vez. También, una viga grande. *To follow one's bent,* Seguir su inclinación, sus gustos.
Bent, *pp.* 1. Dirigido o inclinado a determinado paraje. 2. Determinado, resuelto. *V.* BEND. 3. Inclinado, encorvado, tendido. *To be bent upon,* Tener mucho empeño en; estar determinado o decidido a; no pensar más que en.
Benumb [bę-num'], *va.* Entorpecer, dejar torpe o casi sin movimiento. *Benumbed with cold,* Yerto, traspasado de frío.
Benumbedness [bę-num'-ed-nes], *s.* Entorpecimiento.
Benzene [ben'-zīn], *s.* *V.* BENZOLE.
Benzin, Benzine [ben'-zīn], *s.* Bencina, substancia líquida, incolora, de olor penetrante, inflamable y algo volátil, compuesta de carbono y de hidrógeno; la cual se obtiene de varias materias y principalmente de la brea o del aceite de hulla.
Benzoic [ben-zō'-ic], *a.* Benzoico, perteneciente o relativo al benjuí.
Benzoin [ben-zeín'], *s.* 1. Benjuí o menjuí, especie de resina aromática y medicinal que viene de las Indias orientales. *V.* STYRAX. 2. *V.* SPICE-BUSH. 3. (Quím.) Compuesto cristalizable ($C_{14}H_{12}O_2$) que se obtiene por diversos procedimientos.
Benzole [ben'-zōl] o **Benzol,** *s.* Benzole, líquido volátil, muy inflamable, obtenido por destilación de ácido benzoico. (<benzoin.)
Bepaint [bę-pênt'], *va.* Colorar, dar color, teñir alguna cosa.
Bepinch [bę-pinch'], *va.* Pellizcar, señalar con pellizcos.
Bepowder [bę-pau'-dęr], *va.* Empolvar (los cabellos).
Bepraise [bę-prêz'], *va.* Lisonjear hiperbólicamente.
Bepurple [bę'pūr'-pl], *va.* Purpurar, teñir de púrpura.
Bequeath [be-cwīdh'], *va.* 1. Mandar, legar o donar alguna cosa a otro en testamento. 2. Transmitir a la posteridad.
Bequeather [be-cwīdh'-er], *s.* *V.* TESTATOR.
Bequest [[bę-cwest'], *s.* Manda, donación o legado que alguno deja a otro en su testamento.
Berate [bę-ret'], *va.* Zaherir, reñir, poner a uno como nuevo.
Berber [bęr'-ber], *s.* Berberí o Bereber.
Berberry [bęr'-bęr-i], *s.* Berberís, agracejo. *V.* BARBERRY.
Bere [bīr], *s.* (Esco.) Especie de cebada, farro.
Bereave [bę-rīv'], *va.* 1. Despojar, quitar o privar a alguno de lo que goza y tiene, o desposeerle con violencia de ello; arrebatar. 2. Desolar, acongojar.
Bereavement [bę-rīv'-męnt], *s.* Privación, despojo, desamparo; aflicción.
Beret [bê-rê'], *s.* Boina.
Berg [bęrg], *s.* Gran masa o témpano de hielo.
Bergamot [bęr'-ga-mot], *s.* (Bot.) 1. Bergamota, variedad de pera delicada, llamada así porque procede de Bérgamo en Lombardía. 2. Bergamota, especie de lima muy aromática, de cuya corteza se extrae el aceite esencial de su nombre. 3. Especie de rapé o tabaco en polvo rociado con la esencia de bergamota.
Bergmaster [bęrg'-mąs-tęr], *s.* Burgomaestre, bailío.
Berhyme [be-raim'], *va.* Elogiar a uno en verso rimado.
Berlin [bęr'-lin], *s.* Berlina, coche de dos asientos. *Berlin blue,* Azul de Prusia. *Berlin wool,* Estambre.
Bermuda shorts [Bęr-miū'-da shorts], *s. pl.* Cierto estilo de calzones que llegan a la rodilla.
Bernicle [bęr'-ni-cl], *s.* Bernacho, especie de ánsar.
Berry [ber'-i], *s.* Baya, fruta pequeña, que crían varios árboles y arbustos; grano. *Avignon, French* o *yellow berries,* Granas de Aviñón, pizacantas.
Berry, *vn.* Producir bayas.
Berry-bearing [ber'-i-bêr-ing], *a.* Bacífero, que lleva bayas; dícese de los árboles.
Berth [bęrth], *s.* 1. Camarote de marinero. 2. Anclaje, estación de un buque. 3. (Fam.) Empleo, destino. 4. Cada una de las literas, camas o catres fijos construídos en los camarotes de los buques; cama en coche dormitorio de ferrocarril.
Berth, *va.* Proporcionar o dar un *berth,* ya en sentido literal ya en el de colocación, destino o empleo.
Bertha [bęr'-tha], *s.* 1. Berta, pañoleta de mujer. 2. Berta, nombre propio.
Berthage [bęrth'-ęj], *s.* 1. Derechos de anclaje o de estación de un buque. 2. El lugar destinado a cada buque en un puerto.
Bertram [bęr'-tram], *s.* (Bot.) Agerato o alterreina.
Beryl [ber'-il], *s.* Berilo, piedra preciosa; agua marina.
Berylline [ber'-il-ain], *a.* Lo perteneciente al berilo.
Bescrawl [bę-scrōl'], *va.* Escarabajear, garabatear, garrapatear.
Bescribble [bę-scrib'-l], *va.* Borrajear.
Beseech [bę-sīch'], *va.* Suplicar, rogar, pedir, implorar, hacer instancias, conjurar.
Beseecher [bę-sīch'-ęr], *s.* Rogador, suplicante, implorante.
Beseeching [bę-sīch'-ing], *s.* Ruego, instancia, súplica.
Beseem [bę-sīm'], *va.* Convenir, parecer bien.—*vn.* Aparecerse, parecer.
Beseeming [bę-sīm'-ing], *s.* Gracia, donaire, decencia, decoro, bien parecer, propiedad.—*part. adj.* Conveniente, decoroso.
Beseemly [bę-sīm'-li], *a.* Decoroso, gracioso, decente.
Beset [bę-set'], *va.* (*pret.* y *pp.* BESET). 1. Sitiar, rodear. 2. Acosar, perseguir, acechar, espiar. *Beset with troubles,* Lleno de disgustos. *A besetting sin,* Vicio habitual y dominante, flaco de una persona.
Beside [bę-said'], **Besides** [bę-saidz'], *prep.* 1. Cerca, al lado de otro. 2. Excepto. 3. Sobre; fuera de.—*adv.* Además, a más de esto, por otra parte, aun, fuera de esto o ello, fuera de que. *To be beside one's self,* Estar loco o fuera de sí, haber perdido la cabeza o el juicio; estar desatinado.
Besiege [bę-sīj'], *va.* 1. Sitiar, poner sitio a alguna plaza. 2. (Met.) Sitiar, asediar, acosar a alguno. *Besieged by applicants for office,* Asediado de pretendientes.
Besieger [bę-sīj'-ęr], *s.* Sitiador, el que pone sitio a alguna plaza.
Besieging [bę-sīj'-ing], *s.* Sitio, cerco.
Beslave [bę-slêv'], *va.* Esclavizar.
Beslobber [bę-sleb'-ęr], *va.* Salpicar o ensuciar.
Besmear [bę-smīr'], *va.* 1. Salpicar, ensuciar. 2. Embadurnar.
Besmearer [bę-smīr'-ęr], *s.* Ensuciador.
Besmirch [bę-smęrch'], *va.* 1. Manchar, ensuciar. 2. Deshonrar, despreciar.
Besmoke [bę-smōc'], *va.* 1. Ahumar, llenar de humo alguna cosa. 2. Ahumar, poner al humo alguna cosa para que la cure.
Besmut [bę-smut'], *va.* Tiznar con humo u hollín.
Besnuffed [bę-snuft'], *a.* Manchado con tabaco en polvo o rapé.
Besom [bī'-zum], *s.* Escoba, manojo de ramillas que se usa para barrer.
Besot [bę-set'], *va.* Infatuar, entontecer; embrutecer.
Besottedly [bę-set'-ed-li], *adv.* Tontamente.
Besottedness [bę-set'-ed-nes], *s.* Entontecimiento, fatuidad; embrutecimiento.
Besought [bę-sōt'], *pret.* y *pp.* del verbo *To* BESEECH.
Bespangle [bę-spang'-gl], *va.* Matizar, adornar con matices o con lentejuelas.
Bespatter [bę-spat'-ęr], *va.* 1. Salpicar, manchar con agua, lodo o suciedad. 2. Disfamar, desacreditar.
Bespeak [bę-spīk'], *va.* 1. Encomendar, mandar, ordenar, encargar a otro alguna cosa para que la haga; apalabrar alguna cosa. Mandar hacer; apalabrar. *To bespeak a pair of shoes,* Encargar un par de zapatos. 2. Predecir, adivinar. 3. Hablar a alguno. 4. Demostrar, dar a conocer. *His behaviour bespeaks a composed mind,* Su porte demuestra un ánimo tranquilo. 5. Alquilar. 6. Prevenir, advertir.
Bespeaker [bę-spīk'-ęr], *s.* El que encarga alguna cosa.
Bespeckle [bę-spec'-l], *va.* Abigarrar, gayar, pintorrear o pintarrajear alguna cosa.
Bespew [bę-spiū'], *va.* Ensuciar alguna cosa con vómito.
Bespice [bę-spais'], *va.* Condimentar, sazonar con especias o condimentos.
Bespit [bę-spit'], *va.* Escupir; ensuciar con saliva, escupiduras o gargajos.—*s.* Salivazo.
Bespoke [bę-spōc'], **Bespoken** [bę-spōc'-n], *pret.* y *pp.* del verbo *To* BESPEAK. Mandado, ordenado, alquilado, prevenido; mandado a hacer.
Bespot [bę-spet'], *va.* Abigarrar, salpicar de manchitas.
Bespread [bę-spred'], *va.* Cubrir, tender una cosa sobre otra.
Besprent [bę-sprent'], *a.* (Poét.) Rociado, esparcido.
Besprinkle [bę-spring'-cl], *va.* Rociar, esparcir alguna cosa sobre otra.
Besprinkler [bę-spring'-clęr], *s.* Rociador, el que rocía o esparce.

Besputter [bẹ-sput'-ẹr], *va.* Salpicar o ensuciar con escupiduras o saliva.
Bessemer [bes'-e-mẹr], *s.* Cualquier producto del procedimiento especial descubierto por Henry Bessemer en 1855, para la preparación del hierro y el acero. *Bessemer steel*, Acero de Bessemer. *Bessemer converter* o *apparatus*, Aparato de Bessemer.
Best [best], *a.* Superlativo de *Good* (bueno). Óptimo, superior, lo mejor, lo más bueno.—*adv.* Más bien, mejor y rectamente, más oportunamente. *I love that best of all*, Prefiero aquello a todo lo demás. *To do one's best*, Hacer todo lo que se puede, o cuanto se puede. *The second best*, El segundo en los premios, es decir, el mejor después del primero. *To make the best of a bad game*, Salir de un mal paso o negocio lo mejor posible. *He had the best of it*, Se llevó la mejor parte, sacó para sí toda la ventaja. *At best, at the best*, A lo más, lo más ; cuando mejor.
Bestain [bẹ-stên'], *va.* Manchar, llenar de manchas.
†**Bestead** [bẹ-sted'], *va.* 1. Poner, colocar en condición o circunstancia determinada ; en una posición cualquiera. Se usa casi exclusivamente en el participio pasivo. *Bestead with dangers*, Rodeado de peligros. 2. Servir o hacer favor a alguno.
Bestial [bes'-tial], *a.* Bestial, brutal ; carnal.
Bestiality [bes-ti-al'-i-ti], *s.* Bestialidad, brutalidad, irracionalidad.
Bestialize [bes'-tial-aiz], *va.* Obrar como bestia.
Bestir [bẹ-stẹr'], *va.* Mover, menear, incitar.—*vn.* Removerse, intrigar.
Best man [best man], *s.* Padrino de boda.
Bestow [bẹ-stō'], *va.* 1. Dar, conferir, otorgar. 2. Dar de limosna. 3. Dar en matrimonio. 4. Regalar, dar como presente o dádiva. 5. Emplear, gastar.
Bestowal [bẹ-stō'-al], *s.* Acción de dar, o presentar ; dádiva presentación.
Bestower [bẹ-stō'-ẹr], *s.* Regalador.
Bestraddle [bẹ-strad'-l], **Bestride** [bẹ-straid'], *va.* 1. Montar a horcajadas. 2. Zanquear, atrancar. 3. Atravesar. *V.* STRIDE.—*pret.* BESTRODE, *pp.* BESTRIDDEN.
Bestrew, Bestrow [bẹ-strū', bẹ-strō'], *va.* Rociar, esparcir, derramar sobre.
Bet [bet], *s.* Apuesta, acción de apostar ; cantidad o premio de la apuesta.
Bet, *va.* Apostar. *How much will you bet?* ¿Cuánto quiere V. apostar?
Betake [be-têc'], *va.* (*pret.* BETOOK, *pp.* BETAKEN). 1. Recurrir, acudir. 2. Irse a un lugar o punto determinado. *To betake one's self to study*, Aplicarse o darse al estudio. *To betake one's self to one's heels*, Huir, escapar, tomar las de Villadiego, afufárselas.
Beta particle [bê'-tạ par'-ti-cl], *s.* Partícula beta.
Beta ray [bê'-tạ rê], *s.* Rayo beta.
Betatron [bê'-tạ-tron], *s.* Betatrón.
Betel o **Betle** [bí'-tl], *s.* (Bot.) Betel, planta trepadora, de la familia de las piperáceas, que se cultiva en el extremo Oriente. Sus hojas tienen cierto sabor a menta y se emplean en Filipinas para la composición del buyo, el cual es una mixtura hecha con el fruto de la areca, hojas de betel y cal de conchas marinas, que mascan los naturales.
Bete noire [bêt nwār], *s.* Coco, espantajo ; objeto espantoso que causa terror. (Gal.)
Bethel [beth'-el], *s.* 1. Iglesia o capilla para marineros. 2. En Inglaterra, capilla de los disidentes. 3. Lugar santificado por la presencia de Dios.
Bethink [bẹ-thinc'], *va.* Recapacitar, recordar algo, volver a reflexionar sobre alguna cosa.—*vn.* Considerar, pensar, examinar.
Bethlehem, *s.* *V.* BEDLAM.
Bethlehemite, *s.* *V.* BEDLAMITE.
Bethought [bẹ-thōt'], *pret.* y *pp.* del verbo *To* BETHINK.
Bethump [bẹ-thump'], *va.* Dar de puñadas.
Betide [bẹ-taid'], *vn.* Suceder, acontecer, acaecer, llegar el lance, verificarse alguna cosa.—*va.* Presagiar, indicar.
Betime [be-taim'], **Betimes** [be-taimz'], *adv.* 1. Con tiempo, en sazón. 2. Pronto, antes de mucho. 3. Temprano.
Betoken [bẹ-tō'-kn], *va.* 1. Significar, representar. 2. Anunciar, pronosticar, presagiar. 3. Marcar, designar.
Betokening [bẹ-tō'-kn-ing], *s.* Presagio, pronóstico.
Betony [bet'-o-ni], *s.* (Bot.) Betónica, planta labiada. Stachys Betonica.
Betook [bẹ-tuk'], *pret.* del verbo *To* BETAKE.
Betoss [bẹ-tōs'], *va.* Agitar, mover alguna cosa con violencia.
Betray [bẹ-trê'], *va.* 1. Traicionar, hacer traición, vender a uno o entregarle alevosamente en manos del enemigo. 2. Revelar, descubrir o divulgar algún secreto. 3. Exponer, arriesgar. 4. Mostrar, hacer ver. *His voice betrayed him*, Su propia voz le descubrió o le vendió.
Betrayal [bẹ-trê'-al], *s.* La acción y efecto de traicionar, de revelar, de mostrar, etc. *A betrayal of confidence*, Abuso de confianza.
Betrayed [bẹ-trêd'], *pp.* Vendido, descubierto, engañado alevosamente. *V.* BETRAY.
Betrayer [bẹ-trê'-ẹr], *s.* Traidor.
Betrim [bẹ-trim'], *va.* Acicalar, pulir, adornar.
Betroth [bẹ-trōth'], *va.* 1. Desposar, contraer esponsales. 2. Dar palabra de casamiento.
Betrothal [bẹ-trōth'-al], *s.* Esponsales, promesa de matrimonio ; el acto de contraer esponsales.
Betrothment [bẹ-trōth'-mẹnt], *s.* Esponsales, esponsalicio, el acto de contraer esponsales. (Poco us.)
Better [bet'-ẹr], *a. comp.* Mejor, lo que es superior a otra cosa con que se compara.—*adv.* Mejor, más bien. *So much the better*, Tanto mejor. *To be better*, Estar mejor de salud ; ser de mejor conducta ; valer más. *To make better*, Mejorar una cosa o hacerla de más valor de lo que era ; enmendar, corregir, reformar. *To grow better*, Irse mejorando alguna cosa, enmendarse. *To grow better and better*, Ir de mejor a mejor. *The better way is to*, El mejor modo o medio es. *To be better off*, Estar en mejor posición, más acomodado.
Better, *va.* 1. Mejorar adelantar, reformar, aumentar. 2. Sobrepujar, exceder.
Better, *s.* 1. El mejor o lo mejor, de más suposición ; ventaja, mejoría. 2. Superior, persona de rango más elevado o de mayor mérito. *Our betters*, Nuestros superiores.
Better, *s.* Apostador.
Bettering [bet'-ẹr-ing], *s.* Mejoría.
Betterment [bet'-ẹr-mẹnt], *s.* Mejora, mejoramiento, en especial de bienes raíces.
Betting [bet'-ing], *s.* Apuesta.
Bettor [bet'-er], *s.* Apostador.
Betty [bet'-i], *s.* 1. Maricón, cominero, el hombre que se entremete en los quehaceres de mujeres. 2. (E. U.) Matraz, botella que tiene el cuello muy largo. 3. (Ger.) Pie de cabra, instrumento de hierro para romper y derribar puertas ; ganzúa romana, corchete, garabato.—*n. pr.* Belica, Belita, dim. de *Elizabeth*.
Between [bẹ-twín'], *prep.* 1. Entre, en medio de una y otra cosa. *Between decks*, (Mar.) Entre puentes. 2. Entre, perteneciente a dos que están en compañía. *Between whiles*, (Vulg.) A ratos. *The space between*, Intermedio, espacio, hueco. *Between now and then*, De aquí a allá.
Betwixt [bẹ-twicst'], *prep.* Entre. *V.* BETWEEN.
Bevatron [bev'-a-tron], *s.* (Fís.) Bevatrón.
Bevel [bev'-el], *s.* Cartabón, instrumento que sirve para medir y formar ángulos de toda especie. *Bevel edge*, Bisel, chaflán. *Bevel gear*, Engrane o engranaje cónico; ruedas o piñones cónicos o en ángulo. *Bevel rule*, Falsarregla, falsa escuadra.
Bevel, *va.* Cortar un ángulo al sesgo o en chaflán, chaflanar, achaflanar.
Bevelling [bev'-el-ing], *s.* Sesgadura, chaflán, bisel, bies, corte al sesgo.
Beverage [bev'-ẹr-ẹj], *s.* 1. Brebaje, bebida. 2. Estrena. 3. (Dial. brit.) Propina.
Bevy [bev'-i], *s.* 1. Bandada, número crecido de aves o pájaros que vuelan juntos. 2. Compañía o junta de mujeres ; corro, corrillo.
Bewail [bẹ-wêl'], *va.* Llorar, lamentar, sentir, deplorar.—*vn.* Plañir.
Bewailing [bẹ-wêl'-ing], *s.* Lamentación, lloro, sentimiento, pesar, pena.
Beware [bẹ-wār'], *va.* Cuidar de, mirar por.—*vn.* Guardarse, recelarse y precaverse de algún riesgo o peligro ; recatarse.
Beweep [bẹ-wíp'], *va.* Llorar, lamentar con lágrimas.—*vn.* Plañir.
Bewet [bẹ-wet'], *va.* Mojar, humedecer alguna cosa.
Bewilder [bẹ-wil'-dẹr], *va.* Descaminar, descarriar, separar del camino recto o hacer perder a uno en parajes escabrosos y sin salida.
Bewitch [bẹ-wich'], *va.* 1. Encantar, maleficiar. 2. Encantar, embelesar, cegar, hechizar, arrobar.
Bewitcher [bẹ-wich'-ẹr], *s.* 1. Encantador, brujo, hechicero. 2. Halagador, encantador, hechicero.
Bewitchery [bẹ-wich'-ẹr-i], **Bewitchment** [bẹ-wich'-mẹnt], *s.* Encantamiento, hechizo; embeleso, encanto, gracia.
Bewitching [bẹ-wich'-ing], *s.* Encanto, hechizo ; halago, embeleso.—*a.* Atractivo ; encantador, hechicero.
Bewitchingly [bẹ-wich'-ing-li], *adv.* Halagüeñamente.
Bewray [bẹ-rê'], *va.* (Des.) 1. Traicionar, hacer traición. 2. Hacer ver, descubrir.
Bewrayer [bẹ-rê'-ẹr], *s.* Traidor.
Bey [bê], *s.* Bey, el gobernador entre los turcos.
Beyond [bẹ-yond'], *prep.* 1. Más allá,

a la parte de allá, allende, más adelante. 2. Fuera. *Beyond my reach*, Fuera de mis alcances. *Beyond the hour*, Pasada la hora. *Beyond measure*, Desmesuradamente. *Beyond dispute*, Incontestable. *Beyond doubt*, Fuera de duda. *Beyond comprehension*, Incomprensible.—*adv.* Lejos.

Bezel, Bezil [bez'-el], *s.* Chatón, la parte de un anillo en que se engasta la piedra.

Bezel [bez'-el], *va.* 1. Cortar un ángulo al sesgo. 2. Poner chatón, engarzar.

Bezique [bę-zíc'], *s.* Juego de naipes.

Bezoar [bę-zō'-ar], *s.* Bezar, bezaar o bezoar, piedra medicinal.

Bezoardic [be-zo-ār'-dic], *a.* Bezoárdico.

Bi- [bai], prefijo que significa dos, dos veces o doble. Algunas veces *bin*, por eufonía. (< Lat. bis.)

Biangular [bai-ang'-giu-lar] (preferido) o **Biangulated** [bai-an'-giu-lê-ted], *a.* Biangular, lo que tiene dos ángulos.

Biannual [bai-an'-yū-al], *a.* Semestral, semianual.

Bias [bai'-as], *s.* 1. Sesgo, sentido oblicuo, oblicuidad. 2. Carga o peso que se echa en un lado de un bolo para que al tirarlo se desvíe de la línea recta. 3. Propensión, inclinación, disposición; sesgo. 4. (Fig.) Preocupación, prejuicio.—*adv.* Al sesgo. *To cut on the bias*, Cortar al sesgo.

Bias, *va.* 1. Inclinar, ladear hacia una parte determinada. *Passions bias the judgment*, Las pasiones arrastran o tuercen el juicio. 2. Prevenir, preocupar. 3. Ganar, atraer la voluntad de alguno. (Fig.) Preocupar, inducir a una opinión o juicio sin el debido examen.

Bib [bib], *s.* Babador, babero, un pedazo de lienzo que para más limpieza se pone a los niños en el pecho.

Bib, *va.* Beber frecuentemente, beborrotear.

§**Bibacious** [bai-bé'-shus], *a.* Dado al vicio de beber, bebedor, borracho. (Fam.) Cuero.

Bibasic [bai-bé'-sic], *a.* (Quím.) Bibásico, de dos bases o de doble base.

Bibb [bib] o **Bibcock**, *s.* Grifo, llave curva de agua.

Bible [bai'-bl], *s.* 1. Biblia, la Sagrada Escritura; ejemplar de la Biblia; también, una edición particular de las Escrituras. 2. Los libros sagrados de cualquier pueblo.

Biblical [bib'-li-cal], *a.* 1. Bíblico, que pertenece a la Biblia. 2. En consonancia con la Biblia.

Bibliographer [bib-li-og'-ra-fęr], *s.* Bibliógrafo.

Bibliographical [bib-li-o-graf'-i-cal], *a.* Bibliográfico.

Bibliography [bib-li-og'-ra-fi], *s.* Bibliografía.

Bibliomania [bib-li-o-mé'-ni-a], *s.* Bibliomanía.

Bibliomaniac [bib-li-o-mé'-ni-ac], *s.* Bibliómano.

Bibliophile [bib'-li-o-fail], *s.* Bibliófilo, aficionado a los libros.

Bibliopolist [bib-li-op'-o-list], *s.* Librero.

Bibulous [bib'-yu-lus], *a.* 1. Poroso, esponjoso. *Bibulous paper*, Papel secante, papel de filtro. 2. Bebedor, borrachín.

Bicapsular [bai-cap'-siu-lar], *a.* (Bot.) Bicapsular, la planta cuya cápsula está dividida en dos partes.

Bicarbonate [bai-cār'-bo-nêt], *s.* Bicarbonato, sal que contiene doble cantidad de ácido carbónico que el carbonato neutro.

Bice [bais], *s.* Azul de Armenia.

Bicentenary [bai-sent'-en-a-ri], *s.* Bicentenario.

Bicephalous [bai-sef'-a-lus], *a.* Bicéfalo, de dos cabezas.

Biceps [bai'-seps], *s.* Músculo de dos cabezas. Hay uno en el brazo, el braquial, y otro en el muslo, femoral.

Bichloride [bai-clō'-rid], *s.* (Quím.) Bicloruro. Se llama también DICHLORID.

Bichromate [bai-crō'-mêt], *s.* (Quím.) Bicromato.

Bicipital, Bicipitous [bai-sip'-i-tal, tus], *a.* Bicípite, lo que tiene dos cabezas.

Bicker [bik'-ęr], *vn.* 1. Escaramucear, pelear a veces acometiendo y a veces retirándose; reñir, disputar. 2. Correr rápidamente con algún ruido, como un arroyo; chisporrotear; charlar, gorjear como los pájaros.—*va.* Dar o golpear muchas veces.

Bicker, *s.* (Prov. Ingla. y Esco.) Vasija de madera para alimento y bebidas.

Bickerer [bik'-ęr-ęr], *s.* Escaramuzador, el que pelea haciendo escaramuzas; pendenciero.

Bickering [bik'-ęr-ing], *s.* Escaramuza; pendencia, riña, disputa, contestación.

Bickern [bik'-ęrn], *s.* Pico de bigornia.

Bicolor [bai'-cul-er], *a.* Bicolor, de dos colores.

Biconcave [bai-con'-kêv], *a.* Bicóncavo, de dos caras cóncavas.

Biconvex [bai-con'-vex], *a.* Biconvexo, de dos caras convexas.

Bicornous [bai-cōr'-nus], *a.* Bicorne, que tiene dos cuernos.

Bicorporal [bai-cōr'-po-ral], *a.* Bicorpóreo, de dos cuerpos.

Bicuspid [bai-cus'-pid], *a.* Bicúspide, que tiene dos cúspides.—*s.* La muela inmediata al colmillo.

Bicycle [bai'-si-kl o bai'-sai-kl], *s.* Bicicleta, biciclo, velocípedo de dos ruedas. *Safety bicycle*, Bicicleta de dos ruedas iguales, del mismo diámetro; es la forma usual hoy día.

Bicycling [bai'-si-kling], *s.* Ciclismo, arte y práctica de andar en bicicleta.

Bicyclist, Bicycler [bai'-si-klist, -klęr] *s.* Ciclista.

Bid [bid], *s.* 1. Postura, el precio o valor que se ofrece en una venta, o almoneda pública. 2. La puja o valor que se ofrece sobre otra puja.

Bid, *va.* (*pret.* BADE, BAD, o BID; *pp.* BIDDEN o BID). 1. Pedir, rogar, convidar. 2. Mandar, ordenar. 3. Ofrecer, proponer, dar, pujar. 4. Sobrepujar, exceder. 5. Pronunciar, publicar, declarar. *To bid adieu*, Despedirse. *To bid defiance to*, Atreverse con.

Bidden [bid'-n], *pp.* del verbo *To* BID. Invitado; comandado.

Bidder [bid'-ęr], *s.* El postor, el que ofrece, propone o puja el precio de alguna cosa. *The highest bidder*, El mejor postor.

Bidding [bid'-ing], *s.* 1. Orden, mandato. 2. Ofrecimiento de precio por alguna cosa, postura.

Biddy [bid'-i], *s.* 1. Nombre que se emplea para llamar a las gallinas. 2. (Fam.) Brígida: por extensión, criada irlandesa.

Bide [baid], *va.* Sufrir, aguantar.—*vn.* Residir, vivir de asiento en alguna parte.

Bidental [bai-den'-tal], *a.* Bidentado, que tiene dos dientes.

Bidentate [bai-den'-têt], *a.* De dos dientes, bidentado.

Bidet [bi-det'], *s.* 1. Bidé, bañadera de asiento para uso de las señoras. 2. Jaca, caballo pequeño.

Biding [baid'-ing], *s.* Residencia, mansión.

Biennial [bai-en'-ni-al], *a.* Bienal, que dura dos años o que sucede cada dos años.—*s.* 1. Planta bienal que produce hojas y raíces el primer año, y flores con fruto el segundo, y en seguida muere. 2. Examen que se verifica una vez cada dos años en los colegios.

Bier [bir], *s.* Andas, féretro, el ataúd en que llevan a enterrar los muertos.

Bifarious [bai-fé'-ri-us], *a.* Duplicado; de dos maneras.

Bifer [bai'-fęr], *s.* Planta que produce flores o frutos dos veces al año.

Biferous [bif'-ęr-us], *a.* Que da dos cosechas al año.

Bifocal [bai-fō'-cal], *a.* Bifocal. *Bifocal glasses*, Lentes o anteojos bifocales.

Bifold [bai'-fōld], *a.* Doble.

Biform [bai'-fōrm], **Biformed** [bai'-fōrmd], *a.* Biforme, que tiene dos formas.

Bifurcate [bai-fūr'-kêt] o **Bifurcated** [bai-fūr'-kê-ted], *a.* Bifurcado, que tiene dos cabezas; que está dividido a modo de horca.

Bifurcation [bai-fūr-kê'-shun], *s.* División en dos partes, bifurcación.

Big [big], *a.* 1. Grande, abultado, espeso, lleno, grueso. 2. Preñada. *A woman big with child*, Una mujer preñada o embarazada. 3. Hinchado, inflado. *To talk big*, Echar bravatas. *To look big*, Entonarse. 4. Grande, noble, generoso, valeroso, magnánimo. *Big bug*, (Fam. E. U.) Persona de importancia o que cree serlo. *Big-bellied*, Ventrudo, ventroso; preñado. *Big-bodied*, Grueso, gordo, repleto. *Big-boned*, Huesudo, robusto. *Big-corned*, Lleno de granos muy gruesos. *Big-head*, (Vulg.) Estado de presumido y arrogante. *Big-sounding*, Altisonante. *Big-swoln*, Túmido, hinchado. *Bigwig*, *s.* (Vulg.) Persona de importancia.

Bigg, *s.* (Bot.) Especie de cebada.

Bigamist [big'-a-mist], *s.* Bígamo, el que tiene dos mujeres a un tiempo.

Bigamy [big'-a-mi], *s.* 1. Bigamia, el delito de tener dos mujeres a un tiempo. 2. Bigamia, el estado de ser casado dos veces.

Biggin [big'-in], *s.* 1. Cafetera. 2. Capillo de niño.

Biggish [big'-ish], *a.* Algo grande o grueso.

Bighearted [big-hārt'-ed], *a.* Generoso, magnánimo, de gran corazón.

Bighorn [big'-hōrn], *s.* (Zool.) Carnero de grandes cuernos de las Montañas Roqueñas, América del Norte.

Bight [bait], *s.* (Mar.) 1. Seno de un cabo. 2. Caleta, pequeña ensenada.

Bigly [big'-li], *adv.* Orgullosamente, con orgullo y altivez, extremadamente.

Bigness [big'-nes], *s.* 1. Grandeza, el exceso que tiene alguna cosa sobre lo regular y común. 2. Grandor, espesor, grosor, el tamaño de alguna cosa, sea pequeña o grande.

Bigot [bɪg'-et], *s.* 1. Fanático, el hombre que sigue un partido u opinión religiosa con preocupación y entusiasmo. 2. Beatón, santurrón, hipócrita, mojigato.

Bigoted [bɪg'-et-ed], *a.* Ciegamente preocupado a favor de alguna cosa.

Bigotry [bɪg'-et-rɪ], *s.* 1. Fanatismo, celo indiscreto y excesivo o preocupación en materias religiosas. 2. Hipocresía.

Bikini [bi-ki'-ni], *s.* Bikini, brevísimo traje de baño femenino.

Bilander [bɪl'-an-dẹr], *s.* Embarcación pequeña de dos palos que se usa para portear géneros.

Bilateral [baɪ-lat'-ẹr-al], *a.* Bilateral, de dos lados.

Bilberry [bɪl'-ber-ɪ], *s.* Arándano, fruta silvestre; mirtil.

Bilbo [bɪl'-bō], *s.* Estoque, arma con que sólo se puede herir de punta. (Des.) Toma el nombre de la ciudad española de Bilbao.

Bile [baɪl], *s.* 1. Bilis, humor amarillento o verdoso que secreta el hígado. 2. (Met.) Cólera, ira, enojo; mal genio.

Bile-duct [baɪl'-duct], *s.* Conducto biliar, por donde pasa la bilis.

Bilge [bɪlj], *vn.* (Mar.) Hacer agua.

Bilge, *s.* (Mar.) 1. Pantoque. *Bilge-water,* Agua de pantoque. *Bilge-pumps,* Bombas de carena. 2. Barriga de barril.

Biliary [bɪl'-ɪ-a-rɪ], *a.* Biliario, que pertenece a los órganos que secretan la bilis.

Bilingual [baɪ-lɪŋ'-gwal], *a.* 1. Bilingüe, en dos lenguas. 2. Que habla dos idiomas.

Bilious [bɪl'-yus], *a.* Bilioso, lo que abunda en bilis.

Biliousness [bɪl'-yus-nes], *s.* Biliosidad, estado bilioso.

Bilk [bɪlk], *va.* Engañar, defraudar, pegarla, chasquear, no pagar lo que se debe.

Bilk, *s.* 1. Traición, engaño. 2. (Vulg.) Engañador, trampista, el que defrauda a sus acreedores.

Bill [bɪl], *s.* 1. Pico de ave. 2. Honcejo o podadera corva. *Bill-hook* o *hedging bill,* Podadera corva con dos filos. 3. Papel, escrito, billete, cédula. 4. (Com.) Cuenta, factura. 5. Billete, pagaré, letra. *Bill of exchange,* Letra de cambio. 6. Proyecto de ley o estatuto, que se presenta al Parlamento de Inglaterra o al Congreso de los Estados Unidos para su aprobación. 7. Cartel. 8. Hacha de armas. *Bill-broker,* Corredor de cambios. *Bill of rights,* Una de las leyes fundamentales de Inglaterra. *Play-bill,* Cartel de teatro. *Bill of lading,* Conocimiento de embarque; resguardo de un capitán de buque. *Bill of fare,* Lista de los manjares dispuestos para comer. *Bill of health,* Patente de sanidad. *Bill of mortality,* Lista o relación de los muertos que ha habido en algún distrito en un tiempo determinado. *Bills payable,* Letras pagaderas. *Bills receivable,* Letras a cobrar. *Bill-head,* Encabezamiento de factura.

Bill, *vn.* Arrullar, como las palomas cuando se enamoran; acariciar. —*va.* Avisar al público, o publicar alguna cosa por medio de periódicos, carteles, etc.

Bill of sale [bil ef sêl], *s.* Escritura de venta.

Billboard [bil'-bōrd], *s.* Cartelera, cartel para anuncios.

Billet [bɪl'-et], *s.* 1. Billete, esquela. 2. Zoquete de leña para chimenea u horno. 3. Boleta.

Billet, *va.* Alojar o aposentar soldados.

Billet-doux [bɪl'-ẹ-dū], *s.* Carta o esquela amorosa.

Billfold [bil'-fōld], *s.* Billetera.

Billiards [bɪl'-yardz], *s.* Billar, juego a modo del de los trucos. *Billiard-ball,* Billa, bola de billar. *Billiard-cue,* Taco. *Billiard-cloth,* Paño de billar. *Billiard-pocket,* Tronera de billar. *Billiard-table,* Mesa de billar.

Billion [bɪl'-yun], *s.* (Arit.) 1. Billón, millón de millones. 2. Mil millones, en el sistema de enumeración actual, que es el francés y americano; un millón de millones en el inglés.

Billionaire [bil'-yʊn-ār], *s.* Billonario.

Billionth [bɪl'-yunth], *a.* Billonésimo, cada una de las partes iguales de un todo dividido en mil millones de ellas; la última de estas partes.

Billow [bɪl'-ō], *s.* Oleada, ola grande.

Billow, *vn.* Crecer o hincharse como una ola.

Billowy [bɪl'-o-ɪ], *a.* Hinchado como las olas.

Billy [bɪl'-ɪ], *s.* Palo corto con extremidad gruesa; cachiporra de agente de policía.

Bilobate [baɪ-lō'-bêt], *a.* De dos lóbulos; bilobulado.

Bilocular [baɪ-lec'-yu-lar], *a.* Bilocular, de dos celdillas.

Bimana [baɪ'-ma-na o bɪm'-a-na], *s.* (Zool.) Bimano, el orden más elevado de los mamíferos: es decir, el hombre.

Bimetallic [baɪ-met-al'-ɪc], *a.* Bimetálico, que consiste de dos metales o se refiere a ellos.

Bimetallism [baɪ-met'-al-ɪzm], *s.* Uso concurrente del oro y la plata como dinero, en una razón fija.

Bimonthly [bai-mʊnth'-li], *a.* Bimestral.—*adv.* Bimestralmente.

Bin [bɪn], *s.* 1. El lugar o sitio donde se guarda pan, vino, carbón o granos. 2. Hucha, arcón, arca.

Binary [baɪ'-na-rɪ], *a.* Binario, doble, el número que consta de dos unidades.

Binaural [bin-ō'-ral], *a.* 1. Para los dos oídos. 2. De dos orejas.

Bind [baɪnd], *va.* 1. Atar, apretar, amarrar con cadenas u otra cosa. 2. Ceñir, envolver, ribetear, galonear. 3. Unir, juntar una cosa con otra. 4. Encuadernar. 5. Vendar una herida. 6. Obligar, precisar, constreñir, empeñar. 7. Estreñir, desecar. 8. Impedir, embarazar. 9. Poner a uno a servir. *To bind one apprentice,* Escriturar a alguno como aprendiz de un oficio. 10. *To bind over,* Obligar a comparecer ante el juez.—(For.) Condenar a.—*vn.* 1. Encogerse una cosa poniéndose dura. 2. Astringir, estreñir. 3. Ser obligatorio.

Bind, *s.* Tallo o vástago de lúpulo.

Binder [baɪn'-dẹr], *s.* 1. Encuadernador, el que encuaderna libros. 2. Atadero, lo que sirve para atar alguna cosa. 3. Atador, entre los segadores el que ata los haces en gavillas; en particular, agavilladora, apéndice de una máquina segadora, para agavillar las mieses. 4. (Carp.) Traviesa, ligazón, amarra.

Bindery [baɪnd'-ẹr-ɪ], *s.* Taller de encuadernación.

Binding [baɪn'-dɪng], *s.* 1. Venda, tira, faja, cinta ancha y larga que sirve para atar o ligar cubriendo alguna cosa. *Bindings,* (Mar.) Herrajes de las vigotas. 2. Ribete de costura. 3. Encuadernación.

Binding, *a.* 1. Obligatorio, lo que obliga. 2. Astringente, estíptico, lo que estriñe. *Binding screw,* (Elec.) Tornillo de conexión.

Binnacle [bɪn'-a-cl], *s.* (Mar.) Bitácora, la caja en que se pone la aguja de marear.

Binocle [bɪn'-o-cl], *s.* (Opt.) Binóculo, anteojo doble de larga vista, gemelo.

Binocular [bin-ec'-yū-lar], *a.* Binocular. **Binoculars,** *s. pl.* Gemelos, binóculos.

Binomial [baɪ-nō'-mɪ-al], *s.* (Alg.) Raíz binomia, la que consta de dos partes o números.

Biochemical [baɪ-o-kem'-ɪ-cal], *a.* Bioquímico.

Biochemistry [bai-o-kem'-is-tri], *s.* Bioquímica.

Biodegradable [bai-o-dẹ-grêd'-a-bl], *a.* Hecho de compuestos que se descomponen por la acción de bacterias.

Biodynamics [bai-o-dai-nam'-ics], *s.* Biodinámica.

Bioecology [bai-o-ẹ-cel'-o-ji], *s.* Bioecología.

Biogenesis [bai-o-jen'-ẹ-sis], *s.* Biogénesis, doctrina de que la vida se produce únicamente por medio de seres vivientes.

Biogeny [baɪ-ej'-ẹn-ɪ], *s.* Biogenia, la evolución de los organismos o cosas vivientes.

Biographer [baɪ-eg'-ra-fẹr], *s.* Biógrafo, escritor de vidas.

Biographical [baɪ-o-graf'-ɪ-cal], *a.* Biográfico.

Biography [baɪ-eg'-ra-fɪ], *s.* Biografía.

Biologic, Biological [baɪ-o-lej'-ɪc, al], *a.* Biológico, perteneciente a la biología.

Biology [baɪ-el'-o-jɪ], *s.* Biología, ciencia de la vida, o de los organismos vivientes; comprende la zoología y la botánica.

Biologist [bai-el'-o-jist], *s.* Biólogo.

Bionics [bai-e'-nics], *s.* (Biol.) Biónica.

Bionomy [baɪ-en'-o-mɪ], *s.* Bionomía, ciencia de las leyes a que obedecen las funciones de los seres vivientes.

Biophysical [bai-o-fiz'-i-cal], *a.* Biofísico.

Biophysics [bai-o-fiz'-ics], *s.* Biofísica.

Biopsy [bai'-ep-si], *s.* Biopsia.

Biosphere [bai'-o-sfir], *s.* Biosfera.

Biotin [bai'-o-tin], *s.* Biotina.

Biparous [bip'-a-rʊs], *a.* La hembra que pare dos hijos a un tiempo.

Bipartisan [bai-par'-ti-zan], *a.* Representante de dos partidos políticos.

Bipartition [baɪ-par-tɪsh'-un], *s.* División en dos pedazos o partes.

Bipartite [baɪ-pār'-taɪt], *a.* Que consta de dos partes correspondientes.

Biped [baɪ'-ped], *s.* Bípedo, animal de dos pies.

Bipedal [bɪp'-e-dal], *a.* Bípede, que tiene dos pies.

Bipennated [baɪ-pen'-ê-ted], *a.* Que tiene dos alas.

Bipetalous [baɪ-pet'-a-lus], *a.* Bipétalo, que tiene dos pétalos.

Biplane [bai'-plên], *s.* Biplano.

Bipolar [baɪ-pō'-lar], *a.* Bipolar, que tiene dos polos.

Bipyramidal [baɪ-pɪ-ram'-ɪ-dal], *a.* Bi-

piramidal, formado por dos pirámides, unidas por sus bases.
Biquadrate [bai-cwed'-rêt], **Biquadratic** [bai-cwod-rat'-ic], *s.* (Alg.) Bicuadrática, la cuarta potencia que proviene de la multiplicación del cuadrado por sí mismo.
Birch [bęrch], *s.* (Bot.) 1. Abedul, cualquier árbol o arbusto del género Betula, de las cupulíferas. 2. Varilla de abedul para azotar à los niños. 3. Madera del árbol.
Birchen [bęrch'-en], *a.* Abedulino, perteneciente al abedul; hecho de abedul.
Bird [bęrd], *s.* Ave, término general para todo animal de pluma que vuela; pájaro. *Bird of passage,* Ave de paso. *Bird of prey,* Ave de rapiña. *Song bird,* Pájaro cantor. *Birds of a feather,* Pájaros de una misma pluma, gente de una calaña. *A bird in the hand is worth two in the bush,* Más vale pájaro en mano que ciento volando.
Bird, *vn.* Andar a caza de pájaros.
Bird-bolt [bęrd'-bōlt], *s.* 1. Saetilla o dardo pequeño. 2. *V.* BURBOT.
Bird-cage [bęrd'-kêj], *s.* Jaula de pájaros.
Bird-call [bęrd'-cōl], *s.* Reclamo.
Bird-catcher [bęrd'-cach-ęr], **Birder** [bęrd'-ęr], *s.* Pajarero, el que caza pájaros.
Bird-eyed [bęrd'-aid], *a.* Dotado de ojo vivo como el de los pájaros.
Bird-fancier [bęrd-fan'-si-ęr], *s.* 1. El aficionado a los pájaros. 2. Pajarero, el que se dedica a la cría y venta de pájaros.
Birdie [bęrd'-i], *s.* En el juego de golf, golpe menos de par en un agujero.
Bird-like [bęrd'-laic], *a.* Semejante a pájaro.
Bird-lime [bęrd'-laim], *s.* Liga, materia viscosa con la cual, untando unas varillas o espartos, se cazan pájaros; ajonje.
Bird-limed [bęrd'-laimd], *a.* (Fig.) Cogido como con liga.
Bird-man [bęrd'-man], *s.* Pajarero; dedicado al estudio de las aves.
Bird's-eye [bęrdz'-ai], *s.* (Bot.) Ojo de pájaro. *Bird's-eye view,* Vista de pájaro. *Bird's-eye diaper,* Género moteado (lienzo adamascado). *Bird's-eye maple,* Arce moteado.—*a.* 1. Moteado, salpicado de motas que semejan ojos de pájaro. 2. Visto de una ojeada, y desde lo alto, como ven los pájaros.
Bird's-foot [bęrdz'-fut], *s.* (Bot.) Pie de pájaro, planta del género Ornithopus.
Bird's-nest [bęrdz'-nest], *s.* 1. Nido de ave. 2. (Bot.) Planta.
Birgander [bęr'-gan-dęr], *s.* (Orn.) Ganso silvestre.
Birkie [bęrk'-i], *a.* (Esco.) Vivo, listo.—*s.* Impertinente.
Birr [būr], *s.* Zumbido, ruido continuado, como el que hace el torno al hilar.
Birr, *vn.* Zumbar, moverse con ruido continuado y bronco.
Birt, *s.* *V.* TURBOT.
Birth [bęrth], *s.* 1. Nacimiento, el acto de nacer. 2. Nacimiento, alcurnia, el origen y descendencia de alguna persona en orden a su calidad. *He is a gentleman by birth,* Es caballero de nacimiento. 3. Parto, el feto que ha nacido. 4. Parto, la acción o acto de parir. 5. Camada, lechigada. 6. Causa, principio. *A new birth,* Renacimiento, regeneración.
Birth control [bęrth'-ken-trol], *s.* Control de natalidad.
Birthday [bęrth'-dê], *s.* Cumpleaños, el aniversario del día en que alguno ha nacido. *Birthday present,* Cuelga, regalo.
Birthdom [bęrth'-dum], *s.* Derechos de nacimiento, los privilegios que corresponden a uno por su nacimiento.
Birth-mark [bęrth'-mārc], *s.* Marca o señal corporal de nacimiento.
Birthnight [bęrth'-nait], *s.* La noche en que alguno nace.
Birthplace [bęrth'-plês], *s.* Suelo nativo, el paraje donde uno nace.
Birth rate [berth rêt], *s.* Natalidad.
Birthright [bęrth'-rait], *s.* 1. Derechos de nacimiento, los privilegios que corresponden à uno por su nacimiento. 2. Primogenitura, la prerrogativa del primogénito. 3. Mayorazgo.
Birthwort [bęrth'-wert], *s.* (Bot.) Aristoloquia.
Bis-. Prefijo latino que equivale a dos veces.
Biscayan [bis-kê'-an], *a.* Vizcaíno, de Vizcaya.
Biscuit [bis'-kit], *s.* 1. Galleta o bizcocho, pan que se cuece segunda vez para que dure por mucho tiempo. 2. Bizcocho, masa compuesta de la flor de harina, almendras y azúcar. 3. Porcelana cocida antes de ser vidriada.
Bise. *V.* BICE.
Bisect [bai-sect'], *va.* Dividir en dos partes iguales.
Bisection [bai-sec'-shun], *s.* Bisección, la división de alguna cantidad en dos partes iguales.
Bisector [bai-sec'-ter], *s.* Bisector, bisectriz.
Bisexual [bai-sex'-yu-al], *a.* (Bot.) De dos órganos; flor que tiene estambres y pistilos.
Bishop [bish'-up], *s.* 1. Obispo, prelado. 2. Alfil, pieza del juego de ajedrez. 3. Bebida compuesta de vino, azúcar y zumo de naranjas. *Bishop's lawn,* Linón, batista; especie de tela muy fina.
Bishop, *va.* Confirmar o administrar la confirmación.
Bishop-like [bish'-up-laik], **Bishoply** [bish'-up-li], *a.* Episcopal, lo que es propio de un obispo o pertenece a él.
Bishopric [bish'-up-ric], *s.* Obispado, el territorio o distrito asignado a cada obispo; diócesis.
Bishopsweed [bish'-ups-wīd], **Bishopswort** [bish'-ups-wūrt], *s.* (Bot.) Amijistro.
Bisk [bisc], *s.* Sopa o caldo; guisado a modo de pepitoria.
Bismuth [biz'-muth], *s.* Bismuto, metal de color blanco rojizo. *Magistery of bismuth* o *pearl white,* El nitrato de bismuto.
Bison [bai'-sęn], *s.* Bisonte, o búfalo de la América del Norte, muy parecido al toro: raza casi extinguida.
Bisque [bisk], *s.* Porcelana blanca no vidriada. (De BISCUIT, 3ª acep.)
Bissextile [bi-sex'-til], *s.* y *a.* Bisiesto.
Bister o **Bistre** [bis'-tęr], *s.* Tinta de China: hollín desleído.
Bistort [bis'-tert], *s.* (Bot.) Bistorta, dragoncia o dragúnculo.
Bistoury [bis'-tū-ri], *s.* Bisturí, instrumento de cirujano que sirve para hacer incisiones.
Bisulcous [bai-sul'-cus], *a.* Partihendido, bisulco.
Bisulphate [bai-sul'-fêt], *s.* Bisulfato.
Bit [bit], *s.* 1. Bocado. *Tit-bit,* Trozo delicado. 2. Pedacito, pedazo pequeño de alguna cosa. 3. (Local, E. U.) Real americano de moneda cortada; a menudo el real fuerte español, de 12½ centavos. 4. Barrena de berbiquí. 5. Freno, brida. *Bit of a bridle,* Bocado del freno. *Bit of a key,* Paletón de llave. *Bit of an auger,* Gusanillo de taladro. *Bit of a cable,* (Mar.) Bitadura del cable. *Bits,* (Mar.) *V.* BITTS. *Not a bit,* Nada, ni miaja. *Extension* (ó *expansion*) *bit,* (Mec.) Barrena de extensión. *Taper-bit,* Alisador cónico.
Bit, *va.* 1. Enfrenar, echar el freno al caballo. 2. (Mar.) Tomar la bitadura con el cable, abitar.
Bit, *pret.* y *pp.* del verbo *To* BITE.
Bitch [bich], *sf.* 1. Perra, la hembra del perro. †*A proud bitch,* Perra salida. 2. (Vulg.) Zorra, nombre contumelioso que se da a las mujeres perdidas.
Bite [bait], *va.* (*pret.* BIT, *pp.* BITTEN o BIT). 1. Morder, asir con los dientes haciendo presa con ellos, o cortando y despedazando alguna cosa; roer. *To bite the dust,* Morder el polvo, morir, caer vencido. *To bite the bait,* Picar el anzuelo. 2. Punzar, picar. *This mustard bites my tongue,* Esta mostaza me quema la boca. 3. Murmurar o satirizar, hiriendo la fama de alguno. 4. Engañar, clavar, defraudar.
Bite, *s.* 1. Mordedura, tarascada, la acción de morder. 2. Mordedura, la acción de picar el pez el cebo del anzuelo. 3. Bocado. 4. Engaño. 5. (Ger.) Engañador, impostor, ladrón, ratero.
Biter [bait'-ęr], *s.* 1. Mordedor, el que muerde. 2. Pez que muerde o pica el cebo. 3. Engañador, impostor.
Biting [bait'-ing], *s.* 1. Mordimiento, mordedura, tarascada. 2. El acto de dañar a uno censurándole.—*a.* Mordaz; picante.
Bitingly [bait'-ing-li], *adv.* Mordazmente, con mofa; satíricamente.
Bitt, *s.* *V.* BITTS.
Bitten, *pp.* del verbo *To* BITE.
Bitter [bit'-ęr], *a.* 1. Amargo, áspero, lo que tiene amargor o gusto desapacible. 2. Amargo, cruel, severo. 3. Calamitoso, miserable. 4. Mordaz, satírico, rudo. 5. Penoso, desagradable. *Bitter words,* Palabras mayores, frases picantes, insultos.—*s.* Alguna cosa amarga. *To taste bitter,* Ser de gusto amargo. *A bitter criticism,* o *critique,* Una crítica amarga, severa, mordaz. *Bitter enmity,* Odio encarnizado. *Bitter cold,* Frío picante. *Bitters,* Licor en cuya composición entran diversas plantas y raíces amargas.
Bitterish [bit'-ęr-ish], *a.* Amargoso, ligeramente amargo.
Bitterly [bit'-ęr-li], *adv.* 1. Amargamente, con amargura o sabor amargo. 2. Con angustia o pena. 3. Agriamente, severamente.
Bittern [bit'-ęrn], *s.* 1. (Orn.) Alcaraván o bitor, especie de garza. 2. Agua madre de sal que contiene sulfato de magnesia.
Bitterness [bit'-ęr-nes], *s.* 1. Amargor o amargura, sabor o gusto amargo. 2. Odio, rencor, tirria, ojeriza, mala voluntad. 3. Severidad, dureza de genio. 4. Mordacidad, lenguaje que zahiere. 5. Pena, dolor, angustia, amargura.
Bitters. *V.* BITTER, ad finem.
Bittersweet [bit'-ęr-swīt], *s.* Dulcamara, planta de las solanáceas.
Bitterwort [bit'-ęr-wūrt], *s.* (Bot.) Genciana, una planta.

Bitts, *s. pl.* (Mar.) Bitas, barraganetes, dos pedazos de vigas al rededor de los cuales se asegura el cable cuando se ha aferrado el áncora. *Lining of the bitts*, Forro de las bitas. *Pawl bitts*, Bitas del linguete. *Topsail bitts*, Abitones.
Bitumen [bi-tiū'-men], *s.* Betún, materia combustible, algo semejante a las resinas.
Bituminize [bi-tiū'-min-aiz], *va.* Embetunar, cubrir o impregnar de betún.
Bituminous [bi-tiū'-mi-nus], *a.* Bituminoso, que contiene betún o participa de él.
Bivalence, Bivalency [bai'-vê-lens, lensi], *s.* Equivalencia de dos en los compuestos químicos.
Bivalent [bai'-vé''-lent], *a.* (Quím.) Que tiene el valer o poder de dos, en sus combinaciones.
Bivalve [bai'-valv], **Bivalvular** [baival'-viu-lar], *a.* 1. Bivalvo, de dos conchas, que tiene dos conchas, como las ostras, etc. 2. (Bot.) Vaina de dos ventallas.
Bivouac [biv'-u-ac], *s.* (Mil.) Vivac o vivaque, guardia extraordinaria que se hace de noche para la seguridad de un campo, de una plaza o de un puesto militar.
Bivouac [biv'-u-ac], *vn.* (Mil.) Vivaquear, pasar la noche al sereno o a campo raso.
Biweekly [bai-wic'-li], *a.* Quincenal, cada dos semanas.—*adv.* Quincenalmente.—*s.* Publicación quincenal.
Bizarre [bi-zār'], *a.* Raro, caprichoso.
Blab [blab], *va.* Parlar, revelar, decir o divulgar lo que se debía callar.—*vn.* Chismear.
Blab, Blabber [blab'-er], *s.* Chismoso, el que se emplea en traer y llevar chismes. Hablador.
Blabbing [blab'-ing], *s.* Habladuría.
Black [blac'], *va.* Dar de negro. (Fig.) Denigrar, deshonrar. *V.* BLACKEN.
Black, *s.* 1. Negro, el efecto producido en la vista por la falta de luz. 2. Luto. 3. Negro, el etíope. *Boneblack*, Negro animal. *Ivory black*, Negro de marfil (marfil carbonizado). *Lampblack*, Negro de humo. *Black and blue*, Cardenal, contusión.
Black, *a.* 1. Negro, obscuro. 2. Ceñudo, tétrico, demasiadamente serio, grave y melancólico. 3. Horrible, malvado, atroz. 4. Triste, funesto. *Black and blue*, Lívido, amoratado. *To look black at*, Mirar de través, con ceño.
Blackamoor [blac'-a-mūr], *s.* Negro, el etíope.
Black art [blac' ārt], *s.* Nigromancia, mágica negra.
Blackball [blac'-bōl], *s.* Bola negra para votar.
Blackball, *va.* Echar o dar bola negra; votar en contra.
Blackberry [blac'-ber-i], *s.* 1. (Bot.) Zarza, mata espinosa. 2. Zarzamora, el fruto de la zarza.
Blackbird [blac'-berd], *s.* (Orn.) Mirlo o merla.
Blackboard [blac'-bōrd], *s.* Pizarra, encerado de las escuelas.
Black-browed [blac'-braud], *s.* Cejinegro; triste, tenebroso.
Black-cap [blac'-cap], *s.* 1. El que lleva una gorra negra. 2. Alondra, silvia, de cabeza negra. 3. Frambueso negro y su fruta. 4. Enea, espadaña común.
Black cattle [blac' cat-l], *s.* Ganado vacuno.
Black-cock [blac'-coc], *s.* Gallo silvestre.
Black currant [cur'-ant], *s.* Grosella negra.
Black draught [draft], *s.* Infusión de sen.
Blacken [blac'-n], *va.* 1. Dar de negro o teñir de negro. 2. Tildar, obscurecer o difamar. *To blacken one's character*, Denigrar, quitar a uno la estimación. 3. Negrecer o ennegrecer.
Blackener [blac'-n-er], *s.* Ennegrecedor, el que ennegrece alguna cosa; denigrador.
Black-eyed [blak'-aid], *a.* Ojinegro.
Black-faced [blac'-fēst], **Black-visaged** [blac'-viz-ejd], *a.* Carinegro, moreno.
Black flag [flag], *s.* Bandera negra, pabellón pirata.
Black friars [frai-ars], *s.* 1. Frailes negros, apodo dado a los dominicanos. 2. Nombre de un barrio de Londres.
Blackguard [blag'-ard], *s.* (Fam.) Pillastrón, pelagatos, galopo, tunante, pillo.
Black-haired [blac'-hārd], *a.* Pelinegro.
Blackhead [blac'-hed], *s.* Espinilla.
Blacking [blak'-ing], *s.* Betún, unto o lustre de zapatos; bola.
Blackish [blak'-ish], *a.* Negruzco, lo que tira a negro.
Black-jack [blac'-jac], *s.* 1. Pequeño roble. Quercus nigra. 2. *V.* BLENDE. 3. Pabellón pirata. 4. Cachiporra pequeña. 5. Jarro o escudilla charolada que era antiguamente de piel.
Black-lead [blac'-led], *s.* Lápiz-plomo, mineral que se usa para lapiceros; es el grafito de los mineralogistas.
Blackleg [blac'-leg], *s.* 1. Petardista; fullero, tramposo. (En Inglaterra se aplica también abusivamente al trabajador que no pertenece a los gremios de oficios.) 2. Enfermedad pestilente del ganado vacuno; morriña negra.
Black-letter [blac'-let-er], *s.* Letra gótica antigua de imprenta; impresión en caractéres góticos: p. ej., **Esta línea está en black-letter.**
Black list [blac list], *s.* Lista negra.
Blackly [blac'-li], *adv.* Atrozmente.
Blackmail [blac'-mēl], *s.* Chantaje, extorsión de dinero amenazando con escándalo, denuncia o censura. —*va.* Chantajear, amenazar con chantaje.
Blackmailer [blac'-mē''-ler], *s.* Chantajista, persona que practica el chantaje.
Black market [blac' mar'-ket], *s.* Mercado negro.
Black-mouthed [blac'-maudhd], *a.* Grosero, vil, bajo, el que usa de un lenguaje indecente.
Blackness [blac'-nes], *s.* 1. Negrura, color negro. 2. Obscuridad.
Blackout [blac'-aut], *s.* Oscurecimiento, obscurecimiento. (Mex.) Apagón.
Black-pudding [blac'-pud-ing], *s.* Morcilla.
Black-rod [blac'-red], *s.* Ujier de la vara negra, el que lo es de la orden de la Jarretera, llamado así por llevar en la mano una vara negra.
Black-sheep [ship], *s.* Oveja sarnosa. (Met.) El peor entre todos, el malo entre los buenos.
Blacksmith [blac'-smith], *s.* Herrero.
Blacksnake [blac'-snēk], *s.* 1. Cierta clase de serpiente negra o negruzca. 2. Azote pesado, flexible, hecho de cuero acordonado.
Blackthorn [blac'-thērn], *s.* Endrino, el árbol que lleva las endrinas.
Black vomit [vem'-it], *s.* Vómito negro, de la fiebre amarilla.
Blackwell hall [blac'-wel hōl], *s.* Sala donde se vende paño o telas de lana. *Blackwell-hall factor*, Factor o agente de los fabricantes de lana.
Blad [blād o blad], *va.* (Esco.) Herir, dar; dar una bofetada, golpear; de aquí, maltratar.
Blad, *s.* 1. Pedazo o porción grande. 2. Teleta, papel secante. 3. Manotada, golpe dado con la mano.
Bladder [blad'-er], *s.* 1. Vejiga, bolsa muscular y membranosa que sirve de receptáculo a la orina. 2. Vejiga, ampolla. *Bladder-senna*, (Bot.) Espantalobos.
Bladdered [blad'-erd], *a.* Hinchado como vejiga.
Bladderwort [blad'-er-wūrt], *s.* Utricularia, planta acuática.
Blade [blēd], *s.* 1. La punta tierna del grano antes de granar. 2. Hoja, la parte cortante de alguna arma o instrumento. 3. Pala de remo. 4. Jaquetón, el valentón y guapo. *Cunning blade*, Zorrastrón. *Old blade*, Viejo muy experto y marrullero. *Stout blade*, Bravo, valiente. *Blade of a propeller*, Ala o paleta del hélice. *Blade of grass*, Tallo de hierba.
Blade-bone [blēd'-bōn], *s.* Escápula, espaldilla u omoplato.
Bladed [blēd'-ed], *a.* Entallecido, lo que tiene tallos.
Bladesmith [blēd'-smith], *s.* Espadero, fabricante de espadas.
Blamable [blēm'-a-bl], *a.* Culpable, digno de culpa, vituperable.
Blamableness [blēm'-a-bl-nes], *s.* Culpabilidad.
Blame [blēm], *va.* Culpar, echar la culpa; condenar, vituperar, reprender; censurar; tachar.
Blame, *s.* 1. Culpa, vituperación, imputación de algún delito o defecto, reprobación, censura. 2. Culpa, delito.
Blameful [blēm'-ful], *a.* Reo, culpable.
Blameless [blēm'-les], *a.* Inocente, el que está libre de culpa, irreprensible, puro.
Blamelessly [blēm'-les-li], *adv.* Inocentemente, sin culpa.
Blamelessness [blēm'-les-nes], *s.* Inocencia, carencia de culpa.
Blamer [blēm'-er], *s.* Reprensor, censurador.
Blameworthy [blēm'-wūr-dhi], *a.* Culpable.
Blameworthiness [blēm'-wur-dhi-nes], *s.* Culpabilidad.
Blanch [blanch], *va.* 1. Blanquear, poner blanca alguna cosa. 2. Pelar, mondar, quitar la cascarilla. 3. Dejar o pasar en blanco. 4. Eludir, paliar, colorear, cohonestar.—*vn.* Blanquear, ponerse blanco, perder el color; palidecer.
Blanch, *s.* Mineral de plomo incrustado en la roca.
Blancher [blanch'-er], *s.* Blanqueador, el que blanquea.
Blanching [blan'-ching], *s.* Blanquición, la operación de blanquear la moneda, blanqueo. *Blanching liquor*, Agua de blanquear, solución de cloruro de cal.
Blanc-mange [bla-mānzh'], *s.* (Fr.) Manjar blanco, compuesto de gelatina, musgo marino u otra sustan-

cia viscosa, fécula de maíz, leche, azúcar, etc.
Bland [bland], *a.* Blando, suave, dulce.
Blandation [blan-dé'-shun], *s.* Blandura, lisonja, caricia.
¿**Blandiloquence** [blan-dil'-o-cwens], *s.* Agasajo; blandura; lenguaje lisonjero, cumplimiento, lisonja.
Blandish [blan'-dish], *va.* 1. Ablandar, suavizar. 2. Engatusar, acariciar, halagar, lisonjear.
Blandisher [blan'-dish-ẹr], *s.* Halagador, lisonjero.
Blandishing [blan'-dish-ing], *s.* Blandura, caricia. *V.* BLANDISHMENT.
Blandishment [blan'-dish-mẹnt], *s.* Halago, requiebro, caricia, agasajo, demostración afectuosa, sea de palabra o de obra.
Blank [blank], *a.* 1. Blanco. 2. En blanco, no escrito. 3. (Poét.) Suelto o sin rima, hablando de versos. 4. Confuso, turbado, desconcertado, pálido.—*s.* 1. Blanco, espacio, hueco. 2. Suerte o cédula de la lotería que no gana nada. 3. Papel en blanco. 4. Blanco, la señal fija y determinada a que se tira. 5. Pedazo de plata u oro destinado a la acuñación. 6. Carta blanca, el naipe sin figura. *Blank cards,* Tarjetas. *Blank-book,* Libro en blanco. *Blank cartridge,* Cartucho sin bala.
Blank, *va.* 1. Perturbar, confundir. 2. Anular, cancelar, borrar.
Blanket [blan'-ket], *s.* 1. Manta, frazada, cubierta de lana para la cama y otros usos; cobertor, colcha o cobertura; (Mex.) cobija. 2. Mantilla, envoltura para las criaturas. 3. Mantilla, el cordellate que se pone en las imprentas entre el tímpano y timpanillo.
Blanket, *va.* 1. Cubrir con manta. 2. Mantear, levantar en el aire a alguna persona poniéndola en una manta.
Blanketing [blan'-ket-ing], *s.* Manteamiento, el acto de mantear.
Blankly [blangc'-li], *adv.* En blanco.
Blankness [blangc'-nes], *s.* 1. Blanco, hueco. 2. Turbación, confusión.
Blare [blār], *vn.* Bramar, vociferar. *V.* BELLOW.
Blare, *s.* Ruido, fragor; sonido como de trompeta.
Blarney [blār'-ni], *s.* 1. Aldea y castillo cerca de Cork, en Irlanda. 2. Lenguaje adulador, zalamería, caricia mentida.
Blasé [bla-zé'], *a.* Hastiado de placeres o disipación. (Gal.)
Blaspheme [blas-fīm'], *va.* 1. Blasfemar, hablar con impiedad de Dios y de todo lo sagrado. 2. Hablar mal de alguna persona.—*vn.* Decir blasfemias, jurar.
Blasphemer [blas-fīm'-ẹr], *s.* Blasfemo, blasfemador.
Blaspheming [blas-fīm'-ing], *s.* Blasfemia, la acción de blasfemar.
Blasphemous [blas'-fẹ-mus], *a.* Blasfemo, impío.
Blasphemously [blas'-fẹ-mus-li], *adv.* Blasfemamente, impíamente, con blasfemia o impiedad.
Blasphemy [blas'-fẹ-mi], *s.* Blasfemia, palabra injuriosa contra Dios o cualquiera cosa sagrada.
Blast [blast], *s.* 1. Ráfaga, ventarrón, golpe de aire. 2. Ventolera. 3. Soplo, aire impelido por un fuelle, soplete, etc. 4. Carga de pólvora o dinamita; explosión (de una mina), vuelo. 5. Son de cualquier instrumento músico de viento. 6. Golpe o influjo de astro maligno. 7. Tizón, añublo.
Blast, *va.* 1. Castigar con alguna calamidad repentina. 2. Infamar. 3. Marchitar, secar. 4. Espantar. 5. Volar, dar barreno, abrir las rocas con pólvora. 6. Arruinar. 7. Anieblar, añublar, atizonar los granos.
Blaster [blas'-tẹr], *s.* El que arruina, infama o marchita repentinamente.
Blast furnace [blast' fūr-nẹs] *s.* Alto horno.
Blasting [blas'-ting], *s.* 1. El acto de abrir o hender las rocas. 2. Voladura.
Blastoderm [blas'-to-dẹrm], *s.* Blastoderma, membrana germinal del embrión. (Gr. *blastos,* germen y *derma,* pellejo, piel.)
Blast-off [blast'-ōf], *s.* (Aer.) Despegue.
Blatant [blé'-tant], *a.* Mugiente o bramante a manera de becerro. Vocinglero.
Blate,[2] *a.* (Prov. Ingla. y Esco.) 1. Sin agudeza de ingenio o ánimo; tonto. 2. Atrasado o vergonzoso.
Blather [bladh'-ẹr], *va.* y *vn.* Charlar, hablar mucho sin sustancia; balbucear.—*s.* Charla, desatino, disparate.
Blatherskite [bladh'-ẹr-skait], *s.* (E. U. y Esco.) 1. Matamoros, fanfarrón. 2. Fanfarronada, baladronada.
Blaw [blō], *va.* (Esco.) 1. Jactarse, fanfarronear. 2. Adular, lisonjear.
Blaw, *s.* (Esco.) Flor. *V.* BLOW.
Blaze [blēz], *s.* 1. Llama o llamarada. Fuego, fogata. 2. Publicación o divulgación de alguna cosa. 3. Ruido, rumor. 4. Estrella, la mancha blanca en la frente del caballo o la vaca. 5. Mancha, estrella o señal hecha en los troncos de los árboles, comunmente por los agrimensores y cazadores, para servirles de marca o guía. *A blaze of glory,* Una gloria brillante.
Blaze, *vn.* 1. Encenderse en llama. 2. Brillar, resplandecer, lucir, arder.—*va.* 1. Inflamar o hacer llama. 2. Publicar, divulgar. 3. Marcar los árboles á fuego o con cortes y señales, para que sirvan de guía.
Blazer [blēz'-ẹr], *s.* 1. Prenda de vestir, chaqueta ligera de franela o seda, que se usa comunmente en los juegos al aire libre. 2. Brasero, braserillo. 3. Charlador, cuentero.
Blazing [blēz'-ing], *a.* Flameante, en llamas; resplandeciente, deslumbrador. *Blazing-star,* (1) Cometa. (2) (E. U.) Hierba de las liliáceas. Chamælirium.
Blazon [blēzn'], *va.* 1. Blasonar, disponer los escudos de armas según las reglas del arte. 2. Explicar la significación de los escudos de armas. 3. Adornar, decorar. 4. Celebrar, alabar. 5. Publicar o hacer notorio, explicar.
Blazon, *s.* 1. *V.* BLAZONRY. 2. Divulgación, publicación, celebración.
Blazoner [blē'-zn-ẹr], *s.* 1. Autor de heráldica. 2. Genealogista, heraldo. 3. Difamador, infamador.
Blazonry [blēzn'-ri], *s.* Blasón, el arte de explicar y describir los escudos de armas.
Bleach [blīch], *va.* Blanquear al sol, poner blanca alguna cosa.—*vn.* Blanquear.
Bleacher [blīch'-ẹr], *s.* 1. Blanqueador. *V.* BLEACHERY. 2. *pl.* (E. U.) Gradas o asientos descubiertos para espectadores.
Bleachery [blīch'-ẹr-i], *s.* Blanquería, el sitio donde se ponen las cosas a blanquear.
Bleaching [blīch'-ing], *s.* Blanqueo, blanqueamiento, blanqueadura.
Bleak [blīk], *a.* 1. Abierto, desabrigado, expuesto a la intemperie. 2. Frío, helado.
Bleak, *s.* Albur, pez pequeño de río.
Bleakness [blīk'-nes], *s.* Intemperie, destemplanza; frío, frialdad.
Blear [blīr], **Bleared** [blīrd], *a.* Lagañoso o legañoso.
Blear, *va.* Hacer legañoso; ofuscar la vista.
Blear-eyed [blīr'-aid], *a.* 1. Legañoso. 2. Confuso de entendimiento.
Blearedness [blīr'-ed-nes], *s.* Legaña; ofuscación o turbación que padece la vista.
Bleat [blīt], *s.* Balido, la voz que forman la oveja, el carnero y el cordero.
Bleat, *vn.* Balar, dar balidos la oveja o el cordero.
Bleating [blīt'-ing], *s.* Balido, el acto de balar.
Bleb [bleb], *s.* Ampolla, vejiga.
Bled [bled], *pret.* y *pp.* del verbo *To* BLEED.
Bleed [blīd], *vn.* 1. Sangrar. echar sangre. 2. Morir, fallecer.—*va.* Sangrar, sacar sangre, chorrear sangre. (Fig.) Renovarse, abrirse otra vez, presentarse, hacerse sentir de nuevo. 3. Perder el jugo o la savia (hablando de la vid, o de los árboles).—*va.* Arrancar dinero de una persona. *To bleed to death,* Morir de una hemorragia.
Bleeder [blīd'-ẹr], *s.* Sangrador, el que sangra.
Bleeding [blīd'-ing], *s.* Sangría; flujo de sangre. *A bleeding heart,* Un corazón traspasado de dolor.—*a.* Tierno, afectuoso, simpático.
Bleeding heart, *s.* (Bot.) Dicentra, planta papaverácea, originaria de la China que se da en los jardines; y en Inglaterra, el alhelí doble. (Cheiranthus cheiri.)
Blemish [blem'-ish], *va.* 1. Afear, poner fea alguna cosa, manchar, ensuciar, ajar. 2. Denigrar, deshonrar, infamar, quitar el crédito.
Blemish, *s.* 1. Tacha o defecto físico. 2. Deshonra, infamia, mancha en la reputación, tacha en las cualidades morales. *Without blemish or defect,* Sano y sin tacha.
Blemishless [blem'-ish-les], *a.* Irreprensible, sin tacha o defecto.
Blench [blench], *vn.* 1. Cejar, recular, retroceder; estremecerse. 2. (Obs.) Obstruir, impedir.
Blencher [blen'-chẹr], *s.* El que espanta o sobresalta.
Blend [blend], *va.* (*pret.* BLENDED, *pp.* BLENDED o BLENT). 1. Mezclar, trabar unas cosas con otras o confundirlas. 2. Manchar, echar a perder. 3. (Pint.) Casar colores.—*vn.* Unirse, casarse; se dice de los colores.
Blend, *s.* Acción y efecto de mezclar; mezcla, mixtura—v. g. de tés, de colores o matices, etc.
Blende [blend], *s.* (Min.) Blenda o sulfido o sulfuro de zinc.
Blender [blen'-dẹr], *s.* 1. Mezclador. 2. Brocha para casar.
Blennorrhœa [blen-er-rī'-a], *s.* (Med.) Blenorrea, flujo abundante mucoso; leucorrea.
Blent [blent], *pret.* y *pp.* de BLEND.
Blenny [blen'-i], *s.* (Zool.) Blenia, pez de la familia de los blénidos;

sobre los ojos presenta dos apéndices membranosos en forma de cuernos.

Bless [bles], *va.* 1. Bendecir, prosperar, hacer feliz. 2. Bendecir, desear o pedir la felicidad y prosperidad de otra persona. 3. Alabar, dar alabanzas por los beneficios recibidos.

Bless me [bles' mi], *inter.* ¡Buen Dios! ¡gran Dios! ¡válgame Dios!

Blessed [bles'-ed], *a.* 1. Bendito, santo; dichoso. 2. Bienaventurado, el que goza de la eterna felicidad. *Blessed thistle,* (Bot.) Cardo bendito. *The blessed Virgin,* La Santísima Virgen.

Blessedly [bles'-ed-li], *adv.* Bienaventuradamente, dichosamente, felizmente.

Blessedness [bles'-ed-nes], *s.* Felicidad, santidad, beatitud.

Blesser [bles'-ęr], *s.* El que bendice.

Blessing [bles'-ing], *s.* Bendición, la acción de bendecir; bien, prosperidad; gracias, favores del cielo. *Blessings upon you!* ¡Dios le bendiga! *With the blessing of God,* Con la bendición o la gracia de Dios.

Blest, *part. adj.* *V.* Blessed.

Blet [blet], *vn.* Pasarse, echarse a perder interiormente, como sucede con ciertas frutas cuando están demasiado maduras.

Blet, *s.* Picadura, mancha de una fruta demasiado madura; podredumbre incipiente.

Blethering [bledh'-ęr-ing], *a.* Chirlador, chirladora.

Blew [blū], *pret.* del verbo *To* Blow.

Blight [blait], *s.* 1. Tizón; pulgón. 2. (Agr.) Añublo; alheña, roña. 3. Todo lo que marchita las esperanzas o expectativas.

Blight, *va.* 1. Atizonar, abrasar, esterilizar, anieblar las mieses. 2. Ajar, marchitar.—*vn.* Atizonarse.

Blimp [blimp], *s.* *Blimp,* pequeño dirigible.

Blind [blaind], *a.* 1. Ciego, privado de la vista. *Blind of one eye,* Tuerto. 2. Ignorante, insensato.

Blind, *va.* Cegar, quitar la vista; turbar o extinguir la luz de la razón, deslumbrar.

Blind, *s.* 1. Velo, cualquiera cosa que estorba la vista u ofusca el entendimiento. 2. Escondite. 3. Pretexto. 4. Máscara. 5. Tabla, biombo, etc. para libertarse del calor del fuego. *Window-blind,* Transparente, persianas. *Purblind,* Muy corto de vista. *Blinds, pl.* (For.) Rindajes, especie de defensa hecha por lo común de mimbres, que sirve para cubrir a los trabajadores. *Venetian blinds,* Celosías.

Blind alley [blaind al'-e], *s.* 1. Callejón sin salida. 2. Atolladero, atascadero, obstáculo insuperable.

Blinders [blaind'-ęrs], *s. pl.* Anteojeras, viseras de caballo.

Blind flying [blaind flai-ing], *s.* 1. Vuelo a ciegas, vuelo ciego. 2. Vuelo dirigido por radar.

Blindfold [blaind'-fōld], *va.* Vendar los ojos.

Blindfold, *a.* Que tiene los ojos vendados.

Blindly [blaind'-li], *adv.* Ciegamente, a ciegas, precipitadamente, sin conocimiento ni reflexión.

Blindman's-buff [blaind'-manz-buf], *s.* Juego de la gallina ciega.

Blindness [blaind'-nes], *s.* 1. Ceguedad o ceguera, privación o falta de la vista. 2. Ceguedad, alucinación, afecto que ofusca y obscurece la razón.

Blind side [blaind' said], *s.* Debilidad, fragilidad, flaqueza, el flaco o la parte débil de una persona.

Blind-worm [blaind'-wūrm], *s.* Cecilia, serpiente pequeña que parece ciega.

Blink [bliņk], *vn.* 1. Pestañear, parpadear. 2. Cerrar los ojos, disimular; eludir, evadir.—*va.* 1. Eludir. 2. Paliar, colorear, cohonestar. 3. Guiñar.

Blink, *s.* Ojeada, mirada pronta y ligera; vislumbre. En plural significa las ramas que se rompen cazando.

Blinker [blink'ęr], *s.* Luz intermitente.—*pl.* Anteojeras.

Bliss [blis], *s.* 1. Gloria, bienaventuranza, felicidad eterna. 2. Gusto y placer vehemente.

Blissful [blis'-ful], *a.* Bienaventurado, feliz en sumo grado, dichoso.

Blissfully [blis'-ful-i], *adv.* Felizmente.

Blissfulness [blis'-ful-nes], *s.* Suprema felicidad. *V.* Bliss.

Blissless [blis'-les], *a.* Infeliz, desgraciado.

Blister [blis'-tęr], *s.* 1. Vejiga, ampolla, flictena. 2. Vejigatorio, cantárida. 3. Ampolla o burbuja de aire que se levanta en el esmalte, pintura u otra cosa.

Blister, *vn.* Ampollarse, levantarse ampollas en alguna parte del cuerpo.—*va.* Ampollar, hacer ampollas, aplicar un vejigatorio o cantárida.

Blistering plaster [blis'-tęr-ing plas'-tęr], *s.* Vejigatorio o parche de cantáridas.

Blithe [blaidh o blaith], **Blitheful** [blaith'-ful], *a.* Alegre, contento, gozoso, lleno de alegría natural.

Blithely [blaith'-li], *adv.* Alegremente, con alegría.

Blitheness [blaith'-nes], **Blithesomeness** [blaith'-sum-nes], *s.* Alegría, júbilo, contento del ánimo.

Blithesome, *a.* *V.* Blithe.

Blitzkrieg [blits'-crig], *s.* *Blitzkrieg,* guerra relámpago. (Al.)

Blizzard [bliz'-ard], *s.* (E. U.) 1. Viento huracanado y agudamente frío, con abundante nevada. 2. Descarga ruidosa de armas de fuego; golpe que echa a tierra; desastre repentino.

Bloat [blōt], *va.* Hinchar.—*vn.* Entumecerse, hincharse.

Bloat, *va.* Ahumar, curar por medio del humo, como se hace con el arenque.

†**Bloat,** *a.* Ahumado.

Bloatedness [blōt'-ed-nes], *s.* Turgencia, hinchazón con encendimiento del cutis.

Bloater [blōt'-ęr], *s.* Arenque ahumado.

Blob [blob], *s.* 1. Gota, masa esférica blanda. 2. Burbuja, ampolla de aire. 3. Masa redonda de hierro que sirve de base a un poste de hierro en los buques.

Blobber [blob'-ęr], *s.* Burbuja, la ampolla que se levanta en el agua.

Blobber-lip [blob'-ęr-lip], *s.* Bezo, labio grueso.

Blobber-lipped [blob'-ęr-lipt], **Blob-lipped** [blob'-lipt], *a.* Bezudo, el que es grueso de labios.

Bloc [bloc], *s.* Bloque, agrupación de fuerzas políticas.

Block [bloc], *s.* 1. Zoquete, pedazo de madera grueso y corto. *Hatter's block,* Horma de sombrero. 2. Tajo, pedazo de madera sobre el cual eran degollados los reos. *Chopping-block,* Tajo de cocina. 3. Boliche o bolín, la bola pequeña de que se usa en el juego de bochas. 4. (Mar.) Motón, garrucha de madera de diversas formas y tamaños por donde laborean los cabos. *Block and block,* (Mar.) Abesar. 5. Modrego, el sujeto desmañado y que no tiene habilidad. 6. Obstáculo, impedimento. 7. Canto, piedra, trozo de granito, trozo de mármol sin pulir. 8. Polea, garrucha. 9. Molde. 10. (Mar.) Motón, cuadernal. *Block of houses,* Manzana de casas. *Block and tackle,* Polea con aparejo. *Double block,* Motón de dos ojos. *Single block,* Motón sencillo. *Snatch block,* Pasteca. *Swivel block,* Motón giratorio. *Block letter,* Tipo de madera. *Block pulley,* Carillo, motón, polea.

Block, *va.* Bloquear, poner bloqueo a alguna plaza o costa. *To block up,* Bloquear, obstruir, cerrar, tapiar, condenar una puerta o ventana. (Tip.) Montar una plancha. (Art y Of.) Conformar un sombrero.

Blockade [blok-ēd'], *s.* Cerco que se pone a alguna plaza, bloqueo de un puerto o litoral.

Blockade, *va.* Bloquear, poner bloqueo o cerco a alguna plaza.

Blockhead [bloc' hed], *s.* Bruto, necio, tonto, bolonio.

Blockheaded [bloc'-hed-ed], *a.* Lerdo; tardo, estúpido, tonto.

Blockheadly [bloc'-hed-li], *adv.* Lerdamente, tontamente.

Block-house [bloc'-haus], *s.* Fortaleza colocada en medio de un paso para cerrarlo.

Blockish [blok'-ish], *a.* Estúpido, tonto, bobo, estólido.

Blockishness [blok'-ish-nes], *s.* Estolidez, incapacidad, estupidez, grosería, tontería, necedad; indecencia.

Block-like [bloc'-laic], *a.* Como un tonto; parecido a un zoquete.

Block system [sis'-tęm], *s.* División de una vía férrea en trozos o tramos, para organizar y dirigir el movimiento de los trenes por medio de determinadas señales.

Block tin [bloc-tin'], *s.* Estaño puro, tejo.

Blond, Blonde [blond], *a.* y *s.* Rubio, rubia. (Mex.) Güero, güera.

Blond-lace [blond'-lēs], *s.* Encaje o blonda hecha de seda.

Blood [blud], *s.* 1. Sangre, humor rojo contenido en las arterias y venas del animal. 2. Sangre, alcurnia, linaje o parentesco. 3. Ira, cólera, indignación. 4. Jugo o zumo de alguna cosa. 5. Vida. 6. Asesinato, muerte violenta. 7. Hombre animoso. *To let blood,* Sangrar. *Blue blood,* Casta pura; linaje aristocrático.

Blood, *va.* 1. Ensangrentar, teñir o manchar con sangre. 2. Ensangrentar, exasperar. 3. Sangrar, sacar sangre.

Bloodbank [blud'-bank], *s.* Banco de sangre.

Blood-consuming [blud'-con-siūm-ing], *a.* Lo que gasta sangre.

Blooded [blud'-ed], *a.* 1. Que tiene sangre de tal o cual carácter determinado. *Fishes are cold-blooded,* Los peces tienen la sangre fría. 2. De pura casta, de buena raza.

Blood-flower [blud'-flau-ęr], *s.* (Bot.) Flor de la sangre.

Blood-frozen [blud'-frōz-n], *s.* El que tiene la sangre helada.

Blood-guiltiness [blud'-gil-ti-nes], *s.* Homicidio, asesinato.

Blood-heat [blud'-hît], *s.* El calor natural de la sangre: es decir, 37.6° C. o 100° Fahr.
Blood-horse [blud'-hōrs], *s.* Caballo de buena casta, especialmente de la raza anglo-árabe.
Bloodhound [blud'-haund], *s.* Sabueso, especie de podenco.
Bloodily [blud'-i-li], *adv.* Cruelmente, inhumanamente.
Bloodiness [blud'-i-nes], *s.* 1. El estado de lo que echa sangre o está sanguinolento. 2. Crueldad.
Bloodless [blud'-les], *a.* 1. Exangüe, desangrado, muerto. 2. Sin efusión de sangre.
Bloodletter [blud'-let-ęr], *s.* Sangrador, flebotomista.
Bloodletting [blud'-let-ing], *s.* Sangría, flebotomía, abertura de una vena para sacar sangre.
Blood-money [blud'-mun-i], *s.* Precio que se paga por la comisión de un homicidio por el derramamiento de sangre.
Blood platelet [blud' plēt-let]. *s.* Plaqueta, plaqueta sanguínea.
Blood poisoning [blud poi'-zn-ing], *s.* Envenenamiento de la sangre, septicemia.
Blood pressure [blud presh'-ur], *s.* Presión arterial. *High blood pressure,* Hipertensión, presión alta.
Blood-red [blud'-red], *a.* Encarnado o rojo como la sangre.
Blood-relation [blud-rę-lé'-shun], *s.* Pariente consanguíneo.
Blood-relationship, *s.* Parentesco de consanguinidad.
Blood-root [blud'-rūt], *s.* Sanguinaria, planta medicinal perenne de América. Sanguinaria Canadensis.
Bloodshed [blud'-shed], *s.* Efusión de sangre; matanza.
Bloodshedder [blud'-shed-ęr], *s.* Homicida, asesino.
Bloodshedding [blud'-shed-ing], *s.* Derramamiento de sangre.
Bloodshot [blud'-shet], *a.* Ensangrentado. Inyectado de sangre: dícese, por lo común, de los ojos.
Blood-stained [blud'-stēnd], *a.* Manchado con sangre; cruel.
Bloodstone [blud'-stōn], *s.* Hematites, piedra de color verde con venas o manchas sanguinolentas.
Bloodsucker [blud'-suk-ęr], *s.* 1. Sanguijuela. 2. Homicida, asesino. 3. Avaro.
Bloodsucking [blud'-suk-ing], *a.* Que chupa sangre.
Bloodthirstiness [blud-thęrst'-i-nes], *s.* Inclinación, tendencia y prontitud a derramar sangre.
Bloodthirsty [blud'-thęrs-ti], *a.* Sanguinario, cruel, inclinado a derramar sangre.
Blood transfusion [blud trans-fiū'-shun], *s.* Transfusión de sangre.
Blood-type [blud'-taip], *va.* Determinar el tipo de sangre.
Blood vessels [blud' ves-els], *s. pl.* Vasos sanguíneos.
Blood-warm [blud'-wērm], *a.* A la temperatura de la sangre.
Bloody [blud'-i], *a.* Sangriento, manchado con sangre, ensangrentado; cruel. *Bloody-faced,* El que tiene cara de asesino. *Bloody flux,* Disentería. *Bloody-minded,* Cruel, sanguinario. *Bloody-red,* Sanguíneo, rojo obscuro *Bloody-sceptred,* El de cetro o corona ensangrentada.
Bloody, *va.* Ensangrentar, manchar con sangre.
Bloom [blūm], *s.* 1. Flor de los árboles y plantas. 2. Flor, hablando de la edad; belleza, lindeza, frescura. 3. Changote, trozo de hierro en bruto o después de la primera operación del mazo. 4. Pelusilla muy suave que cubre algunas frutas y hojas. De aquí, todo lo que da apariencia de frescura atractiva; suavidad al tacto, viveza de color.
Bloom, *va.* Echar o producir flor.—*vn.* 1. Florecer. 2. Ser joven.
Bloomery [blūm'-ę-ri], *s.* La primera forjadura del hierro en goas o changotes.
Bloomers [blūm'-ęrs], *s. pl.* Pantalones bombachos de mujer. Deben su nombre a la Sra. Bloomer, de Nueva York, E.U., que fue la primera en proponer esta clase de vestido en 1850.
Bloomingly [blūm'-ing-li], *adv.* Floridamente.
Blossom [bles'-um], *s.* La flor de los árboles y plantas.
Blossom, *vn.* Florecer, echar flor.
Blot [blet], *va.* 1. Borrar, testar o tachar lo escrito. 2. Cancelar. 3. Manchar, ensuciar, empañar. 4. Denigrar. *To blot out,* Rayar lo escrito, testar o borrar.
Blot, *s.* 1. Canceladura de alguna cosa escrita, testadura. 2. Borrón, mancha.
Blotch [blech], *s.* 1. Mancha, borrón, lunar, pintarrajo. 2. Roncha, mancha, el bultillo que se eleva en el cutis.
Blotch, *va.* Marcar o cubrir con manchas o ronchas.
Blotter [blet'-ęr], *s.* 1. Borrador, libro en que los mercaderes y hombres de negocios hacen sus anotaciones. 2. Papel secante.
Blotting [blet'-ing], *s.* El acto de manchar o borronear papel.
Blotting-paper [blet'-ing-pé'-pęr], *s.* Papel secante, teleta.
Blouse [blaus'], *s.* Blusa, prenda de vestir exterior y muy holgada, de uso frecuente entre los niños y en Europa entre los trabajadores y artesanos.
Blow [blō], *s.* 1. Golpe. *Blows of fortune,* Reveses de fortuna. 2. Acaecimiento repentino, desastre, desdicha. 3. Florescencia, estado de florecer las plantas; las flores en general. 4. Ventarrón. 5. Huevo de mosca depositado en carne. Esta voz se expresa a menudo en español por el sufijo -azo, así: *Blow with the fist,* Puñetazo. *Blow with a stick, with a chair,* Bastonazo, silletazo. *To come to blows,* Venir a las manos. *At a blow, at a single blow,* De un golpe, de un solo golpe, de una vez.
Blow, *vn.* (*pret.* BLEW, *pp.* BLOWN). 1. Soplar el viento haciéndose sentir. 2. Jadear, arrojar con vehemencia y congoja el aliento o respiración. 3. Sonar, hacer ruido harmonioso algún instrumento músico de viento. 4. Florecer, abrirse las flores. 5. Pasar.—*va.* 1. Soplar, impeler alguna cosa a fuerza de aire. 2. Inflar, henchir algo de aire. 3. Dar figura a alguna cosa llenándola de aire. 4. Hacer sonar a un instrumento de viento. 5. Calentar algo con el aliento. 6. Divulgar algo. 7. Hacer florecer. *To blow away,* Apartar o llevar soplando. *To blow down,* Hacer caer alguna cosa soplándola; derribar, echar por tierra. *To blow in,* (1) Introducir alguna cosa soplando. (2) (Jerga. E. U.) Gastar inconsideramente, malgastar, despilfarrar. *To blow off,* Disipar con soplos. *To blow out,* Expeler o separar a soplos. *To blow out a candle,* Apagar una vela a soplos o soplarla. *To blow over,* Quitar o echar una cosa a soplos de donde estaba; pasar algo sin causar perjuicio; disiparse, ser olvidado (se usó primeramente con referencia a las caravanas sorprendidas por una tormenta de arena). *To blow up,* Volar o volarse por medio de pólvora; llenar algo de aire aumentando su volumen; henchir o henchirse de orgullo: encender; henchir o llenar de entusiasmo; excitar, levantar. *To blow upon,* Dañar, desacreditar, disfamar. *To blow a trumpet,* Tocar una trompeta. *To blow one's own trumpet,* Alabarse a sí mismo; alabar sus agujas; alabáos, coles, que hay nabos en la olla. *To blow one's nose,* Sonarse las narices. —*v. imp. It blows,* Hace viento. *To blow fresh,* Refrescar el viento.
Blower [blō'-ęr], *s.* Soplador, el que sopla; aventador, fuelle.
Blow-fly [blō'-flai], *s.* Corónida, mosca grande que deposita sus huevos sobre carne. Calliphoria vomitoria.
Blow-gun [blō'-gun], *s.* Bodoquera; cañuto con el cual se puede arrojar una flecha soplando con fuerza; cerbatana.
Blowing [blō'-ing], *s.* Soplo, soplido; sonido de la respiración bronca. Sopleo de vidrio.—*a.* Que sopla. *Blowing weather,* Tiempo tempestuoso. *Blowing-fan,* Aventador.
Blowout [blō'-aut], *s.* Reventón de neumático o de llanta.
Blow-pipe [blō'-paip], *s.* Soplete. *Glass-blower's pipe,* Caña, cañón de soplar.
Blown [blōn], *pp.* del verbo *To* BLOW.
Blowtorch [blō'-tōrch], *s.* Soplete para soldar.
Blowzy [blauz'-i], *a.* 1. Quemado o tostado por el sol. 2. Desaliñado, puerco.
Blubber [blub'-ęr], *s.* 1. Grasa o unto de ballena. 2. Ortiga marina. 3. Gimoteo, acción de gimotear.
Blubber, *vn.* y *a.* Llorar hasta hincharse los carrillos; gimotear.
Blude [blūd], *s.* (Escocés) Sangre.
Bludgeon [bluj'-un], *s.* Cachiporra o porra, palo corto que tiene un extremo grueso.
Blue [blū], *s.* 1. Azul, uno de los siete colores originales. 2. Materia colorante que se emplea para dar un color azul. *The blues,* Esplín, melancolía, abatimiento de espíritu.—*a.* 1. Azul, de color azul; cerúleo. 2. Abatido, desalentado, falto de buen humor; triste, melancólico, desconfiado. 3. Severo, estricto, puritánico. 4. Fiel, leal, genuino. 5. Lívido, amoratado, como por una contusión. 6. Pedante; dícese de las mujeres. 7. Que designa el polo sur de un imán; opuesto a rojo. *Sky blue,* Azul celeste. *To look blue,* Quedarse, confuso, chafado, aturrullado o consternado. *Blue devils, blues,* Dolencia del bazo; hipocondría. *Blue-gum,* Eucalipto, árbol de tronco alto y duro, originario de Australia. *True blue,* Leal, constante, adicto, fiel; sin mezcla, sincero, recto. *Blue grass,* Hierba del género Poa, particularmente la de Kentucky; Poa pratensis. *Blue light,* (1) Luz de señales. (2) Preparación pirotécnica que arde con llama azul resplandeciente. *Blue*

peter, (Mar.) Bandera con cuadro blanco que se usa para indicar que un buque está dispuesto a hacerse a la vela. *Blue-jacket*, Marinero de buque de guerra. *Blue-stone*, Sulfato de cobre.
Blue, *va.* 1. Azular, teñir de azul. 2. Pavonar, dar color azulado obscuro al hierro o acero.
Blue baby [blū bē'-bi], *s.* Niño atacado de cianosis congénita.
Blue-bell [blū'-bel], **Bluebottle** [blū'-bot-l], *s.* (Bot.) Campanilla o coronilla, flor.
Blueberry [blu'-ber'-i], *s.* (Bot.) Arándano azul.
Blue-bird [blū'-bęrd], *s.* Pájaro cantor, muy común en los Estados Unidos; azulejillo, azulejo. Sialia sialis.
Blue-book [blū'-buk], *s.* 1. Publicación parlamentaria; se llama así por el color de sus cubiertas de papel azul. 2. En los Estados Unidos, nombre popular de un registro que contiene los nombres y señas de casa de los empleados del gobierno.
Bluebottle, *s.* (Ent.) Corónida, mosca de vientre azul.
Blue-eyed [blū'-aid], *a.* Ojizarco, ojiazul.
Blue jay [blū'-jē], *s.* (Zool.) El gayo común de los Estados Unidos; azulejo. *V.* JAY.
Blueness [blū'-nes], *s.* 1. Propiedad del color azul. 2. Cardenal.
Blueprint [blū'-print], *s.* 1. Cianotipia, cianotipo; heliografía. 2. Plan detallado.
Blueprint, *va.* Copiar a la cianotipia.
Blues [blūs], *s. pl.* 1. (fam.) Melancolía, tristeza. 2. Canciones con letra triste y ritmo sincopado.
Bluestocking [stek-ing], *s.* Mujer pedante; mujer docta.
Bluff [bluf], *a.* 1. Agreste, áspero, rústico. 2. (Mar.) Obtuso. 3. Rudo, firme. 4. Escarpado, amogotado.
Bluff, *s.* 1. Colina o risco escarpado, por lo general inmediato a las orillas de un río o del mar. 2. Fanfarronada; expresión de confianza en sí mismo para intimidar a otros.
Bluff, *va.* Engañar simulando recursos de que se carece. Alardear, fanfarronear.
Bluffness [bluf'-nes], *s.* Asperidad.
Bluing [blū'-ing], *s.* 1. Substancia colorante azul como el añil, que se emplea en el lavado de ropa; azul en pasta para lavandera. 2. Acto o procedimiento de dar un matiz azul al hierro o acero; el mismo matiz azul.
Bluish [blū'-ish], *a.* Azulado, lo que tira a azul.
Blunder [blun'-dęr], *vn.* 1. Desatinar, disparatar, hacer o decir desatinos o despropósitos. 2. Desatinar, perder el tino.—*va.* Confundir una cosa con otra sin consideración. *To blunder about*, Hacer las cosas a tientas. *To blunder a thing out*, Divulgar alguna cosa inconsideradamente; dejar escapar algún secreto sin pensar. *To blunder upon a thing*, Desatinar sobre algo, razonar sin conocimiento acerca de una cosa.
Blunder, *s.* Desatino, disparate, despropósito, error craso; atolondramiento, ligereza, indiscreción, falta.
Blunderbuss [blun'-dęr-bus], *s.* Trabuco, escopeta corta y de boca ancha que calza muchas balas a un tiempo.
Blunderer [blun'-dęr-ęr], **Blunderhead** [blun'-dęr-hed], *s.* Desatinado, imprudente.
Blunderingly [blun'-dęr-ing-li], *adv.* Desatinadamente.
Blunge [blunj], *va.* (Art. y Of.) Mezclar (arcilla) con agua por medio de un *blunger* o en una artesa. *Cf.* PLUNGE.
Blunger [blun'-jęr], *s.* Paleta para mezclar la pasta. Es en forma de espátula, pero mucho más grande.
Blunt [blunt], *a.* 1. Embotado, falto de filo obtuso. 2. Lerdo, tardo. 3. Bronco, áspero, descortés, tosco, grosero, rudo. *To grow blunt*, Entorpecerse, embrutecerse, hablando de personas; embotarse, hablando de instrumentos.
Blunt, *va.* 1. Embotar, engrosar los filos o puntas de las armas y otros instrumentos cortantes o agudos. 2. Enervar, debilitar. 3. Adormecer, calmar o mitigar un dolor.
Bluntly [blunt'-li], *adv.* 1. Sin filo. 2. Lisa y llanamente, sin artificio; claramente; bruscamente, sin delicadeza. 3. Obtusamente.
Bluntness [blunt'-nes], *s.* 1. Embotadura o embotamiento, falta de filo o punta en alguna arma o instrumento. 2. Grosería, falta de urbanidad; prontitud o viveza de genio con sequedad, aspereza.
Blunt-witted [blunt'-wit-ed], *a.* Estúpido, lerdo.
Blur [blūr], *s.* 1. Apariencia, forma indistinta o confusa. 2. Borrón o mancha.
Blur, *va.* 1. Hacer obscuro o indistinto. 2. Embotar, entorpecer. 3. Manchar.
Blurt [blūrt], *va.* Decir o soltar alguna cosa de una manera abrupta e inesperada. *To blurt out*, Hablar sin consideración.
Blush [blush], *vn.* Abochornarse, sonrojarse, sonrosearse, ponerse colorado, mostrar en la cara rubor, vergüenza o confusión tener empacho o vergüenza.—*va.* Sonrojar, abochornar a alguno.
Blush, *s.* 1. Rubor, bochorno, sonroseo o sonrojo, los colores que la vergüenza pinta en la cara. 2. Color rojo o purpúreo.
Blushing [blush'-ing], *s.* Sonrojo, sonroseo, bochorno.
Blushless [blush'-les], *a.* Desvergonzado, descarado.
Bluster, Blustering [blus'-tęr, ing], *s.* Ruido, tumulto; jactancia. *Blustering weather*, Tempestad, tiempo tempestuoso. *A blustering wind*, Viento fuerte, vehemente o furioso. *A blustering fellow*, Espíritu violento, inquieto o turbulento. *A blustering style*, Estilo hinchado.
Bluster, *vn.* 1. Bramar, hacer ruido tempestuoso. 2. Bravear, echar fieros o bravatas.—*va.* Proferir, articular ruidosa y coléricamente.
Blusterer [blus'-tęr-ęr], *s.* Matasiete, el fanfarrón que se precia de valiente y animoso.
Bo [bō], *inter.* Bú, voz con que se causa terror, miedo o espanto a los niños.
Boa [bō'-a], *s.* 1. Boa, serpiente grande y no venenosa que aplasta la presa entre sus pliegues. 2. Boa, cuello de pieles que usan las mujeres.
Boar [bōr], *s.* Verraco, el cerdo padre. *A wild boar*, Jabalí.
Board [bōrd], *s.* 1. Tabla, pedazo de madera más ancho y largo que grueso. 2. Mesa. 3. La mesa a que se sientan para despachar los ministros de algún tribunal. 4. Tribunal, consejo, junta. *Board of admiralty*, El consejo del almirantazgo. *Board of trade*, Junta de comercio. *Board of trustees*, Junta directiva. *Board of Education*, Junta de Educación. *Board of Health*, Junta de Sanidad; la que, con carácter oficial, cuida de mantener y mejorar las condiciones sanitarias de una población. 5. (Mar.) Bordo, el lado o costado de un navío. Bordada, el camino o derrota que recorre una embarcación entre dos viradas, para ganar el barlovento. *To make a good board*, Barloventear bien. *On board*, A bordo. 6. Alimento; pensión. 7. Cartón. (Enc.) *Bound in boards*, Encartonado. *Bristol-board*, Cartulina de Bristol. *Cardboard*, Cartón. *Free on board* (o abrev. *f. o. b.*), Libre de gastos a bordo.—*pl. Boards*, Las tablas, la escena de un teatro. *Headboard*, Cabecera de cama. *Paddle-boards*, Paletas (de las ruedas). *Straw board*, Cartón de paja. *Chessboard*, Tablero para jugar al ajedrez. *Falling board*, Trampa. *Side-board*, Alacena, bufete. *Sounding-board*, Tornavoz. *To go by the board*, (Mar.) (1) Caer un mástil roto por el costado del buque. (2) Arruinarse por completo.
Board, *va.* 1. (Mar.) Abordar. 2. Acometer, acercarse a. 3. Entablar, entarimar, cubrir el suelo con tarimas o tablas.—*vn.* 1. Estar a pupilaje, pagar en una casa un precio determinado por habitar y mantenerse en ella. 2. Tomar pupilos.
Boardable [bōrd'-a-bl], *a.* Accesible.
Board-wages [bōrd'-wē-jez], *s.* La ración en dinero que se da a los criados para mantenerse.
Boarder [bōrd'-ęr], *s.* Pensionista, huésped, pupilo, el que vive y se mantiene en casa de otro por un tanto al día, mes o año.
Boarding [bōrd'-ing], *s.* (Mar.) Abordaje. *Boarding-pikes*, Chuzos.
Boarding-house [bōrd'-ing-haus], *s.* Casa de pupilos o de huéspedes, posada, casa en que se da de comer y cuarto por precio determinado.
Boarding pupil [bōrd'-ing piū'-pil], *s.* Interno, discípulo pensionista.
Boarding-school [bōrd'-ing-scūl], *s.* Pupilaje, escuela en que los alumnos viven con el maestro; casa-pensión.
Boarish [bōr'-ish], *a.* Brutal, cruel, áspero, bronco.
Boast [bōst], *vn.* Jactarse, vanagloriarse, alabarse, prorrumpir en alabanzas propias.—*va.* 1. Ponderar. 2. Exaltar, magnificar. 3. Alabar excesivamente, decantar.
Boast, *s.* Jactancia, vanidad, vanagloria o arrogancia, expresada con palabras de alabanza propia; ostentación.
Boaster [bōst'-ęr], *s.* Fanfarrón, bocón, jactancioso, vanaglorioso.
Boastful [bōst'-ful], *a.* Jactancioso, copetudo, baladrón.
Boasting [bōst-ing], *s.* Jactancia, expresión de ostentación, vanagloria, bravata.
Boastingly [bōst'-ing-li], *adv.* Jactanciosamente, ostentosamente.
Boastless [bōst'-les], *a.* Simple, sencillo.
Boat [bōt], *s.* Bote, barca o lancha, batel, chalupa. Vapor de río. *Ballast-boat*, (Mar.) Bote de lastrar. *Ferry-boat*, Bote de pasaje. *Fishing boat*, Bote de pescar *Shipwright's boat*, Bote de maestranza. *Boat in*

frame, Bote en piezas de armazón. *To bale the boat,* (Mar.) Achicar el bote. *To trim the boat,* (Mar.) Adrizar el bote. *To moor the boat,* (Mar.) Amarrar el bote. *Boat-rope,* Cordel de bote. *Packet-boat,* Paquebote o paquebot. *Boat-hook,* Bichero, botador. *Boat-house,* Casilla de botes. *Boat-load,* Barcada. *Gun-boat,* Lancha cañonera. *Jolly-boat,* Canoa pequeña y ligera. *Life-boat,* Bote salvavidas. *Steamboat,* Bote de vapor. *Tow-boat* o *tug(boat)* Remolcador.

Boatage [bōt'-êj], *s.* 1. Barcaje, transporte por bote, o el precio o flete que por él se paga. 2. Capacidad o cabida total de los botes de un buque.

Boating [bōt'-ing], *s.* 1. El acto de guiar o manejar un bote, ir en bote. 2. Transporte de carga o pasajeros en bote.

Boatman [bōt'-man], **Boatsman** [bōts'-man], *s.* Barquero.

Boatswain [bōt'-swên o (Mar.) bōs'-n], *s.* Contramaestre. *Boatswain's mate,* Segundo contramaestre.

Bob [bob], *va.* 1. Apalear, golpear con algún objeto redondeado o nudoso. 2. Sacudir con el codo o la mano. 3. *va.* y *vn.* Mover, agitar, mover(se) de un lado a otro, o de arriba abajo, de una manera súbita y rápida. 4. Cortar la cola de un caballo.—*vn.* 1. Bambolear, moverse alguna cosa de un lado a otro sin salir de su sitio; estar pendiente, colgar. 2. Pescar con boya o flotador ligero de corcho o madera.

Bob, *s.* 1. Pingajo o colgajo; pendiente de oreja. 2. Estrambote, copla añadida a alguna composición poética. 3. Golpe. 4. Un toque de campanas. 5. Corcho de caña para pescar. Cebo para pescar. 6. Lenteja, disco o parte más pesada del péndulo. 7. (Fam.) Chelín (en Inglaterra). 8. Balancín de bomba o de máquina de vapor. 9. La cola cortada de un caballo.

Bobbin [bob'-in], *s.* 1. Bolillo, pedacito de palo delgado con una cabecilla. 2. Canilla, en que los tejedores devanan el hilo o la seda; broca entre bordadores; carrete diminuto de algunas máquinas de coser. *Lace bobbins,* Palillos o majaderitos. *Bobbin-work,* Obra o fábrica hecha con palillos, canillas o brocas. 3. Carrete, bobina. (Elec.) Rollo de alambre aislado que contiene generalmente un centro de hierro dulce, el cual se magnetiza cuando atraviesa el alambre una corriente eléctrica.

Bobbinet (o **Bobbin net**) [bob'-in-et], *s.* Punto de bobiné, labor de adorno.

Bobby pin [bob'-i pin], *s.* Variedad de horquilla para el pelo.

Bobby socks [bō'-bi socs], *s. pl.* Tobilleras, medias tobilleras.

Bobcat [bob'-cat], *s.* (Zool.) Variedad de lince.

Bobolink [bob'-o-linc], *s.* Pájaro migratorio famoso por su canto alegre y retozón.

Bob-sled [bob'-sled], *s.* Cada una de las dos rastras cortas, a manera de doble trineo, que van unidas entre sí por medio de una tabla. También se da este nombre al trineo de carga así formado.

Bob-stay [bob'-stê], *s.* (Mar.) Barbiquejo. *Bob-stay-holes,* Grueras de tajamar.

Bobtail [bob'-têl], *s.* Rabón, descolado; cola cortada. *Bobtail car,* (Fam.) Carro urbano pequeño, sin conductor o cobrador y por lo general con un solo caballo.

Bobtailed [bob'-têld], *a.* Rabón, descolado; con cola cortada.

Bob-white [bob'-hwait], *s.* La codorniz común de los Estados Unidos del Norte, o perdiz de los del Sur y su grito. (Imitado.)

Bobwig [bob'-wig], *s.* Peluca redonda; peluquín.

Bocasine [boc'-a-sin], *s.* 1. Especie de bocací delgado. 2. *V.* CALLIMANCO.

Bode [bōd], *va.* Presagiar, pronosticar.—*vn.* Predecir.

Bodement [bōd'-ment], *s.* Presagio, pronóstico.

Bodice [bod'-is], *s.* Corpiño, jubón ajustado al cuerpo, parte del vestido de mujer; almilla atada con cordones.

Bodied [bod'-id], *a.* Corpóreo, lo que tiene cuerpo.

Bodiless [bod'-i-les], *a.* Incorpóreo, lo que no tiene cuerpo.

Bodily [bod'-i-li], *adv.* Corpóreo, corporal, real, verdadero.

Bodily, *adv.* Corporalmente, con el cuerpo.

Boding [bōd'-ing], *s.* Presagio, pronóstico.

Bodkin [bod'-kin], *s.* 1. Punzón de sastre. 2. Agujeta o aguja de jareta. 3. (Ant.) Daga, puñal. 4. Horquilla para los cabellos. 5. (Tipo.) Punzón para sacar tipos de una forma.

Bodle [bō'-dl o bod'-l], *s.* Antigua moneda de cobre escocesa, por valor de un tercio de centavo de peso.

Body [bod'-i], *s.* 1. Cuerpo, la sustancia material del hombre y de los demás animales. 2. Tronco, el cuerpo humano con excepción de la cabeza, brazos y piernas. 3. Materia, en oposición al espíritu. 4. Una persona, un individuo. 5. Realidad, como opuesta a una mera representación. 6. Cuerpo, la masa colectiva o el agregado de las partes que componen un todo. 7. Cuerpo o gremio, el agregado de personas que forman un pueblo, república o comunidad. 8. Cuerpo, la parte principal de alguna cosa. 9. Colección general. 10. Cuerpo, espesor, fortaleza. *A busybody,* Entremetido. *Anybody,* Cualquiera. *Somebody,* Alguien, alguno. *Everybody,* Cada uno, todos. *Nobody,* Ninguno, nadie. *Body of a church,* Nave de una iglesia. *Body of a tree,* Tronco. *The main body of an army,* El grueso de un ejército. *Body-clothes,* Manta, la cubierta que se pone a los caballos. *Body-colour,* Primera mano de color. *Body-guard,* (1) Guardia de corps. (2) (Fig.) Seguridad. Salvaguardia.

Body, *va.* Dar cuerpo, forma u orden a alguna cosa. *Able-bodied,* Sano, robusto, sin tacha.

Bœotian [bi-ō'-shan], *a.* De Beocia, provincia de Grecia; beocio.

Boer [bōr], *s.* Agricultor holandés; persona blanca de raza holandesa en la República del Transvaal.

Bog [bog], *s.* Pantano, lugar o sitio bajo donde se recoge y detiene el agua formando charco cenagoso. *Bog-bean,* (Bot.) Trifolio fibrino. *Bog-moss,* Esfagno, musgo de pantano. *Bog-ore, bog-iron ore,* Limonita, peróxido de hierro hidratado. *Bog-land,* El que vive en país pantanoso. Tierra pantanosa. *Bog-oak,* Lignito de encina. *Bog-trotter,* El que vive entre pantanos.

Bogey o **Bogy** [bō'-gi], *s.* Duende, espantajo.

Boggle [bog'-l], *vn.* 1. Recular, cejar, retroceder. 2. Cejar, fluctuar, titubear, vacilar, balancear.

Boggle, *s.* Fantasma, espectro, objeto espantoso.

Bogglish [bog'-lish], *a.* Irresoluto, indeciso.

Boggy [bog'-i], *a.* Pantanoso, lleno de pantanos.

Bogie [bō'-gi], *s.* Carretilla de cuatro ruedas que se usa para sostener parte de la locomotora al componerla. *Bogie-engine,* Locomotora de balaste.

Bogus [bō'-gus], *a.* Falso, espúreo; postizo. (Fam. E. U. A.)

Bohea [bō-hī'], *s.* Nombre de cierta especie de te que viene de la China; es de calidad inferior.

Bohemian [bō-hī'-mi-an], *a.* Bohemio, bohemiano, de Bohemia.

Boil [boil], *vn.* 1. Hervir, cocer; dícese de todo lo que hierve o cuece. 2. Bullir; dícese de los líquidos. 3. Estar extraordinariamente agitado o hervirle a uno la sangre. 4. Estar lleno de fervor. *To boil away,* Consumir un líquido a fuerza de cocerlo. *To boil down,* Reducir por medio de la cocción. *To boil over,* Bullir o salirse fuera de la vasija con el calor.—*va.* Cocer, sacar la crudeza de alguna cosa poniéndola en agua hirviendo y teniéndola en este estado hasta darle el punto que se requiere.

Boil, *s.* Divieso, furúnculo, tumor doloroso. (Cuba) Nacido. (Mex.) Clacote.

Boiler [boil'-er], *s.* 1. Cocedor, el que cuece alguna cosa. 2. Marmita, olla o caldero. 3. Caldera. *Large boiler,* Cazo, caldera, paila. *Steam-boiler,* Hervidero para vaho; caldera de vapor. *Sugar boilers,* (Cuba) Tachos. *Boiler compound,* Pasta o polvos desincrustadores para las calderas. *Boiler-shell* o *jacket,* Camisa o cubierta de una caldera. *Boiler-iron,* Hierro en planchas para calderas.

Boiler maker [boil'-er mêk'-er], *s.* Calderero.

Boilery [boil'-er-i], *s.* En las salinas, el lugar donde está el caldero para secar la sal.

Boiling [boil'-ing], *s.* Hervor; ebullición; cocción, acción de hervir.

Boiling, *pa.* Hirviendo. *Boiling hot,* Hirviendo a borbollones o borbotones. *Boiling-kettle,* Caldera. *Boiling-point* (del agua), Centígrado, 100°; Fahrenheit, 212°; Réaumur, 80°, al nivel del mar.

Boisterous [bois'-ter-us], *a.* 1. Vocinglero y rudo, clamoroso, ruidoso, tumultuoso. 2. Borrascoso, tempestuoso. *A boisterous youth,* Un aturdido.

Boisterously [bois'-ter-us-li], *adv.* Ruidosamente, tumultuosamente, furiosamente.

Boisterousness [bois'-ter-us-nes], *s.* Turbulencia, tumulto, vocinglería; vehemencia, impetuosidad.

Bold [bōld], *a.* 1. Intrépido, arrojado, ardiente, falto de temor, bravo, valiente. 2. Audaz, atrevido, osado, temerario. 3. Impudente, descarado, desvergonzado. 4. (Mar.) Saltado, alto, escarpado, acantilado; dícese de la ribera del mar.

Bold-face [bōld'-fês], *s.* Descaro, desvergüenza, impudencia.

Bold-faced [bōld'-fēst], *a.* Descarado, desvergonzado. *Bold-faced type,* Letra negra, negrita, como ésta: **Bold-face.** Lo mismo que FULL-FACE.

Boldly [bōld'-li], *adv.* 1. Intrépidamente, audazmente. 2. Descaradamente, con descaro.

Boldness [bōld'-nes], *s.* 1. Arresto, arrojo o determinación para emprender alguna cosa árdua; intrepidez, aliento, ánimo, resolución, valentía. 2. Descaro, desvergüenza. 3. Libertad, atrevimiento, avilantez, osadía. 4. Confianza en Dios.

Bole [bōl], *s.* 1. Tronco, la parte inferior de un árbol. 2. Bol o bolo, especie de tierra que se usa para los tintes, las pinturas y el bruñido de oro. 3. Antigua medida inglesa para grano, de seis fanegas; dos hectólitros.

Bolero [bo-lê'-rō], *s.* 1. Bolero, aire musical popular español y el baile correspondiente. 2. Bolero, chaquetilla corta de señora, abierta al frente.

§**Bolide** [bō'-lid], *s.* Bólido, meteoro ígneo que cruza el espacio con gran velocidad. (Gal.)

Boll [bōl], *s.* Tallo. *Boll of flax* o *hemp,* Tallo o cápsula de lino o cáñamo. *Boll* o *bole of salt,* Medida de sal que consta de dos fanegas.

Boll weevil [bōl wî'-vl], *s.* Picudo, gorgojo del algodón.

Bolognese [bo-lō-nyîs'], *a.* Bolonés, de Bolonia. *Bologna sausage,* Salchichón de Bolonia.

Bolshevik [bōl'-she-vîk], *s.* y *a.* Bolchevique.

Bolshevism [bōl'-she-vizm], *s.* Bolchevismo.

Bolster [bōl'-stẹr], *s.* 1. Travesero, almohadón para recostar la cabeza en la cama. 2. Colcha. 3. Cabezal, lienzo de varios dobleces que se pone encima de la herida y debajo de las vendas. 4. (Mar.) Almohada de los palos. 5. Borrenes, las almohadillas de la silla de montar que se levantan sobre los fustes. 6. Solera de carro. (F. C.) 7. Nabo; canecillo; caballete.

Bolster, *va.* 1. Recostar la cabeza en al travesero. 2. Aplicar el cabezal a una herida. 3. Sostener, mantener, apoyar.

Bolsterer [bōl'-stẹr-ẹr], *s.* Mantenedor, sostenedor.

Bolstering [bōl'-stẹr-ing], *s.* Apoyadero, apoyo.

Bolt [bōlt], *s.* 1. Dardo, flecha. 2. Rayo; proyectil largo y cilíndrico para un cañón; lo que aparece o sobreviene de repente. 3. Cerrojo, pasador de una puerta. 4. Pestillo de cerradura. 5. (E. U.) Disidencia, acto de separarse de un partido político, o de negarse a apoyar a un candidato, medida o política de un partido. 6. Partida o salto repentino. *A bolt for home,* Partida súbita de una persona con rumbo a su casa. 7. Rollo (de tela). 8. (Mar.) Perno, cavillas de hierro. *Bolts,* Grillos, prisiones para los pies. 9. Clavija, perno, tolete. 10. Tamiz muy fino para separar la harina del salvado. *Bolt of cloth,* Rollo. *Bolt and nut,* Perno y tuerca. *Countersunk bolt,* Perno de cabeza perdida. *Round-headed bolt,* Perno de cabeza de hongo. *Square-headed bolt,* Perno de cabeza de diamante. *Bolt upright,* Derecho, recto como un dardo.

Bolt, *va.* 1. Cerrar con cerrojo. 2. Cerner, separar con el cedazo las partes más gruesas de las más finas de cualquiera materia reducida á polvo. 3. Examinar, escudriñar. 4. (E. U.) Rehusar uno su apoyo al partido político a que pertenece; rechazar a un candidato o una medida de partido. 5. Charlar, hablar sin discreción ni tacto, descubrir por imprudencia lo que se debe callar. 6. Engullir, tragar sin mascar. 7. Lanzar, arrojar, echar, expeler de repente. *To bolt together,* Asegurar con pernos.—*vn.* 1. Saltar de repente. 2. Lanzarse, arrojarse. 3. Caer como un rayo. *To bolt in,* Entrar de repente. *To bolt out,* Salir de golpe.

Bolter [bōlt'-ẹr], *s.* 1. Cedazo. 2. Especie de red. 3. El que niega su apoyo a una candidatura debidamente acordada o designada.

Bolthead [bōlt'-hed], *s.* (Quím.) Recipiente.

Bolting [bōlt'-ing], *s.* 1. Cernido o cernidura, la acción de pasar por cedazo. 2. Cerramiento. 3. Acción de negar su apoyo a un candidato o a una medida de partido. *Bolting-cloth,* Cedazo, tamiz, criba. *Bolting-house,* Cernedero. *Bolting-hutch, bolting-tub,* Tina para cerner harina.

Bolus [bō'-lus], *s.* 1. Bolo, píldora gruesa; de aquí, dosis o medicamento difícil de tomar. 2. Cuerpo esférico de cualquiera materia.

Boma [bō'-mā], *s.* Espacio circular rodeado y defendido por troncos, estacas y maleza.

Bomah-nut [bō'-ma-nut], *s.* Fruto de un arbusto tropical africano, que se emplea para curtir.

Bomb [bem], *s.* 1. Estallido, estampido como de bomba. 2. Bomba, bola hueca de hierro, la cual se llena de pólvora y se dispara de un mortero, o cañón, y que estalla en el aire o al caer.

Bomb, *vn.* Zumbar, sonar como bomba.—*va.* Bombardear.

Bomb-chest [bem'-chest], *s.* Caja de bombas que se pone en algún paraje subterráneo para volarlo.

Bomber [bem'-ẹr], *s.* Bombardero, avión de bombardeo.

Bomb-ketch [bem'-kech], **Bomb-vessel** [bem'-ves-el], *s.* (Mar.) Bombarda, embarcación cuyas cubiertas están fuertemente apuntaladas, para que puedan resistir el empuje de la pólvora al disparar los morteros.

†**Bombard** [bēm'-bard], *s.* 1. Bombarda, una máquina militar antigua. 2. (Ant.) Vasija para conservar vino.

Bombard [bem-bārd'], *va.* Bombardear, tirar bombas.

Bombardier [bem-bar-dîr'], *s.* Bombardero. *Bombardier beetle,* Escarabajo bombardero o escopetero, llamado así porque volatiliza, con explosión, el líquido que segregan ciertas glándulas anales.

Bombardment [bem-bārd'-mẹnt], *s.* Bombardeo, el acto de bombardear.

Bombast [bem'-bast], *s.* 1. Hinchazón, estilo hinchado. 2. Especie de estofa blanda y ligera.

Bombast, Bombastic [bem-bas'-tic], *a.* Altisonante, pomposo, retumbante, hinchado.

Bombax [bem'-bax], *s.* Árbol americano de los trópicos, familia de las malváceas; la ceiba de Cuba. Bombax.

Bombazette [bem-ba-zet'], *s.* Alepín.

Bombazine [bem-ba-zîn'], *s.* Alepín, tela fina de lana y seda, que un tiempo se usó mucho para lutos.

Bombic [bem'-bic], *a.* Perteneciente al gusano de seda (bómbice) o que se deriva de él.

Bomb-proof [bem'-prūf], *a.* (Mil.) A prueba de bomba.

Bomb release [bem rẹ-lîs'], *s.* (Aer.) Lanzabombas.

Bombshell [bem'-shel], *s.* 1. Bomba, granada. 2. (fig.) Sorpresa devastadora.

Bomb shelter [bem'-shel-tẹr], *s.* Refugio antiaéreo.

Bombsight [bem-sait], *s.* Mira de bombadero, visor.

Bombyx [bem'-bix], *s.* (Ent.) Gusano de seda en el estado de mariposa, bómbice.

Bona-fide [bō-na-fai'-dî]. (Lat.) De buena fe, sin engaño. (Com.) Verdad sabida, y buena fe guardada.

Bonbon [beñ'-boñ], *s.* Confite, dulce. *V.* SUGAR-PLUM. (Gal.)

Bond [bend], *s.* 1. La cadena o soga con que está atado alguno. 2. Ligadura, vínculo, unión. 3. Prisión, cautiverio. 4. Obligación, la escritura, promesa o cédula que uno hace a favor de otro, de que cumplirá aquello que ofrece o a que se obliga. 5. Bono, obligación; título de la deuda de una corporación o una nación. *To bond,* Poner en depósito. *In bond,* En depósito. 6. Depósito.—*a.* Cautivo, siervo.

Bondage [bend'-ẹj], *s.* Cautiverio, esclavitud, servidumbre, estado a que pasa la persona que, perdida su libertad, vive en poder de otro; obligación.

Bonded [bend'-ed], *pp.* Garantido por obligación escrita; asegurado; depositado. *Bonded goods,* Mercancías en depósito. *Bonded warehouse,* Almacén de depósito. *Bond-holder,* Tenedor de bonos u obligaciones.

Bondmaid [bend'-mêd], *s.* Esclava, sierva, mujer puesta en esclavitud.

Bondman [bend'-man], *s.* Esclavo, siervo.

Bondservant [bend'-sẹr-vant], *s.* El esclavo o esclava que sirve como tal.

Bondservice [bend'-sẹr-vis], *s.* Esclavitud.

Bondslave [bend'-slêv], *s.* *V.* BONDMAN.

Bondsman [bendz'-man], *s.* 1. Fiador, seguridad, el que da fianza por otro. 2. Esclavo.

Bone [bōn], *s.* 1. Hueso, la parte sólida y dura del animal. 2. Raspa o espina del pez. 3. Hueso, fragmento de carne. *To pick a bone,* Roer un hueso. *To have a bone to pick with any one,* Tener que hacer con alguno; tener alguna queja de él, alguna diferencia, o satisfacción que pedirle. *A Spaniard to the backbone,* Español a todo trance, á las derechas. 4. Dado. *The backbone,* La espina dorsal. *The cheekbone,* El hueso malar, apófisis del pómulo. *The jaw-bone,* La quijada. *To be skin and bones,* No tener más que la piel y los huesos. *Whalebone,* Barba de ballenas. *Boneblack,* Negro animal.

Bone, *va.* 1. Desosar, quitar o apartar los huesos de la carne. 2. Emballenar, poner ballenas a un corpiño, corsé, etc. 3. Abonar con huesos pulverizados.

Bone, *va.* Nivelar con un instrumento.

Bone-ache [bōn'-ēk], *s.* Dolor de huesos.
Boned [bōnd], *a.* Osudo, huesudo, ososo; robusto.
Bonelace [bōn'-lēs], *s.* Encaje de hilo.
Boneless [bōn'-les], *s.* Pulposo, sin huesos.
Boneset [bōn'-set], *s.* Eupatorio, hierba medicinal amarga y tónica. Eupatorium perfoliatum.
Bone-setter [bōn'-set-ẹr], *s.* Cirujano, curandero, el que concierta los huesos dislocados.
Bonfire [ben'-fair], *s.* Hoguera o fogata encendida al aire libre, ya para quemar basura, ya por diversión o en señal de regocijo.
Bonito, *s.* Pez semejante al atún.
Bonnet [ben'-et], *s.* 1. Gorra, gorro; sombrero de mujer. 2. Solideo, bonete. 3. (Fort.) Bonete de clérigo, pequeño baluarte avanzado. 4. (Mar.) Bonetas, los pedazos de velas que se añaden por la parte inferior a la vela mayor, mesana y trinquete.
Bonnily [ben'-i-li], *adv.* Bonitamente, alegremente, hermosamente.
Bonny [ben'-i], *a.* 1. Bonito, lindo, galán, gentil. 2. Alegre, festivo. Es voz usada hoy casi exclusivamente en Escocia.
Bon-ton [beñ'-teñ'], *s.* 1. El gran mundo, la alta sociedad. 2. Buen tono, buenas maneras. (Gal.)
Bonus [bō'-nus], *s.* 1. Adehala, lo que se da de gracia sobre el precio principal. 2. Regalo en dinero para obtener un favor, un privilegio o suministro. 3. Prima; bonificación.
Bony [bō'-ni], *a.* Huesudo.
Booby [bū'-bi], *s.* Zote, hombre bobo, necio e ignorante.
Booby trap [bū'-bi trap], *s.* (Mil.) Granada o mina disimulada que estalla al moverse el objeto que la oculta.
Boodle [bū'-dl], *s.* (Ger. E. U.) 1. Dinero, especialmente dinero pagado como soborno; producto de un hurto o malversación. 2. Agregado, totalidad, colección; cuadrilla. Se escribe también *caboodle.* Dícese más comunmente de personas. 3. (Ger.) Moneda falsa.
Boogie-woogie [bu'-gi-wu'-gi], *s.* Forma de tocar *blues* en el piano caracterizada por un ritmo grave y persistente.
Book [buk], *s.* 1. Libro, volumen de papel cosido y cubierto para leer o escribir en él. 2. Libro, las partes principales en que se divide algún volumen o tratado. 3. Libro de asiento, el libro en que un negociante asienta sus cuentas. *Day-book,* Diario. *Invoice-book,* Libro de facturas. *Pocket-book,* Cartera. *Memorandum-book,* Librito de memoria. *Cash-book,* Libro de caja. *Old book,* Maulón, maula. *A paper book,* Libro en blanco. *Second-hand books,* Libros de ocasión. *School books,* Libros de enseñanza.
Book, *va.* Asentar en un libro; notar en un registro. *To book one's place,* Retener un asiento (en un carruaje público, etc.).
Bookbinder [buk'-bain-dẹr], *s.* Encuadernador de libros.
Bookbinding [buk'-bain-ding], *s.* Encuadernación.
Bookcase [buk'-kēs], *s.* Armario o estante para libros; biblioteca.
Bookie [buk'-i], *s.* (fam.) Corredor de apuestas (en las carreras de caballos).
Booking [buk'-ing], *s.* Registro, asiento. *Booking clerk,* (Ingl.) Vendedor de billetes de pasaje o teatro. *Booking office,* (Ingl.) Registro y despacho de pasajes, expendeduría de billetes.
Bookish [buk'-ish], *a.* 1. Estudioso, aficionado a los libros; entendido o versado en libros. 2. Teórico, poco práctico, especulativo.
Bookishness [buk'-ish-nes], *s.* Aplicación intensa a los libros; estudiosidad; falta de sentido práctico.
Bookkeeper [buk'-kīp-ẹr], *s.* Tenedor de libros, el dependiente que en una casa de comercio está encargado de los libros.
Bookkeeping [buk'-kīp-ing], *s.* La teneduría de libros, el arte de hacer los asientos en los libros de comercio.
Book-learned [buk'-lẹrn-ed], *a.* Leído, versado en libros, erudito.
Book-learning [buk'-lẹrn-ing], *s.* Literatura, conocimiento de las letras o ciencias.
Bookless [buk'-les], *a.* Sin libros; desaplicado.
Bookmaker [buk'-mēk-ẹr], *s.* 1. El que compila o escribe libros sólo por la ganancia o lucro; el que los imprime y encuaderna. 2. Apostador de profesión; dícese en especial del que solicita y anota apuestas en las carreras de caballos.
Bookmaking [buk'-mēk-ing], *s.* La ocupación de compilar o escribir libros a destajo.
Bookman [buk'-man], *s.* Hombre estudioso o dedicado al estudio.
Bookmark [buk'-mārc], *s.* Marcador de libros.
Bookmate [buk'-mēt], *s.* Condiscípulo.
Book-muslin [muz'-lin], *s.* Percalina plegada en la pieza a manera de libro.
Bookseller [buk'-sel-ẹr], *s.* Librero, el que vende libros. *Book trade,* El comercio de libros. *Book-store,* Librería, almacén de libros.
Bookstand [buk'-stand], *s.* Puesto de libros.
Bookstore [buk'-stōr], *s.* Librería.
Bookworm [buk'-wūrm], *s.* 1. Polilla o gusano que roe los libros. 2. (Met.) Estudiante demasiadamente aplicado a los libros; buquinista, ratón de biblioteca.
Boom [būm], *s.* 1. (Mar.) Botalón, palo largo con un motón hecho firme en una cabeza para pasar las escotas de las alas. 2. Cadena para cerrar un puerto. 3. Estampido, estrépito, estruendo. 4. Jirafa (de micrófono). 5. Bonanza, auge, prosperidad repentina. *Boom town,* Ciudad que está en auge. *Boom times,* Epoca de gran prosperidad comercial.
Boom, *vn.* 1. Hacer ruido profundo y resonante, como el de las olas del mar, o el estampido de un cañón. 2. Moverse con violencia; ir a velas desplegadas. 3. (Fam. E. U.) Aumentar rápidamente de valor en el mercado o ganar en favor.—*va.* Favorecer, anunciar y fomentar algo muy enérgicamente.
Boomerang [būm'-ẹr-ang], *s.* 1. Bomerang, arma arrojadiza muy singular de los indígenas de Australia y de algunas partes de la India. 2. Todo acto o proceder cuyas malas consecuencias recaen sobre el autor del mismo.
Boon [būn], *s.* Dádiva, presente, regalo; gracia, merced, favor; dicha, bendición.
Boon, *a.* 1. Alegre, festivo. 2. Liberal, generoso. 3. Dichoso, afortunado, próspero.
Boor [būr], *s.* 1. Patán, aldeano, villano.
Boorish [būr'-ish], *a.* Rústico, agreste; grosero.
Boorishly [būr'-ish-li], *adv.* Rústicamente, toscamente.
Boorishness [būr'-ish-nes], *s.* Rusticidad, tosquedad, falta de cultura.
Boose [būz], *s.* (Prov. Ingl.) 1. Boyeriza, establo para los bueyes. 2. Cierta mezcla de tierra y minerales.
Boost [būst], *va.* (Fam. E. U.) Empujar, levantar, alzar desde abajo. —*s.* Alza; ayuda, asistencia.
Booster [būst'-ẹr], *s.* Fomentador, secuaz. *Booster rocket,* Cohete impulsor. *Booster shot,* (Med.) Inyección estimulante.
Boot [būt], *va.* y *vn.* 1. Aprovechar, ser de algún uso o utilidad, valer, servir, ser útil, importar. 2. Calzarse las botas, ganar.
Boot, *s.* 1. Ganancia, provecho, utilidad, ventaja. 2. Bota, botín, todo calzado que cubre parte de la pierna. *Boot-jack,* Sacabotas. *Bootlegs,* Cortes de botas. *Boot-hose,* Calcetones. *Boot-tree,* Horma de bota. (Fam.) *To boot* (Cuba), De ñapa, de contra; de más a más; encima. (Mex.) De ganancia, de pilón. 3. Pesebrón de un coche.
Bootblack [būt'-blac], *s.* Limpiabotas. (Mex.) Bolero.
Booted [būt'-ed], *a.* Puesto de botas, calzado con botas.
Bootee [bū'-ti], *s.* Botita de lana para infantes.
Booth [būdh], *s.* 1. Barraca o casa hecha de tablas, choza, cabaña. 2. Puesto, tabladillo, mesilla de feria o mercado.
Bootleg [būt'-leg], *va.* y *vn.* Contrabandear (esp. en licores).
Bootlegger [būt'-leg-ẹr], *s.* Contrabandista (esp. de licores).
Bootlegging [būt'-leg-ing] *s.* Contrabando (esp. de licores).
Bootless [būt'-les], *a.* 1. Inútil, sin provecho. 2. Sin botas.
Boots [būts], *s.* Limpiabotas (de una fonda).
Booty [bū'-ti], *s.* Botín, presa, saqueo. *To play booty,* Jugar fraudulentamente, o estar de inteligencia con uno para engañar a otro.
Booze [būz], *vn.* Embriagarse, emborracharse.—*s.* Borrachera; bebida espirituosa.
Boozy [būz'-i], *a.* Embriagado, beodo.
Bopeep [bō-pīp'], *s.* 1. El acto de mirar al soslayo, de hurto o de reojo. 2. Escondite.
Boracic acid [bo-ras'-ic as'-id], *s.* Ácido borácico, o bórico.
Boracite [bō'-ra-sait], *s.* (Min.) Borácita o borato de magnesia.
Borate [bō'-rēt], *s.* Borato, sal compuesta de ácido borácico unido a alguna base.
Boratto [bo-rat'-ō], *s.* Tela de seda y lana semejante a bombasí o alepín.
Borax [bō'-rax], *s.* Bórax, atíncar mineral compuesto de borato de sosa y agua.
Borborygm [bōr'-bōr-im], *s.* Borborigmo, ruido de tripas.
Border [bōr'-dẹr], *s.* 1. Orilla, borde, margen o extremidad de alguna

cosa. 2. Frontera, límite o confín de algún país. 3. Guarnición de vestido, florón, ribete, franja, farfalá. 4. Borde o lomo de un jardín plantado de flores.

Border, *vn.* 1. Confinar; lindar. 2. Aproximarse, acercarse. —*va.* 1. Guarnecer, ribetear. 2. Alcanzar, tocar o lindar; limitar. *To border on* o *upon*, Confinar, tocar, limitar. *France borders upon Spain*, Francia confina con España. De aquí, acercarse en carácter, asemejarse.

Bordering [bōr'-dẹr-ing], *s.* Guarnicionado.—*a.* Fronterizo, contiguo, cercano, vecino. *A bordering town*, Ciudad fronteriza.

Borderline [bōr'-dẹr-lain], *s.* Límite, orilla, frontera.— *a.* Incierto, dudoso. *A borderline case*, Caso entre lo normal y subnormal.

Bore [bōr], *va.* Taladrar; barrenar, excavar.—*vn.* 1. Hacer agujeros. 2. Adelantarse avanzar gradualmente. 3. Llevar la cabeza baja los caballos. (Fam.) *To bore*, Molestar, incomodar, jorobar.

Bore, *pret.* del verbo *To* BEAR.

Bore, *s.* 1. Taladro, barreno, el agujero que se hace taladrando o barrenando. 2. Taladro, barreno o barrena, el instrumento con que se taladra o barrena. 3. Calibre, el hueco de un cañón. 4. (Fam.) *A bore*, o *A perfect bore*, Majadero, jorobón, pelma, pesado, molienda, insufrible, pelmazo. 5. Ola que forma la subida de la marea por el cauce de un río.

Boreal [bō'-rẹ-al], *a.* Septentrional, boreal.

Boreas [bō'-rẹ-as], *s.* Norte, uno de los vientos.

Borecole [bōr'-cōl], *s.* (Bot.) Especie de berza.

Boredom [bōr'-dum], *s.* 1. Los pesados, y majaderos, como clase. 2. La condición de verse y estar fastidiado y molestado.

Borer [bōr'-ẹr], *s.* 1. Barreno o taladro. 2. Lo que excava, como escarabajo, polilla o molusco.

Boresome [bōr'-sum], *a.* Fastidioso, aburrido, cansado.

Boric [bō'-ric], *a.* Bórico.

Boring [bōr'-ing], *a.* 1. Fastidioso, aburrido. 2. (fam.) Latoso.

Born [bōrn], *pp.* Nacido; destinado. *To be born*, Nacer. *Since I was born*, Desde que nací. *To be born again*, Renacer. *The first-born*, El primogénito. *High-born*, *low-born*, De elevado, de humilde nacimiento.

Borne [bōrn], *pp.* de *To* BEAR. Llevado, sostenido.

Boron [bō'-ren], *s.* Boro, elemento químico no metálico; origen del ácido bórico.

Borough [bur'-ō], *s.* 1. Ciudad o villa. 2. (Ingl.) Corporación municipal, no una ciudad, dotada por real cédula de ciertos privilegios (*municipal borough*). 3. (Ingl.) Pueblo constituido o no en corporación legal, pero con derecho de representación en el Parlamento (*parliamentary borough*).

Borrow [ber'-ō], *va.* 1. Tomar fiado o prestado. 2. Pedir prestado; lo contrario de *to lend*, prestar. 3. Usar prendas ajenas, servirse de lo que pertenece a otro.

Borrower [ber'-ō-ẹr], *s.* El que pide prestado.

Borrowing [ber'-o-ing], *s.* Empréstito, préstamo, el acto de pedir prestado o la cosa que se pide prestada.

Boscage [bes'-kẹj], *s.* 1. Boscaje, soto, floresta, arboleda, el conjunto de árboles y plantas. 2. (Pint.) Paisaje poblado de árboles.

Bosh [besh], *s.* 1. Galimatías, necedad. 2. Atalaje de alto horno; embudo del cabilote. (< Turco.)

Bosk [besk], *s.* Bosque pequeño; matorral.

Bosket [bes'-kẹt], *s.* Bosquecillo, bosquete, grupo de árboles en un jardín extenso.

Bosnian [bez'-ni-an], *a.* Bosnio, de Bosnia.

Bosom [bū'-zum], *s.* 1. Seno, el pecho, el corazón. 2. Amor, inclinación, afecto, cariño. *Bosom friend*, Amigo íntimo o de la mayor confianza. 3. Pecho, la parte del vestido de mujer que está sobre el pecho. *Bosom of the church*, El gremio de la Iglesia. 4. Pechera, en costura. *Bosom of a shirt*, Pechera de la camisa.

Bosom, *va.* 1. Guardar en el pecho. 2. Ocultar o tener secreta alguna cosa.

Boson, *s.* *V.* BOATSWAIN.

Bosphorus [bos'-fō-rus], *s.* Bósforo, el estrecho, canal o garganta de mar entre dos tierras firmes, por donde un mar se comunica con otro.

Boss [bos], *s.* 1. Clavo o tachón; giba, joroba, corcova, abolladura. *Boss of a bridle*, Copa de freno. *Boss of a book*, Lomo de un libro. 2. Patrón, maestro: capataz de obreros. 3. Dictador o cacique político.

Boss, *va.* 1. Trabajar en relieve. *V.* EMBOSS. 2. (Fam. E. U.) (1) Dirigir obras. (2) Tener y ejercer poder o influencia.

Bossage [bos'-ẹj], *s.* Relieve o proyectura de alguna piedra.

Bossed [best], **Bossy** [bos'-i], *a.* Saltado, tachonado; turgente, abultado, saliente.

Bot [bet], *s.* 1. Larva de estro. 2 Estro. *V.* BOT-FLY.

Botanic, Botanical [bọ-tan'-ic, al], *a* Botánico, que pertenece a la botánica.

Botanically [bọ-tan'-i-cal-i], *adv.* Botánicamente.

Botanist [bet'-an-ist], *s.* Botánico, el que profesa la botánica o tiene conocimiento de las plantas.

Botanize [bet'-an-aiz], *va.* Explorar en busca de ejemplares botánicos o para estudiar la vida de plantas.—*vn.* Herborizar, buscar plantas y estudiarlas; ocuparse en botánica.

Botany [bet'-a-ni], *s.* Botánica, la parte de la biología que trata de las plantas, sus clases, géneros y especies.

Botch [bech], *s.* 1. Roncha, el bultillo que se eleva en el cuerpo del animal. 2. Remiendo, cualquiera cosa mal acabada añadida a otra. 3. Landre, úlcera. 4. (Poét.) Ripio.

Botch, *va.* 1. Remendar ropa chapuceramente. 2. Juntar o unir alguna cosa chabacanamente. 3. Chapuzar, chafallar, hacer un trabajo apresuradamente. 4. (Poét.) Llenar de ripios el verso.

Botcher [bech'-ẹr], *s.* Sastre remendón.

Botchy [bech'-i], *a.* Señalado con ronchas.

Bot-fly [bet'-flai], *s.* Estro, insecto díptero de la familia Oestridæ, de muchas especies diferentes; algunas de ellas son nocivas al caballo, al buey y a la oveja, en cuyos cuerpos depositan sus huevos. Gastrophilus equi.

Both [bōth], *a.* Ambos, los dos, entrambos, ambos a dos. *On both sides*, Por ambos lados, por ambas partes, de uno y otro lado. *Both of them*, Ellos dos. *Both of us*, Nosotros dos. *Both his sons*, Sus dos hijos.

Both, *conj.* Tanto como, así como. *Both in time of peace and war*, Tanto en tiempo de paz como de guerra.

Bother [bedh'-ẹr], *va.* (Fam.) Aturrullar, confundir, perturbar, enojar, aturdir con ruido; molestar, incomodar, jorobar.

Bothnian [beth'-ni-an], *a.* Botniano.

Botryoidal [bet"-ri-eid'-al], *a.* Botrioideo, que tiene la forma de un racimo: se aplica comunmente a los minerales. (Gr. botrys, racimo.)

Bots [bets], *s. pl.* Lombrices en las entrañas de los caballos. Larvas de varias especies de moscas (*bot-fly*), que molestan a las caballerías.

Bottle [bet'-l], *s.* 1. Botella, frasco, redoma de vidrio. 2. Botella, la cantidad de vino que se echa en dicha vasija, que viene a ser algo menos de dos cuartillos. 3. Haz o gavilla de heno o verde. *Bottle friend* o *companion*, Compañero en el beber; bebedor. *Nursing-bottle*, Mamadera, biberón. *Stone bottle*, Botella de greda.

Bottle, *va.* 1. Embotellar, enfrascar, poner alguna cosa en botellas o frascos. 2. Agavillar.

Bottled [bet'-ld], *a.* Embotellado, enfrascado.

Bottleflower [bet'-l-flau-ẹr], *s.* (Bot.) Centaurea.

Bottlegreen [bet'-l-grīn], *s.* Verde botella, un color.

Bottleneck [bet'-l-nek], *s.* 1. Cuello de botella. 2. Cuello de estrangulación (en el tránsito). 3. (fig.) Angostura, obstrucción.

Bottlescrew [bet'-l-scrū], *s.* Tirabuzón o sacatrapos para extraer los tapones de los frascos y botellas.

Bottling [bet'-l-ing], *s.* Embotellamiento.

Bottom [bet'-um], *s.* 1. Fondo, suelo, la parte inferior o más baja de alguna cosa. 2. Zanja, el cimiento o fundamento de alguna cosa. 3. Cañada o valle. 4. Hondonada, ovillo, globo o pelota compuesta de hilo, seda, etc. 5. Embarcación o buque. 6. Fin, designio, motivo. 7. Culo. *The bottom of the belly*, El empeine. 8. Asentaderas, nalgas. 9. Asiento de una silla. 10. Pie; base, fundamento.

Bottom, *va.* 1. Cimentar, fundar, apoyar. 2. Ovillar, devanar un ovillo.—*vn.* Apoyarse.

Bottomed [bet'-umd], *a.* Lo que tiene fondo o suelo. Forrado.

Bottomless [bet'-um-les], *a.* 1. Insondable, lo que no se puede sondear. *Bottomless pit*, Abismo. 2. Excesivo, desmesurado, impenetrable.

Bottomry [bet'-um-ri], *s.* (Mar.) Casco y quilla, el acto de tomar dinero prestado hipotecando todo el barco.

Botulism [bech'-u-lizm], *s.* Botulismo.

Boudoir [bū-dwer'], *s.* Tocador o recámara de señora.

Bouffe [būf], *a.* Cómico. *V.* OPERA.

Bough [bau], *s.* Brazo del árbol, las ramas mayores que parten del tronco.

Bought, *pret.* y *pp.* del verbo *To* BUY.

Bought [bōt], *s.* 1. Torcedura, nudo, corvadura o curvatura. 2. La parte de la honda que contiene la piedra.
Bougie [bū'-zhī], *s.* 1. Candelilla, cilindro flexible para superar obstrucciones de la uretra, esófago u otros conductos del cuerpo, o para dilatarlos en casos de estrechez. 2. Candelilla de gelatina, u otra substancia, impregnada de un medicamento para su introducción en la uretra, u otro conducto. (Gal.)
Bouillon [būl-yeñ'], *s.* Caldo claro de carne. (Gal.)
Boulder o **Bowlder** [bōl'-dẹr], *s.* Peña, piedra desprendida de una masa de roca. Guijarro grande.
Boulder-wall [bōl'-dẹr-wōl], *s.* (Arq.) Muralla o pared compuesta de grandes cantos rodados.
Boulevard [bū'-le-vārd], *s.* Bulevar, avenida ancha o paseo público.
Bounce [bauns], *vn.* 1. Arremeter, acometer con ímpetu. 2. Brincar, saltar, dar un salto repentino. 3. Bravear, echar fieros o bravatas; jactarse.—*va.* 1. Hacer saltar o botar. 2. (Fam. E. U.) Despedir, privar de algún empleo u oficio.
Bounce, *s.* 1. Golpazo, golpe fuerte. 2. Estallido, ruido o estruendo. 3. Bravata, fanfarronada, amenaza con arrogancia para intimidar a otro. 4. Brinco. 5. Bote, salto de una pelota u otro cuerpo elástico. 6. Bola, mentira grosera.
Bouncer [baun'-sẹr], *s.* El guapo que echa bravatas y fieros; fanfarrón.
Bouncing [baun'-sing], *a.* 1. Fuerte, vigoroso, bien formado. *A bouncing baby,* Un niño robusto. 2. Exagerado, desmesurado. 3. Fanfarrón, valentón; mentiroso.
Bound [baund], *s.* 1. Límite, término, confín o lindero. 2. Bote, brinco, corcovo, salto. 3. Resalto, repercusión.
Bound, *va.* 1. Deslindar o poner límites. 2. Confinar. 3. Limitar, ceñir. 4. Hacer saltar.—*vn.* 1. Saltar, dar saltos. 2. Resaltar. 3. Botar.
Bound, *a.; pret.* y *pp.* del verbo *To* BIND. 1. Atado, ligado; confinado. 2. Moralmente o legalmente obligado o forzado. 3. Encuadernado, o que tiene cobertura. 4. (Fam.) Destinado; sentenciado. 5. (Fam. E. U.) Decidido, resuelto. 6. Puesto en aprendizaje. 7. Estreñido, cerrado de vientre.—*a.* Destinado. *Our ship is bound for Venice,* Nuestra embarcación está destinada a Venecia o va a Venecia.
Boundary [baun'-da-ri], *s.* Límite o linde, frontera.
Bounden [baund'-ẹn], *a.* Obligado, precisado; indispensable.
Bounder [baun'-dẹr], *s.* El que pone límites, medidor.
Bounding-stone [baun'-ding-stōn], **Boundstone** [baund'-stōn], *s.* 1. Mojón, piedra que sirve como señal para dividir los términos, lindes o caminos. 2. Piedra de jugar, piedra de saque.
Boundless [baund'-les], *a.* Ilimitado, lo que no tiene límites ni término; infinito.
Boundlessness [baund'-les-nes], *s.* Inmensidad, infinidad de espacio.
Bounteous [baun'-tẹ-us], *a.* Liberal, generoso.
Bounteously [baun'-tẹ-us-li], *adv.* Liberalmente, generosamente.
Bounteousness [baun'-tẹ-us-nes], *s.* Munificencia, liberalidad, generosidad.
Bounteth [baun'-teth], *s.* (Esco.) Propina, recompensa sobre el salario regular.
Bountiful [baun'-ti-ful], *a.* Liberal, generoso, bienhechor.
Bountifully [baun'-ti-ful-i], *adv.* Liberalmente, generosamente, copiosamente.
Bountifulness [baun'-ti-ful-nes], *s.* Generosidad, liberalidad, largueza.
Bounty [baun'-ti], *s.* 1. Generosidad, liberalidad, munificencia, bondad. 2. Premio. 3. Ayuda de costa. *Bounty money,* Enganche.
Bouquet [bū-ké'], *s.* 1. Ramillete de flores. 2. Perfume, aroma del vino.
Bourbon [būr'-bẹn], *s.* 1. Borbón, miembro de la antigua casa de Borbón en Francia; o de sus ramas en España y Nápoles. 2. (Ger. E. U.) Porfiado en sus ideas políticas conservadoras; opuesto al progreso.
Bourdon [būr'-dẹn], *s.* (Fr.) Bordón, registro de órgano.
Bourgeois [būr"-zhwā'], *a.* Burgués, el que pertenece á la clase media o comercial; de aquí, común, ordinario, poco cultivado.—*s.* Burgués, ciudadano de la clase media; vecino de una ciudad; comerciante, tendero. (Gal.)
Bourgeois [būr-jeis'], *s.* Tipo medio entre breviario y entredós; carácter de nueve puntos.
Bourgeoisie [būr-zhwā-zī'], *s.* Burguesía. (Fr.)
Bourgeon [būr'-jun], *vn.* Brotar o echar ramas.—*s.* Yema. (Fr.)
Bourn [bōrn o būrn], *s.* 1. Límite o linde. 2. Arroyo.
Bourse [būrs], *s.* 1. Bolsa, lonja; especialmente la de Paris. 2. (Anat.) Cualquier receptáculo en forma de bolsa, como el pericardio.
Bouse [būz], *vn.* Beber con intemperancia. *V.* BOOZE.
Bousy [bū'-zi], *a.* Borracho, embriagado. *V.* BOOZY.
Bout [baut], *s.* 1. Vez, la relación de una cosa con otra sucesiva o anterior; un rato. 2. Ataque de borrachera, o de enfermedad. 3. Curva o vuelta de una cuerda. *A bout at fencing,* Un asalto de esgrima.
Bovate [bō'-vêt], *s.* El espacio de tierra que puede arar un par de bueyes en un año; medida antigua.
Bovine [bō'-vin o vain], *a.* Bovino, relativo al buey, o al ganado vacuno.
Bow [bau], *va.* 1. Hacer reverencia o cortesía: expresar por medio de la inclinación del cuerpo. 2. Escoltar o acompañar haciendo reverencias. 3. Agobiar, oprimir, agravar. —*vn.* 1. Doblarse, torcerse o encorvarse. 2. Agobiarse. 3. Ceder, someterse. *He bowed his head,* Inclinó la cabeza.
Bow [bau], *s.* 1. Reverencia, cortesía, inclinación del cuerpo o parte de él que se hace en señal de respeto. 2. (Mar.) Proa, toda la figura exterior de la embarcación, de la nave a la roda. *On the bow,* (Mar.) Por la serviola. *Bow-oar, s.* El remo más cercano a la proa de una lancha, o la persona que lo maneja. *To make a bow,* Saludar, hacer un saludo.
Bow [bō], *s.* 1. Arco, arma para disparar flechas. 2. El arco iris. 3. Arco, el instrumento con que se tocan los violines y violones. 4. Lazo, de corbata, de cinta, etc. 5. Arzón de silla.
Bow [bō], *va.* Encorvar en forma de arco; doblar y torcer alguna cosa.
Bow-bent [bō'-bent], *a.* Arqueado.
Bowel [bau'-el], *va.* (Des.) Traspasar las entrañas, destripar, despanzurrar.
Bowel [bau'-el], *s.* 1. Intestino, entraña, tripa. 2. *pl.* Entrañas, lo más escondido o más interior de una cosa. 3. (Ant.) Entrañas, ternura, compasión. *To open the bowels,* Hacer moverse el vientre. *A bowel complaint,* Enfermedad de los intestinos.
Bowelless [bau'-el-les] *a.* Inhumano, sin ternura o compasión.
Bower [bau'-ẹr], *s.* 1. Glorieta, emparrado o enramada de jardín; bóveda. 2. Morada, domicilio; retrete, aposento retirado. *Bower-bird,* Ave de enramada; tilonorinco, pájaro australiano de la familia de los córvidos, notable por la pequeña enramada o choza que construye en el suelo aparte de su nido, y que adorna con conchas, plumas, huesos y objetos de colores brillantes.
Bower [bō'-ẹr], *s.* 1. Tocador con arco. 2. Arquero. *V.* BOWYER.
Bower (del alemán, *bauer*), *s. Right bower, left bower,* Los dos naipes más altos en el juego llamado "euchre."
Bower, *va.* *V.* EMBOWER.
Bower-anchor [bau'-ẹr-ang-kẹr], *s.* (Mar.) Ancla de servidumbre.
Bowery [bau'-ẹr-i], *a.* Lleno de emparrados o enramadas; sombrío.
Bow-hand [bō'-hand], *s.* La mano del arco, la que tiene el arco para herir las cuerdas de los instrumentos músicos.
Bowie-knife [bō'-i-naif], *s.* Cuchillo de monte; puñal largo y ancho.
Bowing [bau'-ing], *a.* Inclinado.
Bow-knot [bō'-net], *s.* Lazo corredizo, o escurridizo.
Bowl [bōl], *s.* 1. Taza, cuenca. 2. Hueco o cóncavo de alguna cosa. 3. Tazón de fuente. 4. Bolo, esfera de madera o hierro que se hace rodar por el suelo para jugar a los bolos o a las bochas. *Bowl of a pipe,* Hornillo de la pipa. *Bowl of a spoon,* Paleta de la cuchara. 5. *pl.* Juego de bolos.
Bowl, *va.* 1. Voltear como una bola. 2. Bolear, tirar los bolos.—*vn.* Jugar a las bochas.
Bowlder. *V.* BOULDER.
Bow-legged [bō'-legd], *a.* Patiestevado, el que tiene las piernas estevadas. *Bowleg,* Pierna corva.
Bowler [bōl'-ẹr], *s.* Jugador de bochas o de bolos.
Bowline [bō'-lin], **Bowling** [bōl'-ing], *s.* (Mar.) Bolina, cabo que se fija en las púas que nacen de las relingas de las velas mayores. *To haul the bowlines,* (Mar.) Bolinear.
Bowling, *s.* El arte o acto de jugar a las bochas; el juego de bolos. *Bowling-alley,* Sitio cubierto para jugar a los bolos. *Bowling-green, Bowling-ground,* Plano para jugar a las bochas, juego de bolos; calle en los jardines cubierta de céspedes.
Bowman [bō'-man], *s.* Arquero, el soldado que peleaba con arco y flechas.
Bownet [bō'-net], *s.* Nasa o cesta para pescar.
Bowse [baus], *vn.* (Mar.) Halar a un tiempo.
Bow-shot [bō'-shet], *s.* La distancia a que una flecha puede ser arrojada del arco.
Bowsprit [bō'-sprit], *s.* (Mar.) Bauprés, palo que sale inclinado de la proa de un bajel.

Bowstring [bō'-string], *s.* Cuerda de arco.
Bow-window [bō'-win-dō], *s.* Ventana arqueada o saliente en forma de arco.
Box [box], *s.* 1. (Bot.) Box o boj, árbol cuya madera se llama también así. 2. Caja, cajita o cajón; excusabaraja; pieza hueca de madera, metal, piedra u otra materia para meter dentro alguna cosa. 3. (Mar.) Bitácora. 4. Palco de teatro. 5. Puñete, manotada o puñada dada en la cabeza. 6. Cuarto muy reducido en una taberna o botillería. 7. Cajetín en las imprentas. *Band-box,* Caja de cartón. *Hat-box,* Sombrerera. *Jewel-box,* Caja para joyas. *Letter-box,* Buzón del correo. *Strong box,* Cofre fuerte. *Box car,* Carro de cajón, furgón. *Christmas-box,* Aguinaldo. *Alms-box,* Cepillo de limosna. *Coach-box,* Pescante de coche. *Dice-box,* Cubilete. *Dust-box,* Salvadera. *Snuff-box,* Tabaquera. *Box of a pump,* Émbolo de una bomba. *Box plaiting,* (Cost.) Plegado que consiste en dobleces o pliegues hechos a derecha e izquierda alternadamente. *Box-elder,* Árbol norteamericano semejante al arce, pero con hojas de tres o cinco hojuelas. Negundo aceroides o Acer negundo.
Box, *va.* 1. Encajonar. 2. Apuñear, dar manotazos.—*vn.* Combatir o pelear a puñadas, andar a trompis. *To box the compass,* (Mar.) Cuartear.
Boxen [bec'-sẹn], *a.* Hecho de boj, o semejante a él.
Boxer [bec'-sẹr], *s.* 1. Púgil, el que combate a puñadas. 2. El que pone géneros en cajas.
Boxhaul [becs'-hōl], *va.* (Mar.) Dar vuelta la nave cuando no se puede virar.
Boxing [bec'-sing], *s.* Boxeo, pugilato.
Box office [bex ef'-is], *s.* Taquilla.
Box seat [bex sît], *s.* Palco (en un teatro).
Boxwood [bex'-wud], *s.* Madera amarillenta del box; también, el mismo árbol.
Boy [bōi], *s.* 1. Muchacho o niño. *His wife was delivered of a boy,* Su mujer parió un varón. 2. Muchacho, el que no ha llegado á la edad adulta y ha pasado de la de niño. 3. Muchacho, voz de desprecio con que se moteja a los jóvenes. 4. Criado, lacayo. *Cabin-boy,* Paje de escoba. *School-boy,* Muchacho de escuela. *Choir-boy,* Niño de coro. *Soldier's boy,* Galopín, galopo. *A little boy,* Muchachito, chico. *My dear boy,* Mi querido niño. *Bad, naughty boy,* Chico travieso. *Boy's-play,* Pasatiempo o juego de muchachos.
Boycott [bei'-cet], *va.* Boicotear. Desacreditar, excluir, coaligarse contra una persona, por ejemplo, un propietario o tendero. (Del capitán Boycott, así tratado en Irlanda en 1880.)
Boycott *s.* Boicoteo. Coalición organizada contra un propietario, comerciante u otra persona, negándose a sostener con ella relaciones sociales o de negocios.
Boyhood [bei'-hud], *s.* Muchachez, el estado de muchacho.
Boyish [bei'-ish], *a.* Pueril, propio de niño.
Boyishly [bei'-ish-li], *adv.* Puerilmente, como niño.
Boyishness [bei'-ish-nes], *s.* Puerilidad, muchachada, niñada o cosa propia de niños.
Boy scout [bei scaut], *s.* Explorador, muchacho o niño explorador.
Brabble [brab'-l], *vn.* Armar camorra.—*s.* Camorra, riña o pendencia; debate.
Braccate [brak'-ẹt], *a.* (Orn.) Paticalzado, el ave que tiene las patas cubiertas de plumas.
Brace [brēs], *va.* 1. Atar, ligar, amarrar. 2. (Mar.) Bracear, halar las brazas o poner las vergas según es menester. 3. Cercar, rodear. 4. Fortificar, vigorizar (los nervios).
Brace, *s.* 1. Abrazadera, laña, grapón, broche, lo que mantiene alguna cosa firme. *Carpenter's brace,* Barbiquejo; berbiquí, barbiquí; tornapunta. *Brace and bits,* Berbiquí con sus barrenas. 2. Tirante, la vigueta que va de solera a solera en una fábrica. 3. Sopanda de coche, cada una de las correas que sostienen la caja. 4. Par. *Brace of partridges,* Un par de perdices. 5. (Imp.) } Corchete, llave, rasgo que abraza dos o más renglones en lo escrito o impreso. 6. (Arq.) Anclaje, silla, mordaza; can, canecillo.—*Braces,* (1) (Mar.) Brazas, los cabos que vienen por los motones de los brazaletes, para poner la braza como conviene. *Braces of a rudder,* (Mar.) Hembras del timón. (2) Tirantes del pantalón.
Bracelet [brēs'-let], *s.* 1. Brazalete, adorno para el brazo. (Méx.) Pulsera, manilla. 2. Brazalete, brazal, armadura del brazo.
Bracer [brē'-sẹr], *s.* 1. Brazal, armadura del brazo. 2. (Med.) Un medicamento tónico, fortificante y astringente. 3. Abrazadera, laña; cinto, venda. 4. Braguero.
Braces [brê'-sez], *s. pl.* Abrazadera, freno para dientes.
Brachial [brak'-i-al], *a.* Braquial, que pertenece o toca al brazo.
Brachiopod [brak'-i-o-ped], *s.* Braquiópodo, ejemplar de la familia de moluscos bivalvos que tienen dos brazos carnosos dotados de extensión y contractilidad, que les sirven para moverse.
Brachium [brak'-i-um], *s.* (*pl.* BRACHIA). El brazo superior o lo que lo representa en cualquier animal.
‡**Brachygrapher** [bra-kig'-ra-fẹr], *s.* Braquiógrafo, el que escribe en abreviatura.
Brachygraphy [bra-kig'-ra-fi], *s.* Braquiografía, el arte de escribir en abreviatura.
Bracing [brēs'-ing], *a.* Fortificante, tónico, confortante.—*s.* (Tec.) Amarra, ligazón, refuerzo, trabazón.
Brack [brac], *s.* Rotura; pelo o mancha en los metales.
Bracken [brak'-n], *s.* (Bot.) 1. Helecho grande de las regiones templadas; en particular la Pteris aquilina. 2. Helechal, sitio poblado de helechos.
Bracket [brak'-et], *s.* 1. Puntal, el madero en cuya corona o cabeza estriba otra cosa; listón, listoncillo; can, repisa. *Cat-head brackets,* (Mar.) Aletas de las serviolas. 2. Paréntesis, angulares; así [ ]. 3. (Mec.) Bloque, garfio. 4. Repisa, rinconera, codillo. 5. Brazo de lámpara.
Brackish [brak'-ish], *a.* Salobre, que por naturaleza tiene sabor de sal; áspero.
Brackishness [brak'-ish-nes], *s.* Sabor salobre; saladura; aspereza.
Bract [bract], *s.* (Bot.) Bráctea, hoja de cuya axila se levanta un tallo de flor, o pedúnculo.
Bractlet [bract'-let], *s.* (Bot.) Bracteola, bractea pequeña o secundaria.
Brad [brad], *s.* Clavo de ala de mosca; puntilla.
Brad-awl [brad-el], *s.* Punzón afilado, lesna.
Brag [brag], *s.* 1. Jactancia. 2. La cosa de que se jacta uno. 3. Un juego de naipes.
Brag, *vn.* Jactarse, fanfarronear.
Braggadocio [brag-a-dō'-shi-ō], *s.* Fanfarrón, el que echa fanfarronadas.
Braggardism [brag'-ard-izm], *s.* Jactancia, vana ostentación.
Braggart [brag'-ārt], *a.* Jactancioso, el que se jacta.
Braggart, Bragger [brag'-ẹr], *s.* Fanfarrón, el que echa fanfarronadas.
Bragget [brag'-et], *s.* Aguamiel, una bebida dulce.
Braggingly [brag'-ing-li], *adv.* Jactanciosamente.
Brahman [brā'-man], *s.* Bracmán, nombre que se da a los filósofos y sacerdotes de la India.
Brahmanical, Braminical [brā-min'i-cal], *a.* Bracmánico, perteneciente a los bracmanes. *V.* BRAHMAN.
Braid [brēd], *va.* 1. Trenzar, hacer trenzas. 2. Acordonar, bordar con cordoncillo o de realce; galonear.
Braid, *s.* 1. Galón, fleco, alamar. 2. Trenza; cordoncillo.—*a.* Astuto, fraudulento, falso. (Esco.) Ancho. *Braidclaith,* Paño ancho.
Brail [brēl], *va.* (Mar.) Cargar las velas; halar por medio de candelizas.
Brails [brēlz], *s.* (Mar.) Candelizas o cargaderas, los cabos pequeños que pasan por los motones.
Brain [brēn], *s.* 1. Cerebro, sesos, la colección de vasos y órganos contenidos en la cavidad del cráneo. 2. Entendimiento, seso, juicio, cordura, talento. *To blow out one's brains,* Levantarse la tapa de los sesos.
Brain, *va.* Descerebrar, matar a uno haciéndole saltar la tapa de los sesos. *Hare-brained,* Aturdido, sin seso. *Scatter-brained* (o *shittle-brained,* ant.), Veleidoso, voltario, ligero, inconstante.
Brainish [brēn'-ish], *a.* Loco, furioso.
Brainless [brēn'-les], *a.* Tonto, insensato.
Brainpan [brēn'-pan], *s.* Cráneo o casco.
Brainsick [brēn'-sic], *a.* Alegre de cascos, inconstante, mala cabeza; frenético.
Brainsickly [brēn'-sic-li], *adv.* Con debilidad de cabeza.
Brainsickness [brēn'-sic-nes], *s.* Inconstancia, instabilidad; vértigo, veleidad, ligereza.
Brainstorm [brēn'-stōrm], *s.* 1. Agitación transitoria. 2. Confusión mental. 3. Repentina idea genial.
Brainwashing [brēn'-wesh'-ing], *s.* "Lavado cerebral," imposición por persuasión o tortura de ciertas ideas políticas.
Brake [brēc], *s.* 1. Helecho del género *Pteris,* particularmente Pteris aquilina. *V.* BRACKEN. 2. Agramadera, instrumento para agramar lino o cáñamo. 3. Maleza, zarzal, matorral. 4. (F. C.) Freno; retranca. 5. (Mar.) Guimbalete de bomba. 6. Amasadera, la artesa de amasar. 7. Bocado de canutillo

para caballo. 8. Palanca, espeque. *Brake beam*, Barra del freno. *Brakeman*, Guardafreno, retranquero. *Air-brake*, Freno atmosférico o de aire. *Automatic brake*, Freno automático.

Brake, *pret.* del verbo *To* BREAK. (Ant.)

Braky [brê'-ki], *a.* Espinoso, áspero, lleno de malezas.

Bramble [bram'-bl], *s.* Zarza u otro cualquier arbusto espinoso.

Brambled [bram'-bld], *a.* Breñoso, zarzoso, cubierto de zarzas o arbustos espinosos.

Brambling [bram'-bling], *s.* Pinzón, especie de pájaro.

Brambly [bram'-bli], *a.* Zarzoso, lleno de zarzas.

Bran [bran], *s.* Salvado, la cáscara del trigo después de molido; afrecho.

Bran-new o **Brand-new** [bran-niū'], *a.* Enteramente nuevo, flamante.

Branch [branch], *s.* 1. Rama o ramo del árbol. 2. Ramo, la parte separada de algún todo con dependencia y relación a él. 3. Brazo, parte de un río que desemboca en otro mayor. 4. Rama, cualquier persona con relación al tronco de que trae su descendencia u origen. 5. Pitón, asta. 6. Cama del freno. 7. Brazo del candelero. 8. Brazo de trompeta. *Vine branch*, Sarmiento. *Branch pease*, Arvejones enramados. 9. Sucursal. 10. (F. C.) Ramal, bifurcación. *Branches*, (colectivamente) Ramas, ramaje.—*a.* Divergente de un tronco o parte principal o tributario de ella.

Branch, *vn.* 1. Ramificarse, esparcirse y dividirse en ramas alguna cosa. 2. Hablar difusamente. 3. Echar pitones, astas o ramas.—*va.* 1. Ramificar, dividir en ramas. 2. Bordar alguna cosa con figuras de ramos.

Brancher [branch'-er], *s.* 1. El que divide en ramos. 2. (Cetr.) Halcón ramero.

Branchery [branch'-er-i], *s.* Las partes vasculosas de algunos frutos.

Branchiæ [bran'-ki-ê], *s. pl.* Branquias, órganos respiratorios de los peces, crustáceos y muchos moluscos.

Branchial [bran'-ki-al], *a.* Branquial.

Branchiness [bran'-chi-nes], *s.* Frondosidad.

Branchless [branch'-les], *a.* Sin ramas; desnudo.

Branchlet [branch'-let], *s. dim.* Rama pequeña, ramilla.

Branchy [bran'-chi], *a.* Ramoso, lo que tiene muchos ramos o ramas.

Brand [brand], *s.* 1. Tizón o tea, palo encendido o propio para encenderse. 2. Espada. 3. Rayo. 4. Marca o sello que se pone a las reses y que se ponía a los reos con un hierro ardiendo. 5. Tizón, nota de infamia. *To cast a brand upon one*, Disfamar a alguno, quitarle la reputación.

Brand, *va.* 1. Herrar, marcar o sellar con un hierro ardiendo. 2. Tiznar, infamar, desdorar, manchar, empañar la reputación. *Branded gray horse*, Caballo con manchas irregulares.

Brand goose [brand' gūs], *s.* Oca silvestre. *V.* BRANT.

Brandiron [brand'-ai-ūrn], *s.* Marca, el hierro para marcar a los animales o a los malhechores.

Brandish [bran'-dish], *va.* Blandir; jugar con; sacudir con la mano.

Brandish, *s.* Floreo; movimiento rápido y de corta duración.

Brandling [brand'-ling], *s.* Especie de gusano que sirve para cebo.

Brandrith [brand'-rith], *s.* Antepecho o brocal de pozo.

Brandy, Brandy-wine [bran'-di, wain], *s.* Aguardiente, coñac.

Brandyshop [bran'-di-shop], *s.* Aguardentería, la tienda en que se vende aguardiente.

§**Brangle** [bran'-gl], *vn.* Vocinglear, disputarse. *V.* WRANGLE.

Brank, *s.* (Dial. ingl.) *V.* BUCKWHEAT.

Brankursine [brangc'-ur-sin], *s.* (Bot.) Branca ursina, acanto.

Branlin [bran'-lin], *s.* Salmón pequeño antes de ir al mar.

Branny [bran'-i], *a.* Casposo, parecido al salvado.

Brant [brant], *s.* Especie de ganso, u oca silvestre. Se llama también *brent.*

Brasen, Brazen [brêz'-n], *a.* Hecho de bronce.

Brash [brash], *a.* Impetuoso; temerario.—*s.* 1. Ramas sueltas de árboles. 2. Enfermedad repentina.

Brasier, Brazier [brê'-zher], *s.* 1. Latonero, el que trabaja en latón, azófar, alambre o cobre. 2. Brasero o copa.

Brasil, Brazil [bra-zil'], *s.* Palo del Brasil.

Brass [bras], *s.* 1. Latón, bronce. 2. Descaro, desvergüenza. 3. (fam.) Altos jefes militares. *Brass band*, Banda de instrumentos de viento, charanga.

Brassfounder [bras'-faun-der], *s.* Fundidor de bronce.

Brassie [bras'-i], *s.* Maza que se emplea en el juego de golf.

Brassière [bra-zîr'], *s.* Brassière, soporte para senos.

Brassiness [bras'-i-nes], *s.* Bronceadura, apariencia de bronce.

Brass-visaged [bras'-viz'-êjd], *a.* Descarado, descocado, desvergonzado.

Brassy [bras'-i], *a.* 1. Que participa de la naturaleza del latón. 2. Descarado, desvergonzado. 3. *V.* BRAZEN.

Brat [brat], *s.* 1. Rapaz, el muchacho pequeño de edad; chulo, chiquillo; angelito. 2. (Despect.) Prole.

Brattle [brat'-l], *vn.* Hacer ruido rápidamente repetido y poco sonoro; correr con estruendo; poner pies en polvorosa.

Brattle, *s.* Ruido resonante, como el de un tambor, el correr de personas o el de un ataque. (Onomatopéyico.)

Bravado [bra-vê'-do], *s.* Bravata, baladronada.

Brave [brêv], *a.* 1. Bravo, valiente, esforzado, animoso, atrevido, intrépido. 2. Garboso, airoso. 3. Bravo, elegante, hábil, honrado.

Brave, *va.* 1. Desafiar, provocar a duelo. 2. Bravear, echar bravatas. 3. Ofender, insultar. 4. Arrostrar.

Brave, *s.* 1. Bravonel, el guapo que echa bravatas y fieros, fanfarrón. 2. Bravata, amenaza con arrogancia.

Bravely [brêv'-li], *adv.* Bravamente, valientemente; perfectamente.

Bravery [brê'-ver-i], *s.* 1. Esfuerzo, valentía, valor, ánimo. 2. Lustre, galantería, esplendor, magnificencia. 3. Pompa, ostentación. 4. Bravata.

Bravingly [brê'-ving-li], *adv.* En desafío.

Bravo [brê'-vo o brā'-vo], *s.* Asesino asalariado.—*inter.* Voz de aplauso. ¡Bueno; bueno; bravo va!

Bravura [brā-vū'-ra], *s.* (Mús.) Aire o canción difícil de cantar.

Braw [brē], *a.* (Esco.) Bravo, garboso, elegantemente vestido; espléndido, hermoso.

Brawl [brēl], *s.* 1. Quimera, alboroto, disputa, camorra. 2. Baile, y la música que lo acompaña.

Brawl, *vn.* 1. Alborotar, armar quimera con voces desentonadas; vocinglear. 2. Hacer ruido.—*va.* Expeler por medio de ruido; aterrar.

Brawler [brēl'-er], *s.* Quimerista o camorrista.

Brawling [brēl'-ing], *s.* Alboroto, el acto de alborotar, vocinglería.

Brawn [brēn], *s.* 1. Pulpa, carne mollar, la parte carnosa y muscular del cuerpo. 2. El brazo, llamado así por ser muy musculoso. 3. Carnosidad, carne maciza y musculosa. 4. Carne de verraco o cerdo padre.

Brawner [brēn'-er], *s.* El verraco que se mata para comer.

Brawniness [brēn'-i-nes], *s.* Fortaleza o dureza de músculos; partes carnosas.

Brawny [brēn'-i], *a.* Carnoso, musculoso, membrudo.

Braxy [brax'-i], *s.* Fiebre carbuncular de los carneros y las ovejas; también una res lanar atacada de este mal.—*a.* Atacado de dicha fiebre.

Bray [brê], *va.* 1. Majar, triturar, moler, machacar o pulverizar. 2. Emitir.—*vn.* 1. Rebuznar. 2. Hacer ruido desapacible.

Bray, *s.* 1. Rebuzno, la voz desapacible del asno. 2. Ruido bronco. 3. Monte de tierra, trinchera. *False bray*, (Mil.) Falsabraga.

Brayer [brê'-er], *s.* 1. Rebuznador. 2. (Imp.) Moledor de tinta.

Braying [brê'-ing], *s.* Grito, clamor; rebuzno.

Braze [brêz], *va.* 1. Soldar con latón o azófar. 2. Broncear. 3. Hacer desvergonzado o descarado a alguno.

Brazen [brê'-zn], *a.* 1. Bronceado; hecho de bronce. 2. Descarado, desvergonzado.

Brazen, *va.* Hacerse descarado. *To brazen out a thing*, Sostener alguna cosa con impudencia. *To brazen one down*, Desconcertar, aturdir, confundir a uno.

Brazen-browed [brê'-zn-braud], **Brazen-faced** [brê'-zn-fêst], *a.* Descarado, desvergonzado, impudente.

Brazen-face [brê'-zn-fês], *s.* Cara de vaqueta, la persona que no tiene vergüenza.

Brazenness [brê'-zn-nes], *s.* Descaro, desvergüenza.

Brazier, *s.* *V.* BRASIER.

Brazil-wood [bra-zil'-wud], *s.* Madera o palo del Brasil.

Braziletto [bra-zi-let'-ō], *s.* Brasilete, madera inferior al brasil.

Breach [brîch], *s.* 1. Rotura o rompimiento, el acto de romper alguna cosa. 2. Brecha, la rotura o abertura que se hace en la muralla. 3. Contravención de alguna ley o contrato, violación; ofensa, perjuicio, detrimento de la honra, reputación, derechos o privilegios. *Breach of trust*, Falta de fidelidad. 4. Rompimiento, desavenencia. *Breach of promise*, Falta de palabra. *Breach of duty*, Violación del deber.

Bread [bred], *s.* 1. Pan, alimento que

se hace de la harina de diversas semillas. 2. Pan, todo lo que en general sirve para el sustento diario del hombre. *To earn one's bread,* Ganarse la vida. *Household bread,* Pan casero, pan bazo. *Light bread,* Pan esponjoso. *Ship bread,* Galleta, bizcocho de mar. *Batch of bread,* Hornada de pan. *Soft bread,* Mollete. *Sow bread,* Criadilla de tierra. *Unleavened bread,* Ázimo. *Breadstuffs,* La harina, trigo, maíz, y en general todos los granos que sirven para hacer pan. *New bread,* Pan tierno. *Stale bread,* Pan duro o sentado. *Rye bread,* Pan de centeno. *Slice of bread,* Rebanada de pan. *Corn bread,* Pan de maíz. *Brown bread,* Pan moreno.

Breadboard [bred'-bōrd], *s.* Tabla para cortar el pan o para amasarlo.

Bread-corn [bred'-cērn], *s.* Pan, la semilla de que se hace pan.

Breaden [bred'-n], *a.* (Poco us.) Hecho de pan.

Bread-fruit [bred'-frūt], *s.* Arbol del pan y su fruto. Artocarpus incisa.

Bread line [bred lain], *s.* Cola que se forma para recibir alimentos gratuitamente.

Bread room [bred'-rūm], *s.* (Mar.) Pañol del pan.

Breadstuff [bred'-stuf], *s.* Material para hacer pan; grano, harina, etc.

Breadth [bredth], *s.* 1. Anchura, la dimensión contrapuesta a lo largo. *The breadth and length of anything,* Lo ancho y largo de alguna cosa. 2. Catolicidad, liberalidad. 3. Paño, lo ancho de una tela. *There are five breadths in that skirt,* Hay cinco paños en esa saya o falda.

Breadthwise [bredth'-waiz], *adv.* A lo ancho.

Bread-winner [bred-win'-ẹr], *s.* El que se mantiene a sí mismo y a otros con su sueldo, jornal o ganancias; productor.

Break [brêk], *va.* (*pret.* BROKE o BRAKE (poét.); *pp.* BROKEN o BROKE). 1. Romper, quebrar, abrir o hender alguna cosa a la fuerza. 2. Vencer, sobrepujar. 3. Abrir brechas batiendo; horadar. 4. Quebrantar o destruir alguna cosa. 5. Abatir el espíritu. 6. Imposibilitar, inutilizar. 7. Domar. 8. Causar quiebra o bancarrota. 9. Quebrantar, violar algún contrato o promesa; quebrantar una ley. 10. Arruinar o destruir a uno; marchitar. 11. Interceptar, interrumpir, impedir.—*vn.* 1. Romperse, dividirse una cosa. 2. Abrirse, reventarse algún tumor, descargando materia. 3. Prorrumpir, exclamar. 4. Quebrar, hacer bancarrota. 5. Decaer, tener la salud o las fuerzas quebrantadas. 6. Romper, enemistarse. 7. Separarse, apartarse con violencia. 8. Entrar de repente, apuntar, abrir (p. ej. el día). 9. Estallar (v. gr. una tempestad). 10. Mudar, perder calidad música, hablando de la voz. *To break asunder,* Partir, dividir, separar en dos partes. *To break cover,* Salir de un bosque, de la espesura (hablando de la caza), de un escondite. *To break down,* Abatir, derribar, demoler, arruinar; (y como neutro) caer, desplomarse, arruinarse; volcar (un carruaje); cortarse (en un discurso). *To break forth,* Brotar, saltar, salir de la tierra. *To break in* o *into,* Arrojarse, asaltar, acometer; horadar; forzar; penetrar adentro, entrar por fuerza; cargar al enemigo o cerrar con él; mezclarse en negocios de otros; interrumpir al que está ocupado. *To break in,* Enseñar, acostumbrar, formar; domar un caballo. *To break off,* Romper; dejar por acabar, sin concluir; desgajar. *To break of,* (una cosa) Corregir, reformar. *To break open,* Romper, fracturar. *To break out,* Desenfrenarse, darse o entregarse a los vicios; salir o dejarse ver; llenarse de úlceras; reventar, rebosar, salir de madre; exclamar, prorrumpir; declararse; encolerizarse; abrir camino; salir con violencia; escalar la cárcel. *To break the law,* Infringir la ley. *To break through,* Pasar por medio de, romper, superar, abrirse camino, vencer dificultades o peligros. *To break up,* 1. *va.* Demoler, derribar, abatir; romper, desgarrar, partir. 2. *vn.* Decampar, levantar el campo, tomar las de Villadiego, poner pies en polvorosa; principiar las vacaciones en las escuelas. 3. Levantar una sesión; interrumpir; disolver, despedir una asamblea. *To break up an officer,* (Mil.) Desaforar a un oficial, echarle del regimiento. *To break up an army,* Licenciar las tropas. *To break the bank,* Hacer saltar la banca (en el juego). *To break open a door,* Desherrajar una puerta. (Mar.) Desbaratar. *To break a business,* Abrir una discusión, proponer un asunto. *To break a custom,* Desacostumbrar, hacer perder algún hábito o costumbre. *To break a horse,* Domar un caballo. *To break a jest,* Decir un chiste de repente. *To break prison,* Forzar o escalar la cárcel. *To break bulk,* Sacar parte de la carga. *To break ground,* Abrir la trinchera; arar. (Fig.) Comenzar una empresa, un trabajo. *To break a lance with,* Oponerse a, entrar en la lucha contra. *To break loose,* Desatar o desatarse, escapar, huir. *To break one's back,* Derrengar. *To break one's fast,* Desayunarse. *To break one's heart,* Matar a pesadumbres. *To die broken-hearted,* Morir de pesadumbre, o de pena. *To break the spirit,* Deprimir, abatir el espíritu o el corazón. *To break one's oath,* Ser traidor o perjuro, faltar al juramento. *To break open a house,* Forzar una casa. *To break with sorrow,* Consumirse de tristeza. *To break wind,* Peer, ventosear, soltar el preso.

Break, *s.* 1. Rotura, abertura. 2. Pausa, parada, intervalo, interrupción, vacío. 3. Una línea que ponen los ingleses al fin de algunas oraciones para denotar que no está completo su sentido. 4. Blanco en los escritos. *The break of the day,* La aurora.

Breakable [brêk'-a-bl], *a.* Quebradizo, frágil.

Breakage [brêk'-ẹj], *s.* 1. Fractura, rotura o quebrantamiento. 2. Objetos quebrados. 3. Indemnización por cosas quebradas.

Breakdown [brêk'-daun], *s.* 1. Parada imprevista, avería repentina, pana. 2. (Med.) Colapso, crisis. 3. Derrumbamiento, falta de éxito o mal éxito, fracaso. 4. (Quím.) Descomposición, análisis.

Breaker [brêk'-ẹr], *s.* 1. El que rompe o labra tierra de labor. 2. Infractor, quebrador, rompedor.—*Breakers, pl.* Embate de las olas, cuando se retiran de los escollos. Reventazones, rompientes.

Break-even point [brêk-ī-vn point], *s.* Punto en que un negocio empieza a cubrir los gastos que ocasiona.

Breakfast [brek'-fast], *vn.* Desayunarse, almorzar.

Breakfast, *s.* Desayuno, almuerzo, el alimento que se toma por la mañana; alimento.

Breaking [brêk'-ing], *s.* 1. Bancarrota. 2. Irrupción; disolución. 3. Rompimiento de tierra. 4. Principio de las vacaciones en las escuelas. 5. Fractura, rompimiento. *Breaking up of the Parliament,* Suspensión de las sesiones del Parlamento.

Breakneck [brêk'-nec], *s.* Despeñadero, paraje en que está alguno expuesto a despeñarse; precipicio, ruina.—*a.* Precipitado, rápido.

Breakthrough [brêk'-thrū], *s.* 1. Descubrimiento o hipótesis que permite un adelanto científico o tecnológico. 2. (Mil.) Ruptura, brecha. 3. Oportunidad.

Breakvow [brêk'-vau], *s.* El que falta a sus votos; embustero.

Breakwater [brêk'-wē-tẹr], *s.* Rompeolas, tajamar, muralla o construcción de piedra a la entrada de un puerto para impedir las oleadas.

Bream [brīm], *s.* Sargo, pez de agua dulce. *Sea bream,* Besugo.

Bream, *va.* Limpiar algo, p. ej. los fondos de un buque, de conchas, algas, fango, etc., por medio de fuego y raedura. *Cf.* BROOM.

Breast [brest], *s.* 1. Pecho, seno, la parte del cuerpo humano desde la garganta hasta el estómago. 2. Testera, los extremos delanteros de las gualderas de una cureña de campaña. 3. Pecho o teta en la mujer. 4. Pecho, el corazón, el interior del hombre. *To beat one's breast,* Darse golpes de pecho. 5. Toro, moldura del pie de la columna. 6. Frente o cara de veta o filón. 7. Comba del cubo de una rueda. *A child at the breast,* Un niño de teta.

Breast, *va.* Acometer de frente o presentarse de frente.

Breastbone [brest'-bōn], *s.* Esternón, el hueso que constituye la parte anterior del pecho.

Breast-deep [brest'-dīp], **Breast-high** [brest'-hai], *a.* Alto hasta el pecho; antepecho.

Breasted [bres'-ted], *a.* Lo que tiene pecho. *Narrow-breasted,* Hundido de pecho. *Pigeon-breasted,* De pecho abultado.

Breasthooks [brest'-huks], *s.* (Mar.) Buzardas, piezas de madera que se colocan en la proa para sujetar la unión de los costados.

Breastknot [brest'-net], *s.* Lazo o lazada, adorno de cintas en forma de lazo que llevan las mujeres al pecho.

Breastpin [brest'-pin], *s.* Broche, alfiler de pecho, sostén y adorno de diferentes formas que llevan las mujeres al pecho.

Breastplate [brest'-plêt], *s.* 1. Peto, armadura del pecho. 2. Pretal de una cabalgadura. 3. Pectoral.

Breast-plow o **Breast-plough** [brest'-plau], *s.* Arado de pecho, especie de arado pequeño que se empuja a fuerza de pecho.

Breast-pump [brest'-pump], *s.* Extractor de leche.

Breastrail [brest'-rêl], *s.* (Mar.) Antepecho.

Breastrope [brest'-rōp], *s.* 1. (Mar.) Guardamancebo de sondar. 2. (Mar.) Nervio de las redes de combate.
Breast-wheel [hwīl], *s.* Rueda hidráulica de costado.
Breastwork [brest'-wūrk], *s.* 1. (Fort.) Parapeto, terraplén que defiende el pecho contra los golpes del enemigo. 2. (Mar.) Propao.
Breath [breth], *s.* 1. Aliento, respiración, resuello, huelgo. 2. Soplo de aire. 3. Vida. 4. Pausa; sobreseimiento. 5. Instante; un momento. *To be short of breath,* Ser corto de resuello, respirar con dificultad. *Under one's breath,* En voz baja. *In a breath,* De un tirón, de una vez. *At every breath,* A cada instante. *To gasp for breath,* Jadear. *To be out of breath,* Estar sin aliento, sofocado. *To run one's self out of breath,* Correr hasta perder el aliento. *Foul breath,* Mal aliento.
Breathable [brīdh'-a-bl], *a.* Respirable, que se puede respirar.
Breathe [brīdh], *vn.* 1. Alentar, respirar o arrojar el aliento. 2. Vivir. 3. Respirar, descansar. 4. Soplar, arrojar el aliento dentro de alguna cosa. 5. Exhalar, echar el aliento hacia fuera. 6. Secar al aire.—*va.* 1. Inspirar, respirar; exhalar; dar aire o desahogo. 2. Decir o revelar secretamente alguna cosa. *To breathe after,* Anhelar, desear, ansiar. *To breathe a vein,* Abrir las venas, sangrar. *To breathe one's last,* Dar el último suspiro, morir.
Breather [brīdh'-ẹr], *s.* 1. El que respira o vive. 2. Revelador. 3. El que inspira.
Breathful [breth'-ful], *a.* Lleno de aire; lleno de olor.
Breathing [brīdh'-ing], *s.* 1. Aspiración. 2. Respiradero, abertura por donde entra o sale el aire.
Breathing-place [brīdh'-ing-plēs], *s.* Pausa, respiradero, descanso, parada.
Breathing spell [brīdh'-ing spel], *s.* Reposo, lapso para descansar.
Breathing-time [brīdh'-ing-taim], *s.* Relajación, reposo; el tiempo de alentar o descansar; descanso, parada; interrupción o cesación del trabajo; intervalo, intermisión, alivio en el dolor.
Breathless [breth'-les], *a.* 1. Falto de aliento, sin aliento; desalentado. 2. Muerto.
Breathlessness [breth'-les-nes], *s.* Desaliento; muerte.
Breathtaking [breth'-tēk-ing], *a.* Fascinador, emocionante, conmovedor.
Breccia [brech'-i-a], *s.* (Min.) Piedras conglutinadas o compuestas, como el mármol colorado.
Brechan [brec'-an], *s.* (Esco.) *V.* BRACKEN.
Bred, *pret.* y *pp.* del verbo *To* BREED.
Breech [brich], *s.* 1. Trasero, nalgas, posaderas. 2. Culata de cañón o fusil; recámara.
Breech, *va.* 1. Poner los calzones a uno. 2. Azotar. 3. Poner culata a un cañón o fusil.
Breeches [brich'-ez], *s. pl.* Calzones, parte del vestido del hombre, que cubre desde la cintura hasta la rodilla. *To wear the breeches,* Ponerse los calzones; dícese de la mujer que gobierna a su marido.
Breeches-buoy, *s.* Aparato salvavidas que consiste en unas bragas de lona aseguradas por la cintura a una boya de salvamento, la cual pende de un cable tendido desde la orilla a un buque náufrago.
Breeching [brich'-ing], *s.* 1. Grupera del arnés. 2. (Mar.) Bragueros de cañón.
Breech-loader [lōd'-ẹr], *s.* Arma de retrocarga, que se carga por la recámara.
Breech-loading [lōd'-ing], *a.* Que se carga por la recámara (hablando de armas).
Breed [brīd], *va.* 1. Criar, procrear, engendrar, multiplicar. 2. Ocasionar, causar, producir. 3. Criar, educar, enseñar.—*vn.* Criar, hacer cría o multiplicarla.
Breed, *s.* 1. Casta, raza, progenie. 2. Progenie, generación.
Breeder [brīd'-ẹr], *s.* 1. Lo que cría o produce alguna cosa. 2. La persona que cría y educa a otro. 3. Paridera, la hembra fecunda de cualquier especie. 4. Criador, el que cría caballos, mulas u otros animales.
Breeder reactor [brīd'-ẹr rī-ac'-tẹr], *s.* Reactor reproductor.
Breeding [brīd'-ing], *s.* 1. Crianza, urbanidad, atención, cortesía. 2. Educación, enseñanza, forma dada a la inteligencia y a los modales. *Breeding-cage,* Jaula de criar, criadera. *Cross breeding,* Cruzamiento de razas. *Good breeding,* Buena educación. *Bad breeding,* Modales groseros, de mal tono.
Breeze [brīz] o **Breeze-fly,** *s.* Tábano, especie de moscón. Se escribe también *breese* y *brize.*
Breeze [brīz], *s.* 1. Brisa, viento suave. 2. (Fam.) Ligera agitación o alarma; confusión, quimera.
Breeze [brīz], *s.* Cenizas calientes, rescoldo. Carboncillo, cisco de *coke.* (Ingl.)
Breezeless [brīz'-les], *a.* Inmoble, sin movimiento o brisa.
Breezy [brīz'-i], *a.* Refrescado con brisas.
Brent [brent], *a.* Liso, no arrugado; también, alto, prominente. (Palabra escocesa.)
Brethren [bredh'-ren], *s. pl.* de BROTHER. Hermanos, en estilo grave o hablando de todos los hombres.
Breton [bret'-ọn], *a.* Natural de la Bretaña francesa, o perteneciente a ella; bretón.—*s.* 1. Un bretón. 2. Idioma de los bretones.
Breve [brīv], *s.* (Mús.) 1. Breve, nota de música, hoy poco usada. 2. *V.* BRIEF.
Brevet [brẹ-vet'], *va.* En el ejército, la milicia y la marina, conceder un grado superior al empleo efectivo; dar un ascenso honorífico.
Brevet [brẹ-vet'], *s.* (Mil.) Nombramiento o comisión honoraria, grado honorífico. *Brevet rank,* Graduación militar sin el sueldo correspondiente ni empleo efectivo. *Brevet colonel,* Coronel graduado.
Breviary [brī'-vi-er-i], *s.* 1. Compendio, extracto, epítome, resumen. 2. Breviario, el libro que contiene el rezo u oficio divino diario de todo el año.
Breviate [brī'-vi-ēt], *s.* 1. Compendio corto. 2. *V.* BRIEF.
Brevier [brẹ-vīr'], *s.* Breviario, grado de letra muy menuda, tipo o carácter de letra de ocho puntos. El de nueve puntos se llama en inglés *bourgeois.*
Brevirostrate, Brevirostral [brev-i-ros'-trēt, tral], *a.* Que tiene pico corto.
Brevity [brev'-i-ti], *s.* Brevedad, concisión.
Brew [brū], *va.* 1. Hacer licores mezclando varios ingredientes. 2. Urdir o tramar algún designio, maquinar, fraguar. 3. Menear a fuerza de brazo; batir, preparar; mezclar. *A storm is brewing,* Se prepara una tempestad; habrá borrasca.—*vn.* Hacer cerveza; fermentar los licores.
Brew, *s.* Mezcla; modo de mezclar o de hacer fermentar los licores.
Brewage [brū'-ēj], *s.* Brebaje, bebida en que entran muchos ingredientes.
Brewer [brū'-ẹr], *s.* Cervecero.
Brewery [brū'-ẹr-i], **Brew-house** [brū'-haus], *s.* Cervecería, la casa o fábrica en que se hace la cerveza.
Brewing [brū'-ing], *s.* 1. La cantidad de cerveza que se hace de una vez. 2. (Mar.) Apariencia de borrasca; reunión de nubes negruzcas.
Brewis [brū'-is], *s.* Rebanada de pan mojada en caldo de vaca salada mientras está hirviendo.
Bribe [braib], *s.* Cohecho, soborno.
Bribe, *va.* Cohechar, sobornar, ganar para un fin malo, corromper.
Briber [braib'-ẹr], *s.* Cohechador, sobornador, corruptor.
Bribery [braib'-ẹr-i], *s.* Cohecho, soborno.
Bric-a-brac, *s.* Bric-a-brac: objetos de arte, artículos curiosos y de gusto.
Brick [bric], *s.* 1. Ladrillo, pedazo de tierra amasado y cocido. 2. Ladrillo de pan; una clase de pan que tiene la figura de un ladrillo. *Sun-dried brick,* (Mex.) Adobe. 3. (Ger.) Un buen sujeto, un real mozo. *Bath* o *Bristol brick,* Piedra hecha de arena muy fina, en forma de ladrillo, para limpiar cuchillos.
Brick, *va.* Enladrillar, solar o cubrir alguna cosa con ladrillos. *To brick a floor,* Enladrillar el suelo.
Brickbat [bric'-bat], *s.* Pedazo de ladrillo.
Brick-clay [bric'-clē], **Brick-earth** [bric'-ẹrth], *s.* Tierra para hacer ladrillos.
Brickdust [bric'-dust], *s.* Ladrillo molido.
Brick-kiln [bric'-kil], *s.* Horno de ladrillo, que se llama también ladrillar o ladrillal.
Bricklayer [bric'-lē-ẹr], *s.* Albañil, el que hace paredes u otras fábricas de ladrillo. *Bricklayer's boy,* Peón de albañil.
Brickmaker [bric'-mēk-ẹr], *s.* Ladrillero, el que hace ladrillos.
Brickwork [brik'-wūrc], *s.* Enladrillado, obra de ladrillos.
Bricky [brik'-i], *a.* Ladrilloso, lleno de ladrillos.
Brickyard [bric'-yard], *s.* Ladrillar.
Bridal [brai'-dal], *a.* Nupcial, perteneciente a las bodas.—*s.* Boda, fiesta nupcial. *Bridal song,* Epitalamio.
Bride [braid], *s.* Novia, desposada, la mujer recién casada, o la que va a casarse. *Bride-bed,* Tálamo, la cama de los desposados. *Bride-cake,* Torta o pan de la boda. *Bride-chamber,* Cámara nupcial.
Bridegroom [braid'-grūm], *s.* Novio el recién casado, o el que va a casarse.
Bridesmaid [braids'-mēd], *sf.* Madrina de boda.
Bridesman [braids'-man], *s.* Padrino de boda, el que acompaña al novio en la ceremonia del matrimonio. Son nombres más usuales los de *best man* y *groomsman.*

Bridge [brij], *s.* 1. Puente, fábrica construída sobre los ríos, fosos, etc., para pasarlos. *Drawbridge,* Puente levadizo. *Bridge of boats,* Puente de barcas. 2. El caballete de la nariz. 3. Puente de violín, violón, guitarra u otro instrumento de cuerda. 4. Balanza de Wheatstone, artificio para medir la resistencia eléctrica. *Cantilever bridge,* Puente de contrapeso. *Suspension bridge,* Puente colgante.

Bridge, *va.* Construir o levantar un puente en algún paraje.

Bridgehead [brij'-hed], *s.* Cabecera de puente, entrada de puente.

Bridgeward [brij'-wgrd], *s.* 1. Custodio de puente. 2. Guarda principal de una llave.

Bridgework [brij'-wurk], *s.* 1. Construcción de puentes. 2. Puente dental.

Bridle [brai'-dl], *s.* 1. Brida o freno. 2. Freno, sujeción. *Bridle-cutter,* El que corta cuero para los silleros y freneros. *Bridle-hand,* Mano izquierda, la mano del jinete que tiene las riendas. *Bridle-path,* Senda angosta, que sólo permite pasar á las caballerías o acémilas una tras otra.

Bridle, *va.* 1. Guiar un caballo con el freno. 2. Embridar, poner la brida a un caballo. 3. Reprimir, refrenar.—*vn.* Levantar la cabeza. *To bridle it,* Remilgarse, erguirse.

Bridles [brai'-dlz], *s. pl.* (Mar.) Poas.

Bridler [brai'-dlgr], *s.* El que gobierna, dirige o refrena.

Brief [brîf], *a.* Breve, conciso, corto, sucinto, sumario ; estrecho.

Brief, *s.* 1. Epítome, resumen o compendio. 2. Alegato, memorial ajustado, informe, el apuntamiento en que se contiene todo el hecho de algún pleito o causa ; auto jurídico. 3. (Mús.) Breve, nota que vale dos compases del tiempo que se llama compasillo. 4. Breve, buleto apostólico. 5. Despacho, sumario, informe. Licencia para pedir socorros públicamente por alguna pérdida o desgracia.

Brief case [brîf kês], *s.* Cartera grande, portafolio.

Briefing [brîf'-ing], *s.* Instrucciones breves.

Briefless [brîf'-les], *a.* Sin causas o pleitos : sin clientes.

Briefly [brîf'-li], *adv.* Brevemente, sucintamente, compendiosamente, en pocas palabras.

Briefness [brîf'-nes], *s.* Brevedad, concisión.

Brier [brai'-gr], *s.* 1. Escaramujo, agavanzo, rosal silvestre. 2. Zarza, mata espinosa.

Briery [brai'-gr-i], *a.* Zarzoso, lleno de zarzas.

Brig, Brigantine [brig, brig'-an-tîn], *s.* (Mar.) Bergantín.

Brigade [brig-êd'], *s.* Brigada, cierto número de batallones o escuadrones.

Brigadier-general [brig'-a-dîr-jen'-gr-al], *s.* Brigadier, el oficial que tiene el grado inmediatamente inferior al de mariscal de campo.

Brigand [brig'-and], *s.* Ladrón público, salteador de caminos, bandido, bandolero.

Brigandine [brig'-an-din], *s.* Cota de malla de que usaban antes los ladrones y rufianes y algunas tropas ligeras.

Brigantine [brig'-an-tin], *s.* *V.* BRIG.

Bright [brait], *a.* 1. Claro, reluciente, luciente, resplandeciente, lustroso, brillante. 2. Claro, evidente. 3. Esclarecido, ilustre. 4. Ingenioso, agudo, perspicaz, vivo. *To make bright,* Pulimentar, poner brillante, reluciente.

Brighten [brai'-tn], *va.* 1. Pulir, bruñir, dar lustre. 2. Avivar, dar viveza. 3. Ilustrar, ennoblecer. 4. Aguzar el ingenío.—*vn.* Aclarar, ponerse claro lo que estaba obscuro, realzar.

Bright-eyed [brait'-aid], *a.* Ojialegre.

Bright-haired [brait'-hārd], *a.* Que tiene los cabellos relucientes.

Bright-harnessed [brait'-hār-nest], *a.* El de armadura brillante.

Brightly [brait'-li], *adv.* Espléndidamente, con esplendor y lustre.

Brightness [brait'-nes], *s.* 1. Lustre, esplendor, brillo, brillantez. 2. Agudeza o viveza de ingenio. 3. Resplandor, claridad.

Brights [braits], *s. pl.* Luces de carretera.

Bright's disease [braits' diz-îz'], *s.* Mal de Bright, nefritis crónica.

Brill [bril], *s.* Mero, pez semejante al rodaballo, muy estimado como alimento. *V.* BRET.

Brilliance [bril'-yans], **Brilliancy** [bril'-yan-si], *s.* Brillantez, brillo, el resplandor o luz que da de sí alguna cosa ; esplendor, lustre.

Brilliant [bril'-yant], *a.* Brillante, lo que brilla.—*s.* 1. Brillante, el diamante abrillantado. 2. El tipo de menor tamaño que se funde y se emplea en la impresión : $3\frac{1}{2}$ puntos. 3. Tela de algodón, con dibujo alzado y tejido.

Brilliantine [bril'-yan-tîn], *s.* Brillantina, tela para vestidos parecida á la alpaca, pero de calidad superior.

Brilliantly [bril'-yant-li], *adv.* Espléndidamente.

Brilliantness [bril'-yant-nes], *s.* Brillantez.

Brills [brilz], *s. pl.* (Des.) Las pestañas del caballo.

Brim [brim], *s.* Borde, extremo u orilla de alguna cosa ; labio de un vaso ; ala de sombrero.

Brim, *va.* Llenar hasta el borde. —*vn.* Estar de bote en bote ; estar llena alguna vasija hasta no caber más.

Brimful [brim'-ful], *a.* Lleno hasta el borde, lleno de bote en bote.

Brimfulness [brim'-ful-nes], *s.* El estado de estar lleno hasta el borde.

Brimless [brim'-les], *a.* Sin labio o borde.

Brimmer [brim'-gr], *s.* Copa o vaso lleno.

Brimming [brim'-ing], *a.* Lleno hasta el borde.

Brimstone [brim'-stōn], *s.* Azufre ; dícese del azufre vivo o amoldado en canelones.

Brindle [brin'-dl], *s.* Variedad de colores como la que tiene el tigre.

Brindled, *a.* Abigarrado. *V.* BRINDED.

Brine [brain], *s.* 1. Salmuera. 2. (Poét.) El mar. 3. Lágrimas.

Brine, *va.* (Agr.) Embeber en salmuera el trigo antes de sembrarlo, para impedir el tizón.

Brinepit [brain'-pit], *s.* Pozo de salina o de agua salada.

Bring [bring], *va.* (*pret.* y *pp.* BROUGHT). 1. Llevar o traer. 2. Traer, hacer venir. 3. Atraer, traer hacia sí alguna cosa ; acarrear ; recoger. 4. Poner en un estado determinado. 5. Inducir, persuadir. *To bring about,* Efectuar, poner por obra, salir con el intento. *To bring again,* Volver, conducir o traer de nuevo. *To bring back to life again,* Volver á la vida, hacer revivir. *To bring away,* Llevarse, quitar, sacar una cosa de donde estaba ; hacer salir ; alzar. *To bring back,* Traer de vuelta, devolver. *To bring by the lee,* (Mar.) Tomar por la luna sobre la arribada. *To bring down,* Abatir, deprimir, humillar ; disminuir ; llevar una cosa baja ; bajar o echar abajo. *To bring down the house,* Promover grandes aplausos. *To bring forth,* Producir, dar de sí ; parir ; dar á luz ; poner de manifiesto. *To bring forward,* Empujar, dar empuje. (Com.) Llevar una suma a otra cuenta. *Brought forward,* Suma y sigue, referencia, partida referente. *To bring in,* Reclamar ; dejar utilidad o ganancia ; reducir ; introducir, meter. Servir (una comida), introducir (una moda). *To bring into,* Comprometer. *To bring off,* Desempeñar o desempeñarse ; rescatar ; desembarazar ; disuadir, desviar, apartar. *To bring on,* Transportar ; aguantar ; empeñar, inducir ; empeñarse, obligarse. *To bring over,* Ganar, atraer a alguno a su partido ; transportar, hacer atravesar. *To bring out,* Salir ; recitar ; mostrar, echar fuera, descubrir ; hacer salir, sacar, extraer. *To bring to,* Someter ; resolver ; llevar a. (Mar.) Ponerse a la capa. *To bring under,* Sojuzgar, sujetar, avasallar, someter a su mando. *To bring up,* Hacer subir, hacer avanzar o adelantarse ; poner a la moda ; llevar en alto ; educar, enseñar. *To bring upon,* Atraer ; exponer. *To bring an action,* Poner una demanda. *To bring dinner in,* Servir la comida. *To bring low,* Abatir, humillar ; debilitar. *To bring to bed,* Parir. *To bring together,* (Fig.) Reconciliar. *To bring word,* Informar, dar noticia. *To bring upon one's self,* Buscarse, causarse, atraerse, procurarse.

Bringer [bring'-gr], *s.* Portador, la persona que lleva o trae alguna cosa. *Bringer in,* El que introduce alguna cosa. *Bringer up,* Instructor. (Mil.) El soldado postrero de cada fila. *Bringing forth,* Producción.

Brinish [brain'-ish], *a.* Salado, lo que tiene sabor de sal.

Brinishness [brain'-ish-nes], *s.* Sabor de sal.

Brink [bringk], *s.* Orilla, margen, borde ; extremidad, extremo. *Brink of a well,* Pozal o brocal de pozo.

Briny [brain'-i], *a.* Salado, del sabor del agua del mar. *The briny deep,* El mar, el océano.

Briquette [bric-et'], *s.* Briqueta, conglomerado de carbón en forma de ladrillo.

Brisk [brisk], *a.* 1. Vivo, alegre, despejado, jovial, festivo, juguetón. 2. Vigoroso, fuerte. 3. Enamorado; alegre de cascos, alegrillo, alumbrado por haber bebido un poco más de lo regular. *A brisk gale of wind,* Viento fresco.

Brisk up, *vn.* Avanzar con viveza, presentarse con garbo y aire ; regocijarse, alegrarse.—*va.* Vivificar, avivar.

Brisket [bris'-ket], *s.* El pecho de un animal o un pedazo cortado de él.

Briskly [brisk'-li], *adv.* Vigorosamente; alegremente.

Briskness [brisk'-nes], *s.* 1. Viveza, actividad, vigor, vivacidad. 2. Viveza, garbo, gallardía. 3. Alegría, humorada. 4. Desenvoltura, desahogo.

Bristle [bris'-l], *s.* 1. Cerda, seta, el pelo duro y recio que crían los cerdos. 2. Pelusa, especie de vello de ciertas plantas.

Bristle, *va.* Erizar, levantar o poner derechas las cerdas o púas el animal que las tiene.—*vn.* Erizarse, ponerse derechas las cerdas o púas de un animal, como las del cerdo y del erizo. *To bristle a thread,* Poner seta al hilo de zapatero.

Bristly [bris'-li], *a.* Cerdoso, lleno de cerdas.

Bristol-board [bris'-tel-bōrd], *s.* Cartulina; calidad fina de cartón satinado. (De Brístol, ciudad inglesa.)

Bristol-stone [bris'-tel-stōn], *s.* Diamante de Brístol.

Brit [brit], *s.* 1. El alimento de las ballenas; consta de entomostráceos y otros animalillos que nadan en la superficie. 2. Arenque pequeño.

Britannia [bri-tan'-ya] (Metal.), *s.* Metal inglés, liga de estaño, antimonio, bismuto y cobre.

Britannic [bri-tan'-ic], *a.* Británico, de la Gran Bretaña.

Brite [brait], *va.* (Prov. Ingl.) Modorrarse, madurarse demasiado; desgranarse las mieses.

British [brit'-ish], *a.* Británico, lo que pertenece a la Gran Bretaña. *The British language,* La lengua de los antiguos celtas de la Gran Bretaña. *British Lion,* El león británico, emblema de la Gran Bretaña. *British Thermal Unit,* Unidad termal británica.

Britisher [brit'-ish-ẹr], *s.* (Fest.) Inglés; particularmente un soldado o marinero inglés.

Briton [brit'-en], *a.* y *s.* El natural de la Gran Bretaña, o lo que pertenece a este país.

Brittle [brit'-l], *a.* Quebradizo, que con facilidad se quiebra, frágil.

Brittleness [brit'-l-nes], *s.* Fragilidad.

Broach [brōch], *s.* 1. Asador. 2. Lezna, punzón. 3. Terraja, herramienta de relojero. 4. Espetón, alfiler con gancho; broche. 5. (Carp.) Brocha, mecha. 6. (Arq.) Aguja, chapitel.

Broach, *va.* 1. Mencionar por primera vez; introducir; hacer público. 2. Espetar, atravesar alguna cosa con otra que sea puntiaguda, como se atraviesa la carne con el asador. 3. Barrenar el tonel u otra vasija que tenga vino o cualquier licor, para sacarlo; barrenar, decentar. 4. Empezar a gastar alguna cosa que se tenía guardada o intacta. 5. Proferir; decir alguna cosa de la que es uno autor; inventar o propagar mentiras; sembrar una especie. 6. *To broach to,* (Mar.) Tomar por la luna, por avante.

Broacher [brōch'-ẹr], *s.* 1. Asador. 2. Autor o inventor de alguna cosa.

Broad [brēd], *a.* 1. Ancho, lo contrapuesto a lo angosto; extenso, amplio. 2. Claro, abierto. 3. Comprensivo; liberal, tolerante, de amplias miras e ideas. 4. Grosero, poco delicado, inmodesto, impuro. 5. Descomedido, atrevido; rudo de habla, que habla un dialecto. *Broad as long,* Igual en todo. *At broad noon,* Al medio día. *To grow broad,* Ensancharse. *To speak broad,* Hablar groseramente. *In broad day,* En pleno día: a la luz del día. *Broad Scotch,* El dialecto escocés fuertemente marcado. *Broad-blown,* Enteramente formado. *Broad-breasted,* Ancho de pechos. *Broad-brimmed,* Que tiene el borde ancho; de alas anchas, hablando de sombreros. *Broad-eyed,* El que tiene vista muy larga. *Broad-faced, Broad-fronted,* Cariancho. *Broad-horned,* Que tiene cuernos grandes o anchos. *Broad-leaved,* (Bot.) Que tiene las hojas anchas. *Broad-shouldered,* Espaldudo, la persona que tiene grandes espaldas, rechoncho. *Broad-tailed,* Cosa o animal de cola ancha.

Broad-axe, *s.* Hacha ancha de carpintero; doladera (de tonelería).

Broad-brim, *s.* 1. Sombrero de ala ancha. 2. (Fam.) Cuákero.

Broadcast [brēd'-cạst], *s.* 1. Radiodifusión. 2. (Agr.) Siembra al vuelo.—*va.* 1. Radiodifundir. 2. (Agr.) Sembrar al vuelo. 3. Esparcir a lo lejos, diseminar a gran distancia.

Broadcaster [brēd'-cạst-ẹr], *s.* Radiodifusor.

Broadcasting [brēd'-cạst-ing], *s.* Radiodifusión.

Broad Church. Partido en la Iglesia de Inglaterra, que profesa el liberalismo y la tolerancia en la doctrina y las prácticas religiosas; el elemento liberal de una iglesia cualquiera o de todas.

Broadcloth [brēd'-clēth], *s.* Paño fino de más de 29 pulgadas de ancho.

Broaden [brēd'-n], *vn.* Ensancharse, ponerse más ancha alguna cosa.

Broad gauge [gêj], *a.* 1. (F. C.) Vía ancha, de más de 56½ pulgadas inglesas. 2. *V.* Broad-minded.

Broadish [brēd'-ish], *a.* Algo ancho.

Broad jump [brēd' jump], *s.* Salto de longitud.

Broadloom [brēd'-lūm], *a.* Tejido en telar ancho. *Broadloom rug,* Alfombra de un solo color.

Broadly [brēd'-li], *adv.* Anchamente.

Broad-minded [brēd-maind'-ẹd], *a.* Tolerante, de ideas liberales.

Broadmindedness [brēd-maind'-ed-nes], *s.* Tolerancia, amplitud de miras.

Broadness [brēd'-nes], *s.* 1. Ancho o anchura. 2. Grosería, falta de urbanidad.

Broadside [brēd'-said], *s.* (Mar.) 1. Costado de un buque. 2. Andanada, la descarga de todos los cañones del costado de un navío hecha de una vez. 3. (Imp.) Cada lado de un pliego de papel.

Broadsword [brēd'-sōrd], *s.* Espada ancha, espadón.

Broadwise [brēd'-waiz], *adv.* A lo ancho, o por lo ancho.

Brocade [brō-kêd'], *s.* Brocado, tela de seda tejida con oro o plata.

Brocade, *va.* Tejer o hacer labor con dibujo de relieve; decorar; adornar como con brocado.

Brocaded [brō-kêd'-ed], *a.* Vestido de brocado; tejido como brocado.

Brocage o **Brokage** [brō'-kêj], *s.* *V.* Brokerage.

Brocatel [brec'-a-tel], *s.* Brocatel, tejido basto adamascado de seda y lana, cáñamo o algodón, que se emplea en muebles y colgaduras.

Broccoli [brec'-o-li], *s.* Bróculi, brécol, especie de bretón.

Brochure [brō'-shūr], *s.* Librito de pocas hojas; folleto. (Fr.)

Brock [brec], *s.* 1. Tejón, animal cuadrúpedo. 2. (Prov. Ingl.) Hombre sucio.

Brocket [brek'-et], *s.* Gamo de dos años.

§**Brodekin** [brōd'-kin], *s.* Borceguí.

Brogan [bro'-gan], *s.* Zapato pesado y basto.

Broggle [bre'-gl], *vn.* Enturbiar el agua para pescar anguilas.

Brogue [brōg], *s.* 1. Especie de calzado. *V.* Brogan. 2. Idioma corrompido, jerigonza, jerga, particularmente de los irlandeses.

Brogue-maker [brōg'-mê-kẹr], *s.* Zapatero.

†**Broidery** [breid'-ẹr-i], *s.* Bordadura, bordado. *V.* Embroidery.

Broil [brēil], *s.* 1. Tumulto, quimera, camorra, riña, disensión. 2. Alboroto, debate; sedición; división.

Broil, *va.* Asar carne sobre las ascuas o en parrillas; soasar.—*vn.* Asarse, padecer calor.

Broiler [breil'-ẹr], *s.* 1. Quimerista. 2. Parrillas. 3. Pollo a propósito para asar.

Broiling [breil'-ing], *a.* Extremamente cálido; tórrido.

Broke [brōk], *pret.* de To Break.—*a.* (vul.) En quiebra, sin dinero. *To be broke,* (Mex.) Estar bruja.

Broken [brō'-kn], *pp.* Quebrado, roto, interrumpido. *Broken English,* Inglés mal pronunciado, chapurrado. *Broken meat,* Fragmentos de viandas, carne cortada. *A broken week,* Una semana que tiene días de fiesta. *A broken voice,* Una voz interrumpida. *Broken-bellied, a.* Quebrado, el que padece hernias (poco usado). *Broken-backed,* (Mar.) Quebrantado. *Broken-down,* Arruinado, quebrantado, descompuesto, deshecho. *Broken-handed,* Manco. *Broken-hearted,* Aburrido de pesadumbre; contrito de corazón, traspasado de dolor. *Broken language,* Lenguaje chapurrado o tosco. *Broken sleep,* Sueño interrumpido. *Broken spirit,* Espíritu decaído, amilanado. *Broken-winded,* Corto de aliento.

Brokenly [brō'-kn-li], *adv.* Interrumpidamente, a ratos y no de seguida.

Brokenness [brō'-kn-nes], *s.* Desigualdad.

Broker [brō'-kẹr], *s.* 1. Corredor, el que por oficio interviene en ajustes, compras y ventas de todo género de cosas. 2. Chamarilero, almonedero, ropavejero, el que vive de comprar y vender cuadros y trastos viejos, o ropa usada. 3. Alcahuete. 4. Trujamán.

Brokerage [brō'-kẹr-êj], *s.* 1. Corretaje, el pago que se da al corredor por su diligencia y trabajo en los ajustes y ventas. 2. Corretaje, el estipendio que se da a los alcahuetes, espías y a otras personas empleadas para algún fin depravado o ilícito. 3. Ropavejería. 4. Comercio de mercancías viejas.

Brokery [brō'-kẹr-i], *s.* Correduría, trujamanía.

Bromate [brō'-mêt], *va.* Combinar con el bromo.—*s.* Sal formada con el ácido brómico.

Bromide [brō'-mid o maid], *s.* Bromuro.

Bromine [brō'-min o min], *s.* Bromo,

elemento químico, que se relaciona con el cloro y el iodo. Es un líquido de olor sofocante.

Bromoform [brō'-mo-fōrm], *s.* Bromoformo: análogo al cloroformo.

Bronchi [broṇ'-kai], *pl.* de BRONCHUS.

Bronchial [breṇ'-ki-al], **Bronchic** [breṇk'-ic], *a.* Bronquial, que pertenece a los bronquios.

Bronchitis [breṇ-kai'- o ki'-tis], *s.* Bronquitis, inflamación de la membrana mucosa que reviste los bronquios.

Bronchopneumonia [bren'-co-niu-mō'-nia], *s.* (Med.) Bronconeumonía.

Bronchotomy [breṇ-cot'-o-mi], *s.* (Cir.) Broncotomía. El acto de cortar la tráquea, o traquearteria.

Bronchus [breṇ'-cus], *pl.* BRONCHI [breṇ'-kai], *s.* Bronquio, ramal de la tráquea y sus subdivisiones. Las más pequeñas se llaman *bronchioles.*

Bronze [bronz], *s.* 1. Bronce, liga de cobre y estaño, de color moreno rojizo; a veces contiene otros metales en pequeña proporción. 2. Figura o estatua en bronce. 3. Color preparado para imitar el bronce.

Bronze, *va.* 1. Broncear, poner moreno, tostar por el sol. 2. Broncear, pavonar.

Broo [brū], *s.* 1. (Esco.) La frente; opinión favorable. 2. Zumo; líquido, caldo.

Brooch [brōch o brūch], *s.* 1. Broche o piocha de diamantes. 2. Aguada, diseño o dibujo hecho de un color.

Brooch, *va.* (Poco us.) Adornar con joyas o diamantes.

Brood [brūd], *vn.* 1. Empollar, ponerse las aves sobre los huevos. 2. Cobijar, tapar los pollos con las alas, como las gallinas. 3. Considerar, pensar o rumiar alguna cosa con cuidado. 4. Madurar alguna cosa con cuidado.—*va.* Criar con cuidado.

Brood, *s.* 1. Progenie, generación, raza, casta, ralea; hablando de personas se toma en mala parte. 2. Nidada, el conjunto de huevos puestos en el nido. 3. Cría, los pajarillos o pollos criados a un tiempo o de una vez. 4. Producción, cualquier cosa producida.

Brooder [brūd'-ẹr], *s.* 1. Incubadora. 2. Gallina clueca.

Broody [brūd'-i], *a.* Clueca o llueca.

Brook [bruc], *s.* Arroyo.

Brook, *va.* Sufrir, aguantar, tolerar, llevar con paciencia.

Brooklet [bruc'-let], *s.* Arroyuelo.

Brooklime [bruc'-laim], *s.* (Bot.) Becabunga o becabunca, especie de planta medicinal.

Brookmint [bruc'-mint], *s.* (Bot.) Menta de agua.

Brooky [bruk'-i], *a.* Lo que tiene muchos arroyos.

Broom [brūm], *s.* 1. (Bot.) Hiniesta, retama. 2. Escoba de hiniesta o retama.

Broom, *va.* (Mar.) *V.* CAREEN.

Broom corn [cōrn], *s.* Millo de escoba. Variedad de sorgo semejante al maíz, de que se usa para hacer escobas.

Broom-land [brūm'-land], *s.* Retamal, el lugar o sitio en que se cría la retama.

Broomstaff [brūm'-stāf], **Broomstick** [brūm'-stic], *s.* Palo de escoba.

Broomy [brūm'-i], *a.* Retamoso, lleno de retamas.

Broth [brōth], *s.* Caldo, el agua en que se ha cocido carne.

Brothel, Brothel-house [broth'-el, haus], *s.* Burdel, la casa pública de mujeres mundanas; mancebía.

Brother [brudh'-ẹr], *sm.* 1. Hermano, el que ha sido engendrado del mismo padre y madre que otro. *Brother-in-law,* Cuñado. *Foster brother,* Hermano de leche. 2. Hermano, el que está íntimamente unido con otro. 3. El que tiene la misma profesión que otro. *Brother lawyer,* (Fam.) Compañero, colega. *Half-brother,* Medio hermano o hermano solamente por parte de padre o de madre.

Brotherhood [brudh'-ẹr-hud], *s.* 1. Hermandad. 2. Fraternidad, el parentesco que hay entre los hermanos. 3. Hermandad, cofradía, reunión de hombres con un mismo objeto y bajo las mismas reglas. 4. Confraternidad.

Brotherless [brudh'-ẹr-les], *a.* Dícese de la persona que no tiene ningún hermano.

Brotherlike [brudh'-ẹr-laic], *a.* Fraternal.

Brotherly [brudh'-ẹr-li], *a.* Fraternal, lo que es propio de hermanos.—*adv.* Fraternalmente.

Brougham [brū'-am], *s.* Coche cerrado de cuatro ruedas, para dos o cuatro personas.

Brought [brōt], *pret.* y *pp.* del verbo *To* BRING. *Brought forward,* Pasa al frente, o suma del frente; suma y sigue. *Brought over,* Suma de la vuelta.

Brow [brau], *s.* 1. Ceja, una porción de pelo corto en figura de arco que guarnece la extremidad superior del cóncavo del ojo. 2. Frente o rostro. 3. Cara o semblante. 4. Ceja, cima, la parte superior o la cumbre del monte o sierra. 5. Atrevimiento. 6. (Met.) *Brow,* Sien, usado siempre en plural. *His brow was encircled with laurel,* Sus sienes estaban coronadas de laurel. *To knit the brows,* Fruncir las cejas, arrugar el entrecejo.

†**Brow,** *va.* Estar al borde o al canto de. (Milton.)

Browbeat [brau'-bīt], *va.* 1. Imponer, intimidar. 2. Mirar con ceño; mirar con fiereza.

Browbeating [brau'-bīt-ing], *s.* El acto de mirar con ceño o desdén.

Browbound [brau'-baund], *a.* Coronado, el que tiene las sienes ceñidas con corona.

Browless [brau'-les], *a.* Descarado.

Brown [braun], *a.* Moreno, castaño, bazo, que tira a encarnado o medio entre encarnado y negro, como el color de la pasa; pardo.—*s.* Color moreno o pardo; el obtenido mezclando rojo, amarillo y negro en diferentes proporciones; matiz de las hojas marchitas. *Brown bear,* Oso pardo. *Brown paper,* Papel de estraza. *Brown-red* o *red ochre, V.* OCHRE. *Brown bread,* Pan bazo o moreno. Pan de harina de centeno con maíz; o de trigo con centeno y maíz. *Brown sugar,* Azúcar terciado. *Brown coal,* Lignito, combustible fósil. *V.* LIGNITE.

Brownian [braun'-i-an], *a.* *V.* BRUNONIAN.

Brownie [brau'-ni], *s.* Especie de duende moreno, bondadoso, del que se supone que frecuenta las granjas y hace labores útiles por la noche. (Fam. de Escocia.)

Brownish [braun'-ish], *a.* Lo que tira a moreno o castaño.

Brown-linnet [braun'-lin-et], *s.* (Orn.) Pardillo.

Brownness [braun'-nes], *s.* Color moreno.

Brown stone [stōn], *s.* Variedad de piedra arenisca, muy usada en la construcción de edificios.

Brownwort [braun'-wūrt], *s.* (Bot.) Escrofularia.

Browse [brauz], *va.* Ramonear, pacer, cortar o comer las ramas, pimpollos o renuevos, como hacen los venados, cabras, etc.—*vn.* Alimentarse.

Browse, *s.* Pimpollos, renuevos o ramillas que sirven de pasto a las cabras.

Browsing [brauz'-ing], *s.* El alimento o comida de los venados.

Browst [braust], *s.* (Esco.) Braceaje, trabajo de preparación de la cerveza.

Brucia, Brucine [brū'-sia, brū'-sin], *s.* Brucina, alcaloide vegetal que se halla en la nuez vómica.

Bruin [brū'-in], *s.* Oso: nombre usado en los cuentos populares.

Bruise [brūz], *va.* Magullar, machacar, abollar, majar; pulverizar.

Bruise, *s.* Magulladura, contusión, golpe, y también el cardenal que queda señalado; confusión.

Bruiser [brūz'-ẹr], *s.* 1. Un instrumento de los ópticos. 2. (Fest.) Púgil.

Bruisewort [brūz'-wūrt], *s.* Consuelda o suelda consuelda.

Bruit [brūt], *s.* 1. Ruido, rumor, noticia, fama. 2. [brū'-i] (Med.) Sonido generalmente irregular y anómalo que se oye por la auscultación.

Bruit, *va.* Esparcir, divulgar, publicar; echar voz, dar fama.

Brumal [brū'-mal], *a.* Brumal, perteneciente al invierno.

Brumous [brū'-mus], *a.* Brumal, nebuloso, brumoso, invernal.

Brunch [brunch], *s.* Combinación de desayuno y almuerzo o comida.

Brunette [brū-net'], *sf.* Morena, trigueña, mujer agraciada de tez morena.

Brunonian [brū-nō'-ni-an], *a.* Lo que pertenece al Doctor John Brown, de Edimburgo: hallado o inventado por él.

Brunswick black [brunz'-wic blac], *s.* Charol negro. Llámase también *Japan black.*

Brunt [brunt], *s.* 1. Choque ó encuentro violento, combate, esfuerzo. 2. Golpe. 3. Desastre, accidente, desgracia.

Brush [brush], *s.* 1. Cepillo, escobilla, brocha, limpiadera, bruza, pincel. 2. Asalto, choque, combate, zacapela, sarracina, riña de voces y golpes. 3. Haz de leña menuda. 4. Matorral, monte, breñal.

Brush, *va.* 1. Acepillar, limpiar con el cepillo o escobilla; restregar; rasar. 2. Pintar con brocha.—*vn.* 1. (Joc.) Mover apresuradamente. 2. Pasar ligeramente por encima. *To brush away,* Quitar, como con cepillo. *To brush by one,* Pasar bruscamente cerca de alguno sin hacer caso de él.

Brusher [brush'-ẹr], *s.* Acepillador, limpiador.

Brushfire war [brush'-fair wōr], *s.* Guerra de escaramuzas, guerra limitada o acción militar menor.

Brushwood [brush'-wud], *s.* Matorral, breñal, zarzal.

Brushy [brush'-i], *a.* Cerdoso, cerdudo; áspero como el cepillo de cerdas; velludo, hablando de personas.

Brusk [brusc, brusk] o **Brusque**, *a.* Aspero, rudo.
Brussels [brus'-elz], *n. pr.* Bruselas, la capital de Bélgica. Da su nombre a varios artículos de comercio: *Brussels carpet*, Alfombra de Bruselas. *Brussels lace*, Encaje de Bruselas.
Brussels sprouts [brus'-elz sprauts], *s. pl.* Colecitas de Bruselas.
Brutal [brū'-tal], *a.* 1. Brutal, lo que pertenece a los brutos. 2. Salvaje, cruel, inhumano.
Brutality [brū-tal'-i-ti], *s.* Brutalidad, la propiedad del bruto.
Brutalize [brū'-tal-aiz], *vn.* Embrutecerse, entorpecerse.
Brutally [brū'-tal-i], *adv.* Brutalmente.
Brute [brūt], *s.* Bruto, animal irracional.
Brute, *a.* Salvaje, silvestre, montaraz, irracional, áspero, feroz, bestial.
Brute, *va.* *V.* BRUIT.
Brutify [brū'-ti-fai], *va.* Embrutecer, entorpecer.
Brutish [brū'-tish], *a.* 1. Brutal, bestial. 2. Brutal, fiero, feroz, salvaje. 3. Brutal, grosero, ignorante. 4. Insensible; frívolo. 5. Sensual.
Brutishly [brū-'tish-li], *adv.* Brutalmente.
Brutishness [brū'-tish-nes], *s.* Brutalidad.
Bryology [brai-el'-o-ji], *s.* La parte de la botánica que trata de los musgos.
Bryozoa [brai-o-zō'-a], *s. pl.* *V.* POLYZOA.
Bub [bub], *s.* 1. Muchachito. 2. (Ger.) Cerveza doble o fuerte.
Bubble [bub'-l], *s.* 1. Burbuja, la ampolla que se levanta en el agua. 2. Bagatela, cosa de poca o ninguna firmeza. 3. Engañifa, apariencia falsa.
Bubble, *vn.* 1. Burbujear, hacer burbujas o ampollas el agua; bullir. 2. Correr con ruido manso.—*va.* Engañar.
Bubbler [bub'-lęr], *s.* Engañador, fullero.
Bubbly [bub'-li], *a.* Espumoso.
Bubby [bub'-i], *s.* 1. Voz cariñosa que se aplica a un muchachito. Es corrupción de *brother.* 2. (Vul.) Teta o pecho de mujer.
Bubo [biū'-bō], *s.* Incordio, bubón, tumor que se forma en la ingle, producido generalmente por el virus venéreo.
Bubonic [biū-bon'-ic], *a.* Bubónico. *Bubonic plague*, Peste bubónica.
Buccal [buc'-al], *a.* Bocal, de la boca.
Buccaneers [buc-a-nīrz'], *s. pl.* Filibusteros, nombre que tuvieron en otro tiempo los piratas de las Antillas.
Bucentaur [biū-sen'-tōr], *s.* 1. Bucentauro, animal mitológico, mitad toro, mitad hombre. 2. Bucentauro, galera del dux de Venecia.
Buchu [biū'-kiū], *s.* Buchú, arbusto del Africa del Sur, con hojas pequeñas usadas en medicina. (Barosma.)
Buck [buc], *s.* 1. Gamo, animal parecido al ciervo. 2. El macho de algunos animales, como el ciervo, el antílope, la liebre, el conejo, etc. Indio o negro varón y adulto. (Fam. E. U. A.) 3. Petimetre atrevido y descarado. 4. Banquillo de aserrador de leña.
Buck, *s.* 1. Lejía o colada en que se limpia y blanquea la ropa. 2. Colada, la porción de ropa que hay en la lejía.
Buck, *va.* 1. Colar, lavar ropa en la colada. 2. (Mil.) Castigar atando entre sí los codos, las muñecas y las rodillas del delincuente, obligándolo a permanecer encorvado y en cuclillas.—*vn.* 1. Juntarse gamo y gama en tiempo de brama. 2. Saltar violentamente, cayendo con las patas delanteras rígidas, y la cabeza lo más baja posible: dícese del caballo o mulo vicioso.—*va.* y *vn.* Romper el mineral con martillo.
Buckbean [buc'-bīn], *s.* Trifolio palustre o trébol de pantano.
Buckboard [buc'-bōrd], *s.* (E. U.) Carretón de cuatro ruedas, sin muelles.
Bucket [buk'-et], *s.* 1. Cubo, pozal, balde, herrada, vasija para sacar agua de los pozos. 2. Cangilón de noria, arcaduz. 3. Paleta de rueda; válvula de bomba.
Bucketful [buk'-et-ful], *s.* Cantidad que puede contener un cubo.
Bucket shop [buk'-et shop], *s.* Agencia informativa para apuestas en la bolsa.
Buckeye [buc'-ai], *s.* Nombre de ciertos árboles y arbustos americanos del género Æsculus y parecidos al castaño de Indias.
Buckle [buc'-l], *s.* 1. Hebilla, pieza de metal que sirve para prender las correas y para otros usos. 2. Bucle, el rizo de pelo en forma de anillo o sortija.
Buckle, *va.* 1. Hebillar, afianzar alguna cosa con hebilla. 2. Afianzar, agarrar, no soltar. 3. Juntar en batalla. 4. Hacer rizos en el pelo.—*vn.* Doblarse, encorvarse. *To buckle to*, Someterse, aplicarse a. *To buckle with*, Empeñarse, encontrarse con. *To buckle for*, Prepararse.
Buckler [buc'-lęr], *s.* Escudo, broquel, adarga, arma defensiva.
Buckmast [buc'-mast], *s.* Fabuco.
Buck private [buc prai'-vet], *s.* (fam.) Soldado raso.
Buckram [buc'-ram], *s.* Bocací, tela de lino engomada.
Bucksaw [buc'-sō], *s.* Sierra de bastidor.
Buckshorn [bucs'-hōrn], *s.* (Bot.) Estrellamar, planta parecida en algo al llantén.
Buckshot [buc'-shot], *s.* Posta, perdigón.
Buckskin [buc'-skin], *s.* Ante, el cuero de gamo curtido; también un cuero flexible, fuerte, pardo amarillento, que hoy se hace principalmente de pieles de carnero.—*a.* Hecho de este cuero.
Buckstall [buc'-stōl], *s.* Red tumbadera.
Buckthorn [buc'-thorn], *s.* (Bot.) Cambrón, espino cerval.
Buckwheat [buc'-hwīt], *s.* Trigo negro o sarraceno.
Bucolic, Bucolical [biū-cel'-ic, al], *a.* Bucólico, pastoril.
Bucolic, *s.* El autor de bucólicas; bucólica.
Bud [bud], *s.* 1. Pimpollo, vástago, botón o yema de las plantas; capullo de una flor. 2. El acto o estado de brotar. 3. (Zool.) Parte parecida a un pimpollo o botón; prominencia semejante a un botón en varios animales, como los pólipos, etc., que se desarrolla y transforma en un nuevo individuo. 4. Lo que se asemeja a un pimpollo. 5. Algo no desarrollado. (Fam.) Una joven al ser presentada por primera vez en sociedad.
Bud, *vn.* 1. Brotar, abotonar, arrojar el árbol o las plantas sus hojas, flores, botones o renuevos. 2. Estar en flor.—*va.* Inocular, ingertar o ingerir, de escudete.
Buddha [bū'-dā], *s.* Buda, dios de la India. Gautama Siddartha, apellidado Buda.
Buddhism [būd'-izm], *s.* Budismo, culto de Buda, doctrina religiosa en Asia.
Buddhist [būd'-ist], *s.* Budista, persona que profesa las doctrinas del Budismo.
Budding [bud'-ing], *s.* Injerto de escudete, la operación de injertar un botón o yema.
Buddle [bud'-l], *s.* Lavadero, artesa grande para lavar el mineral.
Budge [buj], *va.* Mover un poco.—*vn.* Moverse, menearse, mudar de posición; hacer lugar.
Budge, *a.* 1. Guarnecido con piel curtida de cordero o que la lleva. 2. Pomposo, imponente, formal.—*s.* 1. Piel curtida de cordero o cabrito. 2. (Des.) Ratero, ladronzuelo.
Budget [buj'-et], *s.* 1. Talego portátil, mochila. 2. Provisión de alguna cosa. 3. Presupuesto; cómputo de los ingresos y gastos de un estado.
Buff [buf], *s.* 1. Ante, la piel adobada y curtida del búfalo y algunos otros animales, de la cual se hacen ciertas prendas de vestir, cinturones, etc. 2. Búfalo. 3. Coleto de soldado hecho de cuero grueso. 4. Color amarillo ligero. 5. Linfa cuajada.—*a.* 1. De color de ante. 2. Sólido, firme, que no cede.
Buff, *va.* 1. Pulimentar con ante. 2. Adelgazar el cuero. 3. Disminuir la velocidad del movimiento, amortiguar los efectos de un choque. *Buffing-block*, Cojinete o tope para amortiguar el choque entre los vagones de un tren.
Buffalo [buf'-a-lō], *s.* Búfalo, especie de toro salvaje. También se da este nombre al bisonte norteamericano, ya casi extinto.
Buffalo-moth [mōth], *s.* Antreno, insecto coleóptero cuya larva ataca y destruye las alfombras. *Buffalo-robe*, Piel del bisonte norteamericano adobada y con pelo, que se usa como manta de coche y de viaje.
Buffer [buf'-ęr], *s.* 1. Resorte, muelle en espiral. 2. (F. C.) Resortes para choques, tope.
Buffet [buf'-et], *s.* Puñada, el golpe que se da con el puño cerrado.
Buffet [bū-fé'], *s.* 1. Aparador, la mesa en donde está preparado todo lo necesario para el servicio de la comida o cena. 2. Alacena. (Fr.)
Buffet, *vn.* Combatir a puñadas.
Buffeting [buf'-et-ing], *s.* Golpe: puñada.
Buffoon [buf-fūn'], *s.* Bufón, truhán, chocarrero, juglar, que sirve de hazmereir; gracioso en los teatros.
Buffoon, *va.* Burlar, chocarrear, chulear.
Buffoonery [buf-fūn'-ęr-i], **Buffooning** [buf-fūn'-ing], *s.* Bufonada, bufonería, dicho o acción de bufón; chanzas bajas; chocarrería; majadería.
Buffoonlike [buf-fūn'-laic], *a.* Truhanesco, chocarrero, burlesco, licencioso.
Buffy [buf'-i], *a.* De color amarillo ligero; parecido al ante.
Bug [bug], *s.* Chinche, insecto asqueroso y hediondo. Nombre dado

en general en inglés a los insectos hemípteros. *Potato-bug,* Dorysphora. Esta vez se usa también á menudo inexactamente para designar ciertos escarabajos, como *lady-bug* (mariquita o vaquilla de San Martín); o algunos crustáceos, como *sow-bug,* corredera; y aun como sinónimo de insecto en general.
Bugaboo o **Bugbear** [bug'-a-bū, bug-bār], *s.* Fantasma, objeto espantoso que causa terror; espantajo, coco.
Buggy [bug'-i], *a.* Chinchero, chinchoso, lleno de chinches.
Buggy, *s.* Calesín, carruaje ligero de cuatro ruedas.
Bugle, Buglehorn [biū'-gl, hōrn], *s.* Corneta de monte o trompa de caza; instrumento músico militar, corneta de órdenes.
Bugle, *s.* 1. Bolita de vidrio negro. *Bugles,* Abalorios. 2. Búgula o consuelda media; planta.
Bugler [biū'-gler], *s.* Corneta, trompetero.
Bugloss [biū'-glos], *s.* (Bot.) Buglosa, lengua de buey.
Buhl [būl], **Buhlwork** [būl'-wūrk], *s.* Taracea, marquetería decorativa.
Build [bild], *va.* (*pret.* y *pp.* BUILT). 1. Edificar, fabricar, construir, hacer un edificio o fábrica. 2. Cimentar o fundar.—*vn.* Fiarse o apoyarse; contar con algo, confiar en.
Build [bild], *s.* Estructura, la forma o figura de algún edificio o fábrica.
Builder [bild'-ẹr], *s.* Arquitecto, alarife, maestro de obras.
Building [bild'-ing], *s.* Fábrica, edificio. *Ship-building,* Construcción de buques o arquitectura naval. *The art of building,* Arquitectura.
Buildup [bild'-up], *s.* Incremento; publicidad destinada a realzar una persona, producto u organización, popularización.
Built [bilt], *prep.* y *pp.* del verbo TO BUILD. *Built-in,* Empotrado. *Built-in furniture,* Muebles empotrados.
Bulb [bulb], *s.* (Bot.) 1. Bulbo o cebolla, la raíz redonda formada de cascos o cubierta de telas. 2. Cubeta del barómetro. 3. Ampolleta del termómetro.
Bulbar [bul'-bar], *a.* Perteneciente a un bulbo, y especialmente a la medula espinal.
Bulbous [bul'-bus], *a.* Bulboso, lo que tiene bulbos.
Bulgarian [bul-gē'-ri-an], *a.* Búlgaro, de Bulgaria.
Bulge [bulj], *s.* Parte prominente o la más convexa; comba. (Mar.) Abertura de agua.
Bulge, *vn.* 1. (Mar.) Hacer agua la embarcación. 2. (Arq.) Hacer barriga o comba el muro o la pared.
Bulk [bulk], *s.* 1. Tamaño, bulto, masa, volumen, magnitud, grosor, el grandor de alguna cosa. 2. Corpulencia, talle. 3. La mayor parte. 4. Cabida de una fábrica. 5. Capacidad o carga de un buque. *By the bulk,* En grueso, por mayor.
Bulk, *s.* (Ingl.) Barriga o comba en algún edificio; banco delante de las tiendas donde se ponen mercancías a vender.
Bulkhead [bulk'-hed], *s.* (Mar.) Mampara, división de tablas que se forma en diferentes partes de la embarcación.
Bulkiness [bulk'-i-nes], *s.* Volumen o bulto, masa, magnitud. *V.* BULK.
Bulky [bulk'-i], *a.* Voluminoso, corpulento, macizo, repleto, pesado, abultado, grueso, grande.
Bull [bul], *s.* 1. Toro, el padre del ganado vacuno. 2. (Astr.) Tauro, el segundo signo de los doce del zodíaco. 3. Bula pontificia. 4. Disparate, bola, dicho fuera de propósito, dicho absurdo; contradicción manifiesta, incongruidad, inconsecuencia. 5. Alcista, jugador á la alza. *John Bull,* (Fest.) Apodo dado á la nación inglesa.
Bulla [bul'-a], *s.* Flictena, ampolla, vejigüela cutánea transparente, que contiene un humor seroso.
Bullace [bul'-ēs], *s.* Ciruela silvestre o bruna.
Bullary [bul'-a-ri], *s.* Bulario, recopilación de las bulas de los Papas.
Bull-baiting [bul'-bēt-ing], *s.* Combate de toros y perros.
Bull-beef [bul'-bīf], *s.* Carne de toro.
Bull-calf [bul'-caf], *s.* 1. Ternero. 2. El hombre tosco y pusilánime.
Bull-dog [bul'dog], *s.* 1. Alano, perro dogo o de presa. 2. Revólver de calibre grande.
Bulldoze [bul'-dōz], *va.* (Ger. E. U.) Intimidar con amenazas o violencia física: echar fieros.
Bulldozer [bul'-dōz-ẹr], *s.* 1. Niveladora, maquinaria empleada para movimiento y desplazamiento de tierra. 2. (Fam.) Valentón, matón.
Bullen [bul'-en], *s.* Cañamiza; cañamazo.
Bullet [bul'-et], *s.* Bala de metal.
Bulletin [bul'-et-in], *s.* 1. Boletín, anuncio, noticias del día. 2. Publicación periódica sobre asunto ó ramo especial. (Fr.)
Bulletin board [bul'-et-in bōrd], *s.* Tablero para noticias.
Bullet-proof [bul'-et-prūf], *a.* A prueba de bala.
Bull-faced [bul'-fēst], *a.* Cariancho.
Bull-feast [bul'-fīst], **Bull-fight** [bul'-fait], *s.* Corrida de toros o fiesta de toros.
Bullfinch [bul'-finch], *s.* Pinzón real; pájaro cantor del género Pyrrhula.
Bullfrog [bul'-frog], *s.* Rana norteamericana de unas ocho pulgadas de largo, y de estruendoso graznido. Rana catesbiana.
Bull-head [bul'-hed], *s.* 1. Cabeza redonda, el de rudo entendimiento. 2. Gobio, pez. *V.* CATFISH. 3. Chorlito, ave zancuda.
Bullion [bul'-yun], *s.* 1. Oro en tejos, o plata en barras y sin labrar. 2. Canutillo briscado. *Bullion fringe,* Franja de oro.
Bullish [bul'-ish], *a.* Disparatado.
Bullock [bul'-uc], *s.* Buey, en especial el de más de cuatro años.
Bull's-eye [bulz'-ai], *s.* 1. Claraboya, tragaluz, ventana redonda ú ovalada. 2. Linterna sorda. 3. Centro de blanco y tiro que da en el blanco. 4. (Astr.) Aldebarán estrella principal de la constelación de Tauro. 5. (Mar.) Ojo de buey u ojo de ciego.
Bull-weed [bul'-wīd], *s.* (Bot.) Escoba, una mata.
Bully [bul'-i], *s.* Espadachín, el preciado de guapo y valentón, alborotador y amigo de pendencias, quimerista, matón, rufián, tahur.
Bully, *a.* (Ger.) 1. Jovial; vistoso. 2. Magnífico, excelente.
Bully, *va.* Echar plantas, fieros o bravatas; insultar.—*vn.* Reñir, fanfarronear.
Bulrush [bul'-rush], *s.* Junco, enea, planta que se cría en los parajes acuosos.
Bulwark [bul'-warc], *s.* 1. Baluarte, cuerpo de fábrica que en las plazas fortificadas se coloca en los ángulos para defender las murallas. 2. (Met.) Baluarte, lo que sirve de amparo ó defensa.
Bulwark, *va.* Fortificar o fortalecer con baluartes.
Bum [bum], *va.* Hacer girar y zumbar (una peonza).—*vn.* (Fam. E. U.) 1. Holgazanear, estar ocioso o hacer vida disipada (con la preposición *around*). 2. †Beber a pote.
Bum [bum], *s.* 1. Holgazán, vagabundo. 2. (vul.) Nalgas, trasero.
Bumbailiff [bum-bēl'-if], *s.* Corchete, el ministro de justicia que lleva los presos a la cárcel.
Bumble-bee o **Humble-bee** [bum'-bl-bī], *s.* Abejorro, abejón; abeja grande social del género Bombus; se llama así a causa de su zumbido.
Bumboat [bum'-bōt], *s.* (Mar.) Bote vivandero.
Bumkin [bum'-kin], **Boomkin** [būm'-kin], *s.* (Mar.) Pescante de la amura del trinquete.
Bummer [bum'-ẹr], *s.* Holgazán, ocioso, pillo. (Fam. E. U. A. *Cf.* alem. bummler.)
Bump [bump], *s.* Hinchazón o bulto; giba, joroba, corcova, hablando de animales; bollo, chichón, bodoque de golpes dados en la cabeza; abolladura, en el metal; barriga, en una pared.
Bump, *va.* Dar estallido como una bomba. Golpear, dar golpes.
Bumper [bum'-pẹr], *s.* 1. Lo que da golpes. 2. Tope para amortiguar los choques. 3. Defensa o parachoques de un automóvil. *Bumper crop,* (fam.) Cosecha abundante.
Bumpkin [bump'-kin], *s.* Patán, el hombre zafio, tosco y campesino; villano, rústico.
Bumpkinly [bump'-kin-li], *a.* Zafio, rústico.
Bumptious [bump'-shus], *a.* (Fam.) Engreído, envanecido, presuntuoso.
Bun [bun], *s.* Bollo en forma de panecillo.
Bunch [bunch], *s.* 1. Nudo, bulto o tumor, giba, corcova. 2. Racimo, ristra. 3. Manojo, atado, hacecillo, gavilla. 4. Puñado, montón de hierba. 5. Penacho. *Bunch-grass,* Ejemplar de varias plantas gramíneas del Oeste de la América del Norte, que crecen comunmente en grupos; v. g. algunas especies de Stipa y Agropyrum, Poa tenuifolia, Festuca scabrella, etc.
Bunch, *vn.* Formar giba o corcova.
Bunchbacked [bunch'-bact], *a.* Gibado, corcovado.
Bunchiness [bun'-chi-nes], *s.* La calidad de ser racimoso o nudoso.
Bunchy [bun'-chi], *a.* Racimoso, lo que se va formando en racimos; corcovado, gibado, giboso.
Bunco, Bunko [bun'-cō], *s.* 1. Variedad de juego de naipes. 2. Estafa. —*va.* Estafar, engañar.
Buncombe, Bunkum [buṇ'-cum], *s.* Lenguaje o discurso altisonante y ampuloso, sin más objeto que ganar el aplauso del público.
Bundle [bun'-dl], *s.* Atado, lío, mazo, envoltorio.
Bundle, *va.* Liar, atar, hacer un lío o atado; empaquetar, envolver.
Bung [bung], *s.* Tapón o tarugo que se pone en la parte superior de las cubas o barriles.
Bungalow [buṇ'-ga-lō], *s.* En la India inglesa, y en general en Oriente, casa, habitación de un solo piso ro-

deada de galerías o portales cubiertos.

Bunghole [bung'-hōl], *s.* Boca, el agujero por el cual se envasan los licores en las pipas, toneles y barriles, y se tapa con el tapón.

Bungle [buŋ'-gl], *va.* Chapucear, chafallar, hacer alguna cosa chapuceramente; echar a perder una cosa, estropear.—*vn.* Hacer algo chabacanamente.

Bungler [bun'-glẹr], *s.* Chapucero, chambón, el que hace mal y toscamente las cosas de su oficio.

Bunglingly [buŋ'-gling-li], *adv.* Chapuceramente, chabacanamente, groseramente, toscamente.

Bunion o **Bunyon** [bun'-yun], *s.* Juanete del pie.

Bunk [bunc], *s.* 1. Tarima para dormir. 2. (fam.) Palabrería, faramalla.

Bunker [bun'-kẹr], *s.* 1. (Mil.) Fortín. 2. (Mar.) Carbonera.

Bunny [bun'-i], *s.* (Fam.) Un conejo, o una ardilla.

Bunt [bunt], *vn.* (Mar.) Hincharse.

Bunt, *s.* Hinchazón. *Bunt of a sail*, (Mar.) Batidero de vela.

Bunt, *s.* Hongo parásito, especie de tizón que convierte el interior de los granos de trigo en fétido polvo negro. (< burnt.)

Bunt, *s.* 1. Empellón, empujón. 2. Voz usada en el juego de pelota llamado *base-ball.*

Bunt, *va.* 1. Dar o empujar con la cabeza; topetar. 2. (*Base-ball*) Golpear la pelota con la maza de una manera especial.

Bunter [bunt'-ẹr], *s.* Mujercilla, mujer vil y despreciable.

Bunting [bunt'-ing], *s.* (Mar.) Lanilla, tejido del cual se hacen por lo común las banderas.

Bunting, *s.* Pájaro del género Emberiza, del que hay varias especies. Verderón pintado.

Bunting-iron [bunt'-ing-ai-ūrn], *s.* Soplete de vidrio.

Buntlines [bunt'-linz], *s.* (Mar.) Brioles, cuerdas que sirven para cargar o recoger las velas de un buque.

Buoy [bei], *s.* 1. (Mar.) Boya, el palo, corcho u otro objeto que nada sobre el agua, sujeto a algún peso. 2. Boya, señal flotante para señalar la posición de algún objeto situado bajo el agua; o para indicar á los buques la dirección de un paso ó canal. *Can-buoy*, Boya cónica de baliza. *Wooden buoy*, Boya de madera. *Buoy-rope*, Orinque. *Buoy-slings*, Eslingas o guarnimiento de la boya. *Bell-buoy*, Boya de campana. *Whistling buoy*, Boya de pito de alarma. *Life-buoy*, Boya salvavidas; guíndola.

Buoy, *va.* Boyar, mantener sobre el agua. *To buoy the cable*, (Mar.) Boyar el cable. *To buoy one up*, Apoyar o sostener a alguno.

Buoyage [bei'-ẹj], *s.* Conjunto de boyas; sistema de boyas; acción de proveer de boyas.

Buoyancy [bei'-an-si], *s.* Fluctuación, la propiedad de sobrenadar o flotar en el agua o de mantenerse sobre un gas.

Buoyant [bei'-ant], *a.* Boyante, lo que nada sobre el agua y no se va a fondo.

Buprestis [biū-pres'-tis], *s.* Bupresto, insecto coleóptero, notable por la riqueza de sus colores. En estado de larva es muy perjudicial a los árboles.

Bur [būr], *s.* 1. Cadillo o cabeza áspera de alguna planta, como de la cardencha. 2. Envoltura de algunos frutos. *V.* Burr.

Bur, *va.* 1. Desmotar, quitar los cadillos a la lana. 2. Disponer una cavidad con el buril del dentista.

Burbot [būr'-bẹt], *s.* (Ict.) Mustela de río o agua dulce.

Burdelais [būr-de-lê'], *s.* Uva de parra gruesa, morada o blanca, que vulgarmente llaman de San Diego.

Burden [būr'-dn], *s.* 1. Carga, el peso que lleva sobre sí el hombre o la bestia. 2. Carga, cuidados y aflicciones del ánimo. *Life is a burden to him*, Está cansado de vivir. 3. Carga ó cargazón de buque. 4. Estrambote, estribillo, verso o copla que se repite al fin de alguna canción o estancia. *Beast of burden*, Acémila, bestia de carga. *To be a burden on*, Ser una carga para.

Burden, *va.* Cargar, agobiar, embarazar, oprimir.

Burdener [būr'-dn-ẹr], *s.* Cargador, el que carga; opresor, el que oprime.

Burdensome [būr'-dn-sum], *a.* Gravoso, pesado, molesto, incómodo.

Burdensomeness [būr'-dn-sum-nes], *s.* Molestia, pesadez.

Burdock [būr'-doc], *s.* (Bot.) Badana.

Bureau [biū'-rō], *s.* 1. Armario con cajones; escritorio, bufete, papelera, escaparate. 2. Escritorio, oficina, despacho. *The Weather Bureau*, El departamento de Señales Meteorológicas en el Ministerio de Agricultura, Estados Unidos de N. A.

Bureaucracy [biū-rō'-cra-si], *s.* Sistema de gobierno por medio de oficinas departamentales, cada una de ellas bajo el jefe respectivo.

Bureaucratic [biū-rō-crat'-ic], *a.* Perteneciente o relativo á las oficinas públicas, a los empleados en general, y al sistema en que predomina esa clase de gobierno.

Burette [biū-ret'], *s.* (Fr.) Bureta, probeta para dividir los líquidos en partes decimales.

Burg [būrg], *s.* Villa, aldea. *V.* Borough.

Burgage [būr'-gẹj], *s.* Una clase de arriendo de tierras.

Burgamot [būr'-ga-met], *s.* *V.* Bergamot.

Burganet [būr'-ga-net] o **Burgonet** [būr'-go-net], *s.* Borgoñota, armadura antigua de la cabeza.

Burgess [būr'-jes], *s.* 1. Ciudadano, el que goza ciertos privilegios en alguna ciudad. 2. El diputado de la cámara de los comunes que representa uno de los pueblos que gozan del derecho de enviar diputados al Parlamento.

Burgess-ship [būr'-jes-ship], *s.* Oficio y calidad de diputado de villa o ciudad con derecho de representación.

Burgh [būrg], *s.* *V.* Borough.

Burgher [būrg'-ẹr], *s.* Ciudadano, vecino.

Burghership [būrg'-ẹr-ship], *s.* Ciudadanía, privilegio de ciudadano.

Burglar [bur'-glar], *s.* Ladrón, ratero, salteador. *Burglar alarm*, Alarma contra ladrones.

Burglarious [būr-glê'-ri-us], *s.* Lo que pertenece al robo de casas por la noche: del robo en poblado.

Burglary [bur'-gla-ri], *s.* Robo, acción de robar. *Burglary insurance*, Seguro contra robos.

Burgomaster [būr'-go-mgs-tẹr], *s.* Burgomaestre, el primer magistrado de alguna ciudad, particularmente en los Países Bajos.

Burgundy [būr'-gun-di], *s.* Borgoña, antiguo ducado francés. *Burgundy wine*, Vino de Borgoña. *Burgundy helmet*, Celada borgoñona. *Burgundy pitch*, Pez de Borgoña.

Burial [ber'-i-al], *s.* 1. Entierro, el acto de enterrar y dar sepultura a los cuerpos difuntos. 2. Enterramiento, la acción de poner alguna cosa debajo de la tierra. 3. Oficio de difuntos, exequias, las honras funerales que se hacen a los difuntos.

Burial-ground [ber'-i-al-graund] o **Burial-place** [ber'-i-al-plês], *s.* Cementerio.

Burier [ber'-i-ẹr], *s.* Enterrador, sepulturero.

Burin [biū'-rin], *s.* Buril, instrumento para grabar.

Burl [būrl], *va.* Batanar, golpear paños o telas en el batán; desnudar o quitar los nudos en el paño.

Burlap [būr'-lap] o **Burlaps**, *s.* Especie de aspillera; tela basta de cáñamo, jute o lino.

Burler [būr'-lẹr], *s.* El que quita los nudos en el paño.

Burlesque [būr-lesc'], *s.* y *a.* Lengua burlesca; burlesco, lo que mueve a risa.

Burlesque, *va.* Burlar, chasquear, zumbar; disfrazar.

Burlesquer [būr-lesk'-ẹr], *s.* Burlador.

Burletta [būr-let'-a], *s.* Entremés con música. (Ital.)

Burliness [būr'-li-nes], *s.* 1. Tosquedad. 2. Volumen.

Burly [būr'-li], *a.* Voluminoso, túmido; jactancioso; turbulento; nudoso; repleto; gordo.

Burn [būrn], *va.* (*pret.* y *pp.* Burned o Burnt.) 1. Quemar, abrasar o consumir con fuego. 2. Quemar, herir con fuego; incendiar.—*vn.* 1. Quemarse, arder. 2. Estar enardecido por una pasión; secarse, consumirse. 3. Reducirse a cenizas. *To burn away*, Consumir una cosa quemándola. *To burn to ashes*, Reducir a cenizas. *To burn up*, Quemar todo, consumir. *To burn with*, Abrasarse de o en. *He burnt his fingers there*, No le tuvo cuenta allí; se llevó chasco. *They burned his shirt off of his body*, Le quemaron la camisa en el cuerpo. *To burn to do a thing*, Arder en deseo de hacer una cosa.

Burn, *s.* 1. Quemadura, la llaga o herida que hace el fuego ó una cosa muy caliente. 2. (Esco. é Ingl. del Norte) Arroyo, riachuelo. 3. Un incendio y sus consecuencias.

Burnable [būrn'-a-bl], *a.* Combustible.

Burner [būrn'-ẹr], *s.* 1. Quemador, el que quema alguna cosa. 2. Quemador de lámpara, piquera, mechero. *Bat's wing* o *butterfly burner*, Quemador de abanico.

Burnet [būr'-net], *s.* (Bot.) Sanguisorba; pimpinela.

Burning [būrn'-ing], *s.* 1. Ardor, inflamación. 2. Quemadura, abrasamiento, quema, incendio. *Burning-glass*, Espejo o vidrio ustorio.—*a.* Abrasador, ardiente, vehemente. *It is a burning shame*, Es una gran vergüenza.

Burnish [būr'-nish], *va.* Bruñir, pulir o dar lustre a alguna cosa; gratar; satinar.—*vn.* 1. Tomar lustre. 2. Crecer, aumentarse.

Burnisher [būr'-nish-ẹr], *s.* 1. Bruñidor, pulidor, el que bruñe. 2. Bruñidor, instrumento para bruñir; acicalador; satinador.

Burnoose, Burnous [bŏr-nūs'], *s.* Albornoz, capa o capote de los árabes.

Burnt, *pp.* del verbo *To* BURN. 1. Quemado, abrasado. 2. Consumido, reducido á cenizas. 3. Cocido. *A burnt child dreads the fire,* Gato escaldado del agua fría huye.

Burr [bŏr], *s.* 1. El filo delgado, o lomo, dejado por una herramienta al cortar o modelar el metal. 2. El capullo o cáscara de algunos frutos, como de la castaña; cadillo de la cardencha. 3. (Dent.) Buril. 4. (Carp.) Rondana de perno, virola. 5. Lóbulo o pulpejo de la oreja. 6. Raíz de las astas de un ciervo.

Burr, *va.* y *vn.* Pronunciar o hablar con dejo gutural, dejando oir el sonido de la erre.—*s.* 1. Articulación bronca y gutural, como en un dialecto; en particular, el sonido gutural de la erre común en el Norte de Inglaterra. 2. Zumbido, zumbo.

Burrel [bur'-el], *s.* 1. Manteca de oro, especie de pera. (< su color, buriel.) 2. *Burrel fly,* Mosca de burro, especie de mosca muy molesta a los animales; el tábano del ganado: Hypoderma bovis. 3. *Burrel shot,* Especie de metralla.

Burrow [bur'-ō], *s.* 1. Madriguera, conejera. 2. Montón de tierra. 3. (Des.) *V.* BOROUGH.

Burrow, *vn.* Minar como los conejos; esconderse en la madriguera.

Burrowing-owl [bur'-rō-ing-aul], *s.* Buho peculiar de América. Noctua canicularia.

Burr-stone [bŏr'-stōn], *s.* Roca silícea de la cual se obtienen las mejores piedras de molino.

Bursa [bŏr'-sa], *s.* Bolsillo, bolsa o saco; particularmente un hueco sinovial situado entre los tendones y eminencias huesosas.

Bursar [bŏr'-sar], *s.* 1. Tesorero de un colegio. 2. Colegial de beca en los colegios de Escocia.

Bursarship [bŏr'-sar-ship], *s.* Oficio de tesorero de un colegio.

Bursary [bŏr'-sa-ri], *s.* 1. Tesorería de una institución pública o una orden religiosa. 2. Fondo para mantener a los estudiantes necesitados.

Burse [bŏrs], *s.* 1. Bolsa, divisa oficial del Lord Canciller de Inglaterra. 2. Cubierta para cáliz, etc. 3. Fondo para mantener a los estudiantes necesitados.

Burst [bŏrst], *vn.* (*pret.* y *pp.* BURST). Reventar, estallar, abrirse alguna cosa por el impulso de otra interior; rebosar; echarse con violencia; principiar repentinamente; prorrumpir.—*va.* Romper, quebrar alguna cosa, haciéndola reventar o saltar de repente. *To burst out,* Reventar, prorrumpir; brotar. *To burst into tears,* Deshacerse en lágrimas, prorrumpir en llanto.

Burst, *s.* 1. Reventón, estallido, el acto de reventar o abrirse alguna cosa; rebosadura. 2. Esfuerzo repentino, carrera precipitada.

Burster [bŏrst'-ęr], *s.* Rompedor, quebrador.

Burstwort [bŏrst'-wŏrt], *s.* Herniaria, planta que se usaba para curar las hernias.

Burthen [bŏr'-dhęn], *s.* *V.* BURDEN.

Burton [bŏr'-ton], *s.* (Mar.) Aparejo o palanquín de polea y gancho.

Bury [ber'-i], *va.* 1. Enterrar, sepultar, dar sepultura a los cuerpos de los difuntos. 2. Sepultar, esconder, ocultar. *To bury the hatchet,* Poner a un lado las armas de la guerra, y hacer la paz. Débese esta frase a una costumbre de los indios norteamericanos.

Burying [ber'-i-ing], *s.* Entierro; exequias.

Burying-ground o **Burying-place** [ber'-i-ing-plês], *s.* Cementerio, campo santo.

Bus [bʊs], *s.* Autobús, ómnibus.

Bus *va.* Transportar en autobús.

Bush [bush], *s.* 1. Arbusto, mata; espinal, breña; matorral, zarza. 2. Ramo, señal que se pone a las puertas de las tabernas. 3. Cola de zorra. 4. Guedeja.

Bush, *vn.* Crecer espeso o contiguo. —*va.* 1. Aforrar con otro material, como se hace con la cámara del cañón, el cojinete del eje, etc. 2. Apoyar, sostener con matas. 3. Gradar o igualar el terreno arrastrando matas sobre él. 4. Labrar (piedra) a escuadra con un martillo de canto de acero.

Bushel [bush'-el], *s.* Fanega, medida de granos y otras semillas. El *bushel* imperial inglés equivale a 36.35 litros; el americano a 35 litros.

Bushelage [bush'-el-ęj], *s.* Derecho que se paga por fanega.

Bushiness [bush'-i-nes], *s.* 1. Espesor formado por los arbustos. 2. Estado de lo lanudo ó peludo.

Bushing [bush'-ing], *s.* Encaje de una pieza de metal dentro de otra, boquilla, anillo de guía.

Bushy [bush'-i], *a.* 1. Espeso, cerrado como el monte o arboleda cuyos arbustos o ramos están muy juntos y unidos; lleno de arbustos. 2. Lanudo; peludo.

Busily [biz'-i-li], *adv.* Solícitamente, diligentemente; apresuradamente.

Business [biz'-nes], *s.* Empleo, oficio, asunto, negocio, ocupación. *What is your business here?* ¿Qué le trae a Vd. acá? *To do the business for,* Liquidar (una cuenta) completamente; acabar; de aquí, matar o arruinar a alguno. *It is not my business,* Eso no me atañe; nada tengo que ver con eso. *To attend to business,* Aplicarse a los negocios. *To carry on business,* Comerciar. *To do business,* Hacer negocios. *To give up business,* Retirarse del comercio. *Beginning business,* Establecerse. *In business,* Estar establecido. *On business,* Por o para negocios. *Line of business,* Ramo de negocios.

Businessman [biz'-nes-man], *s.* Hombre de negocios, negociante, comerciante.

Businesswoman [biz'-nes-wum'-an], *s.* Mujer de negocios.

Busk [busk], *s.* 1. Palo de cotilla. 2. Ballena de corsé.

Buskin [bus'-kin], *s.* Borceguí, especie de calzado; botín que llega á la mitad de la pierna; coturno.

Buskined [bus'-kind], *a.* Calzado con borceguíes.

Buss [bus], *s.* 1. Beso, el acto o efecto de besarse. 2. (Mar.) Bucha pescadora.

Buss, *va.* (Ant. o Prov.) Besar.

Bust [bust], *s.* 1. Busto, estatua que representa medio cuerpo humano hasta el pecho. 2. El pecho, particularmente el de mujer.

Bustard [bus'-tard], *s.* Avutarda, especie de pavo silvestre.

Bustle [bus'-l], *vn.* Bullir, menearse con extrema viveza; no parar; hacer ruido o estruendo; entremeterse.

Bustle, *s.* 1. Bullicio, ruido, alboroto. 2. Polisón.

Bustler [bus'-lęr], *s.* Bullebulle, hombre inquieto y excesivamente vivo.

†**Busto,** *s.* *V.* BUST.

Busy [biz'-i], *a.* 1. Ocupado, aplicado o empleado en alguna cosa. 2. Bullicioso, entremetido.

Busy, *va.* Ocupar, emplear.—*vn.* Ocuparse.

Busybody [biz'-i-bod'-i], *s.* Entremetido, el que se mete en todo sin ser llamado.

Busybrain [biz'-i-brên], *s.* Ingenio inventivo; proyectista.

But [but], *conj.* 1. Excepto, menos. 2. Pero, mas, sin embargo, no obstante. 3. Solamente, no más que, que no. *I can not but go,* No puedo dejar de ir. *He is but just gone,* No ha hecho más que salir. *But for,* Si no fuera por, a no ser por. *It is but a poor shift,* Es un pobre efugio. *But little,* Muy poco. *But few,* Muy pocos. *But yet,* Sin embargo. *The last but one,* El penúltimo. *But a while since,* Hace poco. *But just now,* Inmediatamente. 4. (Lóg.) Es así que.—*prep.* Sin, excepto.—*adv.* Solamente.—*inter.* Exclamación de sorpresa o admiración.

But o (preferido) **Butt,** *s.* Límite, cabo, fin, término; hito, blanco.

Butcher [buch'-ęr], *s.* 1. Carnicero, el que mata animales y vende su carne. 2. Carnicero, el hombre cruel, sanguinario o inhumano.

Butcher, *va.* Matar atrozmente, hacer una carnicería, hacer pedazos, dar muerte cruel.

Butcher-bird [buch'-ęr-bęrd], *s.* Pegareborda, alcaudón, especie de marica. Llámase así por su costumbre de impalar su presa, avecillas, insectos, etc., en espinas, para devorarla más fácilmente.

Butchering [buch'-ęr-ing], *s.* El acto de matar de un modo cruel; carnicería, matanza.—*a.* Cruel, inhumano.

Butcher's-broom [buch'-ęrz-brūm] o **Knee-holly** [nī'-hel-i], *s.* (Bot.) Brusco, planta perenne.

Butcherliness [buch'-ęr-li-nes], *s.* Crueldad, inhumanidad.

Butcherly [buch'-ęr-li], *a.* Sanguinario, bárbaro, cruel.

Butchery [buch'-ęr-i], *s.* 1. El trato y oficio de carnicero. 2. Carnicería o destrozo, mortandad de gente; degüello. 3. Matadero, el paraje en donde se matan las reses.

Butler [but'-lęr], *s.* 1. Mayordomo que sirve a la mesa. 2. Despensero, el que provee la mesa de vinos y los tiene a su cargo. *Butler's pantry,* Despensa situada entre el comedor y la cocina.

Butlerage [but'-lęr-êj], *s.* 1. Departamento del despensero. 2. (Ingl.) Antiguamente, derecho sobre vinos.

Butlership [but'-lęr-ship], *s.* Oficio de despensero; sumillería.

Butlery [but'-lęr-i], *s.* Despensa.

Butment [but'-męnt], *s.* Estribo de un arco.

Butt [but], *s.* 1. Terrero, el objeto o blanco que se pone para tirar a él. 2. Blanco, hito, el fin u objeto a que se dirigen las acciones de alguno.

3. Hazmerreir, el que es objeto de la irrisión de otros. 4. Bota, pipa. *Butt-leather*, Cuero de buey. *Butt-end*, Cabo o mango de alguna cosa; término más pesado de alguna cosa. Regatón, contera. *Cigar-butt*, Punta de cigarro.

Butt, *va.* Topar o topetar, dar con la cabeza en alguna cosa.

Butt-ends [but-endz'], **Butts** [buts], *s. pl.* Pie de árbol, la unión de los extremos de los tablones.

Butte [biūt o but], *s.* Colina ó altura, aislada por lo general, que se destaca conspicuamente a manera de torre natural. (Fr.)

Butter [but'-ẹr], *s.* 1. Manteca; (Amer.) mantequilla. 2. (Quím.) Manteca, nombre que se daba antiguamente a varias preparaciones por su consistencia semejante a la de la manteca, como manteca de antimonio, arsénico, estaño, etc. *Fresh* o *salt butter*, Manteca fresca o salada. *Drawn butter*, Manteca derretida. *Butter-boat*, Bote o vasija para mantequilla derretida en la mesa.

Butter, *va.* 1. Untar con manteca. 2. Doblar las puestas, en el juego. *His bread is buttered on both sides*, Él come a dos carrillos, o tiene un empleo que le da dobles emolumentos. *He knows on which side his bread is buttered*, Él sabe por dónde va el agua al molino. *His bread is well buttered*, Tiene el riñón bien cubierto, está rico.

Butterbur [but'-ẹr-būr], *s.* (Bot.) Fárfara o uña de caballo.

Buttercup [but'-ẹr-cup], *s.* Ranúnculo, botón de oro.

Butter dish [but'-ẹr dish], *s.* Mantequillera.

Butterfat [but'-ẹr-fat], *s.* 1. Nata de la leche. 2. Grasa de la mantequilla.

Butterfly [but'-ẹr-flai], *s.* Mariposa, nombre general de los lepidópteros diurnos.

Butterin(e) [but'-ẹr-in], *s.* Manteca artificial. *V.* OLEOMARGARINE.

Buttermilk [but'-ẹr-milk], *s.* Suero de manteca.

Buttermold [but'-ẹr-mōld], **Butter-print** [but'-ẹr-print], *s.* Molde para manteca, pieza de madera en que se vacía la figura de lo que se quiere estampar en las mantequillas.

Butternut [but'-ẹr-nut], *s.* Nuez oleaginosa, comestible, del nogal blanco americano; el árbol que la produce. Juglans cinerea.

Butterscotch [but'-er-scoch], *s.* Mezcla de mantequilla y azúcar morena.

Buttertooth [but'-ẹr-tūth], *s.* Diente incisivo.

Butterwife [but'-ẹr-waif], **Butter-woman** [but'-ẹr-wum'-an], *sf.* Mantequera, vendedora de manteca.

Butterwort [but'-ẹr-wūrt], *s.* (Bot.) Sanícula, hierba sin tallo del género Pinguicula. Sus hojas son anchas y gruesas y segregan una substancia oleosa.

Buttery [but'-ẹr-i], *s.* Despensa, el lugar o sitio donde se guardan los comestibles.

Buttery, *a.* Mantecoso, que tiene manteca o se asemeja a ella.

Buttock [but'-ọc], *s.* 1. Nalga, trasero. 2. (Mar.) Cucharros o llenos de popa, la parte de la embarcación comprendida entre el yugo principal y la línea superior del agua.

Button [but'-n], *s.* 1. Botón, el que se pone al canto de los vestidos para que los afiance y abroche. 2. (Art.) Cascabel, el remate en forma casi esférica que tiene por la parte posterior el cañón de artillería. 3. (Prov. Ingl.) Botón o capullo que echan las plantas o flores. 4. Apendice parecido a un nudo, como el término de la cola de la serpiente de cascabel, o la extremidad posterior de las orugas de ciertas mariposas. 5. Toda protuberancia parecida a un botón, como el llamador de un timbre eléctrico o el botón de un florete. 6. Botón, pequeño glóbulo o disco de metal que se halla en el crisol después de la fusión. *Button-hook*, Abotonador, abrochador. *Button-maker*, Botonero.

Button, *va.* Abotonar.—*vn.* Abotonarse.

Button-hole [but'-n-hōl], *s.* Ojal.—*va.* 1. Hacer o abrir ojales. 2. Asir a uno por la solapa a tiempo que se habla con él; fastidiar. *Button-hole scissors*, Tijeras para hacer ojales.

Button-wood [but'-n-wud], *s.* 1. El plátano de América, o de Occidente. 2. Pequeño árbol siempre verde de las Antillas.

Buttress [but'-rẹs], *s.* 1. Contrafuerte, estribo, machón, arbotante, pedazo de pared fuerte a manera de pilar, que se pone arrimado a la misma pared o muralla para sostenerla. 2. Apoyo, sostén.

Buttress, *va.* Estribar, afianzar con estribo.

Butyric [biū-tir'-ic], *a.* Perteneciente a la manteca, o derivado de ella.

Buxom [buc'-sum], *a.* 1. Vivo, alegre, jovial, juguetón. *A buxom lass*, Moza retozona o juguetona. 2. Rollizo, regordete. 3. (Des.) Obediente, obsequioso, dócil; amoroso. (Esta fué la acepción primitiva.)

Buxomly [buc'-sum-li], *adv.* Vivamente, jovialmente; amorosamente.

Buxomness [buc'-sum-nes], *s.* Jovialidad, alegría; dulzura, buen humor, genio festivo.

Buy [bai], *va.* (*pret.* y *pp.* BOUGHT). Comprar, adquirir por dinero el dominio de alguna cosa. *To buy upon trust, upon credit*, Comprar al fiado. —*vn.* Tratar de compra. *To buy one off*, Ganar a alguno con presentes; corromperle, comprarle.

Buyer [bai'-ẹr], *s.* Comprador, el que compra.

Buz [buz], *inter.* Exclamación de disgusto al oir alguna cosa ya sabida.

Buzz, *s.* Susurro, soplo, zumbido, murmurio.

Buzz, *vn.* 1. Zumbar, hacer un ruido sordo, como las abejas y moscardones. 2. Cuchuchear, llevar chismes, o cuchichear, hablar al oido de alguno. —*va.* (Aer.) Bordonear.

Buzzard [buz'-ard], *s.* 1. Buaro, especie de milano. 2. Modrego, majadero. *To be betwixt hawk and buzzard*, No ser ni carne ni pescado, nadar entre dos aguas.

Buzzer [buz'-ẹr], *s.* (Elec.) Zumbador, vibrador.

Buzz saw [buz' sō], *s.* Sierra circular.

By [bai], *prep.* 1. Por, preposición que significa el agente, el instrumento, la causa, el modo y el medio por el cual se ejecuta alguna cosa. 2. A, en algún paraje. *By the river's side*, A la orilla del río. 3. Con, partícula que denota la diferencia de dos cosas cotejadas entre sí. 4. A: de, con, en. *By the laws of Castile*, A ley de Castilla. *By stealth*, A hurtadillas. *By dint of*, A fuerza de. *By all means*, Absolutamente, cueste lo que cueste. *By no means*, De ningún modo. *By much*, Con mucho. *By this time*, En este tiempo. 5. Cerca, junto a. *To sit by the fire*, Sentarse cerca del fuego. 6. A solas. 7. Por, partícula con que se expresa el juramento. *To swear by God*, Jurar por Dios. 8. A la mano. 9. Por, partícula que se usa en los ruegos o súplicas. 10. De. *He is abhorred by everybody*, Es aborrecido de todos. *By this time twelve months*, De aquí a un año. *By day, by night*, De día, de noche. *By proxy*, Por poder, por procuración.—*adv.* 1. Cerca. *My house is hard by*, Mi casa está aquí cerca. 2. Presente, delante. *By and by*, Pronto, luego, de aquí a poco. ahora. 3. Al lado de. *By reason* o *by reason that*, Porque. *By reason of*, A causa de, a fuerza de. *By then*, Para entonces, en ese tiempo, ó antes de él. *By the way*, (1) En el camino, junto al camino, o cerca de él. (2) De paso; entre paréntesis. *By one's self*, Solo, aparte. *Set it by itself*, Póngalo Vd. a un lado, aparte. *By and large*, Por todos conceptos, de todos modos. *To stand by*, (1) Sostener, defender, apoyar. (2) (Mar.) Mantenerse cerca, estar o quedarse allí; estar listo, pronto o preparado.

By, *s.* Asunto accidental o el que no es el objeto principal de la atención. *By the by*, De paso; entre paréntesis: escríbese también, *by the bye*.

By-blow [bai'-blō], *s.* 1. Accidente imprevisto; chiripa. 2. Hijo natural, ilegítimo.

By-book [bai'-buk], *s.* Libro de memoria.

By-corner [bai'-cēr-nẹr], *s.* Esquina retirada.

By-design [bai-dẹ-zain'], *s.* Designio casual o secreto.

Bygone [bai'-gēn], *a.* Pasado. *Let bygones be bygones*, Olvidemos lo pasado.

By-lane [bai'-lên], *s.* Camino retirado y fuera del principal.

By-law [bai'-lē], *s.* Ley privada o particular; estatutos o reglamentos interiores de un cuerpo o una sociedad.

By-matter [bai'-mat-ẹr], *s.* Alguna cosa accidental.

By-name [bai'-nêm], *s.* Apodo.

†**By-name**, *va.* Motejar, apodar.

By-pass [bai'-pas], *s.* Desvío, desviación.—*va.* 1. Desviar. 2. Pasar por alto.

By-past [bai'-past], *a.* Pasado.

By-path [bai'-pāth], *s.* Senda descarriada.

By-play [bai'-plê], *s.* Aparte escénico, acción o palabras de un actor, suponiendo que no le yen ni le oyen los demás.

By-product [bai-prod'-uct], *s.* Subproducto, derivado, producto accesorio. *Coal tar is a by-product in the manufacture of gas*, El alquitrán de hulla es un subproducto de la fabricación de gas.

By-road [bai'-rōd], *s.* Camino apartado o no frecuentado.

By-speech [bai'-spich], *s.* Digresión o arenga pronunciada por incidencia o casualidad.

Byssus [bis'-us], *s.* 1. Lienzo fino de Egipto. 2. Cirro de filamentos sedosos secretados por el pie de algunos moluscos, como los mejillones, y que les sirve para adherirse a las peñas.

Bystander [bai'-stand-ẹr], *s.* Mirón, mirador; uno que está presente.

By-street [bai'-strît], *s.* Calle desviada.

By-town [bai'-taun], *s.* Pueblo que no está en el camino principal o de posta.

By-turning [bai'-tūrn-ing], *s.* Senda obscura; rodeo.

By-view [bai'-viū], *s.* Fin particular o propio interés.

By-walk [bai'-wēc], *s.* Paseo oculto, privado o reservado.

Byway [bai'-wê], *s.* Camino desviado.

By-wipe [bai'-waip], *s.* Sarcasmo de dos sentidos, uno de los cuales es satírico y el otro puede tomarse á buena parte.

By-word [bai'-wūrd], *s.* 1. Locución, persona, etc., que ha llegado á ser objeto de irrisión o escarnio. 2. Apodo, mote. 3. Dicho trillado.

Byzant, Bizantine [biz'-ant, bi-zan'-tain], *s.* Besante, antigua moneda de oro acuñada en Bizancio (ahora Constantinopla), de un valor aproximado de 360 pesetas.

Byzantian, Byzantine [bi-zan'-shan, bi-zan'-tin], *a.* Bizantino, de Bizancio.

C

C [si] Tiene tres sonidos; el primero como la *c* castellana cuando precede á las letras *a, o, u, l, r;* v. g. en *cap, come, coo, clap, crop;* el segundo á modo de una *s* pronunciada con dulzura, como en *cessation, cinder, cypress;* y el tercero cuando la sigue la *h*, semejante á la *ch* castellana, como en *chap, chess, chin, chop, choose, much.* Las letras *ch* en las voces que se derivan del griego ó del latin, se pronuncian generalmente como *c* ó *k*, ó *que, qui*, como en castellano, v. g. *character, christian, monarchy, archæology* (cáracter, crístian, mónarqui, arqueóloyi); y en las tomadas del francés se les da el sonido que tienen en esta lengua, como en *chaise, machine* [shêz, ma'-shîn'].

C, vale ciento en los números romanos. (Mús.) *Do*, nota tónica de la gama natural, sin sostenido ni bemol. *Middle C*, el *do* que se halla en el centro del piano ú órgano entre el soprano y el bajo.

Cab [cab], *s.* 1. Cab, medida hebraica. 2. Cabriolé, coche de alquiler de uno ó dos asientos, con pescante y por lo general de un solo caballo. 3. Garita, casilla del maquinista; la parte cubierta de una locomotora. 4. Taxímetro.

Cabal [ca-bal'], *s.* 1. Cábala, la ciencia secreta de los rabinos. 2. Cábala, junta ó sociedad de personas unidas para alguna conjuración ó intriga. 3. Maquinación, trama, partido, manejo.

Cabal, *vn.* Maquinar, tramar, enredar á uno ó muchos, formar alguna conjuración ó partido.

Cabala [cab'-a-la], *s.* Cábala de los judíos.

Cabalism [cab'-al-izm], *s.* Cabalismo, ciencia de la cábala.

Cabalist [cab'-al-ist], *s.* Cabalista, el que está versado en las tradiciones judaicas.

Cabalistic, Cabalistical [cab-a-lis'-tic, al], *a.* Cabalístico, oculto, secreto.

Cabalistically [cab-a-lis'-tic-al-i], *adv.* Cabalísticamente.

Caballer [ca-bal'-ẹr], *s.* Pandillero, maquinador, sedicioso, pandillista, fomentador de tramas y partidos.

Cabana [ca-ban'-a], *s.* Cabaña.

Cabaret [cab-a-rê'], *s.* Cabaret, club nocturno.

Cabas [cab'-a], *s.* 1. Bolsa de labor de mujer; saco de mano pequeño. 2. En Francia, esportilla o capacho para llevar higos, uvas, etc. (Gal.)

Cabbage [cab'-ẹj], *s.* 1. Berza, col. *A head of cabbage*, Repollo. 2. Los retales que los sastres se apropian de las telas que se les entregan. *Cabbage butterfly*, Mariposa de berza del género Pieris, como Pieris rapæ, cuyas orugas devoran las hojas de la berza, y otras plantas parecidas. *Cabbage fly*, Mosca que en estado de larva ataca las raíces de la berza.

Cabbage, *va.* Cercenar o hurtar retazos, como hacen los sastres; ratear, hurtar. (Ger.)—*vn.* Formar una cabeza redonda como la de las berzas, acogollarse, apiñarse, apretarse las berzas y lechugas.

Cabbage-tree [cab'-ẹj-trî], *s.* (Bot.) Especie de palma, un árbol grande de las Antillas.

Cabbage-worm [cab'-ẹj-wūrm], *s.* Gusano de berza, oruga de algunas especies de falenas y mariposas que devora las hojas de la col.

Cabdriver [cab'-draiv-ẹr], *s.* 1. (Auto) Taxista. 2. (Carruaje) Cochero.

Cabin [cab'-in], *s.* 1. Cabaña, choza. 2. (Mar.) Camarote. *Cabin steward*, Camarero.

Cabin, *vn.* Vivir en cabaña o choza. —*va.* Encerrar en cabaña o choza.

Cabin-boy [cab'-in-boi], *s.* 1. (Mar.) Paje de escoba de la cámara del capitán. 2. Muchacho de cámara.

Cabinet [cab'-i-net], *s.* 1. Gabinete, escritorio, conjunto de cajones y anaqueles en que se guardan cosas curiosas. 2. Gabinete, paraje retirado en una casa para tratar negocios secretos, o para consultas. 3. Gabinete, ministerio, el cuerpo de ministros del Estado. 4. Caja, estuche. *Cabinet organ*, Órgano de salón. *Cabinet piano*, Gran piano vertical. *Cabinet-council*, Consejo privado. *Cabinet-maker*, Ebanista, el que trabaja en ébano y en otras maderas finas. *Cabinet-work*, Ebanistería.

Cabinet, *va.* *V.* ENCLOSE.

Cable [kê'-bl], *s.* 1. (Mar.) Cable, maroma muy gruesa que se asegura al ancla para dar fondo. 2. Cable, medida longitudinal. *V.* CABLE'S-LENGTH. 3. Cualquier maroma pesada de alambre. 4. Cable, conductor eléctrico, subacuático, aéreo o subterráneo, envuelto en una cubierta aisladora. *Best bower cable*, Cable del ayuste. *Small bower cable*, Cable sencillo o de leva. *Sheet cable*, Cable de esperanza. *Stream cable*, Calabrote. *Cable-bit*, Bitadura o media bitadura. *Weather-bit of a cable*, Bitadura entera de cable. *To bit the cable*, Tomar la bitadura con el cable. *To clap a messenger on the cable*, Tomar margarita sobre el cable. *To heave in the cable*, Virar el cable para abordo. *To pay away the cable*, Arriar cable para afuera. *To part the cables*, Partir los cables. *To serve the cable*, Aforrar el cable. *To slip the cable*, Alargar el cable por ojo o por el chicote. *Cable-car*, Carro o vagón que corre sobre carriles movido por tracción de cable. *Cable grip*, Grapa, fiador de cable. *Cable-laid*, Guindareza acalabrotada. *Cable's-length*, Cable, medida longitudinal equivalente al décimo de una milla marina o 120 brazas. *Cable railroad*, Ferrocarril en el cual la fuerza motriz, producida por una máquina fija, se comunica a un cable continuo que está situado debajo del pavimento o en una depresión del mismo. Los carros toman o sueltan el cable por medio de una grapa especial que pasa por una muesca en la calzada. Fué inventado en San Francisco de California. *Submarine cable.* Cable telegráfico submarino.

Cable address [kê'-bl ạd-dres'], *s.* Dirección cablegráfica.

Cable car [kê'-bl cār], *s.* Teleférico.

Cabled [kê'-bld], *a.* Atado o afirmado con cable.

Cablegram [kê'-bl-gram], *s.* (Fam.) Mensaje telegráfico enviado por cable; cablegrama.

Cabman [cab'-mạn], *s.* Cochero de cabriolé; calesero, simón.

Cabob [ca-bob'], *va.* Asar un lomo de carnero.

Cabob, *s.* Pierna de carnero con salsa de arenques. Carne asada, en general.

Caboose [ca-būs'], *s.* 1. (Mar.) El fogón o cocina a bordo de un barco. 2. (F. C.) Carro de conductor enganchado a un tren de mercancías.

Cabotage [cab'-o-têj], *s.* (Mar.) Cabotaje, la navegación o el tráfico que se hace sin desviarse mucho de la costa del mar.

Cabriolet [cab-ri-o-lê'], *s.* Cabriolé, especie de coche ligero de dos ruedas; corresponde también a birlocho, silla volante o carrocín. *V.* CAB y GIG.

Caburn [cab'-ūrn], *s.* (Mar.) Cajeta, trenza de filástica o meollar, de la cual se hacen tomadores y rizos.

Cacao [ca-kê'-ō], *s.* (Bot.) Cacao, árbol de la América tropical y su simiente, una almendra carnosa que se emplea como principal ingrediente del chocolate.

Cachalot [cach'-a-lot], *s.* Cachalote, especie de ballena.

Cache [cạsh], *va.* Depositar en un escondrijo; ocultar en la tierra, o debajo de un montón de piedras.

Cache, *s.* Escondite, escondrijo, lugar recóndito y a propósito para ocultar alguna cosa.

Cachectic, Cachectical [ca-kec'-tic, al], *a.* Caquéctico, el que padece caquexia.

Cachexia [ca-kex'-ia] o **Cachexy** [ca-kex'-i], *s.* Caquexia, estado del cuerpo en el que está impedida la nutrición y por consiguiente debilitadas las funciones vitales y animales.

Cachinnation [cac-i-nê'-shun], *s.* Carcajada, risotada.

Cackle [cac'-l], *vn.* 1. Cacarear, cloquear la gallina, o graznar. 2. Reirse. 3. Chacharear, picotear, hablar mucho y sin sustancia.

Cackle, *s.* 1. Cacareo, la voz de la gallina u otra ave que cacarea. 2. Charla, cháchara.

Cackler [cac'-lẹr], *s.* 1. Cacareador, pájaro o ave que cacarea. 2. Cacareador, hablador, chismoso, parlanchín.

Cackling [cac'-ling], *s.* 1. Cloqueo de la gallina. 2. Cháchara, parla.

Cacochymic, Cacochymical [cac-o-kim'-ic, al], *a.* Cacoquímico, lleno de malos humores.

Cacodemon [cac-o-dí'-men], *s.* Diablo, espíritu maligno.

‡**Cacoethes** [cac-o-í'-thiz], *s.* Mala costumbre; comezón.

Cacography [ca-cog'-ra-fi], *s.* Cacografía, mala ortografía.

Cacophony [ca-cof'-o-ni], *s.* Cacofonía, sonido desagradable al oído.

Cactus [cac'-tus], *s.* (*pl.* CACTI [cac'-tai] o CACTUSES). Cacto, género de plantas vasculares, crasas y perennes, de hojas carnosas y espinosas, familia de las cácteas; tales son la higuera de Indias y el nopal.

Cacumen [ca-kiū'-men], *s.* Ápice, cumbre.

Cacuminate [ca-kiū'-min-êt], *va.* Aguzar, acabar o terminar alguna cosa en punta o figura piramidal.

Cad [cad], *s.* 1. Hombre vulgar y malcriado, cualquiera que sea su posición social. Femenino, CADDESS. 2. Demandadero, mozo de esquina o de cordel. 3. (Ingl.) Conductor de ómnibus.

Cadaver [ca-dê'-ver], *s.* Cadáver, el cuerpo muerto.

Cadaverous [ca-dav'-er-us], *a.* Cadavérico, pálido.

Caddie [cad'-i], *s.* (Esco.) Mensajero, recadero; dícese especialmente del muchacho que en el juego llamado *golf* lleva los bastones o mazas de que se sirven los jugadores.

Caddis [cad'-is], *s.* 1. Jerguilla de lana. 2. Especie de cinta hecha de seda y estambre. 3. Gusano de la paja, larva de la frigana estriada, insecto neuróptero. Se escribe también, en este sentido, *caddis-worm.*

Caddow [cad'-ō], *s.* (Prov. Ingl.) 1. (Orn.) *V.* JACKDAW. 2. Vestidura basta de lana.

Caddy [cad'-i], *s.* Botecito, cajita para té. *V.* CADDIE.

Cade [kêd], *a.* Manso, domesticado, delicado, criado a la mano.

Cade, *s.* 1. (Prov. Ingl.) Barril; banasta. 2. Enebro. *Cade-oil,* Aceite de enebro. (Juniperus oxycedrus.)

Cade, *va.* Criar con blandura, mimar.

Cadence [kê'-dens], *va.* Regular por medida música.

Cadence, *s.* 1. Caída, declinación. 2. Cadencia, en la música, en la poesía o en las frases.

Cadent [kê'-dent], *a.* Cayente.

Cadet [ca-det'], *s.* 1. Cadete, de un cuerpo militar. 2. El hermano menor con relación a otro mayor.

Cadge [caj], *va.* (Prov. Ingl.) Llevar un fardo.

Cadger [caj'-er], *s.* Placero, regatón. *V.* HUCKSTER.

Cadi [kê'-di], *s.* Cadí, un magistrado entre los mahometanos.

Cadmium [cad'-mi-um], *s.* Cadmio, cuerpo simple metálico, parecido al estaño.

Caduceus [ca-diū'-se-us], *s.* Caduceo, la vara de Mercurio.

Caducity [ca-diū'-si-ti], *s.* Caducidad; lo que amenaza ruina; fragilidad.

Caducous [ca-diū'-cus], *a.* 1. Caduco, perecedero, poco durable. 2. En el derecho romano significaba lo que estaba sujeto a las leyes sobre herencias.

Cæcal [sí'-cal], *a.* Cecal, del intestino ciego.

Cæcum [sí'-cum], *s.* Intestino ciego, el mayor de los intestinos gruesos.

Caesarean operation [se-zé'-re-an op-er-ê'-shun], *s.* (Med.) Operación cesárea.

Cæsura [si-ziū'-ra], *s.* (Poét.) Cesura, o pausa en un verso.

Cæsural [si-ziū'-ral], *a.* Lo que pertenece a la cesura.

Café [ca-fê'], *s.* 1. Café, restaurante. 2. Cantina.

Cafeteria [caf-e-tí'-ri-a], *s.* Cafetería, restaurante en que se sirve uno mismo.

Caffein [caf'-e-in], *s.* Cafeína, alcaloide cristalizable que se extrae del café.

Caftan [caf'-tan], *s.* Vestimenta que se estila entre los persas.

Cage [kêj], *s.* 1. Jaula. 2. Jaula para fieras. 3. Jaula o cárcel, trena, prisión.

Cage. *va.* Enjaular, encerrar en jaula.

Cahoots [ca-hūts'], *s. pl.* *In cahoots,* (Coll.) Cómplices, aliados. *To be in cahoots with,* Conspirar con, complotar con.

Caic o **Caique** [cā-íc'], *s.* Caique, esquife destinado al servicio de las galeras; lancha de los cosacos en el Mar Negro.

Caiman [kê'-man], *s.* Caimán, nombre que dan los americanos a una especie de cocodrilo.

Cairn [cārn], *s.* Montón de piedras sobre el sepulcro de alguna persona distinguida.

Caisson [kê'-sen], *s.* 1. Arcón o cajón grande, que sirve en los ejércitos para las municiones, víveres, etc. 2. Cajón dentro del cual se hacen los estribos de los puentes. 3. (Mar.) Camello, aparato para poner un barco a flote, o para levantarlo y carenarlo.

Cajeput, Cajuput [caj'-(e)-u-put], *s.* Cayeput, árbol pequeño de las Molucas, familia de las mirtáceas, del cual se obtiene un aceite que destruye los insectos y se usa contra el dolor de muelas.

Cajole [ca-jōl'], *va.* Lisonjear, adular; requebrar, engatusar, acariciar.

Cajolery [ca-jōl'-er-i], *s.* Adulación, lisonja; requiebro, zalamería.

Cake [kêk], *vn.* 1. Cocer o endurecer, pegarse. 2. Formar costra.

Cake, *s.* Bollo, especie de pan delicado, tortita, hojaldre, pastelillo. *Cake of wax,* Pan de cera. *Bride-cake, wedding cake,* Torta o pastel de boda. *Plum-cake, fruit-cake,* Torta con pasas de Corinto. *Cake walk,* Diversión originaria de los negros del Sur de los Estados Unidos; marcha o paseo en el que se da un pastel como premio a la pareja que mejor y más graciosamente se contonea.

Calabash [cal'-a-bash], *s.* 1. Calabaza, güira, tapara. 2. Calabacera, taparo.

Caladium [ca-lê'-di-um], *s.* Caladio, planta que se da en los terrenos húmedos de la América del Sur. Se cultiva por sus hojas grandes, multicolores y sagitadas.

Calamanco [cal-a-man'-co], *s.* Calamaco, especie de tela de lana.

Calamar, Calamary [cal'-a-mār, cal'-a-mê-ri], *s.* 1. Calamar, molusco que posee una secreción negra llamada tinta. 2. Su concha interior o casco córneo. *V.* SQUID.

Calamine [cal'-a-main], *s.* Calamina o piedra calaminar.

Calamint [cal'-a-mint], *s.* (Bot.) Calamento.

Calamitous [ca-lam'-i-tus], *a.* Calamitoso, miserable, desgraciado, infeliz.

Calamitousness [ca-lam'-i-tus-nes], **Calamity** [ca-lam'-i-ti], *s.* Calamidad, infortunio, trabajo, miseria, desastre, desgracia.

Calamus [cal'-a-mus], *s.* (Bot.) Cálamo aromático.

Calash [ca-lash'], *s.* 1. Calesa, carruaje pequeño. 2. Gorra que llevan las señoras en la cabeza para guardar el peinado.

Calcareous [cal-kê'-ri-us], *a.* Calcáreo, que tiene propiedad de cal.

Calceated [cal'-se-ê-ted], *a.* Calzado, el que tiene puestos los zapatos.

Calcedony [cal-sed'-e-ni], *s.* Calcedonia, piedra preciosa.

Calciferous [cal-sif'-er-us], *a.* Que produce o contiene cal.

Calcification [cal-si-fi-kê'-shun], *s.* Conversión en sustancia pétrea por la deposición de sales de cal; v. gr. una petrificación.

Calcify [cal'-si-fai], *va.* y *vn.* Calcificar, calcificarse.

Calcimine [cal'-si-main], *s.* Pintura de cola, lechada, mezcla de yeso o cal con cola y agua; a menudo se le mezcla también algún color.—*va.* Dar lechada, aplicar esta mezcla a las paredes o techos. Escríbese también KALSOMINE.

Calcinable [cal'-sin-a-bl], *a.* Calcinable, capaz de ser calcinado.

Calcination [cal-si-nê'-shun], *s.* Calcinación, la acción de calcinar.

Calcinatory [cal-sin'-a-to-ri], *s.* Calcinatorio, vasija que se usa para calcinar.

Calcine [cal'-sin], *va.* Calcinar, reducir a cal o ceniza los metales, piedras, etc.; quemar.—*vn.* Calcinarse.

Calcite [cal'-sait], *s.* Espato calcáreo, carbonato de cal.

Calcitrate [cal'-si-trêt], *vn.* Acocear, hollar, patear.

Calcium [cal'-si-um], *s.* Calcio, metal ligero amarillo que combinado con el oxígeno, forma la cal.

Calc-spar [calc'-spar], *s.* Espato calcáreo.

Calculable [cal'-kiu-la-bl], *a.* Calculable.

Calculate [cal'-kiu-lêt], *va.* Calcular, contar, suputar; adaptar.—*vn.* Hacer cálculos. *Well calculated,* (Fam.) Muy a propósito. *It is well calculated,* Es lo que se necesita.

Calculation [cal'-kiu-lê-shun], *s.* Calculación, cálculo.

Calculative [cal'-kiu-le-tiv], *a.* Lo que pertenece al cálculo.

Calculator [cal-kiu-lê'-ter], *s.* 1. Calculador, persona que calcula. 2. Máquina calculadora.

Calculatory [cal'-kiu-le-to-ri], *a.* Lo que pertenece al cálculo.

Calculous [cal'-kiu-lus], **Calculose** [cal'-kiu-lōs], *a.* Pedregoso, arenoso; calculoso.

Calculus [cal'-kiu-lus], *s.* Cálculo, piedra en la vejiga o en los riñones. *Calculi,* Cálculos.

Caldron [cōl'-drun], *s.* Caldera o caldero.

Caledonian [cal-e-dō'-ni-an], *a.* Escocés, natural de, o perteneciente a Escocia.

Calefacient [cal-e-fê'-shient], *a.* Lo que produce calefacción, que da calor.

Calefaction [cal-e-fac'-shun], *s.* Calefacción, la acción y efecto de calentar o calentarse.

Calefactive [cal-e-fac'-tiv], **Calefactory** [cal-e-fac'-to-ri], *a.* Calefaciente, que calienta.

Calefy [cal'-e-fai], *vn.* (Des.) Calentarse, caldearse.—*va.* Calentar.

Calendar [cal'-en-dạr], *s.* 1. Calendario o almanaque. 2. Lista o tabla de los pleitos o causas que están para verse en los tribunales.
Calendar, *va.* Entrar o insertar en el calendario.
Calender, *s.* Calandria o prensa recargada, máquina para dar lustre a las telas de seda o para satinar papel.
Calender, *va.* Prensar con calandria, lustrar el papel o las telas pasándolas entre dos cilindros.
Calenderer [cal'-en-dẹr-ẹr], *s.* Aprensador, el que aprensa con calandria.
Calends [cal'-endz], *s. pl.* Calenda o calendas, el primer día de cada mes en el antiguo cómputo romano.
Calendula [ca-len'-diu-la], *s.* Caléndula, maravilla, planta crisantema del orden de las compuestas.
Calendulin [ca-len'-diu-lin], *s.* Calendulina, goma o sustancia mucilaginosa, que se extrae de la caléndula.
Calenture [cal'-en-tiūr], *s.* Calentura, fiebre tropical violenta.
Calf [cāf], *s.* (*pl.* CALVES [cāvz]). 1. Ternero o ternera; cervatillo. 2. Pantorrilla, la parte posterior de la pierna, la más carnosa y abultada. 3. Tonto; cobarde. *Calf's foot jelly,* Gelatina de manos de ternero.
Calfskin [cāf'-skin], *s.* Becerrillo, becerros o piel de ternero.
Caliber, Calibre [cal'-i-bẹr], *s.* 1. Calibre, la abertura, hueco y diámetro del cañón de un arma de fuego. 2. Grado de capacidad, mérito o facultades intelectuales. 3. Peso total del armamento de un buque.
Calibrate [cal'-i-brêt] *va.* Calibrar.
Calibration [cal-i-brê'-shun], *s.* Calibración.
Calico [cal'-i-cō], *s.* 1. Calicó, indiana, una especie de tela de algodón estampada. 2. Zaraza. (Mex.) Angaripola.
Calico-printer [cal'-i-cō-prin'-tẹr], *s.* Estampador de tela de algodón.
Calid [cal'-id], *a.* (Des.) Caliente; cálido, ardiente.
Calidity [ca-lid'-i-ti], **Calidness** [cal'-id-nes], *s.* (Des.) Calor, encendimiento.
Calif, Caliph [ké'-lif], *s.* Califa, título que tomaron los sucesores de Mahoma.
Californian [cal-i-fōr'-ni-an], *a.* Califórnico, perteneciente a California. —*s.* Californio, california, natural de California.
Caligraphy [ca-lig'-ra-fi], *s.* *V.* CALLIGRAPHY.
Calipash [cal-i-pash'], *s.* Cierta parte de la tortuga próxima a la concha superior; una substancia gelatinosa verdusca.
Calipee [cal-i-pí'], *s.* Parte de la tortuga próxima a la concha inferior; substancia gelatinosa amarillenta.
Caliper [cal'-i-pẹr], *s.* Compás, calibrador. *Inside calipers,* Compás de calibres. *Outside calipers,* Compás de espesores.
Caliphate [cal'-i-fêt], *s.* Califato, dignidad o jurisdicción del califa.
Calisaya [cal-i-sé'-ya], *s.* Variedad de quina de las más estimadas.
Calisthenic, *a.* *V.* CALLISTHENIC.
Caliver [cal'-i-vẹr], *s.* (Ant.) Una especie de escopeta; pedrero, cantero.
Calix [ké'-lix], *s.* 1. Órgano o cavidad en forma de copa. 2. *V.* CALYX.
Calk, Caulk [cōk], *va.* 1. (Mar.) Calafatear un buque. *Calking mallet,* Maceta de calafate. *Calking iron,* Escoplo de calafate. 2. (Vet.) Hacer talones o proyecciones en la herradura del caballo.
Calk [calk], *va.* y *vn.* Marcar con tiza; de aquí, calcar, pasar un dibujo.
Calker [cōk'-ẹr], *s.* Calafate. *Calker's boy,* Calafatín. *Calker's tool-box,* Banqueta de calafate.
Calkin [cōk'-in], *s.* (Vet.) La parte saliente en la herradura de los caballos para impedir que tropiecen.
Calking [cōk'-ing], *s.* Calafateo, acción y efecto de calafatear.
Call [cōl], *va.* 1. Llamar, nombrar. 2. Llamar, decir a uno que venga. 3. Convocar, citar, juntar, congregar. 4. Llamar, inspirar. 5. Invocar o apelar. 6. Proclamar, publicar, pregonar. 7. Poner apodos. 8. Visitar a uno; llamar a uno o darle voces. 9. Excitar, traer a la vista. —*vn.* 1. Pararse un rato: hacer visita. 2. Gritar. *To call after one,* Llamar a alguno a voces. *To call again,* Volver a llamar; hacer volver. *To call aloud,* Dar voces, gritar. *To call aside,* Llamar a parte, sacar a parte. *To call away,* Hacer salir, echar fuera; llevar consigo. *To call back,* Mandar volver, hacer volver, llamar a uno para que vuelva al punto de donde ha salido, o decirle que vuelva. *To call down,* Hacer bajar. *To call for,* Llamar, preguntar por alguno, ir a buscarle. *To call forth,* Hacer salir o venir. *To call in,* Reasumir; volver atrás, llamar a alguno para que entre o hacerlo entrar; introducir; retirar, revocar. *He has called in his money,* Ha retirado sus fondos. *To call in question,* Poner en duda. *To call off,* Disuadir; divertir (la atención). *To call on,* Solicitar; pronunciar con solemnidad el nombre de algún muerto o ausente llamándole; visitar a alguno, ir a ver a alguno. *To call out,* Desafiar; llamar a uno para que salga; llamar fuerte, gritar. *To call over,* Repasar, leer algo, leer alguna lista o catálogo. *To call to account,* Pedir cuentas. *To call to witness,* Tomar por testigo. *To call upon,* Implorar, rogar, pedir; visitar; exhortar, animar; invocar.
Call, *s.* 1. Llamada, la acción de llamar. (Fam.) Visita. *I have some calls to make,* Tengo que hacer algunas visitas. 2. Instancia, llamamiento; vocación. 3. Pretensión o alegación de derecho a alguna cosa. 4. Reclamo, instrumento para llamar los pájaros. *Call-bird,* Pájaro de reclamo. 5. Inspiración divina. 6. (Mar.) Pito de contramaestre. 7. Demanda (de fondos). *Be within call,* Esté Vd. al alcance de la voz. *He had no call to do it,* Él no tenía derecho a hacerlo.
Calla [cal'-a], *s.* (Bot.) Lirio de Egipto, planta parecida al yaro. Richardia ethiopica.
Caller [cōl'-ẹr], *s.* Llamador, el que llama.
‡**Callid** [cal'-id], *a.* Astuto, sagaz.
Calligraph [cal'-i-grạf], *s.* Ejemplar o muestra de buena escritura.
Calligraphic [cal-i-graf'-ic], *a.* Caligráfico, relativo a la caligrafía.
Calligraphy [cal-lig'-ra-fi], *s.* Bella escritura, letra hermosa y elegante; caligrafía en general.
Callimanco, *s.* *V.* CALAMANCO.
Calling [cōl'-ing], *s.* Profesión, vocación, el modo de vida que cada uno tiene, usa y ejerce públicamente; clase; oficio, ejercicio.
Calliope [cal-lai'-o-pi], *s.* Instrumento musical compuesto de una serie de silbatos que tocan mediante un teclado.
Callipers [cal'-i-pẹrz], *s.* Compás calibrador. *V.* CALIPER.
Callisthenic [cal-is-then'-ic], *a.* Calisténico; perteneciente a la calistenia; lo que favorece la gracia y soltura del cuerpo.
Callisthenics [cal-is-then'-ics], *s.* Calistenia, ligeros ejercicios gimnásticos a propósito para las niñas y jóvenes, con objeto de aumentar la agilidad y el donaire del cuerpo.
Callosity [cal-los'-i-ti], **Callousness** [cal'-us-nes], *s.* Callosidad, dureza; insensibilidad.
Callous [cal'-us], *a.* 1. Calloso, endurecido. 2. Insensible.
Callously [cal'-us-li], *adv.* Insensiblemente, duramente.
Callow [cal'-ō], *a.* 1. Pelado, desplumado. 2. Sin experiencia del mundo, joven.
Callus [cal'-us], *s.* Callo, dureza en alguna parte del cuerpo; el punto por donde se unen otra vez los huesos después de rotos.
Calm [cām], *s.* Calma, serenidad, tranquilidad, quietud, bonanza, reposo, sosiego. *Dead calm,* (Mar.) Calma chicha.—*a.* Quieto, tranquilo, sosegado, sereno. *To become calm,* (Mar.) Calmar o comenzar a hacer calma.
Calm, *va.* Tranquilizar, aquietar; apaciguar, calmar; aplacar, sosegar.
Calmer [cām'-ẹr], *s.* Tranquilizador, apaciguador, sosegador, aquietador, pacificador.
Calmly [cām'-li], *adv.* Serenamente, con serenidad.
Calmness [cām'-nes], *s.* Tranquilidad, serenidad, calma.
Calmy [cām'-i], *a.* Tranquilo, pacífico.
Calomel [cal'-o-mel], *s.* Calomelanos, calomel, cloruro mercurioso (Hg_2Cl_2).
Caloric [ca-ler'-ic], *s.* (Quím.) Calórico.
Calorie [cal'-o-ri], *s.* Caloría.
Calorific [cal-o-rif'-ic], *a.* Calorífico.
Calorimeter [cal-o-rim'-e-tẹr], *s.* Calorímetro, instrumento para medir el calor.
Caltha [cal'-tha], *s.* (Bot.) Hierba centella, calta.
Caltrop [cal'-trọp], *s.* 1. (Mil.) Abrojo, pieza de hierro con tres o cuatro puntas, una de las cuales queda siempre hacia arriba; se usa para impedir el paso de infantes y caballos, mutilándoles los pies. 2. (Bot.) Tríbulo, abrojo.
Calumet [cal'-yu-met], *s.* Pipa de los aborígenes de la América del Norte. Tiene la taza o cabeza de piedra y el tubo de caña.
Calumniate [ca-lum'-ni-êt], *va.* y *vn.* Calumniar.
Calumniation [ca-lum-ni-ê'-shun], *s.* Calumnia.
Calumniator [ca-lum'-ni-ê-ter], *s.* Calumniador, el que calumnia o acusa falsamente.
Calumniatory [ca-lum'-ni-a-to-ri], **Calumnious** [ca-lum'-ni-us], *a.* Calumnioso, injurioso.
Calumniously [ca-lum'-ni-us-li], *adv.* Injuriosamente, calumniosamente.
Calumny [cal'-um-ni], *s.* Calumnia.
Calvary [cal'-va-ri], *s.* 1. Calvario, el lugar del suplicio de N. S. Jesucristo. 2. Calvario, Via crucis.

Calve [cāv], *vn.* Parir la vaca.
Calvinism [cal'-vin-izm], *s.* Calvinismo, la doctrina de Calvino.
Calvinist [cal'-vin-ist], *s.* Calvinista.
Calvinize [cal'-vin-aiz], *va.* Enseñar la doctrina de Calvino.
Calvish [cāv'-ish], *a.* Aternerado.
Calvity, *s.* *V.* BALDNESS.
Calx [calx], *s.* (*pl.* CALXES o CALCES). 1. Cenizas o residuos procedentes de la calcinación de minerales. 2. (Anat.) El hueso calcáneo, que forma el talón o calcañar.
Calycle [cal'-i-cl], *s.* Calículo, cáliz accesorio de algunas flores.
Calypso [ca-lip'-so], *s.* 1. (Bot.) Calipso. 2. Calipso, ritmo afroantillano originario de la isla de Trinidad.
Calyx [kē'-lix], *s.* 1. (Bot.) Cáliz, envoltura exterior de las flores. 2. (Anat.) Pelvis del riñón.
Cam [cam], *s.* (Mec.) Álabe, excéntrica, leva.
Camber [cam'-bęr], *s.* (Mar.) Comba, combadura, alabeo de la cubierta. —*vn.* y *va.* Combar, hacer comba o tener arqueo hacia arriba.
Cambist [cam'-bist], *s.* (Com.) 1. Cambista, el que tiene por oficio dar o aceptar letras de cambio. 2. Cambiador, el que cambia las monedas.
Cambium [cam'-bi-um], *s.* (Bot.) Substancia viscosa, que se encuentra entre la albura y la corteza de los árboles.
Cambric [kēm'-bric], *s.* Batista, olán batista.
Came [kēm], *pret.* del verbo *To* COME.
Camel [cam'-el], *s.* 1. Camello, bestia de carga en África y Oriente. *Camel's hair*, Pelo o lana de camello. *Camel's hair pencil*, Pincel de pelo de camello. *Camel's hay*, Esquinante o esquinanto, junco oloroso medicinal. 2. (Mar.) Camello, aparato a manera de bote o barco, herméticamente cerrado, que sirve para levantar buques en los diques y para poner a flote las embarcaciones sumergidas.
Camellia [ca-mel'-i-a], *s.* Camelia, planta y flor.
Camelopard [ca-mel'-o-pārd], *s.* Camello pardal, jirafa, animal algo parecido al camello.
Cameo [cam'-e-o], *s.* Camafeo, piedra preciosa con figuras labradas en relieve.
Camera [cam'-ę-ra], *s.* 1. Cámara, caja en la cual se refleja la imagen de los objetos exteriores sobre una superficie plana, por medio de una lente, o lentes. 2. (Anat.) Cavidad, como las del corazón. 3. (Ley inglesa) Cámara particular para los jueces. *Folding camera*, Cámara plegadiza. *Hand camera*, Cámara (fotográfica) de mano. *Camera stand*, Pie, sostén de la cámara fotográfica. *Stereoscopic camera*, Cámara estereoscópica. *Camera lucida*, Cámara lúcida. *Camera obscura*, Cámara obscura, aparato para mirar, trazar o fotografiar.
Cameral [cam'-ę-ral], *a.* Relativo a una cámara, un cuarto, oficina pública, o tesorería.
Cameralistic [cam-ę-ral-is'-tic], *a.* Perteneciente a la hacienda y rentas del Estado.
Camera man [cam'-ę-ra . man], *s.* Camarógrafo.
‡**Camerated** [cam'-er-ē-ted], *a.* Arqueado, abovedado.
Cameration [cam-ęr-ē'-shun], *s.* Arqueo, abovedación.
Camisado [cam-i-sā'-do], *s.* (Ant.) Encamisada, una estratagema militar.
Camisated [cam'-i-sé-ted], *a.* Encamisado, el que tiene la camisa puesta sobre el vestido.
Camise [ca-mīs'], *s.* Camisa holgada que usan los orientales; también una bata ligera y holgada. *Cf.* CHEMISE.
Camlet [cam'-let], *s.* 1. Camelote o chamelote. 2. Barragán.
Cammock [cam'-oc], *s.* (Bot.) Detienebuey, gatuña. (Ononis.)
Camomile [cam'-o-mail], *s.* (Bot.) Manzanilla, camomila, hierba amarga de flores medicinales.
Camouflage [cam'-ū-flazh], *s.* Camuflaje, simulación, engaño.—*va.* Recurrir al camuflaje, fingir, simular (algo).
Camp [camp], *s.* (Mil.) Campo, campamento (tropa y terreno).
Camp, *vn.* Acampar, colocarse el ejército en tiendas.—*va.* Alojar un ejército; acampar.
Campaign [cam-pēn'], *s.* 1. Campaña, campiña, campo raso, llanura rasa. 2. (Mil.) Campaña, el tiempo que el ejército se mantiene en el campo. *To open the campaign*, Empezar la campaña.
Campaign, *vn.* Servir en campaña.
Campaigner [cam-pēn'-ęr], *s.* Campeador; veterano.
Campaniform [cam-pan'-i-form], **Campanulate** [cam-pan'-yu-lēt], *a.* (Bot.) Campaniforme o campanuda, flor que tiene la figura de campana.
Campanile [cam-pa-nī'-le], *s.* Campanario de iglesia, especialmente cuando la torre se destaca aislada.
Campanology [cam-pa-nel'-o-ji], *s.* Campanología, el arte de tocar o repicar las campanas.
Campanula [cam-pan'-yu-la], *s.* (Bot.) Campánula.
Campanulate [cam-pan'-yu-lēt], *a.* *V.* CAMPANIFORM.
Campeachy-wood [cam-pīch'-i-wud], *s.* Palo de Campeche o Palo campeche.
Campfire [camp'-fair], *s.* Hoguera en un campamento.
Camphine [cam-fīn'], *s.* Aceite de trementina rectificado, que se usó antiguamente para el alumbrado.
Camphor [cam'-fęr], *s.* Alcanfor, substancia blanca, volátil, parecida a la goma, de un olor característico, que se extrae del alcanforado, o laurel-alcanfor. *Camphor-tree*, Alcanforero, alcanforado, o laurel alcanfor. Laurus camphora.
Camphor, Camphorate [cam'-fer-ēt], *va.* Alcanforar, impregnar o lavar con alcanfor.
Camphorate, *a.* Alcanforado.
Camping [camp'-ing], *s.* 1. Campamento. 2. (Des.) Antiguo juego de pelota con los pies.
Campion [cam'-pi-en], *a.* (Bot.) Colleja, hierba de las cariofileas.
Campus [cam'-pus], *s.* (E. U.) Terreno perteneciente a un colegio e inmediato a él, o el patio rodeado por los edificios del colegio o universidad. (Lat.)
Camshaft [cam'-shaft], *s.* (Mec.) Árbol de levas, eje de levas.
Camwood [cam'-wud], *s.* Madera roja de Africa y del Brasil.
Can [can], *s.* Lata, bote. *Can opener*, Abridor de lata, abrelatas.
Can, *vn. irr.* (*pret.* COULD). 1. Poder. *If I can but see him*, Con tal que yo le pueda ver. *As sure as can be*, Sin duda, indudablemente, segurísimamente. *As soon as can be*, Al instante que se pueda; lo más pronto posible. *It can not be*, Es imposible, no puede ser. *He can't* (*can not*) *pay*, Él no puede pagar. *He is as like his father as can be*, Él es tan parecido a su padre que más no puede ser. 2. Saber. *She can read and write*, Ella saber leer y escribir. *Nobody can tell*, Nadie sabe nada.
Can, *va.* Guardar algo en cajas de hoja de lata para conservarlo en buen estado. *Canned goods*, Carne preparada, hortalizas, pescado o frutas encerrados herméticamente en receptáculos de hoja de lata o de vidrio. Llámanse generalmente en la Gran Bretaña, *tinned goods*.
Canada Balsam, *s.* *V.* BALSAM.
Canadian [ca-nē'-di-an], *a.* Canadiense, del Canadá.
Canal [ca-nal'], *s.* 1. Canal; conducto artificial por donde corre el agua. 2. Canal, de navegación. 3. Canal, conducto por donde circulan la sangre y otros humores del cuerpo. 4. (Arq.) Estría, media caña.
Canalage [ca-nal'-ēj], *s.* 1. Construcción de canales. 2. Coste, gastos del transporte por un canal.
Canaliculate [can-a-lic'-yu-lēt], *a.* Acanalado, estriado, abierto en forma de media caña.
Canaliculus [can-a-lic'-yu-lus], *s.* Canal, o tubo, diminuto como los que hay en un hueso.
Canard [ca-nārd'], *s.* Embuste; noticia falsa, principalmente en un periódico.
Canary [ca-nē'-ri], *s.* 1. Vino de Canarias. 2. Canario, un baile antiguo.
Canary-bird [ca-nē'-ri-bęrd], *s.* Canario, pájaro pequeño que canta primorosamente.
Canary-seed [ca-nē'-ri-sīd], *s.* Alpiste.
Canasta [ca-nas'-ta], *s.* Canasta (juego de naipes).
Can-buoy [can'-boi], *s.* (Mar.) Boya cónica de barril.
Can-hooks [can'-hucs], *s. pl.* (Mar.) Gafas.
Cancel [can'-sel], *va.* 1. Cancelar, borrar. 2. Cancelar un escrito. 3. Invalidar, anular. 4. Limitar, encerrar, estrechar, poner límites.
Cancel, *s.* (Imp.) Cartón, cuartilla, la hoja o las páginas que se rehacen, sea por corrección o por errata.
Cancellate [can'-sel-lēt], *a.* Reticular, celular, poroso como algunos huesos.
Cancellation [can-sel-ē'-shun], *s.* Canceladura, cancelación.
Cancer [can'-sęr], *s.* 1. Cáncer, tumor maligno. 2. Cáncer, el signo de solsticio de estío. 3. Cangrejo.
Cancerate [can'-sęr-ēt], *vn.* Cancerarse o encancerarse.
Canceration [can-sęr-ē'-shun], **Cancerousness** [can'-sęr-us-nes], *s.* Principio de cáncer, el estado o calidad cancerosa.
Cancer-fighting [can'-sęr-fait'-ing], *a.* Anticanceroso.
Cancerous [can'-sęr-us], *a.* Canceroso, lo que tiene la malignidad de cáncer; virulento.
Candelabrum [can-de-lē'-brum], *s.* CANDELABRA, *pl.* 1. Hachero, blandón, el pie o soporte en que los antiguos ponían la lámpara. 2. Candelero con varios mecheros, mechero.
Candent [can'-dent], *a.* (Ant.) Candente, que está hecho un ascua.
Candid [can'-did], *a.* 1. Cándido, sencillo, ingenuo, sincero, franco,

íntegro, abierto, sin doblez. 2. (Des.) Blanco.

Candidate [can'-di-dêt], *s.* Candidato, el que aspira a algún empleo; pretendiente, opositor, aspirante.

Candidateship [can'-di-dêt-ship], *s.* Candidatura, estado de candidato.

Candid camera [can'-did cam'-ẹ-rạ], *s.* Pequeña máquina fotográfica utilizada para tomar instantáneas inadvertidamente.

Candidly [can'-did-li], *adv.* Cándidamente, ingenuamente, francamente.

Candidness [can'-did-nes], *s.* Candidez, candor, sinceridad, pureza de ánimo.

Candied [can'-did], *pp.* y *a.* Confitado, bañado en azúcar o conservado en almíbar. *V.* CANDY.

Candle [can'-dl], *s.* 1. Candela, vela. 2. Luz. 3. Bujía. *Candle power,* Fuerza de iluminación de una *standard candle. Standard candle,* (1) Vela de esperma que quema dos granos por minuto: se usa como tipo y medida de la luz. (2) La cantidad de luz que da esa vela o bujía. (3) La cantidad de luz emitida por 1/20 milímetro cuadrado de platino derretido. *Roman candle,* Vela romana, fuego artificial. *The game is not worth the candle,* No vale la pena. *To hold a candle to,* Comparar una persona o cosa con otra. *Candle-ends,* Cabo de vela; fragmentos, sobras; dícese en desprecio. *Candle-holder,* Portavela. *Candle-light,* La luz de una vela, bujía o candela; luz artificial, en general. *At early candle-light,* Al punto de las oraciones; al tiempo preciso de encender las luces. *Candle-snuffers,* Despabiladeras, instrumento para despabilar; cuando se aplica a personas, denota inutilidad o estupidez.

Candleberry-tree [can'-dl-ber-i-trî], *s.* (Bot.) Árbol de la cera.

Candlemas [can'-dl-mas], *s.* Candelaria, fiesta que celebra la iglesia en honra de la Purificación de la Virgen.

Candlepower [can'-dl-pau-ẹr], *s.* (Elec.) Bujías.

Candlestick [can'-dl-stic], *s.* Candelero. *Chamber candlestick,* Palmatoria. *Branched candlestick,* Araña. (Mex.) Candil.

Candor, Candour [can'-dẹr], *s.* Candor, sinceridad, integridad, sencillez, ingenuidad, franqueza.

Candy [can'-di], *va.* 1. Confitar, cubrir las frutas o pastas con un baño de azúcar o cocerlas en almíbar. *Lemon candy,* Caramelos. *Peanut candy,* Pepitoria. *Candied almonds,* Almendras garapiñadas. 2. Garapiñar.—*vn.* Cristalizarse (el azúcar); secarse o endurecerse los dulces.

Candy [can'-di], *s.* Confite, confitura, dulce. *Candy box,* Caja de dulces o confites. *Candy dish,* Confitera. *Candy-pull,* Tertulia en que se hace melcocha estirando la pasta.

Candytuft [can'-di-tuft], *s.* (Bot.) Carraspique ibéride, planta crucífera que se cultiva en los jardines como de adorno.

Cane [kên], *s.* 1. Caña o junco de Indias, caña de Bengala. 2. Caña de azúcar. 3. Lanza, caña. 4. Junco o bastón. 5. Caña, planta hueca y nudosa que se cría en los lugares húmedos. 6. Caña o bastón de caña de Bengala. *Head of a cane,* Puño de bastón. *Cane-brake,* Cañaveral espeso. *Cane-field,* Cañaveral. *Cane-juice,* Zumo de la caña de azúcar, llamado en Cuba guarapo. *Cane-mill,* Ingenio de azúcar.

Cane, *va.* Apalear, dar de palos con un bastón o caña.

Canella [ca-nel'-a], *s.* 1. Canelero, canelo. 2. Canela, corteza aromática.

Canescent [ca-nes'-ent], *a.* Que se pone blanco o cano.

Canicular [ca-nic'-yu-lar], *a.* Canicular, perteneciente a la canícula.

Canine [ca-nain'], *a.* Canino, perruno.

Canister [can'-is-tẹr], *s.* 1. Canastillo, cesta pequeña. 2. Bote, frasco, o caja, de plata u hoja de lata para guardar te, tabaco, etc.

Canker [caṇ'-kẹr], *s.* 1. Una llaga ulcerosa con tendencia a la gangrena; especialmente una pequeña úlcera en la boca. 2. Gangrena, enfermedad que padecen los árboles.

Canker, *vn.* Gangrenarse, corromperse, roerse.—*va.* Gangrenar, roer, corromper; contaminar.

Cankerous [caṇ'-kẹr-us], *a.* Gangrenoso, corrosivo, canceroso.

Cankerworm [caṇ'-ker-wūrm''], *s.* Oruga que destruye los árboles y frutas, especialmente las larvas del género Anisopteryx.

Cannabis [can'-a-bis], *s.* Cáñamo, planta de las cannabíneas, antiguo orden incluido hoy en la familia de las urticáceas.

Canned goods [cand gudz], *s. pl.* Conservas enlatadas, artículos enlatados.

Cannel [can'-nel], *s.* Carbón duro. *V.* COAL.

Canner [can'-ẹr], *s.* El que pone los víveres en cajas de hoja de lata.

Cannery [can'-ẹr-i], *s.* Fábrica para conservar las frutas, etc., en cajas de hoja de lata.

Cannibal [can'-i-bal], *s.* Caníbal, caribe, antropófago, el que come carne humana.

Cannibalism [can'-i-bal-izm], *s.* Canibalismo, carácter y costumbres de los caníbales.

Cannon [can'-un], *s.* 1. Cañón de artillería. 2. (Ingl.) Carambola en el juego de billar. *Within cannon-shot,* A tiro de cañón. *Cannon-ball* o *cannon-shot,* Bala de cañón. *Cannon metal,* Metal para cañones, que es generalmente bronce, pero algunas veces hierro y acero.

Cannon-hole [can'-un-hōl], *s.* (Mar.) Tronera.

Cannon-proof [can'-un-prūf], *a.* A prueba de cañón.

Cannonade [can-un-êd'], *va.* Cañonear o acañonear, batir a cañonazos.—*s.* Cañoneo, acto de cañonear; la repetición de cañonazos.

Cannoneer [can-un-îr'], *va.* Cañonear.

Cannoneer, *s.* Cañonero o artillero, el que carga, apunta y dispara el cañón.

Cannot [can'-ot], *vn.* De *can* y *not.* No poder. *V.* CAN.

Canny, Cannie [can'-i], *a.* (Esco.) 1. Sagaz, prudente, cuerdo. 2. Agradable, placentero; garboso; digno.

Canoe [ca-nū'], *s.* Canoa.

Canon [can'-on], *s.* 1. Canon, regla, ley, estatuto. 2. Canon o cánones, leyes establecidas por los concilios, que tratan de la disciplina eclesiástica. 3. Canónigo, el que posee una prebenda o canongía en las catedrales o colegiatas. 4. Canon, catálogo de los libros sagrados y auténticos aceptados por la Iglesia. 5. Canon, un grado de la letra de imprenta, letra gruesa.

Canoness [can'-on-es], *sf.* Canonesa, la doncella que posee una de las prebendas que hay en algunas partes, destinadas a mujeres.

Canonic, Canonical [ca-non'-ic, al], *a.* Canónico, según los cánones o según las leyes eclesiásticas; espiritual.

Canonically [ca-non'-i-cal-i], *adv.* Canónicamente.

Canonicals [ca-non'-i-calz], *s. pl.* Hábitos eclesiásticos, vestidos clericales.

Canonicate [ca-non'-i-kêt], *s.* Canonicato.

Canonist [can'-on-ist], *s.* Canonista, profesor de derecho canónico.

Canonization [can-on-ai-zê'-shun], *s.* Canonización, declaración del Sumo Pontífice, por la cual se pone en el número de los santos a alguno que ha vivido ejemplarmente.

Canonize [can'-on-aiz], *va.* Canonizar, poner en el número de los santos.

Canonry [can'-on-ri], **Canonship** [can'-on-ship], *s.* Canongía o canonicato; prebenda.

Canopied [can'-o-pid], *a.* Endoselado.

Canopy [can'-o-pi], *s.* Dosel, pabellón. (Aer.) Cabina cerrada transparente. *Canopy of a bed,* Cielo de cama colgada.

Canopy, *va.* Endoselar, cubrir con dosel.

Canorous [ca-nō'-rus], *a.* Canoro, lo que produce un sonido agradable al oído; melodioso, musical.

Can't [cant]. (Fam.) Abreviación de *cannot.* *V.* CAN.

Cant [cant], *s.* 1. Jerigonza, germanía, modo de hablar usado entre gitanos y gente vaga. 2. Hipocresía, fingimiento de piedad, virtud o devoción. 3. Almoneda pública. 4. Sesgo, posición oblicua, desviación de la línea vertical u horizontal. 5. (Ant.) Esquina, ángulo; escuadra.

Cant, *vn.* Hablar en jerigonza o germanía.—*va.* 1. Poner oblicuamente, o al sesgo; inclinar a un lado. 2. Derribar, invertir. 3. Almonedear; engaitar, engatusar.

Cantaloup o **Cantaloupe** [can'-ta-lūp], *s.* *Cantaloup,* variedad de melón de cáscara rugosa y pulpa anaranjada.

Cantankerous [can-taṇ'-kẹr-us], *a.* (Fam.) Quimerista, pendenciero, propenso a poner faltas.

Cantata [can-tā'-ta], *s.* Cantata, canción. (Ital.)

Canted [cant'-ed], *a.* Oblicuo, inclinado.

Canteen [can-tîn'], *s.* 1. (Mil.) Cantina, bote de hoja de lata en que los soldados llevan agua o licor. 2. Cantina, puesto en el campo donde se vende vino, cerveza y licores.

Cantel [can'-tel], *s.* *V.* CANTLE, 1ª acep.

Canter [can'-tẹr], *s.* Medio galope.

Canter, *vn.* Andar el caballo a paso largo y sentado.

Cant-frames [cant'-frêmz], *s. pl.* (Mar.) Cuadernas reviradas. *Cant-timbers,* o *cant-crotches,* Piques capuchinos o revirados.

Cantharides [can-thar'-i-dîz], *s.* Cantáridas.

Canthus [can'-thus], *s.* Canto o ángulo del ojo.

Canticle [can'-ti-cl], *s.* 1. Cántico, canto o canción. 2. El Cantar de los Cantares de Salomón.

Cantilever [can-ti-lev'-er], *s.* (Arq.) Ménsula, viga voladiza.

Cantingly [cant'-ing-li], *adv.* Hipócritamente.

Cantle, Cantlet [cant'-let], *s.* 1. Pedazo, fragmento o residuo. 2. Borrén, trasero del arzón de una silla de montar.

Canto [can'-tō], *s.* Canto, parte de algún poema u obra de poesía.

Canton [can'-ten], *s.* Cantón, porción de territorio con el correspondiente número de habitantes; una de las 22 divisiones de la Confederación Suiza.

Canton, Cantonize [can'-ten-aiz], *va.* Acantonar, acuartelar, distribuir en cuarteles separados.

Cantonment [can'-ten-mẹnt], *s.* Acuartelamiento, acantonamiento.

Cantor [can'-ter], *s.* Chantre, cantor principal.

Canty [can'-ti], *a.* (Esco.) Alegre, jovial, festivo.

Canvas [can'-vas], *s.* 1. Lona, tela tosca y fuerte hecha de cáñamo o algodón. 2. Cañamazo, tela gruesa y clara sobre la que se borda con seda o lana. 3. Lienzo, tela tendida sobre un bastidor y preparada para recibir colores. 4. (Mar.) Lona, vela, velamen.

Canvas-back [can'-vas-bac''], *s.* Pato marino de la América del Norte, muy estimado por su carne. (Aythya.)

Canvass, *s.* 1. El acto de solicitar votos para lograr algún destino; pretensión. 2. Examen, inspección oficial de alguna cosa. 3. Investigación circunstanciada.

Canvass, *va.* 1. Escudriñar, examinar. 2. Disputar, controvertir.—*vn.* Solicitar votos para lograr algún destino, pretender, ser candidato en alguna elección; ambicionar, escudriñar.

Canvasser [can'-vas-ẹr], *s.* 1. Solicitador; particularmente el que solicita comercio o negocios yendo de casa en casa. 2. (E. U.) Agente electoral.

Canyon [can'-yun], *s.* Cañón, desfiladero.

Canzonet [can-zo-net'], *s.* Cancioneta o cancioncilla, canción pequeña.

Caoutchouc [cū' chuc], *s.* Goma elástica, hule; jugo resinoso y lechoso de varios árboles tropicales.

Cap [cap], *s.* 1. Gorro o gorra, que se pone en la cabeza. 2. Birreta o capelo, la insignia de cardenal. 3. Tapa (de lente). 4. (Mar.) Tamboretes, tablones gruesos, que se ponen al remate del palo. 5. Sombrero de mortero. 6. Reverencia hecha con la gorra. 7. Cima, cumbre, el punto más elevado. *Fool's cap*, (1) Nombre de una especie de papel para escribir, cuya dimensión corresponde al marquilla español. (2) (En las escuelas) Orejas de burro. *Percussion cap*, Cápsula, pistón fulminante. *The cap fits*, Viene de perilla. *To set one's cap for*, Proponerse o procurar conquistarse el amor de un hombre; dícese de la mujer que anda en busca de marido. *Cap paper*, Papel a propósito para escribir. *V.* PAPER.

Cap, *va.* 1. Poner cima o remate a; cubrir la punta de. 2. Cubrir la cabeza. 3. Saludar a uno. 4. Dar la última mano, acabar; también, sobrepujar.—*vn.* Quitarse el gorro en señal de reverencia o cortesía. *To cap verses*, Recitar versos.

Capability [kê-pa-bil'-i-ti], *s.* Capacidad, idoneidad, aptitud, inteligencia.

Capable [kê'-pa-bl], *a.* 1. Capaz, idóneo. 2. Capaz, inteligente. 3. Capaz, lo que puede contener alguna cosa. 4. Suficiente, bastante, apto, bueno, propio.

Capableness [kê'-pa-bl-nes], *s.* Capacidad, la propiedad de ser capaz.

Capacious [ca-pê'-shus], *a.* 1. Capaz, ancho. 2. Capaz, extensivo, espacioso, extenso, grande, vasto.

Capaciously [ca-pê'-shus-li], *adv.* Extensivamente.

Capaciousness [ca-pê'-shus-nes], *s.* Capacidad, cabida.

Capacitate [ca-pas'-i-têt], *va.* Habilitar, hacer capaz, investir de autoridad conforme a la ley.

Capacity [ca-pas'-i-ti], *s.* 1. Capacidad, cabida. 2. Inteligencia, poder, habilidad, capacidad, comprehensión, saber. 3. Calidad, estado, condición, carácter. 4. Calidad, empleo, destino.

Cap and gown [cap and gaun], *s.* Toga y birrete.

Cap-a-pie [cap-a-pī'], *adv.* De pies a cabeza, de punta en blanco.

Caparison [ca-par'-i-sun], *s.* Caparazón, cubierta que se pone a los caballos para tapar la silla y el aderezo.

Caparison, *va.* 1. Enjaezar un caballo. 2. (Fam.) Vestir soberbiamente.

Cape [kêp], *s.* 1. Cabo, promontorio o punta de tierra. *To double* o *sail round a cape*, (Mar.) Doblar o montar un cabo. 2. Capa corta, esclavina, manteleta.

Caper [kê'-pẹr], *s.* 1. Cabriola, salto o brinco. 2. Alcaparra, fruta del alcaparro. 3. Corsario holandés del siglo XVII. *Cross capers*, Desgracias, trabajos. *To cut a caper*, Cabriolar, dar un brinco súbito.

Caper, *vn.* 1. Cabriolar, cabriolear, hacer cabriolas. 2. (Fam.) Bailotear, brincar.

Caperbush [kê'-pẹr-bush], *s.* (Bot.) Alcaparra o alcaparro, la mata que produce las alcaparras.

Caperer [kê'-pẹr-ẹr], *s.* Danzador, saltador.

Caper-spurge [kê'-pẹr-spūrj], *s.* (Bot.) Tártago o catapacia menor.

Capias [kê'-pi-as], *s.* Auto ejecutivo o de ejecución. (Lat.)

Capillaceous [cap-i-lê'-shus], *a.* Capilar, delgado, semejante a un cabello.

Capillaire [cap-i-lār'], *s.* Jarabe de culantrillo.

†**Capillament** [ca-pil'-a-mẹnt], *s.* (Fr. Bot.) Estambre o hebra de flor.

Capillarity [cap-i-lar'-i-ti], *s.* Capilaridad, atracción capilar.

Capillary [cap'-i-lẹ-ri], *a.* 1. Semejante a un cabello, capilar, delgado. 2. Que pertenece a los vasos capilares. 3. Que pertenece a los fenómenos que se observan en los líquidos contenidos en tubos muy delgados, y a otros de atracción molecular.—*s.* (Anat.) Vaso capilar.

Capillose [cap'-i-lōs], *a.* Cabelludo.

Capillation [cap-i-lê'-shun], *s.* Ramificación pequeña de vasos.

Capital [cap'-i-tal], *a.* 1. Capital, que pertenece a la cabeza. 2. Criminal, capital. 3. Mayúscula, hablando de letras. 4. Excelente, brillante, magnífico. 5. Principal. —*s.* 1. Capitel o chapitel de una columna. 2. Capital, la ciudad principal o cabeza de algún gobierno. 3. Capital, fondo, principal, caudal productivo.

Capitalism [cap'-i-tal-izm], *s.* Capitalismo.

Capitalist [cap'-i-tal-ist], *s.* Capitalista, el dueño de un capital, fondo o caudal productivo.

Capitalize [cap'-i-tal-aiz], *va.* 1. Capitalizar, agregar al capital el importe de los intereses; reducir la renta al capital. 2. Principiar una palabra con mayúscula.

Capitally [cap'-i-tal-i], *adv.* 1. Excelentemente, admirablemente. 2. Capitalmente con pena de muerte.

Capital punishment [cap'-i-tal pun'-ish-mẹnt], *s.* Pena capital, pena de muerte.

Capitate [cap'-i-têt], *a.* (Bot.) Capitado, dispuesto en forma de cabezuela.

Capitation [cap-i-tê'-shun], *s.* Encabezamiento o empadronamiento.

Capitol [cap'-i-tel], *s.* 1. Capitolio, ciudadela antigua de Roma. 2. Capitolio, palacio del congreso en Washington, Estados Unidos de América; y edificio del poder legislativo en los diferentes Estados de la Unión.

Capitoline [cap'-i-to-lain], *a.* Perteneciente al capitolio romano, capitolino.

Capitular [ca-pit'-yu-lar], *s.* Estatutos capitulares, o el libro capitular en que se ponen.

Capitularly [ca-pit'-yu-lar-li], *adv.* Capitularmente.

Capitulary [ca-pit'-yu-la-ri], *a.* Capitular.

Capitulate [ca-pit'-yu-lêt], *vn.* 1. (Mil.) Capitular, rendirse o entregarse bajo ciertas condiciones. 2. (Des.) Escribir alguna cosa dividiéndola en capítulos.

Capitulation [ca-pit-yu-lê'-shun], *s.* 1. Capitulación, tratado, condición o términos con que se entrega alguna ciudad o plaza. 2. El acto de escribir por capítulos.

Capitulator [ca-pit'-yu-lê-tẹr], *s.* Capitulante, el que capitula.

Capnomancy [cap'-no-man-si], *s.* Capnomancia, pretendida adivinación por medio de las formas y la dirección del humo.

Capon [kê'-pen], *s.* Capón o pollo castrado.

Capot [ca-pet'], *s.* Capote, en varios juegos es cuando un jugador no deja baza al contrario, así como en otros se llama bola.

Capote [ca-pōt'], *s.* Capote, capota.

Cappadine [cap'-a-din], *s.* Cadarzo, seda basta de capullo.

Capparidaceous [cap-a-ri-dê'-shus], *a.* Caparídeo, que se parece o refiere al género alcaparra.

Capper [cap'-ẹr], *s.* 1. Gorrero, el que hace o vende gorras. 2. El que en las fábricas para conservar frutas, etc., solda las tapas sobre los botes de hoja de lata. 3. Herramienta para fijar las cápsulas en la cabeza de una granada.

Capreolate [cap'-re-o-lêt], *a.* (Bot.) Que tiene zarcillos o se asemeja a ellos. Dícese de las vides y otras plantas.

Caprice [ca-prīs'], *s.* Capricho, extravagancia; antojo, humor.

Capricious [ca-prish'-us], *a.* Caprichoso, caprichudo; antojadizo, extravagante.

Capriciously [ca-prish'-us-li], *adv.* Caprichosamente o caprichudamente.

Capriciousness [ca-prish'-us-nes], *s.* Capricho. *V.* CAPRICE.

Capricorn [cap'-ri-cōrn], *s.* (Astr.) Capricornio. *Capricorn-beetle*, (Ent.) Capricornio, especie de escarabajo.

Caprification [cap-ri-fi-kê'-shun], *s.* Caprificación, la acción de impregnar a la higuera hembra con el polen de la higuera macho, para que se madure el fruto.
Capriole [cap'-ri-ōl], *s.* Corveta, cabriola, salto que da un caballo.
Capsicum [cap'-si-cum], *s.* (Bot.) Pimiento, pimentero; pimiento de Guinea.
Capsize [cap'-saiz], *va.* y *vn.* Trabucar, trastornar, volcar, poner patas arriba, volver de arriba abajo, acostar, tumbar, quedar dormido, zozobrar.
Capstan [cap'-stan] o **Capstern** [cap'-stęrn], *s.* 1. Cabrestante, para levantar cosas de peso. 2. (Mar.) Cabrestante, máquina a bordo de un buque, por medio de la cual se levan las áncoras y se descargan los fardos más pesados. *Capstan-barrel*, Cuerpo o eje de cabrestante. *Capstan-whelps*, Guarda-infantes. *Capstan-chocks*, Cuñas de cabrestante. *Capstan-drumhead*, Cabeza de cabrestante. *Capstan - spindle*, Pínola del cabrestante. *Step of the capstan*, Concha o carlinga del cabrestante. *Capstan-bars*, Barras del cabrestante. *Capstan-pins*, Pernillos del cabrestante. *To rig the capstan*, Guarnir el cabrestante. *To heave the capstan*, Virar el cabrestante. *To pawl the capstan*, Pasar linguete. En las minas de Méjico, *Malacate*.
Capstone [cap'-stōn], *s.* Piedra que corona y remata un edificio o monumento.
Capsular [cap'-siu-lar], **Capsulary** [cap'-siu-la-ri], *a.* Capsular, en forma de bolsa o caja.
Capsulate, Capsulated [cap'-siu-lêt, ed], *a.* Cerrado en forma de cápsula.
Capsule [cap'-siūl], *s.* 1. (Bot.) Cápsula, hollejo que cubre el fruto de alguna planta. 2. (Quím.) Crisol para ensayar los minerales. 3. Cajita, bolsita.
Captain [cap'-tęn], *s.* (Mil.) 1. Capitán, el oficial que manda una compañía de soldados. 2. Jefe, comandante. *Captain of a ship of the line*, (Mar.) Capitán de navío. *Captain of the top*, Gaviero mayor.
Captaincy [cap'-ten-si], **Captainship** [cap'-ten-ship], *s.* Capitanía, el grado y empleo de capitán.
Caption [cap'-shun], *s.* 1. Título, rótulo, introducción de un documento legal. 2. Membrete, encabezamiento. 3. Captura, prisión, la acción de prender a alguno.
Captious [cap'-shus], *a.* 1. Susceptible, quisquilloso, caviloso. 2. Capcioso, sofístico, falaz.
Captiousness [cap'-shus-nes], *s.* Espíritu de contradicción; humor pendenciero o querellista.
Captivate [cap'-ti-vêt], *va.* 1. Cautivar, hacer a alguno cautivo; esclavizar. 2. Cautivar, atraer la voluntad.
Captivating [cap'-ti-vêt'-ing], *a.* Encantador, seductor, seductivo, atractivo.
Captivation [cap-ti-vê'-shun], *s.* Captura, la acción de hacer a uno prisionero o cautivo.
Captive [cap'-tiv], *s.* 1. Cautivo o esclavo. 2. Prisionero.—*a.* Cautivo.
Captivity [cap-tiv'-i-ti], *s.* 1. Cautiverio o cautividad, prisión. 2. Sujeción mental; influencia ejercida por una persona sobre la mente o la voluntad de otra.
Captor [cap'-tər], *s.* Apresador, el que coge un prisionero o una presa.
Capture [cap'-chur], *s.* 1. Captura, la acción de prender. 2. Presa, botín, apresamiento.
Capture, *va.* Apresar, capturar.
Capuchin [cap-yu-chīn'], *s.* 1. Capuchino, religioso reformado de la orden de San Francisco. 2. Capucha y capotillo, especie de vestido exterior de señoras, algo parecido al de los capuchinos. 3. (Orn.) Especie de copete de plumas sobre la cabeza de los pájaros, en forma de capucha. 4. Capuchino, mono de la América del Sur, sapajú con el pelo de la cabeza en forma de capucha de fraile.
Capucin [cap'-yu-sin]. 1. Color rojizo anaranjado. 2. Capuchina, planta trepadora, y su flor.
Capulet [cap'-yu-let], *s.* Especie de capucha que usan las labradoras de Francia, cerca de la frontera española.
Car [cār], *s.* 1. (E. U.) Vagón, coche, carro de ferrocarril. 2. Carreta o carro de dos ruedas. 3. Carro militar, en que combatían antiguamente los héroes. 4. Caja de un ascensor. 5. *Car of a balloon*, Barquilla de globo aerostático. *Baggage-car*, Coche de equipaje. *Dining-car*, Coche comedor. *Flat car*, Carro de plataforma. *Express car*, Coche del expreso, para bultos y paquetes. *Sleeping-car*, Coche dormitorio. *Cable-car*, *V.* Cable. *Postal car*, Coche estafeta. *Street car*, Coche de tranvía, carro urbano.
Carabine [car'-a-bain], **Carbine** [cār'-bain], *s.* Carabina, arma de fuego pequeña.
†**Carabineer**, †**Carabinier** [car-a-bin-īr'], *s.* *V.* Carbineer.
Carac [car'-ac], *s.* Carraca, navío grande y tardo en navegar.
Caracole [car'-a-cōl], *s.* 1. Caracol, la vuelta que hace el jinete con el caballo, como en medio torno. 2. Escalera de caracol.
Caracole, *vn.* Caracolear.
Carafe [ca-raf'], *s.* Garrafa, botella de cristal. (Fr.)
Caramel [car'-a-mel], *s.* 1. Caramelo, pasta de azúcar hecho almíbar al fuego y endurecido. 2. Caramelo, azúcar quemado para colorar licores.
Carapace [car'-a-pês], *s.* Carapacho, la concha (superior) de las tortugas y algunos otros animales.
Carat [car'-at], *s.* Quilate, ley, grado de bondad y perfección del oro; peso de cuatro granos con que se pesan los diamantes y perlas.
Caravan [car'-a-van], *s.* 1. Caravana, multitud de viajeros, peregrinos, traficantes, etc., que se juntan en Turquía y Oriente para seguridad en los desiertos y caminos. 2. Caravana, cada una de las cuatro campañas de mar que hacían los caballeros de Malta.
Caravel [car'-a-vel], **Carvel** [cār'-vel], *s.* Carabela, antigua embarcación larga y angosta, de una cubierta, tres mástiles y espolón a proa.
Caraway o **Caraway-seed** [car'-a-wê, sīd], *s.* (Bot.) Alcaravea.
Carbid(e) [cār'-bid], *s.* Carburo, combinación de carbón y un elemento positivo.
Carbine [cār -bain], *s.* Carabina, fusil pequeño.
Carbineer [cār-bin-īr'], *s.* Carabinero, soldado de caballería ligera armado con carabina.
Carbohydrate [cār-bo-hai'-drêt], *s.* Carbohidrato.
Carbolic [cār-bol'-ic], *a.* Perteneciente al aceite de alquitrán. *Carbolic acid*, Ácido carbólico o fénico. Llámase también *phenol*.
Carbolize [cār'-bol-aiz], *va.* Impregnar con ácido carbólico.
Carbon [cār'-bon], *s.* (Quím.) Carbón o carbono.
Carbonate [cār'-bon-êt], *s.* Carbonato, sal formada por el ácido carbónico unido a alguna base.
Carbonated [car'-bon-êt-ed], *a.* Carbonatado.
Carbon copy [cār'-bon cop'-i], *s.* Copia de carbón.
Carbon dioxide [cār'-bon dai-ox'-aid], *s.* (Quím.) Bióxido (o dióxido) de carbono.
Carbon 14 [car'-bun' fōr-tīn'], *s.* Carbono 14.
Carbonic [cār-bon'-ic], *a.* Carbónico.
Carboniferous [car-bon-if'-ęr-us], *a.* Carbonífero, que contiene o da carbón o hulla.
Carbonization [car-bon-i-zê'-shun], *s.* Carbonización, acción y efecto de carbonizar.
Carbonize [cār'-bon-aiz], *va.* 1. Carbonizar, reducir a carbón. 2. Cubrir papel con carbón, negro de humo, etc.
Carbon paper [cār'-bon pê'-pęr], *s.* Papel carbón.
Carborundum [cār-bo-run'-dum], *s.* (Quím.) Carborundo.
Carbuncle [cār'-buŋ-cl], *s.* 1. Carbúnculo o carbunclo, piedra preciosa que brilla en la obscuridad. 2. Carbunco, tumor puntiagudo y maligno con inflamación y dolor.
Carbuncled [cār'-buŋ-cld], *a.* 1. Engastado con carbunclos. 2. Lleno de granos.
Carbuncular [car-buŋ'-kiu-lar], *a.* Encarnado como un carbunclo.
Carburet [cār'-biu-ret], *s.* Carbureto, combinación del carbono con una base. *V.* Carbide.
Carburetor [cār-biu-rê'-tər], *s.* Carburador.
Carburize [cār'-biū-raiz], *va.* Combinar o impregnar con carbón.
Carcanet [cār'-ca-net], *s.* Collar o gargantilla de perlas o de otras piedras.
Carcass, Carcase [cār'-cas], *s.* 1. Res muerta o el cuerpo de un animal muerto; caparazón, hablando de aves. 2. Armazón de una casa. 3. (Mar.) Casco o armazón de una embarcación. 4. (Art.) Carcasa, especie de bomba oblonga.
Carcer [cār'-sęr], *s.* Cárcel, lugar de encierro. (Lat.)
Carceral [cār'-se-ral], *a.* Lo que pertenece a la cárcel.
Carcinogen [car-sin'-ǫ-jęn], *s.* (Med.) Carcinógeno.
Carcinoma [cār-si-nō'-ma], *s.* Carcinoma, cáncer.
Carcinomatous [cār-si-nom'-a-tus], *a.* Carcinomatoso, canceroso.
Card [cārd], *s.* 1. Naipe, carta, cartón pintado con diversos colores y figuras para jugar a varios juegos. *Pack of cards*, Una baraja de naipes. *To shuffle the cards*, Barajar las cartas. *To deal the cards*, Dar cartas. *To cut the cards*, Alzar o cortar las cartas para darlas. *Court card*, Figura. *Small card*, Carta sencilla. *Trump card*, Triunfo. *Card-table*, Mesa de juego. *Postal card*, Tarjeta postal. 2. Rosa naútica, la división que se hace en un círculo de cartón

para señalar los vientos; llámase también rosa de los vientos. 3. Tarjeta. 4. Cardencha, carda, instrumento para cardar lana.
Card, *va.* 1. Cardar lana; mezclar; desenredar. 2. Peinar y limpiar el pelo de los caballos con una carda.
Cardamine [cār'-da-min], *s.* (Bot.) Mastuerzo de prado, hierba de las crucíferas.
Cardamom [cār'-da-mom], *s.* Cardamomo o grana del paraíso.
Cardass [car-das'], *s.* 1. Alanquia, carda grande de peinar seda. 2. Cardencha, carda para la lana.
Cardboard [cārd-bōrd], *s.* Cartón. *Cardboard binding,* Encuadernación en cartoné, encuadernación con pastas de cartón.
Card catalogue, *s.* Catálogo de tarjetas o fichas.
Carder [cārd'-ẹr], *s.* 1. Cardador. 2. *Carder,* o *carder-bee,* Abejorro que carda y fieltra el musgo para su nido. Bombus muscorum.
Cardiac [cār'-di-ac], *a.* Cardiaco, cordial.
Cardialgia, Cardialgy [cār'-di-al-ji], *s.* (Med.) Cardialgia.
Cardigan sweater [car'-di-gan swet'-ẹr], *s.* Suéter o chaqueta tejida con botonadura al frente.
Cardinal [cār'-di-nal], *a.* 1. Cardinal, principal, primero. 2. De color rojo vivo como el ropaje de los cardenales; bermellón.—*s.* 1. Cardenal, prelado de la Iglesia romana que tiene voz activa y pasiva en el cónclave para la elección del Pontífice. 2. Capa de mujer, del siglo XVIII. *Cardinal-bird,* Cardenal, pájaro rojo de la familia de los fringílidos. Cardinalis cardinalis. *Cardinal-flower,* Escurripa, hierba perenne norteamericana con flores de color rojo vivo. Lobelia cardinalis.
Cardinalate [cār'-di-nal-ēt], **Cardinalship** [cār-di-nal-ship], *s.* Cardenalato, empleo o dignidad de cardenal.
Card index, *s.* Fichero, tarjetero.
Carding [cārd'-ing], *s.* 1. El juego de naipes. 2. Cardadura, el acto de cardar lana o algodón.
Cardiograph [cār'-di-o-graf], *s.* Cardiógrafo.
Cardiogram [cār'-di-o-gram], *s.* Cardiograma.
Cardiology [cār-di-ol'-o-ji], *s.* Cardiología.
Cardmaker [cārd'-mē-kẹr], *s.* Fabricante de naipes o de cardenchas.
Cardoon [car-dūn'], *s.* (Bot.) Cardo silvestre.
Card-party [cārd'-pār'-ti], *s.* Partido o partida, el conjunto de los que participan en un juego de naipes.
Carduus benedictus [cār'-diu-us ben-e-dic'-tus], *s.* (Bot.) Cardo santo o bendito. (Lat.)
Care [cār], *s.* 1. Cuidado, solicitud, inquietud, zozobra, desasosiego. 2. Cuidado, cautela. 3. Cuidado, cargo, objeto de cuidado. *To take care,* Tener cuidado. *To cast away care,* Olvidar penas, alegrarse, regocijarse. *Care-crazed,* Consumido de cuidados. *Care-worn,* Devorado de inquietud, lleno de zozobra.
Care, *vn.* 1. Cuidar, tener cuidado o pena, inquietarse o fatigarse de o por alguna cosa. 2. Estimar, apreciar, hacer caso. *What care I?* ¿A mí qué me importa? *Will you come to walk?* ¿Quiere Vd. venir a pasear? *I don't care if I do,* Como Vd. quiera; me importa poco el hacerlo o no; me es indiferente. *I do not care,* No se me da nada; no me importa, no me da cuidado. *He does not care to be seen there,* Él se ríe de que le vean allí. *Not to take care of one,* No hacer caso de alguno, despreciarle, desairarle.
Careen [ca-rīn'], *va.* (Mar.) Carenar o dar carena al navío, dar de lado a un barco para carenarle, o componerle. *Careening gear,* Aparejo de carenar. *Careening wharf,* Muelle de carenaje.—*vn.* Echarse de costado, dar a la banda.
Careening [ca-rīn'-ing], *s.* (Mar.) Carenamiento, el acto y efecto de carenar.
Career [ca-rīr'], *s.* 1. Carrera o curso de alguna cosa. 2. Carrera, el acto de correr rápidamente. 3. Carrera, profesión (armas, letras o ciencias). 4. (Des.) Carrera o estadio, el terreno en que se corre una carrera.
Career, *vn.* Correr a carrera tendida o a todo galope.
Carefree [cār'-frī], *a.* Despreocupado, sin cuidados.
Careful [cār'-ful], *a.* 1. Cuidadoso, ansioso, lleno de cuidados, inquieto. 2. Diligente, cauteloso, vigilante, avisado, prudente, solícito.
Carefully [car'-ful-i], *adv.* Cuidadosamente, con cuidado.
Carefulness [car'-ful-nes], *s.* Cuidado, vigilancia; cautela, atención, diligencia; ansiedad.
Careless [cār'-les], *a.* 1. Descuidado, negligente, omiso, indiferente, abandonado. 2. Alegre, tranquilo. 3. Desenfadado; sencillo. 4. Dejado, flojo, indolente, perezoso. 5. Inconsiderado, hecho o dicho sin reflexión.
Carelessly [cār'-les-li], *adv.* Descuidadamente, negligentemente; con indiferencia.
Carelessness [car'-les-nes], *s.* Descuido, negligencia, abandono, indiferencia, dejadez, flojedad, incuria.
Caress [ca-res'], *va.* Acariciar, halagar.
Caress, *s.* Caricia, halago.
Caret [car'-et o kē'-ret], *s.* Nota de corrección interlineal.
Cargo [cār'-gō], *s.* Carga, cargazón cargamento de un buque.
Caribou [car'-i-bū], *s.* El reno norteamericano. (Francés canadiense.)
Caricature [car-i-ca-chūr], *s.* Caricatura.
Caricature, *va.* Hacer caricaturas, ridiculizar; representar falsamente.
Caricaturist [car'-i-ca-chūr-ist], *s.* El que hace caricaturas.
Caries [kē'-ri-īz], **Cariosity** [kē-ri-os'-i-ti], *s.* Caries, ulceración o corrosión de los huesos o dientes.
Carina [ca-rī'-na], *s.* Carena, pétalo inferior de ciertas flores; prolongación del tallo en las hojas.
Carinate [car'-i-nẹt], *a.* Carenado; dícese de la flor que presenta la forma de una carena o quilla de buque.
Carious [kē'-ri-us], *a.* Carioso, lo que tiene caries.
Cark [cārk], *vn.* (Ant.) Ser muy cuidadoso; estar consumido a fuerza de cuidados.
Carking [cārk'-ing], *a.* Devorador, acerbo, que causa cuidado o inquietud; penoso.
Carl [cārl], *s.* Patán, rústico; hombre ruin, grosero, villano.
Carline, Carling [cār'-lin, ling], *s.* Carlinga, madero fijo sobre la quilla, en el que entra la mecha del palo. (Mar.) Atravesaños de las latas. *Carlings of the hatchways,* (Mar.) Galeotas de las escotillas.
Carload [cār'-lōd], *s.* (F.C.) Furgón entero.
Carlock [cār'-lec], *s.* Variedad de colapez rusa.
Carman [cār'-man], *s.* Carretero, carromatero.
Carmelite [cār'-mel-ait], *s.* 1. Carmelita, religioso o religiosa del Carmen. 2. Tela fina de lana, ordinariamente de color gris. 3. Especie de pera.
Carminative [cār-min'-a-tiv], *a.* Carminante o carminativo, lo que pertenece a los remedios contra los flatos.
Carmine [cār'-min], *s.* Carmín, color rojo muy encendido; la materia colorante de la cochinilla.
Carnage [cār'-nẹj], *s.* Carnicería, mortandad.
Carnal [cār'-nal], *a.* 1. Carnal, lo que pertenece a la carne por contraposición a lo que es espiritual. 2. Carnal, lujurioso, sensual, brutal. *Carnal-minded,* Sensual, mundano.
Carnalist [cār'-nal-ist], *s.* El que es lujurioso o lascivo.
Carnality [car-nal'-i-ti], *s.* 1. Carnalidad, sensualidad, lujuria, concupiscencia, lascivia. 2. Propensión o acto carnal.
Carnalize [cār'-nal-aiz], *va.* Hacer carnal, excitar la sensualidad; atribuir carnalidad.
Carnally [cār'-nal-i], *adv.* Carnalmente.
Carnation [car-nē'-shun], *s.* 1. (Pint.) Encarnación, color natural de la carne. 2. Clavel doble, flor muy fragante y hermosa.
Carnationed [car-nē'-shund], *a.* Encarnado como un clavel.
Carnelian [car-nī'-lian], *s.* Cornerina, piedra preciosa, variedad de calcedonia.
Carneous [cār'-ne-us], *a.* Carnoso, carnudo, lleno de carne.
Carnification [car-ni-fi-kē'-shun], *s.* Carnificación, una alteración patológica de los órganos.
Carnify [cār'-ni-fai], *vn.* Carnificarse, criar carne.
Carnival [cār'-ni-val], *s.* 1. Carnaval 2. Parque de atracciones.
Carnivora [cār-niv'-o-ra], *s. pl.* Carnívoros, orden de animales que se alimentan de carne.—CARNIVOR, uno de los carnívoros.
Carnivorous [car-niv'-o-rus], *a.* Carnívoro, carnicero.
Carnosity [car-nos'-i-ti], *s.* Carnosidad.
Carnous [cār'-nus], *a.* Carnoso, carnudo. *V.* CARNEOUS.
Carob [car'-ob], *s.* (Bot.) 1. Algarroba, árbol, y su fruto. 2. Algarroba, planta anual y su semilla.
Carob-bean [car'-ob-bīn], *s.* Algarroba, el fruto del algarrobo.
Carol [car'-ol], *s.* Villancico de Nochebuena o Navidad, canción alegre y piadosa.
Carol, *va.* Cantar, celebrar la Navidad con canciones o villancicos.
Carom [car'-um], *s.* Carambola (en el juego de billar).
Carotid, Carotidal [ca-rot'-id, al], *a.* Carótidas, dos arterias que nacen del tronco ascendente de la aorta.
Carousal [ca-rau'-zal], *s.* 1. Festín, o función de alboroto y gresca. 2. Francachela, comida alegre entre amigos. 3. Jarana, gresca.
Carouse [ca-rauz'], *va.* y *s.* Jaranear, alborotar. (Fam.) Correrla. Beber excesivamente, embriagarse.

Carouse, *s.* Borrachera, jarana.
Carousel [car'-ū-zel], *s.* 1. *V.* MERRY-GO-ROUND. 2. Liza, justa o torneo. (Fr.)
Carouser [ca-rauz'-ęr], *s.* Bebedor, jaranero.
Carp [cārp], *s.* Carpa, pez de agua dulce.
Carp, *vn.* Censurar, criticar, vituperar, afear; sutilizar; regañar.
Carpal [cār'-pal], *a.* De, o cerca de, la muñeca.—*s.* Hueso de la muñeca.
Carpel [cār'-pel], *s.* (Bot.) Carpelo, cada uno de los frutos o pistilos parciales de una misma flor.
Carpenter [cār'-pen-tęr], *s.* Carpintero. *Ship-carpenter*, Carpintero de ribera o de buque.
Carpentry [cār'-pen-tri], *s.* 1. Carpintería. 2. Maderaje, maderamen. *Carpenter and joiner*, Carpintero ensamblador, ebanista.
Carper [cārp'-ęr], *s.* Regañón, criticón, censurador; maldiciente, murmurador.
Carpet [cār'-pet], *s.* 1. Tapete de mesa. 2. Alfombra o tapiz. *To be on the carpet*, Estar examinándose algún negocio o cuestión; hablarse mucho de alguna cosa; traer a alguna persona o suceso de boca en boca. *Carpet-beetle*, Antreno, escarabajo cuya larva destruye alfombras y telas de lana.
Carpet, *va.* Alfombrar, entapizar.
Carpeting [cār'-pet-ing], *s.* 1. Materia o tela para alfombras; alfombra o tapete, en general. 2. El acto o la acción de alfombrar.
Carpet sweeper [cār'-pet swīp'-ęr], *s.* Barredor de alfombras.
Carpet-walk [cār'-pet-wōk], **Carpet-way** [cār'-pet-wê], *s.* Camino alfombrado o cubierto de césped.
Carphology [cār-fel'-o-ji], *s.* (Med.) Carfología, acción inconsciente de arañar y plegar el enfermo las ropas de la cama; obsérvase en casos de delirio y fiebre lenta y se considera como síntoma mortal.
Carping [cārp'-ing], *a.* Capcioso, porfiado, caviloso.—*s.* Efugio, censura.
Carpingly [cārp'-ing-li], *adv.* Mordazmente.
Car pool [car' pūl], *s.* Transporte colectivo en automóvil a prorrata.
Carport [car'-port], *s.* Cobertizo para automóvil.
Carpus [cār'-pus], *s.* Carpo, muñeca, la parte del cuerpo que está entre el antebrazo y la palma de la mano.
Carrageen [car''-a-gīn'], *s.* Musgo de Irlanda, alga marina abundante en las costas peñascosas. Chondrus crispus.
Carriage [car'-ij], *s.* 1. Porte, conducción, acarreo o transporte de alguna cosa de una parte a otra. 2. Porte, presencia, continente, aire de una persona. 3. Porte, conducta o modo de proceder. 4. Coche, carroza; vehículo. 5. Carga. 6. Cureña de cañón. 7. En la Gran Bretaña, vagón de ferrocarril. 8. Pieza de una máquina sobre la cual descansa y funciona otra, como en los tornos, taladros, etc. *Carriage paid*, Porte pagado. *Carriage free*, Franco de porte. *Carriage and four*, Carroza de cuatro caballos.
Carrier [car'-i-ęr], *s.* 1. Portador, el que lleva alguna cosa. 2. Arriero, ordinario, carretero o conductor de mercaderías. 3. Mensajero, el que lleva algún recado, despacho o noticia de otro. *Carrier-pigeon*, Paloma correo, o mensajera.
Carrion [car'-i-un], *s.* 1. Carroña, la carne corrompida. 2. Carne muerta que no sirve para alimento. 3. Pulpón, pelleja, desollada; dícese de una mujer abandonada.—*a.* Mortecino, podrido.
Carron-oil [car'-en-eil''], *s.* Mezcla de una parte de agua de cal y dos de aceite de linaza: se usa en casos de quemaduras recientes.
Carrot [car'-ęt], *s.* (Bot.) Zanahoria.
Carroty [car'-et-i], *a.* Pelirrojo, el que tiene el pelo de color de zanahoria.
Carry [car'-i], *va.* 1. Llevar, conducir de una parte a otra. 2. Llevar encima, tener consigo. 3. Llevar, arrebatar o quitar. 4. Llevar a efecto alguna cosa. 5. Llevar adelante. 6. Buscar y traer, como hacen los perros de agua. 7. Conseguir, lograr. 8. Contener; importar; mostrar.—*vn.* Alcanzar, llegar (hablando de armas de fuego). *To carry about*, Llevar de un lado a otro, o llevar de una parte a otra. *To carry along*, Alzar, llevarse una cosa. *To carry arms*, (1) Pertenecer al ejército. (2) Llevar o portar armas. (3) (Mil.) Cuadrarse, sosteniendo el fusil, espada u otra arma en posición vertical, a lo largo del cuerpo y apoyada contra el hombro. *To carry away*, Llevarse, quitar, mudar una cosa de un lugar a otro, alzar. *To carry away by force*, Arrebatar, quitar de delante, tomar por fuerza, llevar tras sí con violencia alguna cosa, robar. *To carry back*, Restituir, traer a la mano, volver a llevar, traer o sacar, devolver, acompañar a alguno al paraje de donde se le había sacado. *To carry coals to Newcastle*, Llevar hierro a Vizcaya, o leña al monte; llevar géneros a donde los hay de sobra. *To carry down*, Hacer bajar, descender, conducir, acarrear, portear. *To carry forth*, Sacar, mostrar, hacer parecer, hacer salir de alguna parte, hacer progresar una cosa; sostener una opinión. *To carry in*, Introducir meter o llevar adentro, hacer entrar. *To carry into*, Llevar a efecto, poner en ejecución o en planta. *To carry on*, Mantener, sostener, fomentar. *To carry off*, Alzar, llevarse una cosa; arrastrar, disipar. *To carry on*, Promover; continuar; mantener, sostener, conducir, llevar adelante, empujar; proseguir. *To carry out*, Llevar a cabo, desarrollar, realizar; sacar, mostrar, hacer parecer, hacer salir de alguna parte; hacer progresar alguna cosa; sostener una opinión. *To carry over*, Transportar; hacer atravesar. *To carry to and fro*, Llevar de un lado a otro o llevar de aquí para allí. *To carry through*, Sostener; vencer dificultades, llevar a buen término. *To carry up*, Hacer subir, elevar. *To carry all before one* Hacerse dueño de todo; vencer o sobrepujar todos los obstáculos, apoderarse de todo, alcanzar cuanto se desea. (Fam.) Dejar atrás, echar el pie atrás a. *To carry it high*, Afectar señorío o grandeza, hacer de persona. *To carry the cause*, Ganar la sentencia. *To carry the day*, Quedar victorioso, alcanzar victoria. *To carry one's self well*, Saber vivir, conducirse debidamente, portarse bien. *A pillar that carries false*, Una columna que falsea o se está cayendo. *Carried over* o *forward*, (en las cuentas), Pasa al frente, o pasa a la vuelta; suma y sigue.
Carry, *s.* (Prov.) Movimiento de las nubes.
Carry-all [car'-i-ōl], *s.* (E. U.) Carruaje de familia, ligero, cubierto, de cuatro ruedas y generalmente tirado por un solo caballo.
Cart [cārt], *s.* Carro, carromato, carreta, carruaje. *Cart-horse*, Caballo de tiro. *Cart-wheel*, Rueda de carro. *Garbage* o *Offal cart*, Carro de basura. *Cart-load*, Carretada, carga de carro o carreta. *Cart-rope*, Cuerda gorda. *Cart-way*, Carril, camino carretero.
Cart, *va.* Carretear, acarrear con carros o carretas.—*vn.* Usar carretas o carros.
Cartage [cārt'-ēj], *s.* Carretaje, paga por el uso de un carro.
Carte-blanche [cārt-blańsh'], *s.* 1. Carta blanca, papel o firma en blanco, para que ponga en él lo que quiera la persona a quien se da. 2. Autorización verbal o escrita ilimitada; amplias facultades.
Cartel [cār'-tel], *s.* 1. Cartel, reglas acordadas entre dos enemigos para el rescate, canje o cambio de prisioneros; se llama también así el buque que lleva prisioneros canjeados. 2. Cartel de desafío. 3. Cartel, papel escrito o cartelón impreso; anuncio, tablilla.
Carter [cārt'-ęr], *s.* Carretero.
Cartesian [cār-tī'-zian], *s.* y *a.* Cartesiano, el que sigue el sistema filosófico de Cartesio o Descartes y de sus discípulos.
Carthusian [car-thiū'-zian], *s.* Cartujo, el monje de la orden de San Bruno.
Cartilage [cār'-ti-lēj], *s.* (Anat.) Cartílago, ternilla.
Cartilaginous [car-ti-laj'-in-us], *a.* Cartilaginoso, ternilloso.
Cartographer [car-teg'-ra-fęr], *s.* Véase su equivalente CHARTOGRAPHER.
Cartography [car-teg'-ra-fi], *s.* Cartografía, dibujo de mapas.
Carton [cār'-ten], *s.* Caja de cartón fino, o el cartón para hacer esas cajas.
Cartoon [cār-tūn'], *s.* 1. Cartón, dibujo hecho en papel grueso, que representa el asunto o adorno que después ha de ejecutarse en pintura al fresco, mosaicos, tapices, vidrios, etc. 2. Dibujo o caricatura, por lo general de carácter político o satírico.
Cartouch [cār-tūsh'], *s.* 1. Cartucho de balas o metralla. 2. Cartuchera. 3. Cartón, adorno de diferentes formas con una inscripción en el centro.
Cartridge [cār'-trij], *s.* Cartucho de pólvora para cargar cañones o fusiles. *Cartridge-box*, Cartuchera, caja para llevar cartuchos. *Blank cartridge*, Cartucho sin bala.
Cart-rut [cārt'-rut], *s.* Carril, rodada, el vestigio o señal que deja la rueda de un carro.
Cartulary [cār'-tiu-lę-ri], *s.* 1. Cartulario, el libro donde se asientan y copian los privilegios y donaciones otorgados a favor de una iglesia o convento. 2. Guarda de cartulario. 3. Papelera.
Cartwright [cārt'-rait], *s.* Carretero, el carpintero que hace carros, carretas y carretones.
Caruncle [car'-uŋ-cl], *s.* Carúncula, excrecencia pequeña de carne.

Carve [cārv], *va.* 1. Esculpir en madera o piedra; cincelar, tallar, entallar; abrir de talla; embutir. *Carved work,* Entallado, obra de talla. 2. Trinchar, cortar o dividir las viandas en la mesa. 3. Grabar. 4. Distribuir. 5. Apropiar.—*vn.* 1. Cortar cualquier material. 2. Trinchar.

Carvel [cār'-vel], *s.* (Mar.) Carabela. *V.* CARAVEL.

Carven [cārv'-n], *a.* (Poét.) Esculpido, entallado, grabado.

Carver [cārv'-ęr], *s.* 1. Escultor, el artífice que esculpe en madera o piedra; grabador, entallador, tallista. 2. Trinchante, el que trincha las viandas en la mesa.

Carving [cārv'-ing], *s.* 1. Escultura o figuras esculpidas; talla. 2. El arte de trinchar. 3. La acción de trinchar.

Caryatid [car-i-at'-id], **Caryatides** [car-i-at'-i-dīz], *s. pl.* Cariátide, especie de columna o pilastra en figura de mujer, que sirve para sostener el arquitrabe.

Casal [kē'-sal], *a.* (Gram.) Perteneciente a un caso o casos.

Cascabel [cas'-ca-bel], *s.* 1. Cascabel, remate esférico de la parte posterior del cañón de artillería. 2. Serpiente de cascabel, o el cascabel mismo.

Cascade [cas-kēd'], *s.* Cascada, salto o despeñadero de agua desde un lugar elevado.

Cascara sagrada [cas'-ca-ra sa-gra'-da], *s.* (Bot.) Cáscara sagrada.

Cascarilla [cas-ca-ril'-a], *s.* Cascarilla, corteza aromática de un arbusto de las Antillas.

Case [kēs], *s.* 1. Caso, suceso, acontecimiento. 2. Casualidad, caso, lance, coyuntura. 3. Estado o condición de alguna cosa; situación. 4. Enfermedad, mal. 5. Contingencia. 6. Caso, cuestión relativa a personas o cosas particulares. 7. (Gram.) Caso, las diversas inflexiones de los nombres. *The case in point,* El caso en cuestión, el asunto de que se trata. *In any case,* A todo evento, en todo caso. *In the case of,* En cuanto a, respecto a. *In a sad case,* En una triste posición. *To make out one's case,* Demostrar lo que uno se proponía. *A case in law,* Un proceso, una causa, un pleito. *In case,* Si acaso. (Fam.) Gordo o lucio.

Case [kēs], *s.* 1. Caja, estuche, vaina, funda, cubierta. 2. Caja, y el contenido de ella. 3. Caja de imprenta. *Upper case,* Caja alta, de mayúsculas o versales, versalitas y signos. *Lower case,* Caja baja, de minúsculas, números, puntuación y espacios. *Book-case,* Estante de libros. *Dressing-case,* Tocador. *Jewel-case,* Cofrecito de joyas. *Needle-case,* Alfiletero. *Glass-case,* Vidriera, mostrüario. *Cigar-case,* Tabaquera. *Pillow-case,* Funda de almohada. *Pistol-case,* Pistolera, funda de pistolas. *Case-knife,* Cuchillo de mesa.

Case, *va.* 1. Encajar, poner en caja o estuche alguna cosa. 2. Cubrir, resguardar.

Caseharden [kēs'-hārd-n], *va.* Endurecer por fuera, templar la superficie del hierro, convirtiéndola en acero.

Casein [kē'-sę-in], *s.* 1. Caseína, principio albuminoso de la leche de que se forma el queso. 2. Legúmina, albúmina vegetal.

Casemate [kēs'-mēt], *s.* (Fort.) Casamata, caserna, construcción abovedada para protección de las tropas, depósito de víveres, etc.; también, mampara acorazada de a bordo horadada para los cañones de banda.

Casement [kēs'-męnt], *s.* 1. Puerta ventana. 2. (Fort.) Barbacana. 3. Cubierta, caja.

Casern [ca-zęrn'], *s.* 1. Caserna, alojamiento inmediato al terraplén. 2. Cuartel, edificio donde se alojan los soldados de una guarnición.

Case-shot [kēs'-shot], *s.* Balas encajonadas.

Caseworker [kēs'-wūrk-ęr], *s.* Investigador, estudioso de los antecedentes de un caso sociológico.

Cash [cash], *s.* 1. Dinero contante, dinero contante y sonante. 2. Fondos disponibles. *Cash discount,* Descuento en efectivo.

Cash [cash], *va.* Cambiar, convertir en moneda o dinero contante (un billete, un cupón, etc.); hacer efectiva (una letra).

Cash-book [cash'-buk], *s.* Libro de caja.

Cashew [ca-shū'], *s.* Anacardo, árbol de las Antillas. *Cashew-nut,* Anacardo, fruto medicinal del árbol del mismo nombre.

Cashier [cash-īr'], *s.* Cajero, el que guarda o tiene a su cargo el dinero.

Cashier, *va.* Destituir, quitarle a uno su empleo. (Mil.) Desaforar, esto es, arrojar ignominiosamente de un regimiento o cuerpo a uno de sus oficiales.

Cashier's check [cash-īrz' chec], *s.* Cheque de caja.

Cashmere [cash'-mīr], *s.* 1. Casimir, tela fina y suave de lana para vestidos. 2. Tela fina suave y costosa hecha con lana de cabras de Cachemira, en la India. 3. Mantón o chal de cachemira.

Cash on delivery [cash en dę-liv'-ęr-i], *s.* Entrega contra reembolso, cóbrese al entregar.

Cashoo [ca-shū'], *s.* *V.* CATECHU.

Cash register [cash rej-is-tęr], *s.* Caja registradora.

Casing [kēs'-ing], *s.* 1. Cubierta, lo que recubre o aforra: estuche, envoltura. 2. Guarnición de una ventana o puerta.

Casings [kē'-singz], *s. pl.* (Prov. Ingla.) Boñiga seca para combustible.

Casino [ca-sī'-no], *s.* 1. Casino, salón de baile y de juego. 2. Casino, club social. 3. Variedad de juego de naipes.

Cask [cęsk], *s.* 1. Barril o tonel; cuba; casco. 2. Casco o casquete.

Cask, *va.* Entonelar.

Casket [cęs'-ket], *s.* 1. Cajita para joyas, casquete, estuche. *Wedding-casket,* Las donas. 2. (E. U.) Ataúd de metal o madera, pero de igual anchura en toda su extensión.

Casket, *va.* Poner en cajita.

Caskets [cas'-kets], *s.* (Mar.) *V.* GASKET.

Casque [cęsc], *s.* Casquete o casco, armadura que cubre y protege la cabeza. Antiguamente almete, capacete, morrión, casquete.

Cassation [cas-sē'-shun], *s.* 1. La acción de anular alguna cosa. 2. (For.) Casación, anulación de una sentencia o de un fallo judicial.

Cassava [cas-sā'-va], *s.* (Bot.) Cazabe, harina gruesa de América, hecha con la raíz de la yuca.

Casserole [cas'-ęr-ol], *s.* Cacerola. *Casserole, casserole dish,* Guiso a la cacerola.

Cassia [cash'-i-a], *s.* Casia, especie de canela. *Cassia buds,* Flores de casia.

Cassimere [cas'-i-mīr], *s.* Casimir, casimira o casimiro, tela de lana muy fina.

Cassino [ca-sī'-no], *s.* Un juego de naipes. *V.* CASINO.

Cassiterite [cas-sit'-ęr-ait], *s.* Casiterita, óxido de estaño; el más importante mineral de estaño.

Cassock [cas'-ec], *s.* Sotana o balandrán, vestidura talar que usan los eclesiásticos debajo del manteo.

Cassoon [cas-sūn'], *s.* (Arq.) Artesón, que se pone ordinariamente en las bóvedas o vueltas de los arcos.

Cassowary [cas'-o-wę-ri], *s.* (Zool.) Casoar, ave zancuda parecida al avestruz.

Cassweed [cas'-wīd], *s.* (Bot.) Bolsa de pastor.

Cast [cęst], *va.* (*pret.* y *pp.* CAST). 1. Tirar, arrojar, lanzar alguna cosa con la mano. 2. Tirar alguna cosa como inútil o dañosa. 3. Echar, verter. 4. Tirar dados o echar suertes. 5. Tumbar o derribar a uno luchando con él. 6. Mudar o estar de muda. 7. Desechar ropa. 8. Sobrepujar o exceder en el peso. 9. Ganar el pleito a su adversario. 10. Fundir, derretir. 11. Abortar, hablando de animales. 12. Modelar. 13. Comunicar por reflexión. 14. Ceder enteramente. 15. Imponer una pena. 16. Adicionar (una cuenta), computar, calcular. 17. Distribuir (los papeles de una comedia, etc.)—*vn.* 1. Idear o maquinar alguna cosa, discurriendo los medios para ejecutarla. 2. Amoldarse, recibir otra forma o figura. 3. Alabearse o torcerse la madera. 4. Vomitar. *To cast about,* Esparcir, derramar, arrojar por todos lados; considerar, meditar, revolver proyectos en la imaginación. *To cast against,* Reprochar, dar en rostro, echar en cara, vituperar, afear. *To cast aside,* Desechar, dejar o poner a un lado. *To cast away,* Desechar, dejar, abandonar; desterrar; echar a un lado, arrojar. *To be cast away,* Naufragar. *To cast down,* Abatir, derribar, echar por tierra: (fig.) Afligir, desanimar; abatir, humillar. *To cast forth,* Exhalar; centellear, relumbrar, echar rayos de luz. *To cast off,* Abandonar, desamparar; despojar; mudar la pluma; descartar; echar de sí. *To cast out,* Echar fuera, arrojar; espantar. *To cast up,* Calcular, sumar o ajustar alguna cuenta; vomitar; improperar; exhalar. *To cast up a bank,* Construir un dique. *To cast up one's eyes,* Levantar los ojos. *To cast upon,* Empañar, deslucir; recurrir, acudir. *To cast a fault upon,* Culpar, echar la culpa. *To cast an account,* Ajustar una cuenta. *To cast headlong,* Precipitar. *To cast her young,* Malparir (se dice de los animales). *To cast his coat,* Mudar pellejo. *To cast into a form,* Dar la forma de. *To cast into sleep,* Adormecer. *To cast one behind,* Adelantarse a alguno, dejarle atrás. *To cast scorn upon,* Despréciar. *To cast the eyes on,* Mirar, poner la vista o los ojos; echar la vista o los ojos. *Cast it in his teeth,* Arrójele Vd. eso al rostro, o a la faz. *To cast lots,* Echar suertes. *To cast a glance at* o *on,* Echar una ojeada hacia o sobre. *To cast a statue in bronze,* Vaciar una estatua en bronce. *Casting vote,* Voto decisivo o de calidad. *Casting-house,* Fundería, fundición. *Cast-*

ing-net, Esparavel, red redonda para pescar.
Cast, *s.* 1. Tiro, golpe. 2. Ojeada o mirada. 3. Molde, forma. 4. Aire o modo de presentarse; también, tinte, tono, matiz. 5. Modo de echar o tirar. 6. Echamiento. 7. Tendencia a; apariencia exterior, aspecto, semblante, mirada. 8. Temple. 9. Fundición. 10. La distribución de los papeles para la representación de alguna pieza en el teatro. *That has a greenish cast*, Eso tiene un tinte verdusco. *To have a cast in one's eye*, Bizcar, torcer la vista, mirar bizco o atravesado.
Castanets [cas'-ta-nets], *s. pl.* Castañetas o castañuelas.
Castaway [cgst'-a-wê], *s.* 1. Náufrago. 2. Desecho, zupia, desperdicio. 3. Réprobo.
Caste [cast], *s.* 1. Casta, raza; clase hereditaria del Indostán. 2. Clase social, división de la sociedad en virtud de principios convencionales, como el derecho hereditario, la riqueza, etc.
Castellan [cas'-tel-an], *s.* Castellano, el alcaide de un castillo. *Castellans*, Habitantes de un castillo.
Castellany [cgs'-tg-lg-ni], *s.* Castellanía.
Castellated [cgs'-tg-lg-ted], *a.* Hecho en forma de castillo; encerrado dentro de murallas, encastillado.
Castelry [cgs'-tel-ri], *s.* El gobierno, derecho de posesión o jurisdicción de un castillo; territorio sometido al señor del castillo.
Caster, Castor [cgst'-gr], *s.* 1. Tirador, el que tira. 2. Adivino; calculador. 3. Fundidor. 4. Ruedecilla con eje de eslabón giratorio para rodar por todos lados. 5. Ampolleta destinada a contener aceite, vinagre pimienta o sal para el servicio de la mesa. *Casters*, Vinagreras.
Castigate [cas'-ti-gêt], *va.* Castigar; corregir.
Castigation [cas-ti-gê'-shun], *s.* 1. Castigo o pena. 2. Corrección, enmienda.
Castigator [cas'-ti-gê-ter], *s.* Enmendador, castigador.
Castigatory [cas'-ti-ga-to-ri], *a.* Penal, lo que sirve para castigar.
Castile [cas-tîl'], *s.* Castilla, una provincia de España. *Castile-soap*, Jabón de Castilla.
Castilian [cas-til'-yan], *s.* y *a.* Castellano, habitante o natural de Castilla, y su idioma.
Castilleia [cas-ti-lî'-ya], *s.* Castilleja, género grande de plantas de las escrofulariáceas. (De Castillejo, botánico español.)
Casting [cgst'-ing], *s.* 1. Tiro, el acto de tirar o arrojar. 2. Invención, distribución, arreglo; plan, modelo. 3. Fundición. 4. Moldaje, forma que se da a un metal vaciado; y la operación de dejar correr el metal y vaciarlo. 5. Curalle, medicamento usado en cetrería.
Cast iron [cgst-ai'-ūrn], *a.* 1. Hecho de hierro colado. 2. Parecido al hierro colado; rígido, que no cede, inflexible.
Castle [cas'-l], *s.* 1. Castillo, fortaleza. 2. Palacio, morada de un hombre opulento. 3. Roque o torre, cierta pieza del juego de ajedrez.—*va.* Enrocar (en el juego de ajedrez.)
Castle-builder [cas'-l-bild-gr], *s.* Proyectista imaginario, el que hace castillos en el aire.
Castled [cas'-ld], *a.* Lleno de castillos; fortificado con castillo.
Castleguard [cas'-l-gard], *s.* Especie de feudo.
Castlet [cast'-let], *s.* Castilluelo, castillejo.
Castling [cast'-ling], *s.* Aborto, lo que nace antes de tiempo.
Castor [cgs'-ter], *s.* 1. Castor, animal anfibio. 2. Sombrero fino hecho del pelo de castor. 3. Castóreo. *V.* Castoreum. 4. *V.* Caster.
Castor and Pollux [cas'-ter and pel'-ucs], *s.* (Meteor.) 1. Cástor y Pólux, especie de metéoro que los marineros llaman fuego de Santelmo. 2. Constelación de los Gemelos (Gemini).
Castoreum [cas-tō'-re-um], *s.* Castóreo, substancia aceitosa y de olor fuerte que tiene el castor en bolsas en el vientre.
Castor-oil [cas'-ter-eil], *s.* Aceite de palmacristi o ricino; aceite de castor, usado en la medicina como purgante.
Castrametation [cas-tra-me-tê'-shun], *s.* (Mil.) Castrametación, arte de acampar un ejército con ventaja.
Castrate [cas'-trêt], *va.* 1. Castrar, capar. 2. Expurgar un escrito.
Castration [cas-trê'-shun], *s.* Capadura, la acción de capar.
Castrel [cas'-trel], *s.* (Orn.) Especie de halcón. *V.* Kestrel.
Castrensian [cas-tren'-shan], *a.* (Poco usado) Castrense.
Casual [cazh'-yu-al], *a.* Casual, fortuito, accidental.
Casually [cazh'-yu-al-i], *adv.* Casualmente, fortuitamente.
Casualness [cazh'-yu-al-nes], *s.* Contingencia.
Casualty [cazh'-yu-al-ti], *s.* Casualidad, aventura, contingencia, acaso, accidente.
Casuist [cazh'-yu-ist], *s.* Casuista, el que escribe, trata o estudia casos de conciencia, y los resuelve y determina.
Casuistical [cazh-yu-is'-ti-cal], *a.* Casuístico, lo que pertenece a casos de conciencia.
Casuistry [cazh'-yu-is-tri], *s.* Teología moral, la ciencia de los casuistas.
Casus [kê'-sus o cg'-sus], *s.* (Lat.) Contingencia, acaecimiento, suceso. *Casus belli*, Caso o motivo de guerra.
Cat [cat], *s.* 1. Gato. *A wild cat*, Un gato montés. *To bell the cat*, Poner el cascabel al gato. *Civet-cat*, Algalia. *Polecat*, Veso, animal cuadrúpedo parecido a la garduña, pero de pelo negro. 2. (Mar.) Gata. *Cat-tackle*, (Mar.) Aparejo de gata. *Cat-harpings*, (Mar.) Jaretas. *Cat-heads*, (Mar.) Serviolas. *Cat's-paw*, (Mar.) Soplo. (Fam.) Mano de gato: se aplica al que se deja engañar y sirve, sin conocerlo, de medio o anzuelo para que otro consiga lo que desea. (Fam.) *To make one a cat's-paw*, Sacar las castañas del fuego con mano de gato. *Cat-o'-nine-tails*, Disciplina o azote con nueve ramales. *Cat's-eye*, (Min.) Ojo de gato; especie de ágata. *Cat's-foot*, (Bot.) Hiedra terrestre. Nepeta glechoma.
Catabolism [ca-tab'-o-lizm], *s.* Catabolismo.
Catachresis [cat-a-crî'-sis], *s.* Catacresis, empleo defectuoso de metáforas o epítetos.
Cataclysm [cat'-a-clizm], *s.* Cataclismo, diluvio, inundación.
Cataclysmal, Cataclysmic [cat-a-cliz'-mal, mic], *a.* Lo que se refiere al cataclismo.
Catacombs [cat'-a-cōmz], *s. pl.* Catacumbas, lugares subterráneos y especie de grutas para enterrar á los muertos.
Catacoustics [cat-a-cūs'-tics o caus'-tics], *s.* Catacústica, ciencia de los sonidos reflejos.
Catadioptric, Catadioptrical [cat-a-dai-ep'-tric, al], *a.* Catadióptrico.
Catafalque [cat'-a-falc], *s.* Catafalco, túmulo muy elevado y magnífico para las exequias de altos personajes.
Catalectic [cat-a-lec'-tic], *a.* (Ret.) Cataléctico, verso falto de una sílaba.
Catalepsy [cat-a-lep'-si], *s.* Catalepsia, suspensión de las sensaciones e inmovilidad del cuerpo, debidas a un accidente nervioso repentino.
Cataleptic [cat-a-lep'-tic], *a.* Cataléptico, referente a la catalepsia; que la padece.
Catalogue [cat'-a-leg], *s.* Catálogo, lista o memoria que contiene muchos nombres propios de hombres, títulos de libros u otros objetos. Hoy se escribe a menudo Catalog.
Catalogue, *va.* Catalogar, poner en catálogo.
Catalpa [ca-tal'-pa], *s.* Árbol de adorno, originario de la América del Norte. Tiene hojas ovaladas y acorazonadas de gran tamaño y flores grandes y campaniformes.
Catalysis, *s.* 1. (Quím.) Catalisis, descomposición y nueva combinación de los cuerpos químicos compuestos, efectuadas por un agente que permanece inalterable. 2. (Poco us.) *V.* Dissolution
Catalyst [cat'-g-list], *s.* Catalizador, agente catalítico.
Catalytic [cat-a-lit'-ic], *a.* Catalítico, perteneciente a la catalisis.
Catalyzer [cat'-a-lai-zgr], *s.* (Quím.) Catalizador.
Catamaran [cat-a-ma-ran'], *s.* 1. Almadía larga y estrecha de la India. 2. Embarcación de vela o vapor formada por dos cascos paralelos unidos entre sí.
Catamenia [cat-a-mî'-ni-a], *s.* Menstruación, reglas. (< Gr.)
Catamite [cat'-a-mait], *s.* Catamita, sodomita.
Catamount [cat'-a-maunt], *s.* Gato montés.
Cataphract [cat'-a-fract], *s.* Armadura antigua hecha con chapas de metal a manera de escamas, fijadas sobre cuero, etc.
Cataplasm [cat'-a-plazm], *s.* Cataplasma.
Catapult [cat'-a-pult], *s.* Catapulta, máquina antigua de guerra para arrojar piedras, lanzas, etc.
Cataract [cat'-a-ract], *s.* 1. Cascada. 2. Catarata, opacidad de la lente cristalina del ojo o de su cápsula, que produce la ceguera, parcial o total. (Fam.) *A cataract of tears*, Un diluvio de lágrimas.
Catarrh [ca-tār'], *s.* Catarro, romadizo, resfriado, constipado, fluxión, reuma.
Catarrhal [ca-tār'-al], **Catarrhous** [ca-tār'-us], *a.* Catarral.
Catastrophe [ca-tas'-tro-fg], *s.* 1. Catástrofe, la mutación o revolución imprevista que se hace en un poema dramático y que por lo común le da fin. 2. Catástrofe, por lo común cosa infeliz, desgraciada y funesta.
Catbird [cat'-bgrd], *s.* Tordo mimo (Galeoscoptes carolinensis), de color

de pizarra; se halla desde el Canadá hasta Méjico y Cuba.

Catcall [cat'-cōl], *s.* 1. Silbo, silbido, con que se hace burla de lo que se desaprueba en las representaciones públicas. (Mex.) Chiflido, chiflo y el silbido que sirve para avisar cuando deben correrse o descorrerse los telones. 2. Reclamo.

Catch [cach], *va.* (*pp.* y *pret.* CAUGHT). 1. Coger, agarrar, asir, arrebatar. 2. Coger al vuelo. 3. Coger, alcanzar. 4. Coger o detener alguna cosa para que no caiga. 5. Coger, atrapar. 6. Comprender, discernir. 7. Agradar, dar gusto. 8. Coger algún mal por infección o por contagio. 9. Asir repentinamente o ansiosamente. 10. Pillar; clavar; albardar. 11. Sorprender. 12. Ganar. *To catch a tartar*, Caer en la trampa que se ha puesto para otro.—*vn.* 1. Agarrarse a; con *at.* 2. Cerrarse, enredarse o engancharse algo. 3. Pegarse, ser pegajoso o contagioso. *To catch cold*, Resfriarse. *To catch a distemper*, Inficionarse, contagiarse; enfermar. *To catch one's death*, Causarse la muerte. *To catch at*, Buscar, inquirir, procurar, coger u obtener una cosa, en sentido figurado; y llevar las manos hacia alguna cosa con intención de agarrarla, en sentido propio. *To catch hold of*, Agarrarse a, apoderarse de. *To catch up*, Coger, asir, empuñar; alcanzar. *To catch on*, (Fam.) Entender, comprender. *To catch it*, (Fam.) Ganarse una zurra, una reprimenda, etc.

Catch, *s.* 1. Presa; captura, prisión o prendimiento; es también aprensión, hablando de contrabandos; la acción de prender o coger. 2. Taravilla de picaporte. 3. Provecho, ventaja; atracción. *It is no great catch*, No es gran cosa, no vale la pena. 4. Alzaprima, palanca de rueda. 5. Gancho. 6. Canción con estribillo. 7. Cuaiche, especie de embarcación de dos palos o masteleros. *V.* KETCH. *To be* o *lie upon the catch*, Espiar o acechar la presa.

Catchable [cach'-a-bl], *a.* Expuesto a ser pillado o cogido.

Catchall [cach'-ōl], *s.* (Fam.) Armario, cesto, cajón o saco destinado a recibir indistintamente toda clase de objetos, retazos, etc.

Catcher [cach'-ẹr], *s.* 1. Cogedor, el que coge o con lo que se coge alguna cosa. 2. Agarrador. 3. Jugador de pelota.

Catchfly [cach'-flai], *s.* (Bot.) Especie de colleja.

Catching [cach'-ing], *s.* 1. El endentado de una rueda en que deben entrar o engranar los dientes de otra. 2. Presa, captura.—*a.* Contagioso.

Catchment [cach'-mẹnt], *s.* Desagüe. *Catchment basin*, Cuenca o territorio desaguado por un río.

Catchpenny [cach'-pen-i], *s.* Engañifa, baratija, alguna cosa de poco valor hecha para venderse muy barata.

Catchpoll [cach'-pōl], *s.* Corchete, alguacil.

Catchup [cach'-up], *s.* Salsa picante hecha de setas o tomates. *V.* CATSUP.

Catchword [cach'-wūrd], *s.* 1. Reclamo, la palabra o sílaba que se pone al fin de cada plana, que es la misma con que ha de empezar la plana siguiente. 2. Palabra o frase de efecto destinada a llamar la atención pública.

Catechetic, Catechetical [cat-e-ket'-ic, al], *a.* 1. Catequístico, lo que tiene preguntas y respuestas.

Catechetically [cat-e-ket'-i-cal-i], *adv.* Por preguntas y respuestas.

Catechism [cat'-e-kizm], *s.* 1. Catecismo, compendio de un credo religioso puesto en forma de preguntas y respuestas. 2. Manual de instrucción en forma de diálogo.

Catechist [cat'-e-kist], *s.* Catequista o catequizante.

Catechistical [cat-e-kis'-ti-cal], *s.* Catequístico.

Catechize [cat'-e-kaiz], *va.* 1. Catequizar, preguntar, examinar. 2. Catequizar, instruir en los artículos fundamentales de la religión cristiana.

Catechizer [cat'-e-kaiz-ẹr], *s.* Catequizante.

Catechizing [cat'-e-kaiz-ing], *s.* Examen, interrogación.

Catechu [cat'-e-kiū o chū], *s.* Cato, tierra japónica o catecú, un medicamento astringente.

Catechumen [cat-e-kiū'-men], *s.* Catecúmeno, el que aprende los principios de la religión.

Catechumenical [cat-e-kiu-men'-i-cal], *a.* Catecuménico, lo que pertenece a los catecúmenos.

Categoric, Categorical [cat-e-gor'-ic, al], *a.* Categórico, absoluto, positivo, explícito.

Categorically [cat-e-gor'-ic-al-i], *adv.* Categóricamente.

Category [cat'-e-go-ri], *s.* Categoría, clase; orden de ideas; predicamento.

Catenary [cat'-e-nẹ-ri], *s.* (Geom.) La línea curva formada por una cuerda o cadena perfectamente flexible, suspendida por ambos extremos.

Catenate [cat'-e-nēt], *va.* Encadenar.

Catenation [cat-e-nē'-shun], *s.* Encadenamiento, encadenadura.

Cater [kē'-tẹr], *vn.* Abastecer, proveer de víveres o procurar diversión y entretenimiento.

Cater-cousin [kē'-tẹr-cuz'-n], *s.* 1. Un favorito. 2. Primo cuarto, dícese familiarmente de dos que son parientes en grado muy remoto.

Caterer [kē'-tẹr-ẹr], *s.* Proveedor, abastecedor. En el estilo familiar significa propiamente la persona que va a la plaza a comprar los mejores comestibles; y en el figurado, el sujeto que procura las mejores diversiones, etc.

Cateress [kē'-tẹr-es], *sf.* Proveedora, abastecedora.

Caterpillar [cat'-ẹr-pil-ar], *s.* 1. Oruga, gusanillo muy nocivo que se engendra en las hojas y frutas; larva de un insecto himenóptero. 2. (Bot.) Oruga.

Caterpillar tractor [cat'-er-pil-ar trac'-tẹr], *s.* Tractor de oruga.

Caterwaul [cat'-ẹr-wōl], *vn.* 1. Maullar, como los gatos en celo. 2. Dar chillidos o hacer algún ruido desapacible, como el maullido de los gatos.

Caterwauling [cat'-ẹr-wōl-ing], *s.* El maullido de muchos gatos juntos.

†**Cates** [kēts], *s. pl.* Provisiones en general, y especialmente platos o manjares delicados.

Cat-eyed [cat'-aid], *a.* El que tiene ojos de gato o como gato.

Catfish [cat'-fish], *s.* Siluro, pez de cabeza ancha; barbo.

Catgut [cat'-gut], *s.* 1. Hilo que se forma de tripa de carnero retorcida y sirve en los instrumentos músicos de cuerda. 2. Merli, especie de tela (del siglo XVIII) más basta que la gasa.

Catharine-wheel [cath'-a-rin-hwīl], *s.* (Arq.) 1. Rosa, gran ventana circular, cerrada por lo común con vidrieras de colores. 2. Rueda de fuegos artificiales.

Catharist [cath'-a-rist], *s.* Puritano, persona que hace gran ostentación de pureza de vida o de principios.

Catharsis [ca-thār'-sis], *s.* (Med.) Catarsis, operación de purgar.

Cathartic, Cathartical [ca-thār'-tic, al], *a.* Catártico, purgante.

Cathartic, *s.* Catártico o medicina purgante.

Catharticalness [ca-thār'-ti-cal-nes], *s.* Calidad purgante de alguna cosa.

Cathedra [cath'-ẹ-dra], *s.* 1. Sillón de un obispo en la iglesia catedral de su diócesis. 2. Silla de profesor o catedrático.

Cathedral [ca-thī'-dral], *s.* Catedral, iglesia principal o matriz de un obispado.

Catheter [cath'-e-tẹr], *s.* Catéter, algalia, instrumento hueco de que se usa parar dar curso a la orina, cuando hay retención de ella, o para introducir en otros conductos del cuerpo.

Catheterize [cath'-e-tẹr-aiz], *va.* Introducer el catéter.

Cathetus [cath'-e-tus], *s.* (Geom.) Línea perpendicular imaginaria que pasa por el centro de un cuerpo cilíndrico.

Cathode [cath'-ōd], *s.* Polo negativo de una batería galvánica; opuesto a *anode. Cathode rays*, *cf.* ROENTGEN RAYS. *Cathode-ray tube*, Tubo o válvula de rayos catódicos.

Catholic [cath'-o-lic], *a.* 1. Católico, universal o general; ortodoxo. 2. Perteneciente a la Iglesia romana, a la anglicana, o a la griega. 3. Liberal, de amplias miras e ideas. —*s.* Católico romano, el que profesa la religión católica.

Catholicism [ca-thel'-i-sizm], *s.* Catolicismo, la profesión de la religión católica.

Catholicize [ca-thel'-i-saiz], *vn.* Hacerse católico.

Catholicly [cath'-o-lic-li], *adv.* Católicamente, generalmente.

Catholicness [cath'-o-lic-nes], *s.* (Des.) Universalidad. *V.* CATHOLICITY.

Catkin [cat'-kin], *s.* Trama, amento, flores imperfectas que cuelgan de los árboles a manera de látigo, como se ve en los sauces. *V.* AMENT.

Catlike [cat'-laic], *a.* Gateado, gatuno.

Catling [cat'-ling], *s.* 1. Legra, especie de cuchillo de que se sirven los cirujanos. 2. Cuerdas de violón o guitarra.

Catmint [cat'-mint], **Catnip** [cat'-nip], *s.* (Bot.) Gatera, calamento, calaminta, especie de planta del género Nepeta.

Catnap [cat'-nap], *s.* Siesta, siesta corta, sueño ligero o corto, somnolencia, modorra.

Catnap, *vn.* Adormecerse, dormitar, estar amodorrado.

Catnip [cat'-nip], *s.* Calamento.

Catonian [ca-o kē-tō'-ni-an], *a.* Grave, serio; riguroso.

Catoptrical [ca-tep'-tri-cal], *a.* Catóptrico.

Catoptrics [ca-tep'-trics], *s.* Catóptrica, ciencia que enseña el modo de ver los objetos por medio de la

reflexión de los rayos de la luz en los espejos y otras superficies tersas.
Catsilver, *s.* (Min. Ant.) *V.* MICA.
Cat's-tail [cats'-têl] o **Cattail** [cat'-têl], *s.* (Bot.) Espadaña, hierba acuática.
Catsup [cat'-sup], *s.* Salsa de setas o de tomate. *V.* CATCHUP.
Cattish [cat'-ish], *a.* Gatuno, gatesco.
Cattle [cat'-l], *s.* 1. Ganado, toda especie de bestias que pacen juntas. *Neat cattle, black cattle*, o *horned cattle*, Ganado vacuno. 2. Dícese por desprecio de las personas. *Small cattle*, Ganado lanar y cabrío. *Cattle plague*, Fiebre tifoidea contagiosa que ataca al ganado vacuno: el *rinderpest* de Alemania. *Cattle range*, Terreno dilatado y no cercado para apacentar el ganado mayor.
Catty [cat'-i], *s.* Cati, medida de peso de la China que equivale a 6 hectogramos.
Caucasian [cē-cash'-ian o cē-kê'-shan], *a.* Caucásico, del Cáucaso.
Caucus [cō'-cus], *s.* 1. Conventículo o junta secreta de los directores o accionistas de una compañía, banco, ferrocarril o sociedad, para resolver en todo lo que se relaciona con la empresa. 2. Junta privada para designar candidatos o discutir medidas o asuntos políticos. 3. Entruchada.
Caudad [cō'-dad], *adv.* Hacia la cola.
Caudal [cō'-dal], *a.* Lo que pertenece a la cola.
Caudate, Caudated [cō'-dêt, ed], *a.* Caudato, que tiene cola.
Caudex [cō'-dex], *s.* (*pl.* CAUDICES [cō'-di-sīz]). Tallo en forma de cola; tallo de una palma.
Caudle [cō'-dl], *s.* Bebida confortante, compuesta de vino y otros ingredientes, que se da a las recién paridas y a otros enfermos.
Caudle, *va.* Componer una bebida confortante; confortar.
Cauf [cōf], *s.* Vivero de pescado, canasta o cajón lleno de agujeros en que se tienen peces vivos dentro del agua.
Caught, *pret.* y *pp.* del verbo *To* CATCH.
Caul [cōl], *s.* 1. Redecilla, cofia ó toca, red en que las mujeres recogen el pelo. 2. Redecilla, cualquier red pequeña. 3. Membrana ó tela que cubre la cabeza de algunas criaturas cuando nacen. 4. Omento.
Caulescent [cō-les'-ent], *a.* (Bot.) Caulescente, que tiene un tallo bien definido.
Cauliferous [cō-lif'-er-us], *a.* Colífero; dícese de las plantas que tienen tallos como la coliflor.
Cauliflower [cō'-li-flau-er], *s.* Coliflor, especie de col o berza.
Caulk, *va.* *V.* CALK.
Cauma [cō'-ma], *s.* (Ant.) Calor de fiebre; fiebre.
Caup [cōp], *va.* (Inglaterra del Norte) Cambiar, trocar.
Caup [cōp], *s.* (Esco.) Copa; taza.
Causable [cōz'-a-bl], *a.* Causable.
Causal [cōz'-al], *a.* Causal, perteneciente a una causa.
Causality [cō-zal'-i-ti], **Causation** [co-zê'-shun], *s.* Causa, origen, principio, modo o acción con que se causa u obra un efecto.
Causally [cōz'-al-i], *adv.* De un modo causal.
Causative [cōz'-a-tiv], *a.* Causal, causativo, causante.
Causatively [cōz'-a-tiv-li], *adv.* Efectivamente.
Cause [cōz], *s.* 1. Causa, origen, principio. 2. Autor, causa; motivo, razón; pretexto. 3. Acción o pleito incoado ante un tribunal, y también todo un procedimento judicial. 4. Partido. *The cause is over*, Se ha visto la causa. *To espouse one's cause*, Abrazar la causa de alguno, tomar su partido.
Cause, *va.* Causar, hacer, excitar, producir algún efecto. *To cause love*, Inspirar amor. *To cause sorrow*, Dar pesadumbre. *To cause to*, Hacer hacer, expedir.
Causeless [cōz'-les], *a.* 1. Que tiene su origen en sí mismo y no reconoce causa. 2. Infundado, injusto, sin razón.
Causelessly [cōz'-les-li], *adv.* Infundadamente, sin causa, motivo ni fundamento.
Causelessness [cōz'-les-nes], *s.* Motivo o causa injusta.
Causer [cōz'-er], *s.* 1. Causador. 2. Autor.
Causeway [cōz'-wê], **Causey** [coz'-i], *s.* Arrecife, camino real, o calzada empedrada.
Causidical [co-zid'-i-cal], *a.* Causídico, perteneciente a la prosecución de causas y pleitos.
Caustic, Caustical [cōs'-tic, al], *a.* Cáustico, que quema y destruye todo aquello a que se aplica.
Caustic, *s.* Cáustico, medicamento corrosivo.
Causticity [cōs-tis'-i-ti], *s.* Mordacidad; calidad de caústico.
Causticness [cōs'-tic-nes], *s.* *V.* CAUSTICITY.
†**Cautelous** [cō'-tel-us], *a.* Cauteloso, cauto, astuto, prudente, socarrón.
Cauterant [cō'-ter-ant], *s.* y *a.* Cauterio, medicamento cáustico.
Cauterism [cō'-ter-izm], **Cauterization** [cō-ter-i-zê'-shun], *s.* Cauterización, cauterio.
Cauterize [cō'-ter-aiz], *va.* Cauterizar, dar cauterio.
Cauterizing [cō'-ter-aiz-ing], *s.* Cauterización.
Cautery [cō'-ter-i], *s.* Cauterio.
Caution [cō'-shun], *s.* 1. Caución, cautela, prudencia, precaución, circunspección, atención. 2. Amonestación, prevención, advertencia. 3. Aviso, miramiento, recato.
Caution, *va.* 1. Caucionar, precaver, prevenir, advertir, avisar, amonestar. 2. Caucionar, afianzar, dar fianza.
Cautionary [cō'-shun-e-ri], *a.* 1. Amonestador, admonitorio, avisador; que amonesta. 2. Caucionado, dado en fianza o en rehenes; aviso.
Cautious [cō'-shus], *a.* Cauto, vigilante, circunspecto.
Cautiously [cō'-shus-li], *adv.* Cautamente, prudentemente.
Cautiousness [cō'-shus-nes], *s.* Cautela, vigilancia, circunspección, prevision, prudencia, precaución.
Cavalcade [cav-al-kêd'], *s.* Cabalgata o procesión a caballo.
Cavalier [cav-a-lîr'], *s.* 1. Caballero. Cuando las guerras civiles de Inglaterra en el reinado de Carlos I, se llamaron *Cavaliers* los realistas, y los del partido contrario *Roundheads;* así como en España en el tiempo de las Comunidades llamaron *caballeros* a los que seguían el partido del rey, y *comuneros* a los que seguían el del pueblo. 2. Hombre galante, que sirve de escolta a una dama o de pareja en el baile. 3. Jinete, caballero, y especialmente un jinete armado. 4. (Fort.) Caballero, el terraplén que se levanta para colocar los cañones.—*a.* 1. Caballeresco, bravo, belicoso. 2. Altivo, desdeñoso, alegre, libre.
Cavalierly [cav-a-lîr'-li], *adv.* Altivamente, a lo caballero, caballerosamente.
Cavalry [cav'-al-ri], *s.* Caballería, cuerpo de milicia que va a caballo.
Cavalryman [cav'-al-ri-man], *s.* (Mil.) Soldado de caballería.
Cavatina [cā-va-tī'-na], *s.* Aria corta y sencilla; pieza música cantada por una sola persona.
Cave [kêv], *s.* Cueva, caverna, antro; bodega; cualquier lugar hueco y subterráneo.
Cave, *vn.* 1. Hundirse, abismarse. 2. (Fam.) Ceder, rendirse.—*va.* Excavar. *To cave in*, Caer en un hoyo.
Caveat [kê'-vi-at], *s.* 1. (For.) Intimación o notificación formal hecha a un juez o funcionario público, para que suspenda todo procedimiento ulterior hasta haber oído al peticionario. 2. (E. U.) Descripción de un invento no perfeccionado todavía, archivada en la Oficina de Patentes en Washington.
Cavendish [cav'-en-dish], *s.* Un tabaco norteamericano.
Cavern [cav'-ern], *s.* Caverna, concavidad hecha en la tierra.
Caverned [cav'-ernd], **Cavernous** [cav'-ern-us], *a.* Cavernoso, lleno de cavernas o concavidades. *Caverned*, El que vive en caverna o cueva.
Cavesson [cav'-e-sen], *s.* Cabezón, cabezada con muserola y provista de argolla para rienda o cuerda, por medio de la cual se obliga al caballo a trotar o andar en círculo, en torno del domador.
Caviar [cav-i-ār'], *s.* Cavial, caviar, especie de embuchado que se hace con las huevas de esturión saladas.
Cavil [cav'-il], *s.* Efugio, evasión, cavilación, sofistería, vanas sutilezas, quisquillas; triquiñuelas en el juego; trampa legal.
Cavil, *vn.* Cavilar, querer hallar dificultades donde no las hay; armar pleitos o enredos; sutilizar o buscar escapatorias para salir de alguna dificultad, buscar quisquillas.—*va.* Poner faltas quisquillosamente.
Caviller [cav'-il-er], *s.* Sofista; trapacero, enredador.
Cavilling [cav'-il-ing], *s.* Cavilación, sofistería. *V.* CAVIL.
Cavillingly [cav'-il-ing-li], *adv.* Cavilosamente.
¿**Cavilous** [cav'-il-us], *a.* Caviloso, quisquilloso.
Cavitary [cav'-i-tê''-ri], *a.* Que tiene una cavidad, hueco; que tiene un conducto intestinal, como ciertos gusanos.
Cavity [cav'-i-ti], *s.* Cavidad, espacio cóncavo o vacío.
Cavort [ca-vōrt'], *vn.* (Ger. E. U.) Cabriolar como el caballo.
Caw [cō], *vn.* Graznar, crascitar, como el grajo o el cuervo; jadear.
Cay [kê], *s.* Cayo, peñasco o isleta en las Antillas. (< cayo.) *Cf.* KEY.
Cayenne pepper [kê-en' o kai-en' pep'-er], *s.* (Bot.) Pimentón; pimiento, guindilla.
Cayman [kê'-man], *s.* Caimán, cocodrilo de América.
Cease [sīs], *vn.* 1. Cesar, desistir, parar. 2. Fenecer, acabarse. 3. Descansar.—*va.* Parar, suspender.
Ceaseless [sīs'-les], *a.* Incesante, perpetuo, continuo, perenne.

Ceaselessly [sīs'-les-li], *adv.* Perpetuamente, incesantemente.
Ceasing [sīs'-ing], *s.* Cesación.
Cecils [sī'-silz], *s. pl.* Pisto, picadillo de carne.
Cecity [sī'-si-ti o ses'-i-ti], *s.* Ceguedad, ceguera, privación de la vista.
Cedar [sī'-dar], *s.* Cedro, árbol fragante de las coníferas; también, tuya.
Cedar-bird [sī'-dar-berd], *s.* (Orn.) Pájaro del cedro (de América).
Cedarlike [sī'-dar-laic], *a.* Semejante al cedro.
Cedarn [sī'-darn], *a.* 1. *V.* CEDRINE. 2. Hecho o revestido con cedros.
Cede [sīd], *va.* Ceder, traspasar a otro una cosa o un derecho; transferir territorio.
Cedilla [se-dil'-a], *s.* Zedilla, virgulilla debajo de una *c*, que servía para expresar un sonido parecido al de la zeda.
Cedrine [sī'-drin], *a.* Cedrino, que se refiere o pertenece al cedro.
Ceil [sīl], *va.* Cubrir o techar con cielo raso.
Ceiling [sīl'-ing], *s.* 1. Techo o cielo raso de una habitación. 2. (Mar.) Revestimiento interior de la bodega. 3. (Aer.) Cielo, cielo máximo, techo.
Ceiling price [sīl'-ing prais], *s.* Precio tope.
Celature [sel'-a-tiūr], *s.* Grabado, el arte de grabar sobre los metales.
Celebrant [sel'-e-brant], *s.* Celebrante, el sacerdote que dice la misa.
Celebrate [sel'-e-brêt], *va.* 1. Celebrar, alabar, aplaudir. 2. Celebrar, solemnizar. 3. Hacer elogio o elogiar.
Celebrated [sel'-e-brê-ted], *a.* Célebre, famoso.
Celebration [sel-e-brê'-shun], *s.* 1. Celebración, acción hecha con solemnidad; tiempo de celebrar. 2. Celebración, celebridad, aplauso. 3. Elogio, panegírico, alabanza.
Celebrator [sel'-e-brê-tor], *s.* Celebrador, celebrante.
†**Celebrious** [se-leb'-ri-us], *a.* Célebre, famoso, renombrado.
Celebrity [se-leb'-ri-ti], *s.* 1. Celebridad, fama, renombre. 2. Personaje, persona renombrada.
Celeriac [se-ler'-i-ac], *s.* (Bot.) Apio napiforme.
Celerity [se-ler'-i-ti], *s.* Celeridad, ligereza, prontitud, velocidad, rapidez.
Celery [sel'-e-ri], *s.* (Bot.) Apio.
Celestial [se-les'-chal], *a.* 1. Celestial, célico, celeste. 2. Divino, excelente.—*s.* 1. Habitador del cielo. 2. Chino.
Celestial mechanics [se-les'-chal me-can'-ics], *s.* Mecánica celeste.
Celestialize [se-les'-chal-aiz], *va.* Hacer celestial o celeste.
Celestially [se-les'-chal-i], *adv.* Celestialmente.
Celestins [sel'-es-tinz], *s.* Celestinos, una orden religiosa.
Celiac [sī'-li-ac], *a.* (Med.) Celíaco, perteneciente al vientre. *Celiac axis,* Arteria corta que surte al hígado, al estómago y al bazo.
Celibacy [sel'-i-ba-si], *s.* Celibato, soltería, el estado de los que no están casados.
Celibate [sel'-i-bêt], *a.* ¿Célibe, soltero.—*s.* 1. Celibato, estado de la persona que no ha tomado estado de matrimonio. 2. Célibe.
Cell [sel], *s.* 1. Célula, el elemento mínimo de planta o animal que manifiesta libre acción vital; unidad de estructura. 2. Nicho, cavidad pequeña; alveolo. 3. Celdilla de abejas en los panales. 4. Celda, habitación de un religioso o religiosa. 5. Celdilla, cavidad donde se hallan encerradas ciertas semillas. 6. (Ant.) Cavidad de los tejidos esponjosos. 7. Celda, par de una batería galvánica.
Cellar [sel'-ar], *s.* Sótano, bodega de una casa.
Cellarage [sel'-ar-ĝj], *s.* 1. Cueva, sótano, la parte subterránea de un edificio destinada a poner el carbón, el vino y otras cosas. 2. Alquiler que se paga por poner el vino en la bodega de otro.
Cellarer [sel'-ar-er], **Cellarist** [sel'-ar-ist], *s.* Cillerero, el despensero de un monasterio.
Cellaret [sel'-ar-et], *s.* Frasquera, caja de licores.
Cello [chel'-o], *s.* Violoncelo, bajo; abreviatura de violoncello. (Ital.)
Cellophane [sel'-o-fên], *s.* Celofán.
Cellular [sel'-yu-lar], *a.* Celular, lo que se compone de varias celdillas o cavidades.
Cellule [sel'-yul], *s.* Celdita.
Celluloid [sel'-yu-leid], *s.* Celuloide, compuesto duro elástico, que se forma sometiendo algodón pólvora, alcanfor y otras substancias a presión hidráulica.
Cellulose [sel'-yu-lōs], *s.* Celulosa, substancia insoluble en agua que cubre las células; materia fundamental de las plantas.
Celsitude [sel'-si-tiud], *s.* Celsitud, elevación, altura, alteza.
Celt, Kelt [selt], *s.* Celta, nombre de los antiguos habitantes de la parte occidental de Europa.
Celticism [sel'-ti-sizm], *s.* Celticismo, costumbre de los celtas.
Celtic [selt'-ic], **Keltic** [kelt'-ic], *a.* Céltico, lo que pertenece a los celtas.
Cement [se-ment'], *s.* 1. Cemento, argamasa o mezcla muy fuerte para pegar, tapar, etc. 2. Cal arcillosa que se endurece en el agua. 3. Lo que sirve para unir dos cuerpos entre sí. 4. Enlace o vínculo de amistad.
Cement, *va.* Pegar, unir una cosa con otra por medio de una mezcla; argamasar; asegurar, estrechar, solidar.—*vn.* Unirse, hacer liga.
Cementation [sem-en-tê'-shun], *s.* 1. Ligazón, la acción de unirse una cosa con otra. 2. (Quím.) Cimentación, afinación de un metal por medio de un cemento; se dice particularmente de la transformación del hierro en acero.
Cementer [se-ment'-er], *s.* Ligador, pegador.
Cemetery [sem'-e-ter-i], *s.* Cementerio.
Cenobite [sen'-o-bait], *s.* Cenobita, religioso o monje.
Cenobitic o **Cenobitical** [sen-o-bit'-ic, al], *a.* Cenobítico, el que vive en comunidad.
Cenobium [se-nō'-bi-um], *s.* 1. Morada de cenobitas. 2. (Zool.) Grupo o colonia de protozoarios. 3. (Bot.) Entre las algas unicelulares, colonia de individuos independientes unidos por una matriz común.
Cenotaph [sen'-o-taf], *s.* Cenotafio, monumento sepulcral erigido para honrar la memoria de algún difunto.
Cense [sens], *va.* Incensar, perfumar con incienso.
Censer [sen'-ser], *s.* Incensario, braserillo con que se inciensa.
Censor [sen'-ser], *s.* 1. Censor, magistrado de Roma que formaba el censo y tenía cuidado de la corrección de las costumbres. 2. Censor, el que todo lo censura y critica.
Censorial [sen-so'-ri-al] ¿, **Censorian** [sen-sō'ri-an], *a.* Censorio, lo perteneciente al censor o a su oficio.
Censorious [sen-sō'-ri-us], *a.* Severo, rígido; crítico, maldiciente, sofístico.
Censoriously [sen-sō'-ri-us-li], *adv.* Severamente, críticamente.
Censorship [sen'-sor-ship], *s.* Censura, el oficio o dignidad de censor.
Censual [sen'-shu-al], *a.* Censual, lo perteneciente al censo.
Censurable [sen'-shur-a-bl], *a.* Censurable, digno de censura.
Censurableness [sen'-shur-a-bl-nes], *s.* La calidad de ser censurable.
Censurably [sen'-shur-a-bli], *adv.* Censurablemente.
Censure [sen'-shur], *s.* 1. Censura, reprensión, crítica. 2. Censura, parecer, opinión. 3. Censura, pena espiritual o eclesiástica como la excomunión, suspensión, etc.
Censure, *va.* 1. Censurar, culpar, reprender. 2. Criticar, condenar. 3. Juzgar.
Censurer [sen'-shur-er], *s.* Censurador, censurante.
Censuring [sen'-shur-ing], *s.* Improperio, censura.
Census [sen'-sus], *s.* Censo.
Cent [sent], *s.* 1. Centavo, moneda de cobre de los Estados Unidos, cuyo valor es un centavo o la centésima parte de un peso o *dollar.* 2. Ciento, en la frase *per cent* que quiere decir por ciento. *Six per cent* (interés de), Seis por ciento. 3. Centésima parte de la unidad en otros sistemas monetarios, como céntimo de franco.
Cental [sen'-tal], *s.* Quintal, peso de cien libras.—*a.* Perteneciente a un ciento.
Centare [sāñ-tār'], *s.* Centiárea, la centésima parte de un área, o sea el metro cuadrado, 1⅕ yardas cuadradas.
Centaur [sen'-tōr], *s.* 1. (Poét.) Centauro, monstruo mitad hombre y mitad caballo. 2. Centauro, un signo del zodíaco.
Centaurea [sen-tō'-re-a], *s.* (Bot.) Centaurea, género de plantas compuestas.
Centaury [sen'-tō-ri], *s.* (Bot.) Centaura, o centaurea, planta medicinal.
Centenarian [sen-te-nê'-ri-an], *s.* Centenario, la persona que llega a la edad de cien años.
Centenary [sent'-en-a-ri], *s.* Centena, centenar, centenario, tiempo o plazo de cien años.
Centennial [sen-ten'-i-al], *a.* Centenario.
Center [sen'-ter], *s.* Centro: es la ortografía preferida en los Estados Unidos de América. *V.* CENTRE.
Center-board [sen'-ter-bōrd], *s.* (Mar.) Orza de deriva, usada especialmente en los yates.
Centered [sen'-terd], *pp.* Concentrado, reunido en centro.
Centering [sen'-ter-ing], *s.* 1. Acto o operación de colocar un objeto en el foco del microscopio o anteojo. 2. Acto de practicar un hueco poco profundo en el centro de un objeto. 3. (Arq.) Cimbra de arco o bóveda.

Centesimal [sen-tes'-i-mal], *a.* Centésimo, que llega al número de ciento.
Centifolious [sen-ti-fō'-li-us], *a.* Centifolio, que tiene cien hojas.
Centigrade [sen'-ti-grēd], *a.* Centígrado, de cien grados. En el termómetro centígrado el punto de congelación se marca cero y el de ebullición del agua 100°
Centigram (o **Centigramme**) [sen'-ti-gram], *s.* Centigramo, el peso de la centésima parte de un gramo.
Centiliter o **Centilitre** [sen'-ti-lī-tęr], *s.* Centilitro, la centésima parte de un litro.
Centimeter o **Centimetre** [sen'-ti-mī-tęr], *s.* Centímetro, la centésima parte de un metro.
Centipede [sen'-ti-pīd], *s.* Cientopiés o ciempiés, insecto venenoso.
Centner [sent'-nęr], *s.* 1. Peso de cien libras = 45.36 kilos. 2. En docimástica, una dracma.
Cento [sen'-tō], *s.* Centón, obra literaria compuesta por la mayor parte de pensamientos entresacados de diferentes autores.
Centrad [sen'-trad], *adv.* (Zool.) Hacia el centro.
Central [sen'-tral], *a.* Central, lo que se refiere o pertenece al centro.
Centralism [sen'-tral-izm], *s.* Centralización.
Centrality [sen-tral'-i-ti], *s.* Centralidad, posición central.
Centralization [sen-tral-i-zē'-shun], *s.* Centralización.
Centralize [sen'-tral-aiz], *va.* Centralizar.
Centrally [sen'-tral-i], *adv.* Centralmente.
Centre [sen'-tęr], *s.* 1. Centro, punto que está en medio de una esfera o de una figura circular; el punto medio de otras figuras. 2. Punto de atracción o convergencia; punto focal. 3. Punto de emanación; núcleo, origen. 4. Cimbra.
Centre, Center, *va.* Centrar, colocar o fijar en un centro.—*vn.* 1. Descansar o reposar sobre alguna cosa. 2. Terminar, rematar, confinar; reunirse.—*vr.* Colocarse en el centro o en medio.
Centric, Centrical [sen'-tric, al], *a.* Central.
Centrically [sen'-tric-al-i], *adv.* Centralmente.
Centricalness [sen'-tric-al-nes], *s.* Situación central.
Centrifugal [sen-trif'-yu-gal], *a.* Centrífugo, lo que se aparta o se aleja del centro.
Centripetal [sen-trip'-e-tal], *a.* Centrípeta, lo que se acerca o tiene tendencia al centro.
Centuple [sen'-tiu-pl], *a.* Céntuplo, centuplicado, cien veces tanto.
Centuplicate [sen-tu'-pli-kēt], *va.* Centuplicar, aumentar cien veces más alguna cosa.
Centurial [sen-tiū'-ri-al], *a.* 1. Perteneciente a una centuria del pueblo romano. 2. Secular, referente a un espacio de cien años.
Centuriator [sen-tiū'-ri-ē-tər], **Centurist** [sen'-chu-rist], *s.* El que distingue los tiempos por siglos.
Centurion [sen-tiu- o tū'-ri-un], *s.* Centurión, capitán, oficial militar romano que mandaba cien hombres.
Century [sen'-chu-ri], *s.* 1. Centuria, siglo; el número de cien años. 2. Centuria, cuerpo o fuerza militar romano que un tiempo constó de cien hombres.
Cephalalgia [sef-al-al'-jia], *s.* Cefalalgia, dolor de cabeza.
Cephalic [sef-al'-ic], *a.* Cefálico, útil o perteneciente a la cabeza.
Cephalopod [sef'-a-lo-pod], *a.* Perteneciente a los cefalópodos.
Cephalopoda [sef-a-lep'-o-da], *s. pl.* Cefalópodos, clase de moluscos caracterizados por largos brazos o tentáculos.
Cepheus [sī'-fiūs], *s.* Cefeo, constelación boreal, cerca del Dragón y Casiopea.
Ceraceous [sę-rē'-shūs], *a.* Ceráceo, de la naturaleza de la cera o semejante a ella.
Ceramic [ser-am'-ic], *a.* Cerámico, relativo al arte de la fabricación de objetos de tierra, loza y porcelana. *Ceramic art*, Arte cerámica.
Ceramics [ser-am'-ics], *s.* 1. Arte cerámica, alfarería; el arte de modelar barro, etc. 2. Alfarería, los objetos hechos de barro o porcelana. Se escribe también KERAMICS.
Cerasin [ser'-a-sin], *s.* Cerasina, goma del cerezo, ciruelo, etc.
Cerastes [ser-as'-tīz], *s.* Cerasta o cerastes, una especie de culebra venenosa de África.
Cerate [sī'-rēt], *s.* Cerato, composición de cera, aceite o resina, con medicamentos; permanece siempre sólida.
Cerated [sī'-rē-ted], *a.* Encerado.
Cerberean [ser-bī'-re-an], *a.* Parecido al cancerbero o relativo a él.
Cere [sīr], *va.* Encerar, dar con cera.
Cereal [sī'-re-al], *a.* Cereal, lo que pertenece a los granos farináceos. —*s.* Planta farinácea, como el trigo, centeno, cebada, etc., y el grano que produce.
Cerebellar [ser-ę-bel'-ar], *a.* Relativo o perteneciente al cerebelo.
Cerebellum [ser-e-bel'-um], *s.* Cerebelo, la parte posterior del cerebro.
Cerebral [ser'-e-bral], *a.* Cerebral. *Cerebral palsy*, Parálisis cerebral, diplejía espástica.
Cerebrate [ser'-e-brêt], *vn.* Exhibir actividad mental, pensar.
Cerebration [ser-ę-brē'-shun], *s.* Función cerebral, sea o no consciente y voluntaria.
Cerebrum [ser'-e-brum], *s.* Cerebro o celebro; encéfalo.
Cerecloth [sīr'-clōth], *s.* Encerado, hule, lienzo aderezado con cera, goma o cualquiera otra materia glutinosa.
Ceremonial [ser-ę-mō'-ni-al], *a.* y *s.* Ceremonial; rito externo; conjunto de formalidades o ceremonias de un acto público y solemne.
Ceremonialness [ser-ę-mō'-ni-al-nes], **Ceremoniousness** [ser-ę-mō'-ni-us-nes], *s.* Ceremoniosidad.
Ceremonious [ser-ę-mō'-ni-us], *a.* 1. Ceremonial, lo que toca o pertenece al uso de las ceremonias. 2. Ceremonioso, cumplimentero, etiquetero. 3. Ceremoniático, importuno a fuerza de ceremonias.
Ceremoniously [ser-ę-mō'-ni-us-li], *adv.* Ceremoniosamente.
Ceremony [ser'-ę-mo-ni], *s.* 1. Ceremonia, los ritos y fórmulas que se usan en el culto divino. 2. Ceremonia, cumplido, especie de cortesía que usan los hombres unos con otros. 3. Ceremonias, fórmulas exteriores que se observan por razón de estado. *The book of ceremonies*, Ceremonial. *Without ceremony*, Con franqueza, con toda libertad. *Master of ceremonies*, Maestro de ceremonias.
Cereous [sī'-ri-us], *a.* Hecho de cera o parecido a ella.
Cereus [sī'-rę-us], *s.* Género de los cactos con flores grandes, laterales, tubulares y a menudo nocturnas. El Cereus giganteus, de Arizona, es a veces de sesenta pies de alto y dos de diámetro.
Cerinthian [sī-rin'-thi-an], *s.* Cerintio, el que sigue la herejía de Cerinto, mezcla de cristianismo, judaísmo y paganismo.
Cerite [sī'-rait], *s.* Cerita, silicato de cerio, mineral muy escaso, resinoso.
Cerium [sī'-ri-um], *s.* Cerio, elemento metálico muy escaso, descubierto en 1803 por Berzelius.
Cernuous [sęr'-niu-us], *a.* Que tiene la extremidad superior inclinada; que se dobla e inclina, como una flor.
Cerograph [sī'-re-graf], *s.* Grabado, o escritura sobre cera.
Cerography [sī-reg'-ra-fi], *s.* 1. El arte de grabar o escribir sobre cera. 2. El arte de pintar al encausto, o por medio del fuego, con ceras de colores. 3. Procedimiento de imprimir con cera, clisando matrices o planchas grabadas en cera.
Cerise [sę-rīz'], *a.* De color cereza.
Ceroplastic [sī-ro-plas'-tic], *s.* Ceroplástica, arte de modelar en cera.
Cerris [ser'-is], *s.* (Bot.) Especie de encina.
Certain [sęr'-tęn], *a.* 1. Cierto, claro, evidente, manifiesto, indudable, incontestable, lo que no admite duda. 2. Cierto, alguno, un tal. 3. Cierto, determinado, fijo. 4. Cierto, seguro.
Certainly [sęr'-tęn-li], *adv.* 1. Ciertamente, indudablemente, sin duda, a la verdad. 2. Seguramente, sin falta.
Certainness [sęr'-tęn-nes], **Certainty** [sęr'-tęn-ti], *s.* 1. Certeza, certidumbre, conocimiento cierto de alguna cosa y que excluye toda duda. 2. Seguridad, verdad. *There is no certainty in him*, No se puede tener confianza en él; no hay que fiar en él.
†**Certes** [sęr'-tīs], *adv.* (Ant.) Ciertamente, en verdad.
Certificate [sęr-tif'-i-kēt], **Certification** [sęr-tif-i-kē'-shun], *s.* Certificación, testimonio. *Certificate of baptism*, Fe de bautismo.
Certificate, *va.* Certificar.
Certifier [sęr'-ti-fai-ęr], *s.* Certificador.
Certify [sęr'-ti-fai], *va.* Certificar, atestiguar, afirmar.
Certiorari [sęr-shi-o-rē'-rai], *s.* (For.) Auto de uno de los tribunales superiores de justicia avocando a sí la causa que pende en un tribunal inferior.
Certitude [sęr'-ti-tiūd], *s.* Certidumbre, certeza.
Cerulean [sę-rū'-lę-an], *a.* Cerúleo, azul obscuro.
Cerulific [ser-u-lif'-ic], *a.* Lo que puede dar color cerúleo.
Cerumen [sę-rū'-men], *s.* Cera de los oídos, cerilla.
Ceruse [sī'-rūs], *s.* Cerusa, albayalde.
Cerused [sī'-rūst], *a.* 1. Cosa que tiene albayalde. 2. Mujer que usa el albayalde u otro afeite.
Cervical [sęr'-vi-cal], *a.* Cervical, lo que pertenece al cuello.
Cervix [sęr'-vix], *s.* Cerviz, el cuello, o lo que a él se parece, y en especial la parte posterior del cuello.
§**Cespititious** [ses-pi-tish'-us], *a.* Hecho de césped.

Cespitose [ses'-pi-tōs], *a.* De césped, lo que crece en grupos o espesuras como el césped.
Cess [ses], *va.* Amillarar, repartir las contribuciones por millares.
Cess, *s.* Amillaramiento, repartimiento de las contribuciones por millares.
Cessation [ses-sé'-shun], *s.* Cesación, interrupción, suspensión, intermisión, parada.
Cession [sesh'-un], *s.* Cesión, la acción de ceder o la acción con que un hombre cede a otro el derecho que tiene a alguna cosa.
Cessionary [sesh'-un-ę-ri], *a.* y *s.* Cesionario, que hace cesión.
Cessor [ses'-er], *s.* (For.) 1. El que descuida cumplir con lo que debe dentro del término legal. 2. Asesor. 3. Tasador. 4. Repartidor, amillarador.
Cesspool o **Cesspit** [ses'-pūl], *s.* Sumidero, pozo de letrina, hoyo cubierto para recibir las inmundicias de un edificio.
Cesura, *s.* *V.* CÆSURA.
Cest [sest], *s.* Ceñidor.
Cestus [ses'-tus], *s.* 1. Ceñidor de Vénus. 2. Manopla guarnecida de hierro.
Cetacean [sę-té'-sę-an], *s.* Uno de los cetáceos, como la ballena.
Cetaceous [sę-té'-shus], *a.* Cetáceo, de la especie de la ballena.
Cha [chā], *s.* El té; especie de te arrollado que se usa en el Asia central.
Chablis [shą-blí'], *s.* Nombre de un vino blanco hecho cerca de Chablis, en Francia.
Chafe [chêf], *va.* 1. Frotar, estregar, ludir, escaldar, calentar alguna cosa frotándola. 2. Enojar, enfadar, irritar.—*vn.* Enojarse, enfadarse, acalorarse; fricarse; desollarse.
Chafe, *s.* Acaloramiento, rabia, furor, cólera, ardor.
Chafer [chê'-fęr], *s.* 1. Especie de escarabajo. 2. Escalfador, jarro de metal para calentar agua.
Chafery [chê'-fęr-i], *s.* Fragua o forja en la herrería.
Chaff [chąf], *s.* 1. Zurrón u hollejo, la cáscara del grano que se separa después de trillado y aventado. 2. Arista, cascabillo, gluma, o funda exterior de las gramíneas; también paja menuda. 3. (Met.) Paja, tamo, lo que es de ningún valor o entidad. 4. Befa, burla, zumba.
Chaffer [chaf'-ęr], *vn.* Regatear, baratear.
Chaffinch [chaf'-inch], *s.* (Orn.) Pinzón, pájaro. Fringilla cœlebs.
Chaffless [chąf'-les], *a.* 1. Sin zurrón u hollejo; mondado. 2. Sólido, profundo, lo que no tiene paja.
Chaffy [chąf'-i], *a.* Pajizo, lleno de zurrón u hollejo.
Chafing [chêf'-ing], *s.* Desolladura, escaldadura, fricción.
Chafing dish [chê'-fing dish], *s.* Infiernillo, anafe.
Chagas' disease [cha'-gas diz-íz'], Enfermedad de Chagas.
Chagrin [sha-grín'], *s.* Mal humor o mala condición, enfado, pesadumbre, disgusto, desazón, pena.
Chagrin, *va.* Enfadar o provocar a ira, vejar, entristecer, desazonar, enfadar, amohinar.
Chain [chên], *s.* 1. Cadena, serie de muchos anillos o eslabones unidos unos á otros; serie o sucesión. 2. Encadenamiento, enlace de causas, de ideas, etc. 3. Cadena, grillete. 4. Cadena de agrimensor; también medida de 66 pies ingleses o 20.1164 metros. 5. Cadena entre los tejedores; los hilos por donde pasa la trama. *Chain of rocks*, Arrecife de piedras. En plural es servidumbre, cautiverio, esclavitud. *Chain-gang*, Cadena de presidiarios. *Chain-plates*, (Mar.) Cadenas de las vigotas. *Top-chains*, Cadenas de las vergas. *Chain-pump*, (Mar.) Bomba de cadena. *Chain-shot*, (Art.) Balas encadenadas o balas enramadas.
Chain, *va.* 1. Encadenar. 2. Esclavizar. 3. Poner cadena a alguna cosa. 4. Enlazar, unir, juntar.
Chain reaction [chên ri-ac'-shun], *s.* Reacción en cadena.
Chainwork [chén'-wūrk], *s.* Cadeneta, labor o trabajo hecho en figura de cadena.
Chair [chār], *s.* 1. Silla o taburete, asiento portátil. 2. Silla, asiento de juez u otra persona constituida en autoridad. 3. Silla de manos. 4. Sillón, asiento de la presidencia en una asamblea o cuerpo legislativo: por extensión, presidente (de una asamblea o congreso). *Arm-chair*, Silla de brazos o poltrona. *Privy-chair*, Sillico o servicio. 5. Silla volante. *Hair-bottomed chairs*, Sillas con asientos de crin. *Cane-bottomed chairs*, Sillas de junquillo. *Rocking-chair*, Mecedora. (Cuba) Columpio. *Pivot-chair*, Silla giratoria. 6. Calesín, volanta o volante, quitrín. 7. Cojinete (de ferrocarril). *The chair is taken*, Se ha abierto la sesión. *Professor's chair*, Cátedra. *To be in the chair*, Presidir.
Chair lift [chār' lift], *s.* 1. Telesilla. 2. Montaescaleras.
Chairman [chār'-man], *s.* 1. Presidente de una junta o reunión. 2. Silletero, el que está asalariado para llevar silla de manos; o sillero, el que hace o vende sillas.
Chairmanship [chār'-man-ship], *s.* Presidencia (de un comité, una asamblea, etc.)
Chaise [shêz], *s.* 1. Silla volante. 2. Coche de cuatro ruedas. *Post-chaise*, Silla de posta.
Chaise longue [shêz long'], *s.* Canapé, tipo de sofá muy cómodo.
Chalaza [ca-lê'-za], *s.* 1. (Zool.) Chalaza, cada uno de los ligamentos que unen la yema del huevo a los polos del mismo. 2. (Bot.) Chalaza, cordón de algunas semillas.
Chalcedony [cal-sed'-o-ni], *s.* Calcedonia, cuarzo no cristalizado y muy translúcido.
Chaldaic [cal-dê'-ic], **Chaldean** [cal-dí'-an], *a.* Caldaico, caldeo, lo que pertenece a Caldea.—*s.* **Chaldaic, Chaldee**, idioma caldeo.
Chaldron [chōl'-drun], *s.* Chaldrón, peso o medida de carbón y cok, equivalente en Inglaterra a unas 32 a 36 fanegas, y en los Estados Unidos de América de 2,500 a 2,900 libras.
Chalet [shą''-lé'], *s.* 1. Casita de labrador suizo. 2. Quinta de forma y construcción parecidas a las de las casas suizas.
Chalice [chal'-is], *s.* Cáliz.
Chalk [chōk], *s.* Greda, marga; clarión, tiza. (Amer.) Tizate. *French chalk*, Espuma de mar. Jaboncillo de sastre, esteatita usada para marcar sobre telas. *Chalk-cutter*, Cavador de greda. *Chalk-pit*, Pozo de que se saca la greda. *Chalk-stone*, Pedazo de greda, o tiza.
Chalk, *va.* 1. Engredar. 2. Señalar, marcar o dibujar con lápiz o yeso. 3. Margar, abonar con greda o con marga.
Chalky [chōk'-i], *a.* Gredoso, yesoso, lo que tiene greda o yeso.
Challenge [chal'-enj], *va.* 1. Desafiar, retar, provocar a combate o desafío: poner a prueba. 2. Acusar, imputar. 3. Recusar, tachar o poner excepción a un juez, ministro o testigo. 4. Alegar derecho a alguna cosa; pedir, pretender. 5. Citar a uno para el cumplimiento de alguna condición. 6. (Mil.) Dar el quién vive.
Challenge, *s.* 1. Desafío, el papel, billete o cartel de desafío. 2. Demanda, pretensión, la acción de pedir lo que se debe. 3. Recusación 4. Concurso, de los que se disputan algún premio o destino.
Challengeable [chal'-enj-a-bl], *a.* Sujeto o expuesto a desafío o acusación; recusable.
Challenger [chal'-en-jęr], *s.* Desafiador, duelista, agresor; demandante.
Challis [shal'-i], *s.* Chalí, tela ligera de lana. (Fr.)
Chalumeau [shal-u-mō'], *s.* El registro más bajo del clarinete.
†**Chalybean** [ca-lib'-ę-an], *a.* Calibeado, lo perteneciente a los antiguos calibes en Asia menor, famosos artífices en hierro y acero.
Chalybeate [ca-lib'-i-ēt], *a.* Impregnado con hierro o acero.—*s.* Agua ferruginosa.
Chama [kê'-ma], *s.* El molusco de mayor tamaño conocido hasta el día, que llega a pesar 500 libras.
Chamade [shą-mąd'], *s.* (Mil.) Llamada, señal que se hace con la caja o clarín para parlamentar y a veces para rendirse. (Fr.)
Chamber [chêm'-bęr], *s.* 1. Cámara, cuarto, habitación, aposento, pieza habitable de una casa. *Bed-chamber*, Alcoba, dormitorio. (Mex.) Recámara. *Chamber-pot*, Orinal. 2. Cámara, tribunal o sala de justicia. 3. *Chamber of commerce*, Cámara de Comercio. 4. *Chamber of a pump*, (Mar.) Almacén de una bomba. 5. (Art.) Cámara, la parte hueca del cañón que ocupa la carga. 6. (Art.) Cámara de mina, la cavidad en donde se pone pólvora en una mina. *Chamber of London*, Cámara o ayuntamiento de Londres, o su tesoro público. *Chamber of presence*, Sala de estrado. *Judge's chamber*, Gabinete del juez. *Condensing chamber*, Condensador. *Chamber-council*, (1) Comunicación confidencial. (2) Junta o consejo secreto. *Chamber-counsel*, Jurisconsulto, abogado que da su parecer sin presentarse ante el tribunal. *Chamber-music*, Música de salón. *Chamber-organ*, Órgano portátil. *Chamber-practice*, La práctica del jurisconsulto o consejero que da su parecer sin presentarse en los tribunales.
Chamber, *va.* 1. Hacer la cámara de un cañón. 2. Ajustar a la cámara. —*vn.* 1. Ajustarse de una manera compacta los perdigones de un cartucho. 2. (Ant.) Entregarse a la lascivia.
Chamberer [chêm'-bęr-ęr], *s.* (Ant.) Galancete, hombre faldero, mujeriego y galanteador; libertino, disoluto.
Chamber-fellow [chêm'-bęr-fel'-o], *s.* Compañero de cuarto, el que duerme en la misma pieza que otro.

Chambering [chêm'-bęr-ing], *s.* 1. División en compartimientos. 2. (Des.) Lascivia, liviandad.
Chamberlain [chêm'-bęr-lęn], *s.* 1. Jefe de cámara. *Lord chamberlain*, Gran chambelán; camarlengo o camarero mayor. 2. Recibidor de rentas.
Chamberlainship [chêm'-bęr-lęn-ship], *s.* Oficio de camarero.
Chamber-lye, *s.* *V.* URINE.
Chamber-maid [chêm'-bęr-mêd], *sf.* 1. Doncella de una señora; camarera. 2. Criada de sala.
Chambray [sham'-brê], *s.* Cambray, o batista, lienzo blanco muy delgado.
Chameleon [ca-mī'-lę-en], *s.* Camaleón, especie de lagarto.
Chamfer [cham'-fęr], *va.* Acanalar, arrugar, estriar.
Chamfer, Chamfret [cham'-fret], *s.* Canal, arruga, estría, bisel.
Chamfrain [cham'-frên], *s.* Testera, armadura para la frente de un caballo de guerra o de batalla. *Cf.* CHANFRIN.
Chamois [sham'-ī], *s.* Gamuza, especie de cabra montés.
Chamomile [cam'-o-mail], *s.* Manzanilla, camomila, hierba de flores medicinales. Anthemis nobilis.
Champ [champ], *va.* Morder, mascar, mordiscar.
Champagne [sham-pên'], *s.* Vino de Champaña.
Champaign [sham-pên'], *s.* Campiña, campo descubierto, llanura.
Champaign, *a.* Abierto o llano.
Champak [cham'-pak], *s.* Árbol sagrado del Indostán con flores color de oro y muy fragantes. Pertenece a las magnoliáceas. Michelia champaca.
Champertor [sham'-pęr-ter], *s* Pleitista o litigante que quiere tener parte de la cosa litigada.
Champerty [sham'-pęr-ti], *s.* Mantenimiento de un pleito para recibir parte de la cosa litigada.
Champion [cham'-pi-en], *s.* 1. Defensor de una causa, doctrina o persona. 2. Campeón, el que mantenía contienda o batalla por medio de las armas. 3. Héroe, guerrero.
Championess [cham'-pi-en-es], *s.* Campeona, defensora; abogada.
Chance [chąns], *s.* 1. Fortuna, ventura, suerte. 2. Acaso, suceso, lance, accidente, casualidad, contingencia. 3. Riesgo, peligro. 4. (Mat.) Probabilidades. *Ill chance*, Desdicha. *By chance*, Por ventura, casualmente, por acaso, por casualidad. *There is no chance*, No hay esperanza, remedio, escape. *He met me by chance*, Me encontró por casualidad. *The main chance*, Lo sólido, lo esencial. *To stand a chance*, Tener suerte. *To take one's chance*, Correr el riesgo, aventurarse. *The doctrine of chances*, El cálculo de las probabilidades.
Chance, *a.* Fortuito, casual, accidental.—*adv.* Casualmente, por acaso.
Chance, *vn.* Acaecer, suceder, acontecer. *If my letter should chance to be lost*, Si acaso se perdiese mi carta.
Chance-medley [chąns-med'-li], *s.* (For.) Homicidio casual; propiamente, es el homicidio cometido en defensa propia en una riña repentina.
Chancel [chan'-sel], *s.* Presbiterio en la iglesia.
Chancellor [chąn'-sel-ęr], *s.* Canciller, cancelario. *Chancellor of the Exchequer*, (Ingl.) Ministro de hacienda. *Lord High Chancellor*, Ministro de justicia o gran canciller.
Chancellorship [chąn'-sel-er-ship], *s.* Cancillería, el empleo y la dignidad de canciller.
Chancery [chąn'-sęr-i], *s.* Cancillería.
Chancre [shaŋ'-kęr], *s.* Úlcera venérea. (Vul.) Chancro.
Chancrous [shaŋ'-crus], *a.* Ulceroso.
Chancy [chąn'-si], *a.* (Fam.) Expuesto a riesgo; incierto; aventurado, peligroso.
Chandelier [shan-de-līr'], *s.* Araña de luces, candelero, cornucopia. (Méx.) Candil. (Fr.)
Chandler [chand'-lęr], *s.* Cerero o velero, el que hace o vende velas de cera o sebo. *Chandler's shop*, Lonja, abacería, tienda de víveres. (Am.) Pulpería. (Mex.) Tienda. *Ship-chandler*, Abastecedor de buques. *Wax-chandler*, Cerero. *Tallow-chandler*, Velero. *Corn-chandler*, Triguero, el que vende trigo y granos.
Chandlery [chand'-lęr-i], *s.* Todas las cosas que se venden en las tiendas de granos, velas, etc.; mercería. *Ship-chandlery*, Almacén donde se vende toda especie de artículos necesarios para los barcos.
Chanfrin [shan'-frin], *s.* Frente o faz del caballo.
Change [chênj], *va.* 1. Poner una cosa en lugar de otra. 2. Cambiar, trocar una cosa por otra. 3. Cambiar, reducir una moneda mayor a varias menores. 4. Convertir, transmutar. 5. Mudar de genio o de vida.—*vn.* Mudar, variar, alterarse, corregirse.
Change, *s.* 1. Mudanza, variedad, conversión, variación de estado que tienen las cosas. 2. Vicisitud. 3. Cambio, dinero menudo. 4. Lonja o bolsa, lugar donde se reunen los comerciantes a tratar sus negocios. En este sentido es abreviatura de EXCHANGE. *I have no change*, No tengo suelto o no tengo cambio. *Change of the moon*, Interlunio, cuarto de luna. *Change of clothes*, Muda de ropa. *Change of life*, La edad crítica, cesación final del menstruo.
Changeability [chênj-a-bil'-i-ti], *s.* Mutabilidad.
Changeable [chênj'-a-bl], *a.* 1. Voluble, variable, inconstante, veleidoso. 2. Mudable, lo que se puede mudar. 3. Cambiante, tornasolado, hablando de géneros.
Changeableness [chênj'-a-bl-nes], *s.* Mutabilidad, volubilidad, inconstancia.
Changeably [chênj'-a-bli], *adv.* Inconstantemente.
Changeful [chênj'-ful], *a.* Inconstante, variable, voltario, veleidoso.
Changeless [chênj'-les], *a.* Constante, inmutable.
Changeling [chênj'-ling], *s.* 1. Un niño cambiado por otro, sea por equivocación o de intento. 2. Loco, tonto. 3. Inconstante, el que es mudable, persona irresoluta, sin carácter.
Changer [chênj'-ęr], *s.* 1. Cambiante, cambista, el que cambia dinero. 2. El que muda de parecer.
Channel [chan'-el], *s.* 1. Canal, álveo, la madre de un río. 2. Canal, cualquiera cavidad hecha longitudinalmente. (Arq.) Estría, mediacaña. 3. Canal, trozo de mar estrecho. *British Channel*, El canal de la Mancha. *Channels*, (Mar.) Mesas de guarnición. *Fire-channels*, (Mar.) Canales de fuego. *Channel out of soundings*, (Mar.) Foso. *Channel of a block*, (Mar.) Cajera.
Channel, *va.* 1. Acanalar, estriar; surcar. 2. Conducir o llevar por, o como por un canal.
Channer [chan'-ęr], *vn.* (Esco.) Refunfuñar, quejarse.
Chant [chąnt], *va.* y *vn.* 1. Cantar. 2. Cantar el servicio en una iglesia catedral.
Chant, *s.* Canto; canto llano, melodía.
Chanter [chąnt'-ęr], *s.* 1. Cantor, el que canta. 2. Chantre.
Chantey [chąnt'-ę], *s.* Canto monótono de los marineros cuando halan y en otras maniobras.
Chanticleer [chan'-ti-clīr], *s.* Quiquiriquí, el gallo, así llamado por su modo de cantar.
Chantress [chąnt'-res], *s.* Cantora, cantante, cantatriz.
Chantry [chąnt'-ri], *s.* 1. Capilla, especialmente una dotada para decirse en ella misas diarias. 2. Vallado, enrejado o estructura que contiene una tumba.
Chaos [kê'-os], *s.* 1. Caos, la mezcla confusa en que se hallaban todos los elementos antes de la creación. 2. Caos, confusión, mezcla irregular, desorden.
Chaotic [kê-et'-ic], *a.* Caótico, confuso, desordenado, irregular.
Chap [chap], *va.* Hender, rajar, resquebrajar; abrir grietas o rajas en el cutis, en la madera, etc.—*vn.* 1. Rajarse o hendirse la tierra por el excesivo calor. 2. Hacerse grietas en la cara o en las manos por la frialdad. 3. (Esco.) *V.* CHEAPEN.
Chap, *s.* 1. Grieta, abertura, rendija, hendidura. 2. (Esco.) Golpe seco sobre la puerta; choque. 3. Mozo, joven, muchacho. *Chap-book*, Folleto vendido por un pacotillero. 4. (Fam.) Mozo, chico. En este sentido es abreviatura de "chapman." *A queer chap*, Un original, un hombre extravagante.
Chap [chep], *s.* 1. Mandíbula, quijada inferior o superior de un animal. *V.* CHOP. 2. Quijada de un tornillo de banco.
Chaparral [chap-a-ral'], *s.* (E. U. del Oeste) Chaparral, el sitio poblado de chaparros. (< Español.)
Chape [chêp], *s.* Chapa de cinturón; contera de espada; charnela de hebilla.
Chapel [chap'-el], *s.* 1. Capilla, iglesia pequeña. 2. Capilla, dependencia de una iglesia con su altar. 3. Edificio consagrado al culto de los disidentes. 4. El cuerpo organizado de los cajistas e impresores de una imprenta dada. *Chapel-master*, Maestro de capilla. *V.* KAPELLMEISTER.
Chapeless [chêp'-les], *a.* Sin contera.
Chapelet [chap'-el-et], *s.* 1. (Equit.) Doble estribo. 2. Máquina para elevar agua, o para dragar el fondo de un puerto, por medio de cubos sujetos a una cadena sin fin.
Chapelry [chap'-el-ri], *s.* La jurisdicción o límites de una capilla.
Chaperon [shap'-ęr-ōn], *s.* 1. Señora que acompaña a una o más jóvenes en público, o en reuniones, viajes, etc. Rodrigón, hombre de edad que acompaña a una señora, por el buen parecer. 2. Caperuza, capirote.
Chaperon, *va.* Acompañar a una o

más señoras a las tertulias o reuniones o tener cuidado de ellas.
Chapfallen, Chopfallen [chep'-fōl-n], *a.* Boquihundido, el que tiene hundidos los labios. (Fig.) *To be chapfallen,* Estar triste, abatido, desanimado. (Fam.) Estar con las orejas gachas.
†**Chapiter** [chap'-i-tęr], *s.* (Arq.) Capitel. *V.* CAPITAL.
Chaplain [chap'-len], *s.* 1. Capellán, el sacerdote que se dedica al servicio de una capilla; limosnero. 2. Capellán castrense.
Chaplaincy [chap'-len-si], **Chaplainship** [chap'-len-ship], *s.* Capellanía.
Chapless [chap'-les], *a.* Boquiseco.
Chaplet [chap'-let], *s.* 1. Guirnalda, corona de flores. 2. Rosario. 3. (Arq.) Moldura de cuentas. 4. Penacho. 5. Capilleja.
Chapman [chap'-man], *s.* Buhonero, vendedor, traficante en géneros baratos; pacotillero.
Chapter [chap'-tęr], *s.* 1. Capítulo, una de las partes de que se compone un libro. 2. Capítulo, categoría, lista, serie; asunto de que se trata. 3. Capítulo, cabildo, junta del clero de una catedral. 4. Ramificación o sucursal de una sociedad o confraternidad. *And so on to the end of the chapter,* Y así lo demás. *Chapter-house,* Sala capitular. *To read one a chapter,* (Fig.) Poner a alguno como nuevo, zaherirle. *To the end of the chapter,* Hasta el fin.
Char [chār], *va.* 1. Hacer carbón de leña. 2. Trabajar a jornal.
Char, *s.* 1. (Des.) Jornal, trabajo a jornal. 2. Umbra, especie de pescado de agua dulce.
Character [car'-ac-tęr], *s.* 1. Carácter, la índole, genio y condición de cada uno. 2. Carácter, nombre, fama, calidad, reputación. 3. Informe, testimonio de conducta. 4. Retrato, descripción, representación de una persona o cosa. 5. Personaje, persona, individualidad. 6. Papel, la parte de un actor en el teatro. 7. Carácter, marca, distintivo o señal. 8. Carácter o forma de la letra. *Persons of bad character,* Personas de mala vida o reputación.
Character, *va.* Grabar, esculpir, señalar, imprimir.
Character-assassination [cār'-ac-tęr-as-sas-i-nē'-shun], *s.* Difamación, calumnia, descrédito público.
Characteristic, Characteristical [car-ac-tęr-is'-tic, al], *a.* Característico.
Characteristic, *s.* Característico.
Characteristically [ca-rac-tęr-is'-tic-al-li], *adv.* Característicamente.
Characteristicalness [car-ac-tęr-is'-tic-al-nes], *s.* Propiedad característica.
Characterization [car''-ac-tęr-i-zē'-shun], *s.* El acto, procedimiento o efecto de caracterizar.
Characterize [car'-ac-tęr-aiz], *va.* 1. Caracterizar. 2. Grabar, esculpir, señalar.
Characterless [car'-ac-tęr-les], *a.* Sin carácter.
Charactery [car'-ac-tęr-i], *s.* 1. Carácter, impresión o señal. 2. Sistema de caracteres; representación.
Charade [sha-rēd'], *s.* Charada, especie de enigma, acertijo.
Charbon [shār'-ben], *s.* 1. Fiebre esplénica, ántrax. 2. Mancha negra en los dientes de los caballos después que cierran.
Charcoal [chār'-cōl], *s.* Carbón de leña. *Animal charcoal,* Carbón animal, negro de marfil.
Chard [chārd], *s.* (Bot.) 1. Hoja de alcachofa, o acelga, aporcada. 2. Acelga suiza. Beta cicla.
Chardoon [chār-dūn'], *s.* *V.* CARDOON.
Charge [chārj], *va.* 1. Cargar, poner una carga o peso sobre alguna cosa. 2. Cargar, introducir la carga en un arma de fuego. 3. Encargar, comisionar, confiar al cuidado de alguno. 4. Cargar, poner en cuenta; poner precio, pedir por. 5. Cargar, atarear. 6. Cargar, acometer. 7. Censurar, acusar, imputar, denunciar. 8. Mandar, exhortar, instruir. 9. Hacer gastar.—*vn.* 1. Demandar o fijar precio. 2. Atacar. 3. Agacharse, acuclillarse; dícese de los perros de caza.
Charge, *s.* 1. Carga, tiro, la cantidad de pólvora y balas con que se carga un arma de fuego. 2. Cargo, cuidado. 3. Precio, coste, gasto, partida, cláusula. 4. Precepto, mandato, orden; cargo, comisión. 5. Cargo, acusación. 6. Ataque, embestida. 7. Carga, medicina que se aplica a los caballos. 8. Encargo, depósito. 9. Acto y posición de agacharse los perros de caza o la orden de agacharse.
Chargeable [chārj'-a-bl], *a.* 1. Imputable, lo que se puede imputar, como una deuda o un delito. 2. Acusable, sujeto a cargos y acusaciones. 3. (Ant.) Costoso, caro, dispendioso, lo que cuesta mucho.
Chargeableness [chārj'-a-bl-nes], *s.* Gasto, coste.
Charge account [chārj' a-caunt], *s.* Cuenta corriente.
Charger [chārj'-ęr], *s.* 1. Fuente o plato grande. 2. Corcel, caballo criado para la guerra.
Charily [chār'-i-li], *adv.* Cautelosamente, cuidadosamente.
Chariness [chār'-i-nes], *s.* Cautela, cuidado, precaución.
Chariot [char'-i-ęt], *s.* 1. Carroza de paseo o de ceremonia. (Prov.) Faetón o carrocín. 2. Carro militar, en que combatían antiguamente los héroes. 3. Coche ligero o cochecillo. *Chariot-race,* Carrera de carros.
Charioteer [char-i-ęt-īr'], *s.* Cochero; carretero.
Charitable [char'-i-ta-bl], *a.* 1. Caritativo, limosnero. 2. Benigno.
Charitableness [char'-i-ta-bl-nes], *s.* Caridad.
Charitably [char'-i-ta-bli], *adv.* Caritativamente; benignamente.
Charity [char'-i-ti], *s.* 1. Caridad, ternura, benevolencia, amor. 2. Caridad, virtud teologal que consiste en amar a Dios y al prójimo. 3. Caridad, limosna, el socorro que se da a los pobres. *To be in charity with all men,* Querer a todo el mundo, no desear el mal de nadie. *Charity begins at home,* La caridad bien ordenada empieza por uno mismo.
Charivari [shar''-i-var'-i], *s.* Cencerrada, ruido discorde para dar broma a los recién casados.
Chark [chārk], *va.* Carbonizar, reducir a carbón. *Cf.* CHAR.
Charlatan [shār'-la-tan], *s.* Charlatán, saltimbanco, curandero, empírico.
Charlatanic [shar-la-tan'-ic], *a.* Empírico, propio de un charlatán.
Charlatanry [shār'-la-tan-ri], *s.* Charlatanería, engaño; picotería.
Charles's wain [chārlz'-ez wên], *s.* (Astr.) Osa mayor, constelación boreal.
Charlock [chār'-lec], *s.* (Ingl.) Mostaza silvestre, planta común en los sembrados.
Charlotte [shār'-let], *s.* Compota de fruta, nata, etc., contenida en un molde de bizcocho. *Charlotte russe,* Nata batida o flan en un molde de bizcocho.
Charm [chārm], *s.* 1. Encanto, hechizo o maleficio. 2. Embeleso, atractivo, gracia, hechizo, encanto.
Charm, *va.* 1. Ensalmar, hechizar, encantar. 2. Encantar, embelesar, atraer, hechizar, arrobar; captar o arrebatar la vista, los oídos o el ánimo.—*vn.* Sonar armoniosamente.
Charmed [chārmd], *a.* Encantado; complacido, embelesado.
Charmer [chārm'-ęr], *s.* 1. Encantador, hechicero. 2. Hechicero, la persona que atrae las voluntades.
¿**Charmful** [chārm'-ful], *a.* Lleno de encantos, gracioso.
Charming [chārm'-ing], *a.* Agradable, hechicero, encantador, maravilloso, pasmoso.
Charmingly [chārm'-ing-li], *adv.* Agradablemente, deleitosamente.
Charmingness [chārm'-ing-nes], *s.* Encanto, embeleso, atractivo.
Charnel [chār'-nel], *a.* Del osario, lo que contiene huesos de difuntos.
Charnel-house [chār'-nel-haus], *s.* Carnero, u osario, el paraje en que se ponen los huesos de los difuntos.
Charpie [shār'-pi], *s.* Hilas, las hebras que se van sacando de los trapos de lienzo. (Fr.)
Charr [chār], *s.* Umbra, trucha asalmonada, pez de agua dulce.
Charry [chār'-i], *a.* Carbonoso, de la naturaleza del carbón.
Chart [chārt], *va.* Poner en una carta hidrográfica.—*s.* (Mar.) Carta de navegar o de marear; carta hidrográfica.
Chartaceous [car-tê'-shus], *a.* Que tiene la textura de papel de escribir.
Charter [chār'-tęr], *s.* 1. Escritura auténtica. 2. Cédula, título, privilegio exclusivo. 3. Carta constitucional.
Charter, *va.* 1. Establecer por ley, incorporar o reconocer como un cuerpo legítimo. 2. (Mar.) Fletar un barco por un tanto.
Chartered [chār'-tęrd], *a.* Privilegiado. (Mar.) Fletado.
Charter-party [chār'-tęr-pār'-ti], *s.* Contrata, carta-partida, instrumento o papel con que las partes aseguran algún convenio, quedándose cada una con una copia.
Chartography, Cartography [car-teg'-ra-fi], *s.* Cartografía, arte de construir las cartas marinas o mapas.
Chartreuse [shar-trūz'], *s.* 1. Cartuja, monasterio de cartujos. *V.* CARTHUSIAN. 2. Un licor estomacal.
Chartulary, *s.* *V.* CARTULARY.
Char-woman [chār'-wum-an], *s.* Mujer asalariada para las faenas domésticas por uno o pocos días.
Chary [chār'-i], *a.* Cuidadoso, cauteloso, circunspecto; económico, frugal.
Chasable [chês'-a-bl], *a.* Cazadero, cazable.
Chase [chês], *va.* 1. Cazar. 2. Dar caza, perseguir o seguir al enemigo por mar o tierra. 3. Engastar, montar una piedra preciosa. 4. Cincelar (el oro y la plata). *V.* ENCHASE. 5. Seguir. *To chase away,* Hacer huir, espantar. *To chase after,* Correr tras de, o en seguimiento de.

Chase, *s.* 1. Caza. 2. Caza, seguimiento o la acción de seguir al enemigo. 3. Caza, los animales o aves que se cazan. 4. Cazadero, el sitio en que se hace la caza. 5. Partida de cazadores que van á cazar. 6. (Mar.) Caza. *Bow-chase*, Cañón de mira. *Stern-chase*, Guardatimón, cañón de a popa. *Wild-goose chase*, A caza de ilusiones, en seguimiento de lo inasequible.

Chase, *s.* 1. Rama, cerco de hierro, con que se sujeta el molde en la prensa. 2. Cualquier muesca o encaje. 3. (Art.) Calibre de un cañón.

Chaser [chê'-sęr], *s.* 1. Cazador. 2. Engastador.

Chasing [chê'-sing], *s.* 1. Cinceladura, arte de cincelar; trabajo en relieve. 2. Seguimiento, caza.

Chasm [cazm], *s.* 1. Hendidura, grieta, rajadura, abertura. 2. Vacío, hueco, cóncavo u hondo. 3. En los libros de cuentas, laguna, falta, blanco.

Chasmed [cazmd], *a.* Hendido, rajado, lleno de grietas.

Chassis [shąs'-i], *s.* Chasis, armazón.

Chaste [chêst], *a.* 1. Casto, puro, honesto, continente, púdico, opuesto a la sensualidad. 2. Castizo, neto, limpio y puro; dícese del estilo.

Chaste-eyed [chêst'-aid], *a.* El que tiene el mirar modesto.

Chastely [chêst'-li], *adv.* 1. Castamente; decorosamente. 2. Correctamente, de una manera castiza (hablando del estilo).

Chasten [chê'-sn], *va.* 1. Corregir, castigar. 2. Depurar, limpiar, las faltas o errores; purificar por medio de aflicción. 3. Limpiar, elevar.

Chastener [chê'-sn-ęr], *s.* Castigador, corrector, depurador, limpiador.

Chasteness [chêst'-nes], *s.* Pureza, castidad, continencia.

Chastening [chês'-n-ing], *s.* Castigo, corrección, reprimenda; disciplina.

Chaste-tree [chêst'-trî], *s.* (Bot.) Agnocasto, sauzgatillo o pimiento loco.

Chastisable [chas-taiz'-a-bl], *a.* Punible, castigable.

Chastise [chas-taiz'], *va.* Castigar, reformar, corregir.

Chastisement [chas'-tiz-męnt], *s.* Castigo, pena, corrección.

Chastiser [chas-taiz'-ęr], *s.* Castigador, castigadora.

Chastity [chas'-ti-ti], *s.* Castidad, pureza, continencia.

Chasuble [chas'-yu-bl], *s.* Casulla, vestidura sagrada que se pone el sacerdote sobre el alba; manta sin mangas.

Chat [chat], *vn.* Charlar, parlotear.

Chat, *s.* 1. Charla, locuacidad, cháchara, parla, flujo de hablar, garrulidad. 2. Pájaro de ambos hemisferios: uno es el Collalba, pájaro del grupo de los tenuirrostros, o de pico delgado (Saxicola rubicola); y otro el de cuello amarillo, pájaro cantor americano (Icteria virens). 3. (Prov. Ingl.) Amento. *V.* CATKIN.

Chateau [shą-tō'], *s.* *V.* CASTLE.

Chatelaine [shąt'-ę-lên], *s.* 1. Cadena o cadenas que cuelgan del cinturón de la mujer. (Fr.) 2. Castellana, la señora de un castillo.

Chatellany [shat'-e-len-i], *s.* Castellanía.

Chattel [chat'-el], *s.* Bienes muebles.

Chatter [chat'-ęr], *vn.* 1. Cotorrear, parlar como una cotorra. 2. Rechinar los dientes. 3. Charlar, parlotear, parlar.

Chatter, *s.* 1. Chirrido. 2. Charla, cháchara, parla; conversación ociosa.

Chatterbox [chat'-ęr-box], *s.* Parlero, parlador, charlador, guapetón, hablador; especialmente un niño.

Chatterer [chat'-ęr-ęr], *s.* Charlador o charlante, gárrulo.

Chattering [chat'-ęr-ing], *s.* 1. Chirrido de los pájaros. 2. Rechinamiento de dientes. 3. Garrulidad.

Chattering, *a.* Locuaz, hablanchín.

Chatty [chat'-i], *a.* Dispuesto a hablar.—*s.* (Anglo-indio) Jarra, olla porosa de la India.

Chauffeur [shō'-fęr], *s.* Chofer.

Chauvinism [shō'-vin-izm], *s.* Chauvinismo, patriotería.

Chauvinist [shō'-vin-ist], *s.* El que demuestra celo exagerado por la honra y el buen nombre de su patria.

Chaw [chē], *va.* (Vul.) Mascar, masticar. *V.* CHEW.

Cheap [chîp], *a.* 1. Barato, lo que se vende o compra a poco precio. 2. Barato, lo que no tiene estimación. 3. Común, de poco valor, de poco aprecio.—*s.* (Des.) Mercado; compra, una cosa barata.

Cheapen [chîp'-n], *va.* 1. Regatear alguna cosa antes de comprarla. 2. Abaratar, minorar o rebajar el precio de alguna cosa.

Cheapener [chîp'-n-ęr], *s.* Regatón, traficante.

Cheaply [chîp'-li], *adv.* Barato, a bajo precio.

Cheapness [chîp'-nes], *s.* Baratura.

Cheat [chît], *va.* 1. Engañar, defraudar, estafar, entrampar, cometer fraude o engaño. 2. Trampear, trapacear, no jugar limpio o hacer fullerías en el juego. 3. Chasquear.

Cheat, *s.* 1. Trampa, fraude, impostura, engaño, ratería, droga. 2. Trampista, petardista, droguero. *Cheat-bread*, Pan blanco.

Cheatableness [chît'-a-bl-nes], *s.* Engaño, trapacería, fullería, impostura, fraude.

Cheater [chît'-ęr], *s.* Trampista, bribón, estafador, ratero, petardista, fullero, droguero, trapacero.

Cheatery [chît'-ęr-i], *s.* Fraude sistemático; trampa, fullería (en el juego).

Cheating [chît'-ing], *pa.* y *s.* Engaño, fraude, trampa, añagaza.

Check [chec], *va.* 1. Reprimir, refrenar, moderar, detener, contener, atajar, sofocar, ahogar. 2. Confrontar o examinar un talón de banco, las partidas de una cuenta, los nombres de una lista, etc. 3. Dar jaque en el juego de ajedrez. 4. Poner talón o contraseña a un bulto u objeto, para su expedición. 5. (Ant.) Regañar, reñir, desaprobar algún dicho o hecho.—*vn.* 1. Pararse o detenerse. 2. Meterse o mezclarse en alguna cosa.

Check, *s.* 1. Rechazo, resistencia. 2. Restricción, freno. 3. Obstáculo, impedimento; contratiempo, descalabro, derrota. 4. La persona, cosa o causa que impide; alguna interrupción. 5. Cheque, documento en forma de mandato de pago, para recibir dinero de un banco. 6. Talón, conocimiento o contraseña de que se usa en los ferrocarriles. 7. Contraseña, billete de salida en los entreactos de los teatros. 8. Jaque, en el ajedrez. 9. Listado, lienzo tejido en cuadros o listas de azul y blanco; paño de varios colores. *Check-book*, Libro de cheques o talones. *Check-list*, *check-roll*, Lista para la confrontación de nombres, lista de electores, rol de obreros, etc.

Checkbook [chec'-buk], *s.* Talonario, libro talonario, libro talonado.

Checker o **Chequer** [chek'-ęr], *va.* 1. Taracear, formar cuadros de varios colores. 2. Diversificar.

Checker o **Chequer**, *s.* 1. Una de las piezas usadas en el juego de damas, por lo común un pequeño disco. 2. Uno de los cuadros en una superficie taraceada. 3. Reprensor, amonestador. 4. *pl.* Damas, juego de damas; nombre más común en los Estados Unidos que *draughts*. *V.* DRAUGHTS. *Checker-board*, Tablero.

Checkered [chek'-ęrd], *pp.* y *a.* 1. Dividido en cuadros de diferentes colores; ataraceado. 2. Diversificado, variado entre lo bueno y lo malo.

Checking account [chec'-ing a-caunt], *s.* Cuenta corriente.

Checkless [chek'-les], *a.* Violento, desgobernado.

Checkmate [chec'-mêt], *va.* 1. Dar jaque mate. 2. Deshacer, derrotar completamente al enemigo.—*s.* Mate, jaque mate, el último lance del ajedrez.

Checkpoint [chec'-pēint], *s.* Sitio o lugar de revisión o inspeccíon.

Check room [chec'-rūm], *s.* Guardarropa. *Check-room attendant*, Guardarropa.

Check stub [chec' stub], *s.* Talón. —*pl.* Libro talonario, talonario.

Cheek [chîc], *s.* 1. Carrillo, mejilla, cachete. *Cheeks of a window* o *door*, Jambas de ventana o puerta; derrame. 2. (Art.) Gualdera de cureña. 3. *Cheeks of a mast*, (Mar.) Cacholas, guarnición de madera que se pone sobre el cuello de los palos mayores. *Cheek of the pump*, (Mar.) Picota. *Cheeks of the head*, (Mar.) Tajamar. *Cheek by jowl*, (Vul.) Cara a cara. 4. (Ger.) Descaro, desvergüenza, impudencia. *To have plenty of cheek*, Tener cara de baqueta, ser desvergonzado.

Cheek-bone [chîc'-bōn], *s.* Pómulo, juanete de la mejilla.

Cheep [chîp], *vn.* Piar, chirriar, las aves pequeñas.—*s.* Gorjeo débil.

Cheer [chîr], *s.* 1. Banquete, festín. 2. Convite a un festín o banquete. 3. Alegría, buen humor; ánimo, vigor. 4. Gesto, aire, ademán. 5. Vivas, vítores, aplausos.

Cheer, *va.* 1. Excitar, animar, alentar. 2. Consolar, alegrar, dar consuelo o alegría. 3. Vitorear, aplaudir.—*vn.* Alegrarse, ponerse alegre. *To cheer up*, Tomar o cobrar ánimo. *Cheer up!* ¡Vamos, valor!

Cheerer [chîr'-ęr], *s.* Alegrador, regocijador, vitoreador, aplaudidor.

Cheerful [chîr'-ful], **Cheerly** [chîr'-li], **Cheery** [chîr'-i], *a.* 1. Alegre, vivo, lleno de ánimo. 2. Placentero, jovial.

Cheerfully [chîr'-ful-i], **Cheerily** [chîr'-i-li], **Cheerly** [chîr'-li], *adv.* Alegremente, con alegría.

Cheerfulness [chîr'-ful-nes], *s.* Alegría, buen humor, jovialidad.

Cheerless [chîr'-les], *a.* Triste, melancólico, falto de alegría.

Cheese [chîz], *s.* Queso. *Cream cheese*, Queso fresco. *Cheese curds*, Cuajadas. *Cheese-mite*, Ácaro de queso. *Cheese rennet*, Cuajaleche, gallote, género de plantas rubiáceas. *Cheese-cake*, Quesadilla. *Cheese-monger*, Quesero, el que hace o vende queso. *Cheese-paring*, Raedura de queso. *Cheese-parings and candle-ends*, (Joc.) Gajes del oficio. (Vul.) Buscas. *Cheese-press*, Prensa de queso. *Cheese-vat*, Quesera, la tabla formada a propósito para hacer queso.

Cheeseburger [chîz-burg'-ẹr], *s.* Emparedado de queso y carne molida.

Cheesecake [chîz'-kêk], *s.* 1. Pastel de queso. 2. (fam.) Fotografías que exhiben desnudeces femeninas.

Cheese cloth [chîz clōth], *s.* Estopilla (tela).

Cheesy [chîz'-i], *a.* Caseoso, de la calidad del queso.

Chemical [kem'-i-cal], *a.* Químico.—*s.* Producto químico.

Chemise [she-mîz'], *s.* 1. Camisa de mujer. 2. (Fort.) Camisa o revestimiento exterior de la muralla. 3. (Art. y Of.) La manga de hierro laminado de que se usa para hacer los cañones de escopeta.

Chemisette [shem-i-zet'], *s.* Prenda de ropa interior de mujer, que sólo cubre el cuello y los hombros.

Chemism [kem'-izm], *s.* Afinidad química.

Chemist [kem'-ist], *s.* Químico, el que profesa la química.

Chemistry [kem'-is-tri], *s.* Química.

Chenille [she-nîl'], *s.* Felpilla, cordón tejido con pelo, como la felpa, y hecho de algodón, seda, estambre o lana.

Chenopodium [kî-no-pō'-di-um], *s.* Ceñiglo, hierba común.

Cheque [chek], *s.* Cheque o talón; forma usual en Inglaterra. *V.* CHECK, quinta acepción.

Cherish [cher'-ish], *va.* 1. Criar, mantener, fomentar, proteger. 2. Mantener, preservar vivo; apreciar, estimar; acordarse con placer.

Cherisher [cher'-ish-ẹr], *s.* Fautor, fomentador, protector; amigo de.

Cherishing [cher'-ish-ing], *s.* Apoyo, fomento, protección, estima.

Cheroot [shẹ-rūt'], *s.* Filipino, especie de cigarro puro de perilla cortada.

Cherry [cher'-i], *s.* 1. Cereza, la fruta del cerezo. 2. Cerezo, árbol de varias especies del género Prunus. 3. La madera del cerezo. *Cherry-stone*, Cuesco o hueso de cereza. *Cherry-tree*, Cerezo.

Cherry, *a.* Lo que tiene color de cereza. *Cherry-cheeks*, Mejillas encarnadas. *Cherry-brandy*, Aguardiente de cerezas.

Cherry-pit [cher'-i-pit], *s.* 1. Hueso de cereza. 2. Hoyuelo, juego de niños.

Chert [chẹrt], *s.* (Min.) Horsteno, variedad de cuarzo.

Cherty [chẹrt'-i], *a.* Lo que tiene cuarzo o pedernal.

Cherub [cher'-ub], *s.* Querubín, espíritu angélico. —*pl.* CHERUBIM, Querubines.

Cherubic, Cherubical [che-rū'-bic, al], *a.* Angelical.

Chervil [chẹr'-vil], *s.* (Bot.) Perifollo o cerafolio, hierba semejante al perejil.

Chess [ches], *s.* El juego del ajedrez. *Chess-board*, Ajedrez, el tablero en que se juega a dicho juego. *Chess-man*, Pieza de ajedrez. *Chess-player*, Jugador de ajedrez.

Chess-trees [ches'-trîz], *s. pl.* (Mar.) Castañuelas de las amuras.

Chest [chest], *s.* 1. Arca, caja de madera u otro material. 2. (Art. y Of.) Receptáculo para gases o líquidos: como *steam-chest*, caja de vapor. 3. (Com.) Caja, cantidad determinada. 4. Pecho, tórax. *Chest of drawers*, Cómoda, buró, guardarropa con cajones; armario con gavetas. En los Estados Unidos se llama generalmente *bureau.*

Chest, *va.* Depositar o meter alguna cosa en una cómoda.

Chested [ches'-ted], *a.* De pecho; usado en composición: como, *Narrow-chested*, Estrecho de pecho. *Hollow-chested*, De pecho hundido.

Chestnut [ches'-nut], *s.* 1. Castaña. 2. Color de castaña. 3. Pequeña callosidad en la superficie interior de la pierna del caballo. 4. (E. U., fest.) Broma vetusta, chanza o dicho muy repetido y sabido de todos.

Chestnut-tree [ches'-nut-trî], *s.* (Bot.) Castaño.

Chetah [chî'-tạ], *s.* Leopardo de Asia y norte de África; suele adiestrarse para la caza.

Cheval [shẹ-val'], *s.* Caballo, caballete; apoyo, sostén. *Cheval-glass*, Psiquis, espejo que gira sobre un eje horizontal. *Cheval-de-frise*, *V.* CHEVAUX-DE-FRISE.

Chevalier [shev-a-lîr'], *s.* Caballero.

Chevaux-de-frise [shev'-o-de-frîz'], *s.* (Mil.) Caballo de frisa, madero con púas que se usa como defensa contra la caballería.

Cheveril [shev'-ẹr-il], *s.* (Des.) 1. Cabritillo o cabrito, choto. 2. Cabritilla, la piel del cabrito.

Chevron [shev'-ron], *s.* 1. Cheurrón, figura de dos o tres barras en forma de V, que llevan en las mangas las clases del ejército. 2. Cheurrón, cabrio, la figura o pieza en forma de ángulo que se pone en los escudos.

Chew [chū], *va.* 1. Mascar, masticar o desmenuzar con los dientes. 2. Rumiar, meditar, considerar despacio; reflexionar.—*vn.* Rumiar.

Chew, *s.* Mascadura, y la cosa masticada.

Chewing [chū'-ing], *s.* Masticación.

Chewing gum [chū'-ing gum], *s.* Chicle, goma de mascar.

Chewink [che-wink'], *s.* (Orn.) Emberiza, pájaro negro, blanco y rojizo. Pipilo erythrophthalmus. (Nombre imitativo.)

Chiaroscuro [kiār-es-cū'-rō], *s.* Claroscuro, acertada distribución de la luz y sombras de un cuadro.

Chic [shîc], *a.* 1. Gentil, bonito, bien hecho, bien parecido, elegante. 2. Vivo, listo, impertinente; mono, fino. —*s.* 1. Elegancia, buen tono, originalidad y buen gusto, como en decorar y vestirse. 2. Facilidad y habilidad de ejecución. 3. Viveza, vivacidad y petulancia de maneras.

Chicane [shi-kên'], *s.* Tramoya, enredo, embrollo, cavilación, trampa, artificio. (For.) Trampa legal.

Chicane, *vn.* 1. Entretener, tener a uno en suspenso dilatando la decisión de algún pleito o demanda. 2. Armar enredos, sutilizar, buscar escapatorias.

Chicaner [shi-kên'-ẹr], *s.* Sofista, trampista, enredador, trapacero.

Chicanery [shi-kê'-nẹ-ri], *s.* Sofistería, trapacería, enredo, trapaza, embrollo, trampa legal, efugio, quisquilla, vanas sutilezas.

Chick, Chicken [chik, en], *s.* 1. Polluelo o pollo. 2. (Fig.) Jovencito; niño.

Chickadee [chic'-a-dî''], *s.* Paro americano sin cresta, y con el cuello y parte superior de la cabeza negros. Parus atricapillus. (Nombre imitativo de su canto.)

Chicken-hearted [chik'-en-hārt-ed], *a.* Cobarde, gallina, medroso, mandria.

Chicken-pox [chik'-en-pecs], *s.* Viruelas locas.

Chickling [chic'-ling], *s.* Pollito, polluelo.

Chickpea [chic'-pî], *s.* (Bot.) Garbanzo.

Chickweed [chic'-wîd], *s.* (Bot.) Álsine, planta anual. Stellaria.

Chicle [chic'-l], *s.* (Bot.) Chicle, goma de mascar.

Chicory [chic'-o-ri], *s.* Achicoria; planta cuya raíz se usa para la adulteración del café.

Chide [chaid], *va.* (*pret.* CHID o CHODE, *pp.* CHID o CHIDDEN). Reprobar, culpar, echar en cara, regañar, refunfuñar.—*vn.* Regañar, reñir, alborotar.

†**Chide,** *s.* Murmullo, reprensión, reprimenda.

Chider [chai'-dẹr], *s.* Regañón, regañador.

Chiding [chaid'-ing], *s.* Reprensión, regaño, reprimenda.

Chidingly [chaid'-ing-li], *adv.* Con reprensión o reprimenda.

Chief [chîf], *a.* 1. Principal, capital, eminente, jefe. 2. Superior, supremo. *The chief man in the town*, El primer personaje de la población. *Our chief happiness*, Nuestra mayor felicidad. *Chief-clerk*, Oficial mayor; primer dependiente. *Chief-justice*, Presidente de sala.

Chief, *s.* 1. Jefe, principal; cabeza de tribu, familia, ejército, escuadra, departamento del Estado, etc.; el que tiene autoridad. 2. Actor, agente principal. 3. Parte principal, la mayor parte de una cosa.

Chiefest [chîf'-est], *a. sup.* (Ant.) Principalísimo.

Chiefless [chîf'-les], *a.* Sin jefe o superior.

Chiefly, Chief (Poét.), [chîf'-li], *adv.* Principalmente, particularmente, sobre todo.

Chieftain [chîf'-ten], *s.* 1. Jefe, comandante. 2. Caudillo, capitán; cabeza de bando.

Chieftainship [chîf'-ten-ship], *s.* Jefatura, la dignidad u oficio de jefe.

Chiffer, Chiffre [shif'-ẹr], *s.* Cifra, como en música escrita con números.

Chiffon [shi-fon'], *s.* Gasa, tela de seda muy transparente.

Chiffonier [shif-o-nîr'], *s.* Cómoda, cajonería, guardarropa con cajones.

Chignon [shî'-nyōñ], *s.* Penca o moño de pelo que llevaban las mujeres.

Chigoe [chig'-ō], *s.* Nigua, pulga pequeñísima de las Antillas y Sud América, cuya hembra se introduce bajo la epidermis, especialmente de los pies, produciendo gran escozor y molestia.

Chilblains [chil'-blênz], *s. pl.* Sabañones.

Child [chaild], *s.* (*pl.* CHILDREN). 1. Infante, el niño pequeño y de muy poca edad. 2. Hijo o hija. 3. Parto, el efecto o producto de otra cosa. *From a child*, Desde niño. *With child*, Preñada, embarazada.

Childbearing [chaild'-bār-ing], *s.* Parto.

Childbed [chaild'-bed], *s.* Sobreparto.

Childbirth [chaild'-bẹrth], *s.* Parto o

dolores de parto. *To die in childbirth,* Morir de parto.

Childermas-day [chil'-dęr-mas-dê], *s.* Día de inocentes, el 28 de Diciembre.

Childhood [chaild'-hud], *s.* Infancia, niñez; puerilidad, niñería.

Childish [chaild'-ish], *a.* Frívolo, trivial, pueril, propio de niño. *Childish trick,* Muchachada.

Childishly [chaild'-ish-li], *adv.* Puerilmente.

Childishness [chaild'-ish-nes], *s.* Puerilidad, cosa propia de niños.

Childless [chaild'-les], *a.* Sin hijos, infecundo.

Childlike [chaild'-laic], *a.* Pueril, propio de niño o muchacho.

Children [chil'-dren], *s. pl.* de CHILD. Niños. (Prov.) *Children and fools speak the truth,* Los niños y los locos dicen las verdades.

Chilean [chil'-e-an], *a.* y *s.* Chileno, chileño.

Chiliast [kil'-i-ast], *s.* Milenario, sectario que espera la venida de un período de mil años, en que todo el mundo será justo y vivirá feliz.

Chili sauce [chil'-i sōs], *s.* Salsa de tomate con chile.

Chill [chil], *a.* 1. Frío, friolento. 2. Desanimado, desalentado, abatido; rudo.—*s.* Frío, escalofrío, sensación de frío que a veces precede a la fiebre. (Fig.) Estremecimiento. *To take the chill of,* Quitar el frío. *A chill came over the assembly,* Un estremecimiento recorrió la asamblea.

Chill, *va.* 1. Enfriar, poner fría alguna cosa. 2. Helar. 3. Desanimar, desalentar —*vn.* Escalofriarse.

Chilliness [chil'-i-nes], *s.* Principio o entrada del frío; calofrío, tiritón.

Chillness [chil'-nes], *s.* Frío, falta de calor.

Chilly [chil'-i], *a.* Friolento.—*adv.* Fríamente.

Chimæra, *s.* *V.* CHIMERA.

Chimaphila [cai-maf'-i-la], *s.* Quimafila, género de plantas medicinales y de adorno de las piroláceas.

Chime [chaim], *s.* 1. Armonía de sonidos, como los de las campanas o de un instrumento; melodía; ritmo (de un discurso o poema). 2. Juego de campanas dispuestas de modo que producen sonidos armónicos. 3. Conformidad, analogía.

Chime, *s.* 1. Jable o gárgol de tonel, barril o cuba, salida formada por las extremidades de las duelas. 2. Muesca, ranura de la duela.

Chime, *vn.* 1. Sonar con armonía. 2. Convenir, concordar. 3. Tañer, repicar las campanas.—*va.* Tocar o mover alguna cosa con compás y armonía.

Chimer [chaim'-ęr], *s.* Campanero; repicador o tañedor de campanas.

Chimera [ki-mī'-ra], *s.* 1. Quimera, monstruo fabuloso. 2. Quimera, ilusión, imaginación vana.

Chimere [shi-mīr'], *s.* Sobrepelliz, vestidura exterior y sin mangas de un obispo.

Chimerical [ki-mer'-i-cal], *a.* Quimérico, imaginario.

Chimerically [ki-mer'-i-cal-i], *adv.* Quiméricamente, imaginariamente.

Chimney [chim'-ney], *s.* 1. Cañón de chimenea. 2. Chimenea u hogar, lugar en que se enciende el fuego en las casas. 3. Tubo o cañón de vidrio, para las lámparas. *Flue of a chimney,* Cañón, humero de una chimenea. *Mantlepiece of a chimney,* Campana de la chimenea; repisa.

Chimney-corner [chim'-ni-cōr'-nęr], *s.* Rincón de chimenea.

Chimney-piece [chim'-ni-pīs], *s.* Las jambas y el dintel que sirven para adorno de las chimeneas.

Chimney-sweeper [chim'-ni-swīp'-ęr], *s.* Deshollinador o limpiachimeneas.

Chimney-top [chim'-ni-top], *s.* La parte superior del cañón de la chimenea.

Chimpanzee [chim-pan'-zī], *s.* Chimpancé, mono antropomorfo, de cerca de cinco pies de altura; habita en el oeste de África.

Chin [chin], *s.* Barba. *Chin-cloth* o *bib,* Babero, babador.

China, Chinaware [chai'-na, wār], *s.* China, porcelana, loza de China.

China o **India ink** [ind'-yan ink], *s.* Tinta de China.

China-root [chai'-na-rūt], *s.* (Bot.) China, planta y raíz que se trae de la China.

Chinchilla [chin-chil'-a], *s.* Chinchilla y su piel.

Chincough [chin'-cōf], *s.* (Des.) Tos convulsiva, tos ferina.

Chine [chain], *s.* 1. Espinazo. 2. Lomo en los animales. 3. Solomo.

Chine, *va.* Deslomar, romper por el espinazo.

Chinese [chai-nīs'], *a.* Chino, chinesco, de la China, o parecido a las cosas de aquel país. *Chinese white,* Blanco de China, óxido de cinc.—*s.* 1. Chino, natural de la China. 2. La lengua china.

Chink [chink], *s.* Grieta, hendedura, rajadura, abertura.

Chink, *vn.* Henderse, abrirse; sonar, resonar.

Chinkapin [chin'-ka-pin], *s.* Castaño enano, y su fruto; arbusto del Este de los Estados Unidos.

Chinky [chink'-i], *a.* Hendido, rajado, lleno de hendeduras.

Chinned [chind], *a.* Barbado.

Chinquapin, *s.* *V.* CHINKAPIN.

Chinse [chins], *va.* (Mar.) Calafatear.

Chints, Chintz [chints], *s.* Zaraza, tela de algodón con dibujos en colores.

Chip [chip], *va.* Desmenuzar, hacer pedazos menudos una cosa; es hacer astillas, si se habla de leña o madera, y picar, si de carne.—*vn.* 1. Romperse, abrirse; dícese de los huevos empollados. 2. Quebrarse; dícese de la loza o del vidrio.

Chip, *s.* Brizna, astilla, raspaduras de la corteza del pan; barbas de los libros cuando se igualan sus cortes; viruta de la madera cuando se cepilla, llamada también doladura o cepilladura. *Chip-axe,* Azuela. *Chip-hat,* Sombrero de virutas, o de hoja de palma; sombrero jíbaro. *Chip of the same block,* De tal palo tal astilla.

Chipmunk [chip'-munc], *s.* Ardilla terrícola listada.

Chipper [chip'-ęr], *a.* (E. U. Fam.) Vivo, alegre, jovial; sano, robusto.

Chipping [chip'-ing], *s.* 1. Brizna, la parte pequeña que se separa de alguna cosa. 2. Acto de desmenuzar.

Chirk [chęrk], *a.* (Fam.) Alegre, jovial.

Chirk, *s.* Petrosílex, horsteno. *V.* CHERT.

Chirograph [cai'-ro-graf], *s.* 1. Contrato que se hacía formando dos copias idénticas sobre un mismo pergamino y cortándolas ó separándolas después. 2. Quirógrafo, documento autorizado con una firma autógrafa.

Chirographer [kai-reg'-ra-fęr], *s.* Escribano, escribiente; el vale o escritura hecho de propia mano.

Chirography [kai-reg'-ra-fi], *s.* Quirografía; el arte de escribir, y la atestación de escribir de propia mano; modo de escribir.

Chiromancer [kai'-ro-man-sęr], *s.* Quiromántico, el que profesa la quiromancia.

Chiromancy [kai'-ro-man-si], *s.* Quiromancia, supuesta adivinación por las rayas de la mano.

Chironomy [cai-ren'-o-mi], *s.* Quironomía, arte o teoría de los movimientos y de la gesticulación dramática y oratoria.

Chiropodist [cai-rep'-o-dist], *s.* Pedicuro, el que tiene por oficio la extirpación y curación de los callos y uñeros y otras dolencias de los pies.

Chiropractor [cai'-ro-prac-ter], *s.* Quiropráctico.

Chirp [chęrp], *vn.* Gorjear o piar como los pájaros; chirriar, como los insectos.

Chirp, *s.* 1. Chirrido, gorjeo. 2. Canto.

Chirper [chęrp'-ęr], *s.* Chirriador, el que chirría o gorjea.

Chirping [chęrp'-ing], *s.* Chirrido, el canto sin melodía de los pájaros e insectos.

Chirrup [chir'-up], *va.* y *vn.* Gorjear, con nota sostenida; trinar.

†**Chirurgeon** [kai-rūr'-jun], *s.* Cirujano. *V.* SURGEON.

†**Chirurgery** [cai-rūr'-jęr-i], *s.* Cirugía. *V.* SURGERY.

†**Chirurgical** [cai-rūr'-ji-cal], *a.* Quirúrgico. *V.* SURGICAL.

Chisel [chiz'-el], *s.* Escoplo o cincel, formón.

Chisel, *va.* Escoplear o cincelar, esculpir.

Chiseler [chiz'-el-ęr], *s.* Estafador, oportunista.

Chit [chit], *s.* 1. Chiquilla, muchacha. (Voz ligeramente despectiva.) 2. Tallo, germen, botones, yema, el pitoncillo que arroja el grano. 3. Peca en la cara.

Chit, *va.* Quitar los brotes o tallos tiernos de los bulbos, tubérculos y plantas.—*vn.* Brotar, echar botones o yemas las plantas.

Chitchat [chit'-chat], *s.* Charla. (Fam.) Cuchicheo, palique.

Chitin [cai'-tin (o kit'-in)], *s.* Quitina, la parte esencial del carapacho de los insectos y crustáceos.

Chitinous [cai'-tin-us], *a.* Quitinoso, perteneciente o relativo a la quitina.

Chitterlings [chit'-ęr-lingz], *s. pl.* 1. Despojos; el vientre, asadura, cabeza y manos de las reses que se matan en las carnicerías. 2. Pechera, guirindola o chorrera de camisola.

Chitty [chit'-i], *a.* 1. Lo que tiene gérmenes o botones. 2. (Des.) Pecoso.

Chivalric [shiv'-al-ric], *a.* Caballeresco, perteneciente a la caballería.

Chivalrous [shiv'-al-rus], *a.* Caballeroso, propio de caballero.

Chivalry [shiv'-al-ri], *s.* 1. Caballería, grado y dignidad de caballero milicar. 2. Caballería andante; cortesía, hidalguía. 3. Proeza, hazaña.

Chive [chaiv], *s.* 1. Cebolleta, cebollino, especie de cebolla pequeña. 2. (Des.) Estambre, filamento.

Chlamys [clē'-mis o cla'-mis], *s.* 1. Clámide, capa corta y ligera de los griegos y romanos. 2. Capa pluvial de color de púrpura.

Chloracetic [clō-ra-set'-ic], *a.* (Quím.) Cloracético. *Chloracetic acid,* Ácido cloracético, obtenido por la acción del cloro sobre el ácido acético.

Chloral [clō'-ral], *s.* Cloral, líquido incoloro, aceitoso, con olor penetrante; obtenido por la acción del cloro sobre el alcohol. *Chloral hydrate* (o simplemente *chloral*), Hidrato de cloral, compuesto blanco, cristalizado, picante, que se usa en medicina como narcótico.

Chloramphenicol [clor-am-fen'-i-cōl], *s.* (Med.) Cloramfenicol.

Chlorate [clō'-rēt], *s.* Clorato, sal del ácido clórico.

Chloremia [clōr-ī'-mi-a], *s.* (Med.) Cloremia.

Chloric [clō'-ric], *a.* Clórico, combinado con el cloro. *Chloric acid,* Ácido clórico ($HClO_3$).

Chlorid, Chloride [clō-rid, clō'-rid ó raid], *s.* Cloruro, combinación del cloro con metal o metaloide.

Chlorination [clor-i-nē'-shun], *s.* Tratamiento al cloro.

Chlorine [clō'-rin], *s.* (Quím.) Cloro, gas amarillo verdoso, venenoso, y de olor desagradable.

Chlorite [clō'-rait], *s.* (Min.) Clorita, ejemplar de varios silicatos hidratados, de color verdoso.

Chloroform [clō'-ro-fōrm], *s.* Cloroformo, líquido incoloro, volátil, algo dulce, que se emplea como poderoso anestésico y anodino.—*va.* Administrar cloroformo; cloroformizar.

Chloromycetin [clo-rō-mais'-tin], *s.* (Med.) Cloromicetina.

Chlorophyl, Chlorophyll [clō'-ro-fil], *s.* Clorofila, la materia colorante verde de las hojas de los vegetales.

Chlorosis [clo-rō'-sis], *s.* (Med.) Clorosis, enfermedad de las adolescentes caracterizada por palidez del rostro y empobrecimiento de la sangre, y comunmente por amenorrea.

Chlorotic [clō-ret'-ic], *a.* Clorótico, clorótica, perteneciente o relativo a la clorosis. Dícese de la mujer que la padece.

Chlorous [clō'-rus], *a.* Combinado con el cloro y en especial en su valor de tres.

Chock [chec], *s.* 1. Calzo, cuña, pedazo de madera u otro objeto a propósito para calzar un barril, tonel, etc. 2. (Mar.) Choque, calzo fijo sobre la cubierta de un buque o sobre un muelle, con quijadas por las cuales se puede pasar un cable o cadena. 3. *V.* CHUCK.

Chock [chec], *va.* 1. Afianzar, soportar, proveer con calzos. 2. *vn.* Cerrar, tapar, llenar un hueco o juntura.

Chock-full, Chuck-full [chec'-ful], *a.* Colmado, lleno hasta el tope; de bote en bote.

Chocolate [chec'-o-lēt], *s.* 1. Chocolate, pasta hecha de cacao, azúcar, etc. 2. Chocolate, el compuesto líquido de la pasta desleída por medio de agua caliente o leche.

Choice [cheis], *s.* 1. Escogimiento, elección, preferencia; el acto, facultad o cuidado de elegir, escoger o preferir una cosa a otra. 2. La cosa elegida, lo selecto, lo más escogido (de personas). *Hobson's choice,* O tal cosa, o nada; o tomarlo o dejarlo.

Choice, *a.* 1. Escogido, selecto, exquisito, excelente. 2. Cuidadoso, frugal, parco, económico.

Choiceless [cheis'-les], *a.* Limitado, el que no tiene facultad de elegir.

Choicely [cheis'-li], *adv.* Escogidamente, primorosamente.

Choiceness [cheis'-nes], *s.* Delicadeza; discernimiento en lo que se elige; precio extraordinario; destreza, pericia.

Choir [cwair], *s.* 1. Coro, unión o conjunto de voces. 2. Coro, los que cantan salmos, himnos y otras composiciones sagradas. 3. Coro, la parte de la iglesia en que se juntan los que cantan. *Choir-service,* Oficio de coro.

Choke [chōk], *va.* 1. Ahogar, sofocar, quitar la respiración. 2. Cerrar alguna comunicación o paso. 3. Suprimir, oprimir. *To choke up,* Obstruir, tapar. 4. Atragantarse, atorarse.

Choke, *s.* Hebra de alcachofa.

Choke-full [chōk-ful'], *a.* Lleno enteramente hasta los bordes. *V.* CHOCK-FULL.

Choke-pear [chōc'-pār], *s.* 1. Ahogadera, especie de pera áspera al paladar. 2. †(Met.) Tapaboca, cualquier dicho picante que obliga a alguno a callarse.

Choker [chō'-kęr], *s.* 1. Ahogador, el que ahoga; el que hace callar a otro; tapaboca, argumento sin réplica. 2. Corbata grande.

Choky [chō'-ki], *a.* Lo que puede ahogar; sofocante.

Cholagogue [cel'-a-geg], *s.* Colagogo, medicamento que purga la bilis.

Choler [cel'-ęr], *s.* Ira, enojo.

Cholera [cel'-e-ra], *s.* 1. (Med.) Cólera-morbo, enfermedad aguda, epidémica, causada por un bacilo; cólera asiático. 2. Cólera-morbo, enfermedad no epidémica, esporádica. *Cholera morbus, V.* 2ª acep.

Choleric [cel'-ęr-ic], *a.* Colérico, enojado.

Cholericness [cel'-ęr-ic-nes], *s.* Cólera, ira, enojo.

Cholerine [cel'-ęr-in o in], *s.* 1. Colerina, primer período del cólera epidémico. 2. Tipo ligero de esta enfermedad; diarrea coleriforme.

Cholesterol [col-es'-te-rōl], *s.* (Bioquímica) Colesterol.

Chondroid [cen'-dreid], *a.* Parecido al cartílago.

Choose [chūz], *va.* Escoger, tomar o elegir con preferencia, predestinar. —*vn.* Tener facultad para elegir, hacer o dejar de hacer alguna cosa; preferir, querer. *Why don't you tell me your age?* ¿Por qué no me dice Vd. su edad? *Because I don't choose,* Porque no quiero, porque no me place. *To choose rather,* Preferir. *The chosen ones,* Los mejores, los más granados, los escogidos.

Chooser [chūz'-ęr], *s.* Escogedor; elector.

Choosing [chūz'-ing], *s.* Escogimiento, elección.

Chop [chep], *va.* 1. Tajar, cortar o separar; picar; desbastar un madedero. 2. Rajar, hender. 3. Mudar, trocar; comprar. 4. Articular de un modo rápido y entrecortado.—*vn.* Hacer alguna cosa con movimiento veloz; tropezar. *To chop off,* Tronchar. *To chop at,* Pillar, zampar, atrapar con la boca. *To chop in,* Entrar de repente con la intención de sorprender. *To chop about,* Girar, rodear, mudar. *To chop meat,* Picar la carne. *Chopped hands,* Manos agrietadas.

Chop, *va.* Cambiar, trocar.—*vn.* Cambiar, variar, mudarse; dícese del viento. *Chop-logic,* Argumentación llena de argucias y sutilezas.

Chop, *s.* Porción, parte; tajada de carne; chuleta o costilla de ternera, carnero, etc.; raja.

Chop-fallen. *V.* CHAP-FALLEN.

Chop-house [chep'-haus], *s.* Bodegón, figón.

Chopper [chep'-ęr], *s.* Cuchilla de carnicero.

Chopping [chep'-ing], *a.* 1. Que se cambia de repente a otra dirección (viento). 2. Lleno de olas pequeñas. 3. (Ant.) Rollizo, robusto.—*s.* Tajadura, cortadura. *Chopping-block,* Tajo de cocina, tajadera. *Chopping-board,* Tajador. *Chopping-knife,* Cuchilla, tajadera.

Choppy [chep'-i], *a.* 1. Rajado, hendido, lleno de grietas, agujereado. 2. Lleno de olas pequeñas y agitadas.

Chops [cheps], *s.* (Vul.) Boca; quijadas. *Chops of the channel,* (Mar.) Boca de un canal.

Chop-sticks [chep'-stics], *s. pl.* Varillas delgadas de marfil o madera, de que se sirven los chinos y japoneses para llevar los alimentos á la boca.

Chop suey [chep sū'-i], *s.* Guiso popular en E.U. que se supone de origen chino.

Choral [cō'-ral], *a.* Coral, perteneciente al coro; cantado en coro.

Chord [cōrd], *s.* 1. (Mús.) Cuerda. Cuando esta voz quiere decir cordel o soga se escribe *cord.* 2. (Mús.) Acorde, combinación de sonidos escogidos según las leyes de la armonía. 3. (Geom.) Cuerda, línea recta que une los dos extremos de un arco de círculo.

Chord, *va.* (Mús.) Encordar, poner cuerdas en alguna cosa.

Chore [chōr], *s.* Tarea o trabajo de poco momento; especialmente del servicio doméstico.

Chorea [co-rī'-a], *s.* Corea, baile de San Vito, enfermedad caracterizada por movimientos convulsivos.

Choreograph [cer'-ę-o-graf], *s.* Coreógrafo, maestro de baile.

Choreography [cer-ī-eg'-ra-fi], *s.* Coreografía.

Choree, Choreus [cō'-rī, co-rī'-us], *s.* Coreo, troqueo, pie de verso (— ◡).

Choriambic [co-ri-am'-bic], *s.* Coriambo, pie de verso (— ◡ ◡ —).—*a.* Coriámbico, relativo al coriambo.

Chorion [cō'-ri-en], *s.* (Anat.) Corion, membrana exterior que envuelve el feto en el útero.

Chorographer [co-reg'-ra-fęr], *s.* Corógrafo.

Chorography [co-reg'-ra-fi], *s.* Corografía, ciencia que enseña a formar el mapa particular de una región o provincia.

Choroid [cō'-reid], *a.* Coroideo, parecido al corion.—*s.* Túnica media del ojo.

Chorus [cō'-rus], *s.* 1. Coro. 2. Coro, estrambote o estribillo.

Chose, Chosen, *pret.* y *pp.* del verbo *To* CHOOSE.

Chose [shōz], *s.* (For.) Cada uno de los objetos que constituyen propiedad mueble. *Chose in action,* Derecho de una persona sobre propiedad mueble o dinero no en su posesión pero reivindicable por medio de procedimiento legal. (Fr.)

Chough [chuf], *s.* (Orn.) Chova, especie de grajo de color negro y patas rojas.

Chouse [chaus], *va.* Engañar, embaucar, engatusar.

Chouse, *s.* 1. Primo, tonto, bobalicón, el bobo o simple que se deja engañar. 2. Engaño, fraude, chasco, pieza, burla.
Chousing [chaus'-ing], *s.* Bellaquería, engaño, fraude.
Chow-chow [chau'-chau], *s.* Mezcla, olla podrida; alimentos divididos a la manera china; en especial, encurtidos de diferentes legumbres con mostaza. (Chino.)
Chowder [chau'-dẹr], *s.* Sopa de pescado o de mariscos.
Chow mein [chau mên'], *s.* Guiso de tallarines chinos, carne y verduras. Se supone de origen chino.
Chrestomathy [cres-tem'-a-thi], *s.* Crestomatía, colección de escritos selectos, especialmente la destinada a la enseñanza en un idioma determinado.
Chrism [crizm], *s.* Crisma, aceite consagrado.
Chrismatory [criz'-ma-to-ri], *s.* Crismera.
Christ [craist], *s.* Cristo o Jesucristo, nuestro Salvador.
Christ-cross-row [cris'-cres-rō'], *s.* (Ant.) El Crístus o la cartilla.
Christen [cris'-n], *va.* 1. Dar nombre al tiempo de bautizar. 2. Bautizar, practicar las ceremonias por medio de las cuales uno se hace cristiano. 3. ‖Cristianar, hacer cristiano por medio del bautismo. 4. (Fam.) Estrenar, empezar a usar una cosa.
Christendom [cris'-n-dum], *s.* Cristianismo, cristiandad.
Christening [cris'-n-ing], *s.* Bautismo.—*a.* Bautismal.
Christian [cris'-chan], *s.* Cristiano, el que profesa la fe de Jesucristo.—*a.* Cristiano, lo que pertenece a la religión cristiana o es arreglado a ella. *Christian name*, Nombre de bautismo o de pila.
Christianism [cris'-chan-izm], **Christianity** [cris-chi-an'-i-ti], *s.* Cristianismo.
Christianization [cris-chan-i-zé'-shUn], *s.* Cristianización.
Christianize [cris'-chan-aiz], *va.* Cristianizar, cristianar.
Christianlike [cris'-chan-laic], *a.* Propio de cristiano.
Christianly [cris'-chan-li], *adv.* Cristianamente.
Christless [craist'-les], *a.* Anticristiano, impío, herético.
Christmas [cris'-mas], *s.* 1. La Navidad o Natividad, conmemoración anual del nacimiento de nuestro Señor Jesucristo. 2. El día de Navidad. 3. Aguinaldo o regalo de Navidad. *Christmas carol*, Villancico, cántico de Navidad. *Christmas eve*, Víspera de Navidad. *Christmas holidays*, Vacaciones de Pascuas.
Christmas-box [cris'-mas-bex], *s.* Cajita o arquilla para recoger el aguinaldo; el aguinaldo mismo.
Christmas-flower, *s.* (Bot.) *V.* HELLEBORE.
Christ's-thorn [craists'-thērn], *s.* (Bot.) Espino amarillo.
Chroma [crō'-ma], *s.* Intensidad de color; el mayor o menor grado de color respecto del blanco.
Chromate [crō'-mêt], *s.* Cromato, sal del ácido crómico.
Chromatic [cro-mat'-ic], *a.* 1. Cromático, relativo a los colores. 2. (Mús.) Cromático, que procede por semitonos.—*s.* (Mús.) Nota modificada por un bemol o sostenido.
Chromatics [cro-mat'-ics], *s.* Cromática, ciencia del colorido.
Chromatography [cro-ma-teg'-ra-fi], *s.* Cromatografía, descripción de los colores.
Chrome [crōm], *s.* 1. Cromo. 2. *V.* CHROMIUM.
Chromic [crō'-mic], *a.* Crómico, que pertenece al cromio en su mayor grado de combinación con otros cuerpos. *Chromic acid*, (Quím.) Ácido crómico.
Chromium [crō'-mi-um], *s.* (Quím.) Cromio, metal que se halla mineralizado con plomo, hierro y piedras preciosas.
Chromo [crō'-mō], *s.* *V.* CHROMO-LITHOGRAPH.
Chromo-lithograph [crō'-mō-lith'-o-graf], *s.* Estampa o lámina en colores, obtenida por la cromolitografía.
Chromo-lithography [crō'-mō-li-theg'-ra-fi], *s.* Cromolitografía, el arte de hacer impresiones litográficas en colores.
Chromosome [crō'-mo-sōm], *s.* (Biol.) Cromosoma.
Chronic, Chronical [cren'-ic, al], *a.* 1. Crónico, lo que pertenece al tiempo. 2. (Med.) Crónico, de larga duración.
Chronicity [cro-nis'-i-ti], *s.* Estado o calidad de crónico.
Chronicle [cren'-i-cl], *s.* Crónica, historia compuesta por orden de fechas.
Chronicle, *va.* Formar una crónica.
Chronicler [cren'-i-clẹr], *s.* Cronista, historiador.
Chronogram [cren'-o-gram], *s.* Cronograma, inscripción en la que las letras numerales forman la fecha de algún suceso.
Chronograph [cren'-o-graf], *s.* Cronógrafo, aparato eléctrico indicador del tiempo o duración de un acontecimiento.
Chronographer [cro-neg'-ra-fẹr], *s.* Cronologista.
Chronography [cro-neg'-ra-fi], *s.* Cronografía, descripción del tiempo pasado.
Chronologer [cro-nel'-o-jẹr], **Chronologist** [cro-nel'-o-jist], *s.* Cronologista, cronólogo, el que es versado en la cronología.
Chronologic, Chronological [cren-o-lej'-ic, al], *a.* Cronológico.
Chronologically [cren-o-lej'-i-cal-i], *adv.* Cronológicamente.
Chronology [cro-nel'-o-ji], *s.* 1. Cronología, ciencia que determina el orden y fecha de los sucesos históricos. 2. Manera de computar los tiempos.
Chronometer [cro-nem'-e-tẹr], *s.* Cronómetro, instrumento para medir el tiempo; reloj de longitudes que mide exactamente el tiempo.
Chronometric, Chronometrical [cren'-o-met'-ric, al], *a.* Cronométrico, referente al cronómetro o determinado por medio de él.
Chronometry [cro-nem'-e-tri], *s.* Cronometría, la acción de medir el tiempo; ciencia de la medición del tiempo.
Chronoscope [cron'-o-scōp], *s.* Cronógrafo, u otro instrumento para medir un intervalo muy corto de tiempo.
Chrysalis [cris'-a-lis], *s.* Crisálida, ninfa o dormida, la oruga y otros insectos en su capullo antes de transformarse en mariposas.
Chrysanthemum [cris-an'-the-mum], *s.* (Bot.) Crisantemo, género de plantas compuestas que se cultivan como de adorno.
Chrysoberyl [cris-o-ber'-il], *s.* (Min.) Crisoberilo, piedra preciosa.
Chrysolite [cris'-o-lait], *s.* Crisólito, piedra preciosa.
Chrysoprase [cris'-o-prêz], *s.* (Min.) Crisoprasa o crisopracio, especie de calcedonia de color verde manzana.
Chub [chub], *s.* Coto, pez de agua dulce. *Chub-faced*, Cariancho.
‖**Chubbed** [chubd], *a.* Cabezudo, el que tiene la cabeza grande. *V.* CHUBBY.
Chubby [chub'-i], *a.* Gordo, gordiflón, rechoncho.
Chuck [chuc], *vn.* Cloquear, cacarear la gallina cuando está clueca.—*va.* 1. Dar una sobarbada o golpe debajo de la barba a alguno. 2. Arrojar diestramente. 3. Cloquear, llamar la gallina á sus pollos.
Chuck, *s.* 1. Cloqueo. 2. Cariño. 3. Sobarbada. 4. Rumor repentino.
Chuck, *s.* (Art. y Of.) 1. Mandril, mangote, plato de un torno; invento para asir un objeto de tal manera que pueda girar. 2. Cuña, calzo.
Chuck-farthing [chuc'-fār-dhing], *s.* Hoyuelo, especie de juego de los muchachos en que meten el dinero en un hoyo.
Chuckle [chuk'-l], *vn.* Reir entre dientes; sonreir de satisfacción; fisgar sonriéndose.—*va.* 1. Cloquear, llamar la gallina a sus pollos. 2. Acariciar, hacer fiestas a alguno; requebrar.
Chuckle, *s.* Risa ahogada.—*a.* Grueso o tosco (hablando de la cabeza). *Chuckle-head*, Tonto, estúpido, cabeza de chorlito.
Chuff [chuf], *s.* (Ant.) Patán, rústico.
Chuffily [chuf'-i-li], *adv.* Groseramente.
Chuffiness [chuf'-i-nes], *s.* Rusticidad, falta de urbanidad.
Chuffy [chuf'-i], *a.* Grosero, desatento.
Chum [chum], *vn.* Compartir una habitación con otro; ser íntimo.—*s.* Camarada, compañero; condiscípulo.
Chump [chump], *s.* 1. Tajo, tronco, leño grueso. 2. La extremidad gruesa de alguna cosa, por ejemplo, el lomo del carnero. 3. (Ger.) Leño, tonto, naranjo, mastuerzo.
Chunk [chuņk], *s.* Pedazo grueso y corto; persona o bestia rechoncha. *A chunk of bread*, Un zoquete de pan.
Chunky [chuņk'-i], *a.* Corto, rechoncho, abundante en carnes. (E. U.)
Church [chūrch], *s.* 1. Iglesia, templo, edificio consagrado al culto. 2. Iglesia, la congregación de los fieles; cuerpo determinado de cristianos. 3. Culto público, oficio divino regular. 4. El clero. *The Church of England*, La Iglesia anglicana. *To go to church*, Ir a misa, asistir al oficio divino. **Eastern Church**, La iglesia griega. *V.* GREEK CHURCH. **Western Church**, La iglesia del imperio romano de occidente en la edad media, hoy la Iglesia católica romana. *Church of Jesus Christ of Latter-day Saints*, Título oficial de la iglesia de Mormón, que quiere decir: Iglesia de Jesucristo de los Modernos Santos. *Church militant*, La iglesia militante, congregación de los fieles que viven en este mundo. *Church-ale*, Aniversario o fiesta solemne en memoria de la consagración de una

iglesia. *Church-book, church register,* Registro de parroquia, libro de bautizos. *Church-burial,* Entierro según los ritos de la iglesia. *Church-land,* Tierras beneficiales; bienes eclesiásticos. *Church-music,* Música sagrada. *Church-preferment,* Beneficio o renta eclesiástica. *Church-robbing,* Sacrilegio. *Church-way,* Camino a la iglesia. *Church-work,* La obra del Escorial, dícese de algún trabajo que procede lentamente.

Church, *va.* Purificar, ejecutar las ceremonias de la purificación de una mujer recién parida.

Churchdom [chŏrch'-dum], *s.* Dominio o autoridad de la iglesia.

Churching [chŏrch'-ing], *s.* Salida a misa o saca-a-misa; la misa y ceremonias del día en que una recién parida se presenta en la iglesia con su criatura.

Churchlike [chŏrch'-laik], *a.* Eclesiástico, propio de un sacerdote.

Churchman [church'-man], *s.* Sacerdote, eclesiástico; miembro de la Iglesia anglicana o católica.

Churchwardens [chŏrch'-wōr-denz], *s. pl.* Mayordomos, los que se eligen anualmente para que cuiden de las cosas de la iglesia.

Churchyard [chŏrch'-yārd], *s.* Cementerio de parroquia.

Churl [chŏrl], *s.* Patán, rústico, payo. charro; hombre ruin, miserable tacaño.

Churlish [chŏrl'-ish], *a.* Rudo, agreste; ruin, escaso, rústico, grosero, brutal, avaro.

Churlishly [chŏrl'-ish-li], *adv.* Rudamente, brutalmente.

Churlishness [chŏrl'-ish-nes], *s.* Rusticidad; rudeza, grosería, descortesía.

Churn [chŏrn], *s.* Mantequera, vasija en que se hace la manteca.

Churn, *va.* 1. Agitar o menear alguna cosa con violencia. 2. Batir o menear la nata de la leche para hacer manteca.

Churning [chŏrn'-ing], *s.* Batido.

Churn-staff [chŏrn'-staf], *s.* Batidera, instrumento con el cual se bate la nata en la mantequera.

†**Chuse,** *v.* *V.* CHOOSE.

Chute [shūt], *s.* Caída, plano inclinado o cualquier conducto de arriba hacia abajo. (Fr.)

Chylaceous [kai-lé'-shus], *a.* Quiloso.

Chyle [cail], *s.* Quilo, fluido lechoso que se extrae del quimo y que se mezcla con la sangre.

Chylifaction, Chylification [kai-li-fac'-shun], *s.* Quilificación.

Chylifactive [kai-li-fac'-tiv], *a.* Quilificativo.

Chylopoietic [cai-lo-pei-et'-ic], *a.* Quilopoyético, que tiene poder de hacer quilo.

Chylous [kai'-lus], *a.* Quiloso.

Chyme [kaim], *s.* Quimo, la masa de alimentos disgregados y reblandecidos por la digestión, de que se forma el quilo.

†**Chymic** [kim'-ic], **Chymistry,** etc., *a.* *V.* CHEMIC, etc.

Cibarious [si-bé'-ri-us], *a.* Que pertenece a los alimentos, cibario.

Cibol [sib'-el], *s.* 1. Cebolleta, cebolla gala, o puerro de piedra. 2. Chalota, especie de ajo.

Ciborium [si-bō'-ri-um], *s.* 1. Dosel de altar. 2. Copón, vaso que encierra el Santísimo Sacramento en el sagrario.

Cicada [si-ké'-da], *s.* Cigarra, insecto hemíptero; llámase también *harvest-fly.*

Cicatrice [sic'-a-tris], **Cicatrix** [sic'-a-trics], *s.* Cicatriz.

Cicatrisant [sic-a-trai'-zant], *s.* Cicatrizante.

Cicatrisive [sic-a-trai'-siv], *a.* Cicatrizativo.

Cicatrization [sic-a-tri-zé'-shun], *s.* Cicatrización.

Cicatrize [sic'-a-traiz], *va.* Cicatrizar.

Cicely [sis'-e-li], *s.* Perifollo, cerafollo, planta de las umbelíferas. *Sweet cicely,* Perifollo, planta aromática. Myrrhis odorata en Europa; Osmorrhiza en los Estados Unidos.

Cicerone [chi-chê-rō'-nê o sis-e-rō'-ne], *s.* Guía que enseña los monumentos, las instituciones y cosas dignas de verse en algún lugar. Dícese en plural *ciceroni,* y es voz moderna italiana.

Cicuta [si-kiū'-ta], *s.* Cicuta, hierba umbelífera cuya raíz es venenosa.

Cider [sai'-der], *s.* Sidra, bebida hecha del zumo de manzanas.

Ciderist [sai'-der-ist], *s.* Fabricante o conocedor de sidra.

Ciderkin [sai'-der-kin], *s.* Aguapié, la sidra que se saca de la manzana ya exprimida.

Ci-devant [si-de-vāñ'], *a.* Del tiempo pasado; anterior. antecedente.

Cigar [si-gār'], *s.* Cigarro, puro. *Cigar store,* Cigarrería, tabaquería, estanco de cigarros.

Cigarette [sig-a-ret'], *s.* Cigarrillo, cigarro. *Cigarette case,* Cigarrera. *Cigarette lighter,* Encendedor automático. *Cigarette paper,* Librillo.

Cilia [sil'-i-a], *s.* Plural de CILIUM.

Ciliary [sil'-i-e-ri], *a.* Ciliar, lo que pertenece o se refiere a las pestañas.

Ciliate [sil'-i-ēt], *a.* Ciliado, pestañoso, provisto de pelitos.

Cilicious [si-lish'-us], *a.* Cerdoso.

Cilium [sil'-i-um], *s.* (Más usado en plural.) 1. Pelito, por lo común microscópico, semejante a una pestaña. 2. Pestaña: barbilla de las plantas.

Cima [sai'-ma], *s.* *V.* CYMA.

Cimbric [sim'-bric], *s.* Címbrico, el lenguaje de los antiguos habitantes de Jutlandia.

Cimeter [sim'-e-ter], *s.* Cimitarra, arma de acero a manera de sable, de hoja ancha y corva.

Cimmerian [sim-mi'-ri-an], *a.* Lo perteneciente a los cimerios, pueblos de Italia de los que relata Homero que vivían en obscuridad perpetua. *Cimmerian darkness,* Obscuridad espantosa.

Cinch [sinch], *va.* (Fam. E. U.) Cinchar; apretar, forzar.—*s.* 1. Cincha (de cabalgadura). 2. (Fam.) Cosa segura, cosa hecha; ganga. (<esp.)

Cinchona [sin-cō'-na], *s.* Cinchona, nombre científico de la quina.

Cincture [sinc'-chur], *va.* Ceñir, como con un cinto o ceñidor; cercar, rodear.—*s.* Cinto, ceñidor, cíngulo, cincho; cercado, cerca.

Cinder [sin'-der], *s.* 1. Carbón, cualquier cosa quemada al fuego, pero no reducida a cenizas. 2. Cernada o ceniza gruesa y caliente.

Cinder-wench [sin'-der-wench], **Cinder-woman** [sin'-der-wum'-an], *sf.* Mujer que escarba los montones de ceniza para hallar carbones.

Cinema [sin'-e-ma], *s.* Cinema, cinematógrafo.

Cineraceous [sin-e-ré'-shius], *a.* Cinéreo, de ceniza o parecido á ella.

Cineraria [sin-e-ré'-ri-a], *s.* Cineraria, género de plantas de flores compuestas, natural del África del Sur.

Cinerary [sin'-e-re-ri], *a.* Cinerario, relativo a las cenizas o que contiene cenizas.

Cinereous [si-ni'-ri-us], *a.* Ceniciento, cinéreo.

Cineritious [sin-e-rish'-us], *a.* Cenizoso, cineríceo, de la naturaleza de las cenizas; de su color.

Cingle [sing'-gl], *s.* (Poco us.) Cincha. *V.* SURCINGLE.

Cinnabar [sin'-a-bār], *s.* Cinabrio o bermellón, sulfuro rojo de mercurio (HgS).

Cinnamic [sin-am'-ic], *a.* De la canela, o derivado de canela.

Cinnamon [sin'-a-mun], *s.* Canela, la corteza fragante de un árbol que se cría en la isla de Ceilán. *Cinnamon bag,* Churla de canela.

Cinnamon-tree [sin'-a-mun-tri'], *s.* Árbol de la canela.

Cinquefoil [sinc'-feil], *s.* 1. (Arq.) Pentalóbulo, adorno o ventana de cinco puntas. 2. (Bot.) Cincoenrama, planta del género Potentilla.

Cinque Ports [sink pōrt], *s.* Cinco puertos de Inglaterra situados frente a la costa de Francia, a saber: Hastings, Sandwich, Dover, Romney y Hythe.

†**Cion** [sai'-un], *s.* *V.* SCION.

Cipher [sai'-fer], *s.* 1. Cifra, carácter aritmético. 2. Cero, cifra aritmética que ni por sí, ni puesta antes de otro número, tiene valor alguno. 3. Cifra, carácter arbitrario y convenido con que se escriben dos personas en secreto. 4. Cifra, enlace de letras para expresar un nombre en abreviatura. 5. (Mús.) Prolongación indebida del sonido de un cañón de órgano, causada por el imperfecto funcionamiento de una válvula.

Cipher, *vn.* 1. Numerar, usar de cifras o números para contar o formar algún cómputo. 2. Sonar un cañón de órgano sin que el organista toque la tecla correspondiente.—*va.* Cifrar, escribir en cifra.

Circensial [ser-sen'-shal], **Circensian** [ser-sen'-shan], *a.* Circense, relativo a los juegos o espectáculos de los romanos en el circo.

Circinate [ser'-si-nēt], *a.* (Bot.) Arrollado hacia dentro; aplícase a la vernación.

Circle [ser'-cl], *s.* 1. Círculo, circunferencia, curva plana, cerrada, cuyos puntos equidistan de otro interior llamado centro. 2. Círculo, área o superficie contenida dentro de la circunferencia. 3. Corro, corrillo, el cerco formado por un número de personas reunidas formando círculo. 4. Reunión, asamblea, junta, congreso de muchos en un mismo lugar. 5. Circunlocución, circunloquio, rodeo, ambages.

Circle, *va.* 1. Mover alguna cosa circularmente. 2. Circundar, rodear. 3. Cercar, ceñir, abrazar todo al rededor.—*vn.* Circular, dar vueltas como en círculo.

Circled [ser'-cld], *a.* Redondo, en forma de círculo.

Circlet [ser'-clet], *s.* 1. Círculo pequeño, anillo. 2. Disco; corona.

Circling [ser'-cling], *a.* Circular, redondo.

Circuit [ser'-kit], *s.* 1. Circuito, revolución, la vuelta que se da al rededor de alguna cosa. 2. Circuito, recinto, el espacio contenido dentro de un círculo. 3. (Elec. y Radio) Circuito. *Circuit breaker,* (Elec.) Cortacircuitos.

†Circuit, *vn.* Moverse circularmente. —*va.* Andar al rededor.
‡Circuiteer [sẹr-kit-ír'], *s.* El juez que recorre un distrito para administrar justicia.
Circuitous [sẹr-kiū'-i-tus], *a.* Tortuoso, rodeado, indirecto.
Circuitously [sẹr-kiū'-i-tus-li], *adv.* Tortuosamente.
Circulable [sẹr'-kiu-la-bl], *a.* Capaz de ser puesto en circulación.
Circular [sẹr'-kiu-lar], *a.* 1. Circular, redondo. 2. Circular, lo que siempre vuelve al punto donde empieza. *Circular letter*, Circular, carta, aviso, orden, etc., que se envía á muchas personas a un tiempo, dándoles conocimiento de alguna cosa. —*s.* Circular, carta o aviso circular.
Circularity [sẹr-kiu-lar'-i-ti], *s.* Forma o figura circular.
Circularize [sẹr'-kiu-lar-aiz], *va.* Hacer circular (algo).
Circulate [sẹr'-kiu-lêt], *va.* 1. Hacer circular, esparcir; diseminar; poner en circulación. 2. Cercar, circundar.—*vn.* 1. Circular, dar vueltas como en círculo, moverse al rededor. 2. Circular, pasar de mano en mano, propagarse, esparcirse. 3. Pasar de un sitio a otro por curso indirecto, como el vapor por un sistema de tubos. *Circulating decimal*, Fracción continua o periódica. *Circulating medium*, Moneda corriente. *Circulating library*, Librería circulante, esto es, librería en donde depositando el precio del libro, y por un pequeño interés, se prestan los libros por tiempo determinado.
Circulation [sẹr-kiu-lé'-shun], *s.* 1. Circulación. 2. Mudanza recíproca de sentido. 3. Circulación de moneda.
Circulatory [sẹr'-kiu-la-to-ri], *a.* Circular, circulante.
Circum-. Prefijo latino que significa alrededor.
Circumambiency [sẹr-cum-am'-bi-en-si], *s.* Circumambiencia.
Circumambient [sẹr-cum-am'-bi-ent], *a.* Circumambiente.
Circumambulate [sẹr-cum-am'-biu-lêt], *vn.* Circumambular, pasear o andar al rededor.
Circumcise [sẹr'-cum-saiz], *va.* Circuncidar.
Circumciser [sẹr-cum-sai'-zẹr], *s.* Circuncidador.
Circumcision [sẹr-cum-sizh'-un], *s.* 1. Circuncisión. 2. Purificación espiritual. 3. Los judíos, como pueblo circuncidado.
Circumduct [sẹr-cum-duct'], *va.* 1. Circunducir. 2. Contravenir; anular, revocar, abrogar.
Circumduction [sẹr-cum-duc'-shun], *s.* 1. Anulación, abolición. 2. Circunducción.
Circumference [sẹr-cum'-fẹr-ens], *s.* Circunferencia, periferia; perímetro, cerco, circuito.
Circumferential [sẹr-cum-fẹ-ren'-shal], *a.* Circunferencial.
Circumferentor [sẹr-cum-fẹ-ren'-tẹr], *s.* 1. Grafómetro, instrumento para medir tierras. 2. Plancheta, instrumento para levantar planos.
Circumflex [sẹr'-cum-flex], *s.* Acento circunflejo.—*a.* 1. (Gram.) Pronunciado o marcado con el acento llamado circunflejo. 2. (Anat.) Circunflejo, encorvado en forma curvilínea, arqueado; como algunos vasos y nervios.
Circumflexion [sẹr-cum-flec'-shun], *s.* Encorvamiento, encorvadura, acción de encorvar, de dar a un objeto forma o dirección curvilínea.
Circumfluence [sẹr-cum'-flu-ens], *s.* Acción de correr las aguas en torno de algo, rodeándolo.
Circumfluent [sẹr-cum'-flu-ent], *a.* Circunfluente.
Circumfluous [sẹr-cum'-flu-us], *a.* Lo que rodea o circunda con agua.
Circumfuse [sẹr-cum-fiūz'], *va.* Verter o derramar al derredor.
‡Circumfusile [sẹr-cum-fiū'-sil], *a.* Lo que puede vaciarse o verterse al rededor.
Circumfusion [sẹr-cum-fiū'-zhun], *s.* El acto de esparcir alguna cosa en torno de otra.
Circumgyrate [sẹr-cum-jai'-rêt], *va.* Girar, dar vueltas al rededor.
Circumgyration [sẹr-cum-jai-ré'-shun], *s.* Giro o vuelta al derredor.
Circumjacent [sẹr-cum-jé'-sent], *a.* Lo que está en torno de alguna cosa.
Circumlittoral [sẹr-cum-lit'-to-ral], *a.* Circunlitoral, adyacente a la costa.
Circumlocution [sẹr-cum-lo-kiū'-shun], *s.* Circunlocución, circonloquio, rodeo de palabras, perífrasis.
Circumlocutory [sẹr-cum-loc'-yu-to-ri], *a.* Circunlocutorio.
‡Circummure [sẹr-cum-miūr'], *va.* Rodear de murallas.
Circumnavigable [sẹr-cum-nav'-i-ga-bl], *a.* Navegable al rededor.
Circumnavigate [sẹr-kum-nav'-i-gêt], *va.* Circunnavegar, navegar al rededor.
Circumnavigation [sẹr-cum-nav-i-gé'-shun], *s.* Navegación al rededor.
Circumnavigator [sẹr-cum-nav'-i-gê-tẹr], *s.* El que navega al rededor.
Circumoral [sẹr-cum-ō'-ral], *a.* Que rodea o circunda la boca.
Circumpolar [sẹr-cum-pō'-lar], *a.* Circumpolar, alrededor del polo.
Circumposition [sẹr-cum-po-zish'-un], *s.* (Poco us.) Colocación circular de alguna cosa.
Circumrenal [sẹr-cum-rí'-nal], *a.* Que rodea o circunda los riñones.
Circumrotation [sẹr-cum-ro-té'-shun], *s.* Rotación; circunvolución.
Circumrotatory [sẹr-cum-rō'-ta-to-ri], *a.* Giratorio, lo que se mueve en rotación.
Circumscissile [sẹr-cum-sis'-il], *a.* (Bot.) Dehiscente, separable a manera de cápsula, en una línea transversal circular, de suerte que la parte superior se abre como una tapa; así sucede en la verdolaga común y otras plantas.
Circumscribe [sẹr-cum-scraib'], *va.* Circunscribir.
Circumscription [sẹr-cum-scrip'-shun], *s.* 1. Circunscripción. 2. Limitación. 3. Inscripción circular.
Circumscriptive [sẹr-cum-scrip'-tiv], *a.* Circunscriptivo.
Circumspect [sẹr'-cum-spect], *a.* Circunspecto, prudente, mirado, reservado, discreto, recatado, contenido.
Circumspection [sẹr-cum-spec'-shun], *s.* Circunspección, miramiento, prudencia, reserva, comedimiento, recato, moderación.
Circumspective [sẹr-cum-spec'-tiv], *a.* Circunspecto, mirado.
Circumspectively [sẹr-cum-spec'-tiv-li], **Circumspectly** [sẹr'-cum-spect-li], *adv.* Circunspectamente, con cautela y vigilancia.
Circumspectness [sẹr'-cum-spect-nes], *s.* Cautela, vigilancia, recato.
Circumstance [sẹr'-cum-stans], *s.* 1. Accidente, cosa adventicia, incidente, acontecimiento; lo que sucede o existe incidentalmente. 2. Circunstancia, incidente, estado o condición en que se halla alguna cosa. 3. Circunstancia; tomado absolutamente en plural es el estado o condición de los negocios públicos. *To be in easy circumstances*, Estar acomodado, en buena posición.
Circumstance, *va.* Colocar en buen o mal estado, en una posición cualquiera; se usa comunmente en el participio pasado. *Circumstanced as we were, we could not escape*, En las circunstancias en que nos encontrábamos, era imposible escapar.
Circumstantial [sẹr-cum-stan'-shal], *a.* 1. Accidental, casual; accesorio. 2. Circunstanciado, puesto con todas las circunstancias y menudencias precisas; particular.
Circumstantiality [sẹr-cum-stan-shi-al'-i-ti], *s.* 1. Circunstancialidad. 2. Detalles minuciosos.
Circumstantially [sẹr-cum-stan'-shal-i], *adv.* 1. Circunstanciadamente, con toda menudencia. 2. Eventualmente, según las circunstancias.
Circumstantiate [sẹr-cum-stan'-shi-êt], *va.* 1. Contar, referir o explicar una cosa con todas sus circunstancias. 2. Notar o señalar las circunstancias de cualquiera cosa, circunstanciar, detallar.
Circumterraneous [sẹr-cum-ter-é'-ne-us], *a.* Lo que está al rededor de la tierra.
Circumvallate [sẹr-cum-val'-êt], *va.* Circunvalar, rodear algún paraje con trincheras o fortificaciones.
Circumvallation [sẹr-cum-val-é'-shun], *s.* Circunvalación, cerco o línea de defensa o ataque de una plaza fuerte, campamento, etc.
Circumvent [sẹr-cum-vent'], *va.* Entrampar, enredar, engañar a alguno con artificio.
Circumvention [sẹr-cum-ven'-shun], *s.* Engaño, fraude, impostura, trampa, enredo, embrollo.
Circumventive [sẹr-cum-ven'-tiv], *a.* Engañoso, delusorio.
Circumvest [sẹr-cum-vest'], *va.* 1. Envolver, rodear, con un ropaje o vestidura. 2. Circundar, rodear, cercar.
Circumvolation [sẹr-cum-vo-lé'-shun], *s.* Vuelo al rededor.
Circumvolution [sẹr-cum-vo-lū'-shun], *s.* Circunvolución, la vuelta que en redondo hace una cosa.
Circumvolve [sẹr-cum-volv'], *va.* Enrollar una cosa en torno de otra.
Circus [sẹr'-cus], *s.* 1. Circo, recinto circular destinado a los ejercicios de equitación y de gimnástica. 2. Circo, edificio que servía entre los romanos para carreras, juegos y otros espectáculos.
Cirrhosis [si-rō'-sis], *s.* (Med.) Cirrosis, lesión en las vísceras, especialmente en el hígado. *Cirrhosis of the liver*, Cirrosis del hígado.
Cirripeds, Cirripedia [sir'-i-peds, sir-i-pi'-di-a], *s. pl.* Cirrópodos, orden de crustáceos encerrados en envolturas calcáreas, y que tienen por lo común seis pares de patas cirriformes. Incluye, entre otros, los escaramujos.
Cirro-, forma de combinación. *V.* CIRRUS.
Cirrus [sir'-us], *s.* 1. Cirrus: nombre dado a las nubes que presentan el aspecto de fibras extendidas como los hilos de una madeja. 2. (Bot.) Cirro, zarcillo, el apéndice en forma de espiral que tienen muchas plantas. 3. (Anat.) Apéndice parecido a un zarcillo o hilo, que sirve como

órgano del tacto. *Cirro-cumulus, cirro-stratus*, Nubes que parecen ser mezclas de cirrus con cúmulus o estratus. El primero se llama vulgarmente cielo aborregado.

Cisalpine [sis-al'-pin], *a.* Cisalpino.

Cist [sist], *s.* (Ant.) 1. Cista, o canastillo de ofrendas en los misterios de Eleusis. 2. Caja de metal para contener artículos de tocador. 3. (Des.) *V.* CYST.

Cistercian [sis-tẹr'-shan], *s.* Cisterciense, religioso del orden de San Bernardo.

Cistern [sis'-tẹrn], *s.* 1. Cisterna, aljibe, receptáculo de agua. 2. Arca de agua.

Cistoscope [sis'-to-scōp], *s.* Cistoscopio.

Cistus [sis'-tus], *s.* (Bot.) Cisto, jara, juagarzo, estepa, planta ramosa.

Cit [sit], *s.* (Fam.) Ciudadano. *V.* CITIZEN.

Citable [sai'-ta-bl], *a.* Citable, que se puede citar, o digno de ser citado.

Citadel [sit'-a-del], *s.* Ciudadela.

Citation [sai-té'-shun], *s.* 1. Citación, comparendo, emplazamiento judicial, con señalamiento de tiempo y circunstancias. 2. Cita, la acción de alegar o citar alguna ley o autor. 3. Mención de alguna cosa.

Citatory [sai'-ta-to-ri], *a.* Citatorio, que cita.

Cite [sait], *va.* 1. Citar a juicio, llamar á alguno ante el juez. 2. Alegar alguna ley, autoridad, texto o ejemplo. 3. Citar, referirse a.

Citer [sait'-ẹr], *s.* Citador.

Cithara [sith'-a-ra], *s.* Antigua lira griega, triangular, de 7 a 11 cuerdas.

Cithern [sith'-ẹrn], *s.* Cítara, especie de laúd.

Citified [sit'-i-faid], *a.* Con las maneras propias de la ciudad.

Citizen [sit'-i-zn], *s.* 1. Ciudadano, el que goza de los derechos civiles. 2. Habitante o vecino de una ciudad. *Fellow-citizen*, Conciudadano.

Citizenship [sit'-i-zn-ship], *s.* Ciudadanía, naturalización. *Citizenship papers*, Documentos de naturalización.

Citrate [sit'-rêt], *s.* (Quím.) Citrato, sal formada del ácido cítrico unido a una base.

Citric [sit'-ric], *a.* (Quím.) Cítrico, derivado del limón o frutas semejantes. *Citric acid*, Acido cítrico.

Citrine [sit'-rin], *a.* 1. Cetrino, color de limón. 2. Perteneciente al limón.

Citron [sit'-run], *s.* Cidra, toronja, fruta semejante al limón.

Citron-tree [sit'-run-trî], *s.* Cidro, acitrón, toronjal, árbol que produce las cidras.

Citron-water [sit'-run-wō'-tẹr], *s.* Aguardiente destilado de cidras.

Citrus [sit'-rus], *a.* (Bot.) Auranciáceo, cítrico. *Citrus fruits*, Agrios, frutas agrias (como el limón, la toronja, la naranja, etc.)

City [sit'-i], *s.* Ciudad. En Inglaterra tienen el nombre de *city* todas las poblaciones donde hay silla episcopal; en los Estados Unidos toda población que tiene ayuntamiento establecido por las leyes del respectivo estado.—*a.* Ciudadano.

City hall [sit'-i hōl], *s.* Palacio municipal, ayuntamiento, casa consistorial.

City planning [sit'-i plan'-ing], *s.* urbanización, planificación.

Civet [siv'-et], *s.* 1. Civeta, gato de algalia. 2. Algalia, el perfume que despide de sí la civeta.

Civic [siv'-ic], *a.* Cívico, lo que pertenece o se refiere a una ciudad, a un ciudadano o a la ciudadanía.

Civics [siv'-ics], *s.* Instrucción cívica.

Civil [siv'-il], *a.* 1. Civil, lo que pertenece al gobierno, vida o intereses de los ciudadanos de un estado. 2. Civil, lo contrario a criminal en términos forenses, y lo que no es eclesiástico ni militar. *Civil death*, La privación de los derechos civiles á consecuencia de una sentencia o pena. 3. Civil, intestino, doméstico. 4. Civil, atento, urbano, cortés, afable. *Civil service*, Los departamentos del servicio público que no son militares ni navales. *Civil law*, *V.* LAW.

Civil defense [si-vil di-fens'], *s.* Defensa civil.

Civil disobedience [si-vil dis-o-bi'-di ẹns], *s.* Desobediencia civil.

Civil engineer [siv'-il en-ji-nir'], *s.* Ingeniero civil.

Civilian [si-vil'-yan], *s.* 1. El que no pertenece al ejército, la marina ni el clero. 2. Jurisperito, jurisconsulto, el que está versado en el derecho civil.

Civility [si-vil'-i-ti], *s.* Civilidad, urbanidad, cortesía, buena crianza, política, sociabilidad; decoro, afabilidad, atención.

Civilization [siv-il-i-zé'-shun], *s.* Civilización.

Civilize [siv'-il-aiz], *va.* Civilizar, instruir; suavizar el lenguaje, la condición y las costumbres de alguno; hacer razonables, cultas y sociables a las personas o naciones; humanizar.

Civilized [siv'-il-aizd], *pp.* y *a.* Civilizado, el que ya se ha acostumbrado al lenguaje, usos y modales de la gente culta; en estado de civilización.

Civilizer [siv-il-aiz'-ẹr], *s.* Civilizador, el o lo que civiliza.

Civilly [siv'-il-i], *adv.* Civilmente, cortésmente.

Civism [siv'-izm], *s.* 1. Civismo, patriotismo, devoción al interés público. 2. Ciudadanía.

Clabber, Bonny-clabber [clab'-ẹr, bon'-i-clab'-ẹr], *s.* Cuajo, leche cuajada. —*vn.* Cuajarse, como la leche.

Clack [clac], *s.* Cualquier cosa que hace un ruido o estrépito continuo e importuno.

Clack, *vn.* 1. Cencerrear, hacer un ruido importuno; crujir, restallar; castañetear. 2. Charlar, picotear, hablar demasiado.

Clad [clad], *a.* Vestido, cubierto, aderezado.

Claim [clêm], *va.* Demandar, pedir en juicio, reclamar, reivindicar, pretender como cosa debida.

Claim, *s.* 1. Pretensión, título, derecho, reclamación, reivindicación. 2. Demanda, la acción o propuesta que se hace a un juez para que ponga al demandante en posesión de lo que otro tiene.

Claimable [clẹm'-a-bl], *a.* Lo que se puede demandar o pedir en justicia como debido.

Claimant [clêm'-ant], **Claimer** [clêm'-ẹr], *s.* Demandante, el que demanda o pide.

Clairvoyance [clār-vei'-ans], *s.* Lucidez, facultad atribuida a las personas magnetizadas de ver los objetos distantes u ocultos.

Clairvoyant [clār-vei'-ant], *a.* Lúcido, en estado de lucidez magnética. vidente.

Clam [clam], *s.* Marisco, molusco de dos conchas, muy estimado como alimento.

Clam, *va.* (Prov.) Empastar, pegar con alguna cosa viscosa o glutinosa. —*vn.* 1. Mojarse; hambrear. 2. Excavar para sacar de la playa los moluscos llamados *clams*. 3. (Prov. Ingl.) Repicar, echar las campanas a vuelo.

Clamant [clam'-ant], *a.* 1. Clamante, que da voces lastimosas pidiendo auxilio. 2. (Poét.) Clamoroso; resonante.

Clamber [clam'-bẹr], *vn.* Gatear, trepar, encaramarse.

Clamminess [clam'-i-nes], *s.* Viscosidad, materia viscosa.

Clammy [clam'-i], *a.* Viscoso, pegajoso.

Clamor [clam'-er], *s.* 1. Clamor, grito, vociferación. 2. Clamoreo. 3. Algarabía, alboroto.

Clamor, *vn.* Vociferar, gritar, exclamar.—*va.* Aturdir con ruido. *To clamor against*, Quejarse de.

Clamorous [clam'-ẹr-us], *a.* Clamoroso, ruidoso, tumultuoso, estrepitoso.

Clamorously [clam'-er-us-li], *adv.* Clamorosamente; ruidosamente.

Clamour, *v.* y *s.* (Forma común en Inglaterra.) *V.* CLAMOR.

Clamp [clamp], *s.* 1. Torno de mano, tornillo. 2. Abrazadera, cuchillero. 3. (Med.) Pinza hemostática.

Clamp, *va.* 1. Sujetar con abrazadera. 2. Asegurar con el torno de mano. 3. Imponer. *To clamp down on*, 1. Apretar los tornillos a. 2. Cohibir, refrenar, reprimir.

Clampdown [clamp'-daun], *s.* Cohibición, refrenamiento, represión.

Clan [clan], *s.* 1. Clan. Familia, tribu, casta o raza de muchas personas enlazadas por sangre o parentesco. 2. Secta, grupo.

Clandestine [clan-des'-tin], *a.* Clandestino, secreto, oculto.

Clandestinely [clan-des'-tin-li], *adv.* Clandestinamente.

Clandestineness [clan-des'-tin-nes], *s.* Secreto, estado oculto.

Clang [clang], *s.* 1. Rechino, sonido desapacible resultante del choque de una cosa con otra. 2. Ruido de armas, de cadenas, etc. 3. *V.* CLANG-TINT.

Clang, *vn.* Rechinar, hacer o causar un sonido agudo y retumbante.—*va.* Hacer resonar.

Clangor, Clangour [claŋ'-gẹr], *s.* Ruido estridente, agudo, penetrante; ruido de armas, cadenas o campanas; clamor.

Clang-tint [clang'-tint], *s.* Calidad de sonido; timbre: color acústico. (< Al. Klangfarbe.)

Clank [claŋk], *s.* Rechinamiento, ruido estridente, poco musical, pero no retumbante como el *clang;* producido por el choque de metales entre sí.

Clank, *vn.* Rechinar, producir un ruido agudo y penetrante.—*va.* Hacer rechinar.

Clannish [clan'-ish], *a.* Del *clan* o tribu o semejante a él; estrechamente unido.

Clansman [clanz'-man], *s.* Miembro de un *clan*.

Clap [clap], *va.* 1. Batir, golpear una

cosa contra otra. 2. Pegar, encajar, encasquetar una cosa a otra; juntar, aplicar. 3. Palmear, palmotear, vitorear. †*To clap up*, Concluir una cosa instantáneamente. *To clap up a peace*, Hacer una paz simulada. *To clap up together*, Empaquetar. *To clap in prison*, Encarcelar. *To clap up a bargain*, Rematar un trato o ajuste. *To clap in*, Empujar, hacer entrar por fuerza.—*vn.* 1. Cerrarse ruidosamente. 2. Arrojarse con violencia o impetuosidad en. 3. Aplaudir, dar palmadas. *To clap on all the sails*, Cargar todas las velas. *To clap the door to*, Cerrar la puerta con violencia. *To clap spurs to one's horse*, Poner espuelas al caballo.

Clap, *s.* 1. Estrépito, ruido o golpe causado por el encuentro repentino de dos cuerpos. 2. Trueno, el estruendo o ruido que causa la exhalación eléctrica al dividir el aire. 3. Palmoteo, palmada, el acto de palmotear, aplauso. 4. (Vul.) Gonorrea o purgaciones. *Clap of thunder*, Trueno, rayo.

Clapboard [clap'-bōrd], *s.* Tabla de chilla, comunmente más gruesa en su borde inferior que en el superior.

Clapper [clap'-ẹr]. *s.* 1. Palmoteador, el que palmea o palmotea. 2. Badajo de campana. 3. Taravilla o cítola de molino. 4. Aldaba de una puerta. 5. (Mar.) Chapaleta de la bomba. 6. (Mar.) Chapaletas de los imbornales.

Clapper-claw [clap'-ẹr-clō], *va.* (Vul.) 1. Golpear (con la mano), rascar y desgarrar; atacar con el pico y las uñas. 2. Regañar; maltratar de palabra.

Clapping [clap'-ing], *s.* Aleteo; palmoteo, palmada, aplauso.

Clap-trap [clap'-trap], *a.* Engañador, que causa sensación, pero sin mérito verdadero.—*s.* Recurso, lenguaje, conducta encaminados a evocar aplauso; artificio indigno.

Claque [clac], *s.* (Teat.) Claque, aplaudidores pagados.

Clarabella [clar'-a-bel'-a], *s.* Clarabela, registro melodioso del órgano; se hace de madera.

Clarence [clar'-ens], *s.* Cupé, Clarence, carruaje de cuatro ruedas, provisto comunmente de un frente de vidrio.

Clarendon [clar'-en-den], *s.* Carácter de tipo algo grueso y compacto. La voz CLARENDON a la cabeza de este título está impresa en dicha letra.

Clare-obscure [clār'-ob-skiur'], *s.* Claroscuro.

Claret [clar'-et], *s.* Clarete, vino tinto o rojo; vino tinto de Burdeos.

Clarification [clar-i-fi-kē'-shun], *s.* Clarificación.

Clarify [clar'-i-fai], *va.* 1. Clarificar, aclarar, poner claro lo que está turbio. 2. Ilustrar, dar lustre o esplendor a alguna cosa.

Clarinet [clar'-i-net], *s.* Clarinete, instrumento músico de viento.

Clarinettist [clar-i-net'-ist], *s.* Clarinetista, el que toca el clarinete.

Clarion [clar'-i-en], *s.* Clarín, instrumento de música, especie de trompeta de agudo sonido.

Clarionet [clar'-i-o-net], *s.* *V.* CLARINET.

Clarity [clar'-i-ti], *s.* Claridad, resplandor, luz.

Clary [clē'-ri], *s.* (Bot.) Salvia silvestre.

Clash [clash], *vn.* 1. Chocar, entrechocarse, tropezar o encontrarse con violencia. 2. Encontrarse; contradecir, oponerse.—*va.* Batir, golpear una cosa contra otra.

Clash, *s.* 1. Choque, fragor, crujido, colisión de una cosa contra otra con ruido o estrépito. 2. Oposición, contradicción; disputa, debate, choque.

Clashing [clash'-ing], *s.* Oposición, contradicción, enemistad, contienda; choque, ruido.

Clashingly [clash'-ing-ly], *adv.* En oposición, en contradicción.

Clasp [clqsp], *s.* 1. Broche, chapeta, botoncito, especie de corchete que sirve para abrochar y asegurar alguna cosa; hebilla. 2. Abrazo.

Clasp, *va.* 1. Abrochar, cerrar o unir con broche o corchete. 2. Abrazar, coger alguna cosa entre los brazos. 3. Cercar, incluir.

Clasp-knife [clqsp'-naif], *s.* Navaja, especie de cuchillo que se dobla entrando el corte en el mango.

Class [clqs], *s.* 1. Clase, orden o número de personas del mismo grado, calidad y oficio. 2. Rango, categoría. 3. Clase en las escuelas; conjunto de personas que se han graduado juntas en un colegio o universidad, o que esperan graduarse a la vez; cada clase toma el nombre del año de su graduación, y así se dice, por ejemplo, la clase de 1899. 4. Orden de cosas pertenecientes a una misma especie. 5. (Biol.) Clase, subdivisión intermedia entre reino y género. *The working class*, La clase trabajadora, los artesanos, operarios, etc. *The upper class*, La clase alta, la clase elevada. *The lower class*, La clase baja. *Class-room*, Sala de enseñanza, local de una clase.

Class, *va.* Clasificar, coordinar, ordenar, distribuir.

Classic, Classical [clas'-ic, al], *a.* 1. Clásico, relativo a los antiguos autores griegos y latinos de primer orden, y a los de primer rango entre los modernos. 2. Clásico, de primera clase, en la literatura o arte. 3. Compuesto por los grandes maestros de música.

Classic, *s.* Autor clásico.

Classically [clas'-ic-al-i], *adv.* Clásicamente.

Classicism [clas'-i-sizm], *s.* 1. Clasicismo, estilo o idiotismo clásico. 2. Erudición clásica.

Classicist [clas'-i-sist], *s.* Clásico, el partidario de las obras de la antigüedad; el que sigue las doctrinas del clasicismo.

Classification [clas-i-fi-kē'-shun], *s.* Clasificación, coordinación o distribución de algunas cosas en clases.

Classify [clas'-i-fai], *va.* Clasificar, coordinar o distribuir algunas cosas en clases.

Classis [clas'-is], *s.* 1. Consejo o tribunal en algunas iglesias reformadas. 2. Clase biológica.

Classmate [clas'-mēt], *s.* Condiscípulo, compañero de clase.

Classroom [clas'-rūm], *s.* Sala de clase.

Clastic [clas'-tic], *a.* 1. Que se rompe en partes. 2. Compuesto de fragmentos. (< Gr.)

Clatter [clat'-ẹr], *vn.* 1. Resonar, hacer sonido o ruido. 2. Charlar, picotear; disputar.—*va.* 1. Golpear alguna cosa haciéndola retumbar. 2. Gritar, vocear, reñir.

Clatter, *s.* 1. Ruido, estruendo, fracaso. 2. Gresca, trapisonda, alboroto, bulla y confusión.

Clatterer [clat'-ẹr-ẹr], *s.* El que hace ruido; soplón.

†**Claudicate** [clō'-di-kēt], *vn.* Claudicar, cojear, ser o estar defectuoso.

Clause [clōz], *s.* 1. Cláusula, punto, miembro de un período. 2. Artículo, estipulación particular de un contrato. 3. Condición.

Claustral [clōs'-tral], *a.* Claustral.

‡**Clausure** [clō'-zhur], *s.* 1. Clausura, encierro. 2. Broche para libro.

Clavate [clē'-vēt], **Clavated** [clev'-ē-ted], *a.* 1. Clavado, en forma de maza o clava. 2. Claveteado.

Clavichord [clav'-i-cērd], *s.* Clavicordio, instrumento músico de cuerda que precedió al piano.

Clavicle [clav'-i-cl], *s.* Clavícula, hueso que está sobre el pecho más abajo del cuello.

Clavicular [cla-vic'-yu-lar], *a.* Clavicular, de las clavículas.

Clavier [clē'-vi-ẹr], *s.* 1. (Mús.) Teclado (del órgano). 2. [clq-vīr'] Instrumento con teclado, particularmente el clavicordio o el piano de mesa u horizontal.

Claw [clō], *s.* 1. Garra; garfa. 2. Garra, la mano del hombre; en este sentido es voz despectiva. 3. (Mar.) Uñas de espeque o pie de cabra. 4. (Bot.) Uña de un pétalo. *Claw-bar*, Palanca de uña. *Claw-hammer*, Martillo de orejas. *Claw-hammer coat*, Frac, casaca de cola de bacalao; llámase así por su forma. *Claw for tacks*, Arrancador de puntillas.

Claw, *va.* 1. Desgarrar. 2. Arañar, rasgar, despedazar. 3. Reñir, regañar. 4. (Des.) Lisonjear. 5. *To claw off*, (Mar.) Desempeñarse de una costa; por extensión, escapar, tomar el tole. *To claw it off*, Hacer una cosa con diligencia.

Clawed [clōd], *a.* Armado de garras o zarpas.

Clay [clē], *s.* Arcilla, tierra crasa y pegajosa. *Potter's clay*, Marga, barro de olleros o alfareros. *Clay-stone*, Concreción de diversas formas que se halla en la arcilla aluvial. *Clay-ground*, Tierra arcillosa. *Clay-marl*, Marga, tierra gredosa. *Clay-pit*, Barrizal, el paraje de donde se saca barro, tierra o arcilla.—*a. Clay-cold*, Frío, sin vida.

Clay, *va.* Cubrir alguna cosa con arcilla; abonar las tierras con arcilla.

Clayey [clē'-i], **Clayish** [clē'-ish], *a.* Arcilloso, lleno de arcilla o barro.

Claymore [clē'-mōr], *s.* Espada de dos filos, larga y ancha, de los antiguos escoceses.

Cleading [clīd'-ing], *s.* (Art. y Of.) Cubierta o envoltura exterior de tablas, forro de fieltro, u otro material, para dar mayor resistencia e impermeabilidad. Aplícase a la presa de un molino, a una caldera de vapor, al pozo o galería de un ascensor, etc.

Clean [clīn], *a.* 1. Limpio, claro, exento de suciedad. 2. Limpio, casto, inocente. 3. Curioso, aseado; desembarazado, despejado; claro, distinto. 4. Entero. 5. Diestro. 6. Bien proporcionado, que tiene simetría.—*adv.* Enteramente, perfectamente, completamente. *To make clean*, Limpiar. *To make a clean breast*, Hacer una confesión plena y sin reservas; aliviar el ánimo. *Clean up*, (1) Aseo general. (2) La acción de recoger el oro después de lavado y triturado; y el oro así recogido. *To show a clean pair of heels*, Escapar huyendo, dejar atrás en fuga.

Clean, *va.* Limpiar; asear, desembarazar de toda suciedad o materia extraña; desenlodar; lavar (la vajilla, etc.); desengrasar las telas; depurar (el oro).

Clean-cut [clin'-cut], *a.* 1. Cortado con claridad. 2. Bien definido. *Clean-cut person*, Persona de aspecto nítido y agradable.

Cleaner [clīn'-ęr], *s.* Limpiador, el que limpia.

Cleaning [clīn'-ing], *s.* Limpieza, aseo. *Dry-cleaning*, Tintorería, lavado en seco. *Cleaning rod*, Baqueta para limpiar (armas de fuego).

Cleanliness [clen'-li-nes], *s.* 1. Limpieza, aseo. 2. Curiosidad en el vestir.

Cleanly [clīn'-li], *a.* Limpio, aseado; puro, delicado.—*adv.* Primorosamente, aseadamente.

Cleanness [clīn'-nes], *s.* Limpieza, aseo; pureza, inocencia.

Cleanse [clenz], *va.* 1. Limpiar, purificar. 2. Purgar de algún reato o delito. 3. Librar de malos humores. 4. Fregar, limpiar.

Cleanser [clenz'-ęr], *s.* Evacuante, purgante.

Cleansing [clenz'-ing], *s.* Purificación.

Clear [clīr], *a.* 1. Claro, transparente, diáfano. 2. Alegre, sereno. 3. Evidente, indisputable, palpable. 4. Patente, manifiesto, claro, fácil de comprender. 5. Libre de culpa, puro, inocente, fuera de riesgo. 6. Neto, líquido. 7. Desempeñado, sin deudas. 8. Desenredado. 9. Claro, sonoro. *Clear reputation*, Reputación sin mancha, buen nombre.—*adv.* Claramente; enteramente, absolutamente. *A clear sky*, Un cielo despejado. *A clear style*, Un estilo claro, inteligible. *Clear weather*, Tiempo sereno, apacible.

Clear, *s.* Claro, el espacio no interrumpido entre dos cosas.

Clear, *va.* 1. Clarificar, dar lustre y esplendor a alguna cosa. 2. Aclarar, disipar alguna obscuridad. 3. Justificar, purificar, absolver de una acusación. 4. Desembarazar o librar de lo que ofende. 5. Clarificar, poner claro algún licor. 6. Limpiar, blanquear. 7. Sacar los géneros de la aduana. 8. Desembrollar (un negocio); satisfacer (una hipoteca). 9. Saltar por encima; pasar por encima de algo, sin tocarlo. 10. Cortar o arrancar los árboles y malezas de un terreno; preparar para la labranza; desmontar.—*vn.* 1. Aclararse, volver a ponerse claro lo que estaba obscuro. 2. Desembarazarse, desenredarse. *It clears up*, Va aclarando. *To clear the room*, Desocupar un cuarto, hacer salir de él a los que están dentro. *To clear the table*, Levantar la mesa. *To clear the way*, Abrir camino. *To clear accounts*, Liquidar cuentas. *To clear off*, Desbastar, pulir. *To clear a vessel or merchandise in the custom-house*, Despachar un barco o géneros en la aduana. *To clear a wood*, Desmontar un bosque.

Clearage [clīr'-ęj], *s.* El acto de remover alguna cosa; despejo.

Clearance [clīr'-ans], *s.* 1. Despejo. 2. (Com.) Despacho de aduana. 3. (Com.) Utilidad líquida. 4. (Aer.) Espacio. *Clearance sale*, Liquidación, barata.

Clear-cut [clīr'-cut], *a.* Claro, bien definido.

Clearer [clīr'ęr], *s.* Lo que aclara, purifica o ilumina.

Clearing [clīr'-ing], *s.* 1. Justificación, vindicación. 2. Claro, raso, sitio sin árboles en un bosque. 3. Arreglo, liquidación de los balances en el banco de liquidación.

Clearing house [clīr'-ing haus], *s.* (Com.) Bolsa o banco de compensación.

Clearly [clīr'-li], *adv.* Claramente, evidentemente; libremente; llanamente; abiertamente, sin reserva.

Clearness [clīr'-nes], *s.* 1. Claridad, transparencia; lustre, esplendor; luz. 2. Perspicuidad, perspicacia. 3. Sinceridad. *Clearness of the air*, Serenidad del aire.

Clear-sighted [clīr-sait'-ed], *a.* Previsor, perspicaz, juicioso, despierto, avisado.

Clear-sightedness [clīr-sait'-ed-nes], *s.* Perspicacia, discernimiento, penetración.

Clearstarch [clīr'-stārch], *va.* Almidonar.

Clearstarcher [clīr'-stārch-ęr], *s.* Almidonador, la persona que almidona ropa fina.

Clearstory [clīr'-sto-ri], *s.* 1. Piso más alto de la nave y del coro de una iglesia, con una serie de pequeñas ventanas. 2. Piso semejante en edificios de otro carácter, o sobretecho de un coche de ferrocarril con claraboyas a los costados para darle luz y ventilación.

Clear-voiced [clīr'-veist], *a.* El que tiene la voz clara.

Clearwing [clīr'-wing], *s.* Falena diurna con alas casi transparentes. Ægeria tipuliformis.

Cleat [clīt], *s.* 1. Listón de madera o hierro que se asegura sobre otro material para sujetarlo, cubrirlo, impedir que se deslice, etc. 2. (Mar.) Tojino. 3. (Mar.) Galápago de las palomas.

Cleavage [clīv'-ęj], *s.* 1. La acción de hendirse o el estado de hendido; hendidura, división. 2. Tendencia de una roca o cristal a partirse en determinadas direcciones.

Cleave [clīv], *vn.* 1. Pegarse o unirse una cosa a otra. 2. Ajustarse una cosa con otra. 3. Adherir, arrimarse, atenerse al dictamen o parecer de otro. 4. Abrirse en rajas, dividirse.—*va.* Rajar, hender, partir naturalmente.

Cleaver [clīv'-ęr], *s.* 1. Cuchilla de carnicero. 2. Hacha para rajar madera.

Cleavers [clīv'-ęrz], *s. pl.* (Bot.) Galio. *V.* Bedstraw.

Cleek [clīc], *s.* 1. Gancho. 2. Maza empleada para el juego de golf.

Clef [clef], *s.* (Mús.) Clave, signo que indica el tono al principio de la pauta.

Cleft [cleft], *s.* Rajadura, hendedura, abertura, grieta. *Clefts*, Grietas, aberturas que se forman en los pies de las caballerías.

Cleftgraft [cleft'-graft], *va.* Ingertar en tronco.

Clematis [clem'-a-tis], *s.* (Bot.) Clemátide, género de plantas de las ranunculáceas.

Clemency [clem'-en-si], *s.* Clemencia, misericordia, indulgencia, bondad.

Clement [clem'-ent], *a.* Clemente, piadoso, benigno, indulgente, misericordioso.

Clench [clench], *va.* 1. Asir fuertemente o resueltamente. 2. Cerrar con estrechez o convulsivamente, como el puño o los dientes. 3. Hacer firme, asegurar. 4. *V.* Clinch.—*s.* La acción de asir fuertemente.

Clencher [clench'-ęr], *s.* 1. El que o lo que ase; herramienta para asir. 2. (Fig.) Argumento sin réplica.

Clepsydra [clep'-si-dra], *s.* Clepsidra, reloj de agua.

Clerestory [clīr'-sto-ri], *s.* *V.* Clearstory.

Clergy [clęr'-ji], *s.* Clero.

Clergyman [clęr'-ji-man], *s.* Clérigo, eclesiástico.

Cleric [cler'-ic], *s* Clérigo.—*a.* Clerical.

Clerical [cler'-ic-al], *a.* Clerical, eclesiástico.

Clerk [clęrk y clārk en Ingl.], *s.* 1. Oficial de secretaría; amanuense, escribiente. 2. Dependiente, mancebo de tienda; empleado de oficina. 3. Eclesiástico, clérigo. 4. Escolar, estudiante. *Clerk of a ship*, Contador de navío. *Clerk of a parish*, Sacristán. *The clerk of the king's great wardrobe*, El primer ayuda de cámara del rey. *Clerk of a counting-house or shop*, Dependiente, cajero, mancebo, mozo de tienda o almacén. *Clerk of a court of justice*, Escribano de cámara, o secretario de tribunal.

Clerkly [clęrc'-li], *a.* Diestro, literato.—*adv.* Ingeniosamente.

Clerkship [clęrc'-ship], *s.* 1. Literatura, educación literaria. 2. El oficio, empleo u ocupación de dependiente, clérigo, estudiante o escribiente. 3. Escribanía de cámara, secretaría.

Clever [clev'-ęr], *a.* 1. Diestro, experto, hábil, avisado, mañoso, listo, inteligente, capaz. 2. (Fam. E. U.) Bien dispuesto, complaciente. 3. (Ant.) Justo, apropiado, cómodo, apto, propio.

Cleverly [clev'-ęr-li], *adv.* Diestramente, hábilmente.

Cleverness [clev'-ęr-nes], *s.* Destreza, habilidad, conocimiento, maña; garbo, gracia.

Clevis [clev'-is], *s.* Abrazadera, pieza de hierro sujeta al timón del arado o a las boleas de un coche, y a la cual se asegura la cadena de tiro. (Mec.) Correón.

Clew [clū], *s.* 1. Hilo ovillado, ovillo de hilo, seda o lana. 2. Guía, norte. En sentido de guía escríbese a menudo "clue." *To give a clew to*, Guiar, enseñar el camino. 3. *Clew of a sail*, (Mar.) Puño, extremo o ángulo donde forman gazas las relingas de las velas.

Clew-lines [clū'-lainz], *s. pl.* (Mar.) Chafaldetes de los puños.

Cliché [cli-shé'], *s.* 1. Clisé, pieza de metal de imprenta con letra o dibujo, clisada para imprimir. 2. Negativo fotográfico. (Fr.)

Click [clic], *va.* Retiñir, hacer un ruido acompasado y sucesivo como el del reloj.

Click, *s.* 1. Sonido breve, agudo y seco que es comunmente resultado de un choque o golpe. 2. Linguete, retén o fiador de rueda. 3. Articulación especial a manera de chasquido, que en la lengua hotentote y otras análogas se produce retirando rápidamente la lengua de los dientes y del paladar

Clicker [clik'-ęr], *s.* 1. El que hace o lo que produce el sonido seco llamado *click*. 2. (Impr.) Compaginador. 3. (Vul. Ingl.) El que está a la puerta de un ropavejero invitando a entrar á los que pasan.

†Clicket [clik'-et], *s.* Llamador o aldaba de puerta.

Client [clai'-ent], *s.* 1. Cliente, el litigante que se aconseja con un letrado para que le defienda. 2. Ahijado, hechura, protegido, el que debe su fortuna o empleo a la protección de algún poderoso.

Cliental [clai'-ent al], *a.* Dependiente.

Cliented [clai'-ent-ed], *a.* Provisto de clientes.

Clientele [clai'-en-tîl], *s.* 1. Clientela, conjunto de personas acogidas a la protección de un poderoso o de una institución. 2. Conjunto de personas que se valen de los servicios de un médico o letrado, o que concurren de ordinario a un mismo establecimiento o tienda, hotel, teatro, etc. (Fr.)

Clientship [clai'-ent-ship], *s.* Clientela, patrocinio.

Cliff [clif], *s.* Peñasco, roca escarpada; costa acantilada.

Cliffy [clif'-i], **Clifty** [clift'-i], *a.* Acantilado, escarpado; escabroso.

Clift [clift], *s.* 1. (Ant.) *V.* CLIFF. 2. (Des.) *V.* CLEFT.

Climacteric [cli-mac'-tęr-ic], *s.* Época peligrosa y crítica. *Grand climacteric,* La edad de sesenta y tres años.

Climacteric [cli-mac'-tęr-ic], **Climacterical** [cli-mac-ter'-i-cal], *a.* Climatérico, perteneciente a un clima.

Climate [clai'-mêt], **Climature** [clai'-ma-chur], *s.* 1. Clima, las condiciones atmosféricas de una región. 2. Clima, país diferente de otro por razón de su temperatura, humedad, etc.

Climatic [clai-mat'-ic], **Climatical** [clai-mat'-i-cal], *a.* Del clima, relativo al clima.

Climatology [clai-ma-tol'-o-ji], *s.* Climatología, el estudio o tratado de los climas.

Climax [clai'-macs], *s.* 1. Clímax o gradación, figura retórica por la cual una sentencia o período va ascendiendo por grados. 2. Colmo, culminación, cenit, punto más alto o de mayor intensidad en una progresión ascendente.

Climb [claim], *va.* Trepar, subir ayudándose de pies y manos, o (una planta) por medio de zarcillos; escalar.—*vn.* 1. Trepar, ascender, subir, elevarse. 2. Elevarse, ascender regularmente (en posición o dignidad) por medio de continuo esfuerzo.

Climbable [claim'-a-bl], *a.* Lo que se puede ascender.

Climber [claim'-ęr], *s.* 1. Trepador, escalador. 2. Enredadera, planta trepadora. 3. (Zool.) Trepador, nombre genérico de un orden de pájaros.

Climbing [claim'-ing], *s.* Subida, el acto de subir.

Clime [claim], *s.* (Poét.) 1. Porción o región de la tierra. 2. (Des.) Clima.

Clinch [clinch], *va.* 1. Remachar un clavo. 2. Agarrarse, pelear forcejeando. 3. Afirmar, fijar, afianzar, establecer, confirmar. (Mar.) Entalingar. 4. *V.* CLENCH.—*vn.* 1. Agarrarse. 2. Remacharse, ser remachado.

Clinch, *s.* 1. Remache, o lo que remacha; (fig.) argumento sin réplica. 2. (Mar.) Entalingadura, la parte del cable que se ata al ancla. 3. (E. U.) Forcejeo, lucha cuerpo a cuerpo. 4. (Des.) *V.* PUN.

Clincher [clin'-chęr], *s.* Laña. *V.* CRAMP.

Clinching [clinch'-ing], *s.* (Mar.) Solapadura, especie de calafateo ligero.

Cling [cling], *vn.* (*pret.* y *pp.* CLUNG). 1. Adherirse, pegarse, unirse, fuertemente una cosa a otra. 2. Adherirse, unirse o amistarse por interés o afecto. 3. (Prov.) Secarse, consumirse.—*va.* (Ant.) Encoger, estrechar.

Clingstone [cling'-stōn], *a.* Que se pega al hueso; dícese de un melocotón.—*s.* Pavía, variedad del pérsico, cuya pulpa se pega al hueso.

Clingy [cling'-i], *a.* Colgante, pendiente, adhesivo.

Clinic [clin'-ic], *s.* (Med.) Clínica. *Dental clinic,* Clínica dental.

Clinical [clin'-i-cal], *a.* Un enfermo habitual que guarda cama, y el que le asiste. *Clinical lecture,* Lectura médica hecha a la cabecera de los enfermos.

Clink [clink], *vn.* Retiñir, resonar, retumbar, tañer, tocar.

Clink, *s.* Tañido, retintín, sonido o golpe que deja la campana u otro cuerpo metálico sonoro.

Clinker [cliņk'-ęr], *s.* 1. Lo que retiñe; específicamente, escoria de fundición. 2. Lava irregular porosa, semejante a la escoria de los hornos. 3. Ladrillo refractario. 4. Baldosa de Holanda.

Clinometer [clai-nem'-ę-ter], *s.* Clinómetro, instrumento para medir la inclinación de toda línea o plano con respecto a un plano horizontal.

Clinometric [clai-no-met'-ric], *a.* Clinométrico, del clinómetro y de su medida.

Clinometry [clai-nem'-ę-tri], *s.* Clinometría, arte de medir la inclinación de las capas o estratos.

Clinquant [cliņ'-cant], *a.* Brillante, reluciente.—*s.* Oropel. (Fr.)

Clip [clip], *va.* 1. Trasquilar o cortar con tijeras. 2. Cortar a raíz; escatimar, acortar; omitir sílabas de las palabras; chapurrear, estropear un idioma. 3. Cercenar o minorar alguna cosa. *To clip a coin,* Tallar o cercenar una moneda. 4. Abrazar, dar un abrazo. 5. Confinar, tener agarrado.

Clip, *s.* 1. Tijeretada, tijeretazo, talla. 2. Esquileo, y el producto de esta operación; la acción de esquilar. 3. Cercenadura. 4. (Des.) Abrazo.

Clip, *s.* Pieza o herramienta que sirve para asir o tener firme; grapa, pinza (fotográfica), grapas de resorte, sujetapapeles.

Clipper [clip'-ęr], *s.* 1. Tallador, cercenador de monedas, el que las cercena en circuito para dejarlas en su peso. 2. Maquinilla o aparato que se usa para cortar el pelo, particularmente de los caballos. 3. Esquilador. 4. Barco de vela de mucho andar; clíper.

Clippers [clip'-ęrz], *s. pl.* Maquinilla para cortar el pelo.

Clipping [clip'-ing], *s.* Cercenadura, cortadura, retal; tijereteo. *Clipping-machine.* Maquinilla de atusar. *V.* CLIPPER, 2ª acep.

Clique [clîk], *s.* Corrillo, pandilla, pequeña reunión de personas, por lo común de gente aviesa.

Cloaca [clo-ê'-ca], *s.* 1. (Zool.) Cloaca, cavidad en la que convergen el canal alimenticio y los conductos urinarios y genitales de las aves y de algunos peces, insectos, etc. 2. Cloaca, conducto por donde van las aguas sucias.

Cloak [clōc], *s.* 1. Capa. 2. Capa, cualquiera cosa que tapa o encubre. 3. Pretexto, excusa. †*Cloak-bag,* Portamanteo, especie de maleta para llevar ropa. *Cloak-loop,* Cordoncillo para atar la capa.

Cloak, *va.* 1. Encapotar. 2. Ocultar, encubrir, paliar.

Clock [clec], *s.* 1. Reloj, máquina para medir el tiempo. *Tower clock,* Reloj de torre. *Alarm-clock, V.* ALARM. *What o'clock is it?* ¿Qué hora es? *Nine o'clock in the morning,* Las nueve de la mañana. *To wind up a clock,* Dar cuerda a un reloj. 2. Cuadrado, adorno que se pone en las medias. *Clock-maker,* Relojero. *Clock-setter,* El que da cuerda y arregla el reloj.

Clock, *vn.* (Gran Bretaña) *V.* CLUCK.

Clockwise [clec'-waiz], *a.* y *adv.* Con movimiento circular a la derecha.

Clockwork [clec'-wūrc], *s.* Movimiento causado por medio de pesos y resortes, como el del reloj.—*a.* Que tiene regularidad de movimiento; que se mueve con precisión automática.

Clod [cled], *s.* 1. Terrón, césped; y de aquí tierra, suelo. 2. Masa, trozo de alguna cosa. 3. El cuerpo del hombre. 4. Cualquiera cosa baja, vil y despreciable. 5. Idiota, zoquete. *Clod-crusher,* Desterronador.

Clod, *vn.* Convertirse en terrones.—*va.* Tirar terrones.

Cloddy [cled'-i], *a.* 1. Lleno de terrones. 2. (Fig.) Terrenal, bajo, grosero.

Clodhopper [cled'-hep-ęr], **Clodpoll** [cled'-pōl], *s.* Zoquete, rústico.

Clodpate [cled'-pêt], *s.* Idiota, zoquete.

Clodpated [cled'-pêt-ed], *a.* Negado, necio, ignorante.

Clog [cleg], *va.* Cargar, embarazar, empachar, impedir, cargar con alguna cosa que impide el movimiento.—*vn.* 1. Apiñarse, atestarse, agolparse, estrecharse y unirse una cosa con otra. 2. Embarazarse, hallarse embarazado o impedido.

Clog, *s.* 1. Traba, embarazo, impedimento, obstáculo. 2. Carga, hipoteca. 3. Galocha, especie de calzado como zueco o chapín que se usa para andar por el lodo, la nieve o el agua; zuecos, chanclos.

Clogginess [cleg'-i-nes], *s.* Embarazo, impedimento, obstáculo.

Cloggy [cleg'-i], *a.* Embarazoso.

Cloister [clois'-tęr], *s.* 1. Claustro, galería que cerca el patio. 2. Monasterio, convento.

Cloister, *va.* 1. Enclaustrar, poner a una persona en un convento. 2. Proveer de claustros.

Cloisteral [clois'-tęr-al], **Cloistral,** *a.* Claustral, del claustro; solitario, retirado.

Cloistered [clois'-tęrd], *a.* 1. Solitario, enclaustrado. 2. Cercado de tránsitos, columnas o galerías.

Cloisterer [clois'-tęr-ęr], *s.* Monje, religioso.

Cloisteress [clois'-tęr-es], *sf.* Monja una religiosa.

Cloke [clōk], *v.* y *s.* (Des.) *V.* CLOAK.

†Clomb, *pp.* de *To* CLIMB.

Clonic [clen'-ic], *a.* Clónico, convulsivo, relajante. *Clonic spasm,* Espasmo clónico.

Close [clōz], *va.* 1. Cerrar, juntar, unir, consolidar. 2. Cerrar, ajustar, encajar, poner en contacto, hacer continuo. 3. Concluir, terminar, acabar. 4. Incluir, contener. 5. Unir o juntar los pedazos rotos de alguna cosa. 6. (Ant.) Encerrar. *V.* INCLOSE.—*vn.* 1. Cerrarse, unirse las partes que estaban separadas. 2. Convenirse, estar de acuerdo. 3. Darse á partido. *To close in*, Cercar (un jardín), poner una cerca. *To close round*, Arcar, rodear. *To close with*, Cerrar con el enemigo. *To close with one*, Acordarse ó estar de acuerdo con uno. *To close in with the people*, Ser del partido del pueblo. *To close in*, Encerrar. *To close up*, Cerrar completamente. *To close up a wound*, Cicatrizar una herida.

Close [clōz], *s.* 1. Fin, conclusión, término. 2. Pausa, cesación. 3. Riña, lucha cuerpo a cuerpo. 4. Cierre, la manera de cerrarse. *At the close of the day*, Al concluir el día, a la caída de la tarde.

Close [clōs], *s.* 1. Cercado, huerta, prado u otro sitio rodeado de vallado o tapias. 2. Atrio, el espacio cercado que hay en algunas iglesias y abadías.

Close [clōs], *a.* 1. Cerrado, apretado, perfectamente ajustado, sin abertura. 2. Sofocante, sin respiradero. 3. Compacto, denso. 4. Incomunicado (hablando de un preso). 5. Inmediato, contiguo; unido. 6. Estrecho, angosto; ajustado. 7. Breve, compendioso. 8. Oculto, secreto. 9. Apretado, avaro, interesado, tacaño. 10. Retirado, solitario; aplicado. 11. Nublado, obscuro, cubierto. 12. Reservado, callado. 13. Casi a la par o igual. *A close election*, Una elección muy reñida. 14. (Com. y fam.) Difícil de obtener: se dice del dinero. 15. Limitado a determinadas personas, restringido, o cerrado por la ley; no abierto o libre. 16. Que se ajusta estrechamente. 17. Observador atento, riguroso. *Close study*, Aplicación. *Close connection*, Intimidad. *Close substance*, Sustancia compacta. *Close piece of cloth*, Paño tupido. *Close weather*, Tiempo pesado, sofocante. *Close discourse*, Discurso conciso. *Close-fisted*, Escaso, tacaño, poco dispuesto a dar. *Close-grained*, Denso, compacto, sólido. *Close-hauled*, (Mar.) De bolina, ciñendo el viento. *Close-season*, La época del año en que la ley prohibe la caza o pesca de ciertos animales, para favorecer su propagación.

Close [clōs], *adv.* De cerca, estrechamente, apretadamente. *To live close*, Vivir económicamente. *To study close*, Estudiar con mucha aplicación. *Close to the ground*, Pegado a la tierra, a raíz de la tierra. *Close by*, Muy arrimado, pegado, junto, cerca. *To sail close to the wind*, Ceñir el viento, navegar de bolina.

Close-bodied [clōs-bod'-id], *a.* Ajustado al cuerpo.

Close-curtained [clōs'-cūr'-tind], *a.* Rodeado de cortinas.

Closed-circuit [clōsd-sęr'-kit], *a.* (Elec.) En circuito cerrado.

Closed shop [clōsd shop], *s.* Contrato de trabajo según el cual pueden ocuparse sólo obreros sindicalizados

Close-fisted [clōs-fist'-ed], **Close-handed** [clōs-hand'-ed], *a.* Apretado, avariento, mezquino.

Close-fitting [clōs-fit'-ing], *a.* Entallado, ajustado al cuerpo.

Closely [clōs'-li], *adv.* 1. Estrechamente, contiguamente. 2. Estrechamente, fuertemente, sólidamente. 3. Estrictamente, exactamente. 4. Secretamente, atentamente. *To pursue any one closely*, Irle a uno a los alcances, seguirle de cerca. *Closely packed*, Sólidamente empaquetado. *A page closely printed*, Una página de impresión compacta. *To examine closely*, Examinar atentamente, de cerca.

Closemouthed [clōs-maudhd'], *a.* Reservado, discreto, incomunicativo.

Closeness [clōs'-nes], *s.* 1. Encierro. 2. Estrechez, falta de lugar. 3. Espesura, condensación, apretamiento. 4. Falta de aire o ventilación. 5. Solidez, firmeza. 6. Reclusión, soledad; secreto. 7. Tacañería, avaricia, ruindad. 8. Conexión, dependencia, unión. 9. Amistad, intimidad. 10. Exactitud, fidelidad (de una copia o traducción).

Close-pent [clōs'-pent], *a.* Cerrado estrechamente.

Close quarters [clōs cwōr'-ters], *s. pl.* Espacio limitado, lugar estrecho.

Closer [clōz'-ęr], *s.* El que acaba o concluye.

Close-tongued clōs'-tungd], *a.* Cauteloso en el hablar.

Closet [cloz'-et], *s.* 1. Retrete, cuarto pequeño; habitación retirada de una casa. 2. Gabinete. 3. Secreta, común, excusado, letrina (a la inglesa; abreviación de *water-closet*). *Understairs closet*, Covacha.

Closet, *va.* Encerrar o esconder en un retrete o gabinete; deliberar o conferenciar en gabinete. *To closet one's self* o *to be closeted*, Encerrarse.

Close-up [clōs'-up], *s.* 1. Fotografía de cerca. 2. Algo visto muy de cerca.

Closing [clōz'-ing], *s.* 1. Cierre. 2. Clausura.

Closure [clō'-zhur], *s.* 1. (Neol.) Procedimiento por el cual se pone fin al debate en un cuerpo deliberante. 2. Cierre; cerca. *V.* INCLOSURE. 3. Fin, conclusión. 4. Completamiento de un circuito eléctrico.

Clot [clot], *s.* 1. Grumo, parte de lo líquido que se coagula. 2. Cuajarón de sangre.

Clot, *vn.* 1. Coagularse, cuajarse. 2. Engrumecerse, hacerse grumos el líquido.

Cloth [clōth], *s.* 1. Paño, tela de lana, seda, lino, algodón, etc., tejida en telar. 2. Porción o parte de una de esas telas, como un mantel o manteles. 3. Vestido o ropa clerical; y de aquí, el clero, el conjunto de eclesiásticos en general. *Cloth-prover*, Contador, cuentahilos, microscopio de tejedores para contar el número de hilos en una pulgada cuadrada. *Cloth-yard*, Antigua medida para el paño, de 27 pulgadas. *Cloth-shearer*, Tundidor de paños.

Cloth binding [clōth bain'-ding], *s.* Encuadernación en tela.

Clothe [clōdh], *va.* 1. Vestir, cubrir el cuerpo con vestido, adornar con vestidos. 2. Cubrir; investir. *To clothe with authority*, Investir de autoridad.—*vn.* †Llevar ropa.

Clothes [clōdhz], *s. pl.* 1. Vestido, vestidura, ropaje, vestuario, ropa de toda especie. 2. Ropa de cama. *Cast-off clothes*, Ropa usada. *A suit of clothes*, Un vestido completo. *Clothes-horse*, Percha de colgar ropa. *Clothes-line*, Tendedera. *Clothes-pins*, Ganchos de tendedera. *Clothes-press*, Guardarropa, gabinete para vestidos. *Clothes-wringer*, Exprimidor de ropa.

Clothesbrush [clōdhz'-brush], *s.* Cepillo de ropa.

Clothes hanger [clōdhz hang'-ęr], *s.* Colgador o gancho de ropa.

Clothes line [clōdhz lain], *s.* Tendedero, cuerda para tender la ropa.

Clothesman [clōdhz'-man], *s.* 1. Ropero. 2. Ropavejero.

Clothespin [clōdhz-pin], *s.* Gancho o pinza para tender la ropa.

Clothier [clōdh'-yęr], *s.* Fabricante de paños; pañero.

Clothing [clōdh'-ing], *s.* 1. Vestidos, ropa de toda especie. 2. Revestimiento o cubierta no conductora que envuelve el cilindro de una máquina de vapor, una cañería o una caldera.

Clotted, Clotty [clot'-i], *a.* Grumoso, coagulado.

Cloud [claud], *s.* 1. Nube. 2. Nublado, nublo, nubarrón; dícese de la nube obscura o de tempestad. 3. Nube, manchita, sombra que se nota en algunas piedras preciosas y en otros cuerpos. 4. Cualquiera cosa que obscurece o encubre a otra. 5. Acumulación o hacinamiento parecido al de las nubes: muchedumbre, multitud, montón. *A cloud of witnesses*, Una multitud de testigos.

Cloud, *va.* 1. Anublar, encubrir la luz del sol. 2. Anublar, obscurecer, cegar. 3. Abigarrar con venas obscuras. 4. Manchar, difamar.—*vn.* Anublarse; obscurecerse, tomar aire sombrío y triste.

Cloudberry [claud'-ber-i], *s.* (Bot.) Camemoro.

Cloudburst [claud'-būrst], *s.* Turbión, chaparrón, tormenta de lluvia.

Cloud-capt [claud'-capt], **Cloud-covered** [claud'-cuv'-ęrd], **Cloud-topt** [claud'-topt], *a.* Nublado, cubierto de nubes.

Cloud-dispelling [claud'-dis-pel'-ing], *a.* Lo que disipa y separa las nubes.

Cloud-kissing [claud'-kis-ing], *a.* Lo que es tan alto que llega a las nubes; dícese de las cumbres más elevadas de los montes.

Cloudily [claud'-i-li], *adv.* Obscuramente; con mucha niebla.

Cloudiness [clau'-di-nes], *s.* 1. Nebulosidad, calidad de nebuloso, obscurecido por las nubes. 2. Obscuridad, falta de claridad o brillantez.

Cloudless [claud'-les], *a.* Sin nubes, claro, sereno, despejado.

Cloudy [claud'-i], *a.* 1. Nublado, nubloso, obscurecido por nubes. 2 Obscuro, difícil de entenderse. 3 Tétrico, sombrío, triste, melancólico. 4. Nubarrado, colorido en figura de nubes.

Clout, *va.* 1. Remendar toscamente alguna cosa. 2. Tapar o cubrir con algún paño o trapo. 3. Chapucear. 4. (Vul. Ingl.) Abofetear.

Clove [clōv], *s.* 1. Clavo, especia aromática. 2. Diente de ajo, las partes en que se divide la cabeza del ajo. 3. (Prov.) Peso de siete libras, usado para pesar lana o queso.

Cloven-foot, Cloven-footed [clōv'-n-fut, ed], **Cloven-hoofed** [clov'-n-huft], *a.* Patihendido, el animal que tiene el pie dividido en dos partes. *To betray* o *show the cloven foot*, (Fam.) Enseñar la oreja, sacar la pata.

Clove-gilly-flower [clōv'-jil'-i-flau'-ẹr], *s.* (Bot.) Especie de clavel de flores dobles. Se llama también *Clove-pink.*
Clove-hitch [clōv'-hich], *s.* (Mar.) Trincafía, ballestrinque, nudo de dos cotes.
Clover [clō'-vẹr], *s.* (Bot.) Una de varias especies de trébol. *To be* o *live in clover,* Vivir lujosamente, en la abundancia.
Clovered [clō'-vẹrd], *a.* Cubierto con trébol.
Cloverleaf [clō'-vẹr-lîf], *s.* Hoja de trébol. *Cloverleaf* (*highway intersection*), Hoja de trébol (en la carretera).
Clove-tree [clev'-trî], *s.* Árbol del clavo, clavero.
Clown [claun], *s.* Patán, hombre zafio, rústico y agreste ; el gracioso de teatro ; el payaso de los circos ecuestres.
Clownery [claun'-ẹr-i], *s.* 1. Rusticidad, mala crianza. 2. Bufonada, payasada.
Clownish [claun'-ish], *a.* 1. Villano, rústico, agreste. 2. Rudo, malcriado, grosero. 3. Tosco, basto, desmañado, inculto.
Clownishly [claun'-ish-li], *adv.* Toscamente, groseramente.
Clownishness [claun'-ish-nes], *s.* Rusticidad, falta de crianza, grosería, brutalidad, impolítica, rustiquez.
Cloy [clei], *va.* 1. Saciar, hartar, ahitar. 2. Clavar cañones. 3. (Des.) Tapar, obstruir. 4. Clavar, punzar a un caballo herrándole.
Cloyless [clei'-les], *a.* Ligero, lo que no puede ahitar.
Cloyment [clei'-mẹnt], *s.* Saciedad, hartura.
Club [club], *s.* 1. Clava, cachiporra, garrote, tranca, maza. 2. Basto o bastos, uno de los cuatro palos de que se compone la baraja de naipes. 3. Escote, la parte o cantidad que a prorrata cabe a cada uno de los que se han divertido o comido juntos. 4. Club, junta de personas para elegir los oficiales o funcionarios públicos, o para otras medidas en los asuntos de una sociedad o de una población. 5. Tertulia, junta de cierto número de personas. *Club of hair,* Castaña. *Club-house,* El edificio de un casino o tertulia. *Club-moss,* (Bot.) Camepitios, pinillo. *Indian clubs,* Mazas de hacer gimnasia.
Club, *vn.* Contribuir, o concurrir a gastos comunes, unirse o juntarse para un mismo fin.—*va.* Escotar, pagar a prorrata la parte que a cada uno le toca.
Clubbed [clubd], *a.* En forma de clava o maza, más grueso hacia un extremo : v. g. *Clubbed antennæ,* Antenas en forma de maza.—*pp.* de *To* CLUB.
Clubbist [club'-ist], *s.* Individuo de algún club o junta, reunión o tertulia particular : socio de un casino.
Club-foot [club'-fut], *s.* Pateta, patituerto, el que tiene un torcimiento congénito de los pies.
Club-footed [club'-fut-ed], *a.* Patituerto.
Club-headed [club'-hed-ed], *a.* Cabezudo, cabezorro.
Club-law [club'-lā], *s.* La ley del más fuerte.
Club-room [club'-rum], *s.* La pieza o sala en donde se reune la junta o tertulia llamada *club.*
Cluck [cluc], *vn.* Cloquear la gallina, dar su voz cuando llama a los pollos.—*va.* Cloquear.
Clue [clū], *s.* 1. Guía, norte ; todo lo que sirve de guía en medio de la duda o perplejidad. 2. Cualquier indicio provechoso ; indicación, aviso ; pista, rastro. En sentido náutico y como verbo, *V.* CLEW.
Clump [clump], *s.* 1. Grupo (de árboles o arbustos). 2. Trozo de madera, etc., sin forma ni figura particular.
Clumsily [clum'-zi-li], *adv.* Zafiamente, groseramente.
Clumsiness [clum'-zi-nes], *s.* Zafiedad, falta de destreza ; tosquedad, rusticidad, rustiquez, grosería.
Clumsy [clum'-zi], *a.* Basto, ordinario, tosco, pesado ; inculto, sin arte.
Clung, *pret.* y *pp.* del verbo *To* CLING.
Cluniac [clū'-ni-ac], *s.* Cluniacense, monje benedictino de Cluni en Borgoña.
Cluster [clus'-tẹr], *s.* 1. Racimo. 2. Manada, hato, caterva o multitud de animales que se juntan en un paraje ; enjambre de abejas. 3. Agregado, colección, por regla general de limitado número. 4. Grupo. 5. (Fam.) Piña. *Cluster-cups,* Pequeñas cápsulas amarillentas y por lo general agrupadas, que contienen esporos ; representan una fase de la vida de los hongos parásitos de ciertas plantas.
Cluster, *vn.* Arracimarse, agruparse. —*va.* Apiñar, juntar y estrechar unas cosas con otras.
Clustery [clus'-tẹr-i], *a.* Arracimado ; apiñado ; agrupado.
Clutch [cluch], *va.* 1. Agarrar o asir con la mano. 2. Empuñar, agarrar con el puño cerrado ; apretar.
Clutch, *s.* 1. Toma, presa, apresamiento. 2. Garra, mano. 3. Embrague (de un automóvil). *Clutch pedal,* Pedal del embrague.
Clutter [clut'-ẹr], *s.* (Fam.) 1. Baraúnda, ruido y confusión grande, batahola. 2. Desorden, enredo, confusión.
Clutter, *vn.* Alborotar, hacer ruido o estrépito ; atroparse, reunirse en desorden.
Clyster [clis'-tẹr], *s.* Clístel o clíster, jeringazo ; ayuda, lavativa.
Coach [cōch], *s.* 1. Coche, carroza. 2. Preceptor que prepara a un pupilo para un examen ; el que dirige los ejercicios preparatorios de los que han de participar en regatas, carreras, etc. 3. Coche o carro de viajeros en los ferrocarriles. *Hackney-coach,* Coche de alquiler o coche simón. *Coach and four,* Coche tirado por cuatro caballos. *Coach-box,* Pescante de coche. *Coach-dog,* Perro dalmático, que corre debajo o a lo largo de un coche. *Coach-hire,* Alquiler de coche. *Coach-horse,* Caballo de coche. *Coach-house,* Cochera. *Coach-maker,* Carrocero. *Coach-office,* Administración de diligencias. *Coach-stand,* Estación de carruajes.
C/o, C.o. (Abreviatura de *Care of*), A cargo de (c/o).
Coach, *va.* 1. Instruir, enseñar ; adiestrar. 2. Llevar en coche.—*vn.* 1. Pasearse en coche. 2. Estudiar con un preceptor o adiestrador.
Coachman [cōch'-man], *s.* Cochero.
Coachmanship [cōch'-man-ship], *s.* El arte de cochear.
Coact [co-act'], *va.* Forzar juntamente, compeler o refrenar.—*vn.* (Poco us.) Cooperar, obrar de acuerdo o de concierto.
Coaction [co-ac'-shun], *s.* 1. Coacción, necesidad, fuerza. 2. [cō'-ac-shun] Acción concertada.
Coactive [co-ac'-tiv], *a.* Coactivo ; cooperante.
Coadjument [co-aj'-u-mẹnt], *s.* Mutua y recíproca asistencia.
Coadjutant [co-aj'-ū-tant], *a.* Coadyuvante, auxiliar, lo que coadyuva o auxilia.
Coadjutor [co-a-jū'-tor], *s.* 1. Coadjutor, compañero. 2. Coadjutor, el que ayuda a una persona en dignidad, regularmente eclesiástica, a ejercer sus funciones.
Coadjutrix [co-a-jū'-trics], *sf.* Coadjutora ; abadesa.
Coadjuvancy [co-aj'-u-van-si], *s.* Coadjutoría ; ayuda, socorro.
Coadunation [co-ad-yu-nê'-shun], **Coadunition** [co-ad-yu-nish'-un], *s.* Coadunación, unión.
Coadventurer [co-ad-ven'-chur-ẹr], *s.* Coaventurero.
Coagent [co-ê'-jent], *s.* Coagente, cooperador.
Coagulability [co-ag-yu-la-bil'-i-ti], *s.* La propiedad de coagularse.
Coagulable [co-ag'-yu-la-bl], *a.* Coagulable.
Coagulant [co-ag'-yu-lant], *a.* y *s.* Coagulante, lo que produce la coagulación.
Coagulate [co-ag'-yu-lêt], *va.* Coagular, cuajar, condensar.—*vn.* Coagularse, cuajarse, espesarse.
Coagulation [co-ag-yu-lê'-shun], *s.* Coagulación ; coágulo ; espesamiento.
Coagulative [co-ag'-yu-lê-tiv], *a.* Coagulativo.
Coagulator [co-ag'-yu-lê-tor], *s.* Coágulo, lo que causa la coagulación.
Coagulum [co-ag'-yu-lum], *s.* Coágulo, masa coagulada ; dícese comunmente de un cuajarón de sangre.
Coak [cōk], *s.* 1. Dado o macho de madera dura para unir piezas de la arboladura. 2. (Mar.) Dado de roldana. 3. *V.* COKE.
Coak, *va.* Unir por medio de dados.
Coal [cōl], *s.* 1. Carbón de piedra. *Anthracite coal,* Carbón de antracita, mineral muy duro, sin humo, y de un ardor intenso. *Bituminous coal,* Carbón bituminoso, hulla. *Cannel coal,* Hulla grasa. 2. Brasa, fuego, alguna cosa inflamada o encendida. (Prov.) *To carry coals to Newcastle,* Llevar hierro a Vizcaya, llevar algo allí donde lo hay de sobra. *Coal-black,* Negro como el carbón. *Coal-box,* Caja del carbón, carbonera. *Coal-hole,* Carbonera. *Coal-man,* Carbonero. *Coal-mine,* Mina de carbón. *Coal-miner,* Carbonero. *V.* COLLIER. *Coal-pit,* Carbonera, hoya de donde se saca el carbón de piedra. *Coal-ship,* Barco carbonero. *V.* COLLIER. *Coal-tar,* Alquitrán de hulla. Produce los tintes de anilina, y compuestos semejantes. *Coal-work,* Carbonera, obras en las minas de carbón.
Coal, *va.* 1. Proveer de carbón. 2 Reducir a carbón, carbonizar. 3. ¿Dibujar o señalar con carbón.—*vn.* Hacer provisión de carbón.
Coalesce [cō-a-les'], *vn.* Unirse, juntarse, incorporarse.
Coalescence [cō-a-les'-ens], *s.* Unión, enlace, coyuntura, coalescencia.
Coalheaver [cōl'-hîv-ẹr], *s.* Trabajador que descarga los barcos de carbón.

Coalition [cō-a-lish'-un], *s.* 1. Unión, enlace, o trabazón de unas cosas con otras. 2. Coalición, confederación.
Coaming [cōm'-ing], *s.* Brazola de escotilla ; brocal de un pozo.
Coaptation [co-ap-tē'-shun], *s.* Arreglo, ajuste, el acto de ajustar o proporcionar las partes de un todo para que vengan bien.
Coarctate [co-ārc'-tēt], *a.* Comprimido, estrechado ; contraído, especialmente en la base.
Coarctation [co-arc-tē'-shun], *s.* (Med.) Contracción, estrechamiento de un canal.
Coarse [cōrs], *a.* 1. Basto, ordinario. 2. Tosco, rústico, grosero ; bajo, vil, descortés. 3. Grueso, gordo, basto, hablando de tejidos.
Coarsely [cōrs'-li], *adv.* Toscamente ; groseramente.
Coarseness [cōrs'-nes], *s.* 1. Tosquedad, falta de finura. 2. Grosería, falta de crianza ; bajeza.
Coassume [co-as-siūm'], *va.* Asumir en unión de otro, juntamente.
Coast [cōst], *s.* 1. Costa, ribera u orilla del mar. 2. (Ant.) Término, límite ; lado. *The coast is clear,* Ha pasado el peligro.
Coast, *vn.* 1. (Mar.) Costear, ir navegando por la costa. 2. (E. U.) Bajar una cuesta o declive, v. gr. en una narria o en un trineo.—*va.* Costear algún país o litoral.
Coaster [cōst'-ęr], *s.* 1. Piloto práctico en las costas. 2. Bajel o buque costanero.
Coaster brake [cōst'-ęr brēc], *s.* Freno de bicicleta.
Coasting [cōst'-ing], *s.* Cabotaje, navegación costera.
Coast line [cōst lain], *s.* Costa, litoral.
Coastwise [cōst'-waiz], *a.* y *adv.* A lo largo de la costa.
Coat [cōt], *s.* 1. Levita, casaca, frac ; chaqueta ; prenda de vestir que cubre la parte superior del cuerpo : llevado comunmente por los hombres. 2. Cubierta o envoltura, como el pelo, lana y plumas que cubren a los animales y aves ; túnica del ojo ; capa o mano de pintura, yeso, alquitrán, etc. *Coat of mail,* Cota de malla. *Great-coat, overcoat, top-coat,* Sobretodo, abrigo. *Dress-coat,* Frac, casaca. *Coat of arms,* Escudo de armas. *Frock-coat,* Levita. *To turn one's coat,* (Met.) Volver casaca, mudar de partido, cambiar de opinión.
Coat, *va.* Cubrir, vestir. *Sugar-coated,* Garapiñado, cubierto con azúcar.
Coatee [cōt-ī'], *s.* (Ingl.) Casaquilla, levitín, casaca muy corta.
Coating [cōt'-ing], *s.* Revestimiento, capa, mano de pintura, barniz, cal, etc., sobre una pared u otra superficie cualquiera.
Coax [cōcs], *va.* Engaitar, engatusar, mimar, acariciar, halagar.
Coaxer [cōcs'-ęr], *s.* Engatusador, mimador, gaitero.
Coaxial [cō-ax'-i-al], *a.* Coaxial. *Coaxial cable,* Cable coaxial.
Coaxing [cōcs'-ing], *s.* Engatusamiento, adulación, caricia.
Cob [ceb], *s.* 1. Masa casi redonda, montón ; cabeza. 2. Mazorca de maíz. 3. Jaco, caballo fuerte, rechoncho y de piernas cortas. 4. El cisne. 5. Araña. 6. Peso duro de España. 7. Gaviota de Inglaterra. 8. Mezcla de arcilla y paja para hacer paredes y la pared hecha con ella.
Cob, *va.* (Mar.) Azotar con una paleta. *Cobbing-board,* Paleta de azotar.
Cobalt [cō'-bōlt], *s.* Cobalto, un metal duro, de color gris, estimado por los colores azules que produce.
Cobalt bomb [cō'-bōlt bem], *s.* Bomba de cobalto.
Cobble [ceb'-l], *va.* 1. Chapucear, remendar o hacer alguna cosa sin pulidez. 2. Remendar zapatos.
Cobble o **Cobblestone** [ceb'-l-stōn], *s.* Guijarro, piedra redondeada por la acción del agua.
Cobbler [ceb'-lęr], *s.* 1. Zapatero de viejo, remendón. 2. Chapucero, chambón, mal oficial. 3. Galopín, persona vil y baja.
Cobelligerent [cō-bel-lij'-ęr-ęnt], *a.* y *s.* Cobeligerante, que hace la guerra en unión y de acuerdo con otra potencia.
Cobirons [ceb'-ai-ūrnz], *s. pl.* (Prov.) Morillos, caballetes de hierro que se ponen en el hogar para sustentar la leña o el asador.
Cobishop [cō''-bish'-up], *s.* Obispo coadjutor o auxiliar.
Cobnut [ceb'-nut], *s.* 1. Especie de avellana grande.
Cobra [cō'-bra], *s.* (Zool.) Cobra.
Cobweb [ceb'-web], *s.* 1. Telaraña. 2. Trama, tramoya.
Cobwebbed [ceb'-webd], *a.* Entelarañado, cubierto con telarañas.
Coca [cō'-ca], *s.* Coca, las hojas del arbusto Erythroxylon Coca, estimulante enérgico precedente de la América del Sur.
Cocain, Cocaine [cō'-ca-in], *s.* Cocaína, acaloide blanco, amargo, cristalino, que se halla en la coca : muy empleada en medicina como anestésico local.
Cocainize [cō'-ca-in-aiz], *va.* Poner bajo la influencia anestésica de la cocaína.
Cocciferous [cec-sif'-ęr-us], *a.* Lo que produce o cría bayas.
Cocculus indicus [cec'-yu-lus in'-di-cus], *s.* (Bot.) Baya narcótica y de que se usa para emborrachar los peces.
Coccus [cec'-cus], *s.* 1. Bacteria esférica, o casi esférica. 2. Cóccido, insecto escamoso del orden de los hemípteros.
Coccygeal [cec-sij'-ę-al], *a.* Relativo, o cerca del coxis o la cola.
Coccyx [cec'-six], *s.* Coxis, hueso en que termina la columna vertebral.
Cochineal [cech'-i-nil], *s.* 1. Cochinilla, insecto del cual se obtiene el color de grana. Coccus cacti. 2. Cochinilla, el color que se obtiene de este insecto.
Cochlea [cec'-lę-a], *s.* Cóclea, conducto interior del oído, generalmente de forma espiral.
Cochleary [cec'-lę-ę-ri], **Cochleated** [cec'-lę-ē-ted], *a.* Caracoleado.
Cock [cec], *s.* 1. Gallo, el macho de la gallina. 2. Macho, ave del sexo masculino entre los pájaros ; en este sentido se usa ordinariamente en composición. 3. Veleta, giraldilla, pedazo de hierro que señala el viento que corre. 4. Llave, instrumento de metal que sirve para sacar los licores de las vasijas o el agua de las fuentes ; grifo, grifón, espita. 5. (Ingl.) Caudillo, campeón. 6. Montoncillo de heno. 7. Pie de gato de escopeta ; y la posición en que se halla el gatillo cuando está levantado. 8. Estilo o gnomon de reloj de sol. 9. Armazón de sombrero. 10. Aguja de romana. *A cock and bull story,* Cuento pesado ; embuste. *Cockspurs,* Navajas de gallo. *Cock-sparrow,* Gorrión. *Turkey-cock,* Pavo, guanajo.
Cock, *va.* 1. Enderezar o poner derecho hacia arriba. 2. Encandilar el sombrero, armar el sombrero. 3. Amartillar, preparar un arma de fuego para dispararla. 4. Hacinar o amontonar heno.—*vn.* 1. Entonarse, engreirse. 2. (Raro) Criar o enseñar gallos para pelear. *Cocked hat,* (1) Sombrero de tres picos. (2) Juego de bochas con tres piezas que se ponen en los ángulos de un triángulo. *To knock into a cocked hat,* (Vul.) Aporrear, dar de palos de suerte que algo pierda su forma ; vencer ; demoler.
Cockade [cek-ēd'], *s.* Escarapela o cucarda.
Cockatoo [cec-a-tū'], *s.* (Orn.) Cacatoes, especie de papagayo de la India y Australia, que tiene un copete eréctil.
Cockatrice [cec'-a-trais], *s.* Basilisco ; animal fabuloso.
Cockboat [cec'-bōt], *s.* (Mar.) Bote pequeño de remo.
Cock-brained [cec'-brēnd], *s.* Ligero, temerario, travieso.
Cock-broth [cec'-brōth], *s.* Caldo de gallo.
Cockchafer [cec'-chē-fęr], *s.* (Ento.) Abejorro, escarabajo cuyo nombre científico es Melolonta. Se llama también *May-bug.*
Cock-crowing [cec'-crō-ing], *s.* El canto del gallo ; la aurora.
Cocker [cek'-ęr], *va.* Acariciar, mimar.
Cocker, *s.* 1. Sabueso pequeño que se emplea para cazar la chochaperdiz y otras aves. 2. (Poco us.) El que es aficionado a las peleas de gallos.
Cockerel [cek'-ęr-el], *s.* Gallipollo.
Cockering [cek'-ęr-ing], *s.* Indulgencia excesiva, mimo.
Cocket [cek'-et], *s.* 1. Sello de la aduana. 2. Certificación de pago de la aduana.—*a.* (Des.) Vivo ; atrevido.
Cock-eyed [cek'-aid], *a.* Bizco.
Cock-fight, Cock-fighting [cec'-fait, ing], *s.* 1. Riña o pelea de gallos. 2. Juego de gallos.
Cock-fighter [cec'-fait-ęr], **Cock-master** [cec'-mas-tęr], *s.* Gallero, el que tiene y cría gallos para pelear.
Cock-horse [cec'-hōrs], *s.* Caballito mecedor de juguete ; palo o caña con que juegan los niños montándolo a horcajadas.
Cocking [cek'-ing], *s.* La riña de gallos.
Cockle [cec'-l], *s.* 1. Una especie de caracol de mar comestible. Cardium edule. 2. (Bot.) Vallico, zizaña, joyo, hierba que nace entre los trigos y cebadas.
Cockle, *va.* Arrugar, hacer arrugas ; doblar una cosa en figura espiral.—Plegarse, doblarse.
Cockled [cec'-ld], *a.* Espiral, hecho en figura de caracol.
Cockler [cec'-lęr], *s.* El que vende los caracoles de mar llamados *cockle.*
Cock-loft [cec'-lōft], *s.* Desván, zaquizamí.
Cock-match [cec'-mach], *s.* Riña o pelea de gallos.
Cockney [cec'-ni], *s.* 1. Hijo de Londres, particularmente el que carece de educación. 2. †Hombre afeminado.

Cock-pit [coc'-pit], *s.* 1. Reñidero de gallos. 2. (Mar.) Entarimado del sollado.
Cockroach [coc'-rōch], *s.* Cucaracha, corredera, insecto ortóptero que infesta las cocinas y despensas.
Cockscomb [cocs'-cōm], *s.* (Bot.) 1. Amaranto, moco de pavo, flor. Celosia cristata o Amarantus. 2. *V.* COXCOMB.
Cockspur [coc'-spūr], *s.* 1. Espolón natural o navaja de gallo. 2. (Bot.) Especie de níspero.
Cock-sure [coc'-shūr], *a.* (Vul.) Confiado, cierto, seguro.
Cockswain [coc'-sn], *s.* (Mar.) Patrón de bote. *V.* COXSWAIN.
Cocktail [coc-têl'], *s.* Coctel, bebida alcohólica compuesta.
Cocoa [cō'-cō], *s.* 1. Coco, palma de América. 2. Cacao, árbol de América y la bebida preparada con sus simientes.
Cocoa-nut, Coconut [cō'-co-nut], *s.* 1. Coco, fruto del árbol llamado coco. 2. Cacao, el fruto del cacao.
Cocoon [co-cūn'], *s.* Capullo del gusano de seda, y de otros insectos en estado de oruga.
Coction [coc'-shun], *s.* Cocción, la acción de cocer, el acto de hervir.
Cod, Codfish [cod, cod'-fish], *s.* Abadejo, bacalao. *Cod-liver oil,* Aceite de hígado de bacalao.
Cod, *s.* 1. (Bot.) Vaina, vainilla, la corteza tierna y larga en que están encerradas algunas legumbres o semillas. *V.* POD. 2. (Anat.) Bolsa; panza; el escroto.
Cod, *va.* Envainar, encerrar en vaina u hollejo.
C.O.D. [si ō di]. Abreviatura de *Cash on delivery,* Entrega contra reembolso, cóbrese al entregar.
Coddle [cod -l], *va.* 1. Criar con mucho cuidado o ternura. 2. Cocer a medias.
Code [cōd], *s.* 1. Código, compilación de leyes. 2. Clave, sistema de señales o de caracteres para representar palabras o frases. 3. Colección de preceptos o reglas de conducta: como *Code of honour,* Código de honor.
Codein [cō-dī'-in], *s.* Codeína, alcaloide obtenido del opio.
Codger [coj'-er], *s.* Hombre tacaño y avariento; úsase despreciativamente.
Codicil [cod'-i-sil], *s.* Codicilo, escrito auténtico por el cual se quita o añade algo a un testamento.
Codification [cod-i-fi-kē'-shun], *s.* Codificación (de las leyes).
Codify [cod'-i- ai o cō'-di-fai], *va.* Codificar, compilar leyes, formar código de leyes, señales o reglas.
Codling [cod'-ling], *s.* Manzana medio cocida. *Codling-* (o *codlin*) *moth,* Mariposa tortrícida cuya oruga es el gusano de la manzana. Carcocapsa pomonella.
Coeducation [cō-ed-yu-kē'-shun], *s.* Coeducación.
Coeducational [cō-ed-yu-kē'-shun-al], *a.* Coeducativo.
Coefficiency [co-ef-ish'-en-si], *s.* Cooperación, concurso.
Coefficient [co-ef-ish'-ent], *a.* Coeficiente.
Coefficiently [co-ef-ish'-ent-li], *adv.* Cooperativamente.
Coemption [co-emp'-shun], *s.* Compra mutua, cierta forma de matrimonio en el derecho romano.
Coequal [co-ī'-cwal], *a.* Igual. Coigual, hablando de las personas de la Santísima Trinidad.
Coerce [co-ers'], *va.* 1. Forzar, obligar. 2. Contener, refrenar.
Coercible [co-ers'-i-bl], *a.* Lo que puede o debe ser refrenado.
Coercion [co-er'-shun], *s.* Coerción, violencia, fuerza, sujeción, opresión.
Coercive [co-er'-siv], *a.* Coercitivo; coactivo.
Coessential [cō"-e-sen'-shal], *a.* Coesencial.
Coessentiality [cō"-e-sen-shi-al'-i-ti], *s.* Coesencia.
Coessentially [cō"-e-sen'-shal-i], *adv.* Coesencialmente.
Coestablishment [co-es-tab'-lish-ment], *s.* Establecimiento combinado con otro.
Coetaneous [cō"-e-tē'-ne-us], *a.* Coetáneo, contemporáneo.
Coeternal [cō"-e-ter'-nal], *a.* Coeterno.
Coeternally [cō"-e-ter'-nal-i], *adv.* Coeternamente.
Coeternity [cō"-e-ter'-ni-ti], *s.* Coeternidad.
Coeval [co-ī'-val], *a.* Coevo, contemporáneo.—*s.* *V.* CONTEMPORARY.
Coexist [cō"-eg-zist'], *vn.* Coexistir.
Coexistence [cō"-eg-zist'-ens], *s.* Coexistencia.
Coexistent [cō"-eg-zist'-ent], *a.* Coexistente.
Coextend [cō"-ex-tend'], *va.* Coextenderse.
Coextension [cō"-ex-ten'-shun], *s.* Coextensión.
Coextensive [cō"-ex-ten'-siv], *a.* Coextensivo.
Coextensively [cō"-ex-ten'-siv-li], *adv.* Coextensivamente.
Coffee [cof'-e], *s.* 1. Café, haba o baya del árbol así llamado. 2. Café, bebida hecha con las bayas de café tostadas, molidas e infundidas en agua hirviendo. *Coffee-bean* o *berry.* Grano de café. *Coffee break,* Pausa para tomar café. *Coffee mill,* molinillo de café. *Coffee plantation,* Cafetal, plantillo de café. *Coffee planter* o *seller,* Cafetero. *Coffee store,* Cafetería. *Coffee table,* Mesita para el servicio de café en las salas.
Coffee-house [cof'-e-haus], *s.* Café, casa o sitio donde se vende café.
Coffee-pot [cof'-i-pot], *s.* Cafetera, vasija en que se hace el café.
Coffee-tree [cof'-i-trī], *s.* (Bot.) Cafeto, el árbol que produce el café.
Coffer [cof'-er], *s.* 1. Arca, cofre o caja. 2. †(Fort.) Cofre, cierta excavación que se hace en medio del foso seco, para contener al enemigo al llegar a la contraescarpa. 3. Tesoro; en este sentido se usa más comunmente en plural. 4. (Arq.) Artesón hondo. *V.* CAISSON.
Coffer, *va.* 1. Atesorar o meter dinero en arcas. 2. Adornar con artesones. 3. Proveer de un cofre o cofres.
Coffer-dam [cōf'-er-dam], *s.* Represa encofrada, malecón, construcción que se introduce en el agua para que los trabajadores puedan hacer los estribos de los puentes y otras obras parecidas.
Coffin [cof'-in], *s.* 1. Ataúd. 2. La parte del casco del caballo que cubre un hueso. 3. Cucurucho de papel en que dan envueltos sus géneros los especieros. *Coffin-bone,* El hueso que se halla dentro del casco del caballo.
Coffin-maker [cof'-in-mē'-ker], *s.* El que hace ataudes.
Cofounder [co-faund'-er], *s.* El que funda alguna cosa con otro u otros.
Cog [cog], *va.* 1. Puntear una rueda, ponerle puntos o dientes. 2. Engañar, engaitar, trampear. *To cog a die,* Cargar un dado, poner plomo en él para que se incline a un lado. —*vn.* Mentir, engañar con lisonjas.
Cog, *s.* 1. Punto, diente de rueda con el cual se mueven otras. 2. Fraude, engaño. 3. Ramplón de herradura. 4. Botequín, o barca de pescador.
Cog-wheel [cog'-hwīl], *s.* Rueda dentada.
Cogency [cō'-jen-si], *s.* Fuerza lógica o moral, urgencia, evidencia.
†**Cogenial,** *a.* *V.* CONGENIAL.
Cogent [cō'-jent], *a.* 1. Convincente, poderoso, urgente. 2. Fuerte, potente (en sentido físico).
Cogently [cō'-jent-li], *adv.* Convincentemente.
Cogger [cog'-er], *s.* (Ingl.) Adulador, engañador, lisonjero; fullero, tahur.
Cogging [cog'-ing], *s.* Lisonja, adulación; fullería.
Cogglestone [cog'-l-stōn], *s.* (Prov. Ingl.) Guijarro.
Cogitable [coj'-i-ta-bl], *a.* Cogitable, lo que puede ser objeto del pensamiento.
Cogitate [coj'-i-têt], *vn.* Pensar, meditar, reflexionar.
Cogitation [coj-i-tē'-shun], *s.* Pensamiento, reflexión, meditación.
Cogitative [coj'-i-tē-tiv], *a.* Discursivo, pensativo, reflexivo.
Cognac [cō'-nyac], *s.* Coñac, aguardiente francés.
Cognate [cog'-nêt], *a.* 1. Cognado, consanguíneo. 2. Semejante, análogo. 3. Pariente colateral por la línea femenina.
Cognation [cog-nē'-shun], *s.* Cognación, parentesco de consanguinidad.
Cognition [cog-nish'-un], *s.* Conocimiento, experiencia, convicción.
Cognitive [cog'-ni-tiv], *a.* Cognoscitivo, capaz de conocer.
Cognizable [cog'-ni-za-bl], *a.* 1. Lo que se puede comprender, percibir o conocer. *Cognizable by the senses,* Perceptible por medio de los sentidos. 2. Lo que se puede examinar jurídicamente; de la competencia de.
Cognizance [cog'-ni-zans], *s.* 1. Conocimiento, acto de conocer o juzgar una cosa. 2. Divisa, señal o distintivo con que uno es conocido. 3. (For.) Conocimiento, competencia, derecho a conocer de una causa o negocio.
Cognizant [cog'-ni-zant], *a.* Que nota o advierte; sabedor, que tiene conocimiento.
Cognizee [cog"-ni-zī'], *s.* (For. Ant.) El censualista que tiene derecho de cobrar una multa por la venta o trueque de las tierras o posesiones sujetas al pago del censo.
Cognizor [cog-ni-zor'], *s.* (For. Ant.) El censualista que pasa su derecho de cobrar multas por ventas o trueques o otra persona.
Cognomen [cog-nō'-men], *s.* Apellido o sobrenombre, el último de los tres nombres que llevaban los romanos. Cognombre; es hoy palabra anticuada en castellano.
Cognominal [cog-nom'-i-nal], *a.* Tocayo.
Cognominate, *va.* *V.* DENOMINATE.
Cognomination [cog-nom-i-nē'-shun], *s.* Sobrenombre que se da a alguno a causa de sus virtudes o vicios, v. g. *Alfonso el Sabio.*

Cognosce [cog-nes'], *va.* y *vn.* (Ley escocesa) Conocer o entender jurídicamente, adjudicar.
Cognoscible [cog-nos'-i-bl], *a.* Conocible, cognoscible.
Cognoscitive [cog-nos'-i-tiv], *a.* Cognoscitivo, lo que es capaz de conocer.
Cognovit [cog-nō'-vit], *s.* (For.) Convenio o acuerdo escrito por el cual el demandado reconoce justa la reclamación del demandante, o parte de ella, y acepta la decisión del tribunal. (Lat.)
Cohabit [cō-hab'-it], *vn.* 1. (Ant.) Vivir en compañía de otro. 2. Cohabitar, vivir como marido y mujer.
Cohabitant [cō-hab'-i-tant], *s.* El que es convecino de otro.
Cohabitation [cō-hab-i-tē'-shun], *s.* 1. El estado de vivir en compañía. 2. Cohabitación, vida maridable.
Coheir [cō-ār'], *s.* Coheredero.
Coheiress [co-ār'-es], *sf.* Coheredera.
Cohere [cō-hīr'], *vn.* Adherirse, pegarse, unirse, adaptarse. (Des.) Convenir, conformarse.
Coherence, Coherency [cō-hīr'-ens, i], *s.* Cohesión, coherencia, conexión, unión; consecuencia; consistencia, relación.
Coherent [co-hīr'-ent], *a.* Coherente; consecuente, consiguiente; ligado, unido.
Cohesion [co-hī'-zhun], *s.* 1. Cohesión, coherencia, adherencia. 2. Cohesión, fuerza de adherencia entre las moléculas de un cuerpo. 3. Hilación, enlace, conexión.
Cohesive [co-hī'-siv], *a.* Coherente, adherente.
Cohesively [co-hī'-siv-li], *adv.* Coherentemente.
Cohesiveness [co-hī'-siv-nes], *s.* Calidad o propiedad coherente.
Cohibit [co-hib'-it], *va.* (Raro) Cohibir, refrenar, impedir.
†Cohobate [cō'-ho-bēt], *va.* (Quím.) Destilar repetidas veces una misma cosa.
Cohort [cō'-hert], *s.* Cohorte.
Coif, *va.* Adornar la cabeza con una cofia.
Coifed [coift], *a.* Lo que tiene o está adornado con cofia o escofieta.
Coiffure [coif-fiur'], *s.* Tocado, peinado. V. HEADDRESS.
Coil [coil], *va.* Recoger, doblar en redondo; arrollar en espiral. *To coil a cable,* (Mar.) Adujar un cable. —*vn.* Formar círculos.
Coil, *s.* 1. Rollo, serie de círculos o espiral, que se forma doblando algo en redondo. 2. (Mar.) Adujada, cable o cabo adujado. 3. Pliegue (de serpiente o culebra); lío (de cuerdas). 4. (Elec.) Alambre conductor enrollado en un carrete.
Coiling [coil'-ing], *s.* (Mec.) Arrollamiento.
Coin [coin], *va.* 1. Acuñar moneda. 2. Falsificar, falsear, contrahacer. *To coin words,* Inventar palabras. *To coin a lie,* Forjar una mentira.
Coin, *s.* 1. Moneda acuñada con cuño real o autoridad pública. 2. Pago de dinero contante. 3. (Arq.) Rincón, cuando significa el ángulo entrante; esquina, cuando indica el ángulo saliente. *V.* QUOIN.
Coinage [coin'-ēj], *s.* 1. Acuñación. 2. Moneda, dinero. 3. Braceaje, los gastos de acuñación. 4. Falsificación, la acción de falsear o contrahacer alguna cosa. 5. Invención, cuento forjado.
Coincide [cō-in-said'], *vn.* 1. Coincidir, concurrir, convenir. 2. Con *with;* convenirse, estar o ponerse de acuerdo.
Coincidence [co-in'-si-dens], *s.* 1. Coincidencia, concurrencia. 2. Contemporaneidad.
Coincidency [co-in'-si-den-si], *s.* 1. Concurrencia, acaecimiento o concurso de varios sucesos al mismo tiempo. 2. Tendencia de muchas cosas al mismo fin.
Coincident [co-in'-si-dent], *a.* Coincidente, concurrente.
Coincider [co-in-said'-er], *s.* Lo que coincide con otro.
Coindicant [co-in'-di-cant], *a.* Concurrente, confirmante de otra indicación previa.
Coindication [co-in-di-kē'-shun], *s.* Coindicante.
Coined [coind], *pp.* 1. Acuñado. 2. Inventado, forjado. *Newly coined words,* Palabras nuevamente introducidas, neologismos.
Coiner [coin'-er], *s.* 1. Acuñador de moneda. 2. Monedero falso. 3. Inventor, fabricador.
Coir [coir o cair], *s.* Estopa de coco, la cáscara fibrosa de su nuez y la cuerda hecha con esa fibra.
Coition [co-ish'-un], *s.* La acción de juntarse; especialmente el coito, la cópula.
Cojuror [co-jū'-rer], *s.* Compurgador, el que confirma bajo juramento la declaración de otro.
Coke [cōc], *s.* Cok, coque, hulla calcinada en hornos o retortas.
Coke, *va.* y *vn.* Cambiar o cambiarse en coque.
Colabourer [cō-lē'-ber-er], *s.* Colaborador, el que trabaja con otro.
Colander [cul'-en-der], *s.* Coladera, coladero, colador, cedazo.
Colation [co-lē'-shun], **†Colature** [cel'-a-chur], *s.* Coladura, la acción y efecto de colar.
Colchicum [cel'-chi-cum], *s.* (Bot.) Cólquico, azafrán rumí o bastardo; planta medicinal; (ant.) villorita.
Colcothar [cel'-co-thar], *s.* (Quím.) Colcótar, peróxido de hierro rojo que se prepara calcinando la caparrosa. *Cf.* CROCUS y ROUGE.
Cold [cōld], *a.* 1. Frío. 2. Frío, indiferente, insensible; sereno; casto, sin pasiones. 3. Frío, insulso, soso, desagradable, sin energía ni gracia. 4. Frío, tibio, flojo. 5. Reservado, esquivo, serio, poco tratable, seco en el trato. *To be cold,* Tener frío (hablando de personas); hacer frío (hablando del tiempo). *In cold blood,* A sangre fría. *To turn the cold shoulder,* Proceder con tibieza; ser indiferente. *To throw cold water on,* Desanimar con tibieza o frialdad. *Cold-chisel,* Cortafrío. *Cold-cream,* Pomada o ungüento para el cutis. (El ungüento de agua rosada.)
Cold, *s.* 1. Frío. 2. Frío, frialdad, sensación de frío. 3. Resfriado, constipado. *To catch cold,* Resfriarse, coger un resfriado; constiparse, tener una fluxión. *A cold in the head,* Un romadizo. *To leave out in the cold,* Dejar a uno a la luna de Valencia; menospreciar con premeditación.
Cold-blooded [cōld-blud'-ed], *a.* 1. De sangre fría; deficiente en calor vital. 2. Que tiene una temperatura baja casi igual a la en que viven; dícese de los peces y reptiles. 3. Inhumano, atroz, cruel.
Cold-hearted [cōld'-hārt-ed], *a.* Insensible, desamorado, hurón.
Coldly [cōld'-li], *adv.* Fríamente; indiferentemente.
Coldness [cōld'-nes], *s.* 1. Frialdad. 2. Tibieza, indiferencia, lentitud, descuido. 3. Frialdad, esquivez. 4. Castidad.
Cold storage [cōld stōr'-ēj], *s.* Cámara frigorífica.
Cold war [cōld wōr], *s.* Guerra fría.
Cole [cōl], *s.* (Bot.) Col, berza.
Coleoptera [cel-e-ep'-te-ra o cō-le], *s. pl.* Coleópteros, orden de insectos cuyas alas anteriores son córneas y forman como un estuche; los escarabajos.
Coleopterous [cel-e-ep'-ter-us], *a.* Coleoptéreo, con las alas encerradas en un estuche.
Cole-slaw [cōl'-slō], *s.* Ensalada de col cortada menudamente.
Colessee [cō''-les-sī'], *s.* Mediero, el que toma a medias una finca en arriendo.
Colessor [cō-les'-ōr], *s.* Una de dos o más personas que otorgan un contrato de arrendamiento.
Colewort [cōl'-wūrt], *s.* (Bot.) Especie de berza.
Colic [cel'-ic], *s.* Cólico o dolor cólico. —*a.* Cólico, que afecta el intestino grueso.
Colitis [co-lai'-tis], *s.* (Med.) Colitis.
Collaborate [cel-lab'-o-rēt], *vn.* Colaborar.
Collaboration [cel-lab-o-rē'-shun], *s.* Colaboración.
Collaborator [cel-lab'-o-rē''-ter], *s.* Colaborador.
Collage [cō-lazh], *s.* (Gal.) Arte de colaje.
Collapse [cel-laps'], *va.* Hacer derrumbarse, contraerse o decaer.—*vn.* 1. Desplomarse, derrumbarse, hundirse por completo. 2. Salir con mal éxito; acabarse desastrosamente. 3. Postrarse, debilitarse. 4. Desalentarse, desanimarse; quedar rendido.
Collapse, *s.* 1. Derrumbamiento, desplome, hundimiento, caída completa y simultánea (de un edificio, etc.). 2. (Med.) Colapso, postración repentina de la energía cerebral y de las fuerzas vitales. 3. Fracaso, mal resultado; ruina.
Collar [cel'-ar], *s.* 1. Cuello, parte de ciertas prendas de vestir que rodea el pescuezo; cuello de camisa, frac, levita, etc. 2. Collar, cadena de metal que rodea el pescuezo de esclavos y malhechores; aro de metal o cuero que se pone al cuello de ciertos animales. 3. Collera, el collar para las caballerías de tiro. 4. Collar, insignia que usan los caballeros de varias órdenes militares. 5. (Mar.) Collar, encapilladura. 6. (Arq.) Anillo, moldura convexa. *To slip the collar,* Escaparse, desenlazarse, desenredarse, librarse de alguna dificultad.
Collar, *va.* 1. Agarrar a uno por los cabezones. 2. Proveer de un cuello o collar. *To collar beef,* Arrollar y ceñir un pedazo de carne.
Collar-bone [cel'-ar-bōn], *s.* Clavícula, hueso transversal de la parte superior y anterior del pecho.
Collate [cel-lēt'], *va.* 1. Comparar, confrontar, cotejar una cosa con otra de la misma especie. 2. Colar un beneficio, conferirle canónicamente.
Collateral [cel-lat'-er-al], *a.* 1. Colateral. 2. Colateral, el pariente que lo es por línea transversal. 3. In-

directo, accesorio. **4. Subsidiario.** *Collateral security*, Garantía subsidiaria.

Collaterally [cel-lat'-ẹr-al-i], *adv.* Colateralmente, indirectamente, transversalmente, subsidiariamente.

Collateralness [cel-lat'-ẹr-al-nes], *s.* Colateralidad.

Collation [cel-lé'-shun], *s.* 1. Cotejo, comparación, paralelo de una copia con el original o con otra copia para asegurarse de que se hallan conformes. 2. Colación, título o provisión de un beneficio. 3. Colación, merienda; originalmente, refacción que se solía tomar por la noche cuando se ayunaba.

Collative [cel-lé'-tiv], *a.* Colativo, dícese del patronato en que el patrón y el obispo son la misma persona.

Collator [cel-lé'-ter], *s.* 1. El que coteja copias o manuscritos. 2. Colador de beneficio.

Colleague [cel'-íg], *s.* Colega, compañero, el que está asociado con otro en algún oficio o empleo profesional.

Colleague [cel-íg'], *va.* Unir, juntar, reunir.—*vr.* Coligarse.

Collect [cel-lect'], *va.* 1. Recoger, juntar; coleccionar (plantas, libros, insectos, monedas, etc.). 2. Sumar, juntar muchos números para saber cuánto componen. 3. Cobrar, recaudar. 4. (Des.) Colegir, inferir, deducir. *To collect himself*, Volver en sí; sosegarse, reponerse, reposarse.—*vn.* Congregar, reunirse; acumularse.

Collect [cel'-ect], *s.* Colecta, oración breve.

Collectable, *a.* *V.* COLLECTIBLE.

Collectaneous [cel-lec-té'-nẹ-us], *a.* Congregado, juntado, unido.

Collected [cel-lect'-ed], *a.* 1. Reunido, junto. 2. Sosegado, vuelto en sí.—*pp.* de COLLECT.

Collectedly [cel-lec'-ted-li], *adv.* Juntamente, todo unido á la vista.

Collectedness [cel-lec'-ted-nes], *s.* El acto de rehacerse de una sorpresa.

Collectible [cel-lec'-ti-bl], *a.* Cobrable, que puede cobrarse, recaudarse o recogerse.

Collection [cel-lec'-shun], *s.* 1. Colección, el conjunto de las cosas recogidas. 2. Colección, cobro, recaudación. 3. Cuestación o colecta, petición con objeto piadoso y la suma recogida. 4. Compilación.

Collective [cel-lec'-tiv], *a.* 1. Colectivo, congregado, agregado; opuesto a individual. 2. Lo que siendo en sí singular denota pluralidad. *People, army are collective nouns*, Pueblo, ejército son nombres colectivos. 3. Que puede juntar o unir.

Collectively [cel-lec'-tiv-li], *adv.* Colectivamente, en masa.

Collectivism [cel-lec'-ti-vizm], *s.* Colectivismo.

Collectivization [cel-lec-ti-vi-zé'-shun], *s.* Colectivización.

Collectivize [cel-lec'-ti-vaiz], *va.* Colectivizar.

Collector [cel-lec'-ter], *s.* 1. Colector, el que recoge. 2. Colector, recaudador de contribuciones. 3. Compilador.

Collectorate [cel-lect'-ẹr-ét], **Collectorship** [cel-lec'-ter-ship], *s.* Colecturía, oficio o jurisdicción de colector o recaudador.

College [cel'-ej], *s.* 1. Colegio, casa de educación. 2. Edificio o serie de edificios poseídos y usados por un colegio. 3. Colegio, cuerpo de asociados, colegas o compañeros: como el colegio de cardenales.

College-like [cel'-ej-laic], *a.* Colegial.

Collegial [cel-lí'-ji-al], *a.* Colegial, lo que pertenece á colegio.

Collegian [cel-lí'-ji-an], **Collegiate** [cel-lí-ji-ẹt], *s.* Colegial, miembro o individuo de un colegio.

Collegiate, *a.* Colegiado, lo que pertenece a un colegio.

Collenchyma [cel-len'-ki-ma], *s.* (Bot.) Especie de parenquima de paredes gruesas.

Collet [cel'-et], *s.* 1. Cuello o collar. 2. Engaste, la parte de la sortija en que está engastada la piedra.

Collide [ce-laid'], *vn.* 1. Chocar, ludir, una cosa con otra. 2. Contradecir, estar en oposición.

Collie [cel'-i], *s.* Perro de pastor, muy inteligente, procedente de Escocia.

Collier [cel'-yẹr], *s.* 1. Minero, carbonero o cavador de carbón de piedra. 2. Barco carbonero. 3. Mercader de carbón. 4. Carbonero, el que hace o vende carbón.

Colliery [cel'-yẹr-i], *s.* 1. Carbonera, mina de carbón. 2. Comercio de carbón.

Colliflower [cel'-i-flau-ẹr], *s.* (Des.) Coliflor. *V.* CAULIFLOWER.

Colligate [cel'-i-gét], *va.* Atar, juntar, amarrar, una cosa con otra.

Colligation [cel-i-gé'-shun], *s.* Coligación, la acción y efecto de coligarse.

Collimate [cel'-i-mét], *va.* Poner en línea, como los ejes de dos lentes; hacer paralelos (rayos de luz); ajustar la visual de un telescopio.

Collimation [cel-i-mé'-shun], *s.* Acción de poner en línea recta.

Collimator [cel-i-mé-ter], *s.* 1. Telescopio fijo que se emplea para ajustar otro. 2. Tubo del espectroscopio que hace paralelos los rayos de luz.

Collineate [cel-lin'-ẹ-ẹt], *va.* *V.* COLLIMATE.—*vn.* Hallarse en línea recta.

Collineation [cel-in-ẹ-é'-shun], *s.* Acción o procedimiento de alinear; posición en línea recta.

Collinsia [cel-lin'-si-a], *s.* (Bot.) Género de plantas de las escrofulariáceas, que se cultivan para adorno.

†**Colliquate** [cel'-i-cwét], *va.* Colicuar, derretir.—*vn.* Colicuarse.

Colliquative [cel-lic'-wa-tiv], *a.* Colicuante, colicuativo.

Colliquefaction [cel-lic-wi-fac'-shun], *s.* Colicuefacción, el acto de colicuar o colicuarse muchas cosas juntas.

Collish [cel'-ish], *s.* (Art. y Of.) Herramienta para pulir las suelas de calzado.

Collision [cel-lizh'-un], *s.* 1. Colisión, ludimiento; choque, encuentro. 2. Oposición, contradicción.

Collocate [cel'-o-két], *va.* Colocar.

Collocate, *a.* Colocado; puesto.

Collocation [cel-o-ké'-shun], *s.* Colocación, situación.

§**Collocution** [cel-o-kiú'-shun], *s.* Conferencia, conversación.

§**Collocutor** [cel-lec'-yu-ter], *s.* Interlocutor, dialoguista.

Collodion [cel-ló'-di-en], *s.* Colodio, solución de algodón pólvora en éter y alcohol, que se emplea en cirugía y fotografía.

Colloid [cel'-eid], *s.* y *a.* (Quím.) Coloide.

Collop [cel'-up], *s.* 1. Bocado delicado, tajada pequeña de carne. *A collop of bacon*, Torrezno. 2. Pedacito, pequeña porción de cualquier cosa.

Colloquial [cel-ló'-cwi-al], *a.* Familiar, de uso común, en contraposición al literario.

Colloquialism [cel-ó'-cwi-al-izm], *s.* Vulgarismo, expresión familiar.

Colloquist [cel'-o-cwist], *s.* Interlocutor.

Colloquy [cel'-o-cwi], *s.* Coloquio, conversación, plática.

Collotype [cel'-o-taip], *s.* Colotipia.

Collude [cel-lúd'], *vn.* Obrar de concierto, convenirse o entenderse secretamente con una de las partes litigantes en perjuicio de la otra.

Colluder [cel-lúd'-ẹr], *s.* Colusor, cómplice en un engaño.

Collusion [cel-lú'-zhun], *s.* Colusión, inteligencia fraudulenta entre dos o más personas.

Collusive [cel-lú'-siv], *a.* Colusorio, concertado con fraude y en daño de tercero.

Collusively [cel-lú'-siv-li], *adv.* Colusoriamente.

Collusiveness [cel-lú'-siv-nes], *s.* Convenio fraudulento, colusión.

Collusory [cel-lú'-so-ri], *a.* Colusorio.

Colly, *va.* (Des.) Manchar, ennegrecer o ensuciar con hollín.

Collyrium [cel-lir'-i-um], *s.* Colirio, remedio para los males de los ojos.

Colocynth [cel'-o-sinth], *s.* (Bot.) Coloquíntida, especie de cohombro, y su fruto; purgante violento.

Colon [có'-len], *s.* 1. (Gram.) Colon perfecto o dos puntos (:). 2. (Anat.) Colon, parte del intestino grueso.

Colonel [cŭr'-nel], *s.* Coronel, el jefe de un regimiento.

Colonelcy [cŭr'-nẹl-si], **Colonelship** [cŭr'-nel-ship], *s.* Coronelía.

Colonial [co-ló'-ni-al], *a.* Colonial.

Colonialism [co-ló'-ni-al-izm], *s.* Colonialismo.

Colonialist [co-ló'-ni-al-ist], *s.* & *a.* Colonialista.

Colonist [cel'-o-nist], *s.* Colono, habitante de una colonia.

Colonize [cel'-o-naiz], *va.* Colonizar, formar o establecer colonias.—*vn.* Establecerse en un país lejano.

Colonization [cel-o-ni-zé'-shun], **Colonizing** [cel'-o-nai-zing], *s.* Colonización.

Colonizer [cel'-o-naiz-er], *s.* Colonizador, uno de los fundadores de una colonia.

Colonnade [cel-o-néd'], *s.* Columnario o peristilo, columnata.

Colony [cel'-o-ni], *s.* 1. Colonia, conjunto de colonos. 2. Colonia, el país habitado por colonos.

Colophon [cel'-o-fen], *s.* La fecha de una impresión y el nombre del lugar e impresor puestos al fin del libro; colofón.

Colophony [co-lef'-o-ni], *s.* Colofonia, especie de resina negra.

Color, Colour [cul'-er], *s.* 1. Color. 2. Color, colores, la coloración de la tez, la tez misma. 3. Color o colores, materiales de varios colores que preparan los pintores para pintar. 4. Color, pretexto, motivo, colorido, excusa. 5. Palo, en los naipes. —*Colors, pl.* Bandera, la insignia bajo la cual militan los soldados. *To hoist the colors*, (Mar.) Enarbolar la bandera. *Oil-color*, Color al óleo. *Water-color*, Acuarela. *Under color of*, So color de, bajo capa o con pretexto de. *There was no color of excuse*, No tenía ni sombra de excusa. *With flying colors*, A banderas desplegadas.

Color, *va.* 1. Colorar, colorir, teñir o dar color; dar los colores a lo que se pinta; iluminar un dibujo. 2. Paliar, extenuar.—*vn.* 1. Colorearse, tomar color. 2. Ponerse colorado, ruborizarse, encenderse.
Colorableness [cul'-er-a-bl-nes], *s.* Lo que es plausible.
Colorably [cul'-er-a-bli], *adv.* Plausiblemente, especiosamente.
Coloration [cul-er-é'-shun], *s.* Coloración.
Colorature [cel'-er-a-chur o tiūr], *s.* Floreos, variaciones y cadencias caprichosas en el canto.
Color-blind [cul'-er-blaind], *a.* Daltoniano.
Color blindness [cul'-er blaind'-nes], *s.* Daltonismo.
Colorcast [cul'-er cast], *s.* Un programa de televisión en color.
Colorcast, *va.* Transmitir en color un programa de televisión.
Colored [cul'-erd], *a.* 1. Colorado, que tiene color; pintado o teñido. 2. Persona de color, de origen africano en todo o en parte. 3. Especioso, embellecido, exagerado.
Colorific [cel-o-rif'-ic], *a.* Colorativo, lo que tiene virtud para producir colores.
Colorimeter [cul"-er-im'-e-ter], *s.* Colorímetro, aparato para medir la intensidad de los colores.
Coloring [cul'-er-ing], *s.* 1. Colorante, lo que da color o tinte; coloración, acción de colorar. 2. Estilo o aire particular. 3. (Pint.) Colorido.
Colorist [cul'-er-ist], *s.* Colorista, el que es hábil en dar colorido.
Colorless [cul'-er-les], *a.* Descolorido, sin color, incoloro.
Color-man [cel'-er-man], *s.* El que hace y vende toda especie de colores, barniz, afeite, aceites, etc.
Colossal [co-les'-al], **Colossean** [cel-os-si'-an], *a.* Colosal.
Colosseum [cel-o-si'-um], *s.* Coliseo, el anfiteatro de Vespasiano en Roma.
Colossus [co-les'-us], *s.* Coloso, estatua de magnitud desmesurada.
Colostrum [co-les'-trum], *s.* Calostro, la primera leche de las recién paridas.
Colour, *s.* y *v.* *V.* COLOR. Así se escribe generalmente en Inglaterra.
Colporteur [cel'-pōr-ter], *s.* Agente viajero de una sociedad religiosa que vende o da libremente Biblias, libros y folletos religiosos. (Fr.)
Colt [cōlt], *s.* 1. Potro, caballo nuevo que no pasa de cuatro años. 2. Mozuelo sin juicio. 3. Soga, con un nudo al extremo, para castigar.
Colt's-foot [cōlts'-fut], *s.* (Bot.) Tusílago, fárfara.
Colt's-tooth [cōlts'-tūth], *s.* 1. Diente imperfecto del potro. 2. Niñada o niñadas, placeres pueriles, boberías.
Colter [cōl'-ter], *s.* Cuchilla, reja de arado.
Coltish [cōlt'-ish], *a.* Juguetón, retozón.
Colubrine [cel'-yu-brain], *a.* Culebrino; astuto.
Columbian [co-lum'-bi-an], *a.* 1. Colombiano, de la República de Colombia. 2. Relativo a Cristóbal Colón; colombino.
Columbine [cel'-um-bin], *a.* Parecido a la paloma o perteneciente a ella; columbino.
Columbine [cel'-um-bain], *s.* 1. (Bot.) Aguileña o pajarilla, planta de las ranunculáceas. 2. La actriz que hace el papel de graciosa en las pantomimas.
Columbium [co-lum'-bi-um], *s.* (Min.) Columbio, elemento métalico, de color gris; se llama también niobio.
Columbo [ce-lum'-bō], *s.* Medicamento tónico hecho del columbo o colombo.
Columella [cel-yu-mel'-a], *s.* 1. (Anat. y Zool.) Varita, pequeña columna o eje central; como la varilla central de la cóclea. 2. (Bot.) Eje central, como el de un musgo.
Column [cel'-um], *s.* 1. (Arq.) Columna, especie de pilar cilíndrico, que sirve para sostener o adornar algún edificio, altar, etc. 2. (Fig.) Columna, cantidad de fluido de figura cilíndrica. 3. Algo parecido a una columna; sostén. En anatomía, la espina dorsal. 4. (Imp.) Columna, división perpendicular de una página. 5. (Mil.) Columna, cuerpo de tropas formadas en secciones de poco frente y mucho fondo.
Columnar [co-lum'-nar], *a.* Columnario, en forma de columna; parecido al fuste de columna; con columnas.
Columned [cel'-umd], *a.* Con columnas, o arreglado en columnas.
Columnist [cel'-um-nist], *s.* Articulista encargado de una sección especial de un periódico.
Colure [co-lūr'], *s.* (Astr.) Coluro, uno de los dos círculos máximos que en la esfera se cortan en ángulos rectos por los polos del globo, pasando por los signos Aries y Libra.
Colza [cel'-za], *s.* Colza, especie de berza de que se extrae un aceite estimado.
Com-. Prefijo, que en composición significa con o en compañía de otro.
Coma [cō'-ma], *s.* 1. (Med.) Coma, letargo, sopor profundo con estertor. 2. (Astr.) Cabellera, atmósfera luminosa que rodea o sigue al nucleo de un cometa. 3. (Bot.) Manojito de hebras sedosas que hay al extremo de algunas semillas.
Comate [cō'-mét], *s.* Camarada, compañero.
Comate, *a.* Cabelludo. *V.* HAIRY.
Comatose [cō'-ma-tōs], *a.* Comatoso, letárgico.
Comb [cōm], *s.* 1. Peine, instrumento con que se limpia y compone el pelo. *Carved or cut shell comb*, Peineta de carey calada. *Braid shell comb*, Peineta de carey para rizo. *Carved horn comb*, Peineta de cuerno calada. *Cockscomb*, Cresta de gallo. *Honey-comb*, Panal de miel. *Flax-comb*, Rastrillo. 2. Carda, rastrillo, para preparar el lino, el cáñamo, o la lana. 3. Cresta carnosa o carúncula del gallo o de la gallina. 4. Alvéolo, celdilla donde la abeja deposita su miel. *V.* HONEY-COMB. 5. *V.* CURRY-COMB. *Fine-toothed comb*, Peine fino, lendrera. *Comb-foundation*, Hoja delgada de cera, copia exacta de la pared media del panal, sobre la cual acaban las abejas el panal.
Comb, *va.* Peinar, limpiar y componer el pelo; cardar la lana; rastrillar el lino.
Combat [cem'-bat], *s.* Combate, batalla, pelea, desafío. *Single combat*, Duelo, desafío, combate singular.
Combat, *vn.* Combatir, luchar.—*va.* Resistir, impugnar.
Combatant [cem'-bat-ant], *s.* Combatiente; campeón.—*a.* Dispuesto a pelear.
Combater [cem'-bat-er], *s.* Combatidor, campeador.
Combative [cem'-ba-tiv], *a.* Dispuesto a combatir.
Combativeness [cem'-ba-tiv-nes], *s.* Combatividad, predisposición a la lucha.
Comb-brush [cōm'-brush], *s.* Limpiadera, bruza para limpiar los peines, cepillo de peines.
Comb-maker [cōm'-mé-ker], *s.* Peinero, el que hace peines.
Comber [cōm'-er], *s.* 1. Cardador o peinador de lana. 2. Ola de cresta (o cumbre) larga; marejada. *V.* BREAKER.
Combinable [cem-bain'-a-bl], *a.* Combinable, que se puede combinar.
Combination [cem-bi-né'-shun], *s.* Combinación, unión, liga; mezcla.
Combinative [cem-bai'-na-tiv], *a.* Combinatorio.
Combine [cem-bain'], *va.* Combinar, juntar, unir; ajustar.—*vn.* Unirse, juntarse; maquinar, conspirar.
Combing [cōm'-ing], *s.* 1. La acción de peinar, de cardar, de rastrillar, etc. 2. Postizo, cabello sobrepuesto para cubrir la calva.
Combless [cōm'-les], *a.* Descrestado.
Combo [com'-bo], *s.* Peq eña orquesta de *jazz*, con combinación especial de instrumentos.
Combustibility [cem-bust-i-bil'-i-ti], *s.* Combustibilidad.
Combustible [cem-bust'-i-bl], *a.* Combustible.—*s.* Combustible, todo lo que puede servir para mantener el fuego.
Combustibleness [cem-bust'-i-bl-nes], *s.* Combustibilidad.
Combustion [cem-bus'-chun], *s.* 1. Combustión, quema, incendio, acción del fuego sobre las substancias inflamables. 2. Combustión, combinación química acompañada de calor y luz.
Combustion chamber [cem-bus'-chun chêm-ber], *s.* (Mec.) Cámara de combustión.
Come [cum], *vn.* (*pret.* CAME, *pp.* COME). 1. Venir, llegar, aproximarse. 2. Moverse a la vista; hacerse perceptible. 3. Llegar, estar presente, existir; llegar a ser o conseguir alguna cosa. 4. Proceder, venir. 5. Acontecer, suceder. *To come about*, Girar, rodear; acontecer, acaecer, suceder; efectuar, conseguir; venir por rodeo. *Come*, en imperativo, sirve para llamar la atención o animar. *To come again*, Volver, venir otra vez *To come after*, Seguir, venir detrás, venir después. *To come after one*, Suceder a, o ser sucesor de alguno. *To come asunder*, Deshacerse, hacerse pedazos, desunirse; dislocarse, desnucarse. *To come along*, Andar, caminar con otro. *Come along*, ¡Vamos, ven aprisa! *Come along with me*, Venga Vd. conmigo. *To come at*, Alcanzar, conseguir, adquirir, obtener, tener, ganar, llegar a. *To come away*, Retirarse, irse. *To come back*, Volver, venir otra vez. *To come back again*, Volver a venir. *To come before*, Llegar antes, anteponerse, ponerse delante. *To come between*, Interponerse; intervenir, sobrevenir. *To come by*, Pasar junto, cerca o arrimado a; obtener. *How did he come by it?* ¿Cómo lo ha obtenido? *To come down*, Bajar, descender; desplomarse, desmoronarse. *To come down again*, Volver a bajar. *To come down on* o *upon*, Caerse pesada-

mente. *To come for*, Venir á buscar, venir por. *To come forth*, Salir, aparecer; adelantarse. *To come forward*, Adelantar, aprovechar, hacer progresos; adelantarse, llegar primero. *To come high or low*, Venderse caro o barato. *To come home*, Volver a casa. (Fig.) Dar en la tecla, tocar la cuerda sensible. *To come in*, Entrar, llegar; desembocar; ceder, rendirse, someterse, acceder; venir a parar, hacerse de moda una cosa; llegar a hacerse parte de una cosa; adelantar o medrar en intereses; parir la vaca; empezar a dar leche. *To come in as an heir*, Presentarse como heredero, reclamar una herencia. *To come in the way*, Presentarse al paso, ofrecerse; sobrevenir. *To come in for*, Pretender. *To come in for a share*, Tocar a uno cierta porción de cualquier cosa repartida. *To come into*, Juntarse á socorrer, venir al socorro; consentir, condescender; acordarse o ponerse de acuerdo en una cosa. *To come into business*, Comenzar a negociar; comenzar a tener salida o despacho en la venta de los géneros, o principiar a tener parroquianos, corresponsales, clientes, etc. *To come into trouble*, Meterse en trabajos, tomar algún empeño trabajoso; principiar a ser desafortunado. *To come into danger*, Exponerse al peligro. *To come into the world*, Venir al mundo, nacer. *To come in unto*, Tener coito el hombre con la mujer. *To come it*, (Fam.) Manejar o efectuar algo. *To come near*, Acercarse, allegarse. *To come next*, Venir inmediatamente después, seguir inmediatamente. *To come of*, Proceder, venir de. *To come off*, Librarse, desembarazarse, separarse, salir de un cuidado, negocio, etc.; caer; acontecer, suceder. (Fam. E. U.) Dejarse de necedades; ser razonable. (Úsase en imperativo.) *To come off from*, Dejar, omitir. *To come on*, Adelantarse, avanzar; aprovechar en el estudio; cerrar con el enemigo; engordar. *Come on!* ¡Vamos! ¡adelante! ¡valor! ¡ánimo! expresión que se usa para alentar a alguno. *To come over*, Volver, disiparse, irse; alborotarse. *To come out*, Salir, trascender, parecer; apuntar el día; brotar las plantas; salir algo a luz; descubrirse o hacerse una cosa pública. *To come out with*, Dar salida, dejar escapar, soltar, aflojar. *To come over*, Atravesar, pasar; volver, disiparse, irse. (Fam.) Sorprender, engañar. *To come round*, Venir por rodeos; llegar a ser, conseguir una cosa, obtener el puesto que se esperaba ocupar; convenir, asentir, después de haber hecho oposición; restablecerse, cobrar nuevo vigor. (Fam.) Obrar con doblez. *To come short of*, Faltar, salir mal de, ser desafortunado. *To come to*, Acercarse; llegar a obtener, alcanzar; consentir; llegar a, lograr, conseguir; estar reducido a; pasar a alguna parte; ascender, montar o importar cuando se trata de cantidades; parar en. *To come to an estate*, Heredar, suceder a uno en la posesión de una hacienda. *To come to and fro*, Pasar y repasar. *To come to grief*, Salir mal parado. *To come to hand*, Ser recibido, llegar a manos de; ofrecerse. *To come to himself*, Volver en sí. *To come to nothing*, Reducirse a nada una conversación, discurso, etc.; no quedar en nada, no valer nada, echarse a perder, ir en decadencia. *To come to an end*, Estar a punto de acabarse; morir. *To come to life*, Nacer. *To come to life again*, Resucitar. *To come to mind*, Ocurrir, presentarse a la memoria. *To come to pass*, Acontecer, acaecer, suceder. *To come to terms*, Someterse a algunas condiciones. *To come to one*, Acercarse o llegar a uno, dirigirse a él. *To come short*, Estar bajo la dependencia de otro; ser desafortunado; faltar. *To come together*, Venir juntos, juntarse; casarse. *To come up*, Subir; aparecer; establecerse una cosa; brotar o nacer las plantas. *To come up to*, Acercarse a, llegar a, subir a; juntarse con; abordar un buque. *To come up with*, Alcanzar a uno. *To come upon*, Embestir, atacar, sorprender, coger de repente; agarrar, asir, coger. *To come back*, Volver, retroceder. *To come forward*, Presentarse, salir al frente. *To come across*, Encontrar, hallar por casualidad. *He eats nothing but what comes up*, Vomita cuanto come. *How comes that?* ¿Cómo es eso? *To come*, Por venir. *In time to come*, En tiempo venidero. *In the world to come*, En el otro mundo.

Comedian [co-mí'-di-an], *s.* 1. Comediante, representante, cómico, actor o actriz. 2. Escrito de comedias. *V.* DRAMATIST.

Comedienne [co-mé-di-en'], *s.* Cómica, actriz. (Fr.)

Come-down [cum'-daun], *s.* (Fam.) Cambio desfavorable de circunstancias, descenso en la escala social.

Comedy [com'-e-di], *s.* Comedia.

Comelily [cum'-li-li], *adv.* Donosamente, cortésmente.

Comeliness [cum'-li-nes], *s.* 1. Gracia, donaire, hermosura, garbo, modestia. 2. Honestidad, decencia.

Comely [cum'-li], *a.* Garboso, bien parecido, hermoso, decente, honesto, modesto.—*adv.* 1. *V.* COMELILY. 2. Decentemente.

Come-off [cum'-ef], *s.* Salida, pretexto, excusa, escapatoria.

Comer [cum'-ẹr], *s.* Viniente, el que viene.

Comestible [co-mes'-ti-bl], *a.* Comestible.—*s.* Comestible, mantenimiento.

Comet [com'-et], *s.* 1. Cometa, cuerpo celeste. 2. Cometa, juego de naipes.

Cometarium [com-e-té'-ri-um], *s.* Instrumento para mostrar la revolución de un cometa.

Cometary [com'-e-tẹ-ri], *a.* Perteneciente a un cometa.

Comet-like [com'-et-laic], *a.* Semejante a un cometa; cosa que causa espanto o admiración.

Cometography [com-et-eg'-ra-fi], *s.* Cometografía.

Comfit [cum'-fit], *s.* Confite, pasta hecha de azúcar.

Comfit, *va.* Confitar.

Comfiture [cum'-fi-tiūr], *s.* Confitura.

Comfort [cum'-fẹrt], *va.* 1. Confortar, fortificar, dar fuerza, espíritu y vigor. 2. Animar, alentar, consolar al afligido. 3. Alegrar, divertir, dar gozo y placer al que está triste. 4. (For.) Ayudar, apoyar. *Cf.* ABET.

Comfort, *s.* 1. Confortación, auxilio asistencia, favor, ayuda. 2. Consuelo, alivio, en alguna pena o aflicción; placer, satisfacción. 3. Comodidad, conveniencia, regalo. 4. (For.) Ayuda, apoyo en la perpetración de un crimen.

Comfortable [cum'-fẹrt-a-bl], *a.* Agradable, cómodo, consolador, consolatorio, consolante, dulce.—*s.* (E. U.) Bufanda.

Comfortableness [cum'-fẹrt-a-bl-nes], *s.* 1. Comodidad, bienestar. 2. Consuelo, dulzura, agrado.

Comfortably [cum'-fẹrt-a-bli], *adv.* Agradablemente, cómodamente.

Comforter [cum'-fẹrt-ẹr], *s.* 1. Consolador. 2. El Espíritu Santo. 3. (E. U.) Sobrecama o manta acolchada. 4. Bufanda larga de lana.

Comforting [cum'-fert-ing], *a.* Consolador, confortante.

Comfortless [cum'-fẹrt-les], *a.* Desconsolado, sin consuelo, inconsolable, desesperado, desagradable.

§**Comfortress** [cum'-fẹrt-res], *sf.* Consoladora.

Comic, Comical [com'-ic, al], *a.* Cómico, burlesco, alegre.

Comically [com'-ic-al-i], *adv.* Burlescamente, cómicamente.

Comic strip [com'-ic strip], *s.* Historieta cómica.

Coming [cum'-ing], *s.* 1. Venida, llegada. 2. Advenimiento.

Coming, *a.* 1. El o lo que viene, venidero, viniente. 2. En camino de la celebridad o del poder.

Coming-in [cum'-ing-in'], *s.* 1. Introducción, principio, entrada. 2. Renta. 3. Sumisión.

Comitative [com-i-té'-tiv], *a.* Que indica asociación o acompañamiento.

Comitial [co-mish'-al], *a.* Perteneciente á comicios o asambleas.

Comity [com'-i-ti], *s.* Cortesía, urbanidad.

Comma [com'-a], *s.* 1. Coma, el signo (,) que sirve para dividir los miembros más cortos de la oración o del período. 2. (Mús.) Coma, ligera diferencia en el tono. *Turned comma*, (') Virgulilla. *V.* QUOTATION-MARK.

Command [com-mqnd'], *va.* 1. Mandar, comandar, ordenar, regir, gobernar. 2. Dominar, hablando de un paraje elevado con relación a las llanuras que lo rodean.—*vn.* Tener poder o autoridad suprema, gobernar.

Command, *s.* 1. Mando, poder, dominio, comando. 2. Mandamiento. 3 Autoridad, imperio. 4. Cuerpo de tropas bajo un comandante. 5. Dominación; y de aquí, alcance de vista. 6. Facilidad, recursos. *To have command of* o *over one's self*, Saber dominarse. *Yours to command*, Su seguro servidor.

Commandant [com-an-dqnt'], *s.* Comandante.

Commandeer [com-man-dír'], *va.* (Mil.) Confiscar, expropiar. Reclutar forzosamente.

Commander [com-mqnd'-er], *s.* 1. Comandante. 2. Maza o mazo para empedrar.

Commander in chief [com-mqnd'-ẹr in chíf], *s.* Comandante en jefe.

Commandery [com-mqnd'-ẹr-i], *s.* 1. Comandancia, el cuerpo de los caballeros de Malta de una misma nación. 2. Residencia de algún cuerpo de caballeros. 3. Encomienda, en las órdenes militares.

Commanding [com-mqnd'-ing], *pa.* 1. Dominante, imperativo. 2. Imponente. 3. (Mil.) Comandante. *A commanding presence*, Una presencia imponente. *The commanding officer*, Comandante en jefe.

Commandingly [com-mqnd'-ing-li],

adv. Imperativamente, en tono de mando.
Commandment [cem-mɑnd'-mẹnt], *s.* Mandato, precepto. *Commandments,* Mandamientos de la ley de Dios.
Commando [cem-man'-dō], *s.* Comando, comandos, soldado o tropa entrenados especialmente para misiones difíciles.
Commandress [cem-mɑnd'-res], *sf.* Comendadora, mandante.
Commatism [cem'-ɑ-tizm], *s.* Concisión, brevedad.
Commeasurable [cem-mezh'-iur-ɑ-bl], *a.* Conmensurable.
Commemorable [cem-mem'-er-ɑ-bl], *a.* Memorable, digno de ser recordado.
Commemorate [cem-mem'-o-rêt], *va.* Conmemorar, recordar.
Commemoration [cem-mem-o-rê'-shun], *s.* Conmemoración, recuerdo.
Commemorative [cem-mem'-o-rẹ-tiv], *a.* Conmemorativo.
Commemoratory [cem-mem'-o-rẹ-to-ri], *a.* Conmemoratorio.
Commence [cem-mens'], *vn.* Comenzar, empezar.—*va.* Comenzar, principiar, entablar.
Commencement [cem-mens'-mẹnt], *s.* 1. Principio, comienzo. 2. El día de recibir grados en las universidades y la celebración que hacen los graduandos en ese día.
Commend [cem-mend'], *va.* 1. Encomendar, recomendar, encargar algún negocio o persona al cuidado de otro. 2. Alabar, hablar en favor de alguna persona. 3. Ensalzar. 4. Enviar.
Commendable [cem-men'-dɑ-bl], *a.* Recomendable, loable, digno de alabanza.
Commendably [cem-men'-dɑ-bli], *adv.* Loablemente.
Commendatary [cem-men'-dɑ-tẹ-ri], *s.* Comendatario, beneficiado.
Commendation [cem-men-dê'-shun], *s.* Recomendación, encomio, alabanza.
Commendator [cem-men-dê'-ter], *s.* Comendatario, el eclesiástico que tenía en encomienda algún beneficio.
Commendatory [cem-men'-dɑ-to-ri], *a.* 1. Recomendatorio. 2. Encomendero.—*s.* Encomio, recomendación.
Commender [cem-mend'-ẹr], *s.* La persona que recomienda; alabador.
Commensal [cem-men'-sɑl], *a.* 1. Comensal, el que come a la mesa y a expensas de otro. 2. (Biol.) Asociado a otro o que vive con él, pero no como parásito; por ejemplo, una anémona marina y un cangrejo ermitaño.
Commensalism [com-men'-sal-izm] o **Commensality** [cem-men-sal'-i-ti], *s.* Comensalía, la compañía de casa y mesa.
Commensurability [cem-men-shur-ɑ-bil'-i-ti], **Commensurableness** [cem-men' shur-ɑ-bl-nes], *s.* Conmensurabilidad.
Commensurable [cem-men'-shur-ɑ-bl], *a.* 1. Conmensurable, lo que tiene una medida común. 2. Proporcionado, a propósito.
Commensurate [cem-men'-shur-êt], *va.* Conmensurar, medir o tomar la proporción de alguna cosa reduciéndola a medida común.
Commensurate, *a.* Conmensurativo, proporcionado.
Commensurately [cem-men'-shur-êt-li], *adv.* Proporcionadamente.
Comment [cem'-ent], *va.* 1. (Ant.) Comentar, hacer un comentario, glosar. 2. *vn.* Anotar, hacer notas críticas; explicar.
Comment, *s.* Comento, explicación, glosa, exposición.
Commentary [cem'-en-tẹ-ri], *s.* 1. Comentario, glosa; interpretación. 2. Comentario, relación histórica de alguna expedición. 3. Notas explicatorias del texto, escolio.
‡**Commentate** [cem'-en-têt], *vn.* Glosar, anotar.
Commentator [cem'-en-tê''-ter], **Commenter** [com'-en-tẹr], *s.* Comentador, expositor.
†**Commentitious** [cem-en-tish'-us], *a.* Imaginario, fingido, falso.
Commerce [cem'-mẹrs], *s.* 1. Comercio, negociación, tráfico. 2. Trato familiar, correspondencia, amistad, unión amistosa. 3. Comercio, un juego de naipes. *Foreign commerce,* Comercio exterior. *Domestic commerce,* Comercio interior. *To enter into commerce with,* Entrar en relaciones con. *To carry on a commerce,* Hacer tráfico de, comerciar en.
Commerce [cem-mẹrs'], *vn.* 1. Mantener trato o correspondencia. 2. (Des.) Comerciar, traficar, negociar, tratar con.
Commercial [cem-mẹr'-shɑl], *a.* Comercial, comerciante, mercantil. *Commercial flying,* Aviación comercial.—*s.* Anuncio comercial (en el radio, en la televisión, etc.)
Commercialize [cem-mẹr'-shɑl-ɑiz], *va.* 1. Mercantilizar. 2. Explotar un negocio. 3. Comerciar un producto.
Commercially [cem-mẹr'-shɑl-i], *adv.* Comercialmente.
Commerge [cem-mẹrj'], *va.* y *vn.* Mezclar, unir o unirse.
‡**Commigrate** [cem'-i-grêt], *vn.* Emigrar juntos, en compañía de otros.
Commination [cem-i-nê'-shun], *s.* Conminación, amenaza.
Comminatory [cem-min'-ɑ-to-ri], *a.* Conminatorio.
Commingle [cem-min'-gl], *va.* Mezclar, hacer mezcla de cosas diversas. —*vn.* Mezclarse, unirse una cosa con otra.
Comminute [cem'-i-niūt], *va.* Moler, pulverizar, desmenuzar, romper, quebrar, dividir. *Comminuted fracture,* Fractura conminuta, rotura del hueso en varios fragmentos.
Comminution [cem-i-niū'-shun], *s.* 1. Pulverización; división. 2. (Cir.) Fractura conminuta. 3. Atenuación, pérdida gradual.
Commiserable [cem-miz'-ẹr-ɑ-bl], *a.* Lastimoso, digno de compasión.
Commiserate [cem-miz'-ẹr-êt], *va.* Apiadarse, tener lástima o compasión, compadecerse.
Commiseration [cem-miz''-ẹr-ê'-shun], *s.* Conmiseración, compasión, piedad.
Commiserative [cem-miz'-ẹr-ɑ-tiv], *a.* (Poco usado) Compasivo.
Commiserator [cem-miz'-ẹr-ê''-tẹr], *s.* Apiadador.
Commissariat [cem-i-sê'-ri-at], *s.* 1. Comisaría, el empleo o la oficina del comisario. 2. El cuerpo de Administración Militar, que se encarga de proveer á la subsistencia del ejército. 3. Los víveres y demás artículos necesarios abastecidos por la Administración Militar.
Commissary [cem'-i-sẹ-ri], *s.* 1. Comisario, delegado. 2. (Mil.) Comisario de guerra, oficial que tiene a su cargo el aprovisionamiento de las tropas. *Commissary-general,* Jefe superior de Administración Militar.
Commissaryship [cem'-i-sẹ-ri-ship], *s.* Comisaría, comisariato.
Commission [cem-mish'-un], *s.* 1. Comisión, la acción de cometer a otro alguna cosa. 2. Comisión, encargo. 3. Patente, despacho, nombramiento en virtud del cual se designa o constituye a un oficial en algún empleo militar. 4. Comisionados, cierto número de personas a quienes se les confía alguna comisión. 5. (Com.) Mando o autoridad de algún comisionista o agente. 6. Paga o sueldo de comisionista. 7. Comisión, perpetración. *To put in* o *into commission,* Poner un buque de guerra bajo el mando directo de un oficial determinado para el servicio activo.
Commission, *va.* Comisionar, dar comisión o poder a alguno para que en su virtud obre; autorizar, encargar, apoderar.
Commission agent [cem-mish'-un ê'-jent], *s.* Agente comisionista.
Commissional [cem-mish'-un-ɑl], **Commissionary** [cem-mish'-un-ẹ-ri], *a.* Comisionado.
Commissioner [cẹm-mish'-un-ẹr], *s.* Comisionado, apoderado.
Commissure [cem'-i-shūr], *s.* (Anat.) Comisura, punto de unión de ciertas partes similares del cuerpo, como los labios y los párpados. El adjetivo de este vocablo es *Commissural* [cẹm-mis'-siu-rɑl].
Commit [cẹm-mit'], *va.* 1. Cometer, perpetrar algún delito o yerro. 2. Cometer, confiar. 3. Depositar, entregar. 4. Encarcelar, poner preso. 5. Encargar, encomendar. 6. Aprender de memoria.
Commitment [cẹm-mit'-mẹnt], *s.* 1. Auto de prisión. 2. Fianza, seguridad, prenda. 3. Perpetración (de un delito). 4. Remisión de un proyecto de ley a una comisión.
Committal [cem-mit'-ɑl], *s.* 1. *V.* COMMITMENT, 1ª y 3ª aceps. 2. Consignación. 3. Encarcelamiento.
Committee [cẹm-mit'-ẹ], *s.* Junta de comisión o meramente comisión encargada de un negocio particular. *Committee of arrangements,* Comisión de arreglos, junta o diputación de personas para disponer una función. *Committee,* (For.) Guardián o curador judicial de la persona o bienes de un lunático o un menor.
Committeeship [cẹm-mit'-ẹ-ship], *s.* El empleo de comisión.
Committer [cẹm-mit'-ẹr], *s.* Perpetrador, agresor, el que hace o comete algún delito; autor.
Committible [cẹm-mit'-i-bl], *a.* Lo que se puede cometer.
Commix [cẹm-mix'], *va.* Mezclar.—*vn.* Unir.
Commixture [cẹm-mix'-chur o tiūr], *s.* Mezcla, mixtura, mixtión; compuesto.
Commode [cẹm-mōd'], *s.* 1. Cómoda, mueble con cajones para guardar ropa y otras cosas. 2. Lavabo cubierto con aljofaina, etc. 3. Sillico o servicio. 4. Tocado que usaron las mujeres por los años de 1700. (Fr.)
Commodious [cẹm-mō'-di-us], *a.* Cómodo, conveniente, útil, apropiado para su objeto, especialmente en el sentido de espacioso, dilatado.
Commodiously [cẹm-mō'-di-us-li], *adv.* Cómodamente, aptamente.
Commodiousness [cẹm-mō'-di-us-nes], *s.* Conveniencia, comodidad; extensión.
Commodity [cẹm-med'-i-ti], *s.* 1. Interés, ventaja, utilidad, provecho. 2. Comodidad, conveniencia de tiempo o lugar. 3. *pl.* Géneros,

mercaderías, productos, frutos, producciones.

Commodore [com'-o-dōr], *s.* (Mar.) Comodoro, grado inmediatamente inferior al de contraalmirante ; jefe de escuadra.

Common [com'-un], *a.* 1. Común, corriente, usual. 2. Común, ordinario, vulgar. 3. Público, general. 4. Bajo, inferior, de poco valor.—*adv. V.* COMMONLY. *Common council*, Ayuntamiento, consejo. *Common councilman*, Regidor. *Common hall*, Casa consistorial. *Common Pleas Court*, Uno de los tribunales de justicia para las causas civiles. *Common law*, La ley no escrita (de Inglaterra), costumbre que tiene fuerza de ley. *Common Prayer*, Liturgia de la Iglesia anglicana. *Common sense*, Sentido común, sensatez, inteligencia práctica. *Common crier*, Pregonero. *Common carrier*, Conductor público de mercancías de un lugar a otro ; en particular un ferrocarril, vapor, o compañía de expreso. *Common sewer*, Albañal. *Common soldier*, Soldado raso. *Commonplace topics*, Lugares u observaciones comunes.

Common, *s.* Común, comunal, pastos comunes.

Commonable [com'-un-a-bl], *a.* Común, comunal.

Commonage [com'-un-ej], *s.* Derecho de pastar ganados en terreno común.

Commonality [com-un-al'-i-ti] (Des.), **Commonalty** [com'-un-al-ti], *s.* El común, el vulgo o pueblo ; la mayor parte del género humano ; sociedad, comunidad.

Commoner [com'-un-er], *s.* 1. Plebeyo, el que es del estado llano. 2. Individuo o miembro de la cámara baja o de los comunes en Inglaterra. 3. Estudiante de segunda clase en la universidad inglesa de Oxford. 4. Comunero, el que tiene parte en alguna heredad o pasto común.

Commonly [com'-un-li], *adv.* Comunmente, frecuentemente.

Commonness [com'-un-nes], *s.* 1. Comunidad ; igual participación de una cosa entre muchos. 2. Frecuencia.

Commonplace [com'-un-plēs], *a.* Común, vulgar, trivial.—*s.* 1. Memento, nota. 2. Lugares comunes, en los escritos.

Commonplace, *va.* Escribir en libros de memoria.

Commons [com'-unz], *s. pl.* 1. El vulgo o pueblo bajo. 2. La cámara baja en Inglaterra. 3. Ordinario, la comida usual de todos los días.

Common stock [com'-un stoc], *s.* (Com.) Acciones ordinarias.

Commonwealth [com'-un-welth], *s.* 1. Todo el pueblo del Estado, el cuerpo político. 2. República, gobierno en el cual el poder supremo reside en el pueblo.

Commonwealthsman [com-un-welths'-man], *s.* (Des.) Republicano.

Commorance [com'-o-rans], **Commorancy** [com'-o-ran-si], *s.* (For.) Morada, estancia, residencia.

Commorant [com'-o-rant], *a.* (For.) Residente, habitante, vecino.

Commotion [com-mō'-shun], *s.* 1. Agitación, movimiento del mar ; y de aquí perturbación del ánimo. 2. Conmoción, levantamiento, tumulto, sublevación, sedición.

Commotioner [com-mō'-shun-er], *s.* Conmovedor, perturbador, revolucionario, agitador.

Commove [com-mūv'], *va.* (Poco usado) Conmover, perturbar, turbar, agitar, revolver.

Communal [com'-yu-nal o com-miū'-nal], *a.* 1. Referente a un distrito municipal (de Francia) llamado *commune*. 2. Que pertenece a la comunidad ; comunal, público.

Commune [com'-yūn], *s.* 1. La menor división política de Francia, distrito municipal. 2. Comunidad organizada para gobernarse por sí misma. 3. Plática íntima.

Commune [com-miūn'], *vn.* 1. Conversar, platicar, conferir, hablar familiarmente. 2. Comulgar, recibir la comunión.

Communicability [com-miū"-ni-ca-bil'-i-ti], **Communicableness** [com-miū'-ni-ca-bl-nes], *s.* Comunicabilidad.

Communicable [com-miū'-ni-ca-bl], *a.* 1. Comunicable, lo que se puede comunicar, susceptible de comunicarse o pasar de uno a otro. 2. Distribuído, poseído con otros. 3. *V.* COMMUNICATIVE.

Communicant [com-miū'-ni-cant], *s.* Comunicante, comulgante, el que recibe la comunión.

Communicate [com-miū'-ni-kēt], *va.* 1. Comunicar, decir a otro lo que uno sabe. 2. Descubrir, revelar o enseñar a uno ; participar, transmitir.—*vn.* 1. Comulgar. 2. Comunicarse, tener comunicación.

Communication [com-miū-ni-kē'-shun], *s.* 1. Comunicación. 2. Comunicación, entrada, paso de un lugar a otro. 3. Participación recíproca de lo que se sabe. 4. Trato o correspondencia entre dos o más personas ; plática, conversación.

Communicative [com-miū'-ni-ke-tiv], *a.* 1. Comunicativo, el que tiene aptitud, inclinación y propensión natural a comunicar a otros lo que sabe, o a dividir lo que posee. 2. Franco, sociable, accesible al trato de los demás.

Communicativeness [com-miū'-ni-ke-tiv-nes]. Comunicabilidad.

Communicatory [com-miū'-ni-ca-to-ri], *a.* Comunicatorio, que da a conocer.

Communion [com-miū'-nyen], *s.* 1. Comunión, trato familiar ; relaciones amistosas ; confraternidad. 2. Comunión, el acto de recibir la sagrada eucaristía. 3. Comunión, congregación de muchas personas unidas por una creencia uniforme.

Communiqué [ce-miū-ni-kē'], *s.* Comunicación oficial.

Communism [com'-yu-nizm], *s.* 1. El sistema social de la comunidad de bienes. 2. Comunismo, doctrina que proclama la abolición del derecho de propiedad particular y la absoluta autoridad del cuerpo político para dirigir todo lo relativo al trabajo, la religión, las relaciones sociales, etc.

Communist [com'-yu-nist], *s.* Comunista, el partidario del comunismo.

Communistic [com-yu-nis'-tic], *a.* 1. Perteneciente al comunismo. 2. Dividido en común.

Community [com-miū'-ni-ti], *s.* 1. Comunidad, el cuerpo político, el público ; la sociedad en general. 2. Conjunto de personas que tienen intereses comunes, por ejemplo una comunidad de frailes. 3. Comunidad, propiedad o goce común de una cosa ; igualdad, conformidad.

Community chest [com-miū'-ni-ti chest], *s.* Fondo de caridad para beneficio de la comunidad.

Commutable [com-miū'-ta-bl], *a.* Conmutable.

Commutation [com-miū-tē'-shun], *s.* 1. Mudanza, alteración. 2. Cambio, trueque, el acto de dar una cosa por otra. 3. Conmutación, el trueque de una pena corporal en otra pecuniaria. 4. Iguala, ajuste, el precio que se da por la franquicia de pasar un río, camino, etc., por cierto tiempo. *Commutation ticket*, Billete de abono, válido para viajar por tiempo determinado, a precio reducido.

Commutative [com-miū'-ta-tiv], *a.* Conmutativo.

Commutatively [com-miū'-ta-tiv-li], *adv.* Conmutativamente.

Commutator [com'-yu-tē"-ter], *s.* Conmutador, aparato para cambiar la corriente en una máquina dinamoeléctrica.

Commute [com-miut'], *va.* 1. Conmutar, permutar, trocar, cambiar ; rescatar. 2. Igualarse, ajustarse, pagar un tanto por cierto tiempo por el peaje, pasaje de un río, etc., con el objeto de no tener que hacerlo cada vez.—*vn.* Conmutar, resarcir por medio de conmutación.

Commuter [com-miū'-ter], *s.* La persona que viaja con billete de abono, a precio reducido.

¿**Commutual** [com-miu'-chiu-al], *a.* Mutuo, recíproco.

Comose [cō-mōs'], *a.* Peludo.

Compact [com'-pact], *s.* Pacto, convenio, concierto, ajuste.

Compact [com-pact'], *va.* 1. Consolidar, juntar y unir unas cosas con otras con solidez y firmeza. 2. Pactar, hacer algún pacto o convenio. 3. Compaginar, ordenar y componer unas cosas con otras hasta reducirlas a sistema.

Compact, *vn.* Coligarse, unirse a o con.

Compact, *a.* 1. Compacto, firme, sólido, denso ; cerrado, apretado. 2. Breve, compendioso. 3. Pulido, hermoso. 4. Compuesto o hecho de, consistente en.

Compacted [com-pact'-ed], *a.* Consolidado, apretado, firme.

Compactedly, *adv. V.* COMPACTLY.

Compactedness [com-pact'-ed-nes], *s.* Firmeza, estrechez, solidez, densidad.

Compactible [com-pact'-i-bl], *a.* Lo que se puede unir, estrechar, hacer compacto.

Compactly [com-pact'-li], *adv.* Estrechamente, unidamente, pulidamente, en pocas palabras.

Compactness [com-pact'-nes], *s.* Firmeza, densidad, unión, estrechez, pulidez.

Compages [com-pē'-jez], *s.* Trabazón, juntura, enlazamiento, enlace.

¿**Compaginate** [com-paj'-i-nēt], *va.* Compaginar, juntar, adaptar.

Compagination [com-paj-i-nē'-shun], *s.* Compaginación.

Companion [com-pan'-yun], *s.* 1. Compañero, socio. 2. Compañero, camarada, la persona con quien uno se acompaña. 3. Caballero de una orden. *A boon companion*, Un compañero alegre y jovial.

Companion, *s.* (Mar.) 1. Lumbrera, chupeta de escala en los buques mercantes. 2. Carroza, cubierta de popa. *Companion-ladder*, Escala de toldilla. *Companion-way*, Escalera de la cámara.

Companionable [cem-pan'-yun-a-bl], *a.* Sociable.
Companionably [cem-pan'-yun-a-bli], *adv.* Sociablemente.
Companionship [cem-pan'-yun-ship], *s.* Sociedad, compañía, reunión de amigos.
Company [cum'-pa-ni], *s.* 1. Compañía o sociedad. 2. Compañía, junta o tertulia de personas que se reunen para divertirse o hablar de algún asunto. 3. Compañía, número de personas que se unen para un fin determinado. 4. Compañía de comercio. 5. Gremio, cuerpo. 6. Compañía, cierto número de soldados que militan al mando de un capitán. 7. (Mar.) Tripulación. *To join company,* (Mar.) Incorporarse. *To keep company,* Frecuentar. *To keep company with,* (1) Asociarse, acompañar. (2) (Prov.) Cortejar, galantear o recibir galanteos. *To bear company,* Acompañar, o asistir a. *A joint-stock company,* Una sociedad por acciones. *Limited company,* V. LIABILITY (*limited*). *To part company* (*with*), Separarse. *By companies,* En cuadrilla; en tropel.
†**Company,** *va.* *V.* ACCOMPANY.—*vn.* Asociarse. *V.* ACCOMPANY.
Comparable [cem'-pa-ra-bl], *a.* Comparable.
Comparably [cem'-pa-ra-bli], *adv.* Comparablemente.
Comparate [cem'-pa-rêt], *s.* Una cosa que está comparada con otra.
Comparative [cem-par'-a-tiv], *a.* 1. Comparativo, respectivo, relativo, no absoluto. 2. Comparativo, lo que tiene capacidad para comparar. *Comparative degree,* (Gram.) Comparativo, grado que expresa la mayor o menor intensión de calidad en una cosa que en otra; v. g. Juan es menos hábil que Pedro; la mano derecha es más fuerte que la izquierda.
Comparatively [cem-par'-a-tiv-li], *adv.* Comparativamente, relativamente.
Compare [cem-pār'], *va.* Comparar, cotejar, confrontar, colacionar, comprobar.—*vn.* (Des.) *V.* VIE.
Compare, *s.* (Poét. o Ant.) Comparación, cotejo, comprobación; símil.
Comparer [cem-pār'-er], *s.* Comparador.
Comparing [cem-pār'-ing], *s.* Comparación.
Comparison [cem-par'-i-sen], *s.* 1. Comparación, la acción y efecto de comparar, cotejo, confrontación, comprobación. 2. Símil; parábola. *Beyond comparison,* Sin comparación; sin igual.
Compart [cem-pārt'], *va.* Compartir, dividir, distribuir.
Compartment [cem-pārt'-ment], *s.* 1. Compartimiento, cada una de las partes en que se subdivide un espacio cerrado, por ejemplo el interior de un buque. 2. Compartimiento, división o distribución de una pintura o diseño. 3. Cajoncito, gaveta de un escaparate o cómoda. 4. (Her.) División de un escudo de armas, cuartel.
Compartition [cem-par-tish'-un], *s.* Compartimiento; división.
Compass [cum'-pas], *va.* 1. Conseguir, lograr, alcanzar, obtener. 2. Trazar, idear, maquinar, conspirar contra. 3. Comprender, entender, concebir. 4. (Ant.) Circuir, cercar, rodear, circundar; sitiar.
Compass, *s.* 1. Círculo, circuito, ámbito; alcance; extensión, espacio encerrado entre límites. 2. Circunferencia. 3. Moderación, límites, la justa medida y término razonable que deben tener las cosas. 4. Compás de la voz o de un instrumento. 5. Intención, designio, propósito. 6. Compás, instrumento que sirve para formar círculos, tirar líneas y otros usos. En este sentido se usa generalmente en plural. *Caliber compasses,* Compás de calibres. *Proportional compasses,* Compás de reducción. 7. Compás de mar, brújula, aguja de marear. *Azimuth compass,* Brújula de azimut. *Hanging compass,* Brújula revirada de cámara. *Compass-box,* Caja de brújula. *Compass-card,* Rosa de los vientos. *Compass-timber,* (Mar.) Madera de vuelta. *Compass-saw,* (Carp.) Serrucho angosto para cortar circularmente.
Compassable [cum'-pas-a-bl], *a.* Asequible, que se puede alcanzar u obtener.
Compassion [cem-pash'-un], *s.* Compasión, conmiseración, piedad.
Compassionable [cem-pash'-un-a-bl], *a.* Lastimoso, digno de compasión.
Compassionate [cem-pash'-un-êt], *a.* Compasivo, el que con facilidad se mueve a compasión.
Compassionate, *va.* Compadecer a alguno, sentir con él sus penas y trabajos.
Compassionately [cem-pash'-un-et-li], *adv.* Tiernamente.
§**Compaternity** [cem-pa-ter'-ni-ti], *s.* Compaternidad, compadrazgo.
Compatibility [cem-pat-i-bil'-i-ti], **Compatibleness** [cem-pat'-i-bl-nes], *s.* Compatibilidad, cualidad de las cosas que no se oponen entre sí.
Compatible [cem-pat'-i-bl], *a.* Compatible, que puede coexistir; congruo, apto.
Compatibly [cem-pat'-i-bli], *adv.* Compatiblemente.
Compatriot [cem-pê'-tri-et], *s.* Compatriota.—*a.* Lo que es de la misma patria.
Compeer [cem-pīr'], *s* Compañero, colega; compadre.
Compel [cem-pel'], *va.* 1. Compeler, obligar, constreñir, precisar, forzar. 2. Predominar. 3. Arrancar, tomar por fuerza o con violencia.
Compellable [cem-pel'-a-bl], *a.* Lo que puede ser compelido, obligado o violentado.
Compellably [cem-pel'-a-bli], *adv.* A viva fuerza.
Compellation [cem-pel-lê'-shun], *s.* 1. Tratamiento, el título de cortesía que se da a alguno; apóstrofe. 2. Acción de dirigir la palabra.
Compeller [cem-pel'-er], *s.* Compulsor, el que compele.
Compend [cem'-pend], *s.* Compendio, resumen, epítome, sumario que se hace de un libro, causa o proceso.
†**Compendiarious** [cem-pen-di-ê'-ri-us], *a.* *V.* COMPENDIOUS.
Compendious [cem-pen'-di-us], *a.* 1. Compendioso, breve, sucinto, reducido. 2. (Des.) Directo, sin rodeos.
Compendiously [cem-pen'-di-us-li], *adv.* Compendiosamente.
Compendiousness [cem-pen'-di-us-nes], *s.* Brevedad.
Compendium [cem-pen'-di-um], *s.* Compendio, resumen, epítome, extracto.
†**Compensable** [cem-pen'-sa-bl], *a.* Compensable.
Compensate [cem'-pen-sêt], *va.* Compensar, dar o tomar el equivalente de una cosa; indemnizar, resarcir, reparar.—*vn.* (Con la preposición *for.*) Compensarse las pérdidas con las ganancias, o los males con los bienes.
Compensation [cem-pen-sê'-shun], *s.* Compensación, acción con que una cosa se sustituye y compensa con otra equivalente; indemnización, resarcimiento, reparación. *Compensation balance, bar* o *pendulum,* Volante o balanza, barra o péndulo de compensación de un reloj.
Compensative [cem-pen'-sa-tiv], **Compensatory** [cem-pen'-sa-to-ri], *a.* Equivalente, lo que compensa.
Compensator [cem'-pen-sê-ter], *s.* El que o lo que compensa, compensador, v. g. de una brújula.
†**Compense** [cem-pens'], *va.* *V.* COMPENSATE.
Compete [cem-pīt'], *vn.* Competir, contender dos o más sujetos entre sí, aspirar unos y otros con empeño a una misma cosa. *To compete with,* Competir, rivalizar con.
Competence, Competency [cem'-pe-tens, i], *s.* 1. Lo bastante, lo suficiente; tanto cuanto basta. 2. Lo necesario, bienes suficientes para un mediano pasar. 3. Competencia, la jurisdicción que pertenece a un juez o tribunal.
Competent [cem'-pe-tent], *a.* Competente, adecuado, bastante, suficiente, capaz, propio, apto, calificado.
Competently [cem'-pe-tent-li], *adv.* Competentemente; razonablemente, suficientemente.
†**Competible** [cem-pet'-i-bl], *a.* *V.* COMPATIBLE.
Competition [cem-pe-tish'-un], *s.* Competencia, competición, disputa o contienda entre dos o más personas acerca de alguna cosa que se pretende; rivalidad, concurrencia en un mismo empeño.
Competitive [cem-pet'-i-tiv], *a.* De la competencia, referente a la competencia. *Competitive examination,* Examen de concurso u oposición.
Competitor [cem-pet'-i-ter], *s.* Competidor, rival, antagonista.
Competitress [cem-pet'-i-tres], **Competitrix** [cem-pet'-i-trix], *sf.* Competidora.
Compilation [cem-pi-lê'-shun], *s.* Compilación, colección de varios autores; conjunto de algunas cosas.
†**Compilator** [cem-pi-lê'-ter], **Compiler** [cem-pail'-er], *s.* Compilador; redactor.
Compilatory [cem-pai' la-to-ri], *a.* Perteneciente a un compilador o a una compilación.
Compile [cem-pail'], *va.* Compilar, juntar en un cuerpo varias noticias o materias.
†**Compilement** [cem-pail'-ment], *s.* Compilación.
Complacence, Complacency [cem-plê'-sens, i], *s.* Complacencia, placer, gusto, satisfacción; deferencia al gusto o parecer de otro; condescendencia. *Self-complacency,* Satisfacción de sí mismo.
Complacent [cem-plê'-sent], *a.* Afable, cortés, urbano, condescendiente.
Complacently [cem-plê'-sent-li], *adv.* Afablemente, urbanamente.
Complain [cem-plên'], *vn.* 1. Quejarse, lamentarse, querellarse. 2. (For.) Querellarse, poner acusación contra alguno en justicia, por agravio, injuria o delito; demandar, por daños y perjuicios. 3. Quejarse, afirmar que se siente dolor; estar enfermo.

Complainable [cǫm-plên'-a-bl], *a.* Lastimero.

Complainant [cǫm-plên'-ant], *s.* Querellante, demandante.

Complainer [cǫm-plên'-ęr], *s.* Lamentador.

Complaining [cǫm-plên'-ing], *s.* Lamento.

Complaint [cǫm-plênt'], *s.* 1. Queja, expresión de dolor, pena o sentimiento; lamento, llanto, quejido. 2. Causa u objeto de algún agravio. 3. Mal, enfermedad. 4. Queja, querella. *Ground of complaint,* Motivo de queja. 5. (For.) Demanda. *To lodge a complaint,* Presentar una demanda en justicia.

Complaisance [cǫm'-plê-zǫns''], **Complaisantness** [com'-plê-zant''-nes], *s.* Civilidad, cortesía, urbanidad, cumplimiento, y muchas veces adulación.

Complaisant [com'-plê-zant''], *a.* 1. Cortés, atento, complaciente. 2. Cumplimentero.

Complaisantly [com'-plê-zant''-li], *adv.* Cortésmente.

Complanate [com'-pla-nêt], *va.* Aplanar, allanar.—*a.* Aplanado, llano; que está situado en el mismo plano.

Complected [com-plec'-ted], *a.* Entretejido, enlazado, complicado.

Complement [com'-plę-męnt], *s.* 1. Complemento, perfección o colmo de alguna cosa. 2. Complemento, lo que acaba de completar alguna cosa. (Mil.) Contingente, fuerza numérica. 3. Apéndice, o cosa accesoria que sirve de adorno. 4. Colmo, total. *Complement of the course,* (Mar.) Complemento de la derrota, los puntos que faltan a la derrota para ser igual a noventa grados o a ocho rumbos, que son los que componen el cuarto del compás de la brújula.

Complement, *va.* Suplir una falta, acabar, hacer perfecto o cabal.

Complemental [com-plę-men'-tal], *a.* Completivo, lo que completa o llena.

Complementary [com-plę-men'-ta-ri], *a.* Complementario, que completa, que suple lo que falta.—*s.* Algo que suple lo que falta; color complementario.

Complete [com-plît'], *a.* Completo, acabado, perfecto, cabal, consumado.

Complete, *va.* Completar, acabar, concluir, consumar.

Completely [com-plît'-li], *adv.* Completamente, perfectamente.

†Completement [com-plît'-męnt], *s.* Complemento, acabamiento.

Completeness [com-plît'-nes], *s.* Perfección, complemento.

Completion [com-plî'-shun], *s.* Complemento, acabamiento, colmo.

Completive [com-plî'-tiv], **Completory** [com-plî'-to-ri], } *a.* Completivo.

Completory [com-plî'-to-ri], *s.* Completas. (Ant.) *V.* COMPLIN.

Complex [com'-plecs], *a.* Complexo, compuesto; complicado, enredado.

Complex, *s.* Complicación, suma, total; reunión, colección.

Complexion [com-plec'-shun], *s.* 1. Tez, color de las partes exteriores del cuerpo, y particularmente del rostro. 2. Aspecto general, estado; carácter o calidad. *Political complexion of a legislature,* Carácter político de un cuerpo legislativo. 3. (Ant.) Complexión, temperamento y constitución de los humores del cuerpo humano. 4. (Ant.) Complexo, el conjunto de varias cosas. *A fine complexion,* Un hermoso cutis, un bello color. *A fresh complexion,* Una tez fresca, rosada.

Complexional [com-plec'-shun-al], *a.* Complexional.

Complexionally [com-plec'-shun-al-i], *adv.* Por complexión.

Complexioned [com-plec'-shund], *a.* De tal o cual tez; dotado de cierto color. *Dark-complexioned,* De tez morena.

Complexity [com-plec'-si-ti], **Complexness** [com-plecs'-nes], *s.* Complexidad, estado complexo.

Complexly [com-plecs'-li], *adv.* Complexamente.

Complexus [com-plecs'-us], *s.* 1. Complicación, sistema complicado. 2. Complexo, gran músculo del cuello y de la espalda.

Compliable [com-plai'-a-bl], *a.* Complaciente, rendido, sumiso; acorde, conforme.

Compliance [com-plai'-ans], *s.* 1. Sumisión, obediencia. 2. Cumplimiento, rendimiento, condescendencia, consentimiento, complacencia.

Compliant [com-plai'-ant], *a.* Rendido, sumiso; atento, cortés, condescendiente, fácil, complaciente, oficioso, obsequioso, servicial, galante.

Compliantly [com-plai'-ant-li], *adv.* Rendidamente.

Complicacy [com'-pli-ca-si], *s.* Complicación, lo que es complicado y el estado o la calidad de serlo.

Complicate [com'-pli-kêt], *va.* 1. Complicar, enredar una cosa con otra. 2. Mezclar, confundir; embrollar, crear dificultades.

Complicate, *a.* Complicado, enredado; difícil de entender o explicar.

Complicately [com'-pli-kêt-li], *adv.* Complicadamente.

Complicateness [com'-pli-kêt-nes], *s.* Complicación, perplejidad, enredo.

Complication [com-pli-kê'-shun], *s.* Complicación.

Complicative [com'-pli-kę-tiv], *a.* Que produce, o puede producir, complicaciones.

†Complice [com'-plis], *s.* Cómplice, compañero en el delito.

Complicity [com-plis'-i-ti], *s.* 1. Complicidad, la calidad de cómplice. 2. Estado complexo.

Complier [com-plai'-ęr], *s.* Hombre dócil, condescendiente y complaciente; consentidor, contemporizador.

Compliment [com'-pli-męnt], *s.* 1. Cumplimiento, obsequio, regalo, fineza que se hace por urbanidad o cortesía. 2. Cumplimiento, cumplido, muestra de urbanidad; más usado en plural.

Compliment, *va.* 1. Cumplimentar, dirigir frases de cortesía o afecto; felicitar; hacer un regalo por cumplido o muestra de afecto. 2. Cumplimentar, obsequiar, lisonjear.—*vn.* Hacer cumplimientos, usar de ceremonias.

Complimental [com-pli-men'-tal], *a.* (Ant.) *V.* COMPLIMENTARY.

Complimentary [com-pli-men'-ta-ri], *a.* 1. Cumplido, cortés, obsequioso. 2. Cumplimentero, ceremonioso.

Complimenter [com'-pli-men-tęr], *s.* Adulador, la persona que es muy cumplimentera o amiga de cumplimientos.

Complin, Compline [com'-plin], *s.* Completas, la parte del oficio divino con que terminan las horas canónicas del día.

†Complore [com-plōr'], *vn.* Condolerse.

Complot [com'-plot], *s.* Trama, confederación o conspiración secreta; maquinación, cábala.

Complot [com-plot'], *va.* Tramar, conspirar, conjurar.

Complotment [com-plot'-męnt], *s.* Conjuración, conspiración.

Complotter [com-plot'-ęr], *s.* Conspirador, conjurado.

Comply [cǫm-plai'], *vn.* Cumplir, obedecer, satisfacer, llenar; ceder, condescender, consentir, someterse, conformarse, acomodarse. A menudo va seguido de la preposición *with. To comply with the necessary formalities,* Llenar las formalidades necesarias. *To comply with the times,* Contemporizar.

Component [cǫm-pō'-nent], *a.* Componente, lo que compone o entra en la composición de un todo.—*s.* Parte constitutiva.

Comport [cǫm-pōrt], *vn.* y *va.* 1. Convenir, concordar. 2. (Des.) Sufrir, tolerar, aguantar. 3. Comportarse, portarse.

Comportable [com-pōrt'-a-bl], *a.* Conforme.

†Comportment [com-pōrt'-męnt], *s.* Porte, conducta.

Compose [com-pōz'], *va.* 1. Componer, formar de varias cosas una juntándolas con método. 2. Colocar alguna cosa en su debida forma y según método. 3. Componer, hacer alguna obra de ingenio; escribir, inventar. 4. Apaciguar, sosegar, serenar, calmar. 5. Ajustar, concertar, reglar, ordenar. 6. (Imp.) Componer, formar dicciones colocando las letras o caracteres. 7. Componer, poner alguna cosa en música.—*vn.* Ocuparse en la composición de obras literarias o musicales, o en componer o parar tipo de imprenta. *Composing frame* o *stand,* Chivalete de imprenta. *Composing-rule,* Regleta o filete de cajista. *Composing-stick,* Componedor de cajista.

Composed [com-pōzd'], *a.* Compuesto, sosegado, tranquilo, cachazudo, sereno.—*pp.* de COMPOSE.

Composedly [com-pōz'-ed-li], *adv.* Tranquilamente, serenamente, sosegadamente.

Composedness [com-pōz'-ed-nes], *s.* Compostura, modestia, tranquilidad, serenidad, calma.

Composer [com-pōz'-ęr], *s.* 1. Autor, escritor; compositor (de música); cajista. 2. Conciliador, el que arregla una diferencia; la persona que calma, apacigua y serena.

Compositæ [com-pez'-i-tî], *s. pl.* Compuestas, orden de plantas, el más numeroso de todos.

Composite [com-pez'-it], *a.* 1. Compuesto, formado de partes distintas, mezclado, no sencillo. 2. (Arq.) Compuesto, uno de los cinco órdenes de arquitectura.—*s.* 1. Compuesto, mezcla o unión de varios miembros. 2. (Bot.) Una de las flores o plantas compuestas.

Composition [com-po-zish'-un], *s.* 1. Composición. 2. Compuesto, la masa que resulta de la mezcla de varios ingredientes. 3. Composición, obra compuesta, escrita o impresa. 4. Composición, el acto de quedar el deudor solvente con el acreedor pagándole solamente parte de la deuda. 5. Convención, acomodamiento, ajuste.

Compositive [com-pez'-i-tiv], *a.* Componente, que puede combinar o componer; sintético.

Compositor [com-poz'-i-tɐr], *a.* 1. (Imp.) Compositor, cajista. 2. El que arregla o pone en orden.
Compos mentis [com'-pos men'-tis]. Sano de espíritu, en posesión de su inteligencia. (Lat.)
‖**Compossible** [com-pos'-i-bl], *a.* Que puede existir con otra cosa.
Compost [com'-pōst], *s.* Abono, estiércol; mezcla para abonar la tierra.
Compost [com'-pōst], *va.* Abonar, engrasar, estercolar la tierra.
Composure [com-pō'-zhur], *s.* 1. Compostura, serenidad, tranquilidad, calma, sangre fría, presencia de espíritu. 2. (Des.) Colocación, combinación; hechura. 3. (Des.) Composición o compostura, trato amigable con que se avienen las partes en un pleito o desavenencia.
‖**Compotator** [com-po-tē'-tɐr], *s.* (Poco us.) El que bebe con otros.
Compound [com-paund'], *va.* 1. Componer, formar de varias cosas una mezclándolas; arreglar, acomodar. 2. Componer un pleito o desavenencia. 3. Componerse un deudor con sus acreedores pagándoles solamente parte de la deuda.—*vn.* 1. Componerse, concertarse, rebajando una de las partes o ambas alguna cosa. 2. Ajustar, comprar o vender por entero. 3. Capitular.
Compound [com'-paund], *a.* Compuesto, formado de dos o más ingredientes, de varias partes. (Gram.) Formado de dos o más palabras.—*s.* Mezcla, compuesto, agregado de varias cosas que componen un todo.
Compoundable [com-paund'-a-bl], *a.* Componible, que se puede componer, arreglar o conciliar.
Compounder [com-paund'-ɐr], *s.* 1. Compositor, mezclador. 2. Arbitrador, mediador.
Comprehend [com-prɐ-hend'], *va.* 1. Comprender, contener, encerrar, incluir en sí alguna cosa. 2. Comprender, conocer, entender, penetrar, concebir.
Comprehensible [com-prɐ-hen'-si-bl], *a.* 1. Comprensible, inteligible, fácil de comprender. 2. (Des.) Comprensible, que puede ser comprendido, contenido o incluído en otra cosa.
Comprehensibleness [com-prɐ-hen'-si-bl-nes], *s.* Comprensibilidad.
Comprehensibly [com-prɐ-hen'-si-bli], *adv.* Comprensiblemente.
Comprehension [com-prɐ-hen'-shun], *s.* 1. Comprensión, el acto o propiedad de comprender, contener o incluir. 2. Comprensión, inteligencia, concepción, conocimiento. 3. *V.* COMPREHENSIVENESS.
Comprehensive [com-prɐ-hen'-siv], *a.* 1. Comprensivo, inclusivo, de mucha cabida, de gran alcance de inteligencia, de gran amplitud de simpatías, de miras, etc. 2. Compendioso, corto. 3. (Biol.) Sintético.
Comprehensively [com-prɐ-hen'-siv-li], *adv.* Comprensivamente.
Comprehensiveness [com-prɐ-hen'-siv-nes], *s.* 1. Extensión, alcance, cabida. 2. Comprensión, perspicacia y capacidad para comprender o penetrar. 3. Energía, precisión, brevedad, cualidad de contener mucho en pocas palabras.
Compress [com-pres'], *va.* 1. Comprimir, apretar, estrechar, condensar. 2. Abreviar, reducir, hace breve o acortar una cosa. *Compressed air,* Aire comprimido.
Compress [com'-pres], *s.* Cabezal, compresa, lienzo de varios dobleces que se pone encima de una herida.
Compressibility [com-pres-i-bil'-i-ti], **Compressibleness** [com-pres'-i-bl-nes], *s.* Compresibilidad.
Compressible [com-pres'-i-bl], *a.* Compresible, comprimible.
Compression [com-presh'-un], *s.* Compresión, la acción de estrechar, apretar y unir las partes de un cuerpo con violencia; condensación, construcción.
Compressive [com-pres'-iv], *a.* Compresivo, que puede comprimir.
Compressor [com-pres'-ɐr], *s.* El o lo que comprime; en particular: 1. Máquina o aparato para comprimir el aire, gases u otras substancias, como el heno o algodón. 2. Compresor, instrumento para comprimir los vasos o un miembro, en las operaciones quirúrgicas. 3. Aparato para el microscopio que produce una presión graduada sobre el objeto que se examina. En este sentido se llama a menudo **Compressorium.**
‖**Compressure** [com-presh'-ur], *s.* Compresión.
Comprint [com-print'], *vn.* (Ant.) Imprimir en concurrencia con el impresor del Rey.
Comprisal [cɐm-praiz'-al], *s.* Inclusión, comprensión.
Comprise [cɐm-praiz'], *va.* Comprender, contener, incluir, encerrar.
Compromise [com'-pro-maiz], *s.* Compromiso, el acto y efecto de comprometerse; convenio entre litigantes por el cual ajustan o zanjan su litigio mediante concesiones recíprocas; arreglo.
Compromise, *va.* 1. Comprometer, comprometerse, allanarse o convenir en la decisión de un tercero; terminar un desacuerdo por medio de concesiones mútuas. 2. Comprometer, exponer, arriesgar un negocio por algún acto o declaración.—*vn.* Transigir, someterse a un compromiso.
Compromiser [com'-pro-maiz-ɐr], *s.* Compromisario.
‖**Compromissorial** [com-pro-mi-sō'-ri-al], *a.* Compromisorio.
Compromit, *va.* (Ant.) Comprometer.
Comprovincial [com-pro-vin'-shal], *a.* (Ant.) Comprovincial.
Compt [caunt], *s.* (Des.) Cuenta, cálculo.
Comptrol, *v.* y *s.* *V.* CONTROL.
Comptometer [comp-tom'-ɐ-tɐr], *s.* Contómetro, máquina calculadora.
Comptroller [con-trōl'-ɐr], *s.* Contralor, interventor, inspector.
Comptrollership [con-trōl'-ɐr-ship], *s.* Contraloría.
Compulsative [com-pul'-sa-tiv], **Compulsatory** [com-pul'-sa-to-ri], *a.* Compulsorio, coactivo, que tiene fuerza o autoridad para compeler.
Compulsatively [com-pul'-sa-tiv-li], **Compulsively** [com-pul'-siv-li], *adv.* Por fuerza.
Compulsion [com-pul'-shun], **Compulsiveness** [cɐm-pul'-siv-nes], *s.* Compulsión, apremio, coacción.
Compulsive [cɐm-pul'-siv], **Compulsory** [cɐm-pul'-so-ri], *a.* Compulsorio.
Compulsively [cɐm-pul'-siv-li], **Compulsorily** [cɐm-pul'-so-ri-li], *adv.* Por fuerza.
Compunction [cɐm-punc'-shun], *s.* Compunción, contrición, arrepentimiento, remordimiento.
Compunctious [cɐm-punc'-shus], *a.* Compungido, arrepentido, contrito.
Compurgation [com-pūr-gē'-shun], *s.* Compurgación, justificación de la veracidad de alguno por medio del testimonio de otro.
Compurgator [com-pūr-gē'-tɐr], *s.* Compurgador, el que en la prueba llamada compurgación canónica, afirmaba bajo juramento la inocencia de un acusado.
Computable [com-piū'-ta-bl], *a.* Computable, estimable, que se puede computar o calcular.
Computation [com-piū-tē'-shun], *s.* Computación, cómputo, cuenta, cálculo.
Compute [com-piūt'], *va.* Computar, contar, calcular, estimar.
Computer [com-piū'-tɐr], *s.* Calculador, computador, computista; máquina calculadora.
Computerize [com-piū'-tɐr-aiz], *va.* Habilitar con computadoras.
Comrade [com'-rad], *s.* Camarada, compañero, asociado o amigo.
Comradeship [com'-rad-ship], *s.* Camaradería.
Con [con], *prep.* Con, partícula inseparable, como en *concourse,* Concurso. Toma la forma de COM- antes de c, d, f, g, i, j, n, q, s, t, w. Este prefijo indica en general ya la unión, como en *conjoin,* juntar, ya la compañía de otro, como en *contend,* discutir; *consort,* asociarse. *V.* COM-. (Lat. cum.)
Con, *adv.* Contra. *Neither pro nor con,* Ni a favor ni en contra.
Con, *va.* 1. Estudiar, reflexionar, meditar, fijar en la memoria. 2. (Mar.) Dirigir la acción de gobernar el buque. 3. (Des.) Conocer, saber.
Concamerate [con-cam'-ɐr-ēt], *va.* 1. Dividir en cámaras. 2. (Des.) Abovedar, cubrir con bóveda.
Concamerated [con-cam'-ɐr-ē-ted], *a.* (Zool.) Dividido en cámaras, como una concha o un hueso.
Concameration [con-cam-ɐr-ē'-shun], *s.* (Zool.) 1. División en cámaras, y la cámara misma. 2. ‖Arco, bóveda; firmamento.
Concatenate [con-cat'-e-nēt], *va.* Concatenar, encadenar.
Concatenation [con-cat-e-nē'-shun], *s.* Concatenación, encadenamiento, sucesión, serie.
Concavation [con-ca-vē'-shun], *s.* La acción de ahuecar.
Concave [con'-kēv], *a.* Cóncavo, hueco, vacío, lo contrario de convexo.
Concave, *va.* (Poco us.) Hacer cóncava alguna cosa.
Concave, *s.* Hueco, hondón.
Concaveness [con-kēv'-nes], *s.* Concavidad.
Concavity [con-cav'-i-ti], *s.* Concavidad, profundidad.
Concavo-concave [con-kē'-vo-con'-cēv], *s.* Cóncavo-cóncavo, esto es, por ambos lados.
Concavo-convex [con-kē'-vo-con'-vecs], *s.* Cóncavo-convexo, cóncavo por un lado y convexo por el otro.
Concavous [con-kē'-vus], *a.* (Des.) *V.* CONCAVE.
Concavously [con-kē'-vus-li], *adv.* (Des.) Con hueco.
Conceal [con-sīl'], *va.* Callar, tapar, ocultar, esconder, tener secreto; disimular. *Concealed weapons,* Armas prohibidas que se llevan ocultamente, en violación de la ley.
Concealable [con-sīl' a-bl], *a.* Ocultable, escondible.
Concealedness [con-sīl'-ed-nes], *s.* Obscuridad, secreto, retiro.

Concealer [cen-sîl'-ẹr], *s.* Ocultador, encubridor.
Concealing [cen-sîl'-ing], *s.* 1. Escondimiento, ocultación. 2. Disimulo, acción de ocultar; encubrimiento (de una cosa robada).
Concealment [cen-sîl'-mẹnt], *s.* 1. Ocultación, secreto, encubrimiento. 2. Escondrijo, escondite. 3. Reticencia. 4. Retiro; misterio.
Concede [cen-sîd'], *va.* Conceder, asentir, convenir en lo que otro dice o afirma.—*vn.* Admitir.
Conceit [cen-sît'], *s.* 1. Amor propio, presunción, arrogancia, alto concepto de sí mismo, engreimiento, encaprichamiento. 2. Concepto, capricho, fantasía, imaginación, pensamiento. 3. Concepción, facilidad o aptitud del entendimiento para comprender. 4. Concepción, pensamiento, idea. (Ant. o Amer.) *To be out of conceit with anything,* Perder el gusto por alguna cosa. *Idle conceits,* Boberías, necedades.
Conceit, *va.* Conceptuar, hacer o formar concepto; imaginar, creer; presumir.—*vr.* Encapricharse, engreirse, conceptuarse.
Conceited [cen-sît'-ed], *a.* 1. Afectado, vano, porfiado, vanaglorioso, fantástico, presumido, caprichoso. 2. (Prov.) Conceptuoso, ingenioso.
Conceitedly [cen-sît'-ed-li], *adv.* Vanamente; fantásticamente; afectadamente.
Conceitedness [cen-sît'-ed-nes], *s.* Presunción, amor propio, pertinacia, porfía, obstinación, vanidad.
Conceitless [cen-sît'-les], *a.* Atolondrado, estúpido; sin ideas.
Conceivable [cen-sîv'-a-bl], *a.* Concebible, lo que se puede concebir o imaginar; inteligible, creíble.
Conceivableness [cen-sîv'-a-bl-nes], *s.* Conceptibilidad.
Conceivably [cen-sîv'-a-bli], *adv.* De un modo conceptible.
Conceive [cen-sîv'], *va.* 1. Concebir, formar idea; entender alguna cosa; comprender. 2. Recibir, abrigar en el espíritu ciertas impresiones y afectos. 3. Crear, imaginar, darse cuenta de. 4. Engendrar, originar. 5. Expresar, formular (hablando de palabras).—*vn.* 1. Concebir, imaginar, pensar. 2. Concebir, hacerse preñada la hembra.
Conceiver [cen-sîv'-ẹr], *s.* El que concibe o comprende.
Conceiving [cen-sîv'-ing], *s.* Entendimiento, comprensión, concepción.
†**Concent** [cen-sent'], *s.* Armonía, concento; consonancia.
Concentrate [cen'-sen-trêt o cen-sen'-trêt], *va.* Concentrar; impeler alguna cosa hacia el centro.
Concentration [cen-sen-trê'-shun], *s.* Concentración. *Concentration camp,* Campo de concentración. *Power of concentration,* Poder de concentración.
Concentrator [cen'-sen-trê"-ter], *s.* Concentrador, máquina o aparato para concentrar o separar los minerales.
Concentre [cen-sen'-tẹr], *vn.* Reconcentrarse.—*va.* Concentrar. *Concentred all in self,* Reconcentrado en sí mismo.
Concentric, Concentrical [cen-sen'-tric, al], *a.* Concéntrico.
Concentrically [cen-sen'-tric-al-i], *adv.* Concéntricamente.
Concentricity [cen-sen-tris'-i-ti], *s.* Concentricidad, estado concéntrico.
Concentual [cen-sen'-chu-al], *a.* (Des.) Armonioso.
Concept [cen'-sept], *s.* 1. Concepto, idea general que comprende todos los atributos comunes a los individuos que componen una clase. 2. En acepción menos propia, concepto, idea que concibe o forma la inteligencia.
Conceptacle [cen-sep'-ta-cl], *s.* 1. Receptáculo. 2. Cavidad que contiene esporos reproductores en muchas algas, hongos, helechos, etc.
Conception [cen-sep'-shun], *s.* 1. Concepción, la acción de concebir la hembra. 2. Concepción, idea que se forma; imagen. 3. Concepto, sentimiento. 4. Conocimiento, comprensión.
Conceptive [cen-sep'-tiv], *a.* Conceptible.
Conceptual [cen-sep'-chu-al o tiu-al], *a.* Referente a una concepción o idea general.
Conceptualize [cen-sep'-chu-al-aiz], *va.* Conceptuar.
Concern [cen-sẹrn'], *va.* 1. Concernir, tocar, importar o pertenecer, interesar, incumbir. 2. Mover, excitar alguna de las pasiones humanas; interesar. 3. Inquietar. *To concern one's self about,* Interesarse en. *To be concerned for,* Tomar mucho interés por. *To be much concerned,* Sentir vivamente, en el alma; estar muy interesado. *What does it concern you?* ¿Qué le va o le viene a Vd. en eso? ¿Qué le importa a Vd. eso?
Concern, *s.* 1. Negocio, ocupación. 2. Interés o parte que se tiene en alguna cosa; incumbencia. 3. Empresa; casa de comercio. 4. Importancia, consecuencia. 5. Afecto, amor, cariño. 6. Inquietud, sentimiento, pesar. *That is no concern of mine,* Eso no es cuenta mía, no es de mi incumbencia, o no me concierne.
Concerned [cẹn-sẹrnd'], *a.* 1. Interesado, comprometido. 2. Inquieto, apesarado.
Concernedly [cen-sẹrn'-ed-li], *adv.* Tiernamente, con cariño.
Concerning [cen-sẹrn'-ing], *prep.* Por lo concerniente, tocante a, respecto a.—*s.* (Des.) Negocio; interés.
Concernment [cen-sẹrn'-mẹnt], *s.* Interés, negocio; importancia, momento, entidad; pena, cuidado; pasión; interposición; trato; influencia, relación.
Concert [cen-sẹrt'], *va.* 1. Concertar, acordar, ajustar. 2. Concertar, tomar medida en unión con otros; deliberar de común acuerdo.
Concert [cen'-sẹrt], *s.* 1. Concierto, convenio; comunicación de designios. 2. Concierto de música. *To act in concert with,* Obrar de concierto o de inteligencia con. *Concert pitch, V.* PITCH.
Concertina [cen-sẹr-tî'-na], *s.* Concertina, instrumento músico parecido a un acordeón, pero de forma poligonal.
Concerto [cen-sẹr'-to], *s.* Concierto, composición de música de varios instrumentos, en que uno desempeña la parte principal. (Ital.)
Concession [cen-sesh'-un], *s.* Concesión, gracia, licencia, cesión, privilegio.
Concessionary [cen-sesh'-un-a-ri], *s.* Concesionario, la persona a quien se hace una concesión.—*a.* Otorgado por concesión; de una concesión.
Concessive [cen-ses'-iv], *a.* Que contiene o denota concesión: concedido, implicando concesión o gracia.—*s.* Palabra o cláusula que concede.
Concessively [cen-ses'-iv-li], *adv.* Por vía de concesión.
Concessory [cen-ses'-o-ri], *a.* Concedente, otorgante.
Concetto [cen-set'-o], *s.* Concepto falso o afectado. Es voz italiana, y en plural *concetti.*
Conch [coṇc], *s.* 1. Concha. 2. Caracol marino de gran tamaño que se usa como bocina. 3. (Arq.) Concha, bóveda de concha. 4. *V.* CONCHA.
Concha [coṇ'-ca], *s.* 1. Concha, la cavidad que se halla en el fondo del pabellón de la oreja. 2. Uno de los cornetes o láminas huesosas de la nariz. 3. (Arq.) *V.* CONCH.
†**Conchite** [coṇ'-cait], *s.* Conchita, concha petrificada.
Conchoid [coṇ'-ceid], *s.* Concoide, especie de curva de cuarto grado.
Conchoidal [coṇ-ceid'-al], *a.* Lo que pertenece a la concoide.
Conchologist [cen-cel'-o-jist], *s.* Conquiliólogo, la persona versada en la conquiliología, o estudio y clasificación de las conchas.
Conchology [cen-cel'-o-ji], *s.* (Zool.) Conquiliología, ramo de la zoología que trata de las conchas de los moluscos.
Concierge [cōn-siārzh'], *s. V.* JANITOR. (Fr.)
Conciliate [cen-sil'-i-êt], *va.* Conciliar, grangear, ganar, atraer.
Conciliation [cen-sil-i-ê'-shun], *s.* Conciliación.
Conciliator [cen-sil'-i-ê-tẹr], *s.* Conciliador.
Conciliatory [cen-sil'-i-a-to-ri], *a.* Reconciliatorio.
Concinnity [cen sin'-i-ti], *s.* 1. Aptitud; decencia; propiedad. 2. Armonía; (poco us.) concinidad.
‡**Concinnous** [cen-sin'-us], *a.* Decente; apto; propio; armonioso.
Concise [cen-sais'], *a.* Conciso, breve, compendioso, lacónico, sucinto, corto.
Concisely [cen-sais'-li], *adv.* Concisamente, lacónicamente, en pocas palabras.
Conciseness [cen-sais'-nes], *s.* Concisión, brevedad, laconismo.
Concision [cen-sizh'-un], *s.* 1. Corte, cortadura. 2. Concisión. *V.* CONCISENESS. 3. (Ant. Biblia) Circuncisión.
Concitation [cen-si-tê'-shun], *s.* (Des.) Revuelta, alteración, conmoción.
Conclamation [cen-cla-mê'-shun], *s.* (Poco us.) Clamor, vocería, gritería.
Conclave [cen'-clêv], *s.* 1. Conclave, el lugar en que se hace la elección del Papa, y la asamblea de todos los cardenales para dicha elección. 2. Conclave, junta o congreso de gentes que se reunen para tratar de algún asunto.
Conclude [cẹn-clūd'], *va.* 1. Concluir, inferir por raciocinio. 2. Decidir, determinar. 3. Concluir, terminar, acabar. 4. Restringir, coartar; en derecho, y por lo regular en forma pasiva. 5. (Ant.) Incluir.—*vn.* 1. Finalizar. 2. Argumentar, juzgar, decidir.
Concluder [cen-clūd'-ẹr], *s.* El que determina o decide.
Concludible [cen-clū'-di-bl], *a.* Determinable.
Concludingly [cen-clūd'-ing-li], *adv.* Con evidencia incontrovertible concluyentemente.

Conclusion [con-clū'-zhun], *s.* 1. Conclusión, determinación. 2. Terminación, término, fin o remate de alguna cosa, desenlace, catástrofe. 3. Consecuencia sacada de las premisas.

Conclusive [con-clū'-siv], *a.* Concluyente, decisivo, final, conclusivo.

Conclusively [con-clū'-siv-li], *a.* Concluyentemente.

Conclusiveness [con-clū'-siv-nes], *s.* Resolución o determinación.

Conclusory [cǫn-clū'-so-ri], *a.* *V.* CONCLUSIVE.

Concoct [cǫn-coct'], *va.* 1. Preparar algo mezclando sus ingredientes, como una bebida, una sopa, etc. 2. (Fig.) Trazar, proyectar, urdir. 3. (Des.) Cocer, digerir, purificar con fuego o calor; madurar.

Concoction [cǫn-coc'-shun], *s.* 1. La acción y efecto de mezclar ingredientes, mezcla. 2. Maquinación, trama; trazo.

Concoctive [cǫn-coc'-tiv], *a.* Perteneciente a una mezcla, o un trazo.

Concomitance, Concomitancy [cǫn-com'-i-tans, i], *s.* Concomitancia, concurrencia de una cosa con otra.

Concomitant [con-com'-i-tant], *a.* Concomitante.—*s.* Compañero; persona o cosa concomitante.

Concomitantly [con-com'-i-tant-li], *adv.* Concomitantemente, en compañía de otros.

Concord [coṇ'-cērd], *s.* 1. Concordia, unión. 2. Concordia, paz, unión, armonía, buena inteligencia. 3. Concordancia, armonía en la música. 4. (For.) Pacto, convención, convenio. 5. (Gram.) Concordancia, correspondencia de las palabras según las reglas gramaticales.

Concordal [con-cērd'-al], *a.* (Gram.) Relativo a la concordancia.

Concordance [con-cērd'-ans], *s.* 1. Concordancia, índice alfabético de todas las palabras de la Biblia, con citas de los lugares en que se hallan, para buscar y cotejar lo que convenga. 2. Concordancia, conformidad, unión.

Concordant [con-cērd'-ant], *a.* Concordante, consonante, conforme.—*s.* Correspondiente.

Concordantly [con-cērd'-ant-li], *adv.* Concordemente, de común acuerdo.

Concordat [con-cēr'-dat], *s.* Concordato, el tratado o convenio que hace el gobierno de un Estado con la Santa Sede, acerca de asuntos eclesiásticos.

Concorporate [con-cēr'-po-rêt], *va.* (Des.) Incorporar, mezclar.—*vn.* Unirse, incorporarse.

Concourse [coṇ'-cōrs], *s.* 1. Concurso, confluencia, concurrencia. 2. Junta, el conjunto de personas unidas, multitud, gentío, muchedumbre.

¿**Concrement** [coṇ'-crę-męnt], *s.* Concremento; masa formada por concreción.

Concresce [con-cres'], *vn.* Unirse, aficionarse; estar estrechamente unidos, juntarse en una masa.

Concrescence [con-cres'-ens], *s.* Concrescencia, crecimiento.

Concrescible [con-cres'-i-bl], *a.* Concrescible, susceptible de hacerse concreto; condensable.

Concrescive [con-cres'-iv], *a.* Uniéndose, que forma estrecha unión.

Concrete [con-crīt'], *vn.* Cuajar, unirse o juntarse en una masa.—*va.* 1. Concretar, unir y juntar unas cosas con otras formando de ellas una masa. 2. Poner en forma concreta. 3. Cubrir con cemento o argamasa.

Concrete [con'-crīt], *a.* 1. Concreto; cuajado, formado en una masa por crecimiento o unión. 2. Concreto, que existe actualmente en el sujeto; opuesto a abstracto. 3. Hecho de hormigón, hecho de cemento (Sp. Am.).—*s.* 1. Concreción. 2. Hormigón, concreto (Sp. Am.). 3. Lo concreto. *Concrete mixer*, Hormigonera. *Concrete number*, Número concreto. *Concrete paint*, Pintura para hormigón. *Reinforced concrete*, Hormigón armado.

Concretely [con-crīt'-li], *adv.* Concretamente.

Concreteness [con-crīt'-nes], *s.* Calidad de lo concreto.

Concretion [con-crī'-shun], *s.* 1. Concreción, agregado de diversas partículas en una masa. 2. (Geol.) Agregación de materia inorgánica de nudillo o disco, alrededor de un centro llamado núcleo. 3. (Med.) Concreción, cálculo.

Concretionary [con-crī'-shun-ę-ri], *a.* Perteneciente a una concreción.

Concretive [con-crī'-tiv], *a.* Formando concreciones.

Concubinage [con-kiū'-bi-nêj], *s.* Concubinato, amancebamiento.

Concubine [coṇ'-kiu-bain], *sf.* Concubina.

Concupiscence [con-kiū'-pi-sens], *s.* Concupiscencia, apetito desordenado de placeres deshonestos.

Concupiscent [con-kiū'-pi-sent], *a.* Libidinoso, lascivo.

Concupiscible [con-kiu-pis'-i-bl], *a.* (Poco us.) Concupiscible, libidinoso.

Concur [con-cūr'], *vn.* 1. Concurrir, encontrarse en un mismo punto. 2. Juntarse, obrar juntamente con otros, adunarse. 3. Convenir, conformarse, estar de acuerdo.

Concurrence o **Concurrency** [con-cūr'-ens, i], *s.* 1. Concurrencia, combinación, acuerdo. 2. Concurrencia, auxilio, asistencia, ayuda. 3. Concurrencia, pretensión recíproca de dos o más personas a un mismo empleo u otra cosa a que tienen igual derecho. 4. Consentimiento, relación, aprobación.

Concurrent [con-cur'-ent], *a.* Concurrente; concomitante, coexistente.

Concurrently [con-cur'-ent-li], *adv.* Concurrentemente.

¿**Concuss** [con-cus'], *va.* 1. Afectar o dañar (el cerebro) por concusión. 2. Sacudir, agitar.

Concussion [con-cush'-un], *s.* 1. Concusión, conmoción, impulso. ¿2. Peculado, cohecho.

Concussive [con-cus'-iv], *a.* Lo que conmueve o sacude violentamente.

Cond [cond], *va.* (Des. Mar.) Guiar o gobernar un bajel. *V.* CON. (Mar.)

Condemn [con-dem'], *va.* 1. Desaprobar, censurar, culpar, vituperar, reprobar, afear. 2. Condenar, sentenciar a una pena. 3. Prohibir oficialmente el uso de algo o el consumo de determinados comestibles o bebidas. 4. Ordenar judicialmente la toma de posesión de algo para el uso público: declarar confiscado; expropiar por motivos de utilidad pública.

Condemnable [con-dem'-na-bl], *a.* Culpable, censurable, vituperable, condenable.

Condemnation [con-dem-nê'-shun], *s.* Condenación, acción y efecto de condenar o condenarse.

Condemnatory [con-dem'-na-to-ri], *a.* Condenatorio, que contiene censura o reprensión; que expresa sentencia o condenación.

Condemner [con-dem'-nęr], *s.* Condenador.

Condensable [con-den'-sa-bl], *a.* Condensable.

Condensate [con-den'-sêt], *va.* y *vn.* (¿ o des.) Condensar, condensarse. *V.* CONDENSE.

¿**Condensate**, *a.* Condensado, comprimido, espesado.

Condensation [con-den-sê'-shun], *s.* Condensación.

Condensative [con-den'-sa-tiv], *a.* Lo que tiene poder de condensar.

Condense [con-dens'], *va.* 1. Condensar, comprimir. 2. Hacer más denso, espeso o compacto, consolidar. 3. Abreviar, epitomar.—*vn.* Condensarse, comprimirse, espesarse.

Condensed [con-densd'], *a.* Condensado. *Condensed milk*, Leche condensada.

Condenser [con-den'-sęr], *s.* Condensador; cualquier invento, máquina o aparato para condensar. V. gr. 1. Recipiente de una máquina de vapor de condensación. 2. Recipiente de aire de una bomba. 3. Lente o lentes para concentrar los rayos de luz, en un microscopio, linterna óptica, faro, etc. 4. Aparato para acumular electricidad. 5. Aparato para eliminar las adulteraciones del gas del alumbrado por medio de la condensación. *Bull's-eye condenser*, Lente gruesa plano-convexa para el microscopio.

Condenser pipe [con-den'-ser paip], *s.* Tubo de condensador.

Condensing [con-den'-sing], *pa.* Condensante. *Condensing engine*, Máquina de condensación.

Condensity [con-den'-si-ti], *s.* (Ant.) Densidad.

Conder [con'-dęr], *s.* El que avisa desde la costa a los pescadores de arenques el camino que lleva el cardume.

Condescend [con-dę-send'], *vn.* 1. Condescender, hacer más de lo que requiere la justicia, consentir. 2. Acomodarse a la voluntad de otro, someterse.

Condescendence [con-dę-sen'-dens], **Condescension** [con-dę-sen'-shun], *s.* Condescendencia.

Condescending [con-dę-send'-ing], *s.* Condescendencia.

Condescendingly [con-dę-send'-ing-li], *adv.* Cortésmente, condescendientemente.

Condign [con-dain'], *a.* Condigno, merecido: se dice del castigo.

Condignity [con-dig'-ni-ti] (Teolo.), **Condignness** [con-dain'-nes], *s.* Condignidad, merecimiento.

Condignly [con-dain'-li], *adv.* Merecidamente.

Condiment [con'-di-męnt], *s.* Condimento, aderezo, guiso, salsa.

¿**Condisciple** [con-di-sai'-pl], *s.* Condiscípulo, compañero, discípulo de un mismo maestro.

Condite [con-dait'], *va.* (Des.) Escabechar, adobar, condimentar, sazonar.

Condition [con-dish'-un], *s.* 1. Condición, cualidad. 2. Condición, natural o genio de los hombres. 3. Condición, situación, estado, circunstancias; la naturaleza o constitución de las cosas. 4. Condición, rango, esfera, calidad del nacimiento o estado de alguno. 5. Condicion, artículo o cláusula de alguna escritura. 6. Requisito necesario, dato necesario, condición *sine qua non.*

Condition, *va.* 1. Condicionar. 2. Requerir antes, constituir la condición de algo. 3. Estipular, pactar.

Conditional [cen-dish'-un-al], *a.* Condicional, lo que incluye y lleva consigo alguna condición o requisito; no absoluto.—*s.* Palabra, cláusula, etc., significativa de condición.

Conditionality [cen-dish-un-al'-i-ti], *s.* Limitación.

Conditionally [cen-dish'-un-al-i], *adv.* Condicionalmente.

Conditionary [cen-dish'-un-ẹ-ri], *a.* Estipulado, convenido, pactado.

Conditionate [cen-dish'-un-ēt], *va.* Calificar, regular.

Conditionate, *a.* Condicionado, establecido con alguna condición.

Conditioned [cen-dish'-und], *a.* Acondicionado, en buen o mal estado, de buena o mala condición.

Condolatory [cen-dō'-la-to-ri], *a.* Que expresa pésame o duelo.

Condole [cen-dōl'], *vn.* Condolerse, dolerse con otro, simpatizar con, dar el pésame.—*va.* (Poco us.) Lamentar con otro.

Condolence [cen-dō'-lens], *s.* 1. Compasión, lástima, dolor o pena por la aflicción ajena. 2. El pésame que se da a otro por haber perdido algún pariente o persona querida.

Condoler [cen-dō'-lẹr], *s.* El que da el pésame a otro.

Condominium [cen-do-min'-i-um], *s.* Condominio, cooperativa, propiedad en condominio, propiedad horizontal.

Condonation, **Condonement** [cen-do-né'-shun, cen-dōn'-mẹnt], *s.* Condonación, perdón, indulto.

Condone [cen-dōn'], *va.* Condonar, perdonar o remitir alguna pena.

Condor [cen'-der], *s.* Cóndor, especie de buitre grande que habita en los Andes.

Conduce [cen-diūs'], *vn.* Conducir, convenir, ser a propósito para el logro de alguna cosa (seguido de la preposición *to*).—*va.* (Des.) Conducir, efectuar.

Conducible [cen-diū'-si-bl], *a.* Conducente, útil, ventajoso.

Conducibleness [cen-diū'-si-bl-nès], **Conduciveness** [cen-diū'-siv-nes], *s.* La calidad de conducir o ser a propósito para el logro de alguna cosa; utilidad, conducencia.

Conducibly [cen-diū'-si-bli], *adv.* Conducentemente.

Conducive [cen-diū'-siv], *a.* Conducente, oportuno, útil, conveniente.

Conduct [cen'-duct], *s.* 1. Conducta, manejo, gobierno, economía. 2. Conducción de tropas. 3. Conducta o convoy. 4. Conducta, proceder, porte, manera como uno dirige su vida y acciones.

Conduct [cen-duct'], *va.* 1. Conducir, guiar, dirigir, acompañar. 2. Dirigir, manejar. 3. Mandar un ejército.

Conductible [cen-duct'-i-bl], *a.* Conductible, que se puede conducir.

Conduction [cen-duc'-shun], *s.* Transmisión del sonido, el calórico o la electricidad por medio de un cuerpo conductor, sin movimiento de dicho cuerpo; conducción en general.

Conductive [cen-duct'-iv], *a.* 1. Conductivo, que tiene la facultad de conducir. 2. (Elec.) Que procede por conducción.

Conductivity [cen-duc-tiv'-i-ti], *s.* Conductividad, virtud de conducir; conductibilidad.

Conductor [cen-duc'-tẹr], *s.* 1. Conductor. 2. Jefe o general de un ejército. 3. Conductor, guía, director. 4. (E. U.) Conductor de un tren o de un carro de ferrocarril urbano o tranvía. *Cf.* GUARD. 5. Ductor; instrumento de cirugía. 6. Conductor eléctrico.

Conductress [cen-duc'-tres], *sf.* Conductora.

Conduit [cen'-dit], *s.* 1. Conducto, encañado. 2. Caño, el tubo o cañón por el cual se saca el agua de una fuente.

Conduplicate [cen-diū'-pli-kêt], *va.* Duplicar, replegar.—*a.* Duplicado, replegado.

Conduplication [cen-du-pli-ké'-shun], *s.* Duplicación, duplicado.

Condyle [cen'-dil], *s.* (Anat.) Cóndilo, nudillo de las articulaciones.

Condyloma [cen-di-lō'-ma], *s.* (Med.) Condiloma, excrecencia como una verruga que suele formarse cerca del ano o de los órganos genitales de uno y otro sexo.

Cone [cōn], *s.* 1. Cono, cuerpo sólido que tiene un círculo por base y termina por la parte superior en vértice o punta. 2. Piña, el fruto y simiente de algunas especies de pinos. 3. Cima simétrica de una montaña. *Cone wheel*, Rueda cónica. *Friction cone*, Cono de fricción. *Cone-shaped*, Cónico, en forma de cono.

Coney, *s.* *V.* CONY.

Confab [cen'-fab], *s.* (Fam.) Abreviatura de *confabulation.*

Confabulate [cen-fab'-yu-lêt], *vn.* Confabular, hablar dos o más personas juntas; platicar, hablar familiarmente.

Confabulation [cen-fab-yu-lé'-shun], *s.* Confabulación, plática.

Confabulatory [cen-fab'-yu-la-to-ri], *a.* Lo que pertenece a la confabulación.

Confarreation [cen-far-ẹ-é'-shun], *s.* Confarreación, una de las formas del matrimonio entre los antiguos romanos.

Confate [con-fêt'], *va.* (Poco usado y solamente en forma pasiva) Decretado, determinado al mismo tiempo.

†**Confect** [cen-fect'], *va.* 1. Confitar. 2. Preparar; construir.

Confect [cen'-fect], *s.* Confitura, dulce, confite.

Confection [cen-fec'-shun], *s.* Confitura, confección, dulce; la fruta que está confitada.

Confectionary [cen-fec'-shun-ẹ-ri], *a.* Perteneciente a los confites, o parecido a ellos.

Confectioner [cen-fec'-shun-ẹr], *s.* 1. Confitero, el que tiene por oficio vender y hacer dulces y confituras. 2. Confeccionador.

Confectionery [cen-fec'-shun-er-i], *s.* 1. Confitura, confite, dulce. 2. Confitería, tienda de confitero.

Confederacy [cen-fed'-ẹr-a-si], **Confederation** [cen-fed-ẹr-é'-shun], *s.* Confederación, alianza, liga, unión; cábala.

Confederate [cen-fed'-ẹr-êt], *va.* Confederar, unir, formar una liga o confederación.—*vn.* Confederarse, unirse, aliarse.

Confederate, *a.* y *s.* Confederado, aliado, ligado.

Confer [cẹn-fẹr'], *vn.* Conferencia, conferir, hablar o tratar con otro sobre algún asunto.—*va.* 1. Conferir, comparar, confrontar, cotejar. 2. Conferir; dar. 3. Conducir, convenir, ser conducente o conveniente.

Conference [cen'-fẹr-ens], *s.* 1. Conferencia, conversación formal en que se trata algún asunto o negocio. 2. Cuerpo organizado de predicadores y legos; y en la Iglesia católica, asamblea de clérigos para discutir cuestiones teológicas.

Conferrable [cen-fẹr'-a-bl], *a.* Que puede ser conferido.

Conferrer [cẹn-fẹr'-ẹr], *s.* 1. Conferidor, colador. 2. Regalador, el que regala.

Conferring [cen-fẹr'-ing], *s.* Colación, acción de conferir.

Conferva [cen-fẹr'-va], *s.* (Bot.) Conferva, el tejido de filamentos verdes que sobrenadan en el agua estancada; género de algas, terrestres o de agua dulce.

Confervoid [cen-fẹr'-veid], *a.* Parecido a una conferva.

Confess [cen-fes'], *va.* 1. Confesar, manifestar algún delito; reconocer y declarar una falta. 2. Confesar, oir en confesión, oir las culpas del penitente. 3. Declarar abiertamente; reconocer; probar. *I must confess*, Debo decir.—*vn.* Confesarse.

Confessant, †**Confessary** [cen-fes'-ant, cen-fes'-a-ri], *s.* 1. El que confiesa o hace una confesión. 2. Penitente, el que se confiesa.

Confessed [cen-fest'], *a.* 1. Incontestable, indudable, evidente. 2. Confesado, declarado, manifiesto.

Confessedly [cen-fes'-ed-li], *adv.* 1. Conocidamente, cierta e infaliblemente, sin contradicción. 2. Manifiestamente, por confesión propia.

Confession [cen-fesh'-un], *s.* 1. Confesión, declaración de algún delito. 2. Confesión, profesión de fe. 3. Confesión sacramental. 4. Reconocimiento de una falta.

Confessional [cen-fesh'-un-al], **Confessionary** [cen-fesh'-un-a-ri], *s.* Confesonario, el lugar destinado para oir la confesión sacramental.

Confessionary, *a.* Lo que pertenece a la confesión.

Confessionist [cen-fesh'-un-ist], *s.* (Poco us.) El que hace una profesión de fe.

Confessor [cen-fes'-ẹr], *s.* 1. Confesor, el que declara su fe. 2. Confesor, el sacerdote que oye en confesión. 3. Penitente; confeso, el que confiesa sus delitos.

Confest [cen-fest'], *a.* (Ant. o poét.) Confesado, manifiesto, reconocido por todos. *V.* CONFESSED.

Confetti [cen-fet'-i], *s.* Confeti.

Confidant [cen'-fi-dant], *s.* Confidente, amigo íntimo a quien se confían los secretos.

Confide [cen-faid'], *vn.* Confiar, fiarse, entregarse o referirse a la fidelidad de otro.—*va.* Confiar, depositar, decir o dar a guardar a otro alguna cosa sin otra seguridad que la buena fe.

Confidence [cen'-fi-dens], *s.* 1. Confianza, seguridad fundada en la discreción o probidad de otro. 2. Confianza, ánimo, aliento y valor. 3. Atrevimiento; presunción. 4. Conversación particular; secreto.

Confident [cen'-fi-dent], *a.* 1. Cierto, seguro. 2. Confiado, terco, dogmático. 3. (Ant.) Descarado, atrevido, resuelto.—*s.* Confidente, a quien se confía un secreto.

Confidential [con-fi-den'-shal], *a.* 1. Reservado, secreto, confidencial. 2. Seguro; de confianza, íntimo.

Confidently [con'-fi-dent-li], *adv.* Confidentemente, confidencialmente, secretamente.

Confidentness [con'-fi-dent-nes], *s.* (Poco us.) Confianza, presunción, atrevimiento.

Confider [con-faid'-ẹr], *s.* El que confía.

Confiding [con-faid'-ing], *a.* Fiel, seguro.

Configurate [con-fig'-yu-rêt], *va.* (Poco us.) Configurar, dar forma o figura.—*vn.* Ser congruo o apto.

Configuration [con-fig-yu-ré'-shun], *s.* 1. Configuración, figura, forma exterior. 2. (Astr.) Aspecto, posición relativa de los planetas.

Configure [con-fig'-yur], *va.* (Poco us.) Configurar, dar forma o figura.

Confinable [con-fain'-a-bl], *a.* Limitable, lo que se puede limitar.

Confine [con'-fain], *s.* Confín, límite, término, frontera o línea que divide un territorio de otro.

Confine [con-fain'], *vn.* Confinar, lindar, estar contiguo o inmediato a otro territorio.—*va.* 1. Limitar, poner límite a alguna cosa. 2. Encerrar, aprisionar, poner preso. 3. Restringir, estrechar, reducir. *He is confined to his bed,* No puede dejar la cama, o está enfermo en cama. *To be confined,* Estar de parto.

Confineless [con-fain'-les], *a.* Ilimitado.

Confinement [con-fain'-mẹnt], *s.* 1. Prisión, encierro, destierro, cautividad. 2. Estreñimiento, restricción dentro de determinados límites; abstención de salir por causa de enfermedad. 3. Parto; sobreparto, tiempo que la parida guarda cama.

Confiner [con-fain'-ẹr], *s.* 1. La persona o cosa que limita, encierra, o restringe. 2. (Des.) Vecino; la cosa que está confinante o rayando con otra.

Confinity [con-fin'-i-ti], *s.* (Poco us.) Cercanía, comarca, proximidad, inmediación.

Confirm [con-fẹrm'], *va.* 1. Confirmar, comprobar, corroborar. 2. Confirmar, administrar la confirmación. 3. Establecer; revalidar, ratificar. 4. Confirmar, fortificar, dar mayor firmeza y seguridad.

Confirmable [con-fẹrm'-a-bl], *a.* Capaz de ser confirmado o ratificado.

Confirmation [con-fẹr-mé'-shun], *s.* 1. Confirmación, la acción de confirmar o corroborar la verdad de una cosa; prueba, testimonio convincente. 2. Confirmación, la acción de confirmar por la imposición de manos del obispo. 3. Revalidación.

Confirmative [con-fẹrm'-a-tiv], *a.* Confirmativo.

Confirmator [con-fẹr-mé'-ter], *s.* (Poco us.) Confirmador.

Confirmatory [con-fẹrm'-a-to-ri], *a.* Confirmativo o confirmatorio.

Confirmed [con-fẹrmd'], *a.* y *pp.* 1. Comprobado, corroborado; ratificado. 2. Establecido, demostrado. 3. Inveterado, consumado.

Confirmedness [con-fẹrm'-ed-nes], *s.* Certeza, firmeza.

Confirmer [con-fẹrm'-ẹr], *s.* Confirmador, establecedor.

Confirmingly [con-fẹrm'-ing-li], *adv.* Confirmativamente.

Confiscable [con-fis'-ca-bl], *a.* Confiscable, lo que puede ser confiscado.

Confiscate [con'-fis-kêt], *va.* Confiscar, privar de sus bienes a algún reo y aplicarlos al fisco.

Confiscate, Confiscated [con-fis'-kêt], ed], *a.* Confiscado, entregado al fisco.

Confiscation [con-fis-ké'-shun], *s.* Confiscación, la adjudicación de los bienes de un reo al fisco.

Confiscator [con'-fis-kê-ter], *s.* Confiscador.

Confiscatory [con-fis'-ca-to-ri], *a.* Lo que confisca.

Confiture [con'-fi-chur], *s.* Confitura, dulce. (Fr.)

‖**Confix** [con-fics'], *va.* Atar, ligar, enclavar una cosa con otra.

†**Confixure** [con-fic'-shur], *s.* Atadura, aseguramiento.

Conflagrant [con-flé'-grant], *a.* Incendiado.

Conflagration [con-fla-gré'-shun], *s.* Conflagración, fuego o incendio general.

Conflate [con-flêt'], *va.* Combinar varias lecciones, lecturas o párrafos para componer con ellos una sola lección; úsase en forma pasiva.

Conflation [con-flé'-shun], *s.* 1. Combinación de dos lecciones variantes para formar una nueva lección. 2. (Poco us.) Toque de muchos instrumentos de viento a un tiempo.

Conflict [con-flict'], *vn.* Luchar, contender, combatir; estar en oposición; chocar, entrechocar.

Conflict [con'-flict], *s.* 1. Conflicto, encuentro violento de una cosa con otra; combate, pelea, contienda. 2. Conflicto, combate o angustia de ánimo, pena, dolor, pesar.

Confluence [con'-flu-ens], *s.* 1. Confluencia, el lugar o sitio en que un río se une con otro. 2. Concurso, concurrencia de muchas personas o cosas.

Confluent [con'-flu-ent], *a.* 1. Confluente, que confluye o se junta. 2. Confluente; dícese de la erupción simultánea de granos, pústulas, etc. *Confluent smallpox,* Viruela confluente.—*s.* Corriente que se une con otra; confluencia de un río.

Conflux [con'-flucs], *s.* Confluencia de varios ríos; concurso o concurrencia de muchas personas o cosas.

Confocal [con-fō'-cal], *a.* Que tiene foco o focos comunes.

Conform [con-fōrm'], *va.* Conformar, hacer una cosa conforme o semejante; ajustar, concordar.—*vn.* 1. Conformarse, allanarse, cumplir con algún rito, ceremonia, uso o costumbre. 2. Conformarse, ceder, someterse.

Conformability, Conformableness [con-fōrm-a-bil'-i-ti, bl-nes], *s.* Conformidad, cualidad o estado de lo que es conforme, correspondiente, consistente, armonioso o semejante.

†**Conform, Conformable** [con-fōrm'-a-bl], *a.* Conforme, semejante; conveniente, proporcionado; dócil, obsequioso.

Conformably [con-fōrm'-a-bli], *adv.* Conformemente.

Conformation [con-fer-mé'-shun], *s.* Conformación, figura, arreglo.

Conformer [con-fōrm'-ẹr], *s.* El que conforma.

Conformist [con-fōrm'-ist], *s.* 1. Conformista, el que se conforma con el culto autorizado por las leyes de Inglaterra o con los ritos de la Iglesia anglicana. 2. El que se somete.

Conformity [con-fōrm'-i-ti], *s.* Conformidad, consistencia, conveniencia, igualdad.

Confound [con-faund'], *va.* 1. Confundir. 2. Enredar, embrollar; turbar, consternar. 3. (Ant.) Atolondrar, atontar; desconcertar, avergonzar. 4. (Des.) Destruir, arruinar.

Confounded [con-faund'-ed], *a.* Maldito, abominable, detestable, aborrecible, odioso, enorme.

Confoundedly [con-faund'-ed-li], *adv.* Detestablemente, horriblemente.

Confoundedness [con-faund'-ed-nes], *s.* Abatimiento, confusión.

Confounder [con-faund'-ẹr], *s.* 1. Enredador. 2. Exterminador, desolador.

Confraternity [con-fra-tẹr'-ni-ti], *s.* 1. Cofradía, confraternidad, hermandad, sociedad. 2. Confraternidad, relaciones amistosas entre los individuos de una sociedad.

Confrère [cōñ-frār'], *s.* Compañero, colega. (Gal.)

Confrication [con-fri-ké'-shun], *s.* (Des.) Confricación, acción y efecto de estregar.

Confront [con-frunt'], *va.* 1. Confrontar, afrontar, hacer frente a. 2. Carear. 3. Cotejar o comparar una cosa con otra.

Confrontation [con-frun-té'-shun], *s.* Confrontación, careo.

Confucian [con-fiū'-shan], *a.* Relativo a Confucio, el sabio chino.

Confuse [con-fiūz'], *va.* 1. Confundir, desconcertar, desordenar; obscurecer. 2. Inquietar, atropellar.

Confused [con-fiūzd'], *a.* Confuso, confundido, desorientado, perplejo.

Confusedly [con-fiūz'-ed-li], *adv.* Confusamente, atropelladamente.

Confusedness [con-fiūz'-ed-nes], *s.* Atropellamiento, confusión, desorden.

Confusion [con-fiū'-zhun], *s.* 1. Confusión, desorden, tumulto, caos, embarazo. 2. Perturbación, vergüenza. 3. (Des.) Ruina, destrucción.

Confutable [con-fiūt'-a-bl], *a.* Refutable.

Confutant [con-fiūt'-ant], *s.* Refutador.

Confutation [con-flu-té'-shun], *s.* Confutación, refutación.

Confute [con-fiūt'], *va.* Confutar, impugnar, refutar.

Conga [con'-ga], *s.* Conga, baile y ritmo afro-cubanos.

Congé [cōñ-zhé'], *s.* Salutación, reverencia; el acto de despedir o despedirse, despedida. (Fr.)

Congé-d'Elire [cōñ-zhé'-dé-lír'], *s.* (Hist. de Ingl.) Real permiso que se daba al deán y cabildo *en sede vacante* para elegir obispo.

Congeal [con-jīl'], *va.* 1. Congelar, helar o cuajar alguna cosa líquida. 2. Helar, dejar a uno suspenso, pasmarle, sobrecogerle.—*vn.* Congelarse, helarse, cuajarse alguna cosa líquida.

Congealable [con-jīl'-a-bl], *a.* Congelable, que es capaz de congelarse.

Congealment [con-jīl'-mẹnt], *s.* Congelación.

Congee [con'-jī], *vn.* Despedirse cortésmente; saludar.

Congee [con'-jī], **Conjee**, *s.* (Ind.) Atole o gachas de arroz, maíz, etc.

Congelation [con-jẹ-lé'-shun], *s.* Congelación.

Congener [con'-jẹ-nẹr], **Congeneric** [con-jẹ-nẹr'-ic], ‖**Congenerous** [con-jen'-ẹr-us], *a.* Congénere, idéntico, de la misma especie o género; congenérico.

¿Congeneracy [cen-jen'-ẹr-a-si], **Congenerousness** [cen-jen'-ẹr-us-nes], *s.* Descendencia de un mismo origen, congeneración.

Congenetic [cen-jẹ-net'-ic], *a.* Semejante en origen.

Congenial [cen-jín'-yal], *a.* 1. Congenial, análogo, de especie o naturaleza semejante, cognado. 2. Congenial, de igual genio o inclinaciones. 3. Simpático.

Congeniality [cen-jín-yal'-i-ti], **Congenialness** [cen-jín'-yal-nes], *s.* Semejanza de genio.

Congenital [cen-jen'-it-al], *a.* Congénito, que nace con el individuo o existe desde el nacimiento.

Conger, Conger-eel [ceng'-gẹr, íl''], *s.* Congrio, pescado de mar.

Congeries [cen-jí'-ri-íz], *s.* Congerie, cúmulo o montón de cosas.

Congest [cen-jest'], *vn.* Hacerse obstruido, acumular, amontonar.

Conjested [cen-jest'-ed], *pa.* (Med.) 1. Congestionado, obstruido por sangre o humores. 2. (Fig.) Apretado, apiñado, obstruido por la muchedumbre como sucede en las calles.

Congestible [cen-jest'-i-bl], *a.* Acumulable, amontonable.

Congestion [cen-jes'-chun], *s.* Congestión.

Congestive [cen-jes'-tiv], *a.* (Med.) Perteneciente a la congestión. *Congestive chill*, Escalofrío congestivo.

Congiary [cen'-ji-ẹ-ri], *s.* Congiario, don que solían distribuir al pueblo los emperadores romanos.

Conglobate [cen-glō'-bêt o cen'-glo-bêt], *a.* Conglobado, amontonado en forma esférica más o menos perfecta.

Conglobate, *va.* Conglobar, formar en figura de globo.

Conglobately [cen-glō'-bêt-li], *adv.* Conglobosamente.

Conglobation [cen-glo-bé'-shun], *s.* Conglobación, globo.

Conglobulate [cen-gleb'-yu-lêt], *vn.* Conglobarse.

Conglomerate [cen-glem'-ẹr-êt], *va.* Conglomerar, aglomerar, redondear.

Conglomerate, *a.* Conglomerado; congregado, redondeado.—*s.* 1. Masa o colección de substancias heterogéneas; colección de cosas o de ideas, confusamente acumuladas. 2. Roca compuesta de guijarros redondeados y desgastados por las aguas; llámase también *puddingstone*.

Conglomeration [cen-glem-ẹr-é'-shun], *s.* 1. Conglomeración. 2. Entretejedura, mezcla.

Conglomeritic, Conglomeratic [cen-glem-ẹr-it'-ic], *a.* De una roca conglomerada o parecido á ella; formado por conglomeración.

Conglutinate [cen-glū'-ti-nêt], *va.* y *vn.* Conglutinar; conglutinarse; pegarse.

Conglutinate, *a.* Conglutinado, unido por medio de una substancia viscosa.

Conglutination [cen-glū-ti-né'-shun], *s.* Conglutinación.

Conglutinative [cen-glu'-ti-nê-tiv], *a.* Conglutinativo, que tiene virtud de conglutinar.

Conglutinator [cen-glū'-ti-nê-tẹr], *s.* Conglutinador, agente medicinal que sirve para unir o cerrar los bordes de las heridas.

Congratulant [cen-grat'-yu-lant], *a.* Congratulatorio.

Congratulant [cen-grat'-yu-lant], *a.* Congratulorio, que expresa congratulación.

Congratulate [cen-grat'-yu-lêt], *va.* Congratular, felicitar.—*vn.* (Des.) Congratularse, alegrarse.

Congratulation [cen-grat-yu-lé'-shun], *s.* Congratulación; felicitación.

Congratulator [cen-grat-yu-lé'-tẹr], *s.* Congratulador; congraciador.

Congratulatory [cen-grat'-yu-la-to-ri], *a.* Congratulatorio, que expresa congratulación.

Congregate [ceṇ'-grẹ-gêt], *va.* Congregar, convocar, reunir—*vn.* Juntarse.

Congregate, *a.* Agregado, reunido.

Congregation [ceṇ-grẹ-gé'-shun], *s.* 1. Congregación, concurso, auditorio, asamblea, reunión. 2. Agregado, colección, masa.

Congregational [ceṇ-grẹ-gé'-shun-al], *a.* 1. Lo que pertenece á alguna congregación o asamblea de cristianos. 2. Congregacional, perteneciente a la denominación protestante del congregacionalismo o a los congregacionalistas.

Congregationalism [ceṇ-grẹ-gé'-shun-al-izm], *s.* 1. Congregacionalismo, la forma de gobierno eclesiástico que reconoce como suprema la autoridad de la congregación local dentro de su jurisdicción. 2. Sistema de creencia y práctica de la secta congregacionalista.

Congregationalist [ceṇ-grẹ-gé'-shun-al-ist], *s.* Partidario del congregacionalismo; miembro de la Iglesia congregacionalista.

Congress [ceṇ'-gres], *s.* 1. Congreso, junta de soberanos o ministros para tratar de asuntos comunes. 2. Congreso, cámara de los diputados. En los Estados Unidos del Norte, Cámara de Representantes y Senado, el cuerpo legislativo nacional. 3. Conferencia, entrevista, congreso de varias personas; como acepción especial, ayuntamiento de hombre y mujer.

Congression [ceṇ-gresh'-un], *s.* (Poco us.) Compañía, asamblea.

Congressional [cen-gresh'-un-al], *a.* Del congreso, relativo a un congreso, congresional. *Congressional debates*, Debates del congreso.

Congressive [cen-gres'-iv], *a.* Juntado, unido, pegado.

Congressman [ceṇ'gres-man], *s.* Miembro del Congreso de los Estados Unidos; especialmente uno de los diputados.

Congruence, Congruency [ceṇ'-gru-ens, i], **Congruity** [cen-grū'-i-ti], *s.* Congruencia, congruidad, conformidad.

Congruent [ceṇ'-grū-ent], *a.* Congruente, conveniente, conforme.

Congruous [ceṇ'-gru-us], *a.* Congruo, apto, proporcionado.

Congruously [ceṇ'-gru-us-li], *adv.* Congruentemente.

Conic, Conical [cen'-ic, al], *a.* Cónico.

Conically [cen'-ic-al-i], *adv.* En forma cónica.

Conicalness [cen'-ic-al-nes], *s.* Conicidad, calidad de cónico.

Conic section [cen'-ic sec'-shun], *s.* (Geom.) Sección cónica. *Conics*, La ciencia de medir conos y sus curvas.

Conifer [cen'-i-fẹr], *s.* Conífero, el árbol que produce fruto en forma de cono.

Coniferæ [co-nif'-ẹ-rí], *s. pl.* Coníferas, orden de plantas resinosas, siempre verdes por lo común, que dan el fruto en forma de cono; v. g. el pino, el cedro, el abeto, etc.

Coniferous [co-nif'-er-us], *a.* Conífero, que produce pericarpos de forma cónica.

Coniform [cō'-ni-fōrm], *a.* Coniforme, cónico.

Conirostral [cō-ni-res'-tral], *a.* Conirrostra, ave de pico cónico.

Conium [co-nai'-um], *s.* Cicuta, planta venenosa de las umbelíferas.

Conjecturable [cen-jec'-chur-a-bl], *a.* Conjeturable.

Conjectural [cen-jec'-chur-al], *a.* Conjetural.

Conjecturality [cen-jec-chur-al'-i-ti], *s.* (Poco us.) Cosa fundada en mera conjetura.

Conjecturally [cen-jec'-chur-al-i], *adv.* Conjeturalmente, por conjetura, sin prueba.

Conjecture [cen-jec'-chur o tiūr], *s.* Conjetura, apariencia, suposición, sospecha. *Conjecture was at fault*, Salieron fallidas las conjeturas.

Conjecture, *va.* Conjeturar; sospechar, pronosticar.

Conjecturer [cen-jec'-chur-ẹr], *s.* Conjeturador.

Conjoin [cen-jein'], *va.* 1. Juntar, unir; asociar. 2. Asociar, conectar.—*vn.* Confederarse, unirse, ligarse.

Conjoint [cen-jeint'], *a.* Asociado, confederado.

Conjointly [cen-jeint'-li], *adv.* Unidamente, de mancomún.

Conjugable [cen'-ju-ga-bl], *a.* (Gram.) Que puede ser conjugado.

Conjugal [cen'-ju-gal], *a.* Conyugal, matrimonial.

Conjugally [cen'-ju-gal-i], *adv.* Conyugalmente.

Conjugate [cen'-ju-gêt], *va.* 1. (Gram.) Conjugar, variar las terminaciones de los verbos. 2. (Poco us.) Juntar, unir (en matrimonio).—*vn.* (Biol.) Unirse en conjugación.

Conjugate, *s.* La palabra que tiene la misma derivación que otras. —*a.* 1. Juntado en pares, apareado. 2. (Mat.) Conjugado, recíprocamente coordinado, recíproco.

Conjugation [cen-ju-gé'-shun], *s.* 1. Conjunción, unión. 2. (Gram.) Conjugación. 3. (Biol.) Unión o fusión de dos o más celdillas o individuos para la reproducción, como sucede con los animales y las plantas más sencillos, p. ej. las algas.

Conjunct [cen-juṇct'], *a.* Conjunto, allegado, unido.

Conjunction [cen-juṇc'-shun], *s.* 1. Conjunción, unión, asociación, liga. 2. (Gram.) Conjunción. 3. (Astr.) Conjunción de dos planetas.

Conjunctiva [cen-juṇc-tai'-va o ti'-va], *s.* Conjuntiva, membrana mucosa que cubre la superficie posterior de los párpados y la parte anterior del globo del ojo.

Conjunctival [cen-juṇc-tai'-val], *a.* Relativo a la conjuntiva.

Conjunctive [cen-juṇc'-tiv], *a.* 1. Conjunto; conjuntivo. 2. (Gram.) Subjuntivo. *Conjunctive mode*, Modo subjuntivo.

Conjunctively [cen-juṇc'-tiv-li], *adv.* Conjuntamente, de mancomún.

Conjunctiveness [cen-juṇc'-tiv-nes], *s.* La calidad de juntar o unir.

Conjunctivitis [cen-juṇc-ti-vai'-tis o vi'-tis], *s.* Inflamación de la conjuntiva.

Conjunctly [cen-juṇct'-li], *adv.* Juntamente.

Conjuncture [cen-juṇc'-chur], *s.* 1. Conyuntura. 2. Ocasión, sazón, crisis. 3. Modo de unión, conexión.

Conjuration [cen-ju-ré'-shun], *s.* 1. Deprecación, petición, súplica ardiente. 2. Conjuro, imprecación supersticiosa. 3. Conjuración, conspiración. 4. La forma o acto de citar a alguno en nombre de Dios.
Conjure [cen'-jur], *va.* 1. Hechizar, encantar, efectuar algo por arte mágica. 2. Citar, ahuyentar, por arte supernatural o mágica.—*vn.* Practicar la mágica, hacer juegos de manos. *To conjure away*, Exorcizar. *To conjure up*, Evocar, llamar con invocaciones supersticiosas. *To conjure up difficulties*, Suscitar dificultades u obstáculos.
Conjure [cen-jūr'], *va.* 1. Conjurar o citar en nombre de Dios; pedir con instancia y ruegos. 2. (Des.) Conjurarse, conspirar. 3. (Ant.) Encantar, hechizar.
Conjurer [cen'-jur-ęr], *s.* 1. Conjurador, encantador. 2. (Irón.) Hombre sagaz. *He is not a conjurer*, No es adivino, o no tiene mucho caletre, es un bolo.
Connascence [cen-nas'-ens], *s.* (Poco us.) El acto de nacer o el de ser producido al propio tiempo que otra cosa, y el ser que ha sido producido al mismo tiempo que otro.
Connate [cen-nêt'], *a.* 1. Del mismo parto, nacido con otro. 2. (Bot.) Connato, unido desde su origen, formando un mismo cuerpo. 3. Innato, que se tiene al nacer.
Connation [cen-nê'-shun], *s.* Calidad de connato; unión congénita.
Connatural [cen-nat'-yu-ral], *a.* Connatural.
Connaturality [cen-nat-yu-ral'-i-ti], **Connaturalness** [cen-nat'-yu-ral-nes], *s.* Participación de la misma naturaleza.
Connaturalize [cen-nat'-yu-ral-aiz], *va.* Unir con lazos naturales, con los que impone la naturaleza.
Connaturally [cen-nat'-yu-ral-i], *adv.* Connaturalmente.
Connect [cen-nect'], *va.* 1. Juntar, unir, enlazar, atar, trabar. 2. Coordinar, combinar, poner en orden y método alguna cosa. 3. Aparear, juntar, reunir; (Mec.) engargantar, poner en comunicación dos ruedas, dos piezas de una máquina.—*vn.* Unirse, juntarse; asociarse. *Connecting-link*, Corredera; eslabón, enganche. *Connecting-rod*, Biela, barra de conexión, biela motriz, vástago oscilante de un émbolo.
Connection [cen-nec'-shun], *s.* 1. Conexión, enlace. 2. Atadura, trabazón. 3. Afinidad, parentesco; familia. 4. Conjunto de personas reunidas; compañía; secta o comunión religiosa. 5. Relación, analogía. 6. Empalme, traspaso de un ferrocarril a otro sin demora.
Connective [cen-nec'-tiv], *a.* Conexivo. *Connective tissue*, (Anat.) El tejido fibroso que atraviesa el cuerpo entero y sirve para unir y sostener las diversas partes.—*s.* 1. (Gram.) Conjunción. 2. (Bot.) La parte del estambre que une los lóbulos de la antera. 3. (Zool.) Pieza de conexión.
Connectively [cen-nec'-tiv-li], *adv.* Conjuntamente, unidamente.
Conner [cen'-ęr], *s.* 1. El que examina atentamente; inspector. 2. El que dirige el gobierno y rumbo de un buque desde un punto elevado o conveniente. 3. [cun'-er] (1) Esparo, crenilabro, pez europeo; (2) *V.* CUNNER.
Connexion [cen-nec'-shun], *s.* 1. Conexión, unión, coherencia, ligazón, correspondencia, enlace. 2. (Mar.) Ligazón. *V.* CONNECTION.
Connexive [cen-nec'-siv], *a.* Conexivo, conjuntivo.
Conning tower [con'-ing tau'-ęr], *s.* Caseta blindada del piloto en barco de guerra.
Conniption, conniption fit [cen-nip'-shun fit], *s.* (fam.) Pataleta, rabieta, ataque de histerismo.
Connivance [cen-naiv'-ans], *s.* Connivencia, disimulo, permisión tácita de un delito.
Connive [cen-naiv'], *vn.* 1. Tolerar, disimular una falta; permitir, hacer la vista gorda. 2. Disimular, fingir ceguedad o ignorancia.
†**Connivence**, †**Conniveney**, *s.* *V.* CONNIVANCE.
Connivent [cen-naiv'-ent], *a.* Descuidado, disimulado.
Conniver [cen-naiv'-ęr], *s.* Cómplice, el que está en connivencia con otro.
Connoisseur [cen-i-sūr'], *s.* Perito, conocedor, inteligente. (Fr.)
Connoisseurship [cen-i-sūr'-ship], *s.* Inteligencia, pericia, conocimiento, habilidad por juzgar de una cosa.
Connotate [cen'-o-têt], *va.* 1. Designar indirectamente. 2. (Lóg.) Connotar, significar algo más de lo que las palabras expresan por sí mismas.
Connotation [cen-o-tê'-shun], *s.* (Lóg.) Connotación, designación indirecta.
Connote [cen-nōt'], *va.* (Lóg.) Connotar, significar indirectamente.
Connubial [cen-niū'-bi-al], *a.* Conyugal, matrimonial.
Connumeration [cen-niū-męr-ê'-shun], *s.* Connumeración.
Conoid [cō'-neid], *s.* 1. Conoide, cuerpo que se semeja al cono y cuya base es una elipse. 2. Conoide, sólido formado por la revolución de una sección cónica sobre su eje.
Conoidal [co-neid'-al], **Conoidical** [co-neid'-i-cal], *a.* Conoidal, lo que pertenece al conoide.
Conquer [ceŋ'-kęr], *va.* 1. Conquistar. 2. Vencer, rendir, sujetar, sojuzgar, domar; superar.—*vn.* Vencer, ganar la victoria.
Conquerable [ceŋ'-kęr-a-bl], *a.* Vencible, conquistable, domable.
Conqueress [ceŋ'-kęr-es], *sf.* Conquistadora.
Conquering [ceŋ'-kęr-ing], *a.* Victorioso, triunfador, triunfante.
Conqueror [ceŋ'-kęr-er], *s.* Vencedor, conquistador.
Conquest [cen'-cwest], *s.* 1. Conquista. 2. Conquista, la cosa conquistada. *The Conquest*, La conquista de Inglaterra por Guillermo de Normandía en el siglo XI.
Consanguineous [cen-san-gwin'-ę-us], *a.* 1. Consanguíneo, que tiene parentesco de consanguinidad. 2. Dícese en inglés de los que tienen el mismo padre, pero diferentes madres.
Consanguinity [cen-san-gwin'-i-ti], *s.* Consanguinidad, parentesco natural o de sangre.
Conscience [cen'-shens], *s.* 1. Conciencia, ciencia o conocimiento íntimo e interior del bien que debemos hacer y del mal que debemos evitar. 2. Escrúpulo, dificultad; justicia; veracidad. 3. (Fam.) Razón. *For conscience' sake, to satisfy one's conscience*, Para descargo de la conciencia.
Conscienced [cen'-shenst], *a.* Concienzudo.
Conscientious [cen-shi-en'-shus], *a.* 1. Concienzudo. 2. Escrupuloso. *Conscientious objector*, Objetor de conciencia.
Conscientiously [cen-shi-en'-shus-li], *adv.* Escrupulosamente.
Conscientiousness [cen-shi-en'-shus-nes], *s.* 1. Rectitud de conciencia, equidad, justicia. 2. Escrúpulo.
Conscionable [cen'-shun-a-bl], *a.* Justo, razonable.
Conscionably [cen'-shun-a-bli], *adv.* En conciencia, razonablemente.
Conscious [cen'-shus], *a.* 1. Consciente, sabedor de sus propios pensamientos y acciones; que tiene conciencia de sus actos. 2. Que tiene excesiva conciencia de sí mismo; turbado o cohibido por el sentimiento exagerado de la propia individualidad. 3. *V.* COGNIZANT. *I am conscious of it*, Lo sé muy bien o estoy convencido de ello; estoy cierto de ello, lo conozco.
Consciously [cen'shus-li], *adv.* Con cierta ciencia o conocimiento de sus propias acciones; a sabiendas, sinceramente.
Consciousness [cen'-shus-nes], *s.* Ciencia o conocimiento interior, sentimiento interior. *To recover* o *return to consciousness*, Recobrar el sentido, volver en sí.
Conscript [cen'-script], *a.* Conscripto; registrado, notado en algún registro. *Conscript fathers*, Padres conscriptos, los senadores de la antigua Roma.—*s.* Conscripto, recluta francés.
Conscript [cen-script'], *va.* Reclutar, obligar al servicio militar.
Conscription [cen-scrip'-shun], *s.* Reclutamiento, quinta, alistamiento forzoso en el ejército.
Consecrate [cen'-sę-crêt], *va.* 1. Consagrar, destinar una cosa profana a usos piadosos; dedicar, poner aparte solemnemente. 2. Dedicar o destinar alguna cosa a un fin particular. 3. Canonizar. 4. Hacer reverendo o venerable.
Consecrate, *a.* (Poét.) Consagrado.
Consecration [cen-sę-crê'-shun], *s.* 1. Consagración, el rito de consagrar o destinar alguna cosa al servicio de Dios. 2. Canonización.
Consecrator [cen'-sę-crê-tęr], *s.* Consagrante, consagrador.
‖**Consecratory** [cen'-sę-cra-to-ri], *a.* Sacramental, lo que pertenece a la consagración.
Consecutive [cen-sec'-yu-tiv], *s.* 1. Consecutivo, consiguiente; sucesivo. 2. Consecuente; con la preposición *to*.
Consecutively [cen-sec'-yu-tiv-li], *adv.* Consecutivamente.
Consension [cen-sen'-shun], *s.* (Ant.) Convenio, ajuste, reconocimiento.
Consensual [cen-sen'-shu-al], *a.* 1. (For.) Que existe solamente a causa de aquiescencia o consentimiento. 2. (Fisiol.) Excitado por medio de acción simpática o refleja.
Consensus [cen-sen'-sus], *s.* 1. Consenso, opinión colectiva, consentimiento general. 2. (Fisiol.) La relación simpática de los órganos del cuerpo en la ejecución de una función cualquiera.
Consent [cen-sent'], *s.* 1. Consentimiento, asenso, convenio, correspondencia, conexión; aprobación, permiso, beneplácito, acuerdo. *Silence gives consent*, Quien calla otorga. 2. (Ant.) *V.* CONSENSUS.

Consent, *vn.* Consentir, cooperar; obrar de concierto con otro; conceder, permitir; avenirse.
Consentaneous [cen-sen-tê'-ne-us], *a.* Conforme, conveniente, acorde, consentáneo, de acuerdo con; simultáneo.
Consentaneously [cen-sen-tê'-ne-us-li], *adv.* Conformemente, convenientemente.
Consentaneousness [cen-sen-tê'-ne-us-nes], *s.* Conformidad, proporción, correspondencia.
Consenter [cen-sent'-er], *s.* Consentidor.
Consentient [cen-sen'-shent], *a.* Acorde, unido y convenido en el modo de pensar; uniforme, de opinión unánime.
Consenting [cen-sent'-ing], *s.* Consentimiento.
Consequence [cen'-se-cwens], *s.* 1. Consecuencia, resulta, efecto. 2. Consecuencia, proposición sacada de las premisas de un silogismo. 3. Consecuencia, encadenamiento de causas y efectos. 4. Importancia, momento; influencia, tendencia. *By* o *in consequence,* De consiguiente. *In consequence,* En, a, o por consecuencia.
Consequent [cen'-se-cwent], *a.* 1. Consiguiente, lo que sigue, depende o se deduce de otra cosa. 2. Lógico, lo que está caracterizado por la exactitud del raciocinio.—*s.* 1. Consecuencia, efecto. 2. Consiguiente, la segunda proposición de un entimema.
Consequential [cen-se-cwen'-shal], *a.* 1. Consecutivo, consiguiente, concluyente. 2. Necesario, lógico, producido por el encadenamiento de los efectos con las causas. 3. Pomposo, altivo, importante.
Consequentially [cen-se-cwen'-shal-i], *adv.* Consiguientemente, consecuentemente; pomposamente.
Consequentialness [cen-se-cwen'-shal-nes], *s.* Consecuencia, el método regular o hilo de un discurso.
Consequently [cen'-se-cwent-li], *adv.* Por consiguiente, en consecuencia, necesariamente.
Consequentness [cen'-se-cwent-nes], *s.* Coherencia, conexión.
Conservable [cen-serv'-a-bl], *a.* Lo que se puede conservar.
Conservancy [cen-serv'-an-si], *s.* 1. Conservación. 2. Junta para la conservación y fomento de las pesquerías.
Conservant [cen-serv'-ant], *a.* Lo que conserva.
Conservation [cen-ser-vê'-shun], *s.* Conservación, el acto de conservar, continuar o guardar; preservación, defensa, protección.
Conservatism [cen-serv'-a-tizm], *s.* Disposición a ser conservador, opuesto a la mudanza.
Conservative [cen-serv'-a-tiv], *a.* 1. Conservador, que se adhiere al orden actual de cosas; opuesto a la mudanza y en cierto modo al progreso. 2. Conservativo, preservativo, que tiene el poder de preservar.
Conservator [cen'-ser-vê"-ter], *s.* Conservador, defensor, protector.
Conservatory [cen-serv'-a-to-ri], *a.* Conservatorio, a propósito para conservar.—*s.* 1. Invernáculo, pieza o casa cubierta y abrigada artificialmente para conservar las plantas delicadas. 2. Conservatorio, establecimiento público para enseñar y fomentar la música u otras artes.
Conservatrix [cen'-ser-vê"-trics], *sf.* Conservadora.
Conserve [cen-serv'], *va.* 1. Conservar, cuidar, guardar, mantener alguna cosa para que no se pierda o consuma. 2. Disponer las frutas para hacer conserva.
Conserve [cen'-serv], *s.* 1. Conserva, dulce que se hace con frutas y azúcar. 2. (Farm.) Confección.
Conserver [cen-serv'-er], *s.* Conservador; confitero.
Consider [cen-sid'-er], *va.* 1. Considerar, pensar, meditar, examinar, reflexionar. 2. Recompensar, atender o premiar el trabajo o mérito de alguno. 3. Estimar, querer. 4. Ser de opinión, creer; seguido de una cláusula complemental.—*vn.* 1. Considerar, pensar con madurez. 2. Considerar, deliberar, dudar, resolver consigo mismo. *To consider of,* Examinar, deliberar, discutir o pensar detenidamente. *To consider again,* Pensar o deliberar de nuevo. *To consider one,* Considerar o estimar a alguno, mostrarle consideración. *Consider what you do,* Mire Vd. lo que hace.
Considerable [cen-sid'-er-a-bl], *a.* 1. Considerable, digno de consideración; respetable. 2. Importante, notable. 3. Considerable, cuantioso.
Considerableness [cen-sid'-er-a-bl-nes], *s.* Importancia, entidad, valor.
Considerably [cen-sid'-er-a-bli], *adv.* Considerablemente, importantemente.
Considerance [cen-sid'-er-ans], *s.* (Des.) Consideración, reflexión.
Considerate [cen-sid'-er-et], *a.* Considerado, prudente, mirado, atento; moderado, discreto, circunspecto, tranquilo.
Considerately [cen-sid'-er-et-li], *adv.* Atinadamente, maduramente, juiciosamente, prudentemente.
Considerateness [cen-sid'-er-et-nes], *s.* Prudencia, circunspección, moderación.
Consideration [cen-sid-er-ê'-shun], *s.* 1. Consideración. 2. Consideración, reflexión, miramiento; examen, deliberación. 3. Importancia, valor, mérito, consecuencia. 4. Recompensa, remuneración. 5. (For.) Motivo, respeto, razón, causa; la condición de un contrato sin la cual es nulo. *To take into consideration,* Cuidar de; tomar en consideración.
Considerative [cen-sid'-er-a-tiv], *a.* (Ant.) Considerado.
Considerer [cen-sid'-er-er], *s.* Hombre de reflexión; considerador.
Considering [cen-sid'-er-ing], *prep.* y *conj.* En atención a, en consideración a, a causa de, visto que, en razón a. Por origen es participio. *Considering she is a woman,* Visto que es mujer.—*a.* Pensativo, considerado, juicioso.
Consideringly [cen-sid'-er-ing-li], *adv.* Seriamente, atinadamente.
Consign [cen-sain'], *va.* 1. Consignar o entregar a otro alguna cosa. 2. (For. y Com.) Consignar, enviar, confiar o fiar a otro mercaderías u objetos para vender, transferir o guardar. 3. Ceder, transferir a otro el dominio de alguna cosa; entregar, relegar. *To consign one to punishment,* Castigar a uno; entregarle a la ley.
Consignation [cen-sig-nê'-shun], *s.* 1. Consignación, el acto de consignar o entregar. 2. (Des.) El acto de firmar. 3. En las Iglesias griega, asiria, cóptica y nestoriana, la acción de consagrar o bendecir con la señal de la cruz.
Consignatory [cen-sig'-na-to-ri], *s.* El que firma en unión con otros.
Consignee [cen-sain-i'], *s.* Consignatario, corresponsal, depositario.
Consigner [cen-sain'-er], *s.* (Com.) Consignador. *V.* CONSIGNOR.
Consignification [cen-sig-ni-fi-kê'-shun], *s.* Significación semejante a otra.
Consignify [cen-sig'-ni-fai], *va.* y *vn.* 1. Significar con otro vocablo (el mismo sentido); como "negociar" y "pactar." 2. Significar un sentido, en unión con otra palabra o señal.
Consignment [cen-sain'-ment], *s.* 1. Consignación, la acción de consignar, dar, entregar o ceder. 2. La propiedad o los objetos consignados y la escritura de consignación, cesión o traspaso.
Consignor [cen-si-nōr' o cen-sain'-er], *s.* Consignador. el que consigna sus mercancías o buques a un corresponsal suyo.
Consiliary [cen-sil'-i-e-ri], *a.* Relativo o perteneciente a consejo, aviso o dictamen.
Consimilar [cen-sim'-i-lar], *a.* (Poco us.) Semejante, igual, parecido.
Consist [cen-sist'], *vn.* 1. Consistir, subsistir, permanecer, continuar. 2. Componerse, constar, estar contenido en otra cosa. 3. Coexistir. 4. Convenir, corresponder, acordarse. *Consisting,* Compuesto. *To consist of,* Consistir en, estar compuesto de, componerse de. *To consist with,* Ser compatible, acordarse o estar de acuerdo y conformidad.
Consistence, Consistency [cen-sis'-tens, i], *s.* 1. Consistencia, conformidad; estado o existencia de alguna cosa. 2. Grado de densidad o raridad. 3. Forma substancial. 4. Permanencia, estabilidad. 5. Relación, compatibilidad, conveniencia.
Consistent [cen-sis'-tent], *a.* 1. Consistente, conveniente, conforme. 2. Firme, sólido, estable. 3. Compatible; plausible.
Consistently [cen-sis'-tent-li], *adv.* Conformemente; consecuentemente.
Consistorial [cen-sis-tō'-ri-al], *a.* Consistorial.
Consistory [cen-sis'-to-ri], *s.* 1. Tribunal, sala de justicia de una curia eclesiástica. 2. Consistorio, la junta o consejo que celebra el Papa con asistencia de los cardenales. 3. Junta, asamblea, congreso.
Consociate [cen-sō'-shi-êt], *vn.* Juntar, unir, pegar.—*vn.* Asociarse, unirse, juntarse con otros.
Consociate, *a.* Asociado, confederado, unido.
Consociation [cen-so-shi-ê'-shun], *s.* Alianza, liga; unión, intimidad; asociación, sociedad.
Consol [cen'-sel], *s.* *V.* CONSOLS.
Consolable [cen-sōl'-a-bl], *a.* Consolable.
†**Consolate** [cen'-so-lêt], *va.* Consolar. *V.* CONSOLE.
Consolation [cen-so-lê'-shun], *s.* Consolación, consuelo, alivio.
Consolatory [cen-sel'-a-to-ri], *s.* Consolador, consolatorio, que da consuelo o tiende a consolar.—*s.* Discurso o escrito consolatorio.
Console [cen-sōl'], *va.* Consolar; confortar, aliviar la tristeza o la pena.

Console [con'-sōl], *s.* (Arq.) Cartela, especie de repisa.
Consoler [con-sōl'-ẹr], *s.* Consolador, el o la que consuela.
Consolidant [con-sel'-i-dant], *a.* Consolidativo, lo que tiene virtud de consolidar.
Consolidate [con-sel'-i-dêt], *va.* 1. Consolidar, dar firmeza y solidez a alguna cosa. 2. Reunir dos beneficios.—*vn.* Consolidarse, ponerse firme, dura o sólida alguna cosa. *Consolidated annuities, V.* CONSOLS.
Consolidation [con-sel-i-dé'-shun], *s.* Consolidación, reunión, conjunción.
Consolidative [con-sel'-i-dê-tiv], *a.* Consolidativo.
Consols [con'-selz o con-selz'], *s. pl.* Abreviatura de "*consolidated annuities*"; rentas británicas creadas en varias épocas y consolidadas hoy, para evitar confusiones, en un mismo fondo. Desde 1751 hasta 1888 produjeron interés de tres por ciento; desde entonces 2¾ por ciento, y en 1903, el 2½ por ciento.
Consommé [con-so-mê'], *s.* Consommé, caldo de carne. *Chicken consommé,* Consommé de pollo, caldo de pollo. (Fr.)
Consonance [con'-so-nans], **Consonancy** [con'-so-nan-si], *s.* Consonancia, congruencia, conformidad; rima, armonía; relación.
Consonant [con'-so-nant], *a.* 1. Consonante, conforme, cónsono. 2. *V.* CONSONANTAL.
Consonant, *s.* (Gram.) Consonante, letra que no puede pronunciarse sin el auxilio de alguna vocal.
Consonantal [con-so-nan'-tal], *a.* Perteneciente a una consonante.
Consonantly [con'-so-nant-li], *adv.* Conformemente.
Consonantness [con'-so nant-nes], *s.* Consonancia, conformidad.
Consonous [con'-so-nus], *a.* (Mús.) Cónsono, acorde, armonioso.
†**Consopite** [con'-so-pait], *va.* Adormecer, arrullar para hacer dormir.
Consort [con'-sert], *s.* 1. Consorte, compañero, socio; esposo o esposa. 2. Concurrencia, unión. 3. (Des.) *V.* CONCERT.
Consort [cọn-sōrt'], *vn.* Asociarse, acompañarse.—*va.* 1. Casar, unir el hombre a la mujer por medio del matrimonio. 2. Acompañar, hacer compañía á otro, vivir juntos.
Consortable [con-sōrt'-a-bl], *a.* (Poco us.) Comparable; sociable.
Consortship [con'-sōrt-ship], *s.* Compañía, estado de consorte.
Conspectus [con-spec'-tus], *s.* 1. Ojeada abarcadora y completa; vista general. 2. Resumen, compendio, digesto.
Conspicuity [cọn-spi-kiū'-i-ti], *s.* Claridad, visibilidad; evidencia; eminencia.
Conspicuous [con-spic'-yu-us], *a.* 1. Conspicuo, claro, visible, aparente. 2. Eminente, ilustre, esclarecido, notable, famoso, distinguido.
Conspicuously [con-spic'-yu-us-li], *adv.* 1. Visiblemente, manifiestamente. 2. Claramente, eminentemente.
Conspicuousness [con-spic'-yu-us-nes], *s.* Claridad, celebridad, fama, nombre, reputación.
Conspiracy [con-spir'-a-si], *s.* 1. Conspiración, cooperación, conjuración. 2. Concurrencia.
Conspirant [cọn-spair'-ant], *a.* Conjurado, conspirador.
§**Conspiration** [con-spi-ré'-shun], *s.* Conspiración; unión.
Conspirator [con-spir'-a-ter], *s.* Conspirado, conspirador.
Conspire [con-spair'], *vn.* Conspirar, maquinar; concurrir, convenir; ligarse, conjurarse. *Conspiring,* Conspirante. *Conspiring powers,* (Mec.) Fuerzas conspirantes, todas las que obran simultáneamente para producir un movimiento o un resultado cualquiera.
Conspirer [con-spair'-ẹr], *s.* Conspirador.
Conspiringly [con-spair'-ing-li], *adv.* Conspirando criminalmente.
Constable [cun'-sta-bl], *s.* 1. Condestable. 2. Comisario de barrio. *Constable of the Tower,* Gobernador de la Torre de Londres. En los Estados Unidos *constable* es simplemente un alguacil o esbirro. *First constable,* Alguacil mayor.
Constableship [cun'-sta-bl-ship], *s.* Condestablía.
Constablewick [cun'-sta-bl-wic], *s.* La jurisdicción del condestable o la de un comisario de barrio.
Constabulary [con-stab'-yu-lẹ-ri], *a.* Perteneciente a un alguacil o esbirro; que se compone de ellos.—*s.* El conjunto de alguaciles; fuerza militar de policía.
Constancy [con'-stan-si], *s.* 1. Constancia, perseverancia, firmeza, fuerza, fidelidad, permanencia, estabilidad. 2. Fortaleza de alma, intrepidez. 3. Realidad, veracidad.
Constant [con'-stant], *a.* 1. Constante, firme, sólido; permanente. 2. Firme, resuelto, inmutable, perseverante, invariable; cierto, indudable.
Constantly [con'-stant-li], *adv.* 1. Constantemente, igualmente, invariablemente; asiduamente. 2. Ciertamente, indudablemente.
Constellate [con'-stel-lêt], *vn.* (Ant.) Resplandecer o lucir en grupos, brillar como una constelación.—*va.* Unir o juntar varios cuerpos resplandecientes en uno.
Constellation [con-stel-lé'-shun], *s.* 1. (Astr.) Constelación, grupo de estrellas fijas. 2. Conjunto de resplandores o excelencias.
Consternation [con-stẹr-né'-shun], *s.* Consternación, atolondramiento, aturdimiento, terror, sorpresa.
Constipate [con'-sti-pêt], *va.* 1. Cerrar alguna cosa en paraje estrecho. 2. (Des.) Espesar, condensar; obstruir.—*vn.* 1. Constiparse. 2. Estreñirse el vientre.
Constipation [con-sti-pé'-shun], *s.* 1. Apretura de alguna cosa en paraje estrecho. 2. Estreñimiento de vientre que los médicos suelen llamar constipación. 3. (Des.) Condensación, obstrucción.
Constituent [con-stit'-yu-ent], *s.* 1. Elector, votante. 2. Constituyente (el que diputa o sustituye a otro para que en su nombre haga alguna cosa), comitente, delegante, poderdante. 3. Constitutivo, parte o elemento necesario.—*a.* Constituyente, elemental, esencial.
Constitute [con'-sti-tiūt], *va.* 1. Constituir, formar un todo, o ser de la substancia de; componer. 2. Constituir, señalar. 3. Erigir, establecer. 4. Constituir, diputar, dar poder en forma.
Constituter [con'-sti-tiūt-ẹr], *s.* Constituidor.
Constitution [con-sti-tiū'-shun], *s.* 1. Constitución. 2. Estado, situación o conjunto de circunstancias. 3. Constitución, ley fundamental. 4. Constitución, ley, ordenanza. 5. Complexión, temperamento, constitución, hablando de personas.
Constitutional [con-sti-tiū'-shun-al], *a.* 1. Constitucional, relativo a la constitución o composición de una persona o cosa en general; inherente a la constitución o complexión corporal o al carácter del individuo. 2. Constitucional, legal, conforme á la constitución de un Estado.—*s.* (Fam.) Paseo a pie por motivos de salud, como recurso higiénico.
Constitutionalist [con-sti-tiū'-shun-al-ist], *s.* Constitucional, el partidario de la constitución de un Estado.
Constitutionally [con-sti-tiū'-shun-al-i], *adv.* Constitucionalmente, legalmente.
Constitutionist [con-sti-tiū'-shun-ist], *s.* Constitucional, el defensor celoso de la constitución de su país.
Constitutive [con'-sti-tiu-tiv], *a.* Constitutivo, legislativo; esencial.
Constrain [con-strên'], *va.* 1. Constreñir, obligar, forzar. 2. Restringir, impedir, detener. 3. Comprimir, apretar.
Constrainable [con-strên'-a-bl], *a.* Constreñible.
Constrainedly [con-strên'-ed-li], *adv.* Constreñidamente; por compulsión, por fuerza.
Constrainer [con-strên'-ẹr], *s.* El que obliga o precisa.
Constraint [con-strênt'], *s.* 1. Constreñimiento, coartación, apremio; compulsión, fuerza, violencia, tormento. 2. Incomodidad; necesidad.
Constrict [con-strict'], *va.* 1. Constreñir, apretar, ligar, atar. 2. Constreñir, estrechar, arrugar, encoger. 3. Sofocar o sufocar.
Constriction [con-stric'-shun], *s.* Contracción, encogimiento, constricción, sofocación.
Constrictive [con-stric'-tiv], *a.* Constrictivo, que tiende a constreñir o sofocar.
Constrictor [con-strict'-er], *s.* 1. Constrictor, constringente, sofocante. 2. (Anat.) Constrictor, músculo que estrecha o cierra ciertos conductos o cavidades del cuerpo. 3. (Zool.) Boa constrictor.
Constringe [con-strinj'], *va.* Constreñir, comprimir, estrechar, ligar.
Constringent [con-strin'-jẹnt], *a.* Constrictivo, constringente.
Construct [con-struct'], *va.* 1. Construir, edificar; hacer o formar alguna cosa. 2. Idear, imaginar, componer: v. g. *to construct a theory,* Idear una teoría.
Construct [con'-struct], *a.* Relativo a, o que expresa construcción. *Construct state,* Anexión, estado constructo, en la gramática semítica, expresión de la relación del genitivo.
Constructer, Constructor [con-struct'-ẹr, ẹr], *s.* Constructor, el que construye.
Construction [con-struc'-shun], *s.* 1. Construcción, la acción de construir. 2. (Gram.) Construcción, colocación y régimen de las palabras según las reglas de la sintaxis. 3. Interpretación, explicación, sentido. 4. Modo de describir algún problema geométrico.
Constructional [con-struc'-shun-al], *a.* Lo que pertenece al sentido o a la interpretación.
Constructive [con-struct'-iv], *a.* 1.

Constructivo, que envuelve construcción; que tiene virtud de construir. 2. Que puede deducirse por interpretación. 3. Que resulta en consecuencias positivas; afirmativo.
Constructively [con-struct'-iv-li], *adv.* Constructivamente; por inducción.
Constructiveness [con-struct'-iv-nes], *s.* La facultad de construcción, y particularmente la aptitud mecánica.
Construe [con'-strū], *va.* Construir, expresar la sintaxis de las palabras; interpretar, explicar, colocar las palabras en su orden natural.
Consubsist [con-sub-sist'], *vn.* (Poco us.) Coexistir, existir juntos.
Consubstantial [con-sub-stan'-shal], *a.* Consubstancial, coesencial.
Consubstantialist [con-sub-stan'-shal-ist], *s.* El que cree en la consubstanciación.
Consubstantiality [con-sub-stan-shi-al'-i-ti], *s.* Consubstancialidad, identidad de substancia.
Consubstantiate [con-sub-stan'-shi-ét], *va.* Unir en una misma substancia o naturaleza.—*vn.* (Poco us.) Creer en la consubstanciación.
Consubstantiate, *a.* Unido.
Consubstantiation [con-sub-stan-shi-é'-shun], *s.* Consubstanciación.
Consuetude [con'-swe-tiūd], *s.* Costumbre; (ant.) consuetud; asociación.
Consuetudinary [con-swe-tiū'-di-ne-ri], *a.* Consuetudinario, lo que es de costumbre; lo que viene de uso inmemorial.—*s.* Ritual de las devociones ordinarias o de costumbre.
Consul [con'-sul], *s.* 1. Cónsul, nombre de dos magistrados que tenían la primera autoridad en la república romana. 2. Cónsul, oficial ó empleado público nombrado por el gobierno para proteger el comercio, la navegación y los súbditos o ciudadanos de un país en los puertos y plazas principales de otras naciones.
Consular [con'-siu-lar], *a.* Consular, perteneciente a un cónsul.
Consulate [con'-siu-lét], **Consulship** [con'-sul-ship], *s.* 1. Consulado, el oficio o dignidad de cónsul. 2. (*Consulate* sólo) Consulado, oficina, lugar donde despacha el cónsul.
Consult [con-sult'], *vn.* Consultarse, pedir parecer uno a otro recíprocamente.—*va.* 1. Consultar, pedir parecer, dictamen o consejo a otro. 2. Mirar, escudriñar, examinar. 3. Idear, deliberar, discurrir.—*vn.* Aconsejarse con o de.
†**Consult** [con'-sult], *s.* 1. Consulta, parecer o dictamen que se pide o se da sobre una cosa. 2. Consulta, junta de personas para deliberar y determinar algún asunto.
Consultant [con-sult'-ant], *a.* Consultante.—*s.* Consultante, el que consulta con otro.
Consultation [con-sul-té'-shun], *s.* 1. Consulta, junta, número de personas unidas a quienes se pide parecer. *Consultation of physicians,* Junta de médicos. 2. Deliberación, opinión o parecer dado en consulta.
Consultative, Consultatory [con-sult'-a-tiv, con-sult'-a-to-ry], *a.* Consultivo.
Consulter [con-sult'-er], *s.* Consultante.
Consulting [con-sult'-ing], *a.* Consultor, consultora, el que da su parecer, consultado sobre algún asunto.
Consumable [con-siū'-ma-bl], *a.* Consumible.
Consume [con-siūm'], *va.* Consumir, acabar, destruir, disipar, gastar.—*vn.* Consumirse, deshacerse, acabarse, aniquilarse, perecer.
Consumer [con-siū'-mer], *s.* 1. Consumidor; disipador. 2. (Econ. Polít.) Consumidor, comprador; el que consume un artículo de valor variable.
Consummate [con'-sum-ét o con-sum'-et], *va.* Consumar, acabar, terminar, completar.
Consummate [con-sum'-ét], *a.* Consumado, completo, perfecto, cabal.
Consummately [con-sum'-ét-li], *adv.* Consumadamente.
Consummation [con-sum-é'-shun], *s.* Consumación, perfección completa; desarrollo perfecto, fin.
Consumption [con-sump'-shun], *s.* 1. Consunción, disipación, destrucción, ruina; consumo, gasto. 2. Consunción, tisis, marasmo. 3. (Econ. Polít.) Consumo, destrucción o gasto que se hace de comestibles, telas y otros géneros que ofrece el mercado, para el uso individual. *To be in a consumption,* Estar tísico.
Consumptive [con-sump'-tiv], *a.* Consuntivo, destructivo; hético.
Consumptively [con-sump'-tiv-li], *adv.* A manera de consunción.
Consumptiveness [con-sump'-tiv-nes], *s.* Principio de consunción.
Consute [con-siūt'], *a.* Marcado como por puntos de costura; v. g. los élitros de algunos escarabajos.
Contabescence [con-ta-bes'-ens], *s.* 1. (Med.) Tabes, marasmo, atrofia. 2. (Bot.) Esterilidad de los estambres y el polen; ocurre a menudo en las plantas híbridas.
Contact [con'-tact], *s.* Contacto, tocamiento.
Contact lens [con'-tact lenz], *s.* Lente de contacto.
Contagion [con-té'-jun], *s.* 1. Contagio, peste, pestilencia, infección. 2. Contagio, infición, el daño y corrupción que propagan las malas doctrinas o el mal ejemplo. 3. Contagión, el medio de transmisión de una enfermedad específica.
Contagious [con-té'-jus], *a.* Contagioso, que se pega y comunica por contagio.
Contagiousness [con-té'-jus-nes], *s.* Carácter contagioso.
Contain [con-tén'], *va.* 1. Contener, comprender, caber; incluir, abrazar, encerrar. *That bottle contains six pints,* En aquella botella caben seis cuartillos. 2. Reprimir, contener, refrenar. 3. (Mat.) Ser exactamente divisible.—*vn.* Contenerse, abstenerse, vivir en continencia.
Containable [con-tén'-a-bl], *a.* Contenible.
Container [con-tén'-er], *s.* 1. Envase. 2. Recipiente.
Contaminate [con-tam'-i-nét], *vn.* 1. Contaminar, manchar, corromper; contagiar, inficionar. 2. Corromper, viciar, pervertir.
Contaminate, *a.* Contaminado, manchado, corrompido.
Contamination [con-tam-i-né'-shun], *s.* Contaminación.
Contemn [con-tem'], *va.* Despreciar, menospreciar, desestimar, tener en poco alguna cosa.
†**Contemper** [con-tem'-per], *va.* Contemperar, templar, moderar.
Contemplate [con-tem'-plét o con'-tem-plét], *va.* 1. Contemplar, estudiar, meditar. 2. Proyectar, formar intención.—*vn.* Contemplar, detener el entendimiento en la consideración de alguna cosa; meditar, divagar.
Contemplation [con-tem-plé'-shun], *s.* 1. Contemplación, meditación estudiosa; estudio, consideración. 2. Proyecto; expectación. 3. Meditación sagrada.
Contemplative [con-tem'-pla-tiv], *a.* Contemplativo, estudioso, discursivo.
Contemplatively [con-tem'-pla-tiv-li], *adv.* Con atención y cuidado.
Contemplator [con'-tem-plé"-ter], *s.* Contemplador.
Contemporaneity, Contemporariness [con-tem-po-ra-nī'-i-ti, con-tem'-po-ré"-ri-nes], *s.* Contemporaneidad, sincronismo, existencia al mismo tiempo.
Contemporaneous [con-tem-po-ré'-ne-us], *a.* Contemporáneo, que existe al mismo tiempo que una persona o cosa. *V.* CONTEMPORARY.
Contemporaneously [con-tem-po-ré'-ne-us-li], *adv.* Contemporáneamente, al mismo tiempo, en una misma época.
Contemporary [con-tem'-po-re-ri], *a.* y *s.* Contemporáneo, coetáneo, el que vive al mismo tiempo que otro. *Contemporaneous,* Se dice principalmente de hechos y sucesos; *contemporary,* de personas.
‡**Contemporize** [con-tem'-po-raiz], *va.* Hacer dos o más cosas de un mismo siglo o era; considerar como contemporáneo.
Contempt [con-tempt'], *s.* Desprecio, desdén, menosprecio, vilipendio. *Contempt of court,* Contumacia; rebeldía.
Contemptibility [con-tempt-i-bil'-i-ti], *s.* *V.* CONTEMPTIBLENESS.
Contemptible [con-tempt'-i-bl], *a.* Despreciable, despreciado, desestimado, vil.
Contemptibleness [con-tempt'-i-bl-nes], *s.* Vileza, bajeza, abyección; torpeza.
Contemptibly [con-tempt'-i-bli], *adv.* Vilmente.
Contemptuous [con-temp'-chu-us], *a.* Desdeñoso, altivo, insolente, despreciador. *Contemptuous words,* Palabras ofensivas.
Contemptuously [con-tem'-chu-us-li], *adv.* Desdeñosamente, con menosprecio, con desdén.
Contemptuousness [con-tem'-chu-us-nes], *s.* Desdén, desprecio, altanería.
Contend [con-tend'], *va.* Sostener, afirmar; va seguido de *that* con una cláusula complemental.—*vn.* Contender, pleitear, disputar, pretender; competir, lidiar, altercar. *Contending parties,* Partes contenciosas, o litigantes.
Contendent [con-tend'-ent, **Contender** [con-tend'-er], *s.* Contendedor, competidor, antagonista, rival.
Content [con-tent'], *a.* Contento, satisfecho. En la Cámara de los Pares de Inglaterra, voto afirmativo. *The contents have it,* La proposición queda aprobada.
Content, *va.* Contentar, satisfacer, complacer, agradar.
Content [con-tent'], *s.* 1. Contento, contentamiento, satisfacción, agrado. *Content is the philosopher's stone, that turns all it touches into gold,* El contento es un tesoro, es la verdadera piedra filosofal. 2. [con'-tent] Contenido, lo que se encierra en una cosa; cabida, capacidad; generalmente en plural. 3. (Geom.)

Área contenida, extensión; cabida. *Table of contents*, Tabla de materias de un libro en el orden en que se suceden, lo cual la diferencia de un índice alfabético. *Contents*, El o lo contenido, tabla de materias.

Contented [cen-tent'-ed], *a.* 1. Contento, satisfecho, agradado, tranquilo. 2. Resignado, paciente.

Contentedly [cen-tent'-ed-li], *adv.* Tranquilamente, contentamente.

Contentedness [cen-tent'-ed-nes], *s.* Contento, satisfacción.

†**Contentful** [cen-tent'-ful], *a.* Perfectamente contento, dichoso, feliz.

Contention [cen-ten'-shun], *s.* Contención, contienda, debate, competencia, contestación, altercado; esfuerzo.

Contentious [cen-ten'-shus], *a.* Contencioso, litigioso.

Contentiously [cen-ten'-shus-li], *adv.* Contenciosamente.

Contentless [cen'-tent-les], *a.* 1. Sin contenido o significación. 2. ‖[cen-tent'-les] Descontento, desagradado.

Contentment [cen-tent'-mẹnt], *s.* Contentamiento, contento, gusto, satisfacción.

Conterminable [cen-tẹr'-mi-na-bl], *a.* Lo que es capaz de ser contenido en los mismos límites que otra cosa.

Conterminal [cen-tẹr'-mi-nal], *a.* *V.* CONTERMINOUS.

Conterminate [cen-tẹr'-mi-nêt], *a.* Lo que tiene el mismo límite que otra cosa.

Conterminous [cen-tẹr'-min-us], *a.* 1. Contérmino, vecino, limítrofe. 2. Contenido dentro de los mismos límites, coextensivo. Lo mismo significa *Coterminous.*

Contest [cen-test'], *va.* Contestar, disputar, litigar.—*vn.* Contender, competir; emular.

Contest [cen'-test], *s.* Contienda, disputa, debate, contestación, altercación. *It was a severe contest*, (Mil.) Fué una acción muy reñida; fué una disputa bien sostenida.

Contestable [cen-test'-a-bl], *a.* Contestable, disputable; dudoso, contencioso.

Contestant [cen-test'-ant], *s.* Contestante, disputador, litigante; especialmente el que disputa una elección o un testamento.

†**Contestation** [cen-tes-tê'-shun], *s.* 1. Contestación. 2. Testimonio, prueba.

Contestingly [cen-test'-ing-li], *adv.* Contenciosamente.

Contestless [cen'-test-les], *a.* Indisputable, incontestable.

Context [cen'-tecst], *s.* Contexto, contenido; contextura.

Contextual [cen-tex'-tiu-al], *a.* Del contexto, relativo al contexto.

Contextural [cen-tecs'-chur-al], *a.* Perteneciente a la contextura o entretejido.

Contexture [cen-tecs'-chur], *s.* Contextura, orden o disposición de las partes entre sí, tejido, entretejido, enlazamiento.

†**Contignation** [cen-tig-nê'-shun], *s.* (Arq.) Contignación, trabazón de vigas que forma los pisos y techos. *V.* FRAMEWORK.

Contiguity [cen-ti-giū'-i-ti], *s.* Contigüidad, inmediación de una cosa a otra.

Contiguous [cen-tig'-yu-us], *a.* Contiguo, junto.

Contiguously [cen-tig'-yu-us-li], *adv.* Contiguamente.

Contiguousness [cen-tig'-yu-us-nes], *s.* Contigüidad, vecindad.

Continence o **Continency** [cen'-ti-nens, i], *s.* Continencia, templanza, castidad; dominio sobre sí mismo, especialmente respecto a la pasión sexual.

Continent [cen'-ti-nent], *a.* 1. Continente, casto, puro. 2. (Ant.) Lo que contiene alguna cosa.

Continent, *s.* Continente, gran extensión de tierra, mayor de lo que suelen ser las islas y penínsulas.

Continental [cen-ti-nent'-al], *a.* Continental.

Continently [cen-ti-nent'-li], *adv.* Castamente.

Contingence o **Contingency** [cen-tin'-jens, i], *s.* 1. Contingencia, acontecimiento o cosa que puede suceder o no. 2. Eventualidad, accidente o caso imprevisto.

Contingent [cen-tin'-jent], *s.* 1. Contingencia, casualidad. 2. Contingente, cuota.

Contingent, *a.* Contingente, casual, accidental.

Contingently [cen-tin'-jent-li], *adv.* Contingentemente, casualmente, accidentalmente.

Contingentness [cen-tin'-jent-nes], *s.* Contingencia, casualidad.

Continual [cẹn-tin'-yu-al], *a.* 1. Continuo, frecuente, repetido a menudo. 2. Continuo, que dura o se hace sin interrupción; sin intermisión, incesante.

Continually [cẹn-tin'-yu-al-i], *adv.* Continuamente.

Continualness [cẹn-tin'-yu-al-nes], *s.* Permanencia.

Continuance [cẹn-tin'-yu-ans], *s.* 1. Continuación, permanencia. 2. Demora, duración, dilación, perseverancia. 3. Continuidad o coherencia; plazo. 4. Morada.

Continuate [cen-tin'-yu-et], *a.* (Poco us.) Continuado, unido inmediatamente, no interrumpido.

Continuation [cen-tin-yu-ê'-shun], *s.* Continuación, duración, seguida, serie.

Continuative [cen-tin'-yu-ẹ-tiv], *s.* Expresión que denota continuación o permanencia.

Continuator [cen-tin'-yu-ê-tẹr], *s.* Continuador, el que o lo que continúa o prosigue una obra o sucesión.

Continue [cen-tin'-yū], *vn.* 1. Continuar, durar, ser durable. 2. Permanecer en un estado o lugar. 3. Perseverar; detenerse; persistir, morar.—*va.* Continuar; prolongar, perpetuar.

Continued [cen-tin'-yūd], *a.* Continuo, no interrumpido. *A continued fever*, Fiebre continua.—*pp.* de CONTINUE.

Continuedly [cen-tin'-yūd-li], *adv.* Continuadamente.

Continuer [cen-tin'-yu-ẹr], *s.* Continuador, perseverador.

Continuity [cen-ti-niū'-i-ti], *s.* 1. Continuidad, continuación, coherencia. 2. Unión, enlace, dependencia. *Solution of continuity*, (Med.) Solución de continuidad, la división o destrucción de alguna parte del cuerpo humano.

Continuous [cen-tin'-yu-us], *a.* Continuo, unido o junto, sin espacio intermedio o interrupción aparente.

Contort [cen-tōrt'], *va.* Torcer, contorcer.

Contorted [cen-tōrt'-ed], *a.* y *pp.* 1. Torcido, retorcido. 2. (Bot.) Arrollado, envuelto. *V.* CONVOLUTE.

Contortion [cen-tōr'-shun], *s.* 1. Contorsión, retorcimiento. 2. Dislocación parcial. 3. (Bot.) Retorcimiento irregular del tallo o ramas de las plantas, a causa de interrupción en su crecimiento.

Contortionist [cen-tōr'-shun-ist], *s.* Acróbata ejercitado en retorcer cuerpo o miembros.

Contour [cen-tūr' o cen'-tūr], *s.* Contorno o perfil.

Contra [cen'-tra], *prep. insep.* Contra.

Contraband [cen'-tra-band], *s.* Contrabando, matute. *Contraband goods*, Géneros de contrabando o prohibidos.—*a.* Prohibido, ilegal.

Contrabandism [cen'-tra-band-izm], *s.* Contrabando, importación de géneros prohibidos.

Contrabandist [cen'-tra-band-ist], *s.* Contrabandista, matutero.

Contrabass [cen'-tra-bês], *s.* Contrabajo, instrumento de cuerda, una octava más bajo que el violón.

Contraception [cen-tra-sep'-shun], *s.* Medidas anticoncepcionales.

Contraceptive [cen-tra-sep'-tiv], *s.* y *a.* Contraceptivo, anticoncepcional.

Contract [cen-tract'], *va.* 1. Contraer, apretar, estrechar, encoger, plegar; abreviar, compendiar. 2. Contraer algún vicio, hábito o costumbre. 3. Contratar. 4. Contraer esponsales. —*vn.* 1. Contraerse, encogerse. 2. Contratar, pactar.

Contract [cen'-tract], *s.* 1. Contrato, pacto, convención o convenio entre partes. 2. Esponsales. 3. Contrata, escritura.—*a.* Prometido, afianzado.

Contracted [cen-tract'-ed], *a.* 1. No ancho o amplio; encogido. 2. Contraído, apretado, estrecho.

Contractedly [cen-tract'-ed-li], *adv.* De una manera apretada, contraída.

Contractedness [cen-tract'-ed-nes], *s.* 1. Contracción; apretamiento, opresión. 2. Estrechez de miras, ruindad, mezquindad.

Contractibility [cen-tract-i-bil'-i-ti], **Contractibleness** [cen-tract'-i-bl-nes], *s.* Contractilidad.

Contractible [cen-tract'-i-bl], *a.* Que se puede contraer, susceptible de contracción.

Contractile [cen-trac'-til], *a.* (Med.) Contráctil, lo que puede contraerse; lo que puede producir contracción.

Contracting [cen-tract'-ing], *a.* Contratante. *The contracting parties*, Las partes contratantes, los contrayentes.

Contraction [cen-trac'-shun], *s.* 1. Contracción. 2. (Gram.) La reducción de dos vocales o sílabas en una; abreviatura o abreviación.

Contractor [cen-trac'-tẹr], *s.* 1. Contratante. 2. Contratista, persona que por contrata ejecuta una obra material.

Contra-dance [cen'-tra-dans], *s.* Contradanza y la música de ese baile.

Contradict [cen-tra-dict'], *va.* Contradecir, negar lo que otro da por cierto; oponerse, contrariar.

Contradicter [cen-tra-dict'-ẹr], *s.* Contradictor, el que contradice o se opone.

Contradiction [cen-tra-dic'-shun], *s.* Contradicción, oposición, implicación, contrariedad, incongruencia, repugnancia.

Contradictorily [cen-tra-dic'-to-ri-li], *adv.* Contradictoriamente.

Contradictory [cen-tra-dic'-to-ri], *a.* Contradictorio, contrario, opuesto, que implica contradicción.—*s.* Contrariedad, inconsistencia. (Lóg.)

Contradictoria, una de dos proposiciones, de las cuales la una afirma lo que la otra niega y no pueden ser a un mismo tiempo verdaderas, ni a un mismo tiempo falsas. *Contradictory temper*, Espíritu de contradicción.

Contradistinct [con-tra-dis-tinct'], *a.* Distinguido por calidades opuestas, contradistinto.

Contradistinction [con-tra-dis-tinc'-shun], *s.* Distinción por calidades opuestas. *In contradistinction*, Por oposición, por contradistinción.

Contradistinctive [con-tra-dis-tinc'-tiv], *a.* Contradistintivo.

Contradistinguish [con-tra-dis-tin'-gwish], *va.* Contradistinguir.—*vn.* Poner en oposición, distinguir por calidades opuestas.

Contrafissure [con-tra-fish'-ur], *s.* Contrafractura, abertura del cráneo por la parte opuesta a aquella donde se ha recibido un golpe.

Contrail [con-trêl'], *s.* Estela de vapor.

Contraindicant [con-tra-in'-di-cant], **Contraindication** [con-tra-in-di-ké'-shun], *s.* Contraindicante, contraindicación, síntoma que indica la impropiedad de un remedio dado o tratamiento seguido.

Contraindicate [con-tra-in'-di-kêt], *va.* Contraindicar.

Contralto [con-tral'-to], *s.* y *a.* Contralto, la voz media entre el tiple y el tenor. (Ital.)

Contranatural [con-tra-nach'-ur-al], *a.* (Poco us.) Contranatural.

Contraposition [con-tra-po-zish'-un], *s.* Contraposición.

Contraregularity [con-tra-reg-yu-lar'-i-ti], *s.* Contrariedad.

Contrariant [con-tré'-ri-ant], *a.* (Poco us.) Repugnante, contradictorio.

Contraries [con'-tra-riz], *s. pl.* Contrarios, calidades o proposiciones opuestas o contrarias.

Contrariety [con-tra-rai'-e-ti], *s.* Contrariedad, repugnancia, oposición, inconsistencia, incompatibilidad.

Contrarily [con'-tra-ri-li], *adv.* Contrariamente, en contrario.

Contrariness [con'-tra-ri-nes], *s.* Contrariedad.

Contrariwise [con'-tra-ri-waiz], *adv.* Al contrario, al revés.

Contrary [con'-tra-ri], *a.* Contrario, opuesto, contradictorio, discorde.—*s.* Contrario. *On the contrary*, Al contrario o por el contrario. *I can say nothing to the contrary*, Nada tengo que oponer a eso.

Contrary, *va.* (Prov.) Oponer, contradecir, impedir.

Contrary-minded [con'-tra-ri-maind'-ed], *a.* De diverso parecer.

Contrast [con'-trast], *s.* 1. Contraste, oposición. 2. Oposición, diferencia. 3. (Ret.) *Cf.* ANTITHESIS.

Contrast [con-trast'], *va.* Contrastar, oponer, demostrar desemejanza.—*vn.* Variar, quedar claramente diferenciado de otra cosa por medio de comparación (con la prep. *with*).

Contravallation [con-tra-val-lé'-shun], *s.* Contravalación, construcción de una línea fortificada por el frente de los sitiadores de una plaza.

Contravene [con-tra-vín'], *va.* Contravenir, ir en contra de lo que está mandado y dispuesto, infringir o violar un mandato o una ley.

Contravener [con-tra-vín'-er], *s.* Contraventor, infractor; el que contraviene.

Contravention [con-tra-ven'-shun], *s.* Contravención, infracción, quebrantamiento de lo mandado.

Contraversion [con-tra-ver'-shun], *s.* Vuelta al lado opuesto.

Contrayerva [con-tra-yer'-va], *s.* (Bot.) Contrahierba, dorstenia, planta medicinal de la América tropical.

Contributary [con-trib'-yu-te-ri], *a.* (Poco us.) Contribuyente, contributario.

Contribute [con-trib'-yūt], *va.* Contribuir, dar o pagar cada uno la cuota que le corresponde.—*vn.* Contribuir, ayudar, cooperar o concurrir con otros al logro de algún fin.

Contributer, *s. V.* CONTRIBUTOR.

Contribution [con-tri-biū'-shun], *s.* Cooperación, contribución, la acción de contribuir o suministrar con otros para algún fin; también lo que se contribuye; la cuota o cantidad que se da entre muchos para algún fin público. *Contribution-box*, Caja para recibir dádivas o cuotas, p. ej. en una reunión pública.

Contributive [con-trib'-yu-tiv], *a.* Cooperante, lo que coopera; contribuyente, contribuidor.

Contributor [con-trib'-yu-ter], *s.* Contribuidor, contribuyente.

Contributory [con-trib'-yu-to-ri], *a.* Cooperante o contribuyente.

Contrite [con'-trait], *a.* 1. Contrito, pesaroso, arrepentido, penitente. *Contrite*, entre los teólogos, es el penitente que tiene dolor de contrición, y *attrite*, el que tiene dolor de atrición. 2. (Des.) Quebrantado, machacado, magullado.

Contriteness [con'-trait-nes], *s.* Contrición, arrepentimiento.

Contrition [con-trish'-un], *s.* 1. Contrición, pesar de haber ofendido a Dios por ser quien es. 2. (Des.) Pulverización.

Contriturate [con-trit'-yu-rêt], *va.* Triturar, pulverizar juntamente (con otra cosa).

Contrivable [con-traiv'-a-bl], *a.* Imaginable, que puede inventarse o proyectarse.

Contrivance [con-traiv'-ans], *s.* 1. Idea, plan, designio, discurso, invención. 2. Traza, maña, treta, artificio; concepto, maquinación.

Contrive [con-traiv'], *va.* 1. Idear, inventar, imaginar, discurrir medios para el logro de algún intento, darse maña. 2. Maquinar, tramar.—*vn.* Trazar, delinear, concertar, buscar un medio, maquinar.

Contrivement [con-traiv'-ment], *s.* Traza, invención.

Contriver [con-traiv'-er], *s.* Trazador, autor, inventor.

Control [con-trōl'], *s.* 1. Control, contrarregistro que se tiene en algunas oficinas para servir de comprobante. 2. Sujeción, freno, dominio. 3. Censura, inspección. 4. Poder, autoridad. *Without control*, Sin control, sin límites. *Remote control*, Control remoto. *He has no self-control*, Carece de dominio sobre sí mismo, no puede contenerse. *To control oneself*, Dominarse, contenerse, controlarse. *He is under control*, Lograron dominarlo.

Control, *va.* 1. Reprimir, restringir, predominar; gobernar; refutar. 2. Registrar; examinar, criticar. *Controlling interest*, (Com.) Mayoría, interés predominante.

Controllable [con-trōl'-a-bl], *a.* Sujeto a vista, registro, inspección o examen. *Controllable by*, Sometido al imperio de.

Controller [con-trōl'-er], *s.* Contralor, director, superintendente, mayordomo, veedor, registrador, censurador. *Controller of the Currency*, (E. U.) Funcionario del gobierno que ejerce superintendencia sobre los bancos nacionales.

Controllership [con-trōl'-er-ship], *s.* Contraloría, oficio y oficina de contralor; mayordomía, veeduría.

Controlment [con-trōl'-ment], *s.* Restricción, sujeción.

Control tower [con-trōl' tau-er], *s.* (Aer.) Torre de control.

Controversial [con-tro-ver'-shal], *a.* Perteneciente a las controversias o disputas; polémico, contencioso.

Controversialist [con-tro-ver'-shal-ist], *s.* Controversista, contendor literario.

Controversy [con'-tro-ver-si], *s.* Controversia, disputa, debate, pleito; contradicción.

Controvert [con'-tro-vert], *va.* Controvertir, disputar o altercar sobre alguna cosa.

Controverter [con'-tro-vert-er], **Controvertist** [con'-tro-ver-tist], *s.* Controversista, argumentador.

Controvertible [con-tro-vert'-i-bl], *a.* Controvertible, disputable.

Contumacious [con-tiu-mé'-shus], *a.* Contumaz, rebelde, porfiado, obstinado, terco, tenaz, inflexible.

Contumaciously [con-tiu-mé'-shus-li], *adv.* Contumazmente, pertinazmente.

Contumaciousness [con-tiu-mé'-shus-nes], *s.* Contumacia, obstinación, terquedad.

Contumacy [con'-tiu-me-si], *s.* 1. Contumacia, rebeldía, resistencia a comparecer en juicio o a obedecer la ley. 2. Contumacia, tenacidad, dureza, terquedad; obstinación, porfía.

Contumelious [con-tiu-mí'-li-us], *a.* Contumelioso, sarcástico, afrentoso.

Contumeliousness [con-tiu-mí'-li-us-nes], **Contumely** [con'-tiu-mi-li], *s.* Contumelia, baldón, ultraje, desprecio, injuria, menosprecio, insulto.

Contuse [con-tiūz'], *va.* Contundir, magullar, machacar, causar o hacer contusión.

Contusion [con-tiū'-zhun], *s.* 1. Contusión, magullamiento. 2. Golpe y el cardenal que de él resulta.

Conundrum [co-nun'-drum], *s.* 1. Acertijo, adivinanza. 2. Cuestión o cosa intrincada.

Conure [co-nūr'], *s.* Papagayo americano del género Conurus; a él pertenece la cotorra de la Carolina.

Convalescence o **Convalescency** [con-va-les'-ens, i], *s.* Convalecencia, restablecimiento de la salud, mejoría de una enfermedad.

Convalescent [con-va-les'-ent], *a.* Convaleciente.

Convallaria [con-val-lé'-ri-a o lê'-ri-a], *s.* (Bot.) Convalaria, el lirio de los valles.

Convection [con-vec'-shun], *s.* El acto de llevar o transportar; convección, difusión del calor por un líquido o gas por medio del movimiento de sus partes componentes, lo cual la diferencia de la conducción.

Convective [con-vec'-tiv], *a.* Perteneciente o relativo a la difusión por convección.

Convenable [con-ví'-na-bl], *a.* Lo que puede juntarse.

Convene [con-vín'], *va.* 1. Convocar, congregar, juntar, unir. 2. Citar, emplazar o convocar jurídicamente.—*vn.* Convenir, juntarse.

Convener [con-vīn'-ęr], *s.* Convocador, el que convoca a una reunión.

Convenience o **Conveniency** [con-vīn'-yens, i], *s.* Conveniencia, comodidad, oportunidad, conformidad. *Does it suit your convenience?* ¿Le conviene a Vd.? *It is a great convenience,* Es de gran comodidad.

Convenient [con-vīn'-yent], *a.* Conveniente, apto, cómodo, oportuno, conforme, propio.

Conveniently [con-vīn'-yent-li], *adv.* Cómodamente; convenientemente, útil y oportunamente.

Convening [con-vīn'-ing], *s.* Convención; reunión.

Convent [con'-vent], *s.* 1. Convento; comunidad de personas religiosas que viven en una misma casa. 2. Casa que habita una comunidad.

Convent [con-vent'], *va.* (Des.) Citar o emplazar delante del juez.—*vn.* Concurrir, juntar.

Conventicle [con-ven'-ti-cl], *s.* Conventículo, conciliábulo, junta clandestina e ilícita.

Conventicler [con-ven'-ti-clęr], *s.* El que sostiene o frecuenta conventículos o conciliábulos.

Convention [con-ven'-shun], *s.* 1. Convención, asamblea, congreso, junta. 2. El acto de juntarse; cita, conferencia. 3. Asenso o convenio general o tácito. 4. Contrato, capitulación, tratado.

Conventional [con-ven'-shun-al], *a.* 1. Convencional, estipulado. 2. Convenido, establecido por costumbre, formal. 3. Elegido o considerado arbitrariamente como emblemático de alguna cosa. 4. (Bellas artes) Aceptado como habitual y acostumbrado, pero no necesariamente verdadero y natural; basado sobre la tradición.

Conventionalism [con-ven'-shun-al-izm], *s.* Consideración y respeto para con lo que es de uso y costumbre; artificio, forma o ficción aceptada generalmente.

Conventionality [con-ven''-shun-al'-i-ti], *s.* Carácter artificial; algo establecido y aceptado por costumbre.

Conventionist [con-ven'-shun-ist], *s.* Contratista.

Conventual [con-ven'-chu-al], *s.* Conventual, el que reside en un convento o es individuo de una comunidad.—*a.* Conventual, lo que pertenece al convento.

Converge [con-vęrj'], *vn.* Converger, dirigirse a un mismo punto.

Convergence, Convergency [con-vęr'-jens, jen-si], *s.* Convergencia, tendencia hacia un mismo punto.

Convergent [con-vęrj'-ent], **Converging** [con-vęrj'-ing], *a.* Convergente, que tiende hacia un mismo punto.

Conversable [con-vęrs'-a-bl], *a.* Conversable, sociable.

Conversableness [con-vęrs'-a-bl-nes], *s.* Sociabilidad.

Conversably [con-vęrs'-a-bli], *adv.* Sociablemente, afablemente.

Conversant [con'-vęr-sant], *a.* 1. Versado en, experimentado, familiar, conocedor de. 2. Empleado activamente, ocupado en, interesado.

Conversation [con-vęr-sē'-shun], *s.* 1. Conversación, conferencia, trato, familiaridad. 2. Conducta, porte. 3. Trato carnal.

Conversative [con-vęrs'-a-tiv], *a.* (Poco us.) Conversable, sociable.

Conversazione [con-vęr-sat-si-ō'-nē], *s.* Tertulia. Es voz italiana.

Converse [con-vęrs'], *vn.* 1. Conversar, vivir con otro y tratar con él. 2. Conversar, tener conocimiento con alguno. 3. Platicar, hablar familiarmente sobre algún asunto. 4. Tratar con, tener trato ilícito con persona de otro sexo.

Converse [con'-vęrs], *s.* 1. Conversación, plática, comunicación, familiaridad, trato, comercio. 2. Conversa, proposición opuesta a la directa; lo que existe en relación recíproca a otra cosa.

Conversely [con-vers'-li], *adv.* Mutuamente, recíprocamente.

Conversion [con-vęr'-shun], *s.* 1. Conversión, transmutación de una cosa en otra. 2. Conversión, arrepentimiento. 3. Mudanza de una religión a otra; cambio de opinión, de partido. 4. (For.) Apropiación ilícita de los bienes de otro para uso propio.

Conversive [con-vęrs'-iv], *a.* Conversivo, que causa conversión o que resulta de ella.

Convert [con-vęrt'], *va.* 1. Convertir, transmutar. 2. Convertir, reducir al vicioso a la práctica de las buenas costumbres. 3. Convertir, volver, dirigir una cosa hacia una parte diversa de donde estaba antes. 4. Dar a una cosa destino diverso del que antes tenía. 5. (Com.) Convertir o cambiar en valor de otra forma.—*vn.* Convertirse, mudarse.

Convert [con'-vęrt], *s.* Converso o convertido, la persona que se ha convertido de una religión o parecer a otro diferente. *New convert,* Neófito, recién convertido, converso, convertido; religioso lego.

Converter, Convertor [con-vęrt'-ęr, er], *s.* 1. Convertidor, el que convierte. 2. (Metal) Convertidor, retorta de cementación, aparato de Bessemer para convertir el hierro en acero. 3. Convertidor, transformador eléctrico. *V.* TRANSFORMER.

Convertibility [con-vęrt-i-bil'-i-ti], *s.* Capacidad de conversión.

Convertible [con-vęrt'-i-bl], *a.* Convertible, transmutable.—*s.* Convertible, automóvil convertible.

Convertibly [con-vęrt'-i-bli], *adv.* Recíprocamente, mutuamente.

†**Convertite** [con'-vęrt-ait], *s.* Neófito, recién convertido.

Convex [con'-vecs], *a.* Convexo, que tiene superficie curva más elevada en el centro que en los bordes u orillas; es lo contrario de cóncavo.—*s.* Cuerpo o superficie convexa.

Convexed [con-vecst'], *a.* Convexo, elevado en figura circular.

Convexedly [con-vec'-sed-li], *adv.* En forma o figura convexa.

Convexity [con-vec'-si-ti], *s.* 1. Convexidad, superficie exterior de un cuerpo convexo; forma esférica o convexa. 2. Combadura, comba.

Convexly [con-vecs'-li], *adv.* Convexamente.

Convexness [con-vecs'-nes], *s.* Convexidad.

Convexo-concave [con-vecs'-o-con'-kēv], *a.* Convexo-cóncavo.

Convey [con-vē'], *va.* 1. Transportar, conducir o llevar de una parte a otra. 2. Transmitir, enviar. 3. Transferir, traspasar a otro. 4. Participar, dar parte o noticia de alguna cosa. 5. Comunicar, expresar (el sentido de las palabras). *To convey away,* Quitar del medio, hacer desaparecer, llevarse una cosa, ocultar. *To convey out,* Poner fuera de alcance, salvar. *To convey out of danger,* Sacar del peligro. *To convey his sense,* Expresar su pensamiento.

Conveyable [con-vē'-a-bl], *a.* Capaz de ser transportado o conducido.

Conveyance [con-vē'-ans], *s.* 1. Conducción, transporte. 2. Conducción, modo o manera de conducir o transportar. 3. Entrega. 4. Traspaso o traslación de dominio. 5. Escritura de traspaso.

Conveyancer [con-vē'-an-sęr], *s.* El escribano que hace la escritura de traspaso, enajenación o traslación de dominio.

Conveyancing [con-vē'-an-sing], *s.* El oficio de preparar las escrituras de traspaso, incluyendo la pesquisa de títulos.

Conveyer [con-vē'-ęr], *s.* 1. Conductor, mensajero. 2. Portador, invento mecánico para transportar material, como en molinos, elevadores, etc. 3. (Des.) Truhán, impostor; ladrón.

Conveyor belt [con-vē'-ęr belt], *s.* Correa o cinta transportadora.

Convict [con-vict'], *va.* 1. Convencer, probar la culpabilidad; declarar culpable después de un proceso judicial. 2. Confutar, refutar, destruir los argumentos del contrario.

Convict [con'-vict], *s.* Convicto, el reo a quien legalmente se le ha probado su delito.

Convictible [con-vict'-i-bl], *a.* Convencible.

Conviction [con-vic'-shun], *s.* 1. Convicción, demostración de culpabilidad; juicio basado en pruebas suficientes: proposición firmemente creída. 2. Convicción, la prueba de un delito. 3. Confutación, refutación.

Convictive [con-vic'-tiv], *a.* (Poco us.) Convincente.

Convictively [con-vic'-tiv-li], *adv.* Convincentemente.

Convince [con-vins'], *va.* 1. Convencer, precisar a otro con razones a que mude de dictamen; hacer creer. 2. Poner en evidencia, juzgar. 3. (Des.) Declarar culpable. *V.* CONVICT.

Convincement [con-vins'-męnt], *s.* (Poco us.) Convicción.

Convincer [con-vins'-ęr], *s.* El o lo que convence.

Convincible [con-vins'-i-bl], *a.* Convencible; convincente, incontestable.

Convincingly [con-vins'-ing-li], *adv.* Convincentemente.

Convincingness [con-vins'-ing-nes], *s.* Convicción, evidencia y fuerza de la razón que convence.

Convivial [con-viv'-i-al], *a.* 1. Festivo, relativo a festín o convite. 2. Convivial, festivo, jovial.

Conviviality [con-viv''-i-al'-i-ti], *s.* Jovialidad, buen humor.

Convocate [con'-vo-kēt], *va.* Convocar, citar, llamar a muchos que deben juntarse en un lugar determinado para algún fin.

Convocation [con-vo-kē'-shun], *s.* 1. Convocación, acción de convocar o de reunir. 2. Asamblea así convocada, especialmente junta del clero ó sínodo.

Convoke [con-vōk'], *va.* Convocar, citar, juntar, reunir.

Convolute, Convoluted [con'-vo-lūt o lūt, con'-vo-lū-ted], *a.* Arrollado, envuelto, replegado.—*s.* Lo que está arrollado.

Convolution [con-vo-lū'-shun], *s.* 1. La

acción de arrollar o envolver. 2. Repliegue, enroscadura. (Anat.) Una de las sinuosidades o senos de un órgano, especialmente del cerebro y del intestino.
Convolve [con-volv'], *va.* Arrollar, revolver, retorcer una cosa en sí misma.—*vn.* Revolver o enlazarse sobre sí mismo.
Convolvulaceous [con-vol''-viu-lé'-shus], *a.* (Bot.) Convolvuláceo, semejante ó relativo al convólvulo.
Convolvulus [con-vol'-viu-lus], *s.* Convólvulo, género de plantas cuyo tipo es la correhuela o albohol y que comprende también el dondiego, la batata, la jalapa, etc.
Convoy [con-voi'], *va.* Convoyar, escoltar lo que se conduce por mar o por tierra para que vaya resguardado.
Convoy [con'-voi], *s.* 1. Convoy ó conserva, escolta o guardia que se destina para la segura conducción por mar o por tierra. 2. Convoy, los efectos, valores ó pertrechos que van escoltados. 3. La acción de convoyar; el estado de ser convoyado.
Convulse [con-vuls'], *va.* Convulsar; causar la contracción de los músculos; afectar espasmódicamente; agitar violentamente.—*vr.* Convelerse. convulsarse, irritarse, alterarse o ponerse en convulsión las fibras del cuerpo. *To be convulsed with laughter*, Morirse de risa.
Convulsion [con-vul'-shun], *s.* 1. Convulsión, espasmo. 2. Agitación violenta, inquietud. 3. Conmoción, alboroto, revolución, tumulto. 4. (Geol.) *V.* CATACLYSM.
Convulsionary [con-vul'-shun-e-ri], *a.* De la convulsión; que causa convulsiones o es resultado de ellas.
Convulsive [con-vuls'-iv], *a.* Convulsivo.
Convulsively [con-vuls'-iv-li], *adv.* Tumultuariamente; convulsivamente.
Cony [cō'-ni], *s.* Conejo. *Cony-skins* o *wool*, *V.* RABBIT-SKINS o WOOL.
Cony-burrow [cō'-ni-bur'-ō], *s.* Conejera, vivar o madriguera donde se crían los conejos.
Coo [cū], *vn.* 1. Arrullar, cantar, como paloma o tórtola. 2. Decir ternezas. (Fam.) Enamorar.
Cooing [cū'-ing], *s.* 1. Arrullo de palomas o tórtolas. 2. (Fig.) Arrullo, halago, caricia.
Cook [cuk], *va.* 1. Cocinar, guisar, aderezar las viandas. 2. Falsificar, alterar para engañar.—*vn.* Guisar. *To cook up*, Tramar, maquinar en secreto.
Cook, *s.* Cocinero, cocinera. *Cook's shop*, Bodegón. *Cook-maid*, *sf.* Cocinera. *Cook-room*, *s.* (1) Cocina. (2) (Mar.) Fogón de un buque.
Cookery [cuk'-er-i], *s.* Arte de cocina, el arte de componer las viandas; también, lugar para cocinar.
Cooking [cuk'-ing], *s.* Cocina, arte de cocinar.—*a.* De cocina. *Cooking range, cooking stove*, Estufa, cocina económica. *Cooking utensils*, Batería o enseres de cocina.
Cooky [cuk'-i], *s.* Pequeño bollo dulce.
Cool [cūl], *a.* 1. Frío, fresco. 2. Tibio, flojo, indiferente, poco fervoroso.—*s.* Frescura o fresco.
Cool, *va.* Enfriar, refrescar, entibiar, atemperar, dulcificar, sosegar o templar la ira.—*vn.* Refrescar, enfriarse, templarse, moderarse el enojo o cualquiera pasión. *To cool the heels*, Estar aguardando mucho tiempo, hacer antesala cansada y larga.
Cool-cup [cūl'-cup], *s.* Bebida hecha de vino, agua, azúcar y borraja.
Cooler [cūl'-er], *s.* 1. Enfriadera, garapiñera, garrafa, la vasija en que se enfría alguna cosa. 2. (Med.) Refrigerante.
Cool-headed [cūl'-hed-ed], *a.* Tibio, no fácilmente perturbado o excitado; que obra con calma y deliberación.
Coolie [cū'-li], *s.* Peón chino o de la India que trabaja por contrata.
Cooling [cūl'-ing], *a.* 1. Refrescante, fresco, refrigerativo. 2. Tibio, flojo.
Coolish [cūl'-ish], *a.* Fresco, un poco frío.
Coolly [cūl'-li], *adv.* Frescamente, serenamente, fríamente.
Coolness [cūl'-nes], *s.* 1. Fresco, frío. 2. Frialdad, tibieza. 3. Frescura, serenidad de ánimo.
Coom [cūm], *s.* 1. Hollín de horno. 2. El unto negro que despiden los ejes de las ruedas de carros y coches.
Coomb [cūm], *s.* Antigua medida inglesa de cuatro fanegas.
Coon [cūn], *s.* *V.* RACCOON. *A coon's age*, Mucho tiempo. *An old coon*, Persona astuta y mañosa. *A gone coon*, (Ger. E. U.) Persona o cosa en situación o condición desesperada.
Coop [cūp], *s.* 1. Caponera, gallinero, jaula para capones y otras aves. 2. Redil para ganado lanar. 3. Tonel, barril grande de madera para líquidos. 4. (Esco.) Chirrión. *V.* TUMBREL.
Coop, *va.* Enjaular, encarcelar.
Cooper [cūp'-er], *va.* Hacer o fabricar barriles.
Cooper, *s.* Tonelero, el que hace o fabrica toneles, pipas o cubas.
Cooperage [cūp'-er-ej], *s.* 1. Jornal de tonelero, el dinero que se le da por su trabajo. 2. Todo lo perteneciente a la tonelería.
Co-operant [co-op'-er-ant], *a.* Cooperante, el que o lo que coopera.
Co-operate [co-op'-er-ét], *vn.* 1. Cooperar, obrar de consuno para un mismo fin. 2. Contribuir con algo o de alguna manera para la perfección o consecución de una cosa u objeto.
Co-operation [co-op-er-é'-shun], *s.* Cooperación.
Co-operative [co-op'-er-e-tiv], *a.* Cooperativo; cooperante.
Co-operator [co-op'-er-é''-ter], *s.* Cooperador.
Coopering [cū'-per-ing], *s.* Tonelería, el arte de tonelero.
Co-optate [co-op'-têt], *va.* Adoptar por acción mutua, admitir, agregar.
Co-ordinate [co-ōr'-di-nêt], *a.* Coordinado.
Co-ordinately [co-ōr'-di-nêt-li], *adv.* Coordinadamente.
Co-ordinateness [co-ōr'-di-net-nes]. **Co-ordination** [co-ōr-di-né'-shun], *s.* Coordinación, método, colocación o distribución de alguna cosa.
Coot [cūt], *s.* (Orn.) Negreta, especie de ánade de color muy obscuro.
Cop [cop], *s.* 1. Cima, cumbre, punta. 2. Moño, copa, copete. 3. (Art. y Of.) Penacho, manojito de hilos que se forma sobre el huso de una máquina de hilar.
Cop [cop], *s.* (Ger.) Agente de policía.
Copaiba [co-pé'-ba], **Copayva,** *s.* Copay, copaiba, resina ó bálsamo que se saca de un árbol del Brasil llamado *copayva.*
Copaifera [co-pai'-fe-ra], *s.* Copay o copaiba, género de árboles del Brasil, familia de las leguminosas; varias especies dan el bálsamo copaiba.
Copal [cō'-pal], *s.* Goma copal o ánime; resina dura y transparente empleada para barnices.
Coparcenary [co-pār'-se-ne-ri], **Coparceny** [co-pār'-se-ni], *s.* (For.) Derecho igual por sucesión a alguna herencia.
Copartner [co-pārt'-ner], *s.* Compañero, socio, asociado, el que tiene parte en una empresa o comercio.
Copartnership [co-pārt'-ner-ship], *s.* Compañía, sociedad, asociación; parte o interés en una empresa, negocio, etc.
Cope [cōp], *s.* 1. Lo que cubre formando arco o curva, como la bóveda del cielo, la cima de cúpulas, paredes, etc.; albardilla. 2. Capa pluvial.
Cope [cōp], *va.* (Des.) Contender, disputar, pleitear.—*vn.* Competir o lidiar con otro en condiciones iguales; hacer cara; sobresalir.
Cope, *va.* 1. Cubrir o vestir con capa pluvial. 2. Poner albardilla o caballete sobre un muro. 3. (Ant.) Recompensar, dar en cambio, cambiar, trocar.
Copeck [cō'-pec], *s.* Moneda rusa de un rublo. *V.* KOPEK.
Copernican [cō-per'-ni-can], *a.* Copernicano, lo que pertenece al sistema de Copérnico.
Copestone [cōp'-stōn], *s.* Piedra de una pared que sirve de cima o tope.
Copier [cop'-i-er], *s.* 1. Copiante, copista. 2. Copiador, plagiario.
Coping [cōp'-ing], *s.* Albardilla, el caballete que se forma sobre una pared para que no la penetren y calen las lluvias; cumbre de edificio.
Copious [cō'-pi-us], *a.* Copioso, abundante, difuso, rico.
Copiously [cō'-pi-us-li], *adv.* Copiosamente, ampliamente.
Copiousness [cō'-pi-us-nes], *s.* Abundancia, redundancia; difusión; profusión, copia.
Copivi [co-pī'-vi], *s.* *V.* COPAIBA.
Copped [copt], *a.* Copado, copetudo.
Coppel [cop'-el], *s.* *V.* CUPEL.
Copper [cop'-er], *s.* 1. Cobre, un metal, rojizo y dúctil. 2. Calderón, caldera grande. 3. Vellón, moneda de cobre; centavo, penique. *Copper-coloured*, Color cobrizo; aplícase especialmente a los indios americanos. *Copper-nickel*, *V.* NICCOLITE.
Copper, *va.* 1. Encobrar, cubrir o revestir con hojas de cobre; forrar de cobre un buque. 2. En el juego de faraón, poner un centavo sobre las monedas o las fichas apuntadas a una carta; lo cual significa apostar en contra.
Copperas [cop'-er-as], *s.* Caparrosa, vitriolo verde, sulfato de hierro.
Copperhead [cop'-er-hed], *s.* Culebra norteamericana muy venenosa, parecida a la de cascabel.
Copperish [cop'-er-ish], **Coppery** [cop'-er-i], *a.* Cobrizo, cobreño, lo que contiene cobre, se le asemeja o es de su color.
Copper-plate [cop'-er-plêt], *s.* Lámina de cobre, la plancha de cobre de que se sirven los grabadores para grabar. *Copper-plate prints*, Estampas, láminas ó grabados.

Coppersmith [cep'-gr-smith], *s.* Calderero.
Copper sulphate [cep'-gr sul'-fêt], *s.* Sulfato de cobre, vitriolo azul.
Copper-work [cep'-gr-wūrk], *s.* Fábrica de cobre.
Copperworm [cep'-gr-wūrm], *s.* 1. Broma, gusano que agujerea la madera de los buques. 2. Polilla, insecto que roe la ropa. 3. Arador, insecto que produce comezón en la piel.
Coppice [cep'-is], *s.* Soto, tallar, monte bajo, bosque que se corta a menudo.
Copple-dust [cep'-l-dust], *s.* *V.* CUPEL-DUST.
Coppled [cep'ld], *a.* Lo que se eleva en forma cónica. *V.* COPPED.
Copra [cep'-ra], *s.* Copra, médula del coco de la palma.
Coproprietor [co-pro-prai'-g-ter], *s.* Copropietario, el que posee juntamente con otro alguna cosa.
Copse, *va.* Conservar los bosques recién cortados.
Copsy [cep'-si], *a.* Lo que pertenece a los montes bajos.
Copt [cept], *s.* Copto, descendiente de los antiguos egipcios.
Coptic [cep'-tic], *a.* Cóptico, relativo a los coptos.—*s.* Copto, la lengua antigua de los egipcios cristianos.
Copula [cep'-yu-la], *s.* (Gram. y Lóg.) 1. Cópula, el verbo que une el predicado con el sujeto. 2. En un órgano, *V.* COUPLER. 3. (Anat.) Parte que une o junta.
Copulate [cep'-yu-lêt], *va.* Unir, juntar o estrechar una cosa con otra de modo que no pueda haber mediación o cosa intermedia.—*vn.* Ayuntarse o unirse; tener coito el macho con la hembra o el hombre con la mujer.
Copulation [cep-yu-lê'-shun], *s.* Cópula, coito, unión del macho con la hembra y en particular del hombre con la mujer; conjunción.
Copulative [cep'-yu-lg-tiv], *a.* (Gram.) Copulativo, conjuntivo.—*s.* (Gram.) Conjunción.
Copulatory [cep'-yu-lg-to-ri], *a.* 1. De la cópula o perteneciente á ella. 2. *V.* COPULATIVE.
Copy [cep'-i], *s.* 1. Copia, traslado sacado a la letra de cualquier escrito original. 2. Original, el manuscrito que se da a imprimir. 3. Instrumento legal de entrega. 4. Copia de una pintura o modelo de una estatua. 5. Ejemplar de algún libro. 6. Muestra. *A fair copy,* Copia en limpio. *Rough copy,* Borrador, minuta.
Copy, *va.* Copiar, trasladar algún escrito; imitar.—*vn.* Imitar, contrahacer.
Copy-book [cep'-i-buc], *s.* 1. Cuaderno para planas u otros usos. 2. Cuaderno de escritura; copiador de cartas, libro en que se copian las cartas.
Copyer [cep'-i-gr], **Copyist** [cep'-i-ist]. *V.* COPIER.
Copyhold [cep'-i-hōld], *s.* (For.) Especie de enfiteusis, arrendamiento temporal, tenencia de tierras por censo o por feudo.
Copyholder [cep'-i-hōld'-gr], *s.* 1. Aparato para colocar el original (en las imprentas). 2. El que lee en voz alta al corrector de pruebas. 3. (For.) Arrendador.
Copying [cep'-i-ing], *s.* y *pa.* de *To* COPY. *Copying-ink,* Tinta de copiar, que contiene azúcar, glicerina o substancia parecida, y se usa en la prensa de copiar. *Copying-paper,* Papel muy delgado que se usa en el copiador de cartas. *Copying-press,* Prensa de copiar o copiador de cartas; también, aparato que sirve para sacar numerosas reproducciones de cartas, circulares, etc.
Copyright [cep'-i-rait], *s.* La propiedad de una obra literaria.
Coquet [co-ket'], *va.* y *vn.* 1. Coquetear, hacer coqueterías, tener ademanes o conducta de coqueta. 2. Cocar, hacer cocos, requebrar, cortejar, galantear.
Coquetry [cō'-ket-ri], *s.* Coquetería, afectación en el vestir y hablar para agradar y parecer bien; inconstancia o veleidad en las mujeres.
Coquette [co-ket'], *sf.* 1. Coqueta, dama presumida de hermosa, petimetra. 2. Carantoñera, mujer que gusta de verse cortejada, y hace lo posible para serlo de muchos a un tiempo.
Coquettish [co-ket'-ish], *a.* De coqueta; dispuesta a hacer coqueterías.
Coracle [cer'-a-cl], *s.* Barca de pescadores hecha de cuero, o de encerado sobre un bastidor de mimbre; se usa en Francia, Gales e Irlanda.
Coracoid [cer'-a-ceid], *s.* (Anat.) Coracoides, apófisis del omoplato.
Coral [cer'-al], *s.* 1. Coral, despojo sólido de una agregación de pólipos. 2. Coral, género de pólipo zoofitario cuyo polípero es arborizado.—*a.* Coralino, de coral; parecido al coral.
Coralline [cer'-al-in], *a.* Coralino, lo que tiene coral.—*s.* Coralina, musgo marino, planta de mar; es una concha de zoófitos, así como el coral.
Coralloid, Coralloidal [cer'-al-eid, eid'-al], *a.* Coralino.
Corb [cērb], *s.* Barril de extracción en una mina de carbón.
Corban [cēr'-ban], *s.* 1. Entre los antiguos judíos, ofrenda a Dios, especialmente en cumplimiento de un voto. 2. Cepillo o cestillo para pedir limosna.
Corbeil [cēr'-bel], *s.* (Mil.) Cestón, tejido de mimbres lleno de tierra, para parapetarse contra el fuego del enemigo.
Corbel [cēr'-bel], **Corbil** [cēr'-bil], *s.* 1. (Arq.) Cesta sobre la cabeza de la cariátide. 2. (Arq.) Saledizo fuera de las paredes.
Corbie [cēr'-bi], *s.* (Esco.) Cuervo.
Cord [cērd], *s.* 1. Cuerda, cuerdecita, bramante, cabo; cordel, lazo. 2. Cordoncillo, en los tejidos. 3. Cuerda, haz o montón de leña para quemar, que tiene ocho pies de largo, cuatro de alto y cuatro de ancho. *Spermatic cord, spinal cord, umbilical cord,* véanse los adjetivos.
Cord, *va.* Encordelar, atar o amarrar con cordeles o cuerdas.
Cordage [cērd'-ēj], *s.* Cordaje. *Twice-laid cordage,* Cabos contrahechos. *Plaited cordage,* Cajetas.
Cordate [cēr'-dêt], *a.* Cordiforme, en forma de corazón.
Corded [cērd'-ed], *a.* Hecho de cuerdas.
Cordelier [cerd-e-lîr'], *s.* Fraile franciscano.
Cordial [cēr'-jal o cērd'-yal], *s.* Cordial, remedio confortativo.
Cordial, *a.* 1. Sincero, de corazón, amistoso, afectuoso. 2. Cordial, confortativo.
Cordiality [cerd-yal'-i-ti], *s.* Cordialidad, sinceridad.
Cordially [cērd'-yal-i], *adv.* Cordialmente, sinceramente.
Cordialness [cērd'-yal-nes], *s.* Sinceridad, afecto cordial.
Cordiform [cēr'-di-fērm], *a.* *V.* CORDATE.
Cordite [cērd'-ait], *s.* (Quím.) Cordita.
Cord-maker [cerd'-mê-kgr], *s.* Cordelero, soguero.
Cordon [cēr'-den], *s.* 1. Cordón, serie o línea extensa de hombres o buques, colocados de tal manera que bloqueen una entrada o dominen una frontera. 2. Cordón, cíngulo. 3. (Arq.) Cordón, moldura saliente y horizontal.
Cordovan [cēr'-do-van], **Cordwain** [cerd'-wên], *s.* Cordobán, para hacer zapatos; cuero curtido de caballo.
Corduroy [cēr'-diu-rei], *s.* Pana, tela gruesa y durable de algodón, acordonada o rayada. *Corduroy road,* Camino con piso de troncos.
Cordwainer [cerd'-wên-gr], *s.* Zapatero.
Cord-wood [cērd'-wud], *s.* Cuerda de leña, la porción que está ya medida y hacinada para vender.
Core [cōr], *s.* 1. Corazón; fondo, interior o centro de una cosa. 2. Cuesco o hueso, lo que está debajo de la carne de la fruta y encierra la almendra o semilla. 3. Ánima, macho de un molde. 4. Cascote o roca cilíndrica que se saca con un taladro anular. 5. Corazón, los alambres aislados de conducción de un cable eléctrico. 6. (Prov. Ingl.) Enfermedad del ganado lanar.
Coregency [cō-ri'-jen-si], *s.* Corregencia, calidad del que es regente con otro.
Corelative, *a.* *V.* CORRELATIVE.
Coreopsis [cō-rg-ep'-sis], *s.* (Bot.) Género de plantas americanas de la familia de las compuestas, con hermosas flores amarillas y color de rosa; corcópsida, planta de este género.
Corer [cōr'-gr], *s.* Despepitador; instrumento para quitar las pepitas o los huesos de las frutas.
Corespondent [cō-re-spen'-dent], *s.* 1. (For.) Correspondiente, el que responde con otros. 2. (For.) La persona a quien se acusa como cómplice del demandado en una demanda de divorcio.
Coriaceous [cō-ri-ê'-shus], *a.* Coriáceo, de cuero o parecido al cuero; correoso.
Coriander [cō-ri-an'-dgr], *s.* (Bot.) Cilantro, culantro.
Corinthian [co-rin'-thi-an], *a.* 1. 1. (Arq.) Corintio, el cuarto orden de arquitectura. 2. Libidinoso.
Corival [cō-rai'-val, *s.* Rival, competidor juntamente con dos o más personas.—*va.* Rivalizar.
Cork [cērk], *s.* 1. Alcornoque, árbol parecido a la encina. 2. Corcho, la corteza del alcornoque. 3. Corcho, tapón de botella.
Cork, *va.* Tapar botellas con corchos.
Corkcutter [cērk'-cut-gr], *s.* Taponero, el que hace tapones de corcho; también la herramienta especial que usa.
Corkscrew [cērk'-scrū], *s.* Tirabuzón, sacacorchos, instrumento para sacar los corchos de las botellas. —*a.* En forma de tirabuzón, en espiral.
Cork-tree [cērk'-trî], *s.* Alcornoque.
Cormorant [cēr'-mo-rant], *s.* 1. Corvejón, cuervo marino. 2. (Fig.) Glotón o avaro.

Corn [cērn], *s.* 1. Grano, fruto y semilla de las mieses; en Inglaterra, trigo, cebada, avena y centeno, especialmente el trigo. En Escocia, la avena, por lo general. En América, el maíz, cereal propio del hemisferio occidental. *Green corn*, Mazorca de maíz tierno. (Mex.) Helote. 2. Mies que aun está por segar o trillar. 3. Cualquiera partícula menuda. *Corn-cob*, Mazorca de maíz, la espiga alrededor de la cual crecen los granos del maíz. *Corn-crib*, Granero de rejilla para el maíz. *Corn-meal*, Harina de maíz. *Corn-market*, Precio de los cereales. *Corn-shuck* o *husk*, Cáscara o vaina del maíz. *Corn-starch*, Almidón de maíz, especialmente el purificado para la mesa. *Corn-sheller*, Desgranadora de maíz. *Broom corn*, Millo de escoba. *Indian corn*, Maíz.

Corn, *s.* Callo, dureza que se forma en los pies. (< Fr. *corne*, < lat. *cornu*, cuerno.)

Corn, *va.* 1. Salar. 2. Desmenuzar alguna cosa hasta reducirla a granos pequeños.

Cornage [cērn'-ėj], *s.* La obligación que en lo antiguo tenían ciertas personas de tocar la corneta cuando invadían los enemigos. (Ingl.)

Corn-bind [cērn-baind], *s.* (Bot.) Especie de correhüela.

Cornchandler [cērn'-chand-lęr], *s.* Revendedor de granos.

Corn-crake, *s.* (Orn.) *V.* LAND-RAIL.

Corn-cutter [cērn'-cut-ęr], *s.* 1. Máquina para cortar el maíz. 2. Pedicuro, callista.

Cornea [cēr'-ne-a], *s.* Córnea, la parte anterior transparente del ojo.

Corned [cērnd], *a.* 1. Salado, conservado en salmuera. *Corned beef*, Carne de vaca en media salmuera. 2. (Ger.) Borracho, chispo.

Cornel [cēr'-nel] o **Cornelian-tree** [cer-nīl'-yan-trī], *s.* (Bot.) Cornejo, corno.

Cornelian [cer-nīl'-yan], *s.* Cornerina, piedra preciosa. *V.* CARNELIAN.

Cornemuse [cērn'-miūz], *s.* 1. Cornamusa. 2. Gaita. 3. Oboe.

Corneous [cēr'-nę-us], *a.* 1. Córneo, hecho de cuerno. 2. Calloso.

Corner [cēr'-nęr], *s.* 1. Ángulo, esquina. *The inner corner*, Rincón. *The outer corner*, Esquina. 2. Rincón, escondrijo o lugar retirado. 3. Extremidad, la parte más remota de alguna cosa. 4. Aprieto, apuro, situación difícil. 5. (E. U.) Estado del mercado respecto a un valor o artículo que ha sido monopolizado en gran parte para especular con él. *In all corners of the earth*, Por toda la tierra. *Corner house*, Casa en la esquina de una calle. *Corners of a river*, Vueltas, rodeos o sinuosidades de un río. *In a corner*, Secretamente; en situación difícil.

Corner, *va.* 1. Arrinconar, forzar o empujar hacia un rincón. 2. Poner en situación difícil o embarazosa. 3. (E. U.) Monopolizar, comprar o contratar la compra de ciertos valores o de un artículo de necesario consumo, para dominar el mercado y dictar el precio de dichos valores o mercaderías.—*vn.* Lindar con una esquina.

Cornered [cēr'-nęrd], *a.* Angulado, esquinado. *Three-cornered hat*, Sombrero de tres candiles.

Corner-stone [cēr'-nęr-stōn], *s.* 1. (Arq.) Piedra angular; mocheta. 2. Algo fundamental y de primera importancia.

Cornerwise [cēr'-nęr-waiz], *adv.* Diagonalmente.

Cornet [cēr'-net], *s.* 1. Corneta, instrumento de música y boca. 2. Portaestandarte, oficial de caballería que lleva el estandarte. 3. Toca de mujer. 4. Cucurucho, papel arrollado en forma de cono para envolver géneros menudos. 5. *V.* CORONET, 3ª acep.

Cornetcy [cēr'-net-si], *s.* Empleo y grado de portaestandarte.

Corneter [cēr'-net-ęr], *s.* El que toca la corneta.

Corn-field [cērn'-fīld], *s.* Sembrado, el pedazo de terreno sembrado de granos.

Corn-flag [cērn'-flag], *s.* (Bot.) Gladiolo, gladio o espadaña.

Corn-floor [cērn'-flōr], *s.* Suelo de granero.

Corn-flower [cērn'-flau-ęr], *s.* Azulejo, aciano, coronilla, flores que nacen en los sembrados.

Corn-heap [cērn'-hīp], *s.* Hacina, pila de grano.

Cornice [cer'-nis], *s.* 1. (Arq.) Cornisa. 2. Sobrepuerta.

Cornicle [cer'-ni-cl], *s.* Cuernecito.

Corniculate [cer-nic'-yu-lēt], *a.* (Bot.) Flor corniculada.

Cornific [cer-nif'-ic], *a.* Cornífico, que produce cuernos o substancia córnea.

Cornigerous [cer-nij'-ęr-us], *a.* Cornígero, que tiene cuernos.

Corning-house [cern'-ing-haus], *s.* La casa donde se reduce a grano la pólvora.

Cornish [cer'-nish], *a.* Perteneciente al condado de Cornualles o Cornwall, Inglaterra.—*s.* Antiguo dialecto céltico de Cornualles.

Corn-land [cērn'-land], *s.* Tierra sembrada o destinada y á propósito para sembrar; tierra de pan llevar.

Corn-loft [cērn'-lōft], *s.* Granero, cámara donde se encierran los granos.

Corn-marigold [cern-mar'-i-gōld], *s.* (Bot.) Especie de caléndula.

Corn-meter [cērn'-mī-tęr], *s.* Antiguamente, medidor de granos.

Corn-mill [cērn'-mil], *s.* Molino, máquina para moler trigo y otros granos, o el edificio donde se muelen.

Corn-pipe [cērn'-paip], *s.* Especie de silbato hecho con el tallo del trigo ó de la avena.

Corn-plaster [cērn'-plgs-tęr], *s.* Emplasto para los callos.

Corn-popper [cērn'-pep'-ęr], *s.* Tostador de maíz.

Corn-poppy [cērn'-pep'-i], *s.* (Bot.) Ababa, ababol, amapola, planta que nace en los sembrados. Papaver rhœas.

Corn-rose [cērn'-rōz], *s.* (Bot.) Ababa, ababol, amapola.

Corn-salad [cērn'-sal-ad], *s.* (Bot.) Macha, valerianilla.

Cornucopia [cēr-nu-cō'-pi-a], *s.* 1. Cornucopia, cuerno de la abundancia. 2. Alcartaz, cucurucho.

Cornuted [cer-nūt'-ed], *a.* Cornudo, lo que tiene cuernos; en figura de cuerno.

†**Cornuto** [cer-nū'-to], *s.* Cornudo, el marido cuya mujer ha faltado a la fidelidad conyugal.

Corn-violet [cērn'-vai-o-let], *s.* (Bot.) Especie de campánula.

Corny [cērn'-i], *a.* 1. Hecho de cuerno, córneo, calloso. 2. (Poco us.) Que produce o contiene grano.

Corolla [co-rel'-a], *s.* Corola, cubierta interior o segunda de las flores completas, que presenta generalmente vivos colores. Cada una de las hojas que la forman se llama pétalo. (Esta voz rara vez se escribe *corol.*)

Corollary [cer'-e-lę-ri], *s.* 1. Corolario, consectario. 2. Sobrante.

Corona [co-rō'-na], *s.* 1. (Arq.) Corona de entablamento, una de las partes de que se compone la cornisa. 2. Corona, halo, especie de meteoro circular que aparece alrededor del sol o de la luna. 3. (Bot.) Eminencia parecida a una corona en el ápice de algunos pétalos. (Biol.) Parte o estructura parecida a una corona.

Coronal [cer'-o-nal], *s.* Coronal, el hueso de la frente; corona, guirnalda.—*a.* Coronal, lo perteneciente al hueso coronal.

Coronary [cer'-o-nę-ri], *a.* Coronario, lo que pertenece a la corona.

Coronation [cer-o-nē'-shun], *s.* Coronación.

Coroner [cer'-o-nęr], *s.* Córoner; se llama así un empleado cuyo deber es indagar las causas de las muertes repentinas y violentas, con presencia indispensablemente del cadáver.

Coronet [cer'-o-net], *s.* 1. La corona particular que corresponde á los títulos nobiliarios según su clase. 2. Guirnalda para la cabeza. 3. Margen superior del casco del caballo.

Corporal [cēr'-po-ral], *s.* Cabo o caporal, el que manda una de las escuadras en que se divide la compañía.—*a.* 1. Corporal, corpóreo, lo que pertenece al cuerpo. 2. §Material, no espiritual.

Corporality [cer-po-ral'-i-ti], *s.* Corporalidad, corporeidad.

Corporally [cēr'-po-ral-i], *adv.* Corporalmente.

Corporate [cēr'-pe-rēt], *a.* 1. Formado en cuerpo o en comunidad. 2. General; unido. 3. Perteneciente a una corporación; colectivo.

Corporately [cēr'-po-ret-li], *adv.* 1. Corporalmente; unidamente. 2. En cuerpo.

Corporateness [cēr'-po-ret-nes], *s.* Comunidad, incorporación.

Corporation [cer-po-rē'-shun], *s.* 1. Corporación, cuerpo político ó civil, con capacidad legal para obrar como una sola persona. 2. Cabildo, ayuntamiento, comunidad de personas eclesiásticas o seculares; cuerpo, sociedad, gremio, v. gr. gremio de sastres, zapateros, etc. 3. (Fest.) El cuerpo humano cuando es grande y pesado.

Corporeal [cer-pō'-rę-al], *a.* 1. Corpóreo; material, lo opuesto a inmaterial o espiritual. 2. (For.) Perceptible por los sentidos corporales, substancial y permanente; material, tangible.

Corporealist [cer-pō'-rę-al-ist], *s.* Materialista, el que niega la inmaterialidad del alma.

Corporeality [cer-po-rę-al'-i-ti], *s.* Corporeidad.

Corporeally [cer-pō'-re-al-i], *adv.* Materialmente, corporalmente.

Corporeity [cer-po-rī'-i-ti], *s.* Corporeidad, materialidad.

†**Corporeous** [cer-pō'-rī-us], *a.* Corpóreo.

Corporosity [cer-po-res'-i-ti], *s.* (Ger. E. U.) El cuerpo de una persona; corpulencia, gran barriga.

Corposant [cēr'-po-zant], *s.* (Mar.) Fuego de Santelmo, meteoro de naturaleza eléctrica que aparece en

noches tempestuosas sobre los palos o las vergas de los buques.
Corps [cōr], *s.* Número de personas que obran juntas de algún modo; cuerpo de ejército; cuerpo de guardia. Es voz francesa.
Corpse [cōrps], *s.* Cadáver, el cuerpo muerto de una persona.
Corpulence, Corpulency [cōr'-pu-lens, i], *s.* Corpulencia, la magnitud del cuerpo; gordura, espesor.
Corpulent [cōr'-pu-lent], *a.* Corpulento, gordo, repleto.
Corpus [cōr'-pus], *s.* 1. Cuerpo. 2. (For.) Objeto material, especialmente bienes tangibles, corporales. Los hechos o elementos de un caso legal estimados colectivamente. *Corpus delicti*, El cuerpo del delito, el hecho fundamental y esencial de la perpetración de un crimen.
Corpuscle [cer'-pusl], *s.* 1. Corpúsculo, átomo. 2. Cuerpo diminuto, celdilla, como las de la sangre.
Corpuscular [cer-pus'-kiu-lar], **Corpuscularian** [cer-pus-kiu-lê'-ri-an], *a.* Corpuscular.
Corrade [cer-rêd'], *va.* Desagregar rocas por solución y ludimiento: dícese de los ríos.
Corradiate [cer-rê'-di-êt], *va.* Concentrar los rayos de luz en un mismo punto.
Corradiation [cer-rê-di-ê'-shun], *s.* Unión de los rayos en un mismo punto.
Corral [co-rral'], *s.* Corral.—*va.* Acorralar.
Correct [cer-rect'], *va.* 1. Corregir, rectificar, enmendar lo que está errado. 2. Corregir, reprender, castigar; enmendar, amonestar. 3. Remediar, neutralizar la acción de lo que es perjudicial o dañoso.
Correct, *a.* Correcto, revisto o acabado con exactitud; exacto, justo.
Correction [cer-rec'-shun], *s.* Corrección, castigo, enmienda, lima, reforma; censura, pena. *House of correction*, Casa de corrección, en que se castiga a los adolescentes de uno y otro sexo.
Correctional [cer-rec'-shun-al], *a.* Correccional, lo que conduce a la corrección.
Corrective [cer-rect'-iv], *a.* Correctivo, lo que corrige.—*s.* Correctivo, limitación, restricción, excepción.
Correctly [cer-rect'-li], *adv.* Correctamente.
Correctness [cer-rect'-nes], *s.* Exactitud, corrección.
Corrector [cer-rect'-er], *s.* Corrector, reformador, revisor.
Correlate [cer'-e-lêt], *va.* Poner en correlación o relación recíproca. —*vn.* Tener correlación o relación recíproca.
Correlate, *s.* La persona que tiene correlación con otra.
Correlation [cer-e-lê'-shun], *s.* 1. Correlación, relación recíproca que tienen entre sí dos o más cosas. 2. La acción de poner en unión, correspondencia, o acción intermedia.
Correlative [cer-rel'-a-tiv], *a.* y *s.* Correlativo.
Correlativeness [cer-rel'-a-tiv-nes], *s.* Correlación, correspondencia, analogía o relación recíproca.
Correspond [cer-es-pond'], *vn.* 1. Corresponder, tener proporción una cosa con otra. 2. Estar de acuerdo, o de inteligencia. 3. Corresponderse, tener correspondencia con una persona ausente.
Correspondence, Correspondency [cer-es-pond'-ens, i], *s.* 1. Correspondencia, relación recíproca. 2. Inteligencia. 3. Correspondencia, amistad o comercio mútuo.
Correspondent [cer-es-pend'-ent], *a.* Correspondiente, conforme, conveniente.—*s.* Correspondiente, corresponsal.
Correspondently [cer-es-pend'-ent-li], *adv.* Correspondientemente.
Corridor [cer'-i-dōr], *s.* 1. Corredor, especie de galería alrededor de una casa. 2. (Mil.) Corredor, camino cubierto alrededor de una fortificación. 3. Pasillo.
Corrigent [cer'-i-jent], *a.* (Med.) Correctivo; dulcificante.—*s.* Correctivo, medicamento modificado; adición a una receta para modificar la acción de otros ingredientes.
Corrigible [cer'-i-ji-bl], *a.* Corregible, lo que es capaz de corrección.
Corrival [cer-rai'-val], *a.* Émulo; contrario.—*s.* ¿Competidor, rival.
Corrivalry [cer-rai'-val-ri], *s.* (Poco us.) Competencia, disputa, contienda, rivalidad.
Corroborant [cer-reb'-o-rant], *a.* Corroborante.—*s.* Corroborante, el medicamento que tiene virtud de corroborar o fortificar.
Corroborate [cer-reb'-o-rêt], *va.* Corroborar, confortar, fortalecer; confirmar, fortificar, apoyar.
Corroboration [cer-reb-o-rê'-shun], *s.* Corroboración, confirmación; apoyo.
Corroborative [cer-reb'-o-re-tiv], *a.* Corroborativo, corroborante.—*s.* Confortativo.
Corrode [cer-rōd'], *va.* Corroer, roer poco a poco alguna cosa.
Corrodent [cer-rō'-dent], *a.* y *s.* (Poco us.) Corrosivo.
Corrodibility [cer-rōd-i-bil'-i-ti] o **Corrosibility** [cer-rō-si-bil'-i-ti], *s.* La calidad de ser corrosible.
Corrodible, Corrosible [cer-rōd'-i-bl, cer-rō'-si-bl], *a.* Corrosible, capaz de corrosión.
Corrosibleness, *s.* *V.* CORRODIBILITY.
Corrosion [cer-rō'-zhun], *s.* Corrosión.
Corrosive [cer-rō'-siv], *a.* y *s.* 1. Corrosivo, lo que corroe o destruye. 2. Corrosivo, mordaz, picante. *Corrosive sublimate*, Sublimado corrosivo, solimán, bicloruro de mercurio ($HgCl_2$).
Corrosiveness [cer-rō'-siv-nes], *s.* Calidad de corrosivo o mordicante; también se usa figuradamente con relación al tiempo, al pesar, etc.
Corrugant [cer'-u-gant], *a.* Lo que arruga o hace arrugas.
Corrugate [cer'-u-gêt], *va.* Arrugar, plegar, hacer pliegues o arrugas; acanalar; encarrujar.
Corrugate, *a.* Encogido, arrugado; acanalado.
Corrugated [cer'-u-gêt-ed], *a.* Corrugado, acanalado. *Corrugated carton*, cartón corrugado.
Corrugation [cer-u-gê'-shun], *s.* Corrugación, contracción, encogimiento.
Corrugator [cer'-u-gê-ter], *s.* El o lo que arruga. 1. (Anat.) Contractor, músculo que arruga la piel. 2. Máquina de encarrujar.
Corrupt [cer-rupt'], *a.* 1. Corrompido, corrupto, podrido, en estado de descomposición. 2. (Fig.) Corrompido, depravado, viciado. 3. Seducido, sobornado. 4. Lleno de errores, falsificado, erróneo; v. g. un texto falsificado.
Corrupt, *va.* 1. Corromper, malear, adulterar, viciar una cosa. 2. Corromper, sobornar, seducir, pervertir a una persona. 3. Estragar las costumbres. 4. Infectar, echar a perder, podrir.—*vn.* Corromperse, podrirse.
Corrupter [cer-rupt'-er], *s.* Corruptor, seductor, corrompedor, sobornador.
Corruptibility [cer-rupt-i-bil'-i-ti], *s.* Corruptibilidad.
Corruptible [cer-rupt'-i-bl], *a.* Corruptible, lo que se puede corromper, depravar o viciar.
Corruptibleness [cer-rupt'-i-bl-nes], *s.* Corruptibilidad.
Corruptibly [cer-rupt'-i-bli], *adv.* De un modo corruptible.
Corrupting [cer-rupt'-ing], *s.* Corrupción, adulteración.
Corruption [cer-rup'-shun], *s.* 1. Corrupción, la acción de corromper o el estado de corrompido; destrucción por causa de descomposición, disolución o muerte. 2. Corrupción, vicio, hediondez; podredumbre; depravación, iniquidad, ruindad, maldad. 3. Pus, materia. 4. Seducción, soborno. 5. Corrupción, alteración de un texto o lenguaje, o del buen gusto.
Corruptive [cer-rupt'-iv], *a.* Corruptivo.
Corruptless [cer-rupt'-les], *a.* Incorruptible, íntegro, recto.
Corruptly [cer-rupt'-li], *adv.* Corrompidamente, viciosamente.
Corruptness [cer-rupt'-nes], *s.* Corruptela, corrupción, putrefacción, infección, vicio.
Corruptress [cer-rup'-tres], *sf.* Corrompedora.
Corsage [cōr'-sêj o cōr-sāzh'], *s.* Corpiño, jubón, justillo del vestido de mujer. (Fr.)
Corsair [cōr'-sār], *s.* Corsario, pirata.
Corse [cōrs], *s.* 1. Cinta usada para hábitos y vestiduras. 2. (Ant.) Cadáver, cuerpo muerto.
Corselet [cōrs'-let], *s.* 1. Coselete, peto, armadura que cubre la parte anterior del cuerpo. 2. (Ent.) Coselete, el pecho de todo insecto y artrópodo.
Corset [cōr'-set], *s.* Corsé, especie de cotilla interior con que se ajustan el talle las mujeres. *Corset-maker*, Corsetera, corsetero.
Corsican [cōr'-si-can], *a.* Corso.
Cortège [cōr-têzh'], *s.* Comitiva, séquito, acompañamiento.
Cortes [cōr'-tes], *s.* Cortes, la reunión de los representantes del pueblo español o portugués.
Cortex [cōr'-tecs], *s.* Corteza.
Cortical [cōr'-ti-cal], *a.* 1. Cortical, lo que pertenece a la corteza. 2. (Anat.) Cortical, exterior, de la envoltura exterior.
Corticate [cōr'-ti-kêt], **Corticated** [cōr'-ti-kê-ted], *a.* Cortezudo; que tiene corteza, corticoso.
Corticose [cōr'-ti-cōs], *a.* Corticoso, corticiforme, semejante a o de la naturaleza de la corteza.
Cortisone [cer'-ti-sōn], *s.* (Med.) Cortisona.
Corundum [co-run'-dum], *s.* Corindón, mineral de extrema dureza que se compone casi de alúmina pura (Al_2O_3), y se usa para pulir. Las variedades coloradas son piedras preciosas; v. g. el zafiro, el rubí oriental, el topacio, la esmeralda y la amatista. El esmeril es la variedad granular.

Coruscant [cer-us'-cant], *a.* Coruscante, resplandeciente.
Coruscate [cer'-us-kêt o co-rus'-kêt], *vn.* Relucir, resplandecer.
Coruscation [cer-us-kê'-shun], *s.* 1. Relámpago, especie de metéoro ígneo de una llama muy pronta. 2. Resplandor, brillo.
Corvette [cōr-vet'], *s.* Corbeta, buque de guerra que en orden de tamaño venía después de la fragata.
Corvetto [cōr-vet'-o], *s.* Corveta. *V.* CURVET.
Corvine [cōr'-vin], *a.* Corvino, perteneciente al cuervo; semejante al cuervo.
Corybantes [cer-i-ban'-tîz], *s.* Coribantes, sacerdotes de la diosa Cibeles.
Corybantic [cer-i-ban'-tic], *a.* Lo que pertenece a los coribantes; maniático.
Corymb [cer'-imb], *s.* (Bot.) Corimbo, maceta, una de las especies de inflorescencia o posición de las flores en las plantas.
Corymbiate, Corymbiated [co-rim'-bi-êt-ed], *a.* (Bot.) Corímbeo, en forma de ramillete o corimbo, arbusto cuyas flores forman corimbo.
Corymbiferous [cer-im-bif'-ęr-us], *a.* (Bot.) Corimbífero, lo que lleva corimbo.
Corypheus [cer-i-fî'-us], *s.* Corifeo; director, guía, jefe, principal.
Coryza [cer-ai'-za], *s.* (Med.) Coriza, inflamación de las membranas mucosas de la nariz y las cavidades contiguas.
Coscinomancy [co-sin'-o-man-si], *s.* Adivinación por medio de una criba o cedazo.
Cosecant [co-sî'-cant], *s.* (Geom.) Cosecante.
Cosen, *va.* *V.* COZEN.
Cosentient [co-sen'-shent], *a.* Que percibe o siente con otro.
Cosey [cō'-zi], *a.* *V.* COZY.
Cosher [cesh'-ęr] (Fam.), *va.* Dar de comer dulces y bocados regalados; de aquí, acariciar, mimar.—*vn.* Ser compadre o comadre de; chismear.
Cosine [cō'-sain], *s.* (Geom.) Coseno, el seno de un arco que es el complemento de otro.
Cosmetic [cez-met'-ic], *a.* y *s.* Cosmético, afeite que usan las mujeres para hermosear la cara.
Cosmic, Cosmical [cez'-mic, al], *a.* 1. Cósmico, lo que pertenece al mundo; metódico; opuesto a caótico. 2. Lo que sale con el sol o inmediatamente antes. 3. Perteneciente al universo material; vasto en extensión o duración.
Cosmically [cez'-mic-al-i], *adv.* Con el sol.
Cosmic ray [cez'-mic rê], *s.* Rayo cósmico.
Cosmogony [cez-meg'-o-ni], *s.* Cosmogonía, la ciencia o sistema de la formación del universo.
Cosmogonist [cez-meg'-o-nist], *s.* Cosmogonista, el que sabe o profesa la cosmogonía.
Cosmographer [cez-meg'-ra-fęr], *s.* Cosmógrafo, el que ha escrito, sabe ó enseña la estructura y delineación del mundo.
Cosmographical [cez-mo-graf'-i-cal], *a.* Cosmográfico.
Cosmography [cez-meg'-ra-fi], *s.* Cosmografía, la descripción del mundo, o la ciencia que enseña la figura, construcción y disposición de todas sus partes.
Cosmological [cez-mo-lej'-ic-al], *a.* Cosmológico, referente á la cosmología.
Cosmologist [cez-mel'-o-jist], *s.* Cosmólogo, el que es versado en la cosmología.
Cosmology [cez-mel'-o-ji], *s.* Cosmología, ciencia de las leyes que gobiernan el mundo físico.
Cosmopolitan [cez-mo-pel'-i-tan], **Cosmopolite** [cez-mep'-o-lait], *a.* 1. Cosmopolita, que considera a todo el mundo como patria suya; común a todo el mundo. 2. (Biol.) De extensa distribución; p. ej. un género.—*s.* Cosmopolita, ciudadano del mundo.
Cosmos [cez'-mes], *s.* 1. El mundo o el universo, estimado como sistema perfecto en orden y arreglo; opuesto a caos. 2. Cualquier sistema harmonioso y completo. 3. (Bot.) Planta de las compuestas, y su flor, cultivada como de adorno; de la familia de las dalias. (Gr.)
Cosmotron [cez'-mo-tren], *s.* Cosmotrón.
Cossacks [ces'-acs], *s.* Cosacos, caballería ligera e irregular de Rusia; también es el nombre de los habitantes de algunas provincias del imperio ruso.
Cosset [ces'-et], *s.* Cordero criado sin la madre; se dice también de los terneros y novillos.—*va.* Acariciar, mimar.
Cost [cest], *s.* 1. Coste, precio; expensas, gastos. 2. Costa, daño, pérdida. *To my cost*, A mis expensas. *At cost*, Al costo, o a coste y costas.
Cost, *vn.* Costar, tener alguna cosa un coste o precio. *Cost what it may*, Cueste lo que cueste, o costare. *To cost dear*, Causar grandes gastos, incomodidad o pérdidas y perjuicios de consideración.
Costal [ces'-tal], *a.* Costal, lo perteneciente a las costillas.
Costermonger, Costard-monger, *s.* Buhonero, vendedor ambulante de frutas y legumbres.
Costive [ces'-tiv], *a.* 1. Estreñido de cuerpo o vientre. 2. (Des.) Impervio; dícese de la tierra arcillosa.
Costiveness [ces'-tiv-nes], *s.* Constipación o estreñimiento de vientre.
Costless [cest'-les], *a.* Sin coste o precio, de balde.
Costliness [cest'-li-nes], *s.* Suntuosidad.
Costly [cest'-li], *a.* 1. Costoso, caro, dispendioso. 2. Magnífico, espléndido, suntuoso.
Costmary [cest'-mę-ri], *s.* (Bot.) Especie de tanaceto.
†**Costrel** [ces'-trel], *s.* Botella o frasco (de peregrino) con asas.
Costume [ces'-tiūm o ces-tiūm'], *s.* 1. Traje, vestido; el traje de cierto país, época, clase, etc.; modo de vestir en general. 2. La usanza o estilo de diferentes países a que debe atenerse un pintor o un poeta para guardar propiedad; color local.
Costumer [cos-tiūm'-ęr], *s.* El que hace, vende o alquila trajes para el teatro.
Cosy, *a.* *V.* COZY.
Cot [cet], *s.* 1. Cabaña, choza, casa pequeña o albergue de gente pobre. 2. Hamaca, coy, cama suspendida a bordo de los barcos. 3. Camita, cuna; catre. 4. Dedal. 5. (Irlanda) Barquillo. 6. Desecho o desperdicio de lana.
Cotabulate, *va.* *V.* CONTABULATE.
Cotangent [cō-tan'-jent], *s.* (Geom.) Cotangente.
Cote [cōt], *s.* 1. Corral, redil. 2. Casita para refugio; voz usada sólo en composición, como *dove-cote*, palomar; *sheep-cote*, redil.
Cotemporaneous [co-tem-po-rê'-nę-us], *a.* *V.* CONTEMPORANEOUS.
Cotemporary [co-tem'-po-rę-ri], *a.* Contemporáneo, coetáneo. Es preferible *Contemporary*.
Coterie [cō-te-rî'], *s.* Corrillo, corro, corro de ociosos, tertulia, junta casera de diversión o de amigos.
Coterminous [co-tęr'-mi-nus], *a.* *V.* CONTERMINOUS.
Cothurnus [co-thūr'-nus], *s.* Coturno. *V.* BUSKIN.
Cotillon [co-til'-yęn], *s.* Cotillón, especie de contradanza entre ocho doce o diez y seis personas.
Cotland [cet'-land], *s.* Pedazo de terreno contiguo a una choza.
Cotquean [cet'-cwîn], *s.* Maricón cazolero, maricasera, el hombre que se entremete en los quehaceres de las mujeres.
Cotrustee [co-trus-tî'], *s.* El que ejerce el cargo de síndico, fideicomisario o curador en unión de otra persona.
Cotswold [cets'-wōld], *s.* Redil de campo llano y abierto.
Cotta [cet'-a], *s.* Cota, sobrepelliz corta, vestidura eclesiástica.
Cottage [cet'-êj], *s.* 1. Casa humilde, de un solo piso; también, casa situada en las afueras de una población; casucha. 2. Casa de campo, a veces grande y suntuosa.
Cottage cheese [cet'-êj chîz], *s.* Requesón.
Cottaged [cot'-ęjd], *a.* Poblado de casas humildes o suburbanas.
Cottager [cot'-ę-jęr], **Cotter** [cet'-ęr], *s.* Rústico, aldeano payo. (Cuba) Montero.
Cotter pin [cet'-ęr pin], *s.* (Mec.) Chaveta.
Cotton [cet'-n], *s.* 1. Algodón. 2. Cotonía, una tela de algodón. *Absorbent cotton*, Algodón absorbente, purificado, que se usa en cirugía. *Upland cotton*, Algodón de pellón largo. *Raw cotton*, Algodón en rama. *Cotton bagging*, Lienzo de algodón para sacos. *Cotton balls*, Hilo de algodón en bolas. *Cotton-gin*, Almarraes, desmotadora de algodón. *Cotton jeans*, Coquillos, cotíes de algodón. *Cotton-seed oil*, Aceite de semillas de algodón. *Cotton-waste*, Desperdicios de algodón. *Cotton-plant*, Algodonero, algodonal, la planta que produce el algodón. Gossypium. *Spool-cotton*, Hilo de algodón en carreteles o canillas. *Cotton yarn* (para tejedores), Hilaza de algodón; (para costureras) Hilo de torzal o de pelo. *Cotton cambric*, Muselina finísima. (Amer.) Coco muy fino, estopilla de algodón. *Cotton-wool*, Algodón en rama. (< cotón.)
Cotton, *vn.* 1. Levantar pelusa; cubrirse de pelusa o borra. 2. Acordarse, salir bien.—*va.* Acolchar, rellenar con algodón.
Cottonlike [cet'-n-laik], **Cottony** [cet'-n-i], *a.* Lleno de algodón, semejante al algodón; blando, velloso; acolchado.
Cottonwood [cet'-n-wud], *s.* Cada una de las varias especies americanas del álamo.
Cotyla [cet'-i-la], **Cotyle** [cet-i-li], *s.* (Anat.) Cotila, la cavidad de un hueso que recibe la cabeza de otro hueso.
Cotyledon [cet-i-lî'-dęn], *s.* (Bot.) 1. Cotiledón o paleta de la semilla. 2. Cotiledón, cada uno de los lóbulos que, unidos, forman la placenta.

Cotyloid [cot'-i-leid], *a.* Cotiloidea, en forma de copa; dícese de la cavidad articular de la cadera.

Couch [cauch], *vn.* 1. Acostarse, recostarse, echarse; arrodillarse como las bestias para descansar. 2. Agacharse o inclinarse con intención de ocultarse. 3. Agobiarse, encorvarse de miedo o dolor.—*va.* 1. Colocar sobre una cama u otro sitio de descanso. 2. Colocar una cosa sobre otra en capas o tongadas. 3. Solapar, encubrir o disimular; incluir. 4. (Cir.) Batir las cataratas o nubes de los ojos. *To couch in writing,* Poner por escrito. *To couch the lance,* Enristrar, poner la lanza en ristre.

Couch, *s.* 1. Silla poltrona, silla de descanso; lecho, canapé. 2. Lecho o lechos, tongada, capas o camas de las cosas que se ponen unas sobre otras.

Couchant [cauch'-ant], *a.* Acostado, agachado.

Coucher [cauch'-ẹr], *s.* 1. El que bate las cataratas de los ojos. 2. Cartulario.

Couch-fellow [cauch'-fel-o], *s.* Compañero de cama.

Couching [cauch'-ing], *s.* 1. La operación de batir las cataratas con aguja. 2. Encorvamiento.

Cougar [cū'-gar], *s.* Cuguar, puma, la pantera de América. Felis concolor.

Cough [cōf], *s.* Tos. *Whooping-cough,* Tos ferina, sofocante, o convulsiva.

Cough, *vn.* Toser.—*va.* Arrancar o arrojar del pecho lo que a uno le molesta, a fuerza de toser.

Cough drop [cōf drep], *s.* Pastilla para la tos.

Coughing [cōf'-ing], *s.* Tosidura, acción y efecto de toser. *Fit of coughing,* Acceso de tos.

Could [cud], *pret. imp.* del verbo CAN. *I could not do it,* No pude o no podría hacerlo. *Could you do it?* ¿Pudiera o podría Vd. hacerlo? En los autores antiguos significa también conocido. N. B. *Could,* y su presente *Can,* corresponden frecuentemente a *saber;* v. g. *He did not sign, because he* could *not write,* Él no firmó por no *saber* escribir.

Coulomb [cū-lem'], *s.* Culombio, cantidad de electricidad que, pasando por una disolución de plata, es capaz de separar de ella 1 miligramo y 118 milésimas de este metal; la cantidad de electricidad transmitida por un amperio en un segundo.

Coulter [cōl'-tẹr], *s.* Cuchilla, reja de arado. *V.* COLTER.

Council [caun'-sil], *s.* 1. Concilio o consejo, junta de personas que se unen para consultar y deliberar. 2. Sínodo, junta del clero. *Common council,* Ayuntamiento, cuerpo legislativo municipal. *Councilman,* Concejal, individuo de un consejo municipal.

Council-board [cāun'-sil-bōrd], *s.* Reunión o sesión del consejo.

Councilor, Councillor [caun'-sil-ẹr], *s.* Consejero.

Counsel [caun'-sel], *s.* 1. Consejo, aviso, parecer, dictamen, deliberación, determinación. 2. Prudencia, secreto, sigilo. 3. Trama, designio. 4. Abogado. 5. Consultor.

Counsel, *va.* Aconsejar, dirigir, avisar.

Counsel-keeper [caun'-sel-kīp'-ẹr], *s.* El que guarda un secreto.

Counsellable [caun'-sel-a-bl], *a.* Dócil, dispuesto a recibir y seguir los consejos de otro.

Counsellor [caun'-sel-ẹr], *s.* 1. Consejero, aconsejador. 2. Confidente. 3. Consejero; abogado.

Counsellorship [caun'-sel-ẹr-ship], *s.* El empleo, oficio, plaza o dignidad de consejero.

Count [caunt], *va.* 1. Contar, numerar. 2. Considerar, calcular, reputar. *He counts himself a learned man,* Él se tiene por hombre docto. 3. Imputar, atribuir.—*vn.* 1. Idear, trazar, tramar. 2. Contar, confiar o poner la esperanza en alguna cosa.

Count, *s.* 1. Cuenta o cálculo, partida, cláusula. 2. El acto de dar atención a los detalles; cuidado. 3. (For.) Demanda, cargo, capítulo.

Count [caunt], *s.* Conde, título de nobleza que desde el principio correspondió al de *earl* en Inglaterra.

Countable [caunt'-a-bl], *a.* Contadero, contable.

Countdown [caunt'-daun], *s.* (Aer.) Cuenta inversa. Usase especialmente para explosiones nucleares y lanzamientos de cohetes.

Countenance [caun'-tẹ-nans], *s.* 1. Semblante, cara, rostro, continente, aspecto. 2. Buena o mala cara, en cuanto indica el estado de ánimo de una persona. 3. Patrocinio, amparo, protección, apoyo, favor. 4. Aire de presunción y arrogancia. *Out of countenance,* Abochornado, desconcertado, turbado, consternado, confuso, corrido, chafado. *To be out of countenance, vr.* Abochornarse, correrse, desconcertarse, turbarse, confundirse; sonrojarse. *To give countenance,* Apoyar, favorecer, proteger, auxiliar.

Countenance, *va.* Sostener, patrocinar, apoyar, proteger, fomentar, favorecer, mantener.

Counter [caun'-tẹr], *s.* 1. Contador, contante. 2. Mostrador, tablero, contador. 3. Ficha, tanto, monedilla que sirve para contar. *Counters,* Tantos, fichas, piedras. 4. (Mar.) Bovedilla. *Upper counter,* (Mar.) Bovedilla superior. 5. Lo opuesto, lo contrario. 6. La porción del zapato que ciñe el talón. 7. Pecho del caballo. 8. (Mús.) La parte de canto puesta en contraste inmediato con el tono.

Counter, *adv.* Contra, al contrario, al revés. También es partícula que se usa en composición, y por lo común significa oposición o contrariedad. *To run counter,* Oponerse; violar, faltar a.

Counteract [caun-tẹr-act'], *va.* Contrariar, impedir, estorbar el efecto de alguna cosa; frustrar.

Counteraction [caun-tẹr-ac'-shun], *s.* Oposición; impedimento.

Counteractive [caun''-tẹr-act'-iv], *a.* Que tiende a contrariar o frustrar; contrario, opuesto.—*s.* Opositor.

Counter-approach [caun'-tẹr-ap-prōch'], *s.* (Fort.) Contraaproches o contraataques, trabajos con que los sitiados impiden que los sitiadores se acerquen.

Counterattack [caun'-tẹr-at-tac'], *s.* Contraataque.

Counter-attraction [caun'-tẹr-at-trac'-shun], *s.* Atracción opuesta.

Counterbalance [caun-tẹr-bal'-ans], *va.* Contrapesar, equilibrar, contrabalancear, igualar, compensar.

Counterbalance [caun'-tẹr-bal-ans], *s.* Contrapeso, equilibrio, compensación.

Counter-bond [caun'-tẹr-bend], *s.* Contrafianza, obligación dada a un fiador por la persona a quien fió.

Counterbuff [caun-tẹr-buf'], *va.* Rechazar, repeler.

Counterbuff [caun'-tẹr-buf], *s.* Rechazo.

Counterchange [caun'-tẹr-chênj], *s.* Contracambio, recompensa recíproca.

Counterchange [caun-tẹr-chênj'], *va.* Trocar, cambiar, dar y tomar recíprocamente.

Countercharge [caun'-tẹr-chārj], *s.* Recriminación, acusación del acusado contra el que le acusa.

Countercharge [caun'-tẹr-chārj], *va.* 1. (Mil.) Cargar, atacar a los que dan una carga. 2. Hacer cargos el acusado contra el acusador.

Countercharm [caun'-tẹr-chārm], *s.* Desencanto.

Countercharm [caun-tẹr-chārm'], *va.* Desencantar.

Countercheck [caun-ter-chec'], *va.* Contrastar, contrarrestar.

Countercheck [caun'-tẹr-chec], *s.* Oposición, repulsa.

Counterclaim [caun'-tẹr-clêm], *s.* Contrarreclamación.

Counterclockwise [caun'-ter-clec-wais], *a.* y *adv.* Con movimiento circular a la izquierda.

Countercunning [caun'-tẹr-cun-ing], *s.* Contraastucia, astucia opuesta a otra.

Countercurrent [caun'-tẹr-cur-ent], *s.* Contracorriente, corriente contraria a otra.

Counterdeed [caun'-tẹr-dīd], *s.* Contraescritura, escrito o acto particular que deshace en todo o en parte algún otro acto público.

Counterdistinction, *s.* *V.* CONTRADISTINCTION.

Counterdraw [caun'-ter-drē], *va.* Calcar, pasar un dibujo por medio de un material transparente.

Counterevidence [caun-tẹr-ev'-i-dens], *s.* Contraevidencia, el testimonio de un segundo testigo, opuesto al que otro dió antes.

Counterfeit [caun'-tẹr-fit], *va.* 1. Falsear, contrahacer, copiar alguna cosa con intención de pasarla por original. 2. Imitar, falsificar, forjar; hacer una cosa tan parecida a otra que con dificultad se distingan.—*vn.* Fingir, disimular.

Counterfeit, *s.* 1. Impostura, engaño, falsificación, contrahacimiento. 2. Mentira, disimulo, artimaña, bellaquería, trapacería. 3. Falseador, impostor, falsificador.—*a.* Contrahecho, falsificado, falseado, engañoso, fingido. *Counterfeit coin,* Moneda falsa.

Counterfeiter [caun'-tẹr-fit-ẹr], *s.* Falsario, falsificador, contrahacedor, forjador, falseador, imitador. *Counterfeiter of coin,* Monedero falso.

Counterfeitly [caun'-tẹr-fit-li], *adv.* Falsamente, fingidamente.

Counterguard [caun'-tẹr-gārd], *s.* (Fort.) Contraguardia, obra exterior compuesta de dos caras que forman ángulo, edificada delante de los baluartes.

Counterinfluence [caun'-tẹr-in'-flu-ens], *va.* Influir en contrario.

Counterinfluence, *s.* Influencia opuesta.

Counter-irritant [caun''-tẹr-ir'-i-tant], *s.* Agente medicinal que se emplea para excitar irritación en una parte del cuerpo a fin de aliviar el dolor en otra parte.

Counterlight [caun'-tẹr-lait], *s.* Contraluz, la luz contraria a la pro-

pia para ver el objeto que se presenta.
Countermand [caun''-tẹr-mand'], *va.* Contramandar; revocar, invalidar; retirar las invitaciones para un convite, una junta, etc.
Countermand [caun'-tẹr-mand], *s.* Contramandato, contraorden; nulidad.
Countermarch [caun'-tẹr-mārch], *s.* 1. Contramarcha, retroceso del camino andado. 2. Contramarcha, cambio de frente. 3. Mudanza de ideas o conducta.
Countermarch [caun''-tẹr-mārch'], *vn.* Contramarchar, desandar lo andado.
Countermark [caun'-tẹr-mārc], *s.* 1. Contramarca, segunda o tercera señal que se hace sobre una bala o un fardo de mercaderías. 2. Contramarca del gremio de orífices o plateros en Inglaterra. 3. Cavidad artificial en los dientes de los caballos para ocultar su edad.
Countermine [caun'-tẹr-main], *s.* 1. Contramina, la mina que se hace en oposición á las del enemigo, a fin de inutilizarlas. 2. Contramina, medida adoptada para frustrar el intento de otro.
Countermine [caun''-tẹr-main'], *va.* 1. Contraminar, hacer minas para encontrar las del enemigo. 2. Deshacer o impedir la ejecución de lo que otro intenta, estorbar.
Countermotion [caun''-tẹr-mō'-shun], *s.* 1. Movimiento contrario. 2. Proposición contraria.
Countermove [caun''-tẹr-mūv'], *va.* y *vn.* Mover o moverse en dirección contraria u opuesta a otra.
Countermovement [caun''-tẹr-mūv'-mẹnt], *s.* Movimiento opuesto a otro.
Countermure [caun'-tẹr-miūr], *s.* Contramuro, falsabraga.
Countermure [caun''-tẹr-miūr'], *va.* Contramurar, levantar una contramuralla o falsabraga.
Counternatural [caun''-tẹr-nach'-ur-al], *a.* (Poco us.) Contranatural.
Counternoise [caun'-tẹr-neiz], *s.* Un sonido que impide que se oiga otro.
Counteroffensive [caun'-tẹr-ef-fens'-iv], *s.* Contraofensiva.
Counteropening [caun''-tẹr-ō'-pn-ing], *s.* (Cir.) Contraabertura.
Counterpace [caun'-tẹr-pês], *s.* Contrapaso.
Counterpane [caun'-tẹr-pên], *s.* Colcha de cama, sobrecama; cobertor.
Counterpart [caun'-tẹr-pārt], *s.* Contraparte; duplicado, traslado, copia, imagen.
Counterpetition [caun''-tẹr-pẹ-tish'-un], *s.* Petición opuesta, contrainstancia.
Counterpetition, *vn.* Hacer una petición o súplica contraria a otra.
Counterplea [caun'-tẹr-plī], *s.* Segunda instancia.
Counterplot [caun'-tẹr-plet], *s.* Contratreta, contraastucia, artificio opuesto a otro.
Counterplot [caun''-tẹr-plet'], *va.* Contraminar; oponer una astucia a otra.
Counterplotting [caun''-tẹr-plet'-ing], *s.* Trama inventada para contrarrestar otra.
Counterpoint [caun'-tẹr-peint], *s.* 1. (Mús.) Contrapunto, concordancia harmoniosa de voces contrapuestas. 2. Punto o método opuesto.
Counterpoise [caun''-tẹr-peiz'], *va.* Contrapesar, contrarrestar, contrabalancear.
Counterpoise [caun'-tẹr-peiz], *s.* 1. Contrapeso. 2. Equilibrio. 3. Pilón, pesa movible que corre por el ástil de una romana, y determina el peso de una cosa igualando el fiel.
Counterpoison [caun''-tẹr-pei'-zn], *s.* Contraveneno; antídoto.
Counterpractice [caun''-tẹr-prac'-tis], *s.* Práctica en oposición á otra.
Counterpressure [caun''-tẹr-presh -ur], *s.* Fuerza opuesta o contraria.
Counterproject [caun''-tẹr-prej'-ect], *s.* Proyecto opuesto a otro.
Counterproof [caun'-tẹr-prūf], *s.* Contraprueba, la segunda prueba que sacan los impresores, grabadores y estampadores.
Counterprove [caun''-tẹr-prūv'], *va.* Sacar los perfiles de una estampa o dibujo calcándolo.
Counter-revolution [caun''-tẹr-rev-o-lū'-shun], *s.* Contrarrevolución.
Counter-revolutionist [caun''-tẹr-rev-o-lū'-shun-ist], *s.* Contrarrevolucionario.
Countersalute [caun''-tẹr-sa-lūt'], *s.* Contrasalva, salva en respuesta a otra hecha anteriormente.
Counterscarf [caun'-tẹr-scārf], **Counterscarp** [caun'-tẹr-scārp], *s.* (Fort.) Contraescarpa, el declive hecho junto al foso, al lado de la esplanada y opuesto a la escarpa.
Counterseal [caun''-tẹr-sīl'], *va.* Contrasellar.
Countersecure [caun'-tẹr-sẹ-kiūr], *va.* Asegurar más.
Countersense [caun'-tẹr-sens], *s.* Contrasentido, sentido opuesto.
Countersign [caun'-tẹr-sain], *va.* Refrendar, firmar algún decreto o despacho de alguna autoridad superior para darle mayor autenticidad.
Countersign [caun'-tẹr-sain], *s.* 1. (Mil.) Santo y seña, contraseña. 2. Refrendata, la firma del que subscribe por autoridad pública después del superior.
Countersignal [caun''-tẹr-sig'-nal], *s.* (Mar.) Señal que corresponde a otra.
Countersignature [caun''-tẹr-sig'-na-chur], *s.* *V.* COUNTERSIGN, 2ª acep.
Countersink [caun''-tẹr-sink'], *va.* Avellanar.—*s.* 1. Avellanador. 2. Dilatación de un hueco para recibir la cabeza de un tornillo, de un perno, etc.
Counterstatute [caun''-tẹr-stat'-yūt], *s.* Ordenanza o estatuto contrario a otro.
Counterstroke [caun'-tẹr-strōk], *s.* Golpe retornado.
Countersway [caun'-tẹr-swê], *s.* Influencia que obra en oposición de otra.
Counter-surety, *s.* *V* COUNTERBOND.
Counter-tally [caun'-tẹr-tal-i], *s.* Contratarja.
Counter-taste [caun'-tẹr-têst], *s.* Gusto falso o ficticio.
Counter-tenor [caun-tẹr-ten'-ẹr], *s.* (Mús.) Contralto.
Counter-tide [caun'-tẹr-taid], *s.* (Mar.) Contramarea, una marea contraria á otra.
Countertime [caun'-tẹr-taim], *s.* Defensa, oposición; contratiempo.
Counter-trench [caun'-tẹr-trench], *s.* (Mil.) Contratrinchera.
Counter-turn [caun'-tẹr-tūrn], *s.* Desenlace, desenredo de un lance de comedia.
Countervail [caun-tẹr-vêl'], *va.* Contrapesar, contrarrestar, compensar.
Counter-view [caun'-tẹr-viū], *s.* Postura en que dos personas se miran cara á cara, o se hallan frente a frente.
Counter-vote [caun-tẹr-vōt'], *va.* (Poco us.) Oponer; ganar por pluralidad de votos.
Counter-weigh [caun-tẹr-wê'], *vn.* Contrapesar.
Counterweight [caun'-ter-wêt], *s.* Contrapeso.
Counter-wheel [caun-tẹr-hwīl'], *va.* (Mil.) Evolucionar en diversas direcciones.
Counter-wind [caun'-tẹr-waind], *s.* (Poco us.) Viento contrario.
Counter-work [caun-tẹr-wūrc'], *va.* Contrarrestar, contrariar, resistir o impedir; contraminar.
Countess [caun'-tes], *sf.* Condesa, la esposa del conde, o la que por sí tiene este título.
Counting-house [caunt'-ing-haus], *s.* Despacho, escritorio, en que los comerciantes tienen sus libros y cuentas.
Countless [caunt'-les], *a.* Innumerable, sin número.
Countrified [cun'-tri-faid], *a.* y *pp.* Rústico, campesino.
Countrify [cun'-tri-fai], *va.* Hacer rústico o campesino, especialmente en el aspecto.
Country [cun'-tri], *s.* 1. País, región. 2. Campo, campiña (en oposición a ciudad); provincia, región (en oposición a capital o metrópoli). *To go into the country,* Ir al campo. 3. País, patria, tierra; el país natal o el suelo nativo de alguno. 4. Los habitantes de algún país. 5. (For.) La comunidad donde se convocan o de donde proceden los miembros de un jurado; y de aquí el jurado mismo.—*a.* Rústico, rural, campesino, rudo, agreste, campestre. *Country merchant,* Comerciante del interior, o de tierra adentro.
Country-dance [cun'-tri-dans], *s.* Contradanza. *V.* CONTRA-DANCE.
Countryman [cun'-tri-man] (*pl.* COUNTRYMEN), *s.* 1. Paisano, compatriota, conciudadano. 2. Paisano, aldeano, patán; labrador. 3. Ganso, paleto. (Cuba) Montero, guajiro. (Mex.) Payo.
Country-house [cun'-tri-haus], *s.* Casa de campo, granja, quinta. *The king's country palace,* Real sitio.
Country squire [cun'-tri-scwair], *s.* Caballero de provincia.
Country-woman [cun'-tri-wum''-an], *sf.* Compatriota, paisana; aldeana. *V.* COUNTRYMAN.
County [caun'-ti], *s.* Condado, distrito territorial. En los Estados Unidos, subdivisión civil de un estado; también, sus habitantes. En Inglaterra, se llama también *county* al *shire.* *V.* SHIRE. *County-seat,* Capital de condado o distrito.
Couple [cup'-l], *s.* 1. Par, dos seres o cosas de cualquiera especie, siendo de igual calidad. 2. Par, macho y hembra. *Married couple,* Matrimonio, marido y mujer. 3. Pareja, compañero y compañera, dos personas unidas temporalmente, p. ej. en un baile; dos animales apareados. *The happy couple,* La feliz pareja, los recién casados.
Couple, *va.* 1. Parear, unir, juntar, encadenar, enganchar. 2. Casar, solemnizar el matrimonio, el sacerdote o funcionario autorizado para ello. —*vn.* Tener cópula o coito, unirse ó juntarse carnalmente.
Couple-beggar [cup'-l-beg'-ar], *s.* El

clérigo o funcionario que casa clandestinamente.

Coupler [cup'-lẹr], *s.* Aparato de conexión; enganche, acopladura.

Couplet [cup'-let], *s.* 1. Par, pareja. 2. Copla; pareado, el verso que rima con el que le sigue.

Coupling [cup'-ling], *s.* 1. Ayuntamiento, cópula. 2. Lazo; unión, enganche; ensambladura, conexión. *Coupling-pin,* (F. C.) Pasador del enganche. *Friction-coupling,* Manguito de fricción, unión friccional. *Shaft-coupling,* Embrague, conexión de los ejes de transmisión.

Coupon [cū-pen'], *s.* Cupón, parte de un vale o crédito con interés; parte separable de un billete, etc.

Courage [cur'-ẹj], *s.* Coraje, valor, intrepidez, brío, bravura.

Courageous [cu-ré'-jus], *a.* Animoso, valiente, valeroso, brioso, intrépido.

Courageously [cu-ré'-jus-li], *adv.* Valerosamente.

Courageousness [cu-ré'-jus-nes], *s.* Ánimo, aliento, valor, intrepidez.

Courant [cū-rɑnt'], **Couranto** [cu-rɑnt'-o], *s.* 1. Baile ligero. 2. Diario, noticia, novedad: hoy se emplea solamente como título de periódico.

Courier [cū'-ri-ẹr], *s.* Correo, expreso, ordinario.

Course [cōrs], *s.* 1. Corrida, curso, carrera. 2. Tránsito, paso de un paraje a otro; camino, ruta, tirada, paseo; viaje, correría, excursión. 3. Estadio. 4. (Mar.) Rumbo, derrotero o derrota de una embarcación. 5. Curso, los principios y elementos de alguna ciencia o arte explicados metódicamente. 6. Método o género de vida o modo de obrar; conducta, porte, costumbre. 7. Entrada, servicio, cubierto, el número de platos que se ponen de una vez en la mesa. *Dinner of ten courses,* Comida o mesa de diez entradas. 8. Índole. 9. Estructura regular; serie o hilera de piedras o ladrillos en una pared. 10. Regularidad, orden; marcha, progresión; medios ordenados para alcanzar alguna cosa. 11. Ceremonia, cumplimientos.—*pl.* 1. (Mar.) Papahigos o velas mayores. *To be under the courses,* Andar con los papahigos. 2. (Fam.) Reglas, menstruación. *Of course,* Por supuesto, sin duda, indudablemente, por sabido, por de contado, por consiguiente, de juro. *Matter of course,* Cosa de cajón. *Course of physic,* Método curativo. *Main course,* (Mar.) La vela mayor de un buque. *Words of course,* Ceremonias, cumplimientos. *The last course,* Los postres. *Every one in his course,* Cada uno a su vez. *It is our common course,* Es nuestro modo de obrar, es nuestra costumbre.

Course, *va.* 1. Correr por, o sobre. 2. Hacer correr, excitar a correr. 3. Cazar, dar caza, perseguir.—*vn.* Corretear, andar de casa en casa o de calle en calle; disputar, argumentar. *To course over,* Ir encima de.

Courser [cōrs'-ẹr], *s.* 1. Corcel ligero o veloz. 2. Corredor o cazador de liebres, el que las corre con perros.

Courses, *s. pl.* V. COURSE.

Coursing [cōrs'-ing], *s.* La caza.

Court [cōrt], *s.* 1. Corte, comitiva. 2. Corte, el lugar donde reside el monarca; palacio. 3. Corte, se toma por el soberano y sus ministros, y en esta significación se llama también gabinete. 4. Corte, consejo, tribunal de justicia, el conjunto de jueces que forman un tribunal y la sala donde se juntan a administrar justicia, que también se llama estrados. (For.) *Supreme Court,* Consejo o tribunal supremo; en los Estados Unidos y en cada uno de los estados es el tribunal de último recurso. *Superior Court,* en los Estados Unidos, tribunal de segunda instancia, correspondiente a la Audiencia. *Court of Common Pleas,* Juzgado o tribunal de primera instancia. *Court-martial,* Consejo de guerra, tribunal militar. *Court guide,* Guía de forasteros. 5. Corte, el acompañamiento obsequioso que se hace a alguna persona constituída en dignidad. 6. Corte, cortejo, el obsequio o galanteo que se hace a una mujer. 7. Patio, atrio de una casa.

Court, *va.* 1. Cortejar, enamorar, requebrar, acariciar; hacer la corte; engatusar. 2. Solicitar, adular, rogar.

Court-breeding [cōrt-brīd'-ing], *s.* Educación de corte, cortesanía.

Court-card [cōrt'-cɑ̄rd], *s.* Una figura en los naipes. Es corrupción de *coat-card.*

Court-chaplain [cōrt'-chap-len], *s.* Capellán de palacio.

Court-cupboard [cōrt'-cub-ord], *s.* Especie de alacena.

Court-day [cort'-dê], *s.* 1. Día de junta general de los tribunales de justicia. 2. Día de besamanos.

Court-dress [cōrt'-dres], *s.* Traje de corte.

Court-dresser [cōrt'-dres'-ẹr], *s.* 1. Ayuda de cámara o camarista de las personas de la corte. 2. Lisonjeador.

Courteous [cūr'-tẹ-us o cōrt'-yus], *a.* Cortés, atento, político, civil, sociable, afable, urbano, bien criado; benigno, humano, benévolo; cortesano.

Courteously [cūr'-tẹ-us-li], *adv.* Cortésmente, civilmente.

Courteousness [cūr'-tẹ-us-nes], *s.* Cortesía, cortesanía, atención, agrado, urbanidad, buena crianza, benevolencia.

Courter [cōrt'-ẹr], *s.* 1. Cortejador, cortesano. 2. Pretendiente, aspirante.

Courtesan [cūr'-ti-zan], *sf.* Cortesana, mujer pública.

Courtesy [cūr'-tẹ-si], *s.* 1. Cortesía. 2. Gracia, favor, merced. 3. Bondad, benignidad. 4. [curt'-si] Cortesía, reverencia que hacen las mujeres. *V.* CURTSY.

Courtesy, *vn.* Hacer una cortesía o reverencia.—*va.* Hablar o tratar con cortesía.

Court-fashion [cōrt'-fash-un], *s.* Moda o traje de corte.

Court-favour [cōrt'-fê-vẹr], *s.* Gracia, merced o distinción que dispensa el poder supremo.

Court-hand [cōrt'-hand], *s.* Letra de curia.

Court-house [cōrt'-haus], *s.* Edificio público destinado a los tribunales judiciales. En los estados del sur se llama también así a la capital de condado.

Courtier [cōrt'-yẹr], *s.* Cortesano, palaciego; cortejo, cortejante.

Court-lady [cōrt'-lê-di], *s.* Dama de corte o de palacio.

Courtlike [cōrt'-laic], *a.* Cortesano, propio de corte, elegante, urbano.

Courtliness [cōrt'-li-nes], *s.* Cortesanía, cortesía, urbanidad; elegancia, gracia.

Courtly [cōrt'-li], *a.* Cortesano, elegante, insinuante, cortés.

Court-martial [cōrt'-mɑ̄r'-shal], *s.* Consejo de guerra.

Court-minion [cōrt'-min-yun], *s.* Valido, privado, favorito.

Court-plaster [cōrt'-plɑs-tẹr], *s.* Tafetán inglés.

Courtship [cōrt'-ship], *s.* Corte, cortejo; galantería, obsequio y galanteo; el acto de pretender a una mujer en matrimonio.

Cousin [cuz'-n], *s.* Primo o prima. *Cousin german* o *first cousin,* Primo hermano. *Second cousin,* Primo segundo.

Cove [cōv], *s.* 1. (Mar.) Caleta, ensenada. 2. (Arq.) Bovedilla, toda especie de moldura cóncava. 3. (Ger.) Hombre, mozo, chaval.

Cove, *va.* Abovedar, arquear.

Covenant [cuv'-e-nant], *s.* Contrato, convención, estipulación, pacto, tratado, ajuste; alianza, liga; escritura de contrato. *The new covenant,* El Nuevo Testamento, o la nueva alianza.

Covenant, *va.* Estipular, contratar. —*vn.* Convenir, pactar, estipular.

Covenantee [cuv-e-nant-ī'], *s.* Contratante.

Covenanter, Covenantor [cuv'-e-nant-ẹr, ẹr], *s.* 1. Confederado, coligado, conjurado. 2. Cierta división entre los presbiterianos; covenantario, firmante del covenant o pacto nacional escocés en 1638 hasta 1643; y también, partidario de dicho pacto.

Coventry [cuv'-en-tri], *s.* Nombre de una ciudad en Warwickshire, Inglaterra. *Coventry blue,* Hilo de marcar. *To send to Coventry,* Desterrar, echar de la sociedad.

Cover [cuv'-ẹr], *va.* 1. Cubrir, tender una cosa sobre otra; tapar, ocultar; abrigar, proteger. 2. Empollar, ponerse las aves sobre los huevos para sacar cría. 3. Resarcir, compensar, indemnizar. 4. Apuntar y retener a uno al alcance de un arma de fuego; dominar tropas o cañones. 5. Pasar, atravesar; dícese de un espacio o distancia. 6. Cubrir, juntarse el macho de algunos animales con la hembra. 7. Cubrirse, ponerse el sombrero. 8. Paliar, disfrazar, disimular. *Covered way,* Camino cubierto.

Cover, *s.* 1. Cubierta, tapadera. *Cover of a letter,* Cubierta de una carta, sobre, sobrescrito. 2. Capa o pretexto, velo. 3. Cubierta, lo que cubre o defiende, abrigo, techado, albergue, cobertizo. *Under cover,* (1) Bajo cubierto; al abrigo. (2) Bajo sobre, cerrado (pliego, carta). 4. Cubierto (tenedor, cuchillo y cuchara). 5. Funda (de muebles, de instrumento músico, etc.). 6. Maleza, matorral. *Cover-glass,* Cubierta de vidrio muy delgado para muestras microscópicas.

Coveralls [cuv'-ẹr-ōlz], *s. pl.* Mono.

Coverer [cuv'-ẹr-ẹr], *s.* Lo que cubre o protege.

Covering [cuv'-ẹr-ing], *s.* Ropa o vestido, lo que cubre el cuerpo para abrigarle.

Coverlet, Coverlid [cuv'-ẹr-let, cuv'-ẹr-lid], *s.* Colcha, sobrecama o cobertura de cama.

Coversed sine [cō-vẹrst' sain], *s.* (Mat.) Coseno verso; seno verso del complemento de un ángulo o de un arco.

Covert [cuv'-ẹrt], *s.* 1. Cubierto o cubierta. 2. Refugio, asilo, guarida. 3. Matorral o espesura de matas en que se oculta o se esconde alguno. 4. Bandada, en la caza de aves.—*a.* 1. Cubierto, oculto, tapado, secreto, escondido. 2. Exención legal de la mujer casada de ciertas obligaciones de que es responsable su marido.

Covert-way [cuv'-ert-wê], *s.* (Fort.) Camino cubierto, el espacio que media entre la contraescarpa y la esplanada. Lo mismo que *covered way.*

Covertly [cuv'-ert-li], *adv.* Secretamente, en secreto.

Covertness [cuv'-ert-nes], *s.* Secreto, sigilo; escondrijo.

Coverture [cuv'-er-chur o tiūr], *s.* 1. El estado o condición de una mujer casada, la cual según las leyes de Inglaterra no puede contratar sin permiso de su marido. 2. Escondrijo, escondite; antiguamente, cubierta.

Covet [cuv'-et], *va.* Codiciar, desear con ansia, apetecer, ambicionar.—*vn.* Desear, anhelar, aspirar.

Covetable [cuv'-et-a-bl], *a.* Codiciable.

Coveting [cuv'-et-ing], *s.* Codicia desordenada.

Covetingly [cuv'-et-ing-li], *adv.* Codiciosamente.

Covetous [cuv'-et-us], *a.* Codicioso, avariento, ambicioso, sórdido, interesado, avaro, roñoso, mezquino, mísero, ávido, ansioso.

Covetously [cuv'-et-us-li], *adv.* Codiciosamente.

Covetousness [cuv'-et-us-nes], *s.* Codicia, avaricia; ambición, avidez, mezquindad, miseria, sordidez.

Covey [cuv'-i], *s.* Nidada, pollada; banda o bandada, número crecido de aves o pájaros que vuelan juntos.

Cow [cau], *va.* Acobardar, amedrentar, intimidar, causar o poner miedo.

Cow, *s.* Vaca. *Milch-cow,* Vaca de leche.

Cow-boy [cau'-boi], *s.* 1. Muchacho empleado como pastor de vacas. 2. (E. U.) Vaquero montado.

Cow-catcher [cau'-cach-er], *s.* Botaganado o trompa de locomotora; armazón en forma de cuña que va al frente de la locomotora. *V.* PILOT.

Cow-herd [cau'-herd], *s.* Vaquero, pastor del ganado vacuno.

Cow-house [cau'-haus], *s.* Boyera, boyeriza, el establo en que se guardan vacas o bueyes.

Cow-keeper [cau'-kīp-er], *s.* Vaquero, el que tiene vacas de leche.

Cow-lick [cau'-lic], *s.* Tupé, mechón de cabellos levantado sobre la parte superior de la frente; remolino.

Cow-wheat [cau'-hwīt], *s.* Trigo vacuno.

Coward [cau'-ard], *s.* Cobarde, collón. (Vul.) Pendejo.—*a.* Cobarde, medroso, pusilánime.

Cowardice [cau'-ard-is], **Cowardliness** [cau'-ard-li-nes], *s.* Cobardía, timidez, poquedad de alma, pusilanimidad, pendejada.

Cowardlike [cau'-ard-laic], *a.* Acobardado, amilanado.

Cowardly [cau'-ard-li], *a.* Cobarde, medroso, miedoso, pusilánime, tímido. *Cowardly action,* Acción vil. —*adv.* Cobardemente.

Cowboy [cau'-boi], *s.* Vaquero, gaucho.

Cower [cau'-er], *vn.* Agacharse, bajarse doblando las rodillas.

Cowhide [cau'-haid], *s.* Cuero, piel de vaca curtida—*va.* Azotar, dar azotes con un látigo de cueros.

Cowl [caul], *s.* 1. Cogulla de monje, capuz, capilla, capucha de fraile. *To throw off the cowl,* Colgar los hábitos. 2. Caperuza de chimenea. 3. (Prov. Ingl.) Tina, vasija para agua; cuba, cubeta.

Cowled [cauld], *a.* Lo que tiene cogulla o capucha.

Cowlike [cau'-laic], *a.* Semejante a una vaca.

†**Cowl-staff** [caul'-staf], *s.* Palo para llevar alguna cosa entre dos hombres.

Coworker, *s. V.* FELLOW-LABORER.

Cowpox [cau'-pex], *s.* Vacuna, viruela que sale a las vacas en las tetas. *V.* VACCINE.

Cowry, Cowrie [cau'-ri], *s.* Cauris, concha usada como dinero en Africa y en la India. Cypræa moneta.

Cowslip [cau'-slip], *s.* Prímula o primavera, vellorita.

Coxcomb [cocs'-cōm], *s.* 1. Mequetrefe, mozuelo presumido, pisaverde; currutaco; lechuguino. 2. (Des.) Coronilla, la parte más alta de la cabeza; cresta de gallo.

Coxcombly [cocs'-cōm-li], **Coxcomical** [cocs-com'-i-cal], *a.* Presumido, fantástico, fatuo, impertinente, currutaco.

Coxcombry [cocs'-com-ri], *s.* Presunción, petimetrería, currutaquería.

Coy, Coyish [coi, ish], *a.* Recatado, modesto; reservado, esquivo; retrechero.

Coy, *va.* Halagar, lisonjear, acariciar.—*vn.* (Poco us.) Esquivarse, desdeñarse.

Coyly [coi'-li], *adv.* Con esquivez.

Coyness [coi'-nes], *s.* Esquivez, despego, extrañeza; recato, modestia.

Coyote [cai-ō'-tē], *s.* Coyote.

Coz [cuz], *s.* Voz familiar que significa lo mismo que *cousin. V.* COUSIN.

Cozen [cuz'-n], *va.* Engañar, defraudar.

Cozenage [cuz'-n-ēj], *s.* Fraude, engaño, trampa, supercheria.

Cozener [cuz'-n-er], *s.* Engañador, defraudador.

Cozily [cō'-zi-li], *adv.* Reducida pero cómodamente. Agradablemente.

Cozy [cō'-zi], *a.* Cómodo, manejable, agradable; sociable, tranquilmente instalado. (Escríbese también **Cosey, Cosy** y **Cozey.**)

Crab [crab], *a.* Agrio, áspero.—*s.* 1. Cangrejo. 2. Manzana silvestre. 3. (Poco us.) Hombre de mal genio. 4. (Mar.) Cabrestante sencillo o volante. 5. (Astr.) Cáncer. *Crab-apple,* Manzana pequeña y agria que sirve principalmente para hacer conservas. *V.* 2ª acep. *Crab-louse,* Ladilla. *To catch a crab,* Hundir demasiado el remo, o no tocar con él en el agua, y caerse hacia atrás al dar la remada.

Crabs'-eyes [crabz'-ais], *s. pl.* (Farm.) Ojos de cangrejo. *V.* CRABSTONE.

Crabbed [crab'-ed], *a.* Impertinente, áspero, ceñudo, duro, severo, austero, bronco, tosco; escabroso, desigual.

Crabbedly [crab'-ed-li], *adv.* Impertinentemente; ásperamente, secamente.

Crabbedness [crab'-ed-nes], *s.* 1. Aspereza. 2. Rigidez o austeridad.

Crabsidle [crab'-sai-dl], *vn.* (Fest.) Moverse de lado, como un cangrejo.

Crabstone [crab'-stōn], *s.* Ojo de cangrejo, concreción calcárea que se forma en el estómago de los cangrejos cuando están para mudar la piel.

Crack [crac], *s.* 1. Hendedura, rendija, grieta, raja, quebraja, rotura. 2. Crujido, chasquido, castañetazo, estallido, estampido. 3. Golpe retumbante. 4. Locura, mentecatez. 5. La mudanza de la voz al llegar a la pubertad. 6. Persona de viso en cierto concepto o esfera. 7. (Ant. Ger.) Impureza, cochinada, indecencia.—*a.* (Fam.) De calidad superior; de primer orden.

Crack, *va.* 1. Hender, rajar. 2. Decir alguna cosa con jovialidad. 3. Romper, destruir. *To crack a bottle,* Despachar una botella. 4. Volverle a uno el juicio, volverle loco. (Amer.) Chiflarse.—*vn.* 1. Reventar, saltar, abrirse alguna cosa. 2. (Fam.) Arruinarse. 3. Crujir, dar crujidos o estallidos algún cuerpo cuando se rompe; estallar. 4. (Ant.) Jactarse, echar bravatas o baladronadas.

Crack-brained [crac'-brēnd], *a.* Alocado, alelado, mentecato, estúpido, chiflado.

Cracked [cract], *pp.* de CRACK. *Cracked wheat,* Trigo resquebrajado.

Cracker [crak'-er], *s.* 1. Lo que da crujidos. 2. Cohete de China; triquitraque. 3. (Amer.) Galletica, bizcocho delgado y quebradizo. 4. Ánade de marino o faisán acuátil. 5. El pedacito de papel que se pone en cada rizo para hacerlo.

†**Crack-hemp** [crac'-hemp], †**Crack-rope** [crac'-rōp], *s.* Hombre digno de ser ahorcado.

Crackle [crac'-l], *vn.* Crujir, chasquear, dar chasquidos.

Crackling [crac'-ling], *s.* Estallido, crujido.—*pa.* de CRACKLE.

Cracknel [crac'-nel], *s.* Especie de rosca o bollo duro y quebradizo.

Cradle [crē'-dl], *s.* 1. Cuna. *To rock the cradle,* Mecer o mover la cuna. 2. Niñez, infancia; (fig.) cuna, origen o principio de alguna cosa. 3. (Cir.) Caja o tablilla para un hueso roto. 4. (Agr.) Segadora de mano; arco unido al mango de la guadaña. 5. (Min.) Andamio colgante; artesa móvil para lavar el oro. 6. Carro salvavidas. 7. (Mar.) Cuna, parte del aparato empleado para lanzar un buque al agua. *Cradle scythe,* Hoz de rastra.

Cradle, *va.* 1. Meter en cuna; acostar a un niño en la cuna. 2. Segar las mieses con segadora de mano.—*vn.* Reposar como en cuna.

Cradle-clothes [crē'-dl-clōdhz], *s. pl.* Ropa de cuna.

Craft [craft], *s.* 1. Arte, oficio, el trabajo y ejercicio en que se emplean los artesanos. 2. Arte, maña, artificio, astucia, treta, fraude, engaño. 3. Embarcación, barco; cualquier género de nave. También es el conjunto de naves. *Small craft,* (Mar.) Navichuelos, sean barcos, barcas, bateles, esquifes o lanchas.

Craftily [craft'-i-li], *adv.* Astutamente, artificiosamente, mañosamente.

Craftiness [craft'-i-nes], *s.* Astucia, treta, estratagema, maña.

Craftsman [crafts'-man], *s.* Artífice, artesano.

Craftsmaster [crafts'-mas-ter], *s.* Maestro, el artífice o artesano.

Crafty [craf'-ti], *a.* Astuto, artificioso, taimado.

Crag [crag], *s.* 1. Despeñadero, risco, roca o peñasco lleno de precipicios. 2. Cima de un despeñadero.

Cragged [crag'-ed], *a.* Escabroso, áspero, peñascoso.

Craggedness [crag'-ed-nes], **Cragginess** [crag'-i-nes], *s.* Escabrosidad, desigualdad, aspereza, fragosidad.

Craggy [crag'-i], *a.* Escabroso, áspero, desigual, fragoso, escarpado.
Cram [cram], *va.* 1. Rellenar, henchir. 2. Atestar, llenar demasiado. 3. Atracar, embutir, llenar una cosa hasta no poder más; hartar, atracar de comida. 4. Empujar, meter una cosa en otra con fuerza y violencia.—*vn.* 1. Atracarse de comida. *To cram poultry,* Engordar o cebar capones o pavos. 2. Sobrecargar la inteligencia y la memoria con un cúmulo de conocimientos adquiridos apresuradamente.
Crambo [cram'-bō], *s.* Un juego en el cual dada una palabra hay que hallar un consonante para ella.
Cramming [cram'-ing], *s.* Repaso; término usado en los colegios para designar la acción de preparar a un estudiante para los exámenes.
Cramp [cramp], *s.* 1. Calambre, pasmo o encogimiento de nervios que impide el movimiento. 2. Sujeción, estrechez, aprieto. 3. Laña, especie de grapa de hierro que sirve para unir y trabar dos cosas.—*a.* Dificultoso, nudoso.
Cramp, *va.* 1. Dar o causar calambre. 2. Sujetar, tener en sujeción. 3. Lañar, trabar, asegurar, unir o afianzar con lañas. 4. Constreñir, apretar, enganchar, aferrar. *To cramp out,* Arrancar.
Cramp-fish [cramp'-fish], *s.* Torpedo, tremielga.
Cramp-iron [cramp'-ai-ūrn], *s.* Gatillo de hierro, laña. *V.* CRAMP.
Crampon, Crampoon [cram'-pǫn, cram-pūn'], *s.* 1. Un hierro con garfio en la punta que sirve para levantar con la grúa los maderos, piedras y otras cosas de peso. 2. Raíz aérea para trepar, como en la hiedra. 3. Púa asegurada al calzado para andar sobre el hielo o para escalar postes o muros.
Cranage [crēn'-ẹj], *s.* 1. Permiso para tener pescante o grúa en algún muelle. 2. Derechos de grúa o pescante, el dinero que se paga por sacar géneros de alguna embarcación con la grúa.
Cranberry [cran'-ber-i], *s.* (Bot.) Arándano, planta que nace en lugares pantanosos, y su fruto; éste es ácido y de color escarlata. Vaccinium (macrocarpon).
Crane [crēn], *s.* 1. Grulla, ave de paso, de alto vuelo, con pico largo, recto y agudo. 2. Grúa, máquina para elevar toda clase de pesos. 3. Pescante, instrumento compuesto de poleas, cuerdas y ganchos, para subir y levantar cosas de peso. *Wheel-crane,* Pescante o grúa con rueda. 4. Sifón, cañón o tubo corvo que sirve para sacar licores de una vasija. 5. Cigüeña o aguilón de chimenea. *To crane up, va.* Subir una cosa con la grúa o el pescante.
Crane-fly [crēn'-flai], *s.* (Ent.) Especie de típula; zancudo.
Crane's-bill [crēnz'-bil], *s.* 1. (Bot.) Geranio, pico de cigüeña. 2. Tenazas puntiagudas de los cirujanos.
Cranial [crē'-ni-al], *a.* Del cráneo o perteneciente a él.
Craniology [cre-ni-el'-o-ji], *s.* Craneología.
Cranium [crē'-ni-um], *s.* Cráneo, casco de la cabeza.
Crank [crank], *s.* 1. Biela, manubrio, cigüeña; invento para comunicar movimiento de rotación a un eje, o para convertir el movimiento rotatorio en recíproco, y vice versa. 2. Cigüeña, el hierro a que se asegura el cordel de la campana para tocarla. 3. Capricho, concepto. 4. (E. U. Fam.) Mentecato, maniático. *He is a crank,* Está algo tocado, le falta un tornillo. *Crank-pin,* Botón de manubrio.—*a.* 1. Sano, alegre; vigoroso, dispuesto. 2. (Mar.) *V.* CRANK-SIDED.
Crank, *va.* 1. Poner en marcha (un motor) con biela o manubrio. 2. Encorvar para dar forma de manubrio.
Crankcase [crank'-kēs], *s.* (Mec.) Cárter (de un automóvil).
Crankness [crank'-nes], *s.* Salud, robustez, vigor; alegría vivacidad.
Crankshaft [crank'-shaft], *s.* (Mec.) Cigüeñal.
Crank-sided [crank'-said-ed], *a.* (Mar.) Celoso, el bajel que con facilidad se tumba a la banda y no aguanta la vela, si el viento es algo recio y viene por el costado.
Cranky [crank'-i], *a.* 1. Caprichoso, lleno de extravagancias, lunático. 2. Torcido, corvo. 3. Destartalado, titubeante, expuesto a venirse abajo.
Crannied [cran'-id], *a.* Hendido, abierto, lleno de grietas o aberturas.
Cranny [cran'-i], *s.* Grieta, hendedura, raja, abertura, agujero.
Crape [crēp], *s.* 1. Crespón, tela de seda a modo de gasa. 2. Cendal. (Amer.) Espumilla. *Canton crape,* Burato.
Crape, *va.* 1. Encrespar, rizar el cabello encrespándolo. 2. Revestir con crespón, poner crespón como seña) de luto.
Craps [craps], *s.* Un juego de dados.
Crapshooting [crap-shūt'-ing], *s.* Un juego de dados.
Crapula [crap'-yu-la], *s.* Crápula, glotonería, embriaguez o borrachera.
Crapulent [crap'-yu-lent], **Crapulous** [crap'-yu-lus], *a.* Crapuloso, dado a la crápula; borracho, el que anda en borracheras o comilonas.
Crash [crash], *va.* 1. Estrellar, hacer añicos. 2. (Fam.) Colarse en.—*vn.* 1. (Aer.) Estrellarse. 2. Desplomarse con gran estrépito. 3. Chocar. 4. Dar estallido.
Crash, *s.* 1. Estrépito, estruendo, estampido. 2. Fracaso repentino. 3. Choque. 4. Derrumbe, desplome. 5. Cotí burdo. 6. Crac. 7. (Aer.) Aterrizaje violento.
Crass [cras], *a.* 1. Grueso, gordo; basto, tosco, grosero; espeso. 2. Rudo, torpe, tardo en comprender.
Crassamentum [cras-a-men'-tum], *s.* Parte espesa y coagulable de la sangre.
Crassitude [cras'-i-tiūd], *s.* Crasitud, tosquedad; espesor, espesura.
Crate [crēt], *s.* Cuévano, cesto grande; también la carga o suma de objetos que contiene. *Crate of earthenware,* Canasto de loza. (Mex.) Guacal de loza. (Amer.) Jaba.
Crater [crē'-tẹr], *s.* 1. Cráter, boca de volcán. 2. Copa, en antigüedades clásicas. 3. La Copa, constelación del hemisferio austral.
Cravat [cra-vat'], *s.* Corbata.
Crave [crēv'], *va.* Rogar, suplicar, implorar, pedir encarecidamente, desear con antojo; importunar. *To crave indulgence,* Implorar indulgencia.
Craven [crēv'-n], *s.* Un bajo cobarde.—*a.* Acobardado, pusilánime.
Craven, *va.* Amilanar, acobardar, intimidar.
Craver [crēv'-er], *s.* Pedidor, pedigón, el que es pedigüeño o pide con importunidad.
Craving [crēv'-ing], *s.* Deseo vehemente, ardiente.—*a.* Insaciable; pedigüeño.
Craw [crē], *s.* Buche, bolsa o seno en que reciben las aves la comida.
Crawfish [crē'-fish], *s.* Cangrejo de agua dulce; crustáceo parecido a la langosta. Astacus fluviatilis.—*vn.* (Fam. E. U.) Andar hacia atrás, como el cangrejo; de aquí, recular, retroceder, abandonar la posición o actitud que antes se tenía.
Crawl [crēl], *vn.* 1. Arrastrar, moverse con lentitud. 2. Gatear. *To crawl up,* Trepar. *To crawl forth,* Avanzar rastreando.
Crawl, *s.* 1. Arrastre, movimiento lento. 2. Acto de gatear. 3. Brazada de pecho (en natación).
Crawler [crēl'-ẹr], *s.* Reptil, el que va arrastrándose como los reptiles.
Crayfish [crē'-fish], *s.* Cangrejo de río. *V.* CRAWFISH.
Crayon [crē'-un], *s.* 1. Lápiz, piedra o pasta de varios colores para dibujar al pastel. 2. Dibujo de lápiz. 3. Clarión, tiza.
Craze [crēz], *va.* 1. Alelar, embobar, entontecer. 2. Hacer pequeñas grietas o hendeduras en; literal y figuradamente. 3. (Des.) Quebrantar, debilitar.—*vn.* Henderse, llenarse de grietas la alfarería.
Craze, *s.* 1. Locura, demencia, manía. 2. Extravagancia loca de la moda; capricho. 3. Antojo, capricho, fantasía o manía que no raciocina. 4. Grieta, falta, defecto en el lustre de la alfarería o vajilla de barro.
Crazedness [crēz'-ed-nes], *s.* 1. Calidad de loco. 2. Calidad de grietoso.
Craziness [crē'-i-nes], *s.* Debilidad, sea de cuerpo o entendimiento; locura; enajenación mental; condición de lo desvencijado.
Crazy [crēz'-i], *a.* 1. Lelo, fatuo, simple, loco; acometido de enajenación mental. 2. Quebrantado, decrépito, cascado, caduco. 3. *A crazy thing or article,* Alguna cosa desvencijada, coja o imperfecta; miserable, pobre. 4. (Fam.) Exageradamente deseoso o ansioso; deseoso de un modo insensato.
Creak [crīk], *vn.* Crujir, hacer un ruido áspero; estallar.
Creaking [crīk'-ing], *s.* Crujido, estallido.
Cream [crīm], *s.* 1. Crema, la nata y flor de la leche. 2. Lo mejor, lo más estimado y escogido de alguna cosa. *Cream of tartar,* Crémor tártaro, bitartrato de potasa. *Whipt cream,* Nata batida. *Cold-cream, V.* COLD.
Cream, *vn.* Criar nata, levantar espuma.—*va.* Quitar la crema de la leche o la flor de cualquiera cosa.
Creamery [crīm'-ẹr-i], *s.* 1. El edificio y la habitación donde se conserva la leche a la debida temperatura para obtener la nata. 2. Establecimiento donde se hace la manteca o mantequilla. 3. Lechería, lugar donde se vende la nata.
Creamy [crīm'-i], *a.* Parecido a la crema o nata, o que la contiene.
Crease [crīs], *s.* Pliegue, la doblez o arruga que se hace en alguna cosa; plegadura.
Crease, *va.* Plegar, señalar con pliegues.
Creasote [crī'-a-sōt], *s.* *V.* CREOSOTE.
Create [crẹ-ēt'], *va.* 1. Criar o crear,

producir algo de la nada; dar ser a lo que antes no lo tenía. 2. Criar, producir, ocasionar, causar. 3. Engendrar, procrear. 4. Crear, elevar á alguna nueva dignidad, constituir, elegir.
Creation [crẹ-é'-shun], *s.* 1. Creación, el acto de crear o sacar alguna cosa de la nada. 2. Elevación á nueva dignidad, nombramiento, elección. 3. Creación; el universo. 4. Cualquiera cosa producida o causada; los seres creados; especie.
Creative [crẹ-é'-tiv], *a.* Creativo, creador, lo que puede crear.
Creativeness [crẹ-é'-tiv-nes], *s.* Facultad creadora, genio inventivo.
Creator [crẹ-é'-tẹr], *s.* 1. Creador, Criador, el Ser supremo que creó todas las cosas. 2. Lo que crea o causa.
Creatress [crẹ-é'-tres], *s.* Creadora.
Creature [crí'-chur o tiūr], *s.* 1. Criatura, ente criado o creado. 2. Criatura, voz de desprecio que a veces se aplica a una persona. 3. Criatura, voz que expresa ternura o compasión. *Poor creature!* ¡Pobrecito! 4. Criatura, hechura, el que debe a otro su elevación, empleo o fortuna; dependiente. 5. Bestia, animal. *Our fellow-creatures,* Nuestros semejantes. *Creature comforts,* Las cosas que confortan o refrescan el cuerpo.
Creatureship [crí'-chur-ship], *s.* Estado de criatura.
Credence [crí'-dens], *s.* Creencia, asenso, fe; crédito.
Credendum, *plur.* CREDENDA [crẹ-den'-dum, da], *s.* Creencia; artículos de fe.
Credent [crí'-dent], *a.* (Ant.) Creyente, crédulo, acreditado.
Credential [crẹ-den'-shal], *a.* Credencial.
Credentials [crẹ-den'-shalz], **Credential letters** [crẹ-den'-shal let'-ẹrz], *s. pl.* Cartas de creencia o cartas credenciales.
Credibility [cred-i-bil'-i-ti], *s.* Credibilidad, probabilidad, verosimilitud.
Credible [cred'-i-bl], *a.* Creíble, probable, verosímil; digno de confianza.
Credibleness [cred'-i-bl-nes], *s.* Credibilidad; veracidad.
Credibly [cred'-i-bli], *adv.* Creíblemente, probablemente.
Credit [cred'-it], *s.* 1. Crédito, asenso, fe, creencia. 2. Crédito, reputación, buena opinión; influencia. 3. Confianza, seguridad que uno tiene en otro. 4. Influjo, autoridad, poder, aunque no coactivo. *Letter of credit,* Carta de crédito. *Open credit,* Letra abierta. *To buy goods on credit,* Comprar géneros al fiado. *To sell on credit,* Vender al fiado.
Credit, *va.* 1. Creer, honrar, fiar, confiar, acreditar, dar fama, dar fe. 2. Prestar ó vender á crédito, dar al fiado. 3. (Com.) Acreditar, abonar una partida en el libro de cuentas.
Creditable [cred'-it-a-bl], *a.* Apreciable, estimable, honorífico.
Creditableness [cred'-it-a-bl-nes], *s.* Reputación, estimación.
Creditably [cred'-it-a-bli], *adv.* Honorablemente, honrosamente.
Credit balance [cred'-it bal'-ans], *s.* Saldo acreedor.
Credit card [cred'-it cārd], *s.* Tarjeta de crédito.
Credited cred'-it-ed], *pp.* y *a.* 1. Acreditado, estimado, tenido en buena opinión. 2. Creído. 3. (Com.) Acreditado, abonado en cuenta; pasado al haber.
Creditor [cred'-i-tẹr], *s.* 1. Acreedor. 2. (Com.) Haber, una de las dos partes en que se dividen las cuentas corrientes.
Creditress ó **Creditrix** [cred'-i-tric s], *sf.* (Poco us.) Acreedora.
Credo [crí'-do], *s.* 1. Credo, profesión de fe, especialmente la de los Apóstoles. 2. Música para cantar el credo.
Credulity [crẹ-diū'-li-ti], *s.* Credulidad, demasiada facilidad en creer.
Credulous [cred'-yu-lus], *a.* Crédulo, que cree fácilmente; sin desconfianza.
Credulousness [cred'-yu-lus-nes], *s.* Credulidad.
Creed [crīd], *s.* Credo, creencia, símbolo. *There is my creed,* Esa es mi profesión de fe.
Creek [crīc], *s.* 1. Cala, caleta, ensenada. 2. (E. U.) Corriente formada por la marea creciente, ó que cursa por un valle y cuya dimensión varía entre arroyo y río.
Creek, *n. pr.* Tribu poderosa de indios norteamericanos que en otro tiempo habitaron gran parte de los Estados de Georgia y Alabama.
Creeky [crīk'-i], *a.* Tortuoso, lleno de caletas o entradas.
Creel [crīl], *s.* 1. Cesta de pescador. 2. Jaula de mimbres, para coger langostas. 3. Estizola de urdidor.
Creep [crīp], *vn.* (*pret.* y *pp.* CREPT). 1. Arrastrar, serpear, ratear. 2. Andar lenta ó imperceptiblemente; andar secretamente; insinuarse, entrar á escondidas. 3. Tener sensación nerviosa como de hormigueo sobre la piel. 4. Incensar, lisonjear, adular con bajeza, complacer bajamente. *To creep in* ó *into,* Insinuarse; deslizarse en; (fam.) escaparse de; meterse en, escurrirse. *To creep out,* Salir sin hacer ruido. *To creep on,* Acercarse insensiblemente. *To creep and crouch,* Hacer la gata ensogada. *To creep up,* Trepar á; encaramarse.—*s.* 1. Acción de serpear. 2. *pl.* Sensación nerviosa como de hormigueo sobre la piel.
Creeper [crīp'-ẹr], *s.* 1. El que o lo que anda arrastrándose. 2. (Bot.) Planta enredadera; solano trepador. 3. Un ave pequeña; las hay de varias especies. 4. Garfio, garabato para sacar objetos de un pozo ó estanque. 5. Ramplón de zapato. *Cf.* CRAMPON, acep. 3.
Creep-hole [crīp'-hōl], *s.* 1. Huronera, hueco ó agujero que sirve de refugio á un animal cualquiera. 2. Pretexto, excusa, escapatoria.
Creepingly [crīp'-ing-li], *adv.* Á paso de tortuga, muy lentamente.
Cremate [crī'-mēt], *va.* Quemar (los cadáveres, los desechos, etc.), reducir á cenizas; incinerar.
Cremation [crẹ-mé'-shun], *s.* Cremación, quema, el acto de quemar, especialmente de quemar los cadáveres.
Crematory [crī'-ma-to-ri], *s.* Crematorio, quemadero, lugar para quemar los cadáveres; el edificio y el horno.
Cremona [crẹ-mō'-na], *s.* Violín de hechura y calidad superiores, fabricado en Cremona, en los siglos XVI á XVIII.
Cremor [crī'-mẹr], *s.* Crémor.
Crenate, Crenated [crī'-nēt, ed], *a.* (Bot.) Crenífero, dentado con dientes redondeados.
Crenelate [cren'-el-ēt], *va.* 1. Almenar, cubrir ó coronar de almenas un edificio, muralla, etc. 2. Dentar, festonear, recortar en festón.
Creole [crī'-ōl], *s.* y *a.* Criollo.
Creosote [crī'-e-sōt], *s.* Creosota, líquido oleaginoso, incoloro y transparente, que se destila de la madera y se emplea en medicina. También tiene aplicación en las artes para conservar postes, tablas, etc., y para preservar las carnes.
Crêpe [crēp], *s.* Crespón. *Crêpe de chine,* Crespón de seda.
Crêpe paper [crēp pé'-pẹr], *s.* Papel crepé.
Crepitate [crep'-i-tēt], *vn.* Crepitar, chisporrotear, arder chispeando, como la sal en el fuego; chirriar.
Crept, *pret.* y *pp.* de *To* CREEP.
†**Crepuscule** [crẹ-pus'-kiūl], *s.* Crepúsculo.
Crepuscular, †**Crepusculine** [cre-pus'-kiu-lin], †**Crepusculous** [crẹ-pus'-kiu-lus], *a.* Crepuscular.
Crescendo [cres-shen'-dō], *a.* (Mús.) Que va aumentándose gradualmente en fuerza.—*s.* Aumento gradual del volumen del sonido. Se denota por medio del signo < ó de la abreviatura *cres.* (Ital.)
Crescent [cres'-ent], *a.* Creciente.—*s.* 1. Creciente, el primer cuarto de la luna. 2. Cualquiera cosa que tiene figura semicircular.
Crescive [cres'-iv], *a.* (Ant.) Creciente.
Cress [cres], *s.* (Bot.) Lepidio, mastuerzo. *Water-cress,* Berro.
Cresset [cres'-et], *s.* 1. Fanal o farol. 2. Antorcha, lámpara. 3. Trébedes.
Crest [crest], *s.* 1. Crestón de celada o cimera de morrión; cresta o copete. 2. Orgullo, altanería. *Crest of a horse,* El cuello del caballo. *Crest of a coat of arms,* Cimera sobre el escudo de armas.
Crest, *va.* Señalar alguna cosa con rayas; coronar; encopetar, erguir.
Crested [crest'-ed], *a.* Crestado, encopetado, coronado.
Crestfallen [crest'-fēl-n], *a.* Acobardado, amedrentado, amilanado, abatido de espíritu, caído; con el rabo entre las piernas; con las orejas gachas.
Crestless [crest'-les], *a.* Sin cimera, sin divisa; sin escudo de armas, de humilde estirpe.
Cretaceous [crẹ-té'-shus], *a.* Gredoso, cretáceo, de la naturaleza de la greda.
Cretan [crī'-tan], *a.* Cretense, perteneciente á la isla de Creta.
Cretated [cre-té'-ted], *a.* (Poco us.) Dado de greda.
Cretin [crī'-tin], *s.* Cretino, la persona afectada de cretinismo.
Cretinism [crī'-tin-izm], *s.* Cretinismo, enfermedad incurable, caracterizada por deformidad del cuerpo y alteración de la mente. Ataca á los habitantes de regiones montañosas.
Cretonne [crẹ-ton'], *s.* Cretona, tela de algodón, de superficie mate y estampada en colores.
Cretose [crī'-tōs], *a.* Cretáceo, gredoso.
Crevasse [crẹ-vas'], *s.* 1. Grieta, hendedura profunda en un ventisquero. 2. (E. U.) Brecha en el dique de un río.
Crevice [crev'-is], *s.* Raja, hendedura, grieta, abertura.
Crevice, *va.* *V.* CRACK.
Crew [crū], *s.* 1. Cuadrilla, banda, tropa, reunión de personas congregadas para algún intento, generalmente malo. 2. (Mar.) Tripulación.

Crew, *pret. ant.* del verbo *To* CROW.
Crewcut [crū'-cʊt], *s.* Corte de pelo para que quede como cepillo.
Crewel [cru'-el], *s.* Ovillo de estambre.
Crib [crib], *s.* 1. Pesebre. 2. Camita de niño con barandilla por los lados. *Rattan crib*, Camita de junquillo o bambú. 3. Arcón, arca para las mieses; granero de rejilla. 4. (Min.) Brocal de entibación. 5. (Hid.) Cofre, cajón; balsa pequeña. 6. Fuerte base o estribo flotante. 7. Robo de menor cuantía, y el objeto robado; plagio. 8. (Des.) Choza, casucha, chiribitil.
Crib, *va.* 1. Enjaular, encerrar como en un pesebre. 2. Quitar, hurtar.
Cribbage [crib'-ēj], *s.* Un juego de naipes.
Cribble [crib'-l], *s.* Criba, harnero; aventador.
Cribble, *va.* Cerner, pasar por el cedazo o criba.
Cribriform [crib'-ri-fōrm], *a.* Cribiforme, que tiene forma de criba.
Crick [cric], *s.* 1. Chirrido o chirrío. 2. Calambre, afección espasmódica local del cuello o espalda. *Crick in the neck*, Torticoli.
Cricket [crik'-et], *s.* 1. (Ent.) Grillo. 2. Vilorta, un juego. 3. Cáncana, banquillo, escabelito.
Cricketer [crik'-et-ẹr], *s.* Vilortero.
Crier [craí'-ẹr], *s.* Pregonero.
Crime [craim], *s.* Crimen, delito, culpa.
Criminal [crim'-i-nal], *a.* Criminal, reo. *Crim. con.* o *criminal conversation*, Seducción de una mujer casada; causa por adulterio.
Criminal, *s.* Reo, reo convicto.
Criminality [crim-i-nal'-i-ti], *s.* Criminalidad.
Criminally [crim'-i-nal-i], *adv.* Criminalmente.
Criminalness [crim'-i-nal-nes], *s.* Criminalidad.
Criminate [crim'-i-nēt], *va.* Acriminar, acusar.
Crimination [crim-i-nē'-shun], *s.* Criminación o acriminación.
Criminatory [crim'-i-na-to-ri], *a.* Acriminatorio, acusatorio.
Criminology [crim-i-nel'-o-ji], *s.* Criminología, estudio e investigación científicos de materias referentes a los crímenes y a los delincuentes.
Criminous [crim'-i-nus], *a.* Criminal, malvado, inicuo, criminoso.
†**Criminously** [crim'-i-nus-li], *adv.* Criminalmente.
Crimosin. (Des.) *V.* CRIMSON.
Crimp [crimp], *a.* 1. Quebradizo, desmenuzable, fácil de desmenuzarse. 2. Contradictorio, fácil de contradecir. 3. Tieso, rígido, como almidonado y planchado.
Crimp, *s.* 1. Lo que está encrespado; rizo; se usa en plural. 2. Aparato o instrumento para rizar o encrespar. 3. Sargento que engancha reclutas; también el que con engaño conduce a otros a un sitio determinado para robarlos o maltratarlos.
Crimp, *va.* Torcer, rizar o encrespar; alechugar, dar una forma ondeada.
Crimping [crimp'-ing], *pa.* de *To* CRIMP. *Crimping-iron*, Tenacillas, hierros para rizar. *Crimping-machine*, Máquina de estampar en relieve.
Crimple [crim'-pl], *va.* Encrespar, encoger, arrugar, rizar.
Crimpy [crimp'-i], *a.* Que presenta la apariencia de rizado; encrespado.
Crimson [crim'-zn], *a.* Carmesí.—*s.* Carmesí.
Crimson, *va.* Teñir de carmesí.
Cringe [crinj], *s.* Bajeza.
Cringe, *vn.* Incensar, lisonjear, adular con bajeza.—*va.* Estrechar.
Cringer [crinj'-ẹr], *s.* Adulador servil.
Cringing [crinj'-ing], *a.* Bajo, vil.
Crinigerous [cri-nij'-ẹr-us], *a.* Peludo, lleno de pelo, cabelludo.
Crinite [craí'-nait], *a.* Crinito; peludo.
Crinkle [crin'-cl], *vn.* Serpentear.—*va.* Hacer desigualdades, arrugar.
Crinkle, *s.* Vuelta y revuelta, recodo; sinuosidad.
Crinoid [craí'-neid], *s.* Crinóideo, género de equinodermos.
Crinoline [crin'-o-lin], *s.* 1. Tela de crin. 2. Crinolina, ahuecador o miriñaque de mujer, de tela de crin.
§**Crinose** [crī'-nōs], *a.* Peloso, peludo, cabelludo.
Cripple [crip'-l], *s.* y *a.* Cojo, manco, tullido, estropeado. (Mar.) Desarbolado, desmantelado.
Cripple, *va.* Derrengar, estropear, encojar, tullir, baldar, estropear.
Crisis [craí'-sis], *s.* Crisis; momento crítico; cambio decisivo en una enfermedad, negocio, etc.
Crisp [crisp], *a.* 1. Crespo, rizado. 2. Vivo; quebradizo, frágil. 3. Achicharrado, tostado. *Crisp almonds*, Almendras tostadas.
Crisp, *va.* 1. Crespar, encrespar, torcer, rizar; undular. 2. Hacer quebradizo o frágil. 3. (Poco us.) Trenzar, entrelazar.
Crispate [cris'-pēt], *a.* Desigual, sinuoso, arrugado.
Crispation [cris-pē'-shun], *s.* 1. Contracción ligera o constricción espasmódica; acción de arrugar. 2. (Des.) Encrespadura, crispatura.
Crisping-iron [crisp'-ing-aí'-urn], **Crisping-pin** [crisp'-ing-pin], *s.* Encrespador.
Crispness [crisp'-nes], *s.* Rizado, encrespadura, fragilidad.
Crispy [crisp'-i], *a.* Crespo, rizado, desmenuzable, frágil.
Criss-cross [cris'-crēs], *a.* Cruzado o entrelazado en diferentes direcciones: dícese de líneas, etc.—*s.* 1. Cruz o firma del que no sabe escribir. 2. Líneas cruzadas entre sí. 3. Juego de niños.—*va.* Cruzar líneas,
Criss-cross-row [cris'-cres-ro'], *s.* Cristus, *V.* CHRIST-CROSS-ROW.
Criterion [craí-tí'-ri-ẹn], *s.* Crisis, crítica o criterio.
§**Critic, Critical** [crit'-ic al], *a.* 1. Crítico, exacto, escrupuloso. *Critical affair*, Negocio delicado. 2. (Med.) Crítico, que indica una crisis; difícil, peligroso, decisivo. 3. Crítico, relativo al examen y censura de las obras literarias o de arte. 4. Quisquilloso, caviloso.
Critic, *s.* 1. Crítico, censor. 2. Crítica, observación crítica, examen crítico.
Critically [crit'-ic-al-i], *adv.* Exactamente, rigurosamente.
Criticalness [crit'-ic-al-nes], *s.* Crítica.
Criticism [crit'-i-sizm], *s.* 1. Crítica, juicio fundado en las reglas del arte y del buen gusto. 2. Crítica, censura de las acciones ajenas.
Criticize, Criticise [crit'-i-saiz], *vn.* Criticar.—*va.* Censurar.
Criticizer [crit'-i-saiz-ẹr], *s.* Crítico.
Critique [cri-tíc'], *s.* 1. Crítica, examen crítico de alguna cosa; revista. 2. Crítica, el arte de juzgar el mérito de las obras.
Croak [crōk], *vn.* 1. Graznar, crascitar o crocitar el cuervo; cantar las ranas. 2. Gruñir, murmurar entre dientes, presagiar mal.
Croak, *s.* Graznido de cuervos; canto de ranas.
Croaker [crōk'-ẹr], *s.* Gruñidor, refunfuñador; nombre de desprecio con que se moteja al que da demasiada importancia a los acontecimientos políticos.
Croaking [crōk'-ing], *pa.* de *To* CROAK.—*s.* 1. Graznido del cuervo; canto de la rana. 2. (Fam.) Gruñido, refunfuño.
Croat [crō'-at], *s.* Croata, habitante o natural de la Croacia.
Croatian [crō-ē'-shan], *a.* Croata, de Croacia.
Croceous [crō'-shius], *a.* (Poco us.) Azafranado.
Crochet [crō-shē'], *va.* y *vn.* Tejer con gancho, hacer cierta labor de aguja con hilo de lana, seda o algodón.—*s.* Tejido de gancho. *Crochet needle*, Gancho para tejer.
Crock [crec], *s.* Escudilla, cazuela, orza; olla de barro.
Crockery [crek'-ẹr-i], *s.* Vidriado, loza, todo género de vasijas de barro.
Crocodile [crec'-o-dail], *s.* Cocodrilo, crocodilo o caimán.
Crocus [crō'-cus], *s.* 1. (Bot.) Azafrán. 2. Azafrán croco o de Marte; rojo de pulir.
Croft [creft], *s.* Campo pequeño cercano a una casa; huerta o tierra pequeña cercada.
Cromlech [crem'-lec], *s.* Círculo de piedras verticales, que a menudo rodean un dolman; monumento megalítico. *V.* DOLMEN.
Crone [crōn], *s.* 1. Mujer vieja. (Fam.) Una tía, una comadre. 2. Oveja vieja.
Crony [crō'-ni], *s.* Compinche, camarada, amigo y conocido antiguo. *An old crony*, Un amigo de muchos años; un conocido viejo.
Crook [cruk], *s.* 1. Curvatura, curva; cosa encorvada. 2. Gancho, garfio. 3. Gancho o cayado de pastor. 4. Artificio, trampa. 5. (Fam.) Un criminal de profesión; fullero, petardista.
Crook, *va.* 1. Encorvar, torcer. 2. (Ant.) Pervertir, separar del camino recto.—*vn.* Estar encorvado.
Crook-backed [cruc'-bact], *a.* Jorobado, corcovado, gibado, giboso.
Crooked [cruk'-ed], *a.* 1. Corvo, encorvado, torcido; oblicuo. 2. (Fig.) Perverso, pervertido, malvado. *Crooked legs*, Patituerto o piernas tuertas. *Crooked line*, Línea curva. *To go crooked*, Encorvarse, torcerse.
Crookedly [cruk'ed-li], *adv.* Torcidamente, de través; de mala gana.
Crookedness [cruk'-ed-nes], *s.* 1. Corvadura, corcova. 2. Perversidad, maldad, iniquidad. 3. Vueltas, sinuosidades, anfractuosidades.
Crook-neck [cruk'-nec], *a.* Que tiene el cuello torcido.—*s.* Variedad de calabaza que toma el nombre de su cuello largo y retorcido.
Croon [crūn], *va.* Cantar o canturrear suavemente, con delicadeza.—*vn.* 1. Cantar en tono bajo y monótono. 2. (Poco us.) Gruñir sordamente.
Crop [crep], *s.* 1. Cosecha, agosto, las mieses. 2. Crecimiento de cabellos o barba. 3. Cortadura. 4. Empuñadura de látigo. 5. Caballo desorejado. 6. Buche de ave.

Crop, *va.* 1. Segar o cortar las mieses o hierba. 2. Pacer o roer la hierba. 3. Desorejar, cortar las orejas o los cabellos; esquilar (los perros o las caballerías).
Crop-eared [crep'-ïrd], *a.* Desorejado.
Cropful [crep'-ful], *a.* Harto, hartado, ahito.
Cropper [crep'-ẹr], *s.* Especie de paloma que tiene el buche grande. *V.* POUTER.
Cropping [crep'-ing], *s.* 1. Corta, acción de cortar. 2. Pasto, acción de pastar. 3. Esquileo de los animales. 4. Siega, cultivación de una cosecha. 5. Porción aparente de un estrato en un terreno.
†**Cropsick** [crep'-sic], *a.* Ahito, ahitado, relleno.
Croquet [crō-kê'], *s.* Raqueta, croquet, juego al aire libre con bolas, mazos y arcos de alambre. Pueden jugarlo de dos a ocho personas.—*va.* Hacer cierta jugada especial en el juego de este nombre. (Fr.)
Croquette [crō-ket'], *s.* Croqueta. *Chicken croquettes,* Croquetas de pollo.
Crosier [crō'-zhẹr], *s.* *V.* CROZIER.
Cross [cres], *s.* 1. Cruz, instrumento de suplicio entre los antiguos. 2. Cruz, emblema del cristianismo. 3. Peso, carga, trabajo; oposición; pena, aflicción, desgracia, tormento, revés. 4. Cruz, insignia honorífica de algunas órdenes militares y civiles. 5. Mezcla de las diferentes especies de plantas o de las castas de animales. *Crosses are ladders leading to heaven,* (Prov.) Las cruces llevan al cielo. *The cross on the breast and the devil in action,* La cruz en la frente y el diablo en la mente, o la cruz en la boca y el diablo en la obra. *The Southern Cross,* La Cruz del Sur, constelación del hemisferio austral.
Cross, *a.* 1. Contrario, opuesto, atravesado. 2. Mal humorado, enojado, enfadado, picado; caprichoso, cabezudo, impertinente, revoltoso, regañón. 3. Desgraciado, infausto. 4. Alternado, cruzado; dícese de una raza o linaje. 5. Displicente, desabrido, de mal genio o natural. (For.) *Cross-question, cross-interrogatory,* Repregunta, examen de la parte contraria.
Cross, *prep.* Al través; de una parte a otra.
Cross, *va.* 1. Trazar una línea al través de. 2. Borrar, cancelar, rayar: con las preposiciones *off* o *out.* 3. Cruzar, poner o trazar en forma de cruz. *The two streets cross each other,* Las dos calles se cruzan. 4. Atravesar, cruzar, pasar de una parte a otra. 5. Señalar con la señal de la cruz. 6. Vejar; frustrar; desbaratar. 7. Contradecirse uno a sí mismo. 8. Cruzar, mezclar las castas (sea de los animales o de las plantas).—*vn.* Estar al través, cruzarse. *To cross over,* Atravesar de un lado a otro pasando por encima de una cosa; pasar del lado de allá al de acá.
Cross-armed [crēs'-ārmd], *a.* 1. Cruzado de brazos. 2. (Bot.) Los árboles y arbustos, cuyas ramas se cruzan.
Cross-barred [crēs'-bārd], *a.* Atravesado, atorado.
Cross-bar-shot [crēs'-bār-shet], *s.* (Mar.) Palanqueta.
Cross-bearer [crēs'-bār-ẹr], *s.* Crucífero.
Cross-bill [crēs'-bil], *s.* 1. Escrito ó cargo producido por el demandado contra el demandante. 2. *Cross-bill* o *cross-beak,* (Orn.) Picogordo. Loxia curvirrostra.
Cross-bow [crēs'-bō], *s.* Ballesta.
Cross-bower [crēs'-bō-ẹr], **Cross-bow-man** [crēs'-bō-man], *s.* Ballestero.
Cross-bun [crēs'-bun], *s.* Bollo señalado con una cruz.
Cross-cut [crēs'-cut], *va.* Intersecar, cortar al través.—*s.* Senda traviesa, camino más corto.
Cross-examination [crēs-eg-zam-i-nê'-shun], *s.* (For.) Repreguntas que se hacen a un testigo sobre la declaración que ha dado.
Cross-examine [crēs-eg-zam'-in], *va.* Examinar o repreguntar a un testigo sobre su declaración.
Cross-eye [crēs'-ai], *s.* Estrabismo.
Cross-eyed [cres'-aid], *a.* Bizco, bisojo.
Cross-fertilize [crēs-fẹr'-til-aiz], *va.* Fertilizar una flor por medio del polen de otra.
Cross-flow [crēs-flō'], *vn.* Fluir o correr en dirección contraria, al través de.
Cross-grained [crēs'-grênd], *a.* 1. Vetado ó veteado; (madero) de fibras atravesadas y difícil de cortar y trabajar. 2. (Fig.) Perverso, intratable, desabrido, de mal natural.
Crossing [crēs'-ing], *s.* 1. El acto de señalar con la cruz, oposición. 2. Travesía, paso; lugar donde se puede cruzar, pasar o vadear algo. 3. Cruzado de una tela; encrucijada, cuatro calles; en los ferrocarriles, cruce de vía, vía diagonal.
Cross-jack [crēs'-jac], *s.* (Mar.) Vela seca.
Cross-legged [crēs'-legd], *a.* Patizambo.
Crossly [crēs'-li], *adv.* Contrariamente; enojadamente.
Crossness [crēs'-nes], *s.* 1. Mal humor; enfado, enojo. 2. Malicia, perversidad. 3. Travesía.
Cross-piece [crēs'-pîs], *s.* (Mar.) Cruz de las bitas; (Carp.) travesaño, cruceta. *Cross-piece of the forecastle,* (Mar.) Atravesaño del propao del castillo.
Cross-purpose [cres'-pūr-pus], *s.* 1. Disposición contraria. 2. Enigma, juego, diversión casera.
Cross-question [crēs'-cwes-chun], *va.* (For.) Repreguntar. *V.* CROSS-EXAMINE.
Cross reference [cres ref'-ẹ-rens], *s.* Referencia cruzada, remisión del lector de una parte de un texto a otra.
Cross-road [cres'-rōd], *s.* Atajo, trocha, camino que acorta una distancia. *Cross-roads,* Encrucijada, cuatro caminos; ocurre a menudo en las aldeas pequeñas.
Cross-row [crēs'-rō], *s.* Alfabeto, cartilla.
Cross-section [cres-sec'-shun], *s.* Corte transversal.
Cross-staff [crēs'-stgf]. (Mar.) Ballestilla.
Cross-trees [crēs'-trîs], *s. pl.* (Mar.) Crucetas, baos de gavia.
Cross-way [crēs'-wê], *s.* Senda; camino de travesía. *V.* CROSS-ROAD.
Cross-wind [crēs'-wind], *s.* Viento atravesado.
Crosswise [cres'-waiz], *adv.* 1. De través, al través; de una parte a otra. 2. En forma de cruz.
Crossword puzzle [cres'-wūrd puz'-l], *s.* Crucigrama.
Crosswort [crēs'-wūrt], *s.* (Bot.) Cruciata.
Crotch [crech], *s.* Gancho, corchete; horquilla, cruz.
Crotchet [crech'-et], *s.* 1. Capricho, entusiasmo; idea o pensamiento extravagante. 2. Corchea, nota musical cuyo valor es una cuarta parte de la semibreve. 3. Garfio pequeño. 4. Corchete, carácter o signo de imprenta así [ ]. *V.* BRACKET. 5. Instrumento de obstetricia.
Crotchety [crech'-et-i], *a.* Caprichoso, extravagante, raro.
Crouch [crauch], *vn.* Agacharse, abatirse, bajarse; adular con bajeza.
Croup [crūp], *s.* 1. Obispillo o rabadilla de ave; anca, grupa (de caballo). 2. Crup, garrotillo, enfermedad de los conductos respiratorios que ataca a los niños.
Crow [crō], *s.* 1. Cuervo, ave de rapiña. 2. *Crow, crowbar,* Barra, palanca de hierro; pie de cabra. *As the crow flies,* En línea recta. *To eat crow,* (E. U.) Desdecir uno sus palabras, contradecirse.
Crow, *vn.* 1. Cantar el gallo. 2. Gallear, jactarse, cantar victoria, hacer alarde de. *To crow over one,* Afectar superioridad sobre alguno; bravear, echar plantas, fieros o bravatas.
Crowd [craud], *s.* 1. Tropel, gentío, turba, concurso; apretura; muchedumbre, tumulto, confusión de cosas o personas; populacho, vulgo. 2. Antiguo instrumento músico de Irlanda y Gales, parecido al violín. Fué el primero de su clase que se tocó con arco. *To get through the crowd,* Atravesar o abrirse camino por medio del gentío.
Crowd, *va.* Amontonar, atestar, apretar. *To crowd sail,* (Mar.) Hacer fuerza de vela.—*vn.* Apiñarse, estrecharse o juntarse demasiado unas personas o cosas con otras.
Crowfoot [crō'-fut], *s.* 1. (Bot.) Ranúnculo. 2. (Mar.) Araña. 3. (Mil.) Abrojo. *V.* CALTROP. 4. (Elec.) Cierta clase de cinc de batería que se usa en una celda de gravedad.
Crown [craun], *s.* 1. Corona, ornamento honorífico de los reyes y príncipes soberanos; y por extensión, la monarquía, el poder real y la dignidad de monarca. 2. Premio. 3. Guirnalda de flores. 4. Coronilla, la parte más alta de la cabeza o del sombrero. 5. Copa, cima. 6. Complemento, colmo. 7. Moneda de plata en Inglaterra del valor de cinco chelines. 8. Corona, parte del diente que se halla fuera de la encía. 9. (Arq.) Corona, coronamiento de bóveda o arco; parte de la cornisa que está debajo del cimacio y la gola. *Crown lands,* (Ingl.) Bienes raíces que pertenecen al soberano: en el día casi todos han sido devueltos a la nación, mediante una renta o concesión anual fija (cerca de £375,000 o $1,875,000).
Crown, *va.* Coronar, recompensar, premiar; completar, dar la última mano.
Crownet, *s.* *V.* CORONET.
Crown-glass [craun'-glas], *s.* Vidrio fino para vidrieras. *V.* GLASS.
Crowning [craun'-ing], *s.* (Arq.) Remate.
Crown-wheel [craun'-hwîl], *s.* Rueda superior próxima al volante del reloj.
Crown-works [craun'-wūrks], *s.* Obra coronada, la que está separada del

cuerpo de la plaza para defender algún puesto.
Crow's-foot [crōz'-fut], *s.* 1. Pata de gallo, arruga que se forma en el ángulo externo del ojo. 2. Abrojo. *V.* CALTROP. 3. Punto de hacer bordado.
Crozier [crō'-zhẹr], *a.* Cayado o báculo pastoral del obispo.
Crucial [cru'-shial], *a.* 1. Decisivo, conclusivo, final; que determina absolutamente la verdad o la falsedad de algo. 2. Cruzado, atravesado.
Cruciate [crū'-shi-ẹt], *a.* 1. Cruciforme, en forma de cruz. 2. (Poco us.) Atormentado.
Crucible [crū'-si-bl], *s.* Crisol, vasija que resiste la acción del fuego y sirve para fundir metales y otras cosas.
Cruciferous [crū-sif'-ẹr-us], **Crucigerous** [crū-sij'-ẹr-us], *a.* 1. Crucífero, lo que lleva cruz. 2. (Bot.) Crucíferas, familia de plantas con flores de cuatro pétalos que forman cruz.
Crucifier [crū'-si-fai-ẹr], *s.* Crucificador.
Crucifix [crū'-si-fics], *s.* Crucifijo, la efigie o imagen de nuestro Señor crucificado.
Crucifixion [crū-si-fic'-shun], *s.* Crucifixión.
Cruciform [crū'-si-fōrm], *a.* Cruciforme, en forma de cruz.
Crucify [crū'-si-fai], *va.* 1. Crucificar. 2. Atormentar, enojar.
Crud [crud], *s.* (Prov. Ingl.) *V.* CURD.
Crude [crūd], *a.* 1. Crudo, indigesto, imperfecto. 2. Crudo, no refinado, que no tiene forma regular; en estado que necesita preparación antes de ser usado. 3. (Fig.) Imperfecto, mal elaborado, mal concebido; superficial.
Crudeness [crūd'-nes], **Crudity** [crūd'-i-ti], *s.* Crudeza, falta de madurez, imperfección. *Crudity,* Lo crudo, lo indigesto o informe.
Cruel [crū'-el], *a.* Cruel, inhumano, bárbaro, terrible, feroz, sanguinario, desapiadado, inclemente, atroz.
Cruelly [crū'-el-i], *adv.* Cruelmente, dolorosamente, inhumanamente.
Cruelness [crū'-el-nes], **Cruelty** [crū'-el-ti], *s.* Crueldad, inhumanidad, barbarie; tiranía, dureza.
Cruet [crū'-et], *s.* Ampolleta para aceite o vinagre; vinagrera.
Cruet-stand [crū'-et-stand], *s.* Angarillas, vinagreras, salvilla en que se colocan las ampolletas de aceite, vinagre, mostaza, etc.
Cruise [crūz], *s.* 1. Travesía marítima. 2. Paseo por tierra. 3. Viaje por avión.
Cruise, *vn.* (Mar.) Navegar por el mar o a lo largo de la costa.
Cruiser [crūz'-ẹr], *s.* La persona o nave que hace viaje por mar; especialmente crucero, buque de guerra próximo en fuerza al *battle-ship* o acorazado y más ligero que éste.
Cruising speed [cruz'-ing spīd], *s.* Velocidad de crucero.
Crum o **Crumb** [crum], *s.* Miga, migajón, la parte interior y más blanda del pan.
Crum, Crumb, *va.* 1. Migar, desmigajar, reducir a migajas. 2. Desmenuzar.
Crumble [crum'-bl], *va.* Migar, desmigajar, desmenuzar o partir alguna cosa en porciones pequeñas.—*vn.* Desmigajarse, desmoronarse. *To crumble to pieces,* Irse desmoronando.
Crummy [crum'-i], *a.* Blando, tierno; que tiene mucha miga; que se desmigaja.
Crump [crump'], *a.* 1. *V.* CRISP. 2. (Des.) Corcovado, gibado, giboso, el que tiene giba o corcova.
Crumpet [crum'-pet], *s.* Buñuelo o bollo blando.
Crumple [crum'-pl], *va.* Arrugar, manosear, ajar manoseando.—*vn.* Contraerse, encogerse.
Crumpled [crum'-pld], *pp.* y *a.* Arrugado, ajado; contraído.
Crumpling [crum'-pling], *s.* Manzana pequeña arrugada.
Crunch [crunch], *vn.* Mascar haciendo ruido; crujir, cascar con los dientes.
Cruor [crū'-er], *s.* Cruor, sangre coagulada.
Crupper [crup'-ẹr], *s.* 1. Crupera, ataharre. 2. Grupa.
Crural [crū'-ral], *a.* Crural, perteneciente a la pierna o al muslo. *Crural artery,* Arteria crural.
Crus [crus], *s.* 1. Pierna, la parte del animal que está entre el pie y la rodilla. 2. Parte parecida a la pierna; pedúnculo; comunmente en plural, CRURA.
Crusade [crū-sēd'], **Crusado** [crū-sē'-do], *s.* Cruzada.—*Crusado,* Cruzado, moneda de plata de Portugal que corresponde a 10 reales de vellón.
Crusader [crū-sē'-dẹr], *s.* Cruzado.
Cruse [crūs], *s.* Ampolleta, cantarillo, frasco, redomita, botellita.
Cruset [crū'-set], *s.* Crisol de orífice o platero.
Crush [crush], *va.* 1. Aplastar, machacar, moler. (Fam.) Despachurrar. 2. Apretar, comprimir, oprimir. 3. Amilanar, arruinar, trastornar, destruir; sojuzgar completamente.—*vn.* Estar comprimido; condensarse.
Crush, *s.* Colisión, choque.
Crusher [crush'-ẹr], *s.* 1. Apretador; opresor. 2. Bocarte, triturador, instrumento para machacar el mineral antes de fundirlo.
Crust [crust], *s.* 1. Costra. 2. Corteza. 3. Pedazo o fragmento de pan ya duro. 4. Pasta de una torta, de un pastel. 5. Capa (del globo). 6. Carapacho, concha: el tegumento duro de los cangrejos e insectos.
Crust, *va.* Encostrar, cubrir con costra, revestir, incrustar.—*vn.* Encostrarse.
Crustacea [crus-tē'-shẹ-a], *s. pl.* (Zool.) Crustáceos, clase de animales articulados que comprende langostas, cangrejos, langostines, camarones, percebes y otros.
Crustacean [crus-tē'-shẹ-an], *a.* y *s.* Crustáceo. *V.* CRUSTACEA.
Crustaceous [crus-tē'-shus], *a.* Crustáceo; conchado, cubierto de conchas.
Crustate [crus'-tēt], *a.* Cubierto con corteza o costra.
Crustation [crus-tē'-shun], *s.* Incrustación, cobertura.
Crustily [crust'-i-li], *adv.* Enojadamente, broncamente.
Crustiness [crust'-i-nes], *s.* 1. Dureza de la costra. 2. Mal genio, aspereza de carácter.
Crusty [crust'-i], *s.* 1. Costroso. 2. Bronco, rudo, impertinente, inquieto; brusco, áspero.
Crutch [cruch], *s.* 1. Muleta. 2. (Mar.) Horquilla del cangrejo.—*Crutches,* (Mar.) Horquetas. *Crutched man,* Un cojitranco.
Crutch, *va.* Andar con muletas.
Cry [crai], *vn.* 1. Gritar, vocear, llamar a voces. 2. Pregonar, publicar. 3. Exclamar; lamentarse. 4. Llorar, gimotear. 5. Aullar, bramar.—*va.* Pregonar, publicar la pérdida o hallazgo de alguna cosa. *To cry aloud,* Levantar la voz; llorar a gritos. *To cry down,* Culpar; hacer callar a uno a fuerza de voces; menospreciar; reprimir; rebatir o responder con demasiada violencia; prohibir. *To cry for,* (1) Gritar, pedir llorando. (2) Llorar a causa de. *To cry for joy,* Llorar de alegría. *To cry off,* Renunciar, no querer más. *To cry out,* Gritar fuertemente, vocear, exclamar; llorar dando quejidos; estar de parto; publicar las faltas de alguno. *To cry out upon one,* Avergonzar a alguno. *To cry one's eyes out,* Llorar amargamente. *To cry unto,* Invocar, reclamar. *To cry up,* Aplaudir, alabar; ponderar, exagerar, exaltar. *To cry one up for a saint,* Hacer pasar a alguno por santo.
Cry, *s.* (*pl.* CRIES). 1. Alarido, grito. 2. Lamento, lloro o llanto. 3. Gritería, clamor, grito; aplauso. 4. Pregón, promulgación, publicación. 5. Aclamación. 6. Llamada importuna. 7. Muta, cuadrilla de perros de caza. *A far cry,* Camino largo. *Great cry and little wool,* Mucho ruido y pocas nueces.
Cry-baby [crai-bē'-bi], *s.* Niño llorón.
Cryer [crai'-ẹr], *s.* 1. *V.* CRIER. 2. Halcón gentil, neblí.
Crying [crai'-ing], *s.* Grito, lloro, dolores de parto. *Crying down,* Desestimación, desprecio, hablando de personas; desaprecio, ningún aprecio, hablando de cosas.—*a.* Enorme, atroz, lo que pide venganza al cielo por injusto o tiránico.
Cryogenics [crai-o-jen'-ics], *s.* Criogenía, física de muy bajas temperaturas.
Crypt [cript], *s.* 1. Bóveda subterránea en que antiguamente acostumbraban enterrar los muertos y a la que llamaban cripta. 2. (Anat.) Cripta, pequeño folículo, saquillo secretorio de la piel o de las membranas mucosas.
Cryptic, Cryptical [cript'-ic, al], *a.* Escondido, secreto.
Cryptically [cript'-ic-al-i], *adv.* Ocultamente.
Crypto-, del griego cryptos, oculto; forma de combinación.
Cryptogam [crip'-to-gam], *s.* Criptógama, planta de la clase de ese nombre.
Cryptogamia [crip-to-gē' [o gg'] -mi-a], *s. pl.* Criptogamia, la clase de plantas cuyos órganos sexuales están ocultos o son poco aparentes.
Cryptogram [crip'-to-gram], *s.* Escritura secreta por medio de signos convenidos, cifra.
Cryptography [crip-teg'-ra-fi], *s.* Criptografía; caracteres secretos, el arte de escribir en cifra.
Cryptology [crip-tel'-o-ji], *s.* Criptología, lenguaje enigmático.
Crystal [cris'-tal], *s.* 1. Cristal, forma regular poliedra en que se presentan las sales, piedras, metales y otros cuerpos. 2. Cristal, vidrio incoloro y muy transparente; cristal de roca, cuarzo transparente. 3. *V.* GLASS (Flint). 4. Cristal de reloj.
Crystal, Crystalline [cris'-tal-in], *a.*

1. Cristalino, hecho ó compuesto de cristal. 2. Claro, transparente.

Crystallizable [cris'-tal-aiz''-a-bl], *a.* Cristalizable.

Crystallization [cris-tal-i-zé'-shun], *s.* Cristalización.

Crystallize [cris'-tal-aiz], *va.* Cristalizar.—*vn.* Cristalizarse, formar un sólido cristalino.

Crystallizer [cris'-tal-aiz-ẹr], *s.* Lo que ayuda a cristalizarse; receptáculo para cristalizarse.

Crystalloid [cris'-tal-eid], *a.* Cristaloide, parecido a un cristal.—*s.* Ejemplar de una substancia cristalizable, cuyas soluciones son de fácil difusión; lo opuesto a *colloid.*

Cub [cub], *s.* 1. Cachorro, hijuelo de osa, loba o zorra. 2. Ballenato, el hijuelo de la ballena. 3. Cachorro, voz con que se moteja a un zopenco o a un hombre de modales rudos. 4. (Prov. Ingl.) Establo de ganado.

Cub, *vn.* Parir la osa o zorra.

Cuban [kiū'-ban], *s.* y *a.* Cubano, de Cuba; natural de Cuba.

Cubation [kiū-bé'-shun], *s.* 1. *V.* CUBATURE. 2. (Des.) Acostamiento, el acto de acostarse.

Cubature [kiū'-ba-chur], *s.* (Geom.) Cubicación.

Cubbyhole [cub'-i-hōl], *s.* Casilla, compartimiento pequeño.

Cube [kiūb], *s.* 1. Cubo, el sólido cuyas caras son seis cuadrados perfectos. 2. Cubo, la tercera potencia de una cantidad, el producto de tres factores iguales.—*va.* Cubar, elevar a la tercera potencia. *Cube root,* Raíz cúbica.

Cubeb [kiū-beb], *s.* Cubeba o carpo, semilla aromática.

Cubic, Cubical [kiū'-bic, al], *a.* Cúbico.

Cubically [kiū'-bic-al-i], *adv.* Cúbicamente.

Cubicular [kiu-bic'-yu-lar], *a.* Lo perteneciente a la alcoba.

Cubiform [kiū'-bi-fērm], *a.* Cúbico.

Cubism [kiūb'-ism], *s.* Cubismo.

Cubit [kiū'-bit], *s.* Codo, antigua medida lineal que se tomó de la distancia que media desde el codo a la extremidad de la mano.

Cubital [kiū'-bit-al], *a.* Cubital, lo que tiene la medida de un codo; relativo o perteneciente al codo.

Cubited [kiū'-bit-ed], *a.* Lo que tiene un codo de largo.

Cub scout [cub scaut], *s.* Cachorro, lobato, (de los exploradores).

Cuckold [cuc'-eld], *s.* Cornudo, el marido de una adúltera. Se llama así del cuco o cuclillo, a causa de la costumbre de esa ave de poner sus huevos en el nido de otra.

Cuckold, *va.* Hacer cornudo.

Cuckoldmaker [cuc'-eld-mé'-kẹr], *s.* Encornudador.

Cuckoldom [cuc'-el-dum], *s.* 1. Adulterio, el acto de cometer adulterio. 2. El estado y la calidad de cornudo.

Cuckoldly [cuc'-eld-li], *a.* Vil, despreciable, cobarde.

Cuckoo [cuc'-ū], *s.* (Orn.) Cuclillo o cuco.

Cuckoo-flower [cuc'-ū-flau'-ẹr], *s.* (Bot.) Cardámina.

Cuckoo-spittle [cuc'-ū-spit'-l], *s.* Baba de cuclillo, exudación que se halla sobre algunas plantas y que proviene de las larvas de ciertos insectos.

Cucullate, Cucullated [kiu-cul'-ét, ed], *a.* Cubierto con capilla; en forma de capucho o capucha.

Cucumber [kiu'-cum-bẹr], *s.* Cohombro o pepino.

Cucurbit [kiu-cūr'-bit], *s.* 1. Cucúrbita, retorta de alambique en forma de calabaza. 2. Una planta cualquiera de la familia cuyo tipo es la calabaza.

Cucurbitaceous [kiu-cūr-bi-té'-shus], *s.* (Bot.) Cucurbitáceo.

Cud [cud], *s.* 1. El alimento contenido en el estómago de los animales rumiantes, antes de masticarle por segunda vez. *To chew the cud,* Rumiar, meditar, reflexionar. 2. (Vul.) Chicote, pedazo de tabaco para mascar. *V.* QUID. 3. Rumen, el primer estómago de un rumiante.

Cudbear [cud'-bār], *s.* 1. Tinte purpúreo parecido a la orchilla, que se hace de algunas especies de líquenes, especialmente Lecanora tartarea. 2. El liquen mismo.

Cuddle [cud'-l], *va.* Proteger, acariciar, abrazar.—*vn.* Agacharse, agazaparse, esconder el cuerpo para no ser visto.

Cuddy [cud'-i], *s.* (Mar.) 1. Camarote de proa; carroza de barco abierto. 2. Pañol del cocinero. 3. Rústico, patán.

Cudgel [cuj'-el], *s.* Garrote o palo.

Cudgel, *va.* Apalear, dar golpes con garrote, palo o bastón. *To cudgel one's brains,* Devanarse los sesos.

Cudgel-play [cuj'-el-plé], *s.* Juego con garrotes.

Cudgel-proof [cuj'-el-prūf], *a.* A prueba de garrotazos.

Cudgeller [cuj'-el-ẹr], *s.* Apaleador.

Cudweed [cud'-wīd], **Cudwort** [cud'-wūrt], *s.* (Bot.) Gnafalio, algodonera.

Cue [kiū], *s.* 1. Cola, rabo, la punta o extremidad de alguna cosa; particularmente una larga trenza de cabello. En este sentido se escribe a menudo *queue.* 2. Apunte, el acto de leer o indicar el apuntador al actor lo que ha de decir. 3. Indirecta, sugestión. 4. Genio, humor. 5. Taco de billar.

Cuff [cuf], *s.* 1. Puñada, manotada o bofetón; golpe. 2. Puño de camisa; vuelta o bocamanga de una prenda de vestir. *A cuff on the ear,* Un sopapo. *To go to cuffs,* Principiar a darse golpes. *Handcuffs,* Manillas, esposas con que se maniata a los reos.

Cuff, *va.* Golpear con la mano abierta; dar golpes, abofetear.—*vn.* Dar de puñadas, luchar, boxear; herir con las garras como las aves de rapiña.

Cuff-links [cuf'-lincs], *s. pl.* Gemelos (para los puños de camisa).

Cuirass [cwī rgs'], *s.* Coraza, armadura que cubre el pecho y la espalda.

Cuirassier [cwī-ra-sīr'], *s.* Coracero, soldado armado de coraza.

Cuish [cwish], *s.* Escarcela, quijote, armadura de los muslos.

Cuisine [cwẹ-zīn'], *s.* 1. La cocina, pieza o piezas de una casa destinadas a guisar; el departamento culinario. 2. Cocina, estilo o clase de cocina, manera de guisar. (Fr.)

Culinary [kiū'-li-ne-ri], *a.* Culinario, perteneciente a la cocina.

Cull [cul], *va.* Escoger, elegir, echar mano de lo mejor, entresacar, extraer.

Cullender [cul'-en-dẹr], *s.* *V.* COLANDER.

Culler [cul'-ẹr], *s.* El que escoge o elige.

Cullion [cul'-yun], *s.* 1. Raíz semejante a un bulbo; órquide. 2. (Vul.) Belitre, pícaro, tunante.

Cullis [cul'-is], *s.* 1. Gotera, canalón en un tejado. 2. Muesca, como para un bastidor de teatro.

Cully [cul'-i], *va.* Engaitar, engañar, engatusar.

Cully, *s.* Bobo, el que se deja engañar.

Culm [culm], *s.* 1. (Bot.) Caña, especie particular de tallo propio de las gramas. 2. Carbón de piedra en polvo; cisco.

Culmen, *s.* *V.* SUMMIT.

Culmiferous [cul-mif'-ẹr-us], *a.* Culmífero; dícese de las plantas cuyo tallo está articulado y envainado por la base de las hojas.

Culminate [cul'-mi-nēt], *vn.* 1. Culminar, pasar por el meridiano. 2. Lograr, alcanzar el punto o grado más alto.

Culmination [cul-mi-né'-shun], *s.* 1. Culminación, el punto del paso de un astro por el meridiano. 2. Apogeo, la situación o el punto más alto a que puede llegar una persona o una cosa.

Culpability [cul'-pa-bil'-i-ti], *s.* Culpabilidad.

Culpable [cul'-pa-bl], *a.* Culpable, el que es delincuente, criminal.

Culpableness [cul'-pa-bl-nes], *s.* Culpa, delito.

Culpably [cul'-pa-bli], *adv.* Culpablemente, criminalmente.

Culpatory [cul'-pa-to-ri], *a.* Lo que culpa o reprende.

Culprit [cul'-prit], *s.* Reo, culpado, criminal.

Cult [cult], *s.* 1. Culto, sistema de prácticas religiosas. 2. Adoración de una persona o una cosa; homenaje extravagante. 3. El objeto de gran admiración o devoción.

Cultivable [cul'-ti-va-bl], *a.* Cultivable.

Cultivate [cul'-ti-vēt], *va.* 1. Cultivar, labrar; mejorar la tierra con el cultivo. 2. Adelantar, perfeccionar por el estudio o instrucción y ejercicio. 3. Prestar atención asidua; consagrarse.

Cultivation [cul-ti-vé'-shun], *s.* 1. Cultivación, cultivo; las labores y beneficios que se dan a la tierra y a las plantas. 2. Mejora, adelantamiento. 3. Cultura, el estudio y enseñanza con que se perfecciona y mejora.

Cultivator [cul'-ti-vé-tẹr], *s.* 1. Cultivador, labrador, agricultor. 2. Cultivadora, arado de cultivar; especie de mielga.

Cultural [cul'-chur-al], *a.* Perteneciente a la cultura o al cultivo.

Culture [cul'-chur], *s.* 1. Cultura. 2. Arte de mejorar las tierras, artes, ciencias o costumbres.

Culture, *va.* Educar, enseñar, criar; refinar.

Culverin [cul'-vẹr-in], *s.* Culebrina, pieza de artillería usada en el siglo XVI.

Culvert [cul'-vẹrt], *s.* Alcantarilla, conducto artificial para el paso de las aguas construido debajo de un camino o ferrocarril.

Culvertail, *s.* *V.* DOVETAIL.

Cumbent [cum'-bent], *a.* (Poco us.) Acostado, recostado.

Cumber [cum'-bẹr], *va.* Embarazar, obstruir, embrollar, estorbar; impedir; incomodar; sujetar.

Cumbersome [cum'-bẹr-sum], *a.* Engorroso, embarazoso, enfadoso, pesado, incómodo, fastidioso, molesto.

Cumbersomely [cum'-bẹr-sum-li], *adv.* Embarazosamente.

Cumbersomeness [cum'-bẹr-sum-nes], *s.* Embarazo, impedimento.
Cumbrance [cum'-brans], *s.* Carga, peso, impedimento, obstáculo, molestia.
Cumbrous [cum'-brus], *a.* Engorroso, pesado, confuso.
Cumbrously [cum'-brus-li], *adv.* Pesadamente, fastidiosamente.
Cumfrey [cum'-fri], *s.* (Bot.) Consuelda.
Cumin [cum'-in], *s.* (Bot.) Comino, planta anual que produce semillas de olor aromático y sabor acre. La simiente es medicinal y se usa también como condimento.
Cumulate [kiū'-miu-lêt], *va.* Acumular, cumular, amontonar, hacinar.
Cumulation [kiū-miu-lé'-shun], *s.* Acumulación, amontonamiento, hacinamiento.
Cumulative [kiū'-miu-lê-tiv], *a.* Cumulativo.
†**Cunctation** [cuṇc-té'-shun], *s.* Demora, tardanza, retardo.
Cuneal [kiū'-nẹ-al], *a.* Lo que pertenece a cuña; en forma de cuña.
Cuneiform [kiū-nī'-i-fōrm], *a.* Cuneiforme, en forma de cuña: (1) Nombre de tres huesos del tobillo. (2) Antiguos caracteres asirios inscriptos sobre bronce, hierro, ladrillos, piedra y otros materiales.
Cunner [cun'-ẹr], *s.* Pez lábrido muy abundante en la costa atlántica de Norte América. Ctenolabrus adspersus.
Cunning [cun'-ing], *a.* 1. Sabio, experto. 2. Artificioso, mañoso, astuto, maulero, artero, marrullero, trapacero, sutil, diestro, hábil; disimulado, capcioso, intrigante, sagaz. 3. (E. U.) Fino, gracioso, divertido, mono. *A cunning child,* Un niño gracioso.—*s.* 1. Astucia, ardid, maña, treta, disimulo, artificio, manejo, artimaña, maulería, bellaquería, marrullería, artería, trapaza. 2. (Ant.) Arte, habilidad, destreza, sutileza.
Cunningly [cun'-ing-li], *adv.* Astutamente; expertamente.
Cunningness [cun'-ing-nes], *s.* Astucia, fraude, engaño, maña, treta. *V.* CUNNING.
Cup [cup], *s.* 1. Copa, taza, jícara y el líquido contenido en ellas. *A cup of tea* o *coffee,* Una taza de te o café. *A cup of chocolate,* Una jícara de chocolate. *Cup made of a gourd,* (Cuba) Güiro. (Mex.) Tecomate. *Cup and can,* La maza y la mona. *Cups,* Convite de bebedores. 2. Cáliz, que sirve en la misa para echar el vino que ha de consagrarse; y el vino mismo. 3. (Fig.) Suerte, fortuna; toda aflicción o alegría extraordinaria. 4. Bebida embriagante. 5. Premio, comunmente una copa de oro o plata que se da al vencedor en las carreras o juegos atléticos, tiro al blanco y regatas. 6. Cualquier objeto o cavidad en forma de copa. 7. (Med.) Ventosa. *V.* CUPPING-GLASS. *There's many a slip 'twixt the cup and the lip,* De la mano a la boca se pierde la sopa.
Cup, *va.* 1. Pegar, echar o aplicar ventosas sajadas o secas. 2. (Art. y Of.) Ahuecar en forma de taza.
Cupbearer [cup'-bār-ẹr], *s.* Copero o escanciador.
Cupboard [cub'-ord], *s.* Armario o alacena con anaqueles para guardar loza o comestibles.
Cupel [kiū'-pel], *s.* Copela, vaso pequeño preparado para ensayar y afinar el oro y la plata.
Cupel-dust [kiū'-pel-dust], *s.* Polvo de copela.
Cupellation [kiū-pel-lé'-shun], *s.* (Quím.) Copelación, afinación del oro y de la plata en una copela.
Cupful [cup'-ful], *s.* El contenido de una taza o copa.
Cupid [kiū'-pid], *s.* Cupido, el dios del amor de los antiguos romanos.
Cupidity [kiū-pid'-i-ti], *s.* 1. Apetito, deseo inmoderado de poseer; codicia, avaricia. 2. (Poco us.) Concupiscencia.
Cupola [kiū'-po-la], *s.* 1. Cúpula, bóveda o media esfera que remata algunos grandes edificios. 2. Horno de fundición para el hierro. 3. Torre blindada giratoria, provista de cañones de grueso calibre, v. gr. la de un monitor (buque de guerra).
Cupper [cup'-ẹr], *s.* Aplicador de ventosas sajadas o secas.
Cupping-glass [cup'-ing-glas], *s.* (Cir.) Ventosa, escarificador.
Cupreous [kiū'-pre-us], *a.* Cobrizo, cosa de cobre o que tiene su color.
Cupric [kiū'-pric], *a.* (Quím.) Cúprico, relativo al cobre.
Cuprous [kiū'-prus], *a.* (Quím.) Del cobre en su menor facultad de combinación.
Cup-shaped [cup'-shêpt], *a.* Acopado, en forma de copa.
Cupule [kiū'-piūl], *s.* 1. Hueco acopado o cóncavo. 2. (Bot.) Parte acopada; cúpula o copa, la cascarilla que rodea la base de la bellota, avellana, etc.
Cur [cūr], *s.* 1. Perro inútil o de mala ralea. 2. Perro, hombre vil y despreciable.
Curable [kiūr'-a-bl], *a.* Curable.
Curableness [kiūr'-a-bl-nes], *s.* Capacidad de curarse.
Curacy [kiū'-ra-si], *s.* Tenencia, vicariato, vicaría.
Curare [cū-rā'-rê], *s.* Curare, veneno vegetal muy violento, que preparan y usan los indios de la América del Sur.
Curate [kiū'-ret], *s.* Teniente de cura; beneficiado.
Curateship, *s.* *V.* CURACY.
Curative [kiū'-ra-tiv], *a.* Curativo.
Curator [kiū-rê'-tẹr], *s.* Curador; guardián, conservador.
Curb [cūrb], *s.* 1. Barbada, cadena de hierro que abraza al barboquejo del caballo para sujetarle. 2. Freno, sujeción, restricción. 3. Brocal de pozo: orilla (de una acera). *V.* CURB-STONE.
Curb, *va.* Refrenar, contener, reprimir, poner freno, moderar.
Curbable [cūrb'-a-bl], *a.* (Poco us.) Restringible.
Curbing [cūrb'-ing], *s.* Obstáculo, restricción, freno, oposición.
Curb-stone [cūrb'-stōn], *s.* Cada una de las piedras gruesas, o el conjunto de ellas, que se ponen verticalmente donde termina el empedrado de las calles y que forman el reborde, canto u orilla de la acera; guardacantón.
Curd [cūrd], *s.* 1. Cuajada. 2. Requesón.
Curd, *va.* Cuajar, coagular, condensar.
Curdle [cūrd'-l], *vn.* Cuajarse, coagularse, espesarse, condensarse.—*va.* Coagular, cuajar, espesar.
Curdy [cūrd'-i], *a.* Cuajado, coagulado, espeso.
Cure [kiūr], *s.* 1. Cura; remedio, medicina, medicamento. 2. Cura de almas. 3. Salazón de pescados o carnes.
Cure, *va.* 1. Curar, sanar. 2. Preservar; salar, ahumar; preparar, componer, curar.
Cure-all [kiūr'-ōl], *s.* Panacea, cúralo todo.
Cured [kiūrd], *a.* Salado. *Cured fish,* Pescado salado.
Cureless [kiūr'-les], *a.* Incurable.
Curer [kiūr'-ẹr], *s.* 1. El que prepara alguna cosa para que se conserve. 2. Médico.
Curfew [cūr'-fiū], *s.* Toque de campana que por mandato de Guillermo el Conquistador se daba al anochecer, a fin de que sirviese de aviso para cubrir el fuego y apagar las luces. La retreta, la queda.
Curia [kiū'-ri-a], *s.* Curia, tribunal de justicia.
Curio [kiū'-ri-ō], *s.* Curiosidad, objeto curioso y raro; cosa de bric-a-brac. (Abreviación de *curiosity.*)
Curiosity [kiū-ri-os'-i-ti], *s.* 1. Curiosidad, deseo de saber o averiguar alguna cosa. 2. Curiosidad, objeto curioso y raro, rareza.
Curioso, *s.* *V.* VIRTUOSO.
Curious [kiū'-ri-us], *a.* 1. Curioso, deseoso de saber y averiguar las cosas. 2. Cuidadoso, exacto. 3. Delicado, primoroso, exquisito, admirable, raro, singular, extraño; elegante. 4. (Des.) Difícil de agradar; riguroso.
Curiously [kiū'-ri-us-li], *adv.* 1. Curiosamente, con cuidado. 2. Singularmente, de una manera rara, extraña. 3. Primorosamente, con arte. 4. Elegantemente.
Curiousness [kiū'-ri-us-nes], *s.* Curiosidad, exactitud, delicadeza, primor.
Curl [cūrl], *s.* 1. Bucle o rizo de pelo. 2. Tortuosidad, sinuosidad, ondulación. (Cuba) Crespo. 3. Enfermedad de los melocotones causada por un hongo microscópico, el *Taphrina deformans.* 4. Alabeo (de la madera).
Curl, *va.* 1. Rizar o encrespar el pelo, formar rizos o bucles. 2. Ensortijar, torcer. 3. Ondear, formar ondas u ondulaciones en alguna cosa. *To curl the lip,* Fruncir el labio. —*vn.* Rizarse, ondearse, enroscarse.
Curled pate [cūrld' pêt], **Curly-headed** [cūr'-li-hed-ed], *a.* El que tiene rizado el pelo.
Curlew [cūr'-liū], *s.* Chorlito, ave acuátil.
Curlicue [cūrl'-i-kiū], *s.* 1. Algo ondeado o torcido de un modo raro, como los rasgos o adornos hechos con una pluma. 2. Cabriola, brinco.
Curliness [cūrl'-i-nes], *s.* El estado de las cosas rizadas o formadas en bucles.
Curling-irons [cūrl'-ing-ai-ūrnz], **Curling-tongs** [cūrl'-ing-tōngz], *s.* Encrespador, tenacillas de hierro para rizar el pelo. *Curl-paper,* Papel a propósito para hacer rizos.
Curlingly [cūrl'-ing-li], *adv.* A manera de rizos.
Curly [cūrl'-i], *a.* Lo que cae en forma de rizos o sortijas, y lo que es fácil de rizarse.
Curmudgeon [cūr-muj'-un], *s.* Hombre tacaño, mezquino y miserable.
Curmudgeonly [cūr-muj'-un-li], *a.* Codicioso, mezquino, avariento.
Currant [cur'-ant], *a.* 1. Grosellero, el arbusto que produce la grosella. 2. Grosella, fruta del grosellero. 3. Uva o pasa de Corinto.

Currency [cur'-en-si], *s.* 1. El medio circulante, la moneda que está en circulación, ya sea acuñada o en papel. 2. Circulación. 3. Aceptación general ó uso corriente de alguna cosa. 4. Valor corriente de alguna cosa. *Fractional currency*, Menudo, moneda de valor menor que la moneda tipo, ya sea ésta el peso o *dollar*, el franco, la peseta, etc. *Paper currency*, Papel moneda.

Current [cur'-ent], *a.* 1. Corriente, común; admitido, en boga; general, popular. 2. Presente, del día, de actualidad. *The current year*, El año corriente.—*s.* 1. Corriente, curso de un arroyo, de un río; movimiento progresivo de las aguas, ó del aire. 2. Curso, progresión, marcha.

Currently [cur'-ent-li], *adv.* Corrientemente; generalmente, a la moda.

Currentness [cur'-ent-nes], *s.* Circulación; facilidad en pronunciar; aceptación general.

Curricle [cur'-i-cl], *s.* Carro abierto de dos ruedas, con lanza o pértiga.

Curriculum [cur-ric'-yu-lum], *s.* Curso de estudios en un colegio.

Currier [cur'-i-ẹr], *s.* Curtidor, zurrador.

Currish [cũr'-ish], *a.* 1. Perruno, parecido a un perro; arisco; dispuesto a morder. 2. (Fig.) Brutal, regañón, áspero.

Currishly [cũr'-ish-li], *adv.* Brutalmente, ásperamente.

Currishness [cũr'-ish-nes], *s.* Morosidad, malignidad, mezquindad; carácter arisco.

Curry [cur'-i], *va.* 1. Zurrar, adobar el cuero después de curtido; preparlo para usarlo. 2. Zurrar, dar una zurra. 3. Almohazar, estregar las caballerías con las almohazas para limpiarlas. 4. Hacer cosquillas; agradar, lisonjear. *To curry favour*, Insinuarse, ganar el ánimo o la voluntad de alguno. *To curry with one*, Cortejar a alguno.

Curry, *s.* Curri, salsa picante muy usada en la India; guisado preparado con esta salsa. *Curry-powder*, Polvo de ciertas especias para preparar el curri.

Curry-comb [cur'-i-cōm], *s.* Almohaza, instrumento para limpiar las caballerías.

Currying [cur'-i-ing], *s.* 1. El acto de almohazar. 2. Zurrar, el acto de zurrar las pieles después de curtirlas; remojarlas y desengrasarlas.

Curse [cũrs], *va.* 1. Maldecir, echar maldiciones a alguno. 2. Afligir, atormentar.—*vn.* Imprecar, negar o afirmar con imprecaciones, blasfemar.

Curse, *s.* 1. Maldición, juramento, imprecación, anatema. 2. Castigo, pena, grave aflicción.

Cursed [cũrs'-ed], *a.* Maldito, aborrecible, perverso, malvado, detestable, abominable, execrable; molesto, enfadoso.

Cursedly [cũrs'-ed-li], *adv.* Miserablemente, abominablemente.

Cursedness [cũrs'-ed-nes], *s.* Estado de maldición; malicia, perversidad; abominación.

Curser [cũrs'-ẹr], *s.* Maldiciente.

Curship [cũr'-ship], *s.* Vileza, bajeza, ruindad, brutalidad.

Cursing [cũrs'-ing], *s.* Execración, maldición.

Cursitor [cũr'-si-tẹr], *s.* Antiguamente un empleado en el tribunal de la Chancillería que extendía los originales.

Cursive [cũr'-siv], *a.* y *s.* Cursivo, corriente.

Cursorily [cũr'-so-ri-li], *adv.* Precipitadamente, de paso.

Cursory [cũr'-so-ri], *a.* Precipitado, inconsiderado. *Cursory view*, Vista por encima, o de paso.

†**Curst** [cũrst], *a.* Malavenido, rencilloso, maligno.

Curt [cũrt], *a.* Corto, conciso, lacónico; brusco en su expresión.

Curtail [cũr-tēl'], *va.* Cortar, abreviar, cercenar, mutilar; estrecharse, economizar; desmembrar. *To curtail a privilege*, Restringir un privilegio.

Curtailing [cũr-tēl'-ing], *s.* Abreviatura.

Curtailment [cũr-tēl'-mẹnt], *s.* Reducción, abreviación.

Curtain [cũr'-ten], *s.* 1. Cortina; cualquiera cosa que tapa u oculta como una cortina. *Curtain-lecture*, Reconvención de la mujer a su marido en particular; originalmente, regaño dado en la cama. *To draw the curtain*, Correr la cortina; correr un velo, ocultar. 2. (Fort.) Cortina, el lienzo de muralla que está entre dos bastiones. 3. Telón de boca en los teatros. *Curtain in a play-house*, Telón de teatro. *To raise the curtain*, Levantar el telón. *To drop the curtain*, Correr o bajar el telón.

Curtain, *va.* Rodear o proveer de cortinas.

Curtly [cũrt'-li], *adv.* Brevemente, lacónicamente.

Curtness [cũrt'-nes], *s.* Concisión, brevedad; brusquedad.

Curtsy [cũrt'-si], *s.* Reverencia o saludo especial que solían hacer las mujeres doblando las rodillas.

Curule [kiū'-rūl], *a.* Curul, de la magistratura romana. *Curule chair*, Silla curul, asiento oficial de los magistrados romanos de más alto rango.

Curvate, Curvated [cũr'-va-ted], *a.* Corvo, encorvado.

Curvature [cũr'-va-chur], *s.* Curvatura, comba, combadura, cimbra.

Curve [cũrv], *va.* Encorvar, formar curva o curvatura.

Curve, *a.* Corvo, torcido, encorvado.—*s.* Corva, curva, comba o combadura.

Curvet [cũr'-vet], *s.* 1. Corveta, corcovo, salto que da el caballo. 2. Ventolera, capricho.

Curvet, *vn.* 1. Corcovear, dar corcovos. 2. Cabriolar, hacer cabriolas. 3. Saltar de alegría: ser revoltoso.

Curvilinear [cũr-vi-lin'-ẹ-ar], *a.* Curvilíneo.

Curvity [cũr'-vi-ti], *s.* Curvatura, combadura.

Cushat [cush'-at], *s.* Paloma torcaz. Columba palumbus.

Cushion [cush'-un], *s.* 1. Cojín, almohada, almohadilla de sillón. 2. (Mec.) Cojinete, soporte, chumacera.

Cushion, *va.* 1. Amortiguar, amortecer. 2. Mitigar, disminuir. 3. Colocar sobre cojines.

Cushioned [cush'-und], *a.* Encojinado.

Cushionet [cush'-un-et], *s.* Cojinete, cojinillo.

Cusp [cusp], *s.* 1. Punta o cuerno de la luna u otro astro. 2. Punta o cúspide de un diente, o una planta.

Cuspated [cus'-pa-ted]. *V.* CUSPIDATE.

Cuspidal [cus'-pi-dal], *a.* Puntiagudo, lo que remata en punta.

Cuspidate, *va.* *V.* SHARPEN.

Cuspidate, Cuspidated [cus'-pi-dēt, ed], *a.* Cuspidada ó apuntillada, dícese de las plantas.

Cuspidor [cus'-pi-dōr], *s.* Escupidera.

Cuspis [cus'-pis], *s.* Cúspide, remate puntiagudo.

Cuss [cus]. (Fam. E. U.) Corrupción de CURSE; véase esta palabra, verbo y nombre.

Custard [cus'-tard], *s.* Flan, leche crema o quemada; crema confeccionada con huevos y azúcar.

Custodial [cus-tō'-di-al], *a.* Lo que pertenece a la custodia o guarda.

Custody [cus'-to-di], *s.* Custodia, encierro, prisión, cárcel; cuidado; seguridad.

Custom [cus'-tum], *s.* 1 Costumbre, uso. 2. Costumbre de comprar lo que uno necesita de ciertas personas o en determinadas tiendas; parroquia de una tienda. 3. Venta, salida, despacho. 4. (For.) Consuetud, ley o derecho no escrito, pero establecido por el uso de cien años. 5. *plur.* Derechos de aduana, los que se pagan por la introducción o extracción de los géneros. *Custom-free*, Libre de derechos.

Customable [cus'-tum-a-bl], *a.* Común, habitual.

Customableness [cus'-tum-a-bl-nes], *s.* Frecuencia, costumbre, hábito.

Customably [cus'-tum-a-bli], *adv.* (Poco us.) Según costumbre.

Customarily [cus'-tum-ẹ-ri-li], *adv.* Comunmente, ordinariamente.

Customariness [cus'-tum-ẹ-ri-nes], *s.* Frecuencia, hábito, costumbre.

Customary [cus'-tum-ẹ-ri], *a.* 1. Usual, acostumbrado, habitual, ordinario, usado. 2. (For. Ingl.) Consuetudinario, de costumbre, á fuero.

Custom built [cus'-tum bilt], *a.* Hecho a la orden o a la medida.

Customed [cus'-tumd], *a.* (Poét.) Acostumbrado, ordinario, común, acreditado.

Customer [cus'-tum-ẹr], *s.* 1. Parroquiano, marchante. 2. (Fam.) Persona con quien uno se halla, trata o se encuentra; se usa comunmente con adjetivo. *An ugly customer*, (1) Un bribón, un mal pájaro. (2) Adversario temible, duro de pelar.

Custom-house [cus'-tum-haus], *s.* Aduana. *Custom-house officer*, Aduanero, vista de la aduana.

Custom made [cus'-tum mēd], *a.* Hecho a la orden o a la medida.

Custrel [cus'-trel], *s.* 1. Escudero. 2. Vasija de vino.

Cut [cut], *va.* 1. Cortar, hender; esculpir, entallar. 2. Separar, destruir, estropear, herir, mutilar. 3. Partir, dividir. 4. Picar, preparar por medio de un instrumento cortante. 5. Quitar, separar. *V. To cut away* o *to cut off*. 6. Encontrar o pasar a alguno intencionalmente aparentando no conocerlo. 7. Desunir, interrumpir una relación o conexión. 8. Castrar. 9. Alzar o cortar los naipes.—*vn.* 1. Hacer cortadura, operar por incisión. 2. Ser a propósito para dividir ó dividirse. 3. Cortar, perforar las encías (dícese de los dientes). 4. (Ger.) Tomar soleta, tomar el tole. *To cut across*, Cortar al través, tomar por el atajo. *To cut asunder*, Rasgar, hacer pedazos, destrozar, despedazar, quebrar. *To cut away*, Quitar, cercenar, separar. *To cut down*, Abatir; aserrar: cortar una cosa hasta que caiga al suelo, derribar, echar abajo; destrozar un ejército; exceder, sobrepujar. *To cut off*, Cortar completamente, hacer pedazos, destruir, extirpar; separar, tajar, trinchar; matar a alguno; interceptar; poner fin a una cosa; interrumpir, abreviar; imponer silencio a uno que está hablando. *To cut off a leg*, Amputar una pierna. *To cut off an heir*, Desheredar a alguno. *To cut off all contentions*, Prevenir o impedir toda disputa. *To cut off delays*, Despacharse, apresurarse. *To cut out*, Tajar o cortar; formar, hacer, proporcionar o disponer alguna cosa en debida proporción; proyectar, trazar; adoptar; excluir, privar; exceder, aventajar. *To cut short*, Acortar, cercenar, disminuir; interrumpir, cortar la palabra; abreviar, resumir, compendiar. *To cut to*, Cortar de raíz; picar; afligir, lastimar, herir profundamente. *To cut up*, Cortar, partir, trinchar, hacer tajadas, disecar; arrancar de raíz, desarraigar. (Fam.) Hacer de las suyas, travesear. *To cut capers*, Cabriolar. *To cut small*, Desmenuzar. *To cut to the heart*, Afligir, enojar, enfadar, molestar. *To cut a figure*, Hacer papel o también hacer figura. *To cut the lots*, Echar pajas. *To cut over the face*, Acuchillar la cara. *To cut one's hair too short*, Pelar al rape. *To cut the ground*, Abrir la tierra, labrarla por la primera vez.

Cut, *a.* 1. Cortado, tajado. 2. Interceptado, interrumpido. 3. Trinchado; tallado. 4. Preparado.

Cut, *s.* 1. Corte, cortadura. 2. Atajo de camino. 3. Estampa o grabado. 4. Hechura, forma, figura. 5. Tajada, lonja. 6. Cuchillada, herida; hendedura. 7. Corto pasaje o paso. 8. Desgracia, afrenta.

Cutaneous [kiu-té'-ne-us], *a.* Cutáneo.

Cute [kiūt], *a.* (Contracción de ACUTE). (fam.) Atractivo, gracioso (como un niño).

Cut glass [cut' glas], *s.* Cristal cortado.

Cuticle [kiū'-ti-cl], *s.* 1. Cutícula, epidermis, lapa. 2. Película, viscosidad que cubre algunas plantas; capa que se forma en la superficie de un líquido.

Cuticular [kiu-tic'-yu-lar], *a.* Cuticular, de la epidermis.

Cutlass [cut'-las], *s.* Alfanje, machete.

Cutler [cut'-lẹr], *s.* Cuchillero.

Cutlery [cut'-lẹr-i], *s.* Cuchillería, mercadería o géneros de cuchilleros.

Cutlet [cut'-let], *s.* Chuleta, costilla o costillita asada de carnero, ternera, etc.

Cut-off [cut'-ōf], *s.* (E. U.) 1. Atajo de un camino. 2. Cortavapor, invento para interceptar el vapor en el cilindro en un punto fijo.

Cut-out [cut'-aut], *s.* (Elec.) Desviador o interceptador de la corriente.

Cutpurse [cut'-pūrs], *s.* Cortabolsa, ladrón, un ratero.

Cutter [cut'-ẹr], *s.* 1. Cortador. 2. Lo que corta; herramienta o máquina para cortar. 3. Cúter, embarcación ligera o velera semejante a una falúa. 4. Buque guardacostas. 5. (E. U.) Pequeño trineo.

Cut-throat [cut'-thrōt], *s.* Asesino, el que mata o quita la vida a otro alevosamente.—*a.* Cruel, bárbaro.

Cutting [cut'-ing], *s.* 1. Cortadura; incisión. 2. (Cir.) Talla, operación de la piedra. 3. Alce de naipes. 4. Algo obtenido o hecho por cortadura: recorte; cercenadura, viruta, retazo. *Cutting down*, (Mar.) Astilla muerta. *Cutting-down line*, (Mar.) Arrufo de astilla muerta. *Cutting of the teeth*, Dentición, salida de los dientes.

Cutting, *a.* 1. Cortante, que corta. 2. Helado, picante, áspero. 3. Incisivo, mordaz, picante, satírico.

Cuttle [cut'-l] o **Cuttle-fish** [fish], *s.* Jibia, sepia, molusco marino, voraz, carnívoro, del género de los cefalópodos, del cual se extrae el color llamado sepia. *V.* CUTTLE-BONE.

Cuttle-bone [cut'-l-bōn], *s.* Jibión.

Cut-water [cut'-wō-tẹr], *s.* (Mar.) Tajamar, un tablón algo corvo que sale de la quilla y va endentado en la parte exterior de la roda, cuyo uso es cortar el agua. *Beak of the cut-water*, (Mar.) Espolón del tajamar. *Forepiece of the cut-water*, (Mar.) Azafrán del tajamar. *Doublings of the cut-water*, (Mar.) Batideros de proa.

Cut-work [cut'-wūrc], *s.* 1. Obra de bordadura. 2. Impresión de grabados y láminas.

Cut-worm [cut'-wūrm], *s.* Larva de una mariposa (Agrotis) que por las noches destroza las plantas tiernas, por lo general cerca de la superficie y roe las yemas de los árboles.

Cyanic [sai-an'-ic], *a.* 1. Ciánico, perteneciente al cianógeno. *Cyanic acid*, Ácido ciánico. 2. De, o perteneciente al azul.

Cyanid, Cyanide [sai'-a-nid, naid], *s.* Cianuro, compuesto de cianógeno y un metal.

Cyanogen [sai-an'-o-jen], *s.* Cianógeno, gas incoloro, venenoso y licuable (C_2N_2) de olor semejante al de la almendra y que arde con llama purpúrea. Entra en la composición del azul de Prusia.

Cyanuret [sai-an'-yu-ret], *s.* Antiguo nombre del *cyanide* o cianuro.

Cybernetics [sai-bẹr-nẹt'-ics], *s.* (Med. y Elec.) Cibernética.

Cyclamen [sic'-la-men], *s.* (Bot.) Pamporcino, ciclamino, artanita, planta de adorno.

Cycle [sai' cl], *s.* 1. *V.* CIRCLE. 2. (Astr.) Ciclo, período de tiempo o número de años que, acabados, se vuelven a contar de nuevo, y durante los cuales se reproducen fenómenos idénticos a los del período anterior. 3. Curso. 4. Biciclo o triciclo.

Cyclic, Cyclical [sic'-lic, al], *a.* Cíclico, perteneciente a un ciclo o período.

Cyclist [sai'-clist], *s.* El que va montado en un biciclo o triciclo.

Cycloid [sai'-cloid], *s.* (Geom.) Cicloide, curva geométrica.

Cyclometer [sai-clem'-e-tẹr], *s.* 1. Ciclómetro. 2. Odómetro.

Cyclometry [sai-clem'-e-tri], *s.* El arte de medir ciclos o círculos.

Cyclone [sai'-clōn], *s.* 1. Ciclón, torbellino espiral. 2. (Fam.) Huracán, tifón.

Cyclopædia [sai-clo-pí'-di-a], *s.* Enciclopedia, colección de todas las ciencias.

Cyclopean [sai-clo-pí'-an], **Cyclopic** [sai-clep'-ic], *a.* 1. Gigantesco, enorme; de gran dificultad. 2. Perteneciente a los cíclopes.

Cyclops [sai'-cleps], *s.* Cíclope, gigante fabuloso que tenía un ojo en la frente.

Cyclotron [sai'-clo-tren], *s.* (Elec.) Ciclotrón.

Cygnet [sig'-net], *s.* Pollo del cisne.

Cylinder [sil'-in-dẹr], *s.* Cilindro; rollo, rollete, tambor.

Cylindric, Cylindrical [si-lin'-dric, al], *a.* Cilíndrico.

Cylindroid [sil'-in-dreid], *s.* (Geom.) Cilindroide, cilindro con bases elípticas.

Cyma [sai'-ma], **Cymatium** [si-mé'-shi-um], *s.* (Arq.) Cimacio, moldura.

Cymbal [sim'-bal], *s.* Címbalo, platillo, instrumento de percusión.

Cyme [saim], *s.* 1. (Bot.) Cima, grupo o ramo de flores que en su parte superior forman una superficie plana; corimbo. 2. (Arq.) Cimacio.

Cynegetic [sin-e-jet'-ic], *a.* Perteneciente o relativo a la caza con perros.

Cynic, Cynical [sin'-ic, al], *a.* Cínico.

Cynic, *s.* Cínico, filósofo secuaz de Diógenes; misántropo.

Cynicism [sin'-is-izm], *s.* Cinismo.

Cynosure [sai'-no-shur ó sin'-o-shur], *s.* 1. Objeto o centro de la atención o las miradas de todos. 2. (Astr.) Osa Menor.

Cypher, *s.* *V.* CIPHER.

Cypress [sai'-pres], *s.* (Bot.) Ciprés. *Cypress*, (Fig.) Luto.

Cyprian [sip'-ri-an], *a.* 1. Ciprio, chipriota, de la isla de Chipre. 2. Lascivo.—*s.* 1. Chipriota, natural o el idioma de Chipre. 2. Cortesana.

Cypriote [sip'-ri-ōt], *s.* 1. Ciprio, chipriota, natural o habitante de Chipre. 2. La antigua lengua de Chipre, dialecto del griego.

Cyst, Cystis [sist, is], *s.* Quiste o quisto, saco o vejiga membranosa.

Cystic [sist'-ic], *a.* 1. Cístico, contenido en el quiste. 2. Que tiene quistes.

Cystitis [sis-tai'-tis], *s.* (Med.) Cistitis.

Cytase [sai'-tēs], *s.* Citasa.

Cytisus [sit'-i-sus], *s.* (Bot.) Citiso, cantueso.

Cytological [sait-o-loj'-ic-al], *a.* Citológico.

Cytology [sai-tel'-o-ji], *s.* Citología.

Czar [zār], *s.* Zar, emperador de Rusia.

Czardas [zār'-das o chār'-desh], *s.* Danza nacional de los magiares, en dos tiempos, uno lento y otro rápido.

Czarevitch, Czarowitz [zār'-e-vich, zār'-o-wits], *s.* Zarevitz, título que se da al hijo primogénito del zar de Rusia; antiguamente cualquier hijo del zar.

Czarina [za-rí'-na], *sf.* Zarina o zaritza, la esposa del zar de Rusia.

Czarish [zār'-ish], *a.* Zariano.

D

D [di]. Se pronuncia en inglés como la *d* española en Castilla. La *D* usada como abreviatura, quiere decir, *doctor*; *D. D.*, Doctor en Teología; *LL. D.*, Doctor en Leyes, o en ambos derechos; *D. M.*, Doctor en Medicina; como numeral romano vale 500.

Dab [dab], *va.* Dar o estregar suavemente con alguna cosa húmeda o blanda.

Dab, *s.* 1. Pedazo pequeño de alguna cosa. 2. Salpicadura; cualquier golpe dado con alguna cosa blanda. 3. Barbada, pez marino en figura de rombo. 4. (Vul.) Artista.

Dabber [dab'-ẹr], *s.* El que o lo que da suavemente; clisador del impresor.

Dabbing [dab'-ing], *s.* La acción de indentar la superficie de una piedra.

Dabble [dab'-l], *va.* Rociar, salpicar; mojar, humedecer.—*vn.* Chapotear, golpear en el agua o lodo de modo que salpique; entrometerse, meterse alguno donde no le llaman.

Dabbler [dab'-lęr], *s.* 1. Chapuzador; chapucero. 2. Chisgarabís, el que se mete en lo que no sabe ni debe.

Dabster [dab'-ster], *s.* La persona diestra, hábil, experta.

Dace [dês], *s.* Albur, pez de río. Leuciscus.

Dachshund [dacs'-hunt], *s.* Dachshund, perro tejonero alemán.

Dacker [dak'-er], *vn.* 1. Hacer trabajo de pieza. 2. Trocar, traficar permutando géneros. 3. Asir. 4. V. Loiter. 5. V. Ransack.

Dacron [dê'-cren], *s.* Dacrón (*marca de fábrica*); fibra Acrílica.

Dactyl [dac'-til], *s.* (Poét.) Dáctilo, pie de verso que consta de tres sílabas, la primera larga y las otras dos breves (— ⏑ ⏑).

Dactylic [dac-til'-ic], *a.* Dactílico.

Dactylist [dac'-til-ist], *s.* El que escribe versos con pies dáctilos.

Dactylology [dac-til-ol'-o-ji], *s.* Dactilología, el arte de hablar con los dedos.

Dactylonomy [dac-til-en'-o-mi], *s.* Dactilonomía, la ciencia de contar por los dedos.

Dactyloscopic [dac-til-o-scop'-ic], *a.* Dactiloscópico, relativo a las huellas digitales.

Dad, Daddy [dad, i], *s.* Papá. (Fam.) Tata, taitica, padrecito. Palabra usada solamente entre niños y rústicos.

Dadaism [dū'-da-izm], *s.* Dadaísmo, movimiento literario.

Daddy-long-legs [dad''-i-lōng'-legz], *s.* 1. Arácnido de cuerpo corto y largas patas. Llámase también *harvest-man.* 2. Típula. *V.* CRANE-FLY.

Dado [dū'-dō o dê'-dō], *s.* (Arq.) Dado, cubo.

Dæmon [dī'-men], *s.* Demonio. *V.* DEMON.

Daffodil, Daffodilly [daf'-o-dil, i], *s.* (Bot.) Narciso.

Daft [dqft], *a.* Necio, tonto, cabeza de chorlito, mentecato; imbécil.

Dagger [dag'-ęr], *s.* 1. Daga, puñal. *To look* o *to speak daggers to one,* Comerse a uno con los ojos. 2. (Imp.) Cruz [†].

Dago [dê'-gō], *s.* (Ger. E. U.) Extranjero de piel morena; especialmente un italiano, español o portugués. (< Diego.)

Daguerreotype [da-ger'-o-taip], *s.* Daguerrotipo, procedimiento primitivo para tomar las imágenes obtenidas en la cámara obscura y fijarlas sobre una plancha metálica plateada. También, la imagen misma así obtenida.

Dahlia [dū'-lia], *s.* 1. Dalia, planta y flor. 2. Color violado obtenido del alquitrán de carbón.

Daily [dê'-li], *a.* Diario, cotidiano. —*adv.* Diariamente, cada día; con frecuencia.

Dainties [dên'-tiz], *s.* Chochos, confites, golosinas.

Daintily [dên'-ti-li], *adv.* Regaladamente, delicadamente.

Daintiness [dên'-ti-nes], *s.* Elegancia, pulidez, delicadeza, golosina, afectación.

Dainty [dên'-ti], *a.* 1. Delicado, espléndido, elegante. 2. Regalado, sabroso. 3. Melindroso; afectado. —*s.* Regalo, manjar delicado, bocado exquisito, golosina; usábase antiguamente como expresión de cariño.

Daiquiri [dai'-ki-ri], *s.* Daiquirí, bebida alcohólica compuesta.

Dairy [dê'-ri], *s.* Lechería; lugar donde se prepara la leche para hacer queso y manteca; quesera o quesería, el lugar donde se prepara la leche para hacer quesos. *Dairyman,* Lechero.

Dairymaid [dê'-ri-mêd], *sf.* Lechera, mantequera, la mujer que trabaja en una lechería o vende la leche.

Dais [dê'-is], *s.* 1. Tablado o gradas a la cabecera de un salón. 2. Silla elevada, bajo dosel.

Daisy [dê'-zi], *s.* 1. (Bot.) Margarita, maya. 2. (Ger.) Persona o cosa muy admirada.

Dale [dêl], *s.* Cañada, valle pequeño, llanura de tierra entre montes.

Dalliance [dal'-i-ans], *s.* 1. Regodeo, diversión, fiesta; trato familiar entre los casados; juguete, retozo. 2. Tardanza, dilación.

Dallier [dal'-i-ęr], *s.* Retozón o juguetón.

Dally [dal'-i], *vn.* 1. Bobear, acariciarse, juguetear, requebrar, divertirse; retozar. 2. Burlarse, hacer mofa de; retardarse, retrasarse, tardar.—*va.* Dilatar, suspender; hacer pasar el tiempo con gusto.

Dalmatian [dal-mê'-shian], *a.* y *s.* Dálmata, de la Dalmacia, dalmático.

Dalmatic [dal-mat'-ic], *s.* Dalmática, vestidura sagrada de los diáconos.

Dam [dam], *s.* 1. La madre en los animales; yegua. (Despectivo) Madre, mujer. 2. Presa o represa de agua, dique. 3. Límite, linde.

Dam, *va.* Represar, detener o estancar el agua corriente; cerrar, tapar. *To dam up,* Contener el agua con diques. *To dam a neighbour's lights,* Impedir la libre entrada de la luz en casa de un vecino.

Damage [dam'-ęj], *s.* 1. Daño, perjuicio, detrimento. 2. Resarcimiento de daño. 3. Pérdida; retribución. 4. Desventaja. 5. (Com.) Avería.—*pl.* Daños y perjuicios.

Damage, *va.* Dañar, perjudicar.—*vn.* Dañarse, averiarse.

Damageable [dam'-ej-a-bl], *a.* Susceptible de daño; perjudicial, pernicioso, dañoso, dañino.

Damascene [dam'-as-sīn], *va.* *V.* DAMASKEEN.—*a.* Damasceno, de la ciudad de Damasco.

Damask [dam'-asc], *s.* 1. Damasco, tela de seda o lino bastante doble, con dibujo del mismo color. 2. Damasco, tela de lino que se llama así por la semejanza de sus flores a las del damasco de seda. *Damask tablecloth,* Mantel adamascado o alemanisco. *Damask steel,* Acero damasquino.

Damask, *va.* 1. Adamascar. *V.* DAMASKEEN. 2. Tejer con patrones abundantes en flores. 3. Diversificar, matizar.

Damask-plum [dam'-asc-plum], *s.* Ciruela damascena.

Damask-rose [dam'-asc-rōz], *s.* Rosa de damasco o encarnada.

Damaskeen [dam-as-kīn'], *va.* Adornar con incrustaciones metálicas una superficie de hierro o acero; ataujiar; adornar un metal con líneas ondeantes.

Damaskeening [dam-as-kīn'-ing], *s.* Ataujía, el arte o acto de embutir unos metales en otros.

Damassin [dam'-as-in], *s.* Damasina, tejido de seda parecido al damasco en el dibujo y la labor.

Dame [dêm], *sf.* 1. Dama, señora, ama. (Fam.) Tía. 2. Maestra de niñas.

Dame's-violet [dêmz-vai'-o-let], *s.* (Bot.) Violeta matronal, hespéride, planta aromática de las crucíferas.

Dammar [dam'-ar], *s.* Damar, resina usada en las artes.

Damn [dam], *va.* 1. Condenar, castigar con las penas eternas del infierno. 2. Maldecir, echar maldiciones. 3. Vituperar; silbar o reprobar; mofar, despreciar.—*s.* Maldición.

Damnable [dam'-na-bl], *a.* 1. Damnable, condenable. 2. Detestable, pernicioso; infame.

Damnably [dam'-na-bli], *adv.* Horriblemente, de un modo indigno, infame o abominable.

Damnation [dam-nê'-shun], *s.* Damnación, condenación.

Damnatory [dam'-na-to-ri], *a.* Condenatorio.

Damned [damd], *a.* Condenado; maldito; detestable, aborrecible: reprobado; dañado; silbado.

Damnify [dam'-ni-fai], *va.* Dañar, injuriar; debilitar, malear. (Más usado como voz forense.)

Damp [damp], *a.* 1. Húmedo. 2. Triste, abatido, melancólico, amilanado.—*s.* 1. Niebla, humedad; exhalación nociva. Como exhalación nociva se llama también *Choke-damp.* 2. Desaliento, cobardía, pusilanimidad, abatimiento, aflicción, consternación.

Damp, *va.* 1. Mojar, humedecer. 2. Desanimar, desalentar, abatir, acobardar; entorpecer; entibiar, aflojar, amainar, amortiguar, apagar.

Dampen [damp'-n], *va.* 1. Humedecer, poner húmedo. 2. Enfriar, desanimar, desalentar; poner el apagador sobre algo, apagar.

Dampened [damp'-nd], *a.* 1. Humedecido. 2. Desanimado, desalentado.

Damper [damp'-ęr], *s.* 1. Lo que apaga o reprime; registro, llave del humero de una chimenea para regular el tiro; regulador de tiro. 2. Apagador del piano; sordina. 3. Desalentador, el que desalienta.

Dampish [damp'-ish], *a.* Algo húmedo.

Dampishness [damp'-ish-nes], **Dampness** [damp'-nes], *s.* Humedad.

Damsel [dam'-zel], *sf.* 1. Damisela, señorita; en lo antiguo, doncel y doncella. 2. Reborde de la muela.

Damson [dam'-zęn], *s.* Ciruela damascena.

Dan [dan], *s.* 1. Palabra antigua que equivale a *Master. Cf.* DON. 2. Carretón, en las minas de carbón de piedra.

Dance [dąns], *vn.* 1. Bailar, danzar. 2. Saltar, brincar.—*va.* Hacer bailar; hacer saltar. *To dance attendance,* (Vul.) Servir con prontitud y atención, hacer plantón.

Dance, *s.* Danza, baile.

Dance hall [dąns hōl], *s.* Salón de baile.

Dancer [dąns'-ęr], *s.* 1. Danzador, bailador. 2. Danzarín, bailarín.

Dancing [dąns'-ing], *s.* La acción de danzar o bailar. *Dancing-master,* Maestro de baile o danza. *Dancing-school,* Escuela de baile. *Dancing-room,* Sala de baile.

Dandelion [dan'-dg-lai-en], *s.* (Bot.) Diente de león, o amargón.
Dander [dan'-dgr], *s.* 1. *V.* DANDRUFF. 2. (Vul.) Ira, cólera.
Dandify [dan'-di-fai], *va.* Hacer a otro petimetre o currutaco; vestirlo con elegancia exagerada, a lo lechuguino.
Dandiprat [dan'-di-prat], *s.* (Ant.) Hombrecito; hombrezuelo cachigordete.
Dandle [dan'-dl], *va.* 1. Mecer, menear a un niño en los brazos o sobre las rodillas; hacer saltar sobre las rodillas. 2. Mimar, acariciar; tratar a uno como a un niño. 3. Entretener, dar largas.
Dandler [dan'-dlgr], *s.* Niñero.
Dandruff [dan'-druf], *s.* Caspa, escamilla que se forma en la cabeza.
Dandy [dan'-di], *s.* 1. Petimetre, currutaco, elegante exagerado en el vestir y afectado en sus maneras. 2. (Ger.) Cualquier cosa especialmente fina o agradable en su clase. *V.* DAISY. 3. *Dandy* o *dandy-fever*, *V.* DENGUE.
Dane [dên], *s.* Danés, dinamarqués, natural o ciudadano de Dinamarca. *Great Dane*, Perro danés, de raza grande y fuerte.
Dang [dang], *va.* Maldecir; eufemismo rústico en lugar de *damn*.
Danish [dên'-ish], *a.* Dinamarqués, danés, lo que pertenece a Dinamarca.
Danger [dên'-jgr], *s.* Peligro, riesgo, contingencia. (Fam.) *There is no danger*, No hay miedo, no hay cuidado.
Dangerless [dên'-jgr-les], *a.* Seguro, sin peligro.
Dangerous [dên'-jgr-us], *a.* Peligroso, arriesgado.
Dangerously [dên'-jgr-us-li], *adv.* Peligrosamente.
Dangerousness [dên'-jgr-us-nes], *s.* Peligro, calidad de peligroso.
Dangle [daŋ'-gl], *va.* Colgar algo libremente en el aire.—*vn.* 1. Pender, fluctuar, bambolearse; estar colgado en el aire. 2. Hacer a alguno la corte con adulación.
Dangler [daŋ'-glgr], *s.* Juan de las damas, el que continuamente está haciendo la corte a las damas; Perico entre ellas, Don Precioso.
Danish [dê'-nish], *a.* Danés, dinamarqués, perteneciente a Dinamarca.—*s.* Idioma de Dinamarca.
Dank [dank], *a.* Húmedo. *V.* DAMP.
Dankish [daŋk'-ish], *a.* Algo húmedo.
Dankness, *s.* *V.* DAMPNESS.
Dantesque [dgn-tesc'], *a.* Dantesco, propio y característico del Dante, poeta insigne italiano.
Dap [dap], †**Dape** [dêp], *vn.* Dejar caer alguna cosa muy despacio en el agua; pescar con caña en la superficie del agua.
Daphne [daf'-ne], *s.* 1. Dafne, ninfa de Diana, transformada en laurel. 2. Dafne, género de arbustos de la familia de las timéleas.
Dapper [dap'-gr], *a.* Gentil, bonito, limpio, aseado; gallardo; pequeño y vivaz.
Dapperling [dap'-gr-ling], *s.* Enano, chicuelo, monigote.
Dapple [dap'-l], *va.* Varetear, señalar con varios colores, abigarrar.
Dapple, *a.* Vareteado, rucio. *Dapple-gray horse*, Rucio rodado, o moro azul.
Dare, Dart, *s.* (Local, Ingl.) *V.* DACE.
Dare [dār], *vn.* (*pret.* DURST o DARED; *pp.* DARED). Osar, atreverse, arriesgarse, emprender alguna cosa con atrevimiento.—*va.* 1. Arrostrar, hacer frente. 2. Desafiar, provocar contender o competir con otro. *To dare larks*, (Des.) Coger calandrias con espejo.
Dare, *s.* Desafío. *V.* CHALLENGE.
Dare-devil [dār'-dev''-l], *a.* y *s.* Atrevido, temerario; descuidado, atolondrado.
Dareful [dār'-ful], *a.* Atrevido, osado.
Darer [dār'-gr], *s.* Desafiador.
Darg [dārg], *s.* (Esco.) El trabajo de un día; trabajo cansado.
Daring [dār'-ing], *a.* Osado, atrevido, intrépido, arriesgado, temerario, emprendedor.
Daringly [dār'-ing-li], *adv.* Atrevidamente, osadamente.
Dark [dārk], *a.* 1. Desprovisto de luz, en parte o totalmente; obscuro; opaco. *Dark blue*, Azul obscuro. 2. Moreno, bruno, lo que tira a negro. 3. Obscuro, difícil de entenderse, enigmático; secreto. 4. Ignorante, falto de conocimiento. 5. Triste, melancólico, tétrico. 6. Moreno, de tez morena. 7. (Poét.) Ciego, ignorante. *It grows dark*, Va a anochecer, se hace tarde. *Dark room*, Pieza o cuarto obscuro, falto de luz actínica; a propósito para trabajos fotográficos. *The dark ages*, La época de la superstición y la ignorancia. *A dark saying*, Enigma. *Dark lantern*, Linterna sorda.
Dark, *s.* 1. Obscuridad, tinieblas. 2. Ignorancia, falta de ciencia o conocimiento; mancha. *To leave one in the dark*, Dejar a uno a obscuras.
Darken [dārk'-n], *va.* 1. Obscurecer, poner obscuro, sombrío. 2. Anublar, cubrir de nubes. 3. Confundir, embrollar. 4. Denigrar, manchar. 5. (Fig.) Contristar, entristecer.—*vn.* Obscurecerse.
Darkener [dārk'-n-gr], *s.* El que obscurece o confunde.
Dark-field microscope [dārk'-fīld mai'-cro-scōp], *s.* Ultramicroscopio.
Dark horse [dārk hōrs], *s.* En la política, candidato de transacción que surge inesperadamente.
Darkish [dārk'-ish], *a.* Algo obscuro o fusco.
Darkling [dārk'-ling], *a.* 1. Obscurecido, visto ofuscadamente; lo que está en tinieblas. 2. Incapaz de ver.
Darkly [dārk'-li], *adv.* Obscuramente, secretamente.
Darkness [dārk'-nes], *s.* 1. Obscuridad, tinieblas; densidad, opacidad. 2. Ignorancia; secreto; dominio de Satanás.
Dark room [dārk rūm], *s.* Cuarto obscuro, cámara obscura (para fotografías).
Darksome [dārk'-sum], *a.* (Poét.) Obscuro, opaco, sombrío.
Darling [dār'-ling], *s.* El predilecto, el querido, el favorito.—*a.* Querido, amado.
Darn [dārn], *va.* Zurcir.
Darn, *va.* Maldecir: (forma atenuada de *damn*).
Darnel [dār'-nel], *s.* (Bot.) Zizaña, cizaña, una planta cualquiera del género Lolium.
Darner [dārn'-gr], *s.* Zurcidor o zurcidora.
Darning [dārn'-ing], *s.* Zurcidura.
Dart [dārt], *s.* Dardo; venablo.
Dart, *va.* Lanzar, arrojar, tirar, echar de sí alguna cosa con violencia.—*vn.* Lanzarse, arrojarse, precipitarse; volar como dardo o saeta.
Dartars [dār'-tarz], *s.* Roña o llaga que padecen los corderos.
Darter [dārt'-gr], *s.* 1. El que arroja dardos. 2. Pez pequeño americano, de vivos colores. 3. El pájaro-culebra americano. Plotus anhinga.
Darwinism [dār'-win-izm], *s.* Darwinismo, transformismo, sistema de Darwin que explica el origen de las especies animales mediante la transformación y la selección natural.
Dash [dash], *va.* 1. Arrojar, tirar con ímpetu alguna cosa contra otra. 2. Estrellar, chocar, romper; magullar. 3. Rociar, salpicar con agua u otro líquido. 4. Mezclar, mudar alguna cosa por medio de alguna mezcla. 5. Bosquejar, escribir apresuradamente (con *off*). 6. Confundir, avergonzar; frustrar.—*vn.* 1. Chocar, estrellarse, romperse (olas, etc.). 2. Saltar, dar un salto. 3. Estallar, saltar en pedazos dando un estallido. 4. Zabullirse en el agua de golpe haciéndola saltar. *To dash away*, Desechar, arrojar de sí. *To dash down*, Rechazar; precipitar; volcar, echar por tierra. *To dash out*, Levantar la tapa de los sesos; hacer saltar; borrar o testar lo escrito; salir precipitadamente. *To dash one's confidence*, Turbar a alguno, cortarle, desconcertarle. *To dash to pieces*, Hacerse añicos, hacerse una tortilla.
Dash, *s.* 1. Movimiento repentino hacia adelante; arranque, ataque; incursión. 2. Colisión, choque, encuentro violento de dos cuerpos. 3. Guión (—), raya o línea, señal que se usa en lo escrito y en lo impreso. 4. Ostentación vanagloriosa, gran papel. 5. Infusion, mezcla, tintura. 6. Golpe; rasgo. *Dash of a pen*, Rasgo de pluma.
Dashboard [dash'-bord], *s.* 1. Guardafango. 2. Tablero de instrumentos (en un automóvil o avión).
Dashing [dash'-ing], *a.* Precipitado, arrojado.
Dastard [das'-tard], *s.* Collón, hombre bajo y cobarde.
Dastardize [das'-tard-aiz], *va.* Acobardar, amedrentar.
Dastardly [das'-tard-li], *a.* Cobarde, pusilánime, tímido.
Dastardliness [das'-tard-li-nes], **Dastardy** [das'-tard-i], *s.* Cobardía, pusilanimidad.
Data [dê'-ta], *s. pl.* (de DATUM, *V.* infra). Cosas o principios dados, fijos o determinados; datos.
Data processing [dê'-ta pro-ses-ing], *s.* Procesamiento de información; proceso de acumulación, ordenación y presentación de datos.
Datary [dê'-ta-ri], *s.* Datario; dataría.
Date [dêt], *s.* 1. Data, fecha. 2. Duración, continuación; fin, conclusión. *A thing out of date*, Cosa que no se estila, fuera de uso.
Date, *s.* 1. Dátil, el fruto de la palmera. 2. Palmera. *V.* DATE-PALM.
Date, *va.* Datar, fechar; notar la data de alguna escritura o acaecimiento.—*vn.* Contar, computar.
Dateless [dêt'-les], *a.* Sin data, fecha o tiempo señalado.
Date line [dêt lain], *s.* 1. Línea internacional de cambio de fecha. 2. Fecha de publicación de un periódico, una revista, etc.
Dater [dêt'-gr], *s.* Sello fechador.

Date-palm o **Date-tree** [dêt'-pām o trī], *s.* (Bot.) Palmera, el árbol que produce los dátiles. Phœnix dactylifera.

Dative [dê'-tiv], *a.* y *s.* Dativo, el tercer caso del nombre.—*a.* †(For.) Lo que es dado, en oposición a lo que es hereditario.

Datum [dê'-tum], *s.* Dato, algo asumido o conocido; fundamento para formar juicio o deducir consecuencia.—*pl.* DATA.

Daub [dōb], *va.* 1. Embadurnar; untar con alguna substancia pegajosa; bañar, cubrir con yeso; de aquí, manchar, ensuciar, embarrar. 2. Pintorrear, pintar toscamente. 3. Cubrir, disfrazar. 4. (Des.) Adular con vileza.

Daub, *s.* 1. Aplicación viscosa; mancha grasienta. 2. Argamasa barata. 3. Pintarrajo, mamarracho.

Daubing [dōb'-ing], *s.* Mortero, estuco; afeite.

Dauby [dōb'-i], *a.* Viscoso, glutinoso, pegajoso.

Daughter [dō'-tẹr], *sf.* Hija. *Daughter-in-law,* Nuera. *Grand-daughter,* Nieta. *God-daughter,* Ahijada.

Daughterly [dō'-tẹr-li], *a.* Semejante a hija; obediente.

Daunt [dānt o dōnt], *va.* Acobardar, desanimar; espantar, intimidar, atemorizar.

Dauntless [dānt'-les], *a.* Intrépido.

Dauntlessness [dānt'-les-nes], *s.* Intrepidez, valor.

Dauphin [dō'-fin], *s.* Delfín, título que se daba en otro tiempo al primogénito y heredero del rey de Francia.

Dauphiness [dō'-fin-es], *sf.* Delfina, la mujer del delfín.

Davit [dav'-it], *s.* (Mar.) Pescante de bote; cada una de las pequeñas grúas en forma de efe que van en pares a los costados del buque.

Daw [dō], *s.* Corneja.

Dawdle [dō'-dl], *vn.* Gastar tiempo; holgazanear, haraganear.

Dawn [dōn], *vn.* 1. Amanecer, apuntar el día. 2. Empezar lentamente a manifestar lustre o brillo. 3. Apuntar, comenzar a crecer, a esparcirse, a dar muestras de inteligencia.

Dawn, *s.* 1. Alba, albor. 2. Principio u origen de alguna cosa. *The dawn of reason,* La luz de la razón.

Dawning [dōn'-ing], *s.* Alba, el amanecer.

Day [dê], *s.* 1. Día; luz. 2. Día, el espacio de tiempo que emplea la tierra (o un astro) en dar una vuelta completa sobre su eje. 3. La parte del día destinada al trabajo. 4. Tiempo o período; siglo. 5. Jornada, batalla. 6. Día señalado o en el que ha sucedido alguna cosa extraordinaria. 7. Vida; en este sentido se escribe en plural. *In his days,* En su tiempo. *In our days,* En nuestros tiempos. *To gain the day,* Ganar la batalla. *Daytime,* Día, el tiempo que hay luz natural. *By day,* De día. *From day to day,* De día en día; de un día para otro; sin certeza o continuación. *St. John's Day,* Día de San Juan. *Every other day,* Cada tercer día, un día sí y otro no. *To-day,* Hoy. *To this day,* Hasta el día de hoy. *The day before yesterday,* Antes de ayer, anteayer, antier. *This day week* (o *se'nnight*), Hoy hace ocho días; de hoy en ocho días. *Dog-days,* La canícula. *At daybreak,* Al romper el día, al ser de día. *Days of grace,* Días de gracia o de cortesía, cierto número de días que se conceden para el pago de una letra de cambio después de haber vencido. *The day before,* La víspera. *All day long,* Todo el día. *In the days of old,* En otro tiempo, en la antigüedad. *Good-day!* ¡Buenos días! *To gain the day,* Ganar la batalla. *The Lord's Day,* El domingo, el día del Señor. *Work day,* Día de trabajo. *A meagre day,* Día de vigilia. *A fast-day,* Día de ayuno. *Lay days,* (Mar.) Días de demora o de estadía. *An off day,* Un día de más, no del número.

Day-book [dê'-buc], *s.* Diario, libro de mercaderes o mercantes.

Daybreak [dê'-brêk], *s.* *V.* DAWN.

Daydream [dê'-drīm], *vn.* Soñar despierto, hacerse ilusiones.—*s.* Sueño, ilusión, quimera.

Day-labour [dê'-lê-bẹr], *s.* 1. El trabajo de un día; jornada. 2. Jornal.

Day-labourer [dê'-lê-bẹr-ẹr], *s.* Jornalero, gañán.

Dayletter [dê-let'-ẹr], *s.* Carta telegráfica diurna.

Daylight [dê'-lait], *s.* 1. Luz del día, luz. 2. Amanecer, alba. *To scare the daylights out of,* (Fam.) Meter los monos a.

Daylight-saving time [dê'-lait-sêv'-ing taim], *s.* Hora oficial (para aprovechar mejor la luz del día).

Day nursery [dê nūrs'-ẹr-i], *s.* Guardería, casa cuna para niños cuyas madres trabajan.

Day's run [dêz' run], *s.* (Mar.) Singladura, el camino que hace un buque en 24 horas.

Day-scholar [dê'-scol-ar], *s.* Externo, alumno de una escuela que no vive en ella.

Day school [dê scul], *s.* Escuela diurna.

Day service [dê sẹr'-vis], *s.* Servicio diurno.

Dayspring [dê'-spring], *s.* Alba, primera luz del día.

Day-star [dê'-stār], *s.* Lucero.

Day work [dê wūrk], *s.* Trabajo diurno.

Daze [dêz], *va.* Deslumbrar, ofuscar con una luz demasiado viva.—*s.* Deslumbramiento, ofuscamiento.

Dazzle [daz'-l], *va.* 1. Deslumbrar, ofuscar con luz intensa. 2. Ofuscar, turbar, encantar, v. g. con brillantes promesas o expectativas. (Vul.) Encandilar.

Dazzlement [daz'-l-mẹnt], *s.* Deslumbramiento; desvanecimiento, ofuscamiento.

Dazzling [daz'-ling], *a.* Deslumbrador.

D.D.T. [dī dī tī], *s.* D.D.T.

Deacon [dī'-cn], *s.* 1. Diácono. 2. Sobrestante de pobres, en Escocia.

Deaconry [dī'-cn-ri], **Deaconship** [dī'-cn-ship], *s.* Diaconato.

Deactivate [dī-ac'-ti-vêt], *va.* Desactivar.

Dead [ded], *a.* 1. Muerto, sin vida. 2. Muerto, flojo, entorpecido, pesado. 3. Vacío, lo que está desocupado; inútil, estéril. 4. Apagado, sin fuego; y (fig.) sin espíritu. Desolado, despoblado; marchito, que no está animado. 5. Apagado, sin brillo; mate. 6. Sin variación, plano, monótono. 7. Completo, acabado, absoluto. 8. Cierto, seguro, indudable. 9. No para ser contado. 10. Que no da luz; que no permite abrirse. 11. Que no da movimiento; gastado, frío. 12. Sumido en el pecado. 13. (For.) Desprovisto de la vida civil. 14. (Elec.) Que no transmite corriente. 15. Que ya no fermenta. 16. Sin elasticidad; sin eco, no retumbante (un suelo, techo, etc.). 17. (Tip.) Material muerto o para distribuir.—*s.* 1. Personas muertas. 2. Silencio profundo; el centro o medio de alguna cosa. *A dead calm,* Una calma profunda. (Mar.) Calma chicha. *A dead town,* Una ciudad muerta, sin movimiento, sin animación. *Dead certainty,* Certeza completa. *Dead coal,* Carbón apagado. *Dead-drunk,* Borracho, hecho un cuero.

Deaden [ded'-n], *va.* 1. Amortiguar, amortecer, quitar las fuerzas o espíritu de alguna cosa. 2. Retardar, disminuir la velocidad del movimiento. 3. Hacer incapaz de transmitir el sonido; como una pared o un piso. 4. Apagar o quitar el brillo, la viveza del colorido o del pulimento. 5. Hacer insípido (el vino, la cerveza).

Dead-killing [ded-kil-ing], *a.* Que mata instantáneamente.

Dead-letter office [ded'-let-ẹr ef'-is], *s.* El departamento de la administración general de correos donde se examinan las cartas no reclamadas, para remitirlas a los que las franquearon o para destruirlas, según el caso.

Dead lift [ded' lift], *s.* El acto de alzar algo en peso, sin ayuda alguna; de aquí, esfuerzo inútil o hecho en condiciones adversas.

Dead-lights [ded'-laits], *s.* (Mar.) Postigos o portas de correr que se colocan exteriormente en las ventanas de popa.

Dead line [ded lain], *s.* 1. Fecha u hora de cierre de una publicación. 2. Límite de fecha para terminar alguna operación, transacción; plazo, término.

Deadliness [ded'-li-nes], *s.* Peligro mortal; calidad de venenoso, destructivo o mortífero.

Dead load [ded lōd], *s.* Carga fija o permanente.

Deadlock [ded'-loc], *s.* Paro, interrupción o estancamiento por desacuerdo.

Deadly [ded'-li], *a.* Destructivo, mortal, terrible, implacable.—*adv.* Mortalmente, implacablemente. Úsase a veces como aumentativo.

Deadness [ded'-nes], *s.* Frío, frialdad, debilidad, flojedad, inercia; pérdida de vida; amortiguamiento.

Dead-nettle [ded'-net-l], *s.* (Bot.) Ortiga muerta.

Dead-reckoning [ded-rec'-n-ing], *s.* (Mar.) Estima, juicio que forma el piloto del camino que ha andado la embarcación y del paraje en que se halla, sin observación de los cuerpos celestes, y sólo por medio de la barquilla y corredera.

Dead-rising [ded'-raiz-ing], *s.* (Mar.) Línea del arrufo del cuerpo principal.

Dead-struck [ded'-struc], *a.* Espantado, confundido, aterrado, anonadado.

Dead water [ded' wō-tẹr], *s.* (Mar.) Reveses de las aguas de un bajel.

Dead weight [ded wêt], *s.* 1. Peso muerto. 2. Carga onerosa.

Deadwood [ded'-wud], *s.* 1. Leña seca. 2. Material inutilizable. 3. Miembros ineficientes de una organización.

Dead-work [ded'-wŭrc], *s.* (Mar.) Obras muertas.

Deaf [def], *a.* Sordo, el que está privado del sentido del oído. *To make deaf*, Aturdir, ensordecer, dejar sordo. *To turn a deaf ear*, Hacerse el sordo. *Born deaf*, Sordo de nacimiento.

Deaf, Deafen [def'-n], *va.* Ensordar, ensordecer.

Deafly [def'-li], *adv.* Sordamente; obscuramente.

Deaf-mute [def'-miūt"], *s.* Sordomudo; especialmente el que es mudo a causa de sordera.

Deafness [def'-nes], *s.* Sordera.

Deal [dīl], *s.* 1. Parte; cantidad indefinida, grado de más o menos, poco o mucho. 2. Mano, distribución de las cartas en el juego. 3. Madera de pino, tabla, tabla de chilla. 4. (E. U.) Pacto o convenio secreto en la política o en el comercio, en provecho exclusivo de los interesados. *A great deal*, Mucho. *A good deal*, Bastante. *A great deal better*, Mucho mejor.

Deal, *va.* (*pret.* y *pp.* DEALT). 1. Distribuir, repartir, desparramar, esparcir. 2. Dar, hablando de repartir los naipes en el juego.—*vn.* 1. Traficar, comerciar, tratar, negociar. 2. Intervenir, mediar. 3. Portarse bien o mal en cualquier asunto. *To deal in contraband goods*, Hacer contrabando. *To deal in all sorts of commodities*, Comerciar en todo género de mercancías. *To deal with*, Tratar con; contender con. *To deal by*, Portarse, conducirse de cierto modo; usar de. *To deal in*, Mezclarse en, ocuparse en; usar de; comerciar en.

Dealbate [dę-al'-bêt], *a.* (Bot.) Blanqueado: cubierto con polvo blanco.

Dealer [dīl'-ęr], *s.* 1. Interventor. 2. Comerciante, mercader, negociante, traficante. 3. El que da las cartas en el juego; repartidor. *Plain-dealer*, Hombre sincero. *False dealer*, Hombre doble. *Double-dealer*, Hombre de dos caras, engañador; que come á dos carrillos.

Dealing [dīl'-ing], *s.* 1. Modo de obrar o proceder, conducta. *Honest dealing*, Hombría de bien. 2. Trato, comunicación. 3. Tráfico, comercio, negocio. 4. *pl.* Negocios, relaciones de adquisición y de venta. *Fair dealing*, Buena fe. *Foul dealing*, Doblez.

Dealt [delt], *pret.* y *pp.* de *To* DEAL. *Easy to be dealt with*, Tratable, fácil de contentar. *Hard to be dealt*, Descontentadizo.

Dean [dīn], *s.* 1. Deán, dignidad eclesiástica. En la Iglesia católica, el cabeza del cabildo después del obispo. 2. Decano de un colegio o universidad, o de una facultad.

Deanery [dīn'-ęr-i], **Deanship** [dīn'-ship], *s.* Deanato.

Dear [dīr], *a.* 1. Querido, predilecto, caro, amado. 2. Caro, costoso. 3. Escaso; difícil de hallar. 4. (Des.) Peligroso, fatal. *A dear creature*, Buena alhaja.—*s.* Querido, voz expresiva de cariño. *My dear*, Querido mío, querida mía. *Dear me!* ¡De veras! ¡cierto! ¡Dios mío! ¡Válgame Dios!

Dear-bought [dīr'-bōt], *a.* Caro, lo que ha costado mucho.

Dear-loved [dīr'-luvd], *a.* Muy amado.

Dearly [dīr'-li], *adv.* Caramente, tiernamente, cariñosamente, amorosamente.

Dearness [dīr'-nes], *s.* 1. Cariño, amor, afecto, benevolencia. 2. Carestía, el precio muy subido de las cosas.

Dearth [dęrth], *s.* 1. Carestía. 2. Hambre, carestía y falta de bastimentos; esterilidad.

Dearticulate [dī-ār-tic'-yu-lêt], *va.* Desmembrar, desunir, separar.

Deary [dīr'-i], *s.* Expresión de cariño; queridito.

Death [deth], *s.* 1. Muerte; mortalidad. 2. Mortandad, estrago causado por la muerte. 3. Asesinato. 4. Condenación, muerte eterna. *At the point of death*, En artículo de la muerte. *On pain of death*, Bajo ó so pena de muerte. *To grieve one's self to death*, Morirse de pesadumbre.

Death-bed [deth'-bed], *s.* Lecho de muerte; agonía.

Death-boding [deth'-bōd-ing], *a.* Lo que pronostica la muerte.

Deathful [deth'-ful], *a.* Mortal, mortífero.

Deathfulness [deth'-ful-nes], *s.* Apariencia de muerte.

Deathless [deth'-les], *a.* Inmortal.

Deathlike [deth'-laic], *a.* Quedo, inmóvil, silencioso como la muerte; letárgico; cadavérico.

Death's-door [deths'-dōr], *s.* (Fam.) Las puertas de la muerte, cercanía á la muerte; agonía. *He has been at death's-door*, Ha estado en las garras de la muerte, al borde de la tumba.

Death's-head [deths'-hed], *s.* Calavera, armazón de los huesos de la cabeza. *Death's-head moth*, Atropos, mariposa "cabeza de muerto." (Acad.) Acherontia atropos.

Death's-man [deths'-man], *s.* Verdugo. *Man of death*, Asesino.

Death-shadowed [deth'-shad-ōd], *a.* Rodeado de las sombras de la muerte.

Death-token [deth'-tōk-n], *s.* Presagio de muerte.

Deathward [deth'-ward], *adv.* A la muerte.

Death-warrant [deth'-wer"-ant], *s.* 1. Orden oficial para la ejecución de un reo. 2. El fin de toda esperanza.

Death-watch [deth'-wech], *s.* 1. Últimas horas pasadas acompañando a un moribundo; velación de un cadáver. 2. Guardia que se pone para vigilar al reo antes de su ejecución.

Death-watch [deth'-wech], *s.* (Ento.) Anobio, insecto coleóptero que produce un sonido acompasado parecido al *tic-tac* de un reloj y al que los supersticiosos consideran como precursor de próxima muerte. Anobium.

Death-wound [deth'-wūnd] *s.* Herida mortal.

†**Deaurate** [dę-ō'-ret], *va.* Dorar.

Deaurate, *a.* (Ento.) Dorado.

Debacle [dę-bac'-l], *s.* 1. Desbordamiento de las aguas fuera de sus límites naturales. 2. Terror pánico; caída, ruina. (Fr.)

Debar [dę-bār'], *va.* Excluir, no admitir, privar, prohibir.

Debark [dę-bārk'], *va.* Desembarcar. *V.* DISEMBARK.

Debarkation [dę-bar-kê'-shun], *s.* Desembarco.

Debase [dę-bês'], *va.* 1. Abatir, deprimir, humillar, envilecer; degradar, deshonrar. 2. Adulterar, viciar, falsificar, alterar.

Debasement [dę-bês'-męnt], *s.* Abatimiento, envilecimiento; adulteración, falsificación.

Debaser [dę-bês'-ęr], *s.* El que abate o envilece; falsificador.

Debatable [dę-bêt'-a-bl], *a.* Disputable; discutido, sujeto a controversia.

Debate [dę-bêt'], *s.* 1. Discusión, debate, contienda, disputa, contestación, controversia. 2. (Des.) Querella, conflicto.

Debate, *va.* Debatir, contender, altercar.—*vn.* Deliberar, disputar, agitar, examinar, discutir.

Debateful [dę-bêt'-ful], *a.* Litigioso; reñido.

Debatefully [dę-bêt'-ful-i], *adv.* Litigiosamente.

Debatement [dę-bêt'-męnt], *s.* (Poco us.) Debate, contienda, disputa, controversia.

Debater [dę-bêt'-ęr], *s.* Controversista, el que debate.

Debauch [dę-bēch'], *va.* 1. Corromper, viciar, relajar, pervertir, estragar. 2. Corromper o seducir a una doncella; sobornar o sonsacar criados, dependientes, etc.

Debauch, *s.* 1. Exceso, desorden, desarreglo, especialmente en comer y beber. 2. Vida disoluta, el vicio de la lujuria.

Debauchedly [dę-bēch'-ed-li], *adv.* Licenciosamente, de una manera disoluta.

Debauchedness [dę-bēch'-ed-nes], *s.* Intemperancia, lascivia.

Debauchee [deb-e-shī'], *s.* Hombre libertino, disoluto, licencioso, desarreglado, relajado.

Debaucher [dę-bēch'-ęr], *s.* Seductor, corrompedor.

Debauchery [dę-bēch'-ęr-i], *s.* Disolución, libertinaje, desorden, licencia, relajación.

Debauchment [dę-bēch'-męnt], *s.* Corrupción, corrompimiento.

Debenture [dę-ben'-chur], *s.* (Com.) 1. Vale, acción, obligación, papel que hace constar el crédito que uno tiene contra otro y en cuya virtud lo reclama. 2. Remisión o restitución de los derechos al tiempo de exportar los géneros que se han importado anteriormente. 3. Orden de pago del gobierno.

†**Debile** [deb'-il], *a.* Débil.

Debilitate [dę-bil'-i-têt], *va.* Debilitar, extenuar, enervar.

Debilitation [dę-bil-i-tê'-shun], *s.* Debilitación, extenuación.

Debility [dę-bil'-i-ti], *s.* Debilidad, extenuación, imbecilidad, languidez.

Debit [deb'-it], *s.* Balance o alcance.

Debit, *va.* Adeudar, cargar.

Debit balance [deb'-it bal'-ans], *s.* Saldo deudor.

Debonair [deb-o-nār'], *a.* Garboso, cortés, urbano, bien criado, elegante, político, honrado, dulce, complaciente.

Debonairness [deb-o-nār'-nes], *s.* Civilidad, cortesía.

Debouch [dę-būsh'], *va.* Desembocar, descargar; salir. (Fr. déboucher.)

Debouchure [dê-bū-shūr'], *s.* Salida, boca de un desfiladero, etc. (Fr.)

Debris [deb-rī'], *s.* 1. Resto, ruinas. 2. (Geol.) Despojos, restos de las rocas. (< Fr. débris.)

Debt [det], *s.* 1. Deuda o débito. 2. Obligación, lo que uno debe hacer por buena correspondencia. *A small debt*, Deudilla.

Debted, *a.* *V.* INDEBTED.

Debtless [det'-les], *a.* Sin deuda o débito.

Debtor [det'-ẹr], *s.* 1. Deudor. 2. Cargo, el lado de las cuentas en que se sientan las partidas que debe una persona.
Début [dé'-bü], *s.* Estreno de actor, cantatriz, etc.; primer paso, entrada en la sociedad. (Fr.)
Débutant, *m.* **Débutante**, *f.* Principiante, el que se presenta al público por primera vez.
Decade [dek'-êd], *s.* 1. Decenio, curso de diez años. 2. Década, decena.
Decadence, Decadency [dẹ-ké'-dens, den-si], *s.* Decadencia, descaecimiento.
Decagon [dec'-a-gen], *s.* (Geom.) Decágono.
Decagram, Decagramme [dec'-a-gram], *s.* Decagramo, peso de diez gramos.
Decahedron [dec-a-hí'-dren], *s.* Decaedro, figura que tiene diez caras planas.
Decaliter, Decalitre [dec'-a-lí"-tẹr], *s.* Decalitro, medida de diez litros.
Decalogist [dẹ-cal'-o-jist], *s.* Decalogista, expositor del decálogo.
Decalogue [dec'-a-leg], *s.* Decálogo, los diez mandamientos de la ley de Dios dados a Moisés.
Decameter, Decametre [dec'-a-mí"-tẹr], *s.* Decámetro, medida de diez metros.
Decamp [dẹ-camp'], *vn.* 1. Decampar, levantar el campo; mudar un ejército su campamento. 2. Escapar, tomar las de Villadiego, poner pies en polvorosa.
Decampment [dẹ-camp'-mẹnt], *s.* El acto de levantar un campo o campamento; la acción de decampar.
Decanal [dec'-a-nal], *a.* Lo que pertenece al deanato.
Decant [dẹ-cant'], *va.* Decantar, mudar los licores u otros líquidos de una vasija a otra, quedando las heces en la primera; trasegar.
Decantation [dẹ-can-té'-shun], *s.* Decantación; trasiego.
Decanter [dẹ-can'-tẹr], *s.* 1. Botella para el vino, etc., de cristal, garrafa adornada. 2. Vaso para líquidos trasegados.
Decapitate [dẹ-cap'-i-têt], *va.* Degollar, decapitar.
Decapitation [dẹ-cap-i-té'-shun], *s.* Degüello, decapitación.
Decapod [dec'-a-ped], *s.* Decápodo, crustáceo que tiene diez patas.
Decarbonize, Decarburize [dí-cār'-ben-aiz, dí-cār'-biu-raiz], *va.* Descarbonizar, descarburar.
Decasyllable [dec"-a-sil'-a-bl], *s.* Decasílabo, línea o verso de diez sílabas.
Decay [dẹ-ké'], *vn.* Decaer, descaecer, declinar, empeorar, ir a menos; pudrir, degenerar, pasarse, marchitarse.—*va.* Arruinar, destruir, echar a perder.
Decay, *s.* Descaecimiento, menoscabo, decadencia, declinación, caimiento, diminución; pobreza.
Decayedness, *s.* *V.* DECAY.
Decayer [dẹ-ké'-ẹr], *s.* Lo que produce decadencia.
Decaying [dẹ-ké'-ing], *s.* Decadencia.
Decease [dẹ-sís'], *s.* Muerte, fallecimiento.
Decease, *vn.* Morir, fallecer.
Deceased [dẹ-sist'], *a.* Difunto, muerto, fallecido.—*s.* Finado, difunto, fallecido.
Decedent [dẹ-sí'-dent], *s.* (For.) Una persona fallecida; y en especial una cuyos bienes están en manos de un administrador.
Deceit [dẹ-sít'], *s.* 1. Engaño, dolo, fraude, falacia; impostura, supercheria. 2. Artificio, treta, estratagema.
Deceitful [dẹ-sít'-ful], *a.* Fraudulento, engañoso, falso; ilusorio, falaz.
Deceitfully [dẹ-sít'-ful-i], *adv.* Fraudulentamente, falsamente.
Deceitfulness [dẹ-sít'-ful-nes], *s.* Falsedad; atractivos falaces.
Deceivable [dẹ-sív'-a-bl], *a.* 1. Engañadizo, bobalicón. 2. †Engañoso.
Deceive [dẹ-sív'], *va.* Engañar, alucinar, burlar; defraudar; privar de toda esperanza.
Deceiver [dẹ-sív'-ẹr], *s.* Engañador, impostor.
Deceiving [dẹ-sív'-ing], *a.* Engañador.
Deceleration [dí-sel-ẹr-ê'-shun], *s.* Deceleración, desaceleración.
December [dẹ-sem'-bẹr], *s.* 1. Diciembre, el último mes del año. 2. (Fig.) Época de decadencia; vejez.
Decempedal [dẹ-sem'-pe-dal], *a.* 1. Que tiene diez patas. 2. (Des.) Lo que tiene diez pies de largo.
Decemvir [dí-sem'-vẹr], *s.* (*pl.* VIRS [vẹrz] o VIRI [vi-rai]). 1. Decenviro, uno de los diez magistrados superiores de la antigua Roma. 2. Miembro de un cuerpo cualquiera compuesto de diez personas.
Decemvirate [dẹ-sem'-vi-rêt], *s.* Decemvirato.
Decency [dí'-sen-si], *s.* 1. Decencia, adorno. 2. Recato, modestia, decoro; propiedad.
Decennary [dẹ-sen'-a-ri], *a.* Que contiene diez, o pertenece al diezmo.
Decennial [dẹ-sen'-i-al], *a.* Decenal, lo que comprende o dura diez años; que sucede cada diez años.
Decent [dí'-sent], *a.* Decente, razonable; acomodado, propio, conveniente.
Decently [dí'-sent-li], *adv.* Decentemente.
Decentness [dí'-sent-nes], *s.* Decencia, modestia, decoro; propiedad.
Decentralization [dẹ-sen-tral-i-zé'-shun], *s.* Descentralización.
Decentralize [dẹ-sen'-tral-aiz], *va.* Descentralizar.
Deception [dẹ-sep'-shun], *s.* Decepción, engaño, impostura, superchería, dolo, fraude; charlatanería.
Deceptive [dẹ-sep'-tiv], *a.* Falaz, engañoso.
Deceptively [dẹ-sep'-tiv-li], *adv.* Falazmente de una manera engañosa.
Decern, *va.* 1. (For. esco.) Juzgar, decretar. 2. (Des.) *V.* DISCERN.
Decharm [dẹ-chārm'] *va.* (Poco us.) Desencantar.
Decibel [de'-si-bẹl], *s.* (Fís.) Decibel, decibelio.
Decidable [dẹ-said'-a-bl], *a.* Decidible.
Decide [dẹ-said'], *va.* y *vn.* 1. Decidir, determinar, resolver, juzgar. 2. Acabar o poner término a alguna cosa. 3. Sentenciar algún caso, duda, cuestión o pleito.
Decided [dẹ-sai'-ded], *a.* Decidido, terminado, resuelto, incontestable, indudable.
Decidedly [dẹ-sai'-ded-li], *adv.* 1. Decididamente, con decisión. 2. Determinadamente. 3. Indudablemente.
Decider [dẹ-said'-ẹr], *s.* Arbitro, determinante.
Deciduous [dẹ-sid'-yu-us], *a.* Deciduo, decedente, que se desprende y cae algún tiempo después de su desarrollo; sujeto a desprenderse en épocas periódicas, v. g. las hojas, los cuernos, los dientes, etc.
Deciduousness [dẹ-sid'-yu-us-nes], *s.* La facilidad en ser caedizo o en caer; la caída de las hojas en el otoño.
Decigram, Decigramme [des'-i-gram], *s.* Decigramo, peso de un décimo de gramo: cerca de 1.54 granos.
Deciliter, Decilitre [des'-i-lí"-tẹr], *s.* Decilitro, medida de un décimo de litro.
Decimal [des'-i-mal], *a.* Decimal, cuya base es diez; lo que se aumenta o disminuye por decenas.—*s.* Decimal, fracción decimal.
Decimally [des'-i-mal-i], *adv.* Por decenas; por medio de los decimales.
Decimate [des'-i-mêt], *va.* 1. Matar uno de cada diez; (fam.) destruir gran parte de una población. 2. (Des.) Diezmar.
Decimation [des-i-mé'-shun], *s.* La acción y efecto de matar uno de cada diez; gran destrucción.
Decimator [des'-i-mê-tẹr], *s.* Gran destructor.
Decimeter, Decimetre [des'-i-mí-tẹr], *s.* Decímetro, la décima parte de un metro.
Decimo-sexto [des'-i-mō-secs'-tō], *s.* Libro en dieciseisavo.
Decipher [dẹ-sai'-fẹr], *va.* 1. Descifrar. 2. Cifrar, poner en cifra. 3. Estampar o señalar con caracteres. 4. Desenrollar, desembrollar, desenmarañar. 5. Aclarar o interpretar lo que está obscuro, describir lo oculto, explicar lo dudoso.
Decipherable [dẹ-sai'-fẹr-a-bl], *a.* Descifrable, que se puede descifrar o aclarar.
Decipherer [dẹ-sai'-fẹr-ẹr], *s.* Descifrador.
Decision [dẹ-sizh'-un], *s.* 1. Decisión, determinación, resolución. 2. Vigor, firmeza.
Decisive [dẹ-sai'-siv], *a.* Decisivo; conclusivo, terminante.
Decisively [dẹ-sai'-siv-li], *adv.* Decisivamente.
Decisiveness [dẹ-sai'-siv-nes], *s.* Autoridad decisiva.
‡**Decisory** [dẹ-sai'-so-ri], *a.* Decisorio, decisivo.
Deck [dek], *va.* 1. Cubrir. 2. Ataviar, componer, asear, adornar, embellecer.
Deck, *s.* 1. (Mar.) Cubierta, cada uno de los suelos que dividen las estancias de un buque. *Between decks*, Entre puentes. 2. Tejado de un coche o carro. 3. (Min.) Plataforma de jaula. 4. Baraja, el conjunto de cartas de que consta el juego de naipes. *Gun-deck*, Cubierta principal, batería. *On deck*, Sobre cubierta. *Quarter-deck*, Alcázar, castillo de popa. *Spar-deck*, Cubierta alta o de guindaste. *Deck-hand*, Estibador en buque de vapor.
Deck chair [dek chār], *s.* Silla de cubierta (en un barco).
Decker [dek'-er], *s.* 1. Cubridor, adornador, aseador. 2. Navío, carro, etc., con cubierta; se usa solamente en composición. *A two-decker*, Navío de dos puentes.
Decking [dek'-ing], *s.* Adorno.
Deckle [dek'-l], *s.* 1. En la fabricación de papel, cubierta, bastidor rectangular. 2. Banda de caucho flexible y continua. 3. Barba, borde sin cortar del papel hecho a mano.
Declaim [dẹ-clêm'], *va.* Recitar en público.—*vn.* 1. Declamar, recitar de una manera oratoria, arengar. 2. Recitar (de memoria).

Declaimer, *s.* Declamador.
Declaiming [dẹ-clêm'-ing], *s.* Arenga, oración.
Declamation [dec-la-mé'-shun], *s.* Declamación, arenga.
Declamatory [dẹ-clam'-a-to-ri], *a.* Declamatorio.
Declarable [dẹ-clār'-a-bl], *a.* Lo que se puede declarar.
Declaration [dec-la-ré'-shun], *s.* Declaración, manifestación, publicación; explicación, exposición.
Declarative [dẹ-clār'-a-tiv], *a.* Declaratorio, expositivo.
Declaratorily [dẹ-clār'-a-to"-ri-li], *adv.* En forma de declaración.
Declaratory [dẹ-clar'-a-to-ri], *a.* Declaratorio; afirmativo, demostrativo.
Declare [dẹ-clār'], *va.* 1. Declarar, manifestar. 2. Publicar, proclamar. 3. Afirmar, asegurar, confesar.—*vn.* Declarar, deponer, testificar; decidirse en favor de.
Declaredly [dẹ-clār'-ed-li], *adv.* Declaradamente, abiertamente, explícitamente.
Declarer [dẹ-clār'-ẹr], *s.* Declarador, declarante, deponente.
Declaring [dẹ-clār'-ing], *s.* Declaración.
Declension [dẹ-clen'-shun], *s.* 1. Declinación, decadencia, caimiento, diminución, decremento, menoscabo. 2. (Gram.) Declinación, la serie de los casos del nombre. 3. Inclinación, oblicuidad, declivio.
Declinable [dẹ-clain'-a-bl], *a.* Declinable.
Declination [dec-li-né'-shun], *s.* 1. Declinación; descenso, declive; inclinación. 2. Decadencia, decremento; desvío. 3. (Mar.) Declinación de la aguja de marear, lo que la aguja se aparta de la dirección al polo hacia oriente o poniente. 4. (Gram.) Declinación. 5. Negativa: falta de aceptación, excusa.
Declinator [dec'-li-né"-tẹr], **Declinatory** [dẹ-clai'-na-to-ri], *s.* Declinatorio, instrumento para medir el ángulo de declinación.
Declinatory, *a.* Que envuelve o lleva excusa. *Declinatory plea*, (For.) Declinatoria.
Decline [dẹ-clain'], *va.* 1. Rehusar, rechazar, repulsar. 2. Inclinar una cosa hacia abajo, bajarla. 3. (Gram.) Declinar. 4. (Ant.) Huir, evitar. —*vn.* 1. Rehusar, rechazar. 2. Declinar, inclinarse hacia abajo. 3. Decaer, desmejorar. 4. Huir, eludir, desviar.
Decline, *s.* 1. Declinación, decadencia, caimiento. 2. (Med.) Enfermedad que va cediendo de su violencia. 3. Menoscabo, decadencia de las fuerzas físicas o mentales por causa de enfermedad; (fam.) consunción.
Declivity [dẹ-cliv'-i-ti], *s.* Declive, declivo, pendiente de algún terreno.
Declivitous, Declivous [dẹ-cliv'-i-tus, dec'-li-vus], *a.* Inclinado, que está en declive o en pendiente.
Decoct [dẹ-coct'], *va.* 1. Cocer, hervir. 2. (Ant.) Asimilar, digerir.
Decoction [dẹ-coc'-shun], *s.* 1. Cocción o hervor. 2. Decocción de plantas o drogas para sacar la substancia.
Decocture [dẹ-coc'-chur], *s.* Decocción. *V.* DECOCTION.
Decode [dī-cōd'], *va.* Descifrar (lo escrito en clave).
Decollate [dẹ-col'-ēt], *va.* Degollar.
Decollation [dẹ-col-é'-shun], *s.* Degollación.
Decolor, Decolour, Decolorate [dī-cul'-er, ēt], *va.* Quitar el color, blanquear; clarificar (azúcar).
Decoloration [dī-cul-ẹr-é'-shun], *s.* Descoloramiento.
Decompose [dī-cem-pōz'], *va.* Descomponer, reducir un cuerpo a sus principios, separar las partes de algún cuerpo o mezcla, destruir la unión química de las partículas de los cuerpos; pudrir.—*vn.* Pudrirse, corromperse.
Decomposite [dī-cem-pez'-it], *a.* Compuesto de nuevo. (Bot.)
Decomposition [dī-cem-po-zish'-un], *s.* 1. Descomposición, separación. 2. Segunda composición, combinación de cosas ya compuestas.
Decompound [dī-cem-paund'], *va.* 1. Componer de cosas ya compuestas. 2. (Poco us.) Descomponer, separar cosas compuestas.
Decompound, *a.* (Bot.) Dos veces compuesto.
Decompression [dī-cem-presh'-un], *s.* Descompresión. *Decompression chamber*, Cámara de descompresión.
Decontaminate [dī-cen-tam'-i-nēt], *va.* Descontaminar.
Decontamination [dī-cen-tam-i-né'-shun], *s.* Descontaminación.
Decorate [dec'-o-rēt], *va.* Decorar, hermosear, adornar, pulir.
Decoration [dec-o-ré'-shun], *s.* 1. Decoración, adorno o lustre; ornamento. 2. Divisa (de honor). *Decoration Day*, (E. U.) El 30 de Mayo, día señalado para decorar las sepulturas de los soldados y marinos que murieron en la guerra civil (1861–'65).
Decorator [dec'-o-ré-tẹr], *s.* Decorador, adornista.
Decorous [dẹ-cō'-rus], *a.* Decente, decoroso, honesto; conveniente.
Decorously [dẹ-cō'-rus-li], *adv.* Decorosamente.
Decorousness [dẹ-cō'-rus-nes], *s.* Decoro, circunspección, conveniencia de conducta.
Decorticate [dẹ-cōr'-ti-kēt], *va.* 1. Descortezar. 2. Pelar, mondar.
Decortication [dẹ-cōr-ti-ké'-shun], *s.* Descortezamiento.
Decorum [dẹ-cō'-rum], *s.* Decoro, honor, decencia, compostura; propiedad, conveniencia.
Decoy [dẹ-cei'], *va.* 1. Atraer algún pájaro a la jaula con señuelo o añagaza. 2. Atraer con falsos halagos, embaucar, engañar, pillar, clavar.
Decoy, *s.* 1. Seducción, incitación a hacer alguna cosa mala. 2. Cazadero con señuelo.
Decoy-duck [dẹ-cei'-duc], *s.* Pato de reclamo.
Decrease [dẹ-crīs'], *vn.* Decrecer, menguar, ir a menos, minorarse, disminuir.—*va.* Disminuir, minorar.
Decrease, *s.* 1. Decremento, diminución; descaecimiento, decadencia, descrecimiento, mengua, merma, bajada. 2. Menguante de la luna.
Decree [dẹ-crī'], *vn.* Decretar, mandar por decreto o edicto; determinarse, resolverse.—*va.* Decretar, determinar, mandar, ordenar.
Decree [dẹ-crī'], *s.* 1. Decreto, ley, edicto, mandato; regla establecida. 2. Decreto, resolución, determinación, decisión de algún pleito. 3. Decreto del Papa y sus cardenales.
Decrement [dec'-rẹ-mẹnt], *s.* Decremento, diminución.
Decrepit [dẹ-crep'-it], *a.* Decrépito, cargado de años, consumido por la vejez. (Algunas veces se escribe **Decrepid.**)
Decrepitate [dẹ-crep'-i-tēt], *va.* y *vn.* Decrepitar, henderse o saltar con ruido alguna cosa echada al fuego, como la sal, etc.
Decrepitation [dẹ-crep-i-té'-shun], *s.* (Quím.) Decrepitación.
Decrepitness [dẹ-crep'-it-nes], **Decrepitude** [dẹ-crep'-i-tiūd], *s.* Decrepitud, senectud, caducidad.
Decrescendo [dê-cre-shen'-do], *a.*, *s.* y *adv.* (Ital.) *V.* DIMINUENDO.
Decrescent [dẹ-cres'-ent], *a.* Lo que decrece o mengua.
Decretal [dẹ-crī'-tal], *s.* 1. Decretal, epístola pontificia en la que el Papa declara alguna duda. 2. Decretero, libro de decretos; rescripto.—*a.* Decretal, lo que pertenece a un decreto.
Decretion [dẹ-crī'-shun], *s.* Minoración, merma.
Decretist [dẹ-crī'-tist], *s.* Decretista, decretalista, expositor o intérprete de las decretales.
Decretive [dẹ-crī'-tiv], *a.* Decretal, decretivo, de la naturaleza de un decreto.
Decretorily [dec'-rẹ-to-ri-li], *adv.* Definitivamente.
Decretory [dec'-rẹ-to-ri], *a.* Decretorio, definitivo, decisivo, perentorio; crítico.
Decrial [dẹ-crai'-al], *s.* Gritería y confusión contra alguna persona; insulto.
Decrier [dẹ-crai'-ẹr], *s.* El que censura precipitadamente o ruidosamente.
Decrown [dī-craun'], *va.* *V.* DISCROWN.
Decrustation [dī-crus-té'-shun], *s.* La acción de quitar la costra.
Decry [dẹ-crai'], *va.* Desacreditar, culpar o censurar públicamente; gritar contra alguna persona o cosa.
Decubation [dec-yu-bé'-shun], *s.* El acto de acostarse.
Decubitus [de-kiū'-bi-tus], *s.* Decúbito, posición del cuerpo de una persona echada o recostada; posición del enfermo en la cama.
Decumbence, Decumbency [dẹ-cum-bens, i], *s.* La acción de estar acostado y la postura que se tiene en la cama.
Decumbent [dẹ-cum'-bent], *a.* 1. *V.* RECUMBENT. 2. Echado en la cama; enfermo.
Decumbiture [dẹ-cum'-bi-chur o tiūr], *s.* 1. Tiempo que el enfermo guarda cama. 2. (Astrol.) Pronóstico que se toma del aspecto del cielo para predecir la mejoría o la muerte del enfermo.
Decuple [dec'-yu-pl], *a.* Décuplo, diez veces tanto como otra cantidad.
Decurion [dẹ-kiū'-ri-ọn], *s.* Decurión, el jefe de diez soldados entre los romanos.
Decurrent [dẹ-cur'-ent], *a.* (Bot.) Decurrente; dícese de la hoja cuyo limbo se prolonga a lo largo del tallo, adhiriéndose a él.
Decursive [dẹ-cūr'-siv], *a.* *V.* DECURRENT.
Decussate [dẹ-cus'-ēt], *vn.* Cortarse dos líneas en ángulos agudos o en forma de X; cruzarse como las mallas de una red.—*a.* Entrecruzado; en botánica, decusativo; dícese de las hojas opuestas cuyos pares se cruzan formando ángulo recto.
Decussation [dī"-cus-sé'-shun], *s.* Decusación, el punto donde se cruzan

varias líneas o radios; dícese particularmente de los nervios del ojo.

Dedal, Dædal [dī'-dal], *a.* 1. Primorosamente hecho, intricado, artístico, ingenioso. 2. Artificioso, taimado, engañoso.

Dedicate [ded'-i-ket], *va.* 1. Dedícar, aplicar, consagrar alguna cosa a Dios. 2. Dedicar, destinar una persona a algún empleo u ocupación, o una cosa a alguna persona o uso determinado. 3. Dedicar, ofrecer alguna obra o trabajo de la inteligencia á un personaje para que lo patrocine.

Dedicate, *a.* Consagrado, dedicado.

Dedication [ded-i-kê'-shun], *s.* 1. Dedicación, consagración. 2. Dedicatoria que precede a una obra.

Dedicator [ded'-i-kê-tęr], *s.* Dedicante, el que dedica.

Dedicatory [ded'-i-ca-to-ri], *a.* Que contiene o presenta la forma de dedicatoria; que se refiere o pertenece a la dedicatoria.

Deduce [dę-diūs'], *va.* Deducir, sacar por orden o serie regular y conexa; concluir o inferir por consecuencias legítimas, derivar; substraer.

Deducement [dę-diūs'-męnt], *s.* Deducción, conclusión, consecuencia.

Deducible [dę-diūs'-i-bl], *a.* Deducible, que puede ser deducido, inferido.

Deducive [dę-diū'-siv], *a.* Deductivo; concluyente, ilativo.

Deduct [dę-duct'], *va.* Deducir, substraer, descontar, rebajar, bajar, desfalcar, rebatir.

Deduction [dę-duc'-shun], *s.* 1. Deducción, ilación, consecuencia. 2. Deducción, descuento, rebaja, desfalco.

Deductive [dę-duct'-iv], *a.* Deductivo, que obra o procede por deducción, ilativo.

Deductively [dę-duct'-iv-li], *adv.* Por ilación o consecuencia.

Deed [dīd], *s.* 1. Acción, operación, acto, hecho; realidad. 2. Hazaña, acción heroica. 3. Instrumento auténtico que hace fe. *In deed, in very deed,* De veras, en verdad; de hecho.

Deedless [dīd'-les], *a.* Omiso, descuidado, inerte, obscuro, sin nombre, que no se ha dado a conocer por ningún hecho.

Deedy [dīd'-i], *a.* Activo, industrioso.

Deem [dīm], *va.* y *vn.* Juzgar, hacer o formar dictamen o juicio de alguna cosa, imaginar, suponer, pensar, creer, estimar; determinar.

Deemster [dīm'-stęr], *s.* Juez, magistrado en la isla inglesa de Man.

Deep [dīp], *a.* 1. Hondo, profundo, lo que se considera medido desde lo más alto a lo más bajo. 2. Profundo, lo que profundiza o penetra mucho. 3. Sagaz, hábil, penetrador. 4. Artificioso, insidioso. 5. Grave, obscuro. 6. Profundo, silencioso, taciturno. *Deep in debt,* Cargado de deudas. 7. Obscuro; dícese del color. 8. Grave, en sonido. 9. Cenagoso, lodoso; dícese, p. ej., de un camino.—*s.* 1. Piélago, abismo, lo más profundo del mar o de alguna cosa. 2. Misterio. *Deep of night,* El horror de las tinieblas, la obscuridad más profunda.

Deep-drawing [dīp'-drē-ing], *a.* Que está muy profundo en el agua; de mucho calado.

Deepen [dīp'-n], *va.* 1. Profundizar. 2. Obscurecer. 3. Entristecer.—*vn.* Descender gradualmente; profundizarse.

Deep freeze [dīp frīz'], *s.* Congelación rápida.

Deepfreeze [dīp'-frīz], *va.* Congelar, almacenar en congeladora.

Deeply [dīp'-li], *adv.* 1. Profundamente, muy hondo, a una gran profundidad. 2. Profundamente, sumamente, en sumo grado. 3. Gravemente, tristemente, obscuramente. 4. Sagazmente, con profunda atención.

Deep-mouthed [dīp'-maudhd], *a.* Ronco, el que tiene la voz profunda y bronca.

Deep-musing [dīp'-miūz-ing], *a.* Pensativo, contemplativo.

Deepness [dīp'-nes], *s.* Profundidad, la extensión de cualquiera cosa desde su superficie hasta su fondo.

Deep-read [dīp'-red], *a.* Muy leído, profundamente versado en los libros.

Deep-sea fishing [dīp-sī fish'-ing], *s.* Pesca de alta mar.

Deep-sea-line [dīp'-sī-lain], *s.* (Mar.) Escandallo, sonda o plomada para medir la cantidad de brazas de agua que hay hasta el fondo.

Deep-seated [dīp-sīt'-ed], *a.* Arraigado, profundo.

Deer [dīr], *s.* Ciervo o venado, un animal cualquiera del género cerval. *Fallow deer,* Gamo, gama. *Red deer,* Ciervo común. *Deer-fold,* Parque de ciervos. *Deerhound,* Galgo, perro corredor. *Deer-skin,* Gamuza, piel de gamo. *Deer-stalking,* Caza al acecho.

Deface [dę-fês'], *va.* 1. Desfigurar, mutilar la faz o la superficie de una cosa. 2. Borrar, destruir, afear.

Defacement [dę-fês'-męnt], *s.* Violación, injuria; rasadura, destrucción, ruina.

Defacer [dę-fês'-ęr], *s.* Destructor o destruidor.

De facto [dī o dê fac'-to]. De hecho, actual; en oposición a *de jure.*

Defalcate [dę-fal'-kêt], *va.* Desfalcar, descabalar, deducir, quitar parte o porción de alguna cosa.—*vn.* Tomar para sí, apropiarse uno el dinero que otro le ha confiado; malversar.

Defalcation [def-al-kê'-shun], *s.* 1. Desfalco, malversación, hurto. 2. Deducción, diminución. 3. Déficit.

Defamation [def-a-mê'-shun], *s.* Difamación, disfamación, calumnia.

Defamatory [de-fam'-a-to-ri], *a.* Infamatorio, calumnioso, difamatorio.

Defame [dę-fêm'], *va.* Disfamar, desacreditar, deshonrar, denigrar; calumniar.

Defamer [dę-fêm'-ęr], *s.* Infamador, calumniador.

Defaming, *s.* *V.* DEFAMATION.

Default [dę-fēlt'], *s.* 1. Omisión, descuido, negligencia. 2. Culpa, delito. 3. Defecto, falta. *In default whereof,* En cuyo defecto. 4. (For.) Rebeldía, la acción de no comparecer en juicio dentro del plazo de la citación.

Default, *va.* Faltar, no cumplir algún contrato o estipulación.—*vn.* 1. Caer en rebeldía o contumacia. 2. (Des.) Ofender, ser descuidado.

Defaulter [dę-fēlt'-ęr], *s.* El que falta o no cumple su deber. 1. (For.) Rebelde, contumaz, el que no comparece en juicio dentro del término de la citación. 2. Malversador.

Defeasible [dę-fī'-zi-bl], *a.* Anulable, revocable.

Defeat [dę-fīt'], *s.* Derrota, rota, vencimiento, destrucción o ruina; p. ej. de un ejército o un partido.

Defeat, *va.* 1. Derrotar, vencer, deshacer, destruir. 2. Frustrar, privar a alguno de lo que se le debía o esperaba. 3. (For.) Anular, abrogar. 4. (Des.) Abolir, exterminar.

Defeatism [dę-fīt'-izm], *s.* Derrotismo.

Defeatist [dę-fīt'-ist], *s.* Derrotista.

Defecate [def'-ę-kêt], *va.* Purgar, purificar, limpiar; depurar.—*vn.* 1. Limpiarse de impurezas. 2. Exonerar el vientre, defecar.

Defecate, *a.* Depurado, aclarado.

Defecation [def-ę-kê'-shun], *s.* 1. Defecación, dícese de los líquidos cuando se van aclarando por irse posando las heces en el fondo; purificación, clarificación. 2. Exoneración del vientre, defecación.

Defect [dę-fect'], *s.* Defecto, falta, tacha, imperfección; omisión.

Defectible [dę-fect'-i-bl], *a.* Defectible; imperfecto.

Defection [dę-fec'-shun], *s.* 1. Defección, apostasía; conjuración, rebeldía, desobediencia, levantamiento, sublevación. 2. Separación, deserción, abandono.

Defective [dę-fect'-iv], *a.* Defectivo, defectuoso, imperfecto; culpable.

Defectively [dę-fect'-iv-li], *adv.* Defectuosamente.

Defectiveness [dę-fect'-iv-nes], *s.* Defecto, culpa, falta, delito.

Defence [dę-fens'], *s.* **Defenceless,** etc. Lo mismo que **Defense,** etc.

Defend [dę-fend'], *va.* 1. Defender, preservar, proteger, conservar. 2. Sostener alguna opinión. 3. Fortalecer, asegurar. 4. Repeler.

Defendable [dę-fend'-a-bl], *a.* Defendible.

Defendant [dę-fend'-ant], *a.* Defensivo.—*s.* 1. (For.) El demandado. 2. El que defiende.

Defender [dę-fend'-ęr], *s.* Defensor, abogado; campeón; afirmador; protector, patrón.

Defensative [dę-fen'-sa-tiv], *s.* (Ant.) Defensiva, defensa, guardia; reparo.

Defense, Defence [dę-fens'], *s.* 1. Defensa, la acción y afecto de defender; protección, sostén, apoyo. 2. Defensa, vindicación, justificación, apología. 3. Resistencia, resguardo con que se evita o repele algún riesgo; cualquiera cosa que defiende. 4. (For.) Defensa, la respuesta del demandado.

Defenseless [dę-fens'-les], *a.* Indefenso, sin armas, sin defensa; impotente: incapaz de resistir.

Defenselessness [dę-fens'-les-nes], *s.* Desvalimiento, desamparo, abandono.

Defensible [dę-fen'-si-bl], *a.* Defendible, que se puede defender o sostener.

Defensive [dę-fen'-siv], *a.* Defensivo. —*s.* Defensiva, la situación o estado del que sólo trata de defenderse. *To be* o *to stand upon the defensive,* Estar o ponerse a la defensiva.

Defensively [dę-fen'-siv-li], *adv.* Defensivamente.

Defensory [dę-fen'-so-ri], *a.* Defensivo, justificativo.

Defer [dę-fęr'], *vn.* 1. Diferir, dilatar, suspender, posponer. 2. Deferir, ceder, condescender por atención o respeto.—*va.* 1. Diferir, retardar, atrasar. 2. Remitirse al parecer de otro; ofrecer.

Deference [def'-ęr-ens], *s.* Deferencia, sumisión, respeto, considera-

ción, condescendencia. *Out of deference*, Por deferencia, en consideración a.
Deferent [def'-ẹr-ent], *a.* 1. Deferente, que lleva o se lleva. 2. *V.* Deferential.—*s.* Vehículo, lo que lleva o conduce. (Anat.) Canal deferente, conducto excretor.
Deferential [def''-ẹr-en'-shal], *a.* Deferente, respetuoso.
Deferment [dẹ-fẹr'-mẹnt], *s.* (Poco us.) Dilación, tardanza.
Deferrer [dẹ-fẹr'-ẹr], *s.* Tardador, holgazán; el que difiere o dilata.
Deferring [dẹ-fẹr'-ing], *s.* Dilación, la acción de diferir.
Defiance [dẹ-fai'-ans], *s.* 1. Desafío, cartel o reto, provocación a duelo o combate. 2. El acto de retar a otro a que pruebe una acusación. 3. Expresión de menosprecio o vilipendio. *To bid defiance*, Retar, provocar a desafío; bravear, echar plantas, fieros o bravatas; contradecir, oponerse abiertamente o cara a cara. *To set at defiance*, Befar, hacer befa o mofa.
Defibrinate [dī-fai'-brin-êt], *va.* Desfibrinar, quitar la fibrina de la sangre.
Deficiency, Deficience [dẹ-fish'-ens, i], *s.* 1. Defecto, imperfección. 2. Falta; defecto.
Deficient [dẹ-fish'-ent], *a.* Deficiente, defectuoso, falto, incompleto.
Deficiently [dẹ-fish'-ent-li], *adv.* Defectuosamente.
Deficit [def'-i-sit], *s.* Déficit, la falta, alcance o descubierto que resulta comparando el haber con el fondo puesto en la empresa; o la cantidad que falta para pagar las cargas del Estado; descubierto con el fisco.
Defier [dẹ-fai'-ẹr], *s.* Desafiador, el que desafía.
Defile [dẹ-fail'], *va.* 1. Manchar, ensuciar. 2. Violar, profanar, viciar. 3. Corromper, violar, deshonrar.—*vn.* Desfilar, marchar o ir en filas.
Defile [dẹ-fail' o dī'-fail], *s.* Desfiladero, sitio o pasaje estrecho. *A defile between two hills*, Garganta de montaña.
Defilement [dẹ-fail'-mẹnt], *s.* Contaminación, violación, suciedad, corrupción, profanación.
Defiler [dẹ-fail'-ẹr], *s.* Corruptor, violador, contaminador, profanador.
Defiling [dẹ-fail'-ing], *s.* Contaminación, corrupción, profanamiento.
Definable [dẹ-fain'-a-bl], *a.* Definible, lo que se puede definir.
Define [dẹ-fain'], *va.* 1. Definir, describir. 2. Circunscribir, señalar términos o límites; determinar.—*vn.* Decidir, juzgar.
Definer [dẹ-fain'-ẹr], *s.* Definidor, el que explica o define una cosa.
Definite [def'-i-nit], *a.* Definido, exacto, preciso, determinado, limitado, cierto.—*s.* Definido, la cosa definida.
Definitely [def'-i-nit-li], *adv.* Definitivamente, determinadamente, ciertamente.
Definiteness [def'-i-nit-nes], *s.* Limitación fija de alguna cosa.
Definition [def-i-nish'-un], *s.* 1. Definición, descripción breve y clara. 2. Decisión, determinación. 3. (Opt.) Propiedad de una lente de dar una imagen clara y distinta.
Definitive [dẹ-fin'-i-tiv], *a.* Definitivo, decisivo, perentorio.—*s.* Lo que define.
Definitively [dẹ-fin'-i-tiv-li], *adv.* Definitivamente, decisivamente, resolutivamente.
Definitiveness [dẹ-fin'-i-tiv-nes], *s.* Autoridad decisiva.
Deflagrable [def'-la-gra-bl o dẹ-flê'-gra-bl], *a.* Combustible.
Deflagrate [def'-la-grêt], *va.* Incendiar, abrasar, efectuar una combustión, especialmente si es repentina y rápida.—*vn.* Arder con combustión repentina y rápida; crepitar.
Deflagration [def-la-grê'-shun], *s.* 1. Deflagración, combustión repentina y rápida. 2. Destrucción total por medio del fuego.
Deflagrator [def'-la-grê''-tẹr], *s.* (Elec.) Deflagrador, instrumento para efectuar muy rápida combustión.
Deflate [dẹ-flêt'], *va.* Desinflar.
Deflation [dẹ-flê'-shun], *s.* Desinflación.
Deflect [dẹ-flect'], *va.* Desviar, apartar, separar del camino o curso.—*vn.* Desviarse, apartarse, ladearse, separarse del camino o carrera que se llevaba.
Deflection, Deflexion [dẹ-flec'-shun], *s.* 1. Desvío, rodeo. 2. Declinación de la aguja de marear.
Deflex [dẹ-flex'], *va.* Desviar, ladear, doblar repentinamente hacia abajo.
Deflexure [dẹ-flec'-shur], *s.* Combadura, torcimiento.
Deflorate [dẹ-flō'-rêt], *a.* (Bot.) 1. Se dice de la planta que ha cesado de florecer. 2. Que ha emitido o depositado su polen.
Defloration [def-lo-rê'-shun], *s.* 1. Defloración. 2. Escogimiento, elección de lo más florido o precioso.
Deflower, Deflour [dẹ-flaur'], *va.* 1. Quitar la flor de las plantas. 2. Ajar, deslustrar, quitar la flor o lustre a alguna cosa. 3. Desflorar, estuprar, corromper o forzar a una doncella.
Deflowerer, Deflourer [dẹ-flaur'-ẹr], *s.* Estuprador.
Defluxion [dẹ-fluc'-shun], *s.* Fluxión copiosa o abundante, destilación; derramamiento por demasiada abundancia.
Defoliate [dẹ-fō'-li-êt], *a.* Deshojado, privado de hojas.—*va.* Quitar o privar de las hojas; deshojar.
Defoliation [dẹ-fo-li-ê'-shun], *s.* (Bot.) Época de la caída de las hojas.
Deforce [dẹ-fōrs'], *va.* Usurpar la posesión de bienes raíces.
Deforcement [dẹ-fōrs'-mẹnt], *s.* Usurpación, posesión ilegítima de los bienes de otro.
Deforest [dī-fer'-est], *va.* Desboscar, arrancar árboles, talar bosques.
Deform [dẹ-fōrm'], *va.* 1. Deformar, desfigurar, afear. 2. Deshonrar, quitar el honor, estimación o fama.
Deformation [def-er-mê'-shun], *s.* Deformación, alteración.
Deformed [dẹ-fōrmd'], *a.* 1. Deformado, desfigurado; contrahecho. 2. (Des.) Feo: bajo, vergonzoso.
Deformedness [dẹ-fōrm'-ed-nes], **Deformity** [de-fōrm'-i-ti], *s.* 1. Deformidad, fealdad; ridiculez. 2. Deshonor; acción o idea disparatada y opuesta al buen sentido.
Defraud [dẹ-frōd'], *va.* Defraudar, usurpar fraudulentamente a alguna persona lo que le toca y pertenece de derecho; frustrar.
§**Defraudation** [def-rōd-ê'-shun], *s.* Defraudación.
Defrauder [dẹ-frōd'-ẹr], *s.* Defraudador, engañador.
Defrauding [dẹ-frōd'-ing], **Defraudment** [dẹ-frōd'-mẹnt], *s.* Defraudación, fraude.
Defray [dẹ-frê'], *va.* Costear, hacer el gasto o la costa de alguna cosa; satisfacer.
Defrayer [dẹ-frê'-ẹr], *s.* El que hace la costa o el gasto de alguna cosa.
Defrayment [dẹ-frê'-mẹnt], *s.* Gasto, el pago de lo que se ha gastado.
Defrost [dẹ-frōst'], *va.* Descongelar.
Defroster [dẹ-frōst'-ẹr], *s.* Descongelador.
Deft [deft], *s.* Diestro, gallardo, hábil; mañoso, apto.
Deftness [deft'-nes], *s.* Garbo, gracia, maña en hacer una cosa.
Defunct [dẹ-funct'], *a.* Difunto, muerto.—*s.* Difunto.
Defunctionalize [dī-func'-shun-al-aiz], *va.* Privar de una función o funciones.
Defy [dẹ-fai'], *va.* 1. Desafiar, provocar a singular combate, retar; arrostrar. 2. Despreciar, tratar con desprecio. 3. (Des.) Desdeñar, negar, renunciar.
Degeneracy [dẹ-jen'-ẹr-a-si], *s.* 1. Degeneración, bastardía, abandono. bajeza. 2. Depravación, corrupción, envilecimiento.
Degenerate [dẹ-jen'-ẹr-êt], *vn.* 1. Degenerar, no corresponder a las virtudes de los antepasados. 2. Degenerar, descaecer, desdecir. 3. Degenerar, ir perdiendo una cosa su primera calidad o naturaleza por deteriorarse, como sucede con algunos animales, semillas y plantas.
Degenerate, *a.* Degenerado, el que degenera de sus antepasados; vil, bajo, indigno, infame.
Degenerately [dẹ-jen'-ẹr-et-li], *adv.* Bajamente, indignamente.
Degenerateness [dẹ-jen'-ẹr-et-nes], *s.* Degeneración, abandono.
Degenerating [dẹ-jen'-ẹr-êt-ing], *s.* La acción de degenerar.
Degeneration [dẹ-jen-ẹr-ê'-shun], *s.* Degeneración, empeoramiento, deterioración, envilecimiento.
Deglutinate [dẹ-glū'-ti-net], *va.* 1. Despegar, separar las substancias adheridas entre sí. 2. Extraer o separar el gluten, p. ej. del trigo.
Deglutition [deg-lu-tish'-un], *s.* Deglución, la acción de tragar los alimentos.
Degradation [deg-ra-dê'-shun], *s.* 1. Degradación, privación de grado y honores, deposición. 2. Degeneración. 3. Diminución de fuerza o valor. 4. Envilecimiento, corrupción. 5. (Pint.) Degradación de tintas, colores y sombras.
Degrade [dẹ-grêd'], *va.* 1. Degradar, privar, deponer a alguna persona de las dignidades, honores y privilegios que tenía. 2. Minorar, rebajar, reducir. 3. Envilecer, deshonrar, hacer despreciable una cosa. 4. (Pint.) Degradar, atenuar colores o tintas. 5. (Biol.) Reducir de rango superior a uno inferior.—*vn.* 1. Degenerar. 2. (Biol.) Degenerar, pasar de rango superior a uno inferior.
Degradingly [dẹ-grê'-ding-li], *adv.* Degradantemente.
Degree [dẹ-grī'], *s.* 1. Grado, calidad, estimación de una cosa. 2. Estado, rango, condición. 3. Grado, escalón. 4. Grado de parentesco. 5. Grado, proporción. 6. Grado, la graduación y título que se da a quien ha cursado en alguna universidad. 7. (Gram.) Grado (de comparación). 8. Grado; cada una de

los 360 partes en que se divide el círculo; en álgebra, la potencia de un término; es también la medida del calor, frío, humedad, etc. 9. (Mús.) Grado, línea o espacio del pentagrama. *To take one's degrees,* Graduarse. *By degrees, adv.* Gradualmente.

Dehisce [dẹ-his'], *vn.* Hendirse, abrirse en grietas.

Dehiscence [dẹ-his'-ẹns], *s.* 1. Hendedura, grieta. 2. (Bot.) Dehiscencia, la manera y acto de abrirse los frutos para dar salida a las semillas.

Dehiscent [dẹ-his'-ẹnt], *a.* Dehiscente, (ovario) que se abre espontáneamente.

Dehorn [dî-hōrn'], *va.* Descornar, quitar los cuernos a un animal.

Dehort [dẹ-hōrt'], *va.* Disuadir; desaconsejar.

Dehortation [dẹ-hor-tê'-shun], *s.* Disuasión; distracción.

Dehorter [dẹ-hōrt'-ẹr], *s.* El que disuade.

Dehumanize [dî-hiū'-man-aiz], *va.* Privar de las cualidades o los atributos humanos, embrutecer.

Dehumidify [dî-hiū-mid'-i-fai], *va.* Deshumedecer.

Dehydrate [dî-hai'-drêt], *va.* Deshidratar.

Dehydrogenate [dî-hai-drej'-e-nêt], *va.* Deshidrogenar.

Deice [dî-ais], *va.* Descongelar.

Deictic [daic'-tic], *a.* Lo que prueba por razonamiento directo; lo que es directo. (Gr. δεικτίκος.)

Deific, Deifical [dî-if'-ic, al], *a.* 1. Que deifica. 2. Deífico, de los dioses; divino.

Deification [dî-i-fi-kê'-shun], *s.* Deificación, la acción de deificar; apoteosis.

Deifier [dî'-i-fai-ẹr], *s.* El que deifica; idólatra.

Deiform [dî'-i-fōrm], *a.* Deiforme, divino.

Deify [dî'-i-fai], *va.* 1. Deificar, colocar a alguno en el número de los dioses, adorarle como Dios. 2. Endiosar, divinizar, alabar a alguno hasta ponerle en las nubes. 3. Adorar como a un Dios.

Deign [dên], *va.* Conceder, admitir, permitir; considerar digno.—*vn.* Dignarse, condescender. *He did not deign to speak to me,* Tuvo a menos hablarme.

Deigning [dên'-ing], *s.* El acto de condescender o considerar digno.

Deipara [dî-ip'-a-ra], *a.* Deípara, epíteto de la madre de Dios. Equivale al griego Theotokos.

Deism [dî'-izm], *s.* Deísmo, la opinión de los que creen en un Dios sin admitir la religión revelada ni el cristianismo.

Deist [dî'-ist], *s.* Deísta, partidario del deísmo.

Deistical [dî-ist'-ic-al], *a.* Deístico.

Deity [dî'-i-ti], *s.* 1. Deidad, divinidad, naturaleza divina, calidades divinas. 2. Dios fabuloso; falsa deidad de los idólatras.

Deject [dẹ-ject'], *va.* Abatir, afligir, contristar, entristecer; desanimar, desalentar, acobardar, descorazonar.

†**Deject, Dejected** [dẹ-ject', ed], *a.* Abatido, acobardado, amilanado, desanimado, desalentado, afligido. *To look dejected,* Mostrar en el semblante aflicción o consternación.

Dejecta [dẹ-jec'-ta], *s. pl.* Excrementos; materias evacuadas.

Dejectedly [dẹ-ject'-ed-li], *adv.* Abatidamente, tristemente.

Dejectedness [dẹ-ject'-ed-nes], *s.* Abatimiento, desaliento, amilanamiento.

Dejecter [dẹ-ject'-ẹr], *s.* El que abate, aflige o envilece.

Dejection [dẹ-jec'-shun], *s.* 1. Melancolía, tristeza, aflicción, abatimiento de espíritu. 2. Debilidad, extenuación. 3. (Med.) Deyección, cámara, la deposición de un enfermo.

Dejectory [dẹ-jec'-to-ri], *a.* 1. Que tiende a abatir o descorazonar. 2. (Med.) Lo que produce cámaras o las promueve.

Dejecture [dẹ-jec'-chur], *s.* (Poco us.) (Med.) Excremento, deyección.

Dejeuner [dê-zhū-né'], *s.* Almuerzo, almuerzo-comida. (Gal.)

De jure [dî jū'-ri]. (For.) Legalmente, legítimamente; en contraposición a *de facto.*

Dekagram, Dekaliter, etc. *V.* DECAGRAM, etc.

Delaine [dẹ-lên'], *s.* Muselina de lana; chalí. (< Fr. Mousseline de laine.)

Delapsed [dẹ-lapst'], *a.* (Med.) Caído, inclinado hacia abajo.

Delate [dẹ-lêt'], *va.* 1. (Ley escocesa ecles.) Delatar, denunciar, acusar. 2. (Des.) Llevar, conducir.

Delation [dẹ-lê'-shun], *s.* 1. (For.) Delación, acusación, denunciación. 2. (Ant.) Porte, conducción.

Delator [dẹ-lê'-tẹr], *s.* Delator, delatante, denunciador.

Delay [dẹ-lê'], *va.* 1. Dilatar, diferir, suspender. 2. Retardar, retrasar, estorbar.—*vn.* Detenerse, pararse, cesar de obrar; tardar.

Delay, *s.* 1. Dilación, tardanza, plaza. 2. Detención, demora, retardo, retardación; atraso.

Delayer [dẹ-lê'-ẹr], *s.* Temporizador, entretenedor, que gana tiempo dilatando.

Dele [dî'-li], *va.* (Imp.) Borrar, tachar. (Lat.: imperativo del verbo delere, borrar.)

Deleble [del'-ẹ-bl], *a.* Lo que se puede borrar.

Delectable [dẹ-lect'-a-bl], *a.* Deleitable, delicioso.

Delectableness [dẹ-lect'-a-bl-nes], *s.* Delicia, gusto o placer especial que se percibe en alguna cosa.

Delectably dẹ-lect'-a-bli], *adv.* Deleitosamente.

Delectation [dî''-lec-tê'-shun], *s.* Delectación o deleitación, deleite, placer vivo.

Delegate [del'-e-gêt], *va.* 1. Delegar, diputar, dar sus veces a otro. 2. Enviar a una embajada. 3. Comisionar, señalar o nombrar un representante.

Delegate, *s.* Delegado, diputado, comisionado, comisario. *Court of delegates,* Un tribunal de apelación en Inglaterra.—*a.* Delegado, diputado.

Delegation [del-e-gê'-shun], *s.* Delegación, diputación, comisión.

Delete [dẹ-lît'], *va.* Borrar, testar, tachar algún escrito, letra u otra cosa.

Deleterious [del-e-tî'-ri-us], *a.* Deletéreo, mortal, mortífero, destructivo, emponzoñado, venenoso; pernicioso.

Deletion [dẹ-lî'-shun], *s.* Canceladura, la acción de cancelar o borrar; destrucción, ruina.

Deletory [del'-e-to-ri], *s.* Lo que borra.

Delf [delf], *s.* 1. Desaguadero; zanja de derivación. 2. Césped, hierba menuda y espesa. 3. (Ant.) Mina, cantera.

Delf [delf], **Delft** [delft], *s.* Loza fina que se parece a la china. *Delftware,* Loza vidriada.

Delfic, Delphian [del'-fic, del'-fi-an], *a.* Délfico, referente a Delfos y al célebre oráculo de su templo.

Deliberate [dẹ-lib'-ẹr-êt], *va.* Deliberar, discurrir, considerar, premeditar, determinar alguna cosa con premeditación.—*vn.* Pausar, pensar, dudar.

Deliberate, *a.* 1. Pensado, reflexionado, hecho con reflexión y madurez; circunspecto, cauto. 2. Tardo, lento, pausado. 3. Prudente, avisado.

Deliberately [dẹ-lib'-ẹr-et-li], *adv.* Deliberadamente, prudentemente, gradualmente.

Deliberateness [dẹ-lib'-ẹr-et-nes], *s.* Deliberación, circunspección, cautela, precaución, reflexión, premeditación, sangre fría.

Deliberation [dẹ-lib-ẹr-ê'-shun], *s.* 1. Deliberación, el acto de deliberar. 2. Consulta, el acto de consultar con otro acerca del mejor modo de hacer una cosa.

Deliberative [dẹ-lib'-ẹr-a-tiv], *a.* 1. Deliberativo, de la naturaleza de deliberación. 2. Deliberante, el que delibera.—*s.* Discurso deliberativo.

Delicacy [del'-i-ca-si], *s.* 1. Delicadeza, cualidad de lo que es delicado, fino, frágil o tenue; finura; delicadez, flaqueza, falta de vigor o robustez. 2. Delicadeza, nimiedad, escrupulosidad en el comer. 3. Delicadeza, la cosa que agrada a los sentidos. 4. Hermosura mujeril, blandura. 5. Aseo y gusto en el vestir, elegancia. 6. Urbanidad, cortesía; suavidad, dulzura, consideración para con otros. 7. Ternura; escrupulosidad.

Delicate [del'-i-kẹt], *a.* 1. Delicado; fino y ligero en textura; armonioso en color o figura; hermoso; regalado. 2. Delicado, exquisito, escogido, excelente. 3. Cortés, urbano, suave, que manifiesta consideración para con otros. 4. Afeminado, incapaz de aguantar fatiga o trabajo. 5. Puro, claro; fino; casto. 6. Tierno, sensible; frágil, flaco. 7. Delicado, difícil, expuesto a contingencias.

Delicately [del'-i-kẹt-li], *adv.* Delicadamente, exquisitamente, cortésmente, afeminadamente.

Delicateness [del'-i-kẹt-nes], *s.* Delicadeza, molicie.

Delicatessen [del-i-ca-tes'-en], *s. pl.* Delicadezas, golosinas, manjares delicados. (Al.)

Delicious [dẹ-lish'-us], *a.* Delicioso, ameno, agradable, exquisito.

Deliciously [dẹ-lish'-us-li], *adv.* Deliciosamente, gustosamente.

Deliciousness [dẹ-lish'-us-nes], *s.* Delicia, suavidad, gusto, placer.

Deligation [del-i-gê'-shun], *s.* Ligadura, la acción de ligar.

Delight [dẹ-lait'], *s.* Delicia, deleite, placer, gozo, alegría, satisfacción, encanto. *To take delight in reading,* Tener gusto en leer.

Delight [dẹ-lait'], *va.* Deleitar, agradar, contentar, causar placer, divertir.—*vn.* Deleitarse, tener deleite en alguna cosa; divertirse, complacerse.

§**Delighter** [dẹ-lait'-ẹr], *s.* El que se complace o deleita en alguna cosa.

Delightful [dẹ-lait'-ful], *a.* Delicioso, deleitoso, ameno, agradable, deleitable, grato, divertido, encantador, embelesador, exquisito.

Delightfully [dę-lait'-ful-i], *adv.* Deliciosamente, deleitosamente.

Delightfulness [dę-lait'-ful-nes], *s.* Delicia, suavidad, placer, encanto.

Delightless [dę-lait'-les], *a.* Sin placer o deleite.

Delightsome [dę-lait'-sum], *a.* Delicioso, deleitoso, placentero.

Delightsomely [dę-lait'-sum-li], *adv.* Deliciosamente, deleitablemente.

Delightsomeness [dę-lait'-sum-nes], *s.* Delicia, gusto delicioso, deleite, placer; amenidad.

Delineament [dę-lin'-ę-a-męnt], *s.* Delineamiento, representación por líneas; bosquejo; descripción verbal.

Delineate [dę-lin'-ę-ēt], *va.* 1. Delinear, trazar, diseñar, dibujar. 2. Pintar con diversos colores. 3. Representar alguna cosa como es. 4. Delinear, describir.

Delineation [dę-lin-ę-ē'-shun], *s.* 1. Delineación, delineamiento. 2. Bosquejo, esquicio; descripción, pintura, representación por medio de la palabra.

Delineator [dę-lin'-ę-ē'-tęr], *s.* Delineador, dibujante, descriptor.

Delinquency [dę-lin'-cwen-si], *s.* Descuido u omisión en el cumplimiento del deber; delito, culpa, falta.

Delinquent [dę-lin'-cwent], *a.* 1. Descuidado, negligente en sus deberes, culpable, defectuoso. 2. Debido y no pagado; dícese de las contribuciones de un gobierno, del pago de intereses, censos, etc.—*s.* Delincuente, el que descuida su obligación; criminal.

Deliquate [del'-i-cwēt], *vn.* Derretirse, liquidarse.—*va.* Disolver. *V.* DELIQUESCE.

Deliquation [del-i-cwē'-shun], *s.* Derretimiento, liquidación, el acto de derretir o liquidarse alguna cosa.

Deliquesce [del-i-cwes'], *vn.* Liquidarse, hacerse líquido; deshacerse poco a poco por la acción de la humedad.

Deliquescence [del-i-cwes'-ens], *s.* (Quím.) Derretimiento, delicuescencia, la tendencia de algunas sales a derretirse, y el estado líquido a que se reducen a consecuencia de esta tendencia.

Deliquescent [del-i-cwes'-ent], *a.* Delicuescente, dícese de las sales que se liquidan expuestas al aire.

Deliquiate [dę-lic'-wi-ēt], *vn.* *V.* DELIQUATE.

Deliquium [dę-lic'-wi-um], *s.* 1. Liquidación; estado líquido de alguna sal. 2. Defecto, estado debilitado de la mente. 3. (Des.) Deliquio.

Deliriant [dę-lir'-i-ant], *s.* (Med.) 1. Veneno que produce un delirio persistente. 2. Delirante, el que delira.

Delirious [dę-lir'-i-us], *a.* Delirante, el que delira o desvaría.

Delirium [dę-lir'-i-um], *s.* Delirio, perturbación del cerebro; locura, demencia, destemple de la imaginación o fantasía. *Delirium tremens* [trī'menz], Delírium tremens, enfermedad del cerebro producida por el abuso de bebidas alcohólicas o de narcóticos.

Delitescence [del-i-tes'-ens], *s.* (Ant.) 1. Diminución, repentina de una inflamación. 2. Retiro, obscuridad.

Deliver [dę-liv'-ęr], *va.* 1. Librar, libertar, salvar, soltar a un preso, poner a alguno en libertad, sustraerlo a la sujeción o el predominio de otro. 2. Dar, entregar, ceder, rendir. 3. Partear, ayudar o asistir facultivamente al parto (úsase a menudo con la prep. *of*). 4. Recitar, hablar, decir, relatar. 5. Tirar, arrojar. *To deliver over*, Transmitir; poner entre las manos de otro; pasar. *To deliver up*, Entregar, resignar, abandonar.

Deliverance [dę-liv'-ęr-ans], *s.* 1. Rescate; salida de prisión o cautiverio; preservación de un mal, de un peligro. 2. Prolación, la acción de proferir o pronunciar; expresión de parecer u opinión. *V.* DELIVERY. 3. Parto, el acto de parir.

Deliverer [dę-liv'-ęr-ęr], *s.* 1. El que entrega. 2. Libertador, salvador. 3. Narrador, relator, el que narra o relata.

Delivery [dę-liv'-ęr-i], *s.* 1. Libramiento, rescate, la acción de librar o libertar. 2. Entrega, la acción de dar o entregar. 3. Rendición, el acto de rendir alguna cosa. 4. Alumbramiento, parto, el acto de parir. 5. Prolación, la acción de proferir palabras; el modo de producirse. 6. Expedición, desembarazo, la facilidad en producirse. 7. (For.) Entrega, el acto de poner en posesión. (Com.) Remesa. 8. Distribución (del correo). 9. Proyección, descarga; fuerza propulsora; descarga de un cañón.

Dell [del], *s.* Barranco, paraje profundo; valle hondo, hondonada, foso.

Delphian, *a.* *V.* DELFIC.

Delta [del'-ta], *s.* 1. Delta (Δ, δ), cuarta letra del alfabeto griego que corresponde a la D. 2. Delta, isla de figura triangular formada en la desembocadura de algunos ríos; depósito aluvial.

Deltoid [del'-toid], *a.* Deltoide, triangular, en forma de delta.—*s.* (Anat.) Deltoides; dícese de uno de los músculos que levantan el brazo.

Deludable [dę-lūd'-a-bl], *a.* Engañadizo.

Delude [dę-lūd'], *va.* Engañar, entrampar, chasquear, embaucar; frustrar. *To delude one's self*, Hacerse ilusión.

Deluder [dę-lūd'-ęr], *s.* Delusor, engañador, impostor.

Deluding [dę-lūd'-ing], *s.* Colusión, falsedad, engaño, impostura.

Deluge [del'-iuj], *s.* 1. Diluvio, copiosa abundancia de agua e inundación de la tierra. 2. Creciente, avenida, el aumento de agua que toman los ríos. 3. Golpe, infortunio, calamidad, desgracia o infelicidad repentina.

Deluge, *va.* 1. Diluviar, llover a cántaros. 2. Abrumar, oprimir.

Delusion [dę-lū'-zhun], *s.* 1. Error, el estado del que está engañado. 2. Ilusión, prestigio, falsa imaginación. 3. Dolo, decepción, engaño, acción de engañar.

Delusive [dę-lū'-siv], **Delusory** [dę-lū'-so-ri], *a.* Engañoso, falaz, fraudulento, ilusorio.

De luxe [dę lux'], *a.* De lujo.

Delve [delv], *va.* 1. Cavar, levantar y mover la tierra con la azada o azadón. 2. Sondear, inquirir, rastrear con cautela.

Delve, *s.* Foso, hoyo, barranco, hondón; zanja; madriguera.

Delver [delv'-ęr], *s.* Cavador, el que tiene por oficio cavar la tierra.

Demagnetize [dī-mag'-net-aiz], *va.* Desmagnetizar, privar del magnetismo.

Demagogic [dem-a-gej'-ic], *a.* Demagógico, perteneciente a la demagogia o al demagogo.

Demagogism [dem'-a-geg-izm], *s.* Demagogia, dominación tiránica de la plebe o de una facción popular.

Demagogue [dem'-a-geg], *s.* Demagogo.

Demain [dę-mēn'], **Demesne** [de-mēn' o mīn'], *s.* Tierras patrimoniales, las que uno posee heredadas; tierra solariega.

Demand [dę-mand'], *s.* 1. Demanda, súplica, petición. 2. Alegación de derecho a alguna cosa. 3. (Ant.) Demanda, pregunta, interrogación. 4. Petición jurídica de una deuda. 5. Venta continuada, buen despacho. *In full of all demands*, Ajustadas todas las cuentas.

Demand, *va.* 1. Demandar, reclamar, pedir con autoridad o exigir como de derecho; procesar. 2. Demandar, exigir con urgencia, necesitar. 3. (Ant.) Preguntar, interrogar.

Demandable [dę-mand'-a-bl], *a.* Exigible, demandable.

Demandant [dę-mand'-ant], *s.* (For.) Demandante, demandador.

Demander [dę-mand'-ęr], *s.* 1. Exactor, demandador, el que pide, demanda o requiere alguna cosa con autoridad. 2. Pedigüeño, pedigón, el que pide con importunidad.

Demandress [dę-mand'-res], *sf.* Demandadora.

Demarcation [dę-mār-kē'-shun], *s.* 1. Demarcación, señalamiento de confines o límites; separación, distinción. 2. Límite, confín.

Demarch [dę-mārch'], *s.* (Des.) El paso, el andar o modo de andar.

Demean [dę-mīn'], *va.* y *vr.* 1. Portarse, gobernarse bien o mal, conducirse. 2. (Ant.) Dirigir, conducir; registrar.—*va.* Envilecer, desestimar.

Demean [dę-mīn'], *vr.* Rebajarse, degradarse; acepción errónea de *Demean* .

Demeanor, Demeanour [dę-mīn'-ęr], *s.* Porte, conducta, el modo de gobernarse, portarse o conducirse.

Demency [dę-men'-si], *s.* (Poco us.) *V.* DEMENTIA.

Dement [dę-męnt'], *va.* Enloquecer, volver loco o demente, trastornar a uno el juicio.

§**Dementate** [dę-men'-tēt], *vn.* Dementarse, volverse loco.

Demented [dę-ment'-ed], *pp.* y *a.* Demente, falto de razón, loco.

Dementia [dę-men'-shia], *s.* Demencia, locura; pérdida o trastorno de la facultad de pensar con coherencia.

Demephitize [dī-mef'-i-taiz], *va.* Desinfectar, purificar el aire mefítico o malsano.

Demerit [dę-mer'-it], *s.* Demérito, desmerecimiento; lo que es opuesto al mérito.

†**Demerit**, *va.* Desmerecer, hacerse indigno de algún bien.

Demersed [dę-męrst'], *a.* (Bot.) Sumergido, situado en el agua o que crece en ella.

Demersion [dę-męr'-shun], *s.* 1. (Ant.) Inmersión, sumersión o sufocación en el agua. 2. El acto de poner una medicina en algún menstruo o disolvente.

Demi [dem'-i]. Partícula inseparable que significa la mitad de alguna cosa, y a veces también lo mismo que casi. (Fr. del latín *dimidium*, mitad.)

Demi-devil [dem'-i-dev'-il], *s.* Mediodemonio.

Demi-god [dem'-i-ged], *s.* Semidiós.

Demijohn [dem'-i-jen], *s.* Garrafón, damajuana. (< Fr. damejeanne < Arab. dāmijān.)

Demi-lance [dem'-i-lans], *s.* Lanza ligera.

Demilitarize [di-mil'-i-tar-aiz], *va.* Desmilitarizar.

Demi-monde [dem'-i-mend"], *s.* Cierta clase de personas de reputación equívoca; aplícase en especial a las queridas o concubinas que no son mujeres públicas. (Fr.)

Demi-rep [dem'-i-rep], *sf.* Mujer sospechada, pero no convicta de incontinencia.

Demise [dę-maiz'], *s.* 1. Muerte, fallecimiento, especialmente de un soberano o gran personaje. 2. Transmisión de la corona o de la autoridad real. 3. (For.) Traslación de dominio por arriendo o legado.

Demise, *va.* 1. Legar, dejar en testamento. 2. Transferir, ceder el derecho o dominio que se tiene sobre alguna cosa; arrendar, dar en arriendo.

Demission [dę-mish'-un], *s.* Degradación, destitución de una dignidad, dimisión; decadencia.

Demissory, *a.* *V.* DIMISSORY.

Demit [dę-mit'], *va.* 1. Ceder, renunciar, resignar. 2. (Des.) Soltar; despedir. 3. (Des.) Deprimir, abatir, envilecer, humillar.

Demi-wolf [dem'-i-wulf], *s.* Mediolobo; cruzado de perro y loba.

Demobilize [di-mō'-bil-aiz], *va.* (Mil.) Desmovilizar.

Democracy [dę-mec'-ra-si], *s.* Democracia, gobierno en que el pueblo ejerce la soberanía.

Democrat [dem'-o-crat], *s.* Demócrata, el partidario de la democracia.

Democratic, Democratical [dem-o-crat'-ic, al], *a.* Democrático.

Democratically [dem-o-crat'-ic-al-i], *adv.* Democráticamente.

Democratization [dę-mec-ra-ti-zē'-shun], *s.* Democratización.

Democratize [dę-mec'-ra-taiz], *va.* Democratizar.

Demographic [di-mo-graf'-ic], *a.* Demográfico.

Demography [dę-meg'-ra-fi], *s.* Demografía.

Demoiselle [dem"-wa-zel'], *s.* 1. *V.* DAMSEL. 2. Zaida, grulla de Numidia. Anthropoides virgo.

Demolish [dę-mel'-ish], *va.* Demoler, deshacer, arruinar; arrasar.

Demolisher [dę-mel'-ish-ęr], *s.* Arruinador, destructor, el que demuele.

Demolishment [dę-mel'-ish-męnt], *s.* Destrucción, ruina.

Demolition [dem-o-lish'-un], *s.* Demolición. *Demolition squad*, Cuadrilla de demolición.

Demon [dī'-mun], *s.* Demonio, espíritu maligno, diablo.

Demoness [dī'-mun-es], *sf.* Mujer diabólica.

Demonetize [dī-mun'-ę-taiz], *va.* Desmonetizar, quitar su valor legal a la moneda o papel moneda.

Demoniac, Demoniacal [dę-mō'-ni-ac, dī"-mo-nai'-ac-al], *a.* 1. Demoniaco, perteneciente al demonio. 2. Poseso, obseso, endemoniado, afligido o atormentado por el espíritu maligno.

Demoniac, *s.* Energúmeno, el que está poseído del demonio.

Demonism [dī'-men-izm], *s.* 1. La creencia en demonios. 2. Naturaleza o carácter de demonio.

Demonocracy [dī-men-ec'-ra-si], *s.* Poder o gobierno del demonio.

Demonolatry [dī-men-el'-a-tri], *s.* Culto del demonio.

Demonology [dī-men-el'-o-ji], *s.* Demonología, demonomanía.

Demonstrable [dę-men'-stra-bl], *a.* Demostrable.

Demonstrableness [dę-men'-stra-bl-nes], *s.* Capacidad de demostración.

Demonstrably [dę-men'-stra-bli], *adv.* Demostrablemente, demostrativamente; ciertamente.

Demonstrate [dę-men'-strēt ó dem'-en-strēt], *va.* Demostrar, probar y hacer ver alguna cosa con el mayor grado de certeza.

Demonstration [dem-en-strē'-shun], *s.* 1. Demostración, evidencia, prueba de alguna cosa por principios ciertos. 2. Manifestación, señalamiento. 3. (Mil.) Demostración o despliegue de fuerza: especialmente en un ataque simulado. 4. Manifestación pública, sea aprobatoria o condenatoria; asamblea en masa.

Demonstrative [dę-men'-stra-tiv], *a.* 1. Demostrativo, que prueba de una manera evidente. 2. Demostrativo, el que declara con gran fuerza de expresión sus ideas o sentimientos.

Demonstrator [dem'-en-strē-tęr], *s.* 1. Demostrador, mostrador, enseñador. 2. Manifestante.

Demonstratory [dę-men'-stra-to-ri], *a.* Lo que tiende a demostrar.

Demoralization [dę-mer-al-i-zē'-shun], *s.* Desmoralización; corrupción, estragamiento de costumbres.

Demoralize [dę-mer'-al-aiz], *va.* 1. Desmoralizar, hacer perder la buena moral, corromper las costumbres. 2. Desanimar, descorazonar, acobardar, p. ej. a un ejército, a una multitud.

Demotic [dę-met'-ic], *a.* Demótico, que concierne al pueblo; escrito con caracteres usuales, en contraposición a lo escrito en los jeroglíficos que usaban los sacerdotes egipcios. (Gr.)

Demotion [de-mō'-shun], *s.* 1. (Mil.) Degradación. 2. Descenso de rango o categoría.

Demountable [dę-maunt'-a-bl], *a.* Desarmable, desmontable.

Demulcent [dę-mul'-sent], *a.* (Med.) Emoliente, demulcente, dulcificante.—*s.* Emoliente, medicamento dulcificante, como las substancias mucilaginosas y untuosas.

Demur [dę-mūr'], *vn.* 1. Objetar, poner tachas, objeciones o reparos; suspender el curso de alguna instancia en un tribunal con objeciones y dudas. 2. Vacilar, fluctuar; tener escrúpulo sobre alguna cosa. —*va.* (Ant.) Dudar, tener duda de alguna cosa.

Demur, *s.* Duda, escrúpulo, hesitación, perplejidad, vacilación.

Demure [dę-miūr'], *a.* 1. Sobrio, moderado; reservado; decente. 2. Grave, serio, formal. 3. Gazmoño, modesto con afectación; pacato.

Demurely [dę-miūr'-li], *adv.* Modestamente, con gazmoñería.

Demureness [dę-miūr'-nes], *s.* Gazmoñería, modestia afectada o verdadera, seriedad, gravedad de aspecto.

Demurrage [de-mūr'-ēj], *s.* Demora o gastos de demora, gastos extraordinarios que debe abonar el comerciante al patrón de un buque por el tiempo que se detiene en un puerto fuera de lo estipulado; estadía.

Demurral [dę-mūr'-al], *s.* Demora, detención; sobreseimiento, cesación; interrupción o tardanza en sentenciar un pleito a causa de alguna duda ocurrida.

Demurrer [dę-mūr'-ęr], *s.* 1. El que pone tachas, objeciones o reparos. 2. (For.) Excepción perentoria, cuestión de derecho; alegación que admite los hechos alegados por la parte contraria, pero niega que constituyan causa suficiente de acción.

Demy [dę-mai'], *s.* Marquilla, nombre de una clase de papel.

Den [den], *s.* Caverna, antro; cueva de fieras.

Denary [den'-a-ri], *a.* Lo que contiene diez; decimal.—*s.* Decena.

Denationalize [dī-nash'-un-al-aiz], *va.* Desnacionalizar, quitar a uno los privilegios de la nación a que pertenece.

Denatured [dę-nē'-churd], *a.* Desnaturalizado. *Denatured alcohol*, Alcohol desnaturalizado.

Dendriform [den'-dri-fērm], *a.* *V.* DENDRITIC.

Dendrite [den'-drait], *s.* (Min.) Dendrita, piedra con figuras estampadas de árboles y plantas.

Dendritic [den-drit'-ic], *a.* Dendrítico, con arborizaciones que imitan la forma de un arbusto.

Dendrology [den-drel'-o-ji], *s.* Dendrología, historia natural de los árboles.

Dengue [deŋ'-gē], *s.* Dengue, enfermedad tropical aguda y epidémica. Se llama también *break-bone fever* o *dandy-fever*.

Deniable [dę-nai'-a-bl], *a.* Negable, lo que se puede negar.

Denial [dę'-nai'-al], *s.* Denegación, repulsa. *Self-denial*, Abnegación de sí mismo.

Denier [dę-nai'-ęr], *s.* Contradictor, negador.

Denier [dę-nīr'], *s.* Dinero, antigua moneda de plata en Francia, que valía un penique.

Denigrate [den'-i-grēt], *va.* Denegrecer, denegrir, ennegrecer; denigrar, infamar.

Denim [den'-im], *s.* Mezclilla, tela basta y resistente de algodón.

Denization [den-i-zē'-shun], *s.* Naturalización, ciudadanía, acción de naturalizar a uno en Inglaterra.

Denizen [den'-i-zen], *s.* 1. Ciudadano, habitante, residente. 2. (Der. ingl.) El extranjero naturalizado.

Denizen, *va.* 1. Naturalizar. 2. Eximir, otorgar ciertos privilegios al extranjero naturalizado.

Denominate [dę-nem'-i-nēt], *va.* Denominar, nombrar.

Denomination [dę-nem-i-nē'-shun], *s.* 1. Denominación, título, nombre, designación. 2. Secta, grupo de cristianos que no está de acuerdo con una Iglesia establecida.

Denominative [dę-nem'-i-na-tiv], *a.* Denominativo.

Denominator [dę-nem'-i-nē-tęr], *s.* (Arit.) Denominador.

Denotable [dę-nōt'-a-bl], *a.* Capaz de ser notado o distinguido.

Denotation [dī-no-tē'-shun], *s.* Designación, marca, señal, indicio, notabilidad.

Denote [dę-nōt'], *va.* Denotar, indicar, anunciar, significar, designar, marcar, señalar.

Denotement [dẹ-nōt'-mẹnt], *s.* (Poco us.) Señal, indicación.
Denouement [dê-nū'-mãñ], *s.* Éxito, salida, fin; desenredo, desenlace. (Gal.)
Denounce [dẹ-nauns'], *va.* 1. Denunciar, delatar. 2. Acusar; amenazar; proclamar con amenazas. 3. Promulgar, publicar, declarar alguna cosa solemnemente.
Denouncement [dẹ-nauns'-mẹnt], *s.* Denunciación; acusación o delación.
Denouncer [dẹ-nauns'-ẹr], *s.* 1. Denunciador, acusador. 2. Amenazador.
Dense [dens], *a.* Denso, espeso, compacto, cerrado, apretado.
Densimeter [den-sim'-ẹ-tẹr], *s.* Densímetro, areómetro.
Density [dens'-i-ti], *s.* Densidad, solidez.
Dent [dent], *s.* Abolladura, pequeña depresión que resulta de un golpe; golpe, señal que deja un golpe.
Dent, *va.* Abollar, hacer bollos o huecos poco profundos. *V.* también INDENT.
Dental [den'-tal], *a.* 1. Dental, lo que pertenece a los dientes. 2. (Gram.) Dental, la letra cuya pronunciación requiere que la lengua toque en los dientes, como la d y la th.—*s.* (Ict.) Dentón, pescado.
Dentate, Dentated [den'-têt-ed], *a.* Dentado.
Dentelli, *s.* *V.* MODILLIONS.
Denticle [den'-ti-cl], *s.* Dientecillo, punto saliente.
Denticulate [den-tic'-yu-lêt], **Denticulated** [den-tic'-yu-lê-ted], *a.* (Bot.) Dentado, provisto de pequeños dientes.
Denticulation [den-tic-yu-lé'-shun], *s.* Dentadura, la fila de dientes pequeños que tienen algunas máquinas o instrumentos.
Dentifrice [den'-ti-fris], *s.* Dentífrico, lo que sirve para limpiar los dientes.
Dentil [den'-til], *s.* (Arq.) Dentículo, moldura o adorno en figura de diente.
Dentirostral [den-ti-ros'-tral], *a.* Dentirrostro, (pájaro) de pico dentado.
Dentist [den'-tist], *s.* Dentista.
Dentition [den-tish'-un], *s.* 1. Dentición, el procedimiento o la época de endentecer. 2. Dentadura peculiar a un animal.
Dentoid [den'-toid], *a.* Parecido a un diente; en figura de diente.
Denudate [dẹ-niū'-det], *a.* Desnudo; despojado, quitado; en especial, sin escamas, follaje u otra cubierta.
Denudation [den-yu-dé'-shun], *s.* 1. Despojo de ropa, la acción de desnudar o quitar la ropa. 2. (Cir.) Denudación. 3. (Geol.) Erosión, desprendimiento de la parte sólida de la tierra de suerte que los estratos en otro tiempo cubiertos quedan expuestos a la vista.
Denude [dẹ-niūd'], *va.* Desnudar, despojar, privar.
Denunciate [dẹ-nun'-shi-êt], *vn.* Denunciar, amenazar.
Denunciation [dẹ-nun-shi-é'-shun], *s.* 1. Denunciación, acusación; proceso, autos. 2. Publicación, declaración.
Denunciator [dẹ-nun'-shi-ê-tẹr], *s.* Denunciador, denunciante, delator.
Deny [dẹ-nai'], *va.* 1. Negar, contradecir, desmentir. 2. Rehusar, no conceder. 3. Renunciar, no reconocer, desconocer. 4. Abjurar, renegar, desdecirse. 5. Negarse a, no dejarse ver de.—*vn.* Decir que no; replicar negativamente; declarar algo no verdadero. *To deny one's self,* (1) Hacer abnegación de sí mismo, negarse lo agradable o lo necesario; (2) negarse, no dejarse ver de, no recibir a.
Deobstruct [di-ob-struct'], *va.* Desembarazar, desobstruir, abrir.
Deodand [di'-o-dand], *s.* (Ant. Ley inglesa) El animal o cosa causante de la muerte de una persona y que, por lo mismo, era confiscada a favor de la corona para usos piadosos.
Deodorant [di-ō'-dẹr-ant], *s.* Desodorante, agente que destruye los malos olores.
Deodorize [di-ō'-dẹr-aiz], *va.* Modificar o disipar el olor de algo, p. ej. con el empleo de desinfectantes; dícese especialmente de olores perjudiciales a la salud.
Deontology [di''-on-tol'-o-ji], *s.* Deontología, ciencia que trata de los deberes y obligaciones morales.
Deoxidize [di-oc'-si-daiz], **Deoxidate** [di-oc'-si-dêt], *va.* (Quím.) Desoxigenar, desoxidar.
Deoxyribonucleic acid [di-ox-i-ri-bo-nū-clé'-ic a'-sid], *s.* Acido deoxiribonucleico.
Depaint [dẹ-pênt'], *va.* (Ant.) Pintar, describir, representar una cosa.
Depart [dẹ-pārt'], *vn.* 1. Partir, marcharse, empezar a caminar. 2. Desistir; renunciar o dejar alguna cosa a que uno estaba antes acostumbrado; desviarse. 3. Perderse, desaparecer. 4. Desertar, apostatar. 5. Apartarse de algún intento u opinión. 6. Morir, fallecer.—*va.* (Ant.) Dejar. *To depart from,* Desviarse, alejarse, apartarse, desistir.
Departer [dẹ-pārt'-ẹr], *s.* 1. El que se marcha. 2. Refinador de metales.
Departing [dẹ-pārt'-ing], *s.* Partida, ida.
Department [dẹ-pārt'-mẹnt], *s.* 1. Departamento, parte de un todo muy extenso; subdivisión de una empresa, organización o gobierno; ramo de una ciencia. 2. Negociado, despacho. 3. Departamento, provincia o distrito de algún país; distrito de marina.
Departmental [dẹ-pārt-mẹnt'-al], *a.* Departamental.
Departure [dẹ-pār'-chur], *s.* 1. Partida, el acto de partir, de alejarse de un lugar. 2. Muerte. 3. Desamparo, abandono; desistimiento. 4. (Mar.) Diferencia de meridiano.
Depauperate [dẹ-pō'-pẹr-êt], *va.* Empobrecer, hacer pobre a alguno.
Depend [dẹ-pend'], *vn.* 1. Pender, colgar, estar alguna cosa pendiente de otra. 2. Depender, estar sujeto o dependiente de algún superior. 3. Necesitar del auxilio o apoyo de alguna persona. *To depend on* o *upon,* Contar con, confiar, esperar con confianza, descuidar en una persona, dejar a su cuidado una cosa, estar seguro de.
Dependable [dẹ-pend'-a-bl], *a.* Digno de confianza, seguro.
Dependance, Dependancy, *s.* *V.* DEPENDENCE, DEPENDENCY.
Dependant [dẹ-pend'-ant], **Dependent** [dẹ-pend'-ent], *s.* Dependiente, subalterno.—*a.* 1. Dependiente, subordinado, sujeto. 2. Contingente, casual, accidental. 3. Que necesita socorro o ayuda; necesitado. 4. Pendiente, colgante, que cuelga.
Dependence [dẹ-pend'-ens], *s.* 1. Dependencia, estado de dependiente; de aquí, seguridad, esperanza firme. 2. Dependencia, sujeción, inferioridad. 3. Aquello con que uno cuenta, o en que confía, o en lo que descansa; apoyo. *He was their main dependence,* Él fué su principal apoyo. 4. La acción y efecto de pender o estar una cosa pendiente de otra.
Dependency [dẹ-pend'-en-si], *s.* 1. La cosa dependiente de otra. 2. Lugar, territorio o estado sometido a otro. 3. Edificio auxiliar, cerca del principal. 4. Dependencia, sujeción.
Depender [dẹ-pend'-ẹr], *s.* Dependiente.
Depending [dẹ-pend'-ing], *pa.* Pendiente.
Depersonalize [di-pẹr'-sUn-al-aiz], *va.* Hacer impersonal.
‖**Dephlegmate** [dẹ-fleg'-mêt], *va.* (Quím.) Deflegmar, separar la parte acuosa contenida en los líquidos espirituosos.
Depict [dẹ-pict'], *va.* Pintar, representar, retratar, describir.
Depicture [dẹ-pic'-chur], *va.* Representar por medio de la pintura o de las palabras; pintar, retratar, describir.
Depilate [dep'-i-lêt], *va.* Quitar el vello o pelo.
Depilation [dep-i-lé'-shun], *s.* La acción y el efecto de arrancar o quitar el vello o pelo.
Depilatory [dẹ-pil'-a-to-ri], *s.* Atanquía, ungüento para hacer caer el cabello.—*a.* Depilatorio.
Deplete [dẹ-plit'], *va.* 1. Reducir, disminuir, agotar, disipar; vaciar. 2. Disminuir la cantidad de sangre, p. ej. en los vasos del cuerpo.
Depletion [dẹ-pli'-shun], *s.* 1. Vaciamiento. 2. (Med.) Depleción, la acción de disminuir la cantidad de sangre en los vasos del cuerpo.
Depletive, Depletory [dẹ-pli'-tiv, dep'-lẹ-to-ri], *a.* Depletivo, que causa la depleción o tiende a ella.
Deplorable [dẹ-plōr'-a-bl], *a.* 1. Deplorable, lamentable, miserable. 2. Despreciado; lastimoso.
Deplorableness [dẹ-plōr'-a-bl-nes], *s.* Estado deplorable.
Deplorably [dẹ-plōr'-a-bli], *adv.* Deplorablemente, lastimosamente, infelizmente.
Deplore [dẹ-plōr'], *va.* Deplorar, lamentar, llorar.
Deploredly [dẹ-plōr'-ed-li], *adv.* Vilmente.
Deplorer [dẹ-plōr'-ẹr], *s.* Lamentador, llorón.
Deploy [dẹ-ploi'], *va.* y *vn.* (Mil.) Desplegar, extender el frente de batalla; marchar a la derecha o a la izquierda o por ambos lados.—*s.* Acción de desplegar.
Deplumation [dep-lu-mé'-shun], *s.* 1. Muda, tiempo o acto de mudar las aves sus plumas. 2. Caída de las pestañas.
Deplume [dẹ-plūm'], *va.* Desplumar, quitar las plumas; despojar del plumaje.
Depolarization [di-pō-lar-i-zé'-shun], *s.* Despolarización.
Depone [dẹ-pōn'], *va.* Deponer, testificar, declarar en justicia.
Deponent [dẹ-pō'-nent], *s.* 1. Deponente, declarante. 2. (Gram.) Verbo deponente.
Depopulate [dẹ-pep'-yu-lêt], *va.* Despoblar, devastar, asolar, destruir, arruinar.—*vn.* Despoblarse.
Depopulation [dẹ-pep-yu-lé'-shun], *s.* Despoblación; devastación.

Depopulator [dę-pep'-yu-lê-tęr], *s.* Despoblador, asolador.
Deport [dę-pōrt'], *va.* 1. Deportar, desterrar por castigo á un punto lejano. 2. *vr.* (Con *one's self*) Portarse, conducirse, gobernarse.
Deportation [dī-per-tê'-shun], *s.* Deportación, destierro, estrañamiento de un país.
Deportment [dę-pōrt'-męnt], *s.* Porte, conducta, manejo.
Deposable [dę-pōz'-a-bl], *a.* Capaz de ser depuesto.
Deposal [dę-poz'-al], *s.* (Ant.) Destronamiento, deposición; destitución, degradación de honores.
Depose [dę-pōz'], *va.* 1. Deponer. 2. Destronar, privar del trono. 3. Deponer, degradar o destituir á alguna persona de los empleos, dignidades y honores que tenía. 4. Deponer, testificar.—*vn.* Ser testigo.
Deposer [dę-pōz'-ęr], *s.* 1. Desposeedor, el que depone o degrada. 2. Testigo, deponente.
Deposing [dę-pōz'-ing], *s.* Deposición.
Deposit [dę-poz'-it], *va.* 1. Depositar, resguardar; consignar; apartar. 2. Confiar a la guarda de alguien; poner dinero en un banco.
Deposit, *s.* 1. Depósito, sedimento, poso, heces; precipitado. 2. Depósito, cosa confiada como fianza; fianza, prenda.
Depositary [dę-poz'-i-tę-ri], *s.* 1. Depositario, guardián. 2. Almacén, sitio o paraje donde se hacen los depósitos.
Depositing [dę-poz'-it-ing], *s.* El acto de apartar o depositar.
Deposition [dep-o-zish'-un], *s.* 1. Deposición, testimonio, declaración ante juez o escribano. 2. Deposición, el acto de deponer o desposeer a un príncipe de su corona. 3. Destitución, privación del empleo u honores que gozaba alguna persona.
Depositor [dę-poz'-it-er], *s.* Depositante (en un banco, etc.)
Depository [dę-poz'-i-to-ri], *s.* 1. Depositaría, sitio ó paraje donde se hacen los depósitos. 2. (Poco us.) Depositario.
Depositum, *s.* *V.* DEPOSIT.
Depot [dī'-pō o dę-pō'], *s.* 1. Pósito, almacén público o principal. 2. Despacho, oficina de la administración de diligencias, coches de camino, etc.; en los E. U. del Norte, estación de un ferrocarril. En este sentido la palabra es menos usada que en otro tiempo. 3. Estación, almacén o depósito militar.
Depravation [dep-ra-vê'-shun], *s.* 1. El acto de depravar. 2. Depravación, corrupción, estragamiento del gusto o costumbres.
Deprave [dę-prêv'], *va.* Depravar, pervertir, corromper, viciar, estragar; alterar, falsificar; difamar.
Depraved [dę-prêvd'], *a.* Depravado, viciado, abandonado, corrompido.
Depravedly [dę-prêv'-ed-li], *adv.* Corrompidamente, depravadamente.
Depravedness [dę-prêv'-ed-nes], *s.* Depravación, corrupción, estragamiento, malignidad.
Depraver [dę-prêv'-ęr], *s.* Depravador.
Depraving [dę-prêv'-ing], *s.* Depravación.
Depravity [dę-prav'-i-ti], *s.* Depravación, desorden, estragamiento de costumbres, gusto, etc.; corrupción, desorden; maldad, ruindad, malignidad.
Deprecable [dep'-rę-ca-bl], *a.* Capaz de ser suplicado.
Deprecate [dep'-rę-kêt], *va.* Deprecar, rogar, suplicar, con eficacia ó instancia; pedir o desear que no suceda algún mal o verse libre de él.
Deprecation [dep-rę-kê'-shun], *s.* Súplica para conjurar o evitar los males; deprecación, ruego, petición.
Deprecative [dep'-rę-ca-tiv], **Deprecatory** [dep'-rę-ca-to-ri], *a.* Deprecativo, deprecatorio, suplicante.
Deprecator [dep'-rę-kê"-tęr], *s.* Deprecante.
Depreciate [dę-prī'-shi-êt], *va.* 1. Rebajar el valor o precio de alguna cosa. 2. Despreciar, menospreciar, deprimir. — *vn.* Desvalorizarse, amortizar.
Depreciation [dę-prī-shi-ê'-shun], *s.* Depreciación, descrédito, desestimación; baja, reducción de precio.
Depreciative, Depreciatory [dę-prī'-shi-ę-tiv, ę-to-ri], *a.* Despreciativo, que causa desprecio.
Depreciator [dę-prī'-shi-ę-tęr], *s.* Despreciador.
Depredate [dep'-rę-dêt], *va.* 1. Saquear, robar, pillar. 2. Desolar, destruir, arruinar, asolar.
Depredation [dep-rę-dê'-shun], *s.* Depredación, pillaje, saqueo, saco, devastación.
Depredator [dep'-rę-dê-tęr], *s.* Saqueador; rapiñador, ladrón.
Depredatory [dep"-rę-dê'-to-ri], *a.* Que pilla, roba o saquea.
Depress [dę-pres'], *va.* 1. Bajar, comprimir, apretar hacia abajo; dejar caer. 2. Bajar, minorar, disminuir; reducir el precio. 3. Desalentar, desanimar; entristecer.
Depressed [dę-prest'], *a.* 1. Deprimido, comprimido. 2. Rebajado, disminuído. 3. Desanimado, entristecido. 4. (Biol.) Deprimido, hundido, hondo.
Depression [dę-presh'-un], *s.* 1. Compresión, la acción de comprimir o apretar hacia abajo. 2. Depresión; abatimiento. 3. Lo que está apretado hacia abajo; concavidad ligera, hueco poco profundo.
Depressive [dę-pres'-iv], *a.* Depresivo.
Depressor [dę-pres'-ęr], *s.* 1. Depresor. 2. Opresor.
Deprivation [dep-ri-vê'-shun], *s.* 1. Privación. 2. Pérdida. 3. Amovilidad.
Deprive [dę-praiv'], *va.* 1. Privar, despojar, quitar a uno algo. 2. Excluir; impedir. 3. Librar, libertar.
Depriver [dę-praiv'-ęr], *s.* El que priva, despoja o quita.
Depth [depth], *s.* 1. Hondura, profundidad; abismo. 2. Espesor; extensión o distancia hacia dentro, hacia atrás o hacia arriba (del cielo). 3. Centro, punto medio, corazón, fondo de una cosa. *In the depth of winter*, En el rigor del invierno. 4. Obscuridad, o riqueza, viveza, del color; gravedad del sonido. 5. Sagacidad, penetración, conocimiento. 6. Profundidad, extrema extensión; inmensidad. *Beyond one's depth*, (Fig.) Más allá o fuera, en exceso de las fuerzas o la capacidad de uno.
Depth bomb [depth bem], *s.* Bomba de profundidad.
Depthless [depth'-les], *a.* Superficial, sin profundidad.
Depurant [dep'-yu-rant], *a.* Depuratorio, depurativo.
Depurate [dep'-yu-rêt], *va.* Depurar, limpiar, purgar, purificar.
Depurate, *a.* Depurado, limpio, purificado, puro; libre.
Depuration [dep-yu-rê'-shun], *s.* Depuración.
Depurative [dep'-yu-rę-tiv], *a.* *V.* DEPURANT.
Deputation [dep-yu-tê'-shun], *s.* Diputación; comisión.
Depute [dę-piūt'], *va.* Diputar, destinar, señalar, enviar, detener.
Deputize [dep'-yu-taiz], *va.* (E. U.) Diputar. *V.* DEPUTE.
Deputy [dep'-yu-ti], *s.* Diputado, comisario, delegado, enviado, agente. *Lord deputy*, Virrey. *Deputy governor*, Teniente gobernador.
‡**Deracinate** [dę-ras'-i-nêt], *va.* Desarraigar, arrancar de raíz; abolir, extirpar.
Derail [dī-rêl'], *va.* Hacer descarrilar, echar fuera de los carriles.—*vn.* Descarrilar, o desviarse del carril en las vías férreas.
Derailment [dī-rêl'-męnt], *s.* Descarrilamiento, desvío de los carriles.
Derange [dę-rênj'], *va.* Desarreglar, desordenar. desconcertar.
Derangement [dę-rênj'-męnt], *s.* Desarreglo, desorden; enajenamiento del ánimo; confusión, desbarato.
Derby [dęr'-bi, dār'-bi, en Inglaterra], *s.* 1. Derby, famosa carrera anual de caballos en Epsom, condado de Surrey. 2. (E. U.) Sombrero hongo.
Derelict [der'-ę-lict], *a.* Abandonado voluntariamente.—*s.* (For.) Toda propiedad abandonada voluntariamente al mar.
Dereliction [der-ę-lic'-shun], *s.* Desamparo, abandono; dejación de bienes.
Deride [dę-raid'], *va.* Burlar, mofar, escarnecer; zumbar o dar zumba, poner en ridículo.
Derider [dę-raid'-ęr], *s.* Burlón, zumbón, soflamero.
Deridingly [dę-raid'-ing-li], *adv.* Irrisoriamente, con zumba.
Derision [dę-rizh'-un], *s.* Irrisión, mofa, escarnio, burla, chulada.
Derisive [dę-rai'-siv], **Derisory** [dę-rai'-so-ri], *a.* Irrisorio, hecho por mofa o escarnio.
Derisively [dę-rai'-siv-li], *adv.* Irrisoriamente.
Derivable [dę-raiv'-a-bl], *a.* 1. Lo que se puede adquirir por derecho de descendencia. 2. Derivable, deducible, lo que se puede derivar o deducir.
Derivation [dęr-i-vê'-shun], *s.* 1. Derivación, la acción de derivar. 2. Etimología de una voz. 3. (Biol.) Derivación, descendencia. 4. (Med.) Derivación, reducción de la inflamación por medio de un vejigatorio. 5. (Des.) La acción de sacar o desviar agua de un río para formar una acequia.
Derivative [dę-riv'-a-tiv], *a.* y *s.* Derivativo.
Derive [dę-raiv'], *va.* 1. Derivar, repartir o distribuir el agua de algún canal en otros muchos. 2. Derivar, deducir o sacar una cosa de algún origen, causa o principio: recibir por transmisión. 3. Comunicar.—*vn.* (Con *from*) Derivar, derivarse, nacer; descender, proceder; participar.
Deriver [de-raiv'-ęr], *s.* El que deriva o deduce.
Derm [dęrm], *s.* Dermis, cutis. Equivalentes: DERMA, DERMIS.
Dermal, Dermic [dęr'-mal, dęr'-mic], *a.* Dérmico, cutáneo, perteneciente al cutis.
Derma-, Dermato-, Dermo-. Prefijos o bien formas de combinación en

voces científicas, y que significan cutis.

Dermatologist [dẹr-ma-tel'-o-jist], *s.* Dermatólogo.

Dermatology [dẹr-ma-tel'-o-ji], *s.* Dermatología o dermología, ciencia que trata de la piel y sus enfermedades.

Derogate [der'-o-gêt], *va.* 1. ‖Menospreciar. 2. (Ant.) Derogar, revocar, anular, abrogar, invalidar.—*vn.* (Con *from*) Detraer, detractar.

Derogate, *a.* Derogado; desacreditado, envilecido.

Derogately [der'-o-gêt-li], **Derogatorily** [dẹ-reg'-a-to-ri-li], *adv.* Derogativamente.

Derogation [der-o-gé'-shun], *s.* Derogación; desestimación.

Derogative [dẹ-reg'-a-tiv], *a.* Derogatorio, derogativo.

Derogatoriness [dẹ-reg'-a-to-ri-nes], *s.* Derogación; detracción.

Derogatory [dẹ-reg'-a-to-ri], *a.* Derogatorio.

Derrick [der'-ic], *s.* 1. Grúa. 2. Torre de perforación.

Dervish [dẹr'-vish], *s.* 1. Derviche, fakir, santón mendicante mahometano. 2. (Neol.) Partidario del Madí en el Sudán. (Turco.)

Descant [des'-cant], *s.* 1. (Mús.) Discante, melodía; variación, modulación. 2. Discurso, comentario, paráfrasis, disertación.

Descant [des-cant'], *vn.* Discantar: discurrir, comentar larga y pesadamente.

Descanting [des-cant'-ing], *s.* Conjetura, presunción.

Descend [dẹ-send'], *vn.* 1. Descender, bajar. 2. Descender, derivarse, traer o tomar su origen. 3. Descender, tocar o venir a algún sucesor por orden de herencia. 4. (Con *on* o *upon*) Invadir. 5. Pasar de lo general a lo particular.—*va.* Descender, andar hacia abajo. *To descend to* o *into,* Descender o entrar en; bajarse a. *To descend into one's self,* Entrar en sí mismo.

Descendable, *a.* *V.* DESCENDIBLE.

Descendant [dẹ-send'-ant], *s.* 1. Descendiente. 2. Descendencia, posteridad.

Descendent [dẹ-send'-ent], *a.* 1. Descendente, lo que se cae, hunde o viene abajo. 2. Descendiente, que desciende de otro.

Descendibility [dẹ-send-i-bil'-i-ti], *s.* Cualidad de ser transmisible, como una herencia; conformidad con las leyes de descendencia.

Descendible [dẹ-send'-i-bl], *a.* Lo que puede descender, bajar o bajarse; transmisible.

Descension [dẹ-sen'-shun], *s.* 1. Descendimiento, descensión, descenso; declinación, caída. 2. Degradación.

Descent [dẹ-sent'], *s.* 1. Descenso, bajada, descendimiento; descensión; pendiente, declive. 2. Alcurnia, descendencia, origen, nacimiento, linaje. 3. Descendencia, posteridad, herederos. *Of a noble descent,* De nacimiento ilustre. 4. Descendencia, sucesión. 5. Invasión, acción de invadir el enemigo. 6. Oblicuidad, inclinación; degradación.

Describe [dẹ-scraib'], *va.* Describir, delinear, figurar; explicar, definir; representar.

Describer [dẹ-scraib'-ẹr], *s.* Descriptor.

Descrier [dẹ-scrai'-ẹr], *s.* Descubridor; averiguador.

Description [dẹ-scrip'-shun], *s.* 1. Descripción, representación. 2. Clase, género, naturaleza, calidad.

Descriptive [dẹ-scrip'-tiv], *a.* Descriptivo.

Descry [dẹ-scrai'], *va.* 1. Espiar, observar, reconocer de lejos. 2. Columbrar, avistar, divisar; describir; averiguar.

Desecrate [des'-ẹ-crêt], *va.* Profanar.

Desecration [des-ẹ-cré'-shun], *s.* Profanación. *Desecration of a grave.* Profanación de sepultura.

Desegregate [dẹ-seg'-rẹ-gêt], *va.* Suprimir la segregación.

Desegregation [dẹ-seg-rẹ-gé'-shun], *s.* Supresión de la segregación.

Desert [dez'-ẹrt], *s.* Desierto, yermo; soledad.—*a.* Desierto, desamparado, despoblado, inhabitado, solitario.

Desert [dẹ-zẹrt'], *s.* (Muy usado en plural.) 1. Merecimiento. 2. Mérito, virtud.

Desert [dẹ-zẹrt'], *va.* 1. Desamparar, dejar, abandonar. 2. Desertar.—*vn.* Desertar; ausentarse; apartarse.

Deserter [dẹ-zẹrt'-ẹr], *s.* Desertor, tránsfuga.

Desertion [dẹ-zẹr'-shun], *s.* Deserción; abandono.

Desertless [dẹ-zẹrt'-les], *a.* (Poco us.) Indigno, sin mérito.

‖**Desertlessly** [dẹ-zẹrt'-les-li], *adv.* Desmerecidamente.

Deserve [dẹ-zẹrv'], *va.* Merecer, tener derecho a, ser digno de.

Deservedly [dẹ-zẹrv'-ed-li], *adv.* Merecidamente, dignamente.

Deserving [dẹ-zẹrv'-ing], *a.* Meritorio, digno de recompensa o de elogio.—*s.* Mérito. *V.* DESERT.

Deservingly [dẹ-zẹrv'-ing-li], *adv.* Dignamente, merecidamente.

Desiccant [des'-i-cant o dẹ-sic'-ant], *a.* Desecante, que enjuga o deseca.—*s.* (Med.) Desecante.

Desiccate [des'-i-kêt o dẹ-sic'-kêt], *va.* Desecar, enjugar, quitar la humedad a alguna cosa, hacer evaporar; secar, hacer secar.—*vn.* Secarse.

Desiccative [des'-i-kê-tiv o dẹ-sic'-a-tiv], *a.* Desecativo, que tiene la propiedad de desecar.

Desideratum [dẹ-sid''-ẹ-ré'-tum], *s.* Desiderátum, lo que hace mucha falta o que mucho se desea.

Design [dẹ-zain'], *va.* 1. Proponer, pensar, tener intención de; dedicar. 2. Diseñar, hacer el diseño de alguna cosa. 3. Designar, idear, determinar, proyectar. 4. Tramar, maquinar.—*vn.* 1. Proponerse. 2. Tener por empleo hacer diseños, ya sean artísticos o para la industria.

Design, *s.* 1. Dibujo, diseño, trazo. 2. Designio, mira, intento, intención. 3. Empresa; fin, motivo, objeto. 4. Plan, proyecto; treta en perjuicio de otro. *Through design,* Expresamente, con toda intención, adrede.

Designable [dẹ-zain'-a-bl], *a.* Lo que se puede diseñar o pintar.

Designable [des'-ig-na-bl], *a.* Lo que se puede designar o señalar; distinguible.

Designate, *va.* 1. Apuntar, señalar; distinguir. 2. Designar, nombrar, identificar por el nombre. 3. Designar, destinar alguna persona o cosa para determinado fin.

Designation [des-ig-né'-shun], *s.* 1. Designación, señalamiento, título. 2. Nombramiento, nominación. 3. (Ant.) Descripción, carácter, suerte o clase.

Designative [des'-ig-nê-tiv], *a.* Designativo, especificante.

Designedly [dẹ-zain'-ed-li], *adv.* Adrede, de propósito, de caso pensado, de intento.

Designer [dẹ-zain'-ẹr], *s.* 1. Dibujante, diseñador; inventor; proyectista. 2. Maquinador.

Designing [dẹ-zain'-ing], *a.* Insidioso, mal intencionado; astuto, artero.—*s.* Dibujo, diseño, acto o arte de diseñar.

Designingly [dẹ-zain'-ing-li], *adv.* Insidiosamente.

Designless [dẹ-zain'-les], *a.* Inadvertido; sin intención.

Designlessly [dẹ-zain'-les-li], *adv.* Inadvertidamente.

Desinence [des'-i-nens], *s.* Terminación, sufijo, afijo, desinencia.

Desirability [dẹ-zair''-a-bil'-i-ti], *s.* Calidad de lo apetecible. *V.* DESIRABLENESS.

Desirable [dẹ-zair'-a-bl], *a.* Agradable, gustoso; deseable, apetecible.

Desirableness [dẹ-zair'-a-bl-nes], *s.* Ansia, afán; calidad de apetecible.

Desire [dẹ-zair'], *s.* Deseo, anhelo; ansia, apetito.

Desire, *va.* Desear, apetecer; rogar, suplicar, pedir. *To leave nothing to be desired,* No dejar nada que desear. *I desire you to come immediately,* Ruego a Vd. que venga en seguida.

Desireless [dẹ-zair'-les], *a.* Sin deseo, sin ansia, indiferente.

Desirer [dẹ-zair'-ẹr], *s.* Deseador.

Desiring [dẹ-zair'-ing], *s.* Deseo.

Desirous [dẹ-zair'-us], *a.* Deseoso, ansioso. *To be desirous of honours or riches,* Tener ambición de honores o riquezas.

Desirously [dẹ-zair'-us-li], *adv.* Ansiosamente.

Desirousness [dẹ-zair'-us-nes], *s.* Deseo vivo, anhelo.

Desist [dẹ-zist'], *vn.* Desistir, dejar o cesar de hacer alguna cosa; detenerse.

Desistance [dẹ-zist'-ans], *s.* Desistencia, desistimiento, cesación.

Desk [desc], *s.* 1. Bufete, mesa de escribir, escritorio. 2. Pupitre. *Roll-top desk,* Escritorio de tapa corrediza.

Desmid [des'-mid], *s.* Desmidia, planta de hermoso color verde, tipo de un orden de algas microscópicas.

Desmo-. Forma de combinación, derivada del griego desmos, lazo, ligamento.

Desmography [des-meg'-ra-fi], *s.* Desmografía, descripción de los ligamentos del cuerpo.

Desolate [des'-o-let], *a.* Desolado, desierto, despoblado, solitario; abandonado, arruinado, destruido.

Desolate [des'-o-lêt], *va.* Desolar, despoblar, devastar, arruinar.

Desolately [des'-o-let-li], *adv.* De un modo desolador.

Desolateness [des'-o-let-nes], *s.* Desolación, condición desolada.

Desolater, Desolator [des'-o-lé''-tẹr, tẹr], *s.* Desolador, asolador.

Desolating [des'-o-lêt-ing], *s.* El acto de desolar.

Desolation [des-o-lé'-shun], *s.* 1. Desolación, desolamiento, estrago, ruina, destrucción. 2. Desolación, aflicción, desconsuelo; melancolía; destitución. 3. Desierto.

Despair [dẹ-spär'], *s.* Desconfianza, desesperación.

Despair, *vn.* Desesperar, perder la esperanza.

Despairer [dẹ-spär'-ẹr], *s.* Desesperado.

Despairingly [dẹ-spār'-ing-li], *adv.* Desesperadamente.
Despatch [des-pach'], *va.* 1. Despachar, aviar, enviar con prisa y diligencia. 2. Despachar, matar, quitar la vida. 3. Despachar, abreviar, concluir una cosa con prontitud.
Despatch, Dispatch [des o dis-pach'], *s.* 1. Despacho, embarque. 2. Expedición, prontitud. 3. Despacho, oficio o mensaje enviado rápidamente, generalmente por medio del telégrafo. *Despatch boat,* Aviso, embarcación ligera para llevar despachos del gobierno o de un buque de guerra a otro.—*va.* Despachar, embarcar, remitir, enviar.
Despatcher [dẹ-spach'-ẹr], *s.* 1. Despachador, el que despacha. 2. Expedidor, el que envía géneros de un punto a otro. 3. El que ejecuta algún negocio.
Despatchful [dẹ-spach'-ful], *a.* Diligente, expedito.
Desperado [des-pe-rê'-do o ā'-dō], *s.* Hombre desesperado, atrevido, furioso; un rufián, un perdido. (Esp.)
Desperate [des'-pe-ret], *a.* 1. Desesperado, sin esperanza. 2. Arrojado, arriesgado. 3. Desesperado, lo que no tiene remedio. 4. Furioso, inconsiderado, violento, terrible. 5. (Fam.) Consumado, rematado.—*s.* Perdido, el que es atrevido y no tiene esperanza ni miedo.
Desperately [des'-pe-ret-li], *adv.* Desesperadamente, furiosamente.
Desperateness [des'-pe-ret-nes], *s.* Precipitación, temeridad, arrojo, furia, violencia.
Desperation [des-pe-rê'-shun], *s.* Desesperación, furor, encarnizamiento.
Despicable [des'-pi-ca-bl], *a.* Despreciable, vil, bajo.
Despicableness [des'-pi-ca-bl-nes], *s.* Bajeza, vileza.
Despicably [des'-pi-ca-bli], *adv.* Vilmente, bajamente.
Despisable [dẹ-spaiz'-a-bl], *a.* Despreciable.
Despisal [dẹ-spaiz'-al], *s.* (Poco us.) Desdén, desprecio.
Despise [dẹ-spaiz'], *va.* Despreciar, desestimar, menospreciar; desdeñar.
Despised [dẹ-spaizd'], *a.* Desestimado, despreciado; detestado.
Despisedness [dẹ-spaiz'-ed-nes], *s.* Envilecimiento, bajeza, abatimiento.
Despiser [dẹ-spaiz'-ẹr], *s.* Despreciador.
Despising [dẹ-spaiz'-ing], *s.* Desdén, desprecio.
Despite [dẹ-spait'], *s.* Despecho, ira, enojo; desdén con reto; malicia, malignidad, malevolencia.
Despite, *va.* (Ant.) Molestar, enfadar.
Despite, *prep.* A despecho de, a pesar de.
Despiteful [dẹ-spait'-ful], *a.* Malicioso, rencoroso, vengativo, maligno.
Despitefully [dẹ spait'-ful-i], *adv.* Malignamente, maliciosamente.
Despitefulness [dẹ-spait'-ful-nes], *s.* Malignidad, rencor, odio, mala voluntad, malicia.
Despoil [dẹ-spoil'], *va.* (Con *of*) 1. Despojar; privar. 2. (Ant.) Desnudar.
Despoiler [dẹ-spoil'-ẹr], *s.* Pillador, saqueador, robador.
Despoliation [dẹ-spo-li-ē'-shun], *s.* Despojo, la acción de despojar.
Despond [dẹ-spend'], *vn.* Desconfiar, desalentarse, abatirse; desesperanzar, desesperar, decaer de ánimo.
Despondency [dẹ-spend'-en-si], *s.* Desconfianza, temor; desaliento, desmayo; descaecimiento de ánimo. Escríbese también **Despondence.**
Despondent [dẹ-spend'-ent], *a.* Abatido, melancólico, desanimado.
Desponder [dẹ-spend'-ẹr], *s.* El que no tiene esperanza.
Despondingly [dẹ-spend'-ing-li], *adv.* Desconfiadamente.
Despot [des'-pet], *s.* Déspota, señor absoluto.
Despotic, Despotical [des-pet'-ic, al], *a.* Despótico, absoluto, independiente.
Despotically [des-pet'-ic-al-i], *adv.* Despóticamente, arbitrariamente.
Despoticalness [des-pet'-ic-al-nes], *s.* Despotismo, absolutismo.
Despotism [des'-po-tizm], *s.* Despotismo, tiranía, gobierno arbitrario.
¿**Despumate** [des'-piu-met o dẹ-spiū'-mêt], *vn.* Arrojar, desembarazarse de las impurezas en forma de espuma.—*va.* Espumar, despumar, quitar la espuma de algún líquido.
Despumation [des-piu-mê'-shun], *s.* Despumación.
Desquamate [des'-cwa-mêt], *vn.* Despojarse de las escamas o de la epidermis; exfoliarse.
Desquamation [des-cwa-mê'-shun], *s.* Descamación, exfoliación de la epidermis, como en el sarampión y la escarlatina.
Dessert [dez-zẹrt'], *s.* Postres, las frutas, dulces y otras cosas que se sirven al fin de las comidas; ramillete, en las mesas de lujo.
Destinate [des'-ti-nêt], *va.* (Des.) *V.* DESTINE.
Destination [des-ti-nê'-shun], *s.* Destinación, destino; paradero.
Destine [des'-tin], *va.* 1. Destinar, señalar, determinar. 2. Dedicar, consagrar. 3. Preordinar, predestinar, prescribir, decretar.
Destiny [des'-ti-ni], *s.* Destino, hado, fatalidad, fortuna, suerte; signo, estrella, hablando vulgarmente.
Destitute [des'-ti-tiūt], *a.* Destituído, abandonado, desamparado; falto, desprovisto, privado; olvidado.
Destitution [des-ti-tiū'-shun], *s.* 1. Destitución, privación, desamparo, abandono. 2. Pobreza extrema.
Destroy [dẹ-strei'], *va.* 1. Destruir, asolar, arrasar, demoler, arruinar; matar, quitar la vida; acabar, aniquilar. 2. Demostrar ser falso; confutar.
Destroyable [dẹ-strei'-a-bl], *a.* (Poco us.) Destruíble.
Destroyer [dẹ-strei'-ẹr], *s.* 1. Torpedero de alta mar. 2. Destructor.
Destructibility [dẹ-struct-i-bil'-i-ti], *s.* Destructibilidad.
Destructible [dẹ-struct'-i-bl], *a.* Destruíble, destructible.
Destruction [dẹ-struc'-shun], *s.* 1. Destrucción, ruina, asolamiento. 2. Mortandad, destrozo. 3. Causa de desolación. 4. Perdición, muerte eterna.
Destructive [dẹ-struct'-iv], *a.* Destructivo, destructor, ruinoso, fatal.
Destructively [dẹ-struct'-iv-li], *adv.* Destructivamente.
Destructiveness [dẹ-struct'-iv-nes], *s.* 1. Propiedad de destruir. 2. (Frenol.) Destructibilidad, inclinación a destruir o matar.
Destructor [dẹ-struct'-ẹr], *s.* 1. Horno para quemar los desperdicios. 2. (Des.) Destruidor, consumidor.
Desudation [des-yu-dê'-shun], *s.* Sudor excesivo.
Desuetude [des'-wẹ-tiūd], *s.* Desuso; †desuetud.
Desultoriness [des'-ul-to-ri-nes], *s.* 1. Inconstancia, el estado de ser inconstante, irregular o variable. 2. Variación; falta de ilación, orden y método.
Desultory [des'-ul-to-ri], *a.* 1. Pasajero, mudable, variable, irregular, inconstante. 2. Vago, suelto, inconexo, no seguido.
Detach [dẹ-tach'], *va.* 1. Separar, apartar. 2. Destacar, separar un número de soldados del cuerpo principal.
Detached [dẹ-tacht'], *pp.* de DETACH. —*a.* Suelto, distinto, aparte.
Detaching [dẹ-tach'-ing], *s.* El acto de separar o destacar.
Detachment [dẹ-tach'-mẹnt], *s.* 1. Separación, apartamiento. 2. Lo que está apartado o separado. 3. Destacamento, cuerpo de tropas separadas del ejército, o parte de una escuadra, para servicio especial.
Detail [dẹ-têl'], *va.* Detallar, especificar, particularizar, referir por menor, circunstanciar, contar con sus pelos y señales.
Detail [dī'-têl o dẹ-têl'], *s.* 1. Detalle, pormenor, cuenta circunstanciada de alguna cosa. 2. (Mil.) Destacamento poco numeroso (de tropas). 3. (Arte y Arq.) Porción menor y accesoria de una obra; detalle.
Detain [dẹ-tên'], *va.* 1. Detener, retardar, suspender, impedir. 2. Retener, guardar o conservar lo que pertenece a otro.
Detainer [dẹ-tên'-ẹr], *s.* (For.) Detentador, retenedor; detención.
Detect [dẹ-tect'], *va.* Descubrir, averiguar algún delito, fraude o trama; revelar, declarar, manifestar.
Detecter [dẹ-tect'-ẹr], *s.* Descubridor, averiguador; revelador; delator.
Detection [dẹ-tec'-shun], *s.* Averiguación, descubrimiento; manifestación, revelación, declaración.
Detective [dẹ-tect'-iv], *a.* 1. Con aptitud especial para descubrir lo que es secreto. 2. Denunciador, delator de una cosa secreta; referente a la policía secreta.—*s.* Empleado de la policía secreta; espía asalariado.
Detent [dẹ-tent'], *s.* Fiador, retén, seguro; escape de un reloj.
Detention [dẹ-ten'-shun], *s.* Detención, retención; limitación; encierro, cautividad; tardanza.
Detentive [dẹ-tent'-iv], *a.* Que puede detener, detenedor; o que sirve y se emplea para asir, retener o afianzar.
Deter [dẹ-tẹr'], *va.* 1. Desanimar, desalentar, acobardar. 2. Disuadir, desviar, impedir.
Deterge [dẹ-tẹrj'], *va.* Limpiar una llaga.
Detergent [dẹ-tẹr'-jent], *a.* Detergente, lo que tiene poder de limpiar.—*s.* Detersorio, detergente.
Deteriorate [dẹ-tī'-ri-o-rêt], *va.* Desmejorar, deteriorar.
Deterioration [dẹ-tī''-ri-o-rê'-shun], *s.* Deterioración, deterioro, desmejoramiento.
Determent [dẹ-tẹr'-mẹnt], *s.* La acción y efecto de desanimar; lo que impide o desalienta; desaliento, descaecimiento de ánimo; impedimento.
Determinable [dẹ-tẹr'-min-a-bl], *a.* Determinable, lo que puede determinarse o decidirse.
Determinably [dẹ-tẹr'-min-a-bli], *adv.* Determinadamente, resueltamente.
Determinant [dẹ-tẹr'-mi-nant], *a.* De-

terminante, que hace tomar una determinación.—*s.* 1. Lo que causa una determinación. 2. (Biol.) Una de las unidades secundarias del plasma, del germen o substancia hereditaria.
Determinate [dẹ-tẹr'-min-êt], *a.* 1. Determinado, limitado; decidido, resuelto; establecido. 2. Determinante, concluyente; acordado. 3. (Bot.) De inflorescencia limitada.
Determinately [dẹ-tẹr'-min-êt-li], *adv.* Determinadamente, inmutablemente.
Determination [dẹ-tẹr-mi-né'-shun], *s.* 1. Determinación, resolución, decisión. 2. Resolución, entereza. 3. (For.) Auto definitivo, decisión judicial. 4. (Lóg.) Especificación. 5. (Med.) Congestión, acumulación de sangre o humores en alguna parte del cuerpo. 6. (Ant.) Terminación, término.
Determinative [dẹ-tẹr'-mi-na-tiv], *a.* Determinativo.
Determinator [dẹ-tẹr'-min-é"-tẹr], *s.* Determinante; juez árbitro.
Determine [dẹ-tẹr'-min], *va.* Determinar, fijar; limitar, reglar, establecer; decidir, juzgar, resolver definitivamente. — *vn.* Terminar, acabar, concluir; determinarse, resolverse, decidirse, tomar una resolución.
Determined [dẹ-tẹr'-mind], *a.* Decidido, resuelto.
Determiner [dẹ-tẹr'-min-ẹr], *s.* El que toma alguna determinación.
§**Deterration** [di-tẹr-é'-shun], *s.* Desentierro, desenterramiento.
Deterrence [dẹ-tẹr'-ens], *s.* Disuasión.
Deterrent [dẹ-tẹr'-ent], *a.* Disuasivo; que refrena o impide.—*s.* Elemento disuasivo.
Detersion [dẹ-tẹr'-shun], *s.* Detersión, el acto y efecto de limpiar y purificar, p. ej. una llaga.
Detersive [dẹ-tẹr'-siv], *a.* Detersivo, detersorio, detergente.—*s.* Remedio detersivo.
Detest [dẹ-test'], *va.* Detestar, abominar, aborrecer, odiar, execrar.
Detestable [dẹ-test'-a-bl], *a.* Detestable, aborrecible, abominable, odioso, execrable.
Detestably [dẹ-test'-a-bli], *adv.* Detestablemente.
Detester [dẹ-test'-ẹr], *s.* Aborrecedor, el que aborrece.
Dethrone [dẹ-thrōn'], *va.* Destronar, privar a alguno del trono y la potestad real.
Dethronement [dẹ-thrōn'-mẹnt], *s.* Destronamiento.
Detinue [det'-i-niū], *s.* (For.) Auto contra el detentador de alguna cosa.
Detonate [det'-o-nêt], *va.* Hacer detonar o estallar súbitamente.—*vn.* Detonar, inflamarse súbitamente y con estrépito.
Detonation [det-o-né'-shun], *s.* Detonación, fulminación.
Detonator [det'-o-nêt-er], *s.* Detonador, fulminante.
Detorsion [dẹ-tōr'-shun], *s.* Apartamiento, separación o desvío del primer designio.
Detour [dê-tūr'], *s.* 1. Vuelta, rodeo, revuelta, recodo. 2. Rodeo, tergiversación, subterfugio. (Fr.)
Detract [dẹ-tract'], *va.* Detraer, disminuir, quitar.—*vn.* Detraer, detractar, infamar, quitar el crédito; denigrar: (con *from*, por lo común).
Detracter [dẹ-tract'-ẹr], *s.* Detractor, infamador, murmurador.
Detraction [dẹ-trac'-shun], *s.* 1. La acción de detraer, de quitar parte de alguna cosa. 2. Detracción, maledicencia, murmuración, calumnia, denigración.
Detractive [dẹ-tract'-iv], *a.* Difamatorio, derogatorio, denigrante, que lastima la reputación.
Detractor [dẹ-tract'-ẹr], *s.* Difamador; detractor.
Detractress [dẹ-trac'-tres], *sf.* Detractora, murmuradora.
Detrain [di-trên'], *va.* y *vn.* Salir o hacer salir de un tren.
Detriment [det'-ri-mẹnt], *s.* Detrimento, daño, perjuicio, pérdida.
Detrimental [det-ri-mẹnt'-al], *a.* Perjudicial; desventajoso, dañoso.
Detrital [dẹ-trai'-tal], *a.* Detrítico, compuesto de detritus o perteneciente a ellos.
Detrition [dẹ-trish'-un], *s.* Rozadura, desgaste por frotamiento.
Detritus [dẹ-trai'-tus o tri'-tus], *s.* 1. (Geol.) Detritus, los restos del desgaste de las rocas y del deterioro de los vegetales esparcidos por la superficie de la tierra. 2. Cualquier conjunto de substancias desagregadas; desperdicios; inmundicias.
Detrude [dẹ-trūd'], *va.* Hundir, empujar alguna cosa hacia abajo; precipitar.
Detruncate [dẹ-truṇ'-kêt], *va.* Podar, cortar, quitar las ramas superfluas de los árboles.
Detruncation [di"-truṇ-ké'-shun], *s.* Poda.
Detrusion [dẹ-trū'-zhun], *s.* La acción de precipitar alguna cosa.
Deturbation [dẹ-tūr-bé'-shun], *s.* 1. El acto de arrojar al suelo alguna cosa. 2. Degradación.
Deuce [diūs], *s.* 1. Dos en los juegos, como para decir, dos ases, el dos de espadas; dos puntos en los dados. 2. (Vul.) El demonio, el diantre, dianche. *How the deuce!* ¡Cómo diablos! *The deuce take me if I have not forgotten it!* ¡El diablo me lleve si no lo he olvidado!
Deuterium [diū-ti-rium], *s.* (Quím.) Deuterio.
Deutero-, Deuto-, forma de combinación derivada del griego *deuteros*, segundo.
Deuterogamist [diu-tẹr-og'-a-mist], *s.* Bígamo, deuterógamo, el casado en segundas nupcias.
Deuterogamy [diu-tẹr-og'-a-mi], *s.* Deuterogamia, segundas nupcias.
Deuteronomy [diu-tẹr-on'-o-mi], *s.* Deuteronomio, la segunda ley; nombre del quinto libro del Pentateuco.
Devaluate [dẹ-val'-yu-êt], *va.* 1. Desvalorar. 2. Depreciar (el valor de la moneda).
Devaluation [dẹ-val-yu-é'-shUn], *s.* De(s)valuación, desvalorización.
Devastate [dev'-as-têt], *va.* Devastar, arruinar, asolar; gastar; robar.
Devastation [dev-as-té'-shun], *s.* Devastación, desolación, destrucción, ruina, saqueo.
Develop [dẹ-vel'-ep], *va.* 1. Desenvolver, desarrollar, descoger, abrir, desplegar; descubrir. 2. En fotografía, revelar, desarrollar, hacer visible la imagen latente.—*vn.* 1. Progresar; avanzar, pasar de un estado inferior al superior. 2. Hacerse patente, descubrirse (el enredo de una novela); asomar (la imagen fotográfica).
Developer [dẹ-vel'-ep-ẹr], *s.* Revelador, desarrollador; baño químico para revelar una fotografía.
Development [dẹ-vel'-ep-mẹnt], *s.* 1. Desarrollo, revelación, acción de descubrir lo oculto o secreto. 2. Desarrollo, revelación (fot.). 3. Adelanto, progreso, mejoría, evolución, desarrollo.
Devest [dẹ-vest'], *va.* 1. (Des.) Desnudar. 2. (For.) Privar de los bienes o del título; enajenar.—*vn.* Perderse o enajenarse (el título o la herencia).
Deviate [di'-vi-êt], *vn.* 1. Desviarse, salir del camino derecho. 2. Descarriarse, ir errado; pecar.
Deviation [di-vi-é'-shun], *s.* 1. Desvío, la acción y efecto de desviarse; extravío, error; falta, pecado. 2. Mala conducta. 3. (Astr.) Desviación.
Device [dẹ-vais'], *s.* 1. Plan, proyecto. 2. Dispositivo. 3. Estratagema, ardid. 4. Divisa, lema.
Deviceful [dẹ-vais'-ful], *a.* Inventivo, ingenioso, especulativo.
Devicefully [dẹ-vais'-ful-i], *adv.* Curiosamente ideado.
Devil [dev'-l], *s.* 1. Diablo, demonio, espíritu maligno. 2. Diablo, hombre o mujer de mal natural. 3. Úsase como interjección, para indicar sorpresa o enfado. 4. Aprendiz de impresor. *The devil!* ¡Demonio! ¡diantre! *The devil take you!* ¡El diablo te lleve! ¡Vete al diablo! *Devil-fish*, Animal marino de gran tamaño y repulsivo aspecto, especialmente el octópodo o pulpo. *The devil to pay*, Gran confusión o mala suerte; perplejidad. *To whip the devil round the stump*, La culpa del asno, echarla a la albarda. *To play the devil with*, Causar gran perjuicio o daño. *To go to the devil*, Llevárselo a uno la trampa, arruinarse. *Devil's darning needle*, (1) Caballito del diablo, libélula, insecto neuróptero; (2) Peine de Venus, planta umbelífera.
Devil, *va.* 1. Condimentar, preparar pescados y carnes para la mesa sazonándolos con pimienta, mostaza, etc., y sobreasándolos o friéndolos. 2. Hacer diabólico. *Deviled ham*, Jamón en latas, con salsa muy picante.
Deviled eggs [dev'-ld egs], *s. pl.* Huevos cocidos y rellenos con salsa picante.
Deviling [dev'-il-ing], *s.* Diablillo.
Devilish [dev'-il-ish], *a.* 1. Diabólico. 2. Excesivo; dícese en burla. 3. Epíteto para expresar aborrecimiento o desprecio.
Devilishly [dev'-il-ish-li], *adv.* Diabólicamente, endiabladamente.
Devilishness [dev'-il-ish-nes], *s.* Diablura.
§**Devilkin** [dev'-il-kin], *s.* Diablillo.
Devilship [dev'-il-ship], *s.* Calidad o estado de demonio o diablo.
Deviltry [dev'l-tri], *s.* Diablura, diablería, y el espíritu que conduce al mal.
Devious [di'-vi-us], *a.* Desviado, descarriado, descaminado, extraviado, errado; tortuoso; errante.
Deviously [di'-vi-us-li], *adv.* A través, de una manera torcida; tortuosamente.
Deviousness [di'-vi-us-nes], *s.* Extravío, descarrío; desviación del camino recto.
Devisable [dẹ-vaiz'-a-bl], *a.* 1. Imaginable, lo que se puede trazar o idear. 2. Transmisible, lo que se puede legar por testamento.
Devisal [dẹ-vai'-zal], *s.* El acto de

inventar; el de legar por testamento.
Devise [de-vaiz'], *va.* 1. Trazar, idear, inventar, proyectar, pensar, tener ánimo o intención de alguna cosa. 2. Legar.—*vn.* Pensar, considerar, maquinar.
Devise, *s.* (For.) 1. Legado, manda de bienes raíces. 2. Testamento o cláusula del mismo que lega bienes raíces.
Devisee [dev-i-zí'], *s.* Legatario.
Deviser [de-vaiz'-er], *s.* Inventor, autor.
Devisor [de-vai'-zer], *s.* Testador, el que deja un legado de bienes raíces.
Devitalize [dí-vai'-tal-aiz], *va.* Privar del poder vital o de la fuerza para sostener la vida.
Devoid [de-vеid'], *a.* Vacío, desocupado, desembarazado, libre, exento, privado.
Devoir [dev-wūr'], *s.* 1. Obsequio. 2. Cumplimiento, cumplido. (Gal.)
Devolution [dev-o-lū'-shun], *s.* 1. Mudanza de mano en mano; transmisión, traspaso a un sucesor. (For.) Devolución o derecho devoluto. 2. (Neol.) Degeneración, lo contrario de *evolution.*
Devolve [de-volv'], *va.* 1. Transmitir, traspasar, remitir, pasar de una mano a otra. 2. (Ant.) Rodar hacia abajo o hacia adelante.—*vn.* Recaer en alguno por devolución o derecho devoluto (seguido de *to, on* o *upon*).
Devonian [dev-ō'-ni-an], *a.* Devoniano, perteneciente al condado de Devon en Inglaterra. *Devonian age,* (Geol.) Edad devoniana o de los peces, subsiguiente a la silúrica.
Devote [de-vōt'], *va.* 1. Dedicar, consagrar; aplicar, entregar completamente. 2. Maldecir, execrar.
Devoted [de-vō'-ted], *a.* 1. Dedicado, consagrado, aplicado, destinado. 2. Apegado, aficionado, consagrado á. 3. Infeliz, malhadado, desdichado.
Devotedness [de-vōt'-ed-nes], *s.* 1. Devoción, dedicación, afecto a alguna persona. 2. Sacrificio voluntario.
Devotee [dev-o-tí'], *s.* 1. Devoto, devota, persona dedicada con fervor a una causa, empresa o servicio cualquiera, y especialmente a la religión. 2. Santón, santurrón, mojigato.
Devoter [de-vōt'-er], *s.* 1. El que dedica o consagra. 2. (Des.) Adorador.
Devotion [de-vō'-shun], *s.* 1. Devoción, piedad. 2. Adoración, veneración. 3. Oración. 4. Elevación del alma a Dios reconociéndose su criatura. 5. Disposición. 6. Oblación de caridad. 7. Afecto o amor ardiente. 8. Ardor, anhelo, ansia.
Devotional [de-vō'-shun-al], *a.* Devoto, religioso, piadoso.
Devotionalist [de-vō'-shun-al-ist], *s.* Santón, santurrón.
Devotionist [de-vō'-shun-ist], *s.* Santón; persona piadosa.
Devour [de-vaur'], *va.* 1. Devorar, tragar, engullir; comer con avidez, con voracidad, como un animal carnívoro. 2. Devorar, destruir, consumir, consumir sin reparo, deshacerse temerariamente de algo. 3. Mirar con avidez o deleite, devorar con la vista.
Devourer [de-vaur'-er], *s.* Devorador, tragón; destructor.
Devouringly [de-vaur'-ing-li], *adv.* De un modo devorador.
Devout [de-vaut'], *a.* Devoto, piadoso, fervoroso.—*s. V.* DEVOTEE.
Devoutlessness [de-vaut'-les-nes], *s.* Falta de devoción, tibieza en las cosas espirituales.
Devoutly [de-vaut'-li], *adv.* Devotamente, piadosamente.
Devoutness [de-vaut'-nes], *s.* Piedad, devoción.
Dew [diū], *s.* Rocío, relente, sereno.
Dew, *va.* Rociar, mojar como con rocío; de aquí, apaciguar, refrescar.
Dew-bent [diū'-bent], *a.* Inclinado con el rocío, cargado de rocío.
Dewberry [diū'-ber-i], *s.* (Bot.) Zarzamora, el fruto de la zarza rastrera, y la planta misma. Rubus Canadensis.
Dew-besprent [diū'-be-sprent], *a.* Rociado.
Dewdrop [diū'-drep], *s.* Gota de rocío.
Dew-dropping [diū'-drep-ing], *a.* Lo que cae a gotas como el rocío; lo que deja caer rocío.
Dew-impearled [diū'-im-perld], *a.* Aljofarado, cubierto con las gotas de rocío.
Dewlap [diū'-lap], *s.* Papada de buey o toro.
Dewlapt [diū'-lapt], *a.* Papudo, el que tiene papada.
Dew-plant [diū'-plant], *s.* 1. Planta de adorno con gruesas hojas relucientes, del género Mesembryanthemum. Se llama también *Ice-plant.* 2. Rocío del sol, una planta cualquiera del género Drosera.
Dew-point [diū'-peint], *s.* La temperatura a que se forma el rocío; humedad relativa de cien grados.
Dew-worm [diū'-wūrm], *s.* Lombriz de tierra.
Dewy [diū'-i], *a.* Rociado, humedecido con rocío; semejante a rocío, lleno de rocío.
Dexter [dec'-ster], *a.* 1. Diestro o derecho. 2. Favorable, propicio.
Dexterity [dec-ster'-i-ti], *s.* Destreza, agilidad, habilidad, maña y arte; primor, gracia.
Dexterous [dec'-ster-us], *a.* Diestro, sagaz, hábil, experto.
Dexterously [dec'-ster-us-li], *adv.* Diestramente, hábilmente.
Dexterousness [dec'-ster-us-nes], *s.* Habilidad, conocimiento práctico.
Dextrad [dex'-trad], *adv.* A la derecha; al lado derecho.
Dextral [dec'-stral], *a.* Derecho, diestro.
Dextrality [dec-stral'-i-ti], *s.* Situación a la mano derecha.
Dextrin, Dextrine [dex'-trin], *s.* (Quím.) Dextrina, substancia parecida a la goma, y que se usa en sustitución de la goma arábiga. ($C_{12}H_{20}O_{10}$.)
Dextrose [dex'-trōs], *s.* Dextrosa, glucosa, azúcar de uvas. Azúcar no hidrolizable contenida en la miel de abejas y en muchas frutas. Se utiliza en dulces y en la fermentación del tabaco.
Dey [dé], *s.* Bey o dey, el jefe supremo de Argel antes de la conquista francesa de 1830. Los gobernantes de Túnez y Trípoli.
Diabetes [dai-a-bí'-tíz], *s.* (Med.) Diabetes, enfermedad caracterizada por una secreción abundante de orina más o menos cargada de glucosa.
Diabetic [dai-a-bet'-ic], *a.* Diabético, de la diabetes o relativo á ella.
Diabolic, Diabolical [dai-a-bel'-ic, al], *a.* Diabólico.
Diabolically [dai-a-bel'-ic-al-i], *adv.* Diabólicamente.
Diabolicalness [dai-a-bel'-ic-al-nes], *s.* La calidad de diablo.
Diabolism [dai-ab'-o-lizm], *s.* 1. Diablura. 2. Posesión, el estar poseído por los demonios.
Diachylon [dai-ak'-i-len] o **Diachylum** [dai-ak'-i-lum], *s.* Diaquilón, ungüento con que se hacen emplastos, compuesto de óxido de plomo, aceite y agua.
Diaconal [di-ac'-o-nal], *a.* Diaconal, relativo o perteneciente a un diácono o diaconato.
Diacoustics [dai-a-cūs'-tics], *s.* Diacústica, ciencia que trata de la refracción de los sonidos.
Diacritic, Diacritical [dai-a-crit'-ic, al], *a.* Diacrítico, distinguido por un punto, signo o señal.
Diadem [dai'-a-dem], *s.* Diadema, corona.
Diademed [dai'-a-demd], *a.* 1. Coronado. 2. (Her.) Diademado.
Diæresis o **Dieresis** [dai-er'-i-sis], *s.* (Gram.) Diéresis, figura por la cual se disuelve un diptongo, formando sus vocales dos sílabas en vez de una.
Diagnose [dai-ag-nōz'], *va.* (Med.) Diagnosticar, formar el diagnóstico de una enfermedad.
Diagnosis [dai-ag-nō'-sis], *s.* 1. (Med.) Diagnosis, conocimiento de los síntomas característicos de las enfermedades. 2. Discernimiento entre cosas o condiciones de análoga naturaleza. (<Gr.)
Diagnostic [dai-ag-nes'-tic], *s.* (Med.) Diagnóstico, signo característico por el cual se distingue una enfermedad de otra.—*a.* Diagnóstico, distintivo, característico.
Diagnosticate [dai-ag-nes'-ti-kēt], *va.* Diagnosticar, distinguir entre las enfermedades.
Diagonal [dai-ag'-o-nal], *a.* Diagonal.—*s.* Diagonal.
Diagonally [dai-ag'-o-nal-i], *adv.* Diagonalmente.
Diagram [dai'-a-gram], *s.* Diagrama; perfil, bosquejo, recorte, traza; borrón o diseño de un mapa o de una proyección.
Diagraph [dai'-a-graf], *s.* Diágrafo, instrumento de reducción de una imagen con el que se puede trazar toda clase de líneas y figuras.
Diagraphic o **Diagraphical** [dai-a-graf'-i-cal], *a.* Descriptivo.
Dial [dai'-al], *s.* 1. Reloj de sol. 2. Esfera (de un reloj). 3. Brújula. *Dial phone,* Teléfono automático. *Luminous dial,* Esfera luminosa (de un reloj).
Dial, *va.* Marcar.
Dialect [dai'-a-lect], *s.* Dialecto, lenguaje propio de una provincia o región; variedad de un idioma, a diferencia de la lengua general y literaria.
Dialectic [dai-a-lec'-tic], *s.* Dialéctica.—*a.* Arguyente.
Dialectical [dai-a-lec'-tic-al], *a.* Dialéctico.
Dialectician [dai-a-lec-tish'-an], *s.* Dialéctico.
Dialist [dai'-al-ist], *s.* Constructor de relojes solares.
Dialling [dai'-al-ing], *s.* Gnomónica, la ciencia de hacer relojes de sol o cuadrantes.
Dialog, *s.* y *vn. V.* DIALOGUE.
Dialogism [dai-al'-o-jizm], *s.* Dialogismo, el arte del diálogo.
Dialogist [dai-al'-o-jist], *s.* Dialoguista, el que pone en diálogo una cosa.
Dialogistically [dai-al-o-jist'-i-cal-i], *adv.* A manera de diálogo.
Dialogize [dai-al'-o-jaiz], *vn.* Dialogar, dialogizar, hacer diálogos.

Dialogue [dai'-a-leg], *s.* Diálogo, interlocución; conversación, conferencia, coloquio.

Dialogue, *vn.* Dialogar.

Dialogue-writer [dai'-a-leg-rai'-tẹr], *s.* Dialoguista.

Dial-plate [dai'-al-plêt], *s.* Muestra, de un reloj.

Dial telephone [dai'-al tel'-e-fōn], *s.* Teléfono automático.

Dialysis [dai-al'-i-sis], *s.* 1. Diálisis, separación de partes; solución de continuidad. 2. (Quím.) Diálisis, procedimiento de separación fundado en la propiedad que ciertas substancias poseen de atravesar fácilmente las membranas porosas, en tanto que otras quedan retenidas por dichas membranas. 3. (Gram.) Diéresis, crema. 4. (Ret.) Asíndeton. 5. (Med.) Disolución, languidez, dificultad de mover los miembros. 6. (Cir.) Herida abierta.

Dialytic [dai-a-lit'-ic], *a.* Dialítico, perteneciente a la diálisis.

Dialyze [dai'-al-aiz], *va.* Dialisar, separar las substancias susceptibles de desprenderse de una mezcla.

Dialyzer [dai'-al-aiz'-ẹr], *s.* Dialisador, instrumento propio para practicar la diálisis.

Diamantine [dai-a-man'-tin], *a.* Adamantino, diamantino.

Diameter [dai-am'-e-tẹr], *s.* Diámetro.

Diametral [dai-am'-e-tral], *a.* Diametral; opuesto, contrario.

Diametrical [dai-a-met'-ri-cal], *a.* Diametral.

Diametrically [dai-a-met'-ri-cal-i], *adv.* Diametralmente.

Diamond [dai'-a-mund], *s.* 1. Diamante, piedra preciosa. 2. Punta de diamante, instrumento que sirve para cortar el vidrio. 3. Oros, uno de los palos de que se compone la baraja de naipes. 4. Nombre de un grado muy pequeño de letra de imprenta, próximo a la letra "brillante"; 4 o 4½ puntos, corpus cuatro. 5. (Geom.) Rombo. 6. Rombo del juego de pelota llamado *baseball. Diamond-cutter*, Diamantista. *Diamond-drill*, Taladro de punta de diamante.

Diamond, *a.* Diamantado: adiamantado.

Diapason [dai-a-pé'-sẹn], *s.* 1. Diapasón, registro fundamental del órgano. 2. Diapasón, armonía comprensiva o fundamental; tono justo, acuerdo.

Diaper [dai'-a-pẹr], *s.* 1. Lienzo adamascado; servilleta. 2. Arabesco, adorno en pintura y escultura, hecho con dibujos de flores, figuras geométricas, etc. 3. Pañal, sabanilla de niño.

Diaper, *va.* 1. Matizar una tela de diferentes colores. 2. Adamascar.

Diaphaneity [dai-a-fa-ní'-i-ti], *s.* Diafanidad, transparencia.

Diaphanous [dai-af'-a-nus], *a.* Diáfano, transparente, terso, claro.

Diaphoresis [dai-a-fo-rí'-sis o dí-a-fo-ré'-sis], *s.* (Med.) Diaforesis, transpiración copiosa, sudor (en especial la transpiración artificial).

Diaphoretic, Diaphoretical [dai-a-fo-ret'-ic, al], *a.* Diaforético, sudorífico.

Diaphragm [dai'-a-fram], *s.* 1. Diafragma, músculo que sirve para la respiración y que separa el tórax del abdomen; es característico de los mamíferos. 2. Diafragma; división o separación, como el diafragma vibratorio del teléfono.

Diaphragmatic [dai-a-frag-mat'-ic], *a.* Diafragmático, perteneciente al diafragma.

Diarrhœa [dai-a-rí'-a], *s.* Diarrea, flujo de vientre, cámaras, despeño. (Vul.) Evacuaciones, cursos.

Diarist [dai'-a-rist], *s.* Diarista.

Diary [dai'-a-ri], *s.* Diario, relación de los acontecimientos de cada día.

Diastase [dai'-a-stês], *s.* Diastasa, principio componente de la saliva, que se halla también en los cereales en estado de germinación; es un fermento que convierte el almidón en dextrina y azúcar.

Diastole [dai-as'-to-li], *s.* 1. (Med.) Diástole, dilatación del corazón. 2. (Gram.) Diástole, figura que consiste en usar como larga una sílaba breve.

Diastyle [dai'-a-stail], *s.* (Arq.) Diástilo.

Diatessaron [dai-a-tes'-a-ren], *s.* Diatesarón, al intervalo compuesto de dos tonos, mayor y menor, y de un semitono mayor: también es cuarta en la música.

Diathermy [dai'-a-thẹr-mi], *s.* Diatermia.

Diatom [dai'-a-tem], *s.* Diátomo, planta unicelular del orden de las Diatomáceas, algas microscópicas. Crecen en las aguas dulces y saladas y se distinguen de las desmidias por sus válvulas silicosas y su color aureo pardo u obscuro.

Diatomaceous [dai"-a-to-me'-shus], *a.* Diatomáceo, perteneciente a los diátomos.

Diatomic [dai-a-tem'-ic], *a.* (Quím.) 1. Diatómico, que consiste sólo de dos átomos. 2. Bivalente, cuyo poder de combinación es de dos unidades.

Diatonic [dai-a-ten'-ic], *s.* Diatónico, uno de los tres géneros del sistema músico.

Diatribe [dai'-a-traib], *s.* Diatriba, sátira mordaz.

Dibble [dib'-l], *s.* Plantador, almocafre, instrumento que sirve a los jardineros y hortelanos para plantar.

Dibble, *va.* Plantar con plantador o almocafre.

Dibs [dibz], *s.* 1. Jarabe que se hace en Siria, hirviendo el zumo de uvas o dátiles. (Arab.) 2. (Prov. Ingl.) *V.* DIBSTONE.

Dibstone [dib'-stōn], *s.* Piedra que los niños usan en uno de sus juegos para mover a otras; taba.

Dice [dais], *s. pl.* de DIE. Dados.

Dice, *vn.* Jugar con o a los dados.

Dice-box [dais'-bocs], *s.* Cubilete de dados.

Dicer [dais'-ẹr], *s.* Jugador de dados.

Dichotomize [dai-cet'-o-maiz], *va.* Separar, dividir.

Dichotomous [dai-cet'-o-mus], *a.* Dicotómico, lo que se divide y subdivide por parejas, de dos en dos.

Dichotomy [dai-cet'-o-mi], *s.* Dicotomía, distribución de una cosa en dos partes.

Dickens [dik'-ens], *s.* (Vul.) Diantre, dianche, demonio.

Dicker [dik'-ẹr], *va.* (E. U.) Hacer un trueque sin importancia: regatear.—*s.* 1. Cambio, trueque de poca monta. 2. (Des.) Decenar o decenario.

Dickey [dik'-i], *s.* Peto, pechera.

Dicotyledon [dai-cet-i-lí'-den], *s.* Dicotiledón, vegetal que tiene dos lóbulos o cotiledones.

Dicotyledonous [dai-cet-i-led'-on-us], *a.* Dicotiledóneo. *V.* DICOTYLEDON.

Dictate [dic'-têt], *va.* 1. Dictar, declarar a otro alguna cosa con autoridad. 2. Dictar, decir a otro lo que ha de escribir o hablar.

Dictate, *s.* Dictamen, máxima autorizada, precepto; sugestión; lección, doctrina, documento; dictado, nota.

Dictation [dic-tê'-shun], *s.* 1. Dictado, acción de dictar. 2. Precepto, prescripción.

Dictator [dic-tê'-tẹr], *s.* 1. Dictador, el que ejerce una autoridad absoluta, especialmente en época turbulenta o peligrosa. 2. Dictador, el que dicta o prescribe.

Dictatorial [dic-ta-tō'-ri-al], *a.* Autoritativo, arrogante, altivo, imperioso, absoluto, magistral, dogmático.

Dictatorship [dic-tê'-tẹr-ship], *s.* Dictadura; arrogancia, presunción.

Dictatory [dic'-ta-to-ri], *a.* Dominante, arrogante, dogmático.

Diction [dic'-shun], *s.* Dicción, estilo, expresión; locución, lenguaje.

Dictionary [dic'-shun-ẹ-ri], *s.* Diccionario, colección alfabética de las palabras de una lengua, arte o ciencia, con sus definiciones o explicaciones.

Dictograph [dic'-to-grạf], *s.* Máquina para dictar.

Dictum [dic'-tum], *s.* (*pl.* DICTA). 1. Sentencia o dicho positivo o dogmático. 2. (For.) Fallo, la sentencia de un juez, sobre un punto no esencial a la decisión del juicio principal.

Did, *pret.* del verbo *To* DO, hacer.—DID se emplea como indicación del tiempo pasado de los verbos, particularmente en las frases interrogativas y negativas.

Didactic, Didactical [dai-dac'-tic, al], *a.* Didáctico.

Didapper [did'-ap-ẹr], *s.* Somorgujo, somormujo o somormujón, ave acuática.

Diddle [did'-l], *va.* Engañar, entrampar.—*vn.* (Prov.) Vacilar, anadear.

Didst, *pret. seg. pers.* del verbo *To* Do.

Die [dai], *vn.* (*pa.* DYING, *pret.* y *pp.* DIED). 1. Morir, expirar. 2. Fenecer, acabar del todo. 3. Padecer violentamente algún afecto o pasión; padecer la muerte. 4. Marchitarse, perder el jugo y secarse los vegetales. 5. Evaporar o evaporarse, perder el espíritu y fuerza los licores. 6. (Teol.) Perecer eternamente. 7. Descaecer; desmadejarse; desvanecerse. 8. Cesar, extinguirse (hablando de las pasiones y de afectos morales). *To die away*, Debilitarse gradualmente; extinguirse, caer, cesar; disiparse; borrarse, desaparecer.

Die, *s.* 1. Dado, pieza de hueso u otra materia que se usa para jugar: en este sentido su plural es *dice.* 2. Dado, suerte. *To cog a die*, Cargar un dado para que se ladee o se incline. 3. Cuño, el sello con que se acuña la moneda: su plural on este sentido es *dies.* 4. (Arq.) Cubo. *Die-sinker*, Grabador en hueco.

Dieresis, *s.* *V.* DIÆRESIS.

Diesel engine [dí'-zẹl en'-jin], *s.* Locomotora Diesel.

Diet [dai'-et], *s.* 1. Alimento, comida, manjar, vianda. 2. Dieta, régimen. 3. Ración de víveres. 4. Dieta, asamblea de los príncipes y estados del imperio de Alemania.

Diet, *vn.* Estar a o de dieta, poner a dieta; comer, alimentarse.—*va.* 1. Comer parcamente. 2. Dar de comer.

Dietary [dai'-et-ẹ-ri], *a.* Dietético.—*s.* Dieta medicinal.
Diet-drink [dai'-et-driŋk], *s.* Bebida medicinal.
Dieter [dai'-et-ẹr], *s.* El que da reglas para guardar la dieta.
Dietetic, Dietetical [dai-ẹ-tet'-ic, al], *a.* Dietético.
Dietetics [dai-ẹ-tet'-ics], *s* Dietética.
Dieting [dai'-et-ing], *s.* Adietación.
Diffarreation [di-far-ẹ-é'-shun], *s.* Difarreación, la ceremonia que hacían los romanos de partir un bollo cuando se divorciaban.
Differ [dif'-ẹr], *vn.* 1. Diferenciarse, distinguirse. 2. Contender, lidiar, altercar. 3. Contradecir.—*va.* (Poco us.) Diferenciar, variar.
Difference [dif'-ẹr-ens], *s.* 1. Diferencia, diversidad, distinción, desemejanza, disparidad. 2. Diferencia, riña, pendencia. 3. Distinción.
Difference, *va.* Diferenciar, hacer diferencia, distinguir.
Different [dif'-ẹr-ent], *a.* Diferente, distinto, diverso; desemejante.
Differential [dif-ẹr-en'-shal], *a.* (Mat.) Diferencial. *Differential calculus,* Cálculo diferencial.—*s.* (Mec.) Diferencial.
Differentiate [dif-er-en'-shi-êt], *va.* 1. Diferenciar, hacer diferencia. 2. Constituir diferencia entre; ser señal distintiva. 3. (Biol.) Hacer diferencia, hacer especial en forma o función; desarrollar variación en (plantas que se cultivan, etc.).—*vn.* Adquirir carácter diverso y diferente.
Differentiation [dif-er-en-shi-é'-shun], *s.* La acción, el procedimiento y efecto de diferenciar.
Differently [dif'-ẹr-ent-li], **Differingly** [dif'-ẹr-ing-li], *adv.* Diferentemente.
Difficult [dif'-i-cult], *a.* 1. Difícil, dificultoso, obscuro; penoso. 2. Áspero, agrio de condición, difícil de contentar.
Difficulty [dif'-i-cult-i], *s.* 1. Dificultad. 2. Oposición, obstáculo, repugnancia; calamidad. 3. Dificultad, enredo. 4. Duda, argumento, reparo, objeción.
†**Diffide** [di-faid'], *vn.* Desconfiar, recelarse de alguno.
Diffidence [dif'-i-dens], *s.* Difidencia, desconfianza; timidez, pusilanimidad.
Diffident [dif'-i-dent], *a.* 1. Corto, corto de genio, vergonzoso, tímido. 2. (Ant.) Desconfiado, dudoso, receloso.
Diffidently [dif'-i-dent-li], *adv.* Modestamente, tímidamente.
Diffluence, Diffluency [dif'-lu-ens, i], *s.* Fluidez.
Diffluent [dif'-lu-ent], *a.* Que fluye por todas partes; que difluye o se difunde; que se deslíe o disuelve.
Difform [dif'-fōrm], *a.* Disforme, deforme.
Difformity [dif-fōrm'-i-ti], *s.* Deformidad, irregularidad; diversidad de forma.
Diffraction [dif-frac'-shun], *s.* Difracción, fenómeno luminoso producido por el cambio de dirección que experimentan los rayos solares cuando rozan los bordes de un cuerpo muy tenue o penetran por una hendedura muy estrecha.
Diffranchisement [dif-fran'-chiz-mẹnt], *s.* El acto de privar a alguna ciudad de sus franquicias o privilegios. *V.* DISFRANCHISEMENT.
Diffuse [dif-fiūz'], *va.* Difundir, esparcir, esparramar; derramar, verter; repartir; propagar, publicar.
Diffuse [dif-fiūs'], *a.* Difundido, extendido, dilatado, esparcido; difícil, difuso, prolijo.
Diffused [dif-fiūzd'], *a.* 1. Difundido, extendido, derramado. 2. (Zool.) Que se desvanece por los bordes, como sucede con las manchas o colores de algunos animales; borroso.
Diffusedly [dif-fiūz'-ed-li], *adv.* Difusamente, latamente.
Diffusedness [dif-fiūz'-ed-nes], *s.* Dispersión, esparcimiento, separación.
Diffusely [dif-fiūs'-li], *adv.* Extensivamente, copiosamente, ampliamente, prolijamente.
Diffuser [dif-fiūz'-ẹr], *s.* Difundidor, esparcidor.
Diffusible [dif-fiūz'-i-bl], *a.* Difusivo, capaz de difusión o extensión.
Diffusion [dif-fiū'-zhun], *s.* Difusión, prolijidad; esparcimiento, dispersión, diseminación.
Diffusive [dif-fiūs'-iv], *a.* Difusivo, difundido, difuso, extendido; esparcido.
Diffusively [dif-fiūs'-iv-li], *adv.* Difusamente.
Diffusiveness [dif-fiūs'-iv-nes], *s.* Dispersión; difusión, extensión.
Dig [dig], *va.* (*pret.* y *pp.* DUG o DIGGED). 1. Cavar, ahondar. 2. Cultivar la tierra. 3. Extraer, sacar de la tierra; beneficiar una mina. 4. Penetrar con una punta. 5. (Fig.) Buscar y extraer por medio del trabajo. *To dig again,* Binar. *To dig deeper,* Profundizar. *To dig out* o *up,* Desenterrar. *He dug his way out,* Escapó cavándose una salida.—*vn* Trabajar con azadón o azada.
Digamma [dai-gam'-a], *s.* Digama, la letra F, sexto del alfabeto griego originalmente, pero que muy pronto cayó en desuso.
Digastric [dai-gas'-tric], *a.* Digástrico; dícese de dos músculos de la quijada inferior.
Digest [dai'-jest], *s.* Digesto, recopilación de las decisiones de la jurisprudencia romana; también, resumen o extracto de escritos literarios u otros.
Digest [di-jest'], *va.* 1. Digerir el alimento en el estómago para convertirlo en quimo y quilo. 2. Digerir, pensar, meditar, rumiar. 3. Digerir, sufrir con paciencia, tragar o tolerar una afrenta. 4. Digerir, ordenar, disponer, distribuir, colocar. 5. (Quím.) Digerir, cocer alguna cosa por medio de un calor templado.—*vn.* 1. (Quím.) Ser preparado por medio del calor y de la humedad para ulterior manipulación. 2. (Cir.) Supurar.
Digester [di-jest'-ẹr], *s.* 1. El que digiere lo que come. 2. Digeridor; aparato para reducir los huesos y toda la materia animal o vegetal a jalea o líquido. 3. Cualquier cosa que ayuda la digestión.
Digestible [di-jest'-i-bl], *a.* Digerible, que es fácil de digerir.
Digestion [di-ges'-chun], *s.* 1. Digestión, la acción y efecto de digerir. 2. La acción de ordenar y colocar metódicamente o de reducir a método u orden: recepción y asimilación mentales. 3. (Quím.) Fermentación lenta que se produce por medio de un calor artificial. 4. Maduración de un tumor para que supure, por medio de medicinas.
Digestive [di-jest'-iv], *a.* Digestivo; metódico.—*s.* Medicamento digestivo.
Diggable [dig'-a-bl], *a.* Que puede ser cavado.
Digger [dig'-ẹr], *s.* Cavador. *Gravedigger,* Sepulturero.
Dight [dait], *va.* 1. (Poét. o Prov.) Adornar, embellecer, vestir. 2. Preparar; alisar; limpiar.
Digit [dij'-it], *s.* 1. Dedo (de la mano o del pie). 2. Cualquier número denotado por una cifra solamente. 3. (Astr.) Dígito, la duodécima parte del diámetro del sol o de la luna. 4. Dígito, antigua medida longitudinal de tres cuartos de pulgada.
Digital [dij'-it-al], *a.* Digital.
Digital computer [di-ji-tạl com-piū'-tẹr], *s.* Computadora digital, máquina calculadora digital.
Digitalis [dij-i-té'-lis o tạ'-lis], *s.* Dedalera, digital purpúrea, planta medicinal y sus hojas, usadas como tónico cardíaco.
Digitate [dij'-i-têt], **Digitated** [dij'-i-tê-ted], *a.* Dividido como los dedos.
Digitigrade [dij'-i-ti-grêd], *a.* Digitígrado, que anda sobre los dedos.
Diglyph [dai'-glif], *s.* (Arq.) Diglifo, cartela ornada en su frente con dos muescas, semejantes a las tres del triglifo.
Dignified [dig'-ni-faid], *a.* Dignificado.
Dignify [dig'-ni-fai], *va.* Dignificar, exaltar, condecorar, elevar, promover.
Dignitary [dig'-ni-tẹ-ri], *s.* Dignidad, el que en alguna iglesia catedral obtiene alguna dignidad o beneficio preeminente.
Dignity [dig'-ni-ti], *s.* Dignidad, cargo, empleo; rango, elevación; carácter, aire noble, aire de grandeza.
Digress [di-gres'], *vn.* Hacer digresión, separarse o apartarse del asunto, extraviarse.
Digression [di-gresh'-un], *s.* 1. Digresión. 2. Desvío, separación.
Digressional [di-gresh'-un-al], *a.* Lo que se separa del asunto principal; caracterizado por la digresión.
Digressive [di-gres'-iv], *a.* Digresivo, discursivo.
Digressively [di-gres'-iv-li], *adv* Por vía de digresión.
Dihedral [dai-hí'-dral], *a.* Diedro, (ángulo) formado por dos superficies planas.
§**Dijudicate** [di-jiū'-di-kêt], *va.* 1. Fijar con autoridad, juzgar entre dos partes, decidir. 2. Discernir, distinguir, desarrollar.
Dike [daik], *s.* 1. Dique, malecón, defensa contra el ímpetu de las aguas. 2. (Min.) Vena o pared de otra materia que corta o impide la del mineral en alguna mina. 3. (Ant.) Canal de desagüe.
Dike [daik], *va.* Represar, contener por medio de un dique o represa; abrir un canal de desagüe.
§**Dilacerate** [di-las'-ẹr-êt], *va.* Dilacerar, romper, rasgar, lacerar, despedazar.
§**Dilaceration** [di-las-ẹr-é'-shun], *s* Despedazamiento, dilaceración.
Dilapidate [di-lap'-i-dêt], *va.* Dilapidar, arruinar, destruir, derribar. —*vn.* Arruinarse.
Dilapidation [di-lap-i-dé'-shun], *s.* Dilapidación, destrucción, daño.
Dilapidator [di-lap'-i-dê-tẹr], *s.* Dilapidador.
Dilatability [di-lêt-a-bil'-i-ti], *s.* Dilatabilidad, la capacidad de dilatación.

Dilatable [di-lét'-a-bl], *a.* Dilatable.

Dilatant [di-lé'-tant], *a.* Dilatador, que dilata o extiende.—*s.* Instrumento o substancia usada para dilatar.

Dilatation [dil-a-té'-shun], *s.* Dilatación, extensión.

Dilate [di-lét'], *va.* y *vn.* 1. Dilatar, extender, alargar. 2. Hablar difusamente. 3. Dilatarse, explayarse o extenderse. 4. Dilatarse, ensancharse, extenderse.

Dilated, *pp.* y *a.* 1. Dilatado, extendido. 2. Explayado, prolijo, difuso.

Dilater [di-lé'-tęr], *s.* Dilatador, el que dilata o agranda.

Dilation [di-lé'-shun], *s.* 1. Dilatación. 2. (Des.) Dilación, retardación.

Dilative [di-lé'-tiv], *a.* Dilatativo, que tiene virtud de dilatar o de causar extensión.

Dilator [di-lé'-tęr], *s.* (Cir.) Dilatador, instrumento que dilata, extiende o ensancha.

Dilatorily [dil'-a-to-ri-li], *adv.* Lentamente, perezosamente.

Dilatoriness [dil'-a-to-ri-nes], *a.* Lentitud, tardanza, pesadez.

Dilatory [dil'-a-to-ri], *a.* Tardo, lento, perezoso, pesado; dilatorio.

Dilemma [di-lem'-a], *s.* 1. Dilema. 2. Suspensión, dificultad o duda en escoger o elegir; embarazo.

Dilettante [dil-et-tąn'-té], *s.* Aficionado a las artes y ciencias. Voz italiana cuyo plural es *dilettanti.*

Diligence [dil'-i-jens], *s.* 1. Asiduidad, aplicación al trabajo. 2. Diligencia, cuidado, esmero, exactitud. 3. (Der. escocés) (a) Citación, orden, mandato; (b) embargo, secuestro por deudas.

Diligence [dil'-i-jens o dī''-li-zhāns'], *s.* Diligencia, coche grande dividido en dos o tres departamentos, que cubre la carrera ordinaria con relativa rapidez. Tiran de ella cuatro, seis o más caballos o mulas. (Fr.)

Diligent [dil'-i-jent], *a.* Diligente, aplicado, asiduo, activo, exacto, cuidadoso.

Diligently [dil'-i-jent-li], *adv.* Diligentemente, cuidadosamente.

Dill [dil], *s.* (Bot.) Eneldo, hierba umbelífera anual, con semillas aromáticas. (Peucedanum graveolens.)

Dilly-dally [dil'-i-dal'-i], *vn.* (Fam.) Malgastar el tiempo; entretenerse en bagatelas.

†Dilucidate [di-lū'-si-dét], *va.* Dilucidar, aclarar. *V.* ELUCIDATE.

Diluent [dil'-yu-ent], *a.* y *s.* Diluente, lo que diluye.

Dilute [di-lūt' o liūt'], *va.* 1. Desleír, diluir, deshacer, disolver; atenuar. 2. Templar, debilitar. 3. Remojar, clarificar.—*vn.* Desleírse, deshacerse, hacerse menos concentrado.

Dilute, *a.* Atenuado, diluído; desleído, disuelto, adelgazado, templado.

Diluter [di-lūt'-ęr], *s.* Diluente, lo que diluye.

Dilution [di-lū'-shun o liū'-shun], *s.* Desleidura, diluición.

Diluvial, Diluvian [di-lū'-vi-al, di-lū'-vi-an], *a.* Diluviano, lo que pertenece al diluvio: producido por medio de un diluvio o inundación. *Diluvian,* en sentido geológico significa arcaico, antiguo.

Dim [dim], *a.* 1. Obscuro, opaco, falto de brillo. 2. Confuso, indistinto; sombrío, nublado. 3. Turbio de vista; corto de vista; lerdo, falto de inteligencia, tardo en comprender. 4. Falto de brillantez, deslustrado.

Dim, *va.* Ofuscar, quitar la luz; obscurecer, hacer alguna cosa menos resplandeciente; ofuscar, turbar la inteligencia.

Dimension [di-men'-shun], *s.* 1. Dimensión, medida, extensión. 2. (Alg.) Dimensión, grado de una potencia o ecuación; cantidad que entra como factor de un término algebraico.

Dimensionless [di-men'-shun-les], *a.* Lo que no tiene dimensión determinada.

Dimensity [di-men'-si-ti], *s.* (Poco us.) Extensión, capacidad.

Dimensive [di-men'-siv], *a.* Lo que señala las dimensiones.

Dime [daim], *s.* 1. Moneda de plata de los Estados Unidos cuyo valor es diez centavos o dos reales vellón. 2. Décimo; el número diez.

Dimeter [dim'-e-tęr], *a.* y *s.* Verso que consta de dos medidas o cuatro pies.

Dimidiate [di-mid'-i-ét], *va.* Dimidiar, promediar, partir en dos mitades.

Diminish [di-min'-ish], *va.* 1. Disminuir, minorar. 2. Desmejorar, debilitar.—*vn.* Disminuirse, decrecer; debilitarse; degenerar.

Diminishingly [di-min'-ish-ing-li], *adv.* Escasamente.

Diminuendo [di-min-yu-en'-do], *a.* y *adv.* (Mús.) Que va disminuyendo gradualmente en volumen del sonido; lo opuesto a *crescendo* y denotado por *dim., dimin.* o el signo >. (Ital.)

Diminution [dim-i-niū'-shun], *s.* Diminución; degradación; descrédito.

Diminutive [di-min'-yu-tiv], *s.* y *a.* 1. Diminutivo; pequeño; mezquino. 2. Diminutivo, lo que tiene cualidad de disminuir o reducir a menos alguna cosa.

Diminutively [di-min'-yu-tiv-li], *adv.* Diminutivamente.

Diminutiveness [di-min'-yu-tiv-nes], *s.* Pequeñez.

Dimissory [dim'-i-so-ri], *a.* 1. Dimisorio; adjetivo que sólo se usa en castellano unido al sustantivo cartas. 2. Lo que da permiso para retirarse.

Dimity [dim'-i-ti], *s.* Fustán, cotonía.

Dimly [dim'-li], *adv.* Ofuscadamente, obscuramente.

Dimmed headlight [dimd hed'-lait], *s.* Faro de automóvil con luz amortiguada.

Dimmer [dim'-ęr], *s.* Amortiguador (de la luz de un automóvil).

Dimming [dim'-ing], *s.* Obscuridad.

Dimmish [dim'-ish], *a.* Algo ofuscado, obscuro o turbio.

Dimness [dim'-nes], *s.* 1. Ofuscamiento u obscurecimiento de la vista. 2. Torpeza, estupidez.

Dimorph [dai'-mōrf], *s.* Una de las formas de una substancia dimorfa.

Dimorphism [dai-mōr'-fizm], *s.* Dimorfismo, propiedad de existir en dos formas, como la tienen ciertas substancias cristalizables, ciertos insectos, una palabra de doble ortografía (v. g. *quay* y *key*), etc.

Dimorphous [dai-mōr'-fus], *a.* Dimorfo, lo que existe o se presenta en dos formas; caracterizado por el dimorfismo. (<Gr. <*dis,* dos, *morphe,* forma.)

Dimple [dim'-pl], *s.* Hoyuelo, cavidad pequeña en la mejilla, barba u otra parte.

Dimple, *vn.* Formarse hoyos en alguna parte del cuerpo.

Dimpled [dim'-pld], **Dimply** [dim'-pli], *a.* Lleno de hoyos.

Dims [dimz], *s. pl.* Luces de cruce.

Dim-sighted [dim'-sait-ed], *a.* Cegato.

Din [din], *s.* Ruido violento y continuado; son, sonido.

Din, *va.* Atolondrar o aturdir con ruido.

Dine [dain], *vn.* Hacer o tomar la comida principal del día.—*va.* Dar de comer, proveer con la comida principal, dar un convite.

Diner [dai'-nęr], *s.* (F.C.) Carro comedor.

Ding [ding], *va.* 1. Instar, urgir repetidamente. 2. Arrojar violentamente, chocar con violencia.—*vn.* 1. Echar fieros o bravatas. 2. Resonar a intervalos regulares, como los toques de una campana; repicar.

Ding-dong [ding'-deng], *s.* Dindán, tintín, voz onomatopéyica para imitar el sonido de las campanas.

Dinghy, dingy o **dingey** [din'-ge], *s.* 1. Bote de remos de las Indias Orientales. 2. Esquife. 3. Bote salvavidas.

Dingle [ding'-gl], *s.* Cañada, espacio entre dos alturas.

Dingle-dangle [ding'-gl-dang'-gl], *adv.* (Vul.) Dícese de lo que está mal colgado o que estando pendiente se menea por no estar bien firme.

Dinginess [din'-ji-nes], *s.* La calidad de ser deslustrado o moreno.

Dingy [din'-ji], *a.* 1. Empañado, deslucido; manchado, sucio. 2. Moreno, obscuro, negruzco.

Dining car [dain'-ing cār], *s.* (F.C.) Carro comedor.

Dining-room [dain'-ing-rūm], *s.* Comedor, la pieza destinada para comer; refectorio, en los conventos, colegios, etc.

Dinna [din'-na], *v.* (Esco.) No hacer.

Dinner [din'-ęr], *s.* La comida principal del día; banquete; el acto de comer.

Dinner-time [din'-ęr-taim], *s.* La hora de comer.

Dinosaur [dai'-no-sōr], *s.* Dinosaurio.

Dint [dint], *s.* 1. Abolladura, marca, señal o impresión de un golpe. 2. Fuerza, violencia, poder. 3. (Des.) Golpe, choque. *By dint of argument,* A fuerza de argumentos.

Dint, *va.* *V.* DENT.

Diocesan [dai-es'-ę-san o dai-o-sī'-san], *s.* Diocesano.—*a.* Diocesano.

Diocese [dai'-o-sīs], *s.* Diócesis, distrito o territorio de la jurisdicción espiritual de un obispo; distrito.

Diœcious [dai-ī'-shus], *a.* (Biol.) Dioico, dioica; dícese de las plantas y de los moluscos cuyos sexos se hallan en distintos individuos. (Gr. di, y oikos, casa.)

Dioicous [dai-ei'-cus], *a.* *V.* DIŒCIOUS.

Dioptic, Dioptical [dai-ep'-tic, al], **Dioptric, Dioptrical** [dai-ep'-tric, al], *a.* Dióptrico.

Dioptrics [dai-ep'-trics], *s.* Dióptrica, la ciencia que trata de la refracción de la luz.

Diorama [dai-o-rā'-ma], *s.* Diorama, vistas de perspectiva, y el local donde se enseñan o exponen.

Dioramic [dai-o-rā'-mic], *a.* Diorámico, relativo al diorama.

Diorite [dai'-o-rait], *s.* Diorita, roca plutónica compuesta de feldespato y anfíbol.

Dioxide [dai-ex -id], *s.* (Quím.) Bióxido, óxido de segundo grado. Se llama también *binoxide.*

Dip [dip], *va.* 1. Mojar, remojar, bañar, chapuzar, zampuzar, chapotear, sumergir. 2. Ojear, repasar ligeramente algún libro, escrito, etc.; examinar de prisa alguna cosa. 3. Bajar y volver a alzar un objeto, p. ej. una bandera. 4. Alzar, levantar para vaciar; sacar líquidos. 5. (Des.) Hipotecar, empeñar, dar alguna cosa en hipoteca o prenda. —*vn.* 1. Sumergirse, meterse debajo del agua. 2. Empeñarse o meterse en algún negocio. 3. Declinar, inclinarse hacia abajo. 4. (Geol.) Yacer, quedarse o hallarse formando ángulo con el horizonte; dícese de las capas de terreno, estratos, etc.

Dip, *s.* 1. Inmersión, la acción de sumergir; baño corto. 2. La acción del verbo *dip* en cualquiera de sus acepciones; depresión. 3. Baño, líquido en que algo está sumergido. 4. Inclinación de la aguja magnética (vertical), de una capa o estrato, de un eje de carruaje, etc. 5. Profundidad de inmersión de una rueda de paleta, de un hélice, etc.

Dipetalous [dai-pet'-a-lus], *a.* (Bot.) Dipétalo o dipétala.

Diphtheria [dif'-thí'-ri-a], *s.* Difteria, difteritis, enfermedad caracterizada por la formación de falsas membranas.

Diphthong [dif'-thông, y menos aceptado, dip'-thông], *s.* (Gram.) Diptongo.

Diploe [dip'-lo-i], *s.* 1. Diploe, tejido esponjoso de los huesos del cráneo. 2. (Bot.) Parenquima de una hoja entre dos capas epidérmicas.

Diploma [di-plō'-ma], *s.* Diploma, despacho, privilegio, título, autorizado con sello.

Diplomacy [di-plō'-ma-si], *s.* 1. Diplomacia, conocimiento de los intereses o relaciones de unas potencias con otras. 2. El cuerpo de los embajadores o ministros extranjeros.

Diplomat [dip'-lo-mat], *s.* Diplomático, representante de un Estado soberano en la capital o en la corte de otro; miembro de una legación.

Diplomatic [dip-lo-mat'-ic], *a.* 1. Diplomático, relativo o perteneciente a la diplomacia. 2. Diplomático, lo que pertenece al estudio de los diplomas y documentos antiguos o importantes.

Diplomatics [dip-lo-mat'-ics], *s.* (Arqueología) Diplomática, el arte de conocer y distinguir los diplomas y otros documentos de importancia.

Diplomatist [di-plō'-ma-tist], *s.* 1. *V.* DIPLOMAT. 2. Diplomático, el que es versado y hábil en diplomacia. 3. Dícese de la persona disimulada, astuta y sagaz.

Diplopia [di-plō'-pi-a], *s.* (Med.) Diplopía, visión doble; fenómeno morboso que hace ver dobles los objetos.

Dipper [dip'-ęr], *s.* 1. El que moja, sumerge o baña. 2. Cucharón para sacar líquidos en cantidad. 3. Echa y saca líquidos. 4. (Fam.) Osa mayor.

Dipping-needle [dip'-ing-ní'-dl], *s.* Aguja magnética sobre un eje horizontal.

Dipsas [dip'-sas], *s.* Serpiente fabulosa, cuya mordedura producía una sed inextinguible.

Dipsomania [dip-so-mé'-ni-a], *s.* Dipsomanía, deseo irresistible de bebidas alcohólicas.

Dipterous [dip'-tęr-us], *a.* (Ent.) Díptero; dícese de los insectos que tienen dos alas.

Diptych [dip'-tic], *s.* Díptica, registro de obispos y mártires.

Dire [dair], *a.* Horrendo, horroroso, horrible, espantoso, cruel, inhumano.

Direct [di-rect'], *a.* 1. Directo, derecho. *Direct current,* (Elec.) Corriente continua. *Direct hit,* Blanco directo. 2. Abierto, claro, patente.—*adv.* En línea recta, directamente.

Direct, *va.* 1. Dirigir, apuntar, enseñar, enderezar, guiar. 2. Dirigir, prescribir la dirección. 3. Dirigir, gobernar, regir, reglar, conducir, ordenar.

Direction [di-rec'-shun], *s.* 1. Dirección, la acción y efecto de dirigir, encaminar, etc. 2. Dirección, movimiento causado por algún impulso. 3. Dirección, consejo; orden, instrucción, mandato, 4. Curso de una línea, rumbo, dirección. 5. Designio, mira, fin; tendencia. 6. El sobrescrito o sobre de una carta; señas, dirección, residencia.

Directional signal [di-rec'-shun-al sig'-nal], *s.* Luz intermitente, luz direccional.

Direction indicator [di-rec'-shun in-di-kê-tęr], *s.* (Aer.) Indicador de dirección.

Directive [di-rect'-iv], *s.* Directiva, directorio.—*a.* Directivo, que dirige; indicativo.

Directly [di-rect'-li], *adv.* 1. Directamente, en línea recta. 2. Sin medianero, sin intervención de tercero. 3. Inmediatamente, en seguida; al instante.

Directness [di-rect'-nes], *s.* Derechura, línea recta.

Director [di-rect'-ęr], *s.* 1. Director. 2. Regla, ordenanza. 3. Director, el que dirige o instruye; director espiritual.

Directorate [di-rect'-er-êt], *s.* Dirección, el cuerpo de directores de un ramo, empresa o institución.

Directorial [di-rec-tō'-ri-al], *a.* Directorio, directivo.

Directory [di-rec'-to-ri], *s.* 1. Directorio; guía de forasteros. 2. Añalejo, librito que señala el orden del rezo y oficio divino. 3. Directorio comercial, lista alfabética de los habitantes de una ciudad. 4. Directorio, nombre del poder ejecutivo en Francia en 1795.

Direful [dair'-ful], *a.* Horrible, horrendo, fiero, cruel, inhumano, bárbaro.

Direfulness [dair'-ful-nes], *s.* Horribilidad, espanto; fiereza, crueldad.

Direness [dair'-nes], *s.* Horror, espanto; fiereza.

Dirge [dęrj], *s.* Endecha; canto fúnebre; canción triste y lamentosa.

Dirigible [dir-i'-ji-bl], *s.* Dirigible, globo dirigible.

Dirk [dęrc], *s.* Especie de daga.

Dirt [dęrt], *s.* 1. Cieno, lodo, barro, basura. 2. Excremento. 3. Tierra suelta. 4. Vileza, bajeza.—*a.* (fam.) Hecho de tierra. *Dirt cheap,* (fam.) Excesivamente barato.

Dirtily [dęrt'-i-li], *adv.* Puercamente, suciamente, vilmente, indignamente.

Dirtiness [dęrt'-i-nes], *s.* Suciedad; sordidez, bajeza, villanía.

Dirty [dęrt'-i], *a.* 1. Puerco, sucio, asqueroso, cochino; manchado, enlodado. 2. Sórdido, vil, bajo, despreciable, villano, indigno.

Dirty, *va.* Emporcar, ensuciar, manchar, ciscar, enlodar.

Dis [dis], **Des** [des], partícula prepositiva que quiere decir aparte; denota separación, negación, o fuerza intensiva.

Disability [dis-a-bil'-i-ti], *s.* Impotencia; inhabilidad, incapacidad.

Disable [dis-é'-bl], *va.* 1. Disminuir las fuerzas naturales. 2. Inhabilitar, inutilizar, incapacitar; arruinar. *To disable a ship,* (Mar.) Desaparejar un navío. *To disable the guns of a battery,* Desmontar una batería. 3. Incapacitar legalmente.

Disablement [dis-é'-bl-męnt], *s.* Impedimento legal; inhabilitación.

Disabuse [dis-a-biūz'], *va.* Enmendar, desengañar, sacar de un error.

Disaccommodate [dis-ąc-com'-o-dêt], *va.* (Ant.) Incomodar.

Disaccommodation [dis-a-com'-o-dé-shun], *s.* Ineptitud.

Disaccord [dis-ąc-cōrd'], *va.* Desacordar, discordar.

Disaccustom [dis-ąc-cus'-tęm], *va.* Desacostumbrar, deshabituar.

Disadjust [dis-ąd-just'], *va.* Trastornar el arreglo ordenado de algo; desarreglar, poner en desorden.

†**Disadorn** [dis-a-dōrn'], *va.* Desadornar.

Disadvantage [dis-ad-van'-tej], *s.* 1. Desventaja, menoscabo o pérdida. 2. Diminución de alguna cosa apreciable. 3. Desprevención.

Disadvantage, *va.* Menoscabar, dañar, perjudicar.

Disadvantageous [dis-ad-van-té'-jus], *a.* Desventajoso, desaventajado, incómodo.

Disadvantageously [dis-ad-van-té'-jus-li], *adv.* Desventajosamente.

Disadvantageousness [dis-ad-van-té'-jus-nes], *s.* Menoscabo, desventaja.

Disaffect [dis-af-fect'], *va.* Descontentar; inquietar; tener hastío; enfermar; desaprobar; indisponer, malquistar.

Disaffected [dis-af-fect'-ed], *a.* Desaficionado, desinclinado, disgustado, descontento; mal intencionado.

Disaffectedness [dis-af-fect'-ed-nes], *s.* Desafecto, desamor.

Disaffection [dis-af-fec'-shun], *s.* Desafecto, deslealtad; desamor, descontento.

§**Disaffectionate** [dis-af-fec'-shun-et], *a.* Desaficionado.

Disaffirm [dis-af-fęrm], *va.* 1. Contradecir, negar, impugnar una afirmación. 2. (For.) Invalidar, anular, hacer nulo; desconocer, renunciar, rechazar.

Disaffirmance [dis-af-fęrm'-ans], *s.* Confutación, impugnación.

Disaffirmation [dis-af-fęr-mé'-shun], *s.* *V.* DISAFFIRMANCE.

Disafforest [dis-af-fer'-est], *va.* (Der. inglés) Abrir un bosque o hacerlo de uso común.

Disaggregate [dis-ag'-re-gêt], *va.* Desagregar, separar en sus partes constitutivas.

Disagree [dis-a-grí'], *vn.* 1. Desconvenir; discordar, oponerse mutuamente, desavenirse. 2. Contender, lidiar, ser contrario; altercar. 3. No ser conveniente, no sentar bien, ser dañoso o perjudicial: seguido de *with.*

Disagreeable [dis-a-grí'-a-bl], *a.* 1. Contrario, opuesto. 2. Desagradable, ofensivo.

Disagreeableness [dis-a-grí'-a-bl-nes],

s. Oposición, desagrado, disgusto, desplacer.

Disagreeably [dis-a-grí'-a-bli], *adv.* Desagradablemente.

Disagreement [dis-a-grí'-mẹnt], *s.* 1. Desacuerdo, desavenencia, disensión. 2. Desemejanza, diferencia. 3. Discordia, contrariedad.

Disallow [dis-al-lau'], *va.* 1. Negar la autoridad de alguno. 2. Desaprobar, reprobar, censurar, culpar. —*vn.* Negar o no dar permiso, prohibir.

Disallowable [dis-al-lau'-a-bl], *a.* Negable; inadmisible; culpable, censurable.

Disallowance [dis-al-lau'-ans], *s.* Prohibición, vedamiento.

Disanimate [dis-an'-i-mêt], *va.* 1. (Ant.) Desanimar, desalentar, acobardar. 2. (Des.) Matar.

Disannul [dis-an-nul'], *va.* (Ant.) Anular, invalidar.

Disannuller [dis-an-nul'-ẹr], *s.* Anulador.

Disannulling [dis-an-nul'-ing], *s.* Anulación.

Disannulment [dis-an-nul'-mẹnt], *s.* Anulación.

Disanoint [dis-a-neint'], *va.* Profanar; degradar al que está ordenado.

Disapparel [dis-ap-par'-el], *va.* Desnudar, quitar el vestido; desguarnecer.

Disappear [dis-ap-pír'], *vn.* Desaparecer, perderse de vista; ausentarse.

Disappearance [dis-ap-pír'-ans], **Disappearing** [dis-ap-pír'-ing], *s.* Desaparecimiento, desaparición.

Disappoint [dis-ap-peint'], *va.* Frustrar, privar a alguno de lo que esperaba o dejar sin efecto su intento; faltar a la palabra; engañar; chasquear. *To be disappointed,* Llevarse chasco, salir mal en una empresa; ser contrariado. (Fam.) Quedar o dejar plantado, colgado, o chasqueado; petardear.

Disappointment [dis-ap-peint'-mẹnt], *s.* Chasco; contratiempo, petardo, revés, disgusto.

Disapprobation [dis-ap-pro-bé'-shun], *s.* Desaprobación, reprobación.

Disapprobatory [dis-ap'-pro-ba-to-ri], *s.* Desaprobador, que desaprueba.

Disapproval [dis-ap-prū'-val], *s.* Desaprobación, censura.

Disapprove [dis-ap-prūv'], *va.* 1. Desaprobar, reprobar, condenar, censurar. (Úsase a menudo con *of.*) 2. Invalidar, revocar.

Disarm [dis-ārm'], *va.* 1. Desarmar, despojar de armas. 2. Privar del poder de hacer daño; calmar, apaciguar —*vn.* Desechar o poner a un lado las armas; licenciar tropas o fuerzas marítimas, ponerlas en pie de paz.

Disarmament [dis-ārm'-a-ment], *s.* Desarme. *Nuclear disarmament.* Desarme nuclear. *Total disarmament.* Desarme total.

Disarmer [dis-ārm'-ẹr], *s.* El que desarma.

Disarming [dis-ārm'-ing], *s.* Desarme, desarmadura.

Disarrange [dis-ar-rênj'], *va.* Desarreglar, desordenar.

Disarrangement [dis-ar-rênj'-mẹnt], *s.* Desarreglo, desorden, confusión.

Disarray [dis-ar-ré'], *s.* 1. Desarreglo, desorden, confusión. 2. Ropa de levantar, paños menores, trapillo, desabillé.

Disarray, *va.* Desnudar; desarreglar; derrotar, desordenar.

Disarticulate [dis-ar-tic'-yu-lêt], *va.* Desarticular, separar las articulaciones.—*vn.* Desarticularse, descoyuntarse.

Disassociate [dis-as-sō'-shi-êt], *va.* Desunir.

Disaster [diz-ạs'-tẹr o dis-as'-tẹr], *s.* 1. Desastre, mala estrella. 2. Desgracia, aflicción, miseria, desdicha, infortunio, revés.

Disastrous [diz-ạs'-trus o dis-as'-trus], *a.* Desastroso, infeliz, desgraciado, desastrado, ominoso, calamitoso, infausto, funesto, triste, fatal.

Disastrously [diz-ạs' o dis-as'-trus-li], *adv.* Desastrosamente.

Disastrousness [diz-ạs' o dis-as'-trus-nes], *s.* Desgracia, desdicha.

Disavouch [dis-a-vauch'], *va.* (Ant.) Retractar, desdecirse.

Disavow [dis-a-vau'], *va.* Denegar, negar; desconocer; desaprobar.

Disavowal [dis-a-vau'-al], **Disavowment** [dis-a-vau'-mẹnt], *s.* Denegación.

†**Disauthorize** [dis-ō'-tẹr-aiz], *va.* Desautorizar.

Disband [dis-band'], *va.* Despedir de un servicio colectivo, especialmente licenciar del servicio militar.—*vn.* Retirarse, separarse, desmandarse, desbandarse.

Disbar [dis-bār'], *va.* Excluir del colegio de abogados; privar del derecho de comparecer ante un juez o tribunal como abogado.

Disbarment [dis-bār'-mẹnt], *s.* La acción y efecto de excluir a uno del colegio de abogados.

Disbark [dis-bārc'], *va.* (Mar.) Desembarcar.

Disbelief [dis-bẹ-líf'], *s.* Incredulidad, repugnancia en creer, falta de fe, terquedad en no creer; escepticismo.

Disbelieve [dis-bẹ-lív'], *va.* Descreer; desconfiar, dudar.—*vn.* Rehusar, no consentir en creer (p. ej. una doctrina religiosa).

Disbeliever [dis-bẹ-lív'-ẹr], *s.* Descreído, incrédulo.

Disbench [dis-bench'], *va.* (Der. inglés) Desbancar.

Disbowel [dis-bau'-el], *va.* (Ant.) *V.* DISEMBOWEL.

Disbranch [dis-brạnch'], *va.* (Ant.) Desgajar, arrancar las ramas del tronco.

Disbud [dis-bud'], *va.* Desyemar, desborrar, quitar los botones o tallos a las plantas.

Disburden [dis-būr'-dn], *va.* Descargar, aligerar, desembarazar de un peso.—*vn.* Descargar o aquietar el ánimo.

Disbursable [dis-būrs'-a-bl], *a.* Desembolsable, pagable; que se puede desembolsar.

Disburse [dis-būrs'], *va.* Desembolsar, pagar.

Disbursement [dis-būrs'-mẹnt], *s.* Desembolso; partida de gasto o inversión de una cantidad.

Disburser [dis-būrs'-ẹr], *s.* El que desembolsa, pagador.

Disc, *s.* *V.* DISK.

Discal [disc'-al], *a.* De disco; perteneciente o parecido a un disco.

Discalced [dis-calst'], *a.* Descalzado, descalzo (aplícase a los carmelitas).

Discant [dis'-cant], *v.* y *s.* *V.* DESCANT.

Discard [dis-cārd'], *va.* 1. Descartar, desechar como inútil; despedir o echar a un criado. 2. Descartar, deponer, apear de algún empleo o destino.—*vn.* Descartarse (en el juego de naipes).

Discase [dis-kês'], *va.* (Ant.) Desenvainar, quitar la cubierta; desnudar.

Discern [di-zẹrn'], *va.* 1. Columbrar, alcanzar a ver de lejos. 2. Discernir, conocer, percibir, descubrir.—*vn.* Discernir, distinguir.

Discerner [di-zẹrn'-ẹr], *s.* Discernidor, el que discierne.

Discernible [di-zẹrn'-i-bl], *a.* Perceptible, aparente, visible, sensible.

Discernibleness [di-zẹrn'-i-bl-nes], *s.* Visibilidad, perceptibilidad.

Discernibly [di-zẹrn'-i-bli], *adv.* Perceptiblemente, visiblemente.

Discerning [di-zẹrn'-ing], *a.* Juicioso, sagaz, perspicaz, despierto, avisado, advertido.—*s.* Discernimiento.

Discerningly [di-zẹrn'-ing-li], *adv.* Juiciosamente.

Discernment [di-zẹrn'-mẹnt], *s.* Discernimiento, conocimiento; gusto; agudeza, juicio recto.

Discerp [di-sẹrp'], *va.* (Ant.) Despedazar; separar, escoger.

Discerptible [di-sẹrp'-ti-bl], *a.* Separable.

Discerption [di-sẹrp'-shun], *s.* Despedazamiento; separación.

Discharge [dis-chārj'], *va.* 1. Descargar o aliviar la carga. 2. Descargar o sacar a tierra la carga de una embarcación. 3. Descargar, soltar; disparar. 4. Pagar una deuda. 5. Exonerar, eximir de alguna obligación, dispensar; absolver, dar libertad; desembarazar de alguna dificultad. 6. Ejecutar, cumplir. 7. Cancelar, borrar. 8. Descartar, despedir, privar de algún empleo u oficio; desempeñar, cumplir, llenar bien. 9. Emitir.—*vn.* Descargarse, soltarse. *To discharge the officers and crew,* Despedir la tripulación de un buque. *To discharge one's duty,* Cumplir con su obligación.

Discharge [dis-chārj'], *s.* 1. Descarga. 2. Descargo; finiquito, carta de pago. 3. Dimisión de algún empleo; exención. 4. Descargo, absolución. 5. Perdón de algún delito. 6. Rescate. 7. Ejecución. 8. Derrame, desagüe, cantidad o volumen de agua que sale por un orificio en un tiempo dado.

Discharger [dis-chārj'-ẹr], *s.* Descargador, disparador.

Disciple [di-sai'-pl], *s.* 1. Discípulo, alumno, estudiante. 2. Discípulo, partidario, el que sigue una doctrina.

Disciple, *va.* Disciplinar, criar, amaestrar.

Disciple-like [di-sai'-pl-laic], *a.* Semejante a un discípulo, o propio de él.

Discipleship [di-sai'-pl-ship], *s.* Discipulado, el ejercicio y la calidad de discípulo.

Disciplinable [dis'-i-plin-a-bl], *a.* Disciplinable, lo que es capaz o digno de disciplina o corrección.

Disciplinableness [dis'-i-plin-a-bl-nes], *s.* Capacidad de instrucción o de ser instruído.

Disciplinant [dis'-i-plin-ant], *s.* Disciplinante.

Disciplinarian [dis-i-plin-é'-ri-an], **Disciplinary** [dis'-i-plin-a-ri], *a.* Lo que pertenece a la disciplina.

Disciplinarian, *s.* 1. El que gobierna y enseña con rigor y exactitud. 2. (Des.) Puritano, presbiteriano.

Discipline [dis'-i-plin], *s.* 1. Disciplina, doctrina, instrucción, enseñanza; orden, regla, conducta, educación; arte, ciencia. 2. Rigor, castigo; mortificación, corrección.

Discipline, *va.* 1. Disciplinar, educar, instruir. 2. Reglar, gobernar, tener en orden. 3. Castigar, corregir, reformar.
Disc jockey [disc jek'-i], *s.* Anunciador de programas de radio a base de discos fonográficos.
Disclaim [dis-clêm'], *va.* 1. Negar, desconocer, renunciar, rechazar. 2. (For.) Denegar, renunciar (pretensión, derecho); declinar; negar, desconocer (responsabilidad de un acto).
Disclaimer [dis-clêm'-ęr], *s.* 1. Negador, desconocedor. 2. (For.) Renuncia, abandono; el acto, la declaración o escritura en que se hace renuncia o denegación.
Disclose [dis-clōz'], *vn.* 1. Descubrir, destapar; abrir. 2. Revelar, publicar.
Discloser [dis-clōz'-ęr], *s.* Descubridor, revelador.
Disclosure [dis-clō'-zhur], *s.* Descubrimiento, revelación, declaración.
Discoid [dis'-ceid], **Discoidal** [dis-ceid'-al], *a.* Que tiene la figura de un disco; perteneciente a un disco.
Discolor [dis-cul'-ęr], *va.* 1. Descolorar, amortiguar, quitar o comer el color a una cosa; descolorir. 2. Descolorar, descolorir, apagar, robar el color, dar color no natural; dícese de las cosas y personas.
Discoloration [dis-cul-ęr-ê'-shun], *s.* Descoloramiento; mancha, alteración de color.
Discolored [dis-cul'-ęrd], *a.* Descolorido, descolorado, manchado, emborronado, empañado.
Discolour, Discoloured, modo usual de escribir estas palabras en Inglaterra. *V.* Discolor, etc.
Discomfit [dis-cum'-fit], *va.* 1. Derrotar, vencer, deshacer, romper un ejército o tropas. 2. Turbar, desconcertar.
Discomfiture [dis-cum'-fi-chur o tiūr], *s.* 1. Derrota, vencimiento. 2. Turbación, desconcierto.
Discomfort [dis-cum'-fęrt], *s.* 1. Incomodidad, malestar; inquietud, pesar. 2. Desconsuelo, aflicción.
Discomfort, *va.* Incomodar; desconsolar, apesadumbrar, afligir, entristecer.
Discommend [dis-cem-mend'], *va.* (Ant.) Vituperar, censurar, culpar.
Discommendable [dis-cem-mend'-a-bl], *a.* Culpable, censurable.
Discommendation [dis-cem-men-dê'-shun], *s.* Culpa, censura; oprobio.
Discommender [dis-cem-mend'-ęr], *s.* Censor, censurador.
Discommode [dis-cem-mōd'], *va.* Incomodar, molestar, hacer mala obra.
Discommodious [dis-cem-mō'-di-us], *a.* Incómodo, molesto, importuno.
Discommodity [dis-cem-med'-i-ti], *s.* Incomodidad, inconveniente.
Discommon [dis-cem'-un], *va.* Privar de algún privilegio común.
Discompose [dis-cem-pōz'], *va.* 1. Descomponer, desconcertar, sacar de quicio. 2. Turbar, inmutar, inquietar, ofender. 3. Desordenar, desarreglar.
Discomposure [dis-cem-pō'-zhur], *s.* Descomposición, confusión, desorden, desarreglo; emoción, inquietud.
Disconcert [dis-cen-sęrt'], *va.* Desconcertar, descomponer, confundir, turbar, perturbar; hacer perder a uno el tino; avergonzar, correr, cortar.
Disconcerting [dis-cen-sęrt'-ing], *a.* Desconcertante, perturbador.
Disconformity [dis-cen-fōr'-mi-ti], *s.* (Ant.) Desconformidad, desconveniencia. *V.* Nonconformity.
Discongruity [dis-cen-grū'-i-ti], *s.* Incongruencia, incongruidad. *V.* Incongruity.
Disconnect [dis-cen-nect'], *va.* Desunir, separar.
Disconnection [dis-cen-nec'-shun], *s.* Desunión, separación.
Disconsolate [dis-cen'-so-let], *a.* Desconsolado, apesadumbrado, inconsolable, triste, abatido, afligido.
Disconsolately [dis-cen'-so-let-li], *adv.* Desconsoladamente.
Disconsolateness [dis-cen'-so-let-nes], *s.* Desconsuelo, tristeza.
Discontent [dis-cen-tent'], *s.* Descontento, sinsabor, desagrado.—*a.* Descontento, malcontento, desazonado, disgustado.
Discontent, *va.* Descontentar, desagradar, inquietar.
Discontented [dis-cen-tent'-ed], *a.* Descontentadizo, disgustado; malcontento.
Discontentedly [dis-cen-tent'-ed-li], *adv.* De mala gana, a regañadientes.
Discontentedness [dis-cen-tent'-ed-nes], *s.* Descontento, inquietud.
Discontenting [dis-cen-tent'-ing], *a.* Disgustado, malcontento.
Discontentment [dis-cen-tent'-męnt], *s.* Descontentamiento.
Discontinuance [dis-cen-tin'-yu-ans], *s.* 1. Descontinuación, cesación, interrupción, intermisión. 2. Desunión, separación, división.
Discontinuation [dis-cen-tin-yu-ê'-shun], *s.* 1. Descontinuación, el acto y efecto de descontinuar. 2. Desunión, separación.
Discontinue [dis-cen-tin'-yu], *va.* y *vn.* 1. Descontinuar o discontinuar, interrumpir, separarse, cesar. 2. Cesar de recibir un periódico.
Discontinuity [dis-cen-ti-niū'-i-ti], *s.* Desunión, falta de coherencia o de continuidad.
Discontinuous [dis-cen-tin'-yu-us], *a.* Descontinuo, interrumpido; separado, no continuo, abierto.
Discord [dis'-cērd], *s.* 1. Discordia; disensión. 2. Desacuerdo, discordancia, falta de acuerdo. 3. (Mús.) Discordancia, disonancia, sonido desagradable que ofende al oído.
Discord [dis-cērd'], *vn.* (Poco us.) Discordar, disentir.
Discordance, Discordancy [dis-cērd'-ans, i], *s.* Discordancia, contrariedad, disensión.
Discordant [dis-cērd'-ant], *a.* Discorde, incompatible, incongruo, inconsecuente.
Discordantly [dis-cērd'-ant-li], *adv.* Incongruentemente.
Discotheque [dis-co-tek'], *s.* Discoteca.
Discount [dis-caunt'], *s.* Descuento, rebaja, desfalco.
Discount [dis-caunt'], *va.* 1. Descontar, rebajar. 2. Descontar una letra de cambio.
Discountable [dis-caunt'-a-bl], *a.* (Com.) Descontable, que se puede descontar.
Discountenance [dis-caun'-te-nans], *va.* 1. Poner mala cara, reprobar, condenar, desalentar. 2. (Ant.) Avergonzar, sonrojar; mirar de reojo.
Discountenancer [dis-caun'-te-nans-ęr], *s.* Desalentador, el que desalienta a otro con su mala acogida; un vinagre.
Discounter [dis-caunt'-ęr], *s.* Prestamista, el que presta dinero a interés.
Discourage [dis-cur'-êj], *va.* 1. Desalentar, desanimar; acobardar, amedrentar, intimidar. 2. Reprimir, impedir, frustrar; apartar de un propósito (con *from*).
Discouragement [dis-cur'-êj-męnt], *s.* Desaliento, desánimo, descaecimiento de ánimo; cobardía.
Discourager [dis-cur'-êj-ęr], *s.* Desalentador, desanimador.
Discourse [dis-cōrs'], *s.* 1. Discurso plática, conversación; disertación. 2. (Lóg.) Razonamiento.
Discourse, *vn.* 1. Conversar, hablar. 2. Discurrir.—*va.* Hablar de; pronunciar.
Discoursing [dis-cōrs'-ing], *s.* Discurso, plática, conversación.
Discourteous [dis-cūr'-tę-us], *a.* Descortés, grosero.
Discourteously [dis-cūr'-tę-us-li], *adv.* Descortésmente.
Discourtesy [dis-cūr'-tę-si], *s.* Descortesía, grosería.
Discous [dis'-cus], *a.* Discoidal, discoide, a manera o en forma de disco. *V.* Discoid.
Discover [dis-cuv'-ęr], *va.* 1. Descubrir. 2. Revelar, manifestar; exhibir o exponer a la vista, descorrer el velo, hacer patente. 3. Descubrir, ver alguna cosa a lo lejos o de lejos. *To discover ahead*, (Mar.) Descubrir por la proa.
Discoverable [dis-cuv'-ęr-a-bl], *a.* 1. Lo que se puede descubrir. 2. Patente, manifiesto.
Discoverer [dis-cuv'-ęr-ęr], *s.* Descubridor, explorador.
Discovery [dis-cuv'-ęr-i], *s.* 1. Descubrimiento, invento, hallazgo. 2. Revelación, manifestación.
Discredit [dis-cred'-it], *s.* 1. Descrédito, diminución o pérdida de la reputación; deshonor, oprobio, ignominia. 2. Desconfianza.
Discredit, *va.* 1. Discreer, dudar. 2. Desacreditar, infamar, deshonrar, difamar.
Discreditable [dis-cred'-it-a-bl], *a.* Vergonzoso, ignominioso.
Discreet [dis-crīt'], *a.* Discreto, cuerdo, circunspecto.
Discreetly [dis-crīt'-li], *adv.* Discretamente, cuerdamente.
Discreetness [dis-crīt'-nes], *s.* Discreción, prudencia, juicio, seso.
Discrepance, Discrepancy [dis-crep'-ans, i], *s.* Discrepancia, diferencia; divergencia, desacuerdo. (La forma *Discrepance* es menos usada.)
Discrepant [dis-crep'-ant], *a.* Discrepante.
Discrete [dis-crīt'], *a.* 1. Distinto, desunido, separado, hecho de distintas unidades: (med.) discreto. 2. Descontinuo. 3. Contrario, que denota oposición.
Discretion [dis-cresh'-un], *s.* 1. Discreción, prudencia, miramiento, circunspección. 2. Arbitrio. *Age of discretion*, (For.) La edad legal, cumplida la cual se responde criminalmente ante los tribunales de justicia. Varía en los diferentes países.
Discretional [dis-cresh'-un-al], **Discretionary** [dis-cresh'-un-ę-ri], *a.* Discrecional, arbitrario, ilimitado; que se hace libre y prudencialmente.
Discretionally [dis-cresh'-un-al-i], *adv.* Discrecionalmente, a discreción.
§**Discretive** [dis-crī'-tiv], *a.* 1. Disyuntivo, que denota oposición lógica. 2. Distinto; separado.

Discretively [dis-crî'-tiv-li], *adv.* Disyuntivamente, separadamente, cada cosa de por sí.
Discriminable [dis-crim'-i-na-bl], *a.* Discernible, distinguible.
Discriminate [dis-crim'-i-nêt], *vn.* 1. Discriminar, distinguir. 2. Discriminar.
Discriminate, *a.* 1. Que nota o advierte diferencias; escogedor, que distingue. 2. Distinguido, diferenciado, escogido entre otros.
Discriminately [dis-crim'-i-nêt-li], *adv.* Distintamente; particularmente.
Discriminateness [dis-crim'-i-nẹt-nes], *s.* Diversidad, diferencia.
Discriminating [dis-crim'-i-nêt-ing], *pa.* 1. Capaz de distinguir claramente; mirado, fino. 2. Distintivo, particular, que sirve para distinguir. 3. Lo que establece distinción; diferencial.
Discrimination [dis-crim-i-nê'-shun], *s.* 1. Discriminación, distinción. 2. Discriminación.
Discriminative [dis-crim'-i-na-tiv], *a.* Distintivo, característico.
Discriminatively [dis-crim'-i-na-tiv-li], *adv.* De un modo distintivo.
Discriminatory [dis-crim'-i-na-to-ri], *a.* Discriminador.
Discrown [dis-craun'], *va.* Destronar, privar de la corona.
Discubitory [dis-kiū'-bi-to-ri], *a.* Reclinatorio.
†**Disculpate** [dis-cul'-pêt], *va.* Disculpar. *V.* EXCULPATE.
Discumbency [dis-cum'-ben-si], *s.* (Ant.) Reclinación, acción de recostarse para comer, como lo hacían los antiguos.
†**Discurrent** [dis-cur'-ent], *a.* Estancado, no corriente.
Discursion [dis-cūr'-shun], *s.* 1. ?Razonamiento, el acto de razonar. 2. (Des.) El acto de andar a correr de una parte a otra.
Discursive [dis-cūr'-siv], *a.* 1. Errante, vagabundo; discursivo. 2. Que raciocina; que denota pensamiento conexo.
Discursively [dis-cūr'-siv-li], *adv.* Por ilación, por deducción, por inferencia.
Discursiveness [dis-cūr'-siv-nes], *s.* 1. Calidad de digresivo. 2. El hilo o curso de un argumento.
?**Discursory** [dis-cūr'-so-ri], *a.* Argumentativo, racional, dircursivo.
Discus [dis'-cus], *s.* (*pl.* DISCI [dis'-sai]). 1. Disco, tejo de metal o piedra usado en los juegos gimnásticos. 2. (Biol.) Disco. *V.* DISK.
Discuss [dis-cus'], *va.* 1. Examinar alguna cosa; discutir, agitar o ventilar. 2. (Fam.) Catar; probar o juzgar una cosa comiéndola o bebiéndola; p. ej. una comida.
Discusser [dis-cus'-ẹr], *s.* El que discute o examina.
Discussing [dis-cus'-ing], *s.* Examen; debate.
Discussion [dis-cush'-un], *s.* Discusión, examen, debate.
Discussive [dis-cus'-iv], *a.* (Med.) Discusivo.
Discutient [dis-kiū'-shent], *s.* Resolutivo o resolvente.
Disdain [dis-dên', y menos aceptado diz-dên'], *va.* Desdeñar, menospreciar, despreciar, tener a o en menos.
Disdain, *s.* Desdén, desprecio, menosprecio.
Disdainful [dis-dên'-ful], *a.* Desdeñoso; altivo, altanero.
Disdainfully [dis-dên'-ful-i], *adv.* Desdeñosamente, con desprecio, con desdén, de una manera altiva.
Disdainfulness [dis-dên'-ful-nes], *s.* Desprecio altanero.
Disdaining [dis-dên'-ing], *s.* Vilipendio, desprecio.
Disease [diz-îz'], *s.* 1. Mal, enfermedad, achaque, indisposición. 2. Malestar, sufrimiento.
Disease, *va.* 1. Enfermar, causar enfermedad; contagiar. 2. (Des.) Afligir, incomodar; hacer daño.
Diseasedness [diz-îz'-ed-nes], *s.* Enfermedad, indisposición.
?**Disedge** [dis-ej'], *va.* Desafilar, embotar.
Disembark [diz-em-bārk'], *vn.* Desembarcar.—*va.* Desembarcar, sacar a tierra lo que está embarcado.
Disembarkation, Disembarcation [dis-em-bar-kê'-shun], *s.* Desembarque o desembarco.
Disembarrass [dis-em-bar'-as], *va.* Desembarazar.
Disembarrassment [dis-em-bar'-as-mẹnt], *s.* Desembarazo.
Disembay [dis-em-bê'], *va.* Salir de la bahía.
Disembitter [dis-em-bit'-ẹr], *va.* Dulzurar, dulcificar.
Disembodied [dis-em-bed'-id], *a.* Separado del cuerpo.
Disembody [dis-em-bed'-i], *va.* 1. Librar, separar del cuerpo o de la carnalidad. 2. Licenciar temporalmente algún cuerpo de ejército o de milicias.
Disembogue [dis-em-bōg'], *va.* Desembocar, descargar o desaguar en algún río o en el mar.—*vn.* (Mar.) Desembocar, salir de una bahía o de un estrecho.
?**Disembosom** [dis-em-būz'-um], *va.* Sacar del seno o del fondo del corazón.
Disembowel [dis-em-bau'-el], *va.* Desentrañar.
Disembroil [dis-em-breil'], *va.* Desembrollar, desenredar, desenmarañar.
Disenable [dis-en-ê'-bl], *va.* (Des.) Debilitar, incapacitar.
Disenchant [dis-en-chant'], *va.* Desencantar.
Disenclose [dis-en-clōz'], *va.* Descercar.
Disencumber [dis-en-cum'-bẹr], *va.* Desembarazar, librar de obstáculos o estorbos.
Disencumbrance [dis-en-cum'-brans], *s.* Desembarazo.
Disengage [dis-en-gêj'], *va.* Desunir; desocupar; libertar de algún poder u obligación; desenredar, librar a alguno de un embarazo o peligro. —*vn.* Libertarse de, separarse, desembarazarse.
Disengaged [dis-en-gêjd'], *a.* Desembarazado, libre; desunido; desocupado; sin empeño.
Disengagedness [dis-en-gêj'-ed-nes], *s.* Desembarazo; desocupación.
Disengagement [dis-en-gêj'-mẹnt], *s.* Desempeño, desembarazo; vacío.
Disennoble [dis-en-nō'-bl], *va.* (Ant.) Desennoblecer, degradar, envilecer.
Disenroll [dis-en-rōl'], *va.* (Ant.) Borrar algún nombre de una lista.
Disenslave [dis-en-slêv'], *va.* Rescatar de esclavitud.
Disentangle [dis-en-taṇ'-gl], *va.* Desenredar, desenlazar, desasir; separar cosas revueltas o mezcladas sin orden; desembarazar.
Disentanglement [dis-en-taṇ'-gl-mẹnt], *s.* Desenredo, desembarazo, desempeño.
Disentail [dis-en-têl'], *va.* Anular el vínculo u orden de sucesión; librar del vínculo.
Disenthrall [dis-en-thrēl'], *va.* Libertar, sacar de la esclavitud, librar de la opresión, emancipar. Se escribe también **Disenthral.**
†**Disenthrone** [dis-en-thrōn'], *va.* Destronar.
Disentitle [dis-en-tai'-tl], *va.* Privar de un título o derecho.
Disentrance [dis-en-trans'], *va.* Despertar de un sueño profundo; hacer volver a alguno en sí.
Disepalous [dai-sep'-al-us], *a.* Disépalo, de dos sépalos.
†**Disespouse** [dis-es-pauz'], *va.* (Poét.) Invalidar, anular los esponsales de presente o de futuro.
Disestablish [dis-es-tab'-lish], *va.* Privar del estado o carácter establecido; quitar a una Iglesia el apoyo del Estado.
Disestablishment [dis-es-tab'-lish-mẹnt], *s.* La acción y efecto de privar del apoyo de un Estado.
Disesteem [dis-es-tîm'], *s.* Desestima, desestimación.
Disesteem, *va.* Desestimar, tener en poco, desaprobar, no apreciar alguna cosa.
Disestimation [dis-es-ti-mê'-shun], *s.* Desestimación.
Disfame [dis-fêm'], *s.* Descrédito, infamia, mala reputación.
Disfavor [dis-fê'-vẹr], *va.* Desairar; desfavorecer, privar a alguno del favor que gozaba; desfigurar, afear o poner fea a alguna persona.
Disfavor, *s.* Disfavor, disgusto; fealdad, deformidad.
Disfavorer [dis-fê'-vẹr-ẹr], *s.* Desfavorecedor.
Disfavour, *v.* y *s.* *V.* DISFAVOR. Modo usual de escribir esta palabra en Inglaterra.
Disfiguration [dis-fig-yur-ê'-shun], *s.* Desfiguración, deformidad.
Disfigure [dis-fig'-yur], *va.* Desfigurar, afear.
Disfigurement [dis-fig'-yur-mẹnt], *s* Desfiguración.
Disforest, *va.* 1. Desmontar, privar de árboles. 2. *V.* DISAFFOREST.
Disfranchise [dis-frạn'-chiz o fran'-chaiz], *va.* Privar de los derechos de ciudadano; quitar franquicias, privilegios o inmunidades.
Disfranchisement [dis-frạn'-chiz-mẹnt], *s.* Privación de los derechos de ciudadanía, y de otros privilegios e inmunidades.
Disfurnish [dis-fūr'-nish], *va.* (Ant.) Desproveer, despojar, desamueblar.
Disgarnish [dis-gār'-nish], *va.* (Ant.) Desguarnecer.
?**Disgarrison** [dis-gar'-i-sen], *va.* Desguarnicionar.
Disgorge [dis-gērj'], *va.* 1. Vomitar. 2. Arrojar con violencia. 3. Entregar o devolver por fuerza, necesidad o temor.
Disgorgement [dis-gērj'-mẹnt], *s.* Vómito; entrega, devolución.
Disgrace [dis-grês'], *s.* Ignominia, infamia, oprobio, deshonra.
Disgrace, *va.* 1. Deshonrar, disfamar, atraer vergüenza, causar oprobio. 2. Hacer caer en desgracia; despedir con ignominia.
Disgraceful [dis-grês'-ful], *a.* Vergonzoso, deshonroso, oprobioso, ignominioso.
Disgracefully [dis-grês'-ful-i], *adv.* Vergonzosamente.
Disgracefulness [dis-grês'-ful-nes], *s.* Ignominia, afrenta.

Disgracer [dis-grês'-ẹr], *s.* Deshonrador.
Disgruntle [dis-grun'-tl], *va.* (Fam.) Descontentar; dejar plantado, enfadar (< *dis* y *grunt*).
Disguise, [dis-gaiz'], *va.* 1. Disfrazar, enmascarar. 2. Encubrir, solapar, tapar, ocultar; desfigurar, alterar la forma. 3. Embriagar (eufemismo).
Disguise, *s.* 1. Disfraz, máscara, embozo, velo, simulación, rebozo. 2. Embriaguez (eufemismo).
Disguiser [dis-gaiz'-ẹr], *s.* El que disfraza, encubre, etc.
Disguising [dis-gaiz'-ing], *s.* 1. Máscara. 2. El acto de dar apariencia de verdad a lo que es falso.
Disgust [dis-gust'], *s.* Disgusto, desazón, repugnancia; displicencia, sinsabor; aversión, tedio.
Disgust, *va.* Disgustar, repugnar, enfadar.
Disgustful [dis-gust'-ful], *a.* Desabrido, fastidioso, enfadoso, asqueroso, desagradable.
Disgustingly [dis-gust'-ing-li], *adv.* Desagradablemente, asquerosamente, desabridamente.
Dish [dish], *s.* 1. Fuente, plato grande o platón. 2. Plato, la vianda o manjar que se sirve en los platos. 3. Concavidad de la forma; copera, reborde de llanta. *A chafing-dish*, Chofeta, escalfador. *Side dish*, Un plato de entrada, principio. *Soup-dish*, Sopera.—*pl. Dishes*, Vajilla, servicio de mesa.
Dish, *va.* 1. Servir las viandas en fuente o plato grande. 2. Ponerle copera a una rueda. 3. (Ger.) Atrapar, engañar, dar gato por liebre.
Dishclout [dish'-claut], *s.* Rodilla, el trapo con que se limpian los platos.
Dish-water [dish'-wē-tẹr], *s.* Agua en que se lavan los platos.
Dishabille [dis-a-bil'], *s.* Paños menores, trapillo; ropa de mañana o de casa.
Disharmonious [dis-har-mō'-ni-us], *a.* Desacordado, destemplado, desafinado.
Disharmony [dis-hār'-mo-ni], *s.* Discordancia, disonancia.
Dish cloth [dish clōth], *s.* Paño para lavar los platos.
Dishearten [dis-hārt'-en], *va.* Desanimar, desalentar, descorazonar.
Dished [disht], *pp.* de DISH. 1. Servido en un plato; puesto en la mesa. 2. Dícese de la rueda con copera.
Dishevel [di-shev'-el], *va.* Desgreñar, desmelenar.
Dishful [dish'-ful], *s.* Cantidad que puede contener un plato; el contenido de un plato lleno.
Dishing [dish'-ing], *a.* Cóncavo.
Dishonest [dis- o diz-en'-est], *a.* 1. Pícaro, malo; desleal, falto de integridad, indigno de confianza. 2. Fraudulento, falso, injusto. 3. (Des.) Lascivo, impuro, deshonesto.
Dishonestly [dis-en'-est-li], *adv.* Fraudulentamente, de mala fe; injustamente.
Dishonesty [dis-en'-es-ti], *s.* 1. Picardía, dolo, fraude. 2. Violación de la confianza o del fideicomiso.
Dishonor [dis-en'-ẹr], *s.* Deshonor, deshonra, ignominia.
Dishonor, *va.* 1. Deshonrar, infamar. 2. Desflorar. 3. Despreciar; desadornar.
Dishonorable [dis-en'-ẹr-a-bl], *a.* 1. Deshonroso, afrentoso, indecoroso. 2. Deshonrado, infamado, sin honra; de reputación perdida.
Dishonorably [dis-en'-ẹr-a-bli], *adv.* Ignominiosamente.
Dishonour, Dishonourable, etc. *V.* DISHONOR, etc. Así se escribe usualmente en Inglaterra.
Dishonorer [diz-en'-ẹr-ẹr], *s.* 1. Seductor. 2. Deshonrador.
Dishouse [dis-hauz'], *va.* Privar de la casa: desalojar.
Dish rag [dish rag], *s.* Paño o trapo para lavar los platos.
Dishwasher [dish-wesh'-ẹr], *s.* 1. Lavaplatos, lavador o lavadora de platos. 2. Lavadora de platos (máquina).
Disillusion, Disillusionize [dis-il-lū'-zhun, aiz], *va.* Desencantar, quitar la ilusión; desilusionar.—*s.* Desilusión, pérdida de la ilusión.
‖**Disincarcerate** [dis-in-cār'-sẹr-êt], *va.* Desencarcelar.
Disinclination [dis-in-cli-nê'-shun], *s.* Desafecto, desamor; aversión.
Disincline [dis-in-clain'], *va.* Desinclinar, desviar la inclinación o afecto de alguno.
Disinclined [dis-in-claind'], *a.* Desinclinado, averso, indispuesto con.
Disincorporate [dis-in-cēr'-po-rêt], *va.* 1. Desincorporar, quitar las franquicias de una corporación. 2. Disolver una corporación.
Disincorporation [dis-in-cēr-po-rê'-shun], *s.* La privación de los fueros, derechos y privilegios de una corporación.
Disinfect [dis-in-fect'], *va.* Desinficionar, desinfectar, destruir la infección.
Disinfectant [dis-in-fect'-ant], *a.* Desinfectante.—*s.* Desinfectante, substancia usada para desinfectar; como el cloro, el ácido sulfuroso, o la formalina.
Disinfection [dis-in-fec'-shun], *s.* Desinfección, el acto y efecto de desinfectar.
Disinfector [dis-in-fect'-ẹr], *s.* 1. Agente o aparato desinfectante. 2. Desinfectador, el que desinfecta.
Disingenuous [dis-in-jen'-yu-us], *a.* Doble, falso, disimulado.
Disingenuously [dis-in-jen'-yu-us-li], *adv.* Doblemente, falsamente, traidoramente.
Disinhabited [dis-in-hab'-it-ed], *a.* Despoblado, desierto, deshabitado.
Disinherison [dis-in-her'-i-sun], *s.* Desheredamiento. *V.* DISINHERITANCE.
Disinherit [dis-in-her'-it], *va.* Desheredar.
Disinheritance [dis-in-her'-it-ans], *s.* Desheredación, acción de desheredar.
Disintegrate [dis-in'-tẹ-grêt], *va.* Desagregar, desintegrar, desmoronar. —*vn.* Desmoronarse, desintegrarse, desagregarse, hacerse o caerse a pedazos.
Disintegration [dis-in-tẹ-grê'-shun], *s.* Desagregación, desintegración, desmoronamiento.
Disinter [dis-in-tẹr'], *va.* Exhumar, desenterrar.
Disinterested [dis-in'-tẹr-est-ed], *a.* Desinteresado, neutral, imparcial.
Disinterestedly [dis-in'-tẹr-est-ed-li], *adv.* Desinteresadamente.
Disinterestedness [dis-in'-tẹr-est-ed-nes], *s.* Desinterés, abnegación.
Disinterment [dis-in-tẹr'-mẹnt], *s.* Exhumación, desenterramiento.
Disinthrall, *va.* *V.* DISENTHRALL.
‖**Disintricate** [dis-in'-tri-kêt], *va.* Desenredar.
Disinvolve [dis-in-velv'], *va.* Desenredar; destapar.
Disjoin [dis-jein'], *va.* Desunir, desasir, apartar, separar.
Disjoint [dis-jeint'], *va.* 1. Dislocar, descoyuntar, desencajar, desmembrar. 2. Desunir, separar, desarreglar, desordenar. Trinchar un ave. —*vn.* Desmembrarse, caer a pedazos.
Disjoint, Disjointed [dis-jeint', ed], *a.* Dividido.
Disjointly [dis-jeint'-li], *adv.* Desunidamente.
Disjunct [dis-juṇct'], *a.* Descoyuntado, dislocado.
Disjunction [dis-juṇc'-shun], *s.* Disyunción, descoyuntamiento, dislocación.
Disjunctive [dis-junc'-tiv], *a.* y *s.* Disyuntivo.
Disjunctively [dis-juṇc'-tiv-li], *adv.* Disyuntivamente.
Disk [disk], *s.* 1. Disco, figura circular y plana; superficie circular o casi circular y achatada. 2. (Bot.) Disco, cualquier órgano casi plano y circular; centro de una flor compuesta. 3. Patena, platillo sagrado de la eucaristía. 4. (Anat. y Zool.) Parte o estructura circular y achatada. 5. *V.* DISCUS y QUOIT. 6. (Art. y Of.) Disco; rueda de vidrio de la máquina eléctrica.
Diskindness [dis-kaind'-nes], *s.* (Poco us.) Descariño; agravio ligero.
Dislike [dis-laik'], *s.* Aversión, aborrecimiento, repugnancia, antipatía. *To take a dislike to any one*, Tener o tomar a uno entre ojos o entre ceja y ceja.
Dislike, *va.* Tener aversión a alguna persona; desaprobar.
Disliker [dis-laik'-er], *s.* El que desaprueba algo.
‖**Dislimb** [dis-lim'], *va.* Desmembrar.
Dislimn [dis-lim'], *va.* (Ant.) Borrar una pintura.
Dislocate [dis'-lo-kêt], *va.* Dislocar, descoyuntar.
Dislocation [dis-lo-kê'-shun], *s.* Dislocación, descoyuntamiento.
Dislodge [dis-lej'], *va.* 1. Desalojar, sacar o hacer salir de un lugar a una persona o cosa. 2. Desalojar, echar al enemigo de algún puesto.—*vn.* Desalojar, mudarse a otra parte.
Disloyal [dis-lei'-al], *a.* 1. Desleal. 2. Infiel, falso.
Disloyally [dis-lei'-al-i], *adv.* Deslealmente.
Disloyalty [dis-lei'-al-ti], *s.* Deslealtad, infidelidad; perfidia, inconstancia.
Dismal [diz'-mal], *a.* Triste, funesto, deplorable, espantoso, horrendo, horroroso, terrible, infeliz, aciago.
Dismally [diz'-mal-i], *adv.* Funestamente, tristemente.
Dismalness [diz'-mal-nes], *s.* Tristeza, melancolía; aspecto siniestro, infelicidad.
Disman [dis-man'], *va.* 1. Privar de hombres, desguarnecer. 2. (Des.) *V.* UNMAN.
Dismantle [dis-man'-tl], *va.* Desguarnecer, desamueblar; desmantelar una plaza, desaparejar una embarcación; despojar de adornos, etc.
Dismantling [dis-man'-tling], *s.* El acto de desmantelar.
Dismast [dis-mast'], *va.* Desarbolar un bajel.
Dismay [dis-mê'], *s.* Desmayo, deliquio, congoja; espanto, terror.
Dismay, *va.* Desmayar, espantar, desanimar.
Dismayedness [dis-mê'-ed-nes], *s.* Desmayo, desaliento, aterramiento, espanto, deliquio.

†**Disme**, *s.* *V.* TENTH y DIME.

Dismember [dis-mem'-bęr], *va.* 1. Desmembrar, separar un miembro del cuerpo; despedazar. 2. (Poco us.) Separar del cuerpo de una sociedad, iglesia, etc.

Dismemberment [dis-mem'-bęr-męnt], *s.* Desmembramiento.

Dismettled [dis-met'-ld], *a* (Des.) Desanimado, sin espíritu o animación.

Dismiss [dis-mis'], *va.* 1. Despedir, echar; destituir a un empleado; licenciar a un soldado. 2. Descartar, desechar, despachar, enviar. 3. Disolver una reunión, asamblea, etc. 4. Repudiar, rechazar. *To dismiss abruptly*, Echar a uno con cajas destempladas. *To dismiss*, or *send one about his business*, Enviar a uno a pasear.

Dismissal [dis-mis'-al], *s.* 1. Dimisión. 2. Permiso para salir, marcharse o retirarse.

Dismission [dis-mish'-un], *s.* 1. Despedimiento, despedida. 2. Dimisión; deposición, privación de un empleo.

Dismissory, Dismissive [dis-mis'-o-ri, dis-mis'-iv], *a.* Que despide, destituye o licencia; dimisorio.

Dismount [dis-maunt'], *va.* 1. Desmontar, sacar el caballo de la silla a su jinete. 2. Hacer que los soldados de a caballo presten servicio a pie. 3. Desmontar, desarmar una máquina, un cañón, etc., quitándole su montaje.—*vn.* Desmontar, apearse del caballo; bajar, descender.

Disnaturalize [dis-nach'-ur-al-aiz], *va.* Desnaturalizar.

Disobedience [dis-o-bî'-di-ens], *s.* Desobediencia.

Disobedient [dis-o-bî'-di-ent], *a.* Desobediente.

Disobey [dis-o-bé'], *va.* y *vn.* Desobedecer.

Disoblige [dis-o-blaij'], *va.* Desobligar, disgustar; librar de la obligación.

Disobliger [dis-o-blaij'-ęr], *s.* Ofensor.

Disobliging [dis-o-blaij'-ing], *a.* Desagradable, ofensivo.

Disobligingly [dis-o-blaij'-ing-li], *adv.* Desagradablemente.

Disobligingness [dis-o-blaij'-ing-nes], *s.* Desagrado, desatención.

Disorder [dis-ōr'-dęr], *s.* 1. Desorden, desarreglo, confusión, desconcierto. 2. Indisposición, desazón, disgusto. 3. Enfermedad, indisposición; enajenamiento del ánimo. 4. Motín o tumulto; alboroto.

Disorder [dis-ōr'-dęr], *va.* 1. Desordenar, confundir, descomponer, desconcertar. 2. Causar alguna enfermedad. 3. Inquietar, perturbar el ánimo, enojar, enfadar, alterar.

Disordered [dis-ōr'-dęrd], *a.* Desordenado, disoluto; confuso.

Disorderedness [dis-ōr'-dęrd-nes], *s.* Irregularidad, confusión.

Disorderly [dis-ōr'-dęr-li], *a.* Desordenado, desarreglado, confuso; ilegal. —*adv.* Desordenamente; ilegalmente.

Disorganization [dis-ōr-gan-i-zé'-shun], *s.* Desorganización.

Disorganize [dis-ōr'-gan-aiz], *va.* Desorganizar, destruir o romper la estructura orgánica de; derribar.

Disorganizer [dis-ōr'-gan-aiz-ęr], *s.* Desorganizador.

Disorient, Disorientate [dis-ō'-ri-ent, ēt], *va.* 1. Desviar del este; en especial, construir una iglesia sin el altar al lado oriente. *V.* ORIENTATE. 2. Desorientar, hacer perder el conocimiento de la posición que se ocupa en el terreno; de aquí (fig.) extraviar, confundir, hacer confuso en la mente.

Disorientated [dis-ō'-ri-en-té-ted], *a.* Desorientado, desatentado.

Disown [dis-ōn'], *va.* Negar, desconocer, renunciar, no reconocer.

Disparage [dis-par'-ęj], *va.* 1. Rebajar, difamar, injuriar a alguno por compararle o juntarle con otro inferior; rebajar, disminuir el valor de una cosa comparándola con otra de mala calidad. *V.* BELITTLE. 2. Desdorar, quitar el crédito de alguna persona.

Disparagement [dis-par'-ęj-męnt], *s.* 1. Desdoro; unión o comparación injuriosa de una cosa inferior con otra superior. 2. Censura, infamia. 3. Desprecio, murmuración, conversación denigrativa.

Disparager [dis-par'-ęj-ęr], *s.* El que desdora, mancilla o deslustra.

Disparagingly [dis-par'-ęj-ing-li], *adv.* Desdeñadamente, de un modo que rebaja y desdora.

Disparate [dis'-pa-rēt], *a.* Desigual, discorde; desemejante.

Disparates [dis'-pa-rēts], *s. pl.* Cosas tan desemejantes que no admiten comparación entre sí.

Disparity [dis-par'-i-ti], *s.* Disparidad, desigualdad; desemejanza.

Dispark [dis-pārk'], *va.* (Ant.) Descercar, abrir una cerca.

Dispart [dis-pārt'], *va.* 1. Despartir, apartar, dividir, separar. 2. Señalar el punto de mira en los cañones. —*vn.* Partirse, dividirse, rajarse.

Dispart, *s.* 1. Mira, pieza del cañón que sirve para dirigir la vista y asegurar la puntería. Se llama también DISPART-SIGHT. 2. Vivo de un cañón.

Dispassion [dis-pash'-un], *s.* (Ant.) Calma, serenidad de ánimo.

Dispassionate [dis-pash'-un-ēt], *a.* Desapasionado, sereno, fresco, templado, sosegado; imparcial, moderado.

Dispassionately [dis-pash-un-ēt'-li], *adv.* Serenamente, tranquilamente.

Dispassioned [dis-pash'-und], *a.* (Poco us.) Sereno. *V.* DISPASSIONATE.

Dispatch, *v.* y *s.* *V.* DESPATCH.

Dispel [dis-pel'], *va.* Dispersar, esparcir; disipar; expeler, desechar.

†**Dispend** [dis-pend'], *va.* Gastar.

Dispensable [dis-pen'-sa-bl], *a.* Dispensable.

Dispensableness [dis-pen'-sa-bl-nes], *s.* La calidad de dispensable.

Dispensary [dis-pen'-sa-ri], *s.* 1. Dispensario, lugar donde se conservan y preparan los medicamentos. 2. Casa o botica de barrio o distrito donde los enfermos pobres reciben gratuitamente o a precio barato los auxilios facultativos y los medicamentos que necesitan.

Dispensation [dis-pen-sé'-shun], *s.* 1. Distribución o reparto de alguna cosa. 2. Dispensación, dispensa. 3. Dispensación o ley divina; sistema de principios o ritos prescritos en una religión.

Dispensative [dis-pen'-sa-tiv], *a.* (Ant.) Lo que dispensa.

Dispensator [dis'-pen-sé-tęr], *s.* Dispensador.

Dispensatory [dis-pen'-sa-to-ri], *s.* Farmacopea, el libro que prescribe la composición de las medicinas.—*a.* Lo que tiene poder de dispensar o dar dispensas.

Dispense [dis-pens'], *va.* 1. Dispensar, distribuir, repartir. 2. Componer un medicamento de varios ingredientes. 3. Dispensar, exceptuar; excusar. *To dispense with*, (1) Dispensar de, permitir que no se haga alguna cosa, renunciar la observancia de. (2) Privarse de alguna cosa, ceder, dejar, renunciar a algo.

Dispenser [dis-pens'-ęr], *s.* Dispensador; el que inventa disculpas para no hacer alguna cosa.

Dispeople [dis-pî'-pl], *va.* Despoblar.

Dispeopler [dis-pî'-plęr], *s.* Despoblador.

Dispersal [dis-pęr'-sal], *s.* *V.* DISPERSION.

Disperse [dis-pęrs'], *va.* 1. Dispersar, esparcir, desparramar. 2. Disipar. 3. Distribuir. 4. Separar la luz en sus colores componentes.—*vn.* 1. Dispersarse, separarse, retirarse. 2. Disiparse; desaparecer.

Dispersedly [dis-pęrs'-ed-li], *adv.* Esparcidamente.

Dispersedness [dis-pęrs'-ed-nes], *s.* Dispersión.

Disperser [dis-pęrs'-ęr], *s.* Esparcidor, sembrador.

Dispersion [dis-pęr'-shun], *s.* 1. Dispersión, esparcimiento, acción y efecto de dispersar. 2. Desviación de los rayos de luz.

Dispersive [dis-pęrs'-iv], *a.* Esparcidor, lo que tiene el poder de esparcir.

Dispirit [dis-pir'-it], *va.* Desalentar, desanimar, amilanar.

Dispiritedness [dis-pir'-it-ed-nes], *s.* Desaliento, desánimo.

Displace [dis-plés'], *va.* 1. Dislocar, desordenar. 2. Tomar el lugar de (destituyendo).

Displaced person [dis-plésd' per'-sun], *s.* Persona desplazada.

Displacement [dis-plés'-męnt], *s.* 1. Desarreglo, trastorno, mudanza. 2. Cambio aparente de posición, v. gr. de una estrella. 3. (Mar.) Desplazamiento, el peso del agua que desaloja el casco de un buque. 4. (Quím. y Farm.) Coladura. *V.* PERCOLATION. 5. (Geol.) Falla. *V.* FAULT.

Displacer [dis-plé'-sęr], *s.* 1. El que desordena. 2. (Quím.) Colador. *V.* PERCOLATOR.

Displant [dis-plant'], *va.* Transplantar, trasponer; expeler; arrancar.

Displantation [dis-plan-té'-shun], *s.* 1. Trasplante, trasplantación. 2. (Fig.) Expulsión (de una raza, de un pueblo).

Displanting [dis-plant'-ing], *s.* Deposición, expulsión.

Display [dis-plé'], *va.* 1. Desplegar, descoger; extender, ensanchar. 2. Declarar, explicar, exponer; hablar con despejo y sin rebozo. 3. Ostentar, mostrar, hacer patente una cosa. 4. (Mar.) Enarbolar el pabellón, bandera de paz, etc.

Display, *s.* Despliegue, acción de desplegar o extender; ostentación, manifestación; fausto.

Displayer [dis-plé'-ęr], *s.* Ostentador.

Display window [dis-plé' win'-dō], *s.* Vitrina, aparador.

†**Displeasant** [dis-plez'-ant], *a.* Desagradable, ofensivo.

Displease [dis-plîz'], *va.* y *vn.* Desplacer, enfadar, desazonar, incomodar, inquietar; ofender.

Displeased [dis-plîzd'], *a.* Ofendido, disgustado, incomodado, enojado.

Displeasing [dis-plîz'-ing], *pa.* Displicente, ofensivo.

Displeasingness [dis-plîz'-ing-nes], *s.* Ofensa, displicencia.
Displeasure [dis-plezh'-ur], *s.* Desplacer, disgusto, inquietud, ofensa; indignación, desgracia, disfavor.
Displeasure, *va.* (Ant.) Desagradar, disgustar.
†**Displode** [dis-plōd'], *va. V.* EXPLODE.
Dispondee [dai-spen'-dî], *s.* Dispondeo, pie de verso que consta de dos espondeos o cuatro sílabas largas. (— —, — —.)
Disport [dis-pōrt'], *s.* Diversión, pasatiempo.
Disport, *va.* Juguetear, travesear. —*vn.* Entretenerse, retozar, divertirse, recrearse.
Disposable [dis-pōz'-a-bl], *a.* Disponible.
Disposal [dis-pōz'-al], *s.* 1. Disposición, colocación, arreglo. 2. Venta; donación; desembolso; libramiento. 3. Poder de restringir, gobierno, dirección.
Dispose [dis-pōz'], *va.* 1. Disponer, dar, colocar, adaptar, arreglar. 2. Cultivar el entendimiento. *To dispose of,* Aplicar; transferir; vender; entregar; desembarazarse de; dar; dirigir; conducir; poner en alguna condición. *To dispose of a house,* Ceder, transferir, vender una casa. *To dispose of another man's money,* Servirse del dinero ajeno. *To dispose of one,* Librarse o zafarse de uno. (Fig.) Matar a uno. *To dispose of one's time,* Emplear su tiempo.
Disposed [dis-pōzd'], *pp.* Dispuesto, preparado, inclinado. *Disposed of,* Dado; vendido; alquilado.
Disposer [dis-pōz'-ẹr], *s.* Disponedor, regulador, director.
Disposing [dis-pōz'-ing], *s.* Dirección.—*part. adj.* Disponente.
Disposition [dis-po-zish'-un], *s.* 1. Disposición, orden, método. 2. Aptitud, proporción. 3. Genio, natural, índole. 4. Buena o mala intención. 5. Inclinación dominante. *Disposition of body,* El estado de salud.
Dispossess [dis-pez-zes'], *va.* Desposeer, privar a uno de la posesión o goce de alguna cosa.
Dispossession [dis-pez-zesh'-un], *s.* Desposeimiento, despojo.
†**Disposure** [dis-pō'-zhur], *s. V.* DISPOSAL y DISPOSITION.
Dispraise [dis-prêz'], *va.* (Des.) Vituperar, condenar, afear.
Dispraise, *s.* Desprecio, censura, vituperación, reprobación.
Dispraiser [dis-prêz'-ẹr], *s.* Censor.
Dispraisingly [dis-prêz'-ing-li], *adv.* Vituperiosamente.
Dispread [dis-pred'], *va.* (Poco us.) Desplegar.—*vn.* Extenderse.
Dispreader [dis-pred'-er], *s.* Pregonero, publicador.
Disprize [dis-praiz'], *va.* (Ant.) Despreciar.
Disprofit [dis-pref'-it], *s.* (Ant.) Pérdida, daño.
Disproof [dis-prūf'], *s.* 1. Confutación. 2. Refutación, impugnación.
Disproperty [dis-prep'-ẹr-ti], *va.* (Poco us.) Desaposesionar, desposeer a uno de la posesión o dominio de alguna finca.
Disproportion [dis-pro-pōr'-shun], *s.* Desproporción, desigualdad.
Disproportion, *va.* Desproporcionar.
Disproportionable [dis-pro-pōr'-shun-a-bl], **Disproportional** [dis-pro-pōr'-shun-al], **Disproportionate** [dis-pro-pōr'-shun-et], *a.* 1. Desproporcionado, desigual, falto de proporción y simetría. 2. Insuficiente.
Disproportionableness [dis-pro-pōr'-shun-a-bl-nes], **Disproportionality** [dis-pro-por-shun-al'-i-ti], **Disproportionatenes** [dis-pro-pōr'-shun-et-nes], *s.* Desproporción, desigualdad.
Disproportionably [dis-pro-pōr'-shun-a-bli], **Disproportionally** [dis-pro-pōr'-shun-al-i], **Disproportionately** [dis-pro-pōr'-shun-et-li], *adv.* Desproporcionadamente.
Disprovable [dis-prūv'-a-bl], *a.* Refutable, que puede refutarse o impugnarse.
Disprove [dis-prūv'], *va.* Confutar; desaprobar, impugnar.
Disprover [dis-prūv'-ẹr], *s.* Impugnador; censurador.
Dispunishable [dis-pun'-ish-a-bl], *a.* (Ant.) No punible.
Disputability, Disputableness [dis-piū"-ta-bil'-i-ti, bl-nes], *s.* Disputabilidad, condición que permite controversia.
Disputable [dis'-piu-ta-bl o dis-piū'-ta-bl], *a.* Disputable, controvertible, problemático.
Disputant [dis'-piu-tant], *a.* Disputante.—*s.* Disputador.
Disputation [dis-piu-tê'-shun], *s.* Disputa, controversia.
Disputatious [dis-piu-tê'-shus], **Disputative** [dis-piū'-ta-tiv], *a.* Disputador; quisquilloso, caviloso.
Dispute [dis-piūt'], *vn.* Disputar, controvertir.—*va.* 1. Disputar, pleitear; argüir. 2. Contestar, resistir.
Dispute, *s.* 1. Disputa, controversia. 2. Discusión, debate; contienda, altercación. *Beyond* o *without dispute,* Sin disputa, sin la menor duda.
Disputeless [dis-piūt'-les], *a.* Indisputable.
Disputer [dis-piūt'-ẹr], *s.* Disputador; controversista.
Disputing [dis-piūt'-ing], *s.* Disputa, altercación.
Disqualification [dis-cwel-i-fi-kê'-shun], *s.* Inhabilitación, inhabilidad, incapacidad.
Disqualify [dis-cwel'-i-fai], *va.* Inhabilitar, declarar a uno inhábil para una cosa (incapaz de ejercer los derechos de ciudadano, etc.); imposibilitar; privar.
Disquiet [dis-cwai'-et], *s.* Inquietud, desasosiego, desazón—*a.* ‖Inquieto, desasosegado.
Disquiet, *va.* Inquietar, desasosegar, molestar, atormentar, no dejar en paz.
Disquieter [dis-cwai'-et-ẹr], *s.* Inquietador.
Disquietful [dis-cwai'-et-ful], *a.* Que produce inquietud o molestia.
Disquieting [dis-cwai'-et-ing], *s.* Vejación, molestia.—*pa.* de DISQUIET.
Disquietly [dis-cwai'-et-li], *adv.* Inquietamente.
Disquietness [dis-cwai'-et-nes], **Disquietude** [dis-cwai'-e-tiūd], *s.* Inquietud, desasosiego.
Disquisition [dis-cwi-zish'-un], *s.* Disertación, ensayo, tratado o discurso sistemático sobre cualquiera materia.
Disrate [dis-rêt'], *va.* (Mar.) Degradar, rebajar del grado.
Disregard [dis-rẹ-gārd'], *va.* Desatender, no hacer caso, descuidar, pasar por alto, menospreciar.
Disregard, *s.* Desatención, descuido, omisión, negligencia, desprecio.
Disregarder [dis-rẹ-gārd'-ẹr], *s.* Despreciador, menospreciador.
Disregardful [dis-re-gārd'-ful], *a.* Desatento, negligente.
Disregardfully [dis-rẹ-gārd'-ful-i], *adv.* Desatentamente.
Disrelish [dis-rel'-ish], *s.* 1. Disgusto, desazón, desabrimiento causado en el paladar. 2. Desgana, tedio, hastío, aversión, inapetencia.
Disrelish, *va.* 1. Disgustar, causar disgusto y desabrimiento al paladar. 2. Dar un gusto desabrido o ingrato a alguna cosa; tener tedio o aversión.
Disreputable [dis-rep'-yu-ta-bl], *a.* Deshonroso, dañoso a la reputación; desacreditado, despreciado.
Disrepute [dis-rẹ-piūt'], *s.* Descrédito, ignominia, mala fama, mal nombre.
†**Disrepute,** *va.* Deshonrar, quitar el crédito; desatender.
Disrespect [dis-rẹ-spect'], *s.* Irreverencia, desacato, falta de respeto; desatención.
Disrespect, *va.* (Fam.) Desacatar: desatender, despreciar.
Disrespectful [dis-rẹ-spect'-ful], *a.* Irreverente, descortés, desatento, falto de respeto.
Disrespectfully [dis-re-spect'-ful-i], *adv.* Desacatadamente, irreverentemente, desatentamente.
Disrobe [dis-rōb'], *va.* Desnudar, quitar los vestidos; (fig.) despojar, privar.—*vn.* Desnudarse, quitarse los vestidos.
Disrober [dis-rōb'-ẹr], *s.* Desnudador.
Disroot [dis-rūt'], *va.* Desarraigar, arrancar de raíz; arrancar de los cimientos.
Disrupt [dis-rupt'], *va.* Romper, hacer pedazos, rajar.
Disruption [dis-rup'-shun], *s.* Rompimiento; dilaceración; reventón.
Disruptive [dis-rup'-tiv], *a.* Rajante, que revienta o estalla.
Dissatisfaction [dis-sat-is-fac'-shun], *s.* Descontento, disgusto.
Dissatisfactoriness [dis-sat-is-fac'-to-ri-nes], *s.* Incapacidad de contentar.
Dissatisfactory [dis-sat-is-fac'-to-ri], *a.* Desplaciente, enojoso, fastidioso.
Dissatisfy [dis-sat'-is-fai], *va.* Descontentar, desagradar.
‖**Disseat** [dis-sît'], *va.* Echar del asiento.
Dissect [dis-sect'], *va.* 1. Cortar o dividir en pedazos; dividir y examinar por menor, anatomizar, disecar. 2. (Fig.) Criticar, analizar.
Dissection [dis-sec'-shun], *s.* 1. Disección, anatomía. 2. Examen minucioso de una cosa, análisis. 3. Objeto disecado, preparación anatómica.
Dissector [dis-sect'-ẹr], *s.* Anatómico, disector.
Disseize [dis-sîz'], *va.* (For.) Desposeer, usurpar el dominio.
Disseisin [dis-sîz'-in], *s.* (For.) Usurpación de las tierras o heredades ajenas.
Disseizor [dis-sîz'-ẹr], *s.* (For.) Usurpador, el que desposee a otro de su propiedad.
Dissemblance [dis-sem'-blans], *s.* (Ant.) Desemejanza, disimilitud.
Dissemble [dis-sem'-bl], *va.* Disimular, encubrir, dar a entender lo que no es.—*vn.* Disimular, ocultar, hacer el papel de hipócrita.
Dissembler [dis-sem'-blẹr], *s.* Hipócrita, disimulador.
Dissembling [dis-sem'-bling], *s.* Disimulación.
Dissemblingly [dis-sem'-bling-li], *adv.* Disimuladamente.
Disseminate [dis-sem'-i-nêt], *va.* Diseminar, sembrar, esparcir; (fig.) diseminar, divulgar, promulgar.

Dissemination [dis-sem-i-né'-shun], *s.* Diseminación, sembradura; divulgación.
Disseminator [dis-sem'-i-nê-tęr], *s.* Diseminador; sembrador.
Dissension [dis-sen'-shun], *s.* Disensión, contienda, desunión, pendencia, cizaña, querella, división, discordia; oposición.
‖**Dissensious** [dis-sen'-shus], *a.* *V.* DISSENTIOUS.
Dissent [dis-sent'], *vn.* 1. Disentir, diferir de opinión, variar, diferenciarse, disidir. 2. Rehusar adhesión a una iglesia establecida.
Dissent, *s.* Disensión, oposición, o contrariedad en los pareceres.
Dissentaneous [dis-sen-tê'-nę-us], *a.* Discorde; contrario.
Dissenter [dis-sent'-ęr], *s.* 1. Disidente, el que se separa del modo de pensar del mayor número. 2. Disidente, hereje entre los católicos; no conformista.
Dissentient [dis-sen'-shent], *a.* Desconforme, opuesto.
Dissenting [dis-sent'-ing], *s.* Declaración de un parecer u opinión diferente.
Dissentious [dis-sen'-shus], *a.* Contencioso, pendenciero.
Dissertation [dis-sęr-tê'-shun], *s.* Disertación, discurso en que se presentan razones a favor de una opinión y se impugnan las contrarias.
Dissertator [dis-sęr-tê'-tęr], *s.* Disertador.
Disserve [dis-sęrv'], *va.* Dañar, injuriar, perjudicar.
Disservice [dis-sęr'-vis], *s.* Deservicio, perjuicio.
Disserviceable [dis-sęr'-vis-a-bl], *a.* Perjudicial, dañoso.
Disserviceableness [dis-sęr'-vis-a-bl-nes], *s.* Injuria, daño
†**Dissettle** [dis-set'-l], *va.* Descomponer. *V.* UNSETTLE.
Dissever [dis-sev'-ęr], *va.* Partir, dividir en dos partes, separar, desunir, desmembrar.
Dissevering [dis-sev'-ęr-ing], *s.* Separación, desunión.
Dissidence [dis'-i-dens], *s.* Discordia, disidencia, desunión.
Dissident [dis'-i-dent], *a.* Opuesto, desconforme.
Dissilience, Dissiliency [dis-sil'-i-ens, i], *s.* Reventón, el acto de reventar, o abrirse súbitamente.
Dissilient [dis-sil'-i-ent], *a.* Reventado, lo que se abre en dos partes o revienta.
Dissimilar [dis-sim'-i-lar], *a.* Desemejante, diferente, heterogéneo.
Dissimilarity [dis-sim-i-lar'-i-ti], **Dissimilitude** [dis-si-mil'-i-tiūd], *s.* 1. Desemejanza, disimilitud, diversidad, diferencia. 2. Comparación entre dos cosas contrarias.
Dissimulation [dis-sim-yu-lé'-shun], *s.* Disimulación, hipocresía.
Dissipable [dis'-i-pa-bl], *a.* Disipable, lo que es fácil de disiparse o esparcirse.
Dissipate [dis'-i-pêt], *va.* 1. Disipar, esparcir, dispersar. 2. Desparramar, desperdiciar; malgastar, derrochar.—*vn.* 1. Disiparse, esparcirse, evaporarse, desaparecer. 2. Ser pródigo o disoluto.
Dissipated [dis'-i-pêt-ed], *a.* Disipado, perdido, relajado.—*pp.* de DISSIPATE.
Dissipation [dis-i-pé'-shun], *s.* 1. Disipación, la acción y efecto de disipar; evaporación, pérdida. 2. Distracción, dispersión. 3. Relajación, devaneo, vida relajada, disoluta.
Dissociable [dis-sō'-shi-a-bl], *a.* 1. Que no está bien ordenado o asociado, incongruo; insociable. 2. Que permite separarse o desunirse.
Dissocial [dis-sō'-shal], *a.* Insociable, intratable, huraño.
Dissociate [dis-sō'-shi-êt], *va.* Desunir, disociar, dividir, separar; separar las partes cuya aglomeración forma un cuerpo.
Dissociation [dis-sō-shi-é'-shun], *s.* Disociación, separación, desunión.
Dissoluble [dis'-o-lu-bl en literatura, o dis-sel-'yu-bl (Quím.)], *a.* 1. Disoluble. 2. Separable en partes.
Dissolubility [dis-o-lu-bil'-i-ti], *s.* Disolubilidad.
Dissolute [dis'-o-lūt], *a.* Disoluto, libertino, licencioso.
Dissolutely [dis'-o-lūt-li], *adv.* Disolutamente.
Dissoluteness [dis'-o-lūt-nes], *s.* Disolución, relajación de la vida y costumbres, enviciamiento.
Dissolution [dis-o-lū'-shun], *s.* 1. Disolución, acción de disolver, de desleir. 2. (Quím.) Descomposición, separación de las moléculas que componen un cuerpo; desagregación. 3. Disolución de una sociedad o de un parlamento. 4. Muerte.
Dissolvable, Dissolvible [diz-elv'-a-bl, i-bl], *a.* Disoluble, que se puede disolver o desatar.
Dissolve [diz-elv'], *va.* 1. Disolver, deshacer, desleir. 2. Disolver, terminar una asamblea; levantar una sesión. 3. Desencantar. 4. (For.) Anular, abrogar. 5. Desatar, deshacer un lazo o nudo; separar, desunir; relajar. 6. Destruir.—*vn.* 1. Disolverse, derretirse, evaporarse. 2. Descomponerse. 3. Descaecer, ir a menos, perderse de vista. 4. Languidecer, enervarse, aniquilarse.
Dissolvent [diz-elv'-ent], *a.* y *s.* Disolvente, resolutivo.
Dissolver [diz-elv'-ęr], *s.* 1. Disolvente. 2. El que resuelve una dificultad.
Dissonance, Dissonancy [dis'-o-nans, i], *s.* Disonancia, desconcierto, discordia.
Dissonant [dis'-o-nant], *a.* Disonante, discordante; contrario, diferente, opuesto.
Dissuade [dis-swêd'], *va.* Disuadir, desviar, procurar apartar a uno de su intento o hacerle mudar de dictamen (con *from*).
Dissuader [dis-swêd'-ęr], *s.* Disuadidor.
Dissuasion [dis-swé'-zhun], *s.* Disuasión, consejo o persuasión.
Dissuasive [dis-swé'-siv], *a.* Disuasivo.—*s.* Disuasión, consejo.
Dissyllabic [dis-si-lab'-ic], *a.* Disílabo, que consta de dos sílabas.
Dissyllable [dis-sil'-a-bl], *s.* (Gram.) Disílabo.
Distad [dis'-tad], *adv.* (Anat.) Hacia la periferia o la extremidad.
Distaff [dis'-taf], *s.* 1. Rueca. 2. (Fig.) El sexo femenino.
Distain [dis-tên'], *va.* Manchar, teñir; deslustrar.
Distal [dis'-tal], *a.* Relativamente distante del cuerpo o del punto de adherencia. (< distance + al.)
Distance [dis'-tans], *s.* 1. Distancia, de lugar o tiempo. 2. Alejamiento. 3. Lontananza. 4. Respeto, miramiento. 5. Esquivez, extrañeza; frialdad, altivez. 6. Contrariedad. *At a distance,* De lejos o a lo lejos *Not to come within any distance from any one,* No llegarle al zancajo o a los talones. *To keep at a distance,* Tener a distancia, no tratar con familiaridad.
Distance, *va.* Alejar, apartar, desviar; sobrepasar; espaciar; tomar la delantera, dejar atrás, sobresalir. —*vn.* Adelantarse.
Distant [dis'-tant], *a.* 1. Distante, apartado, lejano, remoto. 2. Esquivo, extraño. *To be distant with one,* Tratar a uno con frialdad. *A distant relative,* Un pariente lejano. *A distant hope,* Una esperanza remota. *Distant manners,* Maneras reservadas.
Distantly [dis'-tant-li], *adv.* A distancia, de lejos; en lontananza.
Distaste [dis-têst'], *s.* Hastío, fastidio, aversión, disgusto, tedio.
Distasteful [dis-têst'-ful], *a.* Desabrido, enfadoso, desagradable; maligno.
Distastefulness [dis-têst'-ful-nes], *s.* Aversión, desagrado.
Distemper [dis-tem'-pęr], *s.* 1. Mal, indisposición, incomodidad, enfermedad; se aplica principalmente a los animales. 2. Perversidad de ánimo. 3. Inquietud, desasosiego. 4. (Pint.) Distemple. 5. Falta de la proporción debida.
Distemper, *va.* Destemplar, desordenar, perturbar; causar una enfermedad.
Distemperature [dis-tem'-pęr-a-chur o tiūr], *s.* 1. Destemplanza, perturbación, confusión, agitación de espíritu, desarreglo. 2. Indisposición, dolencia o desarreglo del cuerpo. 3. Desorden, mezcla de elementos incongruos.
Distend [dis-tend'], *va.* Extender, ensanchar; inflar, hinchar con aire.
Distensible [dis-ten'-si-bl], *a.* Dilatable, que se puede dilatar o extender.
Distension, Distention [dis-ten'-shun], *s.* Ensanche, dilatación, anchura.
Distich [dis'-tic], *s.* Dístico; dos versos que forman sentido completo.
Distil, Distill [dis-til'], *va.* 1. Destilar; extraer o producir por medio de la vaporización y la condensación. 2. Purificar, rectificar. 3. Dar, emitir, exhalar en gotas.—*vn.* 1. Destilar, gotear, caer gota a gota, manar poco a poco. 2. Extraer substancias volátiles por medio de la vaporización y la condensación.
Distillable [dis-til'-a-bl], *a.* Destilable.
Distillate [dis-til'-êt], *s.* Destilado, el producto separado o condensado por la destilación.
Distillation [dis-til-lé'-shun], *s.* Destilación, el acto de destilar o de caer gota a gota.
Distillatory [dis-til'-a-to-ri], *a.* Destilatorio, lo que toca a la destilación. —*s.* Aparato para destilar; alambique.
Distiller [dis-til'-ęr], *s.* Destilador, refinador.
Distillery [dis-til'-ęr-i], *s.* Destilatorio, establecimiento en que se hacen las destilaciones.
Distinct [dis-tinct'], *a.* 1. Distinto, diferente, diverso. 2. Preciso, expreso; formal, exacto, ajustado.
Distinction [dis-tinc'-shun], *s.* 1. Distinción, diferencia. 2. Prerrogativa. 3. Discernimiento, juicio, penetración. 4. Seña o designación de honor. 5. Superioridad de cualquier clase o forma; posición honorífica.

Distinctive [dis-tiṇc'-tiv], *a.* Distintivo, característico.
Distinctively [dis-tiṇc'-tiv-li], **Distinctly** [dis-tinct'-li], *adv.* Distintamente, claramente.
Distinctness [dis-tiṇct'-nes], *s.* Distinción, claridad.
Distinguish [dis-tiṇ'-gwish], *va.* 1. Distinguir, conocer la diferencia que hay entre las cosas. 2. Distinguir, marcar, hacer que una cosa se diferencie de otra. 3. Distinguir, manifestar con el aprecio o estima la preeminencia de alguna cosa. 4. Distinguir, hacer particular estimación de una persona o cosa. 5. Discernir.
Distinguishable [dis-tiṇ'-gwish-a-bl], *a.* Distinguible, que se puede distinguir; perceptible.
Distinguished [dis-tiṇ'-gwisht], *a.* 1. Distinguido, eminente, notable, famoso, ilustre. 2. Especial, marcado, señalado.
Distinguisher [dis-tiṇ'-gwish-ęr], *s.* Hombre de discernimiento.
Distinguishingly [dis-tiṇ'-gwish-ing-li], *adv.* Distintamente.
Distinguishment [dis-tiṇ'-gwish-mẹnt], *s.* Distinción.
Distort [dis-tort'], *va.* Tergiversar, falsear, interpretar o describir falsamente.
Distort, *a.* (Des.) Torcido.
Distortion [dis-tōr'-shun], *s.* 1. Esguince, contorsión, torcimiento. 2. Perversión, alteración de la significación.
Distract [dis-tract'], *va.* 1. Distraer, apartar la atención de. 2. Separar, apartar. 3. Perturbar, enloquecer, poner fuera de sí. 4. Interrumpir.
Distractedly [dis-tract'-ed-li], *adv.* Locamente.
Distractedness [dis-tract'-ed-nes], *s.* 1. Turbación, embarazo. 2. Locura, demencia.
Distracter [dis-tract'-ęr], *s.* Perturbador, interruptor.
Distraction [dis-trac'-shun], *s.* 1. Distracción, confusión. 2. Perturbación de ánimo. 3. Frenesí. 4. Discordia.
Distractive [dis-tract'-iv], *a.* Lo que perturba o confunde.
Distrain [dis-trên'], *va.* y *vn.* (For.) Embargar, secuestrar.
Distrainer [dis-trên'-ęr], *s.* Embargador.
Distraint [dis-trênt'], *s.* Embargo, secuestro.
Distraught [dis-trōt'], *a.* Distraído, atolondrado; turbado, desconcertado.
Distream [dis-trîm'], *vn.* (Des. Poét.) Fluir.
Distress [dis-tres'], *s.* 1. Pena, dolor, sufrimiento agudo. 2. Calamidad, miseria, apuro, conflicto, escasez. 3. (For.) Embargo, secuestro. *To put in in distress,* (Mar.) Entrar de arribada.
Distress, *va.* 1. Angustiar, afligir, congojar. 2. Constreñir, obligar por medio de la miseria o la penuria. 3. (For.) Embargar, secuestrar.
Distressedness [dis-tres'-ed-nes], *s.* Aflicción, congoja, angustia, apuro, conflicto.
Distressful [dis-tres'-ful], *a.* Miserable, desdichado, lleno de trabajos.
Distressfully [dis-tres'-ful-i], *adv.* Miserablemente, infelizmente.
Distressing [dis-tres'-ing], *a.* Penoso, congojoso, aflictivo.
Distribute [dis-trib'-yut], *va.* 1. Distribuir, repartir, dividir. 2. Clasificar, arreglar en orden; separar de una colección y localizar. 3. (Lóg.) Aplicar a todos los miembros de una clase tomados separadamente; opuesto a "usar colectivamente." —*vn.* 1. Hacer distribución; hacer un acto de caridad, dar limosna. 2. (Imp.) Distribuir, deshacer los moldes, repartiendo las letras entre los los cajetines.
Distributer [dis-trib'-yu-tęr], *s.* Distribuidor, repartidor.
Distribution [dis-tri-biū'-shun], *s.* 1. Distribución, repartimiento, división. 2. Arreglo, disposición, colocación oportuna; esparcimiento. 3. Distribución, lo que está distribuído. 4. (Arq.) Colocación y dependencia mutua de las subdivisiones interiores, etc.; en este sentido se distingue de *disposition.*
Distributive [dis-trib'-yu-tiv], *a.* Distributivo.
Distributively [dis-trib'-yu-tiv-li], *adv.* Distributivamente.
Distributiveness [dis-trib'-yu-tiv-nes], *s.* El deseo de distribuir.
Distributor [dis-trib'-yu-tør], *s.* Distribuidor.
District [dis'-trict], *s.* Distrito, comarca o territorio; región, jurisdicción.
Distrust [dis-trust'], *va.* Desconfiar, sospechar; rehusar la confianza en (alguien o algo).
Distrust, *s.* Desconfianza, recelo, sospecha.
Distrustful [dis-trust'-ful], *a.* 1. Desconfiado, receloso; sospechoso. 2. Modesto, que desconfía de sí mismo.
Distrustfully [dis-trust'-ful-i], *adv.* Desconfiadamente.
Distrustfulness [dis-trust'-ful-nes], *s.* Desconfianza, sospecha.
Distrusting [dis-trust'-ing], *s.* Estado de desconfianza.
Distrustless [dis-trust'-les], *a.* Sin sospecha, confiado.
Disturb [dis-tūrb'], *va.* 1. Perturbar, desordenar, estorbar, interrumpir. 2. Molestar, atormentar, inquietar.
Disturbance [dis-tūrb'-ans], *s.* Disturbio, confusión, desorden, alboroto, tumulto; perplejidad, irresolución.
Disturber [dis-tūrb'-ęr], *s* Perturbador, inquietador.
Disulfid, Disulphid, Disulphide [dai-sul'-fid], *s.* Bisulfuro. Equivalente, **Disulphuret** [dai-sul'-fiu-ret].
†**Disuniform** [dis-yū'-ni-fōrm], *a.* Heterogéneo.
Disunion [dis-yūn'-yun], *s.* Desunión, discordia, desavenencia, división, separación.
Disunite [dis-yu-nait'], *va.* Desunir, dividir, separar, enajenar, desavenir.—*vn.* Desunirse, separarse, desavenirse.
Disuniter [dis-yu-nait'-ęr], *s.* El que desune.
Disunity [dis-yū'-ni-ti], *s.* Desunión, separación.
Disusage [dis-yū'-zẹj], *s.* Desuso, falta de uso o ejercicio.
Disuse [dis-yūs'], *s.* Desuso, cesación de algún uso o costumbre.
Disuse [dis-yūz'], *va.* Desusar, desacostumbrar.
Disvaluation [dis-val-yu-ê'-shun], †**Disvalue** [dis-val'-yū], *s.* Desestimación.
†**Disvalue,** *va.* Despreciar.
Disyoke [dis-yōk'], *va.* Quitar el yugo a; desuncir.
Dit [dit], *va.* (Esco.) Cerrar.
Ditch [dich], *s.* 1. Zanja, canal que se hace en la tierra para proteger los sembrados, etc. 2. (Fort.) Foso, zanja que circunda alguna plaza o fortaleza.
Ditch, *va.* Abrir zanjas o fosos.—*vn.* Hacer fosos, especialmente como ocupación habitual.
Ditcher [dich'-ęr], *s.* Cavador de zanjas o fosos.
Ditheism [dai'-the-izm], *s.* Diteísmo, doctrina de los que admiten dos dioses iguales; maniqueísmo; sistema de Zoroastro.
Dithyramb [dith'-i-ramb], *s.* Ditirambo, himno en honor de Baco.
Dithyrambic [dith-i-ram'-bic], *s.* Ditirambo.—*a.* Ditirámbico, en forma de ditirambo; apasionado.
Dittany [dit'-a-ni], *s.* (Bot.) 1. Pequeño arbusto perenne americano. Cunila Mariana. 2. Cualquiera planta del género Dictamnus. *Dittany of Crete,* Díctamo. *White dittany,* Fraxinela.
Dittied [dit'-id], *a.* Cantado, adaptado a la música.
Ditto [dit'-ō], *a.* Dicho o dicha, lo mismo, palabra que se usa más frecuentemente en los libros de comercio y cuentas, y equivale a *ídem.*
Ditty [dit'-i], *s.* Cancioneta, composición música corta y sencilla para cantar.
Diuresis [dai-yu-rî'-sis], *s.* (Med.) Diuresis, secreción excesiva de la orina.
Diuretic [dai-yu-ret'-ic], *a.* y *s.* Diurético, lo que tiene virtud para facilitar la secreción de la orina.
Diurnal [dai-ūr'-nal], *a.* 1. Diurno, diario, cotidiano. 2. Diurno, que pertenece al día. 3. (Zool.) Activo durante el día. 4. (Bot.) (a) Que se abre de día y se cierra por la noche; (b) que dura solamente veinticuatro horas, efímero.—*s.* 1. Diurno, libro del rezo eclesiástico que contiene las horas menores. 2. (Des.) Diario, jornal, libro en que se escribe lo que se hace cada día.
Diurnalist, *s.* *V.* JOURNALIST.
Diurnally [dai-ūr'-nal-i], *adv.* Diariamente.
Diuturnal [dai-yu-tūr'-nal], *a.* Diuturno, que ha durado mucho tiempo.
Diuturnity [dai-yu-tūr'-ni-ti], *s.* Diuturnidad, espacio dilatado de tiempo.
Divan [di-van'], *s.* 1. Diván, el supremo consejo entre los turcos. 2. Cámara del consejo. 3. Café, cuarto de fumar. 4. Diván, especie de sofá sin respaldo y con cojines.
Divaricate [di o dai-var'-i-kêt], *vn.* y *va.* 1. Dividirse en dos partes o ramos. 2. (Biol.) Divergir marcadamente. *V.* DIVERGE.
Divarication [di o dai-var-i-kê'-shun], *s.* División en dos partes; extensión.
Dive [daiv], *vn.* 1. Zabullirse, sumergirse o meterse voluntariamente debajo del agua. 2. Bucear, sacar alguna cosa de lo profundo del agua. 3. Sumergirse, enfrascarse en los negocios, etc. 4. Profundizar o estudiar a fondo alguna cuestión o ciencia.
Dive, *s.* 1. Zabullidura. 2. Buceo, acción de bucear o mantenerse debajo del agua. 3. Enfrascamiento, absorción en los negocios, etc. 4. (Fam.) Timba, leonera; sitio adonde concurre la gente soez para bailar y embriagarse.
Dive bomber [daiv' bem'-ęr], *s.* (Aer.) Bombardero en picada.
Diver [dai'-vęr], *s.* 1. Buzo. 2. Ave

que se zabulle; en especial, el colimbo, especie de mergo.
Diverge [di-vęrj'], *vn.* 1. Divergir, divergirse, apartarse. 2. Desviarse de un rumbo, dirección o modelo dado. 3. *V.* Differ.
Divergence, Divergency [di-vęrj'-ens, i], *s.* Divergencia.
Divergent [di-vęrj'-ent], *a.* Divergente.
Divers [dai'-vęrz], *a.* Varios, diversos, diferentes, muchos, más de uno, pero no numerosos.
Divers-coloured [dai'-vęrz-cul'-ęrd], *a.* De muchos o varios colores.
Diverse [di-vęrs'], *a.* Diverso, diferente, distinto; multiforme, variado.
Diversely [di-vęrs'-li], *adv.* Diversamente, distintamente, en diferentes direcciones.
Diversification [di-vęr-si-fi-ké'-shun], *s.* Diversificación, acción de diversificar; variación o variedad de formas o colores.
Diversify [di-vęr'-si-fai], *va.* Diversificar, variar, cambiar, diferenciar; matizar, abigarrar.
Diversion [di-vęr'-shun], *s.* 1. Desviación. 2. Diversión, entretenimiento, pasatiempo. 3. (Mil.) Diversión.
Diversity [di-vęr'-si-ti], *s.* Diversidad, variedad; diferencia, desemejanza; lo opuesto a *Identity.*
Divert [di-vęrt'], *va.* 1. Desviar, apartar, alejar, divertir. 2. Desviar, distraer. 3. Divertir, regocijar, recrear.
Diverter [di-vęrt'-ęr], *s.* Quitapesares, consuelo, alivio.
†**Diverticle** [di-vęr'-ti-cl], *s.* Camino o senda desviada, vuelta.
Diverticulum [dai-vęr-tic'-yu-lum] (*pl.* la), *s.* (Biol.) Divertículo, apéndice (vertical), bolsillo ciego.
Divertisement [di-vęr'-tiz-męnt], *s.* 1. Diversión, holgura. 2. Intermedio de baile (en los teatros).
Divertive [di-vęr' tiv], *a.* Divertido.
Divest [di-vest'], *va.* Desnudar, privar de autoridad; despojar, desposeer.
Divestiture [di-vest'-i-chur o tiūr], *s.* 1. Despojo. 2. (For.) Desposeimiento, el acto y efecto de privar a alguno de sus bienes o hacienda.
Dividable [di-vaid'-a-bl], *a.* Divisible.
Divide [di-vaid'], *va.* 1. Dividir, distribuir. 2. Desunir, separar, meter cizaña.—*vn.* Romper, reñir con alguno; desunirse, dividirse.
Divide, *s.* Vertiente de una montaña; línea divisoria de las aguas. *The Great Divide,* (Fam. E. U.) La vertiente de las Montañas Roqueñas.
Dividedly [di-vaid'-ed-li], *adv.* Separadamente; por separado.
Dividend [div'-i-dend], *s.* 1. Dividendo, la parte o porción que toca a cada uno en el repartimiento de alguna cosa. 2. (Arit.) Dividendo.
Divider [di-vaid'-ęr], *s.* 1. Partidor, el instrumento que parte. *Dividers,* Compás de división. 2. Partidor, el que parte o divide. 3. (Arit.) Divisor, partidor. 4. Distribuidor, repartidor.
Dividing [di-vaid'-ing], *s.* Separación.
Dividual [di-vid'-yu-al], *a.* (Ant.) Dividido.
Divination [div-i-né'-shun], *s.* Divinación, adivinación.
Divinator [div'-i-né-tęr], *s.* Adivinador, adivino.
Divinatory [di-vin'-a-to-ri], *a.* Divinatorio.
Divine [di-vain'], *a.* 1. Divino, lo que pertenece a Dios o a los falsos dioses. 2. Divino, admirable, sublime. —*s.* Predicador, teólogo.
Divine, *va.* Adivinar.—*vn.* Conjeturar, presentir, pronosticar, profetizar; sospechar.
Divinely [di-vain'-li], *adv.* Divinamente; excelentemente.
Divineness [di-vain'-nes], *s.* 1. Divinidad, participación de la naturaleza divina. 2. Excelencia, perfección.
Diviner [di-vain'-ęr], *s.* Adivino, adivinador, conjeturador.
Diving [daiv'-ing], *s.* 1. Buceo. 2. Zambullimiento, zambullida, zambullidura. 3. Salto. *Diving bell,* Campana de buzo, campana de salvamento. *Diving board,* Trampolín. *Diving suit,* Escafandra.
Divinity [di-vin'-i-ti], *s.* 1. Divinidad. 2. Dios (verdadero o falso). 3. La teología. 4. Atributo, virtud o cualidad que se supone ser de carácter divino.
Divisibility [di-viz-i-bil'-i-ti], **Divisibleness** [di-viz'-i-bl-nes], *s.* Divisibilidad.
Divisible [di-viz'-i-bl], *a.* Divisible.
Division [di-vizh'-un], *s.* 1. División, la acción o efecto de dividir, separar o repartir. 2. División, separación, desunión, discordia. 3. (Arit.) División, partición. 4. (Mil.) División, parte de un ejército o de una armada que obran o marchan separadamente. 5. Lo que separa o divide. 6. Votación de un cuerpo legislativo (como del Parlamento británico).
Divisional, Divisionary [di-vizh'-un-al, ę-ri], *a.* Divisional, referente a la división.
Divisive [di-vai'-siv], *a.* Divisivo, que sirve para dividir.
Divisor [di-vai'-zęr], *s.* (Arit.) Divisor.
Divorce [di-vōrs'], *s.* 1. Divorcio, disolución legal del matrimonio. 2. Divorcio, separación, desunión.
Divorce, *va.* 1. Divorciar, autorizar la separación de dos esposos, pronunciar el divorcio. 2. Divorciar; separar alguna cosa de lo que estaba unido con ella; arrancar violentamente una cosa de otra.
Divorcement [di-vōrs'-męnt], *s.* Divorcio.
Divorcer [di-vōrs'-ęr], *s.* Divorciador; el que o lo que divorcia.
Divorcive [di-vōr'-siv], *a.* Lo que tiene poder de divorciar.
Divulgate [di-vul'-gēt], *va.* (Des.) Divulgar, publicar.
Divulge [di-vulj'], *va.* 1. Divulgar, publicar, descubrir, revelar. 2. (Poco us.) Proclamar, pregonar.
Divulger [di-vulj'-ęr], *s.* Divulgador; pregonero.
Divulsion [di-vul'-shun], *s.* Arranque, la acción y efecto de arrancar.
Divulsive [di-vul'-siv], *a.* (Des.) Divulsivo, lo que tiene poder de arrancar o separar violentamente una cosa de otra.
Diwan [di-wān'], *s.* Colección de poemas cortos de un solo autor; ciclo, antología. (Persa.)
Dixie o **Dixieland** [dix'-i-land], *s.* 1. Región integrada por los estados del sur de E.U. 2. Canto de guerra de dicha región en la Guerra de Secesión.
Dizen [diz'-n], *va.* 1. Ataviar, adornar. 2. Poner el lino en la rueca. (Uso propio. < *dis* en Distaff.)
Dizziness [diz'-i-nes], *s.* Vértigo, vahido; desvanecimiento.
Dizzy [diz'-i], *a.* 1. Vertiginoso. 2. Desvanecido, atacado de un vértigo; que causa vértigo. 3. (Ant.) Ligero, voluble, aturdido.
Dizzy, *va.* Causar vértigos o vahidos de cabeza; girar al rededor. —*vn.* Aturdirse, desvanecerse, írsele a uno la cabeza.
Do [dū], *va.* (*pret.* Did, *pp.* Done). 1. Hacer, ejecutar, obrar. 2. Finalizar, concluir, despachar, rematar. 3. Producir algún efecto; preparar, arreglar; modificar; verter, traducir. 4. Servir, aprovechar; emplear el poder, alargar la mano. 5. (Ger.) Estafar, petardear; engañar; también, injuriar, agraviar, matar. 6. Hacer el papel de. 7. (Fam.) Bastar, ser suficiente para: v. g. *Fifty dollars will do me for the present,* Me bastarán cincuenta pesos por ahora.—*vn.* 1. Conducirse, comportarse, portarse, proceder. 2. Pasarlo, estar, hallarse, cuando se trata de la salud o de un empeño. *V.* Fare. *How do you do?* ¿Cómo le va a Vd.? ¿Cómo se halla Vd.? ¿Cómo está Vd.? 3. Salir bien o mal en una cosa; v. g. *In the drawing I did badly,* Salí mal en el sorteo. *He does well in his new enterprise,* Sale bien en su nuevo empeño. 4. Darse maña, discurrir trazas para adelantar, ingeniarse. 5. Servir al designio de uno; ser a propósito.—Este verbo es auxiliar, y se le emplea como tal en los tiempos presente y pasado para señalar la negación o la interrogación. *I do not read,* No leo. *I did not read,* No leí. *Do I read?* ¿Leo yo? *Did my brother go?* ¿Fué mi hermano?—En las oraciones afirmativas se emplea *To do* para dar más energía a la oración, para expresar con más fuerza la oposición y como expletivo. *I do hate him,* Le aborrezco de veras. *I did love her, but I scorn her now,* La amé ciertamente, mas ahora la aborrezco.—También se usa para evitar repeticiones. *I shall come, but if I do not, go away,* Yo vendré, mas si no vengo, márchate. —Se le emplea también para mandar con imperio o pedir una cosa con ansia. *Make haste, do,* Vamos, dése Vd. prisa, despáchese. *Do, pray, go and tell him I am here,* Tenga Vd. la bondad de ir a decirle que estoy aquí.—*To do again,* Rehacer, volver a hacer. *To do away,* Abolir, llevar, borrar. *To do for,* (1) Ser a propósito, servir para. (2) Tener cuidado de, cuidar del bienestar personal o intereses de. (3) (Ger.) Matar, herir o lastimar mortalmente. *To do for one's self,* Sostenerse sin ayuda ajena, ganarse la vida. *To do off,* Deshacer; quitar; sacar. *To do on,* Poner una cosa sobre otra; meter. *To do over,* (1) Hacer de nuevo, volver a hacer. (2) Cubrir completamente con algún material extendido o disuelto. *To do over with gold,* Dorar. *To do over with silver,* Platear. *To do one's best,* Esmerarse. *To do one's utmost,* Hacer cuanto es posible. *To do up,* (1) Liar, empaquetar. (2) Arreglar, enrollar, como los cabellos. (3) Almidonar y planchar, como una tela. (4) Fatigarse, cansarse. *To do with,* (1) Conducirse, arreglarse para. (2) Disponer de; usar en provecho de. *To do without,* Pasar sin; dispensar

de. *That will do,* Eso es bastante, suficiente o a propósito. *That won't do,* Eso no vale, eso no sirve ; ni por esas. *He is done for,* Han acabado con él. *To have done with,* Dejar o abandonar ; cesar, descontinuar. *Parents wish their children to do well,* Los padres desean que sus hijos prosperen o sean felices.

Do [dō], *s.* Do, primera voz de la escala musical que sustituye al *ut.*

Docibility [des-i-bil'-i-ti], *s.* (Poco us.) Docilidad.

Docible [des'-i-bl], *a.* Dócil, flexible, obediente, deferente ; el que aprende con facilidad lo que le enseñan.

Docile [des'-il o dō'-sil], *a.* Dócil ; apacible.

Docility [do-sil'-i-ti], *s.* Docilidad.

Docimastic [des-i-mas'-tic], *a.* Docimástico, referente a la docimasia.

Docimasy, Docimacy [des'-i-ma-si], *s.* Docimasia, docimástica, el arte de ensayar los minerales para determinar los metales que contienen y en qué proporción.

Dock [doc], *s.* Muelle, desembarcadero. *Dry dock,* Astillero, dique seco.—*va.* 1. Entrar en muelle. 2.Rescindir. *To dock one's wages,* Descontar a alguien parte de su sueldo.

Dock, *va.* 1. Descolar, quitar o cortar la cola al animal 2. Cercenar, cortar, rebajar. 3. (Mar.) Meter o poner una embarcación en el dique.

Dockage [dek'-ĝj], *s.* 1. La acción de poner un buque en el dique. 2. Cantidad que se paga por el uso de un dique.

Docket [dek'-et], *s.* 1. Rótulo, extracto. *To strike a docket,* (Com.) Declarar a un comerciante en bancarrota. 2. (For.) Lista, tablilla, enumeración o registro de los pleitos y causas pendientes. 3. Marbete.

Docket, *va.* 1. Extractar, hacer el sumario de una obra, papeles o documentos. 2. Rotular, poner rótulo o nombre a un cuaderno, paquete, etc., indicando su contenido. 3. Incluir en la lista o registro de las causas y pleitos pendientes.

Dock-yard [dec'-yārd], *s.* (Mar.) Arsenal.

Doctor [dec'-tẹr], *s.* 1. Doctor, médico. 2. Doctor, el que ha recibido en una universidad el grado más alto en una facultad, como derecho, teología, etc. *Doctor's office,* Consultorio del médico o del doctor. *Doctor of Law,* Doctor en Leyes. *Medical doctor,* Doctor en Medicina. *Doctor of Philosophy,* Doctor en Filosofía.

Doctor, *va.* 1. (Fam.) Medicinar, recetar. 2. Alterar y adulterar. 3. Reparar, componer.—*vn.* 1. Tomar medicinas o recibir tratamiento médico. 2. Practicar la medicina.

Doctoral [dec'-tẹr-al], *a.* Doctoral, que pertenece al grado de doctor.

Doctorally [dec'-tẹr-al-i], *adv.* A modo de doctor.

Doctorate [dec'-tẹr-ēt], *s.* Doctorado.

Doctorate, *va.* Doctorar, conferir el grado de doctor.

Doctoress [dec'-tẹr-es], *sf.* Doctora.

Doctors' Commons [dec'-tẹrz com'-unz], *s.* Uno de los colegios de abogados en Londres.

Doctorship [dec'-tẹr-ship], *s.* Doctorado.

Doctrinaire [dec-tri-nār'], *a.* y *s.* Doctrinario.

Doctrinal [dec'-trin-al], *a.* 1. Doctrinal, lo que contiene o pertenece a la doctrina. 2. Didáctico, referente a la enseñanza ; instructivo. —*s.* Parte de doctrina ; doctrinal.

Doctrinally [dec'-trin-al-i], *adv.* Magistralmente.

Doctrine [dec'-trin], *s.* 1. Doctrina, dogma, creencia, especialmente en religión. 2. (Ant.) Enseñanza, erudición, saber.

Document [dec'-yu-mẹnt], *s.* Documento, escritura, testimonio, documento auténtico.

Document, *va.* Documentar, proveer de documentos ; probar por medio de documentos o escrituras.

Documental [dec-yu-mẹnt'-al], *a.* Documental, procedente de los documentos.

Documentary [doc-yu-mẹnt'-a-ri], *a.* Documental.

Documentary [doc-yu-mẹnt'-a-ri], *s.* Documental.

Documentation [dec-yu-men-tē'-shun], *s.* Documentación.

Dodder [ded'-ẹr], *s.* (Bot.) Cuscuta, planta parásita sin hojas, que se uso en medicina.

Doddered [ded'-ẹrd], *a.* Cubierto de cuscuta o plantas parásitas.

Dodecagon [do-dec'-a-gon], *s.* (Geom.) Dodecágono, figura que consta de doce lados iguales.

Dodecahedron [do-dec-a-hī'-dren], *s.* (Geom.) Dodecaedro.

Dodecatemory [do-dec-a-tem'-o-ri], *s.* (Astr.) Dodecatemoria, la duodécima parte de un círculo o signo del zodíaco.

Dodge [dej], *va.* 1. Escabullirse, escapar mediante un cambio súbito de posición ; evadir diestramente. 2. Seguir o perseguir mañosa y evasivamente.—*vn.* Moverse rápidamente a un lado. 2. Trampear, entrampar.

Dodger [dej'-ẹr], *s.* 1. Trampista, el que saca de continuo dinero con engaños y estafas. 2. (E. U.) Cartel o anuncio pequeño.

Dodman [ded'-man], *s.* Especie de pescado ; caracol.

Dodo [dō'-dō], *s.* (Orn.) Dido, ave algo parecida a un palomo de gran tamaño, con alas rudimentarias. Se ha extinguido la especie recientemente.

Dodonian [do-dō'-ni-an], *a.* Dodoneo, lo perteneciente al bosque de Dodona o templo de Júpiter.

Doe [dō], *sf.* Gama, la hembra del gamo, de la liebre, del conejo, del canguro y del antílope.

Doer [dū'-ẹr], *s.* 1. Hacedor, el que hace o ejecuta alguna cosa. *He is a great talker but little doer,* Todo se le va por el pico. 2. Actor, agente. 3. La persona que es activa o valiente. *Evil-doer,* El que hace mal.

Does [duz]. Tercera persona del verbo *To* Do, que también es *doth,* en estilo serio y en lenguaje arcaico.

Doeskin [dō'-skin], *s.* 1. Ante, la piel de una gama. 2. Tejido fino de lana.

Doff [def], *va.* Quitar la ropa, deshacer, sacar. *He doffed the cassock for the cuirass,* Él cambió la sotana por la coraza. (Contracción de *do off.*)

Dog [deg], *s.* 1. Perro, perra. *Bull-dog,* Perro de presa. *Setting-dog,* Podenco. *Lap-dog,* Perro faldero o perrito de faldas. 2. Perro, nombre que se da por ignominia y afrenta o jocosamente a un hombre. 3. Úsase para designar el macho de algunos animales, v. g. *The dog fox,* El zorro. 4. Herramienta, pequeña pieza que sirve para asir y asegurar, fiador, retén. 5. Morillo, caballete de hierro que se pone en el hogar para sostener la leña. 6. Gatillo de un arma de fuego. *To give* o *send to the dogs,* Echar a perros, dar a los diablos. tirar por la ventana, disipar la hacienda, malbaratar. *To go to the dogs,* Estar arruinado. *To make dog's ears in books,* (Fam.) Hacer orejones. *To play the dog in the manger,* Ser como el perro del hortelano.

Dog, *va.* Cazar como un perro, seguir los pasos o pisadas de alguno, espiar.

Dog-bane [deg'-bēn], *s.* (Bot.) Matacán.

Dog-brier [deg'-brai-ẹr], *s.* (Bot.) Zarza perruna, escaramujo.

Dog-cart [deg'-cārt], *s.* Coche de dos ruedas para un caballo, con dos asientos unidos por el respaldo, y espacio para perros debajo de los asientos.

Dog-cheap [deg'-chīp], *a.* Muy barato, a bajo precio, por nada. (Cuba) De guagua.

Dog-days [deg'-dēz], *s. pl.* La canícula, los días caniculares, del 15 de Julio al 25 de Agosto.

Dog-fight [deg'-fait], *s.* Riña de perros.

Dog-fish [deg'-fish], *s.* Tiburón.

Dog-fly [deg'-flai], *s.* Mosca perruna.

Doge [dōj], *s.* Dux, jefe de la antiguas repúblicas de Venecia y Génova.

Dogged [deg'-ed], *a.* 1. Duro, inflexible, tenaz. 2. (Des.) Ceñudo, intratable, áspero.

Doggedly [deg'-ed-li], *adv.* Tenazmente, con dureza.

Doggedness [deg'-ed-nes], *s.* Tenacidad, inflexibilidad.

Dogger [deg'-ẹr], *s.* (Mar.) Barca de pescador.

Doggerel [deg'-ẹr-el], *a.* Prosaico, de bajo estilo, bajo ; hablando de versos.—*s.* Coplas de ciego.

Doggish [deg'-ish], *a.* Perruno, brutal, regañón.

Dog-hearted [deg'-hārt-ed], *a.* Sanguinario, cruel, inhumano.

Dog-hole [deg'-hōl], **Dog-kennel** [deg'-ken-el], *s.* Perrera, casa de perros ; la casa en que se encierran los perros de caza ; tabuco, camaranchón.

Dogie [dō'-gi], *s.* (fam.) Ternero huérfano.

Dog-keeper [deg'-kīp-ẹr], *s.* Perrero.

Dog-Latin [deg'-lat-in], *s.* Latín bárbaro o macarrónico.

Dog-leech [deg'-līch], *s.* El albéitar que cura los males de los perros. Se dice también de los malos médicos o cirujanos, por desprecio.

Dog-louse [deg'-laus], *s.* Piojo perruno.

Dogma [deg'-ma], *s.* Dogma, máxima, axioma ; punto de doctrina.

Dogmatic, Dogmatical [deg-mat'-ic, al], *a.* Dogmático, magistral ; autoritario, arrogante.

Dogmatically [deg-mat'-ic-al-i], *adv.* Dogmáticamente.

Dogmaticalness [deg-mat'-ic-al-nes], *s.* Magisterio ; calidad de dogmático.

Dogmatism [deg'-ma-tizm], *s.* 1. Presunción de los que quieren que sus teorías o aseveraciones, expresadas con imperio y arrogancia, sean aceptadas sin discusión. 2. Escuela filosófica opuesta al escepticismo. 3. Sistema médico de la antigua escuela dogmática.

Dogmatist [deg'-ma-tist], *s.* Dogmatista, dogmatizador, dogmatizante.
Dogmatize [deg'-ma-taiz], *vn.* Dogmatizar; afirmar.
Dogmatizer [deg'-ma-taiz-ẹr], *s.* Dogmatizador.
Dog-rose [dōg'-rōz], *s.* (Bot.) Escaramujo, rosal silvestre.
Dog's-ears [degz'-īrz], *s. pl.* Orejones en los ángulos de las hojas de un libro.
Dog-sick [deg'-sic], *a.* Enfermo o malo como un perro.
Dog-skin [deg'-skin], *a.* Hecho de pellejo de perro.
Dog-sleep [deg'-slīp], *s.* Sueño fingido.
Dog's-meat [degz'-mīt], *s.* Perruna, pan para perros.
Dog-star [deg'-star], *s.* Sirio, canícula, la más brillante de las estrellas fijas; su salida coincide con la del sol en los días caniculares.
Dog's-tongue [degz'-tung], *s.* (Bot.) Cinoglosa, hierba medicinal.
Dog's-tooth [degz'-tūth], *s.* (Bot.) Diente de perro.
Dog-teeth [deg'-tīth], *s. pl.* Dientes caninos.
Dog-tired [deg'-taired], *a.* Rendido de cansancio.
Dog-trick [deg'-tric], *s.* Perrería, tratamiento brutal.
Dog-trot [deg'-tret], *s.* Trote lento, como el de un perro.
Dog-watch [deg'-wēch], *s.* (Mar.) Una de las dos guardias de a bordo, de dos horas cada una, entre las cuatro de la tarde y las ocho de la noche.
Dog-weary [deg'-wī'-ri], *a.* Cansado como un perro.
Doily [dei'-li], *s.* 1. Especie de servilleta pequeña para los postres, o para colocar sobre ellas floreros, jarrones, etc. 2. (Des.) Especie de tela de lana.
Doings [dū'-ingz], *s. pl.* Hechos, acciones; eventos; acontecimientos; bullicio; función.
Doit [deit], *s.* Moneda pequeña de muy poco valor.
Dole [dōl], *s.* 1. Distribución, repartimiento. 2. Parte, porción; dádiva, don. 3. Limosna u otra cosa repartida. 4. Dolor, angustia, congoja. 5. Golpes. 6. (Ant.) Miseria. 7. Límite, linde. 8. Vacío, en la cría de ganado.
Dole, *va.* Repartir, distribuir.
Doleful [dōl'-ful], *a.* Doloroso, lastimoso, lúgubre, triste.
Dolefully [dōl'-ful-i], *adv.* Dolorosamente.
Dolefulness [dōl'-ful-nes], *s.* Tristeza, melancolía; miseria.
†Dolent [dō'-lent], *a.* Doliente.
Dolerite [del'-ẹr-ait], *s.* (Min.) Dolerita, roca granítica de color negruzco.
Dolesome [dōl'-sum], *a.* Lastimoso, triste.
Dolesomely [dōl'-sum-li], *adv.* Desconsoladamente, tristemente.
Do-little [dū'-lit-l], *s.* Capitán araña, manda mucho y no hace nada; nombre despectivo con que se moteja al que hablando mucho obra poco.
Doll [del], *s.* 1. Muñeca. 2. Abreviatura de *Dorothy* o Dorotea.
Dollar [del'-ar], *s.* Moneda de los Estados Unidos de América y el Canadá. *Spanish dollar*, Peso, moneda de España. *Hard dollar*, Peso duro o fuerte. *Current dollar*, Peso sencillo.
Dolly [del'-i], *s.* 1. Muñequita. 2. Remachador. 3. Plataforma con rodillos para cargar cosas pesadas.
Dolman [del'-man], *s.* 1. Dolmán, prenda exterior de vestir de los turcos, larga, abierta por delante y de mangas ceñidas. 2. Dormán, especie de chaqueta corta, adornada con alamares; chaqueta de húsar. 3. Capa de mangas perdidas que usan las mujeres.
Dolmen [del'-men], *s.* Dolmen, monumento druídico consistente en una gran piedra sobrepuesta a dos o más verticales.
Dolomite [del'-o-mait], *s.* Dolomita, caliza magnesiana.
Dolomitic [del-o-mit'-ic], *a.* Dolomítico, que contiene dolomita o es parecido a ella.
Dolor [dō'-lọr], *s.* Dolor, angustia; llanto.
Doloriferous [do-lo-rif'-ẹr-us], **Dolorific**, **Dolorifical** [do-lo-rif'-ic, al], *a.* Doloroso; triste, lúgubre.
Dolorous [del'-o-rus], *s.* Doloroso, lastimoso, lamentable.
Dolour, etc. *V.* DOLOR, etc.
Dolphin [del'-fin], *s.* 1. Delfín, cetáceo. *Cf.* PORPOISE. 2. Pez grande de alta mar, notable por sus cambios de color cuando se le saca del agua. 3. La constelación boreal Delfín.
Dolt [dōlt], *s.* El hombre bobo, tonto o imbécil.
Doltish [dōlt'-ish], *a.* Lerdo, estúpido, mentecato, imbécil.
Doltishness [dōlt'-ish-nes], *s.* Estupidez, tontería, imbecilidad.
Domain [do-mên'], *s.* 1. Dominio, imperio, soberanía. 2. Bienes, estados, posesión de tierras.
Domal [dō'-mal], *a.* Lo perteneciente a la casa; úsase en astrología.
Dome [dōm], *s.* 1. (Arq.) Cúpula, cimborrio, dombo, domo, media naranja. 2. Toda cubierta en forma de copa invertida o de cimborrio. 3. (Poét.) Casa, edificio majestuoso.
Domestic, **Domestical** [do-mes'-tic, al], *a.* 1. Doméstico, de la casa, de la familia; familiar. 2. Civil, intestino. 3. Domesticado, criado y domado por el hombre.
Domestic, *s.* Doméstico, criado, sirviente.
Domestically [do-mes'-ti-cal-i], *adv.* Domésticamente.
Domesticate [do-mes'-ti-kêt], *va.* Domesticar, acostumbrar a un animal salvaje a la vista y compañía del hombre.—*vn.* Adquirir costumbres y gustos domésticos.
Domesticity [do-mes-tis'-i-ti], *s.* Calidad de doméstico, domesticidad.
Domestic science, *s.* Economía doméstica.
Domicile [dem'-i-sil], *s.* Domicilio, casa, habitación permanente de un individuo o una familia.—*va.* Domiciliarse, establecer una residencia fija.
Dominant [dem'-i-nant], *a.* Dominante.
Dominate [dem'-i-nêt], *vn.* Dominar, predominar.—*va.* Gobernar.
Domination [dem-i-nê'-shun], *s.* Dominación, imperio; tiranía; gobierno, autoridad.
Dominative [dem'-i-na-tiv], *a.* Dominativo, dominante; imperioso, altivo.
Dominator [dem'-i-nê"-tọr], *s.* Dominador; gobernador.
Domineer [dem-i-nīr'], *vn.* Dominar, señorear, mandar.—*va.* Gobernar.
Domine [dō'-mi-nẹ], *s.* Clérigo, eclesiástico. (Lat.)
Dominical [do-min'-i-cal], *a.* Dominical, perteneciente a los días consagrados al Señor.—*s.* Domínica.
Dominican [do-min'-i-can], *s.* Dominico, ca.—*a.* Dominicano.
Dominie [dem'-i-ni], *s.* 1. Dómine, maestro de escuela, pedagogo. 2. (Fam.) *V.* DOMINE.
Dominion [do-min'-yun], *s.* 1. Dominio, soberanía, imperio, gobierno; potencia. 2. Territorio, distrito. 3. Predominio, ascendiente.
Domino [dem'-i-nō], *s.* 1. Dominó, traje talar para máscaras. 2. Pieza del juego de dominó. 3. *pl.* DOMINOES. Dominó, juego en que se emplean veinte y ocho fichas rectangulares, numeradas de uno a seis.
Don [den], *va.* Vestir, revestir; ponerse una prenda sobre otra. Abrev. de *Do on.*
Don [den], *s.* Don, antes título honorífico y de dignidad en España, y hoy tratamiento usual y corriente, como Señor, o *Mister* en inglés.
Donary [dō'-na-ri], *s.* (Poco us.) Donación piadosa.
Donate [dō'-nêt], *va.* Donar, hacer una donación o dádiva, particularmente cuando es de considerable valor.
Donation [do-nê'-shun], *s.* Donación; don, dádiva, presente, regalo.
Donatism [den'-a-tizm], *s.* Donatismo, herejía de los donatistas.
Donatist [den'-a-tist], *s.* Donatista.
Donative [den'-a-tiv], *s.* Donativo, don, presente, dádiva.
Donator [do-nê'-tọr], *s.* Donador.
Done [dun], *pp.* del verbo *To* Do. 1. Hecho, ejecutado, llevado a cabo. 2. Acabado, concluído. 3. Bien cocido o asado. 4. Fatigado, consumido; lastimado mortalmente o gravemente enfermo. *That may be done*, Lo que es factible, lo que puede hacerse. *That turkey is not done enough*, Ese pavo no está bastante cocido o asado. *To have done with*, Finalizar, concluir, acabar; cesar de, cortar relaciones.—*adv.* (Fam.) De acuerdo; corriente; convenido, adelante.
Done, *inter.* Cosa hecha, muy bien; ya está; expresión que denota conformidad con lo que alguno dice o propone, o bien la conclusión de alguna cosa.
Donee [do-nī'], *s.* Donatario, el que recibe una donación.
Donjon [dun'-jun], *s.* *V.* DUNGEON.
Donkey [den'-ki], *s.* Asno, burro, borrico.
Donnerd [den'-ẹrd], *s.* (Esco.) Persona perezosa e inútil; diablo.
Donor [dō'-nọr], *s.* Donador, dador.
Donship [den'-ship], *s.* Nobleza, caballería, la calidad o rango de caballero.
Don't [dōnt], *abrev.* de DO NOT.
Donzel [den'-zel], *s.* (Des.) Paje, antiguamente doncel.
Doodle [dū'-dl], *va.* y *vn.* Borrajear, garrapatear.
Doom [dūm], *va.* 1. Sentenciar, mandar, juzgar, ordenar judicialmente. 2. Destinar, determinar, resolver absolutamente.
Doom, *s.* 1. Sentencia, juicio, condena. 2. Determinación. 3. Suerte, destino, hado. 4. Perdición, ruina. *The crack of doom*, La señal del juicio final.
Doomsday [dūmz'-dê], *s.* Día del juicio universal.

Doomsday-book [dūmz'-dê-buk], *s.* Gran catastro de Inglaterra, libro hecho por orden del rey Guillermo I de Inglaterra, en el cual se registraban todas las tierras feudales del reino.
Door [dōr], *s.* 1. Puerta. *To knock at the door,* Tocar o llamar a la puerta. *To turn out of doors,* Echar de casa. 2. Portal o zaguán; entrada, pasillo. 3. Avenida. 4. (Fam.) Casa. *Back door,* Puerta trasera. (Fam.) Puerta falsa. *To lock the door,* Cerrar la puerta con llave; echar llave a la puerta. *Out of doors,* Fuera de casa, en la calle, al aire libre. *Door-bell,* Campanilla de puerta. *Door-jamb,* Jamba de puerta, quicial. *Door-mat,* Felpudo de puerta, estera para limpiarse los pies. *Door-plate,* Plancha con el nombre del que habita una casa. *Door-sill,* Umbral. *To lie at one's door,* Ser carga para alguno, imponerle responsabilidad.
Doorcase [dōr'-kês], *s.* Marco de la puerta.
Doorframe [dōr'-frêm], *s.* Dintel o marco de una puerta.
Doorkeeper [dōr'-kīp'-ẹr], *s.* Portero.
Door-nail [dōr'-nêl], *s.* Clavo sobre el cual golpea el aldabón o llamador de una puerta.
Door-post [dōr'-pōst], *s.* Jamba, puerta.
Doorway [dōr'-wê], *s.* Entrada, puerta; portal.
Dope [dōp], *s.* 1. Narcótico, droga heroica. 2. (fam.) Información, datos sobre alguna cosa. 3. (fam.) Zonzo, tonto.
Dor, Dor-bug [dōr', bug], *s.* Escarabajo estercolero que produce fuerte zumbido al volar.
Dorian [dō'-ri-an], **Doric** [der'-ic], *a.* Dórico, lo que pertenece a los dóricos.
Doricism [der'-i-sizm], **Dorism** [der'-izm], *s.* Frase peculiar del dialecto dórico.
Dormancy [dēr'-man-si], *s.* Quietud, descanso.
Dormant [dēr'-mant], *a.* 1. Durmiente. 2. Secreto, oculto; latente. 3. Sin movimiento, parado, sin giro. 4. Inusitado; ineficaz.
Dormant, Dormer [dēr'-mẹr], *s.* 1. Viga maestra. 2. *Dormer-window,* Buharda, ventana de guardilla o desván.
Dormitory [dēr'-mi-to-ri], *s.* Dormitorio, edificio perteneciente a un colegio o escuela y destinado a estudiar y dormir; también, cualquier pieza de gran tamaño donde duermen varias personas. (Mex.) Recámara.
Dormouse [dēr'-maus], *s.* Lirón; escríbese en plural DORMICE [dēr'-mais].
Dorr [dēr], *s.* *V.* DOR.
Dorsad [dēr'-sad], *adv.* (Anat. y Zool.) Hacia la espalda, atrás.
Dorsal [dēr'-sal], *a.* Dorsal, perteneciente al dorso, espalda o lomo; colocado en o cerca de la espalda.
Dorsel [dēr'-sel], **Dorser** [dēr'-sẹr], *s.* Serón, especie de sera o espuerta.
Dorsiferous [dēr-sif'-ẹr-us], **Dorsiparous** [dēr-sip'-a-rus], *a.* 1. Que lleva algo a la espalda o lomo. 2. (Bot.) Dorsífero, se dice de las plantas que tienen las semillas en el dorso de las hojas.
Dorsum [dēr'-sum], *s.* 1. Dorso, revés o espalda de alguna cosa. 2 Cuesta.
Dosage [dō'-sẹj], *s.* La administración de un medicamento en dosis regulares.
Dose [dōs], *s.* Dosis, porción.
Dose, *va.* Disponer las dosis de un remedio cualquiera; proporcionar un medicamento al estado o fuerza del enfermo.
Dossal, Dosel [des'-al], *s.* Retablo, colgaduras o tapices ricos colocados detrás del altar.
Dost [dust]. Segunda persona del singular del presente de indicativo del verbo *To* Do; forma solemne o arcaica.
Dot [det], *s.* 1. Tilde, virgulita o nota que se pone sobre alguna letra; punto. 2. (Mús.) Punto que puesto después de una nota aumenta o prolonga su valor en una mitad.
Dot, *va.* Tildar, poner tildes a las letras que los deben tener.
Dotage [dō'-têj], *s.* 1. Chochera, chochez, debilidad de juicio. 2. Cariño excesivo. 3. Extravagancia, delirio, visiones, desvarío.
Dotal [dō'-tal], *a.* Dotal, lo que pertenece a la dote.
Dotard [dō'-tard], *s.* El viejo que chochea.
Dotardly [dō'-tard-li], *a.* Estúpido, chocho.
Dotation [do-tê'-shun], *s.* 1. Dotación, la acción y efecto de dotar. 2. Dotación, la consignación de renta perpetua para algún establecimiento, fundación, etc.
Dote [dōt], *vn.* Chochear, caducar. *To dote upon,* Amar con exceso; poner el corazón en alguna persona.
Doter [dō'-tẹr], *s.* El que ama con exceso. *V.* DOTARD.
Doth [duth]. Tercera persona del singular del presente de indicativo del verbo *To* Do; forma solemne o arcaica.
Doting [dōt'-ing], *a.* Chocho, excesivamente cariñoso.
Dotingly [dōt'-ing-li], *adv.* Con cariño excesivo, ciegamente.
Dottard [det'-ard], *s.* (Ant.) Árbol bajo o decaído.
Dotterel [det'-ẹr-el], *s.* (Orn.) Calandria marina.
Double [dub'-l], *a.* 1. Doble, doblado, duplicado. *To be double the age of,* Tener doble edad que. 2. Doble, falso, traidor, engañoso.—*adv.* Dos veces.
Double, *va.* 1. Doblar, duplicar, multiplicar por dos. 2. Doblar, plegar; por lo común con *up, over,* etc. 3. Redoblar, repetir. 4. Ser dos veces otra cosa. *To double a cape,* (Mar.) Doblar o montar un cabo. *To double a ship's bottom,* (Mar.) Embonar.—*vn.* 1. Doblarse, duplicarse. 2. Jugar una mala partida, o pegar petardo. 3. Disimular, usar de artificios, obrar con doblez. 4. Volver atrás.
Double, *s.* 1. Doble, duplo. 2. Pliegue, doblez en la ropa. 3. Doblez; impostura, engaño, treta, artificio. 4. Duplicado, semejanza, homónimo; (fig.) aparecido, fantasma. *His double,* Su mismo retrato.
Double-barreled [dub'-l-bar'-reld], *a.* 1. De dos cañones. 2. (fig.) De dos propósitos.
Double-bass [dub'-l-bês], *s.* Contrabajo, instrumento grande de cuerda, de la figura de un violón.
Double boiler [dub'-l beil'-ẹr], *s.* Baño María.
Double-buttoned [dub'-l-but'-nd], *a* Lo que tiene dos hileras de botones.
Double-charge [dub'-l-chārj'], *va.* Echar doble carga.
Double-chin [dub'-l-chin], *s.* Papada.
Double-dealer [dub'-l-dīl'-ẹr], *s.* Hombre doble, traidor y falso; engañador, embustero.
Double-dealing [dub'-l-dīl-ing], *s.* Doblez, trato doble, simulación, dolo, fraude.
Double-dye [dub-l-dai'], *va.* Reteñir.
Double-eagle [dub'-l-ī'-gl], *s.* Moneda de oro de los Estados Unidos; su valor es de dos águilas o 20 pesos.
Double-edged [dub'-l-ejd], *a.* Instrumento de dos cortes o filos.
Double-ender [dub'-l-end'-ẹr], *s.* Lo que tiene las dos extremidades parecidas, como un vapor de río, una canoa.
Double-entry [dub'-l-en'-tri], *s.* (Com.) Partida doble.
Double-eyed [dub'-l-aid], *a.* El que mostrando bondad en su semblante es áspero y cruel.
Double-faced [dub'-l-fêst], *a.* De dos caras: pérfido, doble.
Double feature [dub'-l fī'-chur], *s.* Dos películas cinematográficas en una sola función.
Double-formed [dub'-l-fērmd], *a.* Biforme.
Double-hearted [dub'-l-hārt'-ed], *a.* Pérfido, doble, disimulado.
Double-lock [dub'-l-lec'], *va.* Echar dos vueltas a la llave.
Double-meaning [dub'-l-mīn'-ing], *s.* Ambigüedad, equívoco, sentido doble.—*a.* Con dos sentidos, ambiguo, de doble sentido.
Double-minded [dub'-l-maind'-ed], *a.* Insidioso, doloso; indeciso, irresoluto. (Fam.) Dos caras.
Doubleness [dub'-l-nes], *s.* Doblez, dobladura.
Double play [dub'-l plê], *s.* Maniobra en el beisbol que pone fuera de juego a dos jugadores.
Double-quick [dub'-l-cwic], *a.* (Mil.) A paso redoblado.—*s.* Marcha o movimiento a razón de unos 165 a 180 pasos por minuto, cada paso de una vara (33 pulgadas). Hoy sustituído en los Estados Unidos por *double-time.*
Doubler [dub'-lẹr], *s.* El que dobla alguna cosa.
Doubles [dub'-lz], *s. pl.* Juego de dobles en el tenis.
Doublet [dub'-let], *s.* 1. Par, pareja. 2. Justillo, almilla; casaca; prenda de vestir de los siglos XV a XVII.
Double time [dub'-l taim], *s.* (Mil.) Paso doble, muy rápido.
Double-tongued [dub'-l-tungd], *a.* Doble, falso, engañoso. (Fam.) Doslenguas.
Doubling [dub'-ling], *s.* Vuelta para huir, rodeo; artificio. *Doubling of the bits,* (Mar.) Almohadas de las bitas. *Doubling of a ship's bottom,* (Mar.) Embón, refuerzo del fondo de un buque. *Doubling of the cutwater,* (Mar.) Batideros de proa.
Doubloon [dub-lūn'], *s.* Doblón, moneda de oro de España, la media onza, por valor de ocho pesos. También se da este nombre a una moneda imaginaria del valor de 60 reales vellón, o tres pesos fuertes.
Doubly [dub'-li], *adv.* 1. Doblemente, en doble, por duplicado. 2. Con doblez, disimuladamente, dolosamente.
Doubt [daut], *vn.* Dudar, temer, recelar, sospechar, vacilar.—*va.* Dudar, temer, desconfiar.
Doubt, *s.* Duda; escrúpulo, sospe-

cha, dificultad, reparo, incertidumbre. *To entertain doubts of, as to,* Recelarse de, concebir dudas sobre.
Doubtable [daut'-a-bl], *a.* Dudable.
Doubter [daut'-ẹr], *s.* El que duda.
Doubtful [daut'-ful], *a.* Dudoso, dudable, ambiguo; incierto, receloso.
Doubtfully [daut'-ful-i], *adv.* Dudosamente, ambiguamente.
Doubtfulness [daut'-ful-nes], *s.* Duda, ambigüedad; incertidumbre, irresolución.
Doubting [daut'-ing], *s.* Duda, dubitación.
Doubtingly [daut'-ing-li], *adv.* Dudosamente.
Doubtless [daut'-les], *a.* Seguro, confiado.—*adv.* Indubitablemente, sin duda.
Doubtlessly [daut'-les-li], *adv.* Indubitablemente.
Douce [dūs], *a.* (Esco.) 1. Serio, reposado, no frívolo. 2. (Des.) Dulce.
†**Doucet** [dū'-set], *s.* Flan, una especie de manjar dulce.
Douceur [dū-sōr'], *s.* Halago, señuelo; cohecho; premio, recompensa; gratificación. (Gal.)
Douche [dūsh], *s.* 1. Ducha, chorro de agua dirigido sobre una parte del cuerpo. 2. Instrumento para administrar la ducha. (Fr.)
Dough [dō], *s.* 1. Masa, amasijo (para hacer pan, bollos, etc.). 2. Masa, mezcla pastosa, como de arcilla, etc. *My cake is dough,* Me he llevado chasco, mi empresa se ha frustrado.
Doughnut [dō'-nʊt], *s.* Especie de rosquilla o buñuelo frito.
Doughtiness [dau'-ti-nes], *s.* Valentía, esfuerzo.
Doughty [dau'-ti], *a.* 1. Bravo, valeroso; esforzado; ilustre, noble. 2. Jactancioso, fanfarrón.
Doughy [dō'-i], *a.* Crudo, blando.
Douse [daus], *va.* 1. Zabullir. *V.* DUCK. 2. Dar, dar golpes. 3. (Mar.) Recoger; arriar. 4. (Ger. de marineros) Extinguir.—*vn.* Zabullirse, caer de repente dentro del agua.
Dove [duv], *s.* Palomo o paloma.
Dove's-foot [duvz'-fut], *s.* (Bot.) Geranio columbino.
Dove-cot [duv'-cot], **Dove-house** [duv'-haus], *s.* Palomar.
Dovelike [duv'-laic], *a.* Columbino.
Dovetail [duv'-têl], *s.* Cola de milano, o de pato.—*va.* Ensamblar a cola de pato o de milano, machihembrar.
Dovetailed [duv'-têld], *a.* Ensamblado.
Dovish [duv'-ish], *a.* (Poco us.) Columbino, inocente como el palomo.
Dowable [dau'-a-bl], *a.* Capaz de ser dotado.
Dowager [dau'-a-jẹr], *s.* La viuda que goza el título de su marido. *Queen dowager,* La reina viuda.
Dowdy [dau'-di], *a.* Zafio, desaliñado, sucio; mal vestido.—*s.* Maritornes, mujer desaliñada.
Dowel [dau'-el], *s.* 1. Botón, macho de madera, espiga de un pie derecho. 2. Trozo de madera introducido en una pared para clavar algo en él.
Dower, Dowery [dau'-ẹr, i], *s.* 1. Dote. 2. Viudedad, porción vitalicia de los bienes del marido (la tercera parte por regla general) que gozan las viudas en ciertos casos en Inglaterra. 3. Dotación, don.
Dowered [dau'-ẹrd], *a.* Dotado.
Dowerless [dau'-ẹr-les], *a.* Sin dote.
Dowie [dau'-i], *a.* (Esco.) Murrio, alicaído, triste.
Dowlas [dau'-las], *s.* Lienzo basto que se usaba antiguamente.

Down [daun], *s.* 1. Plumón, flojel. 2. Vello, lana fina o pelo suave, blando y corto. 3. Llanura. 4. (Ingl.) Cuesta que tiene la cima ancha, sin árboles y cubierta de hierba; el espacio raso en su cima. 5. Duna, montecillo de arena en la costa.
Down, *a.* 1. Que va hacia abajo (literal ó figuradamente): pendiente. 2. Abatido; sombrío, melancólico. —*prep.* Abajo.
Down, *adv.* 1. Abajo, en la parte inferior; hacia abajo. 2. En tierra, por tierra; tendido á la larga. 3. En sujeción, bajo la dependencia de. 4. Bajo el horizonte. 5. Á un volumen menor. 6. A precio o paso reducido. 7. Al contado. 8. En un papel; como *to jot down,* anotar en un papel. 9. (Mar.) Á sotavento o hacia sotavento; como *to put the helm down,* poner el timón a sotavento. 10. En aplicación fija; *to get down to work,* aplicarse resueltamente al trabajo. *Down from,* Desde. *To go down,* (1) Ir abajo, bajar, descender. (2) (Fig.) Tragar, creer sin examen, aceptar. *To be downstairs,* Estar abajo, haber bajado. *Down the river* o *stream,* Río abajo, agua abajo. *Up and down,* De arriba a abajo; acá y allá. *Upside down,* Patas arriba, lo de arriba abajo. *To lie down,* Echarse. *To sit down,* Sentarse. *To set down,* Sentar o notar en un papel. *He had his ups and downs,* Tuvo sus altos y bajos. *This will not go down with me,* Lo que es esa no la trago.—*inter.* ¡Abajo! ¡a tierra! *Down with him!* ¡A tierra con él! *Down to,* Hasta. *Down on your knees!* ¡De rodillas!
Down, *va.* (Fam.) Derribar, echar por tierra; vencer, domar.
Down-bed [daun'-bed], *s.* Cama de plumón.
Downcast [daun'-cast], *a.* Alicaído, apesadumbrado, mustio, cabizbajo, encorvado.—*s.* 1. (Poco us.) Tristeza, abatimiento. 2. (Minería) Galería descendente; pozo de entrada de aire.
Downed [daund'], *a.* Cubierto o henchido con plumón.
Downfall [daun'-fōl], *s.* Caída, ruina, decadencia.
Downfallen [daun'-fōl-n], *a.* Caído, arruinado.
Downgrade [daun'-grêd], *s.* 1. Bajada, cuesta abajo. 2. Descenso a un grado inferior.
Downhaul [daun'-hōl], *s.* (Mar.) Cargadera.
Downhaul-tackle [daun'-hōl-tac'-l], *s.* (Mar.) Aparejo de cargadera.
Down-hearted [daun'-hārt-ed], *a.* Abatido, desmayado, desanimado, alicaído.
Downhill [daun'-hil], *a.* Pendiente, inclinado, en declive.—*s.* Declive o declivio, bajada, rampa.
Down-looking [daun'-luk-ing], *a.* Cabizbajo; murrio, melancólico, triste; duro de genio.
Down-lying [daun'-lai-ing], *a.* Parturiente.—*s.* 1. El tiempo de dormir o reposar. 2. Parto.
Down payment [daun pê'-mẹnt], *s.* Pago inicial. (Mex.) Enganche.
Downpour [daun'-pōr], *s.* Chaparrón, fuerte aguacero.
Downright [daun'-rait], *adv.* Perpendicularmente, a plomo; claramente, llanamente.—*a.* 1. Abierto, manifiesto, patente, claro, palpable, evidente. 2. Derecho, perpendicular. 3. Franco, abierto, sincero. 4. Llano, liso.

Downright booby, Solemnísimo bobo.
Downrightly [daun'-rait-li], *adv.* Llanamente.
Downstairs [daun'-stārz], *s.* 1. Abajo. 2. Piso inferior.
Downstream [daun'-strim], *adv.* Aguas abajo.
Downtown [daun'-taun'], *s.* Centro, parte céntrica de una ciudad.
Downtrod, Downtrodden [daun'-trod, n], *a.* Pisado, pisoteado.
Downward [daun'-ward], **Downwards** [daun'-wardz], *adv.* Hacia abajo.
Downward, *a.* 1. Inclinado, pendiente. 2. Descendente; que va hacia abajo.
Downy [daun'-i], *a.* Velloso, felpudo, blando, suave; dulce, tranquilo.
Dowry [dau'-ri], *s.* 1. Dote. 2. Antiguamente, cantidad o recompensa pagada por una esposa (Gen. xxxiv, 12). 3. Dotación, dádiva o posesión.
Doxological [doc-so-lej'-i-cal], *a.* Lo que se refiere o pertenece a la alabanza de Dios.
Doxology [doc-sel'-o-ji], *s.* Himno de alabanza a Dios; el gloria patri.
Doxy [dec'-si], *s.* (Ger.) Querida, manceba; y a menudo, ramera, prostituta.
Doze [dōz], *vn.* Dormitar, cabecear, estar medio dormido; vivir en la ociosidad o en la inacción.—*va.* Pasar sin darse cuenta de ello, o dormitando.
Doze, *s.* Sueño ligero, sopor, adormecimiento.
Dozen [duz'-n], *s.* Docena. *Baker's dozen,* Docena de fraile, trece.
Doziness [dō'-zi-nes], *s.* Somnolencia, entorpecimiento, modorra.
Dozing [dōz'-ing], *s.* Somnolencia o soñolencia.
Dozy [dōz'-i], *a.* Soñoliento, amodorrado, adormecido.
Drab [drab], *a.* Pardo; de color pardo.—*s.* 1. Color entre gris y amarillento; color pardo. 2. (Ant.) Pelleja, mujercilla. 3. En las salinas, cajón para desaguar la sal; pipa de saladar.
Drab, *va.* Acompañar a mujerzuelas.
Drabbing [drab'-ing], *s.* El acto de asociarse con mujerzuelas.
Drachm [dram], *s.* *V.* DRAM.
Drachma [drac'-ma], *s.* 1. Dracma, moneda de plata entre los griegos, antiguamente del valor de 9 a 17 centavos; hoy de la peseta o franco. 2. Antigua medida de peso. 3. En el griego moderno, gramo.
Draconian [dra-cō'-ni-an], *a.* Draconiano, alusivo a Dracón; inexorable, cruel.
Draff [drạf], *s.* Residuo de los granos que se emplean en las cervecerías y destilatorios; desperdicios; heces.
Draft [drạft], *s.* 1. Giro, libranza, letra de cambio. *Sight draft,* Giro a la vista. 2. Borrador, bosquejo. 3. Diseño, plan.
Draft [drạft], *va.* 1. Bosquejar, delinear los contornos de, trazar; diseñar. 2. Bosquejar, hacer borrador, componer la primera forma (de un escrito). 3. (Mil.) Destacar, separar para cualquier servicio; reclutar; hacer alistamiento forzoso. 4. En tejeduría, hacer pasar entre los lizos del telar.
Draftee [draf-tī'], *s.* Conscripto, quinto, recluta.
Draftsman, Draughtsman [drạfts'-man], *s.* Diseñador, dibujador, delineante.
Drag [drag], *va.* Arrastrar, tirar.

To drag for an anchor, (Mar.) Rastrear un ancla.—*vn.* 1. Arrastrar por el suelo. 2. Ir tirando, avanzar penosa o lentamente.

Drag [drag], *s.* 1. Carretilla. 2. Instrumento con garfio o gancho.

Drag chute [drag' shūt], *s.* (Aer.) Paracaídas de frenado.

Draggle [drag'-l], *va.* Emporcar alguna cosa arrastrándola por el suelo.—*vn.* Ensuciarse alguna cosa por llevarla arrastrando.

Dragman [drag'-man], *s.* Pescador con red barredera.

Drag-net [drag'-net], *s.* Red barredera.

Dragoman [drag'-o-man], *s.* Dragomán, trujamán, intérprete que emplean los viajeros en Levánte, en especial el intérprete de una embajada o consulado.

Dragon [drag'-un], *s.* 1. Dragón. *Dragon's blood* o *gum dragon*, Sangre de dragón, goma de India. 2. Hombre o mujer feroz. 3. (Astr.) Dragón, una de las constelaciones boreales.

Dragon-fly [drag'-un-flai], *s.* (Ent.) Libélula; (fam.) caballito del diablo, insecto volador neuróptero; tiene la cabeza grande y los ojos enormes.

Dragonish [drag'-un-ish], *a.* Dragontino.

Dragon-like [drag'-un-laic], *a.* Fiero, furioso, violento.

Dragonnade [drag''-o-nêd'], *s.* 1. Dragonadas, persecuciones dirigidas contra los calvinistas franceses por los dragones de Luis XIV. 2. Cualquiera persecución militar.

Dragoon [dra-gūn'], *s.* (Mil.) Dragón, soldado de a caballo; originalmente soldado que servía igualmente a pie que a caballo.

Dragoon, *va.* Acosar o perseguir por medio de dragones; gobernar despóticamente; intimidar.

Dragooning [dra-gūn'-ing], *s.* Saqueo, pillaje; asolamiento.

Drain [drên], *va.* 1. Desaguar. 2. Desangrar: empobrecer o agotar poco a poco. 3. Agotar, secar, escurrir, enjugar. *Draining-trough*, (Mar.) Coladera.

Drain, *s.* 1. Desaguadero, canal de desagüe. 2. Tajea, reguera. 3. Zanja de derivación para desecar un terreno. 4. (Mar.) Colador.

Drainable [drên'-a-bl], *a.* Desaguable.

Drainage [drên'-ēj], *s.* 1. La acción u operación de desaguar. 2. Desagüe, desecación. 3. Desecamiento, sistema de desecar las tierras por medio de zanjas y canales de desagüe. 4. Lo que está desaguado; derrame de agua. 5. La superficie desaguada; cuenca de un río.

Drake [drêk], *s.* 1. El ánade macho. 2. Piedra plana que se usa en el juego de *ducks and drakes* (= cabrillas). *V.* Duck.

Dram [dram], *s.* 1. Dracma, la octava parte de una onza, sesenta granos peso farmacéutico o 27.34 del peso comercial (setenta y dos en España). 2. *V.* Drachma. 3. (Fam.) Un trago, una copita de licor espirituoso. 4. ‖Parte o porción pequeña de alguna cosa.

Dram, *vn.* Beber aguardiente u otro licor destilado.

Dram-drinker [dram'-drink-ẹr], *s.* Bebedor de licores espirituosos.

Drama [drā'-ma], *s.* Drama.

Dramatic, Dramatical [dra-mat'-ic, al], *a.* Dramático.

Dramatically [dra-mat'-ic-al-i], *adv.* Dramáticamente.

Dramatist [dram'-a-tist], *s.* Dramático, el autor de composiciones dramáticas.

Dramatize [dram'-a-taiz], *va.* 1. Dramatizar, dar un giro dramático; hacer drama de. 2. Referir o representar de una manera dramática.

Dramaturge, Dramaturgist [dram'-a-tūrj, ist], *s.* Dramaturgo, autor o director de obras dramáticas.

Drank [drank], *pret.* del verbo *To* Drink.

Drap [drap], *v.* y *s.* (Esco.) *V.* Drop.

Drape [drêp], *va.* 1. Cubrir con un ropaje, revestir con telas colgantes. 2. Arreglar, disponer los pliegues de un vestido, de un cortinaje, o el ropaje de una estatua. Diseñar o arreglar colgaduras o ropajes.

Drape [drêp], *s.* Cortina, colgadura. V. Drapery.

Draper [drê'-pẹr], *s.* Pañero, mercader de paños. *Linen-draper*, Lencero, mercader de lienzos.

Drapery [drê'-pẹr-i], *s.* 1. Paños o telas de lana. 2. (Esc. y Pint.) Ropaje, también cortinas, colgaduras, tapicería, etc. 3. Oficio y tráfico de un pañero.

Drastic [dras'-tic], *a.* (Med.) Drástico.

Draught [draft], *s.* 1. Corriente de aire, aire colado. 2. Trago; la porción de cualquier licor que se bebe de una vez. 3. Poción, bebida medicinal, toma, dosis. 4. Tiro, la acción de tirar o arrastrar carruajes. *Draught-horse*, Caballo de tiro. 5. (Pint.) Dibujo, diseño. *Rough draught*, Borrador. *Draught of a ship*, Plano de un buque. 6. (Mil.) Destacamento. 7. (Des.) Sentina, albañal. 8. (Mar.) Cala o calado de un buque, o el fondo que necesita en el agua. 9. Libranza o letra de cambio. *V.* Draft, que es como se escribe siempre en los Estados Unidos. 10. *Draught-hooks*, (Art.) Ganchos de telera. 11. *Draught-hook of a washer*, Gancho de volandera. *Draughts*, (1) Tirantes, las cuerdas o correas que sirven para tirar de un carruaje. (2) Juego de damas. *Draft* tiene mucha aceptación, especialmente en los Estados Unidos.

Draught, *va.* *V.* Draft.

†**Draught-house** [draft'-haus], *s.* Estercolero, sitio para arrojar las inmundicias.

Draughtsman [drafts'-man], *s.* 1. Dibujante, delineante. 2. Peón, pieza del juego de damas.

Draw [drō], *va.* (*pret.* Drew, *pp.* Drawn). 1. Tirar, traer hacia sí; atraer. 2. Atraer, ganar, persuadir. 3. Arrastrar. 4. Chupar, mamar. 5. Aspirar, respirar, inspirar, el aliento. 6. Sacar, extraer, arrancar. 7. Poner de manifiesto, sacar a luz; sacar de. 8. Correr las cortinas, abriéndolas o cerrándolas. 9. Dibujar, bosquejar, delinear, representar. 10. Deducir, inferir. 11. Escribir o extender. 12. Destripar, desentrañar. 13. Tirar, alargar, estirar; a menudo va seguido de *out.* 14. Librar una letra de cambio. 15. Tender (un arco). 16. Preparar por medio de infusión.—*vn.* 1. Tirar, arrastrar como los animales que tiran de un carruaje. 2. Encogerse, arrugarse. 3. Adelantarse, moverse. 4. Dibujar, diseñar. 5. Sortear. 6. Calar una embarcación; hundirse en el agua hasta cierto punto. 7. Moverse libremente a fuerza de succión o atracción: tener libre corriente de aire. 8. Salir algo a fuerza de tirar de ello; ser extraído. 9. Atraer la sangre o los humores a la superficie, como lo hace un vejigatorio. 10. Moverse como si tirasen de ello; venirse, irse; se usa con adverbios, v. g. *to draw nigh*, acercarse. *To draw again*, Volver a tirar. *To draw a bridge*, Levantar un puente. *To draw along*, Arrastrar. *To draw asunder*, Separar, dividir. *To draw away*, Quitar, llevar; disuadir, divertir, distraer; enajenar. *To draw back*, Retroceder, volver hacia atrás; perder terreno, retirarse, ceder, aflojar, desistir; volverse atrás; recular, cejar; hacer retroceder o retirarse; hacer cejar o volver hacia atrás. *To draw forth*, Hacer salir, sacar. *To draw down*, Bajar, tirar hacia abajo; hacer bajar. *To draw forward*, Atraer. *To draw in*, Atraer, seducir, inducir, granjear, ganar; arrastrar tras sí. *To draw near to an end*, Fenecer. *To draw off*, Sacar, extraer; trasegar; distraer, disuadir, separar; retirarse; ganar a alguno a su partido haciéndole abandonar el que seguía antes. *To draw on*, Conducir; causar; incitar, empeñar a alguno, arrastrar a uno a que haga lo que no quiere, obligar; acercarse; estar en el último trance. *To draw out*, (1) Sacar, extraer, tirar. (2) Alargar, dilatar, diferir, extraer, extender, desarrollar. *To draw to an issue*, Acabar, concluir. *To draw together*, Juntar, amontonar, apretar. *To draw over*, Persuadir. *To draw up*, Tirar hacia arriba; componer algún libro, discurso o informe; hacer o extender una escritura; ordenar para el combate. *To draw so many feet of water*, (Mar.) Calar (una embarcación) tantos pies de agua.

Draw, *s.* 1. El acto de tirar, sacar o entresacar. 2. Jugada, suerte o mano. *The second draw*, A la segunda carta, jugada o sorteo. 3. Tablas; empate.

Drawable [drō'-a-bl], *a.* Capaz de ser tirado, sacado o sorteado.

Drawback [drō'-bac], *s.* 1. Rebaja o descuento, cierta cantidad de dinero que se abona al pagador por pagar al contado o antes del tiempo estipulado. 2. Rebaja o descuento de derechos de aduana, la rebaja que se hace al extraer las manufacturas del país o ciertas mercancías extranjeras que ya han pagado los derechos de entrada. 3. Desventaja, menoscabo, lo que detrae.

Drawbridge [drō'-brij], *s.* Puente levadizo.

Drawee [drō-ī'], *s.* La persona a cuyo cargo está girada una letra de cambio.

Drawer [drō'-ẹr], *s.* 1. Gaveta, naveta, cajoncito de un escritorio. 2. (Com.) Librador, el que libra o gira una letra de cambio. 3. (Ant.) Aguador. 4. (Des.) Mozo de taberna. *Drawers*, Calzoncillos. (Prov.) Paños menores.

Draw-head [drō'-hed], *s.* (Ferrocarril) Cabeza de la barra de tracción.

Drawing [drō'-ing], *s.* 1. Dibujo. 2. Tiro. 3. Sorteo (de una lotería).

Drawing-room [drō'-ing-rum], *s.* 1. Salón o sala de estrado. 2. Sala principal de una casa. 3. Corte, el conjunto de personas que acuden al besamanos en palacio.

Drawl [drōl], *vn.* Pronunciar con pesadez y lentitud. *To drawl out*, Arrastrar las palabras. *To drawl out his time*, Haraganear.

Drawl, *s.* El acto de hablar como arrastrando las palabras; articulación tarda, falta de energía.

Drawn [drōn], *pp.* del verbo *To* DRAW. 1. Desenvainado, destripado, desentrañado. 2. Movido, inducido. 3. Tablas, juego nulo, sin resultado. (Mil.) Indeciso, hablando de un encuentro o batalla. 4. Abierto. 5. En estado de fusión, fundido, derretido. *Drawn butter*, Manteca derretida. 6. Desenvainado, desnudo, fuera de.

Draw-well [drō'-wel], *s.* Pozo.

Dray, Dray-cart [drê, cart], *s.* 1. Carro que sirve para llevar cargas; carromato, carretón; por lo común más bajo hacia atrás que al frente. 2. (Ingl.) Narria, rastra.

Drayage [drê'-ẹj], *s.* 1. Acarreo, carretaje, el acto de conducir por carretón. 2. Carretaje, lo que se paga por ese servicio.

Dray-horse [drê'-hōrs], *s.* Caballo de carro.

Drayman [drê'-man], *s.* Carromatero, carretero, el que guía los caballos que tiran de los carros.

Dread [dred], *s.* Miedo, terror, espanto.—*a.* Terrible, espantoso, tremendo, formidable; augusto, respetable.

Dread, *va.* Temer, tener miedo o temor.—*vn.* Temer, recelar.

†**Dreadable** [dred'-a-bl], *a.* Temible, temedero.

Dreader [dred'-ẹr], *s.* Temedor.

Dreadful [dred'-ful], *a.* Terrible, espantoso, horroroso, formidable, espantador.

Dreadfulness [dred'-ful-nes], *s.* Terribilidad, horror.

Dreadfully [dred'-ful-i], *adv.* Terriblemente.

Dreadless [dred'-les], *a.* Intrépido, arrojado.

Dreadlessness [dred'-les-nes], *s.* Intrepidez, arrojo.

Dreadnaught [dred'-nōt], *s.* 1. El que no teme nada. 2. Tela muy doble y el capote de capucha hecho con ella. (< *dread* y *naught*, cero.)

Dream [drīm], *s.* 1. Sueño; ensueño, suceso o especie que se representa en la fantasía de uno mientras duerme. 2. Desvarío, cosa fantástica sin fundamento ni razón.

Dream, *vn.* (*pret.* y *pp.* DREAMED y DREAMT). Soñar; desvariar, discurrir fantásticamente.—*va.* Soñar, ver en sueños.

Dreamer [drīm'-ẹr], *s.* Soñador; visionario, iluso.

Dreamful [drīm'-ful], *a.* El que sueña mucho.

Dreamily, Dreamingly [drīm'-i-li, drīm'-ing-li], *adv.* Negligentemente, perezosamente, lentamente.

Dreamland [drīm'-land], *s.* El reino de los sueños.

Dreamless [drīm'-les], *a.* Sin sueños.

Dreamt [dremt], *pret.* y *pp.* de *To* DREAM.

Dream-world [drīm'-wŭrld], *s.* El mundo de las ilusiones.

Dreamy [drīm'-i], *a.* 1. Desvariado, perteneciente a los ensueños; dado a soñar. 2. Peculiar de los sueños.

Drear [drīr], *a.* (Poét.) *V.* DREARY.

Drearily [drīr'-i-li], *adv.* Funestamente, tristemente.

Dreariness [drīr'-i-nes], *s.* Tristeza; melancolía; aspecto lúgubre o murrio.

Dreary [drīr'-i], *a.* 1. Triste, lúgubre, funesto, melancólico. 2. Fatigante, monótono, inanimado, murrio.

Dredge [drej], *va.* 1. Limpiar, excavar, labrar profundamente por medio de draga; dragar. 2. Rastrear, recoger por medio de la red barredera; pescar con dicha red. 3. Esparcir harina sobre alguna cosa al guisarla; enharinar, polvorear.

Dredge, *s.* 1. Aparato para levantar o sacar algo que se halla debajo del agua: (a) draga, aparato para excavar los puertos, canales, etc.; (b) red barredera. 2. *V.* DREDGER, 3ª acep. 3. (Ant.) Mezcla de cebada y avena sembradas juntamente.

Dredger [drej'-ẹr], *s.* 1. El que draga o rastrea; pescador de ostras. 2. *Dredger* o *dredging-machine*, Draga, máquina y el barco de fondo llano que la lleva para limpiar los puertos o ríos. 3. Cajita para espolvorear harina sobre las viandas.

Dreen [drīn], *v.* y *s.* (Dialecto.) *V.* DRAIN.

Dregginess [dreg'-i-nes], *s.* Posos, heces; feculencia.

Dreggish [dreg'-ish], **Dreggy** [dreg'-i], *a.* Feculento, turbio.

Dregs [dregz], *s. pl.* 1. Heces. 2. Escoria, barreduras, morralla, zupia, desperdicio. *The dregs of the people*, El populacho, la gentuza, la canalla. (Mex.) Los léperos.

Drench [drench], *va.* 1. Empapar, humedecer completamente. 2. (Vet.) Purgar con violencia. 3. Abrevar, bañar, embeber.

Drench, *s.* 1. Tragantada. 2. (Vet.) Bebida purgante que se da a un animal. 3. Volumen de líquido suficiente para ahogar; diluvio. 4. Solución para empapar o remojar.

Drencher [drench'-ẹr], *s.* El que remoja alguna cosa.

Dress [dres], *va.* (*pret.* y *pp.* DRESSED y DREST). 1. Vestir; ataviar, adornar. 2. Curar las heridas. 3. Almohazar. 4. Componer; ajustar; arreglar, poner en orden. 5. Cocinar, guisar, adobar, aderezar, disponer las cosas para comer. 6. Adobar y curtir pieles. 7. Preparar lino o cáñamo. 8. Arreglar o disponer una cosa de modo que sirva para un uso particular. (Albañ.) Allanar, aplanar. 9. Alinear, poner en línea recta, v. gr. a una compañía de soldados.—*vn.* 1. Vestirse. 2. (Mil.) Formar los soldados en hileras; alinearse. *To dress a child*, Mudar de ropa a un niño. *To dress a dead body*, Amortajar. *To dress a garden*, Cultivar un jardín. *To dress a vine*, Podar. *To dress a lady's hair*, Peinar a una señora. (Mil.) *Dress left, right!* ¡A la izquierda, A la derecha, alinearse!

Dress, *s.* 1. Vestido, traje. 2. Vestido de mujer o niña. 3. Atavío, tocado. *Dress affair*, Velada o reunión que requiere traje de gala. *Dress ball*, Baile de gala. *Full dress*, Traje de etiqueta, uniforme completo. *Dress suit*, Frac. *Dress parade*, (Mil.) Parada con uniforme completo.

Dresser [dres'-ẹr], *s.* 1. Ayuda de cámara, moza de cámara. 2. Mesa de cocina. 3. Aparador. 4. Cocinero.

Dressing [dres'-ing], *s.* 1. La acción de vestir, ataviar, adornar; adorno. 2. Lo que se usa para aderezar, etc.: (a) cura, curación, hilas, vendajes, etc.; (b) aderezo (de las telas, de los manjares, de las pieles); (c) (agr.) bina, renda, segunda labor de las viñas; (d) estercoladura, estercuelo; (e) corte, poda, de los árboles; cultivo de tierra, labrantía; (f) encoladura de paños; (g) labrado, talla de los cantos. 3. (Fam.) Castigo o regaño. 4. *pl.* (Arq.) Molduras, adornos. *Dressing-case*, Tocador. *Dressing-gown*, Peinador, bata.

Dressing-room [dres'-ing-rum], *s.* Cámara o gabinete para vestirse.

Dressmaker [dres'-mê-kẹr], *s.* Costurera, modista; la que hace vestidos para las mujeres y niños.

Dressmaking [dres'-mék-ing], *s.* El arte de hacer vestidos, el oficio de costurera.

Dressy [dres'-i], *a.* 1. Acicalado, aficionado a ataviarse, amigo de compostura. 2. Elegante, distinguido en porte y aspecto.

Drest, *pp.* del verbo *To* DRESS.

Drew, *pret.* de *To* DRAW.

Dribble [drib'-l], *vn.* 1. Gotear, caer gota a gota; destilar. 2. Babear. —*va.* Hacer caer gota a gota.

Dribbling [drib'-ling], *s.* El acto de gotear.

Driblet [drib'-let], *s.* 1. Pico, cantidad pequeña de dinero. 2. Quebrado o corto resto de alguna cantidad principal.

Dried [draid], *part.* de *To* DRY.

Drier [drai'-ẹr], *s.* Desecante, lo que tiene la propiedad de desecar: (a) substancia añadida a un color para que se seque más rápidamente; (b) aparato para secar (las frutas, etc.). *Drier, Driest, comp.* y *super.* de DRY.

Drift [drift], *s.* 1. Impulso, violencia. 2. Todo objeto arrastrado por las aguas o arrebatado por el viento. 3. Montón de alguna cosa que junta el viento. 4. Objeto o blanco de algún discurso. 5. Designio, intento. 6. Manejo, entremetimiento. 7. (Mar.) La dirección de una corriente; deriva; ángulo de deriva; cambio a sotavento. 8. (Arq.) Empuje de un arco. 9. (Min.) Socavón, galería, cañón de desagüe. 10. (Art. y Of.) Broca, punzón para taladrar palastro. *Drifts of ice*, Hielos flotantes. *Drifts of sand*, Arena movediza. *To go adrift*, Fluctuar a merced de los vientos. *To set adrift*, Echar o dejar a la ventura. *Drifts of dust*, Nubes de polvo. *Drift-wood*, Madera o tronco flotante o echado a tierra por las aguas.

Drift, *va* Impeler, apilar, amontonar.—*vn.* 1. Ser llevado como por una corriente. 2. Formar en montones; esparcir, salpicar, moverse en varias direcciones.

Drift-way [drift'-wê], *s.* Camino de ganado.

Drift-wind [drift'-wind], *s.* Viento que levanta o amontona alguna cosa.

Drill [dril], *va.* 1. Taladrar, barrenar, agujerear. 2. Sembrar, plantar, en hileras o surcos. 3. (Mil.) Disciplinar reclutas, enseñarles el ejercicio.—*vn.* 1. Estar ocupado en ejercicios militares u otros análogos. 2. Plantar en surcos.

Drill, *va.* y *vn.* Hacer salir gota a gota; fluir lentamente.

Drill *s.* 1. Taladro, instrumento de varios tamaños, para agujerear o taladrar; terraja, parauso, taladro que usan los cerrajeros. 2. Máquina para plantar y cubrir semillas

menudas en hileras; sembradora de granos. 3. Hilera de semillas sembradas o surcos hechos con esa máquina. 4. Una especie de mono. 5. (Mil.) Instrucción de reclutas. *Drill-plough*, Arado sembrador, sementero.
Drilling [dril'-ing]. 1. El acto de usar un taladro o de taladrar. 2. Instrucción de reclutas. 3. Material extraído o excavado por un taladro. 4. Dril, tela fuerte y cruzada de algodón o hilo.
Drink [driŋk], *va.* y *vn.* (*pret.* DRANK, antiguamente DRUNK; *pp.* DRUNK, antig. DRUNKEN). 1. Beber, apagar la sed; embriagarse, emborrachar o emborracharse. 2. Chupar, embeber, absorber. 3. Ser habitualmente un borracho. *To drink away*, Beber a porfía. *To drink away one's time*, Malgastar el tiempo bebiendo. *To drink down*, Tragar; (fig.) borrar el recuerdo de algo bebiendo; emborracharse. *To drink down sorrow*, Ahogar las penas en vino. *To drink hard*, Beber mucho. *To drink huge draughts*, Beber a tragantadas. *To drink in*, Embeber, chupar. *To drink off* o *out* o *up*, Beber hasta la última gota. *To drink one's health*, Brindar, beber a la salud de alguno. *To drink to*, Saludar al beber, incitar a beber.
Drink, *s.* 1. Bebida. 2. Licor alcohólico. 3. Trago, la cantidad que se puede tragar de una vez.
Drinkable [driŋk'-a-bl], *a.* Potable.
Drinker [driŋk'-ẹr], *s.* Bebedor, borracho.
Drinking [driŋk'-ing], *s.* La acción de beber. *Drinking-glass*, Vaso, copa. *Drinking-horn*, Vaso de cuerno. *Drinking-house*, Taberna, tienda de vinos; vinatería. *Drinking-pot*, Jarro.
Drink-money [driŋk'-mun-i], *s.* Dinero para beber.
Drip [drip], *vn.* Gotear, destilar.—*va.* Despedir algún líquido a gotas, hacer gotear.
Drip, *s.* Lo que cae gota a gota.
Dripping [drip'-ing], *s.* Pringue, la grasa que chorrea de cualquier cosa crasa puesta al fuego.
Dripping-pan [drip'-ing-pan], *s.* Grasera, la cazuela en que se recoge el pringue.
Drive [draiv], *va.* y *vn.* (*pret.* DROVE, *pp.* DRIVEN). 1. Impeler, empujar, arrojar; estimular; precisar. 2. Cochear. 3. Llevar, conducir; inducir; forzar a; reducir a. 4. Enclavar, clavar. 5. Ser impelido o empujado. 6. Andar o ir en coche. 7. Apuntar o asestar. 8. Secuestrar. 9. Conducir, llevar, guiar (un tiro de caballos, un carruaje, una manada, un rebaño, etc.). 10. Excavar horizontalmente, v. gr. un túnel. 11. Transferir la fuerza a otra acción mecánica. *To drive along*, Empujar, llevar hacia adelante. *To drive at*, Tener puesta la mira en; rematar, terminar. *To drive away*, (1) Echar fuera, ahuyentar, desterrar. (2) (Fig.) Trabajar diligentemente y con persistencia. *To drive back*, Rechazar. *To drive in* o *into*, Hacer entrar por fuerza, meter o encajar a golpe de martillo, echar adentro o a lo hondo; entrar en alguna parte en coche. *To drive off*, Ahuyentar, arrojar, hacer salir de una parte; silbar, mofar; diferir, dilatar. *To drive on*, Tocar; empujar; apresurar la ejecución de una cosa. *To drive out*, Arrojar, hacer salir, expeler. *To drive out of heart*, Desanimar. *To drive to leeward*, (Mar.) Sotaventear. *To be driven to the wall*, Verse entre la espada y la pared. *To drive mad*, Hacer perder la cabeza, enloquecer.
Drive [draiv], *s.* 1. Accionamiento, impulsión. 2. Paseo en coche o en automóvil. 3. Calzada, paseo. 4. Urgencia, presión. *Drive lever*, Palanca de impulsión.
Drive-in [draiv'-in], *a.* Accesible en automóvil. Aplícase a cines, restaurantes, bancos, etc., en que el automovilista ve o es atendido sin abandonar el vehículo.
Drivel [driv'-l], *vn.* Babear; bobear, chochear.
Drivel, *s.* 1. Baba. 2. Cháchara necia, sandeces, vaciedades.
Driveling [driv'-l-ing], *a.* Baboso.
Driveller [driv'-l-ẹr], *s.* Fatuo, simple.
Driven [driv'-n], *pp.* de *To* DRIVE.
Driver [draiv'-ẹr], *s.* 1. Conductor, el que conduce o guía; cochero, carretero, conductor de locomotora. 2. Rueda o fuerza motriz. 3. (Mar.) Maricangalla o maría-cangalla, especie de vela latina que se pone en la mesana, cuando hay bonanza. *Driver-boom*, (Mar.) Botalón de maricangalla. 4. Arriero; porquero, vaquero o boyero.
Driveway [draiv'-wê], *s.* Entrada para vehículos.
Driving [draiv'-ing], *s.* 1. (Mar.) Garrar, se dice cuando el ancla no hace presa en el fondo. 2. Impulso, el acto de dar movimiento; tendencia a hacer alguna cosa.—*a.* 1. Motor, motriz. 2. Impetuoso, violento. *Driving-whip*, Látigo de cochero. *Driving-shaft*, Árbol motor. *Driving-wheel*, Rueda motriz.
Driving license [draiv'-ing lai'-sens], *s.* Licencia para manejar.
Driving school [draiv'-ing scûl], *s.* Autoescuela.
Drizzle [driz'-l], *vn.* Lloviznar, gotear, caer a gotas.—*va.* Echar o despedir en gotas menudas, rociar. *Drizzling rain*, Llovizna.
Drizzle, *s.* Llovizna.
Drizzly [driz'-li], *a.* Lloviznoso. *Drizzly weather*, Tiempo brumoso, de llovizna.
Droll [drōl], *a.* Festivo, chancero, jocoso, chistoso, gracioso; raro. *Droll saying*, Dicho gracioso. *Droll affair*, Cosa rara.—*s.* 1. Bufón; bufonada. 2. Farsa.
Droll, *vn.* Chocarrear, chancearse.
Drollery [drōl'-ẹr-i], *s.* Chocarrería bufonería o bufonada.
Drollish [drōl'-ish], *a.* Divertido, chistoso o gracioso.
Dromedary [drom'-e-dẹ-ri], *s.* Dromedario, camello de una sola giba.
Drone [drōn], *s.* 1. Zángano de colmena; el macho de la abeja. 2. Zángano, zangandungo, haragán. 3. Roncón de gaita. 4. (Aer.) Avión radioguiado. *Drone-fly*, Eristalis, abejorro.
Drone, *vn.* 1. Zanganear, holgazanear. 2. Producir un sonido sordo.
Dronish [drōn'-ish], *a.* Ocioso, perezoso, lento, tardo, flojo.
Drool [drūl], *vn.* (E. U. and prov. Ingl.) Babear.
Droop [drūp], *vn.* 1. Inclinarse, doblarse hacia el suelo, bajarse como obligado por debilidad o flaqueza. 2. Descaecer, decaer; amilanarse, desanimarse, entristecerse, acabarse, penar, consumirse, marchitarse.—*va.* Permitir caer; inclinar, bajar.
Drooping [drūp'-ing], *s.* Languidez, tristeza, abatimiento.—*a.* Lánguido, triste, afligido.
Drop [drop], *s.* 1. Gota, glóbulo de un líquido cualquiera. 2. Gota, muy pequeña porción de alguna cosa. 3. Pendiente con diamantes pequeños. 4. Caída; pendiente, declive. 5. *pl.* Medicamento líquido dado en gotas. *Drop-curtain*, Telón de boca. *Drop-letter*, Carta que ha de ser entregada al destinatario por la misma estafeta en que fué echada al correo. *Drop by drop*, Gota a gota. *Drop of a sail*, (Mar.) Caída de una vela.
Drop, *va.* 1. Destilar. 2. Soltar, desprender, dejar caer de cualquier modo, literal o figuradamente. *To drop tears*, Derramar lágrimas. 3. Soltar, proferir una palabra casualmente o como por incidencia. 4. Dejar de hacer o cesar en lo que se estaba haciendo; abandonar, renunciar; desistir de. 5. Dejar o desprenderse de algún dependiente o compañero; despedir, echar. 6. Dejar, sufrir que una cosa se pierda o se olvide. 7. Parir los animales. 8. (Fam.) Hacer caer, como con un arma de fuego.—*vn.* 1. Gotear, caer gota a gota; soltar gotas. 2. Caer, bajar de un lugar alto a otro más bajo; caer sin ímpetu. 3. Quedarse muerto o morir de repente. 4. Desvanecerse o disiparse alguna cosa; volverse agua de cerrajas. 5. Sobrevenir, venir de repente. *To drop away*, Morir. *To drop in*, Entrar, introducirse, meterse de rondón. *To drop off*, Decaer, ir en decadencia; perder un empleo o acomodo. *To drop out*, Desaparecer, disiparse algún líquido. *To drop a word unawares*, Soltar alguna expresión incautamente; dejar escapar alguna palabra que no debía decirse. *To drop a courtesy*, Hacer una cortesía. *To drop anchor*, Anclar. *To drop in unexpectedly*, Entrar en alguna parte de improviso. *To drop the curtain*, Correr el telón. (Met.) Encubrir, ocultar.
Drop-forge [drop'-fōrj], *va.* Forjar a martinete.
Drop hammer [drop ham'-ẹr], *s.* Martinete.
Drop kick [drop kic], *s.* En el futbol, puntapié que se da a la pelota al rebotar.
Droplet [drop'-let], *s.* Gotita.
Dropper [drop'-ẹr], *s.* Cuentagotas.
Dropping [drop'-ing], *s.* 1. Lo que cae gota a gota. *Droppings of the nose*, Moquita. 2. El acto de caer en gotas. 3. *pl.* (Fam.) Excrementos de los animales domésticos.
Droppingly [drop'-ing-li], *adv.* A gotas, gota a gota.
Dropstone [drop'-stōn], *s.* Espato en figura de gotas.
Dropsy [drop'-si], *s.* Hidropesía.
Dross [dros], *s.* 1. Escoria de metales; borra; espuma; hez. 2. Orín, moho, herrumbre. 3. Impurezas, residuo, heces.
Drossy [dros'-i], *a.* 1. Lleno de escoria, espuma o heces. 2. Vil, despreciable; impuro, puerco; grosero.
Drought, Drouth [draut, drauth], *s.* 1. Seca, sequedad, sequía. 2. Sed.
Droughtiness [draut'-i-nes], *s.* Sequedad, sequía.
Droughty, Drouthy [draut'-i, drauth'-i], *a.* Seco; sediento; árido.
Drove [drōv], *s.* 1. Manada, hato,

rebaño de ganado lanar. 2. Cualquier conjunto de animales; gentío, multitud, muchedumbre.
Drove, *pret.* de *To* DRIVE.
Drover [drōv'-ẹr], *s.* Ganadero, criador de ganado mayor y traficante en él.
Drown [draun], *va.* 1. Ahogar. 2. Anegar; sumergir. 3. Inundar. 4. Sofocar alguna cosa. *To drown one's sorrow in wine,* Ahogar sus pesares en vino, embriagarse. *To be drowned in tears,* Estar anegado en lágrimas. —*vn.* Anegarse, ahogarse.
Drowner [draun'-ẹr]. Anegador, sofocador.
Drowning [draun'-ing], *s.* 1. Ahogamiento, acción de ahogar o ahogarse. 2. Sumersión, inundación.—*pa.* de *To* DROWN.
Drowse [drauz], *va.* Adormecer, causar pesadez o sueño.—*vn.* 1. Adormecerse. 2. Tener murria, estar murrio o cabizbajo.
Drowsily [drau'-zi-li], *adv.* Soñolientamente; lentamente.
Drowsiness [drau'-zi-nes], *s.* Somnolencia, pereza, indolencia, adormecimiento, lentitud.
Drowsy [drau'-zi], *a.* Soñoliento, soporífero, lerdo, estúpido; pesado, adormecido.
Drowsy-headed [drau'-zi-hed'-ed], *a.* Lerdo, pesado, soñoliento.
Drub [drub], *s.* Golpe, puñada.
Drub, *va.* Apalear, sacudir, pegar.
Drubbing [drub'-ing], *s.* Paliza o zurra; tunda.
Drudge [druj], *vn.* 1. Afanarse, fatigarse, trabajar sin descanso. 2. Afanarse a trabajar en oficios u ocupaciones desagradables o viles, sin provecho ni honra.—*va.* Pasar el tiempo fastidiosamente o con trabajo.
Drudge, *s.* Ganapán; marmitón, grumete, galopín de cocina.
Drudgery [druj'-ẹr-i], *s.* Faena o trabajo vil, desagradable, ingrato.
Drudgingly [druj'-ing-li], *adv.* Laboriosamente, penosamente; desagradablemente.
Drug [drug], *s.* 1. Droga. 2. Cualquiera cosa de difícil salida, sin venta.
Drug, *va.* 1. Mezclar con drogas, hacer narcótico por medio de drogas. 2. Jaropar, dar drogas o medicinas con exceso; sumir en torpor, entumecer.—*vn.* Administrar o recetar drogas.
Druggist [drug'-ist], *s.* Farmacéutico, boticario.
Druid [drū'-id], *s.* Druida, sacerdote de los antiguos bretones y celtas.
Drum [drum], *s.* 1. Tambor, atambor. 2. Tambor, uno de los diversos objetos cilíndricos en figura de tambor: v. g. un aparato para difundir el calor; el cilindro que comunica movimiento a una máquina; un cuñete o barrilito de pescado, de higos u otros frutos, etc. 3. Tímpano del oído.
Drum, *vn.* 1. Tocar el tambor. 2. Tamborilear.—*va.* 1. Batir sobre el tambor; batir sin intermisión. 2. (Mil.) Expeler a toque de tambor; (seguido de *out*). 3. Reiterar; aturdir. 4. Atraer parroquianos. *To drum up,* Congregar o juntar a toque de tambor.
†**Drumble** [drum'-bl], *vn.* 1. Sonar como un tambor. 2. Zanganear, holgazanear.
Drum-major [drum'-mê-jẹr], *s.* Tambor mayor.
Drum-maker [drum'-mê-kẹr], *s.* Tamborero.
Drummer [drum'-ẹr], *s.* 1. Tambor, el que toca el tambor. (Mil.) 2. Tamborilero. 3. (Com. Amer.) Agente vendedor de una casa de comercio.
Drummond light [drum'-end lait], *s.* Luz de oxicalcio.
Drumstick [drum'-stic], *s.* 1. Baqueta, palillo o bolillo de tambor. 2. (Fam.) Lo que se asemeja a una baqueta, como el hueso de la pierna de un pavo.
Drunk [druŋk], *a.* Embriagado, borracho, ebrio.
Drunkard [druŋk'-ard], *s.* Borrachón. (Met.) Cuero, el que bebe mucho.
Drunken [druŋk'-en], *a.* Ebrio, borracho.
Drunkenly [druŋk'-en-li], *adv.* Ebriamente.
Drunkenness [druŋk'-en-nes], *s.* Embriaguez; borrachera habitual.
Drupaceous [dru-pê'-shus], *a.* (Bot.) Drupáceo, que produce drupas o es parecida a ellas.
Dry [drai], *a.* 1. Árido, seco; sin jugo. 2. Sediento. 3. Seco, falto de exornación, estéril, frío. 4. Duro, austero, satírico. 5. Apretado, agarrado, mísero, avariento. 6. Taciturno. 7. Privado de dulzura; seco (hablando de vinos). 8. Que no da leche, v. gr. una vaca. *Dry land,* Tierra firme. *Dry goods,* (1) Tejidos, telas, lienzos, ropa, lencería. (2) (Ingl.) Artículos que se venden por medida de capacidad, áridos; y también, en general, especierías, pinturas (colores), etc., en contraposición a otras mercancías y a los tejidos. *Dry style,* Estilo seco, insípido.
Dry, *va.* 1. Secar, quitar o extraer la humedad. 2. Enjugar. 3. Abrasar con sed. 4. Desangrar, desaguar.—*vn.* Secarse, enjugarse. *To dry up,* Enjugar, desecar, agotar, privar enteramente de la humedad.
Dryad [drai'-ad], *s.* 1. Dríada o dríade, ninfa de los bosques. 2. Lirón: Myoxus dryas.
Dry battery [drai bat'-ẹr-i], *s.* (Elec.) Pila o batería seca.
Dry cell [drai sel], *s.* (Elec.) Pila seca.
Dry cleaning [drai clīn'-ing], *s.* Tintorería.
Dry dock [drai doc], *s.* Dique de carena, dique seco, astillero.
Dryer [drai'-ẹr], *s.* 1. Secante. 2. (Quím.) Desecativo, desecante.
Dry-eyed [drai'-aid], *a.* Ojienjuto.
Dry farming [drai farm'-ing], *s.* Cultivos de secano.
Dry ice [drai' ais], *s.* Hielo seco, bióxido sólido de carbono.
Dryly [drai'-li], *adv.* Secamente, fríamente.
Dryness [drai'-nes], *s.* 1. Sequedad, aridez, cualidad o estado de lo que es seco. 2. Sequedad, tibieza, aridez de estilo.
Dry-nurse [drai'-nūrs], *s.* Ama que cría a un niño sin darle de mamar.
Dry-rot [drai'-ret''], *s.* 1. Carcoma, enfermedad de la madera causada por los ataques de algunas especies de hongos. 2. Enfermedad de los tubérculos de la patata. 3. (Fig.) Corrupción interna y oculta, de las costumbres, de la moralidad, etc.
Dry-rub [drai'-rub], *va.* Estregar o limpiar una cosa sin humedecerla.
Drysalter [drai'-sōlt-ẹr], *s.* Traficante en viandas saladas y secas, aceites, escabeches, materias de tinte, etc.
Dry-shod [drai'-shod], *a.* A pie enjuto.
Dry-wall [drai-wōl], *a.* Con paredes de tipo seco. (Aplícase a construcción.)
Dual [diū'-al], *a.* 1. Doble. *Dual control,* Doble mando, doble volante de mando. 2. (Gram.) Dual, número dual.
Dualism [diū'-al-izm], *s.* 1. *V.* DUALITY. 2. Dualismo, todo sistema filosófico que admite en el universo dos principios activos, la materia y el espíritu, o el genio del bien y el del mal.
Dualist [diū'-al-ist], *s.* Dualista, sectario del dualismo.
Duality [diu-al'-i-ti], *s.* Dualidad, expresión del número dos; estado de ser dos; división, separación.
Dub [dub], *va.* 1. Doblar (una película cinematográfica). 2. Armar a alguno caballero. 3. Conferir cualquiera dignidad. 4. Titular, apodar, dar nombre. 5. Alisar, estregar, aderezar.
Dub, *s.* 1. Golpe. 2. Lodazal.
Dubbed [dubd], *a.* *V.* BLUNT.
Dubious [diū'-bi-us], *a.* 1. Dudoso, irresoluto, indeciso. 2. Dudoso, incierto, equívoco, problemático, obscuro, ambiguo.
Dubiously [diū'-bi-us-li], *adv.* Dudosamente.
Dubiousness [diū'-bi-us-nes], *s.* Duda, incertidumbre.
Dubitable [diū'-bi-ta-bl], *a.* Dubitable, dudable.
Dubitation [diu-bi-tê'-shun], *s.* Dubitación, duda.
Ducal [diū'-cal], *a.* Ducal.
Ducat [duc'-at], *s.* Ducado, moneda de oro o plata y de diverso valor en los varios países en que se ha usado y se usa.
Ducatoon [duc-a-tūn'], *s.* Ducatón, moneda de plata que circuló en Venecia y valía medio ducado.
Duchess [duch'-es], *s.* Duquesa, la esposa o viuda de un duque; o la princesa soberana de un ducado.
Duchy [duch'-i], *s.* El territorio o estado sobre que recae el título de duque.
Duck [duc], *s.* 1. Ánade, pato. También el pato hembra, en contraposición al *drake,* o macho. 2. Cabeceo, la acción de volver la cabeza a un lado y a otro. 3. Cabrillas, juego de muchachos. 4. Mona, querida; es voz de cariño. *A lame duck* (en la bolsa de Nueva York), El corredor, agiotista o especulador que no puede pagar sus pérdidas. *To make* o *to play at ducks and drakes,* (1) Cabrillear, jugar el juego de cabrillas; hacer saltar una piedra sobre el agua. (2) (Fig.) Gastar de una manera pródiga; comprometer inconsideramente. Usado con *of* o *with.*
Duck, *s.* Lienzo fuerte no cruzado de hilo o algodón, más ligero y fino que la lona.—*pl.* (Fam.) Pantalones hechos de este tejido.
Duck, *vn.* Zabullirse, chapuzarse; cabecear; bajar la cabeza, hacer una profunda reverencia.—*va.* Zabullir, sumergir debajo del agua, chapuzar.
Duck-bill [duc'-bil], *s.* 1. (Zool.) Ornitorinco, mamífero acuático y ovíparo de Australia. (Ornithorhynchus paradoxus.) 2. Lo que tiene figura de pico de ánade.
Ducker [duk'-ẹr], *s.* Buzo; quitapelillos, zalamero.

Ducking [duk'-ing], *s.* 1. Zambullidura, zabullidura. 2. (Mar.) Zabullida, especie de castigo que se da a bordo.
Ducking-stool [duk'-ing-stūl], *s.* Silla de madera, fuerte y tosca, a la que ataban una mujer para sumergirla una o más veces en el agua. Antiguo castigo que se daba a las mujeres pendencieras, murmuradoras y gruñonas.
Duck-legged [duc'-legd], *a.* Corto de piernas.
Duckling [duc'-ling], *s.* 1. Anadeja. 2. Monina; voz cariñosa.
Duck-meat [duc'-mīt] o **Duck-weed** [duc'-wīd], *s.* (Bot.) Lenteja acuática.
Duck's-foot [ducs'-fut], *s.* (Bot.) Especie de serpentaria.
Duct [duct], *s.* Conducto, canal, tubo.
Ductile [duc'-til], *a.* 1. Dúctil, flexible, blando, correoso. 2. Tratable, obsequioso.
Ductileness [duc'-til-nes], **Ductility** [duc-til'-i-ti], *s.* Ductilidad; docilidad.
Dud [dud], *s.* 1. Bomba que no estalla. 2. (vul.) Persona o cosa que resulta un fracaso. 3. *Duds, pl.* (vul.) Trapos, andrajos, ropa vieja.
Dude [diūd], *s.* Petimetre, currutaco.
Dudgeon [duj'-un], *s.* 1. Ojeriza, desazón, enojo, cólera. 2. La raíz de boj, cuya madera se usó antiguamente para los puños de las dagas; una madera cualquiera abigarrada o veteada.
Due [diū], *a.* 1. Debido, cumplido, devengado. 2. Debido, apto, propio, conveniente, oportuno; exacto, caído. 3. Aguardado, algo cuya llegada está señalada o prevista. 4. Que se puede atribuir o achacar. *Due west,* (Mar.) Poniente derecho. —*adv.* Exactamente. *V.* DULY.—*s.* Lo que de derecho pertenece a alguno, deuda u obligación; derecho; tributo, impuesto. *King's dues,* Derechos del rey. *In due time,* A su tiempo; a propósito.
Due date [diū' dēt], *s.* Plazo.
Duel [diū'-el], *s.* Duelo.
Duel, *vn.* Combatir en duelo.—*va.* Acometer a otro en duelo o desafío.
Dueller [diū'-el-ẹr], **Duellist** [diū'-el-ist], *s.* Duelista.
Duelling [diū'-el-ing], *s.* Desafío.
†**Dueness** [diū'-nes], *s.* Aptitud. *V.* FITNESS.
Duenna [diu-en'-a], *sf.* Dueña, mujer anciana encargada antiguamente de guardar doncellas.
Duet [diu-et'], *s.* (Mús.) Dúo.
Duffel [duf'-l], *s.* 1. Moletón, tejido velludo de lana. 2. Equipo, pertrechos.
Dug [dug], *s.* Teta o pezón de teta de algún animal.—*Pret.* y *pp.* del verbo *To* DIG.
Dugong [dū'-gong], *s.* Mamífero acuático de la India y Australia. Muy parecido al manatí de la América tropical.
Dugout [dug'-aut], *s.* 1. Piragua. 2. Cueva. 3. Refugio contra bombardeos.
Duke [diūk], *s.* 1. Duque, título de los primeros entre la nobleza. 2. (Ant.) General, capitán.
Dukedom [diūk'-dum], *s.* Ducado.
Dulcet [dul'-set], *a.* 1. Dulce, agradable al paladar. 2. Dulce, suave, armonioso. 3. Agradable a la mente; lo que solaza o consuela.
Dulcification [dul'-si-fi-kē'-shun], *s.* 1. Dulcificación. 2. (Quím.) Dulcificación, la combinación de algún ácido mineral con el alcohol.
Dulcified [dul'-si-faid], *a.* Dulcificado.
Dulcify [dul'-si-fai], *va.* Dulcificar, dulzurar, endulzar.
Dulcimer [dul'-si-mẹr], *s.* Tímpano, salterio, instrumento músico.
Dulcinea [dul-sin'-ẹ-a], *f.* Amada, dama y señora de los pensamientos de uno. (< Dulcinea del Toboso.)
Dulcoration [dul-co-rē'-shun], *s.* Dulcificación.
Dulia [du-lai'-a o diū'-li-a], *s.* Dulía, culto que se da a los santos.
Dull [dul], *a.* 1. Embotado, obtuso, sin filo o corte. 2. No agudo o violento; v. g. *A dull pain,* Un dolor sordo. 3. Lerdo, estúpido, torpe, negado, insípido. 4. Flojo, tardo, perezoso, pesado; lánguido, insensible. 5. Triste, melancólico, pensativo, murrio. 6. Opaco, obscuro, ofuscado, nebuloso. 7. Soñoliento. *Dull of hearing,* Algo sordo, tardo o duro de oído.
Dull, *va.* 1. Embotar, engrosar los filos y puntas de instrumentos cortantes. 2. Entontecer, embotar; entorpecer, obstruir; contristar. 3. Hacer menos agudo, aliviar, moderar, mitigar. 4. Ofuscar, deslumbrar; empañar, deslustrar, deslucir. —*vn.* 1. Embotarse, entontecerse. 2. Ofuscarse; entristecerse; mitigarse; entorpecerse.
Dullard [dul'-ard], *s.* Bestia, estólido.—*a.* Estúpido.
Dull-brained [dul'-brēnd], *a.* Estúpido, tonto.
Dull-browed [dul'-braud], *a.* El que tiene las cejas dispuestas de tal modo que atristan los ojos.
Dulled [duld], *a.* Obscurecido, no claro
Duller [dul'-ẹr], *s.* Lo que hace obscuro, lerdo o flojo.
Dull-eyed [dul'-aid], *a.* El que tiene los ojos naturalmente apagados.
Dull-head [dul'-hed], *s.* Zote, un hombre estúpido.
Dull-witted [dul'-wit-ed], *a.* Lerdo, sin viveza.
Dully [dul'-i], *adv.* Lentamente, torpemente, zafiamente, estúpidamente.
Dulness [dul'-nes], *s.* Estupidez, incapacidad, tontería, estolidez, torpeza, rudeza; somnolencia, negligencia, pereza, entorpecimiento, pesadez; deslustre; embotadura.
Dulse [duls], *s.* Alga marina abundante de color rojo claro, que se come en Escocia y en otros países. Rhodymenia palmata.
Duly [diū'-li], *adv.* Debidamente, regularmente, exactamente, puntualmente, a su tiempo.
Dumb [dum], *a.* Mudo, privado del habla. *To strike one dumb,* Enmudecer a uno. *Dumb-bell,* Halterio, pesas, aparato gimnástico. *Dumb creature,* Bestia, bruto. *Dumb show,* Pantomima por señas; signo, gesto. *Dumb motions,* Señas mudas. *Dumb-waiter,* (1) Ascensor doméstico. (2) (Ingl.) Estante giratorio para vajilla, mesa de servicio.
Dumb, *va.* Imponer silencio, mandar callar.
Dumbly [dum'-li], *adv.* Mudamente.
Dumbness [dum'-nes], *s.* Mudez; silencio.
Dumdum [dum'-dum], **dumdum bullet** [dum'-dum bul'-et], *s.* (Mil.) Bala expansiva.
Dumfound, Dumbfound [dum-faund'], *va.* (Fam.) Confundir, enmudecer a alguno.
Dummy [dum'-i], *s.* 1. (Fest.) Mudo. 2. (Mec.) Locomotora de calles, pequeña y poco ruidosa. También un carro cuya parte delantera es la locomotora y la trasera coche de pasajeros. 3. En el juego de naipes, cuando el juego debe hacerse entre cuatro personas y hay sólo tres, se ponen a un lado las cartas del que falta; a esto los ingleses llaman *dummy.* 4. Maniquí para vestidos, cabeza para pelucas, etc., que sirven de anuncio en las tiendas.
Dummy, *a.* Fingido, falseado, imitado.
Dump [dump], *s.* (Vul.) 1. Murria, tristeza. En este sentido se usa sólo en plural. *To be in the dumps,* Tener murria, esplín; estar triste, alicaído, malhumorado. 2. Arrebato, rapto. 3. Asombro, susto. 4. (E. U.) Lugar donde se echan y amontonan las basuras, cenizas, etc.; y también el montón mismo de basuras.
Dump, *va.* Vaciar de golpe; descargar.
Dump body [dump bod'-i], *s.* Caja de volteo (de un camión).
Dumpish [dump'-ish], *a.* Murrio, mustio, triste, melancólico.
Dumpishness [dump'-ish-nes], *s.* Tristeza, descontento, melancolía.
Dumpling [dump'-ling], *s.* 1. Pudín de pasta rellena de fruta o carne. 2. (Prov. Ingl.) Un enano.
Dumpy [dump'-i], *a.* Gordo.
Dun, *va.* Importunar a un deudor. (Vul.) Moler, jorobar, fastidiar.
Dun, *s.* 1. Acreedor importuno. 2. Altura; seto.
Dunce [duns], *s.* Zote, zopenco, bolo, tonto.
Dunderhead, Dunderpate [dun'-dẹr-hed, pēt], *s.* Zote, zopenco, tonto.
Dune [diūn] *s.* Duna, marisma, médano, montecillo de arena suelta y movediza que se forma en las cercanías del mar.
Dung [dung], *s.* Estiércol, fiemo, excremento animal. *Cow-dung,* Boñiga. *Dog-dung,* Canina. *Goat, rat, mice, dung,* Cagarruta. *Hen-dung,* Gallinaza. *Horse-dung,* Cagajón.
Dung, *va.* Estercolar.—*vn.* Estercolar, echar de sí la bestia el excremento o estiércol.
Dungarees [dun-ga-rīs'], *s. pl.* Pantalones o ropa de trabajo hechos de tela basta.
Dungcart [dung'-cart], *s.* Carro de basura.
Dunged [dungd], *a.* Estercolado, engrasado.
Dungeon [dun'-jun], *s.* Calabozo. (Mex.) Bartolina.
Dungeon, *va.* Encalabozar.
Dung-fork [dung'-fōrc], *s.* Horca o pala para el estiércol.
Dunghill [dung'-hil], *s.* 1. Estercolero, muladar. 2. Vivienda vil y ordinaria; situación vil o baja. *To raise one from the dunghill,* Sacar a alguno de la nada o de la miseria. —*a.* Bajo, vil, indigno.
Dungy [dung'-i], *a.* Lleno de estiércol; vil.
Dungyard [dung'-yārd], *s.* Corral de estiércol o para el estiércol.
Dunner [dun'-ẹr], *s.* Cobrador de deudas atrasadas.
Duo [dū'-o], *s.* Dúo, pieza que se canta o toca por dos voces o instrumentos. *V.* DUET.
Duodecimal [diū-o-des'-i-mal], *a.* Duodecimal, dícese del sistema de nu-

meración que emplea doce caracteres, y cuya base es el número doce.

Duodecimo [diū-o-des'-i-mo], *s.* Libro en dozavo, cuya página es de unas 4½ por 7½ pulgadas.

Duodenal [dū-o-dīn'-gl], *a.* Duodenal. *Duodenal ulcer,* (Med.) Ulcera duodenal.

Duodenum [diū-o-dī'-num], *s.* Duodeno.

Duotype [dū'-o-taip], *s.* Dos fotograbados a media tinta obtenidos del mismo negativo.

Dupe [diūp], *s.* Crédulo; víctima de engaño o dolo.

Dupe, *va.* Engañar, embaucar.

Duple [dū'-pl], *a.* Doble.

Duplex [diū'-plex], *a.* 1. Duplo, doble, dúplice. 2. (Mec.) Dúplice, dúplex, que opera o actúa en dos direcciones, especialmente en las transmisiones opuestas simultáneas; v. g. telégrafo dúplex.

Duplicate [diū'-pli-kēt], *va.* 1. Duplicar, hacer duplicado; reproducir exactamente. 2. (Biol.) Dividirse en dos partes espontáneamente.

Duplicate, *s.* 1. Duplicado. 2. El número doble de un mismo objeto en las colecciones de historia natural, minerales, monedas y otras.—*a.* Duplicado, doble, en pares.

Duplication [diu-pli-kē'-shun], *s.* Duplicación; plegadura, pliegue, doblez.

Duplicative [diū'-pli-kg-tiv], *a.* Que se refiere a la duplicación; que produce la duplicación o está producido por ella.

Duplicature [diu'-pli-ca-chur], *s.* Plegadura, pliegue, doblez.

Duplicity [diu-plis'-i-ti], *s.* Doblez, duplicidad, engaño.

Dura mater [diū'-ra mē'-ter], *s.* (Anat.) Duramáter, membrana que envuelve el cerebro.

Durability [diū-ra-bil'-i-ti], *s.* Estabilidad, cualidad o estado de lo durable; duración.

Durable [diū'-ra-bl], *a.* Durable, duradero.

Durableness [diū'-ra-bl-nes], *s.* Dura, duración.

Durably [diū'-ra-bli], *adv.* Duraderamente.

Durance [diū'-rans], *s.* 1. Cautividad, encarcelación, sujeción personal.

Durant [diū'-rant], *s.* Sempiterna, tejido fuerte de lana.

Duration [diu-rē'-shun], *s.* Duración, continuación, perseverancia.

Duress [diū'-res o du-res'], *s.* Compulsión, coacción, prisión. Encierro, mal trato.

Durham [dūr'-am], *s.* 1. Res de una casta de ganado vacuno de cuernos cortos, notable por la excelencia de su carne. 2. Barca de carga con fondo plano que se impele por medio de largas pértigas.

During [diūr'-ing], *prep.* Mientras, durante el tiempo que, entre tanto, al mismo tiempo.

Durst, *pret. irr.* del verbo *To* DARE.

Dusk [dusk], *a.* (Arcaico o poét.) Obscurecido, fusco, obscuro.—*s.* 1. El anochecer o entre dos luces; crepúsculo vespertino. 2. Principio de obscuridad, color fusco, color negruzco.

Duskily [dusk'-i-li], *adv.* Obscuramente.

Duskiness [dusk'-i-nes], *s.* Principio de la obscuridad.

Duskish [dusk'-ish], *a.* Fusco, obscuro, negruzco, sombrío.

Duskishness [dusk'-ish-nes], *s.* Obscuridad.

†**Duskness** [dusk'-nes], *s.* Ofuscamiento.

Dusky [dusk'-i], *a.* 1. Obscuro, falto de luz. 2. Fusco, obscuro, moreno, de tez morena. 3. (Raro) Murrio, triste, melancólico.

Dust [dust], *s.* 1. Polvo, toda substancia reducida a partes muy menudas. 2. Polvo, parte menuda de la tierra muy seca. 3. Nube, multitud de palabras o argumentos que turba y confunde; confusión, controversia. *To kick up a dust,* (Fig.) Levantar polvareda o cantera, causar disensiones. 4. Restos mortales, cenizas. 5. (Fig.) La tierra, la sepultura; polvo, estado o condición vil. 6. Basura, barreduras; residuos. 7. (Fam.) Oro en polvo; de aquí, dinero en general y dinero contante. *Sawdust,* Serrín o aserraduras. *Pin-dust,* Limaduras de alfileres. *Dust of a house,* Barreduras de una casa. *To kick up* o *to raise a dust,* (Fam.) Levantar polvareda, hacer disturbio. *To bite the dust,* Morder el polvo, morir combatiendo.

Dust, *va.* 1. Despolvorear, sacudir o quitar el polvo. 2. Polvorear, llenar de polvo.

Dust bin [dust bin], *s.* Receptáculo para polvo o ceniza.

Dust-born [dust'-bērn], *s.* Nacido del polvo.

Dust-brush [dust'-brush], *s.* Plumero para quitar el polvo; cepillo.

Duster [dust'-gr], *s.* 1. El que quita el polvo. 2. Plumero, atado de plumas u otro utensilio que sirve para despolvorear. 3. Sobretodo largo de lienzo que protege contra el polvo. 4. Utensilio para espolvorear veneno sobre las plantas con objeto de matar los insectos.

Dustiness [dust'-i-nes], *s.* El estado de lo que se halla cubierto de polvo.

Dustman [dust'-man], *s.* Basurero.

Dust-pan [dust'-pan], *s.* Pala de recoger la basura.

Dust storm [dust stērm], *s.* Tolvanera.

Dusty [dust'-i], *a.* Polvoriento, polvoroso, lleno de polvo.

Dutch [duch], *a.* y *s.* Holandés; lo perteneciente a Holanda; idioma que se habla en Holanda. *Dutch cheese,* Queso de Flandes. *Dutch oven,* Asador de vuelta. *Dutch tiles,* Azulejos.

Dutchman [duch'-man], *s.* 1. Holandés, el natural de Holanda. 2. (Fam. E. U.) Alemán.

Duteous [diū'-tg-us], *a.* Obediente, obsequioso, respetuoso.

Dutiable [diū'-ti-a-bl], *a.* (Der.) Sujeto al pago de impuestos.

Dutiful [diū'-ti-ful], *a.* 1. Obediente, sumiso, rendido o humillado a cualquier superior. 2. Respetuoso, respetoso, reverente, sumiso.

Dutifully [diū'-ti ful-i], *adv.* Obedientemente, respetuosamente.

Dutifulness [diū'-ti-ful-nes], *s.* Obediencia, respeto, sumisión.

Duty [diū'-ti], *s.* 1. Deber, obligación, (ant.) respeto, homenaje. 2. Obligación. 3. Obediencia, sumisión, acatamiento. 4. (Mil.) Facción, acto del servicio militar. 5. Impuesto, los derechos que se pagan por la introducción o extracción de géneros; derechos de aduana o de puertas. 6. (Mec.) Trabajo mecánico, el hecho por una máquina comparado con los combustibles consumidos; efecto útil. *Duty free,* Libre de derechos, exento.

Duumvirate [du-um'-vi-rēt], *s.* Duunvirato.

Dwale [dwēl], *s.* 1. (Bot.) Solano. 2. (Her.) Sable, negro.

Dwarf [dwērf], *s.* 1. Enano o enana. 2. Cualquier animal o planta que no tiene su ordinario grandor. *Dwarf-elder,* Yezgo, especie de saúco.

Dwarf, *va.* 1. Impedir que alguna cosa llegue a su tamaño natural. 2. Hacer aparecer pequeño en comparación con otra cosa.—*vn.* Empequeñecerse, achicarse.

Dwarfish [dwērf'-ish], *a.* Enano, bajo, pequeño.

Dwarfishly [dwērf'-ish-li], *adv.* Como un enano.

Dwarfishness [dwērf'-ish-nes], *s.* Pequeñez de estatura.

Dwell [dwel], *vn.* 1. Habitar, morar, residir, vivir en algún paraje. 2. Hallarse en algún estado o condición. 3. (Con *on* o *upon*) Pararse, detenerse, dilatarse, insistir hablando de cualquier asunto.—*va.* (Des.) Vivir, ocupar.

Dweller [dwel'-gr], *s.* Morador, habitante.

Dwelling [dwel'-ing], *s.* Habitación, domicilio, vivienda.

Dwelling-house [dwel'-ing-haus], *s.* Domicilio, morada; casa.

Dwelling-place [dwel'-ing-plēs], *s.* Residencia, morada, domicilio.

Dwindle [dwin'-dl], *vn.* 1. Mermar, disminuirse. 2. Degenerar; descaecer, decaer. 3. Aniquilarse, consumirse.—*va.* Disminuir, rebajar; romper; disipar.

Dwindled [dwin'-dld], *a.* Contraído, disminuído.

Dye [dai], *va.* Teñir.

Dye, *s.* Tinte; materia colorante, o fluido que se usa para teñir. *Dye-house,* Tintorería. *Dye-works,* Tallar de tintorero.

Dyed-in-the-wool [daid-in-the-wul], *a.* Fanático, ferviente, convencido.

Dyer [dai'-gr], *s.* Tintorero.

Dyeing [dai'-ing], *s.* Tintorería, el arte de teñir; tinta, teñidura, tintura.—*a.* Colorante.

Dyestuff [dai'-stuf], *s.* Materia de tinte, droga.

Dyers'-weed [dai'-grz-wīd], *s.* (Bot.) Gualda.

Dying [dai'-ing], *pa.* 1. Moribundo, agonizante. 2. Mortal, destinado a morir. 3. Mortal, que se refiere a la muerte; en el instante de morir. *To be in a dying state,* Estar a la muerte. *The dying words of one,* Las últimas palabras de alguno. *Dying eyes,* Ojos lánguidos o angustiados, vista desfallecida o desmayada.—*s.* Muerte.

Dyingly [dai'-ing-li], *adv.* A manera de moribundo.

Dyke [daik], *s.* *V.* DIKE.

Dynamic, Dynamical [dai-nam'-ic, al], *a.* 1. Dinámico, referente a la dinámica; opuesto a estática. 2. Referente a una fuerza mecánica de cualquier especie. 3. Motor, motriz, que causa actividad o movimiento; eficaz.

Dynamics [dai-nam'-ics], *s.* Dinámica, la ciencia que trata de la acción de las fuerzas motrices sobre los cuerpos sólidos.

Dynamite [dai'-na-mait], *s.* Dinamita, substancia de enorme fuerza explosiva, compuesta de una materia absorbente y nitroglicerina.

Dynamo [dai'-na-mō], *s.* Dinamo, má-

quina para convertir la fuerza mecánica en fuerza eléctrica; abreviatura de *dynamo-electric machine*, máquina electrodinámica.
Dynamo-electric [dai'-na-mo-e-lec'-tric], *a.* Electrodinámico, que transforma la fuerza mecánica en eléctrica o viceversa.
Dynamometer [dai-na-mom'-e-ter], *s.* Dinamómetro, instrumento para evaluar las fuerzas motrices.
Dynamometric [dai'-na-mo-met''-ric], *a.* Dinamométrico.
Dynasty [dai'-nas-ti], *s.* Dinastía, serie de príncipes de una misma familia.
Dyne [dain], *s.* (Fís.) Dina.
Dyscrasia, Dyscrasy [dis-crê'-si-a, dis cra-si], *s.* Discrasia, mal temperamento.
Dysenteric [dis-en-ter'-ic], *a.* Disentérico.
Dysentery [dis'-en-ter-i], *s.* Disentería, flujo de vientre o cámaras de sangre.
Dyspepsia, Dyspepsy [dis-pep'-si-a], *s.* Dispepsia, digestión laboriosa é imperfecta, por lo general de carácter crónico.
Dyspeptic [dis-pep'-tic], *a.* y *s.* 1. Dispéptico, relativo a la dispepsia. 2. Enfermo de dispepsia; mórbido, quejoso. 3. Que tiende a la dispepsia, indigestible.
Dysphagia [dis-fê'-ji-a], *s.* Disfagia, dificultad de tragar.
Dysphonia, Dysphony [dis-fō'-ni-a, dis'-fo-ni], *s.* Disfonía, dificultad de hablar.
Dyspnœa [disp-nî'-a], *s.* Disnea, dificultad de respirar.
Dyspnœal, Dyspnœic [disp-nî'-al, ic], *a.* Disneico, relativo a la disnea.
Dysuria, Dysury [dis-yū'-ri-a, dis'-yu-ri], *s.* Disuria, dificultad en la expulsión de la orina.

E

E [î]. Esta letra tiene tres sonidos en inglés; uno igual al de la letra *i* en castellano; v. g. en *each* [îch], *eagle* [îguel], y otro como el de la *e* en español; v. g. *men, bed, ten.* El tercero no es más que una variación del segundo, y se representa, según su situación, por los signos e y e; v. g. *elegant* [el'-e-gant], *daughter* [dē'-ter]. Es muda cuando finaliza alguna palabra, excepto en las monosílabas y en las derivadas inmediatamente del griego; y sólo sirve, cuando es final, para prolongar la vocal que precede, como en *mine, fate* [main, fēt]. E. en la rosa náutica denota el este u oriente; en la música, mí. *E flat*, Mí bemol.
Each [îch], *pron.* Cualquier o cualquiera, cada, cada uno. *Each other*, Entrambos, mutuamente, unos a otros, el uno al otro; uno sí y otro no.
Eager [î'-ger], *a.* 1. Ansioso, ahincado, deseoso. 2. Fogoso, ardiente, vehemente, impaciente. 3. Vivo, pronto. 4. Acre, mordaz.
Eagerly [î'-ger-li], *adv.* Ansiosamente, vehementemente, ardientemente; acremente. *To be eagerly busied*, Estar embebido en los negocios.
Eagerness [î'-ger-nes], *s.* 1. Ansia, anhelo, ahinco. 2. Vehemencia, violencia, ardor; apresuramiento. 3. Aspereza, acedía.
Eagle [î'-gl], *s.* 1. Aguila. 2. Águila, insignia de los romanos. 3. Águila, moneda de oro de los Estados Unidos que vale diez pesos.
Eagle-eyed [î'-gl-aid], **Eagle-sighted** [î'-gl-sait'-ed], *a.* De vista de lince.
Eagle-speed [î'-gl-spîd], *s.* Velocidad de águila.
Eagless [î'-gles], *sf.* La hembra del águila.
Eagle-stone [î'-gl-stōn], *s.* Etites, piedra de águila, hierro oxidado moreno.
Eaglet [î'-glet], *s.* Aguilucho.
Eagle-winged [î'-gl-wingd], *a.* Alado como águila.
Eagle-wood [î'-gl-wud], *s.* Madera de águila.
†**Ean**, *vn.* *V.* YEAN.
Ear [îr], *s.* 1. Oreja, órgano del oído; pabellón de la oreja. 2. Oído, sentido del oir. 3. Oído para la música. 4. Oído, la atención que se presta a lo que dice una persona. 5. Asa, asidero. 6. (Bot.) Espiga. *Dog's ears*, (Fam.) Orejones, las puntas de las hojas de los libros dobladas o arrolladas. *By ear*, De, o por oídas; de oído.
Ear, *vn.* Espigar, empezar las semillas a crecer y echar espigas.—*va.* (Des.) Arar. *To set by the ears*, Reñir, pelear.
Earache [îr'-êc], *s.* Dolor de oídos.
Ear-bored [îr'-bōrd], *a.* El o la que tiene las orejas horadadas.
Ear-deafening [îr'-def-n-ing], *a.* Lo que ensordece.
Ear-drop [îr'-drep], *s.* Pendiente, zarcillo. *V.* EAR-RING.
Ear-drum [îr'-drum], *s.* Tímpano del oído.
Eared [îrd], *a.* 1. Lo que tiene orejas u oídos. 2. Espigado, provisto de espigas. 3. (Des.) Arado. 4. De las orejas. *Long-eared*, Orejudo, de orejas largas. *Lap-eared*, De orejas pendientes.
Earing [îr'-ing], *s.* (Ant.) La acción de arar la tierra. *Earing of a sail*, (Mar.) Empuñidura de una vela. *Head-earings*, (Mar.) Empuñiduras de grátil. *Reef-earings*, (Mar.) Empuñiduras de rizos.
Earl [erl], *s.* Conde, título de nobleza, hoy el tercero en Inglaterra. *Earl-marshal*, Dignidad en la corte de Inglaterra que tiene a su cargo la dirección de las solemnidades militares y todos los asuntos respectivos a las armas y honores de las familias.
Earldom [erl'-dum], *s.* Condado, señorío de conde.
Earlap [îr'-lap], *s.* La punta de la oreja.
Earless [îr'-les], *a.* Desorejado; el que no quiere oir.
Earlier, Earliest, comparativo y superlativo de EARLY.
Earliness [er'-li-nes], *s.* 1. Precocidad, anticipación. 2. Presteza, prontitud.
Earlock [îr'-lec], *s.* Una especie de bucle o rizo. *V.* LOVE-LOCK.
Early [er'-li], *a.* 1. Primitivo, del principio. 2. Avanzado, precoz, anticipado. 3. Temprano, matinal; cercano, próximo a suceder o acontecer. *An early fruit*, Un fruto temprano. *To rise early*, Madrugar, levantarse temprano. *Early riser*, Madrugador. *Early in the spring*, Al principio de la primavera. *You are early*, Es Vd. matinal. *From the earliest times*, Desde los primeros tiempos.—*adv.* 1. Temprano, de madrugada. 2. Luego, tan pronto como 3. Al principio de. *Early in the morning*, Muy de mañana, de madrugada. *As early as possible*, Tan pronto como sea posible, a la mayor brevedad.
Ear-mark [îr'-mark], *s.* 1. Señal en la oreja. 2. Toda señal que sirve para identificar.
Ear-mark, *va.* Marcar el ganado en las orejas.
Earmuff [îr'-muf], *s.* Orejera.
Earn [ern], *va.* 1. Ganar, adquirir caudal; obtener, conseguir. 2. Merecer, hacer algo que merece recompensa.
Earnest [ern'-est], *a.* 1. Ardiente, fervoroso, ansioso. 2. Activo, diligente; atento, cuidadoso. 3. Serio, importante; formal, de buena fe. —*s.* 1. Veras, seriedad, gravedad. 2. Buena fe, realidad. 3. Arras, el primer dinero que se recibe por lo que se vende. 4. Prenda segura, seguridad, señal, caparra, la parte de precio que se anticipa en cualquier concierto como prenda de seguridad. *To give earnest*, Dar señal o arras. *In earnest*, De veras. *In good earnest*, De buena fe. (Fam.) Con formalidad, con seriedad.
Earnestly [er'-nest-li], *adv.* Seriamente, de veras; encarecidamente; ansiosamente.
Earnestness [er'-nest-nes], *s.* 1. Ansia, anhelo, vehemencia, ardor, celo. 2. Gravedad, seriedad, formalidad. 3. Solicitud, cuidado, ahinco, diligencia.
Earning [ern'-ing], *s.* Salario, jornal, paga.
Earphone [îr'-fōn], *s.* Audífono.
Ear-pick [îr'-pic], *s.* Mondaorejas, escarbaoídos.
Ear-piercing [îr'-pîrs-ing], *a.* Que penetra el oído (sonido agudo).
Ear-ring [îr'-ring], *s.* Zarcillo, pendiente, arracada. (Cuba y Méx.) Arete.
Earshot [îr'-shet], *s.* Alcance del oído.
Ear specialist [îr spesh'-al-ist], *s.* Otólogo, especialista de oídos.
Earth [erth], *s.* 1. Tierra, el globo terráqueo o terrestre. 2. Tierra, porción sólida de nuestro globo. 3. (Quím.) Tierra, substancia inorgánica y fósil; óxido metálico, como alúmina. *Fuller's earth*, Tierra de batán, greda muy fina. 4. Tierra, espacio de terreno a propósito para el cultivo. 5. Mundo, los que habitan el globo. 6. Madriguera, la cuevecilla en que habitan ciertos animales. *Argillaceous earth*, Tierra arcillosa, greda. *Run to earth*, Cazado hasta la misma madriguera.
Earth, *va.* Enterrar, cubrir con tierra.—*vn.* Retirarse debajo de tierra.
Earth-bank [erth'-banc], *s.* Especie de cercado de tierra para guardar los sembrados.
Earth-board [erth'-bōrd], *s.* Orejera, la parte del arado que abre el surco. (Se llama más comúnmente MOLD-BOARD.)
Earth-born [erth'-bērn], *a.* 1. Terrestre, producido por la tierra. 2. El que es de bajo nacimiento.
Earth-bound [erth'-baund], *a.* Comprimido o apretado con tierra.
Earth-bred [erth'-bred], *a.* Vil, bajo.
Earth-created [erth'-cre-êt-ed], *a.* Formado o hecho de tierra.
Earthen [erth'-n], *a.* Térreo, terreno, terroso; de barro. *Earthenware*, Loza de barro. *Glazed earthenware*, Loza vidriada.

Earth-fed [ẹrth'-fed], *a.* Bajo, vil.
Earth-flax [ẹrth'-flacs], *s.* Amianto, fósil; asbesto.
Earthiness [ẹrth'-i-nes], *s.* Terrenidad; grosería.
Earthliness [ẹrth'-li-nes], *s.* Vanidad mundana.
Earthling [ẹrth'-ling], *s.* Habitante de la tierra, mortal.
Earthly [ẹrth'-li], *a.* 1. Terreno, térreo, terrenal, terrestre, mundano. 2. Temporal, sensual, terrenal. 3. Grosero, basto, tosco.
Earthly-minded [ẹrth'-li-maind'-ed], *a.* Mundano, sensual.
Earthly-mindedness [ẹrth'-li-maind'-ed-nes], *s.* Grosería; sensualidad.
Earth-nut [ẹrth'-nut], *s.* 1. Criadilla de tierra; especie de hongo sin raíz, comestible, que se cría debajo de tierra. 2. Cacahuete, maní. Arachis hypogæa.
Earthquake [ẹrth'-cwêc], *s.* Temblor de tierra, terremoto.
Earth-shaking [ẹrth'-shêk-ing], *a.* Lo que tiene poder de mover la tierra.
Earthwork [ẹrth'-wūrk], *s.* 1. Fortificación hecha en gran parte de tierra. 2. Obra de ingeniería que necesita el movimiento de tierras.
Earthworm [ẹrth'-wūrm], *s.* 1. Lombriz de tierra. 2. Gusano, hombre vil y abatido.
Ear-wax [ír'-wacs], *s.* Cerilla o cera de los oídos.
Earwig [ír'-wig], *s.* 1. Tijereta, gusano del oído. Forfícula. 2. Cuchicheador, el amigo de cuchichear.
Ear-witness [ír'-wit-nes], *s.* Testigo auricular o de oídas.
Ease [íz], *s.* 1. Quietud, tranquilidad, ocio, reposo; conveniencia, descanso, comodidad. 2. Alivio, descanso, desahogo. 3. Facilidad, disposición para entender y hacer las cosas sin trabajo; despejo, desembarazo, donaire. *At ease,* Con desahogo, descansadamente. *With ease,* Con facilidad. *At heart's ease,* A pedir de boca.
Ease *va.* 1. Aliviar, ablandar, mitigar, templar, suavizar, moderar. 2. Dar alivio y descanso de algún trabajo corporal. 3. Desembarazar, quitar algún estorbo o embarazo. *To ease one's self,* Hacer del cuerpo. *Ease the ship,* (Mar.) Orza todo. *To ease off* o *away,* (Mar.) Lascar o arriar.
Easel [í'-zl], *s.* Caballete, bastidor que sirve a los pintores para colocar el lienzo en que pintan.
Easeless [íz'-les], *a.* Inquieto, sin reposo.
Easement [íz'-mẹnt], *s.* 1. (For.) Derecho incorpóreo distinto de la propiedad del suelo, como el que se tiene a una corriente de agua o al aire libre. 2. Alivio, apoyo, ventaja.
Easily [íz'-i-li], *adv.* Fácilmente; sin dificultad, esfuerzo ni trabajo; sin inquietud, pesar o fastidio; quietamente, sosegadamente; prontamente.
Easiness [íz'-i-nes], *s.* 1. Facilidad, presteza, diligencia. 2. Libertad, quietud. 3. Comodidad, bienestar. 4. Despejo, desembarazo, gracia, facilidad de maneras.
East [íst], *s.* 1. Oriente; este. *East wind,* Viento del este o de levante. 2. En el comercio se designan con el nombre de Oriente las regiones y los pueblos del Asia que baña el Océano, y con el de Levante los que están en el Mediterráneo.—*a.* Oriental, de Oriente, del Este.

Easter [íst'-ẹr], *s.* Pascua de resurrección o florida. *Easter Eve,* Sábado santo. *Easter Day,* Día de Pascua. *Eastertide,* Estación o época de la Pascua; tiempo que esta dura.
Easterling [íst'-ẹr-ling], *s.* Natural de algún país al oriente de otro.
Easterly [íst'-ẹr-li], *a.* Oriental, del este, hacia el este, situado al este, o viniendo de él. *Easterly wind,* Aire de levante, solano.
Eastern [íst'-ẹrn], *a.* 1. Oriental, de Oriente, o que habita el Oriente. 2. *V.* EASTERLY.
Eastward [íst'-wạrd], *a.* Que se dirige o tiende hacia el este.—*adv.* Hacia el oriente.
Easy [íz'-i], *a.* 1. Fácil; cómodo, que no exige gran esfuerzo ni trabajo. 2. Fácil; complaciente, condescendiente, cortés, sociable. 3. Libre; tranquilo; contento; aliviado, exento de penas, de cuidados. 4. Acomodado, en buena situación de fortuna. 5. Acomodado, liso, llano. 6. Fácil, natural, que no es forzado. 7. Condescendiente, suave. 8. (Com.) No en gran demanda ni escaso; en libre circulación, como el dinero. *Easy sail,* (Mar.) Poca vela. *Easy labor,* Parto feliz. *Easy rent,* Renta barata o corta. *Easy to be borne,* Soportable, fácil de soportar. *Easy-going,* Inalterable, sereno.
Easy chair [íz'-i chār], *s.* Silla poltrona.
Eat [ít], *va.* (*pret.* ATE o EAT [et], *pp.* EATEN [algunas veces EAT]). 1. Comer; masticar. *To eat one's breakfast, dinner, supper,* Almorzar, comer, cenar. 2. Roer; consumir, usar, gastar. 3. Retractar, desaprobar lo dicho o hecho desdiciéndose de ello.—*vn.* 1. Alimentarse, mantenerse, sustentarse. 2. Desdecirse, retractarse; apacentarse el ganado. 3. (Fam.) Saber a, tener buen o mal gusto. *To eat away,* Comer con ánimo; roer, carcomer, consumir. *To eat up,* Comer, devorar, hartarse; destruir, arruinar.
Eatable [ít'-a-bl], *a.* Comestible, bueno de comer, que se puede comer.—*s.* Comestibles víveres, vituallas, todo género de alimentos.
Eater [ít'-ẹr], *s.* Comedor. *A great eater,* Tragón.
Eating-house [ít'-ing-haus], *s.* Figón, bodegón, hostería.
Eaves [ívz], *s. pl.* Socarrén, alero o ala de tejado.
Eavesdrop [ívz'-drep], *vn.* Escuchar por la ventana lo que se habla dentro de la casa; escuchar a las puertas.
Eavesdropper [ívz'-drep-ẹr], *s.* Escuchador, el que se pone con curiosidad y ocultamente a escuchar lo que otros hablan.
Ebb [eb], *vn.* 1. Menguar o retroceder la marea. 2. Menguar, decaer, disminuir, irse consumiendo alguna cosa.
Ebb, *s.* 1. (Mar.) Menguante, reflujo de la marea. 2. Decadencia o decremento de alguna cosa. *Ebb-tide,* (Mar.) Marea menguante. *The ebb of life,* La vejez. *To be in a low ebb,* Estar pobre.
Ebbing [eb'-ing], *s.* Reflujo, el acto de refluir o menguar. *It is ebbing,* La marea mengua o baja.
Ebionite [eb'-i-o-nait], *s.* Ebionita, hereje que negaba la divinidad de Jesucristo.

Ebon [eb'-ọn], *a.* Hecho de ébano; negro, como el ébano.
Ebonite [eb'-on-ait], *s.* Ebonita, caucho negro endurecido o vulcanizado.
Ebonize [eb'-en-aiz], *va.* Ebonizar, dar a la madera el color del ébano.
Ebony [eb'-o-ni], **Ebon,** *s.* Ébano, madera dura, negra, pesada y de mucho valor.
Ebriety [ẹ-brai'-e-ti], *s.* Ebriedad, embriaguez, borrachera.
Ebullience, Ebulliency [ẹ-bul'-yens, i], *s.* Ebullición.
Ebullient [ẹ-bul'-yent], *a.* Hirviente, lo que está hirviendo.
Ebullition [ẹb-ul-lish'-un], *s.* 1. Ebullición, hervor, fermentación. 2. (Fig.) Emoción profunda, viva agitación o exaltación del ánimo.
Eburnated [eb'-ur-nê''-ted], *a.* Condensado y endurecido como el hueso.
Eburnean [eb-ūr'-nẹ-an], *a.* Ebúrneo, de marfil o que se parece a él.
Eccentric, Eccentrical [ec-sen'-tric, al], *a.* 1. Excéntrico, que está fuera del centro o tiene un centro diferente. 2. Extravagante, disparatado, particular, singular, estrafalario, raro. 3. Apartado o distante del centro nervioso.
Eccentric, *s.* 1. (Mec.) Rueda excéntrica. 2. El desvío del centro; la persona que se desvía del modo común de obrar.
Eccentricity, Excentricity [ec-sen-tris'-i-ti], *s.* 1. Excentricidad. 2. Extravagancia, particularidad, singularidad, rareza, extravagancia.
Ecchymosis [ek-i-mō'-sis], *s.* Equimosis, mancha acardenalada de la piel.
Ecclesiastes [ec-lí-zi-as'-tíz], *s.* Eclesiastés, uno de los libros de la sagrada Escritura.
Ecclesiastic, Ecclesiastical [ec-lí-zi-as'-tic, al], *a.* Eclesiástico, lo que pertenece a la iglesia.
Ecclesiastic, *s.* Eclesiástico, el que está ordenado y dedicado al ministerio de la iglesia.
Ecclesiastically [ec-lí-zi-as'-ti-cal-i], *adv.* Eclesiásticamente.
Echape [e-chêp'], *s.* Caballo hijo de caballo y yegua de diferentes castas.
Echelon [esh'-ẹ-lon], *s.* (Mil.) Escalón.
Echinites [ek'-i-naits], *s.* (Min.) Equino petrificado, botón de mar.
Echin, Echino, formas de combinación.
Echinoderm [ẹ-cai'-no-dẹrm], *a.* *V.* ECHINODERMATOUS.—*s.* Equinodermo, miembro de una división importante del reino animal que comprende las holoturias, las estrellas de mar, los erizos de mar, etc. Esta división se llama ECHINODERMATA.
Echinodermatous [ẹ-cai''-no-dẹr'-ma-tus], *a.* Equinodermo, que tiene la piel erizada de púas, espinas ó tubérculos.
Echinus [e-cai'-nus], *s.* 1. (Arq.) Cuarto bocel, miembro de moldura. 2. Erizo de mar; equino. 3. Erizo, animal cubierto de púas agudas como espinas.
Echo [ec'-o], *s.* Eco.
Echo, *vn.* Resonar, formar eco, repetir.—*va.* Repercutir la voz o rechazarla.
Echometer [e-cem'-ẹ-tẹr], *s.* Ecómetro, instrumento para conocer la duración del sonido y distinguir sus intervalos.

Eclaircissement [ê''-clār''-sīs'-māñ], *s.* Aclaración, explicación, ilustración; noticia. (Gal.)
Eclat [ê-clā'], *s.* 1. Esplendor, lustre, magnificencia. 2. Aclamación, aplauso: renombre, celebridad. (Fr.)
Eclectic [ec-lec'-tic], *a.* 1. Ecléctico; que analiza, escoge y concilia; se aplica al filósofo que elige y admite las opiniones o sistemas más probables. 2. Tolerante en materias de gusto, amplio, liberal.—*s.* Ecléctico, miembro de una secta de filósofos y médicos.
Eclecticism [ec-lec'-ti-sizm], *s.* Eclecticismo, elección de lo mejor de toda doctrina o sistema, especialmente en medicina y filosofía.
Eclipse [e-clips'], *s.* Eclipse, obscurecimiento de un cuerpo celeste por la interposición de otro que impide verlo bien o disminuye su luz.
Eclipse, *va.* 1. Eclipsar, causar un astro la ocultación transitoria y total o parcial de otro, o de su luz, interponiéndose entre él y nuestra vista. 2. Eclipsar, extinguir, anublar; hacer desaparecer.
Ecliptic [e-clip'-tic], *s.* Eclíptica, círculo máximo de la esfera.—*a.* Eclíptico; obscurecido.
Eclogue [ec'-log], *s.* Égloga, poema pastoral.
Ecological [ec-o-loj'-ic-al], *a.* Ecológico.
Ecologist [i-col'-o-jist], *s.* Ecólogo.
Ecology [i-col'-o-ji], *s.* Ecología.
Econometrics [e-con-o-met'-rics], *s.* Econometría.
Economic, Economical [i-co-nom'-ic o ec-o-nom'-ic, al], *a.* 1. Económico, frugal, parco, moderado. 2. Económico, perteneciente o relativo a la ciencia de la economía.
Economically [ec-o-nom'-ic-al-i], *adv.* Económicamente.
Economics [ec-o-nom'-ics], *s.* Economía, la ciencia que trata de la riqueza de las naciones, su producción y distribución, y de los medios y métodos de vivir bien, aplicable así al estado, como a la familia y al individuo; economía política.
Economist [e-con'-o-mist], *s.* 1. Economista, el que maneja con economía sus bienes o rentas. 2. Economista, el que estudia o profesa la economía política.
Economize [e-con'-o-maiz], *va.* Economizar, ahorrar, administrar o manejar con prudencia y discreción.
Economy [e-con'-o-mi], *s.* 1. Economía, régimen y gobierno de una casa o familia. 2. Economía, frugalidad, moderación en los gastos. 3. Economía, disposición, arreglo u orden, sea en sentido moral o físico. *Moral, political* o *rural economy*, Economía moral, política o rural. *Political economy*, *V.* ECONOMICS.
Ecraseur [ê-cra-sūr'], *s.* Instrumento quirúrgico para extirpar los tumores sin efusión de sangre.
Ecstasy [ec'-sta-si], *s.* 1. Éxtasi o éxtasis. 2. Gozo, alegría, entusiasmo. 3. Distracción. 4. Éxtasis, estado exaltado del ánimo que suele preceder inmediatamente a la muerte.
Ecstatic, Ecstatical [ec-stat'-ic, al], *a.* Extático, arrobado, absorto, gozoso.
Ectoderm [ec'-to-derm], *s.* Ectoderma, la capa exterior del tegumento de un organismo.
Ectropium [ec-trō'-pi-um], *s.* Ectropión, inversión del párpado.
Ecumenical [ec-yu-men'-i-cal], *a.* Ecuménico.
Eczema [ec'-ze-ma], *s.* Eccema o eczema, enfermedad inflamatoria del cutis, acompañada de picazón.
Eczematous [ec-zem'-a-tus], *a.* Eccematoso o eczematoso.
Edacious [e-dé'-shus], *a.* Voraz, comedor, glotón.
Edaciousness [e-dé'-shus-nes], **Edacity** [e-das'-i-ti], *s.* Voracidad, glotonería.
Eddish [ed'-ish], *s.* (Prov. Ingl.) Heno tardío.
Eddy [ed'-i], *s.* 1. Reflujo de agua contra la corriente. 2. Remolino; olla de agua. *Eddy of a ship*, (Mar.) Reveses de un buque. *Eddy of the tide*, (Mar.) Reveses de la marea.—*a.* Remolinado.
Eddy-water [ed'-i-wō'-ter], *s.* (Mar.) Estela, agua muerta.
Edelweiss [ê'-del-vais], *s.* (Bot.) *Edelweiss*, flor de los Alpes.
Edema, Œdema [e-di'-ma], *s.* Edema, hidropesía, hinchazón blanda producida por la obstrucción de los vasos linfáticos. (Gr.)
Edematous [e-dem'-a-tus], *a.* Edematoso, hinchado, lleno de humor seroso.
Eden [i'-dn], *s.* Edén, paraíso.
Edenized [i'-dn-aizd], *a.* Admitido en el paraíso.
Edentata [i-den-té'-ta], *s.* (Zool.) Desdentados, orden de los mamíferos que carecen de dientes incisivos; comprende los hormigueros, perezosos, armadillos y pangolines.
Edentate [e-den'-tét], *a.* 1. Desdentado. 2. Perteneciente a los desdentados.
Edge [ej], *s.* 1. Filo, el corte de un instrumento cortante. 2. Punta, el extremo de alguna cosa que remata formando ángulo. 3. Canto, borde, esquina, ángulo, margen, ribete, orilla. 4. Punta, acrimonia. *To set the teeth on edge*, Aguzar los dientes, destemplar los dientes. *Edge of the water*, La flor del agua. *To take off the edge*, Embotar. *To set on edge*, Aguzar, afilar.
Edge, *va.* 1. Afilar, aguzar, adelgazar el corte o punta de un instrumento cortante. 2. Ribetear, guarnecer con franjas alguna cosa. 3. Aguijonear, incitar, hacer vehemente. 4. Avanzar, mover poco a poco de filo o de canto.—*vn.* Resistir, oponerse. *To edge away*, (Mar.) Inclinarse a sotavento. *To edge in*, Hacer entrar. *Two-edged sword*, Espada de dos filos.
Edged [ejd], *a.* Afilado.
Edgeless [ej'-les], *a.* Embotado, obtuso.
Edge-tool [ej'-tūl], *s.* Herramienta afilada, instrumento afilado.
Edgewise [ej'-waiz], *adv.* De filo o de canto, de lado o sesgo.
Edging [ej'-ing], *s.* Orla, orilla, ribete; encaje angosto.
Edible [ed'-i-bl], *a.* Comestible.
Edict [i'-dict], *s.* Edicto, mandato, orden; decreto, ordenanza.
Edificant [e-dif'-i-cant], *a.* Edificador, fabricador.
Edification [ed-i-fi-ké'-shun], *s.* Edificación, aprovechamiento, ilustración, instrucción.
Edificatory [ed'-i-fi-ca-to-ri], *a.* Edificatorio, instructivo.
Edifice [ed'-i-fis], *s.* Edificio, fábrica u obra de casa, palacio o templo, etc.
Edificial [ed-i-fish'-al], *a.* Lo perteneciente a algún edificio o a su apariencia.
Edifier [ed'-i-fai-er], *s.* Edificador, edificante.
Edify [ed'-i-fai], *va.* Edificar, instruir, enseñar, mejorar, en materias de fe, religión y moral.
Edifying [ed'-i-fai-ing], *s.* Edificación, buen ejemplo.
Edifyingly [ed'-i-fai-ing-li], *adv.* Ejemplarmente.
Edile [i'-dail], *s.* Edil, magistrado de Roma.
Edit [ed'-it], *va.* 1. Redactar, poner en orden y por escrito alguna cosa. 2. Preparar para la imprenta. 3. Montar (un film).
Edition [e-dish'-un], *s.* Edición, publicación o impresión de un libro.
Editor [ed'-i-ter], *s.* 1. Editor, el que prepara, compila y revisa alguna obra para su publicación; redactor principal. 2. La persona que redacta una publicación periódica; la que se encarga de su impresión y circulación.
Editorial [ed-i-tō'-ri-al], *a.* Editorial, lo que pertenece al cargo de redactor.—*s.* Editorial, la parte escrita por la redacción en un periódico, el artículo de fondo.
Editorship [ed'-i-ter-ship], *s.* El cargo de redactor.
Educate [ed'-yu-kêt], *va.* Educar, criar; enseñar, instruir.
Education [ed-yu-ké'-shun], *s.* Educación, la crianza y doctrina con que se educan los niños y jóvenes.
Educational [ed-yu-ké'-shun-al], *a.* Educador, educadora, perteneciente a la educación.
Educator [ed'-yu-kê-ter], *s.* Educador, instructor.
Educe [e-diūs'], *va.* Educir, sacar una cosa de otra; sacar a luz, extraer de la obscuridad.
Eduction [e-duc'-shun], *s.* Educción.
Edulcorate [e-dul'-co-rêt], *va.* Edulcorar, dulzurar, endulzar.
Edulcoration [e-dul-co-ré'-shun], *s.* 1. Edulcoración, dulcificación. 2. (Quím.) Purificación de alguna substancia lavándola con agua.
Edulcorative [e-dul'-co-ré-tiv], *a.* Dulcificante.
Ee [i], *s.* (Esco.) *pl.* EEN. Ojo. *Eebree*, (quiere decir *eye-brow*) Ceja.
Eek [ik], *va.* (Des.) *V.* EKE.
Eel [il], *s.* Anguila.
Eel-pie [il'-pai], *s.* Empanada de anguilas.
Eelpout [il'-paut], *s.* *V.* BURBOT.
Eel-spear [il'-spīr], *s.* Tridente o arpón para pescar anguilas.
Een [in], *s. pl.* (Esco.) Ojos.
E'en [in], *adv.* Contracción de EVEN.
E'er [ār o êr], *adv.* Contracción de EVER.
Eery, Eerie [i'-ri], *a.* 1. Que inspira miedo o temor; imponente. 2. Atemorizado, afectado por el miedo.
Effable [ef'-a-bl], *a.* (Ant.) Decible, explicable.
Efface [ef-fês'], *va.* Borrar, cancelar, destruir.
Effaceable [ef-fês'-a-bl], *a.* Deleble, que puede borrarse.
Effacement [ef-fês'-ment], *s.* Canceladura.
Effect [ef-fect'], *s.* 1. Efecto, consecuencia; fin, mira, intento, designio. 2. Fortuna, ventaja. 3. Efecto, realidad. 4. Vigor, operación activa; ejecución. 5. (Mec.) Efecto o trabajo útil de una máquina. *Effects*, *pl.* Efectos, los bienes que alguno posee, sean muebles o raíces; caudal. *To take effect*, Salir bien una cosa, producir su efecto; ser puesto en vigor, hacerse efectivo (v. g. una

ley, un itinerario de trenes), etc. *Of no effect*, Vano, inútil. *To this effect*, Con este intento. *In effect*, Efectivo, en operación, efectivamente.

Effect, *va.* Efectuar, poner por obra, ejecutar, producir.

Effecter, *s.* *V.* EFFECTOR.

Effectible [ef-fect'-i-bl], *a.* Factible, practicable.

Effection [ef-fec'-shun], *s.* (Geom.) Construcción, problema derivado de alguna proposición general.

Effective [ef-fect'-iv], *a.* 1. Eficiente; eficaz; operativo; efectivo, real. 2. Pasmoso, que produce viva impresión.

Effectively [ef-fect'-iv-li], *adv.* Eficientemente, eficazmente; efectivamente, realmente.

Effectiveness [ef-fect'-iv-nes], *s.* 1. Efectividad. 2. Eficiencia, eficacia.

Effectless [ef-fect'-les], *a.* Ineficaz, impotente.

Effector [ef-fect'-ẹr], *s.* Causador, criador, hacedor, autor.

Effectual [ef-fec'-chu-al], *a.* Eficiente; eficaz, activo.

Effectually [ef-fec'-chu-al-i], *adv.* Eficientemente, eficazmente.

Effectuate [ef-fec'-chu-êt], *va.* Efectuar, poner por obra, hacer eficaz, ejecutar.

Effeminacy [ef-fem'-i-na-si], *s.* Afeminación, afeminamiento, molicie, delicadeza afeminada.

Effeminate [ef-fem'-i-net], *a.* Afeminado, mujeril, adamado, enervado.

Effeminate, *va.* Afeminar, enervar, debilitar.—*vn.* Afeminarse, enervarse.

Effeminately [ef-fem'-i-net-li], *adv.* Afeminadamente.

Effeminateness [ef-fem'-i-net-nes], *s.* Afeminamiento, afeminación.

Effendi [ef-fen'-di], *s.* Título de respeto entre los turcos; nombre con que honran a los letrados, a los hombres de ciencia, y a los funcionarios del orden civil; casi igual a Señor o Don.

Effervesce [ef-ẹr-ves'], *vn.* Hervir, fermentar, estar en efervescencia.

Effervescence [ef-ẹr-ves'-ens], *s.* Efervescencia.

Effete [ef-fît'], *a.* 1. Estéril, infructuoso. 2. Usado, gastado, consumido, cascado.

Efficacious [ef-i-kê'-shus], *a.* Eficaz, activo, poderoso para obrar.

Efficaciously [ef-i-kê'-shus-li], *adv.* Eficazmente.

Efficaciousness [ef-i-kê'-shus-nes], *s.* Eficacia.

Efficacy [ef'-i-ca-si], *s.* Eficacia.

Efficience, Efficiency [ef-fish'-ens, i], *s.* Eficiencia, actividad, virtud, influencia.

Efficient [ef-fish'-ent], *a.* Eficiente, eficaz.—*s.* Hacedor, causador.

Efficiently [ef-fish'-ent-li], *adv.* Eficientemente.

†Effigies [ef-fij'-i-îz], **Effigy** [ef'-i-ji], *s.* Efigie, retrato, imagen.

Efflation [ef-flê'-shun], *s.* Insuflación; soplo.

Effloresce [ef-lo-res'], *vn.* (Quím.) Eflorescer, disolverse una sal en polvo al contacto del aire, o cubrirse un cuerpo de partículas salinas en forma de moho.

Efflorescence, Efflorescency [ef-lo-res'-ens, i], *s.* 1. Eflorescencia: cristales salinos que se pulverizan expuestos al aire libre. 2. Roncha, erupción que sale en el cutis. 3. Florescencia, la acción de florecer las plantas. 4. Excrecencia en forma de flor que se nota en algunos cuerpos.

Efflorescent [ef-lo-res'-ent], *a.* Eflorescente: que entra o se halla en eflorescencia; en flor.

Effluence [ef'-lu-ens], *s.* 1. Emanación, efluvio; efusión. 2. (Fís.) Efluencia, emanación de los corpúsculos en los cuerpos eléctricos.

Effluent [ef'-lu-ent], *a.* 1. Efluente. 2. Efluente: epíteto dado a la calentura inflamatoria.

Effluvium [ef-flū'-vi-um], *pl.* EFFLUVIA, *s.* Efluvio, exhalación, emanación de partículas imperceptibles; especialmente las nocivas o hediondas.

Efflux [ef'-lucs], *s.* Efusión, emanación; flujo, derrame.

†Efflux [ef-lucs'], *vn.* Fluir.

Effort [ef'-fẹrt], *s.* Esfuerzo, conato, empeño.

Effrontery [ef-frunt'-e-ri], *s.* Descaro, desvergüenza, impudencia.

Effulge [ef-fulj'], *vn.* Brillar, lucir, resplandecer.

Effulgence [ef-ful'-jens], *s.* Resplandor, lustre, esplendor, fulgor.

Effulgent [ef-ful'-jent], *a.* Resplandeciente, lustroso, brillante, luminoso, efulgente.

Effuse [ef-fūz'], *va.* Derramar, verter, esparcir, desparramar.

Effuse [ef-fūs'], *a.* 1. (Bot.) Divergente; que se extiende mucho y a gran distancia. 2. (Des.) Disipado, extravagante.

Effusion [ef-fū'-zhun], *s.* 1. Efusión, derramamiento, desperdicio. 2. Efusión, manifestación afectuosa y cordial. 3. Flujo de palabras.

Effusive [ef-fū'-siv], *a.* 1. Lleno de sentimiento, de afectos; impetuoso; demostrativo. 2. Difusivo, que derrama.

Eft [eft], *s.* 1. Salamandra acuática. *V.* NEWT. 2. Lagartija.

†Eftsoon, Eftsoons [eft-sūn, s], *adv.* Luego después, prontamente; en seguida, de prisa.

Egg [eg], *s.* 1. Huevo. 2. Huevo, el cuerpecillo que cría la hembra de los peces, los insectos y la mayor parte de los reptiles. *To lay an egg*, Poner un huevo, aovar. *Yolk of an egg*, Yema de huevo. *White of an egg*, Clara de huevo. *New-laid egg*, Huevo fresco. *Addle egg*, Huevo huero. *Egg-glass*, Ampolleta de arena de tres minutos para cocer huevos. *Poached eggs*, Huevos hervidos, echados sin cáscara en agua hirviendo. *Fried eggs*, Huevos fritos o estrellados. *Soft-boiled eggs*, Huevos pasados por agua. *Hard-boiled eggs*, Huevos duros o cocidos. *Egg-laying*, Que pone huevos, ovípara. *Egg-shell*, Cáscara de huevo. *Egg-nog*, Bebida compuesta de leche, huevos, azúcar y un licor espirituoso.

Egg, *va.* Hurgar, incitar, provocar; cebar, atraer. (Islandés, eggja: *V.* EDGE, 3ª acep.)

Egg, *va.* 1. Mezclar o cubrir con huevo. 2. (E. U.) Arrojar huevos a una persona.—*vn.* Coleccionar huevos de aves.

Egg beater [eg' bît'-ẹr], *s.* Batidor de huevos.

Egg cell [eg sel], *s.* Célula embrionaria.

Egg-cup [eg'-cup], *s.* Huevera.

Egger [eg'-ẹr], *s.* Incitador, instigador.

Egging [eg'-ing], *s.* Incitamiento.

Eggnog [eg'-nog], *s.* Ponche de huevo. (Mex. y C.A.) Rompope.

Egg-plant [eg'-plant], *s.* Berenjena, planta y fruto.

Egilops. *V.* ÆGILOPS.

Egis, Ægis [î'-jis], *s.* Escudo, armadura defensiva; una influencia o poder protector cualquiera.

Eglantine [eg'-lan-tain], *s.* (Bot.) 1. Eglantina, flor del escaramujo. 2. Agavanzo.

Egoism [eg'-o- o î'-go-izm], *s.* 1. Egoísmo, el inmoderado y excesivo amor a sí mismo y al bien propio, sin atender al de los demás. 2. Egoísmo, una especie de pirronismo o escepticismo que consiste en dudar de todo menos de la propia existencia.

Egoist [eg'-o- o î'-go-ist], *s.* Egoísta, el partidario del egoísmo en uno y otro sentido.

Egoistic [eg'-o- o î-go-is'-tic], *a.* 1. Egoísta, que sólo mira a su interés propio y no procura el de los demás. 2. Egotista. 3. Relativo al pirronismo o al idealismo subjetivo.

Egotism [î'-go-tizm], *s.* Egotismo, vanidad, prurito de hablar de sí mismo.

Egotist [î'-go-tist], *s.* Egotista.

Egotistical [î-go-tis'-tic-al], *a.* Vanaglorioso, uno que se alaba a sí mismo.

Egotize [î'-go-taiz], *vn.* Hablar mucho de sí mismo.

Egregious [ẹ-grî'-jus], *a.* Egregio, insigne, extraordinario; se echa por lo común a mala parte: famoso; perverso.

Egregiousness [ẹ-grî'-jus-nes], *s.* Eminencia.

Egress [î'-gres], **Egression** [e-gresh'-un], *s.* Salida.

Egret [eg'-ret o î'-gret], *s.* 1. (Orn.) Especie de garza. 2. Pluma o plumaje.

Egyptian [ẹ-jip'-shan], *a.* Egipcio, de Egipto.—*s.* 1. Egipcio; copto, a distinción del árabe. 2. Idioma de Egipto.

Eh [ê o e], *inter.* ¿Qué? ¿hé? interjección interrogativa.

Eider, Eider-duck [ai'-dẹr, duc], *s.* Eider, eidero, especie de ánade grande de los mares helados; tiene casi siempre el plumaje blanco por arriba y negro por debajo. Somateria mollisima.

Eider-down [ai'-dẹr-daun], *s.* Edredón, plumazón de varias aves del norte; almohadón, plumón, cubrepiés.

Eidograph [ai'-do-grạf], *s.* Eidógrafo aparato para copiar y reducir dibujos.

Eidolon [ai-dō'-len], *s.* (*pl.* EIDOLA). 1. Representación, imagen. 2. Fantasma. (Gr. id. imagen.)

Eight [êt], *a.* Ocho.—*s.* 1. Isleta en un río. 2. El número ocho.

Eighteen [êt-în'], *a.* y *s.* Diez y ocho.

Eighteenth [êt-înth'], *a.* Décimoctavo.

Eightfold [êt'-fōld], *a.* Ocho veces tanto.

Eighth [êtth], *a.* Octavo.

Eighthly êtth'-li], *adv.* En el octavo lugar.

Eightieth [êt'-i-eth], *a.* Octogésimo.

Eighty [ê'-ti], *a.* y *s.* Ochenta.

Eirie [ê'-ri], *s.* *V.* AERIE.

Either [î'-dhẹr, por algunos ai'-dhẹr], *a.* y *pron.* Cualquiera, cada uno o cada una, uno de dos, cualquiera de los dos.—*conj.* 1. O, sea, ya. *He is either a knave or a fool*, O es pícaro o tonto. 2. (Fam.) Por cierto, en todo caso, también; (precedido de una negación) tampoco.

Ejaculate [e-jac'-yu-lêt], *va.* 1. Exclamar, pronunciar súbitamente, proferir. 2. (Des. o Med.) Arrojar, despedir, eyacular.

Ejaculation [e-jac-yu-lê'-shun], *s.* 1. Jaculatoria. 2. La acción de arrojar alguna cosa con fuerza. 3. Eyaculación, emisión.

Eject [e-ject'], *va.* Arrojar, expeler, despedir, desechar.

Ejection [e-jec'-shun], *s.* 1. Expulsión; evacuación. 2. Deyección, la materia desechada.

Ejection seat [e-jec'-shun sît], *s.* (Aer.) Asiento expulsor.

Ejectment [e-ject'-ment], *s.* Auto de desahucio; expulsión de una casa, posesión, etc.

Ejector [e-ject'-er], *s.* Eyector, expulsor, desposeedor; el que o lo que expele o desposee.

Eke [îk], *va.* 1. Aumentar, suplir, integrar; ensanchar o añadir ligeramente, de manera que algo sea apenas suficiente; seguido de *out.* 2. Obtener, mantener o producir con dificultad, apenas, escasamente.

Elaborate [e-lab'-o-rêt], *va.* Elaborar, trabajar con esmero y cuidado.

Elaborate, *a.* Elaborado, esmerado, acabado, limado; curioso, primoroso.

Elaborately [e-lab'-o-ret-li], *adv.* Cuidadosamente, con mucho trabajo.

Elaboration [e-lab-o-rê'-shun], *s.* 1. Elaboración, la acción de elaborar o producir con primor y perfección en sus detalles. 2. Obra acabada.

Elapse [e-laps'], *vn.* Pasar, correr el tiempo.

Elastic, Elastical [e-las'-tic, al], *a.* Elástico. *Elastic gum, V.* INDIA-RUBBER. *Elastic fluids,* Fluidos elásticos; llámanse así los vapores y los gases.

Elasticity [el-as- o î"-las-tis'-i-ti], *s.* Elasticidad, la propiedad de una cosa de recobrar su forma o posición original (después de haberse ejercido sobre ella presión, expansión o torcedura).

Elate [e-lêt'], *a.* Exaltado de espíritu, triunfante, gozoso.

Elate, *va.* Exaltar, elevar; engreír, ensoberbecer.

Elatedly [e-lêt'-ed-li], *adv.* Exaltadamente, triunfantemente.

Elation [e-lê'-shun], *s.* Júbilo, exaltación del ánimo, viva alegría.

Elbow [el'-bō], *s.* 1. El codo. 2. Codo, cualquier cosa que forma ángulo saliente. *To be at the elbow,* Estar a la mano, estar muy cerca.

Elbow, *va.* Codear, dar codazos a alguno o empujarle con el codo. —*vn.* Formar recodos o ángulos.

Elbow-grease [el'-bo-grîs], *s.* (Vul.) Ejercicio o trabajo constante que excita la transpiración; trabajo manual, duro esfuerzo.

Elbow-room [el'-bo-rum], *s.* Espacio para el libre movimiento de los codos; (fig.) anchura, alcance, desahogo.

Elder [el'-der], *a.* Mayor, mas viejo, de más edad.—*Comp. irr.* de OLD: es preferido a *older* cuando sólo se comparan dos objetos.—*s.* 1. Mayor, el que tiene más edad que otro. 2. (Ecle.) (a) Príncipe o jefe de una tribu o familia; (b) en el Nuevo Testamento, dignatario de la Iglesia cristiana; (c) en el uso moderno, funcionario eclesiástico de rango y funciones diversos.—*pl.* Ancianos, mayores, antepasados.

Elder, *s.* 1. (Bot.) Saúco, arbusto del género Sambucus. 2. Uno de varios árboles o plantas parecidos al saúco. *Elderberry,* La baya o grano del saúco. *Elder-blow,* La flor del saúco.

Elderly [el'-der-li], *a.* Mayor, el de edad ya madura.

Eldest [el'-dest], *a. sup.* Lo más anciano. *V.* OLDEST.

Elect [e-lect'], *va.* 1. Elegir, escoger, designar entre varios. 2. Elegir, escoger por voto de la mayoría.

Elect, *a.* Elegido, escogido, electo; predestinado.

Election [e-lec'-shun], *s.* 1. Elección 2. (E. U.) Nombramiento por votos. 3. Escogimiento, elección, en general. 4. En teología, predestinación.

Electioneering [e-lec-shun-îr'-ing], *s.* El acto de solicitar personas para que voten por el individuo que el partido propone para un empleo.

Elective [e-lec'-tiv], *a.* Electivo. *Elective attraction,* Atracción electiva o afinidad química.

Electively [e-lec'-tiv-li], *adv.* Electivamente.

Elector [e-lec'-ter], *s.* 1. Elector, el que tiene derecho de elegir. 2. Elector, antiguamente cualquiera de los príncipes del imperio germánico que tenía voto en la elección del emperador.

Electoral [e-lec'-ter-al], *a.* Electoral.

Electoress [e-lec'-ter-es], **Electress** [e-lec'-tres], *sf.* Electriz, la mujer o viuda del elector.

Electric, Electrical [e-lec'-tric, al], *a.* 1. Eléctrico. 2. (fig.) Vivo, fogoso, magnético. *Electric cable,* Cable conductor. *Electric chair,* Silla eléctrica. *Electric eye,* Ojo eléctrico o fotocélula. *Electric fixtures,* Dispositivos eléctricos de instalación fija. *Electric beater,* Batidora eléctrica. *Electric motor,* Motor eléctrico. *Electric plant,* Planta eléctrica. *Electrical engineering,* Ingeniería eléctrica. *Electrical transcription,* Grabación fonográfica eléctrica.

Electric eel [e-lec'-tric îl], *s.* (Zool.) Anguila eléctrica.

Electrician [e-lec-trish'-an], *s.* 1. Individuo versado en la electricidad. 2. El que inventa, hace, abastece o tiene a su cargo aparatos eléctricos.

Electricity [e-lec-tris'-i-ti], *s.* Electricidad, agente natural imponderable, invisible y poderoso, que produce muy variadas manifestaciones de su fuerza.

Electrification [e-lec-tri-fi-kê'-shun], *s.* 1. Electrificación. 2. Electrización.

Electrify [e-lec'-tri-fai], *va.* 1. Electrificar. 2. Electrizar.

Electro-. Forma de combinación que representa la palabra *electric* en composición. Estas palabras son muy numerosas: sólo se insertan aquí algunas de las más usadas.

Electrocardiogram [e-lec'-tro-cār'di-o-gram], *s.* Electrocardiograma.

Electrocardiograph [e-lec-tro-car'-di-o-graf], *s.* Electrocardiógrafo.

Electro-chemical [e-lec-tro-kem'-i-cal], *a.* Electroquímico, relativo a la electroquímica.

Electro-chemistry [kem'-is-tri], *s.* Electroquímica, el ramo de la química que trata de la producción de cambios químicos por medio de la electricidad.

Electrocute [e-lec'-tro-kiūt], *va.* Electrocutar, matar por medio de una corriente eléctrica.

Electrocution [e-lec-tro-kiū'-shun], *s.* Electrocución.

Electro-deposit [de-pez'-it], *va.* Depositar químicamente por medio de una corriente eléctrica.

Electro-dynamic [dai-nam'-ic], *a.* Electrodinámico, que puede producir una corriente eléctrica.

Electrodynamics [e-lec-tro-dai-nam'-ics], *s.* Electrodinámica.

Electrode [e-lec'-trōd], *s.* Electrodo, cado uno de los polos de una batería galvánica o un dinamo; los extremos o cabos metálicos de los conductores que proceden de ambos polos eléctricos.

Electrolysis [e-lec-trel'-i-sis], *s.* Electrolisis, electrolización, análisis o descomposición de un cuerpo por medio de la electricidad.

Electrolyte [e-lec'-tro-lait], *s.* Electrolito, cuerpo que puede descomponerse por la electricidad.

Electrolytic [e-lec-tro-lit'-ic], *a.* Electrolítico, relativo a la electrolisis o a un electrolito.

Electrolyzation [e-lec-trel-i-zê'-shun], *s.* Electrolización.

Electrolyze [e-lec'-tro-laiz], *va.* Electrolizar, analizar o descomponer un cuerpo por medio de la electricidad.

Electro-magnet [e-lec'-tro-mag'-net], *s.* Electroimán, centro de hierro dulce, convertido en imán mediante una corriente eléctrica.

Electro-magnetic [mag-net'-ic], *a.* Electromagnético, relativo al electroimán o al electromagnetismo.

Electro-magnetism [mag'-net-izm], *s.* Electromagnetismo: (1) la imantación o el magnetismo producido por medio de la electricidad; (2) el estudio de las relaciones entre la electricidad y el magnetismo.

Electrometallurgy [e-lec-tro-met'-al-ur-ji], *s.* Electrometalurgia.

Electrometer [e-lec-trem'-e-ter], *s.* Electrómetro, instrumento para medir la cantidad y determinar la calidad de la electricidad.

Electro-motive [mō'-tiv], *a.* Electromotor, electromotriz, que se refiere al movimiento de la electricidad o a las leyes que lo gobiernan. *Electromotive force,* Fuerza electromotriz, la que produce el movimiento de la electricidad por un conductor.

Electro-motor [mō'-ter], *s.* 1. Motor eléctrico. 2. Todo aparato que desarrolla electricidad.

Electron [e-lec'-tren], *s.* Electrón. *Electron microscope,* Microscopio electrónico.

Electronegative [e-lec-tro-neg'-a-tiv], *s.* y *a.* Electronegativo.

Electronic [e-lec-tren'-ic], *a.* Electrónico.

Electronics [e-lec-tren'-ics], *s. pl.* Electrónica.

Electro-plate [plêt], *va.* Plaquear un metal por medio del galvanismo o de un dínamo.

Electroplating [e-lec'-tro-plêt'-ing], *s.* Electrochapeado, electrodeposición, electroplastia.

Electropositive [e-lec'-tro-pez'-i-tiv], *s.* y *a.* Electropositivo.

Electroscope [e-lec'-tro-scōp], *s.* Electroscopio, instrumento para determinar la presencia de la electricidad en un conductor.

Electrostatics [e-lec"-tro-stat'-ics], *s.* Electroestática, el ramo de la ciencia eléctrica que trata de los fenómenos de la electricidad en estado de reposo o la electricidad producida por fricción.

Electrotechnics [e-lec-tro-tec'-nics], *s.* Electrotecnia.

Electro-telegraphy [e-lec'-tro-tel-eg'-ra-fi], *s.* Telegrafía por medio de la electricidad.

Electro-telegraphic [tel-e-graf'-ic], *a.* Electrotelegráfico.

Electro-therapeutic [e-lec"-tro-ther"-a-piū'-tic], *a.* Electroterapéutico, que se refiere a la electricidad considerada como medio terapéutico.

Electro-therapeutics [e-lec"-tro-ther"-a-piū'-tics], *s.* Electroterapéutica, la aplicación de la electricidad a la terapéutica.

Electrotherapy [e-lec-tro-ther'-a-pi], *s.* Electroterapia.

Electrotype [e-lec'-tro-taip], *s.* 1. Electrotipo, grabado tipográfico que se obtiene por medio de la electrotipia. 2. Impresión de dicho grabado.—*va.* Electrotipar, hacer un electrotipo; duplicar por medio de la electrotipia.

Electrotypy [e-lec'-tro-tai'-pi], *s.* Electrotipia, el arte de cubrir de una capa metálica, por medio de la electroquímica, los clisés, monedas y otros objetos semejantes.

Electrum [e-lec'-trum], *s.* 1. Plata alemana, liga de níquel, cinc y cobre; cualquiera otra mezcla semejante. 2. Antiguamente, electro o ámbar.

Electuary [e-lec'-chu (o tiu) -e-ri], *s.* Electuario, confección farmacéutica.

Eleemosynary [el-e-e (o e) -mos'-i-ne-ri], *a.* y *s.* 1. Caritativo, de caridad, de limosna. 2. Mendicante, el que vive de limosna; dado de limosna.

Elegance, Elegancy [el'-e-gans, i], *s.* Elegancia, primor, hermosura; buen gusto, aire, garbo.

Elegant [el'-e-gant], *a.* Elegante, fino, delicado, pulido.

Elegantly [el'-e-gant-li], *adv.* Elegantemente, pulidamente.

Elegiac, Elegiacal [el-i'-ji-ac o el-e-jai'-ac, al], *a.* Elegíaco.

Elegiast [el-i'-ji-ast], **Elegist** [el'-e-jist], *s.* Elegíaco, el que escribe elegías.

Elegy [el'-e-ji], *s.* Elegía, canto fúnebre o melancólico.

Element [el'-e-ment], *s.* 1. Elemento. 2. Elemento, la esfera o situación propia de cualquier cosa. 3. Elemento, ingrediente. 4. (Biol.) Una de las unidades primitivas de un organismo; celdilla o unidad morfológica. 5. (Elec.) Elemento de pila o de batería, par. 6. (Quím.) Cuerpo simple, aquella forma de la materia que no puede descomponerse por ninguno de los medios que conoce la ciencia. El número de elementos conocidos hasta el día es de setenta y dos. *Elements,* (1) Primeros principios o ideas fundamentales; rudimentos. (2) El pan y el vino que se consumen en el sacrificio de la misa.

Elemental [el-e-ment'-al], *a.* Elemental, primordial.

Elementary [el-e-men'-ta-ri], *a.* Elemental, inicial; incipiente.

Elemi [el'-e-mi], *s.* Elemí, resina usada para emplastos y barnices.

Elephant [el-e-fant], *s.* Elefante.

Elephantiasis [el-e-fan-tai'-a-sis], *s.* Elefancía, elefantíasis, especie de lepra.

Elephantine [el-e-fan'-tin], *a.* Elefantino.

Elevate [el'-e-vêt], *va.* 1. Elevar, alzar, levantar. 2. Elevar, exaltar; colocar en dignidad o alto rango: exaltar el carácter; promover, hacer adelantar. 3. Excitar, animar, alegrar; inspirar. 4. Alzar el tono o aumentar la resonancia de la voz o de un instrumento músico.

Elevated [el'-e-vêt-ed], *a.* 1. Elevado, alzado. 2. Exaltado. *Elevated railroad,* Tren elevado.

Elevation [el-e-vé'-shun], *s.* 1. Elevación. 2. Altura, encumbramiento. 3. Elevación de espíritu, grandeza de alma, alteza de pensamientos. 4. (Arq.) Alzado de un edificio. 5. (Astr.) Altura de algún cuerpo celeste.

Elevator [el'-e-ve-ter], *s.* 1. Elevador, ascensor, aparato que sirve para conducir personas o carga de uno a otro piso de un edificio. 2. Máquina a manera de noria para transferir granos desde los buques o carros de ferrocarril a los depósitos o graneros.

Elevator hoist [el'-e-vê-ter hoist], *s.* Montacargas, malacate, ascensor para carga.

Eleven [e-lev'-n], *a.* y *s.* Once.

Eleventh [e-lev'-nth], *a.* Onceno, undécimo.

Elf [elf], *s.* 1. Duende, trasgo o espíritu travieso. 2. Demonio, diablo. 3. Enano. Escríbese en plural *elves.*

Elf-arrow [elf'-ar-ō], *s.* Pedernal en forma de flecha.

Elfin [elf'-in], *a.* Lo perteneciente a duendes.—*s.* Diablillo, niño pequeño, travieso y enredador.

Elfish [elf'-ish], *a.* Aduendado, que pertenece a duendes o demonios; travieso, fantástico.

Elf-locks [elf'-locs], *s. pl.* Greñas de duendes, trenzas de pelo.

Elicit [e-lis'-it], *va.* Sacar de; atraer, sonsacar, obtener, hacer salir como por medio de la atracción; educir o extraer gradualmente y sin violencia.

Elicit, *a.* (Filos.) Que resulta de la volición libre o del escogimiento.

Elide [e-laid'], *va.* Elidir, suprimir una vocal en una o más palabras, v. g. *don't* por *do not,* o *'tis* por *it is,* o *th' heroic* por *the heroic.*

Eligibility [el-i-ji-bil'-i-ti], *s.* Elegibilidad, reunión de cualidades para ser elegido.

Eligible [el'-i-ji-bl], *a.* 1. Elegible, preferible. 2. A propósito, digno de admisión o aceptación, deseable.

Eligibleness [el'-i-ji-bl-nes], *s.* Elegibilidad.

Eliminate [e-lim'-i-nêt], *va.* 1. Rechazar, echar fuera, arrojar, especialmente como perjudicial, dañoso o inútil; eliminar. 2. (Alg.) Eliminar, hacer desaparecer una cantidad de una ecuación.

Elimination [e-lim-i-né'-shun], *s.* Eliminación, acción de eliminar; excreción.

Eliquation [el-i-cwé'-shun], *s.* Separación de dos metales por medio de un grado de calor que pueda derretir al uno y no al otro.

Elision [e-lizh'-un], *s.* 1. (Gram.) Elisión. 2. División.

Elite [ê-lît'], *s.* Lo mejor, lo escogido, lo selecto; la flor, la flor y nata. (Fr.)

Elixir [el-ic'-ser], *s.* 1. Elixir, medicamento o tintura compuesta y extraída de varios ingredientes; cordial. 2. Extracto o quinta esencia de alguna cosa.

Elk [elk], *s.* Alce o anta, cuadrúpedo muy corpulento de la familia del ciervo: habita en los bosques de los países del norte.

Ell [el], *s.* Ana, medida de longitud hoy rara vez usada; en Inglaterra tenía 45 pulgadas y en Escocia 37.

Ellipse [el-lips'], *s.* (Geom.) Elipse, curva cerrada que resulta de cortar un cono con un plano oblicuo a la dirección de su eje; óvalo.

Ellipsis [e-lip'-sis], *s.* (Gram.) Elipsis, la omisión de una o más palabras, necesarias para la recta construcción gramatical, pero sin que por eso se obscurezca el sentido de la oración.

Ellipsoid [el-lip'-soid], *s.* Elipsoide, sólido formado por la revolución de la elipse sobre uno de sus dos ejes.

Elliptic, Elliptical [el-lip'-tic, al], *a.* Elíptico.

Elm [elm], *s.* (Bot.) Olmo, árbol de gran altura, tronco recto y madera fuerte y sólida.

Elocution [el-o-kiū'-shun], *s.* Elocución; habla, manera de hacer uso de la palabra.

Eloge [é'-lōzh], *s.* Oración fúnebre, panegírico. (Gal.)

†**Elogist** [el'-o-jist], *s.* Elogiador. *V.* EULOGIST.

Elogy [el'-o-ji], *s.* Elogio, oración fúnebre; relación biográfica; se usa impropiamente en el sentido de encomio, alabanza.

Elongate [e-lōn'-gêt], *va.* Alargar. —*vn.* 1. Volverse más largo; alargarse, aumentarse. 2. (Poco us.) Alejarse, desviarse un astro.

Elongation [e-lon-gé'-shun], *s.* 1. Prolongación, extensión. 2. El acto de alargarse alguna cosa. 3. (Astr.) Elongación.

Elope [e-lōp'], *vn.* 1. Escapar, huir, evadirse. 2. Fugarse, huir una mujer de su casa en compañía de un amante o un seductor.

Elopement [e-lōp'-ment], *s.* Fuga, huída; evasión, escapada: se usa para expresar que una mujer casada se ha escapado con su seductor, o que una joven ha dejado la casa de sus padres para unirse con su amante.

Eloquence [el'-o-cwens], *s.* Elocuencia, propiedad, pureza, buen empleo y distribución de palabras y pensamientos al hablar y escribir.

Eloquent [el'-o-cwent], *a.* Elocuente.

Eloquently [el'-o-cwent-li], *adv.* Elocuentemente.

Else [els], *a.* Otro. *Nobody else, no one else,* Ningún otro. *Nothing else,* Nada más.—*adv.* 1. Más, además; en vez de. 2. De otro modo o manera; en otro caso; a menudo va precedido de *or* (o); si no.

Elsewhere [els'-hwār], *adv.* En cualquiera otra parte, a otra parte, de otra parte.

Elsen, *s.* (Esco.) *V.* AWL.

Elucidate [e-lū'-si-dêt], *va.* Dilucidar, explicar, aclarar, ilustrar.

Elucidation [e-lu-si-dé'-shun], *s.* Elucidación, explicación, aclaración.

Elucidative, Elucidatory [e-lū'-si-de"-tiv, da-to-ri], *a.* Explicativo, que se puede dilucidar.

Elude [e-lūd'], *va.* 1. Eludir, huir la dificultad. 2. Burlar a alguno huyendo de él.

Eludible [e-lūd'-i-bl], *a.* Evitable.

Elusion [e-lū'-zhun], *s.* Escapatoria; artificio para eludir.

Elusive [e-lū'-siv], *a.* Que tiende a

huir o escaparse; falaz, tenue, difícil de asir o de tener.

Elusoriness [e-lū'-so-ri-nes], *s.* Fraude, engaño; astucia.

Elusory [e-lū'-so-ri], *a.* Falaz, engañador; hábil en artificios y subterfugios. *V.* ELUSIVE.

Elutriation [e-lu-tri-é'-shun], *s.* La acción de lavar o limpiar con agua los minerales pulverizados.

Elutriate [e-lū'-tri-êt], *va.* Decantar; colar.

Elves [elvz], *s. pl.* de ELF. Duendes. *Elve, sing.*, es una antigua forma de ELF.

Elvish, *a.* *V.* ELFISH.

Elysian [e-lizh'-ian], *a.* Ameno, delicioso. *Elysian Fields*, Elíseo, campos elíseos.

Elytron, Elytrum [el'-i-tron, trum], *s.* (*pl.* ELYTRA). Élitro, estuche, cada una de las alas anteriores endurecidas de los coleópteros y ortópteros; también se da este nombre a las anchas escamas dorsales de ciertos gusanos.

Elzevir [el'-ze-ver], *a.* Elzeviriano, de los Elzevirios, célebres inpresores holandeses.

Em [em], *s.* 1. Nombre de la letra M, la décimotercia del alfabeto inglés. 2. (Impr.) Eme, el cuadrado del cuerpo de un tipo, usado como unidad de medida.

'em, *pro.* (Fam.) Elisión de *them*, caso objetivo del pronombre *they.*

Emaciate [e-mé'-shi-êt], *va.* Extenuar, adelgazar.—*vn.* Enflaquecer, ponerse flaco o perder carnes.

Emaciate, *a.* 1. Enflaquecido, flaco. 2. (Med.) Emaciado, extenuado.

Emaciation [e-mê-shi-é'-shun], *s.* Extenuación, flaqueza, enflaquecimiento.

Emanant [em'-a-nant], *a.* Emanante.

Emanate [em'-a-nêt], *vn.* Emanar, preceder, derivarse.

Emanation [em-a-né'-shun], *s.* Emanación; efluvio, efluencia.

Emanative [em'-a-na-tiv], *a.* Emanante.

Emancipate [e-man'-si-pêt], *va.* Emancipar; dar libertad, manumitir, libertar.

Emancipation [e-man-si-pé'-shun], *s.* Emancipación.

Emancipator [e-man'-si-pê-ter], *s.* Libertador, manumisor.

Emarginate [e-mār'-ji-nêt], *va.* 1. Quitar el margen, recortar. 2. (Bot.) Hacer una escotadura en el ápice de una hoja u otro órgano plano de las plantas.

Emarginate, *a.* (Bot.) Escotado, emarginado, que tiene el margen interrumpido o mellado.

Emasculate [e-mas'-kiu-lêt], *va.* 1. Castrar, capar. 2. Afeminar, enervar. 3. Empeorar, desvirtuar una obra literaria suprimiendo parte del texto original.

Emasculate [e-mas'-kiu-let o lêt], *a.* Afeminado, viciado; castrado.

Emasculation [e-mas-kiu-lé'-shun], *s.* Castradura, castración, capadura; afeminación, afeminamiento.

†**Embale** [em-bêl'], *va.* Embalar, enfardar, liar, atar.

Embalm [em-bām'], *va.* 1. Embalsamar, impregnar un cadáver de substancias que impidan la putrefacción. 2. Conservar, impedir el decaimiento de alguna cosa; guardar afectuosamente un recuerdo, salvar del olvido. 3. Embalsamar, llenar de fragancia, aromatizar, perfumar.

Embalmer [em-bām'-er], *s.* 1. Embalsamador. 2. Cualquiera cosa que impide el decaimiento o menoscabo de otra.

Embalmment [em-bām'-ment], *s.* Embalsamamiento, la acción de embalsamar.

Embank [em-bank'], *va.* Represar, contener por medio de una presa o dique.

Embankment [em-bank'-ment], *s.* Presa, dique; terraplén.

Embar [em-bār'], *va.* 1. (Ant.) Barrear, cercar, cerrar. 2. Bloquear.

Embarcation [em-bar-ké'-shun], *s.* (Mar.) Embarco, embarque. *V.* EMBARKATION.

Embargo [em-bār'-gō], *s.* 1. Embargo, secuestro de géneros. 2. Embargo, detención de buques.

Embargo, *va.* Embargar, detener.

Embark [em-bārk'], *va.* (Mar.) Embarcar, poner los géneros o personas a bordo de un buque.—*vn.* 1. (Mar.) Embarcarse, ir a bordo de una embarcación. 2. Empeñarse en algún negocio, dar principio a alguna ocupación; invertir el tiempo o el caudal; aventurarse.

Embarkation [em-bar-ké'-shun], *s.* 1. Embarco, el acto de embarcar o embarcarse personas. 2. Embarque, la acción de embarcar géneros, provisiones, etc. 3. Lo que está embarcado; cargamento, fleto, carga.

Embarrass [em-bar'-as], *va.* 1. Avergonzar, aturdir, desconcertar. 2. Embarazar, enredar.

Embarrassed [em-bar'-asd], *a.* Apenado, cortado, avergonzado.

Embarrassment [em-bar'-as-ment], *s.* 1. Aturdimiento, agitación de ánimo, desconcierto. 2. Embarazo, dificultad, perplejidad, enredo. 3. Embarazo, impedimento, estorbo, atascadero.

Embassador [em-bas'-a-der], *s.* Embajador. *V.* AMBASSADOR.

Embassadress [em-bas'-a-dres], *sf.* Embajadora.

Embassy [em'-ba-si], **Embassage** [em'-ba-sej], *s.* Embajada.

Embattle [em-bat'-l], *va.* 1. Formar en orden de batalla, preparar o equipar para la batalla. 2. Almenar, coronar con almenas.—*vn.* Ponerse en orden de batalla.

Embattled [em-bat'-ld], *a.* 1. En orden de batalla. *Here the embattled farmers stood* (Emerson), Aquí se sostuvieron los labriegos en orden de batalla. 2. Que es o ha sido campo o teatro de un combate. 3. Almenado; cortado, recortado: úsase en arquitectura y en heráldica.

Embattlement [em-bat'-l-ment], *s.* Aspillera; parapeto aspillerado.

Embay [em-bé'], *va.* 1. (Des.) Bañar, mojar, lavar. 2. (Mar.) Empeñar en una bahía. 3. Encerrar, cerrar con brazos protectores de tierra, como en una bahía.

Embed [em-bed'], *va.* Poner, depositar en una cama o lecho; encajonar, encajar, incrustar; empotrar. Equivalente, **Imbed.**

Embellish [em-bel'-ish], *va.* 1. Hermosear, embellecer, adornar una cosa; ribetear, ataviar. 2. Exornar, añadir algo imaginario para realzar el interés, bordar un cuento.

Embellishment [em-bel'-ish-ment], *s.* Adorno, ornato.

Embers [em'-berz], *s. pl.* Rescoldo.

Ember-week [em'-ber-wīc], *s.* Semana de témporas. *Ember-days*, Las cuatro témporas.

Embezzle [em-bez'-l], *va.* Hurtar, apropiar o apropiarse alguna cosa ilícitamente.

Embezzlement [em-bez'-l-ment], *s.* 1. Hurto, robo, el acto de ocultar a hurtadillas alguna cosa puesta al cuidado de uno, con intención de apropiársela. 2. La cosa hurtada o robada de esta manera. 3. (For.) Expilación u ocultación maliciosa de bienes pertenecientes a una herencia que aun no ha sido aceptada por el heredero.

Embezzler [em-bez'-ler], *s.* Malversador, estafador; el que se apropia dinero o bienes que otro ha confiado a su cuidado.

Embitter [em-bit'-er], *va.* 1. Hacer amargo al gusto. 2. Agriar, llenar de amargura, agravar. *V.* IMBITTER, como también se escribe.

Emblaze [em-bléz'], *va.* 1. Adornar con colores brillantes, esmaltar. 2. Proclamar, divulgar; celebrar, alabar. 3. Hacer resplandeciente o brillante.

Emblazon [em-blé'-zun], *va.* 1. Blasonar, disponer el escudo de armas de alguna ciudad o familia según las reglas del arte. 2. Blasonar; esmaltar con colores brillantes; adornar con blasones o piezas del escudo. 3. Blasonar, ensalzar, alabar, engrandecer.

Emblazoner [em-blé'-zun-er], *s.* 1. Blasonador, el que divulga alguna cosa pomposamente. 2. Heraldo, rey de armas.

Emblem [em'-blem], *s.* 1. Emblema, símbolo, signo. 2. Divisa, signo distintivo de una familia, un oficio, etc. 3. Emblema, pintura que encierra una alegoría. 4. Esmalte, labor de varios colores, que se hace sobre oro o plata sobredorada.

Emblematic, Emblematical [em-blem-at'-ic, al], *a.* Emblemático, alusivo, simbólico.

Emblematically [em-blem-at'-ic-al-i], *adv.* Emblemáticamente, figuradamente.

Emblematicize [em-blem-at'-i-saiz], *va.* Dar a alguna cosa carácter emblemático; alegorizar.

Emblematist [em-blem'-a-tist], *s.* Escritor o inventor de emblemas.

Emblematize [em-blem'-a-taiz], *va.* Representar o figurar por emblemas.

Emblements [em'-blem-ents], *s. pl.* (For.) Las rentas, utilidad o beneficio que dejan las tierras o su cultivo.

Emblemize [em'-blem-aiz], *va.* Representar por medio de un emblema, signo o figura.

Embodiment [em-bod'-i-ment], *s.* 1. Incorporación, el acto y efecto de incorporar. 2. Personificación; expresión concreta.

Embody [em-bod'-i], *va.* 1. Dar cuerpo, revestir de materia; expresar concretamente. 2. Incorporar, formar un todo o cuerpo; reunir en colección.—*vn.* Unirse, incorporarse.

Emboguing [em-bōg'-ing], *s.* Desembocadura o desembocadero de un río, canal o pantano, o el paraje por donde desaguan en el mar.

Embolden [em-bōld'-n], *va.* Animar, envalentonar.

Embolism [em'-bo-lizm], *s.* 1. (Astr.) Intercalación de ciertos días para igualar el calendario. 2. (Med.) Embolía, la obstrucción de un vaso sanguíneo por un coágulo arrastrado por la circulación de la sangre.

Embolus [em'-bo-lus], *s.* 1. Émbolo.

2. Cualquier cosa que obra o funciona dentro de otra.

Emborder [em-bōr'-dẹr], *va.* Guarnecer con marco o borde.

Embosom [em-buz'-um], *va.* 1. Poner o meter en el seno, medio o centro de alguna cosa; envolver, encerrar, abrigar. 2. Tomar o recibir en el seno; querer, proteger.

Emboss [em-bes'], *va.* 1. Relevar, formar o fabricar alguna cosa en realce o relieve; realzar, resaltar. 2. Grabar en realce, en hueco, o de relieve.

Embossment [em-bes'-mẹnt], *s.* Realce, relieve, resalte; resalto.

Embouchure [āñ-bū-shūr'], *s.* 1. Boca o embocadura de un instrumento músico. 2. Embocadura, la posición o ajuste de la boca y la lengua al tocar un instrumento de viento. (Fr.)

Embowel [em-bau'-el], *va.* 1. Desentrañar, destripar, sacar las entrañas; hacer reventar. 2. Hundir alguna cosa en otra substancia.

Emboweller [em-bau'-el-ẹr], *s.* Desentrañador.

Embower [em-bau'-ẹr], *va.* Cubrir, encerrar o abrigar con una enramada, emparrado o follaje; emparrar.

Embrace [em-brēs'], *va.* 1. Abrazar, estrechar entre los brazos. 2. Abrazar, rodear, ceñir, contener, comprender. 3. Admitir, recibir; aceptar de buena gana; asir o aprovechar (la ocasión, la oferta, etc.).—*vn.* 1. Abrazarse con alguna cosa. 2. Abrazarse mutuamente.

Embrace, *va.* (For.) Influir o tratar de influir por medio del cohecho o la amenaza en la decisión de un juez, tribunal, árbitro o jurado.

Embrace, Embracement [em-brēs'-mẹnt], *s.* Abrazo; recepción; las caricias conyugales.

Embracer [em-brē'-sẹr], *s.* Abrazador.

Embracery [em-brē'-ser-i], *s.* (For.) El delito de influir en el ánimo del jurado por medios ilegales.

Embracing [em-brē'-sing], *s.* Abrazo.

Embrasure [em-brē'-zhur], *s.* (Fort.) Tronera, abertura; cañonera.

Embrocate [em'-bro-kēt], *va.* Embrocar, derramar algo lentamente sobre la parte enferma y frotarla al mismo tiempo.

Embrocation [em-bro-kē'-shun], *s.* (Med.) Embrocación, linimento.

Embroider [em-brei'-dẹr], *va.* Bordar, adornar y enriquecer formando con la aguja figuras o labores.

Embroiderer, Embroideress [em-brei'-dẹr-ẹr, ess], *s.* Bordador, bordadora.

Embroidery [em-brei'-dẹr-i], *s.* Bordado, bordadura.

Embroil [em-breil'], *va.* Embrollar, enredar; confundir; dividir, desunir.

Embroilment [em-breil'-mẹnt], *s.* Alboroto, confusión; embrollo.

Embrown [em-braun'], *va.* 1. Hacer moreno, castaño. 2. Obscurecer, ofuscar.—*vn.* Volverse moreno u obscuro.

†**Embrue** [em-brū'], *va.* *V.* IMBRUE.

Embryo [em'-bri-ō], *s.* 1. Embrión, el feto que empieza a formarse. 2. El primer rudimento del animal o de la planta. 3. Principio, todavía informe, de una cosa.—*a.* En embrión.

Embryogeny [em-bri-ej'-ẹ-ni], *s.* Embriogenia, la ciencia de la formación y desarrollo de los organismos; la generación de los organismos.

Embryology [em-bri-el'-e-ji], *s.* Embriología, el ramo de la biología que trata de los embriones o del desarrollo de los organismos.

Embryonal [em'-bri-on-al], *a.* Embrionario.

Embryonic [em-bri-en'-ic], *a.* Embrionario, perteneciente a un embrión, o parecido a él; rudimentario, que no está desarrollado.

Emend [ẹ-mend'], *va.* Enmendar, corregir, emendar.

Emendable [ẹ-mend'-a-bl], *a.* Corregible.

Emendator [em'-en-dē-tẹr], *s.* Corrector.

Emendatory [ẹ-mend'-a-to-ri], *a.* Lo que contribuye a enmendar, corregir, etc.

Emerald [em'-ẹr-ald], *s.* 1. Esmeralda, piedra preciosa de color verde; variedad del berilo. 2. Color verde vivo y claro como el de la esmeralda. 3. (Ingl.) Tipo intermedio entre la letra miñona y la nomparell; 6½ puntos.—*a.* 1. Del color verde claro de la esmeralda. 2. Impreso en el tipo llamado *emerald.*

Emerge [ẹ-mẹrj'], *vn.* 1. Salir, surgir como de un fluido; salir de un escondrijo; aparecer, asomarse, presentarse a la vista. 2. Salir de la opresión; salir de la obscuridad, salir a luz.

Emergence [ẹ-mẹrj'-ens], *s.* 1. Emersión, salida; el procedimiento o efecto de salir; aparición, emergencia (en sentido óptico). 2. Emergencia (uso incorrecto). 3. Lo que sale o sobresale; excrecencia.

Emergency [ẹ-mẹr'-jẹn-si], *s.* 1. Emergencia, caso o incidente no previsto. 2. Aprieto, necesidad urgente.

Emergency outlet [ẹ-mẹr'-jẹn-si aut-let], *s.* 1. Salida de emergencia. 2. Válvula de escape. 3. Aliviadero o vertedero.

Emergent [ẹ-mẹr'-jent], *a.* Emergente; repentino, subitáneo.

Emeritus [i-mer'-it-us], *a.* Emérito, jubilado, el que después de haber servido en un cargo o una profesión cierto número de años, se retira gozando los honores y parte del sueldo.

†**Emerods, Emeroids**, *s.* *V.* HEMORRHOIDS.

Emersion [ẹ-mẹr'-shun], *s.* 1. Emersión, el acto de salir de algún fluido o de atrás de alguna cosa. 2. (Astr.) Emersión, reaparición.

Emery [em'-e-ri], *s.* Esmeril, variedad de corindón, piedra muy dura; en polvo se usa para bruñir los metales.

Emetic, Emetical [ẹ-met'-ic, al], *a.* Emético, vomitivo.

Emetic, *s.* Emético, vomitivo.

Emetically [ẹ-met'-ic-al-i], *adv.* A manera de vomitivo.

Emeu o **Emew** [i'-miū], *s.* (Orn.) Dromeo. *V.* EMU.

Emication [em-i-kē'-shun], *s.* (Poco us.) Chispeo.

Emigrant [em'-i-grant], *s.* Emigrado.

Emigrate [em'-i-grēt], *vn.* Emigrar, transmigrar.

‡**Emigrate**, *a.* Emigrado; vago, vagamundo.

Emigration [em-i-grē'-shun], *s.* 1. Emigración, el acto de emigrar. 2. Los emigrados colectivamente. 3. *V.* MIGRATION.

Eminence, Eminency [em'-i-nens, i], *s.* 1. Altura, elevación. 2. Cima, cuesta, sumidad. 3. Eminencia, distinción, excelencia. 4. Altura. 5. Eminencia, título de honor peculiar de los cardenales.

Eminent [em'-i-nent], *a.* 1. Eminente, exaltado, conspicuo, notable, distinguido, ilustre. 2. Independiente de otra autoridad, supremo; v. g. *Eminent domain,* El dominio supremo. 3. (Ant.) Alto, elevado, levantado. *Most eminent,* Eminentísimo.

Eminently [em'-i-nent-li], *adv.* Eminentemente, conspicuamente.

Emir [ẹ-mīr'], *s.* 1. Emir, título de dignidad en Turquía y el Oriente mahometano. 2. Fatimita, descendiente de Fátima, hija de Mahoma.

Emissary [em'-i-sẹ-ri], *s.* 1. Emisario, espía, agente secreto. 2. Canal, desaguadero como para el agua. 3. (Anat.) Conducto excretorio o de comunicación.—*a.* 1. Perteneciente al emisario. 2. Enviado por delante o afuera.

Emission [ẹ-mish'-un], *s.* Emisión.

Emissive [ẹ-mis'-iv], *a.* Emisivo, que lanza o emite; que echa rayos o centellea o despide calórico.

Emissory [em'-i-so-ri], *a.* Que emite o lanza; emisivo.—*s.* Desaguadero.

Emit [ẹ-mit'], *va.* 1. Emitir, echar de sí; arrojar, despedir; exhalar. 2. Emitir, poner en circulación, dar a luz autorizadamente.

Emmanuel, *s.* *V.* IMMANUEL.

Emmenagogue [e-men'-a-gog], *s.* Emenagogo, medicamento para provocar la menstruación detenida.

Emmet [em'-et], *s.* Hormiga.

Emollient [ẹ-mel'-yent], *a.* Emoliente, lo que ablanda.—*s.* Emolientes, una clase de medicamentos, mucilaginosos u oleosos.

Emolument [ẹ-mel'-yu-mẹnt], *s.* Emolumento, gaje, utilidad, provecho.

Emolumental [ẹ-mel-yu-ment'-al], *a.* Útil, provechoso.

Emotion [ẹ-mō'-shun], *s.* 1. Emoción, perturbación o agitación del ánimo, conmoción. 2. La facultad de sentir; sensibilidad; sentimiento racional.

Emotional [ẹ-mō'-shun-al], *a.* 1. Sensible, impresionable, que fácilmente cede a las impresiones o al sentimiento. 2. Lo que expresa la emoción.

Emotionalism [ẹ-mō'-shun-al-izm], *s.* 1. La manifestación oral o la expresión de las emociones, de cualquiera manera que se haga. 2. La tendencia a desarrollar el influjo de las emociones, o a ceder fácilmente a ellas.

Empale [em-pēl'], *va.* 1. Empalar, espetar a uno en un palo como se espeta el ave en el asador. 2. Cercar; rodear, encerrar con una estacada o cerca. 3. Poner uno al lado de otro, como iguales (v. g. en el blasón).

Empalement [em-pēl'-mẹnt], *s.* 1. Empalamiento. 2. Junta de armas en el blasón.

Empanel, *va.* *V.* IMPANEL.

Emparadise, *va.* *V.* IMPARADISE.

Emperor [em'-pe-rẹr], *s.* 1. Emperador, el soberano de un imperio. 2. Nombre de ciertas especies de mariposas diurnas y nocturnas. *Emperor-moth,* Mariposa nocturna grande. Saturnia pavonia.

Empery [em'-pẹr-i], *s.* 1. Soberanía, dominio. 2. Mando, autoridad de un emperador; imperio.

Emphasis [em' fa-sis], *s.* Énfasis.

Emphasize [em'-fa-saiz], *va.* 1. Recalcar, acentuar, pronunciar con fuerza o intención. 2. Destacar,

clara y fuertemente; hacer más distinto, positivo o impresivo.
Emphatic, Emphatical [em-fat'-ic, al], *a.* Enfático; fuerte, enérgico.
Emphatically [em-fat'-ic-al-i], *adv.* Enfáticamente, aparentemente.
Emphysema [em-fi-sí'-ma], *s.* (Med.) Enfisema, tumefacción producida por aire o gas en el tejido celular.
Emphysematous [em-fi-sem'-a-tus], *a.* Enfisematoso, que ofrece o presenta los caracteres del enfisema.
Emphyteutic [em-fi-tiū'-tic], *a.* (For.) Enfitéutico, que se da en enfiteusis o que pertenece a ella.
Empire [em'-pair], *s.* 1. Imperio. 2. Mando, autoridad, dominio.
Empiric [em-pir'-ic], *s.* Empírico, charlatán, medicastro, curandero.
Empiric, Empirical [em-pir'-ic-al], *a.* Empírico.
Empirically [em-pir'-ic-al-i], *adv.* Empíricamente.
Empiricism [em-pir'-i-sizm], *s.* Empirismo; charlatanería.
Emplacement [em-plēs'-ment], *s.* Emplazamiento, la posición destinada a los cañones o a una batería dentro de una fortificación.
Emplastic [em-plas'-tic], *a.* Viscoso, glutinoso, pegajoso.—*s.* 1. Medicamente que estriñe el vientre. 2. Substancia adhesiva, pegajosa.
†**Emplead**, *va.* *V.* IMPLEAD.
Employ [em-ploi'], *va.* 1. Emplear, ocupar. 2. Comisionar. 3. Emplear, llenar de ocupaciones.
Employ, *s.* Empleo, ocupación, puesto, oficio público, cargo.
Employable [em-ploi'-a-bl], *a.* Empleable.
Employee, Employé [em-ploi-í', ān-plwa-yé'] (Fr.), *s.* Empleado, el que está al empleo de otro.
Employer [em-ploi'-er], *s.* Empleador, patrón, dueño, principal, amo.
Employment [em-ploi'-ment], *s.* Empleo, ocupación, aplicación, cargo. (Fam.) *You will not want employment,* No le faltará a Vd. que hacer.
Empoison [em-poi'-zn], *va.* (Ant.) Envenenar, atosigar, emponzoñar.
Emporium [em-pō'-ri-um], *s.* 1. Emporio, cualquier ciudad donde concurren muchos para el tráfico y comercio. 2. Bazar.
Empoverish [em-pov'-er-ish], *va.* Empobrecer; minorar la fertilidad de alguna cosa.
Empoverisher, *s.* *V.* IMPOVERISHER.
Empoverishment, *s.* *V.* IMPOVERISHMENT.
Empower [em-pau'-er], *va.* Autorizar, comisionar, habilitar, dar poder.
Empress [em'-pres], *sf.* Emperatriz, emperadora.
Emprise [em-praiz'], *s.* (Ant.) Empresa.
†**Emprison,** *va.* *V.* IMPRISON.
Emptier [emp'-ti-er], *s.* Vaciador, el que vacía, o instrumento para vaciar.
Emptiness [emp'-ti-nes], *s.* 1. Vaciedad. 2. Vacío o vacuo. 3. Futilidad.
Emptins [empt'-ins], *s.* (Dial. E. U.) *V.* EMPTYINGS.
Empty [emp'-ti], *a.* 1. Vacío, vacuo, hueco; desocupado, desalojado; vaco, vacante. *Empty house,* Una casa por alquilar. 2. Vano, inútil, infructuoso. 3. Corto, ignorante, falto de talento o conocimientos. 4. Hambriento. 5. Ligero, frívolo, superficial.
Empty, *va.* Vaciar, evacuar, agotar, desocupar.—*vn.* Vaciarse.
Emptyings [emp'-ti-ingz], *s. pl.* Heces de la cerveza usadas en vez de levadura.
Empurple [em-pūr'-pl], *va.* Purpurar, teñir de púrpura.
Empyema [em-pai-í'-ma], *s.* (Med.) Empiema, acumulación purulenta en la cavidad de la pleura.
Empyreal [em-pir'-e-al o em-pi-rí'-al], *a.* Empíreo
Empyrean [em-pi-rí'-an], *s.* Empíreo, el cielo de los bienaventurados. —*a.* Empíreo.
Empyreuma [em-pi-rū'-ma], *s.* Empireuma, olor y sabor particulares y desagradables que toman las substancias animales y algunas vegetales sometidas a fuego violento.
Emu [í'-miū], *s.* 1. Dromeo, ave grande de Australia parecida al avestruz. Dromæus novæ-hollandiæ. 2. (Des.) Casoar. *V.* CASSOWARY.
Emulate [em'-yu-lēt], *va.* Emular, competir, imitar.
Emulation [em-yu-lé'-shun], *s.* Emulación, pasión que nos excita a imitar y aun a exceder o superar a otros.
Emulative [em'-yu-la-tiv], *a.* Emulativo, inclinado a la emulación.
Emulator [em'-yu-lē-ter], *s.* Émulo, rival, antagonista, competidor, emulador.
Emulatress [em'-yu-lē-tres], *sf.* Émula, emuladora.
Emulgent [e-mulj'-ent], *a.* Emulgente, que cuela; antes se aplicaba a los vasos renales.
Emulous [em'-yu-lus], *a.* Émulo, competidor, rival. *To be emulous of,* Rivalizar con.
Emulously [em'-yu-lus-li], *adv.* Con emulación, a porfía, a competencia.
Emulsify [e-mul'-si-fai], *va.* Hacer o convertir en emulsión.
Emulsion [e-mul'-shun], *s.* 1. Emulsión, medicamento líquido de color de leche preparado de las almendras o de las semillas de algunas frutas. 2. Cualquier líquido lechoso.
Emulsive [e-mul'-siv], *a.* 1. Emulsivo, capaz de hacer emulsión. 2. De la naturaleza de una emulsión; dulcificante.
Emunctory [e-munc'-to-ri], *a.* (Med.) Excretorio, que sirve para descargar materias excrementicias.—*s.* Emuntorio, el conducto o canal excretorio; emunctorio.
En [en], *s.* 1. Nombre de la letra N, la décimacuarta del alfabeto inglés. 2. (Impr.) La mitad de una eme; la mitad del cuadrado del tipo.
En [en], partícula inseparable derivada del latín; escríbese a veces *en* o *in* indiferentemente.
Enable [en-é'-bl], *vn.* Habilitar, proporcionar, facilitar, permitir; poner en estado de, hacer que.
Enact [en-act'], *va.* 1. Establecer, decretar, ordenar, mandar. 2. Efectuar, poner en ejecución. 3. Hacer papel de, representar.
Enactable [en-act'-a-bl], *a.* Que puede ser establecido, efectuado o representado.
Enactive [en-act'-iv], *a.* Lo que establece o manda.
Enactment [en-act'-ment], *s.* 1. Ley establecida, estatuto. 2. El acto de decretar o establecer una ley.
Enactor [en-act'-er], *s.* Legislador. ejecutor, establecedor.
Enallage [en-al'-a-je], *s.* (Gram.) Enálage, el uso de una parte de la oración por otra.
Enambush [en-am'-bush], *va.* Emboscar, armar celada o trampa.
Enamel [en-am'-el], *va.* Esmaltar, labrar con esmalte de varios colores. *A meadow enamelled with flowers,* Una pradera esmaltada de flores.
Enamel, *s.* 1. Esmalte. 2. Labor que se hace con el esmalte sobre algún metal. 3. Lo que se parece al esmalte en la tersura, como el esmalte de los dientes, una capa de charol, de laca, etc.
Enameler, Enameller [en-am'-el-er], *s.* Esmaltador.
Enamelling [en-am'-el-ing], *s.* El arte de esmaltar.
Enamelware [en-am'-el-wār], *s.* Vasijas esmaltadas.
Enamor. Enamour [en-am'-er], *va.* Enamorar. Se usa raramente fuera del participio pasado, y con *of* o *with; He was enamoured of her,* Estuvo enamorado de ella.
Enarthrosis [en-ar-thrō'-sis], *s* (Anat.) Enártrosis, especie de articulación floja y móvil de una cabeza huesosa que encaja en un alvéolo.
Encage [en-kēj'], *va.* Enjaular, encarcelar.
Encamp [en-camp'], *vn.* Acampar, alojarse un ejército en tiendas de campaña.—*va.* Acampar, alojar a un ejército o parte de él en tiendas de campaña.
Encamping [en-cam'-ping], *s.* Campamento, acampamento.
Encampment [en-camp'-ment], *s.* Campamento, campo.
Encase [en-kēs'], *va.* Encajar, encajonar. *V.* INCASE.
Encave [en-kēv'], *va.* Esconder en una cueva.
Encaustic [en-cōs'-tic], *a.* 1. Encáustico, (pintura) hecha al encausto o con fuego. 2. Pintado con adustión, o por medio del fuego, con ceras de colores.—*s.* Encausto, adustión, combustión. *Encaustic painting,* Pintura encáustica.
Enceinte [an-sant'], *a.* Preñada, embarazada, en cinta. Es voz francesa.—*s.* 1. Recinto, reunión de bastiones y cortinas de muralla de una plaza. 2. Cerca, cercado.
Encenia [en-sí'-ni-a], *s. pl.* Fiestas en aniversario de la consagración de algún templo.
Encephalic [en-sef-al'-ic], *a.* Encefálico; del encéfalo o cerebro.
Encephalitis [en-sef-a-lai'-tis], *s.* (Med.) Encefalitis, inflamación del cerebro.
Encephalogram [en-sef'-a-lō-gram], *s.* Encefalograma.
Encephaloid [en-sef'-a-loid], *a.* Encefaloideo, que se parece al cerebro en la materia o en el aspecto. *Encephaloid cancer,* Cáncer encefaloideo; encefaloidea.
Encephalon [en-sef'-a-len], *s.* Encéfalo, el cerebro.
Encephalous [en-sef'-a-lus], *a.* Que tiene cabeza; p. ej. ciertos moluscos.
Enchain [en-chēn'], *va.* Encadenar; aprisionar.
Enchant [en-chant'], *va.* 1. Encantar, practicar la hechicería, hacer cosas maravillosas en apariencia. 2. Encantar, deleitar en sumo grado.
Enchanter [en-chant'-er], *s.* Encantador, hechicero.
Enchantingly [en-chant'-ing-li], *adv.* Como por encanto.
Enchantment [en-chant'-ment], *s.* Encantación, encanto, magia, embeleso.

Enchantress [en-chgnt'-res], *sf:* 1. Encantadora. 2. Seductora.
†**Encharge** [en-chārj'], *va.* Fiar a, cargar con.
Enchase [en-chês'], *va.* 1. Engastar. 2. Adornar, incrustar, cincelar, adornar con relieves. 3. Grabar, retratar por medio de figuras grabadas o en relieve. 4. Empotrar.
§**Enchiridion** [en-ki-rid'-i-gn], *s.* Enquiridión, manual, libro pequeño; en especial, manual de devoción.
Enchorial [en-cō'-ri-al], *a.* Propio de un país determinado: (1) Demótico; (2) Endémico; (3) Indígena, autóctono.
Encircle [en-sgr'-cl], *va.* Cercar, rodear.
Enclitic [en-clit'-ic], *a.* (Gram.) Enclítico; dícese de la partícula o del vocablo que se liga con el vocablo precedente, formando con él una sola palabra.—*s.* Partícula o voz enclítica.
Encloister [en-clois'-tgr], *va.* Enclaustrar.
Enclose [en-clōz'], *va.* 1. Cercar o circunvalar algún terreno; rodear, circundar. 2. Incluir, poner una cosa dentro de otra. 3. Disfrutar o apropiarse un terreno como por derecho exclusivo. *V.* INCLOSE.
Encloser [en-clōz'-gr], *s.* Cercador.
Enclosure [en-clō'-zhur], *s.* 1. Cercamiento; cercado, vallado, tapia, corral, etc. 2. Cercado, espacio cerrado; el huerto, prado u otro lugar o espacio rodeado de una cerca. 3. La inclusa, lo incluso; dícese de las letras de cambio, cuentas, cartas, etc., contenidas en algún pliego o carta.
Enclothe [en-clōdh'], *va.* *V.* To CLOTHE.
Encoach [en-cōch'], *va.* (Poco us.) Meter en coche.
Encoffin [en-cef'-in], *va.* Meter en un ataúd.
Encomiast [en-cō'-mi-ast], *s.* Encomiasta, panegirista, elogiador, encomiador.
Encomiastic, Encomiastical [en-co-mi-as'-tic, al], *a.* Encomiástico, eulogístico.
Encomium [en-cō'-mi-um], *s.* Encomio, elogio, alabanza, panegírico.
Encompass [en-cum'-pas], *va.* 1. Cercar, circundar, sitiar, rodear. 2. Circuir, encerrar. *To encompass the globe,* Dar la vuelta al mundo.
Encore [an-cōr'], *adv.* Otra vez, de nuevo, aún, además.—*inter.* ¡Otra! ¡otra vez! ¡que se repita! (Fr. < Lat. hanc, *esta* + horam, *hora.*)
Encore, *s.* El acto de pedir el público la repetición de una escena dramática o lírica; y la repetición de la misma por los actores o cantantes.
Encore, *va.* Pedir que un actor repita lo que ha recitado o cantado; gritar "*encore!*"
Encounter [en-caun'-tgr], *s.* 1. Encuentro, choque; entrevista, particularmente cuando es casual e imprevista. 2. Encuentro hostil; escaramuza; duelo, desafío; combate, pelea, batalla, refriega.
Encounter, *va.* 1. Encontrar. 2. Acometer o embestir al enemigo. 3. Tropezar con alguno, hallarle por casualidad.—*vn.* Pelear, combatir; encontrarse cara a cara, venir a las manos; oponerse.
Encounterer [en-caun'-tgr-gr], *s.* Antagonista, adversario.
Encourage [en-cur'-ẹj], *va.* 1. Animar, incitar, alentar; favorecer. 2. Infundir ánimo y valor; inspirar confianza. 3. Fomentar.
Encouragement [en-cur'-ẹj-mgnt], *s.* Estímulo, incentivo; patrocinio, amparo, fomento.
Encourager [en-cur'-ẹj-gr], *s.* Patrón, protector, favorecedor, incitador.
Encouraging [en-cur'-ẹ-jing], *pa.* y *a.* Estimulante, que estimula, que excita y anima.
Encouragingly [en-cur'-ẹ-jing-li], *adv.* De una manera estimulante y animadora.
Encradle [en-crê'-dl], *va.* Meter en la cuna.
Encrimson [en-crim'-zn], *va.* 1. Purpurar, teñir de púrpura. 2. Ruborizar, avergonzar, hacer salir los colores á la cara.
Encrinite [en'-cri-nait], *s.* Encrinita, encrino fósil.
Encroach [en-crōch], *va.* Usurpar, avanzar gradualmente; irse apoderando poco a poco, apropiarse lo ajeno.—*vn.* Pasar los límites de la confianza, etc. *To encroach upon kindness,* Abusar de la bondad de alguno.
Encroacher [en-crōch'-gr], *s.* Usurpador.
Encroachingly [en-crōch'-ing-li], *adv.* Por usurpación o intrusión.
Encroachment [en-crōch'-mgnt], *s.* Usurpación, intrusión.
Encrust, *va.* *V.* INCRUST.
Encumber [en-cum'-bgr], *va.* Embarazar, cargar demasiado, abrumar con un peso; estorbar, poner estorbos o impedimentos.
Encumbrance [en-cum'-brans], *s.* Embarazo, impedimento, cargo, estorbo; pensión, carga, gravamen. *Free from encumbrances,* Libre de toda carga.
Encyclical [en-sic'-li-cal], *a.* Encíclica, carta del Papa a los obispos.
Encyclopædia, Encyclopedia [en-sai-clo-pī'-di-a], *s.* Enciclopedia, colección de todas las ciencias; obra en que se trata de muchas ciencias; o tratado completo de un ramo especial de conocimientos. La distribución de las materias es sistemática y por lo general en orden alfabético.
Encyclopedic, Encyclopædic, Encyclopedical [en-sai'-clo-pī-dic, al], *a.* Enciclopédico, perteneciente a la enciclopedia.
Encyclopedist [en-sai-clo-pī'-dist], *s.* Enciclopedista; compilador de una enciclopedia o el que colabora en ella.
Encysted [en-sist'-ed], *a.* (Cir.) Enquistado, metido en un quiste.
End [end], *s.* 1. Fin, cabo, extremidad, remate. 2. Fin, conclusión, cesación, término. 3. Destino, muerte. 4. Resolución, determinación final. 5. Objeto, mira, intento. 6. Consecuencia inevitable o natural. 7. Pieza, fragmento. 8. Fondo, límite extremo de un objeto. *To the end that,* A fin de que, para que; con el objeto de. *To no end,* Sin efecto, en vano. *On end,* De cabeza, en pie, erguido. (Mar.) En candela, a plomo. *End to end,* Cabeza contra cabeza; topando. *End for end,* Al revés. *End on,* (Mar.) Flechado. *Fag end,* Pestaña. *Gable end,* Socarrén. *At loose ends,* En desorden, desarreglado. *At the end of the month, of next month,* A fines del corriente, del mes próximo. *My hair stands on end,* Se me erizan los cabellos. *In the end,* En fin, al fin. *At the latter end,* A las últimas, al fin. *To make an end of,* Acabar con. *To make both ends meet,* Atar ambos cabos. (Fig.) Hacer que baste la renta propia, sin contraer deudas.
End, *va.* 1. Acabar, terminar, concluir, fenecer. 2. Matar, quitar la vida.—*vn.* Acabarse, finalizarse, terminarse; morir, fenecer.
End-all [end'-ōl], *s.* Último remate, conclusión final.
Endanger [en-dên'-jgr], *va.* Poner en peligro, arriesgar.
Endangerment [en-dên'-jgr-mgnt], *s.* Peligro, riesgo.
Endear [en-dīr'], *va.* 1. Hacer o hacerse amar, o querer. 2. Encarecer.
Endearing [en-dīr'-ing], *s.* Atractivo.
Endearment [en-dīr'-mgnt], *s.* Encarecimiento.
Endeavor, Endeavour [en-dev'-gr], *s.* Esfuerzo, conato, empeño.
Endeavor, Endeavour, *va.* Tentar, probar, experimentar, tratar de, procurar, hacer lo posible. (Por lo general con un infinitivo.)—*vn.* Esforzarse, hacer un esfuerzo.
Endeavorer [en-dev'-gr-gr], *s.* El que procura el logro de una cosa o hace esfuerzos para conseguirla. En especial, miembro de la sociedad llamada *Christian Endeavor,* del Esfuerzo Cristiano.
Endeavour, etc. Esta es la manera usual de escribir estas palabras en Inglaterra.
Endecagon [en-dec'-a-gen], *s.* Endecágono. *V.* HENDECAGON.
Endemial [en-dī'-mi-al]. *V.* ENDEMIC.
Endemic, Endemical [en-dem'-ic, al], *a.* Endémico: se aplica al mal o enfermedad propios de un clima determinado.
§**Endenizen** [en-den'-i-zen], *va.* Naturalizar; franquear, hacer libre.
Ender [end'-gr], *s.* Acabador.
Endermic [en-dgr'-mic], *a.* Endérmico, que cura por medio de la aplicación del medicamento a la piel, sobre todo después de ampollarse ésta.
Endictment [en-dait'-mgnt], *s.* (Des.) Edicto, estatuto. *V.* INDICTMENT.
Ending [end'-ing], *s.* 1. Conclusión, cesación. 2. Desinencia, terminación final de las palabras. 3. Fin de la vida.
Endive [en'-div], *s.* (Bot.) Escarola, endibia.
Endless [end'-les], *a.* Infinito, interminable, perpetuo, continuo.
Endlessly [end'-les-li], *adv.* Infinitamente, sin fin, perpetuamente.
Endlessness [end'-les-nes], *s.* Perpetuidad.
Endlong [end'-leng], *adv.* 1. A lo largo, extendido. 2. En línea recta, continuadamente. 3. De pie, en pie, a plomo.
Endmost [end'-mōst], *a.* Lo más lejos, remoto.
Endo-, end-. Formas de combinación del griego *endon,* dentro.
Endocardiac, Endocardial [en-do-cār'-di-ac, al], *a.* Endocardíaco, perteneciente al endocardio; colocado o situado dentro del corazón.
Endocarditis [en-do-car-dai'-tis], *s.* Endocarditis, inflamación aguda o crónica del endocardio.
Endocardium [en-do-cār'-di-um], *s.* Endocardio, membrana que tapiza las cavidades del corazón.
Endocrine [en'-do-crain], *a.* Endocrino.
Endogen [en'-do-jen], *s.* (Bot.) Vegetal cuyo crecimiento se verifica interiormente é irregularmente, en oposición a los exógenos; endógeno.

Endogenous [en-dej'-ẹ-nus], *a.* 1. (Bot.) Endógeno, endógena, monocotiledóneo; que crece interiormente. 2. Que crece en lo interior de alguna cosa.
Endorse [en-dōrs'], *va.* 1. Rotular, refrendar, rubricar, autorizar. 2. Endosar o endorsar una letra de cambio.
Endorsee [en-der-sī'], *s.* La persona a cuyo favor está endosada una letra de cambio. *V.* INDORSEE.
Endorsement [en-dōrs'-mẹnt], *s.* Sobrescrito, rótulo; endoso de una letra de cambio; ratificación.
Endorser [en-dōrs'-ẹr], *s.* Endosante o endosador.
Endosmose [end'-os''-mōs], *s.* Endósmosis, corriente de fuera a dentro, que se establece cuando dos líquidos de distinta densidad están separados por una membrana; también, corriente en la dirección en que un fluido atraviesa el septo más rápidamente.
Endothelium [en-do-thī'-li-um], *s.* (Anat.) Endotelio, membrana compuesta de celdillas planas y delgadas, que tapiza los vasos sanguíneos, los linfáticos y las cavidades. Su adjetivo es **Endothelial.**
Endothermic [en-do-thẹr'-mic], *a.* Endotérmico.
Endow [en-dau'], *va.* 1. Dotar a una mujer. 2. Dotar a una iglesia, colegio, etc. 3. Dotar, dar la naturaleza prendas, talento o algún otro de sus dones.
Endower [en-dau'-ẹr], *s.* Dotador.
Endowment [en-dau'-mẹnt], *s.* 1. Dote, dotación. 2. Dotes, los dones que recibimos de la naturaleza; prendas, talentos, gracias.
Endue [en-diū'], *va.* Dotar, privilegiar; investir.
Endurable [en-diūr'-a-bl], *a.* Sufrible, tolerable, soportable.
Endurance [en-diūr'-ans], *s.* Duración, continuación; paciencia, sufrimiento.
Endure [en-diūr'], *va.* 1. Soportar, sufrir el peso o la presión; resistir á. 2. Aguantar, sufrir, tolerar, soportar.—*vn.* 1. Durar, perseverar, continuar. 2. Sufrir, tener paciencia.
Endurer [en-diūr'-ẹr], *s.* Sufridor; continuador.
Enduring [en-diūr'-ing], *pa.* 1. Que demuestra duración; durable, permanente; constante. 2. Tolerante, paciente, sufrido.
Endwise [end'-waiz], *adv.* De punta, derecho; con la extremidad anterior.
Enema [en'-ẹ-ma o ẹ-nī'-ma], *s.* Enema, lavativa, ayuda, inyección.
Enemy [en'-ẹ-mi], *s.* Enemigo, antagonista; el diablo; toda cosa dañina o peligrosa.
Energetic, Energetical [en-ẹr-jẹt'-ic, al], *a.* Enérgico, vigoroso; ardiente, activo.
Energetically [en-ẹr-jet'-ic-al-i], *adv.* Enérgicamente.
Energic [en-ẹr'-jic], *a.* (Poco us.) Enérgico; motor, activo.
Energize [en'-ẹr-jaiz], *va.* Hacer obrar con energía, excitar o dar energía, dar vigor o actividad.—*vn.* Obrar con energía.
Energizer [en'-ẹr-jaiz-ẹr], *s.* Confortante, excitante, lo que da energía y fuerza.
Energumen [en-ẹr-giū'-men], *s.* Energúmeno, energúmena, la persona que está poseída del demonio.
Energy [en'-ẹr-ji], *s.* Energía, fuerza, vigor, espíritu, resolución.
Enervate [en'-ẹr-vêt], *va.* 1. Enervar, debilitar, quitar las fuerzas. 2. Dejar sin efecto, hacer ineficaz. 3. Cortar los nervios o los tendones.
Enervate, *a.* Debilitado, enervado.
Enervation [en-ẹr-vé'-shun], *s.* Enervación; afeminación.
Enfeeble [en-fī'-bl], *va.* Debilitar, enervar; afeminar.
Enfeeblement [en-fī'-bl-mẹnt], *s.* Debilidad, desfallecimiento, flojedad.
Enfeoff [en-fef'], *va.* Enfeudar, dar en feudo algún estado.
‡**Enfetter** [en-fet'-ẹr], *va.* Encadenar.
Enfilade [en-fi-lêd'], *s.* 1. Fuego o tiro enfilado, o de enfilada. 2. Ringlera, fila, hilera.
Enfilade, *va.* Enfilar, batir por el costado; tirar a lo largo de un cuerpo de tropas, o en la dirección de proa a popa de un buque.
Enfold. *V.* INFOLD.
Enforce [en-fōrs'], *va.* 1. Esforzar, dar fuerza o vigor; poner en ejecución por la fuerza, como se hace con las leyes. 2. Violentar, ejecutar alguna cosa con violencia; forzar, obtener por fuerza. 3. Esforzar, apretar. 4. Demostrar, presentar fuertemente o convincemente. 5. (Ant.) Compeler, obligar.
Enforceable [en-fōrs'-a-bl], *a.* Lo que es capaz de compeler u obligar.
Enforcedly [en-fōrs'-ed-li], *adv.* Por fuerza, forzosamente.
Enforcement [en-fōrs'-mẹnt], *s.* Compulsión, coacción, fuerza; sanción; aprieto, estrecho.
Enfranchise [en-fran'-chaiz], *va.* 1. Dar o conceder franquicia o privilegio político, como el derecho de votar; conceder los privilegios de la ciudadanía. 2. Poner en libertad, dar soltura al que estaba preso; manumitir, enfranquecer, emancipar. 3. Naturalizar, adoptar, v. g. palabras extranjeras.
Enfranchisement [en-fran'-chiz-mẹnt], *s.* 1. Franquicia, privilegio de ciudadano. 2. Manumisión, emancipación. 3. Libertad dada a un preso.
Enfranchiser [en-fran'-chaiz-ẹr], *s.* 1. Libertador, el que da libertad. 2. Manumisor.
Engage [en-gêj'], *va.* 1. Empeñar, comprometer, constituir a una persona en alguna obligación. 2. Atraer a otro a su partido; unir, traer a sí. 3. Empeñar, obligar, precisar, hacer responsable. 4. Halagar, ganar con halagos. 5. Ocupar, emplear la atención. 6. Acometer, embestir. 7. (Mec.) Engranar, encajar los dientes de una rueda con otra. 8. Empeñar, dar o dejar algo en prenda o seguridad del pago. 9. Apalabrar, mandar hacer, ajustar; alquilar (un cuarto, una casa); obtener promesa del uso de una cosa o de los servicios de una persona.—*vn.* 1. Empeñarse, obligarse, dar palabra, comprometerse a hacer alguna cosa. 2. Aventurarse o meterse en algún asunto o negocio. 3. Pelear, venir a las manos. *She is engaged to Mr. N.*, Ella ha dado palabra de matrimonio al Sr. N. *To be engaged,* (1) Estar ocupado, empeñado o comprometido. (2) Haber dado palabra de matrimonio, ser prometido o prometida de. *To engage deeply in an object,* Empeñarse demasiado. (Fam.) Enfrascarse en.
Engagedly [en-gê'-jed-li], *adv.* Parcialmente; con empeño.
Engagement [en-gêj'-mẹnt], *s.* 1. Empeño. 2. Empeño, comprometimiento, ajuste, contrato; en especial, promesa de casamiento; esponsales. *A new engagement,* Nueva contrata. 3. Empleo de la atención hacia alguna cosa. 4. Batalla, combate, pelea. 5. Obligación, motivo.
Engager [en-gê'-jẹr], *s.* El que se empeña en algún asunto, el que se compromete o constituye en algún empeño u obligación.
Engaging [en-gê'-jing], *a.* Atractivo, agraciado, insinuante, halagüeño; simpático.
Engagingly [en-gêj'-ing-li], *adv.* Atractivamente.
Engarland [en-gār'-land], *va.* Enguirnaldar, coronar con guirnalda.
Engarrison [en-gar'-i-sn], *va.* Guarnecer, póner guarnición en una plaza o fortaleza.
Engender [en-jen'-dẹr], *va.* 1. Engendrar, procrear. 2. Producir, formar, dar origen.—*va.* Engendrarse, producirse, causarse.
Engenderer [en-jen'-dẹr-ẹr], *s.* Engendrador.
Engild [en-gild'], *va.* Aclarar, iluminar.
Engine [en'-jin], *s.* 1. Ingenio, máquina; motor; (f. c.) locomotora. *Steam-engine,* Máquina de vapor. *Fire-engine,* Bomba de incendio, aguatocha. *Pile-engine,* Martinete. 2. Máquina complicada y bien acabada para hacer trabajos difíciles y superiores. 3. Mecanismo o aparato de gran tamaño, especialmente para destruir o desagregar. 4. Instrumento, agente. *Condensing engine,* Máquina condensadora. *Beam-engine,* Máquina de balancín. *Expansion engine,* Máquina de expansión. *Portable engine,* Locomóvil, máquina portátil. *Rotary engine,* Máquina de rotación. *Stationary engine,* Máquina fija. *Engine builder, maker,* Fabricante, constructor de máquinas. *Engine-driver,* (Ingl.) Conductor de locomotora. *Engine-turned work,* Trabajo hecho a máquina.
Engineer [en-ji-nīr'], *s.* Ingeniero; maquinista.
Engine room [en'-jin rūm], *s.* Cuarto de máquinas. *Engine-room log,* Cuaderno de máquinas.
Engird [en-gẹrd'], †**Engirt** [en-gẹrt'], *va.* Ceñir, cercar.
Engirdle [en-gẹr'-dl], *va.* Circundar, rodear, ceñir.
Englify [iṇ'-gli-fai], *va.* Hacer inglés; hacer que alguien o algo imite o se parezca a los ingleses en la figura o en los modales.
English [iṇ'-glish], *a.* Inglés, lo perteneciente a Inglaterra.—*s.* Inglés, el natural de Inglaterra y la lengua inglesa. *The English,* Los ingleses, la nación inglesa.
English, *va.* Traducir al idioma inglés.
English horn, *s.* (Mús.) Corno inglés.
Englishman [iṇ'-glish-man], *s.* 1. Inglés, el natural o ciudadano de Inglaterra; persona de sangre inglesa. 2. Navío o buque inglés.
Englishwoman [iṇ'-glish-wum''-an], *f.* Inglesa; la que es natural de Inglaterra o es de sangre inglesa.
Englut [en-glut'], *va.* 1. Engullir, tragar. 2. Atracar, llenar de comida, hartar.
Engorge [en-gōrj'], *va.* Atracar, en-

gullir, devorar.—*vn.* Comer con ansia y voracidad.
Engraft [en-grąft'], *va.* *V.* INGRAFT.
Engrafted [en-grąft'-ed], *a.* Injertado; plantado.
Engrain [en-grên'], *va.* Teñir, dar color subido a alguna cosa. *V.* INGRAIN.
Engrave [en-grêv'], *va.* 1. Grabar; esculpir; tallar. 2. Grabar en el ánimo, causar impresión o sensación. 3. Enterrar, sepultar.
Engravement [en-grêv'-męnt], *s.* Grabado, acción de grabar.
Engraver [en-grê'-vęr], *s.* Grabador; escultor.
Engraving [en-grê'-ving], *s.* 1. Grabado, el acto, efecto y arte de grabar. 2. Grabado, lámina, estampa, pintura. *Copper-plate engraving,* Grabado en cobre o en talla dulce. *Steel engraving,* Grabado sobre acero. *Wood engraving,* Grabado en madera. *Photo-engraving,* (1) Fotograbado. (2) Grabado fotomecánico o fotoquímico.
Engross [en-grōs'], *va.* 1. Escribir en caracteres grandes y de adorno; hacer transcripción formal de algo. 2. Absorber, ocupar o cautivar, tener posesión de. 3. Antiguamente, monopolizar, agavillar. 4. (Des.) Condensar, espesar, abultar.
Engrosser [en-grōs'-ęr], *s.* 1. Pendolista, el que copia en letras hermosas y de adorno. 2. (Ant.) Monopolista.
Engrossing [en-grōs'-ing], *s.* 1. (For.) Compulsa, copia de un instrumento legal. 2. (Com.) Monopolio de algunos géneros para hacer subir su precio. *Engrossing clerk,* Escribiente de letra grande y hermosa.
Engrossment [en-grōs'-męnt], *s.* 1. Monopolio. 2. Copia de un instrumento escrito. 3. Absorción, embebecimiento, embelesamiento, abstracción.
Engulf [en-gulf'], *va.* Engolfar. *V.* INGULF.
Enhance [en-hąns'], *va.* Encarecer, aumentar la estimación de una cosa; levantar en alto; agravar.
Enhancement [en-hąns'-męnt], *s.* 1. Encarecimiento, subida de valor o estimación. 2. Agravación, el acto de agravar alguna cosa.
Enhancer [en-hąns'-ęr], *s.* Encarecedor.
Enharmonic [en-har-mon'-ic], *a.* Enarmónico, uno de los tres géneros del sistema músico.
Enigma [ę-nig'-ma], *s.* 1. Enigma, dicho o frase cuyo sentido se encubre intencionadamente, haciéndolo obscuro y difícil de entender. 2. Suceso o acto de difícil explicación.
Enigmatic, Enigmatical [ę-nig-mat'-ic, al], *a.* Enigmático.
Enigmatically [ę-nig-mat'-ic-al-i], *adv.* Enigmáticamente.
Enigmatist [ę-nig'-ma-tist], *s.* Enigmatista, el que habla con enigmas.
Enigmatize [ę-nig'-ma-taiz], *vn.* Usar de enigmas.
Enjoin [en-join'], *va.* Mandar, ordenar, encargar, prescribir; advertir.
Enjoiner [en-join'-ęr], *s.* 1. Mandante. 2. El que da encargos, preceptos u órdenes.
Enjoinment [en-join'-męnt], *s.* (Des.) Mandato, precepto, orden; encargo.
Enjoy [en-jōi'], *va.* 1. Gozar, sentir o percibir alguna cosa con gusto, complacencia y alegría. 2. Gozar, tener, poseer. 3. Agradar, alegrar. *To enjoy one's self,* Gozarse, vivir contento y alegre, divertirse.—*vn.* Vivir felizmente.
Enjoyable [en-joi'-a-bl], *a.* Gozable, deleitable, encantador.
Enjoyer [en-joi'-ęr], *s.* Gozador.
Enjoyment [en-joi'-męnt], *s.* Goce, fruición, felicidad, gusto, placer.
Enkindle [en-kin'-dl], *va.* 1. Encender, pegar fuego. 2. Inflamar, enardecer y avivar a uno. 3. Incitar, mover, estimular.
Enlace [en-lés'], *va.* Rodear, circundar con encaje o bordado; atar con un encaje; entrelazar, enredar.
Enlarge [en-lārj'], *va.* 1. Agrandar, engrandecer, aumentar, ensanchar. 2. Dilatar, extender, alargar. 3. Ampliar, amplificar. 4. Soltar, desencarcelar, sacar de la prisión, poner en libertad a uno.—*vn.* Difundirse, extenderse; dilatarse en la narración o explicación de las cosas.
Enlargedly [en-lār'-jed-li], *adv.* Extensamente, ampliamente.
Enlargement [en-lārj'-męnt], *s.* 1. Aumento, incremento, extensión, ampliación. 2. Soltura, libertad, que se da al prisionero. 3. Dilatación, expansión; difusión. 4. Amplificación, plenitud de relación. 5. Ampliación, fotografía mayor que su prueba negativa.
Enlarger [en-lār'-jęr], *s.* Ampliador, amplificador.
Enlarging [en-lār'-jing], *s.* Extensión, ampliación. *Enlarging apparatus,* Aparato para ampliar fotografías.
†**Enlight** [en-lait'], *va.* Alumbrar, iluminar.
Enlighten [en-lait'-n], *va.* 1. (Ant.) Alumbrar, iluminar. 2. Iluminar, instruir, ilustrar; explicar, aclarar; comunicar o dar luz tanto en lo físico como en lo moral.
Enlightener [en-lait'-n-ęr], *s.* Alumbrador; instructor, ilustrador.
Enlightenment [en-lait'-n-męnt], *s.* Ilustración, instrucción, iluminación.
Enlink [en-liŋk'], *va.* Encadenar, eslabonar, ligar.
Enlist [en-list'], *va.* 1. Alistar, sentar o poner a alguno en una lista. 2. Alistar, reclutar soldados. 3. Ganar el interés y apoyo de otro; empeñar.—*vn.* 1. Alistarse, entrar voluntariamente en el servicio militar o naval. (Mil.) Sentar plaza. 2. Adherirse, tomar partido por, empeñarse en algo con interés.
Enliven [en-laiv'-n], *va.* 1. Vivificar, animar. 2. Alentar. 3. Avivar, alegrar, regocijar, causar alegría.
Enlivener [en-laiv'-n-ęr], *s.* Vivificador, animador.
Enlivening [en-laiv'-n-ing], *s.* Lo que hace alegre, jovial o que causa placer.
Enmesh [en-mesh'], *va.* Enredar, enmarañar, hacer caer en la red.
Enmity [en'-mi-ti], *s.* Enemistad, odio, malevolencia; malicia; oposición.
Enmoss [en-mos'], *va.* Cubrir con musgo o con algo como musgo.
Ennead [en'-ę-ad], *s.* El número nueve; sistema o grupo de nueve objetos.
Enneadic [en-e-ad'-ic], *a.* Noveno, novena, relativo a nueve.
Enneagon [en'-ę-a-gon], *s.* (Geom.) Eneágono, polígono de nueve ángulos y nueve lados.
Ennoble [en-nō'-bl], *va.* 1. Ennoblecer. 2. Ilustrar, engrandecer. 3. Elevar, levantar.
Ennoblement [en-nō'-bl-męnt], *s.* Ennoblecimiento.
Ennui [āñ-wī'], *s.* Displicencia, aburrimiento, tedio, enfado. Es voz francesa.
Enorm [ę-nōrm'], *a.* (Ant.) Irregular, enorme; perverso.
Enormity [ę-nōr'-mi-ti], *s.* Enormidad, exceso, demasía; atrocidad, delito enorme; fealdad, ruindad. *Enormities,* Atrocidades horribles.
Enormous [ę-nōr'-mus], *a.* 1. Enorme, irregular, desmesurado; excesivo, demasiado. 2. Perverso, atroz, nefando.
Enormously [ę-nōr'-mus-li], *adv.* Enormemente.
Enormousness [ę-nōr'-mus-nes], *s.* Enormidad.
Enough [ę-nuf'], *a.* Bastante, suficiente.—*s.* Lo bastante, lo suficiente.—*adv.* Bastantemente, suficientemente.—*inter.* ¡Basta!
Enounce [e-nauns'], *va.* Declarar, publicar.
Enow [ę-nau'], *a., s.* y *adv.* (Ant. o Poét.) *V.* ENOUGH.
Enquicken [en-cwic'-n], *va.* (Des.) Avivar.
Enquire [en-cwair'], *va.* Inquirir. *V.* INQUIRE y sus derivados.
Enquirer [en-cwair'-ęr], *s.* *V.* INQUIRER.
Enrage [en-rêj'], *va.* Enfurecer, irritar, provocar, encolerizar.
Enrank [en-raŋk'], *va.* Enfilar.
Enrapt [en-rapt'], *a.* Arrebatado, entusiasmado: transportado, extasiado.
Enrapture [en-rap'-chur], *va.* Arrebatar, elevar, transportar, arrobar, extasiar.
Enravish [en-rav'-ish], *va.* Arrebatar, extasiar, enajenar.
Enravishment [en-rav'-ish-męnt], *s.* Arrobamiento, rapto, enajenamiento, pasmo, alborozo, éxtasis.
Enregister [en-rej'-is-tęr], *va.* Registrar, empadronar.
Enrich [en-rich'], *va.* 1. Enriquecer, hacer rico y opulento. 2. Fecundar, fertilizar. 3. Mejorar la calidad de algo, hacerle adiciones de valor. 4. Enriquecer, adornar, embellecer, aumentar la hermosura de alguna cosa.
Enrichment [en-rich'-męnt], *s.* 1. Enriquecimiento; abono, beneficio que se da a las tierras. 2. Adorno, embellecimiento.
‡**Enridge** [en-rij'], *va.* Formar protuberancias longitudinales; formar surcos.
Enring [en-ring'], *va.* Cercar, rodear con anillos.
Enrobe [en-rōb'], *va.* Vestir, adornar o cubrir con vestidos.
Enroll [en-rōl'], *va.* 1. Alistar, sentar o escribir en una lista. 2. Registrar. 3. Envolver, arrollar. *To enroll one's self a soldier,* Sentar plaza de soldado.
Enroller [en-rōl'-ęr], *s.* Registrador.
Enrolment [en-rōl'-męnt], *s.* Registro, protocolo.
Enroot [en-rūt'], *va.* Arraigar, radicar.
En route [āñ rūt], *adv.* En el camino, en ruta. (Gal.)
Ens [enz], *s.* Ente, ser; entidad.
Ensample [en-sam'-pl], *s.* (Ant.) *V* EXAMPLE.
†**Ensample**, *va.* *V.* EXEMPLIFY.
Ensanguine [en-saŋ'-gwin], *va.* Ensangrentar.
Ensate [en'-sêt], *a.* (Biol.) Ensiforme, en forma de espada.

Enschedule [en-sked'-yul], *va.* Insertar en algún escrito.
Ensconce [en-scons'], *va.* 1. Cubrir, resguardar, poner a cubierto, establecer cómodamente. Se usa a menudo como reflexivo. 2. (Ant.) Defender, proteger con un fortín.
Enseal [en-sîl'], *va.* (Ant.) Imprimir, señalar como con un sello.
Enseam [en-sîm'], *va.* Coser o hacer costura.
Ensemble [an-san'-bl], *s.* 1. El conjunto, el total, la apariencia y efecto generales. 2. Vestido de mujer de más de una pieza.
Ensheathe [en-shîdh'], *va.* Envainar, meter en (o como en) la vaina; encerrar, incluir.
Enshrine [en-shrain'], *va.* Guardar como reliquia.
Enshroud [en-shraud'], *va.* Cubrir, proteger como con una mortaja; y de aquí, envolver, esconder.
Ensiform [en'-si-fōrm], *a.* Ensiforme, en forma de espada.
Ensign [en'-sain], *s.* 1. (Mil.) Bandera, insignia de un regimiento. 2. (Mar.) Bandera de popa. 3. Insignia, divisa. 4. (Mil.) Abanderado, el oficial que lleva la bandera.
†**Ensign** [en-sain'], *va.* Señalar con algún indicio o nota; distinguir por algún adorno o divisa.
Ensign-bearer [en'-sain-bār'-ęr], *s.* Abanderado.
Ensigncy [en'-sain-si], *s.* Empleo o dignidad de abanderado.
Ensilage [en'-si-lęj], *s.* Ensilaje, la acción y efecto de ensilar; y el forraje conservado en un silo o subterráneo.
Enskied [en-skaid'], *a.* (Ant. y Poét.) Celestial; encumbrado, puesto sobre las nubes.
Enslave [en-slêv'], *va.* Esclavizar, cautivar.
Enslavement [en-slêv'-męnt], *s.* Esclavitud, cautiverio, servidumbre.
Enslaver [en-slê'-vęr], *s.* Esclavizador.
Ensnare [en-snār'], *va.* 1. Entrampar, hacer caer a algún animal en una trampa. 2. Engañar, tender un lazo.
Ensphere [en-sfîr'], *va.* Colocar en esfera, redondear.
Enstamp [en-stamp'], *va.* Estampar o imprimir una señal.
Ensue [en-siū'], *vn.* 1. Seguirse, inferirse. 2. Suceder o continuar una cosa a otra por orden, turno o número.—*va.* (Ant.) Seguir, perseguir, ir en seguimiento de alguna cosa. *Seek peace and ensue it,* Buscad la paz, y seguidla.
Ensure [en-shūr'], *va.* 1. Asegurar, dar seguridad y fianza de alguna cosa. 2. Asegurar, dar seguro. *V.* INSURE.
Ensurer [en-shūr'-ęr], *s.* Asegurador.
Entablature [en-tab'-la-chur], **Entablement** [en-tê'-bl-męnt], *s.* (Arq.) Entablamento.
Entad [en'-tad], *adv.* (Anat. y Zool.) Hacia el centro del cuerpo o de un órgano; opuesto a *ectad.*
Entail [ên-têl'], *s.* 1. Vínculo, mayorazgo. 2. Cualquier cosa transmitida como herencia inalienable.
Entail, *va.* 1. Vincular, sujetar los bienes a vínculo. 2. Vincular; asegurar o fundar alguna cosa en otra; perpetuar, continuar, fincar, establecer. 3. Transmitir, legar; imponer, ocasionar, causar; traer sobre otro como consecuencia o legado.
Ental [en'-tal], *a.* (Anat. y Zool.) De lo interior; opuesto a *ectal.*
Entangle [en-taŋ'-gl], *va.* 1. Enredar, emarañar, embrollar, embarazar, intrincar. 2. Multiplicar las dificultades de una obra.
Entanglement [en-tan'-gl-męnt], *s.* Enredo, embarazo, confusión, perplejidad.
Entangler [en-taŋ'-gler], *s.* Enredador, embrollón.
Entender [en-ten'-dęr], *va.* (Ant.) Enternecer, ablandar, poner tierna y blanda una cosa.
Enter [en'-tęr], *va.* 1. Entrar; penetrar. 2. Hacer empezar o emprender alguna cosa; introducir. 3. Asentar o poner por escrito, registrar. 4. Hacerse miembro de; unirse a; ser iniciado. 5. Ingerir, insertar. 6. (Com.) Declarar, hacer una declaración de géneros en la aduana. 7. (For.) Incoar (un procedimiento); notar, archivar.—*vn.* 1. Entrar, ir o venir adentro. 2. Penetrar, alcanzar con el discurso. 3. Meterse en algún asunto; dar principio a una cosa, empeñarse en algo.
Enter, *prefijo. V.* INTER.
Enterclose [en'-tęr-clōs''], *s.* (Arq.) Pasadizo, corredor, pasillo, comunicación entre dos piezas o cuartos.
Enterer [en'-tęr-ęr], *s.* El que entra o principia.
Enteric [en-ter'-ic], *a.* Entérico, perteneciente a los intestinos. *Enteric fever,* Fiebre tifoidea. (< Gr.)
Entering [en'-tęr-ing], *s.* Entrada, paso.
Enteritis [en''-tęr-ai'-tis o î'-tis], *s.* Enteritis, inflamación de la mucosa de los intestinos.
Enterocele [en'-ter-o-sîl], *s.* (Cir.) Enterocele, hernia inguinal o femoral.
Enterocolitis [en''-tęr-o-co-li'-tis ó lai'-tis], *s.* Enterocolitis, inflamación de los intestinos delgados y del colon.
Enteromphalos [en-ter-om'-fa-les], *s.* (Cir.) Enterónfalo, hernia umbilical producida por los intestinos.
Enterotome [en'-ter-o-tōm], *s.* (Med.) Enterótomo, instrumento quirúrgico que sirve para abrir los intestinos.
Enterozoa [en-tęr-o-zō'-a], *s. pl.* Los parásitos intestinales.
Enterprise, Enterprize [en'-tęr-praiz], *s.* 1. Empresa, la determinación de emprender algún negocio arduo; tentativa difícil. 2. Resolución, energía e inventiva en los asuntos prácticos.
Enterprise, *va.* Emprender.
Enterpriser [en'-tęr-praiz-ęr], *s.* Emprendedor.
Enterprising [en'-tęr-praiz-ing], *s.* Empresa.—*a.* Atrevido, enérgico, emprendedor.
Entertain [en-tęr-tên'], *va.* 1. Conversar, hablar, tener conversación con alguno. 2. Convidar; tratar, dar de comer a los que se convida. 3. Hospedar, festejar, agasajar. 4. Mantener, tener alguna persona a su servicio; asistir con o dar asistencias. 5. Concebir, pensar alguna cosa. 6. Entretener, divertir; admitir con satisfacción a alguno.
Entertainable [en-tęr-tên'-a-bl], *a.* Abarcable o contenible en la mente, concebible (como opinión).
Entertainer [en-tęr-tên'-ęr], *s.* 1. Anfitrión, el que convida a otro a comer. 2. El que alegra, regocija o divierte a otros. 3. El que alberga con cordialidad y afecto; huésped.
Entertaining [en-tęr-tên'-ing], *a.* Entretenido, chistoso, alegre, divertido, agradable.
Entertainingly [en-tęr-tên'-ing-li], *adv.* Divertidamente, chistosamente.
Entertainment [en-tęr-tên'-męnt], *s.* 1. Conversación, plática familiar. 2. Convite, agasajo, festín, festejo; mantenimiento. *House of entertainment,* Fonda, posada. 3. Hospedaje, acogida, recibimiento agradable. 4. Empleo, cargo, servicio. 5. Entretenimiento, diversión, pasatiempo en general. 6. Pensamiento, el acto de tener en la mente.
Enthalpy [en'-thal-pi], *s.* Entalpía.
Enthrall [en-thrōl'], *va.* 1. Poner bajo una influencia dominante: dícese del ánimo o de los sentidos. 2. Esclavizar, encadenar; sojuzgar.
Enthrone [en-thrōn'], †**Enthronize** [en-thrō'-naiz], *va.* 1. Entronizar, colocar en el trono. 2. Elevar, instalar como obispo.
Enthronization [en-thro-ni-zé'-shun], *s.* Entronización.
Enthusiasm [en-thū'-zi-azm], *s.* 1. Entusiasmo. 2. Entusiasmo, fantasía, calor o arrebato de la imaginación; pasión a favor de una persona o cosa.
Enthusiast [en-thū'-zi-ast], *s.* Entusiasta; fanático.
Enthusiastic, Enthusiastical [en-thū-zi-as'-tic, al], *a.* Entusiasmado; iluso, fanático, visionario; determinado.
Enthymeme [en'-thi-mîm], *s.* Entimema, silogismo que consta de dos proposiciones; silogismo imperfecto.
Entice [en-tais'], *va.* Halagar, acariciar, atraer con halagos o esperanzas; excitar, inducir. *To entice a girl,* Corromper a una doncella. *To entice away,* Tentar, inducir al mal; sonsacar; robar a una doncella.
Enticement [en-tais'-męnt], *s.* 1. Incitación, instigación, sugestión de hacer alguna cosa mala; seducción. 2. Incitamiento; encantos o atractivos que incitan o inducen al mal.
Enticer [en-tais'-ęr], *s.* Incitador, instigador, seductor.
Enticing [en-tais'-ing], *s.* Incitamiento a hacer algo malo.
Enticingly [en-tais'-ing-li], *adv.* Halagüeñamente, seductoramente.
Entire [en-tair'], *a.* 1. Entero, cabal, cumplido, completo, perfecto. 2. Entero, robusto, sano, fuerte. 3. Entero, constante, firme, fiel, leal, adicto, afecto. 4. Íntegro, imparcial, sincero.
Entirely [en-tair'-li], *adv.* Enteramente, totalmente, absolutamente, fielmente.
Entireness [en-tair'-nes], *s.* 1. Entereza, integridad, totalidad, estado completo. 2. (Ant.) Integridad, honradez.
Entirety [en-tair'-ti], *s.* Totalidad, integridad, entereza.
Entitative [en'-ti-ta-tiv], *a.* (Met.) Lo que se considera por sí mismo separadamente de todas las circunstancias accesorias.
Entitatively [en'-ti-ta-tiv-li], *adv.* (Poco us.) Por sí mismo.
Entitle [en-tai'-tl], *va.* 1. Titular; intitular. 2. Tener derecho, habilitar, conceder o dar algún derecho, privilegio o pretexto; calificar; autorizar.
Entity [en'-ti-ti], *s.* Entidad, ente.
Ento-, Ent-. Formas de combinación: derivadas del griego *entos,* dentro de, interior.

Entomb [en-tūm'], *va.* Enterrar, sepultar, colocar un cadáver en el sepulcro.

Entombment [en-tūm'-mẹnt], *s.* Entierro, sepultura.

Entomological, Entomologic [en-to-mo-lej'-ic, al], *a.* Entomológico, perteneciente a la entomología.

Entomologist [en-to-mel'-o-jist], *s.* Entomólogo, naturalista consagrado a la entomología.

Entomologize [en-to-mel'-o-jaiz], *vn.* Estudiar la entomología; coleccionar insectos para investigación científica.

Entomology [en-to-mel'-o-ji], *s.* 1. Entomología, la parte de la zoología que trata especialmente de los insectos. 2. Tratado sobre esta materia.

Entomophagous [en-to-mef'-a-gus], *a.* Entomófago, insectívoro.

Entozoa [en-to-zō'-a], *s. pl.* Entozoarios, los animales parásitos dentro de los cuerpos de otros.

Entozoan [en-to-zō'-an], *a.* *V.* ENTOZOIC.—*s.* Uno de los entozoarios.

Entozoic [en-to-zō'-ic], *a.* 1. Que vive dentro de otro animal; entozoico, de los entozoarios. 2. (Bot.) Que vive dentro de un animal.

Entozoon [en-to-zō'-en], *s.* (*pl.* ZOA). Uno de los entozoarios.

Entrails [en'-trēlz], *s. pl.* 1. Entrañas, las vísceras contenidas en las cavidades del cuerpo, y se da particularmente este nombre a las del vientre. 2. Lo más interior y oculto de alguna cosa. El singular *entrail* se usa rara vez.

Entrammelled [en-tram'-eld], *a.* Encrespado, enredado.

Entrance [en'-trans], *s.* 1. Entrada, el acto de entrar, en cualquier sentido. 2. Entrada, el sitio por donde se entra a alguna parte (puerta, paso, boca o embocadura de río, etc.). 3. Permiso o facultad de entrar. 4. Principio, el acto de empezar; conocimiento anticipado. 5. Toma de posesión de un empleo o dignidad.

Entrance [en-trgns'], *va.* Extasiar, transportar, suspender o arrebatar el ánimo.

Entrant [en'-trant], *a.* Entrante, que entra; que admite.—*s.* Principiante, el que empieza alguna cosa; novicio.

Entrap [en-trap'], *va.* Entrampar; enmarañar, enredar; engañar.

Entreat [en-trīt'], *va.* Rogar, pedir con instancia, suplicar; vencer o conseguir alguna cosa a fuerza de ruegos o instancias; tratar, comunicar.—*vn.* Hacer una súplica, pedir un favor.

Entreatable [en-trīt'-a-bl], *a.* Tratable; accesible al ruego.

Entreater [en-trīt'-ẹr], *s.* Suplicante.

Entreative [en-trīt'-iv], *a.* Suplicativo.

Entreaty [en-trīt'-i], *s.* Petición, ruego, súplica, instancia, solicitud.

Entrée [āṅ-trē'], *s.* 1. Entrada, el acto de entrar. 2. Privilegio de entrar como visitador. 3. (Coc.) Cada uno de los principios o entradas, platos que se sirven en una mesa entre la sopa y el asado. (Fr.)

Entremets [āṇ-tr-mē'], *s. pl.* 1. Intermedios, platos que se sirven en una mesa entre el asado y los postres. 2. Entremés, intermedio, sainete, farsa. 3. *V.* INTERLUDE. (Fr.)

Entrench [en-trench'], *va.* 1. Atrincherar, proteger con trincheras. 2. Hacer trincheras en o sobre.—*vn.* Invadir, infringir. *V.* ENCROACH. En sentido militar se emplean a menudo las formas *intrench*, *intrenchment*, etc.

Entrenchment [en-trench'-mẹnt], *s.* 1. Atrincheramiento, trinchera; parapeto de tierra. 2. Cualquier defensa o protección. 3. El acto y efecto de atrincherar. 4. Infracción, invasión, transgresión. Véase la nota anterior en cuanto al sentido militar.

Entrepot [āṅ'-tr-pō''], *s.* 1. Centro comercial de distribución. 2. Almacén. *V.* DEPOT.

Entrepreneur [en-trẹ-prẹ-nūr'], *s.* Empresario.

Entropy [en'-tro-pi], *s.* Entropía.

Entrust [en-trust'], *va.* 1. Entregar con confianza, confiar, dar en fideicomiso. 2. Poner a cargo o al cuidado de. (Seguido de *with.*) *To entrust one with a secret*, Confiar un secreto a alguien.

Entry [en'-tri], *s.* 1. Entrada, vestíbulo, portal, pórtico por donde se entra en alguna casa. 2. Entrada, el acto de entrar. 3. El acto de tomar posesión de una propiedad. 4. Asiento, anotación o apuntamiento de alguna cosa por escrito. *A little entry*, El pasadizo, o el pasillo. 5. (Mar.) Registro, declaración de entrada de un barco. 6. (Com.) Partida. *Single entry, double entry*, Partida simple, doble.

Entwine [en-twain'], *va.* Entrelazar torciendo.

Entwist [en-twist'], *va.* Torcer; enroscar.

Enucleate [ẹ-niū'-clẹ-ēt], *va.* 1. Descascarar, extraer el núcleo; en cirujía, extraer de un saco o bolsa, extraer de raíz, extirpar. 2. Desenvolver o desarrollar claramente, aclarar; explicar.

Enucleation [ẹ-niū-clẹ-ē'-shun], *s.* Enucleación, acción de extirpar, de extraer un tumor en su totalidad.

Enumerate [ẹ-niū'-mẹr-ēt], *va.* Enumerar, numerar.

Enumeration [ẹ-niu-mẹr-ē'-shun], *s.* 1. Enumeración, cómputo o cuenta numeral; y de aquí, catálogo. 2. (Ret.) Enumeración, recapitulación.

Enumerative [ẹ-niu'-mẹr-a-tiv], *a.* Enumerativo.

Enunciate [ẹ-nun'-si-ēt o shi-ēt], *va.* 1. Articular, pronunciar. 2. Enunciar, declarar, manifestar.

Enunciation [ẹ'nun-si-ē' (o shi-ē')-shun], *s.* 1. Pronunciación, articulación de sonidos vocales; producción. 2. Enunciación, noticia, conocimiento, declaración pública; expresión en los escritos; prolación.

Enunciative [ẹ-nun'-shi-a-tiv], *a.* Enunciativo, declarativo.

Enunciatively [ẹ-nun'-shi-a-tiv-li], *adv.* Enunciativamente.

Enunciatory [ẹ-nun'-shi-a-tō'-ri], *a.* *V.* ENUNCIATIVE.

Enure [en-yūr'], *vn.* Ponerse en operación; tener efecto; servir para el uso o provecho de. *V.* INURE.

Envelop [en-vel'-up], **Envelope** [en-vel'-ōp], *va.* Envolver, aforrar, esconder.

Envelope [en'-ve-lōp], *s.* 1. Envoltura, envolvedor. 2. Sobre de carta, cubierta, sobrescrito.

Envelopment [en-vel'-up-mẹnt], *s.* Envolvimiento; lo que envuelve, cubierta, envolvedor.

Envenom [en-ven'-um], *va.* Envenenar, atosigar; enfurecer, irritar; hacer odioso.

Enviable [en'-vi-a-bl], *a.* Envidiable.

Envier [en'-vi-ẹr], *s.* Envidiador, el que envidia.

Envious [en'-vi-us], *a.* Envidioso, lleno de envidia.

Enviously [en'-vi-us-li], *adv.* Envidiosamente.

Enviousness [en'-vi-us-nes], *s.* Envidia; carácter envidioso.

Environ [en-vai'-run], *va.* Rodear, cercar, bloquear, sitiar; envolver.

Environment [en-vai'-run-mẹnt], *s.* Ambiente, medio ambiente. Todo lo que cerca y rodea; todas las circunstancias externas de un organismo.

Environmental [en-vai-run-ment'-al], *a.* Ambiental.

Environs [en-vai'-runz], *s. pl.* Contornos, alrededores, cercanías o inmediaciones, el terreno o sitios de que está rodeado cualquier lugar o población; afueras, suburbios.

Envoy [en'-vei], *s.* Enviado, ministro público, inferior al embajador; mensajero.

Envoyship [en'-vei-ship], *s.* Legación, dignidad de enviado.

Envy [en'-vi], *va.* y *vn.* 1. Envidiar, tener envidia, sentir el bien ajeno. 2. Envidiar, desear el goce del mismo bien que otro posee.

Envy, *s.* Envidia; emulación; rencor.

Envying [en'-vi-ing], *s.* Malicia, malignidad.

Enwheel [en-hwīl'], *va.* Rodear, circuir.

Enwomb [en-wūm'], *va.* 1. (Ant. y Poét.) Sepultar o esconder en las entrañas o en lo más profundo de alguna cosa. 2. (Des.) Empreñar.

Enwrap [en-rap'], *va.* Envolver.

Enwrapment [en-rap'-mẹnt], *s.* Cubierta, envolvedor.

Enwreathe [en-rīdh'], *va.* Rodear como con una guirnalda.

Enzymatic, Enzymic [en-ze-mat'-ic, en-zai'-mic], *a.* Enzimático.

Enzyme [en'-zaim], *s.* Enzima.

Enzymology [en-zi-mel'-o-ji], *s.* Enzimología.

Eocene [ī'-o-sīn], *a.* (Geol.) Eoceno, eocena; se dice de la capa más antigua de los terrenos terciarios.—*s.* Época eocena.

Eolian [ẹ-ō'-li-an], **Eolic** [ẹ-el'-ic], *a.* Eólico, uno de los cinco dialectos de la lengua griega. *Eolian harp*, Arpa de Eolo, instrumento músico de cuerdas que suenan movidas por el viento.

Eolipile [ẹ-el'-i-pail], *s.* Eolípila, instrumento de física; esfera hueca de metal con un tubo, que sirve para hacer experimentos con el vapor.

Eon o **Æon** [ī'-en], *s.* Eón, espacio incalculable de tiempo.

Eosin [ī'-o-sin], *s.* Eosina, nombre de una materia colorante rojiza ($C_{20}H_8Br_4O_5$). Se obtiene del alquitrán de hulla.

Epact [ep'-act], *s.* Epacta, el número de días en que el año solar excede al lunar común.

Eparch [ep'-ārc], *s.* 1. Hiparca, sátrapa, gobernador de una provincia griega. 2. Obispo ruso metropolitano u otro.

Epaulet [ep'-ō-let], *s.* (Mil.) Charretera.

Epaulement [ep-ōl'-mẹnt], *s.* (Fort.) Espalda, espaldón.

Epenetic [ep-e-net'-ic], *a.* Laudatorio, panegírico.

Epenthesis [ep-en'-the-sis], *s.* (Gram.)

Epéntesis, interposición de una letra o sílaba en medio de una palabra.
Epergne [ê-pern'], *s.* Centro de mesa, adorno para la mesa del comedor.
Ephah [î'-fa], *s.* Efa, medida hebraica de una fanega.
Ephemera [ef-em'-e-ra], *s.* 1. Efémera o efímera, calentura que dura regularmente sólo un día y que vulgarmente se llama causón. 2. Insecto efímero o que vive un solo día.
Ephemeral [ef-em'-e-ral], **Ephemeric** [ef-e-mer'-ic], *a.* Efímero, lo que empieza y acaba en un mismo día.
Ephemerides [ef-e-mer'-i-dîz], *s. pl.* Efemérides o tablas astronómicas.
Ephemeris [ef-em'-e-ris], *s.* Efemérides, libro o comentario en que se refieren los hechos de cada día; diario.
Ephemerist [ef-em'-e-rist], *s.* Astrólogo.
Ephemerous [ef-em'-e-rus], *a.* (Poco us.) Efímero, efimeral.
Ephesian [e-fî'-zhan], *a.* Efesino, efesina, de Efeso.
Ephialtes [ef-i-al'-tîz], *s.* Pesadilla, opresión nocturna. *V.* NIGHTMARE.
Ephod [ef'-od], *s.* Efod, adorno de los sacerdotes hebreos.
Ephor [ef'-or], *s.* (*pl.* EPHORS y EFORI). Eforo, nombre que se daba en Esparta y otras ciudades dóricas a los cinco magistrados elegidos por el pueblo.
Epi-. Preposición griega usada como prefijo. Quiere decir en, sobre, al lado de, etc. Delante de una vocal se convierte en *ep-* y en *eph-* delante de ' la inspiración fuerte.
Epic [ep'-ic], *a.* Epico, lo que pertenece a la epopeya o poesía heroica.—*s.* Poema épico, epopeya.
Epicarp [ep'-i-cārp], *s.* (Bot.) Epicarpo, la membrana que exteriormente cubre el pericarpio.
Epicede, Epicedium [ep-i-sîd', i-um], *s.* Epicedio, elegía.
Epicedian [ep-i-sîd'-i-an], *a.* Elegíaco.
Epicene [ep'-i-sîn], *a.* (Gram.) Epiceno; de género común.
Epicenter [ep'-i-sen'-ter], *s.* 1. Epicentro. 2. Cualquier punto focal.
Epicure [ep'-i-kiūr], *s.* Epicúreo.
Epicurean [ep-i-kiu-rî'-an], *a.* Epicúreo, el que se entrega a los placeres desordenadamente.—*s.* Sectario de Epicuro.
Epicurism [ep'-i-kiur-izm], *s.* Epicureísmo, sensualidad, la doctrina de Epicuro.
Epicurize [ep'-i-kiur-aiz], *vn.* Seguir la doctrina de Epicuro; deleitarse sensualmente; complacerse en el mal de otro.
Epicycle [ep'-i-sai-cl], *s.* Epiciclo, círculo cuyo centro se supone estar en la circunferencia de otro.
Epicycloid [ep-i-sai'-cloid], *s.* Epicicloide, curva descrita por el movimiento de un círculo sobre la circunferencia de otro.
Epidemic, Epidemical [ep-i-dem'-ic, al], *a.* Epidémico, epidemial; general, universal.—*s.* Epidemia, enfermedad general, que se extiende a lo lejos.
†**Epidemy** [ep'-i-dem-i], *s.* Epidemia.
Epidermal [ep-i-der'-mal], *a.* Epidérmico, cuticular, de la epidermis.
Epidermic, Epidermical [ep-i-der'-mic, al], *a.* Epidérmico, que cubre el cutis; semejante a la epidermis.
Epidermis, Epiderm [ep-i-der'-mis, ep'-i-derm], *s.* 1. Epidermis, cutícula. 2. (Bot.) Epidermis, capa exterior de celdillas que cubre la superficie de una planta.
Epigastric [ep-i-gas'-tric], *a.* Epigástrico.
Epigastrium [ep-i-gas'-tri-um], *s.* Epigastrio, región superior del abdomen, especialmente la que queda sobre el estómago.
Epigee [ep'-i-jî], *s.* Perigeo. *V.* PERIGEE.
Epiglottis [ep-i-glot'-is], *s.* Epiglotis, cartílago elástico, ovalado, que tapa la glotis al tiempo de la deglución.
Epigram [ep'-i-gram], *s.* Epigrama.
Epigrammatic, Epigrammatical [ep-i-gram-mat'-ic, al], *a.* Epigramático.
Epigrammatist [ep-i-gram'-a-tist], *s.* Epigramatista.
Epigraph [ep'-i-graf], *s.* 1. Epígrafe, título, inscripción. 2. Epígrafe, la sentencia que suelen poner los autores a la cabeza de una obra o de sus capítulos.
Epilepsy [ep'-i-lep-si], *s.* Epilepsia, gota coral, mal caduco.
Epileptic, Epileptical [ep-i-lep'-tic, al], *a.* Epiléptico.
Epilogistic [ep-i-lo-jis'-tic], *a.* Epilogal.
Epilogize [e-pil'-o-jaiz], *va.* Dar epílogo; proveer de un epílogo.—*vn.* Epilogar; recitar un epílogo.
Epilogue [ep'-i-log], *s.* Epílogo, conclusión o peroración de un discurso, o de un poema dramático.
Epinicion [ep-i-nis'-i-on], *s.* Himno de victoria.
Epiphany [e-pif'-a-ni], *s.* Epifanía, día de Reyes, festividad que celebra la Iglesia el seis de Enero, en conmemoración de la Adoración de los Reyes.
Epiphonema [ep-i-fo-nî'-ma], *s.* Epifonema, exclamación.
Epiphora [e-pif'-o-ra], *s.* Epífora, lagrimeo involuntario y repentino.
Epiphyllospermous [ep-i-fil-o-sper'-mus], *a.* Epifilospermo o dorsífero; dícese de las plantas que tienen la semilla en el dorso de las hojas.
Epiphysis [e-pif'-i-sis], *s.* (Anat.) Epífisis, eminencia huesosa, separada del cuerpo principal del hueso por una capa cartilaginosa.
Epiphytal [ep-i-fai'-tal], *a.* Epífito, que crece sobre otros vegetales sin que le sirvan de alimento.
Epiphyte [ep'-i-fait], *s.* Epífita, la planta no parásita que crece sobre otros vegetales.
Episcopacy [e-pis'-co-pa-si], *s.* 1. Episcopado, el gobierno de una iglesia por obispos, especialmente por los tres órdenes de obispos, presbíteros y diáconos. 2. Episcopado, dignidad de obispo. 3. El conjunto de los obispos.
Episcopal [e-pis'-co-pal], *a.* 1. Episcopal, aquello cuyo gobierno se confía a los obispos. 2. Episcopal, perteneciente o relativo al obispo.
Episcopalian [e-pis-co-pé'-li-an], *a.* Episcopal, perteneciente a la Iglesia protestante episcopal, sus doctrinas, ceremonial, etc.—*s.* 1. Episcopal, el que no reconoce al Papa, y considera a cada obispo como cabeza de la iglesia. 2. Individuo de la Iglesia protestante episcopal.
Episcopally [e-pis'-co-pal-i], *adv.* Episcopalmente.
Episcopate [e-pis'-co-pêt], *s.* Obispado.
Episcopy [e-pis'-co-pi], *s.* (Poco us.) Pesquisa, inspección.
Episode [ep'-i-sōd], *s.* Episodio, digresión.
Episodic, Episodical [ep-i-sod'-ic, al], *a.* Episódico.
Epispastic [ep-i-spas'-tic], *a.* y *s.* Epispástico; vejigatorio.
Episperm [ep'-i-sperm], *s.* (Bot.) Episperma, tegumento exterior que envuelve la semilla.
Epistaxis [ep-i-stax'-is], *s.* Epistaxis, flujo de sangre por las narices.
Epistemology [e-pis-te-mol'-o-ji], *s.* Epistemología.
Epistle [e-pis'-l], *s.* Epístola, carta. (Voz más formal que *letter*, y aplicada especialmente a las epístolas apostólicas.)
Epistler [e-pis'-ler], *s.* Escritor de cartas; epistolero, el que lee o canta la epístola en el oficio divino.
Epistolary [e-pis'-to-le-ri], **Epistolical** [e-pis-tol'-i-cal], *a.* Epistolar.
Epistrophe [ep-is'-tro-fe], *s.* 1. (Ret.) Conversión. 2. (Mús.) Estribillo.
Epistyle [ep'-i-stail], *s.* Epístilo, arquitrabe.
Epitaph [ep'-i-taf], *s.* Epitafio.
Epitaphian [ep-i-taf'-i-an], **Epitaphic** [ep-i-taf'-ic], *a.* Lo que pertenece al epitafio.
Epitasis [e-pit'-a-sis], *s.* Epítasis, enredo, nudo, parte del poema dramático.
Epithalamium [ep-i-tha-lé'-mi-um], *s.* Epitalamio, himno o canción nupcial.
Epithelial [ep"-i-thî'-li-al], *a.* Epitelial, relativo al epitelio.
Epithelium [ep"-i-thî'-li-um], *s.* (Anat.) Epitelio, capa o cubierta más superficial de las membranas mucosas; también la epidermis.
Epithem [ep'-i-them], *s.* (Med.) Epítima, apósito, confortante.
Epithet [ep'-i-thet], *s.* Epíteto.
Epitome [e-pit'-o-me], *s.* Epítome, resumen, compendio.
Epitomize [i-pit'-o-maiz], *va.* Epitomar, abreviar, compendiar.
Epitomizer [e-pit'-o-maiz-er], **Epitomist** [e-pit'-o-mist], *s.* Abreviador, compendiador.
Epitrope [ep-it'-ro-pi], *s.* (Ret.) Epítrope, concesión, figura por la que se concede una cosa, a fin de hacer admitir otra más importante.
Epizootic [ep-i-zo-ot'-ic], *a.* Epizoótico.—*s.* Epizootia.
Epizooty [ep-i-zō'-o-ti], *s.* Epizootia, enfermedad contagiosa de los ganados.
Epoch [ep'-ec o îp'-ec], **Epocha** [ep'-o-ca], *s.* Epoca, punto fijo y determinado de tiempo desde el cual se comienzan a numerar los años.
Epode [ep'-ōd], *s.* (Poet.) 1. Epodo, epoda, la última parte de la oda; la que sigue a la estrofa y antiestrofa. 2. Especie de composición lírica en la que un verso largo va seguido de uno corto.
Epopee [ep'-o-pî], *s.* Epopeya, poema épico.
Epsom salts [ep'-sum sōlts], *s. pl.* Epsomita, sal de Epsom, sal de Higuera, sulfato de magnesia.
Epulotic [ep-yu-lot'-ic], *a.* Epulótico, cicatrizativo.
Equability [î-cwa-bil'-i-ti], *s.* Igualdad, uniformidad.
Equable [î'-cwa-bl o ec'-wa-bl], *a.* Igual, uniforme.
Equableness [î'-cwa-bl-nes], *s.* *V.* EQUABILITY.
Equably [î'-cwa-bli], *adv.* Igualmente.
Equal [î'-cwal], *a.* 1. Igual, seme-

jante. 2. Adecuado, propio para una cosa, en estado de. 3. Imparcial, justo, recto ; neutral. 4. Indiferente. 5. Lo que es ventajoso a dos partes que tienen intereses contrarios. 6. (Bot.) Que tiene los dos lados semejantes, como las hojas ; simétrico.—*s.* El que no es inferior ni superior a otro ; igual.

Equal, *va.* 1. Igualar, hacer igual una persona o cosa con otra. 2. Recompensar, compensar, satisfacer enteramente. *Not to be equalled*, Sin igual.

Equality [ẹ-cwel'-ɪ-tɪ], *s.* 1. Igualdad, uniformidad, semejanza perfecta. 2. Calidad de nivelado, nivel.

Equalize, Equalise [í'-cwal-aiz], *va.* y *vn.* Igualar.

Equalization, Equalisation [ɪ-cwal-ɪ-zé'-shun], *s.* Igualamiento.

Equally [í'-cwal-ɪ], *adv.* Igualmente ; imparcialmente, uniformemente.

Equalness [í'-cwal-nes], *s.* Uniformidad, igualdad, ecuanimidad.

Equanimity [í''-cwa-nim'-ɪ-tɪ], *s.* Ecuanimidad, igualdad y serenidad de ánimo.

Equanimous [ɪ-cwan'-ɪ-mus], *a.* (Poco us.) Igual, constante.

Equation [ẹ-cwé'-shun], *s.* Ecuación.

Equator [ɪ-cwé'-tẹr], *s.* Ecuador.

Equatorial [ɪ-cwa-tō'-rɪ-al], *a.* Ecuatorial, perteneciente al ecuador ; relativo, cercano o determinado por un ecuador, especialmente el terrestre.—*s.* Ecuatorio, gran telescopio que gira sobre dos ejes en ángulo recto, uno de los cuales es paralelo al eje de la tierra ; así se logra que un objeto dado permanezca constantemente en el campo del telescopio, a pesar del movimiento de rotación de la tierra.

Equerry [ec'-we-rɪ], *s.* 1. Caballerizo del rey. 2. Establo, de un príncipe.

Equestrian [ẹ-cwes'-trɪ-an], *a.* Ecuestre.

Equi- [ɪ-cwɪ]. Forma de combinación. (< Lat. *æquus*, igual.)

Equiangular [ɪ-cwɪ-aṇ'-giu-lar], *a.* Equiángulo.

Equicrural [ɪ-cwɪ-crū'-ral], *a.* Lo que tiene sus miembros o lados iguales ; isósceles.

Equidistance [ɪ-cwɪ-dis'-tans], *s.* Equidistancia.

Equidistant [ɪ-cwɪ-dis'-tant], *a.* Equidistante.

Equidistantly [ɪ-cwɪ-dis'-tant-lɪ], *adv.* A la misma distancia.

Equiformity [ɪ-cwɪ-fōrm'-ɪ-tɪ], *s.* Uniformidad.

Equilateral [ɪ-cwɪ-lat'-ẹr-al], *a.* y *s.* Equilátero, de lados iguales.

Equilibrate [ɪ-cwɪ-laɪ'-brēt], *va.* 1. Equilibrar. 2. Contrapesar.

Equilibration [ɪ-cwɪ-lɪ-bré'-shun], *s.* Equilibración ; equilibrio.

Equilibrious [ɪ-cwɪ-lib'-rɪ-us], *a.* (Estát.) Equilibre, que está equilibrado.

Equilibriously [ɪ-cwɪ-lib'-rɪ-us-lɪ], *adv.* En equilibrio.

Equilibrist [ẹ-cwil'-ɪ-brist], *s.* El que equilibra.

Equilibrity [ɪ-cwɪ-lib'-rɪ-tɪ], *s.* Equilibrio, igualdad de peso.

Equilibrium [ɪ-cwɪ-lib'-rɪ-um], *s.* Equilibrio, la posición igual que guardan los dos extremos de una palanca o balanza ; contrapeso.

Equine [í'-cwin ó í'-cwain], *a.* Caballuno, del caballo, que pertenece o se parece al caballo.—*s.* Caballo o animal parecido a él, como la cebra.

Equinoctial [ɪ-cwɪ-nec'-shal], *a.* Equinoccial, lo perteneciente al equinoccio.—*s.* Línea equinoccial.

Equinoctially [ɪ-cwɪ-nec'-shal-ɪ], *adv.* En dirección equinoccial.

Equinox [í'-cwɪ-necs], *s.* Equinoccio, la entrada del sol en los puntos equinocciales.

‡**Equinumerant** [ɪ-cwɪ-niū'-mẹr-ant], *a.* Igual en número.

Equip [ẹ-cwip'], *va.* Equipar, pertrechar, proveer de lo necesario. *To equip one with money*, Dar a alguno el dinero que necesita. *To equip a ship*, Aprestar un navío.

Equipage [ec'-wɪ-pēj], *s.* 1. Equipaje, los artículos esenciales para un objeto o fin determinado, como el conjunto de ropas y objetos que se llevan en los viajes. *V.* EQUIPMENT, 3ª acep. 2. Carroza. 3. Tren, el aparato de criados, etc., que lleva un personaje en las funciones de pompa y ostentación.

Equipaged [ec'-wɪ-pējd], *a.* (Ant.) Equipado, aparejado ; decorado espléndidamente.

Equipendency [ɪ-cwɪ-pen'-den-sɪ], *s.* Peso igual, equilibrio.

Equipment [ẹ-cwip'-mẹnt], *s.* 1. Equipo, el acto de equipar. 2. Equipaje. 3. Apresto, hablando de buques ; equipo o provisión para un objeto especial. 4. Fornitura, montura, uniformes.

Equipoise [í'-cwɪ-peiz], *s.* 1. Equilibrio, igualdad de peso ó de fuerza. 2. Contrapeso. *V.* COUNTERPOISE.

Equipollence, Equipollency [ɪ-cwɪ-pel'-ens, ɪ], *s.* Equipolencia o equivalencia.

Equipollent [ɪ-cwɪ-pel'-ent], *a.* Equipolente o equivalente.

Equipollently [ɪ-cwɪ-pel'-ent-lɪ], *adv.* De un modo equivalente.

Equiponderance, Equiponderancy [ɪ-cwɪ-pen'-dẹr-ans, ɪ], *s.* Igualdad de peso.

Equiponderant [ɪ-cwɪ-pen'-dẹr-ant], *a.* Equiponderante.

‡**Equiponderate** [ɪ-cwɪ-pen'-der-ēt], *vn.* Equiponderar, tener una cosa igual peso que otra.

Equitable [ec'-wɪ-ta-bl], *a.* Equitativo, justo, imparcial.

Equitableness [ec'-wɪ-ta-bl-nes], *s.* Equidad, imparcialidad, justicia.

Equitably [ec'-wɪ-ta-blɪ], *adv.* Equitativamente.

Equitancy [ec'-wɪ-tan-sɪ], *s.* Equitación.

Equitant [ec'-wɪ-tant], *a.* (Bot.) Acaballado : dícese de la posición de las hojas de algunas plantas.

Equitation [ec-wɪ-té'-shun], *s.* Equitación, el arte de montar a caballo ; el manejo del caballo.

Equity [ec'-wɪ-tɪ], *s.* Equidad, justicia, rectitud, imparcialidad.

Equivalence, Equivalency [ẹ-cwiv'-a-lens, ɪ], *s.* 1. Equivalencia. 2. (Quím.) *V.* VALENCE.

Equivalent [ẹ-cwiv'-a-lent], *a.* Equivalente.—*s.* Equivalente, lo que iguala a otra cosa.

Equivalently [ẹ-cwiv'-a-lent-lɪ], *adv.* Equivalentemente.

Equivocal [ẹ-cwiv'-o-cal], *a.* Equívoco, ambiguo, de doble sentido.—*s.* Equívoco.

Equivocally [ẹ-cwiv'-o-cal-ɪ], *adv.* Equivocadamente, ambiguamente.

Equivocalness [ẹ-cwiv'-o-cal-nes], *s.* Equívoco, voz o frase dudosa.

Equivocate [ẹ-cwiv'-o-kēt], *vn.* Usar de palabras o frases equívocas o de expresiones ambiguas que pueden entenderse de dos maneras ; prevaricar.—*va.* Equivocar.

Equivocation [ẹ-cwiv-o-ké'-shun], *s.* Equívoco, vocablo equívoco de que se usa para engañar o divertir ; sentido equívoco, ambigüedad de una frase, anfibología.

Equivocator [ẹ-cwiv'-o-kē-tẹr], *s.* El que usa de equívocos.

Equivoke [ec'-wɪ-vōc], *s.* Equívoco.

-er [ẹr]. Sufijo usado (1) para formar nombres de cosa o persona agente, como -dor en español. To *do*, hacer : *doer*, hacedor. (2) Para formar el grado comparativo ; *long*, largo ; *longer*, más largo. (3) Para formar los verbos llamados en inglés frecuentativos y diminutivos. (4) Para denotar una persona (agente, etc.), sin derivación de un verbo, v. g. *pensioner*, pensionista.

Era [í'-ra], *s.* Era, época o fecha determinada desde la cual se empiezan a contar los años.

Eradiate [ẹ-rē'-dɪ-ēt], *vn.* Radiar ; centellar, relumbrar.

Eradiation [ẹ-rē-dɪ-ē'-shun], *s.* Radiación ; brillo, centelleo.

Eradicate [ẹ-rad'-ɪ-kēt], *va.* Desarraigar, erradicar, destruir, extirpar.

Eradication [ẹ-rad-ɪ-ké'-shun], *s.* Erradicación, extirpación.

Eradicative [ẹ-rad'-ɪ-ca-tiv], *a.* Erradicativo, lo que tiene la virtud de desarraigar.

Erasable, Erasible [ẹ-ré'-sa(sɪ)-bl], *a.* Borrable, que se puede borrar, rayar, raspar, etc.

Erase [ẹ-rēs'], *va.* 1. Cancelar, borrar, rayar, raspar, testar. 2. (Des.) *V.* RAZE.

Erasement [ẹ-rēs'-mẹnt], *s.* (Ant.) Canceladura, testadura. *V.* ERASURE.

Eraser [ẹ-rē'-sẹr], *s.* 1. Borrador, gomma de borrar. 2. Raspador.

Erasion [ẹ-rē'-zhun], *s.* Raspadura, borradura, canceladura ; acción de borrar.

Erasure [ẹ-rē'-zhur], *s.* Raspadura, acción y efecto de raspar, o lo que se quita de la superficie raspando.

Ere [ēr], *adv.* Antes, más pronto, más presto, antes que, más bien que. —*prep.* Antes de.

Erebus [er'-e-bus], *s.* (Mitol.) Erebo, el infierno ; obscuridad, tenebrosidad.

Erect [ẹ-rect'], *va.* 1. Erigir, levantar, poner a plomo. 2. Construir, edificar ; establecer. 3. Exaltar, elevar, alzar a una posición determinada o más elevada. 4. Dibujar sobre una base o plan, como un diseño arquitectónico o una figura geométrica.—*vn.* Erigirse, enderezarse, ponerse derecho.

Erect [ẹ-rect'], *a.* 1. Derecho, levantado hacia arriba, erguido, vertical. 2. Audaz, osado ; vigoroso ; vigilante, atento. 3. Firme. *To sit erect*, Sentarse derecho. *To stand erect*, Estar en pie.

Erectile [ẹ-rec'-tɪl], *a.* Eréctil, capaz de enderezarse o ponerse en erección.

Erection [ẹ-rec'-shun], *s.* Erección, elevación, el acto o procedimiento de edificar o construir; fundación, construcción ; estructura.

Erective [ẹ-rect'-iv], *a.* Levantado, lo que está alzado.

Erectness [ẹ-rect'-nes], *s.* Erección, postura derecha.

Erector [ẹ-rect'-ẹr], *s.* 1. Erector, el que o lo que erige, levanta o endereza, v. gr. un arquitecto, un músculo. 2. Lente de inversión.

Erelong [êr'-lŏng], *adv.* Antes de mucho, dentro de poco tiempo.
Eremite [er'-e-mait], *s.* Ermitaño.
†**Eremitage** [er'-e-mi-têj], *s.* Ermita.
Eremitic, Eremitical [er-e-mit'-ic, al], *a.* Eremítico, solitario.
Erenow [êr-nau'], *adv.* Antes de ahora.
Ereption [e-rep'-shun], *s.* Arrebato; el acto de arrebatar alguna cosa.
Erethism [er'-eth-izm], *s.* (Med.) Eretismo, exaltación anormal de las propiedades vitales de un órgano.
†**Erewhile,** †**Erewhiles** [ār-hwail', z], *adv.* Rato ha, poco ha.
Erg [erg], *s.* (Fís.) Ergio, unidad medidora de trabajo y energía, que representa el esfuerzo necesario para mover un cuerpo del peso de dos gramos a razón de un centímetro por segundo.
Ergo [er'-go], *adv.* Consiguientemente, luego; la conclusión de un argumento. Es voz latina.
Ergot [er'-get], *s.* 1. Cornezuelo de centeno; honguillo parásito en forma de cuerno o espolón de gallo, que a veces se apodera de los granos del centeno, y que es muy perjudicial a la salud de quien lo come. Se usa como medicamento para contener la hemorragia uterina y para otros usos. Claviceps purpurea. 2. (Vet.) Especie de espolón en las patas de los caballos.
Ergotism [er'-go-tizm], *s.* 1. (Med.) Ergotismo, estado de envenenamiento por el cornezuelo de centeno; enfermedad producida por cantidades excesivas del mismo. 2. (Poco común) Conclusión deducida silogísticamente.
†**Eriach** [er'-i-ac], **Eric** [er'-ic], *s.* Multa pecuniaria.
Erica [er-ai'-ca o i'-ca], *s.* (Bot.) *V.* HEATH.
Erin [i'-rin], *s.* Erín, antiguo nombre de Irlanda.
Erinaceous [er-i-nê'-shius], *a.* Del erizo o parecido a él.
Eringo [e-rin'-go], *s.* (Bot.) Eringe, cardo corredor.
Eristic [er-is'-tic], *a.* 1. Erístico, relativo a la controversia. 2. Pendenciero. (< Gr.)
Ermelin [er'-me-lin], *s.* (Ant.) *V.* ERMINE.
Ermine [er'-min], *s.* 1. Armiño, cuadrúpedo pequeño, de piel muy suave y blanquísima en invierno, con una mancha negra en la punta de la cola. 2. La piel de este animal preparada de suerte que las motas negras se destaquen a intervalos regulares sobre el fondo blanco. Se usa en Europa y especialmente en Inglaterra como adorno de las togas de los jueces. 3. De aquí, toga·oficial o dignidad de un juez; pureza ideal del cargo judicial.
Ermined [er'-mind], *a.* Armiñado.
Erode [e-rōd'], *va.* 1. Corroer, roer; comer. 2. (Geol.) Gastar, por medio de diversos agentes.
Erodent [e-rō'-dent], *a.* (Med.) Corrosivo, cáustico (hablando de un medicamento).
Erosion [e-rō'-zhun], *s.* 1. Erosión; corrosión. 2. (Geol.) La acción de gastar o roer las rocas, como por medio del agua.
Erosive [e-rō'-siv], *a.* Que obra por erosión, que tiene la facultad de roer o gastar; erosivo.
Erotic, Erotical [er-et'-ic, al], *a.* Erótico, amatorio.
Erotomania [er-o-to-mé'-ni-a], *s.* Erotomanía, delirio causado por el amor.
Erpetology [er-pet-el'-o-ji], *s.* (Forma errónea.) *V.* HERPETOLOGY.
Err [er], *vn.* 1. Vagar, errar; desviarse. 2. Extraviarse, apartarse del buen camino, pecar. 3. Errar, no dar en el blanco, no acertar.
†**Errable** [er'-a-bl], *a.* Falible, capaz de errar.
Errand [er'-and], *s.* Recado, mensaje, mandado. *Errand-boy,* Muchacho para hacer mandados.
Errant [er'-ant], *a.* 1. Errante, ambulante, vagabundo, vago. 2. Inconstante; vil, abandonado. *Knight-errant,* Caballero andante.
Errantry [er'-ant-ri], *s.* Vida errante; caballería andante.
Errata [er-rê'-ta], *s. pl.* *V.* ERRATUM.
Erratic Erratical [er-rat'-ic, al], *a.* Errático, errante, vagante, vagabundo; irregular. *Erratic, s.* (Desusado) Pícaro.
Erratically [êr-rat'-ic-al-i], *adv.* Erradamente; irregularmente.
Erratum [er-rê'-tum] (*pl.* ERRATA), *s.* Errata, equivocación que se halla en lo impreso o escrito.—*pl.* Erratas, fe de erratas.
Errhine [er'-in], *s.* Errino, remedio tomado por la nariz.
Erring [er'-ing], *a.* Errado, errante.
Erroneous [er-rō'-ne-us], *a.* 1. Errado, falso, erróneo. 2. Irregular, no de acuerdo con la forma legal.
Erroneously [er-rō'-ne-us-li], *adv.* Erróneamente.
Erroneousness [er-rō'-ne-us-nes], *s.* Error.
Error [er'-er], *s.* Error, yerro, equivocación, engaño, descuido; pecado.
Ersatz [er-zāts'], *a.* Sintético.
Erse [ers], *s.* Lenguaje de los montañeses de Escocia.
Erst [erst], *adv.* (Ant. o Poét.) Primero, primeramente, al principio, antiguamente, antes; hasta entonces; hasta ahora.
†**Erstwhile** [erst'-hwail], *adv.* Hasta entonces; en otro tiempo.
Erubescence, Erubescency [er-u-bes'-ens, i], *s.* Erubescencia, rubor.
Erubescent [er-u-bes'-ent], *a.* Colorado; sonrojado, abochornado.
Eruct [e-ruct'], *va.* Eructar, regoldar.
Eructate [e-ruc'-têt], *va.* (Ant.) Eructar; vomitar.
Eructation [e-ruc-tê'-shun], *s.* Eructación, eructo, regüeldo.
Erudite [er'-u-dait], *a.* Erudito, instruído, sabio.
Erudition [er-u-dish'-un], *s.* Erudición, ciencia, doctrina.
Eruginous [e-rū'-ji-nus], *a.* Ruginoso, de color de cardenillo, o parecido al moho del cobre; lo que participa del cobre.
Erupt [e-rupt'], *vn.* Hacer erupción.
Eruption [e-rup'-shun], *s.* 1. Erupción, emisión, salida. 2. Erupción cutánea. 3. Excursión hostil.
Eruptive [e-rup'-tiv], *a.* 1. Eruptivo, que estalla. 2. De, o perteneciente a, la acción volcánica. 3. (Med.) Eruptivo, que produce una erupción cutánea.
Eryngo [e-rin'-go], *s.* (Bot.) Eringe, cardo corredor.
Erysipelas [er-i-sip'-e-las], *s.* Erisipela, afección inflamatoria exantemática o de la piel.
Erysipelatous [er-i-si-pel'-a-tus], *a.* Erisipelatoso, lo que tiene las calidades de la erisipela o se asemeja a ella.
Erythrocyte [e-rith'-ro-sait], *s.* Eritrocito.
Escadrille [es-ca-dril'], *s.* 1. Escuadrilla naval. 2. Escuadrilla aérea.
Escalade [es-ca-lêd'], *s.* **Escalada, la** acción de escalar o poner escalas en los muros.
Escalate [es'-ca-lêt], *va.* Intensificar, aumentar.
Escalation [es-ca-lê'-shun], *s.* Intensificación, aumento.
Escalator [es-ca-lê'-ter], *s.* Escalera mecánica.
Escalop [es-cel'-up], *s.* 1. (Conq.) Pechina, venera de peregrino. 2. Las desigualdades en forma de puntas o dientes en los bordes de alguna cosa. *V.* SCALLOP.
Escapade [es-ca-pêd'], *s.* 1. Escapada, travesura, campanada, extravagancia, acción inconsiderada. 2. Escapada, salida oculta, fuga, huída. 3. Escapada, el acto de dar manotadas y brincos el caballo que caracolea.
Escape [es-kêp'], *va.* Huir, evitar; escapar; eludir.—*vn.* Escapar, salir de algún aprieto o peligro, sustraerse, evadirse, salvarse.
Escape, *s.* 1. Escapada, huída, fuga. 2. Descuido, inadvertencia. 3. Avería, pérdida, merma de un líquido que sale por una abertura. 4. Escapatoria, los medios de fuga o de rescate.
Escape capsule [es-kêp' cap-sul], *s.* (Aer.) Cápsula de emergencia.
Escapement [es-kêp'-ment], *s.* Escape, en relojería.
Escaper [es-kêp'-er], *s.* El que escapa o evita.
Escaping [es-kêp'-ing], *s.* Escape.
Escapism [es-kêp'-izm], *s.* Escapismo.
Escapist [es-kêp'-ist], *s.* Soñador, fantaseador.
Escarp [es-cārp'], *va.* (Mil.) Escarpar, hacer escarpa.
Escarpment [es-carp'-ment], *s.* Escarpa, el declive áspero de cualquier terreno.
Eschar [es'-cār], *s.* Escara, costra o postilla producida por la mortificación o la cauterización.
Escharotic [es-ca-ret'-ic], *a.* Escaró.tico.—*s.* Cáustico.
Escheat [es-chît'], *s.* (For.) Derecho a la sucesión o herencia de una persona por caducación, confiscación o falta de herederos; desherencia, bien caduco.
Escheat, *va.* 1. Confiscar, caducar a favor del fisco.—*vn.* 2. Adquirir el derecho a la sucesión o a la herencia de una propiedad, por confiscación, caducación o falta de herederos legítimos.
Eschew [es-chū'], *va.* Huir, evitar, evadir.
Escort [es'-cert], *s.* 1. Escolta, convoy. 2. El que por cortesía acompaña a una mujer.
Escort [es-cērt'], *va.* Escoltar, convoyar, resguardar.
Escritoire [es-cri-twār'], *s.* Escritorio, mesa para escribir.
Escrow [es-crō'], *s.* (For.) Plica, escrito sellado referente a alguna condición o requisito, que se pone en manos de una tercera persona para entregarlo al donatario, y que no tiene valor ni efecto hasta hacerse dicha entrega.
Esculapian [es-kiu-lé'-pi-an], *a.* Medicinal, referente a Esculapio, dios de la medicina o al arte de curar.

Esculent [es'-kiu-lent], *a.* y *s.* Comestible; comedero.
Escutcheon [es-cuch'-un], *s.* Escudo de armas.
Escutcheoned [es-cuch'-und], *a.* Blasonado.
Eskimo, Eskimau [es'-ki-mō], *s.* Esquimal, habitante de la región boreal de la América del Norte.
Esophagus [ẹ-sef'-a-gus], *s.* Esófago, conducto por donde pasan la comida y bebida al estómago.
Esopian [ẹ-sō'-pi-an], *a.* Esópico, lo tocante a Esopo.
Esoteric [es-o-ter'-ic], *a.* Esotérico, que se enseña a un número limitado de discípulos y es conocido solamente por ellos: de aquí, oculto, reservado; confidencial.
Esoterism [es'-o-ter-izm], *s.* Doctrinas o principios esotéricos; lo oculto.
Espalier [es-pal'-yẹr], *s.* 1. Espaldera, armazón de madera para servir de apoyo a ciertos árboles y plantas enredaderas. 2. Espaldera, cierta dirección dada a los árboles por medio de la poda.
Espalier, *va.* (Jard.) Hacer o formar espalderas.
Especial [es-pesh'-al], *a.* Especial, particular; principal.
Especially [es-pesh'-al-i], *adv.* Especialmente, principalmente.
Espial [es-pai'-al], *s.* Espía; observación, descubrimiento.
Espier [es-pai'-ẹr], *s.* Espiador, espía, espiante.
Espionage [es'-pi-o-nệj], *s.* Espionaje, la acción de espiar; el empleo de espías.
Esplanade [es-pla-nêd'], *s.* 1. Espacio llano y abierto, en especial a los bordes del agua, para pasear a pie o en coche. 2. (Fort.) Explanada. 3. *V.* LAWN.
Espousal [es-pau'-zal], *s.* 1. Desposorio. 2. Adopción, protección.—*a.* Esponsalicio. *Espousals, pl.* Esponsales.
Espouse [es-pauz'], *va.* y *vn.* 1. Desposar o desposarse, contraer esponsales. 2. Casarse, contraer matrimonio. 3. Defender, sostener, adoptar.
Espouser [es-pauz'-ẹr], *s.* Mantenedor, soportador, defensor de alguna causa.
Esprit [es-prî'], *s.* 1. Espíritu. 2. Chiste, agudeza, gracia. (Gal.)
Espy [es-pai'], *va.* Divisar, acechar; averiguar, percibir, descubrir; espiar.—*vn.* (Des.) Velar, mirar al rededor.
Esquimau (*pl.* ESQUIMAUX), *s.* *V.* ESKIMO.
Esquire [es-cwair'], *s.* 1. Escudero; título de honor tan común en Inglaterra como el de *Don* en España. 2. En Inglaterra, dueño de bienes raíces, propietario de provincia. *V.* SQUIRE.
Esquire, *va.* Servir como escudero.
Essay [es-sê'], *va.* 1. Ensayar, tentar, intentar, probar, examinar. 2. Hacer prueba o ensayo de alguna cosa. 3. (Des.) Hacer inspección y reconocimiento de la calidad y bondad de los metales.
Essay [es'-ê], *s.* 1. Conato, empeño, esfuerzo. 2. Ensayo, tentativa; obra suelta; obra o pieza irregular. 3. Ensaye, prueba, experiencia.
Essayer [es-sê'-ẹr], **Essayist** [es'-ê-ist], *s.* Ensayista, escritor de ensayos u obras sueltas.
Essence [es'-ens], *s.* 1. Esencia, el ser y naturaleza de las cosas. 2. Esencia, cierto licor espirituoso; perfume, aceite volátil.
Essenes [es-sînz'], *s. pl.* Esenianos, una secta de judíos. Practicaban la pobreza voluntaria y la comunidad de bienes y aspiraban a un grado superior de santidad.
Essential [es-sen'-shal], *s.* Esencia. —*a.* Esencial, substancial, principal, importante, notable; puro, rectificado.
Essentiality [es-sen-shi-al'-i-ti], *s.* Esencialidad, naturaleza, los principios constituyentes.
Essentially [es-sen'-shal-i], *adv.* Esencialmente.
Essoin [es-soin'], *s.* (Derecho inglés) Excusa, exención; alegación de una persona legalmente citada para no comparecer en juicio.
Essoin, *va.* (For.) Excusar, disculpar.
Essoiner [es-soin'-ẹr], *s.* (For.) Excusador, disculpador.
Establish [es-tab'-lish], *va.* 1. Establecer, fundar, fijar, erigir. 2. Afirmar, confirmar. 3. Probar, demostrar. 4. Ratificar, sancionar.
Establisher [es-tab'-lish-ẹr], *s.* Establecedor.
Establishment [es-tab'-lish-mẹnt], *s.* 1. Establecimiento, ley, ordenanza, estatuto. 2. Fundación, erección, institución; algo establecido, como la iglesia de un estado, una organización militar o naval, etc. 3. Establecimiento, la colocación o suerte estable de una persona; asiento, domicilio. 4. Renta, salario, fortuna que se da o proporciona a una persona. 5. El modo como está constituída una familia.
Estafet [es-ta-fet'], *s.* Estafeta, correo militar.
Estate [es-têt'], *s.* 1. Estado, el público, el interés general de alguna nación. 2. Estado, rango, la condición o calidad de una persona con respecto a sus circunstancias en general. 3. Caudal, bienes, propiedad, fortuna, hacienda, finca. *Man's estate,* La edad viril. *Personal estate,* Bienes muebles. *Real estate,* Bienes raíces o inmuebles. *Third estate,* El estado llano. *Fourth estate,* (jocoso) La prensa periódica; antiguamente la clase baja del estado llano.
†**Estate,** *va.* Dotar, dar o señalar algún caudal o hacienda; establecer, fijar.
Esteem [es-tîm'], *va.* 1. Estimar, apreciar, considerar, honrar, reputar, contemplar. 2. Pensar, juzgar, ser de opinión.—*vn.* Apreciarse, reputarse, tenerse por.
Esteem, *s.* Estimación, estima, aprecio.
Esteemable [es-tîm'-a-bl], *a.* Estimable.
Esteemer [es-tîm'-ẹr], *s.* Estimador, apreciador.
Ester [es'-tẹr], *s.* (Quím.) Éster.
Esthete, Æsthete [es-thît'], *s.* Esteta, partidario o admirador del arte o de la estética.
Esthetic, Æsthetic [es-thet'-ic], *a.* Estético, estética, perteneciente a la ciencia de lo bello.
Esthetical [es-thet'-ic-al], *a.* *V.* ESTHETIC.
Esthetically, Æsthetically [es-thet'-ic-al-i], *adv.* Estéticamente, de una manera estética.
Esthetics, Æsthetics [es-thet'-ics], *s.* Estética, la ciencia que trata de la investigación y determinación de lo bello en la naturaleza y en el arte.
Estimable [es'-ti-ma-bl], *a.* Estimable, digno de estimación, de aprecio.
Estimableness [es'-ti-ma-bl-nes], *s.* Estimabilidad, aprecio.
Estimate [es'-ti-mêt], *va.* Estimar, apreciar, tasar; calcular, computar.
Estimate, *s.* 1. Estimación, tasa, aprecio. 2. Cálculo, cómputo; concierto; presupuesto. 3. Opinión.
Estimation [es-ti-mê'-shun], *s.* 1. Estimación, calculación, valuación; honra. 2. Estimación. 3. Opinión, juicio.
Estimative [es'-ti-ma-tiv], *a.* 1. Estimativo. 2. Lo que compara el valor o la estimación que debe darse a cosas diferentes entre sí para hallar cuál es la más apreciable o de más valor.
Estimator [es'-ti-mê''-tẹr], *s.* Estimador, computista.
Estival [es'-ti-val ó es-tai'-val], *a.* Estival, lo que pertenece al estío o verano; veraniego; estivo, lo que dura todo el estío.
Estivate [es'-ti-vêt], *vn.* Veranear, pasar el verano.
Estivation [es-ti-vê'-shun], *s.* 1. El acto de pasar el tiempo de estío. 2. (Zool.) Descanso de ciertos animales durante el estío. 3. (Bot.) Prefloración, arreglo de las partes de una flor en la yema.
Estop [es-tep'], *va.* 1. (For.) Impedir en un procedimiento judicial la afirmación de lo que es contrario a los actos y admisiones hechos previamente. 2. Excluir o anular uno mismo su demanda en virtud del propio acto o declaración anterior.
Estoppel [es-tep'-el], *s.* 1. (For.) Impedimento, excepción, la acción o admisión que no puede ser negada legalmente. 2. Obstáculo, oposición.
Estovers [es-tō'-vẹrz], *s. pl.* (Der. inglés) Señalamiento o asignación de asistencias, alimentos, etc., por auto de un tribunal.
Estrade [es-trêd'], *s.* 1. Estrado, tarima. *V.* DAIS. 2. (Mil.) Estrada.
Estrange [es-trênj'], *va.* Extrañar, apartar, enajenar.
Estrangement [es-trênj'-mẹnt], *s.* Enajenamiento, extrañeza, distancia, separación voluntaria.
Estray [es-trê'], *s.* (For.) Animal descarriado del rebaño o manada.
Estreat [es-trît'], *va.* 1. (Der. inglés) Extraer, sacar traslado de un original. 2. Imponer una multa.
Estrepement [es-trîp'-mẹnt], *s.* Deterioración de tierras o bosques con perjuicio del propietario.
Estrogen [es'-tro-jen], *s.* (Biol.) Estrógeno.
Estuary [es'-chu-ẹ-ri], *s.* Estuario, brazo de mar; ría, desembocadura de lago o río.
Estuate [es'-chu-êt], *va.* (Des.) Hervir, causar hervor.
Estuation [es-chu-ê'-shun], *s.* (Des.) Hervor, ebullición.
Étagère [ê-ta-zhār'], *s.* Estante, armario con anaqueles. (Gal.)
Etc, &c. Contracción de las voces latinas *et cætera,* que significan lo mismo que, lo demás, lo que resta, lo que se sigue.
Etch [ech], *va.* 1. Grabar al agua fuerte. 2. Delinear, grabando las líneas por medio de un buril.
Etcher [ech'-ẹr], *s.* Aguafuertista, el que graba al agua fuerte.

Etching [ech'-ing], *s.* Aguafuerte, grabado hecho al agua fuerte y el procedimiento por el cual se hace.
Eternal [e-tēr'-nal], *a.* Eterno, perpetuo, inmortal, inmutable.—*s.* El Eterno, Dios.
Eternalist [e-tēr'-nal-ist], *s.* El que sostiene o defiende la eternidad del mundo.
Eternalize [e-tēr'-nal-aiz], *va.* Eternizar, perpetuar para siempre.
Eternally [e-tēr'-nal-i], *adv.* Eternamente, perennemente.
Eternity [e-tēr'-ni-ti], *s.* Eternidad, duración sin fin.
Eternize [e-tēr'-naiz], *va.* Eternizar, inmortalizar, perpetuar.
Etesian [e-tī'-zhan], *a.* Etesio, anualmente periódico; dícese de un viento.
Ether [ī'-thēr], *s.* 1. Éter, las regiones superiores de la bóveda celeste. 2. (Quím.) Éter, licor volátil formado por la destilación del alcohol con algún ácido; en especial éter sulfúrico. 3. Éter, fluido imponderable que llena el espacio, por el cual se propagan las vibraciones de la luz, del calor y de la electricidad.
Ethereal [e-thī'-ri-al], **Ethereous** [e-thī'-ri-us], *a.* 1. Etéreo, celeste. 2. De la naturaleza del éter o del aire; aéreo, ligero, fino, sutil, exquisito. 3. (Quím.) Etéreo, relativo a un éter.
Etherealize [e-thī'-ri-al-aiz], *va.* 1. Hacer etéreo, espiritualizar. 2. Convertir en éter.—*vn.* Hacerse etéreo.
Etherification [ī''-thēr-if-i-kē'-shun], *s.* Eterificación; la formación del éter.
Etheriform [ī'-thēr-i-fōrm''], *a.* Eteriforme, que tiene el carácter del éter.
Etherify [ī'-thēr-i-fai], *va.* Eterificar, convertir en éter.
Etherization [ī''-thēr-aiz-ē'-shun], *s.* Eterización, la administración del éter por las vías respiratorias para practicar una operación quirúrgica sin dolor.
Etherize, Etherise [ī'-thēr-aiz], *va.* Eterizar, someter a la influencia del éter.
Ethic, Ethical [eth'-ic, al], *a.* Ético, relativo a la moral.
Ethically [eth'-ic-al-i], *adv.* Moralmente.
Ethics [eth'-ics], *s. pl.* Ética, la parte de la filosofía comunmente llamada *filosofía moral.*
Ethiop [ī'-thi-op], *s.* Etíope, negro.
Ethiopian [ī-thi-ō'-pi-an], *a.* Etiópico, Etíope, etiopio; propio o natural de Etiopía.—*s.* Etíope, el natural de Etiopía.
Ethiopic [ī-thi-op'-ic], *s.* Lengua etiópica.
Ethiops mineral [ī'-thi-ops min'-ēr-al], *s.* Etíope mineral.
Ethmoid [eth'-moid], *s.* Etmóides, uno de los huesos de la cabeza, situado detrás de la parte superior de la nariz.
Ethmoidal [eth-moi'-dal], *a.* (Anat.) Etmoidal, etmoides, parecido a una criba.
Ethnic, Ethnical [eth'-nic, al], *a.* Étnico, pagano, gentil.
Ethnicism [eth'-ni-sizm], *s.* Paganismo, gentilismo.
Ethnics [eth'-nics], *s. pl.* Étnicos, los gentiles.
Ethnogeny [eth-noj'-e-ni], *s.* Etnogenía, la parte de la etnología que trata del origen de las razas.
Ethnographer [eth-nog'-ra-fēr], *s.* Etnógrafo.
Ethnographic, Ethnographical [eth-no-graf'-ic, al], *a.* Etnográfico, referente a la etnografía.
Ethnography [eth-nog'-ra-fi], *s.* Etnografía, la parte de la antropología cuyo objeto es el estudio y descripción de los diferentes pueblos del orbe.
Ethnologic, Ethnological [eth-no-loj'-ic, al], *a.* Etnológico, perteneciente a la etnología.
Ethnologist [eth-nol'-o-jist], *s.* Etnólogo.
Ethnology [eth-nol'-o-ji], *s.* Etnología, ciencia que trata del conocimiento del origen, usos, costumbres, etc., de las naciones en general o en particular.
Ethological [eth-o-loj'-i-cal], *a.* Etológico, moral.
Ethology [e-thol'-o-ji], *s.* Etología, la ciencia que trata de la formación del carácter humano.
Ethyl [eth'-il], *s.* y *a.* Etilo, elemento monoatómico (C_2H_5) de la serie de parafinas, que existe en el alcohol común.
Ethylene [eth'-i-līn], *s.* Etileno.
Ethylic [e-thil'-ic], *a.* Etílico.
Etiolate [ī'-ti-o-lēt], *va.* y *vn.* Hacer o hacerse blanco, blanquear o blanquearse, v. g. una planta o persona privada de la luz del sol.
Etiology [ī-ti-ol'-o-ji], *s.* (Med.) Etiología, ciencia de las causas en general, y especialmente de las enfermedades.
Etiquette [et'-i-ket], *s.* Etiqueta, ceremonial de los estilos, usos y costumbres que se deben observar.
Ettle [et'-l], *va.* Ganar. *Ettlings,* Sueldo (en el norte de Inglaterra).
Ettle, *va.* 1. (Esco.) Intentar, designar. 2. Conjeturar, suponer.—*vn.* 1. Apuntar (con *at*). 2. Dirigirse. 3. Hacer conato de. 4. Ser ambicioso.
Etui, Etwee [ē-twī'], *s.* Estuche; caja; bolsa; vaina. (Fr.)
Etymological [et-i-mo-loj'-i-cal], *a.* Etimológico.
Etymologically [et-i-mo-loj'-i-cal-i], *adv.* Etimológicamente.
Etymologist [et-i-mol'-o-jist], *s.* Etimologista.
Etymologize [et-i-mol'-o-jaiz], *va.* Etimologizar.
Etymology [et-i-mol'-o-ji], *s.* Etimología, el origen, raíz o principio de las voces.
Etymon [et'-i-mon], *s.* Forma radical de una palabra, voz primitiva.
Eucalyptus [yū-ca-lip'-tus], *s.* (Bot.) Eucalipto, género de árboles siempre verdes originarios de Australia.
Eucharist [yū'-ca-rist], *s.* Eucaristía, la cena del Señor.
Eucharistic, Eucharistical [yū-ca-ris'-tic, al], *a.* 1. Eucarístico. 2. Expresivo de gracias.
Euchology [yū-col'-o-ji], *s.* Eucologio, formulario del rezo.
Euchre [yū'-kēr], *s.* Cierto juego de naipes. Pueden jugarlo de dos á seis personas.—*va.* En dicho juego, impedir que otro haga cierto número de bazas; y de aquí, sobresalir en astucia, vencer.
Eucrasy, Eucrasia [yū'-cra-si], *s.* Eucrasia, buen temperamento del cuerpo humano.
Euclase [yū'-clēs], *s.* (Min.) Euclasa, piedra verde y muy dura del Perú.
Eudemonic [yū-de-mon'-ic], *a.* Perteneciente a la felicidad, o que tiende a producirla.
Eudemonics [yu-de-mon'-ics], *s.* 1. El ramo de la ética que trata de la felicidad. 2. Los medios de obtener o producir comodidad o felicidad.
Eudiometer [yū-di-om'-e-tēr], *s.* (Quím.) Eudiómetro, instrumento para determinar la pureza del aire o del gas.
Eudiometry [yū-di-om'-e-tri], *s.* Eudiometría, el arte de medir o determinar la pureza o salubridad del aire.
Eugenics [yū-jen'-ics], *s.* Eugenesia.
Eulogic [yu-loj'-ic], *a.* (Ant.) Laudatorio.
Eulogist [yū'-lo-jist], *s.* Elogista, aplaudidor.
Eulogistic [yū-lo-jis'-tic], *a.* Laudatorio, aprobador.
Eulogize [yū'-lo-jaiz], *va.* Elogiar, aplaudir.
Eulogy [yū'-lo-ji], *s.* Elogio, encomio, alabanza; panegírico.
Eunomy [yū'-no-mi], *s.* (Poco us.) Eunomía, gobierno de buenas leyes.
Eunuch [yū'-nuc], *s.* Eunuco, capón, hombre castrado; oficial de un palacio oriental.
Eunuchism [yū'-nuk-izm], *s.* Castradura, calidad y estado de eunuco.
Euonymus [yū-on'-i-mus], *s.* (Bot.) Bonetero, arbusto.
Eupatorium [yū-pa-tō'-ri-um], *s.* (Bot.) Eupatorio, agrimonia; género extenso de plantas compuestas.
Eupepsia [yū-pep'-si-a], *s.* Sana digestión; opuesta a *dyspepsia.*
Eupeptic [yū-pep'-tic], *a.* 1. Perteneciente a la buena digestión. 2. Que favorece la digestión.
Euphemism [yū'-fe-mizm], *s.* Eufemismo, la descripción de una cosa ofensiva con expresiones decorosas; nombre con que se designa delicadamente una cosa desagradable.
Euphemistic, Euphemistical [yū-fe-mis'-tic, al], *a.* Caracterizado por el eufemismo.
Euphone [yu-fō'-ni], *s.* Registro melodioso de órgano.
Euphonic, Euphonical [yu-fon'-ic, al], *a.* Eufónico, músico, agradable al oído.
Euphonious [yū-fō'-ni-us], *a.* Eufónico, agradable al oído, v. gr. una palabra o una frase.
Euphoniously [yū-fō'-ni-us-li], *adv.* Eufónicamente, agradablemente al oído.
Euphonium [yū-fō'-ni-um], *s.* 1. Instrumento de viento de fuerte sonido. 2. Eufono, instrumento músico compuesto de 42 cilindros de vidrio.
Euphony [yū'-fo-ni], *s.* Eufonía, sonido músico y agradable al oído.
Euphorbium [yu-fōr'-bi-um], *s.* 1. (Bot.) Euforbio, planta semejante a la cañaheja; género de plantas muy numerosas. 2. Una especie de goma resinosa.
Euphrasia, Euphrasy [yu-frē'-si-a, yū'-fra-si], *s.* (Bot.) Eufrasia, hierba medicinal.
Euphuism [yū'-fiu-izm], *s.* 1. Culteranismo, afectación de elegancia en el estilo; gongorismo. 2. Elegancia afectada en el vestir.
Euphuistic [yū-fiu-is'-tic], *a.* Culterano, culterana.
Eurasian [yur-ē'-shian], *s.* y *a.* Así europeo como asiático. (Dícese de las plantas y de los animales.)
Eureka [yū-rī'-ka], *inter.* Lema del Estado de California: "¡Lo he hallado!" expresivo de la exultación

que causa un descubrimiento. (Gr. εὕρηκα.)

Euripus [yū'-ri-pus], *s.* Euripo, estrecho de mar.

Euroclydon [yu-roc'-li-don], *s.* Euroclidón, viento del nordeste peligroso en el Mediterráneo.

European [yū-ro-pí'-an], *s.* y *a.* Europeo.

Eurus [yū'-rus], *s.* Euro, viento o aire solano.

Eurythmy [yū-rith'-mi], *s.* Euritmia, majestad y elegancia en alguna obra de las bellas artes.

Eustachian [yū-stê'-ki-an], *a.* De Eustaquio, anatomista italiano. *Eustachian tube,* Trompa de Eustaquio, canal de comunicación entre la faringe y el tímpano del oído.

Eustyle [yū'-stail], *s.* (Arq.) Intercolumnio.

Euthanasia [yū-tha-nê'-zha], ¿**Euthanasy** [yū-than'-a-si], *s.* Eutanasia, muerte tranquila.

Eutychian [yū-tik'-i-an], *a.* Eutiquiano.

Evacuant [e-vac'-yu-ant], *s.* (Med.) Evacuante.

Evacuate [e-vac'-yu-êt], *va.* 1. Evacuar, desocupar, vaciar. 2. Evacuar, desocupar, retirarse de.—*vn.* Vaciarse, fluir hacia afuera.

Evacuation [e-vac-yu-ê'-shun], *s.* Evacuación.

Evacuative [e-vac'-yu-a-tiv], *a.* Purgativo, evacuativo.

Evacuator [e-vac'-yu-ê-ter], *s.* El o lo que desocupa, evacua o se retira de algún lugar.

Evade [e-vêd'], *va.* y *vn.* 1. Evadir, huir, escapar, salvarse. 2. Evadir, eludir, evitar. 3. Eludir, huir de la dificultad.

¿**Evagation** [ev-a-gê'-shun], *s.* Evagación; excursión.

Evaluate [e-val'-yū-êt], *va.* Evaluar, valorar.

Evanesce [ev-a-nes'], *vn.* Desaparecer gradualmente; disiparse; desvanecerse.

Evanescence [ev-a-nes'-ens], *s.* Desaparecimiento, desvanecimiento.

Evanescent [ev-a-nes'-ent], *a.* 1. Imperceptible, lo que se desvanece o desaparece de la vista. 2. A punto de desaparecer. 3. (Mat.) Que se aproxima al cero. 4. (Biol.) No permanente, instable.

Evangel, †**Evangelly** [e-van'-jel, i], *s.* Buena nueva, evangelio.

Evangelic, Evangelical [ev-an-jel'-ic, al], *a.* Evangélico.

Evangelism [e-van'-jel-izm], *s.* La promulgación del evangelio.

Evangelist [e-van'-jel-ist], *s.* 1. Evangelista, cada uno de los cuatro escritores sagrados que escribieron el Evangelio. 2. Predicador del Evangelio que va de un lugar a otro y trata de despertar el fervor religioso de sus oyentes.

Evangelistary [e-van'-jel-is-te-ri], *s.* La colección de los evangelios que deben leerse o cantarse durante el oficio divino en las Iglesias griega y romana.

Evangelize [i-van'-jel-aiz], *va.* Evangelizar.

Evaporable [e-vap'-o-ra-bl], *a.* Evaporable.

Evaporate [e-vap'-o-rêt], *vn.* Evaporarse, disiparse en vapor, despedir los cuerpos sus partes más sutiles o espirituosas.—*va.* 1. Evaporar, despedir vapores. 2. Evaporar, exhalar, dar salida a alguna cosa. 3. Evaporar, hacer despedir a los cuerpos sus partes más sutiles o espirituosas por medio del calor.

Evaporated [e-vap'-o-rêt-ed], *a.* Evaporado. *Evaporated milk,* Leche evaporada.

Evaporation [e-vap-o-rê'-shun], *s.* Evaporación; exhalación del vapor.

Evaporator [e-vap'-o-rê''-ter], *s.* Evaporador, aparato para desecar substancias por medio de la evaporación (v. g. las frutas).

Evasion [e-vê'-zhun], *s.* 1. Evasiva, efugio, escapatoria, excusa. 2. (Des.) Evasión, salida, escape.

Evasive [e-vê'-siv], *a.* Evasivo, sofístico, ambiguo; engañoso.

Evasively [e-vê'-siv-li], *adv.* Sofísticamente.

Eve, Even [ív, n], *s.* Tardecita, la caída de la tarde, cerca del anochecer; vigilia, víspera. *On the eve of,* La víspera de. *Christmas Eve,* Víspera de Navidad. (La forma *Even* es poética o anticuada.)

Evection [e-vec'-shun], *s.* 1. (Astr.) Evección, la mayor desigualdad periódica en el movimiento de la luna, por efecto de la atracción solar. 2. (Des.) Exaltación.

Ev'n [í'-vn]. Contracción de EVEN.

Even, *a.* 1. Llano, liso, igual, raso, suave. 2. Igual por ambos lados o partes; par. *To be even with,* Estar en paz con, estar a mano, no deber nada. 3. Par, que se puede dividir exactamente por 2. 4. Constante, firme; sereno, invariable en la disposición, acción o calidad. 5. Al mismo nivel o en la misma línea. *Even with the ground,* Al nivel de la tierra. *To lay even with the ground,* Arrasar, demoler. *To be even with one,* Cancelar la cuenta con alguno; vengarse, pagar en la misma moneda. *To make even,* Allanar, igualar.

Even, *adv.* 1. Aun. 2. Aun cuando, supuesto que. 3. No obstante, sin embargo. 4. Lisamente, llanamente, regularmente (v. g. los versos). *Even as,* Como. *Even down,* Hacia abajo. *Even now,* Ahora mismo. *Even on,* Derechamente. *Even so,* Lo mismo, de veras, así es; cierto; es verdad. *Not even,* Ni siquiera.

Even, *va.* Igualar, allanar, enrasar, nivelar; unir; desquitar, liquidar cuentas. *To even with the ground,* Arrasar.

†**Evene** [i-vín'], *vn.* Acontecer, acaecer, suceder.

Evener [í'-vn-er], *s.* 1. Reconciliador. 2. (Mec.) Aplanador, igualador.

Evenhand [í'-vn-hand], *s.* Paridad de rango o grado.

Evenhanded [í'-vn-hand-ed], *a.* Imparcial.

Evening [ív'-ning], *s.* Tardecita, el anochecer, el principio de la noche. Se usa frecuentemente en sentido figurado, para significar fin, término. *Last evening,* Ayer tarde. *Saturday evening,* El sábado por la tarde.—*a.* Vespertino. *Evening party,* Tertulia. *Evening-song, V.* EVENSONG. *Evening tide, V.* EVENTIDE. *Evening primrose,* (Bot.) Enotera, onagra, planta americana de flores grandes y amarillas que se abren al caer la tarde. (Œnothera biennis.)

Evening-star [ív'-ning-stār], *s.* Héspero, véspero, estrella vespertina.

Evenly [í'-vn-li], *adv.* 1. Igualmente, llanamente; sin accidentes ni asperezas, de una manera igual, uniforme. 2. Horizontalmente, a nivel. 3. Imparcialmente.

Evenness [í'-vn-nes], *s.* Igualdad, uniformidad, llanura, lisura, imparcialidad, serenidad de ánimo.

Even-song [í'-vn-sōng], *s.* 1. Vísperas, el oficio divino de la tarde o el tiempo de la tarde. 2. Canción vespertina, cantada por la tarde; himno de la tarde.

Event [e-vent'], *s.* 1. Evento, acontecimiento, caso, suceso. 2. Éxito, consecuencia, resulta. *At all events,* Sea lo que fuere, o en todo caso, a todo trance; sobre todo. *In the event of,* En caso de.

Eventerate [e-ven'-ter-êt], *va.* Destripar.

Eventful [e-vent'-ful], *a.* Lleno de acontecimientos, incidentes o sucesos; extraordinario, singular.

Eventide [í'-vn-taid], *s.* La tarde, la caída de la tarde; vigilia.

Eventual [e-ven'-chu-al], *a.* 1. Consiguiente, último, final. 2. Eventual, fortuito.

Eventuality [e-ven''-chu-al'-i-ti], *s.* Eventualidad, casualidad.

Eventually [e-ven'-chu-al-i], *adv.* Eventualmente, finalmente, últimamente; con el tiempo.

Eventuate [e-ven'-chu-êt], *vn.* 1. Tener desenlace, terminarse, concluir. 2. Acontecer, acaecer, suceder.

Ever [ev'-er], *adv.* 1. En cualquier tiempo, siempre; perpetuamente. *For ever and ever,* Por siempre jamás, eternamente. *Forever,* Perpetuamente, para siempre, de por vida. Contráese muchas veces en *e'er. Ever since,* Desde entonces, después. *Ever and anon* o *Every now and then,* De cuando en cuando, de vez en cuando. 2. En cualquier grado; en todo caso; generalmente. *Be he ever so rich,* Por rico que sea. *As ever,* Tanto, tanto como, lo más. *Run as fast as ever you can,* Corra Vd. lo más que pueda. *Ever so,* En cualquier grado o extensión; muy. *He is ever so strong,* Él es muy fuerte. *The patient is ever so much better,* El enfermo se halla muy mejorado. 3. Después de una voz negativa o limitativa, nunca, jamás. *Hardly* o *scarcely ever,* Casi nunca. *I do not know if I shall ever see it,* No sé si jamás lo veré.

Ever-burning [ev'-er-būrn'-ing], *a.* Inextinguible.

Ever-during [ev'-er-diūr'-ing], *a.* Eterno, sempiterno.

Everglade [ev'-er-glêd], *s.* Terreno bajo y pantanoso cubierto en su mayor parte por altas hierbas.

Evergreen [ev'-er-grín], *a.* Siempre verde.—*s.* (Bot.) Siempreviva, planta que mantiene su verdor en todas las estaciones.

Everlasting [ev-er-last'-ing], *a.* Eterno, sempiterno, perpetuo, perdurable.—*s.* 1. Eternidad; ser eterno. 2. Sempiterna, especie de tela de lana. 3. Cualquiera planta cuyas flores conservan sus formas y colores después de recogidas y secadas; como la siempreviva, inmortal, gnafalio, etc. *Everlasting-pea,* (Bot.) Siemprehuele, siemprevivo.

Everlastingly [ev-er-last'-ing-li], *adv.* Eternamente, perpetuamente, sin cesar.

Everlastingness [ev-er-last'-ing-nes], *s.* Eternidad.

Everliving [ev-er-liv'-ing], *a.* Inmortal, eterno, sempiterno.

Evermore [ev-er-mōr'], *adv.* Eternamente, para siempre jamás.

Ever-open [ev'-er-ōp'-n], *a.* Nunca cerrado, siempre abierto.

Everpleasing [ev-er-plíz'-ing], *a.* Lo que deleita siempre.
Eversion [e-ver'-shun], *s.* 1. El acto de volver lo de dentro afuera o hacia atrás. 2. Eversión, trastorno, subversión.
Evert [e-vert'], *va.* 1. Everter, volver de dentro afuera; volver hacia atrás o afuera. 2. (Des.) Subvertir, destruir, arruinar.
Ever-watchful [ev'-er-wech'-ful], *a.* Siempre vigilante.
Every [ev'-ri o ev'-er-i], *a.* Cada uno o cada una; todo, todos. *Every day,* Todos los días, cada día. *Everywhere,* En o por todas partes. *Everybody,* Todos, todo el mundo, cada uno. *Every other day,* Cada dos días o cada tercer día. *Everything,* Todo, cada cosa. *Every whit,* Enteramente.
Every-day [ev''-ri-dé'], *a.* Cotidiano, de todos los días, ordinario.
Ever-young [ev-er-yung'], *a.* Siempre joven; nunca decaído.
Evesdropper [ívz'-drep-er], *s.* (Des.) *V.* EAVESDROPPER.
Evict [e-vict'], *va.* 1. Desposeer o privar a alguno de sus bienes en virtud de una sentencia legal; echar fuera, expulsar. 2. Arrebatar, arrancar, alienar, v. g. los bienes.
Eviction [e-vic'-shun], *s.* Desposesión de bienes por sentencia judicial.
Evidence [ev'-i-dens], *s.* 1. Evidencia, certidumbre manifiesta; demostración. 2. Testimonio, prueba; deposición, declaración. 3. (Des.) Testigo. *Circumstancial evidence,* Prueba circunstancial, indicios vehementes. *State's evidence,* El cómplice que, por librarse del castigo, declara contra los otros. *To give evidence,* (1) Dar testimonio. (2) Deponer, declarar.
Evidence, *va.* Evidenciar, hacer patente, probar.
Evidencer [ev'-i-den-ser], *s.* Testigo.
Evident [ev'-i-dent], *a.* Evidente, claro, patente, notorio, manifiesto. *To be evident,* Constar, ser evidente.
Evidential [ev-i-den'-shal], *a.* Lo que produce evidencia o prueba.
Evidently [ev'-i-dent-li], *adv.* Claramente, evidentemente.
Evil [í'-vl], *a.* Malo, depravado, miserable, dañoso, pernicioso, maligno. *The evil one,* El diablo, Satanás. *Evil communications corrupt good manners,* Las malas conversaciones corrompen las buenas costumbres.—*s.* 1. Maldad, acción malvada; mal, daño, injuria. 2. Desgracia, infortunio, calamidad. 3. Enfermedad. *King's evil,* Escrófula; en otro tiempo se suponía curable por el contacto de un rey. *The social evil,* Impureza sexual, prostitución. —*adv.* Malamente, injuriosamente.
Evil-affected [í'-vl-af-fect'-ed], *a.* Desafecto, maligno.
Evil-doer [í'-vl-dú'-er], *s.* Malhechor.
Evil-eyed [í'-vl-aid], *a.* Lo que tiene la vista dañosa, que mira de mal ojo.
Evil-favoured [ív'-l-fé'-verd], *a.* Disforme. *V.* ILL-FAVOURED.
Evil-favouredness [ív'-l-fé'-verd-nes], *s.* Deformidad.
Evilly [í'-vl-i], *adv.* Malamente.
Evil-minded [ív'-l-maind'-ed], *a.* Malicioso, mal intencionado.
Evilness [í'-vl-nes], *s.* Maldad.
Evil-speaking [ív'-l-spík'-ing], *s.* Maledicencia, murmuración, calumnia.
Evil-wishing [ív'-l-wish'-ing], *a.* Malévolo, el que desea mal a otro.
Evil-worker [ív'-l-wūrk'-er], *s.* Malhechor.
Evince [e-vins'], *va.* Probar, justificar, demostrar, hacer patente y manifiesta alguna cosa.—*vn.* Probar.
Evincible [e-vins'-i-bl], *a.* Demostrable.
Evincibly [e-vins'-i-bli], *adv.* Evidentemente, indudablemente.
Evincive [e-vin'-siv], *a.* Capaz de probar, convincente.
†**Evirate** [ev'-i-rét], *va.* Castrar.
Eviscerate [e-vis'-er-ét], *va.* Destripar, desentrañar, sacar las entrañas.
Evitable [ev'-i-ta-bl], *a.* Evitable.
Eviternal [ev-i-ter'-nal], *a.* Eviterno, sempiterno.
Evocation [ev-o-ké'-shun], *s.* 1. Evocación. 2. (For.) Avocación, la transferencia de un litigio de un tribunal inferior a uno superior.
Evoke [e-vōc'], *va.* 1. Evocar, llamar a alguno para que dé favor o auxilio. 2. (Poco us.) Avocar, remover a un tribunal diferente.
Evolute [ev'-o-lūt o liūt], *s.* (Geom.) Evoluta, curva geométrica de muchos centros.
Evolution [ev-o-lū'-shun], *s.* 1. Desplegadura; evolución, desarrollo. 2. (Biol.) Evolución, desarrollo gradual, transformismo. 3. (Alg.) Extracción de una raíz. 4. (Mil. y Mar.) Evolución, movimientos que hacen las naves o los soldados para mudar de posición y tomar otra nueva.
Evolutional [ev-o-lū'-shun-al], *a.* De la evolución o que resulta de ella.
Evolutionary [ev-o-lū'-shun-e-ri], *a.* Evolutivo, evolucionario, relativo a la evolución, en cualquier sentido.
Evolutionist [ev-o-lū'-shun-ist], *a.* Perteneciente a la evolución biológica. —*s.* 1. Creyente en la evolución biológica o metafísica. 2. Jefe diestro en las evoluciones o maniobras militares.
Evolve [e-velv'], *va.* 1. Desenvolver, desplegar, desenredar, desarrollar. 2. Producir por la evolución. 3. Echar fuera, v. gr. los gases.—*vn.* Abrirse, desplegarse, extenderse, desarrollarse.
Evolvement [e-velv'-ment], *s.* 1. Emanación, producción de gases. 2. Desplegadura, despliegue.
Evolvent [e-vel'-vent], *s.* (Geom.) Evolvente. *V.* INVOLUTE.
Evulsion [e-vul'-shun], *s.* Arranque, la acción de arrancar alguna cosa, sea de raíz o de otra suerte.
Ewe [yū], *sf.* Oveja, la hembra del carnero.
Ewer [yū'-er], *s.* Aguamanil, jarro, cántaro de boca ancha para servir agua.
Ewry [yū'-ri], *s.* (Ant.) Sausería, un oficio de palacio.
Ex [ecs]. Preposición latina que quiere decir fuera, fuera de, afuera, más allá. Se usa muchas veces con fuerza intensiva y también para expresar que una persona o cosa no goza o tiene el empleo u oficio que tenía; v. g. *Exalt, ex*-altar, *re*-alzar; *Ex-general,* Exgeneral, o general que fué. *Ex-captain,* Capitán retirado.
Exacerbate [eg-zas'-er-bét], *va.* Exacerbar, exasperar, irritar.
Exacerbation [eg-zas-er-bé'-shun], *s.* Exacerbación, irritación; paroxismo, aumento momentáneo en la fuerza de la enfermedad.
†**Exacervation** [eg-zas-er-vé'-shun], *s.* Amontonamiento.
Exact [eg-zact'], *a.* Exacto, cabal, metódico, puntual, esmerado, justo, estricto. *The exact truth,* La estricta verdad.
Exact, *va.* Exigir.—*vn.* Cometer exacciones, obtener por fuerza.
Exacter [eg-zact'-er], *s.* Exactor, opresor.
Exaction [eg-zac'-shun], *s.* Exacción, extorsión.
Exactitude [eg-zac'-ti-tiud], *s.* Exactitud, puntualidad y fidelidad.
Exactly [eg-zact'-li], *adv.* Exactamente, cabalmente.
Exactness [eg-zact'-nes], *s.* Exactitud, puntualidad; conducta arreglada.
Exactor [eg-zact'-er], *s.* Exactor, opresor.
Exactress [eg-zact'-res], *sf.* Exactora.
Exaggerate [eg-zaj'-er-ét], *va.* 1. Exagerar, encarecer, abultar, ponderar una cosa, dando de ella idea mayor de la que en realidad merece. 2. Aumentar inmoderadamente; realzar el efecto, dibujo o diseño de una cosa.
Exaggeration [eg-zaj-er-é'-shun], *s.* Exageración.
Exaggeratory [eg-zaj'-er-a-to-ri], *a.* Exagerativo.
Exalt [eg-zēlt'], *va.* 1. Exaltar, elevar, levantar. 2. Alentar, alegrar. 3. Exaltar, alabar. 4. Exaltar, realzar, ilustrar, engrandecer.
Exaltation [eg-zēl-té'-shun], *s.* Exaltación, elevación; dignidad.
Exalted [eg-zēlt'-ed], *pp.* y *a.* Exaltado, elevado; de aquí, eminente, noble, grande, sublime.
Exaltedness [eg-zēlt'-ed-nes], *s.* Exaltación, sublimidad.
Exalter [eg-zēlt'-er], *s.* Loador, exaltador, elevador.
Examinable [eg-zam'-in-a-bl], *a.* Investigable, averiguable.
Examinant [eg-zam'-in-ant], *s.* 1. Examinador. 2. (Des.) Examinando, el que está para ser examinado.
Examinate [eg-zam'-in-ét], *s.* Examinado.
Examination [eg-zam-i-né'-shun], *s.* 1. Examen, acción de examinar. 2. Examen interrogatorio; investigación, indagación, averiguación.
Examine [eg-zam'-in], *va.* 1. Examinar, escudriñar, investigar críticamente. 2. Examinar, tomar declaración al reo; examinar a algún testigo. 3. Investigar, probar o tantear por medio de preguntas y ejercicios la idoneidad y suficiencia de alguien, p. ej. de un discípulo o candidato. 4. Hacer pruebas, ensayar; analizar.
Examiner [eg-zam'-in-er], *s.* Examinador, escudriñador.
Example [eg-zam'-pl], *s.* 1. Ejemplar, original, prototipo, muestra. 2. Caso precedente semejante a otro posterior. 3. Ejemplar, ejemplo, pauta de lo que se debe seguir o imitar. 4. Ejemplo, el que ha sufrido un castigo para escarmiento de los demás. 5. Ejemplo, símil o comparación de que se usa para aclarar o apoyar alguna cosa.
Exanimate [eg-zan'-i-mét], *a.* 1. Exánime, muerto, sin vida, sin vigor. 2. Desmayado, acobardado, sin valor, sin ánimo.
Exanimation [eg-zan-i-mé'-shun], *s.* Muerte, pasmo.
Exanthem, Exanthema, *pl.* EXANTHEMATA [ex-an'-them, ex-an-thí'-ma, ec-san-them'-a-ta], *s.* (Med.) Exantema, erupción, sarpullido. *V.* RASH.

Exanthematous [ec-san-them'-a-tus], *a.* Eruptivo, exantemático.
Exarch [ec'-sārc], *s.* 1. Exarca o exarco, antiguo gobernador de Italia delegado por los emperadores de Oriente. 2. Legado de un patriarca en la Iglesia griega.
Exarchate [ec-sār'-kêt], *s.* 1. Exarcado, distrito sujeto a un exarca. 2. La dignidad y el cargo de exarca.
Exarticulate [ec-sar-tic'-yu-lêt], *va.* 1. Dislocar, descoyuntar. 2. (Cir.) Desarticular, amputar por una coyuntura.
Exarticulation [ec-sar-tic-yu-lé'-shun], *s.* 1. Dislocación, descoyuntamiento. 2. Desarticulación, amputación.
Exasperate [eg-zas'-pęr-êt], *va.* 1. Exasperar, irritar, enojar, provocar. 2. Exasperar, hacer más intenso, agravar, amargar.
†**Exasperate**, *a.* Provocado, exasperado, irritado. (Bot.) Áspero.
Exasperater [eg-zas'-per-ê-tęr], *s.* Provocador, provocante.
Exasperation [eg-zas-pęr-é'-shun], *s.* Exasperación, provocación, irritación; enojo; agravación, recargo.
Excamb [ex-camb'], *va.* (Der. esco.) Cambiar, permutar, trocar, especialmente terrenos por terrenos.
‖**Excandescence, Excandescency** [ex-can-des'-ens, i], *s.* 1. (Quím.) Excandecencia. 2. (Des.) Excandecencia, irritación vehemente, ira. *V.* INCANDESCENCE.
Excarnate [ex-cār'-nêt], *va.* Descarnar, despojar de carne.
Excarnation, Excarnification [ex-car-ni-fi-kê'-shun], *s.* Descarnadura.
Excavate [ex'-ca-vêt], *va.* Excavar, ahondar.
Excavation [ex-ca-vé'-shun], *s.* 1. Excavación, cavidad. 2. (Agr.) Excava.
Excavator [ex'-ca-vê-tęr], *s.* Excavador.
Exceed [ec-sīd'], *va.* Exceder; sobrepujar, sobresalir; pasar los límites regulares o prescritos.—*vn.* Excederse, propasarse; aventajarse.
Exceeder [ec-sīd'-ęr], *s.* El que sobresale o excede.
Exceeding [ec-sīd'-ing], *a.* Excesivo. —*s.* Lo que sobrepuja los límites ordinarios.—*adv.* (Ant.) Eminentemente, en alto grado.
Exceedingly [ec-sīd'-ing-li], *adv.* Excesivamente, sumamente, extremamente.
†**Exceedingness** [ec-sīd'-ing-nes], *s.* Grandeza o tamaño excesivo, magnitud desmesurada; duración extraordinariamente larga; extensión muy grande.
Excel [ec-sel'], *vn.* Sobresalir, sobrepujar, aventajarse a, tener buenas propiedades o calidades en sumo grado.—*va.* Sobresalir, exceder singularmente a otra persona o cosa en cuanto a las buenas propiedades o calidades.
Excellence, Excellency [ec'-sel-ens, i], *s.* 1. Excelencia, dignidad, rango, preeminencia. 2. Excelencia, un título de honor. 3. Pureza, bondad.
Excellent [ec'-sel-ent], *a.* Excelente, selecto, sobresaliente, primoroso.
Excellently [ec'-sel-ent-li], *adv.* Excelentemente, primorosamente.
Excelsior [ec-sel'-si-ōr], *a.* Aun más alto; siempre hacia arriba; lema del Estado de Nueva York.—*s.* Madera en hebras y virutas delgadas para empaquetar y rellenar colchones.
Excentric [ec-sen'-tric], *a.* *V.* ECCENTRIC.
Except [ec-sept'], *va.* Exceptuar, omitir, excluir; particularmente excluir la mención o consideración de alguien o algo.—*vn.* Excepcionar, poner excepciones a lo que se alega; recusar o declinar la jurisdicción de alguno.
Except, *prep.* 1. Excepto, con exclusión de, a excepción de, fuera de, menos. 2. Si no, a menos que.
Excepting [ec-sept'-ing], *prep.* A excepción de, fuera de.
Exception [ec-sep'-shun], *s.* 1. Excepción; la cosa exceptuada. 2. Exclusión. 3. (For.) Excepción, recusación; objeción.
Exceptionable [ec-sep'-shun-a-bl], *a.* Recusable, tachable, expuesto o sujeto a reparos y contradicciones.
Exceptional [ec-sep'-shun-al], *a.* Excepcional, que forma excepción a la regla común; poco común, no usual, superior.
Exceptionless [ec-sep'-shun-les], *a.* Sin excepción, sin tacha, fuera de toda objeción; sin falta.
†**Exceptious** [ec-sep'-shus], *a.* Impertinente, ridículo; litigioso; delicado, resentido.
Exceptiousness [ec-sep'-shus-nes], *s.* Impertinencia.
Exceptive [ec-sep'-tiv], *a.* 1. Exceptivo, excepcional, de la naturaleza de una excepción. 2. Susceptible, quisquilloso, caviloso.
Exceptor [ec-sept'-ęr], *s.* Exceptuador, el que pone excepciones.
Excerpt [ec-sęrpt'], *va.* Sacar, extraer, tomar, como se toma o cita de un libro.—*s.* Extracto, selección, cita de materia escrita o impresa.
Excerption [ec-sęrp'-shun], *s.* El acto de hacer extractos; selecciones, colecciones, extractos.
Excerptive [ec-sęrpt'-iv], *a.* Que extrae o entresaca.
Excerptor [ec-sęrp'-tęr], *s.* El que se aprovecha de los escritos de otros tomando trozos de ellos; plagiario.
Excess [ec-ses'], *s.* 1. Exceso, la parte que excede y pasa más allá de la regla y el orden común. 2. Exceso, la porción o parte que hay de más. 3. Exceso, demasía en el comer o beber; destemplanza; transgresión de los límites debidos, desorden, desarreglo.
Excess baggage [ec-ses' bag'-êj], *s.* Exceso de equipaje.
Excessive [ec-ses'-iv], *a.* Excesivo, vehemente, desarreglado, inmoderado, desmesurado.
Excessively [ec-ses'-iv-li], *adv.* Excesivamente, extremadamente.
Excessiveness [ec-ses'-iv-nes], *s.* Exceso, calidad de excesivo.
Exchange [ex-chênj'], *va.* 1. Cambiar; canjear. 2. Cambiar, trocar, permutar. *To exchange words,* Cambiar, decirse algunas palabras. *To exchange guns, pistols,* o *shots,* Darse o tirarse pistoletazos. *To exchange cards,* Desafiarse. *To exchange prisoners,* Canjear prisioneros de guerra. *To exchange signs,* Hacerse señas.
Exchange, *s.* 1. Cambio, trueque o permuta; canje. 2. La cosa que se da o recibe en cambio de otra. 3. (Com.) Bolsa, lonja, plaza o casa de contratación. 4. (Com.) Cambio, el giro o conmutación de dinero de una parte a otra. 5. (Com.) Cambio, el aumento o diminución de valor que se da a la moneda al tiempo de la paga en los parajes adonde se la destina. 6. (Com.) Cambio, el interés que lleva el cambista o banquero. (Mil.) *Exchange of prisoners,* Canje de prisioneros. 7. Despacho central de teléfonos.
Exchangeable [ex-chênj'-a-bl], *a.* Lo que se puede cambiar.
Exchanger [ex-chênj'-ęr], *s.* Cambista o cambiante de letras o moneda, banquero.
Exchequer [ex-chek'-ęr], *s.* Real hacienda, fisco, tesorería. *Exchequer bills,* Vales de la tesorería que se libran y se pagan cada año; vales reales.
Exchequer, *va.* Procesar en el tribunal de la real hacienda.
Excipient [ec-sip'-i-ent], *s.* (Med.) Excipiente, substancia que sirve para incorporar otras a un medicamento o disolverlas en él.
Excisable [ec-sai'-za-bl], *a.* Sujeto al derecho de sisa.
Excise [ec-saiz'], *s.* Sisa, derecho que se paga sobre los comestibles, y otros géneros.
Excise, *va.* 1. Cortar, extirpar. 2. Sisar; aforar, exigir tributo sobre algo.
Exciseman [ec-saiz'-man], *s.* Sisero, el oficial o guarda que registra los géneros que deben pagar el derecho de sisa.
Excision [ec-sizh'-un], *s.* 1. (Cir.) Separación, corte o remoción de una parte; excisión. 2. Extirpación.
Excitability [ec-sait-a-bil'-i-ti], *s.* Excitabilidad, la capacidad de excitarse o de ser excitado.
Excitable [ec-sait'-a-bl], *a.* Excitable.
Excitant [ecs'-it-ant], *s.* y *a.* Estimulante, excitante.
Excitation [ec-si-té'-shun], *s.* Excitación; instigación, incitamiento.
Excitative, Excitatory [ec-sai'-ta-tiv, to-ri], *a.* Excitativo.
Excite [ec-sait'], *va.* Excitar, mover, animar, estimular. *Exciting cause,* (Med.) Causa ocasional o concausa.
Excitement [ec-sait'-męnt], *s.* Estímulo, incitamiento, instigación, motivo, agitación, conmoción.
Exciter [ec-sait'-ęr], *s.* Motor, incitador, agitador, instigador.
Exciting [ec-sait'-ing], *a.* Estimulador, excitante, emocionante.
Exclaim [ex-clêm'], *vn.* Exclamar, dar gritos y voces, clamar mucho.
†**Exclaim**, *s.* Clamor, gritería.
Exclamation [ex-cla-mé'-shun], *s.* 1. Exclamación, grito, clamor. 2. Expresión precipitada o enfática del pensamiento o del sentido. 3. (Gram.) Interjección. 4. Admiración, el signo ortográfico !
Exclamatory [ex-clam'-a-to-ri], *a.* Exclamatorio.
Exclude [ex-clūd'], *va.* Excluir, echar fuera; exceptuar; rechazar; (Biol.) expeler, arrojar.
Exclusion [ex-clū'-zhun], *s.* Exclusión, exclusiva, excepción; emisión.
Exclusionist [ex-clū'-zhun-ist], *s.* El que quiere excluir a otros.
Exclusive [ex-clū'-siv], *a.* Exclusivo, privativo; exceptuado.
Exclusively [ex-clū'-siv-li], *adv.* Exclusivamente, sin entrar en cuenta.
Exclusiveness [ex-clū'-siv-nes], *s.* Exclusiva, repulsa; calidad de exclusivo.
Exclusivism [ex-clū'-siv-izm], *s.* Sistema de exclusión.
Excogitate [ex-coj'-i-têt], *va.* Excogitar, pensar, imaginar, inventar. —*vn.* Pensar.

Excogitation [ex-cej-i-té'-shun], *s.* Invención, pensamiento.
Excommunicable [ex-com-miūn'-i-ca-bl], *a.* Digno de excomunión.
Excommunicate [ex-com-miūn'-i-kêt], *va.* Excomulgar, descomulgar, anatematizar.
Excommunicate, *a.* y *s.* Excomulgado, el que está apartado y excluído de la comunión de los fieles.
Excommunication [ex-co-miū-ni-ké'-shun], *s.* Excomunión, descomunión, anatema religioso.
Excoriate [ex-cō'-ri-êt], *va.* Desollar; y de aquí, excoriar, gastar, arrancar o corroer el cutis quedando la carne descubierta.
Excoriation [ex-co-ri-é'-shun], *s.* Excoriación, desolladura.
Excortication [ex-cōr-ti-ké'-shun], *s.* Descortezadura, el acto de descortezar.
Excreate [ecs'-cre-êt], *va.* (Des.) Escupir, expectorar.
Excrement [ex'-cre-ment], *s.* Excremento.
Excremental [ex-cre-ment'-al], *a.* Excrementoso.
Excrementitial, Excrementitious [ex-cre-men-tish'-al, tish'-us], *a.* Excrementicio.
Excrescence, Excrescency [ex-cres'-ens, i], *s.* Excrecencia, carnosidad o superfluidad que se cría en animales y plantas.
Excrescent [ex-cres'-ent], *a.* Superfluo, lo que forma una excrecencia.
Excrete [ex-crît'], *va.* Excretar, echar fuera, arrojar los humores o materias fecales.
Excrete [ex'-crêt], *s.* Excreta, lo que se excreta; materia inútil.
Excretion [ex-crî'-shun], *s.* 1. Excreción, la acción de excretar. 2. Excreta, la materia que se excreta.
Excretive [ex-crî'-tiv], *a.* Excretorio, lo que tiene virtud de preparar los fluidos destinados a ser expelidos del cuerpo.
Excretory [ex'-cre-to-ri], *a.* Excretorio, perteneciente a la excreción; que lleva o conduce una materia excretada.—*s.* El órgano excretorio o que sirve para la excreción.
Excruciable [ex-crū'-shi-a-bl], *a.* Sujeto o expuesto a tormentos.
Excruciate [ex-crū'-shi-êt], *va.* Atormentar, afligir o molestar corporalmente a otro.
Excruciating [ex-crū'-shi-ê-ting], *a.* 1. Que atormenta agudamente, que causa el dolor más violento; extremamente doloroso. 2. (Fam. E. U.) Extremadamente remilgado, exigente o presuntuoso.
Excruciation [ex-crū-shi-é'-shun], *s.* Tormento, molestia.
Excubation [ex-cu-bé'-shun], *s.* (Des.) Vela, la acción de pasar toda la noche despierto.
Exculpate [ex-cul'-pêt], *va.* Disculpar, excusar, justificar.
Exculpation [ex-cul-pé'-shun], *s.* Disculpa.
Exculpatory [ex-cul'-pa-to-ri], *a.* Disculpador, justificativo.
Excursion [ex-cōr'-shun], *s.* 1. Paseo, viaje corto o de poca duración. 2. Excursión, correría o entrada en país enemigo. 3. La acción de separarse del camino regular o trillado. 4. Digresión. 5. (Fís.) La mitad del movimiento de oscilación o vibración de un cuerpo. *Excursion ticket, train,* Billete de ida y vuelta, tren de excursión.
Excursionist [ex-cōr'-shun-ist], *s.* El que hace una excursión; el que viaja por curiosidad y distracción.
Excursive [ex-cōr'-siv], *a.* 1. Errante, vagante, paseante. 2. (Fig.) Digresivo, errático, pasajero, mudable.
Excursively [ex-cōr'-siv-li], *adv.* De un modo vago, digresivo o errante.
Excursiveness [ex-cōr'-siv-nes], *s.* El acto de pasar los límites acostumbrados.
Excusable [ex-kiū'-za-bl], *a.* Excusable, disculpable.
Excusableness [ex-kiū'-za-bl-nes], *s.* Excusa, calidad de excusable.
Excusatory [ex-kiū'-za-to-ri], *a.* Apologético, lo que excusa.
Excuse [ex-kiūz'], *va.* 1. Excusar, disculpar, dar excusas. 2. Eximir, libertar, exentar, dispensar. 3. Perdonar, no exigir, remitir, tolerar. 4. Justificar, vindicar.
Excuse [ex-kiūs'], *s.* 1. Excusa, apología, defensa, justificación. 2. Excusa, excusación; disculpa.
Excuseless [ex-kiūs'-les], *a.* Inexcusable.
Excuser [ex-kiūz'-er], *s.* Excusador, intercesor; perdonador; apologista.
Excuss [ex-cus'], *va.* 1. (Ant.) Echar de sí, arrojar. 2. Embargar los bienes a alguno.
Excussion [ex-cush'-un], *s.* (Des.) Ejecución, la aprehensión que se hace de la persona o bienes del que es deudor; embargo de bienes.
Execrable [ec'-se-cra-bl], *a.* Execrable, abominable, detestable, aborrecible.
Execrably [ec'-se-cra-bli], *adv.* Execrablemente.
Execrate [ec'-se-crêt], *va.* Execrar, maldecir, abominar.
Execration [ec-se-cré'-shun], *s.* Execración, maldición, abominación.
Execratory [ec'-se-cra-to-ri], *s.* Juramento execratorio.
Executant [eg-zec'-yu-tant], *s.* El que ejecuta o pone por obra; en especial, ejecutante músico.
Execute [ec'-se-kiūt], *va.* 1. Ejecutar, poner por obra lo que está ideado. 2. Ejecutar, ajusticiar. 3. Matar, asesinar.—*vn.* 1. Ejecutar su deber. 2. Servir una cosa perfectamente para el fin a que se la destina.
Executer [ec'-se-kiū"-ter], *s.* Ejecutor, el que ejecuta o pone por obra alguna cosa.
Execution [ec-se-kiū'-shun], *s.* 1. Ejecución, el acto de ejecutar. 2. Ejecución, embargo, la aprehensión que se hace en la persona o bienes del que es deudor por mandamiento de juez competente. *Writ of execution,* Auto de ejecución. 3. Ejecución, justicia, el acto público de ejecutar en el reo la pena capital. 4. Destrucción, mortandad. 5. Agilidad, destreza para tocar un instrumento o cantar; de aquí, destreza técnica. 6. Trabajo efectivo.
Executioner [ec-se-kiū'-shun-er], *s.* 1. Ejecutor, la persona que pone por obra alguna cosa; especialmente, verdugo. 2. (Poco us.) El instrumento o la agencia que sirve para ejecutar algo.
Executive [eg-zec'-yu-tiv], *a.* Ejecutivo.—*s.* *The executive,* El poder ejecutivo, el gobierno; la corte; la autoridad suprema.
Executor [eg-zec'-yu-ter], *s.* Albacea, testamentario.
Executorship [eg-zec'-yu-ter-ship], *s.* Albaceazgo.
Executory [eg-zec'-yu-to-ri], *a.* 1. Ejecutorio, ejecutivo; administrativo 2. Que se debe ejecutar o poner en vigor y efecto; que llega a tener fuerza y efecto en ocasión futura.
Executress [eg-zec'-yu-tres], **Executrix** [eg-zec'-yu-trics], *sf.* Albacea, ejecutora, la mujer que ha sido nombrada testamentaria.
Exegesis [ec-se-jî'-sis], *s.* Explicación, exposición clara; especialmente de la Sagrada Biblia.
Exegetical [ec-se-jet'-i-cal], *a.* Exegético, explicativo.
Exegetically [ec-se-jet'-i-cal-i], *adv.* Por vía de explicación.
Exemplar [eg-zem'-plar], *s.* Ejemplar, original, modelo.
Exemplarily [eg'-zem-ple-ri-li], *adv.* Ejemplarmente; por ejemplo.
Exemplariness [eg'-zem-ple-ri-nes], *s.* Estado, situación o calidad que debe servir de ejemplar o modelo.
†**Exemplarity** [eg-zem-plar'-i-ti], *s.* Ejemplo digno de imitación.
Exemplary [eg'-zem-ple-ri o eg-zem'-ple-ri], *a.* 1. Ejemplar, lo que merece ser imitado. 2. Que sirve como ejemplo de amonestación o escarmiento.
Exemplification [eg-zem-pli-fi-ké'-shun], *s.* 1. Ejemplar, traslado; ejemplificación, declaración o ilustración hecha con ejemplos. 2. (For.) Copia certificada.
Exemplifier [eg-zem'-pli-fai-er], *s.* El que da ejemplo; el que demuestra con ejemplos.
Exemplify [eg-zem'-pli-fai], *va.* Ejemplificar, declarar, manifestar; trasladar, copiar.
Exempt [eg-zempt'], *va.* Exentar, libertar, eximir, privilegiar a alguna persona o cosa.
Exempt, *a.* Exento; no sujeto, no obligado.
Exemptible [eg-zempt'-i-bl], *a.* Exento, privilegiado, libre.
Exemption [eg-zemp'-shun], *s.* Exención, franquicia.
Exenterate [eg-zen'-ter-êt], *va.* (Poco us.) Desentrañar, destripar.
Exequatur [ec-se-cwé'-tur o cwā'-tur], *s.* Exequátur, la autorización que se da a un cónsul extranjero para que pueda ejercer el cargo de que se halla revestido.
Exequial [ec-zî'-cwi-al], *a.* Lo tocante a las exequias o funerales; antiguamente, exequial.
Exequies [ec'-se-cwiz], *s. pl.* Exequias, honras fúnebres.
Exercisable [ec-ser-saiz'-a-bl], *a.* Ejercitativo.
Exercise [ec'-ser-saiz], *s.* 1. Ejercicio, trabajo. 2. Ejercicio, ensayo; el acto de ejercitar alguna cosa. 3. Tarea. 4. Práctica, empleo o ejercicio de alguna cosa para adquirir conocimiento habitual de ella. 5. Acto de hablar, leer, declamar, etc., como en los actos públicos de las escuelas y en las reuniones religiosas; úsase generalmente en plural. Recreación, recreo. 6. (Ant.) El acto de dar culto a Dios.
Exercise, *vn.* Hacer ejercicio; ejercitarse.—*va.* 1. Ejercitar, formar, adiestrar o habituar. 2. Atarear; ejercer. 3. Emplear. 4. Causar ansiedad de ánimo. 5. Comunicar como efecto; dar parte.—*vr.* Emplearse, adiestrarse, ejercitarse.
Exerciser [ec'-ser-saiz-er], *s.* Ejercitante.
Exercitation [eg-zer-si-té'-shun], *s.* Ejercicio, ejercitación, práctica.

Exergue [ec-zẹrg'], *s.* Exergo, la leyenda que está en las medallas debajo del emblema o figura del anverso.
Exert [eg-zẹrt'], *va.* 1. Esforzar; ejecutar, poner por obra alguna cosa; poner en acción. 2. *vr.* *To exert one's self,* Empeñarse, hacer esfuerzo, apurarse, darse trabajo.
Exertion [eg-zẹr'-shun], *s.* Esfuerzo. *Exertions, pl.* Diligencias, pasos, medios.
Exfoliate [ex-fō'-li-êt], *vn.* 1. (Cir.) Exfoliarse, separarse de los huesos ciertas hojitas o láminas cariadas. 2. Escamarse, separarse de la superficie en hojas o láminas.—*va.* Quitar láminas, hojas o esquirlas de alguna cosa.
Exfoliation [ex-fo-li-é'-shun], *s.* Exfoliación, separación por hojas o láminas, como de las partes cariadas de un hueso, de la corteza, de una lámina de mineral, o de la piel.
Exfoliative [ex-fō'-li-a-tiv], *a.* Exfoliativo: dícese de los remedios que pueden ayudar la exfoliación.
Ex-guardian [ex-gār'-di-an], *s.* Exguardián.
Exhalable [ex-hê'-la-bl], *a.* Exhalable, evaporable.
Exhalation [ex-ha-lé'-shun], *s.* 1. Exhalación. 2. Exhalación, efluvio, vapor.
Exhale [ex-hêl'], *va.* 1. Exhalar, echar de sí vapor o vaho; emitir. 2. Evaporar, hacer evaporarse.—*vn.* Disiparse en vapor; desvanecerse.
Exhalement [ecs-hêl'-mẹnt], *s.* (Des.) Exhalación, vapor o vaho.
Exhaust [eg-zēst'], *va.* 1. Apurar, consumir el agua u otro licor. 2. Agotar; gastar, consumir, disipar. 3. Empobrecer; debilitar, enflaquecer. 4. Cansar. *To be exhausted,* No poder más. *Exhausted receiver,* Recipiente de que se ha extraído el aire.
Exhaust, *s.* Escape, descarga, expulsión. *Exhaust chamber,* Cámara de escape. *Exhaust pipe,* Tubo o caño de escape.
Exhauster [eg-zēst'-ẹr], *s.* Agotador.
Exhaustible [eg-zēst'-i-bl], *a.* Agotable, capaz de ser apurado o agotado.
Exhaustion [eg-zēs'-chun], *s.* Agotamiento.
Exhaustive [eg-zēst'-iv], *a.* Apurador, que tiende a agotar; cabal, completo en su ejecución, detallado.
Exhaustively [eg-zēst'-iv-li], *adv.* Cabalmente, completamente.
Exhaustiveness [eg-zēst'-iv-nes], *s.* Calidad de completo, de cabal.
Exhaustless [eg-zēst'-les], *a.* Inagotable.
§**Exheredate** [ex-her'-ẹ-dêt], *va.* Desheredar.
Exheredation [ex-her-ẹ-dé'-shun], *s.* (For.) Desheredamiento.
Exhibit [eg-zib'-it], *va.* 1. Exhibir, manifestar, ofrecer, mostrar. 2. (Med.) Administrar, recetar un remedio.
Exhibit, *s.* 1. Cualquier objeto o colección de objetos expuestos a la vista pública. 2. Manifestación. 3. (For.) Documento fehaciente presentado en un tribunal de justicia.
Exhibiter, Exhibitor [eg-zib'-it-ẹr], *s.* 1. Exponente, el que exhibe, que muestra alguna cosa en público. 2. El que presenta documento fehaciente en un tribunal de justicia.
Exhibition [eg-zi-bish'-un], *s.* 1. Exhibición, manifestación o presentación de alguna cosa; exposición. 2. Espectáculo, la accion de presentar alguna cosa en público. 3. (Med.) Administración de un remedio. 4. (Ingl.) Beca (de un colegio).
Exhibitioner [eg-zi-bish'-un-ẹr], *s.* Estudiante que disfruta en las universidades de Inglaterra de una pensión para su sostenimiento. Esta palabra equivale a *Beca de merced,* o *pensionado.*
Exhibitive [eg-zib'-it-iv], *a.* Representativo.
Exhibitively [eg-zib'-it-iv-li], *adv.* Representativamente.
Exhibitory [eg-zib'-i-to-ri], *a.* Exhibitorio, lo que exhibe o manifiesta.
Exhilarant [eg-zil'-a-rant], *a.* Alegrador, que causa regocijo o alegría.
Exhilarate [eg-zil'-a-rêt], *va.* Alegrar, causar alegría; causar sensación de viveza en; llenar de alegría.—*vn.* Alegrarse.
Exhilaration [eg-zil-a-ré'-shun], *s.* Alegría, buen humor, regocijo.
Exhort [eg-zōrt'], *va.* Exhortar, inducir y mover con razones; excitar.
Exhortation [eg-zōr-té'-shun], *s.* 1. Exhortación. 2. Aviso, consejo.
Exhortative, Exhortatory [eg-zōrt'-a-tiv, eg-zōrt'-a-to-ri], *a.* Exhortatorio.
Exhorter [eg-zōrt'-ẹr], *s.* Exhortador.
Exhumate [ex-hiū'-mêt], *va.* (Fam.) *V.* EXHUME.
Exhumation [ecs-hiū-mé'-shun], *s.* Exhumación, desentierro de un cadáver.
Exhume [ex-hiūm'], *va.* Exhumar, desenterrar.
Exiccate [ec-sik'-êt], *va.* Desecar, secar. *V.* EXSICCATE.
Exiccation [ec-sik-é'-shun], *s.* Desecación. *V.* EXSICCATION.
Exiccative [ec-sic'-a-tiv], *a.* Desecativo. *V.* EXSICCATIVE.
Exigence, Exigency [ec'-si-jens, i], *s.* Exigencia, falta, necesidad, urgencia, aprieto, apuro, lance apretado; ocasión.
Exigent [ec'-si-jent], *a.* Exigente, urgente, que demanda acción inmediata; exigente, que pide demasiado.—*s.* Urgencia; embarazo, perplejidad; cabo, fin, remate.
Exigible [ec'-si-ji-bl], *a.* Exigible, que puede exigirse.
Exiguity [ec-si-giū'-i-ti], *s.* (Poco us.) Pequeñez, parvedad, modicidad, exigüidad.
Exiguous [eg-zig'-yu-us], *a.* Exiguo, pequeño.
Exile [ex'-ail], *s.* 1. Destierro. 2. Desterrado.
Exile [ex'-ail], *va.* Desterrar, deportar.
Exility [eg-zil'-i-ti], *s.* (Ant.) Tenuidad, pequeñez.
†**Eximious** [ec-sim'-i-us], *a.* Eximio, eminente, excelente.
Exinanition [ec-sin-a-nish'-un], *s.* Exinanición, gran falta de vigor y fuerza.
Exist [eg-zist'], *vn.* Existir.
Existence [eg-zist'-ens], *s.* 1. Existencia. 2. Vida, continuación de ser. 3. Ente.
Existent [eg-zist'-ent], *a.* Existente.
†**Existential** [eg-zis-ten'-shal], *a.* Lo que tiene existencia.
Existentialism [eg-zis-ten'-shal-ism], *s.* (Fil.) Existencialismo.
Exit [ec'-sit], *s.* 1. Sale: palabra que se pone en los argumentos de las comedias para indicar cuando el actor se retira de la escena. 2. Partida, muerte. 3. Salida, éxito.
†**Exitial** [eg-zish'-al], **Exitious** [eg-zish'-us], *a.* Destructivo, pernicioso.
Exode [ec-sōd'], *s.* Exodo, una de las cuatro partes de la tragedia griega que contenía la conclusión trágica o catástrofe.
Exodus [ec'-so-dus], *s.* 1. Salida, emigración, éxodo. 2. Éxodo, el segundo libro del antiguo Testamento.
Exogen [ex'-o-jen], *s.* (Bot.) Planta exógena, aquella cuyo tallo crece por la adición de capas externas concéntricas; dicotiledónea.
Exogenous [ex-ej'-en-us], *a.* Exógeno, exógena, que crece por la adición de capas externas.
Exomphalos [eg-zem'-fa-los], *s.* (Cir.) Exónfalo, hernia umbilical.
Exonerate [eg-zen'-ẹr-êt], *va.* 1. Vindicar de una acusación o censura. 2. Exonerar, descargar; aliviar del peso, cargo u obligación.
Exoneration [eg-zen-ẹr-é'-shun], *s.* 1. Exoneración. 2. Vindicación de una censura o acusación.
Exonerative [eg-zen'-ẹr-a-tiv], *a.* Lo que puede exonerar.
Exorable [ec'-so-ra-bl], *a.* Exorable, el que se mueve por ruegos.
Exorbitance, Exorbitancy [eg-zōr'-bi-tans, i], *s.* Exorbitancia, exceso desorden, enormidad, extravagancia.
Exorbitant [eg-zōr'-bi-tant], *a.* Exorbitante, excesivo, desproporcionado, enorme, extravagante.
Exorbitantly [eg-zōr'-bi-tant-li], *adv.* Exorbitantemente.
Exorcise [ec'-ser-saiz], *va.* Exorcizar, conjurar.
Exorciser [ec'-ser-saiz-ẹr], **Exorcist** [ec'-ser-sist], *s.* Exorcista.
Exorcism [ec'-ser-sizm], *s.* Exorcismo, la acción de exorcizar los espíritus malignos; también conjuro ordenado por la Iglesia contra el espíritu maligno.
Exordium [eg-zōr'-di-um], *s.* Exordio, principio o introducción de un discurso.
Exosmose [ex'-es-mōs], *s.* (Fís.) Exósmosis, corriente de dentro a fuera, que se establece al mismo tiempo que su contraria la endósmosis, cuando dos líquidos de distinta densidad están separados por una membrana.
Exosmotic [ex-es-met'-ic], *a.* Exosmótico, relativo a la exósmosis.
Exosseous [ec-ses'-e-us], *a.* Desosado, sin huesos.
Exostosis [ec-ses-tō'-sis], *s.* Exóstosis, tumor huesoso.
Exoteric, Exoterical [ec-so-ter'-ic, al], *a.* Exotérico, público, común a todos, lo contrario de esotérico.
Exotic, Exotical [ec-set'-ic, al], *a.* Exótico, extranjero; advenedizo.—*s.* (Bot.) Planta exótica.
Exotic fuel [ex-e'-tic fiū'-el], *s.* Combustible inusual, combustible de alta potencia.
Expand [ex-pand'], *va.* 1. Extender, dilatar, alargar, ensanchar la superficie. 2. Extender, desarrollar, esparcir; desplegar.—*vn.* Desarrollarse, dilatarse, ensancharse.
Expanse [ex-pans'], *s.* Extensión, espacio.
Expansibility [ex-pan''-si-bil'-i-ti], *s.* Expansibilidad.
Expansible [ex-pan'-si-bl], *a.* Expansible, capaz de expansión.
Expansion [ex-pan'-shun], *s.* 1. Expansión. 2. Aumento de tamaño, dilatación; anchura, largura; desarrollo. 3. Extensión, inmensidad.

4. Aumento de volumen, como el del vapor. *Triple expansion engine,* Máquina de vapor de triple expansión.

Expansile [ex-pan'-sil], *a.* Capaz de extensión, que tiene poder de dilatarse.

Expansive [ex-pan'-siv], *a.* Expansivo.

Expansiveness [ex-pan'-siv-nes], *s.* Expansibilidad, propiedad de un cuerpo de ocupar mayor espacio.

Ex parte [ex pār'-te]. (For.) De una parte, de una de las partes.

Expatiate [ex-pê'-shi-êt], *vn.* 1. Espaciarse, dilatarse, difundirse, hacer digresiones. 2. Extenderse, discurrir con muchas palabras.—*va.* Dar libre curso o alcance; extender.

Expatiation [ex-pê''-shi-ê'-shun], *s.* Digresión, difusión, prolijidad.

Expatiator [ex-pê'-shi-êt-ẹr], *s.* Amplificador, el que habla larga y profusamente sobre un asunto.

Expatiatory [ex-pê-shi-a-to-ri], *a.* Difuso, prolijo.

Expatriate [ex-pê'-tri-êt], *va.* Expatriar, desterrar.

Expatriation [ex-pê-tri-ê'-shun], *s.* Expatriación, destierro.

Expect [ex-pect'], *va.* 1. Esperar, aguardar. 2. Fiarse, descansar en, contar con, como cosa debida. 3. (Fam.) Suponer, en este sentido es un solecismo familiar. 4. (Ant.) Quedar, esperar.

Expectable [ex-pect'-a-bl], *a.* Expectable, lo que es de esperar o temer.

Expectance, Expectancy [ex-pec'-tans, i], *s.* Expectación, expectativa, esperanza, espera.

Expectant [ex-pect'-ant], *a.* Expectante; dícese del que está en expectación de alguna cosa. *Expectant treatment,* Tratamiento expectante. —*s.* Esperador; el que está en expectación de alguna cosa.

Expectation [ex-pect-ê'-shun], *s.* Expectación, expectativa, esperanza. *A prince of great expectation,* Un príncipe de grandes esperanzas. *Expectation of life,* Probable duración media de la vida desde una edad determinada.

Expectative [ex-pect'-a-tiv], *a.* Expectativo.—*s.* (Des.) Objeto de expectación.

Expecter [ex-pect'-ẹr], *s.* Esperador.

Expectorant [ex-pec'-to-rant], *s.* (Med.) Expectorante, que promueve la expectoración, que hace expectorar.—*s.* Medicamento expectorante.

Expectorate [ex-pec'-to-rêt], *va.* Expectorar, arrancar del pecho y arrojar por la boca flemas y otras materias viscosas.

Expectoration [ex-pec-to-rê'-shun], *s.* Expectoración; esputo, gargajo.

Expectorative [ex-pec'-to-ra-tiv], *a.* Expectorativo, expectorante.

Expedience, Expediency [ex-pî'-di-ens, i], *s.* Aptitud, propiedad; lo más practicable o factible, o lo que más conviene hacer dadas las circunstancias, conveniencia, utilidad, oportunidad.

Expedient [ex-pî'-di-ent], *a.* 1. Oportuno, conveniente; prudente, propio. 2. (Des.) Expedito, pronto.—*s.* Expediente, medio, corte, recurso.

Expediently [ex-pî'-di-ent-li], *adv.* Aptamente, convenientemente.

Expeditate [ex-ped'-i-têt], *va.* Cortar una especie de espolones agudos que cierta clase de perros tienen en las patas y con los cuales desgarran la caza.

Expeditation [ex-ped-i-tê'-shun], *s.* La acción de cortar los espolones y las uñas de las patas de los perros.

Expedite [ex'-pẹ-dait], *va.* 1. Desembarazar, facilitar. 2. Acelerar, apresurar, dar prisa. 3. Expedir, dar curso y despacho a las causas o negocios.

†**Expedite,** *a.* *V.* EXPEDITIOUS.

Expeditely [ex'-pẹ-dait-li], *adv.* Expeditamente.

Expedition [ex-pẹ-dish'-un], *s.* 1. Expedición, prisa, diligencia, celeridad. 2. Caminata, jornada de muchas personas, con un objeto determinado y la colectividad de personas que la emprende. 3. Expedición, empresa de guerra.

Expeditious [ex-pẹ-dish'-us], *a.* Pronto, veloz, expedito.

Expeditiously [ex-pẹ-dish'-us-li], *adv.* Expeditamente, prontamente.

Expel [ex-pel'], *va.* Expeler, arrojar, expulsar, echar fuera por medio de la fuerza o autoridad; desterrar, excluir; despedir.

Expellable [ex-pel'-a-bl], *a.* Expulsable, que puede ser expelido.

Expeller [ex-pel'-ẹr], *s.* El o lo que expele, expulsa, etc.

Expend [ex-pend'], *va.* Expender, gastar, emplear dinero, tiempo, palabras, esfuerzos, etc., en alguna cosa; desembolsar.

Expenditure [ex-pend'-i-chur o -tiūr], *s.* Gasto, desembolso.

Expense [ex-pens'], *s.* Expensas, gasto, coste. *At any expense,* A toda costa. *To be at expense, to go to expense,* Meterse o ponerse en gastos.

Expenseless [ex-pens'-les], *a.* Poco o nada costoso.

Expensive [ex-pens'-iv], *a.* 1. Pródigo, gastador, manirroto, amigo de gastar; liberal, generoso. 2. Costoso; dispendioso, de mucho precio.

Expensively [ex-pens'-iv-li], *adv.* Costosamente.

Expensiveness [ex-pens'-iv-nes], *s.* Prodigalidad, profusión; costa, coste, costo.

Experience [ex-pî'-ri-ens], *s.* 1. Experiencia, conocimiento, práctica. 2. Algo experimentado o gozado. 3. Ejercicio espiritual; conversión. *To learn by experience,* Aprender por experiencia propia; hacer la prueba.

Experience, *va.* Experimentar; conocer y reconocer por medio del uso.

Experienced [ex-pî'-ri-enst], *a.* Experimentado, perito; hábil.

Experiencer [ex-pî'-ri-ens-ẹr], *s.* Experimentador.

Experiment [ex-per'-i-mẹnt], *s.* 1. Experimento, prueba, ensayo. 2. Lo que va pasando por una prueba práctica. *He would not try the experiment,* No quiso hacer la prueba, no quiso exponerse.

Experiment, *vn.* Experimentar, hacer una prueba, un experimento.

Experimental [ex-per-i-ment'-al], *a.* Experimental; sabido y conocido en virtud de repetidas pruebas y experiencias.

Experimentalist [ex-per-i-ment'-al-ist], *s.* Experimentador.

Experimentally [ex-per-i-ment'-al-i], *adv.* Experimentalmente.

Experimentation [ex-per-i-men-tê'-shun], *s.* Experimento, la acción u operación de experimentar.

Experimenter [ex-per'-i-ment-ẹr], *s.* Experimentador.

Experimentist [ex-per'-i-ment-ist], *s.* Experimentador.

Expert [ex-pẹrt'], *a.* Experimentado experto, práctico, pronto, diestro, hábil.

Expertly [ex-pẹrt'-li], *adv.* Diestramente, hábilmente, mañosamente.

Expertness [ex-pẹrt'-nes], *s.* Maña, destreza, habilidad.

Expiable [ex'-pi-a-bl], *a.* Expiable, lo que se puede expiar.

Expiate [ex'-pi-êt], *va.* Expiar, limpiar y borrar un delito; pagar las penas debidas por las culpas, reparar un daño, dar satisfacción.

Expiation [ex-pi-ê'-shun], *s.* Expiación, el acto de expiar; reparación, resarcimiento de un daño cualquiera. *V.* ATONEMENT.

Expiatist, Expiator [ex'-pi-ê-tist, ex'-pi-ê-tẹr], *s.* El que expía o hace expiación.

Expiatory [ex'-pi-a-to-ri], *a.* Expiatorio.

Expiration [ex-pi-rê'-shun], *s.* 1. Espiración, salida del aire aspirado en los pulmones. 2. Muerte, el último suspiro o aliento. 3. Remate, término, fin. 4. Vapor.

Expire [ex-pair'], *va.* 1. Exhalar, despedir exhalaciones o vapores. 2. Expirar, respirar; concluir, acabar. —*vn.* 1. Expirar, morir, dar el último aliento. 2. Acabarse alguna cosa.

Explain [ex-plên'], *va.* Explanar, explicar, aclarar.

Explainable [ex-plên'-a-bl], *a.* Explicable.

Explainer [ex-plên'-ẹr], *s.* Expositor, comentador, intérprete.

Explanation [ex-pla-nê'-shun], *s.* Explanación, explicación, interpretación.

Explanatory, Explanative [ex-plan'-a-to-ri, ex-plan'-a-tiv], *a.* Interpretativo, explicativo, que sirve para explicar o tiende á ello.

Expletive [ex'-plẹ-tiv], *a.* Expletivo, que sirve para hacer más llena o armoniosa la locución, pero que no es necesario para el sentido de la frase. —*s.* 1. Interjección, a menudo profana. 2. Partícula expletiva. 3. Algo que sirve para henchir; añadidura.

Expletory [ex'-plẹ-to-ri], *a.* Que sirve para llenar o henchir.

Explicable [ex'-pli-ca-bl], *a.* Explicable.

Explicate [ex'-pli-kêt], *va.* Explicar, aclarar alguna cosa que está confusa; desenredar, interpretar.

Explication [ex-pli-kê'-shun], *s.* Explicación, ilustración, interpretación.

Explicative [ex'-pli-kẹ-tiv], *a.* Explicativo.

Explicator [ex'-pli-kê''-tẹr], *s.* Expositor, antiguamente exponedor, el que explica; ilustrador.

Explicatory [ex'-pli-ca-to-ri], *a.* Explicativo.

Explicit [ex-plis'-it], *a.* Explícito, claro, formal, categórico.

Explicit [ex'-pli-sit]. (Lat. en vez de *explicitus est,* está terminado.) Antiguamente se ponía esta palabra a lo último de los libros en lugar de la voz *fin* que ahora se usa.

Explicitly [ex-plis'-it-li], *adv.* Explícitamente.

Explicitness [ex-plis'-it-nes], *s.* Claridad en el lenguaje; lucidez en las ideas.

Explode [ex-plōd'], *va.* 1. Hacer explosión, estallar, disparar con estallido. 2. Desacreditar, demostrar la falsedad de algo, disfamar. 3.

Expeler con violencia y estrépito. —*va.* 1. Estallar, dar un estallido, hacer explosión, abrirse con estrépito. 2. Silbar, como la pólvora. 3. Reventar, tener súbito fin; desplomarse. 4. (Fisiol.) Salir o dejarse ver súbitamente.

Exploder [ex-plōd'-ẹr], *s.* Causa cualquiera de una explosión; el que o lo que hace explosión o estalla.

Exploit [ex-pleit'], *s.* Hazaña, hecho heroico ó famoso.

Exploit, *va.* (Neol.) 1. Explotar, sacar todo el beneficio o producto posible de una cosa o persona; utilizar para su interés particular. 2. Buscar. 3. Referir con pormenores.

Exploitable [ex-pleit'-a-bl], *a.* Explotable, que puede ser explotado.

Exploitation [ex-plei-tē'-shun], *s.* 1. Explotación, la acción de explotar, de hacer uso de recursos naturales desatendidos hasta entonces. 2. Utilización en interés particular de alguien.

Exploiting [ex-pleit'-ing], *s.* Explotación.

Exploration [ex-plo-rē'-shun], *s.* Exploración, examen; investigación científica, particularmente geográfica, en regiones poco conocidas.

Explorator [ex'-plo-rē-tẹr], *s.* Explorador, examinador.

Exploratory [ex-plōr'-a-to-ri], *a.* Exploratorio.

Explore [ex-plōr'], *va.* Explorar, averiguar, examinar, sondear, profundizar, observar.

Explosion [ex-plō'-zhun], *s.* Explosión.

Explosive [ex-plō'-siv], *a.* Explosivo, lo que tiene capacidad de hacer explosión.—*s.* Cualquiera substancia que puede causar explosión por su repentina combustión o descomposición.

†**Expoliation** [ex-po-li-ē'-shun], *s.* Despojo; gasto.

Exponent [ex-pō'-nent], *s.* 1. (Mat.) Exponente. 2. Representante.

Export [ex-pōrt'], *va.* Exportar, sacar o extraer géneros de un país para otro.

Exports [ex'-pōrts], *s. pl.* Las mercancías o géneros extraídos de un país para otro.

Exportable [ex-pōrt'-a-bl], *a.* Exportable, lo que puede ser exportado.

Exportation [ex-por-tē'-shun], *s.* Exportación, extracción. *Bounty on exportation,* Prima de exportación. *Channel of exportation,* Punto de salida de géneros.

Exporter [ex-pōrt'-ẹr], *s.* Exportador, el que exporta.

Expose [ex-pōz'], *va.* 1. Exponer, poner de manifiesto alguna cosa, mostrar, descubrir, publicar, manifestar. 2. Exponer, poner en peligro, arriesgar. 3. Manifestar las cualidades de alguna persona de modo que se la exponga a ser censurada, burlada o despreciada; comprometer; ponerse en ridículo; descubrirse, faltar a la decencia. 4. Abandonar una persona o cosa a su suerte. 5. Poner a descubierto, desenmascarar, descubrir y divulgar un enredo, abuso o escándalo.

Exposed [ex-pōzd'], *pp.* y *a.* 1. Expuesto, mostrado, etc. 2. Descubierto, no abrigado.

Exposer [ex-pōz'-ẹr], *s.* Exponente, el que expone.

Exposition [ex-po-zish'-un], *s.* 1. Exposición, la acción de exponer a la vista; exhibición pública de productos industriales, agrícolas, artísticos, etc. 2. Exposición, explicación, interpretación. 3. Análisis retórico. 4. Desenlace de un drama. 5. §Riesgo, peligro.

Expositive [ex-pez'-i-tiv], *a.* Expositivo.

Expositor [ex-pes'-i-tẹr], *s.* Expositor; comentador, intérprete.

Expository [ex-pez'-i-to-ri], *a.* Expositivo, explicativo.

Ex post facto [ex pōst fac'-to]. Expresión latina para calificar la resolución tomada acerca de una cosa que ha sucedido antes; v. gr. se llama una ley *ex post facto,* cuando se aplica a un caso o delito anterior a ella.

Expostulate [ex-pes'-chu (o tiu) -lēt], *vn.* Debatir seriamente, reconvenir a uno amigablemente; representar el error o los inconvenientes de un acto, una medida, etc., procurando hacer cambiar a otro de opinión: seguido de *with.*

Expostulation [ex-pes-chu-lē'-shun], *s.* Debate, reconvención, disuasión.

Expostulator [ex-pes'-chu-lē-tẹr], *s.* El que ventila algún asunto con otro reconviniéndole amigablemente.

Expostulatory [ex-pes'-chu-la-to-ri], *a.* Lo que contiene cargos o reconvenciones amistosas.

Exposure [ex-pō'-zhur], *s.* 1. Manifestación, el acto de exponer. 2. Situación arriesgada o peligrosa. 3. Aspecto; situación o posición con respecto a uno de los puntos cardinales. *The house has a southern exposure,* La casa da o mira al sur. 4. Escándalo; revelación de algo oculto y escandaloso.

Exposure meter [ex-pō'-zhur mī'-ter], *s.* En fotografía, medidor de exposición.

Expound [ex-paund'], *va.* Exponer, declarar, interpretar, comentar.

Expounder [ex-paund'-ẹr], *s.* Expositor, comentador.

Express [ex-pres'], *va.* 1. Expresar; manifestar, dar a entender. 2. Representar, ser símbolo o imagen de alguna cosa. 3. Designar, denotar; declarar el pensamiento de uno, proferir, articular. 4. Exprimir, sacar o extraer el jugo de alguna cosa. 5. Enviar, expedir por expreso o mensajero.

Express, *a.* 1. Expreso, claro, formal, explícito. 2. Pintiparado, copiado, parecido. 3. Hecho o llevado por expreso; pronto, de prisa.—*s.* 1. Expreso, correo, mensajero, propio. 2. Expreso, el mensaje o aviso que lleva algún expreso o correo extraordinario. 3. Expreso, servicio organizado para el rápido transporte de mercancías y paquetes de un punto a otro.

Expressage [ex-pres'-ẹj], *s.* 1. Porte, coste de llevar por expreso. 2. Todo lo que se envía por expreso.

Express car, *s.* Vagón expreso.

Express company, *s.* Empresa de transportes rápidos.

Expressible [ex-pres'-i-bl], *a.* 1. Decible; expresable. 2. Exprimible, que puede exprimirse para sacar el jugo.

Expression [ex-presh'-un], *s.* 1. Expresión; gesto, acción de expresarse; expresión de la fisonomía que manifiesta los sentimientos, las emociones, etc. 2. Expresión, locución, voz o palabra; modo de expresar o hacer extender lo que se quiere o piensa. 3. Verdad y viveza con que están expresados los efectos en las artes. 4. (Farm.) Expresión, el acto de exprimir con prensa el zumo o aceite de las plantas.

Expressive [ex-pres'-iv], *a.* Expresivo, significativo, enérgico, enfático.

Expressively [ex-pres'-iv-li], *adv.* Expresivamente, enérgicamente.

Expressiveness [ex-pres'-iv-nes], *s.* Energía.

Expressly [ex-pres'-li], *adv.* Expresamente.

Expressman [ex-pres'-man], *s.* Mensajero, empleado de una compañía de expreso.

Expressness [ex-pres'-nes], *s.* Calidad de exacto, específico y determinado.

Express train, *s.* Expreso, tren expreso.

Express way [ex-pres' wē], *s.* Autopista.

Exprobrate [ex-prō'-brēt], *va.* (Ant.) Vituperar, afear, echar en cara, dar en rostro.

Expropriate [ex-prō'-pri-ēt], *va.* Enajenar, expropiar.

Expropriation [ex-prō-pri-ē'-shun], *s.* Enajenamiento, expropiación, renuncia o privación de la propiedad de algo.

Expugn [ex-piūn'], *va.* Expugnar, tomar por fuerza o asalto una ciudad o plaza.

Expugnable [ex-pug'-na-bl], *a.* Expugnable, que se puede expugnar.

Expugnation [ex-pug-nē'-shun], *s.* Expugnación, toma por asalto.

Expugner [ex-piūn'-ẹr], *s.* Expugnador.

Expulsion [ex-pul'-shun], *s.* Expulsión.

Expulsive [ex-pul'-siv], *a.* Expulsivo, que tiende a expulsar.

§**Expunction** [ex-punc'-shun], *s.* Borradura, raspadura.

Expunge [ex-punj'], *va.* 1. Borrar, cancelar, rayar. 2. Borrar, lavar las manchas o defectos. 3. Acabar, aniquilar.

Expunging [ex-punj'-ing], *s.* Cancceladura, el acto de cancelar.

Expurgate [ex'-pur-gēt o ex-pūr'-get], *va.* Expurgar, tachar u omitir las palabras o cláusulas censurables de un libro; limpiar, purificar de lo que es nocivo.

Expurgation [ex-pur-gē'-shun], *s.* Expurgación, purificación, expurgo.

Expurgatory [ex-pūr'-ga-to-ri], *a.* Expurgatorio.

Exquisite [ex'-cwi-zit], *a.* 1. Exquisito, exquisitamente bello, de singular primor en su especie; consumado. 2. Intenso, excesivo, atroz. *Exquisite pain,* Dolor excesivo, pena atroz. 3. Remilgado, exigente, quisquilloso, delicadamente sensible o impresionable. 4. Vivo, delicioso. *Exquisite pleasure,* Vivo placer.—*s.* Elegante, petimetre, pisaverde.

Exquisitely [ex'-cwi-zit-li], *adv.* Exquisitamente, completamente.

Exquisiteness [ecs'-cwi-zit-nes], *s.* Primor, delicadeza, excelencia, perfección.

Exsanguinate [ec-san'-gwi-nēt], *va.* Desangrar, quitar la sangre.

Exsanguine [ec-san'-gwin], *a.* Que no tiene sangre; desangrado.

Exscind [ec-sind'], *va.* Cortar, extirpar.

Exsect [ec-sect'], *va.* Cortar, extirpar, quitar.

Exsection [ec-sec'-shun], *s.* Cortadura, corte de una parte de un miembro o una corta extensión de hueso.

Exserted [ec-sert'-ed], *a.* (Bot.) Exserto, que proyecta o sobresale de las partes que lo rodean, como los estambres; sin cubierta.
Exsiccant [ec-sic'-ant], *a.* Desecativo, desecante.
Exsiccate [ec'-sik-êt o ec-sik'-et], *va.* Desecar, secar.
Exsiccation [ec-si-kê'-shun], *s.* Desecación.
Exsiccative [ec-sic'-a-tiv], *a.* Desecativo, desecante.
‡**Exspuition** [ex-piu-ish'-un], *s.* Esputo, saliva.
Exstipulate [ex-stip'-yu-lêt], *a.* (Bot.) Sin estípulas, que carece de estípulas.
Exsuction [ec-suc'-shun], *s.* Chupadura, chupetón.
Extancy [ec'-stan-si], *s.* (Ant.) La parte que sobresale en alguna cosa.
Extant [ec'-stant], *a.* 1. Estante, existente; viviente. 2. (Ant.) Sobresaliente, lo que sobresale sobre las demás partes de la misma especie.
†**Extasy** [ec'-sta-si], *s.* Éxtasi o éxtasis. *V.* ECSTASY.
†**Extatic, Extatical** [ec-stat'-ic, al], *a.* Extático, arrobado, fuera de sí. *V.* ECSTATIC.
Extemporal [ex-tem'-po-ral], *a.* (Des.) *V.* EXTEMPORANEOUS.
Extemporaneous [ex-tem-po-rê'-ne-us], **Extemporary** [ex-tem'-po-re-ri], *a.* 1. Repentino, improviso, ejecutado o hecho sin mucha o ninguna preparación; ocasional. 2. Dado a hablar en público sin apuntes, improvisando.
Extemporaneously [ex-tem-po-rê'-ne-us-li], *adv.* Repentinamente, de improviso.
Extempore [ex-tem'-po-rî o rê], *a.* Sin estudio previo, improvisado.—*adv.* Extemporáneamente, de improviso, de repente, in promptu.
Extemporiness [ex-tem'-po-ri-nes], *s.* Improvisación, la facultad de decir alguna cosa extemporáneamente.
Extemporize [ex-tem'-po-raiz], *va.* Improvisar, hablar, tocar o componer música extemporáneamente o de repente.
Extend [ex-tend'], *va.* 1. Extender, tender, alargar; ensanchar, amplificar; prolongar el tiempo. 2. Alargar el brazo, tender la mano. 3. Conceder, dar, comunicar.—*vn.* Alcanzar o extenderse a alguna distancia. *To extend the arm, the hand,* Alargar el brazo; tender la mano. *To extend trade,* Dar extensión al comercio. *To extend the time of payment,* Dar prórroga, diferir la época del pago. *His power does not extend so far,* Su poder no se extiende tan lejos, no llega a tanto.
Extended [ex-tend'-ed], *a.* y *pp.* 1. Extenso, prolongado en el espacio, tiempo o alcance. 2. (Tip.) Tipo abierto, ancho con relación á su altura; v. g. letra abierta.
Extendedly, *adv.* Extensamente.
Extender [ex-tend'-er], *s.* Extendedor.
Extendible [ex-tend'-i-bl], *a.* Extensivo, capaz de ser extendido.
Extensibility [ex-ten-si-bil'-i-ti], **Extensibleness** [ex-ten'-si-bl-nes], *s.* Extensibilidad.
Extensible [ex-ten'-si-bl], *a.* Extensivo, extensible.
Extension [ex-ten'-shun], *s.* 1. Extensión; aumento, prolongación; despliegue. 2. Anexo; cosa agregada. 3. Extensión, espacio, propiedad de la materia.
‡**Extensional** [ex-ten'-shun-al], *a.* Muy extendido, lo que tiene mucha extensión.
Extensive [ex-ten'-siv], *a.* Extenso, dilatado, espacioso, vasto, grande, de mucha extensión.
Extensively [ex-ten'-siv-li], *adv.* Extensivamente.
Extensiveness [ex-ten'-siv-nes], *s.* Extensión, anchura, capacidad, grandor; extensibilidad.
Extensor [ex-ten'-ser], *s.* (Anat.) Extensor, músculo que sirve para extender.
Extent [ex-tent'], *s.* 1. Extensión, grado, compás, término. 2. Tamaño, magnitud. 3. (For.) Ejecución; embargo. 4. (Des.) Comunicación, distribución. *To a certain extent,* Hasta cierto punto. *To the full extent,* En toda su extensión. *To a great extent,* En sumo grado, grandemente.
Extenuate [ex-ten'-yu-êt], *va.* 1. Disminuir, minorar, mitigar, atenuar, paliar. 2. (Poco us.) Extenuar, desengrosar, adelgazar.
Extenuating [ex-ten'-yu-êt-ing], *a.* Atenuante, paliativo, excusador.
Extenuation [ex-ten-yu-ê'-shun], *s.* Extenuación, mitigación, paliación, atenuación de una falta; excusación.
Exterior [ex-tî'-ri-er], *a.* 1. Exterior, de la parte de afuera. 2. Externo. 3. Distinguido o notado por los sentidos, manifiesto. *s.* Lo exterior; la apariencia o aspecto de una persona o cosa.
Exteriority [ex-tî-ri-er'-i-ti], *s.* (Poco us.) Exterioridad.
Exteriorly [ex-tî'-ri-er-li], *adv.* Exteriormente.
Exterminate [ex-ter'-mi-nêt], *va.* 1. Exterminar, desarraigar, destruir, extirpar. 2. (Álg.) Hacer desaparecer. *V.* ELIMINATE.
Extermination [ex-ter-mi-nê'-shun], *s.* Exterminación, destrucción, desolación, extirpación.
Exterminator [ex-ter'-mi-nê-ter], *s.* Exterminador.
Exterminatory [ex-ter'-mi-na-to-ri], *a.* Lo que extermina.
Extern [ex-tern'], *a.* (Ant.) Externo, exterior; extrínseco.
Extern, Externe, *s.* 1. Alumno externo de una escuela o colegio, el que no es pupilo. 2. Médico o practicante de un hospital que no habita en el edificio.
External [ex-ter'-nal], *a.* 1. Externo, exterior. 2. Extranjero, exterior. *External trade,* Comercio exterior o extranjero.—*s.* Lo exterior, la parte externa; símbolo, ceremonia, rito externo, v. gr. los de una religión.
Externality [ex-ter-nal'-i-ti], *s.* 1. Exterioridad, calidad de lo que es exterior. 2. Percepción externa. 3. Objeto externo; rito, símbolo.
Externalize, Externalise [ex-ter'-nal-aiz], *va.* 1. Dar figura, dar cuerpo, incorporar. 2. Hacer real de una manera exterior y visible.
Externally [ex-ter'-nal-i], *adv.* Exteriormente.
Extersion [ex-ter'-shun], *s.* Borradura, raspadura.
Extinct [ex-tinct'], *a.* 1. Extinto, extinguido, apagado; destruído, desaparecido. 2. Extinto, sin sucesión. 3. Abolido, suprimido. *To become extinct,* Extinguirse, apagarse; morir, desaparecer.
Extinction [ex-tinc'-shun], *s.* 1. Extinción, apagamiento. 2. Destrucción, supresión, aniquilación, abolición.
Extinguish [ex-tin'-gwish], *va.* 1. Extinguir, apagar. 2. Suprimir, destruir; obscurecer.
Extinguishable [ex-tin'-gwish-a-bl], *a.* Extinguible.
Extinguisher [ex-tin'-gwish-er], *s.* Extinguidor, apagador. *Fire extinguisher,* Extinguidor o extintor de incendios.
Extinguishment [ex-tin'-gwish-ment], *s.* 1. Apagamiento, extinción; abolición, aniquilamiento. 2. Anulación; amortización, p. ej. de una deuda pública.
Extirpable [ex-ter'-pa-bl], *a.* Capaz de ser extirpado.
Extirpate [ex'-ter-pêt], *va.* Extirpar, desarraigar.
Extirpation [ex-ter-pê'-shun], *s.* 1. Extirpación, exterminio. 2. (Cir.) Excisión, extirpación, la acción de separar o cortar por completo un órgano, tumor, excrecencia, etc.
Extirpator [ex'-ter-pê''-ter], *s.* Exterminador, extirpador.
Extol [ex-tel'], *va.* Engrandecer, ensalzar, aplaudir, magnificar.
Extoller [ecs-tel'-er], *s.* Ensalzador, alabador, loador.
Extorsive [ex-tōr'-siv], *a.* (Poco us.) Que causa extorsión, que sirve para violentar; inicuo, injusto.
Extorsively [ex-tōr'-siv-li], *adv.* Con extorsión.
Extort [ex-tōrt'], *va.* Sacar u obtener por fuerza alguna cosa; arrancar, adquirir por violencia u opresión.—*vn.* Practicar extorsión.
‡**Extorter** [ex-tōrt'-er], **Extortioner** [ex-tōr'-shun-er], *s.* Opresor, el que causa extorsión; concusionario.
Extortion [ex-tōr'-shun], *s.* 1. Extorsión, el acto y efecto de obtener algo de otro por fuerza e indebidamente. 2. Lo que se ha obtenido por fuerza o violencia. 3. (Der.) Extorsión, el delito que comete un empleado público con exacciones injustas.
Extortionary [ex-tōr'-shun-e-ri], *a.* Lo que tiene el carácter o implica una extorsión o acto ilegal.
Extortionate [ex-tōr'-shun-et], *a.* Opresivo, injusto, violento.
Extortionist [ex-tōr'-shun-ist], *s.* *V.* EXTORTIONER.
Extra [ex'-tra], *a.* Extra, además, doble, de repuesto, adicional, suplementario.—*s.* Algo fuera de lo ordinario o lo exigido. Extra, edición suplementaria de un diario. *Extra work, extra pay,* Trabajo, paga extraordinaria, es decir, además de lo que está convenido. *Extra hand,* Empleado supernumerario.
Extra, *prefijo.* Preposición latina que significa *afuera, más allá,* o *exceso,* y entra en la composición de las voces.
Extract [ex-tract'], *va.* 1. Extraer, sacar algo de un lugar, tirar. 2. Extraer, separar por medio de una operación química. 3. Extractar, compendiar, hacer extractos. 4. (Mat.) Buscar, hallar una raíz. *Many beautiful colours are extracted from coal-tar,* Se sacan muchos colores hermosos del alquitrán de hulla.
Extract [ex'-tract], *s.* 1. Extracto, substancia que se saca de una planta, etc. 2. Pasaje sacado de algún libro.
Extractable, Extractible [ex-tract'-a (o i) -bl], *a.* Extraíble, que puede ser extraído.

Extraction [ex-trac'-shun], *s.* 1. Extracción, origen, descendencia, linaje, alcurnia. 2. (Quím.) Extracción, acción de separar o extraer uno o varios de los diversos elementos que forman los cuerpos compuestos.
Extractive [ex-trac'-tiv], *a.* Extractivo, que puede extraer o ser extraído.—*s.* (Med.) Extractivo, la porción de un extracto que se hace insoluble.
Extractor [ex-tract'-ẹr], *s.* 1. Extractor, extractador. 2. Herramienta para extraer.
Extradite [ex'-tra-dait], *va.* Entregar un reo refugiado en un país a las autoridades de su propia nación.
Extradition [ex-tra-dish'-un], *s.* Extradición acción de entregar un reo, refugiado en país extranjero, al gobierno del suyo propio.
Extrados [ex-trē'-des], *s.* (Arq.) Trasdós, curva exterior de una bóveda.
Extrafoliaceous [ex-tra-fo-li-ē'-shus], *a.* Extrafoliáceo, el órgano que tiene su asiento en cualquier parte distinta del sobaco o axila de las hojas.
Extrajudicial [ex-tra-ju-dish'-al], *a.* Extrajudicial.
Extrajudicially [ex-tra-ju-dish'-al-i], *adv.* Extrajudicialmente.
Extramission [ex-tra-mish'-un], *s.* El acto de echar hacia fuera alguna cosa; emisión.
Extramundane [ex-tra-mun'-dēn], *a.* Lo que está fuera del mundo.
Extramural [ex-tra-miū'-ral], *a.* Extramuros.
Extraneous [ex-trē'-nẹ-us], *a.* Extraño, externo, extranjero, extrínseco.
Extraordinarily [ex-trōr'-di-nẹ-ri-li], *adv.* Extraordinariamente.
Extraordinariness [ex-trōr'-di-nẹ-ri-nes], *s.* Singularidad, estado o cosa extraordinaria.
Extraordinary [ex-trōr'-di-nẹ-ri o ex-tra-ōr'-di-nẹ-ri], *a.* 1. Extraordinario, singular, que no es nada común, que excede al tipo o uso común y normal. 2. Especial.—*s.* Cualquier cosa extraordinaria o no común: úsase igualmente en plural.—*adv.* Extraordinariamente.
Extraparochial [ex-tra-pa-rō'-ki-al], *a.* Extraparroquial.
Extrapolate [ex-tra'-pō-lêt], *va.* y *vn.* Extrapolar.
Extraregular [ex-tra-reg'-yu-lar], *a.* Irregular.
Extrasensory [ex-tra-sen'-so-ri], *a.* Extrasensorio. *Extrasensory perception.* Percepción extrasensoria.
Extraterritorial [ex-tra-ter-i-tō'-ri-al], *a.* Extraterritorial.
Extravagance, Extravagancy [ex-trav'-a-gans, i], *s.* 1. Extravagancia, salida de los límites prescritos; disparate, locura, desarreglo, desorden, desbarro. 2. Disipación, profusión, prodigalidad, gastos excesivos.
Extravagant [ex-trav'-a-gant], *a.* 1. Extravagante, singular, estrafalario; exorbitante, disparatado. 2. Profuso, pródigo, manirroto, gastador, despilfarrado.—*s.* 1. Estrafalario, el que comete extravagancias o es extravagante. 2. *pl.* Extravagantes, ciertas constituciones pontificias.
Extravagantly [ex-trav'-a-gant-li], *adv.* Extravagantemente, profusamente, exorbitantemente, costosamente; locamente.
Extravaganza [ex-trav''-a-gan'-za], *s.* Pieza de música, o composición dramática, extravagante y fantástica.
Extravagate [ex-trav'-a-gêt], *vn.* Vaguear, andar a discreción o más allá de los límites debidos.
Extravagation [ex-trav-a-gē'-shun], *s.* Vagancia.
Extravasate [ex-trav'-a-sêt], *va.* y *vn.* Extravasarse, rebosar o derramarse fuera de los vasos naturales.
Extravasate [ex-trav'-a-sê-ted], *a.* Extravasado.
Extravasation [ex-trav-a-sē'-shun], *s.* (Med.) Extravasación.
Extraversion [ex-tra-vẹr'-shun], *s.* (Des.) El acto de arrojar fuera alguna cosa.
Extravert [ex-tra-vẹrt'], *va.* (Poco us.) Volver hacia afuera o a un lado.
Extreme [ex-trīm'], *a.* 1. Extremo, excesivo, sumo. 2. Último, extremo, postrero. 3. Riguroso, estricto, extremado; radical.—*s.* 1. Extremo, ápice; el grado más elevado de alguna cosa. 2. Fin, cabo.
Extremely [ex-trīm'-li], *adv.* Extremamente, sumamente.
Extremism [ex-trī'-mizm], *s.* Extremismo.
Extremist [ex-trī'-mist], *s.* y *a.* Extremista.
Extremity [ex-trem'-i-ti], *s.* 1. Extremidad. 2. Suma violencia rigor; necesidad, apuro.—*pl.* 1. Medidas extremas. 2. (Zool.) Extremidades; mano, pie, órgano locomotor o un apéndice. *To drive one to extremities,* Apurar a uno la paciencia; ponerle entre la espada y la pared.
Extricable [ex'-tri-ca-bl], *a.* Capaz de ser desenredado, desembarazado; evitable.
Extricate [ex'-tri-kêt], *va.* Desembarazar, desenredar, desembrollar; sacar de un peligro, dificultad o apuro.
Extrication [ex-tri-kē'-shun], *s.* Desembarazo, desenredo.
Extrinsic, Extrinsical [ex-trin'-sic, al], *a.* Extrínseco, exterior, lo que viene de afuera.
Extrinsically [ex-trin'-sic-al-i], *adv.* Extrínsecamente.
Extrorse, Extrorsal [ex-trōrs', -trōr'-sal], *a.* 1. (Bot.) Extrorso, que se abre al lado exterior de la flor; se dice de la antera. 2. (Zool.) Vuelto afuera del cuerpo. (< lat.)
Extrovert [ex'-tro-vẹrt], *s.* Extravertido.
Extrude [ex-trūd'], *va.* Rechazar, expulsar, resistir un cuerpo a otro forzándole a retroceder en su curso o movimiento; empujar, echar adelante.
Extrusion [ex-trū'-zhun], *s.* Rechazo, empuje, expulsión.
Extuberant [ex-tiū'-bẹr-ant], *a.* (Poco us.) *V.* PROTUBERANT.
Extumescence [ex-tiu-mes'-ens], *s.* (Poco us.) Tumefacción, hinchazón.
Exuberance, Exuberancy [ex-yū'-bẹr-ans, i], *s.* Exuberancia, extrema fecundidad; superabundancia.
Exuberant [ex-yū'-bẹr-ant], *a.* Exuberante, abundantísimo.
Exuberantly [ex-yū'-bẹr-ant-li], *adv.* Abundantemente.
Exuberate [ex-yū'-bẹr-êt], *vn.* (Poco us.) Sobreabundar.
Exudation [ex-yu-dē'-shun], *s.* 1. Exudación, la acción y efecto de exudar o rezumarse. 2. Transpiración, sudor; lo exudado, lo rezumado.
Exude [ex-yūd'], *vn.* Sudar, exhalar.—*va.* Transpirar, echar hacia fuera.
Exulceration [eg-zul-sẹr-ē'-shun], *s.* (Ant.) Exulceración, enconamiento; corrosión.
Exulceratory [eg-zul'-sẹr-a-to-ri], *s.* (Ant.) Exulceratorio.
Exult [eg-zult'], *vn.* Triunfar, regocijarse sobremanera, alegrarse hasta lo sumo.
Exultance, Exultancy [eg-zult'-ans, i]. (Poco us.) Regocijo, triunfo, rapto de alegría.
Exultant [eg-zult'-ant], *a.* 1. Triunfante. 2. Regocijado, regocijada, festivo, que indica o muestra gran alegría.
Exultation [eg-zul-tē'-shun], *s.* Triunfo; exultación, regocijo grande, sumo placer; transporte, demostración o expresión de alegría.
Exulting [eg-zult'-ing], *a.* y *part. a.* Transportado, embriagado de alegría; triunfante.
Exuviæ [ex-yū'-vi-ī], *s. pl.* 1. Los despojos de los animales. 2. (Geol.) Los restos animales petrificados o fósiles.
Exuviate [ex-yū'-vi-êt], *va.* Mudar, echar de sí alguna parte; como las plumas de las aves, el pelo, los cuernos, la concha o el carapacho de los crustáceos, etc.
Exuviation [ex-yū-vi-ē'-shun], *s.* La muda de las aves, de los crustáceos.
Eyas [ai'-as], *s.* Halcón niego; halconcillo recién sacado del nido.—*a.* (Des.) Implume.
Eye [ai], *s.* 1. Ojo. 2. Ojo: tómase por la misma vista o el modo de mirar; mirada. 3. Ojo, la atención y vigilancia que se pone en alguna cosa. 4. Miramiento, acatamiento, atención, estimación. 5. La vista; el aspecto, frente o cara. 6. Ojo, el agujero que tienen algunas cosas, como la aguja. 7. Corcheta, la hembra del corchete. 8. Ventana redonda hecha en algún edificio. 9. (Bot.) Yema o botón de las plantas. 10. Matiz ligero de algún color. *One-eyed, blind of one eye,* Tuerto. *Evil eyes,* Ojos malos. *Red eyes,* Ojos encarnizados. *Before one's eyes,* A la vista, en presencia de alguno. *In the twinkling of an eye,* En un abrir y cerrar de ojos. *To have a cast in the eye,* Ser bisojo. *To have a thing in one's eyes,* Aspirar a alguna cosa. *To keep a sharp eye on,* Vigilar de cerca. *Black eye,* (1) Ojo negro. (2) Ojo amoratado por un golpe. *Half an eye,* Ojeada, mirada rápida y ligera. *Eye of the anchor,* (Mar.) Ojo, la parte de la caña del ancla en que entra y se afianza el arganeo. *Eye of a strap,* (Mar.) Ojo de gaza. *Eye of a stay,* (Mar.) Ojo del estay. *An eye must be had to the laws of courtesy,* Se han de observar las reglas de la cortesía. *All in one's eye,* (Ger.) Imaginario. *Eye-opener,* Todo lo que sirve para abrir o hacer abrir los ojos, literal o figuradamente; cuento maravilloso, noticia increíble o inesperada. (Fam.) Lo que permite a uno comprender aquello de que antes no podía darse cuenta.
Eye, *va.* 1. Ojear, echar los ojos y mirar con atención a una parte determinada; contemplar, observar; velar. 2. Hacer un agujero en, como el de la aguja.
Eye-ball [ai'-bōl], *s.* Globo del ojo.
Eye-beam [ai'-bīm], *s.* Ojeada.
Eye-bolt [ai'-bōlt], *s.* (Mar.) Cáncamo del ojo.
Eye-bright [ai'-brait], *s.* (Bot.) Eufrasia.

Eye-brightening [ai'-brait-n-ing], *a.* Lo que aclara la vista.
Eye-brow [ai'-brau], *s.* Ceja.
Eyecup [ai'-cup], *s.* Lavaojos.
Eyed [aid], *a.* Lo que tiene ojos. *Blue-eyed,* Ojizarco, ojiazul, que tiene ojos azules. *Brown-eyed,* Ojimoreno. *Blear-eyed,* Lagañoso.
Eye-drop [ai'-drep], *s.* Lágrima.
Eye-flap [ai'-flap], *s.* Anteojera, cada una de las piezas de vaqueta que caen junto a los ojos de las caballerías de tiro.
Eye-glance [ai'-glqns], *s.* Ojeada, mirada pronta y ligera.
Eye-glass [ai'-glqs], *s.* 1. Ocular, cristal óptico de un anteojo. 2. Ocular, la lente próxima al ojo en el microscopio o telescopio. 3. *Eye-glasses, pl.* Lentes, quevedos.
Eye-hole [ai'-hōl], *s.* 1. Ojete, abertura pequeña y redonda por donde puede pasar un alfiler, un corchete o gancho, un cordón, etc. 2. Atisbadero, rendija o agujero por donde se puede atisbar.
Eye-lash [ai'-lash], *s.* Pestaña.
Eyeless [ai'-les], *a.* Ciego; sin ojos o privado de la vista.
Eyelet [ai'-let], *s.* 1. Resquicio, cualquier abertura por donde entra la luz. 2. Ojete; y en especial un pequeño anillo metálico que protege los bordes de un agujero hecho en el lienzo, cañamazo, papel, etc. *Eyelet-holes of the reefs,* (Mar.) Ollados de drizos.
Eyeleteer [ai-let-īr'], *s.* Punzón para abrir ojetes.
Eye-lid [ai'-lid], *s.* Párpado.
Eye-offending [ai'-ef-fend'-ing], *a.* Lo que hiere u ofende la vista.
Eye-piece [ai'-pīs], *s.* Ocular, lente o combinación de lentes que se halla más próxima al ojo en un anteojo o microscopio.
Eye-pleasing [ai'-plīz-ing], *a.* Agradable a la vista.
Eyer [ai'-ẹr], *s.* Mirador, el que mira atentamente.
Eye-salve [ai'-sāv], *s.* Ungüento para los males de los ojos.
Eye-servant [ai'-sẹr-vant], *s.* El criado que sólo trabaja en presencia de su amo, o cuando sabe que lo vigilan.
Eye-service [ai'-sẹr-vis], *s.* Servicio hecho de mala gana y sólo cuando está presente quien lo manda.
Eye-shade [ai'-shêd], *s.* Visera, guardavista que sirve para proteger los ojos de una luz viva.
Eyeshot [ai'-shet], *s.* Ojeada, alcance del ojo; la vista.
Eyesight [ai'-sait], *s.* 1. Vista, el sentido de la vista. 2. Vista, alcance o extensión de la vista.
Eye-sore [ai'-sōr], *s.* 1. Mal de ojos. 2. Cosa que hiere, ofende u ofusca la vista; (fig.) todo lo que disgusta o desagrada.
Eyespot [ai'-spet], *s.* 1. Órgano visual rudimentario de algunos invertebrados. 2. Mancha en forma de ojo.
Eye-spotted [ai'-spet-ed], *a.* Abigarrado con manchas como ojos.
Eye-stone [ai'-stōn], *s.* Piedra llamada del ojo, gránulo calcáreo que colocado debajo del párpado en el ángulo interno del ojo, sirve para hacer salir de éste las substancias extrañas que lo irritan.
Eyestrain [ai'-strên], *s.* Vista cansada o fatigada.
Eye-string [ai'-string], *s.* Fibra del ojo.
Eye-tooth [ai'-tūth], *s.* Colmillo.
Eye-wash [ai'-wesh], *s.* Loción para los ojos.
Eye-water [ai'-wē-tẹr], *s.* Colirio, loción para los ojos.
Eye-wink [ai'-wink], *s.* Guiñada.
Eye-witness [ai'-wit-nes], *s.* Testigo ocular o presencial.
Eyre [ār], *s.* (Ant.) 1. Vuelta, circuito. 2. Especie de juzgado en Inglaterra compuesto de jueces que iban de un punto a otro.
Eyry [ā'-ri], *s.* Nido de ave de rapiña; el paraje en que pone sus huevos y cría.

F

F [ef]. Esta letra tiene el mismo sonido que en castellano, bien que pronunciado con más fuerza. Por abreviatura la *F.* equivale a *fellow,* miembro, socio; como, F. R. S., Miembro de la Real Sociedad. F. L. S., Miembro de la Sociedad Lineana. F. R. M. S., Miembro de la Real Sociedad de Microscopistas.
Fa [fā]. Cuarta voz de la escala música.
Fabian [fê'-bi-an], *a.* Fabiano, relativo a Fabio; que recurre a la dilación y la astucia, como lo hizo Fabio con Aníbal en la segunda guerra púnica.
Fable [fê'-bl], *s.* 1. Fábula, apólogo, ficción moral o histórica. 2. Fábula, la acción que sirve de asunto a los poemas épicos y dramáticos. 3. Ficción; fábula, mentira, cuento, falsedad.
Fable, *vn.* Fingir, mentir, inventar una fábula.—*va.* Contar fábulas, mentiras o cuentos; fabular.
Fabled [fê'-bld], *a.* Celebrado en fábulas.
Fabler [fê'-blẹr], *s.* 1. Fabulista. 2. Cuentero, mentiroso.
Fabric [fab'-ric], *s.* 1. Fábrica, edificio. 2. Material de uso o de adorno; tejido, tela, fieltro, etc. 3. Manufactura, fábrica; clase de construcción o fabricación, textura. *Fabric-lands,* Tierras o rentas de fábrica, las que sirven para los reparos y gastos de la iglesia.
Fabricate [fab'-ri-kêt], *va.* 1. Fabricar, edificar, construir por medio del trabajo manual o de una de las artes. 2. Forjar, fingir, inventar con falsedad.
Fabrication [fab-ri-kê'-shun], *s.* 1. Fabricación, fábrica, el arte de fabricar, y lo que ha sido fabricado o construído; construcción: edificio; tisú, tejido. 2. Ficción, mentira, fábula.
Fabricator [fab'-ri-kê-tẹr], *s.* Fabricante, fabricador.
Fabricature [fab'-ri-ca-tiūr], *s.* *V.* FABRICATION.
Fabrile [fab'-ril], *a.* Fabril.
Fabulist [fab'-yu-list], *s.* Fabulista, autor de fábulas.
Fabulize, Fabulise [fab'-yu-laiz], *va.* Componer o narrar fábulas.
Fabulous [fab'-yu-lus], *a.* Fabuloso.
Fabulously [fab'-yu-lus-li], *adv.* Fabulosamente.
Fabulousness [fab'-yu-lus-nes], *s.* Invención de mentiras, cuentos o cosas fabulosas.
Facade [fa-sād'], *s.* Fachada, frontispicio de un edificio.
Face [fês], *s.* 1. Cara, rostro, faz. 2. Cara, lado, haz, superficie de una cosa; facie (de un cristal). 3. Semblante o facciones de la cara. *To put on a new face,* Mudar de semblante. *Brazen face,* Cara de vaqueta, desfachatado. 4. Fachada, frontis de un edificio. 5. (Mil.) Frente. 6. Aspecto, semblante, estado o disposición que toman las cosas. 7. Apariencia, aspecto, presencia; conocimiento inmediato, vista. 8. Descaro, atrevimiento, desfachatez. 9. Mueca, gesto. *To make wry faces,* Hacer muecas. 10. Cara, lo que está formalmente declarado en un documento; el valor neto, excluyendo el interés y el descuento. 11. (Tip.) Ojo de la letra. *To fly in the face of,* (fig.) Oponer sin razón y con violencia; hacer befa temerariamente. *Face to face,* Cara a cara. *In face of the sun,* A la faz del sol, o de todo el mundo; públicamente. *In my face,* En mi presencia, en mis barbas. *Face-ache, face-ague,* Neuralgia facial. *Face-card,* Figura en la baraja. *Face-value,* Valor nominal, el que está escrito o impreso en un documento.
Face, *va.* y *vn.* 1. Aparentar, engañar haciendo el hipócrita. 2. Encararse; hacer frente. 3. Cubrir, aforrar. *To face a cloak,* Poner embozo a una capa. *To face about,* Volver la cara. *To face one out o down,* Sostener alguna cosa a presencia de una persona que la niega, o ponerse ante su vista para insultarla descaradamente; turbar a fuerza de descaro. *To face out a lie,* Sostener una mentira con impudencia. *To face out,* Arrostrar, hacer frente, salir del paso a fuerza de descaro. (Mil.) Volver las espaldas. *To face the music,* (Ger. E. U.) Hacer frente intrépidamente a las consecuencias.
Face-cloth [fês'-cleth], *s.* Sudario, lienzo con que se cubre el rostro de un cadáver.
Faced [fêst], *a.* Lo que tiene cara o semblante: úsase casi siempre en composición. *Ill-faced,* Mal encarado o engestado.
Face-guard [fês'-gārd], *s.* Careta, con que se cubre el rostro para protegerlo en ciertos experimentos de química u operaciones mecánicas; máscara que se usa en los ejercicios de esgrima.
Faceless [fês'-les], *a.* Sin cara, sin facha.
Face-painter [fês'-pent-ẹr], *s.* Retratista.
Face-painting [fês'-pênt-ing], *s.* 1. Dar colorete al rostro, usar afeites. 2. (Poco us.) El arte de retratar.
Facer [fê'-sẹr], *s.* Golpe dado en la cara, entre pugilistas; de aquí, cualquier percance que atolondra.
Facet [fas'-et], *va.* Labrar una faceta o facetas sobre algo.—*s.* 1. Faceta, cada uno de los lados labrados de una piedra preciosa. 2. (Arq.) Filete plano pero saliente entre las estrías de una columna. 3. (Zool.) Faceta, cada una de las pequeñas divisiones del ojo compuesto; también, la superficie o córnea de dicho ojo, v. gr. en los insectos.
Faceted [fas'-et-ed], *pp.* y *a.* 1. Labrado en facetas. 2. Que tiene facetas, p. ej. el ojo compuesto.
Facetious [fa-sī'-shus], *a.* Salado, chistoso, alegre, jocoso, gracioso.
Facetiously [fa-sī'-shus-li], *adv.* Chistosamente, alegremente.

Facetiousness [fa-sî'-shus-nes], *s.* Sal, chiste, gracia.

Facial [fê'-shial o fa'-si-al], *a.* Facial, que pertenece a la cara, que la afecta o que está cercano a ella. *Facial angle*, Ángulo facial, el que sirve para medir la inclinación o depresión del cráneo, formado por dos líneas que van respectivamente desde los incisivos superiores a la parte media de la frente y al conducto auditivo.

Facile [fas'-il], *a.* 1. Fácil. 2. Obsequioso, obediente, dócil. 3. Vivo, listo, diestro, hábil. 4. Accesible, afable.

Facilely [fas'-il-li], *adv.* Fácilmente. *V.* EASILY.

Facileness [fas'-il-nes], *s.* Docilidad.

Facilitate [fa-sil'-i-têt], *va.* Facilitar, allanar una dificultad; minorar el trabajo.

Facilitation [fa-sil-i-tê'-shun], *s.* Facilitación.

Facility [fa-sil'-i-ti], *s.* 1. Facilidad, destreza, habilidad. 2. Docilidad, prontitud en someterse a una influencia cualquiera, ya sea buena o mala. 3. Afabilidad. 4. Lo que hace algo más fácil; ayuda, conveniencia.

Facing [fê'-sing], *s.* 1. Paramento. 2. Cubierta.

Fac-simile [fac-sim'-i-li], *s.* Facsímile, copia exacta. Úsase también como adjetivo.

Fact [fact], *s.* 1. Hecho, acción, suceso; lo que se ve como actualmente existente; lo concreto opuesto a lo abstracto. 2. Realidad, verdad; una cosa cualquiera estrictamente verdadera. 3. Dato, motivo. *In fact*, En efecto, en verdad. *In the very fact*, En el mero hecho. *Facts are stubborn things*, No hay nada tan terco como un hecho. *Matter of fact*, Hecho positivo, cierto; verdad. *A matter of fact man*, Un hombre positivo, no imaginativo. *V.* MATTER.

Faction [fac'-shun], *s.* 1. Facción, bando, liga, parcialidad. 2. Alboroto, tumulto.

Factional [fac'-shun-al], *a.* Faccionario, partidario.

Factionist [fac'-shun-ist], *s.* El que excita facciones y discordias.

Factious [fac'-shus], *a.* Faccioso, sedicioso, revoltoso.

Factiously [fac'-shus-li], *adv.* Sediciosamente.

Factiousness [fac'-shus-nes], *s.* Espíritu de partido o facción.

Factitious [fac-tish'-us], *a.* Facticio; artificial, hecho por mano o arte del hombre.

Factor [fac'-ter], *s.* 1. Factor, agente comisionado. 2. (Mat.) Factor, el multiplicador y multiplicando. 3. Una de las causas que producen un resultado.

Factorage [fac'-ter-êj], *s.* 1. (Com.) Comisión o el tanto por ciento que se paga a los comisionistas. 2. Factoría, empleo y cargo de factor.

Factorship [fac'-ter-ship], *s.* Agencia, factoría.

Factory [fac'-to-ri], *s.* 1. Fábrica, manufactura, establecimiento para fabricar alguna cosa. 2. Factoría, establecimiento de comercio, especialmente el instalado en país extranjero.

Factotum [fac-tō'-tum], *s.* 1. Criado que hace a todo. 2. La persona que por su habilidad y circunstancias se hace necesaria en una familia o sociedad.

Factual [fac'-chu-al], *a.* Actual, relativo a hechos precisos.

Facture [fac'-chur], *s.* 1. (Com.) Factura. *V.* INVOICE. 2. (Des.) Hechura.

Facultative [fac'-ul-te-tiv], *a.* 1. Facultativo, que produce o da facultad o poder. 2. Que otorga autoridad o poder. 3. (For.) Potestativo.

Facula [fac'-yu-la], *s.* Fácula, cada una de aquellas partes más brillantes que se observan en el disco del Sol.

Faculty [fac'-ul-ti], *s.* 1. Facultad, potencia o virtud para hacer alguna cosa. 2. Facultad, potencia o virtud natural. 3. Maña, talento, don, destreza, habilidad. 4. Propiedad, eficacia, fuerza. 5. Facultad, poder, autoridad, privilegio. 6. Facultad, el conjunto de doctores y profesores de las ciencias o facultades que se enseñan en las universidades.

†**Facund** [fac'-und], *a.* Facundo, elocuente.

Faddle [fad'-l], *vn.* (Prov. Ingl.) Juguetear, jugar, travesear.

Fade [fêd], *vn.* 1. Desaparecer gradualmente; palidecer, descolorarse. 2. Decaer, marchitarse, acabarse poco a poco; durar poco.—*va.* 1. Marchitar, poner pálido, ofuscar; descolorar. 2. Debilitar, enflaquecer, desmejorar. *Day faded into twilight*, El día palideció hasta convertirse en crepúsculo.

Fadeless [fêd'-les], *a.* Que no palidece o se descolora; que no está mustio ni marchito, que no se pasa o decae.

Fade out [fêd'-aut], *s.* Desvanecimiento gradual de la imagen (cinematógrafo).

Fadge [faj], *vn.* (Ant.) Adaptar; suceder; convenir.

Fading [fêd'-ing], *s.* Decadencia, flojedad.

Fadingness [fêd'-ing-nes], *s.* Tendencia a decaer o marchitarse.

Fady [fêd'-i], *a.* Lo que decae o se marchita.

Fæces [fî'-siz], *s. pl.* Heces, excrementos.

Fæcula, Fecula [fec'-yu-la], *s.* (Quím.) Fécula, almidón que se saca de las plantas farináceas.

Faerie, Faery [fê'-er-i], *a.* (Ant.) *V.* FAIRY. *The Faerie Queene*, Título de un poema romántico de Edmund Spenser.

Fag [fag], *va.* 1. Fatigar, cansar. 2. Emplear como ganapán, galopín o marmitón, exigir de uno faenas groseras.—*vn.* 1. Desfallecer o desmayarse de cansancio. 2. Trabajar o hacer faenas groseras en lugar de otro.

Fag, *s.* 1. Esclavo, trabajador; marmitón, ganapán. 2. Nudo en el paño.

Fag-end [fag-end'], *s.* 1. Cadillos, pestañas, los primeros hilos de la urdimbre de la tela. 2. Desecho, sobra o desperdicio de alguna cosa. 3. (Mar.) Cordón.

Fagot [fag'-ot], *s.* 1. Haz o gavilla de leña. 2. Haz de barras de hierro o acero (de 120 libras de peso). 3. Montón de hierro viejo para fundirlo. 4. El tormento de ser quemado vivo. 5. Montón de pescado acumulado para secarlo o para cubrirlo y protegerlo.

Fagot, *va.* 1. Liar, hacer líos o haces. 2. Recoger, recaudar.

Fahrenheit [fā'-ren-hait], *a.* Que designa, pertenece o se refiere á la escala termométrica en que el punto de congelación se marca a los 32° y el de ebullición a los 212°; es la escala usual en la Gran Bretaña y los Estados Unidos.

Faience [fa-yāns'], *s.* Una variedad de mayólica o loza, por lo general muy adornada.

Fail [fêl], *va.* Faltar a la obligación; abandonar, descuidar o no cumplir con lo que se debe; omitir, olvidar; engañar, chasquear.—*vn.* 1. Faltar, no existir alguna cosa, calidad o circunstancia que debiera haber. 2 Consumirse, acabar, fallecer, desvanecerse, decaer, menguar; perecer, perderse. 3. No corresponder uno a lo que es, o una cosa o efecto a lo que se esperaba; tener mal éxito; salir mal una cosa. 4. Quebrar, hacer bancarrota. 5. Faltar, no cumplir con su obligación. *Not to fail*, No dejar de.

Fail, *s.* Falta, omisión, en la locución *without fail;* sin falta u omisión.

Failing [fêl'-ing], *s.* 1. Falta, desliz, defecto; decadencia, malogro. 2. (Poco us.) El acto de hacer bancarrota; quiebra.

Failure [fêl'-yur], *s.* 1. Falta, culpa, omisión, descuido. 2. Quiebra, bancarrota. 3. Concurso de acreedores. 4. Desliz. *It is a complete failure*, Ha salido completamente mal. 5. Hablando de asuntos literarios, o cosas comunes, se dice: *It was a failure*, Salió un disparate, quedó mal. (Vul.) Salió una plasta, se hizo un pastel. *Failure of issue*, Carencia de descendientes a la muerte de la persona de que se trata.

Fain [fên], *a.* 1. Alegre, contento. 2. Obligado, estrechado, precisado. —*adv.* Gustosamente, voluntariamente, de buena gana, alegremente, con gusto.

Faint [fênt], *vn.* 1. Desmayarse, caer en síncope, pasmarse. 2. Acobardarse, extenuarse, desanimarse; dejarse abatir, desalentarse. 3. Descaecer, desvanecerse. *To faint with thirst, with hunger*, No poder aguantar la sed, el hambre.

Faint, *a.* Lánguido, extenuado; indistinto o mal definido en color o sonido, opaco, obscuro; bajo, cobarde, abatido, perezoso. *Faint heart never won fair lady*, (Prov.) A los cobardes no los ayuda Dios, o Quien no se aventura no pasa la mar. *To grow faint*, Desmayarse, sentirse mal de repente. *To feel faint*, Sufrir un desfallecimiento, empezar o desfallecer. *To be faint with hunger*, Estar exánime, estar muerto de hambre.

Faint-hearted [fênt'-hārt-ed], *a.* Cobarde, medroso, pusilánime, apocado.

Faint-heartedly [fênt'-hārt-ed-li], *adv.* Medrosamente.

Faint-heartedness [fênt'-hārt-ed-nes], *s.* Cobardía, miedo, pusilanimidad.

Fainting [fênt'-ing], *s.* Deliquio, desmayo; desfallecimiento.

Faintish [fênt'-ish], *a.* Flojo; débil; que empieza a ponerse malo. *Are you faintish?* ¿Va Vd. a sentirse mal? ¿Se siente Vd. mal? *V.* FAINT.

Faintly [fênt'-li], *adv.* Desmayadamente, débilmente, obscuramente.

Faintness [fênt'-nes], *s.* Languidez, flaqueza, abatimiento; timidez.

Fainty [fênt'-i], *a.* Lánguido, débil. *V.* FAINTISH.

Fair [fãr], *a.* 1. Claro, sereno, no obscurecido por nubes; favorable, próspero. 2. Blanco, rubio; no moreno ni descolorido. *Fair complexion,* Tez blanca. 3. Hermoso, perfecto, bello. 4. Recto, justo, bueno, natural, sincero, honrado, razonable, abierto, franco, ingenuo. 5. Suave, dulce, blando; cortés, liberal. 6. Favorable, propicio, en buen estado; medianamente bueno o grueso, corriente, pasable, ordinario. 7. Bien formado, distinto; legible. *To play fair,* Jugar limpio. *If the weather holds fair,* Si el tiempo se mantiene despejado. *The fair sex,* El bello sexo. *A fair wind,* Un viento favorable. *A fair name,* Un nombre honrado, sin tacha. *You will make a fair copy of it,* Lo pondrá Vd. en limpio. *To give one a fair hearing,* Oir, escuchar con imparcialidad. *To be in a fair way to succeed,* Estar en buen camino de prosperar. *By fair means,* Por medios rectos, honrados. *A fair man, a fair woman,* Un hombre rubio, una mujer rubia. *Fair and square,* Honrado a carta cabal. *Fair-haired,* De cabellos blondos o rubios. (Equivalente, *light-haired.*) *Fair-complexioned,* De tez blanca. *Fair play,* Buena conducta, proceder leal.—*adv.* Decentemente, cortésmente, felizmente.

Fair, *s.* 1. (Ant. y Poét.) Belleza, beldad, hermosura; honradez. 2. Feria, la concurrencia de mercaderes y negociantes en un lugar y día señalados para vender y comprar. 3. Exposición ocasional o periódica de objetos de arte o de capricho; o de productos de la agricultura, aves, caballos, perros, etc.

Fairground [f r'-graund], *s.* Campo donde se celebra una exposición o feria.

Fairing [fãr'-ing], *s.* Ferias, dádivas o agasajos que se hacen en tiempo de ferias.

Fairish [fãr'-ish], *a.* Razonablemente justo; así, así.

Fairly [fãr'-li], *adv.* 1. Bellamente, con primor y perfección. 2. Cómodamente; suavemente. 3. Justamente. 4. Ingenuamente, claramente. 5. Cabalmente. 6. Medianamente.

Fair-minded [fãr-maind'-ed], *a.* Imparcial, justo, equitativo.

Fairness [fãr'-nes], *s.* 1. Hermosura, belleza. 2. Honradez, candor. 3. Justicia, equidad.

Fair-spoken [fãr'-spōc-n], *a.* Bien hablado, cortés.

Fairway [fãr'-wê], *s.* 1. (Mar.) Canalizo, paso expedito de un canal. *That vessel lies in the fairway,* Ese buque está anclado al través, a lo ancho del canalizo. 2. Parte expedita de un campo de golf.

Fair-weather [fãr'-wedh-ẹr], *a.* Dícese de lo que anuncia prosperidad o buen tiempo. *A fair-weather friend,* Un amigo de los días prósperos.

Fairy [fãr'-i], *s.* 1. Duende, trasgo. 2. Hada, bruja, encantadora.—*a.* Lo que pertenece a los duendes. *The fairy land,* La tierra de los duendes. *Fairy tales,* Cuentos de hadas, o de encantadoras.

Fairylike [fãr'-i-laic], *s.* Aduendado, de las hadas.

Faith [fêth], *s.* 1. Fe, creencia. 2. Fe, confianza en Dios. 3. Fidelidad, sinceridad. 4. Fe, palabra que se da. 5. Exactitud en cumplir con su obligación. *To break faith with one,* Faltar a la palabra dada a alguien. *Upon my faith* (*i' faith*—des.). A fe mía.—*adv.* En verdad.

Faithful [fêth'-ful], *a.* Fiel, leal; justo, recto.

Faithfully [fêth'-ful-i], *adv.* Fielmente, firmemente, exactamente.

Faithfulness [fêth'-ful-nes], *s.* Fidelidad, honradez, lealtad.

Faithless [fêth'-les], *a.* Infiel, sin fe, pérfido, desleal.

Faithlessness [fêth'-les-nes], *s.* Infidencia, traición.

Fake [fêk], *s.* (Mar.) Aduja de cable; cada vuelta que forma el cable al recogerlo o arrollarlo.

Fake, *va.* (Ger.) 1. Ocultar engañosamente los defectos de una cosa. 2. Fingir, inventar falsedades; fantasear. 3. Hurtar.—*s.* 1. Estafa; trampa, engaño; estafador. 2. Noticias ficticias, o inventadas.

Fakir [fê'-kẹr o fa-kîr'], *s.* 1. Alfaquí, religioso mendicante entre los mahometanos y en la India. 2. (Vul.) Buhonero.

Falcade [fal-kêd'], *s.* Falcada, especie de corveta del caballo. *To make falcades,* Falcar, deslizarse un caballo repetidas veces sobre las ancas.

Falcation [fal-kê'-shun], *s.* Encorvadura.

Falchion [fēl'-chun], *s.* Cimitarra.

Falciform [fal'-si-fērm], *a.* Falciforme, que tiene la forma de una falce o de una hoz.

Falcon [fē'-cn ó fal'-cen], *s.* 1. Halcón. 2. (Art.) Falcón, un cañón del siglo XVI.

Falconet [fē'-cn-et], *s.* (Art.) Falconete, cañoncito del siglo XVI.

Falconry [fē'-cn-ri], *s.* Halconería, cetrería.

Faldstool [fēld'-stūl], *s.* 1. Facistol, atril desde el cual se lee la letanía. 2. Faldistorio, asiento pequeño de que usan los obispos en ciertas ceremonias; banquillo sobre el cual se arrodillan los soberanos de Inglaterra en su coronación. 3. Silla de tijera.

Fall [fēl], *vn.* (*pret.* FELL, *pp.* FALLEN). 1. Caer, caerse. 2. Apostatar, apartarse de la fe o de la virtud. 3. Morir repentinamente o de muerte violenta. 4. Caer, perder el poder, empleo o valimiento. 5. Caer, pasar del estado de prosperidad al de desgracia o a un estado peor que el que se tenía antes; disminuir. 6. Pasar el cuerpo o alma a un nuevo estado. *To fall asleep,* Dormirse. *To fall sick,* Enfermar. *To fall in love,* Enamorarse. 7. Aparecerse por casualidad; llegar o hallarse casualmente en alguna parte. 8. Principiar alguna cosa con ardor. 9. Apoderarse de alguno una pasión de ánimo. 10. Tocarle a alguno una propiedad. 11. Bajar, minorarse el precio de alguna cosa. 12. Acontecer, acaecer, suceder, tocar. *To fall to one's lot,* Caber o caer en suerte, tocar.—*va.* 1. Soltar, dejar caer. 2. Hundir, abatir, bajar. 3. Parir la oveja. 4. (Fam.) Derribar, derrocar, echar por tierra, cortar. *To fall away,* Enflaquecer; apostatar; perecer; marchitarse. *To fall back,* Retroceder, retirarse; (fig.) faltar a su palabra, retractarse. (Fam.) Llamarse andana. *To fall backward,* Caer de espaldas. *To fall back on* o *upon,* (1) (Mil.) Retirarse hacia o a (una posición, cuerpo de tropas, etc.). (2) Recurrir a. *To fall behind,* Quedarse atrás, perder terreno. *To fall down,* Prosternarse, postrarse, caer al suelo. *To fall flat,* No corresponder a lo que se esperaba, tener mal éxito. *To fall from,* Abandonar, renunciar a favor de uno, rebelarse. *To fall in,* Concurrir, coincidir; acceder; acordarse, conceder; alinearse los soldados. *To fall in with,* Encontrarse. *To fall into,* Acceder, conceder, entrar en las ideas o proyectos de alguno. *To fall off,* Enflaquecer, menguar; desaparecer, disolverse; perecer; separarse; apostatar, degenerar. *To fall on,* Principiar alguna cosa con empeño; asaltar, embestir, acometer. (Fam.) Echarse sobre, fajar sobre. *To fall on one's feet,* Salir del vado. *To fall over,* Desertarse de un partido a otro. *To fall out,* Reñir, querellar, disputar, desamistarse; acaecer, acontecer, suceder. *To fall to,* Principiar a comer con ansia, tirarse sobre; someterse, ponerse a hacer algo. *To fall under,* Hacerse el objeto de; estar sujeto a; colocarse en, ser del número de, ser considerado como. *To fall under one's displeasure,* Incurrir en la indignación de alguno, caer en desgracia. *To fall upon,* Atacar, invadir, asaltar, embestir. *To fall upon an expedient,* Echar un corte. *To fall short,* Faltar, no corresponder a lo que se esperaba. No conseguir, no lograr, no llegar a, no alcanzar. (Vul.) Quedar chasqueado, llevarse un petardo. *To fall through,* Salir mal una cosa. *To fall aboard,* (Mar.) Abordar, caer sobre un bajel. *To fall astern,* (Mar.) Dejarse caer por la popa. *To fall calm,* (Mar.) Calmar. *To fall to leeward,* (Mar.) Dejarse caer a sotavento. *All the real property fell to the elder brother,* Todos los bienes raíces le tocaron al hermano mayor. *When the note fell due,* Cuando venció el pagaré. *Falling star,* Estrella errante.

Fall, *s.* 1. Caída. 2. Muerte, destrucción, ruina, desolación. 3. Decadencia, declinación. 4. Baja o disminución de precio; caída, pérdida en los fondos públicos. 5. Declive. 6. Desembocadura de un río. 7. Catarata, cascada, salto. 8. Otoño. 9. Corta de leña. *Fall of a tackle,* (Mar.) Tira de aparejo. 10. Cadencia, en la música y en la oratoria; caída o bajada de tono, o disminución del volumen del sonido.—*a.* (E. U.) Del otoño, relativo o perteneciente al otoño. *Fall wheat,* Trigo sembrado en el otoño. *A fall overcoat,* Un sobretodo de medio tiempo.

Fallacious [fal-lê'-shus], *a.* Falaz, sofístico, ilógico; engañoso, vano. ilusorio.

Fallaciously [fal-lê'-shus-li], *adv.* Falazmente, engañosamente.

Fallaciousness [fal-lê'-shus-nes], *s.* Falacia, engaño, fraude, sofisma.

Fallacy [fal'-a-si], *s.* Falacia, sofistería, engaño, error. *To cherish a fallacy,* Acariciar una ilusión; equivocarse, estar equivocado.

Fallen [fēl'-n], *pp.* y *a.* Caído; derribado, trastornado; disfamado; arruinado.

Fallibility [fal-i-bil'-i-ti], *s.* Falibilidad, posibilidad de error.

Fallible [fal'-i-bl], *a.* Falible.

Fallibly [fal'-i-bli], *adv.* Faliblemente.

Falling [fōl'-ing], *s.* y *ger.* de *To* FALL. 1. Concavidad pequeña. 2. Caída y la cosa que cae. 3. (Med.) Caída, descenso; prolapso. *Falling away*, Defección, apostasía; enflaquecimiento. *Falling down*, Postración, prosternación; hundimiento, derrumbe. *Falling in*, Caída, desmoronamiento; hueco (de las mejillas). *Falling off*, Caída, decadencia; apostasía, etc. *V. To fall off* en FALL.

Falling-sickness [fōl'-ing-sic'-nes], *s.* Epilepsia, gota coral, mal caduco.

Fallout [fel'-aut], *s.* 1. Descenso de partículas, frecuentemente radiactivas, excitadas o producidas por una explosión nuclear. 2. Conjunto de dichas partículas.

Fallow [fal'-o], *a.* 1. Flavo, leonado. *Fallow deer*, Corzo. 2. Cultivable pero en descanso; no sembrado. 3. Barbechado, arado. 4. Desocupado, abandonado.—*s.* Barbecho; tierra que descansa. *To let lie fallow*, Dejar en barbecho.

Fallow, *va.* Barbechar.

Fallow-finch [fal'-o-finch], *s.* (Orn.) Triguero.

Fallowness [fal'-o-nes], *s.* Esterilidad de algún terreno.

False [fōls], *a.* 1. Falso, contrario a la verdad o a los hechos. 2. Fingido, postizo, contrahecho, falseado. 3. No conforme a la regla, incorrecto, irregular, ilegal. 4. Mentiroso, falsificador. 5. Engañoso, falaz, pérfido, desleal, infiel, traidor, aleve. 6. (Mec.) Provisional, de substitución, o imitado de; falso. 7. (Biol.) Cuasi, seudo; impropiamente nombrado o titulado; incompleto en su disposición o en sus funciones. 8. (Mús.) Falso, discordante, que hace violencia a las reglas de la armonía.—*adv.* Falsamente, injustamente. *False teeth*, Dientes postizos. *A false claim*, Una pretensión infundada. *False imprisonment*, Prisión, detención ilegal.

False bottom [fels bet'-um], *s.* Doble fondo.

False colors [fōls cul'-rz], *s. pl.* 1. Bandera supuesta que se enarbola para engañar. 2. Fingimiento.

False-faced [fōls'-fēst], *a.* Hipócrita, falso.

False-hearted [fōls-hārt'-ed], *a.* Traidor, pérfido, aleve, falso.

Falsehood [fōls'-hud], *s.* Falsedad, mentira, engaño, perfidia.

Falsely [fōls'-li], *adv.* Falsamente, alevosamente, pérfidamente.

Falseness [fōls'-nes], *s.* Perfidia, falsedad, engaño.

Falsetto [fōl-set'-o], *s.* (Mús.) Falsete, voz de cabeza.

Falsies [fel'-sis], *s. pl.* (vul.) Senos postizos.

Falsifiable [fōl'-si-fai'-a-bl], *a.* Falsificable.

Falsification [fel-si-fi-kē'-shun], *s.* Falsificación; confutación.

Falsifier [fōl'-si-fai-ęr], **Falsificator** [fōl'-si-fi-kē-tęr], *s.* Falsificador, embustero, falsario.

Falsify [fōl'-si-fai], *va.* 1. Falsificar, representar falsamente. 2. Confutar, refutar, desmentir. 3. Falsear, contrahacer, adulterar. 4. (For.) Falsificar, alterar. 5. Violar, ser falso a alguno.—*vn.* Mentir, decir falsedades, fábulas, etc.

Falsity [fōl'-si-ti], *s.* Falsedad, mentira.

Falter [fōl'-tęr], *va.* Balbucear, decir de una manera débil y balbuciente; se usa a menudo con la prep. *out.*—*vn.* Tartamudear; faltar; vacilar.

Faltering [fōl'-tęr-ing], *s.* Debilidad, tartamudeo; vacilación.

Falteringly [fōl'-tęr-ing-li], *adv.* Vacilantemente, de una manera balbuciente.

Fame [fēm], *s.* 1. Fama, celebridad, renombre. 2. (Ant.) Fama, noticia o voz común.

Fame, *va.* 1. Afamar; divulgar. 2. Hacer famoso; celebrar.

Famed [fēmd], *a.* Afamado, celebrado, famoso, renombrado.

Fameless [fēm'-les], *a.* Obscuro.

Familiar [fa-mil'-yar], *a.* 1. Familiar, casero, común, ordinario. 2. Afable, agradable; no violento. 3. Acostumbrado, natural, fácil; versado, instruído (en este sentido va seguido de *with*). 4. Demasiado íntimo.—*s.* 1. Amigo íntimo. 2. Demonio familiar. 3. Familiar, criado o sirviente.

Familiarity [fa-mil-i-ar'-i-ti], *s.* Familiaridad, llaneza, intimidad, confianza.

Familiarize [fa-mil'-yar-aiz], *va.* Familiarizar, acostumbrar.

Familiarly [fa-mil'-yar-li], *adv.* Familiarmente, amistosamente.

Family [fam'-i-li], *s.* 1. Familia (en todos sus sentidos); linaje, sangre, raza. 2. (Biol.) Familia, agrupación de géneros naturales que poseen gran número de caracteres comunes.—*a.* Familiar, de la familia, relativo o perteneciente a ella. *Family man*, Padre de familia; un hombre de costumbres domésticas. *Family tree*, Árbol genealógico. *Family-way*, (Fam.) Embarazo de una mujer. *To be in the family-way*, Estar en cinta, embarazada.

Famine [fam'-in], *s.* Hambre, carestía.

Famish [fam'-ish], *va.* Hambrear, matar de hambre.—*vn.* Hambrear, morirse de hambre, sufrir tormento de hambre y sed.

Famous [fē'-mus], *a.* Famoso, celebrado, afamado.

Famously [fē'-mus-li], *adv.* Famosamente.

Fan [fan], *s.* 1. Abanico. 2. Aventador, el bieldo con que se avienta la paja. 3. (Mec.) Ventilador, aparato para renovar el aire; también, volante que sirve para mantener las aspas de un molino en la dirección del viento. *Fan-blast*, La corriente de aire producida por el fuelle en los altos hornos. *Fan-blower*, Aventador, soplador de abanico. *Fan-shaped*, En forma de abanico. *Fan-palm*, Palmera en forma de abanico; particularmente la Corypha umbraculifera de Ceilán; la Sabal palmetto de Florida y la Chamærops humilis del sur de Europa. *Fan wheel*, Rueda aventadora, rueda de paletas. *Fan window*, Ventana en forma de abanico.

Fan, *va.* 1. Abanicar. 2. Aventar, abalear, aechar, separar la paja del grano con el aventador o bieldo. 3. En beisbol, hacer perder el tanto, cuando el lanzador procura que un jugador falle tres veces consecutivas al tratar de golpear la pelota.

Fanatic [fa-nat'-ic], *s.* Fanático.

Fanatic, Fanatical [fa-nat'-ic-al], *a.* Fanático, entusiasta, visionario.

Fanatically [fa-nat'-ic-al-i], *adv.* Fanáticamente.

Fanaticism [fa-nat'-i-sizm], *s.* Fanatismo; celo, ardor, extravagante o furioso.

Fancied [fan'-sid], *a.* Imaginado imaginario, concebido; no real.

Fancier [fan'-si-ęr], *s.* 1. Aficionado a; criador y vendedor de aves y animales. 2. Apasionado por. 3. Visionario, soñador.

Fanciful [fan'-si-ful], *a.* Antojadizo, imaginativo, caprichoso.

Fancifully [fan'-si-ful-i], *adv.* Caprichosamente.

Fancifulness [fan'-si-ful-nes], *s.* Antojo, capricho.

Fancy [fan'-si], *s.* 1. Fantasía, imaginación. 2. Antojo, capricho ventolera. 3. Imagen, idea, concepción. 4. Inclinación, afición, afecto, amor, gusto. *To take a fancy to a thing*, Antojársele a uno alguna cosa, prendarse de ella. *Fancy ball*, Baile de trajes o difraces. (Mex.) Una Jamaica.

Fancy, *a.* 1. Relativo a la fantasía o el capricho en cualquier sentido: v. g. (1) Adornador, que sirve para adorno u ornamento. (2) Ideal, imaginario; bello, elegante. 2. (Com.) De capricho, o de gusto; caracterizado por la variedad, la delicadeza de la última mano, etc.; opuesto a *staple* (regular, normal). 3. Caprichoso, fantástico; extravagante. *Fancy-framed*, Creado por la fantasía. *Fancy-free*, Libre del poder del amor, sin amor. *Fancy-monger*, Hombre fantástico. *Fancy-sick*, Enfermo imaginario. *Fancy goods*, Géneros de capricho o de gusto.

Fancy, *va.* 1. Creer o suponer sin fundamento; imaginar. 2. Gustar, tener complacencia en, querer. 3. Tener idea, concebir en la fantasía. —*vn.* 1. Apasionarse, aficionarse con exceso a alguna persona o cosa; imaginar, figurarse, fantasear. 2. (Fam. Ingl.) Suponer, creer.

Fancywork [fan'-si-wurk], *s.* Labores manuales.

Fane [fēn], *s.* Templo, antiguamente fano.

Fanfare [fan'-fār], *s.* 1. Tocata o sonata de trompas. 2. Procesión o parada ruidosa u ostentosa. 3. Encuadernación vistosa. (Fr.)

Fanfaronade [fan-fa-ro-nēd'], *s.* Fanfarronada.

Fang [fang], *s.* 1. Colmillo, de jabalí u otro animal. 2. Garra, uña.

Fang, *va.* (Ant.) Asir, agarrar.

Fanged [fangd], *a.* Lo que tiene colmillos o garras.

Fangled [faŋ'-gld], *a.* Poco usado, excepto cuando se une con la voz *new*; como, *New-fangled*, Novelero, aficionado a novedades o a cosas nuevas.

Fangless [fang'-les], *a.* Descolmillado, desdentado.

Fanion [fan'-yun], *s.* Banderola, bandera pequeña como las que usan los agrimensores.

Fanlight [fan'-lait], *s.* *V.* FAN WINDOW en la voz *fan*.

Fanlike [fan'-laik], *a.* Parecido a un abanico; en forma de abanico.

Fannel [fan'-el], *s.* Manípulo.

Fanner [fan'-ęr], *s.* Aventador, abanicador.

Fanning [fan'-ing], *s.* Ventilación.

Fanon [fan'-en], *s.* 1. Uno de los dos colgantes o caídas de la mitra episcopal. 2. Manípulo.

Fantail [fan'-tēl], *s.* 1. Variedad de paloma que despliega la cola en forma de abanico. 2. Cola de abanico, pájaro, el matamoscas de Australia o del Oriente (del género Rhipidu-

ra). 3. Mechero de abanico. 4. Ensambladura de cola de milano.
Fantailed [fan'-têld], *a.* En forma de cola de abanico.
Fantasia [fān-ta-zī'-a o fan-tā'-zi-a], *s.* Fantasía, composición música de forma irregular.
Fantasied [fan'-ta-sid], *a.* Fantástico, quimérico, caprichoso, imaginario.
Fantasm [fan'-tazm], *s.* Fantasma.
Fantastic, Fantastical [fan-tas'-tic, al], *a.* 1. Fantástico, de apariencia caprichosa; grutesco. 2. Caprichoso, caprichudo. 3. Ilusorio, imaginario.
Fantastic, *s.* Fantástico.
Fantastically [fan-tas'-tic-al-i], *adv.* Fantásticamente.
Fantasticalness [fan-tas'-tic-al-nes], *s.* Fantasía, humorada, capricho.
Fantasy [fan'-ta-si], *s.* 1. Fantasía, imaginación, la facultad del ánimo de reproducir por medio de imágenes las cosas pasadas o lejanas. (En este sentido se escribe frecuentemente *phantasy.*) 2. Idea fantástica, humorada, capricho. 3. Dibujo fantástico, como el de un bordado.
Fantasy, *va.* Amar, tomar por fantasía un cariño extremado por alguno.
Fantom, *s.* *V.* PHANTOM.
Faquir [fa-kīr'], *s.* *V.* FAKIR.
Far [fār], *adv.* 1. Lejos, a lo lejos. 2. Lejos, a distancia, lejano de una época cualquiera. 3. En gran parte, en mucha proporción. 4. Desde lejos. *Far better,* Mucho mejor. *Far be it from me,* Lejos de mí, no permita Dios. *Far distant,* Muy distante. *Far and wide,* Por todas partes. *By far,* Con mucho, en mucho. *So far,* Tan lejos, hasta ahí, hasta ese punto. *Far beyond,* Mucho más allá de. *Far off,* A gran distancia, a lo lejos. *As far as I see,* A lo que veo. *As far as, so far as,* o *in so far as,* En tanto que, tanto cuanto. *As far as I can,* En cuanto puedo o pueda. *Far from,* Lejos de; muy lejos de eso, ni con mucho. *Are you happy? Far from it!* ¿Es Vd. feliz? Lejos de eso. *Far greater,* Mucho mayor. *Far inferior,* Mucho menor, muy inferior. *Far other,* Muy diferente. *How far,* Cuánto, cuán lejos, hasta dónde, hasta qué punto. *How far is it? (thither),* ¿Cuánto hay de aquí a allí? *Thus far,* Hasta aquí, hasta ahora; bastante. *Far too much,* Demasiado, en demasía. *Far reaching,* De mucho alcance, que llega, o se extiende a lo lejos.—*a.* 1. Lejano, distante, remoto. 2. Que se extiende a lo lejos; de gran alcance. 3. El más lejano de dos objetos. 4. Muy lejano del pensamiento o de la intención de uno.
†**Far-about** [fār'-a-baut], *s.* Rodeo; digresión.
Far-away [far'-a-wê"], *a.* 1. Lejano, alejado. 2. Abstraído, distraído.
Farad [far'-ad], *s.* Faradio, unidad de medida de la capacidad electromagnética de un cuerpo o de un sistema de cuerpos conductores, que con la carga de un culombio produce un voltio.
Faradic [fa-rad'-ic], *a.* Farádico, de Faraday; relativo a las corrientes inducidas rápidamente alternantes.
Faradization [far-a-di-zé'-shun], *s.* Tratamiento de un nervio o músculo por una corriente farádica; faradización.
Farce [fārs], *va.* 1. Embutir. 2. (Des.) Henchir, esparcir.
Farce, *s.* 1. Farsa, entremés, sainete. 2. Ridiculez, cosa vana, éxito absurdo. 3. Albóndiga.
Farcical [fārs'-i-cal], *a.* Entremesado, burlesco, ridículo.
Farcing [fārs'-ing], *s.* Embutido.
Farcy [fārs'-i], *s.* Muermo, una enfermedad de los caballos. *V.* GLANDERS.
†**Fard** [fārd], *va.* Pintar, colorar.
†**Fardel** [fār'-del], *s.* Fardillo, lío o fardo pequeño.
†**Fardel,** *va.* Enfardelar.
Fare [fār], *vn.* 1. Hallarse en cualquiera situación buena o mala; suceder, acontecer. 2. Comer, surtirse, tratarse en cuanto a la comida. 3. (Ant. o Poét.) Ir, andar, viajar. *He fares like a prince,* Se trata a cuerpo de rey.
Fare, *s.* 1. Pasaje, precio que se paga por un viaje terrestre o marítimo. 2. Vianda, comida. 3. Viaje, pasaje. 4. Viajero. *Fare-box,* Caja de depósito de pasajes (para carros urbanos). *Fare-indicator* o *register,* Contador de pasajes para carros urbanos.
Farewell [fār-wel' o fār'-wel], *inter.* A Dios; páselo Vd. bien, quede Vd. con Dios. Locución de que se usa sólo para despedirse. El verbo y el adverbio están muchas veces separados por el pronombre, v. g. *fare thee well.* (< FARE en imperativo y WELL.)—*a.* Relativo a una partida, a una despedida o un adiós. *A farewell song,* Una canción de despedida. —*s.* Despedida. *Last farewell,* El último adiós, la última despedida. *To bid one farewell* o *take farewell of,* Despedirse de alguien.
Far-famed [fār'-fêmd], *a.* Célebre, famoso y conocido en luengas tierras.
Far-fetched [fār'-fecht], *a.* 1. Traído de lejos. 2. Alambicado, apurado, refinado; no obvio.
Farina [fa-rī'-na], *s.* 1. (E. U.) Harina de maíz, preparada para comerla. 2. Harina de los cereales o raíces amiláceas. 3. Almidón, y antiguamente polen.
Farinaceous [far-i-né'-shus], *a.* Harinoso, farináceo.
Farinose [far'-i-nōs], *a.* 1. Farináceo, que da harina. 2. Cubierto de una especie de substancia blanca, parecida a la harina.
Farm [fārm], *s.* 1. Heredad, finca de labranza; terreno destinado a la agricultura. 2. Sistema de arrendar las rentas o las contribuciones. *Farm-house,* Alquería, cortijo, granja. (Mex.) Hacienda. *Grazing farm.* Hacienda de ganados o de cría. (Cuba) Sitio. *Small farm,* Una pequeña alquería o hacienda; un pequeño cortijo. (Mex.) Rancho. (Cuba) Estancia.
Farm, *va.* 1. Cultivar, dar a la tierra las labores que son necesarias para que fructifique. 2. Arrendar, tomar en arriendo. 3. Arrendar, dar en arrendamiento.
Farmable [fārm'-a-bl], *a.* Arrendable.
Farmer [fārm'-ęr], *s.* 1. Labrador, agricultor, hacendado. 2. Arrendatario; rentero; el recaudador de ciertas contribuciones, derechos, etc., mediante un tanto por ciento. *Small farmer,* Labrador, labriego. (Mex.) Ranchero. (Cuba) Sitiero, estanciero. *Farmer-general,* Arrendador o recaudador encargado de imponer ciertas contribuciones en Francia antes de 1789.—*Farmeress, sf.* (Poco us.) Arrendadora, labradora; lo que dirige una hacienda rural.
Farming [fārm'-ing], *s.* 1. Explotación, cultivo, beneficio de una heredad; agricultura. 2. Recaudación o arrendamiento de las contribuciones o rentas por un tanto por ciento.
Farmost [fār'-most], *adv.* (Poco us.) Lo más lejos o distante.
Farmyard [fārm'-yārd], *s.* Corral de una granja o casa de campo.
Farness [fār'-nes], *s.* Distancia.
Faro [fé'-ro o fār'-o], *s.* Faraón, juego de naipes en el cual los jugadores apuestan contra el que da las cartas, acerca del orden en que irán saliendo éstas al tomarlas de la parte superior de la baraja.
Far-piercing [far'-pīrs-ing], *a.* Lo que penetra mucho.
Farrago [far-ré'-gō], *s.* Fárrago, broza.
Farreation, *s.* *V.* CONFARREATION.
Farrier [far'-i-ęr], *s.* 1. Herrador. 2. Albéitar, el que profesa el arte veterinaria o tiene por oficio curar las enfermedades de las bestias.
Farriery [far'-i-ęr-i], *s.* 1. Albeitería. 2. Taller de herrador.
Farrow [far'-ō], *s.* Lechigada de puercos; parto de la marrana.—*a.* Que no queda preñada en un año dado, horra; también machorra, que no ha parido nunca; aplícase a las vacas y las puercas.
Farrow, *va.* Parir la puerca o marrana.
Far-seeing [fār-sī'-ing], *a.* Que ve a gran distancia; previsor, precavido.
Far-shooting [fār'-shūt-ing], *a.* Lo que es de largo alcance, tratándose de armas.
Far-sighted [fār'-sait-ed], *a.* 1. Que ve de lejos; présbite. 2. Dotado de vista penetrante; presciente.
Farther [fār'-dhęr], *adv.* Más lejos, a mayor distancia; más adelante, además de—demás de.—*a.* 1. Más lejos. 2. Ulterior, más alejado. (< *Far,* propriamente *farer;* la letra *th* proviene de la palabra *further.*)
¿**Farther,** *va.* Adelantar, promover. *V.* FURTHER.
Fartherance [fār'-dhęr-ans], *s.* Adelantamiento. *V.* FURTHERANCE.
Farthermore [fār'-dhęr-mōr], *adv.* Además, a más de. *V.* FURTHERMORE.
Farthest [fār'-dhest], *adv.* A lo más lejos.
Farthest, *a.* Remotísimo.—*adv. V.* FURTHEST.
Farthing [fār'-dhing], *s.* 1. Cuarto de penique. 2. Ardite. (Fam.) Un ochavo. *I don't care a farthing about it,* No se me da un pito o un bledo; se me importa muy poco.
Farthingale [fār'-dhing-gêl], *s.* Verdugado, guardainfante.
Farthings-worth [fār'-dhingz-wūrth], *s.* Lo que se vende por un ochavo.
Fasces [fas'-īz], *s. pl.* Fasces, un hacecillo de varas.
Fascet [fas'-et], *s.* Vara de hierro con que se ponen las botellas en el horno para templarlas.
Fascia [fash'-i-a], *s.* 1. (Anat.) Aponeurosis, membrana que cubre los músculos y los mantiene en su lugar. 2. (Arq.) Faja, banda de arquitrabe. 3. Faja, venda, cinturón. (Astr.) Nubecilla en forma de faja alrededor de un planeta.
Fascial [fash'-i-al], *a.* 1. (Anat.) Fascial, relativo o perteneciente a la

fascia. 2. Perteneciente a las fasces de los lictores romanos.

Fasciated [fash'-i-êt-ed], *a.* Fajado, vendado.

Fascicle [fas'-i-cl], *s.* Racimo, manojo; hacecillo, haz pequeño; división de un libro publicado por entregas.

Fascicled [fas'-i-cld], *a.* Arracimado; fasciculado.

Fascicular [fas-sic'-yu-lar], *a.* Fascicular; unido en forma de copa o racimo.

Fascinate [fas'-i-nêt], *va.* Fascinar, hechizar, encantar, aojar o hacer mal de ojo.

Fascinating [fas'-i-nêt-ing], *a.* Fascinador, encantador.

Fascination [fas-i-nê'-shun], *s.* Fascinación, aojo, hechizo, encanto, alucinación.

Fascine [fa-sîn'], *s.* Fagina.

Fascism [fash'-izm], *s.* Fascismo.

Fash [fash], *va.* (Esco.) Enojar, irritar, enfadar.—*vn.* Irritarse, enfadarse.

Fashion [fash'-un], *s.* 1. Forma, figura, hechura de alguna cosa. 2. Moda, uso, costumbre. 3. Rango, calidad, esfera, condición de nacimiento. *People of fashion,* Gente de tono. (Mex.) Gente de sangre azul. *After* o *in a fashion,* A la manera de. *To be in fashion,* Estar de moda. *It is out of fashion,* Ya no es de moda. *I do not like the fashion of that coat,* No me gusta el corte de esa levita. *After the English fashion,* A la inglesa. *Fashion-pieces,* (Mar.) Aletas, piezas sujetas en los extremos de los yugos.

Fashion, *va.* 1. Formar, amoldar. 2. Adaptar, ajustar. 3. Hacer o formar alguna cosa a la moda.

Fashionable [fash'-un-a-bl], *a.* 1. Establecido, usado, acostumbrado, practicado. 2. Hecho a la moda. *Fashionable hat,* Sombrero a la moda.—*s.* Lechuguino, currutaco, petimetre. *The fashionables,* Gente de porte, o rango. (Vul.) La gente grande.

Fashionableness [fash'-un-a-bl-nes], *s.* 1. Figura, forma y disposición de una cosa con respecto a su apariencia exterior. 2. Gentileza en el porte; la costumbre de ataviarse conforme a las modas predominantes.

Fashionably [fash'-un-a-bli], *adv.* A la moda, según la moda.

Fashioner [fash'-un-er], *s.* Hacedor.

Fashionist [fash'-un-ist], *s.* Lechuguino, petimetre.

Fashion-monger [fash'-un-mun'-ger], *s.* Modista.

Fashion plate [fash'-un plêt], *s.* Figurín, persona que viste con elegancia.

Fast [fast ó fast], *vn.* Ayunar, hacer abstinencia.

Fast, *s.* 1. Ayuno. *To break one's fast,* Desayunarse. 2. Espacio de tiempo designado para el ayuno religioso. 3. (De otra raíz) Lazo, amarra. 4. Hielo fijo o inmóvil a lo largo de la ribera.

Fast, *a.* 1. Firme, seguro, fuerte, inmoble, estable, apretado. 2. Firme, constante, fiel. 3. Difícil de borrar o destruir; duradero. 4. Profundo. 5. Veloz, rápido, pronto, ágil, ligero. 6. Hecho o ejecutado rápidamente. 7. Adelantado, dícese de los relojes. *Your watch is three minutes fast,* Su reloj adelanta tres minutos. 8. Gastador, derrochador; dado a la disipación, disoluto. *A fast friend,* Un amigo seguro. *A fast colour,* Color sólido, de buen tinte, duradero. *A fast knot,* Un nudo apretado, firme. *Fast and loose,* (Prov.) Anden y ténganse.—*adv.* 1. Fuertemente, firmemente; estrechamente, apretadamente. 2. Duraderamente; para siempre. 3. Profundamente. *Fast asleep,* Profundamente dormido. 4. No lejos; cerca de. 5. Aprisa, de prisa. *To come fast on the heels of,* Seguir muy de cerca.

Fast-day [fast'-dê], *s.* Día de ayuno.

Fasten [fas'-n], *va.* 1. Afirmar, asegurar, atar, amarrar; trabar, unir. 2. Fijar, hacer pegarse.—*vn.* Fijarse, establecerse, pararse en alguna parte; agarrarse, asirse, pegarse a alguno. *To fasten a door,* Cerrar una puerta. *To fasten one's eyes on,* Fijar los ojos en. *To fasten in,* Clavar, hincar, fijar, imprimir una cosa en otra. *To fasten upon,* Unir o pegar una cosa a otra; imputar, cargar a alguno con obligaciones.

Fastener [fas'-n-er], *s.* El que afirma o asegura.

Fastening [fas'-n-ing], *s.* 1. (Mar.) Encapilladura. 2. Lo que asegura.

Faster [fast'-er], *s.* Ayunador.

‖**Fast-handed** [fast'-hand-ed], *a.* Agarrado, apretado, mezquino, avariento.

Fastidious [fas-tid'-i-us], *a.* Fastidioso, desdeñoso, despreciador, melindroso, dengoso, descontentadizo.

Fastidiously [fas-tid'-i-us-li], *adv.* Fastidiosamente, melindrosamente.

Fastidiousness [fas-tid'-i-us-nes], *s.* Escrupulosidad, delicadeza (en el vestir, etc.)

Fastigiate [fas-tij'-i-êt], *a.* (Bot.) Llano e igual en la cumbre o en el ápice.

Fasting [fast'-ing], *ger.* Ayunando, haciendo abstinencia. *To go out fasting,* Salir en ayunas.—*s.* Ayuno, abstinencia de alimentos. *Fasting and prayer,* El ayuno y la oración.

Fasting-day [fast'-ing-dê], *s.* Día de ayuno.

Fastness [fast'-nes], *s.* 1. Firmeza, seguridad, solidez; fuerza. 2. Fortaleza o plaza naturalmente fuerte. 3. Celeridad, prontitud, diligencia; velocidad, rapidez. 4. Disipación, lujuria, libertinaje.

Fat [fat], *a.* 1. Gordo, pingüe, corpulento. 2. Tosco, lerdo, grosero. 3. Opulento, rico; ganancioso, provechoso, lucrativo.—*s.* 1. Gordo, el cebo o manteca de la carne del animal; enjundia. 2. La parte más rica o más deseable de alguna cosa. 3. (Ant.) Tina. *V.* VAT.

Fat, *va.* Engordar, nutrir.—*vn.* Engrosarse.

Fatal [fê'-tal], *a.* 1. Fatal, mortal, funesto. 2. Inevitable, necesario.

Fatalism [fê'-tal-izm], *s.* Fatalismo.

Fatalist [fê'-tal-ist], *s.* Fatalista.

Fatality [fa-tal'-i-ti], *s.* 1. Fatalidad, predestinación. 2. Fatalidad, desgracia, infortunio. 3. Acontecimiento final, muerte. 4. Decreto del destino.

Fatally [fê'-tal-i], *adv.* Fatalmente.

Fatalness [fê'-tal-nes], *s.* Fatalidad; necesidad inevitable.

Fat-brained [fat'-brênd], **Fat-headed** [fat'-hed-ed], *a.* Lerdo, tardo, torpe.

Fat-cheeked [fat-chîcd'], *a.* Cachetudo, molletudo, cachetón.

Fate [fêt], *s.* 1. Hado, destino, suerte, fortuna, providencia. 2. Hado, muerte, destrucción. 3. *pl.* Las Parcas; los destinos.

Fated [fê'-ted], *a.* Lo que está dispuesto o decretado por los hados, antiguamente *hadado;* fatal, lo que necesariamente ha de suceder o cumplirse.

Fateful [fêt'-ful], *a.* 1. Determinado por el destino. 2. Fatal, funesto.

Father [fā'-dher], *s.* 1. Padre. 2. El principal y cabeza de una familia. 3. Padre, nombre que se da a un anciano o a un hombre respetable. 4. Confesor, padre de almas, padre espiritual. 5. Padre, la primera persona de la santísima Trinidad; Dios como criador. 6. Padre, título de los senadores romanos. 7. Creador, inventor, autor de algo. *Grandfather,* Abuelo. *Our forefathers,* Nuestros padres, abuelos o antepasados. *God-father,* Padrino. *Foster-father,* Padre adoptivo. *Father-like,* Como si fuera padre, con afecto paternal. *Father in God,* Un obispo.

Father, *va.* 1. Prohijar, adoptar, declarar por hijo. 2. Achacar, imputar o atribuir a uno un hijo o un escrito.

Fatherhood [fā'-dher-hud], *s.* Paternidad.

Father-in-law [fā'-dher-in-lē], *s.* Suegro, el padre del marido respecto de la mujer, o el de la mujer respecto del marido.

Fatherland [fā'-dher-land], *s.* Patria, tierra natal, madre patria.

Fatherless [fā'-dher-les], *a.* 1. Huérfano de padre. 2. Desautorizado, lo que no tiene autoridad bastante para ser creído o para merecer consideración.

Fatherliness [fā'-dher-li-nes], *s.* Ternura o amor paternal.

Fatherly [fā'-dher-li], *a.* Paternal, lo que es propio de un padre.—*adv.* Paternalmente.

Fathom [fadh'-um], *s.* 1. Braza, medida de seis pies de largo. 2. Alcance, penetración, profundidad.

Fathom, *va.* 1. Sondar, sondear. 2. Sondear, rastrear, penetrar, profundizar, examinar a fondo, tantear. 3. (Des.) Abrazar, ceñir con los brazos.

Fathomable [fadh'-um-a-bl], *a.* Sondable, sondeable.

Fathomless [fadh'-um-les], *a.* Insondable; impenetrable.

Fatidical [fa-tid'-i-cal], *a.* Fatídico, profético.

‖**Fatiferous** [fa-tif'-er-us], *a.* Fatal, funesto.

Fatigue [fa-tîg'], *s.* 1. Cansancio. 2. Fatiga, trabajo. 3. *Fatigue* o *fatigue-duty,* (Mil.) Faena, todo trabajo que hacen los militares distinto del manejo de las armas y demás ejercicios de su profesión. *Spent with fatigue,* Rendido de cansancio; aspeado. *Fatigue-party,* Los soldados que están de faena, limpieza, etc.

Fatigue, *va.* Fatigar, cansar, con el trabajo corporal o del entendimiento.

Fatigued [fa-tîgd'], *a.* Fatigado, cansado.

Fatiguing [fa-tîg'-ing], *ger.* y *a.* Cansado, pesado, que produce cansancio.

Fatiscent [fa-tis'-ent], *a.* Lo que puesto al aire se convierte en polvo.

Fatling [fat'-ling], *s.* Cebón, animal que se ceba para comerlo.—*a.* Gordo, grueso, regordete.

Fatly [fat'-li], *adv.* Corpulentamente, toscamente.

Fatness [fat'-nes], *s.* 1. Gordura. 2.

Gordo, grasa. 3. Fertilidad, fecundidad.
Fatten [fat'-n], *va.* 1. Engordar, nutrir, alimentar. 2. Cebar. 3. Fertilizar, fecundar o engrasar la tierra.—*vn.* Criar o echar carnes, engrosarse.
Fattener [fat'-n-ęr], *s.* Cebo, lo que engorda.
Fattiness [fat'-i-nes], *s.* Gordura, pringue.
Fattish [fat'-ish], *a.* Gordiflón, algo gordo; pingüedinoso.
Fatty [fat'-i], *a.* Untoso, craso, pingüe.
Fatuitous [fa-tiū'-i-tus], *a.* 1. Necio, fatuo. 2. Vano, ilusorio.
Fatuity [fa-tiū'-i-ti], *s.* Fatuidad, simpleza.
Fatuous [fat'-yu-us], *a.* Fatuo, insensato, simple, tonto.
Fat-witted [fat'-wit-ed], *a.* Torpe, lerdo, pesado.
Fauces [fō'-sīz], *s. pl.* Fauces, la entrada del esófago; gaznate, garganta.
Faucet [fō'-set], *s.* Espita, canilla, llave, grifo; canilla con una válvula para regular la salida de un líquido.
Faugh, *inter.* Expresión de enfado o menosprecio: ¡puf! ¡bah!
Fault [fōlt], *s.* 1. Falta, culpa, desliz o defecto en obrar. 2. Falta, defecto o privación de algo. 3. (Geol.) Falla, interrupción y dislocación de las capas que forman la corteza terrestre por sacudimientos interiores. 4. (Elec.) Avería accidental. *To find fault,* Tachar, criticar; poner faltas. *I find no fault in their opinion,* No hallo nada reprensible en su modo de pensar. 5. Pérdida de la pista o del rastro; dícese de los perros cazadores.
Fault, *va.* 1. (Geol.) Hacer una falla en. 2. (Raro o fam.) Acusar; echar a uno la culpa de alguna falta o delito.—*vn.* (Des.) Faltar; no tener razón; extraviarse.
Fault-finder [fōlt'-faind-ęr], *s.* Censurador, criticón.
Faultily [fōlt'-i-li], *adv.* Defectuosamente, erradamente.
Faultiness [fōlt'-i-nes], *s.* Culpa, falta, vicio, defecto, ofensa.
Faultless [fōlt'-les], *a.* Sin falta; sin tacha; perfecto, cumplido, acabado.
Faultlessness [fōlt'-les-nes], *s.* Perfección; inculpabilidad.
Faulty [fōlt'-i], *a.* Culpable, defectuoso, imperfecto.
Faun [fōn], *s.* Fauno, especie de dios de las selvas.
Fauna [fō'-na], *s.* (*pl.* FAUNÆ o FAUNAS). (Zool.) Fauna, conjunto de los animales de cada país o región (o su descripción científica).
Faunist [fōn'-ist], *s.* Naturalista que estudia una fauna.
Fautor [fō'-tęr], *s.* (Ant.) Fautor, favorecedor.
†Fautress [fō'-tres], *sf.* Fautora, fomentadora.
Favillous [fa-vil'-us], *a.* Ceniciento.
Favonian [fa-vō'-ni-an], *a.* Que sopla del oeste; perteneciente al favonio; favorable, próspero.
Favor o **Favour** [fē'-vęr], *va.* y *vn.* 1. Favorecer, patrocinar, proteger, ayudar, amparar, socorrer. *Favour me with that,* Hágame V. el favor de eso, favorézcame V. con eso. 2. Favorecer, ayudar, asistir con ventajas o conveniencias. *To favor an opinion,* Apoyar una opinión. 3. (Fam.) Asemejarse, parecerse. *Everybody owns that this gentleman favors his father,* Todo el mundo conviene en que este caballero se parece a su padre. 4. Favorecer, conducir, contribuir, convenir para algún fin. 5. Usar con precaución, v. g. un miembro lastimado; abstenerse de usar, guardar, reservar. 6. (Art.) Atenuar, paliar, mitigar.
Favor, *s.* 1. Favor, fineza, beneficio. 2. Favor, socorro, patrocinio, amparo. 3. Mitigación, lenidad, blandura en el castigo. 4. Gracia, beneficio otorgado a uno con exclusión de otros; parcialidad. 5. Permiso, licencia. 6. Conveniencia para alguna cosa, facilidad. 7. Favor, cinta, flor, etc., recibida de una dama como agasajo; los lazos de cinta que se llevan en Inglaterra en algunas ocasiones en señal de regocijo o como signo de pertenecer a un partido; en particular, una fruslería dada en el cotillón. 8. En la correspondencia (esp. comercial), carta; grata, atenta. 9. (Ant.) Facción, semblante. *With your favor* o *by your favor,* Con licencia o permiso de Vd.
Favorable [fē'-vęr-a-bl], *a.* 1. Favorable, propicio, benévolo. 2. Favorable, benigno. 3. Bien encarado, bien parecido.
Favorableness [fē'-vęr-a-bl-nes], *s.* Agrado, benignidad.
Favorably [fē'-vęr-a-bli], *adv.* Favorablemente, benignamente.
Favored [fē'-vęrd], *a.* Favorecido, protegido, amparado. *Well-favored,* Hermoso, bien parecido. *Ill-favored,* Feo, mal carado.
Favoredly [fē'-vęrd-li], *adv.* Sólo se usa unido a los siguientes adverbios: *Well* o *ill favoredly,* Con buena o mala apariencia.
Favoredness [fē'-vęrd-nes], *s.* (Poco us.) Apariencia, aspecto exterior. *Hard-favoredness,* Dureza en la fisonomía; fealdad.
Favorer [fē'-vęr-ęr], *s.* Favorecedor.
Favorite, Favourite [fē'-vęr-it], *s.* Favorito, predilecto, privado, valido; confidente.—*a.* Amado, favorecido.
Favoritism [fē'-vęr-it-izm], *s.* Favoritismo, la influencia que el afecto por algún favorito o predilecto tiene en las acciones de una persona: tómase comúnmente en mal sentido.
Favorless [fē'-vęr-les], *a.* Desfavorecido, desamparado; adverso, contrario.
Favose [fa-vōs'], *a.* Faveolado, guarnecido de celdillas como los alvéolos del panal.
Favour, Favourable, Favourite, etc. (es la forma común en Inglaterra). *V.* FAVOR, etc.
Fawn [fōn], *s.* 1. Cervato, enodio, el macho pequeño de los ciervos; gamo o gama en su primer año. 2. (Poco us.) Lisonja o adulación servil y baja. 3. Color del cervato.
Fawn, *vn.* 1. Parir la cierva. 2. Halagar o hacer fiestas como el perro a su amo; adular servilmente.
Fawner [fōn'-ęr], *s.* Lisonjero, zalamero, adulador, quitapelillos.
Fawning [fōn'-ing], *s.* Adulación o lisonja vil y baja; bajeza.
Fawningly [fōn'-ing-li], *adv.* Lisonjeramente, zalameramente.
Fay [fē], *s.* Duende. *V.* FAIRY.
Fay, *va.* Empalmar, ajustar una pieza con otra.—*vn.* Cuadrar, venir bien una pieza con otra.
Feaberry [fī'-ber-i], *s.* (Prov. Ingl.) *V.* GOOSEBERRY.
Fealty [fī'-al-ti], *s.* Homenaje, fidelidad, lealtad.
Fear [fīr], *s.* 1. Miedo, perturbación originada por la aprehensión de algún peligro. 2. Miedo, temor, recelo. 3. Causa, motivo de temor; carácter alarmante. 4. Respeto, veneración con relación a la autoridad constituída. *Fear of the world,* Respeto humano. *To be in fear,* Tener miedo. *There is fear,* Hay que temer. *For fear,* Por temor de, por miedo de.
Fear, *va.* 1. Temer, tener miedo. 2. Mirar con temor respetuoso y reverencia. 3. (Ant. y Poét.) Amedrentar, espantar.—*vn.* 1. Temer, tener horror a algo. 2. Temer, estar inquieto o receloso.
Fearful [fīr'-ful], *a.* 1. Medroso, miedoso, temeroso, pusilánime. 2. Tímido, encogido y corto de ánimo. 3. Tremendo, horrendo, espantoso, terrible; respetuoso. 4. Digno de respeto y reverencia.
Fearfully [fīr'-ful-i], *adv.* Medrosamente, temerosamente, con miedo y temor; de un modo digno de reverencia; de una manera espantosa, terriblemente.
Fearfulness [fīr'-ful-nes], *s.* 1. Timidez, temor, miedo, pusilanimidad, encogimiento. 2. Temor, miedo, pasión del ánimo que nos hace evitar las cosas dañosas o peligrosas.
Fearless [fīr'-les], *a.* Impertérrito, intrépido, arrojado, ardiente, bravo, atrevido, audaz.
Fearlessly [fīr'-les-li], *adv.* Intrépidamente, sin miedo.
Fearlessness [fīr'-les-nes], *s.* Intrepidez, arrojo, bravura, valentía.
Fearsome [fīr'-sum], *a.* 1. Temible, espantoso, que infunde miedo. 2. Tímido, miedoso, asustado.
Feasibility [fīz-i-bil'-i-ti], *s.* Posibilidad o capacidad de poderse ejecutar alguna cosa.
Feasible [fīz'-i-bl], *a.* Factible, practicable, asequible, hacedero.
Feasibleness [fīz'-i-bl-nes], *s.* Posibilidad o capacidad de poder ejecutar alguna cosa.
Feasibly [fīz'-i-bli], *adv.* De un modo factible, practicable.
Feast [fīst], *s.* 1. Banquete, festín, convite, comida o cena espléndida. (Fam.) Comilitona, comilona. *A smell-feast,* Perrito de todas bodas. 2. Fiesta solemne, regocijo en día señalado. 3. Cualquier cosa agradable al paladar.
Feast, *va.* 1. Festejar, recibir con agasajo en su casa, regalar al que viene a ella a comer. 2. Atracar de comida y bebida.—*vn.* 1. Comer opíparamente. 2. Gozarse, entretenerse.
Feaster [fīst'-ęr], *s.* 1. Comilitón, goloso. 2. Festejador, el que da banquetes.
Feastful [fīst'-ful], *a.* Festivo, placentero; suntuoso, voluptuoso.
Feasting [fīst'-ing], *s.* Banquete; fiesta.
Feast-rite [fīst'-rait], *s.* El ceremonial de los banquetes.
Feat [fīt], *s.* 1. Hecho, acción o hazaña notables. 2. Juego de manos, ligereza de manos. *Feats,* Suertes. —*a.* (Ant.) 1. Apto, ingenioso. 2. Fino, pulido, galán; por ironía o desprecio. *To do feats,* Hacer maravillas.
Feat, *va.* (Des.) Formar, amoldar.
Feather [fedh'-ęr], *s.* 1. Pluma. 2. Algo que se parece a una pluma o

plumas; particularmente en la mecánica, lengüeta, cuña, rayo; refuerzo de eje. 3. Género, clase, naturaleza, especie. *Birds of a feather*, Pájaros de una misma pluma, lobos de la misma camada. 4. Bagatela, fruslería. 5. Al remar, la acción de volver la pala del remo poniéndola casi horizontal. 6. Cacería de animales de pluma en general. *To cut a feather*, (Mar.) Llevar buen viento, navegar con rapidez. *To show the white feather*, Mostrarse cobarde, volverse atrás (dícese porque el verdadero gallo de pelea no tiene plumas blancas). *To pluck a bird's feathers*, Desplumar. *A plume of feathers*, Plumaje. *To laugh at a feather*, Reirse de nada. *Feather-bed*, Colchón de plumas, plumón. *Imitation feathers*, Plumas de imitación, encrespadas para penachos. *Birds of a feather flock together*, (Prov.) Cada oveja con su pareja; o Dios los cría y ellos se juntan. *To be a feather in one's cap*, Dar realce o importancia a alguna persona o cosa. *Feather-edged*, En bisel, en perfil. *Feather-brain*, Imbécil, tonto, casquivano. *Feather-weight*, Púgil o atleta de mínimo peso; de aquí, persona de escasa importancia. *In high feather*, Vivo, alegre.

Feather, *va.* 1. Emplumar, poner o adornar con plumas. 2. Enriquecer, adornar, como con plumas. 3. Volver la pala del remo al sacarla del agua, poniéndola casi horizontal. 4. (Mec.) Ajustar una lengüeta o rayo en algo. 5. Estabilizar un avión por medio de una forma de rotación de hélices o motores.—*vn.* 1. Cubrirse con plumas. 2. Descomponerse en forma emplumada. *To feather one's nest*, Enriquecerse, particularmente a expensas de otro, juntar mucho caudal, hacer su agosto.

Featherbedding [fedh'-ẹr-bed'-ing), *s.* Imposición por parte de sindicatos de trabajadores innecesarios.

Feather duster [fedh'-ẹr dus'-tẹr], *s.* Plumero.

Feathered [fedh'-ẹrd], *a.* 1. Plumado, emplumado. 2. Que tiene apéndices parecidos a plumas. 3. (Poco us.) Alado; veloz como una flecha. *The feathered tribe*, Los pájaros.

Feather-edged [fedh'-ẹr-ejd], *a.* Achaflanado.

Feathering [fedh'-ẹr-ing], *pa.* de *To* FEATHER y *s.* (Úsase en composición.) *Feathering float, paddle*, Álabe, paleta movible de rueda hidráulica. *Feathering-wheel*, Rueda de paletas movibles.

Featherless [fedh'-ẹr-les], *a.* Desplumado, implume.

Feather-seller [fedh'-ẹr-sel'-ẹr], *s.* Plumajero, vendedor de plumajes.

Featherweight [fedh'-ẹr-wêt], *s.* (Boxeo) Peso pluma.

Feathery [fedh'-ẹr-i], *a.* 1. Plumado, cubierto con plumas. 2. Ligero como una pluma, o parecido a las plumas.

Featness [fît'-nes], *s.* (Poco us.) Pulidez, destreza, gentileza.

Feature [fî'-chur], *s.* 1. Semblante, rostro. 2. Facción del rostro, forma, figura. 3. Rasgo, carácter distintivo.—*pl.* Facciones, rostro, la cara entera.

Feature, *va.* Asemejarse, parecerse en el semblante o cara.

Featured [fî'-churd], *a.* 1. Lo que tiene buenas o malas facciones. 2. Tómase en sentido absoluto por el que tiene hermosas facciones. 3. Lo que se parece en el rostro o en las facciones. *Well-featured*, Bien encarado. *Ill-featured*, Mal encarado o engestado.

Featureless [fî'-chur-les], *a.* Que no tiene rasgos distintos ni fisonomía caracterizada.

Febricula [fẹ-bric'-yu-la], *s.* Calenturilla, fiebre ligera.

Febrific [fe-brif'-ic], *a.* Febrífico, febricitante, que causa fiebre.

Febrifacient [feb-ri-fê'-shient], *a.* Febril, que causa o produce fiebre.

Febrifugal [feb-rif'-yu-gal], *a.* Que tiene la cualidad de calmar la fiebre.

Febrile [fî'-bril o feb'-ril], *a.* (Med.) Febril, lo que indica o proviene de la fiebre.

February [feb'-ru-ẹ-ri], *s.* Febrero.

Februation [feb-ru-ê'-shun], *s.* Purificación o sacrificio entre los paganos.

Fecal [fî'-cal], *a.* Fecal.

Feces [fî'-sez], *s. pl.* Excrementos; heces.

Feck [fec], *a.* (Esco.) Endurecido, fuerte, robusto.—*s.* 1. Fuerza, poder, vigor. 2. Cantidad, número o valor. 3. La parte principal.

Fecula [fec'-yu-la], *s.* 1. Almidón. 2. (Poco us.) *V.* CHLOROPHYL.

Feculence, Feculency [fec'-yu-lens, i], *s.* 1. Feculencia; porquería debida a las heces; la calidad de hacer mucho poso o dejar muchas heces. 2. Posos, heces, sedimento.

Feculent [fec'-yu-lent], *a.* Feculento, heciento, puerco, fecal.

Fecund [fec'-und ó fi-cund'], *a.* Fecundo, fértil, prolífico.

Fecundate [fec'-un-dêt o fẹ-cund'-êt], *va.* Fecundar.

Fecundation [fec-un-dê'-shun], *s.* Fecundación.

Fecundify [fe-cund'-i-fai], *va.* Fecundar, fecundizar.

Fecundity [fẹ-cund'-i-ti], *s.* Fecundidad, fertilidad, abundancia.

Fed [fed], *pret.* y *pp.* del verbo *To* FEED. *To be full fed*, Tener el vientre lleno.

Federal [fed'-ẹr-al], *a.* 1. Federal, perteneciente a liga o contrato. 2. Relativo a una confederación de estados. 3. Partidario de la federación; en especial, partidario de la Unión en la guerra civil norteamericana de 1861–1865.

Federalism [fed'-ẹr-al-izm], *s.* Federalismo; principios de los federales.

Federalist [fed'-ẹr-al-ist], *s.* Federalista, nombre dado en la América del Norte a los partidarios de la constitución de los Estados Unidos.

Federalize, Federalise [fed'-ẹr-al-aiz], *va.* Federalizar, formar una federación.

Federate [fed'-ẹr-êt], *a.* Confederado, aliado.—*va.* *V.* FEDERALIZE.

Federative [fed'-ẹr-a-tiv], *a.* Federativo, unido por una liga.

Federation [fed-ẹr-ê'-shun], *s.* Confederación, liga, federación.

Fedora [fẹ-dō'-ra], *s.* Sombrero de fieltro.

Fee [fî], *s.* 1. Recompensa o premio por algún trabajo. 2. Gratificación, paga extraordinaria que se da a las personas empleadas en los oficios públicos. 3. Derechos honorarios, salario, propina, estipendio que se da a los que ejercen alguna profesión por el ejercicio de ella. 4. (Der.) Bienes, hacienda de patrimonio. 5. (For.) Feudo. *Fee simple*, Hacienda libre de condición.

Fee, *va.* 1. Pagar, recompensar, premiar. 2. Alquilar, tener a sueldo. 3. Cohechar, sobornar. 4. Dar propina.

Feeable [fî'-a-bl], *a.* Recompensable; se dice de la persona a quien se puede dar una retribución o propina.

Feeble [fî'-bl], *a.* Feble, débil, flaco, lánguido; enfermizo; debilitado por la edad o las desgracias. *To grow feeble*, Debilitarse, enflaquecerse.

†**Feeble**, *va.* Debilitar. *V.* ENFEEBLE.

Feeble-minded [fî'-bl-maind'-ed], *a.* 1. Falto de inteligencia, imbécil. 2. Irresoluto, vacilante. *Feeble-mindedness*, Debilidad de entendimiento, idiotez; irresolución.

Feebleness [fî'-bl-nes], *s.* Debilidad, extenuación, flaqueza.

Feebly [fî'-bli], *adv.* Débilmente, flacamente.

Feed [fîd], *va.* 1. Dar de comer. 2. Pacer, apacentarse el ganado. 3. Nutrir, alimentar, v. g. una máquina; proveer, suplir lo que falta a alguna cosa. 4. Alimentar con esperanzas. 5. Deleitar, entretener. —*vn.* 1. Comer, alimentarse. 2. Pastar, comer la hierba del campo. 3. Engordar, cebar. *To feed on o upon*, Alimentarse de.

Feed, *s.* 1. Comida, alimento. 2. Pasto, hierba para alimentar los ganados. 3. (Mec.) Movimiento de empuje, y el material con que se alimenta una máquina; alimentación. *Feed-bag*, Morral de pienso. *Feed-head*, (Mec.) Depósito de agua para la alimentación de una máquina. *Feed-motion*, (Mec.) Movimiento de alimentación. *Feed-pump*, Bomba de alimentación para proveer de agua las máquinas de vapor.

Feedback [fîd'-bac], *s.* (Elec.) Realimentación.

Feeder [fîd'-ẹr], *s.* 1. El que da de comer; particularmente persona o aparato para surtir de material a una máquina. 2. Comedor, el que come; también, gorrista, dependiente, criado. 3. Una cosa cualquiera que suple las necesidades de otra o aumenta su importancia; v. g. el afluente de un río. 4. Atizador, incitador. *Nice feeder*, Melindroso en los manjares. *High* o *greedy feeder*, Comilón, glotón. *Dainty feeder*, Goloso, lamerón.

Feeding [fîd'-ing], *s.* Herbaje, pastura, pasto; comida. *Feeding apparatus*, (Mec.) Aparato de alimentación. *Feeding-bottle*, Mamadera, biberón, botellita que sirve para la lactancia artificial de los niños, corderos, etc.

Fee-farm [fî'-farm], *s.* 1. (For.) Enfiteusis o propiamente arrendamiento de un terreno feudal. 2. Escritura de arrendamiento de tierras feudales.

Feel [fîl], *vn.* 1. Sentir, percibir por el tacto. 2. Tentar, examinar, sondear. 3. Tener sensibilidad pronta para percibir la impresión grata o desagradable que causan los objetos. 4. Producir una cosa impresión al tacto. 5. Palpar, tentar, manosear. 6. Tomar el pulso. 7. Sentir placer o pena física o moralmente. 8. Conocerse. *To feel for*, Condolerse de. *To feel soft*, Ser suave al tacto. *To feel coarse*, Ser áspero al tacto. *To feel mortified*, Abochornarse, correrse, mortificarse. *How do you feel?*

¿Cómo se siente Vd.? ¿cómo se halla Vd.?
Feel, *s.* Tacto, palpamiento.
Feeler [fîl'-ẹr], *s.* 1. Tentador. 2. Un órgano del tacto; antena, cada una de las dos puntas que tienen en la cabeza algunos insectos; tentáculo. 3. Tentativa, acción con que se intenta experimentar, probar o tantear alguna cosa.
Feeling [fîl'-ing], *s.* 1. Tacto, el sentido del tacto, palpamiento. *V.* FEEL. 2. Sensibilidad, ternura, compasión. 3. Sensación, percepción, sentimiento. *To touch one's feelings*, (1) Conmover el ánimo; tocar en lo vivo. (2) Herir el amor propio. *Good, proper feeling*, Buen sentimiento. *Wrong, improper feeling*, Mal sentimiento.—*part. a.* Sensible, tierno, conmovedor, patético.
Feelingly [fîl'-ing-li], *adv.* 1. Vivamente, con mucha expresión, con energía. *He spoke very feelingly*, Habló al alma. 2. Sensiblemente, tiernamente; de un modo conmovedor.
Feet [fît], *s. pl.* de FOOT. Pies.
Feetless [fît'-les], *a.* Sin pies.
Feeze [fîz], *va.* (Esco.) Destorcer el chicote de un cabo, hacer pedazos. —*vn.* 1. Destorcerse, heshacerse. 2. (Fam. E. U.) Enfadarse, inquietarse.
Feign [fên], *va.* 1. Inventar, fingir, idear o imaginar lo que no existe. 2. Pretextar, valerse de algún pretexto. 3. Fingir, disimular.—*vn.* Fingir, referir falsedades imaginadas. *A feigned treble*, (Mús.) Falsete. (Fam.) *To feign ignorance*, Hacerse chiquito.
Feignedly [fên'-ed-li], *adv.* Fingidamente.
Feignedness [fên'-ed-nes], *s.* Ficción, fraude, engaño.
Feigner [fên'-ẹr], *s.* Fingidor.
Feigning [fên'-ing], *s.* Fingimiento, simulación, engaño.
Feint [fênt], *s.* 1. Ficción, disimulación, artificio. 2. Finta, movimiento con la espada para distraer o engañar al contrario.—*vn.* Hacer finta, fingir un golpe o estocada.
Feldspar [feld'-spar], *s.* Feldespato, silicato de alúmina y un álcali, que se encuentra en muchas rocas primitivas. (Escríbese también **Feldspath** y **Felspar.**)
Feldspathic [feld-spath'-ic], *a.* Del feldespato, que lo contiene o se le asemeja.
Felicitate [fẹ-lis'-i-têt], *va.* 1. Felicitar, dar el parabién o la enhorabuena, congratularse de algo con otro. 2. (Des.) Hacer feliz o dichoso a alguno.
Felicitation [fẹ-lis-i-tê'-shun], *s.* Felicitación, congratulación, parabién, enhorabuena.
Felicitous [fẹ-lis'-i-tus], *a.* Feliz, dichoso; bienaventurado.
Felicitously [fẹ-lis'-i-tus-li], *adv.* Felizmente, dichosamente.
Felicity [fẹ-lis'-i-ti], *s.* Felicidad, dicha, bienaventuranza.
Felidæ [fî'-li-dî], *s. pl.* (Zool.) Félidos, familia de mamíferos carnívoros que comprende el león, tigre, gato, etc.
Feline [fî'-lain], *a.* Gatuno, gatesco, que pertenece al género felino.
Fell [fel], *a.* 1. Cruel, bárbaro, inhumano. 2. Fiero, sanguinario, feroz, sangriento.
Fell, *s.* 1. Dobladillo, costura que tiene al lado una tira llana y lisa. 2. Remate del tejido. 3. Pelo, guedejas de pelo. 4. (Ant.) Cuero, piel, pellejo. 5. (Prov. Ingl.) Collado, sierra, peñasco.
Fell, *pret.* de *To* FALL.
Fell, *va.* 1. Derribar, derrocar, echar por tierra; acogotar (las reses). 2. Cortar para echar por tierra alguna cosa, como las cabezas, los árboles, etc. *Felling of wood*, Corta o corte de monte o leña. 3. Dobladillar, hacer un dobladillo.
Fellah [fel'-ā], *s.* (*pl.* FELLAHS o FELLAHEEN). En Egipto, Siria, etc., patán, labriego.
Feller [fel'-ẹr], *s.* 1. Derribante. 2. Pieza accessoria de una máquina de coser para hacer dobladillos; sobrecosedor.
Fellmonger [fel'-muṇ-gẹr], *s.* (Des.) Pellejero, el que trata en pellejos.
Fellness [fel'-nes], *s.* Crueldad, ferocidad, barbarie.
Felloe [fel'-ō], *s.* Pina de la rueda. *V.* FELLY.
Fellow [fel'-ō], *a.* Asociado; parecido, correspondiente. (Úsase frecuentemente para formar voces compuestas.)—*s.* 1. Persona, individuo. 2. Compañero, camarada, socio; igual. 3. Compañero, hermano, la cosa que hace juego con otra. *My cuff-buttons are not fellows*, Mis gemelos no hacen juego o no son iguales. 4. Socio o individuo de algún colegio, sociedad o academia. 5. (Fam.) Hombre, mozo, chico. A veces es expletivo cuando se une a los adjetivos, como, *A brave fellow*, Un valiente. (Fam.) Un buen chico, una buena alhaja. *A worthless fellow*, Un para nada, un pícaro. *Dear little fellow*, Querido. queridito mío. *A young fellow*, Un joven, un mozo, un muchacho. *A clever fellow*, Un mozo listo, entendido, de talento. 6. Pelafustán, hombre vulgar, persona inferior o desacreditada. *Fellow-being* o *creature*, El prójimo, nuestro semejante. V. *F.* como abreviatura. *To be hail fellow, well met*, Tratarse de igual a igual, como compañero.
Fellow, *va.* 1. Hermanar, igualar una cosa con otra. 2. Convenir; hacer pareja; aparear.
Fellow-citizen [fel'-o-sit'-i-zen], *s.* Conciudadano, compatriota.
Fellow-commoner [fel'-o-com'-un-ẹr], *s.* El que tiene los mismos derechos que otro.
Fellow-counsellor [fel'-o-caun'-sel-ẹr], *s.* Individuo del mismo consejo.
Fellow-creature [fel'-o-crî'-chur], *s.* Criatura de la misma especie.
Fellow-feeling [fel'-o-fîl'-ing], *s.* 1. Simpatía, compasión. 2. Interés común.
Fellow-heir [fel-o-ār'], *s.* Coheredero.
Fellow-helper [fel'-o-help'-ẹr], *s.* Coadjutor, coadyuvador.
Fellow-laborer [fel'-o-lé'-bẹr-ẹr], *s.* Colaborador, compañero en algún trabajo.
Fellow-maiden [fel'-o-mêd'-n], *sf.* Doncella que vive o está con otra.
Fellow-member [fel'-o-mem'-bẹr], *s.* Individuo de la misma sociedad; miembro del mismo cuerpo; compañero.
Fellow-minister [fel'-o-min'-is-tẹr], *s.* El que sirve el mismo oficio.
Fellow-partner [fel'-o-pārt'-nẹr], *s.* Consocio en algún negocio o casa de comercio, donde hay más de dos compañeros.
Fellow-peer [fel-o-pîr'], *s.* El que goza los mismos privilegios de nobleza, como sucede en Inglaterra, donde los pares tienen títulos y precedencia diferentes, aunque son iguales en los demás privilegios.
Fellow-prisoner [fel'-o-priz'-un-ẹr], *s.* Preso en la misma cárcel o por la misma causa.
Fellow-scholar [fel'-o-scol'-ar], *s.* Condiscípulo.
Fellow-servant [fel'-o-sẹr'-vant], *s.* Sirviente que tiene el mismo amo que otro.
Fellowship [fel'-o-ship], *s.* 1. Intimidad, confraternidad, compañerismo; comunión. 2. Asociación, comunidad de intereses o de sentimientos; participación. 3. Compañía, cuerpo de individuos asociados. 4. Sociedad, compañía, reunión social. 5. (Ingl.) Beca, plaza de colegial en algún colegio; o (E. U.) fundación en las universidades para sostener a un estudiante que se dedica a una carrera universitaria. 6. (Arit.) Regla de compañía. *Good-fellowship*, Espíritu de paz, de concordia. *Do it for good-fellowship*, Hágalo Vd. en obsequio de la concordia. *The fellowship of the Holy Ghost*, La comunión del Espíritu Santo.
Fellowship, *va.* y *vn.* Admitir, aceptar o unirse con otros en sociedad.
Fellow-soldier [fel'-o-sōl'-jẹr], *s.* Conmilitón: úsase por cariño.
Fellow-student [fel'-o-stū'-dent], *s.* Condiscípulo.
Fellow-subject [fel'-o-sub'-ject], *s.* El que vive bajo el mismo gobierno que otro.
Fellow-sufferer [fel'-o-suf'-ẹr-ẹr], *s.* El que sufre por la misma causa o al propio tiempo que otro.
Fellow-traveller [fel'-o-trav'-el-ẹr], *s.* 1. Compañero de viaje. 2. Comunistoide, simpatizador de los comunistas.
Fellow-worker [fel'-o-wūrk'-ẹr], *s.* El que trabaja con el mismo propósito o en el mismo objeto que otro.
Fellow-workman [fel'-o-wūrk'-man], *s.* Artesano que trabaja en la misma obra que otro.
Fellow-writer [fel'-o-rait'-ẹr], *s.* El que escribe al mismo tiempo o sobre el mismo asunto que otro.
Felly, Felloe [fel'-i, fel'-ō], *s.* Pina, cada uno de los trozos curvos de madera que forman en círculo la rueda de un coche o carro.
Felly, *adv.* Cruelmente, bárbaramente, ferozmente.
Felo-de-se [fî'-lo-de-sî'], *s.* (For.) Suicida.
Felon [fel'-un], *s.* 1. Reo de algún delito capital o grave. 2. Panadizo, panarizo, uñero.—*a.* 1. Adquirido por felonía. 2. Malvado, criminal; traidor.
Felonious [fẹ-lō'-ni-us], *a.* Malvado, perverso, traidor, villano, maligno, pérfido.
Feloniously [fẹ-lō'-ni-us-li], *adv.* Traidoramente, alevosamente, malvadamente.
Felonry [fel'-un-ri], *s.* El conjunto de malhechores; toda la pillería.
Felony [fel'-o-ni], *s.* Crimen o delito que tenía originalmente por pena el embargo de los bienes muebles o inmuebles, y hoy tiene pena capital o la encarcelación en una prisión de estado.
Felsite [fel'-sait], *s.* Mezcla de cuarzo y feldespato. *V.* FELDSPAR.

Felspar [fel'-spār], *s.* Feldespato. *V.* FELDSPAR. (Forma más usada en Inglaterra.)
Felt [felt], *s.* Fieltro, lana no tejida, sino unida e incorporada a fuerza de agua caliente, lejía y goma.—*pret.* del verbo *To* FEEL.
Felt, *va.* Trabajar el fieltro para los sombreros.
Felting [felt'-ing], *s.* 1. Materiales para hacer fieltro. 2. Fieltro en cantidad. 3. Acción de aserrar o cortar la madera en la dirección de la vena.
Felt-maker [felt'-mê-kęr], *s.* El oficial de sombrerero que trabaja el fieltro.
†**Felter** [felt'-ęr], *va.* Unir alguna cosa como si fuese fieltro.
Felucca [fe-luc'-a], *s.* Falucho, falúa, embarcación menor y de remos con dos palos y velas latinas.
Female [fî'-mêl], *a.* 1. Femenino, del sexo femenino. 2. Femenino, propio y especial de las mujeres. 3. (Bot.) Que tiene pistilos.—*s.* 1. Hembra, mujer o animal del sexo femenino. 2. Hembra, en las plantas, la que está provista de un pistilo, y que fecundada por el polen del estambre da fruto. *Female screw*, Tuerca, hembra de tornillo. El uso de la palabra *female* para significar mujer lo desaprueban hoy todos los buenos escritores. *Female* se aplica al sexo de la mujer, *feminine* a sus cualidades, particularmente a las más delicadas, a sus intereses, empleos u ocupaciones, etc. *Female voice*, Voz de mujer. *Feminine voice*, Voz femenina, tal vez la de un hombre.
Femalize [fî'-ma-laiz], *va.* Afeminar, inclinar a uno a parecerse a las mujeres por sus gustos, modales y acciones.
Feme covert [fem cuv'-ęrt], *s.* (For.) Mujer casada. *Feme sole*, (1) Soltera. (2) Mujer que comercia sola o sin auxilio de su marido.
Feminality [fem-i-nal'-i-ti], *s.* Femineidad.
Femineity [fem-i-nî'-i-ti], *s.* *V.* FEMINALITY.
Feminine [fem'-i-nin], *a.* 1. Femenino, femíneo. 2. Femenil, tierno, delicado. 3. Mujeril, afeminado. 4. (Gram.) Del género femenino.
Femininity [fem-i-nin'-i-ti], *s.* 1. Calidad, o estado de femenino. 2. El conjunto de las mujeres.
†**Feminity**, *s.* *V.* FEMINALITY.
†**Feminize** [fem'-i-naiz], *va.* Afeminar.
Femoral [fem'-o-ral], *a.* Femoral, perteneciente al muslo.
Femur [fî'-mur], *s.* (*pl.* FEMURS o FEMORA). 1. (Anat.) Fémur, hueso del muslo. 2. (Ento.) Fémur, la tercera pieza o artejo de las patas de los insectos.
Fen [fen], *s.* 1. Marjal, pantano. 2. Enfermedad mohosa del lúpulo. *Fen-berry*, Especie de zarzamora. *Fen-born*, Nacido en país pantanoso. *Fen-cress*, (Bot.) Berro pantanoso. *Fen-cricket*, Grillotalpa. *Fen-duck*, Especie de ánade silvestre.
Fence [fens], *s.* 1. Defensa, reparo, resguardo. 2. Cerca, palizada, vallado que se pone alrededor de un terreno para dividirlo de otro y resguardarlo. 3. Cercamiento, el acto de cercar. 4. Esgrima, el arte de manejar la espada. *Fence of pales* ó *stakes*, Empalizada, estacada. *A coat of fence* o *mail*, Cota de malla. *Fence-month*, Tiempo de veda, el en que se prohibe la caza. *Fence-keeper*, Prendero comprador de efectos robados.
Fence, *va.* 1. Cercar, avallar un sitio o heredad. 2. Defender, preservar, guardar, custodiar.—*vn.* 1. Esgrimir, pelear. 2. Defenderse, luchar, v. gr. en una discusión.
Fenceful [fens'-ful], *a.* Lo que da defensa o reparo.
Fenceless [fens'-les], *a.* Abierto, lo que no está cercado.
Fencer [fen'-sęr], *s.* 1. Esgrimidor, maestro de esgrima; tirador de florete. 2. Caballo ágil para saltar cercas.
Fencible [fen'-si-bl], *a.* Defendible, capaz de defensa. *Fencibles*, (Mil.) Soldados destinados a la defensa particular del país o para algún servicio o tiempo señalado.
Fencing [fen'-sing], *s.* 1. Esgrima, ciencia de manejar la espada o el florete. 2. Los materiales para cercar o hacer vallados. 3. Conjunto de cercas o vallados.
Fencing-master [fen'-sing-mas'-tęr], *s.* Esgrimidor, maestro de armas o de esgrima.
Fencing-school [fen'-sing-scūl], *s.* Escuela de esgrima.
Fend [fend], *va.* 1. Rechazar, resguardar; defenderse de. 2. Defender, preservar; parar.—*vn.* Esgrimir, defenderse, parar, rechazar los golpes del contrario.
Fender [fend'-ęr], *s.* 1. Guardafango, guardabarros (de un auto). (Mex.) Salpicadera. 2. Enrejado de metal delante de la chimenea. 3. Defensas de trozos de cable al costado de un barco. *Fender-bar* o *Fender-rail*, Batayola de un buque por los costados. *Fender-board*, Guardafangos de escalera de carro. *Fender-pile*, Estacada, empalizada.
Fenestral [fe-nes'-tral], *a.* Lo perteneciente a las ventanas.
Fenestrate [fe-nes'-trêt], *a.* (Ent.) Dícese de las puntas transparentes en las alas de las mariposas.
Fenian [fî'-ni-an], *a.* Perteneciente o relativo a los fenianos.—*s.* 1. Individuo de una sociedad irlandesa llamada la Hermandad Feniana, establecida en Nueva York en 1857. 2. Persona que simpatiza con dicha sociedad.
Fenland [fen'-land], *s.* Tierra húmeda o pantanosa.
Fennel [fen'-el], *s.* (Bot.) Hinojo. Fœniculum. *Fennel-seed*, La simiente de hinojo. *Giant fennel*, (Bot.) Cañaheja, férula.
Fenny [fen'-i], *a.* 1. Palustre, pantanoso. 2. Empantanado.
Fenugreek [fen'-u-grîc], *s.* (Bot.) Fenogreco, alholva.
Feod, Feodal, Feodary, etc. *V.* FEUD, etc.
Feoff [fef], *va.* Enfeudar, investir, dar la investidura de un feudo.
Feoff, *s.* Feudo. *V.* FIEF.
Feoffee [fef-î'], *s.* Feudatario, el que recibe la investidura de un feudo.
Feoffer, Feoffor [fef'-ęr], *s.* El que da la investidura de un feudo.
Feoffment [fef'-męnt], *s.* Investidura, concesión y facultad que el señor da a su vasallo para obtener y poseer un feudo o dignidad. *Feoffment in trust*, (For.) Fideicomiso.
§**Feracious** [fe-rê'-shus], *a.* Feraz, fértil.
§**Feracity** [fe-ras'-i-ti], *s.* Feracidad, fertilidad, fecundidad.
Feral [fî'-ral], *a.* Feral, salvaje, no domesticado, feroz; también silvestre.
†**Fere** [fîr], *s.* Compañero; consorte.
Ferial [fî'-ri-al], *a.* Ferial, lo que pertenece a todos los días de la semana a excepción del domingo.
Ferine [fî'-rain], *a.* 1. Salvaje, no domesticado, silvestre, en estado natural. 2. Maligno: dícese de una enfermedad.—*s.* Fiera, animal feroz.
Ferineness [fî'-rain-nes], **Ferity** [fer'-i-ti], *s.* Barbaridad, fiereza, ferocidad, crueldad.
Ferment [fęr-męnt'], *va.* Hacer fermentar.—*vn.* 1. Fermentar, estar en fermentación. 2. Estar en conmoción, agitarse, estar excitado.
Ferment [fęr'-męnt], *s.* 1. Fermento. 2. Fermento, lo que hace fermentar a un cuerpo, como la levadura. 3. Fermentación, movimiento, agitación intestina; tumulto.
Fermentable [fęr-ment'-a-bl], *a.* Fermentable, capaz de fermentación.
Fermentation [fęr-men-tê'-shun], *s.* 1. (Quím.) Fermentación. 2. (Fig.) Efervescencia, agitación de los ánimos.
Fermentative [fęr-ment'-a-tiv], *a.* Fermentativo, que hace fermentar, que pone en fermentación.
Fermentativeness [fęr-ment'-a-tiv-nes], *s.* Capacidad de fermentar.
Fermentescible [fęr-men-tes'-i-bl], *s.* Materia fermentable.
Fermentible [fęr-ment'-i-bl], *a.* Fermentable. *V.* FERMENTABLE.
†**Fermillet** [fęr-mil'-et], *s.* Hebilla, broche.
Fern [fęrn], *s.* (Bot.) Helecho, planta criptógama, tipo de una familia muy numerosa, que en su mayor parte echa semillas en el envés de las hojas.
Fernery [fęrn'-er-i], *s.* Lugar donde se crían los helechos.
Ferny [fęrn'-i], *a.* Lleno de helechos, cubierto de helechos.
Ferocious [fe-rō'-shus], *a.* Feroz, fiero; salvaje, rapaz, voraz.
Ferociously [fe-rō'-shus-li], *adv.* Ferozmente, fieramente.
Ferociousness [fe-rō'-shus-nes], *s.* Ferocidad, crueldad.
Ferocity [fe-ros'-i-ti], *s.* Ferocidad, fiereza.
Ferreous, Ferrean [fer'-e-us, fer'-e-an], *a.* Férreo, lo que es de hierro; relativo al hierro, o parecido a él.
Ferret [fer'-et], *s.* 1. Hurón, animal que sirve para cazar conejos. 2. Un hierro con que se prueba el metal derretido para ver si está en estado de trabajarle. 3. Listón, especie de cinta angosta. *Ferret* o *ferret ribbon*, (1) Hiladillo, cinta de hiladillo, ribecillo. (Prov.) Esterilla. (2) Seda floja.
Ferret, *va.* 1. Rastrear, indagar, averiguar, hallar después de haber buscado con empeño y persistentemente; suele ir seguido de *out*. 2. Cazar con hurones.
Ferreter [fer'-et-ęr], *s.* Hurón, el que averigua y descubre lo escondido y secreto.
Ferriage, Ferryage [fer'-i-ēj], *s.* Barcaje, derecho por pasar en una barca.
Ferric [fer'-ic], *a.* 1. Perteneciente al hierro; férrico. 2. (Quím.) Férrico, relativo al hierro en sus más altas combinaciones.
Ferricyanide [fer''-i-sai'-a-naid o nid], *s.* Ferrocianuro.
Ferriferous [fe-rif'-ęr-us], *a.* (Min.)

Ferrugiento, que produce hierro: dícese de las rocas.
Ferrocalcite [fer-o-cal'-sait], *s.* Ferrocalcita, especie de tierra calcárea que contiene mucho hierro.
Ferrocyanid, Ferrocyanide [fer''-o-sai'-a-nid, naid], *s.* Ferrocianuro, sal del ácido ferrociánico; ferrocianato. (Á veces se escribe también **Ferrocyanate.**)
Ferrotype [fer'-o-taip], *s.* Ferrotipo; fotografía hecha sobre una placa delgada de hierro esmaltado. Se llama también *tintype.*
Ferrous [fer'-us], *a.* Ferroso, de hierro, relativo al hierro en sus más bajas combinaciones. *Ferrous sulphate,* Caparrosa, sulfato de hierro.
Ferruginous [fer-rū'-ji-nus], *a.* 1. Ferruginoso, lo que tiene propiedades o partículas de hierro. 2. Mohoso, enmohecido, es decir del color de la herrumbre.
Ferrule [fer'-il], *s.* 1. Regatón, virola, casquillo. 2. Zuncho o suncho. 3. Marco de una pizarra para escribir.
Ferry [fer'-i], *va.* Barquear, llevar en barca.—*vn.* Pasar un río en barca.
Ferry, *s.* 1. Sistema u organización para el transporte regular de pasajeros y mercancías por una extensión de agua de poca anchura. 2. El embarcadero. 3. (Mar.) Barco o vapor de transporte. *Ferry-boat,* Barca de pasaje o vapor de río; por lo común con los dos extremos de igual forma.
Ferryman [fer'-i-man], *s.* 1. Barquero, el que gobierna una barca. 2. El que lleva géneros o pasajeros en un barco.
Fertile [fẹr'-til], *a.* Fértil, fecundo, abundante.
Fertilely [fẹr'-til-li], *adv.* Fértilmente, abundantemente.
Fertileness [fẹr'-til-nes], **Fertility** [fẹr-til'-i-ti], *s.* Fertilidad, fecundidad, copia, abundancia.
Fertilization [fẹr-til-i-zé'-shun], *s.* Fertilización, la acción de fertilizar o hacer productivo.
Fertilize [fẹr'-til-aiz], *va.* Fertilizar, hacer fértil.
Fertilizers [fẹr-til-aiz'-ẹrz], *s. pl.* Fertilizantes, abonos.
Ferula [fer'-u-la], *s.* 1. (Bot.) Férula, cañaheja; género de plantas umbelíferas que comprende la asafétida. 2. Cetro de los emperadores romanos de Oriente.
Ferule [fer'-ul], *s.* Férula, palma, palmeta.
Ferule, *va.* Castigar con la férula. —*vn.* Palmetear.
Fervency [fẹr'-ven-si], *s.* 1. Fervor, ardor, calor. 2. Celo, devoción ardiente.
Fervent [fẹr'-vent], *a.* 1. Ferviente, hirviente. 2. Ardiente, fogoso, vehemente. *Fervent temper,* Genio vivo. 3. Fervoroso, que tiene mucho fervor y devoción.
Fervently [fẹr'-vent-li], *adv.* 1. Ansiosamente, vehementemente. 2. Fervorosamente, fervientemente.
Ferventness [fẹr'-vent-nes], *s.* Ardor, fervor, celo.
Fervid [fẹr'-vid], *a.* 1. Ardiente, fogoso, vehemente. 2. Encendido, incandescente.
Fervidity, Fervidness, *s.* V. FERVENCY.
Fervor [fẹr'-vẹr], *s.* Fervor, celo, devoción ardiente; ardor, vehemencia.
Fervour, *s.* (Es la forma preferida en Inglaterra.) *V.* FERVOR.
Fescennine [fes'-en-ain], *a.* Obsceno, licencioso.
Fescennine, *s.* 1. Un poema obsceno. 2. Fesceninos, versos obscenos que se cantaban en Roma en algunas fiestas.
Fescue [fes'-kiū], *s* 1. Puntero, el palillo con que el maestro o el discípulo señalan las letras. 2. (Bot.) Festuca, género de plantas gramíneas. *Fescue-grass,* Cualquier especie de festuca.
†**Fesels** [fes'-elz], *s. pl.* Judías, habichuelas, frijoles, frisoles.
Fess [fes], *s.* (Her.) Faja o lista que ocupa propiamente la tercera parte del escudo de armas.
Festal [fes'-tal], *a.* Festivo, alegre, juguetón.
Fester [fes'-tẹr], *vn.* Enconarse, ulcerarse, ponerse de peor calidad la llaga, herida o parte dañada.—*va.* Enconar, emponzoñar.—*s.* Llaga pequeña o tumorcillo ulceroso.
Festival [fes'-ti-val], *a.* Festivo, lo que pertenece a las fiestas.
Festival, *s.* Fiesta, día festivo; a menudo es en celebración del aniversario de un suceso del orden civil o religioso.
Festive [fes'-tiv], *a.* Festivo, alegre, regocijado, gozoso.
Festivity [fes-tiv'-i-ti], *s.* 1. Regocijo, festividad, animación (en un banquete), alegría. 2. Festividad, fiesta, celebración festiva.
Festoon [fes-tūn'], *s.* 1. Festón. 2. (Arq.) Adorno en forma de festones.
Festucine [fes-tiū'-sin], *a.* 1. Relativo a las hierbas festucas. 2. (Des.) Pajizo, de color de paja.
Festucous [fes-tiū'-cus], *a.* (Des.) Pajizo, pajoso.
Fetal, Fœtal [fī'-tal], *a.* Fetal, relativo o perteneciente al feto.
Fetch [fech], *va.* 1. Ir a traer algo, buscar y traer; también, traer o conducir de una manera cualquiera, literal o figuradamente. 2. Derivar, traer su origen, sacar, deducir. 3. (Fam.) Traer a un arreglo, imponer condiciones a. 4. Herir desde lejos, pegar. 5. Ejecutar, hacer. 6. Obtener algo como precio; producir.—*vn.* Moverse, menearse; de aquí, (Mar.) arribar, llegar. *To fetch a compass,* Hacer un rodeo, ir alrededor de. *To fetch away,* Llevar, quitar; desatarse, v. g. a bordo. *To fetch down,* Bajar; abatir, humillar; enflaquecer o debilitar. *To fetch in* o *within,* Hacer entrar; llevar, traer o meter dentro. *To fetch off,* Sacar, arrancar, llevarse, quitar; disuadir. *To fetch out,* Sacar a luz, mostrar claramente; hacer salir, ir a tomar fuera alguna cosa. *To fetch over,* Engañar, burlar. *To fetch up,* Subir; recuperar, volver a ganar. *To fetch a walk,* Dar un paseo. *To fetch one's breath,* Tomar aliento, respirar. *To fetch a sigh,* Dar un suspiro. *To fetch a leap,* Dar un salto o brinco. *To fetch a blow,* Tirar una estocada. *To fetch a circuit,* Hacer un rodeo. *To fetch way,* (Mar.) Tener juego. *To fetch the pump,* (Mar.) Llamar la bomba.
Fetch, *s.* 1. El acto de traer o de buscar y traer. 2. El espacio o la extensión de terreno por el cual se trae algo. 3. Estratagema, treta, artificio.
Fetcher [fech'-ẹr], *s.* Llevador o traedor.
Fête [fêt], *va.* Festejar, honrar con regocijos.—*s.* Fiesta. (Fr.) *Fête-day,* Día de fiesta, día del santo de alguno, o día de cumpleaños.
Fetial [fī'-shial], *a.* Fecial, perteneciente al heraldo que entre los romanos anunciaba la paz y la guerra.
Fetich [fī'-tish], *s.* *V.* FETISH.
Fetid [fet'-id], *a.* Fétido, hediondo, que huele mal.
Fetidness [fet'-id-nes], *s.* Fetor, hedor, mal olor.
Fetish [fī'-tish o fet'-ish], *s.* 1. Fetiche, ídolo o genio que, según los pueblos de África, puede producir el bien y el mal. 2. Objeto de devoción o de afición ciega.
Fetishism [fī'-tish izm], *s.* Fetichismo, culto de los fetiches.
Fetlock [fet'-loc], *s.* Cerneja, el manojo de cerdas que se cría en la cuartilla del caballo.
Fetor [fī'-tẹr], *s.* Hedor, fetor.
Fetter [fet'-ẹr], *va.* Engrillar, encadenar.
Fetters [fet'-ẹrz], *s. pl.* Grillos, manijas, cierto género de prisiones con que aseguran a los reos. *Fetters for horses,* Trabas para caballos.
Fetterless [fet'-ẹr-les], *a.* Desenfrenado, destrabado.
Fettle [fet'-l], *va.* Alisar, poner liso. —*vn.* (Prov. Ingl.) 1. Poner en buen estado. 2. Hacer poco o nada, emplearse en frioleras.
Fettle, *s.* (Prov. Ingl.) Buen reparo; condición vigorosa o próspera. *Fine fettle,* Buena condición; buen humor, alegría.
Fetus, Fœtus [fī'-tus], *s.* Feto.
Feud [fiūd], *s.* 1. Riña, contienda, desunión, guerra civil, disensión, enemistad. 2. Feudo, tierra que se entrega a la buena fe de otro con carga de homenaje, renta o servicio militar.
Feudal [fiūd'-al], *a.* Feudal.
Feudalism [fiūd'-al-izm], *s.* Feudalismo, sistema feudal.
Feudality [fiu-dal'-i-ti], *s.* Feudalidad.
Feudalize [fiū'-dal-aiz], *va.* Enfeudar, constituir en feudo.
Feudary [fiū'-da-ri], *a.* Feudatario. —*s.* 1. Vasallo, sujeto a pagar un feudo. 2. Antiguamente, procurador del rey en los tribunales feudales.
Feudatary, Feudatory [fiū'-da-tẹ-ri], *a.* y *s.* 1. Feudo. 2. Feudatario.
Feudist [fiūd'-ist], *s.* Feudista.
Feuilleton [fö''-lye-tōñ'], *s.* Folletín, la novela u otra lectura amena que se publica por lo regular en la parte inferior de los periódicos. (Gal.)
Fever [fī'-vẹr], *s.* 1. (Med.) Fiebre, calentura. 2. Agitación, sobreexcitación producida por una causa que influye en las pasiones. *To be in a fever,* Estar con calentura; tener calentura. *Yellow fever,* Fiebre amarilla o tifo icteroides. *Burning fever,* Calentura ardiente. *Spotted fever,* Tabardillo pintado. *Puerperal* o *child-bed fever,* Fiebre puerperal. *That sets one's blood in a fever,* Eso quema la sangre. *Fever-weakened,* Debilitado por la fiebre.
Fever, *va.* Causar calentura.
Fever-cooling [fī'-vẹr-cūl'-ing], *s.* Lo que mitiga la calentura refrescando al que la padece.
Feverfew [fī'-vẹr-fiū], *s.* (Bot.) Matricaria, planta estimada en otro tiempo por sus propiedades tónicas.
Feverish [fī'-vẹr-ish], *a.* 1. Febricitante, calenturiento. 2. Lo que

principia a presentar los síntomas de calentura. 3. Vario, incierto, inconstante; lo que está tan pronto frío como caliente. 4. Caliente, ardiente.

Feverishness [fí'-vęr-ish-nes], *s.* Principio o amago de fiebre o calentura; desasosiego.

Feverous [fí'-vęr-us], *a.* (Poco us.) Calenturiento.

Fever-sick [fí'-vęr-sic], *a.* Calenturiento, febricitante.

Few [fiū], *a.* 1. Poco, en corto número. 2. Unos, algunos. *A few,* (1) Un corto número, algunos. (2) En algún grado, algo. *No few,* No pocos, muchos. *The few,* La minoría. (*Few* se emplea siempre con un nombre en plural.) *In few,* En substancia, en una palabra.

†**Fewel** [fiū'-el], *s.* Leña, carbón. *V.* FUEL.

Fewer [fiū'-ęr], *a.* Comparativo de FEW; menos. *The fewer the better,* Cuantos menos mejor.

Fewness [fiū'-nes], *s.* 1. Pequeño ó corto número de personas ó cosas. 2. Brevedad, concisión, corto número de palabras.

Fey fê], *a.* (Esco.) Moribundo; predestinado á morir de repente.—*va.* (Des.) Limpiar una zanja de lodo.

Fez [fez], *s.* Fez, especie de gorro de lana, sin borde, encarnado por lo común, que se usa en Oriente y en el norte de África.

Fiancé, *m.* **Fiancée,** *f.* [fí-ān-sê'], Prometido, prometida, novio, novia. Desposado, desposada.

Fiasco [fi-ās'-co], *s.* 1. Mal éxito de un espectáculo, etc. 2. Frasco, botella. (Ital.)

Fiat [fai'-at], *s.* Fiat, orden, mandato absoluto.

Fib [fib], *s.* Embuste, bola, falsedad, cuento, fábula; falsedad contada sin mala intención.

Fib, *vn.* Mentir, contar mentiras, trapacear.

Fibber [fib'-ęr], *s.* Embustero, mentiroso, trapacero.

Fiber, Fibre [fai'-bęr], *s.* Fibra, hebra.

Fibril [fai'-bril], *s.* Fibrita.

Fibrin, Fibrine [fai'-brin], *s.* Fibrina, la parte fibrosa de la sangre.

Fibrinous [fai'-brin-us], *a.* Fibrinoso, compuesto o de la naturaleza de la fibrina.

Fibroid [fai'-breid], *a.* Fibroso, de la naturaleza o forma de la fibra.—*s.* (*Fibroid* o también **Fibroma**) Tumor, grosor fibroso.

Fibrous [fai'-brus], **Fibrose** [fai'-brōs], *a.* Fibroso, compuesto de fibras.

Fibula [fib'-yu-la], *s.* 1. (Anat.) Peroné, el hueso exterior y menor de la pierna. 2. (Cir.) Aguja empleada para coser las heridas. 3. (Arqueología) Corchete, broche; fíbula.

Fibular [fib'-yu-lar], *a.* Peroneo, que tiene relación con el peroné.

Fichu [fi-shū'], *s.* Pañoleta triangular llevada al cuello.

Fickle [fic'-l], *a.* Voluble, variable, inconstante, mudable, veleidoso.

Fickleness [fic'-l-nes], *s.* Volubilidad, inconstancia, mutabilidad, veleidad.

Fickly [fic'-li], *adv.* Inconstantemente.

Fictile [fic'-til], *a.* 1. Capaz de ser amoldado, plástico. 2. Cosa hecha de barro o por mano de alfarero.

Fiction [fic'-shun], *s.* 1. Ficción, invención. 2. Literatura novelesca. 3. Ficción, mentira, embuste, falsedad, fábula. 4. Ficción de derecho, acción de admitir o suponer lo que no es literalmente verdadero, a fin de poder pasar más rápidamente sobre lo que no se disputa y llegar a los puntos del litigio.

Fictitious [fic-tish'-us], *a.* Ficticio, contrahecho; fingido; fabuloso.

Fictitiously [fic-tish'-us-li], *adv.* Fingidamente.

Fictitiousness [fic-tish'-us-nes], *s.* Representación fingida.

Fictive [fic'-tiv], *a.* Fingido, ficticio, imaginario.

Fictor [fic'-tęr], *s.* (Poco us.) Artista que modela en cera, barro u otra materia blanda.

Ficus [fai'-cus], *s.* Higuera, extenso género de árboles y arbustos de la familia de las urticáceas.

Fid [fid], *s.* 1. Barra atravesada que sirve de sostén. 2. (Mar.) Pasador ó burel; tarugo grande de madera. *Fid of a topmast,* Cuña de mastelero. *Fid-hole,* Ojo de la cuña de mastelero.

Fiddle [fid'-l], *s.* 1. Violín. 2. Utensilio mecánico; los hay de varias clases. *Fiddle-bow,* Arco de violín. *To play first fiddle,* Llevar la batuta, ser el principal o la cabeza de una reunión, empresa, etc. *Fiddle-block,* Motón de poleas diferenciales.

Fiddle, *vn.* 1. Tocar el violín. 2. Enredar o jugar con las manos sin hacer nada. *Fiddling work,* Trabajo en balde, tiempo perdido.

Fiddle-de-dee [fid'-l-dę-dí], *inter.* ¡Quiá! ¡oiga! ¡qué simpleza!—*s.* Disparate, necedad.

Fiddle-faddle [fid'-l-fad'-l], *s.* (Fam.) Bagatelas, frioleras.

Fiddler [fid'-lęr], *s.* Violinista.

Fiddle-stick [fid'-l-stic], *s.* 1. Arco de violín. 2. Bagatela.

Fiddle-sticks! *inter.* ¡Oiga! ¡vaya! ! vaya pues!

Fiddle-string [fid'-l-string], *s.* Cuerda de violín.

Fidelity [fi-del'-i-ti], *s.* Fidelidad, lealtad, veracidad.

Fidget [fij'-et], *va.* (Fam.) Molestar, inquietar.—*vn.* Moverse con impaciencia; mudar de posición frecuentemente; afanarse por nada.

Fidget, *s.* Afán, agitación continua, ocupación inquieta e inútil.

Fidgety [fij'-et-i], *a.* (Fam.) Inquieto, agitado, impaciente.

Fidicinal [fi-dis'-i-nal], *a.* Perteneciente o referente al arpa, a la viola o a un instrumento de cuerda parecido.

Fiducial [fi-diū'-shal], *a.* 1. Fiduciario, que depende del crédito y confianza que merezca; de confianza práctica. 2. Relativo o referente a un cargo, depósito o cosa confiada; fiduciario. 3. Fiducial; dícese del punto fijo, línea u objeto, real o imaginario, desde el cual se mide o que sirve para determinar la posición de otros objetos. 4. (Ant.) Confiado, lleno de confianza.

Fiducially [fi-diū'-shal-i], *adv.* Confiadamente; confidentemente.

Fiduciary [fi-diū'-shi-ę-ri], *a.* 1. Fiduciario, perteneciente a un guardián o depositario, o a sus deberes como tal. 2. Confiado, resuelto, que no vacila.—*s.* 1. Fideicomisario. (For.) La persona á cuya buena fe y probidad se encomienda la ejecución de una cosa. *V.* TRUSTEE. 2. El que cree que basta la fe sin las obras para salvarse.

Fie! [fai], *inter.* ¡Uf! ¡Quita allá! ¡Qué asco! Expresa impaciencia, desaprobación o repugnancia.

Fief [fíf], *s.* Feudo.

Field [fíld], *s.* 1. Campo, campiña, campaña, llanura de tierra sin cerca ni población. 2. Campo, sembrado, trecho de terreno cultivado. 3. (Mil.) Campo de batalla. 4. Batalla, campaña. 5. Campo, el sitio que ocupa un ejército. 6. Campo, en la pintura y grabado el espacio que no tiene figuras. 7. Campo, extensión o espacio en que cabe alguna cosa; el espacio en que se ve alguna cosa en un telescopio o microscopio. 8. Extensión ó espacio en que se ejerce una fuerza. 9. La colectividad de los competidores en los juegos públicos, apuestas, carreras, etc. *To take the field,* Entrar en o salir a campaña. *Fields of ice,* Bancos de hielo. *Corn-field,* Maizal. *Field-artillery,* Artillería de campaña. *Field-glass,* (1) Anteojo de campaña. (2) Lente interior del ocular de un telescopio ó microscopio. *Field-book,* Manual, cuaderno de agrimensor. *Field-day,* Día de ejercicios atléticos o militares; también, un día de exploración científica al aire libre. *Field-gun,* Cañón de campaña. *Field-magnet,* El imán de una máquina magneto-eléctrica. *Field-basil,* (Bot.) Clinopodio, albahaca silvestre. *Field-bed,* Pabellón, cama de campaña colgada como pabellón. *Field-marshal,* (1) Feldmariscal, el grado más elevado del ejército en Inglaterra. (2) El general en jefe de un ejército. *Field-mouse,* Turón, ratón silvestre. *Field-officer,* Oficial de ejército cuyo mando puede extenderse a un regimiento, como el coronel y el teniente coronel. *Field-piece,* Artillería de campaña, los cañones de pequeño calibre que se usan en los combates. *Field-preacher,* Predicador en los campos o al raso. *Field-preaching,* El acto de predicar o arengar al aire libre. *Field-room,* Espacio abierto. *Field-sports,* Los entretenimientos o diversiones de la caza y de la carrera. *Field-works,* (For.) Obras de campaña, las que levanta un ejército para sitiar una plaza, o los sitiados para defenderse.

Fielded [fíld'-ed], *a.* 1. El que está en un campo de batalla. 2. Acampado.

Fielder [fíld'-ęr], *s.* En los juegos de *baseball* y *cricket,* el que está en pie en el campo para interceptar la pelota.

Fieldfare [fíld'-fār], *s.* (Orn.) Zorzal, pájaro del mismo género que el tordo.

†**Fieldy** [fíld'-i], *a.* Abierto, llano, como un campo.

Fiend [fínd], *s.* 1. Enemigo: por antonomasia, el demonio. 2. Ente infernal; furia.

Fiendful [fínd'-ful], *a.* Endemoniado, perverso.

Fiendish [fínd'-ish], *a.* Diábolico: malo, perverso, malvado; semejante a un ente infernal.

Fiendishness [fínd'-ish-nes], *s.* Maldad, perversidad, malicia infernal.

Fiend-like [fínd'-laic], *a.* Semejante al diablo o a un ente infernal; cruel, atroz, salvaje.

Fierce [fírs], *a.* 1. Fiero, feroz, voraz. 2. Fiero, cruel, violento. 3. Fiero, furioso, vehemente, impetuoso, apasionado.

Fiercely [fírs'-li], *adv.* Fieramente,

furiosamente, ferozmente; con furia, con arrebato.
Fierce-minded [fîrs'-maind-ed], *a.* Arrebatado, que tiene movimientos impetuosos de ira o anhela con ansia el hacer daño.
Fierceness [fîrs'-nes], *s.* Fiereza, ferocidad.
Fieri-facias [fai'-er-i-fé'-shi-as], *s.* (For.) El auto jurídico que manda la ejecución de las decisiones de un tribunal.
Fieriness [fai'-er-i-nes], *s.* 1. Fuego, calor, ardor, arrebato, fogosidad, vehemencia, pasión. 2. Ardimiento y gran viveza de ánimo.
Fiery [fai'-er-i o fair'-i], *a.* 1. Ígneo, cosa de fuego o perteneciente a él. 2. Ardiente, caliente como el fuego; encendido. 3. Ardiente, vehemente, activo. 4. Fogoso, colérico, impaciente, vivo. 5. Fiero, feroz, furibundo, indómito. 6. Que brilla o echa chispas como el fuego. *A fiery furnace,* Un horno ardiente. *A fiery disposition,* Un genio iracundo o violento. *A fiery courser,* Un caballo fogoso. *A fiery red face,* Un rostro muy encendido.
Fife [faif], *s.* Pífano, instrumento militar que suele acompañar á las cajas o tambores.
Fife [faif], *va.* y *vn.* Tocar el pífano.
Fifer [faif'-er], *s.* Pífano, el que lo toca.
Fifteen [fif'-tîn], *a.* Quince.—*s.* Quince, número cardinal compuesto de diez y cinco, o el signo que lo representa. *She is fifteen,* Ella tiene quince años.
Fifteenth [fif'-tînth], *a.* 1. Décimoquinto, el ordinal de quince. 2. Quinceno; dícese de cada una de las quince partes iguales en que está dividida una cosa.—*s.* 1. Quincena; cada una de quince partes iguales; cuociente de la unidad dividida por quince. 2. Quincena, registro del órgano. *The fifteenth century,* El siglo décimoquinto, el siglo quince.
Fifth [fifth], *a.* Quinto, número ordinal de cinco.—*s.* El quinto, cada una de las cinco partes iguales de alguna cosa; cuociente de la unidad dividida por cinco. *Charles the Fifth,* Carlos Quinto.
Fifth column [fifth col'-um], *s.* Quinta columna.
Fifth columnist [fifth col'-um-nist], *s.* Quintacolumnista.
Fifthly [fifth'-li], *adv.* Lo quinto, en quinto lugar.
Fiftieth [fif'-ti-eth], *a.* Quincuagésimo, lo que cumple el número de cincuenta.
Fifty [fif'-ti], *a.* y *s.* Cincuenta.
Fig [fig], *s.* 1. Higuera, el árbol que produce higos. 2. Higo, la fruta que da la higuera. *A green fig,* Higo fresco; breva. *A dry fig,* Higo seco. 3. Berruga en la ranilla de un caballo. *Indian fig,* (Bot.) Tuna, higo chumbo, fruto del nopal o higuera de Indias. *Infernal fig,* (Bot.) Argémone, adormidera espinosa. *To give a fig for one,* Dar una higa a alguno, hacer escarnio de él. *I do not care a fig for it,* No me importa un bledo. *A fig for him,* ¡Vaya enhoramala! *Fig-eater,* (1) Escarabajo grande de color verde (Allorhina nitida) y perjudicial a las frutas maduras. (2) Becafigo. *Fig-pecker,* Becafigo.
Fig, *va.* (Ant.) Insultar o despreciar haciendo higas.—*vn.* (Des.) Moverse acelerada o repentinamente. *To fig up and down,* Vagar.
†**Figary** [fig'-a-ri], *s.* *V.* VAGARY.
Fight [fait], *va.* (*pret.* y *pp.* FOUGHT). 1. Pelear, guerrear, combatir, reñir. 2. Sostener con las armas; alcanzar por la fuerza de las armas; vencer. 3. Luchar, disputar, mantener sostener una contienda cualquiera. 4. Dirigir una batalla. 5. Hacer reñir (v. g. a los gallos).—*vn.* Batirse, defenderse, hacer la guerra. *To fight a battle,* Dar batalla. *To fight another man's battles,* Tomar la defensa de otro. *To fight it out,* Terminar alguna contienda peleando. *To fight one's way,* Hacerse o abrirse paso con las armas.
Fight, *s.* Batalla, lid, combate, pelea. *Sea-fight,* Batalla naval. *Running-fight,* Retirada de las tropas peleando.
Fighter [fait'-er], *s.* Guerrero, combatiente; duelista. *He is a great fighter,* Es un gran espadachín.
Fighter plane [fait'-er plên], *s.* Caza.
Fighting [fait'-ing], *a.* 1. Aguerrido, apto para la guerra; combatiente. 2. Ocupado en guerrear.—*s.* Contención, combate, querella, riña.
Fig-leaf [fig'-lîf], *s.* 1. Hoja de higuera. 2. Cobertura endeble y ligera. *V.* Gen. iii, 7.
Figment [fig'-ment], *s.* Ficción, invención.
Figurable [fig'-yur-a-bl], *a.* Figurable, lo que se puede reducir a determinada forma o figura.
Figural [fig'-yu-ral], *a.* Lo que pertenece a la figura.
Figurate [fig'-yur-êt], *a.* 1. Figurado, que tiene cierta y determinada figura; parecido a un objeto de una forma determinada. 2. (Mús.) Figurado, embellecido.
Figuration [fig-yur-ê'-shun], *s.* Figura, disposición de las partes de una cosa por la cual se diferencia de otras; el acto de dar forma determinada.
Figurative [fig'-yur-a-tiv], *a.* 1. Figurativo, que sirve de representación o figura de otra cosa. 2. Figurativo, que no es literal; metafórico. 3. Figurativo, escrito con expresiones retóricas figuradas.
Figuratively [fig'-yur-a-tiv-li], *adv.* Figuradamente.
Figure [fig'-yur], *s.* 1. Figura, forma exterior. 2. Figura, hechura, semejanza. 3. Figura, presencia, talle o disposición del cuerpo. 4. Figura, papel, viso. *To make a figure in the world,* Hacer papel en el mundo. 5. Figura, estatua, imagen. 6. Figura, pintura que representa alguna cosa. 7. Cifra, guarismo o número. 8. (Ret.) Figura retórica. 9. (Gram.) Figura gramatical, desvío de las reglas de la analogía o sintaxis. 10. (Geom.) Figura que cierra un espacio con una o más líneas. 11. (Astrol.) Horóscopo. 12. (Teol.) Tipo, símbolo.
Figure, *va.* y *vn.* 1. Figurar, disponer, delinear y formar la figura de alguna cosa. 2. Figurar, cubrir o adornar con figuras alguna cosa. *Figured velvet,* Terciopelo estampado. *Figured silk,* Seda floreada. 3. Simbolizar, representar con semejanza simbólica o misteriosa. 4. Figurarse, pasar por la imaginación alguna cosa o formarla en ella. 5. Valerse de figuras retóricas; separarse del sentido literal. 6. Hacer papel.
Figure-head [fig'-yur-hed], *s.* 1. Figura o adorno que suelen tener los buques mercantes y de guerra en la roda, en lo más alto de la proa. 2. Caudillo o cabeza nominal, sin verdadera influencia o poder.
Figuring [fig'-yur-ing], *s.* 1. Computación, acción de computar. 2. Acción de trazar figuras.
F'gurist [fig'-yur-ist], *s.* Figurista, el que emplea o explica las figuras de dicción.
Figwort [fig'-wūrt], *s.* (Bot.) Escrofularia, planta que da su nombre a la familia de las escrofulariáceas; cualquiera planta de esta familia.
Fijian, Feejeean [fî'-ji-an], *a.* De Fijí, perteneciente a las islas de este nombre en el Océano Pacífico. —*s.* Habitante aborigine, o lengua aborigine de las Islas Fijí.
Filaceous [fi-lé'-shus], *a.* Hebroso, fibroso, filamentoso.
Filament [fil'-a-ment], *s.* 1. Hebra, fibra, filamento; hilo muy fino. 2. (Bot.) Filamento, tallo o sostén de la antera.
Filamentous, Filamentose [fil-a-men'-tus], *a.* Filamentoso, compuesto de hilos; semejante a un hilo; que tiene fibras o filamentos; parecido a una franja; fibroso.
Filar [fai'-lar], *a.* 1. Perteneciente al hilo, caracterizado por hilos; semejante a un hilo. 2. Con fibras o hilos muy finos que cruzan el campo de la visual, p. ej. en un microscopio.
Filaria [fi-la'-ri-a], *s.* (Zool.) Filaria.
Filariasis [fil-a-rāi'-a-sis], *s.* (Med.) Filariosis.
Filature [fil'-a-chur o tiūr], *s.* 1. Hilandería, la acción o modo de hilar (la seda, etc.). 2. Hilandería, gran fábrica de hilados.
Filbert [fil'-bert], *s.* 1. Avellana de cáscara delgada. 2. Avellano, árbol. *Filbert-shaped,* De la forma de una avellana.
Filch [filch], *vn.* Ratear, sisar, hurtar con sutileza y destreza cosas de poca monta.
Filcher [filch'-er], *s.* Ratero, ladrón que hurta cosas de poco valor, ladroncillo.
Filchingly [filch'-ing-li], *adv.* Ladronamente, rateramente.
File [fail], *s.* 1. Lima, instrumento de acero para alisar y pulir los metales. *Half-round file,* Lima de media caña. 2. Cualquier aparato destinado a guardar papeles y cartas en orden; punzón para ensartar papeles. 3. Legajo de papeles arreglado sistemáticamente para consultarlo; colección de periódicos dispuestos en orden cronológico. 4. (Mil.) Fila, hilera. 5. Catálogo, lista.
File, *va.* 1. Limar, pulir. 2. Ensartar, enhilar, arreglar sistemáticamente para servir de consulta. 3. Registrar, asentar, notar; archivar; presentar de la manera reglamentaria de modo que vaya en el acta o en la minuta de los procedimientos. 4. Ensuciar, manchar.—*vn.* (Mil.) Marchar en fila. *To file off,* Cortar una cosa limándola. (Mil.) Desfilar.
File case [fail kês], *s.* Archivador.
File-cutter [fail'-cut-er], *s.* Picador de limas.
Filemot [fil'-e-mot], *s.* (Ant.) De color leonado; color de hoja seca.

Filer [fail'-ęr], *s.* Limador, el que lima los metales.

Filial [fil'-yal], *a.* Filial, perteneciente al hijo; debido a los padres. *Filial duty*, Deber filial. *Filial affection*, Cariño filial.

Filially [fil'-yal-i], *adv.* Filialmente.

Filiation [fil-i-é'-shun], *s.* 1. Filiación, relación del hijo con el padre. 2. (Der.) La determinación judicial del parentesco (padres).

Filibuster [fil-i-bus'-tęr], *va.* y *vn.* 1. Ser filibustero y conducirse como tal. 2. (E. U.) Aplazar o impedir la aprobación de leyes, etc., por medio de proposiciones o discursos dilatorios.—*s.* Filibustero, pirata; aventurero que por la fuerza se apodera de territorio ajeno; el que procura impedir la legislación sobre una materia, poniéndole obstáculos.

Filiform [fil'-i-fōrm], *a.* Filiforme, formado como hilo.

Filigrane [fil'-i-grēn], **Filigree** [fil'-i-grî], *s.* Filigrana.

Filigreed [fil'-i-grîd], *a.* Afiligranado.

Filings [fail'-ingz], *s. pl.* Limaduras.

Fill [fil], *va.* 1. Llenar, rellenar, henchir. 2. Llenar, satisfacer, contentar. 3. Llenar, hartar. 4. Llenar una persona o cosa el hueco de otra, ocupar. *To fill the chair*, Ocupar, desempeñar la cátedra. 5. Hinchar. 6. Terraplenar.—*vn.* 1. Echar de beber, dar de beber. 2. Llenarse, hartarse, atracarse. *To fill out*, Echar algún líquido para beber; llenar. *To fill up*, Colmar, llenar completamente, llenar a colmo; proveer un empleo vacante. *To fill one's place in his absence*, Llenar u ocupar el puesto de alguno en su ausencia. *To fill up the time*, Emplear el tiempo.

Fill, *s.* 1. Lo que llena o es suficiente para llenar; terraplén; hartura, abundancia; satisfacción. 2. (Dialecto) El hueco entre las varas de un carro o calesa. *V.* THILL.

Filler [fil'-ęr], *s.* 1. Henchidor, llenador, el que o lo que llena; lo que se emplea para llenar. 2. Embudo. *V.* FUNNEL. *Fillers of tobacco*, Tripas, relleno de tabaco.

Fillet [fil'-et], *s.* 1. Venda, tira o faja, cinta puesta alrededor de alguna cosa. 2. Filete, solomillo; también, tajada de una pierna de ternera o carnero. 3. Carne arrollada y atada con bramante. 4. (Arq.) Filete, el adorno más delgado de una moldura. *Fillet of veal*, Filete de ternera.

Fillet, *va.* 1. Vendar, fajar, atar o ceñir con venda, faja o cinta. 2. (Arq.) Adornar con astrágalos.

Filling [fil'-ing], *s.* 1. Adición, suplemento, relleno. 2. Empastadura u orificación en los dientes.

Filling station [fil'-ing stê'-shun], *s.* Estación de gasolina.

Fillip [fil'-ip], *va.* 1. Dar un papirote. 2. Echar, arrojar, impeler, como con un capirotazo; incitar, estimular.

Fillip, *s.* 1. Papirote, el golpe que se da apoyando el dedo del corazón sobre el pulgar y soltando el del corazón con violencia. 2. Estímulo, aguijón.

Filly [fil'-i], *s.* 1. Potranca, la yegua que no pasa de tres años. 2. Doncellita o muchacha ligera y retozona; úsase despreciativamente.

Film [film], *s.* 1. Película, membrana o piel delgada. *A film on the eye*, Tela o nube en el ojo. 2. (Foto.) Película, una capa muy delgada de materia sensibilizada; placa flexible, como de celuloide, para recibir una capa sensibilizada. *Film-carrier*, Bastidor para mantener plana una película fotográfica.

Film, *va.* Cubrir con una película.

Filminess [fil'-mi-nes], *s.* Calidad de membranoso; apariencia como de una película.

Filmstrip [film'-strip], *s.* Tira de película. Película auxiliar de clases o conferencias.

Filmy [film'-i], *a.* Membranoso, pelicular, compuesto de membranas o películas.

Filose [fai'-lōs], *a.* (Anat.) Filiforme, que remata en hilillos.

Filter [fil'-tęr], *va.* Filtrar, depurar, hacer pasar los líquidos por entre los poros de un cuerpo sólido para purificarlos de las partes crasas o extrañas que contienen.

Filter, *s.* 1. Filtro, la manga, lienzo o papel para filtrar. 2. Filtro, bebida con la cual se pretende excitar el amor. *V.* PHILTER.

Filter-tip [fil'-tęr-tip], *a.* De filtro con boquilla. (Aplícase a los cigarrillos.)

Filth [filth], *s.* 1. Inmundicia, porquería; basura, suciedad, fango. 2. Corrupción, infección, impureza.

Filthily [filth'-i-li], *adv.* Asquerosamente, suciamente.

Filthiness [filth'-i-nes], *s.* Inmundicia, suciedad.

Filthy [filth'-i], *a.* 1. Sucio, puerco, asqueroso. 2. Poluto, inmundo, depravado o corrompido moralmente; obsceno, torpe.

Filtrate [fil'-trêt], *va.* Filtrar.—*s.* El líquido filtrado o separado por medio de la filtración.

Filtration [fil-trê'-shun], *s.* (Quím.) Filtración, la acción de filtrar.

Fimbriate [fim'-bri-êt], *va.* Franjear; ribetear.

Fin [fin], *s.* 1. Aleta que tienen los peces en varias partes del cuerpo y con las cuales se ayudan para nadar. 2. Parte saliente o apéndice de un utensilio. 3. Pescados, peces.

Finable [fain'-a-bl], *a.* Multable, sujeto a multa.

Final [fai'-nal], *a.* 1. Final, último. 2. Final, conclusivo, decisivo. 3. Final, mortal. 4. Lo que pertenece al fin, motivo u objeto con que se hace una cosa. *A final answer*, Respuesta decisiva. *A final stroke*, Golpe decisivo.

Finale [fi-nā'-lê], *s.* 1. Acto último, escena última, final, fin. 2. (Mús.) Final, el último movimiento.

Finality [fi-nal'-i-ti], *s.* Finalidad, estado o calidad de final o completo; lo que es final, acto decisivo.

Finally [fai'-nal-i], *adv.* Finalmente, últimamente, en fin, en conclusión, por último.

Finance [fi-nans'], *s.* 1. Hacienda pública, la ciencia de los negocios monetarios; manejo pecuniario. 2. Renta, utilidad o beneficio que se saca anualmente de alguna posesión; en plural por lo común.—*va.* y *vn.* *V.* FINANCIER.

Financial [fi-nan'-shal], *a.* Rentístico, monetario, que pertenece a la hacienda o rentas públicas.

Financially [fi-nan'-shal-i], *adv.* Rentísticamente, en materia de rentas.

Financier [fin-an-sîr'], *va.* y *vn.* Manejar los negocios monetarios de; conducir operaciones rentísticas.—*s.* Recaudador de rentas públicas y el que las maneja, el cual puede llamarse rentista, hacendista o financiero.

Financing [fi-nan'-sing], *s.* Financiamiento.

Finary [fai'-ne-ri], *s.* *V.* FINERY, 2a.

Fin-back [fin'-bac], *s.* Ballena que tiene una aleta dorsal; se llama también, *rorqual* y *razor-back.*

Finch [finch], *s.* (Orn.) Pinzón, fringilino, pájaro de la familia de los fringílidos; picogordo. *Goldfinch*, Acanta. *Chaffinch*, Pinzón. *Bullfinch*, Pinzón real.

Find [faind], *va.* (*pret.* y *pp.* FOUND). 1. Encontrar, hallar, descubrir lo que se buscaba; tropezar o hallar por casualidad. 2. Encontrar una persona a otra. 3. Hallar una cosa perdida. 4. Hallar, conocer por experiencia, descubrir lo que estaba oculto, resolver, adquirir, saber, reconocer. 5. (For.) Juzgar, declarar, decidir según justicia; aprobar, admitir. 6. Surtir, abastecer, proveer, dar alguna cosa que se necesita. 7. Alimentar, mantener.—*vn.* (Der.) Fallar, dar sentencia. *Seek and ye shall find*, Buscad, y hallareis. *To find fault* o *amiss*, Desaprobar, criticar, hallar que decir. *To find in one's heart*, Tener deseo de alguna cosa; estar de humor. *To find one's self*, Hallarse, estar; mantenerse, alimentarse. *How do you find yourself?* ¿Cómo lo pasa Vd.? ¿cómo se halla Vd.? ¿cómo se siente Vd.? *To find one's way*, Introducirse, conducirse. *To find out*, Solver, desatar o resolver; hallar o descubrir; adivinar, imaginar, inventar, dar con, averiguar. *To find a person out*, Llegar a saber quién es uno, o cual es su verdadero carácter. *To find a verdict for the plaintiff*, Fallar o dar sentencia a favor del querellante o demandante. *To find a verdict for the defendant*, Fallar o sentenciar a favor del demandado o acusado, o bien absolverle del cargo o de la demanda. *To find work for one*, Dar ocupación a alguien.

Find [faind], *s.* Una cosa hallada, especialmente un descubrimiento útil.

Finder [faind'-ęr], *s.* 1. Hallador; descubridor, inventor, el que hace algún nuevo descubrimiento. 2. (Ópt.) Buscador, hallador, el pequeño telescopio que va al lado de uno mayor; buscador, lente suplementario, con espejo, asegurado a una cámara fotográfica para ver el objeto en el campo de la visual; un portaobjetos para el microscopio, rayado con líneas muy finamente graduadas para colocar un objeto o un ejemplar de interés.

†Find-fault [faind'-fōlt], *s.* Censurador, crítico.

Finding [faind'-ing], *s.* 1. Descubrimiento, invención. 2. Fallo, sentencia, decisión de un tribunal o árbitro, o de una comisión. 3. Gasto, mantenimiento. 4. *pl.* Herramientas y avíos de un obrero, y particularmente de un zapatero.

Fine [fain], *a.* Fino, refinado, puro; agudo, cortante; claro, transparente; delicado, primoroso; sagaz, astuto, diestro; galán, lindo; bello, elegante, hermoso, bien parecido; cortés, bien criado, instruído; vistoso, espléndido.—*s.* 1. Multa, pena pecuniaria. 2. (Des.) Fin, conclusión.

In fine, Finalmente, en conclusión, por fin.

Fine, *va.* 1. Afinar, refinar, perfeccionar, purificar; aclarar. 2. Lustrar, dar lustre, esplendor, brillantez o transparencia a alguna cosa. 3. Multar.—*vn.* Pagar una multa.

Fine-draw [fain'-drē], *va.* Zurcir o unir dos pedazos de cualquier tela cosiéndolos sutil y curiosamente.

Fine-drawer [fain'-drē-ẹr], *s.* Zurcidor.

Fine-drawing [fain'-drē-ing], *s.* Zurcidura, la acción de zurcir o la unión y costura de la cosa zurcida.

Fine-fingered [fain'-fing-gẹrd], *a.* Delicado, primoroso, el que es capaz de trabajar cosas primorosas o delicadas.

†**Fineless** [fain'-les], *a.* Sin fin. *V.* ENDLESS.

Finely [fain'-li], *adv.* 1. Primorosamente, con elegancia; agudamente, sutilmente. 2. (Irón.) Miserablemente.

Fineness [fain'-nes], *s.* Fineza, delicadeza, primor, lustre, hermosura, esplendor; agudeza, sutileza, ingenio, finura; pureza, perfección.

Finer [fain'-ẹr], *s.* Refinador de metales.—*a.* Comparativo de *fine;* más fino.

Finery [fain'-ẹr-i], *s.* 1. Primor, vista, esplendor, elegancia; adorno, atavío, aderezo. 2. Antigua especie de fragua, hoy en desuso. *Finery cinder,* Una especie de óxido negro de hierro en láminas pequeñas.

Fine-spoken [fain'-spōk-n], *a.* El que usa palabras o frases muy escogidas o afectadas. Se toma casi siempre irónicamente.

Fine-spun [fain'-spun], *a.* Ingeniosamente ideado o delineado; inventado astutamente. (Fam.) *Fine-spun,* Tirado por los cabellos, alambicado.

Finesse [fi-nes'], *vn.* Valerse de subterfugios y artificios.—*s.* 1. Artificio, treta, estratagema, astucia, sutileza. 2. Calidad de hábil, diestro o mañoso.

Fin-footed [fin'-fut-ed], *a.* Palmeado: aplícase a las aves que tienen los dedos unidos por membranas.

Finger [fiṇ'-gẹr], *s.* 1. Dedo, miembro flexible de la mano. *Index finger,* Dedo índice. *Middle finger,* Dedo de en medio, dedo del corazón. *Ring finger,* Dedo anular. *Little finger,* Dedo meñique. 2. Parte parecida a un dedo; pequeña parte que sale o proyecta. 3. Medida de longitud, anchura del dedo, longitud del dedo medio. 4. Medida de profundidad, igual a la anchura del dedo. 5. Dedo, la mano, el instrumento de alguna obra. *Finger-stall,* Dedal, apoyadedos. *Finger-ring,* Anillo. *Finger-bowl, finger-glass,* Enjuague, enjuagatorio, taza que se pone a cada convidado antes de alzar los manteles para limpiar los dedos y enjuagar la boca. *Finger-breadth,* Anchura de un dedo; medida de longitud. *Finger-end,* Punta del dedo. *Finger-mark,* Marca, mancha hecha con el dedo; impresión del dedo pulgar que sirve para identificar las personas. *Finger-post,* Poste indicador en el cual hay una mano o una flecha que indica el camino. *Finger-reading,* La lectura de letras en relieve por medio del tacto, con las puntas de los dedos, como lo hacen los ciegos. *His fingers are all thumbs,* Usa de sus manos desmañadamente. *To have a finger in the pie,* Meter la cuchara; tomar parte en un asunto.

Finger, *va.* 1. Tocar, manosear; llegar a alguna cosa con la mano con ánimo de quitarla. 2. Tocar, pulsar, poner los dedos en algún instrumento de música; manejar, ejecutar alguna obra diestramente con las manos. *Light-fingered,* Ligero de manos, dado al hurto.

Finger-board [fin'-gẹr-bōrd], *s.* 1. La parte del mástil o mango del violín donde se ponen los dedos para tocar. 2. Teclado del órgano o pianoforte.

Fingered [fiṇ'-gẹrd], *a.* Que tiene dedos.

Fingering [fiṇ'-gẹr-ing], *s.* 1. El acto de tocar ligeramente o de juguetear. 2. Modo de tocar o pulsar un instrumento de música; notación para indicar qué dedos han de emplearse. 3. La obra ejecutada primorosamente con los dedos.

Fingernail [fin'-gẹr-nēl], *s.* Uña del dedo de la mano. *Fingernail polish,* Barniz para las uñas.

Finger prints [fin'-gẹr prints], *s. pl.* Huellas digitales.

Finger wave [fin'-gẹr wêv], *s.* Ondulado del cabello sin calor, ondulado al agua.

†**Fingle-fangle** [fiṇ'-gl-faṇ'-gl], *s.* Bujería, friolera: es voz burlesca.

Finial [fin'-i-al], *s.* (Arq.) Florón de pináculo; pináculo; remate que se dirige hacia arriba. (< Lat. finis, fin.)

Finical [fin'-i-cal], *a.* Delicado, afectado, nimio en el vestir, en los modales, etc.

Finically [fin'-i-cal-i], *adv.* Afectadamente.

Finicalness [fin'-i-cal-nes], *s.* Demasiada delicadeza, afectación propia de un petimetre.

Finikin [fin'-i-kin], *a.* Afectado, nimio en el vestir, en los modales, en el lenguaje, etc. *V.* FINICAL. (< Holandés.)—*s.* Especie de paloma con cresta.

Finish [fin'-ish], *va.* 1. Acabar, terminar, concluir, poner fin. 2. Pulir, perfeccionar, dar la última mano, completar. 3. (Fam.) Matar o hacer impotente; vencer.—*vn.* Llegar al fin; cesar.

Finish, *s.* Acabamiento, colmo; pulimento, la última mano.

Finisher [fin'-ish-ẹr], *s.* Consumador, el que consuma, perfecciona o da la última mano a alguna cosa; lo que acaba o decide alguna cosa. *The finisher of the law,* El ejecutor de la justicia.

Finishing [fin'-ish-ing], *s.* Acabamiento, consumación; colmo, perfección; la última mano o pincelada.—*a.* Que acaba, concluye o consuma. *Finishing blow,* Golpe de gracia. *To give the finishing stroke to,* Dar la última mano a.

Finite [fai'-nait], *a.* Finito, lo que tiene fin; limitado.

Finitely [fai'-nait-li], *adv.* Limitadamente.

Finiteness [fai'-nait-nes], *s.* Limitación, restricción.

Finless [fin'-les], *a.* Sin aletas, desaletado.

Finlike [fin'-laic], *a.* Aletado, que se parece a las aletas del pez.

Finn [fin], *s.* Finlandés, finlandesa, un miembro de la raza finlandesa; natural de Finlandia.

Finned [find], *a.* Aletado, que tiene aletas como el pez.

Finnic [fin'-ic], *a.* Finés, perteneciente a los fineses, y a sus idiomas.—*s.* Lengua finesa, en el sentido más lato.

Finnish [fin'-ish], *a.* Finlandés, perteneciente a Finlandia o a sus habitantes.—*s.* Idioma propio de los finlandeses.

Finny [fin'-i], *a.* 1. Armado de aletas como los peces. 2. Abundante en peces.

Fiord o **fjord** [fyērd], *s.* Fiordo.

Fippenny [fip'-pen-i], *a.* Contracción de *fivepenny;* de cinco peniques. *Fippenny bit,* Real americano, español o mejicano, del valor de 6¼ centavos.

Fir [fẹr], *s.* Abeto, árbol semejante al pino. *Fir-tree,* El árbol llamado abeto. *Spruce-fir,* Pinabete. *Scotch fir,* Pino.

Fire [fair], *s.* 1. Fuego, lumbre; combustión; llama, toda materia combustible que está ardiendo. 2. Descarga de armas de fuego. 3. Fuego, incendio, de algún edificio. 4. Fuego, el ardor que excitan algunas pasiones de ánimo. 5. Fuego, ardor o viveza de la imaginación; actividad intelectual; fuerza de la expresión. 6. La tortura del fuego; los tormentos del infierno. 7. Cualquier desgracia o infortunio pesado; rabia. *Fire of love,* Llama del amor. *Slow fire,* Fuego lento. *Fire is a good servant, but a bad master,* (Prov.) Sírvete del fuego, mas guárdate de él. *Fire-alarm,* Alarma o llamada de incendios, particularmente un sistema telegráfico. *Fire-annihilator, V.* FIRE-EXTINGUISHER. *Fire-back,* La pared posterior de un horno u hogar. *Fire-board,* Delantera de chimenea; mampara o tabla con que se tapan las chimeneas en el verano. *Fire-box,* Hogar, caja de fuego de una locomotora. *Fire-brick,* Ladrillo refractario. *Fire-clay,* Arcilla refractaria que resiste a la acción del fuego más intenso, con la cual se hacen los ladrillos refractarios. *Fire-damp,* Fuego grisú, mofeta, hidrógeno carburado explosible en las minas. *Fire-dog,* Morillo de hogar. *Fire-door,* Puerta de horno u hornillo. *Fire-eater,* (1) Titiritero farsante que finge tragarse brasas ardiendo. (2) Jaque, matamoros, fierabrás; retador de profesión. *Fire-escape,* Aparato de salvamento; escala de seguridad para bajar desde lo alto de un edificio incendiado. *Fire-extinguisher,* Extinguidor o apagador portátil de incendios. (Amer.) Apagafuegos. *The fire of persecution,* La rabia, la violencia de la persecución. *To be on fire,* Estar hecho un ascua, encendido, literal o figuradamente. *To put out the fire,* Apagar el fuego. *To set fire to, to set on fire,* Pegar fuego, quemar, incendiar. *By the fire,* A la lumbre, sentado junto al fuego. *To miss fire,* Hacer fogonazo, no disparar. *He will never set the river on fire,* No inventó la pólvora; es decir, es de cortos alcances. *St. Anthony's fire,* Erisipela. *Out of the frying-pan into the fire* Huir del fuego y dar en las brasas. *Under fire,* Expuesto al fuego de fusil o de cañón; se usa también en sentido figurado. *Fire-arrow,* Saeta incendiaria. *Fire-brush,* Escobilla para barrer el hogar. *Fire-fan,* Abanico de chimenea, pantalla que sirve para evitar que el calor de la lumbre dé en la cara. *Fire-fork*, Hurgón. *Fire-insurance*, Seguro contra incendios. *Fire-kiln*, Hornillo. *Fire-lock*, Fusil, carabina, escopeta. *Fire-maker*, Cohetero. *Fire-master*, Oficial de artillería que cuida de las obras de fuego. *Fire-new*, Flamante, nuevo; recién salido de la fragua. *Fire-office*, Oficina de seguros contra los incendios. *Fire-pan*, Brasero, copa, chofeta para llevar fuego. *Fire-plug*, Tapón de los encañados para apagar los incendios en las calles. *Fire-proof*, A prueba de incendio. *Fire-screen*, Pantalla de chimenea, guardafuego. *Fire-ship*, (Mar.) Brulote, bajel lleno de materias combustibles para quemar a otros. *Fire-shovel*, Paleta, badil, badila. *Fire-stick*, Tizón, tea. *Fire-stone*, Pirita, piedra que puede resistir al fuego. *Fire-wood*, Leña para la lumbre.

Fire, *va.* 1. Encender, abrasar, quemar, inflamar, enardecer; avivar el fuego. 2. Encender, animar, excitar. 3. Cauterizar. *To set on fire* o *a-fire*, Inflamar, incendiar.—*vn.* 1. Encenderse; dejarse dominar de alguna pasión, enojarse, enfadarse. 2. Tirar, disparar, descargar, hacer fuego.

Fire-arm [fair'-ārm], *s.* Arma de fuego.

Fire-ball [fair'-bōl], *s.* Granada real o de mano, globo lleno de pólvora, que revienta donde cae.

Fireboat [fair'-bōt], *s.* Embarcación para combatir incendios.

Firebrand [fair'-brand], *s.* 1. Tizón o tea. 2. Incendiario, zizañero.

Firebug [fair'-bʊg], *s.* Incendiario.

Firecracker [fair'-crak-ẹr], *s.* Cohete

Fire-cross [fair'-crōs], *s.* Símbolo de ataque o alarma en Escocia, que se figuraba con dos tizones encendidos y cruzados.

Fire department [fair dẹ-part'-mẹnt], *s.* Cuerpo de bomberos.

Fire-drake [fair'-drêk], *s.* Serpiente de fuego; especie de meteoro.

Fire-engine [fair'-en-jin], *s.* Bomba de apagar los incendios.

Fire-fly [fair'-flai], *s.* Luciérnaga, lampíride.

Fireless cooker [fair'-les cuk'-ẹr], *s.* Vasija eléctrica para cocinar.

Fireman [fair'-man], *s.* 1. Bombero. 2. Fogonero.

Fire-place [fair'-plês], *s.* Hogar, la parte de la chimenea donde se enciende lumbre.

Firer [fair'-ẹr], *s.* Incendiario.

Fire-side [fair'-said], *s.* Hogar, fogón de chimenea; la casa, el hogar doméstico.

Fire truck [fair truc], *s.* Autocamión de bomberos.

Firework [fair'-wūrk], *s.* Fuego tificial, fiesta de pólvora.

Fireworker [fair'-wūrk-ẹr], *s.* Oficial de artillería inferior al maestro de fuegos.

Firing [fair'-ing], *s.* 1. Leña, carbón, combustible. 2. Descarga.

Firing-iron [fair'-ing-ai'-urn], *s.* Cauterio.

Firing lever [fair'-ing lev'-ẹr], *s.* Palanca del disparador.

Firing party [fair'-ing par'-ti], *s.* (Mil.) Piquete de salvas.

Firkin [fẹr'-kin], *s.* 1. Cuñete, barril pequeño, que puede contener unos 36 cuartillos. 2. Cuñete o barrilete que se emplea para mantequilla y otros varios usos.

Firm [fẹrm], *a.* Firme, fuerte, estable, duro, constante, seguro.—*s.* (Com.) Firma, razón social, la denominación con que una casa de comercio hace sus negocios.

Firmament [fẹr'-ma-mẹnt], *s.* Firmamento.

Firmly [fẹrm'-li], *adv.* Firmemente, fuertemente.

Firm name [fẹrm nêm], *s.* Razón social.

Firmness [fẹrm'-nes], *s.* Firmeza, dureza, consistencia, estabilidad, solidez; entereza, constancia, resolución.

First [fẹrst], *a.* 1. Primero; temprano, delantero, primitivo. 2. Primero, excelente, grande, sobresaliente.—*adv.* Primero, en primer lugar, al principio, en el principio. *At first, at the first*, Desde luego, al principio. *First or last*, Tarde o temprano, un día u otro. *At first blush*, A primera vista, sin madura consideración. *First-begotten, first-born*, Primogénito, el hijo o hija que nace primero. *First-class*, De primera clase, de primer orden. *First-cousin*, Primo hermano, prima hermana. *First-created*, Dícese de la primera cosa criada o producida de su especie. *First-fruits*, Primicia, fruto primero. *First-hand*, Lo que viene directamente del origen o del productor.

First aid [fẹrst êd], *s.* Primeros auxilios.

Firstling [fẹrst'-ling], *s.* 1. Primogénito. 2. La cosa que ha sido producida antes que ninguna otra de su especie.—*a.* 1. Primogénito, dícese del hijo que nace primero y de lo que le pertenece. 2. Primerizo, lo que es primero o se anticipa a otro; lo primero que se hace o piensa.

Firstly [fẹrst'-li], *adv.* En primer lugar.

First mate [fẹrst mêt], *s.* (Mar.) Piloto.

First-rate [fẹrst'-rêt], *a.* Preeminente, de un mérito superior, de primera clase u orden.

Firth [fẹrth], *s.* *V.* FRITH.

Firwood [fẹr'-wud], *s.* Madera de abeto o pino.

Fisc [fisc], *s.* Fisco, el erario público, la tesorería, la real hacienda, la hacienda pública. (Fr.)

Fiscal [fis'-cal], *s.* Ministro o Secretario de hacienda.—*a.* Fiscal, perteneciente al fisco, o al oficio del fiscal; rentístico.

Fish [fish], *s.* 1. Pez. 2. Pescado: dícese de la carne de los peces como opuesta a la de los animales terrestres. 3. (Mar.) Gimelga, gemelo, gaburón; (Mec.) refuerzo. *Food-fish*, Pescado, pez comestible. *Sea-fish*, Pez de mar. *Fresh-water fish*, Pez de agua dulce. *Shell-fish*, Pez de concha o testáceo. *Fish-car*, (1) Vivero, receptáculo sumergido en el agua, en el cual se pueden guardar los peces vivos. (2) Carro de ferrocarril para llevar pescado. *Fish-pond*, Nansa, estanque de peces, vivero. *Flying fish*, Pez volador. (Exocœtus y Dactilopterus.) *A craw-fish*, Cangrejo de río o de agua dulce. *An odd fish*, Un estrambótico, hombre raro. *Fish of an anchor*, (Mar.) Pescante de ancla. *To have other fish to fry*, Tener que atender a cosas más importantes, tener otras cosas en qué pensar.

Fish, *va.* 1. Pescar. 2. Buscar en, y sacar a luz; intentar, obtener una cosa. 3. Aprovechar de (una cosa) para pescar; v. g. una red. 4. Componer o reforzar con una pieza de madera que se llama gemelo o gaburón; empalmar (los rieles, etc.) afirmando planchas a lo largo de ellos.

Fish bait [fish bêt], *s.* Carnada para pescar.

Fish-bone [fish'-bōn], *s.* Espina de pescado.

Fish-culture [fish'-cul"-chur], *s.* La crianza artificial de los peces.

Fish-day [fish'-dê], *s.* Día de abstinencia de carnes.

Fisher [fish'-ẹr], *s.* 1. Pescador. 2. El *pekan*, marta de América. *V.* PEKAN.

Fisher-boat [fish'-ẹr-bōt], *s.* Barca pescadora.

Fisherman [fish'-ẹr-man], *s.* 1. Pescador. 2. Barca pescadora.

Fishery [fish'-ẹr-i], *s.* Pesca, pesquera.

Fish-garth [fish'-gārth], *s.* Pesquera o pesquería, paraje cerrado en un río para pescar.

Fish-glue [fish'-glū], *s.* Cola de pescado, colapez.

Fish-hook [fish'-huk], *s.* Anzuelo, garfio para pescar.

Fishing [fish'-ing], *s.* 1. Pesca, arte o práctica de pescar; pesquera, pesquería. 2. El derecho de pescar, o el paraje donde se concurre a pescar. 3. Amordazamiento, barrotaje de los carriles; acción de enganchar el pescador en la cruz del ancla e izarla. *Fishing-line*, Cordel de pescar. *Fishing-fly*, Mosca artificial para carnada. *Fishing-smack*, Barcolongo ó queche para pescar en el mar. *Fishing village*, Pueblo de pescadores. *Fishing-tackle*, Avíos de pescar, aparejo de pesca.

Fishing-net [fish'-ing-net], *s.* Red de pescar.

Fishing-rod [fish'-ing-rod], *s.* Caña de pescar.

Fish-joint [fish'-joint], *s.* En los ferrocarriles, junta de mordaza; dos planchas de hierro o de acero aseguradas con pernos a los lados exteriores e interiores de dos rieles, donde se juntan los extremos de éstos.

Fish-kettle [fish'-ket-l], *s.* Caldera larga para cocer los peces enteros.

Fishlike [fish'-laic], *a.* Semejante a pescado.

Fish-market [fish'-mār-ket], *s.* Pescadería, el sitio donde se vende el pescado.

Fish-meal [fish'-mīl], *s.* Comida de pescado.

Fishmonger [fish'-mun-gẹr], *s.* Pescadero, el que vende pescado.

Fish-plate [fish'-plêt], *s.* Mordaza, plancha de unión de dos rieles. *V.* FISH-JOINT.

Fish-spear [fish'-spīr], *s.* Arpón, dardo.

Fish-skin [fish'-skin], *s.* 1. Piel de pescado. 2. Zapa, lija o piel de lija.

Fish-story [fish'-stō-ri], *s.* (E. U.) Fábula, cuento increíble.

Fishwife [fish'-waif], **Fish-woman** [fish'-wum-an], *sf.* Pescadera, mujer que vende pescado; mujer de plazuela, disputadora, marimacho.

Fishy [fish'-i], *a.* 1. Lo que tiene las calidades o la figura de pescado. 2. Perteneciente o parecido al pescado; o habitado por pescados. 3. Abundante en pescado.

Fissile [fis'-il], *a.* Hendible, rajadizo.

Fission [fi'-zhun], *s.* 1. Fisión, el acto de henderse, hendimiento. 2. (Biol.) La espontánea división de una celdilla o de un organismo en nuevas celdillas u organismos, a manera de reproducción.

Fissionable [fi'-zhun-a-bel], *a.* Fisionable.

Fissiparous [fi-sip'-a-rus], *s.* y *a.* Físíparo, que se reproduce por la división de su propio cuerpo.

Fissipedal [fi-sip'-e-dal], *a.* (Zool.) Fisípedo, que tiene el pie dividido en muchos dedos.

Fissure [fish'-ur], *s.* Grieta, hendedura, abertura.

Fissure, *va.* Hender, hacer grietas.

Fist [fist], *s.* Puño. *To strike with the fist,* Dar puñetazos. *With clenched fist,* Á puño cerrado.

Fistic [fist'-ic], *a.* Relativo al puño; de pugilato, pugilístico.

Fisticuff [fist'-i-cuf], *s.* Puñada; en plural, pugilato, riña a puñadas.

Fistula [fis'-chu-la o tu-la]. *s.* (Cir.) Fístula.

Fistular [fis'-tu-lar], *a.* Fistular, fistuloso, afistolado.

Fistulate [fis'-chu-lêt], *a.* Hueco como un tubo; afistolado, fistuloso.

Fistulous [fis'-tu-lus], *a.* Fistuloso, lo que tiene la forma de fístula o su semejanza.

Fit [fit], *s.* 1. (Med.) Acceso, paroxismo o parasismo. 2. Mal, enfermedad; mal de madre; pasión histérica; convulsión. 3. Transportamiento, rebato o arrebatamiento pasajero; capricho, humor. 4. Ataque, acceso, ímpetu, rebato, acometimiento repentino de algún mal o de alguna pasión de ánimo. 5. (Ant.) Cantos de un poema o partes de una canción que se repiten. *Fainting-fit,* Desmayo. *By fits,* o *by fits and starts,* Á ratos perdidos, a tontas y a locas, al tuntún; espasmódicamente. *To give one fits,* (E. U. Fam.) Poner a uno como nuevo. *Cold fit,* Escalofrío de una fiebre intermitente; temblor. *A melancholy fit,* Un acceso de melancolía. *To be in fits of laughter,* Desternillarse de risa. *If the fit takes me,* (Fig.) Si me parece, si me da la gana.

Fit, *s.* 1. Forma, corte; ajuste; conveniencia, conformidad, adaptación. 2. Acción de alistar, preparación.

Fit, *a.* 1. Apto, idóneo, a propósito para algo, conveniente, aprestado, dispuesto. 2. Hábil, capaz. 3. Cómodo, justo, juicioso, decente. 4. Listo, en estado de preparación. 5. Como si, casi, cuasi; uso familiar adverbial. *If you think fit,* Si a Vd. le parece. *He was not fit for it,* Él no era propio para ello, o él no era a propósito para el caso.

Fit, *va.* 1. Ajustar, acomodar, conformar; igualar, adaptar una cosa a otra. 2. Surtir, proveer lo que se necesita. 3. Poner en estado o disposición de. 4. Hacer acomodar una cosa a alguno; calzar, vestir. 5. Convenir, venir bien. *V.* Befit. —*vn.* Convenir, ser a propósito, venir, sentar o caer bien o mal. *That suit fits you very well,* Ese vestido le sienta a Vd. bien, o le está bien. *To fit out,* Proveer de todas las cosas necesarias, equipar a uno; tripular; armar. *To fit up,* Ajustar una cosa con otra, acomodar, componer; alhajar, adornar.

Fitchet [fich'-et], **Fitchew** [fich'-u], *s.* (Ingl.) Veso, mamífero europeo de la familia de los mustélidos afín de la marta. Putorius fœtidus. *V.* Polecat.

Fitful [fit'-ful], *a.* Alternado con paroxismos, espasmódico; caprichoso; incierto, vacilante.

Fitfully [fit'-ful-i], *adv.* Por intervalos; caprichosamente, de un modo vacilante.

Fitly [fit'-li], *adv.* Aptamente, cómodamente, justamente.

Fitment [fit'-ment], *s.* 1. Apresto, equipo, provisión. 2. Lo que conviene o es a propósito. 3. Mueblaje, conjunto de muebles.

Fitness [fit'-nes], *s.* Propiedad, aptitud, idoneidad, conveniencia, proporción. *Fitness of time,* Oportunidad.

Fittedness, *s.* *V.* Suitableness.

Fitter [fit'-er], *s.* Acoplador, disponedor, unidor, acomodador.

Fitting [fit'-ing], *a.* Propio para; adecuado, conveniente.—*s.* Guarnición; más usado en plural, herrajes; maniobras. *Fitting-shop,* Taller de ajuste.

Fittingly [fit'-ing-li], *adv.* Propiamente, aptamente.

Fitz [fits], *s.* Hijo: usado solamente en los compuestos de nombres propios, como, *Fitzhugh,* Hijo de Hugo, *Fitzroy,* Hijo del rey.

Five [faiv], *a.* Cinco. *He will tell you how many black beans make five,* Él te dirá cuántas son cinco.

Five-bar [faiv'-bār], **Five-barred** [faiv'-bārd], *a.* Lo que tiene cinco barras o palenques.

Fivefold [faiv'-fōld], *a.* Quíntuplo.

Five-finger [faiv'-fin-ger], **Five-leaf** [faiv'-lif], *s.* (Bot.) Cincoenrama.

Fives [faivz], *s.* Un juego de pelota.

Fix [fics], *va.* 1. Fijar, establecer; parar, detener. 2. Fijar, quitar la variedad que puede haber en alguna cosa. 3. Decidir definitivamente; señalar, determinar, establecer. 4. Tratar de suerte que se evite la acción de perder el color, de volatilizarse, o de deteriorarse. *To fix a negative,* Fijar una prueba negativa fotográfica. 5. Dirigir con constancia hacia el mismo punto. 6. Arreglar el orden, poner en orden, ajustar. 7. (Fam. E. U.) Reparar, componer; colocar bien, de una manera conveniente.—*vn.* 1. Fijarse, determinarse. 2. Fijarse, establecerse en alguna parte determinada. 3. Pasar un cuerpo del estado flúido al de sólido.

Fix, *s.* (Fam.) Dificultad; aprieto, dilema. *To be in a bad fix,* Hallarse en trance apurado.

Fixable [fic'-sa-bl], *a.* Fijable, que puede fijarse.

Fixation [fic'-sê-shun], *s.* 1. Fijación, el acto de fijar. 2. Firmeza, estabilidad. 3. Sujeción, restricción. 4. Residencia fija en algún paraje. 5. Paso de un cuerpo flúido al estado de solidez.

Fixative [fic'-sa-tiv], *a.* Que sirve para fijar o hacer permanente. U. t. c. s.

Fixedly [fic'-sed-li], *adv.* Fijamente, ciertamente.

Fixedness [fic'-sed-nes], *s.* Firmeza, estabilidad.

Fixity [fic'-si-ti], *s.* 1. Firmeza y coherencia de las partes. 2. (Quím.) La calidad de los cuerpos por la cual pueden sostener mucho calor sin volatizarse.

Fixing [fic'-sing], *s.* 1. La acción del verbo *To* Fix en cualquier sentido. 2. (Foto.) La acción de tratar una plancha desarrollada de suerte que no se altere la imagen por la acción ulterior de la luz. 3. *pl.* Adornos, decoraciones o jaeces de cualquier clase; también, cosas preparadas para el uso. *Table-fixings,* Accesorios de la mesa.

Fixture [fics'-chur], *s.* 1. Cosa fija, instalación fija, accesorio. 2. Persona que no se mueve de un lugar. *Fixtures, s. pl.* Muebles fijos. *Light fixtures,* Instalaciones fijas para las luces.

Fizgig [fiz'-gig], *s.* 1. Arpón, dardo. 2. Especie de fuego artificial, cohete pequeño. 3. Gazmoña, coqueta, tontuela.

Fizz, Fizzle [fiz, l], *vn.* Hacer un ruido sibilante; hacer un ruido sordo como la pólvora húmeda. *It is a fizzle,* Ha hecho fiasco completo, se empasteló.

Fizzle [fiz'-l], *s.* 1. (Fam.) Estado acosado o cansado. 2. Mal éxito de alguna cosa.

Fjord [fyōrd], *s.* V. Fiord.

Flabby [flab'-i], *a.* Blando, flojo, lacio.

Flabellate [fla-bel'-lêt], *a.* En forma de abanico.

Flabelliform [fla-bel'-i-fērm], *a.* *V.* Flabellate.

Flaccid [flac'-sid], *a.* 1. Flojo, endeble, débil, flaco, lacio. 2. (Med.) Flácido.

Flaccidity [flac-sid'-i-ti], *s.* Flojedad, flaqueza, debilidad.

Flag [flag], *vn.* 1. Pender, colgar. 2. Flaquear, amilanarse; debilitarse.—*va.* 1. Señalar por medio de una bandera. 2. Poner una bandera sobre algo, por ejemplo encima de un edificio. 3. Enlosar, embaldosar.

Flag, *s.* 1. Bandera; estandarte, insignia militar de los cuerpos de ejército. 2. Bandera o pabellón, insignia militar de las naves de guerra. 3. (Bot.) Gladiolo, espadaña. 4. Losa, baldosa. *Flag of truce, white flag,* Parlamentario, pabellón blanco, bandera de parlamento. *Green flag,* (F. C.) Banderín verde, señal de precaución. *Red flag,* (F. C.) Banderín encarnado, señal de peligro. *Black flag,* Pabellón negro, el de los piratas. *Yellow flag,* Bandera amarilla, insignia de cuarentena, o enfermedad contagiosa. *To strike* o *lower the flag,* Arriar la bandera.

Flag-broom [flag'-brum], *s.* Escoba para barrer los enlosados.

Flagellant [flaj'-e-lant], *a.* Flagelante.—*s. pl.* Flagelantes, secta religiosa.

Flagellate [flaj'-e-lêt], *va.* Azotar, flagelar.

Flagellation [flaj-e-lê'-shun], *s.* Flagelación, disciplina.

Flagelliform [fla-jel'-i-fērm], *a.* Flageliforme, que tiene la forma de un látigo, o del renuevo de una planta.

Flagellum [fla-jel'-um], *s.* 1. (Biol.) Apéndice parecido a un látigo; flagelo. 2. Azote. 3. (Bot.) Renuevo o vástago delgado de las plantas.

Flageolet [flaj'-o-let], *s.* Caramillo, flauta delgada; octavín.

Flagginess [flag'-i-nes], *s.* Flojedad, falta de tirantez o tensión.

Flagging [flag'-ing], *s.* 1. Enlosado, embaldosado. 2. Conjunto de baldosas. 3. La acción de embaldosar o enlosar.—*a.* Lánguido, flojo.—*pa.* de *To* Flag.

Flaggy [flag'-i], *a.* Flojo, lacio, endeble; insípido.
Flagitious [fla-jish'-us], *a.* Facineroso, malvado; vicioso, corrompido; atroz, abominable.
Flag-officer [flag'-ef-i-sęr], *s.* (Mar.) Almirante, vicealmirante o contraalmirante; tiene el privilegio de desplegar un pabellón que indica su rango.
Flagon [flag'-un], *s.* Frasco.
Flagrance [flê'-grans], *s.* Flagrancia, la actualidad de cometer algún delito.
Flagrancy [flê'-gran-si], *s.* 1. Incendio, abrasamiento, calor, ardor, fuego. 2. Impudencia descarada.
Flagrant [flê'-grant], *a.* 1. Ardiente, flagrante. 2. Colorado, encendido, con muchos colores en la cara. 3. Rojo. 4. Notorio, públicamente conocido; grande, insigne.
Flagrantly [flê'-grant-li], *adv.* Ardientemente; notoriamente.
Flag-ship [flag'-ship], *s.* (Mar.) Navío almirante, el buque que monta el que manda una escuadra.
Flagstaff [flag'-staf], *s.* (Mar.) El asta de la bandera o pabellón.
Flag-stone [flag'-stōn], *s.* Losa o baldosa, piedra ancha y llana a propósito para enlosar.
Flail [flêl], *va.* Golpear, azotar.
Flake [flêk], *s.* 1. Cualquier cosa que está en pedacitos sueltos y planos. 2. Copo, vedija de lana, algodón o seda; y copo se dice también de la nieve cuando cae de lo alto. 3. Lámina, capa, tonga, tongada. 4. *Flake of fire*, Centella, chispa. *Flake of ice*, Carámbano. 5. Clavel que tiene rayas de un solo color sobre fondo blanco. *Flake white*, Albayalde.
Flake, *s.* 1. Cañizo, andamio ligero; en particular, secadero de pescado. 2. Faldón de silla para mantener la rodilla del jinete fuera del caballo.
Flake, *va.* Reducir una cosa a copos. —*vn.* Romperse o quebrarse en láminas.
Flaky [flê'-ki], *a.* 1. Vedijoso, vedijudo. 2. Lo que está colocado en capas o lechos. 3. Lo que está roto en pequeñas láminas.
Flam [flam], *s.* 1. Falsedad, mentira, embuste; chasco. 2. Capricho, fantasía.
Flam, *va.* Mentir, engañar mintiendo.
Flambeau [flam'-bō], *s.* 1. Antorcha, hachón. 2. Candelero grande adornado. 3. Gran caldera para azúcar. (Gal.)
Flamboyant [flam-boi'-ant], *a.* 1. Extravagante y llamativo; retumbante. 2. Flamígero, flamante. 3. En forma de llamas. (Fr.)
Flame [flêm], *s.* 1. Llama, llamarada, fuego. 2. Impulso vehemente del ánimo, fuego de la imaginación, ardor del temperamento; fuego del amor. 3. (Fam.) Enamorada, enamorado; persona amada.
Flame, *vn.* 1. Arder, quemarse alguna cosa levantando llama; brillar. 2. Inflamarse en alguna pasión violenta.—*va.* (Des.) Inflamar, excitar.
Flame-colour [flêm'-cul-ęr], *s.* Color de llama.
Flame-coloured [flêm'-cul-urd], *a.* Lo que tiene color de llama.
Flame-eyed [flêm'-aid], *a.* El que tiene los ojos centellantes.
Flameless [flêm'-les], *a.* Sin llama.
Flame thrower [flêm' thrō-ęr], *s.* Lanzallamas.
Flaming [flê'-ming], *a.* 1. Flamante,
Flaming [flê'-ming], *a.* 1. Flamante, que emite llamas. 2. Llamativo, faustoso. 3. Apasionado, que tiende a excitar.
Flamingly [flêm'-ing-li], *adv.* Espléndidamente, radiantemente.
Flamingo [fla-min'-gō], *s.* (Orn.) Flamenco, ave palmípeda mayor que la cigüeña. Phœnicopterus.
Flanch, Flanque [flanch, flank], *s.* (Her.) 1. Figura formada a cada lado del escudo por el segmento de un círculo. 2. Reborde, pestaña.
Flange [flanj], *s.* 1. Realce, borde levantado, para mantener alguna cosa en su lugar; repisa, borde saliente, reborde; reborde de una cañería o un tubo; pestaña de rueda de carro. 2. Plancha para cerrar la boca de un cañón.
Flange, *va.* Proveer de realce o reborde.
Flank [flanc], *s.* 1. Ijada. 2. Lado, costado, porción lateral de cualquier cosa; ala, flanco de escuadra o ejército. 3. (Fort.) Flanco, la parte del baluarte que hace ángulo entrante con la cortina y saliente con la frente. 4. La parte delgada del pellejo que proviene de la ijada de un animal.
Flank, *va.* 1. Lindar, confinar, estar inmediato a un límite; estar a un lado u otro de un confín o a ambos. 2. Atacar el flanco de un ejército o escuadra. 3. (Fort.) Flanquear. 4. Asegurar los flancos.—*vn.* 1. Defender o atacar el flanco. 2. Llegar a, tocar a.
Flanker [flank'-ęr], *s.* 1. (Fort.) Flanco. 2. Flanqueador.
†**Flanker**, *va.* 1. Guarnecer o defender los costados, alas o flancos de un cuerpo, campamento o muralla. 2. Atacar de flanco.
Flannel [flan'-el], *s.* Franela o flanela. *Canton* o *cotton flannel*, Moletón, franela de algodón.
Flannelette [flan-el-et'], *s.* Muletón, tela de franela para ropa interior.
Flap [flap], *s.* 1. Pieza o parte ancha, flexible y que cuelga sueltamente; como falda, faldilla, faldón; válvula; labio de una herida; oreja de zapato. 2. Mosqueador. 3. Cachete; alazo; golpe ligero. 4. La acción de aletear, de agitar. 5. (Aer.) Aleta.
Flap, *va.* 1. Golpear, pegar; agitar, columpiar; mosquear, espantar las moscas con el mosqueador. 2. Dejar caer, rebajar alguna cosa. 3. Despertar, hacer, recordar algo a otro por medio de un ligero golpe. *To flap the wings*, Aletear, sacudir las alas.—*vn.* 1. Columpiarse, o moverse de arriba abajo, como oscilante al viento. 2. Agitarse, menearse, sacudirse.
Flap-dragon, *va.* (Vul.) Comer vorazmente.
Flap-eared [flap'-ird], *a.* Orejudo, el que tiene las orejas grandes.
Flapjack [flap'-jac], *s.* Especie de torta hecha a la sartén.
Flap-mouthed [flap'-maudhd], *s.* Morrudo, bezudo, hocicudo.
Flapper [flap'-ęr], *s.* 1. Agitador, golpeador; el que o lo que sacude. 2. El que hace a otro acordarse de alguna cosa. 3. Avecilla que todavía no puede volar.
Flapping [flap'-ing], *s.* La acción de aletear o de sacudirse.
Flare [flār], *vn.* 1. Lucir, brillar, deslumbrar, relampaguear. 2. Brillar, lucir con colores muy vivos; vestirse de un modo faustoso y desagradable. 3. Abrirse o extenderse hacia fuera, como los bordes de un embudo. *To flare up*, Encenderse; (fig.) encolerizarse. *A flare up*, (Fam.) Cólera, displicencia, incomodidad; jarana, disturbio.
Flash [flash], *s.* 1. Relámpago, llamarada, llama pronta y pasajera. 2. Llamarada, movimiento repentino del ánimo de corta duración. 3. Cualquier situación pasajera y corta. 4. Borbollón, golpe de agua impelida con violencia. *Flash of the eye*, Ojeada. *Flash of wit*, Agudeza, rasgo, dicho pronto y vivo.—*a.* 1. Que tiene relación con ladrones y su habla. *Flash language*, Caló, jerigonza de gitanos y ladrones. *Flash-house*, Casa encubridora de hurtos, donde se acogen los ladrones. 2. Barato y de mal gusto.
Flash, *vn.* 1. Relampaguear. 2. Brillar con un brillo pasajero. 3. Saltar, romper con violencia. 4. Prorrumpir en chistes o agudezas. —*va.* 1. Cubrir el vidrio liso con una capa delgada de vidrio de color. 2. Despedir agua a borbollones.
Flashback [flash'-bac], *s.* Interrupción de la continuidad de un relato; por ej., en una película cinematográfica, para presenter escenas anteriores.
Flashbulb [flash'-bulb], *s.* Bombilla de destello, luz relámpago.
Flasher [flash'-ęr], *s.* 1. Luz intermitente, intermitente. 2. Interruptor intermitente.
Flashily [flash'-i-li], *adv.* Superficialmente, con vana ostentación.
Flashing [flash'-ing], *s.* 1. Producción de destellos. 2. Chorro fuerte de agua. 3. Tapajuntas (en la construcción de edificios).
Flashlight [flash'-lait], *s.* Linterna eléctrica de mano, lámpara portátil. *Flashlight photography*, Fotografía instantánea con luz artificial.
Flashy [flash'-i], *a.* 1. Superficial, aparente, presumido sin mérito. 2. Llamativo en apariencia, pero barato; de relumbrón.
Flask [flask], *s.* 1. Frasco, redoma, botella. 2. Frasco, el recipiente en que se llevaba antes la pólvora.
Flasket [flask'-et], *s.* Fuente o plato grande.
Flat [flat], *s.* 1. Llanura, plano. 2. Plano, lo ancho de algún instrumento cortante. 3. Bajío, escollo. *Flat of an oar*, (Mar.) Pala de remo. *Flat of a floor-timber*, (Mar.) Plan de una varenga. 4. (Mús.) Bemol, el signo ♭ que baja en un semitono la entonación natural de una nota. 5. Cualquier cosa de forma achatada o plana, como una barca, un techo plano, un carro de plataforma, etc. 6. (Fam.) Mentecato, fácil de embaucar. 7. Habitación, conjunto de cuartos en un solo piso.—*a.* 1. Llano, liso, plano; raso, chato, aplastado. 2. Insulso, insípido. *Flat wine*, Vino evaporado. 3. Triste, abatido. 4. Perentorio, absoluto. 5. Tendido, postrado en el suelo. *A flat lie*, Una mentira premeditada. 6. En la lonja, sin interés. 7. (Mús.) (1) Debajo del diapasón; (2) menor, o disminuído. 8. Mate, sin lustre, como una superficie pintada.

Flat, *va.* 1. (Mús.) Bajar, abajar un tono. 2. (Mús.) Hacer sonar (o cantar) una nota un poco más bajo de lo que está indicado o escrito. 3. Allanar, poner llana la superficie de alguna cosa; aplastar, achatar. 4. Evaporar; desazonar. *To flat in*, (Mar.) Acuartelar, abroquelar.—*vn.* 1. (Mús.) Bajar el tono de lo que se canta o toca. 2. Aplastarse, aplanarse. 3. Atontarse.
Flat back [flat bac], *s.* y *a.* Lomo plano (encuadernación).
Flatboat [flat'-bōt], *s.* Chalana.
Flat-bottomed [flat'-bet-umd], *a.* Lo que tiene el fondo plano: dícese de los botes.
Flatcar [flat'-cār], *s.* (F.C.) Plataforma.
Flatfoot [flat'-fut], *s.* Pie plano.
Flat-footed [flat'-fut"-ed], *a.* 1. Que tiene los pies achatados. 2. (Fam.) Inflexible, resuelto, determinado.
Flatiron [flat'-ai'-urn], *s.* Plancha.
Flatlong [flat'-lōng], *adv.* De plano.
Flatly [flat'-li], *adv.* 1. Horizontalmente, llanamente. 2. Fríamente. 3. De plano, absolutamente. *He flatly confessed it*, Lo confesó de plano.
Flatness [flat'-nes], *s.* 1. Llanura, lisura. 2. Desabrimiento, insipidez. 3. Abatimiento, apocamiento. 4. Insulsez, frialdad.
Flat-nosed [flat'-nōzd], *a.* Chato, romo.
Flatten [flat'-n], *va.* 1. Allanar, aplastar, achatar, poner chata una cosa. 2. Derribar, echar a tierra. 3. Evaporar; abatir.—*vn.* 1. Aplanarse, igualarse. 2. Atontarse, perder el espíritu y la viveza. 3. Hacerse plano o achatado en cualquier sentido.
Flatter [flat'-ęr], *s.* Allanador.
Flatter, *va.* 1. Adular, lisonjear. 2. Agradar, causar gusto o placer. 3. Halagar o lisonjear a uno haciéndole formar esperanzas ilusorias.
Flatterer [flat'-ęr-ęr], *s.* Adulador, lisonjero, zalamero.
Flattering [flat'-ęr-ing], *a.* Lisonjero, que lisonjea el amor propio; adulador que prodiga falsas alabanzas.
Flatteringly [flat'-ęr-ing-li], *adv.* Con zalamería, halagadoramente.
Flattery [flat'-ęr-i], *s.* Adulación, lisonja, carantoña, zalamería.
Flatting [flat'-ing], *s.* 1. La acción del verbo *to flat* en sus varias acepciones, como el acto de bajar el tono de una nota musical, el aplanamiento o alisamiento de una cosa, etc. 2. Barniz mate, encoladura para preservar el dorado.
Flat tire [flat tair], *s.* Llanta desinflada, neumático desinflado.
Flattish [flat'-ish], *a.* Chato, lo que está como aplastado.
Flatulency [flat'-yu-len-si], *s.* 1. Flatulencia, ventosidad. 2. Hinchazón, vanidad, presunción.
Flatulent [flat'-yu-lent], *a.* Flatulento; hinchado, vano.
Flatuous [flat'-yu-us], *a.* Ventoso, flatulento.
Flatus [flé'-tus], *s.* 1. Flato, ventosidad en el cuerpo humano. 2. Soplo.
Flatwise [flat'-waiz], *adv.* De llano; dícese del cuerpo que está descansando en el suelo por su parte más plana.
Flaunt [flānt], *vn.* Pavonearse, hacer ostentación de galas o vestidos.
Flaunt, *s.* Borla; cualquier cosa que cuelga airosamente.
Flautist [flōt'-ist], *s.* Flautista.
Flavescent [fla-ves'-ęnt], *a.* Que se vuelve amarillo; amarillento.
Flavor, Flavour [flé'-vęr], *s.* 1. Sabor o gusto suave y delicado de alguna cosa. 2. Sainete, salsa o condimento apetitoso. 3. Calidad estética de una obra literaria.
Flavor, Flavour, *va.* 1. Saborear, comunicar buen sabor, añadir un sainete a un manjar. 2. (Fig.) Comunicar cualquier cualidad distintiva a una cosa.
Flavored [flé'-vęrd], *a.* Sabroso, gustoso.
Flavoring [flé'-vęr-ing], *s.* Sainete, salsa que da buen sabor a los comestibles. También se usa en sentido figurado.
Flavour, *s.* y *v.* *V.* FLAVOR. Manera usual de escribir esta palabra en Inglaterra.
Flavourless, Flavorless [fle'-ver-les], *a.* Sin sabor, insípido, soso.
Flavous [flé'-vus], *a.* (Des.) Flavo, amarillo.
Flaw [flō], *s.* 1. Resquebradura, hendedura, grieta, pelo, paño, paja. 2. Falta, defecto, tacha. 3. (Mar.) Ráfaga, soplo repentino de viento.
Flaw, *va.* 1. Rajar, hender. 2. Hacer grietas en el cutis.
Flawless [flō'-les], *a.* Sano, entero, exento de rajas, grietas u otro defecto.
Flax [flacs], *s.* Lino. *To brake flax*, Agramar lino. *To dress flax*, Rastrillar lino. *Flaxseed*, Grano de lino, linaza. *Flax-brake*, Agramadera. *Flax-dressing*, Rastrilleo del lino.
Flax-comb [flacs'-cōm], *s.* Rastrillo.
Flax-dresser [flacs'-dres-ęr], *s.* Rastrillador.
Flaxen [flac'-sen], **Flaxy** [flac'-si], *a.* 1. De lino, lo que está hecho de lino. 2. Blondo. *Flaxen-haired*, Que tiene los cabellos rubios.
Flaxseed [flax'-sīd], *a.* (Ento.) Parecido a la linaza, como las ninfas del cecidomio.—*s.* Linaza.
Flax-weed [flacs'-wīd], *s.* (Bot.) Linaria. *V.* TOADFLAX.
Flay [flê], *va.* Desollar; descortezar.
Flayer [flê'-ęr], *s.* Desollador; descortezador.
Flea [flī], *s.* 1. Pulga, insecto parásito muy molesto. 2. Uno de ciertos escarabajos y crustáceos pequeños que saltan como las pulgas. *A flea in one's ear*, Una amonestación; algunas veces, desaire, mala acogida.
Flea, *va.* (Poco us.) Espulgar, quitar las pulgas.
Fleabane [flī'-bên], *s.* (Bot.) Coniza, pulguera.
Flea-bite, Flea-biting [flī'-bait, ing], *s.* Picadura o picada de pulga.
Flea-bitten [flī'-bit-n], *a.* 1. Picado de pulgas. 2. Vil, bajo, menospreciable.
Fleam [flīm], *s.* 1. Fleme, especie de lanceta para sangrar las bestias. 2. (Prov. Ingl.) Zanja, arroyo.
Fleawort [flī'-wūrt], *s.* (Bot.) Pulguera, zaragatona.
Fleck o Flecker [flek, ęr], *va.* Abigarrar, varetear, señalar con rayas, manchas o lunares.
Fleck, *s.* 1. Punto o lista; mancha, lunar. 2. Copo, vedija de lana. 3. Lonja (de tocino).
Fleckless [flec'-les], *a.* Sin mancha ni marca; inocente.
Flection [flec'-shun], *s.* 1. Flexión, la acción de doblar; inclinación. 2. La parte encorvada o torcida; corvadura. 3. (Gram.) *V.* INFLECTION. 4. Ojeada o mirada.
Flector, *s.* *V.* FLEXOR.
Fled, *pret.* y *pp.* del verbo *To* FLEE.
Fledge [flej], *va.* (Poco us.) Emplumar.—*vn.* Pelechar, emplumecer, emplumarse.
Fledgling, Fledgeling [flej'-ling], *s.* Pajarito próximo a salir del nido.—*a.* Emplumecido poco ha; de aquí, novel, poco conocido, como un joven poeta o escritor.
Flee [flī], *va.* (*pret.* y *pp.* FLED). Huir, evitar, esquivar, escapar.—*vn.* 1. Huirse, apartarse de algún peligro, fugarse, escaparse. 2. No dejarse ver; cesar de ser visible; desaparecer. *He fled to Denmark*, Huyóse a Dinamarca.
Fleece [flīs], *s.* Vellón. *The order of the Golden Fleece*, La orden del Toisón de Oro. *Fleece-wool*, Vellón, la lana cortada a las reses vivas.
Fleece, *va.* 1. Esquilar la lana o pelo de los animales. 2. Desnudar, despojar a uno de lo que tiene. 3. Blanquear.
Fleeced [flīst], *a.* 1. Velludo. 2. Esquilado.
Fleecer [flīs'-ęr], *s.* Despojador, ladrón.
Fleecy [flīs'-i], *a.* Lanudo, cubierto de lana o parecido al vellón; pálido. *Fleecy clouds*, Nubes aborregadas, a modo de vellones de lana.
Fleer [flīr], *vn.* Mofarse de alguno; hacer muecas o gestos.—*va.* Mofar, burlar.
Fleer, *s.* Burla, mueca; risa falsa.
Fleet [flīt], *s.* 1. Escuadra de navíos de guerra, armada; flota de buques mercantes. 2. Número cabal de buques que pertenecen a una compañía o a un gobierno. 3. Caleta, ensenada, ancón (en palabras compuestas).
Fleet, *a.* Veloz, ligero. *Fleet-footed*, Dotado de pies ligeros; rápido. *Fleet-winged*, Dotado de alas ligeras; que vuela velozmente.
Fleet, *va.* y *vn.* 1. Volar, desvanecerse, apartarse alguna cosa repentinamente de la vista. 2. Pasar, ser una cosa pasajera. 3. Flotar. 4. Pasar el tiempo sin sentir. 5. Vivir o pasar el tiempo alegremente.
Fleet-foot [flīt'-fut], *a.* Veloz o ligero de pies.
Fleeting [flīt'-ing], *a.* Que pasa rápidamente, transitorio, momentáneo, pasajero.
Fleeting-dish [flīt'-ing-dish], *s.* Espumadera.
Fleetly [flīt'-li], *adv.* Velozmente.
Fleetness [flīt'-nes], *s.* Velocidad, ligereza.
Fleg [fleg] (Esco.), *va.* Aterrar, espantar.—*s.* Choque.
Fleming [flem'-ing], *s.* Flamenco, el natural de Flandes.
Flemish [flem'-ish], *a.* Flamenco, el natural de Flandes y lo que pertenece a este país. *Flemish linen*, Holanda, lienzo muy fino.
Flense [flens], *va.* (Mar.) Despedazar una ballena o foca y sacarles la grasa.
Flesh [flesh], *s.* 1. Carne. 2. Carnalidad, sensualidad; las pasiones groseras del hombre. 3. En teología y bíblica, la naturaleza humana, la naturaleza pecaminosa del hombre. 4. La parte material del hombre; el cuerpo, a distinción del

espíritu 5. Carne, pulpa, la parte mollar de las frutas y vegetales. 6. (Ant.) Parentela, parientes cercanos. *After the flesh*, Conforme a la carne, de una manera carnal. *Flesh and blood*, (1) Carne y sangre, la naturaleza carnal. (2) Hijos; progenie, casta; los hermanos y parientes cercanos. *One flesh*, Una misma carne, una sola persona. *Proud flesh*, Tejido granuloso parecido a la carne que se forma en las heridas o llagas que están en vías de curación.

Flesh, *va.* 1. Hartar; saciar. 2. Endurecer, habituar, acostumbrar. 3. Dar muestra o pedazo de carne, como al halcón, al perro, y en sentido figurado, a un arma cualquiera; dar ralea a, cebar; (fig.) mojar en sangre. 4. En las tenerías, descarnar, pelambrar.

Flesh-broth [flesh'-brōth], *s.* Caldo de carne o hecho con carne.

Flesh-brush [flesh'-brush], *s.* Cepillo para frotar la piel.

Flesh-colour [flesh'-cul-ęr], *s.* Color de carne; encarnación.

Flesh-diet [flesh'-dai'-et], *s.* Dieta de carne.

Fleshed [flesht], *a.* Carnudo, carnoso.

Flesh-fly [flesh'-flai], *s.* Mosca carnívora que deposita sus huevos en carne corrompida. Sarcophaga.

‡**Fleshful** [flesh'-ful], *a.* Carnoso, gordo.

Flesh-hook [flesh'-huc], *s.* Gancho o garabato para sacar la carne de la marmita.

Fleshiness [flesh'-i-nes], *s.* Carnosidad.

Fleshings [flesh'-ingz], *s. pl.* 1. Calzón de punto muy ajustado que usan los bailarines, los acróbatas y los actores en algunos papeles. 2. (Ten.) Descarnaduras, piltrafas.

Fleshless [flesh'-les], *a.* Descarnado.

Fleshliness [flesh'-li-nes], *s.* Carnalidad.

Fleshly [flesh'-li], *a.* Carnal, animal, corpóreo.

Flesh-meat [flesh'-mît], *s.* Carne, la de los animales o aves que se prepara para comer.

†**Fleshment** [flesh'-męnt], *s.* Ahinco, ardor, ufanía, por razón del buen éxito.

Fleshmonger [flesh'-mun-gęr], *s.* 1. Carnicero. 2. Alcahuete.

Fleshpot [flesh'-pot], *s.* Marmita.

Fleshy [flesh'-i], *a.* 1. Gordo, grueso, corpulento. 2. Carnoso, mollar, pulposo; suculento. 3. Corporal; carnal, relativo a la naturaleza carnal.

Fletch [flech], *va.* (Des.) Emplumar o empenachar una saeta.

Fletcher [flech'-ęr], *s.* Flechero, el que hace flechas y arcos.

Fleur-de-lis [flūr'-dę-li], *s. sing.* y *pl.* Flor de lis, divisa heráldica de la casa de Borbón. (Fr.)

Fleuron [flū'-rōn], *s.* (Arq.) Florón.

Flew [flū], *pret.* del verbo *To* FLY.

Flewed [flūd], *a.* Boquihendido, que tiene belfos.

Flews [flūz], *s. pl.* Belfos, los labios grandes de un perro belfo.

Flex [flex], *va.* Doblar, doblegar, encorvar.—*s.* Doblez.

Flexibility [flec-si-bil'-i-ti], *s.* 1. Flexibilidad. 2. Flexibilidad, docilidad de genio, condescendencia.

Flexible [flec'-si-bl], *a.* Flexible, correoso; dócil; dúctil; adaptable, conformado fácilmente, plástico; obediente; deferente.

Flexibleness [flec'-si-bl-nes], *s.* Flexibilidad; docilidad.

Flexile [flec'-sil], *a.* Flexible.

Flexion [flec'-shun], *s.* *V.* FLECTION.

Flexor [flec'-sęr], *s.* (Anat.) Músculo flexor, el que sirve para doblar o encorvar ciertas partes del cuerpo.

Flexuous [flex'-yu-us], *a.* 1. Tortuoso, vario, inconstante. 2. (Bot.) Flexuoso, lo que muda de dirección en cada nudo.

Flexure [flex'-yur], *s.* Flexión, juntura, corvadura; zalamería.

Flick [flic], *va.* Tocar o dar ligeramente con un látigo, etc.—*s.* Latigazo súbito y poco fuerte. (<flack.)

Flicker [flik'-ęr], *vn.* 1. Vacilar una llama, reavivarse y luego morir. (Prov. pavesear.) 2. Aletear, menear las alas; fluctuar. *The candle flickers*, La vela pavesea, se está acabando. *Flickering flame*, Llama vacilante. *Flickering fire*, Fuego chispeante, trémulo.

Flicker, *s.* (Orn.) Pico del género Colaptes, común en el este de la América del Norte.

Flies, *s. pl.* de FLY. Moscas.

Flier [flai'-ęr], *s.* 1. Volador, lo que vuela; ave volante, etc. 2. Volante de reloj o de otra máquina cualquiera. 3. Escalón; y en plural, escalones de una escalera que va siempre en línea recta, sin dar vueltas. 4. (Fam.) Lo que se mueve con gran velocidad, como un tren expreso.

Flight [flait], *s.* 1. Vuelo, el acto o la facultad de volar. 2. Bandada de pájaros; el conjunto de aves o de cosas que vuelan moviéndose juntas, como una descarga de flechas. 3. Rapidez, velocidad o movimiento veloz de cualquier manera que sea; también el espacio recorrido por un proyectil, por un ave en su vuelo, etc. 4. Rebato, ímpetu, arranque; fuego o vuelo de la imaginación; elevación de ideas. 5. Escalera, serie continua de peldaños: tramo de escalera. *An arrow-flight*, Vuelo de una flecha.

Flight, *s.* 1. Huída, fuga. 2. (For.) Evasión, escape, el acto de huir de la justicia o de fugarse de una cárcel. *To betake one's self to flight*, Escapar, huir, apelar a la fuga.

Flightiness [flait'-i-nes], *s.* Irregularidad; travesura; ligero delirio.

Flight pattern [flait' pa-tęrn], *s.* Esquema de vuelo.

Flight plan [flait' plan], *s.* Plan de vuelo, hoja de ruta.

Flight-shot [flait'-shot], *s.* El alcance de una flecha o saeta.

Flight strip [flait strip], *s.* Pista para aterrizaje de emergencia al lado de una carretera.

Flighty [flait'-i], *a.* Veloz, acelerado, ligero, travieso, inconstante; delirante.

Flimflam [flim'-flam], *s.* (Ger.) Embuste, ficcioncilla; superchería.—*va.* Engañar con astucia.

Flimsiness [flim'-zi-nes], *s.* Textura débil y ligera; falta de solidez, fuerza o resistencia.

Flimsy [flim'-zi], *a.* Débil, endeble; fútil, insubstancial, poco sólido; ineficaz, frívolo. *A flimsy argument*, Argumento frívolo. *Flimsies*, *s. pl.* Papel delgado de calcar; papel de tela de cebolla.

Flinch [flinch], *vn.* Titubear, vacilar a causa de dolor o peligro; faltar a, echarse con la carga, desviar el cuerpo. (Mex.) Echarse con las petacas. *To flinch away*, Huirse, retirarse. *To flinch back*, Retroceder, volver hacia atrás, abandonar el campo; desdecirse. (Fam.) Rebajarse, echar pie atrás. (Vul.) Llamarse andana. *Without flinching*, Sin titubear, sin vacilar.

Flincher [flinch'-ęr], *s.* El que se echa con la carga; el que se vuelve atrás de lo que había dicho o de lo que había emprendido.

Flinching [flinch'-ing], *s.* Vacilación, titubeo, retroceso.

Flinder [flin'-dęr], *s.* Astilla, pedacito, pequeño fragmento, tira. (< Noru.) *Blown to flinders*, Volado en pedazos menudos.

Fling [fling], *va.* (*pret.* y *pp.* FLUNG). 1. Arrojar, tirar, lanzar, esparcir. 2. Empujar, demoler, arruinar; dar en rostro; despedir. 3. Echar en el suelo, como en la lucha a brazo partido; arrojar de la silla: de aquí, sobrepujar, vencer.—*vn.* 1. Lanzar un arma arrojadiza de cualquiera clase. 2. Escarnecer, mofarse, murmurar entre dientes. 3. Alborotarse, cocear, como el caballo; brincar, saltar. 4. Entregarse a movimientos violentos con impaciencia o pasión; saltar impetuosamente. *To fling away*, Desperdiciar, descartar, desechar; exponer, prodigar; retirarse. *To fling down*, Demoler, arruinar. *To fling off*, Engañar en la caza. *To fling out to one*, Poner a la vista. *To fling out*, (1) Arrojar por la fuerza. (2) Hablar violentamente, echar chispas. Alborotarse, cocear, hablando de caballos. *To fling up*, Abandonar, dejar.

Fling, *s.* 1. Tiro, el acto de tirar. 2. Mueca, gesto, burla, sarcasmo, chufleta, pulla. 3. Salto o coz. 4. Libertad de acción, oportunidad de obrar a discreción, sin trabas. 5. Fogosa libertad de movimiento; bravata, atrevimiento. 6. Baile escocés muy vivo.

Flinger [fling'-ęr], *s.* 1. Tirador, arrojador. 2. Mofador, escarnecedor.

Flint [flint], *s.* 1. Pedernal, piedra de chispa o lumbre. 2. Cualquiera cosa sumamente dura. *Flint glass*, Cristal; vidrio que contiene plomo.

Flint-heart, **Flint-hearted** [flint'-hārt, ed], *a.* Empedernido, cruel, duro, insensible.

Flintiness [flint'-i-nes], *s.* La cualidad o naturaleza del pedernal; dureza excesiva.

Flinty [flint'-i], *a.* 1. Apedernalado, silicoso, de pedernal. 2. Empedernido, endurecido, inexorable, duro, cruel, inflexible.

Flip [flip], *va.* 1. Lanzar ligera y rápidamente; chasquear. 2. Dar o golpear con un movimiento ligero y pronto; quitar por medio de un golpe ligero.—*s.* Papirotada; también *V.* FILLIP y FLICK.

Flip [flip], *s.* Una bebida hecha con cerveza, ron y azúcar.

Flippancy [flip'-an-si], *s.* Petulancia, locuacidad, ligereza, impertinencia, ademanes reprensibles.

Flippant [flip'-ant], *a.* Ligero, petulante, locuaz, impertinente.

Flippantly [flip'-ant-li], *adv.* Locuazmente, impertinentemente.

Flipper [flip'-ęr], *s.* 1. Aleta o miembro ancho y plano que sirve para nadar; pata de tortuga o de foca. 2. (Vul.) La mano. 3. Paleta.

Flirt [flęrt], *vn.* 1. Coquetear, cocar; ser una mujer muy amiga de verse cortejada. 2. Proceder o portarse con ligereza. 3. Corretear, correr continuamente de una parte a otra. 4. Mofar, hacer mofa de alguno.—*va.* 1. Tirar o arrojar alguna cosa con ligereza. 2. Mofar, burlar. 3. Manejar o mover velozmente.

Flirt, *s.* 1. Coqueta, cocadora. 2. Golpe o movimiento ligero; gesto, gesticulación; cualquier juego de manos ejecutado con ligereza y de repente. 3. Mueca, burla.—*a.* (Des.) Vivo, petulante; lascivo.

Flirtation [flęr-tē'-shun], *s.* 1. Coquetería. 2. (Poco us.) Movimiento ligero, ligereza.

Flit [flit], *vn.* 1. Volar, revolotear, pasar rápidamente o lanzarse de un paraje a otro. 2. En Escocia, mudar de domicilio.—*va.* (Esco.) Desposeer; hacer mudar de domicilio.

Flitch [flich], *s.* 1. Hoja de tocino; el costado del cerdo salado y ahumado. 2. Lonja o tira cortada del lado de ciertos pescados, ahumada o a propósito para ahumar. 3. (Carp.) Costera, costanera.

Flite [flait], *vn.* (Prov. Ingl. y Esco.) Reñir, regañar.—*s.* Riña.

Flitter [flit'-ęr], *s.* 1. Harapo, andrajo. 2. *V.* FLINDER. 3. Lentejuela, pedacito de metal brillante que sirve de adorno.

Flitter-mouse [flit'-ęr-maus], *s.* Murciélago, murciégalo o murceguillo.

Flitting [flit'-ing], *s.* Fuga, vuelo rápido; la acción en general del verbo *To* FLIT.—*a.* Pasajero, fugitivo, ligero.

Flix, *s.* Borrilla, pelusilla; forro blando de pieles.

Float [flōt], *vn.* 1. Flotar. 2. Fluctuar. 3. Cernerse las aves. 4. Nadar; ser sostenido o llevado por un líquido o gas.—*va.* 1. Hacer flotar o nadar, hacer sobrenadar. 2. Transportar siguiendo el curso del río. 3. (Com.) Poner en circulación; hallar venta o mercado para una cosa. 4. Estropajear, enlucir o lavar una pared estucada. 5. Inundar, cubrir de agua.

Float, *s.* 1. Cualquier cosa que flota sobre el agua; balsa, boya, masa flotante, almadía. 2. Corcho de una caña de pescar. 3. Flotador de nivel de agua. 4. Regla para pulir o allanar una pared. 5. Plataforma con ruedas que se usa en los espectáculos públicos. *Float-boards,* Tableros de rodezno de agua.

Floatable [flōt'-a-bl], *a.* Flotante, que puede flotar o ser llevado por la corriente.

Floatage [flōt'-ęj], *s.* *V.* FLOTAGE.

Floater [flōt'-er], *s.* Flotante.

Floating [flōt'-ing], *a.* 1. Flotante, boyante. 2. A flote, suelto, no anclado. 3. Movible, variable. 4. Flotante, no consolidado. *Floating debt,* Deuda flotante, *Floating dock,* Dique flotante. *Floating policy,* Póliza flotante.

Floaty [flōt'-i], *a.* Flotante.

Floccillation [flec-sil-ē'-shun], *s.* Carfologia, movimientos desordenados de las manos en el estado de delirio; síntoma grave.

Floccose [flec'-ōs], *a.* 1. (Bot.) Velludo, que tiene pelusa. 2. *V.* FLOCCULENT, 2ª acep.

Flocculence [flec'-yu-lens], *s.* 1. La calidad de ser velludo o lanudo. 2. (Ento.) Substancia blanda y semejante a la cera que excretan ciertos insectos, como los pulgones.

Flocculent [flec'-yu-lent], *a.* 1. Velludo, lanudo. 2. (Orn.) Parecido al plumón de las avecillas. 3. (Ento.) Cubierto con una substancia viscosa.

Flocculose [flec'-yu-lōs], *a.* Que tiene pelusa, algo velludo.

Flock [flec], *s.* 1. Manada, rebaño, grey. 2. Conjunto o concurrencia de muchas personas. 3. Vedija de lana. *A flock of birds,* Bandada de aves. 4. Paño deshilado. *Flock-bed,* Lecho de borra; colchón lleno de lana o crin muy desmenuzada. *Flock-paper,* Papel aterciopelado para cubrir las paredes.

Flock, *vn.* Congregarse, juntar o unirse en manadas, atroparse.

Floe [flō], *s.* Amontamiento de hielos en el mar; masa de hielo flotante.

Flog [fleg], *va.* Azotar.

Flogging [fleg'-ing], *s.* Tunda, felpa, zurra. (Prov.) Azotaina, pela. (Cuba) Monda. (Vul.) Bocabajo.

Flood [flud], *s.* 1. Gran extensión o cantidad de agua, sea mar, río ó laguna. 2. Diluvio, inundación. 3. Flujo o creciente de la mar en oposición al reflujo o menguante. 4. Menstruo excesivo. *Young flood,* Marea baja. *High flood,* Marea alta.

Flood, *va.* Inundar, anegar.

Flood-gate [flud'-gēt], *s.* Compuerta de esclusa.

Flooding [flud'-ing], *s.* Inundación. (Met.) Hemorragia uterina.

Flood lighting [flud lait'-ing], *s.* 1. Alumbrado por proyectores. 2. Luz difusa.

Flood-mark [flud'-mārc], *s.* La señal que deja el mar en el sitio más alto a donde llega en la marea alta.

Flook [flūc], *s.* (Mar.) *V.* FLUKE.

Floor [flōr], *s.* 1. Piso, suelo. 2. Piso de una casa. *The ground floor,* Planta baja, primer piso. *To ask for the floor,* Pedir la palabra.

Floor, *va.* 1. Solar, echar suelo o piso a una habitación. 2. Echar al suelo, tender en el suelo. 3. (fig.) Vencer, superar (en un debate, etc.). (fam.) Abrumar, dejar estupefacto.

Floor-cloth [flōr'-clōth], *s.* Hule para cubrir el suelo.

Flooring [flōr'-ing], *s.* Suelo, piso, pavimento.

Floorwalker [flor-wōk'-ęr], *s.* Dependiente mayor de departamento en las grandes tiendas.

Flop [flep], *va.* 1. Dar un golpe, hacer golpear. 2. Moverse, aletear. —*vn.* 1. Caer, caerse inciertamente, agitarse. V. FLAP. 2. Desplomarse, hundirse. 3. (fam.) Fracasar.—*s.* (fam.) Persona o cosa fracasada.

Flora [flō'-ra], *s.* 1. Flora, conjunto de las plantas indígenas de un país o región. 2. Flora, la diosa de las flores. 3. Flora, uno de los asteroides.

Floral [flō'-ral], *a.* Floral, perteneciente a la diosa Flora o a las flores.

Florence [fler'-ens], *s.* 1. Epecie de vino tinto que proviene de Toscana. 2. Moneda antigua de oro. 3. Tafetán delgado.

Florentine [fler'-en-tin], *s.* 1. Florentina, o Florentín, especie de tela de seda. 2. Florentino, el natural de Florencia.

Floret [flō'-ret], *s.* 1. Florecilla, cada una de las que forman una flor compuesta. 2. Cadarzo; filoseda. 3. (Ant.) Florete de esgrima.

Floriculture [flō'-ri-cul-chur], *s.* Floricultura.

Floriculturist [flō-ri-cul'-chur-ist], *s.* Floricultor.

Florid [fler'-id], *a.* 1. Vivo, brillante; encarnado, de un rojo subido. 2. Embellecido con flores de retórica. 3. Sobrecargado de adornos. 4. Florido, lleno o adornado de flores.

Floridity [flo-rid'-i-ti], **Floridness** [fler'-id-nes], *s.* Frescura de color; estilo florido.

Floridly [fler'-id-li], *adv.* Floridamente.

Floriferous [flo-rif'-ęr-us], *a.* Florífero, florígero.

Florin [fler'-in], *s.* Florín, moneda de diverso valor según los países en que corre.

Florist [flō'-rist], *s.* Florista, el que cultiva flores y las cuida; el que las vende.

Floscule [fles'-kiūl], *s.* Flósculo, cada una de las florecitas que forman una flor compuesta, como en la del girasol.

Flosculous [fles'-cu-lus], *a.* Compuesto de flores.

Floss [fles], *s.* 1. Seda floja; filoseda, la seda más fina, no torcida. 2. La borra o pelusa del maíz y de ciertas otras plantas. 3. (Fund.) Escorias que sobrenadan.

Floss-silk [fles'-silk], *s.* Seda floja, atanquía, borra de seda.

Flota [flō'-ta], *s.* (Mar.) Flota.

Flotage [flō'-tęj], *s.* 1. Flotante, lo que flota sobre el agua. 2. Propiedad de una cosa de flotar o hacer flotar a otra.

Flotation [flo-tē'-shun], *s.* 1. La acción o el estado de flotar. 2. Teoría de los cuerpos flotantes. *Line of flotation,* Línea de flotación.

Flotilla [flo-til'-a], *s.* Flotilla.

Flotsam, Flotson [flet'-sam], *s.* 1. Los géneros lanzados o arrastrados al mar desde una embarcación y que se encuentran flotando. El dueño de esos efectos no pierde su derecho de propiedad. 2. Objetos de cualquiera clase flotantes en el mar.

Flounce [flauns], *vn.* Pernear; saltar de enojo o enfado.—*va.* Guarnecer, adornar vestidos por las extremidades con algo que los hermosee.

Flounce, *s.* Fleco, flueco, farfalá, cairel. (Cuba) Vuelo. (Mex.) Olán.

Flounder [flaun'-dęr], *s.* Lenguado, pez marino de cuerpo aplanado y comestible.

Flounder [flaun'-dęr], *vn.* Patear, revolcarse en agua o cieno; revolverse, tropezar, andar de una manera incierta; se usa muchas veces en sentido figurado.—*s.* Tumbo, tropiezo.

Flour [flaur], *s.* Harina. *Fine flour,* Flor de harina o harina fina.

Flourish [flur'-ish], *vn.* 1. Florecer; gozar de prosperidad. 2. Jactarse, gloriarse, vanagloriarse. 3. Escribir haciendo rasgos y adornos con la pluma. 4. Usar un lenguaje florido; amplificar. 5. Agitar una cosa en el aire moviéndola irregularmente. 6. (Mús.) Florear, tocar sin regla determinada.—*va.* 1. Florear, blandir, mover alguna cosa con la mano con vibraciones aceleradas. 2. Exornar, embellecer. *To flourish a sword,* Vibrar una espada.

Flourish, *s.* 1. Muestra o señal de adorno; fausto, ostentación; cualquier cosa hecha exclusivamente por lucimiento y vano alarde, en especial los dibujos, rasgos, o adornos que se hacen con la pluma. 2. (Mús.) Floreo, preludio. 3. La acción de blandir.

Flourisher [flur'-ish-gr], *s.* 1. La persona que se halla en un estado floreciente o muy próspero. 2. El que hace rasgos de adorno con la pluma.

Flourishing [flur'-ish-ing], *a.* Floreciente, que florece; próspero.

Flourishingly [flur'-ish-ing-li], *adv.* Pomposamente; floridamente; prósperamente.

Floury [flaur'-i], *a.* Harinoso; que se parece a la harina, o está cubierto de ella.

Flout [flaut], *va.* Rechazar con menosprecio; hacer burla, befar, escarnecer.—*vn.* Burlarse, mofarse.

Flout, *s.* Mofa, burla, escarnio.

Flouter [flaut'-gr], *s.* Mofador; burlador.

Floutingly [flaut'-ing-li], *adv.* Insolentemente.

Flow [flō], *vn.* 1. Fluir, correr lo líquido; manar. 2. (Mar.) Crecer la marea. 3. Dimanar, proceder, provenir; seguir como consecuencia. 4. Ondear, flotar. 5. Abundar. 6. Descargar sangre, como en la menstruación.—*va.* Inundar. *The tide flows and ebbs,* Sube y baja la marea. *To flow into,* Desaguar. *To flow away,* Deslizarse, pasar. *Tears flowed from her eyes,* Las lágrimas corrían de sus ojos.

Flow, *s.* 1. (Mar.) Creciente de la marea. 2. Copia, abundancia, muchedumbre. 3. Flujo de palabras; torrente de voces.

Flower [flau'-gr], *s.* 1. Flor. 2. Flor, la parte primera y más floreciente, lo más puro, esmerado y perfecto de alguna cosa; figura retórica. 3. Flor, adorno, belleza. 4. Vigor de la edad viril. 5. *pl.* (Quím.) Flor, la parte más sutil de los cuerpos sólidos que se pega á la cabeza del aludel en forma de polvo fino al tiempo de sublimarlos. *Flower-stalk,* Pedúnculo. *Flower of an hour,* Hibisco. *Flower de luce,* Flor de lis, iris. *Eternal flower,* Perpetua. *Sunflower,* Girasol, perdiguera o flor del sol. *Sultan flower,* Especie de centaura. *Trumpet-flower,* Bignonia, arraigadora. *Wind-flower,* Anémone. *Flower-bed,* Cuadro de jardín, era. *Flower-bud,* Capullo, botón de flor. *Flower-girl,* Florera, ramilletera. *Flower-pot,* Tiesto, florero, maceta de flores. *Bed of flowers,* Lecho de flores. *She was the flower of the family,* Ella era la mejor, la más perfecta de la familia.

Flower, *vn.* 1. Florecer, echar flor los árboles y plantas. 2. Florecer, crecer en prosperidad. 3. (Ant.) Fermentar, hervir.—*va.* Florear, adornar con flores artificiales.

Flower-gentle [flau'-gr-jen'-tl], *s.* (Bot.) Especie de amaranto.

Flower-inwoven [flau'-gr-in-wōv'-n], *a.* Adornado con flores.

Flowerage [flau'-gr-ēj], *s.* 1. Acopio de flores, las flores colectivamente. 2. El acto o estado de florecer.

Floweret [flau'-gr-et], *s.* Florecilla, florecita.

Flower-garden [flau'-gr-gar'-den], *s.* Jardín de flores.

Floweriness [flau'-gr-i-nes], *s.* Abundancia de flores; floreo de palabras.

Flowering [flau'-gr-ing], *a.* Que tiene flores evidentes; fenógamo, opuesto a criptógamo.—*s.* Flor, o el conjunto de flores; también, eflorescencia, el acto o estado de florecer.

Flowering-bush [flau'-gr-ing-bush], *s.* (Bot.) Amaranto.

Flowerless [flau'-gr-les], *a.* Sin flores, que no tiene flores.

Flowery [flau'-gr-i], *a.* Florido, lleno de flores; florido, embellecido con figuras de retórica, poético.

Flowing [flō'-ing], *a.* 1. Corriente; fluctuante; que echa de sí. 2. Ondeante, movido por la brisa; colgante; pendiente, agitándose. 3. (Fig.) Fácil, suelto.—*s.* Derrame, escape de líquidos; flujo, creciente del agua.

Flowingly [flō'-ing-li], *adv.* Abundantemente.

Flowingness [flō'-ing-nes], *s.* Dicción flúida.

Flown [flōn], *pp.* del verbo *To* FLY. 1. Huído, escapado. 2. Hinchado, engreído.

Flu [flū], *s.* Influenza, gripe, resfriado.

Fluctuate [fluc'-chu-ēt], *vn.* 1. Fluctuar, ondear, undular; mover, o moverse como las olas. 2. Fluctuar, avanzar y retroceder; vacilar o dudar en la resolución de alguna cosa; estar indeciso.

Fluctuation [fluc-chu-ē'-shun], *s.* Fluctuación, irresolución, instabilidad, agitación, incertidumbre, duda.

Flue [flū], *s.* 1. Cañón o campana de chimenea, humero. 2. Cañón de órgano con efectos de flauta. 3. Flus, tubo de caldera.

Flue, Flew [flū], *s.* Pelusa, borra, polvillo que se desprende de las telas en las fábricas de tejidos.

Fluency [flū'-en-si], *s.* Fluidez; afluencia, facundia; copia, abundancia; volubilidad.

Fluent [flū'-ent], *a.* 1. Flúido, líquido. 2. Fluente, corriente. 3. Copioso, abundante. 4. Fácil.—*s.* Arroyo, agua corriente.

Fluently [flū'-ent-li], *adv.* Con afluencia, facundia o abundancia de expresiones.

Fluff [fluf], *s.* 1. Pelusa, lanilla; pelillo; vello. 2. Una cosa cualquiera vellosa o plumosa.

Fluff [fluf], *va.* 1. Mullir. 2. Olvidar un pasaje en una representación en el teatro, radio, etc.

Fluffy [fluf'-i], *a.* Que consta o está cubierto de plumón o vello; blando y suelto.

Fluid [flū'-id], *s.* 1. Flúido. 2. Flúido, suco, jugo, los humores del cuerpo humano.—*a.* Flúido.

Fluidity [flū-id'-i-ti], **Fluidness** [flū'-id-nes], *s.* Fluidez.

Fluke [flūc], *s.* 1. Lengüeta de ancla, la parte que se aferra al fondo del anclaje. 2. Cada uno de los lóbulos de la cola de la ballena. 3. (Jerga) Chiripa, bambarria en el juego de billar.

Fluke[2]. 1. Lombriz que se halla en las entrañas del ganado lanar. 2. (Ingl.) Acedía, pez de forma aplanada.

Flume [flūm], *s.* 1. Caño, conducto por lo común de madera, para llevar agua al molino, etc.; caz, canal de esclusa. 2. Cañada o paso angosto por donde sale un torrente. 3. *V.* CHUTE.

Flummery [flum'-gr-i], *s.* 1. Manjar blanco; plato ligero hecho con la harina o almidón de maíz. 2. Originalmente, jalea de harina de avena. 3. Lisonja grosera, hojarasca, patarata, cháchara.

Flung, *pret.* y *pp.* del verbo *To* FLING.

Flunk [flunk], *v.* (vul. E. U.) *va.* Faltar a la obligación; esquivar, evitar.—*vn.* Salir completamente mal; cejar, retroceder; cortarse, turbarse.

Flunky, Flunkey [flunk'-i], *s.* 1. Lacayo. 2. (Fig.) Hombre rastrero, servil.

Fluor [flū'-er], *s.* †1. Fluidez; fluido. †2. Menstruación. *Fluor-spar,* (Min.) Espato fluor.

Fluorescence [flū-o-res'-ens], *s.* Fluorescencia, la cualidad que tienen algunos cuerpos transparentes, cuando están iluminados, de despedir una luz de color diferente del suyo propio y del de la luz que los ilumina.

Fluorescent [flū-o-res'-ent], *a.* Fluorescente. *Fluorescent light,* Luz fluorescente. *Fluorescent lighting,* Alumbrado fluorescente.

Fluoric acid [flū-er'-ic as'-id], *s.* (Quím.) Ácido fluórico.

Fluorid, Fluoride [flū'-o-rid, rid o raid], *s.* (Quím.) Fluoruro.

Fluoridation [flū-ōr-i-dē'-shun], *s.* Fluoruración.

Fluorin, Fluorine [flū'-o-rin, rin o rin], *s.* Fluor, elemento gaseoso de color verde pálido.

Fluorite [flū'-o-rait], *s.* Fluorita.

Fluoroscope [flū-er'-o-scōp], *s.* Fluoróscopo, invento o aparato para observar las sombras de objetos que se hallan incluídos o contenidos en medios opacos a la luz ordinaria, pero transparentes a los rayos de Roentgen; o las sombras de objetos que en sus diferentes partes permiten el paso a los rayos de luz en grados también diferentes.

Flurry [flur'-i], *s.* 1. Ráfaga, soplo repentino de viento. 2. Prisa, precipitación; agitación, conmoción, perturbación.

Flurry, *va.* Confundir, atropellar; alarmar, poner en agitación; agitar, avergonzar.

Flush [flush], *vn.* 1. Fluir con violencia; venir precipitadamente. 2. Ponerse colorado.—*va.* 1. Abochornar, poner colorado, sonrojar. 2. Engreír, dar alas a uno para que se entone. 3. Ser causa de que la sangre se suba a la cabeza. 4. Igualar, nivelar, llenar hasta la superficie (se usa a menudo en este sentido con la palabra *up*).

Flush, *va.* Inundar con agua; echar gran cantidad de agua para limpiar las cloacas.—*vn.* 1. Salirse, arrojarse, derramarse repentinamente. 2. Llenarse de agua.

Flush, *a.* 1. Fresco, robusto, lleno de vigor; afectado. 2. Copioso, abundante; opulento, abundante en riquezas. *Flush-deck,* (Mar.) Puente corrido. 3. Nivelado, a nivel.—*s.* 1. Flujo rápido o copioso. 2. Flux, reunión de cartas o naipes de un mismo palo. 3. Copia, abundancia, afluencia. 4. Bandada de aves espantadas. 5. Frescura, rubor, bochorno. 6. Flor, florescencia.

Flushing [flush'-ing], *s.* 1. Rubor, bochorno o rubicundez de la cara. 2. Acción de echar agua para limpiar un pozo, un albañal, etc.

Fluster [flus'-ter], *va.* 1. Poner a uno colorado á fuerza de beber. 2. Confundir, atropellar; aturdirle a uno la cabeza.

Flustered [flus'-tęrd], *a.* Medio borracho, calamocano, a medio vino o a medios pelos.
Flute [flūt], *s.* 1. Flauta. 2. (Arq.) Estría. 3. Rizado, pliegue.
Flute, *va.* 1. Estriar. 2. Alechugar, rizar, plegar. (Mex.) Encarrujar.—*vn.* Tocar la flauta.
Fluting [flūt'-ing], *s.* 1. (Arq.) Estriadura, acanaladura. 2. Rizado, pliegue, como en ciertas prendas de vestir de las mujeres. 3. El acto de hacer una estría, como en una columna. 4. Conjunto de estrías.
Flutter [flut'-ęr], *vn.* 1. Revolotear. 2. Pavonearse, hacer ostentación del tren o vestidos. 3. Agitarse con movimientos o undulaciones ligeras. 4. Estar agitado; hallarse en un estado de incertidumbre; moverse sin objeto fijo o irregularmente.—*va.* 1. Desordenar o poner en desorden, como se espanta a una bandada de pájaros. 2. Cambiar sin orden alguno el sitio o lugar de una cosa. 3. Agitar, alterar el ánimo. 4. (Mar.) Flamear. 5. Crujir.
Flutter, *s.* Alboroto, tumulto, baraúnda, confusión; agitación, vibración, undulación.
Fluttering [flut'-ęr-ing], *s.* Agitación, perturbación; confusión.
Fluvial [flū'-vi-al], *a.* Fluvial, perteneciente a los ríos o formado por ellos.
Flux [flucs], *s.* 1. Flujo, el acto de fluir. 2. Cambio, mudanza. 3. Concurso, confluencia. 4. Flujo o cámaras de materia líquida; disentería. 5. Fundente, lo que mezclado con un cuerpo lo hace derretir o fundirse. 6. Derretimiento, fusión de metales.—*a.* (Ant.) Inconstante, mudable.
Flux, *va.* 1. Fundir, derretir. 2. Mezclar con un fundente.
Fluxation [fluc-sé'-shun], *s.* El acto de dejar de existir y dar lugar a otros; mudanza.
Fluxibility [fluc-si-bil'-i-ti], *s.* Fluxibilidad; fusibilidad.
Fluxion [fluc'-shun], *s.* 1. (Med.) Fluxión, acumulación de los líquidos en alguna parte del cuerpo a consecuencia de la irritación; la hinchazón dolorosa de un órgano que no llega a supuración. 2. El acto de fluir. 3. (Mat.) Cálculo diferencial.
Fluxional [fluc'-shun-al], *a.* 1. Que se refiere al cálculo diferencial. 2. Que se derrite o fluye fácilmente.
Fluxionary [fluc'-shun-ę-ri], *a.* Perteneciente al cálculo diferencial.
Fluxionist [fluc'-shun-ist], *a.* El matemático que es perito en la ciencia del cálculo diferencial.
Fly [flai], *va.* y *vn.* (*pret.* FLEW [flū], *pp.* FLOWN [flōn]). 1. Volar. 2. Volar, desaparecerse de la vista. 3. Pasar ligeramente; moverse con rapidez. 4. Separar con violencia; hacer caer una cosa separándola de otra. 5. Acometer o embestir de repente. 6. Saltar, reventar, romperse alguna cosa con estallido. 7. Huir, escapar. 8. Fluctuar, sostenerse o ser sostenido en los aires o en el agua; desplegarse. 9. Hacer volar una cometa. *To fly abroad* o *about,* Derramarse; esparcirse, propagarse. *To fly at,* Echarse encima de, arrojarse o lanzarse sobre alguno; †cazar o coger pájaros con halcón. *The woman flew at his face like a tigress,* La mujer le saltó a la cara como una tigre. *To fly away,* Volar, escaparse; dejar, abandonar. *To fly back,* Quedarse parado sin poder andar; tirar coces un caballo; refugiarse, huir de la justicia; volver las espaldas, retroceder; desdecirse. *To fly down,* Bajar volando. *To fly from,* Huir, escapar, evitar. *To fly from a danger,* Evitar un peligro. *To fly in the face,* Obrar o hacer algo atrevidamente, insultar. *To fly into a passion,* Encenderse en cólera. *To fly off,* Tomar un vuelo; desaparecer, evaporarse. *To fly off the handle,* (Fam.) Echar sapos y culebras. *To fly open,* Abrirse una cosa de repente o con violencia. *To fly to pieces,* Romperse en mil pedazos; (fig.) echar chispas o venablos. *To fly on,* Acometer violentamente. *To fly out,* Desenfrenarse, entrar en furor. *To fly to arms,* Recurrir a las armas. *Flying camp,* Campo volante. *Flying coach,* Diligencia. *With flying colours,* Con banderas desplegadas; triunfante. *To let fly,* Dejar marchar o volar; descargar, tirar; desplegar la bandera. *To let fly the top-gallant sheets,* (Mar.) Volar las escotas de los juanetes.
Fly, *s.* 1. Mosca. 2. Volante. *V.* FLYER. 3. Mosca artificial, el anzuelo cubierto de plumas, etc., que imitan un insecto. Se usa para pescar con caña. 4. Cabriolé, calesín, una especie de coche ligero. *Fly of an ensign,* (Mar.) Vuelo de bandera. *Vegetable fly,* Especie de hongo que se cría en las Indias. 5. Adulador. *Gad-fly,* Tábano. *Day-fly,* Mosca efímera. *Spanish-fly,* Cantárida. *Fly-paper,* Papel para coger o matar moscas.
Fly,[2] *s.* 1. Uno de los varios objetos, herramientas o utensilios que se mueven rápidamente por el aire: como, (1) el saca-pliegos de una prensa; (2) brazo de romana; (3) volante de un péndulo o de una máquina; (4) la parte de la veleta que indica de qué lado sopla el viento. 2. Bragueta, trampilla (de los pantalones). 3. Vuelo. *Flies,* (Teat.) Telar.
Fly-bitten [flai'-bit-n], *a.* Manchado o descolorado por las moscas.
Fly-blow [flai'-blō], *s.* Cresa, huevo de mosca.
Fly-blow, *va.* Corromper la carne llenándola de cresas.
Fly-boat [flai'-bōt], *s.* (Mar.) Flibote, especie de embarcación velera.
Fly-catcher [flai'-cach-ęr], *s.* Ave que acostumbra coger insectos al vuelo: papamoscas; moscareta. Muscicapa.
Flyer [flai'-ęr], *s.* 1. Volador. 2. Fugitivo, el que huye. 3. El volante de un torno de asar. *V.* FLIER.
Fly-fishing [flai'-fish-ing], *s.* Pesca con moscas artificiales.
Flying [flai'-ing], *pa.* 1. Volante; volador; apto para el movimiento veloz y fácil. *Flying artillery,* Artillería volante. 2. Flotante, undulante; desplegado. *Flying banners,* Banderas desplegadas o flotantes. 3. Que se extiende más allá de lo ordinario, extra. *Flying-jib,* Petifoque, cuarto foque. *Flying bridge,* Puente volante. *Flying buttress,* (Arq.) Botarel, arbotante. *Flying squadron,* Escuadra ligera.—*s.* Vuelo, el acto de volar. *To shoot flying,* Tirar al vuelo.
Flying-fish [flai'-ing-fish], *s.* Pez volador.
Flying fortress [flai'-ing fōr'-tres], *s.* Fortaleza volante o aérea.
Flying saucer [flai'-ing se'-ser], *s.* Plato volador, disco luminoso volador.
Fly-leaf [flai'-lîf], *s.* Guarda de un libro.
Fly-net [flai'-net], *s.* 1. Red que llevan los caballos para librarlos de las moscas. 2. Mosquitero.
Fly-speck [flai'-spec], *s.* Punto o mancha diminuta que hace el excremento de la mosca u otro insecto: cualquiera cosa insignificante.
Flyweight [flai'-wêt], *s.* (Boxeo) Peso mosca.
Fly-wheel [flai'-hwîl], *s.* Rueda volante, voladora.
Foal [fōl], *s.* Potro; potrillo; buche, el borrico mientras mama. *To be in foal* o *with foal,* Estar preñada la yegua, burra, o camella.
Foal, *va* y *vn.* Parir una yegua o una burra; dar crías, producir potrillos o buches; procrear.
Foal-foot [fōl'-fut], *s. V.* COLTSFOOT.
Foam [fōm], *s.* Espuma. *Foam rubber,* Hule espuma.
Foam, *vn.* 1. Espumar, criar o echar espuma. 2. Echar espumarajos por la boca, estar colérico.—*va.* Arrojar espuma.
Foamy [fōm'-i], *a.* Espumajoso, espumoso.
Fob [fob], *s.* Faltriquera pequeña, como la del reloj.
Fob, *va.* Engañar, defraudar, pegársela a uno; disimular.
F.O.B. [ef ō bî], (Abreviatura de *Free on board*) *a.* y *adv.* L.A.B. Libre a bordo.
Focal [fō'-cal], *a.* Focal, que pertenece al foco; céntrico. *Focal distance* o *length,* Distancia focal, punto donde convergen los rayos luminosos.
Focus [fō'-cus], *s.* Foco, el punto céntrico en que se unen muchos rayos de luz en un espejo u otro cuerpo.
Focus, *va.* Enfocar, afocar, acomodar en foco; poner en foco, hallar el foco. *Focusing-screen,* Pantalla o visera para poner en foco una imagen.
Fodder [fod'-ęr], *s.* Forraje, alimento basto a propósito para los ganados.
Fodder, *va.* Dar forraje a las bestias.
Fodderer [fod'-ęr-ęr], *s.* Forrajeador.
Foe [fō], *s.* Enemigo, perseguidor, antagonista, adversario.
Foelike [fō'-laic], *a.* Que obra o procede con enemistad; como un enemigo, hostil.
Foeman [fō'-man], *s.* Enemigo, antagonista.
Fœtus [fî'-tus], *s.* Feto, la criatura que está perfectamente formada en el vientre de su madre.
Fog [fog], *s.* 1. Niebla, neblina, bruma, calina. 2. Extravío, confusión perplejidad. 3. (Foto.) Niebla o capa que obscurece una plancha revelada. *Fog-horn,* Sirena.
Fog, *va.* 1. Obscurecer; en sentido fotográfico, cubrir como con una niebla.—*vn.* 1. Hacerse brumoso, nebuloso. 2. (Foto.) Hacerse indistinto por una capa o película que obscurece. 3. En Escocia, criar musgo.
Fog, Fogge, Foggage [fog, fog'-êj], *s.* 1. La segunda cosecha de hierba de una estación; también, hierba seca que permanece en el campo durante el invierno. 2. (Esco.) Musgo.

Fogbank [feg'-bank], *s.* Neblina sobre el mar.
Foggily [feg-i-li], *adv.* Obscuramente, con nieblas; brumosamente.
Fogginess [feg'-i-nes], *s.* La obscuridad que produce la niebla.
Foggy [feg'-i], *a.* 1. Nebuloso, brumoso, lleno de nieblas. 2. (Bot.) Mohoso, lleno de musgo. 3. (Foto.) Obscurecido como por niebla.
Fogy [fō'-gi], *s.* Vejestorio, persona de ideas anticuadas.
Fogyism [fō'-gi-izm], *s.* Obscurantismo, afición a las ideas anticuadas.
Foh! [fō], *inter.* ¡Quita allá! expresión de enojo o disgusto.
Foible [fei'-bl], *s.* 1. Debilidad, el flaco; defecto leve de carácter. 2. La porción de una espada o de un florete desde el medio hasta la punta.
Foil [feil], *va.* 1. Hacer nulo, vano; frustrar, deshacer al enemigo aunque sin ganar una completa victoria. 2. Embotar; adormecer.
Foil, *s.* 1. Hoja delgada de metal; pan, u hoja de oro o plata para dorar o platear. 2. Hoja de estaño, la que se pone a un espejo por medio del azogue. 3. El fondo del diamante u otra piedra preciosa, la lentejuela puesta para aumentar el brillo; de aquí, contraste, todo lo que da realce a alguna cosa. 4. (Arq.) Hoja, lóbulo. 5. Florete, espada que se usa en la esgrima.
Foil, *s.* 1. Huella, pista, rastro que deja la caza. 2. Caída imperfecta en la lucha cuerpo a cuerpo. 3. (Des.) Chasco, suceso contrario o adverso.
Foilable [feil'-a-bl], *a.* Vencible; lo que se puede inutilizar o deshacer.
Foiler [feil'-ẹr], *s.* Frustrador.
†**Foin** [fein], *vn.* Dar estocadas en la esgrima.—*va.* Punzar, aguijonear.
Foin, *s.* 1. Garduña, fuina. 2. (Des.) Estocada, golpe dado con la punta de la espada o florete.
Foist [feist], *va.* Insertar alguna voz o cláusula subrepticiamente en un escrito; meterse, introducirse sin razón (seguido de *into* o *upon*). *To foist a candidate upon a party*, Imponer injustamente un candidato a un partido.
Foister [feist'-ẹr], *s.* Falsificador, mentiroso.
Fold [fōld], *s.* 1. Redil, el cercado o corral para encerrar ovejas; hato de ganado lanar; y (fig.) una iglesia o la totalidad de la Iglesia cristiana. 2. Doblez, pliegue, plegadura. 3. Otro tanto. 4. (Des.) Límite, lindero. *Twofold*, Duplo. *Fourfold*, Cuádruplo.
Fold, *va.* 1. Doblar, plegar. 2. Poner una cosa junto a otra, ajustar. 3. Abrazar, enlazar; cerrar, incluir. 4. Envolver, encerrar. 5. Encerrar ganado lanar en el redil; incluir.—*vn.* Doblarse o plegarse una cosa sobre otra, como las vidrieras y puertas plegadizas de dos hojas, ciertas persianas, etc. *To fold the arms*, Cruzar los brazos. *To fold a letter*, Doblar una carta.
Folder [fōld'-ẹr], *s.* 1. Plegador, doblador. 2. Plegadera. 3. Folleto, mapa, etc., plegadizo en forma compacta.
Folderol [fel'-dẹ-rel], *a.* Absurdo, desatinado.—*s.* Desatino, pampirolada, pamplingada.
Folding [fōld'-ing], *a.* Plegadizo, dobladizo.—*s.* 1. La acción de plegar o doblar. 2. El acto de cerrar ganado lanar en tierra labrantía. *Folding door*, Puerta de dos hojas o plegadiza. *Folding camera, folding chair*, Cámara, silla plegadiza. *Folding-machine*, Máquina de plegar, plegadora mecánica. *Folding screen*, Biombo.
Fold-net [fōld'-net], *s.* Arañuelo, red muy delgada para coger pájaros por la noche.
Foliaceous [fō-li-ē'-shus], *a.* 1. Foliáceo, de la naturaleza o forma de una hoja. 2. Laminado, que se presenta en láminas, como ciertos minerales.
Foliage [fō'-li-ẹj], *s.* 1. Follaje, frondosidad. 2. Ramillete de hojas, flores y ramas. 3. Follaje, adorno de escultura y arquitectura.
Foliate [fō'-li-ēt], *va.* 1. Batir hojas de oro, plata u otro metal. 2. Azogar un espejo.
Foliation [fo-li-ē'-shun], *s.* 1. El acto de batir las hojas de oro, plata u otro metal. 2. (Bot.) Foliación, la disposición que guardan las hojas en las plantas. 3. El acto de desenvolverse, salir o apuntar las hojas. 4. Laminación.
Foliature [fō'-li-a-chur], *s.* *V.* FOLIATION en todas sus acepciones.
Folio [fō'-li-o o fōl'-yo], *s.* 1. Infolio, libro o tomo en folio. 2. (Com.) Hoja, folio, página numerada de un libro o registro.
Folk [fōc o folk], *s.* 1. (Fam.) Gente, personas, el género humano. 2. Nación, raza, pueblo (raramente usado en plural). 3. *pl.* La gente; (fam. E. U.) parentesco, parientes, los que son de la misma familia. *Old folks*, Viejos o gente vieja. *I never saw such folks*, Nunca he visto gente semejante. *What will folks say?* ¿Qué dirá la gente?
Folklore [fōc'-lōr], *s.* Folklore, conjunto de las tradiciones, creencias y costumbres populares.
Folk music [fōc miū'-zic], *s.* Música folklórica.
Folk song [fōc sōng], *s.* Canto folklórico, canción o balada folklórica.
Follicle [fel'-i-cl], *s.* 1. (Anat.) Folículo, un saquito o cuerpo pequeño membranoso cuyas paredes secretan un flúido que se derrama por la abertura diminuta que hay en uno de sus extremos. 2. (Bot.) Folículo, hollejo. 3. (Ento.) Capullo.
Follicular [fel-lic'-yu-lar], *a.* Folicular; foliculoso, que tiene o produce folículos.
Follow [fel'-ō], *va.* 1. Seguir, ir detrás de alguien; moverse, andar detrás de alguno en la misma dirección; acompañar, escoltar, ir en compañía. 2. Seguir, venir después, suceder en orden o tiempo. 3. Perseguir. 4. Imitar; obedecer, copiar. 5. Obrar conforme a; ponerse de parte de; tener, sostener las mismas opiniones. 6. Aplicarse, dedicarse a; cuidar sus asuntos; poner en práctica. 7. Observar, tener en vista o en la mente. 8. Resultar, ser consecuencia de algo. 9. Procurar obtener lo que se desea.—*vn.* 1. Seguir, venir una persona o cosa tras otra. 2. Seguirse, suceder y continuarse una cosa a otra. 3. Seguirse, originarse, resultar, provenir. *To follow the law*, Estudiar el derecho. *To follow one's business*, Cuidar de sus negocios. *To follow one's pleasures*, Abandonarse a los placeres. *To follow again*, Volver a seguir. *It follows*, Síguese, resulta, la consecuencia de eso es. *As follows*, Como sigue. *To follow up*, Continuar, proseguir. *To follow on*, Continuar prosiguiendo, perseverar.
Follower [fel'-o-ẹr], *s.* 1. Seguidor; acompañante. 2. Dependiente, criado. 3. Discípulo; imitador, copiador; secuaz, partidario; obsequiante, amante; adherente, allegado, compañero. *Followers, pl.* Comitiva.
Follow-up [fel'-ō-up], *s.* Recordatorio, continuidad. *Follow-up system*, Sistema de cartas recordatorias para la correspondencia comercial, etc.
Folly [fel'-i], *s.* 1. Tontería, ignorancia, extravagancia, locura, patochada, bobería; disparate en lo que se hace o dice. 2. (Des.) Vicio, falta de rectitud. 3. Ligereza, debilidad, indiscreción, fragilidad.
Foment [fo-ment'], *va.* 1. Fomentar, dar calor natural o artificial; dar baños calientes. 2. Fomentar, proteger, patrocinar. 3. Provocar, excitar, instigar a la violencia.
Fomentation [fo-men-tē'-shun], *s.* 1. Fomentación, fomento. 2. Excitación, provocación, instigación.
Fomenter [fo-ment'-ẹr], *s.* Fomentador, instigador.
Fond [fend], *a.* 1. Apasionado, demasiadamente indulgente; enloquecido, atontado o loco de contento. 2. Afectuoso, amoroso, cariñoso. 3. Loco, vano, imprudente, extravagante, frívolo. 4. (Ant.) Disparatado, indiscreto. *To be fond of*, Gustar extraordinariamente de alguna cosa, estar apasionado, enamorado o loco por ella. *A fond mother*, Una madre cariñosa.
Fondle [fend'-l], *va.* Mimar, hacer caricias y halagos a alguno.
Fondler [fend'-lẹr], *s.* Mimador. (Fam.) Mimón.
Fondling [fend'-ling], *s.* 1. Favorito, querido; niño mimado o mal criado. 2. Tonto.
Fondly [fend'-li], *adv.* Locamente, cariñosamente.
Fondness [fend'-nes], *s.* 1. (Ant.) Tontería, locura, debilidad. 2. Terneza, pasión loca, apego poco racional; inclinación, afición, pasión por alguna cosa.
Fonetic, *a.* *V.* PHONETIC.
Font [fent], *s.* 1. (< A.-S. fant < Lat. fon(t)s) Pila de bautismo. 2. Fuente o manantial. 3. (< F. fonte) Fundición, todo el surtido de caracteres de imprenta de un mismo grado.
Fontanel [fen''-ta-nel'], *s.* 1. (Anat.) Fontanela, cada uno de los espacios que, en los niños recién nacidos, median entre algunos huesos del cráneo hasta que se completa su osificación. 2. (Ant.) Fuente. *V.* ISSUE.
Food [fūd], *s.* 1. Alimento, comida; vituallas, víveres; pasto de los animales. 2. Lo que alimenta, mantiene activo o sostiene. *To give food for*, Dar materia para.
Foodful [fūd'-ful], *a.* Fértil, fructífero.
Foodless [fūd'-les], *a.* Estéril, infructuoso.
Foodstuffs [fūd'-stufs], *s. pl.* Comestibles.
Fool [fūl], *s.* 1. Insensato, bobo, idiota, mentecato; tonto, necio. 2. Persona de pocos alcances, sin llegar a ser bobo o idiota. 3. Bufón.

truhán, chocarrero. *To play the fool,* Hacer el bobo. *To make a fool of one,* Mofarse de alguno, hacer burla de él; frustrar. 4. (Teol.) Malvado. 5. Hazmerreir, el que es objeto de la irrisión de otros. Lo mismo significa *April fool. Fool* o *gooseberry fool,* Manjar hecho de grosellas cocidas con crema o nata y azúcar.

Fool, *vn.* Tontear, divertirse, chancear, juguetear diciendo o haciendo tonterías.—*va.* 1. Despreciar, chasquear; infatuar, entontecer. 2. Engañar, defraudar, chupar. *To fool one with promises,* Traer entretenido o embaucado a alguno con vanas esperanzas. *To fool one of his money,* Pelar o desollar a uno, robarle el dinero.

Foolery [fūl'-ẹr-i], *s.* Tontería, bobada, bobería.

†**Fool-happy** [fūl'-hap-i], *a.* Feliz por casualidad y sin haber puesto nada por su parte para serlo.

Foolhardiness [fūl-hard'-i-nes], *s.* Temeridad, locura.

Foolhardy [fūl'-hard-i], *a.* Arrojado, temerariamente audaz, locamente arriesgado.

Foolish [fūl'-ish], *a.* 1. Fatuo, loco, escaso de juicio. 2. Bobo, tonto, indiscreto; malvado, necio.

Foolishly [fūl'-ish-li], *adv.* Fatuamente, bobamente, sin juicio.

Foolishness [fūl'-ish-nes], *s.* Tontería, necedad, bobería.

Foolproof [fūl'-prūf], *a.* Muy sencillo, fácil, a prueba de inexpertos.

Foolscap [fūlz'-cap], *s.* Papel ministro; papel de escribir plegado de modo que haga páginas de casi 13 por 8 pulgadas.

Fool-trap [fūl'-trap], *s.* Engañabobos.

Foot [fut], *s.* (*pl.* FEET). 1. Pie; pata (en los animales). *Hind foot,* Pata trasera. *From head to foot,* De pies a cabeza. 2 Pie, la parte inferior de alguna cosa; base. 3. (Mil.) Infantería; en este sentido no tiene plural. 4. Pie, fundamento, principio o escalón para adquirir otra cosa o ascender a ella. 5. Pie, medida de doce pulgadas, equivalente a 3.05 decímetros. 6. Paso, movimiento, acción. 7. Pie, cierto número de sílabas que constituyen parte de un verso. *On* o *by foot,* A pie. *The enemy disputed the ground foot by foot,* Los enemigos disputaron el campo palmo a palmo. *On foot,* (1) De pie o a pie. (2) En estado de salud, activo. (3) Que va adelantando. *To be on foot,* Estar haciendo alguna cosa; organizarse. *To know the length of one's foot,* Conocer a uno, o comprenderle bien; saber los puntos que calza. *To put one's best foot foremost,* (Fam.) Esmerarse, hacer lo más que se pueda. *To put one's foot down,* (Fam.) Expresarse firmemente; tomar una resolución determinada. *To put one's foot in it,* Hacer un pan como unas hostias, estar con el agua a la boca; hallarse en dificultades, por error o intervención oficiosa. *To set on foot,* Poner en pie, empezar. *Under foot,* (1) Debajo de los pies. (2) (Fig.) En el camino (formando obstáculo); también, en poder de. *To trample* o *tread under foot,* Pisotear.

Foot, *vn.* 1. Bailar, saltar, brincar, andar a pie. 2. (Fam.) Sumar guarismos.—*va.* 1. Patear, tirar coces; pisar o pisotear. 2. Establecer, fijar; poner pies a alguna cosa. 3. (Fam. E. U.) Pagar una cuenta; pagar las costas. 4. Sumar una columna de guarismos y poner la suma al pie.

Foot-ball [fut'-bōl], *s.* 1. Pelota o balón para jugar con los pies. 2. Juego en que dos partidos opuestos procuran llevar la pelota más allá de una meta o término.

Foot-band [fut'-band], *s.* Destacamento de infantería.

Foot-boy [fut'-boi], *s.* Volante, lacayo.

Foot-breadth [fut'-bredth], *s.* El espacio o lugar que puede cubrir un pie.

Foot-bridge [fut'-brij], *s.* Puente angosto por el que pueden pasar solamente gentes a pie.

Foot-cloth [fut'-clōth], *s.* Gualdrapa.

Footed [fut'-ed], *a.* Formado como un pie.

Footfall [fut'-fōl], *s.* El sonido de un paso; paso, pisada.

Foot-fight [fut'-fait], *s.* Batalla de a pie.

Foot-guards [fut'-gārdz], *s. pl.* Guardias del rey que sirven a pie.

Foothill [fut'-hil], *s.* Cerro al pie de una montaña.

Foothold [fut'-hōld], *s.* 1. Paraje o espacio en que cabe el pie; pie, fundamento seguro; posición establecida. *To lose one's foothold,* Resbalar. 2. Chanclo de goma que no cubre el talón.

Footing [fut'-ing], *s.* 1. Pie, base, fundamento, lugar donde se pone el pie. 2. Piso, paso; baile, danza. 3. Establecimiento, estado, condición, posición fija. 4. Pie, fundamento, estribo, zócalo saliente. 5. Suma de una columna. 6. El acto de añadir un pie a alguna cosa. *On a war footing,* Bajo pie de guerra. *We are on equal footing,* Somos o estamos iguales.

Footless, *a.* *V.* FEETLESS.

Foot-lights [fut'-laits], *s. pl.* Candilejas, línea de luces en el proscenio del teatro.

Foot-loose [fut'-lūs], *a.* Libre, sin restricciones ni obligaciones.

Footman [fut'-man], *s.* 1. Lacayo. 2. *V.* FOOT-SOLDIERS.

Footmark [fut'-mārk], *s.* *V.* FOOTPRINT.

Foot-note [fut'-nōt], *s.* Anotación debajo de un escrito, nota al pie.

Foot-pace [fut'-pēs], *s.* Descanso de escalera; paso lento o corto.

Foot-path [fut'-path], *s.* Senda, vereda; acera.

Foot-post [fut'-pōst], *s.* Correo de a pie.

Footprint [fut'-print], *s.* Huella, pisada, vestigio, impresión del pie.

Footrest [fut'-rest], *s.* Escabel, banco para descansar los pies.

Foot-rule [fut'-rūl], *s.* Regla o medida de doce pulgadas.

Foot-soldier [fut-sōl'-jẹr], *s.* Soldado que marcha y pelea a pie.

Footsore [fut'-sor], *a.* Que tiene los pies doloridos o lastimados de tanto andar.

Foot-stalk [fut'-stōc], *s.* (Bot.) Pedúnculo.

Foot-stall [fut'-stōl], *s.* Estribo de mujer para montar.

Footstep [fut'-step], *s.* 1. Paso, la acción del pie al andar; sonido de un paso. 2. Paso, vestigio, señal, indicio, huella.

Foot-stool [fut'-stūl], *s.* Escabelo, escabel, tarimilla.

Footway [fut'-wē], *s.* Sendero.

Footwear [fut'-wār], *s.* Calzado.

Footwork [fut'-wurk], *s.* 1. Movimiento de los pies en el boxeo, el baile, juego de futbol, etc. 2. (fam.) Trabajo que se hace a pie para alguna investigación periodística.

Footworn [fut'-wōrn], *a.* Estropeado por el paso de los pies. *Footworn carpet,* Alfombra gastada por las pisadas. *Footworn traveler,* Viajero cansado de caminar.

Fop [fop], *s.* 1. Petimetre, pisaverde, currutaco, lechuguino. 2. Presumido, casquivano.

Fopling [fop'-ling], *s.* Petimetrillo.

Foppish [fop'-ish], *a.* Vano, ocioso; vanidoso, afectado, presumido.

For [fōr], *prep.* (Palabra de muy amplia aplicación; indica por lo general la razón de un acto o el objeto que se procura o desea.) 1. Por, a causa de. 2. En vista de. en consideración a; con respecto o con relación a; en cuanto a. 3. Para; lo que indica el objeto, el destino o la tendencia. 4. En busca de, según lo que, hacia; en favor o en provecho de; por motivo de; en honor o por el nombre de. 5. Con destino a. *Bound for Vera Cruz,* Destinado a Veracruz. 6. Al grado, punto o número de; en lugar, en vez de; en concepto de. 7. A pesar de. 8. Mientras, durante; desde; por (en sentido futuro).—*conj.* 1. Porque, para que; pues. 2. Por cuanto, en atención a que. *As for me,* Tocante a mí. *For as much,* Respecto a, en cuanto a, por lo tocante a. *For why?* ¿Por qué, para qué? ¿a qué? *For fear,* De miedo. *For pity,* De lástima. *For the present,* Por ahora. *It is impossible for me to do it,* No puedo hacerlo, o me es imposible hacerlo. *For all that,* A pesar de eso; con todo eso. *For ever,* Por o para siempre. *I took it for granted,* Lo tomé por dicho, o por concedido. *To serve for,* Servir de. *For the last five years of his life,* Durante los últimos cinco años de su vida. *For the time to come,* En lo venidero, en lo futuro. *For aught,* En lo que, a lo que. *It is true for aught that I know,* Es verdad a lo que creo. *But for,* Si no fuese por, a no ser por. *I should do it but for her,* Lo haría, si no fuese por ella. *Thus much for,* Esto por lo que a tal o cual cosa se refiere. *For shame!* ¡Qué vergüenza! *For God's sake!* ¡Por Dios, por amor de Dios! *Oh! for better times!* ¡Oh! vengan tiempos mejores! *A remedy for headache,* Un remedio para el dolor de cabeza.

For-. Prefijo que equivale a re- o muy. *Forbreak,* Hacer añicos. *Forspend,* Cansar al extremo, agotar. †*Fordry,* Reseco.

Forage [for'-ẹj], *vn.* 1. Forrajear, andar vagando en busca de forraje, particularmente en tiempo de guerra. 2. Proveer de forraje.—*va.* Recorrer una comarca para obtener forraje y víveres.

Forage, *s.* Forraje, toda especie de alimento para el ganado, particularmente para los caballos en tiempo de guerra.

Forager [for'-ẹj-ẹr], *s.* Forrajeador, (ant.) forrajero.

Foraminifera [fo-ram″-i-nif′-e-ra], *s.pl.* Foraminíferos, protozoarios que forman el primer orden de la clase de los rizópodos. Son todos microscópicos y comprenden las especies primeras que aparecieron en el mundo.
Foraminous [fō-ram′-i-nus], *a.* Agujereado, lleno de agujeros.
Foray [fer′-ê], *s.* Correría, irrupción; saqueo, pillaje.—*va.* Saquear, pillar, despojar.
Forbade [for-bad′], *pret.* del verbo FORBID.
Forbear [fēr-bār′] *vn.* (*pret.* FORBORE [fer-bōr′], *pp.* FORBORNE [fer-bōrn′]). 1. Pararse, detenerse, cesar, interrumpirse. 2. Abstenerse, dejar de, reprimirse, guardarse. 3. (Ant.) Tener paciencia, contenerse. *I can not forbear laughing at it,* No puedo menos de reirme de ello.—*va.* 1. Omitir, dejar de hacer; evitar, abstenerse de; aguantar. 2. Tratar con dulzura.
Forbearance [fēr-bār′-ans], *s.* 1. El acto de evitar y precaver que suceda alguna cosa, antiguamente evitación. 2. Intermisión, interrupción. 3. Cachaza. 4. Dulzura, suavidad, paciencia, indulgencia, clemencia.
Forbearer [fēr-bar′-er], *s.* El que interrumpe o evita.
Forbearing [fer-bār′-ing], *a.* Paciente, indulgente; dispuesto a abstenerse.
Forbid [fēr-bid′], *va.* (*pret.* FORBADE, *pp.* FORBIDDEN, algunas veces también FORBID). 1. Prohibir, vedar; mandar que no se haga una cosa, o la abstención de ella. 2. Impedir, estorbar. *God forbid,* Dios no quiera, no permita Dios.—*vn.* Prohibir.
Forbiddance [fer-bid′-ans], *s.* (Poco us) Prohibición.
Forbiddenly [fer-bid′-n-li], *adv.* Ilícitamente.
Forbiddenness [fer-bid′-n-nes], *s.* La calidad que hace a una cosa digna de prohibición.
Forbidder [fer-bid′-er], *s.* El que prohibe.
Forbidding [fer-bid′-ing], *a.* Aborrecible, repugnante.—*s.* Obstáculo, oposición.
Forbore, *pret.* del verbo *To* FORBEAR.
Forby [for″-bai′], *adv.* y *prep.* (Esco.) 1. Además, a más de esto, fuera que. 2. (Irlan.) Cerca de, más allá de.
Force [fōrs], *s.* 1. Fuerza, vigor, robustez, energía, virtud, poder, eficacia; firmeza de las leyes. 2. Fuerza, violencia, agravio. 3. Toda causa de movimiento. 4. Fuerzas, las armadas y ejércitos de un estado. 5. Necesidad, precisión, hado, destino. *Electromotive force,* Fuerza electromotriz. *Main force,* Fuerza mayor. *Motive, moving force,* Fuerza motriz. *Force pump,* Bomba impelente. *Tensile force,* Fuerza de tensión.
Force, *va.* 1. Forzar, violentar; obligar o precisar por fuerza; coger alguna cosa a la fuerza. 2. Impeler, esforzar; constreñir. 3. Forzar, entrar y sujetar a fuerza de armas alguna plaza. 4. Forzar, dominar por la fuerza; y de aquí, violar, conocer a una mujer carnalmente contra su voluntad. 5. Mechar, rellenar, tratándose de guisados. 6. (Hort.) Forzar, apresurar, hacer madurar temprano. 7. Afinar, purificar los vinos. 8. (Des.) Reforzar un puesto, una guarnición, etc., con soldados. *To force along,* Hacer avanzar o adelantar. *To force away,* Obligar a alejarse. *To force back,* Rechazar, hacer retroceder. *To force down,* Obligar a bajar. *To force from,* Obligar a salir, echar de alguna parte. *To force in,* Clavar, meter un clavo, una espada, etc., romper, penetrar por un escuadrón o por un gentío; entrar por fuerza. *To force out,* Arrancar, sacar u obtener por fuerza o con violencia; hacer prorrumpir en; obligar a salir de alguna parte. *To force up,* Hacer subir por fuerza.
Forced [fōrst], *pp.* y *a.* Forzado, hecho con gran esfuerzo; afectado, exagerado, opuesto a lo natural.
Forcedly [fōrs′-ed-li], *adv.* Forzadamente, de una manera forzada; de un modo contrario a lo natural.
Forcedness [fōrs′-ed-nes], *s.* Constreñimiento, compulsión, apremio.
Forceful [fōrs′-ful], *a.* 1. Fuerte, potente, poderoso. 2. Dado o impelido por la violencia; violento.
Forcefully [fōrs′-ful-i], *adv.* Forzosamente; violentamente.
Forceless [fōrs′-les], *a.* Endeble, débil.
Forcemeat [fōrs′-mît], *s.* Relleno, embutido, salpicón. (Voz culinaria.)
Forceps [fōr′-seps], *s.* Fórceps, pinzas, tenaza. *Artery forceps,* (Cir.) Pinzas de torsión. *Bullet forceps,* Sacabalas. *Dressing forceps,* Pinzas de curación. *Obstetrical forceps,* Fórceps de comadrón, muy usado en los partos laboriosos. *Stage forceps,* Pinzas para la plataforma del microscopio.
Forcer [fōrs′-er], *s.* 1. Forzador; vencedor. 2. Lo que fuerza, impele o violenta. 3. Émbolo, el macho de la bomba impelente.
Forcible [fōrs′-i-bl], *a.* 1. Fuerte, potente; eficaz, poderoso; violento. 2. Enérgico; de gran peso; concluyente; obligatorio.
Forcibleness [fōrs′-i-bl-nes], *s.* Fuerza, violencia.
Forcibly [fōrs′-i-bli], *adv.* Fuertemente, forzadamente; violentamente, por fuerza.
Forcing [fōrs′-ing], *a.* y *gerundio* de FORCE. 1. Impelente. 2. Madurador; clarificador del vino por un procedimiento rápido.—*s.* La acción del verbo *To* FORCE en cualquier sentido. *Forcing-bed, V.* HOT-BED. *Forcing-house,* Invernadero para apresurar el desarrollo de las plantas o hacer salir las flores antes del tiempo natural.
Forcipate [fēr′-si-pêt], *a.* Lo que tiene figura de pinzas o tenazas.
Forcipation [fēr-si-pê′-shun], *s.* El acto de atenacear o despedazar con tenazas; uno de los castigos que usaban antiguamente.
Ford [fōrd], *s.* 1. Vado. 2. (Ant.) Corriente de agua; embarcadero.
Ford, *va.* Vadear.
Fordable [fōrd′-a-bl], *a.* Vadeable.
Fordo [fōr-dū′], *va.* 1. (Poét.) Cansar. 2. (Des.) Arruinar.
Fore [fōr], *a.* Anterior, delantero. *Fore foot,* Pata delantera.—*adv.* 1. Anteriormente, delante, antes. 2. (Mar.) De proa. *Fore and aft,* De popa a proa.
Fore-. Prefijo que significa: (a) delante, ante, antes; (b) por, a causa de, en razón a; (c) en vez de.
Foreallege [fōr-al-lej′], *va.* Citar o mencionar antes.
Foreappoint [fōr-ap-peint′], *vn.* Preordinar.
Foreappointment [fōr-a-peint′-ment], *s.* Preordinación, predestinación.
Forearm [fōr′-arm], *s.* Antebrazo, la parte del brazo que media entre el codo y la mano.
Forearm [fōr-ārm′], *va.* Preparar, aparejar y disponer con anticipación armas y pertrechos. *Forewarned, forearmed,* Hombre prevenido vale por dos.
Forebay [fōr′-bê], *s.* 1. Bocal, canalizo, abertura por donde sale el agua a una rueda hidráulica. 2. La enfermería de un buque.
Forebode [fōr-bōd′], *vn.* y *va.* Pronosticar, saber de antemano, particularmente lo malo, enojoso o desagradable; presentir, antever; presagiar, indicar. (Fam.) *My heart forebodes it,* Me lo dice el corazón.
Forebodement [fōr-bōd′-ment], *s.* (Poco us.) Presentimiento, presagio.
Foreboder [fōr-bōd′-er], *s.* Adivino o pronosticador, generalmente de mal agüero.
Foreboding [fōr-bōd′-ing], *s.* Presentimiento, presagio. (Fam.) Corazonada.
Foreby [fōr-bai′], *prep. V.* FORBY, 2ª.
Forecast [fōr-cast′], *va.* y *vn.* 1. Proyectar, formar o disponer proyectos; arreglar, preparar o trazar de antemano la ejecución de una cosa. 2. Prever, ver con anticipación, conocer o conjeturar de antemano. 3. Predecir, pronosticar
Forecast [fōr′-cast], *s.* 1. Previsión, penetración. 2. Proyecto, idea, plan trazado de antemano. 3. Pronóstico, pronosticación. *Weather forecast,* Pronóstico del tiempo.
Forecaster [fōr-cast′-er], *s.* 1. Previsor; en especial, el observador que predice las condiciones y los fenómenos atmosféricos. 2. El que traza, proyecta o forma la idea de una cosa que se ha de ejecutar después.
Forecastle [fōr′-cas-l o (Mar.) fōc′-sl], *s.* (Mar.) Castillo de proa.
Forechosen [fōr-chōz′-n], *pp.* Preelegido.
Forecited [fōr-sait′-ed], *a.* Precitado, ya citado, arriba citado.
Foreclose [fōr-clōz′], *va.* Cerrar, impedir el paso, excluir; en especial, (for.) vender por orden judicial la cosa hipotecada o privar judicialmente del derecho de redimirla.
Foreclosure [fōr-clō′-zhur], *s.* (For.) Exclusión del derecho de redimir la cosa hipotecada.
Foredate [fōr′-dêt], *va. V* ANTEDATE.
Foredeck [fōr-dec′], *s.* (Mar.) Proa, la parte delantera del navío.
Foredesign [fōr-de-zain′], *va.* Prevenir, proyectar.
Foredoom [fōr-dūm′], *va.* Predestinar, predeterminar.
Fore end [fōr end′], *s.* Delantera, la parte anterior de alguna cosa.
Forefather [fōr′-fā-dher], *s.* Abuelo, ascendiente, antecesor.
Forefinger [fōr′-fin-ger], *s.* Índice, el dedo segundo de la mano.
Forefoot [fōr′-fut], *s.* 1. Mano, pie delantero de cualquier cuadrúpedo. 2. (Mar.) Gorja, tajamar.
Forefront [fōr′-frunt], *s.* La parte más adelantada; la primera fila, el primer puesto. *The forefront of a*

battle, Lo más recio de una batalla.
Foreganger [fōr'-gang-ẹr], *s.* 1. Predecesor. 2. Cuerda de arpón.
Forego [fōr-gō'], *va.* (*pret.* FOREWENT, *pp.* FOREGONE). 1. Ceder, renunciar, perder; hacer dimisión de algo. 2. Anteceder, preceder.
Foregoer [fōr-gō'-ẹr], *s.* Abuelo, progenitor; precursor; el que hace cesión.
Foregoing [fōr-gō'-ing], *s.* Precedente; el que va delante.
Foregone [fōr-gōn'], *pp.* y *a.* Predeterminado, decidido de antemano.
Foreground [fōr'-graund], *s.* Delantera, primer plano, la parte del campo de una pintura que parece estar próximo al que mira.
Forehand [fōr'-hand], *s.* Cuarto delantero del caballo.—*a.* (Esco.) Delantero, hacia adelante.
Forehanded [fōr'-hand-ed], *a.* 1. Temprano, lo que se hace o sucede antes del tiempo ordinario; hecho en tiempo oportuno. 2. (E. U.) Que tiene dinero ahorrado; poseedor de recursos o bienes.
Forehead [fer'-ed], *s.* 1. Frente, el espacio que hay en el rostro desde las cejas hasta el cabello. 2. Descaro, desvergüenza, insolencia.
Forehew [fōr-hiū'], *va.* Cortar alguna cosa por la parte anterior o delantera.
Forehorse [fōr'-hōrs], *s.* (Des.) Caballo delantero.
Foreign [fer'-ẹn], *a.* 1. Extranjero, que pertenece a otra nación, o que tiene relación con otros países. 2. Exótico, exterior; que procede de otro país. 3. Extraño, advenedizo. 4. Ajeno, remoto; excluído. *Foreign trade*, Comercio extranjero. *Foreign Office*, (Ingl.) Ministerio de Estado o de negocios extranjeros. *Foreign products*, Productos exóticos.
Foreign-built [fer'-ẹn-bilt], *a.* Construído en el extranjero.
Foreigner [fer'-ẹn-ẹr], *s.* Extranjero, forastero.
Foreignness [fer'-ẹn-nes], *s.* Inconexión, extrañeza, falta de conexión entre dos cosas.
Forejudge, *va.* *V.* PREJUDGE.
Forejudgment [fōr-juj'-mẹnt], *s.* Juicio formado con antelación al completo conocimiento de una cosa; prevención.
Foreknow [fōr-nō'], *va.* Prever, tener presciencia de alguna cosa, conocer de antemano.
Foreknowable [fōr-nō'-a-bl], *a.* Lo que se puede prever.
Foreknower [fōr-nō'-er], *s.* Previsor, el que conoce o sabe lo que ha de acontecer.
Foreknowledge [fōr-nel'-ej], *s.* Presciencia.
Foreland [fōr'-land], *s.* Cabo, promontorio.
Forelay [fōr-lê'], *va.* Poner asechanzas; prevenir.
Foreleader [fōr-līd'-ẹr], *s.* El que guía a otros con su ejemplo.
Forelock [fōr'-lec], *s.* 1. Melena. 2. (Mar.) Chabeta, cuñita de hierro que entra en el ojo del perno para afianzarlo. *Forelock bolts*, Pernos de chabeta.
Forelook [fōr-luk'], *vn.* Mirar de antemano.
Foreman [fōr'-man], *s.* 1. El presidente del jurado. 2. Capataz; regente de imprenta; jefe (de un taller, de una cuadrilla de trabajadores); dependiente principal de un establecimiento; oficial mayor en las oficinas públicas.
Foremast [fōr'-mast], *s.* (Mar.) Palo de trinquete.
Forementioned [fōr-men'-shund], *a.* Ya citado, arriba citado.
Foremost [fōr'-mōst], *a.* Delantero; primero en situación o dignidad.
Foremother [fōr'-mudh-ẹr], *sf.* Abuela, ascendiente, antepasada.
§**Forename** [fōr'-nêm], *s.* Prenombre, el nombre que precede al de familia, o apellido.
Forenamed [fōr-nêmd'], *a.* Ya nombrado, susodicho.
Forenoon [fōr'-nūn], *s.* La mañana hasta mediodía.
Forensic [fo-ren'-sic], *a.* Forense, lo que pertenece al foro; empleado en los pleitos o las formas judiciales.
Fore-ordain [fōr-ōr-dên'], *va.* Preordinar, predestinar.
Fore-ordination [fōr-er-di-nê'-shun], *s.* Predeterminación.
Forepart [fōr'-pārt], *s.* Delantera; la primera parte. (Forma incorrecta; debe escribirse *Fore part.*)
Forepromise [fōr-prem'-is], *va.* Prometer de antemano.
Foreprize [fōr-praiz'], *va.* Apreciar o estimar de antemano.
Foreran [fōr-ran'], *pret.* de FORERUN.
Fore-rank [fōr'-rank], *s.* Primera fila; frente, hilera del frente.
Forereach [fōr-rīch'], *va.* (Mar.) Navegar delante de otro buque.
Fore-remembered [fōr-rẹ-mem'-bẹrd], *a.* Ya acordado o mencionado.
Forerun [fōr-run'], *va.* (*pret.* FORERAN, *pp.* FORERUN, *ger.* FORERUNNING). 1. Preceder, ir delante como pronóstico o señal de lo que sigue. 2. Adelantarse, llegar antes que otro. 3. Anunciar.
Forerunner [fōr-run'-ẹr], *s.* 1. Precursor, el que va delante de otro; predecesor. 2. Presagio, pronóstico, anuncio, preludio. 3. Corredor, batidor. (Mil.) Explorador.
Foresaid [fōr'-sed], *a.* Ya dicho, antedicho, susodicho.
Foresail [fōr'-sêl o (Mar.) fō'-sl], *s.* Trinquete.
Foresee [fōr-sī'], *va.* (*pret.* FORESAW, *pp.* FORESEEN). Prever, tener presciencia, anticipar.
Foreseer [fōr-sī'-ẹr], *s.* Previsor, el que prevé.
Foreshadow [fōr-shad'-o], *va.* Prefigurar, simbolizar.
Foreship [fōr'-ship], *s.* (Mar.) Proa, la parte delantera de una embarcación.
Foreshorten [fōr-short'-n], *va.* (Pint.) Escorzar, degradar, reducir la longitud de un cuerpo u objeto, según las reglas de la perspectiva.
Foreshow [fōr-shō'], *va.* Exhibir de antemano; predecir, pronosticar.
Foreshower [fōr-shō'-ẹr], *s.* El que predice algún acontecimiento.
Foreside [fōr'-said], *s.* 1. Apariencia superficial. 2. El frente, la parte anterior de una cosa.
Foresight [fōr'-sait], *s.* 1. Previsión, providencia, prevención, cuidado por lo que puede suceder. 2. Presciencia. 3. Entre los agrimensores, croquis de nivel.
†**Foresightful** [fōr-sait'-ful], *a.* Próvido, prevenido, cuidadoso.
Foresignify [fōr-sig'-ni-fai], *va.* Prefigurar, presagiar, simbolizar.
Foreskin [fōr'-skin], *s.* Prepucio.
Foreskirt [fōr'-skẹrt], *s.* Parte delantera de una falda o de un faldón.
Foreslow [fōr-slō'], *va.* (Des.) Tardar, retardar, impedir; omitir.—*vn.* Descuidar; detenerse.
Forespeak [fōr-spīk'], *vn.* 1. (Prov. Ingl.) Predecir; prohibir; consagrar. 2. (Esco.) *V.* BESPEAK.
Forespent [fōr-spent'], *a.* 1. (Ant.) Pasado, gastado, consumido. 2. Cansado, fatigado.
Forespurrer [fōr-spūr'-ẹr], *s.* (Des.) Postillón, el que va a caballo delante de otro.
Forest [fer'-est], *s.* Monte espeso, bosque, selva, floresta. *Forest-tree*, Árbol del bosque, a diferencia de un árbol frutal. *Forest-born*, Salvaje, nacido y criado en los bosques. *To thin a forest*, Despejar o aclarar un bosque.
Forest, *va.* Arbolar; formar un bosque.
Forestaff [fōr'-stạf], *s.* (Mar.) Ballestilla, instrumento que usaban los náuticos para tomar las alturas del sol, la luna y las estrellas.
Forestage [fer'-est-ej], *s.* Un tributo pagado antiguamente en Inglaterra por los que vivían en los montes.
Forestal [fer'-est-al], *a.* Forestal, relativo a las selvas o proveniente de ellas.
Forestall [fōr-stōl'], *va.* 1. Anticipar. 2. Preocupar, prevenir. 3. Monopolizar, acaparar (los géneros de un mercado).
Forestaller [fōr-stel'-ẹr], *s.* Monopolista; acopiador.
Forestalling [fōr-stōl'-ing], *s.* Monopolio, acopio.
Forestation [fer-est-ê'-shun], *s.* Forestación.
Forestay [fōr'-stê], *s.* (Mar.) Estay del trinquete. *Forestay-tackle*, (Mar.) Candeletón.
Forested [fer'-est-ed], *a.* Arbolado, poblado de árboles.
Forester [fer'-est-ẹr], *s.* 1. Guardabosque. 2. Habitante de los bosques. 3. (Poco us.) Árbol del bosque. 4. Mariposa del grupo de los cigénidos cuya oruga se alimenta de las hojas de la vid. Alypia octomaculata.
Forestine [fer'-est-in], *a.* Natural de los bosques o hallado en ellos.
Forestry [fer'-est-ri], *s.* Selvicultura, arte de plantar, cultivar y proteger las selvas.
Foretackle [fōr'-tac-l], *s.* (Mar.) Aparejo del gancho del trinquete.
Foretaste [fōr-têst'], *va.* 1. Tener presciencia o conocimiento previo de alguna cosa. 2. (Poco us.) Catar o gustar antes que otro.
Foretaste [fōr'-têst], *s.* Goce por anticipación.
Foretaster [fōr'-têst-ẹr], *s.* Catador, el que gusta o prueba alguna cosa antes que otro.
Foretell [fōr-tel'], *va.* Predecir, pronunciar, profetizar, presagiar.—*vn.* Profetizar o ser profeta.
Foreteller [fōr-tel'-ẹr], *s.* Profeta.
Foretelling [fōr-tel'-ing], *s.* Predicción, profecía, presagio.
Forethink [fōr-think'], *va.* (Des.) Premeditar, pensar o considerar anticipamente.—*vn.* (Des.) Idear, proyectar, discurrir medios de antemano para el logro de algún intento.
Forethought [fōr'-thōt], *s.* Presciencia, providencia; prevención; premeditación.—*a.* Premeditado, previsto, pensado con anticipación.

Foretoken [fōr-tōk'-n], *va.* Pronosticar; prefigurar.
Foretoken [fōr'-tō-kn], *s.* Pronóstico, presagio.
Foretop [fōr'-tep], *s.* 1. (Mar.) Cofa de trinquete. 2. Tupé.
Forever [fer-ev'-ẹr], *adv.* Siempre; para siempre. (En Inglaterra se suele escribir en dos palabras, *for ever.*) *Forevermore,* Por siempre, para siempre. *Forever and a day,* o *forever and ever,* Para siempre jamás.
Forewarn [fōr-wērn'], *va.* 1. Prevenir o amonestar de antemano. 2. Advertir o avisar a alguno acerca de lo que ha de suceder. 3. Precautelar, precaver o prevenir contra alguna cosa.
Forewind [fōr'-wind], *s.* Viento favorable.
Forewoman [fōr'-wum-an], *s.* Primera oficiala de un taller de mujeres; encargada.
Foreword [fōr'-wurd], *s.* Preámbulo, prólogo.
Foreyard [fōr'-yārd], *s.* (Mar.) Verga del trinquete.
Forfeit [fēr'-fit], *s.* 1. Multa, pena, la cosa perdida por su dueño como castigo de una falta o contravención; pérdida legal de un derecho; decomiso. *To pay the forfeit,* Sufrir la pena de. 2. Prenda, gaje (en los juegos). *Game of forfeits,* Juego de prendas.—*a.* 1. Sujeto a multa o confiscación. 2. Confiscado, perdido.
Forfeit, *va.* 1. Perder el título a una cosa o la posesión de ella por dejar de cumplir alguna obligación o condición. 2. Perder o exponerse a perder alguna cosa por falta, omisión, contravención, etc.; incurrir en la pena de embargo o confiscación.
Forfeitable [fēr'-fit-a-bl], *a.* Confiscable.
Forfeiter [fēr'-fit-ẹr], *s.* 1. El que pierde una cosa por faltar a alguna de las condiciones bajo las cuales la poseía. 2. El que incurre en una pena por dejar de cumplir con su obligación.
Forfeiture [fēr'-fi-chur], *s.* Confiscación; secuestro, decomiso, pérdida de bienes; multa.
Forfend [fōr-fend'], *va.* (Ant.) Impedir; desviar. *Heaven forfend!* ¡Líbreme el cielo!
Forficula [fēr-fic'-yu-la], *s.* *V.* EARWIG.
Forgave [fer-gêv'], *pret.* del verbo *To* FORGIVE.
Forge [fōrj], *s.* 1. Fragua; fábrica de metales. 2. Forja, hornaza. *Forge-hearth,* Atrio, hogar de fábrica.
Forge, *va.* 1. Forjar, fraguar obras de herrería, cerrajería u otros metales. 2. Contrahacer, falsificar, falsear monedas, llaves, sellos, escritos, etc. 3. Forjar palabras, cuentos, etc. 4. Fraguar calumnias, falsedades, etc.; tramar, inventar. *To forge off,* (Mar.) Franquear por cima de una roca o arrecife.
Forger [fōrj'-ẹr], *s.* Forjador, fraguador; falsificador, falsario.
Forgery [fōrj'-ẹr-i], *s.* 1. Falsificación; alteración de lo escrito con intención de defraudar; el acto de hacer moneda falsa; falsedad. 2. (Poco us.) Forjadura, lo que se forja en la fragua.
Forget [fer-get'], *va.* (*pret.* FORGOT, *pp.* FORGOTTEN). 1. Olvidar. 2. Descuidar, dejar de atender.
Forgetful [fer-get'-ful], *a.* Olvidadizo, descuidado, desmemoriado.
Forgetfulness [fer-get'-ful-nes], *s.* Olvido, descuido, negligencia.
Forget-me-not [fēr-get'-mẹ-net"], *s.* Raspilla, miosota, planta y su flor, llamada comúnmente Nomeolvides. Myosotis.
Forgetter [fer-get'-ẹr], *s.* Olvidadizo, el que es negligente o descuidado.
Forgetting [fer-get'-ing], *s.* Olvido, descuido, negligencia.
Forgettingly [fer-get'-ing-li], *adv.* Descuidadamente.
Forging [fōr'-jing], *s.* 1. Defecto de algunas caballerías que golpean un pie con otro al andar o trotar. 2. Forja, forjadura; masa o trozo de metal al que se da forma martilleándolo.
Forgivable [fer-giv'-a-bl], *a.* Perdonable, remisible.
Forgive [fer-giv'], *va.* 1. Perdonar, remitir la injuria. 2. Perdonar, remitir una deuda o pena.
Forgiven [fer-giv'-ẹn], *pp.* del verbo *To* FORGIVE.
Forgiveness [fer-giv'-nes], *s.* Perdón u olvido de alguna injuria; condonación, indulgencia, remisión de multa o pena; clemencia, misericordia, absolución.
Forgiver [fer-giv'-ẹr], *s.* Perdonador.
Forgo [fer-gō'], *va.* y *vn.* (*pret.* FORWENT, *pp.* FORGONE). (Poco us.) *V.* FOREGO.
Forgot [fer-get'], *pret.* y *pp.* de *To* FORGET.
Forgot, Forgotten, *pp.* de *To* FORGET.
Forisfamiliate [fo ris-fa-mil'-i-êt], *va.* (For.) Dar al hijo la posesión de una parte de la herencia durante la vida de su padre.
Fork [fērk], *s.* 1. Tenedor. 2. Horca para aventar o hacinar heno, paja, estiércol, etc. 3. Cualquier cosa de figura ahorquillada: como la punta de una flecha; una púa, etc. 4. Bifurcación; paraje donde un camino se divide en dos; confluencia de un río. 5. (Des.) Horca, el patíbulo.
Fork, *va.* 1. Hacinar, echar, cargar con una horca; ahorquillar. 2. Hacer terminar en punta, o hacer dentado, como una rama.—*vn.* 1. Ahorquillarse, bifurcarse. 2. Brotar en forma de horquillas.
Forked [fērkt o ferk'-ed], *a.* Horcado, lo que tiene la forma de horca u horquilla, ahorquillado, hendido.
Forkedly [fērk'-ed-li], *adv.* En figura de horquilla.
Forkedness [fērk'-ed-nes], *s.* Horcajadura, horcadura, horquilladura.
Forkhead [fērk'-hed], *s.* Lengüeta de saeta o flecha.
Forkiness [fērk'-i-nes], *s.* Horcadura.
Forklift truck [ferk'-lift truc'], *s.* Carretilla elevadora.
Forktail [fērk'-têl], *s.* 1. Milano, ave de rapiña. 2. Tirano, pájaro de la América tropical. Milvulus tyrannus. 3. Salmón en su cuarto año.
Forlorn [fer-lērn'], *a.* 1. Abandonado, destituído, perdido, olvidado, desamparado, desesperado. 2. Pequeño, ruin. *Forlorn hope,* Destacamento militar encargado de un servicio excepcional y en extremo peligroso; también, una empresa desesperada o con muy escasas esperanzas de éxito.—*s.* (Poco us.) Hombre abandonado o desamparado.
Forlornness [fer-lērn -nes], *s.* Desamparo, miseria; soledad, abandono.
Form [fērm], *s.* 1. Forma, figura, modelo; modo. 2. Hermosura, elegancia exterior. 3. Ceremonia, formalidad, orden. 4. Método, práctica establecida. 5. Banco, asiento largo. 6. Forma, molde, patrón. 7. Cama de liebre, surco o ligera depresión en vez de madriguera. 8. Forma, molde que se pone en la prensa para imprimir. 9. La condición y el estado general, p. ej. de un caballo de carrera; de aquí, porte, conducta. 10. Lo que tiene figura o contorno sin cuerpo; aparición, sombra. *For form's sake,* Por pura fórmula, para cumplir con las apariencias, por ceremonia. *In due form,* En toda forma, según las reglas, en debida forma. *Form in a school,* Clase de una escuela.
Form, *va.* 1. Formar, hacer alguna cosa. 2. Formar, dar a las cosas una forma o figura; modelar, idear. 3. Poner en orden, juntar, colocar; asentar, componer, arreglar; hacer, constituir.—*vn.* Formarse, tomar una forma o figura.
Formal [fērm'-al], *a.* 1. Formal, hecho o ejecutado según las reglas; metódico, regular. 2. Exterior; en apariencia, pero sin substancia ni esencia. 3. Ceremonioso, formalista, etiquetero. 4. Formal, que se refiere a la forma, en oposición a la materia. 5. Esencial, constitutivo.
Formaldehyde [fēr-mal'-dẹ-haid], *s.* (Quím.) Formaldehida, la aldehida del ácido fórmico (CH_2O). Es un gas acre y un agente antiséptico de primer orden, muy usado hoy para desinfectar habitaciones, buques, etc.
Formalin [fēr'-ma-lin], *s.* (Quím.) Formalina, nombre de una solución acuosa de la formaldehida, en la proporción de cuarenta por ciento. Agente preservativo muy estimado entre los microscopistas y anatomistas.
Formalist [fēr'-mal-ist], *s.* Ceremoniático, formalista.
Formality [fēr-mal'-i-ti], *s.* 1. Formalidad, ceremonia, etiqueta. 2. Formalidad, regla prescrita para proceder en juicio. 3. Esencia de una cosa.
Formally [fēr'-mal-i], *adv.* Formalmente, con toda solemnidad; realmente. *Forma pauperis,* (For.) Defendido por pobre.
Format [fēr'-mat], *s.* Formato (de una publicación).
Formate [fēr'-mêt], *s.* (Quím.) Formiato, sal formada de ácido fórmico con alguna base.
Formation [fēr-mê'-shun], *s.* 1. Formación, acción de formar; manera en que se forma una cosa; desarrollo. 2. Disposición de las partes par dar individualidad o forma característica. 3. Lo que está formado; (Geol.) formación.
Formation flying [fer-mê'-shun flai'-ing], *s.* Vuelo en formación.
Formative [fērm'-a-tiv], *a.* Formativo, que forma o da la forma.
Former [fērm'-ẹr], *a.* Anterior, primero; pasado, antecedente, precedente.—*s.* Formador; molde, matriz.
Formerly [fēr'-mer-li], *adv.* Antiguamente, en tiempos pasados.
Formic [fērm'-ic], *a.* Fórmico, referente a las hormigas; derivado del ácido fórmico. *Formic acid,* Ácido fórmico o ácido de hormigas.

Formication [fōr-mi-kē'-shun], *s.* Hormigueo, sensación de comezón o picazón entre cuero y carne.
Formidable [fōr'-mi-da-bl], *a.* Formidable, pavoroso, terrible, tremendo.
Formidableness [fōr'-mi-da-bl-nes], *s.* Calidad espantosa o formidable; horror.
Formidably [fōr'-mi-da-bli], *adv.* Formidablemente, horriblemente.
Formless [fōrm'-les], *a.* Informe, disforme.
Form letter [fōrm let'-ęr], *s.* Carta circular.
Formula [fōr'-miu-la], *s.* (*pl.* LAS ó LÆ). 1. Fórmula, forma prescrita. 2. Profesión de fe escrita. 3. (Med.) Receta médica, récipe. 4. Regla expresada en signos algebraicos. 5. (Quím.) Grupo de signos que expresan los elementos constitutivos de un cuerpo o de una substancia compuesta.
Formulary [fōr'-miu-lę-ri], *s.* Formulario, el libro o escrito que contiene las fórmulas que se han de observar para la ejecución de alguna cosa.
Formulate [fōr'-miu-lêt], *va.* Formular, expresar en una fórmula; incluir en una forma exacta y metódica.
Formulize [fōr'-miu-laiz], *va.* 1. Hacer formal, formalizar. 2. Formular. *V.* FORMULATE.
Fornicate [fōr'-ni-kêt], *vn.* Fornicar.
Fornicate, *a.* Arqueado; abovedado, en forma de bóveda.
Fornicated [fōr'-ni-kê-ted], *a.* Abovedado.
Fornication [fōr-ni-kê'-shun], *s.* 1. Fornicación, cópula carnal entre dos personas que no están casadas. 2. (Arq.) Bóveda.
Fornicator [fōr'-ni-kê-tęr], *s.* Fornicador, fornicario.
Fornicatress [fōr'-ni-kê-tres], *sf.* Concubina; manceba.
Fornix [fōr'-nix], *s.* (Anat.) Superficie abovedada. La parte arqueada de una concha bivalva.
Forsake [fer-sêk'], *va.* (*pret.* FORSOOK, *pp.* FORSAKEN). Dejar, abandonar; faltar a, desertar; separarse de; alejarse de; renunciar a.
Forsaker [fer-sê'-ker], *s.* Desertor; apóstata.
Forsaking [fer-sêk'-ing], *s.* Abandono.
Forsooth [fer-sūth'], *adv.* Ciertamente. ¡De veras! ¡vaya! Se usa hoy generalmente en sentido irónico.
Forswear [fēr-swār'], *va.* (*pret.* FORSWORE, *pp.* FORSWORN). Renunciar con juramento; negar con juramento. *To forswear one's self,* Perjurarse.—*vn.* Perjurar, jurar falso.
Forswearer [fēr-swār'-ęr], *s.* Perjurador, perjuro.
Forsworn, *pp.* de FORSWEAR.
Fort [fōrt], *s.* Fuerte, castillo, fortaleza. *Little fort,* Fortín.
Fortalice [fōrt'-a-lis], *s.* Fortín, obra pequeña en lo exterior de una fortificación.
Forte [fōrt], *s.* El fuerte, el lado fuerte de alguno; talento o facultad particular en que uno se distingue o descuella.
Forte [fōr'-tê], *s.* (Mús.) Forte, el trozo donde debe esforzarse el sonido.—*a.* De sonido fuerte.
Forth [fōrth], *adv.* 1. En adelante, hacia adelante, adelante; delante. 2. Fuera, afuera. 3. A la vista, públicamente. 4. Hasta lo último. *And so forth,* Y así de lo demás; etcétera. *To go o come forth,* Irse, salir fuera. *To step forth,* Ir adelante, avanzar. *From that day forth,* Desde aquel día en adelante.—*prep.* Fuera de.
Forthcoming [fōrth-cum'-ing], *a.* Pronto a comparecer, que viene o está viniendo. *He is not forthcoming,* No viene; no es fácil que se presente o que venga.
Forth-issuing [fōrth-ish'-yu-ing], *a.* Dícese de la persona o cosa que sale de donde estaba oculta.
†**Forthright** [fōrth-rait'], *adv.* Todo derecho.—*s.* Senda angosta.
Forthwith [fōrth-with' o fōrth-widh'], *adv.* Inmediatamente, sin dilación, sin tardanza.
Fortieth [fōr'-ti-eth], *s.* Cuadragésimo.
Fortifiable [fōr'-ti-fai'-a-bl], *a.* Fortificable.
Fortification [fer-ti-fi-kê'-shun], *s.* 1. Fortificación, arquitectura militar; acción de fortificar; obra construída para defenderse contra un ataque. 2. Plaza fuerte; fortaleza. 3. Aumento de fuerza.
Fortifier [fōr'-ti-fai-ęr], *s.* 1. Fortificador, ingeniero militar. 2. Fautor.
Fortify [fer'-ti-fai], *va.* 1. Fortificar. 2. Fortalecer, dar vigor o fuerzas a alguna cosa. 3. Corroborar, fijar, establecer, confirmar.
Fortissimo [fer-tis'-i-mō], *a.* y *adv.* (Ital.) Muy fuerte o fortísimo.
Fortitude [fōr'-ti-tiud], *s.* 1. Fortaleza de ánimo para soportar el dolor o la adversidad con valor ó paciencia; resolución, firmeza, grandeza de alma. 2. Fuerza, vigor.
Fortlet [fōrt'-let], *s.* Fortín.
Fortnight [fert'-nait o fōrt'-nit], *s.* Quince días, dos semanas. *A fortnight hence,* De aquí a quince días. *A fortnight ago,* Quince días ha.
Fortnightly [fert'-nait-li], *a.* y *adv.* Una vez cada quince días; que sale a luz, ocurre o se publica cada quincena.
Fortress [fōr'-tres], *s.* Fortaleza, plaza fortificada, castillo, fuerte.
Fortuitous [fer-tiū'-i-tus], *a.* Fortuito, impensado, casual, accidental.
Fortuitously [fer-tiū'-i-tus-li], *adv.* Fortuitamente, por casualidad, accidentalmente.
Fortuitousness [fer-tiū'-i-tus-nes], *s.* Casualidad, acontecimiento impensado.
Fortuity [fer-tiū'-i-ti], *s.* Caso fortuito; accidente.
Fortunate [fōr'-chu (o tiu) -net], *a.* Afortunado, feliz, dichoso.
Fortunately [fōr'-chu (o tiu) -net-li], *adv.* Felizmente, dichosamente.
Fortune [fer'-chun o tiun], *s.* 1. Fortuna, suerte, ventura buena o mala. 2. Fortuna, el estado o condición en que uno vive. 3. Fortuna, suerte, destino, lo que ha de suceder a una persona. 4. Bienes de fortuna, sean raíces o muebles. *Man of fortune,* Hombre rico. 5. Hacienda; dote, el caudal que lleva la mujer al tiempo de casarse. *To make one's fortune,* Hacer su propia fortuna, enriquecerse. *A man of broken fortune,* Un hombre arruinado. *Fortune-hunter,* Buscador de dotes, el que anda en busca de esposa rica. *Fortune-teller,* Sortílego, adivino, nigromante; gitano decidor de la buena ventura.
Fortuned [fōr'-chund], *a.* Afortunado, dichoso.
Fortune-book [fōr'-chun-buk], *s.* Libro de la buena ventura.
Fortuneless [fōr'-chun-les], *a.* Sin fortuna, sin bienes.
Forty [fōr'-ti], *a.* y *s.* 1. Cuarenta. 2. Cuarentena, número indeterminado. *He has turned forty,* Ha cumplido la cuarentena, o los cuarenta. *He is forty,* Tiene cuarenta años.
Forum [fō'-rum], *s.* 1. Foro, plaza pública. 2. Tribunal, juzgado.
Forward [fōr'-ward], *adv.* Adelante, hacia adelante, más allá. *Hence forward,* De aquí en adelante. *From this time forward,* De aquí en adelante, en lo venidero. *From that time forward,* Desde entonces, desde aquel instante. *To go, to move forward,* Ir hacia adelante, adelantar. —*a.* 1. Delantero, que va delante o está al frente. 2. Precoz, adelantado, anterior. 3. Pronto, activo, que va adelante; apresurado, vivo, listo. 4. Audaz, osado, emprendedor, atrevido.
Forward, *va.* 1. Adelantar; hacer crecer; promover, patrocinar. 2. Apresurar, activar, impeler. 3. Expedir, enviar, transmitir.
Forwarder [fōr'-ward-ęr], *s.* Promotor; remitente, el que envía.
Forwarding merchant [fōr'-ward-ing męr'-chant], *s.* Comisionista que recibe efectos para remitirlos a otros puntos.
Forwardly [fōr'-ward-li], *adv.* 1. Anteriormente, en lugar delantero. 2. Con descaro o con muy poca vergüenza.
Forwardness [fōr'-ward-nes], *s.* 1. Adelantamiento, progreso. 2. Ansia, ahinco. 3. Prontitud, apresuramiento, ligereza. 4. Precocidad, madurez anticipada. 5. Confianza excesiva; descaro, atrevimiento, audacia.
Forwards [fōr'-wardz], *adv.* *V.* FORWARD.
Foss, Fosse [fes], *s.* (Fort.) Foso.
Fossa [fes'-a], *s.* (Anat.) Fosa.
Fossil [fes'-il], *a.* Fósil, cavado ó sacado de la tierra.—*s.* 1. Fósil, substancia orgánica y prehistórica, más o menos petrificada, que se extrae de las capas terrestres. 2. Persona o cosa anticuada, fuera de uso, antigualla, vejestorio. 3. (Des.) Fósil, cualquier substancia natural que se saca de las entrañas de la tierra.
Fossiliferous [fes-il-if'-ęr-us], *a.* Fosilífero, que contiene fósiles o restos orgánicos.
Fossilize [fes'-il-aiz], *va.* Fosilizar, convertir en fósil; petrificar; hacer anticuado.—*vn.* Fosilizarse, petrificarse.
Fossorial [fes-sō'-ri-al], *a.* 1. Cavador, el que cava. 2. Apto, a propósito para cavar. *Fossorial wasp,* Avispa cavadora.
Fossway [fes'-wê], *s.* Camino grande con fosos.
Foster [fes'-tęr], *va.* Criar, nutrir, mimar, dar alas; consolar.—*vn.* (Des.) Criarse con otros.
Fosterage [fes'-tęr-ēj], *s.* El cargo de criar niños, como el que tienen las amas de cría.
Foster-brother [fes'-tęr-brudh'-ęr], *s.* Hermano de leche.
Foster-child [fes'-tęr-chaild], *s.* Hijo o hija de leche; también, alumno.
Foster-dam [fes'-tęr-dam], *sf.* Ama de cría o ama de leche, nodriza.
Foster-earth [fes'-tęr-ęrth], *s.* Tierra en que crecen las plantas que se han trasplantado de otra.
Fosterer [fes'-tęr-ęr], *s.* El que cría

al hijo de otro como si fuera suyo; promotor.

Foster-father [fes'-tęr-fā'-dhęr], *s.* El que sirviendo de padre cría y enseña a un hijo ajeno.

Fostering [fes'-tęr-ing], *s.* Alimento, nutrimento.—*pa.* de *To* FOSTER.

Fosterling, *s.* *V.* FOSTER-CHILD.

Foster-mother [fes'-tęr-mudh'-ęr], *sf.* Ama de leche, la que cría hijos ajenos.

Foster-nurse [fes'-tęr-nūrs], *s.* Ama de leche. (Cuba) Criandera. (Mex.) Chichigua.

Foster-son [fes'-tęr-sun], *s.* Hijo de leche; alumno.

Fostress, *sf.* *V.* NURSE.

Fother [fedh'-ęr], *s.* Galápago de plomo que sirve de lastre; masa de plomo de ocho galápagos.

Fother, *va.* (Mar.) Cerrar una abertura en el barco tapándola con estopa.

Fought [fōt], *pret.* y *pp.* del verbo *To* FIGHT.

Foul [faul], *a.* 1. Sucio, puerco; impuro, inmundo, hediondo, ofensivo al sentido físico, a la moral o al pudor; obsceno. 2. Malvado, detestable, vil; injusto, sin derecho. 3. Enredado, atascado, que obstruye o daña, que sirve de obstáculo; infecto, pestífero. 4. (Des.) Feo, horrible. 5. (Imp.) Lleno de faltas. *Foul action*, Bajeza, vileza, acción baja. *Foul dealing*, Supercherías, duplicidad, doblez, mala fe. *Foul copy*, Borrador. *Foul language*, Palabras injuriosas. *Foul means*, Medios indignos, violencia, rigor. *Foul page*, Página llena de faltas, cuando se está imprimiendo. *Foul shame*, Infamia. *Foul stomach*, Estómago sucio. *Foul weather*, Mal tiempo. *Foul words*, Palabras provocativas o injuriosas. *By fair means or foul*, A buenas o a malas. *Foul breath*, Aliento fétido—*s.* 1. La acción de ensuciar, de ludir o enredarse una cosa en otra; violación de las reglas establecidas. 2. En el juego de *base-ball*, falta, golpe que lanza la pelota fuera de las líneas del juego. *To fall foul of*, Abordar un buque.

Foul, *va.* 1. Ensuciar, emporcar. 2. (Mar.) Abordar, chocar con, trabarse dos embarcaciones de modo que se impidan el paso. 3. Violar las reglas establecidas de un juego. —*vn.* 1. Ensuciarse. 2. Chocar, las embarcaciones.

Foulard [fū-lārd'], *s.* 1. Fular, tela de seda fina y suave que se usa para vestidos de señora. 2. Pañuelo de fular.

Foul brood [faul' brūd], *s.* Enfermedad muy contagiosa y destructiva de las larvas de las abejas. La causa el *bacillus alvei* y se distingue por un hedor característico.

Foully [faul'-li], *adv.* Asquerosamente, suciamente.

Foul-mouthed [faul'-maudhd], *a.* Obsceno, malhablado, deslenguado.

Foulness [faul'-nes], *s.* 1. Asquerosidad, porquería, impureza. 2. Fealdad, deformidad. 3. Picardía, atrocidad.

Foul play [faul plē], *s.* 1. Mala jugada. 2. Conducta deshonesta. 3. Engaño, perfidia. 4. Violencia, asesinato.

Foul-spoken [faul'-spōk-n], *a.* Calumnioso, infamatorio.

Found [faund], *va.* 1. Cimentar; apoyar. 2. Edificar, levantar algún edificio. 3. Fundar, establecer; dar principio a alguna cosa; fijar, asegurar. 4. Fundir, derretir o liquidar los metales.

Found, *pret.* y *pp.* de *To* FIND.

Foundation [faun-dē'-shun], *s.* 1. Cimiento, fundación, fundamento. 2. Fundación, principio, origen, erección o establecimiento de alguna cosa. 3. Dotación o renta con que se funda alguna cosa. 4. Fundamento, la razón o motivo en que se funda alguna cosa. *Foundation school*, Escuela dotada, que tiene dotación. *A scholar on the foundation*, Un colegial pensionado, con beca.

Foundationless [faun-dē'-shun-les], *a.* Sin fundamento.

Founder [faund'-ęr], *s.* 1. Fundador. 2. Fundidor.

Founder, *vn.* 1. (Mar.) Irse a pique. 2. Salir mal de alguna empresa. 3. Desplomarse.—*va.* Despear los pies del caballo.

Founderous [faun'-dęr-us], *a.* Arruinado, no practicable: dícese de los caminos.

Foundery [faund'-ęr-i], *s.* *V.* FOUNDRY.

Founding [faund'-ing], *s.* 1. Fundación, establecimiento. 2. Fundición, arte de fundir los metales.

Foundling [faund'-ling], *s.* Hijo de la piedra, niño expósito. *Foundling hospital*, Casa de niños expósitos. Inclusa. (Mex.) La cuna.

Foundress [faund'-res], *sf.* Fundadora.

Foundry [faun'-dri], *s.* Fundición, fábrica en que se funde; el arte de fundir los metales.

Fount [faunt], *s.* 1. Fundición de caracteres de imprenta. 2. V. FONT.

Fountain [faun'-ten], *s.* 1. Fuente. 2. Nacimiento de un río. 3. Fuente, principio, fundamento, origen.

Fountain-head [faun'-tęn-hed], *s.* Manantial de un río o arroyo; de aquí, origen de una cosa.

Fountainless [faun'-tęn-les], *a.* Sin fuente.

Fountain pen [faun'-ten pen], *s.* Pluma fuente, pluma estilográfica.

Four [fōr], *a.* y *s.* Cuatro. *To go upon all fours*, Gatear, andar a gatas. *A coach and four*, Un coche con tiro de cuatro caballos, o con dos tiros. *Four-cornered*, *four-square*, Cuadrangular. *Four-footed*, Cuadrúpedo. *Four-wheeled*, Lo que tiene cuatro ruedas.

Four-flusher [fōr'-flush-ęr], *s.* En el juego de poker, lance con un flux de cuatro naipes. (fig.) Fanfarrón.

Fourfold [fōr'-fōld], *a.* Cuádruplo, repetido cuatro veces.

Four-in-hand [fōr'-in-hand], *s.* 1. Carruaje tirado por cuatro caballos. 2. Corbata larga, anudada de modo que las puntas cuelgan verticalmente.

Four-o'clock [fōr'-o'-clec], *s.* 1. (Bot.) Dondiego de noche, planta originaria del Perú, cuyas flores se abren como a las cuatro de la tarde y se cierran a la mañana siguiente. (Mirabilis Jalapa.) Se llama también *Marvel-of-Peru* y *Afternoon-ladies*. 2. (Zool.) Pájaro de la Oceanía.

Fourscore [fōr'-scōr], *a.* 1. Ochenta. 2. Octogenario.

Four-stage rocket [fōr'-stēj rek'-et], *s.* Cohete de cuatro cuerpos.

Fourteen [fōr'-tīn], *a.* y *s.* Catorce.

Fourteenth [fōr'-tīnth], *a.* Catorceno, décimocuarto. *Fourteenth of July*, El catorce de Julio, aniversario de la toma de la Bastilla, en 1789.

Fourth [fōrth], *a.* Cuarto, la cuarta parte. *Fourth of July*, El cuatro de Julio, aniversario de la independencia de los Estados Unidos.

Fourthly [fōrth'-li], *adv.* En cuarto lugar.

Fowl [faul], *s.* 1. Gallo, gallina; pollo. 2. *pl.* Aves domésticas o de corral. 3. Aves en general. 4. (Anticuado en singular) Ave. *Wild fowls*, Aves silvestres.

Fowl, *vn.* Cazar aves.

Fowling [faul'-ing], *s.* La caza de aves.

Fox [fecs], *s.* 1. Zorra, raposa; zorro. 2. Zorro, hombre astuto y engañoso. 3. (Mar.) Rebenque.

Fox, *vn.* 1. Cazar zorras. 2. Hacer el papel de la zorra, disimular. 3. Agriarse, acedarse el vino, la cerveza u otro licor. 4. Ponerse rojizo, descolorarse; dícese de la madera de construcción, del papel, cuero, etc.—*va.* Atontar; emborrachar.

Fox-case [fecs'-kēs], *s.* Piel de zorra.

Fox-chase [fecs'-chēs], *s.* Caza de zorras.

Fox-evil [fecs'-ī-vl], *s.* Enfermedad que hace caer el cabello.

Foxglove [fecs'-gluv], *s.* (Bot.) Dedalera, digital purpúrea.

Foxhole [fecs'-hōl], *s.* Hoyo practicado en tierra para protegerse uno o dos soldados.

Fox-hound [fex'-haund], *s.* Perro zorrero o raposero, el adiestrado especialmente para la caza de zorras.

Fox-hunter [fecs'-hunt-ęr], *s.* Cazador de zorras.

Foxish [fecs'-ish], **Fox-like** [fecs'-laic], *a.* Astuto o engañoso como el zorro.

Fox-ship [fecs'-ship], *s.* Zorrería.

Foxtail [fex'-tēl], *s.* Cola de zorra, planta gramínea; alopécuro.

Fox-trap [fecs'-trap], *s.* La trampa para coger zorras.

Fox trot [fecs tret], *s.* Fox-trot, ritmo y baile de E.U.

Foxwood [fex'-wud], *s.* Madera deteriorada o descolorida; en especial, la que emite una luz fosforescente.

Foxy [fecs'-i], *a.* 1. Raposuno, zorruno; astuto. 2. Rojizo, de color de zorro. *He is very foxy*, Él es muy astuto.

Foxy, *a.* 1. Agriado, impropiamente fermentado, como el vino. 2. Descolorido, manchado, como una tela mal teñida.

Foyer [fei'-ęr], *s.* (Teat). Foyer, salón de descanso.

Fracas [frē'-cas], *s.* Contienda ruidosa, pelea, tumulto, batahola.

†**Fract** [fract], *va.* Romper, quebrar.

Fraction [frac'-shun], *s.* 1. Rompimiento, rotura. 2. Fracción, número quebrado.

Fractional [frac'-shun-al], *a.* Fraccionario.

Fracture [frac'-chur], *s.* Fractura, rompimiento.

Fracture, *va.* Fracturar, quebrar o romper un hueso: romper alguna cosa.

Fragile [fraj'-il], *a.* 1. Frágil, quebradizo. 2. Frágil, caduco, perecedero. 3. Frágil, débil.

Fragility [fra-jil'-i-ti], **Fragileness**, *s.* Fragilidad; instabilidad; debilidad, flaqueza.

Fragment [frag'-mẹnt], *s.* Fragmento; trozo.
Fragmentary [frag'-men-tẹ-ri], *a.* Fragmentario.
Fragor [frê'-gor], *s.* (Poco us.) Estallido, estampido.
Fragrance, Fragrancy [frê'-grans, i], *s.* Fragancia, buen olor, perfume natural.
Fragrant [frê'-grant], *a.* Fragante, oloroso.
Fragrantly [frê'-grant-li], *adv.* Con fragancia.
Frail [frêl], *a.* 1. Frágil, quebradizo. 2. Frágil, débil; propenso y expuesto a error o engaño.—*s.* Capacho, espuerta de juncos.
Frailness [frêl'-nes], **Frailty** [frêl'-ti], *s.* Fragilidad, flaqueza, debilidad; instabilidad, inconstancia; caducidad.
Framable [frê'-ma-bl], *a.* (Poco us.) Componible; que puede ponerse en marco.
Frame [frêm], *va.* 1. Fabricar, formar, construir. 2. Fabricar, componer, ajustar; arreglar, dirigir. 3. Forjar, inventar, idear. 4. Colocar o encerrar en un marco o cerco.
Frame, *s.* 1. Figura, hechura, forma. 2. Forjadura, construcción mecánica; armazón, maderaje para la construcción de una casa. 3. Fábrica, marco, cerco. 4. Molde; bastidor. *Embroidery frame,* Bastidor, o bastidor para bordar. 5. Arreglo general, orden, constitución de una cosa; condición o estado particular del ánimo. 6. (Mar.) Cuaderna. *Frame-timbers,* Ligazones. *Midship-frame,* Cuaderna maestra. *Stern-frame,* Cuaderna del cuerpo popés.
Framer [frê'-mẹr], *s.* Fabricante de marcos; forjador; inventor, autor.
Framework [frêm'-wūrk], *s.* 1. Armazón, esqueleto, entramado; sostén, lo que sostiene una cosa. 2. Obra de marco o cerco.
Framing [frê'-ming], *s.* El acto de construir; la armazón de una cosa.
Franc [franc], *s.* Franco, moneda francesa de plata que pesa cinco gramos; su valor en los Estados Unidos es de 19.3 centavos; equivale a la peseta española y a la lira italiana.
Franchise [fran'-chaiz o fran'-chiz], *s.* 1. Franquicia, un derecho político o constitucional propio del pueblo. 2. Inmunidad, privilegio, exención, concedidos a una persona o un cuerpo. 3. Jurisdicción. 4. Asilo, santuario.
Franchise, *va.* Franquear, conceder franquicias; exentar.
Franchisement [fran'-chiz-mẹnt], *s.* Franqueza, libertad, exención; soltura.
Franciscan [fran-sis'-can], *s.* y *a.* Franciscano, religioso de la orden de San Francisco.
Frangible [fran'-ji-bl], *a.* Frangible, quebradizo, frágil; perecedero.
Frangipani [fran-ji-pä'-ni], *s.* Perfume que se obtiene del jazmín rojo de las Antillas o que lo imita.
Frank [frank], *a.* 1. Franco, abierto, natural en sus maneras; sincero, ingenuo. 2. Franco, privilegiado, exento de derechos. *Frank-hearted,* Sincero, franco. *Frank-service,* Trabajo libre, ejecutado por hombres libres.—*s.* 1. Franqueo; firma autorizada para exentar las cartas, etc., del pago de porte; también carta franca, la que no paga porte. 2. (Des.) Porqueriza, pocilga.
Frank, *va.* 1. Franquear una carta. 2. (Des.) Encerrar en pocilga o zahurda. 3. (Des.) Cebar, engordar.
Frank-chase [franc'-chês], *s.* Caza libre, privilegio de cazar.
Frankfurter [franc'-fẹr-tẹr], *s.* Variedad de salchicha ahumada.
Frankincense [frank'-in-sens], *s.* Incienso; goma aromática.
Frankish [frank'-ish], *a.* Lo que pertenece a los antiguos franceses; en Levante, lo que se refiere o pertenece a los europeos en general.
Franklin, *s.* *V.* FREEHOLDER.
Frankly [franc'-li], *adv.* Francamente, abiertamente.
Frankness [franc'-nes], *a.* 1. Ingenuidad, sinceridad; franqueza, candor, lisura. 2. (Ant.) Generosidad.
Frank-pledge [franc-plej'], *s.* Juramento de fidelidad al rey que se prestaba antiguamente en Inglaterra.
Franks [francs], *s. pl.* 1. Francos o galos. 2. Francos, nombre que dan los turcos o los moradores de la Europa occidental.
Frantic [fran'-tic], *a.* Frenético, furioso, enfurecido.
Franticly [fran'-tic-li], *adv.* Frenéticamente, furiosamente.
Franticness [fran'-tic-nes], *s.* Frenesí, furor.
Frap [frap], *va.* (Mar.) Atortorar un buque.
Fraternal [fra-tẹr'-nal], *a.* Fraternal.
Fraternally [fra-tẹr'-nal-i], *adv.* Fraternalmente.
Fraternity [fra-tẹr'-ni-ti], *s.* Fraternidad, hermandad; sociedad, junta, gremio, compañía de ciertos artífices, traficantes o estudiantes.
Fraternization [fra-tẹr-ni-zê'-shun], *s.* Hermandad, fraternidad.
Fraternize [frat'-ẹr-naiz], *vn.* Fraternizar, hermanarse, hermanar.
Fratricidal [frat-ri-sai'-dal], *a.* Relativo al fratricidio.
Fratricide [frat'-ri-said], *s.* 1. Fratricidio, el asesinato de un hermano. 2. Fratricida, el que asesina a su hermano.
Frau [frau], *s.* Mujer casada; señora, como título. (Alemán.)
Fraud [frōd], *s.* Fraude, engaño, supercheria, artificio.
Fraudful [frōd'-ful], *a.* Pérfido, engañoso, astuto, artificioso, traidor, de mala fe, engañador; fraudulento.
Fraudfully [frōd'-ful-i], *adv.* Engañosamente, pérfidamente.
Fraudless [frōd'-les], *a.* Libre de todo fraude.
Fraudulence, Fraudulency [frōd'-yu-lens, i], *s.* Fraudulencia, fraude, engaño.
Fraudulent [frōd'-yu-lent], *a.* Fraudulento, engañoso.
Fraudulently [frōd'-yu-lent-li], *adv.* Fraudulentamente, fraudulosamente, traidoramente; artificiosamente.
†**Fraught** [frōt], *va.* Cargar. *V.* FREIGHT.
Fraught [frōt], *a.* Cargado, lleno, atestado de, mezclado con. (Vul.) Preñado de. *Fraught with,* Lleno o cargado de.—*s.* (Des.) Carga, cargazón.
Fräulein [froi'-lain], *s.* Señorita; joven, soltera. (Alemán.)
Fraxinella [frac-si-nel'-a], *s.* (Bot.) Fraxinela, fresnillo, díctamo blanco.
Fray [frê], *s.* Refriega, combate, contienda; riña, disputa, querella. *To part the fray,* Separar a los que riñen, ponerlos en paz.
Fray, *va.* 1. Ludir, rozar la superficie, margen o borde de una cosa. 2. (Ant.) Espantar, ahuyentar.—*vn.* Deshilacharse, destejerse por el margen, deshilarse.
Fraying [frê'-ing], *s.* 1. Rozamiento, desgaste. 2. Deshiladura, acción y efecto de deshilarse.
Freak [frīk], *s.* Fantasía, capricho, visión; extravagancia. *Freak of nature,* Cualquier producto raro, caprichoso o extravagante de la naturaleza.
Freak, *va.* Varetear, formar listas de varios colores en los tejidos; abigarrar, gayar.
Freakish [frīk'-ish], *a.* Caprichoso, fantástico, visionario, extravagante.
Freakishly [frīk'-ish-li], *adv.* Caprichosamente.
Freakishness [frīk'-ish-nes], *s.* La calidad de caprichoso o fantástico.
Freckle [frec'-l], *s.* Peca.
Freckle, *vn.* Tener pecas, ponerse pecoso.
Freckled [frec'-ld], *a.* Pecoso.
Freckle-faced [frec'-l-fêst], *a.* Pecoso, con cara pecosa.
Freckly [frec'-li], *a.* Pecoso, lleno de pecas.
Free [frī], *a.* 1. Libre, independiente. 2. Libre, licencioso, insubordinado; disoluto, torpe, deshonesto; desenfrenado, atrevido. 3. Liberal, generoso, franco, abierto, ingenuo; familiar. 4. Exento, privilegiado, dispensado. 5. Libre, permitido, voluntario. 6. Gratuito, lo que es de balde o de gracia. 7. Inocente. 8. Cortés, airoso; vivo, activo. 9. (Mar.) Zafo, flojo, suelto. *Free reed,* Lengüeta. *Free and easy,* (Fam.) Natural, despejado, no cohibido. *Free-board,* (Mar.) Obra muerta. *Free-born,* Nacido libre, no en esclavitud; libre por herencia. *Free goods,* Mercancías exentas de derechos. *Free-handed,* (1) Libre de manos, exento de trabas. (2) Liberal, dadivoso. *Free-liver,* Comedor, comilón, el que come y bebe mucho. *To make free with,* Usar con mucha o demasiada libertad; tomarse libertades con. *Free on board,* (Com.) Libre de gastos a bordo; comunmente se abrevia así: *f. o. b.* *Free port,* Puerto franco. *This seat is free* Este asiento está vacante. *To ride a free horse to death,* (Fig.) Abusar de la paciencia de alguno.
Free, *va.* 1. Libertar, poner en libertad. 2. Librar, sacar o preservar á otro de algún riesgo. 3. Libertar, eximir. 4. Abrirse camino. *To free the ship,* Achicar el agua del bajel.
Freebooter [frī'-būt'-ẹr], *s.* 1. Ladrón, saqueador. 2. Filibustero, forbante.
Freebooting [frī'-būt-ing], *s.* Saqueo, pillaje.
Freedman [frīd'-man], *s.* Liberto, esclavo manumitido.
Freedom [frī'-dum], *s.* 1. Libertad, independencia. 2. Libertad, falta de sujeción o subordinación; contravención desenfrenada a las leyes o buenas costumbres. 3. Libertad, licencia, franqueza o familiaridad atrevida: se usa muy comúnmente en plural en una y otra lengua para expresar una impudente o criminal llaneza o familiaridad. 4. Libertad, la facultad de hacer lo que no se oponga a las leyes ni a las buenas costumbres. 5. Libertad, facilidad,

comodidad. 6. Libertad, soltura de presos y cautivos. 7. La posesión o concesión de inmunidades o privilegios particulares. *The freedom of a city*, La concesión de inmunidades y privilegios especiales en una ciudad. *The freedom of the press*, La libertad de imprenta. *Freedom of speech*, La libertad de la palabra.

Free flight [frī flait'], *s.* (Aer.) Planeo, vuelo libre.

Free-footed [frī-fut'-ed], *a.* El que puede andar sin ningún impedimento.

Free-for-all [frī-fōr-el'], *s.* (fam.) Pelotera, lucha o contienda general.

Freehand [frī'-hand], *a.* Hecho a pulso, sin ayuda de instrumentos. *Freehand drawing*, Dibujo a pulso.

Freehanded [frī-hand'-ed], *a.* Generoso, magnánimo, liberal.

Free-hearted [frī-hārt'-ed], *s.* Liberal, generoso; franco, cordial.

Freehold [frī'-hōld], *s.* Feudo franco, propiedad absoluta de una casa, hacienda, etc.

Freeholder [frī'-hōld-ẹr], *s.* Dueño, propietario absoluto de una casa, heredad, etc.

Free-lance [frī'-lạns], *a.* Independiente. *Free-lance writer, free-lance actor*, Escritor o actor que trabajan independientemente de algún empleo regular.

Freely [frī'-li], *adv.* 1. Libremente, sin restricción, sin reserva; espontáneamente. 2. Desembarazadamente. 3. Francamente, generosamente, de buena gana.

Freeman [frī'-man], *s.* 1. Hombre libre, independiente. 2. Ciudadano, el que goza de los derechos civiles y políticos. 3. Propietario de tierras entre los antiguos anglosajones.

Freemartin [frī'-mar''-tin], *s.* Ternera nacida al mismo tiempo que un ternero y por lo general incapaz de reproducirse.

Freemason [frī-mē'-sn], *s.* Francmasón.

Freemasonry [frī'-mē''-sn-ri], *s.* Francmasonería.

Free-minded [frī-maind'-ed], *a.* Desembarazado, sin cargas ni cuidados.

Freeness [frī'-nes], *s.* Libertad, franqueza; sinceridad; liberalidad.

Free press [frī pres], *s.* Libertad de imprenta.

Freer [frī'-ẹr], *s.* Libertador.—*a.* Más libre; comparativo de *free*.

Free-school [frī'-scūl], *s.* Escuela gratuita.

Freesoiler [frī'-soil-ẹr], *s.* (Amer.) Abolicionista, partidario de la abolición de la esclavitud.

Free-spoken [frī'-spōk-n], *a.* Dicho sin reserva; franco.

Freestone [frī'-stōn], *s.* 1. Piedra franca, piedra arenosa y blanda. 2. Abridero, durazno cuyo hueso se separa fácilmente de la carne.—*a.* Abridero, abridera, fruta cuyo hueso se desprende fácilmente de la carne.

Free-thinker [frī'-thiṇk-ẹr], *s.* El que piensa con libertad, un filósofo. Esta palabra se toma generalmente en mal sentido, e indica un hombre que no cree la religión revelada, y también un libertino.

Free-thinking [frī'-thiṇk'-ing], *s.* Libertad de pensar; filosofismo, libertinaje, irreligión.—*a.* Que piensa con libertad.

Free trade [frī trēd]. Libre cambio; comercio exento de derechos arancelarios.

Free-trader [frī'-trē''-dẹr], *s.* Libre cambista, partidario de la abolición de los derechos arancelarios.

Free verse [frī vẹrs], *s.* Verso libre.

Freeway [frī'-wē], *s.* Autopista sin cuota de peaje.

Freewheeling [frī-hwīl'-ing], *s.* (Mec.) Marcha de rueda libre.

Free-will [frī'-wil], *s.* Libre albedrío, voluntariedad.—*a.* Hecho o ejecutado sin restricción; voluntario, de buena voluntad.

Freewoman [frī'-wum-an], *sf.* Mujer libre, no esclava.

Freezable [frīz'-a-bl], *a.* Congelable.

Freeze [frīz], *vn.* Helarse, helar.—*va.* 1. Congelar, helar de frío. 2. Pasmar de frío, matar de frío. *To freeze on to* o *to*, (Ger.) Convertirse en sombra de otra persona; tomar posesión de una cosa. *To freeze out*, (Fam. E. U.) Excluir, alejar a una persona tratándola con desvío o frialdad.

Freeze-dry [frīz'-drai], *va.* Secar congelado, secar en estado de congelación.

Freezer [frīz'-ẹr], *s.* Congelador. *Deep freezer*, Congeladora.

Freezing [frīz'-ing], *a.* Glacial, de hielo, refrigerante. *Freezing point*, Punto que marca la congelación del agua en los termómetros. (0° C. y R.; 32° F.)—*s.* Congelamiento, hielo.

Freight [frēt], *va.* 1. Fletar, dar y tomar a flete un buque. 2. Cargar.

Freight, *s.* 1. Carga, el peso que lleva un buque de géneros u otra cosa; cargazón. 2. Flete, el precio que se paga por el transporte de las mercancías. *Freight outwards*, Flete de ida. *Freight home* o *return freight*, Flete de vuelta. *Freight out and in*, Flete por viaje redondo. *Dead freight*, Flete falso. *Freight free*, Libre de flete. *To let to freight*, Dejar a flete. *Freight-car*, Furgón o carro de carga.

Freighter [frēt'-ẹr], *s.* Fletador.

Freight house [frēt haus], *s.* (F.C. y Mar.) Depósito de mercancías.

French [french], *a.* y *s.* 1. Francés. *The French*, Los franceses. *After the French fashion*, A la francesa. *A French girl or woman*, Una joven o una mujer francesa. 2. El idioma francés. *In good* o *plain French*, En buen francés. *French leave*, Despedida a la francesa, a la chita callando, como la del que ha cometido un hurto y toma soleta. *To take French leave*, Tomar el pendingue.

French-bean [french'-bīn], *s.* Judía, habichuela, frisol o frijol.

French-chalk [french'-chēc], *s.* Blanco de Meudón. *V.* CHALK.

French-horn [frênch-hērn'], *s.* Bocina, instrumento músico de viento. Corno. *V.* HORN.

Frenchify [fren'-chi-fai], *va.* Afrancesarse, tomar o afectar las modas y costumbres de Francia, volverse gabacho.

French-like [french'-laik], *a.* Afrancesado, agabachado, el que imita o afecta las costumbres o modas francesas.

Frenchman [french'-man], *s.* Francés, el natural de Francia.

Frenetic [frẹ-net'-ic], *a.* Frenético, furioso.

Frenzy [fren'-zi], *s.* Frenesí, enajenamiento furioso del juicio; locura, extravío, devaneo, desbarro.

Frequency [frī'-cwen-si], *s.* Frecuencia; ocurrencia común. *Frequency modulation*, (Radio) Modulación de frecuencia.

Frequent [frī'-cwent], *a.* 1. Frecuente; ordinario, común, usado. 2. (Des.) Frecuentado, lleno de gente.

Frequent [frẹ-cwent'], *va.* Frecuentar o visitar a menudo algún lugar.

Frequentation [frẹ-cwen-tē'-shun], *s.* Frecuentación.

Frequentative [frẹ-cwen'-ta-tiv], *a.* Frecuentativo.

Frequenter [frẹ-cwent'-ẹr], *s.* Frecuentador.

Frequently [frī'-cwent-li], *adv* Frecuentemente.

Fresco [fres'-cō], *s.* 1. Pintura al *fresco*, la que se hace sobre estuco fresco o acabado de hacer; frescura. 2. (Poco us.) Frescura, umbría; en la locución *al fresco*.

Fresh [fresh], *a.* 1. Fresco, nuevo, reciente; recién llegado. 2. Refrescante; que reanima; refrigerante; que devuelve las fuerzas. 3. Fresco, sano, robusto, vivo, fuerte. 4. Dulce o nuevo, lo contrario de añejo o acecinado. 5. Inexperto. 6. Fresco, lo que no está caliente ni tibio; viento fresco o galeno. 7. Fresco, lo que no está salado ni mustio. 8. Presumido, oficioso, entremetido. 9. (Esco.) (a) Sobrio, no achispado; (b) sin helada; abierto. *Fresh way*, (Mar.) Salida fresca. *Fresh wind*, (Mar.) Viento fresco, el algo rápido y fuerte. *A fresh complexion*, Una tez fresca. *Fresh horses*, Caballos nuevos, de relevo. *A fresh hand*, Un novicio. *Fresh from*, Acabado de.—*s.* 1. Avenida, inundación. 2. Arroyo o manantial de agua dulce. 3. Mezcla de agua dulce y salada en los ríos y bahías; desbordamiento de un río.

†**Fresh**, *va.* *V.* REFRESH.

Fresh-blown [fresh'-blōn], *a.* Lo que acaba de echar flor.

Freshen [fresh'-n], *va.* Refrescar, desalar, refrigerar. *To freshen the hawse*, (Mar.) Refrescar los cables. —*vn.* Refrescarse. *The wind freshens*, (Mar.) Refresca el viento.

Freshly [fresh'-li], *adv.* Frescamente; hace poco, recientemente.

Freshman [fresh'-man], *s.* 1. Estudiante de primer año. 2. (Des.) Novicio.

Freshness [fresh'-nes], *s.* 1. Frescura, frescor, el fresco. 2. Frescura, viveza, hermosura, delicadeza, hablando de la tez o de los colores de las flores. 3. El estado de lo que no envejece o pierde fuerzas; renovación del vigor. 4. El estado de lo que es o está fresco, en oposición a lo salado.

Fresh water [fresh wē'-tẹr], *s.* Agua dulce. *Fresh-water*, *a.* De agua dulce.

Fresh-watered [fresh'-wē-tẹrd], *a.* Provisto de agua dulce.

Fret [fret], *s.* 1. Roce o rozamiento; la acción de gastar alguna cosa estregándola; raspadura. 2. Rozadura, el punto gastado o corroído. 3. Enojo, enfado, apuro. 4. Hervor, agitación de la superficie de un líquido. 5. Empeine, herpes.

Fret, *s.* 1. Traste de guitarra. 2. Obra hecha con cincel, o cualquier obra que forma realce o eminencias sobre un plano. 3. (Arq.) Greca, especie de adorno puesto por lo común cerca de las molduras. *Fret-saw*, Sierra de calados.

Fret, *va.* 1. Rozar, gastar o consumir alguna cosa a fuerza de estregarla. 2. Recamar, bordar en realce; varetear. 3. Agitar, enojar, enfadar. 4. Corroer.—*vn.* 1. Rozarse, gastarse o consumirse, apurarse. incomodarse, impacientarse. 2. Agitarse, enojarse, enfadarse. 3. Afligirse, entristecerse. 4. Fermentar. *Fretted columns*, Columnas caladas o estriadas.

Fretful [fret'-ful], *a.* Enojadizo, colérico, mohino, incómodo, molesto.

Fretfully [fret'-ful-i], *adv.* Con mal humor; de mala gana.

Fretfulness [fret'-ful-nes], *s.* Mal genio, mal humor.

Fretter [fret'-ẹr], *s.* El que o lo que consume o enoja. *Vine-fretter*, Pulgón de la viña.

Fretting [fret'-ing], *s.* Agitación, conmoción; entristecimiento.—*pa.* de *To* FRET.

Fretty [fret'-i], *a.* 1. Realzado, bordado, cincelado. 2. (Fam. E. U.) Enojadizo, mohino; aplícase por lo común a las criaturas.

Fretwork [fret'-wŭrk], *s.* Greca, adorno; (Carp.) calado.

Friability [frai-a-bil'-i-ti], *s.* Friabilidad, la calidad de lo que se puede desmenuzar.

Friable [frai'-a-bl], *a.* Friable, desmenuzable.

Friar [frai'-ar], *s.* 1. Fraile, título que se da a los religiosos de algunas órdenes. *Austin friar*, Fraile agustino. *Black friar*, Dominicano. *Gray friar*, Franciscano. *White friar*, Carmelita. 2. *Friar* o *friar-bird*, Pájaro de Australia, el tropidorinco. *Friar's chicken*, (Esco.) Caldo de gallina y huevos. *Friar's lantern*, Fuego fatuo, metéoro.

Friar-like [frai'-ar-laic], **Friarly** [frai'-ar-li], *a.* Frailesco, frailero.

Friary [frai'-a-ri], *s.* Convento de frailes.—*a.* Frailero.

Fribble [frib'-l], *vn.* Tontear, bobear; vacilar.

Fribble, *a.* Vano, inútil, frívolo. —*s.* Pisaverde frívolo; hombre despreciable.

Fribbler [frib'-lẹr], *s.* Un hombre necio.

Fricassee [fric-as-i'], *s.* Fricasé, fritada, cochifrito.

Fricassee, *va.* Hacer un fricasé o guisar algo a modo de fricasé.

Fricative [fric'-a-tiv], *a.* Caracterizado o producido por la fricción.

Friction [fric'-shun], *s.* 1. Fricción; frotación, frotadura. 2. Friega. *Friction clutch* o *coupling*, Manguito de fricción. *Friction matches*, Fósforos de fricción. *Friction gearing*, Engranaje de fricción.

Friday [frai'-dệ], *s.* Viernes. *Good Friday*, Viernes santo. *Black Friday*, Cualquier viernes memorable por una calamidad pública.

Friend [frend], *s.* 1. Amigo, amiga. 2. Compañero, favorecedor, persona propicia o favorable. 3. Adherente, partidario; aliado. 4. Cuáquero, miembro de la sociedad de los cuáqueros, secta religiosa. *A bosom friend*, Amigo de corazón. *A friend at court*, Amigo que tiene el poder de servir a otro. *To make friends with one*, Reconciliarse, hacer las paces. *A friend in need is a friend indeed*, En la necesidad se conoce al verdadero amigo. *Short reckonings make long friends*, Cuanto más amigos más claros; o las cuentas claras hacen los buenos amigos.

Friendless [frend'-les], *a.* Desamparado, desvalido, sin protección ni amigos.

Friend-like [frend'-laic], **Friendly** [frend'-li], *a.* 1. Amigable, amistoso, como amigo. 2. Servicial, favorable, benévolo, dispuesto a favorecer los intereses de otro. 3. Favorable, propicio.

Friendliness [frend'-li-nes], *s.* Amistad.

Friendship [frend'-ship], *s.* Amistad, intimidad, afecto; favor, socorro, ayuda.

Frieze [friz], *s.* 1. Frisa, tela de lana a modo de bayeta. 2. (Arq.) Friso.

Frieze-like [friz'-laic], *a.* Semejante a la frisa.

Frigate [frig'-et], *s.* (Mar.) Fragata, antiguo bajel de guerra. *Frigate-bird*, Fragata, ave acuática de los mares tropicales. Fregata aquila.

Frigate-built [frig'-et-bilt], *a.* (Mar.) Construído a manera de fragata.

Fright (Poét.), **Frighten** [frait, n], *va.* Espantar, causar horror, miedo o espanto, asustar. *To frighten to death*, Hacer, causar un miedo mortal. *To frighten away*, Ahuyentar, espantar.

Fright, *s.* 1. Susto, espanto, terror repentino. 2. Espantajo, esperpento, lo que causa espanto. *To take fright at*, Asustarse de. *What a fright you have made of yourself!* ¡Está Vd. hecho un espantajo!

Frightful [frait'-ful], *a.* Espantoso, horrible; feísimo, horroroso, espantable.

Frightfully [frait'-ful-i], *adv.* Espantosamente, terriblemente.

Frightfulness [frait'-ful-nes], *s.* Horror, espanto.

Frigid [frij'-id], *a.* 1. Frío, frígido. 2. Indiferente; impotente. 3. Frío, lo que no tiene brío, espíritu ni agudeza.

Frigidity [fri-jid'-i-ti], *s.* 1. Frialdad, falta de calor. 2. Frialdad, flojedad, negligencia, lentitud. 3. Frialdad, despego, indiferencia, tibieza de afectos. 4. Impotencia.

Frigidly [frij'-id-li], *adv.* Fríamente, con frialdad o despego.

Frill [fril], *s.* 1. Escote, vuelo; chorrera, pechera. 2. *pl.* (E. U. Fam.) Aires, ademanes afectados.

Frill, *s.* Tiritón que sufren los halcones y otras aves.

Frill, *va.* 1. Hacer algo en forma de vuelo o chorrera. 2. Guarnecer con vuelos o pecheras.—*vn.* Formar o tener algo la forma de vuelo o chorrera.

Fringe [frinj], *s.* Franja; margen, borde, fleco, rodapié, orla, ribete, orilla, guarnición.

Fringe, *va.* Ribetear, franjear, orillar.

Fringe benefit [frinj ben'-e-fit], *s.* (Com.) Beneficio marginal o adicional.

Fringeless [frinj'-les], *a.* Desprovisto de franjas; sin ribete.

Fringe-maker [frinj'-mê-kẹr], *s.* Fabricante de franjas, cordonero.

Fringe-tree [frinj'-trî], *s.* Árbol pequeño de los Estados Unidos del este, cuyas flores son blancas como la nieve y cuelgan formando franjas. Chionanthus Virginica.

Fringy [frinj'-i], *a.* Adornado con franjas; parecido a un ribete.

Fripper, **Fripperer** [frip'-ẹr, ẹr], *s.* Ropavejero, baratillero; prendero.

Frippery [frip'-ẹr-i], *s.* 1. Ropavejería; baratillo. 2. Ropa vieja, vestidos viejos o desechos. 3. Fruslería, bobería.—*a.* Despreciable, frívolo.

Friseur [fri-zūr'], *s.* Peluquero. (Fr.)

Frisk [frisk], *vn.* Saltar, brincar, cabriolar, estar en continuo movimiento; retozar.

Frisk, *s.* Retozo; gambeta, brinco o salto.

Frisker [frisk'-ẹr], *s.* El que es inconstante o voluble.

Frisket [fris'-ket], *s.* (Impr.) Frasqueta, bastidor de hierro que sujeta el papel en las prensas de mano.

Friskiness [frisk'-i-nes], *s.* Viveza en el trato, alegría, vivacidad.

Frisking [frisk'-ing], *s.* Alegría rústica, baile juguetón.

Friskful [frisk'-ful], **Frisky** [frisk'-i], *a.* Juguetón, alegre, desparpajado, vivaracho, gallardo, vivo.

Frit [frit], *s.* 1. Frita; en las fábricas de vidrio, la mezcla destinada a fundirse en los crisoles. 2. Frita, el material o ingredientes de que se hacen ciertos artículos blandos y plásticos de alfarería.

Frith o **Firth** [frith, fẹrth], *s.* 1. (Esco.) Estrecho o brazo de mar. 2. Nasa, especie de red.

Frithy [frith'-i], *a.* (Des.) Leñoso, selvático.

Fritillary [frit'-il-ẹ-ri], *s.* (Bot.) Fritilaria, planta de las liliáceas.

Fritter [frit'-ẹr], *s.* 1. Tajada, torrezno, fritilla. 2. Fragmento, parte pequeña de alguna cosa. 3. Quesadilla, torta de queso. 4. Buñuelo, hojaldre, fruta de sartén.

Fritter, *va.* 1. Tajar carne para freirla. 2. Desmenuzar, deshacer alguna cosa reduciéndola a piezas y partes menudas.

Frivolity [fri-vel'-i-ti], *s.* Frivolidad.

Frivolous [friv'-o-lus], *a.* Frívolo, vano, inútil.

Frivolously [friv'-o-lus-li], *adv.* Frívolamente, vanamente.

Frivolousness [friv'-o-lus-nes], *s.* Frivolidad.

Frizz, **Frizzle** [friz, friz'-l], *va.* Frisar; rizar, encrespar.

Frizzle, *s.* Rizo, bucle.

Frizzler [friz'-lẹr], *s.* Rizador.

Fro [frō], *adv.* Atrás, hacia atrás. *To go to and fro*, Ir y venir, ir de un lado a otro. *Goings to and fro*, Idas y venidas.

Frock [froc], *s.* 1. Bata de niño o de señora; túnica, vestido exterior de mujer. 2. Blusa. *Frock-coat*, Levita. *Smock frock*, Sayo, especie de camisa de lienzo ordinario, que se pone sobre el vestido para resguardarlo.

Frog [freg], *s.* 1. Rana. 2. Ranilla, hendidura del talón del caballo. 3. Corazón o rana de ferrocarril; parte o sección de la vía en que un carril corta a otro o se separa de él, como sucede en los cambiavías o chuchos. *Frog-plate*, (1) Pieza que sirve para colocar la pata de una rana bajo el microscopio a fin de observar la circulación de la sangre. (2) Bastidor de cambio o de rana en los ferrocarriles. *Tree-frog*, Calamite, sapo verde y pequeño. Hyla viridis.

Frogbit [freg'-bit], *s.* (Bot.) Morena, planta acuática.

Froggy [freg'-i], *a.* Lleno de ranas.

Frogman [freg'-man], *s.* Hombre rana.

Frolic [frel'-ic], *s.* Fantasía, capricho, extravagancia, jarana.—*a.* Alegre, vivo, vivaracho, caprichoso.

Frolic, *vn.* Loquear, juguetear, retozar, estar de chacota, triscar, jaranear.

Frolicsome [frel'-ic-sum], *a.* Juguetón, travieso.
Frolicsomely [frel'-ic-sum-li], *adv.* Alegremente, con humorada o viveza.
Frolicsomeness [frel'-ic-sum-nes], *s.* Viveza, humorada, demasiada alegría.
From [frem], *prep.* 1. De. *From my heart,* De lo íntimo de mi corazón. *From time to time,* De cuando en cuando. 2. Después, desde. *From that time,* Desde entonces, desde aquel tiempo. 3. De, desde, hablando de lugar. *From top to toe,* De pies a cabeza. *From above,* Desde arriba, de lo alto. *From afar,* De lejos. *From amidst,* Del medio de. *From beneath,* De abajo, de lo hondo. *From behind,* Desde atrás. *From beyond,* De más allá. *From far,* Desde lejos, de lejos. *From without,* De fuera. *From among,* De entre. *From off,* Lejos, fuera de. *From on high,* Desde lo alto. *From out,* De, desde, del fondo de. *From under,* De debajo. 4. Por, a causa de, a fuerza de; debido a. *From an honourable motive,* Por un motivo honroso. *Rather from policy than,* Más bien por política que. *There is danger from ignorance,* Hay peligro a causa de la ignorancia. 5. De, de parte de. *He came from the general,* Vino de parte del general. 6. Según, conforme. *From what I hear,* Según lo que oigo, o según oigo. *Painted from nature,* Pintado del natural, conforme al natural. 7. Sobre, en; contra. *Men do not gather figs from thistles,* No se cogen higos en (o entre) los abrojos. *A revolt from the monarchy,* Una rebelión contra la monarquía. 8. Con. *He made a supper from the remains of his dinner,* Cenó con los restos de la comida. Esta preposición frecuentemente se invierte en el estilo familiar, como, *Where do you come from?* ¿De dónde viene Vd.?
Frond [frend], *s.* (Bot.) 1. Fronda, la parte hojosa que sostiene la fructificación de los helechos y las algas. 2. Cualquiera hoja grande de los trópicos, como la de la palmera.
Frondent [fren'-dent], **Frondose** [fren'-dōs], *a.* (Bot.) Frondoso.
Frondescent [fren-des'-ent], *a.* (Bot.) Frondescente: dícese de los vegetales cuando están desplegando sus hojas y de las plantas que llevan fronda.
Frondiferous [fren-dif'-ęr-us], *a.* (Bot.) Frondífero.
Front [frunt], *s.* 1. Frente. 2. Frente, la parte que está en frente de alguno. 3. Faz, cara; la manera de hacer frente a una persona o situación. *Put the best front you can on the matter,* Ponga Vd. en este asunto la mejor cara que pueda. *To stand front to front,* Estar cara a cara. *In front of,* En frente de, cara a cara con. 4. Audacia, atrevimiento, descaro. 5. (Arq.) Frente, frontispicio, fachada; portal, como de una iglesia. 6. Pechera, delantera, camisolín; caña de una bota. *Front door,* Puerta de entrada. *Front bolt,* Pasador que asegura el fusil a la caja.
Front, *a.* 1. Anterior, delantero, lo que está al frente. 2. Frontero, mirado del frente. 3. Medido por el frente. 4. Frontal. *Front room,* Cuarto de frente, cuarto a la calle o en la fachada principal de una casa. *Front view,* Vista al frente.
Front, *va.* 1. Hacer frente, oponerse cara a cara. 2. Estar en frente de alguna cosa.—*vn.* 1. Estar al frente. 2. Dar a, caer a. *This house fronts on the park,* Esta casa da al parque.
Frontage [frunt'-ęj], *s.* Extensión lineal de frente. *The lot has a frontage of seventy feet on Vallejo Street,* El solar tiene un frente de setenta pies en la calle de Vallejo.
Frontal [frent'-al], *a.* 1. Frontero, anterior. 2. Frontal, perteneciente a la frente.—*s.* 1. (Arq.) Tímpano pequeño. 2. Frontero, venda.
Front curtain [frunt cūr'-ten], *s.* (Teat.) Telón de boca.
Frontier [fren-tīr' o fren'-tīr], *s.* Frontera, la raya o término de un territorio.—*a.* Fronterizo, frontero. *Frontier town,* Ciudad fronteriza.
Frontiniac [fren-ti-nyac'], *s.* Vino de Frontiñán en Francia.
Frontispiece [fren'-tis-pīs], *s.* 1. El frontis grabado de un libro. 2. Frontispicio.
Frontless [frunt'-les], *a.* Descarado, desvergonzado, impudente.
Frontlet [frunt'-let], *s.* 1. Venda para la frente. 2. (Art.) Frontón de mira. 3. (Orn.) Margen de la cabeza detrás del pico de las aves que está por lo común cubierto con cerdas.
Front seat [frunt sīt], *s.* Asiento delantero.
Frost [frēst], *s.* Helada, hielo. *Hoar frost, white frost,* Escarcha. *Frost-bite,* Congelación parcial de los dedos o las orejas. *Frost-nail,* Clavo de gancho que se pone en las herraduras del caballo en tiempo de hielos para que no resbale. *Frost-nipped,* Quemado por el hielo.
Frost, *va.* 1. Helar. 2. Escarchar, cubrir un manjar con una composición azucarada, parecida a la escarcha. 3. Dañar por medio del frío o el hielo, quemar. 4. Deslustrar, despulir.
Frosted, *pp.* y *a.* 1. Helado. 2. Deslustrado, despulido; que presenta una superficie áspera y sin brillo.
Frost-bitten [frēst'-bit-n], *a.* Helado, quemado o marchitado por el hielo o la escarcha.
Frostiness [frēst'-i-nes], *s.* Frío, helamiento.
Frosting [frest'-ing], *s.* 1. Clara de huevo batida con azúcar, que forma como una capa de nieve sobre ciertos pasteles. 2. Deslustre, aspereza en la superficie del metal, el cristal o la madera; cualquier superficie que imita la escarcha.
Frost-work [frēst'-wūrk], *s.* Garapiña, garapiñado.
Frosty [frēst'-i], *a.* 1. Helado, frío como el hielo. 2. Frío, indiferente, insensible. 3. Cano, canoso.
Froth [frēth], *s.* 1. Espuma que forma el hervor o agitación de algún líquido. 2. Bambolla, paja.
Froth, *vn.* Espumar, criar espuma. —*va.* Hacer espuma.
Frothily [frēth'-i-li], *adv.* Con espuma; frívolamente, sin substancia.
Frothiness [frēth'-i-nes], *s.* Vaciedad, frivolidad.
Frothy [frēth'-i], *a.* 1. Espumoso, lleno o cubierto de espuma. 2. Frívolo, vano, inútil.
Frounce [frauns], *va.* (Ant.) Rizar, encrespar o ensortijar el cabello.—*vn.* Ponerse ceñudo.
Frouzy [frau'-zi], *a.* *V.* Frowzy.
Frow [frau], *s.* (Fam.) Dama holandesa o alemana; mujer casada.
Froward [frō'-ward], *a.* Indómito, incorregible, díscolo, protervo; insolente, impertinente. *A froward child,* Niño impertinente y difícil de contentar.
Frowardly [frō'-ward-li], *adv.* Indócilmente, arrogantemente, insolentemente.
Frown [fraun], *va.* Mirar con ceño, poner mala cara.—*vn.* 1. Poner mal gesto, ponerse ceñudo, enfurruñarse. *To frown upon one,* Mirar a alguno de mal ojo. *To frown any one down,* Avergonzar a uno, hacerle bajar los ojos, sonrojarle 2. Rechazar a alguno con aspecto amenazador o severo. *He frowned them into silence,* Su expresión amenazadora los redujo al silencio.
Frown, *s.* Ceño, entrecejo, desagrado, enfado o enojo. *Frowns of fortune,* Reveses de fortuna.
Frowning [fraun'-ing], *a.* Ceñudo.
Frowningly [fraun'-ing-li], *adv.* Enojadamente, con ceño, de mal ojo.
Frowzy [frau'-zi], *a.* Desaliñado, desaseado, sucio; mal peinado.
Froze [frōz], *pret.* del verbo Freeze.
Frozen [frōz'-n], *pp.* de *To* Freeze. Helado, congelado; frío.
Fructiferous [fruc-tif'-ęr-us], *a.* Fructífero, que da frutos.
Fructification [fruc'-ti-fi-kē'-shun], *s.* (Bot.) Fructificación; fecundación.
Fructify [fruc'-ti-fai], *va.* Fertilizar, fecundar.—*vn.* Fructificar, dar o producir fruto.
Fructose [fruc'-tos], *s.* Fructosa o levulosa.
Frugal [frū'-gal], *a.* Económico; frugal, sobrio, templado.
Frugality [frū-gal'-i-ti], *s.* Economía; frugalidad, moderación, sobriedad o templanza.
Frugally [frū'-gal-i], *adv.* Frugalmente, sobriamente.
Frugiferous [fru-jif'-ęr-us], *a.* Fructífero.
Frugivorous [frū-jiv'-o-rus], *a.* Frugívoro, que se alimenta de frutos.
Fruit [frūt], *s.* 1. Fruto. 2. Fruta. *Dry fruit,* Fruta seca. *To live upon fruit,* Mantenerse con fruta. 3. Fruto, producto, utilidad, provecho. 4. Prole. 5. Postres. *Fruit-basket,* Cesta para fruta. *Fruit-knife,* Cuchillo de postres. *Fruit-jar,* Vaso o tarro para frutas, en especial el que puede cerrarse herméticamente. *Stone fruit,* Fruta de hueso. *Fruit-bearing,* Frutal, que produce fruta. *Fruit-dryer,* Secadero de frutas. *Fruit-eating,* Frugívoro. *Fruit press,* Aparato para prensar frutas. *Preserved fruit,* Fruta en almíbar. *Candied fruit,* Fruta azucarada.
Fruit, *vn.* Producir fruta, dar fruto.
Fruitage [frūt'-ęj], *s.* 1. Frutas, toda suerte de fruta en general. 2. Fruto, resultado o efecto de alguna acción.
Fruit-bearer [frūt'-bār-ęr], *s.* Frutal; lo que produce fruta.
Fruit-bearing [frūt'-bār-ing], *s.* Fructífero; frutal.
Fruit cake [frūt kēk], *s.* Pastel de frutas.
§**Fruitery** [frūt'-ęr-i], *s.* 1. Fruta. 2. Frutería, lugar destinado a guardar la fruta.
Fruitful [frūt'-ful], *a.* Fructífero, fértil, prolífico, abundante, copioso, fecundo; provechoso, útil, ventajoso.

Fruitfully [frūt'-ful-i], *adv.* Fértilmente, prolíficamente.

Fruitfulness [frūt'-ful-nes], *s.* Fertilidad, fecundidad.

Fruit-groves [frūt'-grōvz], *s. pl.* Vergel de frutales.

Fruition [frū-i'-shun], *s.* 1. Fruición. 2. Fruición, gusto, complacencia.

Fruitless [frūt'-les], *a.* Estéril, infructuoso; inútil, vano.

Fruitlessly [frūt'-les-li], *adv.* Infructuosamente; inútilmente.

Fruitlessness [frūt'-les-nes], *s.* Esterilidad; infructuosidad.

Fruit stand [frūt stand], *s.* Puesto de frutas.

Fruit store [frūt stōr], *s.* Frutería.

Fruit-time [frūt'-taim], *s.* Otoño, cosecha, el tiempo de recoger los frutas.

Fruit-tree [frūt'-trī], *s.* Frutal, árbol que produce fruta.

Fruity [frūt'-i], *a.* Semejante a la fruta en el sabor, el olor o las cualidades.

Frumentaceous [frū-men-té'-shus], *a.* Frumenticio.

Frumenty [frū'-ment-i], *s.* Manjar hecho de trigo cocido con leche.

Frump, *s.* 1. Vieja que se viste a la antigua y es de genio áspero y regañón. 2. (Des.) Chiste, burla, mofa.

†**Frush** [frush], *va.* Romper, magullar, quebrar.

Frush, *s.* (Vet.) Arestín.

Frustrable [frus'-tra-bl], *a.* (Poco us.) Capaz de ser frustrado.

Frustrate [frus'-trét], *va.* 1. Frustrar, privar o defraudar a uno de lo que le tocaba o esperaba; burlar, dejar burlada la intención o esperanza de una persona. 2. Anular, hacer nula una cosa.

Frustrate, *a.* 1. Frustrado, burlado. 2. Inútil, vano, nulo. 3. Desventajoso.

Frustration [frus-tré'-shun], *s.* Contratiempo, chasco; privación.

Frustrative [frus'-tra-tiv], *a.* Falaz, engañoso.

Frustratory [frus'-tra-to-ri], *a.* (For.) Frustratorio, lo que hace nula alguna cosa; frustráneo.

Frustule [frus'-tiūl], *s.* (Bot.) Frústula, el casco silíceo de un diátomo.

Frustum [frus'-tum], *s.* 1. Parte inferior de un cuerpo sólido que se forma cortando la cúspide por un plano paralelo a la base. 2. Trozo, pedazo.

Frutescent [frū-tes'-ent], *a.* (Bot.) Fruticoso: dícese de las plantas que se hacen arbustos o que se parecen a un arbusto.

Fruticose [frū'-ti-cōs], *a.* Fruticoso, relativo a los arbustos; que se parece al arbusto.

Fry [frai], *s.* 1. El conjunto de pececillos que sale del desove o de las huevas. 2. Enjambre, la muchedumbre de cosas juntas o de personas, cuando unas y otras son de poca importancia. 3. Fritada, el conjunto de cosas fritas. 4. (Fam.) Aprieto, brete, estado de molestia o agitación.

Fry, *va.* Freir.—*vn.* Freirse; derretirse de calor; estar agitado o acalorado. *To have other fish to fry,* Tener otras cosas en que pensar.

Frying-pan [frai'-ing-pan], *s.* Sartén. *To jump from the frying-pan into the fire,* Saltar de la sartén y dar en las brasas.

Fucate, Fucated [fiū'-kêt, ed], *a.* Pintado, disfrazado.

Fuchsia [fiū'-shia], *s.* Fucsia, arbusto con flores rojas y purpúreas del mismo nombre, que cuelgan de las axilas; es planta de adorno originaria de la América del Sur.

Fucoid [fiū'-ceid], *a.* Fucóideo, que se parece a los fucos u ovas.—*s.* 1. Alga parecida al fuco. 2. Planta viva o fósil que se asemeja a las algas.

Fucus [fiū'-cus], *s.* 1. Afeite, aderezo y compostura del rostro; disfraz. 2. (Bot.) Fuco, ova. *Fuci,* [fiū'-sai], *pl.* Fucos.

Fuddle [fud'-l], *va.* Emborrachar.—*vn.* Emborracharse.

Fudge [fuj], *s.* Embuste, cuento; se usa más como interjección. ¡Quita de ahí! ¡quita allá!

Fuel [fiū'-el], *s.* 1. Combustible, todo lo que sirve de alimento al fuego. 2. Pábulo, aliciente.

Fuel, *va.* (Ant.) Servir material combustible al fuego; proveer con leña o materiales para el fuego.

Fueling [fiū'-el-ing], *s.* Abastecimiento de combustible.

†**Fueller** [fiū'-el-er], *s.* El que provee con leña; el que enciende.

Fugacious [fiu-gé'-shus], *a.* 1. Fugaz, volátil, instable; transitorio. 2. (Bot.) Fugaz, que se cae o que perece muy temprano.

Fugaciousness [fiu-gé'-shus-nes], **Fugacity** [fiu-gas'-i-ti], *s.* Fugacidad, instabilidad, volatilidad.

Fugh [fu], *inter.* ¡Fo! expresión de asco o enfado.

Fugitive [fiū'-ji-tiv], *a.* Fugitivo, desterrado, expulsado; fugaz, volátil, vagabundo, huidizo; pasajero, perecedero.—*s.* 1. Fugitivo, desertor, tránsfuga, apóstata. 2. Refugiado; contumaz, el que se sustrae por la fuga a la acción de la justicia. *Fugitive pieces,* Folletos sueltos.

Fugitiveness [fiū'-ji-tiv-nes], *s.* Fugacidad, instabilidad.

Fugleman, Fugelman [fiū'-gl-man], *s.* (Mil.) Jefe de fila; el que manda una hilera de soldados. (Ale. flügelmann.)

Fugue [fiūg], *s.* (Mús.) Fuga, composición que gira sobre un tema y su imitación, repetidos con cierto artificio por diferentes tonos.

-ful [ful], *sufijo.* 1. Lleno de; abundante en; que contiene. *Fruitful,* Abundante en frutos. 2. Capacidad, cabida o medida; v. g. *spoonful,* cucharada; *a glassful,* un vaso lleno, el contenido de un vaso. Los nombres que tienen este sufijo forman el plural añadiendo la letra *s*: *cupful, cupfuls.*

Fulcrum [ful'-crum], *s.* 1. (Mec.) Apoyo de palanca o alzaprima. 2. (Bot.) Accesoria, apéndice u órganc de las plantas, como pedúnculo, espina, aguijón, zarcillo, etc.

Fulfil [ful-fil'], *va.* 1. Colmar, llenar abundantemente, llenar hasta arriba. 2. Cumplir, ejecutar lo que se había prometido. 3. Observar con exactitud lo que está mandado. *To fulfil one's duty,* Cumplir con su obligación.

Fulfiller [ful-fil'-er], *s.* El que cumple o llena.

Fulfilling [ful-fil'-ing], *s.* Cumplimiento.

Fulfilment [ful-fil'-ment], *s.* Ejecución completa de alguna cosa.

Fulgency [ful'-jen-si], **Fulgidity** [ful-jid'-i-ti], ‖**Fulgor** [ful'-ger], *s.* Fulgor, resplandor, esplendor.

Fulgent [ful'-jent], †**Fulgid** [ful'-jid], *a.* Fulgente, brillante, fúlgido.

‖**Fulgurate** [ful'-giu-rêt], *vn.* Fulgurar.

Fuliginous [fiu-lij'-i-nus], *a.* Fuliginoso, denegrido, tiznado.

Full [ful], *va.* Dar amplitud a una cosa, fruncir el borde de una tela; hacer espeso o grueso.—*vn.* 1. Hacerse lleno, grueso o espeso; llegar la luna a su plenilunio. 2. Fruncirse, plegarse; mostrar amplitud.

Full, *va.* Abatanar o batanar el paño; hacerlo más espeso y compacto por medio de un procedimiento dado.—*vn.* Hacerse más espeso y compacto.

Full [ful], *a.* 1. Lleno, repleto, surtido de alguna cosa; gordo; amplio, pleno. 2. Harto, saciado; copioso, completo. 3. Maduro, perfecto; fuerte. *Full stop,* Punto final. *Full of sorrow,* Lleno de trabajos, consumido por los pesares. *Full of business,* Abrumado de negocios. *Full of play,* Amigo de retozar, alegre, juguetón. *Full moon,* Plenilunio, luna llena. *Full sail,* Vela llena. *Full sea,* Mar bravío. *Full two years,* Dos años bien cumplidos. *Full powers,* Facultades amplias. *Full weight,* Peso cabal. *Full and by,* (Mar.) A buen viento. *To keep the sails full,* (Mar.) Andar a buena vela.—*s.* 1. Lleno, complemento; colmo; saciedad. 2. Total, el todo que resulta de la unión de muchas cosas.—*adv.* 1. Enteramente, del todo, de lleno. *Full well,* Muy bien. 2. Derechamente, rectamente, exactamente. *Full* se usa a menudo en la composición de algunas voces para denotar que una cosa ha llegado a su complemento o perfección. *Full-blooded,* (1) Pletórico, que tiene plenitud de sangre. (2) De sangre pura; de casta no mezclada. *Full-blown,* (1) Abierto, descogido o desplegado completamente; hablando de las flores. (2) Maduro, cabal; en todo su esplendor o desarrollo. (3) Hinchado completamente por el viento. *Full-butt,* (Fam.) Con un choque súbito y violento. *Full-charged,* Sobrecargado. *Full-cock,* Montado, amartillado; dícese de un arma de fuego. *Full-dress,* Gran gala; vestido de gran gala, de uniforme o como es preciso para presentarse de ceremonia en alguna función. *Full-drive,* A carrera tendida, a toda rienda, al galope. *Full-eared,* Lo que tiene espigas llenas y grandes. *Full-eyed,* De ojos saltones. *Full-faced,* (1) Carilleno, carigordo. (2) (Impr.) Letra negra: los mismo que *bold-face. Full-fed,* Bien alimentado, gordo, grueso. *Full-grown,* Maduro; crecido completamente. *A full-grown man, woman,* Un hombre hecho, una mujer hecha. *Full-hearted,* Elevado, confiado; atrevido, valeroso. *Full length,* De grandor natural, de cuerpo entero. *Full-manned,* Tripulado completamente. *Full-mouthed,* Lo que tiene voz o sonido fuerte. *Full-orbed,* Lo que tiene un orbe o una esfera completa; lo que está tan lleno como la luna durante el plenilunio. *Full-spread,* Extendido a lo largo. *Full-summed,* Completo en todas sus partes. *Full-winged,* Lo que tiene alas grandes; alado.

Fullage [ful'-ej], *s.* Lo que se paga por abatanar el paño.

Fullback [ful'-bac], *s.* Defensa (en el futbol).

Fuller [ful'-ẹr], *s.* Batanero, el que abatana el paño.
Fuller's-earth [ful'-ẹrz-ẹrth], *s.* Tierra de batán, especie de greda que se emplea en los batanes para desengrasar los paños.
Fuller's-thistle [ful'-ẹrz-this'-l], *s.* Capota, cardencha, dipsaco.
Fullery [ful'-ẹr-i], *s.* Batán y oficina del batanero.
Full-fashioned [ful-fash'-ʊnd], *a.* Tejido o confeccionado para que ajuste bien (ropa interior, medias, etc.)
Full-fledged [ful-flejd'], *a.* Completo, acabado. *A full-fledged doctor*, Médico en todo el sentido de la palabra.
Fulling-mill [ful'-ing-mil], *s.* Batán.
Full-length film [ful-length film], *s.* Película de largo metraje.
Full swing, in [ful swing], *adv.* En plena actividad, en todo su apogeo.
Fully [ful'-i], *adv.* Plenamente, completamente.
Fulminant [ful'-mi-nant], *a.* Fulminante.
Fulminate [ful'-mi-nêt], *va.* y *vn.* 1. Hacer explosión, estallar. 2. Tronar, dar un estallido, detonar. 3. Excomulgar, imponer una censura. 4. Fulminar. 5. Censurar, condenar.
Fulminating [ful'-mi-nêt-ing], *pa.* Fulminante. *Fulminating cap*, Cápsula fulminante.
Fulmination [ful-mi-nê'-shun], *s.* Fulminación, el acto de fulminar y su efecto; trueno.
Fulminatory [ful'-mi-na-to-ri], *a.* Fulminante, fulminoso, fulmíneo.
Fulmine [ful'-min], *va.* Fulminar, lanzar con explosión, a manera de relámpago.—*vn.* Tronar; de aquí, hablar de una manera vehemente, con voz de trueno.
Fulness o **Fullness** [ful'-nes], *s.* 1. Plenitud, copia, llenura, abundancia; hartura, saciedad. 2. Complemento. 3. Fuerza o vigor del sonido. *Fulness of the heart*, Abundancia de afecto; llenura del corazón.
Fulsome [ful'-sum], *a.* Que ofende o disgusta por exceso de elogio; de aquí, grosero, bajo, repugnante.
Fulsomely [ful'-sum-li], *adv.* Asquerosamente, indecentemente.
Fulsomeness [ful'-sum-nes], *s.* Asquerosidad.
Fulvous [ful'-vus], **Fulvid** [ful'-vid], *a.* Leonado, color leonado; amarillo obscuro con tinte rojizo.
Fumarole [fiū'-ma-rōl], *s.* Agujero pequeño por donde salen vapores volcánicos. (< Ital. fumaruolo.)
Fumble [fum'-bl], *va.* 1. Chapucear, manosear desmañadamente o sin propósito. 2. Parar o coger una pelota desmañadamente, ocasionando una demora.—*vn.* Emplear las manos desmañadamente; ir a tientas. *To fumble along*, Andar a tientas.
Fumbler [fum'-blẹr], *s.* Chapucero.
Fumblingly [fum'-bling-li], *adv.* Chapuceramente.
Fume [fiūm], *s.* 1. El vapor que exhala alguna cosa que fermenta. 2. Vapor del estómago. 3. Cólera, acaloramiento. 4. Humo, vanidad, presunción. 5. (Ant.) Humo. *Fumes of wine*, Vapores del vino.
Fume, *vn.* 1. Humear, echar o arrojar humo. 2. Exhalar, despedir vapores. 3. Encolerizarse, enojarse. —*va.* 1. Ahumar; sahumar; exponer a los vapores del amoniaco, como en ciertas manipulaciones fotográficas. 2. Exhalar, despedir alguna cosa en vapores. *To fume away*, Evaporarse alguna cosa.
Fumet [fiū'-met], *s.* (Des.) Freza, el estiércol de los venados.
Fumigate [fiū'-mi-gêt], *va.* 1. Desinfectar por la acción del humo o del vapor. 2. Perfumar, sahumar. 3. Ahumar, curar por medio del humo.
Fumigation [fiū-mi-gê'-shun], *s.* 1. Sahumerio, sahumo. 2. (Med.) Fumigación.
Fumigator [fiū'-mi-gê-tẹr], *s.* Fumigador, máquina fumigatoria.
Fuming [fiū'-ming], *s.* El acto de humear; capricho vano.—*a.* Humeante, fumante.
Fumingly [fiū'-ming-li], *adv.* Coléricamente.
Fumish [fiū'-mish], **Fumous** [fiū'-mus], *a.* (Bot.) De color de humo.
Fumitory [fiū'-mi-to-ri], *s.* (Bot.) Fumaria, hierba oficinal de las papaveráceas, cuyo jugo es de sabor amargo. *Climbing fumitory*, Fumaria trepadora, Adlumia cirrhosa. Se llama familiarmente, "*lover's-wreath*," corona de los amantes.
Fumy [fiū'-mi], *a.* Humoso.
Fun [fun], *s.* Diversión, entretenimiento; chanza, chiste, chuscada, burla. *For fun* o *in fun*, En chanza, de burlas, por modo de fiesta, de chacota.
Funambulist [fiu-nam'-biu-list], †**Funambulo** [fiu-nam'-biu-lo], *s.* Funámbulo, volatín.
Function [fuṇc'-shun], *s.* 1. Función, el acto o ejercicio de algún empleo, facultad u oficio. 2. Desempeño o cumplimiento de un deber. 3. Ocupación, ejercicio. 4. Función, el ejercicio de los movimientos vitales de las diferentes partes del cuerpo animal. 5. Potencia, facultad. 6. (Mat.) Cantidad que depende de otra.
Functionary [fuṇc'-shun-ẹr-i], *s.* Funcionario, empleado.
Functionate [fuṇc'-shun-êt], *va.* Ejercer una función; tener oficio; obrar.
Functioning [func'-shʊn-ing], *s.* Funcionamiento.
Fund [fund], *s.* 1. Fondo, caudal de alguna cosa; acopio, reserva. *A great fund of humour*, Un abundante fondo de buen humor. 2. Dinero contante, o capital convertible. 3. *pl.* Fondos públicos; (fam.) dinero. *Sinking fund*, Fondo de amortización.
Fund, *va.* 1. Consolidar una deuda; destinar fondos al pago de los intereses de una deuda. 2. Poner dinero en los fondos públicos, o en los de una compañía o casa de comercio.
Fundament [fun'-da-mẹnt], *s.* 1. Fundamento, principio, cimiento. 2. Ancas, trasero; ano.
Fundamental [fun-da-men'-tal], *a.* Fundamental.—*s.* Fundamento.
Fundamentally [fun-da-men'-tal-i], *adv.* Fundamentalmente.
Funded [fund'-ed], *pp.* y *a.* 1. Consolidado; convertido en préstamo permanente. *Funded debt*, Deuda consolidada. 2. Acumulado e invertido, particularmente en los fondos públicos.
Fundus [fun'-dus], *s.* Fondo, base, la parte trasera o lo hondo de alguna cosa.
Funeral [fiu'-ner-al], *a.* Funeral, fúnebre.—*s.* Funeral, funerales, exequias, pompas fúnebres, entierro. *Funeral director*, Director de pompas fúnebres. *Funeral parlor*, Funeraria.
Funereal [fiu-nī'-rẹ-al], *a.* Fúnebre; triste, funesto.
‖**Funest** [fiu-nest'], *a.* Lúgubre, lamentable.
Fungiform [fun'-ji-form], *a.* Fungóideo, que tiene la forma de un hongo.
Fungosity [fun-gos'-i-ti], *s.* Fungosidad, excrecencia blanda.
Fungous [fun'-gus], *a.* Fungoso, lo que se aproxima a la naturaleza del hongo; esponjoso, poroso.
Fungus [fuṇ'-gus], *s.* (*pl.* FUNGI [fun'jai] o FUNGUSES). 1. (Bot.) Hongo, planta criptógama, de color vario pero nunca verde, que crece rápidamente: como el moho, el tizón, la seta y el agárico. Muchas especies son microscópicas. 2. (Med.) Excrecencia, carnosidad.
Funicle [fiū'-ni-cl], *s.* Cuerdecilla, fibra, ligamento pequeño.
Funk [fuṇk], *s.* 1. (Ger.) Temor, miedo infundado. 2. (Vulg.) Hedor, mal olor.
Funk, *va.* 1. (Vulg.) Emponzoñar con malos olores, apestar. 2. (Esco. o vulg.) Espantar, atemorizar.
Funnel [fun'-el], *s.* 1. Embudo. 2. Cañón, conducto por donde pasa aire, humo u otra cosa. *Funnel of a chimney*, Cañón de chimenea.
Funny [fun'-i], *a.* Cómico, alegre, burlesco, gracioso, chistoso; bufón, mono, chulo.—*s.* (Vulg.) Esquife. *Funny-bone*, (Fam.) Cóndilo interno del húmero junto al cual pasa el nervio ulnar en el codo.
Fur [fūr], *s.* 1. Forro de pieles para poner en los vestidos, o la misma piel sobada y peluda que sirve para manguitos, vestidos y otros usos. 2. Pelo de las bestias. 3. Peletería. 4. Sedimento que se pega a la lengua o a las vasijas metálicas; la pelusa del durazno.
Fur, *va.* 1. Aforrar con pieles finas. 2. Cubrir con alguna cosa blanda y suave. *To fur a ship*, Forrar un navío.
Furacious [fiu-rê'-shus], *a.* Rapaz, inclinado a hurtar.
Furacity [fiu-ras'-i-ti], *s.* Codicia; rapacidad.
Furbelow [fūr'-bẹ-lō], *s.* Farfalá, vuelo.
Furbelow, *va.* Adornar con farfalaes o vuelos.
Furbish [fūr'-bish], *va.* Acicalar, pulir, limpiar.
Furbishable [fūr'-bish-a-bl], *a.* Capaz de ser pulido.
Furbisher [fūr'-bish-ẹr], *a.* Acicalador.
Furcate [fūr'-kẹt], *a.* Ahorquillado, hendido.
Furcation [fūr-kê'-shun], *s.* Horcajadura.
Furcular [fūr'-kiu-lar], *a.* Horcado, que tiene la figura de una horquilla.
Furfur [fūr'-fūr], *s.* (Med.) Caspa; escamitas.
Furious [fiū'-ri-us], *a.* Furioso, frenético, furibundo, violento.
Furiously [fiū'-ri-us-li], *adv.* Furiosamente, violentamente.
Furiousness [fiū'-ri-us-nes], *s.* Furia, frenesí.
Furl [fūrl], *va.* Encoger, contraer. *To furl the sails*, (Mar.) Aferrar velas, recoger las velas y plegarlas encima de las vergas.
Furling-lines [fūrl'-ing-lainz], *s. pl.* (Mar.) Aferravelas.

Furlong [fŭr'-leng], *s.* Estadio, la octava parte de una milla.
Furlough [fŭr'-lō], *s.* (Mil.) Licencia o permiso que se da a un militar para ausentarse de su cuerpo o regimiento.
Furmenty [fŭr'-ment-i], *s.* *V.* FRUMENTY.
Furnace [fŭr'-nẹs], *s.* 1. Horno, hornillo. *Blast-furnace,* Horno u hornillo soplante : úsase en las herrerías. *Reverberatory furnace,* Horno de reverbero. *Wind-furnace,* Horno de aire. 2. Hogar de caldera ; horno. *Furnace-hoist,* Grúa o cabria de horno. *Furnace-rake,* Limpiafuegos, utensilio de vidriería. *Furnace for silver ore,* Buitrón, horno de manga para fundir minerales argentíferos. *Bloom reheating furnace,* Horno de recocido de lupias. *Castilian furnace,* Horno circular para plomo. *Muffle furnace,* Horno de mufla, de copela. *Smelting furnace,* Horno de fundición, alto horno. *To heat the furnace,* Caldear el horno.
Furnish [fŭr'-nish], *va* 1. Surtir, suplir, proveer ; aparejar, equipar ; alhajar, decorar, adornar. *To furnish a house,* Amueblar una casa. *To furnish with arms,* Armar. 2. Proporcionar, procurar. *To furnish any one with an opportunity,* Proporcionar ocasión u oportunidad.
Furnished apartment [fur'-nisht a-pārt'-mẹnt], *s.* Departamento o apartamiento amueblado. *Furnished room for rent,* Se renta cuarto amueblado.
Furnisher [fŭr'-nish-ẹr], *s.* 1. Equipador, decorador. 2. Aparejador, proveedor.
Furnishing [fŭr'-nish-ing], *s.* Muestra. *Furnishings,* Trastos, muebles fijos: (en las cuentas de sastres,etc.), avíos.
Furnishment [fŭr'-nish-mẹnt], *s.* Surtimiento, surtido, la acción de proveer, surtir o equipar de lo que se necesita.
Furniture [fŭr'-ni-chur o tiūr], *s.* 1. Ajuar, los muebles de una casa, mueblaje. 2. Guarnición ; adornos, decoraciones ; accesorios necesarios en las diversas aplicaciones de las artes. 3. (Mar.) Aparejo ; obrajes de un arsenal.
Furniture dealer [fur'-ni-chur dīl'-ẹr], *s.* Mueblista, comerciante en muebles.
Furor, furore [fiū'-rer], *s.* 1. Furia, rabia. 2. Furor, entusiasmo, fervor.
Furred [fŭrd], *a.* 1. Cubierto de piel o de algo parecido a ella. (Med.) Cargado, tomado. 2. Forrado. *Furred tongue,* Lengua cargada o sucia.
Furrier [fŭr'-i-ẹr], *s.* Peletero, el que trata en pieles finas.
Furring [fŭr'-ing], *s.* 1. Forro o guarnición de pieles. 2. Incrustación de una caldera y el procedimiento para limpiarla ; sarro de la lengua. 3. (Carp.) Contrapar de armadura falsa ; pedazos de madera para soportar latas o listones.
Furrow [fur'-ō], *s.* 1. Surco ; (fig.) marca, señal. 2. Surco, cualquier canal largo y estrecho ; encaje, muesca ; estría, mediacaña ; reguera, tajea, canaliza.
Furrow, *va.* 1. Surcar, hacer surcos en la tierra. 2. Estriar. *V.* FLUTE.
Furrow-faced [fur'-o-fēst], *a.* Cara surcada o arrugada.
Furry [fŭr'-i], *a.* Hecho de pieles finas o guarnecido de ellas.
Further [fŭr'-dhẹr], *a.* Ulterior, más distante, más separado. *Till further orders,* Hasta nueva orden.—*adv.* Más lejos, más allá ; además ; aun ; además de eso. *On the further side of the Pyrenees,* Más allá, al otro lado de los Pirineos. *What further need have we of witnesses?* ¿Qué necesidad tenemos de más testigos?
Further, *va.* Adelantar, promover, llevar adelante ; asistir, ayudar, apoyar.
Furtherance [fŭr'-dhẹr-ans], *s.* Adelantamiento, progreso, ayuda, socorro, asistencia, apoyo.
Furtherer [fŭr'-dhẹr-ẹr], *s.* Promotor, fautor, patrón, protector.
Furthermore [fŭr'-dhẹr-mōr], *adv.* Además, a más de esto o de aquello.
Furthest [fŭr'-dhest], *a.* y *adv.* Lo más lejos, muy lejos, lo más remoto, apartado o separado.
Furtive [fŭr'-tiv], *a.* Furtivo, oculto, secreto, hecho de tapadillo o a escondidas.
Furuncle [fiū'-run-cl], *s.* Furúnculo, divieso, grano.
Fury [fiū'-ri], *s.* 1. Furor, locura confirmada. 2. Furia ; ira, rabia, cólera. 3. Furor, arrebatamiento, entusiasmo. *Poetical fury,* Furor o estro poético. 4. Furia, mujer furiosa y turbulenta.
Fury-like [fiū'-ri-laic], *a.* Furibundo, rabioso, furioso.
Furze [fŭrz], *s.* (Bot.) Tojo, hiniesta espinosa ; arbusto de las leguminosas. Llamado también GORSE y WHIN, *q. v.* Ulex europæus.
Furzy [fŭrz'-i], *a.* Lleno de tojos o hiniestas espinosas.
Fuscous [fus'-cus], *a.* 1. De color moreno que tira a gris. 2. Fusco.
Fuse [fiūz], *va.* Fundir, derretir.—*vn.* Fundirse, derretirse.
Fuse, *s.* (Elec.) Fusible. *Fuse box,* Caja de fusibles.
Fusee [fiu-zī'], *s.* 1. Huso, cilindro pequeño alrededor del cual da vuelta la cuerda del reloj. 2. (Art.) Espoleta o espiga, el cañoncillo por donde se pega fuego a la bomba o granada. 3. *V.* FUSE, 1ª acep. 4. (Des.) Escopeta de pistón. *V.* FUSIL.
Fuselage [fiū'-sẹ-lēj], *s.* (Aer.) Fuselaje.
Fusel-oil [fiū'-zel-eil], *s.* Compuesto aceitoso y venenoso consistente en gran parte en alcohol amílico, que se obtiene rectificando el aguardiente de maíz o de uvas.
Fusibility [fiu-zi-bil'-i-ti], *s.* Fusibilidad, calidad de fusible.
Fusible [fiū'-zi-bl], *a.* Fusible, fundible.
Fusiform [fiū'-si-fērm], *a.* Fusiforme, lo que remata en punta.
Fusil [fiū'-zil], *a.* Fundible.—*s.* Escopeta de pistón.
Fusileer o **Fusilier** [fiū"-zi-līr'], *s.* (Mil.) Fusilero.
Fusillade [fiū"-zi-led'], *s.* Tiros de fusil, tirotes a fusilazos. (Fr.)
Fusing [fiūz'-ing], *a.* Fundente ; de fusión. *Fusing point,* Punto de fusión.
Fusion [fiū'-zhun], *s.* 1. Fundición, derretimiento. 2. Fusión, licuación de los metales.
Fuss [fus], *s.* 1. Actividad injustificada y molesta ; desasosiego ; importancia exagerada que suele darse a lo que no la tiene. 2. Alboroto, ruido.
Fuss, *va.* Molestar, perturbar con cosas sin importancia.—*vn.* Agitar se ; afligirse.
Fussy [fus'-i], *a.* Molesto, inquieto, remilgado, minucioso, exigente.
Fust [fust], *s.* 1. Fuste, el cuerpo de la columna. 2. (Prov. Ingl.) Caballete del tejado.
Fustian [fus'-chan], *s.* 1. Fustán, tela de lino y algodón. 2. Palabras retumbantes ; estilo altisonante.—*a.* 1. Hecho de fustán. 2. Altisonante, pomposo, retumbante, campanudo.
Fustic [fus'-tic], *s.* Fustoc, fustete, palo amarillo que sirve para los tintes.
Fustigation [fus-ti-gē'-shun], *s.* Castigo o pena de azotes, palos o latigazos.
Fustiness [fus'-ti-nes], *s.* 1. Enmohecimiento. 2. Hedor, hediondez.
Fusty [fus'-ti], †**Fusted** [fus'-ted], *a.* 1. Mohoso. 2. (E. U. y Prov. Ingl.) Husmeador, fisgón, entrometido, oficioso.
Futile [fiū'-til], *a.* Fútil, frívolo, vano, inútil.
Futility [fiu-til'-i-ti], *s.* Futilidad, insubstancialidad.
Futtock [fut'-ẹc], *s.* (Mar.) Genol, ligazón, barraganete ; arraigada. *Lower futtocks,* Genoles o primeras ligazones. *Futtock-shrouds,* Pernadas de las arraigadas.
Future [fiū'-chur], *a.* Futuro, venidero.—*s.* Lo futuro, lo porvenir.
Futurely [fiū'-chur-li], *adv.* En lo venidero, para lo venidero.
Futurism [fiū'-chur-izm], *s.* Futurismo.
Futurition [fiū-tiu-rish'-un], *s.* Realización en lo futuro de algo profetizado o propuesto.
Futurity [fiu-tiū'-ri-ti], *s.* Futuro, el tiempo que ha de venir ; sucesos venideros ; porvenir. *Full of futurity,* Preñado de consecuencias para lo venidero ; lo que producirá sucesos importantes o de consecuencia en lo sucesivo.
Fuzz [fuz], *vn.* Deshilarse, deshilacharse, desflecarse, volar convertido en partículas, como vello o lanilla.—*s.* Lanilla, pelusa, hilacha menuda.
Fuzz-ball [fuz'-bel], *s.* Bejín, hongo semejante a una bola.
Fuzziness [fuz'-i-nes], *s.* Calidad o estado de velloso.
Fuzzy [fuz'-i], *a.* Provisto de una capa de pelusa o vello ; parecido a lanilla.
Fyke [faik], *s.* Nasa, red de forma cónica ; varias redes sucesivas, de forma cónica y con boca ancha.
Fy [fai], *inter.* ¡ Qué vergüenza !

G

G [jī]. Esta letra tiene dos sonidos en inglés ; uno igual al de la misma letra en castellano antes de *a, o, u, l, r ;* v. g. *gas, go, gun, grass, globe ;* y otro más suave que el anterior antes de *e, i* o *y,* el cual equivale al de la *y consonante* en castellano, pronunciada con alguna más fuerza ; v. g. *gem* (dyem), *gibbet* (dyibbet), *dingy* (dindyi). Delante de las mismas letras, y de la *a* en muchos monosílabos y sus derivados, suena fuerte, y como si tuviese interpuesta una *u ;* v. g. *get* (guet), *give* (guiv), *game* (guem), *gamesome* (guémsom). En las palabras que comienzan con *gh,* sólo se pronuncia la primera; v. g. *ghost* (gost); en las que acaban con las mismas letras éstas se pronuncian como una *f;* v. g. *rough* (rof); bien que en algunas voces son mudas, como en *high* (jái). Antes de *n*, al principio o fin de dicción, es muda; v. g. *gnat* (nat), *reign* (réin).

Gab [gab], *vn.* (Fam.) Parlotear, picotear, charlar.—*va.* Decir; especialmente decir falsedades.

Gab, *s.* 1. (Fam.) Locuacidad, cháchara. 2. Garabato, gancho. *To have the gift of gab*, Tener la lengua muy suelta.

Gabardine [gab-ar-dîn'], **Gaberdine** [gab-ẹr-dîn'], *s.* Gabacha, gabardina.

Gabble [gab'-l], *vn.* 1. Charlar, parlar, parlotear, picotear, hablar mucho sin substancia y fuera de propósito. 2. Cacarear.

Gabble, *s.* 1. Algarabía; charla. 2. Cacareo.

Gabbler [gab'-lẹr], *s.* Charlador, chacharero, parlador, hablador, charlante, picotero.

Gabion [gé'-bi-ẹn], *s.* (Fort.) Gavión, cestón de mimbres lleno de tierra.

Gable [gé'-bl], *s.* Cabo angular o remate de tejado que está hecho con caballete y no aplanado.

Gable-end [gé'-bl-end], *s.* Socarrén, alero.

Gad [gad], *vn.* Andorrear, corretear, callejear, pindonguear. *On the gad*, Callejeando, correteando.

Gad, *s.* 1. Cuña, punzón, aguja de minero. 2. Aguijón, vara con punta. 3. Clavo grande, cuña.

Gadabout [gad'-a-baut''], *a.* Callejero, cantonero.

Gadder [gad'-ẹr], *s.* 1. Callejero o correteador. (Fam. Mex.) Cerero y aplanador. 2. Mujer cantonera, andorrera.

Gadding [gad'-ing], *s.* Vagancia, briba; peregrinación.

Gaddingly [gad'-ing-li], *adv.* Haraganamente, á la briba.

Gadfly [gad'-flai], *s.* Mosca de burro o de caballo, tábano; la hembra es grande y voraz.

Gadget [gaj'-et], *s.* Dispositivo o aparato que facilita las labores manuales.

Gadoid [gé'-deid], *a.* De la familia de los peces cuyo tipo es el bacalao.

Gae [gé], *vn.* (Esco.) (*pret.* GAED, *pp.* GAEN, *ger.* GAEING.) Ir, andar.

Gae, *pret.* *V.* GAVE.

Gaelic, Galic [gé'-lic], *s.* Gaélico o céltico, un dialecto de la lengua céltica.—*a.* Lo perteneciente a dicho dialecto.

Gaff [gaf], *s.* 1. Arpón o garfio grande. 2. Espolón de gallo. *V.* GAFFLE. 3. (Mar.) Botavara, berlinga para extender el borde de ciertas velas.

Gaff-boom [gaf'-būm], *s.* (Mar.) Verga de cangreja.

Gaff-sail [gaf'-sél], *s.* (Mar.) Vela de cangreja.

Gaffer [gaf'-ẹr], *s.* Viejo, vejete; viene a significar casi lo mismo que tío, maese, compadre.

Gaffle [gaf'-l], *s.* Espolón de acero que se pone al gallo para reñir. (Mex.) Navaja de gallo.

Gag [gag], *va.* 1. Tapar la boca con mordaza; hacer callar a la fuerza. 2. Provocar bascas o náuseas. 3. Forzar, abrir por medio de una mordaza.—*vn.* Hacer esfuerzos para vomitar, tener náuseas.

Gag, *s.* 1. Mordaza; cualquier limitación de la libertad de la palabra. 2. Asco; lo que produce bascas. 3. (Cir.) Instrumento para mantener las mandíbulas separadas durante una operación.

Gage [gêj], *s.* 1. Prenda, caución. 2. Variedad de ciruela. *Green gage*, Ciruela verdal (o claudia).

Gage, Gauge [gêj], *s.* 1. Medida, regla de medir. 2. (Mar.) Barlovento.

Gage, *va.* (Ant.) Empeñar una alhaja, darla en prenda.

Gage, Gauge, *va.* 1. Aforar, medir. 2. (Mar.) Arquear, medir una embarcación. 3. Comprometer.

Gager [gêj'-ẹr], *s.* Arqueador. *V.* GAUGER.

Gagger [gag'-er], *s.* 1. El que amordaza la boca de otro. 2. Trozo de hierro que se usa para mantener en su lugar el corazón de un molde.

Gaggle [gag'-l], *vn.* Graznar, como el ánsar. *V.* GABBLE.

Gaiety [gé'-e-ti], *s.* *V.* GAYETY.

Gaily [gé'-li], *adv.* *V.* GAYLY.

Gain [gên], *s.* 1. Ganancia, ventaja, provecho, lucro. 2. (Carp.) Disminución, la que se hace en el espaldar del corte del cartabón. 3. El interés que una persona tiene en cualquiera cosa. 4. Ventaja o ganancia mal adquirida. *Net gain*, Ganancia líquida, neta.

Gain, *va.* 1. Ganar, adquirir caudal. 2. Ganar jugando o apostando; adquirir, llevar la palma; salir victorioso. 3. Ganar, conseguir, lograr, granjear. 4. Llegar a, alcanzar. 5. Conciliar; propiciar, apaciguar. *To gain the wind*, (Mar.) Ganar el barlovento.—*vn.* 1. Enriquecerse. 2. Ganar tierra, adelantar poco a poco; obtener una ventaja, un provecho; prevalecer, sacar fruto; con *on* o *upon*. 3. Ganar, lograr, obtener influjo. 4. Aproximarse, acercarse, extenderse. *To gain credit*, Acreditarse. *To gain one's end*, Alcanzar lo que se desea, lograr su objeto. *To gain over*, Conciliar, atraer al partido o parecer de uno. *The night is gaining upon us*, La noche nos sorprende o nos envuelve.

Gainable [gên'-a-bl], *a.* Capaz de ser adquirido.

Gainer [gên'-ẹr], *s.* Ganador.

Gainful [gên'-ful], *a.* Ganancioso, lucrativo, provechoso, ventajoso.

Gainfully [gên'-ful-i], *adv.* Ventajosamente.

Gainfulness [gên'-ful-nes], *s.* Provecho, ganancia.

Gainless [gên'-les], *a.* Desventajoso, infructuoso.

Gainlessness [gên'-les-nes], *s.* Inutilidad, infructuosidad; falto de provecho.

Gainsay [gên-sé'], *va.* (*pret.* y *pp.* GAINSAID). Contradecir; negar; contrariar.

Gainsayer [gên-sé'-ẹr], *s.* Contradictor, adversario.

Gainsaying [gên-sé'-ing], *s.* Oposición, contradicción.

Gainstand [gên-stand'], *va.* (Ant. y Poét.) Resistir, oponer, combatir, reprimir.

Gairish, *a.* *V.* GARISH.

Gairishly, *adv.* *V.* GARISHLY.

Gairishness [gar'-ish-nes], *s.* Pompa. *V.* GARISHNESS.

Gait [gêt], *s.* Marcha, paso, el modo de andar; porte, continente.

Gaiter [gé'-tẹr], *s.* 1. Borceguí, polaina, calza de paño o cordobán. 2. Botín con elásticos, en lugar de botones o cordones.

Gala [gé'-la], *s.* Gala, fiesta.

Galactic [ga-lac'-tic], *a.* 1. Relativo a la secreción de leche. 2. Relativo a la galaxía.

Galactometer, *s.* *V.* LACTOMETER.

Galangal [ga-lan'-gal], *s.* (Bot.) Galanga.

Galatian [ga-lé'-shan], *a.* y *s.* Gálata, de Galacia.

Galaxy [gal'-ac-si], *s.* 1. Galaxía, la vía láctea. 2. Reunión brillante de personas o cosas.

Galbanum [gal'-ba-num], *s.* Gálbano, resina gomosa y medicinal.

Gale [gél], *s.* 1. Viento fresco, muy fuerte, ventarrón; en especial un viento con velocidad de 40 a 70 millas por hora. *A fresh gale*, (Mar.) Temporal de viento. *A stiff gale*, Fugada recia. 2. Diversión bulliciosa. 3. (Bot.) Galo o cerero de Luisiana, un arbusto oloroso.

Galea [gé'-le-a], *s.* Yelmo, o lo que es de forma parecida á él.

Galeate, Galeated [gé'-le-êt-ed], *a.* 1. Cubierto como con yelmo. 2. (Bot.) Llámanse así las plantas que tienen flores en forma de yelmo, como el acónito.

Galena [ga-lí'-na], *s.* (Min.) Galena, sulfuro de plomo nativo, alquifol.

Galenic, Galenical [ga-len'-ic, al], *a.* 1. Galénico, que contiene galena. 2. Galénico, relativo a Galeno o a los medicamentos que empleaba.

Galenism [gé'-len-izm], *s.* Galenismo, la doctrina de Galeno.

Galenist [gé'-len-ist], *s.* Galenista, el que sigue la doctrina de Galeno.

Galilean [gal-i-lí'-an], *s.* 1. Galileo, natural de Galilea. 2. Galileo, el partidario de una secta entre los judíos enemiga de los romanos.

Galiot [gal'-i-et], *s.* (Mar.) Galeota.

Galipot [gal'-i-pet], *s.* Galipodio, trementina solidificada en los pinos y abetos. Cuando está purificada recibe el nombre de *pez blanca* o de *Borgoña*.

Galium [gé'-li-um], *s.* (Bot.) Cuajaleche, galio, género numeroso de plantas rubiáceas.

Gall [gōl], *s.* 1. Hiel, bilis recogida en una vejiga debajo del hígado. 2. Amargura, aspereza. 3. Hiel, odio, rencor, aversión; enfado; malicia, malignidad. 4. Rozadura o matadura de las caballerías. 5. Agalla, excrecencia dura redonda, debida a ciertos insectos, que se forma en el roble y otros árboles y arbustos. *Gall-apple* o *gall-nut*, Agalla. *Gall-fly*, Cinipo, insecto himenóptero que pica los árboles para depositar sus huevos y produce la agalla. *Gall-stones*, Cálculos en la vejiga de la hiel.

Gall, *va.* y *vn.* 1. Desollar, quitar el pellejo o la piel: desollarse, rozarse, herir o herirse ligeramente levantando un pedacito de pellejo. 2. Gastar, consumiendo poco a poco. 3. Acibarar; fatigar, hostigar; dañar.

Gallant [gal-ant'], *a.* Galante, cortés; galanteador, cortejador de damas.

Gallant [gal'-ant], *a.* 1. Valeroso, animoso, valiente, intrépido, bizarro. 2. (Ant.) Garboso, bizarro, elegante en el vestir.

Gallant [gal-lant'], *s.* 1. Galán; galanteador; cortejo. 2. Galán, mancebo, majo; el favorecido por una mujer en el trato ilícito.

Gallant [gal-lant'], *va.* Galantear.

Gallantly [gal'-ant-li], *adv.* Galanamente, valientemente.
Gallantness [gal'-ant-nes], *s.* (Ant.) Elegancia, bizarría.
Gallantry [gal'-ant-ri], *s.* 1. Espíritu heroico, valeroso; valor, heroísmo. 2. Galanteo, cortejo, obsequio y servicio a los débiles, y particularmente a las mujeres. 3. Amores, trato, amistad; atención excesiva dedicada a las mujeres; trato ilícito entre los dos sexos.
Gallate [gal'-ét], *s.* (Quím.) Galato, sal formada por la combinación del ácido agálico con alguna base.
Gall bladder [gel blad'-ẹr], *s.* Vesícula biliar.
Galleon [gal'-ẹ-ẹn], *s.* Galeón, bajel grande usado antiguamente en España.
Gallery [gal'-ẹr-i], *s.* 1. Galería, corredor. 2. (Mar.) Corredor de navío. *A quarter gallery,* Jardines. 3. (Fort.) Galería, corredor con que se ciega el foso. 4. El corredor más alto de un teatro. 5. Socavón, galería o pozo de una mina. *Drain-gallery,* (Min.) Galería de desagüe. *Picture-gallery,* Galería, colección de pinturas.
Galley [gal'-i], *s.* 1. (Mar.) Galera, embarcación de remos. 2. El fogón de a bordo; cocina. 3. (Impr.) Galera, tabla con dos o tres bordes con sus muescas, en las que entra la volandera: úsase para poner la composición y formar las galeradas. *Galley-tiles,* Azulejos.
Galley proof [gal'-i prūf], *s.* (Impr.) Galerada.
Galley-slave [gal'-i-slêv], *s.* Galeote, el que remaba forzado en las galeras.
†**Galliard** [gal'-yard], *s.* Hombre gallardo, galán.—*a.* Vivo, alegre.
Gallic acid [gal'-ic as'-id], *s.* (Quím.) Ácido agálico o de agallas.
Gallic [gal'-ic], **Gallican** [gal'-i-can], *a.* Galicano.
Gallicism [gal'-i-sizm], *s.* Galicismo, modo de hablar privativo de la lengua francesa.
Gallicize [gal'-i-saiz], *va.* Escribir o hablar de un modo conforme al estilo y giros de la lengua francesa.
Gallimaufry [gal-i-mē'-fri], *s.* Almodrote, jigote, picadillo, ropa vieja; mezcla ridícula de cosas contrarias.
Gallinaceous [gal-i-nê'-shus], *a.* Lo que pertenece a las gallinas.
Gallipot [gal'-i-pet], *s.* Orza, vasija vidriada de barro.
Gall-less [gēl'-les], *a.* Sin hiel o amargura; apacible, sencillo, de genio suave.
Gallon [gal'-ẹn], *s.* 1. Galón, medida de líquidos que contiene nueve cuartillos o cuatro litros y medio. El galón de vino o de Winchester, más usado en los Estados Unidos, contiene 231 pulgadas cúbicas o 3.785 litros. El galón imperial de la Gran Bretaña contiene 277.274 pulgadas cúbicas o 4.543 litros. El galón de cerveza contiene 282 pulgadas cúbicas, igual a 4.621 litros. 2. Medida inglesa de capacidad para áridos, casi la octava parte de una fanega inglesa (*bushel*), o sean siete libras.
Galloon [gal-lūn], *s.* 1. Galón, género de tejido fuerte hecho de seda o hilo de oro o plata. 2. Ribecillo.
Gallop [gal'-up], *s.* Galope, movimiento del caballo más violento y acelerado que el paso y el trote. *Full gallop,* A galope tendido, a rienda suelta. *Hand-gallop,* A media rienda.
Gallop, *vn.* Galopar.
Gallopade [gal-o-pêd'], *s.* 1. Caracoleo, movimiento lateral del caballo. 2. Galope, baile de movimiento muy vivo, y la música del mismo.
Galloper [gal'-up-ẹr], *s.* Hombre o caballo que galopa.
Gallows [gal'-oz], *s.* 1. Horca, instrumento de suplicio en el cual mueren colgados los delincuentes condenados a la última pena. 2. Un aparato cualquiera del que se suspenden las cosas. *Gallows-bird,* El malvado que merece la pena de horca. 3. *pl.* (Fam. E. U.) Tirantes del pantalón.
Gallows-free [gal'-oz-frī], *a.* El que tiene la fortuna de no ser ahorcado mereciéndolo.
Gally [gēl'-i], *a.* Amargo; lo que contiene hiel.
Galore [ga-lōr'], *a.* y *adv.* Muchísimo, abundante; sigue siempre al substantivo. (Irlandés.)
Galosh, Galoche [ga-losh'], *s.* Chanclo, zueco, zapato fuerte que se lleva por lo común sobre otro, y por extensión se llama así algunas veces cualquier calzado; zapatón.
Galvanic [gal-van'-ic], *a.* Galvánico, que pertenece al galvanismo.
Galvanism [gal'-va-nizm], *s.* Galvanismo, la electricidad puesta en acción por el contacto de dos substancias de diferente naturaleza.
Galvanize [gal'-va-naiz], *va.* 1. Galvanizar. 2. Dar, comunicar animación o energía ficticia. 3. *V.* ELECTROPLATE.
Galvanometer [gal-va-nom'-ẹ-tẹr], *s.* Galvanómetro, aparato para medir la fuerza de una corriente eléctrica o la diferencia de la potencial.
Gamma globuline [ga-ma glob'-ū-lin], *s.* (Med.) Gama globulina.
Gambade, Gambado [gam-bêd', gam-bê'-do], *s.* 1. Polaina para proteger contra el lodo. 2. *pl.* Cubiertas de cuero a manera de botas que protegen los pies y sirven de estribos.
Gambit [gam'-bit], *s.* Gambito, lance en el juego de ajedrez por el cual se da mate a las primeras jugadas.
Gamble [gam'-bl], *vn.* Jugar con exceso; jugar puerco o con trampas; garitear, frecuentar los garitos.
Gambler [gam'-blẹr], *s.* Tahur, garitero, fullero.
Gamboge [gam-bōj' o gam-būj'], *s.* Gomaguta o gutagamba.
Gambol [gam'-bẹl], *vn.* Brincar, saltar, caracolear.
Gambol, *s.* Cabriola, brinco de alegría, caracoleo.
Gambrel [gam'-brel], *s.* 1. Pierna trasera del caballo. 2. Palo en forma de cayado en que cuelgan la carne los carniceros. 3. *Gambrel roof,* Techo a la holandesa, de ángulo obtuso.
Game [gêm], *s.* 1. Juego, entretenimiento, pasatiempo. 2. Chanza, burla, mofa. 3. Juego, partida o partido. *Low game cards,* Cartas bajas. 4. Caza, lo que mata el cazador. 5. Juegos públicos. *Game-bag,* Zurrón, morral. *The game is up,* (1) Se ha levantado la caza. (2) (Fam.) El proyecto ha salido mal; se acabó.
Game, *vn.* Jugar, entretenerse con alguna especie de juego; jugar fuerte.
Game-cock [gêm'-coc], *s.* Gallo inglés o de pelea.
Game-keeper [gêm'-kīp-ẹr], *s.* Guarda de coto, el que cuida de la caza.
Game-leg [gêm'-leg], *s.* (Ger.) Pierna estropeada.
Gamesome [gêm'-sum], *a.* Juguetón, retozón.
Gamesomeness [gêm'-sum-nes], *s.* Festividad, alegría, juguete.
Gamesomely [gêm'-sum-li], *adv.* Alegremente.
Gamester [gêm'-stẹr], *s.* 1. Tahur jugador; garitero; fullero. 2. Chocarrero, bufón. 3. (Ant.) Ramera mujer pública.
Game warden [gêm wer'-dn], *s.* Guardabosque.
Gaming [gêm'-ing], **Gambling** [gam-bling], *s.* Juego.
Gaming o **Gambling-house** [gêm'-ing o gam'-bling-haus], *s.* Casa de coima, garito, casa de juego.
Gaming-table [gêm'-ing-tê'-bl], *s.* Mesa de juego.
Gamma ray [ga'-ma rêy], *s.* Rayo gama.
Gammer [gam'-ẹr], *sf.* Una vieja; comadre, tía. Corresponde a *gaffer.* (Lit. abuelo, abuela.)
Gammon [gam'-en], *s.* 1. Jamón, el pernil o nalgada del puerco salada y enjuta. 2. *V.* BACKGAMMON. *Gammoning of the bow-sprit,* (Mar.) Trincas del bauprés. *It is all gammon,* (Fam.) Es una necedad o bobada, habladuría, jarabe de pico.
Gammon, *va.* 1. Engañar, chasquear. 2. Ganar doble partida de chaquete.
Gamopetalous [gam-o-pet'-al-us], *a.* (Bot.) Gamopétalo, monopétalo, dícese de las corolas de una sola pieza o de pétalos más o menos unidos.
Gamut [gam'-ut], *s.* (Mús.) Gama, escala.
Gamy [gê'-mi], *a.* 1. Que tiene el tufillo o sabor de la caza. 2. (Fam.) Animoso, dispuesto a pelear.
Ganch [ganch], *va.* Arrojar a una persona desde lo alto sobre ganchos, especie de castigo bárbaro usado entre los turcos.
Gander [gand'-ẹr], *s.* Ánsar, ganso, el macho de la gansa.
Gang [gang], *s.* 1. Cuadrilla, banda. *Gang of robbers,* Cuadrilla de ladrones. 2. (Mar.) Partida. *Press-gang,* Ronda de matrícula. 3. (Min.) *V.* GANGUE. *Gang-plank,* Pasamano de un navío. *Gang-plough,* Arado de reja múltiple. *Gang-saw,* Sierra múltiple.
Ganglion [gang'-gli-un], *s.* 1. (Anat.) Ganglio, nudillo o tubérculo que se halla en el trayecto de los nervios y vasos linfáticos. 2. (Cir.) Ganglio, pequeño tumor enquistado que procede de un tendón.
Gangrenate [gang'-grẹ-nêt], **Gangrene** [gang'-grīn], *va.* Gangrenar.—*vn.* Gangrenarse.
Gangrene, *s.* Gangrena.
Gangrenous [gang'-grẹ-nus], *a.* Gangrenoso.
Gang-board [gang'-bōrd], *s.* (Mar.) Plancha, andamio.
Gangster [gangs'-tẹr], *s.* Pandillero, miembro de una organización de malhechores.
Gangue [gang], *s.* (Min.) Ganga, materia no metálica que se halla en las venas de las minas.
Gannet [gan'-et], *s.* Bubia, ave acuática de especie afín a la de los pelícanos. Sula bassana.
Gangway [gang'-wê], *s.* (Mar.) Pasamano de un buque, portalón.
Ganoid [gan'-eid], *a.* Perteneciente a los ganoideos, gran división de los peces, que comprende los esturiones y otros muchos.
Gantlet, Gauntlet [gant'-let], *s.* Ba-

quetas, castigo militar. *To run the gantlet*, Pasar o correr baquetas.

Gaol [jêl], *s.* Cárcel. *V.* JAIL.

Gaol, *va.* Encarcelar.

Gaoler [jêl'-ęr], *s.* Carcelero, el que guarda la cárcel.

Gap [gap], *s.* 1. Boquete, portillo o abertura en un cercado. 2. Agujero, brecha, hueco. 3. Quebrada; barranca, hondonada. *To stand in the gap*, Defender, exponerse por proteger a alguno que está en peligro.

Gape [gāp o gêp], *vn.* 1. Bostezar, abrir involuntariamente la boca; boquear. 2. Anhelar, desear, ansiar. 3. Hendirse, rajarse, abrirse en grietas. 4. Estar con la boca abierta; admirarse neciamente de lo que uno ve u oye. *To gape after, at*, o *for*, Ansiar o anhelar alguna cosa. *To gape at*, Embobarse, papar moscas.

Gape [gāp], *s.* 1. Bostezo. 2. Abertura, hendedura; particularmente en zoología, anchura de la boca de un pájaro o de un pez, cuando la abre.

Gaper [gāp'-ęr], *s.* El que bosteza, anhela o se emboba mirando u oyendo alguna cosa; papamoscas.

Gar [gār], *va.* (Esco.) Causar, hacer; forzar.

Gar, *s.* Sollo o belona. *V.* GARPIKE.

Garage [ga-razh'], *s.* Garaje.

Garb [gārb], *s.* 1. Vestido, vestidura, traje; particularmente traje característico. 2. Apariencia, exterior, aspecto, aire.

Garbage [gārb'-ęj], *s.* Tripas, desechos de un animal; basura, desperdicios de un casa.

Garbel [gār'-bel], *s.* (Mar.) Aparadura, la primera traca que se dispone contra el alefrís de la quilla.

Garble [gār'-bl], *va.* 1. Alterar un escrito por supresión o elisión; pervertir, mutilar, falsificar. *A garbled quotation*, Citación mutilada. 2. Entresacar, apartar; antiguamente escoger lo bueno de lo malo.—*s.* (Com.) Desecho de especias y drogas.

Garbler [gār'-blęr], *s.* 1. Alterador, falsificador. 2. El que separa lo bueno de lo malo.

Garboard [gār'-bōrd], *s.* (Mar.) Tabla de la quilla.

Garden [gār'-dn], *s.* 1. Huerta, huerto. 2. Jardín. *Nursery garden*, Plantel, criadero, semillero. *Garden-balsam*, Balsamina de jardín. *Garden-bed*, Cuadro de un jardín. *Garden-mould*, Tierra vegetal. *Garden-plot*, Banco de tierra en un jardín o huerta. *Garden-stuff*, Hortalizas, legumbres, frutas.

Garden, *vn.* Cultivar un jardín o huerto.—*va.* Hacer jardines o huertos.

Gardener [gār'-dn-ęr], *s.* Jardinero, hortelano.

Gardenia [gār-dī'-ni-a], *s.* (Bot.) Gardenia.

Gardening [gār'-dn-ing], *s.* Jardinería.

Gare [gār], *s.* (Prov. Ingl.) Lana de caídas, lana burda que tienen en las piernas las reses de ganado lanar.

Garfish [gār'-fish], *s.* El pez aguja, belona. Belone belone.

Gargarism [gār'-ga-rizm], *s.* Gargarismo.

Gargarize [gār'-ga-raiz], *va.* Gargarizar, hacer gárgaras.

Garget [gār'-get], *s.* 1. Enfermedad del ganado mayor caracterizada por hinchazón de la garganta. 2. Enfermedad de las ubres de las vacas.

Gargle [gār'-gl], *va.* 1. Gargarizar. 2. Gorgoritear, hacer quiebros con la voz en la garganta.

Gargle, *s.* Gargarismo, enjuague para hacer gárgaras.

Gargoyle [gār'-goil], *s.* (Arq.) Gárgola.

Garish [gār'-ish], *a.* 1. Deslumbrante, deslumbrador. 2. Pomposo, ostentoso; extravagante.

Garishly [gār'-ish-li], *adv.* Ostentosamente; desatinadamente.

Garishness [gār'-ish-nes], *s.* Pompa, oropel, ostentación; alegría desatinada.

Garland [gār'-land], *s.* 1. Guirnalda, corona abierta tejida de flores, hojas, etc.; de aquí, señal de honor, dada como símbolo de la victoria o el buen éxito. 2. Colección de joyas literarias. 3. Cosa parecida a una guirnalda; corona, florón. (Mar.) Roñada.

Garland, *va.* Enguirnaldar.

Garlic [gār'-lic], *s.* (Bot.) Ajo.

Garlicky [gār'-lik-i], *a.* Parecido al ajo o que lo contiene; que huele a ajo.

Garment [gār'-męnt], *s.* Prenda de vestir.

Garner [gār'-nęr], *va.* Entrojar, almacenar el grano.

Garner, *s.* Granero; acopio.

Garnet [gār'-net], *s.* 1. Granate, silicato de varias especies, estimadas algunas como piedras preciosas. 2. Color rojo obscuro. 3. (Mar.) Palanca para levantar fardos, candeletón.

Garnish [gār'-nish], *va.* 1. Guarnecer, adornar, ataviar, componer. 2. Aderezar un plato o un manjar para la mesa. 3. (Der.) Prevenir, notificar. 4. (Vul. Ingl.) Aprisionar con grillos.

Garnish, *s.* 1. Guarnición, adorno. 2. Aderezo, de un plato o de un manjar.

Garnishee [gar-nish-ī'], *s.* Persona cuyos bienes se embargan.—*va.* Embargar bienes.

Garnisher [gār'-nish-ęr], *s.* El que pone guarniciones o adornos.

Garnishment [gār'-nish-męnt], *s.* 1. Ornamento, adorno. 2. (For.) Orden judicial que prohibe a un tercero disponer de los fondos que tenga en su poder pertenecientes al demandado.

Garniture [gār'-ni-chur], *s.* Guarnición, adorno.

Garpike [gār'-paik], *s.* 1. Pez americano de agua dulce, parecido al sollo; pertenece a los ganoideos y es de gran tamaño. 2. *V.* GARFISH.

Garret [gar'-et], *s.* Guardilla, la habitación que está contigua al tejado; zaquizamí, desván.

Garrison [gar'-i-sn], *s.* (Mil.) 1. Guarnición, el conjunto de soldados para la defensa de una plaza. 2. Guarnición, plaza de armas guarnecida de tropas.

Garrison, *va.* Guarnecer una plaza con las tropas necesarias para su defensa.

Garrote [gar-rōt'], *va.* 1. Ajusticiar por medio del garrote. 2. Agarrar por la garganta para ahogar y robar.

Garrulity [gar-rū'-li-ti], *s.* Garrulidad, locuacidad, charla.

Garrulous [gar'-u-lus], *a.* Gárrulo, locuaz, parlero.

Garter [gār'-tęr], *s.* 1. Liga, cenojil, atadero con que se aseguran las medias; jarretera. 2. Jarretera, orden de este nombre, la más ilustre de Inglaterra. 3. Insignia de esta orden, la liga que llevan los caballeros en el jarrete de la pierna izquierda. *Garter King-at-arms*, Rey de armas. *Garter-fish*, Lepidopo, género de peces.

Garter, *va.* 1. Atar con liga o cenojil. 2. Investir con la orden de la Jarretera.

Garth [gārth], *s.* Obstrucción artificial de una corriente de agua para coger peces.

Gas [gas], *s.* 1. (Quím.) Gas: nombre genérico para toda especie de flúido elástico permanente. 2. Gas para el alumbrado o la calefacción. 3. Mechero de gas. 4. Gas óxidonitroso. *Gas-fitter*, Instalador de gas. *Gas-burner*, Mechero, quemador de gas. *Gas-holder*, *V.* GASOMETER. *Gas-light*, (1) Luz de gas. (2) Mechero de gas. *Gas-main*, Cañería principal o maestra de gas. *Gas-meter*, Gasómetro o contador de gas. *Gas-pipe*, Tubo de gas. *Gas-works*, Fábrica de gas. *Sewer gas*, Emanaciones de las cloacas.

Gasconade [gas-cęn-éd'], *s.* Gasconada, fanfarronada.

Gasconade, *vn.* Jactarse, fanfarronear.

Gaseous [gaz'-ę-us], *a.* 1. Gaseoso, lo que tiene la naturaleza o la forma del gas; aeriforme. 2. Insubstancial.

Gash [gash], *va.* Dar una cuchillada, acuchillar; hacer un chirlo.

Gash, *s.* 1. Cuchillada, herida larga y honda. 2. Cicatriz, la señal que queda de la herida.

Gashful [gash'-ful], *a.* Lleno de cuchilladas. 2. Terrible, horrendo, espantoso.

Gasify [gas'-i-fai], *va.* Gasificar, convertir en gas.

Gasket [gas'-ket], *s.* 1. (Mec.) Relleno, empaquetadura, sea de caucho, cuero, metal en planchas, cáñamo o plomo. 2. *pl.* (Mar.) Tomadores, unas cajetas largas con que se acaban de aforrar las velas. *Bunt-gaskets*, Tomadores del batidero de una vela.

Gaskins [gas'-kinz], *s. pl.* 1. Empaquetadura o empaque de cáñamo. 2. (Des.) Especie de medias anchas que se usaron en el siglo XVI.

Gasolier [gas-o-lîr'], *s.* Candelabro colgante de varios mecheros para gas.

Gasoline [gas'-o-lin o lîn], *s.* Gasoleno, gasolina, líquido incoloro, volátil, inflamable, que se obtiene destilando el petróleo crudo y se usa como combustible.

Gasometer [gas-em'-ę-tęr], *s.* 1. Gasómetro, aparato que en las fábricas de gas del alumbrado se emplea para que el flúido salga con uniformidad por efecto de una constante presión. 2. (Quím.) Aparato para acumular, conservar o mezclar gases.

Gasp [gasp], *vn.* 1. Boquear, respirar convulsivamente, como por extenuación o temor. 2. Suspirar, anhelar, desear alguna cosa con ansia.—*va.* Hablar o emitir sonidos jadeando, como lo hace una persona aterrorizada o moribunda.

Gasp, *s.* La acción de respirar o echar el aliento convulsiva o entrecortadamente. *He is at the last gasp*, Está dando la última boqueada.

Gas-storage tank [gas-stōr'-êj tank'], *s.* Gasómetro.

Gastric [gas'-tric], *a.* Gástrico, perteneciente al estómago.

Gastriloquous [gas-tril'-o-cwɒs], *a.* Ventrílocuo, el que cuando habla parece que saca la voz del vientre.
Gastritis [gas-traɪ'-tis], *s.* Gastritis, inflamación del estómago.
Gastronomer, Gastronomist [gas-tren'-o-mẹr, mist], *s.* Gastrónomo, persona aficionada a la buena mesa.
Gastronomic [gas-tro-nem'-ic], *a.* Gastronómico.
Gastronomy [gas-tren'-o-mi], *s.* Gastronomía. arte de comer opíparamente.
Gastropod [gas'-tro-ped], *s.* Gastrópodo.
Gastrorectomy [gas-tro-rec'-to-mi], *s.* (Med.) Gastrorrectomía.
Gastrotomy [gas-tret'-o-mi], *s.* Gastrotomía.
Gate [gêt], *s.* 1. Puerta, la entrada de una ciudad o plaza. 2. Barrera, talanquera. 3. Puerta de cercado. 4. Vía, camino. 5. Compuertas de esclusa. *Flood-gate,* Paradera, compuerta del caz de un molino. *Gate-keeper, gateward,* Portero; guardabarrera de ferrocarril.
Gated [gêt'-ed], *a.* Lo que tiene puertas.
Gateway [gêt'-wê], *s.* Entrada por las puertas de algún cercado.
Gather [gadh'-ẹr], *va.* 1. Coger, recoger, amontonar. 2. Rebuscar, recoger los residuos de la viña vendimiada o de otros frutos. 3. Juntar, congregar, unir. 4. Fruncir, recoger la orilla del paño u otra tela. 5. Colegir, inferir. 6. Arrugar, plegar.—*vn.* Condensarse, aumentarse, unirse, juntarse. *To gather breath,* Tomar aliento, descansar. *To gather dust,* Cubrirse de polvo. *To gather flesh,* Criar carnes, engordar. *To gather strength,* Recuperarse, restablecerse, tomar fuerzas. *To gather* o *to come to a head,* Llegar al estado de supuración, madurarse un tumor. *To gather corn,* Hacer el verano, recoger la cosecha. *To gather grapes,* Vendimiar. *To gather together,* Reunir, juntar, congregar. *To gather up,* Alzar, recoger.
Gather, *s.* 1. Pliegue. 2. Deslustre o deslucimiento del paño a fuerza de manosearlo o de hacerle pliegues.
Gatherable [gadh'-ẹr-a-bl], *a.* Deducible.
Gatherer [gadh'-ẹr-ẹr], *s.* Colector, segador, vendimiador.
Gathering [gadh'-ẹr-ing], *s.* 1. Asamblea; amontonamiento de gente. 2. Acumulación, amontonamiento de cosas. 3. Cuesta, demanda, colecta de limosnas o donativos para pobres u objetos piadosos. 4. Acumulación de pus o materia, absceso.
Gaudery [gēd'-ẹr-i], *s.* Lujo ostentoso en el traje o modo de vestir. (Vul.) Charrada.
Gaudily [gēd'-i-li], *adv.* Ostentosamente, fastuosamente.
Gaudiness [gēd'-i-nes], *s.* Oropel, cosa de poco valor y mucho brillo; fausto, pompa; ostentación en el vestir.
Gaudy [gēd'-i], *a.* 1. Brillante, lucido; de aquí, llamativo, charro.
Gauge [gêj], *va.* 1. Aforar, medir y reconocer las vasijas que contienen vino o licores para saber su cabida. 2. Medir, tomar la medida de alguna cosa según su anchura, longitud o profundidad. 3. (Mar.) Medir o arquear los navíos.
Gauge, *s.* La vara, sonda o escandallo con que se afora o mide. *Silver in sheets of suitable gauges,* Plata en planchas de largo y grueso proporcionados. *Gauge-cock,* Llave de prueba, de nivel, puesta en la parte anterior de una caldera. *Gauge-wheel,* (Mec.) Gálibo de contornear. *Axle gauge,* Ajustador de eje.
Gauger [gêj'-ẹr], *s.* Aforador, arqueador.
Gauging [gêj'-ing], *s.* El acto de aforar o medir. *Gauging-rod,* Aforador, instrumento para aforar.
Gaul [gēl], *s.* Galia antigua, Francia.
Gaulish [gēl'-ish], *a.* Lo que pertenece a las Galias, galicano.
Gaunt [gānt], *a.* Flaco, delgado.
Gauntlet [gānt'-let], *s.* 1. Manopla, guantelete, armadura de hierro a modo de guante para la mano. 2. Guantelete, guante con prolongación de la muñeca.
Gauntly [gānt'-li], *adv.* Flacamente, flojamente.
Gauze [gēz], *s.* Gasa, especie de tela a manera de red, muy menuda y transparente. *Silk-gauze,* Gasa de seda. *Thread-gauze,* Gasa de hilo. *Linen-gauze,* Clarín.
Gauzy [gez'-i], *a.* Delgado y diáfano como la gasa.
Gave [gêv], *pret.* de *To* Give.
Gavel [gav'-el], *s.* 1. Mazo de albañil. 2. Mazo que usa el presidente de una asamblea o reunión. 3. Gavilla, manojo de mieses. 4. (Hist.) Gabela, tributo.
Gavelock [gav'-e-lec], *s.* Barra o palanca de hierro.
Gavial [gê'-vi-al], *s.* El cocodrilo del Ganges. Gavialis gangeticus.
Gavot [gav'-ẹt o ga-vet'], *s.* Gavota, baile francés.
Gawk [gēk], *s.* 1. Páparo, bobo. 2. (Esco.) Cuclillo.
Gawky [gēk'-i], *s.* Zote.—*a.* Bobo, tonto, rudo.
Gay [gê]. 1. Alegre, de buen humor, jovial. 2. Gayo, alegre, brillante. lucido; especioso. 3. Aficionado a los placeres, particularmente los vedados; inclinado a la lascivia.—*s.* (Des.) Adorno.
Gayety, Gaiety [gê'-e-ti], *s.* Alegría; muchachada; pompa, ostentación, fausto.
Gayly, Gaily [gê'-li], *adv.* Alegremente, jovialmente; espléndidamente.
Gayness [gê'-nes], *s.* Alegría. pompa.
Gaze [gêz], *vn.* Contemplar, considerar.—*va.* Mirar de hito en hito.
Gaze, *s.* 1. Contemplación, mirada, el acto de contemplar o mirar alguna cosa con atención. 2. El objeto que se mira o contempla con atención.
Gaze-hound [gêz'-haund], *s.* Perro que caza con la vista y no con el olfato; particularmente el galgo.
Gazelle [ga-zel'], *s.* Gacela.
Gazer [gêz'-ẹr], *s.* Mirón, el que mira con demasiada curiosidad.
Gazette [ga-zet'], *s.* Gaceta, papel periódico; en especial se designa con este nombre el órgano oficial del gobierno inglés.
Gazette, *va.* Publicar, anunciar, en la Gaceta o diario oficial. *He was gazetted to a captaincy,* Se publicó en la Gaceta su nombramiento de capitán.
Gazetteer [gaz-et-ir'], *s.* 1. Gacetero, el que compone la gaceta. 2. Nombre de un diccionario geográfico de todos los países, ciudades, ríos y lugares del mundo.
Gazing-stock [gêz'-ing-stec], *s.* 1. Hazmereír, la risa, el desprecio y burla de todos. 2. El objeto que llama mucho la atención de los que lo miran.
Gear [gir], *s.* 1. (Mec.) Engranaje, encaje de una rueda en otra; transmisión de movimiento; juego de piezas motrices. 2. (Mar.) Juego de drizas, cuadernales, etc., usado para manejar una verga, berlinga, o vela. 3. Rueda dentada. 4. Juego, manera como están relacionadas dos o más cosas, de modo que sin separarlas tengan movimiento. 5. Lo que está preparado o sirve para la preparación de alguna cosa; de aquí, los vestidos, adornos o atavíos, herramientas, aperos, utensilios caseros, arneses o aparejos de tiro. *Head-gear,* Cofia, tocado de la cabeza. *Gears,* (Mar.) Drizas. *Main-gears,* Drizas mayores. *Fore-gears,* Drizas de la verga de trinquete. *Gear-block,* Cuadernal de paloma. *In gear,* En juego, encajado. *Out of gear,* Fuera de juego, desencajado; desengranado. *To put in gear,* Relacionar, conexionar, engranar. *To throw into gear,* Poner en juego. *To throw out of gear,* Desencajar; desmontar.
Gear [gir], *va.* 1. Aparejar, poner los aparejos, preparar. 2. (Mec.) Engranar, encajar, conectar.—*vn.* Venir o estar en juego.
Gear box, gear case [gir bex, gir kês], *s.* Caja de engranaje.
Gearing [gir'-ing], *s.* 1. (Mec.) Encaje, engranaje; piezas vivas colectivamente. 2. (Mar.) Sogas y aparejos.
Gearshift [gir'-shift], *s.* (Mec.) Cambio de velocidades. *Gear-shift lever,* Palanca de cambios o de velocidades.
Gear wheel [gir hwil], *s.* Rueda de engranaje, rueda dentada.
Geat [jit], *s.* El agujerito por donde entra en el molde el metal derretido.
Gee [ji], *s.* Nombre de la letra G.
Gee [ji], **Geeho** [ji'-hō], *va.* Hacer que un animal de tiro se dirija a la derecha, apartándose del carretero. —*vn.* Dirigirse un buey o una mula hacia la derecha, alejándose del carretero. En imperativo, arre, anda: voz de los carreteros para avivar y guiar a los caballos.
Geese [gis]. *s. pl.* de Goose.
Geiger counter [gai'-gẹr caun'-tẹr], *s.* Contador Geiger.
Gelatin, Gelatine [jel'-a-tin], *s.* Gelatina, substancia coherente, transparente, insípida, que se extrae de los huesos y cuernos o de las patas de los animales. Es soluble en agua caliente.
Gelatinate, Gelatinize [jel-at'-i-nêt, naiz], *va.* y *vn.* Convertir o convertirse en substancia gelatinosa.
Gelatinous [je-lat'-i-nus], *a.* Gelatinoso, de la gelatina o de su naturaleza; semejante a la gelatina.
Geld [geld], *va.* 1. Castrar, capar, v. gr. a un caballo. 2. Castrar, quitar a las colmenas los panales con miel.
Geld, *s.* Tributo antiguo; multa.
Gelder [geld'-ẹr], *s.* Castrador, capador.
Gelding [geld'-ing], *s.* Capón, cualquier animal capado, particularmente el caballo.
Gelid [jel'-id], *a.* (Poét.) Sumamente frío, helado.
Gelidity [je-lid'-i-ti], **Gelidness** [jel'-id-nes], *s.* Frío extremo.

Gem [jem], *s.* 1. Joya, presea. 2. Cosa preciosa, alhaja; objeto raro y cabal; obra literaria o de arte, corta y muy perfecta. 3. (Des.) Yema.
Gem, *va.* Adornar con piedras preciosas.—*vn.* (Ant.) Abotonar, arrojar los árboles y plantas el botón.
Gemel [jem'-el], *a.* y *s.* Gemelo. *Gemel-ring,* Sortija formada por dos o más anillos.
Geminate [jem'-i-nêt], *a.* (Bot.) Que ocurre en pares; gemelo, de dos en dos.—*va.* (Poco us.) Doblar, duplicar.
Gemination [jem-i-né'-shun], *s.* Duplicación, repetición.
Gemini [jem'-i-nai], *s.* Géminis, el tercer signo del zodíaco.
Gemma [jem'-a], *a.* Botón, yema.
Gemmation [jem-mé'-shun], *s.* 1. (Zool.) Gemación, reproducción asexual por medio de un cuerpo parecido a una yema, el cual llega a ser nuevo individuo. 2. (Bot.) El período del desarrollo de los botones; vernación.
Gemmeous [jem'-e-us], *a.* Lo que se asemeja a una piedra preciosa, o al botón o yema de las plantas.
Gemmule [jem'-miūl], *s.* Botón pequeño.
Gemot [ge-mōt'], *s.* Antiguamente asamblea, reunión pública.
Gender [jen'-der], *s.* 1. Género, la división de los nombres según los diferentes sexos. 2. (Fam.) Sexo.
Gender, *va.* Engendrar; producir, causar.—*vn.* (Ant.) Acción de copularse.
Gene [jin], *s.* (Biol.) Gen. *pl. genes.*
Genealogical [jen-e-a-lej'-i-cal], *a.* Genealógico.
Genealogist [jen-e-al'-o-jist], *s.* Genealogista.
Genealogy [jen-e-al'-o-ji], *s.* Genealogía, la descripción de la estirpe de alguno.
Generable [jen'-er-a-bl], *a.* Generable, que se puede producir por generación.
General [jen'-er-al], *a.* 1. General, indeterminado, extensivo. 2. Público, ordinario, común, usual. 3. Visto como totalidad o conjunto.—*s.* 1. Lo general, la mayor parte; el público, el vulgo. *In general,* Por la mayor parte, en general, por lo común. 2. General, oficial general. 3. Generala, un toque de tambor.
Generalissimo [jen-er-a-lis'-i-mo], *s.* Generalísimo.
Generality [jen-er-al'-i-ti], ‡**Generalty** [jen'-er-al-ti], *s.* Generalidad, la parte principal, la mayor parte, la multitud.
Generalization [jen-er-al-i-zé'-shun], *s.* Generalización.
Generalize [jen'-er-al-aiz], *va.* Generalizar.
Generalness [jen-'er-al-nes], *s.* (Poco us.) Frecuencia, extensión.
Generally [jen'-er-al-i], *adv.* Generalmente, comúnmente, por lo general, en general, extensivamente; por la mayor parte.
Generalship [jen'-er-al-ship], *s.* Generalato.
Generant [jen'-er-ant], *a.* Generativo.—*s.* 1. Generante, principio generativo. 2. *V.* GENERATRIX. 1ª.
Generate [jen'-er-êt], *va.* 1. Engendrar, procrear, propagar. 2. Producir, ocasionar, causar. 3. (Mat.) Producir por el movimiento. *A generating line or surface,* Una línea o una superficie generatriz.
Generation [jen-er-é'-shun], *s.* 1. Generación, el acto o la función de engendrar. 2. Generación, familia, linaje, prole, progenie. 3. Siglo, edad. 4. La formación de una figura o un cuerpo geométrico por el movimiento de un punto, de una línea o de una superficie.
Generative [jen'-er-a-tiv], *a.* Generativo, prolífico, fecundo.
Generator [jen'-er-é''-ter], *s.* 1. Padre, procreador, engendrador. 2. La cosa que engendra, causa o produce. 3. Lo que origina o produce electricidad; máquina electrodinámica.
Generatrix [jen'-er-é''-trix], *s.* 1. (Mat.) Punto, línea o superficie que produce una figura por su movimiento. 2. Máquina electrodinámica. 3. Madre; la que produce.
Generic, Generical [je-ner'-ic, al], *a.* Genérico, lo que comprende el género y es común a muchas especies.
Generically [je-ner'-ic-al-i], *adv.* Genéricamente.
Generosity [jen-er-os'-i-ti], *s.* Generosidad, liberalidad; garbo, bizarría.
Generous [jen'-er-us], *a.* 1. Liberal, bizarro, dadivoso; vigoroso; franco, abierto. 2. Generoso, noble, magnánimo. 3. Que tiene cualidades estimulantes, como el vino.
Generously [jen'-er-us-li], *adv.* Magnánimamente, liberalmente, dadivosamente, bizarramente.
Generousness [jen'-er-us-nes], *s.* Generosidad, magnanimidad, nobleza, bizarría.
Genesis [jen'-e-sis], *s.* 1. Creación, principio. 2. Relato o explicación del origen de alguna cosa. 3. Génesis. el primer libro del Antiguo Testamento. 4. (Geom.) *V.* GENERATION, 4ª acep.
Genet [jen'-et], *s.* Haca, jaca, de España.
Genet [je-net'], *s.* 1. Gineta, mamífero que se parece mucho a la civeta, pero más pequeño. 2. La piel adobada de este animal.
Genethliacs [je-neth'-li-acs], *s.* Genetlíaca, el arte de predecir la buena o mala ventura por el día y hora del nacimiento de un persona.
Genetic [je-net'-ic], *a.* Genesiaco; relativo a la creación, la generación, o el origen de alguna cosa.
Genetics [je-net'-ics], *s.* (Biol.) Genética.
Geneva [je-ní'-va], *s.* 1. Ginebra, ciudad de Suiza. 2. *V.* GIN.
Genevan [je-ní'-van], *a.* Ginebrino, de Ginebra.—*s.* 1. El natural de Ginebra. 2. Calvinista.
Genial [jín'-yal o jí'-ni-al], *a.* 1. Cordial, amistoso, de afables maneras, bondadoso. 2. Que comunica calor suave, da alivio o vida; consolador. 3. Nupcial; relativo al matrimonio; generativo.
Genially [jín'-yal-i], *adv.* Cordialmente; bondadosamente.
Geniculate [je-nic'-yu-lêt], *a.* En forma de ángulo, como la rodilla cuando está doblada.
Geniculated [je-nic'-yu-lêt-ed], *a.* 1. Lo que tiene coyunturas o articulaciones. 2. (Bot.) Arrodillado, articulado.
Geniculation [je-nic-yu-lé'-shun], *s.* 1. Genuflexión. 2. (Bot.) Articulación o nudo en las cañas de las plantas gramíneas; nudosidad.
Genie [jí'-ni], *s.* *V.* JINNEE.
Genii [jí'-ni-ai], *s. pl.* Genios.
Genital [jen'-i-tal]. Genital, perteneciente a la generación.—*Genitals, s. pl.* Los órganos exteriores de la generación, en ambos sexos.
Genitive [jen'-i-tiv], *s.* (Gram.) Genitivo, el segundo caso en la declinación de los nombres.—*a.* Que indica, origen, posesión, etc.
Genitor [jen'-i-ter], *s.* Padre, antiguamente genitor.
Genius [jín'-yus], *s.* (*pl.* GENII). 1. Genio, numen o espíritu bueno o malo según el sistema del gentilismo. 2. Ingenio, talento inventivo, numen. 3. Genio, talento, don, prenda o disposición natural para alguna cosa. 4. Ingenio, la persona que posee grandes talentos. (*pl.* GENIUSES en este sentido.) 5. Genio, índole buena o mala; principio esencial de una cosa. 6. Tipo modelo y acabado de algo; personificación.
Genocide [jen'-o-said], *s.* Genocidio.
Genoese [jen-o-is'], *a.* y *s.* Genovés, genovesa, el natural de Génova o lo que pertenece a esta ciudad.
Genteel [jen-tíl'], *a.* 1. Urbano, cortés, bien criado, señoril. 2. Gentil, lindo, gallardo, galán, airoso, decente, formal, caballeroso. 3. Vestido elegantemente, elegante, a la moda.
Genteelly [jen-tíl'-li], *adv.* Urbanamente, cortésmente, gentilmente.
Genteelness [jen-tíl'-nes], *s.* Gentileza, gracia, garbo, urbanidad, bizarría, gallardía, dulzura de genio, formalidad.
Gentian [jen'-shian], *s.* (Bot.) Genciana, cualquiera planta de la familia de las gencianas. La oficinal o amarilla, abundante en Suiza y el Tirol, tiene propiedades tónicas.
Gentianella [jen-sha-nel'-a], *s.* Especie de color azul.
Gentile [jen'-tail], *a.* 1. Gentílico, perteneciente a un pueblo no judáico; pagano. 2. (Gram.) Gentilicio, nombre que indica la nación o patria. 3. Gentilicio, relativo a una tribu (*gens*) o *clan;* propio de las gentes.—*s.* 1. Gentil, el que no es judío. 2. Nombre gentilicio.
Gentilism [jen'-ti-lizm], *s.* Gentilismo, gentilidad.
Gentilitious [jen-ti-lish'-us], *a.* Gentilicio, de una tribu; hereditario.
Gentility [jen-til'-i-ti], *s.* 1. Nobleza de sangre, buen nacimiento. 2. Gentileza, donosura, gracia, donaire. 3. Gente bien nacida. 4. Gentilidad, gentilismo.
Gentle [jen'-tl], *a.* 1. Suave, blando, apacible, dócil, manso, dulce, moderado, benévolo, tranquilo, benigno. 2. Bien nacido; de noble familia.—*s.* 1. (Ant.) *V.* GENTLEMAN. 2. Halcón adiestrado. 3. (Ingl.) Gusano, larva de mosca que sirve de cebo para pescar.
Gentlefolk [jen'-tl-fōc], *s.* La gente bien nacida.
Gentleman [jen'-tl-man], *sm.* 1. Hombre superior al vulgo ya por su buen nacimiento, aunque no sea noble, ya por su carácter o circunstancias: corresponde en español unas veces a caballero y otras a señor, como términos de cortesía. 2. (Fam.) Hacendado, toda persona que vive de su hacienda o tiene rentas. *An independent gentleman,* Un hacendado, propietario, rentista. *Well, gentlemen!* ¡Muy bien, señores! *A gentleman has asked for you,* Un caballero ha preguntado por Vd. *Gentleman-farmer,* Hacendado agricultor.

Gentleman-like [jen'-tl-man-laic], **Gentlemanly** [jen'-tl-man-li], *a.* Caballeroso, galante, civil, urbano; lo que conviene a un hombre bien nacido o bien criado.

Gentlemanliness [jen'-tl-man-li-nes], **Gentlemanship** [jen'-tl-man-ship], *s.* Porte o calidad de caballero.

Gentleman's agreement [jen'-tl-manz a-grî'-mẹnt], *s.* Pacto de caballeros.

Gentleness [jen'-tl-nes], *s.* 1. Dulzura, blandura, suavidad de carácter, mansedumbre, urbanidad. 2. Conducta caballerosa. 3. Nobleza.

Gentlewoman [jen'-tl-wum-an], *sf.* Señora, dama. *The queen's gentlewomen,* Las damas de honor de la reina.

Gently [jen'-tli], *adv.* 1. Dulcemente, suavemente. 2. Poco a poco, despacio, con tiento, con sentir.

Gentoo [jen-tū'], *s.* El natural de la India oriental.

Gentry [jen'-tri], *s.* 1. La clase de personas superiores al vulgo que no pertenecen a la nobleza: úsase también para expresar en general la clase, carácter o calidad de las familias distinguidas. 2. Cualquier clase de gente determinada: irónico, por lo común; como, *Light-fingered gentry,* Gente ladrona, rateros.

Genuflection [jen-yu-flec'-shun], *s.* Genuflexión.

Genuine [jen'-yu-in], *a.* 1. Genuino, real, sin falsedad, ni falsificación. 2. Sincero, puro, propio; escrito por el autor cuyo nombre lleva. 3. (Zool.) Típico. 4. No afectado, franco, sincero; verdadero.

Genuinely [jen'-yu-in-li], *adv.* Puramente, sinceramente, naturalmente.

Genuineness [jen'-yu-in-nes], *s.* Pureza, la calidad que constituye alguna cosa pura y no adulterada.

Genus [jî'-nus], *s.* 1. Género, lo que es común a varias especies y las comprende. 2. (Biol.) Género, conjunto de especies que poseen en común ciertos caracteres distintivos. 3. (Mús.) Clase, particularmente de escalas.

Geocentric [jî-o-sen'-tric], *a.* Geocéntrico: dícese de los planetas.

Geode [jî'-ōd], *s.* Geoda, piedra que tiene una cavidad tapizada de cristales; y el hueco mismo de dicha piedra.

Geodesic [jẹ-o-des'-ic], *a.* Geodésico. *Geodesic dome,* Cúpula geodésica.

Geodesy [jẹ-od'-es-i], *s.* Geodesia, topografía; la medición y representación gráfica de la tierra por medio de observaciones trigonométricas y astronómicas.

Geodetic, Geodetical [jî-o-det'-ic, al], *a.* *V.* GEODESIC.

Geographer [jẹ-eg'-ra-fẹr], *s.* Geógrafo, el que sabe o enseña la geografía.

Geographical [jẹ-o-graf'-i-cal], *a.* Geográfico.

Geographically [jẹ-o-graf'-i-cal-i], *adv.* Geográficamente.

Geography [jẹ-eg'-ra-fi], *s.* 1. Geografía, descripción del globo terrestre. 2. Libro, particularmente el de texto, que contiene dicha descripción.

Geologic, Geological [jẹ-o-lej'-ic, al], *a.* Geológico.

Geologist [jẹ-el'-o-jist], *s.* Geólogo, persona versada en geología.

Geologize [jẹ-el'-o-jaiz], *vn.* Estudiar la geología, particularmente sobre el terreno, en la sierra o en el campo.

Geology [jẹ-el'-o-ji], *s.* 1. Geología, la ciencia que enseña y explica las propiedades de la tierra, su estructura y su historia. 2. Tratado sobre esta ciencia.

Geomagnetic [jî-o-mag-net'-ic], *a.* Geomagnético.

Geometer [jẹ-em'-e-tẹr], *s.* Geómetra, el que profesa el estudio de la geometría o está versado en ella.

Geometric, Geometrical [jî-o-met'-ric, al], *a.* Geométrico, lo que pertenece a la geometría.

Geometrically [jî-o-met'-ric-al-i], *adv.* Geométricamente.

Geometridæ [jî-o-met'-ri-dî], *s. pl.* (Ent.) Geometrinos, suborden de insectos del orden de los lepidópteros o mariposas, cuyas orugas son los gusanos llamados "medidores," muy nocivos a la vegetación.

Geometrize [jẹ-em'-e-traiz], *vn.* Obrar conforme a las leyes de la geometría.

Geometry [jẹ-em'-e-tri], *s.* Geometría, ciencia que trata de la extensión y de su medida.

Geophysical [jî-o-fiz'-i-cal], *a.* Geofísico. *Geophysical year,* Año geofísico.

Geophysics [jî-o-fiz'-ics], *s.* (Geol.) Geofísica.

Geopolitics [jî-o-pel'-i-tics], *s.* Geopolítica.

Geoponic, Geoponical [jî-o-pen'-ic, al], *a.* Geopónico, perteneciente a la agricultura.

Geoponics [jî-o-pen'-ics], *s.* Geopónica, la ciencia o arte de cultivar la tierra; agricultura; economía rural.

George [jērj], *s.* 1. Figura adornada con piedras preciosas que representa a San Jorge en el acto de matar al dragón; una de las insignias del orden de la Jarretera. 2. Peluca grande del siglo XVIII.

Georgette [jēr-jet'], *s.* Crespón de seda transparente.

Georgian [jer'-ji-an], *a.* 1. Perteneciente a los reinados de los cuatro Jorges de Inglaterra. 2. *a.* y *s.* Georgiano, natural del Estado norteamericano de Georgia o perteneciente a él. 3. Georgiano, lo perteneciente o relativo a la Georgia, país de la Transcaucasia rusa, y a sus habitantes.

Georgics [jērj'-ics], *s.* Geórgica, poema rural tocante a la agricultura.

Geoscopy [jẹ-es'-co-pi], *s.* Geoscopia, especie de conocimiento de la naturaleza y calidad de un terreno, obtenido por la vista de él.

Geranium [jẹ-rê'-ni-um], *s.* (Bot.) 1. Geranio, planta de jardín del género Pelargonium, con muchas especies y variedades procedentes en su mayor parte del Africa austral. 2. Geranio, pico de cigüeña, gran género de plantas de la familia de las geraniáceas.

Geriatrician [jer-i-a-trish'-an], *s.* Geriatra.

Geriatrics [jer-i-at'-rics], *s.* Geriatría.

Germ [jẹrm], *s.* 1. Germen, el elemento rudimental de la vida. (*a*) (Biol.) La fase más primitiva de un organismo; embrión. (*b*) (Bot.) Brote, botón nuevo, germen; embrión; ovario, lo que contiene la semilla. 2. Principio, origen de alguna cosa. 3. Microbio, organismo microscópico. *Germ theory,* La teoría de que el tifo, la tisis y otras enfermedades en que entra el elemento de la fermentación, se deben al desarrollo y la multiplicación de microbios en el cuerpo.

German [jẹr'-man], *a.* Pariente, el que tiene relación de parentesco con otro. *Cousin german,* Primo hermano, primo carnal.

German, *s.* y *a.* Alemán; germánico, tudesco. Idioma alemán. *To speak German,* Hablar alemán. *German paste,* Preparación especial para alimento de los pájaros cantores. *German silver,* Plata alemana, alpaca, metal blanco. *German tinder,* Yesca. *V.* AMADOU.

Germane [jẹr-mên'], *a.* Relacionado con, afín.

Germanity [jẹr-man'-i-ti], *s.* Hermandad.

German measles [jẹr'-man mî'-zels], *s. pl.* (Med.) Sarampión benigno.

Germ cell [jẹrm sel], *s.* Óvulo o espermatozoide, célula embrionaria.

Germicidal [jẹr-mi-sai'-dal], *a.* Germicida, que destruye gérmenes o microbios.

Germicide [jer'-mi-said], *s.* Germicida, lo que destruye microbios o gérmenes o impide su desarrollo.

Germinate [jẹr'-mi-nêt], *vn.* Brotar. —*va.* Germinar.

Germination [jẹr-mi-nê'-shun], *s.* Germinación.

Gerocomy [jẹ-rec'-o-mi], *s.* El régimen conveniente a la vejez.

Gerund [jer'-und], *s.* Gerundio.

Gestation [jes-tê'-shun], *s.* Preñez, preñado; el estado de la hembra preñada y el tiempo que está el feto en el vientre de la madre; embarazo en la mujer.

Gesticulate [jes-tic'-yu-lêt], *vn.* Gesticular, hacer gestos y ademanes; accionar.—*va.* Imitar, remedar.

Gesticulation [jes-tic-yu-lê'-shun], *s.* Gesticulación.

Gesticulator [jes-tic'-yu-lê-tẹr], *s.* Gestero, el que hace gestos.

Gesticulatory [jes-tic'-yu-la-to-ri], *a.* Gesticular, perteneciente al gesto.

Gesture [jes'-chur], *s.* Gesto, acción, movimiento expresivo.

Gesture, *vn.* Accionar; gesticular.

Get [get], *va.* (*pret.* GOT, *pp.* GOT o GOTTEN). 1. Ganar, adquirir, granjear alguna cosa con su trabajo; conseguir, obtener, alcanzar, llevar un premio, una ventaja, una victoria, etc.; recibir. *To get a letter,* Recibir una carta. 2. Obtener o conseguir alguna ventaja a pesar de la oposición de otros; de aquí (fam.) poseer, tener; también, estar obligado, haber de ser. *I have got to go,* Tengo que marcharme. *It has got to be done,* Hay que hacerlo, tiene que hacerse. 3. Aprender de memoria. *To get a lesson,* Aprender una lección. *To get one's part,* Aprender su papel. 4. Engendrar, procrear. 5. Hacer ser, hacer, mandar. *To get the work done,* Disponer o hacer que se haga un trabajo. *To get one's self laughed at,* Hacer que se rían de uno. *To get a carriage made,* Mandar hacer un carruaje. 6. Persuadir, inducir, incitar, procurar, adquirir, conseguir, ganar, granjear, ir a buscar, traer. *Get him to go for us,* Persuádale Vd. a que vaya por nosotros. *I can get him to do it,* Puedo inducirle a que lo haga. *Get you gone!* ¡Váyase Vd.! ¡Largo de aquí! —*vn.* 1. Alcanzar, lograr o conseguir alguna cosa poco a poco y con dificultad; prevalecer; adquirir caudal. 2. Pasar una persona o cosa de una situación o estado a otro diverso;

llegar; llegar a ser, volverse, hallarse. *To get home*, Llegar a casa. *To get better*, Ponerse mejor, ir saliendo de una indisposición. *It gets cold early*, Hace frío temprano. 3. Introducirse, meterse una persona o cosa entre otras. 4. (Fam.) Hallar el tiempo, los medios o la oportunidad. *To get about*, (1) *V.* *To get abroad.* (2) Poder moverse de un punto a otro, como lo hace un convaleciente. *To get above one*, Vencer, sobrepujar a uno. *To get abroad*, Hacer salir; publicarse, divulgarse, hacerse público. *To get along*, Hacer andar, adelantar; arrastrar; hallarse; ir siguiendo, adelantarse o mantenerse. *V.* FARE. *To get among*, Hacerse uno de. *To get at*, Ir a, alcanzar; embestir; descubrir, desenmascarar. *To get at the truth*, Descubrir, alcanzar la verdad. *To get at the man*, Alcanzar al hombre; también, embestirlo, atacarlo. *To get a fall*, Caer. *To get a footing*, Establecerse. *To get a wife* o *to get a husband*, Casarse, tomar estado. *To get away*, Quitar, sacar, apartar; huirse, escaparse, poderse escapar, lograr irse. *To get before*, Prevenir; adelantarse. *To get back*, Recobrar; hacerse devolver; regresar, retroceder. *He got back his watch*, Recobró su reloj. *To get behind*, (1) Penetrar; enterarse de los secretos de alguien. (2) Perder terreno; quedarse atrás. *To get by heart*, Aprender de memoria. *To get children*, Engendrar o procrear hijos. *To get clear*, Salir bien de alguna dificultad o empeño. *To get clear of* o *quit of*, Zafarse, libertarse de alguna cosa. *To get down*, Bajar, descender; descolgar, desprender; tragar. *To get forward*, Adelantarse, aprovechar. *To get in*, Lograr entrar; hacer entrar, empeñar; cerrar, encerrar; insinuarse. *To get off*, Deshacerse de algo, vender o despachar alguna cosa; salir de un asunto; escapar, huir; desprender; sacar de un mal paso; descender (de una caballería). *To get on*, Poner, meter; proceder, suceder, acertar; montar a caballo; entrar en un coche o carro; armonizarse. *To get on with*, Vivir u obrar en concordancia con. *To get out*, Salir; sacar, quitar, arrancar; lograr salir; desembarcar; hacerse público. *To get out of the way*, Apartarse a un lado. *To get over*, Pasar, pasar por encima; poner a un lado; atravesar, vencer o sobrepujar obstáculos; responder. *To get ready*, Aparejarse; preparar, aprestar. *To get rid of*, Zafarse o librarse de algo. *To get the better*, Salir vencedor, sobrepujar, sacar ventaja. (Fam.) Salir pujante. *To get the worse*, Llevar lo peor o salir vencido. (Fam.) Salir con las manos en la cabeza. *To get there*, (Ger.) Llegar al fin que se desea, arribar. *To get through*, Pasar por, salir de, pasar al través o de medio a medio. *To get together*, Juntar, amontonar. *To get up*, Levantar o levantarse, subir; montar a caballo; recurrir; preparar. *To get well again*, Recuperarse, restablecerse, recobrar la salud. *To get with child*, Poner en cinta a una mujer. *To get money of one*, Sacar a uno dinero. *To get the start of*, Adelantarse a. *To get rid of*, Deshacerse de, salir de. *To get out of order*, Descomponerse, desajustarse. *To get wind of*, Recibir un informe o una noticia casualmente.

Get, *s.* El acto de engendrar o lo engendrado; progenie, casta. *The get of a stallion*, Lo engendrado por un caballo padre.

Getter [get'-ẹr] *s.* 1. El que procura, adquiere o consigue una cosa. 2. Engendrador, procreador.

Getting [get'-ing], *s.* Adquisición, ganancia, lucro, provecho.

Gewgaw [giū'-gē], *s.* Chuchería, cosa de poca importancia, aunque pulida y delicada; miriñaque, juguete de niños.

Geyser [gai'-sẹr], *s.* Geiser, manantial caliente que arroja agua o lodo en forma de columna y a veces a gran altura.

G-force [jī'-fōrs], *s.* (Fís.) Grado de aceleración producido por la gravedad.

Ghastliness [gqst'-li-nes], *s.* Palidez, color o cara cadavérica.

Ghastly [gqst'-li], *a.* 1. Lúgubre, parecido á la muerte; semejante a un espectro. 2. Horrible, espantoso.

Gherkin [gẹr'-kin], *s.* Pepinillo en adobo; encurtido.

Ghetto [get'-ō], *s.* 1. Ghetto, barrio judío. 2. Barrio de algún grupo racial.

Ghost [gōst], *s.* 1. Aparecido, muerto aparecido, alma del otro mundo o ánima en pena; fantasma, duende; en estilo noble es sombra, espectro. 2. Alma racional. 3. Sombra, imagen, traza leve. 4. (Foto. y Opt.) Imagen falsa o secundaria; mancha, línea o círculo debido a un defecto en la lente. *The ghosts*, Los manes, las sombras. *To give up the ghost*, Entregar el alma a Dios, morir. *The Holy Ghost*, El Espíritu Santo, la tercera persona de la Santísima Trinidad.

Ghost-like [gōst'-laic], *a.* Seco, marchito; con los ojos hundidos; espantoso, parecido a un espectro.

Ghostliness [gōst'-li-nes], *s.* Espiritualidad.

Ghostly [gōst'-li], *a.* 1. Espiritual, lo perteneciente al espíritu. 2. Espiritual, santo, bueno. 3. Lo perteneciente á los aparecidos.

Ghost writer [gōst rait'-ẹr], *s.* Escritor que escribe bajo la firma de otra persona.

Ghoul [gūl], *s.* Trasgo o demonio del que se supone que roba las tumbas y se come los cadáveres; ogro.

Ghurry [gur'-i], *s.* (Anglo-ind.) 1. Clepsidra, reloj de agua, o su timbre; de aquí, cualquier reloj. 2. Hora; según la costumbre india, la sexagésima parte de un día o de una noche.

G.I., *s.* (fam.) Soldado raso del ejército de E.U.—*a.* (fam.) Relacionado con el ejército de E.U. (Las iniciales provienen de la expresión *Government issue* y se originó en la segunda guerra mundial.)

Giant [jai'-ant], *s.* 1. Gigante. 2. Coloso; persona o cosa de gran tamaño, sea física, mental ó figuradamente; fénix. *Giant-powder*, Dinamita.

Giantess [jai'-ant-es], *sf.* Giganta.

Giant-like [jai'-ant-laik], *a.* Gigantesco, giganteo.

Giantship [jai'-ant-ship], *s.* Calidad de gigante.

Gib [jib ó gib], *s.* Chabeta, cuña, contraclavija; pieza de metal que mantiene á otra en su lugar. *Cotter* (o *key*) *and gib*, Clavija y contraclavija.

Gib, *vn.* Destrizar. *V.* GIP.

Gibber [gib'-ẹr], *vn.* Hablar en jerigonza o en jerga.

Gibberish [gib'-ẹr-ish], *s.* Jerigonza, habladuría incoherente, ininteligible por ser muy rápida, confusa o simulada; guirigay.—*a.* Falto de sentido.

Gibbet [jib'-et], *s.* Horca. *V.* GALLOWS.

Gibbet, *va.* 1. Ahorcar. 2. Colgar un cuerpo muerto en la horca, o exponerle en ella. 3. Colgar alguna cosa en un travesaño.

Gibbous [gib'-us], *a.* 1. Jibado, convexo, encorvado. 2. Jiboso, jorobado, corcovado.

Gibbousness [gib'-us-nes], *s.* Convexidad, corvadura.

Gib-cat [gib'-cat], *s.* Gato, particularmente el castrado.

Gibe [jaib], *vn.* Escarnecer, burlarse, mofar, hacer mofa o burla.—*va.* Improperar; burlar, chasquear, ridiculizar.

Gibe, *s.* Escarnio, mofa, burla; pulla, chufleta.

Giber [jaib'-ẹr], *s.* Escarnecedor, mofador.

Gibingly [jaib'-ing-li], *adv.* Desdeñadamente, de burlas, con desprecio.

Giblet [jib'-let], *s.* 1. Uno de los despojos y menudillos de un ave. 2. *pl.* Andrajos, guiñapos.

Giddily [gid'-i-li], *adv.* Vertiginosamente; inconstantemente, negligentemente.

Giddiness [gid'-i-nes], *s.* 1. Vértigo, vahido, aturdimiento, atolondramiento de cabeza. 2. Instabilidad, inconstancia, veleidad. 3. Vaivén. 4. Devaneos, desvaríos.

Giddy [gid'-i], *a.* 1. Vertiginoso. 2. Veleidoso, voltario, voluble, ligero, inconstante. 3. Descuidado, enajenado, descabezado, desatinado, aturdido. 4. Bobo, necio, pelele. *A giddy girl*, Una muchacha aturdida, casquivana. *Giddy fortune*, Fortuna voluble, inconstante. *My head feels giddy*, Se me va la cabeza; tengo vértigo. *Giddy-brained*, Descuidado: ligero de cascos, con los cascos a la jineta. *Giddy-head, giddy-pate*, El hombre loco, fatuo o necio. *Giddy-headed, giddy-pated*, Inconstante, voluble; imprudente.

Gie [gi], *va.* (*pret.* GA o GIED, *pp.* GIEN). (Esco.) *V.* GIVE.

Gift [gift], *s.* 1. Don, dádiva, gracia, favor, presente, regalo; soborno (en lenguaje bíblico). 2. Donación, el acto de donar. 3. Oblación, ofrenda. 4. Don, dote, prenda, el talento natural para hacer alguna cosa. *Christmas* o *New Year's gift*, Aguinaldo. *Gift by will*, Legado. *A deed of gift*, Un instrumento o contrato de donación.

Gift, *va.* Dotar, adornar la naturaleza a alguno con dotes, prendas o talentos para alguna cosa.

Gifted [gift'-ed], *a.* Dotado, talentoso, hábil.

Giftedness [gift'-ed-nes], *s.* El estado de hallarse dotado de prendas o talentos sobresalientes.

Gig [gig], *s.* 1. Calesa, birlocho, calesín, quitrín. 2. Máquina para tundir paño. 3. Esquife, bote de un navío en que los remeros se sientan en bancos alternados. 4. Trompo, peón, peonza, perinola. 5. *V.* FIZGIG. 6. Chacota; calaverada.

Gigantean [jai-gan-tī'-an], *a.* Gigantesco; irresistible.

Gigantic [jai-gan'-tic], *a.* 1. Giganteo, gigantesco, enorme. 2. Terrible; excesivo, violento, extraordinario.
Giggle [gig'-l], *vn.* Reirse tratando de suprimir ú ocultar la risa, reirse sin motivo; reirse por nada.
Giggle, *s.* Risa falsa, ahogada; risa convulsiva; acción de reirse sin motivo, tontamente.
Gigolo [jig'-o-lō], *s.* 1. Hombre que vive de las mujeres públicas. 2. Compañero de baile o acompañante de mujeres pagado por éstas.
Gigot [jig'-ọt], *s.* 1. Pierna de carnero. 2. (Mar.) Aurica, vela.
Gild [gild], *va.* (*pret.* y *pp.* GILDED o GILT). 1. Dorar; dar una capa de oro; adornar con hojas de oro. 2. Dar un color amarillo, cubrir con reflejos dorados; iluminar. 3. Dar brillo o lustre; dar un barniz superficial y aparente.
Gilder [gild'-ẹr], *s.* 1. Dorador. 2. *V.* GUILDER.
Gilding [gild'-ing], *s.* Doradura; dorado, adorno con objetos dorados.
Gilia [jil'-i-a], *s.* Gilia, género de plantas americanas de numerosas especies, de la familia de las polemoniáceas; algunas se cultivan como de adorno. (De Felipe Gil, botánico español.)
Gill [jil], *s.* 1. Medida de líquidos que contiene la cuarta parte de un cuartillo. 2. Moza; particularmente la que es lasciva; pelandusca. 3. (Bot.) Hiedra terrestre. 4. *Gill* o *gill-beer*, Bebida medicinal hecha de cerveza con infusión de hiedra terrestre.
Gill [gil], *s.* 1. Agalla, branquia, una de las aberturas que tienen los peces en el arranque de la cabeza. *Gill-cover*, Membrana cartilaginosa que cubre las agallas. 2. Papada, la carne que crece debajo de la barba. 3. Barranco; rambla.
Gillyflower, **Gilliflower** [jil'-i-flau'-ẹr], *s.* (Bot.) Alelí.
Gilt, *pret.* y *pp.* de *To* GILD.—*s.* 1. Dorado, oro en hojuelas, el material usado para dorar. 2. Oropel; falso brillo; apariencia ficticia, en oposición al verdadero mérito.
Gilthead [gilt'-hed], *s.* (Zool.) Esparo o espátula.
Gimbals [jim'-balz], *s. pl.* (Mar.) Balancines de la brújula.
Gimcrack [jim'-crac], *s.* Chuchería, obra mecánica de poco valor.
Gimlet [gim'-let], *s.* Barrena pequeña. †GIMBLET.
Gimmick [gim -mic], *s.* 1. Truco secreto de prestidigitador. 2. Dispositivo o ardid ingeniosos para lograr algún fin.
Gimp [gimp], *s.* Bocadillo, alamar. *Gimp nail*, Tachuela para tapicería. —*a.* (Des.) Lindo, precioso.
Gin [jin], *s.* 1. Una de varias máquinas; (a) almarrá, desmotadora de algodón; (b) cabria, o cabrestante portátil; (c) bomba movida por un molino de viento; (d) martinete. 2. Trampa, armadijo para cazar algún animal. (Contracción de ENGINE.) 3. Ginebra, alcohol de semillas aromatizado con bayas de enebro. (Corrupción de GENEVA.) *Gin-mill*, (Ger. E. U.) Despacho de licores. *Gin-palace*, Tienda lujosa donde se venden licores. *Gin-shop*, Despacho de ginebra, taberna.
Gin [jin], *va.* 1. Entrampar, coger en la trampa. 2. Alijar, desmotar el algodón.
Ginger [jin'-jẹr], *s.* (Bot.) Jengibre, ajengibre. *Ginger-ale*, *ginger-beer*, Cerveza de jengibre. *Ginger-pop*, Variedad inferior de cerveza de jengibre. *Ginger-snap*, Galletica de jengibre.
Ginger-bread [jin'-jẹr-bred], *s.* Pan de jengibre. *Ginger-bread work*, Chapucería, obra de adorno barata y de mal gusto.
Gingerly [jin'-jẹr-li], *a.* Cauteloso, escrupuloso o quisquilloso. —*adv.* Cautelosamente. (< sueco.)
Gingham [ging'-am], *s.* Carranclán, guinga. (Amer. guingeto).
Gingival [jin'-ji-val], *a.* Lo perteneciente a las encías.
Gingivitis [jin-ji-vai'-tis], *s.* (Med.) Gingivitis.
Gipsy [jip'-si], *s.* 1. Gitano. 2. Jerga, lengua de los gitanos, que llaman ellos *Romani chiv* y contiene casi 5,000 voces. 3. Persona algo ruda y picaresca, especialmente una muchacha brusca y desparpajada. 4. Nombre despectivo que se aplica á las mujeres de piel muy morena. *Gipsy-winch*, Grúa de soporte lateral. *Gipsy-moth*, Ocneria, falena de los lipáridos, cuya oruga es muy dañina a los pinos.—*a.* Gitanesco, picarón. *V.* GYPSY.
Giraffe [ji-raf'], *s.* 1. (Zool.) Jirafa. 2. La constelación Camelopardalis. 3. (E. U.) Carro en forma de jaula que se usa en las minas y especialmente en las galerías en declive; su armazón es más alta á un extremo que al otro.
Girandole [jir'-an-dōl], *s.* Girándula, candelabro de muchos brazos.
Girasol [jir'-a-sel], *s.* Una especie de ópalo.
Gird [gẹrd], *va.* (*pret.* y *pp.* GIRDED o GIRT). 1. Ceñir, atar alguna cosa alrededor. 2. Cercar, rodear. 3. Vestir. 4. Investir.—*vn.* Mofarse, hacer mofa. *To gird* (o *gird on*) *a sword*, Ceñir espada.
Gird, *s.* 1. Escarnio, mofa. 2. (Des.) Angustia, improperio.
Girder [gẹrd'-ẹr], *s.* 1. (Arq.) Cuartón, madero grueso que sirve para las fábricas y otros usos. 2. Censor satírico.
Girding [gẹrd'-ing], *s.* 1. Ceñidura. 2. Ceñidor.
Girdle [gẹrd'-l], *s.* 1. Cíngulo, cinturón, cinto, ceñidor que rodea la cintura. 2. Circunferencia, cerco, círculo. 3. Zodíaco. 4. (Anat.) La disposición anular de los huesos por medio de la cual se adhieren al tronco las extremidades de un animal vertebrado.
Girdle, *va.* 1. Ceñir, cercar, rodear, circundar; atar con cinto. 2. Hacer una incisión circular en la corteza de un árbol.
Girdle-belt [gẹr'-dl-belt], *s.* Ceñidor.
Girl [gẹrl], *sf.* 1. Muchacha, niña, doncellita; mujer joven, solterita. 2. (Fam.) Moza (de servicio), criada. 3. (Fam.) La joven á quien uno galantea. *Best girl*, La amada de uno, dulce amiga.
Girl guide [gẹrl gaid], *s.* Guía, niña guía, niña exploradora.
Girlhood [gẹrl'-hud], *s.* Doncellez, soltería.
Girlish [gẹrl'-ish], *a.* Juvenil, como una muchacha, propio de una muchacha. *Girlish trick*, Niñada.
Girlishly [gẹrl'-ish-li], *adv.* Como una muchacha.
Girl scout [gẹrl scaut], *s.* Guía, niña guía, niña exploradora.
Girn [gern], *vn.* (Esco.) *V.* GRIN.
Girondist [ji-ron'-dist], *s.* y *a.* Girondino, nombre de un partido político que se formó en Francia en tiempo de la Revolución.
Girt [gẹrt], *pret.* de *To* GIRD: *pp.* y *a.* 1. (Mar.) Amarrado de modo que se contrarreste la acción del viento o de la marea. 2. (Ento.) Braceado, sujetado, como una crisálida.
Girt-line [gẹrt'-lain], *s.* (Mar.) Andarivel.
Girth [gẹrth], *s.* Cincha, la faja con que se asegura la silla á la caballería; circunferencia.
Girth, *va.* Cinchar, asegurar con cincha.
Gist [jist], *s.* La clave, la substancia o el grano de un asunto; punto capital.
Give [giv], *va.* (*pret.* GAVE, *pp.* GIVEN). 1. Dar, donar. 2. Pagar, premiar, recompensar. 3. Conceder; ceder, renunciar; dar licencia. 4. Pronunciar, divulgar. 5. Mostrar, demostrar, explicar, exhibir material o mentalmente. 6. Habilitar, autorizar. 7. Entregarse, aplicarse, dedicarse, emplearse. 8. Rendirse (con *up*). *V. Give up.* 9. Conferir, remitir, entregar. 10. Ceder, dejar. 11. Presumir, suponer. 12. Ofrecer, presentar como producto o resultado. 13. Ser el autor, origen u ocasión de; suplir; conferir, excitar.—*vn.* 1. Dar libremente o de buena gana el título o la posesión de algo que tiene valor. 2. Dar de sí, aflojarse, ablandarse; cejar, recular. 3. Dar, mirar hacia una parte, tener vistas a (galicismo). *To give again*, Volver á dar. *To give away*, Enajenar, transferir, dar o traspasar a otro la posesión de alguna cosa, entregar, abandonar, dar libremente o de buena gana. (Fam.) Divulgar por descuido o tontería; vender una cosa de cualquier modo. *To give up for dead*, Dar a uno por muerto o creerle muerto. *To give away for lost*, Dar algo por perdido. *To give back* o *back again*, Volver lo que se había recibido, restituir, devolver. *To give forth*, Publicar, divulgar, sacar á luz, decir públicamente alguna cosa. *To give in*, Ceder echar a huir, retroceder, retirarse, cejar, recular. *To give in to*, Adoptar, abrazar una opinión, un partido, etc., inclinarse a una cosa con preferencia a otra. *To give it to one*, Dar de palos; poner como nuevo a uno, o ponerle de oro y azul; zurrar o censurar de firme. *To give off*, Arrojar de sí, emitir. *To give over*, Cesar, dejar de ser o de hacer algo, parar, descontinuar, abandonar; detenerse, desistir; darse o entregarse completamente a la voluntad de otro o a alguna pasión vicio, etc.; desahuciar. *To give out*, Publicar, proclamar, divulgar, relatar, extender la voz, esparcir voces o rumores; faltar, consumirse, perderse; aparentar, fingirse uno lo que no es; darse por vencido, cesar en un intento o esfuerzo por agotamiento físico; repartir órdenes o trabajo; distribuir. *To give up*, Dejar, ceder, renunciar, entregar, abandonar, dimitir, resignar, volver, restituir; desasirse; desanimarse; abandonar la esperanza respecto a. *I give it up*, Me doy por vencido. *To give a call*, Llamar. *To give a description*, Describir. *To give a fall*, Caer. *To give a guess*, Adivinar. *To give a look*, Mirar.

To give a person his own, Dar a una persona su merecido o tratarla como se merece. *To give a portion,* Dotar; también, entregar a uno su cuota. *To give content.* Contentar. *To give credit,* Dar fe o crédito, creer; prestar, dar fiado. *To give ear,* Escuchar, dar oídos. *To give evidence,* Atestiguar. *To give fire,* Disparar. *To give for lost,* Dar por perdido. *To give ground,* Retroceder, volver atrás. *To give heed,* Advertir, reparar, hacer caso. *To give like for like,* Pagar en la misma moneda. *To give joy,* Dar el parabién, felicitar. *To give judgment,* Juzgar. *To give leave,* Permitir, dar licencia. *To give notice,* Avisar, advertir, prevenir, hacer saber una cosa con anticipación. *To give one's self for lost,* Darse por perdido, creerse perdido; no tener ninguna esperanza. *To give one's mind,* Entregarse á una cosa, aplicarse, aficionarse. *To give place,* Hacer lugar. *To give the hand,* Dar la mano derecha; dar la preeminencia, reconocerse como inferior. *To give the lie,* Desmentir. *To give the slip,* Sustraerse, huirse. *To give trouble,* Incomodar, dar que hacer. *To give warning,* Advertir, poner sobre aviso. *To give way,* Ceder, flaquear, rendirse; hacer lugar; cesar, desaparecer; empezar a bogar (por lo común en imperativo). *The ground gives way under my feet,* La tierra se hunde bajo mis pies. *He gave not a word,* No dijo una palabra. *To give one's respects,* Dar memorias. *Given under my hand and seal,* (For.) Firmado y sellado de mi mano, o por mí. *To give birth to,* Dar a luz, parir; ser causa de. *To give audience,* Otorgar audiencia. *To give fire,* Mandar tirar; tirar, descargar.

Given [gɪv'-n], *pp.* 1. Dado, inclinado habitualmente, adicto. 2. Dado, fijado; concedido, convenido.

Giver [gɪv'-ęr], *s.* Donador, dador; distribuyente.

Giving [gɪv'-ɪng], *s.* El acto de dar o conferir.

Gizzard [gɪz'-ard], *s.* Molleja de ave. *He frets his gizzard,* (Vul.) Se rompe los cascos, se devana los sesos.

Glabrous [glé'-brus], *a.* Liso, calvo, llano; sin pelo ni pelusa.

Glacé [glę-sé'], *a.* 1. De superficie lisa y lustrosa. (Aplícase a cuero, tela, etc.) 2. Garapiñado. (Aplícase a frutas, nueces, etc.)

Glacial [glé'-shɪal], *a.* Glacial, helado.

Glaciate [glé'-shɪ-ét], *va.* 1. (Geol.) Cubrir con hielo glacial o de ventisquero. 2. (Art. y Of.) Producir sobre una superficie un efecto parecido al hielo.—*vn.* Helarse.

Glaciation [glé-shɪ-é'-shun], *s.* Helamiento, congelación.

Glacier [glé'-shier], *s.* Glaciar, ventisquero.

Glacis [glé'-sɪs], *s.* (Fort.) Glacis o explanada, declive que empieza desde el parapeto de la entrada cubierta y se pierde insensiblemente en el llano.

Glad [glad], *a.* Alegre, contento, gozoso; agradable; agradecido. *To be glad,* Alegrarse, celebrar. *I am glad to see you well,* Me alegro de verlo (a Vd.) bueno. *Glad tidings,* Noticias alegres o agradables.

Glad, (Poét.) **Gladden** [glad'-n], *va.* Alegrar, regocijar.

Glade [gléd], *s.* 1. Claro, raso, sitio sin árboles en un bosque. 2. (Local, E. U.) Extensión lisa de hielo descubierto; espacio abierto que no está helado. 3. *V.* EVERGLADE.

Gladiator [glad'-ɪ-é-tęr], *s.* Gladiador o gladiator, el que en los juegos públicos de los romanos luchaba con otro hasta quitarle la vida o perderla.

Gladiatorial [glad-ɪ-a-tō'-rɪ-al], **Gladiatory** [glad'-ɪ-a-to-rɪ], *a.* Gladiatorio.

Gladiole, Gladiolus [glad'-ɪ-ōl, glad-ɪ-ō'-lus], *s.* Planta del género gladiolo; gladio.

Gladiolus [gla-daɪ'-o-lus], *s.* Espadaña, gladiolo, planta de adorno.

Gladly [glad'-lɪ], *adv.* Alegremente; de buena gana, con placer.

Gladness [glad'-nes], *s.* Alegría, placer, buen humor.

Gladsome [glad'-sum], *a.* Alegre, contento.

Gladsomely [glad'-sum-lɪ], *adv.* Alegremente.

Gladsomeness [glad'-sum-nes], *s.* Alegría, buen humor, gracia, donaire.

Glair [glār], *s.* 1. Clara de huevo: empleada en la encuadernación y en el dorado. 2. Cualquier substancia resbaladiza, viscosa y pegajosa.

Glair, *va.* Dar o untar con clara de huevo.

Glairy [glār'-ɪ], *a.* Parecido a la clara de huevo; viscoso, pegajoso.

Glamor [glam'-ęr], *s.* 1. Encanto, hechizo; ilusión efectuada por el encanto. 2. Encanto, interés artificial, embeleso, fascinación, falsa apariencia.

Glamorize [glam'-ęr-aiz], *va.* Embellecer, hermosear; hacer atrayente una persona, cosa o producto; dar encanto.

Glance [glqns], *s.* 1. Vislumbre o resplandor repentino; relámpago. 2. Ojeada, mirada: de aquí, pensamiento repentino o pasajero. 3. Desvío por herir de refilón u oblicuamente. 4. (Min.) Mineral lustroso. *Copper glance,* Cobre sulfurado vidrioso. *Glance-coal,* Antracita. *At the first glance,* Al primer aspecto, a primera vista.

Glance, *vn.* 1. Centellar, brillar o despedir rayos de luz. 2. Dispararse como una centella. 3. Ojear; mirar alguna cosa de prisa. 4. Rebotar, divergir, desviar, después de tocar o herir oblicuamente. 5. Censurar con indirectas o criticar con ademanes.—*va.* 1. Despedir o disparar alguna cosa en dirección oblicua. 2. Lanzar miradas. *To glance at a book,* Hojear un libro. *To glance over,* Registrar, recorrer o pasar ligeramente la vista por alguna cosa.

Glancing [glqns'-ɪng], *s.* Censura por medio de indirectas.

Glancingly [glqns'-ɪng-lɪ], *adv.* De paso, oblicuamente.

Gland [gland], *s.* 1. (Anat.) Glándula, órgano destinado a secretar de la masa de la sangre un flúido determinado. 2. (Bot.) Glándula, órgano secretorio especial de las plantas. Segrega a menudo un flúido oloroso. 3. Bellota.

Glandered [glan'-dęrd], *a.* Muermoso; se dice de los caballos.

Glanders [glan'-dęrz], *s.* Muermo, enfermedad de los caballos.

Glandiferous [glan-dɪf'-ęr-us], *a.* Glandígero, lo que produce bellotas.

Glandiform [gland'-ɪ-fōrm], *a.* Glandiforme, de la figura de bellotas o glándulas.

Glandular [gland'-yu-lar], **Glandulous** [gland'-yu-lus], *a.* Glanduloso, perteneciente a las glándulas.

Glandule [glan'-diūl], *s.* Glandulilla, glándula pequeña.

Glans [glans], *s.* (*pl.* GLANDES). Bellota, o una parte parecida a la bellota; (Anat.) balano, extremidad del pene o del clítoris. (Lat.)

Glare [glār], *vn.* 1. Relumbrar, brillar. 2. Echar miradas de indignación. 3. Ser excesivamente brillante o charro en color.—*va.* (Poco us.) Deslumbrar.

Glare, *s.* 1. Deslumbramiento; mirada feroz y penetrante. 2. (E. U.) Superficie lisa y vidriosa. *V.* GLAIR, 2ª acep.

Glareous, Glaireous [glār'-ę-us], *a.* *V.* GLAIRY.

Glaring [glār'-ɪng], *a.* 1. Brillante, deslumbrador, deslumbrante. 2. Evidente, notorio. 3. Caracterizado por una mirada feroz y penetrante.

Glaringly [glār'-ɪng-lɪ], *adv.* Notoriamente, evidentemente.

Glass [glqs], *s.* 1. Vidrio. 2. (Quím.) Substancia derretida que se asemeja al vidrio. *Glass of cobalt,* Esmalte, safre, vidrio de cobalto. 3. Cualquier artículo hecho de vidrio, como un vaso para beber, una vidriera, u hoja de cristal o vidrio para ventanas, un espejo, una lente, un anteojo de teatro, etc.; y en plural, anteojos, lentes, quevedos. (Estrictamente quevedos en oposición a gafas.) 4. Vaso, la cantidad de líquido que contiene un vaso para beber. 5. Ampolleta, reloj de arena; de aquí, hilo o duración de la vida del hombre. 6. Termómetro o barómetro. *Crown-glass,* El vidrio que contiene cal; el vidrio más común. *Flint-glass,* Cristal; el vidrio que contiene plomo. *Cut glass,* Cristal tallado. *Burning glass,* Lente de foco corto. *Glass bead,* Abalorio, cuenta de vidrio, chaquira. *Focusing-glass,* Lente de enfocar. *Plate-glass,* Vidrio cilindrado; grueso y muy pulido. *Perspective glass,* Telescopio terrestre. *Drinking-glass,* Vaso para beber. *Magnifying-glass,* Vidrio de aumento. *Looking-glass,* Espejo. *Cupping-glass,* Ventosa. *Hour-glass,* Reloj de una hora. *Window-glass,* Cristal o vidrio para ventanas. *Wine-glass,* Copa o copita de vino o para vino. *Pier-glass,* Espejo grande que se coloca entre dos ventanas. *Spy-glass,* Anteojo de larga vista. *Stained glass,* Vidrio pintado al fundirlo, no exteriormente. *Weather-glass,* Barómetro. *Glasses,* (Mar.) Ampolletas. *To wear glasses,* Usar quevedos o lentes.—*a.* Vítreo, hecho de vidrio. *A glass bottle,* Botella de vidrio.

Glass-blower [glqs'-blō'-ęr], *s.* Soplador de vidrio, vidriero.

Glass case [glqs kés], *s.* Vitrina.

Glassful [glqs'-ful], *s.* Vaso, la cantidad de líquido que puede contener un vaso.

Glass-furnace [glqs'-fōr-nęs], *s.* Horno de vidrio.

Glass-grinder [glqs'-graind-ęr], *s.* Pulidor o bruñidor de cristales.

Glass-house [glqs'-haus], *s.* Vidriería fábrica de vidrio o cristal.

Glassiness [glqs'-ɪ-nes], *s.* Lisura, como la del vidrio; estado de vitrificación.

Glass-like [glqs'-laik], *a.* Transparente como el vidrio.

Glass-maker [glqs'-mé-kęr], *s.* Vidriero, el que hace el vidrio.

Glassman [glqs'-man], *s.* Vidriero, el que vende vidrio.

Glass-metal [glɑs'-met-al], *s.* El vidrio derretido.
Glass-shop [glɑs'-shep], *s.* Vidriería, cristalería, tienda ó almacén de cristales.
Glassware [glɑs' wār], *s.* Vidriería, cristalería, todo género de vidrios y cristales.
Glass-window [glɑs'-win-dō], *s.* Vidriera.
Glasswork [glɑs'-wūrk], *s.* Fábrica de vidrio ó cristales; cristalería, vidriería, todo género de vidrios y cristales.
Glasswort [glɑs'-wūrt], *s.* (Bot.) Sosa, barrilla.
Glassy [glɑs'-i], *a.* Vítreo, cristalino, vidrioso.
Glauber's salt [glō'-bẹrz sēlt], *s.* (Med.) Sal de Glauber, sulfato de sosa.
Glaucoma [glō-cō'-ma], *s.* (Med.) Glaucoma, enfermedad gravísima del globo del ojo, caracterizada por el aumento de los humores intraoculares, que acaba por producir la ceguera.
Glaucous [glō'-cus], *a.* 1. Verdemar, glauco. 2. (Bot.) Cubierto de una pelusa azulada y blanquecina.
Glave, Glaive [glêv], *s.* 1. Arma cortante parecida a la alabarda. 2. (Des.) Espada ancha.
Glaze [glêz], *va.* 1. Poner cristales o vidrios en el bastidor de una ventana. 2. Vidriar, dar cierto género de barniz al barro u otros materiales; barnizar; dar una apariencia vidriosa. *Glazed linen,* Lienzo lustroso o glaseado.
Glaze, *s.* 1. Superficie lisa y lustrosa. 2. Barniz, lustre; cualquier substancia empleada para dar lustre.
Glazier [glê'-zher], *s.* Vidriero, el artífice que hace vidrieras para las ventanas.
Glazing [glê'-zing], *s.* 1. El acto o arte de vidriar o barnizar; o de alisar un lienzo. 2. Barniz, lustre. 3. Vidriería, cristalería, conjunto de objetos de vidrio. 4. Vidriería, oficio del vidriero.
Gleam [glīm], *s.* 1. Relámpago, cualquier fuego, resplandor o brillo muy fugaz. 2. Rayo, centelleo; toda cosa comparada al relámpago. *A gleam of wit,* Agudeza chispeante.
Gleam, *vn.* Relampaguear, brillar, lucir rápidamente.
Gleaming [glīm'-ing], *s.* Relámpago.
Gleamy [glīm'-i], *a.* Centelleante, fulgurante.
Glean [glīn], *va.* 1. Espigar, coger las espigas que los segadores han dejado en el campo después de segadas las mieses. 2. Recoger y juntar algunas cosas esparcidas.
Glean, *s.* Rebusca, rebusco, colección hecha gradualmente.
Gleaner [glīn'-ẹr], *s.* Espigador, rebuscador, recogedor.
Gleaning [glīn'-ing], *s.* Rebusca, rebusco.
Glebe [glīb], *s.* 1. (Ant. ó Poét.) Gleba, césped, terrón. 2. (Gran Bretaña.) Tierras beneficiales, terreno anejo a algún beneficio o curato. 3. Extensión de tierra que contiene mineral.
Glebous [glī'-bus], *a.* Gleboso; abundante en terrones o césped.
Glede [glīd], *s.* Milano, ave de rapiña; también, una de ciertas aves semejantes al milano.
Gledge [glej], *vn.* (Esco.) Mirar a hurtadillas, al soslayo.
Glee [glī], *s.* 1. Alegría, gozo, júbilo, jovialidad. 2. Una especie de canción para tres o más voces, sin acompañamiento.
Glee club [glī club], *s.* Coro, club coral.
Gleeful [glī'-ful], *a.* Alegre, gozoso, jovial.
Gleeman [glī'-man], *s.* Cantor ambulante.
Gleesome [glī'-sum], *a.* *V.* GLEEFUL.
Gleet [glīt], *s.* Gonorrea o blenorragia crónica.
Gleety [glīt'-i], *a.* Blenorrágico.
Glen [glen], *s.* Valle, llanura de tierra entre montes o alturas; cañada.
Glib [glib], *a.* 1. Voluble, corriente, suelto de lengua. 2. (Ant.) Liso, resbaladizo.
Glibly [glib'-li], *adv.* Corrientemente, volublemente.
Glibness [glib'-nes], *s.* Volubilidad, fluidez, facundia.
Glide [glaid], *vn.* Manar suavemente y sin ruido; moverse con velocidad y suavidad; deslizarse, escurrirse.
Glide, *s.* La acción de pasar suavemente de una parte a otra.
Glider [glaid'-ẹr], *s.* (Aer.) Deslizador, planeador.
Gliding [glaid'-ing], *s.* Deslizamiento, planeo.
Gliff [glif], *s.* (Esco.) 1. Susto, espanto. 2. Ojeada rápida; momento.
Glim [glim], *s.* (Ger.) Luz, candela. *To douse the glim,* (Mar.) Apagar la luz.
Glimmer [glim'-ẹr], *s.* 1. Vislumbre, resplandor tenue de la luz, luz débil e incierta. 2. Mirada ligera; aprehensión momentánea. 3. Mica laminar.
Glimmer, *vn.* Vislumbrarse, alumbrar, brillar débilmente y de una manera inconstante; alborear; de aquí, dar señales muy inciertas o ligeras de existencia.
Glimmering [glim'-ẹr-ing], *pa.* Vacilante, que brilla ó alumbra débilmente. *The glimmering dawn,* El alba naciente.—*s.* Luz incierta, débil resplandor; vista imperfecta, aprehensión momentánea.
Glimpse [glimps], *s.* 1. Vislumbre, relámpago. 2. Lustre de poca duración; resplandor fugaz; reflejo, apariencia ligera. 3. Ojeada, mirada rápida y breve.
Glimpse, *va.* Ver con mirada rápida, como un relámpago.—*vn.* 1. Ojear, mirar de prisa. 2. Brillar a intervalos; aparecer por un momento.
Glisten [glis'-n], *vn.* Relucir, comúnmente por reflexión; brillar, resplandecer, relumbrar.
Glister [glis'-tẹr], *vn.* (Ant.) *V.* GLITTER.
Glisteringly [glis'-tẹr-ing-li], *adv.* Espléndidamente, lustrosamente.
Glitter [glit'-ẹr], *vn.* 1. Relucir, resplandecer; chispear, centellear. 2. Lucir, brillar, hacer figura brillante.
Glitter, *s.* Lustre, esplendor, resplandor.
Glittering [glit'-ẹr-ing], *a.* Lustroso, resplandeciente, brillante.—*s.* Relámpago, lustre.
Glitteringly [glit'-ẹr-ing-li], *adv.* Lustrosamente, con lustre.
Gloam [glōm], *va.* y *vn.* Obscurecer u obscurecerse, como sucede en el crepúsculo; anochecer.
Gloaming [glōm'-ing], *s.* Crepúsculo nocturno, la anochecida, el anochecer.
Gloat [glōt], *vn.* Mirar u ojear fijamente con satisfacción baja, mala o cruel; manifestar exultación maligna.
Globate [glō'-bêt], **Globated** [glō'-bêted], *a.* Esférico, hecho en forma de globo.
Globe [glōb], *s.* 1. Esfera. 2. Globo. 3. Bola. 4. Globo, receptáculo redondo, hueco; como una redoma para peces, o el bombillo de una lámpara. *Globe-fish,* Pez globo. Spheroides maculatus. *Globe-valve,* Válvula esférica.
Globetrotter [glōb'-tret'-ẹr], *s.* Trotamundos.
Globose [glō'-bōs], **Globous** (Des.) [glō'-bus], *a.* Globoso, redondo, casi esférico.
Globular [gleb'-yu-lar], *a.* Globular.
Globule [gleb'-yūl], *s.* Glóbulo.
Globulous [gleb'-yu-lus], *a.* Globuloso, en forma de globo o glóbulo.
Glomerate [glem'-ẹr-êt], *va.* Conglomerar, aglomerar, formar cualquiera cosa a manera de ovillo o en forma de bola.
Glomerate, *a.* Aglomerado, conglomerado; dícese de las glándulas que forman un ovillo.
Glomeration [glem-ẹr-ê'-shun], *s.* Conglobación.
Glomerule [glem'-ẹr-ūl], *s.* 1. (Bot.) Glomérula, gavilla o conjunto de flores en forma de cabeza compacta. 2. (Anat.) Masa redonda envuelta; particularmente el cuerpo malpigiano del riñón.
Gloom [glūm], *s.* 1. Tinieblas, obscuridad, lobreguez. 2. Melancolía, tristeza.
Gloom, *vn.* 1. Lucir tenue o confusamente. 2. Encapotarse, obscurecerse. 3. Entristecerse, estar de mal humor.—*va.* Llenar de obscuridad o de tristeza.
Gloomily [glūm'-i-li], *adv.* Obscuramente; tétricamente; tristemente, lúgubremente.
Gloominess [glūm'-i-nes], *s.* Obscuridad, tinieblas; aspecto sombrío, nublado; melancolía, tristeza, abatimiento; adustez.
Gloomy [glūm'-i], *a.* 1. Tenebroso, sombrío, obscuro, lóbrego; nublado, cubierto de nubes. 2. Tétrico, triste, melancólico; abatido, desalentado; adusto.
Gloried [glō'-rid], *a.* (Des.) Ilustre, lleno de gloria.
Glorification [glō-ri-fi-kê'-shun], *s.* Glorificación.
Glorify [glō'-ri-fai], *va.* Glorificar, honrar, alabar, exaltar, celebrar.
Glorious [glō'-ri-us], *a.* Glorioso, ilustre, digno de honor y alabanza; orgulloso, jactancioso, soberbio.
Gloriously [glō'-ri-us-li], *adv.* Gloriosamente.
Gloriousness [glō'-ri-us-nes], *s.* Gloria, esplendor.
Glory [glō'-ri], *s.* 1. Gloria, honra, alabanza, fama, renombre, celebridad; esplendor, magnificencia. 2. Aureola o círculo de luz que se pone sobre la cabeza de las imágenes de los santos. 3. Exaltación, adoración. 4. Calidad de resplandeciente; brillantez, resplandor, lustre. 5. Esplendor de la presencia de Dios; la gloria del Paraíso.
Glory, *vn.* Gloriarse, jactarse, preciarse de alguna cosa, llenarse de orgullo.
Gloss [gles], *s.* 1. Lustre, el viso luciente que despide alguna cosa; brillo. 2. Apariencia falaz.
Gloss, *s.* 1. Glosa, escolio. 2. Dis-

culpa o pretexto para ocultar o paliar una falta o un defecto.

Gloss, *vn.* Glosar, comentar, interpretar, notar.—*va.* 1. Paliar, colorear, dar a alguna palabra, designio o acción mala un colorido que la haga parecer lo que no es; generalmente con la prep. *over.* 2. Barnizar, dar con barniz u otra cosa que produzca lustre.

Glossarist [gles'-a-rist], *s.* Comentador.

Glossary [gles'-a-ri], *s.* Glosario, diccionario que sirve para explicar las palabras obscuras, extranjeras y antiguas de un libro: vocabulario explicativo de un dialecto o de una ciencia.

Glossator [gles-ê'-tęr], **Glossist** [gles'-ist], *s.* Glosador, comentador.

Glosser [gles'-ęr], *s.* 1. Comentador. 2. Pulidor.

Glossiness [gles'-i-nes], *s.* Pulimento, lustre superficial.

Glossographer [gles-eg'-ra-fęr], *s.* Glosógrafo, comentador.

Glossography [gles-eg'-ra-fi], *s.* 1. El arte de escribir comentarios. 2. (Anat.) Descripción de la lengua.

Glossy [gles'-i], *a.* 1. Lustroso, brillante como una superficie lisa que refleja el brillo. 2. Especioso, fino en apariencia, plausible.

Glottis [glet'-is], *s.* Glotis, la abertura de la laringe.

Glove [gluv], *s.* Guante.—*pl.* En especial, guantes para pelear a puñadas. *To be hand and glove,* Ser inseparables, ser uña y carne. *To handle without gloves,* Tratar sin contemplaciones, severamente.

Glove, *va.* Cubrir como con guante; enguantarse.

Glove compartment [gluv' cem-part-ment], *s.* Compartimiento de guantes en un automóvil.

Glover [gluv'-ęr], *s.* Guantero.

Glow [glō], *vn.* 1. Estar encendida alguna cosa sin producir llama. 2. Arder, abrasarse, encenderse, inflamarse; cuando se habla de las pasiones del ánimo. 3. Lucir, relucir, resplandecer.—*va.* Calentar o encender alguna cosa.

Glow, *s.* Calor vivo, encendimiento; viveza de color; vehemencia de una pasión.

Glower [glau'-ęr], *vn.* Mirar con ceño, poner mala cara.

Glowing [glō'-ing], *pa.* Resplandeciente, que esparce luz o color excesivo; ardiente; colorado.

Glowingly [glō'-ing-li], *adv.* De un modo resplandeciente.

Glow-worm [glō'-wūrm], *s.* Luciérnaga.

Gloxinia [glec-sin'-i-a], *s.* Flor hermosa de la familia de las escrofulariáceas.

Gloze [glōz], *vn.* 1. Paliar, colorear, con una explicación especiosa. 2. (Ant.) Adular, lisonjear.

Gloze, *s.* (Ant.) Adulación, lisonja.

Glozing [glōz'-ing], *s.* La explicación o interpretación artificiosa de un hecho, de una frase, etc.

Glucin [glū'-sin], **Glucina** [glū-sai'-na], *s.* (Quím.) Glucina, una de las tierras primitivas.

Glucose [glū'-cōs], *s.* Glucosa, azúcar de uvas o de almidón.

Glue [glū o gliū], *s.* Cola; liga, visco. *Fish-glue,* Colapez, cola de pescado.

Glue, *va.* Encolar, pegar, ligar, unir.

Glue-boiler [glū'-beil-ęr], *s.* El fabricante de cola.

Gluer [glū'-ęr], *s.* El que encola.

Gluey [glū'-i], *a.* Viscoso, pegajoso, glutinoso.

Glueyness [glū'-i-nes], *s.* Viscosidad, glutinosidad.

Gluish [glū'-ish], *a.* Viscoso, pegajoso.

Glum [glum], *a.* De mal humor y callado; moroso, regañón, tétrico, triste.

Glumaceous [glū-mê'-shius], *a.* (Bot.) Glumáceo, glumado; que tiene glumas o se refiere a ellas.

Glume [glūm], *s.* (Bot.) Gluma, cubierta floral de las plantas gramíneas.

Glut [glut], *va.* 1. Atestar, hartar de bebida y comida; atracar, saciar; saturar. 2. Sobrellenar, llenar alguna cosa con más de lo que puede recibir. 3. Colmar, dar en abundancia, dar más de lo que se necesita. —*vn.* Devorar vorazmente, engullirse.

Glut, *s.* 1. Lo que se engulle; hartura, hartazgo, plétora, superabundancia, llenura. 2. Cuña de madera. 3. (Alb.) Ripio de ladrillo.

Gluten [glū'-tn], *s.* (Quím.) Gluten.

Glutinosity [glū-ti-nes'-i-ti], **Glutinousness** [glū'-ti-nus-nes], *s.* Glutinosidad.

Glutinous [glū'-ti-nus], *a.* Glutinoso, viscoso, pegajoso.

Glutted [glut'-ed], *pp.* de GLUT. Harto, repleto.

Glutton [glut'-n], *s.* 1. Glotón, tragón. 2. El que es voraz o insaciable, de cualquiera cosa que se trate. 3. Glotón, carcajú, wolverena, mamífero carnicero. Gulo luscus.

Gluttonize [glut'-n-aiz], *vn.* Glotonear.

Gluttonous [glut'-n-us], *a.* Glotón; goloso.

Gluttonously [glut'-n-us-li], *adv.* Vorazmente.

Gluttony [glut'-n-i], *s.* Glotonería.

Glycerin, Glycerine [glis'-ęr-in], *s.* Glicerina, líquido incoloro, espeso y dulce, que se encuentra en los cuerpos grasos como base de su composición. Su adjetivo es **Glyceric** [glis'-er-ic].

Glycogen [glai'-co-jen], *s.* Glicógeno, compuesto blanco, farináceo, amorfo, que se halla en el hígado y en otros tejidos animales; se llama también "almidón animal."

Glyph [glif], *s.* (Arq.) Glifo, media caña que sirve de adorno.

Glyptic [glip'-tic], *s.* Glíptica, el arte de grabar figuras en piedras preciosas.

Glyptography [glip-teg'-ra-fi], *s.* Gliptografía, conocimiento del grabado en hueco y relieve en las piedras preciosas.

Gnarl [nārl], *vn.* Refunfuñar, gruñir.

Gnarl [nārl], *s.* Nudo, protuberancia sobre un tronco o ramo; nudo duro en la madera.

Gnarled [nārld], **Gnarly** [nārl'-i], *a.* Nudoso, lleno de nudos; retorcido. *A gnarled oak,* Un roble retorcido.

Gnash [nash], *va.* 1. (Ant.) Rechinar o crujir los dientes. 2. Rabiar de cólera rechinando los dientes.

Gnashing [nash'-ing], *s.* Rechinamiento o crujido de los dientes.

Gnat [nat], *s.* Mosquito, cínife; toda clase de mosquitos.

Gnaw [nō], *va.* 1. Roer, comer poco a poco. 2. Morder, mordicar. 3. Corroer, gastar alguna cosa con los dientes.

Gnawer [nō'-ęr], *s.* El que muerde, come o roe.

Gneiss [nais], *s.* Gneis, roca de hojuelas planas u onduladas, compuesta de feldespato, cuarzo y mica u hornblenda. Se distingue del granito por su moderada tendencia a hendirse.

Gneissoid [nais'-eid], *a.* Parecido al gneis.

Gnome [nōm], *s.* 1. Máxima, aforismo. 2. Gnomo, una especie de genio, protector de las minas y de los mineros; trasgo, enano. 3. (Zool.) Cierta especie de colibrí.

Gnomical [nem'-i-cal], *a.* Sentencioso, gnómico.

Gnomology [no-mel'-o-ji], *s.* Colección de aforismos.

Gnomon [nō'-men], *s.* Gnomón, el estilo o varita de hierro que señala las horas en los relojes de sol.

Gnomonic, Gnomonical [no-men'-ic, al], *a.* Gnomónico.

Gnomonics [ne-men'-ics], *s.* Gnomónica, la ciencia que trata y enseña el modo de hacer los relojes de sol.

Gnostic [nes'-tic], *s.* Gnóstico, hereje de los primeros siglos, que creía que sólo ellos conocían el sentido del cristianismo, y acomodaban todas sus opiniones a los sistemas de Pitágoras y Platón.

Gnosticism [nes'-ti-sizm], *s.* Gnosticismo, sistema filosófico y religioso de los primeros siglos del cristianismo, mezcla confusa de diversas creencias.

Gnu [nū], *s.* (Zool.) Bucéfalo, especie de antílope del sur de África, con cabeza parecida a la del búfalo, crin como la del asno y cola de caballo.

Go [gō], *va.* (*pret.* WENT, *pp.* GONE). 1. (Fam.) Tomar, como porción de algo, partir. *To go halves,* Ir a medias. 2. Recibir con aprobación, asentir a, tolerar. 3. Apostar.—*vn.* 1. Ir, irse, moverse, pasar de un paraje a otro. 2. Andar, caminar, partir, partirse, marchar, pasear. 3. Ir en busca de, dirigirse a, acudir, recurrir. 4. Ir, estar o ser. 5. Salir, huir, escapar; ser libertado. 6. Pasar, acabarse una cosa. 7. Seguir, proseguir. 8. Cambiar, mudar de situación, opiniones, etc. 9. Pasar por, ser considerado como. 10. Ser aplicable, convenir; sentar, venir, ir, o caer bien; concernir, tocar a. 11. Estar en cinta o preñada. 12. Influir, tener influencia. 13. Contribuir, concurrir, tender, tener por resultado, reunirse para componer alguna cosa. 14. Irse, morirse, estarse muriendo; decaer, debilitarse. 15. Ser desembolsado, vendido o cambiado. 16. Andar, como una máquina o un reloj. *To go about,* Intentar, procurar, emprender, hacer todo lo posible, esforzarse por; rodear; desviarse; girar, rodar, andar o moverse alrededor o en torno, dar vueltas, andar rodando, andar de acá para allá. (Mar.) Virar de bordo. *Go about your business,* Métase Vd. en lo que le importa; váyase Vd. *To go abroad,* Salir, partir, marcharse; divulgarse o hacerse pública una cosa; correr alguna noticia. *To go after,* Seguir a alguno. *To go against,* Oponerse, contradecir, ir en contra de una persona. *The choice went against him,* No salió elegido. *To go ahead,* Adelantar, proseguir. *To go along,* Continuar, proseguir una cosa comenzada. *To go along with one,*

Acompañar a alguno. *To go astray,* Descarriarse, descaminarse, perder el camino. (Fig.) Faltar a su deber, cometer una falta o delito. *V.* ASTRAY. *To go asunder,* Ir separadamente, marchar separados. *To go away,* Salirse, marcharse. *To go away with a thing,* Llevarse alguna cosa. *To go back,* Retirarse, retroceder; ceder, desistir, volverse atrás de un empeño o designio; volver, volverse, ir otra vez al paraje donde se había estado antes. *To go back of,* Mirar más allá de; poner en tela de juicio. *To go back from one's word,* Desdecirse, retractarse. *To go backward,* Retroceder, volver hacia atrás. *To go before,* Preceder, ir delante, adelantarse. *To go behind,* Seguir a alguno, ir detrás de él; defraudar, engañar. *To go between,* Interponerse, mediar, terciar. *To go beyond,* Pasar o ir más allá de un punto determinado o limitado; sobrepujar, exceder. *To go by,* Pasar por alto, pretermitir; escurrirse, escabullirse, pasar sin ser visto ni oído; sufrir con paciencia; observar alguna cosa como regla o principio, o tomarla como regla, pauta o norma de conducta, arreglarse o ajustarse a algo; dirigirse por; pasar cerca. *To go by the worst,* Llevar lo peor de una cosa. *To go down,* Bajar, descender; ponerse el sol; (fam.) ser bien recibida o aprobada alguna cosa; tragarse, persuadirse de o creer algo sin reflexión; tragar. *To go down the stream,* Ir con la corriente. *To go down the wind,* Ir en decadencia, ir empobreciendo. *To go far,* Valer mucho, tener gran influencia o alcance. *To go for,* Ir por algo; ir a buscar o en busca de; ser reputado o considerado por; declararse en favor de alguna persona o cosa; (Ger.) abrumar, embestir, atacar, particularmente con palabras. *To go forth,* Salir, producir, parecer o aparecer, ser sacado a luz o al público. *To go forward,* Adelantar, proseguir, hacer progresos alguna cosa. *To go from,* Dejar, partirse, separarse, faltar a alguna cosa convenida. *To go from the matter,* Apartarse del asunto de que se trata. *To go from one's word,* Desdecirse. *To go hard,* Pasarlo mal, traer a mal traer. *To go in,* Entrar. *To go in and out,* Estar en libertad. *To go in for,* Favorecer enérgicamente. *To go in to o unto,* (Ant.) Entrar a la presencia de; tener coito con. *To go into,* Participar en (un asunto); investigar, discutir o ventilar. *To go it,* Apresurarse inconsideramente; en imperativo, ¡prosiga Vd.! ¡persista Vd.! ¡adelante! *To go near,* Acercarse, tocar de cerca; correr algún peligro. *To go off,* Morirse; irse, largarse, despedirse; dispararse o salir el tiro de un arma de fuego; seguir su curso, tener efecto, salir bien o mal (v. g. un concierto). *To go on,* Continuar, seguir o proseguir lo comenzado; adelantarse, ir adelante; adelantar, progresar; atacar. *To go over,* Pasar, atravesar; desertar, cambiar de casaca, pasarse a una religión, partido, etc., diverso del que se tenía o se profesaba antes. *To go out,* Salir, ponerse en camino, salir a campaña, darse a la vela; apagarse, morirse la lumbre, la luz o el fuego; extinguirse, apagarse la vida, la imaginación, etc. *To go out of the way,* Apartarse del camino, ponerse a un lado; descarriarse. *To go her time out,* Acabarse el tiempo de la preñez, salir o estar fuera de cuenta; salir de cuidado. *To go through,* Llevar a cabo alguna cosa, ejecutar o hacer ejecutar; pasar, examinar o recorrer completamente algo; determinar definitivamente; sufrir una operación quirúrgica; enhebrar, enhilar, ensartar; hender; pasar o atravesar algún camino; atravesar de parte a parte; salir al cabo de; salir con; conseguir alguna cosa. *Go to!* (Ant.) ¡Vaya! ¡Toma! *Go to grass, go to thunder,* interjecciones despectivas: ¡Vaya Vd. a paseo! ¡Mal rayo te parta! *Go-to-meeting,* (Fam. E. U.) Dícese del traje de los días de fiesta; la ropa dominguera. *To go under,* Quebrar, hacer bancarrota; quedar arruinado, vencido o destruído; también pasar por, ser conocido por tal o cual nombre. *To go up,* Subir. *To go up and down,* Rodar, andorrear, corretear, ir de una parte a otra. *To go upon,* Emprender, fundarse en algo. *To go upon sure grounds,* Estar bien fundado, ir sobre seguro. *To go upon sure tick,* Comprar fiado. *To go with,* Acompañar. *To go with child,* Estar preñada. *To go with the tide,* Bajar con la marea. *To go without,* Estar, arreglarse o pasarlo sin; no obtener una cosa a que se tenía derecho. *To go halves,* Ir a medias con uno. *To go to the shade,* Irse a la sombra. *To go to service,* Ponerse a servir. *To go to the bottom,* Ir o irse a pique. *The bell goes,* Suena la campana. *To let go one's hold,* Soltar la presa. *To go so far as,* Ir hasta, llegar a. *To go the whole length,* Llegar hasta; arriesgarlo todo.

Go, *s.* (Fam.) 1. Moda, auge, furor. *It was all the go,* Eso hacía furor. 2. Energía, actividad, empuje. 3. Giro, marcha, curso de los asuntos; predicamento. 4. Ajuste, pacto; buen éxito, esfuerzo dichoso. 5. Oportunidad, ensayo.

Goad [gōd], *s.* Aguijada, aijada, pincho, aguijón.

Goad, *va.* 1. Aguijar, pinchar o herir con la aguijada. 2. Aguijonear, agarrochear, estimular, incitar.

Go-ahead [gō-a-hed'], *a.* (Fam.) Emprendedor, activo, enérgico. Equivalente, **Go-aheadative.** *Go-ahead! inter.* ¡Adelante!

Goal [gōl], *s.* 1. Meta, término. 2. Fin, objeto, motivo. 3. (Futbol), Gol, meta. *Goalkeeper,* Guardameta, portero (en el futbol).

Goat [gōt], *s.* Cabra, chiva, cabrón. *He-goat,* Cabrón, macho de cabrío. *Young goat,* Cabrito, chivo, choto. *Wild goat,* Cabra montés. *To ride the goat,* (Fest.) Someterse a las ceremonias de iniciación en ciertas sociedades secretas.

Goatbeard [gōt'-bīrd], *s.* (Bot.) Barba cabruna.

Goatee [gō-tī'], *s.* Perilla, mechón de pelos que se deja en la barba.

Goatherd [gōt'-hẹrd], *s.* Cabrero.

Goatish [gōt'-ish], *a.* Cabruno, chotuno; lascivo.

Goat-milker [gōt'-milk-ẹr], **Goat-sucker** [gōt'-suk-ẹr], *s.* (Orn.) Caprimulga.

Goat's-hair [gōts'-hār], *s.* Pelote.

Goat-skin [gōt'-skin], *s.* Piel de cabra.

Goat's-rue [gōts'-rū], *s.* (Bot.) Gálega, ruda cabruna.

Goat's-thorn [gōts'-thōrn], *s.* (Bot.) Tragacanto.

Gob [gob], *s.* 1. Una cantidad pequeña de cualquiera cosa; un bocado. 2. (Prov. Ingl.) La boca.

Gob, Gobbin [gob'-in], *s.* (Min.) Escombrera, explotación abandonada llena de escombros y desechos.

Gobbet [gob'-et], *s.* Bocado; pedacito.

Gobble [gob'-l], *va.* Engullir, tragar bocados enteros, tragar vorazmente. —*vn.* Hacer ruido en la garganta como los pavos.

Gobbledygook [gob'-l-di-guk], *s.* Galimatías propio de ciertos funcionarios públicos.

Gobbler [gob'-lẹr], *s.* 1. Engullidor, glotón, tragón, tragador. 2. (Fam.) El pavo, (Méx.) guajalote, (Cuba) guanajo.

Go-between [gō'-bẹ-twīn], *s.* 1. Mediador, medianero; entremetido. 2. Tercero, correvedile. 3. Alcahuete.

Goblet [gob'-let], *s.* Copa, vaso con pie para beber.

Goblin [gob'-lin], *s.* Espíritu errante, duende.

Go-by [gō'-bai], *s.* 1. Menosprecio, repulsa o desaire. 2. (Des.) Treta, trama, fraude. *To give one the go-by in a race,* Adelantarse a otro, dejarlo atrás.

Go-cart [gō'-cārt], *s.* Carretilla o carretón para enseñar a andar a los niños. (Mex.) Andaderas.

God [god], *s.* 1. Dios, el ser supremo. 2. Dios, la persona o cosa que se adora con pasión desordenada. *God save the king,* Dios guarde al rey. *God forbid,* No quiera Dios. *Thank God,* Gracias a Dios. *God's Day,* Domingo; también la fiesta del Corpus Christi. *God's house,* Iglesia o templo. *God-fearing,* Reverente, temeroso de Dios y observador de sus leyes.

God-send [god'-send], *s.* Un milagro, un don particular de Dios. (Fam.) Ganga, chiripa.

Godchild [god'-chaild], *s.* Ahijado, ahijada.

Goddaughter [god'-dō-tẹr], *sf.* Ahijada.

Goddess [god'-es], *sf.* Diosa.

Goddess-like [god'-es-laic], *a.* Semejante a una diosa, divina.

Godfather [god'-fā-dhẹr], *s.* Padrino

Godhead [god'-hed], *s.* Deidad, divinidad.

Godless [god'-les], *a.* Infiel, impío, sin Dios, ateo.

Godlessness [god'-les-nes], *s.* Estado de perdición.

Godlike [god'-laic], *a.* Divino, semejante a la divinidad.

Godliness [god'-li-nes], *s.* Piedad, devoción, santidad.

Godling [god'-ling], *s.* Diosecillo, divinidad secundaria.

Godly [god'-li], *a.* 1. Piadoso, devoto, religioso. 2. Recto, justificado. —*adv.* Piadosamente, justamente.

Godmother [god'-mudh-ẹr], *sf.* Madrina.

Godown [gō-daun'], *s.* Almacén chino o indio; (término angloindio).

Godship [god'-ship], *s.* Dignidad de un dios.

Godson [god'-sun], *sm.* Ahijado.

Godspeed [god'-spīd], *s.* Deseo de que Dios asista y guarde a alguien; ¡buena suerte! Se escribe a menudo en dos palabras.

Godward [god'-ward], *adv.* Hacia Dios.

Godwit [ged'-wit], *s.* (Orn.) Francolín.
Goer [gō'-ęr], *s.* 1. Andador, paseante, el que va de una parte á otra; vagabundo, ambulante. 2. *V.* Go-BETWEEN. *Goers and comers*, Yentes y vinientes.
Goggle [geg'-l], *vn.* Entornar o hacer girar los ojos, mirar con los ojos muy abiertos o de soslayo.
Goggle, *s.* Mirada entornada, vuelta afectada de los ojos. *Goggles*, Anteojos de camino, para guardar la vista del polvo, o para el estrabismo; llámanse también así las anteojeras que se usan para los caballos espantadizos.—*a.* El que tiene los ojos muy abiertos o prominentes; ojos saltones.
Goggle-eyed, *a.* *V.* GOGGLE, *a.*
Going [gō'-ing], *s.* 1. El paso, el andar, el modo de andar. 2. Preñado, preñez. 3. Partida. 4. Paso, movimiento o acción en el modo de gobernarse y portarse. *The going of a horse*, Andadura de un caballo. *Going forward*, Progreso, lo que está pasando o sucediendo actualmente. *Going down*, Puesta del sol, ocaso; baja de fondos, descenso de las aguas.
Goiter, goitre [gei'-tęr], *s.* (Med.) Papera, coto, bocio.
Goitrous [gei'-trus], *a.* Que se refiere a la papera; que la tiene o padece.
Gola [gō'-la], *s.* (Arq.) Gola, cimacio.
Gold [gōld], *s.* 1. Oro. 2. Oro, dinero, moneda de oro, riqueza. *Gold-leaf*, Oro batido, pan de oro. *Crude mass of gold*, Oro virgen, oro bruto. (Prov.) *It is not all gold that glitters*, No es oro todo lo que reluce.
Gold, en composición; de oro. *Gold-bearing*, Aurífero, productor de oro. *Gold-dust*, Polvo de oro. (Bot.) Alisón, planta crucífera, con flores doradas. *Gold fever*, Fiebre del oro, ansia de emprender la busca de oro. *Gold-field*, Distrito o terreno aurífero. *Gold lace*, Galón de oro. *Leaf-gold*, Oro nativo en láminas u hojas.
Gold-beater [gōld'-bīt-ęr], *s.* Batihoja, batidor de oro.
Gold brick [gōld bric], *s.* (vul.) Engaño, estafa.
Golden [gōld'-n], *a.* 1. Aureo, de oro, hecho de oro. 2. Lustroso, brillante. 3. Excelente, de gran valor, precioso. 4. Feliz. 5. Amarillento, de color de oro. *Golden rule: Do unto others as you would wish to be done unto*, (Met.) Haced a los demás lo que queráis que ellos os hagan. (S. Mateo, vii, 12.)
Golden mean [gōld'-n mīn], *s.* Moderación, término medio.
Golden-number [gōld'-n-num'-bęr], *s.* Número áureo, el que indica el ciclo de la luna.
Golden-thistle [gōld'-n-this'-l], *s.* (Bot.) Cardillo.
Golden wedding [gōld'-n wed'-ing], *s.* Bodas de oro.
Gold-filled [gōld-fīld'], *a.* Enchapado o revestido de oro.
Goldfinch [gōld'-finch], *s.* (Orn.) Jilguero.
Gold-fish [gōld'-fish], *s.* Carpa pequeña de color rojo dorado, originaria de China y que hoy abunda en casi todos los países. Carassius auratus.
Gold foil [gōld feil], *s.* Hojuelas de oro.
Gold-hilted [gōld'-hilt-ed], *a.* Lo que tiene el puño de oro o dorado: aplícase comúnmente a las espadas.
Gold-leaf [gōld'-līf], *s.* Pan u hoja de oro; oro en libritos, oro batido.
Gold mine [gōld main], *s.* 1. Mina de oro. 2. (fig.) Fuente de riqueza.
Gold-proof [gōld'-prūf], *a.* A prueba de oro, capaz de resistir las tentaciones del interés o la codicia.
Gold-size [gōld'-saiz], *s.* Cola o barniz de color de oro.
Goldsmith [gōld'-smith], *s.* Orífice, platero de oro, el artífice que trabaja en oro.
Gold standard [gōld stand'-ard], *s.* Patrón oro.
Gold-stone [gōld'-stōn], *s.* Venturina.
Gold-thread [gōld'-thred], *s.* Hilo de oro.
Goldy-locks [gōld'-i-lecs], *s.* (Bot.) Crisocomo.
Golf [gelf], *s.* Golf, juego de pelota que se juega con palos encorvados en los extremos y varios agujeros en la tierra. *Golf club*, 1. Palo que se emplea en este juego. 2. Club de golf. *Golf links*, Campo de golf.
Gondola [gen'-do-la], *s.* Góndola, barca con remos y toldo que se usa en Venecia.
Gondolier [gen-do-līr'], *s.* Gondolero.
Gone [gēn], *pp.* de *To* GO. Ido; perdido, arruinado; pasado; muerto, fallecido; apagado.
Gonfalon [gen'-fa-len], †**Gonfanon** [gen'-fa-nen], *s.* Confalón, gonfalón, estandarte o pendón llevado en la punta de una lanza.
Gonfalonier [gen-fal-o-nīr'], *s.* Confalonero, nombre del jefe que llevaba el pendón o estandarte de algunas repúblicas de Italia.
Gong [geng], *s.* Batintín, gongo, instrumento músico de percusión usado por los asiáticos.
Goniometer [go-ni-em'-e-tęr], *s.* Goniómetro, medidor de ángulos.
Goniometry [go-ni-em'-e-tri], *s.* Goniometría, el arte de medir los ángulos.
Gonorrhœa [gen-o-rī'-a], *s.* Gonorrea, blenorragia.
Goober [gū'-bęr], *s.* *V.* PEANUT.
Good [gud], *a.* Bueno, saludable; apto, conveniente, ventajoso, útil; completo; precioso; genuino, verdadero, válido; perfecto, virtuoso, religioso, justo; benévolo, bondadoso, clemente, misericordioso; de buena índole, cariñoso, alegre; dichoso, feliz; hábil, sobresaliente en su profesión; grande, considerable; legítimo, no fingido; digno. *My good sir*, Mi buen señor. *A good turn*, Un favor, una gracia. *In good time*, A tiempo, a propósito, con oportunidad. *It is as good as done*, Es cosa hecha, es como si estuviese concluído. *It is a good way thither*, Hay mucho camino de aquí a allá; está muy lejos. *In good earnest*, Seriamente, de veras, de fijo. *To hold good*, Subsistir, continuar en toda su fuerza. *To be as good as one's word; to make one's word good*, Cumplir lo prometido. *Good Friday*, Viernes Santo. *To make good*, Probar o justificar alguna cosa; hacer bueno, abonar; completar, suplir, lo que falta; indemnizar, reparar una falta o una pérdida; defender con buen éxito; acertar, lograr, salir bien en alguna empresa o empeño. *He made good his escape*, Logró evadirse. *To see, to think good*, Hallar bueno, juzgar a propósito. *A good deal*, Bastante, mucho. *A good while*, Un buen rato. *He is good for nothing*, No vale un comino, o un pito, o tres pepinos; no vale nada. *As good as*, Tanto como, como, casi. *He is as good as ruined*, Está casi arruinado.—*s.* Bien, lo que física o moralmente contribuye a la felicidad; prosperidad, adelantamiento, ventaja, realidad.—*pl.* Mercancías. *V.* GOODS. *For good and all*, Seriamente, fuera de chanza, de seguro, sin miedo. *Much good may it do you*, Buen provecho le haga.—*adv.* Bien, rectamente.—*inter.* ¡Bueno! ¡bien! úsase a veces en ironía. *For good*, De cierto, de una vez, para siempre. *He comes for good*, Viene para estarse. *She is gone for good*, Se ha ido de una vez, para no volver. *Good-conditioned*, Bien acondicionado. *Good-day*, Buenos días (saludo acostumbrado al encontrarse o al despedirse). *Good-morning, good-morrow*, Buenos días (saludo matutino). *Good-afternoon, good-even*, Buenas tardes. *Good-night, good-evening*, Buenas noches.
Good-breeding [gud'-brīd'-ing], *s.* Buena crianza, finos modales.
Good-by [gud-bai'], *adv.* A Dios, adiós, vaya Vd. con Dios: úsase en inglés como en castellano. (Contracción de *God be with you.*)
Good cheer [gud chīr], *s.* Alegría, buen humor, jovialidad.
Good-fellow [gud'-fel-o], *s.* Socio o compañero festivo y jovial. (Fam.) Buen chico, buen muchacho.
Good-fellowship [gud-fel'-o-ship], *s.* Compañía o sociedad alegre y festiva.
Good-fortune [gud-fōr'-chun], *s.* Dicha, felicidad.
Good-hearted [gud-hārt'-ed], *a.* De buen corazón, misericordioso.
Good-humor [gud-hiū'-mer], *s.* Buen humor, jovialidad.
Good-humored [gud-hiū'-męrd], *a.* Jocoso, vivo, jovial.
Good-humoredly [gud-hiū'-męrd-li], *adv.* Jocosamente, alegremente.
Gooding [gud'-ing], *s.* Costumbre que hubo en Inglaterra de pedir regalos, limosnas o aguinaldos por Navidad.
Goodish [gud'-ish], *a.* 1. Algo bueno, no malo, ni dañoso. 2. Considerable, algo grande.
Goodliness [gud'-li-nes], *s.* Hermosura, gracia, elegancia.
Good-looking [gud'-luk-ing], *a.* Bien parecido, bonito, de agradables facciones.
Good-luck [gud'-luc], *s.* Suerte o buena suerte, dicha.
Goodly [gud'-li], *a.* 1. Hermoso, bien parecido. 2. De calidad escogida; atractivo, agradable o vistoso. 3. Abultado; considerable; algo numeroso. *A goodly prospect*, Hermosa perspectiva: buenas esperanzas.
Good-manners [gud-man'-ęrz], *s.* Cortesía, modales corteses, buena crianza.
Good-nature [gud-né'-chur], *s.* Bondad, benevolencia, buen natural, buen corazón.
Good-natured [gud-né'-churd], *a.* Benévolo, cariñoso, de buen natural, afable.
Good-naturedly [gud-né'-churd-li], *adv.* Cariñosamente, afablemente.
Goodness [gud'-nes], *s.* 1. Bondad, benevolencia, virtud. 2. Acto o expresión de bondad.
Goods [gudz], *s. pl.* 1. Bienes muebles, muebles de una casa; géneros,

mercaderías. *Consignment of goods*, Consignación de mercaderías. *Goods exported* o *exports*, Géneros de extracción. *Goods imported* o *imports*, Géneros importados. *Goods in demand*, Géneros de buen despacho, muy solicitados. *Parcels of goods*, Partidas de géneros. *Assortment of goods*, Surtido de géneros. *Expediter of goods*, Despachador de géneros. *Goods heavy of sale*, Géneros difíciles de vender o poco buscados. *Green goods*, (E. U.) Papel moneda falso, billetes falsificados. 2. En composición, tiene en Inglaterra el mismo valor que *Freight* en los Estados Unidos. *Goods-shed*, Almacén, depósito de mercancías. *Goods-train*, Tren de mercancías. *Goods-wagon*, Furgón, vagón de mercancías.

Good-sense [gud'-sens], *s.* Juicio sano, buen sentido, perspicacia natural.

Good-sized [gud'-saizd'], *a.* Grande, de buen tamaño.

Good-speed [gud'-spîd], *s.* ¡Buena suerte! frase para mostrar a uno que se desea que logre su objeto.

Good-turn [gud'-tūrn], *s.* Servicio en recompensa de un favor, asistencia, o buenos oficios recibidos.

Good-wife [gud'-waif], *sf.* Ama de la casa.

Good-will [gud-wil'], *s.* 1. Benevolencia, sinceridad, bondad. (En este sentido se escribe de ordinario en dos palabras.) 2. Parroquia y buen crédito de una tienda o establecimiento comercial; clientela.

Good-woman [gud-wu'-man], *sf.* Buena ama, mujer o señora; se usa entre rústicos.

Goody [gud'-i], *a.* Bonachón, pazguato, Juan Lanas, mojigato.—*s.* 1. Término de cortesía usado por algunos criados o personas de baja condición, como en castellano *su merced;* ama vieja y pobre, comadre. 2. Persona bonachona. 3. Confitura, golosina.

Goose [gūs], *s.* (*pl.* GEESE [gîs]). 1. Ganso, ánsar, oca; la gansa, en oposición al ánsar macho o *gander*. *Wild goose*, Ganso bravo, salvaje. 2. Plancha de sastre. 3. Persona inocente, ganso, bobo, necio. 4. Juego de la oca.

Goosberry [gūz'- o gūs'-ber-i], *s.* (Bot.) Uva espín o crespa.

Goose-cap [gūs'-cap], *s.* Bobo, tonto, ganso, pazguato.

Goose-flesh [gūs'-flesh], *s.* Carne de gallina, los granitos que aparecen en la piel cuando uno tiene frío, miedo o terror.

Goose-foot [gūs'-fut], *s.* (Bot.) Cualquier planta del género Chenopodium; chual; llámase así por la figura de sus hojas.

Goose-neck [gūs'-nec], *s.* (Mar.) Gancho de botalones; arbotante, cuello de cisne; pescante de bote.

Goose-quill [gūs'-cwil], *s.* Pluma de ave, cañón, pluma para escribir hecha de los cañones de los gansos.

Goose-wings [gūs'-wingz], *s. pl.* (Mar.) Calzones.

Gopher [gō'-fer], *s.* (Zool.) Geomís, roedor americano que construye madrigueras subterráneas como las del topo. Tiene dos grandes bolsas exteriores que le cuelgan de las mejillas. Geomys.

Gopher-wood [gō'-fer-wud], *s.* (Bot.) 1. Árbol de Kentucky y Tennessee de madera amarilla. 2. Nombre que se da a la madera desconocida con que se construyó el arca de Noé.

Gordian [gōr'-di-an], *a.* Intrincado, difícil: dícese por lo común *gordian-knot*, nudo gordiano, para ponderar alguna dificultad.

Gore [gōr], *s.* Sangre, grumo de sangre, sangre cuajada; (prov. Ingl.) lodo. (Del anglosajón gōr, inmundicia.)

Gore, *s.* 1. Cuchillo, nesga; ensanche triangular del vestido para darle vuelo. 2. Pedazo de terreno de forma triangular. (Anglosajón *gāra*, punta de terreno.)

Gore, *va.* 1. Herir a uno con puñal u otra arma punzante. 2. Herir un animal con sus cuernos a otro. 3. Hacer una nesga o cuchillo; ajustar o ensanchar con cuchillos, como una vela o la falda de un vestido.

Gorge [gōrj], *s.* 1. Gorja, garganta, gaznate. 2. Garganta, desfiladero, cañada. 3. Cuello de una vestidura. 4. La acción de engullir; trago, bocado, lo que se ha tragado. 5. Apretujón, presión como la que hace el hielo.

Gorge, *va.* Engullir, tragar con avidez; hartar, saciar.—*vn.* Hartarse, saciarse, atracarse.

Gorged [gōrjd], *a.* Lo que tiene garganta.

Gorgeous [gōr'-jus], *a.* Primoroso, brillante, vistoso, esplendoroso, grandioso, magnífico.

Gorgeously [gor'-jus-li], *adv.* Primorosamente, esplendorosamente, magníficamente.

Gorgeousness [gōr'-jus-nes], *s.* Esplendor, magnificencia.

Gorget [gōr'-jet], *s.* 1. Gola, golilla. 2. Gorguera de la armadura antigua. 3. (Orn.) Lunar o mancha de color en la garganta de las aves. 4. Instrumento quirúrgico; conductor acanalado o cóncavo

Gorgon [gōr'-gon], *s.* 1. Gorgona, monstruo fabuloso. 2. Alguna cosa muy fea y horrenda.

Gorilla [go-ril'-a], *s.* (Zool.) Gorila, mono de África fuerte y fiero, de estatura igual a la del hombre.

Gormand, Gourmand [gōr'-mand, gūr'-mand], *s.* Glotón, gomia; goloso.

Gormandize [gōr'-man-daiz], *vn.* Glotonear, comer con gula.

Gormandizer [gōr'-man-daiz-er], *s.* Golosazo.

Gorse [gōrs], *s.* (Bot.) Especie de hiniesta espinosa. *V.* FURZE.

Gory [gōr'-i], *a.* Cubierto de sangre grumosa; sangriento.

Goshawk [gos'-hōc], *s.* (Orn.) Azor, especie de halcón. Accipiter palumbarius.

Gosling [goz'-ling], *s.* (Orn.) Gansarón, el pollo del ganso.

Gospel [gos'-pel], *s.* 1. Evangelio. 2. Lo que se considera como infaliblemente verdadero.—*va.* Instruir según el Evangelio; llenar de piedad.

Gospeller [gos'-pel-er], *s.* Evangelista; evangelistero.

Gospellize [gos'-pel-aiz], *va.* Evangelizar.

Gossamer [gos'-a-mer], *s.* 1. Hilo muy tenue de telaraña flotante en el aire; trama o tejido de dichos hilos. 2. (Art. y Of.) Tela de araña, gasa muy sutil y suave, pero fuerte. 3. Impermeable, capa o sobretodo hecho con tela impermeable.

Gossamery [gos'-a-mer-i], *a.* Ligero y delgado como la telaraña.

Gossip [gos'-ip], *s.* 1. Compadre, comadre. 2. Compadre de taberna; un comadrero o comadrera. 3. Charla, charladuría, picotería, parlería, parla. 4. Chisme. 5. Padrino, madrina, persona que saca de pila a una criatura; este fué el sentido primitivo de la palabra.

Gossip, *vn.* Charlar, hablar mucho y sin substancia, parlotear, picotear, chismear.

Gossiping [gos'-ip-ing], *s.* La acción de pasar el tiempo charlando o parloteando; murmuración, chismografía.

Got, *pret.* y *pp.* del verbo *To* GET.

Gothic [goth'-ic], *a.* Gótico, relativo a los godos. *Gothic type*, (Impr.) Letra gótica.

Gothic, *s.* La lengua gótica o goda, el godo.

Gothicism [goth'-i-sizm], *s.* 1. El idioma gótico. 2. Rudeza de maneras; barbarie.

Gothicize [goth'-i-saiz], *va.* Hacer alguna cosa como la hacían los godos.

Gotten, *pp.* de *To* GET.

Gouge [gauj], *s.* Gubia, escoplo de media caña.

Gouge, *va.* 1. Excavar o ahondar como con una gubia. 2. Sacar los ojos del enemigo con el dedo pulgar.

Gouge-channel [gauj-chan'-el], *s.* (Mar.) Gubiadura.

Goulash [gū'-lāsh], *s.* Guiso de carne y verduras de origen húngaro.

Gourd [gōrd o gūrd], *s.* (Bot.) Calabaza.

Gourmand, *s.* *V.* GORMAND.

Gourmandize. *V.* GORMANDIZE.

Gourmet [gūr-mê'], *s.* Gastrónomo.

Gout [gaut], *s.* 1. Gota, inflamación del sistema fibroso y los ligamentos de las articulaciones. 2. (Ant.) Gota, grumo de sangre. *A fit of gout*, Un ataque de gota. *Gout of* o *in the feet*, Podagra.

Gout [gū], *s.* Gusto; inclinación. (Fr.)

Goutiness [gaut'-i-nes], *s.* El dolor de la gota y el estado del que la padece.

Goutwort [gaut'-wūrt], *s.* (Bot.) Angélica.

Gouty [gaut'-i], *a.* Gotoso. *Gouty land*, (Spenser) Tierra pantanosa.

Govern [guv'-ern], *va.* 1. Gobernar, guiar, dirigir, regir. 2. Moderar, dominar, domar. 3. (Gram.) Regir. 4. (Mar.) Dirigir los movimientos de la embarcación.—*vn.* Gobernar, tener dominio.

Governable [guv'-ern-a-bl], *a.* Dócil, sumiso, sujeto, obediente· manejable.

Governance [guv'-ern-ans], *s.* Gobierno, ejercicio del poder, autoridad.

Governess [guv'-ern-es], *sf.* Gobernadora, aya, institutriz. *Daily governess*, Maestra que va a dar lecciones a casa de las discípulas.

Government [guv'-ern-ment], *s.* 1. Gobierno, ministerio, administración pública. 2. Gobierno, conducta, porte. 3. (Gram.) Régimen. 4. Dominio, gobierno, territorio sobre que tiene autoridad un gobierno. 5. El derecho de gobernar; autoridad. *For your government*, (Com.) Para su gobierno.

Governor [guv'-ern-er], *s.* 1. Gobernador, tutor, ayo. 2. (Ant.) Piloto 3. (Art. y Of.) Regulador, moderador; mecanismo que en las máqui nas, particularmente en las de vapor, sirve para regular la velocidad del movimiento.

Gown [gaun], *s.* 1. Vestido talar exterior de mujer; túnica. 2. Toga, vestidura talar que usan los estudiantes en algunas universidades.

Gownman [gaun'-man], **Gownsman** [gaunz'-man], *s.* 1. Togado, individuo de una universidad, clérigo, magistrado u otro que por su estado lleva ropa talar. 2. Ciudadano, civil, en oposición al militar.

Grab [grab], *va.* 1. Arrebatar, apresar, agarrar, prender rudamente; asir con la mano. 2. Tomar posesión repentina, violenta o fraudulamente; apresar.—*s.* 1. (Fam.) Toma, apresamiento; lo que está asido. 2. Gancho o aparato para asir.

Grabble [grab'-l], *va.* Tentar, palpar, examinar y reconocer por medio del tacto.—*vn.* Postrarse.

Grace [grês], *s.* 1. Gracia, influencia favorable de Dios en el alma humana. 2. Gracia, favor, merced, perdón, remisión. 3. Gracia, privilegio. 4. Gracia, garbo, donaire, agrado y despejo en la ejecución de alguna cosa. 5. Gracia, afabilidad en el trato común. 6. Gracia, don natural que hace agradable a quien lo posee. 7. Gracia, diosa del paganismo que se suponía otorgaba la hermosura: en este sentido se usa casi siempre en plural en las dos lenguas. 8. Gracia, atractivo o agrado adquirido. 9. Título de honor que se da en Inglaterra a los arzobispos y a los duques, y así equivale en unos casos al tratamiento de Excelencia y en otros al de Ilustrísima. 10. Gracias, las oraciones que se dicen antes y después de comer. *To say grace before a meal,* Bendecir la mesa. *To say grace after a meal,* Dar gracias después de comer o cenar. *Days of grace,* (Com.) Días de gracia, usualmente tres, el tiempo que se da para el pago de una letra de cambio después de su vencimiento.

Grace, *va.* 1. Adornar, hermosear con adornos. 2. Agraciar, conceder alguna gracia, favorecer. 3. Dar gracia celestial.

Grace-cup [grês'-cup], *s.* El trago o brindis echado después de dar gracias.

Graceful [grês'-ful], *a.* 1. Gracioso, elegante, primoroso; fácil, natural. 2. Gracioso, decoroso, conveniente, cortés.

Gracefully [grês'-ful-i], *adv.* Elegantemente, con gracia.

Gracefulness [grês'-ful-nes], *s.* Gracia, elegancia.

Graceless [grês'-les], *a.* Réprobo, malvado, abandonado, desesperado.

Gracelessly [grês'-les-li], *adv.* Sin elegancia.

Graces [grês'-ez], *s. pl.* Gracias, tres divinidades mitológicas. *Good graces,* Favor, amparo, patrocinio, valimiento.

Gracile [gras'-il], *a.* Delgado, sutil, con gracia.

Gracious [grê'-shus], *a.* 1. Gracioso, benévolo, favorable, humano. 2. Virtuoso, bueno. *Our most gracious sovereign,* Nuestro benignísimo soberano. 3. Primoroso, agradable, cortés.

Graciously [grê'-shus-li], *adv.* Graciosamente, benignamente, agradablemente.

Graciousness [grê'-shus-nes], *s.* Gracia, afabilidad, bondad, dulzura, benignidad.

Grackle [grac'-l], *s.* Especie de estornino; también, un mirlo americano. (Quiscalus.)

Gradation [gra-dê'-shun], *s.* 1. Graduación, el acto y efecto de graduar; paso gradual. 2. (Mús.) Gradación. 3. Grado, rango en una serie.

Gradatory [grad'-a-to-ri], *a.* 1. Graduado o gradual, lo que procede por grados. 2. A propósito para andar.

Grade [grêd], *s.* 1. Grado, graduación, rango, grado o división en cualquier serie o curso. 2. Inclinación respecto a la horizontal, declive de un camino, ferrocarril o superficie; también el grado de esa inclinación. 3. Animal o casta de animales producidos por el cruzamiento con los de una casta superior.

Grade, *va.* 1. Colocar, clasificar por series o grados. 2. Nivelar, o igualar en declive. 3. Mejorar por medio del cruzamiento de castas.

Grade crossing [grêd cres'-ing], *s.* (F.C.) Paso a nivel.

Grade scale [grêd' skêl], *s.* Escalafón.

Grade school [grêd scūl], *s.* Escuela primaria, escuela elemental.

Gradient [grê'-di-ent], *a.* 1. Ambulante, lo que se mueve por grados o pasos. 2. Que baja o se levanta por grados regulares de inclinación.—*s.* 1. Pendiente o declive de un camino o ferrocarril, inclinación. 2. (Meteor.) Grado del aumento o diminución, p. ej. de la temperatura o de la presión atmosférica; o el diagrama que lo representa.

Grading [grêd'-ing], *s.* 1. Graduación, clasificación. 2. Nivelación.

Gradual [grad'-yu-al], *a.* Gradual, que procede por pasos o grados; regular y lento.—*s.* Un libro antiguo de himnos.

Gradually [grad'-yu-al-i], *adv.* Gradualmente.

Graduate [grad'-yu-êt], *va.* 1. Graduar, conferir en una universidad el grado de doctor, licenciado o bachiller. 2. Graduar, dividir y señalar por grados. 3. Adelantar, subir o aumentar de grado en grado; graduar los colores de un cuadro; dar a los flúidos cierto grado de consistencia.—*vn.* 1. Graduarse, ganar un grado en un colegio o universidad (acepción muy usada, pero impropia). 2. Pasar por grados; cambiar gradualmente.

Graduate, *s.* 1. Graduado, el que posee algún grado académico. 2. Vaso graduado para medir líquidos, componer recetas médicas, etc.

Graduation [grad-yu-ê'-shun], *s.* 1. Graduación; acto de conferir u obtener grados académicos. 2. Acción y efecto de modificar o de dividir un espacio en partes regulares.

Graft [graft], *s.* 1. Injerto. 2. (fam.) Peculado, negocios ilícitos que se realizan al amparo de un puesto público.

Graft, *va.* 1. Injertar, ingerir. 2. Incorporar, unir una cosa con otra de una manera vital. 3. (Cir.) Transferir, pasar de un animal á otro, v. gr. un trozo de piel.—*vn.* Hacer injertos.

Grafter [graft'-er], *s.* Injertador de árboles.

Grafting [graft'-ing], *s.* Injertación, injerto, el acto de injertar. *Cleft grafting,* Injerto en púa. *Tongue, whip, grafting,* Injerto de lengüeta.

Graham bread [grê'-am bred], *s.* Acemita, pan de acemite.

Grail [grêl], *s.* Cáliz o taza ancha; en especial, *The Holy Grail,* el cáliz empleado por el Redentor en la última Cena. Según la leyenda, se disipa y desaparece cuando se acerca a él alguien que no es puro y santo.

Grain [grên], *s.* 1. Grano, una sola semilla de cualquiera mies. 2. Grano, el fruto y semilla de las mieses. 3. Semilla de cualquier fruto. 4. Grano, porción o parte menuda de cualquiera cosa. 5. Grano, la parte mínima en que se divide el peso. 6. Veta, la lista o raya que se halla en la madera y otros cuerpos fibrosos. *Against the grain,* Contra pelo, a repelo, con repugnancia. 7. Grana, cualquiera cosa teñida con grana. 8. Genio, disposición, índole. 9. Grano, la suavidad o aspereza que existe en la superficie de alguna cosa. *A grain of allowance,* Indulgencia. *A rogue in grain,* Pícaro rematado. *Cross-grain,* A contrahilo. *Grain-fork,* Bieldo. *Grain-moth,* Mariposa cuya larva ataca los granos entrojados. Tinea granella. *Grain-weevil,* Gorgojo. *Grains of paradise,* Cardamomo, grana del paraíso.

Grain, *va.* 1. Granular, granear, formar en granos. 2. Agranelar, vetear o rayar; pintar o teñir para imitar la madera, el mármol, etc.

Grain alcohol [grên al'-co-hol], *s.* Alcohol de granos, alcohol etílico.

Grain elevator [grên el'-e-vê-ter], *s.* Elevador de granos.

Grainy [grên'-i], *a.* Granado; lleno de grano o semilla.

Gram, Gramme [gram], *s.* Gramo, unidad de peso en el sistema métrico; equivale a 15.43 granos.

Gramineous [gra-min'-e-us], *a.* Gramíneo.

Graminivorous [gram-i-niv'-or-us], *a.* Graminívoro, que se alimenta de hierba.

Grammar [gram'-ar], *s.* 1. Gramática, el arte de hablar y escribir una lengua con propiedad. 2. Gramática, el libro que contiene las reglas de la gramática.

Grammarian [gram-ê'-ri-an], *s.* Gramático, maestro de gramática; dómine; autor de una gramática.

Grammar school [gram'-er scūl], *s.* Escuela primaria, escuela elemental.

Grammatic, Grammatical [gram-at'-ic, al], *a.* Gramatical.

Grammatically [gram-at'-ic-al-i], *adv.* Gramaticalmente.

Grammaticaster [gra-mat'-i-cas-ter], *s.* Gramaticuelo, pedante.

Grammaticize [gra-mat'-i-saiz], *va.* Ajustar a las reglas de la gramática.

Grammatist, *s.* (Poco us.) *V.* GRAMMARIAN.

Gramophone [gram'-o-fōn], *s.* Gramófono, tocadiscos.

Grampus [gram'-pus], *s.* (Zool.) Delfín, un pez.

Granary [gran'-a-ri], *s.* Granero, el sitio o lugar donde se recogen los granos.

Grand [grand], *a.* Grande, ilustre, grandioso; sublime, magnífico, noble; elevado, espléndido, augusto, preeminente; comprensivo. *Grand jury, V.* JURY. *Grand-master,* Gran maestre; dignidad en la francmasonería y otras asociaciones.

Grandam, Grandame [gran'-dam,

gran'-dêm], *sf.* Abuela; una vieja arrugada.
Grand-aunt [grand'-ânt], *sf.* La tía del padre o de la madre; la hermana del abuelo o la abuela.
Grandchild [grand'-chaild], *s.* Nieto o nieta.
Grand-daughter [grand'-dō-tęr], *sf.* Nieta.
Grandee [gran-dî'], *s.* Grande, hombre de distinción, poder o dignidad. *Grandee of Spain*, Grande de España.
Grandeur [gran'-jur], *s.* Grandeza, esplendor, fausto, pompa.
Grandfather [grand'-fū-dhęr], *sm.* Abuelo. *Great-grandfather*, Bisabuelo. *Great-great-grandfather*, Tatarabuelo.
Grandiloquence [gran-dil'-o-cwens], *s.* Grandilocuencia.
Grandiloquous [gran-dil'-o-cwus], *a.* Grandílocuo.
Grand larceny [grand lārs'-ni], *s.* Robo de consideración.
Grandly [grand'-li], *adv.* Grandemente, sublimemente.
Grandmother [grand'-mudh-ęr], *sf.* Abuela. *Great-grandmother*, Bisabuela. *Great-great-grandmother*, Tatarabuela.
Grandnephew [grand-nef'-yu], *sm.* Sobrino nieto de un hermano o de una hermana.
Grandness [grand'-nes], *s.* Grandor, grandeza.
Grandniece [grand'-nîs], *sf.* Sobrina nieta de un hermano o de una hermana.
Grand piano [grand pi-an'-o], *s.* Piano de cola.
Grandsire [grand'-sair], *s.* Abuelo.
Grandson [grand'-sun], *s.* Nieto.
Grandstand [grand'-stand], *s.* Gradería principal para observar espectáculos o pasar revista.
Grand-uncle [grand-uŋ-cl], *sm.* El tío del padre o de la madre; el hermano del abuelo o de la abuela.
Grange [grênj], *s.* 1. Granja, cortijo, alquería, hacienda, casa de labranza. 2. (Ant.) Granero.
Granger [grên'-jer], *s.* (E. U.) 1. Individuo de la sociedad llamada *Patrons of Husbandry* (Patronos de la Agricultura). 2. Patán, labrador (despectivo).
Granite [gran'-it], *s.* (Min.) Granito.
Granitic, Granitical [gra-nit'-i-cal], *a.* Granítico, semejante al granito o formado de él.
Granivorous [gra-niv'-o-rus], *a.* Granívoro, que se alimenta de granos.
Granny [gran'-i], *sf.* (Fest.) Abuela; comadre, vieja.
Grant [grąnt], *va.* 1. Conceder, asentir o convenir en lo que otro dice o afirma. 2. Conceder, dar, otorgar, hacer merced y gracia de alguna cosa. 3. Conferir, transferir, transmitir el título de una propiedad, etc. *To take for granted*, Presuponer, dar por supuesto. *To grant or allow for argument's or peace' sake*, Dar de barato.
Grant, *s.* 1. Concesión, don, dádiva, donación; permiso, privilegio. 2. Concesión, el acto de asentir o convenir en una cosa. 3. (For.) Documento que confiere un privilegio o transmite el título de una propiedad.
Grantable [grąnt'-a-bl], *a.* Capaz de ser concedido; dable, permisible.
Grantee [grąnt-î'], *s.* Concesionario, donatario, el que recibe alguna concesión.
Grantor [grąnt'-ęr], *s.* Cesionario, el que concede alguna cosa.
Granular [gran'-yu-lar], **Granulary** [gran'-yu-lę-ri], *a.* Granular, granoso, granujoso.
Granulate [gran'-yu-lêt], *vn.* Granularse, formarse en granos pequeños. —*va.* Granular, granear, levantar grano en alguna cosa.
Granulation [gran-yu-lê'-shun], *s.* 1. Granulación, la acción de granular o granularse. 2. Superficie granulada. 3. (Med.) Encarnación, desarrollo de tejido en una herida en vías de curación.
Granule [gran'-yūl], *s.* Granillo, gránulo.
Granulous [gran'-yu-lus], *a.* Granuloso, granilloso, granujoso.
Grape [grêp], *s.* 1. Uva. *Bunch of grapes*, Racimo de uvas. 2. Vid, planta trepadora que produce las uvas. 3. (Mil.) *V.* GRAPE-SHOT. *To gather grapes*, Vendimiar. *Grape-sugar*, Glucosa, dextrosa. *Grape-vine*, Vid, parra.
Grapefruit [grêp'-frūt], *s.* Toronja.
Grapeless [grêp'-les], *a.* Sin uva.
Grapery [grê'-pęr-i], *s.* Invernadero o criadero de uvas.
Grape-shot [grêp'-shot], *s.* Balas encadenadas, balas enramadas, metralla.
Grape-stone [grêp'-stōn], *s.* Granuja, la simiente de la uva.
Graph [graf], *s.* Gráfica, diagrama.
Graphic [graf'-ic], **Graphical** [graf'-ic-al], *a.* 1. Gráfico, representado por medio de dibujos o figuras. 2. Delineado o descrito de un modo pintoresco. 3. Notado en letras; escrito, impreso o grabado; que pertenece al arte de escribir.
Graphically [graf'-ic-al-i], *adv.* Gráficamente, de un modo pintoresco.
Graphite [graf'-ait], *s.* (Min.) Grafito, plombagina.
Graphology [gra-fōl'-o-ji], *s.* Grafología, estudio psicológico de la escritura.
Graphometer [gra-fem'-ę-tęr], *s.* Grafómetro, instrumento para levantar planos.
Grapline [grap'-lin], **Grapnel** [grap'-nel], *s.* (Mar.) 1. Anclote, ancla pequeña. 2. Arpeo, cloque, gancho para atracar y abordar.
Grapple [grap'-l], *va.* Agarrar, asir; amarrar, tener firmemente.—*vn.* Agarrarse, venirse a las manos. *To grapple and board*, (Mar.) Atracarse, aferrarse o abordarse para pelear.
Grapple, *s.* 1. Lucha, riña, pelea. 2. Arpeo, instrumento con que se asegura o agarra un buque a otro. 3. Cloque, rastra.
Grappling [grap'-ling], *s.* (Mar.) Rezón. *To warp with graplings*, (Mar.) Espiar con rezones. *Grappling-iron*, Cloque, arpeo de abordaje.
Grasp [grąsp], *va.* 1. Empuñar, asir, agarrar. 2. Apoderarse, tomar y tener en posesión de uno. 3. Alcanzar, comprender, saber.—*vn.* Esforzarse por agarrar; asir. *To grasp at*, Querer alcanzar, intentar, ambicionar. *Grasp all, lose all*, Quien mucho abarca poco aprieta; el que todo lo quiere todo lo pierde.
Grasp, *s.* 1. Asimiento, agarro, la acción de agarrar. 2. Posesión, poder; alcance. 3. Puño, puñado; garras.
Grasper [grąsp'-ęr], *s.* Agarrador.
Grass [grąs], *s.* 1. Hierba, herbaje, plantas con que se alimentan los ganados. 2. Césped, verde. 3. (Bot.) Cualquiera planta de las gramíneas. *Grass cloth*, Batista de Cantón. *Canary grass*, Alpiste. *Grass widow*, Mujer separada temporalmente de su marido, o abandonada por él; también la mujer divorciada. *Grass-widower*, Marido separado de su mujer. *To let the grass grow under one's feet*, Perder el tiempo, haraganear.
Grass, *va.* 1. Cubrir de hierba. 2. Extender sobre el césped; blanquear lino. 3. Apacentar los ganados.—*vn.* (Des.) Criar hierba.
Grass-green [grąs'-grîn], *a.* Verde como la hierba.
Grass-grown [grąs'-grōn], *a.* Cubierto con hierba o herbaje.
Grasshopper [grąs'-hep-ęr], *s.* 1. Langosta, saltamontes, saltón, insecto ortóptero. 2. Palanca de pianoforte.
Grassless [grąs'-les], *a.* Sin hierba.
Grass-plot, Grass-plat [grąs'-plot, plat], *s.* 1. Prado, terreno cubierto de hierba; batey (Cuba). 2. (Poét.) La verde alfombra
Grassy [grąs'-i], *a.* Herboso, abundante y lleno de hierba; herbáceo, parecido a la hierba.
Grate [grêt], *s.* 1. Reja, verja, rejilla, rejado o enrejado. 2. Fogón de rejas, brasero, enrejado de hierro; estufa.
Grate, *va.* 1. Rallar, desmenuzar alguna cosa estregándola con el rallo. 2. Rallar, molestar, fastidiar. 3. Rechinar, formar o hacer ruido desapacible. *To grate the teeth*, Rechinar los dientes. 4. Enrejar.—*vn.* 1. Rozarse o estregarse una cosa con otra de modo que se eche a perder. 2. Producir una impresión desagradable, causar irritación mental. *To grate up*, Cerrar con rejas. *To grate*, (Fam.) Desollar, atormentar.
Grateful [grêt'-ful], *a.* 1. Grato, agradecido, reconocido. 2. Gustoso, agradable, bienvenido.
Gratefully [grêt'-ful-i], *adv.* Agradecidamente; gratamente.
Gratefulness [grêt'-ful-nes], *s.* 1. Gratitud, agradecimiento. 2. Agrado, gusto.
Grater [grêt'-ęr], *s.* Rallo, especie de lima basta.
Gratification [grat-i-fi-kê'-shun], *s.* 1. Gusto, placer, deleite. *For the gratification of*, Por dar gusto a. 2. Gratificación, recompensa.
Gratify [grat'-i-fai], *va.* 1. Satisfacer, cumplir; contentar, dar gusto, agradar. 2. Gratificar, premiar, recompensar.
Grating [grê'-ting], *pa.* Discordante, mal sonante; rudo, duro, penoso; ofensivo, áspero. *It must have been grating to his feelings*, Eso ha debido de serle muy penoso.
Gratings [grêt'-ingz], *s. pl.* (Mar.) Ajedrez o jareta, red de cabos o enrejado de madera debajo del cual se pone la gente para pelear con más resguardo. *Gratings of the head*, (Mar.) Enjaretado de proa. *Iron gratings*, Enrejado de hierro.
Gratingly [grêt'-ing-li], *adv.* Ásperamente.
Gratis [grê'-tis], *adv.* Gratis, de balde.
Gratitude [grat'-i-tiūd], *s.* Gratitud, agradecimiento, reconocimiento.
Gratuitous [gra-tiū'-i-tus], *a.* Gratuito, voluntario, sin prueba.
Gratuitously [gra-tiū'-i-tus-li], *adv.* Gratuitamente, de gracia; sin prueba.

Gratuity [gra-tiū'-i-ti], *s.* Gratificación, recompensa, remuneración.
Gratulate [grat'-yu-lêt], *va.* (Ant.) Congratular, dar el parabién, felicitar.
Gratulation [grat-yu-lê'-shun], *s.* Congratulación, parabién, enhorabuena.
Gratulatory [grat'-yu-la-to-ri], *a.* Congratulatorio. *Gratulatory letters,* Cartas de enhorabuena.
Gravamen [gra-vê'-men], *s.* (For.) Agravio, la parte esencial de una queja.
Grave, *va.* (*pret.* GRAVED, *pp.* GRAVED o GRAVEN). 1. Grabar, esculpir, imprimir alguna cosa. 2. (Mar.) Despalmar, limpiar la embarcación, embrearla y darle sebo.—*vn.* Grabar, dibujar o delinear en alguna cosa dura.
Grave [grêv], *s.* 1. Sepultura, hoya, huesa donde se sepulta un cadáver; sepulcro, tumba. 2. Cualquier sitio de destrucción y ruina. 3. Muerte; en la Biblia, el lugar de los muertos, Hades.
Grave-clothes [grêv'-clodhz], *s. pl.* Mortaja.
Grave-digger [grêv'-dig-ęr], **Grave-maker** [grêv'-mê-kęr], *s.* Sepulturero.
Grave, *a.* 1. Grave, serio, circunspecto. 2. Grave, importante, arduo, difícil. 3. Sencillo, modesto, honesto. 4. (Mús.) Grave, bajo, profundo en tono; de muy lento movimiento. 5. (Gram.) Grave, el acento opuesto al agudo.
Gravel [grav'-el], *s.* 1. Cascajo, arena gruesa. 2. La arenilla que se forma en los riñones o en la vejiga; mal de piedra. *Gravel-pit,* Arenaria, hoyo de donde se extrae el cascajo. *Gravel walk,* Paseo arenoso, cubierto de arena gruesa.
Gravel, *va.* 1. Llenar o cubrir alguna cosa con cascajo. 2. Enmarañar, confundir, inquietar, embarazar. 3. Lastimar el pie del caballo la arena metida entre la herradura.
Graveless [grêv'-les], *a.* Insepulto.
Gravelly [grav'-el-i], *a.* Arenisco, cascajoso.
Gravely [grêv'-li], *adv.* Seriamente, modestamente.
Graven [grê'-vn], *pp. irr.* de *To* GRAVE. Esculpido, grabado.
Graveness [grêv'-nes], *s.* Gravedad, seriedad, circunspección, compostura.
Graver [grêv'-ęr], *s.* 1. Grabador. 2. Buril, instrumento de acero de que usan los grabadores.
Graves [grêvs], *s. pl.* Residuo o sedimento del sebo derretido. (Var. de GREAVES.)
Gravestone [grêv'-stōn], *s.* Lápida sepulcral; monumento fúnebre.
Graveyard [grêv'-yārd], *s.* Cementerio, lugar descubierto destinado a enterrar cadáveres.
Gravid [grav'-id], *a.* Preñada; embarazada, en cinta.
Graving [grêv'-ing], *s.* 1. Grabado. 2. Impresión profunda hecha en el ánimo por cualquiera cosa o suceso.
Gravitate [grav'-i-têt], *vn.* Gravitar, tender un cuerpo al centro de atracción.
Gravitation [grav-i-tê'-shun], *s.* 1. Gravitación, la tendencia de los cuerpos a atraerse mutuamente; la fuerza con que todos los cuerpos se atraen. 2. Tendencia mental o moral hacia algún objeto o idea. 3. Gravedad.
Gravity [grav'-i-ti], *s.* 1. (Fís.) Gravedad, pesantez. 2. Gravedad, enormidad, seriedad. *Gravity feed,* Alimentación a gravedad.
Gravure [gra-viūr'], *s.* Clisé, plancha clisada para imprimir grabados.
Gravy [grê'-vi], *s.* 1. Salsa en general. 2. Jugo que despide de sí la carne cuando no está muy consumida por el fuego; pringue, caldillo, unto.
Gray, Grey [grê], *s.* 1. Gris, color que resulta de la mezcla del blanco y negro. 2. Animal gris; se aplica a los caballos, al tejón, a una especie de salmón, al pardillo, etc.—*a.* 1. Gris, pardo. *Gray cloth,* Paño mezclilla. 2. Cano, encanecido. 3. Obscuro como cuando amanece o anochece. *Dark-gray,* gris obscuro. *Gray-eyed,* De ojos grises. *Gray-headed,* Canoso, encanecido, envejecido. *Gray horse,* Caballo pardo.
Graybeard [grê'-bīrd], *s.* Barbicano: hombre ya entrado en años.
Grayfly [grê'-flai], *s.* Trompetilla, especie de mosca parda.
Grayhound [grê'-haund], *s.* *V.* GREYHOUND.
Grayish [grê'-ish], *a.* Pardusco; entrecano.
Grayling [grê'-ling], *s.* (Ict.) Umbla.
Grayness [grê'-nes], *s.* La calidad de ser gris.
Graze [grez], *vn.* 1. Pacer, apacentarse el ganado. 2. Dar pasto o surtir de hierba. 3. Rozar, tocar ligeramente.—*va.* 1. Pastorear, llevar o conducir el ganado al campo o a pacer, apacentar. 2. Dar hierba a los animales; dar forraje a los caballos. 3. Tocar o herir ligeramente y pasar o ir más allá. 4. Pasar volando, rasar la tierra.
Graze, *s.* 1. Rozamiento, la acción de rozar. 2. Roce o tocamiento ligero; raya ligera, raspadura.
Grazer [grêz'-ęr], *s.* Animal que pace o se apacienta.
Grazier [grê'-zhęr], *s.* Ganadero.
Grease [grīs], *s.* 1. Grasa, la manteca, unto o sebo de cualquier animal. 2. Aguajas, enfermedad en los pies de los caballos. *Grease-box,* Caja de sebo que se usa en varias máquinas.
Grease [grīs o grīz], *va.* 1. Engrasar, pringar, untar, manchar con gordura o grasa. 2. Corromper o sobornar con dádivas o dinero: dícese familiarmente untar o untar las manos.
Greaser [grīs'-ęr], *s.* 1. El que o lo que unta con grasa. 2. (E. U. del Oeste) Mejicano o hispanoamericano; úsase despreciativamente.
Greasily [grīs'-i-li], *adv.* Crasamente.
Greasiness [grīs'-i-nes], *s.* Pringue, gordura.
Greasy [grīs'-i], *a.* 1. Grasiento, craso, pringado, gordo. 2. (Vet.) Atacado de las aguajas. 3. (Des.) Indecente, poco delicado, grosero.
Great [grêt], *a.* 1. De gran volumen, grueso, vasto, enorme, desmedido. 2. Mucho, numeroso. 3. De larga duración, prolongado. 4. Gran, grande, considerable, importante. 5. Principal; poderoso, ilustre, eminente, noble, magnánimo. 6. Familiar, íntimo. 7. Adorable, admirable, maravilloso, sublime. 8. Imponente, orgulloso, amenazador. 9. Lleno, henchido; preñado. 10. Indica la tercera generación ascendente, o de los bisabuelos, y cada una de las que la preceden. *A great deal,* Mucho, gran cantidad. *A great many,* Muchos. *A great while,* Largo tiempo. *To make greater,* Agrandar, ensanchar o hacer mayor una cosa. *The great,* Los grandes. *Great Dane,* El mastín danés, perro de gran tamaño y fuerza. *Great gun,* Cañón de artillería. *Great-grandson,* Biznieto. *Great-granddaughter,* Biznieta. *Great-grandfather,* Bisabuelo. *Great-grandmother,* Bisabuela. *Great-grandchildren,* Biznietos. *Great-great-grandfather,* Tercer abuelo o tatarabuelo. *Great-great-grandmother,* Tercera abuela o tatarabuela.—*s.* (Des.) Todo por junto, por entero. *By the great,* (Des.) Por junto, por mayor.
Great-bellied [grêt'-bel-id], *a.* 1. Barrigudo. 2. Preñada.
Great-coat [grêt'-cōt], *s.* Levitón, sobretodo grueso.
Greaten [grêt'-n], *va.* Agrandar, engrandecer.—*vn.* Crecer, aumentarse.
Great-hearted [grêt'-hārt-ed], *a.* Animado, osado, no abatido; de alma grande.
Greatly [grêt'-li], *adv.* 1. Muy, mucho. 2. Noblemente, ilustremente. 3. Grandemente, magnánimamente.
Greatness [grêt'-nes], *s.* 1. Grandeza, grandor, extensión. 2. Grandeza, majestad, nobleza, dignidad, poder. 3. Magnanimidad, grandeza de alma. 4. Grandeza, fausto.
Greaves [grīvs], *s. pl.* 1. Grebas, canilleras, piezas de armadura que cubrían las piernas. 2. Chicharrones, residuo de la grasa de cerdo derretida y del sebo.
Grebe [grīb], *s.* Colimbo, ave palmípeda con cuatro dedos y sin plumas en la cola.
Grecian [grī'-shan], *s.* 1. Griego. 2. Helenista, judío que sabía la lengua griega. 3. Helenista, el que está bien instruído en el griego.—*a.* Griego.
Grecianize [grī'-shan-aiz], *vn.* Grecizar, greguizar.
Grecize [grī'-saiz], *va.* Grecizar, dar a las palabras o frases forma griega; traducir en griego.—*vn.* Imitar a los griegos, llegar a parecerse a ellos.
Grecism [grī'-sizm], *s.* Grecismo, helenismo, idiotismo de la lengua griega.
Greed [grīd], *s.* 1. Codicia, avaricia. 2. *V.* GREEDINESS.
Greedily [grīd'-i-li], *adv.* Vorazmente, ansiosamente: vehementemente.
Greediness [grīd'-i-nes], *s.* Voracidad, ansia; gula, hambre; codicia.
Greedy [grīd'-i], *a.* 1. Voraz, insaciable, goloso. 2. Ansioso, deseoso, apasionado, avaro. *Greedy-gut,* (Vulg.) Glotón.
Greek [grīk], *s.* 1. Griego, el natural de Grecia. 2. Griego, la lengua de los naturales de Grecia. 3. Helenista, literato versado en el idioma griego. 4. (Fam.) Lenguaje no inteligible. *It is all Greek to me,* Para mí eso es griego o gringo.—*a.* Griego, lo que pertenece a Grecia y a sus habitantes.
Greekess [grīk'-es], *sf.* Griega, mujer natural de Grecia.
Greek-fire [grīk'-fair], *s.* Fuego griego, mixto incendiario que arde sobre el agua, inventado por los griegos para quemar las naves.
Greekish [grīk'-ish], *a.* Griego.
Greekling [grīk'-ling], *s.* Un autor griego de poco mérito: vocablo despectivo.
Green [grīn], *a.* 1. Verde. 2. Verde, lo que aun no está maduro. 3. Ver-

de, floreciente, fresco, reciente, acabado de hacer. 4. Pálido, descolorido. 5. Crudo, lo que no está cocido. 6. Joven, tierno, novicio, inexperto.—*s.* 1. Verde, el color de las plantas: 2. Prado o pradera; lugar cubierto de hierba en un pueblo de campo. 3. Afeite, color o afeite verde o verdoso. *Bottle-green*, Verde botella. *Sea-green*, Verde mar. *Greens*, Verduras, todo género de hortaliza. *Green corn*, Maíz tierno; (Mex.) elote; (Ingl.) trigo en hierba. *Green hand*, Novicio, principiante. *Green-laver* o *green-sloke*, Alga marina comestible, de la familia de las ulváceas. Ulva lactuca. *Green vitriol*, Caparrosa, vitriolo verde, sulfato de hierro. *Green ware*, Loza cruda. *Green-cloth*, Mayordomía, sección del servicio de la casa real inglesa, encargada principalmente del aprovisionamiento de palacio. *Green-colored*, Pálido, enfermizo. *Green-eyed*, Lo que tiene ojos verdes.

Green, *va.* Teñir de verde, dar color verde a alguna cosa, verdear.

Greenback [grīn'-bac], *s.* Papel moneda del gobierno de los Estados Unidos, o de los bancos nacionales; llámase así por el color verde de la impresión en el reverso.

Greenfinch [grīn'-finch], *s.* (Orn.) Verdecillo, verderón o verderol.

Green gage [grīn' gêj], *s.* Ciruela verdal.

Greengrocer [grīn'-gro-sẹr], *s.* Verdulero.

Greenhorn [grīn'-hōrn], *s.* (Fam.) Persona sin experiencia, paleto.

Greening [grīn'-ing], *s.* 1. El acto de volverse verde. 2. Manzana verde de diferentes variedades.

Greenhouse [grīn'-haus], *s.* Conservatorio; invernáculo.

Greenish [grīn'-ish], *a.* Verdoso, verdusco.

Greenly [grīn'-li], *adv.* 1. Nuevamente, recientemente. 2. Sin madurez, antes de madurar.

Greenness [grīn'-nes], *s.* Verdín, verdor, vigor, frescura; falta de experiencia; novedad.

Greenroom [grīn'-rum], *s.* 1. Hogar, salón general de un teatro donde esperan los actores que han de salir a la escena. 2. Cuarto destinado a contener loza cruda o tela acabada de hacer.

Greensand [grīn'-sand], *s.* (Geol.) Arenisca verde; una de las capas del período cretáceo.

Greensickness [grīn'-sic-nes], *s.* Clorosis, colores pálidos, una enfermedad de las jóvenes.

Greenstall [grīn'-stōl], *s.* Puesto o tabla para vender frutas y verduras.

Greenstone [grīn'-stōn], *s.* (Geol.) Diorita o dolerita; voz poco precisa y que va cayendo en desuso.

Greensward [grīn'-swērd], *s.* El césped bien verde y tupido; alfombra de hierba.

Greenwood [grīn'-wud], *s.* Bosque verde; selva frondosa.

Greet [grīt], *va.* Saludar, hablar cortésmente a uno, llamarle. *Greet her in my name*, Salúdela Vd. de mi parte.—*vn.* Encontrarse y saludarse.

Greet, *vn.* (Esco.) Llorar, verter lágrimas, lamentarse.

Greeter [grīt'-ẹr], *s.* Saludador, el que saluda.

Greeting [grīt'-ing], *s.* 1. Salutación, saludes: en los instrumentos públicos, *Salud!* 2. (Esco.) Lloro.

Gregarian [grẹ-gé'-ri-an], *a.* Gregario, gregal.

Gregarious [grẹ-gé'-ri-us], *a.* Gregario, gregal, rebañego.

Gregariously [grẹ-gé'-ri-us-li], *adv.* A manadas, gregariamente.

Gregariousness [grẹ-gé'-ri-us-nes], *s.* La propiedad de andar en manadas o rebaños.

Gregorian [grẹ-gō'-ri-an], *a.* Gregoriano.

¿**Gremial** [grī'-mi-al], *a.* 1. Lo que pertenece al regazo. 2. Perteneciente a gremios.

Grenade [grẹ-nēd'], *s.* Granada, granada real, granada de mano.

Grenadier [gren-a-dīr'], *s.* Granadero.

Grenadine [gren-a-dīn'], *s.* Granadina, tela delgada como la gasa que se usa para los vestidos de mujer.

Grew [grū], *pret.* de *To* GROW.

Grey [grê], *a.* Gris, *V.* GRAY.

Greyhound [grê'-haund], *s.* 1. Galgo, galga; lebrel. 2. (Neol.) Vapor de alta mar muy veloz.

Grice [grais], *s.* Gorrino, lechón, cochinillo; osezno, cachorro.

Grid [grid], *s.* 1. Parrilla, reja, serie de barras paralelas. 2. Criba grande de alambre para cerner el mineral.

Griddle [grid'-l], *s.* 1. Tartera para cocer pasteles. 2. Tapadera para el hornillo de una estufa de cocina. *Griddle-cake*, Pastelillo cocido en una tartera; particularmente fritura ligera de trigo sarraceno.

Gridiron [grid'-ai-urn], *s.* 1. Parrillas. 2. (Mar.) Andamiada, basada de esqueleto, para reparar las embarcaciones.

Grief [grīf], *s.* 1. Pesar, pesadumbre, aflicción, pena; dolor moral, como el causado por una desgracia. 2. Lo que causa pesar o perjuicio. *V.* GRIEVANCE.

Griefless [grīf'-les], *a.* Exento de pesadumbres o penas; sin agravio.

¿**Griefshot** [grīf'-shot], *a.* Traspasado de dolor, apesadumbrado.

Grievance [grīv'-ans], *s.* Pesar, molestia, agravio, injusticia, perjuicio, pesadumbre. *To redress grievances*, Reparar agravios.

Grieve [grīv], *va.* Agraviar, afligir, oprimir; apesadumbrar; herir la delicadeza de alguien.—*vn.* Apesadumbrarse, tomar pesadumbre, entristecerse, afligirse. *It grieves me to hear it*, Lo deploro, siento saberlo. *To grieve one's self to death*, Morirse de pena.

Griever [grīv'-ẹr], *s.* El que causa dolor.

Grievingly [grīv'-ing-li], *adv.* Apesaradamente.

Grievous [grīv'-us], *a.* 1. Penoso, doloroso, lastimoso. 2. Provocativo, ofensivo. 3. Grave, enorme; atroz, cruel.

Grievously [grīv'-us-li], *adv.* 1. Penosamente, con dolor y pena, molestamente. 2. Miserablemente, lastimosamente, tristemente.

Grievousness [grīv'-us-nes], *s.* Dolor, pena, aflicción; atrocidad, calamidad, enormidad.

Griffin [grif'-in], **Griffon** [grif'-ọn], *s.* 1. Grifo, animal fabuloso. 2. Dueña vigilante. 3. Mote que se da en la India a los recién llegados de Inglaterra.

Griffin-like [grif'-in-laic], *a.* Rapaz.

Grig [grig], *s.* 1. Cigarra, grillo. *As merry as a grig*, Alegre como un grillo. 2. Anguila pequeña.

Grill [gril], *va.* 1. Asar en parrillas. 2. Atormentar, molestar.

Grillade [gril-êd'], *s.* Cualquier cosa asada en parrillas; carbonada.

Grille [gril], *s.* Enrejado, reja, calado de adorno. (Fr.)

Grillroom [gril'-rūm], *s.* Restaurante o comedor originalmente para alimentos asados.

Grilse [grils], *s.* (Esco.) Esguín, salmón de poco tiempo, cuando por primera vez regresa del mar y sube por los ríos.

Grim [grim], *a.* 1. Disforme, horrendo. 2. Torvo, ceñudo, severo, regañón. 3. Inflexible; formidable.

Grimace [gri-mês'], *s.* Visaje, mueca, gesto.

Grimalkin [gri-mal'-kin o gri-mēl'-kin], *s.* Gatazo, gato viejo.

Grime [graim], *s.* Tizne, mugre porquería.

Grime, *va.* Ensuciar, llenar de mugre

Grim-faced [grim'-fêst], **Grim-visaged** [grim'-vis-êjd], *a.* Malcarado.

Grimly [grim'-li], *a.* Espantoso, horrible; ceñudo.—*adv.* Horriblemente, ásperamente.

Grimness [grim'-nes], *s.* Grima, horror, espanto.

Grimy [grai'-mi], *a.* Tiznado, sucio, manchado, mugriento.

Grin [grin], *vn.* Gestear, hacer gestos con la boca mostrando los dientes.

Grin, *s.* Mueca, visaje; amplia y burlona sonrisa.

Grind [graind], *va.* (*pret.* y *pp.* GROUND). 1. Moler, pulverizar, quebrantar alguna cosa haciéndola polvo. 2. Amolar, afilar. 3. Estregar, refregar una cosa con otra. 4. Mascar. 5. Moler, molestar, agobiar, oprimir. 6. (Fam.) Estudiar con ahinco; también, burlar a alguno.—*vn.* 1. Hacer andar la rueda de un molino. 2. Moverse o andar en rededor como la rueda de un molino. 3. Pulirse, quedar alisado o afilado por el roce; deslustrar el vidrio. *Steel grinds easily*, El acero se afila (o se pule) fácilmente. *Ground glass*, Vidrio deslustrado, opaco.

Grinder [graind'-ẹr], *s.* 1. Molinero, molendero. 2. Muela, piedra para moler y también la que sirve para afilar instrumentos cortantes. 3. Molino, molinillo. 4. Amolador. 5. Muela, uno de los últimos dientes de la quijada. 6. Diente, en desprecio para denotar los de un tragón.

Grindery [graind'-ẹr-i], *s.* Tienda de amolador, para afilar herramientas, navajas, etc.

Grinding [graind'-ing], *s.* Pulverización, molienda; amoladura; bruñimiento, pulidura.—*pa.* de GRIND. *Grinding lathe*, Torno de pulir. *Grinding plate*, Disco pesado de hierro que gira sobre un eje vertical y se usa para pulir el vidrio cilindrado.

Grindstone [graind'-stōn], *s.* 1. Amoladera. 2. Muela, la piedra en que se afilan los cuchillos, tijeras y otros instrumentos cortantes.

Grinner [grin'-ẹr], *s.* El que se sonríe enseñando los dientes.

Grinningly [grin'-ing-li], *adv.* Con sonrisa como una mueca, enseñando los dientes.

Grip [grip], *s.* 1. Apretón de mano, acción de asir o aprehender. 2. Modo especial de tomar y oprimir la mano, para reconocerse los individuos de ciertas asociaciones. 3. *V.* GRIP-SACK. 4. Asidero, puño, la parte por donde se ase alguna cosa. 5. Garra (fiador, retén), aparato para agarrar el cable de tracción de un ferrocarril o soltarlo. 6. Capacidad de agarrar y retener, o de alcanzar, comprender. *Gripman*, Empleado que maneja el fiador en un carro movido por cable. *Gripsack*, (Fam. E. U.) Saquillo, maleta ligera.

Grip, *va.* Agarrar, empuñar, asir, cerrar.—*vn.* Tener firmemente, v. gr. una ancla.

Gripe [graip], *va.* 1. Agarrar, asir, cerrar, empuñar; pellizcar, dar pellizcos. 2. Dar cólico o retortijones de tripas. 3. Afligir, acongojar el ánimo de alguno, apurarlo.—*vn.* 1. Padecer cólico. 2. Sisar, ganar dinero por medio de exacciones mezquinas.

Gripe, *s.* 1. Toma, la acción de tomar; presa; apretón de la mano. 2. Agarro, la acción de agarrar o asir con la mano o con las garras. 3. Presión, la acción de apretar una cosa con otra. 4. Uña, garra, zarpa. 5. Agarradero, asidero, mango. 6. Opresión, aprieto, apuro. *Gripe of an anchor*, (Mar.) Tenedor de ancla. *Gripes, pl.* (1) Dolor cólico, retortijón de tripas. (2) (Mar.) Obenques o bozas de lancha.

Griper [graip'-ẹr], *s.* Usurero.

Griping [graip'-ing], *s.* Dolor o retortijón de tripas; aflicción.

Gripingly [graip'-ing-li], *adv.* Con dolor de tripas.

Grippe, Grip [grip], *s.* Gripe, influenza, catarro epidémico, acompañado de serios trastornos del cuerpo y seguido de gran debilidad; llámase vulgarmente trancazo o dengue.

Grisette [gri-zet'], *sf.* 1. Griseta, obrera joven de París, amiga de galanteos; particularmente, manceba. 2. Tela parda de lana. (Fr.)

Grisly [griz'-li], *a.* Espantoso, horroroso, terrible.

Grist [grist], *s.* 1. Molienda o grano para moler; de aquí, la harina que se saca de él. 2. Provisión, abasto, suministro. *Grist-mill*, Molino harinero.

Gristle [gris'-l], *s.* Cartílago, ternilla.

Gristly [gris'-li], *a.* Cartilaginoso.

Grit [grit], *s.* 1. Partículas ásperas y duras; arena, cascajo. 2. (Geol.) Variedad de arenisca de veta silicosa. 3. Firmeza de carácter, particularmente en peligro o contra obstáculos; valor, ánimo, (Anglosajón greōt, polvo). 4. Moyuelo. 5. *pl.* Grano mondado y medio molido; sémola, farro. (Anglosajón grytt, harina.)

Grittiness [grit'-i-nes], *s.* 1. Arenosidad. 2. Ánimo.

Gritty [grit'-i], *a.* 1. Arenoso, lleno de partículas duras. 2. Valeroso, esforzado, animoso.

Grizzle [griz'-l], *s.* Gris, color entre blanco y negro; mezclilla.

Grizzled [griz'-ld], *a.* Mezclado con gris; aquel cuyo pelo principia a encanecer.

Grizzly [griz'-li], *a.* Pardusco, mezclado con gris.—*s.* Criba grande para separar piedras gruesas y pequeñas en la explotación hidráulica. *Grizzly bear*, El oso pardo, grande y feroz, de la parte occidental de la América del Norte. Ursus horribilis.

Groan [grōn], *vn.* Gemir, suspirar.

Groan, *s.* Gemido, suspiro.

Groaning [grōn'-ing], *s.* Lamentación, lamento, quejido; mugido.

Groat [grōt], *s.* Moneda de Inglaterra del valor de cuatro peniques: úsase también esta palabra para expresar una cantidad muy pequeña de dinero. *Groats*, Avena o trigo mondado y medio molido.

Groatsworth [grōts'-wōrth], *s.* El valor de un *groat*, cuatro peniques.

Grocer [grō'-sẹr], *s.* Especiero, abacero, el lonjista que vende cacao, te, azúcar, especias, etc. (Cuba) Bodeguero. (Amer.) Pulpero. (Mex.) Tendero. *Grocer's shop*, Lonja de especiero, especiería. (Cuba) Bodega. (Amer.) Pulpería, abacería. (Mex.) Tienda de abarrotes, o tienda.

Grocery [grō'-sẹr-i], *s.* 1. (E. U.) Tienda de comestibles, abacería, lonja. 2. *pl. Groceries*, Especierías, todo género de comestibles que venden los especieros, víveres; (Amer.) abarrotes.

Grog [grog], *s.* Grog, mezcla de aguardiente con agua.

Groggy [grog'-i], *a.* 1. Medio borracho, a medios pelos. 2. Que anda irregularmente, v. gr. un caballo. 3. Vacilante: dícese de los púgiles.

Groin [groin], *s.* 1. Ingle. 2. (Arq.) Arista de encuentro, esquina viva.

Groin, *va.* (Arq.) Formar aristas o esquinas vivas.

Groining [groin'-ing], *s.* (Arq.) Unos ornamentos en el techo interior de las iglesias y edificios llamados góticos.

Grommet [grom'-et], *s.* (Mar.) 1. Anillo de cuerda. 2. Roñada o anillo de las velas de estay. *Grommets of the eye-holes*, (Mar.) Roñadas de los sollados.

Groom [grūm], *s.* 1. Mozo de mulas o caballos; palafrenero; antiguamente cualquier criado. 2. Novio, el hombre recién casado. *Groomsman*, Padrino de boda. *Groom of the bedchamber*, Ayuda de cámara del rey. *Groom in waiting*, Camarero de semana. *Groom of the chamber*, Caballerizo de cámara.

Groom, *va.* Cuidar, almohazar los caballos.

Groove [grūv], *s.* 1. Muesca, encaje, acanaladura, ranura, estría. 2. Rutina, hábito fijo en los actos de la vida diaria.

Groove, *va.* Acanalar; hacer muescas, estrías o ranuras.

Grope [grōp], *vn.* Tentar, andar a tientas.—*va.* 1. Tentar, buscar alguna cosa a obscuras o en donde no se ve. 2. Buscar ciegamente en la obscuridad intelectual, sin guía seguro, ni medios de acierto.

Groper [grōp'-ẹr], *s.* El que tienta o busca a obscuras.

Grosbeak [grōs'-bīk], *s.* 1. Picogordo, ave. Habia ludoviciana. 2. Cardenal, loxia, pájaro.

Grosgrain [grō'-grên], *s.* Gro. *Grosgrain ribbon*, Cinta de gro.

Gross [grōs], *a.* 1. Grueso, corpulento, espeso, denso. 2. Indecoroso, mal visto; vergonzoso, chocante; basto, tosco, craso, grosero, obsceno, descortés. 3. Lerdo, estúpido. *Gross amount*, Importe total.—*s.* (*pl.* Gross, lo mismo.) 1. Grueso, la parte principal de algún todo. 2. El conjunto, el todo. 3. Gruesa, el número de doce docenas. *To buy or sell by the gross*, Vender o comprar por mayor. *In gross, in the gross*, En grueso, por junto, en conjunto. *Great gross*, Doce gruesas o 144 docenas tomadas como unidad. *Small gross*, Diez docenas, o 120.

Grossly [grōs'-li], *adv.* En bruto; toscamente, groseramente.

Gross margin [grōs mār'-jin], *s.* Margen bruto de ganancia.

Grossness [grōs'-nes], *s.* 1. Rudeza, grosería. 2. Grosura.

Gross profit [grōs prof'-it], *s.* Ganancia bruta.

Grot [grot], *s.* (Poét.) *V.* Grotto.

Grotesque [gro-tesc'], *a.* Grotesco o grutesco, incongruo, desproporcionado.

Grotesquely [gro-tesc'-li], *adv.* Fantásticamente.

Grotto [grot'-o], *s.* Gruta, caverna.

Grouch [grauch], *s.* 1. Mal humor. 2. Persona malhumorada, cascarrabias.—*vi.* Refunfuñar, quejarse con mal humor.

Ground [ground], *s.* 1. Tierra, terreno, suelo, pavimento. 2. Tierra, país, región, territorio. 3. Tierra, heredad, posesión. 4. Suelo, el asiento o poso que dejan los líquidos: en este sentido se usa en plural. 5. Baño, la primera mano de color que se da al lienzo que se ha de pintar. 6. Principio, fundamento, razón fundamental; pie, base, causa, motivo. 7. (Mil.) Campo de batalla, el sitio o terreno que ocupa un ejército mientras pelea. 8. Fondo o lo más hondo de alguna cosa. (Mar.) Tenedero. 11. Conexión de una corriente eléctrica con la tierra. *Rocky ground*, Fondo de piedras. *On, upon the ground*, En tierra, en el suelo. *To break ground*, (Fig.) Empezar un trabajo o una empresa. *To be on one's own ground*, Ocuparse en aquello en que está uno muy versado. *To fall to the ground*, Caer al suelo; (fig.) fracasar, no salir bien de un empeño. *To gain ground*, Ganar terreno, adelantar en alguna cosa, hacer progresos. *To give* o *to lose ground*, Perder terreno, retroceder, atrasar. *To stand* o *to keep one's ground*, Mantenerse firme.

Ground, *va.* 1. Fundar, zanjar, cimentar, apoyar. 2. Zanjar, establecer, fijar los principios o elementos de alguna ciencia. 3. Poner o sacar a tierra.—*vn.* (Mar.) Tocar, varar.

Ground, *pp.* de *To* Grind.

Groundage [ground'-ẹj], *s.* (Mar.) Derecho de puerto.

Ground-breaking [ground-brêk'-ing], *s.* Iniciación de una obra, colocación de la primera piedra.

Ground-control approach [ground'-con-trol ap-prōch], *s.* (Aer.) Acceso dirigido desde tierra.

Grounder [ground'-ẹr], *s.* En el beisbol, pelota que rueda después de golpeada.

Ground-floor [ground'-flōr], *s.* El piso bajo de una casa.

Ground hog [ground hog], *s.* (Zool.) Marmota americana.

Grounding [ground'-ing], *s.* (Mar.) El acto de varar o dar en la costa.

Ground installations [ground in-stōl-ê'-shunz], *s. pl.* (Aer.) Infraestructura.

Ground-ivy [ground'-ai-vi], *s.* (Bot.) Hiedra terrestre.

Groundless [ground'-les], *a.* Infundado.

Groundlessly [ground'-les-li], *adv.* Infundadamente, sin razón, sin motivo.

Groundling [ground'-ling], *s.* 1. Lo que habita sobre el suelo, animal terrestre. 2. (Ict.) Loche, loja, especie de espirenque de ríos. 3. Hombre vil y abatido.

Ground-pine [graund'-pain], *s.* (Bot.) Camepitios, pinillo.

Ground-plan [graund'-plan], *s.* Plano horizontal; delineación del piso bajo de un edificio; bosquejo.

Ground-plot [graund'-plot], *s.* 1. Solar, terreno o sitio en que se construye un edificio. 2. Icnografía o delineación de un edificio.

Ground-rent [graund'-rent], *s.* La renta que se paga por el privilegio de levantar un edificio en el terreno de otra persona.

Ground-room [graund'-rūm], *s.* Cuarto bajo de una casa.

Groundsel [graund'-sel] o **Groundsil** [graund'-sil], *s.* 1. Umbral de puerta. 2. (Bot.) Hierba cana.

Groundswell [graund'-swel], *s.* Mar de leva o de fondo.

Ground wire [graund wair], *s.* (Elec.) Alambre de tierra.

Groundwork [graund'-wūrc], *s.* 1. Base, fundamento, cimiento. 2. (Arq.) Infraestructura. 3. Principios, rudimentos. *To lay a groundwork for*, Facilitar.

Group [grūp], *s.* 1. Grupo, el conjunto de varias figuras que forman un todo. 2. Grupo, combinación, conjunto de figuras dispuestas en una obra de arte. 3. Grupo, serie, clase.

Group, *va.* Agrupar.

Group insurance [grūp in-shur'-ens], *s.* Seguro colectivo o de grupo.

Grouse [graus], *s.* (Orn.) Gallina silvestre, urogallo, perdiz o faisán; propiamente dicho, tetrao.

Grout [graut], *s.* 1. Mortero poco espeso mezclado con cascajo. 2. Harina basta; sémola, farro. 3. (Bot.) Especie de manzano. 4. *pl.* Heces, zurrapas, sedimento.

Grouty [graut'-i], *a.* 1. Turbio, fangoso. 2. Regañón, áspero, arisco, intratable.

Grove [grōv], *s.* Arboleda, bosquecillo, boscaje. *Oak grove*, Robledal, robledo. *Pine grove*, Pinar.

Grovel [grev'-l], *vn.* 1. Serpear, arrastrarse, andar arrastrando por la tierra. 2. Envilecerse, bajarse.

Grovy [grōv'-i], *a.* (Poco us.) Arbolado, lleno de arboledas o perteneciente a ellas.

Grow [grō], *va.* (*pret.* GREW, *pp.* GROWN). Cultivar, hacer crecer o nacer algún vegetal.—*vn.* 1. Crecer, aumentarse, tomar aumento, hacerse grandes así las cosas animadas como las inanimadas. 2. Nacer, vegetar, crecer y nutrirse los vegetales. 3. Adelantar, progresar, hacer progresos. 4. Hacerse, ponerse o volverse diferente una cosa de lo que era; pasar de un estado o condición a otro. 5. Subir o llegar progresando sucesivamente a un estado superior al que antes se tenía. 6. Extenderse, dilatarse. 7. Nacer, proceder, provenir de una causa o razón cualquiera. 8. Pegarse, unirse; fijarse, echar raíces (con la prep. *to*). *To grow into fashion*, Hacerse moda. *To grow into a proverb*, Llegar a hacerse proverbial. *To grow into favour with one*, Insinuarse en el favor de una persona, irse haciendo su favorito. *To grow out of esteem*, Perder el crédito. *To grow out of favour*, Perder la amistad. *To grow out of kind*, Degenerar. *To grow out of use*, Caer en desuso. *To grow up*, Crecer, salir de la tierra las plantas, brotar, arrojar, apuntar los vegetales. *To grow less*, Disminuir. *To grow hot*, Acalorarse. *To grow near o on*, Acercarse. *To grow old*, Envejecer. *To grow tame*, Domesticarse. *To grow towards an end*, Ir acabándose. *To grow towards morning*, Empezar a amanecer. *To grow weary*, Cansarse. *To grow well*, Restablecerse. *To grow worse*, Empeorar. *To grow young again*, Remozarse. *To grow better*, Ponerse mejor, enmendarse, corregirse. *To grow big*, Engordar; aumentarse. *To grow childish*, Chochear. *To grow cold*, Enfriarse. *To grow dear*, Encarecer. *To grow easy*, Tranquilizarse. *To grow fat*, Engordar, engruesar. *To grow late*, Hacerse tarde. *It grows late*, Se va haciendo tarde. *To grow poor*, Empobrecerse. *To grow rich*, Enriquecerse. *To grow strong*, Ponerse fuerte, reponerse.

Grower [grō'-ẹr], *s.* 1. El que crece. 2. Arrendador, labrador, productor; cultivador. *Fruit-grower*, Cultivador de frutas.

Growing [grō'-ing], *s.* 1. Crecimiento. 2. Vegetación o nacimiento de las plantas. 3. Extensión, progresión (del tiempo). —*a.* Creciente. *Growing children*, Niños adolescentes.

Growl [graul], *vn.* 1. Regañar, gruñir, rezongar, refunfuñar. 2. Regañar el perro.—*va.* Indicar una cosa por gruñidos o regañando.

Growl, *s.* 1. Regañamiento, refunfuño, gruñido de una persona descontenta. 2. Regañamiento de un perro.

Growler [graul'-er], *s.* 1. Perro arisco, muy gruñidor. 2. Regañón, persona que regaña o refunfuña habitualmente.

Grown [grōn], *a.* y *pp.* 1. Cubierto o lleno de alguna cosa que está creciendo. *Grown with weeds*, Cubierto de maleza. 2. Crecido, hecho, llegado a la estatura a que puede llegar. *A grown man*, Hombre hecho. 3. Prevalente, dominante. *Grown up*, Crecido, adulto.

Growth [grōth], *s.* 1. Crecimiento, crecida, medro en la altura y corpulencia de los animales y plantas. 2. Producto, producción; el origen de las personas o cosas con relación al sitio donde fueron producidas. 3. Vegetación. 4. Crecimiento, acrecentamiento, aumento, subida en el número, tamaño, frecuencia o estatura. 5. Aumento, ampliación, extensión de una cosa. 6. Adelantamiento, aprovechamiento, mejora, progreso. 7. Estatura completa, altura. *This tree is not come to its full growth*, Este árbol está creciendo aún.

Grub [grub], *va.* Rozar o limpiar la tierra de las matas que cría arrancándolas; desarraigar; azadonar.—*vn.* 1. Cavar, labrando la tierra. 2. Emplearse en oficios bajos.

Grub, *s.* 1. Gorgojo, larva. 2. (Vul.) Alimento, comestibles. 3. Hombre desaliñado (en desprecio). 4. (Amer.) Algo desarraigado, v. gr. una raíz. *Grub-ax*, Azadón o legón para limpiar la tierra de las malas hierbas.

Grub Street [grub' strīt], *s.* Nombre antiguo de una calle de Londres donde vivían muchos escritores de coplas y producciones de poco mérito, por lo cual se ha dado posteriormente el nombre de la calle a dicha clase de composiciones. Llámase hoy día *Milton Street*.

Grudge [gruj], *va.* 1. Envidiar ó apetecer secretamente el bien que otro goza. 2. Dar o tomar alguna cosa de mala gana.—*vn.* 1. Murmurar, mostrar disgusto. 2. Repugnar, hacer de mala gana, admitir con dificultad alguna cosa.

Grudge, *s.* 1. Rencor, enemistad antigua, ira envejecida, refunfuño, tirria. *He owes him a grudge*, Le debe una jugada, o una mala partida. 2. Ira, mala voluntad. 3. Envidia, odio, aborrecimiento. 4. †Remordimiento de conciencia. 5. †Cualquier síntoma que indica estar próxima alguna enfermedad.

Grudging [gruj'-ing], *s.* 1. Envidia, descontento, sentimiento del bien ajeno; resentimiento, mala voluntad. 2. Refunfuñadura, refunfuño. 3. Repugnancia, aversión o resistencia a hacer o decir alguna cosa. 4. Deseo secreto de gozar el bien de los demás. 5. (Des.) Los síntomas precursores de un mal.

Grudgingly [gruj'-ing-li], *adv.* Con repugnancia, de mala gana, por pura necesidad.

Gruel [grū'-el], *s.* Especie de caldo espeso hecho de harina de trigo o maíz, bien hervida en agua. (Mex.) Atole.

Gruesome, Grewsome [grū'-sum], *a.* Horrible, horrendo, que sugiere pensamientos horrorosos.

Gruff [gruf], *a.* Ceñudo, grosero, tosco, impolítico, mal engestado.

Gruffly [gruf'-li], *adv.* Ásperamente, severamente.

Gruffness [gruf'-nes], *s.* Aspereza, severidad, dureza en la mirada; rudeza de modales, aspecto y lenguaje.

Grum [grum], *a.* Áspero, severo.

Grumble [grum'-bl], *vn.* Refunfuñar, gruñir, regañar, rezongar, murmurar, quejarse.

Grumbler [grum'-blẹr], *s.* Refunfuñador, gruñidor, regañón, regañador, rezongador.

Grumbling [grum'-bling], *s.* Murmuración, queja, descontento, refunfuñadura.

Grumblingly [grum'-bling-li], *adv.* Agriamente, con queja o descontento.

Grume [grūm], *s.* Grumo, cuajarón; masa espesa, viscosa y semiflúida.

Grumly [grum'-li], *adv.* Asperamente.

Grumous [grū'-mus], *a.* 1. Grumoso, que forma cuajarones; espeso, coagulado. 2. (Bot.) Que consta de granos agrupados.

Grumpy [grump'-i], *a.* Gruñón, quejoso, áspero, rudo de modales, malhumorado.

Grunt [grunt], *vn.* 1. Gruñir, dar gruñidos, producir un sonido gutural. 2. Murmurar, quejarse, refunfuñar.

Grunt, Grunting [grunt'-ing], *s.* 1. Gruñido, la voz del cerdo o un sonido parecido a ella. 2. Hemulón, pogonia, pez comestible de los mares tropicales americanos. Hæmulon.

Grunter [grunt'-ẹr], *s.* Gruñidor.

Gruntingly [grunt'-ing-li], *adv.* Regañando, refunfuñando.

Gruntling [grunt'-ling], *s.* Cochinillo.

Guaiac [guai'-ac], *s.* Guayaco, resina o madera (palo santo).

Guaiacum [gwai'-a-cum], *s.* 1. Guayaco, árbol de la América tropical de la familia de las cigofiláceas, cuya madera da, cocida en agua, un líquido acre y amargo que se usa en medicina como sudorífico muy activo. 2. La resina medicinal que se obtiene de este árbol. *Guaiacum-wood*, Palo santo, lignum-vitæ.

Guanaco [gwā-nā'-cō], *s.* (Zool.) Guanaco, especie de llama.

Guano [guā'-no], *s.* Guano, abono excelente compuesto principalmente de excrementos de aves marítimas.—*va.* Abonar la tierra con guano.

Guarantee [gar-an-tī'], *s.* 1. Lo mismo que GUARANTY, pero así en el sentido ordinario de la palabra como en el forense se prefiere la forma GUARANTY. 2. Fiado, caucionado, la persona por quien otro responde. 3. Común, pero incorrectamente, fiador, garante; lo opuesto a *guarantor*.

Guarantee, *va.* 1. Garantir, afianzar, salir fiador o responsable; tomar sobre sí el cumplimiento de lo que se estipula. 2. Asegurar contra pérdida o daño.

Guarantor [gar'-an-tōr], *s.* Garante, fiador, el que responde por otro.

Guaranty [gar'-an-ti], *s.* 1. (For.) Garantía, caución, fianza. 2. El acto de hacer cierto y seguro, de afianzar.

Guaranty, *va.* *V. To* GUARANTEE.

Guard [gārd], *va.* y *vn.* 1. Guardar, tener cuidado y vigilancia en defensa y seguridad de alguna cosa. 2. Guardar, defender, proteger, conservar. 3. Prevenirse, estar prevenido; estar sobre sí; conservar. 4. (Ant.) Guarnecer, adornar vestidos. 5. Guardarse, ponerse en estado de defensa.

Guard, *s.* 1. Guarda, guardia; protección, custodia o defensa; reunión de gente para custodiar o defender algo o a alguien. 2. Precaución, prevención, cautela. 3. Posición o estado de defensa. 4. Guarnición de un vestido o de una espada; guarda, un expediente o medio cualquiera que sirve de protección o seguridad; v. g. *Dust-guard*, Guardapolvo. *Watch-guard*, Cordón para afianzar un reloj de bolsillo. 5. Conductor de ferrocarril o mayoral de diligencia. *To be on one's guard*, Estar sobre sí; guardarse. *To be off one's guard*, Estar desprevenido. *To mount guard*, Montar la guardia. *To relieve the guard*, Relevar la guardia. *To come off guard*, Salir de guardia. *Advanced guard*, Guardia avanzada. *Rear-guard*, Retaguardia. *Van-guard*, Vanguardia. *On guard*, Alerta. *Guard-chamber*, *V.* GUARD-ROOM. *Guard-rail*, (F. C.) Contracarril. (Mar.) Barandilla. *Guard-room*, (1) Cuarto de guardia. (2) Calabozo. *Guard-ship*, Navío de guardia, de ronda o de estación; buque de guerra puesto en un puerto para su defensa.

Guardable [gārd'-a-bl], *a.* Capaz de ser guardado.

Guardedly [gārd'-ed-li], *adv.* Cautelosamente.

Guardedness [gārd'-ed-nes], *s.* Cautela, precaución.

Guardian [gārd'-i-an], *s.* 1. Guardián, el que guarda o cuida de alguna cosa. 2. Tutor o curador, la persona destinada a cuidar de la educación y administración de los bienes de otra. 3. Guardián, el prelado ordinario de los conventos de San Francisco.—*a.* 1. Lo que guarda. 2. Tutelar, lo que ampara o protege.

Guardianship [gārd'-i-an-ship], *s.* 1. Tutela, curaduría; de aquí, protección, amparo, guarda. 2. Guardianía.

Guardless [gārd'-les], *a.* Desamparado, sin amparo ni defensa.

Guardsman [gārdz'-man], *s.* Centinela, oficial de guardia.

Guava [guā'-va], *s.* Guayabo, árbol; guayaba, su fruto. Psidium guaiava. *Guava-tree*, Guayabo.

Gubernatorial [giū-bẹr-na-tō'-ri-al], *a.* (E. U.) Relativo a un gobernador o a la dignidad de gobernador.

Gudgeon [guj'-un], *s.* 1. Gobio, pez pequeño de río que se deja coger fácilmente. 2. Bobo, el que fácilmente se deja engañar; ganso, zote. (Cuba) Guanajo. 3. Algo que se puede obtener sin esfuerzo. *To swallow a gudgeon*, Tragar una píldora, tener buenas tragaderas.

Gudgeon, *s.* (Mec.) 1. Perno, luchadero o cuello de eje. 2. Pezón metálico en un eje de madera. 3. Cojinete de un eje; gorrón; pernete; (Mar.) hembra (del timón).

Guelder-rose [gel'-dẹr-rōz], *s.* (Bot.) Viburno.

Guelf, Guelph [gwelf], *s.* Güelfo, partidario de los papas contra los emperadores de Alemania, en la edad media. Su adjetivo es *Guelfic* o *Guelphic.*

Guerdon [gūr'-dun], *s.* Recompensa, premio, galardón.

Guernsey [gẹrn'-zi], *s.* Res de una casta de ganado vacuno de la isla de Guernsey, en el canal de la Mancha.

Guerrilla [ge-ri'-la], *s.* Guerrillero. *Guerrilla warfare*, Guerra de guerrillas.

Guess [ges], *va.* y *vn.* 1. Conjeturar, suponer, aventurar una suposición acerca de alguna cosa. 2. Adivinar, acertar, descubrir lo oculto, atinar. 3. (Fam.) Pensar, juzgar, imaginar, creer. *You may guess the rest*, Puede Vd. imaginarse lo demás.

Guess, *s.* Conjetura; adivinación; suposición, sospecha.

Guesser [ges'-ẹr], *s.* Conjeturador, adivinador.

Guessingly [ges'-ing-li], *adv.* Conjeturalmente, por conjetura y sin certeza.

Guesswork [ges'-wūrk], *s.* Conjetura, el acto y efecto de conjeturar; casualidad, obra hecha al acaso o por mera conjetura. *It is mere guess-work*, No es más que una conjetura.

Guest [gest], *s.* 1. Huésped, convidado; forastero, visita. 2. Pensionista o inquilino. 3. Animal parásito.

Guest-chamber [gest'-chêm-bẹr], *s.* Alcoba destinada a los huéspedes de la casa.

Guestrope [gest'-rōp], *s.* (Mar.) Guía de falsa amarra.

Guffaw [guf-fō'], *s.* Carcajada, risotada. (Imitativo.)

Guhr [gūr], *s.* (Geol.) Depósito de marga, ordinariamente calcárea, que deja el agua en el hueco de los peñascos. (Al.)

Guidable [gaid'-a-bl], *a.* Manejable.

Guidance [gaid'-ans], *s.* Gobierno, dirección, conducta; la acción y efecto de guiar, de dirigir, de gobernar.

Guidance beam [gaid'-ẹns bīm], *s.* (Aer.) Rayo electrónico orientador.

Guide [gaid], *va.* Guiar, dirigir, arreglar, gobernar; influir, ajustar, poner en orden. *Guide-book*, Guía del viajero, libro con informes sobre todo aquello de más importancia o interés para el que visita una ciudad o un país extranjero.

Guide, *s.* Guía, director, conductor.

Guide-board [gaid'-bōrd], *s.* Tabla de guía en los caminos. *V.* GUIDE-POST.

Guided missile [gai'-ded mis'-il], *s.* Proyectil dirigido.

Guideless [gaid'-les], *a.* Sin guía ni director; sin gobierno.

Guide-post [gaid'-pōst], *s.* Hito, el poste de piedra o palo que hay donde se cruzan los caminos, con inscripciones para servir de guía a los caminantes.

Guidon [gai'-dẹn], *s.* Guión, banderola de guía de los regimientos de caballería o de artillería montada; y el oficial que lo lleva. (Fr.)

Guild [gild], *s.* 1. Gremio, cuerpo, comunidad, hermandad, corporación. 2. Hermandad, sociedad organizada para ayudar en el trabajo de una iglesia o feligresía. *V.* GILD.

Guilder [gild'-ẹr], *s.* Florín, unidad monetaria en Holanda; equivale a 40.2 centavos o 20 peniques. *Cf.* GULDEN.

Guildhall [gild'-hōl], *s.* Casa consistorial, casa de ayuntamiento.

Guile [gail], *s.* Dolo, engaño, fraude, supercheria; de aquí, estratagema, chasco.

Guileful [gail'-ful], *a.* Insidioso, traidor, aleve, engañoso, impostor.—*s.* Traidor, malsín.

Guilefully [gail'-ful-i], *adv.* Insidiosamente, alevosamente, engañosamente.

Guileless [gail'-les], *a.* Sencillo, franco, sincero; sin dolo ni doblez.

Guilelessness [gail'-les-nes], *s.* Inocencia, franqueza, sencillez, sinceridad.

Guilloche [gi-lōsh'], *s.* Guilloquis, adorno compuesto de franjas que se cruzan simétricamente.

Guillotine [gil'-o-tīn], *s.* 1. Guillotina. 2. Una forma de máquina para cortar papel. 3. Instrumento quirúrgico para cortar las amígdalas.

Guillotine [gil-o-tīn'], *va.* Degollar, guillotinar.

Guilt [gilt], *s.* Delito, transgresión, culpa, crimen, falta; en teología, estado de condenación; maldad.

Guiltily [gilt'-i-li], *adv.* Criminalmente.

Guiltiness [gilt'-i-nes], *s.* Criminalidad, maldad, ruindad, malicia.

Guiltless [gilt'-les], *a.* 1. Inocente, libre de culpa; puro, sin tacha. 2. Nesciente, inexperimentado; extraño a, virgen de. *Guiltless of the alphabet*, Nesciente del abecedario *The teeming earth yet guiltless of the plough*, La tierra fecunda aun virgen del arado.

Guiltlessly [gilt'-les-li], *adv.* Inocentemente.

Guiltlessness [gilt'-les-nes], *s.* Inocencia, inculpabilidad.

Guilty [gilt'-i], *a.* 1. Reo, culpable, delincuente, malvado, vicioso, perverso. 2. (Ant.) Reo, sujeto a la pena (con la preposición *of* antes de pena). *Guilty of death*, Reo de muerte. *To plead guilty*, Confesarse culpable. *To be found guilty*, Ser uno declarado reo del delito de que se acusa.

Guimpe [gañp o gimp], *s.* Camisolín de mujer, que se usa con vestido descotado. (Fr.)

Guinea [gin'-i], *s.* 1. Guinea, unidad

monetaria y antigua moneda inglesa, que vale poco más de cinco pesos fuertes o 25 pesetas y 45 céntimos. 2. *n. pr.* Guinea, región de África.
Guinea, en composición: *Guinea-fowl,* Gallina de Guinea, pintada. *Guinea-hen,* (1) Pintada. (2) (Bot.) Fritilaria. *Guinea-pig,* Conejillo de Indias; cobayo; (Cuba) curiel.
Guinea-pepper [gin'-i-pep'-ęr], *s.* (Bot.) Pimiento de Guinea.
Guise [gaiz], *s.* 1. Modo, manera, modales. 2. Continente, apariencia exterior, ya sea en el porte ya en el traje. 3. Práctica, costumbre. 4. Máscara, capa, color, pretexto. *Under the guise of religion,* Socolor, bajo capa, con la máscara de religión. *In this guise,* De este modo, bajo esta apariencia.
Guitar [gi-tār'], *s.* Guitarra, instrumento músico de seis cuerdas, que se pulsan con los dedos.
Gulch [gulch], *s.* (Amer.) Quebrada, rambla; valle estrecho y peñascoso.
Gules [giūlz], *s.* (Her.) Gules, el color rojo.
Gulf [gulf], *s.* 1. Golfo, brazo de mar que avanza dentro de tierra. 2. Golfo, abismo, vorágine. 3. Olla, remolino de agua. 4. Sima, concavidad profunda. 5. Cualquier cosa insaciable.
Gulf Stream. Gran corriente del Océano Atlántico que lleva sus aguas desde el Golfo de Méjico a lo largo de las costas de los Estados Unidos y después con dirección a la Gran Bretaña y la costa escandinava.
Gulf-weed [gulf'-wīd], *s.* Sargazo, gran alga marina de color aceitunado, provista de vejiguillas axilares llenas de aire. Sargassum bacciferum.
Gull [gul], *va.* Engañar, defraudar; estafar, sisar.
Gull, *s.* 1. (Orn.) Gaviota. 2. Engaño, fraude, petardo, estafa. 3. El que es bobo, de poca capacidad o que con facilidad se deja engañar.
Gull-catcher [gul'-cach-ęr], *s.* Engañador, petardista, impostor.
Gullery [gul'-ęr-i], *s.* Engaño, petardo, fraude, impostura.
Gullet [gul'-et], *s.* 1. Gaznate, tragadero, gola. (Anat.) Esófago. 2. Zanja, trinchera profunda. *V.* GULLY y GUSSET.
Gullibility [gul-i-bil'-i-ti], *s.* Tragadero, tragaderas, credulidad.
Gullible [gul'-i-bl], *a.* Bobo, simple, crédulo, que se deja engañar fácilmente.
Gully [gul'-i], *va.* Acanalar por la acción del agua corriente; cavar canalizas.
Gully, *s.* Rambla, excavación causada por las aguas fluviales; barranca, hondonada; zanja honda.
Gully-hole [gul'-i-hōl], *s.* Sumidero, albañal.
Gulp [gulp], *va.* Engullir, tragar con gula. Se usa frecuentemente con *down.* *To gulp up,* Vomitar, vaciar.
Gulp, *s.* Trago.
Gum [gum], *s.* 1. Goma. 2. Encía, la carne que cubre la quijada y guarnece la dentadura. *Gum-drop,* Pastilla de goma. *Gum-elastic,* Goma elástica, caucho. *Gum lac,* Goma laca. *Resin.* Gomorresina. *Gum-tree,* Cualquier árbol de las diferentes especies que producen goma en los Estados Unidos y en Australia; particularmente la nisa o el tupelo y los numerosos eucaliptos. *Gum-water,* Agua de goma, goma arábiga disuelta en agua.
Gum, *va.* Engomar, untar o unir con goma.
Gum arabic [gum ar'-a-bic], *s.* Goma arábiga.
Gumbo [gum'-bō], *s.* 1. Quingombó, quimbombó, hibisco comestible. *V.* OKRA. Abelmoschus esculentus. 2. Sopa de quingombó o guisado hecho con él. 3. Dialecto criollo en Luisiana.
Gum-boil [gum'-beil], *s.* Flemón, tumor en las encías.
Gumminess [gum'-i-nes], *s.* Gomosidad.
Gummy [gum'-i], **Gummous** [gum'-us], *a.* 1. Gomoso, pegajoso, que se parece a la goma. 2. Engomado, cubierto de goma.
Gump [gump], *s.* (Fam.) Páparo, simplón.
Gumption [gump'-shun], *s.* (Fam.) Conocimiento, habilidad.
Gun [gun], *s.* 1. Arma o boca de fuego, como escopeta, fusil, pistola, etc. 2. Cañón, pieza de artillería. *Air-gun,* Escopeta de viento. *Blow-gun,* Cerbatana; pucuna (de los peruanos). *Breech-loading gun,* Cañón, escopeta o rifle de retrocarga. *Double-barrelled gun,* Escopeta de dos cañones. *Field gun,* Pieza de campaña. *Gatling gun,* Ametralladora de Gatling. *Great gun,* (1) Cañón grueso. (2) (Fam.) Persona de consecuencia. *Great guns!* Exclamación de sorpresa, como ¡Canario! ¡Atiza! *Swivel gun,* Colisa, pedrero. *To spike a gun,* Clavar un cañón. *Gun-barrel,* Cañón de fusil. *Gun-carriage,* Afuste, cureña de cañón. *Gun-deck,* Cubierta principal, batería. *Gun-room,* (Mar.) Santa Bárbara, polvorín. *Gun-stock,* Caja de escopeta.
Gunboat [gun'-bōt], *s.* Cañonero, buque de guerra pequeño y de poco calado, con cañones de grueso calibre. Antes se daba este nombre a la cañonera, barco pequeño o lancha con un solo cañón.
Gun cotton [gun cot'-n], *s.* Piroxilina, pólvora de algodón.
Gun metal [gun met'-al], *s.* 1. Metal para artillería. 2. Antiguo bronce de cañones. 3. Metal pavonado. 4. Color gris-pardo.
Gunner [gun'-ęr], *s.* 1. (Mar.) Condestable; artillero de un navío. 2. Escopetero, el que está armado con escopeta.
Gunner's mate [gun'-ęrz-mēt], *s.* (Mar.) Artillero de segunda clase.
Gunnery [gun'-ęr-i], *s.* Artillería.
Gunny sack [gun'-i sac], *s.* 1. Saco de yute. 2. (fig.) Traje estrecho y simple como un saco.
Gunport-bars [gun'-pōrt-bārz], *s. pl.* (Mar.) Barras de portería.
Gunports [gun'-pōrts], *s. pl.* (Mar.) Portas, las ventanas del navío donde se pone la artillería.
Gunpowder [gun'-pau-dęr], *s.* Pólvora.
Gunshot [gun'-shet], *s.* 1. Tiro de escopeta, cañón u otra arma de fuego. 2. Tiro, la distancia a que alcanzan las armas disparadas. *Within gunshot,* A tiro, al alcance de fusil.
Gunsmith [gun'-smith], *s.* Armero, arcabucero.
Gunstick [gun'-stic], *s.* Atacador, baqueta.
Gunter [gun'-tęr], *n. pr.* Edmund Gunter, matemático e inventor inglés. *Gunter's chain,* Cadena de Gunter, la ordinaria de agrimensor: tiene 66 pies de largo, ó 20.1165 metros y está dividida en 100 eslabones. *According to Gunter,* Según Gunter, es decir, de exactitud garantizada.
Gunwale [gun'-wēl, náu. gun'-el], *s.* Regala de la borda del combés, hilada de tablones que cubre las cabezas de los barraganetes entre los saltillos.
Gurgitation [gūr'-ji-tē'-shun], *s.* El movimiento de un líquido en una vorágine ó en estado de ebullición; borbollón, borbotón.
Gurgle [gūr'-gl], *vn.* Manar o fluir haciendo un ruido semejante al que hace el agua que sale de una botella; o murmurar como un arroyuelo en un lecho pedregoso.—*s.* Salida de un líquido con dicho ruido; murmullo. *Death gurgle,* Estertor.
Gurnard [gūr'-nard], **Gurnet** [gūr'-net], *s.* (Ict.) Trigla, golondrina.
Gush [gush], *va.* Derramar con abundancia.—*vn.* 1. Brotar, fluir o manar con violencia; chorrear, fluir copiosamente. 2. Hacer demostraciones extravagantes de afecto o sentimiento.
Gush, *s.* 1. Chorro, derrame repentino e impetuoso de un líquido. 2. Efusión, manifestación extravagante de sentimiento.
Gusher [gush'-ęr], *s.* Géiser, pozo brotante de petróleo.
Gusset [gus'-et], *s.* 1. Escudete, pedazo de tela de forma triangular que se añade a una prenda de vestir para ensancharla o hacerla más resistente. 2. Codo de hierro, hierro angular.
Gust [gust], *s.* 1. Gusto, el sentido del paladar. 2. Deleite. 3. Inclinación, afición, amor. 4. Soplo fuerte o bocanada de aire. 5. Transporte, acceso de pasión. 6. Gusto, elección, discernimiento.
Gustation [gus-tē'-shun], *s.* Gustación, la acción y efecto de gustar.
Gustatory, Gustative [gus'-ta-to-ri, tiv], *a.* Gustable, que pertenece al gusto, que sirve para gustar.
Gusto [gus'-tō], *s.* Sabor, gusto, afición, placer.
Gusty [gust'-i], *a.* Borrascoso, tempestuoso.
Gut [gut], *s.* 1. Intestino: no se emplea entre personas bien habladas. 2. *pl.* (Vulg.) Estómago, el receptáculo de los alimentos; gula, glotonería. 3. Un paso estrecho. 4. Cuerda de tripa, sea de un animal, sea fibra de un gusano de seda cuando está a punto de hilar su capullo. La fibra del gusano de seda se emplea en la pesca y en cirugía.
Gut, *va.* 1. Desventrar, destripar. 2. Desentrañar, sacar lo interior de alguna cosa.
Gutta-percha [gut'-a-pęr'-cha], *s.* Gutapercha, goma pardo rojiza, sólida, que se ablanda por medio del calor, y se obtiene por la evaporación del jugo de un árbol del archipiélago malayo y de la India.
Gutter [gut'-ęr], *s.* 1. Canalón, gotera; canal hecho por el agua o para que corra ésta. 2. Alcantarilla, cloaca para el desagüe; arroyo de calle. 3. Estría, canal de ebanistería. 4. Zanja, acequia.
Gutter, *va.*—Acanalar, estriar.—*vn.* Caer en gotas.
Guttural [gut'-ęr-al], *a.* 1. Gutural, perteneciente a la garganta. 2. Gutural, lo que se pronuncia o es fuerza con la garganta.

Guy[1] [gai], *s.* (Mar.) Retenida, el cabo que sirve para detener cualquiera cosa pesada, a fin de que no golpee en el costado u otra parte del buque.

Guy[2] [gai], *s.* 1. (Ingl.) Efigie de Guy Fawkes, jefe de la conspiración de la pólvora (5 Nov., 1605). 2. De aquí, persona mal vestida ó de apariencia grotesca.

Guy, *va.* 1. (Mar.) Sujetar ó asegurar con una retenida. 2. (Fam. E. U.) Burlarse, mofarse de alguien.

Guzzle [guz'-l], *va.* y *vn.* 1. Beber mucho o repetidas veces. 2. Tragar vorazmente.—*vn.* Emborracharse.

Guzzler, *s.* Bebedor, discípulo de Baco; borracho; pellejo de vino.

Gym [jim], *s.* V. GYMNASTICS.

Gymnasium [jim-né'-zhi-um], *s.* 1. Gimnasio, edificio o cuarto donde se ejercitan y desarrollan las fuerzas físicas. 2. Liceo, escuela de latín o clásica, en oposición a una puramente técnica. 3. Gimnasio, edificio descubierto en que la juventud griega ejercitaba sus fuerzas.

Gymnast [jim'-nast], *s.* Gimnasta, el que es hábil en los ejercicios gimnásticos; atleta.

Gymnastic, Gymnastical [jim-nas'-tic, al], *a.* Gimnástico, gímnico.

Gymnastics [jim-nas'-tics], *s. pl.* Gimnasia, calisténica.

Gymnosophist [jim-nes'-o-fist], *s.* Gimnosofista, nombre de los brahmanes y alguna de sus sectas.

Gymnosperm [jim'-no-sperm], *s.* Planta gimnosperma, que tiene las semillas o gérmenes desnudos.

Gymnospermous [jim-no-sper'-mus], *a.* (Bot.) Gimnospermo o que tiene la semilla desnuda.

Gynarchy [jin'-ar-ki], **Gynæcocracy** [jin-i-ec'-ra-si], *s.* Ginecocracia, gobierno mujeril.

Gynecologist [jin-e-col'-o-jist], *s.* Ginecólogo, persona versada en la ginecología.

Gynecology [jin-e-col'-o-ji], *s.* Ginecología, la ciencia de las funciones y enfermedades propias de la mujer.

Gypseous [jip'-se-us], **Gypsine** [jip'-sin], *a.* Gipsoso o yesoso.

Gypsum [jip'-sum], *s.* Yeso, sulfato de cal, aljez.

Gypsy [jip'-si], *s.* *V.* GIPSY.

Gyral [jai'-ral], *a.* 1. Giratorio, que da vueltas o se mueve circularmente. 2. (Anat.) Que se refiere a las circunvoluciones del cerebro.

Gyrate [jai'-rét], *vn.* Girar, dar vueltas sobre un eje de rotación; revolver, ejecutar una revolución, particularmente en espiral o hélice.

Gyration [jai-ré'-shun], *s.* La acción y efecto de girar, giro; rotación.

Gyratory [jai'-ra-to-ri], *a.* Giratorio, que gira alrededor.

Gyre [jair], *s.* Giro, girada.

Gyrocompass [jai'-ro-cum'-pas], *s.* Brújula giroscópica.

Gyromancy [jai'-ro-man-si], *s.* Giromancia, adivinación por medio del giro constante de una persona dentro de un círculo.

Gyroscope [jai'-ros-cōp], *s.* (Fís.) Giróscopo o giroscopio.

Gyrostatics [jai-ro-stat'-ics], *s.* Girostática, conjunto de leyes que gobiernan la rotación de los cuerpos sólidos.

Gyve [jaiv], *va.* Encadenar, aprisionar con grillos.

Gyves [jaivz], *s. pl.* Grillos, prisión con que aseguran a los reos en la cárcel.

H

H [éch]. Esta letra tiene casi el sonido gutural de una J en español, aunque más suave, excepto en algunas voces en que es muda, como *hour, heir, honest,* etc.

Ha [hā], *inter.* 1. Ah, interjección que sirve para expresar diversos afectos. 2. Expresión que repetida denota risa: ¡Já, já, já! 3. Exclamación que indica duda, indecisión.

Ha, *vn.* *V.* HAW.

Habeas corpus [hé'-bi-as cōr'-pus], *s.* Habeas corpus. (For.) Fuero particular de las leyes inglesas y americanas, por el cual la persona que ha sido presa ocurre a otro juez o tribunal para que, avocando a sí la causa, haga comparecer al preso y declare si ha habido motivo o razón legal para prenderle.

Haberdasher [hab'-er-dash-er], *s.* 1. Tendero vendedor de artículos para caballeros: camisas, puños, cuellos, corbatas, bastones, gemelos, etc. 2. Mercero, el tendero que vende cintas, cofias y otros géneros de poco valor.

Haberdashery [hab'-er-dash-er-i], *s.* 1. Mercería, pasamanería; objetos pequeños. 2. Tienda de efectos para caballeros.

Habergeon [hab'-er-jen ó ha-ber'-jen], *s.* Coraza pequeña.

Habiliment [ha-bil'-i-ment], *s.* Prenda de vestir, parte del vestido o traje; en plural, vestido, traje, vestidura.

Habilitate [ha-bil'-i-tét], *va.* (E. U.) Pertrechar, habilitar, v. g. para la explotación de una mina.—*vn.* Hacerse apto o idóneo para alguna cosa.

Habit [hab'-it], *s.* 1. Hábito, uso, costumbre. 2. Estado o disposición de alguna cosa; constitución, complexión o disposición particular de alguna persona. 3. Hábito, vestido, traje exterior. 4. En botánica, geología y mineralogía, modo característico del crecimiento o de otras modificaciones físicas. *Riding habit,* Traje de montar. *To get in the habit,* (Fam.) Dar en la flor, tomar el tema, tomar la costumbre.

Habit, *va.* Ataviar, adornar, vestir.

Habitable [hab'-it-a-bl], *a.* Habitable, que puede ser habitado.

Habitableness [hab'-it-a-bl-nes], *s.* La posibilidad de ser habitado.

Habitant [hab'-it-ant], *s.* Habitante, morador.

Habitat [hab'-i-tat], *s.* Habitación; en lenguaje científico se llama así al terreno o a la región donde se hallan o crecen naturalmente los individuos de una especie, animal o vegetal. (Lat.)

Habitation [hab-i-té'-shun], *s.* Habitación, el lugar o casa donde se mora o vive; domicilio, morada.

Habited [hab'-it-ed], *a.* 1. Vestido, ataviado. 2. (Ant.) Habitado. 3. (Des.) Usual, acostumbrado.

Habitual [ha-bit'-yu-al], *a.* Habitual, lo que se hace, se padece o se posee con continuación y por hábito.

Habitually [ha-bit'-yu-al-i], *adv.* Habitualmente.

Habituate [ha-bit'-yu-ét], *va.* y *vn.* Habituar; habituarse, acostumbrarse a alguna cosa.

Habituate, *a.* (Poco us.) Obstinado, inveterado.

Habitude [hab'-i-tiūd], *s.* Familiaridad, costumbre; trato o amistad en alguna casa o con alguna persona.

Habitué [ha-bi'-chiū-é], *s.* Parroquiano, cliente habitual.

Hack [hac], *s.* 1. Caballo de alquiler, rocín, cuartago; alquilón. 2. (E. U.) Un simón o coche de alquiler. 3. Peón, trabajador; (fig.) escritor mercenario. 4. Pico, especie de azadón; azuela. 5. Muesca, corte, cuchillada, golpe con un instrumento cortante. 6. (Fam.) Tos corta y seca. *Hackman,* Simón, cochero de alquiler.

Hack, *va.* 1. Tajar, cortar, dividir una cosa en muchos pedazos pequeños, picar irregularmente. 2. Allanar piedras, picarlas como las amoladeras. 3. Hacer muescas, mellar. —*vn.* 1. Cortar, tajar irregularmente, repetidas veces o sin destreza. 2. Emitir una tos corta y seca. 3. Alquilarse, venderse, prostituirse; trabajar como escritor mercenario.

Hackle [hac'-l], *va.* 1. Rastrillar. *V.* HATCHEL. 2. Hacer pedazos una cosa.

Hackle, *s.* 1. Rastrillo. 2. Fibra no hilada, como la seda en rama. 3. Mosca para pescar.

Hackmatack [hac'-ma-tac''], *s.* El alerce o lárice americano. (Nombre indio.) *V.* TAMARACK.

Hackney [hac'-ni], *s.* 1. Caballo de alquiler. 2. Rocín; cuartago; caballo pequeño que tiene buen paso. 3. Alquilón, lo que se alquila.—*a.* Alquilado; común; prostituído; cansado, gastado. *Hackney-coach,* Coche de alquiler o simón. *Hackney writer,* Escritor mercenario. *Hackney coachman,* Cochero de alquiler o simón.

Hackney, *va.* 1. Ejercitar, usar una cosa con continuación; vulgarizar una cosa, hacerla trivial y manoseada. 2. Llevar en coche de alquiler. *A hackneyed subject,* Un asunto trillado, manoseado.

Hack saw [hac sē], *s.* Sierra de arco para trabajo de metales.

Hacqueton [hak'-e-ton], *s.* Especie de jubón antiguo.

Had [had], *pret.* del verbo *To* HAVE; se usa como auxiliar, equivalente a había o hubo.

Haddock [had'-ec], *s.* Merluza, pescado de la familia de los gádidos.

Hade [héd], *s.* (Min.) Descenso escarpado en una mina.

Hades [hé'-dīz], *s.* 1. Hades, voz tomada del griego que significa el estado y la morada de las almas de los muertos; también, los infiernos. 2. Plutón, Orcus o Dis, el señor del mundo inferior; el mundo inferior mismo.

Haet [hét], *s.* (Esco.) Jota, tilde, punto. *V.* WHIT.

Haft [haft], *s.* Mango, asa, agarradera; puño o guarnición de arma blanca.

Hag [hag], *s.* Vejancona, vejarrona fea; bruja, hechicera.

Hag, *va.* Aterrar, infundir terror y espanto. *Hag-born,* Nacido de bruja. *Hag-ridden,* Cabalgado por brujas; de aquí, bajo el influjo de una pesadilla.

Haggard [hag'-ard], *a.* 1. Consumido, desfigurado, flaco o macilento de aspecto; lleno de zozobra. 2. Zahareño, montaraz, intratable.—*s.* 1. Halcón, en especial, en cetrería, el halcón cogido cuando tiene ya todo su plumaje. 2. Fiera, el que es indómito o feroz. 3. (Esco.) Corral de niara; granero.

Haggardly [hag'-ard-li], *adv.* Fieramente; feamente.
Haggish [hag'-ish], *a.* Feo, horroroso.
Haggle [hag'-l], *va.* Tajar, cortar en tajadas.—*vn.* Regatear, porfiar sobre el precio de alguna cosa.
Haggler [hag'-lęr], *s.* 1. Tajador. 2. Regatón, regatero, el que regatea mucho.
Hagiographal [hê-ji-eg'-ra-fal], *a.* Hagiógrafo, que pertenece a los libros o escritores hagiógrafos.
Hagiographer [hê-ji-eg'-ra-fęr], *s.* Hagiógrafo, autor que trata de los santos o de las cosas sagradas.
Hah [hā], *inter.* *V.* HA.
Ha-ha [hā'-hā], *s.* Cerca hundida; foso con escarpa.
Hail [hêl], *s.* 1. Granizo, la lluvia congelada en el aire. 2. Saludo; grito para llamar la atención.—*inter.* ¡Salve, Dios te guarde! ¡Salud!
Hail, *va.* y *vn.* 1. Granizar, arrojar las nubes granizo. 2. Saludar, hablar a otro cortésmente, llamar a. 3. Recibir, celebrar con aclamaciones. *To hail a ship,* (Mar.) Saludar a la voz, venir a voz. 4. *V.* POUR.
Hail-fellow [hêl'-fel-o], *s.* Compañero.
Hailshot [hêl'-shet], *s.* Perdigones, munición menuda.
Hailstone [hêl'-stōn], *s.* Piedra de granizo.
Hailstorm [hêl'-stērm], *s.* Granizada.
Haily [hêl'-i], *a.* Granujado, lleno de granizo.
Hair [hār], *s.* 1. Pelo, la hebra o hilo delgado que sale de los poros del cuerpo animal; dícese también del vello que cubre ciertas partes del cuerpo humano. 2. (Biol.) Filamentos del cuerpo y de las plantas. 3. Cabello, cabellera, pelo de la cabeza y de la cara. *Against the hair,* Á contrapelo; de mala gana. *False hair,* Pelo postizo. *Hair of the head,* Cabellos. *To a hair,* Exactamente, perfectamente. *A fine head of hair,* Una cabellera hermosa. *Horse-hair,* Crin. *To dress one's hair,* Peinarse. *Hair-button,* Botón de crin. *Hair-broom,* Escoba de cerdas o crines. *Hair-brush,* Cepillo, escobilla, para limpiar el cabello. *Hair-cloth,* (1) Cilicio. (2) Esterilla de cerda para sillas. *Hair-dresser,* Peluquero, peinador. *Hair-dye,* Tinte para el pelo. *Hair-lace,* Cinta o venda para atar el pelo. *Hair-sieve,* Tamiz de cerda para colar. *Hair-splitting,* Quisquilla, distinción de poco momento.—*a.* Quisquilloso, que se para en quisquillas. *Hair-spring,* Pelo, muelle (de reloj) muy fino en espiral.
Hairbreadth [hār'-bredth], *s.* Lo ancho de un pelo; poca cosa, casi nada, el negro de una uña. *To have a hairbreadth escape,* Librarse de buena, salir de un apuro.
Haircut [hār'-cut], *s.* Corte de pelo.
Hairdressing [hār-dres'-ing], *s.* Peinados, peluquería, arte de peinar.
Haired [hārd], *a.* Peludo, cabelludo. *Black-haired,* Pelinegro. *Curly-haired,* Que tiene el pelo rizado o encrespado. *Grey-haired,* Canoso.
Hairhung [hār'-hung], *a.* Suspendido de un cabello.
Hairiness [hār'-i-nes], *s.* Calidad y estado de peludo o peloso.
Hairless [hār'-les], *a.* Pelado, pelón, calvo.
Hair net [hār net], *s.* Redecilla para el cabello.
Hairpin [hār'-pin], *s.* Horquilla, alfiler grande que usan las mujeres para sujetar el cabello.
Hairy [hār'-i], *a.* Peludo, velludo, velloso, cabelludo, cubierto de pelo. *Hairy comet,* Cometa crinito.
Haitian [hê'-ti-an ó hai'-ti-an], *a.* *V.* HAYTIAN.
Hake [hêc], *s.* Merlango, pescado de la familia de los gádidos, semejante a la merluza.
Halberd [hal'-bęrd], *s.* Alabarda.
Halcyon [hal'-si-ęn], *a.* Quieto, apacible, tranquilo, sereno, pacífico. *Halcyon days,* Tiempo de paz y tranquilidad; veranillo de San Martín. —*s.* (Orn.) Alcedón, alción.
Hale [hęl], *a.* Sano, robusto, fuerte, vigoroso; entero, ileso.
Hale, *va.* Tirar a sí con violencia: arrastrar, llevar a uno violentamente de una parte a otra.
Half [hāf], *s.* (*pl.* HALVES). Mitad, la parte media de un todo.—*a.* 1. Medio, lo que no está perfectamente concluído o es la mitad de una cosa. 2. Medio, formado por una mitad. *Half an hour,* Media hora. *Half and half,* Mitad de uno y mitad de otro; mezcla de cervezas u otros licores. *Half-seas over,* Medio borracho, el que está calamocano. *Half* en composición significa semi, casi, cerca de o un poco.
Halfback [hāf'-bak], *s.* Medio (en el juego de futbol).
Half-baked [hāf'-bêkt], *a.* 1. A medio asar. 2. (vul.) Inmaturo, inexperto.
Half-blood [hāf'-blud], *s.* Medio hermano, media hermana.
Half-breed [hāf'-brîd], *a.* y *s.* Mestizo, de sangre mezclada, cualquiera que sea la mezcla.
Half-calf binding [hāf'-cāf' baind'-ing], *s.* Encuadernación a media pasta vitela.
Half-caste [hāf'-cąst], *a.* Mestizo, de sangre mezclada, en especial cuando el padre o la madre es de raza blanca.
Half-cock, *a.* En seguro; dícese de un arma de fuego á medio amartillar.
Half-crown [hāf'-craun], *s.* Moneda inglesa de plata del valor de dos chelines y medio o unos sesenta centavos.
Half-hearted [hāf-hārt'-ed], *a.* Sin ánimo, indiferente.
Half holiday [hāf hel'-i-dê], *s.* Medio día de fiesta.
Half life [haf' laif], *s.* Vida media, período medio.
Half-mast [hāf'-mąst], *s.* A media asta, posición de una bandera en el palo en señal de duelo.—*va.* Poner a media asta.
Half-moon [hāf'-mūn], *s.* Semilunio; lo que tiene figura de media luna.
Halfpenny [hāf'-pen-i, vul. hê'-pen'-i], *s.* (*pl.* HALFPENCE [pens] o HALFPENNIES). Medio penique, moneda de cobre en Inglaterra.
Half-tone [hāf'-tōn], *a.* Perteneciente o relativo a un procedimiento fotográfico para la obtención de láminas o ilustraciones de los textos. Se usa principalmente para la reproducción directa de cuadros o fotografías.—*s.* 1. Lámina obtenida por este procedimiento. 2. (Mús.) Semitono.
Halibut [hel'-i-but], *s.* Mero, hipogloso, pez de los mares septentrionales, perteneciente a la familia de los pleuronéctidos.
Halitosis [hal-i-tō'-sis], *s.* Mal aliento.
Hall [hōl], *s.* 1. Vestíbulo, zaguán; corredor. 2. Salón grande a la entrada de algunas casas; antecámara. 3. Sala, el paraje donde se reunen los magistrados de los tribunales superiores para ejercer su ministerio. 4. Casa de ayuntamiento. 5. Casa de un gremio o corporación. 6. Salón, el paraje donde se reunen los diputados del pueblo o los comisionados de un cuerpo para celebrar sus juntas. 7. Colegio en las universidades de Oxford y Cambridge. *Hall-mark,* Sello o marca oficial del Gremio de Orífices y Plateros (Ingl.) que indica la ley de los artículos de oro y plata.
Hallelujah [hal-ę-lū'-ya], *s.* Aleluya, canto en acción de gracias que significa *alabad al Señor.*
Hallo, Halloa [ha-lō'], *inter.* Voz para llamar la atención o para saludar: ¡hola! ¡oye! ¡oiga! ¡eh!
Halloo [ha-lō' o hę-lū'], *inter.* ¡Sus! ¡Busca! Voz con que los cazadores azuzan á los perros.
Halloo, *va.* y *vn.* 1. Gritar a los perros en la caza o azuzarlos con gritos. 2. Gritar a, dar grita, insultar con clamores y gritos. 3. Llamar a uno gritando o a gritos; avisar a uno o darle aviso por medio de un grito.
Hallooing [ha-lū'-ing], *s.* Grito alto y vehemente.
Hallow [hal'-ō], *va.* Consagrar, santificar; reverenciar.
Halloween [hal'-o-wîn'], *s.* Víspera del día de Todos los Santos. Lo celebran principalmente los niños en los E.U. con fiestas de disfraces.
Hallowmas [hal'-o-mąs], *s.* El día de Todos los Santos, y el de la conmemoración de los fieles difuntos, que son el primero y el dos de Noviembre. *Hallow-eve,* La víspera del día de Todos los Santos; muy celebrada entre los irlandeses.
Hallucinate [hal-lū'-si-nêt], *vn.* Alucinarse, confundirse, equivocarse.
Hallucination [hal-lū-si-nê'-shun], *s.* Alucinación, error, equivocación; disparate.
Halma [hal'-ma], *s.* Juego de salón, con tablero y piezas numerosas y en el que toman parte dos, tres o cuatro personas. (Gr. halma < hallomai, saltar.)
Halo [hê'-lō], *s.* 1. Halo o halón, corona, especie de metéoro que consiste en un círculo alrededor del sol y la luna. 2. Lauréola, auréola.
Haloid [hal'-eid], *a.* Haloideo, parecido á la sal marina.—*s.* Sal haloidea.
Halt [hōlt], *vn.* 1. Cojear, andar cojo. 2. Parar, hacer parada o alto en alguna marcha o viaje. 3. Vacilar, dudar, tartamudear.
Halt, *s.* 1. Cojera, el acto de cojear. 2. Parada, alto.—*a.* Encojado, cojo; estropeado, lisiado.
Halter [hōlt'-ęr], *s.* 1. Cabestro, ronzal, ramal, jáquima. 2. Soga, cuerda con que se ahorca á los malhechores. 3. Cojo, el que cojea.
Halter, *va.* 1. Poner el cabestro, echar el ronzal. 2. Encordar.
Haltingly [hōlt'-ing-li], *adv.* A cox cox, a cox cojita, a la pata coja.
Halve [hāv], *va.* Partir en dos mitades.
Halves [hāvz], *inter.* A la parte me llamo: expresión con que alguno

pide parte de lo que otro se ha encontrado o ha ganado.—*pl.* de HALF. *To go halves,* Ir á medias tener una parte igual.

Halyard [hal'-yard], *s.* (Mar.) Driza. *Peak-halyard,* Driza del pico. *Throat-halyards,* Drizas del foque mayor.

Ham [ham], *s.* 1. Pernil, jamón, el anca y muslo del puerco salado. 2. (Anat.) Corva, la parte de la pierna opuesta a la rodilla.—*n. pr.* Cam, hijo de Noé.

Hamate [hê'-mêt], *a.* Enredado, encorvado, ganchoso.

Hamated [hê'-mê-ted], *a.* Garabateado; lo que está afirmado o clavado con ganchos o garabatos.

Hamburger [ham'-bęrg-ęr], *s.* Hamburguesa, emparedado de carne molida.

Hame [hêm], *s.* 1. Horcate, palo que se pone al pescuezo de las caballerías para el tiro. 2. (Esco.) *V.* HOME.

Hamlet [ham'-let], *s.* Aldea, villorrio, población corta, aldehuela.

Hammam [ham'-am], *s.* En Turquía, casa de baño; de aquí, en los países occidentales, baño turco.

Hammer [ham'-ęr], *s.* Martillo, herramienta de percusión, compuesta de una cabeza, por lo común de hierro, y un mango. *Sledge-hammer,* Macho, mazo grande. *Clench-hammer,* Martillo de presa, de oreja. *Claw-hammer,* Martillo con pala hendida, o de orejas. *Drop-hammer,* Martinete. *Paving-hammer,* Pico de cantero. *Peen hammer,* Martillo de boca. *Piano hammer,* Martinete de piano. *Tack-hammer,* Martillo para puntillas. *Tuning-hammer,* Templador de afinador. *Hammer-dressed,* Escuadrado, labrado a escoda.

Hammer, *va.* 1. Martillar, batir y dar golpes con el martillo. 2. Forjar, trabajar alguna cosa a martillo. 3. Forjar, idear, trabajar alguna cosa con el entendimiento. *To hammer one's brains,* Devanarse los sesos.—*vn.* Trabajar, estar ocupado, agitarse, hallarse en agitación.

Hammercloth [ham'-ęr-clōth], *s.* Paño del pescante de un coche.

Hammerer [ham'-ęr-ęr], *s.* Martillador.

Hammerhead [ham'-ęr-hed], *s.* (Zool.) Cornudilla, pez martillo, especie de tiburón.

Hammering [ham'-ęr-ing], *s.* 1. Martilleo; la acción de fraguar; el ruido que hacen los martillazos. 2. Batido a martillo; superficie repujada de un metal.

Hammerman [ham'-ęr-man], *s.* Martillador.

Hammock [ham'-ęc], *s.* Hamaca, red gruesa y clara que sirve de cama o columpio; coy.

Hamper [ham'-pęr], *s.* 1. Cuévano, canasta, cesto grande y hondo que sirve para varios usos. 2. Aparejo, jarcias y motonería a bordo. 3. Traba, impedimento.

Hamper, *va.* 1. Enmarañar, enredar, embarazar, estorbar. 2. Entrampar, persuadir con engaños o añagazas, embobar. 3. Encestar, recoger en una cesta.

Hamstring [ham'-string], *s.* Tendón de la corva.

Hamstring, *va.* Desjarretar, cortar las piernas por el jarrete o por la corva.

Hanaper [han'-a-pęr], *s.* 1. Canasta o cesta para documentos u objetos de valor. 2. Erario, tesorería, una oficina del tribunal inglés de la Cancillería; se llama así porque algunos de sus legajos se guardaron originalmente en una cesta de mimbres.

Hand [hand], *s.* 1. Mano, parte del cuerpo humano que comienza en la muñeca y acaba en las puntas de los dedos. 2. Maña, destreza, habilidad; también obra mecánica o manual, manos. 3. Mano derecha o izquierda, el lado derecho o izquierdo. 4. Operario, operaria, hombre o mujer que hace trabajo manual. 5. Una persona; gente; agente, instrumento; por lo común en plural. *All hands joined in the sport,* Todos se pusieron a divertirse. 6. La mano como prenda de esponsales. 7. Manecilla o aguja de reloj. 8. Disciplina; influencia; poder, posesión. 9. Forma o carácter de escritura. 10. Palmo, medida de cuatro pulgadas. 11. Mano, en el juego. 12. Acción, trabajo, agencia. *Clean hands,* Manos limpias, es decir, honradez en asuntos de interés. *Light hand,* Dulzura, suavidad. *Heavy hand,* Dureza, opresión. *To bear a light* o *heavy hand,* Tratar con dulzura o con dureza. *To bring up by hand,* Dar de mamar artificialmente a un niño o un animalito. *To get one's hand in,* Estar en vena, adquirir habilidad por medio de la práctica. *To get the upper hand,* Llevar la ventaja, ganar la palmeta. *To come to hand,* Estar o hallarse a la mano, ser recibido. *To have a hand in,* Tener parte en, ser interesado o comprometido en. *To lay hands on,* Echar mano (a alguno), acometer; ordenar por medio de la imposición de las manos. *To lend a hand,* Dar una mano, ayudar. *To set the hand to,* Meter mano en, emprender, embarcarse en un negocio. *To stand one in hand,* Concernir, importar a alguno. *To strike hands,* Tocar la mano en señal de cerrar un contrato. *To shake hands,* Apretar la mano (a alguno) en signo de amistad. *To wash one's hands of,* Lavarse las manos, desentenderse, declinar toda responsabilidad. *To change hands,* Cambiar de dueño. *Hands off!* ¡Manos quedas! *To lay violent hands on,* Dar la muerte. *It is allowed on all hands,* Todo el mundo conviene o todos confiesan. *In hand,* De contado, desde luego, por de pronto, hablando de dinero que se recibe. *At hand* o *near at hand,* A la mano, cerca, al lado, junto. *To hold hand,* Competir. *By the hand,* Por medio de. *Under my hand,* Firmado de mi puño y letra. *On the one hand,* Por una parte o por un lado. *I have it from very good hands,* Lo sé de buen origen. *Keep off your hands,* No me toques. *Hand in hand,* De concierto, de acuerdo, de inteligencia. *Short-hand,* Abreviatura, taquigrafía. *Off-hand,* Pronto, sin detenerse. *On hand,* (1) A manos, en poder, en su legítima posesión; surtido. (2) A la mano, en su lugar, presente, puntual. *To buy at first hand,* Comprar de primera mano. *A good hand at cards,* Buen juego, buenas cartas. *They are hand and glove,* Son uña y carne. *Out of hand,* Luego, inmediatamente. *Hand over head,* Inconsideradamente. *Minute hand,* Minutero. *From hand to mouth,* De manos a boca, esto es, sin economía, sin previsión para lo futuro. *First-rate hand,* (hablando de mecánicos) Un buen oficial, un excelente mecánico. *Second-hand clothes,* Ropa usada. *Second-hand clothes shop,* Ropavejería. *Second-hand bookseller,* Librero de viejo, o de libros usados. *An off-hand sketch,* Diseño improvisado. *To be short of hands,* Carecer de brazos, de operarios. *All hands below!* ¡Abajo todo el mundo! *All hands on deck!* ¡Todo el mundo arriba! *Large hand,* Letra grande. *Round hand,* Letra redonda. *To be one's right hand,* Ser la mano derecha de uno.

Hand, *va.* 1. Alargar, alcanzar algo y darlo a otro. 2. Conducir, guiar por la mano. 3. Agarrar, echar la mano. 4. Manejar una cosa o moverla con la mano.—*vn.* Cooperar, concertarse, ir de acuerdo o inteligencia. *To hand down,* (1) Transmitir, pasar sucesivamente de unos á otros. (2) Bajar, entregar a un cuerpo inferior; pasar de arriba a abajo. *To hand in* (o *into*). Dar la mano para entrar; ayudar a entrar en. *To hand round* o *around,* Hacer pasar, hacer circular, pasar de uno a otro. *To hand the sails,* (Mar.) Aferrar las velas.

Handbag [hand'-bag], *s.* Bolsa de mano.

Hand baggage [hand bag'-êj], *s.* Equipaje de mano.

Handball [hand'-bōl], *s.* 1. Pelota de mano. 2. Juego de este nombre. 3. Bola hueca para rociar, etc.

Handbarrow [hand'-bar-ō], *s.* Angarillas, parihuela.

Hand-basket [hand'-bqs-ket], *s.* Cestilla, cesta pequeña.

Handbell [hand'-bel], *s.* Esquila, campanilla.

Handbill [hand'-bil], *s.* Cartel.

Handbook [hand'-buk], *s.* Manual, guía.

Handbow [hand'-bō], *s.* Arco de mano para disparar flechas.

Handbreadth [hand'-bredth], *s.* Palmo, lo ancho de la mano.

†**Handcraft,** *s.* *V.* HANDICRAFT.

Handcuff [hand'-cuf], *s.* Manilla, esposas.

Handcuff, *va.* Maniatar.

Handed [hand'-ed], *a.* 1. Lo que tiene el uso de la mano. 2. (Des.) Con las manos juntas. En composición: *Right-handed,* Que usa habitualmente de la mano derecha. *Left-handed,* Zurdo, que usa con preferencia de la mano izquierda. *V.* también SCREW. *Four-handed,* A cuatro manos. *Empty-handed,* Con las manos vacías. *Hard-handed,* De manos callosas; de mano pesada. *High-handed,* Arbitrario, imperioso. *One-handed,* Manco. *Open-handed,* Generoso, liberal. *Single-handed,* Con una sola mano; por sí solo.

Hander [hand'-ęr], *s.* El que transmite o envía.

†**Handfast,** *va.* 1. Desposar, casar a uno por palabras de presente. 2. Atar, obligar, precisar por deber.

Handful [hand'-ful], *s.* 1. Puñado manojo, una mano llena. 2. (Des.) El ancho de la mano. *Handful of flour,* Puñado de harina. *Handful of people,* Puñado de gente. *Double handful,* Almuerza.

Hand-gallop [hand-gal-up], *s.* Galope fácil ó corto.

Hand grenade [hand grę-nêd'], *s.* Granada de mano.

Hand-gun [hand-gun], *s.* Escopeta de mano.

Hand-glass [hand'-glas], *s.* 1. Espejo de mano. 2. Lente para leer.
Handicap [hand'-i-cap], *va.* Imponer ciertos impedimentos o desventajas para contrapesar determinadas ventajas; de aquí, poner obstáculos, estorbar, detener.—*s.* 1. Condición que se impone para igualar las probabilidades de éxito de los competidores, p. ej. llevar un exceso de peso o empezar una carrera después que los otros contendientes. 2. Carrera con caballos de peso igualado.
Handicraft [hand'-i-crgft], *s.* 1. Oficio, arte mecánica, obra manual. 2. Menestral, mecánico.
Handicraftsman [hand'-i-crgfts-man], *s.* Artesano, menestral, mecánico, el que ejerce algún arte mecánica o manual.
Handily [hand'-i-li], *adv.* Mañosamente, con destreza.
Handiness [hand'-i-nes], *s.* Maña, habilidad, destreza para hacer alguna cosa.
Handiwork [hand'-i-wūrc], *s.* Obra mecánica o manual.
Handkerchief [han'-kęr-chif], *s.* Pañuelo, pedazo de lienzo, seda o algodón que sirve para limpiarse el sudor y las narices, para cubrirse el cuello y otros usos.
Hand-language [hand'-laņ-gwej], *s.* El arte de entenderse por medio de las manos o de los dedos, por señas.
Handle [han'-dl], *va.* 1. Palpar, tocar con las manos; manosear. 2. Manejar; hacer tratable. 3. Tratar un asunto, una materia, una cuestión, etc. 4. Practicar una profesión o arte. 5. Comerciar en, comprar y vender. 6. Tratar, portarse bien o mal con alguno.—*vn.* 1. Hacer uso de las manos, trabajar con ellas. 2. Ser manejado. *Handle with care*, Frágil; con cuidado.
Handle, *s.* 1. Mango, puño, asa, asidero, manija, cabo. *A fan with ivory handles*, Abanico con varillas de marfil. 2. Cualquier cosa de que se puede echar mano para usarla. 3. (Fam.) Tratamiento, título que da una profesión.
Handle bar [han'-dle bar], *s.* Manubrio (de bicicleta, etc.)
Handless [hand'-les], *a.* Manco, sin mano.
Handling [hand'-ling], *s.* 1. Manejo, el acto de manejar alguna cosa. 2. Toque, en la pintura o escultura. 3. Manejo, treta, astucia, ardid.
Hand-made [hand'-mêd], *a.* Hecho a mano.
Handmaid [hand'-mêd], **Handmaiden** [hand'-mêd-n], *sf.* Criada, asistenta.
Hand-mill [hand'-mil], *s.* Molinillo, molino que se mueve con la mano.
Hand-organ [hand'-ōr-gan], *s.* Organillo, órgano de cigüeña.
Handout [hand'-aut], *s.* 1. (fam.) Ropa o comestibles que se dan de limosna. 2. Volante de distribución gratuita. 3. Noticias o información distribuidas por una agencia de publicidad. 4. Declaración oficial proporcionada a la prensa.
Hand-picked [hand'-pict], *a.* Escogido o seleccionado con cuidado.
Hand-sails [hand'-sêlz], *s. pl.* (Mar.) Velas manuales.
Hand-saw [hand'-sē], *s.* Sierra de mano.
Hand-screw [hand'-scrū], *s.* Gato de mano, cornaquí.
Handsel, Hansel [hand'-sel, han'-sel], *s.* 1. Estrena, el primer dinero que se recibe por lo que se vende o la primera venta de algún objeto; regalo que se da como muestra de benevolencia. 2. Prenda que se da como garantía de una venta o contrato.
Handsel, Hansel, *va.* (Poco us.) Estrenar alguna cosa o estrenarse en ella; dar un regalo o aguinaldo; dar prenda en garantía.
Handshake [hand'-shêk], *s.* Apretón de manos.
Handsome [han'-sum], *a.* 1. Hermoso, perfecto, de buena figura, gentil, lindo, agradable a la vista. 2. Primoroso, excelente. 3. Amplio, liberal, dadivoso. 4. Generoso, noble. 5. Honrado, honesto. 6. Fino, distinguido, correcto. *It is not handsome for you to say so*, No le está a Vd. bien el hablar así. Entre *handsome* y *beautiful* existe precisamente la misma diferencia que en español entre *hermoso* y *bello*. Puede ser un hombre *handsome*, pero no *beautiful*.
Handsomely [han'-sum-li], *adv.* Hermosamente, primorosamente; generosamente.
Handsomeness [han'-sum-nes], *s.* Hermosura, gracia, elegancia; generosidad. "*Handsomeness is the more animal excellence, beauty the more imaginative*," La hermosura es la excelencia más corpórea, la belleza la más espiritual.
Handspring [hand'-spring], *s.* Voltereta.
Handstaff [hand'-stgf], *s.* Jabalina, arma antigua.
Handwork [hand'-wūrc], *s.* Obra hecha a mano y no a máquina; obra manual.
Handwriting [hand-rait'-ing], *s.* 1. Carácter de letra, la forma de ietra que cada uno tiene, quirografía. 2. Escritura, algo escrito.
Handy [hand'-i], *a.* 1. Manual o ejecutado con la mano. 2. Socorrido, de uso conveniente; muy arrimado, junto, cerca, de fácil acceso. 3. Diestro, hábil, mañoso. 4. (Mar.) Manual, lo que es fácil de manejar.
Handygripe [hand'-i-graip], *s.* El acto de agarrar, ya sea con las manos o con las garras.
Handy man [hand'-i man], *s.* 1. Factótum. 2. Persona con facilidad para muchos oficios.
Handywork [hand'-i-wūrc], *s.* Obra mecánica o manual.
Hang [hang], *va.* (*pret.* y *pp* HUNG o HANGED). 1. Colgar, suspender alguna cosa en alto. 2. Inclinar alguna cosa, ponerla más baja de lo que debía estar. 3. Desplegar alguna cosa colgándola. 4. Fijar algo de modo que pueda moverse en determinadas direcciones. 5. Colgar, ahorcar. (En este sentido el participio pasado es *hanged* solamente.) 6. Entapizar, adornar con tapices o telas.—*vn.* 1. Colgar, estar alguna cosa pendiente en el aire. 2. Fluctuar, vacilar. 3. Ser ahorcado, sufrir la pena de horca. 4. Pegarse, agregarse alguno a otro importunamente y sin ser llamado. 5. Colgarse, abrazarse fuertemente al cuello de alguna persona. 6. Continuar en el mismo estado. 7. Quedarse suspenso al oir algo. 8. Depender de la voluntad o dictamen de otro. 9. Formar pendiente. 10. Tardar, dilatar. 11. (E. U.) No poder avenirse los pareceres, p. ej. en un jurado. *Cf.* núm. 6. *To hang around*, Tardar, haraganear. *To hang back*, Rehusar ir adelante, vacilar antes de adelantar. *To hang down*, Bajar; colgar, estar pendiente. *To hang out*, Enarbolar. *To hang up*, Levantar, suspender en el aire. *To hang about one's neck*, Abrazarse estrechamente con alguno. *To hang loose*, Estar colgada una cosa de modo que se pueda mover con facilidad. *To hang over*, Cabecear, inclinarse. *To hang together*, Acordarse. *To hang upon*, Mirar con afecto particular. (Mar.) Cargar sobre. *To hang the rudder*, (Mar.) Montar el timón. *To hang fire*, (Mil.) Suspender el fuego; dícese también de las armas de fuego que no disparan al instante; de aquí, tardarse, no tener lugar, no hacerse al tiempo debido. *To hang a room with tapestry*, Entapizar una pieza. *Hanging knees*, (Mar.) Curvas de alto abajo. *Hang me, if it is not a fib all that he says*, (Fam.) Que me emplumen si no es mentira todo lo que dice. *Hang-bird*, Pájaro que fabrica un nido colgante, como la oropéndola y el oriol de Baltimore; a este último se le llama también familiarmente *fiery hang-bird*.
Hang, *s.* 1. La manera como cuelga o se cuelga una cosa. 2. (Fam.) Uso o conocimiento familiar, maña, destreza. 3. Idea prevalente, conexión, aceptación general. 4. (Mar.) Curva, bajada rápida.
Hangar [hang'-ar], *s.* (Aer.) Hangar.
Hangby [hang'-bai], (Ant.) **Hanger-on** [hang'-ęr-en], *s.* 1. Dependiente: mogollón, gorrista, pegote, moscón, ladilla. 2. Familiar; paseante en corte.
Hangdog [hang'-deg], *a.* De carácter o apariencia vil; bajo, tacaño.—*s.* Hombre vil, ruin e insidioso; mataperros.
Hanging [hang'-ing], *s.* 1. Colgadura; tapices o telas con que se cubren y adornan las paredes interiores de las casas. 2. Muestra, exhibición. 3. Muerte en la horca.—*a.* Digno de ser ahorcado o digno de horca. *Hanging face*, Cara de ahorcado.
Hangman [hang'-man], *s.* Verdugo, el ejecutor de las penas corporales y de la pena capital: úsase también como improperio.
Hangnail [hang'-nêl], *s.* Padrastro, respigón, pedacito de pellejo que se levanta de la carne inmediata a las uñas de la mano.
Hank [haņk], *s.* 1. Madeja de hilo, ovillo. 2. (Vulg.) Lazo, freno; influencia, inclinación, poder. *Hanks*, (Mar.) Anillos o arcos de palo.
Hanker [haņk'-ęr], *vn.* Ansiar, apetecer.
Hankering [haņk'-ęr-ing], *s.* Ansia fuerte o vehemente, antojo, deseo; afición, inclinación, apetencia.
Hankle [han'-cl], *va.* (Esco. y Prov. Ingl.) Torcer, enredar.
Hanger [hang'-ęr], *s.* 1. Soporte colgante, colgadero; lo que mantiene alguna cosa colgada o suspensa en el aire. 2. Alfanje, especie de espada ancha, corta y curva. 3. Colgador o gancho de ropa. *Paper hanger*, Empapelador.
Hangover [hang'-ō-vęr], *s.* 1. Cruda. (Amer.) Resaca, goma, guayabo. 2. Sobrante.
Hanseatic [han-si-at'-ic], *a.* Anseático, lo que pertenece a ciertas ciudades libres de Alemania que se confederaron para protegerse mutuamente.

Hansom, Hansom cab [han'-sǫm], *s.* Cabriolé Hansom, del nombre de su inventor; se usa mucho en Londres y tiene el pescante en alto detrás de la caja del coche.

Ha'n't [hênt]. Contracción vulgar de HAVE NOT.

Hap [hap], *s.* 1. Caso, lance, acaso; casualidad, accidente. 2. Fortuna, buena suerte.

Hap, *vn.* Acontecer, acaecer, suceder.—*va.* (Esco.) Cubrir; vestir.

Ha'penny [hé'-pen-i], *s.* Contracción de HALFPENNY, muy común en Inglaterra.

Haphazard [hap-haz'-ard], *a.* 1. De casualidad. 2. Descuidado, a medias.

Hapless [hap-les], *a.* Desgraciado, desventurado, desamparado, miserable.

Haply [hap'-li], *adv.* 1. Quizá o quizás. 2. Casualmente, por casualidad.

Ha'p'orth [hé'-pǫrth], *s.* (Fam. Ingl.) Lo que se vende por medio penique; porción muy corta. Contracción de HALFPENNY-WORTH.

Happen [hap'-n], *vn.* 1. Acontecer, acaecer; suceder por casualidad; sobrevenir; llegar el caso de. 2. Hallarse en alguna parte. *Whatever happens,* Suceda lo que quiera, venga lo que viniere. *I happened to be there,* Por casualidad me hallaba allí. *It unfortunately happened that I was not there,* Por desgracia no me hallé allí. *To happen in,* (Fam.) Hacer una visita por casualidad. *To happen on,* Encontrar, hallar por acaso. *I happened on other things,* Hallé o me encontré con otras materias.

Happening [hap'-en-ing], *s.* Acontecimiento, suceso.

Happily [hap'-i-li], *adv.* Dichosamente, felizmente; graciosamente.

Happiness [hap'-i-nes], *s.* Felicidad, prosperidad, dicha; gracia natural o no estudiada.

Happy [hap'-i], *a.* 1. Feliz, bienaventurado, dichoso, afortunado. 2. Expedito, desembarazado. *To lead a happy life,* Pasar una vida feliz o dichosa.

Happy-go-lucky [hap'-i-gō-luk'-i], *a.* Despreocupado, contento de su suerte.

Hara-kiri o **Hari-kari** [hā'-rā-kī'-ri], *s.* Procedimiento japonés de suicidio por medio del desentrañamiento.

Harangue [ha-rang'], *s.* Arenga, oración.

Harangue, *vn.* Arengar, decir en público alguna arenga o discurso.—*va.* Hablar arengando.

Haranguer [ha-rang'-ǫr], *s.* Orador.

Harass [har'-as], *va.* 1. Cansar, causar cansancio, acosar, fatigar, hostigar, incomodar. (Vulg.) Moler, jorobar. 2. (Mil.) Hostigar, cansar al enemigo por medio de ataques repetidos.

Harassment [har'-as-mǫnt], *s.* Cansancio, fatiga, hostigamiento.

Harbinger [hār'-bin-jǫr], *s.* Precursor, el que va delante de otro; aposentador; anuncio, presagio.—*va.* Presagiar, anunciar; ser precursor de.

Harbor, Harbour [hār'-bǫr], *s.* 1. Puerto, lugar seguro y defendido de los vientos donde pueden entrar los buques con seguridad. *Harbor-dues,* Derechos de puerto. *Harbor-master,* Capitán de puerto. 2. Asilo lugar de refugio y descanso. 3. (Des.) Albergue, posada.

Harbor, *va.* 1. Abrigar, amparar, defender, resguardar. 2. Albergar, acoger, hospedar, dar albergue u hospedaje; concebir, recibir en la mente. 3. Dar abrigo o ser capa de ladrones.—*vn.* Recibir amparo o protección.

Harborage [hār'-bǫr-ėj], *s.* 1. Puerto, lugar de abrigo para las embarcaciones. 2. Amparo, asilo.

Harborer [hār'-bǫr-ǫr], *s.* 1. Amparador, albergador, acogedor, el que hospeda a alguno, antiguamente huésped. 2. Encubridor de robos o ladrones.

Harbour, Harbourer, etc. Forma usual en Inglaterra. *V.* HARBOR, etc.

Hard [hārd], *a.* 1. Duro, sólido, firme, endurecido. 2. Difícil, dificultoso, arduo, penoso, trabajoso. 3. Obscuro, difícil de entenderse. 4. Insensible, cruel, riguroso, severo, rígido. *A hard winter,* Invierno riguroso. 5. Injusto, contrario a la razón, opresivo, ofensivo. 6. Áspero, bronco, grosero. 7. Escaso; tosco y desagradable al gusto. 8. Mezquino, miserable. 9. Cruda, gorda, que contiene ciertas sales minerales disueltas: dícese del agua. *Hard of bearing,* Medio sordo, teniente o duro de oído. *Hard of belief,* Incrédulo. *Hard to deal with,* Intratable, poco sociable. *Hard words,* Palabras ásperas o palabras injuriosas. *Hard drinking,* Borrachera, la condición de beber a pote.—*adv.* 1. Cerca, a la mano. *Hard by,* Inmediato, arrimado, muy cerca. 2. Diligentemente, con ahinco. *To study hard,* Estudiar con ahinco. 3. Inquietamente, con inquietud: con impaciencia, vejación o pesar. *To go hard,* Traer a mal traer, causar apuros. 4. Aprisa, ligeramente. 5. Dificilmente, con dificultad. 6. Tempestuosamente. 7. Reciamente, con fuerza, con dureza. 8. (Mar.) Todo, al límite extremo. *Hard a-port,* A babor todo. *To drink hard,* Beber con exceso. *To grow hard,* Endurecerse. *It rains hard,* Llueve a cántaros. *Hard and fast,* De cal y canto, o a macha martillo. *Hard cash,* Moneda sonante, numerario; opuesto a papel moneda. *Things go hard with him,* Sus asuntos se hallan en mal estado. *It will go hard with me if I can not prevent him,* Me irá mal si no logro impedírselo. *The poor fellow was hard put to it for a living,* El pobre hombre vivía con mucho trabajo. *To be hard up,* Hallarse en apuros, estar a la cuarta pregunta. *Hard-pressed, hard-pushed,* Escaso o falto de recursos, apurado, reducido a una situación angustiosa.

Hard-and-fast [hārd-and-fast'], *a.* Rígido, estricto. *Hard-and-fast rule,* Disposición inquebrantable.

Hard-bound [hārd'-baund], *a.* Estreñido; estéril.

Hard cider [hārd sai'-dǫr], *s.* Sidra, bebida alcohólica.

Hard coal [hārd cōl], *s.* Antracita.

Hard-earned [hārd'-ǫrnd], *a.* Ganado o adquirido con dificultad.

Harden [hārd'-n], *va.* 1. Endurecer, poner dura y sólida alguna cosa. 2. Endurecer, robustecer, hacer a uno más apto para la fatiga o para el trabajo; curtir. 3. Endurecer; hacer duro, insensible, obstinado, descarado o impudente. 4. Hacer a uno firme y constante.—*vn.* Endurecerse, empedernirse.

Hardener [hārd'-n-ǫr], *s.* El que endurece.

Hard-favoredness [hārd'-fé'-vǫrd-nes], *s.* Fealdad; facciones irregulares.

Hard-fisted [hārd'-fist-ed], *a.* 1. Con las manos callosas o endurecidas. 2. Avaro, miserable. *V.* CLOSE-FISTED.

Hard-fought [hārd'-fōt], *a.* Fuertemente combatido.

Hard-got, Hard-gotten [hārd'-got, n], *a.* Adquirido con mucho trabajo.

Hard-handed [hārd'-hand-ed], *a.* 1. Basto, el que tiene las manos encallecidas por el trabajo; menestral, trabajador. 2. Severo, despótico.

Hard-headed [hārd-hed'-ed], *a.* 1. Testarudo, terco. 2. Astuto, sagaz.

Hard-hearted [hārd'-hārt-ed], *a.* Cruel, severo, bárbaro, inhumano, salvaje, duro de corazón, insensible, inflexible, inexorable.

Hard-heartedness [hārd'-hārt'-ed-nes], *s.* Crueldad, falta de ternura o compasión, insensibilidad, inhumanidad, dureza de corazón.

Hardihood [hārd'-i-hud], *s.* 1. Atrevimiento, valor; atrevimiento inconsiderado, temeridad. 2. Descaro, impudencia, desvergüenza.

Hardiness [hārd'-i-nes], *s.* 1. Ánimo, osadía, valor, intrepidez. 2. Robustez, vigor.

Hard labor [hārd lé'-bǫr], *s.* Trabajos forzados (en una prisión, etc.)

Hard-labored [hārd-lé'-bǫrd], *a.* Elaborado, trabajado.

Hardly [hārd'-li], *adv.* 1. Dificilmente, con dificultad, apenas. 2. No totalmente, casi no, apenas; eufemismo en lugar de no. 3. De mala gana, a viva fuerza. 4. Rigurosamente, con rigor y opresión; ásperamente, con aspereza, duramente, severamente. 5. Improbablemente.

Hard-mouthed [hārd'-maudhd], *a.* Desobediente al freno: dícese de los caballos de boca dura.

Hardness [hārd'-nes], *s.* 1. Dureza, firmeza, solidez. 2. Obscuridad, la dificultad en darse a entender. 3. (Ant.) Dificultad de ejecutarse alguna cosa; pena, trabajo. 4. Escasez, penuria. 5. Obstinación en el mal. 6. Ferocidad, fiereza, crueldad, inhumanidad, severidad, obduración. 7. Rigor o aspereza del frío. *Hardness of heart,* Dureza de corazón.

Hard-pan [hārd'-pan], *s.* 1. (Min.) Capa sólida de detrito debajo de un terreno blando. 2. (Fam. E. U.) Do aquí, fundamento firme; base sólida.

Hard rubber, *s.* *V.* RUBBER.

Hards [hārdz], *s.* 1. Desperdicio o parte basta del lino. 2. Mezcla de alumbre y sal que usan los panaderos para blanquear el pan.

Hardship [hārd'-ship], *s.* 1. Injuria, opresión, gravamen, injusticia. 2. Penalidad, trabajo, molestia, fatiga, pena.

Hardtack [hārd'-tac], *s.* Galleta de munición.

Hardtop [hārd'-top], *s.* Capota dura.

Hardware [hārd'-wār], *s.* Quincallería, ferretería, quinquillería, mercaderías menudas de hierro, acero, cobre y otros metales; también muchos instrumentos de agricultura *Hardware trade,* Quincallería.

Hardwareman [hārd'-wār-man], *s.* Quincallero, buhonero.

Hardwood [hɑrd'-wud], *s.* Madera dura, es decir, la de los árboles que mudan sus hojas, en oposición a los de hojas perennes o en forma de aguja.
Hardy [hɑ̄r'-di], *a.* 1. Osado, atrevido, bravo, intrépido. 2. Fuerte, robusto, endurecido. 3. (Hort.) Que sobrevive en invierno, al aire libre; que aguanta bien el frío.
Hare [hɑ̄r], *s.* 1. Liebre, mamífero roedor con orejas muy largas, del género Lepus. 2. Fibras del cáñamo. *Young hare*, Lebratillo. *Hare and hounds*, Juego al aire libre en que se imita la caza de las liebres por los sabuesos.
Harebell [hɑ̄r'-bel], *s.* (Bot.) 1. Campanilla. 2. (Esco.) Jacinto silvestre.
Hare-brained [hɑ̄r'-brēnd], *a.* Inconstante, volátil, precipitado, ligero de cascos, aturdido.
Harefoot [hɑ̄r'-fut], *s.* 1. (Zool.) Lagópedo, especie de gallina silvestre, del género Lagopus. 2. (Poét.) Corredor ágil. 3. *V.* HARE'S-FOOT.
Hare-footed. (Poét.) Ligero, ágil. *Mad as a March hare*, Extravagante, loco, insensato; por vía de alusión al proceder de la liebre en el mes de marzo, época del celo.
Hare-hearted [hɑ̄r-hɑ̄rt'-ed], *a.* Alebrado, temeroso, medroso, tímido, cobarde.
Harehound [hɑ̄r'-haund], *s.* Lebrel, galgo.
Hare-hunter [hɑ̄r'-hunt'-ęr], *s.* Aficionado a la caza de liebres.
Hare-hunting [hɑ̄r'-hunt-ing], *s.* Montería o caza de liebres.
Harelip [hɑ̄r'-lip], *s.* Hendedura o abertura del labio superior.
Harelipped [hɑ̄r'-lipt], *a.* Labihendido, el que tiene partido el labio superior.
Harem [hē'-rem], *s.* 1. Harén, harem, serrallo, la habitación de las mujeres mahometanas. 2. Conjunto de las mujeres del harén.
Haremint [hɑ̄r'-mint], *s.* (Bot.) Yaro, manto de Santa María.
Harenet [hɑ̄r'-net], *s.* Especie de red para coger liebres.
Harepipe [hɑ̄r'-paip], *s.* Lazo para coger liebres.
Hare's-ear [hɑ̄rz'-īr], *s.* (Bot.) Oreja de liebre, hierba de Europa. Bupleurum.
Hare's-foot [hɑ̄rz'-fut], *s.* (Bot.) Pie de liebre, especie de trébol.
Hareslettuce [hɑ̄rz'-let-is], *s.* (Bot.) Ajonjera.
Harewort [hɑ̄r'-wūrt], *s.* (Bot.) Malva de huerta.
Haricot [har'-i-co], *s.* 1. Especie de guisado de carne con habichuelas. 2. Frijol, judía o habichuela.
Hark [hɑ̄rk], *inter.* ¡Eh! ¡oye! ¡mira!
Hark, *vn.* Escuchar, oir con atención.
Harken, Hearken [hɑ̄rk'-n], *va.* Oir con atención, escuchar.—*vn.* Escuchar, atender; seguir con atención lo que se dice para obedecer; tomar en consideración.
Harl [hɑ̄rl], *s.* Hebras de lino; filamento.
Harlequin [hɑ̄r'-lę-cwin o kin], *s.* Arlequín, gracioso, bufón.
Harlequin, *va.* Bufonear, decir gracias, hacer monerías; chasquear.
Harlequinade [har-lę-kin-ēd'], *s.* Arlequinada, suertes de arlequín; pantomima.
Harlot [hɑ̄r'-lęt], *s.* Ramera, meretriz, prostituta.—*a.* Ruin, vil; meretricio.
Harlot, *vn.* Prostituirse, hacerse ramera.
Harm [hɑrm], *s.* 1. Detrimento, daño, peligro, desgracia, perjuicio, agravio. 2. Maldad, mal.
Harm, *va.* Dañar, injuriar, agraviar, ofender.
Harmattan [hɑ̄r-mat'-an], *s.* Nombre de un viento cálido y seco que sopla del interior de África por la costa occidental, en diciembre, enero y febrero.
Harmful [hɑrm'-ful], *a.* Dañoso, nocivo; peligroso, perjudicial.
Harmfully [hɑrm'-ful-i], *adv.* Dañosamente.
Harmfulness [hɑrm'-ful-nes], *s.* Maldad, daño, acción o disposición nociva.
Harmless [hɑrm'-les], *a.* 1. Sencillo, inocente, que no es nocivo, ni perjudicial. 2. Ileso, libre de daño; sano y salvo. *To hold harmless*, Librar de responsabilidad, conservar sano y salvo.
Harmlessly [hɑrm'-les-li], *adv.* Inocentemente, sin daño.
Harmlessness [hɑrm'-les-nes], *s.* Calidad de no ser nocivo; sencillez, inocencia.
Harmonic, Harmonical [hɑ̄r-men'-ic, al], *a.* Armónico, lo perteneciente a la armonía.
Harmonic, *s.* 1. Armónico, tono secundario; sonido que acompaña a otro fundamental. 2. Tono producido en un instrumento de cuerda oprimiendo ligeramente una de las cuerdas. 3. *pl.* ¿Teoría de los sonidos musicales.
Harmonica [hɑ̄r-men'-i-ca], *s.* Uno de varios instrumentos de música: (1) Armonio con teclas de vidrio; vidrios armónicos; (2) armónica, pequeño instrumento que se toca soplándolo.
Harmonically [hɑ̄r-men'-ic-al-i], *adv.* Armónicamente, con proporción armónica.
Harmonicon [hɑ̄r-men'-i-cen], *s.* 1. Armónicon, instrumento de música parecido al organillo y que imita los sonidos de una orquesta. 2. Armónica, pequeño instrumento de viento.
Harmonious [hɑ̄r-mo'-ni-us], *a.* 1. Armonioso, proporcionado. 2. Armonioso, que tiene armonía; musical.
Harmoniously [hɑ̄r-mo'-ni-us-li], *adv.* Armoniosamente, con armonía musical.
Harmoniousness [hɑ̄r-mo'-ni-us-nes], *s.* Armonía, la consonancia en la música.
Harmonist [hɑ̄r'-mo-nist], *s.* 1. Armonista, músico. 2. *V.* HARMONIZER.
Harmonize o **Harmonise** [hɑ̄r'-mo-naiz], *va.* 1. Armonizar, ajustar, concertar, poner de acuerdo; hacer vivir en buena inteligencia. 2. Armonizar, poner en consonancia música.—*vn.* 1. Armonizarse, concordar, congeniar las personas; convenir, corresponder. 2. Estar en armonía musical.
Harmonizer [hɑ̄r'-mo-naiz-ęr], *s.* 1. Conciliador, el que pone de acuerdo. 2. (Mús.) Armonista. 3. El que reune los pasajes de un libro o escrito que concuerdan entre sí.
Harmony [hɑ̄r'-mo-ni], *s.* 1. Armonía, la conveniente proporción y correspondencia de una cosa con otra. 2. Armonía, la consonancia en la música que resulta de la variedad de sonidos puestos en debida proporción. 3. Armonía, concordia, uniformidad.
Harness [hɑ̄r'-nes], *s.* 1. Atelaje, guarniciones, jaeces, los arreos y paramentos que se ponen a los caballos para tirar de los coches y carrozas. 2. Arnés, el conjunto de armas defensivas con que se armaban antiguamente para pelear. *Harness-maker*, Guarnicionero. 3. (Fig.) Equipo para cualquier empresa u objeto; también, los requisitos y exigencias de un negocio cualquiera; servicio activo. *To die in harness*, Morir en servicio activo, antes de retirarse de los negocios.
Harness, *va.* 1. Enjaezar, atalajar, poner el aderezo a un caballo o las guarniciones, si es de tiro. 2. Armar con el arnés.
Harnesser [hɑ̄r'-nes-ęr], *s.* El que pone jaeces o arneses.
Harp [hɑrp], *s.* 1. Arpa, instrumento músico de cuerda tañido con los dedos. 2. (Astr.) Arpa, constelación.
Harp, *va.* y *vn.* 1. Tocar o tañer el arpa. 2. Excitar o mover alguna pasión, mover los afectos del alma. 3. Machacar, cansar, porfiar con terquedad sobre una misma cosa (úsase con *on* o *upon*).
Harper [hɑrp'-ęr], *s.* Arpista, el que tiene por oficio tocar el arpa.
Harpings [hɑrp'-ingz], *s. pl.* 1. (Mar.) Redondos de la proa. 2. (Mar.) Bagaras o maestras.
Harpist [hɑrp' ist], *s.* Arpista, el que toca el arpa.
Harpoon [hɑ̄r-pūn'], *s.* Arpón, especie de arma arrojadiza que sirve para pescar ballenas.
Harpoon, *va.* Arponear. *Harpoon-gun*, Cañón pequeño para lanzar el arpón.
Harpooner [hɑ̄r-pūn'-ęr], †**Harpooneer** [hɑ̄r-pū-nīr'], *s.* Arponero, el que tira el arpón.
Harpsichord [hɑrp'-si-cērd], *s.* Clave, clavicordio, dulzaina.
Harpy [hɑ̄r'-pi], *s.* 1. Arpía, ave monstruosa. 2. Arpía, el hombre o la mujer muy codiciosos. 3. *Harpy* o *harpy-eagle*, Águila muy grande, con copete, de la América tropical. Thrasætus harpyia.
Harquebuss [hɑ̄r'-cwę-bus], *s.* Arcabuz, arma de fuego que precedió al mosquete.
Harquebussier [hɑ̄r-cwę-bus-īr'], *s.* Arcabucero.
Harridan [har'-i-dan], *s.* Mujer colérica, vieja y fea.
Harrier [har'-i-ęr], *s.* 1. Lebrel, sabueso pequeño adiestrado para cazar liebres. 2. Pillador, asolador; molestador. 3. Ave de rapiña parecida al buaro, milano; se llama así porque pilla (*harries*) las aves de corral.
Harrow [har'-ō], *s.* Grada, rastro, rastrillo.
Harrow, *va.* 1. Gradar, desmenuzar la tierra con grada o rastro. 2. Inquietar, perturbar, atormentar.
Harrower [har'-o-ęr], *s.* 1. El que desmenuza la tierra. 2. *V.* HARRIER, 3ª acepción.
Harrowing [har'-ō-ing], *a.* Horripilante, desgarrador.
Harry [har'-i], *va.* 1. Pillar, asolar, saquear. 2. Molestar, inquietar, cansar.
Harsh [hɑrsh], *a.* 1. Áspero, agrio, bronco, rígido, duro, riguroso, aus-

tero, desagradable. 2. Malcondicionado, desapacible; áspero al tacto, tosco.
Harshly [hārsh'-li], *adv.* Ásperamente, severamente, con violencia, desagradablemente, desapaciblemente. *To speak harshly to*, Hablar con dureza, con lenguaje violento. *To treat* o *use harshly*, Tratar con aspereza, con palabras demasiado duras.
Harshness [hārsh'-nes], *s.* 1. Aspereza, rudeza, austeridad en el trato, genio o costumbres; rigor, severidad, mal humor. 2. Sonido desagradable al oído.
Harslet, *s.* *V.* HASLET.
Hart [hārt], *s.* Ciervo, particularmente después de su quinto año. (Mar.) Motón de vigota.
Hartshorn [hārts'-hērn], *s.* 1. Amoníaco en cualquier forma de preparación; antiguamente lo obtenían de los cuernos de ciervo por medio de la destilación. 2. (Bot.) Especie de llantén.
Hartstongue [hārts'-tung], *s.* (Bot.) Escolopendra, lengua de ciervo, especie de helecho.
Hartwort [hārt'-wūrt], *s.* (Bot.) Tordilum.
Harum-scarum [hār'-um-scār'-um], *a.* 1. Atolondrado, precipitado, como espantado. 2. Al tuntún, boca o patas arriba, confuso, desordenado.
Haruspex, Haruspice [hā-rus'-pex, pis], *s.* Arúspice, sacerdote romano que examinaba las entrañas de las víctimas para adivinar los sucesos.
Harvest [hār'-vest], *s.* 1. Cosecha, agosto, el tiempo que se emplea en la recolección de los granos. 2. Agosto, la misma cosecha de granos. 3. Agosto, el fruto de algún trabajo. *To make harvest*, Hacer agosto. *The harvest is late this year*, La cosecha está atrasada este año. *Harvest-bug*, Mita, arador, insecto que se pega a la piel. *Harvest-fly*, Cicada, cigarra. *Harvest-man*, Insecto llamado vulgarmente *daddy-long-legs;* arácnido de los falángidos. *Harvest moon*, Luna de la cosecha, el plenilunio más próximo al equinoccio de otoño; porque la luna sale casi a la misma hora por varias noches consecutivas. *Harvest-mouse*, Ratón silvestre.
Harvest, *va.* Cosechar, recoger las mieses; hacer agosto.
Harvester [hār'-vest-ẹr], **Harvest-man** [hār'-vest-man], *s.* 1. Agostero, cosechero. 2. (*Harvester* sólo.) Segadora, máquina de segar. *Combined harvester*, Segadora de combinación (es decir, que siega, trilla y aecha a la vez); máquina muy usada en los Estados Unidos del Oeste.
Harvest-home [hār'-vest-hōm], *s.* 1. Fiesta inglesa con que se celebra el fin de la cosecha. 2. La canción de los segadores al tiempo de recoger las mieses.
Harvest-lord [hār'-vest-lērd], *s.* El primer segador de una siega.
Harvest-queen [hār'-vest-cwīn], *s.* Una figura que llevan los segadores al acabar la siega.
Hash [hash], *va.* Picar, hacer pedazos menudos alguna cosa.
Hash, *s.* Picadillo; salpicón, jigote.
Hashish, Hasheesh [hash'-ish], *s.* Hachich, preparación embriagadora que usan los orientales, y que hacen con simiente de cáñamo.
Haslet [has'-let], *s.* Asadura de puerco, conjunto de livianos, como el hígado, bazo, corazón, etc.
Hasp [hqsp], *s.* Aldaba de candado; broche.
Hasp, *va.* Abrochar; cerrar con aldaba.
Hassock [has'-ẹc], *s.* Banqueta, escabel; cojín o estera muy gruesa para arrodillarse.
Hastate [has'-tēt], *a.* 1. (Bot.) Alabardado, en figura de alabarda. 2. De punta aguda.
Haste [hēst], *s.* 1. Prisa, presteza, diligencia, velocidad, precipitación. 2. Precipitación, celeridad indecente o mal aconsejada. *V.* HURRY. 3. Necesidad de apresurarse, urgencia. *The more haste the less speed*, Quien más corre menos vuela. *To make haste*, Darse prisa, apresurarse, despacharse. *To be in haste*, Estar de prisa, tener prisa.
Haste, Hasten [hē'-sn], *vn.* Moverse con velocidad, ser pronto, apresurarse.—*va.* Acelerar, apresurar, precipitar, avivar. *Whither are you hastening?* ¿Adónde va Vd. tan aprisa?
Hastily [hēst'-i-li], *adv.* 1. Aceleradamente, apresuradamente. 2. Temerariamente, precipitadamente. 3. Airadamente.
Hastiness [hēst'-i-nes], *s.* 1. Precipitación, demasiada prisa. 2. Prisa, presteza, prontitud, diligencia. 3. Movimiento repentino de ira o enfado; impaciencia.
Hastings [hēst'-ingz], *s. pl.* 1. Guisantes tempranos. 2. Cualquier fruto temprano. (Se usa también en singular.)
Hasty [hēst'-i], *a.* 1. Pronto, apresurado, ligero. 2. Pronto, vivo de genio. 3. Violento, colérico, petulante, temerario, arrojado. 4. Temprano.
Hasty-pudding [hēst'-i-pud'-ing], *s.* Especie de papilla hecha con agua hirviendo y harina (de maíz); gachas.
Hat [hat], *s.* 1. Sombrero. 2. (Fig.) Capelo, dignidad de cardenal. *Beaver hat*, Sombrero de castor. *Panama hat*, Sombrero de jipijapa. *Round hat*, Sombrero redondo. *Silk hat, high hat* (vulg. *stovepipe hat*), Sombrero de copa, o de copa alta; (fest.) chistera. *Three-cocked hat*, Sombrero de tres picos, tricornio. *Three-cornered hat*, Sombrero de tres candiles. *To put on one's hat*, Ponerse el sombrero. *To take off one's hat*, Quitarse el sombrero. *Hats off!* ¡Fuera sombreros!
Hatable [hēt'-a-bl], *a.* Detestable, aborrecible, odioso.
Hat-band [hat'-band], *s.* Cinta del sombrero.
Hat-box [hat'-bōx], **Hat-case** [hat'-kēs], *s.* Sombrerera. *Hat-money*, (Mar.) Gratificación que se da al patrón de un buque por su cuidado del cargamento.
Hatch [hach], *va.* 1. Criar pollos. 2. Empollar, fomentar los huevos para sacar pollos. 3. Fraguar, idear, tramar, maquinar. 4. Sombrear, poner sombras en la pintura, o cruzar líneas en el grabado.—*vn.* Empollarse, salir del cascarón; madurarse. *The birds are just hatched*, Los pájaros acaban de salir del nido, o del huevo. *To count one's chickens before they are hatched*, Echar la cuenta sin la huéspeda.
Hatch, *s.* 1. Cría, pollada, nidada, pollazón. 2. Salida del cascarón. 3. Media puerta. 4. (Mar.) Cuartel, especie de portezuelas que sirven para cerrar las bocas de las escotillas. *To be under hatches*, Andar a sombra de tejado; de aquí, estar en la miseria, en la cárcel, etc. 5. Paradera, presa, exclusa en una corriente para coger peces.
Hatch-bar [hach'-bār], *s.* (Mar.) Barra para cerrar las escotillas.
Hatchel [hach'-el], *s.* Rastrillo, instrumento con que se limpia el lino o cáñamo.
Hatchel, *va.* 1. Rastrillar, limpiar el lino o cáñamo de la arista y estopa. *Hatchelled flax*, Lino rastrillado. 2. Contrariar, impacientar, fastidiar a alguno.
Hatcheller [hach'-el-ẹr], *s.* Rastrillador.
Hatcher [hach'-ẹr], *s.* Trazador, tramador.
Hatchet [hach'-et], *s.* Destral, hacha pequeña. *To bury the hatchet*, Hacer la paz, olvidar las injurias. *To dig up* (o *take up*) *the hatchet*, Desenterrar el hacha, hacer la guerra. (Locuciones tomadas de los indios norteamericanos.)
Hatchet-face [hach'-et-fēs], *s.* Cara delgada, enjuta. *Hatchet-faced*, De facciones enjutas.
Hatchet-helve [hach'-et-helv], *s.* Ástil de hacha.
Hatching [hach'-ing], *s.* El acto de sombrear, o la sombra hecha en el grabado con líneas transversas.
Hatchment [hach'-mẹnt], *s.* El escudo de armas que se llevaba en los funerales y se solía colocar en las fachadas de las casas de los difuntos.
Hatchway [hach'-wē], *s.* (Mar.) Escotilla, la puerta o abertura hecha en las cubiertas. *Main-hatchway*, Escotilla mayor. *Fore-hatchway*, Escotilla de proa. *Magazine-hatchway*, Escotilla de popa.
Hate [hēt], *va.* Detestar, aborrecer, odiar, abominar.
Hate, *s.* Odio, aborrecimiento, tema, aversión.
Hateful [hēt'-ful], *a.* Aborrecible, maligno, malévolo, odioso, detestable.
Hatefully [hēt'-ful-i], *adv.* Malignamente, detestablemente, con tirria, con mala voluntad.
Hatefulness [hēt'-ful-nes], *s* Odiosidad.
Hater [hēt'-ẹr], *s.* Aborrecedor, el que detesta. *Woman-hater*, Enemigo de las mujeres.
Hath [hath]. Tiene, ha, tercera persona del singular, indicativo presente de *To* HAVE. (Ant.)
Hating [hēt'-ing], *s.* Aversión
Hat-maker, *s.* *V.* HATTER.
Hat-pin [hat'-pin], *s.* Alfiler largo que usan las mujeres para prender y asegurar el sombrero en el pelo
Hatrack [hat'-rac], *s.* Clavijero o percha para sombreros.
Hatred [hē'-tred], *s.* Odio, malignidad, mala voluntad, aborrecimiento, aversión, enemistad.
Hatted [hēt'-ed], *a.* El o la que lleva sombrero.
Hatter [hat'-ẹr], *s.* Sombrerero, el que hace o vende sombreros.
Hauberk [hē'-bẹrk], *s.* Coraza de la edad media, túnica de malla formada por anillos de acero entrelazados.
Haughtily [hē'-ti-li], *adv.* Arrogantemente, con arrogancia, fieramente, orgullosamente.
Haughtiness [hē'-ti-nes], *s.* Altanería, soberbia, orgullo, arrogancia, presunción, altivez.

Haughty [hō'-ti], *a.* Soberbio, altanero, altivo, vanidoso, arrogante, presuntuoso, orgulloso, vano.

Haul [hōl], *va.* 1. Tirar, arrastrar con violencia. 2. (Mar.) Halar. *To haul aft the sheets,* Cazar las escotas. *To haul down the colours,* Arriar la bandera. *Haul home,* Caza y atraca. *To haul up the courses in the brails,* Cargar los mayores sobre las candelizas. *To haul the wind,* Abarloar, ceñir el viento.

Haul, *s.* 1. Estirón, la acción de tirar con fuerza; también lo que se logra tirando de ello. 2. Redada, entre pescadores. 3. La distancia que se hace recorrer a una cosa tirando de ella.

Haulage [hōl'-ĝj], *s.* Acarreo.

Hauling [hōl'-ing], *s.* Estirón, el acto de tirar.

Haulm, Haum [hōm], *s.* Paja, rastrojo.

Haunch [hanch], *s.* 1. Anca, grupa, la parte trasera de un animal. 2. (Arq.) Riñón de una bóveda. *Haunch of venison,* Pierna de venado.

Haunt [hānt o hōnt], *va.* 1. Frecuentar, acudir muy a menudo a algun paraje; visitar muy frecuentemente a alguna persona. 2. Molestar, perseguir recurriendo constantemente a la mente. 3. Rondar, andar alrededor de alguna persona o cosa con el objeto de conseguir algo; visitar con frecuencia, a la manera de los duendes; causar obsesión. 4. Rondar, dar vueltas alrededor de alguna cosa.

Haunt, *s.* 1. Guarida, paraje a que concurre alguno con frecuencia. 2. Hábito, costumbre, querencia.

Haunted [hānt'-ed], *pp.* Frecuentado, visitado con frecuencia, particularmente por duendes y apariciones.

Haunter [hānt'-ẹr], *s.* Frecuentador, el que acude a algún paraje o visita a alguna persona muy a menudo; rondador.

Haunting [hānt'-ing], *s.* Frecuentación, trato, comunicación frecuente con una persona.

Haustellum [hōs-tel'-um], *s.* (*pl.* HAUSTELLA). Nombre científico de la trompa u órgano de succión de las mariposas, las moscas y ciertos crustáceos.

Hautboy [hō'-boi], *s.* 1. Oboe, instrumento músico de viento. 2. Una especie de fresa.

Havana cigar [ha-van'-a si-gār'], *s.* Habano.

Have [hav], *va.* (*pret.* y *pp.* HAD, *ger.* HAVING). 1. Haber, tener; poseer. 2. Contener, comprender, incluir. 3. Traer, llevar, tomar. 4. Obtener, gozar. 5. Experimentar o sentir; padecer, sufrir o gozar. 6. Concebir, tener en la mente. 7. Poner por obra, efectuar. 8. Procurar, mandar hacer; mandar o hacer (con otro infinitivo). *To have a house built,* Mandar construir una casa. 9. Haber de, tener que, deber; estar a punto de. *I have to go,* Tengo que ir. 10. Parir; hablando del padre, engendrar. *She had a child last week,* Parió la semana pasada. 11. Mirar, estimar, apreciar. 12. Saber. *Had like,* Estuvo a punto de. *He had like to have killed himself,* Estuvo a punto de matarse. *Have at,* (Ant.) Hacer cara, provocar a combate, desafiar. *Have at you, sir!* ¡Le tengo a Vd. rencor, señor mío! *To have about one,* Tener, llevar consigo. *I, you* (etc.) *had as lief,* Yo, Vd., etc., quisiera de buena gana (pero sin preferencia). *To have down,* Hacer bajar, bajar. *To have from,* Saber por alguien. *To have in,* Hacer entrar. *To have on,* (Fam.) Llevar (una prenda). *She had on a blue dress,* Llevaba un vestido azul. *To have it out,* Concluir, terminar un negocio; también, hablar sin reserva, decir las verdades. *To have it out of a person,* Pagar en la misma moneda, desquitarse. *To have rather,* Querer más, preferir. (Familiar, pero no elegante; *would rather* es muy preferible.) *To have a foresight,* Preveer. *To have a thing by heart,* Saber una cosa de memoria. *What would you have?* ¿Qué quiere Vd.? ¿qué pide Vd.? *I must have him up,* Es necesario que le haga subir. *We will have a trial at him* o *at it,* Lo experimentaremos o lo probaremos. *Have with you,* Iré con Vd. *Have after you,* Seguiré a Vd. *I will have it so,* Así lo quiero. *As fortune would have it,* Por fortuna. *To have better,* Hacer mejor. *To have a mind,* Tener gana, deseo, pensamiento de hacer algo. *To have nothing to do with him,* No tener nada que ver con él. Este verbo *to have* sirve en la lengua inglesa, así como en otras europeas, de verbo auxiliar para formar los tiempos compuestos. *V.* POSSESS.

Haven [hē'v'-n], *s.* Puerto, abra; abrigo, asilo.

Haver [hav'-ẹr], *s.* 1. Poseedor, tenedor. 2. (Esco.) Avena.

Haversack [hav'-ẹr-sac], *s.* Mochila, saco basto para llevar víveres.

Having [hav'-ing], *s.* Bienes, hacienda, haber; el acto o estado de poseer.

Havoc, †Havock [hav'-ẹc], *s.* Estrago, ruina, destrucción, desolación, asolamiento, tala.—*inter.* Exclamación de matanza o de no dar cuartel.

Havoc, *va.* (Poco us.) Estragar, asolar, destruir, talar.

Haw [hō], *s.* 1. La baya y simiente del espino blanco. 2. Granizo o mancha en el ojo. 3. Cañada, cercado. 4. Dificultad en pronunciar las palabras, balbucencia.

Haw, *va.* Volver o hacer volverse a la izquierda; se usa hablando de los bueyes o las caballerías. Lo opuesto a *gee.* *To haw and gee,* Ir de un lado a otro; vacilar, estar irresoluto.—*vn.* Tartamudear; tartalear; hablar muy despacio.

Hawaiian [ha-wai'-yan], *a.* De Hawaii, archipiélago de Oceanía y nombre de la mayor de sus islas.

Hawhaw [hō-hō'], *s.* 1. *V.* GUFFAW. 2. Especie de zanja o cerca dispuesta de tal modo que no se puede percibir hasta estar sobre ella. *V.* HA-HA.

Hawk [hōk], *s.* Halcón, ave de rapiña.

Hawk, *va.* 1. Cazar con halcón. 2. Pregonar géneros por las calles para venderlos. 3. Hacer esfuerzo para arrojar los esputos; expectorar, gargajear.

Hawker [hōk'-ẹr], *s.* Buhonero, mercachifle.

Hawk-eye [hōk'-ai] *s.* (Fam. E. U.) Ojo de halcón, apodo del natural o habitante del Estado de Iowa; viene del nombre de un antiguo jefe indio de aquella región.

Hawk-eyed [hōk'-aid], *a.* Lince, el que tiene la vista penetrante.

Hawking [hōk'-ing], *s.* Cetrería, el acto de cazar con halcón.

Hawk-nosed [hōk'-nōzd], **Hook-nosed** [huk'-nōzd], *a.* Aguileño, de nariz aguileña.

Hawkmoth [hōk'-mōth], *s.* Esfinge, género de mariposas nocturnas que incluye la atropos o mariposa de cabeza de muerto.

Hawk-owl [hōk'-aul], *s.* (Orn.) Úlula, autillo.

Hawk's-bell [hōks'-bel], *s.* Cascabel.

Hawkweed [hōk'-wīd], *s.* (Bot.) Hieracio o hierba del gavilán.

Hawse [hōz], *s.* 1. Proa del buque en que están los escobenes. 2. Situación de los cables al salir de los escobenes cuando un buque está amarrado con dos anclas; también distancia o longitud de un cable. *Hawse-hole,* Escobén, el agujero de la proa por donde pasan los cables, cuando el bajel está anclado. *Hawse-pipes,* Canales de plomo en los escobenes. *Hawse-plugs,* Tacos de los escobenes.

Hawser [hōz'-ẹr], *s.* (Mar.) Guindaleza.

Hawthorn [hō'-thōrn], *s.* (Bot.) Espino blanco.

Hay [hē], *s.* Heno, hierba segada y seca para forraje. *Hay-cold, hay-fever,* Especie de fiebre intermitente, enfermedad catarral caracterizada por la repetición anual de sus síntomas. *Hay-spreader, hay-tedder,* Heneador (Amer.), máquina con ruedas para cosechar el heno. *Make hay while the sun shines* Al buen día meterle en casa.

Hay (Ant.), *s.* 1. Red para cercar la guarida de un animal. 2. Seto, cercado, vallado. 3. Danza en círculo. *To dance the hay,* Bailar en círculo, en redondo.

†Hay, *vn.* Poner lazos para cazar conejos.

Haycock [hē'-coc], *s.* Pila, montón o niara pequeña de heno.

Hay fever [hē fīv'-ẹr], *s.* Fiebre del heno.

Hayfield [hē'-fīld], *s.* Henar.

Hayfork [hē'-fōrk], *s.* (Agr.) Horca.

Hay-harvest [hē'-hār-vest], *s.* La siega del heno.

Hayloft [hē'-lōft], *s.* Henil, el sitio donde se guarda el heno.

Hay-maker [hē'-mē-kẹr], *s.* El jornalero que pone la hierba o el heno a secar en el campo después de segado.

Hay-market [hē'-mār-ket], *s.* Mercado de heno; nombre de una calle de Londres.

Haymow [hē'-mau], *s.* Henal o henil.

Hayrick [hē'-ric], **Haystack** [hē'-stac], *s.* Niara, montón o pila de heno.

Haytian [hē'-ti-an o hai'-ti-an], *a.* Haitiano, de la república de Haití.

Haywire [hē'-wair], *s.* 1. Alambre para embalar heno. 2. *To go haywire,* (fam.) Volverse loco, perder la cabeza.

Hazard [haz'-ard], *s.* 1. Peligro, riesgo. 2. Casualidad, acaso, accidente, suceso imprevisto. 3. Juego de azar a los dados. 4. Tronera, en el juego inglés de billar.

Hazard, *va.* Arriesgar, poner en riesgo o en peligro.—*vn.* Arriesgarse, probar la suerte; aventurar.

Hazardable [haz'-ard-a-bl], *a.* Osado, peligroso, arriesgado.

Hazarder [haz'-ard-ẹr], *s.* 1. Jugador. 2. El que aventura o arriesga.

Hazardous [haz'-ard-us], *a.* Arriesgado, peligroso, expuesto á riesgos.
Hazardously [haz'-ard-us-li], *adv.* Peligrosamente, arriesgadamente.
Haze [hêz], *s.* 1. Tufo, conjunto de partículas muy finas suspendidas en el aire, a menudo con poca o ninguna humedad. 2. Ofuscamiento mental.
Haze, *vn.* Hacer tufo; estar el tiempo nebuloso o humoso.—*va.* 1. Hacer a uno víctima de petardos, chanzas o chascos; dícese de los estudiantes. 2. Cansar, extenuar á fuerza de trabajo; dícese de los marineros.
Hazel [hê'-zl], *s.* (Bot.) Avellano, el árbol que produce la avellana. *Hazel-nut,* Avellana.
Hazel [hê'-zl], *a.* Castaño, del color de avellana.
Haziness [hê'-zi-nes], *s.* Tufo, obscuridad.
Hazy [hê'-zi], *a.* 1. Anieblado, cargado de humo, nublado, nebuloso. 2. Falto de claridad; confuso, obscuro.
H-bomb [H'-bom], *s* Bomba H, bomba de hidrógeno.
He [hî], *pron.* 1. Él, pronombre personal, masculino, de la tercera persona del singular. 2. Alguien, una persona cualquiera, indefinidamente. *He is an honest man,* Él es un hombre de bien. Algunas veces se usa para determinar el género masculino de un animal. *He-goat,* Macho cabrío. *He-bear,* Oso.
Head [hed], *s.* 1. Cabeza, la parte superior del cuerpo y por extensión de otras muchas cosas. 2. Lo que es análogo a la cabeza de un animal por su figura, posición, etc. *Head of cabbage,* etc., Repollo de col, etc. *Head of a bed,* Cabecera de una cama. *Head of a book,* Título de libro. *Head of a cane,* Puño de bastón. *Head of a cask,* Fondo de un barril. *Head of an arrow,* Punta de un dardo. 3. Jefe, cabeza, el superior que gobierna y a quien los demás están subordinados. 4. Primera fila, la posición o rango de un jefe; frente. 5. Res, cabeza de ganado; (en este sentido *head* es igualmente singular y plural). *Two hundred head of sheep,* Doscientas reses de ganado lanar. 6. Progreso, prosperidad, adelantamiento. 7. Juicio, talento, capacidad. 8. Crisis, mutación crítica. 9. Astas de ciervo o venado; puntas, extremo. *To go ahead,* Ir adelante, proseguir, adelantarse. *To fall headlong,* Caer de cabeza, precipitarse. *From head to foot,* De pies a cabeza. *Two heads are better than one,* (prov.) Más ven cuatro ojos que dos. 10. (Mar.) Cabeza de la nave, la proa con el bauprés que salle de ella; alas de proa. *Too much by the head,* Muy metido a proa. *Head-fast,* Cabo de retenida de proa. *Head-rope,* Relinga de gratil. *A-head,* Por la proa. *Head-sails,* Velas de proa. *Head of a sail,* Gratil. 11. Fuente, manantial. *Head of a river,* Nacimiento de un río. 12. Soltura del freno. *To give a horse his head,* Dar rienda suelta a un caballo. 13. Cofia o cualquier adorno para la cabeza. *Hand over head,* Inconsideradamente. *Head and shoulders,* (1) Por fuerza. (2) En mucho. *Head of a discourse.* Punto principal de un discurso. *On this head,* Sobre este punto, asunto o particular. *To hit the nail on the head,* Dar en el clavo. *To be over head and ears in debt, in love,* Estar comido de deudas; estar enamorado hasta las cachas. *To have neither head nor tail,* No tener pies ni cabeza, no tener sentido común. *To drag in by the head and shoulders,* Tirar por los cabellos. *To draw to a head,* Supurar; recapitular. *To bring a business to a head,* Concluir un negocio. *To make head against one,* Hacer frente a alguno o resistirle, oponerse abiertamente.—*a.* Principal.
Head, *va.* 1. Mandar, gobernar, dirigir. 2. Degollar. 3. Poner cabeza, puño, punta o una parte muy principal a alguna cosa. 4. Podar los árboles. 5. Avanzar y cortar la retirada.—*vn.* 1. Adelantarse en una dirección determinada. 2. Repollar, acogollarse (como un col); anudar, cuajar las flores o frutos. 3. Tomar su origen, provenir de.
Headache [hed'-êk], *s.* Dolor de cabeza. *Migraine headache,* Jaqueca, fuerte dolor de cabeza.
Head-band [hed'-band], *s.* 1. Cabezada de libro. 2. Cinta con que se venda la cabeza.
Head-board [hed'-bōrd], *s.* Cabecera de cama.
Head cheese [hed chîz], *s.* Queso de cerdo.
Head-dress [hed'-dres], *s.* Cofia, tocado, redecilla o escofieta.
Headed [hed'-ed], *a.* Lo que tiene cabeza. *Clear* o *long-headed,* Agudo o profundo. *Thick-headed,* De pocos alcances; mentecato.
Header [hed'-ẹr], *s.* 1. El que pone las cabezas de los clavos, alfileres o cosas semejantes. 2. Caída o zambullida de cabeza. 3. Cabezada, golpe en la cabeza. 4. Descabezador de las mieses. 5. Cabeza, el que dirige un cuerpo o reunión de personas. 6. El primer ladrillo en el ángulo de una pared.
Headfirst [hed'-fẹrst], *adv.* De cabeza.
Head-gear [hed'-gîr], *s.* 1. Tocado o cofia de mujer. 2. Las piezas de los jaeces que rodean la cabeza del caballo. 3. (Mar.) Aparejo de las velas de proa.
Headily [hed'-i-li], *adv.* Obstinadamente, desatinadamente.
Headiness [hed'-i-nes], *s.* Desatino, precipitación, obstinación; sacudida.
Heading [hed'-ing], *s.* 1. Título, encabezamiento, encabezado (de cartas, billetes, recibos, facturas, etc.); membrete. 2. Témpano, tapa de barril o cuba. 3. (Min.) Galería, socavón; frente.
Headland [hed'-land], *s.* 1. Cabo, promontorio, punta. 2. Tierra no arada inmediata a los setos o cercados.
Headless [hed'-les], *a.* 1. Descabezado, degollado; acéfalo. 2. Ignorante, terco, obstinado; inconsiderado.
Headlight [hed'-lait], *s.* 1. Linterna de locomotora. 2. Luz blanca puesta al tope de un vapor en movimiento.
Headline [hed'-lain], *s.* Título o encabezado (de un periódico, etc.)
Headlong [hed'-lōng], *a.* Temerario, inconsiderado, imprudente, precipitado.—*adv.* 1. De cabeza, con la cabeza adelante. 2. Temerariamente, imprudentemente, precipitadamente; a toda prisa, de hoz y de coz, sin consideración o sin reparo; al tuntún. *To cast down headlong,* Precipitar. *To fall headlong,* Caer con la cabeza abajo, caer de cabeza.
Headman [hed'-man], *s.* Jefe.
Head-master [hed'-mas-tẹr], *s.* El director de una escuela.
Head-money [hed'-mun-i], *s.* Capitación.
Head off [hed ef], *va.* Alcanzar, adelantarse para prevenir.
Headphone [hed'-fōn], *s.* Auricular.
Headpiece [hed'-pîs], *s.* 1. Casco, yelmo, armadura de la parte superior de la cabeza. 2. Ingenio, entendimiento, cabeza. 3. Auricular para el teléfono. 4. (Impr.) Viñeta.
Head-post [hed'-pōst], *s.* Pilar de la cabecera de una cama, poste de establo.
Head-quarters [hed'-cwēr-tẹrz], *s.* Cuartel general.
Head-sail [hed'-sêl], *s.* (Mar.) Vela delantera.
Head-sea [hed'-sî], *s.* (Mar.) Mar o marejada de proa.
Headset [hed'-set], *s.* Receptor de cabeza, auricular de casco.
Headship [hed'-ship], *s.* Jefatura, el cargo de jefe o cabeza; autoridad, gobierno.
Headsman [hedz'-man], *s.* Verdugo, degollador.
Head-spring [hed'-spring], *s.* Fuente, origen.
Headstall [hed'-stōl], *s.* Cabezada del freno, testera. (Mex.) Bozal.
Head-stone [hed'-stōn], *s.* Piedra fundamental; piedra sepulcral.
Headstrong [hed'-strōng], *a.* Terco, testarudo, cabezudo, rehacio, indócil, obstinado, encalabrinado, aferrado.
Headtire [hed'-tair], *s.* Escofieta, atavío de la cabeza.
Head waiter [hed wêt'-ẹr], *s.* Mayordomo, jefe de los mozos de un restaurante.
Headwaters [hed'-wē'-tẹrz], *s. pl.* Cabecera (de un río, etc.)
Headway [hed'-wê], *s.* 1. Adelantamiento de un buque, el camino que va haciendo; ímpetu; progreso. 2. El intervalo de tiempo que media entre dos trenes o dos carros consecutivos de una misma línea. *Trains running on ten minutes' headway,* Trenes que salen a intervalos de diez minutos.
Head wind [hed wind], *s.* (Mar.) Viento en contra.
Head-work [hed'-wūrk], *s.* 1. Trabajo mental, obra intelectual. 2. (Arq.) Adorno semejante a la cabeza de un animal, puesto, por ejemplo, sobre la clave de un arco.
Heady [hed'-i], *a.* 1. Temerario, arrojado. 2. Fuerte, el licor que se sube a la cabeza y hace daño. 3. Violento, impetuoso.
Heal [hîl], *va.* 1. Curar, sanar, librar de una dolencia. 2. Reconciliar, componer, ajustar. 3. Purificar, devolver la pureza a.—*vn.* Sanar, recobrar la salud; curar o cicatrizarse una herida o llaga. *To heal up,* Cicatrizarse una herida o llaga.
Healer [hîl'-ẹr], *s.* Sanador, el que sana; curador, el que cura; el que hace profesión de curar las enfermedades.
Healing [hîl'-ing], *s.* Sanativo, curativo, medicinal, saludable; emoliente; conciliador, pacífico.—*s.* 1. Curación. 2. El poder de dar la salud.
Health [helth], *s.* 1. Salud, sanidad.

2. Sanidad de alma, sinceridad, pureza de intención. 3. Brindis, la acción de beber a la salud de otro. *Health officer*, Oficial de sanidad o de cuarentena. *Health-lift*, Máquina de alzar pesos, como ejercicio. *Bill of health*, Patente de sanidad. *Certificate of health*, Certificado de sanidad. *Health-giving*, Salubre, saludable, que da la salud. *Your health, sir*, A su salud, caballero.

Healthful [helth'-ful], *a.* Sano, saludable, salubre.

Healthfully [helth'-ful-i], *adv.* Saludablemente, en buena salud, con salud.

Healthfulness [helth'-ful-nes], *s.* 1. Salud, buena disposición del cuerpo. 2. Sanidad, bondad, salubridad, lo sano o saludable de alguna cosa.

Healthily [helth'-i-li], *adv.* Saludablemente, con salud.

Healthiness [helth'-i-nes], *s.* Sanidad, estado sano, goce de buena salud.

Health insurance [helth in-shūr'-ans], *s.* Seguro de enfermedad.

Healthless [helth'-les], *s.* Enfermo, débil, el que no goza salud.

Health resort [helth rẹ-zōrt'], *s.* Centro o lugar de curaciones.

Healthy [helth'-i], *a.* Sano, libre de enfermedades o achaques; sanativo.

Heap [hīp], *s.* 1. Montón, agregado o junta de muchas cosas puestas en un lugar. 2. (Fam.) Turba, muchedumbre de gente. *In heaps*, A montones.

Heap, *va.* 1. Amontonar, poner unas cosas sobre otras sin orden ni concierto. 2. Acumular, juntar, colmar.

Heaper [hīp'-ẹr], *s.* Amontonador.

Hear [hīr], *va.* (*pret.* y *pp.* HEARD). 1. Oir, percibir por el órgano del oído cualquier sonido. 2. Dar audiencia o permiso para hablar. 3. Oir, entender, escuchar; obedecer. 4. Oir en justicia o judicialmente. —*vn.* Oir, escuchar, saber por relación, tener noticia, estar informado. *I hear he is to come back*, Tengo entendido que vuelve. *Pray let me hear from you now and then*, Sírvase Vd. darme noticias suyas de cuando en cuando. *To hear out*, Oir hasta el fin. *To hear tell of*, (Fam.) Oir o entender por la voz común.

Heard [hẹrd], *pret.* y *pp.* de *To* HEAR.

Hearing [hīr'-ing], *s.* 1. Oído, el sentido de oir. 2. Audiencia; averiguación jurídica de alguna cosa; examen de testigos. 3. La acción de oir. 4. El alcance del oído. *To be hard of hearing*, Ser duro de oído, ser algo sordo. *To be within hearing*, Estar al alcance del oído.

Hearsay [hīr'-sē], *s.* Rumor, voz común, fama, lo que se dice de público y notorio, lo que se sabe o cuenta por dicho de otros. *To know a thing by hearsay*, Saber alguna cosa de oídas.

Hearse [hẹrs], *s.* 1. Carro fúnebre. 2. Ataúd, féretro. 3. (Ant.) Cenotafio, monumento.

Hearse, *va.* Encerrar en el féretro o ataúd.

Hearse-cloth [hẹrs'-clōth], *s.* Cubierta ó paño mortuorio.

Hearse-like [hẹrs'-laic], *a.* Lúgubre, fúnebre.

Heart [hārt], *s.* 1. Corazón, músculo impar que es el órgano central de la circulación de la sangre. 2. Corazón, centro de las pasiones, afectos y sentimientos. 3. Corazón, lo interior, el fondo, el centro o lo fuerte de cualquiera cosa; la parte vital o principal de un asunto. 4. Ánimo, valor, esfuerzo. 5. Voluntad amor, benevolencia; simpatía, caridad, filantropía. 6. Figura de corazón en los naipes que equivale a la figura de copas en los naipes españoles. *He died of a broken heart*, o *broken-hearted*, Murió de pesadumbre, o de tristeza. *With all my heart*. Con toda mi alma. *The heart of a country*, El centro de un país o territorio. *At heart*, En el fondo, esencialmente; en verdad. *By heart*, De memoria. *To learn by heart*, Aprender de memoria. *Heart and hand, heart and soul*, Todo, de una manera entusiástica, con instancia y empeño. *To find in one's heart*, Querer, desear. *To have at heart*, Querer con ternura y predilección; fomentar con empeño. *To lay o take to heart*, Desconsolarse, apesadumbrarse; estar inquieto acerca de algo. *To take the heart out of one*, (Fam.) Desalentar, desanimar a alguno. *To be sick at heart*, Tener la muerte en el alma. *To wear one's heart on one's sleeve*, Llevar el corazón en la mano. *To have the heart in the mouth*, Tener el alma entre los dientes, o estar con el alma en un hilo; no llegarle á uno la camisa al cuerpo. *Heart-chilled*, El que tiene el corazón helado o sin acción. *Heart-clot*, Cuajarón fibrinoso que se forma en el corazón. *Heart-clover, heart-trefoil*, (Bot.) Especie de alfalfa que tiene las hojuelas acorazonadas con manchas purpúreas. Medicago maculata. *Heart-consuming, heart-corroding*, Lo que consume o corroe el corazón. *Heart-deep*, Grabado en el corazón. *Heart-discouraging*, Desconsolador, lo que desanima, amilana o acobarda. *Heart-disease*, Enfermedad del corazón. *Heart-easing*, Lo que serena, tranquiliza ó causa reposo. *Heart-eating*, Lo que corroe el corazón. *Heart-expanding*, Lo que abre el corazón o da alegría y placer. *Heart-grief*, Congoja de corazón, angustia. *Heart-hardened*. Endurecido, impenitente. *Heart-quelling*, Lo que atrae el corazón o causa afición o amor. *Heart-rending*, Agudo, penetrante; lo que parte o despedaza el corazón. *Heart-shaped*, Acorazonado, en forma de corazón. *Heart-sick*, Dolorido, afligido, desconsolado, amilanado. *Heart-sickness*, Mal de corazón. *Heart-sore*, Afligido, apesadumbrado, muy angustiosamente; abatido, agobiado. *Heart-sorrowing*, El que está lleno de angustia. *Heart-strings*, Las fibras del corazón. *Heart-struck*, Fijo en el corazón; desmayado.

Heart, *va.* *V.* HEARTEN.

Heart-ache [hārt'-ēk], *s.* Angustia, aflicción, congoja, pesar, pena, inquietud.

Heart-appalling [hārt'-ạp-pōl'-ing], *a.* Lo que abruma, oprime o hace desmayar el corazón.

Heart attack [hart a-tac'], *s.* Ataque al corazón.

Heartbeat [hārt'-bīt], *s.* Latido del corazón.

Heart-blood [hārt'-blud], *s.* 1. Sangre del corazón. 2. La esencia de alguna cosa. 3. Vida.

Heart-break [hārt'-brēk], *s.* Angustia, disgusto, aflicción, pesar.

Heart-breaking [hārt'-brēk-ing], *a.* Congojoso, doloroso, desolador, lo que causa u ocasiona pena o aflicción.—*s.* Congoja, angustia.

Heart-broken [hārt'-brōk-n], *a.* Penetrado de dolor, de angustia o de congoja.

Heartburn [hārt'-būrn], *s.* Cardialgía, dolor que se siente en la boca del estómago.

Heart-ease [hārt'-īz], *s.* Tranquilidad, sosiego, reposo, quietud, serenidad.

Hearted [hārt'-ed], *a.* 1. Lo que está fijo o tiene su asiento en el corazón. 2. Lo que se emprende con ardor o con todo el corazón. *Faint-hearted*, Tímido, pusilánime.

Hearten [hārt'-n], *va.* 1. Animar, alentar, dar vigor o aliento, fortificar. 2. Abonar, engrasar, estercolar las tierras.

Heartener [hārt'-n-ẹr], *s.* Animador, alentador.

Heartfelt [hārt'-felt], *a.* De corazón, cordial, sincero, sentido en el alma o en el fondo del corazón.

Heart-free [hārt-frī], *a.* Libre, sin ningún amor.

Hearth [hārth y rara vez hẹrth], *s.* 1. Hogar, fogón; hogar de forja o de horno. 2. Anaquel delante de una estufa. 3. Hogar doméstico, la casa de uno.

Hearth-money [hārth'-mun-i], *s.* Fogaje, derecho o tributo que se pagaba por cada casa.

Heartily [hārt'-i-li], *adv.* 1. Sinceramente, cordialmente. *To laugh most heartily*, Reirse a más no poder. 2. Ansiosamente, con ansia.

Heartiness [hārt'-i-nes], *s.* Sinceridad; vigor.

Heartless [hārt'-les], *a.* 1. Falto de corazón; sin piedad ni cariño; falto de simpatía, cruel. 2. Cobarde, tímido, pusilánime, amilanado.

Heartlessly [hārt'-les-li], *adv.* 1. Cruelmente, sin piedad, inhumanamente. 2. Pusilánimemente, tímidamente, sin ánimo.

Heartlessness [hārt'-les-nes], *s.* Falta de simpatía y piedad; falta de ánimo.

Heart's-ease [hārts'-īz], *s.* (Bot.) Trinitaria. *V.* PANSY.

Heart-to-heart [hart-tū-hārt'], *a.* Sincero, de corazón a corazón. *Heart-to-heart talk*, Charla íntima y confidencial.

Heart trouble [hart trub'-l], *s.* Enfermedad del corazón, mal cardíaco.

Heart-whole [hārt'-hōl], *a.* 1. Desamorado, el que no está enamorado. 2. Valiente, intrépido, valeroso. 3. Sincero.

Heart-wounded [hārt'-wūnd'-ed], *a.* 1. Lleno de angustia. 2. Enamorado.

Hearty [hārt'-i], *a.* 1. Sincero, alegre, puro, sencillo. 2. Sano, robusto, vigoroso.

Heat [hīt], *s.* 1. Calor, la impresión que produce el fuego. 2. Calor, el estado de cualquier cuerpo sujeto á la acción del fuego. 3. Calor, lo más fuerte o vivo de alguna acción. 4. Carrera o corrida de un caballo o de muchos. 5. Granos que salen en la cara por efecto del calor. 6. Fogosidad, viveza demasiada; ardor, vehemencia; cólera, odio, animosidad. 7. Celo, apetito a la generación en los irracionales, principalmente en las hembras. 8. Una sola operación de calentar, encender, derretir o fundir metales. 9. Fermentación. *Heat-stroke*, Insolación. *V.* SUNSTROKE. *Heat shield*, Protector contra el calor. *Heat wave*, Ola de calor. *Bottom heat*, Calor artificial bajo las capas de tierra en los invernaderos. *Red heat*, Calor llevado hasta el rojo; de aquí, emoción o pasión fuerte. *White heat*, Candencia, incandescencia; pasión la más intensa. *Prickly heat*, Salpullido. *In heat*, En celo, cachonda, salida.

Heat, *va.* 1. Calentar, encender; causar ardor. 2. Hacer fermentar. —*vn.* 1. Fermentar, ponerse algún cuerpo en movimiento de fermentación. 2. Encolerizarse. 3. Arder o estar poseído de una pasión.

Heater [hît'-ęr], *s.* 1. Calentador. 2. Calorífero. *Hot-air heater*, Calorífero de aire caliente.

Heath [hîth], *s.* 1. (Bot.) Brezo, cualquier arbusto de los géneros Erica o Calluna. 2. Brezal, páramo, matorral.

Heathcock [hîth'-cec], *s.* (Orn.) Gallo silvestre.

Heathen [hîdh'-n], *s.* 1. Gentil, pagano, idólatra. 2. Ateo, ateísta.

Heathen, Heathenish [hîdh'-n-ish], *a.* Gentílico, salvaje, bárbaro, feroz.

Heathenishly [hîdh'-n-ish-li], *adv.* A la manera de los gentiles o de los paganos.

Heathenishness [hîdh'-n-ish-nes], *s.* El estado de pagano; profanidad, irreligiosidad.

Heathenism [hîdh'-n-izm], *s.* Gentilismo, gentilidad, paganismo, idolatría.

Heathenize [hîdh'-n-aiz], *va.* Hacer a uno pagano o idólatra.

Heather [hedh'-er], *s.* Brezo.

Heathery [hedh'-ęr-i] o **Heathy** [hîth'-i], *a.* Lleno de brezos, o parecido a ellos; o cubierto de brezos.

Heating [hît'-ing], *s.* Calefacción, la acción de calentar o calentarse.

Heat lightning [hît lait'-ning], *s.* Relámpago sin truenos.

Heat-resistant [hît'-rę-zist-ant], *a.* Calorífugo.

Heat wave [hît wêv], *s.* Onda cálida, onda de calor.

Heave [hîv], *va.* (*pret.* y *pp.* HEAVED, HOVE. *Hove* está casi limitado al uso náutico). 1. Alzar, levantar alguna cosa pesada; (Mar.) izar. 2. Echar fuera, arrojar. 3. Exhalar, prorrumpir. *To heave the lead*, Escandallar, echar el escandallo. *To heave a sigh*, Exhalar un suspiro. 4. Inflar o hinchar alguna cosa. 5. (Geol.) Fracturar un filón y forzarlo fuera de su posición normal.—*vn.* 1. Levantarse y bajarse alternativa y pesadamente, v. gr. el pecho, el mar; suspirar dando grandes sollozos. 2. Palpitar el corazón; respirar trabajosamente. 3. Trabajar con mucha fuerza. 4. Tener náuseas. (Mar.) Virar. *To heave at the capstan*, (Mar.) Virar al cabrestante. *To heave down*, Descubrir la quilla. *To heave ahead*, Virar para proa. *To heave overboard*, Echar a la mar.

Heave, *s.* 1. Elevación; esfuerzo para levantarse o alzarse. 2. Suspiros de congoja. 3. Estertor, hinchazón o elevación del pecho causada por la dificultad de respirar. 4. Náusea; esfuerzo para vomitar. 5. (Geol.) El grado de desviación de las partes de una veta o filón forzadas fuera de su posición normal.

Heaven [hev'-n], *s.* 1. Cielo, firmamento, región etérea. 2. Cielo, paraíso, la mansión de Dios. 3. Cielo, el poder supremo. 4. Cielo, elevación, sublimidad. *Heaven-aspiring*, El que aspira a ganar el cielo. *Heaven-banished*, Desterrado del cielo. *Heaven-begot*, Procreado por un poder celeste. *Heaven-born*, Nacido descendido del cielo; celeste, divino, angélico. *Heaven-bred*, Criado en los cielos. *Heaven-built*, Construído por los dioses. *Heaven-directed*, Dirigido o elevado hacia el cielo. *Heaven-fallen*, Caído del cielo. *Heaven-gifted*, Dotado por el cielo. *Heaven-inspired*, Inspirado del cielo. *Heaven-instructed*, Instruído por el cielo. *Heaven-kissing*, Tocando al cielo: dícese de las montañas que esconden sus cumbres en las nubes. *Heaven-loved*, Querido del cielo; favorecido de Dios. *Heaven-warring*, El que hace la guerra o lucha contra el cielo.

Heavenliness [hev'-n-li-nes], *s.* Excelencia suprema.

Heavenly [hev'-n-li], *a.* Celeste, divino, celestial.—*adv.* Celestialmente, divinamente.

Heavenward [hev'-n-ward], *adv.* Hacia el cielo.

Heaver [hîv'-ęr], *s.* 1. (Mar.) Alzaprima. 2. Cargador, el que levanta; esta voz se usa para formar palabras compuestas. *Coal-heaver*, Cargador de carbón.

Heaves [hîvs], *s. pl.* Huérfago, enfermedad asmática que ataca a las caballerías; emfisema de los pulmones.

Heavily [hev'-i-li], *adv.* Pesadamente, lentamente; melancólicamente, tristemente. *To complain heavily*, Quejarse amargamente.

Heaviness [hev'-i-nes], *s.* 1. Pesadez, peso, gravedad. 2. Pesadez, tardanza, torpeza, languidez. 3. Abatimiento de ánimo, aflicción, tristeza, angustia. 4. Opresión, carga.

Heaving [hîv'-ing], *s.* 1. Palpitación, movimiento irregular del corazón. 2. Hinchazón u oleada del mar.

Heavy [hev'-i], *a.* 1. Grave, pesado, ponderoso. 2. Grande, fuerte, poderoso, muy vivo, violento. 3. Duro, opresivo, importuno, penoso, molesto, enfadoso. 4. Pesaroso, triste, melancólico. 5. Considerable, importante; que compra o vende en grandes cantidades. 6. Frío, falto de espíritu; tardo, lento, soñoliento, lerdo, estúpido. 7. Pesado, difícil de digerirse. 8. Denso, espeso; fuerte; arcilloso. *Heavy beer, liquor*, Cerveza, licor fuerte. *Heavy road*, Camino pesado o arcilloso.—*adv.* V. HEAVILY.

Heavy-hearted [hev'-i-hārt'-ed], *a.* Abatido, descorazonado.

Heavy water [hev'-i wē'-tęr], *s.* (Quím.) Agua pesada.

Heavyweight [hev'-i-wêt], *s.* (Boxeo). Peso completo.

Heazy [hê'-zi], *a.* (Prov. Ingl.) Jadeante, asmático; ronco. *V.* WHEEZY.

Hebdomad [heb'-do-mad], *s.* Siete; siete cosas cualesquiera, particularmente hebdómada, semana.

Hebdomadal [heb-dem'-a-dal], **Hebdomadary** [heb-dem'-a-dę-ri], *a.* Hebdomadario, semanal.

‡**Hebetate** [heb'-ę-têt], *va.* Atontar, entorpecer, embrutecer.—*a.* (Bot.) Que tiene punta obtusa y blanda.

Hebetation [heb-ę-tê'-shun], *s.* Atontamiento, entorpecimiento, embrutecimiento.

‡**Hebete** [heb'-ît], *a.* Entorpecido, embrutecido, atontado.

Hebetude [heb'-ę-tiūd], *s.* Embotamiento, torpeza de los sentidos.

Hebraism [hî'-bra-izm], *s.* Hebraísmo, giro hebreo en el lenguaje.

Hebraist [hî'-bra-ist], ‡**Hebrician** [hî-brish'-an], *s.* Hebraizante, el erudito en la lengua hebrea.

Hebraize [hî'-bra-aiz], *va.* Hebraizar, hacer hebreo; verter al hebreo.—*vn.* Adoptar las costumbres o la lengua hebreas: volverse hebreo.

Hebrew [hî'-brū], *s.* 1. Hebreo, la lengua hebrea. 2. Hebreo, judío. —*a.* Hebraico.

Hecatomb [hec'-a-tūm o tem], *s.* Hecatombe, antiguo sacrificio griego de cien reses; de aquí, gran carnicería, matanza enorme.

Heck, *s.* 1. Enrejado, verja. (a) Enrejado, especie de trampa para coger peces. (b) Recipiente a modo de enrejado, para forraje. (Prov. Ingl.) (c) Puerta cuya parte superior está enrejada o se mueve independientemente de la puerta misma. 2. Volante de un torno de hilar.

Heckle [hec'-l], *v.* y *s.* *V.* HATCHEL.

Hectare [hec'-tār], *s.* Hectárea, medida de superficie que contiene cien áreas; equivale a 2.471 acres ingleses.

Hectic, Hectical [hec'-tic, al], *a.* Hético, héctico, el que padece calentura hética. *Hectic*, *s.* Hética, consunción, fiebre hética.

Hectically [hec'-tic-al-i], *adv.* Constitucionalmente, hablando de la constitución física; de ordinario denota consunción.

Hecto (o hect-). Prefijo tomado del griego que significa ciento, o cien veces. *Hectogram, hectogramme*, Hectogramo, cien gramos (= onzas 3.5 av.). *Hectoliter, hectolitre*, Hectólitro, cien litros (= 26.5 galones de vino, o 22.01 galones imperiales). *Hectometer, hectometre*, Hectómetro, cien metros (= 328.09 pies ingleses).

Hector [hec'-tęr], *s.* Matasiete, fanfarrón, fierabrás, perdonavidas.

Hedera [hed'-ę-ra], *s.* Hiedra; sólo se conocen dos especies, la hiedra común y la australiana.

Hedge [hej], *s.* Seto, vallado de zarzas. Úsase a veces unido a algunas voces con la significación de bajo, vil o despreciable. *Quickset hedge*, Seto vivo. *Stake hedge*, Seto muerto.

Hedge, *va.* 1. Cercar alguna heredad con un seto. 2. Obstruir, impedir, tapar; defender, proteger, como con un seto o vallado. 3. Circundar; rodear.—*vn.* 1. Ponerse al abrigo, agacharse, esconderse (como detrás de un seto). 2. Apostar a fin de compensar o igualar una apuesta anterior; procurar los medios de evadir la responsabilidad por lo que antes se ha dicho o hecho.

Hedge-born [hej'-bērn], *a.* Obscuro, el que es de linaje bajo y no conocido.

Hedge-creeper [hej'-crîp-ęr], *s.* Vagamundo.

Hedgehog [hej'-heg], *s.* 1. Erizo, animal cubierto de púas. 2. Voz de improperio.

Hedge-hyssop [hej'-his-ep], *s.* (Bot.) Hierba del pobre.

Hedge-mustard [hej'-mus-tard], *s.* (Bot.) Erísimo, jaramago.

Hedge-nettle [hej'-net-l], *s.* (Bot.) Galiopsis.

Hedge-note [hej'-nōt], *s.* Mamotreto, voz de desprecio que se aplica a los malos escritos.

Hedge-priest [hej'-prīst], *s.* Clerizonte, clérigo iliterato y mal mirado.
Hedger [hej'-ęr], *s.* 1. Cercador, el que hace cercados o setos de árboles y arbustos. 2. El que compensa o iguala sus apuestas.
Hedgerow [hej'-rō], *s.* La serie de árboles o arbustos en los cercados o setos.
Hedge-sparrow [hej'-spar-ro], *s.* (Orn.) Curruca, especie de gorrión.
Hedging-bill [hej'-ing-bil], *s.* Podadera corva para cortar los setos vivos.
Hedonism [hed'-o-nizm], *s.* Hedonismo, la doctrina de ciertos filósofos griegos de que el placer es el único bien; en la ética, egoismo, interés personal, indulgencia para consigo mismo.
Heed [hīd], *va.* Atender, prestar atención, estar con cuidado y aplicación a lo que se mira u oye; observar, notar.—*vn.* Considerar.
Heed, *s.* 1. Cuidado, atención, cautela, precaución. 2. Observación, reparo, aprecio. 3. Seriedad, gravedad, sobriedad, regularidad. *Take heed what you do,* Mire Vd. lo que hace. *To take no heed of,* No hacer caso de.
Heedful [hīd'-ful], *a.* Vigilante, atento, cauteloso, cuidadoso, exacto, prudente, circunspecto.
Heedfully [hīd'-ful-i], *adv.* Cautelosamente, atentamente, con circunspección.
Heedfulness [hīd'-ful-nes], *s.* Vigilancia, cautela, atención, cuidado, circunspección.
Heedless [hīd'-les], *a.* Descuidado, negligente, omiso, imprudente, inconsiderado, distraído, atolondrado.
Heedlessly [hīd'-les-li], *adv.* Negligentemente.
Heedlessness [hīd'-les-nes], *s.* Descuido, omisión, negligencia, inadvertencia, imprudencia, distracción.
†**Heedy** [hīd'-i], *a.* Cauteloso.
Heel [hīl], *s.* 1. Talón, la parte posterior del pie; la parte correspondiente del pie en los animales. 2. Talón de toda clase de calzado; tacón. 3. El pie, visto por atrás. 4. Cosa colocada a manera de talón, parte inferior; (Mar.) coz o pie de palo. *To take to one's heels,* Apretar los talones, poner pies en polvorosa, huir. 5. La última parte de algo o de alguna cosa. *To be at the heels of,* Perseguir estrechamente. *From head to heel,* De pies a cabeza. *Heels over head,* Patas arriba. *The heel of his shoe came down,* Se le destalonó el zapato. *Down at the heels,* De aspecto desaliñado, descuidado. *Neck and heels,* (Fam.) De pies a cabeza, del todo. *To cool one's heels,* (Fam.) Hacer antesala, consumirse, esperar largo tiempo. *To kick one's heels,* Tascar el freno, esperar ocasión para hablar u obrar. *To lay by the heels,* Poner grillos, encadenar. *To show the heels* o *a clean pair of heels,* Huir; tomar la delantera, dejar atrás. *To throw up the heels of,* Echar a tierra de una zancadilla: de aquí, frustrar, dejar burlada la intención de alguien.
Heel, *va.* 1. Poner talón (a un par de medias, etc.). 2. Asir, agarrar por los talones. 3. Poner espolones al gallo. 4. (Ger. E. U.) Proveer de dinero.—*vn.* (Mar.) Ladearse, inclinarse, tumbarse hacia un lado.
Heeler [hīl'-ęr], *s.* 1. El gallo que usa con destreza de los espolones contra su contrario. 2. (Ger. E. U.) Subalterno de mala ley de un cacique político; secuaz poco escrupuloso, politicastro.
Heel-maker [hīl'-mé-kęr], *s.* Taconero.
Heel-piece [hīl'-pīs], *s.* Tapa, la suela que se pone debajo del tacón del zapato.
Heel-piece, *va.* Poner o echar tapas á los zapatos.
Heft [heft], *s.* 1. (Fam.) Peso, pesadez. 2. (Fam. E. U.) El bulto, la mayor parte de una cosa; o el punto principal. 3. Mango, asa. *V.* HAFT. (< heave.)
Heft, *va.* (Fam. E. U.) Levantar, alzar en peso, tomar en la mano para probar el peso.—*vn.* (Fam.) Pesar, tener cierto peso.
Hegemonic [hej-ę-men'-ic], *a.* Predominante, dominante.
Hegemony [hī'-ję-mo-ni o hé'-ge-mo-ni], *s.* Hegemonía, preeminencia; en particular la de Atenas, Esparta y Tebas.
Hegira [hej'-i-ra o hę-jai'-ra], *s.* Hégira, égira, la era de los mahometanos, que se cuenta desde el día en que Mahoma huyó de la Meca a Medina: A.D. 622.
Heifer [hef'-ęr], *s.* Vaca joven (que aun no ha parido), novilla. *Heifer calf,* Ternera.
Heigh-ho! [hai'-hō], *inter.* ¡Ay! Voz con que se expresa languidez o inquietud.
Height, Hight [hait], *s.* 1. Altura, elevación sobre alguna base, como la superficie de la tierra o el nivel del mar. 2. Estatura, talla. 3. Lo que es alto; altura, colina, montaña; cima ó cumbre, eminencia. 4. Sumidad, el ápice o extremidad de alguna cosa; extremo. 5. Elevación, altura, dignidad encumbrada. 6. Sublimidad, colmo, el más alto grado de una cosa; excelencia. *In the height of his happiness,* En el colmo de su dicha. *Height between decks,* (Mar.) Altura de entrepuentes. *Mount Popocatepetl is 17,784 feet in height,* El Popocatepetl tiene 17,784 pies (5,425 metros) de altura. *He (she) is about my height,* Él (ella) es poco más o menos de mi estatura. *The height of folly,* El colmo de la locura.
Heighten, Highten [hait'-n], *va.* 1. Realzar, levantar más o poner una cosa más elevada de lo que antes estaba. 2. Adelantar, perfeccionar, mejorar. 3. Agravar, abultar. 4. Realzar, ilustrar, adornar. *To heighten the spirits,* Exaltar la imaginación.
Heightening [hait'-n-ing], *s.* Adorno; aplícase comúnmente a los de la poesía y retórica; la acción del verbo *heighten* en todas sus acepciones.
Heinous [hé'-nus], *a.* Atroz, grave, nefando, malvado en extremo.
Heinously [hé'-nus-li], *adv.* Atrozmente, malvadamente, nefandamente.
Heinousness [hé'-nus-nes], *s.* Atrocidad, enormidad, exceso de malicia o suma malicia.
Heir [ār], *s.* Heredero, el que hereda. *Heir-apparent* o *general,* Heredero forzoso. *Heir-presumptive,* Heredero presuntivo. *Joint heir,* Coheredero. *Heir at law,* Heredero legal.
Heir, *va.* (Poco us.) Heredar.
Heirdom [ār'-dum], *s.* Herencia, los bienes y derechos heredados.
Heiress [ār'-es], *sf.* Heredera, la mujer que hereda.
Heirless [ār'-les], *a.* Sin heredero.
Heirloom [ār'-lūm], *s.* 1. (For.) Bienes muebles vinculados que pasan al heredero con la propiedad inmueble. 2. Prenda que desciende de un antepasado.
Heirship [ār'-ship], *s.* Estado, carácter o privilegio de heredero; herencia.
Heliacal [hę-lai'-a-cal], *a.* (Ast.) Helíaco, del sol o perteneciente a él.
Helibus [hel'-i-bus], *s.* Helicóptero de transporte de pasajeros.
Helical [hel'-i-cal], *a.* Espiral. *Helical line,* Hélice o espira.
Helicoid [hel'-i-ceid], *a.* 1. Helicoide, parecido a una hélice o a la concha de un caracol. 2. Perteneciente a los caracoles.—*s.* (Geom.) Superficie parecida a la de un tornillo, generada por una línea recta uno de cuyos extremos se mueve a lo largo de un eje, mientras que el otro extremo describe una espiral en torno de dicho eje.
Helicopter [hel-i-cop'-tęr], *s.* Helicóptero.
Heliocentric [hī-li-o-sen'-tric], *a.* Heliocéntrico, lo que pertenece al centro del sol.
Heliograph [hī'-li-o-graf], *s.* 1. Heliógrafo, instrumento para fotografiar el sol. 2. Lámina fotográfica tomada por la luz del sol. 3. Heliotropo, helióstato, instrumento que sirve para enviar un rayo solar a un observador colocado a gran distancia.
Heliographic [hī-li-o-graf'-ic], *a.* Heliográfico, relativo al heliógrafo o a la heliografía.
Heliography [hī-li-eg'-ra-fi], *s.* 1. Operación de transmitir señales por medio del heliógrafo. 2. Fotografía, heliografía. 3. Descripción de la superficie del sol.
Heliolatry [hī-li-el'-a-tri], *s.* Culto del sol, sabeísmo.
Heliometer [hī-li-em'-ę-tęr], *s.* Heliómetro, instrumento para medir el diámetro del sol.
Helioscope [hī'-li-o-scōp], *s.* Helioscopio, anteojo para mirar al sol sin que su resplandor ofenda la vista.
Heliospherical [hī-li-o-sfer'-i-cal], *a.* Esférico como el sol.
Heliostat [hī'-li-o-stat], *s.* Helióstato, instrumento para proyectar de una manera invariable el rayo solar.
Heliotherapy [hī-li-o-ther'-a-pi], *s.* Helioterapia.
Heliotrope [hī'-li-o-trōp], *s.* 1. (Bot.) Heliotropo, planta de flor muy olorosa, de la familia de las borragíneas. 2. Color de esta flor. 3. (Fís.) Heliotropo, instrumento para enviar un rayo solar a un observador colocado a gran distancia. 4. (Min.) Heliotropio o heliotropo, variedad de calcedonia de color verde claro o de puerro, con manchas de jaspe rojo.
Heliotype [hī'-li-o-taip], *s.* Heliotipo, especie de fotograbado en una superficie de gelatina, de la cual se imprime después; dicha superficie de impresión y la impresión misma.
Heliotypy [hī'-li-o-tai-pi], *s.* Cierto procedimiento para producir fotograbados de la clase llamada heliotipos.
Heliport [hel'-i-pōrt], *s.* (Aer.) Aeropuerto para helicópteros.

Helispheric, Helispherical [hel-i-sfer'-ic-al], *a.* Espiral, sobre una esfera.

Helix [hí'-lix], *s.* 1. Espira, voluta, hélice. 2. (Anat.) Hélix, borde del pabellón de la oreja en el hombre. 3. Caracol de tierra de la familia de los helícidos.

Hell [hel], *s.* 1. Infierno, el lugar de los condenados; el infierno, los espíritus infernales. 2. Cualquier lugar o estado de tormento o miseria extrema. 3. Infierno, el limbo o seno de Abraham, llamado por los griegos Hades y por los hebreos Sheol. 4. El paraje donde se reunen los jugadores de juegos de azar; lugar en que se depositan los desperdicios o deshechos (como en las imprentas, caja para letras inservibles). *Hell-bender*, Gran salamandra del valle del río Ohio, de vida muy tenaz. *Hell-fire*, Fuego o tormento del infierno. *Hell-gate*, La puerta, el umbral del infierno.

Hell-born [hel'-bōrn], *a.* Nacido en el infierno, infernal.

Hell-cat [hel'-cat], *s.* Bruja.

Hell-doomed [hel'-dūmd], *a.* Réprobo.

Hellebore [hel'-ȩ-bōr], *s.* (Bot.) Eléboro, verdegambre.

Helleborism [hel'-ȩ-bor-izm], *s.* Preparación medicinal del eléboro.

Hellenic [hel-len'-ic], *a.* Helénico, heleno, greciano; gentílico.

Helium [hí'-li-ʊm], *s.* Helio.

Hellenist [hel-en-ist], *s.* 1. Judío greguizante. 2. Helenista, el erudito en la lengua griega.

Hellenistical [hel-en-ist'-ic-al], *a.* Lo que pertenece a los judíos que hablan el griego.

Hellenistically [hel-en-ist'-ic-al-i], *adv.* A la manera de los griegos.

Hellenize [hel'-en-aiz], *vn.* Grecizar.

Hellgrammite [hel'-gram-ait], *s.* Gran larva de un insecto acuático (Corydalus cornutus), que se emplea como carnada en la pesca.

Hell-hag [hel'-hag], *s.* Bruja del infierno.

Hell-hound [hel'-haund], *s.* 1. Perro del infierno, el Cancerbero. 2. Agente infernal; perseguidor fiero y cruel.

Hellish [hel'-ish], †**Helly** [hel'-i], *a.* Infernal, malvado.

Hellishly [hel'-ish-li], *adv.* Malvadamente, detestablemente, diabólicamente.

Hellishness [hel'-ish-nes], *s.* Malicia infernal, diablura.

Hellward [hel'-ward], *adv.* Hacia el infierno.

Helm [helm], *s.* 1. (Mar.) Timón, gobernalle, el conjunto de timón, su caña y rueda; en especial, la barra o caña del timón, gobernalle. *After-piece of the helm*, Azafrán del timón. *Main-piece of the helm*, Madre del timón. *To shift the helm*, Cambiar el timón. *To hang the helm*, Calar el timón. *Play of the helm*, Juego del timón. *Helmsman*, Timonero, timonel, el que gobierna el timón. *A ship which answers the helm readily*, Un buque que obedece fácilmente al timón. 2. Timón, la dirección y gobierno de un negocio; el puesto de autoridad y responsabilidad. 3. (Ant.) *V.* HELMET.

§**Helm**, *va.* (Poét.) 1. Timonear, gobernar el timón; guiar. 2. Cubrir con un yelmo o celada.

Helmed [helmd], **Helmeted** [hel'-met-ed], *a.* Lo que tiene o lleva yelmo o celada.

Helmet [hel'-met], *s.* Yelmo, celada, morrión.

Helmet-flower [hel'-met-flau'-ȩr], *s.* (Bot.) Acónito, matalobos.

Helminthic [hel-min'-thic], *a.* Helmíntico: dícese de los remedios contra las lombrices.

Helminthology [hel-min-thel'-o-ji], *s.* Helmintología, tratado y estudio de las lombrices y de sus efectos; o de los gusanos, especialmente los parásitos.

Helmport [helm'-pōrt]. (Mar.) Limera del timón.

Helmsman [helmz'-man], *s.* (*pl.* MEN) Timonero, el que gobierna el timón en las embarcaciones.

Helot [hel'-ȩt], *s.* Ilota, nombre del esclavo en Lacedemonia.

Helotism [hel'-ȩt-izm], *s.* Ilotismo, condición de los esclavos en la antigua Esparta; esclavitud.

Help [help], *va.* y *vn.* 1. Ayudar, asistir, socorrer, amparar, favorecer, patrocinar, sostener. 2. Servir a la mesa. *Shall I help you to a wing of this capon?* ¿Quiere Vd. que le sirva un ala de este capón? 3. Aliviar, librar de dolor o enfermedad; remediar, reparar. 4. Evitar, dejar de hacer, abstenerse, no poder menos de. *How can I help it?* ¿Cómo evitarlo? ¿Qué quiere Vd. que yo haga?—*vn.* Ayudar, contribuir, concurrir. *It helped much to his reputation*, Eso contribuyó mucho a su reputación. *To help back*, Ayudar a retroceder. *To help out*, Ayudar a salir; sacar de algún peligro o mal paso. *To help down*, Ayudar a alguno a bajar. *To help forward*, Adelantar, activar, promover, ayudar a alguno para que adelante. *To help one another*, Favorecerse mutuamente. *I can not help it*, No puedo remediarlo o no puedo dejar de hacerlo. *I can not help believing that*, No puedo menos de creerlo. *To help to* o *on*, (1) *va.* Servir, ofrecer; proporcionar, promover. (2) *vn.* Contribuir, ayudar, concurrir a la ejecución de una cosa.

Help, *s.* 1. Ayuda, auxilio, asistencia, socorro, remedio, apoyo, arrimo, protección, amparo, favor. 2. Medio, recurso; lo que contribuye a hacer adelantar o mejorar una cosa. 3. (E. U.) Criada; jornalera. 4. (Fam.) Porción de comida tomada de una vez. *To cry out for help*, Pedir socorro, llamar en auxilio. *By the help of*, Con auxilio de, por medio de. *There is no help for it*, No tiene remedio.

Helper [help'-ȩr], *s.* 1. Auxiliador, el que auxilia y ayuda. 2. Socorredor, el que socorre. 3. Un criado destinado a ayudar a los otros, que unas veces se llama *asistente*, otras *ayuda* y algunas *sota*.

Helpful [help'-ful], *a.* Útil, provechoso, sano; saludable.

Helpfulness [help'-ful-nes], *s.* Asistencia, utilidad.

Helpless [help'-les], *a.* 1. Desamparado, destituído, abandonado. 2. Irremediable. 3. Inerte, desmañado, desvalido. 4. Imposibilitado.

Helplessly [help'-les-li], *adv.* Irremediablemente, sin recurso, en el desamparo, en el abandono.

Helplessness [help'-les-nes], *s.* 1. Desamparo, falta de amparo. 2. Falta de fuerzas, de energía; debilidad, impotencia.

Helpmate [help'-mēt], *s.* Compañero, asistente; auxiliar.

Helter-skelter [hel'-tȩr-skelt'-ȩr], *adv.* A trochemoche, a trompa y talega, al tuntún, atropelladamente, sin orden ni concierto, confusamente, en desorden.

Helve [helv], *s.* Astil de hacha o destral, mango. *To throw the helve after the hatchet*, Echar la soga tras el caldero, abandonar una empresa.

Helve, *va.* Echar mango o cabo a una cosa.

Helvetic [hel-vet'-ic], *a.* Helvético, helvecio, de Suiza.

Hem [hem], *s.* 1. Ribete, la guarnición que se echa a la extremidad de la ropa o vestido, repulgo, borde, orilla. 2. El ruido que causa la expiración repentina y violenta del aliento.—*inter.* ¡Eh!

Hem, *va.* 1. Ribetear, echar ribetes; repulgar, poner repulgos a algún vestido, repulgar, orillar, etc. 2. Cercar, rodear o encerrar en un recinto.—*vn.* Hacer ruido espirando con violencia; desahogar las fauces. 3. Fingir tos, o toser de fingido.

Hemal, Hæmal [hí'-mal], *a.* 1. Perteneciente a la sangre o al sistema vascular; de la naturaleza de la sangre. 2. Relativo al lado del cuerpo que contiene el corazón.

Hematin [hem'-a-tin], *s.* 1. (Quím.) Hematina, principio colorante derivado del de la sangre por la acción de los ácidos. 2. *V.* HEMATOXYLIN.

Hematite [hem'-a-tait], *s.* Hematita, (Fe_2O_3), mineral común de hierro.

Hematoxylin [hem'-a-tox'-i-lin], *s.* Hematoxilina, principio colorante del palo de Campeche ($C_{16}H_{14}O_6$).

Hemerobaptist [hem-ȩ-ro-bap'-tist], *s.* Sectario judío de los que practicaban diarias abluciones.

Hemi [hem'-i], *a.* Voz que entra en la composición de varias otras, y equivale a medio o semi.

Hemicrania, Hemicrany [hem'-i-crê-ni-a], *s.* Hemicránea, jaqueca, dolor en un lado o en una parte de la cabeza.

Hemicycle [hem'-i-sai-cl], *s.* Semicírculo.

Hemina [hem'-i-na], *s.* Hemina, una medida antigua; medida usada a veces en la farmacia, que tiene unas diez onzas.

Hemiplegia, Hemiplegy [hem''-i-plí'-ji-a], *s.* Hemiplejia, parálisis de todo un lado del cuerpo.

Hemiplegic [hem-i-plí'-jic], *a.* Hemipléjico, de la hemiplejia.

Hemisphere [hem'-i-sfír], *s.* Hemisferio, la mitad de una esfera, dividida por un plano que pasa por su centro.

Hemispheric, Hemispherical [hem-i-sfer'-ic, al], *a.* Hemisférico.

Hemistich, Hemestic [hem'-i-stic], *s.* Hemistiquio.

Hemlock [hem'-loc], *s.* (Bot.) 1. Pinabete o abeto americano, árbol conífero. Tsuga o Abies Canadensis. 2. Cicuta, hierba umbelífera venenosa. Conium maculatum.

Hemoglobin, Hæmoglobin [hem''-o-glō'-bin], *s.* Hemoglobina, la materia colorante de la sangre. Sirve como medio conductor del oxígeno procedente de los pulmones. Su fórmula es notable, a saber: $C_{712}H_{1130}N_{214}S_2FeO_{245}$.

Hemophilia [hem-o-fil'-ia], *s.* (Med.) Hemofilia.

Hemorrhage [hem'-ȩ-rêj], *s.* Hemorragia, flujo de sangre.

Hemorrhoids [hem'-ȩr-eidz], *s. pl.* Hemorroides, almorranas.

Hemorrhoidal [hem-ẹr-eid'-al], *a.* Hemorroidal.

Hemostatic [hẹ-mos-ta'-tic], *a.* (Med.) Hemostático.

Hemp [hemp], *s.* (Bot.) Cáñamo, planta de cuyas cañas se hacen cuerdas y se tejen telas de varias calidades. *Bastard-hemp*, Cañamón, cáñamo bastardo. *Hemp agrimony*, (Bot.) Eupatorio vulgar. *Raw hemp*, Cáñamo sin peinar. *Indian hemp*, Canabina.

Hemp-beater [hemp'-bît-ẹr], *a.* Espadador o espadillador de cáñamo.

Hemp-breaker [hemp'-brê-kẹr], *s.* Agramador de cáñamo.

Hemp-close [hemp'-clōz], **Hemp-field** [hemp'-fîld], *s.* Cañamar, el terreno sembrado de cáñamo.

Hemp-comb [hemp'-cōm], *s.* Peine para pasar el cáñamo después de rastrillado.

Hempen [hemp'-n], *a.* Cañameño, lo que se hace del hilo del cáñamo.

Hemp-seed [hemp'-sîd], *s.* Cañamón.

Hemstitch [hem'-stich], *va.* Hacer un dobladillo de ojo.—*s.* Dobladillo de ojo.

Hempy [hemp'-i], *a.* Semejante al cáñamo.

Hen [hen], *sf.* 1. Gallina, la hembra del gallo. 2. Ave hembra de cualquier especie. 3. *pl.* Pollos, gallinas, aves domésticas en general sin distinción de sexo. *Brood-hen*, Gallina clueca. *Guinea-hen*, Gallina de Guinea o de Indias; pintada. *Turkey-hen*, Pava. *Moor-hen*, Zarceta, ave acuática.

Henbane [hen'-bên], *s.* (Bot.) Beleño, planta venenosa, particularmente para las aves domésticas. Hyoscyamus niger.

Hence [hens], *adv.* 1. De aquí, desde aquí, a distancia de aquí, fuera de aquí. 2. De aquí, por esto, en consecuencia de esto. *Hence it is that they are all rich*, De aquí es que todos son ricos. *Ten years hence*, De aquí a diez años. *Far hence*, Lejos de aquí. *Not many days hence*, Dentro de unos días. *From hence*, Locución pleonástica y anticuada, lo mismo que HENCE, desde aquí, fuera de aquí. 3. Anda, fuera; voz de mando. *Hence with you*, Quítese Vd. de delante, largo de aquí.

Henceforth [hens'-fōrth], *adv.* De aquí en adelante; en adelante, en lo futuro.

Henceforward [hens-fōr'-ward], *adv.* De aquí en adelante; en lo venidero; para siempre.

Henchman [hench'-man], *s.* 1. Agente servil y subordinado. 2. (Ant.) Criado.

Hencoop [hen'-cūp], *s.* Gallinero.

Hendecagon [hen-dec'-a-gon], *s.* Endecágono, polígono de once lados y once ángulos.

Hendecasyllable [hen-dec-a-sil'-a-bl], *s.* Verso endecasílabo.

Hen-harm [hen'-hārm], **Hen-harrier** [hen'-har-i-ẹr], *s.* (Orn.) Pigargo.

Hen-house [hen'-haus], *s.* Gallinero.

Henna [hen'-a], *s.* Arbusto o árbol pequeño de Oriente, llamado Lawsonia inermis; y una preparación cosmética de sus hojas que da un color anaranjado.

Hennery [hen'-ẹr-i], *s.* Gallinero, lugar donde las gallinas se recogen a dormir.

Henpeck [hen'-pec], *va.* Dominar; molestar, fastidiar, importunar con triquiñuelas; dícese de una mujer que así trata y maneja a su marido.

Henpecked [hen'-pect], *a.* Gurrumino, el que está dominado por su mujer. *Henpecked husband*, El marido cuya mujer lleva los calzones.

Hen-roost [hen'-rūst], *s.* Gallinero.

Henry [hen'-ri], *n. pr.* Enrique.—*s.* (Elec.) Unidad práctica de autoinducción; la autoinducción de una corriente a razón de un amperio por segundo, que produce una fuerza electromotriz de un voltio.

Hep [hep], *s.* Fruto del agavanzo. *V.* HIP. *Hep-bramble, hep-brier, hep-tree*, Escaramujo, agavanzo.

Heparin [hep'-ẹr-in], *s.* (Anticoagulante) Heparina.

Hepatic, Hepatical [hẹ-pat'-ic, al], *a.* 1. Hepático, que pertenece al hígado. 2. De color de hígado.

Hepatica [hẹ-pat'-i-ca], *s.* (Bot.) Hepática, planta de la familia de las ranunculáceas, llamada también *liver-leaf* (hoja de hígado). Anemone hepatica, antiguamente Hepatica triloba.

Hepaticæ [hẹ-pat'-i-sî], *s. pl.* (Bot.) Ciertas plantas parecidas a los musgos.

Hepatite [hep'-a-tait], *s.* (Min.) Hepatita, variedad de barita; debe su nombre al olor fétido que despide al calentarla.

Hepatitis [hẹ-pa-tai'-tis], *s.* (Med.) Hepatitis.

Hepatize [hep'-a-taiz], *va.* 1. Cambiar o transformar en una substancia semejante al hígado; aplícase en medicina particularmente a los pulmones. 2. (Des. Quím.) Llenar de gas hidrógeno sulfurado.

Heptachord [hep'-ta-cōrd], *s.* Heptacordio, instrumento músico de siete cuerdas.

Heptagon [hep'-ta-gon], *s.* 1. Heptágono, figura de siete lados y otros tantos ángulos. 2. (Fort.) Heptágono, fortaleza guarnecida con siete bastiones.

Heptagonal [hep-tag'-o-nal], *a.* Heptagonal, lo que tiene siete ángulos y lados.

Heptameride [hep-tam'-e-rid], *s.* Lo que divide o que consiste en siete partes.

Heptarchy [hep'-tār-ki], *s.* Heptarquía, gobierno de siete personas, reinos o provincias.

Heptateuch [hep'-ta-tiūc], *s.* Heptateuco, los siete primeros libros del Viejo Testamento.

Her [hẹr], *pron.* 1. Caso objetivo o acusativo de SHE. La, ella, a ella. 2. Caso posesivo o genitivo de SHE; también se usa como adjetivo posesivo: su, de ella. *I have not seen her*, No la he visto. *I have not sent the book to her*, No le he enviado el libro. *Cherish her*, Ámela Vd. con ternura. (En inglés, los adjetivos posesivos concuerdan en género con el poseedor.) *Her book, her house*, Su libro, su casa (de ella).

Herald [her'-ald], *s.* 1. Heraldo, rey de armas. 2. Precursor; publicador.

Heraldic [her-al'-dic], *a.* Heráldico, genealógico.

Heraldry [her'-ald-ri], *s.* Heráldica, arte o ciencia que trata del blasón; registro de genealogías.

Heraldship [her'-ald-ship], *s.* Oficio de heraldo.

Herb [ẹrb o hẹrb], *s.* Hierba, nombre genérico que se da a todas las plantas menores cuyo tallo nace todos los años; legumbres. *Sweet herbs*, Hierbas odoríferas, olorosas o de olor. *Physical herbs*, Hierbas medicinales. *Salad-herbs*, Hierbas para ensalada. *Pot-herbs*, Hortalizas.

Herbaceous [hẹr-bê'-shus], *a.* Herbáceo.

Herbage [hẹrb'-ẹj o ẹrb'-ẹj], *s.* Herbaje; pasto.

Herbaged [ẹrb'-ẹjd], *a.* Cubierto de hierba o herbaje.

Herbal [ẹrb'-al], *s.* Herbario.—*a.* Lo que pertenece al herbario.

Herbalist [hẹrb'-al-ist], **Herbarist** [hẹrb'-a-rist], **Herbist** [hẹrb'-ist], *s.* Herbolario, el que entiende de hierbas y plantas.

Herbarious [hẹr-bê'-ri-us], *a.* Herbario.

Herbarium [hẹr-bê'-ri-um], *s.* 1. Herbario, colección de plantas secas colocadas según arte. 2. Libro o estante para contener plantas secas. 3. Edificio en que se conservan plantas secas.

Herbarize [hẹr'-ba-raiz], *vn.* Herborizar, ir al campo en busca de hierbas o plantas.

Herbary [hẹr'-ba-ri], *s.* Jardín que contiene solamente hierbas.

Herbescent [hẹr-bes'-ent], *a.* Parecido a una hierba; que tiende a convertirse en hierba.

Herbiferous [hẹr-bif'-ẹr-us], *a.* Herbífero, que produce hierbas.

Herbivorous [hẹr-biv'-o-rus], *a.* Herbívoro, que se alimenta de hierbas.

Herbless [hẹrb'-les], *a.* Sin hierbas, yermo.

Herborization [hẹr-bor-i-zê'-shun], *s.* Herborización.

Herborize [hẹr'-bo-raiz], *vn.* Herborizar, ir al campo en busca de hierbas o plantas.—*va.* Formar dibujos de plantas o árboles, v. g. en una substancia mineral.

Herborizer [hẹrb'-o-raiz-ẹr], *s.* Herborizador, herborizante.

Herbose [hẹrb'-ōs], **Herbous** [ẹrb'-us o hẹrb'-us], **Herby** [ẹrb'-i o hẹrb'-i], *a.* Herboso, lo que abunda en hierbas.

Herbwoman [ẹrb'-wum-an], *sf.* Herbolaria; verdulera, mujer que vende hierbas.

Herculanean [hẹr-kiu-lê'-nẹ-an], *a.* De Herculano, antigua ciudad romana cerca de Nápoles.

Herculean [hẹr-kiū'-lẹ-an], *a.* Hercúleo, que posee o demanda gran fuerza; trabajoso, muy difícil.

Herd [hẹrd], *s.* 1. Hato, grey, manada, rebaño, ganado, número de animales de una especie que pacen o caminan juntos. 2. Hato, junta o reunión de gente; de aquí gentuza, tropel, multitud, vulgo, chusma. 3. Guarda de ganado. *V.* HERDSMAN. *The common herd*, El vulgo, la gente ordinaria, la gentuza. *A herd of rogues*, Un hato de tunantes. *Herd's-grass*, (E. U.) (1) En algunas partes, la planta gramínea llamada *red-top* (Agrostis vulgaris). (2) (Nueva Ingl.) La planta gramínea llamada *timothy*. Phleum pratense. Ambas plantas dan buen forraje. *Cow-herd*, Vaquero o boyero. *Goat-herd*, Cabrero. *Shepherd*, Pastor de ovejas. *Swine-herd*, Porquero.

Herd, *vn.* Ir en manadas o hatos; ir en compañía de otros; asociarse; pacer juntos.—*va.* Reunir el ganado en hatos o rebaños.

Herdic [hẹr'-dic], *s.* Nombre de un carruaje de dos o cuatro ruedas. Tiene la portezuela en la parte de atrás y asientos a uno y otro lado para dos o más personas.

Herdsman [hẹrdz'-man], *s.* Guarda de ganado, pastor, zagal.

Here [hîr], *adv.* 1. Aquí, en este lugar o en este paraje. 2. Acá, a o hacia este lugar. 3. Por aquí, por allá; en este momento, o este período. *Here I must pause,* En este punto he de detenerme. 4. Hé aquí. *Here I am,* Héme aquí. *Here he is, she is, they are,* Héle aquí, héla aquí, hélos aquí. *Here he comes,* Héle aquí que llega. 5. Aquí, en este mundo, en esta vida. *Here below,* En esta vida, en la tierra. *Here goes,* (Fam.) Voy á empezar; ahora entro yo; va seguido á menudo de *for.* *Here is,* (Fam. *here's*) Hé aquí. *Here's another strike,* Hé aquí otra huelga. *Here is John now,* Hé aquí a Juan. *Here's a pretty how-do-you-do!* (Fam.) ¡Ésta sí que es buena! ¡Ahora sí que la hemos hecho! *Here is to you,* A la salud de Vd. *Here and there,* Aquí y allá, acá y acullá. *Here it is,* Aquí está.

Hereabouts [hîr'-a-bauts], *adv.* Aquí alrededor, en estas cercanías, en estas inmediaciones.

Hereafter [hîr-qf'-tęr], *adv.* En el tiempo venidero, en lo futuro.—*s.* Estado futuro.

Hereat [hîr-at'], *adv.* A esto o esta, por eso.

Hereby [hîr-bai'], *adv.* Por esto; por este medio o por este camino; por la presente.

Hereditable [hę-red'-it-a-bl], *a.* Lo que puede ser heredado, antiguamente hereditable.

Hereditament [her-e-dit'-a-męnt], *s.* Herencia, bienes heredados.

Hereditarily [hę-red'-i-tę-ri-li], *adv.* Por herencia, hereditariamente.

Hereditary [hę-red'-i-tę-ri], *a.* Hereditario, en sus varias acepciones.

Herefrom [hîr frem'], *adv.* De aquí, desde aquí; a causa de esto.

Herein [hîr-in'], **Hereinto** [hîr-in'-tū], *adv.* En esto, aquí dentro.

Hereinafter [hîr-in-qf'-ter], *adv.* Después, más abajo, como se verá o se dice más adelante (en este escrito, libro o documento).

Hereof [hîr-ov'], *adv.* De esto, de eso, de aquí.

Hereon [hîr-en'], *adv.* Sobre esto, sobre este punto.

Heresiarch [her'-e-si-arc o hę-rî'-si-arc], *s.* Heresiarca.

Heresiarchy [her'-e-si-ark-i o hę-rî-si-ark-i], *s.* Gran herejía.

Heresy [her'-e-si], *s.* Herejía.

Heretic [her'-et-ic], *s.* Hereje.

Heretical [hę-ret'-ic-al], *a.* Herético, heretical.

Heretically [hę-ret'-ic-al-i], *adv.* Heréticamente.

Hereto [hîr-tū'], *adv.* A esto.

Heretofore [hîr-tu-fōr'], *adv.* En otro tiempo, antes, antiguamente, en tiempos pasados, hasta aquí, hasta ahora, hasta el día.—*s.* El tiempo pasado, antaño.

Hereunder [hîr-un'-dęr], *adv.* Bajo esto, en virtud de esto.

Hereunto [hîr-un-tū'], *adv.* A esto, a eso.

Hereupon [hîr-up-en'], *adv.* Sobre esto.

Herewith [hîr-with'], *adv.* Con esto, junto con esto.

Heriot [her'-i-ŏt], *s.* Pago que se hacía antiguamente al propietario o señor de tierras poseídas en feudo, cuando moría un feudatario o arrendador.

Heritable [her'-it-a-bl], *a.* Que se puede heredar. *V.* HEREDITABLE.

Heritage [her'-it-ęj], *s.* 1. Herencia, sucesión a todos o alguno de los derechos que el difunto tenía al tiempo de su muerte; bienes patrimoniales. 2. Porción, interés. 3. Condición, suerte o estado heredado.

¿**Hermaphrodeity** [hęr-maf-ro-dî'-i-ti], *s.* Estado de hermafrodita. *V.* HERMAPHRODITISM.

Hermaphrodite [hęr-maf'-ro-dait], *a.* 1. Hermafrodita, que presenta los caracteres distintivos de ambos sexos; en botánica, bisexual, que tiene pistilos y estambres. 2. (Mar.) Con aparejo de cruz hacia la proa y arboladura de goleta a popa.—*s.* 1. Hermafrodita, andrógino, ser que tiene los dos sexos a la vez; como ciertos moluscos y gusanos y la mayor parte de las plantas. 2. (Mar.) Bergantín goleta.

Hermaphroditic, Hermaphroditical [hęr-maf-ro-dit'-ic, al], *a.* Que participa de los dos sexos.

Hermaphroditically [hęr-maf-ro-dit'-ic-al-i], *adv.* Como hermafrodita.

Hermaphroditism, Hermaphrodism [hęr-maf'-ro-dait''-izm], *s.* Hermafrodismo, reunión de ambos sexos en el mismo individuo.

Hermeneutics [hęr-mę-niū'-tics], *s.* Hermeneútica, el arte de interpretar textos, y en especial los textos sagrados.

Hermeneutist [hęr-mę-niū'-tist], *s.* Hermeneútico, interpretador de los textos sagrados.

Hermetic, Hermetical [hęr-met'-ic, al], *a.* 1. Hermético, relativo al Hermes griego, dios de los secretos y de la filosofía oculta; o al Hermes egipcio (Thoth). 2. Hermético, hecho a prueba de aire u otros flúidos, v. g. por medio de la fusión. *Hermetic art,* Alquimia; de aquí, química.

Hermetically [hęr-met'-ic-al-i], *adv.* Herméticamente.

Hermit [hęr'-mit], *s.* Ermitaño, eremita, anacoreta, solitario.

Hermitage [hęr'-mit-ęj], *s.* 1. Ermita, la vivienda del ermitaño. 2. Cierta clase de vino francés.

Hermitary [hęr'-mit-ę-ri], *s.* Celda de ermitaño aneja a un monasterio.

Hermitess [hęr'-mit-es], *sf.* Ermitaña.

Hermitical [hęr-mit'-i-cal], *a.* Eremítico.

Hermodactyl [hęr-mo-dac'-til], *s.* (Bot.) Hermodáctilo, especie de iris o lirio cuya raíz se usaba en medicina.

Hern, *s.* *V.* HERON.

Hernia [hęr'-ni-a], *s.* Hernia, quebradura; (fam.) potra.

Hernial [hęr'-ni-al], *a.* Herniario, relativo a la hernia; herniado, que forma hernia.

Hernshaw [hęrn'-shē], *s.* 1. Garza. 2. (Her.) Figura de una garza u otra ave semejante.

Hero [hî'-rō], *s.* 1. Héroe, hombre eminente por su valor; hombre ilustre y de extraordinario mérito. 2. Semidiós, persona de fuerzas sobrehumanas, etc.; personaje ilustre que los antiguos divinizaban después de muerto. 3. Protagonista o personaje principal de un poema, drama, comedia o novela.

Herodians [hę-rō'-di-anz], *s. pl.* Herodianos, unos sectarios entre los judíos.

Heroic, Heroical [hę-rō'-ic, al], *a.* 1. Heroico, lo que produce héroes. 2. Heroico, noble, grande, sublime, ilustre, valeroso, magnánimo. 3. Heroico, lo perteneciente a los héroes o lo que refiere sus hechos.

Heroically [hę-rō'-ic-al-i], *adv.* Heroicamente.

Heroicomic [hę-rō-i-com'-ic], *a.* Jocoserio, lo que consta de una mezcla de serio y jocoso.

Heroin [her'-o-in], *s.* Heroína (narcótico).

Heroine [her'-o-in], *sf.* Heroína.

Heroism [her'-o-izm], *s.* Heroísmo, heroicidad, grandeza de alma, excelencia en el valor.

Heron [her'-en], *s.* (Orn.) Garza, ave de caza.

Heronry [her'-en-ri], *s.* El lugar en que se crían las garzas.

Heron's-bill [her'-enz-bil], *s.* (Bot.) Pico de garza, planta parecida al pico de la cigueña, del género Erodium. Es muy abundante en California, donde se llama más comúnmente alfilerilla y *clocks.* Erodium cicutarium.

Heroship [hî'-ro-ship], *s.* Calidad de héroe.

Herpes [hęr'-pîz], *s.* (Med.) Herpes, erupción, granitos rojizos y arracimados que salen en el cutis.

Herpetic [hęr-pet'-ic], *a.* Herpético.

Herpetologist [hęr-pe-tel'-o-jist], *s.* Persona versada en la herpetología.

Herpetology [hęr-pe tel'-o-ji], *s.* Herpetología, el ramo de la zoología que trata de los reptiles.

Herring [her'-ing], *s.* Arenque. Clupea. *Herring-casks,* Barriles de arenques. *Herring-fishery,* Pesca de arenques. *Red herring,* Arenque ahumado.

Herringbone [her'-ing-bōn], *s.* Punto de espiguilla (en las telas).

Hers [hęrz], *pron. pos.* Suyo, suya, de ella; el suyo, la suya, los suyos, las suyas. *The child is hers,* El niño es suyo. *Is the house yours?* ¿Es de Vd. la casa? *No, it is hers,* No, es la suya (de ella). *I have no money of hers,* No tengo dinero de ella.

Herse [hęrs], *s.* 1. (Fort.) Especie de rastrillo; caballo de frisia. 2. Especie de enrejado. 3. (Des.) *V.* HEARSE.

Herself [hęr-self'], *pron.* Ella misma. *She spoke of herself,* Ella habló de sí misma.

Hersilion [hęr-sil'-i-en], *s.* (Mil.) Caballo de frisa.

Hesitancy [hes'- o hez'-i-tan-si], *s.* Duda, hesitación, incertidumbre, irresolución.

Hesitate [hes'- o hez'-i-têt], *vn.* 1. Dudar, vacilar, tardar, pausar, titubear. 2. Hablar con lentitud o indecisión; balbucear, tartamudear

Hesitation [hes'- o hez-i-tē'-shun], *s* 1. Hesitación, duda, irresolución, perplejidad, vacilación. 2. Dificultad de pronunciar las palabras, balbucencia.

Hesper [hes'-pęr], *s.* Héspero o Venus, la estrella vespertina.

Hesperian [hes-pî'-ri-an], *a.* Hespérido, del poniente o del oeste; occidental.—*s.* Habitante de un país occidental.

Hessian [hesh'-ian], *a.* Perteneciente al ducado de Hesse, o que se refiere a Hesse.—*s.* Natural o ciudadano de Hesse. *Hessian fly,* Cecidomio, mosca pequeña negruzca (Cecidomyia destructor) nociva al trigo, tal vez introducida en Norte América por las tropas asalariadas de Hesse durante la guerra de la independencia. *Hessian crucible,* Crisol de arcilla refractaria.

†**Hest** [hest], *s.* Orden, mandato, precepto. *V.* BEHEST.

Heter-, Hetero-. Formas de combinación, derivadas del griego *heteros*, otro, diferente.
Heteroclite [het'-ẹr-o-clait], *s.* y *a.* Heteróclito, irregular.
Heterodox [het'-ẹr-o-dex], *a.* Heterodoxo, lo que es contrario á la opinión aceptada generalmente y en particular a una doctrina teológica; herético.
Heterodoxy [het'-ẹr-o-dec-si], *s.* Heterodoxia, oposición a las opiniones dominantes, por lo general en materias religiosas.
Heterodyne [het'-ẹ-ro-dain], *a.* Heterodino.
Heterogamous [het-ẹr-eg'-a-mus], *a.* (Bot.) Heterógamo, ma, que tiene flores monoicas, bioicas o polígamas.
Heterogeneity [het-ẹr-o-jẹ-nî'-i-ti], **Heterogeneousness** [het-ẹr-o-jî'-ni-us-nes], *s.* Heterogeneidad.
Heterogeneous [het-ẹr-o-jî'-ni-us], **Heterogeneal** [het-ẹr-o-jî'-nẹ-al] (poco us.), *a.* Heterogéneo, lo que es de diferente género; lo opuesto a *homogéneo.*
Heteronomous [het-ẹr-en'-o-mus], *a.* 1. (Biol.) Diferente del tipo común. 2. Sujeto a la ley o al dominio de otro.
Heteronym [het'-ẹr-o-nim], *s.* 1. Palabra que tiene la misma ortografía que otra, pero sonido y sentido diferentes, v. g. *wind* [wind] viento, y *wind* [waind] enrollar. 2. (Poco us.) Uno de los dos o más nombres con que se designa una misma cosa; por lo general pertenecen a distintos idiomas. Su adjetivo es HETERONYMOUS.
Heteroscian [het-e-resh'-an], *a.* Literalmente, que tiene diferentes sombras (heteroscio); se aplica a las zonas templadas porque la sombra de los objetos se dirige en sentido inverso en cada hemisferio.—*s.* Habitante de las zonas templadas (por la razón antedicha). *The Japanese and the Australians are heteroscians,* Los japoneses y los australianos son heteroscios.
Hew [hiū], *va.* (*pret.* HEWED, *pp.* HEWN y HEWED). 1. Tajar, cortar, picar. 2. Cortar con hacha u otro instrumento cortante; hachear. 3. Efectuar laboriosamente; trabajar. *To hew a stone,* Picar, trabajar una piedra. *To hew right and left,* Acuchillar a diestro y siniestro. *To hew in pieces,* Destrozar, destroncar. *To hew out,* Hachear, cortar; modelar en bruto; abrir paso. *To hew out a passage sword in hand,* Abrirse paso espada en mano. *To rough-hew,* Descortezar; desbastar; modelar en bruto.
Hewer [hiū'-ẹr], *s.* El que tiene por oficio labrar piedra o madera; cantero; cortador de madera.
Hexachord [hex'-a-cērd], *s.* (Mús.) Hexacordo.
Hexagon [hex'-a-gen], *s.* Hexágono, figura plana que consta de seis ángulos y seis lados.
Hexagonal [hex-ag'-on-al], *a.* Perteneciente al hexágono.
Hexahedron [hex-a-hî'-dron], *s.* Hexaedro.
Hexameter [hex-am'-ẹ-tẹr], *s.* Hexámetro.
Hexametric, Hexametrical [hex-a-met'-ric, al], *a.* Que se compone de hexámetros.
Hexangular [hex-an'-giu-lar], *a.* Hexángulo, que tiene seis ángulos.
Hexapod [hex'-a-ped], *a.* Hexápodo, que tiene seis patas.—*s.* Uno de los hexápodos o insectos propiamente dichos, porque su cualidad distintiva es la de tener seis patas.
Hexapodan, Hexapode [hex-ap'-o-dan, hex'-a-pōd], *a.* y *s.* *V.* HEXAPOD.
Hey [hē], *inter.* 1. ¡He! expresión de alegría y gozo. 2. Lo mismo que eh; interjección para preguntar, llamar, despreciar, reprender y advertir; equivale a arre, anda, para arrear a las caballerías, y sirve también para azuzar los perros.
Heyday [hē'-dē], *s.* Colmo, apogeo de vitalidad y vigor.—*inter.* ¡Hola! (expresa alegría, sorpresa o asombro).
Hiatus [hai-ē'-tus], *s.* 1. Grieta, abertura, raja, hendedura. 2. Hiato, sonido desagradable que resulta de la pronunciación de dos vocablos seguidos, cuando el primero acaba en vocal y el segundo empieza con la misma vocal acentuada.
Hibernal [hai-bẹr'-nal], *a.* Invernizo, hiemal, invernal, lo que pertenece al invierno.
Hibernate [hai'-bẹr-nēt], *vn.* 1. Invernar, pasar la estación del invierno en lugar abrigado y en torpor, como ciertos animales. 2. Pasar el tiempo en el retiro o la inacción.
Hibernation [hai-bẹr-nē'-shun], *s.* Invernada, acción de pasar el invierno (o el tiempo) en un paraje retirado o en la inacción.
Hibernian [hai-bẹr'-ni-an], *s.* Irlandés, de Hibernia.
Hibernianism, Hibernicism [hai-bẹr'-ni-an-izm, hai-bẹr'-ni-sizm], *s.* Idiotismo irlandés, giro o forma de expresión irlandesa.
Hibiscus [hai-bis'-cus o hi-bis'-cus], *s.* Hibisco, género numeroso de plantas de la familia de las malváceas.
Hiccough, Hiccup, Hickup [hic'-up], *s.* Hipo.
Hiccough, Hiccup, Hickup, *vn.* Tener o padecer hipo.
Hickory [hic'-o-ri], *s.* 1. Árbol americano parecido al nogal, del género Carya. 2. Su madera. 3. Algo hecho de la madera de este nogal. (Nombre indio.)
Hick-wall [hic'-wōl], **Hick-way** [hic'-wē], *s.* (Orn.) Especie de picamaderos.
Hid [hid], *pret.* y *pp.* de *To* HIDE. *V.* HIDDEN.
Hidden [hid'-n], *a.* y *pp.* Oculto, recóndito, escondido.
Hiddenly [hid'-n-li], *adv.* Escondidamente, secretamente.
Hide [haid], *s.* 1. Cuero, piel, el pellejo del animal adobado o por adobar: (dícese algunas veces, por desprecio, de la piel humana). *To dress hides,* Adobar y curtir cueros. *To warm, to tan one's hide for him,* Zurrar, calentar el pellejo a alguien, pegarle una tunda. *Raw hide,* Cuero crudo, sin curtir. 2. Antiguamente una cantidad de tierra, bastante para mantener a una familia.
Hide [haid], *va.* (*pret.* HID, *pp.* HIDDEN o HID). 1. Esconder, ocultar, encubrir, guardar o retirar de la vista alguna cosa para que no se vea. 2. Tapar, disimular. 3. Volver (la vista) a otra parte; apartar los ojos de. *Adam and his wife hid themselves from the presence of the Lord God,* Escondiéronse Adán y su mujer de la presencia del Señor Dios. *To hide one's fears,* Disimular, ocultar sus temores. *To hide the face from,* Ocultar el rostro; volverse de espaldas, rechazar la presencia y las atenciones de alguno. —*vn.* Esconderse, ocultarse. *Hide and seek,* Juego del escondite.
Hide, *va.* Pegar a uno una tunda, castigar con un rebenque o vergajo.
Hide-bound [haid'-baund], *a.* 1. El que está muy extenuado y tiene la piel pegada a los huesos. 2. Obstinado, apocado, encogido, mojigato.
Hideous [hid'-ẹ-us], *a.* Horrible, horrendo, espantoso, feo, deforme, repugnante.
Hideously [hid'-ẹ-us-li], *adv.* Horriblemente, espantosamente.
Hideousness [hid'-ẹ-us-nes], *s.* Horror, espanto; fealdad, deformidad.
Hiding [haid'-ing], *s.* 1. Encubrimiento. 2. Retiro, retrete. *Hiding-place,* Sitio de retiro, retrete, escondite. 3. (Fam.) Zurra, paliza.
Hie [hai], *vn.* Darse prisa, apresurarse.—*va.* 1. Activar, apresurar. 2. Correr, pasar con rapidez. *Hie thee,* Date prisa. *Hie thee home,* Apresúrate a volver a casa.
Hierarch [hai'-ẹr-ārc], *s.* Jerarca, prelado, pontífice.
Hierarchal [hai'-ẹr-arc-al], **Hierarchical** [hai-ẹr-ark'-i-cal], *a.* Jerárquico.
Hierarchism [hai'-ẹr-ark-izm], *s.* Jerarquía, los principios y el dominio del gobierno eclesiástico; afecto a ese gobierno.
Hierarchy [hai'-ẹr-ark-i], *s.* 1. Jerarquía, gobierno eclesiástico por orden y grados diversos; y el conjunto de los jerarcas. 2. (Biol.) Orden y diversos grados de seres vivos, como reinos, clases, órdenes, familias, etc.
Hieratic, Hieratical [hai-ẹ-rat'-ic, al], *a.* Jerárquico, sacerdotal; consagrado. *Hieratic writing,* Escritura de los antiguos egipcios, forma más complexa que la demótica, o la común entre el vulgo.
Hieroglyph [hai'-ẹr-o-glif], **Hieroglyphic** [hai-ẹr-o-glif'-ic], *s.* Jeroglífico, símbolo, emblema.
Hieroglyphic, Hieroglyphical [hai-ẹr-o-glif'-ic, al], *a.* Jeroglífico o hieroglífico.
Hierogram [hai'-ẹr-o-gram], *s.* Escritura sagrada, carácter o símbolo de significación sagrada.
Hierogrammatic [hai-ẹr-o-gra-mat'-ic], **Hierographical** [hai-ẹr-o-graf'-i-cal], *a.* Perteneciente á una especie de escritura sagrada.
Hierography [hai-ẹr-eg'-ra-fi], *s.* Escritura sagrada.
Hierologic [hai-ẹr-o-lej'-ic], *a.* Hierológico, perteneciente á la hierología.
Hierology [hai-ẹr-el'-o-ji], *s.* 1. Hierología, la ciencia o el libro que trata de las escrituras e inscripciones sagradas del antiguo Egipto. 2. Hierología, estudio y comparación científicos de todas las religiones del mundo.
Hieromancy [hai'-ẹr-o-man-si], *s.* Hieromancia, adivinación por medio de sacrificios.
Hierophant [hai'-ẹr-o-fant], *s.* Hierofante, el que enseña las reglas de la religión.
Hifalutin, *a.* y *s.* *V.* HIGHFALUTIN.
Hi-fi (High-fidelity) [hai'-fai], *a.* (Mús.) De alta fidelidad.—*s.* Fonógrafo de alta fidelidad.
Higgle [hig'-l], *vn.* Regatear, altercar, porfiar sobre el precio de alguna cosa puesta en venta.
Higgledy-piggledy [hig'-l-di-pig'-l-di], *adv.* (Fam.) Confusamente.
Higgler [hig'-lẹr], *s.* Revendedor de comestibles de puerta en puerta.

High [hai], *a.* 1. Alto, levantado, elevado. 2. Difícil, dificultoso, arduo. 3. Altivo, jactancioso, orgulloso. 4. Severo, opresivo. 5. Fuerte, poderoso. 6. Noble, ilustre, grande, sublime. 7. Violento o tempestuoso (aplicado al viento), vehemente, impetuoso; ardiente, fogoso, vivo; borrascoso (v. gr. aplicado al mar). 8. Solemne. 9. Turbulento, indómito. 10. Lleno, cumplido. 11. Alto, grande, enorme. 12. Caro. 13. (Mús.) Alto, agudo. 14. Maleado, mal oliente, corrompido: se dice de la carne. *High colour,* Color muy vivo o muy subido. *High sauces* o *spices,* Salsas o especias muy fuertes o picantes. *High treason,* Alta traición, delito de lesa majestad. *It was high time to do so,* Ya era hora de hacerlo. *High-water,* Marea alta. *The Most High,* El Altísimo. *High road,* Camino real. *High mass,* Misa mayor. *A high look,* Una mirada altanera. *A high hand,* Audacia, befa del derecho y de la autoridad. *High and dry,* En seco, completamente fuera del agua. *High and mighty,* Poderoso, arrogante. *A high day,* Un gran día, un día solemne, o de fiesta. *A high compliment,* Un gran cumplimiento, de alto carácter. *With a high hand,* Despóticamente, tiránicamente. *High passions,* Pasiones ardientes. *High words,* Palabras altivas, arrogantes. *In high terms,* En términos lisonjeros. *At high noon,* En pleno mediodía. *High-aimed, high-aspiring,* El que tiene grandes designios o aspira a cosas grandes. *High-arched,* Lo que consta de bóvedas altas. *High-blest,* Supremamente feliz. *High-blown,* Inflado, hinchado con aire. *High-born,* Noble, ilustre de nacimiento. *High-built,* Elevado: dícese de los edificios. *High-climbing,* Que sube en alto. *High-coloured,* Subido de color. *High-day,* Fino, primoroso. *High-designing,* El que tiene grandes proyectos. *High-embowed,* Dícese del edificio cuyas bóvedas son muy elevadas. *High-engendered,* Engendrado en el aire. *High-fed,* Atracado. *High-flaming,* Lo que echa llama muy alta. *High-flier,* El que es extravagante en sus opiniones o pretensiones. *High-flown,* Altivo, orgulloso; hinchado; fiero, soberbio, presuntuoso. *High-flushed,* Elevado; henchido, lleno, colmado. *High-flying,* Extravagante en alguna cosa. *High-gazing,* Que mira hacia arriba. *High-grown,* Muy crecido o alto. *High-heaped,* Colmado, amontonado altamente. *High-hearted,* Animoso, de pelo en pecho. *High-heeled,* De tacones altos. *High-hung,* Suspendido en alto, colgado. *High mettled,* Osado, atrevido. *High-placed,* Elevado en situación, posición o grado. *High-principled,* Extravagante en sus opiniones o sentimientos. *High-raised,* (1) De pensamientos elevados. (2) Muy alto o muy levantado. *High-reaching,* Lo que se extiende hacia arriba; ambicioso. *High-reared,* De estructura alta. *High-resolved,* Resuelto, determinado. *High-roofed,* Que tiene el tejado alto (un edificio). *High-seasoned,* Picante, demasiadamente sazonado con especias. *High-seated,* Fijado o asentado arriba. *High-spirited,* Osado, atrevido, valeroso. *High-stomached,* Altivo, obstinado *High-tasted,* Picante. *High-towered,* Lo que tiene torres altas.—*adv.* Arriba, sobre; alto; poderosamente, sumamente, profundamente. *On high,* Arriba; a voces, en alto, particularmente en el cielo; sobre.

Highball [hai'-bōl], *s.* Bebida hecha de un licor espiritoso, comúnmente *whiskey,* y agua. (Mex.) Jaibol.

High beams [hai' bimz], *s. pl.* Luces de carretera.

High blood pressure [hai blud presh'-ur], *s.* Hipertensión arterial, alta presión arterial.

High energy physics [hai en-er-ji fiz'-ics], *s.* Física de altas energías.

Highfalutin [hai-fa-lū'-tin], *a.* (Ger.) E. U.) Hinchado, pomposo, retumbante.—*s.* Estilo altisonante, palabras retumbantes.

High fidelity [hai fi-del'-i-ti], *s.* (Mús.) Alta fidelidad.

High-frequency [hai-frī'-cwen-si], *a.* (Elec.) De alta frecuencia.

High-grade [hai'-grêd], *a.* Excelente, de muy buena calidad.

High-handed [hai-hand'-ed], *a.* Arbitrario soberbio, tiránico.

High-keyed, *a.* 1. (Mús.) Agudo, de sonido alto. 2. Impresionable, de mucho corazón.

High jump [hai jump], *s.* Salto de altura.

Highland [hai'-land], *s.* País de montañas, tierras montañosas.

Highlander [hai'-land-ęr], *s.* 1. Montañés, el que vive en las montañas o es natural de ellas. 2. Montañés escocés; gaelo.

High light [hai lait], *s.* 1. Lo que más descuella en una pintura o dibujo. Lo más interesante.

Highlight [hai'-lait], *va.* Iluminar, llenar de luz, acentuar, destacar.

Highly [hai'-li], *adv.* 1. Altamente, elevadamente. 2. Sumamente, en sumo grado, infinitamente. 3. Altivamente, arrogantemente, ambiciosamente. 4. Con aprecio, con estimación. *I am highly obliged to you,* Le quedo a Vd. sumamente agradecido o reconocido. *To think highly of one,* Estimar altamente a alguno. *To think highly of one's self,* Tener gran concepto de sí mismo.

High-minded [hai'-mainded], *a.* 1. De altos o de elevados pensamientos, magnánimo. 2. (Ant.) Altivo, arrogante, ambicioso, fiero.

Highness [hai'-nes], *s.* 1. Altura, elevación. 2. Alteza, tratamiento que se da a los hijos de los reyes y a otros príncipes.

High-octane [hai-oc'-tên], *a.* De alto octano.

High-pitched [hai-picht'], *a.* Agudo. *High-pitched voice,* Voz chillona.

High-powered [hai-pau'-ęrd], *a.* De alta potencia.

High-pressure [hai-presh'-ur], *a.* De alta presión. *High-pressure salesman,* Vendedor insistente y tenaz.

High-priced [hai-praist'], *a.* Caro, costoso.

High-priest [hai-prīst'], *s.* Jerarca, papa; en especial jerarca del pueblo de Israel.

High school [hai scūl], *s.* Escuela secundaria.

High seas [hai sīz], *s. pl.* Alta mar.

High spirits [hai spir'-its], *s. pl.* Animación, jovialidad.

High-strung [hai'-strung], *a.* Excitable, nervioso.

High-test [hai'-test], *a.* De alta graduación o volatilidad.

High-toned [hai'-tōnd], *a.* 1. Honrado. honroso, de nobles principios. 2. De tono o diapasón alto. 3. (Fam. E. U.) Aristocrático. a la moda.

High-water, *s.* *V.* HIGH.

High-water mark [hai-wō'-tęr mārk], *s.* 1. Marea alta. 2. Pináculo.

Highway [hai'-wê], *s.* Camino real.

Highwayman [hai-wê'-man], *s.* Bandolero, ladrón, salteador de caminos.

Hike [haik], *s.* Excursión a pie, caminata.—*vn.* Ir de excursión a pie, caminar largo trecho.

Hilarious [hai-lē'-ri-us], *a.* Alegre, bullicioso.

Hilarity [hai-lar' i-ti], *s.* Alegría, júbilo y contento de ánimo, regocijo.

Hill [hil], *s.* 1. Collado, altura de tierra que no llega a ser montaña; cuesta, cerro, monte, eminencia, altozano. 2. Montoncillo de tierra, hecho artificialmente, como por los animales o en el cultivo. *Hill of beans,* Montoncillo de habas. *Ant-hill,* Hormiguero. *Little hill,* Colina. *Up-hill work,* Cuesta arriba. *Down-hill,* Cuesta abajo. *To write up-hill,* Escribir torcido. *Up hill and down dale,* Por montes y valles.

Hillock [hil'-ec], *s.* Colina, collado pequeño, loma, montecillo; otero.

Hillside [hil'-said], *s.* Lado de una cuesta o de un collado; ladera.

Hilltop [hil'-tep], *s.* Cima, cumbre de un collado, o de una cuesta.

Hilly [hil'-i], *a.* Montañoso, montuoso.

Hilt [hilt], *s.* Puño o guarnición de espada.

Him [him], *pron.* Le. a él, lo (hablando de un substantivo masculino no personificado); es el caso acusativo (llamado objetivo en inglés) del pronombre *He.* *I shall see him to-morrow,* Le veré mañana. *As for him,* En cuanto a él. *He beats the dog and kills him,* Pega al perro y lo mata. *What do you think of him?* ¿Qué piensa Vd. de él? *Give it to him,* Déselo Vd.

Himalayan [hi-mā'-la-yan o him-a-lē'-yan], *a.* Del Himalaya o que tiene relación con él.

Himself [him-self']. Pronombre que en los casos oblicuos tiene significación recíproca. Él, él mismo, se, sí. *He will go himself,* Él mismo irá, irá en persona. *He thinks himself a great man,* Se tiene por grande hombre. *By himself,* Solo, por sí mismo, de por sí. *It is himself,* Es él mismo, hélo aquí.

Hind [haind], *a.* Trasero, zaguero, posterior.—*s.* 1. Cierva, la hembra del ciervo. 2. Criado, la persona que sirve por un salario. 3. Patán, el hombre zafio, tosco y campesino. (Las acepciones 2 y 3 son anticuadas y se hallan en Shakespeare.) *Hind-wheels,* Juego trasero del coche.

Hinder [hin'-dęr], *va.* Impedir, embarazar, estorbar, detener, poner obstáculos.—*vn.* Causar impedimento, oponerse.

Hinder [haind'-ęr], *a.* Posterior, trasero.

Hinderance [hin'-dęr-ans], **Hindrance** [hin'-drans], *s.* Impedimento, obstáculo, embarazo, estorbo; perjuicio, daño. (*Hindrance* es la forma preferida y más moderna.)

Hindermost [haind'-ęr-mōst], **Hind most** [haind'-mōst], *a.* Postrero, lo que es último en orden.

Hindoo, Hindu [hin'-dū], *s.* 1. Indos-

tano, el natural del Indostán. 2. El idioma indostánico; se deriva del sanscrito. 3. El indostano que profesa el brahmanismo.
Hindustani [hin-dū-stā'-nī], *s.* El idioma oficial y común en la India; una forma del indostánico, mezclado con palabras persas y arábigas.
Hinge [hinj], *s.* 1. Gozne, charnela, bisagra, eje principal, resorte. *Butt-hinge,* Quicio. *Dovetail hinges,* (Mar.) Bisagras a cola de pato. 2. Los dos polos o ejes del mundo. 3. Principio, la razón principal sobre la cual se procede en cualquier asunto. *To be off the hinges,* Salirse de sus casillas.
Hinge, *va.* Engoznar, poner goznes a alguna cosa; fijar; encorvar.—*vn.* Dar vueltas como un gozne.
Hinny, *vn.* *V. To* NEIGH y *To* WHINNY. (Lat. hinnio.)
Hint [hint], *va.* Apuntar, insinuar o tocar ligeramente alguna especie o cosa; sugerir indirectamente.—*vn.* Sugerir, echar una indirecta. *To hint at,* Hacer una alusión velada, hacer entrever, dar a entender. *He never so much as hinted at it,* Ni siquiera hizo alusión a ello.
Hint, *s.* Indirecta, sugestión, alusión lejana o velada, aviso, idea, insinuación.
Hip [hip], *s.* 1. Cadera; la parte del cuerpo que está sobre los muslos. 2. Escaramujo, el fruto de la planta llamada escaramujo; agavanzo. 3. (Arq.) Caballete, el ángulo exterior del techo. *To have* o *catch on the hip,* Tener o llevar ventaja sobre alguno; por alusión a una astucia de los luchadores. *To smite hip and thigh,* Derrotar completamente. *Hip-bath,* Baño de asiento, semicupio. *Hip-bone,* Hueso de la cadera, hueso ilíaco.
Hip, *va.* 1. Descaderar, lastimar o fracturar la cadera. 2. (Arq.) Construir un techo con cubierta a cuatro aguas. 3. Echar el luchador a su antagonista sobre la cadera.
Hip, Hipped, Hippish, *s.* *V.* HYPOCHONDRIAC.
Hip-gout [hip'-gaut], *s.* Ciática.
Hippocampus [hip'-o-cam-pus], *s.* 1. Hipocampo, pez llamado también caballo marino. 2. Nombre de dos eminencias del cerebro.
Hippocentaur [hip-o-sen'-tōr], *s.* Hipocentauro, monstruo fabuloso.
Hippocras [hip'-o-cras], *s.* Hipocrás, antigua bebida que se hacía de vino, azúcar, canela, clavo y otros ingredientes.
Hippocrates'-sleeve [hi-pec'-ra-tīz-slīv'], *s.* Manga o calza de lienzo, tela u otra cosa hecha en figura cónica, para colar líquidos.
Hippocratism [hi-pec'-ra-tizm], *s.* La doctrina médica de Hipócrates.
Hippodrome [hip'-o-drōm], *s.* 1. Hipódromo, circo. 2. Circo moderno.
Hippogriff [hip'-o-grif], *s.* Hipogrifo, caballo con alas.
Hippophagist [hip-pef'-a-jist], *s.* El que come carne de caballo.
Hippophagous [hip-pef'-a-gus], *a.* Hipófago, que se alimenta de carne de caballo.
Hippophagy [hip-pef'-a-ji], *s.* Hipofagia, alimentación con carne de caballo.
Hippopotamus [hip-o-pet'-a-mus], *s.* Hipopótamo, mamífero paquidermo que vive en los grandes ríos de África.
Hippuric [hip-piū'-ric], *a.* Hipúrico, de la orina del caballo, o parecido a esa orina. *Hippuric acid,* Ácido hipúrico.
Hipshot [hip'-shet], *a.* Descaderado, con las caderas lisiadas.
Hipwort [hip'-wūrt], *s.* (Bot.) Escaramujo.
Hircine [hęr'-sin], *a.* Cabrío; particularmente que tiene un olor semejante al de las cabras.
Hire [hair], *va.* 1. Alquilar, tomar en alquiler o arrendamiento alguna cosa. 2. Asalariar. 3. Cohechar, sobornar. 4. Alquilar, arrendar, dar en arriendo. *To hire out,* Alquilar, dar en alquiler. *To hire out one's self,* Alquilarse, ponerse a servir, servir a otro por un salario. Algunas veces se suprime el pronombre; v. g. *To hire out for a year,* Ponerse a servir por un año.
Hire, *s.* 1. Alquiler, el precio que se da por el uso de alguna cosa. 2. Salario, el estipendio que los amos dan a sus criados por su servicio y trabajo.
Hireless [hair'-les], *a.* Sin salario o recompensa.
Hireling [hair'-ling], *s.* 1. Jornalero, el que sirve por jornal o salario. 2. Hombre mercenario; mujer prostituta.—*a.* Mercenario, venal.
Hirer [hair'-ęr], *s.* Alquilador, arrendador, el que alquila o arrienda.
Hirsute [hęr-siūt'], *a.* 1. Hirsuto, velludo, guarnecido de cerdas o cubierto de pelos. 2. (Ant.) Áspero, grosero.
Hirsuteness [hęr-siūt'-nes], *s.* Vellosidad.
His [hiz], *pron.* 1. Caso posesivo o genitivo de HE; de él. 2. *pron. pos. mas.* El suyo, la suya, los suyos, las suyas. 3. Adj. posesivo: Su, sus (debe concordar con el género del poseedor y nunca con la cosa poseída). *This book is his,* Este libro es suyo, o de él. *His daughter,* Su hija (de él).
Hispanic [his-pan'-ic], *a.* Hispánico, hispano.
Hispaniola [his-pan-yō'-la], *s.* Isla de Santo Domingo o Haití.
Hiss [his], *vn.* Silbar; producir un silbo, como la serpiente y otros animales; burlarse, hacer burla.—*va.* 1. Silbar, reprobar alguna cosa, hacer burla de ella. Manifestar desagrado el público por medio de silbidos. 2. Producir un silbido cualquiera, hacer oir un sonido agudo.
Hiss, *s.* 1. Silbido de serpiente. 2. Silbido, escarnio o burla que se hace en los teatros.
Hissing [his'-ing], *s.* 1. Silbido de serpiente. 2. Objeto de burla o escarnio.
Hist [hist], *inter.* Chito o chitón, interjección de que se usa para imponer silencio o mandar callar.
Histologic, Histological [his-to-lej'-ic, al], *a.* Histológico, relativo a la histología.
Histologist [his-tel'-o-jist], *s.* Histólogo o histologista, persona versada en la histología.
Histology [his-tel'-o-ji], *s.* Histología, parte de la anatomía que trata de los tejidos orgánicos; la anatomía microscópica.
Historian [his-tō'-ri-an], *s.* Historiador, el que escribe historia.
Historic, Historical [his-ter'-ic, al], *a.* Histórico, lo perteneciente a la historia.
Historically [his-ter'-i-cal-i], *adv.* Históricamente.
Historiographer [his-to-ri-eg'-ra-fęr], *s.* Historiógrafo, historiador, cronista, el que escribe historia o crónicas.
Historiography [his-to-ri-eg'-ra-fi], *s.* Historiografía, el arte de historiar.
†**Historiology** [his-to-ri-el'-o-ji], *s.* Conocimiento de la historia; comentarios sobre la historia.
History [his'-to-ri], *s.* 1. Historia, narración de las cosas y de los hechos dignos de memoria. 2. Historia, el conocimiento de los hechos y sucesos que ella comprende.
History-piece [his'-to-ri-pīs], *s.* Historia, los cuadros o tapices que contienen episodios históricos.
†**Histrion,** *s.* *V.* PLAYER.
Histrionic, Histrionical [his-tri-en'-ic, al], *a.* Histriónico, lo que pertenece al arte cómico o a los cómicos; teatral.
Histrionically [his-tri-en'-ic-al-i], *adv.* Cómicamente, teatralmente.
Histrionism [his'-tri-en-izm], *s.* Histrionismo, representación dramática; de aquí, afectación.
Hit [hit], *va.* (*pret.* y *pp.* HIT). 1. Dar, pegar, golpear. 2. Atinar, acertar, dar en el hito. *You hit the nail on the head,* Vd. lo acertó, o dió en el hito, o en el clavo. 3. Lograr, conseguir alguna cosa. 4. Tocarle a uno donde le duele o darle en las mataduras.—*vn.* 1. Ludir o rozar una cosa con otra. 2. Acaecer o acontecer felizmente, tener buen éxito por casualidad; salir bien, no malograrse alguna cosa. 3. Tropezar, encontrar por casualidad. 4. Acertar, determinar felizmente. *To hit the mark,* Dar en el blanco. *To hit in the teeth with,* Dar en rostro. *To hit against,* Dar contra alguna cosa; encallar un buque. *To hit together,* Encontrarse por casualidad. *To hit upon,* Hallar, encontrar; acordarse. *To hit off,* Describir breve y hábilmente, expresar exactamente. *To hit out,* Ejecutar. *You hit it right,* Dió Vd. en ello.
Hit, *s.* 1. Golpe, choque de dos cuerpos duros. 2. Suerte feliz, golpe de fortuna; chiste, chanza graciosa. 3. Alcance. *Hit or miss,* (Fam.) A todo riesgo, sea como se fuere, salga pez o salga rana. *A lucky hit,* Golpe de fortuna, ocurrencia feliz; exito, buen suceso.
Hitch [hich], *va.* 1. Atar, ligar por un tiempo, enganchar, sujetar; (Mar.) amarrar. 2. Mover a saltos, adelantar a brincos.—*vn.* 1. Saltar, moverse a saltos. 2. Rozarse, tropezar o golpear con los pies: dícese de los caballos. 3. Caer dentro, enredarse. 4. (Fam.) Obrar o vivir en concordancia con otro: ser compatible, estar de acuerdo y conformidad.
Hitch, *s.* 1. Alto, parada; de aquí, tropiezo, dificultad, impedimento, obstáculo. 2. Acción de coger agarrar o colgar. 3. Acción de tirar de algo hacia arriba. 4. (Mar.) Vuelta de cabo.
Hitchel [hich'-el], *va.* Rastrillar.
Hitchel, *s.* *V.* HATCHEL.
Hitchhike [hich'-haik], *vn.* Avanzar, especialmente cuando se va a pie, consiguiendo ser llevado por tramos en automóviles que pasan.
Hitchhiking [hich'-haik-ing], *s.* Autostop.
Hither [hidh'-ęr], *adv.* 1. Acá, desde otro paraje a este. *Come hither,* Ven acá. 2. A esto fin, para este inten-

to. -*a.* Citerior, lo que está más cercano o de la parte de acá. *On the hither side of,* (1) Del lado de acá, hacia el que habla. (2) Más joven, de menos años. *She is on the hither side of sixty,* Ella tiene menos de sesenta años.

Hithermost [hidh'-ęr-mōst], *a.* Lo más cercano o próximo.

Hitherto [hidh'-ęr-tū], *adv.* Hasta ahora, hasta aquí.

Hive [haiv], *s.* 1. Colmena, especie de caja de corcho o de madera en que se crían las abejas. 2. Enjambre, las abejas que se juntan y pueblan una colmena.

Hive, *va.* Enjambrar, encerrar las abejas en las colmenas.—*vn.* Acogerse o encerrarse en una parte muchas personas juntas; vivir o estar muchos en un mismo lugar.

Hive-dross [haiv'-dres], *s.* Cera cruda o áspera.

Hiver [haiv'-ęr], *s.* Colmenero, el que enjambra.

Hives [haivz], *s.* (Med. Fam.) Nombre familiar de la erupción llamada urticaria, y de otras erupciones ligeras.

Ho, Hoa! [hō], *inter.* 1. ¡Eh! ¡basta! ¡mira, hola! voz con la cual se llama o avisa a alguno. 2. *V.* WHOA!

Hoar [hōr], *a.* Blanco, cano; mohoso; lo que aparece blanco por estar cubierto de nieve o de hielo.—*s.* Antigüedad.

Hoarfrost [hōr'-frōst], *s.* Escarcha blanca.

Hoard [hōrd], *s.* 1. Provisión, montón, cantidad de una cosa acumulada y tenida de reserva. 2. Repuesto oculto de dinero u otra cosa; tesoro escondido.

Hoard, *va.* y *vn.* 1. Atesorar, amontonar, acumular, recoger o guardar tesoros, riquezas u otra cosa. 2. Hacer repuesto o acopio.

Hoarder [hōrd'-ęr], *s.* Atesorador, el que hace repuestos en secreto.

Hoarding [hōrd'-ing], *s.* Amontonamiento.

Hoarhound, Horehound [hōr'-haund], *s.* (Bot.) Marrubio, hierba medicinal de la misma familia que la hierbabuena, el tomillo, etc., que produce tallos vellosos y blanquecinos.

Hoariness [hōr'-i-nes], *s.* 1. Blancura. 2. Moho. 3. Canas de viejo; y la vejez misma.

Hoarse [hōrs], *a.* Ronco, enronquecido, el que tiene ronquera, como uno que está resfriado. *To speak in a hoarse voice,* Hablar ronco.

Hoarsely [hōrs'-li], *adv.* Roncamente.

Hoarseness [hōrs'-nes], *s.* Ronquera, carraspera.

Hoary [hōr'-i], *a.* 1. Blanco, blanquecino. 2. Cano, el que tiene el cabello blanco por la edad. 3. Escarchado, blanco con la escarcha. 4. (Des.) Mohoso, cubierto de moho.

Hoast [hōst], *s.* (Esco.) Tos. *V.* COUGH.

Hoax [hōcs], *s.* Engaño, burla, petardo, broma, mentira.

Hoax, *va.* Engañar, burlar, dar un petardo.

Hob [heb], *s.* 1. Antehogar, anaquel a un lado del hogar, donde se coloca lo que se quiere conservar caliente. 2. Cubo o maza de rueda. 3. Plancha de taladro, para cortar roscas de tornillo. 4. Juego con monedas en Inglaterra. 5. (Des.) Patán; duende. 6. (Prov. Ingl.) Error, paso en falso. *To play hob with,* Trastornar, volver patas arriba, poner en confusión.

Hobble [heb'-l], *va.* y *vn.* 1. Cojear, andar inclinando el cuerpo más a un lado que a otro, o cargar sobre una pierna más que sobre la otra; andar cojeando. 2. Hacer versos desiguales o irregulares. 3. Embarazar, enredar, confundir a uno.

Hobble, *s.* 1. Dificultad, atolladero. *To get* o *thrust one's self into a hobble,* Meterse en un atolladero, en un berengenal. 2. Cojera. 3. Traba, atadura puesta en los pies de los caballos. *V.* HOPPLE.

Hobbledehoy [heb-l-dę-hei'], *s.* Joven entre catorce y veintiún años de edad.

Hobbler [heb'-lęr], *s.* En la edad media, soldado de caballería ligera.

Hobblingly [heb'-ling-li], *adv.* Groseramente.

Hobby [heb'-i], *s.* 1. (Fam.) La ocupación o el objeto favorito de una persona. 2. Haca de Irlanda o de Escocia. 3. Caballico, caballito, la caña o palo con que juegan los niños, montándolo y corriendo sobre él. 4. Zoquete, hombre rudo y torpe. 5. Sacre, especie de halcón.

Hobby-horse [heb'-i-hōrs], *s.* 1. Objeto o empeño predilecto. 2. Caballito con que juegan los niños. 3. Zoquete, hombre tonto.

Hobgoblin [heb-geb'-lin], *s.* Duende, espectro, espíritu.

Hobit [heb' it], *s.* (Mil.) Mortero pequeño.

Hoblike [heb'-laic], *a.* Rústico, grosero.

Hobnail [heb'-nēl], *s.* Clavo de herradura.

Hobnailed [heb'-nēld], *a.* Clavado con clavos de herradura.

Hobo [hō'-bo], *s.* (E. U. del Oeste) Obrero holgazán, sin recursos, vagabundo.

Hobson's choice [heb'-sunz cheis], *s.* Expresión proverbial con que se designa una elección en que no hay alternativa.

Hock [hec], *s.* 1. Vino añejo del Rin, originalmente de Hochheim. 2. Jarrete, corvejón de las bestias.

Hock, *va.* Cortar los jarretes, desjarretar. *V.* HOUGH.

Hockey, *s.* 1. Juego de pelota en el que se emplea un palo encorvado en uno de sus extremos. 2. (Prov. Ingl.) *V.* HARVEST-HOME.

Hockle [hec'-l], *va.* 1. Desjarretar, cortar las piernas por el jarrete o por la corva. 2. Guadañar el rastrojo.

Hocus [hō'-cus], *va.* 1. Engañar, chasquear. 2. Dejar insensible a uno por medio de una bebida narcótica, para robarlo.

Hocus-pocus [hō'-cus-pō'-cus], *s.* 1. Jugador de manos, titiritero. 2. Pasapasa, juego de manos. *To do things by virtue of hocus-pocus,* Hacer las cosas por arte de birlibirloque.

Hod [hed], *s.* El artesón o artesa en que el peón lleva el mortero o los ladrillos al albañil.

Hodge-podge [hej'-pej], *s.* Almodrote, mezcla de ingredientes cocidos juntos.

Hodiernal [ho-di-ęr'-nal], *a.* Lo que es de hoy o de este día.

Hodman [hed'-man], *s.* Peón de albañil.

Hoe [hō], *s.* Azada, azadón.

Hoe, *va.* Cavar la tierra con azada o azadón.

Hog [heg], *s.* 1. Puerco, cerdo. 2. Nombre genérico de todo ganado de cerda. *Hog's bristle,* Cerdas, setas. 3. (Met.) Persona grosera, sucia o avarienta; egoista, indiferente a los derechos de otros. 4. (Mar.) Escoba. 5. (Prov.) Carnero o buey de un año. *Hog's pudding,* Morcillas. *To go the whole hog,* Ir al extremo, llegar hasta el último límite.

Hog, *va.* 1. Limpiar el casco de un buque debajo del agua. 2. (Mar.) Hender o partir una embarcación por el medio. 3. (Fam. E. U.) Tomar posesión de más de lo que a uno le corresponde.—*vn.* Arquearse, combarse, torcerse; se dice de una embarcación.

Hogcote, *s.* *V.* HOGSTY.

Hoggerel [heg'-ęr-el], *s.* (Prov.) Oveja de dos años.

Hoggish [heg'-ish], *a.* Porcuno.

Hoggishly [heg'-ish-li], *adv.* Puercamente, cochinamente; vorazmente, vilmente.

Hoggishness [heg'-ish-nes], *s.* Brutalidad, voracidad; porquería, cochinada.

Hog-herd [heg'-hęrd], *s.* Porquero, porquerizo, el que guarda puercos.

Hogshead [hegz'-hed], *s.* 1. Medida inglesa de líquidos que contiene sesenta galones. 2. Barril grande.

Hog-shearing [heg'-shīr-ing], *s.* Expresión anticuada familiar, que equivale en castellano a la de mucho ruido y pocas nueces.

†**Hogsteer** [heg'-stīr], *s.* Jabalí de tres años.

Hogsty [heg'-stai], *s.* Porqueriza, zahurda, el sitio donde se recogen los puercos.

Hoiden [hei'-dn], *s.* 1. Paya, moza agreste, zafia e ignorante. 2. Payo, patán.—*a.* Rústico, grosero. Escríbese también *hoyden.*

Hoiden, *vn.* Retozar, moverse, saltar o jugar con grosería o descompostura.

Hoist [heist], *va.* 1. Guindar, alzar, levantar en alto. 2. (Mar.) Izar, tirar para levantar o subir en alto las vergas y los masteleros. *Hoist away,* ¡Iza, iza!

Hoist, *s.* 1. Cabria, pescante, aparejo para izar, o levantar fardos de mercancías u otros pesos. 2. El acto de levantar. 3. Altura perpendicular de un pabellón o una vela.

Hoisting [heist'-ing], *s.* Elevación, alzamiento. *Engine-hoisting equipment,* Equipo de izar motores. *Hoisting machinery,* Maquinaria elevadora. *Friction-hoisting machine,* Máquina de fricción para izar. *Hoisting of the flag,* Izamiento de la bandera.

Hoity-toity [hei'-i-tei'-i], *a.* (Vulg.) Voluble, descuidado; juguetón —*inter.* ¡Ola! ¡Tate!

Hold [hōld], *va.* (*pret.* y *pp.* HELD, *pp.* (ant.) HOLDEN). 1. Detener, contener; restringir, estrechar, limitar. 2. Contener en sí alguna cosa; caber. 3. Tener, asir, mantener asida alguna cosa; agarrar. 4. Tener, mantener, sostener. 5. Juzgar, reputar, entender. 6. Tener, poseer, gozar. 7. Apostar, hacer alguna apuesta. 8. Continuar, proseguir; conservar; guardar, no infringir.—*vn.* 1. Valer, ser válido, tener fuerza y solidez. 2. Tenerse, mantenerse en su ser. 3. Durar, continuar 4. Refrenarse, abstenerse. 5. Adherirse a alguna persona o partido. 6. Depender o estar dependiente de alguno. 7. Deducir. *To hold back,*

Retener, resistir. 8. Echarse atrás. *To hold forth*, Sacar a la vista o al público, mostrar, descubrir; predicar, hablar en público, arengar. *To hold in*, Tener en sujeción, refrenar; contenerse, refrenarse; continuar. *To hold in hand*, Entretener con falsas esperanzas. *To hold off*, Apartar, alejar, mantener o mantenerse separado o a cierta distancia; apartarse, alejarse, separarse. *To hold on*, Seguir, proseguir, persistir; continuar, prolongar. *To hold out*, Ofrecer, proponer; sostener; extender; mantenerse firme, no ceder, no rendirse; durar; alargar; ir aguantando o sufriendo alguna cosa, continuar haciendo algo o sufriendo algún mal; proferir. *To hold up*, Levantar, alzar; apoyar, sostener, proteger; entretener con buenas palabras; sostenerse, tenerse firme, mantenerse. *To hold a wager*, Apostar, hacer una apuesta. *To hold fast to*, Afirmarse en. *To hold one's peace* o *one's tongue*, Callar. *To hold one's laughing*, Contener la risa. *To hold together*, Mantenerse o estar juntos o reunidos. *To hold up*, (1) (E. U. del Oeste) Mandar detenerse para robar; v. g. *To hold up a train*, Parar un tren para robarlo. (2) Cesar, dejar de. *The rain will soon hold up*, Pronto cesará la lluvia. *To hold with one*, Ser del partido u opinión de alguna persona; declararse por alguno. *Hold your head up*, Levanta la cabeza.

Hold, *inter.* ¡Tente! ¡pára! ¡quieto!

Hold, *s.* 1. Presa, la acción de prender, asir o agarrar. 2. Agarradero, asidero, la parte por donde se agarra alguna cosa; mango, asa. 3. Cualquiera cosa que agarra como garfio o garabato. 4. Prisión, cárcel; custodia. 5. (Mar.) Bodega, todo el espacio entre la sobrequilla y la cubierta (en este sentido se deriva de HOLE). *Afterhold*, Bodega de popa. *Forehold*, Bodega de proa. *To trim the hold*, Abarrotar. *Depth* o *height of the hold*, Puntal de la bodega. 6. Escondite, paraje oculto, propio para esconderse; fuerte, fortaleza, plaza fuerte. 7. Apresamiento, la acción de apresar; toma, la acción de tomar. 8. Poder o influencia. 9. (Mús.) El signo 𝄐 que significa pausa. 10. Llave (en la lucha). *To lay hold of*, 1. Agarrar. 2. Apoderarse de. 3. Reunir, recoger. 4. Aprovecharse de.

Holdback [hōld'-bac], *s.* 1. Restricción, freno. 2. Cejadero, tirante para cejar los carruajes.

Holder [hōld'-ẹr], *s.* 1. Tenedor, el que tiene alguna cosa en su mano. 2. Agarrador, el que agarra. 3. El que guarda o retiene alguna cosa. 4. Poseedor, el que posee algo. 5. Apoyo, el o lo que sostiene. 6. Arrendador; arrendatario, inquilino de una casa. 7. Asidero, mango, puño, asa. 8. Vasija que contiene algo. 9. (Mar.) Marinero de la bodega. (*Holder* se traduce a veces en español por la palabra porta en composición; v. gr. *pen-holder*, portaplumas; *plate-holder*, portaplacas (de una cámara fotográfica.) *Holder of stock*, Tenedor de acciones o valores. *Holder of a bill*, Tenedor o portador de una letra. *Holder of a share*, Accionista.

Holdfast [hōld'-fạst], *s.* Cualquier cosa que agarra; barrilete, grapón, grapa, laña; apoyo, aquello en que está apoyada alguna persona o cosa; (fam.) hombre muy avaro.

Holding [hōld'-ing], *s.* 1. Tenencia, posesión. 2. Arrendamiento. 3. Poder, influencia. 4. (Des.) Coro, estribillo. *Holding-ground*, (Mar.) Buen fondo, fondo donde el áncora se conserva bien agarrada.

Holding company [hōld'-ing cum'-pa-ni], *s.* Empresa tenedora (de acciones o valores de otras compañías).

Hold-up [hōld'-up], *s.* Salteamiento.

Hole [hōl], *s.* 1. Agujero, agujerito, cavidad, hueco. 2. Cueva, cavidad subterránea; hoyo. 3. Cabaña, choza, vivienda vil y mala. 4. (Fam.) Atolladero, dificultad grande, dilema. 5. *A hole to crawl out of*, Escapatoria, excusa, efugio. *A hole in one's coat*, Mancha en la reputación o defecto en el carácter de alguno. *Armhole*, Sobaco.

Hole, *va.* 1. Cavar, agujerear, perforar. 2. En el juego de billar, meter la bola en la tronera.—*vn.* Entrar o meterse, deslizarse en un agujero; invernar.

Holibut, *s.* *V.* HALIBUT.

Holiday, *s.* 1. Día festivo, de fiesta. 2. Día feriado, de descanso y suspensión del trabajo. 3. Aniversario, fiesta que se hace cada año en día señalado. *Holidays*, Vacaciones. 4. (Mar.) Mancha, punto que queda sin que lo toque la brocha al pintar, alquitranar, etc.—*a.* Alegre, festivo, propio de un día de fiesta.

Holily [hō'-li-li], *adv.* Piadosamente; inviolablemente, santamente.

Holiness [hō'-li-nes], *s.* 1. Santidad, perfección e integridad de costumbres conforme a la ley y a la religión. 2. Santidad, beatitud; tratamiento que se da al sumo pontífice.

Holing [hōl'-ing], *s.* Perforación, taladro para introducir un clavo, perno, cabilla, etc.

Holland [hel'-and], *s.* Holanda, especie de lienzo fino. *Brown holland*, Holanda cruda.

Hollands, *s.* *V.* GIN.

Hollen, *s.* (Prov.) *V.* HOLLY.

Hollo, Holloa [he-lō'], *inter.* ¡Hola! voz usada para llamar a uno que está distante o lejos.—*s.* Grito, grita. *V.* HALLO.

Hollo, *vn.* Gritar altamente.

Hollow [hel'-o], *a.* 1. Hueco, lo que es cóncavo o está vacío. 2. El sonido que resulta de la percusión de un cuerpo hueco. 3. Disimulado, falso, insincero. 4. Hundido, empujado hacia adentro. *Hollow eyes*, Ojos hundidos. *Hollow heart*, Corazón doble, disimulado, traidor.—*s.* Cavidad, caverna, cueva, canal, paso; concavidad, hueco; valle, cañada. *Hollow ware*, Ollas, pucheros y otros utensilios de cocina, hechos de hierro, vidriado o barnizado por dentro.

Hollow, *va.* Excavar, ahondar, ahuecar; escotar.

Hollowly [hel'-o-li], *adv.* 1. Con cavidades. 2. Doblemente, traidoramente.

Hollowness [hel'-o-nes], *s.* 1. Cavidad, hueco. 2. Doblez, simulación, falacia, falta de sinceridad.

Hollow-root [hel'-o-rūt], *s.* (Bot.) Moscatelina, palomilla, hierba almizcleña inglesa.

Holly [hel'-i], *s.* (Bot.) Acebo, árbol silvestre.

Hollyhock [hel'-i-hec], *s.* (Bot.) Malva hortense.

Holm [hōlm], *s.* 1. Isleta de río. 2. Terreno bajo y llano cerca de una corriente. 3. (Bot.) Encina. 4. Acebo. *Holm-oak*, Encina. Quercus ilex.

Holocaust [hel'-o-cēst], *s.* 1. Holocausto, el sacrificio en que se quemaba toda la víctima; de aquí, sacrificio o renunciación completos de algo por causa de consagración. 2. Destrucción en masa a sangre y fuego.

Holograph [hel'-o-graf], *s.* El testamento escrito enteramente de la mano del testador.

Holster [hōl'-stẹr], *s.* Funda de pistola. *Holster-cap*, Caperuza.

†**Holt** [hōlt], *s.* Bosque; monte.

Holy [hō'-li], *a.* 1. Santo, pío; puro, inmaculado. 2. Sagrado, consagrado, santificado. *Holy-cross* o *Holy-rood day*, Día de la exaltación de la Santa Cruz, que es el 14 de Septiembre. *Holy day*, Día de fiesta, día sagrado, como el domingo. *Holy Office*, El Santo Oficio o tribunal de la Inquisición. *Holy Rood*, La Santa Cruz. *Holy Ghost*, *Holy Spirit*, Espíritu Santo. *Holy One*, Solo santo, nombre de Dios o Jesucristo. *Holy Thursday*, (1) Día de la ascensión de Nuestro Señor. (2) Juéves santo. *V.* MAUNDY-THURSDAY. *Holy-water*, Agua bendita. *Holy-water sprinkler*, Hisopo.

Holystone [hō'-li-stōn], *s.* (Mar.) Piedra bendita, trozo de arenisca que se usa para limpiar la cubierta de los buques.—*va.* Limpiar la cubierta con la piedra llamada *holystone*.

Homage [hem'-ẹj], *s.* Homenaje, reverencia, respeto; sumisión que se muestra al superior. *To pay homage*, Rendir homenaje.

Homage, *va.* Reverenciar, honrar, profesar fidelidad a.

Homageable [hem'-ej-a-bl], *a.* Sujeto a homenaje.

Homager [hem'-ẹj-ẹr], *s.* 1. El que posee una cosa a título de homenaje. 2. Homenaje.

Home [hōm], *s.* 1. Hogar, casa propia, morada, mansión o habitación en que uno vive; lares. 2. Patria, el país o tierra de donde uno es natural. 3. Domicilio, residencia. 4. Cualquier lugar de descanso y abrigo; asilo, hospedería, refugio; de aquí, sepulcro; muerte, estado futuro. *One's long home*, El sepulcro, el estado futuro. 5. En los juegos, meta, límite o término. *To come home*, Regresar al hogar, volver a su país. *To take home*, Llevar a casa; (fig.) tomar para sí. *To hit* o *strike home*, Dar en el blanco; herir en lo vivo, llegar al alma. *Home is home, be it never so homely*, Mi casa y mi hogar cien doblas val.—*a.* 1. Doméstico, de casa; de su país, natal; opuesto a extranjero, indígena. 2. Que da en lo vivo o en el hito. *A home-thrust*, Gran golpe, que da en el blanco. 3. En los juegos, que llega al término.—*adv.* 1. A su propia casa o habitación. *He is gone home*, Se ha ido a casa. 2. A su tierra o país. 3. Al propósito, al intento. 4. Intimamente, estrechamente; con fuerza, eficazmente. *At home*, (1) En casa, (en fechas de cartas) casa de Vd. (2) En su patria, en su propio país. (3) Libre, espontáneo, como si estuviese en la propia casa.

To be away from home, Estar fuera de casa, hallarse ausente.
Home-born [hōm'-bērn], *a.* Natural de; doméstico, indígena.
Home-bred [hōm'-bred], *a.* 1. Nativo, natural. 2. Casero, lo que se cría o hace en casa y lo que pertenece a ella. 3. Rudo, agreste, inculto. 4. Doméstico, lo que es propio de la casa o pertenece a ella.
Home-brew [hōm'-brū], *s.* Bebida fermentada en casa.
Home economics [hōm ec-o-nem'-ics], *s.* Economía doméstica.
Home-felt [hōm'-felt], *a.* Privado, interno.
Home-keeping [hōm'-kīp-ing], *a.* Persona de su casa, de gustos y costumbres caseros.
Homeland [hōm'-land], *s.* Patria, tierra natal.
Homeless [hōm'-les], *a.* Destituído; sin casa ni hogar.
Homelike [hōm'-laik], *a.* Semejante al hogar doméstico; sosegado y cómodo, que procura bienestar.
Homeliness [hōm'-li-nes], *s.* Simpleza, sencillez, falta de cultivo; grosería; fealdad.
Homely [hōm'-li], *a.* 1. Casero, doméstico, sencillo. 2. Liso, llano. 3. Feo, no hermoso. 4. Ignorante, rústico, inculto; grosero, vulgar, sin elegancia.—*adv.* Llanamente, simplemente; como de casa; groseramente.
Home-made [hōm'-mêd], *a.* Hecho en casa, fabricado en el país.
Homemaker [hōm'-mê-kẹr], *s.* Ama de casa, dueña de casa.
Homeopathic, Homœopathic [hō-me-o-path'-ic], *a.* Homeopático, relativo a la homeopatía.
Homeopathist, Homœopathist [hō-mẹ-ep'-a-thist], *s.* Homeópata, el partidario de la homeopatía o el que la practica.
Homeopathy, Homœopathy [hō-me-ep'-a-thi], *s.* Homeopatía, sistema médico creado en Alemania por Hahnemann, y que consiste en tratar las enfermedades por medicamentos capaces de producir, en el estado normal, síntomas análogos a los de las mismas enfermedades. Por consiguiente la dosis ha de ser sumamente pequeña.
Homer [hō'-mẹr], *s.* 1. Homer, medida antigua de los judíos. 2. Paloma viajera, paloma correo.
Homeric [hō-mer'-ic], *a.* Homérico, que se refiere á Homero; que tiene el carácter de su poesía.
Home-sick [hōm'-sic], *a.* Nostálgico, que experimenta la nostalgia; que siente vivamente estar separado de su hogar o de su país.
Home-sickness [hōm'-sic-nes], *s.* Nostalgia, mal del país, pena o tristeza profunda de verse ausente de su patria o de su hogar.
Homespun [hōm'-spun], *a.* 1. Casero, lo que se hila o se hace en casa. 2. Liso, llano; basto, grosero. 3. Común, vulgar.
‡**Homestall** [hōm'-stōl], **Homestead** [hōm'-sted], *s.* Sitio de la casa, casa propia.
Home stretch [hōm strech], *s.* 1. Última parte de una carrera (especialmente de caballos). 2. (fig.) Final de alguna actividad u operación.
Homeward, Homewards [hōm'-ward, z], *adv.* Hacia casa, hacia su país; de vuelta. *Homeward bound,* De vuelta, que regresa al punto de donde salió.
Homework [hōm'-wūrk], *s.* Tarea, estudio hecho fuera de la clase.
Homicidal [hem-i-saíd'-al], *a.* 1. Sanguinario, matador; homicida.
Homicide [hem'-i-said], *s.* 1. Homicidio, la muerte causada a una persona por otra. 2. Homicida, el que comete homicidio.
Homiletic, Homiletical [hem-i-let'-ic, al], *a.* 1. Homilético, referente a la homilética.
Homily [hem'-i-li], *s.* Homilía, sermón.
Homing pigeon [hōm'-ing pij'-un], *s.* Paloma mensajera.
Hominy [hem'-i-ni], *s.* Maíz machacado.
Homogen [hō'-mo-jen], *s.* Estructura o parte homogénea.
Homogeneal [ho-mo-jī'-nẹ-al], **Homogeneous** [ho-mo-jī'-nẹ-us], *a.* Homogéneo, lo que es de la misma naturaleza o género que otra cosa.
Homogenealness [ho-mo-jī'-nẹ-al-nes], **Homogeneity** [ho-mo-jẹ-nī'-i-ti], **Homogeneousness** [ho-mo-jī'-nẹ-us-nes], *s.* Homogeneidad, uniformidad o semejanza de las partes de un todo comparadas entre sí.
Homogenize [hō-me'-je-naiz], *va.* Homogeneizar (la leche, etc.)
Homolog, Homologue [hem'-o-leg ó hō'-mo-leg], *s.* Parte homóloga o análoga a otra en posición, estructura, etc.
Homologation [ho-mel-o-gê'-shun], *s.* Confirmación o publicación de un acto de justicia para darle más autoridad.
Homologous [ho-mel'-o-gus], *a.* Homólogo, que tiene una estructura, proporción, valor o posición correspondientes o semejantes; proporcional entre sí.
Homonym [hō'-mo-nim], *s.* Homónimo, palabra cuya pronunciación es igual a otra de un sentido diferente: v. g. *reed,* caña, y *read,* leer; *sea,* el mar, *see,* ver; o en castellano, si y sí, mas y más, hora y ora.
Homonymous [ho-men'-i-mus], *a.* 1. Homónimo; dícese de las voces semejantes que tienen un sentido diferente. 2. Equívoco, ambiguo.
Homonymy [ho-men'-i-mi], *s.* Homonimia; equivocación; ambigüedad.
Homosexual [ho-mo-sex'-yu-al], *s.* & *a.* Homosexual.
Honduran [hen-dū'-ran], *s.* y *a.* Hondureño.
Hone [hōn], *s.* Piedra de afilar navajas de afeitar o cortaplumas.
Honest [en'-est], *a.* 1. Honrado, recto, justo. 2. Honesto, casto, recatado. *A downright honest man,* Hombre de bien a carta cabal. 3. Sincero, íntegro; fiel; leal, equitativo. *An honest judge,* Un juez íntegro. *An honest confession,* Una confesión sincera. *Honest people,* Gente honrada. *Honest dealing,* Proceder leal, buena fe.
Honestly [en'-est-li], *adv.* Honradamente, rectamente; honestamente, modestamente. *To deal honestly,* Tratar con honradez; ser honrado en sus tratos.
Honesty [en'-est-i], *s.* 1. Honradez, justicia, integridad. 2. Honestidad. 3. (Bot.) Lunaria.
Honey [hun'-i], *s.* 1. Miel. 2. Dulzura, la calidad de las cosas dulces. 3. Voz de cariño. *Honey-ant,* Hormiga pequeña del género Myrmecocystis, de los Estados Unidos del Sudoeste; tiene una forma de hormiga obrera que recibe y acopia en el abdomen la miel que recogen las otras hormigas. *Honey-bee,* Abeja de miel.
Honey, *va.* Enmelar, cubrir con miel.—*vn.* Hablar con cariño.
Honey-bag [hun'-i-bag], *s.* El órgano en que la abeja lleva a la colmena la parte que recoge de las flores, con la cual fabrica la miel.
Honey-comb [hun'-i-cōm], *s.* 1. Panal, el cuerpo esponjoso de cera que forman las abejas y en el cual depositan la miel. 2. (Art.) Escarabajos, los huequecillos que quedan en la parte interior de los cañones por defecto del molde o del metal.
Honey-combed [hun'-i-cōmd], *a.* Lleno de perforaciones o de celdillas; dispuesto a manera de panal.
Honey-dew [hun'-i-diū], *s.* Especie de rocío que se nota en las hojas de algunas plantas y que alimenta a los insectos que hay en ellas.
Honeyed [hun'-id], *a.* Dulce, meloso, enmelado, cubierto de miel.
Honeyedness [hun'-id-nes], *s.* Dulzura, halago.
Honey-flower [hun'-i-flau'-ẹr], *s.* (Bot.) Ceriflor.
Honey-harvest [hun'-i-hār'-vest], *s.* Cosecha de la miel.
Honeyless [hun'-i-les], *a.* Sin miel.
Honey-mouthed [hun'-i-maudhd], *a.* Adulador, melifluo.
Honey-moon [hun'-i-mūn], **Honey-month** [hun'-i-munth], *s.* La luna de miel; el primer mes de casados, el tiempo que se supone dura el pan de la boda.
Honey-stalk [hun'-i-stōc], *s.* (Bot.) Trébol. *V.* CLOVER.
Honey-suckle [hun'-i-suc-l], *s.* (Bot.) Madreselva, planta de olorosas flores del género Lonicera, familia de las caprifoliáceas.
Honey-sweet [hun'-i-swīt], *a.* Dulce como la miel.
Honey-tongue [hun'-i-tung], *s.* Lengua melosa.
Honor, Honour [en'-ẹr], *s.* 1. Honra, reverencia, veneración. *I take it as a great honour,* Lo tengo a mucha honra. 2. Fidelidad, rectitud, honradez, probidad, integridad. 3. Gloria, reputación, fama. 4. Pudor, castidad, recato, vergüenza. 5. Honor, dignidad, cargo, empleo. *Act of honour,* (Com.) Acto o protesta de intervención. 6. Grandeza de alma, magnanimidad. 7. Dignidad en el porte o en las acciones. 8. Honor, obsequio público que se hace a alguna persona. 9. Honor, privilegio de clase o de nacimiento. En castellano se usa casi siempre en plural en las dos últimas acepciones. 10. Cortesía, civilidad. 11. Ornamento, decoración. 12. Señorío. 13. Se da el tratamiento de *your honour* al Vicecanciller de Inglaterra y otros dignatarios.—*pl.* 14. Los cuatro naipes más altos en el juego de *whist. Honour bright,* Bajo mi palabra de honor; o como interrogación, ¿de veras? ¿en realidad? *On* o *upon honour,* Por mi honor, bajo mi palabra de honor. *Point of honour,* Pundonor, punto de honor.
Honor, Honour, *va.* 1. Honrar, reverenciar, respetar, estimar, venerar; glorificar. 2. Dar un empleo o cargo de brillo y estimación. 3. Dar honor, lustre o gloria. *To honour a bill of exchange,* Aceptar, honrar una letra de cambio, pagarla.

Honorable, Honourable [en'-ẹr-a-bl], *a.* 1. Ilustre, noble, esclarecido. 2. Grande, magnánimo, generoso. 3. Honrado, honorífico, honroso; equitativo, justo.

Honorableness [en'-ẹr-a-bl-nes], *s.* Honradez; eminencia; honestidad.

Honorably [en'-ẹr-a-bli], *adv.* Honorablemente, honoríficamente; generosamente; decentemente.

Honorarium [hen-o-ré'-ri-um], *s.* 1. Honorarios, emolumentos que se dan a los que ejercen una profesión por el ejercicio de la misma. 2. Paga o recompensa voluntaria en cambio de servicios por los cuales la ley no da derecho a obtener remuneración.

Honorary [en'-ẹr-ẹ-ri], *a.* 1. Honorario, honorífico, que honra o da honor. 2. Honorario, que posee un título o un empleo sin desempeñar sus funciones ni cobrar los emolumentos.—*s.* *V.* HONORARIUM.

Honorer [en'-ẹr-ẹr], *s.* Honrador, el que honra.

Honorless [en'-ẹr-les], *a.* Sin honra, deshonrado.

Honour, Honourable, etc. (Forma usual en que se escriben estas palabras en Inglaterra.) *V.* HONOR, etc., con excepción de HONORARY y HONORARIUM.

Hood [hud], *s.* 1. Caperuza o toca de mujer; muceta de graduados; capilla o capucha de religioso. 2. (Mar.) Caperuza de palo. *Hood* o *companion*, (Mar.) Sombrero de la escalera. *Hood of the chimney*, Sombrero de la chimenea.

hood. Sufijo que significa calidad, estado, condición o totalidad. Muchas veces equivale al sufijo castellano -dad o -ez; v. g. *Brotherhood*, fraternidad; *manhood*, virilidad (también, edad viril; valor, bravura); *maidenhood*, virginidad, doncellez. *Childhood*, Niñez, edad de los niños. *Sisterhood*, Hermandad; congregación de mujeres.

Hood, *va.* 1. Cubrir con caperuza o capirote. 2. Cubrir, tapar, cegar poniendo alguna cosa delante de los ojos.

Hoodlum [hūd'-lum], *s.* 1. Tunante, golfo, matón. 2. Pandillero.

Hoodoo [hū'-dū], *va.* (Fam. E. U.) Hacer a alguno mal de ojo, llevarle la mala suerte, particularmente por la presencia de una persona.—*s.* Causa de mala suerte; persona cuya presencia trae mala fortuna; lo opuesto a *mascot.*

Hoodwink [hud'-wiṇc], *va.* 1. Vendar a uno los ojos. 2. Encubrir, tapar, ocultar. 3. Engañar.

Hoof [hūf], *s.* (*pl.* HOOFS, raramente HOOVES). 1. El casco de las bestias caballares, vacunas, etc. 2. Animal que tiene cascos.

Hoof, *vn.* Andar, moverse muy despacio: dícese de las bestias.

Hoof beat [hūf bit], *s.* Ruido de cascos de las bestias.

Hoof-bound [hūf'-baund], *a.* Estrecho de cascos: dícese de los caballos.

Hoofed [hūft], *a.* Dícese del animal que tiene cascos.

Hook [huk], *s.* 1. Gancho, garabato, garfio. 2. Anzuelo, arponcillo de hierro que sirve para pescar. 3. Atractivo, aliciente. 4. (Mús.) El signo a manera de banderola que sale de una corchea o nota más corta. *By hook or by crook*, De un modo u otro, a tuertas o a derechas, a buenas o a malas. *Off the hooks*, Agitado, distraído; no tenerlas todas consigo.

Hook, *va.* 1. Enganchar, coger alguna cosa con gancho, garfio o anzuelo. 2. Enganchar, atraer a uno con arte, atrapar, engatusar; hacer caer en el garlito. 3. Embestir o lastimar con los cuernos; se dice de una vaca o un toro. 4. (Ger.) Ratear, hurtar cosas de poco valor. *To hook the cat to the anchor*, (Mar.) Enganchar la gata al ancla.

Hook-and-eye [huk-and-ai'], *s.* Macho y hembra. (Aplícase a broches.)

Hooked [hukt], *a.* Enganchado, encorvado, ganchoso.

Hooked rug [hukt rug], *s.* Tapete tejido con gancho.

Hooker [huk'-ẹr], *s.* 1. La cosa que engancha a manera de gancho o garabato. 2. (Mar.) Barco holandés de dos palos.

Hook-nosed [huk'-nōzd], *a.* El que tiene nariz aguileña algo corva en el medio.

Hookup [huk'-up], *s.* 1. (Radio) Radiotransmisión en circuito por una cadena de emisoras. 2. Cadena de estaciones radiotransmisoras. 3. (fam.) Alianza entre dos gobiernos.

Hookworm [huk'-wurm], *s.* Lombriz intestinal.

Hooky [huk'-i], *a.* Lleno de ganchos o perteneciente a ellos.

Hooky, *s.* (Ger. de las escuelas.) *To play hooky*, Hacer novillos, irse de pinta, pintar venados.

Hoop [hūp, hup], *s.* 1. Aro, arco, cerco de barril o tonel. 2. Tontillo, especie de guardapiés ahuecado que usaban las señoras. 3. Arete, zarcillo.

Hoop, *va.* 1. Poner arcos o cercos a una cosa. 2. Cercar, rodear.—*vn.* Gritar, vociferar; ojear. *Hoop-poles*, Cujes. *Lining-hoop*, Aro que refuerza la tapa.

Hooper [hūp'-ẹr], *s.* Tonelero.

Hooping-cough, *s.* *V.* WHOOPING-COUGH.

Hoopoe, Hoopoo [hū'-pō, hū'-pū], *s.* (Orn.) Abubilla, upupa, ave que tiene un penacho de plumas eréctiles en la cabeza.

Hoot [hūt], *vn.* 1. Gritar, burlarse de alguno dando gritos. 2. Gritar como el buho.—*va.* Ojear, espantar los animales á fuerza de gritos.

Hoot, *inter.* (Esco.) ¡Fuera! ¡vaya! ¡puf!

Hoot, *s.* Grito, ruido, clamor.

Hooting [hūt'-ing], *s.* Grito, el acto de dar voces.

Hoove, Hove, Hooven [hūv, hūv'-n], *s.* (Vet.) Enfermedad del ganado vacuno y lanar caracterizada por la distensión del abdomen.

Hop [hep], *vn.* 1. Saltar, dar saltos. 2. Cojear de un pie. 3. Juguetear, brincar.—*va.* Mezclar el lúpulo en la cerveza.

Hop, *s.* 1. Salto, brinco. 2. (Bot.) Lúpulo, u hombrecillo. *Hop pillow*, Almohada rellena de lúpulo para inducir el sueño.

Hope [hōp], *s.* 1. Esperanza, confianza. 2. Apoyo, sostén; el que o lo que es la causa de esperanza o confianza. 3. La cosa esperada o ansiada. *Forlorn hope*, Una empresa sin esperanza.

Hope, *s.* (Prov. Ingl.) Cuesta, subida; declive. Se usa en composición en los nombres de lugares: como Stan*hope*.

Hope, *vn.* Esperar, tener esperanza; confiar, poner la confianza en lo futuro o venidero.—*va.* Esperar con ansia.

Hope chest [hōp chest], *s.* Arca en que las solteras acumulan ropa y mantelería en anticipación a su matrimonio.

Hopeful [hōp'-ful], *a.* 1. Lleno de buenas calidades; de grandes esperanzas o que da grandes esperanzas, que promete mucho. 2. Esperanzado, lleno de esperanzas.

Hopefully [hōp'-ful-i], *adv.* Con esperanza.

Hopefulness [hōp'-ful-nes], *s.* Buena disposición, apariencia o perspectiva de buenos resultados.

Hopeless [hōp'-les], *a.* Desesperado, desahuciado, desesperanzado.

Hopelessly [hōp'-les-li], *adv.* Sin esperanza.

Hop-garden [hep'-gār-dn], **Hop-yard** [hep'-yārd], *s.* Plantío de lúpulos.

Hopingly [hep'-ing-li], *adv.* Con esperanza.

Hopper [hep'-ẹr], *s.* 1. El que da saltos o brincos sobre un pie. 2. Tolva, la caja que está colgada sobre la piedra del molino, donde se echa el grano para molerlo. 3. Sementero, el saco o costal en que se lleva el grano para sembrar.

Hoppers [hep'-ẹrz], *s. pl.* *V.* HOP-SCOTCH.

Hop-picker [hep'-pik-ẹr], *s.* El que hace la recolección del lúpulo.

Hopple [hep'-l], *va.* Atar las patas a un caballo para que no dé brincos. —*s.* Traba, atadura que se pone en las patas de los caballos cuando se les pone a pastar.

Hop-pole [hep'-pōl], *s.* Varal o palo para sostener el lúpulo.

Hop-scotch [hep'-scech''], *s.* El juego de muchachos llamado "a la pata coja" o infernáculo, y en América, rayuela. El jugador salta en un pie por encima de unas rayas trazadas en el suelo, e impulsa con el pie una piedra o un trocito de madera.

Horal [hō'-ral], **Horary** [hō'-ra-ri], *a.* Horario.

Horatian [hō-ré'-shian], *a.* De Horacio, que se refiere o se parece a Horacio o a su poesía.

Horde [hōrd], *s.* Horda, aduar, ranchería: nombre que se da a las tribus de los tártaros o árabes que andan errantes.

Hordeolum [her-dí'-e-lum], *s.* Orzuelo, tumorcillo que sale en el borde de los párpados.

Horizon [ho-rai'-zun], *s.* Horizonte.

Horizontal [her-i-zen'-tal], *a.* Horizontal.

Horizontally [her-i-zen'-tal-i], *adv.* Horizontalmente.

Hormone [hēr'-mōn], *s.* Hormona.

Horn [hērn], *s.* 1. Cuerno, asta, el arma que tienen algunos animales en la cabeza. 2. Cuerna, el asta o cuerno del ciervo o venado; cacho. 3. (Zool.) Tentáculo; palpo o antena. 4. Corneta de monte, trompa de caza; bocina. 5. Cuerno, vaso de cuerno para beber y otros usos. 6. Poder, honor; usado simbólicamente en la Sagrada Escritura. *To wear the horns*, Ser cornudo. *Ink-horn*, Tintero. *Shoe-horn*, Calzador de cuerno. *Horn-fly*, Mosca originaria de Europa, de donde fué llevada a los Estados Unidos hacia 1887; debe ese nombre a su costumbre de posarse en enjambres sobre los cuernos del ganado vacuno.

Hæmatobia serrata. *Horn of plenty*, *V.* CORNUCOPIA.

Horn, *va.* Poner cuernos, hacer a uno cornudo.

Hornbeak [hōrn'-bīc], **Hornfish** [hōrn'-fish], *s.* (Ict.) Aguja.

Hornbeam [hōrn'-bīm], *s.* (Bot.) Carpe u ojaranzo, árbol pequeño de la familia de las cupulíferas. Carpinus.

Hornbill [hōrn'-bil], *s.* Cálao, ave de gran tamaño notable por lo enorme de su pico. (Buceros.)

Hornblende [hōrn'-blend], *s.* (Min.) Hornblenda, especie de anfíbol compuesto de sílice, cal, alúmina, magnesia y protóxido de hierro.

Hornblower [hōrn'-blō-ęr], *s.* El que toca la trompa, trompetero, bocinero.

Hornbook [hōrn'-buc], *s.* Cartilla, el cuaderno que contiene los primeros rudimentos para aprender a leer. Toma el nombre de *hornbook* de la costumbre que hubo en varios puntos de Inglaterra de llevarlo en un estuche de cuerno, así como en Castilla se solía llevar pegado a una tabla pequeña.

Horned [hōrnd], *a.* Cornudo; formado como cuerno. *Horned owl*, (Orn.) Buho norteamericano con dos penachos en la cabeza a manera de cuernos.

Hornedness [hern'-ed-nes], *s.* La cosa que tiene semejanza a cuerno o que tiene puntas como las de los cuernos.

Horner [hōrn'-ęr], *s.* El que trabaja el cuerno o lo vende.

Hornet [her'-net], *s.* Avispón, avispa grande; (Vespa crabro de Europa y Vespa maculata de la América del Norte) con aguijón muy agudo. Llámase también *yellow-jacket*. Hace su nido de una clase de papel que extrae de las hojas y los tallos. *To stir up a hornet's nest*, Meterse en un avispero; excitar la hostilidad de mucha gente.

Hornfoot [hōrn'-fut], *s.* Lo que tiene cascos como los de los caballos.

Hornify [hōrn'-i-fai], *va.* Hacer semejante al cuerno.

Horning [hōrn'-ing], *s.* El aspecto de la luna creciente.

Hornish [hōrn'-ish], *a.* Duro; semejante a cuerno.

Hornless [hōrn'-les], *a.* Lo que no tiene cuernos.

Hornpipe [hōrn'-paip], *s.* 1. Gaita. 2. Baile especial predilecto de los marineros.

Hornsilver [hōrn'-sil-vęr], *s.* (Min.) Cloruro de plata, cerargirita.

Horn-spoon [hōrn'-spūn], *s.* Cuchara de cuerno.

Hornstone [hōrn'-stōn], *s.* (Min.) Hornstenio o piedra de cuerno, especie de feldespato.

Hornwork [hōrn'-wūrk], *s.* (Fort.) Hornabeque u obra a tenaza.

Horny [hōrn'-i], *a.* Hecho de cuerno; parecido al cuerno; calloso.

Horography [ho-reg'-ra-fi], *s.* Gnomónica, el arte de construir relojes de sol.

Horologe [her'-o-lōj], **Horology** [ho-rel'-o-ji], *s.* Reloj ú otro cualquier instrumento que sirve para medir el tiempo.

Horologic, Horological [her''-o-lej'-ic, al], *a.* Que se refiere a la relojería o a la gnomónica.

Horologiography [her-o-lo-ji-eg'-ra-fi], *s.* 1. El conocimiento de los instrumentos que sirven para señalar las horas. 2. Gnomónica, el arte de construir relojes de sol.

Horometry [ho-rem'-e-tri], *s.* Horometría, el arte de medir y dividir las horas.

Horoscope [her'-o-scōp], *s.* Horóscopo, observación supersticiosa que hacían los astrólogos en el nacimiento de alguno, para predecir la suerte y sucesos de su vida en vista de la posición de los astros.

Horrent [her'-ent], *a.* 1. Erizado, que tiene puntas hacia fuera. 2. Horrible, espantoso, que causa detestación.

Horrible [her'-i-bl], *a.* Horrible, espantoso, terrible, horrendo; énorme.

Horribleness [her'-i-bl-nes], *s.* Horribilidad.

Horribly [her'-i-bli], *adv.* Horriblemente, espantosamente, enormemente, terriblemente.

Horrid [her'-id], *a.* Horrible, hórrido, espantoso; áspero; obscuro, tenebroso.

Horridly [her'-id-li], *adv.* Enormemente, horriblemente, espantosamente.

Horridness [her'-id-nes], *s.* Carácter o naturaleza horrible; aspecto horrendo; enormidad, horror.

Horrific [her-rif'-ic], *a.* Horrífico.

Horror [her'-ęr], *s.* 1. Horror, consternación, terror, espanto: detestación. 2. Gran accidente, calamidad. *A railroad horror*, Una catástrofe en la via férrea. *The horrors*, (Fam.) Melancolía, hipocondría; también, delirium tremens.

Hors d'oeuvre [or-dęrv'], *s.* Entremés, canapé.

Horse [hōrs], *s.* 1. Caballo, mamífero solípedo; llámase simplemente *horse* en particular al caballo castrado. *Saddle-horse*, Caballo de silla. *Pack-horse*, Caballo de carga. *Carriage-horse*, Caballo de tiro. *Race-horse*, Caballo de carrera. *Cart-horse*, Caballo de carro. *White horse*, Caballo blanco; (Mex.) tordillo. *Black horse*, Caballo negro. *Fine, shining black horse*, Caballo retinto. *Pie-bald horse*, Caballo moro. *Pied horse*, Caballo picazo. *Chestnut horse*, Caballo castaño. *Bay horse*, Caballo bayo. *Dapple horse*, Tordo rodado. *Gray horse*, Caballo pardo. *Dappled gray* (horse), Pardo rodado. *Sorrel* (horse), Alazán. *Brown sorrel* (horse), Alazán tostado. *Seed horse*, Caballo padre. *Run-away horse*, Caballo desbocado. *To ride a horse*, Montar a caballo. 2. Caballería. *Light horse*, Caballería ligera. 3. Caballete para secar la ropa lavada; bastidor llamado también burro, borrico; tendedor, mesa de papel, etc. 4. Garatura o tabla de descarnar. 5. Caballo de palo o potro en que se castiga a los soldados. 6. Traducción, apuntes u otros medios de que se valen los alumnos para preparar sus lecciones. 7. Manía, tema predilecto. *V.* HOBBY. 8. Trabajo cuyo precio se pide antes de ejecutar aquél. *Horse of the bowsprit*, (Mar.) Guardamancebo del bauprés. *Horse of a yard*, (Mar.) Guardamancebo de una verga. *Horse of a sail*, (Mar.) Nervio de vela. *Hackney, livery horse*, Caballo de alquiler. *Iron horse*, Locomotora. *Blood horse*, Caballo de sangre, de pura raza. *Dark horse*, Caballo del cual nadie espera que gane una carrera; de aquí, en política, competidor desconocido, inesperado. *To groom a horse*, Cuidar, curar un caballo. *To clap spurs to one's horse*, Espolear un caballo. *To put a horse to full speed*, Poner un caballo a rienda suelta, a escape tendido. *As fast as his horse could carry*, A rienda suelta, a escape. *To get on* o *mount the high horse*, Asumir un porte altivo, orgulloso, o arrogante. *To take horse*, (1) Cabalgar, pasear a caballo. (2) Permitir la yegua que la cubra el caballo. La voz *horse* se usa frecuentemente en composición para calificar a una cosa de grosera y grande.

Horse, en composición: *Horse-ant*, La hormiga roja. Formica rufa. *Horse-bean*, (Bot.) Haba panosa o caballuna. *Horse-bot*, Lombriz de caballo; Gasterophilus equi, la mosca y su larva. *V.* BOT-FLY. *Horse-boy*, Mozo de caballos, el que los cuida y limpia. *Horse-box*, (Ingl.) *V.* HORSE-CAR, 2ª acepción. *Horse-breaker*, Picador o domador de caballos. *Horse-car*, (E. U.) (1) Carro de tranvía, tirado por caballos. (2) Carro para transportar caballos por ferrocarril. *Horse-cloth*, Mantilla de caballo. †*Horse-colt*, Potro. *Horse-comb*, Almohaza. *Horse-doctor*, Albéitar; veterinario. *Horse-drench*, Toma de medicina para caballo, y el aparato para administrarla. *Horse-dung*, Cagajón, estiércol de caballos. *Horse-faced*, Que tiene la cara larga y de facciones groseras. *Horse-hair*, Crin de caballo. *Horse-keeper*, Establero, mozo de caballos, el que cuida de ellos. *Horse-laugh*, Gran carcajada, risa grosera. *Horse-leech*, Sanguijuela; albéitar. (Fig.) La persona que constantemente pordiosea o molesta. *Horse-litter*, Litera de dos caballos. *Horse-load*, Carga de caballo. *Horse-mackerel*, Caballa, haleche; atún, y varios otros peces. *Horse-mill*, Molino de sangre, el que mueven hombres o caballerías. *Horse-milliner*, El que vende cintas y otros adornos para los caballos. *Horse-pond*, Estanque para dar de beber o bañar a los caballos. *Horse-race*, Carrera o corrida de caballos. *Horse-stealer*, Cuatrero, ladrón de caballos. *Horse-tail*, (Bot.) Cola de caballo. *Horse-way*, Camino de herradura.

Horse, *va.* 1. Montar a caballo o llevar sobre él. 2. Proveer de caballos, proporcionar caballos. 3. Cabalgar, montar el caballo padre a la yegua o cubrirla. 4. (Mar.) Mandar o hacer trabajar tiránicamente o cruelmente (a los marineros).—*vn.* 1. Cabalgar, andar a caballo. 2. Pedir el precio de un trabajo antes de ejecutarlo.

Horse-aloes [hērs'-al-ōz], *s.* Acíbar caballuno.

Horseback [hērs'-bac], *s.* Lomo de caballo o asiento del jinete. *To get on horseback*, Montar a caballo.

Horse-boat [hērs'-bōt], *s.* Barco para transportar caballos.

Horse-block [hērs'-blec], *s.* Apeadero; montador o montadero, cual quier cosa que sirve para montar.

Horse-chestnut [hērs'-ches-nut], *s.* (Bot.) Castaño de Indias, árbol de la familia de las sapindáceas y su fruto. Æsculus hippocastanum.

Horse-flesh [hērs'-flesh], *s.* 1. Carne de caballo. 2. Conjunto de caballos. 3. Variedad de caoba de las Bahamas.

Horse-fly [hērs'-flai], *s.* 1. Tábano, mosca de caballo. 2. *V.* BOT-FLY. 3. Moscarda, garrapata de caballo.

Horse-guards [hērs'-gūrdz], *s. pl.* 1. Guardias de a caballo. 2. Cuartel general del ejército de la Gran Bretaña.

Horsehide [hērs'-haid], *s.* Cuero de caballo.

Horseman [hērs'-man], *s.* 1. Jinete, el que sabe montar bien a caballo. 2. Soldado de a caballo. 3. Jinete, el que está montado a caballo.

Horsemanship [hērs'-man-ship], *s.* Manejo, el arte de manejar los caballos; equitación.

Horsemint [hērs'-mint], *s.* (Bot.) Mastranzo, planta herbácea de la familia de las labiadas. Monarda.

Horse-play [hērs'-plê], *s.* Chanza pesada.

Horse-power [hērs'-pau-ẹr], *s.* 1. Caballo de fuerza, unidad teórica de la medida del trabajo; equivale al esfuerzo necesario para levantar un peso de 33,000 libras a un pie de altura, en un minuto. 2. Máquina o aparato mecánico para convertir el peso o el tiro de un caballo en fuerza mecánica; motor que funciona por tracción animal.

Horse-radish [hērs-rad'-ish], *s.* (Bot.) Rábano picante o rústico.

Horse-shoe [hērs'-shū], *s.* 1. Herradura de caballo. 2. Lo que se parece a una herradura, por ejemplo la curva que forma un río. 3. (Zool.) Límulo, cangrejo.

Horsewhip [hērs'-hwip], *s.* Látigo. (Cuba) Chucho. (Mex.) Cuarta, azote

Horsewhip, *va.* Azotar, castigar con látigo.

Horsewoman [hērs'-wum-an], *s.* Amazona, mujer que monta a caballo.

Horsing [hērs'-ing], *s.* 1. Tablilla sobre que se sienta el amolador de cuchillos. 2. Tunda, zurra que se da a un muchacho llevado a cuestas por otro.

Horsy, Horsey [hērs'-i], *a.* 1. Caballuno. 2. Aficionado a caballos.

Hortative [hēr'-ta-tiv], *a.* Exhortatorio, que tiende a excitar o animar; de la naturaleza de exhortación.

Hortatory [hēr'-ta-to-ri], *a.* Exhortatorio, que contiene o comunica exhortaciones.

Hortensial [hēr-ten'-shal], *a.* Apto para jardín o huerta, relativo a un jardín.

Horticultural [hēr-ti-cul'-chur-al], *a.* Hortícola, que pertenece al cultivo de los jardines y huertas. *Horticultural Society*, Sociedad hortícola, la establecida para promover la introducción y el cultivo de árboles frutales, de legumbres, etc.

Horticulture [hēr'-ti-cul-chur], *s.* Horticultura, jardinería.

Horticulturist [hēr-ti-cul'-chur-ist], *s.* Horticultor, hortelano, aficionado a cultivar los jardines y las huertas, o diestro en ese arte.

Hortus siccus [hēr'-tus sic'-us], *s.* (Bot.) Herbario seco, conjunto de plantas secas y preservadas con orden.

†**Hortyard** [hērt'-yard], *s.* (Des.) Huerto.

Hosanna [hō-zan'-a], *s.* Hosana, exclamación de alabanza a Dios. (Heb.)

Hose [hōz], *s.* 1. Medias, calcetines; antiguamente bragas, calzones. 2. Manguera, tubo flexible de cuero, de hule, etc., para conducir líquidos; manguera de una bomba de incendios. *Great hose*, Zaragüelles. *Hose nozzles*, Boquereles de manguera. *Hose pipes*, Tubos de manguera. *Lawn hose*, Mangueras de regar prados.

Hosier [hō'-zhẹr], *s.* Mediero, el que vende medias.

Hosiery [hō'-zhẹr-i], *s.* 1. Medias, calcetines, los artículos que vende el mediero. 2. Comercio de medias, etc.

Hospice [hos'-pis], *s.* Hospicio, hospedería, particularmente en los Alpes.

Hospitable [hos'-pi-ta-bl], *a.* Hospitalario, caritativo, benigno y afable con los huéspedes.

Hospitableness [hos'-pi-ta-bl-nes], *s.* Hospitalidad.

Hospitably [hos'-pi-ta-bli], *adv.* Hospitalariamente.

Hospital [hos'-pi-tal], *s.* Hospital, la casa donde recogen y curan a los enfermos o los heridos. 2. (Des.) Hospicio, fonda. *Hospital staff*, El personal, los empleados de un hospital.

Hospitality [hos-pi-tal'-i-ti], *s.* Hospitalidad, el recibimiento caritativo de huéspedes, pasajeros o refugiados.

Hospitalization [hos-pi-tal-i-zê'-shun], *s.* Hospitalización.

Hospitalize [hos'-pi-tal-aiz], *va.* Hospitalizar.

Hospital-ship [hos'-pi-tal-ship], *s.* (Mar.) Barco hospital.

Hospital ward [hos'-pi-tal wērd], *s.* Sala de hospital.

Hospodar [hos'-po-dār], *s.* Título de dignidad que pertenecía antiguamente a varios príncipes europeos y hoy al emperador de Rusia.

Host [hōst], *s.* 1. Patrón, huésped, el que hospeda en su casa a alguno. 2. Mesonero, posadero, el amo de una posada. 3. Hueste, ejército, multitud. 4. Hostia. *To reckon without the host*, Hacer la cuenta sin la huéspeda.

Hostage [host'-ẹj], *s.* Rehén, la persona que queda en poder del enemigo como prenda; prenda, gaje.

Hostel [hos'-tel], *s.* 1. Posada, hostal. 2. En las universidades de Francia e Inglaterra, casa de huéspedes para estudiantes.

Hostelry, Hostlery [hos'-tel-ri], *s.* Posada, mesón, hostería.

Hostess [hōst'-es], *sf.* Posadera, mesonera, patrona, huéspeda, ama.

Hostess-ship [hōst'-es-ship], *s.* Carácter u oficio de posadera o mesonera.

Hostile [hos'-til], *a.* Hostil.

Hostilely [hos'-til-li], *adv.* Hostilmente.

Hostility [hos-til'-i-ti], *s.* Hostilidad.

Hostler [hos'-lẹr], *s.* Mozo de paja y cebada, el que cuida de las caballerías en una posada.

Hot [hot], *a.* 1. Cálido, caliente. *Hot weather*, Tiempo caluroso. 2. Ardiente, fogoso, impaciente, fervoroso. 3. Picante, acre. 4. Violento, furioso, colérico. 5. (Fam.) Intolerable, que causa pena y apuros. *To grow hot*, Calentarse, encenderse. *To make hot*, Calentar. *To be burning hot*, Quemarse; hacer mucho calor, asarse los pájaros. *The summer is now at its hottest*, Estamos en los calores más fuertes del estío. *Hot mustard*, Mostaza muy picante. *Hot blast*, Corriente, tiro de aire caliente. *Hot and heavy*, (Fam.) Furioso, fiero y contundente. *Piping hot*, Caliente hasta hervir o bullir. *To be in hot water*, Estar en ascuas. *Hot-livered*, Irascible, de carácter colérico, botafuego.

Hot-bed [hot'-bed], *s.* Era, cuadro de huerta cubierto con capas de estiércol y abrigado con vidrieras. (Fig.) Foco, plantel. *A hotbed of sedition*, Un foco de sedición.

Hot-blooded [hot-blud'-ed], *a.* Excitable, fogoso.

Hot-brained [hot'-brênd], *a.* Violento, furioso.

Hotch-potch [hoch'-poch], *s.* Almodrote.

Hot-cockles [hot'-coc-lz], *s.* Especie de juego de muchachos.

Hot dog [hot dog], *s.* Emparedado de salchicha popular en E.U.

Hotel [ho-tel'], *s.* 1. Posada, hotel. 2. Palacio, residencia de altos personajes; también, casa ayuntamiento o consistorial, como en Francia.

Hot-headed [hot'-hed-ed], *a.* Vehemente, violento, fogoso, colérico.

Hot-house [hot'-haus], *s.* 1. Invernadero o invernáculo con estufas para guardar las flores en invierno. 2. Estufa, aposento recogido para sudar u otros usos.

Hotly [hot'-li], *adv.* 1. Con calor. 2. Vehementemente. 3. Lascivamente.

Hot-press [hot'-pres], *s.* Prensa recargada.

Hot-press, *va.* Prensar papel o paños con láminas de hierro caliente.

Hot rod [hot rod], *s.* Automóvil reconstruido para que alcance altas velocidades y rápida aceleración.

Hotspur [hot'-spūr], *s.* 1. La persona colérica que con facilidad se enfada. 2. Especie de guisante que se cría en poco tiempo.—*a.* Violento.

Hottentot [hot'-en-tot], *s.* 1. Hotentote, natural de la Hotentocia, en el sur de Africa. 2. Hotentote, salvaje, un hombre brutal o tosco.

Hough [hoc], *va.* Desjarretar, descuadrillar. *V.* HOCK.

Hough, *s.* 1. Jarrete; corvejón de las bestias. *V.* HOCK. 2. (Des.) *V.* HOE.

Hound [haund], *s.* 1. Sabueso, perro de montería. *Blood-hound*, Sabueso ventor. *Greyhound*, Galgo, lebrel. 2. Perro, collón, hombre vil. 3. (Mar.) Cacholas. *V.* CHEEKS. *A pack of hounds*, Una traílla de perros.

Hound, *va.* 1. Cazar, perseguir con perros de caza. 2. Soltar los perros, 3. Seguir la pista.

Hound's-tongue [haundz'-tung], *s.* (Bot.) Cinoglosa, viniebla, lengua de perro.

Hound-tree [haund'-trī], *s.* (Bot.) Cornejo.

Hour [aur], *s.* 1. Hora, sesenta minutos. 2. Hora, tiempo señalado o definido, como la hora de la muerte. 3. *pl.* Horas, rezos de la Iglesia católica que se dicen a ciertas horas del día, como las vísperas y maitines. 4. Jornada o camino de una hora; una legua, poco más o menos. *An hour ago, an hour since*, Hace una hora. *About the eleventh hour*, A eso de las once. *To keep good hours*, Retirarse o volver a la casa temprano. *To keep bad hours*, Volver a deshora.

Hour-glass [aur'-glas], *s.* Ampolleta o reloj de arena.

Hour-hand [aur'-hand], *s.* Horario, la saetilla que indica la hora en el reloj.
Houri [hū'-ri o hau'-ri], *s.* Hurí, ninfa del paraíso mahometano.
Hourly [aur'-li], *adv.* A cada hora, frecuentemente.—*a.* Lo que sucede cada hora, frecuente.
Hour-plate [aur'-plēt], *s.* Muestra de reloj.
House [haus], *s.* 1. Casa, edificio hecho para habitarlo; residencia, domicilio. *Country-house,* Casa de campo. *To keep house,* Tener casa. 2. Casa o comunidad. *V.* HOUSEHOLD. 3. Casa, familia, descendencia, linaje. 4. El género de vida; mesa o modo de tratarse con respecto a los alimentos. 5. Casa, razón social, establecimiento mercantil. 6. La gente que compone el concurso de oyentes, el auditorio. 7. Cámara de un cuerpo legislativo. *House of Lords,* Cámara de los pares en Inglaterra. *House of Commons,* Cámara baja o de los comunes. *House of Representatives,* Cámara de los Representantes (en el Congreso de los Estados Unidos). *Ale-house,* Cervecería. *Coffee-house,* Café. *Pigeon-house,* Palomar. *Workhouse,* (1) Hospicio. (2) Casa de corrección. *Ice-house,* Nevera o nevería. *Town-house,* Casa consistorial o casa ayuntamiento. *Summer-house,* Glorieta. *Engine-house, round-house,* Casa de máquinas, rotonda. *Wheel-house,* Carroza, garita o mirador del timonel. *To bring down the house,* Provocar aplauso general y ruidoso. *House-duty,* (Ingl.) Impuesto sobre las casas.
House [hauz], *va.* 1. Albergar, tener a uno en casa; dar casa o habitación a alguna persona. 2. Entrojar; poner a cubierto. 3. (Mar.) Afianzar o cubrir cuando hay borrasca.—*vn.* Residir.
House-breaker [haus'-brēk'-ẹr], *s.* El ladrón que fuerza de noche las puertas de una casa para robarla.
House-breaking [haus'-brēk-ing], *s.* Robo de noche con quebrantamiento de puertas.
House-dog [haus'-deg], *s.* Mastín, perro de guarda.
Housefly [haus'-flai], *s.* Mosca.
Household [haus'-hōld], *s.* 1. Casa, la familia que vive junta en una casa. *King's household,* La casa real. 2. Manejo doméstico, gobierno de casa. *Household furniture,* El ajuar o menaje de una casa. *Household bread,* Pan casero o bazo.
Householder [haus'-hōld-ẹr], *s.* Amo de casa, padre de familia.
Household-stuff [haus'-hōld-stuf], *s.* Ajuar o muebles de una casa.
Housekeeper [haus'-kīp-ẹr], *s.* 1. Ama de gobierno o ama de llaves, la mujer que tiene el gobierno económico de una casa. 2. La persona casera o que está casi siempre en casa. 3. Amo de casa, padre de familia.
Housekeeping [haus'-kīp-ing], *s.* El manejo de los asuntos domésticos, caseros; cuidado de la casa.—*a.* Doméstico, casero.
House-lamb [haus'-lam], *s.* Cordero criado y engordado en casa.
Houseleek [haus'-līc], *s.* (Bot.) Siempreviva o hierba puntera.
Houseless [haus'-les], *a.* Sin habitación o sin casa.
House-maid [haus'-mēd], *s.* Criada de casa o de escalera abajo. *House-maid's knee,* (Med.) Bolsa que suele formarse delante de las rodillas de personas que, como las criadas de servicio, trabajan mucho arrodilladas.
House of cards [haus ev cārdz], *s.* Castillo de naipes, construcción frágil.
House of correction [haus ev cer-rec'-shʊn], *s.* Casa correccional, reformatorio.
House organ [haus ōr'-gan], *s.* Órgano de publicidad de una institución u organización.
House party [haus pār'-ti], *s.* 1. Fiesta (generalmente en una casa campestre) en que los invitados permanecen más de un día. 2. Los invitados a una casa de campo por más de un día.
House-pigeon [haus'-pij-un], *s.* Paloma mansa o doméstica.
House-rent [haus'-rent], *s.* Alquiler de casa, lo que se paga por ella.
House-room [haus'-rūm], *s.* Cabida de una casa.
House-stuff [haus'-stuf], *s.* Menaje, alhajas.
House-warming [haus'-wōrm-ing], *s.* Recepción y convite que se dan al tiempo de estrenar una casa nueva.
Housewife [haus'-waif], *sf.* 1. Ama de una casa; madre de familia. 2. Ama de gobierno o de llaves. 3. Mujer casera y económica. 4. Costurero, cajita o saquito que contiene alfileres, agujas, tijeras, etc. (Mex.) Almohadilla.
Housewifely [haus'-waif-li], *adv.* Con la economía de una mujer casera. —*a.* Lo que pertenece a la mujer que sabe gobernar bien una casa.
Housework [haus'-wʊrk], *s.* Quehaceres domésticos, labores caseras.
Housing [hauz'-ing], *s.* 1. Mantilla, el adorno que cubre las ancas del caballo, gualdrapa; comúnmente en plural. 2. Habitación; abrigo contra la intemperie. 3. (Arq.) Nicho para colocar una estatua. 4. (Art. y Of.) Muesca, encaje de una vigueta; hueco hecho en una pieza para recibir parte de otra.
Housing, *s.* (Mar.) Piola, cabito de tres filásticas que sirve para varios usos.
Hove [hōv], *pret.* del verbo *To* HEAVE.
Hove, *s.* Enfermedad propia de la raza bovina. *V.* HOOVE.
Hovel [hev'-el], *s.* Cobertizo, choza, cabaña.
Hovel, *va.* Abrigar en cabaña.
Hover [huv'-ẹr o hev'-ẹr], *vn.* 1. Revolotear, aletear; rondar, dar vueltas alrededor de un mismo paraje. 2. Colgar, estar suspenso en el aire. 3. Dudar, estar suspenso, en la incertidumbre.
How [hau], *adv.* Como, de qué modo; cuan, cuanto; a qué precio; hasta qué punto; en qué extensión; por qué. *How far?* ¿A qué distancia? ¿Cuánto dista? *How long?* ¿Cuánto tiempo? *How do you do?* ¿Cómo le va a Vd.? ¿cómo está Vd. de salud? *How so?* ¿Por qué? ¿cómo así? *How great soever,* Por grande que sea. *How d'ye do?* ¿Cómo lo pasa Vd.? ¿qué tal? *How is it?* ¿Cómo es? ¿cómo sucede? *How now?* ¿Pues qué? ¿qué significa eso? *How do you sell raspberries?* ¿A cómo vende Vd. las frambuesas? *To know how,* Saber. *To know how to write,* Saber escribir.
Howbeit [hau-bī'-it], *adv.* Sea como sea, sin embargo, de cualquier modo que.
Howel [hau'-el], *s.* Doladera, azuela de tonelero.
However [hau-ev'-ẹr], *adv.* 1. Como quiera que sea. 2. En todo caso, al menos, a lo menos. 3. No obstante, con todo, sin embargo.
Howitzer [hau'-itz-ẹr], *s.* Obús, especie de mortero.
Howl [haul], *vn.* 1. Aullar: dícese del lobo y el perro. 2. Dar alaridos, quejarse tristemente. 3. Rugir, bramar, como el viento o la tempestad.—*va.* Gritar, chillar, hablar gritando.
Howl, *s.* 1. Aúllo, aullido de los lobos y de los perros. 2. Alarido. 3. Rugido.
Howler [haul'-ẹr], *s.* 1. Aullador, el que aúlla; gritador. 2. Mono de la América tropical de voz muy fuerte y penetrante.
Howlet, *s.* *V.* OWL.
Howling [haul'-ing], *s.* Aullido; grito; lamento. *V.* HOWL.
Howsoever [hau-so-ev'-ẹr], *adv.* Como quiera; aunque.
Hoy [hei], *s.* (Mar.) Buque de pasaje de una cubierta.—*inter.* (Mar.) ¡Hola!
Hub [hub], *s.* 1. Cubo, maza de la rueda. 2. Por extensión, cualquier cosa céntrica por su posición o importancia. 3. Clavo, perno a que se arroja el tejo. *The Hub,* (Jocoso) La ciudad de Boston en Massachusetts, E. U. A.
Hubbub [hub'-ub], *s.* Grito, ruido; alboroto, tumulto, batahola, bulla, enredo.
Hub cap, hub cover [hʊb cap, hʊb cʊv'-er], *s.* Tapacubos.
Huckaback [huc'-a-bac], *s.* Alemanisco, lienzo basto adamascado para servilletas.
Huckle, *s.* *V.* HIP.
Huckle-backed [huc'-l-bact], *a.* Jorobado.
Huckleberry [huc'-l-ber-i], *s.* (Bot.) Arándano, la baya comestible del género Gaylussacia; con menos exactitud, la *blueberry,* el fruto de varias especies de Vaccinium.
Hucklebone [huc'-l-bōn], *s.* Cía, el hueso de la cadera.
Huckster [huc'-stẹr], *s.* 1. Regatón, revendedor, el que revende géneros por menor. 2. Perillán, pícaro astuto y vagamundo.
Huckster, *vn.* Regatonear.
Hucksteress [huc'-stẹr-es], *sf.* Regatona, revendedora.
Huddle [hud'-l], *va.* 1. Tapujar, arrebujar, confundir, mezclar. 2. Hacer las cosas precipitada y confusamente.—*vn.* Venir en tropel o confusamente.
Huddle, *s.* Tropel, confusión, baraúnda, alboroto, desorden.
Huddler [hud'-lẹr], *s.* El que hace o pone las cosas confusamente; chapucero.
Hue [hiū], *s.* 1. Color, tez del rostro; matiz de un color. (< A.-S. hiw.) 2. Clamor, alarma que se da contra un criminal. (< Fr. ant. hu.) En esta última significación *hue* va casi siempre junto con *cry.*
Huff [huf], *s.* Bufido, gruñido; altivez.
Huff, *va.* 1. Hinchar, inflar. 2. Bufar, bravear; maltratar de palabra, tratar con aspereza e insolencia. 3. Soplar una dama en el juego.—*vn.* 1. Hincharse, engreirse. 2. Patear de enfado.
Huffish [huf-ish], *a.* Arrogante, insolente, petulante, impertinente.

Huffishness [huf'-ish-nes], *s.* Petulancia, arrogancia, insolencia, impertinencia.
Huffy [huf'-i], *a.* 1. Arrogante, petulante, que se ofende fácilmente; malhumorado. 2. Hinchado, engreído.
Hug [hug], *va.* 1. Abrazar, acariciar, halagar. 2. Abrazarse a alguna cosa de suerte que no se la suelte. 3. Aplaudirse o felicitarse de una ventaja supuesta. 4. (Mar.) Navegar muy cerca de (la costa). *To hug the wind,* Ceñir el viento.
Hug, *s.* Abrazo apretado. *A Cornish hug,* Una zancadilla.
Huge [hiūj], *a.* Vasto, inmenso, grande, enorme.
Hugely [hiūj'-li], *adv.* Enormemente, extremadamente.
Hugeness [hiūj'-nes], *s.* Magnitud o grandeza enorme.
Huguenot [hiū'-ge-net], *s.* Hugonote: nombre que se dió en Francia a los protestantes.
Hula-hula [hū'-lā-hū'-lā], *s.* Baile típico de Hawaii.
Hulk [hulk], *s.* 1. (Mar.) Casco de la embarcación; particularmente uno viejo y en mal estado; casco abandonado de buque náufrago. 2. Armatoste, cualquiera cosa tosca y pesada; masa, cuerpo abultado.
Hulk, *va.* Desentrañar.
Hull [hul], *s.* 1. Cáscara, la corteza y cubierta de las frutas y de algunas otras cosas. *Hull of a bean,* Vaina o vainilla de las habas. 2. (Mar.) Casco y cuerpo de la embarcación; el buque sin palos ni jarcias. *A-hull,* (Mar.) A palo seco.
Hull, *vn.* (Des.) Navegar a palo seco. —*va.* 1. Mondar, quitar a los frutos su cáscara, vaina o vainilla. 2. Disparar cañonazos contra el casco de un buque.
Hullabaloo [hul''-a-ba-lū'], *s.* Alboroto, batahola, bulla, tumulto.
Huller [hul'-er], *s.* Descascarador.
Hullo [hul-ō'], *v., s.* e *inter.* Lo mismo que Halloo.
Hully [hul'-i], *a.* Cascarudo.
Hulver, *s.* *V.* Holly.
Hum [hum], *va.* y *vn.* 1. Zumbar. 2. Hablar entre dientes, susurrar; decir *hem* al verse sorprendido o desconcertado. *V.* Hem. 3. Roncar; susurrar, hacer un ruido monótono como el zumbido de un moscón. 4. Cantar o hablar en voz baja; canturriar. 5. Engañar.
Hum, *s.* 1. Zumbido, baraúnda; ruido suave. 2. Voz inarticulada (como *hem*) con que se expresa aprobación o disentimiento. 3. Burla, chasco.—*inter.* ¡Ya! interjección con que se da a entender duda o suspensión. *To make things hum,* o *to keep things humming,* (Fam. E. U.) Ejecutar cosas de una manera viva y fogosa; ser muy activo.
Human [hiū'-man], *a.* Humano.
Humane [hiū-mên'], *a.* Humano, apacible, compasivo, afable; benigno; cortés.
Humanely [hiū-mên'-li], *adv.* Humanamente, benignamente.
Humanism [hiū'-man-izm], *s.* Literatura castiza y elegante; cultura derivada de las letras humanas o clásicas.
Humanist [hiū'-man-ist], *s.* Humanista, el que profesa las buenas letras o las humanidades.
Humanitarian [hiu-man-i-tê'-ri-an], *a.* Humanitario.—*s.* 1. Filántropo. 2. El que cree que Jesucristo no fué más que un hombre. 3. El que profesa la doctrina de que los deberes del hombre se limitan a hacer bien a los demás y a procurar la mayor felicidad del género humano.
Humanity [hiū-man'-i-ti], *s.* 1. Humanidad. 2. El género humano colectivamente. 3. Humanidad, benignidad, ternura, dulzura, benevolencia. 4. Humanidades o letras humanas.
Humanize [hiū'-man-aiz], *va.* Humanar, humanizar, quitar la ferocidad, suavizar las costumbres.
Humankind [hiū'-man-kaind], *s.* El linaje humano, la especie humana.
Humanly [hiū'-man-li], *adv.* 1. Humanamente. 2. *V.* Humanely.
Humble [hum'-bl], *a.* Humilde, modesto, sumiso, bajo, casero.
Humble, *va.* 1. Humillar, postrar, abatir el orgullo y la soberbia. 2. Domar, aniquilar, abatir; confundir. *The battle of Waterloo humbled the power of Napoleon,* La batalla de Waterloo aniquiló el poder de Napoleón.
Humble-bee [hum'-bl-bī], *s.* Abeja grande y silvestre. *V.* Bumble-bee.
Humble-mouthed [hum'-bl-maudhd], *a.* Manso, blando.
Humbleness [hum'-bl-nes], *s.* Humildad.
Humble-pie [hum'-bl-pai], *s.* Empanada hecha de los despojos de venado, que solía servirse a los monteros y criados. *To eat humble-pie,* Dar excusas, desdecirse, retractarse.
Humbler [hum'-bler], *s.* Humillador.
Humbles [hum'-blz], *s. pl.* Despojo o entrañas de venado. (En vez de *numbles* < Lat. umbilicus.)
Humbling [hum'-bling], *s.* Humillación, abatimiento, rendimiento.
Humbly [hum'-bli], *adv.* Humildemente.
Humbug [hum'-bug], *s.* 1. Trampantojo, bola, patraña, engañifa, engaño, decepción, trampa, embuste, fraude, dolo. 2. Vaya, cantaleta, zumba.
Humbug, *va.* Embaucar, engañar; chasquear.
Humdrum [hum'-drum], *a.* Torpe, sin interés ni aliciente, monótono, trivial.—*vn.* Pasar el tiempo torpe o monótonamente.—*s.* 1. Fastidio; enojo, fatiga. 2. Habla, dejo o tono fastidioso. 3. Pesadilla, persona cargante, fastidiosa.
Humective [hiu-mec'-tiv], *a.* Humectativo, que humedece.
Humeral [hiu'-mer-al], *a.* Humeral, lo que pertenece al hombro.
Humerus [hiū'-me-rus], *s.* (Anat.) Húmero.
Humid [hiu'-mid], *a.* Húmedo.
Humidifier [hiu-mid'-i-fai-er], *s.* Humedecedor, humectador.
Humidify [hiu-mid'-i-fai], *va.* Humedecer.
Humidistat [hiū-mi'-di-stat], *s.* Regulador de humedad.
Humidity [hiu-mid'-i-ti], *s.* Humedad.
Humidor [hiu'-mi-dōr], *s.* 1. Caja acondicionada para conservar el tabaco humedecido. 2. Dispositivo con esponjas mojadas para conservar el aire humedecido.
Humiliation [hiu-mil-i-é'-shun], *s.* Humillación, mortificación.
Humility [hiu-mil'-i-ti], *s.* Humildad, sumisión, rendimiento.
Hummer [hum'-er], *s.* Zumbón.
Humming [hum'-ing], *s.* Zumbido.
Humming-bird [hum'-ing-berd], *s.* Colibrí, pájaro mosca; (Cent. Amer.) guainambí.
Humor, Humour [hiū'-mer ó yū'-mer], *s.* 1. Humor, substancia tenue y flúida del cuerpo animal. 2. Humor, carácter, genio, índole, natural; humorada, fantasía, capricho; 3. Sal, agudeza; chanza de buen gusto, inofensiva. 4. Erupción cutánea que se supone debida al mal estado de la sangre. *Broad humor,* Farsa, acción jocosa o burlesca. *Dry humor,* Chiste socarrón, dicho agudo. *To be in humor,* Estar de buen humor. *To take one in the humor,* Llegarse a alguno en un momento favorable.
Humor, *va.* 1. Satisfacer, agradar, complacer, dar gusto, acceder; consentir en; mimar. 2. Cumplir, ejecutar lo que a uno se le manda. 3. Adaptarse, acomodarse a; desempeñar bien. *A player who humors his part,* Un actor que desempeña bien su papel. *A good-humored man,* Hombre de buen humor. *To humor a song,* Dar alma y viveza a lo que se canta.
Humoral [hiū'-mer-al], *a.* (Med.) Humoral.
Humoralism, Humorism [hiū'-mer-(al)-izm], *s.* 1. Humorismo, la doctrina médica que hace depender las enfermedades de los humores. 2. El ingenio y la gracia en el decir de un escritor festivo.
Humorist [hiū'-mer-ist], *s.* 1. Humorista, escritor festivo. 2. Chocarrero, bufón.
Humorous [hiū'-mer-us], *a.* 1. Grotesco, extravagante, voluntarioso, caprichoso, antojadizo, caprichudo. 2. Festivo, chistoso, juguetón, placentero.
Humorously [hiū'-mer-us-li], *adv.* Jocosamente; caprichosamente.
Humorousness [hiū'-mer-us-nes], *s.* Inconstancia, antojo, impertinencia; humorada.
Humorsome [hiū'-mer-sum], *a.* Petulante, enojoso, caprichoso, impertinente, voluntarioso.
Hump [hump], *s.* Giba, joroba, corcova.—*va.* 1. Doblar, encorvar la espalda. 2. *vr.* (Ger.) Apurarse, hacer un esfuerzo, tomarse el trabajo.
Humpbacked [hump'-bact], *a.* Jorobado, corcovado, giboso.
Humped [humpt], *a.* Jorobado, corcovado.
Humpy [hump'-i], *a.* Giboso, marcado o caracterizado por protuberancias.
Humus [hiu'-mus], *s.* Humus, mantillo.
Hun [hun], *s.* Huno, pueblo procedente de la Sarmacia asiática.
Hunch [hunch], *va.* 1. Dar de puñadas o de codazos. 2. Hacer a uno giboso o corcovado.
Hunch, *s.* 1. Golpe, puñada, codazo. 2. Giba, corcova.
Hunchbacked [hunch'-bact], *a.* *V.* Humpbacked.
Hundred [hun'-dred], *a.* Ciento.—*s.* 1. Centena o centenar; un ciento. *By hundreds,* A centenares. *A hundred-weight,* Quintal, el peso de cien libras o cuatro arrobas; comúnmente en Inglaterra y antiguamente en los Estados Unidos, peso de 112 libras. *Hundred-fold,* Céntuplo, cien veces una cantidad cualquiera. *To increase a hundred-fold,* Centuplicar. 2. División de los condados en Inglaterra en ciertos distritos.
Hundreder [hun'-dred-er], *s.* 1. Un individuo del jurado, cuando ésto

se reune para decidir sobre la adjudicación de posesiones situadas en el distrito donde se junta el jurado. 2. El que tiene la jurisdicción del distrito llamado en inglés *hundred*.

Hundredth [hun'-dredth], *a.* Centésimo.

Hung [hung], *pret.* y *pp.* del verbo *To* HANG. *Hung beef*, Cecina de vaca.

Hungarian [hun-gé'-ri-an], *a.* Húngaro, de Hungría.

Hungarian goulash [hun-gär'-ian gū'-lāsh], *s.* Guiso de carne y verduras de origen húngaro.

Hungary-water [hun'-ga-ri-wō'-tẹr], *s.* Agua de la Reina de Hungría: nombre de un perfume.

Hunger [hʊn'-gẹr], *s.* 1. Hambre, ganas de comer. 2. Hambre, sed, deseo grande de algo. *Pinched with hunger*, Acosado de hambre. *Starved with hunger*, Muerto de hambre. *Hunger strike*, Huelga de hambre.

Hunger, *vn.* Hambrear; desear con ansia.—*va.* *V.* FAMISH.

Hungerbit, Hungerbitten [hun'-gẹr-bit, n], *a.* Presa del hambre, atormentado por el hambre.

Hungrily [hun'-gri-li], *adv.* Hambrientamente.

Hungry [hun'-gri], *a.* 1. Hambriento, acosado de hambre; voraz. 2. Estéril, infecundo, pobre. *To be hungry, to feel hungry*, Tener hambre.

Hunk [hunk], *s.* (Fam.) Pedazo de buen tamaño, rebanada gruesa.

Hunks [huncs], *s.* Hombre sórdido y avaro.

Hunt [hunt], *va.* 1. Montear, cazar. 2. Seguir, perseguir. 3. Buscar. 4. Guiar los perros en la caza.—*vn.* 1. Cazar; ir de caza. 2. Seguir la pista a, ir en busca de; correr tras de. *To hunt out*, Buscar con empeño, descubrir. *To hunt after*, Buscar, desear con ansia. *To hunt up and down*, Buscar por todos lados. *To hunt after riches*, Correr tras la fortuna, tras las riquezas.

Hunt, *s.* 1. Jauría, cuadrilla de perros podencos para cazar. 2. Caza, la acción y acto de cazar 3. Perseguimiento, acosamiento. 4. Asociación de cazadores.

Hunter [hunt'-ẹr], *s.* 1. Montero, cazador de monte. 2. Podenco, perro que olfatea la caza. 3. Caballo de caza. *Hunter's cap*, Montera o gorra que usan los cazadores.

Hunting [hunt'-ing], *s.* Montería, caza, cacería.

Hunting, en composición: *Hunting-box, hunting-lodge*, Pabellón de caza, punto de cita de los cazadores. *Hunting-case*, Cubierta de saboneta. *Hunting-ground*, Terreno favorable para la caza. *Happy hunting-grounds*, El cielo o paraíso de los indios norteamericanos. *Hunting-horn*, Corneta de montería, trompa de caza. *Hunting-horse*, Caballo de caza. *Hunting-match*, Partida de caza. *Hunting-watch, hunting-case watch*, Reloj de caza, saboneta.

Huntress [hunt'-res], *sf.* Cazadora.

Huntsman [hunts'-man], *s.* Montero, cazador de monte.

Huntsmanship [hunts'-man-ship], *s.* Calidades necesarias para ser buen cazador.

Hunt's-up [hunts'-up], *s.* Toque matinal con la trompa de caza para despertar a los monteros; de aquí, cualquier cosa que despierta.

Hurdies [hur'-diz], *s. pl.* (Esco.) Las nalgas.

Hurdle [hŭrd'-l], *s.* 1. Zarzo, tejido compuesto de varas o mimbres. 2. Fábrica de efectos hechos con varas o mimbres; (Mil.) fagina, haz o cesto de mimbres que se usa para fortificar. 3. Especie de serón en que llevaban los reos a la horca o al suplicio.

Hurdle, *va.* Hacer cercas de palos y mimbres; defender con faginas.

Hurdles [hŭrd'-lz], *s. pl.* Carrera de vallas.

Hurdy-gurdy [hŭr'-di-gŭr-di], *s.* Tiorba, instrumento de cuerda parecido a una guitarra, pero que se toca con manubrio y rueda, como un organillo.

Hurl [hŭrl], *va.* 1. Tirar, precipitar o impeler con violencia, arrojar. 2. Gritar, llamar con vehemencia.—*vn.* 1. Moverse o lanzarse rápidamente. 2. Jugar al palocorvo. *To hurl one's self into ruin*, Arruinarse, perderse. *To hurl out*, Gritar, dar alaridos.

Hurl, *s.* Tiro, el acto de tirar o arrojar; lanzamiento.

Hurlbat [hŭrl'-bat], *s.* Especie de garrote o cachiporra.

Hurler [hŭrl'-ẹr], *s.* El que arroja o impele; el que juega a una especie de juego de pelota llamado *hurling*.

Hurley [hŭr'-li], *s.* (Irlandés) 1. El juego de palocorvo. 2. Palo encorvado para este juego.

Hurling [hŭrl'-ing], *s.* 1. Antiguo juego de pelota semejante al de *foot-ball*. 2. En Irlanda, especie de juego de pelota, palocorvo.

Hurlyburly [hŭr'-li-bŭr-li], **Hurly**, *s.* Baraúnda, alboroto, tumulto, confusión.

Hurrah, Hurra [hur-rā'], *inter.* Exclamación de aplauso o alegría que corresponde casi siempre a ¡viva!—*va.* y *vn.* Animar, alentar con vivas; vitorear, aplaudir. *Hurrah for!* ¡Viva!

Hurricane [hur'-i-kēn], *s.* Huracán, gran tempestad; originalmente, ciclón.

Hurried [hur'-id], *a.* y *pp.* de *To* HURRY. Precipitado, apresurado, hecho de prisa. *A hurried note*, Un billete escrito a escape. *Hurried away*, Llevado por la fuerza, arrastrado, arrebatado.

Hurrier [hur'-i-ẹr], *s.* 1. Acelerador, apresurador. 2. (Gran Bret.) El trabajador que saca un carretón de hulla de una mina de carbón de piedra.

Hurry [hur'-i], *va.* 1. Acelerar, apresurar, dar prisa. 2. Atropellar; precipitar; apremiar, no dar respiro; confundir a fuerza de prisa.—*vn.* 1. Atropellarse, apresurarse. 2. (Gran. Bret.) Arrastrar un carretón en una mina de carbón de piedra. *To hurry away*, Llevar, traer o salir precipitadamente. *To hurry after*, Correr detrás o en pos de. *To hurry back*, Volver (o hacer volver) de prisa; apresurarse a volver. *To hurry in*, Hacer entrar de prisa; entrar con precipitación en. *To hurry into*, Arrastrar, impeler hacia. *To hurry off*, Huir, salir de prisa; hacer partir con precipitación. *To hurry on*, Apresurar, precipitar; impulsar, empujar; apresurarse. *To hurry over*, Hacer pasar rápidamente; despachar, expedir; pasar apresuradamente.

Hurry, *s.* 1 Precipitación, demasiada prisa. 2. Confusión, desorden

Hurry-skurry, Hurry-scurry [hur'-i-scur-i], *adv.* Confusamente, con ruido y tumulto.

Hurst [hŭrst], *s.* Bosquecillo, montecillo poblado de árboles; en el día se emplea casi exclusivamente en composición de nombres de localidades: v. g. Chisel*hurst*, Mid*hurst*.

Hurt [hŭrt], *va.* (*pret.* y *pp.* HURT. 1. Dañar, hacer mal o daño; herir; ofender. 2. Perjudicar a alguien en sus intereses; herir la delicadeza de alguno. *To hurt one's feelings*, Dar que sentir, lastimar. *He has hurt his leg*, Él se ha lastimado la pierna. *She hurt his head*, Ella le hirió en la cabeza. *That does not hurt you*, Eso no le hace a Vd. daño.

Hurt, *s.* 1. Golpe, herida, contusión. 2. Mal, daño, perjuicio. *What hurt is there in that?* ¿Qué hay de malo en eso? *I have done it to my hurt*, Lo he hecho en perjuicio mío.

Hurter [hŭrt'-ẹr], *s.* 1. Dañador, el que daña o hiere. 2. Viga que se pone frente a las ruedas de los cañones para proteger la muralla o parapeto.

Hurtful [hŭrt'-ful], *a.* Pernicioso, dañoso, nocivo, funesto, dañino.

Hurtfully [hŭrt'-ful-i], *adv.* Dañosamente, perniciosamente.

Hurtle [hŭrt'-l], *vn.* Encontrarse; rechinar; arrojarse con violencia hacia adelante; girar.—*va.* Menear, empujar con violencia; dar vueltas; blandir.

Hurtleberry, *s.* *V.* HUCKLEBERRY y WHORTLEBERRY.

Hurtless [hŭrt'-les], *a.* 1. Inocente que no hace daño. 2. Ileso, intacto, que no ha recibido daño.

Hurtlessly [hŭrt'-les-li], *adv* Inocentemente.

Hurtlessness [hŭrt'-les-nes], *s.* Inocencia.

Husband [huz'-band], *s.* 1. Marido, esposo. 2. (Ant.) Hombre económico, comedido, frugal en sus gastos.

Husband, *va.* 1. Gobernar con economía y frugalidad, ahorrar, economizar. 2. Procurar marido a alguna mujer. 3. Ser marido de; hacer el papel de marido; pasar por tal.

Husbandless [huz'-band-les], *a.* Soltera, viuda: dícese de la mujer sin marido.

Husbandman [huz'-band-man], *s.* Labrador, viñador.

Husbandry [huz'-band-ri], *s.* 1. Labranza, agricultura. 2. Frugalidad, economía, parsimonia, ahorro. 3. El gobierno económico de la casa, antiguamente casería.

Hush [hush], *inter.* ¡Chitón! ¡silencio!—*a.* Quieto, callado.

Hush, *va.* 1. Apaciguar, aquietar, sosegar, acallar. 2. Mitigar, calmar. 3. Callar *To hush up*, Ocultar, mantener secreto —*vn* Estar quieto, estar callado.

Hushaby [hush'-a-bai], *inter.* ¡A dormir! ¡vamos a la mu! voz de que se usa para hacer dormir a los niños.—*a.* Propenso a amodorrar o apaciguar.

Hush-money [hush'-mun-i], *s.* El dinero que se da a alguno para comprar su silencio

Husk [husk], *s.* 1. Cáscara, vaina, vainilla, pellejo, hollejo de frutos, legumbres, semillas, etc. 2. Alguna cosa de mínimo valor que cubre la parte útil o esencial; bagazo; desperdicio.

Husk, *va.* Descascarar, desvainar, mondar, despellejar, deshollejar.

Husked [huskt], *a.* Lo que tiene cáscara, vaina o pellejo.
Husker [husk'-ẹr], *s.* El que o lo que descascara, desvaina, etc.; descascaradora, desgranadora, máquina para descascarar el maíz.
Huskiness [husk'-i-nes], *s.* 1. Ronquera. 2. El estado de tener cáscara, vaina o pellejo.
Huskily [husk'-i-li], *adv.* Roncamente, secamente.
Husky [husk'-i], *a.* 1. Lo que abunda en vainas o cáscaras. 2. Ronco; falto de claridad; seco.
Hussar [huz-zār'], *s.* Húsar, soldado de caballería ligera.
Hussy [huz'-i], *s.* 1. Buena maula, buena alhaja, picudilla: dícese a veces en inglés por chanza, como se usa la palabra *picarona* con la misma significación en castellano. 2. Un especie de estuche para poner agujas, hilo, etc. *V.* HOUSEWIFE.
Hustings [hus'-tingz], *s.* 1. El tablado que se levanta para verificar la elección de los individuos de la cámara de los comunes. 2. Consejo o tribunal en la ciudad de Londres. Se usa algunas veces en singular.
Hustle [hus'-l], *va.* Escaramuzar; mezclar, confundir; empujar con fuerza, sacudir.—*vn.* 1. Moverse con dificultad en un tropel; apiñarse, adelantarse dando empujones. 2. (Fam. E. U.) Moverse con prisa y prontitud; demostrar energía y perseverencia.
Hustler [hus'-lẹr], *s.* (Fam. E. U.) Hombre de gran energía y actividad.
†**Huswife** [huz'-if], *sf.* 1. *V.* HOUSEWIFE. 2. *V.* HUSSY.—*va.* Gobernar la casa con economía.
Hut [hut], *s.* Choza, cabaña, barraca.
Hut, *va.* Acumular, almacenar o abrigar en una choza o chozas.—*vn.* Vivir en una choza o chozas; alojarse en chozas.
Hutch [huch], *s.* 1. Arca, cesto, cofre. 2. Trampa para coger ratones. 3. Caja para guardar y alimentar conejos.
Hutch, *va.* Atesorar, recoger.
Huzza [huz-ā'], *inter.* ¡Viva! voz con que se aclama y aplaude.
Huzza, *vn.* Vitorear, victorear, aclamar.—*va.* Recibir a alguno con vivas.
Hyacinth [hai'-a-sinth], *s.* 1. (Bot.) Jacinto. 2. (Min.) Jacinto, piedra preciosa; variedad de zircón de varios colores.
Hyacinthine [hai-a-sinth'-in], *s.* Jacintino, perteneciente al jacinto, o de color semejante al del jacinto.
Hyæna, *s.* *V.* HYENA.
Hyaline [hai'-a-lin], *a.* Cristalino, vidrioso, transparente.
Hybrid, Hybridous [hai'-brid o hib'-rid, us], *a.* Mestizo, híbrido, de dos castas o géneros de animales o plantas.
Hybridize [hai'-brid-aiz], *va.* Producir híbridos, asociar animales o plantas de diversas especies para obtener híbridos; hibridar.—*vn.* 1. Producir o generar híbridos. 2. Ser capaz de cruzamiento.
Hydatid [hai'-da-tid o hid'-at-id], *s.* 1. Hidátide, vejiguilla redonda y llena de agua. 2. Estado enquistado de la larva de una tenia.
Hydra [hai'-dra], *s.* 1. Hidra, monstruo fabuloso con muchas cabezas. 2. Mal de muchas formas y difícil de extirpar. 3. Pólipo de agua dulce del género Hydra.
Hydragogue [hai'-dra-gog], *s.* (Med.) Hidragogo, remedio para arrojar fuera del cuerpo la serosidad que en él se halla derramada o infiltrada.
Hydrangea [hai-dran'-je-a], *s.* (Bot.) Hortensia.
Hydrant [hai'-drant], *s.* Boca de riego.
Hydrate [hai'-drêt], *s.* (Quím.) Hidrato.
Hydraulic, Hydraulical [hai-drel'-ic, al], *a.* Hidráulico.
Hydraulics [hai-dre'-lics], *s. pl.* Hidráulica, la ciencia que trata de los líquidos en movimiento, y particularmente del agua.
Hydrazine [hai'-dra-sin], *s.* Hidrazina (combustible).
Hydric [hai'-dric], *a.* (Quím.) Hídrico, perteneciente al hidrógeno en combinación, o al agua.
Hydriodic [hai-dri-ed'-ic], *a.* (Quím.) Iodo-hídrico.
Hydrocarbon [hai-dro-car'-bon], *s.* (Quím.) Hidrocarburo.
Hydrocephalus [hai-dro-sef'-a-lus], *s.* (Med.) Hidrocéfalo, hidropesía de la cabeza.
Hydrochlorate [hai-dro-clō'-rêt], *s* (Quím.) Clorhidrato, hidroclorato.
Hydrochloric [hai-dro-clō'-ric], *a.* Hidroclórico o clorhídrico.
Hydrodynamics [hai-dro-dai-nam'-ics], *s. pl.* Hidrodinámica, ciencia que aplica los principios de la dinámica para determinar el movimiento o el reposo de los flúidos.
Hydroelectric [hai-dro-ẹ-lec'-tric], *a.* Hidroeléctrico.
Hydrogen [hai'-dro-jen], *s.* (Quím.) Hidrógeno. *Carbureted hydrogen*, Hidrocarburo. *Hydrogen peroxide*, Agua oxigenada, peróxido hidrogenado. *Hydrogen sulphide*, Sulfhídrico.
Hydrogenate [hai-drej'-e-nêt], *va.* Hidrogenar.
Hydrogenation [hai-droj-e-nê'-shUn], *s.* Hidrogenación.
Hydrogen bomb [hai'-dro-jen bom], *s.* Bomba de hidrógeno.
Hydrographer [hai-dreg'-ra-fẹr], *s.* Hidrógrafo, el profesor de hidrografía.
Hydrographical [hai-dro-graf'-ic-al], *a.* Hidrográfico.
Hydrography [hai-dreg'-ra-fi], *s.* Hidrografía, descripción de las aguas navegables.
Hydrokinetic [hai"-dro-ki-net'-ic], *a* Hidromecánico, que se refiere al movimiento de los flúidos y a la energía desarrollada por ese movimiento.
Hydrology [hai-drel'-o-ji], *s.* Hidrología, descripción de las aguas terrestres.
Hydrolysis [hai-drel'-i-sis], *s.* (Quím.) Hidrólisis.
Hydrolyze [hai'-dro-laiz], *va.* Hidrolizar.
Hydromancy [hai'-dro-man-si], *s.* Hidromancia, adivinación por medio del agua.
Hydromel [hai'-dro-mel], *s.* Hidromel, aguamiel.
Hydrometer [hai-drem'-ẹ-tẹr], *s.* 1. Hidrómetro, instrumento para medir la gravedad, densidad, etc., del agua u otros flúidos. 2. Instrumento para medir la corriente de agua en ríos, conductos, etc.; fluviómetro.
Hydronics [hai-dron'-ics], *s.* Hidrónica.
Hydropathy [hai-drep'-a-thi], *s.* Hidropatía, método curativo por medio del agua.
Hydrophobia [hai-dro-fō'-bi-a], **Hydrophoby** [hai-dro-fō'-bi], *s.* Hidrofobia, mal de rabia, sed ardiente con horror al agua.
Hydropic, Hydropical [hai-drep'-ic, al], *a.* Hidrópico.
Hydroplane [hai'-dro-plên], *s.* Hidroplano.
Hydroponics [hai-dro-pon'-ics], *s.* Hidroponia.
Hydropsy [hai'-drep-si], *s.* Hidropesía.
Hydrostat [hai'-dro-stat], *s.* Hidrostato, aparato para impedir la explosión de las calderas de vapor.
Hydrostatic, Hydrostatical [hai-dro-stat'-ic, al], *a.* Hidrostático.
Hydrostatics [hai-dro-stat'-ics], *s. pl.* Hidrostática, la ciencia que enseña y examina la gravedad o peso de los cuerpos líquidos.
Hydrotherapy [hai-dro-ther'-a-pi], *s.* Hidroterapia, método curativo por medio del agua.
Hydroxide [hai-drex'-aid], *s.* (Quím.) Hidróxido.
Hyena [hai-i'-na], *s.* Hiena, mamífero carnicero.
Hyetal [hai'-et-al], *a.* Perteneciente á la lluvia; lluvioso.
Hygiene [hai'-ji-in], *s.* Higiene, la parte de la medicina que trata del modo de conservar la salud.
Hygienic [hai-ji-en'-ic], *a.* Higiénico.
Hygrometer [hai-grem'-ẹ-tẹr], **Hygroscope** [hai'-gro-scōp], *s.* Higrómetro, higroscopio, instrumento que sirve para apreciar la existencia del vapor acuoso en el aire o en un gas cualquiera.
Hygroscopic [hai-gro-scep'-ic], *a.* Higroscópico, perteneciente o relativo al higroscopio; que tiene afinidad con el agua; (Bot.) que aumenta o disminuye según la cantidad de humedad.
Hyla [hai'-la], *s.* Rubeta; rana del género Hyla.
Hylozoic [hai-lo-zō'-ic], *s.* El partidario de una secta antigua que sostenía la animación de la materia.
Hymen [hai'-men], *s.* 1. Himeneo, el dios de las bodas o casamientos. 2. Himen, la membrana virginal.
Hymeneal [hai-me-ni'-al], **Hymenean** [hai-me-ni'-an], *s.* Himeneo.—*a.* Nupcial, que pertenece a las bodas.
Hymn [him], *s.* Himno.
Hymn, *va.* Alabar con himnos.—*vn.* Cantar himnos.
Hymnology [him-nel'-o-ji], *s.* Colección de himnos.
Hyp [hip], *va.* (Fam. poco us.) Melancolizar, entristecer, desanimar.
Hyper [hai'-pẹr]. Sobre: úsase en palabras compuestas.
Hyperbola [hai-pẹr'-bo-la], *s.* (Geom.) Hipérbola, curva geométrica que resulta de la intersección de un cono con un plano.
Hyperbole [hai-pẹr'-bo-li], *s.* Hipérbole, figura retórica que aumenta o disminuye excesivamente la verdad de lo que se habla; exageración.
Hyperbolic, Hyperbolical [hai-pẹr-bel'-ic, al], *a.* 1. Hiperbólico. 2. Perteneciente a la hipérbole.
Hyperbolically [hai-pẹr-bel'-ic-al-i], *adv.* Hiperbólicamente.
Hyperbolist [hai-pẹr'-bo-list], *s.* El que exagera o hace hipérboles; exagerador.
Hyperbolize [hai-pẹr'-bo-laiz], *vn.* Usar de hipérboles, antiguamente hiperbolizar.—*va.* Exagerar.

Hyperborean [hai-pęr-bō'-rę-an], *a.* Hiperbóreo, de las regiones septentrionales.
Hypercritic [hai-pęr-crit'-ic], *s.* Crítico inflexible.—*a.* Crítico.
Hypercritical [hai-pęr-crit'-i-cal], *a.* Crítico severo.
Hyperdulia [hai-pęr-diū'-li-a], **Hyperduly** [hai'-pęr-du-li], *s.* Hiperdulía.
Hypergolic [hai-per-gol'-ic], *a.* Hipergólico, auto-inflamable al contacto de sus componentes, sin chispa u otra ayuda exterior: usado para el combustible de un proyectil dirigido.
Hypericon [hai-per'-i-con], **Hypericum** [hai-per'-i-cum], *s.* (Bot.) Hipericón, hipérico, planta llamada más comúnmente *St. John's wort.*
Hypermeter [hai-pęr'-mę-tęr], *s.* Lo que excede a una medida determinada.
Hypersarcosis [hai-pęr-sar-cō'-sis], *s.* (Cir.) Hipersarcosis, excrecencia carnosa que se forma en las heridas.
Hypersensitive [hai-per-sen'-si-tiv], *a.* Excesivamente impresionable.
Hypersonic [hai-per-son'-ic], *a.* Supersónico, hipersónico.
Hypertension [hai-pęr-ten'-shʊn], *s.* (Med.) Hipertensión.
Hypertrophic [hai-pęr-trof'-ic], *a.* (Med.) Hipertrófico.
Hypertrophy [hai-pęr'-tro-fi], *s.* 1. (Med.) Hipertrofia, aumento excesivo del volumen de un órgano o tejido sin alteración efectiva en su composición. 2. Cualquier aumento excesivo.
Hyphen [hai'-fen], *s.* Guión o guiones, signo que denota la unión de las partes de una voz ; signo de esta forma : - o =.
Hypnosis [hip-nō'-sis], *s.* Hipnosis.
Hypnotic [hip-net'-ic], *s.* Hipnótico, medicamento que produce el sueño.
Hypnotism [hip'-no-tizm], *s.* Hipnotismo o hipnalismo ; sueño artificial producido por el magnetismo o por la contemplación fija y reiterada de ciertos objetos ; estado pasivo de la mente.
Hypnotize [hip'-no-taiz], *va.* Hipnotizar.
Hypocaust [hip'-o-cēst], *s.* 1. Hipocausto, el lugar subterráneo donde ponían los griegos y romanos la lumbre para calentar los baños. 2. El sitio donde está la lumbre que mantiene caliente un invernáculo.
Hypochondria [hip-o o hai''-po-con'-dri-a], **Hypochondriasm** [hip-o-con'-dri-azm], *s.* Hipocondría, melancolía.
Hypochondriac [hip-o o hai''-po-con'-dri-ac], *s.* Hipocondríaco.
Hypocist [hip'-o-sist], *s.* (Bot.) Hipocístide o hipocisto, el retoño del cisto, planta.
Hypocrisy [hi-poc'-ri-si], *s.* Hipocresía, disimulo.
Hypocrite [hip'-o-crit], *s.* Hipócrita.
Hypocritic, Hypocritical [hip-o-crit'-ic, al], *a.* Hipócrita, falso, disimulado.
Hypocritically [hip-o-crit'-ic-al-i], *adv.* Hipócritamente.
Hypodermic [hai-po-dęr'-mic], *a.* Subcutáneo, hipodérmico ; introducido o hallado debajo del cutis.
Hypogastric [hai''-po-gas'-tric o hip-o-gas'-tric], *a.* Hipogástrico : dícese de la región inferior del vientre.
Hypogastrium [hip-o-gas'-tri-um], *s.* Hipogastro.
Hypophosphate [hai-po-fos'-fêt], *s.* (Quím.) Hipofosfato.
Hypophyge [hai-pof'-i-ji], *s.* (Arq.) Imóscapo, nacela, moldura cóncava ; escocia.
Hypostasis [hai-pos'-ta-sis], *s.* (Teol.) 1. Hipóstasis, supuesto o persona : dícese de la Santísima Trinidad. 2. (Med.) Sedimento de la orina.
Hypostatic, Hypostatical [hai-po-stat'-ic, al], *a.* Hipostático ; constitutivo ; personal.
Hyposulphate [hai-po-sʊl'-fêt], *s.* (Quím.) Hiposulfato.
Hyposulphite [hai-po-sʊl'-fait], *s.* (Quím.) Hiposulfito.
Hypotension [hai-po-ten'-shʊn], *s.* Hipotensión.
Hypotenuse, Hypothenuse [hai-pet'-ę-niūs], *s.* Hipotenusa, el lado mayor de un triángulo rectángulo.
Hypothecate [hai-peth'-e-kêt], *va.* Hipotecar, empeñar. *V.* PLEDGE.
Hypothesis [hai-peth'-e-sis], *s.* Hipótesis.
Hypothetic, Hypothetical [hai-po-thet'-ic, al], *a.* Hipotético.
Hypothetically [hai-po-thet'-i-cal-i], *adv.* Condicionalmente.
Hyssop [his'-up], *s.* (Bot.) Hisopo.
Hysterectomy [his-ter-ec'-to-mi], *s.* Histerectomía, extirpación quirúrgica del útero.
Hysteria [his-tī'-ri-a], *s.* (Med.) Histerismo, padecimiento nervioso de la mujer.
Hysteric, Hysterical [his-ter'-ic, al], *a.* Histérico, perteneciente al útero ; perteneciente al histerismo.
Hysterics [his-ter'-ics], *s.* Histérico, paroxismo histérico.
Hythe [haith], *s.* Puerto pequeño.

I

I [ai] en inglés tiene varios sonidos ; uno breve, que corresponde al de la *i* castellana, como en *pin, bid* y *lid ;* y otro largo, muy semejante al del diptongo español *ai,* pronunciado tan rápidamente que forme un solo sonido, como en *sign, mild, find* [sain, maild, faind]. La *i* tiene también otro sonido entre la *e* y *o* españolas en *sir, bird, shirt,* y otras semejantes, y que se aproxima al diptongo oe alemán o eu en francés. En este volumen se indica este sonido por el signo ę. Ninguna voz puramente inglesa acaba en *i.*
I, *pron. pers.* Yo : el pronombre *yo* se escribe siempre con letra mayúscula. I se usa como abreviatura de *id ;* v. g. *i. e.* (id est), esto es.
Iambic [ai-am'-bic], *a.* (Poét.) Yámbico, perteneciente al pie yambo o que lo emplea.—*s.* 1. Pie yámbico. *V.* IAMBUS. 2. Verso (línea, estancia, estrofa) compuesto de yambos.
Iambus [ai-am'-bus], *s.* Yambo, pie de verso compuesto de dos sílabas, la primera breve y la segunda larga ; o en el día, la segunda acentuada.
I-beam [ai'-bīm], *s.* Viga en I o viga doble.
Iberian [ai-bī'-ri-an], *a.* y *s.* Ibérico, ibero.
Ibex [ai'-becs], *s.* Íbice, especie de cabra montés.
Ibis [ai'-bis], *s.* Íbis, ave del orden de las zancudas.
-ic, *sufijo.* 1. Usado para formar adjetivos con la significación de "de," "perteneciente a," "parecido a," como en artist*ic*, artístico ; o como desinencia de substantivos, v. g. en *logic,* lógica. 2. Se emplea en química para expresar una proporción del elemento combinante mayor que la del sufijo *-ous.* V. g. *nitric acid,* ácido nítrico (HNO_3) ; *nitrous acid,* ácido nitroso (HNO_2).
Ice [ais], *s.* 1. Hielo, agua congelada. *Flakes of ice,* Bancos de hielo. *Ice-bound,* Rodeado de hielos. *Ice-spurs,* Patines. 2. Sorbete. 3. Azúcar garapiñado. *V.* FROSTING. *Ice-boat,* (1) Bote que anda sobre el hielo ; casco o armazón con patines y velas que corre sobre el hielo. (2) Barco rompehielos ; vapor con máquinas poderosas para romper el hielo en los canales navegables. *Ice-box, ice-chest,* Nevera, caja para hielo. *Ice-blink,* Resplandor o claridad producida cerca del horizonte por la reflexión lejana de masas de hielo. *Ice-field, ice-float, ice-floe,* Témpano de hielo flotante. *Ice-water,* (1) Agua enfriada por el hielo. (2) Hielo derretido o nieve derretida.
Ice, *va.* Helar, cubrir de hielo. *To ice with sugar,* Cuajar de azúcar, garapiñar, alfeñicar.
Iceberg [ais'-bęrg], *s.* Lurte, gran masa o montaña de hielo que flota en los mares del norte.
Icebuilt [ais'-bilt], *a.* Formado de hielo.
Ice cream [ais crīm], *s.* Helado. *Ice-cream cone,* Barquillo de helado. *Ice-cream parlor,* Heladería, nevería. *Ice-cream sundae,* Helado con salsa de frutas y nueces.
Ice-house [ais'-haus], *s.* Nevería.
Iceland moss [ais'-land mōs], *s.* (Bot.) Liquen o musgo de Islandia.
Ice-pack [ais'-pac], *s.* Aplicaciones de hielo.
Ice-pick [ais'-pic], *s.* Punzón para hielo.
Ice skates [ais' skêts], *s. pl.* Patines para hielo.
Ichneumon [ic-niū'-męn], *s.* 1. Icneumon, mamífero carnicero, especie de fuína o garduña. 2. (Ent.) *V.* *Ichneumon-fly.* *Ichneumon-fly,* Icneumon, insecto himenóptero de la forma de una avispa pero sumamente pequeño. Deposita sus huevos sobre o en otros insectos, de los cuales se alimentan después sus larvas. De este modo destruye muchos insectos nocivos a la agricultura.
Ichnographical [ic-no-graf'-i-cal], *a.* Icnográfico.
Ichnography [ic-neg'-ra-fi], *s.* Icnografía, delineación de la planta de un edificio.
Ichor [ai'-cēr], *s* Icor, serosidad acre de la sangre.
Ichorous [ai'-cęr-us], *a.* Icoroso.
Ichthyocolla [ic-thi-o-col'-a], *s.* Colapez o cola de pescado.
Ichthyology [ic-thi-ol'-o-ji], *s.* Ictiología, la parte de la zoología que trata de los peces.
Icicle [ai'-si-cl], *s.* Cerrión, carámbano.
Icily [ai'-si-li], *adv.* Fríamente, con frialdad ; de una manera frígida.
Iciness, Icyness [ai'-si-nes], *s.* Congelación.
Icing [ai'-sing], *s.* Capa de azúcar garapiñado (para tortas, pasteles, etc.)
Icon [ai'-con], *s.* 1. Imagen, representación ; en la Iglesia griega, cuadro, mosaico sagrado, etc. 2. En los libros científicos, ilustración, grabado.

Iconoclast [ai-cen'-o-clast], *s.* Iconoclasta, hereje que niega el culto á las sagradas imágenes.
Iconoclastic [ai-cen-o-clas'-tic], *a.* Iconoclástico, iconoclasta.
Iconography [ai-co-neg'-ra-fi], *s.* Iconografía, descripción de imágenes o pinturas.
Iconolater [ai-co-nel'-a-tęr], *s.* Iconólatra, el que da culto a las imágenes.
Iconology [ai-co-nel'-o-ji], *s.* Iconología, representación de las virtudes, vicios u otras cosas morales o naturales, con la figura o apariencia de personas.
Iconoscope [ai-cen'-o-scōp], *s.* Iconoscopio.
Icosahedron [ai-co-sg-hi'-dren], *s.* Icosaedro, sólido terminado por veinte caras.
-ics. Sufijo, de forma plural pero singular por su significación, derivado del plural griego neutro *-ika*, y que significa un arte o una ciencia.
Icteric, Icterical [ic-ter'-ic, al], *a.* 1. Ictérico, que padece ictericia. 2. Ictérico, remedio contra la ictericia.
Ictus [ic'-tus], *s.* 1. (Med.) Golpecito; como la pulsación de una arteria, o la picadura de un insecto. 2. Acento tónico o métrico en una sílaba o palabra.
Icy [ai'-si], *a.* 1. Helado, cubierto de hielo. 2. Frío, libre de pasiones. 3. Tardo, lento.
I'd [aid], contracción de I WOULD o I HAD.
Idea [ai-dí'-a], *s.* Idea, imagen mental.
Ideal [ai-dí'-al], *a.* Ideal, mental, intelectual.—*s.* Ideal, el sumo grado de perfección concebible; prototipo, modelo.
Idealism [ai-dí'-al-izm], *s.* 1. Idealismo, sistema filosófico. 2. Idealismo, aptitud del artista, orador, poeta, etc., para elevar sobre la realidad sensible los objetos que describe o representa. 3. Esfuerzo para conseguir o lograr la perfección.
Idealist [ai-dí'-al-ist], *s.* Idealista, partidario del idealismo en todas sus acepciones.
Idealistic [ai-dí-al-is'-tic], *a.* Idealista.
Ideality [ai-dí-al'-i-ti], *s.* 1. Idealidad, calidad de ideal. 2. Sentimiento de lo bello, de lo poético, de lo elocuente.
Idealize, Idealise [ai-dí'-al-aiz], *va.* Hacer ideal, idealizar; exaltar, espiritualizar; dar carácter ideal.—*vn.* Formarse ideales, tipos perfectos.
Ideally [ai-dí'-al-i], *adv.* Idealmente, mentalmente, intelectualmente.
Idem [ai'-dem], *pron.* y *a.* (abreviatura, id.) Ídem, lo mismo.
Identical [ai-den'-tic-al], *a.* Idéntico, el mismo.
Identically [ai-den'-tic-al-i], *adv.* Idénticamente.
Identicalness [ai-den'-tic-al-nes], *s.* V. IDENTITY.
Identification [ai-den-ti-fi-kê'-shun], *s.* Identificación, el acto de identificar. *Identification card*, Tarjeta de identificación, comprobantes o documentos de identificación.
Identify [ai-dent'-i-fai], *va.* 1. Identificar. 2. Establecer la identidad de alguien o algo, afirmar o probar ser lo mismo. 3. Asemejar; considerar como idéntico. 4. Identificarse con; unirse con. 5. Servir como señal por la cual se reconoce una cosa o persona.
Identity [ai-den'-ti-ti], *s.* Identidad.
Ideograph [ai'-dę- (ó id-e-) o-graf], *s.* Jeroglífico; símbolo, pintura.
Ideographic [ai-dę-o-graf'-ic], *a.* Ideográfico, perteneciente a la ideografía, o representación gráfica del pensamiento.
Ideologist [ai-dę-el'-o-jist], *s.* Ideólogo, el que profesa la ideología; idealista.
Ideology [ai-dę-el'-o-ji], *s.* Ideología, ciencia que trata de las ideas.
Ides [aidz], *s.* Idus, el 15 de marzo, mayo, julio y octubre, y el 13 de los demás meses entre los romanos.
Idiocrasy [id-i-ec'-ra-si], *s.* V. IDIOSYNCRASY.
Idiocy [id'-i-o-si], *s.* Idiotez, necedad, falta de entendimiento.
Idiom [id'-i-um], *s.* 1. Idiotismo, el modo de hablar propio y peculiar de una lengua. 2. Idioma, modo particular de hablar de algunos o en algunas ocasiones; jerigonza. 3. Genio, índole de una lengua.
Idiomatic, Idiomatical [id-i-o-mat'-ic, al], *a.* Idiomático.
Idiopathic [id-i-o-path'-ic], *a.* Idiopático; se dice de las enfermedades primitivas o esenciales.
Idiopathy [id-i-ep'-a-thi], *s.* 1. Idiopatía, afección o sensación particular. 2. (Med.) Enfermedad primitiva o peculiar.
Idiosyncrasy [id-i-o-sin'-cra-si], *s.* Idiosincrasia, temperamento o disposición peculiar de una persona.
Idiot [id'-i-ęt], *s.* 1. Idiota, un hombre bobo e imbécil, en quien nunca se ha desarrollado la razón. 2. Necio, bobo, tonto.
Idiotic, Idiotical [id-i-et'-ic, al], *a.* Tonto, bobo, necio; simple.
Idiotism [id'-i-et-izm], *s.* 1. Idiotismo, necedad, ignorancia. 2. Idiotismo, modo de hablar peculiar a una lengua.
Idiotize [id'-i-ot-aiz], *vn.* Volverse tonto o necio, embrutecerse.
Idle [ai'-dl], *a.* 1. Ocioso, perezoso, desocupado, holgazán. 2. Inútil, vano, frívolo; estéril. 3. Fútil, sin importancia; (Mec.) que produce movimiento sin fuerza efectiva. 4. Que proporciona tiempo desocupado, ocio. *An idle life*, Una vida ociosa. *Idle hours*, Horas desocupadas. *Idle efforts*, Vanos esfuerzos. *An idle amusement*, Una diversión frívola. *Idle story*, Cuento de viejas. *An idle thing*, Una bagatela, una cosa fútil. *Idle fellow*, Azotacalles, callejero.
Idle, *vn.* Holgazanear, haraganear, estar ocioso.—*va.* Gastar ociosamente, consumir sin provecho.
Idle-headed [ai'-dl-hed'-ed], *a.* Tonto, desrazonable; infatuado.
Idleness [ai'-dl-nes], *s.* 1. Ociosidad, pereza, holgazanería, negligencia. 2. Trivialidad, frivolidad, inutilidad; indignidad.
Idle-pated [ai'-dl-pêt'-ed], *a.* Tonto, estúpido; majadero.
Idler [aid -lęr], *s.* Haragán, holgazán, poltrón.
Idless, Idlesse [ai'-dles], *s.* (Poét.) V. IDLENESS.
Idly [aid'-li], *adv.* Ociosamente, tontamente; inútilmente, vanamente.
Idol [ai'-dol], *s.* 1. Ídolo, imagen. 2. Ídolo, el objeto excesivamente amado.
Idolater [ai-del'-a-tęr], *s.* Idólatra; amante, admirador.
Idolatress [ai-del'-a-tres], *sf.* 1. Idólatra, la que idolatra. 2. La mujer a quien se idolatra, adora o ama con exceso.
Idolatrous [ai-del'-a-trus], *a.* 1. Idólatra, idolátrico, que adora ídolos o falsas deidades. 2. Idólatra, que ama desordenadamente a una persona o cosa.
Idolatry [ai-del'-a-tri], *s.* Idolatría, adoración de los ídolos.
Idolism [ai'-dęl-izm], *s.* Culto de idolatría y la defensa de este culto.
Idolize [ai'-del-aiz], *va.* Idolatrar; amar con exceso.
Idolizer [ai'-del-aiz-ęr], *s.* El que ama hasta la adoración.
Idyl [ai'-dil], *s.* Idilio; por extensión, poema corto, descriptivo o narrativo, muy embellecido, de estilo artístico. *V.* PASTORAL.
Idyllic [ai-dil'-ic], *a.* Idílico, concerniente al idilio; parecido a el.
I. e. Contrac. de ID EST. Es decir; esto es.
If [if], *conj.* 1. Si, partícula o conjunción condicional. *If it please God*, Si Dios quiere. 2. Aunque, dado que, supuesto que, aun cuando. *As if*, Como si; antes de una cláusula, cual si. *As if one should say*, Como si dijéramos, como quien diría. *If so be*, Con tal que, supuesto que. *If you but* (u *only*) *take my part*, Con tal que Vd. se ponga de mi parte. *Without "ifs" or "buts,"* Sin si ni pero.
I'faith [i-féth], *adv.* por IN FAITH. A fe mía, por mi honor, bajo mi palabra.
Igad [i-gad'], *inter.* *V.* EGAD.
Igneous [ig'-nę-us], *a.* Ígneo.
§**Igniferous** [ig-nif'-ęr-us], *a.* Ignífero, que produce fuego.
Ignify [ig'-ni-fai], *va.* Encender.
Ignipotent [ig-nip'-o-tent], *a.* (Poét.) Ignipotente.
Ignis fatuus [ig'-nis fat'-yu-us], *s.* (*pl.* IGNES FATUI). Fuego fatuo, helena, fuego de San Telmo.
Ignite [ig-nait'], *va.* 1. Encender, pegar fuego. 2. Hacer luminoso, causar una apariencia luminosa.—*vn.* Encenderse, enrojecerse por el calor.
Ignitible, Ignitable [ig-nait'-i-bl], *a.* Inflamable, fácil de encender o de excitar.
Ignition [ig-nish'-un], *s.* 1. Ignición, el acto de encender o poner fuego. 2. (Quím.) Ignición, el acto de poner los metales al fuego para que se hagan ascua.
Ignobility [ig-no-bil'-i-ti], *s.* Villanía, bajeza, la falta de magnanimidad, de grandeza o de elevación de ánimo.
Ignoble [ig-nō'-bl], *a.* 1. Innoble, plebeyo, villano; indigno, bajo, vil; cobarde. 2. De casta inferior; aplícase en cetrería a los halcones de alas cortas.
Ignobleness [ig-nō'-bl-nes], *s.* Bajeza, vileza, falta de dignidad en el porte; falta de nobleza en el nacimiento.
Ignobly [ig-nō'-bli], *adv.* Vilmente, bajamente; villanamente.
Ignominious [ig-no-min'-i-us], *a.* Ignominioso.
Ignominiously [ig-no-min'-i-us-li], *adv.* Ignominiosamente, vilmente.
Ignominy [ig'-no-min-i], *s.* Ignominia, infamia, deshonra, oprobio.
Ignoramus [ig-no-rê'-mus o rā'-mus], *s.* Ignorante, tonto, simple. *Ignoramus* es la palabra con que el gran jurado expresa que no ha lugar a formación de causa.

Ignorance [ig'-no-rans], *s.* Ignorancia; inadvertencia.
Ignorant [ig'-no-rant], *a.* 1. Ignorante; el que carece de conocimientos o instrucción. 2. Ignorado, no descubierto.—*s.* Ignorante, el que ignora.
Ignorantly [ig'-no-rant-li], *adv.* Ignorantemente.
Ignore [ig-nōr'], *va.* 1. Ignorar. 2. (For.) Rechazar, sobreseer; dar un fallo de "no ha lugar."
Iguana [i-gwā'-na], *s.* (Zool.) Iguana, reptil de cuerpo semejante al del lagarto; lagarto grande.
Il-. Prefijo que reemplaza a *in* antes de la letra *l.*
Ileum [il'-e-um], *s.* Íleon, el tercer intestino delgado; comprende las tres quintas partes inferiores del intestino delgado.
Ilex [ai'-lecs], *s.* (Bot.) 1. Nombre científico del acebo y de la familia a que pertenece. 2. Coscoja.
Ilk [ilk], *a.* (Ant. o Esco.) Lo mismo. *Kent of that ilk*, Pájaros de la misma pluma, Kent del lugar del mismo nombre. Úsase impropiamente a menudo como equivalente de *ilk*, raza o género. *Ilk* o *ilka*, (Ant. o Esco.) Cada. *Ilka deal*, Cada parte.
Ill [il], *a.* y *s.* 1. Malo, enfermo, doliente. 2. Malo, contrario al bien; insalubre, malsano. 3. De calidad inferior, grosero, ordinario. 4. Poco diestro, inhábil. 5. Desgraciado, funesto. *Ill-humour*, Mal humor. *Ill weeds grow apace*, La mala hierba crece a la vista. *To put an ill construction*, Tomar una cosa a mal, interpretarla en mal sentido. *Dangerously ill*, Peligrosamente enfermo.—*s.* 1. Mal, maldad. 2. Desgracia, infortunio.—*adv.* Mal, malamente. *To take ill*, Llevar a mal. *Ill* se usa frecuentemente en composición expresando su significación primitiva. *Ill-affected* o *disposed*, Mal intencionado. *Ill-contrived*, Mal pensado, mal dispuesto, mal arreglado; cruel, de malas entrañas, duro. *Ill-fated*, Desgraciado, malaventurado, desdichado. *Ill-gotten*, Mal adquirido o ganado. *Ill-grounded* o *founded*, Mal fundado. *Ill-luck*, Desgracia, desdicha. *Ill-minded*, Maligno, malvado, mal intencionado. *Ill-pleased*, Malcontento. *Ill spoken of*, El que tiene mala reputación. *Ill-advised*, No bien considerado, imprudente. *Ill-favoured*, Disforme, feo. *Ill-nature*, Malevolencia, mala intención, mal genio. *Ill-natured*, Duro o áspero de genio; malévolo, nocivo; descontentadizo. *Ill-starred*, Desdichado, desgraciado. *Ill-temper*, Aspereza de genio, irritabilidad, morosidad. *Ill-will*, Mala voluntad, tirria, aversión; tedio. *To bear* o *to owe a person ill-will*, Tener, guardar rencor o tema a alguno.
I'll [ail]. Contracción familiar de *I shall* o *I will;* formas del futuro.
Illapse [il-laps'], *s.* 1. Entrada gradual de una cosa en otra. 2. Acceso; (fig.) inspiración, descenso, como el del Espíritu Santo.
Illation [il-le'-shun], *s.* Ilación, consecuencia, inferencia.
Illative [il'-a-tiv], *a.* Ilativo, conclusivo.—*s.* Lo que indica alguna ilación.
Illatively [il'-a-tiv-li], *adv.* Por ilación o conclusión.
Illaudable [il-lōd'-a-bl], *a.* Indigno de alabanza.
Illaudably [il-lōd'-a-bli], *adv.* Indignamente.
Ill-bred [il-bred'], *a.* Malcriado, mal educado.
Illegal [il-lī'-gal], *a.* Ilegal, contra ley.
Illegality [il-le-gal'-i-ti], *s.* Ilegalidad, falta de legalidad.
Illegalize [il-lī'-gal-aiz], *va.* Hacer ilegal alguna cosa.
Illegally [il-lī'-gal-i], *adv.* Ilegalmente.
Illegibility [il-lej-i-bil'-i-ti], *s.* Condición o calidad de lo que no se puede leer.
Illegible [il-lej'-i-bl], *a.* Ilegible, lo que no se puede leer o es muy difícil de leer.
Illegibly [il-lej'-i-bli], *adv.* De un modo ilegible.
Illegitimacy [il-le-jit'-i-ma-si], *s.* Ilegitimidad.
Illegitimate [il-le-jit'-i-mēt], *a.* 1. Contrario a la ley, ilegal; especialmente, ilegítimo, bastardo, el nacido o procreado fuera de matrimonio legítimo. 2. Falso, erróneo, ilógico. 3. No autorizado por el uso.
Illegitimate, *va.* Ilegitimar.
Illegitimately [il-le-jit'-i-met-li], *adv.* Ilegítimamente.
Illegitimation [il-le-jit-i-mé'-shun], *s.* 1. Bastardía, ilegitimidad. 2. Suposición, impostura, falsedad.
Illeviable [il-lev'-i-a-bl], *a.* Lo que no puede ser exigido.
Ill-humored [il-hiū'-mẹrd], *a.* Malhumorado, de mal humor.
Illiberal [il-lib'-ẹr-al], *a.* 1. Ruin, tacaño, mezquino, miserable. 2. Escaso de inteligencia, de entendimiento limitado. 3. Indigno de un hombre bien educado; innoble, el que carece de nobleza de alma o de dignidad.
Illiberality [il-lib-ẹr-al'-i-ti], *s.* 1. Tacañería, miseria, ruindad. 2. Poquedad, pusilanimidad, apocamiento, cortedad de ánimo.
Illicit [il-lis'-it], *a.* 1. Ilícito, que no es permitido; ilegal. 2. Que se relaciona con cosas o acciones ilícitas.
Illicitly [il-lis'-it-li], *adv.* Ilegalmente, ilícitamente.
Illicitness [il-lis'-it-nes], *s.* Carácter, naturaleza ilícita; ilegalidad.
Illimitable [il-lim'-it-a-bl], *a.* Ilimitable; infinito; indeterminado.
Illimitably [il-lim'-it-a-bli], *adv.* Ilimitadamente.
Illinois [il-i-noi'], *s. pl.* Nombre genérico de ciertas tribus algonquinas, de los aborígenes norteamericanos, cuyo territorio comprendía el actual Estado de Illinois.
Illiquation [il-i-cwé'-shun], *s.* Acción de fundir una cosa en otra.
Illision [il-lizh'-un], *s.* Choque, golpe, colisión.
Illiteracy [il-lit'-ẹr-a-si], *s.* 1. Analfabetismo. 2. Falta de instrucción, ignorancia.
Illiterate [il-lit'-ẹr-et], *a.* 1. Analfabeta. 2. Ignorante.
Illiterateness [il-lit'-ẹr-et-nes], *s.* La falta de conocimientos.
Illiterature [il-lit'-ẹr-a-chur], *s.* Falta de instrucción, ignorancia.
Ill-lived [il'-laivd], *a.* Malvado.
Ill-looking [il-luk'-ing], *a.* Mal carado.
Ill-mannered [il-man'-ẹrd], *a.* Descortés, malcriado.
Ill-nature, [il-né'-chur], *s.* Malevolencia, mala intención, malicia; mal genio.
Ill-natured [il-né'-churd], *a.* Malévolo, nocivo; duro o áspero de genio, indómito, indomable, malicioso, descontentadizo.
Ill-naturedly [il-né'-churd-li], *adv.* De mala gana; con mala intención, con repugnancia.
Ill-naturedness [il-né'-churd-nes], *s.* Falta de cariño; malicia, mala intención.
Illness [il'-nes], *s.* 1. Mal, enfermedad. 2. Maldad, depravación.
Illogical [il-loj'-i-cal], *a.* Que no es conforme a las reglas de la lógica.
Illogically [il-loj'-i-cal-i], *adv.* En oposición a las reglas de la lógica.
Ill-principled [il-prin'-si-pld], *a.* 1. Inmoral, sin principios. 2. Inicuo, sin creencias.
Ill-satisfied [il-sat'-is-faid], *a.* No satisfecho, descontento.
Ill-shaped [il'-shēpd], *a.* Disforme, irregular, mal hecho, mal formado.
Ill-sounding [il-saund'-ing], *a.* Mal sonante.
Ill-starred [il'-stārd], *a.* Malaventurado, desdichado, desgraciado.
Ill-tempered [il-tem'-pẹrd], *a.* De mal carácter, de mal genio.
Ill-treated [il-trīt'-ed], *a.* Maltratado, injuriado, agraviado.
Illume [il-liūm'], *va.* (Poét.) Iluminar, aclarar.
Illuminate [il-liū'-mi-nēt], *va.* 1. Iluminar, alumbrar con luces; dar luz. 2. Iluminar, ilustrar. 3. Iluminar, inspirar. 4. Adornar una cosa con pinturas o letras iniciales transparentes o iluminadas.
‡**Illuminate**, *a.* Iluminado; instruído.—*s.* El que procura ser mirado como un talento de orden superior. *Illuminati* o *Illuminates*, *s. pl.* Los iluminados, nombre que se dió a ciertos entusiastas del siglo XVIII.
Illumination [il-lu-mi-né'-shun], *s.* 1. Iluminación, alumbrado, alumbramiento. 2. Iluminación, luminarias. 3. Brillo, esplendor. 4. Inspiración. 5. Alumbramiento, luces del cielo en nuestras almas.
Illuminative [il-liū'-mi-na-tiv], *a.* Iluminativo.
Illuminator [il-liū'-mi-nēt-ẹr], *s.* 1. Iluminador, el que o lo que ilumina o alumbra; lámpara, lente, etc., para concentrar la luz sobre objetos o lugares determinados. 2. Iluminador, el que tiene por oficio iluminar libros o manuscritos.
Illumine [il-liū'-min], *va.* Iluminar. *V.* ILLUMINATE.
Illusion [il-liū'-zhun], *s.* Ilusión, engaño, falsa apariencia, errada aprensión, imaginación engañosa.
Illusive [il-liū'-siv], *a.* Ilusivo, falso, engañoso.
Illusively [il-liū'-siv-li], *adv.* Falsamente, aparentemente.
Illusiveness [il-liū'-siv-nes], *s.* Ilusión, engaño, apariencia falsa.
Illusory [il-liū'-so-ri], *a.* Ilusorio, fantástico, aparente; engañoso, artificioso.
Illustrate [il-lus'-trēt], *va.* 1. Ilustrar, elucidar, aclarar por medio de figuras, comparaciones, ejemplos, etc. 2. Ilustrar una obra con pinturas, grabados, etc. 3. (Ant.) Engrandecer, ennoblecer. 4. (Ant.) *V.* ILLUMINATE, 1ª acep.
Illustration [il-lus-tré'-shun], *s.* 1. Ilustración, elucidación. 2. Dibujo, grabado, cuadro. 3. Arte o acción de ilustrar.
Illustrative [il-lus'-tra-tiv], *a.* Ilustrativo, explicativo.

Illustratively [il-lus'-tra-tiv-li], *adv.* Explícitamente.
Illustrator [il'-us-tra-tẹr], *s.* Ilustrador.
Illustrious [il-lus'-tri-us], *a.* Ilustre, conspicuo, esclarecido; insigne, célebre.
Illustriously [il-lus'-tri-us-li], *adv.* Ilustremente, esclarecidamente.
Illustriousness [il-lus'-tri-us-nes], *s.* Eminencia, grandeza, nobleza.
Ill-usage [il-yūz'-ẹj], *s.* Injusticia; crueldad; mal trato.
Ill-will [il-wil'], *s.* Mala voluntad, malevolencia, tirria, aversión.
I'm [aim], contrac. de I AM. Yo soy o estoy.
Im [im]. Úsase en composición en lugar de IN, delante de *b, m,* y *p.* Algunos escritores emplean EM.
Image [im'-ẹj], *s.* 1. Imagen, efigie, estatua; retrato, pintura. 2. Imagen, figura, representación, semejanza de una cosa con otra; apariencia. 3. (Ópt.) Imagen, duplicado de un objeto, producido por medio de la reflexión o refracción. 4. Idea, representación de los objetos en el ánimo.
Image, *va.* 1. Figurar, formar una imagen de; reflejar. 2. Representar en la mente. 3. Parecer.
Image-worship [im'-ẹj-wūr'-ship], *s.* El culto de las imágenes.
Imagery [im'-ẹj-ri], *s.* 1. Acción de formar imágenes, en cualquier sentido; conjunto de imágenes. 2. Exterioridad, apariencia. 3. Imaginación, aprehensión, vuelos de la fantasía, ideas falsas. 4. Forma o hechura exterior de las cosas. 5. Tapicería con figuras o pinturas.
Imaginable [i-maj'-i-na-bl], *a.* Imaginable.
Imaginary [i-maj'-i-nẹ-ri], *a.* Imaginario, fantástico.
Imagination [i-maj-i-nē'-shun], *s.* 1. Imaginación. 2. Imaginación, invención, pensamiento. 3. Imaginación, aprehensión, idea fantástica, visión.
Imaginative [i-maj'-i-na-tiv], *a.* Imaginativo.
Imagine [i-maj'-in], *va.* 1. Imaginar, representarse algo en la imaginación. 2. Imaginar, pensar, concebir, idear, inventar, discurrir alguna cosa. 3. Premeditar, formar de antemano un proyecto en el ánimo. —*vn.* Imaginarse, figurarse.
Imaginer [i-maj'-in-ẹr], *s.* El que imagina, idea o inventa.
Imagining [i-maj'-in-ing], *s.* Imaginación, fantasía.
Imago [i-mē'-gō o -mg'-gō], *s.* (Lat.) Insecto adulto llegado a la perfección, desarrollado sexualmente.
Imam [i-mām'], *s.* 1. Imán, ministro de la religión mahometana, que recita las oraciones. 2. Título de Mahoma y sus cuatro sucesores inmediatos.
Imbank, *va.* Respecto de esta palabra y otras en *im-* que no se hallan aquí, véase *em-*.
Imbarn [im-bārn'], *va.* Entrojar, encerrar en graneros.
Imbecile [im'-bẹ-sil], *a.* Imbécil, necio, débil, tonto.
Imbecility [im-bẹ-sil'-i-ti], *s.* Imbecilidad, debilidad; impotencia.
Imbed [im-bed'], *va.* *V.* EMBED.
Imbibe [im-baib'], *va.* 1. Embeber, atraer y recoger en sí alguna cosa líquida. 2. Empapar, chupar. 3. Embelesar el ánimo con alguna idea: en castellano sólo se usa en este sentido como neutro el verbo embeber, y se dice embeberse o embebecerse.
Imbiber [im-bai'-bẹr], *s.* Embebedor, la persona o cosa que embebe.
Imbibition [im-bi-bish'-un], *s.* Imbibición.
†**Imbitter** [im-bit'-ẹr], *va.* *V.* EMBITTER.
Imbosom [im-būz'-um], *va.* *V.* EMBOSOM.
Imbricate, Imbricated [im'-bri-kêt, ed], *a.* Imbricado, puesto o colocado uno sobre otro como ripias o pizarras.
Imbrication [im-bri-kē'-shun], *s.* Desigualdad cóncava, como la de las conchas.
Imbroglio [im-brō'-lyo], *s.* Embrollo, engaño, complicación de la cual resulta confusión.
Imbrown [im-braun'], *va.* *V.* EMBROWN.
Imbrue [im-brū'], *va.* Remojar, embeber o empapar una cosa en algún líquido. *To imbrue one's hands in blood,* Teñir sus manos en sangre.
Imbrute [im-brūt'], *va.* Embrutecer, degradar a uno o reducirle al estado de los brutos.—*vn.* Reducirse al estado de bruto.
Imbue [im-biū'], *va.* 1. Tinturar, teñir. 2. Imbuir, infundir, llenar o penetrar de una doctrina, una opinión, etc.
Imitability [im-i-ta-bil'-i-ti], *s.* La calidad de ser imitable.
Imitable [im'-i-ta-bl], *a.* Imitable, que se puede imitar.
Imitate [im'-i-têt], *va.* 1. Imitar, tomar por modelo, seguir el ejemplo. 2. Remedar, contrahacer. 3. Copiar.
Imitation [im-i-tē'-shun], *s.* 1. Imitación. 2. Ejemplar, modelo; copia. 3. Método de traducir libremente un escrito o composición.
Imitational [im-i-tē'-shun-al], *a.* (Poco us.) Imitador, referente a la imitación.
Imitative [im'-i-ta-tiv], *a.* Imitativo, imitado.
Imitator [im'-i-tê-tẹr], *s.* Imitador.
Imitatorship [im'-i-tê-tẹr-ship], *s.* Imitación, calidad de ser imitador.
Immaculate [im-mac'-yu-lẹt], *a.* Inmaculado, puro.
Immaculately [im-mac'-yu-lêt-li], *adv.* Inmaculadamente.
Immaculateness [im-mac'-yu-lêt-nes], *s.* Pureza, inocencia.
Immailed [im-mêld'], *a.* Lo que tiene malla o armadura.
Immalleable [im-mal'-ẹ-a-bl], *a.* No maleable.
Immanacle [im-man'-a-cl], *va.* 1. Aprisionar con esposas o grillos. 2. (Fam.) Echar o poner grillos o esposas.
Immane [im-mên], *a.* (Ant.) Vasto, enorme.
Immanely [im-mên'-li], *adv.* Monstruosamente.
Immanence, Immanency [im'-a-nens, i], *s.* La calidad y el estado de inmanente; inherencia.
Immanent [im'-a-nent], *a.* Inmanente, inherente, intrínseco, interno; lo que va unido de un modo inseparable a la esencia de un ser.
Immanuel [im-man'-yu-el], *n. pr.* Nombre bíblico de Jesucristo, que quiere decir Dios con nosotros.
Immask [i-mgsc'], *va.* Enmascarar, disfrazar.
Immaterial [im-a-tī'-ri-al], *a.* 1. Inmaterial, incorpóreo. 2. Frívolo, fútil; indiferente; de ninguna importancia.
Immaterialism [im-a-tī'-ri-al-izm], *s.* 1. Espiritismo. 2. Inmaterialismo; idealismo.
Immaterialist [im-a-tī'-ri-al-ist], *s.* Inmaterialista, nombre dado a unos sectarios que sostenían que todo es espíritu; los partidarios del espiritismo.
Immateriality [im-a-tī-ri-al'-i-ti], *s.* Inmaterialidad, espiritualidad.
Immaterialized [im-a-tī'-ri-al-aizd], *a.* Incorpóreo, espiritual.
Immaterially [im-a-tī'-ri-al-i], *adv.* Espiritualmente.
Immaterialness [im-a-tī'-ri-al-nes], *s.* Inmaterialidad.
Immature [im-a-tiūr'], *a.* 1. Inmaturo, que no ha llegado a la perfección; imperfecto, no desarrollado. 2. Temprano, adelantado, prematuro, precoz.
Immaturely [im-a-tiūr'-li], *adv.* Prematuramente, antes de tiempo o de la completa madurez; demasiado pronto.
Immatureness [im-a-tiūr'-nes], **Immaturity** [im-a-tiūr'-i-ti], *s.* Calidad o estado de inmaturo, en sus dos acepciones.
Immeasurability, Immeasurableness [im-mezh''-ur-a-bil'-i-ti, bl-nes], *s.* Inmensidad, inmensurabilidad, calidad de lo que no puede medirse.
Immeasurable [im-mezh'-ur-a-bl], *a.* Inmensurable, inmenso.
Immeasurably [im-mezh'-ur-a-bli], *adv.* Inmensamente.
Immediacy [im-mī'-di-a-si], *s.* Independencia absoluta, facultad de obrar sin intervención de otro.
Immediate [im-mī'-di-ẹt], *a.* 1. Inmediato, lo que se sigue próximamente; instantáneo, o que no admite dilación. 2. Inmediato, lo que obra por sí sin la mediación de otra cosa; directo. 3. Inmediato, lo que está cercano o contiguo a otra cosa. 4. Intuitivo, perteneciente a una concepción directa. *Immediate truths,* Verdades intuitivas.
Immediately [im-mī'-di-ẹt-li], *adv.* 1. Inmediatamente, luego, al instante, incontinenti o incontinente. 2. Directamente, sin intervención de otra causa; intuitivamente.
Immediateness [im-mī'-di-ẹt-nes], *s.* 1. Calidad o estado de inmediato. 2. Presencia inmediata.
Immedicable [im-med'-i-ca-bl], *a.* Incurable, irremediable.
Immelodious [im-me-lō'-di-us], *a.* Discorde; lo que carece de melodía.
Immemorial [im-mẹ-mō'-ri-al], *a.* Inmemorial o inmemorable, tan antiguo que no hay memoria de cuándo comenzó o sucedió.
Immemorially [im-me-mō'-ri-al-i], *adv.* Inmemorialmente, desde tiempo inmemorial.
Immense [im-mens'], *a.* Inmenso, infinito, ilimitado; vasto; desmedido, que no tiene medida.
Immensely [im-mens'-li], *adv.* Inmensamente, sin medida, ilimitadamente.
Immenseness [im-mens'-nes], *s.* Inmensidad, grandeza ilimitada.
Immensity [im-mens'-i-ti], *s.* Inmensidad, infinidad en extensión o medida.
Immensurability [im-men-shur-a-bil'-i-ti], *s.* Inmensurabilidad.
Immensurable [im-men'-shur-a-bl], **Immensurate** [im-men'-shur-êt], *a.* Inmensurable.

Immerge [im-mẹrj'], *va.* Sumergir, zambullir, meter alguna cosa dentro de un flúido.—*vn.* Ocultarse, perderse de vista, como una estrella ante la luz del sol.

Immerse [im-mẹrs'], *va.* 1. Sumergir, zambullir, meter alguna cosa dentro del agua o cualquier otro flúido. 2. Meter alguna cosa en un sitio muy hondo o en algo muy espeso. 3. Sumergir o anegar en penas, dolor, miseria, etc. 4. Bautizar por medio de la inmersión.

Immersed [im-mẹrst'], *a.* Hundido, sumido, sumergido, agobiado.

Immersion [im-mẹr'-shun], *s.* Inmersión, hundimiento, sumersión.

Immersionist [im-mẹr'-shun-ist], *s.* Inmersionista, el que cree en la necesidad de la inmersión total del cuerpo en el bautismo.

Immesh [im-mesh'], *va.* *V.* ENMESH.

Immethodical [im-me-thed'-i-cal], *a.* Sin método, falto de orden.

Immethodically [im-me-thed'-i-cal-i], *adv.* Confusamente, de una manera falta de orden o método.

Immethodicalness [im-me-thed'-i-cal-nes], *s.* Confusión, falta de orden o método.

Immigrant [im'-mi-grant], *s.* Inmigrante, el que llega a un país con ánimo de establecerse en él.

Immigrate [im'-i-grêt], *vn.* Inmigrar, trasladarse o llegar a un país para establecerse en él.

Immigration [im-i-grê'-shun], *s.* Inmigración.

Imminence [im'-i-nens], *s.* El peligro próximo, inminente o cercano.

Imminent [im'-i-nent], *a.* Inminente, lo que amenaza o está para suceder prontamente.

Immingle [im-miṇ'-gl], *va.* Mezclar, trabar, unir.

Immiscibility [im-mis-i-bil'-i-ti], *s.* (Quím.) Inmiscibilidad, calidad de lo que no es susceptible de mezcla.

Immiscible [im-mis'-i-bl], *a.* Inmiscible, que no se puede mezclar homogéneamente con otra cosa, como el agua y el aceite.

Immission [im-mish'-un], *s.* Introducción, inyección, acto y efecto de inyectar o de hacer entrar; lo opuesto a *emission.*

Immit [im-mit'], *va.* Introducir una cosa en otra, inyectar; opuesto a *emit.*

Immitigable [im-mit'-i-ga-bl], *a.* Inmitigable, lo que no puede ser mitigado.

Immobile [im-mō'-bil], *a.* 1. Inmóvil, inmoble, que no se puede mover. 2. Inmoble, que no se deja afectar por las emociones; constante en sus afectos.

Immobility [im-mo-bil'-i-ti], *s.* Inmovilidad, falta de movimiento, resistencia al movimiento.

Immoderacy [im-med'-ẹr-a-si], *s.* (Poco us.) Exceso, inmoderación.

Immoderate [im-med'-ẹr-ẹt], *a.* Inmoderado, excesivo, irrazonable; intemperante, desarreglado.

Immoderately [im-med'-ẹr-ẹt-li], *adv.* Inmoderadamente.

Immoderateness [im-med'-ẹr-ẹt-nes], *s.* Inmoderación.

Immoderation [im-med-ẹr'-ê-shun], *s.* Inmoderación, exceso, desarreglo.

Immodest [im-med'-est], *a.* 1. Falto de reserva, de decoro, de pudor; inmodesto, impuro, indecente, deshonesto. 2. Impudente, atrevido, insolente. 3. (Ant.) Inmoderado, poco razonable.

Immodestly [im-med'-est-li], *adv.* Inmodestamente, de una manera indecorosa; deshonestamente.

Immodesty [im-med'-es-ti], *s.* Inmodestia, falta de modestia, de decoro; indecencia, deshonestidad; profanidad.

Immolate [im'-o-lêt], *va.* Inmolar, sacrificar.

Immolation [im-o-lê'-shun], *s.* Inmolación, sacrificio (cruento, por regla general).

Immolator [im-e-lêt'-ẹr], *s.* Inmolador, sacrificador.

Immoral [im-mer'-al], *a.* Inmoral, depravado, malvado; desarreglado, licencioso, vicioso, corrompido.

Immorality [im-o-ral'-i-ti], *s.* Inmoralidad, pravedad, iniquidad, perversidad, corrupción de costumbres, desarreglo, desorden.

Immortal [im-mōr'-tal], *a.* 1. Inmortal; perpetuo. 2. Inmortal, digno de eterna fama.

Immortality [im-mer-tal'-i-ti], *s.* 1. Inmortalidad, calidad de inmortal. 2. Inmortalidad, eterna memoria o fama entre los hombres.

Immortalization [im-mer-tal-i-zê'-shun], *s.* El acto de inmortalizar; perpetuación.

Immortalize [im-mer'-tal-aiz], *va.* Inmortalizar, eternizar.

Immortally [im-mōr'-tal-i], *adv.* Inmortalmente, sin fin, para siempre.

Immortelle [im-ōr-tel'], *s.* (Bot.) Una cualquiera de las diversas flores que conservan sus formas y colores largo tiempo; como las siemprevivas, perpetuas, etc. (Fr.)

Immotile [im-mō'-til], *a.* (Biol.) Inmóvil, estacionario.

Immovability [im-mūv-a-bil'-i-ti], *s.* Inmovilidad, incapacidad o imposibilidad de moverse.

Immovable [im-mūv'-a-bl], *a.* 1. Inmóvil, inamovible, fijo, inmoto. 2. Inmoble, inmutable, firme, inflexible en un designio; inalterable. 3. Impasible, insensible, apático. *Immovables, immovable estate,* Inmueble: dícese de los bienes raíces o fincas.

Immovableness [im-mūv'-a-bl-nes], *s.* Inmovilidad; inmutabilidad; inalterabilidad; insensibilidad.

Immovably [im-mūv'-a-bli], *adv.* Inmóvilmente, inmutablemente, de un modo inalterable.

Immune [im-miūn'], *a.* (Med.) Inmune, exento de una enfermedad; especialmente, protegido por la inoculación.

Immunization [im-miū-ni-sê'-shun], *s.* Inmunización.

Immunize [im-miū'-naiz], *va.* Hacer inmune, proteger por la inoculación contra la infección.

Immunity [im-miū'-ni-ti], *s.* Inmunidad, libertad, privilegio, exención de cargas, obligaciones, penas, etc.; franquicia.

Immure [im-miūr'], *va.* Emparedar, tapar o cercar con paredes o muros.

Immutability [im-miūt-a-bil'-i-ti], *s.* Inmutabilidad, firmeza, constancia.

Immutable [im-miūt'-a-bl], *a.* Inmutable, que no puede mudar; inalterable.

Immutableness [im-miūt'-a-bl-nes], *s.* Inmutabilidad.

Immutably [im-miūt'-a-bli], *adv.* Inmutablemente, inalterablemente.

Imp [imp], *s.* 1. Diablillo, duende, trasgo. 2. Diablillo, tunantuelo, muchacho travieso.

Impact [im-pact'], *va.* Empaquetar; unir varias cosas entre sí apretándolas mucho unas con otras.

Impact [im'-pact], *s.* Acción de dar un golpe; choque, colisión de un cuerpo que está en movimiento con otro.

Impaction [im-pac'-shun], *s.* (Med.) Atasco, impedimento de un órgano, como el intestino; también, presión de una parte sobre otra.

Impair [im-pār'], *va.* Empeorar, disminuir en cantidad o en valor; alterar, deteriorar, echar a perder, debilitar.—*vn.* Empeorar, ir una cosa de mal en peor; enflaquecer; gastarse o echarse a perder alguna cosa.

Impairer [im-pār'-ẹr], *s.* Lo que disminuye o empeora.

Impairing [im-pār'-ing], *s.* Diminución, alteración.

Impairment [im-pār'-mẹnt], *s.* Empeoramiento, deterioración, deterioro.

Impale, *va.* *V.* EMPALE.

Impalpability [im-pal-pa-bil'-i-ti], *s.* Impalpabilidad, calidad de lo que es impalpable.

Impalpable [im-pal'-pa-bl], *a.* 1. Impalpable, que no se puede tocar o palpar. 2. Intangible, incomprensible, ininteligible, sin realidad.

Impanate, *va.* (Teol.) Empanar; incorporar en el pan.

Impanation [im-pa-nê'-shun], *s.* Empanación, la subsistencia del pan con el cuerpo de Jesucristo después de la consagración, según los luteranos.

Impanel [im-pan'-el], *va.* 1. Inscribir en la lista de los jurados. 2. Formar la lista de los jurados; hacer prestar juramento, como lo prestan los miembros de un jurado.

Imparadise [im-par'-a-dais], *va.* Colocar en un estado feliz semejante al del paraíso.

Imparity [im-par'-i-ti], *s.* 1. Desigualdad, desproporción. 2. Indivisibilidad, calidad de impartible. 3. Disparidad, diferencia.

Impark, *va.* Encerrar o incluir en un parque; rodear, hacer un parque por medio de cercas.

Impart [im-pārt'], *va.* 1. Dar, conceder, conferir. 2. Comunicar, dar parte, hacer saber.

Impartial [im-pār'-shal], *a.* Imparcial.

Impartiality [im-pār-shi-al'-i-ti], *s.* Imparcialidad, equidad, desinterés.

Impartially [im-pār'-shal-i], *adv.* Imparcialmente, equitativamente.

Impartible [im-pārt'-i-bl], *a.* 1. Impartible, indivisible. 2. Comunicable; concedible.

Impartment, *s.* Acción de dar, de conferir; comunicación.

Impassable [im-pas'-a-bl], *a.* Intransitable, impracticable.

Impassableness [im-pas'-a-bl-nes], *s.* Incapacidad de ser pasado o de admitir pasaje o paso.

Impasse [im'-pas], *s.* 1. Camino intransitable. 2. (fig.) Callejón sin salida, obstáculo insuperable, atolladero, atascadero.

Impassibility [im-pas-i-bil'-i-ti], *s.* 1. Impasibilidad, incapacidad de padecer. 2. Inalterabilidad.

Impassible [im-pas'-i-bl], *a.* 1. Impasible, incapaz de padecer. 2. Apático, insensible, sin emoción.

Impassibleness [im-pas'-i-bl-nes], *s.* Impasibilidad.

Impassion [im-pash'-un], *va.* (Poét.) Mover las pasiones, excitar fuertemente el ánimo.—*vn.* Apasionarse.

Impassionable [im-pash'-un-a-bl], *a.* Conmovible, susceptible de apasionamiento.
Impassionate, *va.* Apasionar; conmover, afectar vivamente.
Impassioned [im-pash'-und], *a.* Apasionado, vehemente; que expresa pasión, ardor, etc.
Impassive [im-pas'-iv], *a.* Lo que está exento de la influencia de las causas externas.
Impassiveness [im-pas'-iv-nes], *s.* El estado de hallarse exento de la influencia de las causas externas.
Impastation [im-pas-tê'-shun], *s.* 1. Una mezcla de substancias de diversos colores y consistencia, unidas entre sí por un cemento y endurecidas por el aire o el fuego. 2. (Pint.) Empaste.
Impaste [im-pêst'], *va.* 1. Hacer pasta o poner una cosa en forma de pasta. 2. (Pint.) Empastar, sobrecargar de colores lo que se ha dibujado.
Impatible [im-pat'-i-bl], *a.* Intolerable.
Impatience [im-pê'-shens], *s.* 1. Impaciencia, desasosiego. 2. Irritabilidad, intolerancia de toda oposición o sujeción; petulancia, ansia, apresuramiento.
Impatient [im-pê'-shent], *a.* 1. Impaciente. 2. Inquieto, irritable, intolerante; apresurado.—*s.* ¿El que es impaciente, el que tiene pasiones fuertes.
Impatiently [im-pê'-shent-li], *adv.* Inquietamente, impacientemente.
Impawn [im-pēn'], *va.* Empeñar, dar o dejar alguna cosa en prenda.
Impeach [im-pích'], *va.* 1. Acusar, denunciar o delatar en virtud de autoridad pública; imputar; dirigir una acusación a un personaje, encausarlo. 2. (For.) Tachar, hacer objeción a, poner tachas.
Impeachable [im-pích'-a-bl], *a.* Delatable, susceptible de acusación; censurable, cuestionable, expuesto a ser tachado.
Impeacher [im-pích'-ęr], *s.* Acusador, denunciador, delator.
Impeachment [im-pích'-męnt], *s.* 1. Reconvención, tacha; desdoro. 2. Acusación pública; la acción de pedir cuentas; en especial, acusación y proceso de un alto funcionario del orden civil. 3. Imputación, delación.
Impearl [im-pęrl'], *va.* 1. Hacer alguna cosa en figura de perlas. 2. Adornar con perlas.
Impeccability [im-pec-a-bil'-i-ti], *s.* Impecabilidad.
Impeccable [im-pec'-a-bl], *a.* Impecable, incapaz de pecar.
Impeccancy [im-pec'-an-si], *s.* Impecabilidad, incapacidad de pecar.
Impeccant [im-pec'-ant], *a.* Exento de pecar; sin tacha.
Impecuniosity [im-pę-kiu-ni-es'-i-ti], *s.* Falta de dinero, de recursos.
Impecunious [im-pę-kiū'-ni-us], *a.* Falto de dinero; habitualmente pobre.
Impede [im-píd'], *va.* Impedir, embarazar con obstáculos, o ser obstáculo; retardar, obstruir.
Impediment [im-ped'-i-męnt], *s.* Impedimento, embarazo, obstáculo; obstrucción.
Impedimental [im-ped-i-ment'-al], *a.* Que impide, detiene o retarda; que sirve de obstáculo para la ejecución de una cosa.
Impeditive [im-ped'-i-tiv], *a.* Impeditivo.
Impel [im-pel'], *va.* 1. Impeler, excitar a obrar, poner en movimiento, hacer avanzar. 2. Impeler, incitar, apretar, apurar.
Impellent [im-pel'-ent], *a.* Impelente; impulsor; que tiende a impeler.—*s.* 1. Empuje o empujo. 2. Motor, móvil, autor.
Impeller [im-pel'-ęr], *s.* Impulsor, el que empuja o impele hacia adelante.
Impen [im-pen'], *va.* *V.* IMPOUND.
Impend [im-pend'], *vn.* Amenazar, amagar, ser inminente.
Impendence [im-pend'-ens], **Impendency** [im-pend'-en-si], *s.* El estado de lo que amenaza o está próximo a caer sobre uno.
Impendent [im-pend'-ent], **Impending** [im-pend'-ing], *a.* Inminente, pendiente, amenazante.
Impenetrability [im-pen-e-tra-bil'-i-ti], *s.* 1. Impenetrabilidad, calidad de lo impenetrable. 2. (Fís.) Impenetrabilidad, propiedad que impide la presencia de un cuerpo en el lugar que otro ocupa.
Impenetrable [im-pen'-e-tra-bl], *a.* 1. Impenetrable, intransitable, que no se puede penetrar; dícese de las cosas materiales. 2. Impenetrable, que no se puede penetrar con la vista ni con la mente; abstruso, difícil de comprender; denso, espeso. *Impenetrable darkness*, Obscuridad densa, impenetrable. 3. (Fís.) Que posee la propiedad física de la impenetrabilidad.
Impenetrableness [im-pen'-e-tra-bl-nes], *s.* Impenetrabilidad.
Impenetrably [im-pen'-e-tra-bli], *adv.* Impenetrablemente.
Impenitence [im-pen'-i-tens], **Impenitency** [im-pen'-i-ten-si], *s.* Impenitencia, endurecimiento de corazón, obstinación en el pecado.
Impenitent [im-pen'-i-tent], *a.* Impenitente, obstinado en la culpa.—*s.* El que es impenitente.
Impenitently [im-pen'-i-tent-li], *adv.* Sin penitencia o contrición, con endurecimiento de corazón.
Impennate [im-pen'-ęt], *a.* Impennado, que tiene alas cortas y con plumas tan pequeñas que parecen escamas, como las alas de los pingüinos o penguinos.
Impennous [im-pen'-us], *a.* Sin alas.
Imperate [im'-pę-rêt], *a.* Lo que nace de voluntad y se hace de buena gana, por una convicción interior de que debe hacerse.
Imperative [im-per'-a-tiv], *a.* Imperativo, imperioso, que expresa un mandato positivo; perentorio.—*s.* 1. Mandato perentorio. 2. (Gram.) Modo imperativo.
Imperatively [im-per'-a-tiv-li], *adv.* Imperativamente, por orden expresa.
Imperceptible [im-pęr-sep'-ti-bl], *a.* Imperceptible, que no se puede percibir.—*s.* Cosa imperceptible o pequeñísima.
Imperceptibleness [im-pęr-sep'-ti-bl-nes], *s.* Imperceptibilidad.
Imperceptibly [im-pęr-sep'-ti-bli], *adv.* Imperceptiblemente.
Imperception [im-pęr-sep'-shun], *s.* Falta de percepción, impercepción.
Imperceptive [im-pęr-sep'-tiv], **Impercipient** [im-pęr-sip'-i-ent], *a.* Lo que no tiene poder de percibir o de percepción.
Imperfect [im-pęr'-fect], *a.* Imperfecto, incompleto, defectuoso.
Imperfection [im-pęr-fec'-shun], *s.* 1. Imperfección. 2. Imperfección, falta o defecto ligero en lo moral.
Imperfectly [im-pęr'-fect-li], *adv.* Imperfectamente.
Imperfectness [im-pęr'-fect-nes], *s.* Imperfección, defecto, falta.
Imperforable [im-pęr'-fo-ra-bl], *a.* Imperforable, lo que no se puede agujerear.
Imperforate, Imperforated [im-pęr'-fo-rêt, ed], *a.* Imperforado, sin perforaciones, cerrado.
Imperforation [im-pęr-fo-rê'-shun], *s.* Imperforación, cerramiento, obstrucción de las partes que deben estar abiertas.
Imperial [im-pí'-ri-al], *a.* 1. Imperial, perteneciente a un imperio o a un emperador o emperatriz. 2. Soberano, predominante. 3. A propósito para un emperador, digno de él; de aquí, superior en volumen o en calidad.—*s.* 1. Pera, perilla, porción de barba que se deja crecer bajo el labio inferior. 2. (Arq.) Cúpula con perfil de cimacio, como las moriscas. 3. Cualquier cosa de tamaño o calidad superior en su clase.
Imperialism [im-pí'-ri-al-izm], *s.* Imperialismo, estado, carácter o espíritu imperial; aspiración a formar un imperio; doctrina de los imperialistas.
Imperialist [im-pí'-ri-al-ist], *s.* Imperial, imperialista, partidario del gobierno imperial; en particular, (1) partidario del antiguo imperio de Alemania; (2) partidario del imperio francés, en oposición así a la república como a la monarquía; bonapartista.
Imperialized [im-pí'-ri-al-aizd], *a.* El que es del partido de un emperador.
Imperially [im-pí'-ri-al-i], *adv.* Imperialmente.
Imperialty [im-pí'-ri-al-ti], *s.* El poder imperial.
Imperil [im-per'-il], *va.* Poner en peligro, en riesgo; arriesgar.
Imperious [im-pí'-ri-us], *a.* 1. Imperioso, altivo, orgulloso, arrogante, fiero, despótico. 2. Urgente, perentorio, irresistible. *An imperious necessity*, Una necesidad urgente, imperiosa.
Imperiously [im-pí'-ri-us-li], *adv.* Imperiosamente, con altivez.
Imperiousness [im-pí'-ri-us-nes], *s.* Autoridad, mando; arrogancia, altivez.
Imperishable [im-per'-ish-a-bl], *a.* Imperecedero; indestructible; eterno.
Impermanence [im-pęr'-ma-nens], **Impermanency** [im-pęr'-ma-nen-si], *s.* Instabilidad.
Impermanent [im-pęr'-ma-nent], *a.* Que no es permanente.
Impermeability [im-pęr-mę-a-bil'-i-ti], *s.* Impermeabilidad.
Impermeable [im-pęr'-mę-a-bl], *a.* Impermeable, impenetrable, que no puede ser penetrado por los flúidos.
Impersonal [im-pęr'-sun-al], *a.* 1. Impersonal, que no tiene ni implica personalidad. 2. Que no se relaciona con una persona o cosa determinada. 3. (Gram.) Impersonal, que tiene o contiene sujeto indeterminado; en inglés, ese sujeto es generalmente el pronombre *it*. *It happened to me to be seated beside her at table*, Me tocó sentarme a su lado en la mesa.
Impersonally [im-pęr'-sun-al-i], *adv.* Impersonalmente.

Impersonate [im-pęr'-sun-êt], *va.* 1. Personificar. 2. Representar, hacer el papel de.
Impersonation [im-pęr-so-nê'-shun], *s.* Representación, papel; personificación.
Imperspicuous [im-pęr-spic'-yu-us], *a.* Obscuro, lo que no es perspicuo o claro.
Impersuadable [im-pęr-swê'-da-bl], **Impersuasible** [im-pęr-swê'-si-bl], *a.* Impersuasible, incapaz de ser persuadido.
Impertinence [im-pęr'-ti-nens], **Impertinency** [im-pęr'-ti-nen-si], *s.* Impertinencia; absurdo; insolencia; extravagancia; importunidad; bagatela, cosa de poca o ninguna importancia.
Impertinent [im-pęr'-ti-nent], *a.* Impertinente, incómodo, importuno, cansado; frívolo; insolente, desvergonzado, atrevido; descortés.—*s.* Un impertinente, el que en todo se mete.
Impertinently [im-pęr'-ti-nent-li], *adv.* Impertinentemente, insolentemente.
Imperturbability [im-pęr-tūrb-a-bil'-i-ti], *s.* Imperturbabilidad, serenidad.
Imperturbable [im-pęr-tūrb'-a-bl], *a.* Imperturbable.
Imperturbably [im-pęr-tūrb'-a-bli], *adv.* Imperturbablemente.
Imperturbation [im-pęr-tūr-bê'-shun], *s.* Tranquilidad, calma, serenidad, frialdad, sangre fría.
Imperturbed [im-pęr-tūrbd'], *a.* Sereno, quieto, tranquilo, sosegado.
Impervious [im-pęr'-vi-us], *a.* Impenetrable, impermeable. *Impervious to air*, Impenetrable al aire.
Imperviously [im-pęr'-vi-us-li], *adv.* Impenetrablemente.
Imperviousness [im-pęr'-vi-us-nes], *s.* Impenetrabilidad.
Impetiginous [im-pę-tij'-i-nus], *a.* Tiñoso, impetiginoso.
Impetigo [im-pę-tai'-go], *s.* Impétigo, afección cutánea contagiosa; tiña. Se llama familiarmente *crusted scall.*
Impetrative [im'-pę-trê-tiv], *a.* Impetrador, que emplea ruegos, o que tiende a obtener (alguna cosa) por la impetración.
Impetuosity [im-pet-yu-es'-i-ti], *s.* Impetuosidad, vehemencia; viveza extremada.
Impetuous [im-pet'-yu-us], *a.* Impetuoso, violento, arrebatado, vehemente.
Impetuously [im-pet'-yu-us-li], *adv.* Impetuosamente.
Impetuousness [im-pet'-yu-us-nes], *s.* Impetuosidad.
Impetus [im'-pę-tus], *s.* 1. Ímpetu, fuerza de impulsión, movimiento violento. 2. (Fig.) Impulso, incentivo.
Imphee [im'-fi], *s.* Caña africana de azúcar; se parece al sorgo o andropogon. Holcus saccharatus.
Impicture [im-pic'-churl, *va.* Pintar, formar un cuadro sobre algo.
Impiety [im-pai'-ę-ti], *s.* Impiedad, irreligión.
Impignorate [im-pig'-no-rêt], *va.* (Ant.) Empeñar, dar o dejar alguna cosa en prenda.
Impinge [im-pinj'], *vn.* Tocar, caer o golpear contra una cosa después de moverse; tropezar.
Impious [im'-pi-us], *a.* Impío, sacrílego, malvado, perverso, irreligioso, profano.
Impiously [im'-pi-us-li], *adv.* Impíamente.
Impiousness [im'-pi-us-nes], *s.* Impiedad, desprecio de la religión.
Impish [imp'-ish], *a.* Travieso, malicioso, parecido a un diablillo.
Implacability [im-plê-ca-bil'-i-ti], *s.* Implacabilidad; perseverancia en el resentimiento; rencor, odio inveterado, intratable, inexorable, irreconciliable.
Implacable [im-plê'-ca-bl], *a.* Implacable, irreconciliable; inexorable.
Implacableness [im-plê'-ca-bl-nes], *s.* Odio implacable.
Implacably [im-plê'-ca-bli], *adv.* Implacablemente.
Implacental, Implacentate [im-pla-sen'-tal, têt], *a.* (Biol.) Que no tiene placenta.—*s.* Mamífero que no tiene placenta.
Implant [im-plant'], *va.* Fijar, plantar, ingerir; inculcar, sembrar.
Implantation [im-plan-tê'-shun], *s.* Injertación, plantación; inculcación.
Implausible [im-plāz'-i-bl], *a.* Que no es plausible.
Implausibly [im-plāz'-i-bli], *adv.* Sin apariencia o probabilidad.
Implead [im-plīd'], *va.* Acusar, demandar ante la justicia; en especial, proceder contra dos o más personas a un tiempo; poner pleito.
Impleader [im-plīd'-ęr], *s.* Acusador, demandante.
Implement [im'-plę-męnt], *s.* 1. Herramienta, cualquier instrumento o útil de que usan los artífices para trabajar en sus obras y labores; utensilio, lo que sirve para comodidad de la vida; arma. 2. Originalmente, suplefaltas, el que llena algún hueco o socorre alguna necesidad; medios.
Implete [im-plīt'], *va.* (Poco us.) Llenar, colmar.
Implicate [im'-pli-kêt], *va.* Implicar, envolver; enredar, embrollar.
Implication [im-pli-kê'-shun], *s.* 1. Implicación, la parte que tiene o se supone tener alguno en la perpetración de un delito. 2. Ilación, deducción; (For.) inducción implícita, la que no se expresa aunque tácitamente se comprende.
Implicative [im'-pli-ca-tiv], *a.* Implicativo, implicante.
Implicatively [im'-pli-ca-tiv-li], *adv.* Por implicación.
Implicit [im-plis'-it], *a.* 1. Implícito, lo que se da a entender sin expresarlo. 2. Fundado en la confianza o fe absolutas, sin reserva, que se tiene en otra persona. *With implicit faith*, Con fe ciega, sin vacilación ni reserva.
Implicitly [im-plis'-it-li], *adv.* Implícitamente, tácitamente; sin reserva, sin dudas ni preguntas.
Implicitness [im-plis'-it-nes], *s.* Calidad de implícito.
Implied [im-plaid'], *a.* y *pp.* de IMPLY. Contenido, incluído, aunque no formalmente expresado; implícito.
Impliedly [im-plai'-ed-li], *adv.* Por implicación o ilación.
Imploration [im-plo-rê'-shun], *s.* Imploración, ruego humilde y ferviente.
Implore [im-plōr'], *va.* Implorar, suplicar, rogar, pedir con instancia.
Implorer [im-plōr'-ęr], *s.* Solicitador.
Imploringly [im-plōr'-ing-li], *adv.* De un modo suplicante, implorante.
Imply [im-plai'], *va.* 1. Dar a entender (una significación no expresada), querer decir; significar, denotar. 2. Implicar, envolver, enredar. 3. Adscribir, atribuir.
Impolicy [im-pel'-i-si], *s.* Imprudencia, poca maña; indiscreción, impolítica.
Impolite [im-po-lait'], *a.* Descortés, grosero, impolítico.
Impoliteness [im-po-lait'-nes], *s.* Impolítica, falta de cortesía.
Impolitic [im-pel'-i-tic], *a.* 1. Imprudente, indiscreto, falto de prudencia y discreción. 2. Impolítico, perjudicial para los intereses pendientes.
Impolitically [im-po-lit'-i-cal-i], **Impoliticly** [im-pel'-i-tic-li], *adv.* Sin previsión ni arte, impolíticamente, indiscretamente.
Imponderability [im-pen"-dęr-a-bil'-i-ti], *s.* Imponderabilidad, carencia de peso.
Imponderable [im-pen'-dęr-a-bl], *a.* Imponderable, que no tiene peso perceptible; como el calor, la luz, la electricidad, etc.
Imporosity [im-po-res'-i-ti], *s.* Falta de poros, densidad.
Imporous [im-pō'-rus], *a.* Sólido, macizo, que no tiene poros.
Import [im-pōrt'], *va.* 1. Importar, introducir géneros extranjeros en un país. 2. Denotar, significar. 3. Importar, ser de entidad, tener importancia, interesar en alto grado. 4. Implicar, envolver; introducir en general.—*vn.* Convenir, importar, ser de entidad.
Import [im'-pōrt], *s.* 1. Tendencia, sentido, significación; dirección. 2. Los géneros importados o que se introducen de un país extranjero; más usado en plural. 3. Importancia; momento, peso, consecuencia, entidad. *Import-duty*, Derechos de entrada.
Importable [im-pōrt'-a-bl], *a.* Importable.
Importance [im-pērt'-ans], *s.* 1. Importancia, momento, consecuencia. 2. Autoridad, crédito, dignidad social. 3. Importunidad, vanidad, presunción.
Important [im-pērt'-ant], *a.* 1. Importante, que es de importancia, consecuencia o valor. 2. De pretensiones, pomposo, afectado.
Importantly [im-pērt'-ant-li], *adv.* Importantemente.
Importation [im-por-tê'-shun], *s.* 1. Importación, entrada o introducción de géneros extranjeros. 2. La persona o cosa importada.
Importer [im-pērt'-ęr], *s.* Introductor de géneros extranjeros.
Importing [im-pōrt'-ing], *a.* Importador.
Importunacy [im-pēr'-chu (o -tịū) -na-si], *s.* Importunidad.
Importunate [im-pēr'-chu (o -tịu) -nęt], *a.* Importuno, pesado, insistente; urgente, apremiante.
Importunately [im-pēr'-chu (o -tịū) -nęt-li], *adv.* Importunamente.
Importunateness [im-per'-chu (o -tịū) -nęt-nes], *s.* Importunidad, solicitación incesante.
Importune [im-per'-tiūn], *va.* Importunar, instar, pedir con instancia; cansar con frecuentes o incesantes solicitaciones.
Importuner [im-pēr-tiūn'-ęr], *s.* Importunador.
Importunity [im-per-tiū'-ni-ti], *s.* Importunación, importunidad.
Imposable [im-pōz'-a-bl], *a.* Pechero, imponible, sujeto a impuestos.

Impose [im-pōz'], *va.* 1. Imponer cargas, obligaciones, leyes, u otra cosa. 2. Colocar por influencia o fuerza; prescribir, infligir. 3. Imponer las manos el obispo. 4. (Impr.) Imponer, colocar en la rama. 5. Engañar, hacer creer y persuadir con engaños alguna falsedad. *To impose on* o *upon*, Engañar, hacer creer una cosa falsa. *I have been imposed upon*, Me han engañado.

Imposer [im-pōz'-ẹr], *s.* El que impone, manda o encarga.

Imposing [im-pōz'-ing], *a.* y *pa.* Imponente, impresivo, que infunde respeto.—*s.* (Impr.) Imposición, la acción de colocar en su debido orden las páginas y los blancos. *Imposing-stone* o *-table*, Piedra, o mesa, de imponer.

Imposition [im-po-zish'-un], *s.* 1. Imposición, la acción de poner una cosa sobre otra. 2. Imposición, la acción de imponer. 3. Imposición, carga, tributo u obligación que se impone. 4. Opresión, violencia. 5. Impostura, ficción, fraude, engaño. 6. La tarea extraordinaria que se da a los jóvenes por castigo. *To prevent imposition*, Para precaverse de toda impostura. *The imposition of hands*, La imposición de las manos del obispo en la confirmación o la ordenación.

Impossibility [im-pos-i-bil'-i-ti], *s.* 1. Imposibilidad. 2. Imposible.

Impossible [im-pos'-i-bl], *a.* Imposible.

Impost [im'-pōst], *s.* 1. Impuesto, tributo, gabela, contribución. 2. (Arq.) Imposta, especie de cornisa sobre que asienta el arco, bóveda, etc.

Impostor [im-pos'-tẹr], *s.* Impostor, el que finge y engaña o el que atribuye a otro falsamente alguna cosa.

Imposture [im-pos'-chur], *s.* Impostura, fraude, engaño, falsedad.

Impotence [im'-po-tens], **Impotency** [im'-po-ten-si], *s.* 1. Impotencia, falta de fuerza física o intelectual; debilidad. 2. Impotencia, incapacidad de procrear. 3. ¿Desenfreno, arrebato, desarreglo de alguna pasión.

Impotent [im'-po-tent], *a.* 1. Impotente, sin potencia, que carece de vigor o de fuerza; (Ant.) imposibilitado por naturaleza o por enfermedad; impedido, tullido o baldado de algún miembro. 2. Impotente, incapaz de engendrar o concebir; aplícase más generalmente al varón o al macho. 3. Desenfrenado, desarreglado, que carece de imperio sobre sí mismo.—*s.* 1. Alfeñique, persona delicada. 2. Hombre impotente, falto de vigor sexual.

Impotently [im'-po-tent-li], *adv.* Impotentemente.

Impound [im-paund'], *va.* 1. Encerrar, acorralar, meter los ganados en el corral; aprisionar, restringir. 2. (For.) Depositar, poner en la custodia de un tribunal de justicia.

Impoverish [im-pov'-ẹr-ish], *va.* 1. Empobrecer, reducir a alguno a la pobreza o la indigencia. 2. Minorar la calidad o la fertilidad de una cosa; deteriorar. *Impoverished blood*, Sangre deteriorada, empobrecida.

Impoverishment [im-pov'-ẹr-ish-mẹnt], *s.* Empobrecimiento.

Impracticability [im-prac-ti-ca-bil'-i-ti], *s.* 1. Impracticabilidad, el estado o la cualidad de no ser hacedero. 2. Cosa no hacedera, no factible, impracticable.

Impracticable [im-prac'-ti-ca-bl], *a.* 1. Impracticable, imposible, infactible, lo que no es hacedero. 2. No práctico, inútil, de ningún servicio. 3. Intratable, irrazonable, con quien no se puede vivir; terco; dícese de las personas que tienen mal genio.

Impracticableness [im-prac'-ti-ca-bl-nes], *s.* 1. Imposibilidad. 2. Terquedad, obstinación.

Imprecate [im'-prẹ-kêt], *va.* Imprecar, maldecir, desear abiertamente algún mal para sí o para otro.

Imprecation [im-prẹ-kê'-shun], *s.* Imprecación, maldición.

Imprecatory [im'-prẹ-ca-to-ri], *a.* Imprecatorio.

Impregnable [im-preg'-na-bl], *a.* 1. Inexpugnable, inconquistable. 2. Impregnable, capaz de impregnación o de impregnarse.

Impregnate [im-preg'-nêt], *va.* 1. Empreñar, hacer concebir a la hembra; fecundar. 2. Impregnar, comunicar las virtudes o calidades de una cosa a otra. 3. Fecundar, imbuir, penetrar con un principio o elemento activo.

Impregnate, *a.* Impregnado; empreñado.

Impregnation [im-preg-nê'-shun], *s.* 1. Fecundación, impregnación; fertilización; infusión. 2. El principio o elemento con el cual se impregna una cosa.

Impresario [im-pre-sā'-ri-ō], *s.* Empresario.

Imprescriptible [im-prẹ-script'-i-bl], *a.* Imprescriptible, que no se puede adquirir ni perder por el uso o la prescripción.

Impress [im-pres'], *va.* 1. Imprimir, estampar; formar o fijar por medio de la presión. 2. Impresionar, fijar en el ánimo. 3. Influir, v. g. para hacer tomar una determinación. 4. Marcar por medio de la presión; mellar. 5. Hacer una leva, reclutar soldados o marineros contra su voluntad.

Impress [im'-pres], *s.* 1. Impresión, señal, marca, figura o imagen producida por medio de la presión. 2. Empresa, divisa, lema, mote. 3. Leva, recluta de soldados o marineros hecha contra su voluntad. 4. Impresión, efecto que causan las cosas espirituales en el ánimo.

Impressibility [im-pres-i-bil'-i-ti], *s.* La capacidad de ser impresionado o de recibir impresiones.

Impressible [im-pres'-i-bl], *a.* Impresionable, capaz de recibir impresiones o de ser impresionado; que puede ser estampado, impreso, marcado (sobre otro cuerpo o cosa).

Impression [im-presh'-un], *s.* 1. Impresión, la acción y efecto de imprimir. 2. Impresión, la marca, señal o huella que una cosa deja sobre otra apretándola. 3. Impresión, el efecto visible o material producido por cualquier agencia. 4. Impresión, efecto que causan las cosas en el ánimo, en los sentidos o en la conciencia. 5. Recuerdo ligero o confuso; creencia que se tiene sin fundamentos suficientes. 6. Impresión, edición, todos los ejemplares de una obra ya impresa; también es la marca o señal del tipo, de los grabados, etc. *The enemy made no impression on the fort*, El enemigo no causó efecto material en el fuerte. *The impression of a seal, of type*, La marca o señal de un sello, del tipo. *I have an impression that the color was lilac*, Creo (ó me parece) que el color era lila.

Impressionable [im-presh'-un-a-bl], *a.* Impresionable, susceptible de recibir impresiones; que se impresiona con facilidad. *V.* EMOTIONAL.

Impressionism [im-presh'-un-izm], *s.* (Art y Lit.) Impresionismo.

Impressive [im-pres'-iv], *a.* Impresivo, que produce impresión o tiene la facultad de producirla; que excita la admiración o la emoción, o que atrae la atención.

Impressively [im-pres'-iv-li], *adv.* De un modo poderoso o eficaz.

Impressiveness [im-pres'-iv-nes], *s.* La calidad de hacer impresión; carácter propio para impresionar, o causar admiración.

Impressment [im-pres'-mẹnt], *s.* Leva, el acto de reclutar forzosamente para la marina o de apropiar para el uso público.

Imprest [im'-prest], *s.* (Ingl.) Pago adelantado de dinero.

Imprimatur [im-pri-mê'-tūr], *s.* 1. Voz latina que significa "Imprímase": decreto que autoriza o permite imprimir un libro. 2. Cédula, permiso, licencia en general.

Imprint [im-print'], *va.* 1. Imprimir, estampar, marcar por medio de presión. 2. Imprimir, señalar o estampar las letras en papel, pergamino o alguna tela. 3. Fijar, grabar en el ánimo o en la memoria.

Imprint [im'-print], *s.* 1. Impresión, la marca o señal que resulta de imprimir, estampar o apretar. 2. Impresión que deja o efecto que causa alguna cosa. 3. Nombre del impresor o del editor puesto en un libro u otra publicación.

Imprison [im-priz'-n], *va.* Encerrar, encarcelar, poner preso, aprisionar.

Imprisonment [im-priz'-n-mẹnt], *s.* Reclusión, prisión, encierro, encarcelación. *False imprisonment*, Prisión ilegal.

Improbability [im-prob-a-bil'-i-ti], *s.* Improbabilidad, inverosimilitud.

Improbable [im-prob'-a-bl], *a.* Improbable, lo que no tiene apariencia de verdad; inverisímil.

Improbably [im-prob'-a-bli], *adv.* Improbablemente.

Improbation [im-pro-bê'-shun], *s.* Desaprobación, reprobación.

Improbity [im-prob'-i-ti], *s.* Falta de probidad, improbidad.

Improficience [im-pro-fish'-ens], *s.* Falta de aprovechamiento o de adelantamiento.

Impromptu [im-promp'-tiū o tū], *a.* Hecho, efectuado o pronunciado sin premeditación; *adv.* de repente, en el acto.—*s.* Un repente, un ímpetu; composición u obra improvisada.

Improper [im-prop'-ẹr], *a.* 1. Impropio, inepto, no justo ni conveniente en vista de las circunstancias. 2. Contrario a las reglas establecidas o a las buenas costumbres; irregular, impolítico; indecente, grosero; incorrecto.

Improperly [im-prop'-ẹr-li], *adv.* Impropiamente; imperfectamente.

Impropriate [im-prō'-pri-êt], *va.* 1. Apropiarse, tomar para sí alguna cosa haciéndose dueño de ella. 2. Secularizar, enajenar la posesión de los bienes o réditos eclesiásticos dándola a los legos o seglares.

Impropriate, *a.* Secularizado: se aplica a los bienes que habiendo pertenecido a la iglesia pasan a manos de seglares.

Impropriation [im-pro-pri-é'-shun], *s.* 1. Posesión exclusiva. 2. Venta o secularización de los bienes eclesiásticos.
Impropriator [im-prō'-pri-a-tẹr], *s.* 1. El que se apropia alguna cosa. 2. El lego o secular que posee bienes eclesiásticos.
Impropriety [im-pro-prai'-e-ti], *s.* Impropiedad, incongruencia, descortesía; cualquier cosa impropia.
Improvability [im-prūv-a-bil'-i-ti], **Improvableness** [im-prūv'-a-bl-nes], *s.* Capacidad de mejorar o perfeccionarse; perfectibilidad; susceptibilidad de emplearse con ventaja.
Improvable [im-prūv'-a-bl], *a.* 1. Mejorable, perfectible; de aquí, laborable, capaz de cultivo y beneficio. 2. Que puede emplearse con ventaja o ser aprovechado.
Improvably [im-prūv'-a-bli], *adv.* De un modo que admite mejora, mejorablemente.
Improve [im-prūv'], *va.* y *vn.* 1. Mejorar, adelantar, aumentar o perfeccionar alguna cosa; beneficiar, abonar (las tierras), embellecer, hermosear; corregir, enmendar, rectificar; cultivar, poner en producción; explotar, trabajar, una mina, una hacienda, etc. 2. Mejorar, adelantar en perfección, aprovechar; utilizar, aprovecharse de, sacar partido de alguna cosa.—*vn.* 1. Mejorarse, adelantarse, hacer progresos. 2. (Com.) Subir, encarecer, aumentar de valor. *The price of wool has improved,* El precio de la lana ha subido. *The markets are improving,* Los mercados están en alza. *To improve an opportunity,* Aprovechar una oportunidad, una ocasión. *Some things improve by being kept,* Hay cosas que se mejoran conservándolas. *We amend a bad, but improve a good thing,* Se corrige lo que es malo, pero se mejora lo que es bueno.
Improvement [im-prūv'-mẹnt], *s.* 1. Mejora, mejoría, medra, progreso, adelantamiento o aumento de alguna cosa. 2. Mejoramiento, mejora; empleo ventajoso, aplicación; cosa de que se saca partido. 3. Instrucción, edificación. 4. Cambios u obras útiles hechos en alguna cosa, como en una fábrica, en los ríos y puertos, etc.
Improver [im-prūv'-ẹr], *s.* 1. Adelantador, mejorador, enmendador. 2. Aprendiza de costurera o modista.
Improvidence [im-prev'-i-dens], *s.* Descuido, falta de previsión.
Improvident [im-prev'-i-dent], *a.* Impróvido, descuidado, inconsiderado, imprudente.
Improvidently [im-prev'-i-dent-li], *adv.* Impróvidamente.
Improvisate [im-prev'-i-sêt], *a.* Improvisado, no premeditado.
Improvisation [im-prev-i-sé'-shun], *s.* 1. Improvisación, acción y efecto de improvisar, de hablar o componer sin preparación anterior. 2. Obra improvisada, particularmente una composición poética.
Improvisator [im-prev-i-sé'-tẹr], *s.* V. IMPROVISER.
Improvisatorial, Improvisatory [im-prev"-i-sa-tō'-ri-al, im-prev'-i-sa-to-ri], *a.* Improvisado, que se refiere a la improvisación.
Improvise [im-pro-vaiz'], *va.* Improvisar, hablar o componer de repente, sin previo estudio ni preparación.
Improviser [im-pro-vai'-zẹr], *s.* Improvisador, el que compone o habla sin previo estudio.
Imprudence [im-prū'-dens], *s.* Imprudencia, indiscreción, inconsideración, irreflexión.
Imprudent [im-prū'-dent], *a.* Imprudente, inconsiderado, indiscreto, irreflexivo.
Imprudently [im-prū'-dent-li], *adv.* Imprudentemente, indiscretamente.
Impudence [im'-piu-dens], *s.* Impudencia, insolencia, inmodestia, desvergüenza, atrevimiento, descaro, avilantez.
Impudent [im'-piu-dent], *a.* 1. Impudente, descarado, audaz, insolente. 2. Impúdico, inmodesto, desvergonzado.
Impudently [im'-piu-dent-li], *adv.* 1. Descaradamente, impudentemente, insolentemente. 2. Impúdicamente, sin recato, inmodestamente.
Impudicity [im-piu-dis'-i-ti], *s.* Impudicicia, inmodestia, deshonestidad.
Impugn [im-piūn'], *va.* Impugnar, oponerse a lo que otro dice o hace; poner en tela de juicio, contradecir, contrariar.
Impugnable [im-piūn'-a-bl], *a.* Impugnable, que puede impugnarse.
Impugner [im-piūn'-ẹr], *s.* Impugnador.
Impulse [im'-puls], *s.* 1. Impulso, impulsión, movimiento comunicado de repente. 2. Impulso, ímpetu o estímulo, instigación, motivo. 3. Fuerza muy grande que obra o se ejerce muy poco tiempo; ímpetu, momento mecánico, debido a una fuerza.
Impulsion [im-pul'-shun], *s.* Impulsión, impulso, ímpetu.
Impulsive [im-pul'-siv], *a.* y *s.* 1. Impulsivo, que obra por impulso o emoción, más bien que por reflexión. 2. Impulsivo, que procede del impulso; que tiene fuerza impelente.
Impulsively [im-pul'-siv-li], *adv.* Por impulso, impulsivamente.
Impunity [im-piū'-ni-ti], *s.* Impunidad, falta de castigo, exención de daño o perjuicio.
Impure [im-piūr'], *a.* 1. Impuro, sucio, poco limpio; adulterado, echado a perder por la mezcla de alguna cosa extraña y perjudicial. 2. Impuro, impúdico, deshonesto, inmundo; manchado por el pecado. 3. Que contiene tachas gramaticales o idiotismos extranjeros. 4. Profano, no apto para usos religiosos.
Impurely [im-piūr'-li], *adv.* Impuramente.
Impureness [im-piūr'-nes], **Impurity** [im-piu'-ri-ti], *s.* 1. Impureza; adulteración. 2. Impureza, liviandad, deshonestidad.
Impurple [im-pūr'-pl], *a.* Purpurar, teñir de púrpura.
Imputable [im-piūt'-a-bl], *a.* Imputable, que se puede imputar o atribuir a otro.
Imputableness [im-piūt'-a-bl-nes], *s.* Imputabilidad.
Imputation [im-piu-tê'-shun], *s.* 1. Imputación, acción de imputar, achacar o atribuir a otro. 2. Acusación; reconvención, censura.
Imputative [im-piū'-ta-tiv], *a.* Imputable, transferido por imputación.
Impute [im-piūt'], *va.* Imputar, atribuir, achacar.
Imputer [im-piūt'-ẹr], *s.* Imputador.
In [in]. Preposición relativa al lugar, estado o disposición en que se hallan las cosas, al tiempo en que se hacen o sucedieron, al modo con que se hacen, etc.; y corresponde en castellano a *en, por, a, de, durante, bajo, con.* 1. En (indicando lugar). *He is in Spain,* Está en España. 2. En, de, por, con (indicando estado presente). *In his sleep,* Durante el sueño, o mientras dormía. *He is the best writer in England,* Es el mejor escritor de Inglaterra. *Crippled in his hands,* Baldado de manos. *In time,* Con tiempo. *I am in the right,* Tengo razón, estoy en mi derecho. *To be in great hopes,* Abrigar grandes esperanzas. *In writing,* Por escrito. 3. De, durante, por (indicando duración o espacio de tiempo). *In the night,* Durante la noche, de noche. *In the daytime,* De día. *In the afternoon,* Por la tarde o durante la tarde. *In a few years,* Dentro de, o a la vuelta de pocos años. *In the reign of Elizabeth,* En el reinado, o bajo el reinado, o reinando Isabel. *In the morning,* Por la mañana o a la mañana. 4. Por, a fin de, con (indicando causa). *In obedience to you,* Por obediencia a Vd. *In order to,* A fin de. *In order that,* A fin que. *In defiance of all right,* Con menosprecio de toda justicia. *In* denota también el poder o aptitud de hacer una cosa, y en este caso se traduce generalmente cambiando el giro de la oración en castellano. *It is not in him to do it,* No puede hacerlo o no es capaz de hacerlo. También expresa la proporción que hay entre dos cosas, y entonces corresponde a en, de o entre. *Not one in a hundred will do it,* No hay uno en ciento o entre ciento que lo haga. *Inasmuch as,* En cuanto, por cuanto; puesto que, en vista de. *In that,* (Ant.) Porque, a causa de. *In the meantime* o *in the meanwhile,* Entre tanto. *In so far,* Hasta allí. *In so far as,* En cuanto a, a medida que, tocante a. —*adv.* 1. Dentro, adentro. 2. En casa, en su casa; ahí, aquí o allí. *Are you in?* ¿Está Vd. ahí? *To be in,* Estar aquí o allí. 3. En poder de, en su lugar. *He drove the nail in,* Clavó el clavo en su lugar. *When the tide was in,* En la bajamar. *To go in, to come in,* o *to walk in,* Entrar. *In* está muy a menudo unido a los verbos y muda casi siempre su sentido recto. *Walk in,* Entre Vd. o pase Vd. adelante. *In* se usa en composición, expresando generalmente negación o privación. *To be in for it,* (1) Estar deseoso de algo en particular, o comprometido a seguir una conducta determinada. (2) (Fam.) Al revés me la vestí, y ándese así; no tener medios de evitar una cosa, v. g. un castigo. *To be in it,* (Ger.) Participar en una cosa, especialmente si es próspera o afortunada; por lo general con negación. *To be in with,* (Fam.) Ser íntimo o estar en favor con alguien. *In-and-in, adv.* (1) De una misma casta o raza. (2) (Fig.) Con un movimiento continuo recíproco. *To breed in-and-in,* Aparear, juntar animales de la misma casta.
Inability [in-a-bil'-i-ti], *s.* Inhabilidad, incapacidad, ineptitud, insuficiencia; impotencia, falta de fuerza; falta de medios suficientes.
Inabusively [in-a-biū'-siv-li], *adv.* Sin abuso.

Inaccessibility [in-ac-ses-i-bil'-i-ti], *s.* Inaccesibilidad.
Inaccessible [in-ac-ses'-i-bl], *a.* Inaccesible.
Inaccessibly [in-ac-ses'-i-bli], *adv.* Inaccesiblemente.
Inaccuracy [in-ac'-yu-ra-si], *s.* 1. Inexactitud, falta de exactitud. 2. Falta, defecto, error; impropiedad de una expresión.
Inaccurate [in-ac'-yu-ret], *a.* Inexacto, erróneo, incorrecto.
Inaccurately [in-ac'-yu-ret-li], *adv.* Incorrectamente; inexactamente.
Inaction [in-ac'-shun], *s.* Inacción, abstención de trabajo, descanso; holgazanería.
Inactive [in-ac'-tiv], *a.* 1. Inactivo. 2. Indolente, flojo, negligente; perezoso. 3. Inerte; que no tiene la facultad de moverse.
Inactively [in-ac'-tiv-li], *adv.* Inactivamente, indolentemente; perezosamente; en estado de inercia.
Inactivity [in-ac-tiv'-i-ti], *s.* 1. Inactividad. 2. Ociosidad, desidia, flojedad.
Inadequacy [in-ad'-e-cwe-si], *s.* 1. Insuficiencia; desproporción. 2. Estado incompleto; imperfección.
Inadequate [in-ad'-e-cwet], *a.* Inadecuado, insuficiente, desproporcionado, incompleto.
Inadequately [in-ad'-e-cwet-li], *adv.* Inadecuadamente, incompletamente, sin medios suficientes.
Inadequateness [in-ad'-e-cwet-nes], *s.* Defecto de proporción; imperfección.
Inadmissible [in-ad-mis'-i-bl], *a.* Inadmisible, que no puede admitirse, recibirse ni permitirse.
Inadvertence [in-ad-vert'-ens], **Inadvertency** [in-ad-ver'-ten-si], *s.* Inadvertencia.
Inadvertent [in-ad-vert'-ent], *a.* 1. Inadvertido, hecho sin intención, sin designio, accidental. 2. Atolondrado, negligente, descuidado.
Inadvertently [in-ad-vert'-ent-li], *adv.* Inadvertidamente, por falta de atención, no hecho adrede; atolondradamente.
Inadvisable [in-ad-vaiz'a-bl], *a.* Falto de prudencia, impropio, inconveniente.
‡**Inaffability** [in-af-a-bil'-i-ti], *s.* Reserva, cautela en la conversación.
Inaffable [in-af'-a-bl], *a.* Reservado; descortés; desamorado, poco afable o cariñoso.
Inalienable [in-él'-yen-a-bl], *a.* Inalienable o inajenable.
Inalienably [in-él'-yen-a-bli], *adv.* De un modo inalienable.
Inalterability [in-ōl-ter-a-bil'-i-ti], *s.* Inalterabilidad.
Inalterable [in-ōl'-ter-a-bl], *a.* Inalterable. *V.* UNALTERABLE.
Inamorata [in-ā-mo-rā'-ta], *f.* Enamorada, dulce amiga; la mujer de quién alguien está enamorado.
Inamorato [in-ā-mo-rā'-tō], *s.* El que está enamorado: voces tomadas del italiano.
Inane [in-ēn], *a.* 1. Turulato, atontado, falto de inteligencia, mentecato. 2. Inane, lo que está vacío o desocupado.—*s.* Vacío, espacio desocupado.
Inanimate, Inanimated [in-an'-i-mēt, ed], *a.* 1. Desprovisto de vida animal. 2. Inanimado, falto de animación o de vida; exánime; sin alma ni espíritu.
Inanimateness, Inanimation [in-an'-i-mēt-nes, in-an-i-mé'-shun], *s.* Falta de animación, de vida, de espíritu.
Inanition [in-a-nish'-un], *s.* Inanición, debilidad por falta de alimento; condición de hallarse vacío o desocupado.
Inanity [in-an'-i-ti], *s.* Vacuidad; vanidad; inutilidad, nulidad.
Inappeasable [in-ap-píz'-a-bl], *a.* Incapaz de apaciguarse o aplacarse; que no puede ser satisfecho.
Inappetence [in-ap'-e-tens], **Inappetency** [in-ap'-e-ten-si], *s.* Inapetencia.
Inapplicability [in-ap-li-ca-bil'-i-ti], *s.* Ineptitud para algún objeto particular.
Inapplicable [in-ap'-li-ca-bl], *a.* Inaplicable.
Inapplication [in-ap-li-ké'-shun], *s.* Inaplicación, desaplicación, desidia, indolencia.
Inapposite [in-ap'-o-zit], *a.* No pertinente, fuera de propósito, no apropiado, poco conveniente.
Inappreciable [in-ap-prí'-shi-a-bl], *a.* Inapreciable, inestimable.
Inapprehensible [in-ap-pre-hen'-si-ble], *a.* Ininteligible, incapaz de comprenderse.
Inapprehension [in-ap-pre-hen'-shun], *s.* Falta de aprensión.
Inapprehensive [in-ap-pre-hen'-siv], *a.* Negligente, descuidado, indolente.
Inapproachable [in-ap-prōch'-a-bl], *a.* Inaccesible, de difícil acceso; aquello a que uno no se puede acercar.
Inappropriate [in-ap-prō'-pri-ēt], *a.* Poco apropiado, inadecuado, que no conviene a una cosa, impropio.
Inappropriately [in-ap-prō'-pri-ēt-li], *adv.* Impropiamente, fuera del caso.
Inappropriateness [in-ap-prō'-pri-ēt-nes], *s.* Impropiedad, falta de conveniencia.
Inaptitude [in-apt'-i-tud], *s.* Ineptitud, insuficiencia.
Inarable [in-ar'-a-bl], *a.* Incultivable, no arable.
Inarch [in-ārch'], *va.* Injertar o juntar dos ramas de árboles diferentes; injertar por aproximación.
Inarticulate [in-ar-tic'-yu-let], *a.* 1. Inarticulado, articulado o pronunciado confusa o indistintamente; mudo, incapaz de hablar articuladamente. 2. (Zool.) Inarticulado, que no tiene articulaciones o segmentos.
Inarticulately [in-ar-tic'-yu-let-li], *adv.* De un modo inarticulado.
Inarticulateness [in-ar-tic'-yu-let-nes], *s.* Inarticulación.
Inarticulation [in-ar-tic-yu-lé'-shun], *s.* Falta de claridad en la articulación de las palabras.
Inartificial [in-ar-ti-fish'-al], *a.* 1. Lo que es contrario a las reglas del arte; construído sin plan ni maña. 2. Natural, simple, sencillo, sin artificio.
Inasmuch [in-az-much'], *adv.* Visto, o puesto que, en vista de, ya que; en cuanto a, a medida que. Va siempre seguido de *as.*
Inattention [in-at-ten'-shun], *s.* Desatención, descuido, distracción, inadvertencia.
Inattentive [in-at-ten'-tiv], *a.* Desatento, descuidado, atolondrado.
Inattentively [in-at-ten'-tiv-li], *adv.* Descuidadamente, sin atención.
Inaudibility, Inaudibleness [in-ō-di-bil'-i-ti, in-ō'-di-bl-nes], *s.* Dificultad o incapacidad de ser oído.
Inaudible [in-ō'-di-bl], *a.* Inaudible, no oíble, que no puede oirse, o que no se deja oir.
Inaugural [in-ō'-giu-ral], *a.* Inaugural, relativo a una inauguración.
Inaugurate [in-ō'-giu-rēt], *va.* 1. Inaugurar, consagrar, dedicar. 2. Investir de un cargo con las ceremonias acostumbradas; instalar. 3. Principiar, originar, poner en operación o en movimiento.
Inauguration [in-ō-giu-ré'-shun], *s.* Inauguración, instalación, exaltación; el acto o la ceremonia de inaugurar, de investir con un cargo, de poner en operación, etc., hecha con cierto aparato.
Inauguratory [in-ō'-giu-ra-to-ri], *a.* Inauguratorio, que pertenece a la inauguración.
Inauspicious [in-ōs-pish'-us], *a.* Poco propicio, desfavorable, que pronostica mal, infeliz.
Inauspiciously [in-ōs-pish'-us-li], *adv.* Desgraciadamente, bajo malos auspicios.
Inauspiciousness [in-ōs-pish'-us-nes], *s.* Infelicidad, malos auspicios.
Inbeing [in-bí'-ing], *s.* Inherencia, inseparabilidad.
Inboard [in'-bōrd], *a.* y *adv.* 1. (Mar.) Interior al casco; dentro del casco. 2. (Mec.) Hacia el interior.
Inborn [in'-bērn], *a.* Ínsito, innato, connatural, de nacimiento.
Inbreathe [in-brídh'], *va.* Inspirar, infundir por inspiración.
Inbred [in'-bred], *a.* Ínsito, innato, natural, nacido dentro de nosotros mismos.
Inbreed [in-bríd'], *vn.* Producir, crear.
Inca [in'-ca], *s.* Inca, título de los soberanos que reinaron en el Perú hasta la conquista de Pizarro.
Incage [in-kéj'], *va.* 1. Enjaular, encerrar, poner dentro de una jaula. 2. Encerrar dentro de un espacio muy estrecho.
Incagement [in-kéj'-ment], *s.* El acto de enjaular.
Incalculable [in-cal'-kiu-la-bl], *a.* Incalculable.
Incalescence [in-ca-les'-ens], **Incalescency** [in-ca-les'-en-si], *s.* Principio de calor, calor incipiente, progresivo.
Incalescent [in-ca-les'-ent], *a.* Cuyo calor va aumentando.
Incandescence [in-can-des'-ens], *s.* Incandescencia, candencia, el estado de un cuerpo hecho ascua.
Incandescent [in-can-des'-ent], *a.* Incandescente, candente, hecho ascua. *Incandescent lamp,* Lámpara eléctrica incandescente; también lámpara para gas cuya luz se aumenta mediante la incandescencia de una redecilla de material refractario.
Incantation [in-can-té'-shun], *s.* Encantación, encantamiento, encanto, arte mágica.
Incantatory [in-can'-ta-to-ri], *a.* Mágico; lo que pertenece a los encantamientos.
Incanton [in-can'-ten], *va.* Agregar un distrito a otro: dícese regularmente de los cantones suizos, y entonces significa agregar a uno de los cantones un país que antes no estaba unido a ninguno de ellos.
Incapability [in-ké-pa-bil'-i-ti], **Incapableness** [in-ké'-pa-bl-nes], *s.* Inhabilidad, incapacidad, falta de capacidad.
Incapable [in-ké'-pa-bl], *a.* 1. Incapaz, inhábil. 2. Incapaz, inepto, falto de talento, que no puede comprender o entender algo. 3. Incapaz de una acción baja, de mentir, de hurtar, etc. 4. Inhabilitado o declarado inhábil o incapaz de go-

zar algún derecho, prerrogativa, etc.

Incapacious [in-ca-pe'-shus], *a.* Estrecho, angosto, poco capaz.

Incapaciousness [in-ca-pê'-shus-nes], *s.* Estrechez, angostura.

Incapacitate [in-ca-pas'-i-têt], *va.* 1. Inhabilitar, imposibilitar a uno para alguna cosa; debilitar. 2. Inhabilitar, declarar a uno incapaz de gozar alguna cosa.

Incapacitation [in-ca-pas-i-tê'-shun], *s.* Inhabilitación, la acción y efecto de inhabilitar.

Incapacity [in-ca-pas'-i-ti], *s.* Incapacidad, falta de capacidad, insuficiencia.

Incarcerate [in-cār'-sẹr-êt], *va.* Encarcelar, aprisionar, meter o poner a uno en la cárcel.

Incarcerate, *a.* Encarcelado, preso.

Incarceration [in-car-sẹr-ê'-shun], *s.* 1. Encarcelamiento, prisión. 2. (Cir.) Estrangulación, v. g. de una hernia.

Incarnadine [in-cār'-na-din], *va.* Encarnar, dar color de carne.—*a.* Encarnadino, color encarnado claro; color de carne.

Incarnate [in-cār'-nẹt], *va.* Encarnar, vestir de carne.

Incarnate, *a.* 1. Encarnado, vestido o incorporado con carne. 2. Encarnado, de color de carne.

Incarnation [in-cār-nê'-shun], *s.* 1. Encarnación, encarnadura. 2. (Cir.) Encarnación, desarrollo de tejido en una herida cuando está en vías de curación.

Incarnative [in-cār'-na-tiv], *s.* Encarnativo, remedio que se usa con el objeto de apresurar la cicatrización de las heridas.

Incase [in-kês'], *va.* Encajar, incluir, encerrar, encajonar. *V.* ENCASE.

Incask [in-cqsc'], *va.* Entonelar.

Incastellated [in-cas'-tel-ê-ted], *a.* Encastillado, confinado o encerrado dentro de un castillo.

Incautious [in-cō'-shus], *a.* Incauto, descuidado, negligente, imprudente.

Incautiously [in-cō'-shus-li], *adv.* Incautamente, descuidadamente.

Incautiousness [in-cō'-shus-nes], *s.* Falta de cautela, descuido, negligencia.

Incavation [in-ca-vê'-shun], *s.* Ahuecamiento, la acción de cavar y también la excavación misma.

Incendiarism [in-sen'-di-a-rizm], *s.* Acto de incendiar maliciosamente, de pegar fuego adrede.

Incendiary [in-sen'-di-ẹ-ri], *s.* Incendiario, el que maliciosamente incendia algún edificio, mieses, etc.—*a.* 1. Incendiario, relativo al incendio criminal. 2. Que sirve para pegar fuego. 3. Inflamatorio, que tiende a inflamar las pasiones o suscitar sediciones; cizañero, sedicioso, revoltoso.

Incense [in'-sens], *s.* 1. Incienso. 2. Incienso, alabanza lisonjera. 3. Cualquier perfume agradable.

Incense [in-sens'], *va.* 1. Exasperar, irritar, sulfurar, encolerizar. 2. [in'-sens] Incensar, perfumar con incienso.

Incensement [in-sens'-mẹnt], *s.* Rabia, ira, furia, cólera, arrebato.

Incension [in-sen'-shun], *s.* (Poco us.) Encendimiento, el acto de encender, de pegar fuego, o el de estar ardiendo y abrasándose.

Incensive [in-sen'-siv], *a.* Incitativo; que tiende a excitar o provocar.

Incensor [in-sen'-sẹr], *s.* Incitador, el que provoca la ira o inflama las pasiones.

Incensory [in-sen'-so-ri], *s.* Incensario, el braserillo en que se quema el incienso para incensar.

Incentive [in-sen'-tiv], *s.* Incentivo, estímulo, impulso, motivo.—*a.* Incitativo, que anima o impele.

Inception [in-sep'-shun], *s.* El principio de alguna cosa; período inicial; estreno.

Inceptive [in-sep'-tiv], *a.* Incipiente, incoativo, que principia o comienza.

Inceptor [in-sep'-tẹr], *s.* 1. Principiante. 2. Nombre que se da en las universidades inglesas a la persona admitida a sufrir el examen necesario para recibir el grado de maestro en artes.

Inceration [in-sẹ-rê'-shun], *s.* Enceramiento, la acción de cubrir alguna cosa con cera.

Incerative [in'-se-rê-tiv], *a.* Lo que se pega como cera.

Incertitude [in-ser'-ti-tiūd], *s.* 1. Incertidumbre, duda. 2. Obscuridad.

Incessable [in-ses'-a-bl], *a.* Incesable, continuo, incesante, constante.

Incessant [in-ses'-ant], *a.* Incesante, constante, incesable.

Incessantly [in-ses'-ant-li], *adv.* Incesantemente.

Incest [in'-sest], *s.* Incesto.

Incestuous [in-ses'-chu (o -tịu) -us], *a.* Incestuoso.

Incestuously [in-ses'-chu (o -tịu) -us-li], *adv.* Incestuosamente.

Incestuousness [in-ses'-chu (o -tịu) -us-nes], *s.* El estado de ser incestuosa una persona o cosa.

Inch [inch], *s.* 1. Pulgada, la duodécima parte de un pie: (= 25.4 milímetros). 2. Pizca, una porción mínima o muy pequeña de alguna cosa. *Within an inch,* Poco más o menos. *Within an inch of,* A dos dedos de. *Inch by inch,* Palmo a palmo o a pulgadas. *By inches* o *inch by inch,* (Fam.) A pedacitos. *Every inch,* Cabalmente. *Every inch a man,* Hombre hecho y derecho. *Miners' inch,* Pulgada de fontanero. *V.* WATER-INCH. *Inch-pound,* El esfuerzo necesario para elevar una libra de peso a una pulgada de altura en el espacio de un segundo.

Inch, *va.* Arrojar o echar a uno de donde estaba poco a poco o a palmos; hacer valer una cosa todo lo posible; medir por pulgadas. En general este verbo va unido en su significación activa con la preposición *out.*—*vn.* Avanzar o retirarse poco a poco y haciendo paradas.

Inchamber [in-chêm'-bẹr], *va.* (Poco us.) Encerrar en un aposento o habitación.

Inched [incht], *a.* 1. Marcado o dividido en pulgadas. 2. De tantas pulgadas. *A five-inched cable,* Un cable de cinco pulgadas.

Inchoate [in'-co-ẹt], *a.* Principiado, comenzado, incoado, empezado.—*va.* (Poco us.) Incoar, principiar, empezar.

Inchoately [in'-co-ẹt-li], *adv.* En el primer grado.

Inchoation [in-co-ê'-shun], *s.* Principio.

Inchoative [in-co'-a-tiv], *a.* Incipiente, incoativo.

Incidence [in'-si-dens], *s.* 1. Incidencia, la dirección en que una línea, un plano o un cuerpo se encuentra con otro. 2. Carga, como la de una contribución, que recae o grava desigualmente.

Incident [in'-si-dent], *a.* 1. Incidente, que cae sobre o dentro de algo, que toca o choca desde afuera. 2. Probable, acontecedero. 3. Casual, fortuito; concomitante, dependiente de.

Incident, *s.* 1. Incidente, casualidad, acontecimiento. 2. Episodio, digresión.

Incidental [in-si-dent'-al], *a.* 1. Contingente; concomitante, que sobreviene en el curso de otra cosa, que la acompaña. 2. Casual, que sobreviene o acontece sin designio o irregularmente.

Incidentally [in-si-dent'-al-i], *adv.* Incidentemente.

Incidently [in'-si-dent-li], *adv.* Ocasionalmente, casualmente.

Incinerate [in-sin'-ẹr-êt], *va.* Incinerar, reducir una cosa a cenizas, consumir por medio del fuego.

Incineration [in-sin-ẹr-ê'-shun], *s.* Incineración.

Incipiency [in-sip'-i-en-si], *s.* Principio.

Incipient [in-sip'-i-ent], *a.* Incipiente.

Incircle, *va.* *V. To* ENCIRCLE.

Incircumscriptible [in-sẹr-cum-script'-i-bl], *a.* (Poco us.) Que no puede ser circunscripto.

Incircumspection [in-sẹr-cum-spec'-shun], *s.* Inadvertencia, falta de advertencia; falta de circunspección o de prudencia.

Incise [in-saiz'], *va.* Tajar, hacer incisión, cortar en, grabar, esculpir en hueco.

Incised [in-saizd'], *a.* Inciso, cortado.

Incision [in-sizh'-un], *s.* Incisión; corte, recorte.

Incisive [in-sai'-siv], *a.* Incisivo, incisorio; agudo; mordaz. *An incisive style,* Estilo agudo, mordaz.

Incisor [in-sai'-sẹr], *a.* Incisivo, apto para cortar.—*s.* Incisivos, los cuatro dientes delanteros en cada mandíbula, así llamados porque cortan los alimentos.

Incisorial, Incisory [in-sai-sō'-ri-al, in-sai'-so-ri], *a.* Incisorio.

Incisure [in-saiz'-ūr], *s.* (Poco us.) Incisión, cortadura, corte.

Incitation [in-si-tê'-shun], *s.* Incitación, instigación.

Incite [in-sait'], *va.* Incitar, mover, estimular, aguijonear.

Incitement [in-sait'-mẹnt], *s.* Incitamento, incitamiento, estímulo, aguijón; lo que induce a ejecutar una cosa.

Inciter [in-sait'-ẹr], *s.* Incitador; instigador.

Incitingly [in-sait'-ing-li], *adv.* De un modo estimulante o alentador; incitantemente.

Incivility [in-si-vil'-i-ti], *s.* Incivilidad, inurbanidad, descortesía, desatención.

Inclasp [in-clqsp'], *va.* Estrechar, abrazar; agarrar; abrochar.

Inclavated [in'-cla-vê-ted], *a.* Enclavado, fijo.

Inclemency [in-clem'-en-si], *s.* 1. Inclemencia, rigor de la estación; aprieto, aflicción, apuro. 2. Crueldad, severidad.

Inclement [in-clem'-ent], *a.* 1. Inclemente, severo, duro. 2. Inclemente, riguroso, borrascoso, tempestuoso. 3. Adverso, contrario, malandante; dícese de las circunstancias.

Inclinable [in-clain'-a-bl], *a.* Favorable, inclinado a alguna cosa.

Inclination [in-cli-nê'-shun], *s.* 1. Inclinación; tendencia mutua de dos líneas, superficies o cuerpos el uno hacia el òtro. 2. La superficie inclinada; declive, declivio, descenso. 3. Inclinación, acatamiento, reverencia bajando la cabeza. 4. Inclinación, afición, amor, afecto. 5. Inclinación de la aguja magnética. *V.* DIP. 6. (Farm.) Decantación. *V.* DECANTATION.

Inclinatory [in-clai'-na-to-ri], *a.* Ladeado.

Incline [in-clain'], *va.* 1. Inclinar, enderezar alguna cosa hacia una parte determinada. 2. Ladear, torcer; doblar, doblegar. 3. Inclinar el cuerpo o la cabeza por respeto o reverencia.—*vn.* 1. Inclinarse, torcerse un poco hacia abajo alguna cosa. 2. Inclinarse, hacer reverencia o acatamiento. 3. Inclinarse, sentir disposición favorable hacia alguna persona o cosa; hablando de colores, tirar a. *A hue which inclines to green,* Un matiz que tira al verde. *Inclined plane,* Plano inclinado.—*s.* Declivio; declive de una vía férrea.

Incloister [in-clois'-tẹr], *va.* Enclaustrar.

Inclose [in-clōz'], *va.* 1. Encerrar, cerrar; poner bajo sobre (una carta). 2. Cercar, rodear, incluir, circuir. *V.* ENCLOSE.

Inclosure [in-clō'-zhur], *s.* *V.* ENCLOSURE.

Incloud [in-claud'], *va.* (Poco us.) Obscurecer, ocultar como con nubes.

Include [in-clūd' o cliūd], *va.* 1. Incluir, encerrar. 2. Comprender, como parte componente; abrazar, contener.

Inclusion [in-clū'-zhun], *s.* 1. Inclusión, restricción, limitación. 2. Lo que está incluído o contenido; especialmente un gas o líquido contenido en un mineral.

Inclusive [in-clū'-siv], *a.* Inclusivo.

Inclusively [in-clū'-siv-li], *adv.* Inclusivamente, inclusive.

Incoagulable [in-co-ag'-yu-la-bl], *a.* Incoagulable.

Incoercible [in-co-ẹrs'-i-bl], *a.* Que no puede ni debe ser constreñido.

Incog [in-ceg'], *a., s.* y *adv.* *V.* INCOGNITO.

Incogitable [in-cej'-it-a-bl], *a.* Insabible, inconcebible.

Incogitancy [in-cej'-i-tan-si], *s.* Irreflexión, falta de reflexión.

Incogitantly [in-cej'-i-tant-li], *adv.* Inadvertidamente.

Incognito [in-ceg'-ni-to], *adv.* y *a.* Incógnito o de incógnito.—*s.* 1. La acción de asumir un nombre, papel, tipo o carácter fingidos. 2. Persona que vive, viaja o pasa de incógnito.

Incognizable [in-ceg'-ni-za-bl], *a.* No cognoscible, que no puede reconocerse o distinguirse, particularmente por el hombre.

Incoherence [in-co-hir'-ens], **Incoherency** [in-co-hir'-en-si], *s.* Incoherencia; inconsecuencia.

Incoherent [in-co-hir'-ent], *a.* Incoherente, inconsecuente, inconexo; no adherente, suelto.

Incoherently [in-co-hir'-ent-li], *adv.* Con incoherencia, sin conexión.

Incombustibility [in-cẹm-bus-ti-bil'-i-ti], *s.* Incombustibilidad, la cualidad de resistir al fuego.

Incombustible [in-cẹm-bus'-ti-bl], *a.* Incombustible.

Incombustibleness [in-cẹm-bus'-ti-bl-nes], *s.* Incombustibilidad, la calidad de ser incombustible.

Income [in'-cum], *s.* Renta, entrada, utilidad y beneficio que rinde una cosa anualmente (o en un plazo determinado). *To live up to one's income,* Gastar uno lo que gana.

Incomer [in'-cum-ẹr], *s.* Recién llegado; el que entra o llega; inquilino o tendero que sucede a otro.

Income tax [in'-cum tax], *s.* Impuesto sobre la renta.

Incoming [in'-cum-ing], *a.* Entrante, que llega o está por llegar. *An incoming tenant,* Inquilino entrante o que toma posesión. *Incoming steamer,* Vapor que está por llegar.

Incommensurability [in-cẹm-men-shur-a-bil'-i-ti], *s.* Inconmensurabilidad, la calidad de lo que no es mensurable.

Incommensurable [in-cem-men'-shur-a-bl], *a.* Inconmensurable, no conmensurable.

Incommensurate [in-cem-men'-shur-êt], *a.* Desproporcionado, insuficiente, que no admite una medida común.

Incommensurately [in-cem-men'-shu-ret-li], *adv.* Desproporcionadamente, de un modo desproporcionado.

Incommode [in-cem-mōd'], *va.* Incomodar, fastidiar, hacer mala obra, molestar.

Incommodious [in-cẹm-mō'-di-us], *a.* Incómodo, inconveniente, que no proporciona espacio o comodidad suficiente; estrecho.

Incommodiously [in-cẹm-mō'-di-us-li], *adv.* Incómodamente.

Incommodiousness [in-cẹm-mō'-di-us-nes], **Incommodity** [in-cẹm-med'-i-ti], *s.* Incomodidad, inconveniencia, molestia.

Incommunicability [in-cẹm-miu-ni-ca-bil'-i-ti], *s.* Incomunicabilidad.

Incommunicable [in-cẹm-miū'-ni-ca-bl], *a.* Incomunicable, indecible.

Incommunicableness [in-cẹm-miū'-ni-ca-bl-nes], *s.* Incomunicabilidad.

Incommunicably [in-cẹm-miū'-ni-ca-bli], *adv.* Sin comunicación, de un modo incomunicable.

†**Incommunicating** [in-cẹm-miū'-ni-kêt-ing], *a.* Incomunicado, que no tiene comunicación.

Incommunicative [in-cẹm-miū'-ni-ca-tiv], *a.* Adusto, poco comunicativo, intratable, insociable.

Incommunicativeness [in-cẹm-miū'-ni-ca-tiv-nes], *s.* Calidad o estado de intratable o poco comunicativo; adustez.

Incommutability [in-cẹm-miut-a-bil'-i-ti], *s.* Inconmutabilidad.

Incommutable [in-cẹm-miūt'-a-bl], *a.* Inconmutable.

Incommutably [in-cẹm-miūt'-a-bli], *adv.* Inconmutablemente.

Incomparable [in-cem'-pa-ra-bl], *a.* Incomparable, sin igual.

Incomparableness [in-cem'-pa-ra-bl-nes], *s.* Excelencia superior a toda comparación.

Incomparably [in-cem'-par-a-bli], *adv.* Incomparablemente, sin comparación.

Incompassionate [in-cẹm-pash'-un-ẹt], *a.* Incompasivo, desapiadado.

Incompassionately [in-cẹm-pash'-un-ẹt-li], *adv.* Sin compasión o misericordia, desapiadadamente.

Incompatibility [in-cem-pat-i-bil'-i-ti], *s.* Incompatibilidad, contrariedad.

Incompatible [in-cem-pat'-i-bl], *a.* Incompatible.

Incompatibly [in-cem-pat'-i-bli], *adv.* Incongruentemente, opuestamente.

Incompetence, Incompetency [in-cem'-pẹ-tens, ten-si], *s.* Incompetencia, inhabilidad, insuficiencia.

Incompetent [in-cem'-pẹ-tent], *a.* 1. Incompetente, que no tiene las cualidades necesarias; insuficiente, que no basta. 2. (For.) Inadmisible, que no puede invocarse en derecho; incompetente.

Incompetently [in-cem'-pẹ-tent-li], *adv.* Incompetentemente.

Incomplete [in-cem-plit'], *a.* Incompleto, falto, imperfecto.

Incompleteness [in-cem-plit'-nes], *s.* Falta, imperfección.

Incompliance [in-cem-plai'-ans], *s.* Contrariedad de genio; desobediencia, indocilidad.

Incomprehensibility [in-cem-prẹ-hen-si-bil'-i-ti], *s.* Incomprensibilidad, obscuridad de una cosa que hace que no se pueda entender.

Incomprehensible [in-cem-prẹ-hen'-si-bl], *a.* Incomprensible.

Incomprehensibleness [in-cem-prẹ-hen'-si-bl-nes], *s.* Incomprensibilidad.

Incomprehensibly [in-cem-prẹ-hen'-si-bli], *adv.* De un modo incomprensible, incomprensiblemente.

Incomprehension [in-cem-prẹ-hen'-shun], *s.* Falta de comprensión.

Incomprehensive [in-cem-prẹ-hen'-siv], *a.* Lo que no tiene la extensión necesaria o no comprende lo que debe.

Incomprehensiveness [in-cem-prẹ-hen'-siv-nes], *s.* Incomprensibilidad.

Incompressibility [in-cem-pres-i-bil'-i-ti], *s.* El estado o la calidad de lo que es incomprimible.

Incompressible [in-cem-pres'-i-bl], *a.* Incomprimible.

Inconcealable [in-cen-sil'-a-bl], *a.* Lo que no se puede ocultar o encubrir.

Inconceivable [in-cen-siv'-a-bl], *a.* 1. Inconcebible, incomprensible. 2. Contradictor, que encierra una contradicción; inherentemente contradictorio.

Inconceivableness [in-cen-siv'-a-bl-nes], *s.* Incomprensibilidad, calidad de lo que es inconcebible o que encierra una contradicción.

Inconceivably [in-cen-siv'-a-bli], *adv.* Incomprensiblemente, de un modo inconcebible.

Inconclusive [in-cen-clū'-siv], *a.* Que no concluye ni hace fuerza, ineficaz; que no presenta razones concluyentes; indeciso, que no prueba.

Inconclusively [in-cen-clū'-siv-li], *adv.* Sin conclusión o evidencia decisiva.

Inconclusiveness [in-cen-clū'-siv-nes], *s.* Carencia de conclusión o decisión, calidad de lo que es poco concluyente.

Inconcussible [in-cen-cus'-i-bl], *a.* Incapaz de ser movido.

Incondite [in-cen'-dait o in'-cen-dait], *a.* Mal construído, irregular, no acabado.

Incongealable [in-cen-jil'-a-bl], *a.* Incapaz de congelarse.

Incongruence [in-cen'-gru-ens], **Incongruity** [in-cen-grū'-i-ti], *s.* Incongruencia, incongruidad; desproporción, falta de relación, falta de conveniencia.

Incongruent [in-cen'-gru-ent], *a.* Incongruente, falto de congruencia.

Incongruous [in-cen'-gru-us], *a.* Incongruo, desproporcionado, inconexo; compuesto de partes discordantes o heterogéneas.

Incongruously [in-cen'-gru-us-li], *adv.* Incongruamente.

Incongruousness [in-cen'-gru-us-nes], *s.* Incongruencia.

Inconsequence [in-cen'-sẹ-cwens], *s.* Inconsecuencia.

Inconsequent [in-cen'-sẹ-cwent], *a.* 1. Inconsecuente, inconsiguiente, que no es consiguiente a otra cosa, que no resulta del modo acostumbrado. 2. Inconsecuente, inconsistente, ilógico, informal.

Inconsequential [in-cen-sẹ-cwen'-shal], *a.* Inconsecuente, falto de consecuencia.

Inconsiderable [in-cen-sid'-ẹr-a-bl], *a.* Inconsiderable, insignificante, de poca importancia o consideración; frívolo.

Inconsiderableness [in-cẹn-sid'-ẹr-a-bl-nes], *s.* Falta de importancia, frivolidad.

Inconsiderate [in-cẹn-sid'-ẹr-ĝt], *a.* Inconsiderado, inadvertido; irreflexivo, falto de miramiento y consideración.

Inconsiderately [in-cẹn-sid'-ẹr-ĝt-li], *adv.* Inconsideradamente, irreflexivamente.

Inconsiderateness [in-cẹn-sid'-ẹr-ĝt-nes], **Inconsideration** [in-cẹn-sid-ẹr-é'-shun], *s.* Inconsideración, inadvertencia.

Inconsistence [in-cẹn-sist'-ens], **Inconsistency** [in-cẹn-sist'-en-si], *s.* 1. Incompatibilidad, contradicción, incongruencia. 2. Inconsistencia, mutabilidad, volubilidad, inconsecuencia.

Inconsistent [in-cẹn-sist'-ent], *a.* 1. Inconsistente, incompatible, contradictorio. 2. Implicatorio, inconsecuente. 3. Inconstante, variable, mudable, veleidoso.

Inconsistently [in-cẹn-sist'-ent-li], *adv.* Incongruamente, contradictoriamente.

Inconsolable [in-cẹn-sōl'-a-bl], *a.* Inconsolable.

Inconsonance, Inconsonancy [in-cen'-so-nans, nan-si], *s.* Falta de consonancia; también, falta de harmonía, disonancia de los sonidos entre sí; implicación en los términos o entre sí.

Inconspicuous [in-cẹn-spic'-yu-us], *a.* No conspicuo, poco visible; tan pequeño u obscuro que no puede fácilmente apreciarse con la vista; sin importancia.

Inconstancy [in-cen'-stan-si], *s.* Inconstancia; diversidad.

Inconstant [in-cen'-stant], *a.* Inconstante, mudable, voluble, variable.

Inconstantly [in-cen'-stant-li], *adv.* Inconstantemente.

Inconsumable [in-cen-siūm'-a-bl], *a.* Que no se puede consumir.

Incontestable [in-cen-test'-a-bl], *a.* Incontestable, indisputable, irrecusable, irrefragable.

Incontestably [in-cen-test'-a-bli], *adv.* Incontestablemente, irrecusablemente.

Incontiguous [in-cen-tig'-yu-us], *a.* Separado, que no está contiguo.

Incontinence [in-cen'-ti-nens], **Incontinency** [in-cen'-ti-nen-si], *s.* 1. Incontinencia, falta de recato y dominio en las pasiones y particularmente en los apetitos carnales; lascivia. 2. Incontinencia, flujo no contenido (v. g. de palabras). 3. (Med.) Incontinencia, incapacidad de contener las evacuaciones naturales.

Incontinent [in-cen'-ti-nent], *a.* 1. Incontinente, desenfrenado en las pasiones de la carne. 2. (Med.) Incontinente, incapaz de retener una evacuación natural.—*s.* Un incontinente, el que no domina sus pasiones.

Incontinently [in-cen'-ti-nent-li], *adv.* 1. Incontinentemente. 2. Inmediatamente, al instante, incontinenti.

Incontrollable [in-cẹn-trōl'-a-bl], *a.* Irresistible, incontrastable.

Incontrollably [in-cẹn-trōl'-a-bli], *adv.* Sin restricción.

Incontrovertible [in-cen"-tro-vẹrt'-i-bl], *a.* Incontrovertible, incontrastable, irrefragable, indisputable.

Incontrovertibly [in-cen"-tro-vẹrt'-i-bli], *adv.* Indisputablemente, sin disputa.

Inconvenience [in-cẹn-vín'-yens], **Inconveniency** [in-cẹn-vín'-yen-si], *s.* 1. Inconveniencia, falta de conveniencia. 2. Inconveniente, incomodidad, embarazo, estorbo, desventaja, dificultad.

Inconvenience, *va.* Causar inconvenientes; embarazar, incomodar, estorbar.

Inconvenient [in-cẹn-vín'-yent], *a.* 1. Incómodo, embarazoso, molesto, fastidioso. 2. Inconveniente, impropio; inoportuno, no a propósito.

Inconveniently [in-cẹn-vín'-yent-li], *adv.* Incómodamente, importunamente.

Inconversable [in-cẹn-vẹr'-sa-bl], *a.* Inconversable, intratable, insociable.

Inconvertible [in-cẹn-vẹrt'-i-bl], *a.* Inconvertible.

Inconvincible [in-cẹn-vins'-i-bl], *a.* Inconvencible.

Incorporate [in-cōr'-po-rêt], *va.* 1. Agregar, unir dos o más cosas para que formen un todo. 2. Dar cuerpo o forma material, revestir de materia. 3. Incorporar; formar una corporación legal, un gremio o cuerpo político; asociar.—*vn.* Incorporarse, agregarse o unirse para formar un todo.

Incorporate, *a.* 1. Incorporado, asociado, unido, mezclado. 2. Incorporal, inmaterial. 3. No constituído en corporación o asociación.

Incorporation [in-cōr-po-ré'-shun], *s.* Incorporación, formación de un gremio o cuerpo político; adopción, asociación.

Incorporeal [in-cōr-pō'-rẹ-al], *a.* Incorpóreo.

Incorporeally [in-cōr-pō'-rẹ-al-i], *adv.* Incorporalmente.

Incorrect [in-cer-rect'], *a.* Incorrecto, inexacto, erróneo; inmoral.

Incorrectly [in-cer-rect'-li], *adv.* Incorrectamente, inexactamente.

Incorrectness [in-cer-rect'-nes], *s.* Inexactitud; incorrección; impropiedad, inconveniencia; descuido.

Incorrigible [in-cer'-i-ji-bl], *a.* Incorregible, indócil, obstinado, terco.

Incorrigibility [in-cer-i-ji-bil'-i-ti], **Incorrigibleness** [in-cer'-i-ji-bl-nes], *s.* Incorregibilidad, indocilidad, terquedad de genio, dureza de carácter.

Incorrigibly [in-cer'-i-ji-bli], *adv.* Incorregiblemente, obstinadamente.

Incorrupt [in-cer-rupt'], *a.* 1. Incorrupto, libre de corrupción, lo que no se corrompe o no padece corrupción. 2. Incorrupto, íntegro, recto.

Incorruptibility [in-cer-rupt-i-bil'-i-ti], *s.* Incorruptibilidad.

Incorruptible [in-cer-rupt'-i-bl], *a.* 1. Incorruptible, cosa no corruptible. 2. Incorruptible, incorrupto, persona incapaz de dejarse corromper o cohechar.

Incorruption [in-cer-rup'-shun], *s.* Incorrupción.

Incorruptive [in-cer-rup'-tiv], *s.* Incorrupto.

Incorruptness [in-cer-rupt'-nes], *s.* 1. Incorrupción, pureza de vida o costumbres. 2. Incorrupción, el estado de una cosa que no se corrompe o no puede corromperse.

Incrassate [in-cras'-êt], *va.* Espesar, condensar, encrasar, engrosar; en especial, espesar un flúido como por medio de una mezcla o por evaporación.—*vn.* Espesarse, condensarse, engrosarse.

Incrassate, *a.* Encrasado, que se va aumentando hacia la extremidad, como las antenas y los fémures de ciertos insectos y las hojas de la hierba puntera.

Incrassation [in-cras-é'-shun], *s.* Espesura, condensación: dícese de los líquidos y de los flúidos; también, engrasación, hinchazón a causa de gordura.

Incrassative [in-cras'-a-tiv], *a.* Espesativo, incrasante.

Increasable [in-crís'-a-bl], *a.* Aumentable.

Increase [in-crís'], *va.* Acrecentar, aumentar; abultar, alargar.—*vn.* Crecer, tomar aumento, acrecentarse, multiplicarse; engrandecer.

Increase [in'-crís], *s.* 1. Aumento, acrecentamiento, adelantamiento, incremento. 2. Producto, cosecha; provecho, ganancia, interés. 3. Generación, progenie. 4. Creciente (de la luna); crecida (de las aguas).

Increaser [in-crís'-ẹr], *s.* Aumentador, acrecentador; productor.

Increasing [in-crís'-ing], *a.* Creciente.

Increasingly [in-crís'-ing-li], *adv.* En vías de aumento; en creciente.

Increate [in'-crẹ-êt], *a.* (Poét.) Increado.

Incredibility [in-cred'-i-bil-i-ti], *s.* Incredibilidad.

Incredible [in-cred'-i-bl], *a.* Increíble, lo que no se puede creer.

Incredibleness [in-cred'-i-bl-nes], *s.* Incredibilidad.

Incredibly [in-cred'-i-bli], *adv.* Increíblemente.

Incredulity [in-crẹ-diū'-li-ti], *s.* Incredulidad, repugnancia a, o dificultad en creer; escepticismo.

Incredulous [in-cred'-yu-lus], *a.* Incrédulo, el que cree con dificultad, o repugna creer lo que es creíble; escéptico.

Incredulousness [in-cred'-yu-lus-nes], *s.* Incredulidad.

Incremate [in'-crẹ-mêt], *va.* *V.* CREMATE.

Increment [in'-crẹ-mẹnt], *s.* 1. Incremento, aumento en el crecer; producto. 2. Adición, añadidura, agregación. 3. (Mat.) Cantidad diferencial. 4. (Ret.) Gradación, clímax.

Increpate [in'-crẹ-pêt], *va.* (Des.) Increpar, reprender con dureza y severidad.

Increscent [in-cres'-ent], *a.* Creciente; se dice de la luna.

Incriminate [in-crim'-i-nêt], *va.* Incriminar, acusar de un crimen o delito; acriminar.

Incrust [in-crust'], **Incrustate** [in-crus'-têt], *va.* Encostrar; incrustar; adornar con incrustaciones o embutidos. *A vessel incrusted with salt*, Una vasija encostrada de sal. Se escribe *encrust* en sentido figurado y poético, pero rara vez en las acepciones mecánica y literal.

Incrustation [in-crus-té'-shun], *s.* Incrustación, embutido; encostradura.

Incubate [in'-kiu-bêt], *vn.* Empollar, ponerse las aves sobre los huevos.

Incubation [in-kiu-bé'-shun], *s.* 1. Incubación, empolladura, la acción de empollar por cualesquiera medios. 2. (Med.) Incubación, el tiempo que media entre la impresión de las causas morbosas y la invasión o principio de las enfermedades.

Incubator [in'-kiu-bê"-tęr], *s.* Lo que incuba o empolla; incubadora, aparato para efectuar la incubación artificial.

Incubus [in'-kiu-bus], *s.* 1. Una cosa cualquiera que tiende a sobrecargar u oprimir; carga, cuidado, aflicción; desánimo. 2. Íncubo, pesadilla. 3. (Ant.) Demonio íncubo.

Inculcate [in-cul'-kêt], *va.* Inculcar, introducir algo en la memoria o entendimiento a fuerza de repetirlo.

Inculcation [in-cul-ké'-shun], *s.* Inculcación, el acto y efecto de inculcar.

Inculcator [in-cul'-kê"-tęr], *s.* Inculcador, el que inculca.

Inculcatory [in-cul'-ca-to-ri], *a.* Inculcador, que inculca o sirve para inculcar.

Inculpable [in-cul'-pa-bl], *a.* Inculpable, irreprensible, exento de culpa; inocente.

Inculpableness [in-cul'-pa-bl-nes], *s.* Inculpabilidad.

Inculpably [in-cul'-pa-bli], *adv.* Inculpablemente.

Inculpate [in-cul'-pet], *va.* Culpar, imputar falta a alguien; inculpar.

Inculpation [in-cul-pé'-shun], *s.* Inculpación, acción de inculpar.

Inculpatory [in-cul'-pa-to-ri], *a.* Inculpador, imputador.

Incumbency [in-cum'-ben-si], *s.* 1. La posesión o goce de un cargo, particularmente de un beneficio eclesiástico; y el período durante el cual se ocupa o ejerce dicho cargo. 2. (Poco us.) Incumbencia, obligación y cargo de hacer una cosa.

Incumbent [in-cum'-bent], *a.* 1. Echado; obligatorio, preciso, exigido, demandado. 2. Sostenido por; que se apoya en algo, como una antera en un filamento. *To serve God is incumbent on all men,* Servir a Dios es deber de todos los hombres.—*s.* Beneficiado, el que está en actual posesión de algún empleo público o de un beneficio eclesiástico.

Incumber [in-cum'-bęr], *va.* *V.* ENCUMBER.

Incumbrance [in-cum'-brans], *s.* Impedimento, embarazo, obstáculo, carga, imposición. *V* ENCUMBRANCE.

Incur [in-cör'], *va.* Incurrir, merecer las penas señaladas por una ley; atraerse, causarse. *To incur a debt,* Contraer una deuda.

Incurability [in-kiūr-a-bil'-i-ti], *s.* La calidad que constituye un mal incurable.

Incurable [in-kiūr'-a-bl], *a.* Incurable, irreparable, que no tiene remedio.—*s.* Incurable.

Incurableness [in-kiūr'-a-bl-nes], *s.* El estado del cuerpo o alma que no admite remedio.

Incurably [in-kiūr'-a-bli], *adv* De un modo incurable.

Incuriosity [in-kiu-ri-es'-i-ti], *s* Falta de curiosidad, indiferencia.

Incurious [in-kiū'-ri-us], *a.* Incurioso, descuidado, negligente, dejado, omiso.

Incuriously [in-kiū'-ri-us-li], *adv.* Sin curiosidad, negligentemente.

Incuriousness [in-kiū'-ri-us-nes], *s.* Negligencia, descuido, incuria, omisión.

Incursion [in-cör'-shun], *s.* Incursión, correría; acometimiento.

Incurvate [in-cör'-vêt], **Incurve** [in-cörv'], *va.* Encorvar, doblar o torcer alguna cosa.

Incurvate, *a.* Encorvado, doblado.

Incurvation [in-cör-vé'-shun], *s.* 1. Encorvadura, encorvamiento; (dícese particularmente de las uñas). 2. Reverencia, inclinación del cuerpo en señal de respeto.

Incurvity [in-cör'-vi-ti], *s.* Corvadura, inflexión.

Incus [in'-cus], *s.* Yunque, uno de los huesecillos del oído medio.

Incussion [in-cush'-un], *s.* Sacudimiento violento.

Indart [in-dārt'], *va.* Lanzar alguna cosa hacia dentro.

Indebted [in-det'-ed], *a.* 1. Adeudado, endeudado, empeñado; el que tiene deudas. *He is indebted over head and ears,* Está empeñado hasta los ojos. 2. Obligado, reconocido. *I am indebted to him for many favours,* Le debo muchos favores.

Indebtedness [in-det'-ed-nes], *s.* 1. Calidad y estado de deudor, de endeudado. 2. Deuda pasiva, importe o suma de las deudas de alguien.

Indebtment [in-det'-męnt], *s.* Estado de adeudado.

Indecency [in-dí'-sen-si], *s.* Indecencia, inmodestia; grosería, vulgaridad.

Indecent [in-dí'-sent], *a.* 1. Indecente, grosero, torpe, obsceno. 2. Inconveniente, impropio.

Indecently [in-dí'-sent-li], *adv.* Indecentemente, torpemente.

Indecimable [in-des'-i-ma-bl], *a.* Lo que no debe pagar diezmo, o no está sujeto a su pago.

Indecision [in-dę-sizh'-un], *s.* Indecisión, irresolución.

Indecisive [in-dę-sai'-siv], *a.* 1. Indeciso, que no es decisivo. 2. Dudoso, indeterminado, irresoluto.

Indecisiveness [in-dę-sai'-siv-nes], *s.* La calidad o el estado de indecisión o irresolución.

Indeclinable [in-dę-clain'-a-bl], *a.* Indeclinable.—*s.* Nombre que no se declina.

Indeclinably [in-dę-clain'-a-bli], *adv.* De un modo indeclinable, sin variación.

Indecorous [in-de-cō'-rus], *a.* Indecoroso, vil, indigno, indecente.

Indecorously [in-de-cō'-rus-li], *adv.* Indecorosamente.

Indecorousness [in-de-cō'-rus-nes], *s.* Indecoro.

Indecorum [in-dę-cō'-rum], *s.* Indecoro, ignominia, indecencia.

Indeed [in-díd'], *adv.* Verdaderamente, realmente, bien que, de veras, a la verdad, sí. ¿De veras? ¡De veras! ¡Vaya, vaya! *But indeed,* Pero bien reflexionado. *Though indeed,* Aunque considerado todo. *Then indeed,* Entonces sí. *That indeed,* Eso sí. *Indeed* se usa muy a menudo de un modo expletivo para dar más fuerza al sentido de la frase o de la oración, y entonces corresponde casi siempre en castellano a "ciertamente, muy o verdaderamente." *Indeed? can you suppose it?* ¿De veras? ¿puede Vd. suponerlo?

Indefatigability [in-dę-fat-i-ga-bil'-i-ti], *s.* Estado, calidad o condición de ser uno infatigable o incansable.

Indefatigable [in-dę-fat'-i-ga-bl], *a.* Infatigable, incansable.

Indefatigableness [in-dę-fat'-i-ga-bl-nes], *s.* La calidad de ser infatigable.

Indefatigably [in-dę-fat'-i-ga-bli], *adv.* Infatigablemente, incansablemente, sin cansarse.

Indefeasibility [in-de-fí"-zi-bil'-i-ti], *s.* Calidad de lo inabrogable, de lo que no puede ser anulado.

Indefeasible [in-dę-fí'-zi-bl], *a.* (For.) Incapaz de ser abrogado o anulado; inabrogable, irrevocable.

Indefectibility [in-dę-fect-i-bil'-i-ti], *s.* Indefectibilidad, imposibilidad de faltar o fenecer.

Indefectible [in-dę-fect'-i-bl], *a.* Indefectible.

Indefensible [in-dę-fens'-i-bl], *a.* Indefendible, indefensible, que no puede ser defendido.

Indefensive [in-dę-fens'-iv], *a.* Indefenso, que no tiene defensa o no se puede defender.

Indefinable [in-dę-fain'-a-bl], *a.* Indefinible.

Indefinite [in-def'-i-nit], *a.* Indefinido, indeterminado, incierto; sutil, imperceptible.

Indefinitely [in-def'-i-nit-li], *adv.* Indefinidamente, por un tiempo o espacio indeterminado; de un modo incierto o vago.

Indefiniteness [in-def'-i-nit-nes], *s.* Estado o calidad de lo que es indefinido.

Indehiscence [in-dę-his'-ens], *s.* (Bot.) Indehiscencia, incapacidad de abrirse natural o espontáneamente.

Indehiscent [in-dę-his'-ent], *a.* (Bot.) Indehiscente, que no se abre o hiende espontáneamente.

Indeliberate, Indeliberated [in-dę-lib'-ęr-et, ed], *a.* Indeliberado; no premeditado, hecho sin reflexión.

Indelibility [in-del-i-bil'-i-ti], *s.* La calidad de ser indeleble.

Indelible [in-del'-i-bl], *a.* 1. Indeleble, que no se puede borrar. 2. Irrevocable, que no se puede revocar o anular.

Indelibly [in-del'-i-bli], *adv.* Indeleblemente, irrevocablemente.

Indelicacy [in-del'-i-ca-si], *s.* Falta de delicadeza, de decoro; grosería, inurbanidad.

Indelicate [in-del'-i-ket], *a.* Falto de decoro, no delicado, inmodesto; grosero, inurbano.

Indemnification [in-dem-ni-fi-ké'-shun], *s.* Indemnización, resarcimiento.

Indemnify [in-dem'-ni-fai], *va.* 1. Indemnizar, resarcir los daños y perjuicios sufridos. 2. Asegurar a alguno el resarcimiento de una pérdida o pena.

Indemnity [in-dem'-ni-ti], *s.* 1. Indemnización, resarcimiento. 2. Indemnidad, contrafianza, garantía contra pérdidas.

Indemonstrable [in-dę-men'-stra-bl], *a:* Indemostrable, incapaz de demostración, que no es demostrable.

Indenize [in-den'-aiz], *va.* Dar libertad. *V.* ENDENIZE y sus derivados.

Indent [in-dent'], *va.* 1. Dentar, endentar, cortar en forma de una carrera de dientes; mellar el borde de. 2. *V.* INDENTURE, verbo. 3. En lo escrito o lo impreso, sangrar, empezar una línea más adentro que las otras.—*vn.* 1. Mellarse, hacerse o ponerse dentado. 2. (Ant.) Hacer un contrato, pactar.

Indent, *s.* 1. Mella, diente, abertura parecida a una mella. 2. *V.* IN-

DENTURE, substantivo. 3. (Des.) Desigualdad; impresión.
Indentation [in-den-té'-shun], *s.* 1. La acción de dentar o cortar en puntas. 2. Cortadura dentada, la que está hecha en figura de dientes de sierra; mella.
Indented [in-dent'-ed], *a.* y *pp.* Dentado; (Bot.) dentellado.
Indention [in-den'-shun], *s.* 1. Abolladura, desigualdad. *V.* DENT. 2. Sangría de una línea en lo escrito o impreso.
Indenture [in-den'-chur], *s.* 1. (For.) Carta partida, la escritura o contrato que se hace formando dos copias unidas y semejantes entre sí, cortándolas después por el medio para que la una sirva de contraseña a la otra. 2. Acción y efecto de dentar o cortar en forma de dientes.
Indenture, *va.* Ligar, obligar, por medio de un contrato de aprendizaje hecho por duplicado.
Independence [in-dę-pend'-ens], **Independency** [in-dę-pend'-en-si], *s.* 1. Independencia, libertad de obrar, autonomía. 2. Situación económica desahogada, bienestar. Independencia, en las mismas acepciones que tiene en castellano. 3. Espíritu de confianza en sí mismo. *Independence Day,* En los Estados Unidos, el 4 de Julio.
Independent [in-dę-pend'-ent], *a.* 1. Independiente, que no depende de otra persona o cosa para su gobierno o sustento. 2. Que posee los medios de independencia o de libertad de acción; también, que vive de sus rentas. 3. Libre, fácil, cómodo; intrépido. 4. Separado, desunido (con la prep. *of*). *The soul may exist independent of matter,* El alma puede existir separada de la materia. *An independent gentleman,* Propietario, rentista, hombre que vive de sus rentas.—*s.* Una clase de sectarios llamados independientes, que no reconocen autoridad eclesiástica alguna.
Independently [in-dę-pend'-ent-li], *adv.* Independientemente.
Indeprecable [in-dep'-rę-ca-bl], *a.* Indeprecable, inexorable, que no puede ser deprecado.
Indeprivable [in-dę-prai'-va-bl], *a.* Aquello de que no se puede privar a uno.
Indescribable [in-dę-scraib'-a-bl], *a.* Indescriptible.
Indestructibility [in-dę-struct-i-bil'-i-ti], *s.* Indestructibilidad.
Indestructible [in-dę-struct'-i-bl], *a.* Indestructible.
Indeterminable [in-dę-tęr'-mi-na-bl], *a.* 1. Indeterminable, lo que no se puede determinar. 2. (Hist. Nat.) Que no admite clasificación ni nombre a causa de su mala o imperfecta condición.
Indeterminate [in-dę-tęr'-mi-net], *a.* Indeterminado, no exacto, indefinido.
Indeterminately [in-dę-tęr'-mi-net-li], *adv.* Indeterminadamente.
Indeterminateness [in-dę-tęr'-mi-net-nes], *s.* Indeterminación, irresolución.
Indetermination [in-dę-tęr-mi-né'-shun], *s.* Indeterminación, duda, irresolución.
Indetermined [in-de-tęr'-mind], *a.* Indeterminado, vacilante, irresoluto, irresuelto.
Index [in'-dex], *s.* (*pl.* INDEXES, INDICES [in'-di-siz]). 1. Indicio o señal de alguna cosa; una cosa cualquiera que marca o señala, o manifiesta. 2. Índice, el dedo segundo de la mano. 3. Índice o tabla de materias de un libro dispuestas en orden alfabético, indicando donde se halla cada tema o asunto. 4. Manecilla de reloj; manecilla en la imprenta, el signo ☞ 5. Índice expurgatorio.
Index, *va.* Poner un índice alfabético a un libro.
Indexical [in-dex'-i-cal], *a.* 1. Que tiene la forma de índice. 2. Que sirve para indicar, indicativo.
Indexterity [in-dex-ter'-i-ti], *s.* Desmaña, falta de destreza.
India [in'-di-a], *s.* India, Indias, vasta región del sur de Asia. *India-ink,* Tinta de la China, o tinta China. *India-paper,* Papel de China; papel delgado, absorbente, para imprimir; se emplea para obtener las pruebas más delicadas de planchas grabadas. *India-proof,* Prueba original y escogida hecha en papel de China con una plancha grabada.
Indiaman [in'-di-a-man], *s.* Buque que hace el comercio con la India.
Indian [in'-di-an], *a.* 1. Indio, natural de la India (oriental u occidental) o relativo a ella. 2. (E. U. A.) Hecho de maíz.—*s.* 1. Indio, el natural de la India oriental. 2. Indio, el antiguo poblador o aborigen de todo el continente americano. 3. El natural de las Antillas o el naturalizado y residente en ellas. 4. El europeo que ha residido en la India; anglo-indiano. *Indian-berries* [ber'-iz], Cocas de Levante. *Indian-corn* [in'-di-an-cērn'], Maíz, trigo de la América, trigo de Turquía. *Indian-meal,* Harina de maíz.
Indian-cress [in'-di-an-cres'], *s.* (Bot.) Capuchina; se llama más común y familiarmente *nasturtium.*
Indian-millet [in'-di-an-mil'-et], *s.* (Bot.) Alcandía.
Indian-pink [in'-di-an-pinc'], *s.* (Bot.) Clavelón de Indias: úsase en medicina contra las lombrices. Ipomæa quamoclit.
India-rubber [in'-di-a-rub'-ęr], *s.* Caucho, cauchuco, goma elástica. (Mex.) Hule.
Indian-summer [in'-di-an-sum'-ęr], *s.* (E. U.) Veranillo de San Martín. Días de calor y calma en noviembre.
Indicant [in'-di-cant], *a.* Indicante.
Indicate [in'-di-kēt], *va.* Indicar, señalar, designar, dar a entender, anunciar.
Indication [in-di-ké'-shun], *s.* 1. Indicación, indicio; señal; signo. 2. Manifestación; (Med.) indicación que dan los síntomas de una enfermedad en lo relativo al tratamiento que ha de seguirse.
Indicative [in-dic'-a-tiv], *a.* Indicativo. *Indicative mode* (o *mood*), Modo indicativo.
Indicatively [in-dic'-a-tiv-li], *adv.* Indicativamente.
Indicator [in'-di-kē-tęr], *s.* Indicador, señalador, apuntador, el que o lo que indica. Indicador, manómetro; instrumento para recibir de un telégrafo de cuadrante.
Indicatory [in'-di-ca-to-ri], *a* Demostrativo, indicatorio.
Indices [in'-di-siz], *s.* Plural de *Index;* se usa especialmente en las ciencias y en las matemáticas.
Indict [in-dait'], *va.* 1. Acusar por escrito ante el juez. (For.) Procesar, demandar judicialmente. 2. (Ant.) Componer, escribir o dictar.
Indictable [in-dait'-a-bl], *a.* (For.) Procesable, denunciable; expuesto a ser denunciado o juzgado, sujeto a denuncia.
Indictee [in-dait'-í], *s.* La persona acusada de un delito o demandada en juicio.
Indicter [in-dait'-ęr], *s.* (For.) Denunciante, fiscal, acusador, denunciador.
Indiction [in-dic'-shun], *s.* 1. Indicción, período de quince años, instituido por Constantino y adoptado por los papas, como parte de su sistema cronológico. 2. Dicho período o uno cualquiera de sus años.
Indictment [in-dait'-męnt], *s.* (For.) Acusación de alguna ofensa criminal o delito; particularmente la formulada por el Gran Jurado bajo juramento y por escrito, como base para el procesamiento del acusado.
Indifference [in-dif'-ęr-ens], **Indifferency** [in-dif'-ęr-en-si], *s.* 1. Indiferencia, imparcialidad. 2. Indiferencia, descuido, frialdad, tibieza 3. Indiferencia, desinterés, desapego del ánimo a las cosas.
Indifferent [in-dif'-ęr-ent], *a.* 1. Indiferente, que no interesa. 2. Indiferente, que no se toma interés por ninguna cosa, que no se mueve por nada. 3. Imparcial, desapasionado. 4. Pasadero, mediano, pasable, tal cual, ni bueno ni malo; ordinario.
Indifferently [in-dif'-ęr-ent-li], *adv.* 1 Indiferentemente, imparcialmente, con indiferencia, sin preferencia. 2. Pasablemente, medianamente, ni bien ni mal.
Indigence [in'-di-jens], **Indigency** [in'-di-jen-si], *s.* Indigencia, pobreza, necesidad.
Indigene, *a.* y *s.* *V.* INDIGENOUS.
Indigenous [in-dij'-i-nus], *a.* 1. Indígena, el que es natural de un país o lugar determinado; lo opuesto a exótico; de aquí, innato. 2. (Geol.) Producido por deposición en la superficie de la tierra, como por un sedimento.
Indigent [in'-di-jent], *a.* Indigente, pobre, necesitado; falto.
Indigested [in-di-jest'-ed], *a.* 1. Indigesto, mal digerido; dícese de las obras escritas sin orden ni método. 2. Indigesto, mal digerido, crudo difícil de digerir.
Indigestible [in-di-jes'-ti-bl], *a.* Indigestible, indigesto.
Indigestion [in-di-jes'-chun], *s.* Indigestión.
Indignance, Indignancy, *s* *V* INDIGNATION.
Indignant [in-dig'-nant], *a.* Indignado, conmovido a la vez por la cólera y el desdén.
Indignantly [in-dig'-nant-li], *adv* Con indignación.
Indignation [in-dig-né'-shun], *s.* Indignación, sentimiento de cólera y desprecio, excitado por la injusticia, la mezquindad, la inhumanidad, etc.; despecho, cólera.
Indignity [in-dig'-ni-ti], *s.* Indignidad, ultraje, afrenta; oprobio.
Indigo [in'-di-gō], *s.* 1. Añil, índigo, planta de cuyo jugo se hace una pasta que sirve para teñir, y que recibe el mismo nombre. 2. Color azul obscuro algo violado.
Indirect [in-di-rect'], *a.* 1. Indirecto, oblicuo, torcido. 2. Torcido, doloso, inicuo, falto de rectitud y honradez.

Indirection [in-di-rec'-shun], *s.* 1. Oblicuidad, rodeo, tortuosidad. 2. Efugio, medio tortuoso o siniestro; vía indirecta; segunda intención.
Indirectly [in-di-rect'-li], *adv.* Indirectamente, oblicuamente; siniestramente.
Indirectness [in-di-rect'-nes], *s.* 1. Oblicuidad, tortuosidad. 2. Rodeo, efugio o excusa falsa, doblez, manejo fraudulento.
Indiscernible [in-di-zẹrn'-i-bl], *a.* Indiscernible, imperceptible.
Indiscernibleness [in-di-zẹrn'-i-bl-nes], *s.* La incapacidad de discernir; carácter de lo indiscernible.
Indiscernibly [in-di-zẹrn'-i-bli], *adv.* Imperceptiblemente.
Indisciplinable [in-dis'-i-plin-a-bl], *a.* Indisciplinable.
Indiscoverable [in-dis-cuv'-ẹr-a-bl], *a.* Indescubrible.
Indiscreet [in-dis-crît'], *a.* Indiscreto, imprudente, inconsiderado, incauto.
Indiscreetly [in-dis-crît'-li], *adv.* Indiscretamente, imprudentemente.
Indiscrete [in-dis-crît'], *a.* Que no está separado o desunido.
Indiscretion [in-dis-cresh'-un], *s.* Indiscreción, inconsideración, imprudencia.
Indiscriminate [in-dis-crim'-i-net], *a.* 1. Que no hace distinciones. 2. Indistinto, confuso, promiscuo, general.
Indiscriminately [in-dis-crim'-i-net-li], *adv.* Indistintamente, promiscuamente.
Indiscriminating, Indiscriminative [in-dis-crim'-i-nêt-ing, iv], *a.* Indiscriminado; que no hace distinción alguna.
Indiscrimination [in-dis-crim-i-nê'-shun], *s.* Falta de distinción o claridad.
Indispensability [in-dis-pen-sa-bil'-i-ti], *s.* Indispensabilidad.
Indispensable [in-dis-pen'-sa-bl], *a.* Indispensable, imprescindible; preciso.
Indispensableness [in-dis-pen'-sa-bl-nes], *s.* Indispensabilidad, necesidad.
Indispensably [in-dis-pen'-sa-bli], *adv.* Indispensablemente, precisamente.
Indispose [in-dis-pōz'], *va.* 1. Indisponer, hacer a uno contrario o desfavorable a una cosa. 2. Hacer poco apto para o incapaz de. 3. Indisponer, malquistar, poner a uno mal con otro. 4. Indisponer, causar algún ligero quebranto en la salud.
Indisposedness [in-dis-pō'-zed-nes], *s.* Desazón, desavenencia, indisposición, repugnancia.
Indisposition [in-dis-po-zi'-shun], *s.* 1. Indisposición, desazón, falta de salud. 2. Desafecto, desavenencia; aborrecimiento.
Indisputable [in-dis'-piu-ta-bl], *a.* Indisputable.
Indisputableness [in-dis'-piu-ta-bl-nes], *s.* Certeza.
Indisputably [in-dis'-piu-ta-bli], *adv.* Indisputablemente, ciertamente.
Indissolvable [in-diz-elv'-a-bl], *a.* Indisoluble; permanente, obligatorio.
Indissolubility [in-dis-o-lu-bil'-i-ti], *s.* Indisolubilidad.
Indissoluble [in-dis'-o-lu-bl], *a.* Indisoluble, firme, estable.
Indissolubleness [in-dis'-o-lu-bl-nes], *s.* Indisolubilidad.
Indissolubly [in-dis'-o-lu-bli], *adv.* Indisolublemente.
Indistinct [in-dis-tinct'], *a.* Indistinto, confuso; obscuro, vago.
Indistinction, *s.* 1. Indistinción; obscuridad, falta de claridad, confusión. 2. Igualdad de rango o condición.
Indistinctly [in-dis-tinct'-li], *adv.* Indistintamente, confusamente, vagamente.
Indistinctness [in-dis-tinct'-nes], *s.* Confusión, obscuridad, incertidumbre.
Indistinguishable [in-dis-tin'-gwish-a-bl], *a.* Indistinguible.
Indite [in-dait'], *va.* 1. Poner por escrito; componer, escribir. 2. (Ant.) Dictar, dirigir. 3. (Des.) *V.* INDICT.
Inditement [in-dait'-mẹnt], *s.* Composición; escritura.
Inditer [in-dait'-ẹr], *s.* Autor.
Indium [in'-di-um], *s.* Indio, metal parecido al estaño, color de plata y maleable, descubierto en 1863.
Individual [in-di-vid'-yu-al], *a.* 1. Solo, único. 2. Individual, particular, individuo, que pertenece a uno solo. *An individual soul,* Un alma única.—*s.* 1. Individuo, el particular de su especie, una sola persona, cosa ó animal; especialmente persona humana, la propia persona. 2. Particular, persona privada, en oposición a una sociedad ó corporación.
Individualism [in-di-vid'-yu-al-izm], *s.* 1. Individualismo; sistema de refinado egoísmo, de aislamiento en los estudios, trabajos y existencia. 2. Sistema que no reconoce más realidad que la del individuo y en él cree encontrar el fundamento y fin de todas las leyes, etc. 3. Sistema que ensancha la esfera de acción y derechos del individuo a expensas de las funciones sociales.
Individualistic [in-di-vid-yu-a-lis'-tic], *a.* Individualista.
Individuality [in-di-vid-yu-al'-i-ti], *s.* Individualidad.
Individualize [in-di-vid'-yu-al-aiz], *va.* Individualizar, particularizar.
Individually [in-di-vid'-yu-al-i], *adv.* Individualmente.
Individuate [in-di-vid'-yu-êt], *va.* Individualizar, particularizar.—*a.* 1. Convertido en individuos. 2. Individual, que posee diferencia é identidad numéricas.
Individuation [in-di-vid-yu-ê'-shun], *s.* 1. La acción de individuar o especificar. 2. Producción de individuos.
Indivisibility [in-di-viz-i-bil'-i-ti], **Indivisibleness** [in-di-viz'-i-bl-nes], *s.* Indivisibilidad.
Indivisible [in-di-viz'-i-bl], *a.* Indivisible.—*s.* Incapaz de división.
Indivisibly [in-di-viz'-i-bli], *adv.* Indivisiblemente.
Indocile [in-des'-il], *a.* Indócil, cerril.
Indocility [in-do-sil'-i-ti], *s.* Indocilidad, pertinacia, dureza, aspereza.
Indoctrinate [in-dec'-trin-êt], *va.* Doctrinar, enseñar, disciplinar, instruir.
Indoctrination [in-doc-tri-nê'-shun], *s.* Instrucción, enseñanza.
Indo-European [in"-dō-yu-ro-pî'-an], *a.* Indoeuropeo, indoeuropea; indogermánico, ario.
Indolence [in'-do-lens], *s.* 1. Indolencia, pereza. 2. (Med.) Ausencia de dolor o sufrimiento.
Indolent [in'-do-lent], *a.* 1. Indolente, perezoso, indiferente a todo. 2. (Med.) Indolente, sin dolor, que no causa sufrimiento.
Indolently [in'-do-lent-li], *adv.* Indolentemente, perezosamente, con indolencia.
Indomitable [in-dem'-it-a-bl], *a.* Indomable, que no se puede domar.
Indoor [in'-dōr], *a.* Interno, interior; de puertas adentro. *Indoor work,* Trabajo interior.
Indoors [in-dōrs'], *adv.* Adentro; en el interior de un edificio; en casa, o en la habitación.
Indorsable [in-dōrs'-a-bl], *a.* Endosable, endorsable.
Indorse [in-dōrs'], *va.* 1. Endorsar, escribir en el dorso, respaldar un documento (para archivarlo). 2. Endosar, escribir al dorso de una letra de cambio, vale ó libranza, para cederla a otro o para garantizar su pago. 3. Dar sanción a, aprobar, confirmar. *V.* ENDORSE.
Indorsee [in-dor-sî'], *s.* Endosado, portador; la persona a cuya orden se ha endosado una libranza, pagaré, etc.
Indorsement [in-dōrs'-mẹnt], *s.* 1. Endoso de una letra de cambio, vale ó libranza. 2. Traspaso de un vale ó pagaré. 3. Rótulo, sobrescrito. 4. Sanción, aprobación, ratificación.
Indorser, Indorsor [in-ders'-ẹr], *s.* Endosante, endosador, el que endosa.
Indraft, Indraught [in'-draft], *s.* Entrada, el acto de atraer ó de inspirar, y lo que es atraído.
Indrawn [in'-drēn], *a.* Atraído, inspirado; con voz ahogada; de aquí, abstraído, distraído.
Indubious [in-diū'-bi-us], *a.* Indudable, cierto, seguro.
Indubitable [in-diū'-bit-a-bl], *a.* Indudable, indubitable, lo que no se puede dudar.
Indubitableness [in-diū'-bit-a-bl-nes], *s.* El estado de lo que es indudable.
Indubitably [in-diū'-bit-a-bli], *adv.* Indudablemente, indubitablemente.
Induce [in-diūs'], *va.* 1. Inducir, aconsejar ó persuadir a uno a que ejecute alguna cosa; instigar, incitar. 2. Inferir, sacar consecuencias. 3. Producir, causar, ocasionar, efectuar gradualmente, inspirar. 4. (Fís.) Producir por la inducción eléctrica o magnética.
Inducement [in-diūs'-mẹnt], *s.* Incitamento, móvil, inducimiento, aliciente, lo que induce ó persuade a alguna cosa, persuasión.
Inducer [in-diūs'-ẹr], *s.* Inducidor, persuadidor, inspirador.
Inducible [in-diūs'-i-bl], *a.* Deducible, que puede sacarse por inducción ó ilación.
Induct [in-duct'], *va.* 1. Introducir. 2. Instalar, dar posesión al que ha obtenido algún beneficio ó empleo. 3. Obtener por inducción.
Inductance [in-duc'-tans], *s.* Inductancia.
Induction [in-duc'-shun], *s.* Inducción (en todos sus significados). *Induction coil,* (Elec.) Bobina de inducción. *Induction coefficient,* Coeficiente de inducción. *Series-wound induction coil,* Bobina de inducción en serie. *Vibrator-type induction coil,* Bobina de inducción con temblador. *Cross induction,* Induccion transversal.
Inductive [in-duc'-tiv], *a.* 1. Inductivo. 2. Ilativo. 3. (Elec.) Inductivo, capaz de inducción; producido por la inducción, ó que obra por ella.
Inductively [in-duc'-tiv-li], *adv.* In-

ductivamente, por inducción, por ilación o inferencia.

Inductor [in-duc'-tęr], *s.* 1. El que instala o da posesión de algún beneficio eclesiástico. 2. (Elec.) Inductor, cualquier parte de un aparato eléctrico que obra sobre otra por inducción.

Indue [in-diū'], *va.* 1. Vestir, cubrir con vestido, investir. 2. Dotar a alguno con algún don o excelencia.

Indulge [in-dulj'], *va.* 1. Consentir, por lo común fuera de propósito o poco prudentemente; no oponerse a la ejecución de alguna cosa; condescender, gratificar, dar gusto, tolerar; contentar, satisfacer. 2. Conceder, dar gratuitamente; permitir. 3. Favorecer, animar. *To indulge to,* Entregarse, darse a. *To indulge in,* Lisonjearse.—*vn.* Entregarse a, abandonarse a; satisfacer un deseo sin restricción; se usa con la preposición *in. To indulge one's self,* Darse gusto; obrar con toda comodidad; beber de codos.

Indulgence [in-dul'-jens], **Indulgency** [in-dul'-jen-si], *s.* 1. Indulgencia, cariño, afecto, halago, condescendencia, gratificación, satisfacción, goce. 2. Abandono, acción de entregarse a sus pasiones. 3. Indulgencia, disimulo, inclinación a perdonar y sufrir; facilidad, placer, bondad. 4. Favor, gracia concedida, complacencia; (Com.) permiso para aplazar un pago. 5. Indulgencia, gracia concedida en la Iglesia romana por el Papa y los obispos, en remisión de las penitencias canónicas.

Indulgent [in-dul'-jent], *a.* 1. Indulgente, tierno, clemente, favorable. 2. Indulgente, condescendiente, complaciente, fácil.

Indulgently [in-dul'-jent-li], *adv.* Indulgentemente.

Indulger [in-dulj'-ęr], *s.* Indulgente, el que es complaciente o fácil en acomodarse al gusto de los demás.

Indult [in-dult'], †**Indulto** [in-dul'-to], *s.* Indulto, gracia, o privilegio concedido por el Papa; exención.

Indurate [in'-diu-rêt], *va.* 1. Endurecer una cosa. 2. Endurecer a uno, hacer duro, insensible u obstinado. —*vn.* Endurecerse, empedernirse.

Indurate, *a.* Impenitente, obstinado en la culpa o el mal; duro, endurecido.

Induration [in-diu-rê'-shun], *s.* 1. Endurecimiento, la acción, el acto de endurecer; estado de lo que se halla endurecido. 2. Dureza de corazón.

Industrial [in-dus'-tri-al], *a.* Industrial, que pertenece a la industria. *Industrial exhibition,* Exposición de la industria, fabril, etc. *Industrial psychology,* Psicología industrial. *Industrial school,* Escuela industrial, de artes y oficios; también, escuela donde se instruye y corrige a niños pobres cuya educación ha sido descuidada.

Industrialism [in-dus'-tri-al-izm], *s.* 1. Industrialismo, el sistema moderno industrial; sistema social que considera la industria como el más importante de los fines humanos. 2. Industria, trabajo.

Industrialist [in-dus'-tri-al-ist], *s.* Industrialista.

Industrialization [in-dus-tri-al-i-zê'-shun], *s.* Industrialización.

Industrialize [in-dus'-tri-al-aiz], *va.* Industrializar.

Industrious [in-dus'-tri-us], *a.* 1. Industrioso, diligente, laborioso, aplicado. 2. Industrioso, hecho con industria o mucho arte.

Industriously [in-dus'-tri-us-li], *adv.* 1. Industriosamente. 2. Industriosamente, de industria, de propósito, de intento, adrede.

Industry [in'-dus-tri], *s.* 1. Industria, esmero, diligencia, destreza. 2. Labor, trabajo útil en general (particularmente de la industria manufacturera). 3. Cualquier ramo aislado de la actividad productiva.

Indwell [in-dwel'], *va.* y *vn.* Existir interiormente; morar dentro, habitar; morar permanentemente en el alma.

Indweller [in'-dwel-ęr], *s.* Un habitante.

Indwelling [in-dwel'-ing], *pa.* Morador, ra, que existe dentro.—*s.* Existencia interior, presencia.

Inebriant [in-i'-bri-ant], *a.* Embriagador, que embriaga.—*s.* Substancia embriagadora.

Inebriate [in-i'-bri-êt], *va.* 1. Embriagar, emborrachar. 2. Infatuar, cegar, desvanecer.—*vn.* 1. Embriagarse o emborracharse. 2. Infatuarse. —*s.* Borracho.

Inebriation [in-i-bri-ê'-shun], *s.* Embriaguez, borrachera.

Inedited [in-ed'-it-ęd], *a.* 1. Inédito. 2. No redactado aún.

Ineffable [in-ef'-a-bl], *a.* 1. Inefable, que no se puede expresar con palabras. 2. Aplícase a aquellas cosas de que no se debe hablar, v. g. el nombre de Jehová.

Ineffableness [in-ef'-a-bl-nes], *s.* Inefabilidad.

Ineffably [in-ef'-a-bli], *adv.* Inefablemente, indeciblemente.

Ineffaceable [in-ef-fês'-a-bl], *a.* Indeleble, imborrable, que no se puede borrar.

Ineffaceably [in-ef-fês'-a-bli], *adv.* Indeleblemente, imborrablemente.

Ineffective [in-ef-fec'-tiv], *a.* Ineficaz; vano, inútil; impotente.

Ineffectual [in-ef-fec'-chu-al], *a.* Ineficaz; sin efecto, incapaz de producir el efecto deseado. *To prove ineffectual,* No tener resultado, quedar sin efecto.

Ineffectually [in-ef-fec'-chu-al-i], *adv.* Ineficazmente; sin resultado.

Ineffectualness [in-ef-fec'-chu-al-nes], *s.* Ineficacia.

Inefficacious [in-ef-i-kê'-shus], *a.* Ineficaz.

Inefficaciousness [in-ef-i-kê'-shus-nes], *s.* Ineficacia.

Inefficacy [in-ef'-i-ca-si], **Inefficiency** [in-e-fish'-en-si], *s.* Ineficacia, falta de eficacia.

Inefficient [in-ef-fish'-ent], *a.* Ineficaz.

Inelastic [in-ę-las'-tic], *a.* Falto de elasticidad.

Inelasticity [in-ę-las-tis'-i-ti], *s.* Carencia de elasticidad.

Inelegance [in-el'-ę-gans], **Inelegancy** [in-el'-ę-gan-si], *s.* Inelegancia, falta de elegancia.

Inelegant [in-el'-ę-gant], *a.* Inelegante, falto de elegancia, de buen gusto.

Inelegantly [in-el'-ę-gant-li], *adv.* Sin elegancia, de un modo falto de elegancia.

Ineligibility [in-el-i-ji-bil'-i-ti], *s.* Estado o calidad de lo que no puede ser elegido.

Ineligible [in-el'-i-ji-bl], *a.* 1. Excluído de elección, incapaz de ser elegido. 2. Que no conviene escoger; poco deseable.

Ineluctable [in-ę-luc'-ta-bl], *a.* Inevitable, irresistible, ineluctable.

Inept [in-ept'], *a.* 1. Inepto; no idóneo. 2. Absurdo, tonto, inconsistente con la razón.

Ineptitude [in-ept'-i-tiūd], †**Ineptness** [in-ept'-nes], *s.* Ineptitud, incapacidad.

Ineptly [in-ept'-li], *adv.* Ineptamente, neciamente.

Inequal [in-i'-cwal], *a.* (Ento.) Desigual; dícese de una superficie.

Inequality [in-ę-cwōl'-i-ti], *s.* 1. Desigualdad, diferencia en cosas de la misma clase; disparidad, desemejanza. 2. Desigualdad, falta de regularidad, o de proporción; superficie escabrosa. 3. Desigualdad, variedad o inconstancia; desviación en el movimiento de un astro. 4. Insuficiencia; incompetencia. 5. Injusticia.

Inequitable [in-ec'-wi-ta-bl], *a.* Que no es equitativo o justo.

Ineradicable [in-ę-rad'-i-ca-bl], *a.* Que no se puede desarraigar ni extirpar.

Inerrable [in-er'-a-bl], *a.* Inerrable, libre de error.

Inerrant [in-er'-ant], *a.* Exento de error, infalible.

Inert [in-ęrt'], *a.* Inerte, flojo, que carece de fuerza inherente para moverse o resistir a una fuerza impulsante; inanimado, sin vida.

Inertia [in-ęr'-shi-a], *s.* 1. Flojedad, inacción, desidia. 2. (Fís.) Inercia, propiedad que tienen los cuerpos de permanecer en el estado de movimiento o de reposo en que se encuentran, hasta que una acción exterior obra sobre ellos con suficiente energía.

Inertial guidance [in-er-shi-al gaid'-ens], *s.* Orientación por inercia.

Inertly [in-ęrt'-li], *adv.* Pesadamente, flojamente, indolentemente.

Inertness [in-ęrt'-nes], *s.* Flojedad, inacción.

Inescutcheon [in-es-cuch'-un], *s.* (Her.) Escudo de armas pequeño dentro de otro mayor.

Inestimable [in-es'-ti-ma-bl], *a.* Inestimable, inapreciable, lo que no se puede estimar dignamente.

Inestimably [in-es'-ti-ma-bli], *adv.* De un modo inestimable.

Inevitable [in-ev'-it-a-bl], *a.* Inevitable: (fam.) de ene.

Inevitability [in-ev-it-a-bil'-i-ti], **Inevitableness** [in-ev'-it-a-bl-nes], *s.* El estado o calidad de lo que es inevitable.

Inevitably [in-ev'-it-a-bli], *adv.* Inevitablemente.

Inexact [in-eg-zact'], *a.* Inexacto, falto de exactitud o de verdad; incorrecto.

Inexcusable [in-ex-kiūz'-a-bl], *a.* Inexcusable, injustificable, imperdonable.

Inexcusableness [in-ex-kiūz'-a-bl-nes], *s.* Enormidad o atrocidad que no merece excusa, disculpa o perdón.

Inexcusably [in-ex-kiūz'-a-bli], *adv.* Inexcusablemente, sin excusa.

Inexhaustible [in-eg-zōst'-i-bl], **Inexhaustive** [in-eg-zōst'-iv], *a.* Inexhausto, inagotable.

Inexhaustibleness [in-eg-zōst'-i-bl-nes], *s.* El estado o calidad de lo que es inagotable.

Inexistence [in-eg-zist'-ens], *s.* Inexistencia.

Inexistent [in-eg-zist'-ent], *a.* Inexistente.

Inexorable [in-ec'-so-ra-bl], *a.* Inexorable, duro, inflexible.

Inexorability [in-ec-so-ra-bil'-i-ti], **Inexorableness** [in-ec'-so-ra-bl-nes], *s.* Inflexibilidad.

Inexorably [in-ec'-so-ra-bli], *adv.* Inflexiblemente.

Inexpansible [in-ex-pan'-si-bl], *a.* Poco expansible, incapaz de expansión.

Inexpedience, Inexpediency [in-ex-pí'-di-ens, en-si], *s.* Inoportunidad, impropiedad, falta de conveniencia en el orden, tiempo ó circunstancias en que se hace o se proyecta hacer una cosa.

Inexpedient [in-ex-pí'-di-ent], *a.* Impropio, inoportuno, que no viene al caso o está fuera de propósito.

Inexpensive [in-ex-pen'-siv], *a.* Poco costoso, que no exige grandes gastos; barato.

Inexperience [in-ex-pí'-ri-ens], *s.* Inexperiencia, impericia.

Inexperienced [in-ex-pí'-ri-enst], *a.* Inexperimentado, falto de experiencia.

Inexpert [in-ex-pert'], *a.* Inexperto, poco mañoso, inhábil.

Inexpiable [in-ex'-pi-a-bl], *a.* Inexpiable, lo que no puede ser perdonado o satisfecho, expiado o lavado, hablando de culpas o delitos.

Inexpiableness [in-ex'-pi-a-bl-nes], *s.* El estado ó calidad de lo que es inexpiable o no se puede purgar o satisfacer.

Inexpiably [in-ex'-pi-a-bli], *adv.* De un modo inexpiable, en un grado que no admite expiación.

Inexplicable [in-ex'-pli-ca-bl], *a.* Inexplicable, que no se puede explicar.

Inexplicability, Inexplicableness [in-ex-pli-ca-bil'-i-ti, bl-nes], *s.* El estado ó calidad de lo que es inexplicable.

Inexplicably [in-ex'-pli-ca-bli], *adv.* Inexplicablemente.

Inexplorable [in-ex-plōr'-a-bl], *a.* Que no se puede explorar.

Inexpressible [in-ex-pres'-i-bl], *a.* Indecible, lo que no se puede expresar.—*Inexpressibles, s. pl.* (Fest.) Los pantalones.

Inexpressibly [in-ex-pres'-i-bli], *adv.* Indeciblemente.

Inexpressive [in-ex-pres'-iv], *a.* 1. Falto de expresión en el hablar o en la fisonomía. 2. (Poét.) Indecible.

Inexpugnable [in-ex-pug'-na-bl], *a.* 1. Inexpugnable, lo que no se puede tomar o conquistar. 2. Inexpugnable, el que no se deja vencer fácilmente.

Inextensible [in-ex-ten'-si-bl], *a.* Incapaz de ser extendido; invariable en longitud o superficie.

Inextinct [in-ex-tinct'], *a.* Que no está extinto o apagado.

Inextinguishability [in-ex-tin-gwish-a-bil'-i-ti], *s.* La calidad de lo que es inextinguible.

Inextinguishable [in-ex-tin'-gwish-a-bl], *a.* Inextinguible, lo que no se puede extinguir; implacable, que no se puede apaciguar.

Inextricable [in-ex'-tri-ca-bl], *a.* Intrincado, confuso, enmarañado.

Inextricableness [in-ex'-tri-ca-bl-nes], *s.* El estado de lo que es intrincado o confuso.

Inextricably [in-ex'-tri-ca-bli], *adv.* Intrincadamente, enmarañadamente.

Infallibility [in-fal-i-bil'-i-ti], **Infallibleness** [in-fal'-i-bl-nes], *s.* Infalibilidad, suma certeza, incapacidad de engañar o engañarse.

Infallible [in-fal'-i-bl], *a.* 1. Infalible. 2. Infalible, seguro, cierto, indefectible.

Infallibly [in-fal'-i-bli], *adv.* Infaliblemente, seguramente.

Infamous [in'-fa-mus], *a.* 1. Infame, ignominioso, desacreditado, vil, mal reputado; vergonzoso. 2. Infamante, infamatorio, que infama ó que merece la infamia; odioso, aborrecible, notoriamente injusto o malvado.

Infamously [in'-fa-mus-li], *adv.* Infamemente, ignominiosamente.

Infamousness [in'-fa-mus-nes], **Infamy** [in'-fa-mi], *s.* Infamia, descrédito, deshonra, oprobio, baldón.

Infancy [in'-fan-si], *s.* 1. Infancia, la edad del hombre hasta que tiene uso de razón. 2. Infancia, los primeros años. 3. Infancia, el principio u origen de alguna cosa. 4. (Der.) Menor edad, minoridad, período de la vida antes de la mayor edad (esto es, antes de la capacidad legal).

†**Infangthef** [in-fang'-thef], *s.* Un privilegio de que gozaban antiguamente los señores de juzgar a los malhechores que robaban en sus estados; derecho muy semejante al llamado de horca y cuchillo en España.

Infant [in'-fant], *s.* 1. Infante, niño o niña de tierna edad; criatura. 2. Menor, la persona que aun no ha llegado a la edad que determinan las leyes en los diferentes países para gobernar su hacienda y disponer libremente de su persona; (en los Estados Unidos, la Gran Bretaña y otros países esta edad es de 21 años).—*a.* 1. *V.* INFANTILE. 2. De menor edad. 3. (Fig.) Joven, naciente, que no ha llegado a la madurez. *Infant industries,* Industrias nacientes.

Infanticidal [in-fan-ti-sai'-dal], *a.* Que se refiere al infanticidio.

Infanticide [in-fan'-ti-said], *s.* 1. Infanticidio, homicidio de un niño o criatura. 2. Infanticida, la persona que comete este homicidio.

Infantile [in'-fan-tail], *a.* Infantil, pueril. *Infantile paralysis,* parálisis infantil, poliomielitis.

Infantine [in'-fan-tin o tain], *a.* Infantil, propio de niño.

Infant-like [in'-fant-laic], *a.* Semejante a un niño.

Infantry [in'-fant-ri], *s.* Infantería, peones, infantes.

Infarct [in-fārct'], *s.* Infarto, lo que forma una hinchazón u obstrucción en un órgano.

Infarction [in-fārc'-shun], *s.* (Med.) Obstrucción por repleción; infartamiento, infartación.

Infatuate [in-fat'-yu-ēt], *va.* Infatuar, embobar, privar del uso de razón, preocupar.

Infatuate, Infatuated [in-fat'-yu-ēt-ed], *a.* Infatuado.

Infatuating [in-fat'-yu-ēt-ing], *a.* Que infatúa o entontece.

Infatuation [in-fat-yu-ē'-shun], *s.* Infatuación, preocupación ciega, encaprichamiento.

Infeasibility [in-fīz-i-bil'-i-ti], **Infeasibleness** [in-fīz'-i-bl-nes], *s.* Impracticabilidad.

Infeasible [in-fīz'-i-bl], *a.* Impracticable.

Infect [in-fect'], *va.* 1. Infectar, apestar, inficionar, corromper. 2. (For.) Tachar de ilegalidad.

Infection [in-fec'-shun], *s.* 1. Infección, la acción de infectar; comunicación de una enfermedad por medio del contacto, del aire, del agua o de las ropas. 2. Lo que inficiona, materia morbífica e infecta, como los miasmas. 3. (For.) Acción de tachar de ilegalidad.

Infectious [in-fec'-shus], *a.* 1. Infecto, inficionado; corruptor. 2. (Med.) Pestilente, comunicable por vía de infección o indirectamente; distinto de contagioso. 3. (For.) Tachado de ilegalidad.

Infectiously [in-fec'-shus-li], *adv.* Por infección.

Infectiousness [in-fec'-shus-nes], *s.* Calidad o propiedad de inficionar.

Infective [in-fec'-tiv], *a.* Infectivo, pestilente.

Infecund [in-fec'-und], *a.* Infecundo, estéril.

Infecundity [in-fe-cun'-di-ti], *s.* Infecundidad, esterilidad.

Infelicitous [in-fe-lis'-i-tus], *a.* 1. Inepto, poco apropiado, poco conveniente. 2. Infeliz, desdichado, desgraciado.

Infelicity [in-fe-lis'-i-ti], *s.* 1. Infelicidad, desgracia, desdicha, infortunio. 2. Ineptitud, falta de idoneidad, de conveniencia. 3. Palabra o expresión fuera de propósito, poco conveniente.

Infer [in-fer'], *va.* 1. Inferir, deducir, concluir. 2. Mostrar, implicar. —*vn.* Sacar una consecuencia.

Inferable [in-fer'-a-bl], *a.* Deducible. *V.* INFERRIBLE.

Inference [in'-fer-ens], *s.* Inferencia, ilación, consecuencia, inducción.

Inferential [in-fer-en'-shal], *a.* Ilativo: de la naturaleza de una inferencia.

Inferior [in-fí'-ri-er], *a.* 1. Inferior, lo que es menos que otra cosa en cantidad o calidad. 2. Inferior, debajo de otra cosa o más bajo que ella. 3. (Mús.) De tono más bajo. 4. Inferior, el que está sujeto a otro o el que es menos que otra persona en saber, valer, poder, puesto o mando; subordinado, subalterno. 5. (Impr.) Inferior, que está debajo del nivel de la línea.—*s.* Inferior, el que está subordinado a un superior.

Inferiority [in-fí-ri-er'-i-ti], **Inferiorness** [in-fí'-ri-er-nes], *s.* Inferioridad. *Inferiority complex,* Complejo de inferioridad.

Infernal [in-fer'-nal], *a.* Infernal, cosa del infierno ó perteneciente á él.

Infernalness [in-fer'-nal-nes], *s.* El estado de lo que es infernal.

Inferrible [in-fer'-i-bl], *a.* Que se puede deducir o inferir.

Infertile [in-fer'-til], *a.* Infecundo, infértil, estéril.

Infertility [in-fer-til'-i-ti], *s.* Infecundidad, infertilidad, esterilidad.

Infest [in-fest'], *va.* 1. Infestar, incomodar, trabajar; inficionar, apestar. 2. Infestar, causar el enemigo daños y estragos con hostilidades y correrías.

Infestation [in-fes-tē'-shun], *s.* Infestación; molestia, disturbio.

Infested [in-fest'-ed], *a.* Infestado; molestado, acosado.

Infestive [in-fes'-tiv], *a.* Triste, melancólico.

Infeudation [in-fiu-dē'-shun], *s.* Enfeudación, el acto de enfeudar.

Infidel [in'-fi-del], *s.* Infiel, gentil, pagano.—*a.* Infiel; desleal, fementido, pérfido.

Infidelity [in-fi-del'-i-ti], *s.* 1. Infidelidad, falta de fe, escepticismo respecto de la religión generalmente reconocida; falta de buena fe, infidelidad conyugal. 2. Deslealtad, alevosía, perfidia.

Infiltrate [in-fil'-trêt], *va.* Infiltrar, hacer que un líquido o gas penetre por los poros o intersticios.—*vn.* Infiltrarse, recalar, entrar penetrando por los poros.

Infiltration [in-fil-trê'-shun], *s.* 1. Infiltración, el acto de infiltrar. 2. Lo que está infiltrado; (Med.) infarto blando.

Infinite [in'-fi-nit], *a.* 1. Infinito, lo que no tiene fin ni término; ilimitado. 2. Infinito, innumerable; muy grande. 3. Que lo contiene todo; cabal y perfecto; que comprende todas las perfecciones.

Infinitely [in'-fi-nit-li], *adv.* Infinitamente, ilimitadamente.

Infiniteness [in'-fi-nit-nes], *s.* Infinidad, cualidad de lo infinito.

Infinitesimal [in-fi-ni-tes'-i-mal], *a.* (Mat.) Infinitesimal: dícese del cálculo o cantidad.—*s.* Infinitésima, parte infinitamente pequeña de cualquiera cantidad.

Infinitive [in-fin'-i-tiv], *a.* Infinitivo.—*s.* Modo infinitivo.

Infinitude [in-fin'-i-tiūd], *s.* Infinidad; muchedumbre innumerable o infinita.

Infinity [in-fin'-i-ti], *s.* 1. Infinidad, extensión ilimitada; espacio sin límites, inmensidad. 2. Estado o cualidad de lo infinito; perfección.

Infirm [in-fẹrm'], *a.* 1. Enfermizo, inválido, doliente, achacoso. (Fam.) Enclenque. 2. Enfermo, frágil, débil. 3. Instable, poco firme y seguro; irresoluto. 4. (For.) Anulable; que se puede invalidar.

Infirmary [in-fẹr'-ma-ri], *s.* Enfermería.

Infirmity [in-fẹr'-mi-ti], *s.* 1. Flaqueza, fragilidad, falta cometida por la debilidad natural del sexo, de la edad, del genio, etc. 2. Falta, desliz, traspié. 3. Enfermedad, dolencia, achaque, mal, indisposición o falta de salud.

Infirmness [in-fẹrm'-nes], *s.* Debilidad, extenuación, flaqueza.

Infix [in-fics'], *va.* 1. Clavar, introducir alguna cosa puntiaguda en otra. 2. Imprimir, inculcar, grabar en el alma alguna cosa.—*s.* (Gram.) Partícula que va interpuesta en una palabra para modificar su significación. *Cf.* PREFIX y SUFFIX.

Inflame [in-flêm'], *va.* 1. Inflamar, encender, hacer arder. 2. Inflamar, encender, enardecer el ánimo o las pasiones, acalorar, azuzar, provocar, irritar. 3. Exagerar, agravar.—*vn.* (Med.) Inflamarse, hincharse.

Inflamed [in-flêmd'], *a.* Encendido, irritado, acalorado, enardecido.

Inflamer [in-flêm'-ẹr], *s.* Inflamador, enardecedor, el que inflama, lo que enciende o enardece.

Inflaming [in-flêm'-ing], *s.* Inflamación, enardecimiento.

Inflammability [in-flam-a-bil'-i-ti], *s.* Inflamabilidad, calidad o propiedad de lo que es inflamable; aptitud o disposición a inflamarse.

Inflammable [in-flam'-a-bl], *a.* Inflamable. *Inflammable air,* (Des.) Aire inflamable o gas hidrógeno.

Inflammableness [in-flam'-a-bl-nes], *s.* Inflamación, enardecimiento; la calidad de lo que es inflamable.

Inflammation [in-fla-mê'-shun], *s.* 1. Inflamación, encendimiento. 2. Inflamación, enardecimiento de las pasiones y de los afectos del ánimo. 3. (Med.) Inflamación, estado mórbido de alguna parte del cuerpo, que produce en ella rubicundez, tumefacción, calor y dolor.

Inflammative [in-flam'-a-tiv], (Poco us.) **Inflammatory** [in-flam'-a-to-ri], *a.* Inflamatorio, que produce o es propio para producir inflamación, tumulto, o sedición; incendiario. 2. Inflamatorio, que se relaciona con una inflamación.

Inflate [in-flêt'], *va.* 1. Inflar, hinchar, entumecer. 2. Hinchar, engreir, envanecer. 3. Soplar.

Inflated [in-flêt'-ed], *a.* Hinchado, inflado, entumecido, engreído.

Inflation [in-flê'-shun], *s.* 1. Inflación, hinchazón, entumecimiento. 2. Hinchazón, engreimiento, envanecimiento.

Inflect [in-flect'], *va.* 1. Torcer, doblar, encorvar, mudar, variar. 2. (Gram.) Declinar, conjugar.

Inflection [in-flec'-shun], *s.* 1. Inflexión, dobladura. 2. Inflexión, modulación de la voz. 3. (Gram.) Inflexión, la variación de las terminaciones en los nombres o verbos.

Inflective [in-flec'-tiv], *a.* Lo que tiene virtud para doblar o torcer.

Inflex [in-flecs'], *va.* Encorvar, torcer, doblar.

Inflexibility [in-flec-si-bil'-i-ti], **Inflexibleness** [in-flec'-si-bl-nes], *s.* Inflexibilidad, dureza, pertinacia, obstinación.

Inflexible [in-flec'-si-bl], *a.* 1. Inexorable. 2. Inflexible. 3. Inalterable.

Inflexibly [in-flec'-si-bli], *adv.* Inflexiblemente; inexorablemente.

Inflexion, *s.* *V.* INFLECTION.

Inflict [in-flict'], *va.* 1. Castigar, infligir, imponer penas corporales. 2. Cubrir de. *To inflict disgrace,* Cubrir de oprobio, de vergüenza.

Inflicter [in-flict'-ẹr], *s.* Castigador.

Infliction [in-flic'-shun], *s.* Imposición o castigo de una pena corporal; inflicción.

Inflictive [in-flic'-tiv], *a.* Inflictiva, la pena que se impone al delincuente, o la que se ha de imponer.

Inflorescence [in-flo-res'-ens], *s.* 1. (Bot.) Inflorescencia, disposición general de las flores en los vegetales. 2. Florescencia, acción de florecer; conjunto de las flores del mismo género.

Inflow [in'-flō], *s.* Afluencia.

Influence [in'-flu-ens], *s.* Influencia; influjo, en sus acepciones castellanas, la eléctrica inclusive.

Influence, *va.* Influir: (1) causar ciertos efectos unos cuerpos en otros. (2) Intervenir, tener parte en algún negocio. (3) Comunicar Dios algún efecto o don de su gracia. (4) Tener ascendiente o autoridad moral sobre alguien. (5) Modificar, cambiar la manera de ser.

Influencing [in'-flu-ens-ing], *s.* Influencia, influjo.

Influent [in'-flu-ent], *a.* Que fluye hacia dentro.

Influential [in-flu-en'-shal], *a.* Que influye, que tiene influencia ó influjo.

Influentially [in-flu-en'-shal-i], *adv.* Por medio de influencia o influjo.

Influenza [in-flu-en'-za], *s.* Catarro o fluxión epidémica, acompañada de fiebre.

Influx [in'-flux], *s.* 1. Influjo, el acto de influir en alguna cosa. 2. Infusión, el acto de infundir Dios en el alma algún efecto o gracia. 3. Instilación, intromisión. 4. Desembocadura, paraje por donde desemboca un río, canal, etc.

Influxion [in-fluc'-shun], *s.* Infusión de alguna gracia o don divino.

Infold [in-fōld'], *va.* 1. Envolver, arrollar. 2. Abrazar, apretar, estrechar entre los brazos.

Inform [in-fōrm'], *va.* 1. Informar, dar noticias a alguno; instruir, enseñar. 2. Delatar, acusar ante el juez. 3. Dar forma a, animar, infundir vida o fuerza.—*vn.* Informar, dar parte. *To inform against one,* Delatar a uno.

Informal [in-fōrm'-al], *a.* 1. Informal, irregular, que no está conforme a lo establecido. 2. Informal, que carece de formas oficiales, sin ceremonia.

Informality [in-fōr-mal'-i-ti], *s.* 1. Informalidad, irregularidad, falta de la forma establecida, regular o legal. 2. Hecho o acción informal.

Informally [in-fōr'-mal-i], *adv.* Irregularmente, sin ceremonia.

Informant [in-fōr'-mant], *s.* Informante, denunciador, persona que informa o hace saber. Se diferencia del *informer* o delator.

Information [in-fōr-mê'-shun], *s.* 1. Informe, información, instrucción, aviso, noticia; saber, conocimientos sacados del estudio, de la observación, etc. 2. Acusación, delación, denunciación. 3. Información, el acto de informar.

Information bureau, *s.* Oficina o centro de información.

Informative [in-fōr'-ma-tiv], *a.* Informativo, didáctico.

Informed [in-fōrmd'], *a.* 1. Instruído, inteligente. 2. Informe.

Informer [in-fōrm'-ẹr], *s.* 1. Delator, denunciador; espía, soplón. 2. Informante, el que informa. *V.* INFORMANT. 3. El que forma, amolda o anima. *To turn informer,* Hacerse delator.

Infossous [in-fes'-us], *a.* (Bot.) Deprimido de manera que forma canal, v. gr. las venas en ciertas hojas.

Infra-. Prefijo que significa bajo, debajo de; en la parte inferior.

Infract [in-fract'], *va.* (Poco us.) Romper, quebrantar.

Infracted [in-fract'-ed], *s.* Roto, quebrado, quebrantado.

Infraction [in-frac'-shun], *s.* 1. Quebrantamiento, rompimiento. 2. Infracción, quebrantamiento, transgresión, contravención de una ley, bando o edicto; violación de un tratado.

Infractor [in-frac'-tẹr], *s.* Infractor, transgresor, contraventor.

Infralapsarian [in-fra-lap-sê'-ri-an], *a.* y *s.* (Teol.) Epíteto dado a ciertos calvinistas que pretenden que Dios no proporciona a los hombres los medios de salvarse.

Inframammary [in''-fra-mam'-a-ri], *a.* Situado debajo de los pechos.

Inframaxillary [in''-fra-mac'-sil-lẹ-ri], *a.* Perteneciente a la quijada inferior.—*s.* Quijada inferior.

Infrangible [in-franj'-i-bl], *a.* Infrangible, inquebrantable.

Infrangibleness [in-franj'-i-bl-nes], *s.* El estado de lo que es infrangible.

Infraorbital [in-fra-ōr'-bit-al], *a.* Situado debajo de la órbita del ojo.

Infrared [in-fra-red'], *a.* Infrarrojo.
Infrequency [in-frí'-cwen-si], **Infrequence** [in-frí'-cwens], *s.* Rareza, raridad.
Infrequent [in-frí'-cwent], *a.* Raro, infrecuente, poco común, que ocurre o acaece a largos intervalos.
Infringe [in-frinj'], *va.* 1. Infringir, quebrantar, violar una ley o pacto, contravenir a; entrar sin derecho sobre. 2. Destruir, impedir, embarazar, estorbar.—*vn.* Violar derechos y privilegios. *To infringe on a patent-right,* Violar una patente, imitar o falsificar un artículo que tiene privilegio de invención.
Infringement [in-frinj'-mgnt], *s.* Infracción, violación, transgresión, contravención, quebrantamiento de la ley, de una obligación, de un privilegio o derecho.
Infringer [in-frinj'-gr], *s.* Violador, contraventor, quebrantador, infractor de una ley o convenio.
Infumed [in-fiūmd'], *a.* Desecado al humo.
Infundibular, Infundibuliform [in-fun-dib'-yu-lar, dib'-yu-li-fōrm], *a.* Infundibuliforme, en forma de embudo.
Infuriate [in-fiū'-ri-êt], *a.* Enfurecido, furioso, rabioso.
Infuriate, *va.* Enfurecer, irritar, enojar; hacer, volver o poner rabioso.
Infuscation [in-fus-kê'-shun], *s.* Obscurecimiento.
Infuse [in-fiūz'], *va.* 1. Infundir, echar en infusión, poner un simple en algún licor por cierto tiempo para extraer sus virtudes. 2. Infundir, causar algún efecto en el ánimo o mover alguna pasión. 3. Echar un licor en alguna cosa que pueda contenerle. 4. Infundir, inculcar, instilar, como principios o calidades: con *into. To infuse zeal into his pupils,* Infundir estímulo en sus discípulos.
Infused [in-fiūzd'], *a.* Infuso, infundido.
Infuser [in-fiūz'-gr], *s.* El que infunde o introduce en el ánimo.
Infusible [in-fiūz'-i-bl], *a.* 1. Infundible, lo que no se puede fundir, derretir o liquidar; lo que no sufre fusión. 2. (Poco us.) Capaz de infusión.
Infusion [in-fiū'-zhun], *s.* 1. Infusión, la acción de infundir. 2. Infusión, el acto de poner una substancia en un líquido, con el objeto de extraer sus propiedades o alguna de ellas, y el mismo líquido después de hecha la operación. 3. El acto de embeber o empapar una cosa en un líquido. 4. Infusión, inspiración, gracia infusa en el alma.
Infusive [in-fiū'-siv], *a.* Lo que puede ser infundido o lo que es capaz de infundir.
Infusoria [in-fiū-sō'-ri-a], *s.* Infusorios, nombre genérico de los animálculos que se desarrollan en las infusiones animales o vegetales, y sólo son perceptibles con el microscopio.
Infusorial [in-fiū-sō'-ri-al], *a.* Infusorio, que contiene infusorios, o perteneciente a ellos. *Infusorial earth,* Substancia terrosa muy fina que consiste principalmente en esqueletos silíceos de diátomos; sirve como polvos de bruñir, y como absorbente de la nitroglicerina.
Infusorian [in-fiu-sō'-ri-an], *a.* V. INFUSORIAL.—*s.* Uno de los infusorios. Lo mismo (adjetivo y nombre) significa INFUSORY.
Ingate [in'-gêt], *s.* 1. En la fundición, bebedero, agujero por donde entra el metal derretido. 2. Entrada que comunica el pozo de la mina con una galería lateral.
Ingathering [in'-gadh-gr-ing], *s.* Cosecha; el acto de recoger los productos de la tierra.
Ingelable [in-jel'-a-bl], *a.* Lo que no puede ser congelado.
Ingeminate [in-jem'-i-nêt], *a.* Reduplicado, duplicado, repetido.
Ingeminate, *va.* Reduplicar, duplicar, repetir.
Ingemination [in-jem-i-nê'-shun], *s.* Reduplicación.
Ingenerable [in-jen'-gr-a-bl], *a.* Ingenerable, que puede ser producido dentro, en el interior.
Ingenerate [in-jen'-gr-êt], *va.* Procrear, producir, engendrar.
Ingenerate, *a.* Innato; ingénito.
Ingenious [in-jīn'-yus], *a.* 1. Ingenioso, hábil, sutil, que tiene facultad inventiva; apto para discurrir o inventar. 2. Apto; bien formado, bien concebido o proyectado; mañoso.
Ingeniously [in-jīn'-yus-li], *adv.* Ingeniosamente.
Ingeniousness [in-jīn'-yus-nes], *s.* Ingeniosidad, sutileza, industria, destreza.
Ingenuity [in-je-niū'-i-ti], *s.* 1. Ingeniosidad, facultad inventiva. 2. Maña, habilidad, destreza para construir, idear o hacer algo.
Ingenuous [in-jen'-yu-us], *a.* Ingenuo, real, sincero, sin doblez, franco.
Ingenuously [in-jen'-yu-us-li], *adv.* Ingenuamente.
Ingenuousness [in-jen'-yu-us-nes], *s.* Ingenuidad, sinceridad.
Ingest [in-jest'], *va.* Introducir o ingerir en el estómago alguna cosa.
Ingesta [in-jes'-ta], *s. pl.* Alimentos tomados o tragados; (fig.) cosas incorporadas.
Ingestion [in-jes'-chun], *s.* Introducción de una cosa en el estómago.
Ingle [in'-gl], *s.* (Esco.) Fuego, llama. *Ingleside,* Hogar.
Inglorious [in-glō'-ri-us], *a.* 1. Vil, afrentoso, ignominioso, bajo, deshonroso, vergonzoso. 2. Insensible al honor, a la ambición o a la gloria.
Ingloriously [in-glō'-ri-us-li], *adv.* Ignominiosamente.
Ingloriousness [in-glō'-ri-us-nes], *s.* 1. Ignominia, vileza, deshonra. 2. Insensibilidad o falta de ansia por adquirir fama, reputación o gloria.
Ingluvies [in-gliū'-vi-īz], *s.* El buche de las aves granívoras.
Ingoing [in'-gō-ing], *a.* Entrante, que entra.—*s.* Entrada.
Ingot [in'-got], *s.* 1. Riel, barra de oro, plata u otro metal en bruto; lingote. *Ingot of gold,* Tejo de oro. *Ingot of copper,* Galápago de cobre. 2. Cualquier barra o pedazo de metal sin labrar, y a veces se ha llamado así el molde donde se labra el metal.
Ingraft [in-graft'], *va.* 1. Injertar o enjertar. *V.* GRAFT. 2. Imprimir, grabar, inspirar o fijar profundamente en el ánimo ideas, sentimientos, máximas, etc.
Ingrafting [in-graft'-ing], *s.* Injertación, enjertación, el acto de injertar o enjertar.
Ingraftment [in-graft'-ment], *s.* Injerto o enjerto.
Ingrain [in'-grên], *a.* Teñido en rama; fijado, impreso o grabado profundamente en el alma.—*s.* Alfombra teñida en rama.
Ingrain [in-grên'], *va.* 1. Teñir en rama; particularmente, teñir con grana o cochinilla. 2. Fijar o impregnar profundamente.
Ingrate [in'-grêt], *a.* Ingrato, desagradecido; desapacible.—*s.* Una persona ingrata.
Ingratiate [in-grê'-shi-êt], *vn.* Insinuarse, captar, ganar la voluntad de alguno; congraciarse, solicitar la benevolencia de una persona o granjearse su favor.
Ingratiating [in-grê'-shi-êt-ing], *s.* El acto de granjearse el favor o la benevolencia de una persona.
Ingratitude [in-grat'-i-tiūd], *s.* Ingratitud, desagradecimiento.
Ingredient [in-grī'-di-ent], *s.* Ingrediente, lo que entra en la composición de alguna cosa.
Ingress [in'-gres], *s.* 1. Ingreso, entrada. 2. Acceso, facultad de entrar; también el lugar de entrada.
Ingression [in-gresh'-un], *s.* Ingreso, entrada.
Ingrown [in'-grōn], *a.* Que crece hacia adentro. *Ingrown toenail,* Uñero.
Inguinal [in'-gwi-nal], *a.* Inguinal, lo que pertenece a las ingles.
Ingulf [in-gulf'], *va.* 1. Embocar, sumir, precipitar, hacer entrar violentamente una cosa en un boquete estrecho o sumidero. 2. Engolfar, hacer que alguno se arrebate con un pensamiento o afecto. Úsase casi siempre como neutro en ambos sentidos en castellano.
Ingurgitate [in-gūr'-ji-têt], *va.* (Ant.) Tragar, beber, engullir.—*vn.* Beber o tragar copiosamente; hartarse.
Ingurgitation [in-gūr-ji-tê'-shun], *s.* Voracidad, glotonería.
Inhabit [in-hab'-it], *va.* Habitar, ocupar alguna habitación.—*vn.* (Ant.) Habitar, vivir, residir en algún paraje.
Inhabitability [in-hab-it-a-bil'-i-ti], *s.* Habitabilidad, calidad de habitable.
Inhabitable [in-hab'-it-a-bl], *a.* 1. Habitable. 2. (Des.) Inhabitable, no habitable.
Inhabitance [in-hab'-it-ans], *s.* Habitación, morada permanente, residencia en un lugar.
Inhabitant [in-hab'-it-ant], *s.* Habitador, habitante, vecino, morador.
Inhabitation [in-hab-i-tê'-shun], *s.* Habitación, domicilio, morada.
Inhabited [in-hab'-it-ed], *a.* Poblado, habitado.
Inhabiter [in-hab'-it-gr], *s.* Habitador, habitante, morador, vecino.
†**Inhabitress** [in-hab'-it-res], *sf.* Habitadora.
Inhalation [in-ha-lê'-shun], *s.* 1. Inspiración, el acto de inspirar. 2. (Med.) Inhalación, vapor medicamentoso para aspiraciones.
Inhale [in-hêl'], *va.* Inspirar, aspirar, introducir en el pulmón dilatando el pecho, como se hace con el aire exterior.
Inharmonic, Inharmonical [in-hār-mon'-ic, al], *a.* Dísono o disonante, inarmónico.
Inharmonious [in-hār-mō'-ni-us], *a.* 1. Poco armonioso, falto de armonía; discordante. 2. Falto de concordancia, recíprocamente opuesto.
Inhaul [in'-hōl], *s.* (Mar.) Cabo o jarcia que sirve para halar o atraer una berlinga, v. g. el botalón de foque.

Inhere [in-hír'], *vn.* Inherir, adherir, ser inherente, tener unión íntima con otra cosa.
Inherence [in-hí'-rens], **Inherency** [in-hí'-ren-si], *s.* 1. Inherencia. 2. Cualidad de estar relacionado con otra cosa como elemento, atributo, propiedad o condición.
Inherent [in-hí'-rent], *a.* Inherente; innato, intrínseco.
Inherently [in-hí'-rent-li], *adv.* Inherentemente.
Inherit [in-her'-it], *va.* 1. Heredar, tener uno las cualidades físicas o mentales de sus antepasados. 2. Heredar, adquirir una herencia por disposición testamentaria o legal.—*vn.* Suceder como heredero o por derecho de sucesión.
Inheritable [in-her'-it-a-bl], *a.* Heredable, heredítable.
Inheritance [in-her'-it-ans], *s.* 1. Herencia, patrimonio. 2. Herencia, la posesión de los bienes heredados. *Inheritance tax,* Impuesto sobre la herencia.
Inheritor [in-her'-it-ẹr], *s.* Heredero.
Inheritress [in-her'-it-res], **Inheritrix** [in-her'-it-rix], *sf.* Heredera.
Inhesion [in-hí'-zhun], *s.* Inherencia, unión, adhesión.
Inhibit [in-hib'-it], *va.* 1. Inhibir, contener, detener, impedir. 2. Prohibir, vedar. 3. Prohibir a un sacerdote que ejerza sus funciones espirituales.
Inhibition [in-hi-bish'-un], *s.* 1. Inhibición, prohibición, impedimento. 2. (For.) Inhibición, prohibición a un juez del conocimiento de alguna causa.
Inhibitory [in-hib'-i-to-ri], **Inhibitive** [in-hib'-it-iv], *a.* Inhibitorio, que prohibe, restringe, o impide.
Inhive [in-haiv'], *va.* Enjambrar, reunir las abejas que andan esparcidas y meterlas en colmenas.
Inhospitable [in-hos'-pi-ta-bl], *a.* Inhospitalario, inhospitable.
Inhospitableness [in-hos'-pit-a-bl-nes], **Inhospitality** [in-hos-pi-tal'-i-ti], *s.* Inhospitalidad, falta de hospitalidad o de caridad.
Inhospitably [in-hos'-pit-a-bli], *adv.* Sin hospitalidad.
Inhuman [in-hiú'-man], *a.* Inhumano, cruel, riguroso, desapiadado.
Inhumanity [in-hiu-man'-i-ti], *s.* Inhumanidad, suma crueldad, barbarie.
Inhumanly [in-hiú'-man-li], *adv.* Inhumanamente.
Inhume [in-hiúm'], **Inhumate** [in-hiú'-mêt], *va.* 1. Inhumar, enterrar, sepultar. 2. (Quím.) Exponer a un calor constante enterrando el recipiente en tierra o estiércol caliente.
Inhumation [in-hiu-mê'-shun], *s.* Entierro, sepultura.
Inimaginable [in-i-maj'-in-a-bl], *a.* Inimaginable. *V.* UNIMAGINABLE.
Inimical [in-im'-i-cal], *a.* Enemigo, contrario, opuesto, dañoso, perjudicial.
Inimically [in-im'-i-cal-i], *adv.* Enemigamente, con enemistad, hostilmente; dañosamente.
Inimitability [in-im-it-a-bil'-i-ti], *s.* Imposibilidad o incapacidad de ser imitado.
Inimitable [in-im'-it-a-bl], *a.* Inimitable.
Inimitableness [in-im'-it-a-bl-nes], *s.* Calidad o estado de lo que es inimitable.
Inimitably [in-im'-it-a-bli], *adv.* Inimitablemente.
Iniquitous [in-ic'-wi-tus], †**Iniquous** [in-ic'-wus], *a.* Inicuo, malvado, facineroso, injusto.
Iniquity [in-ic'-wi-ti], *s.* Iniquidad, injusticia, perfidia, maldad, picardía.
Initial [in-ish'-al], *a.* 1. Inicial, lo que está al principio. 2. Incipiente. *Initials,* (1) Letras iniciales, como *D. A. & Co.* por Daniel Appleton y Compañía. (2) Letras iniciales de un capítulo, verso, etc., particularmente cuando son de adorno.
Initially [in-ish'-al-i], *adv.* De un modo incipiente.
Initiate [in-ish'-i-êt], *va.* 1. Iniciar; instruir en los rudimentos o principios; introducir en una sociedad o culto religioso, admitir a la participación de ciertos misterios. 2. Tomar la iniciativa, poner en pie, empezar.
Initiated [in-ish'-i-êt-ed], *a.* Iniciado, instruído, admitido a la participación, uso o conocimiento de alguna cosa.
Initiating [in-ish'-i-êt-ing], *a.* Iniciativo.—*s.* 1. El acto de instruir a alguno en los elementos de un arte o ciencia. 2. La introducción de una persona en cualquiera parte.
Initiative [in-ish'-i-a-tiv], *a.* Iniciativo, que sirve para iniciar.—*s.* 1. Primer paso o acción; acto introductivo. 2. Facultad de poner en pie, de empezar, o de iniciar. 3. Iniciativa, derecho de proponer leyes, etc.
Initiatory [in-ish'-i-a-to-ri], *a.* Iniciativo.
Initiation [in-ish-i-ê'-shun], *s.* 1. Estreno, principio, primer uso o el acto de ejercer o poner por obra alguna cosa. 2. Iniciación en los ritos o misterios.
Inject [in-ject'], *va.* 1. Inyectar, introducir o echar alguna cosa por fuerza, y particularmente por medio de inyección. 2. Introducir sin razón o sin necesidad. *V. To* INTERJECT. 3. (Des.) Echar sobre, aglomerar.
Injected [in-ject'-ed], *a.* Inyectado, introducido por medio de inyección; también, demasiado cargado de sangre.
Injection [in-jec'-shun], *s.* 1. Inyección, acción y efecto de inyectar, y el líquido inyectado. 2. (Med.) Inyección, lavativa; ayuda, el acto de introducir algún líquido en el cuerpo por medio de jeringa u otro instrumento. 3. (Mec.) Inyección, acción de echar agua en el condensador de una máquina de vapor.
Injection pump [in-jec'-shun pump], *s.* Bomba inyectora.
Injector [in-ject'-ẹr], *s.* Inyector, el que o lo que inyecta; particularmente aparato de las máquinas de vapor.
Injudicable [in-jiú'-di-ca-bl], *a.* (Poco us.) Ilegal, que no puede ser objeto del conocimiento de un juez.
Injudicial [in-ju-dish'-al], *a.* (Poco us.) Informal, informe, ilegal.
Injudicious [in ju-dish'-us], *a.* Indiscreto, sin discreción; poco juicioso, imprudente.
Injudiciously [in-ju-dish'-us-li], *adv.* Tontamente, sin juicio.
Injudiciousness [in-ju-dish'-us-nes], *s.* Indiscreción, imprudencia.
Injunction [in-junc'-shun], *s.* 1. Mandato, precepto, mandamiento, orden expresa. 2. Auto interlocutorio del tribunal de equidad o Cancillería, en virtud del cual se ordena, y más generalmente se prohibe hacer una cosa determinada.
Injure [in'-jur], *va.* 1. Injuriar, agraviar, ofender. 2. Molestar, hacer mala obra, perjudicar.
Injurer [in'-jur-ẹr], *s.* Injuriador, el que injuria a otro; ofensor, el que ofende.
Injurious [in-jú'-ri-us], *a.* 1. Injurioso, injusto, dañoso, perjudicial. 2. (Ant.) Contumelioso, detractivo, ofensivo.
Injuriously [in-jú'-ri-us-li], *adv.* Injuriosamente.
Injuriousness [in-jú'-ri-us-nes], *s.* Injuria, calidad de lo injurioso.
Injury [in'-ju-ri], *s.* 1. Injuria, daño, agravio sin razón, perjuicio, mal, detrimento, molestia. 2. Injuria, afrenta, baldón, insulto.
Injustice [in-jus'-tis], *s.* Injusticia, agravio.
Ink [ink], *s.* 1. Tinta, líquido negro o de otro color, y en ciertos casos substancia viscosa, que se emplea para escribir, imprimir o dibujar. 2. El líquido opaco secretado por la jibia. *Indelible ink* o *marking-ink,* Tinta indeleble o de marcar.
Ink, *va.* Entintar, teñir o tiznar con tinta; dar tinta. *To ink the forms,* Dar tinta a los moldes; (Impr.) entintar la forma. *To ink one's fingers,* Untarse de tinta los dedos.
Inkbottle [ink'-bet-l], *s.* Botellita de tinta, que sirve de tintero.
Inkhorn [ink'-hōrn], *s.* Tintero de bolsillo, hecho originalmente de cuerno. *V.* INKSTAND.—*a.* Pedantesco, pomposo.
Inkiness [ink'-i-nes], *s.* Entintamiento; mancha de tinta.
Inkle [in'-kl], *s.* Cinta angosta.
Inkling [ink'-ling], *s.* Insinuación o aviso secreto de alguna cosa.
Inkmaker [ink'-mê-kẹr], *s.* El que hace tinta para escribir o imprimir.
Inknot [in-net'], *va.* Atar o añudar.
Inkstand [ink'-stand], *s.* Tintero.
Inkwell [ink'-wel], *s.* Tintero.
Inky [ink'-i], *a.* Que se compone de tinta; semejante o parecido a la tinta; manchado de tinta.
Inlace [in-lês'], *va.* Adornar con cordones, encordonar o acordonar.
Inlaid [in-lêd'], *pret.* y *pp.* de INLAY.
Inland [in'-land], *a.* 1. Interior, lo que está tierra adentro o distante del mar. 2. No extranjero, doméstico; transportado de un punto a otro del mismo país.—*s.* El interior de un país.—*adv.* Tierra adentro.
Inlander [in'-land-ẹr], *s.* El que habita tierra adentro o lejos del mar. (Amer.) Tierradentreño.
Inlay [in-lé'], *va.* (*pret.* y *pp.* INLAID). Embutir, meter una cosa dentro de otra; en especial, ataracear, taracear, hacer embutidos de varios colores en madera u otra materia; formar mosaico; incrustar. *Inlaid work,* Embutido, taracea, ataracea; incrustación, ataujía.
Inlay [in'-lê], *s.* 1. Materia con que se ataracea o embute. 2. Ataracea, embutido; dibujo producido por el acto de embutir.
Inlayer [in-lê'-ẹr], *s.* El que ataracea o embute; operario en embutidos o taracea.
Inlaying [in-lê'-ing], *s.* El arte o acto de ataracear o embutir.
Inlet [in'-let], *s.* 1. Entrada, paso para entrar en un paraje cerrado.

2. Cuerpo pequeño de agua que da entrada a otro mayor: (1) abra, cala; (2) arroyo o río que alimenta a un lago.
Inlock [in-loc'], *va.* Cerrar, encajar, poner una cosa dentro de otra.
Inly [in'-li], *adv.* Interiormente.
Inmate [in'-mêt], *s.* Habitador, inquilino, el que vive en una casa con otro; huésped, persona alojada en una casa, fábrica u hospital; cualquier ocupante.
Inmost [in'-mōst], *a.* 1. Íntimo, lo más interior o interno de alguna cosa; lo más lejano de la parte exterior, lo más profundo. 2. El más recóndito, secreto, oculto.
Inn [in], *s.* Posada, fonda, mesón. *Inns of court,* (Ingl.) Colegios de abogados o jurisconsultos a que sólo pertenecen los que han sido admitidos por voto general de la junta y presidente que los gobiernan; son cuatro, a saber: Inner Temple, Middle Temple, Lincoln's Inn, y Gray's Inn.
Innate, Innated [in-nêt', ed], *a.* Innato, natural, propio.
Innately [in-nêt'-li], *adv.* Naturalmente.
Innateness [in-nêt'-nes], *s.* El estado o calidad de lo que es innato.
Innavigable [in-nav'-i-ga-bl], *a.* Innavegable.
Inner [in'-er], *a.* Interior. *Inner tube,* Cámara interior o neumática (de una llanta de automóvil).
Innermost [in'-er-mōst], *a.* Íntimo. *V.* INMOST.
Innervate [in-nerv'-et], *va.* Proveer de nervios; comunicar estímulo nervioso a.
Innervation [in'-er-vê'-shun], *s.* (Fís.) 1. Inervación, acción de dar estímulo nervioso a un órgano. 2. Disposición de los filamentos nerviosos en cualquier parte del cuerpo animal.
Innerve [in-nerv'], *va.* Dar vigor, nervio, fuerza.
Inning [in'-ing], *s.* 1. En los juegos llamados *base-ball, cricket,* etc., término para expresar que toca a uno de los jugadores coger la maza o pala; de aquí, el período durante el cual un partido o un sujeto ejerce poder, autoridad o acción. 2. Los terrenos que un tiempo estuvieron cubiertos por las aguas del mar.
Innkeeper [in'-kîp-er], *s.* Posadero, mesonero, fondista, huésped.
Innocence [in'-o-sens], **Innocency** [in'-o-sen-si], *s.* 1. Inocencia, pureza. 2. Inocencia, estado del que se halla inocente del delito que se le imputa. 3. Sencillez, simplicidad. 4. Cualidad de lo que no es nocivo, de lo innocuo.
Innocent [in'-o-sent], *a.* 1. Inocente. 2. Inocente, simple, tonto, idiota. 3. No nocivo, innocuo.—*s.* 1. Inocente, el niño que no tiene uso de razón. 2. Inocente, el que está libre de culpa, absuelto.
Innocently [in'-o-sent-li], *adv.* Inocentemente.
Innocuous [in-nec'-yu-us], *a.* Innocuo, inofensivo, inocente, innocivo, que no hace daño; sencillo.
Innocuously [in-nec'-yu-us-li], *adv.* Inocentemente.
Innocuousness [in-nec'-yu-us-nes], *s.* Inocencia; estado y calidad de lo que no hace daño.
Innominable [in-nem'-i-na-bl], *a.* (Ant.) Innominable, innombrable.
Innominate [in-nem'-i-nêt], *a.* 1. Innominado, que no tiene nombre especial: se emplea en anatomía; hueso innominado, arteria innominada. 2. Anónimo, sin autor conocido.
Innovate [in'-o-vêt], *va.* Innovar, hacer innovaciones; introducir cosas nuevas.
Innovating [in'-o-vêt-ing], *a.* Innovador; tómase comúnmente en mal sentido.
Innovation [in-o-vê'-shun], *s.* Innovación.
Innovator [in'-o-vê-ter], *s.* Innovador, el que innova o introduce novedades y también el que hace esfuerzos para introducirlas. *V.* INNOVATING.
Innoxious [in-nec'-shus], *a.* 1. Innocivo, innocuo, que no es nocivo. 2. (Ant.) Inocente, libre, exento de culpa.
Innoxiously [in-nec'-shus-li], *adv.* Sin daño, innocuamente.
Innoxiousness [in-nec'-shus-nes], *s.* Incapacidad de hacer daño.
Innuendo [in-yu-en'-do], *s.* Indirecta, insinuación, pulla.
Innumerability [in-niu-mer-a-bil'-i-ti], *s.* Innumerabilidad.
Innumerable [in-niū'-mer-a-bl], *a.* Innumerable.
Innumerableness [in-niū'-mer-a-bl-nes], *s.* Innumerabilidad, muchedumbre grande y excesiva.
Innumerably [in-niū'-mer-a-bli], *adv.* Innumerablemente.
Innumerous [in-niū'-mer-us], *a.* Innumerable.
Innutrition [in-niu-trish'-un], *s.* Falta de nutrición.
Innutritious [in-niu-trish'-us], *a.* No nutritivo, que carece de propiedades nutritivas.
Inobservable [in-ob-zerv'-a-bl], *a.* Inobservable.
Inobservance [in-ob-zerv'-ans], *s.* Inobservancia.
Inobservation [in-ob-zer-vê'-shun], *s.* Inobservación.
Inoculate [in-oc'-yu-lêt], *va.* 1. Inocular, comunicar una enfermedad infecciosa por contacto o por medios artificiales. 2. Injertar un botón en (un árbol) para propagarlo. 3. (Fig.) Imbuir, infundir; infectar, inficionar.—*vn.* 1. Comunicar una enfermedad por medio de inoculación. 2. Inocular, injertar, propagar una planta por medio del injerto de un botón.
Inoculation [in-oc-yu-lê'-shun], *s.* 1. Injertación, inoculación, el acto de injertar los árboles. 2. Inoculación, la inserción de un virus, como el de la viruela. 3. Contaminación, infección.
Inoculator [in-oc'-yu-lê-ter], *s.* Inoculador, el que practica la inoculación.
Inodorous [in-o'-der-us], *a.* Inodoro, que carece de olor, que no despide olor.
Inoffensive [in-ef-fen'-siv], *a.* Inofensivo, que no ofende.
Inoffensively [in-ef-fen'-siv-li], *adv.* Inofensivamente, pacíficamente.
Inoffensiveness [in-ef-fen'-siv-nes], *s.* La calidad de lo que no ofende, innocuidad; inocencia.
Inofficial [in-ef-fish'-al], *a.* *V.* UNOFFICIAL.
Inoperable [in-op'-er-a-bl], *a.* (Cir.) Inoperable, que no puede ser operado.
Inoperative [in-op'-er-ê-tiv], *a.* Falto de efecto, ineficaz.
Inopportune [in-op-er-tiūn'], *a.* Inconveniente, inoportuno.
Inopportunely [in-op-er-tiūn'-li], *adv.* Inoportunamente.
Inopportuneness [in-op-er-tiūn'-nes], *s.* Inoportunidad.
Inordinacy [in-ōr'-di-na-si], *s.* Desarreglo, desorden; exceso más allá de lo razonable y lo derecho; naturaleza excesiva.
Inordinate [in-ōr'-di-nêt], *a.* Desordenado, irregular, desarreglado.
Inordinately [in-ōr'-di-nêt-li], *adv.* Desordenadamente.
Inordinateness [in-ōr'-di-net-nes], *s.* Desorden, exceso, demasía.
Inorganic, Inorganical [in-ōr-gan'-ic, al], *a.* Inorgánico.
Inosculate [in-es'-kiu-lêt], *va.* Unir una cosa con otra por contacto físico de aberturas; unir por anastomosis.—*vn.* Anastomarse; comunicar mutuamente.
Inosculation [in-es-kiu-lê'-shun], *s.* Unión de una cosa con otra por algo parecido a un tubo o canal; anastomosis; unión que implica continuidad.
Input [in'-put], *s.* 1. (Elec.) Entrada. 2. (Fig.) Gasto.
Inquest [in'-cwest], *s.* 1. Indagación, averiguación, examen, información o pesquisa judicial con ayuda de un jurado. 2. El jurado u otro cuerpo que hace dicha pesquisa. 3. Examen ante el juez para determinar valores o daños y perjuicios. 4. (Poco us.) Escudriñamiento, examen diligente de alguna cosa. *Coroner's inquest,* La investigación o pesquisa que hace el jurado presidido por el empleado público llamado *Coroner,* para indagar la causa de las muertas repentinas, y de las debidas a un acto de violencia.
Inquietude [in-cwai'-e-tiūd], *s.* Inquietud, desasosiego, descontento.
Inquirable [in-cwair'-a-bl], *a.* Investigable, que puede ser inquirido o examinado.
Inquire [in-cwair'], *vn.* Inquirir, averiguar, examinar; informarse, buscar información por medio de preguntas.—*va.* Preguntar alguna cosa. *To inquire about,* Hacer preguntas sobre alguna cosa; preguntar por alguno. *To inquire after* o *for,* Preguntar por algo. *To inquire into,* Investigar alguna cosa, tratar de saber algo con toda certidumbre.
Inquirer [in-cwair'-er], *s.* Inquiridor, investigador, examinador, preguntón.
Inquiry [in-cwair'-i], *s.* 1. Interrogación, examinación, indagación. 2. Pesquisa, escudriñamiento, información, investigación. 3. Pregunta.
Inquisition [in-cwi-zish'-un], *s.* 1. Inquisición, escudriñamiento. 2. Inquisición, tribunal eclesiástico que inquiría y castigaba los delitos contra la fe católica; el Santo Oficio. 3. Investigación.
Inquisitional [in-cwi-zish'-un-al], *a.* Inquisitorial, perteneciente a la inquisición.
Inquisitive [in-cwiz'-i-tiv], *a.* Inquisitivo, preguntón, curioso, investigador. *An inquisitive mind,* Una mente investigadora; un natural curioso.
Inquisitively [in-cwiz'-i-tiv-li], *adv.* Inquisitivamente.
Inquisitiveness [in-cwiz'-i-tiv-nes], *s.* Curiosidad, deseo de saber y averiguar alguna cosa.
Inquisitor [in-cwiz'-i-ter], *s.* 1. Inquisidor, el que inquiere: juez in-

vestigador. 2. Inquisidor, juez eclesiástico que entendía en las causas sobre asuntos de fe en algunos países católicos. 3. Persona curiosa.

Inquisitorial [in-cwiz-i-tō'-ri-al], *a.* Inquisitorial, a la manera de un inquiridor o de un inquisidor.

Inracinate [in-ras'-i-nēt], *va.* Arraigar, implantar ; fijar.

Inroad [in'-rōd], *s.* Incursión, correría ; invasión, tala.

Inrush [in'-rush], *s.* Empuje, como el de la marea ; invasión.

Insalivate [in-sal'-i-vēt], *va.* Insalivar, mezclar (el alimento) con saliva.

Insalivation [in-sal-i-vē'-shun], *s.* Insalivación.

Insalubrious [in-sa-lū'-bri-us], *a.* Insalubre, malsano.

Insalubrity [in-sa-lū'-bri-ti], *s.* Insalubridad.

Insane [in-sēn'], *a.* 1. Insano, loco, demente, que ha perdido la razón, acometido de enajenación mental; insensato. 2. Usado o puesto aparte para los locos. *Insane asylum*, Casa de locos, asilo para los locos.

Insanity [in-san'-i-ti], *s.* Locura, manía, demencia, insania, enajenación mental.

Insatiable [in-sē'-shi-a-bl], *a.* Insaciable.

Insatiableness [in-sē'-shi-a-bl-nes], *s.* Insaciabilidad.

Insatiably [in-sē'-shi-a-bli], *adv.* Insaciablemente.

Insatiate [in-sē'-shi-ēt], *a.* Insaciable.

Insatiately [in-sē'-shi-ēt-li], *adv.* Insaciablemente.

Inscribe [in-scraib'], *va.* 1. Inscribir. 2. (Geom.) Inscribir, formar una figura dentro de otra. 3. Dedicar una composición o escrito a una persona.

Inscriber [in-scraib'-ęr], *s.* El que inscribe o dedica.

Inscription [in-scrip'-shun], *s.* 1. Inscripción; cualquier leyenda o letrero en caracteres permanentes. 2. Inscripción, registro en una lista o rol. 3. La dedicatoria de un escrito hecha a alguna persona. 4. (For.) Obligación que contrae el acusador de sufrir la pena misma que la ley prescribe al delito de que acusa, si no puede probar que ha sido cometido.

Inscriptive [in-scrip'-tiv], *a.* De la naturaleza de una inscripción; inscrito, inscripto.

Inscrutability [in-scrū-ta-bil'-i-ti], *s.* Inescrutabilidad.

Inscrutable [in-scrū'-ta-bl], *a.* Inescrutable, inescudriñable, incomprensible.

Inscrutably [in-scrū'-ta-bli], *adv.* Inescrutablemente.

Inseam [in-sīm'], *va.* Señalar o marcar con alguna señal, costura, filón o vena.

Inseam, *s.* Costura interior: dícese de los zapatos o vestidos.

Insect [in'-sect], *s.* Insecto, nombre genérico de una clase de animales cuyo cuerpo está dividido en segmentos; los verdaderos insectos son hexápodos, artrópodos de seis patas. *Insect-powder*, Polvos insecticidas; obtenidos por lo común de las flores de ciertas especies de Pyrethrum.

Insectean [in-sec'-tę-an], **Insectile** [in-sec'-til], *a.* Que pertenece a la clase de insectos, antiguamente insectil; ***insectile*** significa también, parecido **a un insecto.**

Insecticide [in-sec'-ti-said], *s.* Insecticida, el que o lo que mata los insectos.

Insectivorous [in-sec-tiv'-o-rus], *a.* Insectívoro, que come insectos o se alimenta de ellos.

Insecure [in-sę-kiūr'], *a.* 1. Inseguro, que no está o no es seguro; lo que está en peligro; poco sólido, poco firme. 2. Expuesto a pérdida, daño o riesgo.

Insecurely [in-si-kiūr'-li], *adv.* Inseguramente.

Insecurity [in-si-kiū'-ri-ti], *s.* Inseguridad, incertidumbre; peligro, riesgo.

Inseminate [in-sem'-i-nēt], *va.* 1. Emitir el semen; con menos exactitud se usa también en el sentido de engendrar, fecundar. 2. (Des.) Sembrar.

Insensate [in-sen'-sēt], *a.* Insensato.

Insensibility [in-sen-si-bil'-i-ti], *s.* 1. Insensibilidad, falta de sentimiento. 2. Estupidez, insensatez, falta de comprensión. 3. Torpeza, adormecimiento de algún sentido corporal.

Insensible [in-sen'-si-bl], *a.* 1. Insensible, imperceptible. 2. Insensible, indiferente. 3. Insensible, duro de corazón.

Insensibleness [in-sen'-si-bl-nes], *s.* Insensibilidad.

Insensibly [in-sen'-si-bli], *adv.* 1. Insensiblemente. 2. Gradualmente, lentamente, poco a poco.

Insentient [in-sen'-shent], *a.* Insensible, lo que no siente o percibe.

Inseparability [in-sep-a-ra-bil'-i-ti], **Inseparableness** [in-sep'-a-ra-bl-nes], *s.* Inseparabilidad.

Inseparable [in-sep'-a-ra-bl], *a.* Inseparable.

Inseparably [in-sep'-a-ra-bli], *adv.* Inseparablemente.

Inseparate [in-sep'-a-rḙt], *a.* No separado, unido.

Insert [in-sęrt'], *va.* Insertar, ingerir una cosa entre otras, colocar en medio de; intercalar; hacer insertar. *To insert a notice in a newspaper*, Insertar un anuncio en un periódico.

Insertion [in-sęr'-shun], *s.* 1. Inserción, la acción de ingerir o insertar; la cosa inserta o insertada. 2. Tira bordada o labrada. (Cuba) Antolar; entredós. 3. Paraje o modo de ligadura o inserción; inserción de una hoja en una rama o inserción de un músculo.

Inserviceable [in-sęr'-vis-a-bl], *a.* Inservible.

Inessorial [in-ses-ō'-ri-al], *a.* Perchador, a propósito para perchar; ave perchadora.

Inset [in-set'], *va.* Meter en; fijar, plantar.

Inset [in'-set], *s.* 1. Adición, hoja u hojas insertadas, v. g. en un libro o periódico. 2. Flujo hacia la orilla, como el de la marea.

Inshelter [in-shel'-tęr], *va.* Poner una cosa bajo la protección de otra.

Inshore [in'-shōr], *a.* 1. Que está o sucede cerca de la orilla. 2. En dirección a tierra.—*adv.* Hacia la orilla o cerca de ella.

Inshrine [in-shrain'], *va.* *V.* ENSHRINE.

Insiccation [in-sik-ē'-shun], *s.* Desecación.

Inside [in'-said], *s.* 1. Interior, lo que está en la parte de adentro. 2. Contenido, lo que está contenido. 3. Viajero, pasajero del interior.—*a.* Interior, de la parte de adentro. —*adv.* Dentro, adentro, en el interior. *Inside out*, De dentro afuera; al revés.

Insider [in-said'-ęr], *s.* El que posee información de primera mano.

Insides [in'-saidz], *s. pl.* Entrañas.

Insidious [in-sid'-i-us], *a.* Insidioso, engañoso.

Insidiously [in-sid'-i-us-li], *adv.* Insidiosamente, engañosamente.

Insidiousness [in-sid'-i-us-nes], *s.* El estado o calidad de lo que es insidioso.

Insight [in'-sait], *s.* 1. Conocimiento profundo de alguna cosa; discernimiento intelectual. 2. Percepción de la naturaleza interior de una cosa.

Insignia [in-sig'-ni-a], *s. pl.* Insignias, divisas honoríficas; estandartes.

Insignificance [in-sig-nif'-i-cans], **Insignificancy** [in-sig-nif'-i-can-si], *s.* 1. Falta de sentido o significación; obscuridad. 2. Friolera, poca importancia; nulidad.

Insignificant [in-sig-nif'-i-cant], *a.* Insignificante, insignificativo, frívolo, nulo.

Insignificantly [in-sig-nif'-i-cant-li], *adv.* Insignificantemente, frívolamente.

Insignificative [in-sig-nif'-i-ca-tiv], *a.* Insignificativo.

Insincere [in-sin-sīr'], *a.* 1. Doble, hipócrita, poco sincero. 2. Turbado; corrompido; agitado.

Insincerely [in-sin-sīr'-li], *adv.* Con doblez, con segunda intención.

Insincerity [in-sin-ser'-i-ti], *s.* Doblez, disimulación.

Insinuate [in-sin'-yu-ēt], *va.* 1. Insinuar. 2. Apuntar, insinuar, dar a entender alguna cosa. *To insinuate one's self*, Insinuarse, introducirse con maña y habilidad en la amistad de alguno.—*vn.* Insinuarse, ganar la voluntad de otro poco a poco y con maña; envolver.

Insinuating [in-sin'-yu-ēt-ing], *a.* El que sabe captar o granjear la voluntad de otro por medio de insinuaciones.

Insinuation [in-sin-yu-ē'-shun], *s.* 1. Insinuación, artificio con que alguno va suavemente atrayendo a sí la atención y benevolencia de otro. 2. Insinuacion, indirecta.

Insinuative [in-sin'-yu-ḙ-tiv], *a.* Insinuante, lo que se insinúa o granjea el afecto de alguien.

Insinuator [in-sin'-yu-ḙ-tęr], *s.* Insinuador, insinuante, el que insinúa algo por medio de indirectas.

Insipid [in-sip'-id], *a.* 1. Insípido, desabrido. 2. Insulso, soso.

Insipidity [in-si-pid'-i-ti], **Insipidness** [in-sip'-id-nes], *s.* 1. Insipidez, desabor. 2. Insulsez, sosería.

Insipidly [in-sip'-id-li], *adv.* Insulsamente.

Insist [in-sist'], *vn.* 1. Insistir, instar o persistir en una cosa. 2. Descansar una cosa en otra; hallar apoyo. *Insist* se usa con *on* o *upon.*

Insistence [in-sist'-ens], **Insistency** [in-sist'-en-si], *s.* Insistencia.

Insistent [in-sis'-tent], *a.* 1. Insistente, que insiste, insta o persiste. 2. Conspicuo. 3. Que se apoya o descansa en alguna cosa.

Insition [in-sish'-un], *s.* Injertación, el acto de injertar.

Insnare [in-snār'], *va.* *V.* ENSNARE.

Insnarl, *va.* *V.* SNARL y ENSNARL.

Insobriety [in-so-brai'-i-ti], *s.* Em-

briaguez, borrachera; falta de sobriedad.
Insolate [in'-so-lêt], *va.* Insolar, secar al sol.
Insolation [in-so-lé'-shun], *s.* 1. Insolación, el acto de poner alguna cosa al sol para que se seque o fermente. 2. Insolación, una enfermedad. *V.* SUNSTROKE.
Insole [in'-sōl], *s.* Plantilla (del zapato).
Insolence [in'-so-lens], **Insolency** [in'-so-len-si], *s.* Insolencia, orgullo, desprecio orgulloso, altanería; atrevimiento.
Insolent [in'-so-lent], *a.* Insolente, arrogante, atrevido, orgulloso.
Insolently [in'-so-lent-li], *adv.* Insolentemente.
Insoluble [in-sel'-yu-bl], *a.* 1. Insoluble; indisoluble. 2. Que no puede resolverse ni explicarse.
Insolubleness [in-sel'-yu-bl-nes], *s.* Indisolubilidad, la incapacidad de disolverse.
Insolvable [in-selv'-a-bl], *a.* 1. Inexplicable, que no admite explicación. 2. Indisoluble, que no se puede desatar o resolver. 3. Que no se puede pagar o saldar.
Insolvency [in-sel'-ven-si], *s.* Insolvencia, imposibilidad de pagar las deudas.
Insolvent [in-sel'-vent], *a.* Insolvente, el que no tiene para pagar sus deudas. *Insolvent debtor,* El deudor que no tiene recursos con que pagar a sus acreedores.
Insomnia [in-sem'-ni-a], *s.* Insomnio, desvelo, incapacidad crónica de dormir.
Insomnious [in-sem'-ni-us], *a.* Insomne, que está desvelado, que no duerme.
Insomnolence [in-sem'-no-lens], *s.* Falta de sueño.
Insomuch [in-so-much'], *conj.* De manera que, de suerte que, de modo que.
Inspect [in-spect'], *va.* Reconocer, examinar, inspeccionar con cuidado; investigar y probar oficialmente.
Inspection [in-spec'-shun], *s.* Inspección, la acción y efecto de reconocer y examinar atentamente alguna cosa; particularmente, examen oficial.
Inspector [in-spec'-tẹr], *s.* 1. Inspector, superintendente. 2. Oficial de la policía en muchas ciudades.
Inspectorate [in-spect'-ẹr-ḙt], *s.* 1. El distrito que corresponde a un inspector. 2. Cargo o empleo de un inspector.
Insphere [in-sfír'], *va.* Colocar en una esfera o globo.
Inspiration [in-spi-ré'-shun], *s.* Inspiración; en los mismos sentidos que en castellano.
Inspirationist [in-spi-ré'-shun-ist], *s.* Defensor de la doctrina de la inspiración.
Inspiratory [in-spair'-a-to-ri], *a.* Inspirador, que aspira aire en los pulmones; inspiratorio, que sirve o concierne a la inspiración.
Inspire [in-spair'], *vn.* 1. Inspirar, introducir el aire exterior en los pulmones. 2. Soplar suavemente. —*va.* 1. Inspirar el aire. 2. Inspirar, sugerir, comunicar al ánimo algún movimiento o idea. 3. Inspirar, iluminar Dios el entendimiento o mover la voluntad.
Inspirer [in-spair'-ẹr], *s.* Inspirador.
Inspirit [in-spir'-it], *va.* Alentar, animar, vigorizar, infundir espíritu.
Inspissate [in-spis'-êt], *va.* Espesar, condensar.—*adj.* Espeso.
Inspissation [in-spis-é'-shun], *s.* Condensación, el acto de condensar o espesar alguna cosa líquida.
Instability [in-sta-bil'-i-ti], *s.* Instabilidad, inestabilidad, inconstancia.
Instable [in-sté'-bl], *a.* Inconstante, vario, variable, mudable.
Install [in-stōl'], *va.* Instalar, poner en posesión al que ha obtenido algún empleo, cargo o beneficio.
Installation [in-stōl-é'-shun], *s.* 1. Instalación, el acto o la ceremonia de dar posesión de un cargo o destino. 2. Emplazamiento y montaje de máquinas o aparatos.
Instalment, Installment [in-stōl'-mẹnt], *s.* 1. Pago parcial; pago en plazos determinados; plazo. 2. Parte o porción de algo que se da, reparte o publica en plazos determinados. *An instalment of a story,* Entrega, porción de una novela, etc., que se publica de una vez. 3. Instalación, acto de instalar.
Instance [in'-stans], *s.* 1. Ejemplo; suceso determinado, caso; prueba. 2. Instancia, ruego, solicitación. 3. Nueva razón u objeción con que se urge algún argumento, pleito o dificultad. 4. (For.) Instancia, expediente, el curso legal de la acción hasta la sentencia definitiva. *For instance,* Por ejemplo. *We have no instance of it,* No hay ejemplo de ello.
Instance, *va.* Ofrecer como ejemplo; citar como ejemplo o prueba.
Instanced [in'-stanst], *a.* Presentado como prueba, dado como ejemplo.
Instancy [in'-stan-si], *s.* Urgencia, instancia, insistencia, solicitación porfiada.
Instant [in'-stant], *a.* 1. Inminente, al instante; pronto, presente; importuno. 2. (Ant.) Urgente, activo; importuno.—*s.* 1. Instante, momento, duración indivisible, tiempo señalado. 2. El mes corriente o presente. *The fifth instant,* El cinco del corriente.
Instantaneity [in-stan-ta-ní'-i-ti], *s.* Instantáneo, la calidad de ser instantáneo.
Instantaneous [in-stan-té'-ne-us], *a.* Instantáneo, o que dura un instante; hecho en un instante.
Instantaneously [in-stan-té'-ne-us-li], *adv.* Instantáneamente.
Instantaneousness, *s.* *V.* INSTANTANEITY.
Instanter [in-stan'-tẹr], *adv.* Al instante, inmediatamente.
Instantly [in'-stant-li], *adv.* 1. Instantáneamente, en un momento. 2. (Ant.) Con instancia o porfía.
Instate [in-stêt'], *va.* Colocar en algún orden o clase.
Instead [in-sted'], *adv.* En lugar de, en vez de; originalmente dos palabras.
Instep [in'-step], *s.* 1. Empeine o garganta del pie. 2. La parte anterior de la pata de atrás de una caballería.
Instigate [in'-sti-gêt], *va.* Instigar, mover, excitar, incitar; poner por obra mediante el incitamento.
Instigation [in-sti-gé'-shun], *s.* Instigación, sugestión, provocación a hacer daño.
Instigator [in'-sti-gê-tẹr], *s.* Instigador, incitador.
Instil, Instill [in-stil'], *va.* 1. Instilar, echar poco a poco o gota a gota algún líquido. 2. Instilar, insinuar, introducir, inculcar, infundir en el ánimo algún afecto.
Instillation [in-stil-é'-shun], *s.* 1. Instilación, el acto de echar los líquidos gota a gota o de introducir insensiblemente alguna cosa en el ánimo; insinuación. 2. La cosa instilada o introducida.
Instiller [in-stil'-ẹr], *s.* El que instila o insinúa; insinuante.
Instilment, Instillment [in-stil'-mẹnt] *s.* Cualquier cosa instilada.
Instinct [in-stinct'], *a.* Animado desde adentro; movido por impulso interior: úsase con *with. Instinct with pity,* Movido por la piedad.
Instinct [in'-stinct], *s.* 1. Instinto, sagacidad natural de los animales. 2. Instinto, el movimiento natural que hace obrar a las personas sin que tenga parte la reflexión.
Instinctive [in-stinc'-tiv], *a.* Instintivo, determinado por un impulso natural; espontáneo.
Instinctively [in-stinc'-tiv-li], *adv.* Por instinto.
Institute [in'-sti-tiūt], *va.* 1. Instituir, establecer, fundar. 2. Poner por obra, poner en operación, empezar. 3. Conferir canónicamente un beneficio eclesiástico. 4. (Des.) Instruir, educar.
Institute, *s.* 1. Instituto, establecimiento. 2. Regla, principio, máxima. *Institutes of Justinian,* Instituta de Justiniano, libro que contiene los principios del derecho romano. *Teachers' institute,* (E. U. A.) Asamblea de maestros para instrucción y auxilio mutuo.
Institution [in-sti-tiū'-shun], *s.* 1. Institución; establecimiento. 2. Ley positiva, derecho positivo. 3. Instrucción, educación, enseñanza. 4. Institución canónica, el acto de poner a alguno en posesión de un beneficio eclesiástico.
Institutional [in-sti-tiū'-shun-al], *a.* 1. Prescrito, instituído por la autoridad. 2. Elemental.
Institutionalize [in-sti-tiū'-shun-al-aiz], *va.* Institucionalizar, establecer.
Institutionary [in-sti-tiū'-shun-ẹ-ri], *a.* Elemental, que contiene los principios de alguna ciencia o doctrina.
Institutive [in'-sti-tiū-tiv], *a.* 1. Instituente, instituidor, capaz de establecer o instituir. 2. Establecido, instituído.
Institutor [in'-sti-tiū"-tẹr], *s.* Instituidor, fundador, el que funda o pone por obra.
Instruct [in-struct'], *va.* 1. Instruir, enseñar, doctrinar; modelar o formar el ánimo. 2. Instruir, dar a conocer a uno el estado de una cosa o informarle de ella. 3. Dar instrucciones, órdenes a; mandar.
Instruction [in-struc'-shun], *s.* 1. Instrucción, enseñanza. 2. Instrucción, conocimiento o saber adquirido. 3. Instrucción, orden particular que da un superior a su subalterno o comisionado para su dirección y gobierno, y también el documento o consejo que se da a otro.
Instructive [in-struc'-tiv], *a.* Instructivo.
Instructively [in-struc'-tiv-li], *adv.* Instructivamente.
Instructiveness [in-struc'-tiv-nes], *s.* El poder o la capacidad de instruir.

Instructor [in-struct'-er], *s.* 1. Instructor, maestro. 2. En los colegios norteamericanos, instructor, maestro de categoría algo más baja que la de un profesor.
Instructress [in-struc'-tres], *sf.* Instructora.
Instrument [in'-stru-ment], *s.* 1. Instrumento, aquello de que nos servimos para hacer una cosa; herramienta o máquina que se usa para trabajar. 2. Instrumento, agente, persona que obra según el dictado o el capricho de otra. 3. (For.) Escritura, acta, documento, instrumento con que se justifica alguna cosa o que contiene un contrato. *V.* DEED. *A wind instrument*, Instrumento de viento. *A stringed instrument*, Instrumento de cuerda. *Instrument approach*, (Aer.) Aproximación por instrumentos. *Instrument board*, Tablero de instrumentos. *Instrument flying*, (Aer.) Vuelo a ciegas, vuelo con instrumentos. *Instruments and supplies of war*, Pertrechos.
Instrumental [in-stru-men'-tal], *a.* 1. Instrumental, lo que conduce a la consecución de algún fin. 2. Instrumental, lo que pertenece a los instrumentos.
Instrumentality [in-stru-men-tal'-i-ti], *s.* El acto de servir de instrumento para una cosa y la calidad de lo que sirve de instrumento.
Instrumentally [in-stru-men'-tal-i], *adv.* Instrumentalmente; con instrumentos de música.
Instrumentalness [in-stru-men'-tal-nes], *s.* La utilidad de una cosa para servir de instrumento en el logro de un fin.
Instrumentation [in-stru-men-tê'-shun], *s.* Instrumentación.
Insubjection [in-sub-jec'-shun], *s.* Inobediencia.
Insubordinate [in-sub-ōr'-di-nęt], *a.* Insubordinado.
Insubordination [in-sub-ōr-di-nê'-shun], *s.* Insubordinación.
Insufferable [in-suf'-ęr-a-bl], *a.* Insufrible, insoportable, detestable.
Insufferably [in-suf'-ęr-a-bli], *adv.* Insufriblemente, insoportablemente.
Insufficiency, ‡Insufficience [in-suf-fish'-en-si], *s.* Insuficiencia, incapacidad.
Insufficient [in-suf-fish'-ent], *a.* Insuficiente; impotente; incapaz, inhábil; mal a propósito.
Insufficiently [in-suf-fish'-ent-li], *adv.* Insuficientemente.
Insufflate [in-suf'-lêt], *va.* 1. Insuflar, soplar en o sobre; tratar por la insuflación. 2. Respirar sobre otra persona; acto simbólico en ciertas ceremonias religiosas. 3. (Med.) Insuflar, introducir á soplos en un organo o en una cavidad un gas, un líquido o una substancia pulverizada.
Insufflation [in-suf-lê'-shun], *s.* 1. Soplo. 2. Insuflación, como ceremonia religiosa. 3. (Med.) Insuflación, operación por medio de la cual se introduce aire libre en los pulmones de los asfixiados, o una substancia pulverizada en una cavidad.
Insular [in'-siu-lar], *a.* 1. Insular, isleño; aislado. 2. Estrecho de miras, iliberal; escaso.
Insularity [in-siu-lar'-i-ti], *s.* Estado o cualidad de ser insular o isleño; de aquí, estrechez de miras.
Insulate [in'-siu-lêt], *va.* 1. Aislar. 2. (Elec.) Aislar de otros cuerpos conductores, como por medio de un soporte o de una cubierta de material mal conductor; impedir que se escape la electricidad.
Insulated [in'-siu-lêt-ed], *a.* Aislado, apartado; escueto, exento, solitario.
Insulating [in'-siu-lê-ting], *a.* (Elec.) Aislante.
Insulation [in-siu-lê'-shun], *s.* 1. Aislamiento, acción de aislar estado de hallarse aislado. 2. Acción de rodear un cuerpo con otros no conductores. 3. (Elec.) Materias, materiales usados para aislar.
Insulator [in'-siu-lê-tęr], *s.* Aislador, el cuerpo que aisla o interrumpe la comunicación de la electricidad con los cuerpos que le rodean.
Insulin [in'-siu-lin], *s.* Insulina.
Insult [in'-sult], *s.* 1. Insulto, ultraje, denuesto; injuria. 2. (Des.) Salto, el acto de saltar sobre algo; de aquí, el acto de cubrir el macho a la hembra. Decíase del ganado vacuno y caballar.
Insult [in-sult'], *va.* 1. Insultar, ultrajar, ajar, injuriar. 2. Despreciar, pisar.
Insulter [in-sult'-ęr], *s.* Insultador, denostador.
Insulting [in-sult'-ing], *a.* Insultante, ultrajante; insolente.
Insultingly [in-sult'-ing-li], *adv.* Insolentemente.
Insuperability [in-siu-pęr-a-bil'-i-ti], *s.* La calidad de ser insuperable.
Insuperable [in-siū'-pęr-a-bl], *a.* Insuperable, lo que no se puede superar.
Insuperableness [in-siū'-pęr-a-bl-nes], *s.* Invencibilidad.
Insuperably [in-siū'-pęr-a-bli], *adv.* Invenciblemente.
Insupportable [in-sup-pōrt'-a-bl], *a.* 1. Insoportable, inaguantable. 2. Insufrible, intolerable.
Insupportably [in-sup-pōrt'-a-bli], *adv.* Insoportablemente.
Insuppressible [in-sup-pres'-i-bl], *a.* Lo que no puede ser ocultado o suprimido.
Insurable [in-shūr'-a-bl], *a.* Capaz de ser asegurado, contra pérdida de la vida, contra incendios, etc.
Insurance [in-shūr'-ans], *s.* 1. Seguro, contrato o escritura con que se asegura la vida o los objetos y caudales que corren algún riesgo en mar o tierra. En la Gran Bretaña se escribe a menudo *assurance*. 2. Sistema de seguros. 3. Prima o premio del seguro, cantidad que paga el asegurado al asegurador. 4. Cantidad total que se obliga a pagar el asegurador al asegurado. *Insurance company*, Compañía de seguros. *Endowment insurance*, Seguro dotal. *Liability insurance*, Contrato por el cual una compañía de seguros asume, mediante el pago de un premio, la responsabilidad legal de un individuo ó una corporación. *Life insurance*, Seguro de vida. *Fire insurance*, Seguro contra incendio. *Accident insurance*, Seguro contra accidentes o percances.
Insurance policy [in-shūr'-ans pol'-i-si], *s.* Póliza.
Insure [in-shūr'], *va.* 1. Asegurar, responder el asegurador, mediante el precio convenido, de todos o de alguno de los daños que puedan sobrevenir a una cosa o persona. 2. Obtener seguros, hacer negocios de seguros, asegurar; garantizar, afianzar.—*vn.* 1. Asegurarse, tomar una póliza de seguro. 2. Tener por ocupación habitual la de hacer u obtener seguros.
Insurer [in-shūr'-ęr], *s.* Asegurador.
Insurgent [in-sūr'-jent], *s.* Insurgente, sublevado, rebelde contra una autoridad legalmente establecida.
Insurmountable [in-sūr-maunt'-a-bl], *a.* Insuperable, insalvable.
Insurmountably [in-sūr-maunt'-a-bli] *adv.* Invenciblemente.
Insurrection [in-sur-rec'-shun], *s.* Insurrección, levantamiento, conjuración, sedición, tumulto.
Insurrectional [in-sur-rec'-shun-al], **Insurrectionary** [in-sur-rec'-shun-ę-ri], *a.* Insurreccional, tumultuoso.
Insusceptible [in-sus-sept'-i-bl], *a.* No susceptible, insensible; incapaz de recibir modificación o impresión.
Intact [in-tact'], *a.* Intacto, que no ha sufrido menoscabo; que está entero.
Intaglio [in-tal'-yō o in-tā'-lyō], *s.* Obra de entalladura.
Intake [in'-têk], *s.* 1. Acceso de aire. 2. Orificio de entrada o acceso de agua. 3. Canal de alimentación. 4. Válvula de aspiración. 5. Cosa tomada o cantidad de ella (como energía eléctrica). *Intake manifold*, Válvula múltiple de admisión.
Intangibility, Intangibleness [in-tan-ji-bil'-i-ti, in-tan'-ji-bl-nes], *s.* Cualidad o estado de lo que es intangible.
Intangible [in-tan'-ji-bl], *a.* Intangible, que no debe o no puede ser tocado; (fig.) incomprensible a la mente.
Integer [in'-tę-jęr], *s.* Entero, un todo, total.
Integral [in'-tę-gral], *a.* 1. Íntegro, total, completo. 2. Entero, perfecto; sano; lo que no está dividido en fracciones o quebrados.—*s.* El todo de una cosa considerado con relación a las partes que la componen.
Integrally [in'-tę-gral-i], *adv.* Integralmente.
Integrant [in'-tę-grant], *a.* Integrante, integral; aplícase por lo común a las partes que entran en la composición de un todo. *Integrant molecule*, Molécula integrante.
Integrate [in'-tę-grêt], *va.* 1. Integrar, formar un todo. 2. Indicar la suma. 3. (Mat.) Integrar.—*vn.* Integrarse, completarse, volverse entero.
Integration [in-tę-grê'-shun], *s.* Reintegro, el acto de reintegrar.
Integrity [in-teg'-ri-ti], *s.* 1. Integridad, entereza, hombría de bien. 2. Pureza.
Integument [in-teg'-yu-ment], *s.* Tegumento, integumento, cubierta natural de un animal o de una semilla
Integumentary, Integumental [in-teg-yu-men'-ta-ri, tal], *a.* Integumentario, que sirve de integumento o pertenece a el.
Intellect [in'-tel-ect], *s.* Entendimiento, inteligencia.
Intellective [in-tel-lec'-tiv], *a.* Intelectivo, que tiene la facultad de entender; intelectual.
Intellectual [in-te-lec'-chu-al], *a.* Intelectual, mental, ideal.—*s.* (Ant.) Entendimiento.
Intellectuality [in-te-lec-chu-al'-i-ti], *s.* Entendimiento en la acepción de potencia, facultad intelectual; antiguamente, intelectualidad.
Intelligence [in-tel'-i-jens], *s.* 1.

Inteligencia, conocimiento, comprensión, el acto de entender, penetración. 2. Informe, noticia, aviso. *To give intelligence*, Dar aviso. 3. Inteligencia, correspondencia mutua, armonía, amistad recíproca. 4. Un ser inteligente. 5. Servicio secreto, espionaje. *Intelligence quotient, I.Q.*, Cociente intelectual.

Intelligencer [in-tel'-i-jen-sẹr], *s.* El que comunica o envía avisos ó noticias secretas o interesantes; noticiero, mensajero.

Intelligence test, *s.* Prueba o examen para medir la inteligencia.

Intelligent [in-tel'-i-jent], *a.* 1. Inteligente, sabio, perito, instruído. 2. Sabio; distinguido por la inteligencia; bien informado. 3. Dotado de facultad intelectiva; que comprende y raciocina.

Intelligentsia [in-tel-i-gent'-si-a], *s.* Círculo de los intelectuales, la clase intelectual.

Intelligibility [in-tel-i-ji-bil'-i-ti], *s.* La posibilidad de ser comprendido o entendido; perspicuidad, claridad.

Intelligible [in-tel'-i-ji-bl], *a.* Inteligible.

Intelligibleness [in-tel'-i-ji-bl-nes], *s.* Comprensibilidad, perspicuidad, claridad.

Intelligibly [in-tel'-i-ji-bli], *adv.* Inteligiblemente.

Intemperance [in-tem'-pẹr-ans], *s.* Intemperancia, destemplanza, exceso, desarreglo; particularmente el uso inmoderado de las bebidas alcohólicas.

Intemperate [in-tem'-pẹr-et], *a.* 1. Destemplado; inmoderado, desenfrenado, desmandado, desarreglado. 2. Intemperante, dado al uso excesivo de las bebidas alcohólicas. 3. Excesivo en carácter o grado.

Intemperately [in-tem'-pẹr-et-li], *adv.* Destempladamente, inmoderadamente, desarregladamente.

Intemperateness [in-tem'-pẹr-et-nes], *s.* 1. Calidad de lo destemplado o lo intemperante; inmoderación, exceso, demasía. 2. Intemperie.

Intend [in-tend'], *va.* 1. Intentar, tener ánimo o designio de ejecutar alguna cosa; destinar, aplicar, determinar, proyectar hacer, designar, proponerse. *I did not intend it*, No era esa mi intención. 2. Dar a entender, significar, señalar. 3. (Ant.) Fijar en un curso dado, dirigir; cuidar, mirar por.

Intendancy [in-tend'-an-si], *s.* Intendencia, empleo de intendente.

Intendant [in-tend'-ant], *s.* Intendente, el que tiene a su cargo la intendencia o dirección de algún ramo particular del servicio público. *Intendant of a province*, Intendente o gobernador de una provincia o territorio.

Intended [in-tend'-ed], *s.* (Fam.) Desposado, da; novio, novia; siempre con pronombre posesivo.

Intendedly [in-tend'-ed-li], *adv.* Adrede, con intención.

Intendment [in-tend'-mẹnt], *s.* 1. (For.) El verdadero intento o la significación correcta de la ley. 2. (Ant.) Intento, designio, intención.

Inteneration [in-ten-ẹr-é'-shun], *s.* Enternecimiento, el acto de enternecer.

Intense [in-tens'], *a.* 1. Intenso, estirado, que tiene tensión, esforzado en alto grado; vivo, ardiente, fogoso. 2. Excesivo, vehemente, violento; extremado, sumo. *Intense sufferings*, Padecimientos excesivos, violentos. 3. Intenso, que hace esfuerzos activos. 4. (Foto.) *V.* DENSE.

Intensely [in-tens'-li], *adv.* Intensamente.

Intenseness [in-tens'-nes], *s.* Intensidad, vehemencia, fuerza, vigor; ardor; fogosidad. *V.* INTENSITY.

Intensifier [in-ten'-si-fai''-ẹr], *s.* El que o lo que hace más intenso; disolución química usada en fotografía para hacer más intensas las imágenes negativas.

Intensify [in-ten'-si-fai], *va.* 1. Hacer o volver más intenso. 2. (Foto.) Aumentar la densidad de una película para obtener más marcados contrastes.—*vn.* Volverse intenso.

Intension [in-ten'-shun], *s.* 1. Intensión; grado. 2. Tensión. 3. (Lógica) El contenido.

Intensity [in-ten'-si-ti], *s.* 1. Intensidad, exceso, fuerza, rigor. 2. Tensión, estado de lo que se halla tenso o estirado. 3. (Fís.) Intensidad, grado de actividad y fuerza de cualquier agente físico. 4. Fogosidad, ardor; aplicación constante del ánimo. 5. (Foto.) Contraste fuerte entre las luces y las sombras en una prueba negativa.

Intensive [in-ten'-siv], *a.* 1. Intensivo, que sirve para aumentar o hacer intenso; en gramática, que da énfasis. 2. Capaz de hacerse intenso. 3. Entero, completo. 4. (Lógica) Relativo al contenido.

Intensively [in-ten'-siv-li], *adv.* Intensivamente.

Intent [in-tent'], *a.* Atento, cuidadoso, aplicado con ahinco.—*s.* Intento, designio, deseo, intención, ánimo. *To all intents and purposes*, En todos sentidos, para el caso. (For.) Para todos los casos y efectos que haya lugar. *To be intent on* o *upon*, Estar absorto en, aplicado a. *To be wholly intent on*, Pensar sólo en.

Intention [in-ten'-shun], *s.* 1. Intención, determinación de la voluntad en un sentido determinado. 2. Intención, ánimo, designio, mira, fin. 3. (For.) Propósito consciente de cometer una acción criminal. 4. (Cir.) Curso o procedimiento natural. *Healing by first intention*, Cura de primera intención, sin supuración. *Healing by second intention*, Cura por cicatrización, después de la supuración.

Intentional [in-ten'-shun-al], *a.* Intencional.

Intentionally [in-ten'-shun-al-i], *adv.* Intencionalmente.

Intently [in-tent'-li], *adv.* Ansiosamente; atentamente.

Intentness [in-tent'-nes], *s.* Aplicación ansiosa, atención, afición.

Inter [in-tẹr'], *va.* Enterrar, soterrar, sepultar.

Inter- [in'-tẹr]. Prefijo; preposición latina que significa *entre, en medio* ó *mutuamente;* entra en la composición de muchas voces.

Interact [in-tẹr-act'], *va.* Obrar entre sí, recíprocamente; afectar el uno al otro.

Interact [in'-tẹr-act], *s.* Entreacto, intermedio, el espacio de tiempo entre los actos de las representaciones dramáticas.

Interaction [in-tẹr-ac'-shun], *s.* 1. Acción o influencia recíproca. 2. Acción intermedia.

Interadditive [in-tẹr-ad'-i-tiv], *a.* Intercalar, ingerido ó añadido a otra cosa; puesto entre paréntesis.

Interamnian [in-tẹr-am'-ni-an], *a.* Situado entre ríos.

Interarticular [in-tẹr-ar-tic'-yu-lar], *a.* Interarticular, que está situado entre las articulaciones.

Interbreed [in-tẹr-brīd'], *va.* y *vn.* *V.* HYBRIDIZE.

Intercalary [in-tẹr'-ca-lẹ-ri], *a.* Intercalar, lo que se pone o introduce entre otras cosas, como sucede con el día 29 de febrero, que en el año bisiesto es día intercalar.

Intercalate [in-tẹr'-ca-lêt], *va.* Intercalar, interponer.

Intercalation [in-tẹr-ca-lé'-shun], *s.* Intercalación.

Intercede [in-tẹr-sīd'], *vn.* 1. Interceder, mediar. 2. Interponerse, ponerse una cosa entre otras.

Interceder, *s.* *V.* INTERCESSOR.

Interceding [in-tẹr-sīd'-ing], *s.* Mediación, intercesión.

Intercept [in-tẹr-sept'], *va.* 1. Interceptar, coger, sorprender alguna carta o pliego antes de llegar a su destino. 2. Obstruir, cerrar el paso, impedir que vaya adelante alguna persona o cosa, o detenerla en su movimiento.

Interceptor [in-ter-sep'-tẹr], *s.* Interceptor. *Interceptor missile*, (Mil.) Proyectil interceptor.

Interception [in-tẹr-sep'-shun], *s.* Intercepción, interrupción de movimiento.

Intercession [in-tẹr-sesh'-un], *s.* 1. Intercesión, mediación. 2. (Liturgia) Oración u oraciones para personas de diferente condición.

Intercessor [in-tẹr-ses'-ẹr], *s.* 1. Intercesor, mediador. 2. Administrador (antiguamente intercesor), obispo que en sede vacante administra la diócesis hasta la llegada del nuevo prelado.

Intercessory [in-tẹr-ses'-o-ri], *s.* Intercesorio.

Interchain [in-tẹr-chên'], *va.* Encadenar, entrelazar.

Interchange [in-tẹr-chênj'], *va.* 1. Alternar, variar una cosa repitiéndola sucesivamente. 2. Cambiar, trocar, permutar.—*vn.* Suceder alternativamente, con alternación.

Interchange [in'-tẹr-chênj], *s.* 1. Comercio, negociación, tráfico, permuta de géneros. 2. Sucesión mutua, vicisitud. 3. Donación recíproca o la acción de dar y recibir al mismo tiempo. 4. Intercambio. *Interchange of compliments*, Cortesías mutuas. *Interchange of gifts*, Presentes o regalos recíprocos.

Interchangeability [in-tẹr-chênj-a-bil'-i-ti], *s.* Permutabilidad.

Interchangeable [in-tẹr-chênj'-a-bl], *a.* Permutable; sucesivo; mutuo, recíproco.

Interchangeableness [in-tẹr-chênj'-a-bl-nes], *s.* Cambio, permuta; sucesión alternativa.

Interchangeably [in-tẹr-chênj'-a-bli], *adv.* Alternativamente, mutuamente, recíprocamente.

Interchapter [in-tẹr-chap'-tẹr], *s.* Capítulo interpuesto.

Intercipient [in-tẹr-sip'-i-ent], *a.* Interceptador, que intercepta u obstruye algo.—*s.* La cosa que intercepta.

Interclude [in-tẹr-clūd'], *va.* Obstruir o interceptar; ocultar a la vista.

Interclusion [in-tẹr-clū'-zhun], *s.* Intercepción, obstrucción.

Intercollegiate [in-tȩr-col-lí'-ji-ėt], *a.* Interuniversitario.

Intercolumnar [in-tȩr-co-lum'-nar], *a.* Colocado entre columnas; intercolumnar.

Intercommon [in-tȩr-com'-un], *va.* (Hist. de Ingl.) Proscribir a uno por sostener comunicación con malhechores o reos, o por albergarlos.—*vn.* 1. Tener unos mismos prados en común, cuando se habla de pueblos; alimentarse en los mismos prados, hablando de animales. 2. (Poco us.) Comer en comunidad, a la misma mesa que otros, en mesa redonda.

Intercommunicate [in-tȩr-com-miú'-ni-kêt], *vn.* Comunicar con otro; sostener comunicación.

Intercommunication [in-tȩr-com-miu-ni-ké'-shun], *s.* Comunicación mutua o recíproca.

Intercontinental [in'-tȩr-con-ti-nen'-tal], *a.* Intercontinental. *Intercontinental ballistic missile,* Proyectil de alcance intercontinental.

Intercostal [in-tȩr-cos'-tal], *a.* Intercostal.

Intercourse [in'-tȩr-cōrs], *s.* 1. Comercio, tráfico; cambios comerciales entre varios países. 2. Comunicación, correspondencia, trato. *Intercourse of trade,* Giro de comercio. *Sexual intercourse,* Cópula, coito.

Intercross [in-tȩr-cros'], *va.* 1. Entrecruzar, cruzarse mutuamente, como las líneas. 2. Cruzar castas o razas de animales o de plantas; hibridar.

Intercurrence [in-tȩr-cur'-ens], *s.* Intercurrente, paso o tránsito entre dos parajes; intervención, ocurrencia.

Intercurrent [in-tȩr-cur'-ent], *a.* Lo que corre entre dos parajes; lo que interviene u ocurre mientras se está haciendo alguna cosa.

Intercutaneous [in-tȩr-kiu-té'-nȩ-us], *a.* Intercutáneo.

Interdenominational [in-tȩr-dȩ-nom-i-nê'-shun-al], *a.* Intersectario.

Interdependence [in-tȩr-dȩ-pend'-ens], *s.* Dependencia mutua.

Interdependent [in-tȩr-dȩ-pend'-ent], *a.* Que depende recíprocamente.

Interdict [in-tȩr-dict'], *va.* 1. Prohibir, vedar (antiguamente entredecir o interdecir). 2. Entredecir, poner entredicho.

Interdict [in'-tȩr-dict], *s.* 1. Prohibición, mandato prohibitorio. 2. Interdicción, entredicho, censura eclesiástica.

Interdiction [in-tȩr-dic'-shun], *s.* Interdicción, prohibición.

Interdictive [in-tȩr-dic'-tiv], *a.* Lo que entredice o tiene poder de prohibir o de entredecir.

Interdictory [in-tȩr-dic'-to-ri], *a.* Lo que pertenece a prohibición o entredicho.

Interdigital [in-tȩr-dij'-i-tal], *a.* Interdigital, situado entre los dedos.

Interest [in'-tȩr-est], *va.* 1. Interesar, hacer tomar parte en alguna cosa. 2. Interesar, empeñar, hacer tomar parte a la voluntad o al corazón en algo.—*vn.* Interesarse, tomar parte.

Interest, *s.* 1. Interés, provecho, utilidad. 2. Interés, la parte que se toma en el logro de alguna cosa; influjo, empeño. 3. Interés, la parte que se toma en alguna negociación lucrativa; lucro del capital; cantidad que se paga por el uso del dinero. 4. Propiedad parcial; porción o derecho copropietario. 5. Influencia, el poder de procurar favorable consideración, influjo. 6. Viva simpatía, curiosidad. *Compound interest,* Interés compuesto. *To put out on interest,* Dar a interés. *To bear five per cent. interest,* Producir cinco por ciento de interés.

Interesting [in'-tȩr-est-ing], *a.* Interesante, atractivo. *In an interesting condition,* En estado interesante, en cinta.

Interfere [in-tȩr-fír'], *vn.* 1. Interponerse, meterse, mezclarse, intervenir; especialmente, embarazar, poner obstáculos, impedir; algunas veces, entremeterse. 2. Chocar, oponerse mutuamente. 3. (Vet.) Rozarse o herirse un pie con el otro al andar; dícese de los caballos.

Interference [in-tȩr-fír'-ens], *s.* 1. Estorbo, obstáculo. 2. Ingerencia, entremetimiento. 3. Interposición, intervención. 4. Interferencia. 5. Ruidos parásitos. *Interference filter,* Antiparásito.

Interfering [in-tȩr-fír'-ing], *s.* 1. Oposición, contrariedad. 2. Alcance, rozadura, hablando de caballos.

Interfluent [in-tȩr'-flu-ent], **Interfluous** [in-tȩr'-flu-us], *a.* Lo que fluye por medio de otra cosa.

Interfulgent [in-tȩr-ful'-jent], *a.* Lo que luce o resplandece entre otras cosas.

Interfuse [in-tȩr-fiūz'], *va.* 1. Hacer fluir juntamente, como dos flúidos; hacer pasar al través de los poros. 2. Entremezclar, producir una mezcla.—*vn.* Fluir uno en otro; mezclarse.

Interim [in'-tȩr-im], *s.* Intermedio, ínterin, el espacio que hay entre un tiempo y otro. *In this interim,* En el ínterin, entre tanto, mientras esto sucedía.

Interior [in-tí'-ri-ȩr], *a.* Interior, interno, lo que está de la parte de adentro.—*s.* El interior.

Interiorly [in-tí'-ri-ȩr-li], *adv.* Interiormente.

Interjacent [in-tȩr-jé'-sent], *a.* Interyacente, interpuesto, situado en medio de otras cosas.

Interject [in-tȩr-ject'], *va.* Poner en medio, insertar.—*vn.* Interponer, intervenir.

Interjection [in-tȩr-jec'-shun], *s.* 1. Interjección, una de las partes de la oración. 2. Intervención, interposición.

Interjoin [in-tȩr-join'], *va.* Unir mutuamente; también, casar entre sí a cuatro o más personas de dos familias.

Interlace [in-tȩr-lés'], *va.* Entrelazar, entremezclar.

Interlard [in-tȩr-lārd'], *va.* 1. Mechar, introducir mechas o rajitas de tocino gordo en la carne de las aves u otras viandas. 2. Entreponer, insertar. 3. Entremezclar, entretejer.

Interleave [in-tȩr-lív'], *va.* Interpolar o interponer hojas blancas entre las escritas o impresas de un libro.

Interline [in-tȩr-lain'], *va.* Interlinear, entrerrenglonar, insertar escribiendo entre renglones, sea o no para corregir.

Interlinear [in-tȩr-lin'-ȩ-ar], **Interlineary** [in-tȩr-lin'-ȩ-a-ri], *a.* Interlineal.

Interlineation [in-tȩr-lin-ȩ-é'-shun], *s.* Interlineación, corrección interlineal.

Interlining [in-tȩr-lain'-ing], *s.* 1. Entretela. 2. Interlineación, corrección interlineal.

Interlink [in-tȩr-linc'], *va.* Eslabonar, encadenar.

‡Interlocation [in-tȩr-lo-ké'-shun], *s.* Interposición.

Interlock [in-tȩr-lec'], *va.* y *vn.* Trabar, unir uno con otro por mutua acción; unirse, entrelazarse una cosa con otra.

Interlocution [in-tȩr-lo-kiū'-shun], *s.* 1. Interlocución, plática o conferencia alternada entre dos o más personas. 2. Auto interlocutorio.

Interlocutor [in-tȩr-loc'-yu-tȩr], *s.* Interlocutor.

Interlocutory [in-tȩr-loc'-yu-to-ri], *a.* 1. Dialogístico, que se compone de diálogos o conferencias entre dos o más personas. 2. Interlocutorio, auto o sentencia interlocutoria.

Interlope [in-tȩr-lōp'], *vn.* Entremeterse sin derecho; mezclarse en partidos o bandos; traficar sin licencia.

Interloper [in-tȩr-lōp'-ȩr], *s.* 1. Entremetido, el que se mete en asuntos que no le atañen. 2. El que trafica en un comercio que por derecho pertenece a otros; intérlope.

Interlude [in'-tȩr-lūd], *s.* 1. Intermedio, baile, sainete, farsa, etc., representada entre los actos o jornadas de una pieza dramática. 2. Pasaje musical corto que se toca, como intervalo o transición, entre las partes de un himno, de una composición sagrada, etc.

Interlunar [in-tȩr-lū'-nar], **Interlunary** [in-tȩr-lū'-na-ri], *a.* Perteneciente al interlunio.

Intermarriage [in-tȩr-mar'-ij], *s.* Matrimonio o casamiento mutuo que se celebra entre dos familias; v. g. dos hermanos con dos hermanas.

Intermarry [in-tȩr-mar'-i], *vn.* Casarse mutuamente cuatro o más personas de dos familias.

Intermeddle [in-tȩr-med'-l], *vn.* Entremeterse, meterse uno o ingerirse donde no le llaman o mezclarse en lo que no le toca.—*va.* Entremezclar, mezclar.

Intermeddler [in-tȩr-med'-lȩr], *s.* Entremetido.

Intermedial [in-tȩr-mí'-di-al], **Intermediate** [in-tȩr-mí'-di-ct], *a.* Intermedio, lo que está entre dos cosas.

Intermediary [in-tȩr-mí'-di-ȩ-ri], *a.* Intermedio, intermediado.—*s.* 1. Agente intermedio; algunas veces, medio o médium espiritista. 2. *V.* INTERMEDIATION.

Intermediate [in-ter-mi'-di-et], *a.* Intermedio, mediano. *Intermediate range ballistic missile,* (Mil.) Proyectil de alcance intermedio.

Intermediation [in-tȩr-mí-di-é'-shun], *s.* Intervención, mediación.

Intermedium [in-tȩr-mí'-di-um], *s.* Intermedio; agente intermedio.

Interment [in-tȩr'-mȩnt], *s.* Entierro, sepultura, funeral.

Intermigration [in-tȩr-mai-gré'-shun], *s.* Mudanza recíproca de una parte a otra.

Interminable [in-tȩr'-mi-na-bl], *a.* Interminable, ilimitado.—*s.* El Ser infinito, Dios.

Interminate [in-tȩr'-mi-nȩt], *a.* Interminable, ilimitado.

Intermingle [in-tȩr-miṇ'-gl], *va.* Entremezclar.—*vn.* Mezclarse.

Intermission [in-tȩr-mish'-un], *s.* 1. Intermisión, interrupción. 2. Intermisión, tiempo intermedio.

Intermissive [in-tȩr-mis'-iv], *a.* Intermitente.

Intermit [in-tȩr-mit'], *va.* Intermitir.—*vn.* Descontinuar o cesar la calen-

ī *ida*; ē *hé*; ā *ala*; e *por*; ō *oro*; u *uno*.—i *idea*; e *esté*; a *así*; o *osó*; u *opa*; ū como en *leur* (Fr.).—ai *aire*; ei *voy*; au *aula*;

tura; cesar o parar un rato alguna acción o movimiento para principiar otra vez después; suspender.

Intermittent [in-tęr-mit'-ent], *a.* Intermitente.

Intermix [in-tęr-mics'], *va.* Entremezclar, mezclar unas cosas con otras.—*vn.* Entremezclarse, mezclarse.

Intermixture [in-tęr-mics'-chur], *s.* 1. Mezcla de una cosa con otra. 2. Masa de ingredientes mezclados. 3. Un ingrediente adicional; mezcla, cantidad añadida.

Intermundane [in-tęr-mun'-dên], *a.* Entremundano, situado entre mundos, como el espacio.

Intermural [in-tęr-miū'-ral], *a.* Entremural, emparedado: colocado entre muros.

Intern [in-tęrn'], *a.* (Poco us.) Interno, intestino.—*s.* Médico o cirujano residente en un hospital.

Intern, *va.* Internar, encerrar en un lugar determinado, poner bajo vigilancia.—*vn.* Trabajar en un hospital como médico interno.

Internal [in-tęr'-nal], *a.* 1. Interno, interior, doméstico. 2. Intrínseco, real, inherente, basado en la misma cosa; derivado de lo interior o de la substancia: como *internal evidence*, prueba íntima, testimonio derivado de la cosa misma. 3. Interior, intestino, que se halla dentro del cuerpo social.

Internally [in-tęr'-nal-i], *adv.* Internamente; mentalmente, intelectualmente.

International [in-tęr-nash'-un-al], *a.* Internacional, lo concerniente a dos o más naciones entre sí. *International law*, Derecho internacional.

Internationalize [in-tęr-nash'-un-al-aiz], *va.* Internacionalizar.

Internecine [in-tęr-nî'-sin], *a.* Lo que es recíprocamente destructivo. *Internecine war*, Guerra a muerte.

Internode, Internodium [in-tęr-nōd', i-um], *s.* 1. (Bot.) Internodio, entrenudo, espacio o intervalo entre los nudos de las plantas o de los árboles. 2. (Anat.) Parte situada entre dos articulaciones.

Internship [in'-tęrn-ship], *s.* Internado (en un hospital, etc.)

Internuncio [in-tęr-nun'-shi-o], *s.* 1. Internuncio, el que habla por otro o lleva mensajes de una parte a otra. 2. Internuncio, ministro pontificio que hace veces de nuncio.

Interpellate [in-tęr-pel'-êt], *va.* Interpelar; dirigir una excitación al gobierno para que dé explicaciones sobre un hecho o sobre su conducta en circunstancias especiales.

Interpellation [in-tęr-pel-ê'-shun], *s.* 1. Interpelación, acción de interpelar; excitación hecha a un gobierno o a una persona para que dé explicaciones. 2. Interrupción. 3. Ruego o súplica ardiente. 4. Interpelación, citación que se hace en justicia para que responda o comparezca un reo.

Interpenetrate [in-tęr-pen'-ę-trêt], *va.* y *vn.* Penetrar completamente; penetrarse mutuamente, formar unión por medio de la penetración.

Interplanetary [in-tęr-plan'-et-ę-ri], *a.* Interplanetario.

Interplay [in-tęr-plê'], *s.* 1. Acción o influencia mutuas. 2. Acción o efecto recíprocos.

Interplead [in-tęr-plîd'], *vn.* (For.) Litigar entre sí dos o más demandantes, para que el tribunal resuelva sobre la propiedad de una cosa.

Interpleader [in-tęr-plîd'-ęr], *s.* (For.) Procedimiento para determinar cuál entre dos o más personas es el dueño legal de la cosa litigada.

Interpledge [in-tęr-plej'], *va.* Dar y tomar recíprocamente una cosa como prenda.

Interpolate [in-tęr'-po-lêt], *va.* 1. Interpolar, insertar una palabra, cláusula o frase en un escrito, sea para completar, sea para alterar el sentido; falsificar. 2. Interpolar, interponer una cosa entre otras.

Interpolation [in-tęr-po-lê'-shun], *s.* Interpolación, añadidura o entrerrenglonadura de una palabra o frase en un manuscrito antiguo.

Interpolator [in-tęr'-po-lê-tęr], *s.* Interpolador, el que añade subrepticiamente alguna palabra o frase a un manuscrito antiguo.

Interposal [in-tęr-pōz'-al], *s.* 1. Interposición, mediación de alguna persona entre otras dos. 2. Intervención, asistencia.

Interpose [in-tęr-pōz'], *va.* 1. Interponer, entreponer. 2. Interponer el favor, crédito, autoridad, etc., en beneficio de alguno.—*vn.* 1. Interponerse, mediar entre dos personas desavenidas para componerlas entre sí. 2. Intervenir; interponerse una cosa entre otras. 3. Interrumpir a alguno, hacer objeción.

Interposer [in-tęr-pōz'-ęr], *s.* El que interpone, mediador.

Interpret [in-tęr'-pret], *va.* 1. Interpretar, explicar o explanar el sentido de alguna cosa. 2. Dar sentido a lo que no lo tiene; descifrar. 3. Representar, ilustrar. 4. Traducir oralmente, como intérprete.

Interpretable [in-tęr'-pret-a-bl], *a.* Interpretable, que es capaz de interpretación o explanación.

Interpretation [in-tęr-pre-tê'-shun], *s.* 1. Interpretación, acción de interpretar. 2. Explicación, exposición; el sentido dado por un intérprete o un expositor.

Interpretative [in-tęr'-pre-ta-tiv], *a.* Interpretativo.

Interpreter [in-tęr'-pre-tęr], *s.* Intérprete; traductor, el que interpreta o traduce de un idioma a otro, en especial el que lo hace oralmente.

Interregnum, Interreign [in-tę-reg'-num, in-tę-rên'], *s.* 1. Interregno, espacio de tiempo en que un trono está vacante. 2. Suspensión de la autoridad ejecutiva a causa de un cambio de gobierno. 3. Cualquier período de espera, transición o desorden.

Interrelated [in-ter-rę-lê'-ted], *a.* Correlativo, con relación recíproca.

Interrogate [in-ter'-o-gêt], *va.* Interrogar, preguntar, examinar.—*vn.* Interrogar, hacer un interrogatorio.

Interrogation [in-ter-o-gê'-shun], *s.* 1. Interrogación, pregunta, pesquisa. 2. Interrogación, signo interrogativo (?).

Interrogative [in-tęr-eg'-a-tiv], *s.* Pronombre interrogativo, que se usa cuando se pregunta alguna cosa, como *who? what?* ¿quién? ¿qué?—*a.* Interrogativo.

Interrogatively [in-tęr-eg'-a-tiv-li], *adv.* Interrogativamente.

Interrogator [in-ter'-o-gê-tęr], *s.* Interrogante.

Interrogatory [in-tęr-eg'-a-to-ri], *s.* Interrogatorio, la serie de preguntas que se hacen al acusado o parte y a los testigos.—*a.* Interrogativo, que expresa una pregunta.

Interrupt [in-tęr-rupt'], *va.* 1. Interrumpir, estorbar, impedir la continuación de una cosa. 2. Dividir, separar; entrecortar, romper la continuidad o la sucesión de.

Interruptedly [in-tęr-rupt'-ed-li], *adv.* Interrumpidamente.

Interrupter [in-tęr-rupt'-ęr], *s.* Interruptor, el que interrumpe o impide de alguna cosa; útil para interrumpir la corriente eléctrica.

Interruption [in-tęr-rup'-shun], *s.* Interrupción, embarazo, obstáculo; interposición; intermisión.

Interscapular [in-tęr-scap'-yu-lar], *a.* Interescapular, que está situado entre ambas escápulas.

Interscholastic [in-tęr-sco-las'-tic], *a.* Interescolar.

Intersect [in-tęr-sect'], *va.* Entrecortar.—*vn.* (Geom.) Intersecarse, cortarse dos líneas.

Intersection [in-tęr-sec'-shun], *s.* Intersección.

Interspace [in'-tęr-spês], *s.* Intervalo, intersticio, espacio que media entre varios cuerpos.

Interspace [in-tęr-spês'], *va.* Hacer intervalos entre dos o más cuerpos; ocupar los intersticios entre ellos.

Intersperse [in-tęr-spęrs'], *va.* Esparcir una cosa entre otras; entremezclar; diseminar.

Interspersion [in-tęr-spęr'-shun], *s.* El acto de esparcir una cosa entre otras.

Interspinal [in-tęr-spai'-nal], **Interspinous** [in-tęr-spai'-nus], *a.* Interespinoso, interespinal, situado entre las apófisis de las vértebras.

Interstate [in'-tęr-stêt], *a.* Que se refiere a las relaciones y al tráfico entre diferentes estados; se aplica particularmente a los estados que forman la confederación norteamericana. *Interstate commerce*, Comercio interior, entre los varios estados.

Interstellar [in-tęr-stel'-ar], *a.* Que está situado entre las estrellas; interestelar.

Interstice [in'-tęr-stis o in-tęr'-stis], *s.* 1. Intersticio, intervalo o espacio que hay de una cosa a otra. 2. Intersticio, intermedio, intervalo, el espacio de tiempo que media entre un acto y otro.

Intertexture [in-tęr-tex'-chur], *s.* El entretejido o enlazamiento de una cosa con otra.

Intertwine [in-tęr-twain'], **Intertwist** [in-tęr-twist'], *va.* Entretejer, entrelazar o tejer una cosa con otra.

Interurban [in-tęr-ur'-ban], *a.* Interurbano.

Interval [in'-tęr-val], *s.* 1. Intervalo, intersticio, distancia de un lugar a otro. 2. Intervalo, el tiempo que pasa entre una cosa y otra. 3. (Mús.) Intervalo, distancia que media de un tono a otro. 4. Remisión o intermisión de algún mal. *Lucid interval*, Intervalo lúcido, el espacio de tiempo en que los delirantes gozan algún alivio en su mal.

Interveined [in-tęr-vênd'], *a.* Interpolado o cortado como las venas.

Intervene [in-tęr-vîn'], *vn.* 1. Intervenir, mediar, ponerse por medio, interponerse; ocurrir, sobrevenir. 2. Interponer con algún fin. 3. Sobrevenir algo de manera que sirva de obstáculo o impedimento. *I shall come if nothing intervenes*, Vendré si nada ocurre que lo impida.

Intervenient [in-tęr-vî'-ni-ent], *a.* Interpuesto; ocurrido.

Intervention [in-tęr-ven'-shun], *s.* 1. Intervención, asistencia, concurrencia en algún negocio. 2. Interposición, mediación.

Intervertebral [in-tęr-vęr'-tę-bral], *a.* Intervertebral, que se halla situado entre las vértebras.

Interview [in'-tęr-viū], *s.* 1. Vistas, entrevista, conferencia, el encuentro ó concurrencia de personas citadas para verse y conferenciar. 2. Abocamiento, conferencia verbal, cita entre dos ó más personas para conferenciar mutuamente: particularmente en el periodismo, conferencia con alguien cuya opinión ó cuyos informes se solicitan para publicarlos; y el relato de lo dicho ú ocurrido en esa conferencia.

Interview, *va.* Celebrar una entrevista con alguno; en el periodismo, interrogar á una persona para obtener de ella informes destinados á la publicación.

Interviewer [in'-tęr-viū"-ęr], *s.* Periodista que se avista y conferencia con los hombres de Estado, artistas y otras personas que por cualquier concepto llaman la atención pública.

Intervolve [in-tęr-velv'], *va.* Envolver una cosa dentro de otra.

Interweave [in-tęr-wīv'], *va.* Entretejer, enlazar, entremeter ó meter una cosa entre otra.

Interweaving [in-tęr-wīv'-ing], *s.* Entretejedura.

Interwreathe [in-tęr-rīdh], *va.* Tejer en forma de guirnalda.

Intestable [in-tes'-ta-bl], *a.* El que legalmente no puede testar ó hacer testamento.

Intestacy [in-tes'-ta-si], *s.* La falta de testamento.

Intestate [in-tes'-têt], *a.* Intestado, el que muere sin hacer testamento.

Intestinal [in-tes'-ti-nal], *a.* 1. Intestinal, de los intestinos. 2. Interior, intestino.

Intestine [in-tes'-tin], *a.* Interior, intestino, doméstico.—*s.* Intestino, tripa: úsase por lo común en plural.

Intextured [in-tex'-churd], *a.* Entretejido; labrado, adornado con labores.

Inthrall [in-thrōl'], *va* Esclavizar. *V.* Enthrall.

Inthralment [in-thrōl'-męnt], *s.* Esclavitud.

Inthrone, *va.* *V.* Enthrone, etc.

Intimacy [in'-ti-ma-si], *s.* Intimidad, familiaridad, confianza.

Intimate [in'-ti-met], *a.* 1. Íntimo, interior; cordial, familiar. 2. Que se adhiere estrechamente. 3. Interno, que procede de lo interior.—*s.* Amigo íntimo ó de toda confianza.

Intimate [in'-ti-mêt], *va.* Insinuar, dar á entender alguna cosa indirectamente ó por medio de rodeos.

Intimately [in'-ti-met-li], *adv.* 1. Íntimamente, estrechamente, familiarmente. 2. En el fondo del alma; con afecto particular.

Intimation [in-ti-mê'-shun], *s.* Insinuación, indirecta, prevención; aviso indirecto, ligero indicio.

Intimidate [in-tim'-i-dêt], *va.* Intimidar, poner ó causar miedo ó temor; aterrar, espantar.

Intimidation [in-tim-i-dê'-shun], *s.* Intimidación.

Intimidatory [in-tim'-i-da-to-ri], *a.* Intimidador, que intimida.

Into [in'-tū], *prep.* 1. En, dentro, adentro, hacia el interior de. Denota: (1) entrada en, (2) penetración al través de algo, (3) inserción, inclusión, (4) cambio de estado, (5) por, multiplicado por. 2. Además de. *Into the bargain*, Además del trato, por demás, como adición.

Intolerable [in-tel'-ęr-a-bl], *a.* Intolerable, lo que no se puede sufrir ó tolerar.

Intolerableness [in-tel'-ęr-a-bl-nes], *s.* Intolerabilidad.

Intolerably [in-tel'-ęr-a-bli], *adv.* Intolerablemente.

Intolerance [in-tel'-ęr-ans], *s.* Intolerancia.

Intolerant [in-tel'-ęr-ant], *a.* Intolerante, falto de tolerancia.—*s.* El que no aguanta ni sufre; el que no puede aguantar ó sufrir.

Intolerated [in-tel'-ęr-êt-ed], *a.* Lo que no es tolerado.

Intoleration [in-tel-ęr-ê'-shun], *s.* Intolerantismo.

Intomb [in-tūm'], *va.* Enterrar, sepultar, poner en un sepulcro.

Intonate [in'-to-nêt], *vn.* 1. Entonar, solfear, cantar. 2. (Des.) Tronar.

Intonation [in-to-nê'-shun], *s.* 1. La modulación de la voz al hablar. 2. Entonación; la acción de entonar.

Intone [in-tōn'], *va.* y *vn.* 1. Entonar, dar tono á las voces. 2. Recitar monótonamente, salmodiar; cantar el oficio de la iglesia.

Intorsion, *s.* *V.* Intortion.

Intort [in-tōrt'], *va.* Torcer, dar vueltas á una cosa en torno, apretándola.

Intortion [in-tōr'-shun], *s.* Torcedura; vuelta de una planta hacia uno ú otro lado.

Intoxicant [in-tex'-i-cant], *s.* Lo que emborracha ó embriaga, como el alcohol y el opio.

Intoxicate [in-tex'-i-kêt], *va.* 1. Embriagar, emborrachar. 2. Excitar hasta el frenesí. 3. (Med.) Envenenar, atosigar, intoxicar, emponzoñar.

Intoxicate, *a.* Emborrachado, borracho, embriagado.

Intoxicated [in-tex'-i-kêt-ed], *a.* Ebrio, borracho. *Intoxicated with joy*, Frenético de alegría.

Intoxication [in-tex-i-kê'-shun], *s.* 1. Embriaguez, borrachera. 2. Trasportamiento, arrebatamiento, entusiasmo. 3. (Med.) Intoxicación, envenenamiento.

Intra- [in'-tra]. Prefijo; preposición latina que significa dentro.

Intractable [in-trac'-ta-bl], *a.* Intratable, áspero, terco.

Intractableness [in-trac'-ta-bl-nes], *s.* Obstinación, porfía, terquedad.

Intractably [in-trac'-ta-bli], *adv.* Obstinadamente, porfiadamente.

Intramural [in-tra-miū'-ral], *a.* Intramuros, que se halla dentro de los muros.

Intranquillity [in-tran-cwil'-i-ti], *s.* Desasosiego, falta de tranquilidad; intranquilidad.

Intransient [in-tran'-shent], *a.* Permanente, que no se muda ó cambia fácilmente; inmutable.

Intransitive [in-tran'-si-tiv], *a.* Intransitivo.

Intransitively [in-tran'-si-tiv-li], *adv.* Intransitivamente.

Intransmutability [in-trans-miu-ta-bil'-i-ti], *s.* Intransmutabilidad.

Intransmutable [in-trans-miū'-ta-bl], *a.* Intransmutable, lo que no se puede mudar.

Intrant [in'-trant], *a.* Entrante, que entra.

Intravenous [in-tra-vī'-nus], *a.* Intravenoso. *Intravenous shot*, Inyección intravenosa.

Intrench [in-trench'], *vn.* Invadir, usurpar, quitar á otro lo que es suyo.—*va.* 1. Atrincherar. 2. Llenar de hoyos ó cortes alguna cosa. *V.* Entrench.

Intrenchment [in-trench'-męnt], *s.* Atrincheramiento, trinchera.

Intrepid [in-trep'-id], *a.* Intrépido, arrojado, osado.

Intrepidity [in-trę-pid'-i-ti], *s.* Intrepidez, arrojo, osadía.

Intrepidly [in-trep'-id-li], *adv.* Intrépidamente.

Intricacy [in'-tri-ca-si], *s.* Embrollo, confusión, embarazo, dificultad.

Intricate [in'-tri-ket], *a.* Intrincado, confuso, enredado, complicado.

Intricate, *va.* (Poco us.) Intrincar, enredar, confundir, embrollar.

Intricately [in'-tri-ket-li], *adv.* Intrincadamente.

Intricateness [in'-tri-ket-nes], *s.* Embrollo, perplejidad, obscuridad.

Intrigue [in-trīg'], *s.* 1. Intriga, manejo, trama; arte ó amaño secreto para lograr un fin. 2. Intriga amorosa, galanteo, trato secreto entre dos amantes. 3. Embrollo, confusión. 4. Enredo ó maraña de una comedia.

Intrigue, *vn.* Intrigar: tramar, manejar ó negociar secretamente un asunto; tramar galanteos secretos. —*va.* Embarazar, turbar, intrincar.

Intriguer [in-trīg'-ęr], *s.* 1. Intrigante, embrollador, entremetido, zaramullo. 2. Amante, la persona que galantea en secreto á una mujer.

Intriguingly [in-trīg'-ing-li], *adv.* Por medio de intrigas ó manejos secretos.

Intrinsic, Intrinsical [in-trin'-sic, al], *a.* 1. Intrínseco, inherente, esencial, verdadero. 2. Intrínseco, interno, interior.

Intrinsically [in-trin'-sic-al-i], *adv.* Intrínsecamente, esencialmente, interiormente.

Intrinsicalness [in-trin'-sic-al-nes], *s.* Realidad; mérito intrínseco.

Introduce [in-tro-diūs'], *va.* 1. Introducir, meter dentro ó dar entrada á uno en algún lugar. 2. Introducir, facilitar ó proporcionar la gracia ó amistad de alguno. 3. Introducir, insertar algo en un escrito ó discurso. 4. Ocasionar, dar motivo. 5. Empezar, establecer; poner en uso ó noticia. 6. Proponer, presentar. *To introduce a bill, a friend*, Presentar un proyecto de ley, presentar á un amigo.

Introducer [in-tro-diūs'-ęr], *s.* Introductor.

Introduction [in-tro-duc'-shun], *s.* 1. Introducción. 2. Introducción, prólogo ó proemio de un libro. 3. Presentación, el acto de presentar á dos ó más personas para que se conozcan.

Introductive [in-tro-duc'-tiv], *a.* Introductivo, lo que sirve de medio para hacer alguna cosa, ó de introducción.

Introductor [in-tro-duc'-tęr], *s.* Introductor.

Introductory [in-tro-duc'-to-ri], *a.* Preliminar, proemial, introductivo.

Introgression [in-tro-gresh'-un], *s.* Entrada.

Introit [in-trō'-it], *s.* Introito de la misa ó del oficio divino.

Intromission [in-tro-mish'-un], *s.* Introducción, admisión.

Intromit [in-tro-mit'], *va.* Introducir

ó dar entrada á alguna cosa, admitir.—*vn.* Tomar posesión de los bienes de otro por fuerza; entremeterse, mezclarse uno en lo que no le atañe.

Intromittent [in-tro-mit'-ent], *a.* 1. Que introduce ó echa dentro. 2. Que se emplea en el coito.

Introreception [in-tro-re-sep'-shun], *s.* Recepción, el acto de recibir ó admitir dentro, en lo interior.

Introspect [in-tro-spect'], *va.* Mirar adentro, mirar lo interior de alguna cosa.

Introspection [in-tro-spec'-shun], *s.* Examen de lo interior de alguna cosa.

Introsusception [in-tro-sus-ep'-shun], *s.* 1. El acto de recibir dentro, en lo interior. 2. Intususcepción, invaginación. *V.* INTUSSUSCEPTION.

Introversion [in-tro-ver'-shun], *s.* El acto de volver ó dirigir hacia dentro; introversión.

Introvert [in'-trō-vert], *s.* y *a.* Introvertido.—*va.* 1. Volver hacia el interior. 2. V. INVERT.

Intrude [in-trūd'], *vn.* Entremeterse, introducirse sin permiso en alguna parte; mezclarse en lo que á uno no le toca; entrar ó aparecer intempestivamente, donde á uno no le llaman.—*va.* 1. Presentar ó introducir indebidamente á alguna persona. *To intrude one's self into a company,* Intrusarse, presentarse en una reunión ó tertulia sin ser invitado. 2. Introducir alguna cosa á viva fuerza.

Intruder [in-trūd'-er], *s.* Intruso, entremetido, el que se entrusa.

Intrusion [in-trū'-zhun], *s.* 1. Intrusión, entremetimiento; la acción de intrusarse, de meterse en alguna parte sin ser llamado. 2. Intrusión en alguna dignidad ú oficio. 3. (Geol.) Intrusión de rocas volcánicas entre otras preexistentes.

Intrusional [in-trū'-zhun-al], *a.* Intruso, relativo á la intrusión.

Intrusive [in-trū'-siv], *a.* Intruso, que viene sin licencia ni permiso; fuera de orden regular; importuno, fastidioso. *V.* OBTRUSIVE.

Intrusiveness [in-trū'-siv-nes], *s.* Intrusión, importunidad, fastidio.

Intrust [in-trust'], *va.* 1. Confiar ó fiar, hacer confianza de otro. 2. Poner en depósito. 3. Confiar un negocio; dar una comisión secreta.

Intuition [in-tiu-i'-shun], *s.* Intuición; conocimiento infuso ó no adquirido, íntimo.

Intuitive [in-tiū'-i-tiv], *a.* Intuitivo, perteneciente á la intuición; que tiene la facultad de descubrir la verdad sin necesidad del raciocinio.

Intuitively [in-tiū'-i-tiv-li], *adv.* Intuitivamente.

Intumesce [in-tiu-mes'], *vn.* Hincharse, entumecerse.

Intumescence [in-tiu-mes'-ens], **Intumescency** [in-tiu-mes'-en-si], *s.* Intumescencia, entumecimiento, levantamiento, la acción de entumecerse, hincharse ó levantarse alguna cosa; tumor, hinchazón.

Intumescent [in-tiu-mes'-ent], *a.* Intumescente; hinchado.

Intussusception [in-tus-sus-sep'-shun], *s.* Calidad y estado de ser recibido dentro: (1) Intususcepción, inversión de una porción de intestino en otra inmediata. (2) Intususcepción, modo de aumentar y crecer los animales y vegetales por los elementos que toman interiormente.

Intwine [in-twain'], *va.* Entrelazar, enlazar, una cosa con otra torciéndolas. *V.* ENTWINE.

Inula [in'-yu-la], *s.* (Bot.) Énula ó énula campana, ínula.

Inulin [in'-yu-lin], *s.* Inulina, substancia parecida al almidón extraída de la raíz de la énula campana.

Inumbrate [in-um'-brēt], *va.* Sombrear, echar sombra sobre.

Inunction [in-unc'-shun], *s.* Untura, untadura, untamiento de un medicamento en la piel.

Inundant [in-und'-ant], *a.* (Poco us.) Inundante.

Inundate [in-un'-dēt], *va.* Inundar; abrumar.

Inundation [in-un-dē'-shun], *s.* 1. Inundación, avenida de aguas. 2. Inundación, multitud excesiva de cualquiera cosa.

Inurbane [in-ūr-bēn'], *a.* Inurbano, descortés, rudo.

Inurbaneness, Inurbanity [in-ūr-ben'-nes, in-ūr-ban'-i-ti], *s.* Inurbanidad.

Inure [in-yūr'], *va.* Endurecer por el uso, acostumbrar, habituar.—*vn.* Tener efecto; ser aplicado á, servir para el provecho de, devolver por la ley.

Inurement [in-yūr'-ment], *s.* Práctica, hábito, uso, costumbre.

Inurn [in-ūrn'], *va.* Introducir ó poner en una urna cineraria.

Inutility [in-yu-til'-i-ti], *s.* Inutilidad.

Invade [in-vēd'], *va.* Invadir, acometer, asaltar, embestir; violar. *To invade one's rights,* Violar los derechos de alguno. *The disease invades the lungs,* La enfermedad invade los pulmones.

Invader [in-vēd'-er], *s.* Invasor, asaltador; acometedor, agresor, violador.

Invaginate [in-vaj'-i-nēt], *va.* Envainar, meter ó recibir en una vaina, como una parte de un tubo en otra; invaginar. *V.* INTROVERT.

Invagination [in-vaj-i-nē'-shun], *s.* Invaginación; intususcepción; bolsa formada por la inversión de una membrana.

Invalid [in-val'-id], *a.* Inválido, nulo, írrito.

Invalid [in'-va-lid], *s.* Inválido, persona baldada ó achacosa; en especial, soldado ó marinero estropeado.

Invalid [in'-va-lid ó in-va-lid'], *va.* 1. Matricular en el registro de inválidos. 2. Invalidar, estropear á uno.

Invalidate [in-val'-i-dēt], *va.* Invalidar, anular; particularmente, privar de valor legal.

Invalidation [in-val-i-dē'-shun], *s.* Invalidación.

Invalidity [in-va-lid'-i-ti], **Invalidness** [in-val'-id-nes], *s.* 1. Invalidación, nulidad de un auto. 2. Debilidad, falta de fuerzas corporales.

Invaluable [in-val'-yu-a-bl], *a.* Invaluable, inestimable, inapreciable.

Invaluably [in-val'-yu-a-bli], *adv.* Invaluablemente.

Invariability [in-vē-ri-a-bil'-i-ti], *s.* Invariabilidad, la subsistencia permanente y sin variación de alguna cosa.

Invariable [in-vē'-ri-a-bl], *a.* Invariable.

Invariableness [in-vē'-ri-a-bl-nes], *s.* Inmutabilidad, constancia.

Invariably [in-vē'-ri-a-bli], *adv.* Invariablemente.

Invasion [in-vē'-zhun], *s.* 1. Invasión, acometimiento, acción de invadir. 2. (Med.) Principio de una enfermedad. 3. Infracción, violación de derechos ajenos.

Invasive [in-vē'-siv], *a.* Hostil; invasor, que invade.

Invective [in-vec'-tiv], *s.* Invectiva, escrito ó discurso injurioso.—*a.* Ultrajante, abusivo, acre.

Invectively [in-vec'-tiv-li], *adv.* Injuriosamente, ultrajosamente.

Inveigh [in-vē'], *vn.* Prorrumpir en invectivas, desencadenarse contra alguno; antiguamente invehir. (Con la prep. *against.*)

Inveigher [in-vē'-er], *s.* Declamador vehemente; ultrajador.

Inveigle [in-vī'-gl ó vē'-gl], *va.* Seducir, engañar con arte y maña, persuadir al mal con palabras seductoras.

Inveiglement [in-vī'- ó vē'-gl-ment], *s.* Engañifa, seducción.

Inveigler [in-vī'-gler], *s.* Seductor.

Inveiled [in-vēld'], *a.* Cubierto como con un velo.

Invent [in-vent'], *va.* 1. Inventar, descubrir. 2. Inventar, forjar, fraguar, fingir.

Inventer [in-vent'-er], *s.* (Des.) *V.* INVENTOR.

Inventful [in-vent'-ful], *a.* (Des.) Inventivo, el que tiene disposición para inventar.

Inventible [in-vent'-i-bl], *a.* Lo que puede ser inventado.

Invention [in-ven'-shun], *s.* 1. Invención, inventiva, maña ó ingenio para inventar. 2. Invención, invento; la cosa inventada. 3. Invención, ficción, mentira, falsedad, etc. 4. (Ant.) Invención, descubrimiento, hallazgo.

Inventive [in-ven'-tiv], *a.* 1. Inventivo, hábil para inventar, fecundo en expedientes, ingenioso. 2. Inventivo, que demuestra invención ó maña para inventar.

Inventiveness [in-ven'-tiv-nes], *s.* Inventiva, ingenio.

Inventor [in-vent'-er], *s.* 1. Inventor, el primero que discurre algún arte ó secreto; también el que dedica su tiempo á la invención. 2. Inventor, invencionero, el que forja ó finge alguna cosa.

Inventorial [in-ven-tō'-ri-al], *a.* Lo perteneciente al inventario.

Inventorially [in-ven-tō'-ri-al-i], *adv.* Por ó con inventario.

Inventory [in'-ven-to-ri], *s.* Inventario, catálogo ó lista de muebles, mercancías ú otros objetos ó bienes.

Inventory, *va.* Inventariar, hacer un inventario.

Inventress [in-ven'-tres], *sf.* Inventora, la mujer que inventa.

Inverse [in-vers'], *a.* Inverso, invertido, trastrocado, trastornado.

Inversely [in-vers'-li], *adv.* Inversamente.

Inversion [in-ver'-shun], *s.* Inversión, transmutación de orden ó tiempo; cambio del orden natural de las cosas, sea de las palabras ó los términos de una proporción, ó de la estructura molecular. (Mús.) Imitación que consiste en reproducir una melodía tomando las notas en orden opuesto.

Invert [in-vert'], *va.* Invertir, poner al revés ó en sentido inverso, trastornar, trastrocar, mudar el orden de las cosas, transponer.

Invertebral [in-ver'-te-bral], *a.* *V.* INVERTEBRATE.

Invertebrate [in-ver'-te-brēt], *a.* Invertebrado, que carece de columna vertebral.—*s.* Animal invertebrado.

Invertedly [in-vẹrt'-ed-li], *adv.* Al revés.
Invest [in-vest'], *va.* 1. Vestir, cubrir y adornar el cuerpo con el vestido. 2. Investir, dar la investidura de algún feudo, señorío o dignidad. 3. Conferir, dar. 4. Sitiar, cercar o cerrar con tropas una plaza fuerte, un puesto fortificado, etc. 5. Cercar o rodear a una persona. 6. (Com.) Invertir, emplear o imponer dinero en valores o propiedades.
Investigable [in-ves'-ti-ga-bl], *a.* Averiguable, investigable.
Investigate [in-ves'-ti-gêt], *va.* Investigar, indagar, buscar, averiguar; examinar con cuidado.
Investigation [in-ves-ti-gé'-shun], *s.* 1. Investigación, pesquisa, averiguación. 2. Escrutinio, examen diligente o cuidadoso.
Investigative [in-ves'-ti-ga-tiv], *a.* Dispuesto a investigar, investigador.
Investigator [in-ves'-ti-gê-tẹr], *s.* Investigador, indagador, averiguador.
Investiture [in-ves'-ti-chur], *s.* 1. Investidura, el acto solemne por el cual se confiere un feudo, señorío o dignidad. 2. Instalación. *V.* INSTALLATION.
Investment [in-vest'-mẹnt], *s.* 1. (Com.) La inversión, colocación o empleo de un capital; el dinero invertido y los bienes comprados. 2. Cerco, acción de cercar una plaza para sitiarla. 3. Instalación, concesión de autoridad. 4. Cubierta; envoltura en su sentido biológico.
Investor [in-ves'-tẹr], *s.* Inversionista.
Inveteracy [in-vet'-ẹr-a-si], **Inveterateness** [in-vet'-ẹr-et-nes], *s.* Perseverancia o continuación prolongada de un mal físico o moral.
Inveterate [in-vet'-ẹr-et], *a.* Inveterado, lo que se ha arraigado o ha tomado raíces: dícese de los males físicos o morales.
Inveteration [in-vet-ẹr-é'-shun], *s.* (Poco us.) Endurecimiento; estado inveterado.
Invidious [in-vid'-i-us], *a.* Envidioso, odioso, aborrecible.
Invidiousness [in-vid'-i-us-nes], *s.* Calidad o propiedad que excita la envidia o el odio.
Invigorate [in-vig'-or-êt], *va.* Vigorizar, dar vigor.
Invigoration [in-vig-or-é'-shun], *s.* 1. El acto de vigorizar. 2. Corroboración, esfuerzo o vigor infundido por algún medio.
Invincibility [in-vin-si-bil'-i-ti], *s.* La calidad que constituye invencible a alguno o a alguna cosa.
Invincible [in-vin'-si-bl], *a.* Invencible.
Invincibly [in-vin'-si-bli], *adv.* Invenciblemente.
Inviolability [in-vai-o-la-bil'-i-ti], *s.* Inviolabilidad.
Inviolable [in-vai'-o-la-bl], *a.* Inviolable, que no se debe o no se puede violar ni profanar.
Inviolableness [in-vai'-o-la-bl-nes], *s.* Inviolabilidad.
Inviolably [in-vai'-o-la-bli], *adv.* Inviolablemente.
Inviolate [in-vai'-o-let], *a.* Inviolado, entero, incorrupto, íntegro.
Inviolated [in-vai'-o-lêt-ed], *a.* Inviolado, incorrupto.
Inviscate [in-vis'-kêt], *va.* (Poco us.) Encolar una cosa, hacerla viscosa; de aquí, coger con liga.
Invisibility [in-viz-i-bil'-i-ti], **Invisibleness** [in-viz'-i-bl-nes], *s.* Invisibilidad.
Invisible [in-viz'-i-bl], *a.* Invisible.
Invisibly [in-viz'-i-bli], *adv.* Invisiblemente.
Invitation [in-vi-té'-shun], *s.* Invitación, convite; llamamiento, instancia; cebo para atraer a alguno.
Invitatory [in-vai'-ta-to-ri], *a.* Invitador, que invita.—*s.* Invitatorio, una antífona.
Invite [in-vait'], *va.* Convidar, invitar; mover, incitar, tentar; llamar; instar, estimular a la ejecución de alguna cosa.
Inviter [in-vait'-ẹr], *s.* Convidador.
Inviting [in-vait'-ing], *a.* Halagador, seductivo, seductor, incitante. —*s.* Convite.
Invitingly [in-vait'-ing-li], *adv.* Halagüeñamente.
Invitingness [in-vait'-ing-nes], *s.* El poder o la calidad de convidar, halagar o incitar.
Invocate [in'-vo-kêt], *va.* (Ant.) Invocar, implorar auxilio o ayuda.
Invocation [in-vo-ké'-shun], *s.* 1. Invocación. 2. (For.) Citación, demanda u orden judicial.
Invoice [in'-vois], *s.* Factura, la nota con precios de los géneros que un comerciante envía a otro. *Invoice-book,* Libro de facturas.
Invoke [in-vōc'], *va.* Invocar, llamar, implorar, suplicar, rogar.
Involucel [in-vel'-yu-sel o in-vo-lū'-sel], *s.* (Bot.) Involucrillo o involucro secundario.
Involucral [in-vo-lū'-cral], *a.* Involucral, que pertenece al involucro; provisto de un involucro.
Involucrate, Involucred [in-vo-lū'-crêt, in'-vo-lū-kẹrd], *a.* Involucrado, provisto de un involucro; que forma involucro.
Involucre [in-vo-lū'-kẹr], **Involucrum** [in-vo-lū'-crum], *s.* 1. (Bot.) Involucro, verticilo de brácteas, situado en el arranque del conjunto de varias flores agrupadas, como en la zanahoria. 2. (Anat.) Envoltura, membrana que envuelve un órgano.
Involuntarily [in-vel'-un-tẹ-ri-li], *adv.* Involuntariamente.
Involuntariness [in-vel'-un-tẹ-ri-nes], *s.* Involuntariedad.
Involuntary [in-vel'-un-tẹ-ri], *a.* Involuntario.
Involute [in'-vo-liut o lūt], *a.* Encorvado o torcido hacia dentro.—*s.* (Geom.) Evolvente, involuta, cierta curva.
Involution [in-vo-lū'-shun], *s.* 1. Envolvimiento, la acción de envolver. 2. Complicación. 3. (Med.) Restitución de un órgano a su volumen normal después de haber sido ensanchado. 4. Envolvedero, envolvedor. 5. Enredo, embrollo, embolismo.
Involve [in-velv'], *va.* 1. Envolver, arrollar. 2. Envolver, implicar, comprometer. 3. Torcer, retorcer. 4. Envolver, implicar, enredar. *To involve one's self in troubles,* Meterse en embrollos. 5. Intrincar, enmarañar, complicar. 6. Revolver, mezclar. 7. Multiplicar una cantidad por sí misma.
Involvedness [in-velv'-ed-nes], *s.* El estado o la calidad de envuelto, arrollado, etc.; envolvimiento.
Invulnerability [in-vul-nẹr-a-bil'-i-ti], **Invulnerableness** [in-vul'-nẹr-a-bl-nes], *s.* Invulnerabilidad, el estado o la calidad que constituye invulnerable alguna cosa.
Invulnerable [in-vul'-nẹr-a-bl], *a.* Invulnerable, que no puede ser herido.
Inwall [in-wōl'], *va.* (Poco us.) Emparedar, tapiar, cercar o rodear con pared, tapia o muro.
Inward, Inwards [in'-ward, z], *adv.* Hacia dentro, hacia lo interior; interiormente; adentro, en lo interior.
Inward, *a.* 1. Interior, lo que está de la parte de adentro. 2. Interno, doméstico. 3. Secreto, oculto.—*s.* El interior; lo que está dentro; en plural, entrañas.
Inwardly [in'-ward-li], *adv.* Interiormente, internamente.
Inwardness [in'-ward-nes], *s.* 1. Calidad, naturaleza o estado interior. 2. Estado de ser interior, efectiva o figuradamente. 3. (Des.) Intimidad, familiaridad.
Inweave [in-wīv'], *va.* Entretejer, enlazar.
§**Inwheel** [in-hwīl'], *va.* Circundar, cercar.
Inwork [in-wūrk'], *va.* Labrar en o dentro; entretejer.—*vn.* Producir efecto en el interior, especialmente en el ánimo o en la mente.
Inwrought [in-rōt'], *a.* Labrado, adornado con labores.
Iodic [ai-od'-ic], *a.* Yodado, que contiene o se refiere al yodo.
Iodid, Iodide [ai'-o-did, ai'-o-did o daid], *s.* Yoduro, combinación del yodo con un metaloide o metal.
Iodin, Iodine [ai'-o-din], *s.* (Quím.) Yodo, cuerpo simple de color azul negruzco y lustre metálico, y que da vapores de color violado; úsase en medicina y en la fotografía.
Iodism [ai'-o-dizm], *s.* (Med.) Yodismo, estado mórbido especial ocasionado por el uso prolongado del yodo.
Iodize [ai'-o-daiz], *va.* 1. (Med.) Someter a la influencia del yodo. 2. (Foto.) Echar yodo a; exponer a los vapores del yodo.
Iodoform [ai-od'-o-fērm], *s.* Yodoformo, compuesto cristalizable de color amarillo claro y de olor característico. Se emplea en la cirugía.
Ion [ai'-en], *s.* Substancia que resulta de la descomposición electroquímica, o uno de los componentes de dicha substancia.
Ionic [ai-en'-ic], *a.* Jónico.
Ionization [ai-en-i-zé'-shun], *s.* (Elec.) Ionización.
Ionize [ai'-en-aiz], *va.* Ionizar.
Ionosphere [ai-en'-o-sfir], *s.* Ionosfera.
Iota [ai-ō'-ta], *s.* Jota, ápice, tilde, punto. *Not a single iota,* Ni tan siquiera una tilde; ni siquiera un punto, ni miaja.
Ipecac [ip'-e-cac], *s.* *V.* IPECACUANHA.
Ipecacuanha [ip-ẹ-cac-yu-an'-a], *s.* Ipecacuana, raíz medicinal de América, llamada por otro nombre *bejuquillo.*
Ipomœa [ip-o-mī'-a], *s.* Ipomea, vasto género de plantas tropicales de la familia de las convolvuláceas. La batata, la jalapa y la patata silvestre son muy conocidas.
Iranian [ai-ré'-ni-an], *a.* Iranio, referente a Irán o Persia.
Irascibility [i-ras-i-bil'-i-ti], *s.* Iracundia, la propensión a encolerizarse o airarse.
Irascible [i-ras'-i-bl], *a.* Irascible.
Irate [ai-rêt'], *a.* Encolerizado, enfurecido, airado.
Ire [air], *s.* Ira, iracundia, enojo, enfado.
Ireful [air'-ful], *a.* Iracundo, colérico.

Irefully [air'-ful-i], *adv.* Airadamente, enojadamente.
Irenarch [ai'-ren-ārc], *s.* Irenarca, un empleado que tenía a su cargo la conservación de la tranquilidad pública entre los griegos del bajo imperio.
Irenic, Irenical [ai-ren'-ic, al], *a.* Pacífico, conciliador.
Iridescence [ir-i-des'-ens], *s.* Iridación, estado de lo iridescente.
Iridescent [ir-i-des'-ent], *a.* Iridescente, que refleja los colores del iris; irisado.
Iridium [i-rid'-i-um], *s.* (Quím.) Iridio, elemento metálico de color de plata, quebradizo, que se halla en la naturaleza, mezclado con el platino y el rodio.
Iris [ai'-ris], *s.* 1. (Anat.) Iris, círculo de varios colores en cuyo centro se halla la pupila del ojo. 2. Iris o arco iris. 3. (Bot.) Iris, género de plantas que es el tipo de la familia de las irídeas; flor de lis. Se llama vulgarmente lirio, pero el tipo de las irídeas y el de las liliáceas es bastante distinto.
Irish [ai'-rish], *a.* Irlandés, natural de Irlanda, y lo perteneciente a esta isla.—*s.* 1. Irlandés, el natural de Irlanda. 2. Irlandés, la lengua nativa céltica de Irlanda. 3. Acento especial del idioma inglés en Irlanda, caracterizado por la pronunciación llamada "*brogue*" o "*broad.*" *Irishman,* Irlandés. *Irish girl,* Joven irlandesa. *Irishwoman,* Irlandesa. *Irish moss,* Musgo de Irlanda.
Irishism [ai'-rish-izm], *s.* 1. Locución irlandesa. 2. Carácter o rasgos irlandeses colectivamente.
Iritis [ai-rai'-tis o i-ri'-tis], *s.* Iritis, inflamación del iris del ojo.
Irk [ẹrc], *va.* Fastidiar. *It irks me,* Me fastidia, estoy cansado de ello. Este verbo se usa casi siempre impersonalmente.
Irksome [ẹrc'-sum], *a.* Tedioso, fastidioso, enfadoso, cansado.
Irksomeness [ẹrc'-sum-nes], *s.* Tedio, fastidio, molestia, cansancio.
Iron [ai'-urn], *s.* 1. Hierro, metal duro que se funde y amartilla; el más importante de los elementos metálicos. *Bar iron,* Hierro en barras. *Cast iron,* Hierro colado. *Forged iron,* Hierro forjado. *Round iron,* Hierro vergajón o cabilla. *Flat iron,* Hierro en planchuela. *Flat-iron, sad-iron,* Plancha, utensilio de hierro para planchar la ropa. *Wrought iron,* Hierro forjado. *Smoothing-iron,* Hierro de planchar; plancha de sastre. *Curling-irons,* Hierros o tenacillas para rizar el pelo. *One-inch square iron,* Hierro cuadradillo. 2. Hierro, cualquier cosa hecha de hierro. 3. Hierros, prisiones. *To put in irons,* Aprisionar, echar grillos.—*a.* 1. Férreo, lo que es de hierro o tiene sus propiedades. *Iron chest,* Arca o caja de hierro para guardar los libros de comercio o dinero. *Iron horse,* (Mar.) Batayora. *Iron-mill,* Herrería o ferrería. *Iron-work,* Herraje. *Iron-work of the rudder,* (Mar.) Herraje del timón. 2. Duro, áspero, severo. 3. Férreo, duro, impenetrable. *Iron plate,* Palastro, plancha de hierro batido. *Iron wire,* Hilo de hierro. *Iron pot,* Olla ó marmita de hierro. *Iron ware,* Trastos de hierro. *To have the iron enter into one's soul,* Estar como en un potro: apurar la copa del dolor hasta las heces. *To have too many irons in the fire,* Tener demasiados asuntos entre manos.
Iron, *va.* 1. Aplanchar, alisar alguna cosa con plancha de hierro. (Vulg.) Planchar. *To iron linen,* Planchar ropa blanca. 2. Aprisionar, poner en prisiones.
Iron, en composición: *Iron-bound,* (1) Rodeado de arcos de hierro. (2) Erizado o rodeado de rocas. (3) Difícil de alterar; inflexible. *Ironclad,* (1) Blindado con armadura de hierro o de acero, como los buques de guerra. (2) Riguroso, que no puede evadirse. (3) Capaz de resistir, fuerte. *Iron-founder,* Fundidor de hierro. *Iron-rust, V.* RUST. *Iron-works,* Fundición de hierro, establecimiento para la manufactura de artículos de hierro de gran peso y tamaño.
Ironclad [ai'-urn-clad], *a.* 1. Armado de hierro. 2. (fam.) Rígido. *An ironclad alibi,* Una coartada indiscutible.—*s.* Buque de guerra blindado.
Iron curtain [ai'-urn cur'-ten], *s.* Telón de acero, cortina de hierro.
Ironed [ai'-urnd], *a.* 1. Planchado, aplanchado. 2. Engrillado; armado.
Ironer [ai'-urn-ẹr], *s.* Planchadora, la persona o la máquina que plancha.
Iron-hearted [ai'-urn-hārt'-ed], *a.* Duro, áspero, severo.
Ironic, Ironical [ai-ren'-ic, al], *a.* Irónico.
Ironically [ai-ren'-ic-al-i], *adv.* Irónicamente.
Ironing board [ai'-urn-ing bōrd], *s.* Tabla de planchar.
Iron lung [ai'-urn lung], *s.* Pulmón de acero.
Ironmonger [ai'-urn-muṇ'-gẹr], *s.* Mercader ó traficante en hierro. (Amer.) Quinquillero, ferretero. *Ironmonger's shop,* Tienda de hierro. (Amer.) Quinquillería, ferretería.
Ironmongery [ai'-urn-muṇ''-ger-i], *s.* Ferretería, cerrajería, el conjunto de los artículos de hierro.
Iron-mould [ai'-urn-mōld], *s.* Mancha de herrumbre o de orín de hierro en el lienzo o paño.
Ironside, Ironsides [ai'-urn-said, saidz], *a.* Lo que tiene un lado o lados de hierro; fuerte, enérgico, terrible en la guerra; soldado del ejército de Cromwell.
Ironware [ai'-urn-wār], *s.* Artículos de ferretería.
Iron-wood [ai'-urn-wud], *s.* Madera de hierro, especie de madera muy dura y pesada. (Amer.) Palo hacha.
Iron-work [ai'-urn-wūrk], *s.* Herraje, obra u objeto de hierro.
Irony [ai'-ro-ni], *s.* Ironía, figura con que se quiere dar á entender que se siente lo contrario de lo que se dice.—[ai'-urn-i], *a.* Férreo.
Irradiance, Irradiancy [ir-rē'-di-ans, an-si], *s.* Irradiación; rayos de luz.
Irradiate [ir-rē'-di-ēt], *va.* 1. Irradiar, herir el sol u otro cuerpo luminoso con sus rayos alguna cosa iluminándola. 2. Iluminar, inspirar. 3. Animar con fuego, calor o luz. 4. Adornar con cosas que den brillo.—*vn.* Lucir sobre una cosa.
Irradiate, *a.* (Poét.) Resplandeciente, iluminado.
Irradiation [ir-rē-di-ē'-shun], *s.* 1. Irradiación. 2. Iluminación. 3. (Fís.) Ampliación aparente de un objeto luminoso cuando se ve contra un fondo obscuro.
Irradicate [ir-rad'-i-kēt], *va.* Arraigar firme o profundamente.
Irrational [ir-rash'-un-al], *a.* 1. Irracional, que carece de razon o de inteligencia. 2. Irracional, absurdo, desrazonable. 3. (Álg.) Irracional, que no tiene medida conocida, ni número cierto.
Irrationality [ir-rash-un-al'-i-ti], *s.* Irracionalidad.
Irrationally [ir-rash'-un-al-i], *adv.* Irracionalmente.
Irreclaimable [ir-rẹ-clêm'-a-bl], *a.* Indómito, incorregible, obstinado; que no se puede redimir.
Irreclaimably [ir-rẹ-clêm'-a-bli], *adv.* Incorregiblemente.
Irreconcilable [ir-rec-en-sail'-a-bl], *a.* Irreconciliable, incomponible, implacable; incompatible.
Irreconcilableness [ir-rec-en-sail'-a-bl-nes], *s.* Imposibilidad de reconciliarse.
Irreconcilably [ir-rec-en-sai' a-bli], *adv.* Irreconciliablemente.
Irreconciled [ir-rec'-en-saild], *a* Dícese de la maldad, delito o culpa que no se ha expiado.
Irreconcilement [ir-rec'-en-sail-mẹnt], **Irreconciliation** [ir-rec-en-sil-i-ê'-shun], *s.* Falta de reconciliación, discordia.
Irrecoverable [ir-rẹ-cuv'-ẹr-a-bl], *a.* Irreparable, perdido sin recurso; irrecuperable, irremediable; incobrable.
Irrecoverableness [ir-rẹ-cuv'-ẹr-a-bl-nes], *s.* El estado y la calidad de lo que no se puede recobrar o es irrecuperable.
Irrecoverably [ir-rẹ-cuv'-ẹr-a-bli], *adv.* Irremediablemente, sin recurso, irreparablemente.
Irrecuperable [ir-rẹ-kiū'-pẹr-a-bl], *a.* Irrecuperable, irremediable.
Irredeemable [ir-rẹ-dîm'-a-bl], *a.* Irredimible.
Irredeemably [ir-rẹ-dîm'-a-bli], *adv.* De un modo irredimible.
Irreducible [ir-rẹ-diūs'-i-bl], *a.* 1. Irreducible, que no se puede reducir; que no se puede llevar al estado, a la forma o al arreglo deseados. 2. (Cir.) Que no cede al tratamiento; dícese de una hernia o fractura.
Irreflective [ir-rẹ-flec'-tiv], *a.* Irreflexivo, que carece de reflexión.
Irrefragable [ir-ref'-ra-ga-bl], *a.* Irrefragable, que no se puede impugnar ni contradecir.
Irrefutable [ir-rẹ-fiūt'-a-bl], *a.* Irrefragable, indubitable, cierto, indisputable.
Irregular [ir-reg'-yu-lar], *a.* 1. Irregular, falto de regularidad. 2. Desordenado, que desdice de alguna virtud o se opone a ella; desarreglado. 3. Irregular, que no sigue regla, disciplina o sistema determinados. 4. (Zool.) Irregular, que se aparta de up tipo establecido.—*s.* El que no sigue regla determinada; soldado de tropas irregulares; empírico, charlatán.
Irregularity [ir-reg-yu-lar'-i-ti], *s.* 1. Irregularidad. 2. Desorden, demasía, exceso.
Irregularly [ir-reg'-yu-lar-li], *adv.* Irregularmente.
Irrelative [ir-rel'-a-tiv], *a.* Absoluto; inconexo, sin relación alguna; sin regla, sin orden.
Irrelatively [ir-rel'-a-tiv-li], *adv.* De un modo inconexo.
Irrelevancy [ir-rel'-e-van-si], *s.* El

estado de lo que no es aplicable o a propósito.
Irrelevant [ir-rel'-e-vant], *a.* Que no es aplicable o a propósito; que no prueba nada, no concluye o no es del caso.
Irrelevantly [ir-rel'-e-vant-li], *adv.* Fuera de propósito.
Irrelievable [ir-re-lív'-a-bl], *a.* Irremediable, irreparable.
Irreligion [ir-re-lij'-un], *s.* Irreligión, ateísmo, impiedad.
Irreligious [ir-re-lij'-us], *a.* Irreligioso, que no tiene religión; contrario a la religión; impío, profano.
Irreligiously [ir-re-lij'-us-li], *adv.* Irreligiosamente.
Irremediable [ir-re-míd'-i-a-bl], *a.* 1. Irremediable, irreparable. 2. Incurable; incorregible.
Irremediableness [ir-re-míd'-i-a-bl-nes], *s.* El estado o la condición de lo que no tiene remedio.
Irremediably [ir-re-míd'-i-a-bli], *adv.* Irremediablemente.
Irremissible [ir-re-mis'-i-bl], *a.* Irremisible, incapaz de perdón.
Irremissibleness [ir-re-mis'-i-bl-nes], *s.* La calidad que hace a una cosa irremisible.
Irremissibly [ir-re-mís'-i-bli], *adv.* Irremisiblemente.
Irremovable [ir-re-mūv'-a-bl], *a.* 1. Inamovible, que no puede ser removido; que no puede ser privado de su empleo, ni trasladado a otro. 2. Inmutable.
§**Irremunerable** [ir-re-miū'-ner-a-bl], *a.* Incapaz de ser remunerado o premiado.
Irreparability [ir-rep-a-ra-bil'-i-ti], *s.* El estado de lo que es irreparable.
Irreparable [ir-rep'-a-ra-bl], *a.* Irreparable.
Irreparably [ir-rep'-a-ra-bli], *adv.* Irreparablemente.
Irrepealable [ir-re-píl'-a-bl], *a.* Inabrogable, que no puede ser abrogado, anulado o revocado.
Irreplaceable [ir-re-plês'-a-bl], *a.* Irremplazable.
Irreprehensible [ir-rep-re-hen'-si-bl], *a.* Irreprensible.
Irreprehensibly [ir-rep-re-hen'-si-bli], *adv.* Irreprensiblemente.
Irrepresentable [ir-rep-re-zent'-a-bl], *a.* Lo que no se puede poner a la vista por medio de alguna representación o figura.
Irrepressible [ir-re-pres'-i-bl], *a.* Lo que no puede ser oprimido ni reprimido.
Irreproachable [ir-re-prōch'-a-bl], *a.* Intachable, incensurable.
Irreproachably [ir-re-prōch'-a-bli], *adv.* Irreprensiblemente.
Irreprovable [ir-re-prūv'-a-bl], *a.* Irreprensible.
Irreprovably [ir-re-prūv'-a-bli], *adv.* Sin tacha, sin cometer falta ninguna.
Irresistance [ir-re-zist'-ans], *s.* Falta de propensión a hacer oposición o resistir; paciencia para sufrir las injurias.
Irresistibility [ir-re-zist-i-bil'-i-ti], *s.* Fuerza o poder irresistible, lo que no se puede resistir o contrarrestar.
Irresistible [ir-re-zist'-i-bl], *a.* Irresistible.
Irresistibleness [ir-re-zist'-i-bl-nes], *s.* Poder o calidad irresistibles.
Irresistibly [ir-re-zist'-i-bli], *adv.* Irresistiblemente.
Iressoluble [ir-rez'-o-lu-bl], *a.* Irresoluble, que no se puede resolver o determinar.
Irresolubleness [ir-rez'-o-lu-bl-nes], *s.* Solidez o resistencia de un cuerpo a la separación de sus partes.
Irresolute [ir-rez'-o-lūt ó liūt], *a.* Irresoluto, irresuelto, vacilante, indeciso.
Irresolutely [ir-rez'-o-lūt-li], *adv.* Irresolutamente.
Irresoluteness [ir-rez'-o-lūt-nes], *s.* Irresolución.
Irresolution [ir-rez-o-lū'- ó liū'-shun], *s.* Irresolución, vacilación, duda.
Irrespective [ir-re-spec'-tiv], *a.* Inconsiderado, independiente de condiciones; que carece de relación, que no hace al caso. Se usa por lo común con la prep. *of. Irrespective of ability*, Independiente de la habilidad o capacidad.
Irrespectively [ir-re-spec'-tiv-li], *adv.* Inconsideradamente.
Irrespirable [ir-re-spair'-a-bl ó ir-res'-pi-ra-bl], *a.* Irrespirable; impropio para la respiración.
Irresponsibility [ir-re-spon-si-bil'-i-ti], *s.* Irresponsabilidad, falta de responsabilidad.
Irresponsible [ir-re-spon'-si-bl], *a.* Irresponsable, exento de responsabilidad.
Irretraceable [ir-re-três'-a-bl], *a.* Se aplica al camino por donde se va y no se puede volver; que no puede ser puesto de nuevo en su estado anterior.
Irretrievable [ir-re-trív'-a-bl], *a.* Irrecuperable, irreparable; incobrable.
Irretrievably [ir-re-trív'-a-bli], *adv.* Irreparablemente.
Irreturnable [ir-re-tūrn'-a-bl], *a.* Incapaz de volver o retornar.
Irreverence [ir-rev'-er-ens], *s.* Irreverencia, falta de reverencia, de veneración, particularmente hacia cosas sagradas.
Irreverent [ir-rev'-er-ent], *a.* Irreverente, falto de reverencia, de veneración; irrespetuoso, desatento.
Irreverently [ir-rev'-er-ent-li], *adv.* Irreverentemente.
Irreversible [ir-re-vers'-i-bl], *a.* 1. Que no se puede volver al revés; que no puede ser mudado o puesto en lugar de otra cosa. 2. Irrevocable.
Irreversibleness [ir-re-vers'-i-bl-nes], *s.* El estado de lo que es irrevocable.
Irreversibly [ir-re-vers'-i-bli], *adv.* Sin poder ser revocado.
Irrevocability [ir-rev'-o-ca-bil''-i-ti], *s.* Irrevocabilidad.
Irrevocable [ir-rev'-o-ca-bl], *a.* Irrevocable.
Irrevocableness [ir-rev'-o-ca-bl-nes], *s.* El estado o la calidad irrevocable de una cosa.
Irrevocably [ir-rev'-o-ca-bli], *adv.* Irrevocablemente.
Irrigant [ir'-ri-gant], *a.* Regador, que sirve para regar.
Irrigate [ir'-i-gêt], *va.* 1. Regar, conducir el agua por medio de acequias o canales para fertilizar la tierra. 2. Mojar, humedecer; irrigar una llaga.
Irrigation [ir-i-gé'-shun], *s.* Riego, regamiento.
Irrision [ir-rizh'-un], *s.* Irrisión, desprecio, burla.
Irritability [ir-i-ta-bil'-i-ti], *s.* 1. Irritabilidad, una de las calidades exclusivamente propias de los cuerpos organizados; propiedad de responder a un estímulo. 2. Propensión a irritarse fácilmente.
Irritable [ir'-i-ta-bl], *a.* 1. Irritable, irascible, que es capaz de irritación. 2. Irritable, que está dotado de irritabilidad.
Irritableness [ir'-i-ta-bl-nes], *s.* Iracundia, irritabilidad, con propensión a irritarse.
Irritant [ir'-i-tant], *a.* 1. (For.) Irritante, írrito, lo que anula o invalida. 2. Irritante, lo que irrita.
Irritate [ir'-i-têt], *va.* 1. Irritar, exasperar. 2. Irritar, agitar.
Irritation [ir-i-té'-shun], *s.* 1. Irritación, provocación, movimiento de cólera. 2. Irritación, conmoción violenta de algunos humores.
Irritative [ir'-ri-ta-tiv], *a.* Irritador, irritante, que sirve para causar irritación; acompañado de irritación.
Irruption [ir-rup'-shun], *s.* Irrupción, entrada violenta o forzada; invasión.
Irruptive [ir-rup'-tiv], *a.* Invasor, que comete o hace alguna irrupción.
Is [iz]. Es o está, tercera persona singular del presente de indicativo del verbo *To* Be.
Isabel [iz'-a-bel], *s.* Color isabela o isabelino, amarillo parduzco; color de arena.—*n. pr.* Isabel.
Isagogical [is-a-gej'-i-cal], *a.* Isagógico, que pertenece a la introducción de los libros de la Biblia, su historia literaria, inspiración, etc.
Isagon [is'-a-gen], *s.* (Geom.) Iságono, figura de ángulos iguales.
Isaiah [ai-zé'-ya ó i-zg'-ya], *s.* Isaías, libro del Viejo Testamento.
Ischiatic [is-ki-at'-ic], *a.* Isquiático, perteneciente o relacionado con el hueso isquion.
Ischium [is'-ki-um], *s.* Isquion, parte inferior y posterior del hueso loxal o innominado.
Ischury [is'-kiu-ri], *s.* Iscuria, retención de orina.
Ischuretic [is-kiu-ret'-ic], *s.* Cualquier remedio para hacer salir la orina detenida o suprimida.
Iserine [ai'-zer-in], *s.* (Min.) Iserina, especie de minera o quijo de titanio.
-ish [ish]. Terminación inglesa que sirve para expresar diminución en la calidad del substantivo a que se añade, o para hacer adjetivos gentilicios o patronímicos, como *bluish*, azulado, de *blue*, azul; *sickish*, enfermizo, de *sick*, enfermo; *Spanish*, español, de *Spain*, España.
Isinglass [ai'-zin-glas], *s.* Colapiscis, colapez, o cola de pescado.
Islam [is'-lām], *s.* 1. Islam, islamismo, la religión de Mahoma. 2. Islam, conjunto de los hombres y pueblos que creen y aceptan esta religión.
Island [ai'-land], *s.* Isla, tierra rodeada enteramente de agua.
Islander [ai'-land-er], *s.* Isleño, el natural de alguna isla o el que vive en ella.
Isle [ail], *s.* Isla pequeña (generalmente voz poética).
Islet [ai'-let], *s.* Isleta.
Ism [izm], *s.* Doctrina; úsase a menudo por burla o desprecio.
Iso-. Forma de combinación, del griego *isos*, igual.
Isobaric [ai-so-bār'-ic], *a.* Isobárico.
Isochromatic [ai''-so-cro-mat'-ic], *a.* 1. Isocromático, que tiene o denota el mismo color. 2. *V.* Orthochromatic.
Isochronal [ai-sec'-ro-nal], **Isochronous** [ai-sec'-ro-nus], *a.* Isócrono.
Isogloss [ai'-so-gles], *s.* Isoglos, línea de demarcación entre regiones de diferencias lingüísticas.

Isolate [is'-o-lêt o ai'-so-lêt], *va.* 1. Aislar, separar, apartar, poner solo. 2. (Elec.) Aislar. 3. (Quím.) Eliminar de una substancia toda combinación.
Isolation [is-o-lê'-shun], *s.* Aislamiento, separación; estado de soledad.
Isolationism [ais-o-lê'-shun-izm], *s.* Aislacionismo.
Isolationist [ais-o-lê'-shun-ist], *s.* Aislacionista, partidario del aislacionismo en las relaciones internacionales.
Isomerism [ai-som'-er-izm], *s.* (Quím.) Isomerismo, identidad de elementos y proporciones con propiedades diferentes.
Isometric [ai-so-me'-tric], *a.* Isométrico.
Isometrics [ai-so-me'-trics], *s.* Isometría.
Isomorphic [ai-so-mōr'-fic], *a.* Isomorfo.
Isomorphism [ai-so-mōr'-fizm], *s.* (Min.) Isomorfismo, isomorfia, estado de los cuerpos que, difiriendo en su composición, presentan al cristalizar formas iguales.
Isomorphous [ai-so-mōr'-fus], *a.* Isomorfo.
Isoperimetrical [ai-so-per-i-met'-ri-cal], *a.* Isoperimétrico.
Isosceles [ai-sos'-e-liz], *a.* Isósceles.
Isotherm [ai'-so-therm], *s.* Línea isoterma, la que pasa por los puntos de la tierra en que es la misma la temperatura media.
Isothermal [ai-so-ther'-mal], *a.* Isotermo, isotérmico.
Isotope [ai'-so-top], *s.* (Fís. y Quím.) Isótopo.
Israeli [iz-rê'-li], *a. & s.* Israelí.
Israelite [iz'-ra-el-ait], *s.* Israelita, descendiente de Israel (o Jacob); hebreo, judío.
Issuable [ish'-ū-a-bl], *a.* Lo que es capaz de llevar o conducir una cosa hasta su terminación.
Issue [ish'-ū], *s.* 1. Salida, el acto de salir. 2. Salida, la parte por donde se sale fuera de algún sitio o lugar. 3. Lo que se produce, emite o publica: (a) edición, v. g. la de un periódico; (b) prole, progenie, sucesión; (c) emisión de valores; (d) rentas, réditos. *He died without issue,* Murió sin sucesión. 4. Evento, consecuencia, resultado, fin, término, conclusión. 5. Fuente, cauterio, una llaga pequeña que se mantiene abierta artificialmente con varios objetos. 6. Decisión, conclusión. *Issue of blood,* Pérdida de sangre. *Issue in a wall,* Cuarteadura. *A cause at issue,* Una causa que está para verse o sentenciarse. *Feigned issue,* (For.) Expediente formado con el consentimiento de ambas partes para la decisión del punto en cuestión, sin pasar por los trámites judiciales. *Point at issue,* Materia de que se trata, punto en cuestión; asunto; proceso. *To join issue,* Tomar partes opuestas en una discusión o un pleito; tener pareceres contrarios sobre una proposición; contradecirse mutuamente.
Issue, *vn.* 1. Salir, pasar de la parte de adentro a la de afuera. 2. Prorrumpir, brotar. 3. Venir, proceder, traer su origen. 4. Provenir, salir o proceder de algún fondo. 5. Acabarse, terminarse, resolverse; esparcirse en líneas.—*va.* 1. Echar, brotar, arrojar para afuera. 2. Expedir, despachar alguna cosa judicialmente. 3. Emitir, poner en circulación. 4. Dar a luz, publicar.
Issueless [ish'-ū-les], *a.* Sin sucesión.
Issuing [ish'-ū-ing], *s.* Salida.
Isthmian games [ist'-mi-an gêmz], *s. pl.* Juegos ístmicos de la antigua Grecia.
Isthmus [ist'-mus o is'-mus], *s.* Istmo, lengua de tierra entre dos mares que une dos continentes o una península a un continente.
It [it]. Pronombre inglés que se pone en lugar de los nombres de cosas inanimadas, y aun de los animales cuyo sexo no puede determinarse; por consiguiente corresponde en español a *él, ella, ello, lo, la, le,* según los géneros y casos de las cosas a que se refiere: v. g. *He will not have it* (con referencia a un *libro*), Él no *le* quiere; (con referencia a una *manzana*), él no *la* quiere. *She caught the butterfly, and preserved it,* Ella cogió la mariposa, y *la* conservó. Cuando *it* es objeto de los verbos, se traduce por medio del pronombre *lo,* o se omite, según la frase; como, *He saw it,* Él lo vió. *They know nothing of it,* Ellos no saben nada, o nada de ello. *It,* en las frases impersonales, y cuando se usa en lugar del sujeto que se pospone al verbo, no se traduce; v. g. *It is warm,* Hace calor. *It is a matter of constant experience that bodily exercise is conducive to health,* Es materia de constante experiencia, que el ejercicio corporal es conducente a la salud. Tampoco se traduce en las preguntas o respuestas de la misma clase; v. g. *It was he who did it,* Él fué quien lo hizo. *It* se usa para preguntar por el estado de una persona o cosa. *How is it with our general?* ¿Cómo está nuestro general? Se usa algunas veces después de los verbos neutros para dar énfasis a su significación.
Italian [i-tal'-yan], *s.* Italiano, el natural de Italia y la lengua de este país.—*a.* Italiano.
Italianize [i-tal'-yan-aiz], *va.* 1. Hacer italiano; conformar al carácter, costumbres o lengua italianos. 2. Convertir abejas en la clase de las llamadas italianas, dándoles una reina italiana.
Italic [i-tal'-ic], *a.* Bastardilla, carácter de letra. *It is printed in italics,* Está impreso en letra bastardilla.
Italicize [i-tal'-i-saiz], *va.* Distinguir con letras bastardillas; de aquí, dar énfasis.
Itch [ich], *s.* 1. Sarna, enfermedad cutánea. 2. Comezón, picazón. 3. Sarna, el deseo vehemente de conseguir alguna cosa; prurito, flujo. *Itch-insect,* (Ent.) Ácaro, arador, insecto que se engendra en las postillas sarnosas.
Itch, *vn.* 1. Picar, sentir picazón o comezón. *My arm itches,* Me pica el brazo. 2. Antojarse, padecer antojo o deseo vehemente de alguna cosa, tener prurito por algo.
Itchiness [ich'-i-nes], *s.* 1. Escozor, picazón. 2. Sarnosidad.
Itching [ich'-ing], *s.* 1. Escozor, picazón; irritación de la piel. 2. Deseo ardiente, prurito.
Itchy [ich'-i], *a.* 1. Sarnoso. 2. Lo que produce comezón o picazón; picante.
Item [ai'-tem], *adv.* Ítem; otro sí, aun más: úsase para distinguir los diversos artículos en un escrito.—*s.* 1. Cada uno de los artículos separados por el adverbio ítem en algun escrito. 2. Partida, artículo, párrafo.
Itemize [ai'-tem-aiz], *va.* Sentar alguna cosa por artículos; apuntar cada artículo.
Iterable [it'-er-a-bl], *a.* Iterable, capaz de repetirse.
Iterate [it'-er-êt], *va.* Iterar, repetir, reiterar; inculcar.
Iteration [it-er-ê'-shun], *s.* Iteración, la repetición de un acto.
Iterative [it'-er-a-tiv], *a.* 1. Iterativo, que se reitera o repite. 2. (Gram.) Frecuentativo.
Itinerant [ai-tin'-er-ant], *a.* Itinerante, viandante; vago; ambulante, errante.
Itinerary [ai-tin'-er-e-ri], *s.* 1. Itinerario, derrotero y dirección de un camino por donde se debe pasar haciendo un viaje. 2. Viaje de exploración, su plan o su relato. 3. Guía (libro).—*a.* Itinerario, hecho en viaje, perteneciente a viaje.
Itinerate [ai-tin'-er-êt], *vn.* Viajar.
-itis [i'-tis]. Sufijo que denota inflamación.
Its [its]. El genitivo del pronombre *It.* Su (de él, de ella, de ello). *A house and its furniture,* Una casa con sus muebles.
It's. Abreviatura de *it is.*
Itself [it-self'], *pron.* El mismo, la misma, lo mismo; pronombre recíproco que se aplica solamente a las cosas, como *himself* y *herself* se aplican a las personas. *It moves of itself,* Eso se mueve por sí mismo. *She is virtue itself,* Es la virtud misma.
I've [aiv]. Contracción familiar de *I have,* yo hé, yo tengo. *I've seen it!* ¡Lo he visto!
-ive [iv]. Sufijo equivalente a -or o -ivo en español; que sirve para ejecutar la acción del verbo. *Expulsive,* Expulsivo.
Ivied [ai'-vid], *a.* Cubierto de hiedra.
Ivory [ai'-vo-ri], *s.* 1. Marfil, el colmillo del elefante. 2. Substancia que se parece al marfil. 3. *pl.* Cosas hechas de marfil. 4. (Fest.) *pl.* Dientes.—*a.* Ebúrneo, lo que está hecho de marfil, o se parece a él; blanco, duro.
Ivy [ai'-vi], *s.* 1. (Bot.) Hiedra. *Ground ivy,* Hiedra terrestre. 2. Unas de varias otras plantas trepadoras, como la ampelopsis o *Virginia creeper* y la *German ivy,* hiedra alemana (Senecio scandens), planta de hojas de color verde claro. *Poison ivy,* Arbusto trepador, especie de zumaque, con tres hojuelas dentadas.
†**Iwis** [i-wis'], *adv.* Ciertamente; à saber. *V.* Ywis.
-ize, -ise. Sufijo usado en la formación de verbos que significan hacer, dar, practicar.
Izzard [iz'-ard], *s.* La letra Z; nombre antiguo, usado en la locución: *from A to izzard,* de cabo a rabo, desde el principio hasta fin, completamente.

J

J [jê]. Esta letra tiene siempre en inglés un sonido semejante al de la *y* consonante castellana, aunque mucho más fuerte, igual al de la sílaba *gi* en italiano, como en *giorno, giocoso.* Puede representarse por *dy*; v. g. *jade* [dyêd]; pero en este diccionario conserva su propia forma inglesa.

Jab [jab, dyab], *va.* (Fam.) Pinchar con violencia; golpear rudamente. —*s.* Punzada; golpe a manera de pinchazo.

Jabber [jab'-ẹr], *vn.* 1. Charlar, hablar mucho y sin substancia. 2. Farfullar, parlar precipitadamente. 3. (Fam.) Hablar en jerigonza, hablar en griego, marmotear. 4. Mascar o farfullar las palabras.

Jabberer [jab'-ẹr-ẹr], *s.* Farfullador, parlanchín.

Jabberment [jab'-ẹr-mẹnt], *s.* (Poco us.) Charla, farfulla, jerga, algarabía, guirigay.

Jaborandi [jab-o-ran'-di], *s.* Jaborandi, pilocarpo, planta medicinal del Brasil cuyas hojas son diaforéticas. Pilocarpus.

Jacent [jé'-sent], *a.* Yacente, que está echado o tendido.

Jacinth, *s.* 1. (Bot.) *V.* HYACINTH. 2. (Min.) *V.* ZIRCON.

Jack [jac], *s.* 1. Juanito, Juanillo, diminutivo de *John*, Juan; hombre; marinero. 2. Sacabotas u otro cualquier instrumento que se supone hace lo que debía hacer un muchacho. 3. Martinete, el palillo del clavicordio que hiere las cuerdas. 4. Torno de asador. 5. Jarro o vaso de cuero negro encerado. 6. Cota de malla. 7. Boliche o bola pequeña que se echa en el juego de las bolas para que sirva de señal a los jugadores. 8. Macho, el animal del sexo masculino. 9. Burro, armazón con que los aserradores afianzan el madero que se ha de aserrar. 10. (Mar.) Bandera de proa. 11. (Ict.) Lucio o luso pequeño, un pez. 12. La sota entre los naipes. *Jack-o'-lantern*, Fuego fatuo, o de San Telmo, helena. *Jack-boots*, Botas grandes y fuertes. *Jack of the clock-house*, Estatua de reloj que da la hora con un mazo. *Jack by the hedge*, (Bot.) Erísimo. *Jack sauce*, Hombre descarado. *To be jack of all trades*, (1) Aprendiz de todo y oficial de nada. (2) Sábelo todo. *Jack-o'-lent*, *Jackalent*, Maniquí, efigie de Judas Iscariote que solían llevar en las procesiones de cuaresma en Inglaterra y a la que apedreaban después. *Jack-in-the-pulpit*, *V.* INDIAN TURNIP. *Jack-plane*. Garlopa, cepillo grande de carpintero. *Jack-pudding*, Arlequín, bufón, titiritero, payaso. *Jack-rabbit*, Liebre americana de orejas y piernas muy largas.

Jackal [jac'-ẹl], *s.* Chacal o adive, animal semejante al perro.

Jackanapes [jac'-a-nêps], *s.* 1. Pisaverde, mequetrefe; un impertinente. 2. Salvaje, necio, tonto. *Hatter's jack*, Carda.

Jackass [jac'-as], *s.* 1. Garañón, asno, borrico. 2. (Fig.) Asno, tonto, necio, imbécil.

Jackdaw [jac'-dō], *s.* (Orn.) Corneja pequeña, ave parecida al cuervo y al grajo. Corvus monedula.

Jacket [jak'-et], *s.* 1. Chaqueta, saco. 2. (Mec.) Chaqueta, cubierta del cilindro. *Jacket (of a book)*, Forro de un libro.

Jackhammer [jac'-ham-ẹr], *s.* Perforadora.

Jack Ketch [jac' kech], *s.* Verdugo.

Jack-knife [jac'-naif], *s.* Navaja sevillana, navaja fuerte de bolsillo.

Jackscrew [jac'-scrū], *s.* (Mar.) Gato cornaquí.

Jacksmith [jac'-smith], *s.* El que hace tornos de asador.

Jackstaff [jac'-staf], *s.* (Mar.) Asta de bandera.

Jackstone [jac'-stōn], *s.* Una de las piedrecitas o piezas de metal usadas en un juego de niños.

Jackstraw [jac'-strē], *s.* 1. Efigie de paja; de aquí, hombre insignificante, sin influencia. 2. *pl.* Juego con pajitas o astillas de madera, hueso, etc. En singular, una de esas pajas o astillas.

Jack-tree [jac'-tri], *s.* Artocarpo, árbol de cultivo, semejante al árbol del pan.

Jacobean [jac-o-bí'-an o ja-cō'-bẹ-an], *a.* Que se refiere al tiempo de Jacobo 1°, rey de Inglaterra.

Jacobin [jac'-o-bin], *s.* 1. Dominico o fraile dominicano. 2. Jacobino, demócrata, antimonárquico. 3. Irreligioso. 4. Pichón con copete.

Jacobin, Jacobinical [jac-o-bin'-i-cal], *a.* Jacobínico.

Jacobinism [jac'-o-bin-izm], *s.* Jacobinismo, los principios de los jacobinos.

Jacobinize [jac'-o-bin-aiz], *va.* Infundir o propagar los principios o máximas de los jacobinos.

Jacobite [jac'-o-bait], *s.* 1. Hereje. 2. Jacobita, el partidario del rey Jacobo II de Inglaterra.

Jacob's-ladder [jé'-cọbz-lad'-ẹr], *s.* 1. (Bot.) Polemonio azul. Polemonium cæruleum. 2. (Mar.) Escala de jarcias para subir a las cofas.

Jacob's-staff [jé'-cọbz-staf], *s.* 1. Bordón de peregrino; bastón con estoque. 2. (Mar.) Báculo de Jacob, astrolabio.

Jacobus [ja-cō'-bus], *s.* Moneda de oro, del tiempo de Jaime I., de valor de unos 6 pesos.

Jaconet, Jacconet [jac'-o-net], *s.* Chaconá, chaconada, especie de tela de algodón muy fina que usan las mujeres para vestidos de verano.

Jactitation [jac-ti-té'-shun], *s.* Agitación, inquietud.

Jaculate [jac'-yu-lêt], *va.* Lanzar, arrojar.

Jaculation [jac-yu-lé'-shun], *s.* (Ant.) Lanzamiento.

Jaculatory [jac'-yu-la-to-ri], *a.* 1. Arrojado o disparado de pronto. 2. Jaculatorio, breve y fervoroso.

Jade [jêd], *s.* 1. Rocín, caballo alquilón y de mala traza. 2. Mujercilla, picarona, buena alhaja: término de desprecio. 3. (Min.) Piedra nefrítica. 4. Jade, especie de esmeralda.

Jade, *va.* Cansar, acosar; sujetar, maltratar, tiranizar.—*vn.* Desanimarse, desalentarse.

Jadery [jéd'-ẹr-i], *s.* (Poco us.) Burla pesada.

Jadish [jêd'-ish], *a.* 1. Vicioso: dícese de las yeguas. 2. Incontinente; dícese de las mujeres.

Jag [jag], *va.* Dentar, formar dientes en alguna cosa.

Jag, *s.* 1. Diente, las puntas que se hacen en ciertos instrumentos como las sierras, hoces, etc.; punta saliente. 2. (Prov. Ingl. y E. U.) Carga para un solo caballo; de aquí, licor fuerte en cantidad bastante para embriagar.

Jagged [jag'-ed], *a.* Dentado; recortado en los bordes de un modo desigual.

Jaggedness [jag'-ed-nes], *s.* El estado de lo que está dentellado o dentado.

Jaggy [jag'-i], *a.* Dentado, dentellado.

Jaghir [jā'-gīr], *s.* Rentas del gobierno de la India inglesa, cuya recaudación se encomienda a un empleado especial.

Jai Alai [hai' a-lai], *s.* Jai Alai, frontón, juego de pelota vasca.

Jail [jêl], *s.* Cárcel, prisión. *Jail fever*, Tifo, fiebre de las cárceles.

Jail-bird [jél'-bẹrd], *s.* El que ha sido encarcelado, tal vez con frecuencia; criminal.

Jailer [jél'-ẹr], *s.* Carcelero, alcaide de una cárcel.

Jalap [jal'-ap], *s.* Jalapa.

Jalopy [jal-ep'-i], *s.* Auto viejo y destartalado.

Jam [jam], *s.* 1. Conserva o marmelada de frutas. 2. Aprieto, apretura causada por mucha gente o por muchos objetos; apretadura, apiñadura. 3. Apuro, Eualquier situación difícil.

Jam, *va.* Apiñar; acuñar o apretar, estrechar, apachurrar. 2. Llenar y cerrar algo apretando y apiñando. 3. (Rad.) Enredar la difusión de una difusora.—*vn.* Quedarse inmóvil por efecto de apretadura o acumulación.

Jamaican [ja-mé'-can], *a.* Jamaicano, perteneciente a la isla de Jamaica.

Jamaica pepper [ja-mé'-ca pep'-ẹr], *s.* (Bot.) Pimienta.

Jamaica wood [ja-mé'-ca wud], *s.* 1. Palo de Campeche. 2. Brasilete. 3. Caoba fina.

Jamb [jam], *s.* Quicial, el madero que asegura y afianza las puertas y ventanas.

Jamboree [jam-bo-rí'], *s.* 1. (fam.) Jolgorio, ruidoso festival. 2. Reunión nacional o internacional de muchachos exploradores.

Jane [jên], *s.* Moneda de Génova.

Jam session [jam' se-shun], *s.* Reunión de músicos para improvisar música popular.

Jangle [jaŋ'-gl], *vn.* Reñir, altercar; charlar.—*va.* Hacer sonar desapaciblemente alguna cosa.

Jangle, *s.* Sonido discordante; de aquí, disputa, querella, altercado.

Jangler [jaŋ'-glẹr], *s.* Un charlatán; parlanchín, disputador.

Jangling [jaŋ'-gling], *s.* Sonido discordante; riña, pendencia; charla.

Janitor [jan'-i-tẹr], *s.* Portero; bedel, en los colegios y universidades.

Janizary [jan'-i-zẹ-ri], *s.* Genízaro, soldado de la antigua guardia del Gran Turco.

Jannock [jan'-ẹc], *s.* Pan de avena.

Jansenism [jan'-sen-izm], *s.* Jansenismo: las doctrinas de Jansenio respecto de la gracia, condenadas por la silla apostólica como contrarias al dogma.

Jant, Janty. *V.* JAUNT, JAUNTY.

January [jan'-yu-ẹ-ri], *s.* Enero, el primer mes del año.

Japan [ja-pan'], *s.* Charol, obra charolada; barniz. *Japan earth*, Tierra japónica.

Japan, *va.* 1. Charolar, embarnizar. 2. Limpiar y dar lustre al calzado.

Japanese [jap-a-nís' o níz'], *a.* Japonés, natural del Japón, o perteneciente a él.—*s.* 1. Natural del Japón. 2. Idioma japonés, lengua aglutinante.

Japhetic [ja-fet'-ic], *a.* Jafético, descendiente de Jafet, hijo de Noé, o que se refiere a él.

Jar [jār], *vn.* 1. Chocar o ludir una cosa con otra. 2. (Mús.) Discordar, desentonar. 3. Reñir, desavenirse, disputar, descompadrar, contender, cruzar. 4. Sonar alguna cosa con un sonido o vibración igual, como el tic-tac de un reloj.—*va.* 1. Hacer discordar o desentonar. 2. Agitar, sacudir.

Jar, *s.* 1. Jarro o jarra; tinaja, cántaro, tarro, orza, botija. 2. Choque, pendencia, disensión, riña. 3. Sonido desapacible y repetido. 4. Balanceo, como el de una puerta sobre sus goznes; se emplea solamente en la locución *on a jar, on the jar,* entreabierto. *V.* AJAR.

Jardinière [zhār-dī-nyār'], *s.* Jardinera, mueble para colocar en él macetas con plantas.

Jargon [jār'-gen], *s.* 1. Jerga, jerigonza, guirigay, monserga. 2. Caló. *V.* CANT y LINGO.

Jargon, Jargoon [jār'-gen, jar-gūn'], *s.* (Min.) Jacinto, una especie de piedra preciosa. *V.* JACINTH.

Jargonelle [jar-go-nel'], *s.* Especie de pera tempranera.

Jarl [yārl], *s.* (Hist. escand.) 1. Noble, hidalgo. 2. Jefe, caudillo.

Jarring [jār'-ing], *s.* Riña, contienda.

Jashawk [jas'-hēc], *s.* Halconcillo.

Jasmine [jas'-min], **Jessamine** [jes'-a-min], *s.* (Bot.) Jazmín. *American jasmine,* Jazmín americano. Ipomœa o Quamoclit coccinea. *Carolina* o *yellow jasmine* (o *jessamine*), Jazmín amarillo. Gelsemium sempervirens, planta medicinal.

Jasper, Jasperite [jas'-per], *s.* 1. Jaspe, variedad opaca e impura de cuarzo, de uno o varios colores. 2. (Biblia) Piedra preciosa en el pectoral del gran sacerdote de los judíos. (< Gr. iaspis < Arab.)

Jato [jē'-tō], *s.* (Aer.) Propulsión auxiliar para el despegue de aviones.

Jaundice [jān'-dis], *s.* 1. Ictericia. (Vulg.) Tiricia, una enfermedad. 2. Celos, prevención, preocupación del ánimo.—*va.* Afectar con ictericia; de aquí, preocupar, predisponer el ánimo contra alguien o algo.

Jaundiced [jān'-dist], *pp.* y *a.* Ictérico, ictericiado.

Jaunt [jānt], *vn.* Corretear, andar de una parte a otra, ir y venir.

Jaunt [jānt], *s.* 1. Excursión, caminata, paseata. 2. Llanta, pina. *V.* FELLOES.

Jauntiness [jān'-ti-nes], *s.* Viveza, gentileza, garbo, ligereza.

Jaunty [jān'-ti], *a.* Ostentoso, vistoso, delicado, gentil, galán, airoso.

Javanese [jav-a-nīs'], *a.* Javanés, javo, de la isla de Java o perteneciente a ella.—*s.* 1. Natural o habitante de Java. 2. Lengua del centro de Java.

Javelin [jav'-lin], *s.* Jabalina, especie de media lanza.

Jaw [jō], *s.* 1. Quijada, mandíbula; hueso maxilar; órgano análogo en los invertebrados. 2. (Art. y Of.) Boca, quijada. 3. Boca; (fig.) abismo, garras. *The jaws of death,* Las garras de la muerte. 4. (Vulg.) Vituperio o insulto hecho con palabras groseras. *Jaw-teeth,* Las muelas. *The jaws of hell,* La boca del infierno. *Jaw of a vise,* Telera.

Jawbreaker [jō'-brēk-er], *s.* Trabalenguas, palabra kilométrica.

Jawed [jōd], *a.* Lo que tiene la apariencia de las quijadas o es semejante a ellas.

Jay [jē], *s.* (Orn.) Gayo, ave parecida al cuervo en su forma, pero con plumaje matizado de colores claros, en América de azul principalmente. El gayo europeo es Garrulus glandarius; el *blue jay* de América es Cyanocitta cristata o (en Florida y California) una especie de Aphelocoma.

Jaywalk [jē'-wōk], *vn.* Cruzar imprudentemente a pie calles de intenso tráfico.

Jazz [jaz], *s.* Jazz, música popular sincopada originaria de E.U.A. *Progressive jazz,* Jazz progresivo.

Jealous [jel'-us], *a.* 1. Celoso. 2. Envidioso. 3. Receloso, el que teme. 4. Desconfiado, el que desconfía. 5. Suspicaz.

Jealously [jel'-us-li], *adv.* Celosamente, sospechosamente.

Jealousy [jel'-us-i], *s.* 1. Celos, sospecha, inquietud, recelo, suspicacia. 2. Desconfianza; emulación.

Jealousness [jel'-us-nes], *s.* Vigilancia, sospecha; celos.

Jean [jīn], *s.* Mezclilla, tela burda de algodón. *Jeans, pl.* Pantalones de mezclilla.

Jeep [jīp], *s.* Jeep, automóvil pequeño de transporte.

Jeer [jīr], *vn.* Befar, mofar, escarnecer.—*va.* Escarnecer, tratar con escarnio.

Jeer, *s.* 1. Befa, mofa, escarnio, burla. 2. *pl. Jeers* o *jears,* (Mar.) Guindaste con sus drizas.

Jeerer [jīr'-er], *s.* Mofador, escarnecedor, burlador.

Jeering [jīr'-ing], *s.* Burla, escarnio.

Jeeringly [jīr'-ing-li], *adv.* Con escarnio.

Jehovah [je-hō'-va], *s.* Jehová, nombre hebreo de Dios.

Jehu [jī'-hiu], *s.* 1. Aficionado a guiar caballos; cochero que guía veloz o furiosamente. 2. Cochero en general. (< Jehu, Biblia, Libro de los Reyes.) *To drive like Jehu,* Ir desempedrando las calles.

Jejuneness, Jejunity [je-jūn'-nes, je-jū'-ni-ti], *s.* Carestía, esterilidad; pobreza, tibieza, aridez de estilo.

Jejunum [je-jū'-num], *s.* (Anat.) Yeyuno, el segundo de los intestinos delgados.

Jellied [jel'-id], *a.* Gelatinoso, convertido en jalea; dulce como una jalea.

Jelly [jel'-i], *s.* Jalea, jaletina. *Currant jelly,* Jalea de grosellas. *Jelly broth,* Consumado.

Jellyfish [jel'-i-fish], *s.* 1. Aguamar, medusa. 2. (Fam.) Calzonazos.

Jemmy, *a. V.* SPRUCE.—*s.* Pie de cabra corto. *V.* JIMMY.

Jennet [jen'-et], *s.* Jaca, caballo chico de España.

Jenny [jen'-i], *s.* 1. Torno, máquina para hilar. 2. Una hembra; particularmente, asna, burra, borrica. 3. (Orn.) Troglodita.

Jeopard [jep'-ard], *va.* Arriesgar, exponer a pérdida o daño.

Jeopardize [jep'-ard-aiz], *va. V.* JEOPARD.

Jeopardy [jep'-ard-i], *s.* Riesgo, peligro.

Jerboa [jer'-bo-a o jer-bō'-a], *s.* Gerbo, cuadrúpedo roedor. Dipus ægypticus.

Jeremiad [jer-e-mai'-ad], *s.* Jeremiada, lamentación, a veces sarcástica, sobre la maldad o la depravación de otros.

Jerk [jerk], *s.* 1. Tirón o empellón repentino; sacudida, sobarbada, sacudimiento, vibración. 2. La sacudida o golpe repentino que dan las cosas elásticas cuando se rompen o saltan. 3. Salto o brinco. 4. Tasajo, charqui.

Jerk, *va.* 1. Tirar o arrojar con impulso violento y repentino, dar un tirón repentino y brusco; mover a tirones; emitir de una manera convulsiva. 2. Tasajear, charquear, cortar la carne (de buey) en lonjas largas y secarlas al sol sin salarlas. *Jerked beef,* Tasajo, charqui.—*vn.* Sacudir; vibrar.

Jerker [jerk'-er], *s.* Sacudidor, tirador.

Jerkin [jer'-kin], *s.* 1. Coleto de ante sin mangas. *V.* JACKET. 2. (Orn.) Especie de halcón.

Jersey [jer'-zi], *s.* 1. Estambre fino. 2. Camisa fuerte hecha de punto de lana fina. 3. Jubón o chaqueta elástica muy ajustada al cuerpo, hecha de lana o de seda. 4. Res de ganado mayor oriundo de la isla de Jersey, en el canal de la Mancha.

Jerusalem artichoke [je-rū'-sa-lem ār'-ti-chōk], *s.* (Bot.) Pataca, aguaturma.

Jess [jes], *s.* Grillos de halcón, correilla que se ataba a la pata del halcón.

Jessamine [jes'-a-min], *s.* (Bot.) Jazmín. *V.* JASMINE.

Jesse [jes'-i], *s.* 1. Araña o candelero sin pie con muchos mecheros. 2. (Ger.) Reprensión, zaherimiento. *To give one (particular) Jesse,* Ponerlo a uno como nuevo.

Jest [jest], *vn.* Bufonearse, burlarse, chancearse, zumbar, chulear.

Jest, *s.* 1. Chanza, burla, broma, zumba; chiste. 2. Hazmerreir. *A piercing jest,* Broma pesada, chasco.

Jester [jest'-er], *s.* Gracioso, mofador, bufón, burlón, chancero.

Jesting [jest'-ing], *s.* Mofadura, chanza, bufonería.

Jestingly [jest'-ing-li], *adv.* De burlas.

Jesuit [jez'-yu-it], *s.* Jesuita.

Jesuitic, Jesuitical [jez-yu-it'-ic, al], *a.* Jesuítico.

Jesuits' bark [jez'-yu-its bārc], *s.* Quina, cascarilla.

Jesus [jī'-zus], *s.* Jesús, el Hijo de Dios.

Jesus Christ [jī'-zus craist], *s.* Jesucristo.

Jet [jet], *s.* 1. Azabache. 2. Surtidor; mechero para gas; tubo que sirve para dar salida a un flúido. 3. Objeto, blanco, antiguamente escopo. *Jet of water,* Chorro de agua. 4. Salidizo. *V.* JUT. *Jet-black,* Negro como el azabache.

Jet, *vn.* Echar, arrojar fuera, lanzar; contonearse, inflarse; traquear, vacilar; correr de una parte a otra. *To jet it along,* Andar con orgullo. *To jet out,* Sobresalir.

Jet plane [jet plēn], *s.* Avión de retropropulsión, avión a chorro.

Jet propulsion [jet pro-pul'-shun], *s.* Propulsión a chorro, propulsión por reacción, retropropulsión.

Jetsam [jet'-sam], o **Jetson** [jet'-sun], *s.* 1. (Mar.) Echazón. 2. Parte de la carga de un buque cuando hay necesidad de aligerarla; en derecho, los géneros echados al mar que quedan debajo del agua; en contraposición a *flotsam,* los que sobrenadan.

Jettee, *s. V.* JETTY.

Jettison [jet'-i-sun], *va.* Arrojar al

mar fardos de mercancías y otros objetos para aligerar un buque en peligro.—*s.* 1. Echazón. 2. *V.* JETSAM, 2ª acepción.

Jetty, *a.* Hecho de azabache, azabachado, negro.—*s.* 1. Salidizo. 2. Muelle. *V.* JUTTY.

Jew [jū], *s.* Judío.

Jewel [jū'-el], *s.* 1. Joya. 2. Piedra preciosa. *Jewels*, Pedrería. 3. Prenda, expresión de cariño.

Jewel, *va.* Adornar con piedras preciosas.

Jewel-like [jū'-el-laic], *a.* Brillante como pedrería.

Jeweller [jū'-el-ẹr], *s.* Joyero, diamantista.

Jewess [jū'-es], *sf.* Judía.

Jewish [jū'-ish], *a.* Judaico, judío

Jewishness [jū'-ish-nes], *s.* Ritos religiosos de los judíos.

Jewry [jū'-ri], *s.* 1. Judea. 2. Judería.

Jews'-ears [jūz'-îrz], *s.* (Bot.) Orejas de Judas, especie de hongo.

Jews'-harp [jūz'-hārp], *s.* Birimbao. (Amer.) Marímbula, trompa.

Jezebel [jez'-e-bel], *s.* Mujer presumida, jamona é impertinente.

Jib [jib], *s.* (Mar.) Maraguto o foque. *Flying-jib*, Petifoque o cuarto foque. *Standing-jib*, Contrafoque. *Middle-jib*, Segundo foque. *Jib-boom*, Botalón de foque. *Jib-iron*, Arraca.

Jibe [jaib], *va.* (Mar.) Mudar un botavante.

Jiffy [jif'-i], *s.* (Fam.) Instante, momento.

Jig [jig], *s.* 1. Cualquier baile y música vivos y alegres; por lo común en el compás de 6/8 o 12/8. 2. Trampa, petardo. 3. (Min.) Criba. 4. Anzuelo que tiene el astil cargado de plomo. 5. (Mec.) Conductor o guía para fabricar piezas idénticas. *Jig-saw*, Sierra de vaivén.

Jig, *va.* 1. Cantar o tocar música en el compás de 6/8. 2. Sacudir de abajo hacia arriba; separar minerales con una criba. 3. Formar ó adaptar por medio de guías.—*vn.* 1. Bailar sin maestro; bailar mal o con poca gracia. 2. Pescar con el anzuelo emplomado llamado *jig*.

Jigger [jig'-ẹr], *s.* 1. El que baila; lo que va y viene. 2. Cualquier utensilio que tiene movimiento de vaivén; v. g. criba para minerales; rueda de alfarero; (Mar.) aparejuelo, el palanquín de socaire.

Jigger, *s.* 1. Nigua, insecto muy parecido a la pulga que se introduce bajo la epidermis de los pies (en el Perú, se llama *pique*). *V.* CHIGOE. 2. Pulga, garrapata u otra sabandija.

Jigjog [jig'-jog], *s.* (Vulg.) Empujón, sacudimiento.

Jigsaw [jig'-sō], *s.* Sierra de vaivén o de calar.

Jigsaw puzzle [jig'-sō puz'-l], *s.* Rompecabezas que consiste en pedazos de cartón cortados con sierra de vaivén.

Jill [jil], *s.* 1. Una joven; querida; a menudo significa manceba, concubina. 2. Hurón hembra. 3. Taza, jícara. *Jill-flirt*, Mujer ligera y coqueta.

Jilt [jilt], *s.* La mujer que caprichosamente despide a un pretendiente; dícese también algunas veces del hombre que no corresponde al amor de una mujer.

Jilt, *va.* Engañar una mujer a sus amantes; lisonjear una mujer a un hombre traidoramente dándole esperanzas falsas. (Fam.) Plantar, dejar colgado. *To jilt a man*, Despedirle. (Met.) Darle calabazas, enviarle noramala, o a pasear.—*vn.* Hacer una mujer el papel de coqueta u ocuparse en intrigas amorosas.

Jimmy [jim'-i], *s.* Pie de cabra de los salteadores en poblado.

Jingle [jiṇ'-gl], *vn.* 1. Retiñir, sonar o resonar. 2. Hacer eco; rimar.—*va.* Producir un sonido agudo, como de pequeños objetos metálicos.

Jingle, *s.* 1. Retintín, sonido de campanas pequeñas o pedazos de metal. 2. Cualquier sucesión agradable de sonidos rítmicos; rima pueril, aleluya.

Jingo [jiṇ'-gō], *s.* (Fam.) Miembro de un partido de la Gran Bretaña que favorece una política exterior agresiva y vigorosa; todo el que favorece dicha política.

Jingoism [jin'-gō-izm], *s.* Jingoísmo, patriotería exaltada.

Jingoist [jin'-gō-ist], *s.* y *a.* Jingoísta.

Jinnee [jin'-i], *s.* (*pl.* JINN). Genio, en la mitología árabe; demonio, espíritu bueno o malo de quienes se supone haber sido creados dos mil años antes de Adán.

Jinx [jincs], *s.* Cenizo, portador de la mala suerte.

Jippo [jip'-o], *s.* Jubón, jaqueta o chaqueta sin mangas; una especie de cotilla.

Jitterbug [jit'-ẹr-bug], *s.* Bailador, en forma exagerada, de música sincopada (jazz).

Jive [jaiv], *s.* 1. Cierta música sincopada. 2. Jerga de músicos. 3. Galimatías.

Job [job], *s.* 1. Tarea; labor o trabajo hecho o que ha de hacerse como un todo; destajo, remiendo. 2. Negocio u ocupación lucrativa a expensas del público, engañifa; cucaña, ganga, el negocio o empleo que es muy lucrativo con poco trabajo. 3. (Fam.) Empleo, obtención de trabajo. 4. (Fam.) Suceso, circunstancia; negocio. 5. La herida hecha de repente con arma punzante, que en castellano se llama familiarmente mojada. *V.* JAB. *Job-printing*, Impresión de remiendos. *Odd job*, Trabajo de poca monta, friolera, bagatela.

Job, *va.* 1. Comprar en grueso al importador o fabricante y vender a los comerciantes. 2. Hacer al destajo, por ajuste; trabajar al destajo. 3. Dar una mojada o herir repentinamente con arma punzante.—*vn.* Negociar en los fondos públicos; cambalachear o chalanear.

Jobber [job'-ẹr], *s.* 1. Agiotador, agiotista, el que negocia en los fondos públicos. 2. Destajero, destajista; (Com.) corredor. *V.* MIDDLEMAN. 3. (Fam.) El que se emplea en negocios bajos. 4. Remendero, remendón, el que hace obras de poca monta.

Jobbery [job'-ẹr-i], *s.* Engañifa, manejos bajos para fines políticos.

Jobbing [job'-ing], *pa.* y *s.* Acción del verbo *to job*. *Jobbing house*, Casa que compra a importadores o fabricantes y vende a detalladores.

Jobless [job'-les], *a.* Cesante, sin empleo, sin trabajo.

Job lot [job lot], *s.* Colección miscelánea de mercancías que se supone de calidad inferior.

Job seeker [job sîk'-ẹr], *s.* El que busca empleo.

Jockey [jok-i], *s.* 1. El jinete que corre a caballo en las carreras públicas. 2. Chalán, el que trata en caballos. 3. Engañabobos, el que usa de embustes y trampas.

Jockey, *va.* 1. Atropellar a uno con un caballo. 2. Trampear, engañar con trampas o fraudes.

Jocose [jo-cōs'], *a.* Jocoso, festivo, chancero, burlesco, jovial.

Jocosely [jo-cōs'-li], *adv.* Jocosamente, en burla, en chanza.

Jocoseness [jo-cōs'-nes], **Jocosity** [jo-cos'-i-ti], *s.* Jocosidad, festividad, alegría, chanza.

Jocular [joc'-yu-lar], *a.* Jocoso, chistoso, divertido; burlesco.

Jocularity [joc-yu-lar'-i-ti], *s.* Festividad, jocosidad.

Jocularly [joc'-yu-lar-li], *adv.* Jocosamente.

Joculatory [joc'-yu-la-to-ri], *a.* Chistoso, gracioso, chancero, divertido.

Jocund [joc'-und], *a.* Alegre, festivo, plácido, agradable.

Joe Miller [jō mil'-ẹr]. (Fam.) Chanza muy sabida, chiste que data de mucho tiempo; libro de chistes.

Jog [jog], *va.* 1. Empujar; dar un golpe suave a alguno para llamar su atención; sacudir con el codo o la mano. 2. (Fig.) Excitar suavemente, estimular. *To jog the memory*, Estimular la memoria.—*vn.* Traquearse, bambolearse, moverse suavemente. *To jog on*, Empujar a alguno hacia adelante; moverse hacia adelante con un movimiento suave; andar a saltos.

Jog, *s.* 1. Empellón, sacudimiento ligero, movimiento irregular. 2. Traqueo, zangoloteo, bazuqueo: dícese del movimiento de un coche o carruaje.

Jogging [jog'-ing], *s.* Sacudimiento, traqueo.

Joggle [jog'-l], *vn.* 1. Moverse o agitarse con movimiento trémulo. 2. Vacilar.—*va.* Empujar.

John [jon], *n. pr.* Juan; muchacho; tipo nacional. *John Bull*, (1) Apodo dado al inglés típico; de aquí, el pueblo inglés. Su traducción literal es Juan Toro. (2) Juego con peniques. *John Chinaman*, Un chino; los chinos en general.

John-apple [jon'-ap-l], *s.* (Bot.) Especie de manzana tardía. *St. John's Gospel*, El evangelio de San Juan. *St. John's bread*, (Bot.) Garrofa o algarroba, fruto del árbol llamado algarrobo. *St. John's bread tree*, Algarrobo. *St. John's wort*, Hipérico, corazoncillo. *John-dory*, Dorado, fabro, pez de mar de forma comprimida. (Zeus faber.)

Johnny [jon'-i], *n. pr.* Juanito, dim. de Juan; apodo dado a los confederados por los soldados de los Estados Unidos del Norte durante la guerra civil.

Jonny-cake [jon'-i-kēk], *s.* (E. U.) Torta de maíz.

Join [join], *va.* 1. Juntar, unir, añadir, trabar. 2. Juntar, unir a una persona con otra en alianza o en matrimonio; asociar. 3. Juntarse o unirse a; empeñarse juntos, por lo general en sentido hostil contra otro u otros; chocar, embestir. *To join battle*, Empezar la batalla.—*vn.* 1. Unirse, juntarse; ser contiguo o próximo a. 2. Unirse, aliarse, confederarse por alianza o por matrimonio. 3. Agregarse, asociarse. *To join with one*, Asociarse a alguno o tener parte en lo que alguno ha hecho.

Joinder [join'-dẹr], *s.* (For.) Junta, unión, asociación.

Joiner [join'-ẹr], *s.* Ensamblador, carpintero de obra prima.

Joinery [join'-ẹr-i], *s.* Ensambladura, juntura ; el arte del ensamblador.

Joining [join'-ing], *s.* Coyuntura ; bisagra ; juntura.

Joint [joint], *s.* 1. Coyuntura, articulación. 2. Gozne, bisagra ; charnela. 3. Cuarto, uno de los miembros de un animal cortado para aderezarlo y comerlo ; uno de esos trozos de carne puesto sobre la mesa. 4. Ensambladura. 5. Nudo ó articulación de una planta. *Out of joint*, Lujado ; desunido, despegado ; desordenado, confuso, desconcertado, descoyuntado.—*a.* 1. Distribuído, dividido, repartido. 2. Participante, el que tiene parte en alguna cosa ; común a muchos, solidario. *Joint heir*, Coheredero. 3. Unido, combinado, indiviso. *With joint consent*, De común acuerdo. *Joint responsibility*, Responsabilidad solidaria. *Joint property*, Propiedad indivisa. *Joint-stock*, Capital social, fondos en común. *Joint-stock company*, Compañía por acciones. *Joint tenant*, Inquilino en común con otro ; terrateniente pro indiviso.

Joint, *va.* 1. Juntar, unir, agregar. 2. Formar nudos, articulaciones o coyunturas. 3. Descuartizar. 4. Confederar, hacer alianza.

Jointed [joint'-ed], *a.* Nudoso, lo que está lleno de nudos ó junturas ; de o con coyunturas ; de movimiento.

Jointer [joint'-ẹr], *s.* Juntera, instrumento de carpintería.

Jointly [joint'-li], *adv.* Juntamente, unidamente, mancomunadamente. *Jointly and severally*, Todos y cada uno de por sí.

Jointress [joint'-res], *sf.* Mujer que posee alguna cosa por derecho de viudedad.

Joint-stool [joint'-stūl], *s.* Asiento o banquillo plegadizo, silla de tijera.

Jointure [join'-chur ó joint'-yūr], *s.* Viudedad, lo que ha de poseer la mujer después de la muerte de su marido, señalado ya en la vida de éste.

Jointure, *va.* Asignar bienes o rentas a una mujer en las capitulaciones matrimoniales.

Joist [joist], *s.* Viga o vigueta de bovedilla o suelo.

Joke [jōc], *s.* Chanza, dicho o hecho burlesco, burla, chocarrería. *In joke*, En chanza, de burlas, en zumba. *A ready joke*, Un dichito al caso. *A practical joke*, Un bromazo, un petardo, una mala pasada. *A sorry joke*, Una broma pesada. *To crack a joke*, Decir un chiste, una agudeza ; hacer el gracioso.

Joke, *vn.* Chancear, chancearse, usar de chanzas.

Joker [jōk'-ẹr], *s.* 1. Burlón, chancero, deudor. 2. En algunas formas del juego de naipes llamado *euchre*, naipe adicional que es siempre el triunfo más alto.

Joking [jōk'-ing], *s.* Chanza, burla, chiste.

Jokingly [jōk'-ing-li], *adv.* De burlas, en chanza, chistosamente.

Jollily [jel'-i-li], *adv.* Alegremente.

Jolliness [jel'-i-nes], **Jollity** [jel'-i-ti], *s.* Viveza ; alegría, regocijo.

Jolly [jel'-i], *a.* 1. Alegre, festivo, airoso, gallardo, vivo, placentero, agradable. 2. Rollizo, lleno, robusto.

Jolly-boat [jel'-i-bōt], *s.* (Mar.) Botequín, serení.

Jolt [jōlt], *vn.* Traquearse, bambolearse.—*va.* Traquear, sacudir ; menear repentinamente de arriba abajo.

Jolt, *s.* Vaivén, traqueo, salto.

Jolter [jōlt'-ẹr], *s.* Lo que traquea o sacude.

Jolthead [jelt'-hed], *s.* Cabeza redonda, zote, bolonio.

Jonathan [jen'-a-than], *n. pr.* Jonatán. *Brother Jonathan*, Apodo que dan los igleses al pueblo de los Estados Unidos o a un individuo típico de esa nación.

Jonquil [jen'-cwil], *s.* (Bot.) Junquillo, planta de jardín de flores amarillas.

Joss [jes], *s.* Ídolo o dios chino. *Joss-house*, Templo o lugar para ídolos chinos. *Joss-paper*, Papel dorado ó plateado que queman los chinos en los funerales y en ciertos ejercicios religiosos. *Joss-stick*, Pajuela perfumada, cubierta con polvos de maderas olorosas, que los chinos queman ante sus ídolos.

Jostle [jes'-l], *va.* Rempujar, apretar, codear.—*vn.* Dar un tropezón con otro, empujarse.

Jot [jet], *s.* Jota, ápice, tilde, punto, una cosa mínima. *Every jot*, Todo. *V.* Iota.

Jot, *va.* Apuntar, tomar notas.

Jotting [jet'-ing], *s.* Apunte, nota.

Joule [jaul], *s.* Julio, unidad de medida del trabajo eléctrico, equivalente al producto de un voltio por un culombio ; el esfuerzo necesario para mantener la resistencia de un amperio contra la de un ohmio durante un segundo.

Jounce [jauns], *va.* y *vn.* (Fam.) Sacudir o sacudirse, traquear.—*s.* Sacudimiento repentino o violento.

Journal [jūr'-nal], *s.* 1. Diario, relación de lo que sucede cada día. 2. Diario, papel periódico que se da al público cada día. 3. Jornal, libro en que los mercaderes hacen los asientos de sus operaciones ó negocios por días, desde el borrador o diario, para anotarlos después en el libro mayor. 4. (Mec.) Luchadero, manga de eje, cilindro que termina un árbol de rotación, sostenido por un cojinete. *Journal-bearing*, Cojinete.

Journalism [jūr'-nal-izm], *s.* Periodismo, profesión y ocupación de periodista.

Journalist [jūr'-nal-ist], *s.* Diarista, periodista.

Journalize [jūr'-nal-aiz], *va.* (Com.) Pasar al jornal, por vía de preparación para el libro mayor.—*vn.* Apuntar en un diario.

Journey [jūr'-ni], *s.* 1. Jornada. 2. Viaje por tierra, a distinción de navegación o viaje por mar. 3. Tránsito, el paso o acto de pasar de un paraje a otro.

Journey, *va.* Viajar, ir de viaje de una parte a otra.

Journeyman [jūr'-ni-man], *s.* Jornalero, el que trabaja por un jornal. *Journeyman tailor*, Oficial de sastre.

Journey-work [jūr'-ni-wūrc], *s.* Jornal, trabajo del jornalero.

Joust [just], *s.* Justa, torneo, regocijo público entre los antiguos caballeros.

Joust, *vn.* Justar, combatir en una justa.

Jovial [jō'-vi-al], *a.* Jovial, alegre, festivo.

Joviality, Jovialness [jo-vi-al'-i-ti, jō'-vi-al-nes], *s.* Jovialidad, festividad, buen humor, regocijo.

Jovially [jō'-vi-al-i], *adv.* Alegremente, con alegría y jovialidad.

Jowl [jōl], *s.* Carrillo o quijada ; de aquí, cabeza de pescado aderezada o cocida.

Jowler [jōl'-ẹr ó jaul'-ẹr], *s.* Nombre dado a una especie de perros de caza.

Joy [jei], *s.* 1. Alegría, júbilo, alborozo, regocijo. 2. Gozo, gusto, complacencia, deleite, la cosa que causa deleite. *I wish you joy*, Le doy a Vd. la enhorabuena. *To wish one joy*, Desear prosperidad a alguno, dar la enhorabuena. *Joy, joy !* ¡ Albricias, albricias ! *Joy-bells*, *s. pl.* Campaneo en señal de regocijo.

Joy, *vn.* (Poét.) Regocijarse, recrearse.—*va.* (Des.) 1. Congratular, felicitar, dar el parabién o la enhorabuena a otro por la felicidad que ha logrado. 2. Gozar, poseer.

Joyful [jei'-ful], *a.* Alegre, gozoso.

Joyfully [jei'-ful-i], *adv.* Alegremente.

Joyfulness [jei'-ful-nes], *s.* Alegría, gozo, júbilo.

Joyless [jei'-les], *a.* Triste, sin alegría, insulso.

Joylessly [jei'-les-li], *adv.* Tristemente, insulsamente.

Joylessness [jei'-les-nes], *s.* Tristeza, melancolía.

Joyous [jei'-us], *a.* Alegre, festivo, gozoso.

Joyously [jei'-us-li], *adv.* Alegremente, gozosamente.

Joyousness [jei'-us-nes], *s.* Condicion o estado de gozoso.

Jubilant [jū'-bi-lant], *a.* El que se regocija cantando himnos de alegría.

Jubilate [jū'-bi-lêt], *vn.* Alegrarse, proferir sonidos o voces de alegría.

Jubilation [jū-bi-lé'-shun], *s.* Júbilo, regocijo, alegría.

Jubilee [jū'-bi-lī], *s.* 1. Jubileo, cierta fiesta que celebran los israelitas cada cincuenta años. 2. El quincuagésimo aniversario de cualquier evento y el año en que ocurre ese aniversario. 3. Jubileo, una solemnidad y ceremonia eclesiásticas de la Iglesia católica.

Judaic, Judaical [jū-dé'-ic, al], *a.* Judío, judaico.

Judaically [jū-dé'-i-cal-i], *adv.* A manera de judío.

Judaism [jū'-dẹ-izm], *s.* Judaísmo.

Judaize [jū'-dẹ-aiz], *vn.* Judaizar, abrazar la religión de los judíos.

Judaizer [jū'-da-aiz-ẹr], *s.* Judaizante, el que judaiza.

Judas-tree [jū'-das-trī], *s.* (Bot.) Árbol del amor, árbol de Judas, algarrobo loco.

Judean [jū-dī'-an], *a.* Judaico, que se refiere a la Judea.

Judge [juj], *s.* 1. Juez, magistrado revestido de autoridad para administrar justicia. 2. Juez árbitro, el que es designado para resolver una duda o contienda ; el que es capaz de discernir el mérito de alguna cosa. *To be no judge of*, No ser juez en la materia, no entender de.

Judge, *vn.* 1. Juzgar, sentenciar, fallar como juez. 2. Juzgar, hacer buen o mal juicio de alguna cosa. 3. Censurar, criticar. 4. Discernir, distinguir.

Judgment, Judgement [juj'-mẹnt], *s.* 1. Juicio, discernimiento. 2. Juicio, decisión, fallo; sentencia del juez. 3. Juicio, voto, sentir, opinión, dictamen. 4. Altos juicios de Dios, castigo de Dios; juicio final. *A man of judgment,* Hombre de discernimiento. *In my judgment he is greatly mistaken,* Yo creo que se engaña mucho. *Judgment-seat,* Tribunal. *To the best of one's judgment,* Según el leal saber y entender de uno.

Judger [juj'-ẹr], *s.* Juez, el que juzga.

Judgeship [juj'-ship], *s.* Oficio o dignidad de juez; magistratura.

Judicable [jū'-di-ca-bl], *a.* Que puede ser probado o juzgado.

Judicative [jū'-di-ca-tiv], *a.* Judicativo, que tiene facultad para juzgar.

Judicatory [jū'-di-ca-to-ri], *s.* 1. Justicia. 2. Tribunal de justicia.—*a.* Judicial, que administra justicia.

Judicature [jū'-di-ca-chur], *s.* 1. Judicatura, magistratura. 2. Tribunal de justicia.

Judicial [ju-dish'-al], *a.* 1. Judicial, lo que pertenece al juicio o a la administración de justicia. 2. Penal, lo que se impone como pena o castigo por un delito.

Judicially [ju-dish'-al-i], *adv.* Judicialmente.

Judiciary [ju-dish'-i-ẹ-ri], *a.* Judiciario; judicial.

Judicious [ju-dish'-us], *a.* Juicioso, prudente, circunspecto, mirado.

Judiciously [ju-dish'-us-li], *adv.* Juiciosamente, con juicio.

Judiciousness [ju-dish'-us-nes], *s.* El estado o la calidad que constituye a uno juicioso.

Jug [jug], *va.* 1. Introducir o cocer en una botija o cacharro. 2. (Vulg.) Encarcelar.—*vn.* Lanzar cierta nota especial, como lo hacen el ruiseñor y algunos otros pájaros. (Voz onomatopéyica.)—*s.* 1. (E. U.) Jarro, cacharro, por lo general de barro y con tapón, de boca estrecha y cuerpo ancho, para conservar o conducir líquidos. 2. Jarro, botija, porrón.

Juggle [jug'-l], *vn.* Hacer juegos de manos; engañar, fingir, hacer trampas.

Juggle, *s.* 1. Juego de manos. 2. Impostura, engaño, truhanería.

Juggler [jug'-lẹr], *s.* 1. Juglar, truhán, titiritero. 2. Impostor, el que finge y engaña con apariencias de verdad. 3. Prestidigitador, jugador de manos.

Juggling [jug'-ling], *s.* Engaño, impostura, trampa, truhanería.

Jugglingly [jug'-ling-li], *adv.* Engañosamente.

Jugular [jū'-giu-lar], *a.* 1. Yugular, perteneciente a la garganta. 2. Yugular, que se relaciona con la vena yugular.—*s.* 1. Vena yugular. 2. (Ict.) Yugular, orden de peces que tienen las aletas ventrales delante de las pectorales.

Jugulate [jū'-giu-lēt], *va.* Degollar, cortar la garganta.

Jugulation [jū'-giu-lē-shun], *s.* Degollación, degüello.

Juice [jūs], *s.* 1. Zumo, el líquido que se saca de algunas plantas y frutas exprimiéndolas. 2. Jugo, la substancia que se saca de alguna cosa cociéndola. *Juice of the sugar-cane,* Zumo de caña; (Cuba) guarapo. 3. Jugo, la substancia de las hierbas. 4. Suco, el humor de que se alimentan los animales y plantas. *Expressed juice,* Zumo. *Boiled juice,* Jugo. (Mex.) *The unfermented juice of the maguey,* Aguamiel.

Juiceless [jūs'-les], *a.* Seco, sin zumo, sin jugo, sin sucos.

Juiciness [jū'-si-nes], *s.* Jugosidad.

Juicy [jū'-si], *a.* Jugoso, zumoso, suculento.

Jujitsu [jū-jit'-sū], *s.* Jiu-jitsu, arte japonés de lucha sin armas.

Juke box [jūk bex], *s.* Sinfonola. (Mex.) Tragadieces, tragaveintes.

Julep [jū'-lep], *s.* 1. Bebida compuesta de aguardiente o whisky, azúcar, hielo y menta. 2. Julepe, bebida dulce que se usa para tomar en ella un medicamento.

Julienne [zhü-li-en'], *s.* Caldo claro de carne que contiene zanahorias y otras legumbres picadas; sopa de hierbas.

July [ju-lai'], *s.* Julio, el séptimo mes del año.

Jumble [jum'-bl], *va.* Mezclar y revolver confusamente unas cosas con otras.—*vn.* Mezclarse, revolverse, confundirse.

Jumble, *s.* 1. Mezcla, revoltillo, bazuqueo, enredo, embrollo, confusión. 2. Bollito delgado y dulce.

Jumbler [jum'-blẹr], *s.* Mezclador, embrollón, el que mezcla confusamente unas cosas con otras.

†**Jument** [jū'-mẹnt], *s.* Acémila, jumento, cualquier bestia de carga.

Jump [jump], *vn.* 1. Saltar, brincar, cruzar una distancia. 2. Traquearse, sacudirse; moverse a saltos. 3. Convenir, concordar.—*va.* 1. Arriesgar, aventurar inconsideradamente. 2. (Ger., E. U. y Austral.) Usurpar, tomar posesión por fuerza o en ausencia del propietario (v. g. de una mina). 3. Pasar por, omitir. 4. En el juego de damas, tomar o comer un peón del adversario. *To jump over,* Saltar de un lado a otro por encima de alguna cosa. *To jump at,* Apresurarse a aceptar. *To jump on one,* (Fam.) Poner a uno de oro y azul. *To jump to a conclusion,* Apresurarse a deducir.

Jump, *s.* 1. Salto, brinco. 2. Distancia o extensión de un salto. 3. (Min.) Falla de una vena. *On the jump,* (E. U.) A paso rápido; enérgicamente.

Jumper [jump'-ẹr], *s.* 1. Saltador, brincador. 2. (E. U.) Especie de zamarra o camiseta fuerte exterior que llega hasta las caderas, hecha de algodón cruzado o de lienzo basto; la usan los marineros, estivadores, carreteros y otros. 3. (Mec.) Mecanismo que funciona con un movimiento como de salto.

Junction [junc'-shun], *s.* 1. Junta, unión, agregación y adición de unas cosas a otras. 2. Paraje de unión; empalme, punto en que se unen dos ferrocarriles; estación de empalme.

Juncture [junc'-chur], *s.* 1. Juntura. 2. Juntura, coyuntura, articulación. 3. Unión, amistad. 4. Coyuntura, sazón, oportunidad; momento crítico.

June [jūn], *s.* Junio, el sexto mes del año. *June-bug,* Insecto coleóptero que empieza a volar a principios de junio.

Jungle [juṇ'-gl], *s.* Soto espeso tropical; matorral, zarzal; red de hierbas gigantescas (en África); pantano intransitable o impenetrable. *Jungle-fever,* Fiebre intermitente característica de las selvas del Indostán y de África.

Junior [jūn'-yẹr], *a.* 1. Más mozo, más joven que otro; hijo, el menor. 2. Menos antiguo; más bajo en grado. *A junior partner,* Socio menos antiguo. *Samuel Adams, junior,* Samuel Adams, hijo.

Junior college [jūn'-yẹr col'-ej], *s.* Los dos primeros años en un colegio universitario.

Junior high school [jūn'-yẹr hai scūl], *s.* Primeros años de escuela secundaria.

Juniority [jūn-yer'-i-ti], *s.* El estado de ser más joven que otro.

Juniper [jū'-ni-pẹr], *s.* (Bot.) Enebro, el árbol que produce las nebrinas o bayas de enebro. *Juniper-berries,* Bayas de enebro.

Junk [juṇc], *s.* 1. (Mar.) Junco, cierta embarcación del oriente o de la China. 2. Trozada, trozos de cable viejo; desecho de cualquier clase que puede usarse de nuevo, como hierro viejo, botellas usadas, etc.

Junket [juṇk'-et], *s.* 1. Festín, comida a escote. 2. Golosina, manjar delicado hecho de cuajadas. 3. Dulce seco; cualquier género de cosa confitada en seco.

Junket, *vn.* Tener o dar un convite, o una comida a escote.

Junkman [junc'-man], *s.* Chatarrero.

Junta [jun'-ta], *s.* Junta, asamblea o reunión de personas para tratar de algún negocio.

Jupiter [jū'-pi-tẹr], *s.* (Astr.) 1. Júpiter, uno de los planetas. 2. Júpiter, dios de los antiguos griegos y romanos.

Jupon [ju-pon'], *s.* 1. Especie de casaca corta, jubón de los siglos XIV y XV. 2. Tela francesa de urdimbre de algodón, con trama de lana cardada.

Jurat [jū'-rat], *s.* 1. Jurado, magistrado de algunas poblaciones. 2. Cláusula de un certificado oficial que da fe de un juramento.

Juratory [jū'-ra-to-ri], *a.* Juratorio, lo que está acompañado de juramento: úsase en la expresión *fianza juratoria.*

Juridical [ju-rid'-i-cal], *a.* Jurídico, judicial.

Juridically [ju-rid'-i-cal-i], *adv.* Jurídicamente.

Jurisconsult [jū"-ris-con'-sult], *s.* Jurisconsulto, abogado.

Jurisdiction [jū"-ris-dic'-shun], *s.* 1. Jurisdicción, derecho, o facultad legal de ejercer autoridad. 2. Límite, territorio en que puede ejercerse dicha autoridad.

Jurisdictional [jū"-ris-dic'-shun-al], *a.* Jurisdiccional.

Jurisdictive [jū-ris-dic'-tiv], *a.* Que tiene jurisdicción.

Jurisprudence [jū-ris-prū'-dens], *s.* Jurisprudencia, la ciencia del derecho.

Jurisprudent [jū-ris-prū'-dent], *a.* Jurisperito, jurisprudente, abogado.

Jurist [jū'-rist], *s.* Jurista, legista, profesor de derecho, jurisperito.

Juror [jū'-rẹr], *s.* 1. (For.) Jurado, cada uno de los miembros que componen la institución jurídica del mismo nombre. 2. Jurado, individuo de una comisión o junta encargada de adjudicar premios, decidir en las oposiciones o los certámenes, etc.

Jury [jū'-ri], *s.* Jurado, reunión de personas congregadas para decidir, bajo juramento, si de los hechos que se les presentan resulta que se ha cometido un delito, o si es culpable de él la persona acusada. *Grand jury*, El gran jurado, jurado de acusación; consiste de doce a veintitres miembros, doce de los cuales por lo menos han de estar de acuerdo para que haya acusación con fuerza legal. *Petty* o *petit jury*, Jurado de juicio, encargado de declarar y determinar el hecho. Entre los anglosajones lo componen doce individuos, cuyo fallo ha de ser unánime para que haya veredicto. *Jury-box*, Lugar que ocupan los jurados en la sala del tribunal.

Juryman, *s.* *V.* JUROR.

Jurymast [jū'-ri-mast], *s.* (Mar.) Bandola, palo que se arbola provisionalmente en alta mar en lugar de un mástil tronchado o perdido. *To pitch* o *set up a jurymast*, Armar una bandola.

Just [just], *a.* 1. Justo, que es conforme a justicia, equitativo, verdadero. 2. Recto, íntegro, honrado, virtuoso, puro, inocente. 3. Justo, exacto; cabal, aquello á que nada sobra ni falta. 4. Ordenado, colocado en orden; exactamente proporcionado. *A just judge*, Un juez íntegro, recto. *Just dealing*, Buena fe. *A just charge*, Una acusación fundada; una admonición justa, imparcial.—*adv.* 1. Justamente, exactamente, cabalmente. 2. Apuradamente, tasadamente. 3. Casi o cuasi. 4. No más que, apenas; en el mismo instante; sólo, solamente. 5. Poco ha o hace, dentro de un momento; nuevamente, de nuevo. *Just as*, Al momento que, luego que, al tiempo que; cuando; no bien. *Just as* (like), Lo mismo que, semejante a. *Just now*, Ahora mismo, en este mismo instante, poco hace, recientemente, últimamente. *Just by*, Aquí cerca. *Just as I came in*, En el momento mismo o al tiempo de entrar yo. *Just as you please*, Como Vd. guste. *Just beyond*, Un poco más allá. *That will just do*, Eso hará precisamente al caso; eso convendrá exactamente. *To have but just time*, Tener justamente el tiempo necesario.

Just, Joust [just], *s.* Justa, combate singular á caballo y con lanza.

Just, Joust, *vn.* Justar, lidiar, combatir en una justa.

Justice [jus'-tis], *s.* 1. Justicia, virtud que consiste en dar a cada uno lo que le pertenece; equidad. 2. Justicia, el acto de ejecutar en el reo la pena impuesta por sentencia. 3. Justicia, razón, derecho. 4. Justicia, el ministro que por su autoridad la ejerce. *Justice of the peace*, Juez de paz, alcalde, magistrado de jurisdicción limitada.

Justiceship [jus'-tis-ship], *s.* El puesto, empleo o dignidad de justicia, antiguamente justiciazgo.

Justiciable [jus-tish'-i-a-bl], *a.* Lo que debe examinarse en los tribunales de justicia.

Justiciary [jus-tish'-i-ẹ-ri], *s.* Juez, el que administra justicia; alto magistrado.

Justifiable [jus'-ti-fai-a-bl], *a.* Justificable, conforme a la razón, según justicia.

Justifiableness [jus'-ti-fai-a-bl-nes], *s.* Rectitud; la posibilidad de ser justificado.

Justifiably [jus'-ti-fai-a-bli], *adv.* Justificadamente.

Justification [jus-ti-fi-kē'-shun], *s.* 1. Justificación. 2. Descargo, defensa, los motivos que expone el acusado en un tribunal para defenderse de los cargos que se le hacen.

Justificative [jus'-ti-fi-kē"-tiv o jus-tif'-i-ca-tiv], *a.* Justificativo.

Justificator [jus'-ti-fi-kē"-tẹr], *s.* Defensor; justificador.

Justificatory [jus-tif'-i-ca-to-ri], *a.* Justificativo, defensivo.

Justifier [jus'-ti-fai-ẹr], *s.* Justificador; justificante.

Justify [jus'-ti-fai], *va.* 1. Justificar, sacar a uno inocente del delito que se le imputa, o absolverle de la acusación. 2. Justificar, probar en justicia alguna cosa; defender; absolver. 3. (Teol.) Absolver, perdonar una falta, reinstalar en la gracia de Dios. 4. (Impr.) Justificar, espaciar bien, ajustar a una misma medida las líneas de una plana.

Justle, *s.* y *v.* *V.* JOSTLE.

Justly [just'-li], *adv.* Justamente, rectamente; cabal y exactamente, precisamente.

Justness [just'-nes], *s.* 1. Justicia, equidad, precisión. 2. Exactitud, la propiedad con que está hecha alguna cosa; regularidad; primor.

Jut [jut], *vn.* Sobresalir, extenderse más allá de la parte principal de alguna cosa; úsase frecuentemente con la prep. *out;* combarse. —*s.* Salidizo, vuelo, proyección. *To jut out*, Sobresalir.

Jute [jūt], *s.* 1. Hierba anua asiática del género Corchorus, familia de las tiliáceas. 2. Yute, cáñamo chino o de las Indias, fibra textil obtenida de la corteza interior de dicha planta.

Jut-window [jut'-win-dō], *s.* Ventana saliente, mirador.

Juvenile [jū'-ve-nil], *a.* 1. Juvenil, lo que conviene a la mocedad. 2. Joven, característico de la juventud, de pocos años.

Juvenility [jū-ve-nil'-i-ti], *s.* 1. Mocedad, juventud. 2. Ligereza, ardor o fuego de la juventud.

Juvenescence [jū-vẹ-nes'-ens], *s.* Renovación de la juventud. *V.* REJUVENESCENCE.

Juvenescent [jū-vẹ-nes'-ent], *a.* Rejuveneciente, que se remoza.

Juxtaposition [juc-sta-po-zish'-un], *s.* Yuxtaposición, el modo de aumentar de volumen los cuerpos por la incorporación de los elementos que se les agregan exteriormente.

K

K [kē], undécima letra del abecedario inglés; se pronuncia en inglés siempre como la *c* antes de *a* en castellano; v. g. *kali* (cáli), *ken* (quen). Antes de *n* no se pronuncia; v. g. *knight* (náit).

K., abreviatura significa potasio (kalio). K. o Kt., *Knight*, Caballero.

Kaaba [kā'-a-ba], *s.* Caaba, Caba, templo venerado en la Meca, que contiene una piedra sagrada.

Kafir, Kaffir [kaf'-ẹr], *s.* 1. Cafre, miembro de una de las tribus bantus, del sur de África. 2. Idioma de los cafres sudafricanos. 3. Natural del Kafiristán, región del Afganistán. 4. Infiel, el que no profesa la fe mahometana.

Kafta [kaf'-ta], *s.* Las hojas de un arbusto de Arabia usadas en substitución del té y el café; artículo de comercio. Catha edulis.

Kaiak, Kayak [kai'-ak o kē'-yak], *s.* Canoa de los esquimales.

Kail ó **Kale** [kēl], *s.* (Bot.) Bretón, especie de berza; col rizada.

Kaiser [kai'-zẹr], *s.* Káiser, antiguo emperador de Alemania.

Kaleidoscope [ka-lai'-do-scōp], *s.* Caleidoscopio, aparato óptico, con espejos inclinados que al menor movimiento presentan una nueva imagen.

Kaleidoscopic [ka-lai'-do-scep"-ic], *a.* Caleidoscópico, perteneciente al caleidoscopio; de aquí, variado, pintoresco.

Kali [kā'-li], *s.* Barrilla, hierba.

Kalmia [kal'-mi-a], *s.* (Bot.) Kalmia, un género norteamericano de plantas fruticosas siempre verdes, con umbelas de flores azules, purpúreas o blancas.

Kalmuck [kal'-muc], *s.* 1. Calmuco, raza mongola del Asia central. 2. Su idioma.

Kalsomine, *v.* y *s.* *V.* CALCIMINE. Es ortografía incorrecta.

Kana [kā'-na], *s.* Escritura japonesa propia; tiene 48 caracteres.

Kanaka [ka-nā'-ka o ka-nak'-a], *s.* Natural de las islas de Hawai; por extensión, cualquier habitante de las islas del Pacífico.

Kangaroo [can-ga-rū'], *s.* Canguro, mamífero del orden de los marsupiales.

Kantianism [kant'-i-an-izm], *s.* Kantismo, doctrina del filósofo Kant.

Kaolin [kē'-o-lin], *s.* Caolín, arcilla blanca muy pura con que se hace la porcelana fina.

Kapellmeister [ka-pel'-mai-stẹr], *s.* Maestro de capilla; director de una orquesta o de un coro. (Al.)

Karakul [kar'-a-kūl], *s.* Astracán, piel de astracán.

Karma [kār'-ma], *s.* (Sanscrito) Efecto de cualquier acto, religioso u otro; retribución ineludible.

Karn [kārn], *s.* Montón de piedras. *V.* CAIRN. (Ingl.)

Kat [kat], *s.* *V.* KAFTA.

Kata-, *prefijo.* *V.* CATA.

Katydid [kē'-ti-did], *s.* Insecto arbóreo, verde y con largas antenas, del orden de los ortópteros. (Nombre imitativo.) Cyrtophyllum concavum.

Kebboc [keb'-ec], *s.* (Esco.) Un queso.

Keck [kec], *vn.* Querer vomitar, tener náuseas.—*s.* Tallo de cicuta.

Keckle [kec'-l], *va.* (Mar.) Aforrar un cable.

Kecksy, *s.* *V.* KEX.

Kedge [kej], *s.* (Mar.) Anclote; ancla pequeña.

Kedger [kej'-ẹr], *s.* Anclote; pescadero.

Keel [kīl], *s.* 1. (Mar.) Quilla, pieza de madera o hierro, que va de popa á proa por la parte inferior del barco. *False keel*, Zapata de quilla. *Rabbit of the keel*, Alefriz de quilla. *Scarfs of the keel*, Juntas de quilla. *Sheathing of the keel*, Embón de quilla. 2. (Bot.) Quilla, pétalo inferior de una flor papilionácea que incluye los estambres y el pistilo.

Keel, *va.* Enfriar; refrescar.—†*vn.* Resfriar, desanimar.

Keelage [kīl'-ej], *s.* (Mar.) Derechos de quilla.

Keelfat [kīl'-fat], *s.* Garapiñera, vasija grande en que se pone a enfriar algún líquido.

Keelhale [kīl'-hēl], *va.* (Mar.) Pasar por la quilla.

Keelhaul [kīl'-hōl"], *va.* Aplicar a los marineros el antiguo castigo que consistía en zambullir y sacar varias veces del mar a un delincuente, atado con una cuerda.
Keeling [kīl'-ing], *s.* (Ict.) Especie de merluza.
Keelrope [kīl'-rōp], *s.* (Mar.) Cabo imbornalero de las varengas.
Keelson [kīl'-sun], *s.* (Mar.) Sobrequilla, pieza de madera de casi todo el largo del buque, colocada directamente encima de la quilla.
Keen [kīn], *a.* 1. Afilado; aguzado. 2. Agudo, penetrante, sutil, vivo. 3. Ansioso, vehemente. 4. Acre, desabrido, mordaz, satírico, picante. *Keen-sighted*, El que tiene vista perspicaz. *Keen appetite*, Gran apetito.
Keenly [kīn'-li], *adv.* Agudamente, sutilmente.
Keenness [kīn'-nes], *s.* 1. Agudeza, sutileza o delicadeza de filo. 2. Agudeza, perspicacia, viveza o sutileza de ingenio. 3. Rigor o aspereza del frío. 4. Ansia, anhelo, deseo vehemente. 5. Aspereza de genio, acrimonia.
Keep [kīp], *va.* (*pret.* y *pp.* KEPT). 1. Tener, mantener, retener. 2. Preservar, librar, guardar. 3. Cuidar, proteger, defender. 4. Impedir, detener, entretener. 5. Conservar, reservar, ocultar. 6. Poner por escrito o de otra manera para referencia; apuntar; llevar (los libros de comercio), 7. Mantener, proveer del alimento necesario. 8. Sostener algo para que no se caiga. 9. Proseguir voluntariamente en lo que se está haciendo; ser fiel a. 10. Observar, guardar o cumplir exactamente alguna cosa. 11. Solemnizar.—*vn.* 1. Mantenerse, perseverar o subsistir en un mismo estado. 2. Acostumbrar, soler. 3. Mantenerse, proveerse del alimento necesario. 4. Continuar en alguna situación, quedar. 5. Vivir, residir. 6. Tener cuidado de alguna cosa. *To keep along*, Continuar en la misma situación; seguir una senda. *To keep aloof*, Apartarse, ponerse á un lado, no entremeterse. *To keep asunder*, Tener separado o desunido; estar ó vivir separado o desunido. *To keep at it*, (Fam.) Perseverar, persistir. *To keep at home*, Quedarse en casa. *To keep away*, Tener o retener a alguno apartado o alejado; estar o vivir apartado o alejado; mantenerse ausente. *To keep back*, Retener, detener, ocultar, impedir; preservar, guardar, reservar; restringir. *To keep down*, Sujetar; tener humillado. *To keep from*, Guardar o guardarse; defender; impedir. *To keep in*, Reprimir, refrenar, moderar, contener, tener en sujeción; esconder, ocultar. *To keep in awe*, Hacerse temer, darse a respetar o hacerse respetar. *To keep off*, Impedir, detener, tener separado o alejado; desanimar; estar o mantenerse separado o alejado; mantener a distancia, no admitir a alguno. *To keep on*, Ir adelante, proseguir, adelantar. *To keep out*, Impedir a uno que entre; estar o mantenerse fuera de algún sitio; no querer entrar. *To keep out of sight*, Esconder, quitar de delante; estar o mantenerse oculto. *To keep to*, Adherirse estrictamente a alguna cosa; detenerse. *To keep under*, Sujetar, tener debajo o en sujeción. *To keep up*, Mantener, conservar, continuar; mantenerse con resolución en alguna situación o estado; no descaecer; no ceder, no cesar; estar de jarana. *He keeps up his usual retinue*, Mantiene su tren acostumbrado. *To keep it up*, (Fam.) Persistir en una acción. *To keep company*, Acompañar o estar frecuentemente con alguno; tener trato familiar con una persona. *To keep books*, Llevar los libros de comercio. *To keep cash*, Tener o guardar la caja o el dinero de una casa de comercio, ser cajero. *To keep holidays*, Guardar las fiestas. *To keep Lent*, Observar la cuaresma o los preceptos de la religión pertenecientes a los ayunos, etc., en tiempo de cuaresma. *To keep one's bed*, Guardar cama. *To keep one at bay*, Divertir a alguno; entretenerle con buenas palabras o promesas. *To keep one hungry*, Hacer padecer hambre a alguno. *To keep one's ground*, Mantenerse firme, defender su terreno. *To keep one's temper*, Tener calma, ser dueño de sí mismo, contenerse. *To keep a woman*, Mantener una manceba. *To keep the land aboard*, (Mar.) Mantenerse inmediato a la tierra. *To keep off*, (Mar.) Mantenerse distante de la tierra, no arrimarse. *To keep the sea*, (Mar.) Mantenerse mar afuera.
Keep, *s.* 1. Mantenimiento, medios de subsistencia; guarda, guardia, custodia, cuidado. 2. Torre, la parte más fuerte de los castillos antiguos; torreón; de aquí, castillo, alcázar. 3. Construcción en que se conserva algo. *For keeps*, (Fam. E. U.) Para guardar o retener, para siempre.
Keeper [kīp'-ęr], *s.* 1. Defensor, defendedor. 2. Tenedor, el que tiene a su cargo alguna cosa, por lo regular en nombre de otro; guardián, guardador, el que guarda. 3. Carcelero. 4. Guardabosque. 5. Guarda, el que tiene a su cargo o cuidado la conservación de alguna cosa. *Keeper of the great seal*, Guardasellos del rey. *Book-keeper*, Tenedor de libros.
Keepership [kīp'-ęr-ship], *s.* Oficio o empleo de guarda; alcaidía, oficio o empleo de carcelero.
Keeping [kīp'-ing], *s.* 1. Cargo, custodia, mantenimiento; cuidado, preservación, defensa; guarda. 2. Congruencia; razón o relación justa o recta. *Not in keeping*, No congruente, mal avenido. *Woman in keeping*, Manceba. *Book-keeping*, Teneduría de libros.
Keepsake [kīp'-sēc], *s.* Dádiva, regalo, o presente hecho para que el que lo recibe lo conserve en memoria del que lo da.
Keeve [kīv], *s.* Cuba o tina, vasija en que fermenta la cerveza antes de envasarla.
Keever [kīv'-ęr], *s.* Enfriadera de cerveza. *V.* BACK.
Keg [keg], *s.* Cuñete, barrilito.
Keir ó Kier [kīr], *s.* Cuba, tanque de blanquear.
Kell [kel], *s.* Una membrana o telilla que sacan algunas criaturas en la cabeza al nacer. *V.* CAUL.
Kelp [kelp], *s.* 1. Las especies de alga marina cuyas cenizas sirven para hacer vidrio o preparar yodo; las grandes algas bastas, de cualquier especie, como las laminariáceas y las fucáceas. 2. Las cenizas de algas.
Kelpie ó Kelpy [kel'-pi], *s.* Un duende, fantasma o espectro que los escoceses suponen anda sobre el agua.
Kelson [kel'-sun], *s.* (Mar.) Sobrequilla. *V.* KEELSON.
Kelt, Keltic [kelt, ic]. *V.* CELT.
Kelter [kel'-tęr], *s.* Buen orden o estado para trabajar. *V.* KILTER.
Ken [ken], *va.* 1. (Ant. o esco.) Divisar, espiar o reconocer de lejos, ver a una gran distancia, ver de lejos. 2. (Ant. o esco.) Saber, conocer, alcanzar, comprender.—*vn.* (Des.) Mirar alrededor.
Ken, *s.* Vista, la distancia hasta donde se alcanza a ver alguna cosa.
Kendal-green [ken'-dal-grīn], *s.* Especie de paño verde. (Se fabricó primero en Kendal.)
Kennel [ken'-el], *s.* 1. Perrera, el lugar o sitio donde se guardan o encierran los perros de caza o un perro. 2. Jauría; traílla, cuadrilla de perros podencos en una cacería. 3. Zorrera, la cueva de la zorra. 4. Habitación sórdida. 5. Conducto o canal para dar curso ó salida á las aguas en las calles cuando llueve; arroyo.
Kennel, *vn.* Encamarse, echarse o estar en la cama: dícese regularmente de los animales, y por desprecio algunas veces de los hombres. —*va.* Tener en perrera.
Keno [kī'-nō], *s.* Quinterno en la lotería; juego de azar.
Kentle [ken'-tl], *s.* *V.* QUINTAL.
Kentledge [kent'-lej], *s.* (Mar.) Lingotes de hierro para lastre, puestos permanentemente encima de la sobrequilla.
Kept, *pret.* y *pp.* del verbo *To* KEEP.
Keramic [kęr-am'-ic], *a.* *V.* CERAMIC.
Kerb-stone [cũrb'-stōn], *s.* 1. Brocal de pozo. 2. Guardacantón, piedra grande o poste puesto a las esquinas de las casas para resguardarlas de los golpes de los carros o carruajes. 3. *V.* CURB-STONE.
Kerchief [kęr'-chif], *s.* Cofia, tocado de mujer; pañuelo.
Kerchiefed [kęr'-chift], *a.* Adornado, vestido.
Kerf [kęrf], *s.* 1. La abertura que hace la sierra en la madera. 2. La cortadura que hace una máquina de esquilar o tundir.
Kermes [kęr'-mīz], *s.* 1. Quermes, el gusanillo que se engendra dentro del coco de la grana. *Kermes oak*, Coscoja. 2. Quermes mineral, hidro-sulfureto de antimonio, una preparación de antimonio.
Kermess [kęr'-mes], *s.* En los Países Bajos, fiesta, romería fuera de casa; originalmente una fiesta religiosa.
Kern [kęrn], *s.* (Esco. e Ingl. del Norte) 1. La última gavilla del agosto, fin de cosecha, y la fiesta con que se celebra. 2. (Impr.) Hombro de una letra de imprenta que sobresale, como en una *f* bastardilla. 3. Patán. 4. Soldado irlandés. 3 y 4 se derivan de otra raíz. *Kern* o *corn baby*, Una figura o muñeco que los agosteros conducen con gran regocijo al concluir el agosto.
Kern, *vn.* 1. Granar, formarse completamente el grano cuando llega a madurar. 2. Formarse en granos.
Kerned [kęrnd], *a.* (Impr.) Dícese del tipo que tiene hombro.
Kernel [kęr'-nel], *s.* 1. Almendra, la

pepita, meollo o simiente que se encuentra en las frutas de hueso, que se llama cuesco, grano, semilla, etc., según las frutas. *Kernel of a walnut,* El meollo de la nuez. *Kernel of an apple,* La pepita de la manzana. 2. La parte central de alguna cosa. 3. Haba, cierto género de roncha que sale en el cutis. 4. Concreción dura en la carne.

Kernel, *vn.* Madurar las almendras, pepitas o cuescos de las frutas.

Kernelly [kẹr'-nel-ī], *a.* Almendrado; que está lleno de almendras.

Kernelwort [kẹr'-nel-wūrt], *s.* (Bot.) Escrofularia, ruda canina.

Kerosene [ker'-o-sīn], *s.* Querosina, petróleo, aceite destilado de nafta cruda.

Kersey [kẹr'-zī], *s.* Una especie de tela basta de lana.

Kerseymere [kẹr'-zī-mīr] o **Cassimere** [cas'-ī-mīr], *s.* Casimiro o casimira, tela de lana muy fina.

Kerve [kẹrv], *va.* En las minas de carbón del norte de Inglaterra es minar debajo de.

Kestrel [kes'-trel], *s.* (Orn.) Cernícalo.

Ketch [kech], *s.* (Mar.) Quaiche o queche, especie de embarcación de dos palos o masteleros.

Ketchup, *s.* *V.* CATCHUP.

Ketone [kī'-tōn], *s.* (Quím.) Cuerpo de una clase de compuestos orgánicos, en los cuales el grupo llamado carbonilo (CHO,CO), une dos radicales alcohólicos. (Var. de *acetone.*)

Kettle [ket'-l], *s.* Caldera, vasija en que se cuece algún licor o cosa líquida. *A large kettle,* Calderón. *A small kettle,* Calderico, calderilla. *A tea-kettle,* Tetera.

Kettledrum [ket'-l-drum], *s.* 1. Timbal, atabal. *Kettledrummer,* Timbalero, atabalero. 2. Sarao, te, reunión informal de las señoras por la tarde.

Kettlepins [ket'-l-pinz], *s.* Juego de bolos.

Kevel [kev'-el], *s.* 1. (Mar.) Manigueta o maniguetón, el extremo de los palos que están en la borda del alcázar. 2. (Zool.) Gacela, antílope de África. *Kevel-head,* Escalamote, abitón.

Key [kī], *va.* 1. Enchabetar, calzar, acuñar; sujetar con una llave. 2. Proveer con llaves. 3. Afinar, templar un instrumento de música con una llave.

Key [kī], *s.* 1. Llave, instrumento de metal que sirve para abrir y cerrar puertas, etc. 2. Llave, destornillador, cierto instrumento que se usa para quitar o poner tornillos. 3. Clave o llave de una cifra o de un enigma. 4. (Art. y Of.) Chabeta; cuña; clavija (en la encuadernación): sotrozo. 5. Llave, conmutador de una máquina telegráfica. 6. Tecla, cualquiera de las piezas para los dedos en las máquinas de escribir o en las de componer y distribuir tipos. 7. (Mús.) Tecla. 8. (Mús.) Clave, llave, conjunto o sistema de tonos relacionados entre sí. 9. Cualidad, intensidad o diapasón del tono al hablar. *She spoke in a high key,* Ella habló en tono alto. 10. (Bot.) La cáscara que contiene la simiente de algunas plantas. *To be under lock and key,* Estar bajo llave o cerrado con llave; estar bien guardado. *Skeleton-key, pass-key,* Ganzúa, llave maestra. *In key,* Templado, de acuerdo, en armonía. *Key-action,* El teclado de un órgano o piano y el mecanismo relacionado con él. *Natural key,* (Mús.) (1) Cualquier tecla blanca del teclado de un órgano o piano. (2) Clave de C ♮ tocada en las teclas blancas.

Key [kī], *s.* Cayo, isleta particularmente de coral y cercana á la costa.

Keyboard [kī'-bōrd], *s.* Teclado, como el de un piano o de una máquina para escribir.

Keyed [kīd], *a.* 1. Teclado, que tiene teclas; que tiene llave. *An eight-keyed flute,* Una flauta con ocho llaves. 2. Estirado, puesto en estado de tensión, como una cuerda. 3. Templado, como un instrumento de música.

Keyhole [kī'-hōl], *s.* Agujero de la cerradura, la parte por donde entra en ella la llave.

Key ring [kī' ring], *s.* Llavero.

Keystone [kī'-stōn], *s.* Clave o llave de un arco o bóveda, la última piedra con que se cierra.

Key-word [kī'-wūrd], *s.* Palabra clave.

Khaki [kā'-kī], *s.* y *a.* Color caqui.

Khan [kān], *s.* 1. Kan o Khan, jefe o gobernador entre los tártaros; caballero, en la India. (< Per.) 2. Posada o mesón en Turquía.

Khedive [ked-īv'], *s.* Jedive o kedive, nombre del virrey de Egipto.

Kibitzer [kib'-it-sẹr], *s.* 1. Mirón, espectador en un juego de naipes. 2. (fam.) Camasquince, entremetido.

Kick [kic], *va.* Acocear, cocear, dar o tirar coces.—*vn.* 1. Patear, dar patadas o puntapiés. *To kick one out of the house,* Echar a alguno a puntapiés. 2. Ofrecer resistencia, como por medio de coces; oponerse, quejarse: es uso vulgar.

Kick, *s.* 1. Puntapié, patada; coz. 2. (Ger.) Oposición, protesta.

Kicker [kik'-ẹr], *s.* Acoceador, coceador, el que da o tira coces; el que hace objeciones.

Kicking [kik'-ing], *s.* Coceadura, la acción y efecto de cocear; pateamiento, pateadura.

Kickshaw [kik'-shō], *s.* 1. Patarata, ridiculez, monada, fruslería, bagatela. 2. Almodrote, especie de guisado.

Kid [kid], *s.* 1. Cabrito, la cría de la cabra. 2. Cabritilla. *Kid upper leathers,* Capelladas de cabritilla. 3. La carne de cabrito. 4. *pl.* Guantes o zapatos hechos de cabritilla. 5. (Ger.) Niño, niña; muchachito, muchachita.

Kid, *vn.* Parir cabritos.

Kidded [kid'-ed], *a.* Nacido, hablando de cabritos.

Kickback [kic'-bac], *s.* Retroceso, movimiento de retroceso cuando un motor o maquinaria da marcha atrás.

Kiddle [kid'-l], *s.* Presa o represa en un río.

Kiddow [kid'-o], *s.* (Orn.) Especie de colimbo, ave marítima.

Kidling [kid'-ling], *s.* Cabritillo.

Kidnap [kid'-nap], *va.* Plagiar, hurtar o robar niños, y también hombres.

Kidnapper [kid'-nap-ẹr], *s.* Ladrón de niños, el que hurta o roba niños u hombres.

Kidney [kid'-nī], *s.* 1. Riñón. 2. (Ant.) Afectos, pasiones. 3. Calaña; índole, temperamento. *Kidney-vetch,* (Bot.) Vulneraria. *Kidneywort,* (Bot.) Ombligo.

Kidney-bean [kid'-nī-bīn], *s.* Judía, habichuela, frijol; se usa generalmente en plural.

Kilerg [kil'-ẹrg], *s.* Unidad de trabajo o energía: 1,000 *ergs.*

Kill [kil], *va.* 1. Matar, quitar la vida. *To kill one's self,* Matarse; tomarse mucho trabajo, fatigarse demasiado (animal o vegetal), por cualquier medio que sea; hacer morir. 2. Destruir, privar de vigor, de eficacia o de utilidad; amortiguar; neutralizar. 3. Descartar; suprimir. 4. Hacer una carnicería.

Kill [kil], *s.* Riachuelo, arroyo, caleta; forma parte de muchos nombres geográficos en los Estados Unidos, como Peeks*kill,* Fish*kill.* (< Holan. kil.)

Killer [kil'-ẹr], *s.* Matador.

Kill-joy [kil'-joi], *s.* Aguafiestas.

Killow [kil'-o], *s.* Tierra gallinera o negruzca.

Kiln [kil], *s.* Horno, fábrica hecha en forma de bóveda que sirve para secar, quemar o calcinar alguna cosa. *Brick-kiln,* Ladrillera o ladrillal. *Lime-kiln,* Calera.

Kilo [kil'-ō]. Prefijo y abreviatura de *kilogram.*

Kilocalorie [kil'-o-cal''-o-ri], *s.* (Fís.) Kilocaloría.

Kilocycle [kil'-o-sai''-cl], *s.* (Elec. y Radio) Kilociclo.

Kilogram, Kilogramme [kil'-o-gram], *s.* Kilogramo, peso de mil gramos: = 2.204 libras.

Kiloliter [kil'-o-lī''-tẹr], *s.* Kilolitro, mil litros.

Kilometer [kil'-o-mī''-tẹr], *s.* Kilómetro, longitud de mil metros: = 0.621 o cinco octavas partes de una milla inglesa.

Kilometric [kil-o-met'-ric], *a.* Kilométrico.

Kiloton [ki'-lo-ton], *s.* Kilotonelada, kilotón.

Kilovolt [kil'-o-volt], *s.* (Elec.) Kilovoltio.

Kilowatt [kil'-o-wat], *s.* (Elec.) Kilovatio. *Kilowatt-hour,* Kilovatio-hora.

Kilt [kilt], *s.* Túnica corta que usan los montañeses de Escocia.

Kilter, Kelter [kil'-tẹr, kel'-tẹr], *s.* (Prov. E. U. e Ingl.) Estado propio para trabajar; buena condición.

Kimono [ki-mō'-no], *s.* Quimono, túnica japonesa.

Kin [kin], *s.* 1. Parentesco, vínculo, conexión. 2. Parientes, los que son de la misma familia o linaje. 3. Género, especie, clase. *They are all of a kin,* Son todos de una misma especie, son lobos de una camada. 4. Terminación diminutiva, como *manikin,* Hombrezuelo. *Next of kin,* Pariente próximo, el primero en el orden de parentesco.—*a.* Congenial; de la misma naturaleza.

Kind [kaind], *a.* Benévolo, benigno, bondadoso, benéfico, favorable, afable, cariñoso. *She is very kind to me,* Me trata con mucho cariño o es muy cariñosa conmigo. *You are very kind,* Vd. tiene mucha bondad, o Vd. me trata con sobrada bondad. *Kind-hearted,* Benévolo.—*s.* 1. Género, especie, clase. 2. Naturaleza, la esencia y propio ser de cada cosa. 3. Modo, manera; especie, calidad. *In such a kind,* De tal suerte, de tal manera. *This kind of men,* Este linaje de hombres. *The human kind,* El género humano. *A different kind of plant,* Una planta de especie diferente. *A kind reception*, Una acogida favorable, bondadosa. *Kind-hearted*, Dotado de buen corazón. *Kind-heartedness*, Bondad de corazón. *Kind of*, (Fam. E. U.) Algo; de un modo, como si.

Kindergarten [kin'-dẹr-gār"-tn], *s.* Jardín infantil, escuela de niños del sistema Froebel. (Alemán.)

Kindle [kin'-dl], *va.* 1. Encender, hacer que una cosa se inflame y arda. 2. Inflamar, enardecer y avivar a uno. 3. (Des. ó Prov. Ingl.) Parir; se dice sólo de la liebre y algunos otros animales.—*vn.* Arder, quemarse alguna cosa levantando llama.

Kindler [kin'-dlẹr], *s.* Incendiario; incitador, agitador; el que fomenta disturbios ó revoluciones.

Kindliness [kaind'-li-nes], *s.* Favor, benevolencia; índole; curso natural de las estaciones, etc.

Kindling wood [kin'-dling wud], *s.* Leña fácilmente inflamable.

Kindly [kaind'-li], *adv.* Benignamente, naturalmente, propiamente.—*a.* 1. Benigno, cariñoso, suave, tratable. 2. Beneficioso, provechoso. 3. (Ant.) Natural, idóneo, propio.

Kindness [kaind'-nes], *s.* 1. Benevolencia, beneficencia, buena voluntad, cariño, afecto, humanidad. 2. Favor, gracia, beneficio, atención, fineza.

Kindred [kin'-dred], *s.* 1. Parentesco, conexión por consanguinidad o afinidad. 2. Parentela, casta.—*a.* Emparentado, el que tiene parentesco con otro. *The stirrups are of no kindred*, Los estribos no son parejos.

Kine [kain], *s.* Antiguo plural de *cow.* Vacas.

Kinematics [kin-ẹ-mat'-ics], *s.* (Fís.) Cinemática, parte de la mecánica que trata del movimiento sin considerar las fuerzas que lo producen.

Kinescope [kai'-ne-scōp], *s.* Cinescopio, kinoscopio.

Kinetic [ki-net'-ic], *a.* Cinético. *Kinetic energy*, Energía cinética.

Kinetics [ki-net'-ics], *s.* Dinámica, ciencia que trata de las fuerzas que dan movimiento a los cuerpos o lo modifican.

King [king], *s.* 1. Rey, el soberano o monarca de un reino. *God save the king*, Dios guarde al rey. 2. Rey, la carta o naipe que tiene figura de rey. *King's yellow*, Color amarillo hecho de oropimente.

King, en composición: *King-bolt*, Perno pinzote, perno real. *King-crab*, Límulo, animal crustáceo. *King-cup*, (Bot.) Botón de oro, especie de ranúnculo. *King James' version* o *Bible*, *V.* VERSION. *King-pin*, (1) *V.* KING-BOLT. (2) En el juego de bolos, el que se coloca delante de los otros. (3) (Fam. E. U.) Persona de gran importancia.

King, *va.* 1. Dar un rey al reino que no le tenía: se usa casi siempre en sentido jocoso. 2. Elevar a alguno a la dignidad real. 3. Coronar un peón haciéndole dama, en el juego de las damas.

King-bird [king'-bẹrd], *s.* (Orn.) Tirano, muscícapa. Tyrannus tyrannus.

Kingcraft [king'-craft], *s.* Arte de gobernar, arte de reinar o mandar como rey.

Kingdom [king'-dum], *s.* 1. Reino, los territorios o dominios sujetos a un rey. 2. Reino, la clase u orden diferente de seres o cosas, especialmente en la historia natural. 3. Región, una extensión cualquiera de tierra.

Kingfisher [king'-fish-ẹr], *s.* Alción, íspida o martín pescador.

Kinghood [king'-hud], *s.* Soberanía, estado, oficio o dignidad de rey.

Kinglet [king'-let], *s.* 1. Reyezuelo, rey insignificante. 2. (Orn.) Abadejo, régulo.

Kinglike [king'-laic], **Kingly** [king'-li], *a.* 1. Real, soberano, monárquico. 2. Regio, noble, augusto, pomposo, majestuoso.

Kingly, *adv.* Majestuosamente, con majestad.

Kingpin [king'-pin], *s.* 1. En el juego de bolos, el bolo central. 2. (fam.) Cabeza de un grupo o empresa. 3. Pivote.

Kingship [king'-ship], *s.* Majestad, la dignidad real, y por metáfora el trono o cetro: monarquía.

King-size [king'-saiz], *a.* De tamaño grande. (Aplícase generalmente a cigarrillos.)

Kingspear [king'-spīr], *s.* (Bot.) Gamón.

Kink [kiṇk], *s.* 1. Torcedura, vuelta que forma un cabo o un hilo de metal al desdoblarse; ojal, coca. 2. (Fam. E. U.) Capricho infundado.

Kink, *va.* y *vn.* 1. Formar cocas, como una soga. 2. Torcerse, enredarse.

Kinky [kiṇk'-i], *a.* 1. Que tiende a formar cocas u ojales. 2. Que tiene cocas u ojales; pasudo; dícese de la lana y de los cabellos lanosos.

Kinkhaust [kiṇc'-hōst], *s.* Tos violenta.

Kino [kai'-no o kī'-no], *s.* Quino, un extracto vegetal que se usa en la medicina como astringente.

Kinsfolk [kinz'-fōc], *s.* Parentela, parientes.

Kinsman [kinz -man], *s.* Pariente, el que es de la misma familia que otro.

Kinswoman [kinz'-wum-an], *sf.* Parienta.

Kiosk [ki-esk'], *s.* Kiosco, pequeño pabellón de gusto oriental abierto por todos lados a manera de mirador. (Palabra turca.)

Kip [kip], *s.* Pellejo no curtido de un ternero, o del ganado vacuno de talla menos que mediana. *Kip-leather*, *kip-skin*, Becerro, pellejo curtido de dichos animales.

Kipper [kip'-ẹr], *a.* Término aplicado a los salmones cuando están desovando o poco después del tiempo del desove.

Kirk [kẹrk], *s.* Iglesia: úsase en Escocia.

Kirtle [kẹr'-tl], *s.* Manto, capa; chupa larga.

Kismet [kis'-met], *s.* Hado, destino. (Tur. < Arab, qismat.)

Kiss [kis], *va.* 1. Besar. 2. Acariciar, hacer caricias y halagos. 3. Besar, tocar suavemente, rozar. 4. Retrucar, hacer retruque en el juego de billar.

Kiss, *s.* 1. Beso, ósculo. 2. Toque o rozamiento suaves. 3. Merengue, dulce. 4. Retruco, retruque, en el juego de billar.

Kisser [kis'-ẹr], *s.* Besucador, besador, amigo de besar.

Kissing-crust [kis'-ing-crust], *s.* Beso, la parte del pan que se tocó con otro al cocerse en el horno.

Kist, *s.* (Ingl. del Norte y Esco.) Cofrecillo, caja.

Kit [kit], *s.* 1. Vasija para salmón o caballa; colodra, como para mantequilla. 2. Violín pequeño de tres cuerdas. 3. Aparejo, apresto, conjunto de artículos y herramientas para un fin particular. 4. (Foto.) Marquito, un marco interior para sostener una placa más pequeña que la que corresponde al marco.

Kitcat [kit'-cat], *a.* 1. Término que se aplica a una tertulia o junta de personas que hablan de política, y a los retratos de poco menos de medio cuerpo. 2. *Kitcat* o *kitcat-roll*, Rodillo para las tierras de labranza, formado por dos conos unidos por sus bases.

Kitchen [kich'-en], *s.* Cocina. *Kitchen furniture* o *utensils*, El ajuar de la cocina, que también se dice batería; el cobre o la espetera, cuando las piezas son de cobre o hierro. *Kitchen-garden*, Huerta, el sitio o paraje donde se plantan hortalizas y legumbres. *Kitchen-maid*, Criada que sirve en la cocina y ayuda a la cocinera. *Kitchen-stuff*, (1) Material de cocina; también, hierbas de cocina, legumbres. (2) Grasa, la manteca o pringue que da de sí la carne cocida o asada. *Kitchen-wench*, Fregona, fregatriz.

Kitchenette [kitch-en-et'], *s.* Cocina pequeña que se combina con el comedor y la despensa. *Kitchenette apartment*, Pequeño departamento en que una cocina diminuta se combina con el resto de la habitación.

Kitchen police [kitch'-en po-līs'], *s.* (Mil.) 1. Trabajo de cocina en un campamento. 2. Soldados ayudantes de cocina.

Kitchen range [kitch'-en rênj], *s.* Estufa, cocina económica.

Kite [kait], *s.* 1. Milano, ave de rapiña. 2. Cometa, (prov.) barrilete, (Cuba) papalote, armazón de papel y cañas que echan a volar los muchachos por diversión. 3. (Mar.) Sobrejuanete, foque volante. *Kite-flying*, (1) Acción de remontar una cometa. (2) (Ger.) Acción de poner en circulación pagarés sin valor.

Kith [kith], *s.* Los conocidos o amigos de alguien; sólo se usa en la locución *kith and kin*, parientes y amigos.

Kitten [kit'-n], **Kitling** [kit'-ling], *s.* Gatito, gatico.

Kitten, *vn.* Parir las gatas.

Kitty [kit'-i], *s.* Gatito; voz de que se usa para llamar al gato, como miz y minino.

Kleptomania [klep-to-mé'-ni-a], *s.* Cleptomanía, aberración mental que se manifiesta por una tendencia irresistible al robo.

Kleptomaniac [klep-to-mê'-ni-ac], *s.* Cleptómano.

Klick [clic], *v.* y *s.* *V.* CLICK.

Knack [nac], *s.* 1. Maña, destreza, habilidad, prontitud, gracia, arte para ejecutar alguna cosa; treta astuta. 2. Costumbre, hábito, uso. *To get the knack*, Dar en la tecla. *To have a knack for*, Tener el don de.

Knack, *vn.* 1. Crujir, estallar, rechinar. 2. Hablar culto o con afectación; antiguamente, cultiparlar.

Knaggy [nag'-i], *a.* Nudoso; áspero.

Knap [nap], *s.* (Des. o prov. Ingl.) Bulto que sobresale en alguna parte del cuerpo; cerro, montecillo, cumbre; cualquier eminencia pequeña que sobresale en una cosa llana.

Knap, *va.* (Ant.) 1. Morder, romper con los dientes. 2. Golpear alguna cosa haciendo ruido.—*vn.* Crujir, estallar, rechinar; chasquear o dar chasquidos la madera.

Knapsack [nap'-sac], *s.* Mochila, la talega en que los soldados llevan su ropa y algunas provisiones.

Knapweed [nap'-wîd], *s.* (Bot.) Cabezuela; varias especies de centáurea.

Knave [nêv], *s.* 1. Bribón, pícaro, bellaco. 2. La sota de los naipes castellanos. 3. †(Ant.) Muchacho; criado; siervo.

Knavery [nêv'-ẹr-i], *s.* 1. Picardía, bellaquería, bribonada. 2. Travesura.

Knavish [nêv'-ish], *a.* 1. Fraudulento, malicioso, ratero, pícaro. 2. Travieso.

Knavishly [nêv'-ish-li], *adv.* Fraudulentamente, picaramente. *To look knavishly,* Tener cara de ahorcado.

Knavishness [nêv'-ish-nes], *s.* El estado o la calidad que constituye a uno pícaro, ratero o travieso.

†**Knaw,** *v.* *V.* GNAW.

Knead [nîd], *va.* Amasar, formar o hacer una masa, como la del pan.

Kneader [nîd'-ẹr], *s.* Panadero, amasador.

Kneading [nîd'-ing], *s.* Amasadura, acción de amasar. *Kneading-trough* [trōf], Amasadera, la artesa en que se amasa.

Knee [nî], *s.* 1. Rodilla, la parte de la pierna que la une con el muslo. 2. (Mar.) Curva, pieza de madera ó de metal que por la parte exterior forma un ángulo y por la interior una línea curva. *Knee of the head,* (Mar.) Curva capuchina. *Upper part of the knee,* (Mar.) Brazo superior de la curva. *Hanging knees,* (Mar.) Curvas de peralto o de abajo. *Lodging-knees,* (Mar.) Curvas valonas. *Helmport-knees,* (Mar.) Curvas del contrayugo. *Wing-transom-knees,* (Mar.) Curvas del yugo principal. *Deck-transom-knees,* (Mar.) Curvas de la cubierta. *Small-knees,* (Mar.) Curvatones. *Knee-crooking,* Obsequioso. *Knee-deep,* Metido hasta las rodillas, subido hasta las rodillas. *Knee-high,* Hasta la rodilla. *Knee-high to a grasshopper,* (Fest. E. U.) Muy corto, muy pequeño. *Knee-joint,* (1) Juntura, articulación de la rodilla. (2) (Art. y Of.) Codo, ángulo, escuadra. (3) Junta de codillo. *Knee-jointed,* Encorvado o angular como la rodilla. *Knee-timber,* Madera a propósito para hacer piezas curvas o rodillas. *Knee-tribute,* Genuflexión, la acción de ponerse de rodillas para mostrar obediencia o respeto.

Knee, *va.* Suplicar algo de rodillas. —*vn.* Arrodillarse para pedir.

Kneecap [nî'-cap], *s.* Rótula, choquezuela.

†**Kneeholly** [nî'-hol-i], **Kneeholm** [nî'-hōlm], *s.* (Bot.) Brusco.

Kneel [nîl], *vn.* Arrodillarse, hincar la rodilla, hincarse de rodillas, ponerse de hinojos.

Kneeler [nîl'-ẹr], *s.* El que se arrodilla.

Kneepan [nî'-pan], *s.* (Anat.) Rótula o choquezuela, el hueso en la parte anterior de la articulación de la tibia con el fémur. *V.* PATELLA.

Knell [nel], *s.* Doble, tañido fúnebre, el sonido de las campanas cuando tocan a muerto; de aquí, mal agüero.

Knell, *va.* y *vn.* 1. (Poét.) Doblar, tocar las campanas a muerto; convocar por medio de ese toque. 2. Dar un sonido lúgubre, o un toque de aviso.

Knew [niū], *pret.* de *To* KNOW.

Knickerbocker [nik'-ẹr-bek'-ẹr], *s.* 1. Descendiente de una de las primeras familias holandesas que se establecieron en Nueva York, E.U. 2. *Knickers, knickerbockers,* Calzón corto y ancho, ceñido debajo de la rodilla, que antiguamente llevaban los muchachos y los ciclistas.

Knickers [nik'-ẹrz], *s. pl.* V. KNICKERBOCKER, *pl.*

Knick-knack [nic'-nac], *s.* (Fam.) Bujería, juguete.

Knife [naif], *s.* (*pl.* KNIVES [naivz]). 1. Cuchillo, cuchilla, navaja. *Carving-knife,* Trinchante, cuchillo de trinchar. *Chopping-knife,* Cuchilla de carnicero. *Clasp-knife,* Cuchillo grande que se cierra; cuchillo de caza. *Pocket-knife,* Navaja. *Table-knife,* Cuchillo de mesa. *Dessert-knife,* Cuchillo de postre. *Pruning-knife,* Podadera. *Pen-knife,* Cortaplumas. *Shoemaker's paring-knife,* Trinchete de zapatero. *Flemish knife,* Navaja flamenca. 2. Puñal, espada. 3. Cuchilla, hoja de cuchillo que forma parte de una herramienta o de una máquina.

Knife, *va.* (Ger.) 1. Cortar o matar con un cuchillo. 2. (E. U. Fig.) Deshacer o arruinar por medio de oposición secreta.

Knight [nait], *s.* 1. Caballero; campeón. *Knight of the Order of the Garter,* Caballero de la orden de la jarretera. *Knight-errant,* Caballero andante. *Knight of the shire,* Diputado por un condado en el parlamento inglés. 2. Caballo, pieza del juego del ajedrez. *Knight of St. Crispin,* Zapatero. *Knight of the shears,* (Fest.) Sastre.

Knight, *va.* Crear o hacer a uno caballero; armar caballero.

Knight-errantry [nait-er'-ant-ri], *s.* Caballería andante.

Knighthead [nait'-hed], *s.* (Mar.) Tragante exterior del bauprés. *Knighthead of the windlass,* (Mar.) Cepos o bitas del molinete. *Knightheads of the gears,* (Mar.) Guindastes.

Knighthood [nait'-hud], *s.* Caballería, la dignidad de caballero; honor o grado de nobleza concedido para recompensar un mérito.

Knightly [nait'-li], *a.* Propio o digno de caballero.—*adv.* Caballerosamente, caballerescamente.

Knit [nit], *va.* y *vn.* 1. Enlazar, unir, entretejer; trabajar a punto de aguja; hilar, hacer malla. *To knit stockings,* Hacer media o calceta con agujas. 2. Atar, juntar, anudar, unir; unirse. *The bones knit,* Los huesos se unen. 3. Contraer. 4. Entretejer o tejer con las manos. *To knit the eyebrows,* Fruncir las cejas.

Knit, *s.* Tejido o tela hecha a mano. *Knit stockings,* Medias de punto.

Knittable [nit'-a-bl], *a.* Capaz de ser tejido, unido o atado.

Knitter [nit'-ẹr], *s.* Calcetero, mediero.

Knitting [nit'-ing], *s.* 1. Unión, junta. 2. Acción u ocupación de hacer calceta; trabajo de punto. *Knitting-machine,* Máquina para hacer calceta. *Knitting-needle* [nî'-dl], Aguja de hacer medias de punto. *Knitting-work,* Trabajo de punto.

Knittle [nit'-l], *s.* 1. (Mar.) Sardineta. 2. Cordoncillo de bolsa.

Knives [naivz], *s. pl.* de KNIFE.

Knob [neb], *s.* 1. Prominencia, bulto o eminencia que sobresale en alguna cosa; nudo en la madera. 2. Borlita o borlilla que está unida a una cosa para adornarla. 3. Perilla, botón. 4. Manecilla o bola para tirar de una puerta y cerrarla, botón, gorrón. 5. (Arq.) Abollón.

Knobbed [nebd], *a.* Lo que tiene bultos o eminencias.

Knobbiness [neb'-i-nes], *s.* Calidad de lo que tiene bultos.

Knobby [neb'-i], *a.* 1. Lleno de bultos, lleno de nudos. 2. Obstinado, terco.

Knock [nek], *va.* y *vn.* 1. Chocar, encontrarse, tropezar una cosa con otra. 2. Golpear, tocar, llamar a una puerta. *V. To* RAP. 3. Golpear, dar o pegar golpes. 4. Pegar, dar con una cosa contra otra causando estallido o ruido; aporrear, macear. *To knock down,* Derribar, echar por tierra de un golpe. *To knock down to the highest bidder,* Rematar al mejor postor. *To knock in,* Martillar o amartillar; hacer entrar en una parte alguna persona o cosa a fuerza de golpes. *To knock off,* (1) Hacer saltar una cosa a fuerza de golpes. (2) Cesar, descontinuar, suspender el trabajo. (3) (Fam.) Hacer o ejecutar prontamente. (4) Rebajar, descontar. *To knock on the head,* (1) Romper la cabeza; matar de un golpe. (2) Frustrar, hacer ineficaz. *To knock out,* Hacer salir a fuerza de golpes; acogotar, hacer caer a uno desvanecido de un golpe en el cuello, como sucede a veces en las luchas de púgiles; de aquí, vencer completamente. *To knock together,* Construir algo toscamente o de prisa. *To knock under,* Someterse, rendirse. *To knock up,* (1) Hacer levantar a uno a golpes. (2) Cansar en extremo, extenuar con el excesivo trabajo.

Knock, *s.* Choque, golpe; llamada.

Knocker [nek'-ẹr], *s.* 1. Golpeador. 2. El que cae al suelo de un golpe. 3. Llamador, la aldaba o el aldabón con que se llamaba a las puertas y en lugar del cual se usa hoy el timbre o campanilla.

Knocking [nek'-ing], *s.* Aldabazo, aldabonazo, toque de puerta; el acto de tocar o llamar a la puerta.

Knock-kneed [nek'-nîd], *a.* Patizambo.

Knockout [nek'-aut], *s.* 1. Golpe decisivo en una pelea. 2. (fam.) Persona o cosa sumamente atractiva.

Knoll [nōl], *va.* Doblar, tocar las campanas a muerto.—*vn.* Sonar como campana.

Knoll, *s.* 1. Colina o montecillo redondeado; también, cumbre o cima de una colina. 2. El doblar de las campanas.

Knop, *s.* 1. (Ant.) *V.* KNOB. 2. (Arq.) Florón, ramo de flores hecho de realce.

Knot[1] [net], *s.* 1. Nudo, atadura o ligadura que se hace en cualquier hilo, cuerda o cinta. 2. Lazo, cualquier figura cuyas líneas se cruzan mutuamente. 3. Nudo, vínculo, lazo, del matrimonio, de la amistad, etc. 4. Nudo de la madera o de los árboles y plantas. 5. Enredo, maraña, en las composiciones dramáticas, antiguamente nudo. 6. Confusión, embrollo, dificultad, intriga. 7. Asociación, confederación, colección, reunión. 8. Nudo, el punto más arduo y embarazoso de una cosa. 9. Milla náutica. *To sail twelve knots an hour*, Correr doce millas por hora. *Knots of the log-line*, Señales de la corredera. 10. *V.* SHOULDER-KNOT. *Hard knot*, Nudo apretado. *Loose knot*, Nudo flojo. *Running knot, slip-knot*, Nudo corredizo.

Knot,[2] *s.* Canuto, tríngido, ave de la familia de lasescolopácidas. Tringa canutus.

Knot, *va.* Anudar, enredar, juntar; intrincar, unir.—*vn.* 1. Hechar nudos las plantas. 2. Hacer nudos para adornar los vestidos.

Knotgrass [net'-gras], *s.* 1. Centinodia. Polyganum aviculare. 2. Polígono. 3. Grama, trigo rastrero.

Knothole [net'-hōl], *s.* Hoyo correspondiente a un nudo de la madera.

Knotless [net'-les], *a.* Sin nudos.

Knotted [net'-ed], *a.* Lleno de lazos; nudoso.

Knottiness [net'-i-nes], *s.* Abundancia de nudos; desigualdad; dificultad; bulto.

Knotty [net'-i], *a.* Nudoso; duro, áspero; intrincado, difícil.

Knout [naut], *s.* Instrumento de suplicio usado antes en Rusia, azote hecho de correas de cuero, trenzadas a menudo con alambres.

Know [nō], *va.* 1. Conocer. saber. 2. Distinguir, discernir. 3. Reconocer, hacerse cargo, caer en algo. 4. Saber, no ignorar, estar familiarizado con, estar al corriente de. 5. (Ant.) Conocer carnalmente, tener acto carnal con persona de otro sexo. *To know how many black beans make five*, (prov.) Saber cuántas son cinco.—*vn.* 1. Comprender, conocer, saber de cierto; tener noticia de alguna cosa; estar informado, informarse. 2. Tomar nota de; obtener experiencia o instrucción.

Knowable [nō'-a-bl], *a.* Conocible.

Knower [nō'-ẹr], *s.* Sabio, el que tiene sabiduría; conocedor, el que tiene mucho conocimiento.

Know-how [nō'-hau], *s.* Capacidad, habilidad.

Knowing [nō'-ing], *a.* Instruído, inteligente, hábil, entendido; diestro.—*s.* Conocimiento, inteligencia. *A thing worth knowing*, Una cosa digna de saberse.

Knowingly [nō'-ing-li], *adv.* Hábilmente; a sabiendas, de intento, adrede, a proposito.

Know-it-all [nō'-it-ōl], *s.* (Fam.) Sábelotodo.

Knowledge [nel'-ej], *s.* 1. Conocimiento, erudición, ciencia, saber, instrucción, noticia. 2. Inteligencia, destreza, habilidad, experiencia práctica de alguna cosa. *Not to my knowledge*, No que yo sepa. *Carnal knowledge*, Acto carnal. *Without his knowledge*, Sin su conocimiento, sin saberlo. *To the best of my knowledge*, Según mi leal saber y entender. *To our knowledge*, Que sepamos.

Known [nōn], *pp.* de *To* KNOW. Conocido, sabido, reconocido, comprendido. *To make known*, Hacer saber, declarar, participar. *As is well known*, Como es bien sabido, como ya se sabe.

Knuckle [nuc'-l], *s.* 1. Nudillo, artejo, juntura de los dedos. 2. Jarrete de ternero. 3. Juntura o articulación de las plantas.

Knuckle, *vn.* Someterse, rendirse; abandonar la partida.

Knuckled [nuc'-ld], *a.* Nudoso; lo que tiene articulaciones.

Knur [nūr], **Knurl** [nūrl], *s.* 1. Nudo, protuberancia. 2. Substancia dura.

Knurled [nūrld], †**Knurry** [nūr'-i], *a.* Nudoso. lleno de nudos.

Kodak [Kódæk], *s.* (foto.) Marca de fábrica. Se aplica a cámaras portátil para instantáneas y a otros productos.—*va.* (foto.) sacar una instantánea.

Koran [kō-rān' o cō'-ran], *s.* Alcorán o Corán, el libro sagrado de los mahometanos.

Kosher [kō'-shẹr], *a.* 1. Autorizado para los judíos. (Aplícase a alimentos.) 2. (fam.) Genuino, legítimo, correcto.

Kotow [kō-tau'], *s.* Reverencia que hacen los chinos hincándose de rodillas y tocando el suelo con la frente.—*vn.* Hacer esa clase de reverencia.

Kraal [krāl], *s.* 1. Población de hotentotes en el sur de África; reunión de barracas. 2. Corral, redil.

Kraft, Kraft paper [kraft pê'-pẹr], *s.* Papel de estraza, papel basto de envolver.

Kremlin [krem'-lin], *s.* Kremlín, fortaleza de una ciudad rusa; en especial, la de Moscow.

Kumiss o **Koomiss** [kū'-mis], *s.* Caracosmos, leche fermentada de yegua, que beben los calmucos; o una bebida ligeramente alcohólica hecha en los países occidentales con leche de vaca, azúcar y levadura. Kumys.

Kyanize, Kyanise [kai'-an-aiz], *va.* Impedir que se pudra la madera dándole un baño de sublimado corrosivo. (< Kyan, inventor del procedimiento.)

Ky, Kye, Kie [kai], *s. pl.* (Esco.) Vacas.

L

LA pronunciación de la *l* es la misma que en castellano, excepto cuando está seguida de *f*, *k* o *m*, pues entonces no se pronuncia; v. g. *palm* [pām]. En las voces monosílabas se duplica al fin, como en *wall*, *mill*, si la *l* no está después de un diptongo, pues en este caso no se duplica.—La *L*, como abreviatura, quiere decir libra esterlina; y también 50 como número romano. *LL. B.* o *D.*, Bachiller o Doctor en ambos derechos.

La [lā], *s.* La, sexta voz de la escala música en el solfeo.

La [lō], *inter.* (Des. o bajo) He aquí, ved aquí, mirad, pues, ya; sí; ya se ve; ¡vamos!

Labarum [lab'-a-rum], *s.* Lábaro, el estandarte imperial en que Constantino hizo poner la cruz, y la cifra del nombre de N. S. Jesucristo.

Labdanum [lab'-da-num], *s.* Ládano. *V.* LADANUM.

Labefaction [lab-ẹ-fac'-shun], *s.* Decadencia, decaimiento; enflaquecimiento; declinación.

Label [lê'-bel], *s.* 1. Marbete, pedacito de papel pegado al extremo de las piezas de tela o paño en el que está escrito el número de varas que tiene la pieza, etc.; rótulo, rotulata, membrete, letrero. 2. El pedazo de papel y a veces de pergamino pegado a un escrito, que contiene comúnmente el sello.

Label, *va.* Rotular o señalar alguna cosa con un rótulo que exprese lo que contiene, su dueño, etc.; de aquí, designar, clasificar.

Labellum [la-bel'-um], *s.* 1. (Bot.) Pétalo inferior, á menudo ensanchado o de varias figuras, de una flor orquídea. 2. (Ento.) Parte de la trompa o probóscide de un insecto díptero.

Labial [lê'-bi-al], *a.* 1. Labial, perteneciente a los labios; formado o modificado juntando los labios. 2. Que tiene labios o bordes, v. gr. un cañón de órgano.—*s.* 1. Letra labial, como p, b, v, w. 2. Cañón de órgano provisto de comisuras a manera de labios.

Labiate [lê'-bi-êt], *a.* (Bot.) Labiado, en forma de labios.—*s.* Cualquier planta de la familia de las labiadas, de corolas gamopétalas.

Labiated [lê'-bi-êt-ed], *a.* Dividido a modo de labios.

Labiodental [lê-bi-o-den'-tal], *a.* Labiodental, pronunciado por la cooperación de los labios y dientes.

Labium [lê'-bi-um], *s.* (*pl.* LABIA). Labio, o algo en forma de labio; labio inferior de los insectos, o labio de una flor.

Labor, Labour [lê'-bẹr], *s.* 1. Trabajo, labor, pena, fatiga. 2. Obra o trabajo que se tiene que hacer o está ya hecho. 3. Ejercicio, quehacer. 4. Dolores de parto. *His wife is in labor*, Su mujer está de parto. 5. Violento balanceo y cabeceo de un buque. *Hard labor*, Trabajo arduo, rudo; trabajo forzado en una prisión. *Labor-saving*, Que ahorra trabajo; propio para disminuir un trabajo. *To have one's labor for one's pains*, Trabajar en balde, trabajar para el Gran Turco.

Labor, *vn.* 1. Trabajar, afanarse, esforzarse. 2. Hacer algo con dificultad o mediante esfuerzo doloroso; (des.) tener algún mal o enfermedad. 3. Estar sufriendo agravios, injurias, persecuciones, etc. 4. Estar de parto. 5. (Mar.) Trabajar en mar y viento grandes.—*va.* 1. Elaborar, formar con trabajo y cuidado; pulir, perfeccionar. 2. Labrar, cultivar o arar la tierra. 3. Hacer trabajar, activar. 4. (Des.) Trabajar, zurrar, golpear, sacudir. *A ship that labors much*, Un buque que balancea mucho.

Laboratory [lab'-o-ra-to-ri], *s.* 1. Laboratorio, la oficina en que se hacen las operaciones químicas o farmacéuticas, los experimentos físicos, etc. 2. (Mil.) Taller en un arsenal donde se hacen cebos fulminantes, cartuchos, torpedos, etc.

Laborer [lê'-bẹr-ẹr], *s.* Peón, gañán, jornalero.

Laboring [lê'-bẹr-ing], *s.* Trabajo, esfuerzo. *A laboring beast*, Una bestia de carga.

Laborious [la-bō'-ri-us], *a.* Laborioso, trabajoso, penoso; difícil; diligente.

Laboriously [la-bō'-ri-us-li], *adv.* Laboriosamente.

Laboriousness [la-bō'-ri-us-nes], *s.* Laboriosidad, afán, trabajo, diligencia, aplicación; dificultad.

Laborsome, Laboursome [lê'-bẹr-sum], *a.* Trabajoso, penoso.

Labor union [lê'-bər yūn'-yʊn], *s.* Sindicato obrero.
Labour [lê'-bər], *s.* *V.* LABOR. Forma usual en Inglaterra, y lo mismo con sus derivados, *labourer*, etc.
Labra, *pl.* de LABRUM.
Labradorite [lab'-ra-dōr-ait], *s.* (Min.) Labradorita, feldespato laminar de color gris, translúcido, iridiscente, que entra en la composición de diferentes rocas.
Labrum [lê'-brʊm], *s.* (Zool.) Labro, labio exterior o superior (de los insectos). (Plural, LABRA o LABRUMS.)
Laburnum [la-bōr'-nʊm], *s.* (Bot.) Codeso o ébano de los Alpes. Cytisus laburnum.
Labyrinth [lab'-i-rinth], *s.* 1. Laberinto. 2. (Anat.) Laberinto, los canales sinuosos del oído interno.
Labyrinthian [lab-i-rinth'-i-an], *a.* 1. Lo perteneciente al laberinto. 2. Intrincado, confuso, enmarañado.
Lac [lac], *s.* 1. Laca, especie de resina dura, encarnada, transparente y quebradiza, que sirve para teñir de escarlata y para hacer lacre y barnices. *Stick, seed* o *shell lac*, Laca en palillos, en granos o en tablillas. 2. *V.* LACQUER.
Lac, Lakh [lak], *s.* 1. La suma de (100,000) cien mil; por sí solo, cien mil rupias. 2. Gran número o multitud.
Lace [lês], *s.* 1. Encaje, randa, pasamano, galón de oro o plata. 2. Cuerda, cordón, cinta. 3. (Des.) Lazo, trampa. *Black silk lace*, Blonda negra. *Thread-lace*, Encaje de hilo, puntas de hilo. *Twisted* o *plaited laces*, Cordones, torzales. *Lace-pillow*, Almohadilla para hacer encajes. *Point-lace*, Punta; encaje de origen italiano, costoso, y hecho completamente a mano, con aguja.
Lace, *va.* 1. Abrochar, cerrar, unir y afianzar los vestidos u otra cosa con lazos o cordones; atar; encordonar, enlazar. 2. Galonear, guarnecer y adornar los vestidos con galones. 3. *V.* INTERLACE. 4. Rayar con líneas muy finas. 5. (Fam.) *V. To* LASH. *Lace-frame*, Telar para encajes. *Lace-woman*, Vendedora de encajes, randas, etc.; pasamanera. *Lace-man*, Pasamanero, el que trata en encajes, galones, randas, etc. *Lace-winged*, Provisto de alas como de gasa o encaje.
Laced [lêst], *a.* y *pp.* Atado con un lazo o cordón.
Lacedæmonian [las-e-de-mō'-ni-an], *a.* Lacedemonio, de Esparta.
Lacerable [las'-er-a-bl], *a.* Que se puede lacerar.
Lacerate [las'-er-êt], *va.* Lacerar, rasgar, despedazar, hacer pedazos; lastimar.
Laceration [las-er-ê'-shun], *s.* Laceración, desgarradura, desgarrón, rasgón.
Lacertian [la-ser'-shan], *a.* Lacertídeo, parecido a un lagarto.—*s.* Lagarto, lacerto, reptil terrestre.
Lacewing [lês'-wing], *s.* Crisopo, insecto neuróptero, con alas transparentes y como de encaje; a sus larvas se les da el nombre de *aphis-lions* (leones, comedores de pulgones).
Lachrymal [lac'-ri-mal], *a.* Lacrimal. *V.* LACRIMAL.
Lachrymary, etc. *V.* LACRIMARY, etc.
Lachrymose [lac'-ri-mōs], *a.* Lacrimoso.
Lacing [lê'-sing], *s.* 1. Enlace, enlazamiento, la acción de enlazar o atar con un lazo; en particular el uso de corsés. 2. Cordón, cordoncillo, cuerda para atar alguna cosa. 3. Algo que enlaza o refuerza, pieza de espaldar, como una curva de barco. 4. (Fam.) Zurra, tunda.
Laciniate [la-sin'-i-êt], *a.* Serrado, dentado.
Lack [lac], *va.* y *vn.* Carecer, necesitar, tener o padecer falta de alguna cosa, estar o hallarse necesitado, faltar algo.
Lack, *s.* Falta, menester, carencia o necesidad de alguna cosa.
Lackadaisical [lac-a-dê'-zi-cal], *a.* Sentimental, pensativo con afectación, lánguido.
Lack-a-day [lac'-a-dê], *inter.* ¡Mal día! ¡día aciago! exclamación de dolor, con la cual se expresa que el día en que ha sucedido una cosa, ha sido de mala ventura.
Lackbrain [lac'-brên], *s.* Un tonto, una persona falta de entendimiento.
Lacker [lak'-er], *s.* 1. El que hace falta. 2. *V.* LACQUER.
Lacker, *va.* Barnizar.
Lackey [lak'-i], *s.* Lacayo.
Lackey, *va.* Servir como criado; servir bajamente a alguna persona en cualquier negocio.—*vn.* Ser criado de alguno, andar en torno de una persona por interés.
Lacklinen [lac'-lin-en], *a.* Descamisado, falto de camisa.
Lacklove [lac'-luv], *s.* Desamorado.
Lackluster [lac'-lus-ter], *a.* Deslustrado, falto de brillo.
Laconic, Laconical [la-con'-ic, al], *a.* Lacónico, breve, conciso, compendioso.
Laconically [la-con'-ic-al-i], *adv.* Lacónicamente, en breve.
Laconism [lac'-o-nizm], *s.* Laconismo, estilo lacónico.
Lacquer [lak'-er], *va.* Barnizar; dar una capa de laca.—*s.* 1. Barniz hecho desleyendo laca en hojuelas en alcohol. 2. *Lacquer* o *lacquer-work*, Construcción de madera, particularmente china o japonesa, pulida con barniz duro y brillante y a menudo incrustada con oro, plata, marfil, etc.
Lacquer, *s.* Laca. *Lacquer red*, Rojo lacre.—*va.* Barnizar, dar una capa de laca.
Lacquering [lak'-er-ing], *s.* 1. Arte o acción de barnizar con laca. 2. Adorno de barniz abrillantado; capa de barniz de laca.
Lacrimal [lac'-ri-mal], *a.* Lacrimal. —*s.* Hueso lacrimal.
Lacrimary [lac'-ri-me-ri], *a.* Que contiene lágrimas o está destinado a contenerlas.
Lacrimation, Lachrymation [lac-ri-mê'-shun], *s.* Efusión o derramamiento de lágrimas, antiguamente lacrimación.
Lacrimatory [lac'-ri-ma-to-ri], *s.* Lacrimatorio, vaso en que los antiguos recogían las lágrimas que vertían por los difuntos.
Lacrimose, Lachrymose [lac'-ri-mōs], *a.* Llorón, lloroso, plañidero; que hace llorar.
Lacrosse [la-cres'], *s.* Cierto juego de pelota de origen indio, común en el Canadá; se juega con una especie de raqueta.
§**Lactage** [lac'-têj], *s.* La cantidad de leche que dan los animales.
Lactary [lac'-ta-ri], *a.* Lácteo, lactario.—*s.* Lechería.
Lactate [lac'-têt], *s.* Lactato, sal formada de ácido láctico con alguna base.
Lactation [lac-te'-shun], *s.* 1. Lactancia, acción de mamar, y el tiempo que dura la lactancia; lactación. 2. Secreción de la leche.
Lacteal [lac'-te-al], *a.* 1. Lácteo, lo que es de leche o tiene sus propiedades. 2. Quilífero, lo que lleva el quilo o lo conduce; aplícase a los vasos linfáticos de los intestinos.
Lacteous [lac'-te-us], *a.* Lácteo.
Lactescence [lac-tes'-ens], *s.* Semejanza con la leche.
Lactescent [lac-tes'-ent], *a.* Lácteo, lactario, lo que es semejante a la leche.
Lactic [lac'-tic], *a.* Lácteo, perteneciente a la leche. *Lactic acid*, (Quím.) Acido láctico.
Lactiferous [lac-tif'-er-us], *a.* Lactífero, lo que da o tiene leche.
Lactometer [lac-tem'-e-ter], *s.* Lactómetro, galactómetro, probeta graduada para determinar la calidad de la leche.
Lactose [lac'-tōs], *s.* Lactosa, azúcar de la leche.
Lacuna [la-kiū'-na], *s.* (*pl* LACUNÆ). 1. Laguna, blanco, claro, falta (en un texto); abertura, espacio que carece de algo. 2. Hoyo o hueco pequeño; pequeña abertura, como en los huesos y en los vegetales.
Lacunar, Lacunal [la-kiū'-nar, nal], *a.* Que tiene lagunas u hoyos, o les pertenece.
Lacunar, *s.* (Arq.) Lagunar, artesonado.
Lacustrine, Lacustral [la-cus'-trin, tral], *a.* 1. Lacustre, perteneciente a los lagos o pantanos. 2. Hallado en los lagos o que se cría en ellos.
Lad [lad], *s.* Mozo, joven, muchacho, mozalbete. *Come, my lads!* ¡Vamos, muchachos! ¡vamos, compañeros!
Ladanum [lad'-a-num], *a.* Ládano, resina de color obscuro que destila la jara. (Cistus ladaniferus o creticus).
Ladder [lad'-er], *s.* 1. Escala o escalera portátil. *Step of a ladder*, Peldaño de escalera. *Accommodation-ladder*, (Mar.) Escala real. *Quarter* o *poop ladder*, (Mar.) Escala de popa o de la toldilla. *Quarter-deck ladder*, (Mar.) Escala del alcázar. 2. Escalón, grado que se sube en dignidad o el paso que se adelanta en las aspiraciones o pretensiones de uno.
Lade [lêd], *s.* 1 Desaguadero, canal de desagüe. 2. Embocadero, desembocadero.
Lade [lêd], *va.* (*pp.* LADED ó LADEN). 1. Cargar, poner una cosa sobre otra; cargar un macho, un burro, etc. *V. To* LOAD. *Laden in bulk*, (Mar.) Buque cargado con cosas echadas á granel en la bodega. 2. Sacar agua; sacar, o echar en un líquido con un cucharón, un jarro, un cubo, etc.; vaciar; echar en.—*vn.* (Mar.) Hacer agua una embarcación, abrir agua.
Lading [lêd'-ing], *s.* Carga, cargamento, flete, cargazón. *Bill of lading*, Conocimiento, póliza.
Ladkin [lad'-kin], *s.* Jovencito, mozuelo.
Ladle [lê'-dl], *s.* 1. Cucharón, cuchara grande. *Pitch-ladle*, (Mar.) Cucharón de brea. 2. Álabe, una de las paletas cóncavas de que se compone el rodezno de los molinos

de agua. 3. Vertedor para achicar el agua de un bote. 4. (Art.) Cuchara, instrumento que sirve para sacar la carga de un cañón.

Ladle, *va.* Achicar, sacar, vaciar el agua u otro líquido con un cucharón.

Ladleful [lé'-dl-ful], *s.* Cucharada.

Lady [lé'-di], *sf.* Señora, señorita, dama. *Lady* es voz de tratamiento que se usa sólo delante de los nombres o apellidos, cuando la señora de quien se habla es mujer de un par de Inglaterra, de un *baronet*, de un caballero o de un hijo de par que tenga título, o cuando es hija de un duque, marqués o conde. Tomada en sentido absoluto, la voz *lady* se aplica a cualquier mujer bien educada, de buen porte. *The lady of the house*, El ama o la señora de la casa. *My lady*, Señora. *Lady love*, Dama. (Fam.) Querida, amante, cortejo. *Lady in waiting*, Dama de una reina o princesa. *Lady's-bower*, (Bot.) La especie británica de clemátide. *Lady's-finger*, El bizcocho llamado suspiro. *Lady's-mantle*, (Bot.) Alquímila, pie de león. *Lady's-slipper*, Zueco, planta orquídea, común en América; cualquier especie del género Cipripidio. *Lady's-smock*, (Bot.) Cardamina. *Lady's-tresses*, (Bot.) Planta orquídea; cualquier especie del género Spiranthus.

Lady-bird [lé'-di-bęrd], **Lady-bug** [lé'-di-bug], **Lady-cow** [lé'-di-cau], **Lady-fly** [lé'-di-flai], *s.* (Ento.) Coquito de San Antón, mariquita; coccinela, insecto coleóptero. Coccinella.

Lady-day [lé'-di-dé], *s.* El día de la Anunciación de Nuestra Señora.

Lady-fern [lé'-di-fęrn], *s.* Aspidio, helecho hembra. Aspidium filix-femina.

Lady-killer [lé'-di-kil''-ęr], *s.* (Fest.) Un Don Juan, un Tenorio; galanteador de oficio, hombre de quien se supone que agrada a las mujeres.

Lady-like [lé'-di-laic], *a.* Delicado, afeminado; tierno, elegante, señoril, aseñorado, político; afectado.

Lady-love [lé'-di-luv], *s.* Amada, la mujer querida.

Ladyship [lé'-di-ship], *sf.* Señoría, tratamiento de cortesía y respeto que se da a las mujeres de los marqueses, condes, vizcondes o barones en Inglaterra, a las de los *baronets*, de los caballeros, y a todas las hijas de los duques, marqueses y condes: corresponde en castellano unas veces a Excelencia y otras a Señoría.

Lag [lag], *a.* (Poco us.) Trasero, postrero, zaguero, último; posterior, lo que está o viene detrás.

Lag, *vn.* 1. Remolonear, roncear, tardar en hacer lo que se debe, rezagarse; moverse lentamente. 2. Quedarse atrás, detenerse, tardar. —*s.* 1. (Mec.) Retardación de movimiento por cualquier causa y la medida de esa retardación. 2. Listón de madera; parte de una capa de cascajo.

Lager [lā'-gęr], *s.* Especie de cerveza. *V.* BEER.

Laggard [lag'-ard], *a.* Tardío, perezoso, holgazán.

Lagger [lag'-ęr], *s.* Haragán, holgazán.

Lagoon (o LAGUNE, poco us.) [la-gūn'], *s.* 1. Laguna; agua poco profunda, como en la desembocadura de algunos ríos. 2. Laguna, el agua tranquila dentro de un atolón o isleta de coral. 3. Concavidad en las altas mesas de los E. U. del Oeste.

Laic [lé'-ic], *s.* y *a.* Laico, lego, seglar.

Laical [lé'-i-cal], *a.* Laical, laico, lego, secular, seglar.

Laid [léd], *pret.* y *pp.* del verbo *To* LAY.

Laidly [léd'-li], *a.* (Esco.) Feo, asqueroso.

Lain [lén], *pp.* del verbo *To* LIE.

Lair [lār], *s.* 1. Cubil, la cama en que se recogen las fieras y otros animales salvajes. 2. (Esco.) Espacio de terreno destinado a la inhumación de cadáveres.

Laird [lārd], *s.* (Esco.) Lord; hacendado; a veces, un propietario.

Laity [lé'-i-ti], *s.* El estado seglar, en contraposición al estado eclesiástico.

Lake [lék], *s.* 1. Lago, laguna. 2. Charco, pantano, depósito artificial de agua. 3. Color rojo obscuro preparado con grana o rubia para pintar.

Lake, *vn.* (Prov.) Jugar.

Lakelet [lék'-let], *s.* Lago pequeño, laguito.

Lakh [lac], *s.* Cien mil. *V.* LAC[2].

Lallation [lal-lé'-shun], *s.* Imperfección en la pronunciación que consiste en dar a la erre el sonido de ele.

Laky [lék'-i], *a.* (Poco us.) Lagunoso, perteneciente a lagos o lagunas.

Lama [lā'-ma], *s.* 1. Sacerdote, monje o monja budista de Tibet. 2. *V.* LLAMA.

Lamb [lam], *s.* 1. Cordero, el hijo de la oveja. (Mex.) Borrego. *A yearling lamb*, Borrego, borrega; borro, borra. 2. El Salvador del mundo. 3. Persona apacible o inocente.

Lamb, *vn.* Parir corderos.

Lamb-ale [lam'-él], *s.* (Ingl.) Fiesta que se celebra al tiempo del esquileo de los corderos.

Lambative [lam'-ba-tiv], *a.* Lo que se lame.—*s.* Cualquier medicina que se toma lamiéndola.

Lambdoidal [lam-deid'-al], *a.* Lo que está formado como la lamda griega, que tiene esta figura, Λ.

Lambent [lam'-bent], *a.* Ligero, ondulante, que se mueve de una manera suave y lenta. *Lambent flame*, Fuego fatuo, llama ligera.

Lamb-like [lam'-laic], *a.* Manso, inocente, semejante a un cordero.

Lambkin [lam'-kin], *s.* Corderito.

Lambrequin [lam'-bęr-kin], *s.* 1. Guardamalleta, pieza de adorno que pende sobre el cortinaje por la parte superior y que permanece fija. 2. Cubierta de adorno de paño, etc., que se ponía al yelmo. (< Fr.)

Lamb's-wool [lamz'-wul], *s.* Lana de cordero. *Lambskin*, Corderina. *Lamb's-lettuce*, (Bot.) Macha, valerianilla; se llama también, *cornsalad*. Valerianella olitoria. *Lamb's-wool*, Cerveza mezclada con manzanas asadas, nuez moscada y azúcar.

Lame [lém], *a.* Lisiado, estropeado, defectuoso en algún miembro del cuerpo; cojo, renco; imperfecto. *To go lame*, Cojear, andar cojeando. *Lame expression*, Expresión manca. *Lame comparison*, Comparación defectuosa. *Lame excuse*, Disculpa frívola. *Lame verses*, Versos cojos o defectuosos. *A lame account*, Una relación imperfecta. *A lame excuse*, Una mala excusa. *Lame duck*, (Ger.) Especulador que no cumple sus compromisos.

Lame, *va.* Lisiar, estropear.

Lamella [la-mel'-a], *s.* (*pl.* LAMELLÆ). Laminilla; la hoja, lámina o concha muy delgada; hoja delgada de los hongos.

Lamellar [lam'-el-ar o la-mel'-ar], *a.* Compuesto de láminas.

Lamellate, Lamellated [lam'-el-ét, ed], *a.* Laminado, hecho o compuesto de láminas; hojaldrado.

Lamelliform [la-mel'-i-fōrm], *a.* Lameliforme, en forma de láminas u hojas.

Lamely [lém'-li], *adv.* Con cojera; imperfectamente, defectuosamente; debilmente.

Lameness [lém'-nes], *s.* Cojera; falta, defecto, imperfección: el estado de una persona lisiada o estropeada.

Lament [la-męnt'], *va.* y *vn.* Lamentar o lamentarse, sentir con llanto o gemido alguna cosa; afligir y afligirse.

Lament, *s.* Lamento, expresión de pesar.

Lamentable [lam'-en-ta-bl], *a.* Lamentable, lamentoso, deplorable, lastimoso.

Lamentably [lam'-en-ta-bli], *adv.* Lamentablemente.

Lamentation [lam-en-té'-shun], *s.* Lamentación, duelo, gemido, lamento.

Lamenting [la-ment'-ing], *s.* Lamentación, acto de lamentar.

Lamia [lé'-mi-a], *s.* 1. Lamia, especie de demonio. 2. (Zool.) Género de coleópteros, de la familia de los cerambícidos.

Lamina [lam'-i-na], *s.* Lámina, planchita, hoja o capa delgada que encaja en otra; en plural, LAMINÆ.

Laminable [lam'-i-na-bl], *a.* Laminable, susceptible de ser reducido a láminas u hojas.

Laminar [lam'-i-nar], *a.* Laminar, compuesto de hojas o láminas.

Laminate, Laminated [lam'-i-nét, ed], *a.* Laminado, dispuesto en láminas, reducido a láminas u hojas delgadas.

Lammas [lam'-as], *s.* El día primero de agosto.

Lamp [lamp], *s.* 1. Lámpara, y a veces farol o velón. *Argand lamp*, Especie de lámpara en cuyo interior circula el aire; se conoce en España con el nombre de quinqué (de su primer fabricante francés). *Astral lamp*, Lámpara de aceite o gas, que por medio de un globo de vidrio difunde la luz con más claridad. 2. Lo que esparce luz. *Lamp-chimney*, Tubo de lámpara, bombillo. *Lamp-holder*, Porta-lámparas. *Lamplighter*, (1) Farolero, lamparero. (2) Lo que sirve para encender lámparas, como un fósforo de cartón o un aparato eléctrico. *Lamp-post*, Peana, poste, pie de farol en la calle. *Lamp-shade*, Pantalla de lámpara. *Lamp-wick*, Mecha, torcida.

Lampass [lam'-pas], *s.* *V.* LAMPERS.

Lampblack [lamp'-blac], *s.* Hollín de resina, humo de pez, negro de humo. (Mex.) Humo de ocote, que sirve para hacer la tinta que usan los impresores.

Lampers [lam'-perz], *s.* (Vet.) Bulto de carne, acompañado de inflamación, en la parte superior de la boca de los caballos.

Lamplight [lamp'-lait], *s.* Luz de una lámpara; luz artificial.

Lampoon [lam-pūn'], *s.* Sátira o escrito insultante y denigrativo, libelo; pasquín.

Lampoon, *va.* Satirizar, escribir sátiras o zaherir y motejar con ellas; hacer coplas contra alguno o coplearle.

Lampooner [lam-pūn'-ẹr], *s.* Satirizante, escritor de sátiras personales.

Lamprey [lam'-pri], *s.* (Zool.) Lamprea.

Lampron [lam'-prun], *s.* 1. (Zool.) Especie de lamprea. 2. (Zool.) Especie de anguila larga.

Lanary [lé'-na-ri], *s.* Almacén para lana.

Lanate, Lanated [lé'-nêt, ed], *a.* Lanoso. (Bot.) Lanudo.

Lance [lạns], *s.* 1. Lanza, arma blanca. 2. Lanceta. 3. Lancetada, lancetazo, lanzada. 4. *m.* Lanza, el que usa de una lanza. 5. Llamarada.

Lance, *va.* 1. Lancear, dar una lanzada; penetrar, cortar. 2. Abrir una apostema con lanceta o bisturí.

Lanceolate [lan'-sẹ-o-lẹt], *a.* Lanceolado, formado como lanza o lanceta.

Lancer [lạns'-ẹr], *s.* 1. El que lancea. 2. Lancero, soldado de a caballo armado de lanza. 3. *pl. V.* LANCIERS.

Lancet [lạn'-set], *s.* 1. Lanceta. 2. (Arq.) Arco puntiagudo, bóveda gótica. 3. Trompetilla de los mosquitos, tábanos y otros dípteros.

Lancewood [lạns'-wud], *s.* 1. Palo de lanza. 2. Cualquier árbol que produce esta madera, especie de chirimoyo; anona.

Lanch [lanch], *va.* Lanzar. *V.* LAUNCH.

Lanciers [lan'-sirz], *s. pl.* (Fr.) Lanceros, forma moderna de la contradanza, y la música de eso baile.

Lancinate [lan'-si-nêt], *va.* Lacerar, despedazar.

Lancination [lan-si-né'-shun], *s.* Laceración; dolor agudo.

Land [land], *s.* 1. Tierra, en contraposición al agua; la porción sólida de nuestro globo. 2. Terreno, sitio o espacio de tierra. 3. Suelo, terruño; bienes raíces, hacienda. 4. País, región, reino, provincia, territorio considerado como habitación del hombre; nación. 5. Continente, tierra firme. *To travel by land,* Viajar por tierra. *To go on land,* Tomar tierra, ir a tierra, desembarcar. *Law of the land,* Ley nacional. *Arable land,* Tierra labrantía o de labranza. *To make (the) land,* Descubrir tierra, acercar la nave a la costa. *To see how the land lies,* Sondar el terreno. *To know how the land lies,* (Fig.) Estar al corriente de un asunto; saber a qué atenerse. *Land-agent,* Corredor de fincas rurales. *Land-breeze,* Brisa de tierra. *Land forces,* Fuerzas terrestres, tropas de tierra. *Land-jobbing,* Especulación en la compra y venta de bienes raíces. *Land-hunger,* Codicia de poseer tierras. *Land-office,* Oficina del catastro. *Land-poor, a.* Poseedor de muchas tierras que dan rentas insuficientes para pagar los gastos. *Land-surveying,* Agrimensura.

Land, *va.* 1. Desembarcar. 2. Coger (un pez).—*vn.* 1. (Mar.) Aterrarse, saltar en tierra, abordar. 2. (Aer.) Aterrizar. *To land on the moon,* Alunizar.

de coche con imperial que se puede abrir o cerrar.

Landed [land'-ed], *a.* Hacendado, el que tiene hacienda o patrimonio en tierras.—*pp.* Desembarcado.

Landfall [land'-fōl], *s.* 1. Herencia de tierras por muerte del anterior poseedor. 2. (Mar.) Recalada.

Landgrave [land'-grêv], *s.* Langrave, título de algunos príncipes de Alemania.

Landgraviate [land-gré'-vi-êt], *s.* Langraviado, título de algunos principados de Alemania.

Landholder [land'-hōld-ẹr], *s.* Hacendado, el que tiene hacienda en tierras.

Landing [land'-ing], *s.* 1. Desembarco. 2. Aterrizaje de un avión. 3. Pasillo o descanso de escalera. *Landing craft,* Equipo o aparato de aterrizaje. *Landing field,* Campo de aterrizaje. *Landing gear,* Tren de aterrizaje. *Landing net,* Red para pescado. *Landing place.* Desembarcadero.

Landjobber [land'-job-ẹr], *s.* Corredor de bienes raíces, el que compra o vende tierras por otro.

Landlady [land'-lé-di], *sf.* 1. Ama, casera, la mujer que arrienda o da alguna cosa en arrendamiento. 2. Huéspeda, mesonera, posadera, patrona.

Landless [land'-les], *a.* Sin bienes o sin tierras; sin fortuna, pobre.

Landlocked [land'-lect], *a.* Cercado de tierra, resguardado o abrigado de los vientos por la tierra.

Landlord [land'-lōrd], *s.* 1. El propietario o dueño de tierras o casas. 2. Amo, huésped posadero; casero, patrón.

Landlordism [land'-lōrd-izm], *s.* 1. Acción, conducta u opiniones propias del propietario, huésped o casero; autoridad del propietario. 2. El conjunto de los propietarios en general.

Landlubber [land'-lub-ẹr], *s.* Término de desprecio usado por los marinos para motejar a los que no son de su profesión.

Landmark [land'-mārk], *s.* Mojón, marca, la señal que se pone para dividir los términos, lindes y caminos. *Landmarks,* (Mar.) Marcas.

Landscape [land'-skêp], *s.* 1. País, la extensión de terreno que se descubre de una sola mirada. 2. Paisaje, país. *Landscape gardening,* Arquitectura de jardines y parques.

Landscape [land'-scêp], *va.* Mejorar el terreno: todo lo referente a embellecer el paisaje por medios humanos, ya en pequeños jardines, ya en vastas extensiones.

Landslide [land'-slaid], **Landslip** [land'slip], *s.* 1. Derrumbamiento, derrumbe, desprendimiento de tierra; (Méx.) desliz. 2. La masa de tierra que se ha derrumbado.

Landslide, *s.* En la política, abrumadora mayoría de votos.

Land-surveyor [land'-sūr-vé'-ẹr], *s.* Agrimensor.

Land-tax [land'-tax], *s.* Tributo sobre tierras y sobre el terreno que ocupan las casas.

Land-waiter [land'-wê-tẹr], *s.* Guarda de puerto, empleado de la aduana que vigila el desembarque de los géneros en los puertos.

Landward [land'-ward], *adv.* Hacia la tierra.

Lane [lên], *s.* 1. Senda, vereda, calle, el camino estrecho que hay entre dos setos. 2. Callejuela, calle angosta. 3. Calle o paso formado por dos hileras de personas.

Language [lan'-gwẹj], *s.* 1. Habla, lenguaje. 2. Lengua, lenguaje, el idioma particular de cada nación o provincia. 3. Lenguaje, expresión por medio de signos; o por sonidos inarticulados, como los de las aves. 4. Vocabulario de una ciencia, lenguaje particular de algún ramo de negocio, etc. 5. *V.* LANGUET. *Language-master,* Maestro de idiomas.

Languaged [lan'-gwẹjd], *a.* Lengüetero, dícese del que sabe muchas lenguas.

Languet [lan'-get], *s.* 1. Lengüeta, cualquier cosa cortada en figura de lengua pequeña. 2. Orejeta, lengüeta, como la de los instrumentos de viento; orejeta o lengüeta de la guarnición de una arma.

Languid [lan'-gwid], *a.* Lánguido, débil, flaco; sin animación ni interés; descaecido.

Languidly [lan'-gwid-li], *adv.* Lánguidamente.

Languidness [lan'-gwid-nes], *s.* Languidez, caimiento, falta de fuerza.

Languish [lan'-gwish], *va.* y *vn.* 1. Descaecer, enflaquecer, extenuarse, consumirse, penar o padecer lentamente; adolecer. 2. Agostarse, ponerse mustio. 3. Aflojar, entibiarse. 4. Mirar con ternura. 5. Debilitar, consumir.

Languisher [lan'-gwish-ẹr], *s.* El que se consume o se aflige.

Languishing [lan'-gwish-ing], *s.* Languidez, flaqueza.—*a.* Lánguido, descaecido, afligido; enamorado o derretido, hablando de amantes.

Languishingly [lan'-gwish-ing-li], *adv.* Lánguidamente.

Languishment [lan'-gwish-mẹnt], *s.* 1. Languidez, debilidad. 2. Consumimiento, angustia, hablando de lo que sufren los que desean o esperan con ansia alguna cosa.

Languor [lan'-gẹr o gwẹr], *s.* Desfallecimiento, diminución de ánimo, flojedad, descaecimiento.

Languorous [lan'-gẹr-us], *a.* Lánguido, flojo, que induce o sugiere descaecimiento.

Laniard [lan'-yard], *s.* (Mar.) Acolladr. *V.* LANYARD.

Laniary [lé'-ni-ẹ-ri], *a.* Propio para lacerar, como los dientes caninos.—*s.* Colmillo, diente canino.

Lank [lanc], *a.* 1. Flojo, flaco, descarnado, delgado, desfallecido. 2. Largo y recto. *Lank hair,* Cabellos largos y lacios.

Lankly [lanc'-li], *adv.* Flojamente, sueltamente.

Lankness [lanc'-nes], *s.* Flaqueza, flojedad.

Lanky [lank'-i], *a.* (Fam.) Larguirucho, alto y delgado: dícese de las personas.

Lanner [lan'-ẹr], *s.* (Orn.) Alcotán. *Lanneret,* Alcotanillo.

Lanolin [lan'-o-lin], *s.* Lanolina, manteca o gordura clarificada de oveja o de carnero; se usa en farmacia como base de ungüentos.

Lansquenet [lans'-kẹ-net], *s.* 1. Sacanete, un juego de naipes. 2. (Ant.) Soldado de a pie.

Lantern [lan'-tẹrn], *s.* 1. Linterna, farol. *Dark-lantern,* Farol de ronda, linterna sorda, que deja o no ver la luz a voluntad del que la lleva. *Poop-lantern,* (Mar.) Farol de popa. *Top-lantern,* (Mar.) Farol de la cofa. *Battle or hand lantern,* (Mar.) Farol de combate. *Signal lanterns,* (Mar.) Faroles de señales. *Lantern-maker,* Linternero. 2. Faro, fanal, que sirve de guía a los marinos. 3. (Arq.) Linterna, fábrica de figura redonda con ventanas para dar entrada a la luz.

Lantern-jaws [lan'-tęrn-jōz], *s.* Quijadas de farol: apodo con que se moteja al que es chupado de cara.

Lantern slide [lan'-tęrn slaid], *s.* Diapositiva, fotografía positiva en cristal.

Lanyard [lan'-yard], *s.* (Mar.) Acollador, cabo delgado que sirve para tener tiesos y estirados los obenques, brandales y estays. *Lanyards of the stoppers,* (Mar.) Mojeles de las hozas. *Lanyards of the buoy,* (Mar.) Rebenques de cabeza de la boya.

Lap[1] [lap], *s.* 1. Faldas, regazo; faldón, faldones. 2. Rodillas; (fig.) seno. 3. (Mec.) Longitud o extensión determinada. 4. Presilla, oreja de bolsillo, etc. 5. (Mec.) Rueda de metal blando, madera o cuero, que usan los lapidarios para labrar joyas y bruñir metales duros. *Lapstone,* Piedra sobre la cual baten el cuero los zapateros. *Lap-dog,* Perro de faldas, perrillo faldero.

Lap,[2] *s.* Salidizo, la parte saliente de un objeto o cuerpo que cubre a otro. 2. Pliegue, doblez; solapadura, avance.

Lap,[1] *va.* 1. Arrollar, envolver; plegar, hacer pliegues; doblar una cosa sobre sí misma. 2. Caer, recaer, replegarse sobre; cruzar; exceder, hacer salidizo.—*vn.* Doblarse alguna cosa torciéndose sobre sí misma; estar replegado; estar echado o tendido al lado de otra cosa.

Lap,[2] *va.* 1. Lamer, beber a lengüetadas, alimentarse o comer lamiendo los alimentos. 2. Bañar, tocar el agua, o hacer ondulaciones en una orilla.—*vn.* 1. Lamer. 2. Hacer un sonido como de lamido o toque suave.

Laparotomy [lap"-a-ret'-o-mi], *s.* Laparotomía, operación quirúrgica, incisión abdominal hecha por el costado.

Lapel [la-pel'], *s.* Solapa, la parte de la levita que cae sobre el pecho y que se dobla hacia atrás.

Lapful [lap'-ful], *s.* Lo que puede caber en el regazo o enfaldo.

Lapidary [lap'-i-dę-ri], *s.* Lapidario, el que trabaja y labra las piedras preciosas o comercia en ellas.—*a.* 1. Lapidario, perteneciente al arte de labrar las piedras preciosas. 2. Inscripto sobre piedra. 3. Lapídeo.

Lapidate [lap'-i-dēt], *va.* 1. Labrar las piedras finas y preciosas. 2. (Poco us.) Apedrear, matar a pedradas.

Lapidation [lap-i-dé'-shun], *s.* Lapidación, apedreamiento.

Lapidescence [lap-i-des'-ens], *s.* Concreción de piedra.

Lapidescent [lap-i-des'-ent], *a.* Lo que se petrifica o vuelve piedra.

Lapidification [la-pid-i-fi-kē'-shun], *s.* Lapidificación.

Lapidist [lap'-i-dist], *s.* Lapidario.

Lapis [lé'-pis], *s.* 1. Procedimiento para estampar indianas con añil. 2. Piedra: se usa solamente en composición. *Lapis infernalis,* Piedra infernal, nitrato de plata.

Lapis lazuli [lé'-pis laz'-yu-lai], *s.* Lapislázuli, mineral exquisito de color azul, duro como el acero y acompañado frecuentemente por pirita de hierro.

Laplander [lap'-land-ęr], *s.* *V.* LAPP.

Lapling [lap'-ling], *s.* Apodo que se aplica al hombre que gusta mucho de los placeres sensuales; voz despectiva.

Lapp, Lap [lap], *s.* 1. Lapón, natural de Laponia. 2. Idioma de los lapones.

Lapper [lap'-ęr], *s.* El que lame, arrolla o pliega alguna cosa.

Lappet [lap'-et], *s.* Caídas de toca o escofieta, aquellas partes de la misma que penden como adorno.

Lapsable [laps'-a-bl], *a.* Prescriptible; que puede sufrir traslación de derecho; susceptible de caer o deslizarse.

Lapse [laps], *s.* 1. Caída, la acción de caer; movimiento imperceptible hacia adelante o hacia abajo; de aquí, intervalo de tiempo. 2. Desliz, traspié, yerro, falta ligera. 3. (For.) Prescripción, traslación de derecho o dominio. *In the lapse of time,* Con el transcurso del tiempo, o andando el tiempo.

Lapse, *vn.* 1. Escurrir, manar o fluir poco a poco. 2. Deslizarse, decir o hacer alguna cosa irreflexivamente. 3. Caer en algún defecto, desliz o error. 4. (For.) Prescribir, caducar.—*va.* 1. Dejar caer. 2. (Des.) Acusar; convencer.

Lapsed [lapst], *a.* Caído; deslizado; omitido; prescrito.

Lapwing [lap'-wing], *s.* (Orn.) Avefría, frailecillo.

Lapwork [lap'-wūrk], *s.* Obra entrelazada o entretejida.

Lar [lār], *s.* Lar, dios doméstico: por lo común en plural, LARES.

Larboard [lār'-bōrd], *s.* (Mar.) Babor, el lado o costado izquierdo del buque mirando de popa a proa. (Para evitar confusión con *starboard* se usa hoy día la voz *port* con preferencia.)

Larcener, Larcenist [lār'-sę-nęr, nist], *s.* Ladrón, ratero.

Larceny [lār'-se-ni], *s.* (For.) Ratería, hurto de cosas de poca importancia; acción de robar y llevarse consigo los bienes personales de otro contra la voluntad de su dueño. *Petty larceny,* Hurto cuyo monto sólo llega a un valor determinado. *Grand larceny,* El que pasa de dicho valor.

Larch [lārch], *s.* (Bot.) Alerce, lárice.

Lard [lārd], *s.* Manteca de puerco o de cerdo; lardo, tocino gordo. *Lard-oil,* Aceite espeso que se extrae del lardo.

Lard, *va.* 1. Mechar. 2. Engordar. 3. Entreverar, mezclar alguna cosa con otra para mejorarla. *Larding-pin,* Mechera, aguja de mechar.

Lardaceous [lār-dé'-shus], *a.* 1. Lardoso, grasiento. 2. (Med.) Que indica degeneración crasa de un órgano.

Larder [lārd'-ęr], *s.* Despensa.

Larderer [lārd'-ęr-ęr], *s.* Despensero.

Large [lārj], *a.* 1. Grande, abultado, grueso. 2. Ancho, amplio, vasto, espacioso, extenso. 3. Largo, franco, liberal, espléndido. 4. Dilatado, difuso, copioso. *At large,* Sin limitación; a lo largo; difusamente, por extenso; en general; en libertad, libre en sus movimientos. —*adv.* 1. Con viento a la cuadra. 2. (Fam.) Con jactancia. *To sail large,* (Mar.) Navegar con viento largo o con viento a la cuadra. *To talk large,* Darse tono; presumir de gran señor.

Large-heartedness [lārj'-hārt-ed-nes], *s.* Liberalidad, largueza, generosidad.

Largely [lārj'-li], *adv.* Largamente, latamente, liberalmente, ampliamente.

Largeness [lārj'-nes], *s.* 1. Grandor, extensión, anchura, amplitud. 2. Liberalidad, generosidad. 3. Grandeza de ánimo.

Large-scale [lārj'-skēl], *a.* En gran escala.

Largess [lār'-jes], *s.* 1. Don, dádiva, liberal; presente. 2. (Ant.) Liberalidad.

Larghetto [lār-get'-o], *a.* (Mús.) Lento, a compás algo menos lento que "*largo.*"—*s.* Música en dicho compás. (Ital.)

Largo [lār'-gō], *adv.* (Mús.) Largo, lento.

Lariat [lar'-i-at], *s.* 1. Reata. 2. Lazo. *V.* LASSO. (< la reata.)

Lark[1] [lārk], *s.* (Orn.) Alondra, calandria. *Meadow-lark, tit-lark,* Alondra de los prados. Alauda.

Lark,[2] *s.* (Fam.) Calaverada, travesura. *To be on a lark,* Hacer una travesura; hacer de las suyas, andar de picos pardos, andar de holgorio.

Larker [lark'-ęr], *s.* Cazador de alondras.

Lark-like [lark'-laik], *a.* Semejante a la alondra.

Larksheel, *s.* (Bot.) *V.* NASTURTIUM.

Larkspur [lārk'-spūr], *s.* (Bot.) Espuela de caballero, delfinio; planta y su flor. Delphinium.

Larrup [lar'-up], *va.* (Fam.) Zurrar, tundir, zurriagar.

Larum [lar'-um], *s.* (Des. o poét.) Alarma, ruido que indica riesgo o peligro. *V.* ALARM.

Larva [lār'-va], *s.* (Zool.) Larva u oruga; la primera forma de algunos animales; insecto después de salir del huevo y antes de su primera transformación.

Larval [lār'-val], *a.* Larval, que pertenece a la larva.

Larvate, Larvated [lār'-vēt, ed], *a.* Larval, encubierto, que tiene larva o máscara.

Laryngeal [la-rin'-ję-al o la-rin-ji'-al], *a.* Laríngeo, relativo a la laringe.

Laryngitis [la-rin-jai'-tis], *s.* (Med.) Laringitis.

Laryngoscope [la-riṇ'-go-scōp], *s.* Laringoscopio, instrumento que sirve para explorar la laringe.

Laryngoscopy [la-riṇ-ges'-co-pi], *s.* Laringoscopia.

Laryngotomy [la-rin-get'-o-mi], *s.* (Cir.) Laringotomía, la operación de cortar la traquiarteria a fin de dar paso al aire y evitar la sufocación.

Larynx [lar'-incs], *s.* Laringe, la cabeza o boca de la tráquea.

Lascivious [las-siv'-i-us], *a.* Lascivo, incontinente, lujurioso, lúbrico; propio para provocar deseos carnales.

Lasciviousness [las-siv'-i-us-nes], *s.* Lascivia, incontinencia, lujuria.

Laser [lé'-zęr], *s.* Laser, amplificación de luz por estímulo de emisiones de radiación.

Lash [lash], *s.* 1. La punta del látigo, fusta, etc., con que se da un latigazo. 2. Latigazo, golpe dado con un látigo u otra cosa flexible. 3. Sarcasmo, invectiva, dicho satírico y picante. 4. Pestaña. *Drooping lashes,* Pestañas caídas.

Lash, *va.* 1. Dar latigazos; azotar. 2. Mover alguna cosa violentamente haciendo ruido. 3. Satirizar, zaherir con sátiras o invectivas. 4. (Mar.) Amarrar, ligar o trincar.—*vn.* Latiguear, andar chasqueando el látigo. *To lash out*, Desenfrenarse, desordenarse, hacerse extravagante en el trato o en las costumbres.

Lasher [lash'-ẹr], s. Azotador.

Lash-free [lash'-frî], *a.* Lo que está libre o no tiene peligro de que lo satiricen.

Lashing [lash'-ing], *s.* 1. Ligadura, lazo, cabo de cuerda que sirve para atar una cosa con otra; (Mar.) amarra, amarradura. 2. Castigo de azotes; acción de satirizar o de lanzar invectivas. *Lashings of the long-boat*, (Mar.) Obenques de la lancha. *Lashing-rings*, (Mar.) Argollas de amura.

Lasket [las'-ket], *s.* (Mar.) Badaza de boneta.

Lass [las], *sf.* Doncella, mujer joven y soltera; moza, muchacha: aplícase comúnmente a las campesinas o aldeanas.

Lassie [las'-i], *f.* Muchachita, mozuela.

Lassitude [las'-i-tiūd], *s.* Lasitud, cansancio, fatiga.

Lasso [las'-ō], *va.* Coger con un lazo.—*s.* Lazo, larga tira de cuero trenzado que termina en un lazo corredizo; se usa para coger caballos y toros salvajes.

Last [lạst], *a.* Ultimo, postrero, pasado. *At last*, Al fin, finalmente. *To the last*, Hasta lo último. *Last week*, La semana pasada. *Last night*, Anoche. *The last but one*, El penúltimo. *The last but two*, El antepenúltimo. *To be on one's last legs*, Estar en apuros. *That is the last straw*, Eso es el colmo. *The last word*, La última palabra, lo mejor, la última moda.—*adv.* De último, al final. —*s.* Horma para zapatos.

Last, *vn.* 1. Durar, permanecer, continuar existiendo. 2. Conservarse, guardarse, continuar en buen estado. 3. Sostenerse, no rendirse a los sitiadores.

Lastage [lạst'-ẹj], *s.* 1. Espacio para el cargamento de un buque. 2. Lastre.

Lasting [lạst'-ing], *a.* Duradero, perpetuo, perdurable, durable, permanente, constante.—*s.* 1. Sempiternas, tejido fuerte de lana y estambre. 2. Acción de ahormar las palas de un zapato.

Lastingly [lạst'-ing-li], *adv.* Perpetuamente, para siempre.

Lastingness [lạst'-ing-nes], *s.* Duración, continuación.

Lastly [lạst'-li], *adv.* Últimamente, en conclusión, por fin, finalmente, por último.

Lastmaker [lạst'-mê-kẹr], *s.* Hormero.

Latch [lach], *s.* Aldaba de puerta; picaporte. *Latch-string*, Cordón de aldaba. *The latch-string is (always) out*, Sea Vd. bienvenido; está Vd. en su casa.

Latch, *va.* Cerrar con aldaba; ajustar, unir.

Latchet [lach'-et], *s.* Agujeta de zapato.

Late [lêt], *a.* 1. Tardío; remoto, lejano; tardo, lento. 2. Último, el postrero en algún oficio o empleo. 3. Difunto, la persona que acabó la vida temporal; o que ha ejercido una dignidad o cargo. *Late Professor of Latin*, Professor que ha sido de la lengua latina. 4. Reciente, o comparativamente reciente.—*adv.* 1. Tarde, fuera de tiempo, pasado mucho tiempo. 2. Poco ha, últimamente, antes. *Of late*, De poco tiempo acá, de poco tiempo a esta parte. *Better late than never*, Más vale tarde que nunca. *Late in the year*, Al fin del año. *You are late*, Llega Vd. tarde. *What made you so late?* ¿Qué le ha retardado a Vd.? *To keep late hours*, Acostarse tarde, volver a deshora. *It was late in the season*, La estación estaba ya adelantada. *Too late*, Demasiado tarde; después del tiempo señalado.

Lateen [la-tîn'], *a.* Latino, voz que significa un palo corto, percha larga y vela triangular. *Lateen-sail*, (Mar.) Vela latina o de burro.

Lately [lêt'-li], *adv.* Poco ha, no ha mucho, recientemente, poco tiempo hace.

Latency [lê'-ten-si], *s.* El estado de lo que se halla oculto; obscuridad, confusión.

Lateness [lêt'-nes], *s.* 1. Tiempo o edad avanzada. 2. Tiempo moderno en contraposición a otro más antiguo.

Latent [lê'-tent], *a.* Latente, escondido, oculto.

Later [lê'-tẹr], *adv.* y *a.* (*comp.* de LATE). Más tarde; más adelantado, más tardío, subsecuente. *Sooner or later*, Tarde o temprano. *A later development*, Manifestación o suceso más reciente.

Lateral [lat'-ẹr-al], *a.* Lateral, ladeado.

Laterally [lat'-ẹr-al-i], *adv.* Lateralmente.

Laterite [lat'-ẹr-ait], *s.* Una arcilla roja y ferruginosa, muy abundante en algunos países tropicales.

Latescent [la-tes'-ent], *a.* Que se va obscureciendo u ocultando.

Latest [lê'-test], *a.* y *adv.* Superlativo de *late*, el último, últimamente. *At the latest*, A más tardar.

Latex [lê'-tex], *s.* (Bot.) Látex, jugo lechoso de algunas plantas, del que se obtiene caucho, resinas, etc.

Lath [lạth], *s.* Lata, listón, palo que sirve para formar las techumbres y para colocar en ellas las tejas y pizarras. *Lath of a bed*, Varilla de cama.

Lath, *va.* Poner latas en los techos.

Lathe [lêdh], *s.* 1. Torno, máquina que usa el tornero para tornear su obra. 2. Lecho, cama de telar. *V.* LAY.

Lather [ladh'-ẹr], *vn.* Espumar, formar espuma, hacer o formar espuma como el jabón.—*va.* Bañar con espuma de jabón y agua.

Lather, *s.* Jabonaduras, la espuma que se forma al jabonar o batir el agua con jabón.

Lathwork [lạth'-wurk], *s.* Enlistonado (en carpintería).

Lathy [lạth'-i], *a.* Delgado como lata.

Latidentate [lat-i-den'-têt], *a.* Latidentado, de dientes anchos.

Latin [lat'-in], *a.* Latino.—*s.* El latín o la lengua latina.

Latin American [lat'-in a-mer'-i-can], *s.* y *a.* Latinoamericano.

Latinism [lat'-in-izm], *s.* Latinismo.

Latinist [lat'-in-ist], *s.* Latinista, persona que cultiva la lengua y literatura latinas.

Latinity [la-tin'-i-ti], *s.* Latinidad; estilo latino, modo de emplear la lengua latina.

Latinize [lat'-in-aiz], *va.* 1. Latinizar, traducir en latín. 2. Dar forma latina a las palabras de otra lengua.—*vn.* Servirse de palabras o locuciones sacadas del latín.

Latish [lêt'-ish], *a.* (Fam.) Algo tarde, retardado.

Latirostrous [lat-i-ros'-trus], *a.* Latirrostra, que tiene el pico ancho; dícese de las aves.

Latitat [lat'-i-tat], *s.* (For. Ingl.) Auto judicial para comparecer ante el tribunal llamado Banco del rey.

Latitude [lat'-i-tiūd], *s.* 1. Latitud, la distancia que hay desde cualquier lugar o paraje al ecuador. 2. Latitud, anchura, extensión; difusión. 3. Acepción ilimitada de una cosa; laxitud en las opiniones. 4. Latitud, exención de las reglas fijas o apartamiento de ellas.

Latitudinal [lat-i-tiū'-di-nal], *a.* Latitudinal, relativo o referente a la latitud.

Latitudinarian [lat-i-tiūd-i-nê'-ri-an], *a.* 1. Libre, sin freno o regla; de vasto alcance o extensión; de aquí, no exacto ni preciso. 2. Libre en materias concernientes a las opiniones religiosas.—*s.* La persona que es libre en sus opiniones religiosas.

Latria [la-trai'-a], *s.* Culto de latría, adoración debida sólo a Dios.

Latten [lat'-en], *s.* Latón, azófar, un metal cuando está en planchas u hojas, pues cuando está en masa se llama *brass*.

Latter [lat'-ẹr], *a.* 1. Posterior, más reciente, que viene después de otra cosa; moderno. 2. Éste o esto, el último de quien se habla, si se trata de dos, a distinción de *former*, anterior, *aquél* o *aquello*. 3. (Des.) Último. *Latter-day*, Del presente; de un período reciente. *Latter-day Saints*, El pueblo mormón. (Variedad de LATER.)

Latterly [lat'-ẹr-li], *adv.* Recientemente, poco ha, de poco tiempo acá.

§**Lattermath** [lat'-ẹr-math], *s.* (Agric.) *V.* AFTERMATH.

Lattice [lat'-is], *s.* Celosía, rastel, enrejado de listoncillos de madera o hierro puesto en una ventana; cualquier cosa hecha con esa clase de enrejado, como una ventana o un biombo.

Lattice, *va.* Enrejar, hacer un enrejado a manera de celosía.

Laud [lōd], *s.* Alabanza, elogio. *Lauds*, Laudes, una parte del oficio divino.

Laud, *va.* Alabar, celebrar, loar.

Laudability [lōd-a-bil'-i-ti], *s.* *V.* LAUDABLENESS.

Laudable [lōd'-a-bl], *a.* Laudable, loable, digno de alabanza.

Laudableness [lōd'-a-bl-nes], *s.* El estado de lo que merece alabanza; la propiedad o calidad laudable de una cosa.

Laudably [lōd'-a-bli], *adv.* Laudablemente, loablemente, con elogio.

Laudanum [lō'-da-num], *s.* Láudano, tintura de opio, una medicina.

Laudative [lōd'-a-tiv], **Laudatory** [lōd'-a-to-ri], *a.* Laudatorio.—*s.* Panegírico.

Lauder [lōd'-ẹr], *s.* Loador.

Laugh [lạf], *vn.* 1. Reir; también estar contento. 2. Sonreir; mostrarse alegre, animado o retozón.—*va.* Mofar, burlar, escarnecer. *To laugh at*, Reirse de, mofarse, ridiculizar, poner en ridículo; divertirse a costa ajena. *To laugh at one to his face*, Reírsele a uno en las barbas. *To laugh at a feather*, Reirse de nada o por nada. *To laugh out*, Reirse a carcajadas; echarse a reir. *To laugh* *in one's sleeve,* Reirse interiormente. *To laugh down,* Ridiculizar, hacer desistir a otro de un plan o propósito por medio del ridículo; hacer callar a un orador a carcajadas. *To laugh out of the other side of the mouth,* Llevarse chasco o petardo, particularmente después de jactarse de algo. *There is nothing to laugh at,* No hay motivo de risa.

Laugh, *s.* Risa, risada. *Horse-laugh,* Carcajada, risotada. *Laugh-and-lay-down,* Un juego de naipes. *To carry off the laugh,* Ser el último en reirse. *To turn off with a laugh,* Hacer burla de una cosa, tomarla a broma.

Laughable [lqf'-a-bl], *a.* Risible, ridículo; divertido, que excita la risa.

Laughing [lqf'-ing], *a.* Risueño; que ríe, reidor.—*s.* Risa, alegría. *Laughing eyes,* Ojos alegres, reidores. *Laughing-gas,* Gas exhilarante, protóxido de ázoe.

Laughingly [lqf'-ing-li], *adv.* Alegremente, con risa.

Laughing-stock [lqf'-ing-stec], *s.* Hazmerreir, el que es objeto de la irrisión de otros, juguete de todos, vaca de la boda.

Laughter [lqf'-tęr], *s.* Risa, risada.

Launch [lānch], *vn.* 1. Arrojarse, echarse, tirarse al agua. 2. Extenderse, dilatarse; alargarse; vagar o andar vagando. 3. Lanzarse.—*va.* 1. Botar o echar al agua. 2. Llevar adelante, empezar una empresa o una profesión. 3. Lanzar o arrojar alguna cosa con ímpetu y violencia.

Launch, *s.* 1. El acto de botar un barco al agua. 2. Botadura al agua de un buque recién construído. 3. (Mar.) Lancha, chalupa; el mayor de los botes de un buque de guerra. 4. Lancha de recreo, impulsada por fuerza motriz, como vapor, nafta o electricidad.

Launching pad [lanch'-ing pad], *s.* (Aer.) Torre de lanzamiento, plataforma de lanzamiento.

Launder [lān'-dęr], *va.* Lavar la ropa.

Laundress [lān'-dres], *sf.* Lavandera.

Launderer [lān'-der-er], *s.* Lavandero.

Laundromat [lān'-dro-mat], *s.* Lavandería automática.

Laundry [len'-dri], *s.* 1. Lavandería. 2. Lavado de ropa. 3. Ropa sucia para lavar.

Laundryman [lēn'-dri-man], *s.* Lavandero.

Laureate [lō'-ri-ēt], *a.* Laureado. *Poet-laureate,* Poeta del rey o laureado.

Laureation [lō-rg-ē'-shun], *s.* El acto de recibir algún grado académico.

Laurel [lō'-rel], *s.* 1. (Bot.) Laurel guindo o laurel regio. *Alexandria laurel,* Laurel alejandrino. 2. (E. U.) Arbusto siempre verde de los géneros Kalmia o Rhododendron. 3. Corona o guirnalda de laurel; honor, distinción.

Laurelled [lō'-reld], *a.* Laureado.

Laurentian [lō-ren'-shian], *a.* 1. (Geol.) Lorenziano, perteneciente al río San Lorenzo; roca de las más antiguas. 2. Relativo a Lorenzo de Médicis o a la Laurentina.

Lava [lā'-va], *s.* Lava, la materia que arrojan los volcanes al tiempo de su erupción.

Lavabo [la-vē'-bō], *s.* 1. Lavabo litúrgico. 2. Lavamanos.

Lavaliere [lā-vg-lier'], *s.* Pendiente, medallón.

Lavatory [lav'-a-to-ri], *s.* Lavatorio, lavadero; loción.

Lave [lēv], *va.* y *vn.* 1. Lavar, bañar. 2. Lavarse, bañarse. *To lave water,* Sacar agua.

Lavement [lēv'-męnt], *s.* 1. Lavado, acción de lavar. 2. Enema, lavativa, ayuda.

Lavender [lav'-en-dęr], *s.* (Bot.) Espliego, alhucema, lavándula. *Lavender cotton,* Santolina.

Laver [lē'-vęr], *s.* Lavadero, aguamanil, vasija para lavarse.

Laver, *s.* Ova, cualquier alga comestible del género Porphyra, o un plato preparado con ella. *Green laver* (ova verde), Ulva latissima.

Lavish [lav'-ish], *a.* Pródigo, profuso, descabellado, despilfarrado.

Lavish, *va.* 1. Desparramar, disipar, malbaratar, malgastar, gastar con profusión. 2. Prodigar cumplimientos, alabanzas, etc. 3. Sacrificar, despreciar su sangre, su vida, etc.

Lavishly [lav'-ish-li], *adv.* Pródigamente, profusamente.

Lavishment [lav'-ish-męnt], **Lavishness** [lav'-ish-nes], *s.* (Poco us.) Despilfarro, prodigalidad, profusión, disipación.

Law [lō], *s.* 1. Ley, regla y norma de conducta. 2. Ley, constitución o estatuto. 3. Ley, regla o principio convencional. 4. Derecho. *According to law,* Según derecho. *Civil law,* Derecho civil. 5. Litigio judicial entre partes. 6. Jurisprudencia. 7. (Bib.) Tora, libro de la ley judía. 8. Ley de la naturaleza, la ocurrencia uniforme de los fenómenos naturales de un mismo modo, bajo las mismas condiciones. *To go to law with one,* Poner pleito a uno. *To follow the law,* Estudiar las leyes. *Father, son, daughter* o *brother-in-law,* Suegro, yerno, nuera o cuñado. (Fam.) Padre, hijo o hermano político, hija política. *In point of law,* Desde el punto de vista legal. *Ceremonial law,* La ley eclesiástica contenida en el Antiguo Testamento. *Law of nations,* Derecho internacional. *Gresham's law,* La ley económica según la cual donde hay dos formas de moneda corriente la inferior o peor excluye de la circulación a la mejor; "el mal dinero expele al bueno." *To take the law in one's own hands,* Hacerse justicia por sí mismo.

Law-breaker [lō'-brēk"-ęr], *s.* Transgresor, el que viola la ley.

Law-day [lō'-dē], *s.* Día en que están abiertos los tribunales.

Lawful [lō'-ful], *a.* Legal, según derecho, conforme a la ley; permitido, legítimo, justo, válido, lícito. *A lawful prize,* Una presa legítima. *Lawful goods,* Géneros permitidos o lícitos.

Lawfully [lō'-ful-i], *adv.* Legalmente, legítimamente.

Lawfulness [lō'-ful-nes], *s.* Legalidad, legitimidad.

Lawgiver [lō'-giv-ęr], *s.* Legislador.

Lawgiving [lō'-giv-ing], *a.* Legislativo.

Lawless [lō'-les], *a.* No sujeto a la ley; ilegal; desordenado, desarreglado.

Lawlessly [lō'-les-li], *adv.* Ilegalmente, contra las leyes.

Lawlessness [lō'-les-nes], *s.* Desorden, desobediencia.

Lawmaker [lō'-mē-kęr], *s.* Legislador.

Lawmonger [lō'-mun-gęr], *s.* Término de desprecio que se aplica al que hace comercio de la ley de un modo bajo.

Lawn [lōn], *s.* 1. Prado, campo abierto entre bosques o casas. 2. Linón, tela fina de lino. *Long lawn,* Estopilla.—*a.* Hecho de linón. *Lawn-mower,* Segadora de mano para prados. *Lawn-sprinkler,* Regadera para prados. *Lawn-sleeve,* Manga de línón, parte esencial del traje oficial de los obispos anglicanos.

Lawnmower [lōn'-mō-ęr], *s.* Cortacésped.

Lawn tennis [lōn ten'-is], *s.* Variedad del juego de tenis.

Lawsuit [lō'-siūt], *s.* Pleito, proceso, litigio, causa. (For.) Lite.

Lawyer [lō'-yęr], *s.* Abogado, jurista, jurisconsulto. (Mex. y C. A.) Licenciado. *Lawyer's office,* Bufete de abogado.

Lawyerly [lō'-yęr-li], *a.* Judicial.

Lax [lacs], *a.* 1. Laxo, suelto, flojo, desatado. 2. Vago, indeterminado. 3. Corriente de vientre.—*s.* (Poco us.) Despeño, cámaras, flujo de vientre, diarrea.

Laxation [lac-sē'-shun], *s.* Laxación.

Laxative [lax'-a-tiv], *a.* Laxativo, laxante.—*s.* Laxante, purgante.

Laxity [lac'-si-ti], **Laxness** [lax'-nes], *s.* 1. Aflojamiento, la acción y efecto de aflojar; laxitud, flojedad. 2. Relajamiento de nervios, etc.; relajación de costumbres, etc. 3. Anchura, soltura, desahogo. 4. Despeño, diarrea, cursos, cámaras.

Laxly [lax'-li], *adv.* Flojamente, sueltamente.

Lay [lē], *pret.* del verbo *To* LIE.

Lay [lē], *va.* (*pret.* y *pp.* LAID). 1. Poner, fijar, colocar alguna cosa. 2. Tender, extender o echar a lo largo en el suelo; echar o tumbar por tierra; impedir que se levante alguna cosa que está caída; hacer doblar las espigas o la hierba hacia el suelo. 3. Matar el polvo. 4. Enterrar. 5. Pintar, representar algo por medio de figuras. 6. Calmar, aquietar, sosegar, apaciguar. 7. Prepagar las plantas enterrando sus vástagos. 8. Añadir, juntar. 9. Imponer cargas, obligaciones u otra cosa. 10. Proyectar, trazar, discurrir. 11. Imputar. 12. Mandar, ordenar como una obligación. 13. Abatir, derrocar, derribar. 14. Apostar. 15. Exhibir, presentar, manifestar alguna cosa.—*vn.* 1. Poner huevos las hembras de las aves y otros animales. 2. Tramar, formar un plan. 3. (Mar.) Venir o ir como mandado; como *to lay aloft,* ir arriba. 4. Estar situado; uso incorrecto por *lie.* *To lay about,* Hacer todos los esfuerzos posibles por el logro de algún objeto, mover cielo y tierra por conseguir alguna cosa; dar golpes a ciegas o sin concierto. *To lay against,* Acusar. *To lay aft,* Ir a popa. *To lay apart,* Reservar, poner a parte. *To lay aside,* Desechar, echar o poner a un lado, arrinconar, poner en olvido, despreciar, descuidar, omitir, abandonar; separar, reservar. poner a parte. *To lay at,* Intentar, dar golpes y también golpear. *To lay away,* Dejar, echar a un lado. *To lay before,* Exponer a la vista, desplegar, mostrar, manifestar; representar ante alguna autoridad exponiendo daños, quejas o agravios. *To lay by,* Reservar, guardar, conservar alguna cosa para tiempo oportuno; deponer o apear de algún empleo o cargo; despedir, despachar, echar fuera; omitir; arrimar, arrinconar.

To lay down, Sentar y sostener una opinión o parecer; apostar; poner en depósito como prenda o equivalente; pagar, devolver, restituir; perder; rendir las armas. *To lay down a garden*, Delinear un jardín. *To lay for*, (Fam.) Asechar, poner asechanzas. *To lay forth*, Extenderse; poner o colocar a un muerto de un modo decente. *To lay hold of*, Asir, agarrar, coger; prender. *To lay in*, Atesorar; comprar. *To lay in for*, Hacer proposiciones con un objeto insidioso o doble. *To lay on*, Aplicar con violencia alguna cosa; obrar con vehemencia; imponer cargas u obligaciones; extender una cosa sobre la superficie de otra. *To lay open*, Descubrir, poner al descubierto, hacer ver, demostrar. *To lay over*, Cubrir una cosa con otra; desembolsar. *To lay out*, Gastar, emplear, desembolsar; ajustar, hacer divisiones; disponer, esforzarse; desplegar; descartarse en el juego. *To lay to*, Acusar; acometer; aplicarse con energía a algo; sentar una proposición; empeñar, consignar o depositar alguna cosa; renunciar; reposar. *To lay to heart*, Tomar a pechos, resentir vivamente. *To lay under*, Someter, sojuzgar. *To lay up*, Guardar, acumular, atesorar, amontonar, juntar, encerrar; cerrar, apretar; guardar cama por estar enfermo; prender o meter a uno en la cárcel o en paraje seguro. *To lay upon*, Imponer, cargar; poner algo sobre otra cosa. *To lay a bet*, Apostar, hacer una apuesta. *To lay eggs*, Aovar, poner huevos las aves u otros animales ovíparos. *To lay claim*, Reclamar, pretender. *To lay hands on one*, Sentar la mano, pegar a alguno. *To lay hands on one's self*, Matarse, cometer suicidio. *To lay level*, Igualar, allanar, destruir, arruinar. *To lay the blame on another*, Echar la culpa a otro. *To lay ropes*, (Mar.) Colchar cabos. *To lay waste*, Asolar. *Laying on of hands*, Imposición de manos. *To lay a bill on the table* (hablando de la cámara de representantes o del senado), Dar carpetazo a un proyecto de ley u otra providencia.

Lay [lê], *s.* 1. Caída, la manera como está situada o colocada alguna cosa; dirección relativa, contorno. 2. Negocio particular. 3. Cantidad determinada de hilo. 4. Marco oscilante de telar. 5. Ganancia o parte de ganancia. 6. Lecho, tongada, capa o cama con que se ponen algunas cosas sobre otras. *Lay-days*, (Mar.) Días de demora o estadía. *Over-lay-days, demurrage*, (Mar.) Sobreestalas, días de detención.

Lay [lê], *s.* Canción, balada, poema narrativo en estilo llano y sencillo.

Lay [lê], *a.* Secular, lego, seglar; no eclesiástico; no profesional. *A lay opinion*, Opinión no profesional. *Lay brother*, Hermano o fraile lego. *Lay clerk*, Capiscol, sochantre de una iglesia. *Lay reader*, Lego autorizado para leer las oraciones en una iglesia. *Lay land*, Baldío, campo que está inculto. *V.* LEA.

Layer [lê'-ẹr], *s.* 1. Lecho, capa, cama, tonga, tongada. 2 Vástago, pimpollo, renuevo de alguna planta; acodo. 3. Gallina que pone. *Layer out*, Mayordomo. *Layer up*, Tesorero.

Layer, *va.* Acodar, propagar plantas por medio de acodos.

Lay-figure [lê'-fig-yur], *s.* Maniquí, figura movible que se puede poner en varias actitudes.

Laying [lê'-ing], *s.* 1. El acto de colocar o poner alguna cosa. 2. Capa, costra.—*a.* Situado, colocado. (Mar.) Anclado.

Layman [lê'-man], *s.* Lego, el seglar que no goza fuero eclesiástico.

Layoff [lê'-ōf], *s.* Despedida del trabajo.—*va.* Cesar o despedir de un trabajo.

Lay of the land [lê ev dhi land], *s.* 1. Disposición o plano de un terreno. 2. Estado de algún asunto o circunstancias prevalecientes del mismo.

Layout [lê'-aut], *s.* 1. Plan, esquema. 2. Disposición, distribución.

Layover [lê'-ov-ẹr], *s.* Permanencia de pasada en algún lugar.

Lazar [lê'-zar], *s.* Lázaro, leproso.

Lazaret [laz'-ar-et], **Lazaretto** [laz-ar-et'-o], **Lazar-house** [lê'-zar-haus], *s.* Lazareto, hospital o casa donde hacen la cuarentena los que vienen de parajes sospechosos de peste.

Lazarwort [lê'-zẹr-wūrt], *s.* (Bot.) Laserpicio.

Lazily [lêz'-i-li], *adv.* Perezosamente, pesadamente.

Laziness [lê'-zi-nes], *s.* Pereza, desidia, ociosidad, haraganería.

Lazuli, *s.* *V.* LAPIS LAZULI.

Lazy [lê'-zi], *a.* 1. Perezoso, ocioso, flojo, desidioso, haragán. 2. Tardo, pesado.

Lea [lī], *s.* Prado, pradera; llanura.

Leach [līch], *va.* Lavar las cenizas de lejía para extraer el álcali; lixiviar.—*s.* 1. Cenizas de lejía, y la disolución obtenida por la lixiviación. 2. Lixiviación. 3. *Leach* o *leach-tub*, Cubo o tina donde se ponen las cenizas para hacer la colada.

Lead [led], *s.* 1. Plomo, metal blando, pesado, flexible y correoso. *Leads*, Techo emplomado. *Lead-mine*, Mina de plomo. *Black-lead*, Lápiz-plomo, plombagina, grafito. *White-lead*, Albayalde. *Red-lead*, Almagra o almagre; también se da este nombre al minio o azarcón. *Yellow-lead*, Albayalde calcinado. *V.* MASSICOT. *Lead-pencil*, Lápiz. *Sugar of lead*, Azúcar de plomo, acetato de plomo. 2. Interlínea, regleta. 3. (Mar.) Sondalesa, escandallo. *Hand-lead*, Sondalesa de mano. *Deep-sea-lead*, Escandallo mayor. *To heave the lead*, Echar la sonda. *The lead constantly going*, Sondeando constantemente.

Lead [led], *va.* (*pret.* y *pp.* LEADED). 1. Emplomar, forrar o guarnecer con plomo. 2. (Impr.) Interlinear, poner una regleta entre las líneas.

Lead [līd], *s.* 1. Primacía, primer lugar. *To take the lead*, Llevarse la primacía; tomar la delantera. 2. Mano, el que juega primero en las partidas de naipes. 3. Salida, el palo que juega el que es mano en algunos juegos de naipes.

Lead [līd], *va.* (*pret.* y *pp.* LED). 1. Llevar de la mano. 2. Conducir, guiar o dirigir a otro. 3. Mandar, regir, gobernar. 4. Guiar, ir delante. 5. Enseñar, amaestrar. 6. Halagar, atraer, inducir, mover, motivar. 7. Gastar o emplear el tiempo en alguna cosa.—*vn.* 1. Mandar en jefe. 2. Guiar, enseñar el camino; conducir; dominar. 3. Ser mano en el juego de naipes. *To lead along*, Conducir, acompañar. *To lead astray*, Llevar fuera del camino recto, extraviar; seducir. *To lead away*, Llevar o traer de una parte a otra, hacer una persona que otra la acompañe. *To lead back*, Acompañar de vuelta, volver a conducir a una persona al paraje de donde se la había traído antes. *To lead a horse to water*, Llevar a abrevar un caballo. *To lead in* o *into*, Introducir. *To lead off* o *out of*, Desviar, estorbar, impedir; principiar. *To lead one a dance*, Hacer dar a uno muchos pasos o gastar doble tiempo del necesario. *To lead out of the way*, Descarriar. *To lead a good life*, Vivir bien. *To lead a new life*, Enmendarse. *To lead the way*, Mostrar el camino, tomar la delantera.

Leaded [led'-ed], *pp.* y *a.* 1. Interlineado. 2. Emplomado, plomado; guarnecido de plomo o engastado en plomo o grafito.

Leaden [led'-n], *a.* 1. Hecho de plomo. 2. Aplomado, de color de plomo. 3. Pesado, tardo, lento, estúpido. *Leaden-hearted*, Duro, insensible, que tiene corazón de mármol. *Leaden-heeled*, Lento, tardo.

Leader [līd'-ẹr], *s.* 1. Guía, conductor, la persona que encamina y enseña el camino. 2. Jefe, general, capitán, comandante, el superior que dirige un ejército o parte de él; caudillo, corifeo, cabeza, principal de una facción, reunión, etc. 3. Guión, el que va delante. *Leader of a dance*, Guión, director de una danza o un baile. *Ringleader*, Jefe de partido. (Fam.) Cabecilla, cabeza de bando.

Leadership [lī'-dẹr-ship], *s.* Dirección, estado, condición del que conduce, guía o dirige.

Leading [līd'-ing], *a.* Principal, primero; capital. *To have the leading hands at cards*, Ser mano en el juego. *Leading man*, Jefe de partido. *Leading-strings*, (1) Andadores, los cordones o cintas con que se sostiene al niño que empieza a andar. (2) De aquí, dirección, refrenamiento, especialmente si es desagradable o estorba. *Leading word*, La primera palabra.—*s.* Guía, conducción.

Leadsman [ledz'-man], *s.* (Mar.) Sondeador.

Leady [led'-i], *a.* Aplomado, parecido al plomo o que lo contiene.

Leaf [līf], *s.* (*pl.* LEAVES [līvs]). 1. (Bot.) Hoja. 2. Hoja, la parte de un libro que se compone de dos páginas o llanas. 3. Hoja de puerta, o de mesa que se dobla. 4. Hoja, plancha batida y muy delgada. *A leaf of gold* o *silver*, Hoja o pan de oro o plata. *Leaf brass*, Oropel. *Over the leaf* o *turn the leaf*, A la vuelta. *Fly-leaf*, (Impr.) Guarda, hoja blanca. *To turn down a leaf*, Hacer un pliegue a una hoja. *To turn over a new leaf*, Doblar la hoja, enmendar uno su conducta o sus costumbres. *Leaf-bud*, Yema, botón de una planta que se desarrolla en una rama frondosa. *Leaf-hopper*, Insecto hemíptero saltador que se alimenta de las hojas de ciertas plantas; v. gr. el Erythroneura vitis. *Leaf-lard*, Manteca en rama. *Leaf-stalk*, Peciolo, pezón.

Leaf, *vn.* Echar hojas.

Leafage [līf'-ẹj], *s.* Follaje, la abundancia de hoja.

Leafed [līft], **Leafy** [līf'-i], *a.* Frondoso, poblado de hoja: dícese de los árboles; hojoso.

Leafiness [lîf'-i-nes], *s.* Follaje, abundancia de hojas.

Leafless [lîf'-les], *a.* Sin follaje, que no echa hojas; deshojado.

Leaflet [lîf'-let], *s. dim.* Hojilla, hojuela.

Leaf tobacco [lîf to-bac'-o], *s.* Tabaco en rama.

League [lîg], *s.* 1. Liga, alianza, confederación; unión, asociación entre dos o varias personas, partidos, estados, etc. 2. Legua, medida de tierra de tres millas geográficas poco más o menos. La legua marina es de veinte al grado, o tres millas náuticas.

League, *vn.* Confederarse, ligarse, aliarse, unirse.

Leagued [lîgd], *a.* Confederado, ligado, aliado.

Leaguer [lîg'-ẹr], *s.* 1. (Poco us.) Coligado, conjurado. 2. (Mil.) Campamento.

Leak [lîk], *s.* 1. Rendija, grieta, raja por donde entra o se escapa el agua; (Mar.) vía de agua. 2. Goteo, filtración, paso de un flúido por una grieta, rendija o cualquier abertura. *To spring a leak*, (Mar.) Hacer agua, o abrir agua un barco. *To fother a leak*, (Mar.) Atajar una corriente, cegar una vía de agua.

Leak, *vn.* Gotear, hacer agua; derramarse, rezumarse. *The ship leaks*, (Mar.) El navío hace agua. *A barrel that leaks*, Barril que se rezuma.

Leakage [lîk'-ẹj], *s.* 1. Goteo, filtración. 2. Avería, pérdida, merma de un líquido que sale por una abertura. 3. Merma, derrame, la rebaja que se hace por lo que se rezuman las vasijas o medidas de los líquidos.

Leak proof [lîk prûf], *a.* 1. Que no se gotea. 2. A prueba de escape.

Leaky [lîk'-i], *a.* 1. Roto; haciendo agua; que se rezuma. 2. (Fam.) Locuaz, indiscreto, la persona propensa a revelar secretos.

Leal [lîl], *a.* (Poét., Prov. Ingl. y Esco.) Leal, fiel, sincero. *The land of the leal*, La morada de los fieles, el cielo.

Lean [lîn], *vn.* 1. Apoyarse, recostarse contra alguna cosa, reclinarse, repantigarse. 2. Inclinarse, torcerse un poco hacia abajo, encorvarse. 3. Inclinarse, tener propensión a alguna cosa.—*va.* Inclinar, torcer algo hacia abajo, encorvar. *To lean against*, Apoyarse en, arrimarse a. *To lean over*, Adelantarse hacia alguna parte.

Lean, *a.* Flaco, magro; mezquino, necesitado.—*s.* 1. Carne mollar, carne magra sin gordura. 2. *Lean* o *leaning*, Inclinación, disposición, propensión.

Leanly [lîn'-li], *adv.* Pobremente; sin gordura.

Leanness [lîn'-nes], *s.* Flaqueza, magrura; pobreza.

Lean-to [lîn'-tū], *s.* Colgadizo.

Lean-witted [lîn'-wit-ed], *a.* Tonto, necio.

Leap [lîp], *vn.* 1. Saltar, brincar. 2. Correr hacia alguna parte con precipitación y de repente. 3. Saltar, brotar, salir con ímpetu. 4. Palpitar el corazón.—*va.* 1. Saltar, brincar. 2. Cubrir, tener coito el macho cuadrúpedo con la hembra. *To leap again*, Volver a saltar. *To leap for joy*, Saltar de alegría, de gozo.

Leap, *s.* 1. Salto, el acto de saltar. 2. Salto, el espacio de tierra que mide un salto. 3. Salto, tránsito desproporcionado de una cosa a otra, paso repentino o súbito. 4. Asalto o acometimiento de algún animal feroz. 5. El ayuntamiento o coito de los animales. 6. Salto o tránsito desproporcionado de una cosa a otra. 7. (Prov. Ingl.) Cestón para pescado.

Leaper [lîp'-ẹr], *s.* 1. Saltador, brincador. 2. El caballo que pasa saltando todos los obstáculos que encuentra en la carrera.

Leap-frog [lîp'-frog], *s.* A la una la mula, juego de muchachos, llamado también (Amer.) carga o salta la burra.

Leaping [lîp'-ing], *s.* Salto, el acto de saltar.

Leapingly [lîp-ing-li], *adv.* A brincos, a saltos.

Leap-year [lîp'-yîr], *s.* Año bisiesto o intercalar.

Learn [lẹrn], *va.* (*pret.* y *pp.* LEARNED o LEARNT). 1. Aprender, adquirir el conocimiento de alguna cosa por medio del estudio; fijar en la mente. 2. (Des.) Instruir, enseñar; informar.—*vn.* 1. Aprender siguiendo el ejemplo de otro; instruirse. 2. Saber, recibir una noticia. *We learn that he is dead*, Sabemos, recibimos la noticia de que ha muerto.

Learnable [lẹrn'-a-bl], *a.* Que puede aprenderse.

Learned [lẹrn'-ed], *a.* 1. Docto, erudito. 2. Sabio, inteligente. 3. Hábil, diestro; versado en, perito, experto. *The learned*, Los doctos, los sabios, los literatos. *The learned world*, La república de las letras. *My learned brother*, Mi ilustrado colega.

Learnedly [lẹrn'-ed-li], *adv.* Sabiamente, doctamente.

Learner [lẹrn'-ẹr], *s.* Tirón, el que es bisoño en un arte o ciencia; escolar, estudiante; aprendiz; discípulo, principiante.

Learning [lẹrn'-ing], *s.* 1. Literatura, el conocimiento y ciencia de las letras; saber, ciencia, erudición, estudio. 2. Conocimiento de alguna cosa.

Leasable [lîs'-a-bl], *a.* Arrendable.

Lease [lîs], *s.* 1. Arriendo, escritura de arrendamiento, el contrato por el cual se adquiere por determinado número de años la posesión de casas o tierras pagando una cantidad convenida, ora adelantada, ora a ciertos plazos o períodos. 2. Posesión de una cosa cualquiera. 3. En los tejidos, paso, cruce.

Lease, *va.* Arrendar, dar en arriendo la posesión de casas o tierras por tiempo fijo de años.—*vn.* (Poco us.) Espigar, coger las espigas que han dejado de segar los segadores o las que han quedado en el campo.

Leaser [lîs'-ẹr], *s.* 1. Espigador. 2. (Des.) Embustero.

Leaseholder [lîs'-hōld'-ẹr], *s.* Arrendatario.

Leash [lîsh], *s.* 1. Pihuela, traílla, correa. 2. Tres, par y medio. *Leash of hares*, Tres liebres. *Leash of partridges*, Tres perdices. 3. Cualquiera cosa con que está atada otra. 4. Lizo, entre los tejedores.

Leash, *va.* Atar con cuerda o correa.

†**Leasing** [lîs'-ing], *s.* Mentira, falsedad.

Least [lîst], *a.* (*sup.* de LITTLE). Mínimo; el menor, el mínimo, el más pequeño. *The least space*, El menor espacio. *The least of the apostles*, El menor de los apóstoles.—*adv.* Lo menos. *At least*, A lo menos. *At the least* o *at leastwise*, En la menor cantidad posible. *Not in the least*, Ni en lo más mínimo; de ninguna manera. *Be not in the least uneasy*, No tenga Vd. el menor cuidado.

Leat [lît], *s.* (Ant.) El cauce o canal que conduce el agua a un molino o por donde sale de él.

Leather [ledh'-ẹr], *s.* 1. Cuero, cordobán, pellejo. 2. Pieza, porción o artículo hecho de cuero. 3. Cuero, pellejo o piel de racional: en este último sentido se usa sólo hablando con ironía o desprecio. *Alum leather, tawed leather*, Cuero blanco, curtido con alumbre y sal. *Patent leather, enamelled leather*, Charol. *Sheep's leather*, Badana. *Wash leather*, Gamuza. *Alligator leather*, Cuero de caimán (cocodrilo). *Russia leather*, *V.* RUSSIA.—*a.* *V.* LEATHERN. *Leather-winged*, Que tiene alas como de cuero; se dice de algunos insectos.

Leather, *va.* 1. Forrar, guarnecer con cuero. 2. Hacer cuero, cambiar en cuero. 3. Golpear, pegar, zurrar con una correa de cuero.—*vn.* Batir, sacudir; dar tundas.

Leather-coat [ledh'-ẹr-cōt], *s.* Especie de manzana; una cosa cualquiera cubierta con una corteza correosa.

Leather-cutter [ledh'-ẹr-cut'-ẹr], *s.* El que vende cuero curtido por menor.

Leather-dresser [ledh'-ẹr-dres'-ẹr], *s.* Curtidor, pellejero.

Leatherette [ledh''-ẹr-et'], *s.* Cuero artificial; imitación de cuero hecha con papel o tela.

Leatherhead [ledh'-ẹr-hed''], *s.* 1. Tropidorinco. *V.* FRIAR-BIRD. 2. Un tonto, un estúpido.

Leathern [ledh'-ẹrn], *a.* De cuero, hecho de cuero o cordobán.

Leathery [ledh'-ẹr-i], *a.* Lo que se parece al cuero, correoso.

Leave [lîv], *s.* 1. Licencia, permiso, venia. *By your leave*, Con el permiso de Vd., con licencia de Vd. *Give me leave to tell you*, Permítame Vd. que le diga. 2. Despedida, la acción de despedirse; dícese también **Leave-taking**. *To take leave of one's friends*, Despedirse de los amigos. *To be absent on leave*, Hallarse ausente con permiso o licencia. *To take French leave*, Despedirse a la francesa. *V.* FRENCH.

Leave, *va.* y *vn.* (*pret.* y *pp.* LEFT). 1. Dejar, permitir la permanencia; no alejar. 2. Dejar o legar alguna cosa después de muerto. *To leave issue*, Dejar hijos o sucesión. 3. Dejar, desamparar, abandonar. 4. Dejar, separarse de una persona o lugar. 5. Dejar; dar, ceder o renunciar una cosa a favor de otro. 6. Dejar, despojarse, renunciar. 7. Dejar, cesar, desistir de un empeño, de una obra, etc. 8. Referirse a alguien o a algo; entregar, confiar en depósito. *To leave off*, Cesar, parar, descontinuar. *To leave out*, Omitir, olvidar, descuidar, desatender; excluir. *To be left till called for*, En la lista del correo. *To leave behind*, Dejar atrás; dejar en pos de sí a su muerte. *I leave the reader to judge*, Dejo juez al lector. *To leave off a garment*, Quitarse una prenda de ropa. *Nothing was left out*, No se omitió nada.

Leaved [lîvd], *a.* Hojoso, hecho de hojas.

Leaven [lev'-n], *s.* 1. Levadura, fermento. *Leavened bread,* Pan de levadura. 2. Toda cosa que ejerciendo una influencia latente y poderosa, ocasiona un cambio general.

Leaven, *va.* 1. Fermentar, leudar, poner en movimiento intestino las partículas de un cuerpo. 2. Corromper, contaminar, pervertir, viciar. 3. Imbuir buenas máximas, buenos principios, etc.

Leavening [lev'-n-ing], *s.* Fermento.

Leavenous [lev'-n-us], *a.* Lo que contiene fermento; corrompido.

Leaver [lîv'-ẹr], *s.* El que abandona o deja.

Leaves [lîvz], *s. pl.* de LEAF, hoja. *Marbled leaves,* Cortes jaspeados. *Gilt leaves,* Cortes dorados, hablando de libros.

Leaving [lîv'-ing], *s.* 1. Partida, acción de partir de un lugar. 2. *pl.* Sobras, relieves; desechos; desperdicios; residuo, sobra.

Leavy, *a.* (Ant.) *V.* LEAFY.

Lecher [lech'-ẹr], s. Hombre putañero, disoluto, libertino.

Lecherous [lech'-ẹr-us], *a.* Lujurioso, impúdico, lascivo.

Lecherousness [lech'-ẹr-us-nes], **Lechery** [lech'-ẹr-i], *s.* Lujuria, el apetito desordenado de los deleites carnales.

Lectern [lec'-tẹrn], *s.* Atril, facistol de iglesia.

Lection [lec'-shun], *s.* 1. Lección, lectura que se hace en la celebración del oficio divino. 2. Lección, la letra o texto de alguna obra.

Lectionary [lec'-shun-ẹ-ri], *s.* Leccionario, libro que contiene las lecciones del oficio divino.

Lecture [lec'-chur], *s.* 1. Discurso, razonamiento o plática razonada sobre alguna materia; discurso moral o religioso; particularmente explicación de los principios de alguna ciencia. 2. Fraterna, corrección; reprensión pedantesca.

Lecture, *va.* 1. Enseñar, instruir, por medio de razonamientos. 2. Enseñar alguna cosa de un modo pedantesco.—*vn.* Dar explicaciones públicas sobre los principios de alguna ciencia.

Lecturer [lec'-chur-ẹr], *s.* Lector, instructor; teniente de cura de alguna parroquia.

Lectureship [lec'-chur-ship], *s.* El empleo de uno que da lecciones o explicaciones; el de un teniente de cura.

Lecturn, *s.* *V.* LECTERN.

Led, *pp.* y *pret.* del verbo *To* LEAD.

Led-captain [led-cap'-ten], *s.* El que obtiene el favor de una persona por medio de obsequios humildes y bajos.

Ledge [lej], *s.* 1. Anaquel, moldura saliente, o parte parecida a un anaquel; capa, tonga, tongada; arrecife. *Ledge of rocks,* Arrecife de piedras o peñas. 2. (Mar.) Latas de los baos. *Ledges of the gratings,* (Mar.) Barrotes de los enjaretados.

Ledger [lej'-ẹr], *s.* 1. Libro mayor, el libro principal en que los comerciantes asientan sus cuentas. *Alphabet of the ledger,* Índice alfabético del libro mayor. 2. Alguna cosa, como una barra o piedra, que ha de yacer o tenderse llana o quedarse en una posición fija; como solera de emparrillado, traviesa de andamio.—*a.* Ligero. *V.* LEGER.

Led-horse [led'-hōrs], *s.* Caballo de mano.

Lee [lî], *s.* 1. (Mar.) Sotavento, el costado del navío opuesto a la parte por donde da el viento. 2. Paraje resguardado, al abrigo de los vientos. (No tiene plural.)—*a.* 1. (Mar.) Sotaventado, expuesto al sotavento; opuesto a *weather* (barlovento). 2. (Esco.) Solitario. *Lee shore,* (Mar.) Costa de sotavento. *Lee side,* (Mar.) Banda de sotavento. *Leeway,* (Mar.) Abatimiento o derriba. *Lee braces,* (Mar.) Brazos de sotavento. *Under the lee,* (Mar.) A sotavento. *To have lee o sea room,* Tener buen sotavento. *Lee tide,* Marea de donde viene el viento. *On the lee beam,* A la banda de sotavento.

Leech [lîch], *s.* 1. Sanguijuela. 2. (Ant.) Médico, el que sabe y profesa el arte de la medicina o de curar. *Horse-leech,* Albéitar. 3. Instrumento para sangrar, como escarificador, ventosa, etc., llamado *artificial leach.* 4. (Mar.) Caídas. *Leech-lines,* (Mar.) Apagapenoles. *Leech-rope,* (Mar.) Relinga de las caídas.

Leech, *va.* 1. *V.* LEACH. 2. (Ant.) Curar, sanar.

†Leechcraft [lîch'-craft], *s.* (Des.) Arte de curar.

Leek [lîc], *s.* (Bot.) Puerro.

Leer [lîr], *s.* 1. Ojeada, mirada de reojo, que puede ser maliciosa, amorosa o equívoca. 2. Templador, especie de horno que sirve para templar y enfriar el cristal y vidrio después de vaciado.—*a.* (Des. o prov. Ingl.) Vacío, frívolo, sin juicio.

Leer, *vn.* Ojear o mirar de soslayo o de reojo.—*va.* Atraer con risa, engañar con miradas.

Leeringly [lîr'-ing-li], *adv.* Con risa engañosa o mirada de desprecio.

Lees [lîz], *s. pl.* Heces, sedimento, poso. (Antiguamente se empleaba también en singular, *lee;* hez, zupia.)

Leet [lît], o **Court-leet** [cōrt'-lît], *s.* Un tribunal de justicia en tiempos antiguos, y el día en que se reunía.

Leeward [lî'-ward, lū'-ard entre los marineros], *a.* (Mar.) Sotavento. *Leeward ship,* (Mar.) Navío sotaventeador. *Leeward Islands,* Islas de sotavento. *Leeward-tide,* (Mar.) Marea en la dirección del viento. *To leeward,* (Mar.) A sotavento.

Leeway [lî'-wê], *s.* 1. (Mar.) Deriva, abatimiento del rumbo; ángulo de deriva. 2. De aquí en general desviación de un rumbo fijo.

Left [left], *pp.* y *pret.* del verbo *To* LEAVE. *This package is to be left at Mr. N.'s,* Este paquete deberá entregarse o dejarse en casa del Sr. N. *Left-off,* Puesto a un lado, desechado.

Left, *a.* Siniestro, izquierdo, lo que no está a la mano derecha. *To the left,* A la izquierda. *Left hand,* Mano izquierda. *Over the left,* (Vulg.) Exactamente lo opuesto.

Left-hand [left'-hand''], *a.* 1. Zurdo, situado al lado izquierdo. 2. Que da vueltas, rueda, se abre o se mueve hacia la mano izquierda. *Left-handed,* (1) Zurdo. (2) Poco diestro, desmañado. (3) Indirecto, insincero, malicioso. (4) Que da vueltas en sentido contrario al movimiento de las manecillas de un reloj; que gira el plano de polarización hacia la izquierda. (5) (Des.) Desgraciado; intempestivo. *Left-handed screw,* Tornillo zurdo. *Left-handedness,* El uso habitual de la mano izquierda. *Left-handiness,* Costumbre zafia.

Leftist [lef'-tist], *a.* & *s.* Izquierdista.

Leftovers [left-ō'-vẹrz], *s. pl.* Sobras (de comida).

Leg [leg], *s.* 1. Pierna; pata de las aves y animales. 2. Pie, la base sobre que se mantiene el cuerpo de alguna cosa; pata. *Leg of a table,* Pata de una mesa. 3. La parte de una prenda de ropa que cubre la pierna; caña de media. 4. (Mar.) Espacio recorrido por un buque en una bordada. 5. Lado de un triángulo que no es su base. *Leg-bail,* (Vulg.) Huída, fuga de la cárcel o custodia. *To take leg-bail,* Tomar las de Villadiego. *On one's last legs,* A la muerte, agonizante, literal y figuradamente; exhausto de recursos. *On* o *upon its legs,* En pie, firmemente establecido. *To get on one's legs,* (1) Levantarse para dirigir la palabra a una cámara o concurso. (2) Recobrar la salud. *To give a leg to,* Ayudar a montar un caballo afirmando la pierna. *Not to have a leg to stand on,* Hallarse enteramente sin recursos; no saber por qué lado echar. *Not to leave one a leg to stand on,* Poner a uno entre la espada y la pared. *To pull one's leg,* (Ger.) Obtener dinero o favores de una persona por dolo o engaño.

Legacy [leg'-a-si], *s.* Legado, manda.

Legacy-hunter [leg'-a-si-hunt'-ẹr], *s.* El que anda a caza de herencias.

Legal [lî'-gal], *a.* 1. Legal, jurídico, legítimo; lícito, permitido por la ley. 2. Definido, provisto por la ley; que puede remediarse apelando a la ley.

Legality [lẹ-gal'-i-ti], *s.* Legalidad, legitimidad.

Legalize [lî'-gal-aiz], *va.* Legalizar, autorizar, legitimar.

Legally [lî'-gal-i], *adv.* Legalmente.

Legal tender [lî'-gal ten'-dẹr], *s.* Moneda legal.

Legate [leg'-êt], *s.* 1. Legado, diputado. 2. Legado, cardenal u obispo enviado por el Papa con una misión.

Legatee [leg-a-tî'], *s.* Legatario, la persona a quien por testamento se deja algún legado.

Legateship [leg'-êt-ship], *s.* Legacía, el empleo de legado.

Legatine [leg'-a-tin o tain], *a.* Hecho por un legado o que pertenece a él.

Legation [lẹ-gê'-shun], *s.* Legación, embajada.

Legato [lê-gā'-tō], *adv.* (Mús.) Ligado, de un modo igual y conexo; lo opuesto a *staccato.* (Ital.)

Legator [le-gê'-tẹr o leg-a-tor'], *s.* El que hace testamento dejando legados.

Legend [lej'-end], *s.* 1. Leyenda o legenda, crónica o registro de las vidas de los santos. 2. Relación, narración. 3. Letrero, la inscripción que tienen las medallas o monedas. 4. Narrativa increíble y no auténtica, fábula.

Legendary [lej'-end-ẹ-ri], *a.* Fabuloso, quijotesco.—*s.* 1. Legendario, el libro de las actas y vidas de los santos. 2. Hagiógrafo, el escritor de vidas de los santos.

Leger [lej'-ẹr], *a.* 1. Ligero y delicado, como una línea. 2. (Des.) Residente, permanente. *Leger-lines,* Líneas adicionales para escribir no-

tas de música. *Leger space*, Espacio comprendido por una de esas líneas adicionales.—*s. V.* LEDGER.

Legerdemain [lej-gr-de-mên'], *s.* Ligereza de manos, juego de manos, engaños a ojos vista, el que usan los saltimbancos.

Legged [legd], *a.* Lo que tiene piernas; empernado. Se usa en composición; como *a three-legged stool*, Banqueta, banquillo de tres pies.

Legging, Leggin [leg'-ing, leg'-in], *s.* Polaina larga que llega a la rodilla; guardapierna.

Leghorn [leg'-hōrn], *s.* 1. Sombrero de paja de Italia; y el tejido fino hecho con esta paja. 2. Casta o raza de gallinas.

Legibility [lej-i-bil'-i-ti], *s.* La calidad de lo que puede ser leído fácilmente.

Legible [lej'-i-bl], *a.* Legible; patente, manifiesto.

Legibleness [lej'-i-bl-nes], *s.* El estado o calidad de lo que es legible.

Legibly [lej'-i-bli], *adv.* Legiblemente.

Legion [lī'-jun], *s.* 1. Legión, un cuerpo de tropas romanas, que según los tiempos se componía de tres á cuatro mil hombres de caballería é infantería. 2. Legión, un gran número; tropa, multitud.

Legionary [lī'-jun-g-ri], *a.* y *s.* Legionario.

Legislate [lej'-is-lêt], *vn.* Legislar, dar leyes.

Legislation [lej-is-lé'-shun], *s.* Legislación, la facultad legislativa.

Legislative [lej'-is-la-tiv], *a.* Legislativo.

Legislator [lej'-is-lé-tgr], *s.* Legislador.

Legislatorial [lej-is-la-tō'-ri-al], *a.* Perteneciente o relativo a la legislación o a una legislatura.

Legislatorship [lej is-lé'-tgr-ship], *s.* El oficio o dignidad de legislador; el poder o facultad de hacer leyes.

Legislatress [lej-is-lé'-tres], *sf.* Legisladora.

Legislature [lej'-is-lé-chur], *s.* Legislatura, cuerpo legislativo.

Legist [lī'-jist], *s.* Legista, jurisconsulto.

Legitimacy [le-jit'-i-ma-si], *s.* 1. Legitimidad, conformidad con la ley o con la lógica; legalidad. 2. Nacimiento legítimo. 3. Pureza, estado exento de falsificación.

Legitimate [le-jit'-i-met], *a.* 1. Legítimo; legal, lícito, permitido por la ley y costumbre. 2. Nacido legalmente durante el matrimonio. 3. Legítimo, justo, resultante de consecuencias naturales o regulares.

Legitimate, *va.* Legitimar, hacer legítimo; conferir los derechos de hijo legítimo al que nació fuera del matrimonio.

Legitimately [le-jit'-i-met-li], *adv.* Legítimamente.

Legitimateness [le-jit'-i-met-nes], *s.* Legitimidad, legalidad.

Legitimation [le-jit-i-mé'-shun], *s.* 1. Legitimación, el acto de legitimar a un hijo natural. 2. En Europa, legitimación (para residir, etc.).

Legitimist [le-jit'-i-mist], *s.* Legitimista, partidario de cierta autoridad como legítima.

Legitimize [le-jit'-i-maiz], *va. V. To* LEGITIMATE.

Legume [leg'-yum o le-giūm'], **Legumen** [le-giū'-men], *s.* (Bot.) Legumbre, vaina, fruto bivalvo unicelular de la familia de las leguminosas (habas, frijoles, guisantes, etc.).

Leguminous [le-giū'-min-us], *a.* (Bot.) Leguminoso, lo que pertenece a la familia de las leguminosas.

†**Leisurable** [līzh'-ur-a-bl], *a.* Hecho o ejecutado despacio y sin precipitación.

Leisure [lī'-zhur], *s.* 1. Ocio, tiempo desocupado y de descanso; desocupación, ociosidad. 2. Comodidad. *At leisure*, Despacio, con comodidad o cómodamente, con sosiego. *To be at leisure*, Estar desocupado.—*a.* Conveniente; libre de negocios o asuntos. *Leisure hours*, Las horas desocupadas, o destinadas al descanso o al reposo.

Leisurely [lī'-zhur-li], *a.* Pausado, deliberado.—*adv.* Despacio, con cachaza; deliberadamente.

†**Leman** [lī'-man], *s.* Amante, galán; cortejo; concubina, manceba.

Lemma [lem'-a], *s.* Lema, proposición que se suele poner para demostrar otras que se siguen.

Lemming [lem'-ing], *s.* (Zool.) Turón de Noruega; arvícola.

Lemna [lem'-na], *s.* (Bot.) Lentícula (lenteja de agua).

Lemon [lem'-gn], *s.* Limón, el fruto del *Lemon-tree*, limonero. *Candied lemon*, Acitrón, dulce hecho con las cáscaras del limón. *Pickled lemon*, Limón encurtido o salado. *Lemon-peel*, Corteza de cidra. *Lemon-squeezer*, Exprimidor de limón.—*a.* 1. Sazonado con limón o que contiene limón. 2. De color de limón.

Lemonade [lem-gn-éd'], *s.* Limonada, bebida compuesta de agua, azúcar y zumo de limón.

Lemon drops [lem'-gn drops], *s. pl.* Pastillas de limón.

Lemur [lī'-mur], *s.* Lémur, animal parecido al mono, uno de los prosimios o lemúridos. Vive en Madagascar e islas vecinas.

Lemures [lem'-yu-rīz], *s. pl.* Fantasmas, sombras de los muertos, almas de los malos que según los gentiles vagaban bajo feísimas formas.

Lend [lend], *va.* 1. Prestar, dar alguna cosa con la obligación de que sea restituída. 2. Dar, conceder. *To lend aid*, Dar ayuda o auxilio. *To lend a hand (to)*, Dar o echar una mano, ayudar.

Lendable [lend'-a-bl], *a.* Prestadizo, prestable.

Lender [lend'-gr], *s.* Prestador, prestamista; logrero.

Lending [lend'-ing], *s.* Empréstito, préstamo.

Lene [lī'-nī ó lé'-né], *a.* (Gram.) Suave, no aspirado.—*s.* Consonante no aspirada; aspiración suave '.

Length [length], *s.* 1. Longitud, largura, lo largo de alguna cosa. *A picture in full length*, Retrato de cuerpo entero. 2. Espacio o duración de tiempo. 3. Extensión, dilatación, distancia. 4. Alcance (de un tiro, etc.), capacidad de llegar; punto, grado. *At length*, (1) Al fin, finalmente, en conclusión. (2) Extensamente, sin abreviación ni omisión. *At full length*, A lo largo, de todo el largo. *Length of days*, Lo largo de la vida, la existencia prolongada.

†**Lengthen** [length'-en], *va.* Alargar, extender, prolongar, dilatar.—*vn.* Aumentarse, alargarse, prolongarse o dilatarse alguna cosa. *To lengthen out*, Estirar, dilatar, alargar.

Lengthening [length'-en-ing], *s.* Alargamiento, continuación, prolongación.

Lengthwise [length'-waiz], *adv.* Longitudinalmente; según lo largo, á lo largo.

Lengthy [length'-i], *a.* Bastante largo, indebidamente largo; algo difuso, v. gr. un discurso o sermón.

Lenient [lī'-ni-ent], *a.* y *s.* 1. Benigno, clemente, misericordioso. 2. (Poco us.) Leniente, emoliente; laxativo, lenitivo.

Lenify [len'-i-fai], *va.* Lenificar, suavizar, mitigar, ablandar.

Lenitive [len'-i-tiv], *a.* Lenitivo.—*s.* 1. Lenitivo, la medicina o remedio que ablanda. 2. Lenitivo, cualquier medio para suavizar o aplacar las pasiones del ánimo.

Lenity [len'-i-ti], *s.* Lenidad, blandura, suavidad.

Lens [lenz], *s.* (*pl.* LENSES). 1. Lente, vidrio generalmente de forma circular, convexo o cóncavo, de que se usa en los instrumentos ópticos. 2. Cristalino, cuerpo transparente situado inmediatamente detrás del iris del ojo. 3. Objetivo.

Lent [lent], *pret.* y *pp.* del verbo *To* LEND. Prestado.

Lent, *s.* Cuaresma, los cuarenta días seguidos de abstinencia en las iglesias anglicana, católica romana y otras. *Lent dinner*, Comida de viernes.

Lenten [lent'-en], *a.* 1. Cuaresmal, cuadragesimal, lo que pertenece a la cuaresma. 2. Escaso.

Lenticel [len'-ti-sel], *s.* (Bot.) Lentejuela, tuberculillo que pertenece a la capa de corcho de las plantas.

Lenticula [len-tic'-yu-la], *s.* 1. (Ópt.) Lente pequeño. 2. (Med.) *V.* FRECKLE. 3. (Bot.) *V.* LENTICEL.

Lenticular [len-tic'-yu-lar], **Lentiform** [len'-ti-fōrm], *a.* Lenticular, semejante a las lentejas.

Lentiginous [len-tij'-i-nus], *a.* (Bot. y Zool.) Pecoso; que presenta la apariencia de haber sido polvoreado como con granillos.

Lentil [len'-til], *s.* (Bot.) Lenteja.

Lentiscus [len-tis'-cus], **Lentisk** [len'-tisc], *s.* (Bot.) Lentisco.

Leo [lī'-o], *s.* (Astr.) 1. León, el quinto signo del zodíaco. 2. Constelación que antiguamente se hallaba en este signo, pero que está hoy en el signo Virgo.

Leonine [lī'-o-nin o nain], *a.* 1. Leonino, lo que toca o pertenece al león o participa de sus propiedades. 2. Leonino, clase de versos latinos.

Leopard [lep'-ard], *s.* Leopardo, mamífero carnicero.

Leopard's-bane [lep'-ardz-bên], *s.* (Bot.) Dorónico.

Leper [lep'-gr], *s.* Un leproso, el que padece lepra.

Leperous [lep'-gr-us], *a. V.* LEPROUS.

Lepidoptera [lep"-i-dep'-te-ra], *s.* (Ent.) Lepidópteros, orden de insectos que tienen una trompa chupadora, cuatro alas cubiertas de un polvo escamoso, y metamorfosis completa; las mariposas, falenas, etc.

Lepidopterous [lep-i-dep'-tgr-us], *a.* Lepidóptero, perteneciente a los insectos llamados lepidópteros.

Leporine [lep'-o-rin o rain], *a.* Lebruno, lo que pertenece a la liebre.

Leprose [lep'-rōs], *a.* (Bot.) Casposo, escamoso; cubierto de escamas delgadas.

Leprosity [lep-res'-i-ti], *s.* La calidad de ser escamoso.

Leprosy [lep'-ro-si], *s.* Lepra, elefancía.
Leprous [lep'-rus], *a.* Leproso.
Leprousness [lep'-rus-nes], *s.* Leprosidad.
Lepus [lī'-pus], *s.* Liebre, una constelación del hemisferio austral.
Lesbian [lez'-bi-an], *a.* & *s.* Lesbiano, Lesbio.
Lese-majesty [līz-maj'-es-ti], *s.* Lesa majestad.
Lesion [lī'-zhun], *s.* Lesión, en sus acepciones médicas y forenses.
Less [les], *a.* (*comp.* de LITTLE). Menor, menos, inferior.—*s.* Una cantidad más pequeña que otra.—*adv.* Menos, en grado más pequeño; en grado más bajo. *Much less,* Mucho menos. *More or less,* Más o menos. *Less and less,* De menos en menos. *To grow less,* Disminuirse, achicarse. *To make less,* Aminorar, disminuir, escatimar. *So much the less,* Tanto menos cuanto. *The less . . . . the less,* Cuanto menos . . . . menos.
less, *sufijo.* Terminación negativa o privativa, que expresa la privación o falta de una cosa; sin. *Childless,* sin hijos; *hopeless,* sin esperanza, etc. *Penniless,* Sin un cuarto, sin un céntimo.
Lessee [les-ī'], *s.* Arrendatario, el que toma en arrendamiento alguna cosa.
Lessen [les'-n], *va.* 1. Minorar, achicar, disminuir, acortar, reducir a menos. 2. Degradar, privar a alguno de sus honores, grados o dignidad.—*vn.* 1. Mermar, disminuirse. 2. Degradarse, bajarse.
Lesser [les'-ẹr], *a.* (*comp.* de LITTLE). Menor, más pequeño: úsase *lesser* con los nombres colectivos o en plural, y *less* con los nombres en singular. *The lesser prophets,* Los profetas menores.
Lesson [les'-n], *s.* 1. Lección, enseñanza, instrucción, precepto, lectura. 2. Fraterna, corrección, reprensión. 3. Lección, pasaje de la Sagrada Escritura que se lee en los oficios divinos. 4. Lección, saber, conocimiento obtenido, v. g. por la experiencia.
Lesson, *va.* (Poco us.) Enseñar, instruir.
Lessor [les'-ẹr], *s.* Arrendador, el que da una cosa en arrendamiento.
Lest [lest], *conj.* Para que no, por miedo de o de miedo que, por recelo de, a fin de que, no sea que.
-let, *sufijo.* Terminación que forma diminutivos de los nombres ingleses y franceses; como *tablet,* tablilla, tablita; *gimlet,* barrena pequeña.
Let [let], *va.* (*pret.* y *pp.* LET). 1. Dejar, conceder, permitir. 2. Arrendar, dar en arrendamiento alguna renta, casa, heredad o posesión; alquilar. 3. Dejar, no impedir. *Let me alone,* Déjeme Vd. en paz. *Let me sit,* Déjeme Vd. sentar o permita Vd. que me siente. *Let me go,* Déjeme Vd. ir o permita Vd. que me vaya. 4. (Ant.) Impedir, estorbar. *Oftentimes I purposed to come unto you, but was let hitherto,* Muchas veces me he propuesto venir a vosotros, empero hasta ahora he sido estorbado. (Rom. i, 13.)—*vn.* Ser alquilado o arrendado. *A house to let,* Una casa por alquilar. *The house lets for forty dollars,* La casa se alquila por cuarenta pesos. *To let alone,* Dejar solo, dejar a un lado; dejar hacer, abandonar. *To let down,* Dejar caer; dejar bajar; bajar, descender. *To let in,* Dejar entrar, admitir, recibir, introducir, hacer entrar. *To let into,* Dejar entrar en; dejar conocer; hacer entrar. *To let loose,* Soltar, aflojar; desatar, desencadenar. *To let off,* Disparar, descargar, tirar un tiro. *To let out,* Dejar salir; poner en libertad, soltar; hacer salir; arrendar, alquilar. *To let out to use,* Poner dinero a interés. *To let up,* Dejar subir; (fam. E. U.) cesar, parar, disminuir en severidad. *To let be,* Dejar que una cosa sea lo que es; no entremeterse en un asunto o negocio. *To let blood,* Sangrar; hacerse sangrar. *To let know,* Advertir, hacer presente, hacer saber, dar a conocer. *To let fly,* (Fam.) Disparar, dejar salir el tiro de una arma de fuego; decir disparates. *To let fall a word,* Soltar inadvertidamente una palabra. *To let go,* Soltar. *To* LET tiene el pretérito y participio *let* en todas sus significaciones, excepto en la de impedir o estorbar, pues entonces es *letted. Let* es auxiliar del modo imperativo, como en *Let us go,* Vámonos. *Let Peter read,* Que lea Pedro.
Let, *s.* (Poco us.) Estorbo, obstáculo, impedimento. De ordinario sólo se usa en la locución, *Without let or hindrance,* Sin estorbo ni obstáculo.
Letch [lech], *va.* y *s.* *V.* LEACH.
Letdown [let'-daun], *s.* 1. Aflojamiento. 2. (fam.) Decepción, abatimiento.
Lethal [lī'-thal], *a.* Letal, mortal.
‡**Lethality** [lī-thal'-i-ti], *s.* Mortalidad.
Lethargic, Lethargical [lẹ-thār'-jic, al], *a.* Letárgico, lo que pertenece al estado de letargo.
Lethargied [leth'-ar-jid], *a.* Aletargado.
Lethargize, Lethargise [leth'-ar-jaiz], *va.* Aletargar.
Lethargy [leth'-ar-ji], *s.* 1. (Med.) Letargo. 2. Letargo, torpeza, enajenamiento del ánimo. 3. Entorpecimiento producido por la invernada.
Lethe [lī'-thī], *s.* Olvido. (Mit.) El río Leteo.
Lethean [lī-thī'-an], †**Letheed** [lī'-thīd], *a.* Léteo.
Letter [let-ẹr], *s.* 1. El que deja o permite. 2. Letra, carácter. *Letter* o *bill of exchange,* Letra de cambio. *Letter of license,* Moratoria, espera. *Letters patent,* Letras patentes. *Letters of safe conduct,* Guía, salvoconducto. *Letter of attorney,* Poder, procuración. 3. Carta, carta misiva. *Letters inclosed,* Cartas inclusas o adjuntas. *To frank letters,* Franquear las cartas. *Direction of letters,* Sobre o sobrescrito de cartas. *Letter of credit,* Carta de crédito. *Letter rogatory,* (For.) Suplicatoria. *Letter of marque,* Patente de corso. 4. Letra, el sentido gramatical de una frase, sentencia o discurso. 5. *pl.* Letras, literatura, erudición. *Man of letters,* Hombre de letras, hombre erudito, literato. *Letter-book,* Copiador de cartas, el libro en que las conservan o copian los comerciantes. *Letter-box,* (1) Buzón. (2) Caja de correspondencia; taquilla, caja cerrada para recibir cartas, en el correo o a la puerta de una casa. *Letter-carrier,* Cartero, el que reparte las cartas. *Letter-case,* Cartera; escribanía portátil. *Letter-drop,* Buzón, agujero por donde se echan las cartas en el correo, o en un carro postal. *Letter-file,* Guardacartas, cualquier mueble o aparato para archivar las cartas. *Letter-founder,* Fundidor de letras. *V.* TYPE-FOUNDER. *Letter-founding,* Fundición, acto de fundir letras. *Letter-foundry,* Fundición, lugar donde se funden tipos de imprenta. *Letter-paper,* Papel de cartas, papel de escribir (mayor que el papel para esquelas). *Silent letters,* Letras mudas o que no se pronuncian, como *ugh* en *though* y *k* en *knee.*
Letter, *va.* Estampar con letras; escribir, poner un rótulo. *To letter a book,* Rotular un libro.
Lettered [let'-ẹrd], *a.* Letrado, instruído, erudito, literato, docto.
Letterhead [let'-ẹr-hed], *s.* Membrete.
Lettering [let'-ẹr-ing], *s.* 1. El acto u oficio de poner rótulos o de hacer letras. 2. Letrero, inscripción, rótulo; estampilla.
Letter-perfect [let'-ẹr-pẹr'-fect], *a.* Preciso, que se sabe a la perfección.
Letterpress [let'-ẹr-pres], *s.* Impresión, la obra impresa, en contraposición a la grabada; el texto de un libro, en oposición a los grabados.
Lettuce [let'-is], *s.* (Bot.) Lechuga.
Leucocyte [liū'-co-sait], *s.* Leucocito, corpúsculo blanco de la sangre y de la linfa.
Leucoma [liū-kō'-ma], *s.* (Med.) Leucoma, mancha corneal.
Leucorrhea [liū-cor-rī'-a], *s.* Leucorrea.
Leukemia [liū-kī'-mi-a], *s.* Leucemia.
Levant [lẹ-vant'], *s.* Levante, oriente, las costas del Mediterráneo.—*a.* Oriental. *Levanter,* Viento de levante. *Levant trade,* Comercio de levante.
Levantine [lẹ-van'-tin o lev'-an-tin], *a.* Levantino. *Levantines,* Levantín, sarga de Cantón. *Levantine handkerchiefs,* Pañuelos de Cantón.
Levator [lẹ-vé'-tẹr], *s.* 1. Músculo elevador. 2. Levantador, instrumento de cirugía.
Levee [lev'-ī], *s.* 1. (Des.) El tiempo de levantarse por la mañana. 2. Corte, el concurso de gente que hace la corte a algún personaje, y se toma por lo que comúnmente se llama en español día de corte. 3. Recepción sin ceremonia en las habitaciones particulares de una persona. 4. [lev'-ī o lev-ī'] Dique para detener el agua.
Level [lev'-el], *a.* 1. Llano, igual; nivelado, a nivel, allanado. 2. Casi horizontal, no en declive 3. Igual a otra cosa. 4. Apuntado o moviéndose en línea recta; de aquí, honrado, probo. 5. (Fam.) De buen juicio, avisado, bien equilibrado. *To be level,* Estar el nivel; estar al alcance del entendimiento. *To make level,* Allanar, nivelar. *Everything lies level to our wish,* Todo va a medida de nuestros deseos.
Level, *s.* 1. Llano, llanura. 2. Plano, superficie plana, ras, nivel. 3. Igualdad de rango, moralidad, educación, etc. 4. Nivel, instrumento de los agrimensores. 5. Nivel, la altura media de una cosa. *Sea level,* Nivel del mar. 6. La línea de dirección de una bala o cualquiera otra cosa disparada. 7. La línea de la vista.
Level, *va.* 1. Igualar, aplanar, alla-

nar. 2. Nivelar. 3. Arrasar, hacer caer, derribar. 4. Apuntar, asestar. 5. Dirigir, encaminar. 6. Proporcionar, adaptar, ajustar. 7. Igualar, hacer igual una cosa con otra.—*vn.* 1. Asestar, apuntar el cañón u otra arma. 2. Emplear el nivel en la agrimensura. 3. (Raro) Acordar, concordar, conformar, convenir una cosa con otra.

Leveler, Leveller [lev'-el-ẹr], *s.* 1. Allanador, igualador, aplanador, nivelador. 2. El que quiere hacer a todos iguales sin distinción de personas ni de clases.

Level-headed [lev'-el-hed'-ed], *a.* Sensato, juicioso.

Leveling, Levelling [lev'-el-ing], *s.* 1. Nivelación, acción de nivelar. 2. Igualación de rangos o condiciones.

Levelness [lev'-el-nes], *s.* Igualdad, allanamiento, nivel.

Lever [lev'-ẹr o lí'-vẹr], *s.* 1. Palanca. 2. Escape de reloj.

Leveret [lev'-ẹr-et], *s.* Lebratillo, el hijuelo de la liebre.

Leviable [lev'-i-a-bl], *a.* Exigible.

Leviathan [le-vai'-a-than], *s.* Leviatán, un animal enorme del mar; supuesto monstruo marino.

Levigate [lev'-i-gêt], *va.* 1. Reducir cualquier substancia sólida a polvo impalpable. 2. (Des.) Pulir, alisar; acepillar.

Levigate, *a.* Aligerado, alisado, reducido a polvo.

Levigation [lev-i-gé'-shun], *s.* Reducción a polvo impalpable.

Levitation [lev-i-té'-shun], *s.* El acto o calidad de hacer ligera alguna cosa.

Levite [lí'-vait], *s.* Levita, de la tribu de Leví; sacerdote (despreciativo).

Levitical [le-vit'-i-cal], *a.* Levítico, lo perteneciente a los levitas o sacerdotes judíos.

Levity [lev'-i-ti], *s.* 1. Levedad, ligereza. 2. Inconstancia, veleidad. 3. Vanidad. 4. Alegría loca o inconsiderada ligereza.

Levulose [lev'-yu-lōs], *s.* Levulosa, variedad de azúcar que se halla en la miel y en varias frutas; distínguese de la dextrosa por su propiedad de inclinar el plano de polarización hacia la izquierda.

Levy [lev'-i], *va.* Hacer leva, levantar gente; exigir tributos. (For.) Embargar y vender los bienes de un deudor para pagar al acreedor.

Levy, *s.* 1. Leva, alistamiento de tropas. 2. Colectación, recaudación, exacción de tributos. 3. Embargo de bienes.

Lewd [liūd o lūd], *a.* 1. Lujurioso, lascivo, deshonesto, disoluto, libertino. 2. (Ant.) Malvado, perverso, depravado. 3. (Des.) Lego, ignorante.

Lewdly [liūd'-li o lūd'-li], *adv.* Malvadamente, lascivamente; tontamente, ignorantemente.

Lewdness [liūd'-nes], *s.* Lascivia, incontinencia, relajación, licencia, disolución de vida o costumbres: libertinaje, desenfreno; prostitución, en las mujeres.

Lewis o **Lewisson** [liū'-is], *s.* Clavija para mover o alzar piedras, castañuela de cantera; grapa, retén.

Lexical [lex'-i-cal], *a.* 1. Relativo a las palabras de un idioma, y no a su construcción gramatical. 2. Lexicográfico.

Lexicographer [lex-i-cog'-ra-fẹr], *s.* Lexicógrafo, escritor de diccionarios.

Lexicographic [lex-i-co-graf'-ic], *a.* Lexicográfico.

Lexicography [lex-i-cog'-ra-fi], *s.* Lexicografía.

Lexicon [lex'-i-cọn], *s.* Léxico o lexicón; diccionario del idioma latino, griego o hebreo.

Liability [lai-a-bil'-i-ti], *s.* 1. Condición de estar sujeto o expuesto, como a un accidente, daño, etc. 2. Responsabilidad; deuda pasiva; pasivo. *Legal liability insurance,* Seguro por el cual se asume la responsabilidad legal de una persona o corporación. 3. Propensión.

Liable [lai'-a-bl], *a.* 1. Sujeto, expuesto a una pena, a las costas, al pago de daños y perjuicios, etc. 2. Responsable, deudor, justa o legalmente. 3. Propenso, con tendencia a (en sentido desfavorable).

Liableness [lai'-a-bl-nes], *s.* 1. Propensión, inclinación a alguna cosa. 2. Responsabilidad.

Liaison officer [li-é-zọn' ef'-i-sẹr], *s.* (Mil.) Oficial de intercomunicación.

Liar [lai'-ar], *s.* Embustero, mentiroso, el que dice una mentira.

Lias [lai'-as], *s.* (Geol.) Lías, sistema de rocas calcáreas y arcillosas, del terreno jurásico.

Lib [lib], *va.* (Prov. Ingl. y Escocia) Castrar, capar.

Libation [lai-bé'-shun], *s.* Libación.

Libel [lai'-bel], *s.* 1. Libelo, el papel o escrito satírico y denigrativo. 2. (For.) Libelo, cargo que se hace por escrito y en derecho contra alguna persona.

Libel, *va.* y *vn.* 1. Satirizar, escribir sátiras o zaherir y motejar con ellas. 2. Difamar, calumniar o quitar el crédito por medio de libelos infamatorios o de sátiras denigrativas.

Libelant, Libellant [lai'-bel-ant], *s.* (For.) El actor o demandante en las acciones ante el tribunal de la Chancillería o del Almirantazgo.

Libeler, Libeller [lai'-bel-ẹr], *s.* Libelista, el autor de libelos; infamador.

Libeling, Libelling [lai'-bel-ing], *s.* Difamación.

Libellous [lai'-bel-us], *a.* Infamatorio, difamatorio.

Liber [lai'-bẹr o lí'-bẹr], *s.* 1. Libro, volumen de instrumentos auténticos, archivos o hipotecas. 2. (Bot.) Líber, corteza interior de los vegetales.

Liberal [lib'-ẹr-al], *a.* 1. Liberal, generoso, dadivoso, bizarro; (fam.) campechano, desprendido, que no es mezquino ni miserable. 2. Liberal, honorífico, caballeroso. 3. Liberal, libre; propenso a ideas democráticas o republicanas; libre de fanatismo o de sumisión a una autoridad o un dogma. 4. Abundante. 5. Libre, que no es estricto ni a la letra. 6. Noble, bien nacido.

Liberal arts [lib'-ẹr-al ārts], *s.* Letras (humanas), humanidades, artes liberales.

Liberalism [lib'-ẹr-al-izm], *s.* Liberalismo en los principios políticos y religiosos.

Liberality [lib-ẹr-al'-i-ti], *s.* Liberalidad, generosidad, bizarría, munificencia.

Liberalize [lib'-ẹr-al-aiz], *va.* Liberalizar, hacer liberal, generoso, tolerante.

Liberally [lib'-ẹr-al-i], *adv.* Liberalmente, dadivosamente.

Liberal-minded [lib'-ẹr-al-maind'-ed], *a.* Liberal, de ideas tolerantes.

Liberate [lib'-ẹr-êt], *va.* Libertar, librar; manumitir.

Liberation [lib-ẹr-é'-shun], *s.* El acto de libertar.

Liberator [lib-ẹr-é'-tẹr], *s.* Libertador, librador.

Libertinage [lib'-ẹr-tin-ẹj], *s.* *V.* LIBERTINISM.

Libertine [lib'-ẹr-tin], *s.* 1. Libertino, hombre disoluto. 2. (For.) En la historia romana, libertino, el hijo de liberto.—*a.* Libertino, disoluto.

Liberty [lib'-ẹr-ti], *s.* 1. Libertad, condición del que es o está libre. 2. Libertad, libre albedrío. 3. Exención, privilegio, prerrogativa, inmunidad, franquicia. 4. Libertad, poder de obrar conforme a las leyes. 5. Libertad, franqueza, llaneza demasiada de una persona. 6. Libertad, soltura de presos o cautivos. 7. Licencia, permiso.

Libidinist [li-bid'-in-ist], *s.* (Poco us.) Mico, el que es libidinoso.

Libidinous [li-bid'-in-us], *a.* Libidinoso, liviano, deshonesto, lascivo, lujurioso, disoluto, impúdico.

Libidinously [li-bid'-in-us-li], *adv.* Libidinosamente, lascivamente.

Libra [lai'-bra], *s.* (Astr.) Libra, un signo del zodíaco.

Libral [lai'-bral], *a.* (Poco us.) Relativo a la libra romana.

Librarian [lai-bré'-ri-an], *s.* 1. Bibliotecario. 2. (Des.) Copiante.

Librarianship [lai-bré'-ri-an-ship], *s.* El empleo u oficio de bibliotecario.

Library [lai'-bra-ri], *s.* 1. Biblioteca, librería, conjunto de libros, folletos, etc. 2. El edificio o la pieza que contiene la biblioteca.

Librate [lai'-brêt], *va.* Balancear, poner en equilibrio.

Libration [lai-bré'-shun], *s.* Libración, balance; equilibrio.

Libratory [lai'-bra-to-ri], *a.* Lo que balancea.

Libretto [li-bret'-ō], *s.* (Mús.) Libreto (de una ópera, etc.)

Lice, *s. pl.* de LOUSE. Piojos.

Licebane [lais'-bên], *s.* (Bot.) Albarraz, hierba piojera.

License, Licence [lai'-sens], *s.* 1. Licencia, permiso. 2. Despacho, cédula, título; diploma; certificado escrito o impreso que contiene un permiso, una autorización. 3. Licencia, libertinaje, libertad inmoderada o desordenada, desorden, desarreglo, desenfreno de costumbres.

License, *va.* 1. Licenciar, dar licencia o permiso; autorizar; dar cédula, despacho o privilegio. 2. Soltar, dar soltura.

Licensee, licencee [lai-sen-sí'], *s.* Concesionario, el que obtiene una licencia.

Licentiate [lai-sen'-shi-êt], *s.* 1. El que usa de licencia. 2. Licenciado, el que ha recibido en alguna universidad el grado así llamado. 3. Licenciado, el que tiene licencia para predicar o practicar una profesión.

Licentious [lai-sen'-shus], *a.* Licencioso, desordenado, libertino, disoluto.

Licentiously [lai-sen'-shus-li], *adv.* Licenciosamente.

Licentiousness [lai-sen'-shus-nes], *s.* Licencia, libertad inmoderada; disolución, desarreglo o desenfreno de vida o costumbres.

Lich [lich], *s.* (Des.) Cadáver, un

cuerpo muerto. *Lich-gate*, Sotechado que proyecta sobre la entrada de un cementerio. *Lich-owl*, Lechuza, especie de buho, del que se cree vulgarmente que pronostica la muerte.

Lichen [lai'-ken], *s.* (Bot.) Liquen, empeine, planta criptógama.

Licit [lis'-it], *a.* Lícito, permitido.

Licitly [lis'-it-li], *adv.* Lícitamente.

Licitness [lis'-it-nes], *s.* Calidad o condición de lícito.

Lick [lic], *va.* 1. Lamer, chupar. 2. (Vulg.) Cascar, aporrear, golpear; dar una tunda o felpa. 3. (Vulg.) Sobresalir, sobrepujar, vencer. *To lick up*, Devorar, consumir.

Lick, *s.* 1. Lamedura, lametada, lengüetada. 2. Lengüetada, la cantidad que se puede lamer de una vez. 3. (E. U.) Depósito de sal, al que acuden ciertos animales que la lamen. 4. (Fam.) Mojicón, cachete, bofetón.

Licker [lik'-ęr], *s.* Lamedor, el que lame.

Lickerish [lik'-ęr-ish], †**Lickerous** [lik'-ęr-us], *a.* Regalado, delicado, apetitoso, sabroso.

Lickerishness [lik'-ęr-ish-nes], *s.* Delicadeza de paladar, regalo.

Lickerishly [lic'-ęr-ish-li], *adv.* Deliciosamente.

Lickspittle [lic'-spit''-l], *s.* Quitapelillos, parásito, hombre servil.

Licorice, Liquorice [lic'-er-is], *s.* (Bot.) Regaliz, regaliza, orozuz. *Licorice-juice* o *Spanish-licorice*, Zumo de orozuz, regaliz en pasta.

Lictor [lic'-tęr], *s.* Lictor.

Lid [lid], *s.* 1. Tapa, la parte superior que cierra las cajas, etc. 2. Párpado, el pellejo blando que cubre los ojos.

Lie [lai], *s.* 1. Mentira, ficción, embuste. 2. Desmentida, mentís. 3. Error, vanidad, lo que sirve para engañar ó que crea una impresión falsa.

Lie [lai], *s.* 1. Posición en que está echada una cosa; caída. 2. Cubil, cama de un animal salvaje. *The lie of the land*, La caída, la situación relativa del terreno.

Lie, *vn.* (*pret.* y *pp.* LIED, *pa.* LYING). Mentir, levantar falsos testimonios; decir o hacer falsedades con intento de engañar.

Lie, *vn.* (*pret.* LAY, *pp.* LAIN). 1. Echarse, tumbarse, tenderse a la larga. 2. Descansar recostado, apoyarse. 3. Reposar, acostarse, estar acostado. 4. Yacer, estar echado o tendido; úsase comúnmente hablando de los muertos. 5. Yacer, existir de algún modo, estar alguna persona o cosa en un lugar, o estar situada una cosa en algún paraje. 6. Residir, morar, habitar. 7. Apretarse, estrecharse. 8. Consistir, depender; estar en la mano alguna cosa; tocar o pertenecer a alguno la ejecución de un empeño, negocio, etc. 9. Costar. 10. Estar pendiente una acusación contra alguno. *To lie at*, Importunar, molestar; estar expuesto. *To lie at heart*, Tener clavada una cosa en el corazón; sentir mucho y por largo tiempo alguna desgracia o contratiempo. *To lie at the point of death*, Estar expirando. *To lie at stake*, Estar muy interesado en algo. *To lie about*, Estar esparcido. *To lie by*, Reposar; estar tranquilo o quieto. *To lie down*, Acostarse, reposar; yacer en el sepulcro. *To lie in*, Estar de parto. *To lie in the way*, (1) Ser obstáculo o impedimento. (2) Presentarse convenientemente. *To lie in wait*, Espiar, observar, reconocer y notar con disimulo y secreto; asechar. *To lie out*, Dormir fuera de casa. *To lie out at length*, Tenderse a la larga. *To lie under*, Estar sujeto a, hallarse expuesto, acusado o atacado; estar sumido. *To lie up and down*, Estar en desorden. *To lie upon*, Hacer alguna cosa un deber u obligación para alguno; ser un deber la ejecución de algo. *To lie with*, Estar acostado con otro; hablar con alguno en la cama; tener coito, conocer carnalmente. *To lie in one's way*, Hallarse en el camino que otro lleva, presentarse a alguno, estar cómodo; ser un obstáculo, impedir. *To lie sick*, Guardar cama. *To lie on*, (Mar.) Estar en carga. *To lie to*, (Mar.) Estar a la capa. *To lie along*, (Mar.) Dar a la banda.

Lief [lif], *adv.* De buena gana, de buena voluntad.—*a.* (Des.) 1. Agradable, querido. 2. Bien dispuesto; inclinado.

Liege [lij], *s.* 1. Ligio: dícese del feudo que imponía al vasallo el ser vicio de bienes y persona, y del vasallo sujeto al tal servicio; feudatario. 2. Soberano. 3. Vasallo, súbdito.—*s.* (Des.) Soberano, señor de vasallos.

Lien [li'-en; en los E. U. de A. se pronuncia a menudo lin], *s.* 1. Derecho de retención. 2. De aquí, una demanda que ha de ser atendida; obligación imperativa.—*part.* antiguo del verbo *To* LIE.

Lientery [lai'-en-ter-i], *s.* Lientería, flujo de vientre en el cual se echan los alimentos a medio digerir.

Lier [li'-ęr], *s.* (Ant.) El que descansa o yace; el que está oculto o escondido.

Lieu [liū], *s.* Lugar, en la locución *In lieu of*, En lugar de, en vez de. (Fr.)

Lieutenancy [liu-ten'-an-si], *s.* 1. Tenencia, lugartenencia, el cargo u oficio de teniente. 2. (Des.) El cuerpo de tenientes.

Lieutenant [liu-ten'-ant], *s.* 1. Teniente o lugarteniente. 2. (Mil.) Teniente, el que ocupa el puesto inmediato al de un superior.

Lieutenantship [liu-ten'-ant-ship], *s.* Tenencia, el cargo u oficio de teniente.

Lieve [liv], *adv.* (Des.) *V.* LIEF.

Life [laif], *s.* 1. Vida. 2. Vida, el acto de vivir o la permanencia en la unión del alma y del cuerpo. 3. Vida, el principio de nutrición en los animales y vegetales. 4. Vida, el espacio de tiempo desde el nacimiento hasta la muerte. 5. Vida, conducta, el modo de vivir; el modo de pasar la vida con respecto a sus comodidades e incomodidades. 6. Vida, la relación o historia de las acciones de una persona. 7. Viveza, prontitud, vivacidad, fuego, ardor; espíritu. 8. Vida: expresión de cariño. 9. Semejanza exacta; la forma viva y exacta; el carácter real y verdadero. 10. Espíritu, la idea central y esencial. 11. Mundo, lo que pasa en él; el curso de los asuntos o sucesos humanos. 12. Vida, figuradamente se entiende de los seres organizados. *Life-annuity*, Renta vitalicia. *Life-insurance* o *assurance*, Seguro sobre la vida o de vida. *To depart this life*, Morir. *To have life*, Vivir. *For life*, Por toda la vida. *A pension for life*, Una pensión vitalicia. *To call one into question for his life*, Acusar a una persona de un delito que merece pena capital. *I would lay my life upon it*, Pondría mi cabeza a que es así. *Life-belt*, Cinto de salvamento, para sostenerse en el agua. *Life-boat*, Lancha salvavidas. *Life-buoy*, Boya o guíndola salvavidas. *Life-interest*, Renta o hacienda vitalicia. *Life-line*, Cuerda salvavida; andarivel horizontal de verga. *Life-preserver*, Salvavidas, aparato, chaqueta o cinto flotante, etc., que sirve para sobrenadar.

Life-blood [laif'-blud], *s.* Sangre vital; alma, nervio, lo que constituye la fuerza o la energía.

Lifeboat [laif'-bōt], *s.* Bote de salvamento.

Life-giving [laif'-giv-ing], *a.* Vivificante, lo que da vida.

Lifeguard [laif'-gärd], *s.* Vigilante de playa, guardia, salvavidas.

Life insurance [laif' in-shūr'-ans], *s.* Seguro sobre la vida.

Lifeless [laif'-les], *a.* 1. Muerto, inanimado, amortiguado. 2. Falto de fuerza, espíritu, o vigor; flojo. 3. Inhabitado por hombres y animales; sin vida aparente.

Lifelessly [laif'-les-li], *adv.* Sin vigor, sin espíritu.

Life-like [laif'-laic], *a.* Que parece estar vivo.

Lifelong [laif'-long''], *a.* Que dura toda la vida.

Life raft [laif raft], *s.* Balsa salvavidas.

Life-size [laif'-saiz], *a.* De tamaño natural (de una persona).

Lifestring [laif'-string], *s.* Nervio o cordón en el organismo humano por donde se suponía que los órganos recibían su vitalidad.

Lifetime [laif'-taim], *s.* Durante el tiempo de la vida. *In his lifetime*, En su vida.

Life-weary [laif'-wī-ri], *a.* Infeliz, cansado de la vida.

Lift [lift], *va.* 1. Alzar, elevar, levantar. 2. Exaltar, ensalzar, elevar, levantar. 3. Engreir, envanecer, ensoberbecer. 4. Quitar la presión de (alguna cosa). 5. (Fam.) Hurtar; quitar, llevarse.—*vn.* 1. Hacer fuerza o esforzarse para levantar alguna cosa. 2. Alzarse y disiparse en la atmósfera. *To lift up*, Levantar o alzar alguna cosa. *To lift the hat*, Quitarse el sombrero para saludar. *To lift the feet*, Acudir presuroso al socorro de alguno. *To lift the eyes*, Levantar los ojos, fijar la atención en. *To lift the face*, Levantar la cara como para suplicar. *To lift up the hand*, (Fig.) (1) Jurar. (2) Orar, suplicar. *To lift up the heel against*, Tratar con insolencia y desprecio. *To lift the horn*, (1) Tratar con insolencia, con desdén. (2) Establecer en autoridad. *To lift up the voice*, Levantar la voz; gritar.

Lift, *s.* 1. El esfuerzo que se hace para levantar alguna cosa pesada. 2. Alzamiento, la acción y efecto de alzar. 3. El modo de alzar alguna cosa. 4. El acto de levantar o hacer levantar algo. 5. Máquina o utensilio para alzar; (Ingl.) elevador, ascensor. 6. Alza. 7. (Prov. Ingl.) Cielo, atmósfera. *To give one a lift*, Ayudar a uno a levantarse o hacer algo. *At one lift*, De un golpe. *Lifts*, (Mar.) Amantillos, cabos que sirven para levantar las vergas por una parte bajándolas por otra. *Topping-lifts*, (Mar.) Amantillos de la botaborra. *Handing-lifts*, (Mar.) Mostachos.

Lifter [lift'-er], *s.* 1. El que levanta. 2. Ladrón. *V.* SHOPLIFTER.

Lifting [lift'-ing], *s.* El acto de levantar; la ayuda o auxilio que se da a uno para que se levante.

Lift-off [lift'-ōf], *s.* Despegue de un cohete.

Ligament [lig'-a-ment], *s.* Ligamento; ligazón, ligadura.

Ligation [li-gê'-shun], *s.* Ligación, la acción y efecto de ligar.

Ligature [lig'-a-chur o tiūr], *s.* 1. Ligadura, en sus acepciones médica, musical y mecánica. 2. Ligación, la acción de ligar. 3. (Impr.) Ligadas, como fi, fl, etc.

Light [lait], *s.* 1. Luz; claridad, claro, resplandor. 2. Luz, vela, bujía, lámpara, farol; emisión de luz. 3. Vista, ventana o cuadro de vidrio. 4. Luz, ilustración, conocimiento; explicación de alguna cosa obscura. 5. Luz, noticia, aviso, estado de visibilidad; publicidad; aspecto, punto de vista. 6. Luz, el punto o centro desde donde se iluminan y alumbran los objetos pintados en un cuadro. 7. Vista, poder de visión; percepción; inteligencia. 8. Día; alba, amanecer. —*a.* 1. Ligero, leve. 2. Llevadero, lo que fácilmente se puede sufrir o aguantar. 3. Fácil de ejecutarse; fútil, de poco valor o consideración; frívolo, superficial. 4. Ligero, ágil, desembarazado. 5. Leve, inconstante, mudable. 6. Gayo, alegre, vivo. 7. Liviano, incontinente. 8. Claro, resplandeciente, brillante, reluciente. 9. (Mar.) Boyante, la embarcación que no está cargada o no tiene lastre suficiente. 10. Claro, que no es de color muy subido; blondo, rubio: dícese del pelo o de la tez. *Light brown*, Castaño claro. *Light complexion*, Tez blonda. *Light supper*, Colación. *Light of belief*, Crédulo. *To make light of a thing*, Burlarse de una cosa, tomarla en chanza. *Northern lights*, Aurora boreal.—*adv. V.* LIGHTLY.

Light, *va.* 1. Encender. *To light a fire*, Encender lumbre. 2. Alumbrar, dar luz, iluminar. *Light me home*, Alumbréme V. hasta mi casa. 3. (Mar.) Aligerar, hacer más ligera una embarcación.—*vn.* 1. Tropezar, hallar, encontrar por casualidad. 2. Desmontarse, apearse de la caballería o carruaje; desembarcar; salir del coche u otra parte. 3. Parar, descansar. *Light-wave*, Onda u ondulación de luz. *Light-armed*, Armado levemente o a la ligera. *Light-borne*, Llevado, traído por la luz o en medio de la luz. *Light-fingered*, Largo de uñas, ligero de dedos; el que tiene habilidad para hurtar.

Light-brain [lait'-brên], *s.* Hombre frívolo e ignorante, o con los cascos a la jineta.

Lighten [lait'-n], *vn.* 1. Relampaguear. 2. Brillar. 3. Hablar con vehemencia. 4. Caer, descender sobre.—*va.* 1. Iluminar, alumbrar. 2. Exonerar, descargar. 3. Aligerar, hacer menos pesada una cosa. *To lighten a ship*, (Mar.) Aligerar un bajel. 4. Alegrar, infundir, alegría.

Lighter [lait'-er], *s.* 1. (Mar.) Alijador, lanchón o gabarra. *Ballast-lighter*, Lanchón de lastrar. 2. Cualquier cosa que comunica luz o claridad. 3. Encendedor, utensilio para encender el gas; mecha, pedazo de papel torcido o antorcha para encender las luces.

Lighterage [lait'-er-ēj], *s.* Gabarraje, el flete de las gabarras.

Lighterman [lait'-er-man], *s.* (Mar.) Lanchonero, el que gobierna el alijador o lanchón.

Light-faced type [lait-fêst taip], *s.* (Impr.) Letra o tipo delgado.

Light-foot, Light-footed [lait'-fut-ed], *a.* Ligero de pies.

Light-headed [lait'-hed-ed], *a.* 1. Ligero de cascos, casquivano. 2. Delirante, el que delira, dice disparates o despropósitos. 3. Atolondrado, aturdido.

Light-headedness [lait'-hed-ed-nes], *s.* Delirio, atolondramiento, aturdimiento.

Light-hearted [lait'-hārt-ed], *a.* Alegre, festivo.

Light heavyweight [lait hev'-i-wêt], *s.* (Boxeo) Peso semicompleto.

Light-horse [lait'-hōrs], *s.* Caballería ligera.

Lighthouse [lait'-haus], *s.* (Mar.) Faro, fanal o torre de luces que sirve de guía a los navegantes.

Lighting [lait'-ing], *s.* Iluminación artificial, alumbrado. *Electric lighting*, Alumbrado eléctrico.

Light-keeper [lait'-kîp"-er], *s.* Torrero; farolero.

Lightless [lait'-les], *a.* Obscuro, falto de luz, sin luz, sin claridad.

Lightly [lait'-li], *adv.* 1. Ligeramente, levemente. 2. Fácilmente; prontamente. 3. Sin razón, sin motivo. 4. Alegremente, con alegría, airosamente. 5. Deshonestamente, livianamente.

Light-minded [lait'-maind-ed], *a.* Voluble, inconstante, variable, atolondrado.

Light-money [lait'-mun-i], *s.* Derechos de faro o de fuego.

Lightness [lait'-nes], *s.* 1. Levedad, ligereza; agilidad, velocidad. 2. Inconstancia. 3. Liviandad, deshonestidad.

Lightning [lait'-ning], *s.* 1. Relámpago; rayo, la descarga eléctrica. 2. Aligeramiento. *As quick as lightning*, (Fam.) Como una pólvora, o como un relámpago.

Lightning bug [lait'-ning bʊg], *s.* Luciérnaga.

Lightning rod, *s.* Pararrayo.

Light-room [lait'-rum], *s.* (Mar.) Caja de faroles del pañol de pólvora o lampión.

Lightship [lait'-ship], *s.* Buque fanal o buque faro.

Lightsome [lait'-sum], *a.* 1. Alegre, festivo, airoso. 2. (Poét.) Luminoso, claro.

Lightweight [lait'-wêt], *s.* (Boxeo) Peso ligero.—*a.* De poco peso, liviano.

Light-year [lait'-yir], *s.* (Astr.) Año luz.

Ligneous [lig'-ne-us], **Lignous** [lig'-nus], *a.* Leñoso, hecho de madera o semejante a ella.

Ligniferous [lig-nif'-er-us], *a.* Leñífero, que produce madera.

Lignify [lig'-ni-fai], *va.* y *vn.* Convertir o convertirse en madera.

Lignite [lig'-nait], *s.* Lignito, combustible fósil.

Ligulate [lig'-yu-lêt], *a.* (Bot.) Acintillada, semiflosculosa o ligulada: dícese de la flor compuesta que consta de cintillas o semiflósculos.

Ligule [lig'-yūl], *s.* (Bot.) Florecilla acintillada, lígula o semiflósculo.

Ligure [lig'-yur], *s.* Ligurio, piedra preciosa mencionada en el Éxodo.

Like [laik], *a.* 1. Semejante, parecido; igual, lo mismo que. 2. Creíble, probable, verisímil o verosímil. —*s.* Semejante, semejanza.—*adv.* 1. Como, del mismo modo que. 2. Verisímilmente, probablemente. Se usa muy a menudo esta voz en composición para expresar semejanza. *To give like for like*, Pagar en la misma moneda. *He has not his like*, No tiene igual. *Like master, like man*, (prov.) Tal para cual. *To be of like force*, Ser de la misma fuerza. *In like manner*, Del mismo modo. *Like nothing else*, Que no se parece a nada. *To look like*, Parecerse a, tener el aspecto de. *To be as like as two peas*, Parecerse como dos gotas de agua.

Like, *va.* y *vn.* 1. Hallar agrado en, a su gusto; contentarse con; estar contento de. 2. Querer, amar; gustar, agradar alguna cosa. *As you like it*, Como Vd. quiera, o como Vd. guste. *I should like to see*, Yo quisiera ver, me gustaría ver. *Do you like this tea?* ¿Le gusta a Vd. este te? *How do you like her?* ¿Cómo la halla Vd.?

Likelihood [laik'-li-hud], **Likeliness** [laik'-li-nes], *s.* Probabilidad, verisimilitud, posibilidad.

Likely [laik'-li], *a.* 1. Probable, verisímil; creíble, plausible. 2. Bien parecido; placentero; loable; que da buenas esperanzas. 3. Apto, idóneo, a propósito.—*adv.* Probablemente, según todas las apariencias. *Likely enough*, No sería extraño. *Most likely*, Es regular.

Liken [laik'-n], *va.* Asemejar, comparar.

Likeness [laik'-nes], *s.* 1. Semejanza, conformidad, igualdad. 2. Viso, forma, apariencia, aire. 3. Semejante, la cosa que se semeja á otra. 4. Retrato fiel o vivo de una persona.

Likewise [laik'-waiz], *adv.* También, asimismo, además, igualmente.

Liking [laik'-ing], *s.* 1. Inclinación, gusto, agrado, deseo; aprobación, preferencia. 2. (Ant.) Semblante, apariencia, en lo que se refiere a la salud de una persona.

Lilac [lai'-lac], *s.* (Bot.) Lila o lilas, arbusto.—*a.* Del color de la lila común.

Liliaceous [lil-i-ê'-shius], *a.* (Bot.) Liliáceo, perteneciente a la familia de los lirios (las liliáceas).

Lilliputian [lil-li-piū'-shian], *a.* Liliputiense, muy pequeño y endeble: es alusión a los fantásticos personajes de Liliput imaginados por el novelista Swift, en sus "Viajes de Gulliver." U. t. c. s.

Lilt [lilt], *vn.* 1. (Prov. Ingl.) Hacer alguna cosa diestramente. 2. Cantar, bailar, saltar alegremente.

Lily [lil'-i], *s.* 1. Lirio, azucena, planta de adorno del género Lilium o su flor. 2. Planta o flor parecida a ésta; como *water-lily*, ninfea, nenúfar; *day-lily*, hemerocálide; funkia. 3. Flor de lis. *Lily of the valley*, Lirio de los valles, muguete. Convallaria majalis. *White lily*, Azucena.

Lily-handed [lil'-i-hand-ed], *a.* Manos de alabastro, el que tiene las manos muy blancas.

Lily-livered [lil'-i-liv-ęrd], *a.* Cobarde; doble.

Lilywort [lil'-i-wŭrt], *s.* Una planta cualquiera de las liliáceas.

Lima [lai'-ma o li'-ma], *n. pr.* Lima, capital del Perú. *Lima beans*, Habas de Lima, grandes y aplastadas; variedad de haba trepadora, faséolo. Phaseolus lunatus. *Lima wood*, Brasilete.

Limaceous [li-mé'-shus], *a.* Limáceo, parecido a la limaza o babosa.

Limb[1] [lim], *s.* 1. Miembro, parte del cuerpo, como un brazo, una pierna, un ala, etc. 2. Rama de árbol; vástago que brota del tallo o tronco principal. 3. Orilla, extremo o remate de una cosa. 4. (Fam.) Travieso, turbulento, enredador, malévolo. (< Anglosajón lim.)

Limb[2] [lim], *s.* Limbo; dícese de la orilla o borde del disco del sol y de la luna. (< Fr. limbe.)

Limb, *va.* 1. Poner miembros o cosa que se les asemeje. 2. Desmembrar, despedazar, hacer pedazos.

Limbed [limd], *a.* Membrudo, fornido.

Limber [lim'-bęr], *a.* Manejable, flexible, blando.—*s.* 1. Avantrén de cureña, armón, juego delantero de un furgón de artillería. 2. (Mar.) Groera del canal del agua.

Limber, *va.* 1. Poner flexible o manejable. 2. Poner o colocar el armón; poner el avantrén a una cureña; úsase con la prep. *up.*

Limber-boards [lim'-bęr-bōrdz], *s. pl.* (Mar.) Panas imbornaleras de las varengas. *Limber-holes*, (Mar.) Imbornales de las varengas. *Limber-rope*, (Mar.) Cabo imbornalero de las varengas.

Limberness [lim'-bęr-nes], *s.* Flexibilidad.

Limbless [lim'-les], *a.* Inmembre, que no tiene miembros.

Limbo [lim'-bō], *s.* 1. Limbo, el lugar a donde se dice que van las almas de los niños que mueren sin bautismo. 2. Cualquier paraje donde hay miseria y falta de libertad. (Fest.) *To be in limbo*, Estar en Babia.

Lime[1] [laim], *s.* 1. Cal. *Quicklime*, Cal viva. *Lime-light*, Luz de calcio. *Lime-kiln* [kil], Calera, horno de cal. *Lime-water*, Agua de cal. 2. Liga, materia viscosa y pegajosa que sirve para cazar pájaros, untando con ella unas varillas o espartos. *V.* Bird-lime. *Lime-twig*, Vareta, varilla untada con liga. *Lime-twigged*, Lo que tiene varetas o palitos untados con liga. 3. Agua de cal.

Lime[2] [laim], *s.* 1. (Bot.) Lima, una especie de limón más pequeño y redondo que los demás; y limero, el árbol que produce las limas. Hay dos variedades: la agria y la dulce. Citrus medica. *Lime-juice*, Zumo de lima, remedio contra el escorbuto. 2. *V.* Linden.

Lime, *va.* 1. Enredar, enmarañar. 2. Untar con liga. 3. Unir con betún, argamasa, mortero o mezcla. 4. Abonar la tierra con cal.

Lime-burner [laim'-bŭrn-ęr], *s.* Calero, el que hace cal.

Limehound [laim'-haund], *s.* Perro grande para cazar jabalíes; sabueso.

Limelight [laim'-lait], *s.* 1. Rayo de luz concentrada que se proyecta sobre el escenario. 2. Lugar que ilumina esta luz. 3. Posición brillante a los ojos del público.

Limestone [laim'-stōn], *s.* Piedra de cal o piedra caliza.

Limit [lim'-it], *s.* 1. Límite, término, fin; lindero, linde; frontera, raya, confín. 2. Lo que impide o restriñe; obstáculo, impedimento, freno. 3. (Mat.) Una cantidad determinada.

Limit, *va.* Limitar, fijar; restringir. *Limited, limited liability*, *V.* Company.

Limitation [lim-i-té'-shun], *s.* Limitación, modificación, restricción.

Limiter [lim'-it-ęr], *s.* Limitador.

Limitless [lim'-it-les], *a.* Ilimitado.

Limn [lim], *va.* (Ant. o Poét.) Pintar; dibujar; retratar.

Limner [lim'-nęr], *s.* (Ant. o Poét.) Pintor; dibujador; retratista.

Limning [lim'-ning], *s.* Pintura.

Limous [lai'-mus], *a.* Cenagoso.

Limousine [lim'-u-zin], *s.* Vehículo de lujo y cerrado. Generalmente lleva y trae pasajeros de avión.

Limp [limp], *s.* Cojera.—*a.* 1. Débil, flexible, falto de rigidez. 2. Insípido, falto de espíritu, sin firmeza de carácter.

Limp, *vn.* 1. Cojear. 2. (Mec.) Cojear, agotar irregularmente, v. g. una máquina de vapor.

Limper [limp'-ęr], *s.* Cojo.

Limpet [lim'-pet], *s.* Lepada o lepas, molusco común.

Limpid [lim'-pid], *a* Limpio, claro, transparente.

Limpidity, Limpidness [lim-pid'-i-ti, lim'-pid-nes], *s.* Claridad; limpieza.

Limping [limp'-ing], *pa.* Cojera.

Limpingly [limp'-ing-li], *adv.* Con cojera.

Limy [lai'-mi], *a.* 1. Viscoso, glutinoso, pegajoso. 2. Calizo.

Linchpin [linch'-pin], *s.* Sotrozo, perno, pasador; (Art.) pezonero.

‡**Lincture** [linc'-chur], **Linctus** [linc'-tus], *s.* Lamedor, jarabe.

Lind [lind], *s.* (Des.) *V.* Linden.

Linden, Linden-tree [lin'-den, tri], *s.* (Bot.) Tilo, teja.

Line [lain], *s.* 1. (Mat.) Línea, longitud que se considera sin latitud o con una sola dimensión. 2. (Mil.) Línea, las defensas que levanta y forma en el campo un ejército; línea de batalla. 3. Línea, vía (de ferrocarril o de vapores). 4. Línea, serie o sucesión de parientes de diferentes grados que descienden todos del mismo tronco. 5. Línea, raya: dícese de las señaladas en la palma de la mano y en la cara; rasgo, arruga; esquicio, contorno, trazo, croquis. 6. Línea o línea equinoccial, el ecuador. 7. Línea, renglón, raya, hablando de un manuscrito o impreso. *To send a line* o *a few lines*, Enviar cuatro líneas o cuatro renglones; escribir una carta muy corta. 8. Línea, la duodécima parte de la pulgada. 9. Línea, término, límite. 10. Cualquier cordón muy delgado; cuerda, cordel; (Mar.) vaivén. 11. Ramo de negocios. 12. Surtido, cantidad de géneros de una clase particular. 13. Curso de pensamiento y acción. *Fishing-line*, Sedal para pescar. *Tarred line*, (Mar.) Vaivén alquitranado. *Lead-line*, (Mar.) Sondalesa. *Leech-lines*, (Mar.) Apagapenoles. *Log-line*, (Mar.) Corredera.—*Lines, pl.* Versos. *Lines drawn up and down on paper for accounts*, Cajilleros. *Head-line*, Encabezamiento, título corriente. *Branch line*, (F. C.) Ramal, vía lateral. *Junction line*, (F. C.) Línea de empalme. *Isothermal line*, Línea isotérmica. *Tape-line*, Lienza, cinta de medir. *Tow-line, towing-line*, Remolque, estacha, sirga. *Hard lines*, (Fam.) Apuro, situación angustiosa.

Line,[1] *va.* 1. Linear, trazar líneas, hacer líneas sobre. 2. Alinear; poner en su propia relación, v. g. las partes de una máquina. 3. Leer en voz clara, línea por línea. 4. Hacer concebir: úsase comúnmente hablando de los animales.—*vn.* Estar en línea; colocarse en posición, como para jugar a la pelota.

Line,[2] *va.* 1. Forrar, aforrar; llenar lo interior de. 2. Revestir; cubrir o fortalecer la muralla o pared. 3. Colocar, disponer personas o cosas a lo largo, en hileras.

Lineage [lin'-ę-ęj], *s.* Linaje, línea, descendencia de una familia.

Lineal [lin'-ę-al], *a.* 1. Lineal, lo perteneciente a la línea; hecho con líneas. 2. Descendiente, emparentado; hereditario.

Lineally [lin'-ę-al-i], *adv.* En línea recta.

Lineament [lin'-ę-a-męnt], *s.* Lineamento, facción del rostro.

Linear [lin'-ę-ar], *a.* Lineal, compuesto de líneas.

Lineate [lin-ę-ét], *a.* Señalado con líneas.

Lineation [lin-ę-é'-shun], *s.* Dibujo de línea o líneas.

Linemen [lain'-men], *s. pl.* Delanteros (en el futbol).

Linen [lin'-en], *s.* Lienzo, lino; tela hecha de lino o cáñamo. *Linen*, Ropa blanca. *Linen cambric*, Olán batista, cambray. (Méx.) Cambray superfino. *Clean linen*, Ropa limpia. *Bleached linen*, Lienzo blanqueado. *Baby-linen*, Pañales. *Table-linen*, Mantelería. *A change of linen*, Muda de ropa. *Linen collars, cuffs*, Cuellos, puños de hilo. *Linen damask*, Damasco de hilo, alemanisco. *Linen hose*, Mangueras de lienzo. *Linen hosiery*, Medias de hilo. *Linen-prover*, Cuentahilos.

Linen-draper [lin'-en-dré-pęr], *s.* Lencero, mercader de lienzos.

Linen trade [lin'-en tréd], *s.* Lencería.

Linen-weaver [lin'-en-wiv'-ęr], *s.* Tejedor de lienzos.

Liner [lain'-ęr], *s.* Trasatlántico (avión o barco).

Ling [ling], *s.* 1. (Bot.) Brezo. 2. (Zool.) Molva, lota, merluza, pez de la familia de los gádidos.

-ling, *sufijo.* Se usa para formar diminutivos; v. g. *stripling*, mozuelo, jovencito; *duckling*, anadeja; *gosling*, gansarón, el pollo del ganso.

Linger [liŋ'-gęr], *vn.* 1. Consumirse, penar, padecer poco a poco o lentamente. 2. Estar en expectación de alguna cosa por mucho tiempo. 3. Ir pasando, tardar mucho en llegar a alguna parte o en conseguir algún fin. 4. Estar parado, quedar o estar suspenso.—*va.* Prolongar, dilatar, pasar el tiempo en expectación; se usa con *out* o *away.*

Lingerer [liŋ'-gęr-ęr], *s.* El que tarda, prolonga o está suspenso.

Lingering [liŋ'-gęr-ing], *a.* Lento, pesado, tardo, lánguido.—*s.* Tardanza, dilación; prolongación.

Linget [liŋ'-get], *s.* *V.* Lingot.

Lingle [liŋ'-gl], *s.* Sedal o hilo de zapatero.

Lingo [liṇ'-gō], *s.* (Vulg.) Algarabía, greguería, dialecto.
Linguadental [liṇ-gwa-den'-tal], *a.* Linguodental, articulado con la lengua y los dientes.
Lingual [liṇ'-gwal], *a.* 1. Lingual, que pertenece o se refiere a la lengua. 2. Pronunciado principalmente con la extremidad de la lengua. —*s.* Letra lingual, como la *l*, *t*, etc.
Linguist [liṇ'-gwist], *s.* Linguista, el que sabe y habla varias o muchas lenguas.
Linguistic [lin-gwis'-tic], *a.* Lingüístico.—*Linguistics*, *s.* Lingüística, la ciencia del lenguaje o el estudio comparativo de los idiomas.
Liniment [lin'-i-mẹnt], *s.* Linimento.
Lining [lain'-ing], *s.* 1. Forro, aforro. 2. Cualquier cosa que sirve para cubrir la parte interior de otra.
Link [liṇc], *s.* 1. Eslabón o anillo de cadena. 2. Cadena, enlace. 3. Hacha de viento. *Link-motion*, Cuadrante de la corredera, el conjunto de las piezas que sirven para operar las válvulas de una locomotora u otra máquina semejante.
Link, *va.* 1. Enlazar, unir y trabar una cosa con otra. 2. Juntar o reunir por confederación o contrato. 3. Ensartar, encadenar.—*vn.* Tener conexión una cosa con otra.
Links [liṇks], *s. pl.* Terreno dispuesto para el juego de *golf*. (< Anglosajón hlinc, cuesta.)
Linkup [linc'-up], *s.* Enlace, conexión, unión.
Linnet [lin'-et], *s.* (Orn.) Pájaro de una de las diversas especies de la familia de los fringílidos; particularmente el pardillo (Linota cannabina) y el acanta.
Linoleum [li-nō'-lẹ-um], *s.* Linoleo, preparación de aceite de linaza endurecida por un procedimiento de oxidación. Sustituye al caucho, o mezclada con corcho pulverizado y sometida a fuerte presión sobre lona forma un hule para piso muy resistente.
Linotype [lin'-o-taip], *s.* 1. Linotipo, línea de tipos de molde fundida en una sola pieza. *Linotype machine*, Linotipia. *Linotype operator*, Linotipista.
Linseed [lin'-sīd], *s.* Linaza.
Linstock, Lintstock [lin'-stoc], *s.* Botafuego, disparador.
Lint [lint], *s.* 1. Lino. 2. Hila.
Lintel [lin'-tel], *s.* Lintel o dintel, tranquero.
Lion [lai'-un], *s.* 1. León. 2. Hombre de valor conspicuo. 3. Objeto de interés y curiosidad. 4. León, signo del zodíaco. *Lion's share*, La parte del león; el todo o la mayor parte. *Lion's-foot*, (Bot.) Pie de león, alquemila. *Lion-leaf*, (Bot.) Lóntice leontopétalo. *Lion's-tail*, (Bot.) Leonuro.
Lioness [lai'-un-es], *sf.* Leona.
Lion-like [lai'-un-laic], †**Lionly** [lai'-un-li], *a.* Aleonado.
Lip [lip], *s.* 1. Labio: dícese no sólo de los de la boca sino también de los que forman las llagas o heridas. 2. Los órganos del lenguaje; la boca; el habla. 3. Extremidad o borde de alguna cosa. 4. Pico o pezón de una ampolleta. *Great lip*, Bezudo. *To make a lip*, Befar, hacer befa, hacer muecas, hacer gestos. *Lip-glue*, Cola de boca. *Lip-devotion*, Devoción de boca; devoto de boca. *Lip-good*, Dícese del que tiene buenas palabras y malas obras, farisáico. *Lip-labour*, Jarabe de pico, palabras vanas, cumplimientos de corte, vanas ofertas. *Lip-reading*, La comprensión o interpretación de lo que quiere expresar una persona observando el movimiento de sus labios, como sucede entre los sordomudos. *Lip-salve*, Ungüento para los labios. *Lip-service*, Servicio de boca. *Lip-wisdom*, Charla, habladuría sin substancia.
Lipped [lipt], *a.* Que tiene labios. *Blubber-lipped*, Belfo, morrudo, hocicudo.
Lipstick [lip'-stic], *s.* Lápiz de labios, lápiz labial, tubo de labios.
Liquate [lai'-cwêt], *vn.* Derretirse, licuarse, liquidarse, fundirse.
Liquation [lai-cwé'-shun], *s.* 1. Licuación, licuefacción, liquidación; conversión de un cuerpo sólido en líquido. 2. La propiedad de derretirse o disolverse.
Liquefaction [lic-wẹ-fac'-shun], *s.* Licuación, liquidación, licuefacción.
Liquefiable [lic'-wẹ-fai"-a-bl], *a.* Liquidable, licuable.
Liquefy [lic'-wẹ-fai], *va.* Licuar, derretir o liquidar alguna cosa sólida. —*vn.* Liquidarse, derretirse.
Liquescent [li-cwes'-ent], *a.* (Fís.) Licuescente lo que es capaz de licuarse, derretirse o liquidarse.
Liqueur [li-cūr'], *s.* Licor, bebida fuerte, dulce y aromática. (< Fr.)
Liquid [lic'-wid], *a.* 1. Líquido, flúido. 2. Claro, transparente. *Liquid air*, Aire líquido o licuado (generalmente para refrigerantes). *Liquid fire*, (Mil.) Fuego líquido (que se arroja de un lanzallamas). *Liquid hydrogen*, Hidrógeno líquido. *Liquid measure*, Medida para líquidos.—*s.* Líquido.
Liquidambar [lic'-wid-am'-bar], *s.* Liquidámbar, resina odorífera producida por un árbol del mismo nombre.
Liquidate [lic'-wi-dêt], *va.* Liquidar, ajustar las cuentas.
Liquidation [lic-wi-dé'-shun], *s.* Liquidación, la acción y efecto de liquidar.
Liquidity [lic-wid'-i-ti], *s.* Sutileza; raleza; liquidez, fluidez.
Liquidizer [lic-wid-ai'-zẹr], *s.* Licuadora.
Liquidness [lic'-wid-nes], *s.* Liquidez; fluidez.
Liquor [lic'-ẹr], *s.* 1. Licor, el cuerpo líquido o flúido. 2. Licor, licor alcohólico, bebida fuerte. 3. Una de las diferentes disoluciones que se emplean en las artes y oficios; licor. *Tan liquor*, Baño de casca. *Malt liquor*, Cerveza. *Liquor-case*, Cantina, frasquera.
Liquor [lai'-cwer o li'-cwer], *s.* En la farmacopea de los Estados Unidos, disolución acuosa de una substancia no volátil, con exclusión de los jarabes, las infusiones y las decocciones.
Lira [li'-ra], *s.* 1. Lira, nombre de una moneda italiana de plata, de valor igual al de la peseta y el franco. 2. Moneda turca de oro.
Lisbon [liz'-bẹn], *s.* 1. Vino blanco de Lisboa. 2. (Des.) Una especie de azúcar.
Lisle [lail], *s.* Hilo de algodón especial que se usa generalmente para calcetines.
Lisp [lisp], *vn.* Tartamudear, cecear. —*va.* Pronunciar las palabras ceceando.
Lisp, *s.* Tartamudeo, ceceo.
Lisper [lisp'-ẹr], *s.* El que cecea o tartamudea.
Lispingly [lisp'-ing-li], *adv.* Con ceceo.
Lissom, Lissome [lis'-um], *a.* *V.* LITHESOME.
List [list], *s.* 1. Lista, nómina, cédula de personas o cosas; catálogo. (< Fr. liste.) 2. (Mar.) Falsa banda, bandeo, inclinación de un buque sobre un costado. 3. (Des.) Deseo, gana; voluntad; elección. (2 y 3 < Anglosajón lust, placer.) 4. El terreno cercado en que se tienen justas, torneos o combates. *List of topics*, Temario. *To have a list*, Dar a la banda.
List,[2] *s.* 1. Lista, tira o pedazo de cualquier tela; cenefa. 2. (Arq.) Filete, listelo, orla. 3. Listón, barandal. 4. (Poét.) Borde exterior, cabo, límite. (< Anglosajón list.)
List, *vn.* 1. (Mar.) Inclinarse a la banda. 2. (Ant.) Querer, desear, inclinarse, gustar.—*va.* 1. Registrar, poner o inscribir en un registro o en una lista. 2. (Mil.) Alistar. 3. Cercar una liza para torneos. 4. Guarnecer con listones de diferentes colores. 5. (Poét.) Escuchar. 6. (Mec.) Hacer disminuir la anchura de alguna cosa. 7. (Mar.) Dar carena al buque.
Listed [list'-ed], *a.* Listado, listeado.
Listel [lis'-tel], *s.* (Arq.) Listel, filete.
Listen [lis'-n], *va.* y *vn.* 1. Escuchar, atender. 2. Seguir un consejo; obedecer, conformarse con una opinión.
Listener [lis'-n-ẹr], *s.* Escuchante, escuchador, espía, escucha.
Listerine [lis'-tẹr-in], *s.* Listerina (marca de fábrica de un antiséptico).
Listerism [lis'-tẹr-izm], *s.* Listerismo, el procedimiento quirúrgico antiséptico, como lo practicó por primera vez Sir José Lister (nacido en 1827).
Listing [list'-ing], *s.* 1. Orilla de paño, tira, cenefa. *V.* LIST [2], 1ª acep. 2. (E. U.) Apuntar, acción de poner en un catálogo o lista.
Listless [list'-les], *a.* Indiferente, descuidado, omiso, negligente.
Listlessly [list'-les-li], *adv.* Indiferentemente, negligentemente.
Listlessness [list'-les-nes], *s.* Descuido, omisión, indiferencia, negligencia.
List price [list prais], *s.* Precio de catálogo.
Lit [lit], *pret.* y *pp.* del verbo *To* LIGHT. Acontecido; alumbrado, encendido o inflamado.
Litany [lit'-a-ni], *s.* Letanía.
Liter [li'-tẹr], *s.* Litro, medida de capacidad; decímetro cúbico.
Literal [lit'-ẹr-al], *a.* Literal.—*s.* Sentido literal.
Literalist [lit'-ẹr-al-ist], *s.* El que se adhiere a la letra o al sentido literal.
Literally [lit'-ẹr-al-i], *adv.* Literalmente, conforme a la letra o al sentido literal.
Literalness [lit'-er-al-nes], *s.* Significación original, primaria o literal; conformidad con la letra, exactitud.
Literary [lit'-ẹr-ẹ-ri], *a.* Literario.
Literate [lit'-ẹr-et], *a.* Literato.
Literati [lit-ẹr-é'-tai o ā'-ti], *s. pl.* Literatos, sabios, doctos, eruditos.

Literatim [lit-er-é'-tim o ɡ'-tim], *adv.* Letra por letra, á la letra; literalmente.

Literator [lit'-ɡr-ê-tɡr], *a.* Maestro de escuela: dícese despreciativamente.

Literature [lit'-ɡr-a-chur], *s.* 1. Literatura. 2. Las obras literarias de una nación o época. 3. Trabajo literario. 4. Conocimiento de las letras o libros.

Litharge [lith'-arj], *s.* Litargirio, litarge, almártaga.

Lithate [lith'-êt], *s.* Urato. *V.* URATE.

Lithe [laidh], *a.* Flexible, delgado, blando, manejable.

Litheness [laidh'-nes], *s.* Flexibilidad, flojedad; blandura.

Lither [lai'-dher], *a.* (Prov. Ingl.) Blando, flexible, manejable.

Litherly [lidh'-ɡr-li], *a.* (Prov. Ingl.) Artificioso, malicioso; travieso, enredador.—*adv.* (Des.) Tardamente, perezosamente.

Lithesome [laidh'-sum], *a.* (Poét.) Flexible, que se dobla fácilmente; activo, ligero, listo.

Lithia [lith'-i-a], *s.* Litina, óxido alcalino de litio.

Lithic [lith'-ic], *a.* Lítico, perteneciente a (1) cálculo de la vejiga; (2) a la piedra; (3) al litio.

Lithium [lith'-i-um], *s.* (Quím.) Litio, elemento metálico, blando, blanco de plata, y tan ligero que flota sobre el agua.

Litho-, Lith-. Formas de combinación, derivadas del griego *lithos*, piedra.

Lithocolla [lith-o-cel'-a], *s.* Litocola, una especie de betún.

Lithograph [lith'-o-grɡf], *va.* Litografiar.—*s.* Litografía, estampa de un dibujo en piedra.

Lithographer [lith-eg'-ra-fɡr], *s.* Litógrafo.

Lithographic [lith-o-grɡf'-ic], *a.* Litográfico, relativo a la litografía.

Lithography [lith-eg'-ra-fi], *s.* Litografía, el arte de grabar sobre piedra.

Lithoid, Lithoidal [lith'-eid, lith-ei'-dal], *a.* Litoideo, que tiene aspecto pétreo.

Litholapaxy [lith-o-la-pax'-i], *s.* Litolapaxia, la operación de pulverizar un cálculo dentro de la vejiga y a la vez de extraer los fragmentos con un tubo por medio de la succión. Es la operación preferida.

Lithologic, Lithological [lith-o-lej'-ic, al], *a.* Litológico, concerniente a la litología.

Lithology [lith-el'-o-ji], *s.* 1. Litología, historia natural de las piedras. 2. Tratado sobre los cálculos que se encuentran en el cuerpo humano y su curación.

Lithophyte [lith'-o-fait], *s.* Litófito, especie de zoófito.

Lithosphere [lith'-o-sfir], *s.* (Geol.) Litosfera.

Lithotomist [lith-et'-o-mist], *s.* (Cir.) Litotomista, el que extrae la piedra de la vejiga.

Lithotomy [lith-et'-o-mi], *s.* Litotomía, talla, la operación para extraer la piedra de la vejiga.

Lithotrity [lith-et'-ri-ti ó lith-o-trai'-ti], *s.* Litotricia, operación de reducir a pedazos la piedra dentro de la vejiga.

Lithotrite [lith'-o-trait], *s.* Litotrictor, instrumento para hacer la operación de la litotricia.

Lithuanian [lith-yu-é'-ni-an], *a.* Lituano, perteneciente a la Lituania.

Litigant [lit'-i-gant], *s.* y *a.* Litigante.

Litigate [lit'-i-gêt], *va.* Litigar o pleitear.—*vn.* Litigar, tener pleito pendiente.

Litigation [lit-i-gé'-shun], *s.* Litigio, pleito pendiente.

Litigious [li-tij'-us], *a.* Litigioso.

Litigiously [li-tij'-us-li], *adv.* De un modo litigioso.

Litmus [lit'-mus], *s.* Tornasol en pasta, especie de orchilla.

Litre [li'-tɡr], *s.* *V.* LITER. (< Fr.)

Litter [lit'-ɡr], *s.* 1. Litera, cama portátil; antiguamente también vehículo llevado por dos caballerías. 2. Cama, la paja que se pone en las cuadras para que se echen las caballerías y demás animales. 3. Lechigada, camada, ventregada, el número de animalillos que nacen de un parto. 4. Desechos, cachos, fragmentos esparcidos; estado de desorden.

Litter, *va.* 1. Parir o dar a luz los animales. 2. Desordenar; cubrir algún sitio con cosas esparcidas sin orden ni concierto. 3. Cubrir de paja o con paja algún paraje. 4. Preparar algún sitio con paja para que descanse en él el ganado lanar. —*vn.* 1. Tenderse, echarse o dormir en la paja, como el ganado. 2. Parir la puerca y otros animales.

Litterbug [lit'-ɡr-bug], *s.* Persona que ensucia parques dejando tirados papeles, etc.

Little [lit'-l], *a.* (*comp.* LESS y a veces LESSER; *super.* LEAST). 1. Poco, escaso, limitado y corto en cantidad; pequeño, chico. 2. De poca importancia, insignificante; mediano, ligero; de aquí, despreciable, mezquino. *This has done me little or no service*, Esto me ha servido de poco o nada. *A little one*, Un niño. *By little and little*, Poco a poco. *Be it ever so little*, Por poco que sea. *Little* se traduce a menudo en español por una desinencia diminutiva: *a little house*, casita; *a little one*, chiquillo, chiquitín.—*s.* Poco, parte o porción pequeña de alguna cosa. *A little sleep*, Un poco de sueño.—*adv.* Poco. *Sing a little*, Cante Vd. un poco.

Littleness [lit'-l-nes], *s.* Pequeñez, bajeza, apocamiento de espíritu; falta de dignidad.

Littoral [lit'-o-ral], *a.* Litoral, perteneciente a la ribera, costa o playa.

Liturgic, Liturgical [li-tūr'-jic, al], *a.* Litúrgico.

Liturgy [lit'-ur-ji], *s.* Liturgia, el orden aprobado por la Iglesia para celebrar los oficios divinos.

Livable [liv'-a-bl], *a.* 1. Digno de la vida; que vale la pena de vivir. 2. Aguantable, soportable.

Live [liv], *va.* 1. Pasar, llevar; pasar la vida de cierto modo. 2. Conformarse habitualmente a alguna cosa.—*vn.* 1. Vivir. 2. Mantenerse, subsistir. 3. Morar, habitar. 4. (Mar.) Estar, quedarse á flote; escapar a la destrucción. *To live at rest*, Pasar tranquilamente la vida. *To live by one's self*, Hacer corro o rancho aparte. *To live from hand to mouth*, Vivir al día, de un modo precario. *To live up to*, Vivir en conformidad con. *To live up to one's income*, Comerse todas sus rentas. *To live down*, Sobrevivir a; refutar una calumnia, borrar una falta.

Live [laiv], *a.* 1. Vivo, en vida. 2. Que manifiesta vida o energía: (1) listo, preparado para el uso, efectivo; (2) ardiente, abrasador, vivo, brillante; (3) útil para imprimir. *Live steam*, Vapor efectivo. *A live coal*, Una brasa, un carbón ardiente. 3. (E. U.) Vivo, fogoso, que tiene viveza, interés o animación. *Live-box*, (1) Porta-animálculos, celdilla de vidrio para examinar los objetos vivos con el microscopio. *Live circuit* o *wire*, Circuito o alambre por el cual está pasando una corriente eléctrica. *Live stock*, Ganadería, conjunto de los animales domésticos de una finca o hacienda.

Live broadcast [laiv brōd'-cɡst], *s.* Transmisión directa por radio o televisión, en contraste con las grabadas en cinta.

Livelihood [laiv'-li-hud], *s.* 1. Vida, modo de vivir o de ganar la vida; mantenimiento, subsistencia. 2. Apariencia de vida.

Liveliness [laiv'-li-nes], *s.* Vida, viveza, prontitud, agilidad, vivacidad, actividad.

Livelong [liv'-leng], *a.* Tedioso, fastidioso, enfadoso, molesto, cansado; largo.

Lively [laiv'-li], *a.* 1. Vivo, vigoroso, brioso. 2. Gallardo, airoso, galán. 3. Animado, vivificado. 4. Eficaz.—*adv.* Vigorosamente; enérgicamente; vivamente, muy a lo vivo.

Live-oak [laiv'-ōk], *s.* Encina americana notable por su dureza, con hojas siempre verdes; hay varias especies, entre ellas Quercus chrysolepis y Quercus virens.

Liver [liv'-ɡr], *s.* 1. Viviente. *Good liver*, El que se da buena vida. 2. Hígado.

Livered [liv'-ɡrd], *a.* El que tiene hígado. *White-livered* o *lily-livered*, Cobarde, bajo, mezquino, pérfido, que tiene malos hígados o mala voluntad.

Liveried [liv'-er-id], *a.* Que lleva una librea.

Liverwort [liv'-ɡr-wūrt], *s.* (Bot.) Hepática.

Livery [liv'-ɡr-i], *s.* 1. Librea, el vestido que se da a algunos criados. 2. Cualquier vestido que se lleva en señal de alguna cosa o a consecuencia de algún acontecimiento. 3. El cuerpo de ciudadanos de Londres. *Liveryman*, Ciudadano de Londres, individuo de algún gremio. *Liverymen*, Criados de librea. *Livery stable*, Caballeriza donde se tienen caballos para alquilar, o donde se mantienen y cuidan caballos por un precio determinado; pensión de caballos. *To keep horses at livery*, Tener caballos de alquiler. 4. Entrega, el acto de dar o tomar posesión.

Lives [laivz], *pl.* de LIFE.

Livestock [laiv'-stek], *s.* Ganadería.

Live wire [laiv wair], *s.* 1. Alambre cargado. 2. (fam.) Persona muy activa y llena de vida. 3. Muchacho muy travieso.

Livid [liv'-id], *a.* Lívido, cárdeno, acardenalado, amoratado.

Lividness [liv'-id-nes], *s.* Lo cárdeno, lo amoratado; el color lívido, cárdeno o amoratado.

Living [liv'-ing], *s.* 1. Modo de vivir o de ganar la vida, subsistencia, mantenimiento. 2. Vida, potencia vital. 3. Beneficio eclesiástico.—*a.* Vivo, vigoroso; que tiene movimiento y vida. *Living coals*, Brasas.

Livingly [liv'-ing-li], *adv.* En estado de vida, vivo.
Living room [liv'-ing rūm], *s.* Sala, estancia.
Living wage [liv'-ing wêj], *s.* Jornal adecuado para la subsistencia.
Lixivial [lix-iv'-i-al], *a.* Lejivial; aplícase a la sal alcalina sacada de las cenizas por medio de la loción.
Lixivium [lics-iv'-i-um], *s.* Lejía, agua impregnada de sales alcalinas.
Lizard [liz'-ard], *s.* Lagarto. (Mex.) Lagartija.
Llama [lā'-ma], *s.* Llama del Perú, animal rumiante. Auchenia llama.
LL. D. Abrev. de *legum doctor*, o doctor en ambos derechos.
Lloyd's [leidz], *s.* Nombre de una asociación inglesa de corredores de seguros marítimos. *Lloyd's List*, Lista de Lloyd, publicación que da noticias sobre el comercio marítimo. *Lloyd's Register*, Registro de Lloyd, catálogo clasificado de los buques de todas las naciones.
Lo [lō], *inter.* Hé aquí, ved aquí, mirad.
Load [lōd], *s.* 1. Carga; medida; peso. 2. Carga, gravamen; de aquí, opresión. 3. Fardo. 4. La resistencia que una máquina opone al motor que la impele. 5. Peso, presión hacia abajo sobre una construcción. *Ship-load*, Cargamento de un buque. *Load-line, load-water line*, Línea de flotación. *Cart-load*, Carretada. *Boat-load*, Barcada.
Load, *va.* 1. Cargar, poner o echar algún peso sobre el hombre, sobre las bestias, etc. 2. Embarazar, impedir. 3. Cargar un arma de fuego. 4. Colmar; llenar, agobiar. 5. Falsificar, adulterar. 6. Hacer pesado, cargar (como con plomo). *A loaded whip*, Látigo emplomado.—*vn.* Tomar una carga o cargamento; a veces con la prep. *up*. *To load with favours*, Colmar de favores. *To load with reproaches*, Llenar de reconvenciones.
Loader [lōd'-ẹr], *s.* Cargador, embarcador.
Loadstone [lōd'-stōn], *s.* Imán. *V.* LODESTONE.
Loaf [lōf], *s.* Pan, la masa de harina que se forma para cocer en el horno. *A large loaf*, Hogaza. *A small loaf*, Panecillo. *A loaf of sugar*, Pilón de azúcar. *Loaf sugar*, Azúcar de pilón. *Penny loaf*, Rollo, bollo.
Loaf, *va.* Pasar en la ociosidad; se usa con la prep. *away*. *To loaf one's time away*, Pasar su tiempo en la ociosidad.—*vn.* Haraganear, holgazanear. (< Al. laufen, correr.)
Loafer [lōf'-ẹr], *s.* Haragán, holgazán; tunante, pelafustán.
Loam [lōm], *s.* 1. Marga, mezcla no cohesiva de arena y arcilla, que contiene substancias orgánicas; tierra labrantía. 2. En fundición, tierra de moldeo.
Loamy [lōm'-i], *a.* Terroso, margoso.
Loan [lōn], *s.* 1. Préstamo; empréstito. 2. Permiso para usar.
Loath [lōth], *a.* Repugnante, desinclinado, disgustado, poco dispuesto a. *I was loath to come away*, Estaba poco dispuesto a irme.
Loathe [lōdh], *va.* 1. Aborrecer, detestar. 2. Tener hastío, aborrecer alguna cosa por estar harto de ella. —*vn.* Fastidiar. causar o sentir fastidio, disgusto o aborrecimiento.
Loather [lōdh'-ẹr], *s.* El que está disgustado, fastidiado o lleno de tedio.
Loathful [lōdh'-ful], *a.* (Poco us.) Fastidiado, lleno de tedio; aborrecido, odiado.
Loathing [lōdh'-ing], *s.* Disgusto, aversión, asco, repugnancia.
Loathingly [lōdh'-ing-li], *adv.* De mala gana, con disgusto.
Loathsome [lōdh'-sum], *a.* Aborrecible, detestable, fastidioso, asqueroso.
Loathsomeness [lōdh'-sum-nes], *s.* La calidad o propiedad de lo que causa asco o fastidio.
Loaves [lōvz], *pl.* de LOAF.
Lob [lǝb], *s.* 1. Lombriz grande. *V.* LOBWORM. 2. Masa, mezcla blanda y espesa. 3. Meta, término de los juegos de pelota y vilorta. 4. (Ant.) Pelmazo, el sujeto tardo y pesado en sus acciones.
Lob, *va.* Soltar o dejar caer alguna cosa por torpeza o falta de maña.
Lobar [lō'-bar], *a.* Lobular. *Lobar pneumonia*, Neumonía de un lóbulo entero (como ocurre comúnmente entre los adultos).
Lobate, Lobated [lō'-bêt, ed], *a.* Lobulado, en forma de lóbulo, o provisto de lóbulos.
Lobby [leb'-i], *s.* Paso, pasillo o corredor que hay delante de la puerta de una sala u otra pieza de una casa; antecámara, vestíbulo, pórtico, galería, tribuna.
Lobby, *va.* y *vn.* (E. U.) Procurar la aprobación de una medida o proyecto de ley, tratando de obtener en su favor los votos de los legisladores.
Lobbying [leb'-i-ing], *s.* Cabildeo. (Mex. coll.) Coyoteo.
Lobe [lōb], *s.* 1. (Zool. y Bot.) Lóbulo; lobo. 2. Lóbulo, parte más marcada del esquema de señales que aparece en la pantalla.
Lobelia [lo-bī'-lia], *s.* Lobelia, extenso género de plantas con flores muy vistosas; planta de este género.
Lobscouse [leb'-scaus], **Loblolly** [leb'-lel-i], *s.* Almodrote, vianda usada en el mar; polenta. *Loblolly boy*, Criado del cirujano de un buque.
Lobster [leb'-stẹr], *s.* Langosta de mar, crustáceo comestible. Homarus vulgaris o americanus.
Lobule [leb'-yūl], *s. dim.* Lobulillo.
Local [lō'-cal], *a.* Local, relativo a determinado lugar. *Local remedies*, Remedios externos, tópicos.—*s.* 1. (Fam. E. U.) Noticia de interés local. 2. (E. U.) Tren de escala; (Ingl.) tren suburbano. 3. Batería o circuito local.
Localism [lō'-cal-izm], *s.* 1. Costumbre o idiotismo particular de un lugar; locución local. 2. Provincialismo; estado local.
Locality [lo-cal'-i-ti], *s.* 1. Localidad, paraje determinado; posición, situación topográfica. 2. Particularidad o circunstancia local.
Localize [lō'-cal-aiz], *va.* Localizar, orientar.
Locally [lō'-cal-i], *adv.* Localmente.
Local option [lō'-cal ep'-shun], *s.* Derecho de una ciudad, distrito, etc. a permitir o no la venta de bebidas alcohólicas.
Locate [lō'-kêt], *va.* Poner, colocar, situar; trazar la línea de un ferrocarril.
Location [lo-kê'-shun], *s.* Colocación, localidad, situación, ubicación.
Loch [lēj o leн: esta *j* suena como en español, o como la *ch* alemana], *s.* (Esco.) Lago; también ensenada marina.
Lochia [lō'-ki-a], *s. pl.* Loquios, líquido que sale por los órganos de la mujer durante el puerperio.
Lock [lec], *s.* 1. Cerradura, cerraja. *Spring-lock*, Cerradura de muelle. *Padlock*, Candado. 2. Llave, la parte de las armas de fuego que sirve para dispararlas. 3. Abrazo estrecho y apretado. 4. Cercado, cerca, vallado. 5. Vedija de lana; bucle, rizo, trenza, guedeja, hablando del pelo; ramillete, borla. 6. Esclusa, represa de río o canal navegable; compuerta. 7. Trabas, maniotas, para las manos de los caballos. *Under lock and key*, Bajo llave.
Lock, *va.* 1. Cerrar. 2. Tener debajo de llave. 3. Abrazar, coger alguna cosa entre los brazos.—*vn.* 1. Estar una cosa cerrada; tener alguna cosa bajo de llave. *The door does not lock*, La puerta no cierra. 2. Unirse o entrelazarse una cosa con otra. *To lock in*, Encerrar, poner bajo llave; abrazar. *To lock up*, Cerrar, encerrar. *To lock one out*, Cerrar la puerta a uno para que no entre.
Lockage [lek'-êj], *s.* 1. Materiales para la construcción de una esclusa. 2. Diferencia de nivel en un canal de esclusas. 3. Portazgo de esclusa, derecho que se paga por pasar.
Locked [lect], *a.* 1. Cerrado con llave. 2. Entrelazado, enganchado.
Locker [lek'-ẹr], *s.* 1. Cajón, gaveta o cosa semejante cerrada con llave; armario. 2. (Mar.) Cajón o alacena de cámara. *Shot-locker*, (Mar.) Chillera.
Locket [lek'-et], *s.* Guardapelo, medallón pequeño.
Lockjaw [lec'-jō], *s.* (Med.) Trismo, tétanos.
Lockout [lec'-aut], *s.* (Econ. polít.) Cierre de una fábrica u otro establecimiento por los dueños del mismo; (correlativo de huelga).
Lockram [lec'-ram], *s.* Estopa, especie de lienzo basto o tela grosera.
Locksmith [lec'-smith], *s.* Cerrajero.
Lockstitch [lec'-stich], *s.* Punto de cadeneta.
Locomotion [lō-co-mō'-shun], *s.* Locomoción, mudanza de lugar; potencia locomotriz.
Locomotive [lō-co-mō'-tiv], *a.* Locomotivo, capaz de moverse y de mudarse de lugar.—*s.* Locomotora, máquina motriz de los ferrocarriles.
Locomotor [lō-co-mō'-tẹr], *a.* Locomotor, locomotriz, perteneciente a la locomoción.
Locust [lō'-cust], *s.* (Ent.) 1. Langosta, saltamontes. 2. (E. U.) Cigarra, cicada. 3. *Locust* o *locust-tree*, Llámanse así vulgarmente el algarrobo, la acacia y otros árboles. Robinia pseudacacia.
Locution [lo-kiū'-shun], *s.* Locución, modo de hablar; frase.
Locular [lec'-yu-lar], *a.* (Bot.) Locular, loculado, dividido en celdillas.
Loculicidal [lec-yu-li-sai'-dal], *a.* (Bot.) Loculicida; dícese de la dehiscencia que se efectúa por la sutura media de las celdillas de un pericarpio.
Lode [lōd], *s.* 1. Filón, vena metálica (metalífera). 2. Extensión de agua detenida, como en una acequia.
Lodestar [lōd'-stār], *s.* Cinosura, estrella del norte, estrella de guía.

Lodestone [lōd'-stōn], *s.* Imán natural, piedra imán.

Lodge [lej], *va.* 1. Alojar, aposentar, poner en alojamiento. 2. Colocar, poner alguna cosa en paraje determinado. 3. Dar hospedaje o alojamiento por breve tiempo. 4. Fijar alguna cosa en la memoria. 5. Abrigar, cubrir. 6. Derribar, echar abajo.—*vn.* 1. Residir, habitar, vivir, morar en algún lugar o casa. *Where do you lodge?* ¿Dónde vive Vd.? 2. Alojarse u hospedarse de noche. 3. Tenderse, echarse. *Lodging-knees,* (Mar.) Curvas valonas. *To lodge a complaint against,* Dar una queja contra alguien.

Lodge, *s.* 1. Casa de guarda en el bosque o monte. 2. Cualquier casita pequeña pegada a otra mayor y formando parte de ella. *Porter's lodge,* Covacha o cuarto del portero. 3. Logia, la reunión o subdivisión local de ciertas sociedades secretas y la casa en que se juntan.

Lodgment [lej'-mgnt], *s.* 1. Amontonamiento. 2. (Mil.) Atrincheramiento, trinchera.

Lodger [lej'-er], *s.* Huésped, inquilino, morador.

Lodging [lej'-ing], *s.* 1. Posada, habitación, vivienda; cuartos alquilados. 2. Alojamiento, cuando se habla de tropas. 3. Morada, residencia temporal. *Private lodging,* Habitación o cuarto en una casa particular. *Board and lodging,* Mesa y habitación; casa de huéspedes. *Lodging-house,* Casa de huéspedes amueblada, pensión.

Loft [lōft], *s.* 1. Suelo, piso. 2. Sobrado, desván. *Hayloft,* Henil. (Voz islandesa.)

Loftily [lōft'-i-li], *adv.* 1. En alto. 2. Altivamente, pomposamente.

Loftiness [lōft'-i-nes], *s.* 1. Altura, elevación. 2. Sublimidad o elevación. 3. Altivez, soberbia, orgullo; majestad.

Lofty [lōf'-ti], *s.* 1. Alto, elevado, levantado. 2. Sublime, grande, excelso. 3. Altivo, orgulloso, soberbio.

Log [log], *s.* 1. Leño, trozo de árbol o madera sin figura particular. *A log of mahogany,* Una toza de caoba. 2. (Mar.) Barquilla, cierto palito en figura de barca que sirve para obrar con la corredera y carretel. *Log-board,* (Mar.) Tableta de bitácora. *Log-line,* (Mar.) Corredera. *Log-book,* (Mar.) Diario de navegación. *Log-reel,* (Mar.) Carretel. *Log-cabin, log-hut,* Cabaña hecha con maderos o troncos de árboles.

Loganberry [lō'-gan-ber'-i], *s.* (Bot.) Variedad de zarzamora.

Logarithm [log'-a-rithm], *s.* Logaritmo.

Logarithmic, Logarithmical [log-a-rith'-mic, al], *a.* Logarítmico.

Loggerhead [log'-gr-hed], *s.* 1. Zote, necio. 2. Cierta tortuga marina de gran tamaño. 3. Pegareborda de los Estados Unidos. *To fall* o *to go to loggerheads,* Reñir sin armas, estar de cuerno con uno.

Loggerheaded [log'-gr-hed-ed], *a.* Necio, tonto, zote.

Logic [lej'-ic], *s.* Lógica, la ciencia que enseña a discurrir con exactitud.

Logical [lej'-ic-al], *a.* Lógico, perteneciente a la lógica.

Logically [lej'-ic-al-i], *adv.* Lógicamente.

Logician [lo-jish'-un], *s.* Lógico, el que profesa o enseña la lógica.

Logistics [lo-jis'-tics], *s. pl.* (Mil.) Logística, ramo del arte militar que trata de los movimientos y el abastecimiento de tropas y de la dirección general de una campaña.

Logogram [log'-o-gram], *s.* 1. Abreviatura u otro signo que indica una palabra, como *lb.* por libra, *$* por peso o dólar. 2. Logogrifo, enigma en verso.

Logograph [log'-o-graf], *s.* Palabra escrita.

Logogriph [log'-o-grif], *s.* Logogrifo, enigma.

Logomachy [lo-gem'-a-ki], *s.* 1. Logomaquia, altercación sobre voces o palabras. 2. Juego que consiste en formar nuevos vocablos con las letras de una palabra dada.

Logwood [log'-wud], *s.* Palo de Campeche o de tinte.

Loin [lein], *s.* Ijada, ijar, la parte del cuerpo situada entre las costillas falsas y los huesos de las caderas. *Loins,* Lomos.

Loiter [lei'-tgr], *vn.* Haraganear, perder el tiempo, tardar.—*va.* Malgastar el tiempo.

Loiterer [lei'-tgr-gr], *s.* Haragán, el holgazán, perezoso o negligente.

Loll [lel], *vn.* 1. Apoyarse, recostarse o tenderse con dejadez y flojedad en alguna cosa. 2. Colgar hacia fuera.—*va.* Sacar la lengua de la boca.

Lollard [lel'-ard], †**Loller** [lel'-gr], *s.* Lolardo, nombre dado en Inglaterra a algunos reformadores.

Lollypop [lel'-i-pep], *s.* (Ingl.) Variedad de melcocha o arropía.

Lombardic [lem-bārd'-ic], *a.* Lombárdico: dícese de un alfabeto usado por los lombardos.

Loment [lō'-mgnt], *s.* (Bot.) Lomento, pericarpio (legumbre) indehiscente, con divisiones o articulaciones transversales entre las semillas.

London [lun'-dun], *n. pr.* Londres. *London-pride,* (1) Una saxífraga irlandesa cultivada en los jardines ingleses de campo. (2) (o *London-tuft*) Clavel barbudo, clavel de poeta.

Londoner [lun'-dun-gr], *s.* Londinense, el natural o habitante de Londres.

Londonism [lun'-dun-izm], *s.* Londonismo; costumbre, locución o giro propios de los habitantes de Londres.

Lone [lōn], *a.* 1. Solitario, solo, aislado. 2. Soltero o soltera. 3. (Ant.) No frecuentado.

Loneliness [lōn'-li-nes], *s.* Soledad.

Lonely [lōn'-li], *a.* 1. Solitario; solo; abandonado. 2. Amante de la soledad.

Loneness [lōn'-nes], *s.* (Poco us.) Soledad, retiro y poca afición a estar en compañía.

Lonesome [lōn'-sum], *a.* Solitario, desierto.

Lonesomely [lōn'-sum-li], *adv.* Solitariamente.

Lonesomeness [lōn'-sum-nes], *s.* Estado o calidad del que está solo.

Long [lōng], *a.* 1. Largo, extenso en espacio o en duración; de largo, de longitud. *Longer,* Más largo. *Longest,* El más largo. *Longest liver,* Sobreviviente. *A long way about,* Un gran rodeo. *A piece of timber seventy feet long,* Un madero de setenta pies de largo. *Two inches long,* Dos pulgadas de largo o de longitud. *Long measure,* Medida de longitud. 2. Dilatorio, tardo, lento; enfadoso, afectadamente circunspecto. 3. Extenso, prolongado; continuo. 4. (Com.) Que retiene en su poder acciones o valores esperando que ocurra un alza en los precios: dícese de un corredor y es lo contrario de *short.*—*adv.* 1. A una gran distancia; mucho. *Long after,* Mucho después. *Long ago, long since,* Mucho tiempo ha. *Ere long,* Antes de mucho. *As long as I live,* Mientras viva o para mientras viva. *So long as,* Mientras que, en tanto que. *All my life long,* Toda mi vida. *How long is it since?* ¿Cuánto hace o cuánto tiempo hace? *Not long before,* Poco antes o poco tiempo antes. *Longer,* Más largo tiempo. 2. En consecuencia de, debido a.—*s.* Longa, una antigua nota de música. *The long and the short,* Lo largo y lo corto, es decir, el todo; la substancia, el resumen. *Long clothes,* Las primeras ropas de una criatura, vestido largo que se extiende más allá de los pies. *Long-drawn,* Prolongado; fastidioso. *Long-headed,* Astuto, sagaz, prudente. *Long primer,* (Impr.) Entredós, filosofía, letra de diez puntos. *Long staple,* De fibra larga; dícese del algodón.

Long, *vn.* 1. Desear con vehemencia alguna cosa, anhelar, ansiar, suspirar por algo. *I long to see him,* Tengo mucho deseo de verle. 2. Antojarse; (fam.) pirrarse.

Longanimity [long-ga-nim'-i-ti], *s.* (Jocoso) Longanimidad, constancia de ánimo en las adversidades.

Long-boat [lōng'-bōt], *s.* (Mar.) Lancha, falúa o faluca.

Long-distance [lōng-dis'-tans], *a.* De larga distancia. *Long-distance call,* Llamada telefónica de larga distancia.

Longe [lunj], *s.* 1. Estocada, golpe. 2. Terreno en que se trabajan y adiestran los caballos para las carreras.

Longevity [len-jev'-i-ti], *s.* Longevidad, ancianidad, duración larga de la vida.

Longhand [lōng'-hand], *s.* La escritura ordinaria, sin abreviación de las palabras, a diferencia de la estenografía o taquigrafía.

Longhorn [lōng'-hōrn], *s.* Animal de cuernos largos, especialmente un tipo de ganado de origen español, ahora prácticamente extinto.

Longicorn [len'-ji-cern], *a.* y *s.* Longicornio, de largas antenas, familia de insectos coleópteros. Las larvas del capricornio y otras especies horadan las maderas más duras.

Longimetry [lōn-jim'-e-tri], *s.* Longimetría, arte de medir las distancias.

Longing [lōng'-ing], *s.* Antojo, deseo vehemente, anhelo, ansia; saudad. *A woman's longing,* Un capricho de mujer.

Longingly [lōng'-ing-li], *adv.* Vehementemente; impacientemente.

Longish [lōng'-ish], *a.* Algo largo, un poco largo.

Longitude [len'-ji-tiūd], *s.* 1. Longitud. 2. (Geog.) Longitud, la distancia que hay de un lugar cualquiera del globo al primer meridiano.

Longitudinal [len-ji-tiū'-di-nal], *a.* Longitudinal, perteneciente a la longitud o hecho con arreglo a ella.

Long-legged [lōng'-leg-ed], **Long-shanked** [lōng'-shanct], *a.* Zanquilargo.

Long-lived [lŏng'-laivd], *a.* Longevo, de larga vida; de mucha vida.
Longly [lŏng'-li], *adv.* 1. Por mucho tiempo, prolijamente. 2. (Des.) Ansiosamente, ardientemente.
Longness [lŏng'-nes], *s.* Largura.
Long-pepper [lŏng'-pep-ẹr], *s.* Pimienta larga.
Long-playing [lŏng-plê'-ing], *a.* De larga duración.
Longshoreman [leng-shōr'-man], *s.* 1. Estivador, trabajador de muelle. 2. El hombre que vive a orillas del mar y subsiste de la pesca, o como remero, etc.
Long-sighted [leng'-sait-ed], *a.* 1. Que ve a gran distancia; de aquí, sagaz, previsor, precavido. 2. Présbite, que ve mejor de lejos que de cerca.
Longspun [lŏng'-spun], *a.* Prolijo, dilatado. (Fam.) Tirado por fuerza, o por los cabellos.
Long-standing [lŏng-stand'-ing], *a.* De larga duración.
Long-suffering, *a.* Paciente, sufrido.
Long-term [leng'-tẹrm], *a.* De largo plazo.
Longways [lŏng'-wêz], *adv.* (Fam.) *V.* LENGTHWISE.
Long-winded [lŏng-wind'-ed], *a.* Largo, pesado, prolijo.
Loo, Lu [lū], *s.* Juego de naipes, en el que puede participar un número cualquiera de jugadores, con tres o cinco naipes cada uno.
Loo, *va.* Ganar todas las bazas en el juego de naipes; dar capote; dar bola.
Loof [lūf], *s.* (Mar.) Lof, la parte circular de la proa desde las amuras hasta la roda.
Look [luk], *va.* y *vn.* 1. Mirar, dirigir la vista hacia algún objeto o poner la vista en él. 2. Mirar, considerar, pensar, contemplar; esperar. 3. Mirar, poner cuidado, tener cuidado. 4. Mirar, dar, caer, estar situada una cosa frente de otra. *The front of the house looks on* o *toward the garden*, La fachada de la casa mira al jardín, o hacia el jardín. 5. Parecerse a alguno, darse un aire; parecer, tener apariencia o traza de. 6. Mirar, buscar. 7. Mirar, dar una mirada. *To look about*, Mirar alrededor; cuidar, tener cuidado de. *To look about one*, Estar alerta, tener vigilancia. *To look after*, Cuidar; tener cuidado; prestar atención; buscar, inquirir, investigar alguna cosa. *To look at*, Mirar a; considerar; atender. *To look back*, Reflexionar. *To look down upon*, Despreciar. *To look down upon one with scorn*, Mirar á alguno de arriba abajo, con desprecio. *To look for*, Esperar, buscar. *To look into*, Examinar, considerar; tomar conocimiento de una cosa, inspeccionar atentamente. *To look nine ways*, Ser bisojo, torcer la vista. *To look on*, Considerar, concebir, pensar, imaginarse; mirar, ver; dar, caer; ser espectador indiferente; estimar. *These windows look on the river*, Estas ventanas dan al río. *To look out*, Buscar; cuidar de; estar alerta; mirar por; descubrir alguna cosa a fuerza de investigaciones o encontrarla a fuerza de buscarla. *To look over*, Examinar alguna cosa en todos sus pormenores. *To look to*, Cuidar de, velar, guardar; observar, considerar, contemplar. *Look to it*, Esté Vd. con cuidado, esté Vd. sobre sí. *To look up to*, Esperar o tener esperanza en la protección de alguno. *To look black*, Tener ceño, estar ceñudo, tener mala cara por estar enfadado. *To look big*, Entonarse. *To look ill*, Tener malas trazas o tener mala cara por presentar la apariencia de enfermo. *To look like*, Semejarse. *To look sharp*, (1) (Fam.) Estar muy alerta, tener mucho cuidado. (2) Apresurarse, ser muy pronto y despierto. *To look well*, Tener buenas trazas o buena cara por tener la apariencia de salud. *To look out after a fleet of ships*, (Mar.) Vigiar una escuadra. *Look before you leap*, (prov.) Antes que te cases, mira lo que haces. *They went away looking daggers*, (Fam.) Se fueron echando chispas.
Look, *s.* 1. Aspecto, semblante, cara, aire, ademán. 2. Mirada. *The look-out*, (Mar.) Vigía.—*inter.* Mira, atiende; he aquí, ¡cuidado!
Looker [luk'-ẹr], *s.* Mirador, el que mira; mirón, el que está mirando alguna cosa.
Looking [luk'-ing], *s.* 1. Miramiento, el acto de mirar, o considerar alguna cosa; mirada. 2. Expectación, el anhelo con que se espera alguna cosa.
Looking-glass [luk'-ing-glas], *s.* Espejo. *Paper looking-glasses*, Tocadores, o espejitos de cartón.
Lookout [luk'-aut], *s.* 1. Vigía, atenta vigilancia. 2. Mirador, garita, torrecilla de observación, atalaya; la persona que vigila, guardia. 3. Toda cosa que ha de ser bien cuidada y guardada.
Loom [lūm], *s.* 1. Telar. *Stocking-loom*, Telar de medias. 2. Guión del remo. *Loom-gale*, (Mar.) Fugada bonancible.
Loom, *vn.* 1. Asomar, ir apareciendo o alzándose gradualmente. 2. Lucir, relucir.
Looming [lūm'-ing], *s.* Ilusión optica que parece elevar y prolongar la imagen de un objeto cualquiera, particularmente al través del agua.
Loon [lūn], *s.* 1. Bobo, necio, estúpido. 2. (Orn.) Somorgujo, ave acuática palmípeda. Urinator imber y Colymbus arcticus.
Loop [lūp], *s.* 1. Anillo, gaza, lazo; ojal, presilla. 2. Curva, comba de cualquier clase. 3. (Mec.) Abrazadera, anilla.
Loop, *va.* 1. Atar o asegurar con una presilla. 2. Hacer gazas, enlazar, formar curvas.—*vn.* Andar haciendo curvas, como ciertas larvas (orugas).
Looped [lūpt], *a.* Ojalado, lleno de ojales.
Loophole [lūp'-hōl], *s.* 1. Abertura, mirador, tronera; una especie de cornisa ancha. 2. Escapatoria, efugio, excusa. 3. (Mar.) Tronera.
Loopholed [lūp'-hōld], *a.* Lo que tiene muchos agujeros o cavidades.
Loop-lace [lūp'-lês], *s.* Los adornos puestos alrededor de los ojales.
Loop-maker [lūp'-mê-kẹr], *s.* Ojaladero, presillero.
Loose [lūs], *va.* 1. Desatar, desprender y desenlazar una cosa de otra, desliar. 2. Desapretar, aflojar. 3. Aliviar, dar alivio o descanso. 4. Soltar al que estaba preso. 5. Libertar de alguna obligación o riesgo; sacar de algún mal paso, desenredar; desocupar. *To loose one's hold*, Abandonar, soltar lo que se había tomado.
Loose, *a.* 1. Suelto, desatado. 2. Flojo, movible, lo que no está bien apretado. 3. Vago, indeterminado, falto de precisión. 4. Suelto de vientre. 5. Libre, relajado. 6. Suelto, puesto en libertad. 7. Disoluto. 8. Desenredado. 9. Descuidado, negligente. *To grow loose*, Desbandarse. *To break loose*, Ponerse en libertad; recobrar la libertad venciendo obstáculos; desencadenarse. *To get loose from one*, Desembarazarse de alguno. *To hang loose*, Colgar, flotar. *To let loose*, Libertar, poner en libertad.—*s.* Libertad; soltura. *A loose gown*, Un vestido flotante. *Loose morals*, Moral relajada. *Loose reasoning*, Raciocinio vago. *A loose liver*, Un libertino. *To be loose in the bowels*, Andar suelto de vientre. *To give loose to*, Dar rienda suelta a.
Loose-leaf [lūs'-līf], *a.* De hojas sueltas o insertables.
Loosely [lūs'-li], *adv.* Sueltamente, con desenvoltura, negligentemente.
Loosen [lūs'-en], *vn.* Desunirse, desatarse, separarse.—*va.* 1. Aflojar, laxar, soltar, desliar. *To loosen the sails*, (Mar.) Largar o descargar las velas. 2. Librar, libertar, desatar. 3. Soltar el vientre.
Looseness [lūs'-nes], *s.* 1. Aflojamiento, flojedad. 2. Relajación de costumbres, libertad, licencia, desgarro. 3. Soltura. 4. Flujo de vientre, diarrea, cursos.
Loosening [lūs'-en-ing], *a.* Laxante.
Loot [lūt], *va.* Saquear, pillar; llevarse como botín.—*s.* Botín, pillaje de un ejército vencedor.
Lop [lep], *va.* Desmochar, cortar las ramas superfluas de los árboles. *To lop vines*, Podar viñas.
Lop, *s.* 1. La rama podada. 2. Pulga.
Lopper [lep'-ẹr], *s.* Podador de árboles.
Loppered [lep'-ẹrd], *a.* Coagulado.
Loppings [lep'-ingz], *s. pl.* Ramas cortadas.
Lopsided [lep'-said-ed], *a.* 1. Que se inclina demasiado a un lado; más pesado de un lado que de otro. 2. De aquí, maniático, lleno de temas o rarezas.
Loquacious [lo-cwê'-shus], *a.* Locuaz, charlador, parlador o hablador.
Loquaciousness [lo-cwê'-shus-nes], **Loquacity** [lo-cwas'-i-ti], *s.* Locuacidad, habladuría, flujo de hablar, charla, parla.
Loran [lo'-ran], *s.* Loran. (Contracción de LOng RAnge NAvigation, sistema electrónico de navegación.)
Lord [lērd], *s.* 1. Señor, monarca. 2. Dios, el Ser Supremo; también, Nuestro Señor Jesucristo. 3. Señor, amo, dueño. 4. Marido. 5. Lord, nombre genérico que se da a los pares de Inglaterra, y por cortesía o de gracia se da también á todos los hijos de los duques y marqueses y a los hijos mayores de los condes. 6. Barón, para distinguir a los que gozan este título en Inglaterra, de los duques, marqueses, condes o vizcondes. 7. Título que se añade a la denominación de algunos empleos de palacio que regularmente están servidos por pares. *Lord Chamberlain*, Camarero mayor. *Lord High Steward*, Mayordomo mayor. También se añade este título a las denominaciones de

otros empleos, como *Lord Chief Justice*, El Presidente del tribunal supremo de Inglaterra; *Lord Mayor*, El Alcalde o Corregidor de Londres. *Lord's day*, Domingo, el día del Señor. *Lord's Supper*, La Última Cena, el Sacramento de la Eucaristía. *Lord's table*, Altar de la sagrada comunión; la misma comunión, Eucaristía.

Lord, *vn.* Señorear, dominar, mandar despóticamente.—*va.* Investir a uno con la dignidad y privilegios de par de Inglaterra.

Lording [lōrd'-ing], *s.* Hidalguillo, hidalgo de gotera, señor de poco más o menos.

Lord-like [lōrd'-laic], *a.* 1. Como un lord o semejante a un lord. 2. Altivo, orgulloso, insolente.

Lordliness [lōrd'-li-nes], *s.* 1. Dignidad, señorío. 2. Altivez, orgullo.

Lordling [lōrd'-ling], *s.* Un lord pequeño (término de desprecio).

Lordly [lōrd'-li], *a.* 1. Cosa perteneciente a un lord; señoril. 2. Altivo, orgulloso, imperioso.—*adv.* Imperiosamente, altivamente.

Lordship [lōrd'-ship], *s.* 1. Señorío, dominio, poder. 2. Señoría, tratamiento de respeto y cortesía que se da en Inglaterra a los pares que no son duques, a los que tienen el título de lord de gracia y a algunos otros empleados públicos; corresponde en castellano unas veces a Excelencia, y otras a Usía.

Lore [lōr], *s.* 1. Erudición, saber, ciencia; la erudición propia de un pueblo o de un siglo. 2. (Ant.) Lección, doctrina, enseñanza, instrucción.

Lorgnette [lōr-nyet'], *s.* Anteojos con mango largo, dentro del cual se doblan y guardan cuando no se usan. (Fr.)

Lorica [lo-rai'-ca o lo-rī'-ca], *s.* 1. (Ant.) Peto, coselete. 2. (Zool.) Cubierta protectora, como las de los infusorios y rotíferos. 3. Brasca o luten para proteger los crisoles, etc., de la acción del fuego.

Loricate [ler'-i-kêt], *va.* Planchear, cubrir alguna cosa con hojas o planchas protectoras.

Loricate, *a.* Plancheado, cubierto con hojas o planchas.

Lorication [ler-i-kê'-shun], *s.* Superficie cubierta con alguna cosa.

Loriot [ler'-i-et], *s.* (Orn.) Oropéndola de Europa.

Loris [lō'-ris], *s.* (Zool.) Loris, animal pequeño y arbóreo, de la familia de los lemúridos.

Lorn [lōrn], *a.* Dejado, abandonado, sin parentesco ni amigos: (ant.) perdido.

Lory [lō'-ri], *s.* Loro, pagagayo de color escarlata.

Losable, Loseable [lūz'-a-bl], *a.* Que se puede perder.

Lose [lūz], *va.* 1. Perder. 2. Perder, no conseguir lo que se deseaba. 3. Perder, desperdiciar, disipar, malgastar. 4, Exponer a la pérdida de. 5. Entregar a la ignominia o a la ruina. 6. Hacer perder.—*vn.* 1. Perderse, errar el camino que se llevaba o no encontrarle. 2. Declinar, decaer. *To lose ground*, Perder terreno. *To lose one's way*, Perderse, no acertar con el camino que se quiere llevar. *That stroke lost him many friends*, Esa acción le hizo perder muchos amigos.

Loser [lūz'-ẹr], *s.* Perdedor, el que pierde, sea del modo que fuere. *You shall be no loser by it*, Nada perderá Vd. en ello.

Losing [lūz'-ing], *s.* Pérdida, diminución.

Loss [les o lōs], *s.* 1. Pérdida, daño, menoscabo; privación, destrucción; mal éxito. 2. Desperdicio, disipación, mal uso de algo. *To be at a loss*, Desatinar, perder el rastro, la huella o el rumbo; no atinar, no acertar, no poder dar en la tecla; verse embarazado para hacer o decir una cosa; no saber qué hacer.

Lost [lest o lōst], *pp.* y *pret.* de *To* Lose. 1. Perdido. 2. Perdido, no obtenido; malgastado, desperdiciado. 3. Desorientado, perplejo, confuso, embarazado; incapaz de hallar el buen camino. 4. Arruinado, perdido; sin remedio; perdido en sentido espiritual. *Like to be lost*, En peligro de perderse. (Fam.) *He lost his heart to her*, Él se enamoró de ella, le entregó su corazón. *This remark was not lost upon Mr. N.*, El Sr. N. no dejó de advertir esta observación.

Lot [let], *s.* 1. Suerte, el estado o modo de vivir que a cada uno le toca. 2. Lote, suerte, fortuna, el dado u otra cosa que se usa para determinar si uno ha de perder o ganar. *To cast lots*, Echar suertes. 3. Cuota, la cantidad que a alguno le toca de una contribución, repartimiento, gasto, etc.; partija, parte, porción. 4. Solar, extensión de terreno medido y destinado a la venta o a edificar en él. 5. (Fam.) Gran cantidad; mucho. *A lot of money*, Gran cantidad de dinero. *Lots of trouble*, (Fam.) Muchas molestias, angustias o penas.

Lot, *va.* Asignar, destinar, repartir, distribuir en cuotas.

Lotah [lō'-tā], *s.* Vasija pequeña de bronce o cobre que usan los naturales de la India y los mahometanos para beber y para sus abluciones.

Lote [lōt], *s.* (Bot.) 1. *V.* Lotus, 2ª acep. 2. (Zool.) *V.* Burbot.

Loth [lōth], *a.* *V.* Loath.

Lothario [lo-thé'-ri-ō o thg'-ri-o], *s.* Libertino, tuno.

Lotion [lō'-shun], *s.* Loción, ablución.

Lotos o **Lotus** [lō'-tus], *s.* 1. (Bot.) Loto, planta acuática. 2. Loto, almez; cualquier árbol cuyo fruto se supone ser el loto de la antigua fábula. 3. Azufaifo.

Lottery [let'-ẹr-i], *s.* Lotería, rifa.

Lotto [let'-ō], *s.* Lotería, juego casero.

Loud [laud], *a.* 1. Ruidoso, alto. *To speak loud*, Hablar alto. 2. Clamoroso, turbulento, estrepitoso, alborotado. 3. (Fam.) Urgente. 4. (Fam.) Ostentoso sin gusto ni esmero; llamativo. *A loud laugh*, Una risa estrepitosa. *A loud voice*, Una voz fuerte, alta.—*adv.* Ruidosamente, en alta voz, con ruido.

Loudly [laud'-li], *adv.* Ruidosamente, alborotadamente; con mucho ruido.

Loudness [laud'-nes], *s.* Ruido, mucho volumen de sonido, retumbo; alboroto, turbulencia.

Loudspeaker [laud-spīk'-ẹr], *s.* Altoparlante.

Lough [leн], *s.* Lago, laguna.

Lounge [launj], *vn.* 1. Haraganear, holgazanear, corretear, callejear; andar acá y acullá sin objeto fijo. 2. Repantigarse; ponerse uno a sus anchas. *V.* Loll.

Lounge, *s.* 1. Haraganería, holgazanería; acción de repantigarse o tenderse. 2. Lugar que se escoge para descansar. 3. Canapé, sofá.

Lounger [launj'-ẹr], *s.* Haragán, holgazán, ocioso.

Lounging room [launj'-ing rūm], *s.* Sala de espera, sala de descanso y esparcimiento.

Lourdan, *s.* *V.* Lurdan.

Louse [laus], *s.* (*pl.* Lice [lais]). Piojo. *Crab-louse*, Ladilla. *Plant-louse*, Pulgón, áfido.

Louse [lauz], *va.* Despiojar.

Lousewort [laus'-wūrt], *s.* (Bot.) Hierba piojera.

Lousily [lauz'-i-li], *adv.* Con piojería, de un modo vil y bajo, mezquinamente.

Lousiness [lauz'-i-nes], *s.* Piojería. (Mex.) Zicatería.

Lousy [lauz'-i], *a.* 1. Piojoso, piojento. 2. Piojoso, miserable, mezquino, apocado, soez, vil, bajo. (Mex.) Zicatero.

Lout [laut], *s.* Patán, rústico, zafio.

Lout, *vn.* 1. Tardar, perder el tiempo, callejear. 2. (Ant.) Doblarse, encorvarse, someterse, hacer reverencia.

Loutish [laut'-ish], *a.* Rudo, rústico, tosco, grosero.

Louver [lū'-vẹr], *s.* Abertura en el cielo de un edificio, lumbrera, tronera, provista de tejadillos inclinados para impedir que entre la lluvia. *Louver-boards*, Tejadillos.

Lovable [luv'-a-bl], *a.* Amable.

Love [luv], *va.* 1. Amar, tener amor. 2. Amar, querer, tener cariño. 3. Gustar, tener inclinación a alguna cosa que agrada.—*vn.* Deleitarse, tener gusto en. *To love one another*, Amarse unos a otros. *To love to see*, Gustar de ver.

Love, *s.* 1. Amor. 2. Amor, el objeto amado. 3. Amor, expresión de cariño. 4. Amor, cariño, inclinación o afecto a alguna persona o cosa; amistad. 5. Galanteo. *To make love*, Galantear, cortejar. 6. Amor, una divinidad entre los gentiles. *To be in love with one*, Estar enamorado de alguno. *To fall in love*, Enamorarse. *Self-love*, Amor propio. (*Not*) *for love or money*, Ni por amor ni por dinero. *Labour of love*, Lo que se hace por amor a otro, sin esperanza de recompensa. *To marry for love*, Casarse por amor. *To be out of love with a thing*, Tener despego, repugnancia por una cosa.

Love-apple [luv'-ap-l], *s.* (Bot.) Tomate (nombre antiguo). *V.* Tomato.

Lovebird [luv'-bẹrd], *s.* Periquito. Debe su nombre en inglés al gran afecto que se demuestran las parejas.

Love-favour [luv'-fê-vẹr], *s.* Favor, expresión de agrado hecha por una dama.

Love-feast [luv'-fīst], *s.* Agapas, comidas de los primeros cristianos en las iglesias.

Love-fit [luv'-fit], *s.* Transporte o arrebato de amor.

Love-knot [luv'-not], *s.* Nudo o lazo de amor.

Love-lass [luv'-las], *f.* Cortejo, amada.

Loveless [luv'-les], *a.* Desamorado, falto de amor, sin cariño, insensible, hurón.

Love-letter [luv'-let-ẹr], *s.* Esquela, billete o carta amorosa.

Love-lies-bleeding [luv'-laiz-blīd'-ing], *s.* (Bot.) Una especie de amaranto.
Loveliness [luv'-li-nes], *s.* Amabilidad, agrado; belleza.
Love-look [luv'-luc], *s.* Rizo largo con lazo de cinta en su extremo que se usaba en el siglo XVII.
Lovelorn [luv'-lōrn], *a.* Abandonado o desamparado por su amante.
Lovely [luv'-li], *a.* 1. Amable, hermoso, agradable, cariñoso. 2. (Fam.) Atractivo. 3. (Fam.) Ameno, deleitoso.—*adv.* Hermosamente, con agrado, con cariño, con alegría.
Love-making [luv-mêk'-ing], *s.* Enamoramiento.
Love-potion [luv'-pō-shun], *s.* Filtro.
Lover [luv'-er], *s.* 1. Amante, galán, cortejo. 2. Amante, el que tiene afición a alguna cosa; amigo.
Love-secret [luv'-si-cret], *s.* Secreto entre amantes.
Love-shaft [luv'-shaft], *s.* Flecha de Cupido.
Love-sick [luv'-sic], *a.* Enamorado, enamoricado, herido de amor.
Lovesome [luv'-sum], *a.* Amable.
Love-song [luv'-sōng], *s.* Canción amorosa.
Love-suit [luv'-siūt], *s.* Cortejo, galanteo, enamoramiento, trato amoroso.
Love-tale [luv'-têl], *s.* Cuentos de amor o de enamorados; requiebros.
Love-thought [luv'-thōt], *s.* Pensamiento amoroso.
Love-token [luv'-tō-cn], *s.* Regalo en señal de amor.
Love-tricks [luv'-trics], *s. pl.* Tretas de amantes o enamorados.
Loving [luv'-ing], *pa.* 1. Amante. 2. Afectuoso, amoroso, cariñoso, aficionado. 3. Benigno, apacible.
Loving-kindness [luv'-ing-kaind'-nes], *s.* Cariño, favor; misericordia.
Lovingly [luv'-ing-li], *adv.* Afectuosamente, amorosamente.
Lovingness [luv'-ing-nes], *s.* Afección, cariño, afecto, terneza, afabilidad.
Low [lō], *a.* 1. Bajo, pequeño. 2. Hondo, poco elevado. *Low-water*, (Mar.) Bajamar, marea menguante o vaciante. 3. Bajo, lo que no mete ruido. 4. Abatido, débil, desanimado, amilanado. 5. Bajo, menospreciable, vil, ruin. 6. Bajo, lo que no es sublime ni elevado. 7. Pobre, falto de bienes. 8. Último, hablando de tiempo. 9. Deshonroso. 10. Reverente, sumiso. *Low latitude*, Latitud cercana a la línea. *In a low tone*, En tono bajo. *The patient is very low*, El enfermo está muy débil. *A low fever*, Una calentura lenta. *You seem in low spirits*, Parece que está Vd. abatido. *A low trick*, Una mala partida. *Low expressions*, Expresiones vulgares, bajas. *Low-lived*, De modales groseros, innoble. *Low-necked*, Escotado; dícese de los vestidos de mujer. *Low pressure*, Baja presión.—*adv.* 1. Abajo, cerca del suelo, en la parte inferior. 2. Barato, a precio bajo. 3. Bajamente; vilmente; sumisamente. 4. En voz baja; también en tono profundo.
Low, *vn.* Mugir, dar mugidos el toro, la vaca o el buey.—*va.* (Des.) Bajar, poner una cosa más baja de lo que estaba.
Low [lau], *s.* (Prov.) Llama, fuego.
Low beams [lō' bīmz], *s. pl.* Luces de cruce.

Lowbell [lō'-bel], *s.* Un modo de coger pájaros por la noche, por medio de una campanilla que los despierta, y una luz que los hace caer en el lazo.
Low-church [lō'-chūrch], *a.* Opuesto al ritualismo; que considera los principios establecidos sobre la organización eclesiástica como de importancia secundaria.
Lower [lō'-er], *va.* 1. Abajar, humillar, abatir. 2. Bajar, poner en lugar inferior lo que estaba en alto. 3. Bajar, minorar, disminuir. *To lower the sails*, (Mar.) Arriar las velas. *To lower away gradually*, (Mar.) Arriar poco a poco.—*vn.* Bajar, minorarse, disminuirse alguna cosa.
Lower [lau'-er], *vn.* 1. Encapotarse o encubrirse el cielo. 2. Mirar con ceño, poner mala cara.
Lower [lō'-er], *a.* Comp. de *Low*, más bajo. *Lower berth*, Cama o litera baja (en un tren, etc.). *Lower case*, 1. Caja baja, la que contiene las letras minúsculas. 2. Letras minúsculas.
Lowering [lau'-er-ing], *a.* Sombrío, nebuloso; amenazador.
Lowermost [lō'-er-mōst] o **Lowest** [lō'-est], *a.* El más bajo, bajísimo, ínfimo.
Lowing [lō'-ing], *s.* Mugido, bramido.
Lowland [lō'-land], *s.* Tierra baja. *The Lowlands*, Las tierras bajas en el sur y el oeste de Escocia.
Lowlander [lō'-land-er], *s.* Habitante de la parte baja de un país, particularmente de las tierras bajas de Escocia.
Lowlily [lō'-li-li], *adv.* Bajamente; vilmente.
Lowliness [lō'-li-nes], *s.* 1. Humildad. 2. Bajeza, vileza, ruindad.
Lowly [lō'-li], *a.* 1. Humilde, sumiso. 2. Vil, bajo, ruin, despreciable. 3. Bajo, humilde, rastrero, hablando del estilo o de los modales.—*adv.* Humildemente, modestamente; vilmente.
Lown [laun], *s.* Pícaro, bobo, el que es tonto o necio.
Lowness [lō'-nes], *s.* 1. Pequeñez. 2. Bajeza de condición o de carácter. 3. Bajeza de ánimo, apocamiento o poquedad de ánimo, abatimiento. 4. Humildad, sencillez en el estilo o pensamientos. 5. Sumisión. *Lowness of spirits*, Abatimiento o caimiento de ánimo; tristeza. 6. Disminución de precio o de valor. 7. Gravedad del sonido o tono; suavidad, debilidad del sonido.
Low-spirited [lō-spir'-it-ed], *a.* Abatido, amilanado, desanimado, acobardado, descorazonado.
Low-temperature physics [lō tem'-per-chūr fiz'-ics], *s.* Física de bajas temperaturas.
Low-thoughted [lō-thōt'-ed], *a.* El que tiene pensamientos bajos.
Lox [lex], *s.* Oxígeno líquido.
Loxodrome [lex'-o-drōm], *s.* Línea loxodrómica.
Loxodromic [lex"-o-drem'-ic], *a.* Loxodrómico, que se refiere a la loxodromía. *Loxodromic line*, Línea loxodrómica, curva que forma un mismo ángulo en su intersección con todos los meridianos y sirve para navegar con rumbo constante.
Loyal [lei'-al], *a.* Leal, constante, fiel.
Loyalist [lei'-al-ist], *s.* Realista: nombre dado en Inglaterra a los partidarios del rey en algunas guerras civiles, y a los partidarios de la metrópoli en las guerras con las colonias.
Loyally [lei'-al-i], *adv.* Lealmente.
Loyalty [lei'-al-ti], *s.* Lealtad.
Lozenge [lez'-enj], *s.* 1. (Geom.) Rombo. 2. Pastilla de boca. 3. (Her.) Losanje, lisonja, la figura de rombo.
Lozenged [lez'-enjd], *a.* Que tiene forma de losanje o rombo.
Lozengy [lez'-en-ji], *a.* Lisonjado, el escudo blasonado en forma de losanjes.
Lu, *s.* *V.* Loo.
Lubbard [lub'-ard], *s.* (Poco us.) *V.* LUBBER.
Lubber [lub'-er], *s.* Tomajón, haragán, persona gorda y perezosa, un bobo; en especial, marinero de agua dulce; joven sin experiencia.
Lubberly [lub'-er-li], *a.* Poltrón, perezoso, haragán, holgazán.—*adv* Toscamente, zafiamente.
Lube [lūb], *s.* (Mech.) Aceite lubricante.
Lubricant [lū'-bri-cant o liū'-bri-cant], *s.* Lubricante, como aceite, grasa, etc., para la maquinaria.
Lubricate [lū'-bri-kêt], *va.* Hacer lúbrica o resbaladiza alguna cosa, antiguamente lubricar o lubrificar; untar con alguna materia crasa.
Lubricating [lū-bri-kêt'-ing], *a.* Lubricante.
Lubrication [lū-bri-kê'-shun], *s.* Lubricación.
Lubricator [lū-bri-kêt'-er], *s.* Lubricador.
Lubricity [lū-bris'-i-ti], *s.* 1. Lubricidad, la lisura de alguna superficie. 2. Inconstancia, incertidumbre, ligereza, instabilidad. 3. Lubricidad, lujuria, lascivia, incontinencia.
Lubrifaction [lū-bri-fac'-shun] o **Lubrification** [lū-bri-fi-kê'-shun], *s.* El acto de hacer más tersa o lúbrica alguna cosa.
Luce [liūs ó lūs], *s.* (Ict.) Lucio.
Lucern [lū-sern'], *s.* (Bot.) Alfalfa, mielga, especie de trébol.
Lucid [lū'-sid], *a.* 1. Luciente, diáfano, transparente, brillante, luminoso. 2. Lúcido, se aplica al intervalo de tiempo en que los locos hablan con alguna razón.
Lucidity [lū-sid'-i-ti], *s.* Perspicuidad, claridad en materias intelectuales.
Lucidness [lū'-sid-nes], *s.* Claridad, transparencia; esplendor, resplandor.
Lucifer [lū'-si-fer], *s.* 1. Lucero, la estrella del alba. 2. Lucifer, el príncipe de las tinieblas. 3. *Lucifer* o *lucifer-match*, Fósforo de fricción.
Luciferian [lū-si-fī'-ri-an], *a.* 1. Luciferino, diabólico, endiablado. 2. Lo perteneciente a la herejía de Lucífero, obispo de Cerdeña.
Luciferous [lū-sif'-er-us], *a.* Luminoso, lucífero, resplandeciente.
Lucific [lū-sif'-ic], *a.* Luciente, lúcido, lucífero.
Luciform [lū'-si-fōrm], *a.* Luciforme.
Luck [luc], *s.* Acaso, casualidad, accidente o suceso feliz o infeliz, fortuna, suerte. *Good luck*, Fortuna, dicha, feliz casualidad. *I wish you good luck*, Le deseo a Vd. toda felicidad. *To bring one luck*, Traerle a uno la fortuna. *To take pot luck*, Comer lo que haya, sin ceremonia.
Luckily [luk'-i-li], *adv.* Por fortuna, por dicha, dichosamente.

Luckiness [luk'-i-nes], *s.* Dicha, buena fortuna o suerte, felicidad.
Luckless [luk -les], *a.* Malaventurado, infeliz, desgraciado, desdichado, desventurado.
Lucky [luk'-i], *a.* Afortunado, feliz, dichoso, venturoso; propicio, favorable. *A lucky man,* Un hombre feliz.
Lucrative [lū'-(o liū'-) cra-tiv], *a.* Lucrativo, ganancioso.
Lucre [lū'-kẹr], *s.* Lucro; ganancia; usura.
Lucubrate [lū'-kiu-brêt], *va.* Lucubrar, trabajar velando y con aplicación en obras de ingenio.
Luculent [lū'-kiu-lent], *a.* Luciente, claro; evidente, cierto, indubitable.
Ludicrous [lū'-(o liū'-) di-crus], *a.* Burlesco, jocoso, alegre, ridículo, cómico, risible.
Ludicrously [lū'-di-crus-li], *adv.* Jocosamente, en chanza.
Ludicrousness [lū'-di-crus-nes], *s.* Ridiculez, extravagancia.
Luff [luf], *s.* 1. Gratil. 2. Acción de orzar, orzada. 3. Cachete de proa. *Luff-tackle,* (Mar.) Aparejo de bolinear.
Luff, *va.* (Mar.) Ceñir el viento, orzar, bolinear. *Keep your luff,* (Mar.) Orza. *To luff round,* (Mar.) Meter todo a lof. *To luff up,* (Mar.) Tomar por avante. *To spring the luff,* (Mar.) Partir el puño.
Lug [lug], *s.* (Fam.) 1. Tirón, estirón, el acto de tirar; la cosa tirada, una cosa lenta y pesada. 2. (Mar.) Vela al tercio.
Lug, *s.* 1. Oreja, lóbulo de la oreja. 2. De aquí, prominencia parecida á veces a la oreja: (1) agarradera, asa; (2) jamba de chimenea; (3) correa de las varas de un carruaje. 3. (Prov. Ingl.) Pértiga, vara larga.
Lug, *va.* 1. Tirar alguna cosa hacia sí. 2. (Mar.) Halar, tirar de los cabos. *To lug away, to lug off,* Arrastrar, arrebatar. *To lug in* o *into,* Arrastrar hacia dentro; (fam.) introducir, v. g. alguna cosa no pedida. *To lug out,* (Vulg.) Desenvainar una espada, sacar la espada.
Luggage [lug'-ej], *s.* 1. Originalmente, cualquier cosa pesada y embarazosa que hay que conducir de una parte a otra. 2. (Ingl.) Equipaje, trastos de un viajero.
Lugger [lug'-ẹr], *s.* (Mar.) Lugre, especie de embarcación pesada con vela cuadrada.
Lug-sail [lūg'-sêl], *s.* (Mar.) Vela al tercio.
Lugubrious [lū-giū'-bri-us], *a.* Lúgubre, triste, funesto, melancólico.
Lugworm [lug'-wūrm], *s.* Arenícola, lombriz de las riberas y costas, que sirve de cebo para pescar. Se llama también *lobworm* y *lugbait.*
Lukewarm [lūc'-wērm], *a.* 1. Tibio, templado. 2. Tibio, indiferente, falto de celo y fervor, frío.
Lukewarmly [lūc'-wērm-li], *adv.* Tibiamente, indiferentemente.
Lukewarmness [lūc'-wērm-nes], *s.* 1. Calor moderado. 2. Indiferencia, tibieza, frialdad.
Lull [lul], *va.* 1. Arrullar, cantar a los niños, para que se duerman. 2. Adormecer, aquietar, sosegar, calmar, mitigar.
Lull, *s.* La calidad o el poder de calmar.
Lullaby [lul'-a-bai], *s.* Arrullo, la cantilena con que el ama adormece al niño.
Luller [lul'-ẹr], *s.* Niñero, el que mima a los niños.
Lum [lum], *s.* (Esco. y prov. Ingl.) Chimenea de cabaña.
Lumbago [lum-bê'-gō], *s.* Lumbago, dolor reumático en los lomos.
Lumbar [lum'-bar], *a.* Lumbar, lo que pertenece a los lomos.
Lumber [lum'-bẹr], *s.* 1. Tablazón, maderaje, madera, tablas, tablones, latas, duelas y otras maderas de construcción. 2. Armatoste, cualquier mueble inútil o engorroso. 3. (Fam.) Trastos o muebles inútiles o de poco uso. 4. (Prov. Ingl.) Daño. *Lumber-room,* Camaranchón, cuarto de trastos, o muebles inútiles. *Lumber-yard,* Depósito de maderas de construcción.
Lumber, *va.* Amontonar trastos inútiles unos sobre otros sin orden ni método.—*vn.* 1. Andar pesadamente. 2. Avanzar con ruido sordo.
Lumbering [lum'-bẹr-ing], *s.* Embarazado por su propio volumen o bulto: pesado y enorme; también, que produce un ruido sordo y prolongado.
Lumberjack [lum'-bẹr-jak], *s.* 1. Hachero. 2. Maderero, comerciante en maderas.
Lumber jacket [lum'-bẹr jak'-et], *s.* Chamarra.
Lumberman [lum'-bẹr-man], *s.* Maderero.
Lumbrical [lum'-bri-cal], *a.* Dícese de algunos músculos pequeños de las manos y pies.
Luminary [lū'-mi-nẹ-ri], *s.* 1. Luminar, lumbrera, cualquiera de los astros que despide luz o claridad; cualquiera cuerpo que da luz o es luminoso. 2. Lumbrera, el hombre insigne que edifica e instruye al mundo con sus virtudes o sus doctrinas.
Luminosity [lū-mi-nos'-i-ti], *s.* 1. Cualidad de lo luminoso. 2. Intensidad de la luz en un color, medida por la fotometría.
Luminous [lū'-mi-nus], *a.* 1. Luminoso, resplandeciente. 2. Iluminado, luciente. 3. Perspicuo, lúcido, de fácil inteligencia.
Luminously [lū'-mi-nus-li], *adv.* De un modo luminoso.
Luminousness [lū'-mi-nus-nes], *s.* Resplandor, brillo, brillantez.
Lump [lump], *s.* 1. Masa informe de alguna cosa, particularmente pedazo, o masa pequeña. 2. El conjunto de cosas diversas que forman una masa. 3. Protuberancia, hinchazón. *To sell* o *buy by the lump,* Vender o comprar por grueso o por junto; vender o comprar alguna cosa á ojo, sin medir o pesar. *Lump sugar,* Azúcar de terrón o en terrones. *A lump of sugar,* Un terrón de azúcar.
Lump, *va.* 1. Amontonar sin orden ni método. 2. Tomar alguna cosa por junto o por mayor.—*vn.* 1. Trabajar como estivador. 2. Tomar una forma desigual, con protuberancias.
Lump-fish [lump -fish], *s.* (Ict.) Lumpo jibado.
Lumping [lump'-ing], *a.* (Vulg.) Grande, pesado, largo.
Lumpish [lump'-ish], *a.* Pesado, tardo, lento, torpe, lerdo, grosero; grave, macizo; tosco.
Lumpishly [lump'-ish-li], *adv.* Lerdamente, estúpidamente, pesadamente, groseramente.
Lumpishness [lump'-ish-nes], *s.* Pesadez, tardanza; majadería, tontería.
Lumpy [lump'-i], *a.* Lleno de terrones o de masas endurecidas.
Lunacy [lū'-na-si], *s.* Locura intermitente, frenesí; trastorno de las facultades intelectuales.
Lunar [lū'-nar], *a.* 1. Lunar, perteneciente a la luna, o medido por las revoluciones de la luna. 2. Luniforme. *V.* LUNATE. 3. Causado por la luna o atribuído a ella; lunático. 4. En alquimia y medicina, relativo a la plata. *Lunar caustic,* Lunar cáustico, nitrato de plata. *Lunar year,* Año lunar, doce meses lunares, o 354⅓ días.
Lunar landing [lū'-nar land'-ing], *s.* Alunizaje.
Lunary [lū'-na-ri], *a.* Lunar, que se refiere a la luna.—*s.* (Bot.) Hierba de la plata, lunaria anual.
Lunate [lū'-nêt], *a.* Lunar, luniforme, en forma de media luna.
Lunatic [lū'-na-tic], *a.* Lunático, frenético, alunado.—*s.* Un lunático, un loco.
Lunation [lu-nê'-shun], *s.* Lunación, intervalo entre dos lunas nuevas, es decir 29½ días.
Lunch [lunch], **Luncheon** [lun'-chun], *s.* 1. Puñado de comida, la cantidad de ella que puede caber en la mano. 2. El alimento tomado entre el almuerzo y la comida; refección, merienda. *To take a luncheon,* Hacer o tomar las once, tomar un bocado.
Lunch, *va.* Tomar las once, merendar; tomar un bocado.
Lune [lūn], *s.* 1. Lúnula, figura limitada por dos arcos de círculo. 2. La luna.
Lunette [lu-net'], *s.* Una cosa en forma de media luna, como la luneta de una fortificación, un lente cóncavo-convexo, etc.
Lung [lung], *s.* Pulmón, cada uno de los órganos situados en el pecho que son los principales agentes de la respiración; llámanse también bofes o livianos, principalmente cuando se habla de los animales. *To sing at the top of one's lungs,* (Fam.) Cantar a gaznate tendido, a todo gritar.
Lunge [lunj], *s.* 1. Estocada. 2. (Fam.) Movimiento brusco hacia adelante.
Lunge, *vn.* 1. Dar un bote, un empuje. 2. Arrojarse, echarse hacia adelante.
Lung-grown [lung'-grōn], *a.* Que tiene los pulmones pegados al pecho.
Lungwort [lung'-wūrt], *s.* (Bot.) Pulmonaria oficinal.
Lunisolar [lū-ni-sō'-lar], *a.* Lunisolar, compuesto de la revolución del sol y de la luna.
Lunt [lunt], *s.* 1. (Esco.) Bocanada de humo. 2. (Des.) Mecha de cañón.
Lunulate [lū'-niu-lêt], *a.* Lunado, formado como una media luna.
Lunule [lū'-niūl], *s.* 1. Figura o construcción en forma de luna creciente. 2. (Geom.) Lúnula. *V.* LUNE.
Lupine [lū'-pin], *s.* (Bot.) Altramuz, lupino.—*a.* 1. Lupino, de lobo; como un lobo, voraz. 2. (Zool.) Perteneciente a la familia que comprende los perros y los lobos.
Lupuline [lū'-piu-lin], *s.* Lupulino, polvo resinoso y amarillo que se halla en los frutos del lúpulo, y se emplea en medicina.
Lupus [lū'-pus], *s.* 1. (Astr.) El Lobo, una constelación austral. 2.

(Med.) Lupia, lobanillo, excrecencia de carácter tuberculoso, que se presenta en la piel y comúnmente cerca de la nariz.

Lurch [lūrch], *s.* 1. Abandono. *To leave one in the lurch,* Abandonar a uno; dejarle en el atolladero, o en las astas del toro. 2. Partida doble en algunos juegos. 3. Vaivén o balance brusco (como de un buque o de un vagón de ferrocarril).

Lurch, *va.* 1. (Ant.) Privar a uno de lo que esperaba, dar chasco, engañar. 2. Ganar una partida doble.

Lurch, *vn.* Torcerse, dar un vaivén o balance repentino hacia un lado, como un buque en mar alborotado; balancearse.

Lurcher [lūrch'-ẹr], *s.* 1. El que está en acecho o espía la ocasión favorable para cometer una mala acción. 2. Perro de caza. 3. (Des.) Glotón.

Lurching [lūrch'-ing], *s.* Celada.

Lurdan [lūr'-dan], *a.* (Ant.) Estúpido, incapaz.—*s.* (Des.) Patán.

Lure [liūr], *s.* 1. Señuelo, añagaza, armadijo para engañar y cazar pájaros. 2. Añagaza, cebo, engaño, para atraer a uno y engañarle.

Lure, *vn.* Llamar a los halcones con señuelo.—*va.* Atraer, persuadir, inducir.

Lurid [liū'-rid], *a.* Lóbrego, triste; pálido, cárdeno.

Lurk [lūrk], *vn.* 1. Espiar, acechar, ponerse en emboscada para hacer algo malo. 2. Ocultarse a las miradas del público.

Lurker [lūrk'-ẹr], *s.* Acechador, espía, el que está en acecho para hacer daño.

Lurking-place [lūrk'-ing-plês], *s.* Escondite, escondrijo, guarida, rincón; emboscada.

Lurry [lur'-i], *s.* 1. (Min.) Carretón especial que se usa en las minas. 2. (Ant.) Sonido confuso, inarticulado.

Luscious [lush'-us], *a.* 1. Dulzaino, empalagoso. 2. Azucarado, almibarado, meloso. 3. Grato, agradable, delicioso.

Lusciously [lush'-us-li], *adv.* Dulcemente, melosamente.

Lusciousness [lush'-us-nes], *s.* Dulzura que empalaga, melosidad.

Lush [lush], *a.* 1. Suculento, jugoso; fresco y lozano. 2. Fácil de arar, poco duro, pulverizado, como el terreno.

Lust [lust], *s.* 1. Deseo, inclinación y voluntad, vehementes, vivos, desordenados. *The lust of conquest,* Deseo ciego de conquistas. 2. Lujuria, sensualidad, incontinencia, concupiscencia, lascivia, impudicicia, deshonestidad.

Lust, *vn.* 1. Lujuriar, cometer el pecado de lujuria. 2. Codiciar, desear con ansia alguna cosa. 3. Desordenarse, desarreglarse.

Luster [lus'-tẹr], *s.* 1. Lustre, brillantez. 2. Araña de cristal. 3. Lucimiento, esplendor. 4. Lustro, el espacio de cinco años.

Lusterless [lus'-tẹr-les], *a.* Sin brillo.

Lustful [lust'-ful], *a.* 1. Lujurioso, sensual, voluptuoso. 2. Deshonesto, impúdico, lascivo, incontinente.

Lustfully [lust'-ful-li], *adv.* Lujuriosamente, lascivamente, sensualmente.

Lustfulness [lust'-ful-nes], *s.* Lascivia, incontinencia, deshonestidad, impudicicia, lubricidad.

Lustily [lust'-i-li], *adv.* Fuertemente, vigorosamente, con fuerza.

Lustiness [lust'-i-nes], *s.* Lozanía, vigor, robustez.

Lustral [lus'-tral], *a.* Lustral, lo que se usa en las purificaciones.

Lustrate [lus'-trêt], *va.* (Des.) Lustrar, purificar.

Lustration [lus-trê'-shun], *s.* Lustración.

Lustre [lus'-tẹr], *s.* *V.* LUSTER.

Lustring [lus'-tring], *s.* Lustrina, tela de mucho lustre.

Lustrous [lus'-trus], *a.* Lustroso, brillante.

Lustrum [lus'-trum], *s.* 1. Lustro, período de cinco años. 2. Lustración, ceremonia de purificación de todo el pueblo romano que se efectuaba cada cinco años.

Lustwort [lust'-wūrt], *s.* (Bot.) Rocío del sol. *V.* SUN-DEW.

Lusty [lust'-i], *a.* 1. Lozano, fornido, fuerte, robusto, vigoroso. 2. (Des.) Hermoso; deleitoso.

Lutanist [liū'-ta-nist], *s.* El que toca el laúd.

Lutation [liū-tê'-shun], *s.* Lutación, el acto de tapar o embarrar las vasijas con el luten.

Lute [liūt], *s.* 1. Laúd, instrumento músico de cuerdas. 2. Luten, mezcla de claras de huevo, argamasa u otra substancia, con que se tapan las aberturas y junturas de los vasos químicos. 3. En los ladrillales, raspador con filo cortante para embarrar con luten el secadero o lugar donde se secan los ladrillos.

Lute, *va.* Tapar, enlodar o embarrar con luten.

Luter [liūt'-ẹr], **Lutist** [liūt'-ist], *s.* El que tañe el laúd.

Lutestring [liūt'-string], *s.* 1. Cuerda de laúd. 2. (Ento.) Mariposa nocturna, cuyas alas tienen líneas semejantes a las cuerdas de un laúd. 3. Lustrina, especie de tela de seda (corrupción de *lustring*).

Lutheran [liū'-thẹr-an], *s.* y *a.* Luterano, que sigue la doctrina de Lutero.

Lutheranism [liū'-thẹr-an-izm], *s.* Luteranismo.

Luthern [liū'-thẹrn], *s.* (Arq.) Especie de lumbrera o ventanilla de guardilla o desván.

Lutose [liū'-tōs], *a.* Cubierto con arcilla, lodoso, cenagoso.

Lux [lux], *va.* (Des.) *V.* LUXATE.

Luxate [lux'-êt], *va.* Dislocar, desencajar, desconcertar, descoyuntar.

Luxation [lux-ê'-shun], *s.* Luxación, dislocación, descoyuntamiento.

Luxuriance [lug-zhū'-ri-ans o lux-yū'-ri-ans], **Luxuriancy** [lug-zhū'-ri-an-si], *s.* Exuberancia, lozanía, suma abundancia, superabundancia, frondosidad, vicio.

Luxuriant [lug-zhū'-ri-ant o lux-yū'-ri-ant], *a.* Exuberante, lozano, superabundante, sobreabundante; muy fértil; frondoso, vicioso.

Luxuriantly [lug-zhū'-ri-ant-li], *adv.* Abundantemente, con mucha fecundidad, con profusión.

Luxuriate [lug-zhū'-ri-êt o lux-yū'-ri-êt], *vn.* 1. Lozanear, ostentar lozanía o brillar con ella. 2. Crecer o brotar con exuberancia. 3. Vivir con lujo. 4. (Fig.) Gloriarse, jactarse, complacerse.

Luxurious [lux-yū' o lug-zhū'-ri-us], *a.* 1. Un glotón o regalón. 2. Exuberante, sobreabundante; frondoso; faustoso. 3. (Des.) Lujurioso, impúdico, libidinoso.

Luxuriously [lug-zhū'-ri-us-li], *adv.* Con lozanía o exuberancia; frondosamente; lozanamente; con lujo o fausto.

Luxuriousness [lug-zhū'-ri-us-nes], *s.* El estado que constituye a una persona lujuriosa o voluptuosa; nimiedad excesiva en la elección de manjares.

Luxury [luc'-shu-ri], *s.* 1. Lujo, exceso y demasía en la pompa o regalo; fausto, molicie; gastos superfluos. 2. Manjar delicioso; una cosa cualquiera que procura placer y gusto, pero es innecesaria en realidad. 3. (Des.) Exuberancia, suma abundancia. 4. (Des.) Lujuria, lascivia, sensualidad, incontinencia, voluptuosidad.

-ly [li]. Sufijo que se emplea para formar (1) adjetivos que expresan semejanza; parecido a; como *manly,* de *man,* hombre; viril, varonil (como un varón). (2) Adverbios de modo, y en tales casos equivale a -mente. *Clear,* claro; *clearly,* claramente.

Lycanthropy [lai-can'-thro-pi], *s.* Licantropía, un género de melancolía o manía en el cual el enfermo se cree transformado en lobo.

Lyceum [lai-sī'-um], *s.* 1. Liceo, paraje situado cerca de Atenas en el que Aristóteles enseñaba la filosofía. 2. (E. U.) Liceo, asociación para la instrucción por medio de lecturas, discusiones o cursos públicos; y su edificio. 3. Escuela de segunda enseñanza.

Lychnis [lic'-nis], *s.* (Bot.) Licnide, nombre genérico de plantas cariofíleas.

Lycopodium [lai-co-pō'-di-um], *s.* Licopodio, polvo de una especie de musgo que es muy inflamable.

Lydian [lid'-i-an], *a.* Lidio, que se refiere a la antigua Lidia, famosa por su riqueza y su cultivo de la música.

Lye [lai], *s.* 1. Lejía. 2. (Ingl.) Ramal, empalme lateral de un ferrocarril.

Lying [lai'-ing], *pa.* Echado. *A ship lying along,* (Mar.) Bajel tendido sobre la banda. *Lying to,* (Mar.) Al pairo o en facha. *Lying-in hospital,* Hospital de parturientes, casa refugio. (Amer.) Casa de maternidad. *Lying-in woman,* Mujer parida.—*s.* La práctica o costumbre de mentir; mentira, embuste.

Lyingly [lai'-ing-li], *adv.* Mentirosamente, falsamente.

Lymph [limf], *s.* 1. Linfa, humor acuoso que se halla en varias partes del cuerpo. 2. Exudación coagulable de los vasos en las inflamaciones. 3. Virus, o cultura del virus de una enfermedad, que se emplea en la vacunación o inoculación. *Lymph-duct,* Vaso linfático.

Lymphatic [lim-fat'-ic], *s.* Linfático: dícese de los vasos que conducen la linfa.—*a.* 1. Linfático. 2. Flemático.

Lymphoid [lim'-feid], *a.* Parecido a la linfa o a una glándula linfática.

Lynch [linch], *va.* Linchar, castigar con la llamada ley de Lynch; por lo común, ahorcar.

Lynch-law [linch'-lō], *s.* Ley de Lynch, suplicio impuesto sin procedimiento ni forma legal, por personas que no tienen derecho para hacerse justicia por su mano. Voz debida al nombre de un hacendado de la Virginia llamado *Lynch,* que durante la guerra de la independencia norteamericana solía hacerse justicia por su mano.

Lynx [liŋcs], *s.* (Zool.) Lince, mamífero carnicero.
Lyrate [lai'-rêt], *a.* Formado como la lira antigua.
Lyre [lair], *s.* Lira, instrumento músico de cuerdas que se usaba en lo antiguo; arpa.
Lyre-bird [lair'-bẹrd], *s.* (Orn.) Menura o menura-lira, ave de Australia cuya cola tiene la forma de una lira antigua.
Lyric, Lyrical [lir'-ic, al], *a.* 1. Lírico, lo que pertenece a la lira, o se compone para cantar al son de la lira. 2. Perteneciente o relativo a la poesía lírica.
Lyric, *s.* 1. Poema lírico. 2. (Poco us.) Poeta lírico.
Lyrist [lair'-ist], *s.* 1. El que toca la lira. 2. Poeta lírico.
Lysin [lai'-sin], *s.* Lisina.
Lysis [lai'-sis], *s.* (Med.) Lisis, cesación gradual de una enfermedad, en contraposición a *crisis*.
Lysozyme [lai'-so-zaim], *s.* Lisozima.
Lyssa [lis'-a], *s.* Rabia canina.

M

M [em] nunca es muda en inglés, y se pronuncia como en español, aunque con más fuerza. No va nunca seguida de otra consonante al principio de las voces o sílabas en las palabras puramente inglesas; y cuando está seguida de *n* al fin de algunas voces, hace muda a esta última letra. *M* como numeral romano equivale a mil. Como abreviatura, M. A. es Maestro en Artes; M. B., Bachiller en Medicina; M. C., Miembro del Congreso o de la Cámara de los Representantes; M. P., Miembro del Parlamento; MS., Manuscrito, y MSS. Manuscritos.
Ma'am [mām o mam], *s.* Contracción de *madam*, señora.
Mac. Prefijo, que en los nombres de origen escocés o irlandés significa "hijo de." (Se abrevia a menudo tomando las formas de Mc o M'.)
Macabre [ma-cā'-br], *a.* Macabro.
Macadam [mac-ad'-am], *s.* Piedras trituradas para macadamizar; calzada empedrada con ellas.
Macadamize [mac-ad'-am-aiz], *va.* Macadamizar, empedrar con trozos de piedra sobre una base dura o blanda, según los casos; toma su nombre de Juan L. MacAdam, ingeniero escocés.
Macaroni [mac-a-rō'-ni], *s.* 1. Macarrones, pasta alimenticia, en figura de canuto largo. 2. Una especie de muñeca. 3. Pisaverde; gracioso.
Macaronic [mac-a-ren'-ic], *s.* Montón confuso o mezcla de muchas cosas. —*a.* 1. Macarrónico, consistente en una mezcla confusa de palabras de diferentes idiomas; mezclado. 2. Macarrónico, referente a los macarrones.
Macaroon [mac-a-rūn'], *s.* Almendrado, especie de pasta hecha de harina, almendras, huevos y azúcar; mostachón de almendras.
Macassar [ma-cas'-ar], *s.* Macasar, aceite perfumado para el cabello.
Macaw [ma-cē'], *s.* (Orn.) Guacamayo, papagayo de cola larga. Ara macao y Ara ararauna.
Mace [mês], *s.* 1. Maza, la insignia que llevan los maceros delante de los magistrados y otras personas de autoridad en los actos públicos. 2. Maza, clava o porra de metal. 3. Macis o macías, la corteza sutil y olorosa que cubre la nuez moscada.
Mace-bearer [mês'-bār-ẹr], *s.* Macero.
Macerate [mas'-ẹr-êt], *va.* 1. Macerar, poner en infusión algún cuerpo y prepararlo para la disolución o destilación. 2. (Ant.) Enflaquecer, debilitar, mortificar el cuerpo.
Maceration [mas-ẹr-ê'-shun], *s.* Maceración, el acto de macerar o infundir una cosa sólida en algún líquido para ablandarla.
Machete [mạ-she'-ti], *s.* Machete.
Machiavellian, Machiavelian [mak-i-a-vel'-i-an o vil'-yan], *s.* Maquiavelista, partidario del maquiavelismo. —*a.* Maquiavélico.
Machiavelism [mak'-i-a-vel-izm], *s.* Maquiavelismo, sistema político de Maquiavelo; tiranía astuta; engaño, fraude, astucia; conducta zorrastrona.
Machicolation [mach"-i-co-lê'-shun], *s.* (Arq.) Matacán o ladronera, abertura entre un muro y un parapeto.
Machinate [mak'-i-nêt], *vn.* Maquinar, tramar, fraguar, trazar, discurrir o idear medios para lograr algún fin, particularmente con avieso designio.
Machination [mak-i-nê'-shun], *s.* Maquinación, conjuración, trama, asechanza oculta.
Machinator [mak'-i-nê-tọr], *s.* Maquinador, maquinante.
Machine [ma-shīn'], *s.* 1. Máquina con que se da juego o movimiento a alguna cosa. 2. El que obra sin intención o de un modo meramente mecánico. 3. La organización de los poderes de un cuerpo complexo. 4. La parte que los entes sobrenaturales tienen en la acción de un poema. 5. (Gran Bret.) Vehículo, coche, calesa. 6. (E. U.) Organización dentro de un partido político a fin de apropiarse y dirigir el repartimiento de cargos y destinos. *Machine-shop*, Taller de maquinaria. *Machine-tool*, Herramienta de máquina; máquina para operar con herramientas cortantes, o para modelar.
Machine gun [ma-shīn' gun], *s.* Ametralladora.
Machine-gun [ma-shīn'-gun], *va.* Ametrallar.
Machinery [ma-shīn'-ẹr-i], *s.* 1. Maquinaria, mecánica; las piezas de una máquina, o el conjunto de máquinas y sus útiles y herramientas colectivamente. 2. (Ant.) El conjunto de entes sobrenaturales introducidos en un poema.
Machinist [ma-shīn'-ist], *s.* Maquinista.
Mach-number [mac num'-bẹr], *s.* Número Mach; relación de la velocidad de un cuerpo con la del sonido.
Mackerel [mak'-ẹr-el], *s.* (Zool.) Escombro. *Horse-mackerel*, (Zool.) Caballa, haleche. *Mackerel sky*, Cielo aborregado
Mackinaw [mak'-i-nē], *s.* Chamarra.
Mackintosh [mak'-in-tesh], *s.* 1. Traje, levitón o sobretodo impermeables. 2. Tela delgada forrada interiormente de caucho. (Del nombre de su inventor.)
Mackle [mac'-l], *va.* (Impr.) Repintar, macular.—*s.* Maculatura.
Macrobian [mac-rō'-bi-an], *s.* Macrobiano, persona de muy larga vida, particularmente de más de cien años.
Macrocosm [mac'-ro-cezm], *s.* Macrocosmo, el mundo entero.
Macroeconomics [mac"-ro-ec-o-nem'-ics], *s.* Macroeconomía.
Macromolecule [mac"-ro-mel'-ẹ-kiūl], *s.* Macromolécula.
Macula [mac' yu-la], **Macule** [mac'-yul], *s.* Mácula, mancha, tacha, lunar. *Solar macula*, Mácula del sol.
Maculate [mac'-yu-lêt], *va.* Macular, manchar.
Maculate, *a.* Manchado, maculado.
Mad [mad], *a.* 1. Loco, demente, perturbado. 2. Furioso, rabioso, insensato, desesperado, furibundo. *Mad-apple*, Berengena. *Madbrain*, *mad-brained*, Loco, insensato, furioso; aturdido. *Madcap*, Locarias, orate, el sujeto de poco juicio.
Mad, *va.* (Poco us.) Enloquecer, enfurecer.—*vn.* Enloquecerse, enfurecerse, desenfrenarse; estar loco.
Madam [mad'-am], *s.* Madama, señora: tratamiento de cortesía.
Madden [mad'-n], *va.* Enloquecer, hacer que uno se vuelva loco.—*vn.* Enloquecerse, volverse loco.
Madder [mad'-ẹr], *s.* (Bot.) Rubia, una planta cuya raíz sirve para teñir de rojo. *Madder-roots*, Rubia en raíz o graneada.
Made [mêd], *pret.* y *pp.* del verbo *To* MAKE. 1. Fabricado; producido, particularmente con arte. 2. En posición desahogada, próspero. *Made-up*, (1) Artificial, ficticio. (2) Completado, acabado.
Madeira Wine [ma-dê'-ra wain], *s.* Vino de Madera.
Made-to-order [mêd-tū-ēr'-dẹr], *a.* Hecho a la orden, hecho a la medida.
Mad-headed [mad'-hed-ed], *a.* Fogoso, antojadizo.
Madhouse [mad'-haus], *s.* Manicomio, casa de locos o de orates, el hospital donde se curan o encierran los locos.
Madly [mad'-li], *adv.* Furiosamente locamente.
Madman [mad'-man], *s.* Un loco, un maniático, un orate.
Madness [mad'-nes], *s.* 1. Locura, demencia, manía, extravagancia. 2. Furor, arrebato de ira o cólera, enajenación mental; rabia.
Madonna [ma-den'-a], *s.* 1. Señora, madama; antigua voz italiana de tratamiento. 2. Dícese de las imágenes de la Virgen.
Madras [ma-drạs'], *s.* 1. Madrás, tela fina de algodón que se usa generalmente para camisas de hombre. 2. Pañoleta de seda o de algodón de colores vivos.
Madrepore [mad'-re-pōr], *s.* (Zool.) Madrépora, pólipo de los mares intertropicales, y su polipero, que llega a formar escollos e islas.
Madrigal [mad'-ri-gal], *s.* 1. Madrigal, una composición poética. 2. Canción pastoral. 3. Canto amoroso.
Madwort [mad'-wūrt], *s.* (Bot.) Marrubio, aliso.
Maelstrom [mêl'-strẹm], *s.* 1. Malstrom, peligroso remolino que forman las aguas junto a la costa de Noruega. 2. Cualquier fuerza o influencia poderosa que arruina y destruye.
Magazine [mag'-a-zin], *s.* 1. Revista, publicación ilustrada. 2. Almacén para guardar géneros o cosas vendibles. 3. Cámara para cartuchos en un rifle de repetición. 4. Pañol de pólvora o Santabárbara.

Magdalen [mag'-da-len], *s.* Ramera arrepentida.—*n. pr.* Magdalena.

Mage [mêj], *s.* Mago. *V.* MAGICIAN.

Magenta [ma-jen'-ta], *s.* Nombre de una materia de tinte obtenida de la anilina, y de un rico color purpúreo rojizo.

Maggot [mag'-et], *s.* 1. Gusano, larva de una mosca. 2. (Vulg.) Capricho, fantasía, antojo.

Maggoty [mag'-et-i], *a.* 1. Gusaniento, lleno de gusanos. 2. (Vulg.) Caprichoso, fantástico.

Magi [mê'-jai], *s. pl.* Magos o sabios del oriente.

Magian [mê'-ji-an], *a.* Lo perteneciente a los magos o sabios del oriente.

Magic [maj'-ic], *s.* Magia negra. *Natural magic,* Magia blanca.—*a.* Mágico, encantador. *Magic lantern,* Linterna mágica u óptica.

Magical [maj'-ic-al], *a.* Mágico; encantado.

Magically [maj'-ic-al-i], *adv.* Mágicamente, por magia, por arte de encantamiento.

Magician [ma-jish'-an], *s.* Mago, mágico, nigromante.

Magilp, Megilp [ma-gilp'], *s.* Secante, aceite secante, compuesto de que se sirven los artistas para secar pronto los colores.

Magisterial [maj-is-tî'-ri-al], *a.* Magistral, magisterial; imperioso, arrogante, absoluto.

Magisterially [maj-is-tî'-ri-al-i], *adv.* Magistralmente.

Magistery [maj'-is-ter-i], *s.* 1. Decreto magisterial. 2. Panacea. 3. (Quím.) Magisterio, precipitado de composición no conocida.

Magistracy [maj'-is-tra-si], *s.* Magistratura.

Magistral [maj'-is-tral], *a.* Magistral, magisterial.

Magistrate [maj'-is-trêt], *s.* 1. Magistrado. 2. Juez de paz.

Magistratic [maj-is-trat'-ic], *a.* Lo que pertenece a la autoridad de magistrado.

Magma [mag'-ma], *s.* Cualquier masa blanda, como la de harina.

Magna Charta [mag'-na cär'-ta], *s.* La Carta Magna que contiene los privilegios de la nación inglesa.

Magnanimity [mag-na-nim'-i-ti], *s.* Magnanimidad.

Magnanimous [mag-nan'-i-mus], *a.* Magnánimo.

Magnanimously [mag-nan'-i-mus-li], *adv.* Magnánimamente.

Magnate [mag'-nêt], *s.* 1. Magnate, noble. 2. Grande del reino de Hungría.

Magnesia [mag-nî'-shi-a], *s.* Magnesia, tierra muy fina y blanca, usada en medicina: óxido de magnesio.

Magnesian [mag-nî'-shian], *a.* Magnésico, que contiene magnesia.

Magnesium [mag-nî'-shium], *s.* Magnesio, metal blanco y maleable, que se usa a menudo en la fotografía para procurar una luz brillante.

Magnet [mag'-net], *s.* 1. Imán, piedra imán; particularmente un imán artificial. 2. Persona o cosa muy atractiva.

Magnetic, Magnetical [mag-net'-ic, al], *a.* 1. Magnético. 2. Dotado de magnetismo personal; que ejerce una fuerza moral atractiva.

Magnetically [mag-net'-ic-a-li], *adv.* De un modo atractivo.

Magneticalness [mag-net'-ic-al-nes], †**Magneticness** [mag-net'-ic-nes], *s.* La calidad de lo que es magnético.

Magnetism [mag'-net-izm], *s.* Magnetismo.

Magnetizable [mag-net-aiz'-a-bl], *a.* Magnetizable.

Magnetize [mag'-net-aiz], *va.* 1. Magnetizar, imantar o imanar. 2. Atraer por medio de la simpatía e influencia personales. 3. Someter al hipnotismo.—*vn.* Imanarse, adquirir propiedades magnéticas.

Magneto-electric [mag-net'-o-ę-lec'-tric], *a.* Magneto-eléctrico.

Magneto-electricity [mag-net'-o-ę-lec-tris'-i-ti], *s.* Electromagnetismo.

Magnetohydrodynamics [mag-net'-o-hai-dro-dai-nam'-ics], *s.* Magnetohidrodinámica.

Magnetometer [mag-net-om'-ę-tęr], *s.* Magnetómetro, instrumento para medir la fuerza magnética por medio de una balanza de torsión.

Magnetron [mag'-nę-tron], *s.* Magnetrón.

Magnifiable [mag'-ni-fai''-a-bl], *a.* Capaz de ser engrandecido.

Magnification [mag-ni-fi-kê'-shun], *s.* 1. Amplificación, poder de aumento de una lente. 2. Alabanza, glorificación; exageración.

Magnificence [mag-nif'-i-sens], *s.* Magnificencia, grandeza, esplendor.

Magnificent [mag-nif'-i-sent], *a.* Magnífico, espléndido, lucido.

Magnificently [mag-nif'-i-sent-li], *adv.* Magníficamente.

Magnifier [mag'-ni-fai-ęr], *s.* 1. Microscopio, vidrio de aumento, lente. 2. El que magnifica, ensalza o alaba con exageración; panegirista.

Magnify [mag'-ni-fai], *va.* 1. Aumentar la magnitud de los objetos a la vista. 2. Magnificar, exaltar, exagerar. *Magnifying glass,* Lupa, vidrio de aumento, lente.

Magniloquence [mag-nil'-o-cwens], *s.* Altilocuencia; fanfarronada.

Magnitude [mag'-ni-tiūd], *s.* 1. Magnitud, grandeza, tamaño, grandor, importancia. 2. Extensión en altura, anchura y espesor o profundidad.

Magnolia [mag-nō'-li-a], *s.* (Bot.) Magnolia, árbol originario de América, con hojas perennes y flores hermosísimas.

Magpie [mag'-pai], *s.* Marica, urraca, picaza; pega.

Maguey [ma-gey'], *s.* (Bot.) Maguey.

Magyar [maj-ār'], *s.* Magiar o Magyar; dícese de la raza predominante en Hungría y Transilvania y de su lengua.

Mahaut [ma-haut' o ma-hūt'], *s.* Guarda y guía de un elefante.

Mahlstick, Maulstick [māl'-stic, mēl'-stic], *s.* Tiento, bastoncillo en que el pintor apoya la mano derecha.

Mahogany [ma-heg'-a-ni], *s.* Caoba o caobana, madera de un árbol grande de América, muy estimada en mueblería.

Mahometan, Mahomedan, etc. *V.* MOHAMMEDAN, etc.

Maid [mêd], **Maiden** [mêd'-n], *sf.* 1. Doncella, soltera; virgen. *Old maid,* Solterona, doncella jamona. 2. Hembra. 3. Criada. *Maid of honour in waiting,* Dama de honor de una reina o princesa. 4. (Ict.) Especie de lija.

Maiden, *a.* 1. Virgíneo, virginal, lo que pertenece a las vírgenes o doncellas; soltero, soltera. *A maiden aunt.* Una tía soltera. 2. Nuevo, inicial, intacto, que no se ha usado o no se ha tocado. *Maiden speech,* El primer discurso público hecho por un nuevo representante o miembro de una asamblea.

Maidenhair [mêd'-n-hār], *s.* (Bot.) Culantrillo.

Maidenhead [mêd'-n-hed], **Maidenhood** [mêd'-n-hud], *sf.* Doncellez, virginidad; el estado de alguna cosa intacta.

Maidenliness [mêd'-n-li-nes], *s.* Modestia, dulzura y conducta como la que debe tener una doncella.

Maidenly [mêd'-n-li], **Maiden-like** [mêd'-n-laic], *a.* Virginal, modesto, púdico, reservado.—*adv.* Modestamente.

Maidhood [mêd'-hud], *s.* Virginidad.

Maid-marian [mêd'-mar'-i-an], *s.* Primero fué una especie de baile rústico, y después, un bufón: de aquí, maritornes, marimacho, o mujer impúdica.

Maid-servant [mêd'-sęr-vant], *sf.* Doncella de servicio, criada.

Mail [mêl], *s.* 1. Correo, servicio público para la conducción de la correspondencia; y también, correo, valija, el conjunto de cartas, etc., que se reciben o se despachan. 2. Maleta, valija a propósito para guardar o llevar ropas, etc. (<Fr. malle.) 3. Cota de malla, jacerina. (<Fr. maille.) 4. †Renta; mancha. *V.* BLACKMAIL. *Mail-bag,* Mala, valija del correo. *Mail-catcher,* Garra para asir los sacos del correo y depositarlos en un carro o vagón en movimiento. *Mail-sack,* Saco de lona para periódicos y paquetes.

Mail, *va.* 1. Armar con cota de malla, antiguamente mallar. 2. (E. U.) Depositar en un buzón para cartas; echar al correo. 3. (Ant.) Atar las alas.

Mailable [mêl'-a-bl], *a.* Que puede ser enviado por el correo.

Mail box [mêl' bex], *s.* Buzón para el correo.

Mailed [mêld], *a.* Cubierto con cota de malla.—*pp.* del verbo *To* MAIL.

Mailman [mêl'-man], *s.* Cartero.

Mail order [mêl ōr'-dęr], *s.* Pedido postal. *Mail-order house,* Casa que vende mediante pedidos postales.

Mailplane [mêl'-plên], *s.* Avión postal.

Maim [mêm], *va.* Mutilar, cortar, cercenar alguna parte del cuerpo; estropear, lisiar.

Maim, *s.* Mutilación, manquera, daño, defecto.

Maimedness [mêm'-ed-nes], *s.* Mutilación, mancamiento, defecto.

Main [mên], *a.* 1. Principal. 2. Violento, fuerte. 3. Mayor, lo que tiene la parte principal. 4. Importante, esencial, lo que importa. *Main hatchway,* (Mar.) Escotilla mayor. *Main braces,* (Mar.) Brazos mayores. *Main-top braces,* (Mar.) Brazos de gavia. *Main-top-gallant braces,* (Mar.) Brazos de juanete mayor. *Main yard,* Verga mayor. —*s.* 1. Océano o alta mar; de aquí, continente, porción principal de la tierra. 2. Cañería maestra, conducto principal, como para agua o gas. 3. Fuerza, violencia. 4. Partida o pareja de gallos. 5. (Ant.) Grueso, la mayor parte o la más principal y fuerte de alguna cosa. *With might and main,* Con todas sus fuerzas. *Upon the main,* Al fin.

Mainland [mên'-land], *s.* Continente, tierra firme.

Mainly [mên'-li], *adv.* Principalmente, primeramente; poderosamente.
Mainmast [mên'-mast], *s.* (Mar.) Palo mayor de un bajel.
Main office [mên ef'-is], *s.* Casa matriz, oficina principal.
Mainsail [mên'-sêl], *s.* (Mar.) Vela mayor. *Main-top sail,* Vela de gavia. *Main-top-gallant sail,* Vela de juanete mayor. *Main-top-gallant royal,* Vela de sobrejuanete mayor.
Main-sheet [mên'-shît], *s.* (Mar.) Escota mayor.
Mainspring [mên'-spring], *s.* Muelle real (de reloj, etc.).
Mainstay [mên'-stê], *s.* (Mar.) 1. Estay mayor. 2. Sostén principal.
Maintain [mên-tên'], *va.* 1. Tener, guardar, conservar. 2. Mantener, sostener alguna opinión; vindicar, defender. 3. Mantener, hacer el gasto de alguna cosa. 4. Mantener, proveer a alguno de lo necesario para la vida. *To maintain secrecy,* Observar el secreto.
Maintainable [mên-tên'-a-bl], *a.* Defendible, sostenible.
Maintainer [mên-tên'-ẹr], *s.* Mantenedor; defensor, patrón.
Maintenance [mên'-ten-ans], *s.* Mantenimiento, apoyo, protección; sustento; continuación.
Main-top [mên'-tep], *s.* (Mar.) Cofa mayor o de gavia. *Main-top-mast,* Mastelero mayor. *Main-top gallant,* Mastelero de juanete mayor. *Main-top yard,* Verga de gavia. *Main-top-gallant yard,* Verga de juanete mayor. *Main-top-gallant-royal yard,* Verga de sobrejuanete mayor.
Maize [mêz], *s.* Maíz (y maiza, la planta). Por lo general en los Estados Unidos se llama solamente *corn.* Zea mays.
Majestic, Majestical [ma-jes'-tic, al], *a.* Majestuoso, augusto; pomposo, elevado, sublime, grande.
Majestically [ma-jes'-tic-al-i], *adv.* Majestuosamente.
Majesty [maj'-es-ti], *s.* 1. Majestad, poder, soberanía. 2. Majestad, título que se da a reyes y emperadores.
Majolica, Maiolica [ma-jel'-i-ca, mā-yō'-li-ca], *s.* Mayólica, variedad de loza con esmalte metálico.
Major [mé'-jẹr], *a.* 1. Mayor; más grande en número, en cantidad, en extensión. 2. Mayor, más grande en dignidad o importancia; de primera consideración; principal. 3. (Mús.) Mayor, normal; que contiene la tercera, la sexta y la séptima mayores.—*s.* 1. (Mil.) Sargento mayor de regimiento, comandante, jefe de batallón, oficial de rango inmediatamente superior al de capitán. 2. (For.) El mayor de edad. 3. Mayor, la primera proposición de un silogismo.
Major-General [mé'-jẹr-jen'-ẹr-al], *s.* (Mil.) Mariscal de campo.
Majority [ma-jer'-i-ti], *s.* 1. Mayoría, la ventaja en que una cosa excede a otra. 2. Pluralidad, el mayor número. 3. Mayoría, mayor edad. 4. Sargentía mayor de un regimiento.
Make [mêk], *va.* (*pret.* y *pp.* MADE). 1. Hacer, crear, producir; causar, ocasionar; formar, fabricar; componer, trabajar; hablar, pronunciar, relatar. 2. Hacer, ejecutar, practicar, efectuar. 3. Hacer, disponer, aderezar. 4. Obtener, procurar, adquirir, ganar; granjear, proporcionar. 5. Hacer, dar el ser intelectual o formar algo con la imaginación. 6. Obligar, forzar, compeler. 7. Contribuir, constituir; disponer o inclinar a; alcanzar. 8. Atravesar, pasar por, cruzar. 9. (Mar.) Descubrir, avistar, llegar a, alcanzar. 10. Contar por, mirar como, decidir a otro. 11. Poner en estado o forma conveniente, arreglar. *To make a bed,* Arreglar, hacer una cama. *To make one's toilet,* Hacer su tocador. 12. Poner fin á, completar, acabar. 13. Hacer fortuna. 14. Inferir por raciocinio, concluir; pensar. 15. (Ant.) Intentar, tener intención de; estar a punto de.—*vn.* 1. Hacerse, volverse. 2. Ir, dirigirse o encaminarse a algún paraje determinado; tender. 3. Tener efecto, contribuir, servir; corresponder, concordar, venir bien una cosa con otra. 4. Hacer de o hacer él o la, fingir alguna cosa, aparentar ser una cosa diferente de la realidad. 5. Fluir o levantarse como la marea. *To make after,* Tratar de coger, seguir. *To make again,* Rehacer, hacer de nuevo. *To make against,* Estar en oposición a, ser contrario a; ser nocivo o dañoso a. *To make angry,* Enfadar. sulfurar. *To make as if,* Aparentar, fingir, hacer como. *To make at,* Arremeter. *To make away,* Huirse; gastar; transferir el dominio de una cosa; matar, destruir; derrochar, disipar. *To make away with,* Derrochar; hurtar; matar. *To make believe,* Fingir, pretender. *To make for,* Dirigirse a; aprovecharse, tener utilidad, sacar ventaja o provecho de una cosa. *To make for a place,* Ir hacia una parte, tomar rumbo hacia un lugar determinado. *To make little* (o *nothing*) *of,* Hacer poco o ningún caso de, despreciar; hacer con facilidad; comprender poco, o no comprender nada. *To make much of,* Hacer mucho caso de; acariciar, halagar, mostrar amistad o cariño; regalar, festejar; economizar, sacar de una cosa toda la utilidad posible; estimar, apreciar. *To make no difference* o *no matter,* Ser indiferente, no importar. *That makes no difference,* Eso no importa. *To make merry,* Divertirse; comer opíparamente. *To make of,* Sacar utilidad o ventaja, aprovecharse; considerar, estimar, hacer caso; entender algo en. *I knew not what to make of,* No pude entenderlo. *To make off,* Irse, huirse, tomar las de Villadiego. *To make off with,* Llevarse, quitar de delante; arrebatar. *To make one's way,* (1) Avanzar, progresar, abrirse paso. (2) Obtener buen éxito; salir bien. *To make out,* Llegar á comprender, descifrar, descubrir; establecer por testimonio, probar, justificar con pruebas; suplir, abastecer de lleno, completar; componer, redactar, o completar (los documentos legales, expedientes, etc.); estar o ser próspero, tener buen éxito. *We will make out the deeds at once,* Redactaremos las actas auténticas en seguida. *To make out a case,* Probar su pleito, justificar uno su demanda; llegar a comprender. *To make over,* (1) Rehacer, hacer de nuevo. (2) Ceder, traspasar o transferir el dominio de una cosa; depositar alguna cosa en poder de personas abonadas; confiar. *To make towards,* Arrimarse á uno para cogerle. *To make up,* Acabar, concluir; completar, juntar hasta el completo de una cosa; reparar, suplir; colmar; plegar; recompensar; formar; ajustar una cuenta; recuperarse de una pérdida; indemnizar, resarcir; conciliar, apaciguar; fabricar, contar fábulas ó mentiras; componerse con afeites como un actor; compaginar, arreglar en columnas o páginas (término de imprenta); enumerar, contar. *To make up a lip,* Estar de hocico, amohinarse. *To make up to one,* Acercarse a uno. *To make up for,* Compensar, poner una cosa en lugar de otra perdida. *To make up one's mind,* Resolverse, hacer ánimo, tener determinado. *To make a doubt,* Dudar. *To make a figure,* Hacer papel, hacer figura. *To make a fool of,* Burlarse o reirse de uno; dar chasco; divertirse á costa de alguna persona. *To make a jest of,* Poner en ridículo. *To make a litter,* Ensuciar, desordenar. *To make a man,* Hacer la fortuna o la suerte de una persona. *To make a man of a person,* Hacer valiente á alguno. *To make a mistake,* Equivocarse, engañarse. *To make a pass,* Tirar una estocada. *To make a pen,* Tajar una pluma. *To make a wonder,* Admirar, admirarse. *To make account,* Calcular; creer; echarse la cuenta. *To make account of,* Estimar, tener consideración o tratar con consideración, hacer caso. *To make amends,* Indemnizar, resarcir, reparar, compensar. *To make angry,* Enfadar, enojar, irritar, poner de mal humor a alguno. *To make clean,* Limpiar. *To make fast,* (Mar.) Amarrar, afianzar. *To make free,* Libertar, poner en libertad. *To make free with,* Tratar sin ceremonia; no gastar cumplimientos; estar como en su casa; coger una cosa sin pedirla. *To make gain of,* Ganar. *To make good,* Mantener, defender; hacer bueno, probar; mejorar, cumplir; garantizar, responder de, salir fiador; lograr. *To make good one's word or promise,* Cumplir su palabra, promesa o empeño. *To make good a loss,* Reparar, resarcir una pérdida. *He made good his escape,* Logró escaparse. *To make haste,* Apresurarse, darse prisa. *To make hay,* Revolver y extender el heno segado para que se seque. *To make head against,* Hacer frente a, resistir. *To make hot,* Acalorar. *To make interest,* Empeñarse. *To make it good to one,* Indemnizar, resarcir, reparar. *To make it up,* Hacer las amistades, hacer las paces. (Fam.) Contentarse, volver a ser amigos, olvidar lo pasado. *To make known,* Publicar, hacer saber, notificar. *To make lean,* Poner flaco. *To make less,* Minorar, adelgazar, hacer más pequeña o delgada alguna cosa. *To make level,* Allanar. *To make liable,* Hacer responsable; sujetar. *To make light of,* Menospreciar, tratar con desprecio, no hacer caso. *To make love,* Enamorar, cortejar, galantear. *To make many words,* Altercar, disputar, porfiar sobre una cosa. *To make merry,* Divertirse, regalarse, pasarlo alegremente. *To make money,* Ganar dinero. *There is money to be made,* Hay dinero que ganar. *To make no doubt,* No dudar. *To make one out of his wits,* Sacar de quicio, hacer perder la paciencia, poner a una persona fuera de sí o sacarla de sus casillas. *To make one's escape,* Escaparse, huirse, evadirse, salvarse huyendo. *To make*

one's fortune, Hacer hombre, hacer rico o enriquecer a alguno. *To make one's self known*, Darse a conocer. *To make one's self miserable*, Hacerse infeliz, entristecerse, afligirse. *To make ready*, Preparar, tener pronta alguna cosa. *To make sail*, Dar a la vela. *To make sense of*, Hallar sentido a. *To make no sense of*, No hallar sentido a, hallar confuso u obscuro un escrito, lenguaje, etc. *To make shift with*, Sacar el mejor partido de una cosa poco favorable. *To make speed*, Apresurarse, darse prisa. *To make sure of*, Estar seguro, tener por cierto, asegurarse en la posesión de una cosa; contar con una cosa; considerar como seguro y cierto. *To make the most of it*, Aprovecharlo todo; sacar todas las ventajas posibles. *To make use*, Servirse de una cosa o hacer uso de ella. *To make water*, (1) (Mar.) Hacer agua o abrir una vía de agua. (2) Hacer aguas, mear, orinar. *Make yourself easy*, Pierda Vd. cuidado. *He will make nothing of it at last*, Al cabo nada sacará de ello. *To make more sail*, (Mar.) Largar las velas. *To make sternway*, (Mar.) Hacer camino para popa. *To make headway*, (Mar.) Hacer camino para avante. *To make the land*, (Mar.) Tomar tierra, descubrir la tierra.

Make, *s.* 1. Hechura, forma, figura; estructura. 2. Fábrica, producción, manufactura. 3. Producto.

Makable [mēk'-a-bl], *a.* (Poco us.) Factible, practicable.

Make-believe [mēk'-bg-līv"], *a.* Fingido, falso, imaginado; no real.—*s.* Ficción, cosa imaginada; pretexto.

Make-peace [mēk'-pīs], *s.* Pacificador, conciliador.

Maker [mēk'-ęr], *s.* 1. Criador, hacedor supremo. 2. Artífice, fabricante. 3. Hacedor, el que hace alguna cosa. 4. Poeta; autor.

Make-up [mēk'-up], *s.* 1. Combinación de las partes de que consiste un todo. 2. (Impr.) Imposición de los tipos. 3. Carácter, modo de ser. 4. Maquillaje.

Makeweight [mēk'-wēt], *s.* Cualquier cosa pequeña que se pone en una balanza para igualar el peso.

Making [mēk'-ing], *s.* 1. Composición, estructura, forma, hechura, trabajo. 2. (Des.) Poema.

Making-iron [mēk'-ing-ai'-ūrn], *s.* (Mar.) Hierro de sentar.

Mal-. Prefijo que significa malo o falto, defectuoso. *Maladjustment*, Ajuste malo, defectuoso. *Maladministration*, Mala administración.

Malachite [mal'-a-kait], *s.* Malaquita, piedra de color verde, con todos los grados de transparencia hasta la opacidad perfecta; carbonato de cobre ($H_2Cu_2CO_5$).

Malacology [mal-a-cel'-o-ji], *s.* Malacología, la parte de la zoología que trata de los moluscos.

Maladdress [mal-ad-dres'], *s.* Grosería, poca maña o descortesía en el habla o en los modales; falta de finura.

Maladjustment [mal-ad-just'-ment], *s.* 1. Mal ajuste. 2. Inadaptación.

Maladroit [mal-a-droit'], *a.* Desmañado, torpe.

Malady [mal'-a-di], *s.* 1. Mal, enfermedad, dolencia. 2. Mal mental; cualquier condición de desarreglo.

Malaga [mal'-a-ga], *s.* Vino o uva de Málaga.

Malaise [mal-ēz'], *s.* Indisposición, enfermedad ligera o pasajera. (<Fr.)

Malanders [mal'-an-dęrz], *s.* (Vet.) Ajuagas, esparavanes.

Malapert [mal'-a-pęrt], *a.* Desvergonzado, descomedido, descarado.

Malapertness [mal'-a-pęrt-nes], *s.* Insolencia, atrevimiento, impudencia.

Malapropos [mal-a"-pro-pō'], *a.* Mal a propósito, fuera de propósito.

Malar [mē'-lar], *a.* Malar, perteneciente a la mejilla. *Malar bone*, Hueso malar, pómulo.

Malaria [ma-lē'-ri-a], *s.* 1. Aire malsano, exhalación nociva; en especial las emanaciones de los pantanos o de materias animales o vegetales en estado de descomposición. 2. Enfermedad producida por dicho aire malsano o emanaciones nocivas; fiebre intermitente; calentura maligna; aria cattiva de los italianos.

Malarial [ma-lē'-ri-al], *a.* Afectado por la malaria o fiebre intermitente, o causado por ella; de la naturaleza de una calentura intermitente o maligna; malsano, palúdico.

Malarious [ma-lē'-ri-us], *a.* Que contiene aire malsano o malaria; que produce calenturas intermitentes o malignas.

Malate [mē'-lēt], *s.* (Quím.) Malato, sal formada por la combinación del ácido málico con alguna base.

Malay, Malayan [ma-lē', an], *a.* Malayo.

Malcontent [mal-con-tent'], *a.* Malcontento; perturbador del orden público.

Male [mēl], *a.* 1. Masculino; varón, macho. *Male issue*, Hijos varones, sucesión masculina. 2. Compuesto de varones. *A male quartet*, Cuarteto de varones. 3. (Bot.) Estaminado, provisto de estambres. 4. Que denota un útil, instrumento u objeto que tiene un correlativo conocido con el nombre de hembra: *male screw*, tornillo; *female screw*, hembra del tornillo, tuerca.—*s.* Macho, animal del sexo masculino o viril.

Malediction [mal-e-dic'-shun], *s.* Maldición.

Malefaction [mal-e-fac'-shun], *s.* (Poco us.) Delito, culpa.

Malefactor [mal-e-fac'-tęr], *s.* Malhechor.

Malefic [ma-lef'-ic], *a.* Maléfico, dañoso.

Maleficent [ma-lef'-i-sent], *a.* Maléfico, maligno.

Maleficiation [mal-e-fish-i-ē'-shun], *s.* Hechicería.

Malepractice [mal-prac'-tis], *s.* (Des.) *V.* MALPRACTICE.

Malevolence [ma-lev'-o-lens], *s.* Malevolencia, aversión, mala voluntad, odio, tirria.

Malevolent [ma-lev'-o-lent], †**Malevolous** [ma-lev'-o-lus], *a.* Malévolo, maligno; mal intencionado.

Malevolently [ma-lev'-o-lent-li], *adv.* Malignamente.

Malfeasance [mal-fī'-zans], *s.* 1. Comisión de un acto malo y contrario a la ley. 2. Malhecho; acto ilegal; malversación.

Malformation [mal-for-mē'-shun], *s.* Hechura o formación defectuosa; cualquiera irregularidad congénita de un organismo.

Malformed [mal-fōrmd'], *a.* Mal formado, malhecho, contrahecho.

Malic [mē'-lic], *a.* Málico, concerniente a las manzanas. *Malic acid*, Ácido málico.

Malice [mal'-is], *s.* Malicia, mala intención, malignidad, maldad, ruindad.

Malicious [ma-lish'-us], *a.* Malicioso, maligno.

Maliciously [ma-lish'-us-li], *adv.* Maliciosamente.

Maliciousness [ma-lish'-us-nes], *s* Mala intención, malicia.

Malign [ma-lain'], *a.* 1. Maligno, malicioso, mal inclinado. 2. Maligno, contagioso: dícese de las enfermedades.

Malign, *va.* Envidiar, dañar, perjudicar; censurar.—*vn.* (Des.) Tener malicia.

Malignancy [ma-lig'-nan-si], *s.* Malignidad, malicia, malevolencia.

Malignant [ma-lig'-nant], *a.* Maligno, malicioso; nocivo; envidioso. *Malignant fever*, Calentura maligna. —*s.* Hombre maligno, mal intencionado o envidioso.

Malignantly [ma-lig'-nant-li], *adv.* Malignamente.

Maligner [ma-lain'-ęr], *s.* Hombre mordaz, maligno o mal intencionado; detractor, difamador.

Malignity [ma-lig'-ni-ti], *s.* Malignidad, perversidad.

Malignly [ma-lain'-li], *adv.* Malignamente.

Malinger [ma-liņ'-gęr], *vn.* Fingirse enfermo para evitarse algún trabajo o servicio.

Malingerer [ma-lin'-gęr-ęr], *s.* Maula, el que se finge enfermo para que se le dispense de algún servicio.

Malison [mal'-i-sun], *s.* (Poét.) Maldición.

Malkin [mōl'-kin], *s.* 1. Aljofifa; deshollinador de horno. 2. Gorrona, mujer soez y vil, criada sucia. 3. Espantajo en figura de mujer. 4. Gato. *V.* GRIMALKIN.

Mall [mōl], *s.* 1. Mazo, mallo. 2. (Des.) Bote, golpe.

Mall, *va.* *V.* MAUL.

Mall [mal o mel], *s.* Alameda, paseo público nivelado y con árboles.

Mallard [mal'-ard], *s.* (Orn.) Lavanco, ánade silvestre. Anas boschas.

Malleability [mal-ę-a-bil'-i-ti], **Malleableness** [mal'-ę-a-bl-nes], *s.* Maleabilidad.

Malleable [mal'-ę-a-bl], *a.* Maleable, lo que se puede extender a golpe de martillo.

Malleate [mal'-ę-ēt], *va.* Martillar, trabajar a martillo, y formar en planchas.

Mallet [mal'-et], *s.* Mazo, mallo; mallete, martillo ligero. *Serving-mallet*, (Mar.) Maceta de aforrar. *Calking-mallet*, Maceta de calafate. *Driving-mallet*, Maceta de ajustar.

Malleus [mal'-ę-us], *s.* Martillo, uno de los huesecillos del oído, contenidos en la caja del tímpano.

Mallow, Mallows [mal'-ō, z], *s.* (Bot.) Malva, malvas.

Malmsey [mam'-zi], *s.* Malvasía, cierta especie de uva y el vino que se saca de ella.

Malnutrition [mal-niu-trish'-un], *s.* Desnutrición, mala nutrición.

Malodorous [mal-ō'-dęr-us], *a.* Fétido, mal oliente.

Malpighian [mal-pī'-gi-an], *a.* Malpigiáceo, de Malpighi, nombre de un anatomista y botánico italiano del siglo XVII.

Malpractise, Malpractice [mal-prac-tis], *s.* 1. En medicina y cirugía, tratamiento erróneo, perjudicial o ilegal. 2. Mala conducta, mala dirección.

Malt [mǒlt], *s.* 1. Cebada preparada para hacer cerveza. 2. *V.* MALT-LIQUOR. *Malt-dust,* Polvo que despide la cebada preparada al molerla para hacer cerveza; úsase como abono para la tierra. *Malt-floor,* Suelo para germinar y secar cebada. *Malt-horse,* Zote: voz de desprecio. *Malt-house,* La casa o paraje en donde se prepara y guarda la cebada para hacer cerveza. *Malt-kiln,* Horno para secar la cebada germinada. *Malt-liquor,* Cerveza, cualquier bebida preparada con cebada. *V.* ALE, BEER, PORTER. *Malt-mill,* Molino para moler la cebada germinada.
Malt, *va.* Hacer germinar la cebada, prepararla para hacer cerveza.—*vn.* Germinar la cebada para convertirse en cerveza.
Maltha [mal'-tha], *s.* Especie de betún hecho con pez y cera.
Maltman [mǒlt'-man], **Maltster** [mǒlt'-stęr], *s.* El que prepara y dispone la cebada para hacer cerveza.
Maltose [mǒl-tōs], *s.* Maltosa, azúcar cristalizable.
Maltreat [mal-trît'], *va.* Maltratar.
Malvaceous [mal-vê'-shus], *a.* Malváceo, que pertenece a la malva.
Malversation [mal-vęr-sê'-shun], *s.* Malversación, mala administración, falta de fidelidad, particularmente en las funciones públicas.
Mameluke o **Mamaluke** [mam'-e-lūc], *s.* Mameluco.
Mama, Mamma [ma-mā'], *s.* Mamá, madre.
Mamma [mam'-a], *s.* Mama de los mamíferos; teta.
Mammal [mam'-al], *s.* Mamífero, animal que tiene mamas y da de mamar a sus pequeñuelos.
Mammalia [ma-mê'-li-a], *s.* Mamíferos, la clase primera de los animales cuyas hembras tienen tetas.
Mammalian, [mam-mê'-li-an], *a.* Mamífero.
Mammalogy [mam-mal'-o-ji], *s.* Mamalogía, el ramo de la zoología que trata de los mamíferos.
Mammary [mam'-a-ri], *a.* Mamario, perteneciente a la teta o mama, o de la naturaleza de ella.
Mammee-tree [mam-mî'-tri], *s.* (Bot.) Mamey, árbol de América cuya fruta tiene el mismo nombre.
Mammet [mam'-et], *s.* *V.* MAUMET.
Mammiform [mam'-i-fōrm], *a.* Mamiforme, que tiene la figura de mamilas o tetas.
Mammillary [mam'-il-ę-ri], *a.* Mamilar.
Mammillate, Mammillated [mam'-i-lêt, ed], *a.* Lo que tiene tetas.
Mammon [mam'-ǫn], *s.* 1. El espíritu de la codicia. 2. El dios siríaco de las riquezas.
Mammonist [mam'-ǫn-ist], *s.* Mundano, avaro.
Mammoth [mam'-eth], *a.* Enorme, gigantesco.—*s.* Mamut, elefante fósil primitivo, ahora desaparecido.
Mammy [mam'-i], *s.* 1. (Fam.) Madre, mamá. 2. (E. U. del Sur) Negra, ama de leche para los niños blancos. 3. (Ingl.) Abuela.
Man [man], *s.* 1. Hombre, animal racional, acepción genérica bajo la cual se comprende toda la especie humana. 2. Hombre, varón, respecto de la mujer o hembra y respecto también de un muchacho o joven. 3. Hombre: voz muy familiar con que se dirige la palabra a alguno. 4. Criado, servidor (varón). 5. Peón, una de las piezas delanteras del juego del ajedrez, o la pieza movible con que se juega a las damas. 6. Alguien; cualquiera. 7. (Mar. y solamente en composición) Buque, navío: *man-of-war,* buque de guerra; *merchant-man,* buque mercante. *A man in an instant may discover it,* Cualquiera puede descubrirlo en un instante. *He is not his own man,* Está fuera de sí o no está en sus sentidos. *To be one's own man,* No depender más que de sí, ser independiente. *The creditors went against it to a man,* Los acreedores, sin faltar uno solo, se opusieron a ello. *So much a man,* Tanto por cabeza o tanto por barba. *Where is my man?* ¿Dónde está mi criado? *Man and wife,* Marido y mujer. *Man's estate,* Edad viril. *Man-eater,* Antropófago, caribe. *Man-Friday,* Criado que sirve para todo (como el de Robinson Crusoe, del mismo nombre). *Man-hater,* Misántropo; también el que o la que aborrece al sexo masculino. *Man-milliner,* Hombre que comercia en artículos de modista. *The sick man,* La Turquía, el imperio turco. nombre debido a sus continuas dificultades rentísticas y políticas. *To a man,* Hasta el último, como un solo hombre, de acuerdo unánime. *Man-killer,* Homicida, asesino. *Man-midwife,* Partero, comadrón. *Man of straw,* Testaferro, maniquí que no figura más que de nombre en una cosa.
Man, *va.* 1. (Mar.) Tripular, poner gente en; armar. *To man the capstan,* (Mar.) Armar o guarnir el cabrestante. 2. Guarnecer o fortalecer con gente una plaza o fortaleza. 3. (Poco us.) Amaestrar, adiestrar un halcón. *To man the yards,* Disponer la gente sobre las vergas para poder maniobrar con las velas.
Manacle [man'-a-cl], *s.* Manilla, el anillo de hierro que por prisión se echa a la muñeca. *Manacles, pl.* Esposas, las dos manillas emparejadas con que se aseguran ambas manos.
Manacle, *va.* Maniatar, atar las manos con esposas o manillas; atar las manos de las bestias con maniotas.
Manage [man'-ej], *va.* y *vn.* 1. Manejar, conducir, gobernar, dirigir, administrar o disponer de alguna cosa. 2. Manejar, usar o traer entre manos una cosa. 3. Manejar, dirigir o llevar bien un asunto o una dependencia. 4. Manejar, hablando de caballos, es gobernarlos o usar de ellos según arte. 5. Amansar, domar.—*vn.* Ingeniarse para, darse maña para alcanzar o conseguir alguna cosa; usar de medios prudentes; arreglarse para.
†**Manage,** *s.* 1. Manejo. 2. *V.* BEHAVIOR. 3. *V.* MANÈGE.
Manageable [man'-ĝj-a-bl], *a.* Manejable; dócil, tratable.
Manageableness [man'-ĝj-a-bl-nes], *s.* Docilidad; flexibilidad, mansedumbre.
Management [man'-ĝj-męnt], *s.* Manejo, administración, negociación; prudencia, destreza; directores o empresarios colectivamente.
Manager [man'-a-jęr], *s.* 1. Administrador, director; empresario. 2. Hombre económico, el que sabe manejar su hacienda; buen padre de familia. 3. Proyectista diestro, intrigante.
Managing editor [man'-ej-ing ed'-i-tęr], *s.* Subdirector (de una publicación, etc.).
Manatee [man-a-tî'], *s.* (Zool.) Manatí, vaca marina, mamífero pisciforme de la familia de los sirenios.
Manche [mānsh], *s.* (Her.) Armas parecidas a un mango. (Fr.)
Manchet [man'-chet], *s.* (Ant.) Panecillo, pan pequeño de flor de harina, bodigo, mollete.
Manchineel [man-chi-nîl'], *s.* (Bot.) Manzanillo, árbol grande de las Antillas cuya fruta es venenosa y la sombra muy nociva.
Mancipation [man-si-pê'-shun], *s.* (Der. rom.) 1. Enajenación de bienes por venta. 2. Emancipación, acto por el cual daba un padre libertad a su hijo. 3. (Des.) Esclavitud.
Manciple [man'-si-pl], *s.* El mayordomo o administrador de un colegio o comunidad de cualquier clase.
Mandamus [man-dê'-mus], *s.* (For.) Mandamiento, orden de un tribunal superior a otro inferior, o a una corporación o persona particular, para que hagan alguna cosa que están obligados a ejecutar.
Mandarin [man-da-rîn'], *s.* 1. Mandarín, título de dignidad en la China, funcionario civil o militar. 2. Mandarina, lengua sabia y oficial de la China. 3. Amarillo de mandarín. 4. Naranja mandarina.
Mandatary [man'-da-tę-ri], *s.* 1. Mandatario, el sujeto que por encargo o mandato de otro entiende en algún asunto. 2. Mandante.
Mandate [man'-dêt], *s.* 1. Mandato, orden, precepto. 2. Encargo, poder que da uno a otro, comisión.
Mandator [man-dê'-tęr], *s.* Director.
Mandatory [man'-da-to-ri], *a.* (For.) Preceptivo, que expresa un mandato positivo y no un permiso.—*s.* Mandatario.
Mandible [man'-di-bl], *s.* Mandíbula, quijada o su equivalente en los pájaros y en los insectos.
Mandibular [man-dib'-yu-lar], *a.* Mandibular.
Mandolin, Mandoline [man'-do-lin], *s.* Bandolin o mandolina, instrumento músico de cuerdas metálicas, y cuya caja es de forma parecida a la almendra.
Mandragora [man-drag'-o-ra], **Mandrake** [man'-drêk], *s.* (Bot.) 1. Mandrágora. 2. *Mandrake,* (E. U.) Planta común de los bosques, llamada también *May-apple* (manzana de mayo), notable por sus grandes hojas. Se emplea en medicina. Podophyllum peltatum.
Mandrel [man'-drel], *s.* Polea de madera de que usan los torneros en sus tornos, mandril; y el parahuso o taladro de los cerrajeros.
Mandrill [man'-dril], *s.* (Zool.) Mandril, mormón, mono de la familia de los cinocéfalos, del oeste de África.
§**Manducate** [man'-diu-kêt], *va.* Comer, mascar, manducar.
Manducation [man-diu-kê'-shun], *s.* Manducación, mascadura.
Mane [mên], *s.* Crin o clin de caballo.
Man-eater [man'-ît-ęr], *s.* Antropófago.
Maned [mênd], *a.* Crinado, crinito.
Manège [ma-nêzh'], *s.* 1. Picadero, el lugar o sitio donde los picadores adiestran los caballos. 2. Escuela de equitación, lugar donde se enseña a montar a caballo. (Fr.)
Manequin [man'-e-kin], *s.* *V.* MANIKIN.

Manes [mé'-niz], *s.* Manes, las sombras o almas de los muertos.

Maneuver, Manœuvre [ma-nū'-vẹr], *s.* 1. Maniobra, evolución. 2. Movimiento hecho con destreza.

Maneuver, Manœuvre, *va.* 1. Maniobrar, hacer maniobras de tropas o de buques. 2. Llevar a un paraje determinado por medio de maniobras.—*vn.* 1. Maniobrar las tropas o una flota. 2. Intrigar, tramar, negociar artificiosamente.

Manful [man'-ful], *a.* Bravo, valiente, animoso, esforzado, atrevido.

Manfully [man'-ful-i], *adv.* Valerosamente, valientemente.

Manfulness [man'-ful-nes], *s.* Valentía, esfuerzo, aliento, valor, ánimo.

Manganate [man'-ga-nêt], *s.* Manganato, sal formada por la combinación del ácido mangánico con una base.

Manganese [maŋ-ga-nîs'], *s.* Manganeso, metal duro de color gris, blanquizco y quebradizo, de que se usa en la manufactura del vidrio y de las pinturas.

Manganic [man-gan'-ic], *a.* Mangánico, relativo al manganeso, particularmente en su grado más alto de oxidación.

Manganous [maŋ'-ga-nus], *a.* Manganoso, relativo al manganeso en su más bajo grado de oxidación.

Mange [mênj], *s.* Roña, sarna perruna, especie de sarna que da a los animales.

Manger [mên'-jẹr], *s.* 1. Pesebre. 2. (Mar.) Caja de agua.

Manginess [mênj'-i-nes], *s.* Sarnazo, roña, infección roñosa; comezón.

Mangle [man'-gl], *va.* 1. Mutilar, estropear; desfigurar, desgarrar cortando, lacerar. 2. (Fig.) Chafallar, hacer algo desatinadamente; arruinar. 3. Lustrar, dar prensa y lustre a las telas, alisarlas, darles calandria o pasarlas por la calandria.

Mangle, *s.* Planchadora eléctrica.

Mangler [maŋ'-glẹr], *s.* 1. Destrozador, despedazador. 2. El que prensa y da lustre a las telas por medio de la calandria.

Mangling [man'-gling], *s.* 1. Despedazamiento. 2. El acto de prensar y dar lustre a las telas con la calandria.

Mango [maŋ'-go], *s.* Mango, árbol originario de la India, de fruta muy estimada y abundante en las Antillas. Mangifera Indica.

Mangonel [maŋ'-go-nel], *s.* Máquina para arrojar piedras grandes; catapulta de la edad media.

Mangrove [man'-grōv], *s.* (Bot.) Mangle, árbol que se cría en agua salada.

Mangy [mên'-ji], *a.* Sarnoso, el que padece de sarna.

Manhandle [man-han'-dl], *va.* Maltratar.

Manhole [man'-hōl], *s.* Entrada de pozo, abertura por donde puede entrar un hombre en una caldera, tanque, alcantarilla, etc.

Manhood [man'-hud], *s.* 1. Naturaleza humana. 2. Virilidad o edad viril. 3. (For.) Masculinidad. 4. Fortaleza, valor, valentía, espíritu, resolución.

Mania [mé'-ni-a], *s.* 1. Manía, locura furiosa. 2. Frenesí, acción disparatada, manía.

Maniac, Maniacal [mé'-ni-ac, ma-nai'-a-cal], *a.* Maniático, maníaco.

Maniac, *s.* Loco, maniático o maníaco.

Manicheism [man-i-kí'-izm], *s.* Maniqueísmo, la herejía de los Maniqueos persas; especie de dualismo que prevaleció en los siglos tercero a séptimo.

Manichord [man-i-cōrd], *s.* Manicordio, instrumento músico parecido al clave o clavicordio.

Manicure [man'-i-kiūr], *s.* (Neol.) El cuidado y tratamiento de las manos y uñas; manicuro, manicura, la persona que se dedica a esa profesión. —*va.* Cuidar, curar y hermosear un manicuro las manos y las uñas de sus clientes.

Manicurist [man-i-kiū'-rist], *s.* Manicuro, manicurista.

Manifest [man'-i-fest], *a.* Manifiesto, descubierto, patente, aparente, evidente.—*s.* 1. Manifiesto, declaración; la exhibición que un capitán hace en la aduana de todos los géneros y mercaderías que trae a bordo. 2. Por extensión, conocimiento, hoja de ruta.

Manifest, *va.* Manifestar, hacer patente, hacer ver; declarar; demostrar, revelar.

Manifestable [man-i-fest'-a-bl], *a.* Mostrable, demostrable.

Manifestation [man-i-fes-té'-shun], *s.* Manifestación, acción de hacer patente; demostración evidente, ostensión, revelación.

Manifestly [man'-i-fest-li], *adv.* Manifiestamente, evidentemente.

Manifestness [man'-i-fest-nes], *s.* Evidencia clara o patente; perspicuidad.

Manifesto [man-i-fes'-tō], *s.* Manifiesto, el escrito en que se justifica y declara al público alguna cosa.

Manifold [man'-i-fōld], *a.* 1. Múltiple, multíplice, vario, de diversos géneros; numeroso. 2. Manifestado de muchos modos.

Manifold, *va.* Sacar más de una copia a un tiempo, como se hace en las máquinas de escribir.

Manifoldly [man'-i-fōld-li], *adv.* De muchos modos, de diferentes maneras.

Manifoldness [man'-i-fōld-nes], *s.* Multiplicidad.

Maniglions [ma-nil'-yunz], *s. pl.* (Art.) Mangos de un cañón de artillería.

Manihot [man'-i-het], **Manioc** [man'-i-ec o mé'-ni-ec], *s.* (Bot.) Yuca, arbusto de América de cuya raíz se hace una especie de torta o pan llamado cazabe o casabe.

Manikin [man'-i-kin], *s.* 1. Maniquí, figura artificial del cuerpo humano para hace ver la estructura anatómica, etc. 2. Maniquí, modelo de la figura humana para uso de los artistas. 3. Hombrecillo, hombre pequeño.

Manila, Manilla [ma-nil'-a], *s.* 1. Filipino, especie de cigarro que viene de Manila. 2. Abacá, cáñamo de Manila.

Manille [ma-nil'], **Manilio** [ma-nil'-yo], *s.* 1. Manilla, especie de anillo o ajorca para adornar brazos y piernas. 2. Malilla, juego de naipes.

Manioc [man'-i-ec], *s.* Manioca, yuca.

Maniple [man'-i-pl], *s.* 1. Manípulo, ornamento sacerdotal que se ciñe al brazo izquierdo. 2. Manípulo, la compañía de soldados en las cohortes romanas. 3. (Raro) Puñado.

Manipular [ma-nip'-yu-lar], *a.* Lo que pertenece al manípulo.

Manipulate [ma-nip'-yu-lêt], *va.* Manipular, operar con las manos; de aquí, manejar, influir artificiosamente.—*vn.* Trabajar con las manos.

Manipulation [ma-nip-yu-lé-shun], *s.* Manipulación, acción y efecto de operar con las manos o manipular.

Manipulative [ma-nip'-yu-la-tiv], **Manipulatory** [ma-nip'-yu-la-to"-ri], *a.* Manipulante, perteneciente a la manipulación; que se lleva a cabo por medio de la manipulación o es a propósito para ella.

Manipulator [ma-nip'-yu-lé"-tẹr], *s.* Manipulador, el que manipula.

Mankind [man-kaind'], *s.* 1. El género humano, la especie humana. 2. Los hombres, en contraposición a las mujeres.

Manlike [man'-laik], *a.* Varonil, de hombre, animoso.

Manless [man'-les], *a.* Sin hombres, sin gente.

Manliness [man'-li-nes], *s.* Hombrada, valentía, valor, brío, ánimo, fuerza, bravura.

Manly [man'-li], *a.* Varonil, valiente, valeroso, lleno de dignidad.—*adv.* Varonilmente.

Man-made satellite [man-mêd' sat'-el-ait], *s.* Satélite artificial.

Manna [man'-a], *s.* 1. Maná, mangla, licor o goma que se usa como purgante. 2. Maná, substancia con que Dios sustentó milagrosamente al pueblo de Israel.

Manned flight [mand flait'], *s.* Vuelo tripulado.

Mannequin [man'-e-kin], *s.* Maniquí.

Manner [man'-ẹr], *s.* 1. Manera, modo, método. 2. Maña, costumbre, hábito, moda. 3. Manera, porte o modales de una persona. 4. Suerte, género, especie. 5. Traza, aire, ademán, modo o manera de mirar. 6. *pl.* Modales, urbanidad, crianza. *In the same manner as,* Del mismo modo que, así como. *After* o *in this manner,* Así, de este modo. *Paul, as his manner was,* Pablo, como tenía por costumbre. *By all manner of means,* De todos modos; en todo caso; de cualquier modo posible. *To take in* o *with the manner,* Coger o atrapar en el acto de cometer el delito; ser cogido en fragante o en el hecho. *Good manners,* Buena crianza, buenas maneras, modales. *He has no manners,* Es un mal criado, no tiene crianza. *I shall teach you better manners,* Yo te enseñaré a portarte mejor.

Mannered [man'-ẹrd], *a.* Bien criado, de buenos modales; úsase en palabras compuestas. *Ill-mannered,* Descortés, brusco.

Mannerism [man'-ẹr-izm], *s.* Adhesión pronunciada a una manera o a un estilo (literario o artístico); estilo amanerado, modismo.

Mannerliness [man'-ẹr-li-nes], *s.* Urbanidad, cortesía, política, cortesanía.

Mannerly [man'-ẹr-li], *a.* Cortés, urbano, atento.—*adv.* Urbanamente.

Mannikin [man'-i-kin], *s.* *V.* MANIKIN.

Mannish [man'-ish], *a.* 1. Masculino, que tiene trazas de hombre, que remeda a los hombres. *A mannish woman,* Marimacho. 2. (Des.) Hombruno, varonil.

Man of the world [man ev dhi wūrld], *s.* Hombre de mundo.

Manometer [ma-nem'-e-tẹr], *s.* Manómetro, instrumento para hacer ver o medir la fuerza elástica de los gases.

Manor [man'-ẹr], *s.* 1 Señorío o jurisdicción territorial, feudo. 2. **Manor-house** [man'-ẹr-haus], **Manor-seat** [man'-ẹr-sît], *s.* Casa solariega, mansión o morada del señor de una jurisdicción o del poseedor de un señorío.

Manorial [ma-nō'-ri-al], *a.* Señorial, perteneciente al señor de vasallos o de un feudo.

Manpower [man'-pau-ẹr], *s.* 1. Brazos de que se dispone. 2. Conjunto de elementos humanos de que dispone una nación para su defensa.

Mansard (roof) [man'-sārd], *s.* Techo de boardilla, aboardillado.

Manse [mans], *s.* 1. Cortijo, granja, quinta, alquería. (Mex.) Hacienda. 2. Casa rectoral, la morada del párroco, abadía en algunas provincias.

Mansion [man'-shun], *s.* Mansión, morada, residencia. *Mansion-house,* Casa grande que sirve de habitación; palacio del Lord Mayor o alcalde de Londres.

Manslaughter [man'-slē-tẹr], *s.* Homicidio casual, bien que con alguna culpa por parte del que lo comete.

Man-slayer [man'-slê-ẹr], *s.* Homicida.

Man-stealer [man'-stîl-ẹr], *s.* El que hurta y vende hombres.

Man-stealing [man'-stîl-ing], *s.* La acción de hurtar hombres para venderlos.

†**Mansuetude** [man'-swẹ-tiūd], *s.* Mansedumbre.

Mantel [man'-tl], *s.* Manto, frente de la campana de una chimenea. *Mantel-piece,* Repisa de chimenea, la parte que sobresale de la campana encima del hogar.

Mantelet [man'-tel-et], *s.* 1. Capotillo, manteleta de mujer. 2. (Mil.) Mantelete, parapeto portátil cubierto para que sirva de defensa a los minadores.

Mantilla [man-til'-a], *s.* Mantilla.

Mantis [man'-tis], *s.* Mántide (f.), mantis, insecto ortóptero de muy rara figura; se llama vulgarmente rezadora. Mantis religiosa.

Mantle [man'-tl], *s.* 1. Manto, manteo, capa, manteleta, mantilla, mantellina. 2. (Zool.) Manto, palio, capa, lo que encubre u oculta un órgano. 3. Caperuza o tapa compuesta de las sales de ciertas substancias terrosas muy escasas, que se pone sobre la llama del gas para aumentar su brillo por medio de la incandescencia.

Mantle, *va.* y *vn.* 1. Cubrir, tapar, ocultar, disfrazar. 2. Extender las alas. 3. Extenderse mucho por la superficie; bañar, desparramarse.

Mantling [man'-tling], *s.* (Blas.) Mantelete, manto o ropaje alrededor de un escudo de armas.

Mantua [man'-tu-a], *s.* Manto de señora.

Manual [man'-yu-al], *a.* Manual. *Manual work,* Trabajo, obra manual. *Sign manual,* Firma.—*s.* 1. Manual, libro compendioso. 2. Teclado de órgano para las manos. 3. (Mil.) Ejercicio sistemático en el manejo de algún arma.

Manual training [man'-yu-al trên'-ing], *s.* Instrucción en trabajo o labores manuales. Enseñanza de artes y oficios.

Manubrium [ma-nu'-bri-um], *s.* 1. Manubrio, la empuñadura o mango de un instrumento. 2. (Biol.) Manubrio, una parte o eminencia comparable a un mango.

Manuductor [man-yu-duc'-tẹr], *s.* Guía, guiador, conductor.

Manufactory [man-yu-fac'-to-ri], *s.* Fábrica, manufactura, edificio o lugar donde se fabrican mercancías.

Manufacture [man-yu-fac'-chur], *s.* 1. Fabricación, el acto de fabricar. 2. Manufactura, fábrica, artefacto, obra; una cosa cualquiera manufacturada.

Manufacture, *va.* Fabricar, manufacturar; hacer una cosa por medios mecánicos.—*vn.* Estar ocupado en alguna manufactura.

Manufacturer [man-yu-fac'-chur-ẹr], *s.* Fabricante, fabriquero, el que trabaja la materia prima; el propietario de una fábrica o manufactura.

Manufacturing [man-yu-fac'-chur-ing], *pa.* Fabricante, manufacturero, que se refiere a la manufactura; fabril.

†**Manumise,** *va.* *V. To* MANUMIT.

Manumission [man-yu-mish'-un], *s.* Manumisión, el acto de libertar al esclavo.

Manumit [man-yu-mit'], *va.* Manumitir, dar libertad al esclavo.

Manumotor [man-yu-mō'-tẹr], *s.* Cochecito movido a mano por el que va en él; lo usan los inválidos.

Manurable [ma-niūr'-a-bl], *a.* 1. Que puede ser fertilizado con abono. 2. (Des.) Labrantío, de labor, cultivable.

Manure [ma-niūr'], *va.* 1. Abonar, engrasar, estercolar. 2. (Des.) Cultivar, labrar la tierra.

Manure, *s.* Abono, el estiércol o cosa equivalente que se echa a las tierras para beneficiarlas; fiemo, basura.

Manus [mê'-nus], *s.* La mano, o la parte correspondiente terminal del miembro torácico.

Manuscript [man'-yu-script], *s.* Manuscrito.—*a.* Manuscrito, que está escrito con la mano.

Manutyper [man'-yu-taip-ẹr], *s.* El o la que imprime a mano por medio de una máquina de escribir; y la máquina de escribir misma.

Manx [manx], *a.* y *s.* De la isla inglesa de Man; el lenguaje, y en sentido colectivo, el pueblo de dicha isla.

Many [men'-i], *a.* (*comp.* MORE, *sup.* MOST). Muchos, muchas; varios, diversos. *Many a, an,* o *another,* Significa gran número pero como un todo aislado, y va seguido de nombre en singular. *Many a man,* Muchos hombres. *Many a time,* Muchas veces. *Many times,* Muchas veces, frecuentemente. *Too many,* Demasiados. *They were too many for us,* Eran demasiado fuertes para nosotros. *One too many,* Uno de más o de sobra. *Twice as many,* El doble, dos veces tantos. *How many?* ¿Cuántos, cuántas? *A great many,* Un gran número, muchos. *So many,* Tantos. *Many-coloured,* De muchos colores, abigarrado. *Many-cornered,* Polígono, que tiene muchos lados. *Many-headed,* Que tiene muchas cabezas. *Many-languaged,* Que tiene muchas lenguas o idiomas. *Many-minded,* De mudable parecer; voluble, versátil. *Many-peopled,* Numeroso, populoso. *Many-sided,* Multilátero.—*s.* Muchedumbre, multitud, gente; familia, criados; servidumbre, hablando de reyes.

Manyplies [men'-i-plaiz], *s.* Omaso, salterio, el tercer estómago de los rumiantes, cuya membrana interior forma numerosos pliegues longitudinales.

Manzanita [man-za-nî'-ta], *s.* Manzanita, arbusto o árbol pequeño de los Estados Unidos del Oeste, con fruto rojizo. Se asemeja al madroño. Arctostaphylos manzanita.

Maoism [mau'-izm], *s.* Maoísmo.

Map [map], *s.* Mapa, plano topográfico. *Map maker,* Cartógrafo.

Map, *va.* Delinear mapas, sean geográficos o topográficos.

Maple [mê'-pl], *s.* (Bot.) Arce, plátano falso; cualquier árbol del género Acer.

Mappery [map'-ẹr-i], *s.* Dibujo de mapas.

Mar [mār], *va.* Echar a perder alguna cosa, dañar, desfigurar, corromper.

Mar, *s.* Mancha, borrón, injuria.

Marabou [mar'-a-bū], *s.* (Zool.) Marabú, ave del género cigüeña, originaria de África, que tiene en las alas unas plumas muy hermosas y delicadas del mismo nombre, muy apreciadas para adorno.

Marabout [mar-'a-būt], *s.* Morabito, ermita, santón mahometano entre los bereberes.

Maranatha [ma-ra-nā'-tha], *s.* Maranata, fórmula de excomunión entre los judíos.

Maraschino [mar-as-kî'-nō], *s.* Licor marrasquino. *Maraschino cherries,* Cerezas conservadas en licor marrasquino.

Marasmus [ma-raz'-mus], *s.* (Med.) Marasmo, flaqueza y consunción de la substancia del cuerpo.

Maraud [ma-rēd'], *va.* Merodear, pillar, robar.

Marauder [ma-rēd' ẹr], *s.* Merodeador, soldado que sale a robar en el campo enemigo; pillador.

Marauding [ma-rēd'-ing], *a.* Dícese del soldado que merodea.—*s.* Merodeo, pecorea, pillaje.

Maravedi [mar-a-vê'-di], *s.* Maravedí, la moneda más pequeña de cobre de España.

Marble [mār'-bl], *s.* 1. Mármol. 2. *Marbles, pl.* Canicas, bolillas de mármol, de barro cocido, de vidrio o porcelana con que juegan los niños.—*a.* Marmóreo, de mármol. *Marble-cutter,* Marmolista, obrero que trabaja en mármol. *Marble works,* Marmolería.

Marble, *va.* Jaspear, pintar imitando los colores del jaspe o mármol. *Marbled paper,* Papel jaspeado. *Marbled leaves,* Cortes jaspeados.

Marble-hearted [mār'-bl-hārt'-ed], *a.* Duro, insensible, que tiene corazón de mármol.

Marbleize [mār'-bl-aiz], *va.* Jaspear.

Marc [mārc], *s.* Orujo, el hollejo de la uva después de exprimida.

Marcasite [mār'-ca-sait], *s.* Marquesita, marcasita, pirita blanca.

Marcel wave [mār-sel' wêv] *s.* Ondulado Marcel (para el cabello).

March [mārch], *vn.* Marchar, caminar; andar con aire de majestad; limitar.—*va.* Poner en marcha, hacer marchar. *To march back,* Volverse atrás; hacer volver. *To march in,* Entrar, seguir. *To march off,* Irse, partirse, retirarse; desalojar. *To march on,* Marchar, caminar. *To march out,* Salir o hacer salir. *To march up,* Avanzar, adelantar; hacer avanzar, adelantar.

March, *s.* 1. Marzo, el tercer mes del año. 2. (Mil.) Marcha, la acción de marchar los soldados de un paraje a otro; la acción de marchar, modo de andar con cierta dignidad. 3. (Mil.) Marcha, el son que toca el tambor o el clarín para que se pongan en marcha los soldados. 4. Marcha, pieza de música que sirve para regularizar el paso de los que marchan. *To strike up a march*, Tocar una marcha. 5. Adelanto, progreso. *Marches, pl.* Frontera, raya, límite, término.

Marcher [mārch'-ẹr], *s.* Jefe militar o señor que antiguamente defendía los límites de una frontera.

Marching [mārch'-ing], *s.* Marcha, movimiento militar, paso de tropas. —*pa.* Marchando, dispuesto a caminar; de marcha. *Marching order*, Orden de marcha.

Marchioness [mār'-shun-es], *sf.* Marquesa.

Marchpane [mārch'-pên], *s.* Mazapán.

Marcid [mār'-sid], *a.* Macilento, magro, flaco; extenuado, descarnado.

Mare [mār], *sf.* Yegua, la hembra del caballo. *Mare's nest*, Agua de cerrajas, algo que al principio pareció ser importante, y que resulta ser inútil, menguado o falso.

Mare's-tail [mārz'-têl], *s.* (Bot.) Cola de caballo; planta acuática.

Margaric [mar-gar'-ic], *a.* Margárico, perteneciente a la perla. *Margaric acid*, Mezcla de los ácidos esteárico y palmítico; ácido margárico.

Margarin, Margarine [mār'-ga-rin], *s.* (Quím.) Margarina.

Margarite [mār'-ga-rait], *s.* Margarita, perla.

Marge [mārj], *s.* (Poét.) *V.* MARGIN. (Fr.)

Margin [mār'-jin], *s.* 1. Margen, borde, orilla o extremidad de alguna cosa. 2. Margen, la porción del papel que se deja en blanco a una y otra parte de lo escrito o impreso. 3. Provisión o reserva que se hace para atender a futuras contingencias o cambios. 4. Alcance. 5. (Com.) (1) La diferencia entre el precio de compra y el de venta de las mercancías. (2) Cantidad de dinero depositado en manos de un agente de cambio, para protegerle contra posibles pérdidas en el curso de sus operaciones por cuenta de su principal.

Margin, *va.* 1. Marginar, margenar, escribir algo en el margen de un escrito o impreso. 2. Lindar, poner borde o margen; formar el borde de.—*vn.* Depositar fondos de reserva en manos de un agente de cambio.

Marginal [mār'-jin-al], *a.* Marginal, escrito o anotado al margen.

Marginally [mār'-jin-al-i], *adv.* Al margen.

Marginate, Marginated [mār'-jin-êt, ed], *a.* Marginado.

Margrave [mār'-grêv], *s.* Margrave, título que gozan algunos príncipes de Alemania.

Mariet [mar'-i-et], *s.* (Bot.) Especie de campanilla.

Marigold [mar'-i-gōld], *s.* (Bot.) Caléndula, flamenquilla.

Marihuana, marijuana [mar-i-hwa'-na], *s.* Mariguana o marihuana.

Marimba [ma-rim'-ba], *s.* (Mús.) Marimba.

Marina [ma-rín'-a], *s.* 1. Estación de gasolina para los botes. 2. Dársena abrigada para embarcaciones con servicio de verdadero o grúas para izarlas.

Marinate [mar'-i-nêt], *va.* Escabechar pescado.

Marine [ma-rín'], *a.* Marino, de mar; oceánico; náutico; naval. *Marine engine*, Máquina de vapor marítima. —*s.* 1. Marino, soldado de marina. 2. Marina, fuerza naval; buques o bajeles en general. 3. Marina, pintura o cuadro que representa el mar.

Mariner [mar'-i-nẹr], *s.* Marinero. *Mariner's compass*, Brújula, compás para la navegación.

Marionette [mar-i-o-net'], *s.* Títere.

†**Marish** [ma'-rish], *s.* *V.* MARSH.—*a.* (Des.) Pantanoso. *V.* MARSHY.

Marital [mar'-i-tal], *a.* Marital.

Maritime [mar'-i-tim], *a.* Marítimo, naval, cercano al mar; que pertenece al mar, marino.

Marked man [mārkt man], *s.* Individuo sentenciado por sus enemigos.

Marjoram [mār'-jo-ram], *s.* (Bot.) Mejorana, almoradux, hierba del género Origanum.

Mark [mārk], *s.* 1. Marca, señal, nota, impresión, huella. 2. Prueba, evidencia; observación, nota. 3. Blanco, señal fija y determinada a que se tira. *To hit the mark*, Dar en el blanco. 4. La cruz u otra señal que hace en lugar de firma el que no sabe escribir. 5. Marco, moneda de plata, unidad monetaria de Alemania, equivalente a unos veinticinco centavos; antigua moneda de Inglaterra que valía trece chelines y cuatro peniques. 6. La señal por la cual se sabe la edad de un caballo. 7. Señal característica. 8. Eminencia, distinción. 9. Regla, norma. 10. *V.* MARQUE. *St. Mark's gospel*, Evangelio de S. Marcos. *Open marks*, Señales evidentes.

Mark, *va.* Marcar, señalar; notar, advertir, observar; mirar como válido o importante.—*vn.* Advertir, notar, reparar. *To mark down*, (1) Anotar, poner por escrito. (2) Marcar a un precio más bajo. *To mark out*, Mostrar, señalar; elegir, escoger; cancelar, borrar.

Markdown [mārk'-daun], *s.* Subprecio.

Marker [mārk'-ẹr], *s.* 1. Marcador. 2. Marcador, tanteador, en los juegos, etc.

Market [mār'-ket], *s.* 1. Mercado, plaza de mercado o gran edificio en que se ponen a la venta los víveres o provisiones de boca y otros géneros. 2. Venta, tráfico, estado del comercio en cuanto a los precios, o a la oferta y la demanda; precio, curso. 3. Localidad o país en que se puede comprar o vender alguna cosa. 4. Mercado, concurrencia de gente en un paraje determinado para comprar y vender géneros. *Market rate*, Tipo del mercado. *The market price of silver*, El precio corriente de la plata. *The cotton market is firm*, Los precios del algodón se mantienen firmes. *Money market*, Mercado monetario. *Markets are cheaper*, Han bajado los precios. *Market-garden*, Huerto o huerta, terreno donde se cultivan legumbres y frutas menores. *Market price, market rate*, El precio del mercado, precio corriente de las mercancías. *Market-town*, Pueblo de mercado. *Market-man*, Placero, el que va al mercado a vender o comprar. *Market-bell*, (Ingl.) Campana de mercado. *Market-cross*, Cruz del mercado. *Market-day*, Día de mercado, o de plaza.

Market, *va.* Mercar, comprar o vender en mercado.

Marketable [mār'-ket-a-bl], *a.* Vendible, corriente, pedido, de venta.

Marketing [mār'-ket-ing], *s.* 1. Compra. 2. Venta. 3. Mercadotecnia. *Marketing research*, Análisis de mercados, mercadotecnia.

Market-place [mār'-ket-plês], *s.* Mercado o plaza de mercado, el sitio donde se celebra el mercado.

Marking [mārk'-ing], *s.* y *pa.* Marcación, la acción de marcar. *Marking-ink*, Tinta de marcar. *Marking-iron*, Hierro de marcar. *Marking-machine*, Máquina de marcar, de acordonar monedas. *Marking-nut*, Agalla de caoba; su jugo mezclado con cal viva hace una tinta indeleble.

Marksman [mārcs'-man], *s.* 1. Tirador, el que tira con acierto al blanco. 2. ¿El que no sabe escribir su nombre y hace una señal.

Marksmanship [mārcs'-man-ship], *s.* Puntería.

Mark time [mārk taim], *vn.* 1. Llevar el compás de la música. 2. Quedar inactivo en espera de alguna actividad futura.

Markup [mārk'-up], *s.* Sobreprecio.

Marl [mārl], *s.* Marga, depósito de carbonato de cal, arcilla y arena que sirve para abonar los terrenos. *Marl-pit*, Marguera, gredal, margal.

Marl, *va.* 1. Margar, abonar la tierra con marga. 2. (Mar.) Trincafiar, envolver con merlín anudado a cada vuelta.

Marlaceous [mār-lé'-shius], *a.* Margoso, que contiene marga o se parece a ella.

Marline [mār'-lin], *s.* (Mar.) Merlín, cuerdas delgadas de cáñamo sin retorcer que se empapan en pez y sirven para liarlas alrededor de los cables.

Marmalade [mār'-ma-lêd], *s.* Mermelada, conserva de frutas ácidas o amargas hecha con azúcar.

Marmoration [mār-mo-ré'-shun], *s.* Incrustación de mármol.

Marmoreal [mar-mō'-rẹ-al], **Marmorean** [mār-mō'-rẹ-an], *a.* Marmóreo.

Marmoset [mār'-mo-zet], *s.* Mono muy pequeño de la América del Sur.

Marmot [mār'-mot], *s.* Marmota, animal roedor. Arctomys marmotta.

Maroon [ma-rūn'], *va.* Abandonar, castigar a un marinero dejándolo en una costa desierta.

Maroon, *a.* De color purpúreo o rojo obscuro.—*s.* 1. Color rojo obscuro. 2. Materia de tinte obtenida del alquitrán de hulla.

Maroon [ma-rūn'], *s.* 1. Cimarrón, negro esclavo de las Antillas que se refugiaba en los bosques. 2. Persona abandonada en una isla.

Marplot [mār'-plot], *s.* Cizañero, revolvedor, el que con su intervención e intrigas hace malograr un proyecto.

Marque [mārk], *s.* Licencia para tomar represalias. *Letter of marque*, Patente de corso.

Marquee [mār-kī'], *s.* 1. Marquesina. 2. Gran tienda de campaña. 3. Toldo para una ventana.

Marquess, *s.* *V.* MARQUIS.

Marquetry [mār'-ket-ri], *s.* Marquetería, ataracea.

Marquis [mār'-cwis], *s.* Marqués, título de dignidad.

Marquisate [mār'-cwis-ēt], *s.* Marquesado.
Marquisette [mār-ki-zet'], *s.* Tejido fino de malla.
Marrer [mār'-ẹr], *s.* El que echa á perder o el que daña a alguna persona o cosa.
Marriage [mar'-ij], *s.* 1. Matrimonio, maridaje. 2. Casamiento (el estado y el acto), matrimonio. 3. Boda. 4. (Fig.) Enlace, íntima unión. *The marriage articles,* El contrato matrimonial o los contratos esponsalicios. *Marriage-song,* Epitalamio. *The marriage-bed,* El lecho nupcial. *The marriage-day,* El día de la boda. *Marriage-bell,* Toque de campanas con motivo de una boda. *Marriage-license,* Licencia para casarse; cédula oficial concedida según la ley para que se casen las personas nombradas en ella. *Marriage-portion,* Dote.
Marriageable [mar'-ij-a-bl], *a.* Casadero, núbil, capaz de contraer matrimonio. *She is not yet marriageable,* No ha llegado aún a la edad de tomar estado, o a la edad de matrimonio.
Married [mar'-id], *a.* Casado, matrimonial, conyugal, connubial. *A married couple,* Cónyuges, marido y mujer, casados. *To get married,* Casarse. *The married state,* El estado matrimonial.
Marron [ma-rūn'], *s.* 1. Petardo pirotécnico. 2. Color castaño. 3. Gran castaña dulce del sur de Europa; se usa como alimento y para confitura.
Marrow [mar'-ō], *s.* 1. Tuétano, medula. 2. Meollo, medula, la substancia interior de alguna cosa; la esencia. *Vegetable marrow,* Medula vegetal, variedad de la calabaza. Cucurbita ovífera.
Marrow-bone [mar'-o-bōn], *s.* Caña o hueso medular. *Marrow-bones,* (Fest.) Las rodillas.
Marrowfat [mar'-o-fat], *s.* (Bot.) Guisante, especie de legumbre.
Marrowish [mar'-o-ish], *a.* Meduloso.
Marrowless [mar'-o-les], *a.* Falto de medula o tuétano.
Marrowy [mar'-o-i], *a.* Lleno de tuétano, meduloso; medular, de tuétano.
Marry [mar'-i], *va.* 1. Casar, unir en matrimonio a un hombre y una mujer. 2. Casar, dar por esposo o esposa. 3. Tomar por marido o por mujer; desposar. 4. Casar, disponer algunas cosas de modo que hagan juego; (Mar.) ayustar los cabos sin aumentar el diámetro.—*vn.* Casar o casarse, contraer matrimonio. *To marry again,* Volverse a casar, casarse de nuevo. *Marry in haste and repent at leisure,* Tal se casa de prisa y se arrepiente despacio.
Marry [mar'-i], *inter.* ¡De cierto, cabal, lo dicho! (Corrupción del nombre de María; antigua interjección á manera de juramento.)
Mars [mārz], *s.* 1. Marte, uno de los planetas; el cuarto en orden de la distancia desde el sol (♂). 2. El dios romano de la guerra y de la fertilidad. 3. (Des.) Hierro.
Marseilles [mār-sēlz'], *s.* Tela tupida de algodón con un dibujo en relieve. (Fr. < Marsella.)
Marsh [mārsh], *s.* Pantano, tremedal, ciénaga, marjal. *Marsh-elder,* (Bot.) Especie de guelde. *Marsh-mallow,* (1) (Bot.) Malvavisco, altea. (2) Confite hecho con altea. *Marsh-marigold,* (Bot.) Hierba centella. *Marsh-rocket,* (Bot.) Especie de berro.
Marshal [mār'-shal], *s.* 1. Mariscal. 2. Bastonero ó maestro de ceremonias. 3. Mariscal de campo, militar del más alto rango. 4. (E. U.) (1) Oficial de los tribunales de justicia de los Estados Unidos. (2) Jefe de la policía ó del departamento de incendios en algunas ciudades. 5. Precursor, aposentador de camino; mariscal de logis.
Marshal, *va.* Ordenar, poner en orden; guiar como director de alguna función, disciplinar.—*vn.* Juntarse y ordenarse, v. g. los ejércitos; reunirse.
Marshaller [mār'-shal-ẹr], *s.* El que arregla, ordena y pone en orden alguna cosa: ordenador.
Marshalship [mār'-shal-ship], *s.* Mariscalía, mariscalato.
Marshy [mārsh'-i], *a.* Pantanoso, cenagoso.
Marsupial [mār-siū'-pi-al], *a.* Marsupial, que tiene una bolsa para llevar sus pequeñuelos.—*s.* Animal marsupial que tiene dicha bolsa.
Mart [mārt], *s.* 1. Emporio, lugar donde concurren para comerciar gentes de diversas naciones; mercado público. 2. (Des.) Tráfico, compra y venta.
Martel [mār'-tel], *s.* (Her.) Martillo, maza de armas.
Marten [mār'-ten], *s.* 1. Marta, fuína, garduña, animal carnívoro cuya piel es muy estimada. 2. Piel de fuína. 3. (Orn.) Avión, vencejo.
Martial [mār'-shal], *a.* 1. Marcial, belicoso, guerrero. 2. Marcial, militar. *Court-martial,* Consejo de guerra. *Martial music,* Música marcial. *Martial array,* Orden de batalla.
Martialism [mār'-shal-izm], *s.* Marcialidad; valentía.
Martialist [mār'-shal-ist], *s.* Guerreador, guerrero.
Martian [mār'-shian], *a.* De Marte (el planeta o el dios mitológico).
Martin [mār'-tin], **Martinet** [mār'-ti-net], **Martlet** [mārt'-let], *s.* Avión, especie de golondrina; vencejo.
Martinet [mār-ti-net'], *s.* 1. El militar muy riguroso en la disciplina. 2. [mār'-ti-net] (Mar.) Apagapenoles.
Martingale [mārt'-in-gēl], *s.* 1. Martingala; gamarra. 2. (Mar.) Moco del bauprés.
Martini [mar-ti'-ni], *s.* Martini, bebida alcohólica compuesta.
Martinmas [mār'-tin-mas], *s.* Día de S. Martín, el once de noviembre.
Martyr [mār'-tẹr], *s.* 1. Mártir, el que padece muerte por la verdad o en defensa de la religión. 2. Mártir, el que sufre muerte o persecución por cualquier causa. 3. El que padece mucho tiempo, v. g. por falta de salud.
Martyr, *va.* 1. Martirizar; hacer sufrir el martirio. 2. Perseguir con crueldad, atormentar.
Martyrdom [mār'-tẹr-dum], *s.* Martirio.
Martyrize [mār'-tẹr-aiz], *va.* Martirizar.
Martyrological [mār-tẹr-o-loj'-i-cal], *a.* Lo perteneciente al martirologio.
Martyrologist [mār-tẹr-ol'-o-jist], *s.* Escritor de martirologios.
Martyrology [mar-tẹr-ol'-o-ji], *s.* Martirologio.
Marvel [mār'-vel], *s.* Maravilla, prodigio, lo que causa admiración. *Marvel of Peru,* (Bot.) Maravilla del Perú. Mirabilis jalapa. *V.* FOUR-O'CLOCK.
Marvel, *vn.* Maravillar, maravillarse, admirar, admirarse, llenarse de admiración, pasmarse de alguna cosa.
Marvellous [mār'-vel-us], *a.* Maravilloso, pasmoso, admirable, prodigioso, asombroso, estupendo.
Marvellously [mār'-vel-us-li], *adv.* Maravillosamente, pasmosamente.
Marvellousness [mār'-vel-us-nes], *s.* Maravilla, extrañeza, singularidad; lo maravilloso, lo extraordinario.
Marxianism, Marxism [mārc'-sian-izm, mārc'-sizm], *s.* Marxismo, doctrina de Carlos Marx.
Marxist [mārk'-sist], *s.* Marxista, partidario de la doctrina de Carlos Marx.
Mascara [mas-car'-a], *s.* Tinte para obscurecer las pestañas.
Mascle [mas'-cl], *s.* (Her.) Macle, losanje hueco o abierto.
Mascot [mas'-cot], *s.* (Fam.) Alguna cosa de la que se supone que trae buena fortuna a su dueño.
Masculine [mas'-kiu-lin], *a.* 1. Masculino, varonil. 2. (Gram.) Del género masculino (por su sexo o en sentido gramatical). *Masculine woman,* Marimacho, mujer varonil.
Masculineness [mas'-kiu-lin-nes], *s.* Masculinidad; virilidad.
Maser [mê'-ser], *s.* Maser, amplificación de microondas por estímulo de emisiones de radiación.
Mash [mash], *s.* 1. Amasijo, masa de alguna cosa ablandada, como afrecho amasado con agua. 2. Malta, el grano machacado o molido e infundido en agua caliente para hacer cerveza. 3. (Des.) Baturrillo, fárrago. *Mash* o *mashing-tub,* Tina, vaso grande para mezclar cebada y agua.
Mash, *va.* 1. Amasar, magullar, majar, poner blanda una cosa machacándola. 2. Amasar o mezclar la cebada molida con agua hirviendo para hacer cerveza. 3. (Ger.) Hacer cocos, cocar con persona del otro sexo.
Mashy [mash'-i], *a.* Producido por magullación: magullado, abollado.
Mask [mąsk], *s.* 1. Máscara, carátula, disfraz, carantoña, careta, mascarilla; mojiganga. 2. Velo, capa, pretexto, disimulación, disimulo, apariencia, color. *To put on a mask,* Ponerse una máscara o careta. *To take off the mask,* Quitarse la máscara. 3. Molde que se obtiene de las facciones de una persona muerta. 4. Mascarada. *V.* MASQUERADE. 5. Representación dramática antiguamente en voga en la que los actores asumían el papel de deidades mitológicas. 6. Máscara, persona que se disfraza. 7. (Mil.) Cubierta de ramaje para ocultar una batería.
Mask, *va.* 1. Enmascarar, disfrazar y cubrir el rostro con máscara. *To mask a ship,* (Mar.) Disfrazar la bandera. 2. Encubrir, disimular, enmascarar, ocultar.—*vn.* Andar enmascarado. *Mask-ball* o *masked ball,* Baile de máscaras, en que los concurrentes están disfrazados.
Masker [mąsk'-ẹr], *s.* Máscara, el que se enmascara.
Masking [mąsk'-ing], *s.* El acto de llevar máscara.—*pa.* de MASK.
Maslin [maz'-lin], *s.* (Prov. Ingl.)

Mezcla de granos; comuña, tranquillón.

Mason [mê'-sn], *s.* 1. Albañil. 2. Francmasón. 3. Abeja albañila, que hace para su morada agujeros en la tierra endurecida y en las tapias. *Mason-wasp*, Avispa muy notable por las celdas de barro que construye.

Masonic [ma-sen'-ic], *a.* 1. Masónico, lo que pertenece a la sociedad de los francmasones. 2. Albañil, relativo a la albañilería.

Masonry [mê'-sen-ri], *s.* 1. Albañilería, el arte u oficio del albañil. 2. Construcción de albañilería. 3. Francmasonería.

Masorite [mas'-o-rait], *s.* Escritor del Masora.

Masque [mɑsc], *s.* *V.* MASK.

Masquerade [mas-kɐr-êd'], *s.* 1. Mascarada, máscara, sarao de personas que se disfrazan con máscaras. 2. Mojiganga, disfraz, artificio para disimular. 3. Fiesta de cañas.

Masquerade, *vn.* Enmascararse, disfrazarse, ir disfrazado; asistir á algún sarao con máscara.

Masquerader [mas-kɐr-êd'-ɐr], *s.* Máscara, bufón.

Mass [mɑs], *s.* 1. Masa, montón, congerie, mole, conjunto de cosas que forman colectivamente un solo cuerpo. 2. Cuerpo informe; masa de materia concreta. 3. La parte principal de alguna cosa. 4. Bulto, volumen. *In mass* o *in the mass*, Como un todo, en conjunto. *The masses*, El vulgo, la plebe, la gente con exclusión de los ricos y de las clases privilegiadas.

Mass, *s.* 1. Misa, en la Iglesia católica. 2. Misa, la música que se compone para una misa solemne. (<Anglosajón, masse <Lat. missa.) *High mass*, Misa mayor. *Low mass*, Misa rezada. *A mass for the dead*, Misa de réquiem o de ánima. *A mass-book*, Misal, libro de misa.

Mass, *va.* Formar, reunir en una masa o todo.—*vn.* Formarse, juntarse en masas.

Massacre [mas'-a-kɐr], *s.* Carnicería, matanza, mortandad grande, particularmente de seres humanos que oponen poca o ninguna resistencia.

Massacre, *va.* Matar atrozmente, hacer una carnicería, destrozar.

Massacrer [mas'-a-crɐr], *s.* Matador, asesino.

Massage [mɑs-sūzh'], *s.* Masaje.—*va.* Dar masajes, sobar el cuerpo.

Masseter [mas-sî'-tɐr], *s.* Masetero, músculo masticatorio poderoso de la quijada inferior.

Masseur [mɑ-sɐr'], *s.* Masajista (hombre).

Masseuse [mɑ-sɐz'], *s.* Masajista (mujer).

Massicot [mas'-i-cet], *s.* Albayalde calcinado, el óxido amarillo de plomo.

Massiness [mɑs'-i-nes], **Massiveness** [mɑs'-iv-nes], *s.* Peso, bulto, mole; solidez.

Massive [mɑs'-iv], *a.* 1. Macizo, pesado, abultado, sólido. 2. (Min.) Sin forma definida de cristalización.

Mass-meeting [mɑs-mît'-ing], *s.* Asamblea en masa; reunión pública a la que todos pueden concurrir.

Mass production [mɑs pro-duc'-shʊn], *s.* Fabricación en serie o en gran escala.

Massy [mɑs'-i], *a.* Abultado, pesado, ponderoso, grueso, grande

Mast [mɑst], *s.* 1. Palo de una embarcación; mástil. *Lower* o *standing mast*, (Mar.) Palos principales. *Topmasts*, (Mar.) Masteleros. *Mainmast*, Palo mayor. *Foremast*, Palo de trinquete. *Mizzen-mast*, Palo de mesana. *Main-topmast*, Mastelero mayor o de gavia. *Main-top-gallant mast*, Mastelero de juanete mayor. *Fore-topmast*, Mastelero de proa. *Fore-top-gallant mast*, Mastelero de juanete de proa. *Mizzen-topmast*, Mastelero de sobremesana. *Mizzen-top-gallant mast*, Mastelero de velacho de sobremesana. *Pole-mast*, Palo de una pieza. *Made mast*, Palo compuesto. *Fished mast*, Palo reforzado. *Mast sprung*, Palo rendido. *To spend a mast*, (Mar.) Perder un palo. 2. Bellota, fabuco, el fruto del roble y de la haya; avellana; en este sentido no tiene plural.

Mast, *va.* 1. (Mar.) Arbolar un palo. 2. Cebar con bellotas, fabucos, etc., como a los cerdos.

Master [mɑs'-tɐr], *s.* 1. Amo. 2. Amo, dueño, señor, el poseedor de una cosa. 3. Maestro, en contraposición a discípulo o aprendiz. 4. Director, gobernador, jefe. 5. Término de respeto que se usa como nombre genérico para designar a los señoritos muy jóvenes, o delante de los apellidos de estos mismos señoritos, como *Master Laight*, El señorito Laight. 6. Hombre entendido y diestro en alguna cosa. *Dancing-master*, Maestro de baile. *Fencing-master*, Maestro de esgrima. *Master of the horse*, Caballerizo mayor. *Master of the ordnance*, Director general de artillería o ingenieros. *Master-warden of the mint*, El director de la casa de moneda. *Master of the rolls*, Archivero mayor o gran archivero, la segunda dignidad judicial en Inglaterra. *Master of arts*, Maestro en artes o doctor en filosofía. *Master of a merchant vessel*, (Mar.) Capitán, maestre, o patrón. *Past master*, (1) En muchas sociedades benéficas, el que ha tenido el oficio de director. (2) De aquí, el que es muy experto o hábil en alguna cosa. *Master-hand*, Mano maestra, maestría. *Master-key*, Llave maestra. *Master-stroke*, Golpe maestro, golpe diestro.—*a.* Magistral, superior, principal. *Master builder*, Constructor principal, jefe de construcción. *Master workman*, Maestro, capataz.

Master, *va.* 1. Vencer, sujetar, domar; gobernar, dominar. 2. Ejecutar alguna cosa con maestría o destreza; comprender en todos sus detalles.—*vn.* Ser superior en alguna cosa.

Masterdom [mɑs'-tɐr-dum], *s.* Dominio, mando.

Masterful [mɑs'-tɐr-ful], *a.* 1. Imperioso, ufano; violento. 2. Hábil; diestro, capaz.

Masterliness [mɑs'-tɐr-li-nes], *s.* Maestría, destreza.

Masterly [mɑs'-tɐr-li], *a.* 1. Magistral, que se ejecuta con maestría; digno de un maestro, hecho como por un maestro. 2. Ufano, imperioso, dominante.—*adv.* Magistralmente, con maestría.

Master of ceremonies [mɑs'-tɐr ev ser'-e-mō-nis], *s.* Maestro de ceremonias.

Masterpiece [mɑs'-tɐr-pîs], *s.* Obra o pieza maestra, obra magistral.

Mastership [mɑs'-tɐr-ship], *s.* 1. Dominio, poder, gobierno. 2. Maestría, destreza. 3. Superioridad, preeminencia, conocimiento. 4 Magisterio, rectoría de un colegio u hospicio; la dignidad de ser el superior de un establecimiento público. 5. Tratamiento irónico de respeto.

Masterwork [mɑs'-tɐr-wūrk], *s.* *V.* MASTERPIECE.

Masterwort [mɑs'-tɐr-wūrt], *s.* (Bot.) Imperatoria.

Mastery [mɑs'-tɐr-i], *s.* 1. Magisterio. 2. Dominio, poder, gobierno. 3. Preeminencia, superioridad. 4. Maestría, destreza, habilidad. 5. Adquisición de conocimientos, de superioridad o de poder.

Mastful [mɑst'-ful], *a.* Lo que abunda en bellotas, fabucos o castañas.

Masthead [mɑst'-hed], *s.* 1. (Mar.) Tope o remate del mástil. 2. Vigía, el marinero que vigila desde el mástil.—*va.* 1. Alzar al tope del mástil. 2. Enviar a un marinero al tope del mástil por castigo.

Mastic [mas'-tic], *s.* Almáciga o almástiga, resina que destila el lentisco; materia pegajosa o betún.

Masticate [mas'-ti-kêt], *va.* Masticar, mascar, desmenuzar con los dientes.

Mastication [mas-ti-kê'-shun], *s.* Masticación.

Masticator [mas'-ti-kê"-ter], *s.* 1. Mascador, el que masca. 2. Masticador, una máquina para preparar el caucho crudo o la gutapercha.

Masticatory [mas'-ti-ca-to-ri], *s.* Masticatorio, especie de medicamento.

Mastiff [mɑs'-tif], *s.* Mastín.

Mastitis [mas-tî'-tis], *s.* Mastitis, inflamación de la mama en las mujeres preñadas o parturientes.

Mastless [mɑst'-les], *a.* 1. Lo que no produce bellotas, fabucos o castañas. 2. (Mar.) Desarbolado, sin palo o árbol.

Mastodon [mas'-to-den], *s.* Mastodonte, elefante ya extinto, cuyos restos se han encontrado en estado fósil.

Mastoid [mas'-teid], *a.* Mastoideo, que tiene forma de teta o pezón; que se refiere a la apófisis mastoidea del hueso temporal.—*s.* La apófisis mastoidea.

Mastology [mas-tel'-o-ji], *s.* *V.* MAMMALOGY.

Masturbate [mas'-tur-bêt], *vn.* Practicar la masturbación.

Masturbation [mas-tur-bê'-shun], *s.* Masturbación, onanismo.

Mat [mat], *s.* 1. Estera, esterilla, petate, ruedo, felpudo hecho de esparto o de otra materia. *Sheep-skin mat*, Zalea. 2. (Mar.) Palleta o pallete, empalletado, andullo para impedir el roce. 3. Borde de cartón puesto alrededor de un cuadro, grabado, etc. *Chafed-mat*, (Mar.) Palleta afelpada.

Mat, *va.* Esterar, cubrir con esteras; tejer.

Mat, *va.* Producir (en los metales) una superficie mate, no pulida.—*a.* Mate, no pulido.—*s.* Herramienta para producir una superficie sin brillo. *V.* MATT.

Matador [mat'-a-dōr], *s.* Matador, espada (en las corridas de toros).

Matadore [mat-a-dōr'], *s.* Mate o matador, dase este nombre en ciertos juegos a las tres cartas mayores o de estuche.

Match [mach], *s.* 1. Mecha, pajuela, cualquiera cosa a que se pega fuego con facilidad. 2. (Art.) Mecha, cuerdamecha, cuerdacalada. 3. Cerilla, fósforo. *Match-box*, Fosforera. (Fr. ant. mesche < Gr. myxa.) †*Locofoco matches*, Pajuelas de fricción.

Match, *s.* 1. Compañero, pareja, una de las personas o cosas que forman un par. 2. Contrincante, el que compite con otro; igual, semejante. 3. Partido. 4. Juego, contienda, lucha de agilidad o fuerza. 5. Casamiento, alianza, boda. *Match at tennis*, Partido a la pelota. *He has met with his match*, Ha encontrado la horma de su zapato. *A rich match*, Alianza rica o ventajosa. *A running match*, Apuesta a la carrera. *An even match*, Una partida igual. *To be a bad match*, Ir mal juntos, no emparejar. (Anglosajón gemæcca, compañera.)

Match, *va.* 1. Igualar a, hacer conveniente, proporcionar. 2. Competir, entrar en competencia con otro. 3. Hermanar, aparear. *To match a pair of buckles*, Hermanar un par de hebillas. *To match horses*, Emparejar caballos. 4. Casar, dar en matrimonio.—*vn.* 1. Casar, contraer matrimonio. 2. Hermanarse, ser una cosa igual a otra. *His stockings do not match*, Sus medias no son parejas o iguales.

Matchable [mach'-a-bl], *a.* Adaptable, igual, correspondiente, proporcionado.

Matchbook [mach'-buk], *s.* Pequeño paquete de fósforos.

Matchless [mach'-les], *a.* Incomparable, sin igual, sin par.

Matchlessly [mach'-les-li], *adv.* Incomparablemente.

Matchlessness [mach'-les-nes], *s.* El estado, calidad o propiedad de lo que no tiene igual.

Matchlock [mach'-lec], *s.* Llave de los mosquetes antiguos que tenía una mecha.

Match-maker [mach'-mê-kẹr], *s.* 1. Casamentero. 2. Pajuelero, fabricante de pajuelas o fósforos.

Match-making [mach'-mêk-ing], *s.* 1. Acción de meterse en hacer bodas, 2. Fabricación de pajuelas o fósforos.

Mate [mêt], *s.* 1. Consorte, marido o mujer. 2. Compañero, compañera; camarada. 3. Macho o hembra entre los animales. 4. Comensal, el que come a la mesa con otro. 5. Mate, en el juego del ajedrez. 6. (Mar.) Contramaestre, oficial de rango inferior al del capitán. *Boatswain's mate*, (Mar.) Guardián del contramaestre. *Steward's mate*, (Mar.) Ayudante del despensero.

Mate, *va.* 1. Casar, desposar. 2. Igualar; aparear. 3. Competir; asombrar, asustar. 4. En el juego de ajedrez, dar jaque mate. 5. (Des.) Abrumar, confundir; vencer.

Mateless [mêt'-les], *a.* Solo, sin compañero, falto de consorte.

Material [ma-tî'-ri-al], *a.* 1. Material; corpóreo. 2. Importante, que es de consecuencia o entidad, principal, esencial, potente; serio, grave. *Nothing material*, Nada de interesante o de importancia. 3. Material, lo contrapuesto a formal. *Most material to*, De la mayor importancia para.—*s.* 1. Material, ingrediente. 2. El material de que se compone una obra. *Building materials*, Materiales de construcción.

Materialism [ma-tî'-ri-al-izm], *s.* Materialismo.

Materialist [ma-tî'-ri-al-ist], *s.* Materialista, el sectario del materialismo; el que admite como única substancia la materia, negando la espiritualidad.

Materiality [ma-tî-ri-al'-i-ti], *s.* Materialidad, corporeidad, existencia meramente material.

Materialize [ma-tî'-ri-al-aiz], *va.* 1. Hacer material alguna cosa; reducir a materia; considerar como materia. 2. Realizar, hacer visible y real. 3. Hacer común o vulgar.—*vn.* Realizarse, llegar a ser objeto de observación, tomar forma perceptible.

Materially [ma-tî'-ri-al-i], *adv.* 1. Materialmente. 2. Esencialmente, de una manera importante. 3. Desde el punto de vista físico.

Materialness [ma-tî'-ri-al-nes], *s.* Materialidad, importancia.

Maternal [ma-tẹr'-nal], *a.* Maternal, materno.

Maternity [ma-tẹr'-ni-ti], *s.* 1. Maternidad. 2. Hospital de parturientes: (Amer.) casa de maternidad.

Math [math], *s.* La siega del heno: úsase en composición, como *Aftermath*, Retoño del heno.

Mathematic, Mathematical [math-e-mat'-ic, al], *a.* Matemático.

Mathematically [math-e-mat'-ic-al-i], *adv.* Matemáticamente.

Mathematics [math-e-mat'-ics], *s. pl.* Matemática, matemáticas, ciencia que trata de la cantidad.

Mathematician [math-e-ma-tish'-an], *s.* Matemático.

Mathesis [ma-thî'-sis], *s.* (Ant.) Matemática, la doctrina o ciencia matemática.

Matin [mat'-in], *s.* Mañana.—*a.* Matutino.

Matinée [mat-i-nê'], *s.* Matiné, función de la tarde. *Matinée idol*, Actor que goza temporalmente de la adoración femenina.

Matins [mat'-inz], *s. pl.* Maitines.

Matrass [mat'-ras], *s.* (Quím.) Matraz, una especie de retorta.

Matriarch [mê'-tri-ark], *s.* Madre que gobierna a su familia.

Matrices [mat'-ri-sîz], *s. pl.* de MATRIX.

Matricidal [mat-ri-sai'-dal], *a.* Que se refiere al matricidio.

Matricide [mat'-ri-said], *s.* Matricidio; matricida.

Matricula [ma-tric'-yu-la], *s.* Matrícula, lista, catálogo, de un colegio o universidad.

Matriculate [ma-tric'-yu-lêt], *va.* y *vn.* Matricular, sentar en la matrícula; admitir o ser admitido en un colegio o en una universidad.

Matriculate, *s.* y *a.* Matriculado.

Matriculation [ma-tric-yu-lê'-shun], *s.* Matriculación, el acto de matricular en algún colegio o universidad.

Matrimonial [mat-ri-mō'-ni-al], *a.* Matrimonial, conyugal; marital.

Matrimonially [mat-ri-mō'-ni-al-i], *adv.* Matrimonialmente.

Matrimony [mat'-ri-mo-ni], *s.* 1. Matrimonio, el estado de los casados; himeneo. 2. Casamiento, nupcias. 3. Juego de naipes entre cinco o más personas.

Matrix [mê'-trix o mat'-rix], *s.* 1. (Anat.) Matriz, útero. 2. (Biol.) Substancia intercelular. 3. Matriz, molde. 4. Quijo, la piedra sólida en que se cría el metal en las minas.

Matron [mê'-tron], *sf.* 1. Matrona, mujer casada, madre de familia; mujer de edad y respetable. 2. Ama de llaves, o directora de un instituto o corporación.

Matronal [mê'-tren-al o mat'-ren-al], *a.* Matronal, lo perteneciente a la matrona.

Matronize [mê'-tren aiz], *va.* 1. Dar la apariencia o las cualidades de matrona. 2. Acompañar a una joven a las tertulias o a reuniones públicas.

Matron-like [mê'-tren-laic], *a.* Semejante a una matrona; grave, modesta.

Matronly [mê'-tren-li], *a.* Como matrona, seria, grave.

Matronymic [mat-ro-nim'-ic], *a.* Perteneciente al nombre de la madre o derivado de él.—*s.* Nombre así derivado.

Matt [mat], *a.* Mate, sin brillo, sin pulimento. *A matt surface*, Superficie mate, sin brillo.—*s.* Superficie no bruñida.

Matte [mat], *s.* Mate, producto metálico sin purificar que contiene azufre; se obtiene especialmente del cobre.

Matter [mat'-ẹr], *s.* 1. Materia, cuerpo. 2. Materia o material con que se hace alguna cosa. 3. Materia, asunto, objeto de que se habla o de que se trata. 4. Cosas, asuntos, negocios, quehacer, dependencia. 5. Cuestión, proposición sobre que se disputa o trata. 6. Importancia, consecuencia, entidad. 7. Cualquiera cosa o razón por la cual se siente alguna inquietud o cuidado. 8. Materia, pus. *What is the matter with you?* ¿Qué tiene Vd.? *It is no matter*, No importa. *What is the matter?* ¿De qué se trata? *What is the matter that you are so sad?* ¿Por qué está Vd. tan triste? *I make no matter of it*, No hago caso de ello: familiarmente, maldito el caso que hago de tal cosa. *A matter of seven miles*, Cosa de siete millas. *A matter of course*, Una cosa de cajón.—*a.* Natural, que ha de esperarse. *It is a matter of fact*, Es un hecho; cosa positiva, realidad. *A matter of fact man*, La persona que se atiene estrictamente a lo que resulta de los hechos. *He only believes what he sees*, (Vulg.) Santo Tomás, ver y creer. *Off-hand matters*, Cosas o asuntos de cada día.

Matter, *vn.* 1. Importar, convenir o hacer al caso alguna cosa: úsase solamente después de *it, this, that* o *what*. *It matters not*, No importa, y familiarmente, no vale la pena. *What matters it?* ¿Qué importa eso? *It matters much*, Importa mucho. 2. Supurar, formarse materia o pus en una úlcera o llaga.—*va.* Hacer caso.

Matterless [mat'-ẹr-les], *a.* Fútil, falto de interés, de importancia ó de objeto.

Matting [mat'-ing], *s.* 1. Esterado, tejido de juncos para entapizar. 2. *V.* MAT, 3ª acep. 3. Empalletado para impedir el roce.

Mattock [mat'-ec], *s.* Azadón de peto; zapapico, piqueta.

Mattress [mat'-res], *s.* 1. Colchón, cojín grande para descansar o dormir sobre él. 2. Empalletado, enlazado de ramaje, pértigas, etc., para proteger los diques y escolleras.

Maturation [mat-yu-rê'-shun], *s.* 1. Maduración, progreso hacia la madurez. 2. (Med.) Supuración.

Mature [ma-tiūr'], *a.* 1. Maduro, sazonado. 2. Maduro, prudente, juicioso, sesudo. *Upon a more mature deliberation*, Después de haberlo reflexionado detenidamente. 3. Acabado, elaborado. 4. (Com.) Vencido, pagadero. *To grow mature*, Madurarse.

Mature, *va.* 1. Madurar, disponer los medios para facilitar el logro de algún fin; adelantar hacia la conclusión. 2. Madurar, sazonar las frutas, etc.—*vn.* 1. Madurar o madurarse. 2. Ir madurando, tomando asiento o entrando en seso. 3. (Com.) Vencer, cumplirse un plazo.

Maturely [ma-tiūr'-li], *adv.* Maduramente; con anticipación, con mucha reflexión.

Matureness [ma-tiūr'-nes], *s.* Madurez, estado de perfección.

Maturity [ma-tiū' ri-ti], *s.* 1. Madurez; edad madura. 2. Estado de perfección; a veces, la pubertad. 3. (Com.) Vencimiento (de un pagaré).

Matutinal [ma-tiū'-ti-nal o mat-yu-tai'-nal], *a.* 1. Matutino, lo que pertenece á la mañana. 2. Matutinal, aplícase a las misas que se dicen a la aurora.

Maudlin [mēd'-lin], *a.* 1. Entontecido por la embriaguez. 2. Lloroso y calamocano, que tiene el vino triste.—*s. V.* YARROW.

†**Maugre** [mē'-gęr], *adv.* A pesar de, no obstante. (< Fr.)

Maukin [mē'-kin], *s.* Trapo; espantajo. *V.* MALKIN.

Maul [mēl], *va.* 1. Apalear, maltratar a golpes, aporrear; tratar rudamente, abusar. 2. Hender por medio de un mazo y cuñas.

Maul, *s.* 1. Mazo o martillo grande de madera. 2. (Mar.) Bandarria, mandarria.

Maul-stick [mēl'-stic], *s. V.* MAHL-STICK.

Maun [mēn], *vn.* (Esco.) Deber, ser menester. *V.* MUST.

Mauna [mē'-na]. (Esco.) No ser menester.

Maund [mānd o mēnd], *s.* (Prov. Ingl.) Canastillo, cesto pequeño, cuévano.

Maunder [mēnd'-ęr], *vn.* 1. Gruñir, murmurar, rezongar, refunfuñar. 2. (Des.) Mendigar.

Maunderer [mānd'-ęr-ęr], *s.* Gruñidor, murmurador.

Maundering [mānd'-ęr-ing], *s.* Queja, quejido, gruñido, murmuración.

Maundy [mēnd'-i], *s.* Mandato, la ceremonia eclesiástica de lavar los pies a doce personas. *Maundy Thursday*, Jueves santo, o jueves del mandato, la víspera del Viernes Santo.

Maurandia [mē-ran'-di-a], *s.* (Bot.) Nombre de un género de hierbas perennes de las escrofulariáceas; son trepadoras, indígenas de Méjico, Texas y Arizona, y tienen hermosas flores muy estimadas. (< Dr. Maurandy, botánico español.)

Mausolean [mē-so-lī'-an], *a.* Sepulcral, lo que pertenece al sepulcro o al mausoleo.

Mausoleum [mē-so-lī'-um], *s.* Mausoleo, sepulcro magnífico y suntuoso.

Mauve [mōv], *s.* Color purpúreo delicado o lila; substancia purpúrea de tinte. (< Fr.)

Maverick [mav'-e-ric], *s.* 1. Animal sin marca de hierro. 2. Becerro sin madre. 3. (fam.) Disidente.

Mavis [mē'-vis], *s.* (Orn.) Malvís, zorzal.

Maw [mē], *s.* 1. Buche o molleja de las aves. 2. Cuajar, la parte del animal que corresponde al ventrículo o estómago en el hombre. 3. Vejiga de aire en los peces.

Mawk [mēk], *s.* (Prov. Ingl.) 1. Gusano. *V.* MAGGOT. 2. Mujer desaliñada; también se llama *mawks*. *V.* SLATTERN.

Mawkish [mēk'-ish], *a.* Fastidioso, empalagoso, desagradable al paladar; insípido o asqueroso.

Mawkishness [mēk'-ish-nes], *s.* La calidad o propiedad de causar hastío o repugnancia; asquerosidad.

Mawky [mēk'-i], *a.* Gusaniento.

Maw-worm [mē'-wūrm], *s.* 1. Lombriz. 2. *V.* BOT.

Maxilla [max-il'-a], *s.* Hueso maxilar, uno de los huesos de la quijada, particularmente de la superior.

Maxillar [max'-il-ar], **Maxillary** [max'-il-ę-ri], *a.* Maxilar, perteneciente a las mejillas o quijadas.

Maxim [max'-im], *s.* 1. Máxima, sentencia, o dicho sentencioso, aforismo, regla. 2. Principio aceptado, teórico o práctico. 3. (Ant.) Axioma.

Maximum [max'-i-mum], *s.* Lo sumo, lo más alto, lo último a que puede subir alguna cosa.

May [mê], *vr. irr.* y *def.* (*pret.* MIGHT). 1. Tener licencia, libertad, facultad o permiso, tener el poder moral; ser lícito, permitido. *If it may be*, Si puede ser. *If I may say so*, Si me es permitido decirlo o si puedo decirlo. 2. Ser posible dadas ciertas circunstancias; poderse. *As much as may be*, Tanto como se pueda. *As soon as may be*, Lo mas pronto posible. *It may be*. Puede ser. 3. Suceder, sea lo que sea: úsase elípticamente. *Be the pain what it may*, Cualquiera que sea el dolor. 4. Denota deseo vivo, y se traduce por ojalá, Dios quiera, o se omite, y el verbo se pone en el modo optativo inglés, correspondiente al subjuntivo en castellano. *May I live long enough to see my country*, Ojalá que yo viva hasta que pueda ver mi patria. *May you live long and happy*, Viva Vd. largos y felices años. *May it please the court*, Dígnese el tribunal (o el consejo) atender a mi súplica o solicitud.

May [mé], *s.* 1. Mayo, el quinto mes del año. 2. Primavera de la vida. 3. (Des.) Virgen, doncella. 4. *V.* HAWTHORN. *May-apple*, Podofilo, la planta y su fruto. *V.* MANDRAKE, 2ª acep. *May-bloom*, (Bot.) Maya, espina blanca. *May-bug*, (Ent.) Especie de escarabajo. *May-lady*, *May-queen*, Maya, la joven que sus compañeras elijen para que presida la fiesta de mayo. *May-lily*, (Bot.) Lirio de los valles. *May-pole*, Mayo, el árbol cortado y adornado que se pone en los pueblos en algún lugar público para bailar y divertirse alrededor de él en el primer día de mayo. *May-weed*, (Bot.) Manzanilla loca.

May, *vn.* Coger flores la mañana del día primero de mayo.

Maya [mā'-ya], *a.* y *s.* Maya, Quiché, nombre de la lengua indígena del Yucatán y Guatemala y de la antigua civilización de estos países.

May-day [mê'-dê], *s.* El día primero de mayo. *May-duke*, Variedad de la cereza ordinaria (corrupción de Médoc).

May-flower [mê'-flau-ęr], *s.* (Bot.) 1. Maya; las flores que se hallan en mayo. 2. (E. U.) Planta rastrera primaveral; la Epigæa repens. *V. Arbutus, trailing.*

May-fly [mê'-flai], *s.* (Ent.) Mosca de mayo o de pescadores; mosca de un día, insecto efímero.

May-game [mê'-gêm], *s.* Juego, fiesta o diversión del día primero de mayo.

Maybe, **Mayhap** [mê'-bī], *adv.* Acaso, quizá, por ventura.

Mayhem [mê'-hem], *s.* (For.) Mutilación, la acción de privar con violencia a una persona de uno de los miembros que le son necesarios para su defensa, o de desfigurar el cuerpo de cualquier manera.

Maying [mê'-ing], *s.* El acto de celebrar la antigua festividad del primero de mayo con guirnaldas, flores, bailes, etc.

Mayonnaise [mê''-ęn-êz'], *s.* Mayonesa, salsa fría de yemas de huevo y aceite, batidos y sazonados a voluntad. (Fr.)

Mayor [mê'-er], *s.* Alcalde, corregidor, el magistrado principal de una ciudad; en Londres, Liverpool, Manchester y York se le llama *lord mayor*.

Mayoralty [mê'-ęr-al-ti], *s.* Corregimiento, el empleo y oficio del corregidor.

Mayoress [mê'-ęr-es], *sf.* Corregidora, la mujer del corregidor.

Mazarine [maz-a-rīn'], *s.* 1. Color azul subido. 2. Un modo particular de guisar aves. 3. Plato pequeño puesto dentro de otro mayor. *Mazarine blue*, Color azul subido; del nombre del cardenal Mazarino.

Mazda lamp [maz'-da lamp], *s.* Lámpara de tungsteno.

Maze [mêz], *s.* 1. Laberinto, lugar compuesto de varias calles o encrucijadas de difícil salida. 2. Laberinto, embolismo, enredo, duda, perplejidad, confusión. *To be in a maze*, Estar perplejo, dudoso, confuso o sorprendido, estar metido en un laberinto.

Maze, *va.* 1. Descarriar, extraviar, meter en un laberinto. 2. Asombrar, confundir, causar confusión. —*vn.* Serpentear de una manera irregular y confusa.

Mazer [mê'-zęr], *s.* Taza de arce u otra madera.

Maziness [mê'-zi-nes], *s.* Perplejidad, enredo.

Mazurka [ma-zūr'-ka], *s.* Mazurca, especie de polca, y su música.

Mazy [mêz'-i], *a.* Confuso, perplejo, asombrado, embrollado, enredado, confundido.

Me [mī], *pron.* Me, el caso oblicuo de *I*, Yo; mí, después de una preposición. *As for me*, En cuanto a mí. *For me*, Para mí, en mi sentir. *With me*, Conmigo. *Do me the favour*, Hágame Vd. el favor.

Mead [mīd], *s.* Aguamiel, licor fermentado compuesto de miel y agua, aromatizado con especias.

Mead (Poét.), **Meadow** [med'-o], *s.* Pradera, pradería, vega, prado; por lo común produce el heno. *Meadow-lark*, Alondra de los prados; pájaro cantor americano del género Sturnella. Sturnella magna.

Meadow-saffron [med'-o-saf'-run], *s.* (Bot.) Villorita, quitameriendas.

Meadow-sweet [med'-o-swīt], **Meadow-wort** [med'-o-wūrt], *s.* (Bot.) Ulmaria, barba de cabra.

Meadowy [med'-o-i], *a.* De pradera; parecido a un prado; lleno de prados.

Meager, Meagre [mí'-gẹr], *a.* 1. Magro, flaco, enjuto; insuficiente. 2. Pobre, hambriento, falto de fertilidad o de riqueza. 3. Cuaresmal, propio de la cuaresma. *Meager soup*, Sopa de viernes.

Meagerly, Meagrely [mí'-gẹr-li], *adv.* Pobremente, flacamente.

Meagerness, Meagreness [mí'-gẹr-nes], *s.* Flaqueza, falta de carnes; escasez.

Meal [mîl], *s.* 1. Comida, el sustento que se toma de una vez. 2. Harina, el grano comestible no muy molido.

Mealman [mîl'-man], *s.* Harinero, el que comercia en harina.

Mealy [mîl'-i], *a.* Harinoso, farináceo.

Mealy-mouthed [mîl'-i-maudhd], *a.* Pacato, tímido y modesto en apariencia, doble, falso, que engaña con apariencia de bondad y palabras blandas.

Mealy-mouthedness [mîl'-i-maudh-ed-nes], *s.* Melosidad, hipocresía en el hablar.

Mean [mîn], *a.* 1. Humilde, mediano; basto, inferior, pobre. 2. Bajo, vil, ruin, indigno, obscuro, despreciable, abatido. *A mean action*, Bajeza, bastardía, vileza, ruindad. *That was mean*, Fué una vileza. 3. Mezquino, sórdido; pobre. 4. De poco valor o eficacia. (< Anglosajón mæne, malvado.) *No mean foes*, No despreciables enemigos.

Mean, *a.* 1. Medio, del medio. 2. Intermedio, en cuanto al volumen, al grado, a la calidad o al tiempo. (< Fr. ant. meien < Lat. medianus.) *In the meantime, meanwhile*, Ínterin, entre tanto, mientras tanto. *Mean time*, (Astr.) Tiempo medio.

Mean, *s.* 1. Medio, lo que está entre los extremos; de aquí, mediocridad, medianidad, medianía. 2. Medio, modo, forma, instrumento, expediente, diligencia o acción conveniente para el logro de alguna cosa. 3. *pl.* Medios, instrumento; lo que sirve para hacer una cosa; se usa a menudo con el verbo en singular. 4. *pl.* Medios, caudal, rentas, recursos, riquezas. 5. Término medio de un silogismo. *By all means*, Positivamente, sin duda, sin falta. *By no means*, De ningún modo, de ninguna manera. *By fair means*, Por medios lícitos; sin gatuperio; a buenas, por buenos modos, por dulzura. *By foul means*, Por malos medios, por medios injustos, por la fuerza. *By this means*, Por este medio. *By some means*, De una manera u otra. *To live on one's means*, Vivir de sus rentas.

Mean, *vn.* (*pret.* y *pp.* MEANT). Hacer intención, hacer ánimo, pensar, proponerse o tener propósito de hacer alguna cosa. *I mean to go by daybreak*, Me propongo partir al romper el día. *I mean to go to-morrow*, Estoy en ir mañana.—*va.* 1. Significar, querer decir, dar a entender. 2. Intentar, pretender. *What do you mean by that?* ¿Qué quiere Vd. decir con eso? *What do you mean to do?* ¿Qué pretende Vd. hacer? *He is a little rough, but he means well*, Es un poco tosco, pero tiene buen corazón, o buenas intenciones. *What do you mean!* ¡Cómo se entiende! *What do you mean by taking it?* ¿Cómo se atreve Vd. a coger eso? *To mean what one says*, Pensar lo que se dice. *He did not mean to do it*, Lo hizo sin querer, sin pensar. *A well-meaning man*, Un hombre de buena fe o buenos sentimientos; sincero, cándido, bien intencionado.

Meander [mẹ-an'-dẹr], *s.* Laberinto, camino tortuoso y lleno de vueltas y revueltas.

Meander, *va.* Rodear, hacer una cosa tortuosa o intrincada.—*vn.* Serpentear, voltear, tornar.

Meandrian [mẹ-an'-dri-an], †**Meandry** [mî-an'-dri], *a.* Serpentino, tortuoso.

Meandrous [mẹ-an'-drus], *a.* (Poco us.) Tortuoso, serpentino.

Meaning [mîn'-ing], *s.* 1. Ánimo, intención, voluntad, designio. 2. Sentido, significado, acepción, significación de una palabra o sentencia. *Double meaning*, Ambigüedad, equívoco, sentido doble. (Vulg.) Retruécano. *There is no meaning in what he says*, Es cháchara todo lo que dice; no tiene el menor fundamento cuanto dice.

Meaningless [mîn'-ing-les], *a.* Vacío de sentido, sin objeto ni importancia.

Meaningly [mîn'-ing-li], *adv.* De una manera significativa, con intención.

Meanly [mîn'-li], *adv.* 1. Sin dignidad. *Meanly born*, Nacido de baja estofa. 2. Mediocremente. 3. Bajamente, vilmente. 4. Con desprecio; pobremente, miserablemente. *To think meanly of*, Despreciar, hacer poco caso de.

Meanness [mîn'-nes], *s.* 1. Bajeza, pobreza. 2. Bajeza, vileza, villanía, infamia, bastardía. 3. Tacañería, miseria, ruindad, roñería, mezquindad.

Meant [ment], *pret.* y *pp.* del verbo *To* MEAN.

Meantime, Meanwhile [mîn'-taim, mîn'-hwail], *adv.* Mientras tanto, entre tanto, en el intervalo.—*s.* Ínterin.

Mease [mîs], *s.* (Prov. Ingl.) La cantidad de quinientos. *A mease of herrings*, Quinientos arenques.

Measled [mî'-zld], **Measly** [mîz'-li], *a.* 1. Atacado del sarampión o que tiene sarampión. 2. Roñoso (dícese de los cerdos). 3. (Bajo) Despreciable, vil; que no debe tocarse.

Measles [mî'-zlz], *s.* 1. Sarampión, una fiebre eruptiva del cuerpo humano. 2. Roña de los cerdos y otros animales, enfermedad causada por la lombriz solitaria. 3. Cáncer, enfermedad de los árboles.

Measurable [mezh'-ur-a-bl], *a.* Mensurable; limitado y corto en cantidad.

Measurableness [mezh'-ur-a-bl-nes], *s.* Mensurabilidad.

Measurably [mezh'-ur-a-bli], *adv.* Mesuradamente.

Measure [mezh'-ur], *s.* 1. Medida. 2. Unidad de medida; tipo, modelo. *Dry measure*, Medida para áridos. *Liquid measure*, Medida para líquidos. 3. Medida, proporción, correspondencia que guarda una cosa con otra. 4. Medida, la cantidad de sílabas de los versos. 5. Compás, metro, cadencia. 6. Modo, grado, cantidad. 7. Moderación. 8. Medida, disposición, providencia; medios, expediente que se toma para conseguir algún fin. 9. Acto o procedimiento determinado; en especial, propuesta de ley. 10. (Mat.) Cantidad que se toma como unidad para expresar las relaciones con otras cantidades. 11. (Mús.) Porción de música entre dos barras de la pauta. 12. *pl.* (Geol.) Serie de capas relacionadas que tienen algún rasgo común entre sí. *To have hard measure*, Ser tratado con rigor. *In some measure*, De algún modo. *In a great measure*, En gran manera, en mucha parte. *Beyond measure, out of measure*, Con exceso. *Common measure*, Compás ordinario; lleva el signo 𝄴 o $\frac{4}{4}$. *To take measures*, Tomar las medidas necesarias.

Measure, *va.* 1. Medir. 2. Ajustar, proporcionar. 3. Medir, señalar, distribuir. 4. Formar juicio de la cantidad o extensión de una cosa. 5. Estimar, juzgar; valuar. 6. Atravesar midiendo.—*vn.* 1. Tomar la medida de alguna cosa. 2. Tener ciertas dimensiones. *Measure your desires by your fortune*, Proporcionad vuestros deseos a vuestra fortuna.

Measured [mezh'-urd], *pp.* y *a.* 1. Medido, calculado, determinado por un tipo o una regla. 2. Uniforme, lento, rítmico. 3. Limitado, restringido.

Measureless [mezh'-ur-les], *a.* Inmenso, inmensurable.

Measurement [mezh'-ur-mẹnt], *s.* Medida, la acción de medir. *Measurement-bill*, (Mar.) Certificación del porte de los buques.

Measurer [mezh'-ur-ẹr], *s.* Medidor.

Measuring [mezh'-ur-ing], *s.* Medición, medida, el acto de medir.—*pa.* of MEASURE. *Measuring-worm*, Cualquier oruga que se encoge y alarga alternativamente al andar; geómetra, oruga nociva.

Meat [mît], *s.* 1. Carne, la parte de los animales a propósito para comerse. 2. Vianda, la comida y sustento de los racionales. *Boiled meat*, Cocido. *Stewed meat*, Estofado. *Minced meat*, Picadillo. *Roast meat*, Asado. *Baked meat*, Carne asada al horno. *Fried meat*, Carne frita. *Broiled meat*, Carne asada en parrillas. *Cold meat*, Carne fiambre. *Hashed meat*, Guisado. *Preserved meats*, Viandas conservadas. *One man's meat is another man's poison*, (prov.) Lo que a uno cura a otro mata. *Meat-fly*, Mosca de carne; *V.* FLESH-FLY.

Meat ball [mît'-bōl], *s.* Pelota de carne molida, especie de albóndiga.

Meated [mît'-ed], *a.* Alimentado, comido, sustentado.

Meat market [mît mār'-ket], *s.* Carnicería.

Meatus [mẹ-ê'-tus], *s.* Meato, cada uno de ciertos orificios o conductos del cuerpo humano.

Meaty [mît'-i], *a.* Carnoso.

Meazling [mîz'-ling], *a.* Lo que cae o se destila a modo de llovizna. *V.* MIZZLING.

Mechanic [mẹ-can'-ic], *a.* 1. Mecánico, perteneciente a la ciencia mecánica, que está hecho o construido según las leyes y reglas de la mecánica. 2. Materialista, atomístico.

Mechanic, *s.* Mecánico, artesano.

Mechanical [mẹ-can'-ic-al], *a.* 1. Mecánico, que se refiere a las máquinas; producido por una máquina o por maquinaria. 2. Materialista. 3. Mecánico, que pertenece a los oficios y obras de los menestrales; de artesano. 4. Que tiene talento inventivo o para la construcción.

5. Maquinal, que obra por una fuerza mecánica, o sin reflexión; hecho por costumbre. *A mechanical motion*, Un movimiento maquinal.

Mechanically [mẹ-can'-ic-al-i], *adv.* Mecánicamente.

Mechanicalness [mẹ-can'-ic-al-nes], *s.* 1. Conformidad con las leyes de la mecánica. 2. Bajeza.

Mechanician [mec-a-nish'-an], *s.* Mecánico, maquinista; persona hábil en mecánica.

Mechanics [mẹ-can'-ics], *s.* Mecánica, la mecánica o la maquinaria.

Mechanism [mec'-an-izm], *s.* 1. Máquina. 2. Mecanismo. 3. Dispositivo. 4. (Fil.) Mecanicismo.

Mechanist [mec'-an-ist], *s.* Mecanista.

Mechanization [mec-a-ni-zé'-shun], *s.* Mecanización.

Mechanize [mec'-a-naiz], *va.* Mecanizar, hacer maquinal; convertir en máquina.

Mechlin [mec'-lin], *a.* Encaje o puntas de Malinas.

Mechoacan [mẹ-chō'-a-can], *s.* (Bot.) Mechoacán.

Meconic [mẹ-cen'-ic], *a.* Mecónico, obtenido de las adormideras.

Meconium [mẹ-cō'-ni-um], *s.* 1. Meconio, alhorre, el primer excremento que arrojan los niños recién nacidos. 2. (Des.) Meconio, opio.

Medal [med'-al], *s.* 1. Medalla. 2. Medalla o moneda antigua. *Medal without a title*, Medalla anepígrafa, la que no tiene título ni inscripción.

Medallic [mẹ-dal'-ic], *a.* Numismático, que pertenece a las medallas.

Medallion [mẹ-dal'-yun], *s.* 1. Medallón, medalla grande. 2. Medallón, caja pequeña y de forma comprimida, donde se colocan retratos, rizos u otros objetos. 3. (Arq.) Medallón, cierto relieve bajo de forma redonda u ovalada.

Medalist, Medallist [med'-al-ist], *s.* 1. Numismático, el inteligente en medallas o monedas antiguas; el colector de medallas; el que ha escrito un tratado sobre numismática. 2. Grabador de medallas. 3. El que ha obtenido una medalla como recompensa.

Meddle [med'-l], *vn.* 1. Meterse, entremeterse, ingerirse uno donde no le llaman; tocar o manosear una cosa sin permiso o sin derecho. 2. (Des.) Tener que hacer en alguna cosa.—*va.* (Des.) Mezclar o trabar una cosa con otra.

Meddler [med'-lẹr], *s.* Entremetido, intrigante.

Meddlesome [med'-l-sum], *a.* Entremetido, oficioso, intruso.

Meddlesomeness [med'-l-sum-nes], *s.* Entremetimiento.

Meddling [med'-ling], *s.* Interposición impertinente y oficiosa.

Media [mí'-di-a], *s.* 1. (Anat.) La túnica media de un vaso. 2. *pl.* de MEDIUM: medios.

Medial [mí'-di-al], *a.* Medio, del centro.

Median [mí'-di-an], *a.* Del medio, situado en el centro.

Mediastinum [mí-di-as-tai'-num], *s.* (Anat.) Mediastino, espacio comprendido entre las pleuras.

Mediate [mí'-di-ēt], *vn.* 1. Mediar, interponerse entre dos o más personas que contienden, procurando reconciliarlas. 2. Mediar, existir o estar una cosa en medio de otras.—*va.* 1. Procurar o facilitar por medio de la mediación. 2. Diligenciar, poner los medios o las diligencias.

Mediate, *a.* 1. Mediato, lo que en tiempo y lugar está en conexión con alguna cosa, mediando otra entre las dos. 2. Medio entre dos extremos. 3. Interpuesto.

Mediately [mí'-di-ēt-li], *adv.* Mediatamente.

Mediation [mí-di-é'-shun], *s.* Mediación, intercesión; interposición, intervención.

Mediator [mí'-di-é''-tẹr], *s.* Mediador, intercesor, medianero; tercero.

Mediatorial [mí-di-a-tō'-ri-al], **Mediatory** [mí'-di-a-to-ri], *a.* (Poco us.) Medianero.

Mediatorship [mí-di-é'-tẹr-ship], *s.* El oficio de mediador

Medic [med'-ic], *s.* (Bot.) Alfalfa, mielga. Medicago.

Medicable [med'-i-ca-bl], *a.* Medicable, no incurable.

Medical [med'-i-cal], *a.* 1. Médico, medical, que pertenece a la medicina; de medicina. 2. Medicinal, que tiene propiedades curativas. *Medical school*, Escuela de medicina. *Medical services*, Servicios médicos. *Medical transplant*, Injerto, trasplante de órganos en medicina.

Medically [med'-i-cal-i], *adv.* Médicamente.

Medicament [med'-i-ca-mẹnt], *s.* 1. Medicamento. 2. Agencia, tendencia o poder para sanar.

Medicamental [med-i-ca-ment'-al], *a.* Medicamentoso, sanador; que tiene propiedades curativas.

Medicamentally [med-i-ca-ment'-al-i], *adv.* Como medicamento o en calidad de medicina.

Medicaster [med'-i-cas''-tẹr], *s.* Medicastro, empírico, curandero, charlatán.

Medicate [med'-i-kēt], *va.* 1. Medicinar, tratar con medicamentos. 2. Hacer medicinal alguna cosa.

Medication [med-i-ké'-shun], *s.* 1. El acto de hacer alguna cosa medicinal. 2. El acto de medicinar, medicación.

Medicative [med'-i-kẹ-tiv], *a.* (Med.) Medicinal.

Medicinal [me-dis'-i-nal], *a.* 1. Medicinal, que tiene virtud curativa. 2. (Ant.) Médico, lo perteneciente a la medicina.

Medicinally [me-dis'-i-nal-i], *adv.* Médicamente, según el método y reglas de la medicina.

Medicine [med'-i-sin], *s.* 1. Medicina, medicamento, pócima, remedio. 2. Medicina, el arte o ciencia de conservar la salud y curar las enfermedades. *Medicine-chest*, Botiquín, caja para medicamentos; farmacia portátil. *Medicine-lodge*, Casilla o tienda cónica destinada a ciertas ceremonias místicas en un pueblo indio. *Medicine-man*, Entre los salvajes, exorcista, hechizador. *Patent medicines*, Remedios de patente, con privilegio.

Medicine ball, *s.* Pelota grande de cuero usada en los gimnasios.

Medicolegal [med'-i-co-lí'-gal], *a.* Médicolegal, que se refiere a la ciencia de la medicina en sus relaciones con los preceptos legales.

Medieval, Mediæval [mí-di-í'-val], *a.* De la edad media; relativo a o descriptivo de la edad media.

Medievalism [mí-di-í'-val-izm], *s.* El espíritu o los usos de la edad media.

Mediocre [mí'-di-o-kẹr], *a.* Mediano, mediocre; ordinario, vulgar, trivial.

Mediocrist [mí'-di-o-crist], *s.* El de mediano talento.

Mediocrity [mí-di-oc'-ri-ti], *s.* Mediocridad; moderación, templanza.

Meditate [med'-i-tēt], *va.* Meditar, idear, proyectar, premeditar, tramar, pensar.—*vn.* 1. Contemplar, meditar sobre una cosa. 2. Reflexionar, rumiar; proponerse, tener en vista una cosa.

Meditation [med-i-té'-shun] *s.* Meditación; discurso, reflexión.

Meditative [med'-i-ta-tiv], *a.* 1. Meditativo, contemplativo. 2. Que procede de la meditación, o que la expresa.

Mediterranean [med-i-ter-é'-nẹ-an], **Mediterraneous** [med-i-ter-é'-nẹ-us], *a.* Mediterráneo.

Medium [mí'-di-um], *s.* (*pl.* MEDIUMS o MEDIA). 1. Medio; expediente; lo que sirve de instrumento intermedio. 2. (Fís.) El éter al través del cual pasan la luz y el calor; también medio, cualquier substancia a través de la cual o en la cual puede moverse, vivir, o ser llevada alguna cosa. 3. (Pint.) Vehículo líquido, como el aceite. 4. Objeto o estado intermedio. 5. Medium, persona a propósito para que en ella se manifiesten los fenómenos del magnetismo, o para comunicar con los espíritus.—*a.* Mediano, intermedio; mediocre. *Medium-sized*, De grandor o talla medianos. *Circulating medium*, Moneda corriente. *At a medium*, Uno con otro.

Medlar [med'-lar], *s.* 1. (Bot.) Níspero, árbol. 2. Níspero, níspera o níspola, el fruto del níspero.

Medley [med'-li], *s.* Miscelánea, la mezcla, unión y entretejimiento de unas cosas con otras.—*a.* Mixto, mezclado, confuso. (Fam.) Mescolanza.

Medullar [mẹ-dul'-ar], **Medullary** [med'-ul-ẹ-ri], *a.* Medular, tocante o perteneciente a la medula o tuétano.

Medusa [mẹ-diū'-sa], *s.* 1. Medusa, hechicera fabulosa, una de las tres Gorgonas. 2. (Zool. *pl.* MEDUSÆ) Medusa, aguamar. *V.* JELLY-FISH.

Meed [míd], *s.* Premio, recompensa dada al mérito.

Meek [mík], *a.* 1. Apacible, mego, manso, tratable, halagüeño, dulce; que sufre pacientemente las injurias. 2. Humilde, sumiso; que no es orgulloso.

†**Meek**, †**Meeken** [mík'-n], *va.* Amansar, suavizar.

Meekly [mík'-li], *adv.* Mansamente, suavemente, modestamente.

Meekness [mík'-nes], *s.* Mansedumbre, suavidad; modestia; dulzura.

†**Meer**, *a.* y *s.* *V.* MERE.

Meerschaum [mír'-shēm o mēr'-shaum], *s.* 1. Espuma de mar, un hidrosilicato blando y ligero de magnesia. 2. Pipa de espuma de mar.

Meet [mít], *va.* (*pret.* y *pp.* MET). 1. Encontrar, hallar; llegar donde está alguno (que viene en dirección diferente). 2. Tropezar, hallar casualmente. 3. Tocar una cosa a otra. 4. Hacer frente, refutar, destruir con argumentos. *To meet expenses*, Hacer frente a los gastos. *To meet a charge*, Refutar, responder a una acusación. 5. Estar, hacer, o tener lugar en conformidad con. *That will meet my wishes*, Eso se conformará a mis deseos. 6. Satisfacer, saldar una cuenta. 7. Batirse, pelear con. *When Greek meets Greek*, Cuando un griego se bate con otro. 8. Verse, empezar a conocer, entrar en trato. *I met her at the seaside*, Hice conocimiento con ella a orillas del mar.—*vn.* 1. Encontrar, tropezar una persona con otra. 2. Encontrarse, hallarse y concurrir juntas en un mismo lugar dos o más personas, abocarse con alguno, tener una entrevista con él. 3. Encontrarse, oponerse, enemistarse; chocar, pelear, combatir. 4. Unirse, juntarse, congregarse. 5. Adelantarse un sujeto á medio camino para encontrar a otro que viene a buscarle. 6. Confluir. *To meet with*, Encontrar lo que se buscaba; hallar lo que no se buscaba; juntarse, unirse; encontrarse inesperadamente con algún mal; combatir, venir a las manos; obviar, evitar, huir, apartar o quitar del medio lo que puede ser contrario: (en este último sentido es latinismo). *To meet with one*, Desquitarse, corresponder, hacer otro tanto, pagar en la misma moneda. *To meet one full in the face*, Encararse con. *Till we meet again*, Hasta más ver.

Meet, *a.* Apto, idóneo, propio, a propósito, conveniente.

Meet, *s.* 1. Reunión de cazadores para una cacería. 2. Conjunto de personas que se reunen. 3. Cita, lugar de reunión.

Meeting [mît'-ing], *s.* 1. Junta, asamblea o congreso de varias personas. *Meeting of creditors*, Concurso de acreedores. *To call a meeting*, Llamar a junta o convocar una junta. 2. Reunión; conventículo, sesión. 3. Confluencia o concurrencia de dos ríos. 4. Encuentro, duelo. *Take measures to prevent their meeting*, Tome Vd. medidas para impedir que se encuentren, o que se batan.

Meeting-house [mît'-ing-haus], *s.* Capilla o iglesia de los noconformistas y particularmente de los cuáqueros.

Meetly [mît'-li], *adv.* Convenientemente.

Meetness [mît'-nes], *s.* Aptitud, propiedad, conveniencia.

Mega-, Megalo-. Formas de combinación, derivadas de la griega *megas*, grande.

Megacosm [meg'-a-cozm], *s.* Megacosmo, el mundo grande; el universo.

Megacycle [meg'-a-sai-cl], *s.* Megaciclo.

Megalith [meg'-a-lith], *s.* Monumento megalítico, piedra grande, de remota antigüedad. *Cf.* CROMLECH y DOLMEN.

Megalomania [meg-a-lo-mê'-nia], *s.* Megalomanía, delirio de grandeza.

Megaphone [meg'-a-fōn], *s.* Megáfono, instrumento que sirve para llevar la voz a larga distancia.

Megascope [meg'-a-scōp], *s.* Megascopio, una modificación del microscopio solar, que permite ver cuerpos de grandes dimensiones.

Megaton [meg'-a-ton], *s.* Megatonelada, megatón.

Megrim [mî'-grim], *s.* Hemicránea, especie de jaqueca.

Meikle, *a.* y *s.* *V.* MICKLE.

†Meiny [mî'-ni], *s.* Familia, tren, criados domésticos.

Meiocene, *a.* y *s.* *V.* MIOCENE.

Melancholic [mel''-an-col'-ic], *a.* Melancólico, abatido, que siente tristeza: hipocondríaco; triste, lúgubre, infeliz, desgraciado.—*s.* Melancólico, hipocondríaco.

Melancholically [mel-an-col'-i-cal-i], *adv.* De una manera melancólica.

Melancholiness [mel'-an-col-i-nes], *s.* Melancolía, hipocondría.

Melancholy [mel'-an-col-i], *s.* Melancolía, hipocondría, delirio; tristeza. —*a.* Melancólico, triste, hipocondríaco, tétrico.

Melange [mê-lānzh', mel'-ānj], *s.* Mezcla: es voz francesa. *V.* MEDLEY.

Melanosis [mel-a-nō'-sis], *s.* (Med.) Melanosis, cáncer negro.

Melanospermous [mel''-a-no-sper'-mus], *a.* Melanospermo, de frutos negros.

Melee [mê'-lê], *s.* Pelotera, revuelta.

Melic [mel'-ic], *a.* Mélico, lírico, propio para el canto: dícese de la poesía.

Meliceris [mel-i-sî'-ris], *s.* (Cir.) Melíceris, nombre de una especie de lupia o tumor enquistado.

Melilot [mel'-i-lot], *s.* (Bot.) Meliloto, trébol dulce.

Meliorate [mîl'-yo-rêt], *va.* Mejorar; hacer más soportable o menos penoso; adelantar; bonificar.—*vn.* Mejorarse.

Melioration [mîl-yo-rê'-shun], *s.* Mejoramiento, medra, mejora, adelanto.

Melissa [me-lis'-a], *s.* (Bot.) Melisa, abejera, toronjil; planta herbácea medicinal.

Melliferous [mel-lif'-er-us], *a.* Melífero, que produce miel.

Mellification [mel-i-fi-kê'-shun], *s.* (Poco us.) El acto o arte de melificar.

Mellifluence [me-lif'-lu-ens], *s.* Melifluidad, dulzura, suavidad y delicadeza.

Mellifluent [me-lif'-lu-ent], **Mellifluous** [me-lif'-lu-us], *a.* 1. Melífluo, que mana miel. 2. Melífluo, dulce y tierno en su expresión.

Mellow [mel'-ō], *a.* 1. Maduro, sazonado. 2. Meloso; tierno, blando, suave. 3. Suave, mantecoso; agradable a los sentidos, armonioso. 4. Blando, friable, poco duro, como ciertos terrenos. 5. Medio borracho, alegrado por la bebida.

Mellow, *va.* Sazonar, madurar, ablandar.—*vn.* Madurar, madurarse.

Mellowness [mel'-o-nes], *s.* 1. Madurez de los frutos. 2. Madurez de la edad. 3. Habla melosa, melosidad.

Mellowy [mel'-o-i], *a.* Blando, suave; untuoso.

Melocoton, Melacotoon [mel'-o-co-tūn], *s.* 1. Membrillo o membrillero. 2. Melocotón. *V.* PEACH.

Melodic [mel-od'-ic], *a.* Melódico, perteneciente a la melodía o que la contiene.

Melodious [me-lō'-di-us], *a.* Melodioso, dulce y suave al oído; musical.

Melodiously [me-lō'-di-us-li], *adv.* Melodiosamente.

Melodiousness [me-lō'-di-us-nes], *s.* Melodía; calidad de lo que es agradable al oído por una sucesión suave de sonidos.

Melodist [mel'-o-dist], *s.* 1. Melodista, compositor o cantor de melodías. 2. Colección de melodías.

Melodize [mel'-o-daiz], *va.* Hacer melodioso.—*vn.* Hacer melodía o melodías.

Melodrama [mel''-o-drā'-ma], **Melodrame** [mel'-o-dram], *s.* Melodrama, representación dramática mezclada con canciones.

Melodramatic [mel-o-dra-mat'-ic], *a.* Melodramático, propio del melodrama.

Melodramatist [mel-o-dram'-a-tist], *s.* Autor de melodramas.

Melody [mel'-o-di], *s.* 1. Melodía, cualidad del canto agradable. 2. Canción o poema armonioso, puesto en música. 3. Aire, la parte vocal principal. 4. Dulzura al hablar.

Melon [mel'-un] *s.* (Bot.) Melón, planta herbácea anual de la familia de las cucurbitáceas, y su fruto. *Water-melon*, Sandía o zandía, melón de agua. *Musk-melon*, Melón almizcleño. (Caracas) Patilla. *Melon-beetle*, Diabrótico, insecto coleóptero muy nocivo a las hojas del melón y de plantas semejantes.

Melrose [mel'-rōz], *s.* Miel de rosas.

Melt [melt], *va.* 1. Derretir, fundir, liquidar; disolver. 2. Ablandar, enternecer, mover con cariño, aplacar. 3. Consumir, gastar, disolver, evaporar.—*vn.* 1. Derretirse, liquidarse. 2. Ablandarse, moverse a compasión. 3. Llenarse de aflicción, amilanarse; estar abatido. *To melt into tears*, Deshacerse en lágrimas; llorar a lágrima viva. 4. Confundirse, mezclarse, unirse con otra cosa; disiparse.

Melt, *s.* *V.* MILT.

Melter [melt'-er], *s.* 1. Fundidor. 2. Crisol.

Melting [melt'-ing], *a.* Lo que se derrite o enternece; fundente.—*s.* Derretimiento, fundición, fusión; enternecimiento, cariño; el acto de ablandar o enternecer. *Melting-cone*, Cono fusorio, vasija de figura cónica, para recibir y precipitar los metales fundidos. *Melting-point*, Punto de fusión. *Melting-pot*, Crisol.

Meltingly [melt'-ing-li], *adv.* Tiernamente, derretidamente.

Melton [mel'-tun], *s.* Paño Melton, paño tupido de lana; úsase particularmente para sobretodos.

Member [mem'-ber], *s.* 1. Miembro, parte del cuerpo. 2. Miembro, cláusula o parte de un discurso; parte o elemento de un todo. 3. Miembro, individuo, de algún cuerpo o comunidad.

Membered [mem'-berd], *a.* 1. Membrudo, fortachón, fornido de miembros. 2. (Her.) Membrado, se dice de las piernas de las águilas y otros animales cuando son de diverso color que el cuerpo.

Membership [mem'-ber-ship], *s.* 1. Personal de socios. 2. Número o nómina de socios.

Membranaceous [mem-bra-nê'-shus], **Membranous** [mem'-bra-nus], *a.* Membranoso.

Membrane [mem'-brên], *s.* 1. Membrana. 2. Trozo de pergamino.

Membraniform [mem-brê'-ni-form], *a.* Membraniforme.

Memento [me-men'-tō], *s.* Recuerdo, memento; memoria que se da de alguna cosa.

Memoir [mem'-wer], *s.* 1. Memoria, relación, narrativa. 2. *pl.* Memorias, recuerdos de una persona publicados juntos, en general o con relación a una época particular. 3. Memorial, relación biográfica. (Fr.)

Memorabilia [mem-o-ra-bil'-i-a], *s. pl.* Cosas notables y dignas de recuerdo.

Memorable [mem'-o-ra-bl], *a.* Memorable, memorando, digno de memoria.

Memorably [mem'-o-ra-bli], *adv.* Memorablemente.

Memorandum [mem-o-ran'-dum], *s.* Memoria, nota, apuntes de una cosa para recuerdo y gobierno de alguno. *Memorandum-book,* Libro de memoria.

Memorative [mem'-o-ra-tiv], *a.* (Ant. y poco us.) Conmemorativo.

Memorial [me-mō'-ri-al], *a.* Conmemorador de una persona fallecida o de un suceso. *A memorial window,* Ventana conmemorativa en un templo u otro edificio, en recuerdo de una persona fallecida, o de un acontecimiento.—*s.* 1. Memoria; monumento, recuerdo. 2. Nota diplomática de carácter semioficial. 3. Memorial, petición, papel o escrito pidiendo alguna gracia o justicia. 4. (For.) Nota, apuntamiento que se archiva como protocolo.

Memorialist [me-mō'-ri-al-ist], *s.* Memorialista, el que escribe o presenta un memorial; pretendiente.

Memorialize [me-mō'-ri-al-aiz], *va.* 1. Presentar una petición, un memorial. 2. Conmemorar.

Memorize [mem'-o-raiz], *va.* 1. Aprender de memoria, confiar a la memoria. 2. Recordar, conservar memoria de.

Memory [mem'-o-ri], *s.* 1. Memoria. *To call to memory,* Traer a la memoria. *Weak memory,* Memoria de gallo o de grillo, mala memoria. 2. Memoria, fama, gloria, lo que liberta del olvido. 3. Memoria, recuerdo, reminiscencia. *To commit to memory,* Confiar a la memoria, aprender de memoria. *Of sound and disposing mind and memory,* (For.) En el goce pleno y cabal de sus facultades mentales; legalmente apto para testar.

Men, *s. pl.* de MAN.

Men-pleaser [men'-plīz-er], *s.* La persona que pone demasiado cuidado en agradar a otras.

Menace [men'-ēs], *va.* 1. Amenazar, intimidar con amenazas. 2. Mostrar o pronosticar algún mal.—*vn.* Hacerse amenazador.

Menace, Menacing [men'-ēs-ing], *s.* Amenaza; presagio o pronóstico de un mal venidero.

Menacer [men'-ēs-er], *s.* Amenazador.

Ménage [mē-nazh'], *s.* 1. Familia de una casa. 2. Manejo de una familia; economía doméstica. 3. (Des.) *V.* MENAGERIE. (Fr.)

Menagerie [men-aj' (o -azh') -er-i], *s.* Colección de animales salvajes; casa de fieras, de animales raros.

Mend [mend], *va.* 1. Recomponer, reparar, remendar. 2. Mejorar, reparar una cosa, darle nueva o mejor forma. 3. Corregir, enmendar, reformar las costumbres, hábitos, etc. 4. Adelantar, aprovechar, aumentar.—*vn.* 1. Corregirse, enmendarse, reformarse. 2. Restablecerse, curarse; mejorar de salud. *To mend one's pace,* Apresurar el paso. *To mend the pen,* Cortar la pluma con que se ha escrito ya.—*s.* El acto de curarse, de enmendarse.

Mendable [mend'-a-bl], *a.* Reparable, componible.

Mendacious [men-dē'-shus], *a.* Mentiroso, embustero, falso.

Mendacity [men-das'-i-ti], *s.* Falsedad, mentira; carácter falso y mentiroso.

Mender [mend'-er], *s.* Enmendador, reformador; reparador; remendón. *Mender of old clothes,* Sastre remendón, el que compone vestidos viejos.

Mendicancy [men'-di-can-si], *s.* Mendiguez, mendicidad.

Menhaden [men-hē'-dn], *s.* Pez marino parecido al sábalo; es del género Brevoortia y abunda en las costas del nordeste de los Estados Unidos. Se obtiene de él aceite y sirve para abono. (Nombre indio.) Llámase también *whitefish.*

Mendicant [men'-di-cant], *a.* Mendicante.—*s.* Mendicante, mendigo.

Mendicity [men-dis'-i-ti], *s.* Mendicidad, mendiguez.

Menial [mī'-ni-al], *a.* 1. Doméstico, de criado. 2. Servil, bajo.—*s.* Criado doméstico, lacayo; por lo general, término de desprecio.

Meningeal [me-nin'-je-al], *a.* Perteneciente a las meninges o situado cerca de ellas.

Meninges [me-nin'-jīz], *s. pl* de MENINX. Meninges, tres membranas que envuelven el cerebro y la medula espinal, llamadas duramáter, piamáter y aracnoides.

Meningitis [men-in-jai'-tis o gī'-tis], *s.* Meningitis, inflamación de las meninges.

Meninx [mī'-ninx], *s.* Meninge, membrana que envuelve el cerebro y la medula espinal; úsase por lo común en plural.

Meniscus [me-nis'-cus], *s.* 1. Lúnula. 2. Menisco, un vidrio o lente convexo por un lado y cóncavo por el otro. 3. La superficie de una columna líquida hecha convexa o cóncava por la capilaridad.

Menology [me-nol'-o-ji], *s.* Menologio, el martirologio de los griegos.

Menopause [men'-o-pōz], *s.* (Med.) Menopausa, cesación del menstruo en las mujeres.

Menow [men'-ō], *s.* *V.* MINNOW.

§**Mensal** [men'-sal], *a.* 1. Lo perteneciente a la mesa. 2. Mensual, de cada mes.

Mense [mens], *s.* (Esco. y prov. Ingl.) Decoro, buena crianza, decencia.

Menseful [mens'-ful], *a.* (Esco. y prov. Ingl.) Primoroso, gracioso, cortés, urbano.

Menses [men'-sīz], *s. pl.* Menstruo, reglas; flujo periódico de la matriz de las mujeres y de las hembras de ciertos animales.

Menstrual [men'-stru-al], *a.* Menstrual; mensual.

Menstruate [men'-stru-ēt], *vn.* Menstruar, tener la hembra la evacuación menstrual.

Menstruation [men-stru-ē'-shun], *s.* Menstruación.

Menstruous [men'-stru-us], *a.* 1. Menstruo, menstruoso, menstruosa. 2. (Bot.) Que dura un mes.

Menstruum [men'-stru-um], *s.* (*pl.* MENSTRUUMS o MENSTRUA). (Quím.) Menstruo, disolvente.

Mensurability [men-shur-a-bil'-i-ti], *s.* Mensurabilidad.

Mensurable [men'-shur-a-bl], *a.* Mensurable, que se puede medir.

Mensural [men'-shur-al], *a.* 1. Perteneciente a la medida. 2. Relativo a la primera forma de la música.

Mensuration [men-shur-ē'-shun], *s.* 1. Medición, acción de medir. 2. Medida; mensura, ramo de las matemáticas.

-ment. Sufijo de los substantivos verbales que denota el efecto, la condición, la acción o la agencia, equivalente al castellano -mento o -miento, y algunas veces a -ción. *Acknowledgment,* Reconocimiento. *Atonement,* Expiación. *Predicament,* Predicamento.

Mental [men'-tal], *a.* 1. Mental, intelectual. 2. Efectuado por la mente, en especial sin el auxilio de símbolos escritos.

Mentally [men'-tal-i], *adv.* Mentalmente; con el pensamiento.

Mentha [men'-tha], *s.* Menta, género de hierbas odoríferas, familia de las labiadas, que comprende la hierbabuena y la menta verde.

Menthol [men'-thōl], *s.* Mentol, compuesto blanco y cristalizable, de olor como el del aceite de hierbabuena; se usa contra la jaqueca, etc.

Mentholated [men-thōl-ēt'-ed], *a.* Que contiene mentol.

Mention [men'-shun], *s.* Mención, recuerdo, alusión.

Mention, *va.* Mencionar, hacer mención de; aludir, nombrar sin describir, hablar de.

Mentionable [men'-shun-a-bl], *a.* Mencionable, que se puede mencionar.

Mentor [men'-ter], *s.* Mentor, guía, consejero y amigo sabio, honrado y prudente.

Menu [me-nü'], *s.* Lista de los platos de una comida; por extensión, la comida misma.

Meow [me-au'], *s.* y *vn.* MEW.

Mephitic, Mephitical [me-fit'-ic, al], *a.* Mefítico, infecto, pestífero, pestilente, nocivo a la vida; se usa a menudo en sentido figurado.

Mephitis [me-fai'-tis o fī'-tis], *s.* Mefitis, vapor fétido, cualquier gas pestilente o destructivo; mofeta de una mina, etc.

Mercantile [mer'-can-til], *a.* Mercantil, de comercio.

Mercenariness [mer'-se-ne-ri-nes], *s.* Venalidad, calidad de ser una cosa vendible o expuesta a la venta; vicio de la persona que se deja sobornar con dádivas.

Mercenary [mer'-se-nē-ri], *a.* Mercenario, venal. *A mercenary man,* Hombre venal.—*s.* 1. Mercenario, el que trabaja por un estipendio; jornalero, el que trabaja a jornal o por un tanto. 2. Mercenario, interesado, el que obra sólo por interés.

Mercer [mer'-ser], *s.* Sedero, mercero, mercader de sedas, cintas, etc.

Mercerized [mer'-ser-aizd], *a.* Mercerizado.

Mercership [mer'-ser-ship], *s.* Sedería, mediería, el trato o comercio en sedas y artículos menores.

Mercery [mer'-ser-i], *s.* 1. Mercería, mercaderías y artículos en que tratan los merceros. 2. Sedería, medieria.

Merchandise [mer'-chan-daiz], *s.* Mercadería, mercancía; todo género vendible.

Merchandise, *vn.* Traficar, comerciar, negociar.

Merchant [mer'-chant], *a.* Mercante, mercantil; apto para el comercio o empleado en él.—*s.* Mercader, comerciante, negociante. *Merchant captain,* Capitán de un buque mercante. *Merchant service,* Marina mercante. *Merchant tailor,* Sastre mercader, sastre que vende y pone el paño de los trajes que hace.

Merchant-like [mer'-chant-laic], *a.* Mercantil, como negociante.

Merchantman [mer'-chant-man], *s.*

Barco o buque mercantil, embarcación de comercio o mercante.
Merciful [mẹr'-si-ful], *a.* Misericordioso, piadoso, benigno, clemente, humano.
Mercifully [mẹr'-si-ful-i], *adv.* Misericordiosamente, piadosamente.
Mercifulness [mẹr'-si-ful-nes], *s.* Misericordia, compasión, clemencia, piedad.
Merciless [mẹr'-si-les], *a.* Cruel, inhumano, desalmado; sin misericordia, sin clemencia.
Mercilessly [mẹr'-si-les-li], *adv.* Cruelmente, inhumanamente.
Mercilessness [mẹr'-si-les-nes], *s.* Crueldad, inhumanidad.
Mercurial [mẹr-kiū'-ri-al], *a.* 1. Mercurial, perteneciente al dios Mercurio; de aquí, vivo, activo, jovial; volátil. 2. Mercurial, relativo al azogue. 3. Lo que sirve de dirección en alguna cosa.—*s.* 1. (Des.) Hombre vivo, alegre, activo e inconstante. 2. (Med.) Preparación química de azogue.
Mercurialist [mẹr-kiū'-ri-al-ist], *s.* Persona voluble, voltaria, versátil, activa, alegre e inconstante.
Mercurialize [mẹr-kiū'-ri-al-aiz], *va.* 1. (Med.) Someter a un tratamiento mercurial; salivar. 2. (Foto.) Emplear azogue en el desarrollo de las pruebas negativas.—*vn.* Ser chistoso, festivo o inconstante.
Mercurification [mẹr-kiū-ri-fi-ké'-shun], *s.* (Poco us.) Mezcla de mercurio con otras cosas; la operación de extraer el mercurio de los minerales.
Mercurochrome [mẹr-kiū'-ro-krōm], *s.* (Med.) Mercurocromo.
Mercury [mẹr'-kiū-ri], *s.* 1. Mercurio, azogue, metal flúido. 2. Viveza, vivacidad, desparpajo, desembarazo. 3. Mercurio, el menor de los planetas principales, próximo al sol. 4. Gaceta o papel periódico. 5. Mensajero, gacetero; corredor de oreja. 6. (Bot.) Mercurial. 7. Mercurio, uno de los dioses del paganismo, patrono de los heraldos, de los mensajeros, de los mercaderes y de los ladrones. *Mercury's wand,* Caduceo.
Mercy [mẹr'-si], *s.* 1. Misericordia, clemencia, piedad; merced, remisión de una falta, gracia, perdón. 2. Arbitrio, discreción, poder, capricho, voluntad. *For mercy, for mercy's sake,* Por gracia, por Dios; ¡ten misericordia! *To cry mercy,* Pedir gracia, misericordia. *To show mercy,* Mostrar misericordia. *Sisters of Mercy,* Las monjas de la Merced, en la Iglesia católica, comunidad de religiosas que se dedican a obras de piedad.
Mercy-seat [mẹr'-si-sīt], *s.* Propiciatorio, lámina de oro que según la antigua ley se colocaba sobre el arca del Testamento.
†**Merd** [mẹrd], *s.* Estiércol, mierda.
Mere [mīr], *a.* Mero, puro, simple; solo, no más que (lo mencionado).—*s.* 1. (Raro en los E. U.) Lago, laguna grande. 2. (Esco.) El mar. 3. (Ingl.) Lindero, límite.
Merely [mīr'-li], *adv.* Solamente, meramente; simplemente; puramente.
Meretricious [mer-e-trish'-us], *a.* 1. Meretricio. 2. Subido, chillón, de mal gusto, artificiosamente atractivo.
Meretriciousness [mer-e-trish'-us-nes], *s.* Calidad o condición de meretricio o chillón; putería, putañería.
Merganser [mẹr-gan'-sẹr], *s.* (Orn.) Mergo, mergánsar, cuervo marino que tiene la parte superior del pico dentada en sus bordes.
Merge [mẹrj], *va.* Sumergir la identidad o la individualidad de.—*vn.* Estar sumergido, hundirse, perderse, absorberse.
Merger [mẹrj'-ẹr], *s.* Consolidación, fusión de empresas comerciales o industriales.
Meridian [me-rid'-i-an], *s.* 1. Mediodía. 2. Meridiano, círculo máximo que pasa por los polos del mundo, dividiendo la esfera en dos hemisferios; meridiana. 3. Cenit, auge, el punto más elevado de gloria o poder.—*a.* 1. Meridiano, que está al mediodía; que se refiere al meridiano geográfico. 2. Elevado a lo sumo.
Meridional [me-rid'-i-o-nal], *a.* 1. Meridional, situado en el meridiano, en lo más elevado. 2. Meridional, del mediodía, del sur.
Meridionality [me-rid-i-o-nal'-i-ti], *s.* Situación meridional.
Meridionally [me-rid'-i-o-nal-i], *adv.* Hacia el mediodía.
Meringue [me-rang'], *s.* Merengue, dulce. (Fr.)
Merino [me-rī'-no], *a.* Merino.—*s.* Paño merino. (Esp.)
Merit [mer'-it], *s.* 1. Mérito, virtud, excelencia. 2. Mérito, merecimiento, lo que hace nuestras obras dignas de premio o castigo. 3. Premio.
Merit, *va.* Merecer, ser digno de, tener derecho a, ya sea como premio o como castigo.
†**Meritable** [mer'-it-a-bl], **Meritorious** [mer-i-tō'-ri-us], *a.* Meritorio, digno de recompensa.
Merited [mer'-it-ed], *a.* Meritorio, merecido.
Meritoriously [mer-i-tō'-ri-us-li], *adv.* Meritoriamente.
Meritoriousness [mer-i-tō'-ri-us-nes], *s.* Merecimiento, mérito.
†**Meritory** [mer'-i-to-ri], *a.* Meritorio.
Merle [mẹrl], *s.* (Orn.) Merla, mirlo.
Merlin [mẹr'-lin], *s.* (Orn.) Esmerejón.
Merlon [mẹr'-lọn], *s.* (Fort.) Merlón, trozo de parapeto entre tronera y tronera.
Mermaid [mẹr'-mêd], *s.* Sirena, ser fabuloso con hermosas facciones y busto de mujer, terminado en cola de pez.
Merman [mẹr'-man], *s.* El macho de la sirena, ser fabuloso mitad hombre y mitad pez.
Merops [mī'-reps], *s.* Abejarruco, ave que persigue a las abejas.
Merovingian [mer-o-vin'-ji-an], *a.* Merovingio, perteneciente a la dinastía de los primeros reyes de Francia.
Merrily [mer'-i-li], *adv.* Alegremente, jovialmente.
Merrimake [mer'-i-mêk], *s.* Gaudeamus, concurso de algunas personas para comer, beber y divertirse; fiesta, regocijo.
Merrimake, *vn.* Alegrarse, divertirse.
Merriment [mer'-i-mẹnt], *s.* Alegría, júbilo, diversión; fiesta, regocijo.
Merriness [mer'-i-nes], *s.* (Poco us.) La disposición a alegrarse o regocijarse.
Merry [mer'-i], *a.* 1. Alegre, apacible. 2 Risueño, placentero, agradable, jovial, festivo, divertido. *To make merry,* Divertirse, recrearse. *To be a little merry,* Estar alegre por haber bebido con algún exceso. *To live a merry life,* Vivir alegremente. *Merry-Andrew,* Bufón, truhán, chocarrero. *Merry-go-round,* Tío vivo, caballitos, diversión consistente en figuras de caballos y otros animales de madera que giran al rededor de un eje y sirven de montura al público, y en especial a los niños. *Merry-making, merry-meeting,* Fiesta, reunión jovial, jarana. (Amer.) Holgorio, un gaudeamus. *Merry-thought,* Hueso de la pechuga de las aves.
Mersion [mẹr'-shun], *s.* Inmersión.
Mesentery [mes'-en-ter-i], *s.* (Anat.) Mesenterio, entresijo.
Meseraic [mes-e-rê'-ic], *a.* Meseraico o mesentérico.
Mesh [mesh], *s.* 1. Malla, la abertura que tiene la red entre nudo y nudo. 2. Obra de malla; randa, particularmente en plural. 3. Una cosa cualquiera que enreda o envuelve; trampa, lazo. 4. (Mec.) Engrane.
Mesh, *va.* Enredar, meter o coger en la red.
Meshy [mesh'-i], *a.* Reticular, hecho de malla como red.
Mesial [mes'-i-al o mī'-zi-al], *a.* Mediano, del medio, dirigido hacia el medio. *Mesial plane,* Plano mediano del cuerpo.
Meslin [mez'-lin], *s.* Tranquillón, la mezcla de granos cereales.
Mesmeric [mes-mer'-ic], *a.* Mesmeriano, relativo al mesmerismo.
Mesmerism [mes'-mẹr-izm], *s.* Mesmerismo, magnetismo animal, sugestión hipnótica.
Mesmerist [mes'-mẹr-ist], *s.* 1. Partidario del mesmerismo, mesmeriano. 2. Magnetizador.
Mesmerize [mes'-mer-aiz], *va.* 1. Influir o dirigir por el mesmerismo; practicar el hipnotismo. 2. Fascinar, hechizar.
Meso-. Forma de combinación que significa del medio.
Mesocolon [mes-o-cō'-lọn], *s.* (Anat.) Mesocolon.
Mesoderm [mes'-o-dẹrm], *s.* (Zool.) Mesodermo.
Mesologarithm [mes-o-log'-a-ridhm], *s.* Mesologaritmo, logaritmo de la tangente.
Meson [mê'-son], *s.* (Fís. y Quím.) Mesón.
Mesozoic [mes-o-zō'-ic], *a.* (Geol.) Mesozoico, de la edad media; secundario.
Mesquit [mes-kīt'], *s.* Mezquite, algarrobo, árbol de América.
Mess [mes], *s.* 1. Plato, la cantidad de vianda o manjar que se sirve de una vez en la mesa. 2. Rancho, reunión de varias personas que comen juntas. *Steward of the mess,* (Mar.) Ranchero. 3. Ración, porción.
Mess, *s.* (Fam.) Estado de desorden, desorden sucio.
Mess, *vn.* Comer en rancho o hacer rancho; comer a escote.—*va.* Dar de comer, proveer comidas para.
Mess, *va.* 1. Mezclar en confusión, desordenar. 2. Hacer sucio, ensuciar.—*vn.* Formar desorden sucio o mezcla.
Message [mes'-ẹj], *s.* 1. Mensaje, el recado que envía una persona a otra de palabra o por escrito; parte, anuncio. 2. Comunicación ofi-

cial del que ejerce el poder ejecutivo á una asamblea legislativa.

Messenger [mes'-en-jẹr], *s.* 1. Mensajero. 2. Portero, en los tribunales. 3. (Mar.) Aparejo para levar el ancla. *To clap a messenger on the cable,* (Mar.) Coser un aparejo al cable.

Mess hall, mess room [mes hel, mes rūm], *s.* Comedor para soldados, marineros, etc.

Messiah [me-saí'-a], *s.* Mesías, Cristo.

Messieurs [mesh'-yūrz], *s. pl.* Señores: es palabra de cortesía en el trato civil, y se usa como plural de *mister;* se escribe por lo común *Messrs.*, en abreviatura.

Messmate [mes'-mêt], *s.* Comensal, el que come con otro a una misma mesa.

Messuage [mes'-wẹj], *s.* Menaje, ajuar de casa.

Mestizo, Mestino [mes-tī'-zō], *s.* Mestizo; en América, persona de raza española e india.

Met, *pret.* y *pp.* del verbo MEET.

Metabola [me-tab'-o-la], *s.* (Med.) Mudanza de tiempo, aire o enfermedad.

Metabolic [met-a-bel'-ic], *a.* Metabólico, que se refiere al metabolismo.

Metabolism [mẹ-tab'-o-lizm], *s.* 1. (Biol.) Metabolismo, procedimiento de asimilación por el cual los alimentos inanimados se convierten en substancia viviente, al paso que por la descomposición de ciertos elementos vivos toman éstos, subdivididos, una forma más sencilla dentro de una celdilla u organismo. 2. (Ento.) Metabología, metamorfosis. 3. Cambio de un metro poético a otro.

Metacarpal [met-a-cār'-pal], *a.* Metacarpiano, que pertenece al metacarpo.

Metacarpus [met-a-cār'-pus], *s.* (Anat.) Metacarpo, parte de la mano comprendida entre el carpo y los dedos.

Metachronism [me-tac'-ro-nizm], *s.* Metacronismo, anacronismo en poner un hecho antes o después del tiempo en que sucedió.

Metage [mīt'-ẹj], *s.* Medida o el acto de medir el carbón de piedra.

Metagrammatism [met-a-gram'-a-tizm], *s.* El arte o la práctica de hacer anagramas.

Metal [met'-al], *s.* 1. Metal, cuerpo simple, por lo común duro, pesado, lustroso, maleable y dúctil, buen conductor del calórico y de la electricidad y que forma una base en combinación con el oxígeno. 2. Algo compuesto de uno o más elementos metálicos, o que se parece á ellos. (1) Liga, mezcla. (2) Piedra triturada que se emplea en la superficie de los caminos o para el terraplenaje. (3) Vidrio en fusión. 3. Substancia constitutiva, cualidad esencial. *Babbitt metal,* Metal blando y blanco resistente a la fricción. *Dutch metal,* Metal holandés, similor.

Metalepsis [met-a-lep'-sis], *s.* Metalepsis, figura retórica, conjunción de dos o más tropos en la misma palabra.

Metaleptically [met-a-lep'-ti-cal-i], *adv.* Por transposición.

Metalled [met'-ald], *a.* Macadamizado; terraplenado, afirmado (dícese de una vía férrea).

Metallic [me-tal'-ic], *a.* Metálico.

Metalliferous [met-a-lif'-ẹr-us], *a.* Metalífero.

Metalline [met'-al-in o ain], *a.* Metálico.

Metallist [met'-al-ist], *s.* 1. Metalario, el artífice que tiene conocimiento de los metales. 2. Partidario del uso de la moneda en metálico, en contraposición al papel moneda.

Metallize [met'-al-aiz], *va.* Metalizar, transformar en metal.

Metallography [met-a-leg'-ra-fi], *s.* Metalografía.

Metalloid [met'-al-eid], *a.* (Quím.) Metaloide, semejante a un metal.—*s.* Metaloide, cuerpo simple sin brillo metálico y mal conductor del calórico y de la electricidad, como el arsénico y el antimonio.

Metallurgic, Metallurgical [met-al-ūr'-jic, al], *a.* Metalúrgico.

Metallurgist [met'-al-ūr''-jist], *s.* Metalario, metalúrgico.

Metallurgy [met'-al-ūr-ji], *s.* Metalurgia, el arte de beneficiar los minerales y de extraer económicamente los metales que contienen.

Metalman [met'-al-man], *s.* El que trabaja los metales; calderero, hojalatero, estañero.

Metal shears [met'-al shīrz], *s. pl.* Cizalla.

Metameric [met-a-mer'-ic], *a.* 1. (Quím.) Metamérico, que presenta una variedad del isomerismo en que los compuestos no sólo tienen sus elementos componentes en igual proporción, sino también el mismo peso molecular. 2. (Zool.) Perteneciente a uno de la serie de segmentos homólogos que forman el cuerpo de un animal vertebrado o articulado.

Metamorphic [met-a-mōr'-fic], *a.* 1. Metamórfico, que produce el metamorfismo. 2. Metamórfico, que presenta metamorfismo o se refiere á él.

Metamorphism [met-a-mōr'-fizm], *s.* 1. (Geol.) Metamorfismo, transformación natural ocurrida en las rocas mediante una nueva cristalización de sus elementos constitutivos, con cambio químico o sin él. 2. Cualquier metamorfosis.

Metamorphize [met-a-mōr'-faiz], *va.* *V.* METAMORPHOSE.

Metamorphose [met-a-mōr'-fōz], *va.* 1. Metamorfosear, transformar, cambiar la forma de una cosa; hacerle asumir un carácter diferente. 2. (Geol.) Cambiar por medio del metamorfismo.

Metamorphosis [met-a-mōr'-fo-sis], *s.* 1. Metamorfosis o metamorfosi, transformación, cambio de forma o de estructura. 2. Acción química, causada por la presencia de una substancia particular, como de un fermento, y que resulta en la descomposición de un compuesto.

Metaphor [met'-a-fẹr], *s.* Metáfora, figura retórica.

Metaphoric, Metaphorical [met-a-fer'-ic, al], *a.* Metafórico.

Metaphorically [met-a-fer'-ic-al-i], *adv.* Metafóricamente.

Metaphorist [mẹ-taf'-o-rist], *s.* Metaforista.

Metaphrase [met'-a-frêz], *s.* Metafrasis, traducción literal.

Metaphysic, Metaphysical [met-a-fiz'-ic, al], *a.* 1. Metafísico. 2. Sobrenatural.

Metaphysically [met-a-fiz'-ic-al-i], *adv.* Metafísicamente.

Metaphysician [met-a-fi-zish'-an], *s.* Metafísico.

Metaphysics [met-a-fiz'-ics], *s.* Metafísica, la ciencia que trata de los primeros principios del conocimiento humano, de las ideas universales y de los seres espirituales; ontología.

Metaplasm [met'-a-plazm], *s.* (Gram.) Metaplasmo, cambio operado en una palabra por el aumento, la disminución o sustitución de una letra o sílaba.

Metastasis [mẹ-tas'-ta-sis], *s.* (Med.) Metástasis, mudanza del sitio de una enfermedad.

Metastasize [mẹ-tas'-ta-saiz], *vn.* Metasticizar, diseminarse por metastasis.

Metatarsal [met-a-tār'-sal], *a.* Metatársico, metatarsiano, perteneciente al metatarso.

Metatarsus [met-a-tār'-sus], *s.* (Anat.) Metatarso, parte del pie situada entre el tarso y los dedos.

Metathesis [mẹ-tath'-e-sis], *s.* (Ret.) Metátesis, transposición.

Mete [mīt], *va.* 1. Distribuir, conforme a medida; prorratear. 2. (Ant.) Medir.

Mete [mīt], *s.* 1. (Ant.) Límite, con fin. 2. Medida.

Metempsychosis [mẹ-temp-si-cō'-sis], *s.* Metempsícosis, transmigración de las almas de un cuerpo a otro.

Meteor [mī'-tẹ-ẹr], *s.* Meteoro, fenómeno repentino y luminoso, como una estrella o un cuerpo brillante que cruza por los aires; estrella errante. En sentido técnico significa cualquier fenómeno atmósferico.

Meteoric [mī-tẹ-er'-ic], *a.* 1. Meteórico; perteneciente a los meteoros, compuesto de meteoros. 2. Atmosférico, meteorológico. 3. Brillante temporalmente. *Meteoric iron,* Hierro meteórico. *V.* METEORITE. *Meteoric showers,* Lluvia de estrellas errantes que ocurre periódicamente, en particular en los meses de agosto y noviembre.

Meteorite, Meteorolite [mī'-tẹ-er-ait, mī-te-er'-o-lait], *s.* Aerolito, meteorito, masa pétrea o metálica que cae sobre la tierra desde las regiones planetarias, acompañada de fenómenos luminosos o de alguna detonación.

Meteoroid [mī'-tẹ-er-eid], *s.* Uno de los innumerables fragmentos de materia que se mueven en el espacio y que por su contacto con nuestra atmósfera forman los meteoros.

Meteorological [mī-tẹ-ẹr-el-ej'-ic-al], *a.* Meteorológico, que pertenece a la atmósfera o a la ciencia de la meteorología.

Meteorologist [mī-tẹ-ẹr-el'-o-jist], *s.* Meteorologista, versado en la meteorología.

Meteorology [mī-tẹ-er-el'-o-ji], *s.* Meteorología, ciencia que trata de los meteoros, es decir, de los fenómenos de la atmósfera con especial relación al clima y a la temperatura y estado del aire (tiempo).

Meteorous [mẹ-tī'-o-rus], *a.* Meteórico, lo que pertenece a los meteoros.

Meter [mī'-tẹr], *s.* 1. Medidor, el que mide. 2. Contador, instrumento para medir. *Gas-meter,* Contador de gas. *Water-meter,* Medidor mecánico del agua.

Meter, Metre [mī'-tẹr], *s.* 1. Metro, la medida del verso; el verso. 2. Metro, unidad de medida longitudinal del sistema métrico-decimal; palabra de origen francés. Equivale a la diez millonésima parte del arco del meridiano terrestre comprendido entre el polo y el ecuador.

Methane [meth'-ên], *s.* Gas incoloro (CH_4) formado por la descomposición de materias vegetales; es importante elemento del gas del alumbrado. Se llama también *marsh-gas*, gas de pantano.
Methinks [mẹ-thinḳs'], *v. impers.* Me parece, soy de parecer, creo, pienso.
Method [meth'-ud], *s.* 1. Método, el modo de obrar o proceder. 2. Orden, regla, regularidad. 3. Método, el orden que se sigue en las ciencias para hallar la verdad y enseñarla. 4. La clasificación de los cuerpos según sus cualidades comunes características. 5. Sistema de instrucción musical; libro para el estudio de un arte, una lengua, etc.; (Mús.) manera o estilo de ejecución; técnica.
Methodic, Methodical [meth-ed'-ic, al], *a.* Metódico, dispuesto y arreglado con método; que usa de orden y método.
Methodically [meth-ed'-ic-al-i], *adv.* Metódicamente, con método.
Methodism [meth'-o-dizm], *s.* Metodismo, la doctrina de la secta metodista.
Methodist [meth'-o-dist], *s.* 1. Metodista, la persona que es metódica o procede con arte y método. 2. Metodista, el médico que pertenecía a la secta del metodismo. 3. Metodista, los individuos de una secta religiosa llamada metodismo.
Methodistical [meth-o-dist'-i-cal], *a.* Metodístico.
Methodize [meth'-o-daiz], *va.* Metodizar, regularizar, arreglar metódicamente.
Methought, *pret.* del verbo METHINKS.
Methyl [meth'-il], *s.* (Quím.) Metilo, radical orgánico (CH_3), que existe sólo en combinación, como en el alcohol metílico (CH_3HO), etc.
Methylene [meth'-i-lîn], *s.* Metileno, carburo de hidrógeno, radical orgánico (CH_2) que se conoce solamente en combinación. *Methylene blue*, Material de tinte.
Metonymical [met-o-nim'-i-cal], *a.* Metonímico.
Metonymically [met-o-nim'-i-cal-i], *adv.* Metonímicamente, por metonimia.
Metonymy [mẹ-ten'-i-mi], *s.* Metonimia, figura que se comete tomando la causa por el efecto y el continente por el contenido.
Metope [met'-o-pi], *s.* (Arq.) Metopa, distancia entre los triglifos del friso en el orden dórico.
Metoposcopy [mi-to-pes'-co-pi], *s.* Metoposcopia, arte de adivinar el porvenir o las inclinaciones del hombre por las líneas del rostro.
Metre [mî'-tẹr], *s.* *V.* METER.
Metric, Metrical [met'-ri-cal], *a.* Métrico, que consta de versos; perteneciente al metro, a la medida.
Metrician [mẹ-trish'-an], **Metrist** [mi'-trist], *s.* Versificador, metrista.
Metromania [met-ro-mê'-ni-a], *s.* Metromanía, manía de hacer versos.
Metronome [met'-ro-nōm], *s.* Metrónomo, máquina a manera de reloj con péndulo cronométrico, para marcar el compás de la música.
Metropolis [mẹ-trep'-o-lis], *s.* Metrópoli, ciudad principal de algún país; a menudo es la capital.
Metropolitan [met-ro-pel'-i-tan], *a.* Metropolitano, perteneciente a la metrópoli o al arzobispo.—*s.* 1. Metropolitano, el arzobispo respecto de sus obispos sufragáneos. 2. Ciudadano de una metrópoli, en contraposición al colono.
Metropolitical [met-ro-po-lit'-ic-al], *a.* Metropolitano.
-metry [mẹ-tri]. Sufijo que denota la acción, la ciencia o el arte de medir. (< Gr.)
Mettle [met'-l], *s.* Materia de que se compone una cosa; en especial, disposición constitutiva, brío, bizarría, valor, coraje, firmeza; vivacidad, fuego. *To put one on* (o *to*) *his mettle*, Picar el amor propio de alguno, estimularle.
Mettled [met'-ld], **Mettlesome** [met'-l-sum], *a.* Brioso, vivo, fogoso, ardiente.
Mettlesomely [met'-l-sum-li], *adv.* Briosamente, vivamente.
Mettlesomeness [met'-l-sum-nes], *s.* Brío, fuego, vivacidad.
Mew [miū], *s.* 1. Jaula, encierro para las aves cuando mudan las plumas; cualquier cercado o corral. 2. *pl.* Establo, caballeriza. 3. Maullido, maúllo, maído, la voz natural del gato. 4. (Orn.) Gaviota, ave marina de la familia de los láridos. La rus canus.
Mew, *va.* 1. Enjaular, encerrar, encarcelar. 2. (Des.) Mudar las aves sus plumas.—*vn.* 1. Maullar o miar como el gato. 2. (Des.) Mudar o estar de muda los animales.
Mewing [miū'-ing], *s.* 1. Maullido, maído de los gatos. 2. (Des.) Muda, el acto de mudar las aves sus plumas.
Mewl [miūl], *vn.* Chillar, gritar o llorar como un niño.
Mews [miūz], *s. pl.* Las caballerizas reales de Londres; de aquí, cualquier caballeriza urbana.
Mexican [mex'-i-can], *a.* Mejicano, perteneciente a Méjico.—*s.* Natural o ciudadano de los Estados Unidos Mejicanos.
Mezereon [me-zî'-re-en], *s.* (Bot.) Mecereón, laurel hembra.
Mezzanine [mez'-a-nin], *s.* Mezanina, entresuelo.
Mezzo-rilievo [med'-zo-ri-lyê'-vō], *s.* Medio relieve.
Mezzotint, Mezzotinto [mez'-o-tint, med'-zo-tin'-to], *s.* Estampa de humo, media tinta.
Mi [mî], *s.* 1. Mi, la tercera nota de la escala música; se usa en el solfeo. 2. La nota E.
Miasm [mai'-azm], **Miasma** [mi-az'-ma], *s.* Miasma, exhalación morbífica de las materias animales o vegetales en estado de putrefacción; el virus de la malaria.
Miasmal [mi-az'-mal o mai-az'-mal], *a.* Abundante en miasmas.
Miasmatic [mai-az-mat'-ic], *a.* Miasmático, infecto, relativo a los miasmas o a la malaria, o producido por ellos. *V.* MALARIOUS.
Mica [mai'-ca], *s.* (Min.) Mica, mineral escamoso, lustroso, folicular, que se puede dividir en hojuelas muy delgadas. Las micas son silicatos de composición complicada, principalmente de alúmina con un álcali. *Mica-schist* [shist], Micasquisto, micacito, roca compuesta de mica con algún cuarzo.
Micaceous [mai-kê'-shus], *a.* Micáceo, que es de mica o pertenece a ella.
Mice [mais], *s. pl.* de MOUSE.
Michaelmas [mik'-el-mas], *s.* Día de San Miguel, fiesta que se celebra el veinte y nueve de septiembre.
Mickle [mic'-l], *a.* (Ant. o Esco.) Mucho, grande.
Microampere [mi-crō-am'-pîr], *s.* Microamperio.
Microbalance [mi-crō-bal'-ans], *s.* Microbalanza.
Microbe [mai'-crōb], *s.* Microbio.
Microbial [mi-crō'-bi-al], **Microbic** [mi-crō'-bic], *a.* Micróbico.
Microbicide [mi-crō'-bi-said], *s.* Microbicida.
Microbiology [mai-cro-bai-el'-o-ji], *s.* Microbiología.
Microbus [mai'-cro-bus], *s.* Microómnibus, microbús.
Microcircuit [mai'-cro-ser-kit], *s.* Microcircuito.
Micrococcus [mai-cro-cec'-us], *s.* Micrococo, microbio de forma esférica.
Microcosm [mai'-cro-cezm o mic'-ro-cezm], *s.* Microcosmo, el mundo en pequeño; llámase así el hombre.
Microfilm [mai'-cro-film], *s.* Microfilm, rollo de película fotográfica con reproducciones en tamaño muy reducido.
Micrography [mai-creg'-ra-fi], *s.* Micrografía, la descripción de los objetos tan pequeños que sólo se pueden distinguir con el microscopio.
Microgroove [mai'-cro-grūv], *s.* Microsurco, microestría.
Micrometer [mai-crem'-ẹ-tẹr], *s.* Micrómetro, instrumento que se aplica al telescopio y al microscopio para medir las dimensiones o ángulos pequeños.
Micrometric, Micrometrical [mai-cro-met'-ric, al], *a.* Micrométrico, relativo al micrómetro o hecho con él.
Micrometry [mai-crem'-e-tri], *s.* Micrometría, el arte de medir dimensiones pequeñas con el micrómetro.
Micron [mai'-cren], *s.* Micra, la millonésima parte de un metro.
Microorganism [mi-cro-er'-gan-izm], *s.* Microorganismo.
Microphone [mai'-cro-fōn], *s.* Micrófono.
Microphotograph [mi-cro-fō'-to-graf], **Microphotography** [mi-cro-fo-teg'-ra-fi], *s.* Microfotografía.
Microphysics [mi-cro-fiz'-ics], *s.* Microfísica.
Micropyle [mai'-cro-pail], *s.* Micrópilo.
Microscope [mai'-cro-scōp], *s.* Microscopio, instrumento dióptrico que sirve para hacer perceptible lo que no lo es a la simple vista.
Microscopic, Microscopical [mai-cro-scep'-ic, al], *a.* Microscópico, relativo al microscopio; hecho o como hecho con el microscopio; extremamente pequeño, que no se puede ver sino con el microscopio.
Microscopist [mai'-cro-scō''-pist o mi-cres'-co-pist], *s.* Microscopista, la persona versada en el uso del microscopio.
Microscopy [mai'-cro-sco-pi o mi-cres'-co-pi], *s.* Microscopia, microscópica, el arte de servirse del microscopio.
Microwave [mai'-cro-wêv], *s.* Microonda.
Micturition [mic-tiu-rish'-un], *s.* Micturición, micción, acción de orinar (frecuentemente).
Mid [mid], *a.* Medio: úsase en composición.—*prep.* (Poét.) Entre, en medio de. *V.* AMID. *Mid-age*, La edad media de la vida. *Mid-course*, Media carrera o medio camino. *Mid-heaven*, El medio del cielo, meridiano superior. *Mid-lent*, Media cuaresma. *Mid-week*, Que está en medio de la semana.
Mida [mai'-da], *s.* Mida, saltón o gu-

sanillo que se halla en la flor del haba.

Midday [mid'-dê], *s.* Mediodía.—*a.* Meridional, del mediodía.

Middle [mid'-l], *a.* Medio, intermedio. *Middle finger*, Dedo de en medio o dedo del corazón.—*s.* Medio, intermedio, centro. *About the middle of June*, A mediados de junio. *In the middle of the way*, A medio camino. *Middle class*, La clase media, burguesía. *Middle Kingdom*, El imperio chino. *Middle voice*, Voz media: se dice en griego de la clase de verbos que en las demás lenguas se llaman reflexivos. *Middle-aged*, De mediana edad. *Middle-sized*, De mediana estatura o tamaño.

Middle ear [mid'-l ir], *s.* Tímpano del oído.

Middleman [mid'-l-man], *s.* 1. (Com.) Agente de negocios; corredor. 2. Burgués, ciudadano de la clase media.

Middlemost [mid'-l-mōst], *a.* Colocado en el medio, lo más céntrico.

Middleweight [mid'-l-wêt], *s.* (Boxeo) Peso medio.

Middling [mid'-ling], *a.* 1. Mediano, mediocre, pasadero. 2. De salud pasadera, pero no buena; (fam.) no muy católico.—*s. pl.* Salvado.

Middy (blouse) [mid'-i blaus], *s.* Blusa marinera.

Midge [mij], *s.* 1. Mosquito, o más bien, una mosca pequeña que no pica y tiene larvas acuáticas. 2. Enano.

Midget [mij'-et], *s.* 1. Pequeña mosca. 2. Enano pequeño. 3. Niño activo o inquieto.

Midland [mid'-land], *a.* 1. Mediterráneo, rodeado de tierras. 2. Lo que está tierra adentro o en lo interior de un país.

Midmost [mid'-mōst], *a.* En el medio, del medio.

Midnight [mid'-nait], *s.* Media noche, las doce de la noche.—*a.* Lo que pasa o se hace a media noche.

Midriff [mid'-rif], *s.* Diafragma, músculo que separa la cavidad del pecho de la del vientre.

Midship [mid'-ship], *a.* Que está en medio del buque.—*s. pl.* Bao o cuaderna maestra. *Midship beam*, Bao maestro.

Midshipman [mid'-ship-man], *s.* (Mar.) Guardia marina.

Midst [midst], *s.* Medio, da parte central; (fig.) lo crudo, lo fuerte. *In the midst of winter*, En el rigor, en lo crudo del invierno.—*adv.* En medio.—*prep. V.* AMIDST.

Midstream [mid'-strim], *s.* El medio de una corriente.

Midsummer [mid'-sum-ẹr], *s.* Solsticio estival, la época del solsticio o el 21 de junio; el rigor del estío. *Midsummer day*, El día de San Juan, el 24 de junio.

Midway [mid'-wê], *s.* Medio camino, la mitad del camino.—*a.* Que está en el medio, a mitad del camino.—*adv.* En medio del camino, a medio camino.

Midwife [mid'-waif], *sf.* (*pl.* MIDWIVES [mid'-waivz]). Comadre, partera. *Man-midwife*, Comadrón, partero.—*va.* Partear.—*vn.* Hacer o ejercer el oficio de partera o comadrón.

Midwifery [mid'-waif-ri], *s.* 1. Obstetricia, el arte de partear. 2. El acto de producir o sacar a luz.

Midwinter [mid'-win-tẹr], *s.* Solsticio hiemal; lo recio del invierno.

Mien [mîn], *s.* Semblante, aire, porte.

Miff [mif], *s.* (Fam.) Disgusto, mal humor, descontento.—*va.* Desagradar, ofender ligeramente, enojar; úsase por lo común en pasiva. *To be a little miffed*, (Fam.) Enojarse o incomodarse un poco; amoscarse.

Might [mait], *s.* Poder, fuerza. *With all my might*, Con todas mis fuerzas. *With might and main*, Con todas sus fuerzas, a más no poder.

Might [mait], *pret.* de MAY. *He died that we might live*, Murió para que pudiéramos vivir. *If it might be*, Si eso pudiera ser. *There might be a hundred persons in the room*, Podía haber unas cien personas en la pieza.

Mightily [mait'-i-li], *adv.* Poderosamente.

Mightiness [mait'-i-nes], *s.* Poder, potencia, fuerza; grandeza.

Mighty [mait'-i], *a.* Fuerte, valiente, potente, poderoso, vigoroso; grande; violento; enorme; excelente; eficaz, importante. —*adv.* (Irón.) Extremamente, sumamente.

Mignonette [min-yo-net'], *s.* Reseda, clavellina, planta cultivada por su fragancia. Reseda odorata.

Migraine, migraine headache, [mai'-grên hed'-êk], *s.* Jaqueca.

Migrant [mai'-grant], *a.* Migratorio, de paso.—*s.* Planta o ave migratoria.

Migrate [mai'-grêt], *vn.* Emigrar, pasar de un país a otro, especialmente en grupos o familias.

Migration [mai-grê'-shun], *s.* Emigración, acción de pasar de un país a otro en grupos; cambio de morada, viaje periódico de ciertos animales, aves o insectos.

Migratory [mai'-gra-to-ri], *a.* Migratorio, que se muda de una parte a otra.

Mikado [mi-kā'-dō], *s.* Micado, nombre del emperador del Japón.

Milch [milch], *a.* Lactífera, lechera, que da leche. *Milch-cow*, Vaca de leche.

Mild [maild], *a.* 1. Moderado, indulgente, blando, dulce, apacible, suave, tierno, de buen genio. 2. Nuevo; dícese de las cervezas; suave, no fuerte. *Mild tobacco*, Tabaco suave.

Mildew [mil'-diū], *s.* Añublo, moho, pelusilla, borra; tizón, tizoncillo.

Mildew, *va.* y *vn.* Atizonarse el trigo o los otros granos.

Mildly [maild'-li], *adv.* Suavemente, dulcemente; con indulgencia.

Mildness [maild'-nes], *s.* Benignidad, clemencia, dulzura, blandura, bondad, indulgencia.

Mile [mail], *s.* Milla, medida de distancia que comprende mil pasos geométricos o 5,280 pies ingleses = 1,609.3 metros. *Geographical* o *nautical mile*, La sexagésima parte de un grado, o 1.852 metros.

Mileage [mail'-ệj], *s.* 1. Kilometraje, la longitud de alguna cosa en millas (o en kilómetros). 2. Derecho de peaje por milla. 3. Gastos de viaje proporcionados según el número de millas recorridas.

Milesian [mi-li'-shian], *a.* 1. Milesiano. 2. Irlandés, hibernés, hibérnico.

Mile-post [mail'-pōst], **Mile-stone** [mail'-stōn], *s.* Mijero, piedra millera, el poste que señala las millas en los caminos.

Miliary [mil'-i-ẹ-ri], *a.* Miliar, semejante a los granos de mijo; dícese de una fiebre eruptiva y de algunas glándulas.

Militancy [mil'-i-tan-si], *s.* Combate, guerra; se dice en contraposición a *industrialism.*

Militant [mil'-i-tant], *a.* 1. Militante, combatiente; v. g. *The Church militant*, La Iglesia militante. 2. De un temperamento belicoso o guerrero.

Militarism [mil'-i-ta-rizm], *s.* Militarismo, predominio del elemento militar en el gobierno del Estado; el sistema de mantener grandes ejércitos permanentes.

Militarization [mil-i-tar-i-zê'-shun], *s.* Militarización.

Militarize [mil'-i-tar-aiz], *va.* Militarizar.

Military [mil'-i-tẹ-ri], *a.* Militar, soldadesco, belicoso, guerrero. *A military man*, Un militar. *Military stores*, Municiones de guerra.—*s.* Soldadesca, el conjunto de los soldados; la gente de guerra, la milicia.

Military police, *s.* Policía militar.

Military staff, *s.* Estado mayor.

Militate [mil'-i-têt], *vn.* 1. Militar, haber o concurrir en cualquiera cosa alguna razón o circunstancia particular. 2. (Ant.) Combatir. *To militate against*, Obrar en oposición a, oponerse a.

Militia [mi-lish'-a], *s.* Milicia, el ejército o la guardia nacional, en oposición al ejército regular y permanente. *Militiaman*, Miliciano, el que forma parte de la milicia.

Milk [milk], *s.* 1. Leche. *Cow's milk*, Leche de vaca. *Ass's milk*, Leche de burra. 2. Leche, licor que se saca de algunas pepitas o semillas machacándolas; o el jugo blanco o lechoso de ciertas plantas. *Milk-abscess*, Absceso del pecho. *Milk-and-water*, (Fam.) Vacilante y débil; incierto. *Milk diet*, Régimen lácteo. *Milk-duct*, Conducto de leche, vaso lactífero. *Milk-fever*, Fiebre láctea. *Milk-food*, Lacticinio. *Milk-leg*, Inflamación de las extremidades inferiores que suelen sufrir las mujeres parturientes. *Milk-livered*, Cobarde, mezquino. *Milk-maid*, Lechera; mantequera. *Milk-man*, Lechero, el que vende leche. *Milk-pail*, Colodra. *Milk-pan*, Lechera, vasija en que se guarda la leche para hacer queso y manteca. *Milk-pottage*, Sopa de leche. *Milk-room*, Lechería, cuarto o casa donde se conserva la leche. *Milk-thistle*, (Bot.) Titímalo, cardo lechero o sílibo. Silybum Marianum. *Milk-tooth*, Diente incisivo. *Milk-vetch*, Astrágalo, regaliz silvestre. *Milk-warm*, Tibio, caliente como la leche que se acaba de ordeñar.

Milk, *va.* 1. Ordeñar, exprimir las tetas de la hembra para sacar leche. 2. (Fam.) Desaguar, apurar, agotar; extraer de.

Milker [milk'-ẹr], *s.* Ordeñador.

Milkiness [mil'-ki-nes], *s.* 1. Dulzura, suavidad. 2. Calidad o propiedad láctea.

Milk shake [milk' shêk], *s.* Batido de leche.

Milksop [milk'-sop], *s.* Marica, el hombre afeminado y de pocos bríos.

Milkweed [milk'-wîd], *s.* (Bot.) Asclepias, planta vivaz de América; llámase así por su jugo lechoso. Las semillas tienen filamentos sedosos, circunstancia que da origen a otro nombre, *silkweed.*

Milk-white [milk'-hwait], *a.* Blanco como la leche.

Milkwort [milk'-wŭrt], *s.* (Bot.) Cualquier planta del género polígala; nombre dado antiguamente porque se suponía que aumentaba la secreción de la leche en los animales.

Milky [milk'-i], *a.* 1. Lácteo, lactífero. 2. Lechoso. 3. Lacticinoso, lechal. 4. Blando, tierno, suave, dulce; tímido.

Milky Way [milk'-i-wê], *s.* (Astr.) Galaxia, vía láctea, vulgarmente Camino de Santiago.

Mill[1] [mil], *s.* 1. Molino. 2. Taller, fábrica, edificio provisto de maquinaria para fabricar o manufacturar. *Cotton mill*, Hilandería de algodón. 3. Máquina que funciona con movimiento de rotación, como la rueda de un lapidario. 4. (Vulg.) Lucha a puñetazos. *Water-mill*, Molino de agua, aceña. *Wind-mill*, Molino de viento. *Horse-mill*, Tahona. *Fulling* o *tuck mill*, Batán. *A forge-mill*, Molino de herrería o fragua. *Hand-mill*, Molino de mano, molinete o molinillo. *Paper-mill*, Molino de papel. *Rolling-mill*, Laminador. *Stamping-mill*, Molino de estampar. *Tan* o *bark-mill*, Molino de corteza de roble. *Pepper-mill*, Molinillo para moler la pimienta. *Coffee-mill*, Molinillo de café. *Copper* o *lead-mill*, Molino de cobre o plomo. *Sugar-mill*, Trapiche o ingenio de azúcar. *Sawing-mill*, Molino de aserrar. *Mill-board*, Cartón muy grueso que usan los encuadernadores de libros. *Mill-clack*, Taravilla, cítola. *Mill-course*, Canal o cañal de agua de un molino. *Mill-dam*, Esclusa o represa de molino; dique. *Mill-dust*, Harija. *Mill-hopper*, Tolva de molino. *Mill-horse*, Caballo de tahona. *Mill-hand*, Obrero u obrera en una fábrica. *Mill-race*, Canal o conducto de molino de agua. *Mill-work*, Maquinaria de molino; construcción de un molino. *To go through the mill*, Saber por completo una cosa.

Mill,[2] *s.* La milésima parte; en los Estados Unidos, la décima parte de un centavo.

Mill, *va.* 1. Moler, desmenuzar. 2. Batir el chocolate con el molinillo. 3. Acordonar, labrar el canto o cordoncillo de las monedas.

Millenarian [mil-e-nê'-ri-an], †**Millenist** [mil'-e-nist], *a.* Milenario, perteneciente al millar o al número mil.—*s.* Milenario, sectario que cree que el reino de Cristo después de su segunda venida durará mil años en la tierra.

Millenary [mil'-e-nę-ri], *s.* Milenario; el espacio de mil años.—*a.* Milenario. *V.* MILLENARIAN.

Millennial [mil-len'-i-al], *a.* Milenario, perteneciente a un milenario o a un período de mil años.

Millennium [mil-len'-i-um], *s.* 1. Mileño, el espacio de mil años. 2. Los mil años del reino de Jesucristo en la tierra, con relación al Apocalipsis xx, 1-5.

Milleped [mil'-e-ped], *s.* Ciempiés, cientopiés, escolopendra, miriápodo con numerosos segmentos y patas.

Millepore [mil'-e-pōr], *s.* Milépóro, género de políperos pétreos cuya superficie tiene una multitud de poros.

Miller [mil'-ęr], *s.* 1. Molinero. 2. Mariposa nocturna, generalmente blanquizca y de alas empolvadas como con harina. Llámase comúnmente *moth-miller*. *Miller's Thumb*, (Ict.) Cota.

Millerite [mil'-ęr-ait], *s.* Milerita, níquel sulfurado nativo (NiS) que cristaliza en el sistema hexagonal.

Millesimal [mi-les'-i-mal], *a.* Milésimo.

Millet [mil'-et], *s.* (Bot.) Mijo.

Milliard [mil'-iard], *s.* Mil millones; mil millones de francos. (Fr.)

Milligram, **Milligramme** [mil'-i-gram], *s.* Miligramo, milésima parte de un gramo.

Milliliter, **Millilitre** [mil'-i-li-tęr], *s.* Mililitro, milésima parte de un litro.

Millimeter, **Millimetre** [mil'-i-mi-tęr], *s.* Milímetro, milésima parte de un metro.

Milliner [mil'-i-nęr], *s.* Modista, mujer que confecciona y vende sombreros, gorros, etc., para señoras; en Inglaterra, la persona que vende o hace vestidos o adornos para las señoras.

Millinery [mil'-i-ner-i], *s.* 1. Los géneros que se emplean para hacer o adornar los sombreros, gorros, etc., de las señoras; cintas, lazos, flores artificiales, etc. 2. La ocupación o la tienda de una modista.

Milling [mil'-ing], *s.* 1. Molienda, acción de moler o machacar, de convertir el grano en harina. 2. Acción de acordonar las monedas, y el cordoncillo mismo.

Million [mil'-yun], *s.* 1. Millón, cuento, mil veces mil, un millar de millares. 2. Un número muy grande indeterminado.—*a.* Que consta de un millón.

Millionaire [mil''-yun-ār'], *s.* Millonario, la persona cuyas riquezas se valúan en un millón o más (de pesos, de pesetas, etc.).

Millioned [mil'-yund], *a.* Multiplicado por millones.

Millionth [mil'-yunth], *a.* Millonésimo, que completa un millón o es una parte de él.

Mill-pond [mil'-pond], *s.* Alcubilla, alberca de agua para mover un molino.

Millstone [mil'-stōn], *s.* Muela, piedra de molino; molar, piedra molar. *To see into* o *through a mill-stone*, Ver al través de una pared; tener mucha penetración.

Millwright [mil'-rait], *s.* Constructor de molinos.

Milreis [mil'-rīs o rê'-is], *s.* Milreis, moneda brasileña de plata que vale 2.48 francos; moneda de oro en Portugal por valor de 5.59 francos.

Milt [milt], *s.* 1. Bazo, parte del cuerpo que está en el hipocondrio izquierdo. 2. Lechecillas de los peces, la parte de los peces machos en que se contiene el semen.

Milt, *va.* Impregnar las huevas de los peces.

Milter [milt'-ęr], *s.* Pez macho. *Milter and spawner*, Pez macho y hembra.

Miltwaste [milt'-wêst], *s.* (Bot.) Doradilla.

Mime [maim], *s.* 1. Mimo, truhán, bufón, gracioso, pantomimo, farsante. 2. Pantomima, farsa; mimo, especie de farsa entre los antiguos.

Mime, *vn.* 1. Bufonearse. 2. Remedar, representar una pantomima.

Mimeograph [mim'-ę-o-graf], *s.* Mimeógrafo, aparato en que un papel fibroso delgado y cubierto de parafina sirve como plancha de estarcir para sacar copias de lo escrito a mano o a máquina.

Mimetical [mi-met'-i-cal], *a.* Imitativo, mímico.

Mimic [mim'-ic], *va.* 1. Remedar, imitar burlescamente. 2. Imitar exactamente, contrahacer. 3. (Biol.) Asumir la forma o el color de algo, por vía de protección.

Mimic, *s.* 1. Mimo, imitador, truhán, bufón. 2. Remedo servil o bajo.—*a.* Mímico, imitativo; chancero, burlesco.

Mimical [mim'-ic-al], *a.* Burlesco.

Mimically [mim'-ic-al-i], *adv.* Burlescamente, mímicamente.

Mimicry [mim'-ic-ri], *s.* 1. Bufonada, bufonería, remedo o imitación burlesca. 2. (Zool.) Parecido, semejanza imitativa de un animal a otro o a un objeto inanimado.

Mimosa [mi-mō'-sa o mai-mō'-sa], *s.* (Bot.) Mimosa, sensitiva.

Mimulus [mim'-yu-lus], *s.* (Bot.) Mímulo, género de plantas escrofulariáceas con hermosas flores de varios colores.

Minaret [min'-a-ret], *s.* (Arq.) Minarete, torre de las mezquitas mahometanas.

Minatory [min'-a-to-ri], *a.* Amenazante, lo que amenaza.

Mince [mins], *va.* 1. Desmenuzar; picar la carne. 2. Decir una cosa muy poco a poco y por partes. 3. Paliar, atenuar. 4. Afectar, hablar con afectación.—*vn.* 1. Andar a pasitos cortos, afectadamente. 2. Hablar con dengue o con melindre. —*s.* 1. *V. Mince-meat.* 2. Afectación en el andar o hablar. *Mince-meat*, (1) Carne picada, jigote. (2) Mezcla de carne, manzanas, grasa, frutas secas y especias picadas, para rellenar el pastel llamado *mince-pie* [pai].

Mincingly [mins'-ing-li], *adv.* A pedacitos; con afectación; ligeramente, superficialmente.

Mind [maind], *s.* 1. Mente, entendimiento. 2. Gusto, propensión, elección, inclinación, afición, afecto. 3. Voluntad, gana, designio, intención, resolución, deseo. 4. Pensamiento, opinión, parecer, dictamen. 5. Memoria. 6. Espíritu, ánimo. *Of one mind*, Unánimes. *With one mind*, Unánimemente. *I have made up my mind*, Estoy resuelto o decidido; he tomado un partido. *To call to mind*, Traer a la memoria. *Out of mind*, Olvidado. *Time out of mind*, Tiempo inmemorial. *It will not be out of my mind*, No lo podré olvidar. *To put in mind*, Acordar, recordar. *To speak one's mind*, Decir su parecer. *To be out of one's mind*, Haber perdido el juicio. *To be easy in one's mind*, Tener el espíritu tranquilo. *To have half a mind to*, Tener ligera inclinación, estar dispuesto a hacer una cosa. *Mind-reading*, Adivinación del pensamiento de otra persona, sin intervención de los sentidos y a menudo desde gran distancia.

Mind, *va.* 1. Notar, observar, considerar, atender, prestar atención. 2. Cuidar; vigilar sobre. 3. Obedecer. 4. Estar alerta, resguardarse contra. 5. (Fam.) Recordar, acordar, refrescar la memoria. *Mind your business*, Métase Vd. en lo que le importa; no se meta Vd. donde no le llaman. *Mind him*, Ten cuidado con él. *Never mind*, No haga

Vd. caso; no importa.—*vn.* 1. Inclinarse o tener inclinación a una cosa; estar dispuesto. 2. Ser obediente. 3. Acordarse. *To have a mind to*, Darle a uno la gana. (Fam.) Pedírselo el cuerpo. *To mind one's p's and q's*, Poner los puntos sobre las íes, tener mucho cuidado con lo que se hace o dice. *Not to mind a thing*, No hacer caso de una cosa.

Minded [maind'-ed], *a.* Inclinado, dispuesto, propenso. *High-minded*, De pensamientos elevados. *Evil-minded*, Mal intencionado. *Low-minded*, De bajos pensamientos.

Mindful [maind'-ful], *a.* Atento, cuidadoso, diligente, vigilante, el que tiene presente alguna cosa. *To be mindful*, Tener presente, no olvidar, acordarse.

Mindfully [maind'-ful-i], *adv.* Atentamente, cuidadosamente, con diligencia.

Mindfulness [maind'-ful-nes], *s.* Atención, cuidado.

Mindless [maind'-les], *a.* Descuidado, negligente; necio, insensato.

Mind reading [maind rid'-ing], *s.* Lectura del pensamiento.

Mine [main], *pron. pos.* Mío, mía, lo mío; (Ant.) mí. *This pen is mine*, Esta pluma es mía. *It is mine to search*, A mí me toca buscar. *Your faith and mine*, Su fe y la mía. *Mine eye*, (Ant.) Mi ojo.

Mine, *s.* (Minería) 1. Mina. *A copper mine*, Una mina de cobre. *Shaft of a mine*, Pozo de una mina. 2. (Mil.) Mina. *Mine field*, Campo minado. *Mine layer* (Mar.) Plantaminas. *Mine sweeper* (Mar.) Dragaminas.

Mine, *vn.* 1. Minar, cavar o hacer minas. 2. Zapar, arruinar, hacer algún daño por medios ocultos.—*va.* 1. Minar, obtener cavando; explotar una mina. 2. Zapar, destruir; (fig.) poco a poco, por medio de minas. 3. Dañar secretamente.

Miner [main'-ẹr], *s.* 1. Minador, el que hace minas en las fortificaciones. 2. Minero, el que trabaja en las minas para sacar los metales o minerales. (Mex.) Barretero. *Miner's pick*, Pico de hoja de salvia. *Corps of sappers and miners*, Cuerpo de zapadores-minadores.

Mineral [min'-ẹr-al], *a.* Mineral, inorgánico. *Mineral kingdom*, Reino mineral. *Mineral oil*, Aceite mineral. *Mineral water*, Agua mineral. —*s.* 1. Mineral. 2. Roca, fósil.

Mineralization [min''-ẹr-al-aiz-é'-shun], *s.* Mineralización.

Mineralize [min'-ẹr-al-aiz], *va.* Mineralizar, reducir un metal a forma de mineral.

Mineralizer [min-ẹr-al-aiz'-ẹr], *s.* Cuerpo simple que puede formar combinación con los metales.

Mineralogical, Mineralogic [min-ẹr-al-ej'-ic-al], *a.* Mineralógico, perteneciente a la mineralogía.

Mineralogist [min-ẹr-al'-o-jist], *s.* Mineralogista, el que está versado o es inteligente en el conocimiento de los minerales.

Mineralogize [min-ẹr-al'-o-jaiz], *va.* Estudiar y recoger minerales; hacer excursiones mineralógicas.

Mineralogy [min-ẹr-al'-o-ji], *s.* Mineralogía, la ciencia que trata de los minerales.

Minever [min'-e-vẹr], *s.* Forro de pieles blancas con manchas negras.

Mingle [miŋ'-gl], *va.* 1. Mezclar, unir, incorporar; juntar cosas diversas. 2. Confundir.—*vn.* Mezclarse, juntarse, unirse, formar una mezcla.

Mingle-mangle [miŋ'-gl-maŋ'-gl], *s.* Miscelánea, almodrote.

Mingledly [miŋ'-gld-li], *adv.* Confusamente.

Mingler [miŋ'-glẹr], *s.* Mezclador, el que mezcla.

Miniate [min'-i-ét], *a.* Del color de bermellón.—*va.* (Des.) Pintar con bermellón.

Miniature [min'-i-a-chur o tiūr], *a.* De tamaño mucho menor que el natural o normal; en miniatura.—*s.* 1. Miniatura, pintura en pequeño. 2. Dibujo en pequeño; cosa de tamaño reducido. 3. (Des.) Rúbrica.

Miniaturization [min-i-a-chur-i-zé'-shun], *s.* Miniaturización.

Minify [min'-i-fai], *va.* 1. Empequeñecer, disminuir. 2. Disminuir el valor de; despreciar, denigrar.

Minikin [min'-i-kin], *a.* (Ant.) Pequeño, menudo.—*s.* Cosa muy menuda o delgada; alfilerito.

Minim [min'-im], *s.* 1. Medida flúida usada en farmacia que equivale a 0.95 grano de agua; casi una gota. 2. (Mús.) Mínima, mitad de la semibreve o compasillo. 3. Enano, hombre pequeño. 4. Mínimo, religioso de la orden de los mínimos.

Minimal [min'-i-mal], *a.* Mínimo, lo menor.

Minimize [min'-i-maiz], *va.* Reducir al mínimo; menospreciar, no hacer caso alguno de.

Minimum [min'-i-mum], *s.* Lo mínimo, el último grado a que se puede reducir una cantidad.—*a.* Mínimo, lo menos posible. *Minimum wage*, Salario o jornal mínimo.

Mining [main'-ing], *s.* Minería, trabajo del minero, arte de explotar las minas.—*a.* De mina. *Mining-camp*, Minería, reunión temporal de los que explotan una mina. *Gold-mining*, Minería de oro.

Minion [min'-yun], *s.* 1. Privado, valido, favorito, el predilecto. 2. (Impr.) Miñona, glosilla, letra de siete puntos; (la de esta línea).

Minion-like [min'-yun-laic], **Minionly** [min'-yun-li], *adv.* Regaladamente, afectadamente.

Minish [min'-ish], *va.* Disminuir, minorar.

Minister [min'-is-tẹr], *s.* 1. Ministro, ejecutor, instrumento que sirve para ejecutar lo que otro le manda. 2. Ministro de estado o del despacho. 3. Sacerdote, párroco, cura. 4. Delegado, agente, substituto. 5. Ministro, el agente de una potencia extranjera.

Minister, *va.* y *vn.* 1. Dar, ministrar, administrar, surtir, proveer, socorrer, dar socorros. 2. Ministrar, servir o ejercitar algún oficio. 3. Oficiar, celebrar los oficios divinos. 4. Ministrar o administrar medicinas.

Ministerial [min-is-tí'-ri-al], *a.* Ministerial, perteneciente a los secretarios de estado o del despacho; subalterno, subordinado; eclesiástico, sacerdotal, parroquial. *The ministerial benches*, En Inglaterra, España y otros países los bancos del Parlamento, del Congreso de los Diputados, etc., donde se sientan los ministros de la corona y los partidarios del gobierno; de aquí, el gobierno mismo.

Ministerially [min-is-tí'-ri-al-i], *adv.* Ministerialmente.

Ministrant [min'-is-trant], *a.* Subordinado, subalterno.

Ministration [min-is-tré'-shun], *s.* 1. El acto de cumplir un servicio como ministro o subordinado; servicio, agencia, comisión. 2. Ministerio u oficio eclesiástico.

Ministress [min'-is-tres], *sf.* Ministra.

Ministry [min'-is-tri], *s.* 1. Ministerio, cargo, incumbencia, oficio, servicio. 2. Ministerio eclesiástico, el clero. 3. Ayuda, intervención. 4. Ministerio, el gobierno de un ministro de estado, y se usa también como voz colectiva para expresar el cuerpo de los ministros o secretarios del despacho.

Minium [min'-i-um], *s.* (Quím.) Minio, azarcón, óxido rojo de plomo.

Miniver [min'-i-vẹr], *s.* 1. Ardilla de Siberia y su piel. 2. Piel de abrigo blanca con motas negras.

Mink [miŋk], *s.* Visón, mamífero de los mustélidos, cuya piel es muy estimada. Putorius vison.

Minnesinger [min'-e-sing-ẹr], *s.* Poeta lírico de Alemania en la edad media. *Cf.* TROUBADOUR.

Minnow [min'-ō], *s.* Vario, un pez pequeño de río. Se le llama también, *minnie*. Phoxinus aphya.

Minor [mai'-nẹr], *a.* 1. Menor, más pequeño, menor de edad. 2. Secundario, inferior. 3. (Mús.) Menor, del tono cuya tercera es menor; medio tono más bajo.—*s.* 1. Menor o menor de edad. 2. Menor, la proposición segunda de un silogismo. 3. Franciscano, menor, el fraile de la orden de San Francisco. *V.* MINORITE. 4. Menor, tono cuya tercera es menor; se usa en las composiciones solemnes o fúnebres. La tercera menor consta de un tono y un semitono. *Minor key*, Tono menor.

Minorite [mai'-nẹr-ait], *s.* Menor, mínimo, fraile franciscano.

Minority [mi-ner'-i-ti], *s.* 1. Minoridad o menor edad. 2. Minoría, el menor número, los menos.

Minotaur [min'-o-tōr], *s.* Minotauro, monstruo fabuloso.

Minster [min'-stẹr], *s.* Monasterio; iglesia catedral.

Minstrel [min'-strel], *s.* 1. Ministril, músico ambulante que en la edad media componía versos y se acompañaba con el arpa; trovador. 2. Originalmente, persona que tenía por oficio tocar instrumentos músicos para recreo de su señor. 3. (E. U.) Miembro de una compañía de cómicos que hacen papeles de negros, cantan las canciones de esa raza y dicen chistes y cuchufletas. 4. (Poét.) Bardo, poeta lírico.

Minstrelsy [min'-strel-si], *s.* Música de instrumentos; orquesta o reunión de músicos que tocan instrumentos según las reglas del arte.

Mint [mint], *s.* 1. Casa de moneda. 2. Mina, tesoro; manantial, provisión abundante de cualquier cosa. *Master of the mint*, Director de la casa de moneda. 3. (Bot.) Menta, hierbabuena, sándalo; ejemplar de una de las varias hierbas aromáticas de la familia de las labiadas.

Mint, *va.* 1. Acuñar, batir, fabricar monedas. 2. Inventar, forjar, falsificar.

Mintage [mint'-ẹj], *s.* Moneda acuñada; braceaje, derechos de cuño.

Minter [mint'-ẹr], *s.* Acuñador; inventor.

Mint-master [mint'-mas-tẹr], *s.* 1. Su-

perintendente de una casa de moneda. 2. (Ant.) Inventor, fabricador.
Minuend [min'-yu-end], *s.* Minuendo, cantidad mayor de que ha de restarse otra.
Minuet [min'-yu-et], *s.* Minué, minuete, antiguo baile de origen francés, serio y garboso, de compás ternario.
Minus [mai'-nus], *a.* 1. Menos (una cantidad determinada); indicado por el signo — ; negativo. 2. Desprovisto de, sin, falto de; sin valor positivo. *A knife minus an edge,* Un cuchillo sin filo.
Minute [mi-niūt'], *a.* 1. Menudo, pequeño, diminuto. 2. Muy exacto, minucioso.
Minute [min'-it], *s.* 1. Minuto, la sexagésima parte de una hora o de un grado geográfico. 2. Momento, minuto, instante. 3. Minuta, nota, apuntamiento, un extracto sucinto de alguna cosa. *Minutes,* Minutas, actas de un cuerpo deliberante; memoria auténtica. *Minute-book,* Libro de minutas. *Minute-glass,* Ampolleta o reloj de arena que dura un minuto. *Minute-gun,* Disparos de cañón hechos de minuto en minuto. *Minute-hand,* Minutero. *Minute-man,* Soldado de la guardia nacional pronto para prestar servicio en el acto. *Minute-watch,* Reloj de minutero, el que señala los minutos.
Minute, *va.* Minutar, hacer la minuta de algún instrumento o contrato.
Minutely [mi-niūt'-li], *adv.* Por menor; a cada minuto.
Minutely [min'-it-li], *adv.* A intervalos de un minuto.
Minuteness [mi-niūt'-nes], *s.* Minucia, menudencia, cortedad, pequeñez.
Minutia [mi-niū'-shi-a, *pl.* i], *s.* (*pl.* MINUTIÆ). Minucia, particularidad pequeñísima; detalle minucioso; más usado en plural.
Minx [mincs], *s.* Moza atrevida y libre: antiguamente fué voz de cariño.
Miny [mai'-ni], *a.* Subterráneo, lo perteneciente a las minas o cavernas.
Miocene [mai'-o-sīn], *a.* (Geol.) Mioceno; dícese de la división media de las capas terciarias.
Miracle [mir'-a-cl], *s.* 1. Milagro, maravilla; prodigio. 2. (Teol.) Acontecimiento en el orden natural, pero fuera del orden establecido; obra divina, hecho sobrenatural. 3. Espectáculo teatral de la edad media en el que se representaban escenas de las vidas de los santos. *Miracle-monger,* El que finge que puede hacer milagros, impostor, embustero.
Miraculous [mi-rac'-yu-lus], *a.* 1. Sobrenatural, efectuado por agencia o poder divinos. 2. Milagroso, maravilloso.
Miraculously [mi-rac'-yu-lus-li], *adv.* Por milagro, sobrenaturalmente; milagrosamente.
Miraculousness [mi-rac'-yu-lus-nes], *s.* Lo maravilloso; lo extraordinario.
Mirage [mi-rāzh'], *s.* Espejismo o espejeo, por el cual los objetos distantes dan una imagen en lo alto de la atmósfera, y por lo regular invertida. Es frecuente en las llanuras de los países cálidos y en el mar. (Fr.)
Mire [mair], *s.* Cieno, lodo, fango, limo; lodazal, lugar lleno de cieno, cenagal.
Mire, *va.* Encenegar, enlodar.
Miriness [mair'-i-nes], *s.* Cualidad de fangoso o condición de estar cubierto de lodo.
Mirk, Mirky [mūrk'-i], *a.* *V.* MURKY.
Mirk [merk], *a.* (Esco.) Tenebroso, lóbrego.
Mirror [mir'-er], *s.* 1. Espejo (de vidrio azogado posteriormente o de metal pulimentado). 2. Ejemplar, modelo; lo que refleja o representa claramente.
Mirror, *va.* Reflejar, espejear.
Mirth [merth], *s.* Alegría, regocijo, gozo, júbilo, contento.
Mirthful [merth'-ful], *a.* Alegre, jovial, gozoso, contento.
Mirthfully [merth'-ful-i], *adv.* Alegremente, jovialmente.
Mirthless [merth'-les], *a.* Triste, melancólico.
Miry [mair'-i], *a.* Cenagoso, lodoso, que contiene cieno.
Mis- [mis]. Prefijo que indica culpa, sin razón; mal: también, partícula inseparable negativa o despreciativa.
Misacceptation [mis-ac-sep-tē'-shun], *s.* Mala inteligencia, el acto de entender alguna cosa al revés; de echar algo a mala parte.
Misadventure [mis-ad-ven'-chur], *s.* Desgracia, desventura, revés, infortunio.
Misalliance [mis-al-lai'-ans], *s.* Asociación, unión o alianza impropias o fuera del orden regular.
Misallied [mis-al-laid'], *a.* Lo que forma una unión o asociación impropia e irregular con otra cosa.
Misanthrope [mis'-an-thrōp] o **Misanthropist** [mis-an'-thro-pist], *s.* Misántropo, el que huye y aborrece el trato y compañía de los hombres.
Misanthropic, Misanthropical [mis-an-threp'-ic, al], *a.* Misantrópico, lo que pertenece a la misantropía.
Misanthropy [mis-an'-thro-pi], *s.* Misantropía, aborrecimiento del género humano o aversión al trato humano.
Misapplication [mis-ap-li-kē'-shun], *s.* Mala aplicación o mal uso de una cosa.
Misapply [mis-ap-plai'], *va.* Usar de alguna cosa impropiamente o hacer mal uso de ella.
Misapprehend [mis-ap-pre-hend'], *va.* Entender mal o no comprender alguna cosa como se debe.
Misapprehension [mis-ap-pre-hen'-shun], *s.* Error, equivocación, yerro, engaño, aprehensión o falso concepto formado de alguna cosa en la imaginación.
Misappropriate [mis-ap-prō'-pri-ēt], *va.* Invertir malamente, v. g. los fondos públicos; malversar.
Misbecome [mis-be-cum'], *vn.* Desconvenir, no convenir; no estar bien o no sentar una cosa; no sentar bien; ser poco conveniente. *Levity misbecomes his years,* La levedad no conviene a sus años. *That hat misbecomes her,* Ese sombrero no le está bien, no le sienta, le cae mal.
Misbecoming [mis-be-cum'-ing], *a.* Desproporcionado; indecoroso, impropio, indecente.
Misbecomingness [mis-be-cum'-ing-nes], *s.* Desproporción; impropiedad, indecencia.
Misbegot, Misbegotten [mis-be-got', n], *a.* Ilegítimo, nacido fuera de matrimonio, bastardo.
Misbehave [mis-be-hēv'], *va.* Obrar o proceder mal.—*vn.* Portarse mal, conducirse mal.
Misbehaved [mis-be-hēvd'], *a.* Descortés, malcriado, impolítico.
Misbehavior [mis-be-hēv'-yer], *s.* Mala conducta, mal modo de portarse, mal paso o mala acción.
Misbelief [mis-be-līf'], *s.* 1. Error, opinión falsa o equivocada. 2. Heterodoxia, incredulidad, irreligión
Misbelieve [mis-be-līv'], *vn.* Estar en error, tener opiniones falsas en cualquier asunto y principalmente en materias de religión.
Misbeliever [mis-be-līv'-er], *s.* Incrédulo, el que duda en materias de religión.
Misbelieving [mis-be-līv'-ing], *pa.* Heterodoxo; infiel.
Misbeseem [mis-be-sīm'], *vn.* Venir mal alguna cosa; no convenir una cosa, no ser decente o propia.
Misbode [mis-bōd'], *va.* Sugerir o predecir el mal venidero; ser de mal agüero.
Miscalculate [mis-cal'-kiu-lēt], *va.* Calcular mal.
Miscalculation [mis-cal-kiu-lē'-shun], *s.* Mal cálculo; cuenta errada.
Miscall [mis-cōl'], *va.* 1. Nombrar erradamente o dar un nombre impropio a. 2. Ultrajar, difamar.
Miscarriage [mis-car'-ij], *s.* 1. El éxito infeliz o desgraciado de alguna empresa; mala conducta o mal porte; falta. 2. Aborto, parto prematuro, malparto. 3. Extravío.
Miscarry [mis-car'-i], *vn.* 1. Frustrarse, malograrse alguna cosa, salir mal de un empeño. 2. Abortar, malparir. 3. Extraviarse.
Miscast [mis-cast'], *va.* Tomar mal la cuenta de alguna cosa, contar mal.
Miscegenation [mis-se-je-nē'-shun], *s.* Mezcla de razas, particularmente de las razas negra y blanca.
Miscellanea [mis-el-lē'-ne-a], *s. pl.* Miscelánea, en especial las misceláneas literarias.
Miscellaneous [mis-e-lē'-ne-us], *a.* Misceláneo, mixto, mezclado o compuesto de varios géneros; diverso.
Miscellany [mis'-el-ē-ni], **Miscellaneousness** [mis-e-lē'-ni-us-nes], *s.* 1. Colección de composiciones literarias sobre diversas materias. 2. Miscelánea.
Mischance [mis-chans'], *s.* Desgracia, desdicha, desventura, infortunio, desastre, fatalidad.
Mischarge [mis-chārj'], *va.* Cargar o poner en una cuenta lo que no debía ponerse.
Mischief [mis'-chif], *s.* 1. Mal, daño, perjuicio, pérdida, agravio; mala consecuencia, mala resulta. 2. Travesura, diablura. 3. La persona que molesta o veja. *To play the mischief,* Causar daño. *He did it from downright mischief,* Él lo hizo por pura maldad.
Mischief-maker [mis'-chif-mē-ker], *s.* Dañador, el que causa daño o perjuicio a otro.
Mischief-making [mis'-chif-mē-king], *a.* Que causa daño, dañino.
Mischievous [mis'-chi-vus], *a.* 1. Dañino, dañoso. perjudicial; perverso. 2. Malicioso, malévolo; enredador, travieso, juguetón.
Mischievously [mis'-chi-vus-li], *adv.* Perversamente, de una manera traviesa, juguetona; perjudicialmente, dañosamente.
Mischievousness [mis'-chi-vus-nes], *s.* Malicia, malignidad, maldad, perversidad; picardía, travesura; carácter juguetón; carácter pernicioso y dañino.

Mischna [mish'-na], *s.* *V.* MISHNA.
Miscibility [mis-i-bil'-i-ti], *s.* Cualidad de lo que se puede mezclar o incorporar con otra cosa.
Miscible [mis'-i-bl], *a.* Mezclable, incorporable.
Miscitation [mis-sai-tê'-shun], *s.* Cita falsa o errónea.
Miscite [mis-sait'], *va.* Citar falsa o equivocadamente.
Misclaim [mis-clêm'], *s.* Pretensión mal fundada o sin justicia.
Miscomputation [mis-com-piu-tê'-shun], *s.* Cómputo falso.
Misconceit [mis-con-sît'], **Misconception** [mis-con-sep'-shun], *s.* Concepto equivocado, idea falsa, error, equivocación, engaño; mala inteligencia.
Misconceive [mis-con-sîv'], *va.* y *vn.* 1. Formar concepto erróneo, juzgar mal. 2. Concebir una idea falsa.
Misconduct [mis-con'-duct], *s.* Mala conducta, mal manejo, mal porte.
Misconduct [mis-con-duct'], *va.* Desacertar, obrar sin acierto, conducirse o portarse mal en algún asunto.
Misconstruction [mis-con-struc'-shun], *s.* Mala construcción, interpretación siniestra de palabras o acciones; mal sentido.
Misconstrue [mis-con'-strū], *va.* Interpretar siniestramente, dar mal sentido o mal color a alguna acción o palabra.
Misconstruer [mis-con'-stru-ęr], *s.* El que interpreta siniestramente alguna cosa.
Miscount [mis-caunt'], *va.* Contar mal.—*vn.* Equivocarse en la cuenta.
Miscreancy [mis'-crę-an-si], *s.* Infidelidad, incredulidad, irreligión, adhesión a una religión falsa.
Miscreant [mis'-crę-ant], *s.* Descreído, infiel, mal creyente, incrédulo, impío; hombre malvado o perverso; hombre despreciable.
†**Miscreate, Miscreated** [mis-crę-êt', ed], *a.* Mal formado, contrahecho.
Miscue [mis-kiū'], *s.* En el juego de billar, jugada en falso o desacertada por haberse deslizado el taco.
Misdate [mis-dêt'], *va.* Fechar falsamente, o poner fecha equivocada a un escrito o documento.
Misdeed [mis-dîd'], *s.* Mala acción, mal hecho, crimen, delito, iniquidad; transgresión, violación o quebrantamiento de un deber.
Misdeem [mis-dîm'], *va.* Formar malos juicios; juzgar mal; tener mala opinión de alguno; equivocar.
Misdemean [mis-dę-mîn'], *vn.* Portarse o conducirse mal, tener mala conducta.
Misdemeanor [mis-dę-mîn'-ęr], *s.* 1. Mal proceder, mala conducta. 2. (For.) Delito, crimen de menor cuantía; transgresión de una ley no comprendida entre las que la jurisprudencia inglesa llama *felony.*
Misdirect [mis-di-rect'], *va.* Dirigir erradamente.
Misdirection [mis-di-rec'-shun], *s.* 1. Mala dirección; informe falso; acción de guiar por una vía equivocada. 2. Error que comete un juez en el resumen del juicio o proceso que hace para información de los miembros del jurado.
Misdisposition [mis-dis-po-zish'-un], *s.* (Poco us.) La inclinación al mal.
Misdo [mis-dū'], *va.* Errar, obrar mal a propósito, delinquir.—*vn.* Errar, cometer faltas y yerros.
Misdoer [mis-dū'-ęr], *s.* Malhechor, criminal.
Misdoing [mis-dū'-ing], *s.* Ofensa, yerro, falta, mala acción.
Misdoubt [mis-daut'], *va.* (Ant.) Recelar, temer, sospechar; dudar sin razón o sin fundamento.
Misdoubt, *s.* (Ant.) Recelo, duda, irresolución, perplejidad, vacilación.
Misemploy [mis-em-plei'], *va.* Abusar; emplear o dar a una cosa un destino que no le conviene.
Misemployment [mis-em-plei'-męnt], *s.* Abuso.
Miser [mai'-zęr], *s.* Tacaño, avariento, hombre sórdidamente interesado.
Miser, Mizer, *s.* Aparato tubular para abrir pozos; tiene una válvula y un tornillo de rosca para empujar la tierra hacia arriba.
Miserable [miz'-ęr-a-bl], *a.* 1. Miserable, desdichado, infeliz, pobre. 2. Sin valor; despreciable. 3. Digno de lástima. 4. (Ant. ó Esco.) *V.* MISERLY.
Miserableness [miz'-ęr-a-bl-nes], *s.* Miseria; desesperación.
Miserably [miz'-ęr-a-bli], *adv.* Miserablemente, mezquinamente.
Misery [miz'-ęr-i], *s.* 1. Miseria, infelicidad, desdicha. 2. Calamidad, infortunio, desventura. 3. Sufrimiento, padecimiento; (E. U. del Sur) dolor continuo.
Miserere [miz-ęr-î'-ri], *s.* 1. Miserere, el salmo penitencial que comienza con dicha palabra. 2. (Arq.) Repisa en algunas iglesias de la edad media.
Misericorde [miz''-ęr-i-cōrd'], *s.* Puñal pequeño de que se usó en la edad media para dar muerte a un caballero caído.
Misfashion [mis-fash'-un], *va.* Hacer alguna cosa al revés de lo que debería ser; ejecutar algo fuera de orden.
Misfeasance [mis-fîz'-ans], *s.* (For.) 1. La ejecución de un hecho legal de una manera ilegal, especialmente cuando media negligencia. 2. Infidencia.
Misfit [mis-fit], *va.* 1. Hacer que algo no siente bien; ajustar mal. 2. No sentar bien, no ser a propósito, ni propio para el caso.—*s.* Lo que no sienta bien.
Misform [mis-fōrm'], *va.* Desfigurar.
Misfortune [mis-fōr'-chūn o tiūn], *s.* 1. Desgracia, infortunio, desventura, desdicha. 2. Desastre, calamidad.
Misgive [mis-giv'], *va.* Llenar de dudas o recelos; hacer temer o dudar.—*vn.* 1. Ser receloso, tímido. 2. Faltar a. ***My heart misgives me,*** Me falta corazón.
Misgiving [mis-giv'-ing], *s.* Recelo, duda, presentimiento; desconfianza, temor.
Misgotten [mis-got'-n], *a.* Mal ganado, mal adquirido o adquirido injustamente.
Misgovern [mis-guv'-ęrn], *va.* Desgobernar, gobernar mal; administrar deslealmente.
Misgoverned [mis-guv'-ęrnd], *a.* 1. Mal gobernado, mal administrado. 2. Rudo, rústico, tosco, grosero.
Misgovernment [mis-guv'-ęrn-męnt], *s.* 1. Desgobierno, mala administración o mala dirección, particularmente de los negocios públicos. 2. Desbarato, mala conducta.
Misgraft [mis-grąft'], *va.* Ingerir o ingertar mal.
Misgrowth [mis-grōth'], *s.* Crecimiento anormal; desarrollo defectuoso.
Misguidance [mis-gaid'-ans], *s.* Dirección errada o falsa; extravío, error.
Misguide [mis-gaid'], *va.* 1. Descaminar, descarriar, extraviar. 2. Inducir en error; tratar mal.
Mishap [mis-hap'], *s.* Desgracia, desventura, calamidad, desastre.
Mishappen [mis-hap'-n], *vn.* Acontecer en mala hora alguna cosa; llegar fuera de tiempo.
Mishear [mis-hîr'], *va.* y *vn.* Oir mal, entender mal o imperfectamente.
Mishna [mish'-na], *s.* 1. Misna, la primera parte del Talmud, colección de tradiciones rabínicas. 2. Párrafo de esta colección.
Misinform [mis-in-fōrm'], *va.* y *vn.* 1. Informar o enterar mal, dar alguna información o informe falsa o erradamente. 2. Engañar u ofuscar a alguno dándole falsos informes o falsas noticias sobre alguna cosa.
Misinformation [mis-in-fęr-mê'-shun], *s.* Aviso erróneo, noticia falsa.
Misinformer, Misinformant [mis-in-fōrm'-ęr], *s.* El que engaña dando noticias o informes falsos.
Misinterpret [mis-in-tęr'-pret], *va.* Interpretar mal o siniestramente; entender mal, tomar en sentido erróneo.
Misinterpretation [mis-in-tęr-prę-tê'-shun], *s.* Mala o falsa interpretación; contrasentido.
Misinterpreter [mis-in-tęr'-pret-ęr], *s.* El que interpreta falsa o erradamente.
Misjoin [mis-join'], *va.* Unir mal o impropiamente una cosa a otra; adecuar, acomodar o ajustar mal unas cosas con otras.
Misjudge [mis-juj'], *vn.* Juzgar mal, formar conceptos erróneos. — *va.* Errar, juzgar mal.
Misjudgment [mis-juj'-męnt], *s.* Juicio o determinación injusta; opinión o parecer errado.
Mislay [mis-lê'], *va.* Colocar mal, extraviar, poner una cosa fuera de su lugar o en donde no debe estar. *To mislay papers,* Extraviar papeles.
Mislayer [mis-lê'-ęr], *s.* El que pone o deja alguna cosa fuera de su lugar.
Misle [miz'-l], *vn.* *V.* MIZZLE.
Mislead [mis-lîd'], *va.* Extraviar, descaminar, descarriar; alucinar, engañar, seducir; hacer ejecutar lo que no es justo ni bien hecho.
Misleader [mis-lîd'-ęr], *s.* Seductor, corruptor.
Mislen [miz'-len], *s.* Tranquillón, la mezcla de granos, como de trigo y avena.
Misletoe [mis'-l-tō], *s.* *V.* MISTLETOE.
Mislike [mis-laik'], *va.* (Poco us.) Desaprobar.—*vn.* (Des.) No gustar o no tener afición a alguna cosa.
Mismanage [mis-man'-ęj], *va.* Manejar o conducir mal alguna cosa.
Mismanagement [mis-man'-ęj-męnt], *s.* Mala conducta, desarreglo, despilfarro; mala administración.
Mismanager [mis-man'-a-jęr], *s.* Mal administrador, mal gerente; persona que dirige mal.
Mismatch [mis-mach'], *va.* Desigualar; deshermanar, desajustar.
Mismate [mis-mêt'], *va.* Aparear, juntar o casar de una manera poco acertada o conveniente.
Misname [mis-nêm'], *va.* Trasnombrar, dar un nombre equivocado o falso a alguna cosa.

Misnomer [mis-nō'-mẹr], *s.* Nombre aplicado sin razón, designación inaplicable; el acto de poner a una persona un nombre equivocado en un documento legal.

Misogamist [mis-eg'-a-mist], *s.* Misógamo, aborrecedor del estado del matrimonio.

Misogamy [mis-eg'-a-mi], *s.* Misogamia, aborrecimiento del matrimonio.

Misogynist [mis-ej'-i-nist], *s.* Misógino, aborrecedor de las mujeres.

Misogyny [mis-ej'-i-ni], *s.* Misoginia, aborrecimiento de las mujeres.

Misperception [mis-pẹr-sep'-shun], *s.* Percepción errónea.

Mispickel [mis-pik'-ẹl], *s.* (Min.) Mispiquelio, hierro sulfurado (o cobaltífero) mezclado con arsénico (Fe AsS).

Misplace [mis-plês'], *va.* Traspapelar, extraviar, colocar mal, poner algo fuera de su lugar.

Misplacement [mis-plês'-mẹnt], *s.* Extravío.

Mispoint [mis-peint'], *va.* Puntuar mal algún escrito.

Misprint [mis-print'], *va.* Imprimir mal, cometer erratas en la impresión.

Misprint, *s.* Errata de un libro.

†**Misprise, Misprize** [mis-praiz'], *va.* 1. Errar, equivocar. 2. Menospreciar, no hacer caso.

Misprision [mis-prizh'-un], *s.* 1. La ocultación de un crimen o delito, particularmente traición o felonía. 2. (Ant.) Idea falsa, interpretación errónea; error. *Misprision of felony*, El acto de dejar escapar a un preso acusado de felonía, antes de ser juzgado.

Mispronounce [mis-pro-nauns'], *vn.* Pronunciar mal, hablar sin exactitud.—*va.* Pronunciar impropiamente.

Misproportion [mis-pro-pōr'-shun], *va.* Desproporcionar, proporcionar mal una cosa con otra.

Misquotation [mis-cwo-té'-shun], *s.* Cita falsa o equivocada.

Misquote [mis-cwōt'], *va.* Citar en falso o equivocadamente.

Misrate [mis-rêt'], *va.* Valuar erradamente, dar una estimación o valor mayor o menor del que en realidad tiene una cosa.

Misrelate [mis-rẹ-lêt'], *va.* Referir o relatar inexactamente una cosa.

Misremember [mis-rẹ-mem'-bẹr], *va.* Acordarse mal de algo.

Misreport [mis-rẹ-pōrt'], *va.* Esparcir una noticia falsa o faltar a la verdad al referir o describir una cosa; propagar chismes.

Misreport, *s.* Informe falso, relación inexacta, errónea, falsa.

Misrepresent [mis-rep-rẹ-zent'], *va.* Representar mal o falsamente, o presentar una cosa bajo falsos colores; disfrazar, falsificar.

Misrepresentation [mis-rep-rẹ-zen-té'-shun], *s.* Falsedad, representación falsa, noticia o relación falsa y maliciosa; chisme.

Misrule [mis-rūl'], *s.* Tumulto, desorden, desarreglo, desgobierno, confusión.

Miss [mis], *sf.* 1. Señorita; término de cortesía que precede al nombre o apellido de una joven o de una mujer soltera. 2. Muchacha, joven; una señorita. 3. (Des.) Manceba. Cuando este término de cortesía se aplica a dos o más personas del mismo nombre, se pone en plural el título o el nombre, a discreción. *The Misses Brown* o *the Miss Browns*, Las Señoritas Brown. La primera forma es muy preferible a la última.

Miss, *va.* 1. Errar, no acertar, equivocar. 2. Errar el tiro, errar el golpe; no dar en el blanco. 3. Perder; no conseguir o no obtener lo que se desea; no hallar lo que se busca. 4. Echar de menos alguna cosa; echar de ver que falta algo. 5. Pasar sin alguna cosa o abstenerse de ella; carecer. 6. Omitir, dejar de hacer.—*vn.* 1. Frustrarse, desgraciarse, salir mal un negocio, un empeño, etc. 2. Faltar, caer en falta. 3. Acertar con algo por casualidad. *We can not miss of it*, No podemos dejar de saberlo o de hallarlo. *To miss one's mark*, Errar el blanco. *To miss fire*, Errar, faltar el tiro. *I missed money from the cash-box*, Noté que faltaba dinero en la caja, o de la caja. *She missed a glove*, Ella perdió un guante. *To miss stays*, (Mar.) Faltar la virada, no virar. *Three volumes are missing*, Faltan tres volúmenes.

Miss, *s.* 1. El acto de no acertar, de no hallar, o no obtener, de echar de menos, etc. 2. (Des.) Pérdida, falta.

Missal [mis'-al], *s.* Misal, el libro que contiene el orden y modo de celebrar la misa.

†**Missel**, †**Misselden**, †**Misseldine**, *s.* (Bot.) *V.* MISTLETOE.

Missel-thrush [mis'-l-thrush], *s.* Tordo grande de Europa que se alimenta mucho de las bayas de muérdago. Turdus viscivorus.

Missend [mis-send'], *va.* (*pret.* y *pp.* MISSENT). Enviar en dirección equivocada; dirigir mal una carta, un paquete, etc.

Misshape [mis-shêp'], *va.* Deformar, desfigurar, afear.

Missile [mis'-il], *a.* Arrojadizo. *Missile weapons*, Armas arrojadizas.

Missing [mis'-ing], *s.* El acto de omitir o echar de menos alguna cosa; el estado de lo que se halla ausente o de lo que falta.—*a.* Extraviado, perdido; ausente, que falta.

Mission [mish'-un], *s.* 1. Envío, acción de enviar. 2. Misión, comisión. 3. Misión, cierto número de eclesiásticos enviados para instruir a los fieles o convertir a los infieles, y el sitio o paraje donde se establecen. 4. El destino voluntario o forzoso de una persona; la meta de sus esfuerzos. 5. Embajada, el cargo y la comisión de un representante diplomático en el extranjero.

Missionary [mish'-un-ẹ-ri], *s.* 1. Misionero. 2. Persona enviada con un encargo o misión.—*a.* Misionero, perteneciente a las misiones.

Missis, Missus [mis'-iz], *s.* 1. Señora; modo usual de pronunciar la palabra *Mistress*, cuya abreviatura es *Mrs.* 2. (Fam. y dial.) Mujer, esposa.

Missive [mis'-iv], *a.* Misivo, que se puede enviar o se destina a ser enviado.—*s.* Carta, misiva, comunicación escrita.

Misspell [mis-spel'], *va.* Deletrear mal, escribir con mala ortografía.

Misspelling [mis-spel'-ing], *s.* Ortografía incorrecta, viciosa.

Misspend [mis-spend'], *va.* Malgastar, derrochar, disipar; hacer mal uso, emplear mal.

Misspender [mis-spend'-ẹr], *s.* Malbaratador, disipador.

Misstate [mis-stêt'], *va.* Establecer o sentar mal una cuestión, una tesis; representar o relatar falsamente.

Misstatement [mis-stêt'-mẹnt], *s.* Relación equivocada o falsa, error.

Misstep [mis-step'], *vn.* Dar un paso en falso, tropezar.—*s.* Paso falso o erróneo, real o figuradamente; tropiezo; falta, culpa.

Missy [mis'-i], *s.* (Ingl. y E. U. del Sur) Señorita.

Mist [mist], *s.* 1. Niebla, neblina, vapor espeso, llovizna. 2. Velo o venda que tapa los ojos del cuerpo o de la razón; niebla, confusión u obscuridad que no deja formar juicio recto de las cosas. *To be in a mist*, Estar desconcertado. *A Scotch mist*, Neblina muy espesa como las del oeste de Escocia; de aquí, (fest.) lluvia.

Mist, *va.* Anieblar, anublar, obscurecer.—*vn.* Lloviznar, caer en gotas muy menudas.

Mistakable [mis-té'-ka-bl], *a.* Susceptible de error; que se puede entender o interpretar mal; que puede ser equivocado.

Mistake [mis-ték'], *va.* (*pret.* MISTOOK, *pp.* MISTAKEN). Equivocar, comprender mal; tomar una cosa por otra. *You mistake me*, Vd. no me comprende bien.—*vn.* Equivocarse, engañarse. *To mistake one's way*, Descarriarse. *To be mistaken*, Estar engañado, haberse equivocado. *My opinion is mistaken*, No han comprendido bien cuál es mi parecer. *You are mistaken*, Vd. se engaña.

Mistake, *s.* Equivocación, yerro, engaño. *Book full of mistakes*, Libro lleno de yerros o de erratas.

Mistaken [mis-têk'-n], *pp.* de *To* MISTAKE. 1. Erróneo, incorrecto. 2. Errado, engañado, en error. 3. Comprendido mal, tomado en sentido erróneo.

Mistakenly [mis-têk'-n-li], *adv.* Equivocadamente.

Mistaking [mis-têk'-ing], *s.* Yerro, equivocación, engaño.

Mistakingly [mis-têk'-ing-li], *adv.* Erróneamente, equivocadamente.

Mistaught, *pret.* y *pp.* de *To* MISTEACH.

Misteach [mis-tích'], *va.* (*pret.* y *pp.* MISTAUGHT). Enseñar o instruir mal.

Mistemper [mis-tem'-pẹr], *va.* Destemplar, templar mal; desordenar.

Mister [mis'-tẹr], *s.* Señor, término de cortesía que se antepone al apellido y corresponde unas veces a *Señor* y otras a *Don* o a *Señor Don* en castellano. Se escribe por lo general en abreviatura, *Mr.*

Misterm [mis-tẹrm'], *va.* Nombrar o dar a una persona o cosa un nombre que no le conviene.

Mistful [mist'-ful], *a.* Obscuro, nebuloso, anublado.

§**Misthink** [mis-think'], *va.* Pensar mal o erróneamente.

Mistily [mis'-ti-li], *adv.* Obscuramente, anubladamente.

Mistime [mis-taim'], *va.* Hacer alguna cosa fuera de tiempo; dejar pasar el tiempo oportuno o la ocasión favorable.

Mistimed [mis-taimd'], *pp.* y *a.* Inoportuno; fuera de tiempo.

Mistiness [mis'-ti-nes], *s.* Vapor; el estado de lo que se halla en forma de niebla o vapor.

Mistletoe [miz'-l-tō o mis'-l-tō], *s.*

(Bot.) Muérdago, liga, visco; planta que los antiguos celtas tenían en gran veneración. *Mistletoe-berry,* Baya de muérdago.
Mist-like [mist'-laic], *a.* Nebuloso.
Mistold, *pret.* y *pp.* de *To* MISTELL.
Mistook [mis-tuk'], *pret.* y *pp.* de *To* MISTAKE.
Mistrain [mis-trên'], *va.* Educar o criar mal.
Mistral [mis'-tral], *s.* Nombre de un viento frío, seco y violento que sopla del nordoeste en el golfo de Lión.
Mistranslate [mis-trans-lêt'], *va.* Traducir mal.
Mistranslation [mis-trans lê'-shun], *s.* Traducción mal hecha o infiel.
Mistress [mis'-tres], *sf.* 1. Ama, dueña, caboza o señora de la casa. 2. Señora, término de cortesía que se da a las casadas o viudas y equivale en español a Señora, a Doña, o a Señora Doña. Se escribe *Mrs.* y se pronuncia mis'-iz. 3. Mujer diestra en alguna cosa. *She is mistress of the English language,* Posee o domina la lengua inglesa. *Mistress of the Robes,* Camarera mayor de una reina o princesa. 4. Maestra. 5. Cortejo, la mujer cortejada. 6. Concubina, amiga, querida. *Kept-mistress,* Manceba. *She is mistress of herself,* Ella es dueña de sus acciones, es independiente.
Mistrial [mis-trai'-al], *s.* Pleito viciado de nulidad por causa de error o por empate o desacuerdo del jurado.
Mistrust [mis-trust'], *s.* Desconfianza, sospecha, recelo.
Mistrust, *va.* 1. Desconfiar, recelar, sospechar. 2. Sospechar como probable, imaginarse, conjeturar; tener aprensión o sospecha de.
Mistrustful [mis-trust'-ful], *a.* Desconfiado, receloso, sospechoso.
Mistrustfully [mis-trust'-ful-i], *adv.* Desconfiadamente.
Mistrustfulness [mis-trust'-ful-nes], *s.* Desconfianza.
Mistrustingly [mis-trust'-ing-li], *adv.* Con desconfianza.
Mistune [mis-tiūn'], *va.* Desentonar.
Misty [mis'-ti], *a.* Nebuloso, nublado.
Misunderstand [mis-un-dęr-stand'], *va.* Entender mal, comprender mal una cosa, equivocarse; tomar en sentido erróneo.
Misunderstanding [mis-un-dęr-stand'-ing], *s.* 1. Concepto falso, idea equivocada, equivocación, engaño, error, mala inteligencia. 2. Desavenencia, disensión; tibieza, frialdad en el amor y la amistad.
Misusage [mis-yūz'-ęj], *s.* 1. Abuso, mal uso. 2. Uso erróneo o impropio, mala applicación.
Misuse [mis-yūz'], *va.* Maltratar, tratar mal; abusar de algo.
Misword [mis-wūrd'], *va.* Expresar en palabras o términos erróneos. *The telegram was misworded,* El telegrama estaba equivocado.
Miswrought [mis-rōt'], *a.* Mal trabajado.
Misyoke [mis-yōk'], *va.* Unir o juntar mal.—*vr.* Unirse o juntarse mal.
Mit, *s.* *V.* MITT.
Mite [mait], *s.* Ácaro, insecto arácnoide muy diminuto, como el ácaro del queso o el arador.
Mite, *s.* 1. Pizca, la porción mínima de alguna cosa; blanca, ardite; nada o casi nada. 2. Antigua moneda muy pequeña de Palestina: cualquier moneda muy diminuta o pequeña cantidad de dinero. (< Holandés, mijt.)
Miter, Mitre [mai'-tęr], *s.* 1. Mitra, toca alta y apuntada que usan los arzobispos y obispos en ocasiones solemnes; de aquí, dignidad de obispo, etc. 2. (Mec.) Unión de dos cuerpos en un ángulo dividido igualmente; inglete. 3. Obturador para chimenea. *Miter-box, miter-block,* Caja de ingletes. *Miter-joint,* Inglete, ensambladura a hebra. *Miter-shell,* Concha univalva mitriforme muy hermosa.
Miter, Mitre, *va.* 1. Conferir una mitra. 2. Adornar con mitra. 3. Hacer o juntar con inglete.
Mithridate [mith'-ri-dêt], *s.* Mitridato, antídoto y composición de varias drogas.
Mitigable [mit'-i-ga-bl], *a.* Capaz de ser mitigado.
Mitigant [mit'-i-gant], *a.* Mitigante, lenitivo.
Mitigate [mit'-i-gêt], *va.* 1. Mitigar, moderar, hacer menos riguroso; suavizar. 2. ¿Aplacar, calmar.
Mitigation [mit-i-gê'-shun], *s.* Mitigación de los dolores, rebaja de las cargas o impuestos, minoración de cualquier trabajo o penalidad.
Mitigative, Mitigatory [mit'-i-gę-tiv, ga-to'-ri], *a.* Mitigativo.
Mitigator [mit'-i-gê-tęr], *s.* Mitigador.
Mitochondrion [mait-o-con'-dri-on], *s.* Mitocondrio.
Mitosis [mai-tō'-sis], *s.* (Biol.) Mitosis.
Mitre [mai'-tęr]. *V.* MITER, *v.* y *s.*
Mitred [mai'-tęrd], *a.* Mitrado.
Mitt [mit], *s.* 1. Mitón, confortante, especie de guante sin dedos. 2. *V.* MITTEN.
Mitten [mit'-n], *s.* 1. Puño, mitón, guante con dedo para el pulgar, pero sin separaciones para los otros cuatros dedos. 2. Confortante. *V.* MITT. 3. (Fam.) Calabazas, repulsa de un amante. *To get* o *to give the mitten,* Ser despedido un pretendiente, darle calabazas; es decir que se obtiene solamente el mitón, y no la deseada mano.
Mittimus [mit'-i-mus], *s.* (For.) Auto o decreto de prisión.
Mix [mix], *va.* 1. Mezclar, juntar o incorporar una cosa con otra. 2. Asociar, unir con. 3. Confundir; producir mezclando.—*vn.* 1. Unirse promiscuamente. 2. Mezclarse; tomar parte.
Mixer [mix'-ęr], *s.* 1. Mezclador. 2. Mezcladora (máquina). *Concrete mixer,* Mezcladora de hormigón. *A good mixer,* Persona sociable que congenia fácilmente con otra.
Mixt [mixt], *pp. irr.* de *To* MIX. Mezclado, mixto.
Mixtion [mix'-chun], *s.* Mixtión, mezcla.
Mixture [mix'-chur], *s.* Mistura, mezcla, unión y enlace de una cosa con otra.
Mizen o **Mizzen** [miz'-n], *s.* (Mar.) Mesana. *Mizzen-mast,* Palo de mesana. *Mizzen-shrouds,* Jarcia de mesana. *To change the mizzen,* Cambiar la mesana. *To balance the mizzen,* Tomar rizos en la mesana.
Mizmaze [miz'-mêz], *s.* 1. Laberinto. 2. Laberinto, confusión.
Mizzle [miz'-l], *vn.* Lloviznar, molliznar.
Mizzling [miz'-ling], *pa.* Lloviznando ligeramente.
Mnemonic [nę-men'-ic], *a.* Mnemotécnico, relativo a la memoria, que ayuda a la memoria.
Mnemonics [nę-men'-ics], *s.* Mnemónica, el arte de la memoria; conjunto de preceptos y reglas para ayudar a la memoria.
-mo. Sufijo puesto a los números para designar en cuántas hojas está doblado un pliego de papel; v. g. *12mo,* En dozavo.
Moabite [mō'-ab-ait], *s.* y *a.* Moabita, pueblo descendiente de Moab, hijo de Lot.
Moan [mōn], *s.* Lamento, quejido, gemido, queja.
Moan, *va.* Lamentar, gemir.—*vn.* Lamentarse, afligirse, quejarse; producir un sonido sordo y lúgubre: dícese de los objetos inanimados.
Moanful [mōn'-ful], *a.* Lamentable, triste, lúgubre.
Moanfully [mōn'-ful-i], *a.* Lamentablemente.
Moat [mōt], *s.* Mota, ribazo de tierra para contener el agua o cerrar un campo; foso o canal que rodea una casa o castillo para su defensa. *Dry moat,* Foso seco.
Moat, *va.* Rodear con fosos o canales de agua.
Mob [mob], *s.* 1. Populacho, gentuza, canalla, la gente baja y ruin. 2. Moño, cofia, toca o tocado de mujer. 3. Tumulto, desorden.
Mob, *va.* 1. Tumultuar, levantar algún tumulto, motín o desorden, incitar a la plebe a que cometa excesos. 2. Atropellar, correr a alguno.
Mobbish [mob'-ish], *a.* Vil, bajo, ruin, tumultuoso.
Mobile [mō'-bil], *a.* 1. Movible, móvil. *Mobile kitchen,* Cocina ambulante. 2. Inconstante, variable.
Mobile [mob'-i-li], *s.* 1. Alguna cosa movible; término usado en filosofía. 2. (Des.) Populacho, plebe.
Mobility [mo-bil'-i-ti], *s.* 1. Movilidad, agilidad. 2. Inconstancia, volubilidad, instabilidad, ligereza.
Mobilization [mō-bi-li-zê'-shun], *s.* Movilización
Mobilize [mō'-bil-aiz], *va.* Movilizar, poner en acción, en movimiento, v. g. un ejército.
Mobster [mob'-stęr], *s.* Pandillero, pandillista.
Moccasin [moc'-a-sin], *s.* 1. Mocasín, calzado hecho de cuero flexible o de piel de gamo que usaban los indios de la América del Norte. 2. Mocasín, serpiente venenosa de la familia de los crotálidos que se halla en los Estados Unidos del Sur.
Mocha [mō'-ca], *s.* 1. Moca, especie de café muy estimado; estrictamente el traído de Moca, en Arabia. 2. Un peso de Abisinia, equivalente a una onza de los metales preciosos. *Mocha-stone, V.* MOSS-AGATE.
Mock [moc], *va.* 1. Mofar, escarnecer, hacer mofa o burla de otro. 2. Remedar. 3. Imitar de una manera despreciativa, poner en ridículo. 4. Frustrar, dejar sin efecto algún intento; engañar, burlar.—*vn.* Burlarse de, reírse de (con *at*). *They mocked at him,* Se burlaron de él.
Mock, *s.* Mofa, escarnio, burla; risada, mímica.—*a.* Ficticio, falso, fingido, cómico, burlesco. *Mock praise,* Alabanza irónica. *Mock prophet,* Profeta falso.
Mocker [mok'-ęr], *s.* 1. Mofador, es-

carnecedor, burlador. 2. Cerción, sinsonte, censontli. *V.* MOCKING-BIRD.

Mockery [mek'-ẹr-i], *s.* 1. Mofa, burla, irrisión, ridículo; zumba. 2. Remedo.

Mocking-bird [mek'-ing-bẹrd], **Mock-bird** [mec'-bẹrd], *s.* (Orn.) Cerción, pájaro americano del género Mimus, muy notable por su canto, y su extraordinaria habilidad en imitar otros sonidos. (Amer.) Sinsonte, censontli. Mimus polyglottus.

Mockingly [mek'-ing-li], *adv.* Con mofa, con burla.

Mocking-stock [mek'-ing-stec], *s.* Juguete.

Mocking-thrush, *s.* Mirlo burlón; pájaro mimo, el Harporhynchus rufus.

Mock-orange [mec'-er''-ẹnj], *s.* Arbusto de la familia de las saxífragas que tiene flores parecidas a las del naranjo en forma y fragancia. Llámase también *false syringa.* Philadelphus coronarius.

Mock-privet [mec'-priv-et], **Mock-willow** [mec'-wil-ō], *s.* (Bot.) Ladierno, labiérnago.

Modal [mō'-dal], *a.* Modal, perteneciente al modo o la manera, particularmente a un modo gramatical o lógico.—*s.* Proposición que contiene algunas condiciones o restricciones.

Modality [mo-dal'-i-ti], *s.* Diferencia accidental.

Mode [mōd], *s.* 1. Modo, forma, accidente, diferencia accidental. 2. Manera, método. 3. Moda, uso o costumbre general. 4. Graduación, grado. 5. (Gram.) Modo, cada una de las maneras generales de manifestarse la significación del verbo en la conjugación. 6. (Fil.) Modo, manera de ser en cuanto no es esencial; estado, cualidad accidental o contingente. 7. (Mús.) Disposición de los sonidos en la escala determinada por el lugar del semitono. *Major mode,* Modo mayor. *Minor mode,* Modo menor; equivalente al modo eólico griego y gregoriano. 8. Variedad de seda. *V.* ALAMODE.

Model [med'-el], *s.* 1. Modelo. 2. Modelo o patrón que sirve de original. 3. Modelo, patrón, dechado para imitar o trabajar sobre él. 4. Molde, pieza hueca que da su figura a lo que en sí encierra. 5. Pauta, cualquier instrumento que sirve para gobernarse en la ejecución de alguna cosa.—*a.* Modelo, que se puede copiar o imitar. *A model school,* Una escuela modelo.

Model, *va.* 1. Modelar, formar según modelo; dar forma á, moldear. 2. Dibujar en relieve.—*vn.* Modelar, hacer un patrón.

Modeling, Modelling [med'-el-ing], *s.* 1. Acción de trazar un modelo según el cual se ha de ejecutar una obra. 2. Arte de construir en cera o en arcilla un modelo que ha de hacerse después en piedra o metal.

Modeller [med'-el-ẹr], *s.* Modelador, trazador, dibujador, dibujante, diseñador.

Modena [med'-ẹ-na o mo-dí'-na], *s.* Color que se asemeja al carmesí.

Modenese [mō-den-ís], *a.* Modenés, relativo a la ciudad de Módena, o natural de ella.

Moderate [med'-ẹr-ẹt o et], *a.* Moderado, templado, parco; pacato, quieto, tranquilo; mediano, mediocre; razonable no extremo, no radical, sobrio; apacible, suave; módico (en precio); (fam.) habitualmente lento o pausado en el pensar, hablar o accionar.

Moderate [med'-ẹr-ét], *va.* 1. Moderar, limitar, restringir, reprimir; mantener en ciertos límites. 2. Moderar, templar, modificar, calmar. —*vn.* 1. Moderarse, hacerse menos intenso, menos violento; calmarse, apaciguarse. 2. Presidir, ejercer las funciones de presidente en una reunión.

Moderately [med'-ẹr-ẹt-li], *adv.* Moderadamente; con moderación, con suavidad; sin exceso; razonablemente; módicamente; medianamente.

Moderateness [med'-ẹr-ẹt-nes], *s.* Moderación, templanza; modicidad (de precio).

Moderation [med-ẹr-é'-shun], *s.* 1. Moderación, ecuanimidad, calma, templanza en los afectos o pasiones.

Moderato [med-é-rā'-to], *adv.* (Mus.) Palabra italiana que indica un tiempo entre el andante y el alegro.

Moderator [med'-ẹr-é''-tẹr], *s.* 1. Moderador, el que gobierna, árbitro. 2. Presidente de una reunión o asamblea; hoy sólo se emplea este término en las iglesias presbiteriana y congregacional. 3. Examinador en las universidades inglesas. 4. Moderador, pantalla translúcida que sirve para moderar y esparcir la luz que pasa a un objeto en el microscopio.

Modern [med'-ẹrn], *a.* Moderno, nuevo, reciente; que no es antiguo ni desusado. *Moderns, s. pl.* Modernos, los que viven o han vivido en nuestros tiempos, en contraposición a los antiguos.

Modernism [med'-ẹrn-izm], *s.* 1. Modernismo, uso moderno, práctica moderna. 2. Neologismo.

Modernist [med'-ẹrn-ist], *s.* El que gusta de las cosas modernas.

Modernity [mo-dẹr'-ni-ti], *s.* La condición o calidad de lo moderno; uso moderno o cosa moderna.

Modernization [med-ẹrn-i-zé'-shun], *s.* Modernización.

Modernize [med'-ern-aiz], *va.* Modernizar, hacer moderna una cosa; poner en lenguaje moderno algo que está en lenguaje antiguo; arreglar al gusto del día.

Modernness [med'-ẹrn-nes], *s.* Novedad, el estado de las cosas recién hechas u ocurridas.

Modest [med'-est], *a.* 1. Modesto, contenido, recatado, casto, púdico. 2. Moderado; sencillo, sin presunción. *A modest estimate,* Un cálculo moderado. *A modest woman,* Una mujer modesta, púdica.

Modestly [med'-est-li], *adv.* Modestamente, con modestia, con recato, con pudor; humildemente, sin presunción.

Modesty [med'-est-i], *s.* Modestia, decencia, pudor, reserva; humildad; castidad y pureza de costumbres.

Modesty-piece [med'-est-i-pís], *s.* Bobillo, encaje de costilla, una blonda que se pone a los vestidos en la parte superior del pecho.

Modicum [med'-i-cum], *s.* Pitanza, bocado, porción pequeña; poco.

Modifiable [med-i-fai'-a-bl], †**Modificable** [med'-i-fi-ca-bl], *a.* Lo que se puede modificar o lo que es susceptible de modificación; modificable.

Modification [med-i-fi-ké'-shun], *s.* Modificación; forma o manera particular.

Modificative [mo-dif'-i-ca-tiv], *a.* Modificativo.

Modify [med'-i-fai], *va.* 1. Modificar, hacer algo diferente; cambiar más o menos. 2. Modificar, reducir las cosas a términos justos; moderar, templar.

Modillion, Modillon [mo-dil'-yun], *s.* (Arq.) Modillón, parte de la cornisa.

Modish [mōd'-ish], *a.* (Ant.) Hecho a la moda; conforme a la moda.

Modishly [mōd'-ish-li], *adv.* A la moda, según la moda.

Modishness [mōd'-ish-nes], *s.* Inclinación a seguir la moda, culto de la moda.

Modular [med'-yu-lar], *a.* Modular, perteneciente a un modo o a una modulación.

Modulate [med'-yu-lét], *va.* 1. Modular, cambiar de tono, diapasón o inflexión del sonido. 2. (Mús.) Cambiar a otra clave o escala.

Modulation [med-yu-lé'-shun], *s.* 1. (Mús.) Modulación. 2. Modificación; adaptación.

Modulator [med'-yu-lé-tẹr], *s.* Modulador.

Module [med'-yūl], *s.* 1. (Arq.) Módulo, medida de proporción entre las partes de un orden clásico. 2. (Des.) Molde, modelo.

Modus [mō'-dus], *s.* El acto de pagar un tanto o cantidad alzada como equivalente del diezmo.

Mogul [mo-gul'], *s.* 1. Mogol. 2. Naipe de la mejor calidad. 3. Nombre de una clase de locomotoras de gran tamaño.

Mohair [mō'-hār], *s.* Pelo de camello; hilo o tela hechos de pelo de camello.

Mohammed [mo-ham'-ed], *s.* Mahoma.

Mohammedan [mo-ham'-ẹ-dan], *s.* Mahometano.

Mohammedanism [mo-ham'-ẹ-dan-izm], **Mohammedism** [mo-ham'-ed-izm], *s.* Mahometismo.

Mohammedanize [mo-ham'-ed-an-aiz], *va.* Hacer conforme al mahometismo o convertir a esa religión.

Mohican, Mohegan [mō-hí'-can, mō-hí'-gan], *s.* Miembro de una tribu de indios belicosos que habitaban parte de los Estados de Connecticut y Nueva York hasta el río Hudson.

Mohur [mō'-hūr], *s.* Moneda de oro en la India inglesa que vale libra y media o unas 39 pesetas.

Moidore [mei'-dōr], *s.* Moidoro, moneda de oro de Portugal que vale veinte y siete chelines, u ocho pesos fuertes.

Moil [meil], *va.* 1. Enlodar, ensuciar. 2. Cansar, fatigar.—*vn.* Afanarse, fatigarse, inquietarse, desasosegarse.

Moire, Moiré [mwār, mwa-ré'], *s.* Moaré, muaré, seda con aguas o visos.

Moist [meist], *a.* 1. Húmedo, que contiene humedad o está algo mojado. 2. Jugoso, suculento.

Moisten [mei'-sn], *va.* Humedecer; mojar ligeramente.

Moistener [mei'-sn-ẹr], *s.* Humedecedor; antiguamente, humectante.

§**Moistful** [meist'-ful], *a.* Húmedo, muy húmedo.

Moistness [meist'-nes], **Moisture** [meis'-chur], *s.* Humedad. *The moisture of plants,* Los jugos de las plantas.

Molar [mō'-lar], *a.* Molar. *Molar teeth*, Muelas, dientes molares.
Molary [mō'-la-ri], *a.* *V.* MOLAR.
Molasses [mo-las'-ez], *s.* Melaza, melote, miel.
Mold [mōld], *s.* Molde; tierra; moho. *V.* MOULD.
Mold, Mould [mōld], *va.* *V.* MOULD.
Moldavian [mel-dé'-vi-an], *a.* y *s.* Moldavo, de Moldavia.
Moldboard [mōld'-bōrd], *s.* Vertedera del arado.
Molding, Moldy. *V.* MOULDING, MOULDY.
Mole [mōl], *s.* 1. Mola, pedazo de carne informe que se engendra en el útero de la mujer. 2. Lunar. 3. Muelle, dique. 4. Topo, roedor semejante al ratón y que habita debajo de tierra. *Mole furs* o *skins*, La peletería o pieles de topo. (Amer.) Piel de tusa. 5. ¿Entre los romanos, mausoleo de grandes proporciones en forma de torre. *Mole-cast*, Montoncillo de tierra. *V.* *Mole-hill*. *Mole-catcher*, Cazador de topos. *Mole-cricket*, Grillotalpa o topogrillo. *Mole-hill*, Los montoncillos de tierra que levantan los topos escarbando. *Mole-eyed*, Cegato, que tiene ojos de topo, de vista muy débil. *Mole-rat*, Ratón-topo, roedor del Antiguo Mundo del género Spalax, que vive en galerías subterráneas, como el topo.
Molecular [mo-lec'-yu-lar], *a.* 1. Molecular, perteneciente a la molécula. 2. Resultante de la acción de las moléculas. *Molecular changes*, Cambios moleculares, los que resultan de la acción de las moléculas.
Molecular biology [me-lec'-yū-lar bai-el'-o-ji], *s.* Biología molecular.
Molecularity [mo-lec'-yu-lar'-i-ti], *s.* Estado o cualidad de molecular.
Molecule [mel'-e-kiūl], *s.* Molécula, corpúsculo, parte pequeña de un cuerpo.
Moleskin [mōl'-skin], *s.* 1. Piel de topo. 2. Ratina, especie de paño de frisa.
Molest [mo-lest'], *va.* Molestar, inquietar, atormentar, vejar, hostigar, perseguir, oprimir.
Molestation [mel-es-té'-shun], *s.* Molestia, incomodidad, enfado, enojo, pena; persecución, importunidad, vejación, hostigamiento.
Moletrack [mōl'-trac], *s.* Topera, la excavación que hacen los topos por debajo de tierra.
Molewarp [mōl'-wērp], *s.* Topo. *V.* MOLE.
Molinism [mō'-li-nizm], *s.* Molinismo, doctrina teológica de Molina, jesuita español.
Mollah [mel'-a], *s.* Título de cortesía que dan los mahometanos a los altos dignatarios de su religión.
Mollient [mel'-i-ent], *a.* (Poco us.) Emoliente, lo que ablanda.
Mollifiable [mel'-i-fai-a-bl], *a.* Molificable, que se puede ablandar.
Mollification [mel-i-fi-ké'-shun], *s.* Molificación, ablandamiento; suavización, mitigación, alivio.
Mollifier [mel'-i-fai''-er], *s.* 1. Molificador, mitigador, pacificador. 2. Emoliente, lo que ablanda.
Mollify [mel'-i-fai], *va.* 1. Molificar, ablandar; apaciguar, aquietar. 2. Aliviar, aligerar el peso o pena de alguna cosa; suavizar, mitigar.
Mollusc, *s.* *V.* MOLLUSK.
Mollusca [mel-lus'-ca], *s. pl.* (Zool.) Moluscos, división de los animales invertebrados que comprende las jibias, los caracoles y los conchados.
Molluscan [mel-lus'-can], *a.* y *s.* Molusco.
Mollusk [mel'-usk], *s.* Uno de los moluscos.
Mollycoddle [mel'-i-ced'-l], *s.* (Vulg.) Hombre afeminado; niño mimado; se abrevia a veces en *moll* o *molly*.
Moloch [mō'-lec], *s.* Nombre de un dios de los fenicios al que sacrificaban víctimas humanas, niños principalmente.
Molossus [mo-lus'-us], *s.* Moloso, pie de verso que consta de tres sílabas largas (— — —).
Molt, *v.* y *s.* *V.* MOULT.
Molten, *a.* y *pp. irr.* de *To* MELT.
Molting, *s.* *V.* MOULTING.
Moly [mō'-li], *s.* (Bot.) 1. Planta fabulosa de mágicas virtudes, citada por Homero. 2. Moli, especie de ajo silvestre.
Molybdate [mo-lib'-dét], *s.* Molibdato, sal del ácido molíbdico.
Molybdenum, Molybdena [mo-lib'-de-num, mel-ib-dī'-na], *s.* (Min.) Molibdena, metal duro, blanco como la plata e infusible.
Molybdenous [mo-lib'-de-nus], *a.* Molibdoso, perteneciente a la molibdena, especialmente en su menor equivalencia.
Mome [mōm], *a.* (Ingl. del Norte) Blando, liso.
Moment [mō'-ment], *s.* 1. Momento, minuto, instante, espacio brevísimo de tiempo. *For a moment*, Por de pronto. 2. El tiempo presente. 3. Momento, importancia, consecuencia, entidad. 4. Fuerza, impulso. 5. La cosa que origina o causa; principio de movimiento o de desarrollo.
Momental [mo-ment'-al], *a.* Relativo al ímpetu.
Momentarily [mo'-ment-e-ri-li], *adv.* Momentáneamente.
Momentariness [mo'-ment-e-ri-nes], *s.* Momentaneidad.
Momentous [mo-ment'-us], *a.* Importante, de mucha importancia; grave, de consecuencia.
Momentously [mo-men'-tus-li], *adv.* Con importancia, con gravedad.
Momentousness [mo-men'-tus-nes], *s.* Importancia.
Momentum [mo-men'-tum], *s.* 1. Momento, la propensión que tiene un cuerpo grave a bajar hacia el centro. 2. Ímpetu, fuerza o cantidad de movimiento.
Mon [men], *s.* (Esco. y prov. Ingl.) Hombre.
Mon-. Prefijo. *V.* MONO-.
Monachal [men'-a-cal], *a.* Monacal, monástico.
Monachism [men'-a-kizm], *s.* Monaquismo, monacato.
Monad [men'-ad], *s.* 1. Mónada o mónade, ente simple y sin partes, de que se componen los demás seres o substancias, según el sistema de Leibnitz. 2. (Biol.) Organismo muy pequeño de una sola celdilla; infusorio flagelado. 3. (Quím.) Átomo, radical o elemento con facultad de combinación que vale uno. 4. El espíritu, ser uno e indivisible, cuya totalidad constituye el universo (doctrina de Leibnitz).—*a.* Que se refiere o consta de una mónada; en química, que tiene facultad de combinación equivalente a uno.
Monarch [men'-arc], *s.* Monarca, potentado; originalmente el único jefe de una nación, como rey, reina, o emperador: hoy es en general soberano hereditario constitucional.
Monarchal [me-nārc'-al], *a.* Monárquico, real, imperial.
Monarchical, Monarchial [mo-nārk'-i-cal], *a.* Monárquico.
Monarchism [men'-ar-kizm], *s.* Monarquismo, los principios monárquicos; la adhesión que se profesa a la monarquía.
Monarchist [men'-ark-ist], *s.* Monarquista.
Monarchy [men'-ar-ki], *s.* 1. Monarquía, el gobierno monárquico. 2. Monarquía, el reino o imperio gobernado por un monarca.
Monastery [men'-as-ter-i], *s.* Monasterio, la casa donde viven los monjes.
Monastic, Monastical [men-as'-tic, al], *a.* Monástico, perteneciente al estado de los monjes.
Monastic [men-as'-tic], *s.* Monje.
Monastically [men-as'-tic-al-i], *adv.* Monásticamente, monacalmente.
Monday [mun'-dé], *s.* Lunes, el segundo día de la semana.
Monde [mōnd], *s.* 1. Mundo, en locuciones francesas, como *beau monde*, *demi-monde*. 2. Mundo, globo o esfera con una cruz.
Monetary [mun'-e-te-ri o men'-e-te-ri], *a.* Monetario, perteneciente a la moneda; que consta de dinero; pecuniario.
Monetize [mun'-e-taiz], *va.* 1. Monetizar, legalizar como dinero. 2. Acuñar (un metal) en moneda.
Money [mun'-e], *s.* 1. Moneda, dinero, metal acuñado para comerciar con él; moneda legal, papel moneda; cualquier medio de cambio o medida del valor. 2. Propiedad vendible, caudal, riqueza. 3. Sistema de acuñación. 4. *pl.* Pagos o recibos al contado. *Ready money*, Dinero contante o dinero al contado. *Money governs the world*, Quien tiene dineros pinta panderos. *To advance money*, Adelantar dinero. *Bank-money*, Billete de banco. *Paper-money*, Papel moneda. *To put out money*, Poner dinero a interés o a ganancia. *To take up money*, Tomar prestado. *Hard money*, Numerario, efectivo, moneda acuñada. *Earnest money*, Prenda, arras, señal. *Copper money*, Calderilla, moneda de cobre o de vellón. *Money makes the mare go*, (prov.) Por dinero baila el perro. *Money-bag*, Talega para guardar dinero. *Money-bags*, (Ger.) Un hombre rico, de muchas talegas. *Money-bill*, Ley de hacienda. *Money-box*, Caja, hucha para dinero. *Money-broker*, Corredor de cambios. *Money-changer*, Cambista de dinero. *Money-drawer*, Gaveta, particularmente en las tiendas, que sirve para recibir el dinero de las ventas y para hacer cambio. *Money-lender*, Prestamista. *Money-making*, *a.* (1) Resuelto a enriquecerse, que se complace en amontonar riquezas. (2) Ganancioso, lucrativo, provechoso. —*s.* El acto de acumular riquezas. *Money-matters*, Cuentas de débito y crédito; negocio de dinero. *Money-order*, Libranza postal. *Money-scrivener*, Corredor de dinero. *Money's-worth*, (1) Cualquier cosa que vale dinero. (2) El valor cabal del dinero que se paga por una cosa.
Money, *va.* Acuñar, hacer moneda, convertir en moneda.
Moneyed [mun'-ed], *a.* Adinerado,

el que tiene mucho dinero. *A moneyed man*, Un capitalista.

Moneyer [mun'-ẹ-ẹr], *s.* (Poco us.) 1. Monedero, el que fabrica, forma y acuña la moneda. 2. Banquero, cambista.

Moneyless [mun'-i-les], *a.* Falto de dinero, pobre.

Moneywort [mun'-ẹ-wūrt], *s.* (Bot.) Lisimaquia numularia, hierba de la moneda.

Monger [muṇ'-gẹr], *s.* Tratante, traficante. *Fishmonger*, Pescadero. *Newsmonger*, Novelero, el que anda a caza de noticias. *Whoremonger*, Alcahuete. *Ironmonger*, Ferretero, quincallero.

Mongol [meṇ'-gel], *a.* Mogol, mogólico, de la Mogolia china.—*s.* Mogol; úsase a veces para designar a los chinos en general.

Mongolian [meṇ-gō'-li-an], *a.* 1. *V.* MONGOL. 2. Perteneciente a las razas amarillas de Asia.—*s.* 1. Mogol; también, chino. 2. Idioma mogólico.

Mongoos, Mongoose [men'-gūs], *s.* 1. Mangosta, mamífero pequeño carnicero, notable porque mata las serpientes más venenosas; de aquí que lo domestiquen frecuentemente en la India. Herpestes mungo. 2. Un lemúrido blanco. Lemur mongoz.

Mongrel [muṇ'-grel], *a.* y *s.* Mestizo, nacido de padre y madre de diferentes castas, híbrido.

Monism [men'-izm], *s.* 1. Monismo, teoría que pretende explicar todos los fenómenos cosmológicos refiriéndolos a un solo principio. 2. (Biol.) Unidad de origen. V. MONOGENESIS.

Monition [mo-nish'-un], *s.* Amonestación, consejo, aviso, prevención, advertencia, exhortación.

Monitor [men'-i-tẹr], *s.* 1. Amonestador, instructor, monitor, admonitor. 2. Tipo de buque blindado de mucho calado y bajo de borda, con una o dos torres que contienen cañones de gran calibre.

Monitor [men'-i-ter], *va.* Controlar, vigilar, detectar.

Monitory [men'-i-to-ri], *a.* Instructivo, monitorio.—*s.* Amonestación, aviso eclesiástico.

Monk [muṇk], *s.* Monje, fraile.

Monkey [muṇk'-i], *s.* 1. Mono. 2. Cualquier animal cuadrumano, sea mono, cinocéfalo, marmoseto o lemúrido. 3. Mono o mona: voz de desprecio unas veces, y otras de cariño. 4. Cada uno de varios artículos pequeños, como un fiador del martinete o un pequeño crisol para fundir el vidrio. *To play the monkey*, Hacer monadas. *Monkey tricks*, Monerías. *Monkey-flower*, Mímulo. *V.* MIMULUS. *Monkey-jacket*, Capote o capotón de piloto. *Monkey-wrench*, Llave inglesa.

Monkhood [muṇc'-hud], *s.* Monacato, el estado de los monjes.

Monk's-hood [muṇks'-hud], *s.* (Bot.) 1. Acónito, nombre genérico de plantas. 2. Napelo, acónito napelo.

Mono- [men'-o]. Prefijo que se deriva del griego *monos*, sólo, único, uno.

Monoceros [mo-nes'-ẹ-res], *s.* El unicornio, monoceronte.

Monochlamydeous [men'-o-cla-mid'-ẹ-us], *a.* (Bot.) Monoclamídeo, que tiene una sola cubierta floral.

Monochord [men'-o-cērd], *s.* Monacordio, instrumento antiguo de música.

Monochromatic [men-o-cro-mat'-ic], *a.* Monocromático, de un solo color.

Monochrome [men'-o-crōm], *s.* Monócromo, pintura de un solo color.

Monocle [men'-o-cl], *s.* Monóculo, lente para un solo ojo.

Monoclinal [men-o-claī'-nal], *a.* (Geol.) Que se inclina solamente en una dirección.

Monoclinic [men-o-clin'-ic], *a.* (Min.) Monoclínico, caracterizado por tres ejes oblicuos sobrepuestos, dos iguales y uno desigual.

Monocotyledon [men-o-cet-i-lī'-den], *s.* (Bot.) Monocotiledón o planta monocotiledónea.

Monocotyledonous [men-o-cet-i-led'-o-nus], *a.* (Bot.) Monocotiledóneo, monocotiledón.

Monocular [men-ec'-yu-lar], **Monoculous** [mo-nec'-yu-lus], *a.* 1. Monóculo, que no tiene más que un ojo. 2. De o para un ojo.

Monodactylous [men-o-dac'-ti-lus], *a.* Monodáctilo, que no tiene más que un dedo.

Monody [men'-o-di], *s.* 1. Monodia, poema griego de carácter triste. 2. Composición literaria y triste, con un solo tema. 3. Canto en que una sola voz tiene la parte principal.

Monogamist [mo-neg'-a-mist], *s.* Monógamo, el casado con una sola mujer, o casado una vez solamente; el que desaprueba las segundas nupcias.

Monogamous [men-eg'-a-mus], *a.* 1. Monógamo, casado una vez solamente. 2. (Bot.) Monógamo, de flores que tienen los estambres unidos.

Monogamy [mon-eg'-a-mi], *s.* Monogamia, el estado de los que se han casado una sola vez.

Monogenesis [men-o-jen'-e-sis], *s.* 1. Unidad de origen: la doctrina de la descendencia de todos los seres vivos de una sola celdilla. 2. Reproducción asexual.

Monogenism [men-ej'-ẹ-nizm], *s.* La doctrina de que toda la raza humana es de una misma sangre o especie.

Monogram [men'-o-gram], *s.* 1. Monograma, cifra que contiene las letras, generalmente las iniciales, del nombre de una persona o cosa. 2. Una sola señal o carácter escrito que representa una palabra.

Monograph [men'-o-graf], *s.* Monografía, descripción sistemática de una sola cosa, o de una clase de cosas.

Monographic [men-o-graf'-ic], *a.* Monográfico, dibujado de un rasgo; relativo a una monografía; dibujado con líneas sin colores.

Monography [men-eg'-ra-fi], *s.* 1. Figura hecha con líneas, sin colores. 2. (Des.) Monografía, descripción de un solo asunto. *V.* MONOGRAPH.

Monolith [men'-o-lith], *s.* Monolito, monumento de piedra de una sola pieza.

Monolithic [men-o-lith'-ic], *a.* Monolítico.

Monologian [men-o-lō'-ji-an], **Monologist** [mo-nel'-o-jist], *s.* Monologista, el que recita monólogos ó soliloquios.

Monologue [men'-o-leg], *s.* Monólogo, soliloquio.

Monomachy [mo-nem'-a-ki], *s.* Monomaquia, desafío o duelo singular de uno a uno.

Monomania [men-o-mé'-ni-a], *s.* 1 Monomanía, idea fija, forma de locura. 2. Manía, insensatez.

Monomaniac [men-o-mé'-ni-ac], *a.* Monomaniaco, monomaniático.—*s.* Monómano.

Monome [men'-ōm], *s.* Monomio. *V.* MONOMIAL.

Monomial [men-ō'-mi-al], *a.* (Álg.) Que consta de un solo término.—*s.* Monomio, expresión algebraica de un solo término.

Monopetalous [men-o-pet'-al-us], *a.* Monopétalo, flor que tiene un solo pétalo. *V.* GAMOPETALOUS.

Monoplane [men'-o-plên], *s.* Monoplano.

Monopolist [men-ep'-o-list], *s.* Monopolista, agavillador.

Monopolize [men-ep'-o-laiz], *va.* 1. Monopolizar, hacer monopolios. 2. Agavillar, tomarlo todo para sí. *To monopolize the conversation*, Monopolizar la conversación, no dejar hablar a los demás.

Monopolizer [men-ep'-o-laiz-ẹr], *s.* Monopolista.

Monopoly [men-ep'-o-li], *s.* 1. Monopolio, aprovechamiento exclusivo de alguna industria o comercio, ya provenga de un privilegio o de otra causa. 2. Compañía en posesión de un monopolio. 3. Estanco.

Monopteron [men-ep'-ter-en], *s.* (Arq.) Monopterio.

Monoptic [men-ep'-tic], *s.* El que ve con un solo ojo.

Monopyrenous [men-o-pir'-ẹ-nus], *a.* (Bot.) Monopireno o de una sola semilla o cuesco.

Monosepalous [men-o-sep'-a-lus], *a.* (Bot.) Monosépalo, de sépalos unidos por el borde. *V.* GAMOSEPALOUS.

Monospermous [men-o-spẹr'-mus], *a.* (Bot.) Monospermo, flor que tiene una sola simiente.

Monospherical [men-o-sfer'-i-cal], *a.* Que consta de una esfera.

Monostich [men'-o-stic], *s.* Monóstico, monostiquio, composición poética de un solo verso.

Monostichous [men-es'-ti-cus], *a.* (Bot.) Monóstico, dispuesto en una sola fila o línea vertical.

Monosyllabic, Monosyllabical [men-o-si-lab'-ic, al], *a.* Monosilábico, monosílabo.

Monosyllable [men-o-sil'-a-bl], *a.* Monosílabo, la voz de una sola sílaba.

Monotheism [men'-o-thi-izm], *s.* Monoteísmo, doctrina teológica de los que reconocen un solo Dios.

Monotheist [men'-o-thi-ist], *s.* Monoteísta, el que cree en un Dios único

Monotheistic [men-o-thi-is'-tic], *a.* Monoteísta, partidario del monoteísmo.

Monotone [men'-o-tōn], *s.* Monotonía, ya en la expresión y tono de la voz, ya en la música, la forma de composición, el estilo, etc.

Monotonic, Monotonical [men-o-ten'-ic, al], *a.* Monótono.

Monotonous [men-et'-o-nus], *a.* Monótono, uniforme en el tono.

Monotony [men-et'-o-ni], *s.* Monotonía, el estado o la cualidad de lo monótono; uniformidad fastidiosa del tono; falta de variedad en la cadencia o en la dicción.

Monotriglyph [men-o-traī'-glif], *s.* (Arq.) Monotriglifo, espacio de triglifo entre dos columnas o pilastras.

Monotype, monotyping [men'-o-taip, men-o-taip'-ing], *s.* (Impr.) Monotipia.

Monoxide, Monoxid [men-ex'-id], *s.* Compuesto que contiene un solo átomo de oxígeno.

Monsoon [men-sūn'], *s.* Monzón, viento periódico y general que corre hacia una misma parte en determinado tiempo.

Monster [men'-stęr], *s.* 1. Monstruo, animal fabuloso, parto o producción contra el orden regular de la naturaleza. 2. Monstruo, lo que es sumamente feo y también el que es sumamente perverso.—*a.* Enorme, prodigioso, extraordinario. *A monster meeting,* Una reunión numerosísima, enorme.

Monstrance [men'-strans], *a.* (Ecle.) Custodia, viril.

Monstrosity [men-stres'-i-ti], *s.* Monstruosidad, suma fealdad.

Monstrous [men'-strus], *a.* 1. Monstruoso, contrario al orden de la naturaleza. 2. Extraño, prodigioso, maravilloso. 3. Monstruoso, disforme, horrendo.—*adv.* (Fam.) Excesivamente.

Monstrously [men'-strus-li], *adv.* Monstruosamente, prodigiosamente.

Monstrousness [men'-strus-nes], *s.* Monstruosidad, enormidad.

Montage [men-tāzh'], *s.* Montage, arte de montaje.

Montanic [men-tan'-ic], *a.* Montañoso.

Montanist [men'-tan-ist], *s.* Montanista, hereje sectario de Montano.

Montant [men'-tant], *s.* Montante, término de esgrima y de carpintería.

Monteith [men-tīth'], *s.* Una ponchera de adorno, se llama así del nombre de su inventor.

Month [munth], *s.* Mes, originalmente un mes lunar, hoy una de las doce partes en que se divide el año. *A month ago,* Hace un mes. *Once a month,* Una vez al mes. *What day of the month is it?* ¿Qué día del mes es hoy? *Lunar month, solar month,* Mes lunar, mes solar. *A month of Sundays,* Literalmente, un mes de domingos; tiempo que parece muy largo, como si cada día fuese una semana.

Monthly [munth'-li], *a.* Mensual, que continúa durante un mes o que acontece una vez al mes.—*s.* 1. Publicación que sale a luz regularmente una vez al mes. 2. *pl.* Las reglas, la indisposición periódica de las mujeres.—*adv.* Mensualmente.

Monticle [men'-ti-cl], *s.* (Poco us.) Montecillo.

Monticulous [men-tic'-yu-lus], *a.* (Poco us.) Lo que tiene muchos montecillos.

Monument [men'-yu-męnt], *s.* 1. Monumento conmemorativo; columna, pilar, estatua, puestos encima de una tumba. 2. Monumento, memoria, recuerdo. 3. Piedra u otra señal permanente puesta por los agrimensores para marcar un límite o un ángulo.

Monumental [men-yu-ment'-al], *a.* Monumental, hecho en memoria o para conservar la memoria de alguna persona o acontecimiento; conmemorativo.

Monumentally [men-yu-men'-tal-i], *adv.* 1. Como recuerdo. 2. Por medio de monumentos.

Mood [mūd], *s.* 1. Disposición de animo, genio o natural; humor, capricho. 2. Modo silogístico, la debida disposición de las varias proposiciones de un silogismo. 3. (Gram.) Modo en la conjugación de los verbos. *V.* MODE. Esta forma es preferible. *To be in a cheerful mood,* Estar de buen humor. *To be in the mood to do,* Estar de humor para hacer algo.

Moodily [mūd'-i-li], *adv.* Caprichosamente.

Moodiness [mūd'-i-nes], *s.* Capricho, extravagancia; mal humor; tristeza, cavilación, melancolía.

Moody [mūd'-i], *a.* Fantástico, caprichoso, raro, extravagante; irritable, de mal humor; caviloso, triste, melancólico, taciturno.

Moon [mūn], *s.* 1. Luna, satélite de la tierra. 2. Satélite de cualquier planeta. 3. Mes lunar. *To bay the moon,* Ladrar a la luna, meter la mar en un pozo. *Moonbeam,* Rayo lunar. *Moon-blind,* Cegato, corto de vista. *Moon-blasted,* Echado a perder por la influencia de la luna. *Moon-calf,* Mola, monstruo; bobo, tonto. *Moon-daisy,* (Bot.) Margarita mayor o crisantemo floriblanco. *Moon-dial,* Reloj lunar. *Moon-fern,* (Bot.) Botriquio, especie de helecho común en Europa. Botrychium lunaria.

Mooned [mūnd], *a.* Lunado, lo que tiene figura de media luna.

Moon-eyed [mūn'-aid], *a.* Ojizaino; bizco, bisojo; de ojos lunáticos.

Moonflower [mūn'-flau-ęr], *s.* Especie de ipomea con grandes y blancas flores que se abren por la noche. Ipomœa bona-nox.

Moonless [mūn'-les], *a.* Falto de la luz de la luna.

Moonlight [mūn'-lait], *s.* Luz de la luna.—*a.* Iluminado por la luna.

Moonlit [mūn'-lit], *a.* Iluminado por la luna.

Moonseed [mūn'-sīd], *s.* Cualquier planta del género Menispermo, la familia de las menispermáceas; llámase así por la figura de las semillas.

Moonshee [mūn'-shī], *s.* Nombre que se da en la India a un maestro, y en especial a un mahometano profesor de idiomas; también, intérprete, secretario.

Moonshine [mūn'-shain], *s.* 1. Claridad de la luna. 2. Falta de realidad, ficción; disparate. 3. (Prov.) Licores fuertes matuteados o destilados ilegalmente.—*a.* o *Moonshiny,* Claro, lo que participa de la claridad de la luna.

Moonshiner [mūn'-shai-nęr], *s.* (E. U.) El que destila los licores espirituosos ilícitamente; contrabandista, matutero, particularmente de licores espirituosos.

Moonstruck [mūn'-struc], *a.* Lunático, loco.

Moonwort [mūn'-wūrt], *s.* (Bot.) 1. Lunaria, especie de flor. 2. Botriquio.

Moony [mūn'-i], *a.* 1. *V.* MOONSTRUCK. 2. Parecido a la claridad de la luna. 3. (Her. des.) Lunado. —*s.* Bobo, simplón.

Moor [mūr], *s.* 1. (Gran Bret.) Páramo, a veces cubierto de brezos, a menudo elevado, pantanoso y abundante en turba; frezal, marjal. 2. Moro, sarraceno, árabe; negro, etíope.

Moor, *va.* Amarrar, atar con anclas, cables u otra cosa. *To moor by the stern,* Amarrar con una reguera. *To moor by the head,* Amarrar con las amarras de proa. *To moor with a spring,* Amarrar con codera sobre el cable.—*vn.* Situarse en algún paraje. *Where the ship moored,* En donde estaba surto el barco.

Moor-buzzard [mūr'-buz-ard], *s.* (Orn.) Especie de halcón.

Moor-cock [mūr'-coc], *s.* (Orn.) El macho de la cerceta, el lagópedo rojo de Escocia. Lagopus scoticus.

Moor-hen [mūr'-hen], *sf.* (Orn.) Cerceta, zarceta, gallineta o gallina de río.

Mooring [mūr-ing], *s.* (Mar.) Amarra, amarre, amarradura. *Mooring mast,* (Mar.) Poste de amarre. *Mooring rings,* (Mar.) Argollas de amarrar.

Moorish [mūr'-ish], *a.* 1. Pantanoso, charcoso, cenagoso. 2. Morisco, moro.

Moorland [mūr'-land], *s.* Marjal; brezal; erial, tierra arenisca y ligera.

Moorstone [mūr'-stōn], *s.* Especie de granito.

Moory [mūr'-i], *a.* Que pertenece al marjal; pantanoso: dícese también de la tierra llana y abierta que contiene turba, brezo o hiniesta espinosa.

Moose [mūs], *s.* Mosa, anta, la forma americana del alce. Alces machlis.

Moot [mūt], *va.* Disputar acerca de materias legales; ejercitarse en el arte de defender cualquier punto relacionado con los pleitos o causas criminales; discutir judicialmente.

Moot, *s.* Una proposición o caso de jurisprudencia que los legistas sientan para discutir o disputar sobre él. *Moot case* o *moot point,* El caso o proposición legal que sirve como tema de discusión; pleito fingido. *Moot-court,* Conferencia en las escuelas de derecho; supuesto tribunal en el que los estudiantes de jurisprudencia se ejercitan en la práctica forense.

Mooter [mūt'-ęr], *s.* 1. El que se ejercita o ensaya en defender pleitos. 2. (Mar.) El que hace los toletes o escálamos.

Mop [mep], *s.* 1. Aljofifa, estropajo, rodilla para limpiar con agua estregando, o para sacudir el polvo. 2. Mechón, copete, puñado de cabellos, cerdas, hilachas, etc.

Mop, *s.* 1. Mueca. 2. Una joven; una muchacha mimada o ceñuda.

Mop, *va.* Aljofifar, limpiar alguna cosa estregándola con una aljofifa o un estropajo empapado en agua, o sacudir el polvo con rodilla, estropajo o aljofifa.—*vn.* (Prov. Ingl.) Hacer muecas.

Mopboard [mep'-bōrd], *s.* Banda de madera en la parte baja de las paredes de un cuarto.

Mope [mōp], *s.* El hombre abatido, atontado o estúpido.

Mope, *vn.* Dormitar, entontecerse, estar triste y pensativo, estar melancólico.—*va.* Atontar, privar de las potencias naturales; poner estúpido a uno; desanimar.

Mope-eyed [mōp'-aid], *a.* Tuerto, falto de un ojo; cegato.

Mopish [mōp'-ish], *a.* Atontado, estúpido, adormecido, medio dormido; distraído, que no presta atención.

Mopishness [mōp'-ish-nes], *s.* Abatimiento, adormecimiento.

Moppet [mep'-et], *s.* 1. Muñeca, figura de muchacho o muchacha hecha de trapos. 2. (Fam.) Gachona: voz de cariño que se da a una niña. 3. Mueca.

Mopsical [mep'-si-cal], *a.* Cegato. *V.* MOPE-EYED.

Mopstick [mep'-stic], *s.* Mango de estropajo o aljofija.
Moquette [mo-ket'], *s.* Moqueta, alfombra con trama de cáñamo.
Moqui [mō'-kī o mō'-cwī], *s.* Nombre de una tribu de indios de Arizona.
Moraine [mo-rēn'], *s.* (Fr.) Chancal, los despojos de rocas y tierra que se hallan al pie de un ventisquero distribuidos en montones.
Moral [mer'-al], *a.* 1. Moral, perteneciente a las buenas costumbres y acciones lícitas; ético. 2. Conforme a razón, virtuoso; particularmente casto, púdico; honrado. 3. Que obra según los dictados de la razón o del derecho en el hombre. 4. (Lóg.) Probable, como opuesto a demostrativo; v. g. *moral certainty*, certidumbre moral.—*s.* 1. Moralidad, moraleja, deducción o enseñanza moral contenida en una fábula o narración. 2. *pl.* 1. Costumbres, práctica de los deberes de la vida; conducta, manera de vivir con referencia al bien y al mal; en especial, honestidad, castidad. 2. Ética, los principios de la moral y obligaciones del hombre.
Morale [mo-ral'], *s.* Moral, animación, entusiasmo.
Moralist [mer'-al-ist], *s.* Moralista.
Morality [mo-ral'-i-ti], *s.* 1. Ética, moralidad, doctrina o enseñanza acerca de las buenas costumbres o del arreglo de vida. 2. Moralidad, reflexión o sentencia moral. 3. Moralidad de las acciones humanas, la cualidad de lo moral. 4. Moralidad, el sentido moral de una cosa. 5. Un antiguo drama alegórico del siglo XIV.
Moralization [mer-al-i-zé'-shun], *s.* Moralización.
Moralize, Moralise [mer'-al-aiz], *va.* y *vn.* 1. Moralizar, discurrir acerca de las buenas costumbres y del arreglo de vida. 2. Moralizar, hablar o escribir sobre asuntos morales. 3. Hacer moral o virtuoso.
Moralizer [mer'-al-aiz-er], *s.* Moralizador.
Morally [mer'-al-i], *adv.* 1. Moralmente, en sentido moral, conforme a las reglas de la moral. 2. Virtuosamente, honradamente. 3. Según las reglas de la razón y del juicio práctico; prácticamente.
Moral support [mer'-al sup-pōrt'], *s.* Apoyo moral.
Morass [mo-ras'], *s.* Cenagal, ciénaga, tremedal, pantano.
Morat [mō'-rat], *s.* Bebida hecha de miel con el jugo de moras. (< Ital. morato.)
Moratorium [mer-a-tō-ri-um], *s.* Moratoria, plazo para pagar una deuda vencida.
Moravian [mo-rē'-vi-an], *a.* Moravo, relativo a la Moravia o a sus habitantes.—*s.* 1. Moravo, natural de Moravia. 2. Miembro de una secta religiosa que se llama también de los Hermanos Unidos y Herrnhüter.
Morbid [mōr'-bid], *a.* 1. Mórbido, morboso, que no está sano. 2. Causado por enfermedad o que denota un estado insano del cuerpo o de la mente; patológico.
Morbidness [mōr'-bid-nes], **Morbidity** [mōr-bid'-i-ti], *s.* Estado de enfermedad o la situación del que se halla enfermo; estado mórbido.
Morbific, Morbifical [mōr-bif'-ic, al], *a.* Morbífico, que causa enfermedades o que lleva consigo el germen de las enfermedades.
Morbose [mōr-bōs'], *a.* (Des.) Morboso, malsano, enfermizo.
Morceau [mōr-sō'], *s.* Pedacito; en música y en literatura, una composición corta. (Fr.)
Morchella [mōr-kel'-a], *s.* Morilla, múrgura, hongo de sabor agradable. Morchilla esculenta.
Mordacious [mōr-dé'-shus], *a.* (Ant.) Mordaz, maldiciente, satírico.
Mordant [mōr'-dant], *s.* Mordiente, mordente, substancia para preparar telas o maderas que se quieren teñir.—*a.* 1. Mordiente, que muerde, acre, mordaz. 2. Mordiente, que sirve para fijar los colores.—*va.* Aplicar un mordiente para fijar los colores.
Mordent [mōr'-dent], *s.* (Mús.) Mordente, alternación rápida de dos notas contiguas, especie de trino.
More [mōr], *a.*, (*comp.* de MUCH, MANY). Mayor, más, más numeroso, adicional.—*adv.* 1. Más, con mayor exceso o intensión. 2. Más, término comparativo. *Never more*, Nunca más o jamás. *Once more*, Otra vez. *More and more*, De más en más o cada vez más. *So much the more*, Tanto más, cuanto más, tanto mejor. *To make more of a thing than it is*, Exagerar una cosa. 3. Más, antes bien. *No more*, No más; lo que no existe o ya se acabó. *He fell ill and is no more*, Le sobrevino una enfermedad y se murió. *More* sirve para formar el comparativo de los adjetivos. *The more he spends the less he saves*, Cuanto más gasta, menos ahorra. *The more, the merrier*, Cuantos más locos hay, más se ríe.—*s.* La cantidad o grado mayor de alguna cosa; otra cosa.
Moreen [mo-rīn'], *s.* Filipichín; tela de lana muy fuerte de que se usa para cortinas de ventana.
Moreland [mōr'-land], *s.* Tierra montuosa. *V.* MOORLAND.
Morelle [mō-rel'], *s.* Hierba mora, especie de solano.
Morello [mo-rel'-o], *s.* (Bot.) Especie de cereza de la que se hacen cerezas pasas.
Moreover [mōr-ō'-ver], *adv.* Además, además de eso, por otra parte, a más de lo que se ha dicho.—*conj.* También.
Moresk [mo-resc'], **Morisco** [mo-ris'-cō], *s.* Arabesco. *V.* MORESQUE.
Moresque [mō-resc'], *s.* Arabesco: dícese de ciertas labores de escultura, dibujos y pinturas al estilo de los moros.
Morganatic [mōr-ga-nat'-ic], *a.* Morganático: dícese del matrimonio en que un hombre se casa con una mujer de rango inferior al suyo.
Morgue [mōrg], *s.* Depósito de cadáveres no identificados.
Moribund [mer'-i-bund], *a.* Moribundo.
Morion [mō'-ri-en], *s.* 1. Morrión, antigua armadura de la cabeza. 2. Variedad de cuarzo humoso, casi negro.
Morisco [mo-ris'-cō], *s.* 1. Morisco. 2. Arábigo, la lengua de los moros. 3. Danza morisca. 4. Arabesco.
Mormon [mōr'-men], *s.* Mormón, sectario que admite y profesa, junto con la Biblia, las doctrinas religiosas y demás preceptos contenidos en el llamado Libro de Mormón. Hasta 1890 practicaron los miembros de esta secta la poligamia y en esa fecha la abandonaron abiertamente. *Book of Mormon*, Libro de Mormón, supuesta crónica de los aborígenes de América, que según los mormones fué traducido de planchas de oro por José Smith (1830).
Mormonism [mōr'-mon-izm], *s.* Mormonismo, las doctrinas y sistema de gobierno de los mormones.
Morn [mōrn], **Morning** [mōrn'-ing], *s.* 1. Mañana, la parte del día desde que amanece hasta las doce del mediodía; la primera parte del día. 2. Cualquier parte temprana. *I wish you a good morning*, Tenga Vd. buenos días. *Early in the morning*, Temprano, muy de mañana. *To-morrow morning*, Mañana por la mañana. *Every morning*, Todas las mañanas. *Morning-dress*, Traje de mañana, el vestido de trapillo que se lleva por la mañana. *Morning-glory*, Dondiego de día, planta enredadera del género Ipomea de las convolvuláceas, particularmente la Ipomea purpúrea, con flores de varios colores en forma de embudo; vulgarmente se llama también maravilla. *Morning-gown*, Bata. *Morning-star*, (Astr.) El lucero de la mañana.—*a.* Matutino, matinal.
Moroccan [mo-rek'-an], *s.* y *a.* Marroquí, marroquín.
Morocco [mo-rec'-ō], *s.* 1. Marroquí, tafilete. 2. *n. p.* Marruecos.
Moron [mō'-ren], *s.* Retrasado mental.
Morose [mo-rōs'], *a.* Moroso; áspero de genio, bronco, cabezudo; fantástico; triste.
Morosely [mo-rōs'-li], *adv.* Broncamente; morosamente.
Moroseness [mo-rōs'-nes], *s.* Morosidad; mal humor o aspereza de genio; capricho.
Morpheus [mōr'-fiūs o mōr'-fe-us], *s.* (Mitol.)Morfeo, dios del sueño.
Morphia, Morphin, Morphine [mōr'-fi-a, mōr'-fin, mōr'-fīn], *s.* Morfina, alcaloide vegetal, amargo, cristalizable, que se extrae del opio; es el principal de sus alcaloides y se emplea en medicina.
Morpho-. Forma que se usa en la composición de palabras, y significa forma, figura.
Morphology [mōr-fel'-o-ji], *s.* 1. Morfología, la parte de la biología que trata de la forma y estructura de los animales y de las plantas. 2. La ciencia de las formas o estructura del lenguaje.
Morphological [mōr-fo-lej'-ic-al], *a.* Morfológico, referente a la morfología.
Morphosis [mōr-fō'-sis], *s.* (Biol.) Morfosis, el orden o modo de formación de un órgano o de un organismo.
Morris chair [mer'-is chār], *s.* Poltrona.
Morris-dance [mer'-is-dans], *s.* Danza morisca, baile de los moros; mojiganga.
Morrow [mer'-ō], *s.* Mañana, el día que sigue al de hoy. *On the morrow*, En el día de mañana. *After to-morrow*, Pasado mañana.
Morse code [mōrs cōd], *s.* Clave telegráfica de Morse.
Morsel [mōr'-sel], *s.* Bocado, la porción de alimento que naturalmente cabe de una vez en la boca.
Mort [mōrt], *s.* 1. Muerte. 2. El toque de la trompa de caza al morir la res en las cacerías. (Fr.)
Mortal [mōr'-tal], *a.* 1. Mortal. 2.

Mortal, que ocasiona o puede ocasionar la muerte, fatal. 3. Mortal, humano, lo que es propio de la especie humana. 4. Mortal, que no es venial. 5. (Fam.) Mortal, extremo, violento. 6. Prolijo, fastidioso.—*s.* Mortal, un ser sujeto a la muerte, particularmente un ser humano.

Mortality [mōr-tal'-i-ti], *s.* 1. Mortalidad, capacidad de morir o padecer la muerte. 2. Muerte, la separación del alma del cuerpo. 3. Mortandad, proporción en que ocurren los fallecimientos con relación al número de habitantes. 4. Especie humana; naturaleza mortal.

Mortally [mōr'-tal-i], *adv.* 1. Mortalmente. 2. (Vulg.) Extremamente, sumamente.

Mortar [mōr'-tar], *s.* 1. Mortero, almirez. 2. Mortero, máquina de artillería de gran calibre, para disparar bombas. 3. Argamasa, mezcla, mortero, la cal y arena amasadas para unir piedras o ladrillos.

Mortarboard [mōr'-tar-bōrd], *s.* 1. Esparavel de los albañiles. 2. Birrete o bonete académico.

Mortar-piece [mōr'-tar-pīs], *s.* Mortero para disparar bombas.

Mortgage [mōr'-gēj], *s.* 1. Hipoteca, gravamen que se impone sobre bienes inmuebles u otra clase de propiedad, para responder del cumplimiento de una obligación o del pago de una deuda. 2. El acta o instrumento legal en que consta dicho gravamen. *Covered by a mortgage,* Gravado con una hipoteca. *To pay off a mortgage,* Redimir o levantar una hipoteca.

Mortgage, *va.* Hipotecar, asegurar un pago dando en fianza o hipoteca alguna finca o bienes raíces.

Mortgagee [mōr-gēj-ī'], *s.* Acreedor hipotecario, aquel a quien se le ha hipotecado un inmueble.

Mortgager, Mortgagor [mōr'-gēj-ẹr, ẹr], *s.* Deudor hipotecario, el que hipoteca una propiedad.

Mortician [mōr-tish'-an], *s.* Agente funerario, director de pompas fúnebres. (Cuba) Zacateca.

Mortiferous [mōr-tif'-ẹr-us], *a.* Mortífero, mortal.

Mortification [mōr-ti-fi-kē'-shun], *s.* 1. Mortificación, gangrena, la muerte de una de las partes del cuerpo, continuando vivas las restantes. 2. Maceración, mortificación, el acto de castigar al cuerpo con aspereza y rigor; humillación. 3. Mortificación, aflicción.

Mortify [mōr'-ti-fai], *va.* 1. Mortificar, humillar, herir el orgullo o amor propio; afligir, desazonar o causar pesadumbre o molestia. 2. Mortificar, macerar o castigar la carne; subyugar, domar las pasiones o los apetitos por la abstinencia o la elevación del espíritu. 3. Mortificar, destruir el tejido orgánico y las funciones vitales de una parte de un animal vivo.—*vn.* 1. Mortificarse una parte del cuerpo perdiendo su vitalidad; gangrenarse, corromperse. 2. Estar domado, subyugado.

Mortise [mōr'-tis], *s.* Cotana o muesca. *Mortise-lock,* Cerradura embutida.

Mortise, *va.* Encajar un madero en la cotana o muesca que se ha hecho en otro, lo que en algunas ocasiones se llama enmechar.

Mortmain [mōrt'-mēn], *s.* Manos muertas; dícese de los cuerpos eclesiásticos y obras pías cuyas posesiones no se pueden enajenar.

Mortuary [mōr'-chu-ẹ-ri], *a.* Mortuario, que se refiere a la sepultura de los muertos.—*s.* 1. Manda o legado que hace alguno en compensación de los diezmos que ha dejado de pagar. 2. Depósito de cadáveres; lugar para recibirlos provisionalmente. 3. Cementerio.

Mosaic [mo-zē'-ic], *a.* y *s.* Mosaico, obra taraceada de vidrio, esmalte o piedras de varios colores que parece pintura.—*a.* Mosaico, lo que pertenece a Moisés.

Moslem [mos'-lem o moz'-lem], *a.* Muslime, mahometano.—*s.* Musulmán, mahometano. (< Arab. muslim.) Sin. **Muslim.**

Mosque [mosc], *s.* Mezquita, templo de los mahometanos.

Mosquito [mos-kī'-tō], *s.* Mosquito. *Mosquito net,* Mosquitero.

Moss [mōs], *s.* (Bot.) 1. Musgo, musco, moho. 2. Especie de heno o zacate que sirve para llenar colchones, cojines, etc. 3. Tremedal, terreno pantanoso que produce la turba. *A rolling stone gathers no moss,* (prov.) Piedra movediza nunca moho la cobija. *Iceland moss,* Liquen de Islandia, musgo comestible. *Irish moss, V.* CARRAGEEN. *Moss-agate,* Ágata musgosa, piedra parecida al ágata, especie de dendrita. *Moss-rose,* Rosa musgosa. *Moss-trooper,* Bandido, bandolero.

Moss, *va.* Cubrir de musgo, moho.

Moss-grown [mōs'-grōn], *a.* Mohoso; cubierto de musgo.

Mossiness [mōs'-i-nes], *s.* El estado de lo que se halla cubierto de musgo o de moho.

Mossy [mōs'-i], *a.* Mohoso; cubierto de musgo. *Mossy ground,* Terreno cubierto de hierba menuda y fina.

Most [mōst], *a. superl.* Lo más, los más, la mayor parte de. *Most of the arts and sciences,* Las más de las artes y ciencias. *Most of his money,* La mayor parte de su dinero, o casi todo su dinero.—*adv.* Sumamente, en sumo grado, muy.—*s.* 1. Los más, el mayor número. 2. Lo o el más, el mayor valor. *At most,* A lo más.

Mostly [mōst'-li], *adv.* Por la mayor parte, por lo común, ordinariamente.

Mote [mōt], *s.* 1. Mota, átomo; punto. 2. Úsase en composición con la significación de junta, asamblea o tribunal; v. g. folk*mote.*

Motel [mō-tel'], *s.* Hotel para automovilistas.

Motet [mō-tet'], *s.* (Mús.) Motete.

Moth [mōth], *s.* 1. Mariposa nocturna, insecto lepidóptero heterócero; noctuela, noctuino, falena. *Hawk-moth,* Esfinge. *Silkworm-moth,* Bombix, mariposa del gusano de seda. 2. Polilla, insecto que se cría en la ropa y la destruye. *Moth-miller,* Noctuela blanquecina, polilla.

Moth ball [mōth bōl], *s.* Bola de naftalina contra la polilla.

Moth-eaten [mōth'-īt-n], *a.* Apolillado.

Mother [mudh'-ẹr], *sf.* 1. Madre; también animal hembra que ha parido. *Mother-in-law,* Suegra. *Grand-mother,* Abuela. *Step-mother,* Madrastra. 2. Causa, origen, lo que produce algo; también, la persona que cuida de las más jóvenes y débiles. 3. Religiosa, abadesa. 4. Madre, tía, mujer vieja; término de aprecio. 5. Instinto, sensibilidad de madre. 6. Madre, la materia más crasa del mosto u otro licor que queda en el fondo de las vasijas.—*a.* 1. Natural, nativo, natal, materno; vernáculo. *Mother-tongue,* Lengua madre o vernácula. 2. Materno, nacional, metropolitano. *Mother church,* Iglesia metropolitana.

Mother, *va.* Servir de madre a.—*vn.* Criar madre, como el vino u otro licor.

Mother-country [mudh'-ẹr-cun-tri], *s.* Patria, el país en que uno ha nacido.

Mother-of-pearl [mudh'-ẹr-ev-pẹrl], *s.* Madreperla, la cubierta interior de la concha en que se engendra la perla. *Mother of thyme,* (Bot.) Sérpol.

Motherhood [mudh'-ẹr-hud], *s.* Maternidad; estado o calidad de madre.

Mothering [mudh'-ẹr-ing], *s.* Visita que los ingleses habitantes del campo acostumbran hacer a sus padres a mediados de la cuaresma, cuando están ausentes.

Motherless [mudh'-ẹr-les], *a.* Sin madre. *Motherless child,* Huérfano o huérfana de madre.

Motherliness [mudh'-ẹr-li-nes], *s.* Maternidad, la calidad de madre.

Motherly [mudh'-ẹr-li], *a.* Maternal, materno —*adv.* Maternalmente.

Motif [mō'-tif], *s.* Motivo, asunto, tema. (Fr.)

Motile [mō'-til], *a.* Movible, que puede moverse espontáneamente.

Motion [mō'-shun], *s.* 1. Movimiento. 2. Movimiento, moción, vitalidad. 3. Aire, ademán, modo de andar o moverse. 4. Movimiento, el que hace un ejército o un cuerpo de tropas mudando de posición. 5 Movimiento, ímpetu, agitación o impulso del ánimo. 6. Movimiento, impulso o dirección dada a una cosa para que mude de situación o de estado. 7. Proposición o propuesta que se hace para que se decida o resuelva alguna cosa. 8. Ocurrencia, especie que se presenta de repente a la imaginación. 9. Evacuación del vientre. *To put in motion,* Agitar, mover, poner en movimiento. *To make a motion,* Proponer, hacer una proposición en alguna junta o congreso para que se acuerde sobre ella, o bien hacer una propuesta a alguno. *Dumb motions,* Señas. *Reciprocating motion,* Movimiento recíproco, alternativo o de vaivén. *To do a thing of one's own motion,* Hacer alguna cosa por inspiración o impulso propio.

Motion, *va.* 1. Proponer, presentar una moción, hacer una proposición o propuesta. 2. (Raro) Aconsejar, proponer planes o medios para conseguir un fin.—*vn.* Hacer una señal, hacer señas significativas para dirigir o para indicar algo.

Motionless [mō'-shun-les], *a.* Inmóvil, inmoble, inmovible.

Motion picture [mō'-shun pic'-tiūr], *s.* Película cinematográfica.—*s. pl.* Cine, cinematógrafo. *Motion picture camera,* Tomavistas.

Motivate [mō'-ti-vēt], *va.* Motivar.

Motive [mō'-tiv], *a.* Motor, motriz, que mueve o tiene eficacia o virtud para mover.—*s.* 1. Motivo, causa o razón que mueve a hacer alguna cosa; aguijón, estímulo. 2. Idea,

concepción predominante; sujeto, tema, designio; motivo músico.
Motivity [mō-tiv'-i-ti], *s.* Potencia motriz.
Motley [met'-li], *a.* 1. Abigarrado, gayado, pintado de colores varios y extraños, pintorreado, pintarrajado. 2. Mezclado, variado, diverso; que consta de elementos heterogéneos o incongruentes.
Motor [mō'-ter], *s.* Motor, movedor, móvil, lo que mueve ó que imprime movimiento; particularmente una máquina motriz. *Electric motor,* Motor eléctrico; aparato que convierte la fuerza eléctrica en fuerza mecánica; lo contrario del dínamo.—*a.* Motor, móvil, que da o imprime movimiento. *Motor nerve,* Nervio motor.
Motorbike [me'-ter-baic], *s.* Ciclomotor.
Motor boat [mō'-ter bōt], **Motor launch** [mō'-ter lānch], *s.* Gasolinera, lancha de motor.
Motorbus [mō'-ter-bus], *s.* Autobús.
Motorcade [mō'-ter-kēd], *s.* Caravana de vehículos.
Motor car [mō'-ter cār], *s.* Automóvil.
Motorcycle [mō-ter-sai'-cl], *s.* Motocicleta.
Motorist [mō'-ter-ist], *s.* Automovilista.
Motorization [mō-ter-i-zē'-shun], *s.* Motorización.
Motorize [mō'-ter-aiz], *va.* Motorizar.
Motorman [mō'-ter-man], *s.* Motorista (de un tranvía, etc.)
Motor ship [mō'-ter ship], *s.* Motonave.
Motor truck [mō'-ter truc], *s.* Autocamión. camión.
Mottle [met'-l], *va.* Marcar con manchas de diferentes colores, o con diversos matices; variegar, abigarrar.
Motto [met'-o], *s.* Mote, sentencia notable que se pone en alguna inscripción; lema, divisa.
Mould, Mold [mōld], *s.* 1. Moho, el vello que se cría en el pan y otras cosas por estar mucho tiempo en lugares húmedos. 2. Tierra vegetal, suelo, el terreno en que nace alguna cosa. 3. Molde, matriz. (Mex.) En los trapiches o ingenios de azúcar, formas. 4. La materia de que está hecha alguna cosa.
Mould, Mold, *va.* 1. Enmohecer, cubrir con moho alguna cosa. 2. Cubrir con tierra. 3. Moldar, amoldar, moldear. 4. Amasar, formar masa de alguna cosa. 5. (Mar.) Galivar.—*vn.* Enmohecerse, llenarse de moho o criar moho. (Obs.) En Inglaterra se escribe comúnmente con u, y sin ella en los Estados Unidos. Lo mismo sucede con sus derivados.
Moulder, Molder, *vn.* Convertirse en polvo, reducirse a polvo; consumirse, irse disminuyendo o consumiendo.—*va.* Convertir en polvo, consumir, destruir.
Mouldiness [mōld'-i-nes], *s.* Moho, el estado de lo que se halla mohoso.
Moulding, Molding [mōld'-ing], *s.* Moldura.—*pa.* Lo que forma o modela; lo que causa moho o enmohece.
Mouldy, Moldy [mōld'-i], *a.* Mohoso.
Moulin [mū-lañ'], *s.* Pozo casi vertical que forma en un ventisquero el agua que gotea desde la superficie por una grieta. (Fr.)
Moult, Molt [mōlt], *vn.* Mudar la pluma como las aves; mudar o echar el integumento exterior, como la piel, las plumas o los cuernos.
Moulting, Molting [mōlt'-ing], *s.* Muda, el acto de mudar el integumento exterior o sus pertenencias.
Mound [maund], *s.* 1. Montón de tierra, artificial o natural; terraplén, baluarte. 2. (Her.) Mundo, esfera que, como el cetro, forma parte de los atributos de un monarca. *Mound-builder,* Individuo de la raza que construyó ciertos montones de tierra y piedra hallados en muchas partes del mundo.
Mound, *va.* Atrincherar, fortalecer.
Mount [maunt], *s.* 1. Monte, montaña, cuesta. 2. Baluarte, terraplén de una fortificación que domina el terreno cercano.
Mount, *s.* 1. Montadura, objeto que sirve para preparar una cosa o para exhibirla; v. g. el cartón sobre que está colocado un dibujo. 2. Caballería. 3. Apeadero. 4. Monta, toque de clarín para montar a caballo.
Mount, *vn.* 1. Subir, subirse o ascender. 2. Subir, elevarse a una altura considerable. 3. Subir o montar a caballo. 4. Subir, montar, importar, ascender a, hablando de una cuenta, una renta, etc.—*va.* 1. Subir, levantar, hacer una cosa más alta de lo que era, como cuando se habla de una pared, torre, etc.; o aumentar su fuerza, como cuando se habla de la voz. 2. Subir, llevar las cosas arriba. 3. Subir una escalera, una cuesta, etc. 4. Proveer de caballos; poner a caballo. 5. Montar o engastar las piedras preciosas; preparar una cosa para usarla, hacerla servir de adorno, mostrarla, examinarla o conservarla. 6. Alzar, elevar; exaltar. 7. Llevar, portar, ir equipado con. *This ship mounts sixteen guns,* Este navío porta diez y seis cañones. *To mount a fan,* Montar un abanico. *To mount guard,* (Mil.) Montar la guardia. *To mount a cannon,* (Art.) Montar un cañón.
Mountable [maunt'-a-bl], *a.* Que se puede montar o subir.
Mountain [maun'-ten], *s.* 1. Monte, sierra, montaña. 2. Montón, masa enorme. *Mountain chain,* Sierra, cadena de montañas. *Mountain road,* Camino por país montañoso. —*a.* Montés.
Mountain-ash [maun'-ten-ash], *s.* (Bot.) Mostajo, serbal de cazadores.
Mountaineer [maun-ten-īr'], *s.* 1. Montañés, el que vive en las montañas. 2. Salteador de caminos, bandido. 3. Salvaje, el que es montaraz, o tiene genio y propiedades agrestes y groseras.
Mountainous [maun'-ten-us], *a.* 1. Montañoso, país o tierra de montañas. 2. Montuoso, grande, abultado como una montaña. 3. Montaraz. el habitante de las montañas.
Mountebank [maun'-te-banc], *s.* 1. Charlatán, el que vende supuestos medicamentos infalibles. 2. De aquí, saltimbanco, juglar, truhán.
Mounting [maunt'-ing], *s.* 1. Subida; lo que sirve para subir a alguna parte. 2. Montura, engaste, los ornamentos que hermosean y adornan una obra. *V.* MOUNT,[2] 1ª acep. 3. El acto o el arte de preparar una cosa para usarla o exhibirla.
Mourn [mōrn], *vn.* 1. Lamentarse, quejarse, apesadumbrarse, afligirse; plañir; hacer duelo y sentimiento. 2. Vestirse de luto ó llevar luto. —*va.* Deplorar, lamentar, llorar. *To mourn for one,* Llorar a alguno; llevar luto por alguien.
Mourner [mōrn'-er], *s.* 1. Lamentador, el que lamenta. 2. Llorón. 3. El que hace el duelo en algún entierro, vestido de luto; plañidera. *Chief mourner,* Dolorido, el que recibe los pésames y guía el duelo en un entierro. (Amer.) Doliente.—*a.* Lo que se usa en los entierros o lo que sirve para expresar duelo o tristeza.
Mournful [mōrn'-ful], *a.* 1. Triste, melancólico. 2. Funesto, deplorable. 3. Apesadumbrado; lúgubre, triste.
Mournfully [mōrn'-ful-e], *adv.* Tristemente, melancólicamente.
Mournfulness [mōrn'-ful-nes], *s.* 1. Pesar. 2. Tristeza, melancolía, aflicción, desconsuelo, duelo, sentimiento.
Mourning [mōrn'-ing], *a.* Lamentoso, deplorable.—*s.* 1. Lamento, llanto, gemido, aflicción, tristeza. 2. Duelo; plañido. 3. Luto, el vestido que usan en señal de dolor los parientes o amigos de un difunto. *In mourning,* De luto. *Half mourning,* Medio luto. *Mourning-bride, mourning-widow,* Escabiosa, planta herbácea y su flor. Scabiosa. *Mourning-dove,* Paloma de la Carolina. Zenaidura macrura.
Mouse [maus], *s.* 1. Ratón. 2. (Mar.) Barrilete.
Mouse [mauz], *vn.* Cazar o coger ratones.—*va.* 1. Cazar a hurtadillas y con paciencia, como el gato al ratón. 2. Desgarrar, hacer trizas, como un gato. 3. (Mar.) Amarrar, abarbetar, hacer barriletes. *To mouse a hook,* Amarrar un gancho.
Mouse-ear [maus'-īr], *s.* (Bot.) Velosilla, pelosilla oficinal; miosotis.
Mouse-hole [maus'-hōl], *s.* Agujero pequeño.
Mouse-hunt [maus'-hunt], *s.* Caza de ratones.
Mouser [mauz'-er], *s.* Cazador de ratones.
Mouse-tail [maus'-tēl], *s.* (Bot.) Misuro, cola de ratón, nombre genérico de plantas.
Mouse-trap [maus'-trap], *s.* Ratonera.
Mousseline [mū-se-līn'], *s.* 1. Muselina fina francesa. 2. Vidrio de muselina, un vidrio muy delgado que imita los dibujos del encaje.
Moustache, *s.* *V.* MUSTACHE.
Mouth [mauth], *s.* 1. Boca. 2. Boca, entrada; abertura, agujero. 3. Orificio, abertura de un vaso. 4. Embocadero, embocadura o desembocadura de un río. 5. Boca, lengua, tomadas como instrumentos de la voz. 6. Gesto o mueca que se hace con la boca. *Down in the mouth,* Cabizbajo, melancólico. *To make one's mouth water,* Hacer venir el agua a la boca. *To stop the mouth,* Cerrar la boca; (fig.) imponer silencio. quitar el habla. *The mouths of the Nile,* Las bocas del Nilo. *To be born with a silver spoon in one's mouth,* Nacer de pies, nacer rico.
Mouth [maudh], *vn.* Vociferar, hablar a gritos.—*va.* 1. Pronunciar de una manera extravagante; vocear, hablar alto. 2. Mascar, comer. 3. Agarrar con la boca o en la boca. 4. Insultar con palabras descomedidas.

Mouthed [maudhd], *a.* Lo que tiene boca. *Wide-mouthed,* Bocudo o que tiene la boca grande. *Wry-mouthed,* El que tiene la boca torcida. *Foul-mouthed,* Mal hablado, maldiciente. *Mealy-mouthed,* Dulce, melifluo; tímido.

Mouthful [mauth'-ful], *s.* 1. Bocado. 2. Miaja o migaja, parte o porción pequeña de alguna cosa.

Mouthing [maudh'-ing], *a.* El que está vociferando, hablando alto o haciendo ademanes.

Mouthless [mauth'-les], *a.* Desbocado, sin boca.

Mouth-made [mauth'-mêd], *a.* Lo dicho con la boca sin sentirlo el corazón.

Mouth organ [mauth er'-gan], *s.* Armónica.

Mouthpiece [mauth'-pîs], *s.* 1. Boquilla, embocadura, estrangul de un instrumento de música; boquilla de cualquier herramienta o instrumento. 2. El que está encargado de expresar los sentimientos de muchas personas reunidas con un mismo objeto, o el que lleva la palabra por ellas.

Mouth wash [mauth wesh], *s.* Lavado bucal.

Movable, Moveable [mūv'-a-bl], *a.* Movible, movedizo, que puede moverse; que puede cambiar de un tiempo a otro.

Movables [mūv'-a-blz], *s. pl.* Muebles, los bienes que se pueden mover y llevar de una parte a otra, a distinción de los bienes raíces.

Move [mūv], *s.* 1. Movimiento, acción de mover. 2. Paso, acto en la prosecución de un plan o en la ejecución de algo. 3. En varios juegos, suerte, jugada, mano, el derecho de cambiar el lugar de una pieza. *To miss a move,* Errar una jugada, una suerte. *Masterly move,* Jugada maestra. *It is your move,* A Vd. le toca jugar. *A wise move,* Una acción, un paso acertado.

Move, *va.* 1. Mover. 2. Mover o menear una parte del cuerpo; hacer mudar de postura. 3. Mover, impeler, dar o causar movimiento o impulso. 4. Proponer, hacer una proposición o propuesta; recomendar o pedir a uno que se encargue del cuidado de algún asunto. 5. Mover, excitar, incitar o disponer el ánimo para alguna cosa; persuadir, inclinar. 6. Mover a piedad, a lágrimas, etc., conmover, causar u ocasionar una pasión de ánimo. 7. Hacer mover el vientre.—*vn.* 1. Moverse, menearse, mudar de lugar, de postura. 2. Andar, ponerse en movimiento, en camino. 3. Marchar un ejército o cuerpo militar. 4. Entrar en acción, empezar a obrar. 5. Mudar de residencia, marchar, partir. 6. Avanzar, progresar de cierto modo. 7. Exonerarse el vientre. *To move off,* Decampar; poner pies en polvorosa, tomar las de Villadiego, tomar viento. *To move to laughter,* Hacer reir, causar o excitar la risa. *To move to anger,* Enojar, irritar, conmover, provocar. *To move away,* Alejarse; irse, marcharse; mudar de casa. *To move forward,* Adelantarse, avanzar. *To move in,* Entrar; entrar a habitar una casa. *To move round,* 1. Dar vueltas a. 2. Recorrer. *To move up,* 1. Anticipar (una fecha). 2. Ascender, adelantar.

Moveless [mūv'-les], *a.* Inmóvil.

Movement [mūv'-ment], *s.* 1. Movimiento, moción; meneo; marcha. 2. Serie de actos o incidentes que tienden a algún fin. *The temperance movement,* La propaganda o cruzada en favor de la templanza. 3. En literatura, acción, incidente. 4. Movimiento, conjunto de las piezas que hacen andar a un reloj u otra acción mecánica. 5. (Mús.) Movimiento, el compás o tiempo en que mejor efecto produce una composición músical; como *allegretto,* etc. 6. Cámara, evacuación del vientre, cagada.

Mover [mūv'-er], *s.* Motor, movedor, móvil; el autor de una proposición o propuesta. *Prime mover,* Principio motor, motor primordial; fuerza motriz; agencia de la naturaleza.

Movie [mūv'-i], *s.* (fam.) Película cinematográfica.

Movies [mūv'-iz], *s. pl.* (fam.) Cine, cinematógrafo.

Moving [mūv'-ing], *s.* 1. Movimiento. 2. Motivo, impulso.—*a.* Patético, tierno, persuasivo, sensible, afectuoso, lastimero.

Movingly [mūv'-ing-li], *adv.* Patéticamente.

Movingness [mūv'-ing-nes], *s.* El poder de excitar los afectos del ánimo; ternura, persuasión, unción.

Moving picture [mūv'-ing pic'-tiūr], *s.* Película cinematográfica.—*pl.* Cine, cinematógrafo.

Mow [mau], *s.* Granero, hórreo, troj, cámara; henil, el sitio donde se guarda el heno.—*va.* Entrojar, encerrar el heno, etc., en las trojes, paneras o graneros.

Mow [mō], *va.* (*pp.* MOWED y MOWN [mōn]). 1. Guadañar. 2. Segar, cortar con prisa y violencia, o sin distinción.

Mow [mau o mō], *vn.* Hacer muecas; burlarse de.—*s.* Mueca.

Mowburn [mau'-būrn], *vn.* Calentarse o fermentar el grano o heno por no estar bien seco al tiempo de entrojarlo.

Mower [mō'-er], *s.* Dallador, guadañero; guadañadora, máquina de cortar hierba.

Mowing [mō'-ing], *s.* 1. Siega. 2. Gesto, mueca. 3. (Des.) Habilidad. *Mowing-machine,* Máquina para corta la hierba, guadañadora.

Mown [mōn], *pp. irr.* de MOW. Guadañado, cortado.

Moxa [mex'-a], *s.* (Med.) 1. Moxa, cilindro de algodón que se quema encima de la piel. 2. (Bot.) Moxa, ajenjo de la India oriental que queman sobre la piel después de seco para curar varias enfermedades.

Much [much], *a.* 1. Mucho, abundante, excesivo; largo de duración. 2. (Ant.) Er. gran número. *Much people,* Mucha gente, muchas personas.—*adv.* 1. Mucho, excesivamente, en gran manera, con mucho. *As much,* Tanto, tan, otro tanto. *As much as,* Tanto como. *How much?* ¿Cuánto? *So much,* Tanto. *So much the better,* Tanto mejor. *So much the worse,* Tanto peor. *Too much,* Demasiado, excesivo. *Very much,* Mucho, extremamente. *For as much as,* Por cuanto. *As much more,* Otro tanto más. 2. Casi, cuasi, poco más o menos. *It is much the same,* Es o está casi lo mismo; poco más o menos lo mismo. 3. Muy. *He is much afflicted,* Está muy afligido. 4. Muchas veces; por largo tiempo.—*s.* 1. Muchedumbre, copia, abundancia, multitud. 2. Cosa extraña o poco común. *To make much of,* Festejar, tratar a uno con cariño y estimación, acariciarle, tenerle en mucho. *He is much of a gentleman,* Es todo un caballero. *I am much of your opinion,* Soy casi de la misma opinión que Vd. *Much ado about nothing,* Ganas de quejarse; nada entre dos platos; poco mal y bien quejado; más es el ruido que las nueces. *Much at one,* Casi de igual valor o influencia. *Much about,* Alrededor, por ahí. *Much of a muchness,* (Fam.) Casi lo mismo; poco más o menos lo mismo.

Muchness [much'-nes], *s.* Cantidad, y vulgarmente calidad.

†**Muchwhat** [much'-hwet], *adv.* Casi, poco más o menos.

Mucid [miū'-sid], *a.* Viscoso, mohoso, glutinoso; mucilaginoso.

Mucidness [miū'-sid-nes], *s.* (Poco us.) Viscosidad, mucosidad.

Mucilage [miū'-si-lêj], *s.* Mucílago.

Mucilaginous [miū-si-laj'-i-nus], *a.* Mucilaginoso, viscoso.

Mucin [miū'-sin], *s.* Mucina, substancia mucilaginosa secretada por las membranas mucosas.

Mucivorous [miū-siv'-o-rus], *a.* Mucívoro, que se alimenta de mucosidades, de los jugos de plantas.

Muck [muc], *s.* 1. Abono, el estiércol que se echa a las tierras para beneficiarlas. 2. Tierra vegetal, despojos vegetales corrompidos y mezclados con tierra. 3. Porquería, basura, cualquiera cosa baja, vil y asquerosa. 4. Dinero: en sentido despreciativo. *To run a muck,* Atropellar por todo sin consideración. *V.* AMUCK. *Muck-fork,* Horquilla para estiércol.

Muck, *va.* Estercolar, echar estiércol en la tierra.

†**Muckender** [muk'-en-der], *s.* Mocador, moquero, pañuelo para los mocos.

Muckhill [muc'-hil], *s.* Estercolero.

Muckiness [muk'-i-nes], *s.* Suciedad, porquería, inmundicia.

Mucking [muk'-ing], *s.* El acto de abonar con estiércol.

Muckle, *s.* *V.* MICKLE.

Muck-sweat [muc'-swet], *s.* (Med.) Sudor copioso.

Muck-worm [muc'-wūrm], *s.* 1. Gusano de estercolero o muladar. 2. Cicatero, ruin, miserable, mezquino.

Mucky [muk'-i], *a.* Puerco, sucio, asqueroso.

Mucoid [miū'-ceid], *a.* Mucoso, semejante a mucosidad.

Mucor [miū'-cēr], *s.* 1. Moco, mucosidad de los animales. 2. Estado de lo que se halla enmohecido. 3. Nombre de un género de hongos.

Mucous [miū'-cus], *a.* Mocoso, viscoso, glutinoso, pegajoso.

Mucousness [miū'-cus-nes], *s.* Mucosidad, viscosidad.

Mucro [miū'-crō], *s.* Punta.

Mucronate, Mucronated [miū'-crō-nêt-ed], *a.* Puntiagudo, mucronato.

Mucus [miū'-cus], *s.* 1. Mucosidad, substancia parecida al mucílago vegetal, secretado por las membranas mucosas; mocos de las narices. 2. Mucosidad.

Mud [mud], *s.* 1. Fango, limo, légamo del mar, de un estanque, de un charco, etc. 2. Cieno, lodo. 3. Barro, la masa que resulta de la unión de la tierra con el agua. *To stick in the mud,* Atollarse, enfangarse; estar en un cenagal. *Mud-*

dauber, Pelopeo, matador de arañas, avispa que construye para sus larvas celdas de barro a las cuales lleva arañas u orugas para alimento de las larvas. *Mud-lighter*, Gánguil, lancha de draga. *Mud-bath*, Baño de cieno en ciertos manantiales medicinales, en que se sumergen los reumáticos hasta el cuello. *Mud-sucker*, Somormujo, ave acuática. *Mud-volcano*, Cono volcánico que arroja cieno. (Mex.) Hornito.

Mud, *va.* 1. Encenagar, meter o meterse en cieno. 2. Enturbiar, ensuciar.

Muddily [mud'-i-li], *adv.* Turbiamente.

Muddiness [mud'-i-nes], *s.* 1. Turbiedad, suciedad. 2. Confusión de ideas.

Muddle [mud'-l], *va.* 1. Enturbiar. 2. Embriagar, atontar, entontecer, embotar.—*vn.* Estar algo atontado; estar confuso.

Muddy [mud'-i], *a.* 1. Cenagoso, lodoso, sucio, enturbiado, turbio. 2. Grosero, compuesto de tierra o barro, impuro. 3. Tonto, estúpido, confuso.

Muddy, *va.* 1. Enturbiar, ensuciar. 2. Entontecer, obscurecer, turbar.

Muddy-headed [mud'-i-hed-ed], *a.* Turbio o torpe de entendimiento.

Mudguard [mud'-gārd], *s.* Guardafango, guardabarros.

Mud-scow [mud'-scau], *s.* Pontón con que se limpia el río.

Mudsill [mud'-sil], *s.* 1. Madero de construcción puesto inmediatamente sobre el suelo. 2. (E. U.) Persona de baja condición social.

Mud-wall [mud'-wōl], *s.* Tapia, pared formada de tierra sola.

Mud-walled [mud'-wōld], *a.* Tapiado, hecho de tapias.

Mudwort [mud'-wūrt], *s.* (Bot.) Limosela, nombre genérico de plantas. *Common mudwort*, Limosela acuática.

Muezzin [miū-ez'-in], *s.* Muecín, el que desde los minaretes de las mezquitas anuncia la hora de la oración; almuédano, almuecín.

Muff [muf], *s.* Manguito; estufilla.

Muff. Acción poco diestra; en el juego de la pelota, falta, dejar escapar o caer la pelota en vez de cogerla.—*va.* Hacer algo poco diestramente; dejar escapar la pelota en vez de cogerla.

Muffin [muf'-in], *s.* Mollete, bodigo, panecillo.

Muffle [muf'-l], *s.* 1. (Quím.) Mufla, cubierta de barro que se pone encima de los hornillos, copelas, etc. 2. Horno de esmaltar, horno de arcilla para cocer la alfarería; también horno de copela.

Muffle, *va.* 1. Embozar, encubrir el rostro y defenderlo del frío. 2. Vendar a uno los ojos. 3. Envolver, encubrir, ocultar, tapar, para disminuir el sonido. *To muffle a drum*, Enfundar, enlutar un tambor. *Muffled oars*, Remos cubiertos de tela o trapos para ensordecer su ruido.—*vn.* Hablar confusamente.

Muffler [muf'-lẹr], *s.* 1. Bufanda. 2. Sordina. 3. Silenciador (de un automóvil).

Mufti [muf'-ti], *s.* Mufti, el sumo sacerdote de los mahometanos.

Mug [mug], *s.* 1. Cubilete, vasito sin pie y con asa para beber; pichel. 2. (Bajo) La cara o la boca; mueca.

Muggy [mug'-i], **Muggish** [mug'-ish], *a.* Húmedo, caluroso y sofocante (del tiempo): húmedo y mohoso (v. g. el heno).

Mug-house [mug'-haus], *s.* (Vulg.) Cervecería, el sitio o casa donde se vende cerveza.

Mugweed [mug'-wīd], *s.* (Bot.) Cuajaleche cruzado, una planta británica.

Mugwort [mug'-wūrt], *s.* (Bot.) Artemisa o artemisa vulgar.

Mugwump [mug'-wump], *s.* (Política de los E. U.) Elector que de ordinario vota con un partido, pero que se reserva el derecho de votar con entera independencia, llegado el caso.

Mulatto [miu-lat'-ō], *s.* Mulato, la persona que ha nacido de negra y blanco o al contrario.

Mulberry [mul'-ber-i], *s.* Mora, el fruto de la morera. *Mulberry-tree*, Morera o moral, el árbol que produce las moras.

Mulch [mulch], *va.* Cubrir (las plantas, hierbas, etc.) con paja y estiércol.—*s.* El estiércol y la paja, que se echa alrededor de los tallos de las plantas para abrigar sus raíces.

Mulct [mulct], *s.* Multa, pena pecuniaria.

Mulct, *va.* Multar, cargar o imponer alguna pena pecuniaria.

Mulctuary [mulc'-chu-ẹ-ri], *a.* Lo que pertenece á multa.

Mule [miūl], *s.* 1. Mulo, macho, mula, animal engendrado de caballo y burra o de burro y yegua. *She-mule*, Mula. 2. Una planta cualquiera proveniente de una semilla fecundada por el polen de otra especie; cualquier híbrido. 3. Telar que tira del hilo, lo pone tenso y lo tuerce en una sola operación. *Mule-jenny*, Telar para tejer algodón. *V.* 3ª acep. *Mule-twist*, Algodón tejido con el telar llamado "*mule-jenny.*"

Muleteer [miū-let-īr'], **Mule-driver** [miūl'-draiv-ẹr], *s.* Mulero, muletero o mulatero; mozo de mulas.

Muliebrity [miū-li-eb'-ri-ti], *s.* Las costumbres, carácter y demás cualidades propias de las mujeres.

Mulier [miū'-li-ẹr], *s.* 1. (Der. civil.) Mujer casada. 2. (For.) El hijo que ha nacido después que sus padres contrajeron matrimonio, a distinción del que ha nacido anteriormente, de los mismos padres.

Mulish [miūl'-ish], *a.* Obstinado o terco como una mula.

Mull [mul], *s.* 1. (Ingl.) Estado confuso, enredo, desorden. 2. Muselina clara, tela delgada y suave de algodón.

Mull, *s.* 1. (Esco.) Cabo, promontorio. 2. Tabaquera de cuerno.

Mull, *va.* Calentar cualquier licor sazonándolo al mismo tiempo con substancias aromáticas.—*vn.* 1. Afanarse mucho y efectuar poco.

Mull [mul], *va.* 1. Moler, desmenuzar, reducir a polvo. 2. Confundir, aturrullar.

Mullein, Mullen [mul'-en], *s.* (Bot.) Gordolobo, verbasco. Verbascum Thapsus.

Muller [mul'-ẹr], *s.* 1. Moleta (de los pintores). 2. Una piedra que usan varios artífices para moler con la mano y reducir a polvo alguna cosa sobre otra piedra horizontal.

Mullet, *s.* 1. (Ict.) Múgil, mújol. 2. Barbo de mar. Mullus barbatus. 3. (Her.) Estrellita de espuela; espolín.

Mulligrubs [mul'-i-grubz], *s.* 1. (Vulg.) Retortijón de tripas; mal humor. 2. Pasión ilíaca; cólico.

Mullion [mul'-yun], *s.* (Arq.) Columna o pie derecho que divide el bastidor de una ventana.

Mullion, *va.* Dividir (una ventana) por medio de una columna o pie derecho.

Mulse [muls], *s.* Clarea, bebida que se hace de vino cocido con miel o azúcar.

Multangular [mul-taŋ'-giu-lar], *a.* Polígono, lo que consta de muchos lados o muchos ángulos.

Multangularly [mul-taŋ'-giu-lar-li], *adv.* En figura de polígono.

Multangularness [mul-taŋ'-giu-lar-nes], *s.* La propiedad de tener un cuerpo muchos lados o muchos ángulos.

Multicapsular [mul-ti-cap'-su-lar], *a.* Repartido en muchas cápsulas o celdillas.

Multidentate [mul-ti-den'-têt], *a.* Multidentado, provisto de muchos dientes.

Multifarious [mul-ti-fê'-ri-us], *a.* 1. Multifario, vario, diverso, multiplicado, diferente. 2. (Bot. y Zool.) Dispuesto en varias filas o líneas verticales.

Multifariousness [mul-ti-fê'-ri-us-nes], *s.* Diversidad; variedad, desemejanza, diferencia.

Multifid, Multifidious [mul'-ti-fid, mul-tif'-i-dus], *a.* Dividido en muchas partes; abierto o hendido en muchos lóbulos o porciones.

Multiflorous [mul''-ti-flō'-rus], *a.* Multífloro, de muchas flores.

Multiform [mul'-ti-fōrm], *a.* Multiforme.

Multiformity [mul-ti-fōrm'-i-ti], *s.* Multiformidad, diversidad en las figuras, formas, cualidades o propiedades de una cosa.

Multigenerous [mul-ti-jen'-ẹr-us], *a.* Lo que es de muchos géneros.

Multigraph [mul'-ti-grqf], *s.* Multígrafo.

Multilateral [mul-ti-lat'-ẹr-al], *a.* (Geom.) Multilátero, que consta de más de cuatro lados.

Multilineal [mul-ti-lin'-ẹ-al], *a.* Que tiene muchas líneas.

Multilocular [mul-ti-loc'-yu-lar], *a.* Multilocular, de muchas celdillas.

Multimillionaire [mul-ti-mil'-yun-ār], *s.* Multimillonario.

Multinodous [mul-ti-nō'-dus], *a.* Nudoso, que tiene muchos nudos.

Multinomial [mul-ti-nō'-mi-al], *a.* 1. Lo que tiene muchos nombres. 2. Multinomio: dícese en álgebra de la cantidad que tiene muchos términos.

Multiparous [mul-tip'-a-rus], *a.* Multípara, la hembra que pare muchos hijos a la vez.

Multipartite [mul-ti-pār'-tait], *a.* Que consta de muchas partes.

Multiped [mul'-ti-ped], *a.* Multípedo, que tiene muchas patas.—*s.* Ciempiés, escolopendra, animalillo articulado que tiene numerosas patas.

Multiple [mul'-ti-pl], *a.* Múltiplice, múltiple, que contiene más de uno; repetido más de una vez.—*s.* Múltiplice o múltiplo.

Multiple sclerosis [mul-ti-pl sclerō'-sis], *s.* (Med.) Esclerosis múltiple.

Multiplex [mul'-ti-plex], *a.* 1. Múltiplice, que consta de muchas partes. 2. *V.* MULTIPLICATE, 2ª acep.

Multipliable [mul-ti-plai'-a-bl], **Mul-**

tiplicable [mul'-ti-pli-ca-bl], *a.* Multiplicable.
Multipliableness [mul-ti-plai'-a-bl-nes], *s.* La capacidad de ser multiplicado o la calidad de ser multiplicable.
Multiplicand [mul-ti-pli-cand'], *s.* Multiplicando.
Multiplicate [mul-tip'-li-kêt], *a.* 1. Multiplicado, aumentado en cantidad o en número. 2. (Bot.) Plegado en muchos pliegues.
Multiplication [mul-ti-pli-kê'-shun], *s.* 1. Multiplicación. 2. (Arit.) Multiplicación, la regla que enseña a multiplicar un número por otro.
Multiplicative [mul'-ti-pli-kê''-tiv], *a.* Multiplicador, multiplicativo.
Multiplicator [mul'-ti-pli-kê-tẹr], *s.* Multiplicador.
Multiplicity [mul-ti-plis'-i-ti], *s.* Multiplicidad, muchedumbre.
Multiplier [mul'-ti-plai-ẹr], *s.* 1. Multiplicador. 2. Multiplicador, espiral plana de alambre conductor que sirve para aumentar el efecto de una corriente eléctrica sobre una aguja. 3. Máquina que sirve para multiplicar.
Multiply [mul'-ti-plai], *va.* 1. Multiplicar. 2. Multiplicar un número por otro.—*vn.* 1. Multiplicar o multiplicarse, aumentarse por medio de la generación. 2. Cundir, propagarse.
Multiplying-glass [mul'-ti-plai-ing-glas], *s.* Disposición especial de espejos diminutos, que multiplica el número de las imágenes. *Multiplying-lens*, Lente de muchas facetas, lente multiplicadora.
Multipolar [mul''-ti-pō'-lar], *a.* Multipolar, que tiene más de dos polos; dícese de ciertas celdillas de nervio y de aparatos eléctricos.
Multipresence [mul-ti-prez'-ẹns], *s.* La facultad de hallarse presente en varios parajes a un mismo tiempo.
Multisiliquous [mul-ti-sil'-i-cwus], *a.* (Bot.) Multisilicuoso, que tiene muchas vainas.
Multisonous [mul-tis'-o-nus], *a.* Que tiene muchos sonidos.
Multi-stage rocket [mul-ti stêj rek'-et], *s.* (Aer.) Cohete de ignición múltiple.
Multisyllable [mul''-ti-sil'-a-bl], *s.* Multisílabo, palabra compuesta de más de tres sílabas. *V.* POLYSYLLABLE.
Multitude [mul'-ti-tiūd], *s.* 1. Multitud, muchedumbre, gran número de personas o cosas juntas. 2. Muchedumbre, pueblo, vulgo, turba, el común de la gente.
Multitudinous [mul-ti-tiū'-di-nus], *a.* Numeroso; muchos; varios.
Multivalve [mul'-ti-valv], *a.* Multivalvo; dícese de las conchas que resultan de la reunión de más de dos valvas.—*s.* Multivalva, género de conchas de muchas almejas.
Multocular [mult-oc'-yū-lar], *a.* Que tiene muchos ojos.
Multure [mul'-chur], *s.* 1. Maquila, la porción de grano que corresponde al molinero por la molienda; molienda, el grano que se ha molido de una vez. 2. Tanto por ciento que se paga al dueño de un pulverizador de minerales.
Mum [mum], *inter.* ¡Chito! ¡chitón! ¡silencio! interjección de que se usa para imponer silencio.—*s.* Cerveza muy fuerte de trigo.—*a.* Callado, silencioso.
Mum [mum], *va.* y *vn.* Enmascarar, enmascararse; disfrazarse.
Mumble [mum'-bl], *vn.* 1. Gruñir, murmullar entre dientes mostrando disgusto. 2. Murmurar o mormurar, decir alguna cosa entre dientes, muy quedo. 3. Farfullar, hablar precipitadamente. 4. Mascar o comer poco a poco y con los labios cerrados.—*va.* 1. Musitar, barbotar, hablar entre dientes; barbullar. 2. Agarrar con la boca.
Mumbler [mum'-blẹr], *s.* Farfulla, farfullador; gruñidor.
Mumbling [mum'-bling], *s.* El acto de farfullar; mascadura con los labios cerrados.
Mumblingly [mum'-bling-li], *adv.* Con pronunciación mal articulada; farfullando.
Mum-chance [mum'-chans], *s.* 1. Silencio. 2. (Des.) Un juego de dados.
Mummer [mum'-ẹr], *s.* Máscara, el que está enmascarado o disfrazado.
Mummery [mum'-ẹr-i], **Mumming** [mum'-ing], *s.* Momería, mojiganga, trampantojo, disfraz.
Mummification [mum-i-fi-kê'-shun], *s.* Momificación, conversión en momia.
Mummiform [mum'-i-fōrm], *a.* Momiforme, que se parece a una momia.
Mummify [mum'-i-fai], *va.* Momificar, convertir en momia un cadáver; embalsamar; preservar secando.
Mummy [mum'-i], *s.* 1. Momia, cuerpo embalsamado por los egipcios de un modo particular. *To beat to a mummy*, Moler a palos. 2. Especie de cera o betún que usan los jardineros para plantar o ingertar árboles.
Mump [mump], *va.* 1. Mordiscar, morder o mascar. 2. Farfullar, hablar precipitadamente. 3. (Vulg.) Mendigar, pedir limosna de puerta en puerta.
Mumper [mump'-ẹr], *s.* Mendigo.
Mumping [mump'-ing], *s.* El acto de mascar con la boca cerrada; mendiguez.
Mumpish [mump'-ish], *a.* Moroso, intratable, malcontento, malhumorado.
Mumpishness [mump'-ish-nes], *s.* Ceño; morosidad; insociabilidad.
Mumps [mumps], *s.* 1. Tumores glandulosos del cuello; paperas, parótidas. 2. (Raro) Murria, mal humor.
Munch [munch], *va.* Mascar despacio y con ruido; mascar a dos carrillos.
Muncher [mun'-chẹr], *s.* Tragón, comilón.
Mundane [mun'-dên], *a.* Mundano; lo opuesto a espiritual o celestial.
‖**Mundanity** [mun-dan'-i-ti], *s.* (Raro) La calidad de lo que es mundano, mundanalidad.
Mundic [mun'-dic], *s.* Especie de marquesita que se halla en las minas de estaño.
‖**Mundify** [mun'-di-fai], *va.* Mundificar, limpiar, purgar, purificar.
‖**Mundivagant** [mun-div'-a-gant], *a.* Vagamundo o vagabundo.
Munerary [miū'-nẹr-ẹ-ri], *a.* (Poco us.) De la naturaleza de un regalo o dádiva.
Mungoose [mun'-gus], *s.* *V.* MONGOOSE.
†**Mungrel** [mun'-grel], *a.* y *s.* *V.* MONGREL.
Municipal [miu-nis'-i-pal], *a.* Municipal, lo que toca o pertenece a los derechos o costumbres de un pueblo o país.
Municipality [miu-nis-i-pal'-i-ti], *s.* El partido o distrito de la jurisdicción del ayuntamiento de un pueblo.
Muniferous [miu-nif'-ẹr-us], *a.* Dadivoso, liberal, generoso.
Munificence [miu-nif'-i-sens], *s.* Munificencia, liberalidad, generosidad, largueza.
Munificent [miu-nif'-i-sent], *a.* Munífico, liberal, generoso.
Munificently [miu-nif'-i-sent-li], *adv.* Liberalmente, muníficamente.
Muniment [miū'-ni-mẹnt], *s.* 1. Fortaleza; apoyo, defensa. 2. Títulos, documentos, papeles o escritos que se guardan en un archivo.
Munition [miu-nish'-un], *s.* 1. Fortificación, fortaleza. 2. Municiones, los pertrechos y bastimentos necesarios para la manutención de un ejército o plaza. *Munition-bread*, Pan de munición. *Munition-ship*, Navío almacén.
Munjeet [mun-jīt'], *s.* Rubia que se saca de la raíz de la Rubia cordifolia, planta de la India.
†**Munnion** [mun'-yun], *s.* (Arq. Des.) *V.* MULLION.
Muntjack, **Muntjak** [munt'-jac], *s.* Animal de la familia del ciervo que se encuentra en la isla de Java. Cervulus muntjac.
Murage [miū'-rẹj], *s.* Un tributo que antiguamente se pagaba para el reparo de los muros.
Mural [miū'-ral], *a.* 1. Mural, lo que se refiere a los muros o paredes; apoyado en una pared. 2. Que se asemeja a una pared; escarpado, vertical. *Mural crown*, Corona mural. *Mural circle*, (Ast.) Círculo mural. *V.* CIRCLE. *Mural tablet*, Tablilla fijada en una pared.
Murc [mūrc], *s.* Orujo, hollejo de la uva y otras frutas después de exprimidas.
Murder [mūr'-dẹr], *s.* Asesinato, homicidio con premeditación.
Murder, *va.* 1. Asesinar, matar alevosamente. 2. (Fig.) Mutilar, desfigurar, echar a perder, arruinar. 3. Destruir, exterminar, acabar con alguien o algo.
Murderer [mūr'-dẹr-ẹr], *s.* Asesino.
Murderess [mūr'-dẹr-es], *sf.* La mujer que comete un asesinato.
Murderous [mūr'-dẹr-us], *a.* 1. Homicida, matador. 2. Sanguinario, cruel, bárbaro; asesino.
Murderously [mūr'-dẹr-us-li], *adv.* Sanguinariamente.
†**Mure** [miūr], *va.* Murar, cercar con murallas.
Murex [miū'-rex], *s.* (Zool.) Múrice, nombre genérico de unos caracoles de mar cuya boca termina en una canal recta.
Muriate [miū'-ri-êt], *s.* Muriato, nombre que antes se daba a un hidroclorato o cloruro.
Muriatic [miū-ri-at'-ic], *a.* Muriático; hidroclórico; nombre antiguo.
Muricate o **Muricated** [miū'-ri-kêt, ed], *a.* Punzante, espinoso.
Muricide [miū'-ri-said], *s.* Matador de ratones.
Muridæ [miū'-ri-dī], *s. pl.* Múridos, familia del orden de los roedores, entre cuyas especies se cuentan el ratón y la rata.
Muriform [miū'-ri-fōrm], *a.* (Bot.) Dispuesto del mismo modo que los ladrillos de un muro o pared; dícese de las celdillas de las plantas.
Murk [mūrk], *a.* *V.* MURKY.—*s.* 1. (Ant.) Obscuridad, lobreguez. 2. *V.* MURC.

Murky [mŭrk'-i], *a.* Obscuro, lóbrego.
Murmur [mŭr'-mur], *s.* 1. Murmullo, murmurio, susurro. 2. Murmullo, rumor. 3. Murmuración, queja, descontento.
Murmur, *vn.* 1. Murmurar, susurrar, hablando de arroyos, hojas, abejas, etc. 2. Murmullar, gruñir, quejarse. En este último sentido se usa con *at* delante de cosas, y *against* delante de personas. *Murmur not at your sickness*, No te quejes de tu enfermedad. *Murmur not against government*, No te quejes del gobierno.
Murmurer [mŭr'-mur-ẹr], *s.* Gruñidor, murmurador.
Murmuring [mur'-mur-ing], *s.* Murmullo; murmuración.
Murmuringly [mur'-mur-ing-li], *adv.* Con murmullo; con queja.
Murrain [mur'-ẹn], *s.* Morriña, enfermedad epidémica que causa mucha mortandad en el ganado.
Murre, Murr [mŭr], *s.* 1. Ave marina, particularmente la uria. 2. Ave del género Alca. *V.* AUK.
Murrey [mur'-ẹ], *a.* Morado, color mezcla de rojo y negro.
†**Murther**, *s.* *V.* MURDER.
Musa [miū'-za], *s.* Nombre latino del bananero o plátano y de otras plantas musáceas.
Muscadel [mus'-ca-del], **Muscat** [mus'-cat], **Muscatel**, *s.* Moscatel, especie de uva, de vino y de pera dulces.
Muscadine [mus'-ca-din], *s.* (E. U.) La vid silvestre de los Estados Unidos del Sur. Vitis rotundifolia.
Muscardine [mus'-car-din], *s.* Muscardina, enfermedad de los gusanos de seda que destruye la cosecha de capullos. Su causa es un hongo parásito llamado Botrytis Bassiana.
Muscle [mus'-l], *s.* 1. Músculo. 2. La fuerza de los músculos. 3. *V.* MUSSEL.
Muscle-bound [mus'-l-baund], *a.* Con los músculos rígidos (debido a excesiva actividad en los deportes).
Muscoid [mus'-ceid], *a.* Parecido al musgo.—*s.* Planta que se asemeja al musgo.
Muscosity [mus-ces'-i-ti], *s.* El estado de lo que se halla cubierto de moho o de musgo.
Muscovado [mus-co-vé'-dō o -vq'-dō], *s.* Mascabado, azúcar que desde el tacho se pasa directamente a los bocoyes de envase.
Muscovite [mus'-co-vait], *a.* Moscovita, moscovítico, ruso.
Muscovy [mus'-co-vi], *s.* Ánade americano mayor que el ánade ordinario. Se domestica mucho. Cairina moschata.
Muscular [mus'-kiū-lar], *a.* 1. Muscular. 2. Poderoso, vigoroso. *Muscular dystrophy*, Distrofia muscular.
Muscularity [mus-kiu-lar'-i-ti], *s.* El estado de lo que tiene músculos.
Musculature [mus'-kiu-la-tiūr], *s.* Musculatura, el conjunto o la disposición de los músculos.
Muse [miūz], *s.* 1. Musa, nombre de las nueve deidades del Parnaso. 2. Meditación profunda, atención intensa. 3. Musa, numen o ingenio poético. 4. Senda de liebres o conejos.
Muse, *vn.* 1. Meditar, aplicar el pensamiento con intensidad a la consideración de alguna cosa, pensar o reflexionar profundamente. 2. Pasmarse, quedar suspenso o admirado. 3. Distraerse, dejarse llevar de la fantasía; estar meditando o ideando; estar distraído o pensativo.
Museful [miūz'-ful], *a.* Cogitabundo, muy pensativo, muy distraído.
Museless [miūz'-les], *a.* Que es insensible a los halagos de la poesía.
Muser [miūz'-ẹr], *s.* El que está muy pensativo y absorto.
Muset [miū'-zet], *s.* Senda de conejos, y de la caza en general.
Museum [miū-zī'-um], *s.* Museo, gabinete de historia natural, de obras de arte, de las de la antigüedad o de curiosidades instructivas; y el edificio que contiene dicha colección.
Mush [mush], *s.* (E. U.) 1. Potaje espeso o pudín que se hace cociendo harina de maíz en agua o leche. 2. Una cosa cualquiera blanda y mollar. 3. Mineral de hierro de primera calidad.
Mushroom [mush'-rūm], *s.* 1. (Bot.) Seta, hongo, champiñón. 2. Persona que surge de la noche a la mañana.—*vn.* Crecer rápidamente, surgir de repente.
Mushy [mush'-i], *a.* Mollar, pulposo.
Music [miū'-zic], *s.* 1. Música, el arte de combinar los sonidos armoniosos de la voz humana, de los instrumentos, o de una y otros, que comprende la melodía y la armonía. 2. Composición musical. 3. Sonido acorde y modulado o sucesión de dichos sonidos. 4. (Zool.)Estridor de varios insectos. *Music of the spheres*, La armonía de las esferas celestes que según la teoría de Platón podían oir sólo los dioses. *Music-book*, Libro de música; libro o cuaderno que contiene trozos de música. *Music-box* o *musical box*, Caja de música. *Music-hall*, Salón de conciertos. *Music-stand*, (1) Pupitre para papeles de música. (2) Tablado para una orquesta. *Music-stool*, Taburete o banqueta de piano. *Music-rack*, Atril para música.
Musical [miū'-zi-cal], *a.* 1. Musical, que pertenece a la música. 2. Armonioso, melodioso.
Musical comedy [miū'-zi-cal cem'-e-di], *s.* Comedia o revista musical.
Musicale [miu'-zi-kạl], *s.* Velada musical.
Musically [miū'-zi-cal-i], *adv.* Con armonía y consonancia.
Musicalness [miū'-zi-cal-nes], *s.* Armonía, melodía.
Musician [miū-zish'-an], *s.* Músico.
Music-master [miū'-zic-mạs-tẹr], *s.* Maestro de música.
Musing [miū'-zing], *a.* Contemplativo, pensativo, absorto en la meditación.—*s.* Reflexión profunda, meditación, ensueño.
Musk [musk], *s.* 1. Musco, almizcle, substancia muy odorífera que se saca de la bolsa que el almizclero tiene en el vientre. 2. (Bot.) Almizcleña. 3. El olor de almizcle o una substancia de parecido olor. 4. *V.* *Musk-deer*. *Musk-apple*, Camuesa o manzana almizcleña. *Musk-cat*, Desmán. *V.* CIVET. *Musk-cherry*, (Bot.) Cereza almizcleña. *Musk-deer*, Almizclero, animal rumiante muy parecido al corzo común por su tamaño y figura. Tiene en lo bajo del vientre una bolsa redondeada algo saliente que produce el almizcle. Habita en casi toda el Asia. *Musk-grape*, Moscatel. *Musk-pear*, Mosqueruela, pera amizcleña. *Musk-rose*, Rosa amizcleña. *Musk-seed*, Grano de ambarilla. *Musk-thistle*, (Bot.) Cardo nutante, una planta.
Musk, *va.* Almizclar, perfumar con almizcle.
Musked [musct], *a.* Almizclado.
Musket [mus'-kẹt], *s.* 1. Mosquete. 2. Gavilán macho, un ave.
Musketeer [mus-kẹt-īr'], *s.* Mosquetero, el soldado que sirve con mosquete.
Musketoon [mus-kẹt-ūn'], *s.* Trabuco, una especie de escopeta que tiene la boca muy ancha.
Muskiness [musk'-i-nes], *s.* Olor de almizcle.
Muskmelon [musc'-mel-en], *s.* Melón almizcleño, muy fragante. (Prov. Esp.) Melón de Castilla.
Muskrat [musk'-rat], *s.* Rata almizclada o almizclera, especie de roedor americano que se parece a la rata y que despide un olor como el del almizcle. Su piel es muy estimada para abrigos.
Musky [musk'-i], *a.* Almizcleño, lo que huele a almizcle; almizclado.
Muslim, *s.* *V.* MOSLEM.
Muslin [muz'-lin], *s.* 1. Muselina, tela fina hecha de algodón, llamada también bengala. 2. Tela de algodón propia para ropa interior y sábanas.—*a.* Hecho de muselina.
Musquash [mus'-cwesh], *s.* Almizclera. Fiber zibethicus. (Nombre indígena.) *V.* MUSKRAT.
Musqueteer, *s.* *V.* MUSKETEER.
Muss [mus], *s.* 1. (Fam. E. U.) Estado de desorden, confusión. 2. (Vulg.) Arrebatiña, sarracina, riña.—*va.* (Fam. E. U.) 1. Poner en confusión, desarreglar, arrugar. 2. Ensuciar. *V.* MESS.
Mussel [mus'-l], *s.* Pequeño marisco comestible. Mytilus edulis.
Mussing [mus'-ing], *s.* 1. Manoseo. 2. Desarreglo.
Mussulman [mus'-ul-man], *s.* Musulmán.
Must [must], *v. imp.* Deber; ser o estar obligado o precisado; ser preciso, ser menester, ser necesario, convenir, haber de hacerse alguna cosa. *I must have done it*, Yo hubiera debido hacerlo. *It must be*, Ha de ser o debe ser. *I must go and see it*, Es preciso que yo vaya a verlo. *You must take the air oftener*, Debe Vd. de tomar el aire más a menudo.
Must, *s.* 1. Mosto, el zumo exprimido de la uva antes de hacerse vino. 2. La pulpa de patatas preparada para la fermentación.
Must, *s.* *V.* MUSTINESS.
Must, *va.* Enmohecer.—*vn.* Enmohecerse.
Mustache [mus-tạsh'], *s.* 1. Mostachos, bigotes. 2. Mono llamado cercopiteco que habita en el oeste de África. 3. Soldado.
Mustang [mus'-tang], *s.* Caballo medio salvaje de las llanuras americanas, de raza española. (< mesteño.)
Mustard [mus'-tard], *s.* Mostaza. *Mustard gas*, Gas de mostaza (empleado como gas venenoso en la primera guerra mundial). *Mustard plaster*, Cataplasma de mostaza. *Mustard-pot*, Mostacera, salsera para la mostaza.
Musteline, Musteloid [mus'-tẹ-lain o lin, mus'-tẹ-leid], *a.* Mustelino, parecido a la comadreja.
Muster [mus'-tẹr], *vn.* (Mil.) Juntarse o unirse para formar un ejército; pasar lista.—*va.* 1. (Mil.) Pa-

sar revista de tropas. 2. Agregar, congregar; recobrar o mostrar, v. gr. hablando del ánimo.

Muster, *s.* (Mil.) Revista; reseña. *To pass muster*, Pasar revista; valer algo o servir de algo. *Such excuses will not pass muster with God*, Semejantes disculpas nada valdrán para con Dios.

Muster-book [mus'-tẹr-buc], *s.* Libro de revistas.

Muster-master [mus'-tẹr-mas-tẹr], *s.* Comisario de revistas.

Muster-roll [mus'-tẹr-rōl], *s.* 1. Matrícula de revista. 2. (Mar.) Rol de la tripulación.

Mustily [mus'-ti-li], *adv.* Con moho.

Mustiness [mus'-ti-nes], *s.* Husmo, olor a estadizo u olor que despiden las cosas que ya empiezan a pasarse; moho.

Musty [mus'-ti], *a.* 1. Mohoso, enmohecido. 2. Añejo, añejado. 3. Mustio, triste.

Mutability [miu-ta-bil'-i-ti], *s.* Mutabilidad, inconstancia, instabilidad.

Mutable [miū'-ta-bl], *a.* Mudable, alterable, inconstante, instable.

Mutableness [miū'-ta-bl-nes], *s.* Mutabilidad, inconstancia.

Mutably [miū'-ta-bli], *adv.* Instablemente.

Mutation [miū-tê'-shun], *s.* Mudanza, alteración; mutación.

Mutch [much], *s.* (Esco.) Gorra con muchos pliegues, para mujer.

Mute [miūt], *a.* 1. Mudo, silencioso, que no habla; en derecho, que se niega a responder ante la justicia. 2. Mudo, privado de la facultad de hablar. 3. (Gram.) Mudo, que no se pronuncia; también, que se produce contrayendo o estrechando los órganos de la boca.—*s.* 1. Mudo, el que no puede hablar. 2. Letra muda. 3. (Mús.) Sordina, tablita de madera que se pone sobre los puentecillos de los instrumentos de cuerda para ensordecerlos. 4. Funcionario turco que ejerce de verdugo en las ejecuciones de personas de alto rango.

†**Mute**, *vn.* (Des. o Prov.) Tullir, arrojar las aves los excrementos.

Mutely [miūt'-li], *adv.* Mudamente, sin hablar palabra.

Muteness [miūt'-nes], *s.* Silencio, aversión á hablar.

Mutilate [miū'-ti-lêt], *va.* 1. Mutilar. 2. Mutilar, cortar ó separar una parte esencial.

Mutilation [miū'-ti-lê-shun], *s.* Mutilación.

Mutilator [miū'-ti-lê-tẹr], *s.* Mutilador.

Mutineer [miū-ti-nīr'], *s.* Amotinador, amotinado, sedicioso.

Muting [miūt'-ing], *s.* 1. Acción de poner sordina a un instrumento de música. 2. (Des.) Tullidura, el estiércol de ave.

Mutinous [miū'-tin-us], *a.* Amotinado, sedicioso, turbulento, faccioso.

Mutinously [miū'-tin-us-li], *adv.* Amotinadamente.

Mutinousness [miū'-tin-us-nes], *s.* Amotinamiento, sedición, rebelión.

Mutiny [miū'-ti-ni], *vn.* Amotinarse, rebelarse.

Mutiny, *s.* 1. Motín, amotinamiento, insurrección de soldados o de marineros contra sus jefes. 2. (Gran Bret.) Rebelión, sedición.

Mutism [miū'-tizm], *s.* Mudez, impedimento en el habla, imposibilidad de hablar.

Mutter [mut'-ẹr], *vn.* Pronunciar palabras en voz baja y con la boca casi cerrada, o con tono de mal humor o de queja; gruñir, refunfuñar, rezongar, murmurar.—*va.* Musitar, hablar entre dientes, hablar en voz baja e indistinta.

Mutter, *s.* 1. Murmuración, queja, regañamiento. 2. El acto de musitar o hablar entre dientes.

Mutterer [mut'-ẹr-ẹr], *s.* Rezongador, gruñón.

Muttering [mut'-ẹr-ing], *s.* Refunfuño.

Mutteringly [mut'-ẹr-ing-li], *adv.* En voz baja, inarticuladamente.

Mutton [mut'-n], *s.* 1. Carnero, la carne del animal así llamado. 2. (Fest.) Carnero, el mismo animal.

Mutton-broth [mut'-n-brēth], *s.* Caldo de carnero.

Mutton-chop [mut'-n-chep], *s.* Costilla de carnero, chuleta.

Mutton-pie [mut'-n-pai], *s.* Empanada de carnero.

Mutual [miū'-chu-al], *a.* Mutuo, recíproco. *Mutual aid*, Apoyo mutuo, ayuda mutua. *Mutual aid association*, 1. Asociación de ayuda mutua. 2. Mutualidad.

Mutuality [miū-chu-al'-i-ti], *s.* Reciprocidad, reciprocación.

Mutually [miū'-chu-al-i], *adv.* Mutuamente, recíprocamente.

Mutule [miū'-tiūl], *s.* (Arq.) Modillón.

Muzhik [mū-zhik'], *s.* Labriego ruso, o el que fué siervo.

Muzzle [muz'-l], *s.* 1. Boca, entrada o abertura de alguna cosa. 2. Bozal, frenillo, lo que se pone a algunos animales para que no muerdan; risuelo, el frenillo que se pone a los hurones. 3. Boca de una persona, en desprecio; hocico, jeta, de los animales. *Muzzle-loader*, Escopeta o cañón, que se carga por la boca; lo opuesto a *breech-loader*. *Muzzle-loading*, *a.* Que se carga por la boca. *Muzzle-moulding*, Adornos de las bocas de los cañones. *Muzzle-ring*, Anillo de las bocas de los cañones. *Muzzle-velocity*, Velocidad inicial.

Muzzle, *va.* 1. Embozar, abozalar, poner bozal a algún animal. 2. Imponer silencio, impedir que uno publique o arengue. 3. Se aplica figuradamente a las cosas con la significación de impedir que una cosa haga daño.—*vn.* Acercar el hocico los animales o ponerlo cerca de algo para oler.

Muzzy [muz'-i], *a.* (Vulg.) Distraído, olvidadizo, enajenado, descuidado, negligente; borracho.

My [mai], *adj. posses.* y *pron.* Caso posesivo o genitivo de *I*, yo; mi, mis, lo que es mío o me pertenece. *My house*, Mi casa; *my houses*, mis casas. *My children*, Mis hijos. *My own*, Mío, propio. *My own book*, Mi propio libro. *Cf.* MINE.

Mycelium [mi-sī'-li-um], *s.* (Bot.) Micelión, substancia blanca y filamentosa que parece ser el estado rudimentario, o más bien vegetativo, de los hongos.

Mycology [mi-cel'-o-ji], *s.* Micetología, micología, tratado sobre los hongos.

Mynheer [min-hīr'], *s.* 1. Señor, título de cortesía en Holanda. 2. Holandés.

Myocarditis [mai-o-kār-dai'-tis], *s.* (Med.) Miocarditis.

Myocardium [mai-o-kar'-di-um], *s.* Miocardio.

Myography [mai-eg'-ra-fi], **Myology** [mai-el'-o-ji], *s.* Miografía o miología, descripción científica de los músculos.

Myopathy [mai-ep'-a-thi], *s.* Enfermedad de los músculos.

Myope [mai'-ōp], **Myops** [mai'-eps], *s.* Miope, el que es corto de vista.

Myopia, Myopy [mai-ō'-pi-a, mai'-o-pi], *s.* Miopía, cortedad de vista.

Myopic [mai-ep'-ic], *a.* Miope, corto de vista.

Myriad [mir'-i-ad], *s.* 1 El número de diez mil entre los anticuarios. 2. Millares, se usa proverbialmente para expresar un gran número.

Myosotis [mai-o-sō'-tis], *s.* Miosotis o miosótide, planta de la familia de las borragíneas cuyo nombre familiar es "Nomeolvides."

Myriarch [mir'-i-ārc], *s.* El jefe de diez mil hombres.

Myrmidon [mẹr'-mi-den], *s.* Esbirro, rufián, nombre dado a los hombres groseros y bajos que sirven de instrumento en las maquinaciones de otros por interés.

Myrobalan [mi-reb'-a-lan], *s.* Mirabolanos, especie de fruta parecida al dátil.

Myropolist [mi-rep'-o-list], *s.* Vendedor de ungüentos y perfumes.

Myrrh [mẹr], *s.* Mirra, goma resinosa.

Myrrhic [mẹr'-ic], *a.* Mirrado, perteneciente a la mirra.

Myrrhin [mẹr'-in], *s.* Principio resinoso contenido en la mirra.

Myrtiform [mẹr'-ti-ferm], *a.* Mirtiforme, en figura de bayas de mirto.

Myrtle [mẹr'-tl], *s.* (Bot.) 1. Mirto, arrayán, arbusto o árbol pequeño siempre verde. 2. Cualquiera de otras varias plantas parecidas al mirto; a veces se le da indebidamente en los Estados Unidos a la pervinca el nombre de *myrtle*.

Myrtle-berry [mẹr'-tl-ber-i], *s.* Murtón, la baya o fruto del mirto.

Myself [mai-self'], *pron.* Yo mismo; me, a mí, mí mismo. *I could not direct myself*, No podía dirigirme a mí mismo.

Mystagogical [mis-ta-gej'-i-cal], *a.* Lo que pertenece al intérprete de los misterios de la religión.

Mystagogue [mis'-ta-geg], *s.* Mistagoga, sacerdote griego que iniciaba en los misterios de la religión; el que cuida de las reliquias de alguna iglesia.

Mysterious [mis-tī'-ri-us, †**Mysterial** [mis-tī'-ri-al], *a.* 1. Misterioso, impenetrable al entendimiento. 2. Misterioso, el que hace misterio de alguna cosa.

Mysteriously [mis-tī'-ri-us-li], *adv.* Misteriosamente.

Mysteriousness [mis-tī'-ri-us-nes], *s.* 1. Impenetrabilidad de la cosas sagradas. 2. El acto de hacer misterio de alguna cosa.

Mystery [mis'-tẹr-i], *s.* 1. Misterio: dícese de los de la religión. 2. Misterio, lo que está oculto y es muy difícil de comprender. 3. Enigma. 4. Autos sacramentales. 5. (Ant.) Oficio, profesión, ejercicio.

Mystic, Mystical [mis'-tic, al], *a.* Místico, misterioso, emblemático.

Mystic [mis'-tic], *s.* Místico, el que pretende recibir inspiración divina directa; partidario del misticismo.

Mystically [mis'-tic-al-i], *adv.* Místicamente, en sentido místico.

Mysticalness [mis'-tic-al-nes], *s.* Mística, calidad de místico.

Mysticism [mis'-ti-sizm], *s.* 1. Misticismo, calidad de místico. 2. Misticismo, doctrina de los místicos que pretenden estar en relación directa con la divinidad.
Mystification [mis-ti-fi-ké'-shun], *s.* El acto de hacer obscura una cosa; el de desconcertar intencionalmente a alguien.
Mystify [mis'-ti-fai], *va.* 1. Confundir intencionalmente, desconcertar a una persona. 2. Hacer obscuro, o tratar algo obscuramente.
Myth [mith], *s.* Mito, fábula, ficción alegórica, principalmente en asuntos religiosos.
Mythical [mith'-ic-al], *a.* Mítico; fabuloso, imaginario.
Mythological [mith-o-lej'-ic-al], *a.* Mitológico, relativo a la mitología.
Mythologically [mith-o-lej'-ic-al-i], *adv.* Mitológicamente.
Mythologist [mith-el'-o-jist], *s.* Mitologista, el autor de una obra mitológica; el versado en mitología.
Mythology [mith-el'-o-ji], *s.* 1. Mitología, la historia de los dioses y héroes fabulosos del gentilismo. 2. Estudio crítico de los diversos mitos y religiones.
Myxomycetes [mix-o-mai-sí'-tiz], *s. pl.* Mixomicetes, seres considerados ya como animales, ya como plantas, parecidos á los hongos microscópicos.

N

N [en]. Letra décimacuarta del alfabeto inglés. Se pronuncia como en español, aunque en general un poco más fuerte, excepto delante de la *g*, pues en este caso ambas letras pierden algo de su fuerza.—La *n* final es muda cuando la precede una *m* o una *l*.—Al principio de las voces o sílabas las únicas consonantes que pueden seguirla o precederla inmediatamente son la *g*, *k*, y *s*, como en *gnaw*, *know*, *snow*.
Nab [nab], *va.* (Fam.) Prender o coger de repente, atrapar.
Nabob [né'-bob], *s.* 1. Nabab o nabob, título de los príncipes y gobernadores de las provincias mahometanas de la India. 2. Persona muy rica y fastuosa; indiano.
Nacelle [na-sel'], *s.* (Aer.) 1. Cabina. 2. Navecilla. 3. Cápsula que recubre el motor.
Nacre [né'-kẹr], *s.* Nácar, madreperla, substancia con reflejos irisados que tapiza la superficie interior de varias conchas.
Nacreous [né'-kẹr-us], *a.* Nacarado; nacarino.
Nadir [né'-dẹr], *s.* Nadir, el punto de la esfera celeste opuesto al cenit.
Nævose [ní'-vōs], *a.* Manchado, pecoso.
Nævus [ní'-vus], *s.* Lunar, mancha natural en alguna parte del cuerpo.
Nag [nag], *s.* Haca, jaca, caballo pequeño.
Naiad [né'-yad], *s.* (Mitol.) Náyade, ninfa de los ríos y fuentes.
Naif [nā-íf'], *a.* 1. La forma masculina de *Naive.* V. 2. Lustroso antes de haber sido tallado o cortado: naife.
Nail [nél], *s.* 1. Uña. 2. Uña, pezuña; garra de los animales carniceros y de las aves. 3. Clavo, pedazo de hierro largo y delgado con cabeza y punta. *To hit the nail on the head,* Dar en el clavo. 4. Medida de dos pulgadas y cuarto, o la dieciseisava parte de una vara. 5. Tachón, roblón. *Clout-nails,* (Mar.) Clavos sin cabeza. *Brass-headed nails,* Clavos con cabeza de latón. *Clasp-nails,* (Mar.) Clavos de ala de mosca. *Sheathing-nails,* (Mar.) Clavos de entablar. *Clincher-nails,* (Mar.) Clavos de tinglar. *Pump-nails,* (Mar.) Clavos de bomba. *On the nail,* Luego, al instante, sobre la marcha. *Nail-brush,* Cepillo para las uñas. *Nail-extractor, nail-puller,* Arrancaclavos, desclavador. *Nail-file,* Lima para las uñas. *Nail-plate,* Metal en plancha para clavos.
Nail, *va.* 1. Clavar. *To nail to the wall,* Clavar en la pared. 2. Clavetear, guarnecer o adornar con clavos. *To nail a lie,* Demostrar que una cosa es mentira, poner término a la circulación de un embuste. *To nail down* o *nail up,* Sujetar con clavos; condenar una ventana, puerta, etc., clavándola.
Nailer [nél'-ẹr], *s.* Chapucero, el fabricante de clavos.
Nailery [nél'-ẹr-i], *s.* Fábrica de clavos.
Nailing [nél'-ing], *s.* Clavadura, el acto de clavar.
Nainsook [nén'-suk], *s.* Nansú, nanzué, muselina de India, rayada a lo largo o lisa.
Naissant [né'-sant], *a.* (Her.) Naciente: se dice del animal cuya cabeza y cuello salen por encima de una pieza del escudo.
Naive [nā-ív', no né'-iv], *a.* Ingenuo, candoroso, sencillo, natural, sin arte ni afectación.
Naiveté [nā"-iv-té'], *s.* Simplicidad; ingenuidad; gracia. (Fr.)
Naked [né'-kẹd], *a.* 1. Desnudo, en cueros; también, en lo antiguo, insuficientemente vestido. 2. Desarmado, sin defensa. 3. Expuesto a la vista; patente, claro, evidente, mero. 4. Puro, simple. *The naked truth,* La verdad pura o desnuda. 5. (Zool.) Desnudo, privado de cubiertas epidérmicas, como de pelo, escamas, plumas, etc. *Stark naked,* Completamente desnudo, en cueros. *A naked sword,* Una espada desnuda, desenvainada.
Nakedly [né'-kẹd-li], *adv.* Desnudamente, meramente, claramente.
Nakedness [né'-kẹd-nes], *s.* 1. Desnudez; desabrigo; falta de defensa. 2. Claridad, evidencia; simplicidad.
Namable, Nameable [ném'-a-bl], *a.* Que puede recibir un nombre.
Namby-pamby [nam'-bi-pam-bi], *a.* Insípido, afectado.—*s.* Pamplina; dícese hablando de versos para expresar que no son buenos.
Name [ném], *s.* 1. Nombre. 2. Nombre, el título de alguna cosa por el cual es conocida. *Christian name,* Nombre de bautismo, de pila. *In God's name,* En nombre de Dios, por el amor de Dios. 3. Nombre, nombradía, fama, opinión, reputación, crédito. *To get a good name,* Tener buena fama. 4. Nombre, autoridad, poder o virtud con que se ejecuta alguna cosa por otro como si él mismo la hiciera. 5. Apodo, mal nombre. *To call one names,* Poner apodos a uno. 6. Pretexto. *By the name of,* Bajo el nombre de. *An inventor, Marconi by name,* Un inventor llamado Marconi. *Name-plate,* Plancha con un nombre grabado o pintado; suele ser de metal para las puertas, de vidrio para las ventanas.
Name, *va.* 1. Nombrar. 2. Mencionar, hacer mención; proferir. 3. Especificar, elegir, señalar, designar, distinguir a una persona o cosa por su nombre. *Do not name it,* No vale la pena de hablar de ello; no hay de que.
Nameless [ném'-les], *a.* Innominado, anónimo; desconocido.
Namely [ném'-li], *adv.* Señaladamente, particularmente, especialmente; a saber.
Name plate [ném plét], *s.* Placa con el nombre de una persona. (Generalmente se coloca en los escritorios de oficina.)
Namesake [ném'-séc], *s.* Tocayo; (ant.) colombroño.
Naming [ném'-ing], *s.* 1. Nombramiento, el acto de nombrar. 2. El documento o título del nombramiento.
Nankeen [nan-kín'], **Nankin** [nan-kín'], *s.* Mahón, nanquín, tela de algodón, de color anteado, que viene de la China.
Nap [nap], *s.* 1. Sueño ligero, sueño de corta duración; siesta. *To take an afternoon nap,* Dormir la siesta. 2. Vello de las plantas; lanilla, la pelusa que queda en las telas o tejidos de lana por la haz. *Cf.* PILE, 7ª acep. 3. Golpecito, toque ligero. 4. (Prov. Ingl.) Cima, pico o punta de una roca.
Nap, *vn.* Dormitar, tener sueño.—*va.* Hacer lanillas en el paño.
Nape [nép], *s.* Nuca, la parte superior de la cerviz, unión del espinazo con la cabeza.
Napery [né'-pẹr-i], *s.* Ropa blanca, artículo de lienzo; mantelería.
Naphtha [naf'-tha], *s.* Nafta, un aceite ligero, incoloro, volátil e inflamable que hoy día se distila principalmente del petróleo. Su gravedad específica es de .885.
Naphthalene [naf'-tha-lín], *s.* (Quím.) Naftalina, substancia sólida y cristalizable ($C_{10}H_8$) que se encuentra en estado natural y también se extrae del alquitrán de carbón.
Napiform [né'-pi-fōrm], *a.* Que tiene forma de nabo.
Napkin [nap'-kin], *s.* Servilleta.
Napless [nap'-les], *a.* Raído, que no tiene pelusa, vello o lanilla.
Napoleon [na-pō'-lẹ-en], *s.* Nombre de una moneda francesa de oro del valor de veinte francos o $4; ya no se acuña.
Nappiness [nap'-i-nes], *s.* La propiedad de tener pelusa, vello o lanilla.
Nappy [nap'-i], *a.* 1. Espumoso. 2. Velloso.
Narcissine [nār-sis'-in], *a.* Perteneciente a la planta llamada narciso, o parecido al narciso.
Narcissus [nār-sis'-us], *s.* (Bot.) Narciso, planta herbácea de flores olorosas.
Narcosis [nar-cō'-sis], *s.* (Med.) Narcotismo, conjunto de los efectos producidos por los narcóticos.
Narcotic [nār-cet'-ic], *a.* Narcótico, que adormece o entorpece los sentidos. Soporífero, soporífico.—*s.* Narcótico.—*s. pl.* Estupefacientes.
Nard [nārd], *s.* (Bot.) 1. Nardo, dícese de la planta, el aceite o el ungüento. 2. Especie de valeriana empleada antiguamente en medicina.

Nardine [nār'-din], *s.* Nardino, compuesto con nardo o que participa de sus cualidades.

Nares [né'-riz], *s. pl.* de NARIS. Las ventanas de la nariz; narices.

Narrate [nar'-rêt], *va.* Narrar, relacionar, relatar.

Narrating [nar-rêt'-ing], *s.* El acto de narrar, contar o relatar.

Narration [nar-ré'-shun], *s.* Narración, relación de alguna cosa.

Narrative [nar'-ra-tiv], *a.* Narrativo. —*s.* Narrativa, relato.

Narratively [nar'-ra-tiv-li], *adv.* Narrativamente.

Narrator [nar-rêt'-ẹr], *s.* Relator, narrador, el que narra o relata.

Narrow [nar'-ō], *a.* 1. Angosto, estrecho, reducido, corto. 2. Apretado, ruin, avariento. 3. Estrecho, limitado. 4. Próximo, inmediato. 5. Vigilante, atento, escrupuloso. 6. De cerca, apenas suficiente para librarse de un daño, peligro o fiasco. *A narrow escape,* Una escapada difícil. *By a narrow plurality,* Por escasa mayoría. *A narrow-minded man,* Un hombre de ideas mezquinas, avariento, de entendimiento limitado, de pocos alcances o de poco talento. *A narrow-spirited* o *a narrow-souled man,* Un hombre apocado o encogido, de poca resolución o de cortos alcances; innoble, mezquino, bajo. *To bring into a narrow compass,* Compendiar. *Narrow circumstances,* Escasez pecuniaria, cortos posibles. *Narrow-gauge,* Ferrocarril de vía estrecha, de menos de 56½ pulgadas. *Narrow-minded,* Apocado, encogido, mezquino; santurrón, mojigato.—*s.* Estrecho, pasaje angosto; desfiladero; úsase a menudo en plural.

Narrow, *va.* 1. Estrechar, angostar, encoger. 2. Bajar, humillar. 3. Disminuir, limitar.—*vn.* Andar los caballos con las patas muy juntas.

Narrow-hearted [nar'ō-härt-ed], *a.* Corto de ánimo, mezquino, cobarde, poquito.

Narrowing [nar'-ō-ing], *s.* Estrechamiento, estrechura.

Narrowly [nar'-ō-li], *adv.* 1. Estrechamente. 2. Exactamente. 3. Por poco. *We narrowly escaped being drowned,* Por poco nos ahogamos. 4. Escasamente, mezquinamente.

Narrowness [nar'-o-nes], *s.* 1. Angostura. 2. Estrechez, falta de capacidad; apretura. 3. Pobreza, miseria, bajeza.

Narwhal [nār'-hwal], *s.* Narval, unicornio marino.

Nasal [né'-zal o ng'-sal], *a.* Nasal, lo que pertenece a la nariz.—*s.* 1. Errinos, los remedios que se usan para el interior de la nariz; los medicamentos que se toman por la nariz. 2. Letra nasal.

Nasalize [né'-zal-aiz], *va.* Ganguear, pronunciar con sonido nasal.

Nasally [né'-zal-i], *adv.* Con gangueo, con sonido nasal.

Nascent [nas'-ẹnt], *a.* Naciente, creciente.

Nastily [nas'-ti-li], *adv.* Suciamente.

Nastiness [nas'-ti-nes], *s.* Suciedad, porquería, obscenidad.

Nasturtion [nas-tōr'-shun], *s.* (Bot.) Capuchina. *V.* NASTURTIUM.

Nasturtium [nas-tur'-shi-um], *s.* (Bot.) 1. Nasturcio, género de plantas crucíferas; berro o berra. 2. Capuchina, planta geraniácea trepadora o baja.

Nasty [nas'-ti], *a.* 1. Sucio, puerco. 2. Sucio, obsceno, deshonesto, hablando de acciones o palabras. 3. Impuro, sórdido. 4. (Fam.) Desagradable; de aquí, tempestuoso; lodoso, cenagoso.

Natal [né'-tal], *a.* Nativo; natal.

Natalitial [né-ta-lish'-al], **Natalitious** [né-ta-lish'-us], *a.* Natalicio, natal, lo que pertenece al día o fiesta del nacimiento.

Natant [né'-tant], *a.* 1. (Bot.) Nadando, flotando en la superficie del agua. 2. (Her.) Dícese de un pez representado en el escudo de armas horizontalmente o de través.

Natation [ne-té'-shun], *s.* Nadadura, el acto de nadar.

Natatorial [né-ta-tō'-ri-al], *a.* Nadador, natátil, o apto para nadar.

Natatory [né'-ta-to-ri], *a.* Natatorio, que sirve para nadar.

Nates [né'-tiz], *s. pl.* Nalgas, trasero.

Nation [né'-shun], *s.* 1. Nación. 2. Se usa enfáticamente para expresar un gran número o muchedumbre.

National [nash'-un-al], *a.* 1. Nacional; general, público. 2. Aficionado a su propio país, idioma o costumbres; patriótico. 3. Autorizado por un gobierno nacional. *The national debt, church,* La deuda, la iglesia nacional.

Nationalism [nash'-un-al-izm], *s.* 1. Nacionalismo, devoción a toda la nación más bien que a una parte de ella. 2. Forma reciente del socialismo que propone que la nación imponga a todos los jornaleros igual cantidad de trabajo, por los mismos jornales. 3. Deseo de obtener o de mantener la independencia nacional. 4. Idiotismo, costumbre, rasgo característico nacional.

Nationality [nash-un-al'-i-ti], *s.* Nacionalidad.

Nationalization [nash-un-al-i-zé'-shun], *s.* Nacionalización.

Nationalize [nash'-un-al-aiz], *va.* Nacionalizar, hacer nacional.

Nationally [nash'-un-al-i], *adv.* Nacionalmente.

Native [né'-tiv], *a.* 1. Nativo. 2. Nativo, lo perteneciente al nacimiento de cada uno; natural, originario de algún país. 3. Lo que ha nacido al mismo tiempo que otra cosa o tiene conexión íntima con ella. 4. Original, originario.—*s.* 1. Natural. 2. La consecuencia o resultado de alguna causa. *Native place,* Lugar natal. *Native inhabitants,* Habitantes indígenas.

Natively [né'-tiv-li], *adv.* Naturalmente, originalmente, originariamente.

Nativeness [né'-tiv-nes], *s.* El estado de la cosa producida por la naturaleza.

Nativity [na-tiv'-i-ti], *s.* 1. Nacimiento, el acto de nacer. 2. Nacimiento, el origen o principio desde donde empezó a existir una cosa. 3. Horóscopo.

Natron [né'-tron], *s.* (Quím.) Natrón, carbonato de sosa usado en las fábricas de jabón, vidrio y tintes.

Natty [nat'-i], *a.* (Fam.) Elegante, fino; vestido con esmero.

Natural [nach'-ur-al], *a.* 1. Natural, producido o causado por la naturaleza. 2. Conforme al orden establecido. 3. Afectuoso, cariñoso, tierno, humano. 4. Natural, hecho sin artificio. 5. Natural, sencillo. 6. Natural, verdadero. 7. Natural, ilegítimo. 8. (Mús.) Natural, sin sostenidos ni bemoles.—*s.* 1. (Mús.) Becuadro; también el signo ♮ que anula el sostenido o bemol anterior. 2. Tecla blanca; nota natural. 3. Idiota, simplón.

Natural gas [nach'-ur-al gas], *s.* Gas natural.

Naturalism [nach'-ur-al-izm], *s.* Naturalismo, el sistema de religión en que todo se atribuye a la naturaleza.

Naturalist [nach'-ur-al-ist], *s.* Naturalista.

Naturalization [nach-ur-al-i-zé'-shun], *s.* Naturalización, el derecho que concede el gobierno a los extranjeros para que gocen de los privilegios de los naturales del país.

Naturalize [nach'-ur-al-aiz], *va.* 1. Naturalizar, conceder o dar a los extranjeros el privilegio de la naturalización. 2. Naturalizar, habituar; aclimatar hombres, animales o plantas.

Naturally [nach'-ur-al-i], *adv.* Naturalmente.

Naturalness [nach'-ur-al-nes], *s.* 1. Naturalidad. 2. Ingenuidad, sencillez.

Natural science [nach'-ur-al sai'-ens], *s.* Ciencias naturales.

Nature [né'-chur], *s.* 1. Naturaleza. 2. Naturaleza, la propiedad esencial de cada cosa. 3. Natural, índole, genio, inclinación de cada uno. 4. Naturaleza, el orden y concierto de las cosas criadas. 5. Naturaleza, especie, género, clase. 6. Naturaleza, la constitución de un cuerpo animado; complexión. *Good-nature,* Mansedumbre, benignidad, benevolencia, humanidad, afabilidad.

Natured [né'-churd], *a.* Úsase sólo en la formación de palabras compuestas. *Good-natured,* De buen natural. *Ill-natured,* De mal carácter, mal intencionado.

Naught [nōt], *s.* Nada; cero, la cifra 0. *To set at naught,* Hacer poco caso de, tener en poco; desdeñar, despreciar.—*a.* 1. De ningún valor. 2. (Des.) Malo, perverso, indigno, inicuo.

Naughtily [nō'-ti-li], *adv.* Malvadamente, perversamente, inicuamente.

Naughtiness [nō'-ti-nes], *s.* Maldad, iniquidad, perversidad, malignidad.

Naughty [nō'-ti], *a.* 1. Perverso, desobediente, díscolo, pícaro. 2. (Ant.) Malo, malvado, inicuo. *A naughty fellow,* Un malvado. *A naughty boy,* Un picarón o picaruelo; pillo, pillastrón. *A naughty trick,* Una picardigüela; una pillada, una gatada.

Nausea [nō'-she-a], *s.* Náusea, bascas, gana de vomitar.

Nauseant [nō'-she-ant], *a.* Nauseabundo.—*s.* Substancia nauseabunda.

Nauseate [nō'-she-êt], *vn.* Nausear, tener bascas, tener asco; sentir disgusto, aversión o antipatía.—*va.* Dar asco o disgusto; causar aversión o antipatía.

Nauseative [nō'-she-a-tiv], *a.* Nauseativo, nauseoso.

Nauseous [nō'-shus], *a.* Fastidioso, asqueroso.

Nauseously [nō'-shus-li], *adv.* Fastidiosamente.

Nauseousness [nō'-shus-nes], *s.* Náusea.

Nautch [nēch], *s.* Baile de la India. *Nautch-girl*, Bailarina india.
Nautical [nō'-tic-al], *a.* Náutico, lo que pertenece a la navegación.
Nautilus [nō'-ti-lus], *s.* 1. Nautilo, nauclero, caracol hermoso de mar de concha univalva. 2. Argonauta, molusco cefalópodo. 3. Fisalia, acalefo de los mares tropicales, llamado en inglés *Portuguese man-of-war*.
Naval [nê-val], *a.* Naval. *Naval officer*, Oficial de marina; capitán de puerto. *Naval stores*, Alquitrán, trementina y otras resinas. *Naval tactics*, Táctica naval, evoluciones marítimas.
Navarchy [nê'-vark-i], *s.* Pilotaje.
Nave [nêv], *s.* 1. Cubo, maza, pieza gruesa de madera en el centro de las ruedas de los carruajes. 2. Nave, parte principal del cuerpo de la iglesia.
Nave-line [nêv'-lain], *s.* (Mar.) Perigallo de racamento.
Navel [nê'-vl], *s.* 1. Ombligo. 2. Centro, medio, la parte más interior de una cosa. 3. Nombre de una variedad de naranja procedente de Bahía en Brasil. *Navel-gall*, (Vet.) Matadura. *Navel-ill*, (Vet.) Inflamación del ombligo en los becerros y corderos. *Navel-string*, Cordón umbilical.
Naveled [nê'-vẹld], *a.* Que tiene ombligo; a manera de ombligo.
Navelwort * [nê'-vl-wŭrt], *s.* (Bot.) Oreja de monje.
Navigable [nav'-i-ga-bl], *a.* Navegable.
Navigableness [nav'-i-ga-bl-nes], *s.* El estado navegable de una extensión de agua, sea mar, río o lago.
Navigate [nav'-i-gêt], *vn.* Navegar, viajar por el agua.—*va.* Navegar, pasar el agua en barco.
Navigation [nav-i-gê'-shun], *s.* 1. Navegación, náutica, el arte de navegar. 2. Navegación, la acción de navegar y el viaje que hace la embarcación. 3. (Poét.) Marina, las embarcaciones en general.
Navigation lights [nav-i-gê'-shun laits], *s. pl.* (Aer.) Luces de posición.
Navigator [nav'-i-gêt-ẹr], *s.* Navegador, navegante, marino hábil en el arte de navegar.
Navvy [nav'-i], *s.* (Ingl.) Peón que trabaja en obras de canales, ferrocarriles, etc.
Navy [nê'-vi], *s.* Marina, se dice en general del cuerpo de oficiales, tropa, marineros, y aun de los buques que forman la fuerza naval de un estado; armada de una potencia. *The royal navy*, La real armada. *Navy-office*, Almirantazgo. *Navy-yard*, Arsenal de puerto.
Navy bean [nê'-vi bīn], *s.* Frijol blanco.
Navy-blue [nê'-vi-blū], *a.* Azul marino.
Nawab [nẹ-wōb'], *s.* Nabab, gobernador mahometano de una provincia en la India.
Nay [nê], *adv.* 1. No, no sólo, sino; no sólo eso; pero o sino; también; aun más, además, y aun. *Nay verily*, No ciertamente. 2. Sirve para exagerar y dar énfasis, y corresponde en castellano a aun, aun más, también. *He has enough, nay, too much*, Tiene bastante y aun demasiado.—*s.* 1. El que hace oposición votando en contra, y el mismo voto negativo. 2. Denegación, repulsión, repulsa.
Nazarene [naz-a-rīn'], *a.* y *s.* Nazareno, y de aquí, cristiano.
Nazarite [naz'-a-rait], *s.* Nazareísta, nazareo, o nazareno, el hebreo que se consagraba al culto divino de un modo particular; los nazarenos no tomaban bebidas embriagadoras y no se cortaban el cabello ni la barba.
Naze [nêz], *s.* Cabo, promontorio; roca escarpada. (Anglosajón, næss.)
Nazi [nat'-si], *s.* y *a.* Nazi (del partido nacionalsocialista alemán).
Neaf [nīf], *s.* (Esco. y Prov. Ingl.) Puño, la mano cerrada.
‡**Neal** [nīl], *va.* (Des.) Templar, dar temple a alguna cosa por medio de un calor gradual. *V. To* ANNEAL.—*vn.* Templarse al fuego.
Neap [nīp], *a.* Bajo, lo más bajo, ínfimo.—*s.* 1. Bajo, menguante. *Neap tide*, Marea la más baja. 2. En algunas partes de los Estados Unidos, lanza de carretón.
Neapolitan [nī-a-pel'-i-tan], *a.* y *s.* Napolitano, de Nápoles.
Near [nīr], *prep.* Cerca de, inmediato a, junto a, próximo a.—*adv.* 1. Casi o cuasi. 2. Cerca, próxima o inmediatamente. 3. Cerca de. *Near five thousand*, Cerca de cinco mil o unos cinco mil.—*a.* 1. Cercano, próximo, inmediato. 2. Cercano, allegado, el que tiene parentesco inmediato con otro. *A near relation*, Pariente cercano. 3. Íntimo, cordial, estrecho, hablando de amigos o parientes. 4. Interesante, que afecta o se refiere a la felicidad o al bienestar de uno mismo. 5. Cicatero, tacaño, mezquino. 6. Conforme en un todo al original, exacto, literal. 7. A la izquierda, de la izquierda. *The near ox*, El buey de la izquierda. 8. Corto, directo. *The nearest way*, El camino más corto. *Come near me*, Acércate, ven cerca de mí. *Near at hand*, A la mano, cerca, al primer golpe o de primer golpe, inmediatamente. *A near concern*, Un interés que toca de cerca. *Near Quito*, Cerca de Quito. *To come, to draw near*, Acercar, acercarse. *Quite near*, Muy cerca, contiguo.
Near, *va.* Acercar.—*vn.* Acercarse.
Nearly [nīr'-li], *adv.* 1. Cercanamente, a poca distancia. 2. Estrechamente. 3. Miserablemente, mezquinamente. 4. Casi, poco más o menos. 5. Íntimamente, de cerca. *That nearly concerns you*, Eso le toca a Vd. de cerca. 6. Muy aproximadamente, casi literalmente.
Nearness [nīr'-nes], *s.* 1. Proximidad, propincuidad, cercanía. 2. Proximidad, parentesco cercano. 3. Amistad estrecha. 4. Tacañería, ruindad, mezquindad.
Near-sighted [nīr-sait'-ed], *a.* Corto de vista, miope.
Neat [nīt], *a.* 1. Limpio, aseado, primoroso. 2. Bonito, pulido, lindo. 3. Puro, casto, natural, sin mezcla. 4. Gallardo, esmerado, de buenas proporciones, de forma graciosa. 5. (Com.) Neto. *V.* NET. (< Fr. net.)—*s.* Ganado vacuno; vaca o buey. *Neat's leather*, Cuero de ganado vacuno. *Neat's tongue*, Lengua de vaca. *Neat's oil*, Aceite de manitas. *Neat-cattle*, Ganado mayor. (< A.-S. neāt.)
Neat-handed [nīt-hand'-ed], *a.* Limpio, diestro.
'neath [nīth o nīdh], *prep.* Debajo de. *V.* BENEATH.
Neatherd [nīt'-hẹrd], *s.* Vaquero, el pastor de ganado vacuno.
Neatly [nīt'-li], *adv.* Pulidamente, con primor; limpiamente; aseadamente; elegantemente; diestramente, mañosamente.
Neatness [nīt'-nes], *s.* 1. Hermosura, pulidez, elegancia. 2. Limpieza, aseo. 3. Delicadeza.
Neb [neb], *s.* 1. Nariz, pico, boca. 2. Pico, punta, cabo. *V.* NIB.
Nebula [neb'-yu-la], *s.* 1. (Ast.) Nebulosa, mancha blanquecina formada por una aglomeración de estrellas, que sólo con el telescopio pueden observarse separadamente. 2. Nube en los ojos.
Nebular [neb'-yu-lar], *a.* Nebuloso, perteneciente a una nebulosa.
Nebulizer [neb'-yu-lai-zẹr], *s.* Rociador, aparato que sirve para convertir en rocío finísimo un medicamento líquido o un perfume.
Nebulosity [neb-yu-les'-i-ti], *s.* 1. Estado nebuloso de la atmósfera. 2. Nebulosidad, apariencia como de nebulosa.
Nebulous [neb'-yu-lus], *a.* 1. Nebuloso, parecido a una nebulosa (de estrellas). 2. Que tiene sus diversas partes confundidas o mezcladas.
Necessaries [nes'-es-ẹ-riz], *s. pl.* Necesario. *The necessaries of life*, Lo necesario para vivir.
Necessarily [nes'-es-ẹ-ri-li], *adv.* Necesariamente, indispensablemente.
Necessariness [nes'-es-ẹ-ri-nes], *s.* Necesidad.
Necessary [nes'-es-ẹ-ri], *a.* 1. Necesario: decisivo, conclusivo; preciso, forzoso; menester. 2. Esencial, inevitable como conclusión o resultado; ineluctable. 3. Intuitivo.—*s.* 1. Lo necesario. 2. Necesaria, letrina.
Necessitate [nẹ-ses'-i-tẹt], *va.* Necesitar, obligar, precisar.
Necessitous [nẹ-ses'-i-tus], *a.* Necesitado, indigente, pobre.
Necessitousness [nẹ-ses'-i-tus-nes], *s.* Necesidad, pobreza, indigencia.
Necessity [nẹ-ses'-i-ti], *s.* 1. Necesidad; fatalidad. 2. Necesidad. *Necessity knows no law*, La necesidad carece de ley. (Fam.) La necesidad tiene cara de hereje. 3. Consecuencia necesaria e inevitable. 4. Violencia, compulsión; exigencia. 5. Pobreza, indigencia, penuria.
Neck [nek], *s.* 1. Cuello. 2. Parte de un órgano que está oprimida o constreñida; cosa parecida a un cuello; cuello, gollete (de una botella); clavijero (de guitarra o violín); degüello; collarino de una columna; la parte de un vestido que cubre el cuello y el seno. 3. Istmo, desfiladero, península. *Neck of mutton*, Pescuezo de carnero. *Neck of land*, Lengua de tierra. *On the neck*, Luego, inmediatamente, después. *To break the neck*, (Met.) Tener una cosa medio acabada; impedir la ejecución de alguna cosa. *Low-necked*, Muy escotado (hablando de un vestido de mujer). *Neck and crop*, Todo junto y a un tiempo; al momento. *To harden the neck*, Obstinarse en una cosa. *Neck and neck*, Con igual rapidez en una carrera. *Neck or nothing*, A todo correr; cueste lo que cueste. *On the neck of*, ú *over the neck of*, Luego, inmediatamente después.
Neckband [nec'-band], *s.* Cabezón o cuello de camisa.

Neck-beef [nec'-bīf], *s.* Carne de pescuezo.
Neckcloth [nec'-clōth], *s.* Corbata, corbatín.
Neckerchief [nek'-ẹr-chif], **Neck-handkerchief** [nec'-haṇ'-kẹr-chif], *s.* 1. Corbata, corbatín, pañuelo de cuello. 2. Bobillo, encaje que llevaban las mujeres prendido alrededor del escote.
Necklace [nec'-lệs], *s.* Collar, gargantilla.
Necktie [nec'-tai], *s.* Corbata.
Neckwear [nek'-wār], *s.* Corbatas, cuellos, bufandas, etc.
Necro- [nec'-rō]. Forma de combinación derivada del griego, y que significa muerto, cadáver.
Necrologic, Necrological [nec-ro-lej'-ic, al], *a.* Necrológico, que se refiere a los muertos.
Necrologist [nec-rel'-o-jist], *s.* Necrologista, registrador de defunciones; también, el que escribe noticias obituarias.
Necrology [nec-rel'-e-ji], *s.* Necrología, registro o lista de muertos.
Necromancer [nec'-ro-man-sẹr], *s.* Nigromante. (Vulg.) Brujo.
Necromancy [nec'-ro-man-si], *s.* Nigromancia, magia negra. (Vulg.) Brujería.
Necromantic [nec'-ro-man-tic], *a.* Nigromántico.
Necropolis [nec-rep'-o-lis], *s.* Necrópolis, ciudad de los muertos; particularmente, cementerio antiguo.
Necrosis [nec-rō'-sis], *s.* Necrosis, gangrena o mortificación del tejido óseo.
Nectar [nec'-tar], *s.* Néctar, en sus varios sentidos.
Nectarean [nec-tê'-rẹ-an], **Nectareous** [nec-tê'-rẹ-us], **Nectarine** [nec'-ta-rin], *a.* Nectáreo, dulce como el néctar.
Nectarial [nec-tê'-ri-al], *a.* (Bot.) Que se refiere al nectario; nectáreo.
Nectarine, *s.* Abridor liso; se diferencia del melocotón por su envoltura lisa y por su carne sólida y aromática.
Nectarine-tree [nec'-ta-rin-trī], *s.* (Bot.) Abridor.
Nectary [nec'-ta-ri], *s.* 1. Nectario, la parte que en algunas plantas contiene el néctar o la miel. 2. (Ento.) Tubo para miel.
Née [nê], *a.* Nacida; se usa para designar el apellido de una mujer antes de casarse. (Fr.)
Need [nīd], *s.* 1. Necesidad, urgencia. 2. Necesidad, pobreza, miseria. 3. Necesidad, falta de alguna cosa. *If need be*, Si hubiese necesidad o si fuese necesario. *I stand much in need of your advice*, Me hace mucha falta el consejo de Vd. *Address in case of need*, En caso necesario: indicación que se pone en las letras de cambio de una casa, a la que puede acudirse para su cobro, si no fueren pagadas por aquella contra la que están giradas.
Need, *va.* Pedir, requerir lo que es necesario y conveniente; necesitar. —*vn.* 1. Necesitar, haber menester o tener necesidad o precisión de alguna cosa, hacer falta; carecer. 2. Tener que, haber de. *They needed not to fear*, Nada tenían que temer. *He said, "we need but rise,"* Dijo, "no tenemos más que levantarnos." (El verbo neutro *need* se emplea a veces, quedando invariable. *She need not go*, Ella no tiene necesidad de ir.)
Needer [nīd'-ẹr], *s.* Necesitado.
Needful [nīd'-ful], *a.* Necesario, indispensable, preciso.
Needfully [nīd'-ful-i], *adv.* Necesariamente, indispensablemente.
Needfulness [nīd'-ful-nes], *s.* Pobreza, falta, necesidad.
Needily [nīd'-i-li], *adv.* Pobremente.
Neediness [nīd'-i-nes], *s.* 1. Indigencia, pobreza, necesidad. 2. Falta, vacío.
Needle [nī'-dl], *s.* 1. Aguja. 2. Palillo (de hueso, madera, etc.) para hacer medias. *Pack-needle*, Aguja de ensalmar. *Needle of a dial*, Estilo de un reloj de sol; mano, índice. *Needle*, (Mar.) Aguja de marear, brújula. *Sail-needle*, (Mar.) Aguja capotera. *Bolt-rope-needle*, (Mar.) Aguja de relinga. *Knitting-needle*, Aguja de hacer medias, o de malla. *Shepherd's needle*, (Bot.) Aguja de pastor. *Needle of a balance*, Lengüeta, fiel de la balanza. *Crochet, darning needle*, Aguja de crochet, de zurcir. *Sewing-machine needle*, Aguja de máquina de coser. *Needle-gun*, Fusil de aguja. *Needle-holder*, Porta-agujas. *Needle-shaped*, *a.* Acicular, de la forma de una aguja.
Needle-case [nī'-dl-kês], *s.* Alfiletero, cañuto para guardar las agujas.
Needleful [nī'-dl-ful], *s.* Hebra de hilo.
Needle-maker [nī'-dl-mêk-ẹr], **Needler** [nī'-dlẹr], *s.* Agujero, el que hace agujas.
Needle point [nī'-dl peint], *s.* Punto de cruz, bordado de tapicería.
Needless [nīd'-les], *a.* Supérfluo, inútil.
Needlessly [nīd'-les-li], *adv.* En balde; inútilmente.
Needlessness [nīd'-les-nes], *s.* Superfluidad, inutilidad.
Needlewoman [nī'-dl-wum''-an], *sf.* La que hace labores de aguja; costurera.
Needlework [nī'-dl-wūrc], *s.* Costura; bordado de aguja; obra de punto.
Needs [nīdz], *adv.* Necesariamente, indispensablemente. Se usa a menudo con *must: If it must needs be, we will go*, Si es absolutamente necesario, iremos.
Needy [nīd'-i], *a.* Indigente, necesitado, pobre.
Ne'er [nêr o nār], *adv.* *V.* NEVER.
Nefarious [nẹ-fê'-ri-us], *a.* Nefario, sumamente malo, atroz.
Negation [nẹ-gê'-shun], *s.* 1. Negación, la acción de negar. 2. (Lóg.) Negación, carencia de una calidad en un objeto que es incapaz de ella.
Negative [neg'-a-tiv], *a.* 1. Negativo. 2. (Foto.) Negativo, que presenta los claros y los obscuros invertidos. 3. (Elec.) Negativo, de potencia o fuerza relativamente baja.—*s.* 1. Negativa, una partícula en la gramática y una proposición en la lógica. 2. Negativa, denegación, repulsa de lo que se pide. 3. Veto, derecho de rehusar. 4. Negativo, prueba negativa en fotografía. 5. Electricidad negativa.
Negative, *va.* 1. Denegar, desaprobar, negar. 2. Oponerse a, votar en contra; poner su veto a.
Negatively [neg'-a-tiv-li], *adv.* Negativamente.
Neglect [neg-lect'], *s.* 1. Descuido, dejadez, negligencia, olvido. 2. Desprecio, menosprecio, desdén, frialdad, indiferencia. 3. Desuso. *To fall into neglect*, Caer en desuso.
Neglect, *va.* 1. Descuidar, desatender. 2. Descuidar, olvidar, dejar de hacer lo que se debe; diferir; dilatar. 3. Menospreciar, despreciar, no hacer caso, desdeñar, tener en menos. *To neglect one's duties*, Descuidar sus deberes, faltar a su obligación.
Neglecter [neg-lect'-ẹr], *s.* 1. Descuidado, negligente. 2. Despreciador.
Neglectful [neg-lect'-ful], *a.* Negligente, descuidado, omiso.
Neglectfully [neg-lect'-ful-i], *adv.* Negligentemente, descuidadamente.
Neglectfulness [neg-lect'-ful-nes], *s.* Descuido, negligencia.
Negligee [neg-li-zhê'], *s.* Traje casero y cómodo, el que usan las señoras dentro de casa antes de vestirse. —*a.* Desaliñado, descuidado en el vestir.
Negligence [neg'-li-jens], *s.* Negligencia, descuido, omisión, incuria; dejadez, flojedad.
Negligent [neg'-li-jẹnt], *a.* Negligente, descuidado, dejado, flojo, perezoso.
Negligently [neg'-li-jẹnt-li], *adv.* Descuidadamente, negligentemente.
Negligible [neg'-li-ji-bl], *a.* Desatendible, lo que se puede desatender, descuidar, omitir o pasar por alto.
Negotiable [nẹ-gō'-shi-a-bl], *a.* Capaz de ser negociado.
Negotiate [nẹ-gō'-shi-êt], *vn.* 1. Negociar, tratar y comerciar comprando, vendiendo o cambiando géneros, mercaderías o dinero. 2. Negociar, ajustar o manejar políticamente las pretensiones o negocios. *A busy negotiating woman*, Una mujer entremetida o trafagona.—*va.* Negociar letras, vales u otros efectos comerciales. *To negotiate a bill*, Negociar una letra de cambio.
Negotiating [nẹ-gō'-shi-êt-ing], *a.* Negociante, contratante.
Negotiation [nẹ-gō-shi-ê'-shun], *s.* Negociación, negocio.
Negotiator [nẹ-gō'-shi-ê-tẹr], *s.* Negociador.
Negotiatrix [nẹ-gō-shi-ê'-trics], *sf.* Negociadora.
Negress [nī'-gres], *sf.* Negra, mujer negra.
Negrillo [nê-grī'-lyō], *s.* 1. Negro africano de raza enana. 2. *V.* NEGRITO.
Negrito [nê-grī'-tō], *s.* Negrito, uno de los pueblos malayos de raza enana parecidos a los negros. (Esp.)
Negro [nī'-gro], *s.* Negro, etíope.
Negroid [nī'-greid], *a.* Parecido o referente á los negros.
Negundo [nẹ-gun'-dō], *s.* Nombre indígena de un árbol americano muy parecido al arce, pero con hojas pinadas y flores dioicas.
Negus [nī'-gus], *s.* Carraspada, bebida hecha con vino, agua, azúcar, canela y nuez de especia.
Neigh [nê], *vn.* Relinchar.
Neigh, *s.* Relincho, la voz del caballo o la yegua.
Neighbor, Neighbour [nê'-bẹr], *s.* 1. Vecino. 2. Confidente, familiar. 3. Prójimo.—*a.* (Ant.) *V.* NEIGHBORING.
Neighbor, *va.* Confinar, estar vecino o cercano; ser vecino de alguien, vivir cerca de otro.
Neighborhood, Neighbourhood [nê'-bẹr-hud], *s.* 1. Vecindad. 2. Vecindario, los que viven cerca unos de otros. 3. Cercanía, inmediación, proximidad.
Neighboring, Neighbouring [nê'

bẹr-ing], *a.* Vecino, cercano a, próximo, adyacente.

Neighborliness [nê'-bẹr-li-nes], *s.* Urbanidad, cortesía de vecindad; buena vecindad.

Neighborly nê'-bẹr-li], *a.* Urbano, atento.—*adv.* Civilmente.

Neighbour, etc. Forma usual en Inglaterra. *V.* NEIGHBOR, etc.

Neighing [nê'-ing], *s.* Relincho.

Neither [nî'-dhẹr; por unos pocos, naí'-dhẹr], *conj.* 1. Ni; correlativo ordinario de *nor*, ni. *Neither one nor the other*, Ni uno ni otro, ni el uno ni el otro. 2. Tampoco, aun no, nada de eso; después de una negación se reemplaza por *either*, excepto en el uso vulgar. *Neither will I do it*, Yo tampoco lo haré. *Nor then either* (*neither*), Ni entonces tampoco. —*pron.* Ninguno, ni uno ni otro. *To be on neither side*, Ser o permanecer neutral; no tomar parte a favor de uno ni de otro.—*a.* Ninguno, na. *Neither girl sings well*, Ninguna muchacha canta bien.

Nem. con. [nem con]. Abreviatura de *nemine contradicente* o *nemine discrepante.*

Nemesis [nem'-ẹ-sis], *s.* 1. Nemesis, diosa de la venganza. 2. Justicia retributiva.

Neo-. Prefijo del griego que significa nuevo o reciente.

Neo-Catholic [nî-o-cath'-el-ic], *a.* Neocatólico.

Neogamist [nẹ-eg'-a-mist], *s.* Novio, el recién casado.

Neolithic [nî-o-lith'-ic], *a.* Neolítico, de la segunda edad de piedra.

Neological, Neologic [nî-o-lej'-i-cal], *a.* Neológico, lo que pertenece a las voces o locuciones nuevas.

Neologism [nẹ-el'-o-jizm], *s.* 1. Neologismo, vocablo o giro nuevo en una lengua. 2. Uso de estos vocablos o giros nuevos. 3. Nueva doctrina.

Neology [nẹ-el'-o-ji], *s.* Neología, la invención o creación de voces nuevas en una lengua.

Neomenia [nî-o-mî'-ni-a], *s.* Neomenia, el primer día de la luna.

Neon [nî'-en], *s.* Neón. *Neon lamp*, Lámpara neón. *Neon sign*, Anuncio luminoso de neón.

Neophyte [nî'-o-fait], *s.* Neófito, el recién convertido a la verdadera religión.

Neoplatonism [nî-o-plé'-to-nizm], *s.* Neoplatonicismo, escuela filosófica cuya doctrina combinaba las ideas de Platón con las del misticismo oriental.

Neoteric [nî-o-ter'-ic], *a.* Neotérico, moderno.

Neozoic [nî-o-zō'-ic], *a.* (Geol.) Neozoico.

Nepaulese [nep-ē-lîs'], *s.* Natural de Nepal, en el Indostán.

Nepenthes, Nepenthe [nẹ-pen'-thîz, nẹ-pen'-thî], *s.* 1. Nepente, remedio que gozaba de una gran reputación entre los antiguos para remediar las pasiones de ánimo. 2. Nepenta, género de plantas de la India que se llaman *pitcher-plants*, plantas de urna, por razón de la forma de los apéndices de sus hojas.

Nephew [nef'-iu o nev'-yu], *s.* Sobrino.

Nephology [nef-el'-o-ji], *s.* La parte de la meteorología que trata de las nubes.

Nephoscope [nef'-o-scōp], *s.* Instrumento que indica la dirección, elevación, etc., de las nubes.

Nephrite [nef'-rait], *s.* Nefrita, (ant.) ceraunita, variedad de jade.

Nephritic [nef-rit'-ic], *a.* 1. Nefrítico: referente a los riñones. 2. Atacado de nefritis. *Nephritic wood*, Palo nefrítico.

Nephritis [nef-raí'-tis o rî'-tis], *s.* Nefritis, inflamación de los riñones.

Nephrotomy [nef-ret'-o-mi], *s.* Nefrotomía, incisión de un riñón para extraer los cálculos o dar salida a un depósito purulento.

Nepotism [nep'-o-tizm], *s.* Nepotismo, desmedida preferencia dada a los parientes en la distribución de gracias y empleos.

Neptune [nep'-tiūn], *s.* 1. Neptuno, dios del mar; de aquí, océano. 2. Neptuno, el planeta más distante del sol, y que con mayor lentitud se mueve alrededor de este luminar.

Neptunian [nep-tiū'-ni-an], *a.* 1. Neptuniano, referente a Neptuno, o al océano. 2. (Geol.) Formado por el agua.

Nereid [nî'-rẹ-id], *s.* Nereida, ninfa que vivía en el mar.

Nerval [nẹrv'-al], *a.* Nervioso, referente a los nervios.

Nervate [nẹrv'-êt], *a.* (Bot.) Nervado.

Nervation, Nervature [nẹrv-ê'-shun, nẹrv'-a-tiur], *s.* Nervadura, distribución de las fibras de las hojas o de las ramificaciones en las alas de los insectos.

Nerve [nẹrv], *s.* 1. Nervio. 2. Nervio, fortaleza, vigor. 3. Tendón o cuerda. 4. (Bot.) Nervio, vena, fibra muy tenue que corre a lo largo de las hojas de las plantas. 5. Vena del ala de un insecto. 6. *pl.* Excitabilidad nerviosa.

Nerve, *va.* Vigorizar, dar fuerza; animar, alentar.

Nerved [nẹrvd], *a.* Nervudo; venoso, marcado con venas.

Nerviduct [nẹrv'-i-duct], *s.* Conducto óseo para dar paso a un nervio.

Nervine [nẹrv'-in], *a.* 1. Nervioso, nervoso. 2. Nervino, que fortifica y suaviza los nervios.—*s.* Medicamento que afecta los nervios.

Nerveless [nẹrv'-les], *a.* Enervado, débil, falto de fuerzas.

Nervous [nẹrv'-us], *a.* 1. Nervioso, nervoso; nervudo. 2. Que se agita o altera fácilmente. 3. Nervioso, que muestra vigor en las ideas, escritos, discursos, etc.

Nervously [nẹrv'-us-li], *adv.* Nerviosamente.

Nervousness [nẹrv'-us-nes], *s.* Nerviosidad, nervosidad, vigor, fuerza; estado nervioso, irritable.

Nervure [nẹr'-viur], *s.* 1. (Arq.) Costilla. 2. (Bot.) Nervura, conjunto de las venas más gruesas de las hojas. 3. (Ento.) Vena, nervadura de las alas de un insecto.

Nescience [nesh'-ẹns], *s.* Ignorancia, nesciencia, necedad.

-ness. Sufijo de origen anglosajón que expresa una cualidad o el estado de una cosa; como dark*ness*, obscuridad, great*ness*, grandeza, humane*ness*, mansedumbre, benignidad.

Ness [nes], *s.* Promontorio, cabo; se emplea como terminación en ciertos nombres de lugares, como Sheerness, Inverness.

Nest [nest], *s.* 1. Nido. *Nest of birds*, Nidada. 2. (Vulg.) Nido, lugar donde se reune gente de mala conducta. *Nest of thieves*, Nido o guarida de ladrones. 3. Casa, habitación, morada, residencia, generalmente en mal sentido. 4. El conjunto de nichos de un escritorio en que encajan las gavetas; anaquel, gaveta. 5. Juego, serie; particularmente en mecánica, engranaje, conexión de pequeñas ruedas dentadas, resortes, etc. 6. (Geol.) Depósito aislado de mineral en una roca. *To make a nest*, Hacer un nido, anidar. *A mare's nest*, Descubrimiento fraudulento o embuste.

Nest, *vn.* 1. Nidificar, anidar, hacerse un nido. 2. Buscar nidos.—*va.* 1. Anidar; alojar, fijar como en un nido. 2. Anidarse, establecerse, proveer de nido. 3. Colocar una serie de objetos uno dentro de otro.

Nest-egg [nest'-eg], *s.* Nidal, el huevo que se deja en el nido para que la gallina ponga en él.

Nestle [nes'-l], *vn.* 1. Anidarse, enjaular, enjaularse, alojándose en algún cuarto, vivienda o paraje estrecho. 2. Estar abrigado, como en un nido; apiñarse.—*va.* 1. Abrigar, poner como en un nido. 2. Acariciar, mimar, abrazar estrechamente.

Nestling [nes'-ling], *s.* Pollo, el ave recién salida del nido.

Nestorian [nes-tō'-ri-an], *s.* Nestoriano, nombre de unos herejes.

Net [net], *s.* Red; malla.

Net, *a.* 1. Neto. 2. Limpio, líquido. *Net income*, Ingreso neto. *Net profit*, Utilidad neta. *Net weight*, Peso neto.—*s.* Cantidad neta.

Net, *vn.* Hacer redes.—*va.* 1. Enredar, prender o coger con red. 2. (Com.) Sacar el producto neto de alguna cosa.

Nether [nedh'-ẹr], *a.* Inferior, lo que está más bajo en situación. *The Netherlands*, Los Países Bajos.

Nethermost [nedh'-ẹr-mōst], *a.* Lo más inferior o más bajo.

Netmaker [net'-mêk-ẹr], *s.* Redero, el que hace redes.

Netted [net'-ẹd], *a.* 1. Cubierto o protegido por una red. 2. Hecho en forma de red o redecilla.

Netting [net'-ing], *s.* 1. Randa, obra de malla. 2. El acto o la operación de hacer redes o redecillas. *Nettings*, *pl.* (Mar.) Enjaretados, especie de enrejado que usan para defenderse en los abordajes; empavesadas de una nave. *Quarter-nettings*, (Mar.) Redes de combate.

Nettle [net'-l], *s.* (Bot.) Ortiga. *Great nettle*, Ortiga mayor u ortiga dioica. *Roman nettle*, Ortiga pilulífera. *Small nettle*, Ortiga menor o picante. *Dead nettle*, Ortiga muerta o lamio blanco. *Red dead nettle*, Lamio purpúreo. *Nettle-fever*, *nettle-rash*, Urticaria, erupción de la piel que causa gran comezón.

Nettle, *va.* Picar como ortiga; irritar, provocar.

Nettle-tree [net'-l-trî], *s.* (Bot.) Almez, almezo.

Nettling [net'-ling], *s.* Provocación, irritación.

Network [net'-wurk] *s.* 1. Malla, randa. 2. Red de estaciones radiodifusoras. 3. Red, cadena de ferrocarriles.

Neural [niū'-ral], *a.* 1. Nervioso, referente al sistema nervioso. 2. Colocado en el lado que contiene el eje del sistema nervioso central; perteneciente a la medula espinal.

Neuralgia [niur-al'-ji-a], *s.* Neuralgia, dolor vivo a lo largo de un nervio, sin calentura.

Neuralgic [niur-al'-jic], *a.* Neurálgico, relativo a la neuralgia.
Neurasthenia [niū-ras-thī'-ni-a], *s.* (Med.) Neurastenia.
Neuritis [niū-rait'-is], *s.* (Med.) Neuritis.
Neurology [niū-rel'-o-ji], *s.* Neurología, tratado o discurso sobre los nervios.
Neuron, neurone [niū'-ren], *s.* (Anat.) Neurona, célula nerviosa.
Neuropterous, Neuropteral [niu-rep'-tęr-us, al], *a.* Neuróptero, perteneciente al orden de los neurópteros.
Neurosis [niu-rō'-sis], *s.* Neurosis, enfermedad de los nervios (sin lesión).
Neurotic [niū-ret'-ic], *a.* (Med.) Neurótico, que influye principalmente sobre los nervios.
Neuter [niū'-tęr], *a.* 1. (Gram.) Neutro, ni masculino, ni femenino; sin sexo; verbo intransitivo. 2. (Bot. y Zool.) Sin sexo, o sin sexo determinado, como las hormigas obreras. 3. (Ant.) Ni uno ni otro; neutral.
Neutral [niū'-tral], *a.* 1. Neutral, neutro; ni bueno ni malo, indiferente, inactivo. 2. Indefinido, mediano; sin síntoma característico ni color predominante; pardusco o azulado. 3. (Biol.) Neutro, asexual, sin estambres ni pistilos; sin sexo. 4. Neutro, ni ácido ni alcalino.—*s.* Neutral, el que se mantiene indiferente entre dos partidos opuestos.
Neutrality [niū-tral'-i-ti], *s.* 1. Neutralidad, indiferencia, el acto de no tomar partido por algo. 2. Calidad de neutro, ni ácido ni alcalino.
Neutralize [niū'-tral-aiz], *va.* Neutralizar.
Neutrally [niū'-tral-i], *adv.* Neutralmente.
Neutrino [niu-trī'-no], *s.* (Fís. & Quím.) Neutrino.
Neutron [niū'-tren], *s.* (Fís. y Quím.) Neutrón.
Never [nev'-ęr], *adv.* 1. Nunca, jamás, en ningún tiempo; de ningún modo. *I shall never be the better of it,* Nada adelantaré con eso. *Never a one,* Ni aun uno. *Never a whit,* Nada absolutamente, ni pizca. 2. No. *Never mind,* No importa, no haga Vd. caso. *Never fear,* No hay cuidado, no hay miedo. 3. Por; por más que. *Were the world never so unfriendly,* Por más hostil que fuese el mundo. *Never so great* o *little,* Por grande o pequeño que sea.
Never-ceasing [nev-ęr-sīs'-ing], *a.* Continuo, perpetuo.
Never-ending [nev-ęr-end'-ing], *a.* Perpetuo, sin fin, eterno.
Never-erring [nev-ęr-ęr'-ing], *a.* Infalible.
Never-fading [nev-ęr-fēd'-ing], *a.* Inmarcesible.
Never-failing [nev-ęr-fēl'-ing], *a.* Inagotable, infalible.
Nevermore [nev-ęr-mōr'], *adv.* Jamás, nunca.
Nevertheless [nev-ęr-dhę-les'], *adv.* No obstante que, con todo eso, sin embargo, todavía, a pesar de eso.
New [niū], *a.* 1. Nuevo, fresco, reciente, moderno. 2. Nuevo, no acostumbrado, no habituado, tierno. 3. Moderno; renovado.—*adv.* Nuevamente, recientemente. *The New-year,* El año nuevo, el primer día del año. *New bread,* Pan fresco, tierno. *Bran new, spick and span new,* Flamante, nuevecito. *This is something new for me,* Esto es nuevo para mí, esto me sorprende. *To put on the new man,* Transformarse en otro hombre. *The New World,* El Nuevo Mundo, el hemisferio occidental.
New-blown [niū'-blōn], *a.* Lo que acaba de florecer o echar flor.
New-born [niū'-bērn], *a.* Recién nacido.
Newcomer [niū-cum'-ęr], *s.* Recién llegado.
New-created [niū-cre-ēt'-ed], *a.* Recién criado.
New-delivered [niū-dę-liv'-ęrd], *a.* Recién parida.
Newel [niū'-el], *s.* 1. Pilar de escalera de caracol. 2. Poste o pilar en la parte superior e inferior de una escalera, que sostiene el pasamano.
New-fallen [niū-fēl'-n], *a.* Recién caído.
New-fangled [niū-fan'-gld], *a.* Novel, recién inventado.
New-fashion [niū-fash'-un], *s.* La última moda.
New-fashioned [niū-fash'-und], *a.* Hecho a la última moda.
New-formed [niū'-fērmd], *a.* Reformado; formado de nuevo.
New-found [niū'-faund], *a.* Recién hallado, recién descubierto. *Newfoundland,* (1) Terranova. (2) Perro grande originario de Terranova. *Newfoundland fish,* Bacalao o bacallao, abadejo.
New-grown [niū'-grōn], *a.* Recién crecido; recién salido.
New-healed [niū'-hīld], *a.* Dícese del que acaba de salir de una enfermedad.
Newish [niū'-ish], *a.* Nuevo, reciente.
New-kindled [niū-kin'-dld], *a.* Encendido de nuevo.
New-laid [niū'-lēd], *a.* Recién puesto o tendido.
Newly [niū'-li], *adv.* Nuevamente, recientemente, hace poco. *Newly come,* Recién venido.
Newlywed [niū'-li-wed], *s.* y *a.* Recién casado.
New-made [niū'-mēd], *a.* Nuevo.
New-married [niū-mar'-id], *a.* Novio, recién casado.
New-moulded [niū-mōld'-ed], *a.* Amoldado de nuevo, recién hecho.
Newness [niū'-nes], *s.* 1. La cualidad de lo que es nuevo o reciente; novedad, cosa moderna; innovación. 2. Falta de práctica; la situación del que tiene que hacer por primera vez alguna cosa.
News [niūz], *s.* 1. Noticias, novedades, nuevas. 2. Noticia, aviso que se da de alguna cosa; informe. En este sentido es siempre singular aunque tiene forma plural. *What is the news?* ¿Qué hay de nuevo? ¿qué noticias hay? *This was news to me,* Me cogió de nuevo. *No news is good news,* Falta de noticias, buena señal. *News-agent,* Vendedor de periódicos. *News-boy,* Repartidor o vendedor de periódicos. *News-room,* Gabinete de lectura.—*va.* (E. U. y Prov. Ingl.) Dar a luz, divulgar, publicar como noticia.
Newscast [niūz'-cast], *s.* Noticiario. (Mex.) Noticiero.
News-monger [niūz'-mun-gęr], *s.* Novelero, amigo de noticias.
Newspaper [niūz'-pē-pęr], *s.* Diario, periódico (por lo general cotidiano o semanal), gaceta. *Newspaper clipping,* Recorte de periódico.
Newsprint [niūz'-print], *s.* Papel para periódicos.
Newsreel [niūz'-rīl], *s.* Noticiario. (Mex.) Noticiero.
Newsstand [niūz'-stand], *s.* Puesto de periódicos, revistas, etc.
News-writer [niūz'-rait-ęr], *s.* Gacetero.
Newsy [niūz'-i], *a.* Abundante en noticias.
Newt [niūt], *s.* Lagartija acuática, batracio pequeño.
Newtonian [niū-tō'-ni-an], *a.* Neutoniano, lo perteneciente a la filosofía de Newton.
New-year's Gift [niū'-yīrz gift], *s.* Aguinaldo, regalo que se da el día de año nuevo.
New Yorker [niū yōrk'-ęr], *s.* y *a.* Neoyorquino.
Next [next], *a.* 1. Inmediato, contiguo. *The next house,* La casa vecina. 2. Próximo, lo más cercano. 3. Siguiente; sucesivo, que sigue inmediatamente en tiempo u orden. *The next day,* El día siguiente. *The next day before,* La víspera. *I'll do better next time,* Lo haré mejor en lo venidero. *Next to,* (1) Primero después de otra persona o cosa. *He is next to the president,* Es el primero después del presidente. (2) Casi, poco más o menos. *Next to impossible,* Casi imposible. *What next?* ¿Y luego, qué? *Next year,* El año que viene, el año próximo venidero. *Next Sunday,* El domingo que viene. *The next life,* La otra vida, la vida venidera. *That is a difficulty next to impossible,* Esa es una dificultad casi imposible o que raya en lo imposible.—*adv.* Luego, inmediatamente después.
Nexus [nex'-us], *s.* Nexo, lazo o vínculo de una cosa con otra.
Niacin [nai-a-sin], *s.* Niacina.
Nib [nib], *s.* 1. Pico, el extremo de la cabeza del ave. 2. Pico, punta, el extremo de cualquiera cosa; punto de la pluma de acero, o tajo de la de ave.
Nib, *va.* Hacer punta; aguzar, afilar la punta de.
Nibble [nib'-l], *va.* Picar, morder pedacitos de, roer, comer a bocaditos; morder, como muerde el pez el anzuelo; rozar, pacer.—*vn.* 1. Morder, mordiscar. 2. Satirizar, criticar; (con la prep. *at*).
Nibble, *s.* 1. Roedura, la acción de roer, de comer poco a poco, a pedacitos menudos; el acto de morder algo con cautela. 2. Pedacito roído casi todo o en parte.
Nibbler [nib'-lęr], *s.* El que pica o come poco a la vez; criticastro.
Niccolite [nic'-el-ait], *s.* Niquelina, arseniuro de níquel. Llámase también *copper-nickel* por su color rojizo.
Nice [nais], *a.* 1. Delicado, mirado, exacto, diligente, solícito. 2. Circunspecto, cauto en extremo. 3. Tierno, delicado, lo que con facilidad se aja o deteriora. 4. Fino, primoroso, refinado, elegante, esmerado. 5. Fastidioso, escrupuloso, fácil de resentirse, vidrioso. 6. (Fam.) Gustoso, agradable de cualquier modo, delicioso, exquisito, bueno; gentil, amable. *To be nice,* Hacer melindres, hacer dengues. *To make nice,* Ser escrupuloso o delicado. *A nice point,* Un punto delicado. *A nice distinction,* Una distinción exacta, sutil. *She is a nice girl,* Es una muchacha gentil, amable. *A nice bit,* Un buen bocado; un trozo escogido.
Nicene, Nicæan [nai'-sin, nai-sī'-an], *a.* Niceno, perteneciente a Nicea, ciu-

dad de Bitinia. *The Nicene Creed,* El Credo niceno.

Nicely [nais'-li], *adv.* 1. Exactamente, con esmero. 2. Delicadamente. 3. Primorosamente.

Niceness [nais'-nes], *s.* 1. Exactitud, esmero. 2. Delicadeza, nimiedad.

Nicety [nai'-se-ti], *s.* 1. Cualidad de lo que es delicado, agradable, primoroso; exactitud, esmero en la ejecución de alguna cosa. 2. Delicadeza, sutileza, afeminación. 3. Circunspección, discreción, discernimiento; refinamiento, argucia; carácter prolijo de una observación o distinción. *The niceties of logic, of politics,* Las sutilezas de la lógica, las argucias de la política. *Nicety of honour,* La delicadeza del honor, el pundonor. *Meat done to a nicety,* Carne, manjar guisado a punto. *To a nicety,* Con la mayor precisión. *The niceties of a woman,* Los melindres o arrumacos de una mujer. *Niceties,* Golosinas, manjares delicados.

Niche [nich], *s.* Nicho, concavidad formada para colocar en ella una estatua, urna, florero, etc.

Nick [nic], *s.* 1. Punto crítico, ocasión oportuna, tiempo preciso. 2. Muesca. 3. Escote. 4. Tarja. *In the nick of time,* Al tiempo preciso, a buen tiempo, a punto fijo.

Nick, *n. pr.* (abreviatura de Nicolás). *Old Nick,* El diablo.

Nick, *va.* 1. Acertar, dar en el clavo; llegar a tiempo. 2. Cortar en muescas. 3. Tarjar, señalar números en tarjas. 4. (Des.) Engañar, pegársela a uno.

Nickel [nik'-el], *s.* 1. (Quím.) Níquel, metal duro, maleable, blanco argentino, magnético, difícil de fundir y oxidar. 2. (Fam.) Moneda de cinco centavos de los Estados Unidos, hecha de una aleación de níquel y cobre. *Nickel-plated,* Niquelado, que tiene una capa galvánica de níquel. *Nickel-plate, va.* Niquelar, cubrir otro metal con una capa de níquel, por medio de la galvanoplastia.

Nicknack [nic'-nac], *s.* Friolera, cosa de poco valor. *Sundry nicknacks,* Varias chucherías.

Nickname [nic'-nēm], *s.* Apodo, mote, mal nombre.

Nickname, *va.* Motejar, poner apodos.

Nicotian [ni-cō'-shi-an], *a.* Nicociano, relativo al tabaco o derivado de él.

Nicotin, Nicotine [nic'-o-tin, tīn], *s.* Nicotina, alcaloide muy venenoso que contienen las hojas del tabaco ($C_{10}H_{14}N_2$).

Nictitate [nic'-ti-tēt], *vn.* Pestañear, parpadear. *Nictitating membrane,* Membrana de pestañeo, el tercer párpado, o párpado lateral de las aves, de los cocodrilos, etc.

Nictitation [nic-ti-tē'-shun], *s.* Pestañeo; en patología, pestañeo rápido e involuntario, debido a un desarreglo nervioso.

Nidificant [nid'-i-fi-cant], *a.* Que hace nidos, como un ave.

Nidification [nid-i-fi-cē'-shun], *s.* Nidificación, el acto de hacer nidos las aves.

Nidify [nid'-i-fai], *vn.* Nidificar, anidar.

Nidor [nai'-dẹr], *s.* Olor, sabor, como de manjar cocido, o a socarrado.

§**Nidorosity** [nai-do-res'-i-ti], *s.* Eructo o regüeldo.

Nidorous [nai'-do-rus], *a.* Lo que huele a carne o grasa asada; y en medicina lo que huele o sabe a huevo podrido.

Nidulate [nid'-yu-lēt], *va.* *V.* NIDIFY.

Nidulation [nid-yu-lē'-shun], *s.* El tiempo de quedar en el nido.

Niece [nīs], *sf.* Sobrina.

Niello [ni-el'-ō], *s.* Niel, labor que se hace con el buril o el cincel en los metales.—*va.* Nielar, entallar o abrir a buril varias labores en metal, rellenando los huecos con otro metal diferente, o con una aleación negra.

Nig [nig], *va.* 1. Cortar el borde de algo, v. g. de una moneda. 2. Labrar a pico (hablando de piedra).

Nigella [ni-jel'-a], *s.* (Bot.) Neguilla.

Niggard [nig'-ard], *s.* Tacaño, avaro y mezquino.—*a.* 1. Avariento, avaro, miserable, ruin. 2. Escaso, económico, mezquino.

Niggard, *va.* (Poco us.) Escasear.

Niggardish [nig'-ard-ish], *a.* Avariento, ruin, mezquino.

Niggardliness [nig'-ard-li-nes], **Niggardness** [nig'-ard-nes], *s.* Tacañería, miseria, ruindad.

Niggardly [nig'-ard-li], *adv.* Tacañamente, ruinmente.

Niggle [nig'-l], *vn.* Jugar, travesear o retozar; burlarse de.

Nigh [nai], *prep.* Cerca, no lejos, a proximidad. *Nigh at hand,* Cerca a la mano. *Nigh to death,* Próximo a morir.—*adv.* Cerca, inmediato, junto a; casi, cuasi. *Draw nigh,* Acérquese Vd.—*a.* 1. Cercano, próximo, vecino, poco lejano. 2. A la izquierda, de la izquierda; dícese de una yunta de bueyes o caballos. 3. (E. U. y Prov. Ingl.) Apretado, mezquino. 4. Allegado, pariente; íntimo.

Nighness [nai'-nes], *s.* Cercanía, proximidad.

Night [nait], *s.* 1. Noche, todo el tiempo que el sol permanece fuera de nuestro horizonte. 2. Caída de la tarde, término del día. 3. Noche, tinieblas, obscuridad; ceguedad física; falta de inteligencia; tristeza, aflicción. 4. La muerte, la sepultura, o la vejez muy avanzada. *By night,* De noche. *To wish one a good-night,* Darle a uno las buenas noches. *Wednesday night,* Miércoles por la noche. *To-night,* Esta noche, a la noche. *Last night,* La noche pasada, ayer noche. *To-morrow night,* Mañana por la noche. *Night,* en composición: *Night-bell,* Campanilla para llamar por la noche. *Night-bird,* Pájaro nocturno. *Night-blindness,* Defecto del nervio óptico que sólo permite ver los objetos durante el día. *Night-brawler,* Alborotador nocturno. *Night-clothes,* Camisa de dormir, traje de dormir. *Night-chair, V. Night-stool. Night-dew,* Sereno de la noche. *Night-dog,* Perro que caza de noche. *Night-dress,* Vestido de noche. *Night-fire,* Fuego fatuo, helena, santelmo. *Night-fly,* Polilla que vuela de noche. *Night-foundered,* Perdido de noche. *Night-glass,* Anteojo para observaciones nocturnas. *Night-hag,* Bruja nocturna. *Night-hawk,* (1) Chotacabras, pájaro nocturno. Chordeiles virginianus. (2) La chotacabras europea. Caprimulgus europæus. *Night-jar,* Chotacabras europea. *Night-lamp, night-light,* Mariposa, candelilla para conservar luz de noche. *Night-piece,* La pintura en que se representa la noche o una escena nocturna. *Night-raven,* (Orn.) Ave de mal agüero que canta de noche. *Night-rest,* El reposo de la noche. *Night-robber,* Ladrón nocturno. *Night-robe,* Camisa de dormir. *Night-school,* Escuela nocturna; por lo común, escuela gratis para los que trabajan durante el día. *Night-shining,* Que reluce o da resplandor de noche. *Night-shriek,* Chillido que se oye de noche. *Night-soil,* El contenido de las letrinas; llámase así porque su extracción se verifica ordinariamente de noche. *Night-spell,* Encanto para librarse de percances por la noche. *Night-stool,* Sillico; la silla agujereada bajo la cual se pone el sillico. *Night sweat,* Sudor nocturno. *Night-time,* Noche, el tiempo que media desde el anochecer hasta el alba. *Night-tripping,* Lo que vaga de noche. *Night-vision,* Sueño, visión nocturna. *Night-walk,* Paseo de noche. *Night-walker,* (1) Noctívago, sonámbulo. (2) El que anda rondando por la noche con mal intento; particularmente prostituta, mujer pública. *Night-walking,* Paseante de noche; sonámbulo.—*s.* Sonambulismo; paseo nocturno; solicitación de prostituta. *Night-wanderer,* El que vaga de noche. *Night-wandering,* Noctívago. *Night-warbling,* El que canta por la noche. *Night-watch,* (1) Centinela o ronda de noche. (2) La hora en que se mudan los serenos o las rondas de noche. *Night-work,* (1) Trabajo nocturno. (2) Extracción de letrinas.

Nightcap [nait'-cap], *s.* 1. Gorro de dormir. 2. (Fam.) Trago de vino u otro licor antes de acostarse.

Nighted [nait'-ed], *a.* Negro, obscuro.

Nightfall [nait'-fōl], *s.* El anochecer.

Nightfaring [nait'-fār-ing], *a.* Que viaja de noche.

Nightgown [nait'-gaun], *s.* Bata que se usa de noche; traje de dormir.

Nightingale [nait'-in-gēl], *s.* (Orn.) Ruiseñor.

Night letter [nait let'-ẹr], *s.* Carta telegráfica nocturna.

Nightly [nait'-li], *adv.* Por las noches, todas las noches.—*a.* Nocturno, de noche; que ocurre o aparece durante la noche.

Nightman [nait'-man], *s.* Empleado que trabaja de noche.

Nightmare [nait'-mār], *s.* Pesadilla.

Night school [nait scūl], *s.* Escuela nocturna.

Night service [nait sẹr'-vis], *s.* Servicio nocturno.

Nightshade [nait'-shēd], *s.* (Bot.) Una de las varias plantas del género Solanum, como la belladona, el beleño y particularmente la hierbamora.

Nightward [nait'-ward], *a.* Lo que suele hacerse al acercarse la noche.

Nigrescence [nig-res'-ens], *s.* La acción de ennegrecer y la negrura producida.

Nigrescent [nig-res'-ẹnt], *a.* Ennegrecido; negruzco.

Nigrification [nig-ri-fi-kē'-shun], *s.* Ennegrecimiento.

Nigrify [nig'-ri-fai], *va.* Hacer negro, ennegrecer.

Nihil [nai'-hil], *s.* (Lat.) Nada.

Nihilism [nai'-hil-izm], *s.* 1. Nihilismo, negación de toda creencia. 2. Nihilismo; fué en Rusia, en su origen, la negación de todo principio religioso, político y social; y es hoy un partido revolucionario secreto que tiende a subvertir las instituciones existentes.

Nihilist [nai'-hil-ist], *s.* 1. Nihilista, partidario del nihilismo. 2. En Rusia, revolucionario.

Nihility [nai-hil'-i-ti], *s.* Estado de lo que no existe; la nada.

Nil, Nill [nil], *s.* Nada.

Nilgau, Nilghau [nil'-gau], *s.* Tragélafo, rumiante parecido al antílope pero de menor tamaño. Presenta siempre unas líneas o dibujos de formas extrañas, a los que el animal debe el nombre de *jeroglífico*, con que en algunas partes se le conoce. (< Per. *nil*, azul, y *gau*, vaca.) Boselaphus tragocamelus.

†**Nill** [nil], *va.* Rehusar, no querer. *Will he, nill he,* A buenas o a malas, que quiera que no quiera.

Nill, *s.* Chispa de bronce fundido.

Nilometer [nai-lem'-e-ter], *s.* Nilómetro, niloscopo, instrumento para medir las aguas del Nilo.

Nimbiferous [nim-bif'-er-us], *a.* Que trae nubes, lluvia o tempestades.

Nimble [nim'-bl], *a.* Ligero, vivo, activo, listo, ágil.

Nimble-footed [nim'-bl-fut'-ed], *a.* Ligero de pies.

Nimbleness [nim'-bl-nes], *s.* Ligereza, velocidad, actividad, agilidad, celeridad; expedición, destreza.

Nimble-witted [nim'-bl-wit'-ed], *a.* Pronto en hablar; penetrante, de inteligencia viva.

Nimbly [nim'-bli], *adv.* Prontamente, ágilmente.

Nimbosity [nim-bes'-i-ti], *s.* Tormenta.

Nimbus [nim'-bus], *s.* 1. Nube obscura y espesa desde la cual cae o está al caer la lluvia. 2. Aureola, diadema o círculo de luz que se pone sobre la cabeza de los santos.

Nimmer [nim'-er], *s.* (Poco us.) Gato, ladrón, ratero.

Nincompoop [nin'-cum-pūp], *s.* (Fam.) Badulaque, simplón, tonto.

Nine [nain], *a.* Nueve.—*s.* 1. Nueve. 2. (Poét.) Las musas, las nueve hermanas. *Nine men's morris, V.* Morris.

Ninefold [nain'-fōld], *a.* y *adv.* Nueve veces.

Ninepence [nain'-pens], *s.* 1. Nueve peniques. 2. Término que en la Nueva Inglaterra significaba el real fuerte o media peseta; en Nueva York se llamaba *shilling*, y en los Estados del Oeste y del Sur, *bit.*

Ninepins [nain'-pinz], *s.* Juego de bolos.

Ninescore [nain'-scōr], *a.* y *s.* Nueve veces veinte.

Nineteen [nain'-tīn], *a.* y *s.* Diez y nueve.

Nineteenth [nain'-tīnth], *a.* Décimonono.

Ninetieth [nain'-ti-eth], *a.* Nonagésimo.

Ninety [nain'-ti], *a.* y *s.* Noventa.

Ninny, Ninnyhammer [nin'-i, ham'-er], *s.* Un simple, un mentecato, un nene, un imbécil, un bobo, zote.

Ninth [nainth], *a.* Nono, noveno.

Ninthly [nainth'-li], *adv.* Noveno o en nono lugar.

Nip [nip], *va.* 1. Arañar, rasguñar de repente; pellizcar; morder, cortar con las uñas o los dientes. 2. Quebrar, pellizcar, o desgarrar la superficie o extremo de. 3. Helar o secar los frutos antes de madurarse; marchitar, hacer perecer en germen. *To nip in the bud* o *blossom,* Destruir en germen, en el principio. 4. Tocar de cerca, interesar. *To nip off,* Cortar alguna cosa fácil de separarse de donde estaba unida.

Nip, *s.* 1. Pellizco, acción y efecto de pellizcar; porción pequeña, pedacito; trago, traguito; uñada, dentellada. 2. Helada, escarcha. 3. Cogida; la situación de lo que está cogido entre los hielos o encerrado en ellos. 4. Daño repentino que sufren las plantas o los sembrados. *Nip and tuck,* (Fam. E. U.) Caso de igualdad, de empate. 5. (Des.) Sátira, dicho picante y mordaz.

Nipper [nip'-er], *s.* Lo que pellizca o muerde: pinza; la garra grande de un cangrejo; pala, diente delantero del caballo. *V.* Nippers.

Nippers [nip'-erz], *s. pl.* 1. Alicates, tenazas. 2. (Mar.) Mojelas, badernas.

Nipping [nip'-ing], *s.* Araño, rasguño, mordedura. *Nipping jest,* Chanza pesada, dicho picante, sátira mordaz.

Nippingly [nip'-ing-li], *adv.* Mordazmente.

Nipple [nip'-l], *s.* 1. Pezón, la punta que sobresale en los pechos o tetas. 2. Chimenea de un arma de fuego de percusión. 3. Pezón artificial que se emplea con un biberón o para proteger un pezón lastimado. *Nipple shield,* Pezonera.

Nipplewort [nip'-l-wūrt], *s.* (Bot.) Lapsana común.

Nirvana [nir-vā'-na], *s.* Nirvana; en el brahmanismo, la libertad y felicidad espirituales; en el budismo, el aniquilamiento y abandono que constituyen la perfección suprema.

Nisi Prius [nai'-sai prai'-us], *s.* (For.) 1. Nombre de uno de los tribunales ingleses. 2. Palabras con que se encabeza la orden que se da para que se conozca en la materia, a *no ser que* los jueces hayan dispuesto de ella antes.

Nit [nit], *s.* 1. Liendre, el huevo del piojo. 2. Punto pequeño.

Nitency [nai'-ten-si], *s.* (Poco us.) Lustre, esplendor, brillantez.

Niter, Nitre [nai'-ter], *s.* Nitro, salitre, nitrato de potasa.

Nitrate [nai'-trēt], *s.* (Quím.) Nitrato, sal formada de ácido nítrico con alguna base.

Nitre [nai'-ter], *s.* *V.* Niter.

Nitric [nai'-tric], *a.* Nítrico, azoico.

Nitrite [nai'-trait], *s.* Nitrito, sal formada de ácido nitroso con alguna base.

Nitrogen [nai'-tro-jen], *s.* Nitrógeno, el ázoe, gas incoloro, principio constitutivo del aire y de las substancias minerales, vegetales y animales. Su fórmula es N.

Nitrogenize [nai'-tro-jen-aiz ó nai-troj'-en-aiz], *va.* Tratar por el nitrógeno o combinar con él.

Nitrogenous [nai-troj'-en-us], *a.* Nitrogenado, que contiene nitrógeno, le pertenece o se relaciona con él.

Nitroglycerin [nai-tro-glis'-er-in], *s.* Nitroglicerina, líquido aceitoso, amarillo claro, de tremenda fuerza explosiva; se mezcla comúnmente con una substancia neutra para formar la dinamita.

Nitrous [nai'-trus], **Nitry** [nai'-tri], *a.* Nitroso.

Nitrous oxide [nai'-trus ex'-aid], *s.* Óxido nitroso, gas hilarante.

Nitty [nit'-i], *a.* Lendroso, lleno de liendres.

Nival [nai'-val], *a.* 1. Nevoso. 2. Que crece debajo de la nieve.

Niveous [niv'-e-us], *a.* Blanco como la nieve o lo que se parece a la nieve.

Nix [nix], **Nixie** [nix'-i], *s.* Genio de las aguas en la mitología alemana.

Nix, *s.* (Germ. E. U.) Nada. (< Al. nichts.)

Nizam [ni-zam'], *s.* Soberano indígena de Hiderabad en el Indostán.

No [nō], *adv.* No. *Whether or no,* Sea o no sea; que . . . no. *No more of this,* Basta, bastante, no hablemos más de eso.—*a.* Ningún, ninguno. *By no means,* De ninguna manera, de ningún modo. *No matter, it is no matter,* No importa. *To no purpose,* Sin razón alguna, sin objeto, en vano, inútilmente. *You shall come to no harm,* No le sucederá a Vd. nada de malo. *No one,* Nadie. *To wrong no one,* No hacer daño a nadie. *No-account,* Sin valor, despreciable, vil, bajo.

Noah's Ark [nō'-az ārc], *s.* Arca de Noé; cajón de sastre.

Noachian [no-ē'-ki-an], *a.* Relativo a Noé.

Nob [neb], *s.* 1. (Fest.) La cabeza. 2. *V.* Knob. 3. (Germ.) Persona de distinción social, de buen tono.

Nobby [neb'-i], *a.* (Germ.) Llamativo; ostentoso, a la moda.

Nobiliary [no-bil'-i-e-ri], *a.* Nobiliario.

Nobility [no-bil'-i-ti], *s.* 1. Nobleza. 2. Nobleza, se toma colectivamente por el brazo o cuerpo de nobles. 3. Nobleza, dignidad, grandeza, sublimidad de alma, de sentimientos, de estilo, etc.

Noble [nō'-bl], *a.* 1. Noble, hidalgo, que pertenece al cuerpo de la nobleza. 2. Noble, insigne, esclarecido, majestuoso. 3. Noble, elevado, sublime. 4. Magnífico, generoso. 5. Liberal.—*s.* 1. Noble, la persona que pertenece a la nobleza. 2. Noble, moneda antigua cuyo valor ascendía a seis chelines y ocho peniques, o sea $1.60. *They are of noble extraction,* Son de noble alcurnia, o de sangre azul. *To make noble,* Ennoblecer. *Noble metals,* Metales nobles, es decir, el oro, la plata y el platino.

Nobleman [nō'-bl-man], *s.* Noble, hidalgo. *V.* Noble, 1ª acep.

Nobleness [nō'-bl-nes], *s.* 1. Nobleza, dignidad, grandeza. 2. Lustre, esplendor.

Noblesse [nō-bles'], *s.* 1. Nobleza, el conjunto o cuerpo de los nobles. 2. (Ant.) Nobleza, alcurnia noble.

Noblewoman [nō'-bl-wum'-an], *s.* Mujer noble, hidalga.

Nobly [nō'-bli], *adv.* Noblemente. *Nobly born,* Noble de nacimiento.

Nobody [nō'-bed-i], *s.* 1. Nadie, ninguna persona, ninguno. 2. Persona de ninguna estimación, un Don Nadie, un cero a la izquierda. *To be nobody at all,* No ser nada absolutamente. *Nobody else,* Nadie más, ningún otro.

Nock [nec], *s.* 1. (Mar.) Puño de la boca (de una vela). 2. (Des.) Muesca, abertura. *V.* Notch.

Noctiluca [nec-ti-lū'-ca], *s.* Noctiluco, protozoario infusorio, animalillo marino microscópico; es la causa ordinaria de la fosforescencia del mar.

Noctivagant [nec-tiv'-a-gant], *a.* (Poco us.) Noctívago, el que anda vagando por la noche.
Noctivagation [nec-tiv-a-gé'-shun], *s.* El acto de vagar de noche.
Noctuary [nec'-chu-ẹ-ri], *s.* Relación de lo que sucede por la noche.
Noctuidæ [nec-tū'-i-dī], *s. pl.* Noctuinos, mariposas nocturnas, el tercer suborden de los lepidópteros, de cuerpo y palpos gruesos.
Nocturn [nec'-tūrn], *s.* 1. Nocturno, parte del oficio divino de la noche. 2. *V.* NOCTURNE, 1ª acep.
Nocturnal [nec-tūr'-nal], *a.* 1. Nocturnal, nocturno; hecho o sucedido de noche. 2. Activo de noche, que busca su alimento por la noche, como los buhos, los noctuinos, etc.
Nocturnal, *s.* Nocturlabio, antiguo instrumento para medir de noche la latitud por la altura de las estrellas.
Nocturne [nec'-tūrn], *s.* 1. Cuadro, pintura que representa una escena nocturna. 2. (Mús.) Nocturno, composición música de melodía dulce y sentimental. (Fr.)
Nod [ned], *vn.* 1. Cabecear. 2. Hacer un movimiento con la cabeza inclinándola hacia abajo, en señal de respeto o de afecto. 3. Hacer una señal con la cabeza. 4. Amodorrarse, adormecerse.—*va.* 1. Mover la cabeza, dar cabezadas. 2. Indicar, hacer saber, con una inclinación de la cabeza. 3. Inclinar la cima o parte superior, como de una flor o de un árbol.
Nod, *s.* 1. Cabeceo. 2. Cabeceo, el movimiento de la cabeza cuando uno se duerme. 3. Reverencia, mocha, inclinación de la cabeza en señal de cortesía. 4. Cualquiera señal hecha con la cabeza.
Nodal [nō'-dal], *a.* 1. Nodal, que se refiere a los nodos de una superficie vibrante. 2. Nudoso, referente a uno o varios nudos.
Nodder [ned'-ẹr], *s.* El que cabecea o da cabezadas.
Nodding [ned'-ing], *pa.* (Bot.) Nutante, cuya parte superior se inclina o cuelga hacia abajo.—*s.* 1. Cabeceo. 2. Dormitación.
Noddle [ned'-l], *s.* Mollera, cabeza: úsase despreciativamente.
Noddy [ned'-i], *s.* 1. Un simple, un tonto, zote. 2. Carruaje ligero de dos ruedas. 3. Ave de una de las varias especies de pájaros bobos.
Node [nōd], *s.* 1. Nudo. 2. (Cir.) Nodo, nudo, un tumor o dureza de los huesos. 3. (Astr.) Nodo, cualquiera de los dos puntos opuestos en que la órbita de un planeta corta la eclíptica. 4. (Bot.) Nudo, punto del tallo por donde frotan las ramas o de donde nacen las hojas. 5. Nodo, el punto en que una curva se corta a sí misma. 6. Enredo, nudo, intriga de una novela o drama.
Nodose [nō'-dōs], *a.* Nudoso, que tiene nudos o junturas salientes.
Nodosity [nō-des'-i-ti], *s.* Nudosidad, complicación o abundancia de nudos.
Nodular [ned'-yu-lar], *a.* Parecido a un nudo; que tiene nudos.
Nodule [ned'-yūl], *s.* Nudillo; bulto o elevación pequeña de cualquier especie.
Noduled [ned'-yūld], *a.* Lo que tiene nudillos o elevaciones.
Noetic [no-et'-ic], *a.* Mental, concebido por la mente; intuitivo. (Gr.)
Nog [neg], *s.* 1. Baldosa cuadrada de madera. 2. (Mar.) Cabilla para escotas; clavija de madera.
Nog, *s.* (Prov. Ingl.) 1. Pucherito, cantarito. 2. Una cerveza fuerte. *Egg-nog,* Bebida que se hace con leche, huevos, azúcar y algún licor espirituoso.
Noggin [neg'-in], *s.* (Prov.) Vasija de madera; también, jarro y su contenido. *V.* MUG.
Nogging [neg'-ing], *s.* Tabique.
Noise [neiz], *s.* 1. Ruido, sonido, estruendo. 2. Bulla, clamor, gritería. 3. Ruido, rumor, y por extensión fama, nombre, noticia o novedad. *Noise in one's ears,* Zumbido de oídos.
Noise, *va.* 1. Esparcir, divulgar o extender alguna noticia. 2. Turbar con gritos o con estruendo.
Noiseful [neiz'-ful], *a.* Ruidoso.
Noiseless [neiz'-les], *a.* Quedo, sin ruido, tranquilo, callado.
Noisiness [neiz'-i-nes], *s.* Estrépito, ruido, tumulto, alboroto.
Noisome [nei'-sum], *a.* 1. Ofensivo, asqueroso, desagradable, repugnante, particularmente al sentido del olfato. 2. (Ant.) Dañoso, nocivo, malsano.
Noisomely [nei'-sum-li], *adv.* Fétido, asqueroso, infeccionable.
Noisomeness [nei'-sum-nes], *s.* 1. Fastidio, náusea. 2. Malsano, repugnante; asquerosidad, infección.
Noisy [neiz'-i], *a.* Ruidoso, clamoroso, turbulento, estrepitoso.
Nolens-volens [nō'-lenz-vō'-lenz], *adv.* Velisnolis, de buena o mala gana, de grado o por fuerza, quieras o no.
Noli-me-tangere [nō'-lai-mī-tan'-jẹ-rẹ], *s.* 1. (Bot.) Nometoca o impaciente nometoca, balsamina, planta de las geraniáceas. Impatiens balsamina e Impatiens noli-me-tangere. 2. (Med.) Nolimetángere, nometoques, úlcera maligna en la cara, a menudo cancerosa.
Nolition [no-lish'-un], *s.* (Teol.) Nolición, el acto de la voluntad con que no se quiere alguna cosa.
Nolle prosequi [nel'-ẹ pres'-ẹ-cwai o prō'-se-cwī], *loc. lat.* (For.) Término jurídico para indicar que el acusador o demandante desiste de proseguir su acción civil o criminal; abandono de un litigio.
Nomad, Nomadic [nem'-ad, no-mad'-ic], *a.* Nómada, errante, que no tiene asiento ni habitación fija.—*s.* Nómada, miembro de una tribu errante.
¿**Nomancy** [nō'-man-si], *s.* (Poco us.) Supuesta adivinación por las letras del nombre de alguna persona.
Nomarch [nem'-ārc], *s.* Nomarca, gobernador de un nomo en el antiguo Egipto y en la Grecia moderna.
Nome [nōm], *s.* 1. Provincia, nomo, prefectura del antiguo Egipto o de la Grecia moderna. 2. Expresión, cantidad algebraica.
Nomenclator [no-men-clé'-tẹr], *s.* 1. Nomenclator, el que pone nombres propios a personas o cosas. 2. Lista de nombres.
Nomenclature [nō-men-clé'-chur], *s.* Nomenclatura, sistema de nombres o procedimiento para nombrar; el conjunto de las voces técnicas de una facultad o ciencia.
Nominal [nem'-i-nal], *a.* 1. Nominal, que existe más en el nombre que en realidad. *A nominal king,* Rey de nombre. 2. Nominal, que pertenece a un nombre.
Nominalism [nem'-i-nal-izm], *s.* Nominalismo, antiguo sistema que negaba toda realidad a los términos genéricos y consideraba los nombres individuales y particulares como los únicos verdaderamente reales.
Nominalist [nem'-i-nal-ist], *s.* Nominales, escolásticos opuestos a los realistas.
Nominally [nem'-i-nal-i], *adv.* Nominalmente.
Nominate [nem'-i-nêt], *va.* Nombrar, elegir, señalar.
Nomination [nem-i-nê'-shun], *s.* Nombramiento, nominación.
Nominative [nem'-i-na-tiv], *s.* (Gram.) Nominativo, el primer caso del nombre; sujeto.
Nominator [nem'-i-nê-tẹr], *s.* Nominador, nombrador.
Nominee [nem-i-nī'], *s.* Nombrado, provisto, el que es nombrado para algún empleo u oficio.
Nominor [nem'-i-nōr], *s.* Electo, el nombrado para alguna dignidad o empleo.
Nomography [no-meg'-ra-fi], *s.* Nomografía, tratado de jurisprudencia.
Nomothetical [nem-o-thet'-i-cal], *a.* Legislativo.
-nomy. Sufijo que indica una ciencia y corresponde a -nomía en español. *Astronomy,* Astronomía.
Non- [nen]. Partícula negativa que corresponde a los prefijos españoles *in, no:* se une por un guión a la palabra siguiente: *Non-ability,* Inhabilidad, excepción legal. *Non-acceptance,* Falta de aceptación; repulsa. *Non-acid,* No ácido, que no tiene las propiedades de un ácido. *Non-actinic,* No actínico, que no efectúa cambios químicos; dícese de ciertos rayos de luz. *Non-admission,* Denegación, falta de admisión. *Non-appearance* (For.) Contumacia, rebeldía, no comparecencia en juicio; falta. *Non-arrival,* Falta de llegada o arribo. *Non assumpsit,* (For.) La alegación de que una persona no ha hecho alguna promesa. *Non-attendance,* Falta de asistencia. *Non-attention,* Desatención. *Non-commissioned,* Sin título, sin despacho. *Non-commissioned officer,* Clase; sargento o cabo. *Non-concurrence,* Falta de unión o combinación. *Non-conducting,* No conductivo. *Non-conductor,* No conductor, substancia que se opone al paso de una fuerza cualquiera, como el calórico y la electricidad. *Non-contagious,* No contagioso. *Non-content,* Oponente; en la cámara británica de los pares se llama así al lord que vota en contra. *Non-delivery,* Falta de remisión, descuido en hacer un envío, una entrega. *Non-essential,* No esencial. *Non-exportation,* Falta o suspensión de la extracción de géneros. *Non-importation,* Falta o suspensión de la entrada de géneros. *Non-juring,* No juramentado, que rehusa prestar juramento de fidelidad. *V* NONJUROR. *Non-natural,* (Med.) No natural. *Non-payment,* Falta de pago. *Non-performance,* Falta de ejecución. *Non-residence,* Ausencia, falta de residencia en el que tiene obligación de residir en alguna parte. *Non-resident,* Ausente, no residente. *Non-resistance,* Obediencia pasiva. *Non-sensitive,* Falto de percepción o de sensibilidad. *Non-solution,* Insolvencia. *Non-tenure,* (For.) Alegación de estar exento de una jurisdicción.

Nonage [nen'-ẹj], *s.* Minoridad, edad menor.

Nonagenarian [nen-a-jẹ-né'-ri-an], *a.* y *s.* Nonagenario, de noventa o más años de edad.

Nonagesimal [nen-a-jes'-i-mal], *a.* Nonagésimo.

Nonagon [nen'-a-gen], *s.* Nonágono, la figura de nueve ángulos.

Nonce [nens], *s.* Hogaño, el tiempo o la ocasión presente ; la actualidad. *For the nonce,* Al presente, actualmente, hoy día.

Nonchalance [nōñ''-sha-lāns' o nen'-sha-lans], *s.* Estado de indiferencia o incuria ; descuido. (Fr.)

Nonchalant [nen'-sha-lant], *a.* Descuidado, incurioso, negligente. (Fr.)

Non compos mentis [nen cem'-pes men'-tis], *a.* Insano, falto de razón o juicio.

Non-combatant [cem'-bat-ant], *s.* 1. No combatiente, como el médico militar y el capellán castrense. 2. En tiempo de guerra, el que no pertenece al ejército ; como las mujeres, los niños y otros no combatientes.

Non-conformist [nen-cen-fērm'-ist], *s.* No conformista o disidente, el que no se conforma con los ritos de la Iglesia anglicana.

Non-conformity [nen-cen-fēr'-mi-ti], *s.* Desconformidad, disidencia, oposición, repugnancia a conformarse con los ritos de la Iglesia anglicana.

Nondescript [nen'-dẹ-script], *a.* Que no está descrito; fantástico. *V.* ODD. Úsase también como substantivo para designar un objeto de historia natural que no ha sido nunca descrito.

None [nun], *pron.* 1. Nadie, ninguno. *None will be excepted,* No se exceptuará a nadie. *He has none,* No tiene ninguno. 2. Nada, nada de ; fuera. *None of that,* Nada de eso. *Come now, none of your mischief,* Vamos, dejarse de travesuras. 3. *adv.* No. *He was none the worse,* No se hallaba peor. *We have none,* No tenemos. *None-so-pretty,* (Bot.) *V.* LONDON PRIDE. Saxifraga.

Nonentity [nen-en'-ti-ti], **Non-existence** [nen-egz-ist'-ens], *s.* Nada, la nada ; la falta de existencia.

Nones [nōnz], *s. pl.* 1. Nonas ; en el calendario romano el nono día antes de los idus ; el séptimo día de marzo, mayo, julio, y octubre y el quinto de los demás meses. 2. Nona, hora menor del rezo eclesiástico (entre las doce y las tres).

Nonesuch [nun'-such], *s.* Sin igual, sin par.

Nonillion [no-nil'-yun], *s.* Nonilión, un número cardinal : en la numeración francesa, la unidad con treinta ceros ; en la inglesa, unidad seguida de cincuenta y cuatro ceros.

Nonjuror [nen-jū'-rẹr], *s.* El inglés que no quiso prestar el juramento de fidelidad a la dinastía actual de Inglaterra a su advenimiento al trono.

Nonpareil [nen-pa-rel'], *s.* 1. Sin par, bondad sin igual. 2. Especie de camuesa. 3. (Impr.) Nomparel, un grado de letra muy pequeña que usan los impresores ; es de seis puntos. Doce líneas de nomparel hacen una pulgada inglesa. 4. Nombre de varias clases de pájaros ; variedades de pinzón y de loro.—*a.* Sin igual, sobresaliente, que no tiene par.

Nonplus [nen'-plus], *s.* Embarazo, perplejidad, estado de no poder decidir ni avanzar ; dificultad inquietante. *He was left at a nonplus,* No supo qué responder, se quedó cortado, perplejo.

Nonplus, *va.* Confundir, atascar, cortar, arrinconar, estrechar en una disputa.

Nonsense [nen'-sens], *s.* 1. Disparate, desatino, absurdo, necedad. 2. (Fam.) Bagatelas, fruslerías, cosas sin importancia, jerigonza. *Nonsense verses,* Versos de buena forma, pero de sentido desatinado y absurdo.

Nonsensical [nen-sen'-sic-al], *a.* Absurdo, desatinado, impertinente.

Nonsensically [nen-sen'-sic-al-i], *adv.* Disparatadamente.

Nonsensicalness [nen-sen'-sic-al-nes], *s.* Absurdidad ; disparate.

Nonskid [nen-skid'], *a.* Antideslizante.

Nonsuit [nen'-siūt], *s.* (For.) 1. El abandono de un pleito por el demandante. 2. El acto de declarar que el demandante en un juicio ha perdido el derecho de continuar en su demanda por no haber cumplido lo que prescriben las leyes.

Nonsuit, *va.* (For.) Absolver de la instancia, declarar que un demandante en juicio ha perdido el derecho de seguir en su demanda por no haber cumplido lo que prescriben las leyes.

Noodle [nū'-dl], *s.* Simplón, mentecato, idiota.

Noodle, *s.* Tallarín, tira hecha con pasta de macarrones ; se emplea para sopa y es muy estimada entre los alemanes y germanoamericanos.

Nook [nuc], *s.* 1. Rincón, lugar estrecho y retirado, escondrijo. 2. (Esco.) Ángulo, encuentro.

Noon [nūn], *s.* 1. Mediodía, hora en que está el sol en el meridiano. 2. Culminación, apogeo. *High noon,* El mediodía en punto, las doce en punto.

Noonday [nūn'-dé], *s.* Mediodía.—*a.* Meridional.

Nooning [nūn'-ing], *s.* Siesta, el descanso de mediodía.

Noontide [nūn'-taid], *a.* Meridional. —*s.* 1. La hora de mediodía. 2. Período de apogeo o culminación.

Noose [nūs o nūz], *s.* Lazo corredizo. *Noose snare,* Trampa.

Noose [nūs], *va.* 1. Enlazar, apretar con lazo corredizo. 2. Entrampar, hacer caer en la trampa.

Nor [nēr], *conj.* Ni, no, tampoco ; partícula correlativa de *neither* o *not,* pero en el uso poético o retórico, estas últimas palabras se omiten algunas veces. *I did not go, nor did I intend it,* No fuí ni tuve intención de ir. *I neither love nor fẹar thee,* Ni te amo ni te temo. *Nor was this all,* Pero esto no fué todo.

Norm [nērm], *s.* 1. Norma, regla, tipo normal o modelo. 2. (Biol.) Unidad típica de conformación o estructura.

Normal [nēr'-mal], *a.* (Geom.) 1. Perpendicular, lo que forma un ángulo recto. 2. Normal, según las reglas o principios ; que enseña las reglas o principios ; conforme a un tipo o regla. *Normal schools,* Escuelas para enseñar a los maestros cómo han de desempeñar su obligación.

Norman [nēr'-man], *a.* Normando, perteneciente a Normandía.—*s.* 1. Normando, el natural de Normandía. 2. (Mar.) Burel del molinete.

Norse [nērs], *a.* Escandinavo, perteneciente a los países o a los idiomas escandinavos.—*s.* Idiomas escandinavos, particularmente el de Islanda.

Norseman [nērs'-man], *s.* Hombre del Norte, el antiguo escandinavo.

North [nērth], *s.* 1. Norte, punto cardinal opuesto al Sur ; septentrión. 2. Región o distrito al norte de un punto dado ; particularmente en los Estados Unidos, la región que se halla al norte de los estados donde existió la esclavitud.—*a.* Septentrional, del norte. *The North Pole,* El Polo Norte, polo ártico. *North by east,* Norte, cuarto nordeste. *North by west,* Norte, cuarto noroeste. *North star,* Estrella polar, estrella del norte.

Northeast [nērth-īst'], *s.* y *a.* Nordeste.

Northeaster [nērth-īst'-ẹr], *s.* Temporal, ventarrón del nordeste.

Northeasterly [nērth-īst'-ẹr-li], *a.* Dirigido hacia al nordeste o que viene del nordeste.

Northeastern [nērth-īst'-ẹrn], *a.* Situado en el nordeste, perteneciente a esta dirección.

Norther [nērdh'-ẹr], *s.* Viento fuerte del norte ; suele ser frío en Texas ; en California a veces muy cálido y seco.

Northerly [nērdh'-ẹr-li], **Northern** [nērdh'-ẹrn], *a.* Septentrional. *Northerly winds,* Vientos del norte. *Northern lights,* Aurora boreal.

Northing [nērdh'-ing], *s.* (Mar.) La diferencia de latitud de un buque en su rumbo.

Northman [nērth'-man], *s.* Escandinavo. *V.* NORSEMAN.

Northward, **Northwards** [nērth'-ward, z], *adv.* Hacia el norte.

Northwest [nērth-west'], *s.* y *a.* Nordovest, noroeste, norueste.

Northwesterly [nērth-west'-ẹr-li], *a.* Dirigido hacia el noroeste o que viene del noroeste.

Northwestern [nērth-west'-ẹrn], *a.* Perteneciente o situado al noroeste.

North Wind [nērth' wind], *s.* Norte, el viento septentrional.

Norwegian [nēr-wī'-ji-an], *s.* y *a.* Noruego, perteneciente a Noruega, natural de Noruega.

Nose [nōz], *s.* 1. Nariz, órgano del olfato y de la respiración ; hocico de ciertos animales. 2. Olfato, sagacidad. 3. Lo que se asemeja a una nariz : (1) la proa de un buque ; (2) tobera, cañuto del fuelle ; pico, boca (de cafetera o de cántaro). *A flat nose,* Nariz chata, roma o aplastada. *To lead by the nose,* Arrastrar como por fuerza ; llevar tras sí, atraer ciegamente uno a otro á su dictamen o voluntad. *To thrust the nose into,* Entremeterse. *To put the nose out of joint,* Suplantar, desquiciar. *Pug nose,* Nariz roma, achatada. *To bleed at the nose,* Echar sangre por las narices. *To blow one's nose,* Sonarse las narices. *To pick one's nose,* Hurgarse las narices. *To speak through the nose,* Ganguear. *Under one's nose,* A las barbas de uno, en su presencia. *Nose-bag,* Morral de hocico ; cebadera.

Nose, *va.* 1. Oler, olfatear. 2. Descubrir espiando o acechando ; se usa con la prep. *out.* 3. Encararse ; oponerse, hacer frente.

Noseband [nōz'-band], *s.* Muserola, correa que echan a los caballos por las quijadas ; sobarba.

Nosebleed [nōz'-blīd], *s.* 1. Sangre que

sale por las narices, hemorragia nasal. 2. (Bot.) Milenrama.

Nosegay [nōz'-gê], *s.* Ramillete; manojo de flores.

Nosel [noz'-l], *s.* *V.* NOZLE.

Noseless [nōz'-les], *a.* Desnarigado.

Nose-piece [nōz'-pîs], *s.* 1. Sobarba, muserola. 2. Remate del microscopio al cual se asegura el objetivo; porta-objetivos, anillo que sirve á este objeto. 3. Extremo, boquerel de manguera o de tubo.

Nosology [nos-ol'-ō-ji], *s.* Nosología, la descripción y clasificación de las enfermedades. Su adjetivo es *nosological*, nosológico.

Nostalgia [nos-tal'-ji-a], *s.* Nostalgia.

Nostoc [nos'-toc], *s.* Nostoc, género de algas de agua dulce. Forma masas gelatinosas o membranosas de color verde.

Nostologic [nos-to-loj'-ic], *a.* Senil, relativo a la vejez avanzada o segunda niñez.

Nostril [nos'-tril], *s.* Ventana de la nariz.

Nostrum [nos'-trum], *s.* 1. Secreto, remedio o medicina secreta. 2. Proyecto de charlatán o politicastro. 3. Remedio predilecto.

Not [not], *adv.* No, partícula con que se niega o rehusa alguna cosa. *Not at all*, De ningún modo. *Not but, not that*, No que, no es (decir) que. *Not but that I shall go*, No es decir que no iré. *Not that I say*, No es que yo lo diga. *Not to say*, Por no decir. *Not so much as*, Ni siquiera. *They had not so much as heard*, Ni siquiera habían oído. *I think not*, No lo creo; creo que no. *Does* (pro.) *not?* ¿No es verdad? *She sings well, does she not?* Ella canta bien, ¿no es así?

Notability [nō-ta-bil'-i-ti], *s.* 1. Notabilidad, carácter notable. 2. Notabilidad, persona de consecuencia, notable.

Notableness [nō-ta-bl-nes], *s.* Notabilidad, cualidad de lo que es notable; carácter notable.

Notable [nō'-ta-bl], *a.* Notable, digno de nota, reparo o atención; memorable. *A notable example*, Ejemplo notable, memorable.

Notable [not'-a-bl], *a.* Eminentemente cuidadoso o arreglado en sus gastos; hábil. *A notable housewife*, Una cuidadosa ama de casa.

Notably [nō'-ta-bli], *adv.* Notablemente, importantemente.

Notarial [no-tê'-ri-al], *a.* Perteneciente a un notario; ejecutado o hecho ante notario.

Notary [nō'-ta-ri], **Notary-public** [nō'-ta-ri-pub'-lic], *s.* Notario, escribano público, funcionario autorizado para dar fe en los instrumentos auténticos y otros actos extrajudiciales.

Notation [no-tē'-shun], *s.* 1. Notación, anotación; sentido, significación. 2. Notación, numeración escrita; sistema de signos, cifras o abreviaturas empleado en una ciencia o arte. Notación aritmética, musical, química, lógica.

Notch [noch], *s.* Muesca, abertura o corte que se hace en alguna cosa; ranura, mortaja, tajadura; hendidura; malla.

Notch, *va.* Hacer muescas; dentar, ranurar, ruñar.

Note [nōt], *s.* 1. Nota, marca, señal. 2. Caso, aprecio. 3. Nota, censura o reparo de las acciones de alguno. 4. Nota, tacha o defecto grave y reparable. 5. Nota, apuntación, apunte. 6. Nota, reparo o explicación que se hace sobre lo contenido en algún libro o escrito. 7. Carácter, reputación, consecuencia. 8. Aviso, noticia, advertencia. 9. (Mús.) Nota, la señal del tono que se ha de seguir; un sonido musical cualquiera; también una tecla. *The note F*, La tecla F. 10. Sonido melodioso o vocal, tono, voz, acento; modo de hablar; canto de las aves. 11. Nota, el estado de ser o poder ser observado. 12. Indirecta. 13. Esquela, billete. 14. Vale, pagaré, papel que se da en reconocimiento de alguna deuda. *Bank-note*, Billete de banco. *Note of hand* o *promissory note*, Pagaré. *To take note*, Hacer cargo; tomar nota, hacer apuntes, anotar; notar, advertir algo. *Foot-note*, Nota al pie (de la página). *Half note*, (Mús.) Mínima, la mitad de la semibreve. *Whole note*, Semibreve, nota que vale un compás menor. *Note-book*, Libro de memoria o de apuntaciones. *Leading note*, Nota o tecla subtónica, la séptima de la escala.

Note, *va.* 1. Notar, marcar, distinguir. 2. Reparar, observar, advertir. 3. Anotar, notar, apuntar brevemente alguna cosa; poner por escrito, registrar. *To note a bill of exchange*, Anotar una letra de cambio. 4. Censurar, imputar alguna culpa o delito. 5 Componer, hacer composiciones, musicales, notando los tonos.

Noted [nōt'-ed], *a.* Afamado, célebre, insigne, eminente.

Notedly [nōt'-ed-li], *adv.* Notablemente; con nota.

Notedness [nōt'-ed-nes], *s.* Celebridad, fama, reputación.

Noteless [nōt'-les], *a.* Obscuro, sin celebridad, reputación o fama.

Noter [nōt'-er], *s.* Notador, observador.

Noteworthy [nōt'-wūr-dhi], *a.* Notable, digno de nota, de atención, de observación.

Nothing [nuth'-ing], *s.* 1. Nada, ninguna cosa. 2. Nadería, cosa de poca entidad, friolera. 3. Estado de lo que no tiene existencia; la nada. 4. La cifra 0; cero. *That is nothing to me*, Eso nada me importa. *It is good for nothing*, Para nada sirve. *He had nothing to live upon*, No tenía nada con que mantenerse. *It signifies nothing*, Eso no significa nada, nada quiere decir. *He made nothing of his labour*, Nada sacó de su trabajo. *To make nothing of*, (1) No hacer caso de, despreciar, tomar una cosa a burla. (2) No comprender, no poder entender. *I could make nothing of his talk*, No pude entender su charla. *To come to nothing*, Anonadarse, aniquilarse. *To reduce to nothing*, Reducir a la nada. *For nothing*, De balde, por nada, gratuitamente. *A multiplication of nothings*, Un montón de bagatelas. *A good-for-nothing fellow*, Un para nada.—*adv.* De ningún grado o medida.

Nothingness [nuth'-ing-nes], *s.* Nonada, nadería, cosa de poca entidad; nada.

Notice [nō'-tis], *s.* 1. Nota, reparo, observación; atención. *Worthy of notice*, Digno de observación, de atención. 2. Aviso, noticia, informe. 3. Noticia, tratamiento respetuoso; corta noticia literaria. 4. Notificación, orden que se comunica a alguien. *To give notice*, Advertir, hacer saber, avisar, dar aviso, informar. *Take no notice of it*, No haga Vd. caso de ello; haga Vd. como si no viese nada. *To take notice of*, Hacer caso, atender, tener cuidado; notar, observar; cuidarse de. *To give short notice*, Conceder un corto plazo. *He has had notice of it by letter*, Ha sido advertido o informado por carta. *Notice to quit*, Aviso de despedida. *At the shortest notice*, Al momento, tan pronto como sea posible.

Notice, *va.* 1. Notar, observar, mirar, reparar. 2. Hacerse cargo de, atender a, cuidar de; apercibirse de. 3. Mentar, hacer mención de. 4. Tener miramientos, tratar con atención, con finura. *The children were much noticed*, A los niños se les dedicó mucha atención.

Noticeable [nō'-tis-a-bl], *a.* Digno de atención, notable; perceptible.

Noticeably [nō'-tis-a-bli], *adv.* Notablemente, de un modo notable o perceptible.

Notification [no-ti-fi-kē'-shun], *s.* 1. Notificación, el acto de notificar o hacer saber alguna cosa. 2. Aviso, advertencia, citación, cita.

Notify [nō'-ti-fai], *va.* 1. Notificar, advertir, avisar; dar á conocer, informar por cualesquiera medios. 2. Dar a luz, dar noticias de, publicar.

Noting [nōt'-ing], *s.* Notificación, aviso, el acto de notar o tomar notas; el acto de anotar una letra de cambio.

Notion [nō'-shun], *s.* 1. Noción; concepción mental, idea, pensamiento. 2. Parecer, voto, dictamen, opinión. 3. Entendimiento, sentido. 4. (Fam.) Intención, inclinación, designio. 5. (Fam.) Novedad, artículo vendible de poca monta.

Notional [nō'-shun-al], *a.* 1. Imaginario, ideal. 2. Quimérico, fantástico; que se recrea con quimeras; caprichudo, afectado, demasiado aficionado a pequeñeces. *A notional old bachelor*, Un solterón viejo y maniático.

Notionality [nō-shun-al'-i-ti], *s.* La opinión o parecer que no tiene fundamento o nada en que fundarse.

Notionally [nō'-shun-al-i], *adv.* Idealmente.

Notoriety [no-to-rai'-e-ti], *s.* Notoriedad, noticia pública; conocimiento que todos tienen de una cosa.

Notorious [no-tō'-ri-us], *a.* Notorio, público, conocido, manifiesto, aparente, evidente. Úsase casi siempre en inglés para designar una persona o cosa notoriamente mala, y corresponde algunas veces a desacreditado o desestimado.

Notoriously [no-tō'-ri-us-li], *adv.* Notoriamente.

Notoriousness [no-tō'-ri-us-nes], *s.* Notoriedad, noticia pública.

Notus [nō'-tus], *s.* Noto, austro.

Not-wheat [not'-hwît], *s.* (Bot.) Trigo chamorro, trigo cuya espiga no tiene raspas.

Notwithstanding [not-widh-stand'-ing], *conj.* No obstante, sin embargo, aunque, con todo, bien que; por más que.—*adv.* A despecho, sin relación a, a pesar de.

Nought [nōt], *s.* Nada. *V.* NAUGHT.

Noun [naun], *s.* (Gram.) Nombre, substantivo.

Nourish [nur'-ish], *va.* 1. Nutrir. 2. Alimentar, sustentar, mantener. 3.

Alentar, fomentar. 4. Criar, educar.—*vn.* Favorecer el crecimiento o desarrollo de.

Nourishable [nur'-ish-a-bl], *a.* 1. Que se puede alimentar, sustentar o fomentar. 2. (Des.) Nutricio.

Nourisher [nur'-ish-ẹr], *s.* Nutridor, nutriente, alimentador.

Nourishment [nur'-ish-mẹnt], *s.* 1. Nutrimento, alimento, sustento; lo que sustenta o promueve el crecimiento de una manera cualquiera. 2. La acción de nutrir. 3. Lo que favorece el desarrollo de una cosa.

Nous [nūs o naus], *s.* Inteligencia, conocimiento, penetración, sentido. (Gr.)

Novation [no-vé'-shun], *s.* (For.) Novación, renovación de una obligación contraída anteriormente.

Novel [nev'-el], *a.* Novel, nuevo, moderno.—*s.* 1. Novela, historia fingida. 2. (For.) Novela, cualquiera ley de los emperadores añadida al código de Justiniano.

Novelette [nev''-el-et'], *s.* Novela corta.

Novelist [nev'-el-ist], *s.* 1. Novelista, novelador, el que escribe novelas. 2. (Des.) Novator, inventor de novedades.

Novelistic [nev-el-is'-tic], *a.* Novelesco, propio de una novela.

Novelize [nev'-el-aiz], *va.* 1. Poner en forma de novela. 2. (Des.) Innovar.

Novelty [nev'-el-ti], *s.* 1. Novedad, cosa nueva, extraña o poco común. 2. Calidad de nuevo. .. Innovación.

November [no-vem'-bẹr], *s.* Noviembre.

Novenary [nev'-en-ẹ-ri], *a.* Novenario, el número de nueve.

Novennial [no-ven'-i-al], *a.* Que ocurre cada noveno año o que dura nueve años.

Novercal [no-vẹr'-cal], *a.* (Ant.) Propio de madrastra.

Novice [nev'-is], *s.* 1. Novicio, el principiante en cualquier arte o facultad. 2. Novicio, el que en la religión no ha hecho aún profesión de sus reglas y votos.

‡**Noviceship** [nev'-is-ship], *s.* 1. Noviciado, aprendizaje de algún arte, oficio, etc. 2. Noviciado, el tiempo destinado para la probación antes de profesar en las órdenes religiosas.

Novitiate, *s.* 1. *V.* NOVICESHIP, 2ª acep. 2. El novicio mismo.

Novocaine [ne'-ve-kên], *s.* Novocaína, procaína.

Now [nau], *adv.* 1. Ahora, en el tiempo o momento presente, actualmente. 2. Ahora, poco ha. 3. Después de esto, de aquí a poco. 4. Ahora bien, esto supuesto; ¡vamos! *Now and then,* De vez en cuando, de cuando en cuando, algunas veces; aquí y allá. *Just now,* Ahora mismo, inmediatamente. *Just now* se expresa en español a menudo por el verbo "acabar de"; v. gr. *I have just now received a telegram,* Acabo de recibir un telegrama. *How now?* ¿Cómo? ¿qué tal? *Before now,* Antes de ahora. 5. Aun, todavía: ya, en otro tiempo. *It has happened before now,* Ha sucedido ya, o en otro tiempo. *Until* o *till now,* Hasta ahora, hasta este momento. *King Albert is now living,* El rey Alberto vive todavía. *Now . . . now . . .* Ya . . . ya; ora . . . ora, alternativamente. *Now soft, now loud,* Ya suave, ya estrepitoso. *Now rich, now poor,* Alternativamente rico y pobre; ora rico, ora pobre. *Now! what do you think?* ¡Vamos! ¿qué piensa Vd.? ¿qué le parece a Vd.?—*conj.* Mas, pero, pues. *Now it is true,* Pues bien, verdad es.—*s.* Actualidad, el momento presente.

Nowadays [nau'-a-dêz], *adv.* En nuestros días, en nuestros tiempos, hoy día.

Noway [nō'-wê], **Noways** [nō'-wêz], *adv.* De ningún modo.

Nowhere [nō'-hwãr], *adv.* En ninguna parte. *Nowhere else,* En ninguna otra parte.

Nowhither [nō'-hwidh-ẹr], *adv.* Hacia ningún lugar determinado; hacia ninguna parte.

Nowise [nō'-waiz], *adv.* De ningún modo, de ninguna manera, de modo alguno.

Noxious [nec'-shus], *a.* 1. Nocivo, dañoso, pernicioso. 2. (Poco us.) Culpable, delincuente.

Noxiously [nec'-shus-li], *adv.* Perniciosamente.

Noxiousness [nec'-shus-nes], *s.* La calidad que constituye a una cosa perniciosa, dañosa o perjudicial; daño.

Nozle, Nozzle [nez'-l], *s.* 1. Boquerel (de manguera); boquilla, gollete rígido al extremo de un tubo, para desaguar; canuto, tobera. 2. (Prov. Ingl.) Nariz de un animal.

Nuance [nū'-ans], *s.* Ligera diferencia; matiz.

Nubbin [nub'-in], *s.* (Fam. E. U.) Espiga de maíz imperfectamente desarrollada.

Nubian [nū'-bi-an], *a.* Nubio, que pertenece a la Nubia.

Nubile [niū'-bil], *a.* Núbil, persona que por su edad es apta para contraer matrimonio; doncella casadera.

Nubilous [niū'-bi-lus], **Nubilose** [niū'-bi-lōs], *a.* Nubloso, nubiloso.

Nuclear [niū'-cle-ar], *a.* Nuclear, nucleario. *Nuclear physics,* Física nuclear. *Nuclear fission,* Fisión nuclear, fisura nuclear. *Nuclear reactor,* (Fís.) Reactor nuclear. *Nuclear war,* Guerra nuclear.

Nucleate [niū'-cle-êt], *va.* y *vn.* Formar un núcleo; juntarse formando núcleo.

Nucleic [niū-clê'-ic], *a.* Nucleico.

Nucleolus [niu-clí'-o-lus], *s.* (*dim.* de NUCLEUS). Nucléolo, punto bien definido dentro del núcleo de una celdilla, muy susceptible a la influencia de las materias colorantes; núcleo muy pequeño.

Nucleon [niū'-cle-on], *s.* Nucleón.

Nucleus [niū'-cle-us], *s.* 1. Núcleo, punto céntrico del desarrollo. 2. (Biol.) Cuerpo redondo u ovalado, de carácter determinado, encerrado en una celdilla o bien, masa de bioplasma; núcleo. 3. Punto parecido a una estrella que se ve a la cabeza de un cometa.

Nudation [niu-dé'-shun], *s.* El acto de desnudar, de poner algo desnudo.

Nude [niūd], *a.* 1. Desnudo, nudo. 2. (Der.) Hecho sin compensación; nulo.

Nudge [nuj], *va.* Tocar ligeramente para advertir, como se hace con el codo.—*s.* Toque ligero dado con el codo para llamar la atención.

Nudity [niū'-di-ti], *s.* Desnudez.

Nugation [niū-gé'-shun], *s.* Fruslería, nonada.

Nugatory [niū'-ga-to-ri], *a.* Nugatorio, frustráneo, fútil, frívolo, fruslero.

Nugget [nug'-et], *s.* Pedazo; en especial, pepita de oro o de otro metal precioso.

Nuggety [nug'-et-i], *a.* Hallado en forma de pepitas; de la figura de una pepita.

Nuisance [niū'-sans], *s.* 1. Lo que molesta, enoja u ofende; persona o cosa cansada, fastidiosa; incomodidad, molestia, estorbo. 2. Indecencia, porquería. *Nuisance* como término legal es el perjuicio o daño que se causa ilegalmente a la propiedad de uno o más individuos, o la incomodidad que se ocasiona sin derecho para ello. *Commit no nuisance,* Se prohibe hacer aguas, o depositar inmundicias. 3. (Fig.) Suplicio, fastidio, tormento, peste. *What a nuisance!* ¡Qué fastidio! ¡qué suplicio!

Null [nul], *vn.* 1. Tornear algo en forma de rosario. 2. Torcerse como una soga. *Nulled work,* Madera trabajada en la forma de las cuentas de un rosario.

Null, *a.* Nulo, inválido, írrito, sin fuerza legal.—*s.* 1. Cosa que no tiene fuerza ni sentido alguno; nonada, cero. 2. Pieza de madera que sale del torno en la forma de las cuentas de un rosario.

Nullifidian [nul-i-fid'-i-an], *s.* (Ant.) Persona sin fe, religión o creencia; nulo en todo.

Nullify [nul'-i-fai], *va.* Anular, invalidar, abrogar.

Nullity [nul'-i-ti], *s.* Nulidad; falta de existencia.

Numb [num], *a.* Entorpecido, adormecido, privado de sensibilidad; entumecido de frío; aturdido.

Numb, *va.* Entorpecer, causar torpor.

‡**Numbedness** [num'-ed-nes], *s.* *V.* NUMBNESS.

Number [num'-bẹr], *va.* 1. Numerar, contar; computar. 2. Estimar, contar como uno en una reunión o colección. 3. Numerar, dar o poner número a una cosa. *Numbering machine,* Máquina numeradora.

Number, *s.* 1. Número, cantidad, multitud. 2. Armonía; poesía, versos; cadencia. 3. (Gram.) Número, en los nombres y verbos. *Numbers,* Números, un libro del Antiguo Testamento. 4. La ciencia de los números o guarismos. 5. Entrega, cada uno de los cuadernos de un libro o periódico que se publica por partes. *Back number,* Ejemplar no muy reciente de un periódico; de aquí, persona o cosa atrasada, avejentada, que no está al día. *Broken number,* Quebrado, fracción. *Number one,* (Fam.) Uno mismo, sí mismo. *To look out for number one,* Cuidar de sí mismo. *Round numbers,* Números redondos o pares.

Numberer [num'-bẹr-ẹr], *s.* Numerador, contador.

Numberless [num'-bẹr-les], *a.* Innumerable, sin número.

Numbfish [num'-fish], *s.* Torpedo.

†**Numbles** [num'-blz], *s.* Entrañas de venado.

Numbness [num'-nes], *s.* Torpor, entorpecimiento, adormecimiento.

Numerable [niū'-mẹr-a-bl], *a.* Numerable.

Numeral [niū'-mẹr-al], *a.* Numeral; numérico.—*s.* Guarismo. *Arabic numerals*, Guarismos arábigos.
Numerally [niū'-mẹr-al-i], *adv.* Numéricamente.
Numerary [niū'-mẹr-ẹ-ri], *a.* Numerario.
Numerate [niū'-mẹr-ēt], *va.* Numerar, contar.
Numeration [niū-mẹr-ē'-shun], *s.* Numeración.
Numerator [niū'-mẹr-ē-tẹr], *s.* Contador; numerador.
Numeric [niū-mer'-ic], *a.* Numérico.
Numerical [niu-mer'-ic-al], *a.* Numérico.
Numerically [niu-mer'-i-cal-i], *adv.* Numéricamente.
Numerosity [niu-mẹr-es'-i-ti], *s.* 1. Numerosidad, multitud. 2. (Ant.) Cadencia o armonía en las cláusulas, períodos o versos.
Numerous [niū'-mẹr-us], *a.* 1. Numeroso; muchos, muchas. 2. (Des.) Numeroso, armonioso, rítmico. *Numerous things to do*, (Fam.) Muchas cosas que hacer.
Numerousness [niū'-mẹr-us-nes], *s.* Numerosidad, muchedumbre.
Numismatic [niu-mis-mat'-ic], *a.* Numismático, que se refiere a las monedas o medallas.
Numismatics [niu-mis-mat'-ics], *s.* Numismática, la ciencia que trata de las medallas y monedas desde el punto de vista histórico. Se llama también **Numismatology**.
Numismatography [niu-mis-ma-teg'-ra-fi], *s.* Numismática, el conocimiento de monedas y medallas antiguas.
¿**Nummary** [num'-a-ri], *a.* *V.* NUMMULAR.
Nummular [num'-yu-lar], *a.* 1. Pecuniario. 2. (Med.) Numuláceo, parecido a una moneda. *Nummular sputa*, Esputos numuláceos.
Numskull [num'-scul], *s.* Zote, bobote.
Numskulled [num'-sculd], *a.* Lerdo, zote, bobo.
Nun [nun], *s.* 1. Monja, religiosa, mujer que habita en un convento. 2. Una de varias clases de aves; paro, harla, variedad blanca de pichón doméstico con moño o copete, etc. *Nun-buoy*, Boya de barrilete, en figura de dos conos unidos por sus bases. *Nun's veiling*, Velo de monja, tejido de lana muy suave y delgado; se usa para velos y también para trajes.
Nun [nūn], *s.* Letra de los abecedarios árabe y hebreo que corresponde a la *n*.
Nuncio [nun'-shi-ō], *s.* 1. Nuncio, enviado. 2. Nuncio, el embajador que envía el Papa a los príncipes católicos.
†**Nuncupate** [nun'-kiū-pēt], *va.* Declarar abiertamente.
Nuncupative [nun-kiu'-pa-tiv o nun'-kiu-pē-tiv], **Nuncupatory** [nun-kiū'-pa-to-ri], *a.* Nuncupativo, verbal, hecho de viva voz; dícese especialmente de un testamento.
Nundinal [nun'-di-nal], ¿**Nundinary** [nun'-di-nẹ-ri], *a.* Lo que pertenece a los mercados o ferias.
Nunnery [nun'-ẹr-i], *s.* Convento o monasterio de monjas.
Nunnish [nun'-ish], *a.* Monjil, perteneciente o parecido a las monjas; característico de ellas.
Nuptial [nup'-shal], *a.* Nupcial, que pertenece á las bodas. *Nuptial song*, Epitalamio. *Nuptial plumaje*, Plumaje de un ave en la estación de la cría, el cual es muy a menudo pasajero y raro.
Nuptials [nup'-shalz], *s. pl.* Nupcias, boda.
Nurl [nūrl], *va.* Acordonar una moneda; hacerle el cordoncillo. *Nurling-tool*, En tonelería, porta-moleta.
Nurse [nūrs], *s.* 1. Ama de cría, nodriza; niñera, la persona encargada de cuidar niños. *Wet nurse*, Ama de leche. (Mex.) Chichigua. (Cuba) Criandera. *Nurse-child*, Niño de teta. 2. Enfermera, enfermero, la mujer u hombre que cuida de un enfermo. 3. La persona o cosa que cría, educa o protege; lo que favorece el crecimiento. 4. Una especie de tiburón. *Monthly nurse*, Enfermera que por un estipendio se encarga de cuidar a una mujer parida. *Nurse-bee*, Abeja de menos de dieciseis días.
Nurse, *va.* 1. Criar criaturas o animales; dar de mamar. 2. Criar, alimentar, mantener. 3. Cuidar enfermos o asistirlos. 4. Fomentar, dar alas.—*vn.* 1. Cuidar de un enfermo; dar de mamar a un niño. 2. Mamar, chupar la leche de los pechos.
Nurse-maid [nūrs'-mēd], **Nursery-maid** [nūrs'-ẹr-i-mēd], *sf.* La criada que cuida de los niños; niñera; criandera, ama.
Nurser [nūrs'-ẹr], *s.* La persona que cría; promotor.
Nursery [nūrs'-ẹr-i], *s.* 1. Crianza. 2. Plantel, almáciga. 3. El jardín o huerta donde se crían flores o plantas para trasplantarlas, que casi siempre corresponde a lo que se llama en castellano criadero o semillero. 4. Plantel, semillero; un estado cualquiera que favorece el crecimiento. *The nursery of arts*, El plantel de las artes. *A luxurious court is a nursery of diseases*, Una corte corrompida es un semillero de males. 5. El cuarto o habitación de los niños pequeños. 6. Asistencia a los enfermos o el acto de asistirlos y cuidarlos. *Nursery-man*, Jardinero que cuida de los planteles, criaderos o semilleros. *Nursery-tales*, Cuentos de niños.
Nursery school [nurs'-ẹr-i scūl], *s.* Escuela pre-Kindergarten.
Nursing [nūrs'-ing], *s.* El acto de criar niños o el de mamar los niños. *Nursing-bottle*, Mamadera, biberón.
Nursling [nūrs'-ling], *s.* Niño criado o acabado de criarse.
Nurture [nūr'-chur], *s.* 1. El acto de nutrir, de alimentar, de promover el crecimiento. 2. Nutrimento. 3. Educación, crianza.
Nurture, *va.* Criar, educar, enseñar, promover.
Nut [nut], *s.* 1. Nuez, el fruto de ciertos árboles que se compone de almendra o meollo cubierto de una cáscara dura. *Hazelnut*, Avellana. *Walnut*, Nuez de nogal. 2. Piñón o rueda punteada. 3. Tuerca, matriz, hembra de tornillo. 4. El extremo movible del arco de violín por medio del cual se aflojan o se aprietan las cuerdas. 5. Puente, tablilla colocada en la parte superior de los instrumentos de cuerda, que sirve para levantar las cuerdas. *Nut of an anchor*, (Mar.) Oreja de ancla. *A hard nut*, (Fam.) Persona dura, áspera, no impresionable. *To give a hard nut to crack*, (Fig.) Dar que roer, que hacer. *Brazil-nut*, *Pará nut*, Nuez del Brasil, el fruto de la Bertholletia excelsa. *Cashew nut*, Anacardo (el fruto). *Gallnut*, Agalla. *Hickory nuts*, Nueces de Carya, fruto del nogal de América. *Pecan nuts*, Pecanas o pacanas. *Check-nut*, *jam-nut*, Contratuerca. *Finger-nut*, *thumb-nut*, *wing-nut*, Tuerca con orejetas. *Nut-oil*, Aceite de nueces. *To be nuts on*, (Fam.) Estar enamorado o ser admirador de una persona o cosa.
Nut, *vn.* Coger nueces.
Nutant [niū'-tant], *a.* Nutante; dícese particularmente de las flores. *V.* NODDING.
Nutation [niu-tē'-shun], *s.* Nutación, movimiento del eje de la tierra por el que se inclina más o menos sobre el plano de la eclíptica.
Nutbrown [nut'-braun], *a.* Avellanado, del color de la cáscara de una avellana madura
Nutcracker [nut'-crak-ẹr], *s.* Cascanueces, partidor.
Nutgall [nut'-gēl], *s.* Agalla de monte.
Nuthatch [nut'-hach], **Nutpecker** [nut'-pek-ẹr], *s.* (Orn.) Picamadero; pájaro dentirrostro del género sita. Sitta.
Nuthook [nut'-huc], *s.* Horquilla para hacer caer las nueces de los árboles.
Nutmeg [nut'-meg], *s.* Nuez moscada.
Nutria [niū'-tri-a], *s.* (Zool.) Coipú, mamífero roedor de la América del Sur, y su piel. Myopotamus coypus.
Nutrient [niū'-tri-ent], *a.* 1. Nutricio, nutritivo. 2. Nutriente, que sirve para conducir el alimento o nutrición; v. g. una arteria.—*s.* Alimento nutritivo; lo que alimenta.
Nutriment [niū'-tri-mẹnt], *s.* Nutrimento, alimento.
Nutrimental [niu-tri-ment'-al], *a.* Nutrimental.
Nutrition [niu-trish'-un], *s.* Nutrición; nutrimento.
Nutritious [niu-trish'-us], **Nutritive** [niū'-tri-tiv], *a.* Nutritivo, nutricio, alimentoso.
Nutshell [nut'-shel], *s.* 1. Cáscara de nuez o avellana. 2. Alguna cosa de muy pequeño volumen, que contiene muy poco. *In a nutshell*, En pocas palabras, en resumidas cuentas.
Nut-tree [nut'-trī], *s.* (Bot.) Avellano.
Nutty [nut'-i], *a.* 1. Abundante en nueces. 2. Que tiene sabor de nueces, o se parece a ellas.
Nux-vomica [nux-vem'-i-ca], *s.* Nuez vómica, semilla muy venenosa; se emplea en medicina.
†**Nuzzle** [nuz'-l], *va.* 1. (Prov. o des.) Criar, fomentar; acariciar. 2. Anidarse; esconderse.—*vn.* Andar con el hocico hacia abajo como los cochinos. *To nuzzle in the blankets*, Meterse o esconderse debajo de las sábanas.
Nyctalopy [nic-tal'-o-pi], *s.* Nictalopia, defecto de la vista que consiste en ver de noche mejor que de día; antiguamente era lo contrario.
Nyctalops [nic'-ta-leps], *s.* Nictálope, el que ve mejor de noche que de día.
Nylghau, *s.* *V.* NILGAU.
Nylon [nai'-len], *s.* Nylon o nilón (fibra sintética de carbón, aire y agua). *Nylon fabric*, Tela de nylon o nilón.
Nymph [nimf], *s.* 1. Ninfa, deidad

fabulosa. 2. Mujer hermosa, dama; aldeana. 3. Ninfa, palomilla, crisálida de los insectos.

Nympha [nim'-fa], *s.* 1. (Anat.) Labio pequeño de la vulva. 2. (Zool.) Ninfa, crisálida, insecto no completamente desarrollado.

Nymphæa [nim-fí'-a], *s.* Ninfea, nenúfar, la planta llamada comúnmente en inglés *water-lily*, lirio acuático.

Nymphean [nim-fí'-an], *a.* Lo perteneciente a las ninfas.

Nymphomania, Nymphomany [nim'-fo-mé''-ni], *s.* (Med.) Ninfomanía, furor uterino.

Nyssa [nis'-a], *s.* (Bot.) Nisa, género de arbustos, de flores polígamas, hojas alternas, fruto del tamaño de una ciruela, negro e insípido. Crece en la América boreal.

O

O [o]. 1. Décimaquinta letra del alfabeto inglés. Tiene diversos sonidos: uno en que se pronuncia lo mismo que la *o* española muy breve, como en *not, got, lot;* otro en que su pronunciación tira algo al diptongo *ou* español, como en *no, note, bone, alone;* otro cuando se pronuncia lo mismo que la *u* en español, como en *do, prove, move;* otro semejante al de la *o* española muy larga como en *for, nor,* y el último lo mismo que el de la *u* española muy breve, como en *woman, bosom, wolf.* 2. Ovalo o círculo; punto, lentejuela.

O. 1. Oh! interjección para exclamar, exhortar, etc. 2. Ojalá. *O! that morning would come!* ¡Ojalá que apuntara el día!

Oaf [ōf], *s.* 1. Un niño estúpido que se supone han dejado los duendes o brujas, llevándose en cambio otro más listo. 2. Idiota, zoquete, zote.

Oafish [ōf'-ish], *a.* (Poco us.) Lerdo, estúpido, tonto.

Oafishness [ōf'-ish-nes], *s.* (Poco us.) Torpeza, rudeza, estupidez.

Oak [ōc], *s.* 1. (Bot.) Roble, cualquier árbol o arbusto del género *Quercus;* se cuentan casi 300 especies. *Evergreen oak, holm-oak,* (Bot.) Encina, carrasco. (Quercus ilex.) *Scarlet oak,* (Bot.) Coscoja. 2. Roble, la madera del árbol así llamado. *Live-oak, holly-leaved oak,* Encina siempre verde de California y Méjico. (Quercus agrifolia.) *Cork-oak,* Roble de corcho, alcornoque. (Quercus suber.) *Spanish oak, Turkey oak,* Roble español, la *Quercus falcata* de los Estados Unidos del Sur. *Italian oak,* Roble de bellotas dulces: Quercus æsculus del sur de Europa. *White oak,* Roble blanco, gran árbol americano de madera muy estimada. *Turkey oak,* En Europa, roble de Borgoña, el Quercus cerris; en los Estados Unidos, la Quercus falcata. *V. Spanish oak. Oak-apple,* Especie de agalla. *Oak-bark,* Corteza de roble. *Oak-grove,* Robledo, robledal, bosque de robles. *Oak-leaf,* Hoja de roble. *Oak-leather,* (1) Cuero curtido con cáscara de roble. (2) Hongo duro y correoso que se cría en las grietas de los robles viejos y se parece a la cabritilla blanca. *Oak-tanned,* Curtido con corteza de roble. *Quartered oak, V.* QUARTER. *Oak-wood,* Madera de roble. *Oak-tree,* (Bot.) Roble. *Oak timber,* Madera de roble para construcciones.

Oaken [ōc'-n], *a.* Hecho de roble; compuesto de robles o de las hojas y ramas del roble. *An oaken garland,* Guirnalda de hojas de roble.

Oakling [ōc'-ling], *s.* Roble tierno o de poco tiempo.

Oakum [ōk'-um], *s.* (Mar.) Estopa, para calafatear.

Oaky [ōk'-i], *a.* Parecido a un roble; duro, fuerte.

Oar [ōr], *s.* 1. Remo, instrumento de madera que sirve para impulsar las embarcaciones, haciendo fuerza en el agua. 2. Remero. 3. Entre ciertas lombrices, apéndice natatorio que se asemeja a un remo. *Oar-lock,* Chumacera, escalamera. *Flat of an oar,* Pala de remo. *To ship the oars,* Armar los remos. *Hold on your oars,* Alza los remos. *To lie on the oars,* Cesar de remar, aguantar los remos; de aquí, familiarmente, descansar del trabajo.

Oar, *vn.* Remar.—*va.* Bogar, conducir a remo.

Oarage [ōr'-ĝj], *s.* El conjunto de remos de una lancha o un bote.

Oared [ōrd], *a.* 1. Provisto de remos (por lo común, en composición): *Eight-oared,* De ocho remos. 2. (Zool.) Que tiene pies parecidos a remos, o apéndices natatorios.

Oar-finned [ōr'-find], *a.* Lo que tiene remos.

Oarsman [ōrs'-man], *s.* Remero.

Oary [ōr'-i], *a.* Formado como remo; remado.

Oasis [ō'-a-sis u o-ē'-sis], *s.* Oasis, espacio de tierra fértil en un desierto arenoso. (*pl.* OASES.)

Oast [ōst], *s.* Horno para lúpulo.

Oat, Oats [ōt], *s.* Avena. *Wild oat,* Avena loca o silvestre. Avena fatua. *Wild oats,* (1) Avena silvestre. (2) Excesos de la juventud. *To sow one's wild oats,* Pasar las mocedades, correrla. *Off one's oats,* Indispuesto, desganado. *Rolled oats,* Avena, descortezada, cilindrada y sometida a la acción del vapor y que sirve de alimento. *Oats-peas-beans,* Juego de niños que bailan y cantan en corro. *Potato oat,* Avena geórgica. *Tartarian oat,* Avena oriental. *Oat* se usa muy rara vez en singular excepto en composición; como *oat-straw,* paja de avena.

Oat-cake [ōt'-kēc], *s.* Torta de harina de avena.

Oaten [ōt'-n], *a.* Aveníceo, hecho de avena; lo que produce avena.

Oath [ōth], *s.* 1. Juramento, afirmación o declaración solemne poniendo por testigo a Dios, en sí mismo o en sus criaturas. 2. Juramento, blasfemia, uso frívolo del nombre de Dios o de algún objeto sagrado. *To put upon oath,* Hacer prestar juramento. *To take an oath,* Prestar juramento. *On* o *upon oath,* Bajo juramento. *Oath-breaking,* Violación de juramento, perjurio.

Oatmeal [ōt'-mīl], *s.* Harina de avena; gachas, puches de ella.

Obconical, Obconic [ob-cen'-ic-al], *a.* (Bot.) Obcónico, que tiene la forma de un cono invertido.

Obcordate, Obcordiform [ob-cōr'-dēt, ob-cōr'-di-fōrm], *a.* (Biol.) Obcordado, que tiene la forma de un corazón invertido.

Obduce [ob-diūs'], *va.* (Des.) Cubrir, tapar.

Obduracy [ob'-diu-ra-si], *s.* Obduración, obcecación; obstinación; endurecimiento, dureza de corazón.

Obdurate [ob'-diu-ret, ob-diū'-rēt entre ciertos poetas ingleses], *a.* Endurecido, terco, áspero, duro, insensible, obstinado.

Obdurately [ob'-diu-ret-li], *adv.* Tercamente, obstinadamente.

Obdurateness [ob'-diu-ret-nes], **†Obduration** [ob-diu-rē'-shun], *s.* Impenitencia, endurecimiento, obstinación, dureza de corazón.

Obedience [o-bī'-di-ens], *s.* Obediencia, sujeción, sumisión a una orden; prohibición, ley conocida, deber o regla de conducta.

Obedient [o-bī'-di-ent], *a.* Obediente, sumiso.

Obediently [o-bī'-di-ent-li], *adv.* Obedientemente.

Obeisance [o-bī'-sans u o-bē'-sans], *s.* Cortesía, reverencia, saludo respetuoso.

Obeliscal [ob-el-is'-cal], *a.* De la forma de un obelisco.

Obelisk [ob'-el-isk], *s.* 1. Obelisco, pirámide que va adelgazándose poco a poco hasta la punta. 2. (Tip.) Cruz (obelisco), el signo † inserto en el texto para referir al lector a una nota o para indicar una palabra fuera de uso; y antes de fechas biográficas, para denotar el año del fallecimiento. Se llama más comúnmente *dagger.*

Obelus [ob'-el-us], *s.* Obelisco, señal, como — ÷ o †, que se solía poner en la margen de los antiguos manuscritos para señalar un pasaje determinado.

Obese [o-bīs'], *a.* Obeso, gordo, muy corpulento.

Obeseness [o-bīs'-nes], **Obesity** [o-bes'-i-ti], *s.* Obesidad, crasitud.

Obey [o-bē'], *va.* 1. Obedecer, someterse a las órdenes de otro; hacer uno lo que se le ha mandado. 2. Obedecer, estar sujeto a, estar bajo el dominio de. 3. Ser gobernado por, ceder a. *The ship obeys the helm,* El navío obedece al timón.

Obfuscate, *va.* Confundir la mente, ofuscar el entendimiento.

Obi [ō'-bi], *s.* Suerte de magia practicada por los negros de las Antillas; también, *fetish:* véase ésta.

Obit [ō'-bit], *s.* 1. El fallecimiento, o fecha de la muerte de una persona. 2. Exequias, las honras que se celebran en el aniversario de un fallecimiento.

Obituary [o-bit'-yu-e-ri], *a.* Mortuorio, relativo a la muerte.—*s.* 1. Necrología, noticia biográfica de una persona recién fallecida. 2. En la Iglesia catolica romana, obituario, libro de partidas de entierros.

Object [ob'-ject], *s.* 1. Objeto, lo que se percibe con alguno de los sentidos, o por las facultades mentales. 2. Objeto, término o fin de los actos de las potencias. 3. Objeto, fin, intento; blanco, punto. 4. (Gram.) Complemento, régimen directo.

Object [ob-ject'], *va.* 1. Objetar, presentar en oposición, poner reparos a alguna opinión o razón para refutarla. 2. Hacer cargos.—*vn.* Dar en rostro, echar en cara, poner tachas o reparos. *No one objected to his title,* Nadie discutió su derecho.

Objectable [ob-ject'-a-bl], *a.* *V.* OBJECTIONABLE.

Object-glass [ob'-ject-glas], *s.* (Ópt.) Objetivo, la lente o la combinación de lentes en los telescopios, microscopios y otros instrumentos ópticos, que recibe primero los rayos de luz del objeto que se quiere observar.

Objection [ǫb-jec'-shun], *s.* Objeción, oposición, reparo, réplica; tacha. *I have no objection*, No tengo inconveniente en ello, o no tengo nada que decir a eso. *To meet an objection*, Hacer frente a una objeción. *To raise an objection*, Hacer una objeción.

Objectionable [eb-jec'-shun-a-bl], *a.* Reparable, susceptible de objeción, censurable, reprensible; perjudicial.

Objectionableness [eb-jec'-shun-a-bl-nes], *s.* El estado de lo que está expuesto a objeciones o reparos.

Objective [eb-jec'-tiv], *a.* 1. Objetivo, perteneciente a un objeto. 2. Dirigido hacia los objetos y que corresponde a ellos. 3. Existente por sí mismo, independiente por su propia autoridad; lo opuesto a subjetivo. 4. (Gram.) Acusativo; se dice del caso que expresa el complemento de los verbos.—*s.* 1. El caso acusativo. 2. Objetivo. *V.* OBJECT-GLASS. 3. Punto objetivo, destinación.

Objectively [eb-jec'-tiv-li], *adv.* Objetivamente.

Objectiveness [eb-jec'-tiv-nes], *s.* Calidad de objeto, de lo que puede percibirse por los sentidos.

Objectless [eb'-ject-les], *a.* Sin objeto, sin fin.

Objector [eb-ject'-ǫr], *s.* Impugnador, el que objeta, replica, o presenta objeciones.

Objurgate [ǫb-jūr'-gêt], *va.* Reprender, censurar, desaprobar.

Objurgation [ǫb-jūr-gé'-shun], *s.* Reprensión, censura, desaprobación.

Objurgatory [ǫb-jūr'-ga-to-ri], *a.* Reprobatorio.

Oblate [eb-lêt'], *a.* Achatado por los polos; dícese de un esferoide.

Oblation [eb-lé'-shun], *s.* 1. Oblación, ofrenda y sacrificio que se hace a Dios; la eucaristía. 2. En la antigua Iglesia cristiana, don u ofrenda para el clero y los pobres, o para los gastos de la Cena.

Obligate [eb'-li-gêt], *va.* 1. Obligar, ligar por contrato en sentido legal o moral. 2. Obligar a cumplir con un deber.

Obligation [eb-li-gé'-shun], *s.* 1. Obligación, vínculo; contrato que lleva una condición y penalidad en caso de no cumplirse. 2. La fuerza coercitiva de la conciencia que impele a uno a cumplir un voto, promesa, juramento, o ley. 3. Obligación, la correspondencia que uno debe manifestar por los beneficios, favores, mercedes o gracias, etc., que ha recibido. *I am under many obligations to him*, Le debo muchos favores. 4. Obligación, la escritura en que uno se obliga a cumplir lo que ofrece; título de deuda pública, del Estado o de una compañía, por el cual se cobra cierto interés anual.

Obligatoriness [eb'-li-ga-to''-ri-nes], *s.* El estado o calidad de lo que impone obligación.

Obligatory [eb'-li-ga-to-ri u eb-lig'-a-to-ri], *a.* Obligatorio.

Oblige [o-blaij'], *va.* 1. Obligar, precisar, ligar, imponer la obligación de hacer alguna cosa. 2. Complacer, agradar, servir, favorecer, hacer favor o merced a alguno. *You will greatly oblige me by writing to me*, Le estimaré a Vd. mucho que me escriba. *I am much obliged to you*, Le estoy a Vd. muy reconocido. *I did it to oblige him*, Lo hice por favorecerle.

Obligee [eb-li-jī'], *s.* (For.) Obligado.

Obliger [o-blaij'-ǫr], *s.* El que obliga por contrato.

Obliging [o-blaij'-ing], *a.* Servicial, servidor, favorecedor, galante; obsequioso, cortesano, oficioso, comedido.

Obligingly [o-blaij'-ing-li], *adv.* Cortésmente, atentamente.

Obligingness [o-blaij'-ing-nes], *s.* Obligación, cortesía, obsequio.

Obligor [eb''-li-gōr'], *s.* (For.) Deudor, el que contrae una obligación para con otro.

Oblique [eb-līc' u eb-laic'], *a.* 1. Oblicuo, sesgado, torcido, atravesado. 2. (Gram.) Oblicuo; cualquiera de los casos excepto el nominativo y el vocativo. 3. Torcido, indirecto, doloso, siniestro. 4. Colateral, el pariente que no lo es por línea recta.

Obliquely [ǫb-līc'-li u eb-laic'-li], *adv.* 1. Oblicuamente, al sesgo. 2. Indirectamente, por rodeos.

Obliqueness [ǫb-līc'-nes], **Obliquity** [ǫb-lic'-wi-ti], *s.* 1. Oblicuidad, desvío de la línea horizontal o perpendicular. 2. Desvío o declinación de lo recto y justo.

Obliterate [ǫb-lit'-ǫr-êt], *va.* 1. Borrar, testar o tachar lo escrito. 2. Consumir, destruir, arrasar; borrar insensiblemente la memoria de alguna cosa, irla olvidando; hacer imperceptible. *To become obliterated*, Borrarse, apagarse.

Obliteration [ǫb-lit-ǫr-é'-shun], *s.* Obliteración, canceladura, el acto de borrar un escrito o de borrar de la memoria o abolir; extinción.

Oblivion [ǫb-liv'-i-ǫn], *s.* Olvido. *Act of oblivion*, Amnistía, olvido general.

Oblivious [eb-liv'-i-us], *a.* 1. Olvidadizo, desmemoriado. 2. Abstraído, absorto. 3. Que causa olvido.

Oblong [eb'-leng], *a.* Oblongo, más largo que ancho.—*s.* Rectángulo que tiene los lados contiguos desiguales.

Oblongly [eb'-leng-li], *adv.* En figura oblonga.

Oblongness [eb'-leng-nes], *s.* El estado de lo que es oblongo o más largo que ancho.

Obloquy [eb'-lo-cwi], *s.* 1. Murmuración, detracción, maledicencia. 2. Infamia, deshonra, tacha o nota de acción fea. *He scorns the public obloquy*, Se burla del qué dirán.

Obmutescence [eb-miu-tes'-ǫns], *s.* Mudez, pérdida de la facultad de hablar; taciturnidad.

Obnoxious [ǫb-nec'-shus], *a.* 1. Ofensivo, aborrecible, detestable, que causa aversión. *A law obnoxious to the people*, Una ley detestable para el pueblo. 2. Sujeto, expuesto a; delincuente, culpable, responsable.

Obnoxiously [ǫb-nec'-shus-li], *adv.* En estado de sujeción; o en el de uno que está expuesto a ser castigado; odiosamente.

Obnoxiousness [ǫb-nec'-shus-nes], *s.* El estado del que está expuesto a contingencias o castigos; carácter ofensivo o aborrecible.

Obnubilation [eb-niu-bi-lé'-shun], *s.* 1. (Med.) Ofuscamiento de la vista; estado de confusión, como de vértigo o vahido. 2. (Des.) Obscurecimiento.

Oboe [ō'-bo-e], *s.* Oboe, instrumento músico de viento con lengüeta doble.

Obol, Obolus [eb'-o-lus], *s.* Óbolo, antigua moneda ateniense que valía unos seis maravedises.

Obovate [eb-ō'-vêt], *a.* Obovoide, inversamente aovado. OBOVAL, menos usado, significa lo mismo.

Obreption [eb-rep'-shun], *s.* (Poco us.) Obrepción; introducción en alguna parte por sorpresa y secretamente.

Obreptitious [eb-rep-tish'-us], *a.* Obrepticio, hecho por obrepción.

Obscene [eb-sīn'], *a.* 1. Obsceno, impúdico, sucio, torpe, indecente. 2. (Poét.) Asqueroso; (des.) de mal agüero, siniestro.

Obscenely [eb-sīn'-li], *adv.* Obscenamente.

Obsceneness [eb-sīn'-nes], **Obscenity** [eb-sen'-i-ti], *s.* Obscenidad, impureza, suciedad, torpeza.

Obscuration [eb-skiu-ré'-shun], *s.* Obscurecimiento, acción y efecto de obscurecer.

Obscure [eb-skiūr'], *a.* 1. Obscuro, lóbrego; tenebroso. 2. Obscuro, abstruso, ininteligible. 3. Obscuro, desconocido, humilde, retirado. 4. Obscuramente señalado; meramente indicado.

Obscure, *va.* 1. Obscurecer, privar de la luz, hacer menos visible; cubrir de nubes. 2. Obscurecer, ofuscar la razón alterando y confundiendo la verdad o realidad de las cosas. 3. Obscurecer, deslustrar, empañar la fama, reputación, nombre o gloria. *Time has obscured the writing*, El tiempo ha hecho menos legible lo escrito.

Obscurely [eb-skiūr'-li], *adv.* 1. Obscuramente. 2. Obscuramente, sin hacer papel en el mundo. 3. Confusamente, entre sombras.

Obscureness [eb-skiūr'-nes], **Obscurity** [ǫb-skiūr'-i-ti], *s.* 1. Obscuridad, lobreguez, falta de luz y claridad. 2. Obscuridad, confusión, sombras. 3. Obscuridad, humildad o bajeza de nacimiento, estado o situación. 4. Obscuridad, falta de claridad en lo que se habla o escribe.

†**Obsecrate** [eb'-sę-crêt], *va.* Suplicar ansiosamente; obsecrar.

Obsecration [eb-sę-cré'-shun], *s.* 1. Cualquiera de los rezos de la letanía que comienza con *by* en inglés o *per* en latín. 2. Obsecración, figura retórica por la cual el orador implora la asistencia de Dios o la de alguna persona. 3. †Ruego, súplica.

Obsequial [eb-sī'-cwi-al], *a.* Funeral, fúnebre, que se refiere a exequias o funerales.

Obsequies [eb'-sę-cwiz], *s. pl.* Exequias, funeral, ritos fúnebres.

Obsequious [ǫb-sī'-cwi-us], *a.* 1. Zalamero, empalagoso. 2. (Ant.) Obsequioso, rendido, sujeto a hacer la voluntad de otro.

Obsequiously [ǫb-sī'-cwi-us-li], *adv.* Zalameramente; obsequiosamente.

Obsequiousness [ǫb-sī'-cwi-us-nes], *s.* 1. Complacencia baja o excesiva, zalamería. 2. (Ant.) Obsequio, obediencia, rendimiento.

†**Obsequy** [ǫb'-sę-cwi], *s.* Úsase solamente en plural. *V.* OBSEQUIES.

Observable [ǫb-zǫrv'-a-bl], *a.* 1. Observable, que se puede observar; perceptible a la vista o por medio de la observación. 2. Notable, conspicuo, eminente. 3. Acostumbrado, ordinario, de observancia usual.

Observableness [ǫb-zęrv'-a-bl-nes], *s.* Calidad de notable.
Observably [ǫb-zęrv'-a-bli], *adv.* Notablemente, conspicuamente.
Observance [ǫb-zęrv'-ans], *s.* 1. Observancia, reverencia, acatamiento, honor. 2. Observancia, cumplimiento exacto y puntual de un deber. 3. Rito o ceremonia religiosa; costumbre, práctica, uso. 4. Observación, atención; respeto, cuidado exacto.
†**Observancy** [ǫb-zęrv'-an-si], *s.* Atención.
Observant [ǫb-zęrv'-ant], *a.* 1. Observador, vigilante, atento, exacto. 2. Observador de las reglas y leyes, respetuoso, obsequioso, sumiso.
Observation [ǫb-zęr-vé'-shun], *s.* 1. Observación, la acción de observar, de advertir con atención. 2. Escrutinio, examen científico de un fenómeno natural; observación astronómica o meteorológica. 3. Reflexión, experiencia adquirida por la observación. 4. (Poco us.) Observación, nota o reparo crítico sobre alguna cosa. 5. Observancia, el cumplimiento de alguna orden, ley o precepto.
Observatory [ǫb-zęrv'-a-to-ri], *s.* 1. Observatorio, cúpula o edificio elevado propio para las observaciones astronómicas. 2. Atalaya, torre edificada para observar desde ella una gran extensión de terreno; cualquier punto desde el cual se descubre mucho espacio de tierra o mar.
Observe [ǫb-zęrv'], *va.* 1. Observar, mirar, advertir con atención. 2. Observar, notar, reparar. 3. Observar, guardar y cumplir exactamente lo que se ejecuta y ordena. 4. Notar, expresar (una opinión, etc.) incidentalmente.—*vn.* 1. (Des.) Ser mirado o circunspecto. 2. ¿Hacer observaciones o poner reparos. *It is to be observed,* Es de notar.
Observer [ǫb-zęrv'-ęr], *s.* 1. Observador, el que observa, particularmente con instrumentos de precisión. 2. Observador, observante, el que guarda y cumple lo que es de su obligación o se le manda.
Observing [ǫb-zęrv'-ing], *a.* Observador, atento, cuidadoso, pronto a percibir; que presta atención particular a una cosa.
Observingly [ǫb-zęrv'-ing-li], *adv.* Cuidadosamente, atentamente.
Obsession [ǫb-sesh'-un], *s.* 1. Sitio, el acto de sitiar alguna plaza. 2. Obsesión, el estado de una persona atormentada por el espíritu maligno, o por una idea fija.
Obsidian [ǫb-sid'-i-an], *s.* (Min.) Obsidiana, mineral volcánico y vítreo.
Obsidional [ǫb-sid'-i-o-nal], *a.* Obsidional, lo que pertenece al sitio de una plaza.
Obsolesce [ǫb''-so-les'], *vn.* Caer en desuso.
Obsolescence [ǫb-so-les'-ens], *s.* Estado o acto de caer en desuso.
Obsolescent [ǫb-so-les'-ęnt], *a.* Lo que va haciéndose anticuado o fuera de uso.
Obsolete [ǫb'-so-lît], *a.* 1. Obsoleto, desusado, fuera de uso. 2. (Biol.) Atrofiado, imperfectamente desarrollado, obscuro o suprimido.
Obsoleteness [ǫb'-so-lît-nes], *s.* 1. Desuso, el estado de haber caído en desuso. 2. (Biol.) Falta de desarrollo.
Obstacle [ǫb'-sta-cl], *s.* Obstáculo. impedimento, embarazo, inconveniente.
Obstetric, Obstetrical [ǫb-stet'-ric, al], *a.* Obstétrico, referente a la obstetricia.
Obstetrician [ǫb-ste-trish'-an], *s.* Partero, comadrón.
Obstetrics [ǫb-stet'-rics], *s.* Obstetricia, parte de la medicina que trata de la gestación, el parto y el puerperio. *V.* MIDWIFERY.
Obstinacy [ǫb'-sti-na-si], *s.* 1. Obstinación, pertinacia, porfía, terquedad; apego firme y por lo regular infundado a la propia opinión o proyecto. 2. (Med.) Carácter obstinado, resistencia.
Obstinate [ǫb'-sti-net], *a.* 1. Obstinado, terco, porfiado, temoso, tenaz. 2. Difícil de subyugar o curar, rebelde.
Obstinately [ǫb'-sti-net-li], *adv.* Obstinadamente, tercamente.
Obstinateness [ǫb'-sti-net-nes], *s.* Obstinación, terquedad.
Obstreperous [ǫb-strep'-ęr-us], *a.* Estrepitoso, ruidoso, turbulento, que hace mucho ruido.
Obstreperously [ǫb-strep'-ęr-us-li], *adv.* Estrepitosamente.
Obstreperousness [ǫb-strep'-ęr-us-nes], *s.* Estrépito, bulla.
Obstriction [ǫb-stric'-shun], *s.* (Ant.) Obligación, constreñimiento.
Obstruct [ǫb-struct'], *va.* 1. Obstruir, llenar de obstáculos; cerrar. 2. Impedir, retardar, estorbar; detener, no dejar pasar. *Plowing* (o *ploughing*) *was obstructed by rain,* La lluvia retardó la aradura.
Obstructer [ǫb-struct'-ęr], *s.* Estorbador.
Obstruction [ǫb-struc'-shun], *s.* 1. Obstrucción de alguna vía natural. 2. Estorbo, obstáculo, impedimento, dificultad.
Obstructionist [ǫb-struc'-shun-ist], *s.* Estorbador, el que pone obstáculos, particularmente en asuntos legislativos.
Obstructive [ǫb-struc'-tiv], *a.* Obstructivo.—*s.* Embarazo.
Obstructiveness [ǫb-struc'-tiv-nes], *s.* La calidad que hace a una cosa obstructiva o capaz de causar obstrucciones.
Obstruent [ǫb'-stru-ęnt], *a.* Obstructivo; se emplea particularmente en medicina.
Obtain [ǫb-tên'], *va.* 1. Obtener, adquirir, conseguir. 2. (Ant.) Alcanzar, lograr.—*vn.* 1. Estar establecido, mantenerse en uso o en práctica; existir alguna ley, calidad o condición en una cosa. 2. Prevalecer, tener ventaja.
Obtainable [ǫb-tên'-a-bl], *a.* Asequible.
Obtainer [ǫb-tên'-ęr], *s.* El que obtiene.
Obtainment [ǫb-tên'-męnt], *s.* Obtención, consecución.
Obtemper [ǫb-tem'-pęr], *va.* Obedecer, sujetarse a los preceptos de otro.
†**Obtend** [ǫb-tend'], *va.* 1. Pretender, alegar como razón. 2. Oponer.
†**Obtest** [ǫb-test'], *va.* Rogar, suplicar, conjurar; encarecer; implorar.
Obtestation [ǫb-tes-té'-shun], *s.* Encarecimiento; ruego, súplica.
Obtrude [ǫb-trūd'], *va.* Imponer, establecer o introducir a una persona o cosa con violencia o fraude en alguna parte; colocar en posición prominente no debida. *To obtrude one's self,* Entrometerse, meterse uno donde no le llaman.—*vn.* Entrometerse; ser importuno.
Obtruder [ǫb-trūd'-ęr], *s.* Un entremetido, un intruso.
Obtruncate [ǫb-trun'-kęt], *va.* Cortar un miembro; podar o desmochar un árbol.
Obtruncation [ǫb-trun-ké'-shun], *s.* Desmoche.
Obtrusion [ǫb-trū'-zhun], *s.* Intrusión, entremetimiento.
Obtrusive [ǫb-trū'-siv], *a.* Intruso, entremetido; importuno.
Obtund [ǫb-tund'], *va.* Embotar, entorpecer, amortiguar.
Obturation [ǫb-tiu-ré'-shun], *s.* El acto de cerrar o tapar alguna cosa con otra puesta encima de ella.
Obturator [ǫb'-tiu-ré''-tęr], *s.* 1. (Anat.) Obturador; el órgano, membrana, vaso, etc., que cierra o tapa una cavidad o un conducto. 2. Obturador, instrumento para cerrar las aberturas producidas por una llaga o enfermedad.
Obtusangular [ǫb-tius-an'-giu-lar], *a.* Obtusángulo.
Obtuse [ǫb-tiūs'], *a.* 1. Obtuso, mayor que un ángulo recto; más de 90°. 2. Obtuso, romo, sin punta, embotado en la extremidad. 3. Obtuso, lerdo, torpe, tardo. 4. Sordo, hablando de ruido. *Obtuse-angled,* Obtusángulo, que tiene ángulos obtusos.
Obtusely [ǫb-tiūs'-li], *adv.* Obtusamente; lerdamente.
Obtuseness [ǫb-tiūs'-nes], *s.* Embotadura, embotamiento, torpeza.
Obtusion [ǫb-tiū'-shun], *s.* Embotamiento.
†**Obversant** [ǫb-vęr'-sant], *a.* Familiar.
Obverse [ǫb'-vęrs], *s.* Anverso, en las medallas o cuños la cara en que está el busto.—*a.* Del anverso, que denota la cara de una medalla o moneda.
Obvert [ǫb-vęrt'], *va.* Volver hacia o dirigir alguna cosa a paraje determinado.
Obviate [ǫb'-vi-êt], *va.* Obviar, evitar o apartar inconvenientes o dificultades.
Obvious [ǫb'-vi-us], *a.* Obvio, manifiesto, claro, evidente.
Obviously [ǫb'-vi-us-li], *adv.* Obviamente, patentemente, claramente.
Obviousness [ǫb'-vi-us-nes], *s.* Claridad, evidencia.
Oc-. Prefijo, la forma de *ob,* antes de *c.*
Oca [ō'-ca], *s.* Oca, planta indígena del Perú. Hay dos especies; una que se cultiva por sus tubérculos y la otra por los pecíolos de sus hojas. Oxalis crenata y Oxalis tuberosa.
Occasion [ǫc-ké'-zhun], *s.* 1. Ocasión, ocurrencia, casualidad; acaecimiento, acontecimiento. 2. Ocasión, sazón, coyuntura, tiempo oportuno. 3. Ocasión, motivo, causa, origen, razón. 4. Necesidad, falta. *To have occasion,* Ofrecerse, tener que. *Upon occasion,* Cuando se ofrece, ocasionalmente. *To take occasion,* Valerse de la ocasión, aprovechar la oportunidad. *By occasion of,* A consecuencia de. *On occasion,* En su oportunidad, su debido tiempo. *As occasion requires,* En caso necesario, para cuando llegue la ocasión. *There was no further occasion for his services,* No hubo más necesidad de sus servicios.
Occasion, *va.* Ocasionar, causar, excitar.

Occasionable [ǫc-kḗ-zhun-a-bl], *a.* Lo que puede ser causado, producido u ocasionado.
Occasional [ǫc-kḗ-zhun-al], *a.* 1. Que ocurre más o menos frecuentemente, pero no a intervalos fijos y regulares; de circunstancia. 2. Ocasional, casual, contingente; fortuito, accidental. *Occasional visits*, Visitas que sólo se hacen de vez en cuando.
Occasionally [ǫc-kḗ-zhun-al-i], *adv.* Ocasionalmente, por contingencia; de vez en cuando.
Occasioner [ǫc-kḗ-zhun-ǫr], *s.* Motor, causador, causa, motivo.
Occident [ec'-si-dǫnt], *s.* 1. Occidente, la Europa occidental, los países que están al oeste del Asia y los dominios turcos. 2. Occidente, oeste.
Occidental [ec-si-den'-tal], †**Occiduous** [ec-sid'-yu-us], *a.* Occidental.
Occipital [ec-sip'-i-tal], *a.* Occipital, perteneciente al occipucio. *Occipital bone*, El hueso occipital.
Occiput [ec'-si-put], *s.* Colodrillo, occipucio, la parte posterior e inferior de la cabeza.
Occlude [ec-clūd'], *va.* 1. Cerrar, tapar. 2. Absorber, como un metal absorbe un gas.
Occlusion [ec-clū'-zhun], *s.* 1. (Med.) Cerradura, cerramiento, obstrucción de un poro, conducto o cavidad. 2. Absorción de gases por los metales.
Occult [ec-cult'], *a.* 1. Oculto, escondido, ignorado; misterioso. 2. No conocido inmediata ni fácilmente. 3. Visible sólo para los que tienen visión espiritual; término de teosofía.
Occultation [ec-cul-tḗ-shun], *s.* (Astr.) Ocultación, desaparición pasajera de una estrella o planeta ocultado por la luna.
Occultism [ec-cult'-izm], *s.* 1. La investigación de las cosas misteriosas, particularmente de lo sobrenatural. 2. Pretensión de poseer un poder sobrenatural; astrología. 3. Teosofía moderna.
Occultness [ec-cult'-nes], *s.* 1. Ocultación. 2. Ocultación, secreto por el cual se calla una cosa que se sabe, debiendo decirla.
Occupancy [ec'-yu-pan-si], *s.* Ocupación, toma de posesión.
Occupant [ec'-yu-pant], *s.* Ocupador, ocupante, la persona que ocupa; en especial, inquilino que tiene posesión, a distinción del dueño.
Occupation [ec-yu-pḗ-shun], *s.* 1. Ocupación, el acto de tomar posesión de un país o de otra cosa. 2. Manera o tiempo de poseer. *V.* TENURE. 3. Ocupación, trabajo, oficio, empleo, profesión.
Occupier [ec'-yu-pai-ǫr], *s.* 1. Ocupador. 2. El que está empleado en algún destino, arte u oficio.
Occupy [ec'-yu-pai], *va.* 1. Ocupar; ocuparse en; llenar el espacio, el tiempo o la capacidad de; usar de una manera exclusiva. 2. Ocupar, tomar posesión de, apoderarse de. 3. Emplear, dar empleo o trabajo a. *To be occupied with a thing*, Ocuparse en alguna cosa.—*vn.* (Des.) Traficar.
Occur [ec-cǖr'], *vn.* 1. Encontrarse o hallarse aquí y allí; aparecer; de aquí, suceder, acaecer, acontecer. 2. Ocurrir, venir a la imaginación o a la memoria. *The thought did not occur to him*, No se le ocurrió tal idea. *The word glass occurs but once in the Old Testament*, La palabra vidrio se encuentra una sola vez en el Antiguo Testamento.
Occurrence [ec-cǖr'-ǫns], *s.* Ocurrencia, incidente, suceso casual; acontecimiento, acaecimiento, lance. *To be of actual occurrence*, Haber sucedido realmente. *To be of frequent occurrence*, Suceder a menudo.
Ocean [ō'-shan], *s.* 1. Océano, el mar que rodea la tierra. 2. Océano, piélago, una de las partes del océano, como el Atlántico, el Pacífico, etc. 3. Inmensidad, expansión sin límites.
Oceanic [ō-shę-an'-ic], *a.* 1. Oceánico, que pertenece al océano. 2. Inmenso. 3. (Zool.) Pelágico, que vive en el océano.
Ocean liner [ō'-shan lain'-ǫr], *s.* Transatlántico o trasatlántico.
Oceanography [ō-shan-eg'-ra-fi], *s.* Oceanografíah.
Ocellated, Ocellate [es-el'-ēt-ǫd], *a.* 1. Ojoso, que tiene manchas que se parecen a ojos. 2. Que tiene una mancha de un color dentro de un círculo de otro. 3. Manchado.
Ocelot [ō'-sel-et], *s.* Ocelote, leopardo o tigre de Méjico, de color leonado. Se halla desde Arkansas, hasta la Patagonia. Felix pardalis.
Ochlocracy [ec-lec'-ra-si], *s.* Oclocracia, gobierno de la canalla, o muchedumbre baja.
Ochra [ō'-cra], *s.* *V.* OKRA y GUMBO.
Ocher, Ochre [ō'-kǫr], *s.* 1. Ocre, cierta tierra para pintar de amarillo. 2. Cualquier óxido de metal que se encuentra en forma de tierra o polvo. *Yellow ocher*, Ocre amarillo. *Brown ocher*, Ocre carmelita. *Red ocher*, Ocre rojo o encarnado, ocre quemado, almagre, almazarrón.
Ocherous, Ochreous [ō'-kǫr-us], **Ochery** [ō'-kǫr-i], *a.* Ocroso, de la naturaleza o del color del ocre o que lo contiene.
O'clock [o-clec'], *loc.* Contracción de *of the clock*, que significa (la hora) según el reloj. *What o'clock is it?* ¿Qué hora es? *It is eight o'clock*, Son las ocho.
Octagon [ec'-ta-gen], *s.* Octágono, la figura que consta de ocho lados y ocho ángulos.
Octagonal [ec-tag'-o-nal], *a.* Octagonal.
Octahedral [ec-ta-hī'-dral], *a.* Octaédrico, que tiene los caracteres del octaedro.
Octahedron [ec-ta-hī'-drǫn], *s.* Octaedro.
Octandria [ec-tan'-dria], *s.* Octandria, la clase octava de los vegetales en el sistema de Linneo; las plantas que tienen ocho estambres.
Octangular [ec-taŋ'-giu-lar], *a.* Octangular.
Octant [ec'-tant], *a.* y *s.* 1. La octava parte de un círculo; la medida de cuarenta y cinco grados. 2. (Astr.) Octante, instrumento astronómico para tomar la altura del sol.
Octateuch [ec'-ta-tiuc], *s.* Octateuco, los ocho primeros libros del Viejo Testamento.
Octave [ec'-têv], *s.* 1. Octava, el día octavo de alguna festividad; los ocho días que inmediatamente se siguen a alguna festividad. 2. (Mús.) Octava, intervalo de ocho tonos, o de siete grados; una nota o tecla a este intervalo sobre o debajo de otra. *Octave coupler*, Doblemano, mecanismo de los órganos modernos, para hacer que con la tecla baje la de la octava superior.
Octave, *a.* Octavo, perteneciente al número ocho.
Octavo [ec-tḗ'-vō], *a.* 1. En octavo, la forma que tienen los libros cuando el pliego de impresión tiene ocho hojas. 2. Que denota cierto tamaño de la página, comúnmente 6 × 9½ pulgadas.—*s.* Libro, folleto, etc., en que un pliego está doblado en ocho hojas. Escríbese por lo común, 8vo.
Octennial [ec-ten'-i-al], *a.* Que dura ocho años.
Octet [ec-tet'], *s.* 1. Composición musical, compuesta para ocho ejecutantes. 2. Coro de ocho voces u orquesta de ocho ejecutantes.
Octillion [ec-til'-yun], *s.* Octillón, número cardinal; en la numeración francesa, la novena potencia de un mil; el número uno con 27 ceros; en la numeración inglesa, la octava potencia de un millón, uno (1) con 48 ceros.
October [ec-tō'-bǫr], *s.* 1. Octubre, el décimo mes del año. 2. Cerveza o sidra hecha en octubre.
Octodecimo [ec-to-des'-i-mō], *a.* En décimo-octavo; dícese de una forma en que el pliego se dobla en diez y ocho hojas, o treinta y seis páginas. Escríbese por lo común 18mo y se llama *eighteenmo*.
Octoedrical [ec-tō-ī'-dric-al], *a.* Octoédrico, que tiene ocho lados. *V.* OCTAHEDRAL.
Octogenarian [ec-to-jǫ-nḗ'-ri-an], **Octogenary** [ec-tej'-ǫ-nǫ-ri], *a.* y *s.* Octogenario, que tiene ochenta años.
Octonocular [ec-to-nec'-yu-lar], *a.* Que tiene ocho ojos.
Octopetalous [ec-to-pet'-a-lus], *a.* Octopétala, flor que tiene ocho hojas.
Octopus [ec'-to-pus u ec-tō'-pus], *s.* 1. Pulpo, molusco cefalópodo octópodo; jibia octópoda. 2. (Fig.) Organización a la que se atribuyen grandes facultades para hacer daño.
Octoroon [ec-to-rūn'], *s.* La persona que tiene una octava parte de sangre negra y siete octavas blancas; hijo de un cuarterón o una cuarterona y una persona blanca.
Octostyle [ec'-to-stail], *s.* (Arq.) Octóstilo, el edificio que tiene ocho columnas en su frontispicio.
Octosyllabic [ec-to-si-lab'-ic], *a.* Octosílabo, que está compuesto de ocho sílabas.
Octuple [ec'-tiu-pl], *a.* Óctuplo, lo que contiene ocho veces tanto.
Ocular [ec'-yu-lar], *a.* Ocular, perteneciente al ojo; derivado del ojo o que se refiere a él; visual.—*s.* Ocular, la combinación de lentes en un instrumento óptico por medio de la cual se ve aumentada la imagen.
Ocularly [ec'-yu-lar-li], *adv.* Ocularmente, visiblemente.
Oculate [ec'-yu-lēt], *a.* Ocular, que tiene ojos.
Oculist [ec'-yu-list], *s.* Oculista, oftalmólogo.
Odalisk [ō'-da-lisk], *s.* Odalisca, esclava o concubina del sultán que forma parte del harem.
Odd [ed], *a.* 1. Impar, que no puede dividirse en dos porciones sin fracción. 2. Marcado con un número impar. 3. Lo que queda de un número dado o lo que falta para completarlo. 4. Tanto, pico; número

indeterminado que excede ó sobra después del definido. *An odd card*, Una carta sobrante, o de más. 5. Particular, extraordinario, singular, raro, extraño; fantástico. *To play at odd and even*, Jugar a pares y nones. *Odd apparel*, Traje fantástico, singular. *It is an odd affair*, Es una cosa rara. *An odd character*, Un ente singular; (fam.) pájaro, pajarraco. *Three hundred and odd pounds*, Trescientas y tantas libras. *Havana has two hundred thousand and odd inhabitants*, La Habana tiene doscientos mil y pico de habitantes. 6. Solo, único, singular; que pertenece a un par o a una serie de la que falta el resto; desemparejado. *An odd glove*, Un guante sin pareja; un solo guante. *An odd volume*, Tomo suelto, un solo libro. 7. (Ant.) Desviado; lejano. *Odds and ends*, Picos y cabos pendientes. *It is very odd that it was not thought of sooner*, Es muy extraño que no se haya pensado antes en ello.

Oddity [ed'-i-ti], *s.* 1. Singularidad, particularidad, rareza. 2. Ente singular; (fam.) pajarraco.

Oddly [ed'-li], *adv.* Desigualmente, extrañamente, singularmente; de un modo extraño; en número impar.

Oddness [ed'-nes], *s.* 1. Disparidad, desigualdad. 2. Singularidad, extravagancia, rareza en el obrar, hablar, vestir, etc.

Odds [edz], *s. pl.* (y a veces *singular*). 1. Desigualdad, diferencia, disparidad. *That does not make any odds*, Eso no hace diferencia alguna; eso no importa. *The odds were against me*, Tuve que vérmelas con uno más fuerte que yo. *To lay the odds with one*, Hacer una apuesta desigual. 2. Partido desigual, apuesta desigual. 3. Ventaja, superioridad, exceso. 4. Riña, pendencia, disputa. *They are at odds*, Están siempre riñendo. (Fam.) Están de cuernos, están de punta. *To set at odds*, Desunir, descomponer, malquistar. *To fight against odds*, Luchar contra una fuerza superior.

Ode [ōd], *s.* Oda, poema lírico; poema corto, de gran elevación de tema y forma particular.

Odeon [o-dī'-en], *s.* 1. En la antigua Grecia, teatro con techo. 2. ¿Teatro o salón de música.

Odic [ō'-dic], *a.* Ódico, perteneciente a una oda.

Odious [ō'-di-us], *a.* 1. Odioso, abominable, aborrecible. 2. Asqueroso, detestable, aborrecido.

Odiously [ō'-di-us-li], *adv.* Odiosamente, abominablemente.

Odiousness [ō'-di-us-nes], **Odium** [ō'-di-um], *s.* 1. Odiosidad. 2. Odio; carácter odioso.

Odometer [o-dem'-e-ter], *s.* Odómetro, instrumento para medir la distancia que se recorre en coche, a pie o en bicicleta.

Odometrical [o-do-met'-ric-al], *a.* Odométrico, relativo a un odómetro o hecho por él.

Odontalgia [ō-den-tal'-ji-a], *s.* Odontalgia, dolor de dientes o muelas.

Odontalgic [ō-den-tal'-jic], *a.* Odontálgico, que pertenece al dolor de dientes.

Odontograph [o-den'-to-graf], *s.* Odontógrafo, instrumento para formar los dientes de las ruedas.

Odontoid [o-den'-teid], *a.* Odontóideo, que tiene la forma de un diente.

Odontologist [ō-den-tel'-o-jist], *s.* Odontólogo, dentista.

Odor [ō'-der], *s.* Olor; fragancia, olor suave; aroma.

Odoriferous [ō-der-if-er-us], *a.* Odorífero, fragante, perfumado.

Odorless, Odourless [ō'-der-les], *a.* Inodoro, que carece de olor.

Odorous [ō'-der-us], *s.* Oloroso, fragante.

Odour, etc. *V.* Odor, etc. Manera usual de escribir estas palabras en Inglaterra.

Odyl [ō'-dil], *s.* Fuerza hipotética de la que se supone que explica los fenómenos del magnetismo animal.

Odyssey [ed'-is-i], *s.* Odisea o Ulixea, poema épico de Homero.

Œ [ī]. Para las palabras que comienzan por este diptongo y no se hallan aquí, véase la letra E.

Œconomics [ec-o-nem'-ics], *s.* Economía política, el buen uso y regla en el régimen y gobierno de los estados, las familias y los individuos; la ciencia que trata de la producción y de la distribución de la riqueza.

Œcumenical [ec-yu-men'-i-cal], *a.* Ecuménico, universal.

Œdema [e-dī'-ma], *s.* Edema, hidropesía.

Œdematous [e-dim'-a-tus], *a.* Edematoso, perteneciente al edema.

O'er [ōr]. Contracción poética de Over.

Œsophagus [e-sef'-a-gus], *s.* Esófago, tragadero.

Œstrus [es'-trus], *s.* Estro, tábano, insecto díptero muy molesto a las caballerías y al ganado mayor. *V.* Gadfly.

Of [ev], *prep.* 1. De, asociado con; expresa una causa. *Of the*, Del, de la, de los, de las. *The value of land*, El precio o el valor de las tierras. 2. Desde, fuera de, proveniente de; expresa relación de instrumento, movimiento, separación o efecto. *To rid the town of a villain*, Echar de la población a un malvado. 3. Tocante. *All entertain this opinion of the war*, Todos son de esta opinión tocante o con respecto a la guerra. 4. De, según. *Of custom*, De costumbre o según costumbre. 5. Por; (pocas veces para). *Of his great mercy*, Por su gran misericordia. 6. En, entre; sobre. *Of old*, En otro tiempo, antiguamente. *A doctor of law or divinity*, Doctor en leyes o en teología. *Of all things*, Entre o ante todas las cosas; sobre todas las cosas. *I shall think of it*, Pensaré en ello. *It is well done of him*, Ha hecho bien o ha obrado como debía. *Of himself*, De por sí, espontáneamente. *A friend of mine*, Un amigo mío, uno de mis amigos. *Of old*, Antiguamente, en otro tiempo, antaño. *A friend of old*, Un amigo antiguo. *Of course*, Por supuesto, bien entendido. *Of late*, Últimamente, desde hace poco. *That was very unkind of her*, Eso fué una descortesía por parte de ella. *The city of Havana*, La ciudad de la Habana.

Off [ōf]. Adverbio y preposición que generalmente se une a los verbos para modificar o cambiar su significación, y ya unido, ya separado, sirve para expresar separación, ausencia, privación o distancia; lejos, a distancia, fuera de aquí. A veces corresponde al prefijo español *des.* *West of this forest scarcely off a mile*, Escasamente una milla al poniente de este bosque. *A great way off*, Muy lejos. *How far is it off?* ¿Cuánto hay desde aquí á allí? ó de aquí allá? *Far off*, Lejos. *The match is off*, Se ha deshecho la boda. *He is off*, Se va, se marcha. *I saw him off*, Le ví marcharse. *Either off or on*, Ni en pro ni en contra. *The child had his stockings off*, El niño tenía quitadas las medias. *The locomotive ran off the track*, La locomotora descarriló. *The lock is off*, Está quitada la cerradura. *The water is turned off*, El agua no corre; han cortado el agua. *Two per cent. off for cash*, Descuento de dos por ciento por pago al contado. *Off and on*, De vez en cuando, algunas veces; á intervalos; ya bien ya mal; dentro ó fuera. *To be well off*, Salir bien de alguna dificultad; estar bien ó tener con que pasarlo bien; (fam.) tener el riñón bien cubierto. *Well off, badly off*, Bien, mal en sus negocios. *We are no worse off than before*, No estamos peor que antes. *To be off from one*, Reñir con alguno, abandonarle ó separarse de él. *I am off*, Lo dejo; me desdigo; me marcho. *Off-hand*, De repente, de improviso, sin pensarlo. (Mar.) *To be off Cadiz*, Estar sobre Cádiz ó á la altura de Cádiz. *Off color*, (1) De color poco satisfactorio; dícese de una joya. (2) (Ger.) Malo, indecente, verde.—*inter.* ¡Fuera! *Off from hence*, Fuera de aquí. *Off with your hat*, Quítese Vd. el sombrero, ó fuera ese sombrero. *Off with his head!* ¡Que le corten la cabeza!

Off [ōf], *a.* 1. Más distante, á mayor distancia, más lejano; el lado derecho de una yunta ó una pareja de animales; á la derecha, lo opuesto á *nigh* ó *near*. 2. Desviado del camino principal. 3. De descanso, que denota una interrupción. *An off day*, Un día de descanso. 4. (Fam.) En desacuerdo con la realidad; falso, incorrecto. *Off in his calculations*, Errado en sus cálculos. *Off side*, (1) El lado derecho. (2) En el juego de pelota, falta, mala jugada.

Offal [ef'-al], *s.* 1. Asadura, despojos de las reses muertas. 2. Desecho, desperdicio de alguna cosa. Se emplea también como adjetivo.

Offence, Offenceless. *V.* Offense.

Offend [of-fend'], *va.* y *vn.* 1. Ofender, enfadar, irritar, provocar. 2. †Acometer, embestir. 3. Violar, quebrantar alguna ley ó precepto; pecar. 4. Ofender, agraviar, injuriar; desagradar, causar disgusto. 5. Delinquir, quebrantar la ley de Dios ó sus preceptos.

Offender [ef-fend'-er], *s.* Delincuente, transgresor, ofensor.

¿**Offendress** [ef-fend'-res], *sf.* Ofensora; pecadora.

Offense [of-fens'], *s.* 1. Ofensa, quebrantamiento de la ley divina ó humana; pecado; cualquier delito ó culpa; crimen, agresión. 2. Ofensa, injuria, agravio hecho á alguno. 3. Ofensa, ataque, acometimiento. *To take offense*, Ofenderse de alguna cosa, darse por sentido. *No offense*, Sin ofender á Vd.

Offenseless [of-fens'-les], *a.* Inofensivo, que no ofende.

Offensive [ef-fens'-iv], *a.* 1. Ofensivo, injurioso, ultrajante. 2. Desagradable, que causa disgusto. 3. Perjudicial. *Offensive warfare*, Guerra ofensiva. *An offensive odor*, Un olor desagradable.—*s.* Ofensiva, ataque.

Offensively [ef-fens'-iv-li], *adv.* Ofensivamente.

Offensiveness [ef-fens'-iv-nes], *s.* Ofensa, desazón; cualidad perjudicial; causa de asco.

Offer [ef'-ęr], *va.* 1. Ofrecer; hacer patente, dar a conocer, poner en conocimiento del público. 2. Sacrificar, inmolar. 3. Ofrecer, prometer alguna cosa voluntariamente. 4. Atentar. 5. Ofrecer, proponer. —*vn.* 1. Ofrecerse, ocurrir o sobrevenir. 2. Intentar, tratar de. *Do not offer to do it*, Guárdese Vd. de hacerlo.

Offer, *s.* 1. Oferta, ofrecimiento, palabra, promesa. 2. Propuesta; declaración de amor; primeras proposiciones o preliminares para un convenio. 3. Oferta, el precio que se ofrece por una cosa. 4. Esfuerzo. 5. Donativo, don, que se hace por vía de gratificación. *To close with an offer*, Aceptar una oferta. *She has received many offers of marriage*, Han pedido su mano muchas veces.

Offering [ef'-ęr-ing], *s.* 1. Ofrecimiento, el acto de ofrecer. 2. Sacrificio, ofrenda, oblación. 3. Ofrenda, ofertorio, lo que se ofrece, lo que es presentado en el culto divino. *Peace-offering*, Sacrificio propiciatorio. *Burnt-offering*, Holocausto. *Votive offering*, Exvoto, presentalla.

Offertory [ef'-ęr-to-ri], *s.* 1. Ofertorio, ofrecimiento, el acto de ofrecer alguna cosa. 2. Ofrenda, lo que se ofrece en el culto divino. 3. Ofertorio, parte de la misa; y la antífona cantada o pieza compuesta para órgano y ejecutada entre el *Credo* y el *Sanctus*.

Offhand [ōf'-hand], *a.* 1. Hecho o ejecutado sin preparación. 2. No ceremonioso, informal.—*adv.* 1. Sin premeditación, sobre la marcha; sin estudio ni vacilación. 2. Sin apoyo artificial. *To shoot offhand*, Tirar sin apoyo artificial.

Office [ef'-is], *s.* 1. Oficio, la obligación en que cada uno está constituido según su clase y estado. 2. Oficio, empleo, ejercicio, cargo público. 3. Oficio, operación o función. 4. Oficio, servicio que uno hace a otro. 5. Oficios, las funciones solemnes pertenecientes al altar; oficio, rezo. 6. Oficina, despacho, cuarto destinado al despacho de asuntos particulares. 7. La gente de oficina colectivamente. 8. *pl.* (Ingl.) Lugar o sitio donde se guardan la vajilla y las provisiones. *Good office*, Favor. *Office-seeker*, Pretendiente. *To be in office*, Tener un empleo, estar colocado, estar en el poder. *To do the office of*, Hacer el oficio de, servir de, hacer el papel de. *Booking office*, Oficina de registro. *Ticket-office*, Despacho de billetes o papeletas. *Printing office*, Imprenta. *The office of a lawyer, of an attorney*, El bufete, el estudio de un abogado, de un procurador. *Post-office*, Administración de correos, estafeta, casa de correo. *Office-holder*, Empleado público, particularmente del gobierno.

Officer [ef'-i-sęr], *s.* 1. Oficial, el que tiene cualquier cargo público. 2. Oficial, empleado, dependiente en cualquier oficina. 3. Oficial, en la milicia desde alférez arriba. *Half-pay officer*, Oficial retirado, a media paga. 4. Alguacil o ministro inferior de justicia. *Police officer*, Agente de policía. *Commissioned officer*, Oficial nombrado por el Gobierno. *Non-commissioned officer*, Oficial nombrado por el jefe de un cuerpo. *Flag officer*, Oficial general de marina. *Staff officer*, Oficial de estado mayor.

Officer, *va.* 1. Mandar. 2. Proveer de oficiales. *An army well officered*, Un ejército con buena oficialidad.

Official [ef-fish'-al], *a.* 1. Oficial, perteneciente a algún cargo o empleo público. 2. Oficial, hecho o comunicado en virtud de autoridad. 3. Propio, autorizado para usarlo en medicina. *Official letters*, Pliegos de oficio.—*s.* 1. Oficial público; funcionario. 2. (Ingl.) Provisor o juez eclesiástico; juez de la curia.

Officialism [ef-fish'-al-izm], *s.* 1. Estado, condición, costumbres oficiales. 2. Formalismo, apego a las formas oficiales.

Officially [ef-fish'-al-i], *adv.* De oficio, oficialmente.

Office supplies [ef'-is sup-plaiz'], *s. pl.* Enseres de oficina.

Officiate [ef-fish'-i-ēt], *va.* Hacer alguna cosa de oficio.—*vn.* 1. Oficiar, celebrar la misa y demás servicios divinos. 2. Sustituir a otro.

Officinal [ef-fis'-i-nal o ęf-fi-sai'-nal], *a.* 1. Oficinal, hecho en la botica; preparado y en almacén. 2. (Bot.) Empleado en las artes o como medicamento.

Officious [ęf-fish'-us], *a.* 1. Oficioso, entremetido. 2. Oficioso, obsequioso, agasajador.

Officiously [ęf-fish'-us-li], *adv.* Oficiosamente.

Officiousness [ęf-fish'-us-nes], *s.* Oficiosidad, obsequio voluntario y muchas veces excesivo.

Offing [ōf'-ing], *s.* Largo, aquella parte del mar visible que está lejana de la costa y más allá del lugar de anclaje: ensenada. *To gain the offing*, Tomar el largo. *To stand for the offing*, (Mar.) Correr a lo largo.

Offish [ōf'-ish], *a.* Intratable, poco sociable, de maneras reservadas.

Offscouring [ōf'-scaur-ing], *s.* Hez, recremento, desecho, basura, lavaduras.

Offscum [ōf'-scum], *s.* y *a.* Dejado; vil, bajísimo.

Offset [ōf'-set], *s.* 1. Balance, compensación, suma o valor puesto como equivalente. 2. Pimpollo, el vástago o tallo nuevo que echa la planta. 3. En agrimensura, cierta línea auxiliar que sirve en la medición y división de los terrenos. 4. (Impr.) Offset. *Offset printing*, Impresión con máquina Offset.

Offset [ōf-set'], *va.* 1. Balancear, compensar; comparar una suma o valor con otro. 2. Medir la tierra por el procedimiento de ordenadas. 3. Hacer un voladizo en.

Offshoot [ōf'-shūt], *s.* Ramo, vástago; cosa secundaria o accesoria.

Offshore [ōf'-shōr], *a.* Costanero.—*adv.* En la cercanía de la costa.

Offspring [ōf'-spring], *s.* 1. Prole, linaje, hijos, descendencia, casta. 2. Producción de cualquier especie, renuevo. 3. Cauce, venero.

Off stage [ōf stēj], *a.* y *adv.* (Teat.) Entre bastidores, que sucede fuera del escenario.

Offward [ōf'-ward], *adv.* (Mar.) Al largo de la costa.

Oft [ōft] *a.* (Poét.) Frecuente.—*adv.* Muchas veces, a menudo.

Often [ōf'-n], **Ofttimes** [ōft'-taimz], **Oftentimes** [ōf'-n-taimz], *adv.* Frecuentemente, muchas veces, á menudo. *As often as*, Siempre que. *How often*, Cuántas veces. *So often*, Tantas veces. *Not often*, Rara vez. *Too often*, Demasiado á menudo.

Ogdoastich [eg-do-as'-tic], *s.* El epigrama de ocho versos.

Ogee [o-jī'], *s.* (Arq.) Cimacio, moldura ó bóveda en forma de S.

Ogive [ō'-jiv ú ō'-jaiv], *s.* (Arq.) 1. Ojiva, curva saliente de una bóveda gótica. 2. Ojiva, arco apuntado.

Ogle [ō'-gl], *va.* Guiñar, mirar al soslayo en señal de cariño ó para no ser observado.

Ogle, *s.* Guiñada, mirada al soslayo, ojeada.

Ogler [ō'-glęr], *s.* Guiñador, el que mira al soslayo.

Ogling [ō'-gling], *s.* El acto de guiñar el ojo mirando con cariño.

Oglio [ō'-li-o], *s.* *V.* OLIO.

Ogre [ō'-gęr], *s.* Ogro, monstruo imaginario del que se suponía que se alimentaba de carne humana.

Ogress [ō'-gres], *f.* Ogro hembra.

Oh ! [ō], *inter.* ¡Oh! exclamación que denota pena, asombro, admiración, alegría ó cualquier emoción repentina.

Ohm [ōm], *s.* Ohmio, unidad de resistencia eléctrica; la resistencia que, á cero grados, opone al paso de una corriente eléctrica una columna de mercurio de un milímetro cuadrado de sección y 106.3 centímetros de longitud; casi equivalente á la resistencia de 400 pies del alambre telegráfico común (de hierro).

Oho [o-hō'], *inter.* ¡Ajá! interjección que expresa asombro verdadero ó fingido, ó burla.

Oil [eil], *s.* Aceite; óleo. *Linseed-oil*, Aceite de linaza. *Nut-oil*, Aceite de nueces. *Salad-oil*, Aceite de comer. *Palm-oil*, Aceite del Senegal. *Neat's-foot oil*, Aceite de manitas. *Olive-oil*, Aceite de oliva. *Cod-liver oil*, Aceite de hígado de bacalao. *Castor-oil*, Aceite de ricino. *Rapeseed oil*, Aceite de colza. *Kerosene-oil, petroleum*, Kerosina, petróleo refinado. *Oil-colours*, Colores al óleo. *Oil cars*, Carros de tanque para petróleo. *Oil-bag*, Glándula oleífera. *Oil-beetle*, Méloe, insecto coleóptero que se emplea como vejigatorio. *Oil-painting*, Pintura al óleo, cuadro pintado con colores al óleo; el arte de pintar con colores al óleo. *Oil-paints*, Tintas, pinturas al óleo. *To burn the midnight oil*, Quemarse las cejas. *To strike oil*, Encontrar una capa de petróleo; de aquí, (E. U.) hacerse rico de súbito. *Oil-bottle*, Aceitera, alcuza, vasija para el aceite. *Oil-cake*, Los asientos de la linaza después de exprimido el aceite. *Oil-cloth*, Encerado, hule. *Oil-colour*, Color molido con aceite. *Oil-mill, oil-press*, Molino de aceite. *Oil-shop*, Aceitería tienda de aceite.

Oil, *va.* 1. Aceitar, engrasar; untar con aceite; de aquí, hacer liso, suave y agradable. 2. Ungir, olear.

Oiler [eil'-ęr], *s.* 1. El ó lo que engrasa ó aceita; obrero que unta la maquinaria con aceite. 2. Aceitera, aceitador; utensilio para untar con aceite. 3. Aceitera, vasija en que

se tiene el aceite para llevarlo de un punto a otro; alcuza.
Oilet [eil'-et], **Oilet-hole** [eil'-et-hōl], *s.* 1. (Arq.) Tronera, mirador. 2. (Des.) Ojete.
Oiliness [eil'-i-nes], *s.* Oleaginosidad, untuosidad.
Oilman [eil'-man], *s.* Aceitero.
Oil paper [eil pê'-pęr], *s.* Papel encerado.
Oily [eil'-i], *a.* Aceitoso, oleoso, oleaginoso.
Oily-grain [eil'-i-grên], *s.* (Bot.) Ajonjolí, alegría, sésamo oriental.
Oily-palm [eil'-i-pām], *s.* (Bot.) Palma del Senegal.
Ointment [eint'-męnt], *s.* Ungüento.
Okra [ō'-kra], *s.* Abelmosco, hibisco comestible, quimbombó; planta malvácea que sirve para sopa. Abelmoschus esculentus.
Old [ōld], *a.* 1. Viejo. *An old man,* Hombre anciano. 2. Viejo, antiguo; anticuado. *Old age,* Vejez. *How old are you?* ¿Cuántos años tiene Vd.? *I am twenty years old,* Tengo veinte años. *To grow old,* Envejecer. *Of old,* Antiguamente, mucho tiempo ha. *To be old enough,* Tener bastante edad; no ser niño. 3. Usado, gastado con el tiempo; que no es nuevo o que ya no está en uso; conocido desde hace mucho tiempo. 4. De costumbre, familiar; lo que hace mucho tiempo se produjo; del año anterior. *Old wine, old wheat,* Vino añejo, trigo añejo. *Old shoes,* Zapatos usados. *Old clothes,* Ropa vieja, usada. *An old castle,* Un castillo antiguo. *Old bachelor,* Solterón. *Old maid,* (1) Solterona. (2) La mona, cierto juego de naipes. *Old-maidish,* Que se parece a una solterona, peripuesto, formal; puesto de veinticinco alfileres. *Old-style,* (Impr.) Estilo antiguo; tipo de forma antigua. Este es estilo antiguo. *Old world,* Del viejo mundo; también del prehistórico.
Olden [ōld'-n], *a.* (Poét.) Viejo, antiguo. *The olden time,* Los tiempos pasados o antiguos.—*vn.* Envejecer, hacerse viejo.
Old-fashioned [ōld-fash'-und], *a.* Hecho a la antigua; del tiempo de Maricastaña.
Old hand [ōld hand], *s.* Experto, perito.
Oldish [ōld'-ish], *a.* Algo viejo o anciano; avejentado.
Old-line [ōld'-lain], *a.* Conservador, anticuado.
Oldness [ōld'-nes], *s.* Ancianidad, vejez, antigüedad.
Old school [ōld scūl], *s.* Grupo conservador de ideas anticuadas.
Old wife [ōld' waif], *s.* Vieja: úsase despreciativamente para designar a una mujer habladora.
Oleaceous [ō-lę-ê'-shus], *a.* Oleáceo, de las plantas gamopétalas cuyas especies más notables son el olivo y el fresno.
Oleaginous [ō-lę-aj'-i-nus], *a.* Oleaginoso, aceitoso.
Oleander [ō-lę-an'-dęr], *s.* (Bot.) Adelfa, baladre, arbusto siempre verde de adorno. Nerium oleander.
Oleaster [ō-lę-as'-tęr], *s.* (Bot.) Olivo silvestre o acebuche.
Oleate [ō'-lę-êt], *s.* Oleato, sal formada por la combinación del ácido oleico con una base.
Olefiant [o-lī'-fi-ant], *a.* Olefiante, dícese de un gas compuesto de un átomo de carbono y un átomo de hidrógeno; se llamó así porque forma con el cloro un líquido oleaginoso; hoy se llama etileno.
Oleic [o-lī'-ic u ō'-lę-ic], *a.* Oleico; derivado del aceite, o perteneciente a él.
Olein [ō'-lę-in], *s.* Oleína, substancia incolora, que se halla en todos los aceites vegetales, y en algunas grasas ($C_{57}H_{104}O_6$).
Oleomargarine [ō'-li-o-mār'-ga-rin], *s.* Oleomargarina.
Oleose [ō'-lę-ōs], **Oleous** [ō'-lę-us], *a.* (Poco us.) Oleoso.
Oleraceous [o-lę-rê'-shus], *a.* Semejante a hortaliza.
Olfactory [el-fac'-to-ri], *a.* Olfatorio, perteneciente al olfato.
Olibanum [o-lib'-a-num], *s.* Incienso, olíbano, goma aromática.
Oligarchy [el'-i-gār-ki], *s.* Oligarquía, gobierno de pocos.
Olio [ō'-li-ō], *s.* 1. Mezcla, miscelánea. 2. Olla podrida.
Olitory [el'-i-to-ri], *s.* Huerta de hortalizas.
Olivaceous [el-iv-ę'-shus], *a.* Oliváceo, aceitunado.
Olivary [el'-iv-ę-ri], *a.* Oliviforme, de la forma de una oliva; parecido a una aceituna.
Olive [el'-iv], *s.* 1. (Bot.) Olivo, el árbol que produce las aceitunas. 2. Aceituna, oliva.—*a.* Aceitunado, que tiene color de aceituna.
Olive-bearing [el'-iv-bār-ing], *a.* Olivífero.
Olive Branch [el'-iv branch], *s.* Rama de olivo; emblema de paz.
Olive-colour [el'-iv-cul-ęr], *s.* Aceitunado.
Olive-drab [el'-iv-drab], *a.* De color aceitunado (de los uniformes militares de E. U.)
Olive-grove [el'-iv-grōv], **Olive-yard** [el'-iv-yard], *s.* Olivar.
Olive-oil [el'-iv-eil], *s.* El aceite de oliva o de mesa.
Olive-tree [el'-iv-trī], *s.* Olivo.
Olla [el'-la], *s.* 1. Olla. 2. Marmita, olla.
Olympiad [o-lim'-pi-ad], *s.* Olimpiada, período de cuatro años entre los antiguos griegos.
Olympian [o-lim'-pi-an], *a.* 1. Perteneciente a los dioses del Olimpo, y especialmente a Zeus (Júpiter); olímpico. 2. Referente a los juegos olímpicos.
Olympic [o-lim'-pic], *a.* Olímpico.
Olympus [o-lim'-pus], *s.* Olimpo; el cielo.
Om [ōm], *s.* Nombre solemne del Ser Supremo entre los bracmanes.
Omasum [o-mê'-sum u o-mę'-sum], *s.* Omaso, ventrículo o tercer estómago de los rumiantes.
Ombre [ōm'-bęr], *s.* El tresillo o juego del hombre.
Ombrometer [em-brem'-ę-tęr], *s.* Un instrumento que sirve para medir la cantidad de lluvia que cae.
Omega [o-mī'-ga u ō'-mę-ga], *s.* Omega, la letra vigésima cuarta y última del alfabeto griego; fin.
Omelet [em'-ę-let], *s.* Tortilla de huevos; fritada de huevos.
Omen [ō'-men], *s.* Agüero, pronóstico, presagio o anuncio de un mal o de un bien.
Omentum [o-men'-tum], *s.* Omento, el redaño que cubre las entrañas.
Omer [ō'-męr], *s.* Homer, medida hebraica de capacidad, equivalente a 5.1 pintas.
Ominous [em'-i-nus], *a.* 1. Ominoso, azaroso, siniestro, fatal. 2. De buen agüero, pronosticador en general.
Ominously [em'-i-nus-li], *adv.* Ominosamente; por vía de presagio.
Ominousness [em'-i-nus-nes], *s.* La calidad que constituye a una cosa ominosa o de mal agüero.
Omissible [o-mis'-i-bl], *a.* Que se puede omitir o excluir.
Omission [o-mish'-un], *s.* 1. Omisión; flojedad, descuido. 2. Alguna cosa omitida o que queda por hacer; olvido de insertar o mencionar. *Errors and omissions excepted,* Salvo error u omisión.
Omissive [o-mis'-iv], *a.* Que omite, excluye, o descuida insertar o mencionar.
Omit [o-mit'], *va.* 1. Omitir, dejar de hacer o usar alguna cosa; descuidar, excluir, desechar. 2. Omitir, pasar en silencio, olvidar la inserción o mención de.
Omnibus [em'-ni-bus], *s.* Ómnibus, coche de gran capacidad, con cuatro ruedas, entrada por detrás y dos bancos laterales corridos.—*a.* Que comprende muchos casos diferentes o una gran variedad de objetos. *An omnibus bill,* Estatuto que comprende muchos asuntos diferentes.
Omnifarious [em-ni-fê'-ri-us], *a.* De todo género y especie.
Omniferous [em-nif'-ęr-us], *a.* Que puede producir todas las cosas.
Omniform [em'-ni-fērm], *a.* Omniforme, que tiene todas las formas o figuras.
Omniformity [em-ni-fērm'-i-ti], *s.* Omniformidad, la calidad de lo que tiene todas las formas o figuras.
Omnigenous [em-nij'-ę-nus], *a.* Omnígeno, que consta de todos los géneros.
§**Omniparient** [em-ni-pê'-ri-ęnt], **Omniparous** [em-nip'-a-rus], *a.* Omníparo, que produce todas las cosas.
Omnipercipiency [em-ni-pęr-sip'-i-ęn-si], *s.* Percepción de todas las cosas.
Omnipotence [em-nip'-o-tęns], **Omnipotency** [em-nip'-o-ten-si], *s.* Omnipotencia.
Omnipotent [em-nip'-o-tęnt], *a.* y *s.* Omnipotente, todopoderoso.
Omnipresence [em-ni-prez'-ęns], *s.* Ubicuidad, omnipresencia.
Omnipresent [em-ni-prez'-ęnt], *a.* Omnipresente, presente en todas partes; ubicuo, en todas partes a la vez.
Omniscience [em-nish'-ęns], **Omnisciency** [em-nish'-ęn-si], *s.* Omnisciencia.
Omniscient [em-nish'-ęnt], *a.* Omnisciente, infinitamente sabio, que todo lo sabe, omnisapiente.
Omnium [em'-ni-um], *s.* 1. (Ingl.) El agregado de diversas acciones en los fondos públicos. 2. Estante para bric-a-brac. *Omnium gatherum,* (Fam.) Miscelánea, mezcla confusa, mare mágnum.
Omnivorous [em-niv'-o-rus], *a.* 1. Omnívoro, que todo lo devora; que se alimenta indistintamente de toda clase de substancias. 2. (Zool.) Omnívoro, que se alimenta de substancias animales y vegetales; aplícase a los osos, cuervos, etc. 3. (Fig.) Que lee toda clase de libros.
Omoplate [em'-o-plêt], *s.* (Anat.) Omoplato, espaldilla.
Omphalic [em-fal'-ic], *a.* Umbilical, que se refiere al ombligo.
On [en], *prep.* Sobre, encima, en; de; a. 1. Sobre, en contacto con la superficie superior de una cosa; que

viene o cae en tal contacto; suspendido de o soportado por; por medio de; además de; por la autoridad de. 2. En seguida, después de; tras, detrás de; con motivo de, por razón de; al cargo de; en conformidad con, según. 3. Con dirección a, hacia, a, al lado de, cerca. 4. En el acto de; bajo la influencia de, bajo. 5. En; en interés o favor de; en, se emplea con el participio presente; en el momento de; *on* no se traduce en castellano delante del nombre de un día o de una fecha. *On the fifth of May*, El cinco de mayo. 6. Por lo concerniente, respecto a, tocante a, acerca. 7. En estado o calidad de; como, *On record*, En calidad de archivado, registrado. 8. Por; y a veces para. *On an average*, Por término medio. *It lies on the table*, Está sobre o encima de la mesa. *On the right hand*, A la mano derecha. *On pain of death*, So pena de muerte. *On his arrival*, A su llegada. *On my return*, A mi vuelta. *On horseback*, A caballo. *On foot*, A pie. *On purpose*, De intento, adrede, a propósito, expresamente. *On high*, En alto. *On the contrary*, Por el contrario. *On my part*, De mi parte o por mi parte; en cuanto a mí. *On condition that you come*, Con tal que Vd. venga. *To be off and on*, Estar indeciso. *To play on the violin*, Tocar el violín. *On a sudden*, De golpe, de repente, de improviso. *My shoes are on*, Estoy calzado. *On account of*, A causa de. *On no account* o *consideration*, Por ningún concepto, por nada en el mundo. *On second thoughts*, Bien pensado el caso, después de maduro examen. *On returning from the theater I went to my room*, Al regresar del teatro fuí a mi habitación. *On leaving the harbour of San Francisco*, Al salir del puerto de San Francisco. *To be on guard*, Estar de guardia. *To be on his guard*, Estar en guardia. *On every side*, Por todas partes.—*inter.* ¡Vamos! ¡adelante! ¡marchen!

On, *adv.* 1. En contacto con una cosa que sirve de apoyo y sostén; encima, sobre; en posición o condición de adherencia. 2. En la misma dirección o manera, adelante; sin cesar; a lo largo. 3. En o hacia el propio y debido lugar de acción. 4. En existencia u operación. Frecuentemente *on* sirve para modificar el sentido de un verbo, *Go on*, Prosiga Vd.; continúe Vd.; ¡marchen! ¡adelante! *To have on*, Tener, llevar, puesto. *To have one's hat on*, Tener puesto el sombrero, tener la cabeza cubierta. *To have one's clothes on*, Tener puesto el vestido, estar vestido. *To look on*, Mirar, considerar. *Lead on*, Enseñad el camino. *Play on*, Continuad jugando. *On and off*, A intervalos, de vez en cuando. *And so on*, Y así de lo demás; (fam.) y otras hierbas.

Onager [on'-a-jẹr], *s.* Onagro, asno silvestre del Asia central.

Onanism [ō'-nan-izm], *s.* (Med.) Onanismo, masturbación.

Once [wuns], *adv.* 1. Una vez. *Once for all*, Una vez para siempre. *At once*, A un tiempo, de una vez, de un golpe. *All at once*, De repente. *Once more*, Más todavía, otra vez. 2. En otro tiempo, otras veces, antiguamente. *For once*, Una vez siquiera; últimamente, al fin. *Once in a way*, (Fam.) Una vez siquiera. *Once upon a time*, En otro tiempo; érase; mucho tiempo ha (a veces, en tiempo de Maricastaña, o del rey que rabió).

Oncoming [en-cum'-ing], *a.* Venidero, próximo.

One [wun], *a.* Un, uno; solo, único; uno solo, una sola. *One boy*, Un muchacho. *One girl*, Una muchacha. *One hundred and forty dollars*, Ciento cuarenta pesos. *One while he laughs and another he cries*, Ora ríe, ora llora. *One-horse*, De un caballo, tirado por un caballo; de aquí, de escasa capacidad, de poca importancia, pequeño, inferior. *One-story*, De un solo piso. *It is all one to me*, Lo mismo me da; me es lo mismo. *One or other*, Uno u otro. *With one accord*, De común acuerdo, unánimemente.—*pro.* Uno, una persona; el uno, la una; él, la; se, sí. *Every one*, Cada uno. *One by one*, Uno á uno, uno por uno. *Such a one*, Uno, cierto sujeto o cierta persona, fulano. *Every one of them*, Todos. *One* se usa frecuentemente en inglés como nombre general e indefinido, que se une con los adjetivos que no tienen substantivo expreso con que concertar, y en este caso casi nunca es necesario traducirlo en español. *This is a good one*, Este es bueno. *My little one*, Mi niño, mi hijo, mi chiquito. *They are but little ones*, Son pequeños, son chiquitos. *One's*, Su, sus. *To live according to one's estate*, Vivir arreglado a lo que se tiene. *One another*, El uno al otro. *To love one another*, Amarse unos a otros. *One knows that*, Sabido es que. *One sees how*, Se ve cómo. *How shall one do it?* ¿Cómo se ha de hacer? *Any one*, Alguien, quienquiera; todo el mundo. *Any one who says so is mistaken*, Quienquiera que lo diga se equivoca.

One-eyed [wun'-aid], *a.* Tuerto.

One-handed [wun'-hand-ed], *a.* Manco.

Oneness [wun'-nes], *s.* Unidad, singularidad de número, o la calidad que constituye el número uno como singular e indivisible.

Onerary [en'-ẹr-ẹ-ri], *a.* (Poco us.) Propio para carga o conducción.

Onerous [en'-ẹr-us], *a.* Oneroso, opresivo, pesado, molesto, gravoso.

Oneself, One's self [wun-self', wun'z self'], *pro.* Se, sí, sí mismo. *To come to oneself*, Volver en sí.

One-sided [wun'-sai"-dẹd], *a.* 1. De un solo lado; parcial, injusto; incompleto. 2. (Bot.) De lados desiguales, inclinado a un lado.

One-step [wun'-step], *s.* 1. Variedad de baile de salón. 2. Ritmo musical de dicho baile.

One-time [wun'-taim], *a.* Antiguo, anterior.—*adv.* En otros tiempos.

One-track [wun-trac'], *a.* (F. C.) De una sola vía. *One-track mind*, Mente estrecha, que sólo puede percibir una cosa a la vez.

One-way [wun-wê'], *a.* De una sola vía. *One-way street*, Tránsito en un solo sentido.

Onion [un'-yun], *s.* (Bot.) Cebolla. *Onion porridge* o *broth*, Sopa, potaje o caldo de cebollas. *Bunch of onions*, Ristra de cebollas. *Onion-bed*, Cebollar.

Onionskin [un'-yun-skin], *s.* Papel transparente satinado para copias.

Onlooker [en'-luk-ẹr], *s.* Espectador, asistente.

Only [ōn'-li], *a.* Único, solo; singular, raro.—*adv.* Solamente, únicamente, sino, no más que.

Onomatechny [en-o-ma-tec'-ni], *s.* Onomancia, el arte de adivinar algo por las letras del nombre de alguna persona.

Onomantic, Onomantical [en-o-man'-tic, al], *a.* (Poco us.) Onomántico.

Onomatopœia [en-o-mat-o-pî'-ya], *s.* 1. Onomatopeya, imitación del sonido de una cosa en el vocablo que se forma para significarla, p. ej. *Whizz*, Chirrido, chisporroteo. 2. El mismo vocablo que imita el sonido de la cosa nombrada con él. 3. Figura retórica de este nombre.

Onondagas [en'-en-dō'-gaz], *s.pl.* Nombre de una tribu de indios norteamericanos; una de las Cinco Naciones.

Onrush [en'-rush], *s.* *V.* Onset.

Onset [en'-set], *s.* 1. Embestida, primer ímpetu, ataque. *To give a fresh onset*, Volver a la carga. 2. Primer acceso de una enfermedad; estreno; principio de una pasión.

Onslaught [en'-slēt], *s.* Ataque furioso, embestida violenta, asalto.

Onto [en'-tū], *prep.* Por encima de, sobre; uso incorrecto en vez de *on*.

Ontologist [en-tel'-o-jist], *s.* Ontologista, metafísico.

Ontology [en-tel'-o-ji], *s.* Ontología, ciencia o tratado del ser en general.

Onward [en'-ward], *a.* Avanzado, progresivo, aumentado, adelantado.

Onward, Onwards, *adv.* 1. Adelante, hacia el frente, progresivamente. 2. En adelante, en lo venidero. *To come onward*, Acercarse.

Onyx [ō'-nix], *s.* 1. Ónice, ónique u ónix, piedra preciosa con fajas blanquecinas sobre fondo azulado. 2. Uña. 3. Una especie de absceso en el ojo.

Oolite [ō'-o-lait], *s.* (Min.) Oolita, piedra calcárea compuesta de pequeñas concreciones en forma de huevos de pescado.

Oology [ō-el'-o-ji], *s.* Oología, la parte de la ornitología que trata de los huevos y de la nidificación de las aves.

Oolong [ū'-lēng], *s.* Nombre de una variedad de té negro.

Ooze [ūz], *s.* 1. Fango, limo, cieno, légamo, cama de un estanque, de un río, etc.; tierra muy mojada o esponjosa. 2. Chorro suave de agua u otro líquido. 3. Adobe o adobo de curtidor.

Ooze, *vn.* Manar o correr algún líquido suavemente; pasar lentamente como al través de poros o intersticios; filtrar.

Oozy [ūz'-i], *a.* Cenagoso. *Oozy ground*, (Mar.) Baza.

Opacity [o-pas'-i-ti], *s.* Opacidad, cualidad de lo opaco, falta de transparencia; obscuridad.

Opal [ō'-pal], *s.* Ópalo, mineral silíceo con algo de agua, de lustre resinoso, quebradizo, translúcido u opaco (SiO_2nH_2O). *Fire opal*, Ópalo de fuego. *Precious opal*, Ópalo noble, precioso.

Opalesce [ō-pal-es'], *vn.* Emitir reflejos como los colores del ópalo.

Opalescence [ō-pal-es'-ens], *s.* Opalescencia, reflexión y refracción de la luz de color perla, como la del ópalo.

Opalescent [ō-pal-es'-ent], *a.* Opalino, que tiene reflejos de ópalo.

Opaline [ō'-pal-in], *a.* Opalino, de color lechoso y azulado, con reflejos de ópalo.

Opaque [o-pêc'], *a.* 1. Opaco, impenetrable a la luz; no diáfano ni transparente. 2. (Bot. y Ento.) Que no tiene brillo, obscuro, mate.

Ope [ōp], *va.* (Poét.) *V. To* OPEN. —*vn.* Abrirse; ladrar.

Open [ōp'-n], *va.* 1. Abrir, descubrir o destapar lo que estaba cerrado, tapado o unido; deshacer, desempaquetar, quitar alguna cosa que cubre a otra. 2. Abrir, desprender, alejar, dar paso a, remover obstáculos. 3. Hacer público o de libre acceso. 4. Descubrir, hallar. 5. Abrir, hender, rajar; romper. 6. Abrir, empezar, dar principio a alguna cosa. *To open a campaign*, Abrir una campaña, dar principio a ella. 7. Descubrir, revelar, manifestar lo que estaba secreto; mostrar, hacer saber; interpretar, explicar. 8. Ensanchar, aumentar.—*vn.* 1. Abrirse lo que estaba cerrado. 2. Abrirse, descubrirse, declararse con alguno. 3. Dividirse, entreabrirse. 4. Aparecer, hacerse visible, asomar. 5. Desarrollarse, llegar a ser receptivo, como la mente de un niño. 6. Comenzar, estrenar; comenzar a ladrar a la caza. *The shares opened at par*, Las acciones comenzaron (a venderse) á la par. 7. Dar. *To open a little*, Entreabrir, medio abrir, no abrir bien ó del todo *Her windows open upon a garden*, Sus ventanas caen, dan o miran a un jardín.

Open, *a.* 1. Abierto, extendido, desplegado; que no está cercado; sin sellar; desempaquetado, sin atar; destapado; descubierto; raso; libre, que no está obstruído, libre para todos los que vienen; abierto, que no está protegido, expuesto a un ataque; desnudo, a la vista. 2. Receptivo, dispuesto a recibir o a ser modificado o influido por lo que se acerca o se envía; listo, pronto, aparejado, preparado, dispuesto para los negocios, para la ocupación, etc.; dispuesto a escuchar y acoger lo que se dice; (Com.) abierto, sin arreglar, sin haberse hecho el saldo; no decidido, pendiente. 3. Patente, manifiesto, claro, evidente; sincero, franco, declarado. 4. Suave; más caliente que lo ordinario; abierto, libre de hielo. 5. Abierto, que tiene aberturas o agujeros; no tupido. 6. (Mús.) No pulsada con el dedo; dícese de una cuerda: cuyo remate superior está abierto; dícese de un cañón de órgano. 7. Pronunciado con los órganos vocales sin obstrucción; que no termina en consonante. *A little open*, Entreabierto. *In the open field*, A campo raso. *In the open street*, En medio de la calle. *To lie in the open air*, Dormir o quedarse al raso, dormir en el mesón de la estrella. *To set, to throw open*, Abrir. *With open force*, A mano armada, a viva fuerza. *An open winter*, Un invierno templado, sin heladas. *Open shame*, Vergüenza pública. *An open look*, Una mirada franca, abierta. *In open court*, En pleno tribunal. *To keep open house*, Tener casa abierta para todos. *To keep the bowels open*, Tener el vientre libre. *To cut open*, Abrir, cortar. *An open question*, Una cuestión pendiente. *Open-eyed*, Alerta, vigilante, cuidadoso, activo. *Open-handed*, Generoso, dadivoso, liberal, benéfico. *Open-hearted*, Ingenuo, franco, sincero, abierto, sencillo. *Open-mouthed*, Voraz, ávido; con la boca abierta.

Open-air [ōp'-n-ār], *a.* Abierto, al aire libre.

Opener [ōp'-n-ẹr], *s.* Abridor, el que abre; intérprete. *Can-opener*, Abridor de cajas de lata.

Open-heartedness [ō'-pn-hārt-ed-nes], *s.* Liberalidad, generosidad, franqueza, ingenuidad.

Opening [ō'-pn-ing], *s.* 1. Abertura, hendedura; camino abierto. 2. Vislumbre, conjetura, sospecha, indicio, noticia remota o dudosa. 3. Entrada, tronera, abertura.—*a.* Aperitivo

Open letter, *s.* Carta abierta (en un periódico o publicación) generalmente de súplica o protesta.

Openly [ō'-pn-li], *adv.* Abiertamente.

Openness [ō'-pn-nes], *s.* 1. Claridad. 2. Franqueza, sinceridad, ingenuidád, candor. *Openness of weather*, Blandura del tiempo.

Open question, *s.* Asunto discutible.

Open secret [ōp'-n sī'-cret], *s.* Secreto a voces.

Open-sesame [o-pn-ses'-a-mẹ], *s.* Ábrete, sésamo; conjuro mágico para abrir puertas secretas y para obtener entrada.

Open shop, *s.* Contrato de trabajo según el cual pueden ocuparse obreros sindicalizados o no.

Openwork [ō'-pn-wūrk], *s.* Calado, cualquier obra manual que contiene numerosas aberturas pequeñas.

Opera [op'-ẹr-a], *s.* Ópera, pieza dramática en música, y también el teatro en que se representa. *Opera-glass*, Gemelos de teatro. *Opera-house*, Sala o teatro de la ópera. *Opera bouffe*, Ópera cómica o bufa.

Operable [op'-ẹra-bl], *a.* Operable.

Operate [op'-ẹr-ēt], *va.* 1. Poner en acción y gobernar el movimiento de (v. g. una máquina); hacer funcionar. 2. Dirigir, manejar los negocios de. 3. Efectuar.—*vn.* 1. Obrar, operar. 2. Obtener un resultado determinado. 3. Producir el efecto propio o propuesto (v. g. un medicamento). 4. Exonerar, descargar el vientre, hacer del cuerpo. 5. Operar, hacer una operación quirúrgica con el fin de curar. 6. Especular en valores de ferrocarriles, minas, etc.

Operatic, Operatical [op-ẹr-at'-ic, al], *a.* De ópera, que pertenece á la ópera.

Operating [op'-ẹr-ēt-ing], *a.* 1. (Cir.) Operatorio. 2. (Mil.) Operacional. *Operating room*, Quirófano, sala de operaciones. *Operating surgeon*, Operador. *Operating table*, Mesa de operaciones.

Operation [op-ẹr-ē'-shun], *s.* 1. Operación, la acción y el efecto de operar. 2. (Cir.) Operación, el acto de cortar, abrir o separar una parte del cuerpo, con el fin de curar una enfermedad o de prevenir algún mal inminente. 3. Operación, acción, efecto; procedimiento, manipulación, movimiento.

Operative [op'-ẹr-a-tiv], *a.* Operativo, eficaz, activo.—*s.* Operario, trabajador, obrero en una manufactura.

Operator [op'-ẹr-ē-tẹr], *s.* 1. Operario, el que trabaja en alguna cosa. 2. (Cir.) Operador, el que ejecuta las operaciones quirúrgicas. 3. Agente, corredor de cambios o valores.

Opercular [o-pẹr'-kiu-lar], *a.* Opercular, que cierra una cavidad á manera de tapa.

Operculate [o-pẹr'-kiu-let ó lēt], *a.* Operculado, que cierra o cubre un opérculo; operculífero, que tiene un opérculo.

Operculum [o-pẹr'-kiu-lum], *s.* (Biol.) Opérculo, especie de cubierta, válvula o tapa, que cubre y cierra algún hueco, poro, celdilla o concavidad y que figura en uno de los tres reinos de la naturaleza.

Operetta [op-ẹr-et'-a], *s.* Opereta, ópera corta con diálogo; zarzuela.

Ophicleide [ef'-i-claid], *s.* (Mús.) Instrumento músico de viento, parecido a la corneta pero con mayor número de llaves.

Ophidian [o-fid'-i-an], *a.* y *s.* Ofidiano, perteneciente a los ofidios o serpientes; la serpiente misma, ofidio, un orden de reptiles.

Ophioglossum [o-fi-o-gles'-um], *s.* (Bot.) Ofiglosa, lengua de serpiente, género de plantas criptógamas.

Ophthalmia [ef-thal'-mi-a], **Ophthalmy** [ef-thal'-mi], *s.* Oftalmia, la inflamación de los ojos.

Ophthalmic [ef-thal'-mic], *a.* Oftálmico, referente al ojo.

Ophthalmology [ef-thal-mel'-o-ji], *s.* Oftalmología, parte de la patología que trata de las enfermedades de los ojos.

Opiate [ō'-pi-ēt], *s.* Opiata, medicamento que contiene opio; bebida para hacer dormir.—*a.* Narcótico, soporífico.

‡**Opiate**, *va.* 1. Hacer dormir por medio del opio. 2. Mezclar, o componer con opio.

Opinable [o-pain'-a-bl], *a.* Opinable, que se puede defender en uno y otro sentido.

Opine [o-pain'], *vn.* (Ant.) Opinar, pensar, ser de parecer.

Opinion [o-pin'-yun], *s.* 1. Opinión, dictamen, sentir o juicio que se forma de alguna cosa; pensamiento, idea. *This is my opinion*, Esto es lo que yo pienso. *He has a high opinion of himself*, Está muy pagado de sí mismo. 2. Opinión, fama o concepto que se forma con relación a personas o cosas. 3. Estimación, reputación; buena opinión, juicio favorable.

†**Opinionate, Opinionated** [o-pin'-yun-ēt, ed], *a.* Porfiado, obstinado, terco, pertinaz.

Opinionately [o-pin'-yun-ēt-li], *adv.* Porfiadamente.

Opinionative [o-pin'-yun-a-tiv], *a.* (Ant.) Terco, obstinado, porfiado, pertinaz.

Opinionatively [o-pin'-yun-a-tiv-li], *adv.* Tercamente.

Opinionativeness [o-pin'-yun-a-tiv-nes], *s.* Porfía, terquedad, obstinación.

Opinioned [o-pin'-yund], *a.* Presumido, pagado de sí mismo; obstinado.

Opinionist [o-pin'-yun-ist], *s.* 1. Opinante. 2. El que está adherido a su propia opinión o muy pagado de sí mismo.

Opium [ō'-pi-um], *s.* Opio, el zumo de las adormideras; narcótico.

Opobalsam [op-o-bēl'-sam], *s.* Opobálsamo, resina astringente y medicinal.

Opopanax [o-pep'-a-nacs], *s.* Opopónaco, especie de goma empleada antiguamente en medicina.

Opossum [o-pes'-um], *s.* Zorra mochilera, cuadrúpedo carnívoro de ambas Américas. Es notable la hembra por tener en la parte inferior del vientre una bolsa, cuya entrada abre y cierra á voluntad, y en ella lleva y guarda los hijuelos hasta que son algo crecidos.

Oppidan [op'-i-dan], *a.* Relativo a una ciudad, cívico.—*s.* Alumno externo del colegio de Eton en Inglaterra.

Oppilation [op-i-lé'-shun], *s.* Opilación, obstrucción.

Opponency [op-pō'-nen-si], *s.* Oposición; ejercicio para recibir un grado académico; exposición de los argumentos en contra de una proposición.

Opponent [op-pō'-nent], *s.* Antagonista; contrincante, arguyente contrario; lo opuesto a *respondent* o *defendant;* parte adversa.—*a.* 1. Opuesto, contrario. 2. (Anat.) Oponente, que sirve para contraponer una parte en frente de otra.

Opportune [op-er-tiūn'], *a.* Oportuno, conveniente, hecho a tiempo o cuando conviene.

Opportunely [op-er-tiūn'-li], *adv.* Oportunamente, cómodamente, a tiempo.

Opportuneness [op-er-tiūn'-nes], *s.* El estado de lo que es oportuno, oportunidad.

Opportunism [op-er-tiūn'-izm], *s.* Oportunismo (generalmente en la política).

Opportunity [op-er-tiū'-ni-ti], *s.* Oportunidad, comodidad, sazón; ocasión, circunstancia favorable. *Opportunity makes the thief,* La ocasión hace al ladrón.

Opposable [op-pōz'-a-bl], *a.* Oponible; (1) que se puede oponer a otra cosa; (2) que puede ser objeto de oposición.

Oppose [op-pōz'], *va.* 1. Oponer, poner impedimento a una cosa, obrar en oposición a, resistir a, combatir. 2. Oponer, contraponer, poner una cosa enfrente de otra; colocar opuestamente o en contraste. 3. Oponer, objetar una razón, un argumento, etc.—*vn.* 1. Oponer u oponerse, contrariar, resistir. 2. Argüir, oponerse u objetar por medio de argumentos a lo que otro dice.

Opposeless [op-pōz'-les], *a.* Irresistible.

Opposer [op-pōz'-er], *s.* Opositor, antagonista, rival.

Opposite [op'-o-zit], *a.* 1. Fronterizo, opuesto, lo que está enfrente de otra cosa. 2. Opuesto, adverso, repugnante, contrario, antagónico; otro, diferente. *Opposite leaves,* Hojas opuestas. *The opposite sex,* El otro sexo, el sexo opuesto.—*s.* 1. Antagonista, adversario. 2. Lo opuesto, lo contrario.

Oppositely [op'-o-zit-li], *adv.* Enfrente, opuestamente.

Oppositeness [op'-o-zit-nes], *s.* Contrariedad, estado contrario.

Opposition [op-o-zish'-un], *s.* 1. Oposición, la disposición de algunas cosas de modo que estén enfrente de otras. 2. Oposición, contrariedad. 3. Oposición, resistencia, contradicción. 4. Oposición, óbice, impedimento. 5. Oposición, el partido antiministerial o los individuos de un cuerpo legislativo que se oponen generalmente a las medidas del gobierno. 6. (Astr.) Situación relativa de dos cuerpos celestes cuando distan 180° uno de otro. *To meet with opposition,* Encontrar oposición.

Oppositional [op-o-zish'-un-al], *a.* De la naturaleza de oposición; perteneciente a un partido antiministerial.

Oppositionist [op-o-zish'-un-ist], *s.* Miembro de la oposición; miembro del partido que combate al ministerio o a la administración.

Oppositive [op-poz'-i-tiv], *a.* Capaz de ser puesto en oposición.

Oppress [op-pres'], *va.* 1. Oprimir, apretar, aquejar o afligir a uno; sobrecargar; agobiar con impuestos excesivos; tratar con dureza injusta. 2. Oprimir, apretar o comprimir una cosa.

Oppression [op-presh'-un], *s.* 1. Opresión, crueldad, tiranía; acción de oprimir. 2. Miseria, calamidad; calidad de oprimido, sobrecargado, afligido o aquejado. 3. Opresión de ánimo; fatiga; opresión o apretura de una parte del cuerpo; sensación de pesadez o de constricción.

Oppressive [op-pres'-iv], *a.* 1. Opresivo, cruel, inhumano, tiránico. 2. Pesado, molesto.

Oppressively [op-pres'-iv-li], *adv.* Opresivamente.

Oppressiveness [op-pres'-iv-nes], *s.* Opresión.

Oppressor [op-pres'-er], *s.* Opresor.

Opprobrious [op-prō'-bri-us], *a.* 1. Oprobioso, ignominioso, infamante. 2. Injurioso, ultrajante.

Opprobriously [op-prō'-bri-us-li], *adv.* Ignominiosamente.

Opprobriousness [op-prō'-bri-us-nes], *s.* Oprobio, ignominia.

Opprobrium [op-prō'-bri-um], *s.* Oprobio, ignominia, deshonra, infamia.

Oppugn [op-piūn'], *va.* Opugnar, hacer resistencia; contrariar, combatir.

Oppugnancy [op-pug'-nan-si], *s.* Opugnación, oposición, contradicción.

Oppugnation [op-pug-né'-shun], *s.* (Poco us.) Resistencia.

Oppugner [op-piūn'-er], *s.* Opugnador, resistidor.

Opsimathy [op-sim'-a-thi], *s.* (Ant.) La educación que se recibe después de pasada la niñez.

Optative [op'-ta-tiv], *a.* Optativo; que expresa deseo o elección. Se aplica en especial a un modo del verbo griego.—*s.* Optativo; modo optativo o subjuntivo.

Optic, Optical [op'-tic, al], *a.* 1. Óptico, de la vista, que pertenece a los órganos de la visión. 2. Óptico, que pertenece a la óptica: *optical* significa además lo que ayuda a la visión. *Optic angle,* Ángulo óptico. *Optic nerve,* Nervio óptico. *Optical instruments,* Instrumentos ópticos. —*s.* Cualquier órgano que sirve para ver.

Optician [op-tish'-an], *s.* 1. Óptico, el que fabrica o vende anteojos y otros instrumentos ópticos. 2. (Poco us.) El que es versado en la óptica o la profesa.

Optics [op'-tics], *s.* Óptica, ciencia físico-matemática que trata de la luz y de las leyes de la visión.

§**Optimacy** [op'-ti-ma-si], *s.* Nobleza, el conjunto o cuerpo de los nobles.

Optimism [op'-ti-mizm], *s.* 1. Optimismo, el sistema de los que afirman que todo lo que sucede es bueno en sumo grado. 2. Disposición a considerar las cosas bajo su aspecto más favorable.

Optimist [op'-ti-mist], *s.* 1. Optimista, el que sigue y defiende el optimismo. 2. El que espera que sucederá lo mejor y más favorable que pueda ocurrir; el que lo ve todo de color de rosa.

Optimist, Optimistic [op'-ti-mis'-tic], *a.* Optimista.

Option [op'-shun], *s.* 1. Opción, la facultad de elegir; derecho o libertad de escoger; preferencia, escogimiento. 2. (Com.) El derecho que se adquiere por un tanto y razón de comprar o vender una cosa por un precio dado, dentro de un plazo determinado.

Optional [op'-shun-al], *a.* Que tiene o da la facultad de elegir, que proviene de la elección. *To be optional with,* Tener la elección de.

Optometry [op-tom'-e-tri], *s.* Optometría, medición de la vista.

Opulence [op'-yu-lens], **Opulency** [op'-yu-len-si], *s.* Opulencia, abundancia de bienes, riqueza; lozanía, copia.

Opulent [op'-yu-lent], *a.* Opulento.

Opulently [op'-yu-lent-li], *adv.* Opulentamente.

Opus [ō'-pus], *s.* (*pl.* OPERA [op'-e-ra]). Obra o composición literaria o música.

Opuscle [o-pus'-l], *s.* Opúsculo.

Or [ōr], *conj.* 1. O, partícula disyuntiva que denota distribución u oposición y que se cambia en *u* cuando la palabra que sigue empieza con *o* u *ho.* Es a menudo correlativa de *whether* o *either.* Si la precede una negación, ni. 2. O, alias, por otro nombre. *I could not see either justice or reason in it,* No pude ver en ello ni justicia ni razón. *Either . . . or,* O . . . o, ya . . . ya; sea . . . sea; ni . . . ni. *Either by land or water,* O por tierra o por agua. *Either misery or opulence,* O pobreza u opulencia. *He must either fall or fly,* O ha de perecer o ha de huir.—*adv.* Antes. *Or ever,* Antes de todo.

Or, *s.* (Her.) Color de oro. (Fr. < lat. *aurum,* oro.)

-or. Sufijo que sirve para formar; (1) los nombres que indican agencia, como *actor,* actor; *competitor,* competidor; (2) los comparativos de origen latino, como *junior,* menor, más joven; *major,* mayor; (3) substantivos abstractos y concretos de origen latino: *honour,* honor; *terror,* terror.

Orach [ō'-rac], *s.* (Bot.) Nombre genérico que Gerard dió a diferentes especies de cañiglo y de armuelle. *White orach,* Armuelle o armuelle hortense. *Purple orach,* Cañiglo rojo. *Wild orach,* Armuelle verdolagueño o averdolagado. *Sea orach,* Armuelle laciniado. *Stinking orach,* Cañiglo hediondo o sardinera.

Oracle [er'-a-cl], *s.* 1. Oráculo, la deidad que consultaban los gentiles y también la respuesta que daba. 2. Oráculo, el lugar donde se tributa culto a una deidad determinada, como el templo u oráculo de Apolo en Delfos. 3. Oráculo, cosa revelada y contenida en la Escritura o declarada por la Iglesia. 4. Oráculo, la persona a quien todos escuchan con respeto por su mucha sabiduría.

Oracular [o-rac'-yu-lar], §**Oraculous** [o-rac'-yu-lus], *a.* 1. Lo que revela oráculos. 2. Positivo, magistral, dogmático. 3. Obscuro, ambiguo.

Oracularly [o-rac'-yu-lus-li], *adv.* A modo de oráculo.

Oral [ō'-ral], *a.* 1. Oral, verbal, hablado, no escrito. 2. Oral, perteneciente a la boca; cercano de, o alrededor de la boca, o en ella.

Oral contraceptive [er-al con-tra-sep'-tiv], *s.* Contraceptivo bucal u oral.

Orally [ō'-ral-i], *adv.* Verbalmente, de palabra.

Orang-outang, Orang-utan [o-rang'-ū-tang], *s.* Orangután, especie de mono grande. Simia satyrus.

Orange [er'-ẹnj], *s.* 1. (Bot.) Naranjo, el árbol que produce las naranjas. 2. Naranja. *China oranges,* Naranjas chinas. 3. Color de naranja. *Seville* o *bitter orange,* Naranja amarga. *Washington* o *navel orange,* Naranja con muy pocas o ninguna semilla. Es oriunda de Bahía, en el Brasil. *Orange-blossom,* Azahar, flor del naranjo de la cual se extrae el agua de azahar; se usa mucho como adorno nupcial. *Orange-dog,* Oruga de la mariposa Papilio cresphontes, muy nociva a los naranjos en los Estados Unidos del Sur. *Orange-scale,* Insecto cóccido que se cría en el naranjo; o el Aspidiotus aurantii o el Mitilaspis citricola. *Orange-colour,* Color de naranja. *Orange-dew,* Rocío de naranja, especie de rocío que en la primavera cae de las hojas de los naranjos y limones. *Orangeman,* Orangista, miembro de una sociedad instituida en Irlanda, para oponerse a la religión católica. *Orange-musk,* Pera anaranjada, especie de pera. *Orange-peel,* Cáscara de naranja. *Orange-wife, orange-woman,* Naranjera, vendedora de naranjas.—*a.* Lo perteneciente a las naranjas; anaranjado.

Orangeade [er-ẹnj-ēd'], *s.* Naranjada, agua de naranja.

Orangery [er'-ẹnj-ri], *s.* Naranjal.

Orange-tawny, *s.* y *a.* *V.* ORANGE, 3ª acep.

Orate [ō'-rēt], *vn.* (Fest.) Pronunciar una oración en público, arengar.

Oration [o-rē'-shun], *s.* Oración, razonamiento, locución, arenga, declamación.

Orator [er'-a-tẹr], *s.* 1. Orador. 2. Suplicante en el tribunal del Canciller de Inglaterra.

†**Oratorial** [er-a-tō'-ri-al], †**Oratorious** [o-ra-tō'-ri-us], *a.* Retórico, oratorio.

Oratorian [er-a-tō'-ri-an], *s.* Sacerdote que pertenece a un oratorio. *V.* ORATORY, 3ª acep.

Oratorical [er-a-ter'-ic-al], *a.* Oratorio, retórico.

Oratorio [er-a-tō'-ri-o], *s.* 1. Oratorio, representación teatral de asuntos sagrados, con música. 2. Concierto de música seria dado en domingo.

Oratory [er'-a-to-ri], *s.* 1. Oratoria, el arte que enseña a hacer oraciones retóricas; elocuencia, ejercicio de elocuencia. 2. Oratorio, lugar destinado para retirarse a hacer oración: capilla pequeña, principalmente en las casas particulares. 3. Oratorio, congregación de personas devotas que forman una especie de monasterio y viven en comunidad.

Oratress [er'-a-tres], **Oratrix** [er'-a-trics], *sf.* (Poco us.) Oradora.

Orb [ōrb], *s.* 1. Orbe, esfera, globo, cuerpo esférico; astro. 2. Círculo, rueda. 3. (Poco us.) Período de tiempo.

Orb, *va.* Formar en, cercar o encerrar en círculo.

Orbed [ōrbd], *a.* 1. Redondo, circular; esférico; en forma de órbita. 2. Redondeado; lleno. *The orbed moon,* Luna llena. 3. Que tiene ojos; se usa en composición. *A bright-orbed maid,* Una doncella de ojos vivos.

Orbicular [ōr-bic'-yu-lar], *a.* Orbicular, redondo.

Orbit [ōr'-bit], *s.* 1. Órbita, la línea que describe un planeta en su movimiento de traslación. 2. Órbita, la cuenca del ojo.

Orbit [ōr'-bit], *vn.* Describir órbitas.

Orbital [ōr'-bit-al], *a.* Orbital, referente a una órbita en todas sus acepciones; orbitario, que se refiere a la órbita del ojo.

Orc [ōrc], *s.* Orca, orco, especie de cetáceo.

Orcanet [ōr'-ca-net], *s.* (Bot.) Ancusa tintórea, palomilla de tinte, una planta. *V.* ALKANET.

Orchard [ōr'-chard], *s.* Huerto, huerta, colección o plantío de árboles frutales; verjel. (< A.-S. orcerd.)

Orchardist [ōr'-chạrd-ist], *s.* Hortelano, cultivador de árboles frutales.

Orchesis [ōr'-ke-sis], *s.* Orquesis.

Orchestra [ōr'-kes-tra], *s.* 1. Orquesta, el conjunto de músicos que tocan en los teatros o conciertos y también el lugar que en ellos les está destinado. En la orquesta predominan los instrumentos de cuerda. 2. En los teatros griegos y romanos, espacio semicircular, reservado en los griegos para el coro, y en los romanos para los asientos de los senadores y otros personajes.

Orchestral [ōr'-kes-tral u ōr-kes'-tral], *a.* De orquesta, perteneciente a la orquesta: compuesto para, o ejecutado por una orquesta.

Orchestra seat [ōr'-kes-tra sīt], *s.* (Teat.) Luneta.

Orchestration [er-kes-trē'-shun], *s.* (Mús.) Orquestación.

Orchid [ōr'-kid], *s.* Una planta cualquiera de la familia de las orquídeas; nombre genérico.

Orchidaceous [ōr-ki-dē'-shus], *a.* Orquídeo, relativo o semejante a las plantas orquídeas.

Orchil [ōr'-kil], *s.* (Bot.) Orchilla de Canarias. *V.* ARCHIL.

Orchis [ōr'-kis], *s.* (Bot.) 1. Órquide, planta monocotiledónea del Antiguo Mundo. 2. Cada una de las plantas del género Orchis; e inexactamente cualquier planta orquídea *V.* ORCHID. Satirión abejera o hierba de la abejera. *Monkey orchis,* Órquide trefosanto. *Lizard orchis,* Órquide chotuno. *Frog orchis,* Órquide verde. *Green-man orchis,* Abejera antropófora. *Bee orchis,* Abejera abejeña. *Drone orchis,* Abejera zanganera. *Bog orchis,* Abejera paludosa. *Late-spider orchis,* Abejera arañerada.

Orchotomy [ōr'-cot'-o-mi], *s.* (Cir.) Orcotomía, la amputación de los testículos.

Orcin, Orcine [ōr'-sin], *s.* Orcina, compuesto incoloro y cristalizable $(C_7H_8O_2)$, que se obtiene de ciertos líquenes y del áloe.

†**Ord** [ōrd], *s.* 1. Filo, corte. 2. Principio (anticuado).

Ordain [ōr-dēn'], *va.* 1. Ordenar, mandar, prescribir; decretar, establecer, instituir. 2. Ordenar, conferir las órdenes sagradas a alguno.

Ordainability [ōr-dēn-a-bil'-i-ti], *s.* La calidad de lo que puede ser ordenado o arreglado para que llene un objeto.

Ordainable [ōr-dēn'-a-bl], *a.* Que es capaz de ser ordenado o decretado.

Ordainer [ōr-dēn'-ẹr], *s.* Ordenador.

Ordeal [ōr'-dẹ-al], *s.* 1. Prueba rigurosa del valor de una persona, de su paciencia, conciencia, etc.; experiencia penosa, o una serie de ellas. 2. Ordalía, prueba que se hacía en tiempos antiguos de la inocencia de alguna persona, haciendo uso del fuego, del agua hirviendo, del veneno o de la lucha.

Order [ōr'-dẹr], *s.* 1. Orden, regla, método, arreglo. 2. Orden, mandato. 3. Orden, serie, clase, estado. 4. Medida, medio que se toma para conseguir alguna cosa. 5. (Com.) Pedido, encargo de una partida de mercancías; comisión de surtir, comprar o vender una cosa. 6. Orden, en botánica la subdivisión de una clase. 7. Uso establecido, procedimiento regular; el estado existente de las cosas. 8. Orden, condecoración honorífica. 9. Orden o posición social. 10. Instituto religioso; rito, sacramento; orden. 11. Orden de arquitectura. 12. *Orders, pl.* La jerarquía eclesiástica; el oficio de clérigo. *To confer holy orders,* Ordenar, conferir a alguno las órdenes sagradas. *To put out of order,* Poner en confusión, desordenar, descomponer. *In order to,* Para, a fin de, con intención de, para que. *In order to do it,* Para hacerlo, con el fin o con el objeto de hacerlo, a fin de hacerlo. *Out of order,* En mal estado, descompuesto, que anda o funcion mal. *To be out of order,* Descomponerse, desarreglarse una cosa; no atenerse a los reglamentos, no tener derecho a hablar en una reunión o asamblea. *The order of the day,* La orden del día. *Till further orders,* Hasta nueva orden. *Order-book,* Libro de pedidos. *To give an order,* Hacer un pedido. *Sailing orders,* Últimas instrucciones dadas al capitán de un buque. *Lower orders,* Las clases bajas. *Higher orders,* Las clases altas o elevadas. *Order of the Garter,* La orden de la Jarretera. *In holy orders,* Revestido de funciones sacerdotales.

Order, *va.* 1. Ordenar, poner en orden, disponer, arreglar, dar método u orden a alguna cosa. 2. Ordenar, mandar. 3. Ordenar, conferir las órdenes sagradas. 4. Ordenar, encaminar y dirigir a algún fin. 5. (Com.) Mandar, pedir, mandarse hacer. *To order one's life,* Arreglar su vida. *To order a bill of goods,* Pedir una factura de géneros. *To order arms,* (Mil.) Poner el fusil perpendicularmente contra el lado derecho, descansando la culata en el suelo. *To order away,* Despedir a uno, decirle que se vaya. *To order in,* Mandar entrar, mandar traer. *To order out,* Mandar salir; mandar llevar; poner de patitas en la calle.

Orderer [ōr'-dẹr-ẹr], *s.* Ordenador.

Ordering [ōr'-dẹr-ing], *s.* Manejo, dirección, disposición.

Orderless [ōr'-dẹr-les], *a.* Desordenado, confuso, sin orden; irregular.

Orderliness [ōr'-dẹr-li-nes], *s.* Regularidad, orden, método, buena dirección o buena conducta.

Orderly [ōr-dẹr-li], *a.* 1. Ordenado, metódico, regular. 2. Bien arreglado, quieto, tranquilo. *Orderly,* (1) (Mil.) Asistente, ordenanza, el soldado que se halla al servicio inmediato de un superior. (2) Practicante, asistente en un hospital.—*adv.* Ordenadamente, regularmente, metódicamente, en orden.

Orders [ōr'-dẹrz] o **Holy Orders,** *s. pl.* *V.* ORDER (12ª acep.).

Ordinal [ōr'-di-nal], *a.* 1. Ordinal, lo

que señala el orden de las cosas. 2. Perteneciente a un orden de animales o plantas.—*s.* 1. Número ordinal, el que indica el orden en que están puestas las cosas. 2. Ritual que contiene y enseña el modo de rezar y hacer los divinos oficios.

Ordinance [ōr'-di-nans], *s.* 1. Ordenanza, ley, mandato, reglamento, estatuto. 2. Rito, ceremonia del culto. 3. (Arq.) Sistema de arreglo, disposición.

Ordinarily [ōr'-di-ne-ri-li], *adv.* Ordinariamente, regularmente.

Ordinary [ōr'-di-ne-ri], *a.* 1. Ordinario, común, usual, regular. 2. Ordenado, metódico, normal. 3. Ordinario, bajo, vulgar, mediano, de bajo nacimiento. 4. (Bajo o des.) Feo; de mala disposición; algunas veces, por contracción, *ornery.*—*s.* 1. Ordinario, juez eclesiástico; juez (civil) que tiene autoridad para tomar conocimiento de las causas por derecho propio y no por delegación. 2. Fonda a precio fijo; mesa redonda. 3. (Her.) Figura ordinaria del escudo. 4. Capellán. *In ordinary,* (1) En actual servicio, con ejercicio. (2) (Mar.) Puesto en lugar seguro; fuera de uso, desarmado. *Painter in ordinary to the king,* Pintor de cámara del rey. *Vessels in ordinary,* (Mar.) Buques desarmados.

Ordinate [ōr'-di-nēt], *a.* Ordenado, metódico.—*s.* (Geom.) Ordenada o aplicada, distancia entre un punto dado y el eje de abscisas.

Ordination [ōr-di-nē'-shun], *s.* 1. Ordenación, disposición. 2. Ordenación, el acto de conferir orden sacerdotal.

Ordnance [ōrd'-nans], *s.* Nombre genérico de todas las armas de guerra; en especial, artillería, cañones. *The master general of the ordnance,* El director general de artillería. *Ordnance supplies* u *ordnance stores,* Todas las armas de guerra, con las municiones y el conjunto de los equipos militares.

Ordonnance [ōr'-den-ans], *s.* 1. La disposición de las figuras y demás piezas de que se compone una pintura. 2. Ley, ordenanza, estatuto.

Ordure [ōrd'-yūr u ōr'-jur], *s.* Basura, porquería, excremento.

Ore [ōr], *s.* Quijo, ganga, mineral, el metal conforme se saca de la mina.

Oread [ō'-re-ad], *s.* Oréade, ninfa de los bosques.

Oregonian [er-e-gō'-ni-an], *a.* Oregoniano, perteneciente a Oregón, uno de los estados de la Unión norteamericana.

Oreweed [ōr'-wīd], **Orewood** [ōr'-wud], *s.* Alga; las plantas arrojadas a la playa por las olas.

†**Orfrays** [ōr'-frēz], *s.* *V.* ORPHREY.

Orgal [ōr'-gal], *s.* Las heces secas de vino. *V.* ARGAL.

Organ [ōr'-gan], *s.* 1. Órgano, cualquiera de las partes constitutivas del animal o vegetal que ejercen alguna función. 2. Órgano, instrumento músico de viento, compuesto de varios cañones, de un teclado con registros, y fuelles que comunican el aire. 3. Sistema de cañones de un órgano que tiene su propio teclado. 4. Instrumento músico que se parece en algo a un órgano; organillo de cilindro. *The ear is the organ of hearing,* La oreja es el órgano del oído. *Great organ,* Gran órgano. *Organ-grinder,* El que toca un organillo.

Organ-builder [ōr-gan-bil'-der], *s.* Organero.

Organdy [ōr'-gan-di], *s.* Organdí, especie de muselina muy fina, a menudo con dibujos.

Organic, Organical [ōr-gan'-ic, al], *a.* 1. Orgánico, relativo a un órgano u órganos; de la naturaleza de seres vivientes; que sirve para el mismo objeto que un órgano. 2. (Quím.) Que contiene carbono como parte constitutiva esencial. 3. Organizado, que se compone de órganos; sistematizado. 4. Constitutivo, fundamental. *Organic remains,* Restos orgánicos. *Organic chemistry,* Química orgánica. *Organic laws,* Leyes orgánicas, fundamentales.

Organically [ōr-gan'-ic-al-i], *adv.* Orgánicamente.

Organicalness [ōr-gan'-ic-al-nes], *s.* El estado de lo que es orgánico.

Organism [ōr'-gan-izm], *s.* 1. Organismo, un ser organizado o viviente; un animal o una planta. 2. Estructura orgánica; también, un órgano cualquiera. 3. Organismo, cualquier cosa análoga al organismo físico.

Organist [ōr'-gan-ist], *s.* Organista, el que toca el órgano.

Organization [ōr-gan-i-zē'-shun], *s.* 1. Organización, la acción de organizar, o el estado de un cuerpo organizado. 2. Lo que está organizado: (1) un organismo animal o vegetal; (2) sociedad, unión de varias personas para un mismo fin. 3. Cualquier combinación o correspondencia de partes o de fuerzas.

Organize [ōr'-gan-aiz], *va.* 1. Organizar, poner en correspondencia las diversas partes de un todo; disponer, arreglar de tal manera que una parte pueda cooperar con otra. 2. Prepararse una asamblea deliberante para empezar sus trabajos, eligiendo la mesa, los que han de dirigirla. 3. (Biol.) Organizar, proveer de órganos.—*vn.* Organizarse, unirse en compañía o sociedad.

Organ-loft [ōr'-gan-lōft], *s.* Tribuna para el órgano, sitio donde se coloca el órgano.

Organ-pipe [ōr'-gan-paip], *s.* Cañón o tubo de órgano.

Organography [ōr-gan-eg'-ra-fi], *s.* (Biol.) Organografía, la descripción científica de los órganos de un ser viviente.

Organology [ōr-gan-el'-o-ji], *s.* Organología, parte de la biología que trata de los órganos del cuerpo.

Organzine, Organzin [ōr'-gan-zīn o zin], *s.* 1. Hilo de seda hecho con varios otros hilos torcidos. 2. Tela que se hace con ese hilo.

Orgasm [ōr'-gazm], *s.* 1. Excitación excesiva o conducta inmoderada. 2. (Med.) Orgasmo, tensión violenta y pasajera del tejido eréctil (particularmente en el coito).

Orgeat [ōr'-zhat], *s.* Jarabe de horchata, que se hace con almendras, agua de azahar y azúcar.

Orgies [ōr'-jiz], *s. pl.* Orgías, fiestas bacanales.—*sing.* **Orgy,** Orgía.

Orichalch [er'-e-calc], **Orichalcum** [er-e-cal'-cum], *s.* Latón, antiguamente oricalco.

Oriel [ō'-ri-el], *s.* 1. Ventana circular. 2. Alcoba cerca de la sala principal.

Orient [ō'-ri-ent], *a.* 1. Naciente como el sol. 2. Oriental. 3. Brillante, resplandeciente.—*s.* Oriente, Este.

Orient, *va.* 1. Orientar, determinar la posición de una cosa con respecto al este. 2. Colocar algo de tal manera que el frente mire al este.

Oriental [ō-ri-en'-tal], *a.* Oriental, que pertenece al oriente.—*s.* Oriental: habitante de Asia.

Orientalism [ō-ri-en'-tal-izm], *s.* Estilo oriental, orientalismo.

Orientalist [ō-ri-en'-tal-ist], *s.* 1. Habitador o natural del oriente. 2. El que sabe las lenguas orientales.

Orientalize [ō-ri-en'-tal-aiz], *va.* Orientalizar, conformar a las costumbres y al carácter del oriente.

Orientate [ō''-ri-en'-tēt], *va.* 1. Orientar, colocar de modo que el frente esté hacia el este. 2. Colocar un cristal en posición tal que presente simetría.—*vn.* Caer, mirar, hacia el este.

Orientation [ō-ri-en-tē'-shun], *s.* 1. Orientación, dirección al este; construcción con referencia al este, como en el caso del altar de una iglesia. 2. Colocación con relación a los puntos cardinales. 3. Cualquier procedimiento de agrimensura para determinar la dirección. 4. (Zool.) El instinto de dirigirse hacia el lugar nativo, como lo hacen las palomas.

Orifice [er'-i-fis], *s.* Orificio, boca de alguna cosa; abertura de un conducto.

Oriflamme [er'-i-flam], *s.* 1. Oriflama, antiguo estandarte de los reyes de Francia. 2. Cualquier pabellón real o símbolo glorioso.

Origan [er'-i-gan], **Origanum** [o-rig'-a-num], *s.* (Bot.) Orégano, mejorana silvestre, planta labiada.

Origin [er'-i-jin], *s.* 1. Origen, primera existencia. 2. Origen, principio, manantial, causa moral, nacimiento de alguna cosa. 3. Origen, ascendencia, familia.

Original, *a.* Original, primitivo, primero.—*s.* 1. Original, prototipo o primera forma de alguna cosa; primer escrito, composición o invención que se hace de una cosa para que de ella se saquen las demás. 2. Original, el idioma en que un documento o libro se escribió primeramente. 3. Persona de carácter o índole como no hay otros.

Originality [o-rij-i-nal'-i-ti], *s.* Originalidad; facultad de inventar.

Originally [o-rij'-i-nal-i], *adv.* Originalmente, originariamente.

¿**Originary** [o-rij'-i-ne-ri], *a.* Productivo; originario, primitivo.

Originate [o-rij'-i-net], *va.* Originar, causar, inventar, ser principio y origen de alguna cosa.—*vn.* Originarse, traer su origen, emanar de.

Origination [o-rij-i-nē'-shun], *s.* 1. Origen, primera producción de alguna cosa. 2. Modo de propagar o de producir.

Orillon [o-ril'-en], *s.* (Fort.) Orejón, obra que se hace sobre el tercio del flanco del baluarte, al lado del ángulo de la espalda.

Oriole [ō'-ri-ōl], *s.* 1. Oriol, oropéndola. Oriolus galbula. 2. Pájaro de América, de varias especies, cuyos colores son principalmente negro y amarillo o anaranjado. *Baltimore oriole,* La oropéndola americana; se llama así, porque los colores del macho, anaranjado y negro, fueron los de las armas de Lord Baltimore.

Orion [o-rai'-en], *s.* (Astr.) Orión, constelación notable por sus tres brillantes estrellas en línea recta y por su nebulosa, perceptible a la simple vista.

Orison [er'-i-zun o sen], *s.* Oración, petición, súplica devota. (Fr.)

Orle [erl], *s.* 1. (Arq.) Orla, filete o listón. 2. (Her.) Orla, alrededor del escudo.

Orlon [er'-len], *s.* Orlón (*marca de fábrica*); fibra de Poliestireno.

Orlop [ōr'-lep], *s.* (Mar.) Sollado o entarimado de una embarcación. *Orlop-beam*, (Mar.) Bao vacío o bao del sollado.

Ormolu [ōr'-mo-lū], *s.* 1. Aleación de cobre, cinc y estaño. 2. Oro molido, para dorar bronce. 3. Mercadería metálica, dorada o bronceada. (< Fr.)

Ornament [ōr'-na-ment], *s.* 1. Ornamento, adorno, ornato, compostura o atavío de alguna cosa. 2. Ornamento, las prendas que recomiendan a una persona. 3. Decoración, señal de distinción.

Ornament, *va.* Ornamentar, adornar; embellecer.

Ornamental [ōr-na-men'-tal], *a.* Que sirve de adorno; de la naturaleza de adorno.

Ornamentally [ōr-na-men'-tal-i], *adv.* Ornadamente.

Ornamentation [ōr-na-men-tē'-shun], *s.* Ornamentación, acto de adornar, o calidad de adornado; manera de disponer los adornos; conjunto de cosas que sirven de adorno.

Ornamented [ōr'-na-ment-ed], **Ornate** [ōr'-nēt], *a.* Ornado, ornamentado, adornado, ataviado.

Ornateness [er'-nēt-nes], *s.* Ornato, ornamento, adorno, atavío, aparato.

Ornithological [er-ni-tho-lej'-i-cal], *a.* Ornitológico, concerniente a la ornitología.

Ornithologist [ōr-ni-thel'-o-jist], *s.* Ornitólogo, el que se dedica al estudio y conocimiento de las aves.

Ornithology [ōr-ni-thel'-o-ji], *s.* Ornitología, la parte de la zoología que trata de las aves.

Ornithomancy [er-nith'-o-man-si], *s.* Ornitomancia, adivinación por medio de las aves.

Orographic [er-o-graf'-ic], *a.* Orográfico, perteneciente a la orografía.

Orography [er-eg'-ra-fi], *s.* Orografía, descripción del desarrollo y relaciones de las montañas.

Oroide [ō'-ro-aid], *s.* Oroide, aleación de cobre, cinc, estaño y otros metales que tiene apariencia de oro.

Orology [o-rel'-o-ji], *s.* Orología, el estudio y conocimiento de las montañas; tratado sobre ellas.

Orphan [ōr'-fan], *s.* Huérfano, hijo o hija que carece de padre o madre ó de ambos.—*a.* Huérfano, destituido de padres, niño desamparado.

Orphan [ōr'-fan], *va.* Privar a uno de sus padres. *Orphaned*, *pp.* Huérfano; sin padres.

Orphanage [ōr'-fan-ēj], *s.* 1. Orfandad; los huérfanos colectivamente. 2. Asilo para huérfanos.

Orphanhood [ōr'-fan-hud], *s.* Orfandad.

Orphean [ōr-fī'-an u ōr'-fī-an], *a.* Lo que pertenece a Orfeo; poético o músico.

Orphic [ōr'-fic], *a.* Órfico, relativo a Orfeo; se aplica particularmente a una hermandad mística de Atenas, del siglo sexto antes de J. C.

Orpiment [ōr'-pi-ment], *s.* Oropimente, sulfuro amarillo de arsénico (As_2S_3).

Orpine [ōr'-pin], *s.* 1. (Bot.) Telefio, fabacrasa. *V.* STONECROP. 2. Color de pintura, rojo o amarillo.

Orrery [er'-er-i], *s.* Planetario, instrumento que con muchos movimientos representa las revoluciones de los cuerpos celestes.

Orris [er'-is], *s.* 1. (Bot.) Lirio de Florencia, cualquier especie del género Iris que tiene raíz perfumada. Corrupción de *Iris*. *Orris-root*, Raíz de lirio o iris florentina. 2. Bocadillo y galón; y (des.) especie de encaje de oro y plata.

Orthochromatic [ōr-tho-cro-mat'-ic], *a.* Ortocromático, que representa, en la fotografía, los colores en sus verdaderas relaciones, y difiere en esto del procedimiento común, en el que el azul tira al blanco y el amarillo al negro.

Orthodontist [ōr-tho-den'-tist], *s.* Ortodóntico.

Orthodox [ōr'-tho-decs], *a.* 1. Ortodoxo, libre de herejía. 2. Perteneciente a la Iglesia Griega. 3. Aprobado; recibido; convencional.

Orthodoxy [ōr'-tho-dec-si], *s.* Ortodoxia, sana doctrina, pureza de doctrina, conformidad con la fe o doctrina predominante; en especial, doctrina trinitaria.

Orthodromics [ōr-tho-drem'-ics], **Orthodromy** [er'-tho-dro-mi], *s.* (Mar.) Ortodromía, navegación en línea recta, en contraposición a la loxodromía.

Orthoepic, **Orthoepical** [ōr-tho-ep'-ic, al], *a.* Ortológico, perteneciente a la ortología, propio de ella.

Orthoepist [ōr'-tho-ep''-ist], *s.* Ortólogo, el que es versado en el arte de pronunciar correctamente.

Orthoepy [ōr'-tho-ep-i], *s.* Ortología, el arte de pronunciar bien.

Orthogon [ōr'-tho-gen], *s.* Ortogonio, figura rectangular.

Orthogonal [ōr-theg'-o-nal], *a.* Rectángulo.

Orthographer [ōr-theg'-ra-fer], *s.* Ortógrafo, el que sigue las reglas de la ortografía.

Orthographic, **Orthographical** [ōr-tho-graf'-ic, al], *a.* Ortográfico, que pertenece a la ortografía.

Orthographically [ōr-tho-graf'-i-cal-i], *adv.* Ortográficamente.

Orthographist [ōr-theg'-ra-fist], *s.* Ortógrafo, autor que trata de la ortografía.

Orthography [ōr-theg'-ra-fi], *s.* Ortografía, la parte de la gramática que enseña cómo se ha de escribir correctamente.

Orthology [ōr-thel'-o-ji], *s.* (Ant.) Ortología, descripción verdadera de las cosas.

Orthometry [ōr-them'-e-tri], *s.* Ortometría, leyes o reglas para componer versos.

Orthopedia, **Orthopædia**, **Orthopedy** [ōr-tho-pī'-di a, ōr'-tho-pī''-di], *s.* Ortopedia, el arte de corregir las deformidades del cuerpo, principalmente en los niños.

Orthopedic, **Orthopædic** [ōr-tho-pī'-dic], *a.* Ortopédico.

Orthopedist [er-tho-pī'-dist], *s.* Ortopedista.

Orthopnœa [ōr-thep-nī'-a], *s.* (Med.) Ortopnea, opresión de pecho que impide la respiración a no ser que el enfermo esté en pie.

Orthoptera [ōr-thep'-te-ra], *s. pl.* Ortópteros, orden de insectos mascadores, con un par de alas membranosas plegadas longitudinalmente y con antenas de más de once artejos. Comprende las langostas, grillos, cucarachas, tijeretas, etc.

Orthopterous [ōr-thep'-ter-us], *a.* Ortóptero, relativo a los ortópteros; cuyas alas anteriores están plegadas a lo largo.

Orcive [ōr'-tiv], *a.* (Astr.) Ortivo, que equivale a oriental.

Ortolan [ōr'-to-lan], *s.* (Orn.) Hortelano; verderol de los cañaverales, emberiza. Emberiza hortulana. También *V.* BOBOLINK.

Orvietan [ōr-vi-ī'-tan], *s.* (Ant.) Supuesto antídoto contra veneno.

Oryx [er'-ix u ō'-rix], *s.* (Zool.) Órix, antílope abisinio.

Osage Orange [ō'-sēj er'-enj], *s.* Árbol americano de las urticáceas, con fruto parecido a la naranja. Este árbol se emplea mucho para formar setos, y es originario de las Montañas Osage, en Arkansas. Maclura aurantiaca.

Oscillate [es'-il-ēt], *va.* Hacer oscilar.—*vn.* Oscilar, vibrar; moverse alternativamente en dos sentidos contrarios.

Oscillation [es'-il-ē-shun], *s.* Oscilación, vibración, balanceo.

Oscillatory [es'-il-a-to-ri], *a.* Oscilatorio, oscilante.

Oscitancy [os'-it-an-si], *s.* (Ant.) 1. Bostezo. 2. Descuido, negligencia.

Oscitant [es'-i-tant], *a.* (Ant.) Bostezante, soñoliento; pesado, negligente.

Oscitate [es'-i-tēt], *vn.* (Ant.) Bostezar.

Osculant [es'-kiu-lant], *a.* 1. En biología, de carácter intermedio entre dos grupos. 2. Que se adhiere fuertemente; que se aferra, como ciertas orugas.

Osculation [es-kiu-lē'-shun], *s.* 1. Beso, el acto de besar; ósculo. 2. (Geom.) Osculación.

Osculatory [ōs'-kiu-la-to-ri], *a.* 1. Relativo a la acción de besar. 2. Osculatorio, perteneciente a la osculación.

Osier [ō'-zher], *s.* (Bot.) Mimbrera, el arbusto cuyas ramas tiernas cortadas se usan como mimbres. *Common osier*, Sauce mimbrero o mimbrera propiamente dicha. *Golden osier*, Sauce vitelino, mimbrera ama.

Osmazome [es'-ma-zōm], *s.* Osmazoma u osmazomo, substancia contenida en la carne que da olor y sabor a los caldos.

Osmic [es'-mic u ez'-mic], *a.* Ósmico, perteneciente al osmio o que lo contiene. *Osmic acid*, Ácido ósmico, un óxido de osmio (OsO_4) de propiedades venenosas; es incoloro y volátil.

Osmium [ez'-mi-um], *s.* (Min.) Osmio, un metal que se halla mezclado con el platino y el iridio.

Osmose [ez'-mōs u es'-mōs], **Osmosis** [es-mō'-sis], *s.* Osmosis, el acto de mezclarse, o la tendencia a mezclarse, de dos líquidos o gases, pasando al través de una membrana separadora o de un tabique poroso.

Osmotic [es-met'-ic], *a.* Osmótico, que se refiere a la osmosis.

Osprey [es'-prē], *s.* (Orn.) Águila marina, halieto, osífraga. Pandion haliaetus.

Osseous [es'-e-us], *a.* Huesoso, óseo, ososo.

Ossicle [es'-i-cl], *s.* Huesecillo, hueso pequeño.

Ossiferous [es-if'-ẹr-us], *a.* Osífero, que contiene huesos.
Ossific [es-if'-ic], *a.* Osífico, que convierte en hueso o que forma hueso.
Ossification [eṣ-i-fi-kê'-shun], *s.* Osificación, la conversión insensible de las partes ternillosas en hueso.
Ossified [es'-i-faid], *a.* Osificado.
Ossifrage [es'-i-frêj], *s.* (Orn.) Osífraga, quebrantahuesos.
Ossify [es'-i-fai], *va.* Osificar, convertir en hueso.
Ossivorous [es-iv'-ẹr-us], *a.* Osívoro, que come huesos; o que destruye los huesos atacando su substancia, como ciertos tumores.
Ossuary [es'-yu-ẹ-ri], *s.* Osario, osar.
Ostensible [es-ten'-si-bl], *a.* 1. Profesado u ofrecido como verdadero; aparente, disfrazado. 2. (Poco us.) Ostensible, manifestable. *Ostensible purpose,* Designio aparente, que puede ser verdadero o fingido.
Ostensibly [es-ten'-si-bli], *adv.* Ostensiblemente; aparentemente.
Ostensive [es-ten'-siv], *a.* Ostensivo, que muestra.
Ostentation [es-ten-tê'-shun], *s.* Ostentación, gala, jactancia, fausto.
Ostentatious [es-ten-tê'-shus], *a.* Ostentador, lleno de ostentación, ostentoso, jactancioso, vanaglorioso, fastuoso.
Ostentatiously [es-ten-tê'-shus-li], *adv.* Pomposamente.
Ostentatiousness [es-ten-tê'-shus-nes], *s.* Ostentación, vanidad, vanagloria, jactancia.
Osteocolla [es-tẹ-o-col'-a], *s.* Osteocola, cal carbonatada, incrustante, que se deposita sobre los vegetales.
Osteocope [es'-tẹ-o-cōp], *s.* Dolor osteócopo o dolor fijo y muy violento en los huesos.
Osteocopic [es-tẹ-o-cep'-ic], *a.* (Med.) Osteócopo.
Osteography [es-tẹ-eg'-ra-fi], *s.* Osteografía, descripción de los huesos.
Osteologist [es-tẹ-el'-o-jist], *s.* Osteólogo, el que sabe o profesa la osteología.
Osteology [es-tẹ-el'-o-ji], *s.* Osteología, la parte de la anatomía que trata de los huesos.
Osteopathy [es-tẹ-ō'-path-i], *s.* (Med.) Osteopatía.
Ostiary [es'-ti-ẹ-ri], *s.* 1. Ostiario, el que tiene uno de los grados eclesiásticos así llamado. 2. (Poco us.) Ostial, la boca de un río o canal, o el sitio de su desembocadura.
Ostler [es'-lẹr], *s.* *V.* HOSTLER.
Ostmen [ōst'-men], *s. pl.* Los primitivos colonos daneses establecidos en Irlanda; significa hombres del este.
Ostosis [es-tō'-sis], *s.* Una formación de hueso; osificación.
Ostracean [es-trê'-sẹ-an], *a.* Ostráceo, referente a la ostra.—*s.* Ostra.
Ostraceous [es-trê'-shus], *a.* Ostráceo, perteneciente a las ostras.
Ostracism [es'-tra-sizm], *s.* 1. Exclusión del trato o favor, p. ej. en sociedad o en la política; expulsión. 2. Ostracismo, destierro político entre los griegos.
Ostracite [es'-tra-sait], *s.* Ostracita, concha de ostra petrificada o parecida a ella.
Ostracize [es'-tra-saiz], *va.* Desterrar por voto del pueblo.
Ostrich [es'-trich], *s.* (Orn.) Avestruz, la mayor de las aves existentes; habita en África y Arabia. *Ostrich plume, feather,* Pluma de avestruz.
Ostrogoth [es'-tro-geth], *s.* Ostrogodo, pueblo bárbaro proveniente de la Escandinavia que se estableció en Italia en el siglo V; Godo del Este. *Cf.* VISIGOTH.
Otacoustic [ō-ta-cūs'-tic], *a.* Otacústico, propio para perfeccionar el sentido del oído.—*s.* Trompetilla, instrumento a modo de trompeta para ayudar al sentido del oído.
Otalgia [o-tal'-ji-a], *s.* Otalgia, dolor de oído.
Other [udh'-ẹr], *pron.* 1. Otro, la persona o cosa diferente o distinta de aquella de que se habla. 2. El segundo de dos; el opuesto. *This book or the other,* Este libro u otro. *Every other day,* Un día sí y otro no; cada dos días. *On the other side,* Del otro lado.—*s.* Otra persona o cosa. *Others, pl.* Los otros, los demás.—*a.* 1. Otro, diferente, no el mismo. 2. Adicional, además de. 3. Segundo; opuesto, contrario. *The other side,* El otro lado, el partido opuesto. *The other day,* El otro día; poco ha, recientemente.
Otherwise [udh'-ẹr-waiz], *adv.* De otra manera, de otro modo, por otra parte.—*a.* Otro, diferente.
Otic [ō'-tic], *a.* Ótico, que se refiere a la oreja, o que está situado cerca de la oreja.
Otiose [ō'-shi-ōs], *a.* Ocioso, que está en reposo; también perezoso, holgazán.
Otolith [ō'-to-lith], *s.* Otolito, concreción calcárea que se encuentra en el oído interno de animales vertebrados e invertebrados.
Otologist [o-tel'-o-jist], *s.* Otólogo, el que es versado en otología; aurista.
Otology [ō-tel'-o-ji], *s.* (Med.) Otología, la ciencia que trata del oído y sus enfermedades.
Otorrhea, Otorrhœa [ō-ter-ri'-a], *s.* Otorrea, flujo por el oído.
Ottar [et'-ar], **Otto** [et'-ō], *s.* Aceite esencial. *Ottar of roses,* Aceite esencial de rosas. *V.* ATTAR.
Otter [et'-ẹr], *s.* 1. Nutra o nutria, mamífero carnicero y anfibio. *Otter-skin,* Piel de nutria. 2. Nutria de mar. 3. Oruga de una mariposa nocturna, la Epialus humuli, que ataca los lúpulos.
Otter-hunting [et'-ẹr-hunt-ing], *s.* Caza de nutrias.
Otter-pike [et'-ẹr-paic], *s.* (Ict.) Dragón marino.
Ottoman [et'-o-man], *a.* Otomano, nombre que se da al imperio de los turcos.—*s.* 1. Otomano, turco. 2. Escaño con cojín y sin respaldo. 3. Escabel movible cubierto con alfombra.
Ouch [auch], *s.* 1. Engaste de una piedra preciosa. 2. Adorno de oro, particularmente un broche o corchete. (En vez de *nouch.*)
Ouch, *inter.* ¡Huy! interjección que indica un dolor ligero.
Ought [ēt], *s.* y *adv.* Algo, alguna cosa. *For ought I know,* Por lo que yo puedo comprender; en cuanto yo alcanzo o sé. Con más propiedad se escribe *aught.* *V.* AUGHT.
Ought, *s.* Nada; corrupción de *naught.*
Ought [ēt], *v. def.* y *auxiliar.* 1. Deber, tener la obligación moral de satisfacer alguna cosa. 2. Ser menester, necesario; convenir, ser conveniente. *You ought to remember that,* Vd. debe acordarse de eso. *It ought to be so,* Conviene que así sea, o así debe ser. *I ought to,* Es menester que yo; debo, debía, deberé. *You ought to have come sooner,* Vd. hubiera debido venir antes.—*Ought* tiene más fuerza que *should.*
Ounce [auns], *s.* 1. Onza, la décimasexta parte de una libra común (= 28.35 gramos) o de la libra *troy* (= 31.1 gramos). 2. Onza, mamífero carnicero de la India y Persia. 3. Otro felino semejante de América, como el jaguar. 4. Onza, moneda de oro española de valor de 320 reales vellón o $16; pertenece a la primitiva historia del oro en California.
-our. Sufijo, lo mismo que *-or.*
Our, Ours [aur], *a.* y *pron. poss.* Nuestro, lo que a nosotros pertenece. *Our parents,* Nuestros padres. *Our country,* Nuestro país. *Our church,* Nuestra iglesia. *Your house is larger than ours,* La casa de Vd. es mayor que la nuestra. *This is ours,* Esto es nuestro o de nosotros.
Ouranography [ū-ran-eg'-ra-fi], *s.* Uranografía, descripción de los cielos.
Ourself [aur-self'], *pron.* Yo mismo, yo misma; se usa solamente en el estilo oficial o regio.
Ourselves [aur-selvz'], *pron. recip.* Nosotros mismos.
-ous [us]. Sufijo que corresponde a las desinencias castellanas oso, osa, uoso, uosa, y a veces a otras que indican la presencia de una cualidad en cualquier grado. También indica el compuesto químico del grado inferior al que termina en -ic.
Ousel [ū'-zl], *s.* (Orn.) Mirlo, mirla. *V.* OUZEL.
Oust [aust], *va.* Desposeer; echar fuera, despedir.
Ouster [aust'-ẹr], *s.* (For.) Desposeimiento, despojo.
Out [aut], *adv.* 1. Fuera, afuera, a la parte exterior. 2. En lo exterior, en condición de haber salido, ausente. 3. No conforme, no de moda o de uso; destituido, que no tiene ya empleo, que ha perdido el poder; en error, que no tiene razón. 4. Descubierto, que ya no está oculto; publicado, aparecido; en condición de haber perdido, faltado, de haber salido mal; extinguido, agotado, acabado; con pérdida (de tanto). 5. De una manera libre, abierta, franca; completamente, enteramente. 6. Libre de algo que obstruye, molesta o sirve de obstáculo. 7. Hasta el cabo, de cabo a cabo; hasta la extinción o el agotamiento; hasta obtener buen éxito. 8. En alta voz, distintamente, de un modo claro. *Throw it out,* Échelo Vd. afuera. *To go out,* Salir, partir, marcharse. *He is out,* Está fuera de casa. *Out at the elbows,* Agujereado, roto por los codos. *Out at the heels,* Con zapatos rotos. *To set out,* (1) Partir; (2) plantar, introducir en la tierra. *V.* SET. *A way out,* Salida, lugar por donde se sale. *The story is out,* Se acabó, se concluyó el cuento. *The book has just come out,* El libro acaba de publicarse. *To be out at interest,* Estar puesto a interés. *He was out one hundred francs,* Perdió cien francos. *The soup was out,* Se había acabado la sopa. *The time is out,* El tiempo ha pasado; el plazo ha expirado. *To be out,* Estar fuera de su propio lugar o ausente; no estar en casa; no estar de moda o en boga; verse despedido de un cargo o empleo; sin poder jugar en ciertos juegos, por haber perdido; cortarse, quedarse cortado; haber perdido una suma de

dineró; estar apagado, apagarse; acabar de publicarse, etc. *Out of,* (1) Fuera de. (2) Más allá, además de; de; en, sobre. (3) Sin. (4) Por (indicando la causa). *Out of sight,* (1) Fuera del alcance de la vista; (2) (Germ. E. U.) de calidad superior, muy excelente, notable. *Out of breath,* Sin aliento. *Out of character,* Impropio, fuera de carácter, no conveniente o poco á propósito. *To copy out of an author,* Copiar de un autor. *Out of sorts,* (1) Indispuesto, no muy bien de salud. (2) Descontento, poco satisfecho. (3) (Impr.) Falto de ejemplares suficientes de un tipo o letra. *Out of the woods,* Fuera del vado, libre de dudas y dificultades; seguro.—En numerosos verbos compuestos, *out* añade el sentido de ir más allá, de sobrepujar o exceder. *Out of danger,* En salvo, fuera de peligro. *Out of doubt,* Indudable. *Let him out,* Déjele Vd. salir. *Out of place,* Desacomodado. *Out of fashion,* No usado, desusado. *Time out of mind,* Tiempo inmemorial. *To be out of patience,* Perder la paciencia. *He is much out in this point,* Está muy equivocado acerca de esto. *The candle is out,* La vela está apagada. *To be out of trim,* Estar de mal humor; no tenerlas todas consigo. *Out of trim,* (Mar.) Mal estivado. *Out of tune,* Desentonado; destemplado. *To fall out with one,* Reñir con uno. *Out of hand,* Luego, al punto. *Out of friendship,* Por amistad. *Out of spite,* Por despique. *Out of pity,* Por compasión. *Out of order,* Desordenado, descompuesto; desarreglado. *To drink out of a glass,* Beber de un vaso o con un vaso. *Out of hope,* Desesperanzado, sin esperanza. *Out of humour,* De mal humor, enojado. *Out of measure,* Desmesurado. *Out of his wits,* Fuera de sí, insensato. *A book out of print,* Un libro del que no se hallan ejemplares de venta. *Out of favour,* Desvalido, desgraciado. *Pray, hear me out,* Sírvase Vd. escucharme hasta que concluya. *Speak out,* Hable Vd. cuanto tenga que decir. *It will out,* Ello dirá; allá se verá; se descubrirá. *Murder will out,* El asesinato se descubrirá. *A voyage out and home,* Viaje redondo. *Out* se usa en inglés muy frecuentemente para modificar o cambiar la significación primitiva de los verbos.—*inter.* Fuera. *Out with it,* Fuera con ello. Hable Vd. francamente, sin rodeos. *Out upon thee!* ¡Maldito seas!

Out, *s.* 1. El exterior o la parte exterior de alguna cosa; esquina, lugar exterior; también, el aspecto exterior de un asunto. 2. El que no tiene ya un empleo; en plural, los que han perdido el poder, la oposición. 3. Olvido, omisión que comete el cajista en la composición. 4. En algunos juegos, como el de *base-ball,* el efecto de echar a un jugador del lugar que ocupaba.

Out, *va.* Expeler, desposeer, despojar.

Outact [aut-act'], *va.* Propasar, pasar más adelante de lo que se debía; ir más allá.

Out-and-out [aut'-and-aut''], *a.* Cabal, entero, sin calificación; verdadero. Completamente, verdaderamente.

Outargue [aut-ār'-giū], *va.* Sobresalir en la argumentación; imponer por la razón.

Outbalance [aut-bal'-ans], *va.* Preponderar, exceder en algo.

Outbid [aut-bid'], *va.* Pujar, aumentar el precio puesto a alguna cosa que se vende o arrienda; sobrepujar.

Outbidder [aut-bid'-ẹr], *s.* Pujador, el que hace puja en lo que se vende o arrienda.

Outboard [aut'-bōrd], *a.* y *adv.* Fuera de la borda del barco.

Outbound [aut'-baund], *a.* Destinado a un viaje distante o a algún país extranjero.

Outbrag [aut'-brag], *va.* Exceder, sobrepujar en fanfarronadas.

Outbrave [aut-brēv'], *va.* 1. Exceder, ser superior en valentía o audacia. 2. Arrostrar los peligros. 3. Exceder en magnificencia o garbo.

Outbreak [aut'-brēc], *s.* Erupción; ataque violento, pasión, tumulto.

Outbreathe [aut-brīdh'], *va.* 1. Exhalar, emitir, echar el aliento. 2. Exhalar, echar de sí. 3. (Poco us.) Exceder a alguno en la carrera o en otro género de fatiga por poder sufrir la falta de aliento mejor que él.

Outbuilding [aut-bild'-ing], *s.* Dependencia, construcción exterior.

Outburst [aut'-bŭrst], *s.* Explosión, erupción.—*vn.* (Ant.) Prorrumpir, brotar.

Outcast [aut'-cast], *a.* 1. Desechado, arrojado, inútil. 2. Desterrado, expulso, proscripto; perdido.—*s.* Un desterrado.

Outclass [aut-clas'], *va.* Exceder en habilidad, en calidad o en facultades.

Outcome [aut'-cum], *s.* Éxito, resultado visible, consecuencia.

Outcrop [aut-crep'], *vn.* Asomar; en geología, aparecer en la superficie o encima de la superficie del terreno, v. g. una roca.

Outcrop [aut'-crep], *s.* Aparición, porción visible de un estrato sobre la superficie de un terreno.

Outcry [aut'-crai], *s.* Clamor, voz lastimosa que indica aflicción o pasión de ánimo; ruido, alboroto, gritería, vocería.

Outdare [aut-dār'], *va.* Osar, emprender alguna cosa con atrevimiento, atreverse demasiado o más que otro.

Out-dated [aut-dēt'-ed], *a.* Anticuado, pasado de moda.

Outdo [aut-dū'], *va.* Exceder a otro en alguna cosa; sobrepujar, eclipsar, dejar deslucido.

Outdoor [aut'-dōr''], *a.* 1. Externo, que está al raso, hecho al aire libre; fuera de la casa, de lo exterior. 2. Externo de ciertas instituciones públicas, como un hospital u hospicio. *Outdoor exercise,* Ejercicio al aire libre. *Outdoor sports,* Juegos al aire libre, en campo abierto.

Outdoors [aut-dōrz'], *s.* El raso, el mundo de puertas afuera.—*adv.* Fuera de casa, al raso.

Outdrink [aut-drinc'], *va.* Beber más que otro.

Outer [aut'-er], *a.* Exterior, externo

Outer space [aut'-ẹr spēs], *s.* Espacio interastral.

Outerly [aut'-ẹr-li], *adv.* Hacia fuera, exteriormente.

Outermost [aut'-ẹr-mōst], *a.* Extremo; lo más exterior.

Outface [aut-fēs'], *va.* Humillar a otro haciendo de generoso o magnánimo; mantener cara a cara.

Outfall [aut'-fōl], *s.* 1. Canal para regar; desembocadura. 2. Riña, disensión.

Outfit [aut'-fit], *s.* 1. Equipo, apresto. 2. Habilitación, desembolso; el gasto hecho para equipar un barco, o dar principio o fomento a una empresa, particularmente a un viaje. 3. Pertrechos, avíos, menesteres de alguna ocupación.

Outfitter [aut'-fit'-ẹr], *s.* Armador de una embarcación; abastecedor, proveedor, habilitador de todo lo necesario para un viaje, empresa o negocio.

Outflank [aut-flanc'], *va.* Extenderse un ejército o cuerpo de ejército más que las alas o flancos del enemigo, lo que modernamente se ha expresado por la voz flanquear; también, llevar la ventaja, ganar la palmeta.

Outflow [aut'-flō], *s.* Efusión, derrame, flujo; salida.—*vn.* [aut-flō'] (Poét.) Correr, manar hacia afuera.

Outfly [aut-flai'], *va.* Exceder en el vuelo, volar más o mejor.

†**Outgate** [aut'-gēt], *s.* Salida, puerta exterior.

Outgeneral [aut-jen'-ẹr-al], *va.* Exceder a uno en táctica militar.

Outgive [aut-giv'], *va.* Dar más que otro, exceder en generosidad.

Outgo [aut-gō'], *va.* Exceder, vencer; adelantarse, tomar la delantera.

Outgo [aut'-go], *s.* Gasto, lo que se ha gastado; expendio, costas, lo opuesto a *income.*

Outgoing [aut'-go-ing], *s.* Salida; la acción de partir.—*a.* Que sale o se retira de un empleo; saliente, aquel cuyo cargo termina.

Outgrow [aut-grō'], *va.* 1. Sobrecrecer, crecer más que otro. 2. Hacerse demasiado grande o viejo para algo. *The boy has outgrown his clothes,* El muchacho ha crecido tanto que la ropa le está corta.

Outgrowth [aut'-grōth], *s.* 1. Excrecencia, lo que crece en el exterior de otra cosa. 2. Resultado o efecto natural; consecuencia.

Outguard [aut'-gārd], *s.* (Mil.) Guardia avanzada.

Outhouse [aut'-haus], *s.* Casa pequeña de los criados o dependientes de una alquería, hacienda u otra posesión rural, a corta distancia de la del dueño; dependencia de una casa.

Outing [aut'-ing], *s.* Salida; paseo, viaje corto para divertirse, excursión.

Outland [aut'-land], *s.* Terreno situado más allá de los límites de ocupación o cultivación.

Outlandish [aut-land'-ish], *a.* 1. Extranjero, remoto. 2. Grosero, rústico, bárbaro en aspecto o acciones.

Outlast [aut-last'], *va.* Durar más que otra cosa, excederla en duración; sobrevivir a.

Outlaw [aut'-lō], *s.* 1. Proscripto. 2. Bandido, bandolero.

Outlaw, *va.* Proscribir, privar a uno de la protección de las leyes; sentenciar en rebeldía.

Outlawry [aut'-lō-ri], *s.* Proscripción, la sentencia con que se condena a uno o muchas personas, privándolas de la protección de las leyes.

Outlay [aut'-lē], *s.* Desembolso, gasto; expendio.

Outleap [aut-līp'], *va.* Pasar saltando, saltar más allá del término señalado.

Outlearn [aut-lẹrn'], *va.* Adelantar a otro en lo que se aprende.

Outlet [aut'-let], *s.* Salida, orificio de salida, desagüe; desaguadero; portillo. *Outlets*, (Des.) Contornos.
Outlie [aut-lai'], *va.* Mentir más que otro, excederle en decir o inventar mentiras.—*vn.* Dormir al raso, acampar en tiendas.
Outlier [aut'-lai-ẹr], *s.* Aquel cuya residencia no está en el mismo lugar en que se hallan su oficina o sus negocios.
Outline [aut'-lain], *s.* Contorno, perfil, diseño, bosquejo, traza, recorte; plan general.
Outline [aut'-lain], *va.* Dibujar los contornos de, bosquejar, delinear; describir en términos generales.
Outlive [aut-liv'], *va.* Sobrevivir a; exceder en duración.
Outlook [aut'-luc], *s.* 1. Vista, perspectiva, lo que se alcanza a ver desde un balcón, ventana o punto elevado; de aquí, la condición o aspecto de alguna cosa, la perspectiva de un negocio o empresa. 2. Vigilancia, previsión. 3. Atalaya, vigía; garita. 4. Centinela, guardia.
Outlook [aut-luc'], *va.* Desconcertar, turbar por medio de conducta atrevida o descarada; ver más lejos, alcanzar a mayor distancia con la vista.
Outluster, Outlustre [aut-lus'-tẹr], *va.* Exceder en brillantez.
Outlying [aut'-lai-ing], *a.* 1. Distante de, lejos de alguna cosa; extrínseco. 2. Exterior, fuera de límites o fronteras, forastero.
Outmaneuver [aut-ma-nū'-vẹr], *va.* Mostrarse superior en táctica militar.
Outmarch [aut-mārch'], *va.* Dejar atrás a otro en un paseo, viaje o marcha.
Outmatch [aut-mach'], *va.* Mostrarse superior a otro en alguna actividad.
Outmeasure [aut-mezh'-ur], *va.* Exceder en medida.
Outmoded [aut'-mōd'-ed], *a.* Anticuado, pasado de moda.
Outmost [aut'-mōst], *a.* Lo más exterior; lo más lejano.
Outnumber [aut-num'-bẹr], *va.* Exceder en número.
Out-of-door(s) [aut-ev-dōrz'], *a.* y *adv.* Al aire libre, afuera.
Out-of-print [aut-ev-print'], *a.* Agotado (el libro, la edición, etc.)
Out-of-stock [aut-ev-stek'], *a.* Agotada (la existencia).
Out-of-the-way [aut'-ev-dhẹ-wē''], *a.* 1. Lejano, de difícil acceso, apartado, desviado. 2. Fuera de lo ordinario, singular, extraño, particular.
Outparish [aut'-par-ish], *s.* Parroquia situada extramuros.
Outpart [aut'-pārt], *s.* Parte exterior; extremidad, la parte o partes que están más distantes del centro de alguna cosa.
Outpatient [aut'-pē''-shẹnt], *s.* Enfermo, paciente externo, no residente en un hospital o casa de salud.
Outpensioner [aut'-pen-shun-ẹr], *s.* Pensionista externo.
Outporch [aut'-pōrch], *s.* Pórtico exterior.
Outport [aut'-pōrt], *s.* 1. Un puerto de mar algo distante de la aduana principal. 2. Punto de exportación; puerto de mar.
Outpost [aut'-pōst], *s.* Avanzada, guardia o puesto avanzado.
Outpour [aut-pōr'], *va.* Chorrear, verter, despedir un líquido a chorros.—*s.* Chorreo. efusión libre:
Outpouring [aut'-pōr''-ing], *s.* Efusión abundante, chorro; emanación.
Output [aut'-put], *s.* 1. Producción total de algo, cantidad obtenida o producida y pronta para venderse o distribuirse en fecha determinada. 2. Lo que se expele por los pulmones, los riñones o la piel. 3. La fuerza eléctrica de un dínamo; se expresa comúnmente en vatios.
Outrage [aut'-rēj], *va.* Ultrajar, ajar o injuriar; maltratar, violentar, violar, abusar atrozmente; cometer rapto.
Outrage, *s.* Ultraje, afrenta, violencia, tropelía; barbarie, tiranía.
Outrageous [aut-rē'-jus], *a.* 1. Violento. 2. Ultrajoso, de porte chocante, ofensivo. 3. Atroz, desenfrenado, desaforado.
Outrageously [aut-rē'-jus-li], *adv.* Violentamente, atrozmente.
Outrageousness [aut-rē'-jus-nes], *s.* Furia, violencia.
Outrank [aut-rank'], *va.* Exceder en rango o posición.
Outreach [aut-rīch'], *va.* Pasar más adelante que otro o tomarle la delantera; pasar más allá de lo que se debe.
Outreason [aut-rīz'-n], *va.* Discurrir mejor que otro.
Outride [aut-raid'], *va.* Ganar la delantera a caballo, andar a caballo más que otro.—*vn.* Andar a caballo o en carruaje de una parte a otra.
Outrider [aut'-raid-ẹr], *s.* 1. Volante, el lacayo que va á pie o a caballo delante del coche. 2. Batidor, el soldado o criado que va a caballo delante del coche de su jefe o amo. 3. (Des.) Receptor, oficial comisionado por un tribunal para ciertas diligencias.
Outrigger [aut-rig' ẹr], *s.* 1. Horqueta, vuelo, parte de una embarcación o máquina que sobresale y sirve de apoyo o punto de enganche. 2. Batanga, refuerzo de cañas gruesas de bambú, amadrinadas a lo largo de las canoas filipinas y de otras islas del Pacífico. 3. (Mar.) Pescante de banda para carenar; puntal de tope. *Outriggers of the tops*, (Mar.) Pescantes de las cofas.
Outright [aut-rait'], *a.* Sincero, franco, sin segunda intención.—*adv.* 1 Sin reserva ni limitación; completamente, abiertamente. 2. Sin tardanza, al momento, luego, cumplidamente. *To laugh outright*, Reir a carcajadas, desternillarse de risa, morirse de risa.
Outrival [aut-rai'-val], *va.* Sobrepujar en excelencia.
Outroot [aut-rūt'], *va.* 1. Arraigar más y mejor que otra cosa. 2. (Ant.) Desarraigar, extirpar, arrancar de raíz.
Outrun [aut-run'], *va.* 1. Correr más que otro, ganarle a correr. 2. Ganar, exceder. *To outrun the constable*, Gastar más de lo que uno tiene, comerse los frutos antes de la cosecha.
Outs [auts], *s. pl.* *To be on the outs*, (Fam.) Estar de monos.
Outsell [aut-sel'], *va.* Vender á mayor precio o más caro que otro; vender más rápidamente.
Outset [aut'-set], *s.* Principio; estreno.
Outshine [aut-shain'], *va.* 1. Brillar, resplandecer. 2. Exceder en brillantez, dejar deslucido, eclipsar.
Outshoot [aut-shūt'], *va.* Ganar a uno a tirar; tirar más lejos que otro.
Outside [aut'-said], *a.* 1. Exterior, superficial. 2. Extraño, extrínseco. 3. Extremo, que alcanza al límite. 4. Ajeno, neutral, que no tiene parte ni interés.—*s.* 1. Superficie, parte externa o exterior. *Outside shutter*, Contraventana. 2. Extremidad, la parte más remota del centro; lo último, lo extremo. 3. Exterior. 4. Apariencia superficial. 5. Costera, en las resmas de papel. —*adv.* Afuera, fuera.—*prep.* Fuera de, más allá de.
Outsider [aut-sai'-dẹr], *s.* El que está fuera; entremetido, intruso, el que no tiene parte ni interés en alguna cosa.
Outsit [aut-sit'], *va.* Estar sentado más tiempo que lo preciso.
Outskirt [aut'-skẹrt], *s.* Parte exterior; borde, linde, orilla; lugar cercano al confín; arrabal de una población; suburbio.
Outsleep [aut-slīp'], *va.* Dormir más tiempo del que se ha fijado, o más de lo que se debe.
Outspeak [aut-spīc'], *va.* 1. Hablar en alta voz; explicarse claramente, 2. Hablar mejor o más tiempo que otro.—*vn.* Hablar atrevidamente, osar hablar.
Outspread [aut-spred'], *va.* Extender, difundir.
Outstand [aut-stand'], *va.* ‖Sostener, resistir.—*vn.* Hacer barriga o comba; salir fuera de la línea señalada; subsistir en una parte más de lo regular.
Outstanding [aut-stand'-ing], *a.* 1. Salidizo, saliente. 2. Sobresaliente, extraordinario, fuera de lo común. 3. Pendiente, no pagado. *Outstanding account*, Cuenta pendiente por pagar.
Outstare [aut-stār'], *va.* Mirar a uno de hito en hito; desconcertar a una persona; mantener una cosa a la cara o en presencia de otro que la niega.
Outstay [aut-stē'], *va.* 1. Permanecer más tiempo que otros. 2. Resistir más que otros.
Outstretch [aut-strech'], *va.* Extenderse, alargar.
Outstrip [aut-strip'], *va.* Avanzar más que otro, dejar atrás; rezagar, sobrepujar, aventajar, ganar.
Outtalk [aut-tōc'], ‖**Outtongue** [aut-tung'], *va.* Aturdir con voces; hablar más que otro.
Outvalue [aut-val'-yū], *va.* Subir de precio, exceder en valor.
Outvote [aut-vōt'], *va.* Ganar a uno en el número de votos.
Outwalk [aut-wōc'], *va.* Andar más que otro, dejarle atrás; cansar a uno, rendirle a fuerza de andar.
Outwall [aut'-wōl], *s.* 1. Pared exterior; antemural. 2. Lo exterior, la parte externa; apariencia.
Outward [aut'-ward], *a.* 1. Exterior, externo, visible. *An outward friendship*, Una amistad superficial. 2. Extranjero, extraño. 3. Exterior, extrínseco. 4. (Teol.) Carnal, corpóreo.—*adv.* 1. Fuera, afuera, exteriormente. 2. Sobre la superficie, superficialmente. 3. Desde el puerto, hacia otro país, para el extranjero. *Outward bound*, Fletado para el extranjero, con rumbo a un puer to extranjero. *A ship bound outward*, Embarcación destinada a otro país.—*s.* (Poco us.) La figura exterior.
Outwardly [aut'-ward-li], *adv.* Exte-

riormente, extrínsecamente; en apariencia, superficialmente.

Outwards [aut'-wardz], *adv.* Hacia fuera, por fuera. *V.* OUTWARD.

Outwatch [aut-wēch'], *va.* Vigilar o velar más que otro.

Outwear [aut-wêr'], *va.* 1. Durar más tiempo que. 2. Gastar, consumir, usar hasta el fin.

Outweigh [aut-wê'], *va.* 1. Preponderar; pesar más que. 2. Sobrepujar, exceder en valor, en influjo, en excelencia.

Outwit [aut-wit'], *va.* Engañar a uno a fuerza de tretas; sobrepujar en astucia.

Outwork [aut-wūrk'], *va.* Trabajar más que otro.

Outwork [aut'-wūrk], *s.* (Fort.) Obra de una plaza fuerte situada fuera de las murallas: (ant.) obra avanzada, obra exterior.

Outworn [aut-wōrn'], *a.* Ajado, gastado, destruido de puro usado.

Ouzel [ū'-zl], *s.* Uno de varios pájaros túrdidos; mirlo, mirla o merla. Merula merula; turdus torquatus. *Water-ouzel,* Mirlo de agua. Cinclus aquaticus.

Oval [ō'-val], *s.* Óvalo, figura plana muy parecida a la elipse.—*a.* Oval, ovalado.

Ovally [ō'-val-l], *adv.* En figura de óvalo.

Ovarian, Ovarial§ [o-vê'-ri-an], *a.* Ovárico, perteneciente o relativo al ovario.

Ovariotomy [o-vê-ri-ot'-o-mi], *s.* Ovariotomía, operación quirúrgica para extraer un ovario enfermo.

§**Ovarious** [ō-vê'-ri-us], *a.* Lo que se compone de huevos.

Ovary [ō'-va-ri], *s.* 1. Ovario, órgano interno de la fecundación en las hembras; overa de los animales ovíparos. 2. (Bot.) Ovario, parte inferior del pistilo que contiene el rudimento de la semilla.

Ovate o **Ovated** [ō'-vêt, ed], *a.* Ovado, formado a manera de huevo, con una extremidad más dilatada que la otra.

Ovation [o-vê'-shun], *s.* 1. Manifestación espontánea del entusiasmo público hacia una persona. 2. Ovación, uno de los triunfos menores entre los romanos.

Oven [uv'-n], *s.* Horno para cocer pan o pastelería, para templar y secar ciertas substancias. *Oven-fork,* Hurgón. *Oven full,* Hornada. *Oven-peel,* Pala de horno.

Over [ō'-vęr], *prep.* 1. Sobre, encima, por encima de: expresa superioridad de lugar; lo contrario de *under,* debajo, bajo de. *Over the gate was an inscription,* Había una inscripción encima de la puerta. 2. Expresa superioridad en dignidad, poder, estado; sobre. "*Shall Saul reign over us?*" "¿Reinará Saúl sobre nosotros?" 3. A pesar de. *The bill was passed over the veto,* El proyecto de ley fué aprobado a pesar del veto. 4. Por encima, cubriendo o cubierto de; moviéndose sobre la superficie de; de un lado a otro; al otro lado de. 5. Más de. *Over five hundred dollars,* Más de quinientos pesos. 6. Mientras, durante. *The ice kept over the summer,* El hielo se conservó durante todo el verano. 7. Por, en. *To be over head and ears in debt,* Estar endeudado hasta los ojos; deber mucho. *Over the way,* Al otro lado de la calle. *Over the hills,* Más allá, al otro lado de las colinas o collados. *All over,* Por todas partes, por todos lados. *All the world over,* Por todo el mundo.—*adv.* 1. De un lado a otro, al lado opuesto. *He was completely won over,* Fué atraído al lado contrario, se pasó al enemigo; quedó persuadido. 2. De ancho, a lo ancho. 3. De arriba abajo, al revés, patas arriba, trastocado. 4. Encima, sobre. 5. Más, demás; completamente, desde el principio al fin. 6. Otra vez. 7. Demasiado, excesivamente. 8. En estado de hecho, al fin. *It is all over,* Acabóse. *Over and above,* Además de, por demás. *Over against,* Enfrente. *Over and over,* Repetidas veces, una y otra vez. *Over again,* Otra vez, segunda vez. *To be over,* Cesar, pasar, concluirse, acabar. *To run over,* Rebosar, derramarse por encima; recorrer, registrar a la ligera, al paso; pasar por encima (un coche, un tren, etc.); aplastar. *Over* se une con mucha frecuencia a los verbos para modificar su significación, y se usa también en composición delante de los nombres y verbos.

Overabound [ō-vęr-a-baund'], *vn.* Superabundar, abundar con exceso.

Overabundance [ō'-vęr-a-bun'-dans], *s.* Superabundancia.

Overact [ō-vęr-act'], *va.* Llevar una cosa al extremo o más allá de lo justo y razonable.

Overalls [ō'-vęr-ōlz], *s. pl.* Zaragüelles, pantalones que se ponen sobre los otros para resguardarlos.

Overanxious [ō-vęr-anc'-shus], *a.* Demasiado ansioso.

Overarch [ō-vęr-ārch'], *va.* Cubrir con una bóveda o arco, abovedar; formar una bóveda encima de.

Overawe [ō-vęr-ē'], *va.* Tener bajo freno; imponer respeto; intimidar, sobrecoger.

Overbalance [ō-vęr-bal'-ans], *va.* y *vn.* Preponderar; echar más peso a un lado que a otro; llevar ventaja.

Overbalance [ō'-vęr-bal-ans], *s.* Preponderancia, exceso de peso o de valor.

Overbear [ō-vęr-bār'], *va.* (*pret.* OVERBORE, *pp.* OVERBORNE). 1. Sojuzgar, sujetar, reprimir. 2. Subyugar, oprimir, abrumar, agobiar.—*vn.* Llevar demasiado fruto.

Overbearing [ō-ver-bār'-ing], *a.* Ultrajoso, despótico; insufrible; insuperable.

Overbid [ō-vęr-bid'], *va.* 1. Ofrecer más, pujar. 2. Ofrecer demasiado por algo, pagar excesivamente.

Overbidding [ō-vęr-bid'-ing], *s.* Puja.

Overbig [ō-vęr-big'], *a.* Demasiado grande o grueso.

Overblow [ō-vęr blō'], *vn.* 1. (Mar.) Soplar con violencia excesiva. 2. (Des.) Pasar la borrasca; calmar el viento.—*va.* 1. Disipar soplando, como el aire disipa las nubes. 2. (Ant.) Cubrir con flores; esparcir flores sobre algo.

Overboard [ō'-vęr-bōrd], *adv.* (Mar.) Al mar, fuera del barco. *To heave overboard,* (Mar.) Echar a la mar. *To fall overboard,* Caer al agua desde una embarcación.

Overboil [ō-vęr-boil'], *va.* Hervir o cocer demasiado.

Overbold [ō-vęr-bōld'], *a.* Temerario, descarado, presuntuoso.

Overborne [ō-vęr-bōrn'], *a.* y *pp.* Abatido ó sujetado por alguna influencia superior. *V.* OVERBEAR.

Overburden [ō-vęr-būr'-dn], *va.* Sobrecargar; oprimir.

Overcapitalization [ō-vęr-cap-i-tal-i-zê'-shun], *s.* 1. Capitalización excesiva. 2. Cálculo exagerado del capital de una corporación.

Overcare [ō'-vęr-cār], *s.* Solicitud, demasiado cuidado.

Overcareful [ō-vęr-cār'-ful], *a.* Demasiado cuidadoso.

Overcarry [ō-vęr-car'-i], *va.* Precipitar a una persona o instigarla a que obre sin precaución o precipitadamente; llevar alguna cosa más allá de lo regular.

Overcast [o-vęr-cast'], *va.* 1. Anublar, obscurecer; entristecer. 2. Cubrir. 3. Hilvanar; coser la orilla de una tela con puntadas envolventes, en forma espiral.

Overcautious [ō-vęr-cō'-shus], *a.* Demasiado circunspecto o precavido.

Overcharge [ō-vęr-chārj'], *va.* 1. Poner alguna cosa a precio muy subido. 2. Sobrecargar (un arma de fuego). 3. Oprimir. 4. Exagerar. 5. Hacer una acusación exagerada o fantástica contra alguien.

Overcheck [ō-vęr-chec'], *s.* Falsarrienda que pasa por encima de la cabeza del caballo, entre las orejas.

Overcloud [ō-vęr-claud'], *va.* Cubrir de nubes.

Overcloy [ō-vęr-cloi'], *va.* Saciar o llenar demasiado.

Overcoat [ō'-vęr-cōt], *s.* Sobretodo, gabán, levitón, abrigo.

Overcome [ō-vęr-cum'], *va.* 1. Vencer, rendir, sujetar, domar, sojuzgar, conquistar, triunfar de. 2. Superar, vencer.—*vn.* Alcanzar superioridad sobre alguno; sobreponerse; hacerse superior a alguna cosa.

Overcomer [ō-vęr-cum'-ęr], *s.* Vencedor.

Overconfidence [ō-vęr-con'-fi-dens], *s.* Presunción, demasiada confianza.

Overconfident [ō-vęr-con'-fi-dent], *a.* Demasiado confiado, confiado fuera de razón.

Overcount [ō-vęr-caunt'], *va.* Tasar o apreciar alguna cosa en más de lo que vale.

Overcredulous [ō'-vęr-cred'-yu-lus], *a.* Demasiado crédulo.

Overcrowd [ō'-vęr-craud], *s.* Excedente (de concurrentes, etc.)—*va.* Apiñar, atestar, llenar (algún aposento) demasiado.

Overcurious [ō-vęr-kiū'-ri-us], *a.* Demasiado curioso, nimio o delicado.

Overdiligent [ō-vęr-dil'-i-jent], *a.* Diligente en exceso.

Overdo [ō-vęr-dū'], *vn.* (*pret.* OVERDID, *pp.* OVERDONE). Hacer más de lo necesario.—*va.* 1. Llevar al exceso; fatigar excesivamente; agobiar, abrumar de trabajo. 2. Exagerar. 3. Cocer, asar demasiado; socarrar. 4. (Poét.) Eclipsar, dejar deslucido. *To overdo one's self,* Atarearse, perjudicarse a puro trabajar. *That meat is overdone,* Esa carne está muy asada o muy cocida.

Overdone [ō-vęr-dun'], *pp.* Pasado, demasiadamente asado o cocido; rendido, cansado.

Overdose [ō-vęr-dōs'], *va.* Dar una dosis excesiva.—*s.* Dosis excesiva o tóxica.

Overdraft [ō'-vęr-draft], *s.* (Com.) Giro, libranza en exceso de los fondos o el crédito disponibles; y el acto de hacer ese giro.

Overdraw [ō'-vęr-drē], *va.* (*pret.* OVERDREW, *pp.* OVERDRAWN). 1. (Com.) Exceder, en un giro, del crédito disponible. 2. Estirar, tirar excesivamente. 3. Exagerar, ya sea en la escritura, narración, dibujo, ademanes o acciones.

Overdress [ō-vẹr-dres'], *va.* y *vr.* Adornar con demasía, engalanar con exceso.

Overdrink [ō-vẹr-drịnc'], *vn.* Beber con exceso. *To overdrink one's self,* Emborracharse.

Overdrive [ō'vẹr-draiv], *s.* Sobremarcha de un automóvil, capacidad adicional de propulsión.—*va.* Arrear demasiado, fatigar a los animales.

Overdue [ō-vẹr-diū'], *a.* Que ha pasado del tiempo debido; (1) no pagado al vencimiento; (2) no llegado al tiempo debido.

Overeager [ō-vẹr-ī'-gẹr], *a.* Demasiado ansioso o celoso.

Overearnest [ō-vẹr-ẹr'-nest], *a.* Demasiado ardiente.

Overeat [ō-vẹr-īt'], *vn.* Tupirse, hartarse de algún manjar o bebida, comer o beber demasiado.

Overestimate [ō-vẹr-es'-ti-mêt], *va.* Estimar en valor excesivo; tener opinión demasiado alta de alguien o algo.

Overexposure [ō-vẹr-ex-pō'-zhur], *s.* Exposición excesiva.

Overfatigue [ō-vẹr-fa-tīg'], *va.* Fatigar demasiado.

Overfeed [ō-vẹr-fīd'], *va.* Dar de comer en demasía.

Overfierce [ō-vẹr-fīrs'], *a.* Demasiado atrevido o soberbio; temerario.

Overfill [ō-vẹr-fil'], *va.* Sobrellenar, llenar con exceso.

Overflourish [ō-vẹr-flur'-ish], *va.* Adornar, florear o engalanar alguna cosa en demasía.

Overflow [ō-vẹr-flō'], *vn.* Salir de madre; rebosar.—*va.* 1. Sobrellenar, llenar alguna cosa hasta que se vierta. 2. Inundar.

Overflow [ō'-vẹr-flō], *s.* Inundación, diluvio; exceso, superabundancia.

Overflowing [ō-vẹr-flō'-ing], *s.* Superabundancia, inundación.

Overflowingly [ō-vẹr-flō'-ing-li], *adv.* Superabundantemente.

Overfly [ō-vẹr-flai'], *va.* Pasar a vuelo, alcanzar mayores alturas que otra cosa.

Overfond [ō-vẹr-fend'], *a.* El que quiere o gusta excesivamente de alguna cosa.

Overforward [ō-vẹr-fōr'-ward], *a.* Demasiado ardiente o apresurado; muy vivo.

Overfraught [ō-vẹr-frēt'], *a.* Sobrecargado.

Overfree [ō-vẹr-frī'], *a.* Demasiado libre.

Overfreight [ō-vẹr-frêt'], *va.* Sobrecargar, poner excesivo peso.

Overfruitful [ō-vẹr-frūt'-ful], *a.* Demasiado rico; prolífico en demasía.

Overgild [ō-vẹr-gild'], *va.* Sobredorar.

Overgird [ō-vẹr-gẹrd'], *va.* Atar muy apretado.

Overgo [ō-vẹr-gō'], *va.* Sobrepujar, exceder, sobresalir.

Overgreedy [ō-vẹr-grīd'-i], *a.* Codicioso en demasía.

Overgrow [ō-vẹr-grō'], *va.* (*pret.* OVERGREW, *pp.* OVERGROWN). 1. Cubrir con plantas o hierba; entapizar; remontarse sobre. 2. Crecer demasiado, hacerse demasiado grande para. *V.* OUTGROW.—*vn.* Crecer o desarrollarse con exceso. Se usa más en el participio pasado, *overgrown: A garden overgrown with weeds,* Un jardín cubierto o lleno de mala hierba. *An overgrown child,* Un niño que se ha desarrollado demasiado, o muy rápidamente.

Overgrowth [ō'-vẹr-grōth], *s.* 1. Vegetación exuberante. 2. Crecimiento, producción sobre o encima de alguna cosa.

Overhang [ō-vẹr-hang'], *va.* 1. Sobresalir por encima de alguna cosa; estar pendiente o colgando sobre ella; salir algo fuera del nivel de un edificio. 2. Mirar a, dar a, caer a. *This window overhangs the street,* Esta ventana da a la calle. 3. Ser inminente, amenazar. 4. Poner demasiadas colgaduras. *The walls were overhung,* Las paredes tenían demasiadas colgaduras.

Overhard [ō-vẹr-hārd'], *a.* Duro en demasía.

Overharden [ō-vẹr-hārd'-n], *va.* Endurecer excesivamente.

Overhasty [ō-vẹr-hêst'-i], *a.* Demasiado apresurado.

Overhaul [ō-vẹr-hōl'], *va.* 1. Desparramar alguna cosa; registrar, examinar; volver las cosas de arriba abajo. 2. (Mar.) Alcanzar, o ir ganando un barco en la persecución de otro. 3. (Mar.) Recorrer, registrar, tiramollar. *To overhaul the tacks and sheets,* (Mar.) Tiramollar las amuras y escotas. *To overhaul accounts,* Reexaminar o revisar las cuentas.

Overhead [ō-vẹr-hed'], *adv.* Encima, arriba, en lo alto, sobre la cabeza.

Overhead, overhead expense, *s.* Gastos generales (de un negocio, etc.).

Overhear [ō-vẹr-hīr'], *va.* Oir por casualidad y de paso; escuchar palabras no destinadas a quien las oye.

Overheat [ō-vẹr-hīt'], *va.* Acalorar.

Overhours [ō'-vẹr-aurs''], *s. pl.* 1. Horas extraordinarias, horas de trabajo además de las de reglamento. 2. Horas de trabajo demasiado largas.

Overindulge [ō'-vẹr-in-dulj'], *va.* 1. Mimar demasiado. 2. Darse uno demasiado gusto. 3. Excederse (en la bebida, etc.).

Overjoy [ō-vẹr-jei'], *va.* Arrebatar o enajenar de alegría, alegrar demasiado.

Overjoy [ō'-vẹr-jei], *s.* Arrebato de alegría, éxtasis, enajenamiento.

Overjoyed [ō-vẹr-jeid'], *a.* Lleno de alegría.

Overkind [ō-vẹr-kaind'], *a.* Excesivamente cariñoso o bondadoso.

Overland [ō'-vẹr-land], *a.* y *adv.* Que pasa o se ejecuta por tierra. *Overland route,* Ruta, camino, rumbo, por tierra.

Overlap [ō''-vẹr-lap'], *va.* 1. Tapar o cubrir en parte, extenderse sobre. 2. Hacer doblar o plegarse sobre.—*vn.* Extenderse de manera que descanse en parte sobre lo que está inmediato.

Overlap [ō'-vẹr-lap], *s.* Estado o condición de extenderse sobre, de cubrir en parte; también la parte que cubre o descansa sobre lo que está inmediato.

Overlarge [ō-vẹr-lārj'], *a.* Demasiado grande.

Overlay [ō-vẹr-lê'], *va.* 1. Echar encima, colocar sobre, cubrir de. 2. (Impr.) Calzar, aplicar pedacitos de papel llamados *overlays* al tímpano para corregir un hueco en el cuadro. 3. Anublar, obscurecer. 4. Echar un puente sobre. *To overlay ivory with gold,* Incrustar, cubrir el marfil con oro.

Overlaying [ō-vẹr-lê'-ing], *s.* Capa o cubierta superficial de una substancia, colocada de modo que cubra enteramente otro cuerpo de diferente material.

Overleap [ō-vẹr-līp'], *va.* Pasar de un salto de una parte a otra.

Overlie [ō''-vẹr-lai'], *va.* 1. Descansar o extenderse encima de o sobre. 2. Sofocar echándose encima, como sucede, por ejemplo, con un niño pequeño. En este sentido se usa a veces incorrectamente el verbo *overlay.*

Overlive [ō-vẹr-liv'], *va.* Sobrevivir. —*vn.* Vivir demasiado.

Overload [ō-vẹr-lōd'], *s.* Sobrecarga, recargo.—*va.* Sobrecargar.

Overlong [ō-vẹr-lōng'], *a.* Demasiado largo.

Overlook [ō-vẹr-luk'], *va.* 1. Mirar desde lo alto; tener vista a, dominar con la vista una extensión de terreno. 2. Examinar una cosa. 3. Rever, volver a ver o examinar con cuidado; repasar. 4. Celar, dirigir, tener la dirección de. 5. Pasar por alto, disimular, tolerar; juzgar con indulgencia, hacer la vista gorda. 6. Descuidar, no hacer caso; desdeñar, mirar con desdén, menospreciar. 7. Mirar, dar, caer a. *The window overlooks the river,* La ventana mira al río. *To overlook a slight,* Perdonar un desaire, pasarlo por alto. *To overlook the construction of a building,* Celar, dirigir la construcción de un edificio.

Overlook [ō'-vẹr-luk], *s.* 1. Mirada desde lo alto. 2. Altura, punto de vista elevado, como una montaña. 3. Planta trepadora de las leguminosas, con tres hojuelas. Canavalia gladiata.

Overlooker [ō-vẹr-luk'-ẹr], *s.* Sobrestante, celador, inspector, veedor.

Overlying [ō''-ver-lai'-ing], *a.* Que está colocado encima, que yace sobre algo.

Overmaster [ō-vẹr-mast'-ẹr], *va.* Señorear, dominar o gobernar con mucho imperio y autoridad.

Overmatch [ō-vẹr-mach'], *va.* Sobrepujar, vencer o superar a otro.

Overmatch [ō'-vẹr-mach], *s.* 1. El que puede más que otro. 2. Contienda en que un partido vence a otro.

Overmeasure [ō'-vẹr-mezh-yur], *s.* Colmo, la porción que sobresale de la medida justa.

Overmeasure [ō-vẹr-mezh'-yur], *va.* Dar demasiada importancia, estimación o valor a alguna cosa.

Overmuch [ō-vẹr-much'], *a.* y *adv.* Demasiado, más de lo suficiente; en demasía.

Overnight [ō'-vẹr-nait], *a.* Que permanece en la noche. *Overnight guests,* Invitados que se quedan a dormir.

Overofficious [ō-vẹr-ef-fish'-us], *a.* Demasiado entremetido, muy oficioso.

Overpass [ō-vẹr-pas'], *va.* 1. Atravesar, salvar. 2. Mirar con indiferencia, menospreciar. 3. Pasar por alto; omitir; dejar de contar alguna partida en una cuenta. 4. Sobrepujar, exceder. 5. Rever, repasar, considerar.

Overpass [ō'-vẹr-pas], *s.* Paso superior (en las carreteras).

Overpay [ō-vẹr-pê'], *va.* Pagar o premiar demasiado.

Overpeople [ō''-vẹr-pī'-pl], *va.* Atestar de habitantes; poblar demasiado.

Overpersuade [ō-vẹr-pẹr-swēd'], *va.* Persuadir a alguno á despecho de sus opiniones e inclinaciones.

Overplus [ō'-vẹr-plus], *s.* Sobrante.

Overply [ō-vẹr-plai'], *va.* Cargar de trabajo.

Overpopulated [ō-ver-pop'-yu-lêt-ed], *a.* Superpoblado.

Overpower [ō-vẹr-pau'-ẹr], *va.* Predominar, subyugar, vencer, superar, sobrepujar; supeditar, oprimir, abrumar; colmar.

Overpoweringly [ō-vẹr-pau'-ẹr-ing-li], *adv.* Con fuerza superior; de una manera incontrastable.

Overpress [ō-vẹr-pres'], *va.* Oprimir, abrumar.

Overprize [o-vẹr-praiz'], *va.* Sobrestimar.

Overproduction [o-vẹr-pro-duc'-shun], *s.* Sobreproducción, superproducción.

Overpromptness [ō-vẹr-prompt'-nes], *s.* Precipitación.

Overrake [ō-ver-rêk'], *va.* (Mar.) Barrer de popa a proa un buque al ancla, como lo hacen las olas.

Overrate [ō-vẹr-rêt'], *va.* Encarecer, apreciar o valuar alguna cosa en más de lo que vale.

Overreach [ō-vẹr-rīch'], *va.* 1. Estafar, trampear, engañar astutamente. 2. Extender, alargar demasiado (una de las extremidades o el cuerpo entero). 3. Ir, pasar, extenderse más allá. 4. Extenderse sobre, de manera que cubra.—*vn.* 1. Golpear con el pie de atrás contra el pie delantero; dícese de las caballerías. 2. (Mar.) Dar una bordada o virada más allá de lo necesario.

Overreach [ō'-vẹr-rīch], *s.* Coz, rozadura que ha recibido una caballería sobre el casco.

Overreckon [ō-vẹr-rec'-un], *va.* Calcular en más de la cuenta, hacer cálculos exagerados.

Override [ō-vẹr-raid'], *va.* 1. Pasar por encima del cuerpo de; vencer, como pisando debajo de los pies del caballo de uno. 2. Poner a un lado, rechazar arbitrariamente; anular. 3. Fatigar un caballo con exceso.

Overripe [ō-vẹr-raip'], *a.* Demasiado maduro.

Overripen [ō-vẹr-raip'-n], *va.* Madurar demasiado.

Overroast [ō-vẹr-rōst'], *va.* Tostar, asar demasiado.

Overrule [ō-vẹr-rūl'], *va.* 1. Predominar, dominar; ganar, alcanzar superioridad sobre alguno. 2. (For.) Denegar, no admitir un alegato. 3. Gobernar, dirigir, regir. *There is an overruling Providence,* Hay una Providencia que todo lo dirige.

Overruler [ō-vẹr-rūl'-ẹr], *s.* Director, gobernador.

Overrun [ō-vẹr-run'], *va.* 1. Invadir, hacer correrías en algún territorio. 2. Adelantarse, tomar o ganar la delantera; ir o pasar más allá de los límites debidos, de cualquier clase que sean. 3. Cubrir enteramente alguna cosa. 4. Infestar, plagarse de, llenarse de. 5. Retocar o repasar los caracteres con que se imprime. 6. *V. To* OUTRUN. 7. (Des.) Injuriar alguna cosa pisándola.—*vn.* Rebosar, salirse el agua ú otro licor por la boca o bordes de los límites que la contienen por estar demasiado llenos; inundar; estar muy abundante.

Overscrupulous [ō-vẹr-scrū'-piu-lus], *a.* Demasiado escrupuloso.

Overseas [ō-vẹr-sīs'], *a.* De ultramar.—*adv.* Allende el mar.

Oversee [ō-vẹr-sī'], *va.* (*pret.* OVERSAW, *pp.* OVERSEEN). 1. Inspeccionar, revistar, vigilar, celar, tener la inspección o superintendencia de alguna cosa. 2. Pasar, omitir, no reparar en alguna cosa, pasarla por alto. 3. Ver demasiado bien o claramente.

Overseen [ō-vẹr-sīn'], *pp.* Engañado, cegado, equivocado.

Overseer [ō-vẹr-sīr' ú ō-vẹr-sī'-ẹr], *s.* 1. Sobrestante, superintendente, celador; director. (Amer.) Mayoral, administrador. 2. Nombre de un cargo parroquial en Inglaterra cuya obligación es dar a los pobres los socorros que perciben de los fondos de la parroquia.

Overseership [ō-vẹr-sīr'-ship], *s.* Cargo, oficio de superintendente.

Overset [ō-vẹr-set'], *va.* 1. Volcar, derribar, torcer o trastornar alguna cosa hacia un lado de modo que caiga. 2. Trastornar, invertir el orden de alguna cosa: subvertir, arruinar.—*vn.* Volcarse, caerse.

Overshade [ō-vẹr-shêd'], *va.* Obscurecer, echar sombra sobre algo; hacer sombra desde lo alto.

Overshadow [ō-vẹr-shad'-o], *va.* 1. Asombrar, hacer sombra una cosa a otra. 2. Eclipsar, hacer insignificante por comparación. 3. (Ant.) Abrigar, amparar, patrocinar, proteger.

Overshoe [ō'-vẹr-shū], *s.* Chanclo, calzado (zapato) que se lleva sobre otro; ordinariamente de caucho o de fieltro.

Overshoot [ō-vẹr-shūt'], *va.* (*pp.* y *pret.* OVERSHOT). 1. Tirar más allá del blanco. 2. Ir más allá de, exceder. 3. Pasar rápidamente por encima.—*vn.* Pasar de raya, llegar más allá del término que estaba señalado.

Overshot [ō'-vẹr-shot'], *pa.* 1. Excedido, de cualquier manera que sea. 2. Que se hace pasando por encima de algo. *Overshot wheel,* Rueda hidráulica de arcaduces o artesas.

Oversight [ō'-vẹr-sait], *s.* 1. Yerro, equivocación, inadvertencia, olvido, omisión. 2. Vigilancia, inspección; dirección atenta; superintendencia.

Overskip [ō-vẹr-skip'], *va.* 1. Pasar saltando. 2. Pasar alguna cosa sin reparar; omitir, saltar; evitar.

Overskirt [ō'-vẹr-skẹrt], *s.* Sobrefalda, saya que se lleva sobre la falda del vestido (de mujer).

Oversleep [ō-vẹr-slīp'], *vn.* Dormir demasiado.

Oversoon [ō-vẹr-sun'], *adv.* Demasiado pronto.

†**Overspent** [ō-vẹr-spent'], *a.* Agotado, apurado.

Overspread [ō-vẹr-spred'], *va.* 1. Desparramar, extender alguna cosa por el suelo, cubrir. 2. Estar echado sobre.

Overstate [ō-vẹr-stêt'], *vn.* Exagerar, referir o relatar usando términos demasiado fuertes.

Overstatement [ō-vẹr-stêt'-mẹnt], *s.* Exageración en lo dicho, declaración exagerada.

Overstep [ō-vẹr-step'], *va.* Propasar, pasar de los límites, ir más allá; exceder.

Overstock [ō-vẹr-stoc'], *va.* Atestar, colmar, llenar alguna cosa con exceso.

Overstore [ō-vẹr-stōr'], *va.* Surtir o proveer en demasía.

Overstrain [ō-vẹr-strên'], *vn.* Esforzarse demasiado, hacer grandes esfuerzos.—*va.* Apretar o estirar demasiado.

Overstretch [ō-vẹr-strech'], *va.* Estirar demasiado.

Overstrew, Overstrow [ō-vẹr-strū', strō], *va.* Esparcir, derramar sobre.

Overstrung [ō''-vẹr-strung'], *a.* 1. Templado con exceso; demasiado excitable, muy sensible. 2. Que tiene dos juegos de cuerdas cruzadas oblicuamente.

Overstuff [ō'-vẹr-stuf], *va.* 1. Llenar en exceso. 2. Tapizar completamente (un mueble).

Oversway [ō-vẹr-swê'], *va.* Predominar, dominar, mandar con tiranía.

Overswell [ō-vẹr-swel'], *va.* Hincharse por arriba.

Overt [ō'-vẹrt], *a.* Abierto, público, manifiesto, claro, patente.

Overtly [ō'-vẹrt-li], *adv.* Abiertamente, manifiestamente.

Overtake [ō-vẹr-têk'], *va.* 1. Alcanzar, seguir a alguna persona o cosa hasta encontrarla. 2. Coger o pillar en el hecho, sorprender en el acto, y familiarmente, coger en la trampa, en el garlito, o con las manos en la masa.

Overtask [ō-vẹr-tqsc'], *va.* Atarear demasiado.

Overtax [ō-vẹr-tacs'], *va.* Oprimir con tributos.

Overthrow [ō-vẹr-thrō'], *va.* 1. Trastornar, volver alguna cosa de arriba abajo. 2. Demoler, derribar, echar por tierra. 3. Vencer, ganar la victoria. 4. Destruir, aniquilar.

Overthrow [ō'-vẹr-thrō], *s.* 1. Trastornamiento, trastornadura. 2. Trastorno; ruina, destrucción, derrota. 3. Degradación.

Overthrower [ō-vẹr-thrō'-ẹr], *s.* Trastornador; derrocador.

Overthwart [ō-vẹr-thwērt'], *a.* (Ant.) 1. Fronterizo, opuesto. 2. Contrario, adverso. 3. Terco, porfiado. 4. Lo que cruza otra cosa.—*prep.* (Poco us.) Por encima.

Overtime [ō'-vẹr-taim], *s.* Horas adicionales, es decir, horas de trabajo además de las de reglamento.—*adv.* Fuera del tiempo estipulado.

Overtire [ō-vẹr-tair'], *va.* Fatigar demasiado.

Overtop [ō-vẹr-top'], *va.* 1. Elevarse sobre otra cosa, estar más elevado, dominar, mirar desde lo alto. 2. Sobresalir, exceder.

Overtrade [ō-vẹr-trêd'], *vn.* Hacer un comercio demasiado grande; emprender especulaciones comerciales demasiado arriesgadas.

Overtrip [ō-vẹr trip'], *va.* Pasar ligeramente por encima de alguna cosa.

Overture [ō'-vẹr-chur ú ō'-vẹrt-yūr], *s.* 1. Insinuación, declaración, proposición, propuesta. 2. (Mús.) La introducción musical de una ópera u oratorio. 3. (Poco us.) Revelación, descubrimiento. 4. (Des.) Abertura, hendedura.

Overturn [ō-vẹr-tūrn'], *va.* 1. Subvertir, trastornar; trastrocar, volver al revés, mudar lo de arriba abajo. 2. Sobrepujar, vencer.

Overvalue [ō-vẹr-val'-yu], *va.* 1. Apreciar o estimar demasiado alguna cosa. 2. Encarecer, ponderar o exagerar el valor de una cosa.

Overviolent [ō-vẹr-vai'-o-lẹnt], *a.* Muy violento.

Overwatch [ō-vẹr-wēch'], *vn.* Cansar a fuerza de vigilias.

Overweak [ō-vẹr-wīc'], *a.* Demasiado endeble.

Overweary [ō-vẹr-wī'-ri], *va.* Domar por la fatiga.

Overweening [ō-vẹr-wīn'-ing], *s.* Presunción.—*a.* Presuntuoso, arrogante, altanero.

Overweeningly [ō-vẹr-wīn'-ing-li], *adv.* Presuntuosamente, con arrogancia.

Overweigh [ō-vẹr-wē'], *va.* 1. Pesar más, preponderar. 2. Prevalecer, tener más fuerza.

Overweight [ō'-vẹr-wêt], *s.* 1. Preponderancia, exceso en el peso. 2. Superioridad, crédito.

Overwhelm [ō-vẹr-hwelm'], *va.* Abrumar, oprimir, abatir; sumergir; soterrar.

Overwhelming [ō-vẹr-hwelm'-ing], *a.* y *a. part.* Abrumador, opresor; irresistible, dominante.

Overwhelmingly [ō-vẹr-hwelm'-ing-li], *adv.* Opresivamente; irresistiblemente.

Overwise [ō-vẹr-waiz'], *a.* Sabihondo, sabio con afectación.—*s.* (Fam.) Un sábelo todo, un pedante.

Overwiseness [ō-vẹr-waiz'-nes], *s.* Sabiduría afectada; pedantería.

Overwork [ō-vẹr-wūrk'], *va.* 1. Hacer trabajar con exceso; fatigar, cansar con el trabajo; exigir esfuerzo superior a las facultades de uno. 2. Elaborar la superficie de (una cosa). —*vn.* Trabajar más allá de lo que permiten las fuerzas.

Overwork [ō'-vẹr-wūrk], *s.* 1. Trabajo excesivo. 2. Trabajo hecho a deshora, fuera de las horas reglamentarias.

Overworn [ō-vẹr-wōrn'], *a.* Gastado por el trabajo; abrumado de fatiga.

Overwrought [ō-vẹr-rōt'], *a.* 1. Excitado, estimulado, conmovido excesivamente. 2. Elaborado, labrado por todas partes, como con calados y encajes. 3. Demasiadamente trabajado, demasiado esmerado. 4. Cansado, fatigado por el exceso de trabajo.

Overzealous [ō-vẹr-zel'-us], *a.* Demasiado celoso o ardiente.

Ovicular [o-vic'-yu-lar], *a.* Ovicular, oval, perteneciente a un huevo.

Ovidian [o-vid'-i-an], *a.* Referente al poeta latino Ovidio, o conforme a su estilo.

Oviduct [ō'-vi-duct], *s.* Oviducto, el conducto por el cual pasa el huevo fecundado del ovario al útero, o al exterior de un animal.

Oviferous [ō-vif'-ẹr-us], **Ovigerous** [ō-vij'-er-us], *a.* Ovífero, que contiene huevos.

Oviform ō'-vi-fōrm], *a.* Aovado, que tiene forma o figura de huevo.

Ovine [ō'-vin], *a.* Lanar, ovejuno, cabruno, relativo a las ovejas o a las cabras.

Oviparous [ō-vip'-a-rus], *a.* Ovíparo, dícese de los animales cuyas hembras ponen huevos.

Oviposit [ō-vi-pez'-it], *va.* Poner huevos, particularmente entre ciertos insectos por medio del órgano que termina el abdomen de las hembras y forma un taladro o un aguijón.

Ovipositor [ō-vi-pes'-it-ẹr], *s.* Órgano compuesto de piezas acanaladas que termina el abdomen de las hembras de muchos insectos y les sirve para depositar sus huevos.

Ovoid, Ovoidal [ō'-void, o-void'-al], *a.* Ovoide, aovado, que tiene la figura o forma de un huevo.

Ovolo [ō'-vo-lo], *s.* (Arq.) Óvol equino, cuarto bocel.

Ovule [ō'-viūl], *s.* Óvulo, germen contenido en el ovario antes de la fecundación; en botánica, rudimento de la semilla.

Ovum [ō'-vum], *s.* (*pl.* OVA). 1. Celdilla con núcleo formada en el ovario de la hembra; huevo en su más amplio sentido. 2. (Arq.) Óvolo, equino, ornamento en forma de huevo.

Owe [ō], *va.* (*pa.* OWING, *pp.* OWED; antiguamente OWN u OUGHT). 1. Deber, estar endeudado, tener deudas. 2. Deber, estar obligado; ser debido a; ser causado por. *I owe him many favours,* Le debo muchos favores. *To be owing,* Ser debido, que se debe; resultado, que es efecto de; imputable, atribuible a; por causa de, por. *To pay what is owing,* Pagar lo que es debido. *To what is it owing?* ¿A qué se le debe atribuir o imputar?

Owl [aul], *s.* (Orn.) Lechuza, buho, mochuelo, ave nocturna de rapiña de la familia de las estrígidas. *Barn-owl,* Lechuza. *Screech-owl,* Buho, zumaya, autillo. *Long-eared owl,* Mochuelo común. *Snowy owl,* Harfango.

Owl, *vn.* (For.) Hacer contrabando.

Owlet [aul'-et], *s.* 1. Buho, lechuza pequeña. 2. Hijuelo del buho. 3. *V. Owlet-moth. Owlet-moth,* Insecto de varias clases de mariposas nocturnas.

Owl-light [aul'-lait], *s.* Crepúsculo.

Owlish [aul'-ish], **Owl-like** [aul'-laic], *a.* Semejante a la lechuza.

Own [ōn], *a.* 1. Propio, lo que pertenece a uno propio, particular. 2. Del grado más cercano, real. *He wrote it with his own hand,* Lo escribió de su propio puño. *To be one's own man,* Ser dueño de sí mismo, no depender de nadie. *My own-self,* Yo mismo. *Own cousin,* Primo hermano, prima hermana. *My own brother,* Mi propio hermano. *'Tis his own fault,* Es culpa suya. *Own* sirve para dar énfasis y acompaña a los adjetivos y pronombres posesivos. *I do not want your hat, I want my own,* No quiero su sombrero de Vd., sino el mío propio. *He has nothing of his own,* No tiene nada que pueda llamar suyo. *He came to his own, and his own received him not,* A lo suyo vino y los suyos no le recibieron.

Own, *va.* 1. Poseer, ser dueño legítimo de alguna cosa. *Who owns this house?* ¿De quién es esta casa? 2. Reconocer, dar por suyo o confesar que una cosa es suya o le pertenece. 3. Confesar, aseverar.

Owner [ōn'-ẹr], *s.* Dueño, poseedor, propietario, el que tiene el título legal. *Owner of a ship,* Naviero.

Ownership [ōn'-ẹr-ship], *s.* Dominio, propiedad, posesión legítima.

Owning [ōn'-ing], *s.* Confesión, reconocimiento.

Ox [ex], *s.* Buey.—*pl.* OXEN, Bueyes. *Ox-eye,* (Mar. y Bot.) Ojo de buey. (Orn.) Pajarito. *Ox-bow,* Yugo de buey. *Ox-cheek,* Quijada de buey. *Ox-eyed,* Que tiene ojos grandes, como los del buey. *Ox-fly,* Tábano. *Ox-goad,* Aguijada de bueyes. *Ox-house, ox-stall,* Boyera, boyeriza, establo para los bueyes. *Ox-like,* Semejante al buey. *Ox-tongue,* (Bot.) Buglosa.

Oxalate [ex'-al-êt], *s.* (Quím.) Oxalato, sal formada de ácido oxálico con alguna base.

Oxalic [ex-al'-ic], *a.* Oxálico, perteneciente a la acedera; dícese de un ácido muy abundante en el reino vegetal.

Oxen, *s. pl.* de Ox.

Oxidate [ex'-i-dêt], *va.* *V.* OXIDIZE.

Oxidation [ex-i-dé'-shun], *s.* Oxidación, acción y efecto de oxidar y oxidarse.

Oxide [ex'-id], *s.* (Quím.) Óxido.

Oxidize [ex'-id-aiz], *va.* Oxidar, combinar el oxígeno con algún cuerpo sin que de la combinación resulte un ácido.

Oxidizement [ex'-i-daiz-mẹnt], *s.* Oxidación.

Oxlip [ex'-lip], *s.* (Bot.) Prímula descollada, una planta.

Oxonian [ex-ō'-ni-an], *a.* Perteneciente a Oxford en Inglaterra o a su universidad.—*s.* Natural, habitante de Oxford o estudiante de su universidad.

Oxychloride [ex"-i-clō'-rid o raid], *s.* Oxicloruro, combinación de un cloruro con un óxido.

Oxygen [ex'-i-jen], *s.* (Quím.) Oxígeno, gas simple, sin olor, color, ni sabor, esencial a la respiración, y uno de los principios constitutivos del agua, del aire, de los óxidos, de muchos ácidos, etc.

Oxygenate [ex'-i-jen-êt], *va.* Oxigenar, combinar con el oxígeno, oxidar.

Oxygenation [ex-i-jen-ē'-shun], *s.* Oxigenación, oxidación, el acto o procedimiento de oxigenar.

Oxygenic, Oxygenous [ex-i-jen'-ic, ex-ij'-ẹ-nus], *a.* De oxígeno, perteneciente al oxígeno o que lo contiene.

Oxygenize [ex'-i-jen-aiz], *va.* Oxigenar.

Oxygen tent [ex'-i-jen tent], *s.* Tienda de oxígeno.

Oxygon [ex'-i-gen], *s.* (Geom.) Oxigonio, acutángulo.

Oxygonal [ex-ig'-o-nal], **Oxygonial** [ex-i-gō'-ni-al], *a.* Que pertenece o se refiere al oxigonio.

Oxyhydrogen torch [ex-i-hai'-dro-jen torch], *s.* Soplete oxhídrico.

Oxymel [ex'-i-mel], *s.* Ojimiel, composición que se hace de miel y vinagre.

Oxytone [ex'-i-tōn], *a.* 1. Que tiene acento agudo en la última sílaba. 2. Que hace que una palabra precedente tome el acento agudo.—*s.* Palabra que lleva dicho acento, vocablo agudo.

Oyer [ō'-yẹr], *s.* (For.) Audición, vista de un pleito o una causa. Audiencia o tribunal en donde se oyen y determinan causas. *Oyer and terminer,* Tribunal inglés que se reune dos veces al año en cada condado; en algunos estados norteamericanos, tribunal de más alta jurisdicción criminal.

Oyes, Oyez [ō'-yes], *inter.* (For.) Oid, escuchad: voz de los ujieres de los tribunales para llamar la atención.

Oylet, *s.* *V.* EYELET.

Oyster [ois'-tẹr], *s.* Ostra, marisco que se cría en una concha bivalva, muy estimado como alimento. *Pickled oysters,* Ostras escabechadas. *Oyster-shells,* Conchas de ostra. *Oyster-bed,* Banco de ostras. *Oyster-farm,* Espacio en el fondo de una bahía donde se cultivan las ostras. *Oyster-cocktail,* Ostras crudas puestas en un vaso pequeño y cubiertas con salsa picante. *Oyster-fishery,* Pesquería de ostras. *Oyster-plant,*

Salsifí. *Oyster-green*, Ulva verde, alga marina. Ulva lactuca o Ulva latissima.

Oyster-woman [ois'-tẹr-wum' an], *sf.* Ostrera, la mujer que vende ostras.

Ozæna [o-zí'-na], *s.* Ocena, úlcera fétida en la nariz.

Ozone [ō'-zōn], *s.* (Quím.) Ozono, gas incoloro muy oxidante que tiene un olor fuerte parecido al del cloro. Se le considera como una alotropía del oxígeno producida por la electricidad.

Ozonic, Ozonous [ō-zō'-nic u ō-zen'-ic, ō-zō'-nus], *a.* Ozónico, perteneciente al ozono, o que lo contiene.

P

P [pî]. Décimasexta letra del alfabeto inglés, que se pronuncia en inglés más fuerte que en español. Es muda cuando precede a la *s* y á la *t* al principio de una palabra, como en *psalm, ptisan.* Cuando la *p* está antes de la *h* pierde su sonido, y se pronuncian las dos letras como *f*, según sucedía antiguamente en español. *P., p.*, es abreviatura de *page*, página; y de *piano*, con tono suave, dulce.

Pa [pā], *s.* Papá; voz que emplean los niños.

Pabular [pab'-yu-lar], *a.* Alimentoso, que alimenta o puede alimentar; nutritivo, que sustenta.

Pabulum [pab'-yu-lum], *s.* 1. Pábulo, alimento, pasto para la subsistencia o conservación. 2. Pábulo, sustento, mantenimiento, hablando de las cosas inmateriales.

Paca [pg'-ca ó pê'-ca], *s.* Paca, mamífero roedor de América, de carne muy estimada y algo mayor que la liebre.

¿**Pacated** [pê'-kê-ted], *a* Pacato, pacífico, tranquilo.

Pace [pês], *s.* 1. Paso. 2. Paso, modo de andar; grado de celeridad. 3. Paso, la diligencia que se usa en la prosecución de algún negocio. 4. Paso, el movimiento regular con que caminan las caballerías. 5. Portante, paso especial del caballo, en el cual mueve a un tiempo la mano y el pie del mismo lado. 6. Medida de tres o 3.3 pies. 7. (Arq.) Estrado, tablado, parte del suelo algo elevado sobre el nivel general. *To keep pace with*, Andar al mismo paso que otro; ir, seguir a un paso igual, llevar el mismo paso.

Pace, *vn.* 1. Pasear, andar poco a poco, a pasos regulares. 2. Ir a paso de andadura las caballerías; andar el caballo alzando a la vez el pie y la mano del mismo lado.—*va.* 1. Andar a pasos medidos. 2. Medir a pasos. 3. Enseñar a andar.

Pacemaker [pês'-mêk'-ẹr], *s.* El que establece el paso o la marcha (en las carreras).

Pacer [pê'-sẹr], *s.* 1. El que mide a pasos. 2. Caballo de paso de andadura; caballería que va alzando a la vez la mano y el pie del mismo lado.

Pacha [pa-shā'], *s.* *V* PASHA.

Pachyderm [pak'-i-dẹrm], *a.* Paquidermo, de piel gruesa y dura.

Pachydermatous, Pachydermous [pak-i-dẹr'-ma-tus, mus], *a.* Paquidermo.

Pacific [pa-sif'-ic], †**Pacifical** [pa-sif'-ic-al], **Pacificatory** [pa-sif'-i-ca-to-ri], *a.* 1. Pacífico, pacificador, dispuesto a hacer o a restablecer la paz. 2. Quieto, sosegado, tranquilo.

Pacificate [pa-sif'-i-kêt], *va.* Pacificar, apaciguar.

Pacification [pas-i-fi-kê'-shun], *s.* Pacificación, apaciguamiento.

Pacificator [pas-i-fi-kê'-tẹr], **Pacifier** [pas'-i-fai-ẹr], *s.* Pacificador.

Pacificator [pa-sif'-i-kê-tẹr], *s.* Pacificador, el que restablece la paz o pacifica los que están opuestos y enemistados.

Pacifist [pa'-si-fist], *s.* Pacifista.

Pacify [pas'-i-fai], *va.* Pacificar, poner paz, sosegar, aquietar, calmar, tranquilizar.

Pacing [pês'-ing], *s.* Paso, andadura.

Pack [pac], *s.* 1. Lío, fardo, carga. 2. Baraja de naipes. 3. Muta, perrada, conjunto de perros de caza. 4. Conjunto de hombres o animales que van en compañía; vuelo de perdices; hatajo o cuadrilla de malhechores, manga de pícaros. *Pack of robbers*, Cuadrilla de ladrones. 5. Gran extensión de hielos flotantes. 6. Cubierta de sábanas mojadas, que se usa en ciertos casos de enfermedad.

Pack, *va.* 1. Enfardelar, embalar, envasar; encajonar, poner en cajas; disponer en buen orden para llevar. 2. Meter en cualquier receptáculo. 3. Apretar, juntar algo apretando; colmar. 4. Despachar, enviar de prisa. 5. Cargar, poner la carga a una acémila. 6. Llevar sobre la espalda o el lomo. 7. Envolver a un enfermo en sábanas mojadas, con cubiertas secas al exterior. 8. Empandillar el naipe o poner un naipe junto con otros para hacer alguna trampa. 9. Juntar o unir personas escogidas para algún mal fin.—*vn.* 1. Empaquetar; hacer el baúl, arreglar el equipaje. 2. Reunirse en una masa firme. *Ground packs after a rain*, El terreno se consolida después de la lluvia. 3. Enfardelarse, empaquetarse, encajonarse. 4. Marcharse o irse corriendo. *To pack away, off* o *one's tools*, Largarse, huir, tomar las de Villadiego. *To pack off*, Despedir, despachar; poner de patitas en la calle. *To send one packing*, Enviar a uno a pasear.

Package [pak'-ẹj], *s.* Fardo, paquete; embalaje, gasto de embalar o empaquetar géneros o mercancías.

Pack animal [pac an'-i-mal], *s.* Acémila, animal de carga.

Pack-cloth [pac'-clōth], *s.* Arpillera.

Packer [pak'-ẹr], *s.* Embalador, empaquetador.

Packet [pak'-et], *s.* 1. Paquete, fardo pequeño. 2. Paquete de cartas; mala, la valija del correo de posta. 3. (Mar.) Paquebot o paquebote, correo marítimo o buque que sirve de correo.

Packet, *va.* Empaquetar, enfardelar.

Packet-boat [pak'-et-bōt], *s.* Paquebot o paquebote, correo marítimo, embarcación que sirve para llevar los correos de una parte a otra.

Pack-horse [pac'-hōrs], *s.* Caballo de carga.

Packing [pak'-ing], *s.* 1. Embalaje, envase, enfardeladura. 2. Empaque, empaquetadura, relleno de estopa, grasa, etc., para hacer impermeable al agua u otro flúido, v. g. a un émbolo; o para llenar un espacio vacío. 3. (Alb.) Relleno, enripiado, cascajo. 4. (Des.) Fraude, engaño. *Packing-box, packing-case*, Caja de embalaje; envase. *Packing leather*, Cuero para empaquetadura.

Packing house [pak'-ing haus], *s.* 1. Empacadora. 2. Frigorífico.

Packman [pac'-man], *s.* Buhonero, vendedor ambulante.

Pack-saddle [pac'-sad-l], *s.* Albarda, una de las piezas que componen el aparejo de las bestias de carga.

Packstaff [pac'-stqf], *s.* Palo de buhonero.

Packthread [pac'-thred], *s.* Bramante, hilo de acarreto, guita, hilo gordo o cordel muy delgado hecho de cáñamo.

Pack train [pac trên], *s.* Recua (de animales de carga).

Pact [pact], ¿**Paction** [pac'-shun], *s.* Pacto, contrato, convenio, tratado, composición, convención, ajuste, trato.

Pad [pad], *s.* 1. Cojín, almohadilla, colchoncillo lleno de alguna substancia elástica para evitar la vibración o el roce; peto, coraza acolchada (para la esgrima); útil que sirve para aplicar tinta. 2. Cuaderno, conjunto de pliegos de papel engomados por dos cantos, que forman como un libro. 3. Hoja grande y flotante de una planta acuática. (Var. de *pod.*)

Pad, *s.* (Prov.) 1. Haca, caballo de camino. 2. Salteador de caminos a pie: dícese comúnmente *footpad*. 3. Senda, camino estrecho. (Var. de *path.*)

Pad, *va.* 1. Poner una almohada para que esté más blando el asiento; forrar, rellenar de pelote o paja. 2. Aumentar (un libro) con material superfluo. 3. Encolar, pegar pliegos de papel por los cantos, de manera que formen cuadernos.

Padded [pad'-ed], *a.* Acojinado, rellenado (con paja, papel, algodón, etc.)

Padder [pad'-ẹr], *s.* 1. Rellenador; el que hace almohadillas. 2. (Des.) Salteador de caminos que va a pie.

Padding [pad'-ing], *s.* 1. El acto de rellenar, de formar un colchoncillo o almohadilla. 2. Guata, (Amer. huata) lo que sirve para rellenar, o para hacer una almohadilla. 3. Lo que se inserta o introduce únicamente para aumentar el volumen de algo.

Paddle [pad'-l], *vn.* 1. Remar. 2. Chapotear, golpear el agua con los pies o las manos de modo que salpique.—*va.* 1. Impeler con un canalete. 2. Manosear, tentar y tocar con las manos alguna cosa, dar repetidas palmaditas. 3. (Fam.) Golpear con un canalete.

Paddle, *s.* Canalete, especie de remo; paleta. *Paddle-board, paddle-float*, Paleta de rueda hidráulica. *Paddle-wheel*, Rueda de paleta. *Paddle-wheel steamer*, Vapor de ruedas.

Paddle, Paddlestaff [pad'-l-stqf], *s.* Cualquier palo con un extremo de hierro puntiagudo; béstola o arrejada, instrumento que se usa para desbrozar el arado.

Paddler [pad'-lẹr], *s.* Remero.

Paddock [pad'-ẹc], *s.* 1. Dehesa, cercado para ejercitar los caballos. 2. (Prov. y Esco.) Escuerzo, sapo.

Paddock-stool [pad'-uc-stūl], *s.* Especie de hongo.

Paddy [pad'-i], *s.* 1. Un irlandés;

apodo derivado del nombre propio *Patrick*, muy común entre los irlandeses. 2. Un ánade de la América del Norte. 3. Taladro para pozos con perforadores de expansión.
Paddy, *s.* Arroz en cáscara, palay (nombre angloindio). *Paddy-field*, Arrozal, campo de arroz.
Padesoy [pad'-e-soi], *s.* *V.* PADUASOY.
Padlock [pad'-lec], *s.* Candado.
Padlock, *va.* Echar el candado, cerrar con candado.
Padra [pā'-dra], *s.* Nombre de un te negro de superior calidad.
Paduasoy [pad'-yu-a-soi], *s.* Seda de Padua, tela de seda fuerte y rica del siglo XVIII; entonces la usaban las personas de uno y otro sexo.
Pæan [pī'-an], *s.* Canto o himno de triunfo.
Pædobaptism [pī-do-bap'-tizm], *s.* Bautismo de niños.
Pagan [pé'-gan], *s.* Pagano, gentil. —*a.* Pagano, gentil, étnico.
Paganish [pé'-gan-ish], *a.* Pagano, idólatra.
Paganism [pé'-gan-izm], *s.* Paganismo, idolatría.
Paganize [pé'-gan-aiz], *va.* y *vn.* Hacer o hacerse pagano.
Page [péj], *s.* 1. Página. 2. Libro, escrito: cualquier fuente de conocimientos. 3. Paje, criado, asistente; jovencito al servicio de algún alto personaje.
Page, *va.* Foliar, paginar.
Pageant [paj'-ant], *s.* 1. Espectáculo público; carro o arco triunfal; trofeo. 2. Apariencia, exterioridad.—*a.* Ostentoso, vistoso, pomposo; superficial.
Pageantry [paj'-ant-ri], *s.* 1. Fasto, fausto, pompa. 2. Exterioridad.
Pagehood [péj'-hud], *s.* Estado o servicio de paje.
Page proof [péj prūf], *s.* (Impr.) Prueba de plana
†**Paginal** [paj'-i-nal], *a.* Compuesto de páginas.
Paginate [paj'-i-nét], *va.* Paginar (un libro, etc.).
Paging [pé'-jing], *s.* Paginación, acción y efecto de numerar las páginas de un libro; el orden de las páginas. *Paging-machine*, Máquina para numerar páginas.
Pagoda [pa-gō'-da], *s.* Pagoda, templo de la India oriental; una moneda del mismo país.
Paid [péd], *pret.* y *pp.* de *To* PAY.
Paidology [pai-dol'-o-ji], *s.* (Neologismo) Estudio científico del niño por especialistas instruidos al efecto.
Paid-up [péd-up'], *a.* Acabado de pagar. *Paid-up policy*, Póliza (de seguros) pagada.
Pail [pél], *s.* Cubo, colodra; pozal, cubeta. (Mar.) Balde.
Pailful [pél'-ful], *s.* Cubada o cubetada, la cantidad que cabe en un cubo.
Pain [pén], *va.* 1. Causar dolor, atormentar, hacer padecer físicamente. 2. Acongojar, causar una pena, un daño moral, angustiar, afligir, inquietar. El verbo *pain*, activo en inglés, hay que traducirlo a veces en español por doler (neutro), particularmente con los nombres de las partes del cuerpo. *My eye pains me*, Me duele el ojo.
Pain, *s.* 1. Pena, castigo. *On pain of death*, So pena de muerte. 2. Pena, dolor, tormento, trabajo. 3. Inquietud, pesadumbre, sentimiento. *Pains*, *pl.* (1) Trabajo, incomodidad, fatiga. (2) Ansiedad, inquietud, solicitud. (3) Dolores de parto. *A pain in the knee*, Un dolor de rodilla. *To be in pain*, Estar con mucho cuidado, estar inquieto; doler, padecer. *To be in pain all over*, Dolerle a uno todo el cuerpo. *To feel pain*, Sentir dolor. *Where do you feel pain?* ¿Dónde le duele á Vd.? *To be at the pains of*, Tomarse el trabajo de, poner cuidado. aplicarse, cuidar. *To take great pains*, Afanarse, empeñarse, esmerarse en algo. *No gains without pains*, No hay ganancia sin trabajo. *It gives pain to see*, Duele verlo.
Painful [pén'-ful], *a.* 1. Dolorido, afligido, desconsolado, atormentado. 2. Doloroso, aflictivo. 3. Penoso, difícil, laborioso, trabajoso. 4. Industrioso, aplicado.
Painfully [pén'-ful-i], *adv.* 1. Dolorosamente. 2. Penosamente. 3. Laboriosamente.
Painfulness [pén'-ful-nes], *s.* Dolor, aflicción, pena, trabajo, fatiga; industria.
†**Painim**, *a.* y *s.* *V.* PAYNIM.
Painless [pén'-les], *a.* Sin pena o trabajo; libre de dolor.
Painlessness [pén'-les-nes], *s.* Ausencia de dolor.
Painstaker [pénz'-ték-er], *s.* Trabajador, afanador.
Painstaking [pénz'-ték-ing], *a.* Cuidadoso, industrioso; afanoso, fiel en ejecución.
Paint [pént], *va.* 1. Pintar, cubrir de colores; en sentido más amplio, dar una capa delgada de algún líquido. 2. Pintar, representar o delinear una figura con colores. 3. Pintar, describir por escrito o de palabra alguna cosa.—*vn.* Afeitarse, aderezarse o componerse con afeites. *To paint the town red*, (Germ. E. U.) Cometer diabluras, divertirse de una manera turbulenta, correr la tuna como embriagado, alborotar.
Paint, *s.* 1. Pintura, el color con que se pinta; material preparado para pintar o dar capas sobre otro, ya seco, ya mezclado con aceite, agua, etc. 2. Pintura, descripción o narración de alguna cosa. 3. Afeite, colorete. *Paint-box*, Caja de colores o pinturas. *Paint-brush*, Brocha, pincel. *Oil paints*, Pinturas, colores al óleo.
Painter [pént'-er], *s.* 1. Pintor. 2. (Mar.) Amarra del bote o de la lancha. *House-painter*, Pintor de casas. *Ornamental painter*, Pintor decorador. *Sign-painter*, Pintor de muestras.
Painting [pént'-ing], *s.* 1. Pintura, el arte de pintar; también, el acto u oficio de dar capas de colores con una brocha. 2. Pintura, el cuadro pintado. 3. Pintura, la narración o descripción que se hace de alguna cosa por escrito o de palabra.
Paintress [pént'-res], *sf.* Pintora.
Pair [pār], *s.* 1. Par, el conjunto de dos cosas de una misma especie; dos personas o animales unidos o asociados. 2. Una sola cosa que tiene dos partes semejantes dependientes una de otra. *A pair of scissors, of spectacles*, Un par de tijeras, de anteojos. 3. Par, tómase en inglés muy comúnmente por el marido y la mujer; macho y hembra de los animales, cuando están apareados. 3. Juego de cosas semejantes que forman un todo; escalera. 4. Dos miembros de una asamblea legislativa de opiniones contrarias, que convienen en abstenerse de votar y así anulan mutuamente su voto.
Pair, *vn.* 1. Aparearse, hacer pareja. 2. Hermanarse, igualarse una cosa con otra.—*va.* 1. Parear. 2. Hermanar, igualar una cosa con otra. *To pair off*, (1) Hablando de las votaciones del parlamento, es salir del local dos diputados de opiniones contrarias antes de la votación. (2) Retirarse de una reunión en parejas. *To pair with*, Hacer pareja dos personas.
Pajamas o **pyjamas** [pa-jā'-maz, pi-jā'-maz], *s. pl.* Pijamas o piyamas.
Pal [pal], *s.* (Vulg.) Compañero, confederado.
Palace [pal'-és], *s.* Palacio; edificio suntuoso.
†**Palacious** [pa-lé'-shus]. *V.* PALATIAL.
Paladin [pal'-a-din], *s.* Paladín, uno de los doce pares de Carlomagno; de aquí, modelo de caballería.
Palæography, Palæontology, *s.* *V* PALEOGRAPHY, PALEONTOLOGY.
Palanquin [pal-an-kīn'], *s.* Palanquín, especie de litera cubierta.
Palatable [pal'-a-ta-bl], *a.* Sabroso, gustoso al paladar.
Palatal [pal'-a-tal], *a.* y *s.* Paladial, que se refiere al paladar; (consonante) pronunciada con el auxilio del paladar, como la *k*, la *ñ*, la *y*.
Palate [pal'-et], *s.* 1. Paladar, el órgano del sentido del gusto. 2. Paladar, el apetito o deseo de cualquier cosa inmaterial o espiritual.
Palatial [pa-lé'-shal], *a.* Palaciego, palatino, que pertenece a palacio; magnífico, suntuoso.
Palatic [pa-lat'-ic], *a.* (Poco us.) Paladial: dícese de las letras que se pronuncian tocando el paladar con la lengua. *V.* PALATAL.
Palatinate [pa-lat'-i-nét], *s.* Palatinado, provincia o dominios de un príncipe palatino.
Palatine [pal'-a-tin], *a.* 1. Palatino, dotado de privilegios reales. *A count palatine*, Conde palatino. *A county palatine*, Palatinado. 2. Paladial, perteneciente al paladar.
Palaver [pa-lā'-ver], *s.* 1. Charla frívola, palabrería, particularmente zalamería, lisonja; embustes. 2. Plática larga; conferencia o discusión pública.—*va.* y *vn.* 1. Adular, lisonjear, usar de zalamerías, engatusar. 2. Charlar, hablar mucho sin substancia. (< pg. palavra, esp. palabra.)
Pale [pél], *a.* 1. Pálido, descolorido. 2. Claro o que no es de muy subido color. *Pale wine*, Vino clarete. *Pale green*, Verde claro. 3. Pálido, lo que no brilla ni tiene lustre. *To grow pale*, Volverse pálido, palidecer.
Pale [pél], *s.* 1. Estaca, palo puntiagudo para clavarlo en tierra. 2. Palizada, empalizada, defensa de estacas. 3. Palizada, el sitio cercado de estacas. 4. Distrito, territorio limitado; mojón, límite. 5. Espacio cerrado, literal o figuradamente; esfera, seno, gremio, sociedad. 6. (Her.) Palo de escudo. *Pale of the church*, Gremio de la iglesia, bajo la protección o autoridad de la iglesia.
Pale, *va.* 1. Empalizar. 2. Cercar, rodear. 3. Poner pálido, hacer empalidecer a una persona. 4. Descolorar, quitar o amortiguar el color de una cosa.

Palea [pé'-lę-a], *s.* (Bot.) Glumilla, arista, cubierta floral de las gramíneas. (Lat.)

Paleaceous pé-lę-é'-shus], *a.* Aristoso, que tiene aristas o pajas.

Pale-eyed [pēl'-aid], *a.* Que tiene la vista turbia o los ojos pálidos.

Paleface [pēl'-fēs], *s.* Persona blanca o caucásica; nombre que dan los indios a los blancos.

Pale-faced [pēl'-fēst], *a.* Pálido, descolorido de cara.

Palely [pēl'-li], *adv.* Con palidez.

Paleness [pēl'-nes], *s.* Palidez.

Paleograph [pé'-lę-o-graf], *s.* Manuscrito antiguo.

Paleography [pa-lę-eg'-ra-fi], *s.* Paleografía, conocimiento de las escrituras antiguas.

Paleolithic [pē-lę-o-lith'-ic], *a.* (Geol.) Paleolítico, relativo a la primera edad de la piedra.

Paleologist [pē-lę-el'-o-jist], *s.* Paleólogo, el que es versado en paleología.

Paleology [pē-lę-el'-o-ji], *s.* Paleología, arqueología, el estudio de la antigüedad o antigüedades.

Paleontology [pē-lę-en-tel'-o-ji], *s.* Paleontología, ciencia que trata de los restos orgánicos fósiles y de cuanto tuvo vida en la superficie del globo en las épocas geológicas. *Paleontologist,* Paleontologista.

Paleozoic [pē-lę-o-zō'-ic o pel-e-o-zō'-ic], *a.* Paleozoico, perteneciente a la época geológica más antigua.

Palette [pal'-et], *s.* Paleta, tabla pequeña en que el pintor tiene los colores dispuestos para pintar.

Palfrey [pōl'-fri], *s.* Palafrén, caballo pequeño y manso para señoras.

Palfreyed [pōl'-frid], *a.* Dícese de las señoras que tienen palafrén o van a caballo en él.

Palimpsest [pal'-imp-sest], *s.* Palimpsesto, manuscrito en pergamino en el que se escribía dos veces, la segunda después de borrarse total o parcialmente el texto original.

Palindrome [pal'-in-drōm], *s.* Palindromia, palabra o sentencia que dice lo mismo leída al revés que al derecho; v. g. *ama; Yreka Bakery* (nombre califórnico).

Paling [pél'-ing], *s.* Estacada, palizada.

Palingenesis, Palingenesia [pal-in-jen'-e-sis, pal-in-jen-í'-si-a], *s.* Regeneración, renacimiento.

Palinode [pal'-in-ōd], †**Palinody** [pal-in-o-di], *s.* Palinodia, retractación pública de lo que antes se había dicho. *To sing a palinode* o *to make his palinode,* Cantar la palinodia. (Fam.) Llamarse antana o andana.

Palisade [pal-i-sēd'], **Palisado** [pal-i-sé'-do], *s.* 1. Palizada, empalizada. 2. *pl.* Peñasco largo, precipicio de rocas. Extensa serie de rocas que forman precipicio, por lo general a orillas de un río.

Palish [pēl'-ish], *a.* Algo pálido, paliducho.

Pall [pōl], *s.* 1. Paño de ataúd, paño mortuorio; (fig.) lo que ocasiona aflicción o tristeza. 2. Cubierta de cáliz; también, palio de arzobispo. 3. (Des.) Manto real. *Pall-bearers,* Los que en un funeral acompañan y rodean el cadáver en calidad de principales dolientes.

Pall, *vn.* Hacerse insípido o sin sabor; cesar de producir interés o dar placer.—*va.* 1. Evaporar, desvirtuar. 2. Desalentar, desanimar. 3. Saciar, ahitar, hartar

Palladium [pal-lé'-di-um], *s.* 1. Paladión; en Troya, imagen de Palas o Minerva, a la que se consideraba como garantía de la salud pública; de aquí, cualquier garantía o prenda de seguridad, salvaguardia. 2. (Min.) Paladio, metal raro que se halla mezclado con la platina.

Pallet [pal'-et], *s.* 1. Paleta de reloj, fiador de rueda, retén, linguete. *V.* PAWL. 2. Uno de los discos en la cadena sin fin de una bomba de cadena. 3. (Mar.) Caja de lastre. 4. Torno de alfarero; también, paleta, instrumento de albañilería. 5. Paleta de pintor. 6. Herramienta empleada para dorar o inscribir los lomos de los libros. 7. Válvula de cañón de órgano. 8. Jergón, camilla, cama pequeña y pobre.

Pallial [pal'-i-al], *a.* Que se refiere al palio o manto de los moluscos.

Palliate [pal'-i-ēt], *va.* 1. Excusar, disculpar, extenuar o minorar una falta con disculpas. 2. Paliar un mal, no curarle de raíz, mitigar, reducir la severidad de algo, v. g. de una enfermedad.

Palliation [pal-i-é'-shun], *s.* 1. Paliación, mitigación, alivio. 2. Cura paliativa o imperfecta.

Palliative [pal'-i-a-tiv], *a.* Paliativo, paliatorio, mitigador, aliviador.—*s.* Paliativo, lo que mitiga.

Pallid [pal'-id], *a.* Pálido, descolorido.

Pallidity [pa-lid'-i-ti], **Pallidness** [pal'-id-nes], *s.* Palidez.

Pallium [pal'-i-um], *s.* 1. Palio. 2. Palio, clámide, de los antiguos griegos y romanos. 3. Palio, manto, de un molusco o de una gaviota.

Pall-mall [pel'-mel], *s.* Mallo, un juego; el mallo con que se empuja la bola en este juego y el sitio donde se juega.

Pallor [pal'-ęr], *s.* Palidez, disminución del color natural; falta de color.

Palm [pām], *s.* 1. (Bot.) Palma, palmera, familia de plantas endógenas, que crecen principalmente en las regiones cálidas. *Palm-Sunday,* Domingo de Ramos. *Palm-oil,* Aceite de palma. 2. Palma, rama de la palmera. 3. Palma, victoria. *To bear* o *carry away the palm,* Alcanzar la palma, la victoria. 4. Palma, la parte interior y cóncava de la mano. 5. Palma, el ancho de la mano, medida de tres y a veces cuatro pulgadas. 6. (Mar.) Rempujo, especie de dedal que se usa para coser las velas. *Palm-bird,* Pájaro que habita en las palmeras; en especial, el llamado tejedor. Ploceus. *Palm-cabbage,* Hojas tiernas comestibles que crecen en la cima de ciertas especies de palmeras. *Palm-tree,* Palmera, palma, cualquier árbol de esta familia. *Palm-wine,* Vino de palmera, la savia fermentada del cocotero, etc.

Palm, *va.* 1. Escamotar, esconder en la mano como hacen los prestidigitadores. 2. Escamotar, engañar, defraudar a alguno con destreza. 3. Manejar, tomar en la mano; manosear, tentar y tocar con la mano. 4. (Fam.) Encajar, dar como verdadero lo que no lo es. 5 Cubrir de ramas de palmera.

Palma [pal'-ma], *s.* Palma de la mano o la parte correspondiente a ella en los animales e insectos.

Palma-christi [pal''-ma-cris'-ti], *s.* (Bot.) Palmacristi o higuera infernal

Palmar [pal'-mar], *a.* Palmar, colocado cerca de la palma de la mano.

Palmary [pal'-ma-ri], *a.* Principal, palmario, claro, palmar.

Palmate, Palmated [pal'-mēt, ed], *a.* Palmeado, parecido a una mano abierta; palmado, que tiene lóbulos (cinco por lo común) que divergen como los dedos de una mano.

Palmately [pal'-met-li], *adv.* De un modo palmado o palmeado.

Palmer [pām'-ęr], *s.* Palmero, peregrino, romero.

Palmer-worm [pām'-ęr-wūrm], *s.* 1. Oruga velluda que es una plaga destructora. 2. Larva de cualquier coleóptero destructivo, como el gorgojo.

Palmetto [pal-met'-o], *s.* 1 Palmera de la Carolina, cualquiera de las varias palmeras de copa en forma de abanico, especialmente la Sabal palmetto de los Estados Unidos. 2. Sombrero hecho de las hojas de esta palmera. (< palmito.) *Palmetto State,* Carolina del Sur.

Palmiferous [pal-mif'-ęr-us], *a.* Palmífero, que produce palmas.

Palmiped [pal'-mi-ped], *a.* Palmeado, palmípedo, que tiene los dedos de los pies unidos con una membrana, como las aves acuáticas.

Palmister [pal'-mis-tęr], *s.* Quiromántico, el que pretende adivinar por la inspección de las palmas de las manos.

Palmistry [pal'-mis-tri], *s.* Quiromancia, pretendida adivinación por la inspección de las palmas de las manos.

Palmitic [pal-mit'-ic], *a.* Palmítico, de la palmera, sacado de la palmera. *Palmitic acid,* Ácido palmítico ($C_{16}H_{32}O_2$), compuesto cristalizable contenido en numerosos aceites y grasas animales y vegetales.

Palmy [pām'-i], *a.* 1. Próspero, floreciente; triunfal, de triunfo. 2. Palmar, lleno de palmas o palmeras.

Palp, Palpus [palp, pal'-pus], *s.* Palpo, órgano del tacto colocado en la parte inferior de la boca de ciertos insectos; apéndice oral de moluscos bivalvos.—*pl.* PALPI.

Palpability [pal-pa-bil'-i-ti], *s.* Palpabilidad, evidencia.

Palpable [pal'-pa-bl], *a.* 1. Palpable. 2. Palpable, evidente, patente, obvio.

Palpableness [pal'-pa-bl-nes], *s.* El estado de lo que es palpable.

Palpably [pal'-pa-bli], *adv.* Palpablemente, claramente.

Palpation [pal-pé'-shun], *s.* Palpamiento, palpadura; (Med.) exploración por medio de las manos.

Palpebra [pal'-pę-bra], *s.* Pálpebra. párpado.

Palpebral [pal'-pę-bral], *a.* Palpebral, perteneciente a los párpados.

Palpitate [pal'-pi-tēt], *vn.* Palpitar, latir, agitarse el corazón; agitarse o moverse irregularmente.

Palpitation [pal-pi-té'-shun], *s* Palpitación, latido.

Palsied [pōl'-zid], *a.* Paralítico

Palsy [pōl'-zi], *s.* 1. Parálisis, perlesía. 2. Flaqueza de acción, ineficacia.

Palsy [pōl'-zi], *va.* 1. Paralizar, afectar con parálisis. 2. Paralizar, impedir la acción moral de alguna cosa.

Palter [pōl'-tęr], *vn* Jugar o burlarse de alguno, pegar petardos; usar de rodeos y circunlocuciones.—*va.* (Des.) Desperdiciar, malgastar.

Palterer [pōl'-tęr-ęr], *s.* Petardista, engañador; el que usa de rodeos para lograr un fin.

Paltriness [pōl'-tri-nes], *s.* Vileza, bajeza, mezquindad.

Paltry [pōl'-tri], *a.* Vil, despreciable, miserable, mezquino.

Paludal [pa-liū'-dal], **Palustral** [pa-lus'-tral], *a.* Palúdico, palustre, perteneciente a lagunas o pantanos; también se dice de la fiebre que suelen ocasionar los miasmas de los pantanos.

Paly [pé'-li], *a.* 1. (Poét.) Pálido, marchito, que carece de colores y frescura. 2. (Her.) Dividido en partes iguales por medio de líneas o barras verticales.

Pampas [pam'-paz], *s. pl.* Pampas, llanuras (de la Argentina, etc.).

Pamper [pam'-pęr], *va.* Atracar, llenar de comida, engordar; tratar con mucho regalo, mimar, acariciar.

Pamperer [pam'-pęr-ęr], *s.* Acariciador.

Pamphlet [pam'-flet], *s.* Folleto; papelucho.

Pamphleteer [pam-flet-ir'], *s.* Folletista.

Pan [pan], *s.* 1. Cualquier vasija de metal o de barro ancha y honda destinada a componer o guardar la comida; paila de cerero; cazo, cuenco. 2. Gamella, cazo de hierro para ensayar arenas auríferas. 3. Cazoleta de un arma de fuego. 4. (Mec. Quicio, rangua. 5. Cráneo. 6. Subsuelo muy duro, capa de arcilla. *Stewing-pan*, Cazuela. *Frying-pan*, Sartén. *Warming-pan*, Calentador. *Baking-pan*, Tartera. *Sauce-pan*, Cazo, cacerola. *Perfuming-pan*, Perfumador. *Dripping-pan*, Grasera. *Earthen pan*, Cazuela de barro, barreño pequeño, lebrillo, cuenco. *Snuffer-pan*, Platillo para las despabiladeras. *Pan-pudding*, Una especie de pudín cocido en el horno. *Brain-pan*, El cráneo. *Knee-pan*, Rótula, choquezuela. *Pan of a gun-lock*, Cazoleta de escopeta. *A flash in the pan*, El acto de dar higa un arma de fuego. *V.* FLASH.

Pan, *va.* 1. Separar el oro sacudiendo la tierra o arena que lo contiene con agua en un cazo metálico. 2. (Fam.) Alcanzar, ensacar, enredar, lograr de cualquier modo. 3. Cocer y servir en una cazuela.—*vn.* 1. Con *out*, dar oro la tierra o arena; aparecer oro en un cazo; de aquí, (fam.) dar buen resultado o provecho. 2. Procurar obtener oro usando del cazo. 3. Girar la cámera fotográfica.

Panacea [pan-a-sí'-a], *s.* 1. Panacea. 2. (Bot.) Pánace, planta medicinal.

Panada [pa-né'-da], *s.* Panetela, substancia de pan que se da a los enfermos.

Panama hat [pan'-a-mā hat], *s.* Sombrero panamá o de jipijapa.

Pan-American [pan-a-mer'-i-can], *a.* Panamericano, perteneciente a ambas Américas del Norte y del Sur.

Pan-Americanism [pan-a-mer'-i-can-izm], *s.* Panamericanismo.

Panary [pan'-a-ri], *a.* Lo que pertenece al pan, panado.

Pancake [pan'-kék], *s.* Fruta de sartén; buñuelo.

Panchromatic [pan-kro-mat'-ic], *a.* Pancromático (en fotografía).

Pancratic, Pancratical [pan-crat'-ic, al], *a.* Pancracial, que pertenece a ciertos ejercicios gimnásticos de los griegos; muy atletico, muy fuerte en los ejercicios gimnásticos.

Pancreas [pan'-crę-as], *s.* (Anat.) Páncreas, un cuerpo glanduloso situado en el abdomen detrás del estómago.

Pancreatic [pan-crę-at'-ic], *a.* Pancreático, que pertenece al pancreas.

Pandean [pan-dí'-an], *a.* Que se refiere al dios Pan.

Pandect [pan'-dect], *s.* 1. El tratado que comprende todo lo que se sabe en alguna ciencia. 2. *Pandects, pl.* Pandectas, la recopilación de varias obras. 3. La recopilación de las leyes del derecho civil hecha por Justiniano.

Pandemonium [pan-dę-mō'-ni-um], *s.* 1. Pandemonio, el lugar de reunión de los demonios. 2. Tumulto, batahola diabólica.

Pandemic [pan-dem'-ic], *a.* Pandémico, que ataca a todo un pueblo, muy epidémico.

Pander [pan'-dęr], *s.* 1. Alcahuete. 2. Tercero, alcahuete, el que ministra a las pasiones bajas o a las tendencias degradantes de otros.

Pander, *va.* 1. Alcahuetear. 2. Ministrar a las pasiones o a las prevenciones de otro.

Panderism [pan'-dęr-izm], *s.* Alcahuetería.

Pandiculated [pan-dic'-yu-lét-ed], *a.* Extendido, abierto.

Pandore [pan-dōr'], *s.* Bandola, instrumento músico de cuerdas de alambre.

Pandour, Pandur [pan'-dūr], *s.* Panduro, soldado húngaro de infantería que antiguamente tenía fama de cruel y sanguinario.

Pandowdy [pan-dau'-di], *s.* Postre de manzanas cortadas en rebanadas y cocidas en una vasija honda, con o sin pasta.

Pane [pén], *s.* 1. Cuadro de vidrio: tómase por cada uno de los vidrios o cristales de una vidriera. 2. Cuadro, cada una de las piezas de ciertas obras hechas de pedazos cuadrados. 3. Una superficie plana o llana en un objeto que tiene varios lados. *V.* PANEL.

Paned [pénd], *a.* Dícese de la obra que contiene pedacitos cuadrados de diversos géneros.

Panegyric [pan-ę-jir'-ic], *s.* Panegírico, discurso en alabanza de alguno.—*a.* Panegírico, perteneciente a la alabanza o elogio.

Panegyrical [pan-ę-jir'-i-cal], *a.* Panegírico.

Panegyrist [pan-ę-jir'-ist], *s.* Panegirista.

Panel [pan'-el], *s.* 1. Entrepaño, tablero, pieza rectangular puesta en un bastidor. 2. Tabla preparada para hacer un cuadro. 3. Superficie llana, cara de la piedra labrada. 4. Paño de otra tela insertado a lo largo de un vestido de mujer.

Panel, *s.* Panel, grupo de personas seleccionadas para un fin especial: jurados, oradores, especialistas, etc. *Panel discussion*, Discusión a cargo de un panel.

Panel, *va.* Hacer alguna cosa en forma de tableros o cuarterones; labrar en artesones.

Paneling, Panelling [pan'-el-ing], *s.* Artesón, artesonado; conjunto de entrepaños.

Paneless [pén'-les], *a.* Dícese de las cosas hechas en cuadritos, cuarterones o pedazos de diversa figura cuando les faltan uno o más de ellos. *A paneless window*, Una vidriera a la que le faltan algunos vidrios ó cristales.

Panful [pan'-ful], *s.* Cazada, el contenido de un cazo.

Pang [pang], *s.* Angustia, dolor, congoja, tormento, pena. *The pangs of death*, Las ansias de la muerte, la agonía. *The pangs of childbirth*, Los dolores de parto.

Pang, *va.* Atormentar, afligir, angustiar, acongojar.

Panhandler [pan'-han-dlęr], *s.* Limosnero, pordiosero.

Pan-Hellenism [pan-hel'-ęn-izm], *s.* Panhelenismo, la aspiración de reunir a todos los griegos en un solo cuerpo político.

Panic [pan'-ic], *a.* Pánico.

Panic, *s.* 1. Miedo o terror ciego, cobardía extrema. 2. Pánico comercial, que suele producir quiebras y desastres en el mundo de los negocios, precipitando bancarrotas. *Panic-stricken, panic-struck*, Sobrecogido de terror.

Panic, Panic-grass, *s.* (Bot.) Panizo, nombre dado a un género de plantas gramíneas.

Panicle [pan'-i-cl], *s.* (Bot.) Panículo, panoja, variedad de inflorescencia compuesta.

Paniculate, Paniculated [pa-nic'-yu-lét, ed], *a.* (Bot.) Apanojado: dícese de las plantas cuyo tallo o flores están dispuestos en forma de panoja.

Panier, *s.* *V.* PANNIER.

Panniculus, Pannicle [pan-nic'-yu-lus, pan'-i-cl], *s.* (Biol.) Panículo, membrana delgada, cubierta parecida a una sábana.

Pannier [pan'-yęr], *s.* 1. Cuévano, uno de los dos canastos que llevan las acémilas. 2. Cesto grande, serón, canasto, canastón. 3. Cestón, gabión. 4. (Arq.) *V.* CORBEL. 5. Tontillo que llevaban las mujeres en tiempo pasado.

Panoply [pan'-o-pli], *s.* Panoplia, armadura completa.

Panorama [pan-o-rā'-ma], *s.* Panorama, pintura en que se ven los objetos como si fuesen reales.

Pansy [pan'-zi], *s.* (Bot.) Trinitaria o violeta tricolor, pensamiento, planta cuyas flores presentan variedad de colores.

Pant [pgnt], *vn.* 1. Jadear, anhelar, respirar con vehemencia y congoja. 2. Anhelar, desear vivamente, estar ansioso por. 3. Palpitar, moverse y agitarse el pecho. *To pant for* o *after*, Suspirar por, desear con ansia. 4. (Poét.) Moverse lánguidamente. *The breeze pants on the leaves*, (Poét.) El céfiro juguetea con las hojas.

Pant, *s.* Palpitación.

Pantalets [pan''-ta-lets'], *s. pl.* Pantalón, perniles largos que llevaban en otro tiempo las mujeres y los niños.

Pantaloon [pan-ta-lūn'], *s.* 1. Arlequín, gracioso, bufón en las pantomimas o comedias. 2. *pl.* Pantalones, calzones. *A pair of pantaloons*, Unos pantalones, un par de pantalones. *Pantaloon stripes*, Listado para pantalones.

Pantelegraph [pan-tel'-ę-graf], *s.* Pantelégrafo, instrumento para transmitir por telégrafo autógrafos, dibujos, etc., en facsímile.

Panter [pgnt'-ęr], *s.* 1. Anheloso, el que respira con dificultad; jadeante; persona que desea con ansia. 2. (Des.) Red para ciervos; trampa.

Pantheology [pan-thẹ-el'-o-ji], *s.* Panteología, sistema completo acerca de la divinidad.
Pantheist [pan'-thẹ-ist], *s.* Panteísta, el que confunde a Dios con el universo.
Pantheon [pan'-thẹ-ǫn], *s.* Panteón, templo dedicado al culto de todos los dioses.
Panther [pan'-thẹr], *s.* 1. Pantera, leopardo. 2. Puma de América.
Pantherine [pan'-thẹr-in], *a.* Panterino.
Panties [pan'-tiz], *s. pl.* Pantaletas, breve pantalón íntimo de mujer.
Pantile [pan'-tail], *s.* Teja, canalón.
Panting [pąnt'-ing], *a.* Sin aliento, sin respiración.—*s.* Palpitación.
Pantingly [pąnt'-ing-li], *adv.* Con palpitación, anhelantemente.
Pantler [pant'-lẹr], *s.* 1. El criado que en una casa grande tiene el cuidado del pan. 2. Panetero, el empleado en la panetería de la casa real.
Pantofle [pan'-to-fl], *s.* Chinela, pantuflo.
Pantograph, Pantagraph [pan'-to-grąf], *s.* 1. Pantógrafo, instrumento para reducir un dibujo. 2. Compás de proporción.
Pantographic, Pantagraphic [pan-to (o ta) -graf'-ic], *a.* Pantográfico, relativo al pantógrafo.
Pantometer [pan-tem'-e-tẹr], *s.* Pantómetro, instrumento para medir toda clase de ángulos.
Pantomime [pan'-to-maim], *s.* 1. Serie de gestos y ademanes que se hacen para darse a entender; lenguaje de signos. 2. Pantomima, representación teatral que se reduce a gestos y remedos.
Pantomimic [pan-to-mim'-ic], *a.* Pantomímico, perteneciente a la pantomima.
Pantomimist [pan-to-mai'-mist], *s.* Pantomimo, actor mudo.
Pantry [pan'-tri], *s.* Despensa, el lugar o sitio en donde se guardan los comestibles.
Pants [pants], *s. pl.* Pantalones.
Panzer [pūnt'-sẹr], *s.* Ejército motorizado.
Pap [pap], *s.* 1. Pezón, la punta que sobresale en los pechos o tetas de los animales por donde los hijos chupan la leche. 2. Papas, papilla, las sopas blandas que se dan a los niños. 3. Carne, la parte mollar de la fruta.
Papa [pa-pū' o pa'-pa], *s.* Papá, voz de que usan los niños en varios idiomas para llamar a su padre.
Papacy [pê'-pa-si], *s.* Papado, la dignidad de Papa.
Papal [pê'-pal], *a.* Papal, relativo o perteneciente al Papa.
Papaverous [pa-pav'-ẹr-us], *a.* Amapolado, papaveráceo, de la naturaleza de la adormidera.
Papaw [pa-pē'], *s.* 1. Papayo, árbol tropical indígena de la América. Carica Papaya. 2. Papaya, su fruta. El jugo de ésta tiene la notable propiedad de ablandar la carne más dura. 3. Asimina, pequeño árbol de la familia de las anonáceas que se cría en los Estados Unidos. Tiene un fruto amarillento, mollar, de tres o cuatro pulgadas de largo. Asimina triloba.
Paper [pê'-pẹr], *s.* 1. Papel. 2. Hoja de papel. 3. Papel auténtico, documento, relato formal, escrito o impreso; en plural, cartas de valor, papeles, apuntes; autos. 4. Diario, periódico. *V.* NEWSPAPER. 5. Ensayo literario, escrito, disertación. 6. Valor, vale comercial. 7. Paquete envuelto en papel, que contiene una cantidad o número limitado de algo. *A paper of tacks*, Un paquete de tachuelas. *Leaf of paper*, Hoja de papel. *Sheet of paper*, Pliego de papel. *Quire of paper*, Mano de papel. *Ream of paper*, Resma de papel. *Brown paper*, Papel de estraza. *Stamped paper*, Papel sellado. *Blotting-paper*, Teleta, papel secante. *Fly-paper*, Papel para coger moscas. *Marbled paper*, Papel jaspeado. *Outside quires of paper*, Costeras, papel quebrado. *Large paper*, Papel marquilla o papel grande con relación al ordinario en que se tira casi el todo de una edición. *Vellum paper*, Papel avitelado. *Waste paper*, Papel viejo, el que se destina por inútil a envolver y otros usos semejantes. *Cap paper*, Papel de escribir de varios tamaños. *Demy paper*, Papel de unas 16 por 21 pulgadas. *Filter-paper*, Papel de filtrar. *Emery-paper*, Papel de lija o esmeril. *Music-paper*, Papel pautado para música. *Laid paper*, Papel acanillado. *Litmus paper*, Papel de tornasol. *India paper*, Papel de China. *Tissue-paper*, Papel de seda, papel muy delgado y de varios colores. *Toilet-paper*, Papel para excusados. *Unsized paper*, Papel sin cola. *Wall-paper*, Papel para empapelar habitaciones. *Wove paper*, Papel avitelado. *Wrapping-paper*, Papel de envolver. *Paper bag*, Saco de papel. *Paper-case*, Papelera. *Paper-clip*, Abrazadera para papeles. *Paper-cutter*, (1) Cortapapel, cuchillo para abrir libros. (2) Máquina usada por los impresores para cortar papel. *Paper currency*, Papel moneda. *Paper-folder*, Plegadera. *Paper-hanger*, Empapelador. *Paper kite*, Cometa de papel. *Paper-knife*, Cuchillo de palo, hueso o metal, para cortar papel; cortapapel. *Paper-machine, paper-making machine*, Máquina para hacer papel continuo. *Paper-pulp*, Pulpa, pasta de que se hace el papel. *Paper-stainer*, Fabricante de papeles pintados. *Paper-wasp*, Avispa, particularmente la que fabrica una substancia parecida al papel. *Paper weight*, Pisapapel, prensapapeles. *On paper*, Escrito o impreso.—*a.* Hecho de papel; delgado como un pliego de papel. *A paper wheel*, Rueda hecha de papel prensado.
Paper [pê'-pẹr], *va.* Empapelar una pieza, forrarla con papel.
Paper-hangings [pê'-pẹr-hang-ingz], *s. pl.* 1. Colgaduras de papel pintado. 2. Papel pintado para empapelar.
Paper-maker [pê'-pẹr-mê-kẹr], *s.* Papelero, el que fabrica papel.
Paper-mill [pê'-pẹr-mil], *s.* Molino de papel.
Paper money [pê'-pẹr mʊn'-ẹ], *s.* Papel moneda.
Paper-office [pê'-pẹr-ef'-is], *s.* El archivo u oficina donde se guardan los documentos o papeles concernientes a algún negociado.
Paper-staining [pê'-pẹr-stên'-ing], *s.* El acto de pintar papel; mercadería de papel pintado o jaspeado.
Papery [pê'-pẹr-i], *a.* Parecido al papel, de la naturaleza del papel; papiráceo.
Papescent [pa-pes'-ent], *a.* Pulposo. carnoso.
Paphian [pê'-fi-an], *a.* Pafio, de Pafos, ciprio.
Papier-maché [pą-piê'-ma-shê], *s.* Papel majado, substancia plástica hecha de pasta de papel con goma, aceite, resina, etc. Humedecido se moldea y sirve para hacer multitud de objetos.
Papilio [pa-pil'-yo], *s.* Mariposa; un género de mariposas.
Papilla [pa-pil'-a], *s.* 1. Teta, pezón. 2. Papila, los pezoncillos que se levantan sobre la lengua.
Papillary [pap'-i-lẹ-ri], **Papillous** [pa-pil'-us], *a.* Papilar, mamilar.
†**Papism, Papistry.** *V.* POPERY.
Papist [pê'-pist], *s.* Papista, nombre que los protestantes dan a los católicos romanos.
Papistic, Papistical [pa-pis'-tic, al], *a.* Papal, papístico.
Papoose, Pappoose [pap-ūs'], *s.* Niño de los indios norteamericanos.
Pappose [pap'-os], **Pappous** [pap'-us], *a.* Velloso, velludo.
Pappus [pap'-us], *s.* (Bot.) Vilano, apéndice de filamentos que tienen las semillas de muchas plantas compuestas, y les sirve para ser transportadas por el aire.
Pappy [pap'-i], *a.* Mollar, jugoso.
Paprika [pap'-ri-ka], *s.* Pimentón.
Papula, Papule [pap'-yu-la, pap'-yūl], *s.* 1. Pápula, especie de erupción en la piel, caracterizada por un tumorcillo sin serosidad ni pus. 2. Papila.
Papular [pap'-yu-lar], *a.* Papuloso, cubierto de pápulas.
Papulous [pap'-yu-lus], *a.* Lleno de pápulas.
Papyrus [pa-pai'-rus], *s.* 1. El papel de escribir de los antiguos egipcios, hecho del papiro. 2. Lo escrito sobre el papiro. 3. Papiro, planta parecida a un junco de que antiguamente se hacía papel. Cyperus Papyrus o Papyrus antiquorum.
Par [par], *s.* 1. Equivalencia, paridad, nivel. 2. Igualdad de cambio; equivalente sin prima ni descuento. *To be at par with one*, Hallarse en situación igual a la de otro. *At par*, A la par, término del cambio mercantil. *On a par*, Igual, de cantidad o valor iguales. 3. (Golf) Par.
Parable [par'-a-bl], *s.* Parábola, instrucción alegórica.
Parabola [par-ab'-o-la], *s.* (Geom.) Parábola, sección cónica.
Parabolic, Parabolical [par-a-bel'-ic, al], *a.* 1. Parabólico, que incluye parábolas. 2. Perteneciente a la parábola geométrica.
Parabolically [par-a-bel'-i-cal-i], *adv* Parabólicamente.
Paraboloid [par-ab'-o-leid], *s.* Paraboloide, sólido engendrado por la rotación de una parábola alrededor de su eje.
Paracentric, Paracentrical [par-a-sen'-tric, al], *a.* Paracéntrico, lo que se desvía del centro.
Parachronism [par-ac'-ro-nizm], *s.* Paracronismo, error cronológico, que se comete poniendo un suceso después del tiempo en que acaeció.
Parachute [par'-a-shūt], *s.* Paracaídas. *Parachute jumper*, Paracaidista.
Parachutist [par-a-shūt'-ist], *s.* Paracaidista.
Paraclete [par'-a-clît], *s.* Paráclito o paracleto, nombre del Espíritu Santo, como consolador de los fieles.

Parade [pa-rêd'], *s.* 1. (Mil.) Parada, muestra o revista de tropas. 2. Ostentación, pompa, alarde, gala, fachenda. 3. Procesión. 4. (Ingl.) Un paseo público. 5. (Esg.) Parada, repulsa. *Parade-ground,* Plaza de armas, lugar de ejercicio para las tropas.

Parade, *vn.* 1. Marchar la tropa en orden militar. 2. Reunirse la tropa ya sea para formar en parada, para que la revisten o para hacer el ejercicio. 3. Fachendear, hacer gala, pasear, alardear.—*va.* 1. Convocar a una revista. 2. Poner o arreglar como en orden militar.

Paradigm [par'-a-dim], *s.* Paradigma, modelo gramatical; ejemplo, ejemplar.

Paradise [par'-a-dais], *s.* 1. Paraíso terrenal. 2. Cielo. 3. Paraíso, cualquier sitio o lugar ameno.

Paradisiacal, Paradisaic [par-a-di-sai'-ac-al, par-a-di-sê'-ic], *a.* Paradisiaco, perteneciente al paraíso.

Paradox [par'-a-dex], *s.* Paradoja, especie que está fuera de la común opinión y sentir de los hombres; aserción que parece estar en contradicción consigo misma.

Paradoxical [par-a-dex'-i-cal], *a.* Paradójico, paradojo.

Paradoxically [par-a-dex'-i-cal-i], *adv.* Paradójicamente.

Paraffin, Paraffine [par'-af-fin], *s.* Parafina, substancia sólida, translúcida e incolora que se extrae del alquitrán; es una mezcla de hidrocarbonos, fundible entre 32° y 80° centígrados.

Parage [pār'-êj o par'-êj], *s.* 1. Igualdad de sangre, de dignidad o terreno (entre los coherederos). 2. (For.) Ser coheredero, heredero con otro.

Paragoge [par-a-gō'-je], *s.* Paragoge, adición de una letra o sonido al fin de una palabra.

Paragogic [par-a-gej'-ic], *a.* Paragógico, relativo a la paragoge.

Paragon [par'-a-gen], *s.* 1. Modelo, muestra de excelencia. 2. (Impr.) Paragona, grado de letra la mayor después de gran canon y de casi 20 puntos. 3. (Ant.) Par, compañero, rival. *Paragon of beauty,* Hermosura sin par, modelo de hermosura.

Paragraph [par'-a-graf], *va.* Dividir en párrafos.

Paragraph, *s.* 1. Párrafo, división de un capítulo o discurso que comienza con una nueva línea. 2. Párrafo, artículo corto en un diario. 3. Párrafo, el signo de esta forma ¶, que sirve para denotar la división de los párrafos, o como signo de referencia.

Paragraphic, Paragraphically [par-a-graf'-ic, al], *a.* Perteneciente a los párrafos, que consiste en, o es abundante en párrafos.

Paraguayan [par'-a-gwê-an o par-a-gwai'-an], *a.* y *s.* Paraguayo, paraguayano.

Paraleipsis [par-a-laip'-sis], **Paralepsis** [par-a-lep'-sis], *s.* (Ret.) Paralipse, supuesta omisión de lo que realmente se dice.

Parallactic, Parallactical [par-a-lac'-tic, al], *a.* Paraláctico, que pertenece a la paralaje.

Parallax [par'-a-lacs], *s.* Paralaje o paralaxis, la diferencia entre el lugar verdadero y el aparente de un astro.

Parallel [par'-a-lel], *a.* Paralelo; igual, semejante.—*s.* 1. Líneas paralelas, dirección paralela. 2. Paralelo, grado de latitud sobre el globo. 3. Paralelo, cotejo. 4. Conformidad, semejanza. 5. Par, igual, contraparte, copia. 6. (Mil.) Paralela, línea de comunicación de una trinchera a otra en el ataque de una plaza. 7. (Impr.) Signo de esta forma ‖ que sirve como señal de referencia. *Parallel ruler,* Regla para trazar líneas paralelas. *To run parallel,* Guardar una distancia igual, andar en línea paralela.

Parallel, *va.* 1. Paralelizar, hacer paralelas. 2. Parangonar, cotejar, poner en paralelo.

Parallelable [par-a-lel'-a-bl], *a.* Que puede ser igualado o puesto en paralelo.

Parallelism [par'-a-lel-izm], *s.* Paralelismo.

Parallelly [par'-a-lel-li], *adv.* Con paralelismo.

Parallelogram [par-a-lel'-o-gram], *s.* Paralelogramo, una figura de cuatro lados en la que los dos opuestos son paralelos.

Parallelogramic, Parallelogramical [par-a-lel-o-gram'-ic, al], *a.* Perteneciente al paralelogramo.

Parallelopiped [par-a-lel-o-pai'-ped], *s.* Paralelepípedo, cuerpo sólido terminado por seis paralelogramos, siendo iguales y paralelos cada dos opuestos entre sí.

Paralogism [pa-ral'-o-jizm], **Paralogy** [pa-ral'-o-ji], *s.* (Lógica) Paralogismo, discurso falaz o conclusión falsa.

Paralysis [par-al'-i-sis], *s.* 1. (Med.) Parálisis, privación o diminución notable del movimiento voluntario y algunas veces de la sensibilidad. 2. (Fig.) Cesación de las funciones normales. (Mex. Fam.) Insulto.

Paralytic, Paralytical [par-a-lit'-ic, al], *a.* Paralítico, perlático.

Paralytic, *s.* El que padece parálisis; paralítico, perlático. (Mex. Fam.) Insultado.

Paralyze, Paralyse [par'-a-laiz], *va.* 1. Paralizar, causar parálisis. 2. Privar de la facultad de obrar.

Paramagnetic [par-a-mag-net'-ic], *a.* Paramagnético, que exhibe la polaridad magnética en la misma dirección que la fuerza magnetizante.

Parameter [par-am'-e-ter], *s.* (Mat.) Parámetro, línea invariable que entra en la ecuación y formación de una curva.

Paramilitary [pār-a-mil'-i-te-ri], *a.* Paramilitar.

Paramorphism [par"-a-mōrf-izm], *s.* La transformación de un mineral en otro que tiene la misma composición química, pero diferente estructura molecular y otras propiedades físicas.

Paramount [par'-a-maunt], *a.* Superior a los demás, supremo, eminente; de primer orden, en primera línea. *Our paramount duty,* Nuestro primer deber.—*s.* Jefe, el superior.

Paramour [par'-a-mūr], *s.* Amante, querido o querida; la persona con quien se tienen relaciones amorosas ilícitas.

Paranoia [par-a-nei'-a], *s.* Paranoia, monomanía.

Paranoiac [pār-a-nōi'-ac], *s.* Paranoico.

Paranymph [par'-a-nimf], *s.* 1. Paraninfo, el padrino de la boda. 2. El que ayuda, favorece o sostiene a otro.

Parapet [par'-a-pet], *s.* 1. (Arq.) Baranda, barandilla, parapeto. 2. Parapeto, baluarte o elevación de tierra para poner a los soldados a cubierto del fuego del enemigo.

Paraphernalia [par-a-fer-nê'-li-a], *s. pl.* 1. Atavíos, adornos accesorios. 2. Insignias. *V.* REGALIA. 3. (For.) Bienes parafernales, los que lleva la mujer al matrimonio fuera de la dote.

Paraphrase [par'-a-frêz], *s.* 1. Paráfrasis, la explicación de un texto más clara y difusa por lo general que el texto mismo; traducción libre. 2. En las iglesias escocesas, versión poética de un pasaje de la Sagrada Escritura.

Paraphrase, *va.* Parafrasear, explicar un texto, traducir libremente.

Paraphrast [par'-a-frast], *s.* Parafraste, autor de paráfrasis.

Paraphrastic, Paraphrastical [par-a-fras'-tic, al], *a.* Parafrástico.

Paraphrastically [par-a-fras'-tic-al-i], *adv.* Parafrásticamente.

§**Paraphrenitis** [par-a-fre-nai'-tis], *s.* Parafrenitis.

Paraplegia [par-a-pli'-ji-a], *s.* Paraplejia, parálisis de la mitad inferior del cuerpo, debida a enfermedad o lesión de la medula espinal.

Paraplegic [pār-a-pli'-jic], *s.* (Med.) Parapléjico.

Parapsychology [pār-a-sai-kel'-o-ji], *s.* Parapsicología.

Parasite [par'-a-sait], *s.* 1. Parásito, animal o vegetal que vive asido a otro o dentro de él y del cual saca su alimento. 2. Pájaro que pone sus huevos en el nido de otro. 3. Parásito, gorrista.

Parasitic, Parasitical [par-a-sit'-ic, al], *a.* 1. Parásito, que vive en otro organismo y que se alimenta de él. 2. Adulatorio, lisonjero, gorrístico. 3. (Med.) Parasítico, perteneciente a los parásitos, causado por ellos; de la naturaleza del parásito.

Parasitically [par-a-sit'-i-cal-i], *adv.* Lisonjeramente.

Parasitism [par'-a-sai-tizm], *s.* Parasitismo, la manera de ser de un parásito; estado o condición de un ser organizado que vive en otro cuerpo vivo a expensas de él.

Parasitology [par-a-si-tol'-o-ji], *s.* Parasitología.

Parasitosis [par-a-si-to'-sis], *s.* Parasitosis.

Parasol [par'-a-sel], *s.* Parasol, quitasol.

Paratyphoid [par'-a-tai'-feid], *s.* (Med.) Paratifoidea.

Parboil [pār'-beil], *va.* 1. Medio cocer, salcochar, cocer ligeramente. 2. Formar, producir vejiguillas o vesículas en la piel por medio del calor.

Parbuckle [pār'-buc"-l], *s.* Tiravira, cuerda fuerte que sirve para hacer subir o bajar objetos pesados por un plano inclinado.—*va.* Levantar o bajar por medio de una tiravira.

Parcel [pār'-sel], *s.* 1. Paquete, lío o atado pequeño. 2. Un conjunto indeterminado de personas. *A parcel of rascals,* Una cuadrilla de tunantes. 3. Porción, cantidad. *Parcel of ground,* Lote de terreno, solar. 4. (Amer.) Paño de tierra. *Part and parcel,* Carne y hueso.

Parcel, *va.* 1. Partir, dividir. 2. Empaquetar, formar un paquete de alguna cosa.

Parcenary [pār'-se-ne-ri], *s.* La herencia que corresponde a muchos herederos y no está aún dividida.

Parcener [pār'-sen-er], *s.* Coheredero.

Parch [pärch], *va.* 1. Desecar, enjugar, agotar. 2. Tostar, quemar, abrasar.—*vn.* Tostarse, quemarse, abrasarse. *I am parched with thirst,* Me muero de sed.

Parcheesi [par-chí'-si], *s.* Especie de juego de chaquete.

Parching [pärch'-ing], *a.* Abrasador, ardiente, secante. *A parching wind,* Un viento abrasador.

Parchment [pärch'-ment], *s.* 1. Pergamino. 2. Lo escrito en pergamino.

Parchment-maker [pärch'-ment-mé-ker], *s.* Pergaminero.

Pard [pärd], *s.* 1. (Ant.) Leopardo. 2. (Germ. E. U.) Socio, compañero, asociado. *V.* PARTNER.

Pardon [pär'-dun], *va.* 1. Perdonar, absolver; hacer gracia de la pena correspondiente a un pecado, falta o delito. 2. Disculpar, dispensar, excusar. *Pardon me,* Perdone Vd., Vd. dispense. *To pardon a criminal,* Conceder gracia a un criminal.

Pardon, *s.* Perdón, remisión de injuria, delito, pecado, deuda u otra cosa. *I beg your pardon,* Vd. dispense, perdone Vd. (fórmula de cortesía).

Pardonable [pär'-dun-a-bl], *a.* Perdonable, excusable; venial.

Pardonably [pär'-dun-a-bli], *adv.* Venialmente.

Pardoner [pär'-dun-er], *s.* Perdonador.

Pardoning [pär'-dun-ing], *a.* Indulgente.

Pare [pêr o pär], *va.* 1. Recortar, cortar o cercenar alguna cosa. 2. Mondar, quitar la cáscara a las frutas, pelar patatas, etc. 3. Cercenar, escatimar, reducir disminuyendo poco a poco. *To pare the nails,* Cortar las uñas. *To pare a horse's foot,* Despalmar el casco de una caballería para que siente la herradura. *To pare bread,* Raspar la corteza del pan. *To pare an apple,* Mondar una manzana.

Paregoric [par-e-ger'-ic], *a.* Paregórico, calmante.—*s.* Elixir paregórico, tintura alcanforada de opio; abreviación de *paregoric elixir.*

Parenchyma [pa-ren'-ki-ma], *s.* 1. (Anat.) Parénquima, tejido propio de los órganos glandulosos en los animales. 2. (Bot.) La substancia blanda y esponjosa de las plantas.

Parenchymal [pa-ren'-ki-mal], *a.* Parenquimal, que es de la naturaleza del parénquima.

Parenchymous [pa-ren'-ki-mus], **Parenchymatous** [pa-ren-kim'-a-tus], *a.* Parenquimatoso.

¿**Parenesis** [pa-ren'-e-sis], *s.* Parénesis, discurso moral, exhortación o amonestación.

Parenetic [par-e-net'-ic], *a.* Parenético, persuasivo.

Parent [pär'-ent], *s.* 1. El padre o la madre. *Parents, pl.* Padres. 2. Cualquier ser organizado que engendra a otro. 3. Autor, productor, causa, origen.—*a.* Que tiene la relación de autor u origen. *Parent speech,* Lengua madre, aquella de que han nacido o se han derivado otras.

Parentage [pär'-ent-éj], *s.* Parentela, nacimiento, origen y descendencia de una persona.

Parental [pa-rent'-al], *a.* Paternal, lo que pertenece a los padres.

Parenthesis [pa-ren'-the-sis], *s.* Paréntesis, una breve digresión introducida en un discurso o escrito: y el signo ortográfico ( ) con que se indica comúnmente dicha digresión.

Parenthetical, Parenthetic [pa-ren-thet'-i-cal], *a.* Que pertenece al paréntesis, de la naturaleza de un paréntesis; entre o por paréntesis.

Parenthood [pär'-ent-hud], *s.* Calidad de padre o madre.

Parenticide [pa-ren'-ti-said], *s.* Parricidio.

Parentless [pär'-ent-les], *a.* Huérfano.

Parer [pär'-er], *s.* Instrumento para recortar o mondar. *A smith's o farrier's parer,* Pujavante. *Apple-parer,* Mondador de manzanas.

Paresis [par'-e-sis], *s.* Paresia, parálisis parcial que sólo priva al paciente de la facultad de moverse.

Parget, *va.* Enyesar, cubrir o decorar con yeso; dar lechada.—*s.* 1. Yeso. *V.* GYPSUM. 2. Mortero, argamasa, para cubrir el interior de las chimeneas. 3. Enlucido. *V.* PARGETING.

Pargeting [pär'-jet-ing], *s.* 1. Enlucido; obra de yeso: en particular, trabajo en estuco, escayola, adornos de estuco en relieve. 2. Argamasa. *V.* PARGET, 2ª acep.

Parhelion [pär-hí'-li-en], *s.* Parelia o parelio, una especie de meteoro.

Pariah [pé'-ri-a o pä'-ri-a], *s.* 1. Natural del Indostán, de la casta ínfima, que sirve de criado o peón. 2. Un proscrito de la India oriental; de aquí, cualquier persona rechazada, expulsada de todas partes.

Parian [pé'-ri-an], *a.* Pario, de Paros, isla del mar Egeo: se aplica particularmente a su mármol blanco.

Parietal [pa-rai'-e-tal], *s.* (Anat.) Parietal, un hueso del cráneo.—*a.* 1. Paredaño, que está pared por medio; que forma las paredes de cualquier cavidad del cuerpo o pertenece a ellas. 2. Parietal, perteneciente o relativo a la pared; relativo a la residencia dentro de paredes, v. g. en un colegio; residencial. 3. (Bot.) Parietal, sostenido por una división a modo de pared, como algunos óvulos.

Parietes [pa-rai'-e-tíz], *s. pl.* (Anat.) Los lados de la cabeza.

Pari-mutuel [pe-ri-miú'-chiu-el], *s.* 1. Sistema para apostar en las carreras de caballos. 2. Máquina en que se registran las apuestas.

Paring [pär'-ing], *s.* Raedura, peladura, mondadura, pellejo, corteza.—*a.* Para cortar o pelar. *Paring knife,* Cuchillito para pelar legumbres.

Paris green [par'-is grin], *s.* Cardenillo, verde de París.

Parish [par'-ish], *s.* 1. Parroquia, feligresía, curato. 2. Parroquia, el conjunto de los fieles que están gobernados en lo espiritual por un párroco. 3. En el Estado de Luisiana, división civil correspondiente a un condado (*county*).—*a.* Parroquial. *Parish clerk,* Sacristán de parroquia.

Parishioner [pa-rish'-un-er], *s.* Parroquiano.

Parisian [pa-riz'-i-an], *a.* Parisiense, perteneciente a París.—*s.* Natural o habitante de París.

Parity [par'-i-ti], *s.* Paridad, semejanza, igualdad.

Park [pärc], *s.* 1. Parque, bosque cerrado, lugar público de recreo en las ciudades. 2. Campiña, campo abierto. 3. En las Montañas Roqueñas, valle o llano pintoresco, escaso de árboles.

Park, *va.* 1. Estacionar. 2. Aparcar, parquear (Sp. Am.). 3. (Mil.) Aparcar.

Parking [pärk'-ing], *s.* Estacionamiento, aparcamiento. *Parking lights,* Luces de población. *Parking space,* Aparcamiento. *Parking lot,* Estacionamiento de automóviles.

Parkway [pärk'-wê], *s.* 1. Avenida, alameda, carretera o avenida principal arbolada. 2. Calzada arbolada.

Parlance [pär'-lans], *s.* Modo de hablar, locución, habla; conversación.

Parley [pär'-li], *vn.* Parlamentar; discutir; conversar unos con otros; conferenciar verbalmente con un enemigo.

Parley, *s.* 1. Conferencia, plática, como con un enemigo en el campo de batalla. 2. Parlamento, la acción de parlamentar. *To beat* o *sound a parley,* Hacer oir el toque de parlamento.

Parliament [pär'-li-ment], *s.* Parlamento, el cuerpo legislativo de la Gran Bretaña, compuesto del rey, pares del reino y diputados nombrados por el pueblo: cuerpo legislativo en general.

Parliamentarian [pär-li-men-té'-ri-an], *s.* 1. Parlamentario, el que es versado en la ley parlamentaria. 2. Parlamentario: dan este nombre los ingleses a los que en sus guerras civiles siguieron el partido del parlamento contra el rey.

Parliamentary [pär-li-men'-ta-ri], *a.* 1. Parlamentario, perteneciente al parlamento, o hecho por el parlamento. 2. Conforme a las reglas y usos de las asambleas legislativas.

Parliament-house [pär'-li-ment-haus], *s.* El sitio donde el parlamento celebra sus sesiones.

Parliament-man [pär'-li-ment-man], *s.* Diputado, individuo del parlamento.

Parlor, Parlour [pär'-ler], *s.* 1. Sala de recibo. 2. Parlatorio, locutorio.

Parlor car [pär'-ler cär], *s.* (F. C.) Vagón-salón.

Parlous [par'-lus], *a.* 1. (Ant.) Peligroso, medroso, que infunde temor de un peligro. 2. (Des.) Astuto, chocarrero.

Parmesan [pär-me-zan'], *a.* Parmesano, de Parma.—*s.* Queso parmesano.

Parnassian [par-nas'-i-an], *a.* Parnáside, que pertenece o se refiere al Parnaso.

Parnassus [pär-nas'-us], *s.* Parnaso, el monte de la Fócide, morada principal de las musas.

Parochial [pa-rō'-ki-al], *a.* 1. Parroquial. 2. Sostenido por una parroquia o limitado a ella; estrecho.

Parochially [pa-rō'-ki-al-i], *adv.* Por parroquias.

Parody [par'-o-di], *s.* 1. Parodia. 2. Trova burlesca, imitativa. 3. (Des.) Refrán.

Parody, *va.* Parodiar; trovar, convertir una obra seria en burlesca.

Parol [pa-rōl'], *a.* (For.) 1. Verbal, dado de viva voz, oral. 2. Escrito, pero no bajo sello.

Parole [pa-rōl'], *s.* 1. (Mil.) Palabra, promesa de honor de un prisionero de guerra de no intentar escaparse o no volver a tomar armas contra sus captores hasta después de canjeado. 2. Libertad bajo caución, libertad condicional.

Parolee [pa-rōl-ī'], *s.* 1. (Mil.) Prisionero libre bajo su palabra de honor 2. Preso libre bajo caución.
Paronomasia [par-o-no-mē'-zhi-a], *s.* Paronomasia, figura retórica en que se emplean los parónimos.
Paronomastic [par-o-no-mas'-tic], *a.* Paronímico.
Paronym [par'-o-nim], *s.* 1. Parónimo, voz de igual etimología que otra. 2. Parónimo, palabra que se asemeja a otra en el sonido, pero que tiene otra significación y se escribe de modo diferente, v. g. *ale*, cerveza, y *ail*, sufrir, o indisposición.
Paronymous, Paronymic [pa-ren'-i-mus, par-o-nim'-ic], *a.* Paronímico, relativo al parónimo: (1) Derivado de la misma raíz, como *civil* del latin *civilis;* (2) semejante en sonido, pero escrito de diferente modo y con sentido también diferente, como *fair*, rubio, bello, y *fare*, precio de pasaje, manjares.
Paroquet [par'-o-ket], *s.* *V.* PARRAKEET.
Parotid [pa-rot'-id], *a.* Parótido, situado cerca de la oreja.—*s.* Parótida, glándula salival situada debajo del oído.
Paroxysm [par'-ox-izm], *s.* Paroxismo o parasismo.
Paroxysmal [par-ox-iz'-mal], *a.* 1. Paroxismal, que pertenece o procede del paroxismo. 2. (Geol.) Que resulta de una convulsión de las fuerzas naturales.
Parquet [par-kê'], *s.* (Teat.) Piso de las lunetas. *Parquet, parquet floor*, Piso de parqué (mosaico de madera).
Parquetry [pār'-ket-ri], *s.* Entarimado, mosaico de madera, para suelos o muebles.
Parrakeet [par'-a-kit], *s.* Periquito, papagayo pequeño, cotorra, particularmente el que tiene la cola en forma de cuña.
Parrel [par'-el], *s.* 1. Manto de chimenea. 2. (Mar.) Racamento, el compuesto de vertellos, liebres y bastardo que pasa por ellos, y con que se une y atraca la verga con el palo. *Parrel-rope*, Bastardo. *Ribs of the parrel*, Liebres del racamento. *Parrel-trucks*, (Mar.) Vertellos del racamento.
Parrhesia [pa-ri'-zhi-a o si-a], *s.* Libertad u osadía en el uso de la palabra.
Parricidal [par-i-sai'-dal], †**Parricidious** [par-i-sid'-i-us], *a.* Parricida.
Parricide [par'-i-said], *s.* 1. Parricida, el que mata a su padre o madre. 2. Parricidio, el delito cometido por el parricida.
Parrot [par'-ẹt], *s.* 1. Papagayo, loro, ave del orden de las trepadoras, de pico encorvado y de plumaje amarillo, encarnado y verde. 2. De aquí, el que repite o imita sin comprender. *Parrot-fish, parrot-wrasse* [ras], Escaro, pez cubierto de grandes escamas de color más o menos rojo.
Parroted [par'-ẹt-ed], *a.* Dícese de la persona a quien han enseñado a repetir las palabras como un papagayo.
Parry [par'-i], *vn.* 1. Esgrimir. 2. Parar, rechazar, desviar los golpes del contrario.
Parrying [par'-i-ing], *s.* El acto de parar, evitar o desviar los golpes del contrario.
Parse [pārs], *va.* Analizar alguna sentencia.
Parsee, Parsi [pār'-si], *s.* 1. Parsi adorador del fuego, que profesa la religión de Zoroastro. 2. Idioma primitivo de los persas: parsi.
Parseeism, Parsism [pār'-si-izm], *s.* Parsismo, religión de Zoroastro.
Parsimonious [pār-si-mō'-ni-us], *a.* Ahorrativo, avaro, mezquino, sumamente o indebidamente económico en sus gastos.
Parsimoniously [pār-si-mō'-ni-us-li], *adv.* Parcamente.
Parsimoniousness [pār-si-mō'-ni-us-nes], *s.* Parcidad, miseria.
Parsimony [pār'-si-mo-ni], *s.* Parsimonia; tacañería, mezquindad.
Parsing [pārs'-ing], *s.* Análisis de alguna oración o frase.
Parsley [pārs'-li], *s.* (Bot.) Perejil, planta hortense.
Parsnip [pārs'-nip], *s.* (Bot.) Chirivía, planta hortense de raíz comestible.
Parson [pār'-sn], *s.* 1. Clérigo. 2. (Ingl.) Párroco, cura, rector.
Parsonage [pār'-sun-ẹj], *s.* 1. Curato. 2. Beneficio curado. 3. Curato o casa del cura.
Parsonage-house [pār'-sun-ẹj-haus], *s.* La casa del párroco.
Part [pārt], *s.* 1. Parte, porción, cantidad especial o determinada de una cosa o de un todo. 2. Parte esencial de un cuerpo u organismo; miembro. 3. Parte, región, lugar, sitio. 4. Parte, la porción que corresponde a alguno en un reparto; papel que representa un actor. *He acted the part of an emperor*, Hizo el papel de emperador. 5. Interés, cuidado, lo que concierne o atañe. 6. Parte, partido, el lado a que alguno se inclina. 7. Obligación, deber. 8. (Mús.) Parte, melodía o música escrita para una sola voz o instrumento. 9. Entrega de un libro o periódico. 10. Raya del cabello.—*Parts, pl.* Partes, las prendas, calidades y dotes naturales que adornan a alguno; talentos. *A man of parts*, Hombre de buenas prendas. *For my part*, Por lo que a mí toca, por mi parte, en cuanto a mí. *To take part*, Tomar parte en, participar. *To take part with one*, Tomar la defensa o el partido de una persona. *Part and parcel*, Uña y carne. *Foreign parts*, Parajes, países extranjeros. *Do your part*, Cumpla Vd. con su obligación. *The part of a wise man is to*, Es obligación de un hombre cuerdo. *To play a part*, Representar un papel, hacer el papel. *Part owner*, Condueño, propietario de una parte. *In good or ill part*, En buena o mala parte, por bien o por mal.
Part, *va.* 1. Partir, repartir, distribuir. 2. Separar, desunir, dividir. 3. Partir, romper. 4. Apartar a dos que riñen. 5. Rayar, disponer con una línea de, división entre dos partes; tener o llevar en dos porciones. *To part the hair*, Partir el pelo, hacerse la raya.—*vn.* 1. Partirse, desunirse, separarse. 2. Despedirse. 3. Partir, irse. 4. Tener parte en alguna cosa; ir a la parte. 5. (Mar.) Apartarse del ancla. *To part with*, Deshacerse de alguna cosa, ceder, dejar, vender, enajenar. *He parted with his house and lot*, Enajenó, se deshizo de su casa y solar. *To part from*, Despedirse, decir adiós. *He parted from his wife and children*, Se despidió de su esposa e hijos.
Partable [pārt'-a-bl], *a.* Partible.
Partage [pārt'-ẹj], *s.* Repartimiento.
Partake [pār-têk'], *va.* (*pret.* PARTOOK, *pp.* PARTAKEN). Repartir, tener parte en.—*vn.* 1. Participar; tomar parte en. 2. Tener, poseer algo de la naturaleza, propiedad o función de.
Partaken, *pp.* de *To* PARTAKE.
Partaker [pār-têk'-ẹr], *s.* Participante; cómplice.
Parter [pārt'-ẹr], *s.* Partidor.
Parterre [pār-tār'], *s.* 1. Era de un huerto, cuadro de jardín, división de tierra completamente igual y por lo común adornada con flores puestas con orden. 2. En los Estados Unidos el patio de un teatro, el área y los asientos que quedan debajo de las galería y detrás de las lunetas o butacas. (Fr.)
Parthenogenesis [pār-then-o-jen'-e-sis], *s.* Partenogénesis, reproducción sin unión sexual, como por medio de huevos, semillas o esporos no fertilizados.
Parthenon [pār'-then-en], *s.* Partenón, templo de Minerva en Atenas.
Partial [pār'-shal], *a.* 1. Parcial, que pertenece a la parte de un todo. 2. Parcial, el que sigue el partido de otro. 3. Parcial, que tiene parcialidad o demasiado afecto a alguna persona o cosa; aficionado a, amante de. 4. Particular, individual, no general.
†**Partialist** [pār'-shal-ist], *s.* Partidario; muy apasionado.
Partiality [pār-shi-al'-i-ti], *s.* 1. Parcialidad; afecto excesivo. 2. Prevención, falta de equidad. 3. Predilección, gusto más pronunciado por una cosa que por otra; gusto particular.
Partially [pār'-shal-i], *adv.* 1. Parcialmente, en parte, no del todo. 2. Parcialmente, con parcialidad.
Partibility [pār-ti-bil'-i-ti], *s.* Divisibilidad.
Partible [pār'-ti-bl], *a.* Partible, divisible.
Participable [pār-tis'-i-pa-bl], *a.* Participable.
Participant [pār-tis'-i-pant], *a.* Participante, partícipe.
Participate [pār-tis'-i-pêt], *va.* y *vn.* Participar, recibir o tomar parte de alguna cosa.
Participation [pār-tis-i-pê'-shun], *s.* Participación; distribución, repartimiento.
Participial [pār-ti-sip'-i-al], *a.* Participial.
Participially [pār-ti-sip'-i-al-i], *adv.* Participialmente.
Participle [pār'-ti-si-pl], *s.* (Gram.) Participio, cierta forma del verbo que participa de la índole del verbo y del adjetivo. El participio presente del idioma inglés corresponde al gerundio español, y expresa el tiempo presente. Su desinencia es *-ing*. *The leaves are falling*, Las hojas están cayendo. El participio pasado termina en *d, ed, en, n,* o *t;* y expresa tiempo pretérito. *Chafed*, estregado, rozado; *parted*, separado; *risen*, levantado, subido; *hurt*, herido, lastimado.
Particle [pār'-ti-cl], *s.* 1. Partícula, parte o porción pequeña de alguna cosa; cantidad o grado pequeño. 2. (Gram.) Partícula, la palabra o voz de pocas sílabas que no se declina ni conjuga. 3. (Mec.) Canti-

dad de alguna substancia tan pequeña que se la considera como un punto, aunque tiene todavía inercia y atracción.

Particular [pār-tic'-yu-lar], *a.* 1. Particular, peculiar. 2. Particular, singular, extraordinario, poco común; notable. 3. Preciso, exacto, delicado o escrupuloso en el examen de alguna cosa. *A particular friend*, Un amigo íntimo. 4. Particular, detallado, circunstanciado. 5. Exigente, quisquilloso, delicado en sus gustos. *A particular account*, Relación circunstanciada o con todas sus menudencias. 6. Extravagante, extraño.—*s.* 1. Particular, el punto o materia de que se está tratando. 2. Particularidad, circunstancia o detalle particular; una persona o cosa determinada entre otras muchas. 3. Relación circunstanciada, dato, artículo. 4. Interés propio. *In particular*, Particularmente.

Particularity [pār-tic-yu-lar'-i-ti], *s.* Particularidad, cualidad o estado de lo particular, lo especial.

Particularize [pār-tic'-yu-lar-aiz], *va.* Particularizar.

Particularly [pār-tic'-yu-lar-li], *adv.* Particularmente.

Parting [pārt'-ing], *s.* 1. Separación, división, reparto: (Quím.) la acción de separar el oro de la plata. 2. Separación, partida, despedida, adiós. 3. Ruptura, v. g. la de un cable. 4. Paraje, línea o superficie de separación o división.—*pa.* 1. Que se refiere a una despedida, partida o separación. 2. Que se acaba, que se va. 3. Divisible, partible. *The parting hour*, La hora de la despedida. *A parting kiss*, Un beso de despedida. *The knell of parting day*, El toque del día que declina.

Partisan, *a.* y *s.* *V.* PARTIZAN.

Partition [pār-tish'-un], *s.* 1. Partición, repartimiento, división, la acción de dividir. 2. Separación, distinción, división; linde, línea de división. 3. Tabique, pared, (Mar.) mampara. 4. (Bot.) Pared interior que separa células o cavidades. *Partition-wall*, Tabique, pared medianera.

Partition, *va.* Partir, dividir o separar.

Partitive [pār'-ti-tiv], *a.* 1. Partitivo, que separa en partes o divisiones. 2. (Gram.) Partitivo, que significa una de las partes en que se puede dividir un todo; también, distributivo.—*s.* Palabra o caso partitivo.

Partizan, Partisan [pār'-ti-zan], *a.* 1. Partidario, que se refiere o adhiere a un partido. *A partizan vote*, Una votación de partido. 2. Que se refiere a guerrilleros o partidarios; llevado adelante por ellos.

Partizan, Partisan [pār'-ti-zan], *s.* 1. Partidario, secuaz. 2. Partidario, el oficial que manda una partida o cuerpo destacado en campaña.

Partizan, Partisan, *s.* 1. Partesana, especie de pica o alabarda; soldado que la lleva. 2. Bastón de mando.

Partizanship, Partisanship [pār'-ti-zan-ship], *s.* Calidad de partidario; adhesión ciega a un partido.

Partly [pārt'-li], *adv.* En parte, en cierto modo.

Partner [pārt'-ner], *s.* 1. Socio, compañero, compañera (en los negocios, en el juego, o para otro fin); socio, asociado, copropietario en una empresa. *Sleeping partner*, Socio comanditario. 2. Pareja, se llama en los bailes el par de personas que bailan juntas. 3. (Mar.) Malletes o fogonaduras. *Partners of the main-mast*, (Mar.) Fogonaduras del palo mayor. *Partners of the capstan*, (Mar.) Malletes del cabrestante.

†**Partner**, *va.* Asociarse con otro.

Partnership [pārt'-ner-ship], *s.* 1. Sociedad, interés social, propiedad común a varias personas. 2. Asociación de dos o más personas para negocios, fundada en un contrato; sociedad.

Partook, *pret.* de *To* PARTAKE.

Partridge [pār'-trij], *s.* (Orn.) Perdiz. *A young partridge*, Perdigón. *A covey of partridges*, Un vuelo de perdices.

Parturient [pār-tiū'-ri-ent], *a.* Parturiente, que está de parto; que se refiere al parto.

Parturition [par-tiu-rish'-un], *s.* Parto, el acto de parir; alumbramiento; el estado de la hembra que está con los dolores de parto.

Party [pār'-ti], *s.* 1. Partido, el conjunto de personas que siguen una misma facción u opinión. 2. Partido, parcialidad o coligación; facción. 3. Parte, cualquiera de los litigantes en un pleito. 4. Interesado. *He, too, was a party to the affair*, Él tomó también parte en el asunto, o estuvo interesado en él. 5. Partida, función, convite, tertulia, reunión escogida de personas para comer juntas o divertirse. *Party of pleasure*, Día de campo. (Amer.) Día de jarana o de diversión. *A hunting, fishing, or riding party*, Una partida de caza, de pesca, una cabalgata. *To go (out) to a party*, Ir de tertulia. *To join the party*, Agregarse a la partida; también, afiliarse a un partido. 6. Partida, cierto número de soldados. 7. (Fam. o bajo) Persona, individuo.

Party-coloured [pār'-ti-cul'-ġrd], *a.* Abigarrado.

Party-jury [pār'-ti-jū'-ri], *s.* Jurado compuesto por mitad de ingleses y de personas de cualquier otra nación.

Party line [pār'-ti lain], *s.* 1. Línea telefónica que sirve a varios suscriptores. 2. Linde. 3. Política y normas fijadas por un partido político

Party-man [pār'-ti-man], *s.* Partidario, parcial, hombre de partido.

Party-wall [pār'-ti-wōl], *s.* Pared medianera.

Parvenu [pār'-ve-niū], *s.* y *a.* Medrado, el que desde condición obscura ha hecho gran fortuna o ha obtenido posición y honores superiores a sus méritos.

Parvis [pār'-vis], *s.* 1. (Arq.) El atrio delante de la puerta principal de una iglesia; el espacio alrededor del tabernáculo de los judíos. 2. †Controversia académica.

Pas [pā], *s.* 1. Paso. 2. Baile. 3. Precedencia. *V.* PRECEDENCE.

Paschal [pas'-cal], *a.* Pascual.

†**Pash**, *va.* Herir, golpear.

Pasha [pa-shā' o pash'-ē], *s.* Bajá, gobernador, general o almirante turco o egipcio; funcionario de alta clase.

Pasque-flower [pasc'-flau'-ġr], *s.* (Bot.) Anémone pulsatila, planta que florece por pascua.

Pasquinade [pas-cwin-ēd'], **Pasquil** [pas'-cwil], **Pasquin** [pas'-cwin], *s.* Pasquín, pasquinada.

Pass [pas], *va.* 1. Pasar, llevar o conducir de un lugar a otro. 2. Pasar, ir más allá del punto determinado. 3. Pasar, atravesar, traspasar, cruzar. 4. Pasar, aprobar un cuerpo deliberante algún proyecto de ley, decreto u otra cosa. 5. Pasar la vida, el tiempo, las horas, etc. 6. Pasar, transferir o trasladar una cosa de un sujeto a otro. 7. Pasar, colar, cerner. 8. Pasar, exceder, aventajar, superar. 9. Pasar, no poner reparo, censura o tacha en alguna cosa. 10. Pasar, hacer tener una cosa por otra. 11. Pasar, enviar.—*vn.* 1. Pasar, ir a alguna parte y transitar caminando por ella. 2. Pasar, cesar, disiparse, desvanecerse o acabarse alguna cosa; morir. 3. Pasar de un estado o situación a otro diverso. 4. Propasarse o excederse. 5. Pasar, ocurrir, suceder. 6. Pasar, ser admitida sin reparo la moneda, y por extensión se dice de otras muchas cosas; obtener aceptación general. 7. Pasar, admitirse o aprobarse alguna opinión, hecho, etc. 8. Omitir, dejar de hacer una cosa. 9. Pasar, vivir con alguna comodidad. 10. Pasar, salir con una exoneración del vientre. 11. Pasar, dar una estocada, hacer un pase en la esgrima. 12. En los juegos de naipes, dar al próximo jugador el derecho de elegir entre dos jugadas. 13. Arrojar una pelota a otro, como ejercicio. *To pass along*, Pasar a lo largo. *As I passed along*, Al pasar yo. *To pass away*, Gastar, desperdiciar; consumir, desvanecer, disipar; pasarse, irse consumiendo una cosa; fallecer. *To pass by*, Pasar, excusar, olvidar, perdonar; omitir, pasar por o cerca de alguna cosa; ir más allá de un punto determinado. *To pass by in silence*, Pasar en silencio, pasar por alto. *To pass for*, Pasar por, ser tenido o reputado. *To pass off*, Dar o circular como legítimo lo que no es; pasar, seguir su curso; disiparse. *To pass on* o *upon*, Entregar al próximo; engañar o abusar de alguien; formar juicio sobre, examinar y decidir sobre; (des.) pasar su camino. *To pass out*, Salir. *To pass up*, Subir, volver o subir. *To pass over*, Atravesar, cruzar; pasar por alto, excusar, perdonar; no hacer caso; olvidar. *To pass a trick*, Jugar una pieza. *To pass censures*, Censurar. *To pass compliments*, Hacer cumplimientos; dirigir alabanzas o elogios. *To pass sentence* o *judgment*, Pronunciar sentencia. *To pass one's word for another*, Empeñar su palabra por otro. *To come to pass*, Suceder, acontecer. *To let pass*, Dejar pasar, permitir, conceder entrada; excusar, no hacer caso, olvidar, perdonar. *To make a pass to*, Tirar una puñalada a uno. *To bring to pass*, Traer a efecto, hacer suceder, efectuar.

Pass, *s.* 1. Pasillo; paso, pasaje, lugar por donde se pasa; desfiladero, garganta, desembocadero; curso de las aguas. 2. Pase, licencia o permiso para pasar, o para ir y venir; billete de favor; a veces, pasaporte. 3. Estado, condición; crisis. 4. Salida feliz de un examen, prueba o inspección. 5. Gesto que hacen con la mano o con una varilla los magnetizadores. 6. Estocada. *Pass-book*, Libro de cuenta y razón. *Pass-key*, Llave maestra, ganzúa. *Pass-parole*, (Mil.) Circule el santo y seña.

Passable [pɑs'-a-bl], *a.* 1. Pasadero, transitable. 2. Pasadero, que se puede tolerar. 3. Pasadero, que es medianamente bueno.

Passably [pɑs'-a-bli], *adv.* Tolerablemente, medianamente.

Passage [pas'-ẹj], *s.* 1. Pasaje; travesía. 2. Pasadizo; callejón, corredor. 3. Pasaje, paso, sitio o lugar por donde se pasa, camino. 4. Pasaje, porción corta de algún libro, escrito o discurso. 5. Ocurrencia, acontecimiento. *Passage-boat*, Bote de pasaje. 6. Derecho de pasaje; libertad o facultad de pasar; entrada, salida, o tránsito libres. 7. Adopción de una ley. 8. Encuentro personal, pelea, disputa. 9. Migración, viaje periódico, particularmente de las aves. 10. Cámara, cagada, exoneración del vientre.

Passageway [pas'-ẹj-wê], *s.* Pasadizo, pasillo.

Passed [pɑst], *pp.* y *a.* 1. Que ha pasado un examen para el ascenso. 2. Anterior, de otro tiempo. 3. Decretado, promulgado. *V.* Pass.

Passenger [pas'-en-jẹr], *s.* Pasajero, transeunte; viajero.

Passer [pɑs'-ẹr], *s.* El que pasa; viandante.

Passerine [pas'-ẹr-in], *a.* Paserino, parecido a los gorriones, o propio de ellos.

Passibility [pas-i-bil'-i-ti], **Passibleness** [pas'-i-bl-nes], *s.* Pasibilidad, la capacidad de recibir impresiones de los agentes externos.

Passim [pas'-im], *adv.* Aquí y allá, repetidas veces, en varios pasajes de un libro o escrito. (Lat.)

Passing [pɑs'-ing], *a.* 1. Pasajero, transitorio, momentáneo. 2. Pasando, sucediendo, ocurriendo. 3. (Ant.) Sobresaliente, eminente.—*adv.* Eminentemente, perfectamente.—*s.* 1. Paso, pasaje; salida; de aquí, muerte. 2. Adopción de un proyecto de ley; dictado de una sentencia. *Passing-place*, Desviadero de los ferrocarriles.

Passing-bell [pɑs'-ing-bel], *s.* La campana que toca a muerto.

Passion [pash'-un], *s.* 1. Pasión. 2. Impresión, el efecto o alteración que causa en un cuerpo otro extraño. 3. Ira, cólera, enojo. *To put into a passion*, Encolerizar, irritar, sacar de sus casillas. 4. Pasión, fuerte afición a una cosa con preferencia a las demás; amor, afecto; celo, ardor. 5. Pasión, los últimos tormentos y muerte que padeció el Redentor del mundo. *Passion-week*, Semana de pasión.

Passion-flower [pash'-un-flau"-ẹr], *s.* (Bot.) Pasionaria, pasiflora; se llama ñorbo en el Perú, donde es indígena.

Passionate [pash'-un-et], *a.* Apasionado; colérico; arrebatado, berrinchudo, mohino; ardiente; vivo, impetuoso, intenso. *A passionate lover*, Un amante apasionado, ardiente. *Passionate longing*, Antojo, anhelo vivo o intenso.

Passionately [pash'-un-et-li], *adv.* Apasionadamente; ardientemente; impetuosamente; coléricamente, enojosamente. *To be passionately in love*, Amar perdidamente.

Passionateness [pash'-un-et-nes], *s.* La disposición a encolerizarse; vehemencia de afectos; impetuosidad.

Passionless [pash'-un-les], *a.* Frío, soso, desamorado; insensible, sin pasiones.

Passive [pas'-iv], *a.* 1. Pasivo, que es objeto de una acción sin cooperar en ella. 2. Quieto; inactivo, inerte. 3. Pasivo, que recibe o padece sin resistencia. 4. En sentido pasivo. —*s.* La voz pasiva.

Passively [pas'-iv-li], *adv.* Pasivamente.

Passiveness [pas'-iv-nes], **Passivity** [pas-iv'-i-ti], *s.* 1. Pasibilidad. 2. Sensibilidad. 3. Calma, paciencia.

Passover [pɑs'-o-vẹr], *s.* Pascua de los hebreos, conmemorativa de la noche en que el ángel del Señor pasó sobre las casas de los israelitas en Egipto. (< *pass* + *over*, pasar + encima.)

Passport [pɑs'-pōrt], *s.* Pasaporte.

Password [pɑs'-wūrd], *s.* Palabra de pase, santo y seña, contraseña.

Past [pɑst], *a.* 1. Pasado, transcurrido, último. *These six days past*, Estos seis últimos días. *At half-past five o'clock*, A las cinco y media dadas. 2. Concluído, terminado; consumado.—*s.* 1. Lo pasado, el tiempo que pasó. 2. (Gram.) Pretérito. 3. Los antecedentes, la historia de alguien o de una nación. —*prep.* 1. Más de, después (tiempo). 2. Más allá de, fuera de (lugar). 3. Fuera de alcance, sin. *It is past four*, Son más de las cuatro. *He is past recovery*, No hay esperanzas de que se cure. *Past the strait*, Más allá del estrecho. *Past feeling*, Fuera de sentido, sin sentido. *Past a doubt*, Fuera de duda. *Past bearing*, Insoportable; infecundo. *Past president*, Presidente que fué. *Past cure*, Incurable. *Past dispute*, Incontestable, fuera de duda. *Past*, con referencia a empleos, se traduce *ex*, o *que fué.*

Paste [pêst], *s.* 1. Pasta, masa formada y unida de manera que forme un cuerpo viscoso. 2. Engrudo, la masa que se hace de harina para pegar una cosa. 3. Pasta, la masa de que se hacen fideos, tallarines y otras cosas que sirven para sopa. 4. Una mezcla artificial hecha a imitación de las piedras preciosas. 5. Pasta, confección hecha de azúcar, goma, etc., con los zumos de frutas.

Paste, *va.* Engrudar, pegar alguna cosa con engrudo.

Pasteboard [pêst'-bōrd], *s.* Cartón fuerte. *Pasteboard binding*, Encuadernación en cartoné.

Pastel [pas'-tel], *s.* 1. Pastel, especie de dibujo hecho con lápices especiales de varios colores. 2. Lápiz de arcilla dura, de varios colores; clarioncillo. 3. (Bot.) Hierba pastel o glasto, planta; o su tinte azul.

Pastern [pas'-tẹrn], *s.* 1. Cuartilla del caballo. 2. Atadura para los pies de un caballo.

Pasteurize [pas'-tẹr-aiz], *va.* Pasterizar (la leche, etc.)

Pasteurization [pas-tẹr-i-zê'-shun], *s.* Pasterización (de la leche, etc.)

Pastil [pas'-til], *s.* 1. Pastilla de olor, pasta para sahumerios. 2. Pastilla de boca. 3. En pirotecnia, el tubo de papel donde se contiene la pólvora que hace girar las ruedas y otros fuegos de artificio. 4. Pastel. *V.* Pastel.

Pastime [pɑs'-taim], *s.* Pasatiempo, diversión, recreación.

Past master [pɑst mɑs'-tẹr], *s.* 1. Ex funcionario de una logia masónica. 2. Autoridad o experto (en alguna materia).

Pastor [pɑs'-tẹr], *s.* 1. Pastor espiritual, ministro del Evangelio que tiene a su cargo una iglesia, congregación o cura de almas. 2. Estornino con copete del género Pastor, particularmente Pastor roseus. 3. (Des.) Pastor, zagal.

Pastoral [pɑs'-tẹr-al], *a.* 1. Pastoril, que pertenece a los pastores de ganado. 2. Pastoral, que se refiere a un pastor o a la cura de almas.—*s.* 1. Pastoral, pastoril, bucólica; idilio. 2. Obra de arte que representa escenas campestres. 3. Pastoral, carta pastoral. 4. Pastorela.

Pastorate [pɑs'-tẹr-ẹt], *s.* 1. Oficio, estado o dignidad de un pastor; la cura de almas. 2. Tiempo que dura su cargo o curato.

Pastorship [pɑs'-tẹr-ship], *s.* *V.* Pastorate.

Pastry [pê'-stri], *s.* Pastelería, pasteles, pastas.

Pastry-cook [pês'-tri-cuk], *s.* Pastelero.

Pasturable [pɑs'-chur-a-bl], *a.* Bueno para pasto.

Pasturage [pɑs'-chur-ẹj], *s.* 1. Pastos, las hierbas que sirven para alimentar a los animales. 2. Pasturaje, el lugar de pasto abierto o común. 3. Ganadería, el tráfico en ganados.

Pasture [pɑs'-chur], *s.* 1. Apacentadero, dehesa. 2. Pastura, pasto; apacentamiento. *Pasture-ground*, Dehesa, pradera, apacentadero; pasturaje.

Pasture, *va.* Pastar, apacentar.—*vn.* Pastar, pacer o comer la hierba del campo los ganados.

Pasty [pês'-ti], *a.* Pastoso, semejante a la pasta, o de la consistencia de ésta.—*s.* Pastel de carne.

Pat [pat], *a.* Apto, conveniente, propio, bueno, cómodo.—*s.* 1. Pasagonzalo, golpecillo ligero y acariciador dado con la mano o con los dedos. 2. Pastilla, masa pequeña moldeada o formada con los dedos.—*adv.* Aptamente, convenientemente.

Pat, *va.* Dar golpecillos, tocar ligeramente con la mano, de una manera suave y cariñosa.

Patch [pach], *va.* 1. Remendar, apedazar, echar remiendos o pedazos a alguna cosa rota. 2. Adornar el rostro con lunares o parches de tafetán negro. 3. Chafallar, hacer o remendar alguna cosa sin arte ni aseo. 4. Componer una cosa con retazos de diversos géneros; se usa generalmente con *up* (denotando, el resultado) o *together* (indicando los materiales).—*vn.* Echar remiendos, hacer labor de retazos.

Patch, *s.* 1. Remiendo. 2. Pieza embutida en obra mosaica. 3. Lunar, parche de tafetán negro con el cual las señoras solían adornar sus rostros. 4. Terreno, pedazo de tierra. *Patch of land* o *ground*, Pedazo de terreno.

Patcher [pach'-ẹr], *s.* Chafallón; remendón.

Patchwork [pach'-wūrk], *s.* Obra o labor de retacitos; taracea de paño o lienzo.

Pate [pêt], *s.* (Fest.) 1. La cabeza. 2. (Fort.) Especie de media luna.

Pated [pêt'-ed], *a.* Lo que tiene cabeza. *Long-pated man,* Hombre de entendimiento, hombre de gran cabeza.
Patella [pa-tel'-a], *s.* 1. Rótula o choquezuela de la rodilla. 2. (Zool.) Parte semejante a una copa. 3. Vasija o cazo pequeño.
Paten [pat'-en], *s.* Plato; en especial, patena, el platillo en donde se pone la hostia en la misa.
Patent [pat'-ent o pê'-tent], *a.* Patente, manifiesto, visible; público.—*s.* 1. Patente, privilegio exclusivo; privilegio de invención, documento que garantiza al inventor, durante cierto número de años, el derecho exclusivo de explotar un invento nuevo. 2. Cédula oficial, como de tierras, de privilegio, título o franquicia. *Patent Office,* Oficina de los privilegios de invención, o de patentes.
Patent [pat'-ent], *va.* 1. Obtener una patente o privilegio exclusivo. 2. Conceder por cartas patentes, por privilegio.
Patentable [pat'-ent-a-bl], *a.* Que puede ser objeto de privilegio exclusivo.
Patentee [pat-en-tî'], *s.* Privilegiado, el que tiene una patente, que disfruta un privilegio exclusivo.
Patent leather [pat'-ent ledh'-er], *s.* Charol.
Patent medicine [pat'-ent med'-i-sin], *s.* Medicina de patente.
Patera [pat'-e-ra], *s.* 1. Patera, taza que se usaba en los sacrificios de los gentiles. 2. Ornamento de arquitectura en forma de plato.
Paternal [pa-ter'-nal], *a.* Paternal, paterno.
Paternity [pa-ter'-ni-ti], *s.* 1. Paternidad, cualidad de padre. 2. Linaje, alcurnia por parte de padre. 3. Origen en general.
Pater-noster [pê'-ter nos'-ter], *s.* 1. Paternóster, "padre nuestro," la oración dominical. 2. Rosario; (Arq.) contera.
Path [path], *s.* 1. Senda, sendero, vereda; camino estrecho para personas o animales. 2. Por extensión, camino, vía. 3. Paso, huella, curso, espacio; de aquí, método de vida o de conducta.
Pathetic, Pathetical [pa-thet'-ic, al], *a.* 1. Patético, tierno, conmovedor, que mueve a compasión y simpatía; que excita las emociones tiernas. 2. Apasionado, animado.
Pathetically [pa-thet'-ic-al-i], *adv.* Patéticamente, tiernamente.
Pathfinder [path-faind'-er], *s.* Explorador que descubre un nuevo sendero.
Pathless [path'-les], *a.* Intransitable, sin senda.
Pathogenic [path-o-jen'-ic], *a.* 1. Patógeno. 2. Patogénico.
Pathognomonic [pa-thog-no-mon'-ic], *s.* Patognomónico: aplícase en medicina a los signos que caracterizan una enfermedad.
Pathological, Pathologic [path-o-loj'-ic-al], *a.* Patológico.
Pathologist [pa-thol'-o-jist], *s.* (Med.) Patólogo.
Pathology [pa-thol'-o-ji], *s.* Patología, la parte de la medicina que trata de las enfermedades y de su naturaleza, causas y síntomas.
Pathos [pê'-thos], *s.* Lo patético, lo tierno; lo que excita las pasiones y las emociones tiernas; lástima.
Pathway [path'-wê], *s.* Senda, vereda, camino estrecho. *V.* PATH.
¿**Patibulary** [pa-tib'-u-le-ri], *a.* Lo que pertenece al patíbulo o a la horca; patibulario.
Patience [pê'-shens], *s.* 1. Paciencia, resignación y tolerancia en los trabajos. 2. Paciencia, reposo, sosiego en lo que se desea. 3. (Bot.) Romaza, planta. *To be out of patience,* Perder la paciencia, perder los estribos, salirse de sus casillas. *You wear out my patience,* Vd. pone a prueba mi paciencia. (Fam.) Me fastidias o eres muy majadero.
Patient [pê'-shent], *a.* 1. Paciente, sufrido, asiduo, constante, que sufre con calma los males, injusticias y ofensas. 2. Constante, perseverante en sus esfuerzos. 3. Tolerante, tierno, y que no se desalienta al ayudar a otros. 4. Que espera con calma, tranquilamente. 5. Sufrido, paciente en cuanto a las fatigas del cuerpo.—*s.* 1. Paciente, sujeto pasivo; persona o cosa que recibe impresiones externas. 2. Paciente, enfermo, el que padece alguna enfermedad o dolencia.
Patiently [pê'-shent-li], *adv.* Pacientemente.
Patina [pat'-i-na], *s.* Pátina.
Patio [pa'-tio], *s.* Patio estilo español.
Patness [pat'-nes], *s.* Aptitud, conveniencia.
Patois [pa-twā'], *s.* Jerga, lenguaje corrompido y provincial. (Fr.)
Patriarch [pê'-tri-ārc], *s.* 1. Patriarca, jefe de una familia, el que gobierna por derecho paterno. 2. Hombre anciano y venerable; de aquí, cualquier objeto digno de veneración.
Patriarchal [pê'-tri-ārc'-al], *a.* Patriarcal.
Patriarchate [pê'-tri-ārk'-êt], **Patriarchship** [pê'-tri-ārc-ship], **Patriarchy** [pê'-tri-ārk-i], *s.* Patriarcado.
Patrician [pa-trish'-an], *a.* Patricio, noble, de alcurnia aristocrática.—*s.* 1. Patricio, miembro de la nobleza de Roma. 2. Persona de alta clase. 3. Título de honor.
Patricide [pat'-ri-said], *s.* V. PARRICIDE.
Patrimonial [pat-ri-mō'-ni-al], *a.* Patrimonial.
Patrimony [pat'-ri-mo-ni], *s.* Patrimonio, los bienes y hacienda que el hijo tiene heredados de su padre.
Patriot [pê'-tri-et o pat'-ri-et], *s.* Patriota.—*a.* Patriótico.
Patriotic [pê-tri-ot'-ic], *a.* Patriótico, inspirado por el amor al país natal, a la patria; que tiene en mira el bien de su país.
Patriotism [pê'-tri-et-izm], *s.* Patriotismo, celo patriótico, amor a la patria.
Patristic, Patristical [pa-tris'-tic, al], *a.* Patrístico, que se refiere a los antiguos Padres de la Iglesia cristiana.
Patrol [pa-trōl'], *s.* 1. El acto de patrullar. 2. Patrulla, el número de soldados que con un cabo salen a rondar. 3. Ronda del resguardo o de la policía.
Patrol, *va.* y *vn.* Patrullar, rondar; hacer la ronda.
Patrolman [pa-trol'-man], *s.* Policía o vigilante rondador.
Patrol wagon [pa-trōl' wag'-un], *s.* Camión de policía.
Patron [pê'-trun o pat'-run], *s.* 1. Patrón, patrono, protector, defensor, amparador. 2. Patrón, el santo que se elige como especial protector. 3. Abogado, defensor. 4. Patrono, el que tiene el derecho del patronato eclesiástico.
Patronage [pat'-run-ej], *s.* 1. Patrocinio, amparo, protección. 2. Patronato, patronazgo, el derecho de presentar personas idóneas para empleos civiles o eclesiásticos. 3. El patrocinio de un santo.
Patroness [pê'-trun-es], *sf.* Patrona, protectora; señora, patrona de una obra de caridad o de una función social.
Patronize [pat'-run-aiz], *va.* 1. Patrocinar, proteger; apoyar, favorecer, alentar una empresa. 2. Condescender con arrogancia. 3. (Fam.) Hacerse parroquiano de una tienda. *A patronizing manner,* Aires o maneras condescendientes. *What bookstore do you patronize?* ¿De qué librería es Vd. parroquiano?
Patronizer [pat'-run-aiz-er], *s.* Patrón, patrocinador.
Patronless [pê'-trun-les], *a.* Desamparado, despatronado.
Patronymic [pat-ro-nim'-ic], *s.* y *a.* Patronímico, nombre de familia.
Patted [pat'-ed], *a.* Golpeado ligeramente, con la mano.
Patten [pat'-en], *s.* 1. Galocha, zueco, especie de calzado de madera con la parte inferior muy gruesa. 2. Base de columna; cimiento, fundamento de una pared o muro.
Patter [pat'-er], *vn.* 1. Hacer ruido con una rápida sucesión de sonidos ligeros, como la lluvia. 2. *To patter with the feet,* Patalear, patear; hacer ruido dando patadas.
Patter, *s.* 1. Sucesión de golpecitos o palmaditas. 2. Habla rápida y voluble. 3. Charla, habladuría, parlería. 4. (Bajo) Dialecto, jerga.
Pattern [pat'-ern], *s.* 1. Modelo, dechado, norma. 2. Ejemplar, caso, suceso o hecho que se pone por modelo. 3. Muestra, la porción corta de alguna mercadería que se da para reconocer su calidad. 4. Patrón, dechado, cualquiera cosa cortada en papel o en paño para imitar o trabajar sobre ella. *Goods of good patterns,* Géneros de gusto o de moda.
Pattern, *va.* Copiar, imitar; servir de ejemplo.
Patty [pat'-i], *s.* Pastelillo, pastel pequeño. *Patty-pan,* Tortera o tartera.
Patulous [pat'-u-lus], *a.* Abierto, extendido, un poco divergente.
Paucity [pē'-si-ti], *s.* Poquedad, escasez, pequeño número, pequeña cantidad.
Pauline [pēl'-in], *a.* Paulista, que se refiere a San Pablo.
Paulist [pēl'-ist], *s.* Miembro de la orden de los Padres Paulistas, hermandad moderna americana en la Iglesia católica romana. Se ocupan en trabajos misioneros y literarios.
Paulownia [pē-lō'-ni-a], *s.* Paulonia, árbol del Japón que se cultiva en muchos países.
Paunch [pēnch o pānch], *s.* 1. Panza, vientre. 2. El *rumen* o primer estómago de los rumiantes. 3. Borde de una campana. 4. (Mar.) Pallete, jimelga de frente.
†**Paunch,** *va.* Desbarrigar, romper o herir el vientre.
Pauper [pē'-per], *s.* Pobre, indigente, el que depende de la caridad, que no tiene para vivir más que los

socorros de la parroquia o de la ciudad.

Pauperism [pō'-pęr-izm], *s.* Pauperismo, indigencia, mucha pobreza, falta de medios de existencia.

Pauperize, Pauperise [pō'-pęr-aiz], *va.* Reducir a la indigencia.

Pause [pōz], *s.* 1. Pausa; duda, suspensión, interrupción del movimiento, acción o ejercicio. 2. Intervalo, tiempo de parada; interrupción o fin de párrafo. 3. Hesitación, irresolución, vacilación. 4. Signo que indica una pausa en música o puntuación. *I only require some pause,* No pido más que un poco de reposo.

Pause, *vn.* 1. Pausar, cesar, detenerse, interrumpirse, hacer una pausa; cesar de hablar por cualquier causa. 2. Tardar, pausar; vacilar. 3. Aguardar, estar en expectación. 4. Deliberar. *Pause a day or two,* Aguarde Vd. uno o dos días.

Pauser [pōz'-ęr], *s.* El que se detiene; el que reflexiona o delibera.

Pavan [pav'-an], *s.* Pavana, baile antiguo.

Pave [pêv], *va.* 1. Pavimentar, enladrillar, empedrar, enlosar, embaldosar. 2. Allanar el camino. *To pave the way for,* Facilitar o allanar el camino para. *Paved road,* Camino pavimentado.

Pavement [pêv'-męnt], **Paving** [pêv'-ing], *s.* 1. Pavimento, suelo de losas o baldosas; empedrado de calle. 2. Camino o sendero empedrado. 3. El material con que está empedrada una superficie; pavimento. *Mosaic, tessellated pavement,* Pavimento de mosaico.

Paver [pêv'-ęr], **Pavier** [pêv'-yęr], *s.* Empedrador; solador.

Pavilion [pa-vil'-yun], *s.* 1. Pabellón, tienda de campaña; habitación movible y temporal; cenador de jardín. 2. (Arq.) Pabellón, construcción que forma parte del edificio principal. 3. Dosel, pabellón. 4. La oreja, el oído externo. 5. Pabellón, bandera.

Pavilion, *va.* Proveer de pabellones; cobijar bajo un pabellón.

Paving [pê'-ving], *s.* Empedrado, acción de empedrar; y empedrado, pavimento, la superficie empedrada. *Paving-stone,* Adoquín. *Paving-tile,* Loseta.

Pavonine [pav'-o-nin], *a.* Relativo o que pertenece al pavo real; (poco us.) irisado.

Paw [pō], *s.* 1. Garra, la mano o pata de un animal que tiene garfas o uñas corvas, como el perro y el gato. 2. (Fest.) Garra, mano tosca del hombre.

Paw, *vn.* Patear el caballo o escarbar la tierra con un pie delantero.—*va.* 1. Herir con el pie delantero. 2. Manosear alguna cosa con poca maña o ajándola.

Pawed [pōd], *a.* Armado de garras; patiancho.

Pawl [pōl], *s.* Linguete, fiador de rueda, paleta de reloj, diente de encaje, retén, seguro. *Pawl of the capstan,* Linguete del cabrestante. *Supporter of the pawl,* (Mar.) Descanso del linguete. *Hanging pawls,* (Mar.) Linguete de por alto.

Pawn [pōn], *va.* Empeñar, dar o dejar alguna cosa en prenda.

Pawn, *s.* 1. Prenda, la alhaja que se entrega para la seguridad de alguna deuda o contrato. 2. Prenda, la condición de ser tenido como garantía del dinero prestado. *In pawn,* En prenda. 3. Peón, pieza del juego de ajedrez.

Pawnbroker [pōn'-brok-ęr], *s.* 1. Prestamista, prendero, el que presta dinero y recibe prendas en seguridad de la deuda. 2. (For.) Comodatario.

Pawnee [pō-nī'], *s.* 1. Prestador, prestamista sobre prendas. 2. (Siempre con mayúscula) Nombre de una tribu de indios norteamericanos, que habitó en otro tiempo en Nebraska y Kansas, hoy en el Territorio de los Indios.

Pawnshop [pōn'-shop], *s.* Montepío, monte de piedad, casa de empeño.

Pax [pacs], *s.* Paz, en la misa.

Pay [pê], *va.* (*pret.* y *pp.* PAID). 1. Pagar; remunerar, recompensar. 2. Gastar, desembolsar; cubrir o pagar los gastos de; distribuir en pagos. 3. Dar tributo, ofrecer algo a uno; dar, hacer. 4. Ser provechoso a, aprovechar a. 5. Pagar, sufrir el castigo o la pena por alguna falta, culpa, olvido, etc. 6. Pagar, corresponder a los beneficios que se reciben.—*vn.* 1. Pagar, satisfacer una deuda. 2. Producir adecuada ganancia, dar provecho. *To pay in full,* Pagar por completo. *To pay back,* Pagar; volver lo que se ha recibido; restituir. *To pay down,* Pagar en dinero contante o al contado. *To pay for,* Pagar una cosa que se compra; espiar, satisfacer, purgar culpas, pecados o yerros. *To pay attention to,* (1) Dar, prestar atención a. (2) Dedicar atenciones a una mujer, cortejarla, galantearla. *To pay one's addresses to,* Cortejar, pretender en matrimonio a una mujer. *To pay due honour to,* Tributar a uno los honores que le son debidos. *Pay him my respects,* Hágale Vd. presentes mis respetos. *He will get paid,* Hará que le paguen. *He must be paid,* Es menester pagarle. *To rob Peter to pay Paul,* Ganar el cielo con rosario ajeno: literalmente, robar a Pedro para pagar a Pablo. *To pay off,* (1) Pagar el sueldo completo. (2) Despedir, despachar. (3) Retornar, desquitar, pagar en la misma moneda. *To pay a visit,* Pagar o hacer una visita. *To pay one's self,* Tomarse la paga por su mano. *To pay in cash,* Pagar al contado. *To pay by instalments,* Pagar a plazos. *To pay on account,* Pagar a buena cuenta. *To pay out a cable,* (Mar.) Arriar el cable.

Pay, *va.* Embrear. *To pay a ship's bottom,* (Mar.) Despalmar, embrear y alquitranar la embarcación. *To pay the seams,* (Mar.) Embrear las costuras. (Fr. ant. peier < L. pico < pix, pez.)

Pay, *s.* 1. Paga; sueldo, salario. (Mil.) Prest o pre, la paga diaria del soldado. 2. Compensación, recompensa; equivalente. 3. Recompensa, merecido, pena. *Half-pay,* Medio sueldo. *Half-pay officer,* Oficial retirado. *Pay-clerk,* Empleado pagador. *Pay-dirt, pay-gravel,* Tierra o arena que da cantidad provechosa de oro.

Payable [pê'-a-bl], *a.* Pagadero. *Bill payable in March,* Letra que vence en marzo.

Pay-day [pê'-dê], *s.* Día de paga.

Payee [pê-ī'], *s.* (For.) La persona a quien se paga una letra de cambio; aquel a quien debe hacerse un pago.

Payer [pê'-ęr], *s.* Pagador.

Paying [pê'-ing], *s.* 1. El acto de despedir a alguno. 2. El acto de alquitranar o embrear. 3. Sacudimiento, apaleamiento. *Paying away* o *out,* (Mar.) El acto de arriar un cabo. *Paying off,* El acto de pagar a alguno que servía o hacía alguna cosa por dinero, con o sin el objeto de despedirle. *Paying teller,* Empleado pagador de un banco.

Payload [pê'-lōd] *s.* Carga útil.

Paymaster [pê'-mas-tęr], *s.* Pagador. (Mil.) Habilitado.

Payment [pê'-męnt], *s.* 1. Pago, paga, pagamento. 2. Pago, recompensa, premio. 3. Paliza, zurra. *To take goods in payment,* Tomar mercancías en pago. *To stop payment,* Suspender los pagos, dar punto a los negocios. *Cash payment,* Pago al contado, en especie. *Payment in full (of all demands),* Saldo de cuenta. *To delay, to defer the payment,* Diferir, aplazar el pago. *To sue for payment,* Perseguir el pago. *To meet a payment,* Hacer frente a un pago. *On the payment of,* Mediante el pago de.

Paynim, Painim [pê'-nim], *a.* y *s.* (Ant.) Pagano, gentílico; mahometano. Paganismo, gentilismo.

Payoff [pê'-ōf], *s.* 1. Acto de pagar salarios o sueldos. 2. Retribución. 3. (fam.) Desenlace.

Payroll [pê-'rōl], *s.* Nómina de sueldos. (Mex.) Lista de raya.

Pea [pī], *s.* (*pl.* PEAS o PEASE). Guisante, chícharo, especie de legumbre; planta anual de la familia de las leguminosas, y su fruto. Pisum sativum. *Canned peas,* Guisantes en latas. *Chick-pea,* Garbanzo. *Pea-chafer, V. Pea-weevil. Pea-green,* Verde, color de guisante tierno. *Pea-gun,* Cerbatana. *Pea-pod, pea-shell,* Vaina de guisante. *Pea-soup,* Sopa de guisantes. *Pea-weevil,* Gorgojo, coleóptero cuyo gusano roe los guisantes tiernos. *Sweet pea,* Látiro oloroso, guisante de olor, planta trepadora de adorno, y su flor.

Pea [pī], *s.* Pavón o pava real.

Peace [pīs], *s.* 1. Paz. 2. Paz, reposo, tranquilidad, sosiego. 3. Paz, descanso eterno. 4. Silencio, quietud. 5. Estado de reconciliación, concordia, buena inteligencia, armonía.—*inter.* ¡Paz! ¡silencio! *To keep the peace,* No turbar la paz pública. *To hold one's peace,* Guardar silencio, no hablar, callarse. *Peace establishment* o *footing,* (Mil.) Pie de paz. *Justice of the peace,* Juez de paz, alcalde. *V.* JUSTICE. *Peace-offering,* Sacrificio propiciatorio. *Peace-officer,* El ministro de justicia que está encargado de la tranquilidad pública; guardia civil.

Peaceable [pīs'-a-bl], *a.* Tranquilo, sosegado, pacífico, apacible.

Peaceableness [pīs'-a-bl-nes], *s.* Quietud, tranquilidad; carácter pacífico.

Peaceably [pīs'-a-bli], *adv.* Pacíficamente, apaciblemente.

Peaceful [pīs'-ful], *a.* Tranquilo, quieto, sosegado, pacífico.

Peacefully [pīs'-ful-i], *adv.* Tranquilamente, apaciblemente.

Peacefulness [pīs'-ful-nes], *s.* Quietud, calma, tranquilidad, sosiego.

Peace-maker [pīs'-mê-kęr], *s.* Pacificador.

Peace pipe [pīs paip], *s.* Pipa de paz de las ceremonias de los indios de E. U.

Peach [pīch], *s.* (Bot.) Melocotón, durazno, pérsico, albérchigo; también melocotonero, durazno, pérsico, el árbol que produce estas frutas. *Freestone peach*, Abridero; pérsico cuya carne no está adherida al hueso. *Clingstone peach*, Albérchigo o pavía. *Dried peaches*, Orejones. *Peach-borer*, (1) Mariposa nocturna azul, con manchas transparentes en las alas, cuya larva horada la madera blanda y las raíces del melocotonero. Ægeria exitiosa. (2) Bupréstide, cuya larva tiene parecidas costumbres. *Peach-yellows*, Una enfermedad de los melocotoneros que causa la madurez prematura del fruto y pone amarillas las hojas.

Peach, *vn.* (Fam.) Hacerse delator de un cómplice.

Peach-coloured [pîch'-cul-ẹrd], *a.* Que tiene color de melocotón.

Peach-tree [pîch'-trî], *s.* Melocotonero, pérsico, un árbol.

Peacock, Peafowl [pî'-coc], *s.* Pavón o pavo real.

Peahen [pî'-hen], *sf.* Pava real, la hembra del pavón.

Peajacket [pî'-jak"-et], *s.* Marsellés, chaquetón de paño burdo que llevan los marineros en tiempo borrascoso. Se llama también *pilot-jacket.* (< D. *pig*, paño burdo + jacket.)

Peak [pîc], *s.* 1. Cima o cumbre, pico, montaña que termina en punta y sobresale de las otras. 2. Pico, cualquier cosa que remata en punta. 3. (Mar.) Pena o penol, pico, espiga de vela. *Peak-halliards*, (Mar.) Drizas de la pena.

Peak, *vn.* Tener apariencia de enfermo.—*va.* (Mar.) Amantillar el pico, levantar una verga contra el mástil.

Peaked [pîk'-ẹd], *a.* 1. Puntiagudo; con caballete, como un tejado. 2. (Fam.) Enfermizo o flaco en apariencia.

Peaking [pîk'-ing], *a.* 1. Enfermizo, flaco, lánguido; ignoble. 2. (Fam.) Enfermizo, malucho.

Peakish [pîk'-ish], *a.* Perteneciente a la cima o cumbre de una montaña o á cualquier cosa que termina en pico o punta.

Peaky [pîk'-i], *a.* 1. Abundante en picos o cumbres. 2. (Fam.) De apariencia enfermiza.

Peal [pîl], *s.* 1. Repique de campanas. 2. Estruendo como el de los truenos o cañones; estrépito. *To ring the bells in a peal*, Tocar las campanas a vuelo. *The last peal*, El último repique o toque, la última llamada. *Peal of laughter*, Carcajada, risotada.

Peal, *vn.* Tocar con mucho ruido. —*va.* 1. Aturdir haciendo ruido muy grande. 2. Moverse alguna cosa con mucha agitación.

Peanut [pî'-nʊt], *s.* Cacahué, cacahuete. (Mex.) Cacahuate. (Cuba) Maní. *Peanut brittle*, Crocante de cacahuate o de maní. (Mex.) Pepitoria. *Peanut butter*, Mantequilla de cacahuate o de maní.

Pear [pãr], *s.* Pera, el fruto del peral; también el peral mismo. *Pear-blight*, Tizón, enfermedad de los perales. *Pear-shaped*, Piriforme, en forma de pera. *Pear-tree*, Peral.

Pearl [pẹrl], *s.* 1. Perla, concreción depositada en las conchas de varios moluscos, muy estimada en joyería. 2. Perla, alguna cosa parecida a una perla, como una gota de rocío, una lágrima; cosa preciosa o exquisita en su clase; también, madreperla, nacar. 3. (Impr.) Perla, tipo o letra de 5 puntos. *Mother-of-pearl*, Nácar, madreperla. *Pearl seed* o *seed pearl*, Aljófar, rostrillo. *Pearl buttons*, Botones de madreperla. *Paste pearl*, Perla de papelillo. 4. Nube o catarata en el ojo. 5. (Her.) Perla, blanco o plata. *Pearl-ash*, Potasa purificada, álcali vegetal refinado. *Pearl-barley*, Cebada mondada, perlada. *Pearl-eyed*, El que tiene una nube en el ojo. *Pearl-grass*, *pearl-plant*, *pearlwort*, (Bot.) Un nombre genérico de plantas que se da a todas las especies de saginia, que son una clase de hierbas muy pequeñas. *Pearl-oyster*, Molusco parecido a la ostra que produce perlas; la Meleagrina margaritífera. *Pearl-powder*, *pearl-white*, Blanco de perla, oxicloruro de bismuto.

Pearled [pẹrld], *a.* Aljofarado; guarnecido de perlas.

Pearly [pẹr'-li], *a.* Que consta de perlas o es semejante a ellas.

Pearmain [pãr'-mên], *s.* Pero, una variedad de la manzana común.

Peart [pîrt], *a.* (Fam.) Jovial, en buena salud y buen humor; alegre; vivaracho, activo.

Peasant [pez'-ant], *s.* Labriego, patán, el aldeano y labrador rústico. —*a.* Aldeano, campesino, rústico, agreste. *Peasant-like*, Campesino, agreste.

Peasantry [pez'-an-tri], *s.* La gente del campo, los aldeanos, los lugareños.

Peascod [pîz'-cod], **Pea-shell** [pî'-shel], *s.* La vaina de los guisantes.

Pease [pîz], *s. pl.* Guisantes, chícharos, en cantidad o colectivamente.

Peat [pît], *s.* 1. Turba, tierra bituminosa, que sirve de combustible. 2. Turba o césped de tierra de que se hace carbón. *Peat-bog*, Pantano turboso. *Peat-charcoal*, Carbón de turba. *Peat-moss*, (1) Musgo de pantano, particularmente del género Sphagnum (esfagno). (2) (Prov.) Pantano turboso.

Peaty [pît'-i], *a.* Turboso; parecido a la turba o que la contiene.

Pebble, Pebble-stone [peb'-l, stōn], *s.* 1. Guija, china; piedra redondeada por las aguas, de tamaño menor que un guijarro. 2. Cuero abollonado. 3. Pólvora gruesa. 4. Lente de cristal de roca.

Pebble, *va.* y *vn.* Granular, abollonar la superficie del cuero; presentar apariencia áspera.

Pebbled [peb'-ld], *a.* Lleno de guijas.

Pebble-ground [peb'-l-ground], *s.* (Mar.) Fondo de cascajo.

Pebbly [peb'-li], *a.* Abundante en guijas o chinas; guijoso.

Pecan [pẹ-can'], *s.* Pacana, pecana, árbol americano parecido al nogal y su fruto. Carya olivæformis o Hicoria pecan.

Peccability [pec-a-bil'-i-ti], *s.* Fragilidad, disposición a pecar.

Peccable [pec'-a-bl], *a.* Pecable, capaz de pecar.

Peccadillo [pec-a-dil'-o], *s.* Pecadillo, pecado leve o venial.

Peccancy [pec'-an-si], *s.* 1. Vicio, la mala calidad o el defecto y daño físico en las cosas. 2. Vicio, el defecto moral en las acciones.

Peccant [pec'-ant], *a.* 1. Pecador, culpable de pecado, que peca. 2. Corrompido, ofensivo, dañoso, física o moralmente; mórbido, enfermizo. 3. Delincuente, vicioso, defectuoso.

Peccary [pec'-a-ri], *s.* Pecarí, especie de cerdo silvestre que se encuentra desde Méjico hasta el Paraguay. Tiene en el dorso una glándula almizcleña.

Peccavi [pek-é'-vai], *s.* La confesión de un delito: es voz latina.

Peck [pec], *s.* 1. Medida de áridos en Inglaterra que es la cuarta parte de la medida llamada *bushel*, y equivale a 9.08 litros o poco menos de dos celemines; celemín, en general. 2. (Fest.) Montón, gran cantidad. *To get into a peck of troubles*, Encontrarse con mil dificultades. 3. Picotazo, picotada, golpe con el pico.

Peck, *va.* 1. Picotear, golpear o herir con el pico. 2. Picar, herir con algún instrumento punzante. *To peck at*, Regañar de continuo. 3. Recoger (alimento) con el pico.—*vn.* Picotear, dar golpes con el pico.

Pecker [pek'-ẹr], *s.* 1. El que pica o picotea. 2. (Orn.) Picoverde, un ave.

Pecten [pec'-ten], *s.* (*pl.* PECTINES [pec'-ti-nîz]). 1. Peine, o algo parecido a él; en las aves, membrana vascular y colorida del globo del ojo. 2. Festón de una concha.

Pectin, Pectine [pec'-tin], *s.* Pectina, substancia blanca que se extrae de las peras y otras muchas frutas.

Pectinate, Pectinated [pec'-ti-nêt, ed], *a.* Dentado como un peine, parecido a las púas de un peine.

Pectination [pec-ti-né'-shun], *s.* El estado de lo que tiene dientes o púas como los peines.

Pectoral [pec'-to-ral], *a.* Pectoral, que pertenece al pecho.—*s.* 1. Pectoral, la insignia que llevan al pecho los prelados eclesiásticos. 2. Peto, armadura del pecho. 3. Medicamento pectoral o que se emplea en las enfermedades del pecho.

Peculate [pec'-yu-lêt], *vn.* 1. Apropiarse los caudales públicos, cometer peculado. 2. Ratear, hurtar, robar.

Peculation [pec-yu-lé'-shun], *s.* Peculado, la acción o delito de dedicar los caudales públicos al uso propio; malversación.

Peculator [pec'-yu-lê-tẹr], *s.* Peculador, el que comete peculado; malversador.

Peculiar [pẹ-kiūl'-yar], *a.* 1. Peculiar, particular, singular, propio; que pertenece a una cosa con singularidad. 2. Escogido, especial, separado, distinguido. 3. Singular, raro, extraordinario. *A style peculiar to one's self*, Estilo propio de uno mismo. *A peculiar man*, Un hombre singular, raro.—*s.* 1. La propiedad particular de cada uno. 2. (Der. canónico) La parroquia que no está sujeta a la jurisdicción del ordinario.

Peculiarity [pẹ-kiū-li-ar'-i-ti], **Peculiarness** [pẹ-kiūl'-yar-nes], *s.* Particularidad, singularidad; rasgo característico, lo que singulariza á una persona o cosa, haciéndola digna de atención o reparo; individualidad. *A peculiarity of speech*, Una particularidad en el modo de hablar, y también en el idioma, idiotismo.

Peculiarize [pẹ-kiūl'-yar-aiz], *va.* Particularizar, apropiar.

Peculiarly [pẹ-kiūl'-yar-li], *adv.* Peculiarmente, particularmente; separadamente; en particular, especialmente.

Peculium [pẹ-kiū'-li-um], *s.* Peculio.

Pecuniarily [pe-kiū'-ni-ẹ-ri-li], *adv.*

Pecuniariamente ; con referencia al dinero.

Pecuniary [pe-kiū'-ni-e-ri], *a.* Pecuniario, que consta de dinero ; referente al dinero, monetario.

Pecunious [pe-kiū'-ni-us], *a.* Rico, adinerado.

Pedagogic, Pedagogical [ped-a-gej'-ic, al], *a.* Pedagógico, perteneciente a la enseñanza de los niños, y lo que es propio de un pedagogo.

Pedagogics [ped-a-gej'-ics], *s.* Pedagogía, el arte y la ciencia de enseñar o educar.

Pedagogism [ped'-a-go-jizm], *s.* Pedagogismo, la naturaleza o el oficio de un pedagogo, y particularmente de un pedante.

Pedagogue [ped'-a-gog], *s.* 1. Pedagogo, el ayo que cuida de los niños y los enseña. 2. Maestro de escuela. 3. Pedante.

Pedagogy [ped'-a-gō''-ji], *s.* 1. Pedagogía. 2. Pedagogismo.

Pedal [ped'-al o pī'-dal], *a.* Perteneciente al pie o a una parte semejante al pie ; del pie ; relativo a un pedal. *Pedal pipe*, Cañón del órgano de grueso calibre cuyas teclas se mueven con los pies.

Pedal [ped'-al], *s.* 1. Pedal, palanca para el pie, aplicada sólo a ciertos instrumentos músicos, bicicletas o biciclos, triciclos, máquinas de coser y a la maquinaria ligera. 2. Bajo fijo, en la música.

Pedal pushers [ped'-al push'-ers], *s. pl.* Pantalones cortos de mujer que ajustan debajo de la rodilla.

Pedant [ped'-ant], *s.* 1. Pedante, el que hace vano alarde de erudición y el que se precia de sabio teniendo escasos conocimientos. 2. (Des.) Dómine, maestro de niños.

Pedantic, Pedantical [pe-dant'-ic, al], *a.* Pedantesco, que hace vano alarde de su erudición.

Pedantically [pe-dant'-i-cal-i], *adv.* Con pedantería.

Pedantism [ped'-ant-izm], **Pedantry** [ped'-ant-ri], *s.* Pedantería, pedantismo.

‡**Pedantize** [ped'-ant-aiz], *vn.* Regentear, hacer de maestro, doctorear, pedantear, hablar magistralmente.

Pedate [ped'-ēt], *a.* 1. (Zool.) Parecido a un pie o que tiene sus funciones. 2. (Bot.) Que se divide o parte en forma palmar ; dícese particularmente de las hojas.

Peddle [ped'-l], *va.* 1. Vender géneros en cortas cantidades, llevándolos de casa en casa. 2. Distribuir poco a poco.—*vn.* Recorrer los países vendiendo chucherías ; ocuparse en friolerás.

Peddler [ped'-ler], *s.* *V.* Pedler.

Pedesis [pe-dī'-sis], *s.* Pédesis, agitación de las partículas microscópicas contenidas en un líquido. (Gr. < πήδησις, salto.)

Pedestal [ped'-es-tal], *s.* Pedestal, peana.

Pedestrian [pe-des'-tri-an], *s.* Andador, peón, el que anda a pie ; paseador, paseante.—*a.* Pedestre.

Pediatrician [pī-di-at-rish'-an], *s.* (Med.) Pediatra, médico especialista de niños.

Pediatrics [pī-di-at'-rics], *s.* (Med.) Pediatria, la parte de la medicina que se refiere al cuidado higiénico de los niños y al tratamiento de las enfermedades de la niñez.

Pedicel [ped'-i-sel], *s.* Pedúnculo, pedicelo, cabillo de una sola flor ; pedúnculo de un animal.

Pedicellate [ped'-i-sel''-ēt], *a.* Pedicelado, con pedicelo ; sostenido por un pedicelo.

Pedicle [ped'-i-cl], *s.* 1. (Bot.) Pedúnculo o el cabillo de la flor. 2. (Med.) Pedículo, la base angosta y reducida de un tumor.

Pedicular [pe-dic'-yu-lar], **Pediculous** [pe-dic'-yu-lus], *a.* Pedicular : se aplica a la enfermedad en que el enfermo se plaga de piojos.

Pedigree [ped'-i-grī], *s.* Genealogía, la descripción de la estirpe de alguno ; árbol genealógico.

Pediluvium [ped-i-lū'-vi-um], *s.* Pediluvio, baño de pies.

Pediment [ped'-i-ment], *s.* (Arq.) 1. Frontón, témpano. 2. Adorno de molduras en forma triangular que se pone encima de las puertas o ventanas.

Pedler [ped'-ler], *s.* Buhonero, vendedor ambulante, que lleva sus mercancías de casa en casa. (Amer.) Baratillero, el que lleva y vende cosas de buhonería.

Pedlery [ped'-ler-i], *s.* Buhonería, la tienda portátil que el buhonero lleva colgada de los hombros y las baratijas que hay en ella.

Pedling [ped'-ling], *a.* Frívolo, que es de poca monta.

Pedometer [ped-om'-e-ter], *s.* Podómetro, instrumento en forma de reloj que nota cada paso de un andarín.

Peduncle [ped-un'-cl o pe-dun'-cl], *s.* 1. (Bot.) Pedúnculo, parte de la planta que sostiene una flor o muchas. 2. (Anat.) Pedúnculo, tallo o apéndice de un órgano por el cual se adhiere al cuerpo principal ; parte del animal que le sirve de pie.

Peduncular [ped-un'-kiu-lar], *a.* Peduncular, perteneciente a un pedúnculo.

Pedunculate, Pedunculated [pe-dun'-kiu-lêt, ed], *a.* (Bot.) Pedunculado, que tiene un pedúnculo o sostén.

Peek [pīc], *vn.* (Fam.) Mirar por una hendidura, mirar a hurtadillas. *V.* Peep.

Peel [pīl], *va.* 1. Descortezar, pelar, mondar, descascarar, deshollejar. *To peel an orange*, Mondar una naranja. 2. (Ant.) Pillar, hurtar, robar.

Peel, *s.* 1. Corteza, cáscara, pellejo de algunas frutas ; hollejo de uvas, telilla de cebolla. 2. Pala de horno. 3. (Mar.) Palo del remo. 4. (Des.) Espito, colgador, instrumento para extender las hojas impresas.

Peeler [pīl'-er], *s.* 1. Pelador, mondador, el que pela, monda o descorteza. 2. (Ger. Ingl.) Agente de policía ; (derivado del nombre de Sir Robert Peel, reorganizador del sistema de la policía municipal).

Peeling [pīl'-ing], *s.* Peladura, mondadura, los pellejos de las frutas que se pelan o mondan.

Peen [pīn], *s.* El extremo del martillo opuesto a la cara del mismo, cuando es de forma redondeada, cónica o a modo de cuña. *Peen-hammer*, Martillo de punta.

Peep [pīp], *vn.* 1. Asomar, empezar a mostrarse alguna cosa. 2. Atisbar, mirar por un agujero sin ser visto ; mirar a escondidas, furtivamente. *To peep in*, Atisbar lo que pasa dentro de alguna parte. *To peep out*, Atisbar lo que pasa fuera ; mirar hacia fuera ; asomar, salir. 3. Piar los pollos o los pájaros ; chirriar.

Peep, *s.* 1. Asomo, indicio o señal de alguna cosa. *At the peep of day*, Al romper del alba. 2. Ojeada, mirada furtiva. 3. Piada de las aves.

Peeper [pīp'-er], *s.* 1. Atisbador, el que atisba. 2. El pollito que empieza a romper la cáscara.

Peep-hole [pīp'-hōl], **Peeping-hole** [pīp'-ing-hōl], *s.* Atisbadero, agujero por donde uno puede ver sin ser visto.

Peeping [pīp'-ing], *s.* 1. Atisbadura ; ojeada. 2. Piada, chirrido.

Peeping, *a.* Que atisba. *Peeping Tom*, Fisgón, atisbador.—*s.* 1. Atisbadura, ojeada. 2. Piada, chirrido.

Peer [pīr], *vn.* 1. Atisbar, mirar con cuidado, como indagando o investigando. 2. (Poét.) Asomar, empezar a mostrarse, aparecer.

Peer, *s.* 1. Par, igual, uno de la misma clase ; compañero. 2. Par, grande, noble, de Inglaterra. *House of Peers*, Cámara de los pares o lores.

Peerage [pīr'-ej], *s.* La dignidad de par ; el conjunto o cuerpo de los pares.

Peeress [pīr'-es], *sf.* 1. La mujer de un par. 2. La que tiene uno de los títulos que pueden ser heredados por mujeres en Inglaterra.

Peerless [pīr'-les], *a.* Sin par, incomparable, que no admite comparación, que no tiene igual.

Peerlessly [pīr'-les-li], *adv.* Incomparablemente, sin igual, sin par.

Peerlessness [pīr'-les-nes], *s.* Superioridad o excelencia incomparable o el estado de lo que no tiene igual.

Peevish [pīv'-ish], *a.* Impertinente, enfadoso, regañón, de mal humor ; enojadizo, enojoso.

Peevishly [pīv'-ish-li], *adv.* Con impertinencia.

Peevishness [pīv'-ish-nes], *s.* Petulancia, impertinencia, mal humor, mal genio.

Peg [peg], *s.* 1. Clavija, estaca, estaquilla ; pedacito de madera que pasa por un agujero para asegurar alguna cosa ; en un instrumento, clavija en que se aseguran y arrollan las cuerdas para templarlas. 2. Escarpia, colgador, clavija introducida parcialmente en una pared o una tabla y que sirve para colgar de ella alguna cosa. 3. Pretexto o excusa. 4. (Fam.) Grado en la posición social de una persona. *To take one down a peg*, Bajarle a uno los humos. *Peg-top*, Peonza hecha de madera con punta de hierro ; juguete al que se hace dar vueltas por medio de un bramante.

Peg, *va.* Estaquillar, clavar, asegurar alguna cosa con clavijas o estaquillas.

Pegasus [peg'-a-sus], *s.* Pegaso.

Pejorative [pe-jer'-a-tiv], *a.* Que empeora el efecto o la significación.

Pekan [pek'-an], *s.* Especie de mustela (Mustela Pennanti) de la América del Norte, algo parecida a la zorra.

Pekoe [pī'-kō], *s.* (Com.) Una especie de té negro.

Pelagic, Pelagian [pel-aj'-ic, pel-ē'-ji-an], *a.* 1. Pelágico, oceánico, que vive en el mar lejos de la tierra. 2. Flotante en la superficie del mar.

Pelargonium [pel-ar-gō'-ni-um], *s.* Pelargonio, género de plantas de adorno de la familia de las geraniáceas, y llamadas comúnmente geranios.

Pele [pī'-lī], *s.* Nombre de una diosa de las islas Hawai, que se supone habita el cráter del volcán Kilauea *Pele's hair*, Vidrio volcánico en fibras como cabellos.

Pelerine [pel'-ẹr-in], *s.* Esclavina, prenda de vestir que llevan las mujeres al cuello y sobre los hombros y suele terminar en punta por delante.

Pelf [pelf], *s.* Dinero, riquezas; significa a menudo riquezas mal adquiridas.

Pelican [pel'-i-can], *s.* 1. (Orn.) Pelícano, alcatraz, ave acuática del orden de las palmípedas que se alimenta de peces. 2. Alambique, vasija de vidrio con doble tubo de que se sirven los químicos para purificar los licores. 3. Pulicán, un instrumento para sacar muelas.

Pelisse [pe-līs'], *s.* Ropón, capote forrado en pieles: en Inglaterra se llama así un vestido muy usado en Rusia. (Fr.)

Pell [pel], *s.* Pellejo, cuero; de aquí, rollo de pergamino. *V.* PELT. *Pell-rolls*, Rollos de pergamino en que se asientan los gastos y recibos de la real hacienda en Inglaterra.

Pellagra [pel'-a-gra o pel-é'-gra], *s.* (Med.) Pelagra, cierta inflamación escamosa en las partes del cuerpo expuestas al sol y al aire.

Pellet [pel'-et], *s.* Pelotilla; bala, bolita.

Pelleted [pel'-et-ed], *a.* Compuesto de balas.

Pellicle [pel'-i-cl], *s.* 1. Película, piel o membrana delgada y delicada; hollejo. 2. Lapa, la telilla que se forma en la superficie del vino y otros licores.

Pellitory [pel'-i-to-ri], *s.* Cualquier especie de parietaria, planta urticácea. *Common wall pellitory*, Parietaria oficinal. *Pellitory of Spain*, Pelitre, una hierba oficinal conocida en las boticas con el nombre de manzanilla pelitre.

Pellmell [pel-mel'], *adv.* Confusamente, atropelladamente, a trochemoche, al tuntún.

Pellucid [pel-lū'-sid], *a.* Transparente, diáfano.

Pellucidity [pel-lū-sid'-i-ti], **Pellucidness** [pel-lū'-sid-nes], *s.* Transparencia, diafanidad.

Pelt [pelt], *s.* 1. Pellejo, cuero, zalea; también, pelada. 2. Un golpe dado por una cosa arrojada.

Pelt, *va.* Atacar, acometer arrojando piedras u otras cosas, tirar, arrojar.—*vn.* Arrojar alguna cosa; descender violentamente, como el granizo.

Peltate, Peltated [pel'-têt, ed], *a.* Peltado, en forma de pelta o escudo; (Bot.) que tiene su pecíolo inserto casi en medio del disco.

Pelting [pelt'-ing], *s.* Acometimiento, violencia.

Peltry [pelt'-ri], *s.* Peletería, pieles, pellejos.

Pelt-wool [pelt'-wul], *s.* Lana de pellejo.

Pelvic [pel'-vic], *a.* Pélvico, referente a la pelvis.

Pelvis [pel'-vis], *s.* 1. Pelvis, cavidad del cuerpo en la parte inferior del tronco, o en la parte posterior del tronco en los irracionales; parte del esqueleto. 2. Pelvis, receptáculo membranoso en forma de embudo que se halla en cada riñón, y es el principio del uréter.

Pemmican [pem'-i-can], *s.* 1. Al principio, carne mollar de venado en tiras, seca y machacada con gordo y algunas bayas hasta formar una pasta. 2. Alimento semejante que hoy se hace con carne de vaca y frutas secas. (Nombre indio.)

Pen [pen], *s.* 1. Pluma; en otro tiempo cañón para escribir; hoy día, instrumento casi siempre de metal que sirve para escribir con una tinta flúida. 2. Pluma, estilo o habilidad y destreza en escribir. 3. Pluma, escritor. 4. Jaula, caponera, alcahaz. *Gold pen, quill pen, steel pen*, Pluma de oro, de ave, de acero. *Slip of the pen*, Error de pluma. *Fountain pen*, Pluma estilográfica. Pluma fuente.

Pen, *va.* 1. Enjaular, alcahazar, encerrar, poner dentro de la jaula o del alcahaz. 2. Escribir, poner por escrito, componer. Este verbo tiene el pretérito y participio pasado *pent*, además de la forma regular, *penned.*

Penal [pī'-nal], *a.* 1. Penal, que toca y pertenece a la pena o la incluye. 2. Que castiga. 3. Penal, provisto por la ley penal; que señala penas. *Penal servitude*, Presidio, pena de trabajos forzados.

Penalty [pen'-al-ti], *s.* 1. Pena, castigo. 2. Multa, pena pecuniaria.

Penance [pen'-ans], *s.* Penitencia, la pena que se impone en satisfacción del pecado.

Pencase [pen'-kês], *s.* Estuche.

Pence [pens], *s. pl.* de PENNY.

Pencil [pen'-sil], *s.* 1. Lápiz. 2. Pincel, instrumento con que el pintor asienta los colores en el lienzo. *Pencil-case*, Lapicero. *Black-lead pencil*, Lápiz negro. *Red-lead pencil*, Lápiz rojo. 3. Haccecillo de rayos de luz.

Pencil, *va.* Marcar, dibujar, colorir o escribir con un lápiz; lapizar.

Pencil sharpener [pen'-sil shār'-pn-ẹr], *s.* Tajalápices.

Pendant [pend'-ant], *s.* 1. Pendiente, lo que está pendiente o cuelga de otra cosa para adorno o uso; v. g. el adorno que colgado de un arillo se ponen las mujeres en las orejas. 2. (Arq.) Adorno que cuelga de un techo. 3. Uno de los objetos que forman un par; cuadro u objeto de arte que se coloca de manera que corresponda con otro. 4. (Mar.) (1) Amante, maroma corta; (2) gallardete, cierto género de banderilla partida que se pone en lo alto de los masteleros de un navío. *Broad pendant*, (Mar.) Corneta o gallardetón. *Brace pendants*, (Mar.) Brazalotes. *Fish-pendant*, (Mar.) Amante o cañas del aparejo de pescante. *Reeftackle-pendants*, (Mar.) Amantes de aparejuelos de rizos. *Rudder-pendants*, (Mar.) Barones del timón.

Pendency [pend'-en-si], *s.* Suspensión, dilación, demora.

Pendent [pend'-ent], *a.* 1. Pendiente, colgante. 2. Sobresaliente, que proyecta. 3. (Bot.) Pendiente, que cuelga con el ápice hacia abajo.

Pendicle [pen'-di-cl], *s.* 1. Miembro o porción inferior, accesorio; adjunto. 2. (Esco.) *V.* CROFT.

Pending [pend'-ing], *a.* Pendiente, indeciso.—*prep.* 1. Durante. 2. Hasta; mientras, en el intervalo.

Pendular [pend'-yu-lar], *a.* Péndulo, perteneciente a un péndulo o a una péndola.

Pendulosity [pend-yu-les'-i-ti], **Pendulousness** [pend'-yu-lus-nes], *s.* Suspensión, el estado de lo que no está fijado en otra cosa.

Pendulous [pend'-yu-lus], *a.* Péndulo, pendiente.

Pendulum [pend'-yu-lum], *s.* Péndulo, cuerpo suspendido de un punto fijo que puede moverse libremente con vaivenes u oscilaciones; péndulo o péndola de reloj. *Compensated* o *compensation pendulum*, Péndulo de compensación. *Mercurial pendulum*, Péndulo compensador de mercurio.

Penetrability [pen-ẹ-tra-bil'-i-ti], **Penetrableness** [pen'-ẹ-tra-bl-nes], *s.* Penetrabilidad.

Penetrable [pen'-ẹ-tra-bl], *a.* Penetrable, que se puede penetrar, por una fuerza física, moral o intelectual.

Penetrant [pen'-ẹ-trant], *a.* Penetrante, penetrativo, sutil; persuasivo.

Penetrate [pen'-ẹ-trêt], *va.* 1. Penetrar, introducir un cuerpo en otro; horadar, entrar; atravesar, pasar al través. 2. Penetrar, comprender. 3. Penetrar el ánimo, llegar al corazón los sentimientos, afectar vivamente.—*vn.* Introducirse, penetrar.

Penetrating [pen'-ẹ-trêt-ing], **Penetrative** [pen'-ẹ-tra-tiv], *a.* Penetrativo, penetrante; agudo, astuto, sagaz, penetrador.

Penetration [pen-ẹ-trê'-shun], *s.* 1. Penetración, el acto o la propiedad de penetrar físicamente. 2. Penetración, inteligencia cabal de una cosa difícil; agudeza, sagacidad, perspicacia de ingenio.

Penetrativeness [pen'-ẹ-tra-tiv-nes], *s.* La aptitud de penetrar.

Penful [pen'-ful], *s.* Plumada, la cantidad de tinta que puede contener una pluma.

Penguin [pen'-gwin], *s.* 1. (Orn.) Penguín, alca o pájaro bobo, ave palmípeda del tamaño de un ganso grande. Vive en el hemisferio austral. Aptenodytes patagonica. 2. (Bot.) *V.* PINGUIN.

Penholder [pen'-hōld-ẹr], *s.* Portapluma, mango o cabo de pluma.

Penicillate [pen-i-sil'-êt o pen'-i-sil''-êt], *a.* (Biol.) Penicilado, en forma de pincel; guarnecido de hebras finas.

Penicillin [pen-i-sil'-in], *s.* (Med.) Penicilina.

Peninsula [pen-in'-shiu-la], *s.* Península. *The Peninsula* o *the Iberian Peninsula*, Iberia; España y Portugal.

Peninsular [pen-in'-siu-lar], *a.* Peninsular, lo concerniente a una península.

Penis [pī'-nis], *s.* Pene, el miembro viril.

Penitence [pen'-i-tens], *s.* Penitencia, dolor por haber pecado, con el propósito de no pecar más; arrepentimiento, contrición.

Penitent [pen'-i-tent], *a.* Penitente, arrepentido, contrito.—*s.* Penitente, la persona que se arrepiente de sus faltas o pecados.

Penitential [pen-i-ten'-shal], *a.* Penitencial, de arrepentimiento; que pertenece a la penitencia o la incluye; que se refiere a la penitencia como castigo. *The seven penitential psalms*, Los siete salmos penitenciales.—*s.* Libro de penitencias.

Penitentiary [pen-i-ten'-sha-ri], *a.* 1. Penitenciario, que expresa el arrepentimiento; de penitencia, de castigo. 2. Penitenciario, referente al castigo y a la disciplina de los prisioneros.—*s.* 1. Penitenciaría, cása de corrección, cárcel modelo cuyo régimen conduce a la enmienda y mejora de los presidiarios, y donde se les obliga a trabajar. 2. Penitenciario, en sentido eclesiástico; confesor.

Penitently [pen'-i-tent-li], *adv.* Con arrepentimiento, con penitencia.

Penknife [pen'-naif], *s.* Cortaplumas, navaja pequeña; se llama así porque en otro tiempo se empleaba para cortar o tajar las plumas.

Penman [pen'-man], *s.* Pendolista, calígrafo; maestro de escritura; el que tiene por oficio escribir.

Penmanship [pen'-man-ship], *s.* Escritura, el acto de escribir, el arte de escribir.

Pen name [pen nêm], *s.* Seudónimo, nombre ficticio de un escritor.

Pennant [pen'-ant], *s.* 1. Flámula, gallardete. *V.* STREAMER. 2. (Mar.) Amante, maroma corta. *V.* PENDANT.

Pennate, Pennated [pen'-ét, ed], *a.* 1. Alado, que tiene alas. 2. (Bot.) Lo que tiene la figura de pluma. *V.* PINNATE.

Penned [pend], *a.* Escrito; enjaulado.

Penner [pen'-ęr], *s.* 1. Autor, escritor, el que escribe. 2. Plumero, estuche o vaso en que se guardaban antiguamente las plumas de escribir.

Penniferous, Pennigerous [pen-if'-ęr-us, pen-ij'-ęr-us], *a.* Penígero, que tiene plumas.

Penniform [pen'-i-fērm], *a.* Peniforme, parecido a una pluma.

Penniless [pen'-i-les], *a.* Sin dinero, sin un ochavo o sin blanca; muy pobre.

Pennon [pen'-ęn], *s.* Pendoncito, flámula, bandera pequeña acabada en punta.

Penny [pen'-i], *s.* (*pl.* PENNIES, para designar el número de las piezas, y PENCE, cuando se trata de su valor monetario). 1. Penique, moneda de cobre de Inglaterra que vale la duodécima parte de un chelín. *I have not a single penny,* No tengo un cuarto. 2. (Fam. E. U.) Centavo. 3. Dinero, hablando en general. 4. Coste; se emplea en composición, como *sixpenny. Two pennies,* Dos piezas de dos cuartos. *Twopence,* Cuatro cuartos, veinte céntimos. *A halfpenny,* Un medio penique, un cuarto, cinco céntimos. *To turn an honest penny,* (Fam.) Ganar el dinero honradamente. *A pretty penny,* (Fam.) Bastante dinero, regular suma de dinero.

Penny-a-liner [pen'-i-a-lain'-ęr], *s.* El sujeto que escribe para los papeles públicos a razón de un penique por línea.

Penny-post [pen'-i-pōst], *s.* Cartero, correo interior.

Pennyroyal [pen-i-rei'-al], *s.* (Bot.) Poleo, cierta hierba medicinal del género menta y muy común. (En vez de *Puliol-royal* < lat. puleium regium.)

Pennyweight [pen'-i-wêt], *s.* 1. Escrúpulo español, equivalente a veinte y cuatro granos; peso empleado para los metales preciosos y las joyas. 2. Peso del antiguo penique de plata.

Penny-wise [pen'-i-waiz], *a.* Dícese del que por ahorrar poco se expone a perder mucho. *Penny-wise and pound-foolish,* Que escatima en los gastos pequeños y derrocha sumas cuantiosas.

Pennyworth [pen'-i-wūrth], *s.* 1. El valor de un penique o la cosa que se compra por un penique. 2. Cualquier cosa que se compra por dinero. 3. Una cantidad pequeña de cualquier cosa.

Penological [pę-no-lej'-ic-al], *a.* Penológico, referente a la ciencia de la penología.

Penology [pę-nel'-o-ji], *s.* Penología, la ciencia que trata del castigo y de la prevención de los crímenes, y del manejo de las casas de corrección; parte de la sociología.

Pensile [pen'-sil], *a.* Pensil, colgado, suspenso, pendiente en el aire.

Pensileness [pen'-sil-nes], *s.* El estado de lo que se halla suspenso o colgado.

Pension [pen'-shun], *s.* Pensión, cantidad que se concede periódicamente por un acto o servicio meritorio, particularmente por un gobierno; pensión de retiro.

Pension, *va.* Dar una pensión, pensionar.

Pensionary [pen'-shun-ę-ri], *a.* Pensionado, dícese del que goza de alguna pensión.—*s.* Pensionado, pensionista.

Pensioner [pen'-shun-ęr], *s.* 1. Pensionista, pensionado; (Mil. y Mar.) inválido. 2. El que depende de la liberalidad de otro. 3. Estudiante ordinario en Cambridge; corresponde a *commoner* en Oxford.

Pensive [pen'-siv], *a.* Pensativo, meditabundo; melancólico, triste.

Pensively [pen'-siv-li], *adv.* Pensativamente, melancólicamente, tristemente.

Pensiveness [pen'-siv-nes], *s.* Melancolía, tristeza; meditación profunda.

Penstock [pen'-stec], *s.* 1. La esclusa de la represa de los molinos. 2. Paradera (del caz). 3. Portaplumа.

Pent [pent], *a.* y *pp.* de PEN. Acorralado, enjaulado, encerrado. "*Here in the body pent,*" Aquí, encerrado en el cuerpo.

Penta-, Pent-. Formas derivadas del griego *pente,* cinco.

Pentacapsular [pen-ta-cap'-siu-lar], *a.* (Bot.) Pentacapsular, de cinco cápsulas.

Pentachord [pen'-ta-cērd], *s.* Pentacordio, lira de cinco cuerdas.

Pentacle [pen'-ta-cl], *s.* Figura compuesta de cinco líneas rectas formando una estrella que incluye un pentágono, ⛤.

Pentad [pen'-tad], *s.* 1. El número cinco; grupo de cinco cosas. 2. Lustro, espacio de cinco años. 3. (Quím.) Átomo, radical, o elemento que tiene fuerza de combinación de cinco. Se usa también como adjetivo.

Pentagon [pen'-ta-gen], *s.* Pentágono, polígono de cinco ángulos y de cinco lados.

Pentagonal [pen-tag'-o-nal], **Pentagonous** [pen-tag'-o-nus], *a.* Pentagonal, pentangular.

Pentagraph [pen'-ta-graf], *s.* Pentágrafo, instrumento para copiar diseños y pinturas en cualquier proporción.

Pentahedron [pen-ta-hi'-drǫn], *s.* Pentaedro.

Pentahedral, Pentahedrous [pen-ta-hi'-dral, drus], *a.* Pentaédrico, que tiene cinco caras.

Pentameter [pen-tam'-ę-tęr], *s.* Pentámetro.

Pentangle [pent'-aŋ-gl], *s.* Pentángulo.

Pentangular [pent-aŋ'-gu-lar], *a.* Pentangular.

Pentapetalous [pen-ta-pet'-a-lus], *a.* Pentapétalo, que tiene cinco pétalos u hojas.

Pentaphyllous [pen-ta-fil'-us o pen-taf'-il-us], *a.* Pentáfilo, que tiene cinco hojas.

Pentastyle [pen'-ta-stail], *s.* Pentástilo, obra de cinco órdenes de columnas.

Pentateuch [pen'-ta-tiūc], *s.* Pentateuco, los cinco libros de Moisés, que son los primeros del Antiguo Testamento.

Pentecost [pen'-tę-cest], *s.* 1. Pentecostés, fiesta de los judíos, que se celebraba el quincuagésimo día después de Pascua. 2. Pentecostés, la festividad de la venida del Espíritu Santo sobre los Apóstoles.

Pentecostal [pen'-tę-cest-al], *a.* Perteneciente a la pascua de Pentecostés.

Penthouse [pent'-haus], *s.* 1. Tejaroz, tejadillo, colgadizo o cobertizo que sale de una pared con caída hacia fuera. 2. (Mil.) Mantelete (corrupción de *Pentice*). 3. Alguna cosa que se parece a un cobertizo.

Pentice [pen'-tis], *s.* Cualquier techo inclinado; tejado, tejadillo, sotechado.

Pentile [pen'-tail], *s.* Teja cóncava. *V.* PANTILE.

Pent-up [pent'-up], *a.* Cerrado, encerrado, contenido dentro de una cosa.

Penult [pi'-nult o pę-nult'], *s.* *V.* PENULTIMA.

Penultima [pę-nul'-ti-ma], *s.* (Gram.) Penúltima, la sílaba anterior a la última en una palabra.

Penultimate [pę-nul'-ti-mêt], *a.* Penúltimo.

Penumbra [pę-num'-bra], *s.* 1. (Astr.) Penumbra, sombra parcial en los eclipses entre lo iluminado y la parte obscurecida. 2. (Pint.) El punto o línea de un cuadro en que se confunde la sombra con la luz. 3. La franja obscura alrededor del punto céntrico de una mácula del sol.

Penurious [pę-niū'-ri-us], *a.* 1. Tacaño, ruin, avaro, miserable. 2. Escaso; indigente.

Penuriously [pę-niū'-ri-us-li], *adv.* Escasamente, con escasez, miserablemente.

Penuriousness [pę-niū'-ri-us-nes], *s.* Tacañería, ruindad, miseria; cortedad de ánimo; escasez.

Penury [pen'-yu-ri], *s.* Penuria, pobreza; carestía, falta de alguna cosa muy necesaria.

Pen-wiper [pen'-wai"-pęr], *s.* Limpiaplumas.

Peon [pi'-en], *s.* Soldado de a pie en la India; criado; peón.

Peony [pi'-o-ni], *s.* (Bot.) Peonía, cualquier planta del género *Pæonia,* de la familia de las ranunculáceas, y su flor.

People [pi'-pl], *s.* 1. Pueblo, nación, todas las personas que se hallan bajo el mismo gobierno, que hablan el mismo idioma, o que son de la misma sangre. 2. Población, habitantes. 3. Populacho, la gente común, el vulgo. 4. Gente, pluralidad de personas; tomando el verbo en el plural. *What will people say?* ¿Qué dirá la gente? ¿qué dirán? *Common people,* Gentualla, gentuza.

Chosen people, El pueblo elegido, los Israelitas. *The people of Mexico*, Los habitantes de Méjico; la nación mejicana. *Country people*, La gente del campo, los campesinos. *Young people*, Los jóvenes. *People think that*, Se cree que, piensan que.
People, *va.* Poblar.
Pep [pep] *s.* (Fam.) Energía, vigor, entusiasmo, espíritu.
Pepastic [pep-as'-tic], *a.* (Med.) Madurativo, que tiene virtud de madurar.
Pepper [pep'-er], *s.* 1. Pimienta, fruto del pimentero. 2. Pimentero, arbusto que da la pimienta. Piper nigrum. 3. Pimiento, ají, chile; cualquier planta del género Capsicum o su fruto. *Black pepper*, Pimienta de Castilla. *Long pepper*, Pimienta larga. *Red* o *Cayenne pepper*, Pimiento. (Amer.) Ají, guindilla. (Mex.) Chile. *The small red pepper*, Chiltipiquín.
Pepper, *va.* 1. Rociar o sazonar con pimienta o ají. 2. Golpear; herir a uno con un tiro de perdigones u otra munición menuda.
Pepper-box, Pepper-pot [pep'-er-box], *s.* Pimentero.
Pepper-corn [pep'-er-cōrn], *s.* Bagatela, niñería, chuchería.
Peppering [pep'-er-ing], *a.* Caliente, fogoso, colérico.—*s.* Perdigonada, tiro de perdigones.
Peppermint [pep'-er-mint], *s.* (Bot.) Menta piperita, hierbabuena o yerbabuena, planta aromática de la familia de las labiadas. Se emplea en medicina y en dulcería. *Peppermint drop*, Pastilla de menta.
Pepperwort [pep'-er-wūrt], *s.* (Bot.) Lepidio.
Pepsin, Pepsine [pep'-sin], *s.* Pepsina, substancia orgánica secretada por ciertas glándulas del estómago y que forma el fermento digestivo del jugo gástrico.
Peptic [pep'-tic], *a.* Digestivo.
Peptone [pep'-tōn], *s.* Peptona, substancia debida a la transformación de los principios albuminoideos por la acción del jugo gástrico sobre los alimentos.
Peptonize [pep'-ton-aiz], *va.* Peptonizar, convertir en peptona.
Peptonic [pep-ton'-ic], *a.* Peptónico, perteneciente a la peptona o derivado de ella.
Per [per], *prep.* Por. *Per annum*, Al año. *Per capita*, Por cabeza, por persona. *Per cent.*, Por ciento. *Per se*, Por sí mismo, por su propia naturaleza.
Peracute [per-a-kiūt'], *a.* Muy agudo, muy violento.
Peradventure [per-ad-ven'-chur], *adv.* Quizá, acaso, por acaso, por ventura.—*s.* Posibilidad de error; duda, cuestión.
Perambulate [per-am'-biu-lēt], *va.* Pasar por alguna parte, transitar, recorrer algún territorio; ver, visitar.—*vn.* Ir paseando, andar.
Perambulation [per-am-biu-lé'-shun], *s.* La acción de caminar o transitar por alguna parte.
Perambulator [per-am'-biu-lēt-er], *s.* 1. Cochecillo de niño. 2. Odómetro, máquina o rueda para medir los caminos.
Percale [per-cal' o per-kēl'], *s.* Percal, cierta tela de algodón, blanca o pintada, que sirve para vestidos de mujer.
Percarbureted [per-cār'-biu-ret-ed], *a.* Percarburado, combinado con la mayor cantidad posible de carbono.
Perceivable [per-sīv'-a-bl], *a.* Perceptible, que se puede percibir.
Perceivably [per-sīv'-a-bli], *adv.* Perceptiblemente.
Perceive [per-sīv'], *va.* 1. Percibir, comprender, entender; conocer. 2. Percibir, recibir por alguno de los sentidos las impresiones de los objetos. 3. Recibir una cosa la impresión de otra. *To perceive beforehand*, Presentir.
Percentage [per-sent'-éj], *s.* 1. Razón por ciento. 2. Tanto por ciento, interés por ciento; premio o estipendio de comisionista.
Perceptibility [per-sep-ti-bil'-i-ti], *s.* Perceptibilidad, facultad de ser percibido; raramente, la facultad de percibir.
Perceptible [per-sep'-ti-bl], *a.* Perceptible, sensible; que puede percibirse.
Perceptibly [per-sep'-ti-bli], *adv.* Perceptiblemente, sensiblemente, visiblemente.
Perception [per-sep'-shun], *s.* 1. Percepción, acción y efecto de percibir; conocimiento de las cosas exteriores obtenido por las impresiones sobre los sentidos; aprehensión, saber. 2. Facultad de percibir, de adquirir conocimiento de algo. 3. (For.) Toma, recibimiento, de cosechas o de ganancias.
Perceptive [per-sep'-tiv], *a.* Perceptivo, que tiene la facultad de percibir.
Perceptivity [per-sep-tiv'-i-ti], *s.* Perceptibilidad.
Perch [perch], *s.* 1. Perca, pez de agua dulce. 2. Pértica, medida de tierra de cinco varas y media. 3. Alcándara, percha.
Perch, *vn.* Posarse, sentarse, pararse, empingorotarse, encaramarse; descansar las aves, ponerse en percha.—*va.* Emperchar, empingorotar.
Perchance [per-chans'], *adv.* Acaso, quizá, por ventura.
Percher [perch'-er], *s.* 1. El ave que se pone en percha. 2. (Des.) Vela grande, cirio.
Percheron [per'-she-ren], *a.* y *s.* Percherón, caballo de tiro que proviene del Perche, región de la Francia septentrional.
Perchglue [perch'-glū], *s.* Cola fina de perca.
Perchloric [per-clō'-ric], *a.* (Quím.) Perclórico. *Perchloric acid*, Ácido perclórico.
Perchlorid, Perchloride [per-clō'-rid, per-clō'-rid o raid], *s.* Percloruro, combinación del cloro con los demás cuerpos en toda intensidad de que es susceptible aquél.
Percipient [per-sip'-i-ent], *a.* Percipiente, lo que tiene la virtud de percibir.—*s.* Percipiente, el ser que tiene la facultad de percibir.
Perclose [per-clōz'], *s.* (Arq.) Barandilla o enverjado que encierra un lugar u objeto, como un altar o una capilla.
Percoid [per'-ceid], *a.* Percoide, que se parece a la perca.
Percolate [per'-co-lēt], *va.* y *vn.* Colar, filtrar, pasar, o hacer pasar al través de pequeños intersticios.
Percolation [per-co-lé'-shun], *s.* Coladura, filtración.
Percolator [per'-co-lé"-ter], *s.* 1. Filtro, colador. 2. Cafetera filtradora.
Percuss [per-cus'], *va.* Herir, golpear rápidamente; percutir, emplear la percusión como medio de exploración médica.
Percussion [per-cush'-un], *s.* 1. Percusión, golpe. 2. Resonación, el sonido causado por la repercusión; el choque producido por el encuentro de dos cuerpos. 3. (Med.) Percusión, acción de percutir el pecho o el abdomen para producir sonidos que ayudan a reconocer el estado del órgano subyacente. *Percussion caps*, Cebo de golpe o fulminante para las armas de fuego; pistón, cápsula.
Percussion section [per-cush'-un sec'-shun], *s.* (Mús.) Batería.
Percussive [per-cus'-iv], *a.* Que golpea contra otra cosa.
Percutient [per-kiū'-shent], *a.* Percuciente; se dice de lo que hiere o causa impresión en otra cosa.
Perdition [per-dish'-un], *s.* Perdición, destrucción, pérdida, ruina.
Perdurable [per'-diu-ra-bl o per-diū'-ra-bl], *a.* Perdurable, muy duradero.
Perdurably [per'-diu-ra-bli], *adv.* Perdurablemente.
Peregrinate [per-e-gri-nēt], *vn.* 1. Peregrinar, viajar de un país o de un lugar a otro. 2. (Des.) Vivir en países extranjeros.
Peregrination [per-e-gri-né'-shun], *s.* Peregrinación, viaje por países extranjeros, o de un lugar a otro.
Peregrine [per'-e-grin], *a.* 1. Peregrino, migratorio, pasajero, como las aves. 2. Extranjero, que no es indígena.
Peremptorily [per'-emp-to-ri-li], *adv.* Perentoriamente; absolutamente.
Peremptoriness [per'-emp-to-ri-nes], *s.* Tono dogmático o magistral, juicio o decisión absolutos o decisivos; obstinación.
Peremptory [per'-emp-to-ri], *a.* Perentorio; absoluto, decisivo, definitivo; dogmático, magistral. *Peremptory orders*, Órdenes perentorias. *Peremptory sale*, Venta forzosa.
Perennial [per-en'-i-al], *a.* 1. Perenne, perennal; continuo, incesante, permanente, perpetuo. 2. (Biol.) Que crece continuamente: (1) (Bot.) Perenne, que sobrevive más de dos años; (2) (Ento.) que sobrevive más de un año, o que forma colonias que duran varios años.—*s.* (Bot.) Planta perenne, que dura varios años, produciendo comúnmente flores y frutos cada año.
Perfect [per'-fect], *a.* 1. Perfecto, acabado, que no tiene defecto ni falta; hábil, diestro, cabal, consumado. 2. (Bot.) Completo, provisto de estambres y pistilos. 3. (Gram.) Perfecto, que expresa un acto cumplido. 4. (Fam.) Puro, muy grande, excesivo. *She has a perfect horror of spiders*, Ella tiene horror ciego a las arañas.—*s.* Tiempo perfecto.
Perfect [per-fect' o per'-fect], *va.* 1. Perfeccionar, hacer perfecto; acabar enteramente. 2. Perfeccionar, instruir enteramente.
Perfecter [per'-fect-er o per-fect'-er], *s.* Perfeccionador.
Perfectibility [per-fect'-i-bil-i-ti], *s.* Perfectibilidad, cualidad de lo perfectible.
Perfectible [per-fect'-i-bl], *a.* Perfectible, que puede ser perfeccionado.
Perfection [per-fec'-shun], *s.* 1. Perfección, estado de lo perfecto, suprema excelencia. 2. El grado más

alto de una cosa; lo extremo, lo supremo.

Perfective [pẹr-fec'-tiv], *a.* Perfectivo, que da o puede dar perfección.

Perfectionate [pẹr-fec'-shun-ēt], *va.* (Ant.) Perfeccionar.

Perfectionist [pẹr-fec'-shun-ist], *s.* Perfeccionista, puritano.

Perfectively [pẹr-fec'-tiv-li], *adv.* Con perfección.

Perfectly [pẹr'-fect-li], *adv.* Perfectamente, cabalmente.

Perfectness [pẹr'-fect-nes], *s.* Perfección, habilidad, capacidad; excelencia.

Perfervid [pẹr-fẹr'-vid], *a.* Muy férvido, ardiente o celoso.

Perfidious [pẹr-fid'-i-us], *a.* Pérfido, desleal, traidor, fementido; infiel, que viola la fe.

Perfidiously [pẹr-fid'-i-us-li], *adv.* Traidoramente, pérfidamente.

Perfidiousness [pẹr-fid'-i-us-nes], **Perfidy** [pẹr'-fi-di], *s.* Perfidia, deslealtad, traición.

Perfoliate, Perfoliated [pẹr-fō'-li-ēt, ed], *a.* (Bot.) Perfoliado; se dice de una hoja que rodea el tallo y parece estar perforada por él.

Perforate [pẹr'-fo-rēt], *va.* Perforar, horadar, penetrar alguna cosa agujereándola de una parte a otra; calar.

Perforation [pẹr-fo-rē'-shun], *s.* 1. Perforación, el acto de horadar, taladrar o barrenar. 2. Cala.

Perforator [pẹr'-fo-rē-tẹr], *s.* Perforador, el que o lo que perfora: (1) barrena, taladro; (2) perforador, instrumento de obstetricia.

Perforce [pẹr-fōrs'], *adv.* Por fuerza, por necesidad.—*s.* Compulsión, apremio.

Perform [pẹr-fōrm'], *va.* 1. Ejecutar, hacer, poner por obra alguna cosa; efectuar. 2. Desempeñar, llenar. *To perform one's promise,* Cumplir con su palabra. *To perform one's duties,* Llenar sus deberes, cumplir con su obligación.—*vn.* 1. Representar, hacer papel; cantar; tocar un instrumento músico; salir bien en una empresa o empeño.

Performable [pẹr-fōrm'-a-bl], *a.* Ejecutable, practicable.

Performance [pẹr-fōrm'-ans], *s.* 1. Ejecución; cumplimiento. 2. Composición, obra. 3. Acción, hecho, hazaña. 4. Representación teatral o ante espectadores.

Performer [pẹr-fōrm'-ẹr], *s.* 1. Ejecutor, el que ejecuta o pone por obra alguna cosa. 2. El que ejecuta alguna habilidad en público; actor, representante, músico, sinfonista, acróbata.

Perfume [pẹr'-fiūm o per-fiūm'], *s.* 1. Perfume. 2. Olor de perfume, olor fragante, fragancia. (Perú) Agua rica, toda especie de perfumes o aguas de olor.

Perfume [pẹr-fiūm'], *va.* Perfumar, sahumar, aromatizar alguna cosa; incensar.

Perfumer [pẹr-fiūm'-ẹr], *s.* Perfumador, perfumero, perfumista.

Perfumery [pẹr-fiūm'-ẹ-ri], *s.* Los perfumes en general; perfumería, la preparación de los perfumes.

Perfunctorily [pẹr-fuṇc'-to-ri-li], *adv.* Descuidadamente, sin interés, superficialmente, por encima.

Perfunctoriness [pẹr-fuṇc'-to-ri-nes], *s.* Descuido, negligencia.

Perfunctory [pẹr-fuṇc'-to-ri], *a.* Perfunctorio, superficial, hecho meramente para poner fin a alguna cosa; indolente, negligente.

Perfuse [pẹr-fiūz'], *va.* (Poco us.) Tinturar; colmar, llenar demasiado; difundir, extender sobre.

Perfusion [pẹr-fiū'-zhun], *s.* Tintura, el acto de difundir o derramar.

Pergola [pẹr'-go-la], *s.* Pérgola, emparrado.

Perhaps [pẹr-haps'], *adv.* Puede ser, quizá, quizás, acaso, por ventura.

Peri [pī'-ri o pé'-ri], *s.* Peri, hada hermosa y bienhechora de la mitología persa.

Peri. Prefijo griego que significa cerca de, alrededor.

Perianth, Perianthium [per-i-anth', thi-um], *s.* (Bot.) Periantio, el cáliz y la corola combinados cuando se parecen tanto que son casi indistinguibles; también, involucro exterior de la flor.

Pericardial, Pericardiac [per-i-cār'-di-al, ac], **Pericardian** [per-i-cār'-di-an], *a.* Pericardino, referente al pericardio.

Pericarditis [per-i-car-dai'-tis o dī'-tis], *s.* Pericarditis, inflamación del pericardio.

Pericardium [per-i-cār'-di-um], *s.* Pericardio, bolsa membranosa que rodea y protege el corazón.

Pericarp, Pericarpium [per-i-cār'-pi-um], *s.* Pericarpio, película que cubre el fruto de las semillas de varias plantas; la pared del ovario después de madurado el fruto.

Pericarpial, Pericarpic [per-i-cār'-pi-al, pic], *a.* Pericarpial, que pertenece al pericarpio.

Pericranium [per-i-crē'-ni-um], *s.* Pericráneo, membrana que cubre exteriormente los huesos del cráneo.

Peridrome [per'-i-drōm], *s.* (Arq.) Peridromo, galería entre las columnas y la pared.

Periecians, Periœcians [per-i-ī'-shans], *s. pl.* Periecos, los que viven en puntos diametralmente opuestos de un mismo paralelo de latitud.

Perigee [per'-i-jī], **Perigeum** [per-i-jī'-um], *s.* (Astr.) Perigeo, punto en la órbita de la luna (rara vez en la de un planeta) en que se halla más próxima a la tierra.

Perihelion, Perihelium [per-i-hī'-li-ẹn], *s.* (Astr.) Perihelio, punto en que un planeta se halla más inmediato al sol.

Peril [per'-il], *s.* Peligro, riesgo, contingencia, acaso.

Peril, *va.* Exponer al peligro, poner en peligro; arriesgar.—*vn.* Peligrar; estar en peligro.

Perilous [per'-il-us], *a.* Peligroso, aventurado.

Perilously [per'-il-us-li], *adv.* Peligrosamente, arriesgadamente.

Perilousness [per'-il-us-nes], *s.* La situación peligrosa o arriesgada de una cosa.

Perimeter [per-im'-e-tẹr], *s.* Perímetro, el ámbito o circunferencia de algún espacio, figura o lugar.

Perineal [per-i-nī'-al], *a.* Perineal, relativo al perineo.

Perineum [per-i-nī'-um], *s.* (Anat.) Perineo, el espacio entre el ano y los órganos de la generación.

Period [pī'-ri-ẹd], *s.* 1. Período, circuito, revolución. 2. Período, ciclo, tiempo en que se acaba alguna cosa de suerte que empieza de nuevo del mismo modo. 3. Período, cierto y determinado número de años, meses, días, etc. 4. Fin, conclusión; el último punto a que puede llegar alguna cosa. 5. (Gram.) Período, cláusula entera. 6. (Med.) Período, fase particular de una enfermedad. 7. (Mús.) Período, frase de cierto número de compases uniformes y regulares. 8. Período, punto final, signo de puntuación. 9. *The period,* El día de hoy, el presente tiempo.—*pl.* Las reglas, la menstruación.

Periodic, Periodical [pī-ri-ōd'-ic, al], *a.* Periódico.

Periodically [pī-ri-ed'-ic-al-i], *adv.* Periódicamente.

Periodicalness [pī-ri-ed'-ic-al-nes], *s.* Periodicidad, calidad de periódico.

Periœci [per-i-ī'-sai], *s. pl.* Periecos. *V.* PERIECIANS.

Periosteum [per-i-es'-te-um], *s.* Periostio, membrana vascular y nerviosa que cubre los huesos.

Peripatetic [per-i-pa-tet'-ic], *a.* 1. El que anda a pie desde un lugar a otro. 2. Peripatético, el secuaz de Aristóteles. *Peripatetic philosophy,* Peripatetismo.

Peripetia [per-i-pet-ai'-a], *s.* Peripecia, desenredo, desenlace de una pieza dramática.

Peripheral [per-if'-ẹr-al], *a.* 1. Periférico, periferal, perteneciente a una periferia. 2. Distante de un centro. *V.* DISTAL.

Peripheric, Peripherical [per-if'-ẹr-ic, per-i-fer'-ic-al], *a.* *V.* PERIPHERAL.

Periphery [per-if'-ẹr-i], *s.* 1. La superficie exterior. 2. Periferia, circunferencia.

Periphrase [per'-i-frēz], *va.* Perifrasear, hacer circunlocuciones.

Periphrasis, Periphrase [per-if'-ra-sis], *s.* Perífrasis, circunlocución.

Periphrastic, Periphrastical [per-i-fras'-tic, al], *a.* Perifraseado.

Periphrastically [per-i-fras'-tic-al-i], *adv.* Con perífrasis.

Periscii [pẹ-rish'-i-ai], *s. pl.* Periscios, los habitantes de las zonas polares.

Periscope [per'-i-scōp], *s.* Periscopio.

Periscopic [per-i-scop'-ic], *a.* Periscópico, que tiene vista a todos lados. *Periscopic lens,* Lente periscópico, que por todos sus puntos transmite las imágenes de los objetos.

Perish [per'-ish], *vn.* Perecer, acabar, fenecer, morir: marchitarse, pasarse. *To perish with hunger,* Perecer de hambre.

Perishable [per'-ish-a-bl], *a.* Perecedero.

Perishableness [per'-ish-a-bl-nes], *s.* La calidad de perecedero.

Perisperm [per'-i-spẹrm], *s.* (Bot.) Perispermo, envoltura de un óvulo o semilla rudimentaria.

Peristalsis [per-i-stal'-sis], *s.* Movimiento peristáltico o vermicular de un órgano hueco del cuerpo, particularmente del intestino.

Peristaltic [per-i-stal'-tic], *a.* Peristáltico, vermicular.

Peristerion [per-is-tī'-ri-en], *s.* (Bot.) Verbena.

Peristome [per'-i-stōm], *s.* 1. (Bot.) Perístomo, franja de dientes menudos, generalmente un múltiplo de cuatro, que rodea el orificio de la cápsula de los musgos. 2. (Zool.) Las partes que rodean la boca de un marisco univalvo, un zoófito o un insecto díptero.

Peristyle [per'-i-stail], *s.* (Arq.) Peristilo, galería de columnas que rodea un edificio o parte de él.

Perisystole [per-i-sis'-to-le], *s.* (Med.)

Perisístole, el intervalo entre la sístole y la diástole.
Peritoneal [per-i-to-nī'-al], *a.* Peritoneal, perteneciente o relativo al peritoneo.
Peritoneum [per-i-to-nī'-um], *s.* (Anat.) Peritoneo, membrana serosa que cubre interiormente la cavidad abdominal.
Peritonitis [per-i-to-naī'-tis o nī'-tis], *s.* Peritonitis, inflamación del peritoneo.
Peritroch [per-i-trec'], *s.* (Zool.) Anillo, círculo pequeño de pelillos o pestañas.
Periwig [pgr'-i-wig], *s.* Peluca, peluquín; cabellera postiza.
Periwig [per'-i-wig], *va.* (Poco us.) Ponerse peluca o peluquín.
Periwinkle [per'-i-wiŋ-cl], *s.* 1. Litorina, género de moluscos gasterópodos. Littorina littorea o palliata. 2. (Bot.) Pervencha, pervinca, planta de la familia de las apocíneas, y su flor, azul por regla general. Vinca minor y major.
Perjure [per'-jur], *va.* y *vn.* Perjurar, jurar en falso.
Perjurer [pgr'-jur-gr], *s.* Perjurador, perjuro.
Perjury [pgr'-ju-ri], *s.* Perjurio. *To commit perjury,* Jurar en falso.
Perk [pgrc], *vn.* Erguirse, levantar la cabeza con afectación de viveza. —*va.* 1. Adornar, decorar, vestir. 2. Erguir, levantar la oreja o la cabeza.
Perk, Perky [pgrk'-i], *a.* Que tiene la cabeza erguida con gentileza; gallardo.
Permanence [pgr'-ma-nens], *s.* Permanencia, duración firme, continuación en el mismo estado, fijeza.
Permanency [pgr'-ma-nen-si], *s.* 1. Permanencia. 2. Alguna cosa permanente, muy duradera, o indestructible.
Permanent [pgr'-ma-nent], *a.* Permanente, que permanece estable, duradero, que continúa sin cambio.
Permanently [pgr'-ma-nent-li], *adv.* Permanentemente.
Permanent wave [pgr'-ma-nent wêv], *s.* Ondulado permanente (del cabello).
Permanganate [pgr-maŋ'-ga-nêt], *s.* (Quím.) Permanganato, compuesto del ácido permangánico con una base salificable.
Permeability [pgr-mg-a-bil'-i-ti], *s.* Permeabilidad, calidad o condición de permeable.
Permeable [pgr'-mg-a-bl], *a.* (Fís.) Permeable, dícese de todo cuerpo por donde puede penetrar fácilmente el aire, la luz o cualquier otro flúido rezumable; penetrable.
Permeant [pgr'-mg-ant], *a.* *V.* PERMEATIVE.
Permeate [pgr'-mg-êt], *va.* Penetrar, atravesar, pasar por medio.
Permeation [pgr-mg-ê'-shun], *s.* Pasaje o penetración al través de los intersticios o poros de un cuerpo.
Permeative [pgr'-mg-a-tiv], *a.* Penetrativo, permeativo, que penetra por entre los poros.
Permissible [pgr-mis'-i-bl], *a.* Permisible, que se puede permitir o consentir.
Permission [pgr-mish'-un], *s.* Permisión, permiso, licencia.
Permissive [pgr-mis'-iv], *a.* Permisivo, permitido, tolerado, consentido.
Permissively [pgr-mis'-iv-li], *adv.* Permisivamente.
Permit [pgr-mit'], *va.* 1. Permitir, consentir, tolerar, autorizar tácitamente o no poniendo obstáculos. 2. Permitir, conceder permiso o libertad de hacer, autorizar.
Permit [pgr'-mit], *s.* Permiso, licencia.
Permittance [pgr-mit'-ans], *s.* 1. Capacidad electroestática. 2. Permisión, el acto de permitir.
Permittivity [pgr-mit-iv'-i-ti], *s.* Capacidad específica de inducción eléctrica expresada por una razón numérica entre el cuerpo eléctrico y el aire.
Permutation [pgr-miu-tê'-shun], *s.* 1. Permutación, permuta, cambio recíproco. 2. (Mat.) Permutación, combinación en que se atiende al número y términos que se comparan y a la diferencia resultante de los lugares en que se colocan.
Permute [pgr-miūt'], *va.* Permutar, trocar, cambiar entre sí.
Permuter [pgr-miūt'-gr], *s.* La persona que permuta, cambia o trueca.
Pern [pgrn], *s.* (Orn.) Buaro del género Pernis.
Pernicious [pgr-nish'-us], *a.* 1. Pernicioso, gravemente dañoso o perjudicial, funesto, fatal. 2. (Des.) Veloz.
Perniciously [pgr-nish'-us-li], *adv.* Perniciosamente, perjudicialmente.
Perniciousness [pgr-nish'-us-nes], *s.* Malignidad, la calidad maligna o perniciosa de alguna cosa.
†**Pernoctation** [pgr-nec-tê'-shun], *s.* Pernoctación, el acto de dormir al raso; el acto de pasar en vela toda la noche.
Peroration [per-o-rê'-shun], *s.* Peroración, la conclusión de alguna oración o discurso.
Peroxid, Peroxide [pgr-ex'-id, id o aid], *s.* Peróxido, grado mayor de oxidación.
Perpend [pgr-pend'], *va.* (Ant.) Reflexionar, pensar cuidadosamente, examinar o pesar las razones en que se funda una opinión.
Perpend, Perpend-stone [pgr'-pend, stōn], **Perpender** [pgr-pend'-gr], *s.* Perpiaño, piedra que atraviesa toda la pared.
†**Perpendicle** [pgr-pend'-i-cl], *s.* Cualquiera cosa que cuelga perpendicularmente.
Perpendicular [pgr-pen-dic'-yu-lar], *a.* Perpendicular, dícese de la línea o plano que cae sobre otro plano o línea formando ángulos rectos.—*s.* Línea perpendicular.
Perpendicularity [pgr-pen-dic-yu-lar'-i-ti], *s.* La calidad y estado de lo que es perpendicular.
Perpendicularly [pgr-pen-dic'-yu-lar-li], *adv.* Perpendicularmente.
Perpetrate [pgr'-pg-trêt], *va.* Perpetrar, cometer algún delito o culpa grave; hacer, ejecutar; se usa también en sentido festivo.
Perpetration [pgr-pg-trê'-shun], *s.* Perpetración, el acto de cometer algún delito.
Perpetrator [pgr'-pg-trê''-tgr], *s.* Perpetrador.
Perpetual [pgr-pet'-yu-al], *a.* Perpetuo; continuo, incesante, eterno; vitalicio. *Perpetual motion,* Movimiento continuo, perpetuo, eterno.
Perpetually [pgr-pet'-yu-al-i], *adv.* Perpetuamente, continuamente.
Perpetuate [pgr-pet'-yu-êt], *va.* Perpetuar, eternizar; proseguir sin intermisión.
Perpetuation [pgr-pet-yu-ê'-shun], *s.* Perpetuación, la acción de perpetuar.
Perpetuity [pgr-pg-tiū'-i-ti], *s.* Perpetuidad, duración sin fin.
Perplex [pgr-plex'], *va.* 1. Confundir, perturbar, dejar a uno perplejo y lleno de dudas. 2. Intrincar, embrollar, enredar, enmarañar alguna cosa. 3. Atormentar.—*a.* Intrincado, enredado.
Perplexed [pgr-plecst'], *a.* Perplejo, dudoso, irresoluto; confuso.
Perplexedly [pêr-plex'-ed-li], *adv* Perplejamente, confusamente.
Perplexedness [pgr-plex'-ed-nes], **Perplexity** [pgr-plex'-i-ti], *s.* Perplejidad, duda, irresolución; confusión, inquietud.
Perquisite [pgr'-cwi-zit], *s.* Percance, gajes, buscas, propinas, los emolumentos o utilidades que se adquieren por algún empleo u ocupación además del salario o sueldo señalado.
Perquisition [pgr-cwi-zish'-un], *s.* (Poco us.) Pesquisa, indagación, investigación.
Perron [per'-en], *s.* (Arq.) Grada o escalera abierta en la parte exterior de un edificio.
Perry [per'-i], *s.* Sidra de peras.
Persalt [pgr'-sōlt], *s.* (Quím.) Sal formada por la combinación de una base ácida con un peróxido.
Persecute [pgr'-sg-kiūt], *va.* 1. Perseguir, molestar, hostigar, vejar; particularmente perseguir o afligir por motivo de las creencias religiosas de uno. 2. Molestar, fatigar, importunar.
Persecution [pgr-sg-kiū'-shun], *s.* Persecución, vejación; molestia.
Persecutive [pgr'-sg-kiū-tiv], *a.* Perseguidor, que persigue.
Persecutor [pgr'-sg-kiū-tgr], *s.* Perseguidor, dañador.
Perseverance [pgr-sg-vīr'-ans], *s.* Perseverancia, el acto o la costumbre de perseverar; persistencia, constancia.
Perseverant [pgr-sg-vīr'-ant], *a.* (Poco us.) Perseverante, constante, firme.
Persevere [pgr-sg-vīr'], *vn.* Perseverar, persistir.
Persevering [pgr-sg-vīr'-ing], *pa.* Perseverante, persistente.
Perseveringly [pgr-sg-vīr'-ing-li], *adv.* Perseverantemente, constantemente.
Persian [pgr'-shan], *a.* Persa, persiano, perteneciente a Persia.—*s.* 1. Persa, persiano, el natural de Persia. 2. Persiana, tela delgada de seda. 3. Persa, persiano, la lengua de Persia. *Persian blinds,* Celosías. *Persian Gulf,* El Golfo Pérsico. *Persian wheel,* Azuda, máquina con que se saca agua de los ríos para regar los campos.
Persic [pgr'-sic], *a.* Pérsico, persa.—*s.* Idioma persa.
Persiflage [pgr'-si-flāzh], *s.* Choteo, guasa, pitorreo.
Persimmon [per-sim'-gn], *s.* 1. Fruto globular, anaranjado, que se parece a una ciruela, del dióspiro, árbol americano de la familia de las ebenáceas; es de gusto muy áspero y astringente hasta haber estado expuesto a la escarcha; entonces se pone dulce y comestible. 2. Dióspiro, árbol que da este fruto. Diospyros Virginiana. *Japanese persimmon,* Fruto muy estimado en el Oriente, y que hoy se obtiene ya en California y Florida: el Diospyros Kaki. (Nombre indio.)

Persist [pęr-sist'], *vn.* Persistir, permanecer; empeñarse, insistir.

Persistence [pęr-sis'-tens], **Persistency** [pęr-sist'-en-si], *s.* 1. Persistencia, permanencia o firmeza en la ejecución de alguna cosa, constancia. 2. Obstinación, contumacia. 3. Continuación, duración.

Persistent, Persisting, Persistive [pęr-sist'-iv], *a.* 1. Persistente, firme, determinado, resuelto. 2. Permanente, invariable, continuo. 3. (Biol.) Persistente, que no cae o no se marchita.

Person [per'-sun o pęr'-sn], *s.* 1. Persona, individuo o sujeto de la naturaleza humana. 2. Persona, disposición o figura del cuerpo. 3. Persona de la Trinidad. 4. (Gram.) Persona, el nombre o pronombre que rige a un verbo o es regido por él. 5. (Biol.) Individuo. 6. (Ant.) Papel de un actor; por extensión, el sujeto que tiene alguna representación por cualquier concepto. *In person,* Personalmente o en persona.

Personable [pęr'-sun-a-bl], *a.* 1. Hermoso, de buena presencia. 2. (Der. ant.) Capaz de mantener una alegación en los tribunales.

Personage [pęr'-sun-ėj], *s.* 1. Personaje, hombre o mujer de distinción o calidad. 2. Personaje, papel, carácter.

Personal [pęr'-sun-al], *a.* Personal; directo, en persona; corporal; exterior. *Personal estate,* Bienes muebles. *Personal property,* Propiedad mueble. *Personal appearance,* (1) Aspecto, apariencia personal. (2) Comparecencia en persona.

Personality [pęr-sun-al'-i-ti], *s.* 1. Personalidad, lo que constituye a una persona distinta de otra; también lo que constituye un individuo. 2. Personalidad, lo que se dice tocante a una persona determinada, particularmente una expresión injuriosa.

Personalize [pęr'-sun-al-aiz], *va.* 1. Personalizar, hacer personal. 2. (Ret.) Personificar.

Personally [pęr-sun-al-i], *adv.* Personalmente.

Personate [pęr'-sun-ėt], *va.* 1. Representar, subrogarse en los derechos, autoridad o bienes de otro. 2. Contrahacer, remedar. 3. Representar, fingir, hacer el papel de alguna cosa o persona.—*vn.* Representar, ser actor en una pieza dramática.

Personation [pęr-sun-é'-shun], *s.* Disfraz, artificio con que una persona pasa por otra.

Personator [pęr'-sun-ė-tęr], *s.* 1. El que representa a otra persona. 2. Ejecutor, el que hace o ejecuta alguna cosa.

Personification [pęr-sen-i-fi-kė'-shun], *s.* Personificación, prosopopeya, figura por la cual se hace hablar o accionar a personas fingidas o cosas inanimadas.

Personify [pęr-sen'-i-fai], *va.* Personificar, atribuir a las cosas inanimadas o abstractas las pasiones o afectos de las personas.

Personnel [pęr-sę-nel'], *s.* Personal, cuerpo de empleados.

Perspective [pęr-spec'-tiv], *s.* 1. Perspectiva, arte que enseña a delinear en una superficie los objetos con tal arte que aparezcan a la vista como verdaderos; y la obra ejecutada con este arte. 2. Perspectiva, vista o aspecto de diversos objetos juntos mirados de lejos. 3. Vista, importancia relativa de sucesos o materias desde un punto de vista especial.—*a.* (Pint.) Perspectivo, perteneciente al arte de la perspectiva; que representa un objeto en perspectiva.

Perspectively [pęr-spec'-tiv-li], *adv.* Por representación.

Perspicacious [pęr-spi-kė'-shus], *a.* Perspicaz, penetrante.

Perspicaciousness [pęr-spi-kė'-shus-nes], **Perspicacity** [pęr-spi-cas'-i-ti], *s.* 1. Perspicacia; penetración o viveza de ingenio. 2. (Ant.) Agudeza de vista.

Perspicuity [pęr-spi-kiū'-i-ti], *s.* Perspicuidad, claridad, transparencia.

Perspicuous [pęr-spic'-yu-us], *a.* 1. Perspicuo, claramente expresado, inteligible. 2. (Des.) Perspicuo, claro, transparente.

Perspicuously [pęr-spic'-yu-us-li], *adv.* Perspicuamente, claramente.

Perspicuousness [pęr-spic'-yu-us-nes], *s.* Perspicuidad, claridad de estilo.

Perspirable [pęr-spair'-a-bl], *a.* Transpirable.

Perspiration [pęr-spi-rė'-shun], *s.* 1. Transpiración, exhalación de un flúido acuoso por las glándulas excretorias de la piel. 2. Sudor, transpiración, serosidad que se exhala por los poros de los animales.

Perspirative [pęr-spair'-a-tiv], *a.* Lo que transpira.

Perspiratory [pęr-spair'-a-to-ri], *a.* Transpiratorio, lo que pertenece a la transpiración.

Perspire [pęr-spair'], *vn.* Transpirar, evaporar los humores insensiblemente; exhalar flúido por los poros.—*va.* Exhalar, excretar. *A fir-tree perspires balsam,* Un abeto excreta el bálsamo.

Persuadable [pęr-swėd'-a-bl], *a.* Persuasible.

Persuade [pęr-swėd'], *va.* Persuadir, atraer a uno con razones; excitar, mover a alguno a la ejecución de una cosa.

Persuader [pęr-swėd'-ęr], *s.* Persuasor, persuadidor.

Persuasible [pęr-swé'-si-bl], *a.* Persuasible.

Persuasibleness [pęr-swė'-si-bl-nes], *s.* Flexibilidad, facilidad en dejarse persuadir.

Persuasion [pęr-swė'-zhun], *s.* 1. Persuasión, acción y efecto de persuadir. 2. Persuasión, la idea o el juicio que se forma en virtud de algún fundamento. 3. Creencia, opinión religiosa, creencia fija; de aquí, partido, secta, o denominación. 4. Persuasiva, facultad de persuadir.

Persuasive [pęr-swė'-siv], *a.* Persuasivo.—*s.* Persuasiva, eficacia y destreza en persuadir.

Persuasively [pęr-swė'-siv-li], *adv.* De un modo persuasivo.

Persuasiveness [pęr-swė'-siv-nes], *s.* Persuasiva, eficacia para persuadir.

Persuasory [pęr-swė'-so-ri], *a.* Persuasivo.

Persulfate, Persulphate [pęr-sul'-fėt], *s.* (Quím.) Persulfato, combinación de ácido sulfúrico con un peróxido.

Pert [pęrt], *a.* 1. Petulante, atrevido, descocado. 2. (Des.) Listo, vivo.

Pertain [pęr-tėn'], *vn.* 1. Pertenecer, tocar a alguno como atributo, derecho, deber, propiedad, cualidad o adjunto. 2. Concernir, referirse a.

Pertinacious [pęr-ti-nė'-shus], *a.* 1. Pertinaz, obstinado, terco, tenaz. 2. Constante, incesante, continuo.

Pertinaciously [pęr-ti-nė'-shus-li], *adv.* Pertinazmente, obstinadamente.

Pertinaciousness [pęr-ti-nė'-shus-nes], **Pertinacity** [pęr-ti-nas'-i-ti], †**Pertinacy** [pęr'-ti-na-si], *s.* 1. Pertinacia, obstinación, terquedad, tenacidad. 2. Perseverancia, constancia; resolución, firmeza.

Pertinence [pęr'-ti-nens], **Pertinency** [pęr'-ti-nens-si], *s.* Pertinencia, conexión, relación de una cosa con otra.

Pertinent [pęr'-ti-nent], *a.* 1. Pertinente, que viene a propósito. 2. Perteneciente, pertinente.

Pertinently [pęr'-ti-nent-li], *adv.* Pertinentemente, oportunamente.

Pertly [pęrt'-li], *adv.* 1. Insolentemente, descaradamente, descocadamente. 2. (Des.) Vivamente, prontamente.

Pertness [pęrt'-nes], *s.* Petulancia, descaro, atrevimiento, impertinencia.

Perturb [pęr-tūrb'], *va.* Perturbar, inquietar, poner en desorden.

Perturbable [pęr-tūrb'-a-bl], *a.* Perturbable, que se puede perturbar.

Perturbation, Perturbance [pęr-tūr-bė'-shun, pęr-tūrb'-ans], *s.* 1. Perturbación, desorden, agitación de ánimo; efecto de perturbar. 2. Perturbación, desviación en el movimiento de un cuerpo celeste.

Perturbator [pęr'-tūr-bė-tęr], *s.* Perturbador, agitador.

Perturber [pęr-tūrb'-ęr], *s.* Perturbador, agitador.

Pertuse [per-tiūs'], *a.* 1. Horadado con punzón, agujereado. 2. (Bot.) Perforado.

‖**Pertusion** [pęr-tiū'-zhun], *s.* 1. El acto de taladrar. 2. Taladro, el agujero hecho con el taladro o la barrena.

Pertussis [pęr-tus'-is], *s.* (Med.) Tos convulsiva; en particular tos ferina. *V.* WHOOPING-COUGH.

Peruke [per-ūk' o per'-ūk], *s.* Peluca, cabello postizo. *Peruke-maker,* Peluquero.

Perusal [pe-rū'-zal], *s.* Lectura, lección, acción de leer.

Peruse [pe-rūz'], *va.* 1. Leer; leer con atención, leer hasta el fin. 2. (Ant.) Observar, examinar atentamente.

Peruser [pe-rūz'-ęr], *s.* Lector; revisor, examinador.

Peruvian [pe-rū'-vi-an], *a.* Peruano, del Perú. *Peruvian bark,* Quina, cascarilla.

Pervade [pęr-vėd'], *va.* Atravesar, esparcirse por todas partes, penetrar, ocupar, llenar.

Pervasion [pęr-vė'-zhun], *s.* Esparcimiento, el acto de esparcirse alguna cosa por todas partes.

Pervasive [pęr-vė'-siv], *a.* Que se esparce por todas partes; penetrativo, penetrante.

Perverse [pęr-vęrs'], *a.* 1. Perverso, depravado, malo, intratable. 2. Contrario, refractario, obstinado, terco. 3. Enfadoso, molesto, vejador.

Perversely [pęr-vęrs'-li], *adv.* Perversamente.

Perverseness [pęr-vęrs'-nes], *s.* Perversidad, maldad; terquedad, obstinación.

Perversion [pęr-vęr'-shun], *s.* Perversión, pervertimiento, depravación.

Perversity [pęr-vęr'-si-ti], *s.* Perversidad, conducta o naturaleza perversa; obstinación, terquedad.

Perversive [pẹr-vẹr'-siv], *a.* Perversivo.

Pervert [pẹr-vẹrt'], *va.* 1. Pervertir, corromper. 2. Pervertir, falsear, viciar, dirigir mal o interpretar mal, desnaturalizar.—*vn.* 1. Apartarse, desviarse del camino recto. 2. Hacerse renegado, apostatar. *To pervert manners,* Echar a perder las maneras. *To pervert the meaning,* Desnaturalizar el sentido.

Pervert [pẹr'-vẹrt], *s.* Renegado, apóstata; pervertido en oposición a convertido.

Perverter [pẹr-vẹrt'-ẹr], *s.* Pervertidor.

Pervertible [pẹr-vẹrt'-i-bl], *a.* Pervertible, lo que es fácil de corromper o pervertir.

Pervious [pẹr'-vi-us], *a.* Penetrable; permeable. *Pervious to light,* Que permite el paso á la luz.

Perviousness [pẹr'-vi-us-nes], *s.* Penetrabilidad, permeabilidad.

§**Pesade** [pe-sēd'], *s.* Movimiento de un caballo de silla que levanta las patas delanteras sin mover las de atrás. (Fr.)

Peshito, Peshitto [pe-shī'-tō], *s.* 1. Nombre de la versión siríaca más antigua de la Biblia, hecha, según se cree, en el siglo segundo. 2. Una pequeña letra siríaca.

Pesky [pes'-ki], *a.* (Fam. E. U.) Molesto, incómodo; también, apestado, excesivo.

Pessary [pes'-a-ri], *s.* (Cir.) Pesario, instrumento para corregir los prolapsos del útero y mantener este órgano en posición normal.

Pessimism [pes'-i-mizm], *s.* 1. Pesimismo, propensión a verlo todo bajo el aspecto más siniestro. 2. Cinismo, la tendencia a despreciar lo bueno y suponer lo malo. 3. Pesimismo, sistema de filosofía que considera la existencia como un mal.

Pessimist [pes'-i-mist], *s.* Pesimista, persona que todo lo ve bajo el aspecto más desfavorable; partidario del pesimismo, o que desea el exceso del mal como medio de llegar al bien.

Pessimistic [pes-i-mis'-tic], *a.* Pesimista.

Pessimistically [pes-i-mist'-ic-al-i], *adv.* En tono pesimista.

Pest [pest], *s.* 1. Peste, pestilencia. 2. Peste: dícese de las personas o cosas muy dañosas a las buenas costumbres. *Pest-house,* Lazareto.

Pester [pes'-tẹr], *va.* Moler, molestar, vejar, cansar, atormentar, importunar. (Fam.) Jorobar. *He pesters me with his letters,* Me muele a cartas.

Pesterable [pes'-ẹr-a-bl], *a.* Molesto.

Pesterer [pes'-tẹr-ẹr], *s.* Moledor. (Vulg.) Majadero, joroba, moscón, pejiguera.

Pestiferous [pes-tif'-ẹr-us], *a.* Pestífero, pestilente; pernicioso.

Pestilence [pes'-ti-lens], *s.* Pestilencia, peste, enfermedad contagiosa; también en sentido figurado.

Pestilent [pes'-ti-lent], *a.* 1. Pestilente, pestífero, que produce una enfermedad contagiosa. 2. Pernicioso, de influencia maligna, de efecto perjudicial. 3. Importuno, atormentador.

Pestilential [pes-ti-len'-shal], *a.* Pestilencial, pernicioso, dañoso en sumo grado.

Pestilentialness [pes-ti-len'-shal-nes], *s.* Calidad de pestilente.

Pestilently [pes'-ti-lent-li], *adv.* Pestilencialmente.

Pestle [pes'-l], *s.* Mano de almirez, majador de mortero.—*va.* Majar, moler o mezclar en un mortero.

Pet [pet], *a.* Acariciado, mimado; favorito; domesticado. *Pet name,* Nombre cariñoso, a menudo un diminutivo. *Pet lamb,* Cordero criado en la casa, sin madre.—*s.* 1. Enojo, enfado, despecho, acceso de mal humor. 2. Cualquier animal domesticado y acariciado. 3. Favorito. *He is a great pet,* Es el favorito, el mimado, el querido. (Mex.) Chiqueado, amamantado. *To go away in a pet,* Irse enojado o enfadado. *To get in a pet,* Atufarse, enojarse. *He is in a great pet,* Toma el cielo con las manos.

Pet, *va.* Mimar, echar a perder con mimos.

Petal [pet'-al], *s.* (Bot.) Pétalo, cada una de las hojas que forman la corola de la flor.

Petalism [pet'-al-izm], *s.* Petalismo, una especie de destierro entre los antiguos siracusanos.

Petaled, Petalous [pet'-ald, pet'-al-us], *a.* (Bot.) Provisto de pétalos.

Petaliferous [pet-al-if'-ẹr-us], *a.* Que tiene pétalos.

Petaloid [pet'-al-oid], *a.* Petaloideo, semejante a los pétalos o que consta de ellos.

Petard [pe-tārd'], *s.* Petardo, antigua máquina militar.

Petardeer [pet-ār-dīr'], *s.* Petardero.

Petechiæ [pẹ-tek'-i-ī], *s. pl.* Petequias, pintas a manera de picaduras de pulga que salen en algunas calenturas malignas.

Petechial [pẹ-tek'-i-al], *a.* Petequial.

Peter [pī'-tẹr], *vn.* Disminuir, desaparecer una veta o filón en una mina; con la prep. *out.*

Peter's Pence, Peter-pence [pī'-tẹr-pens], *s.* Dinero de San Pedro, un tributo que antiguamente se pagaba al Papa en Inglaterra.

Petiolar [pet'-i-ō"-lar], *a.* Peciolado, perteneciente a un pecíolo, o sostenido por él.

Petiolate [pet'-i-o-lēt], *a.* (Bot.) Peciolado, aplícase a las hojas que tienen pecíolo.

Petiole [pet'-i-ōl], *s.* (Bot.) Pecíolo, pezón o rabillo de la hoja.

Petit [pet'-i; en el derecho, pet'-it], *a.* Pequeño; menor. (Desusado a no ser en frases forenses o tomadas del francés.) *V.* Petty.

Petition [pẹ-tish'-un], *s.* 1. Memorial, representación. 2. Pedimento, petición, demanda. 3. Petición, súplica dirigida al Ser Supremo.

Petition, *va.* Suplicar, orar, rogar; dirigir una petición.

Petitionary [pẹ-tish'-un-ẹ-ri], *a.* 1. Demandante, la parte que demanda en justicia. 2. Suplicante, el que pide o suplica.

Petitioner [pẹ-tish'-un-ẹr], *s.* Suplicante; memorialista, representante.

Petitory [pet'-i-to-ri], *a.* Petitorio, solicitante o solicitado por petición.

Pet name [pet nêm'], *s.* Apodo, nombre cariñoso.

Petong [pẹ-tong'], *s.* Cobre blanco de China; aleación de cobre y níquel.

§**Petrean** [pẹ-trī'-an], *a.* Pétreo, de roca, de la naturaleza de la roca.

Petrel [pet'-rel o pī'-trel], *s.* Procelario, petrel, ave de mar llamada también ave de San Pedro o de las tempestades. Procellaria pelagica.

Petrescence [pẹ-tres'-ens], *s.* Petrificación, acción de convertirse en piedra.

Petrescent [pẹ-tres'-ent], *a.* Que se petrifica.

Petrifaction [pet-ri-fac'-shun], *s.* 1. Petrificación. 2. Petrificación, el cuerpo petrificado.

Petrifactive [pet-ri-fac'-tiv], **Petrific** [pẹ-trif'-ic], *a.* Petrífico, petrificante.

Petrification [pet-ri-fi-kē'-shun], *s.* 1. Petrificación, el cuerpo petrificado. 2. Endurecimiento del corazón.

Petrify [pet'-ri-fai], *va.* 1. Petrificar, transformar en piedra. 2. Endurecer el corazón, hacer a alguno sordo a los remordimientos.—*vn.* Petrificar, endurecerse alguna cosa de modo que parezca piedra.

Petrine [pī'-trin o train], *a.* Referente a San Pedro apóstol.

Petrochemistry [pẹ-tro-kem'-is-tri], *s.* Petroquímica.

Petrography [pet-rog'-ra-fi], *s.* Petrografía, estudio de los caracteres de las rocas.

Petrolatum [pet-ro-lē'-tum], *s.* Mezcla semisólida de los hidrocarbonos de la parafina, que se obtiene destilando las partes más volátiles del petróleo americano y purificando el resto. Se conoce en el comercio con los nombres, de cosmolina, vaselina, saxolina y petrolina.

Petroleum [pẹ-trō'-lẹ-um], *s.* Petróleo, carburo de hidrógeno, principio líquido de los betunes blandos y viscosos.

Petrology [pet-rel'-o-ji], *s.* Petrología, petrognosia, la ciencia de las rocas, su origen y distribución.

Petronel [pet'-ro-nel], *s.* *V.* Pistol.

Petrous [pet'-rus o pī'-trus], *a.* Petroso, pétreo, endurecido como la piedra.

Petticoat [pet'-i-cōt], *s.* Guardapiés, zagalejo; enaguas, basquiña. *Quilted o embroidered petticoat,* Zagalejo picado.—*a.* Lo que pertenece a las mujeres o es propio de ellas. *Petticoat government,* Úsase para expresar la influencia de las mujeres en el gobierno o dirección de una cosa o negocio.

Pettifog [pet'-i-fog], *vn.* Ejercer malamente la abogacía.

Pettifogger [pet'-i-fog-ẹr], *s.* 1. Abogado de guardilla. 2. Picapleitos.

Pettifoggery [pet'-i-fog-ẹr-i], *s.* Los embrollos y enredos de los malos abogados.

Pettiness [pet'-i-nes], *s.* Pequeñez, mezquindad.

Pettish [pet'-ish], *a.* Enojadizo, bronco, áspero, insociable, caprichudo, regañón.

Pettishly [pet'-ish-li], *adv.* Caprichosamente, ásperamente, broncamente.

Pettishness [pet'-ish-nes], *s.* Enojo, aspereza de genio, capricho.

Pettitoes [pet'-i-tōz], *s.* Manos o pies de lechoncillo.

Petto [pet'-o], *s.* Pecho. (Ital.) *In petto,* En lo interior del pecho.

Petty [pet'-i], *a.* 1. Pequeño, corto, menudo. 2. Despreciable, mezquino. *Petty cash,* Efectivo para gastos menores. *Petty king,* Reyezuelo. *Petty larceny,* Robo de cosas de poco valor. *Petty jury,* V. Jury.

Petulance [pet'-yu-lans], **Petulancy** [pet'-yu-lan-si], *s.* Mal humor, mal genio, enfado pasajero, impaciencia, despego en el trato.

Petulant [pet'-yu-lant o pech'-u-lant], *a.* 1. Enojadizo, de mal humor, que

muestra impaciencia caprichuda o despego en el trato. 2. (Des.) Petulante, descarado.
Petulantly [pet'-yu-lant-li], *adv.* Con impaciencia, con aspereza, de mal humor.
Petunia [pe-tiu'-ni-a], *s.* (Bot.) Petunia.
Petuntze, Petunse [pe-tun'-tse, pi-tuns'], *s.* Petonce, feldespato foliado que se usa en China para la fabricación de la porcelana.
Pew [piū], *s.* Banco, asiento, de iglesia; antiguamente un lugar cerrado a manera de cajón.—*pl.* Los dueños o arrendadores de los bancos de iglesia; la congregación.
‡**Pew**, *va.* Proporcionar asientos o bancos particulares en las iglesias.
Pewee [pi'-wi], *s.* (E. U.) Pájaro pequeño de color verde-oliva, una de las varias especies de tirano, particlarmente el pájaro llamado *phœbe*, por la nota de su voz.
Pewholder [piū'-hōld''-er], *s.* El que posee en propiedad o alquila un asiento o banco de iglesia.
Pewit, Peewit [pi'-wit], *s.* Una de varias aves: (1) *V.* PEWEE. (2) Avefría, frailecillo. (3) Laro de cabeza negra, el pájaro reidor.
Pew-opener [piū'-o-pn-er], *s.* (Ingl.) El que abre o guarda los asientos en la iglesia.
Pewter [piū'-ter], *s.* 1. Peltre, especie de metal compuesto de estaño y plomo. 2. Peltre, el conjunto de platos, fuentes y otras vasijas de dicho metal.
Pewterer [piū'-ter-er], *s.* Peltrero, el que trabaja en objetos de peltre, estañador.
Phænogam [fi'-no-gam], *s.* Planta que tiene flores; planta fanerógama. *V.* PHANEROGAM.
Phaeton [fé'-e-ten], *s.* 1. Faetón, coche ligero de cuatro ruedas y uno o dos asientos transversales, provisto comúnmente de cubierta o dosel. 2. Meliteo, mariposa grande de América que tiene las alas negras con manchas rojizas anaranjadas. Melitæa phaeton.
Phagocytes [fag'-o-saits], *s. pl.* Fagocitos, tipo de glóbulos blancos.
Phalangean [fa-lan'-je-an], *a.* Falangético, falángido, que pertenece a la falange.
Phalanges [fa-lan'-jīz], *s. pl.* de PHALANX.
Phalanx [fé'-lanx o fal'-anx], *s.* (*pl.* PHALANGES o PHALANXES, excepto en anatomía y botánica). 1. Falange, cuerpo de infantería de la antigua Grecia. 2. Cualquier cuerpo compacto y numeroso de personas unidas con un mismo fin. 3. Falange, cada uno de los huesos que hay en los dedos de la mano y el pie. 4. Coyuntura del tarso de los insectos.
Phanerogam [fan'-er-o-gam], *s.* Planta fanerógama, que produce flores, es decir que tiene estambres y pistilos.
Phanerogamous, Phanerogamic o **Phanerogamian** [fan-er-og'-a-mus, fan-er-o-gam'-ic, gé'-mi-an], *a.* Fanerógamo, que tiene flores; provisto de estambres y pistilos distintos.
Phantasm [fan'-tasm], **Phantasma** [fan-taz'-ma], *s.* Fantasma.
Phantasmagoria [fan-tas-ma-gō'-ri-a], *s.* 1. Fantasmas incoherentes de un sueño. 2. Fantasmagoría, arte de representar fantasmas por medio de una ilusión óptica; y la misma linterna empleada para ese objeto.
Phantasmagorial, Phantasmagoric [fan-tas-ma-gō'-ri-al, ger'-ic], *a.* Fantasmagórico; ilusorio.
Phantasy [fan'-ta-si], *s.* *V.* FANTASY, y todas las voces que se derivan de ella.
Phantom [fan'-tem], *s.* Fantasma, espectro horrible. *V.* FANTOM.
Pharaonic [fār-a-en'-ic], *a.* Faraónico, concerniente a los Faraones.
Pharisaic, Pharisaical [far-i-sé'-ic, al], *a.* Farisaico.
Pharisaically [far-i-sé'-ic-al-i], *adv.* De un modo farisaico.
Pharisaicalness [far-i-sé'-ic-al-nes], *s.* Farisaísmo.
Pharisee [far'-i-si], *s.* Fariseo.
Pharmaceutic, Pharmaceutical [fār-ma-siū'-tic, al], *a.* Farmacéutico.
Pharmacist [fār'-ma-sist], *s.* Farmacéutico, boticario.
Pharmacology [fār-ma-cel'-o-ji], *s.* Farmacología, conocimiento de los medicamentos.
Pharmacopœia [fār-ma-co-pi'-ya], *s.* Farmacopea, el libro que contiene las reglas para la composición de las medicinas.
Pharmacopolist [fār-ma-cep'-o-list], *s.* Boticario.
Pharmacy [fār'-ma-si], *s.* 1. Farmacia, el arte de preparar los medicamentos. 2. Botica.
Pharos [fé'-res], *s.* Faro, torre alta con luces en la parte superior para servir de guía a los navegantes.
Pharyngeal [far-in-ji'-al o fa-rin'-je-al], *a.* Faríngeo, perteneciente á la faringe.
Pharyngitis [far-in-jai'-tis], *s.* (Med.) Faringitis.
Pharyngotomy [far-in-get'-o-mi], *s.* Faringotomía, incisión de la faringe.
Pharynx [far'-inx], *s.* Faringe, la parte superior del esófago.
Phase [fēz], *s.* 1. Fase, aspecto, cada uno de los cambios que se notan en ciertos objetos. 2. (Astr.) Fase, cada una de las diversas figuras en que vemos la luna y los planetas.
Phasis [fé'-sis], *s.* (Astr.) Fase.
Pheasant [fez'-ant], *s.* (Orn.) Faisán, ave del orden de las gallináceas, muy hermosa y de carne apreciada.
Phenacetin [fe-nas'-e-tin], *s.* Fenacetina, compuesto blanco cristalizable empleado en medicina como antipirético. (< phenol + acetic.)
Phenix [fi'-nix], *s.* 1. Fénix, ave fabulosa, que se creía ser única y que renacía de sus cenizas; emblema de la inmortalidad. 2. Cosa extraordinaria, prodigio. 3. Constelación austral.
Phenogam, etc. *V.* PHÆNOGAM, etc.
Phenol [fi'-nōl], *s.* 1. Cada uno de una serie de cuerpos derivados de la benzola. 2. Fenol, ácido fénico (C_6H_5OH), desinfectante blanco, cristalino, que se extrae del alquitrán de hulla. Su adjetivo es *phenic*, fénico.
Phenomenal [fe-nem'-en-al], *a.* Fenomenal.
Phenomenon [fe-nem'-e-nen], *s.* 1. Fenómeno. 2. Fenómeno, todo lo que admira por su novedad o rareza. Escríbese en plural PHENOMENA.
Phial [fai'-al], *s.* Redomilla. Lo mismo que VIAL.
Philadelphian [fil-a-del'-fi-an], *a.* Filadelfo, de Filadelfia; también de Ptolomeo Filadelfo.
Philander [fi-lan'-der], *vn.* Hacer cocos, divertirse en galantear a una mujer.—*s.* Amante, pretendiente.
Philanthropic, Philanthropical [fil-an-threp'-ic, al], *a.* Filantrópico.
Philanthropist [fi-lan'-thro-pist], *s.* Filántropo, amigo de los hombres; el que se ocupa en hacerles bien.
Philanthropy [fi-lan'-thro-pi], *s.* Filantropía, humanidad, amor natural del género humano.
Philatelic [fil-a-tel'-ic], *a.* Filatélico.
Philatelist [fi-lat'-e-list], *s.* Filatelista.
Philately [fi-lat'-e-li], *s.* Filatelia, ocupación o tarea de coleccionar sellos de franqueo de diversos países, para estudiarlos o formar colecciones.
Philharmonic [fil-hār-men'-ic], *a.* Filarmónico, apasionado por la música; úsase en los nombres de sociedades musicales.
Philhellenic [fil-hel-en'-ic], *a.* Amigo de los griegos y de lo que les concierne.
Philippic [fi-lip'-ic], *s.* 1. Filípica, cada una de las doce arengas de Demóstenes contra Filipo de Macedonia. 2. Filípica, declamación, invectiva.
Philistine [fi-lis'-tin], *s.* y *a.* 1. Filisteo, individuo de un pueblo antiguo y guerrero de la Siria, enemigo de los israelitas. 2. Ciego partidario a las ideas generalmente admitidas; persona venal, de ideas mezquinas.
Philologist [fi-lel'-o-jist] o **Philologer** [fi-lel'-o-jer], *s.* Filólogo, el que estudia y profesa la filología.
Philologic, Philological [fil-o-lej'-ic, al], *a.* Filológico.
Philologize [fi-lel'-o-jaiz], *vn.* (Poco us.) Practicar la crítica y la filología.
Philology [fi-lel'-o-ji], *s.* Filología, erudición en las letras humanas.
Philomel [fil'-o-mel], **Philomela** [fil-o-mi'-la], *s.* (Poét.) Filomela, ruiseñor.
Philopena [fil-o-pi'-na], *s.* 1. Juego casero en que una persona paga una prenda a otra bajo ciertas condiciones. 2. El regalo hecho en pago de prenda, o las almendras que se reparten en este juego. (< Alem. vielliebchen, muy querido.)
Philosophaster [fi-les'-o-fas-ter], *s.* Filosofastro.
Philosopher [fi-les'-o-fer], *s.* Filósofo. *Philosopher's stone*, Piedra filosofal.
Philosophic, Philosophical [fil-o-sef'-ic, al], *a.* 1. Filosófico, relativo a la filosofía. 2. Filosófico, racional, sereno, calmoso.
Philosophically [fil-o-sef'-i-cal-i], *adv.* Filosóficamente.
Philosophism [fi-les'-o-fizm], *s.* Filosofismo, secta o doctrina de los falsos filósofos.
Philosophist [fi-les'-o-fist], *s.* Seudofilósofo, filósofo falso.
Philosophize [fi-les'-o-faiz], *vn.* Filosofar.
Philosophy [fi-les'-o-fi], *s.* 1. Filosofía, ciencia natural o moral; amor a la ciencia. 2. Filosofía, estudio de los principios y de las causas; sistema de principios científicos; sistema particular de filosofía; razonamiento, discurso. 3. Filosofía, fortaleza de ánimo. 4. Tratado sobre algún sistema de filosofía.
†**Philostorgy** [fil-o-stōr'-ji], *s.* El amor natural entre padres e hijos.
†**Philotechnic** [fil-o-tec'-nic], *a.* Aficionado a las artes.

Philter [fil'-tẹr], *s.* Filtro, hechizo amatorio.
Philter, *va.* Hechizar con filtro.
Phiz [fiz], *s.* (Vulg.) Facha, cara, fisonomía.
Phlebotomist [flẹ-bet'-o-mist], *s.* Flebótomo, flebotomiano, sangrador.
Phlebotomize [flẹ-bet'-o-maiz], *va.* Sangrar, abrir una vena como medio curativo.
Phlebotomy [flẹ-bet'-o-mi], *s.* Flebotomía, el arte de sangrar.
Phlegm [flem], *s.* 1. Flema, mucosidad pegajosa que se arroja por la boca. 2. Flema, tardanza y lentitud en las operaciones; apatía, indiferencia, genio cachazudo.
Phlegmasia [fleg-mé'-zhi-a], *s.* Inflamación.
Phlegmatic, Phlegmatical [fleg-mat'-ic, al], *a.* 1. Flegmático o flemático. 2. Cachazudo, lento, indiferente, linfático.
Phlegmon [fleg'-men], *s.* (Med.) Flemón, inflamación del tejido celular, con tendencia a formar pus.
Phlegmonous [fleg'-mo-nus], *a.* Flemonoso, de la naturaleza de un flemón.
Phloem [flō'-em], *s.* (Bot.) Parte externa de la corteza interior que contiene los tubos llamados "de tamiz" (*sieve-tubes*). (< Gr. φλοιός, corteza.)
Phlox [flex], *s.* (Bot.) Flox, género de plantas y de flores norteamericanas, tipo de la familia de las polemoniáceas. (Gr.)
Phoca [fō'-ca], *s.* Foca. *V.* SEAL.
Phœbe, Pœbe-bird [fí'-bí, bẹrd], *s.* Febe, pájaro pequeño de los Estados Unidos del Este; nombre imitativo de su canto. Sayornis phœbe.
Phœnix [fí'-nics], *s.* 1. (Orn.) Fénix. 2. (Bot.) Palma.
Phonation [fo-né'-shun], *s.* Fonación, emisión de la voz o palabra.
Phone [fōn], *s.* (Fam.) Abreviatura familiar de *telephone*, teléfono.
Phonetic, Phonetical [fo-net'-ic, al], *a.* Fonético, que representa sonidos o se refiere a ellos o a la voz.
Phonetics, Phonics [fen'-ics], *s.* Fonología, fonética, estudio de los sonidos de la voz humana.
Phonic [fen'-ic o fō'-nic], *a.* Fónico, concerniente al sonido, o de la naturaleza del sonido.
Phonogram [fō'-no-gram], *s.* 1. Carácter, tipo que simboliza un sonido. 2. Fonograma, el trazo producido por un fonógrafo y por medio del cual se reproducen los sonidos articulados.
Phonograph [fō'-no-graf], *s.* Fonógrafo. *Phonograph record,* Disco fonográfico.
Phonographer [fo-neg'-ra-fẹr], *s.* 1. Taquígrafo fonético, persona versada en la fonografía. 2. Persona versada en el uso del fonógrafo.
Phonographic, Phonographical [fō"-no-graf'-ic, al], *a.* Fonográfico, relativo a la fonografía o al fonógrafo.
Phonography [fo-neg'-ra-fi], *s.* 1. Fonografía, el arte o la ciencia de escribir según los sonidos; una forma de la taquigrafía. 2. Fonografía, representación de los sonidos por medio de signos. 3. El arte de construir o de usar los fonógrafos.
Phonologic, Phonological [fō-no-lej'-ic, al], *a.* Fonológico, referente a la fonología.
Phonology [fo-nel'-o-ji], *s.* Fonología, parte de la ciencia del lenguaje, que estudia las leyes de la fonación en uno o varios idiomas.
Phonometer [fo-nem'-ẹ-tẹr], *s.* Fonómetro, instrumento para medir la intensidad de la voz o del sonido.
Phonometric [fo-no-met'-ric], *a.* Fonométrico, que se refiere al fonómetro.
Phonotype [fō'-no-taip], *s.* Fonotipo, carácter empleado en la impresión fonotípica.
Phonotypy [fo-no-tai'-pi o fo-net'-i-pi], *s.* Fonotipia, sistema de impresión en que cada sonido de la voz está representado por una letra o un carácter distinto.
Phosgene [fes-jin'], *s.* (Quím.) Fosgeno, oxicloruro de carbono.
Phosphate [fes'-fét], *s.* (Quím.) Fosfato, sal formada con ácido fosfórico y alguna base.
Phosphatic [fes-fat'-ic], *a.* Fosfático, que contiene algún fosfato.
Phosphid, Phosphide [fes'-fid, fes'-faid], *s.* Fosfuro, nombre genérico de las combinaciones del fósforo, no ácidas, con otro cuerpo simple.
Phosphite [fes'-fait], *s.* (Quím.) Fosfito, sal formada de ácido fosforoso con alguna base.
Phosphor [fes'-fẹr], *s.* 1. Fósforo, la estrella matutina. 2. *V.* PHOSPHORUS.
Phosphorate [fes'-fer-ét], *va.* Combinar con el fósforo, impregnar de fósforo. *Phosphorated oil,* Aceite fosforado.
Phosphoresce [fes-fer-es'], *vn.* Ser fosforescente, fosforescer, despedir luz en la obscuridad como hace el fósforo.
Phosphorescence [fes-fo-res'-ens], *s.* Fosforescencia.
Phosphorescent [fes-fo-res'-ent], *a.* Fosforescente.
Phosphoric [fes-fer'-ic], *a.* 1. Fosfórico. 2. Fosforescente.
Phosphorous [fes'-fer-us], *a.* Fosforoso, sacado del fósforo en sus más bajas combinaciones. *Phosphorous acid,* Ácido fosforoso (H_3PO_3).
Phosphorus [fes'-fer-us], *s.* Fósforo, metaloide muy combustible, de color blanco amarillento, que luce en la obscuridad cuando se pone en contacto con el aire, y se inflama fácilmente.
Photic [fō'-tic], *a.* Relativo a la luz y a la producción de la luz.
Photo [fō'-tō], *s.* (Fam.) Estampa fotográfica.
Photoelectric [fō-to-ẹ-lec'-tric], *a.* Fotoeléctrico.
Photoengraving [fō"-to-en-gré'-ving], *s.* Fotograbado (así el arte como la estampa).
Photofinish [fō'-tō-fin'-ish], *s.* 1. En carreras de caballos, el triunfo reñidísimo que hay que decidir mediante fotografía tomada al efecto. 2. Esta fotografía.
Photoflash lamp [fō'-to-flash lamp], *s.* Lámpara, lamparilla o bombilla de magnesio, o de destello.
Photogenic [fō-to-jen'-ic], *a.* Fotogénico, que favorece la acción química de la luz; producido por la acción de la luz.
Photograph [fō'-to-graf], *va.* Fotografiar, reproducir por medio de la fotografía; también en sentido figurado.—*s.* Fotografía, estampa obtenida por el arte fotográfico.
Photographer [fō-teg'-ra-fẹr], *s.* Fotógrafo, el que ejerce la fotografía.
Photographic, Photographical [fō-to-graf'-ic, al], *a.* 1. Fotográfico, relativo a la fotografía, o producido por este arte. 2. Semejante a una imagen fotográfica; representado con vigor y fidelidad.
Photography [fo-teg'-ra-fi], *s.* Fotografía, arte o procedimiento de fijar las imágenes de la cámara obscura sobre una placa sensible a la acción de la luz.
Photogravure [fō"-to-gra-viūr'], *s.* Fotograbado, el procedimiento de producir una plancha en hueco para imprimir, en la cual no hay líneas grabadas sino concavidades muy diminutas; y la estampa obtenida de dicha plancha.
Photometer [fo-tem'-ẹ-tẹr], *s.* Fotómetro, instrumento para medir la intensidad de la luz.
Photometric [fō-to-met'-ric], *a.* Fotométrico, relativo a la fotometría.
Photoplay [fō'-tō-plé], *s.* Comedia cinematográfica.
Photosphere [fō'-to-sfír], *s.* Fotosfera, la atmósfera luminosa del sol, o (rara vez) de una estrella fija.
Photostatic [fō-tō-stat'-ic], *a.* Fotostático.
Photosynthesis [fō-tō-sin'-the-sis] *s.* Fotosíntesis.
Phototype [fō'-tō-taip], *s.* Fototipia.
Phrase [fréz], *s.* 1. Frase, la construcción de algunas palabras que forman un sentido perfecto. 2. Frase, estilo, el modo particular con que expresa sus pensamientos cada escritor y la índole y forma especial de las oraciones en cada lengua. *As the phrase goes,* (Fam.) Como suele decirse; vamos al decir.
Phrase, *va.* Llamar, nombrar, intitular.
Phrase-book [fréz'-buc], *s.* Libro de frases o modismos peculiares de cada lengua.
†**Phraseless** [fréz'-les], *a.* Indescriptible.
Phraseologist [fré-zẹ-el'-o-jist], *s.* Fraseologista, el que habla en frases hechas, con afectación.
Phraseology [fré-zi-el'-o-ji], *s.* 1. Fraseología, dicción, construcción, estilo. 2. Libro de frases hechas.
Phrenetic [frẹ-net'-ic], *a.* Frenético, loco.
Phrenologist [frẹ-nel'-o-jist], *s.* Frenólogo, el que profesa la frenología.
Phrenology [frẹ-nel'-o-ji], *s.* Frenología, sistema que atribuye a cada porción del cerebro diversa facultad intelectual, instinto, pasión o afecto.
†**Phrensy** [fren'-zi], *s.* *V.* FRENZY.
Phrygian [frij'-i-an], *a.* y *s.* Frigio, perteneciente a la Frigia.
Phthisic, Phthisical [tiz'-ic, al], *a.* 1. Tísico, hético, que padece de tisis. 2. Asmático.
Phthisis [thai'-sis o thi'-sis], *s.* Tisis, tuberculosis pulmonar.
Phycology [fi-cel'-o-ji], *s.* Algología, ciencia de las algas marinas.
Phylacter, Phylactery [fi-lac'-tẹr, i], *s.* Filacteria, faja que llevan los judíos y en la que están escritos algunos textos de la Biblia.
Phylactered [fi-lac'-tẹrd], *a* Filactérico.
Phyllis [fil'-is], *s.* Muchacha campesina, pastora amada. (De Filis, nombre poético de mujer.)
Phyllium [fil'-i-um], *s.* Insecto parecido a una hoja; género Phyllium
Phyllotaxis [fil-o-tax'-is], *s.* (Bot.) Filotaxia, arreglo o disposición de las hojas sobre el tallo, y las reglas a que obedece.

Phylloxera [fi-lex-i'-ra], *s.* 1. Filoxera, insecto pequeño parecido al pulgón que destruye las raíces y hojas de la vid ; se le cree oriundo de la América del Norte. 2. Enfermedad de la viña, causada por dicho insecto.

Physic [fiz'-ic], *va.* Medicinar y particularmente purgar.

Physic, *s.* 1. Medicina, la ciencia que enseña a precaver y curar las enfermedades del cuerpo humano. 2. Medicamentos, remedios. 3. Purgante o purga.

Physical [fiz'-i-cal], *a.* 1. Físico, perteneciente al universo material o a la ciencia de la física. 2. Material ; corporal, corpóreo. 3. Físico, perteneciente a los fenómenos de que trata la física ; obvio a los sentidos, externo.

Physical chemistry [fiz'-i-cal kem'-is-tri], *s.* Fisicoquímica.

Physical education [fiz'-i-cal ed-yu-kê'-shUn], *s.* Educación física.

Physical examination [fiz'-i-cal eg-zam-i-nê'-shUn], *s.* Reconocimiento médico.

Physically [fiz'-i-cal-i], *adv.* Físicamente ; naturalmente ; materialmente ; corporalmente ; externamente.

Physical science [fiz'-i-cal sai'-ens], *s.* Ciencias físicas.

Physician [fi-zish'-an], *s.* Médico, el que profesa la medicina.

Physicist [fiz'-i-sist], *s.* 1. Físico, persona versada en la física. 2. Partidario de la doctrina de que los fenómenos vitales son puramente físicos y químicos.

Physicochemical [fiz'-i-co-kem'-i-cal], *a.* Fisicoquímico.

Physics [fiz'-ics], *s. pl.* Física, la ciencia que estudia y enseña la naturaleza y las propiedades de los cuerpos.

Physiognomist [fiz-i-eg'-no-mist], *s.* Fisonomista, fisónomo, la persona dedicada al estudio de la fisonomía y sabe juzgar por ella a las personas.

Physiognomy [fiz-i-eg'-no-mi], *s.* 1. Fisonomía, el arte que da reglas para conjeturar por las facciones del rostro el temperamento y las buenas o malas inclinaciones de una persona. 2. Fisonomía, rostro, semblante, aspecto particular de cada persona.

Physiographic, Physiographical [fiz-i-o-graf'-ic, al], *a.* Fisiográfico, relativo a la fisiografía.

Physiography [fiz-i-eg'-ra-fi], *s.* Fisiografía, descripción de (las producciones de) la naturaleza.

Physiologic, Physiological [fiz-i-o-lej'-ic, al], *a.* Fisiológico, perteneciente a la fisiología.

Physiologist [fiz-i-el'-o-jist], *s.* Fisiologista, fisiólogo, el que estudia la fisiología.

Physiology [fiz-i-el'-o-ji], *s.* Fisiología, la ciencia que trata de las funciones orgánicas de los seres vivientes, sean animales o vegetales.

Physiotherapy [fiz-i-o-ther'-a-pi], *s.* Fisioterapia.

Physique [fi-zic'], *s.* Físico, constitución, complexión.

Phytology [fai-tel'-o-ji], *s.* Botánica, la ciencia que trata de las plantas y sus propiedades.

Phytophagous [fai-tef'-a-gus], *a.* Fitófago, que se alimenta de plantas.

Pi, Pie [pai], *va.* Mezclar confusamente letras de imprenta.—*s.* Pastel, mezcla confusa de tipos de imprenta. (Prob. < pica.)

Piacular [pai-ac'-yu-lar], ‡**Piaculous** [pai-ac'-yu-lus], *a.* 1. Expiatorio, satisfactorio. 2. Criminal, atroz.

Pia-mater [pai-a-mê'-ter], *s.* Piamáter, la primera o más interna de las membranas que cubren el cerebro y la medula espinal.

Pianissimo [pi-a-nis'-i-mō], *adv.* y *a.* (Mús.) Muy suavemente ; pianísimo, con fuerza apenas perceptible. En abreviatura, *pp.*

Pianist [pi-an'-ist], *s.* Pianista, el que toca el piano.

Piano [pi-ā'-no], *a.* y *adv.* (Mús.) Dulcemente, piano, bajo, con sonido débil.

Piano [pi-an'-o], *s.* (Fam.) Piano. *V.* PIANOFORTE.

Pianoforte [pi-an''-o-fōr'-tê], *s.* Pianoforte, piano, instrumento músico de teclado y percusión. *Cabinet, upright, piano(forte)*, Piano vertical. *Grand piano(forte)*, Piano de cola. *Square piano*, Piano de mesa.

Pianola [pia-nō'-la], *s.* Pianola, piano mecánico.

Piaster, Piastre [pi-as'-ter], *s.* 1. Escudo, moneda italiana. 2. Peso o peso duro, moneda española.

Piazza [pi-az'-a], *s.* 1. Pórtico o columnata. 2. Galería, corredor cubierto.

Pibroch [pai'-breH], *s.* 1. Música marcial que tocan los montañeses de Escocia con la gaita. 2. (Poét.) Gaita o zampoña.

Pica [pai'-ca], *s.* 1. Lectura, cícero, letra de doce puntos. *Small pica*, Lecturita, letra de unos diez u once puntos. 2. (Med.) Depravación del apetito, afición a comer arcilla, yeso, etc.

Picador [pic'-a-dōr], *s.* Picador, torero de a caballo.

Picaresque [pic-a-resk'], *a.* Picaresco.

Picaroon [pic-a-rūn'], *s.* Picarón ; ladrón, el que roba o hurta.

Picayune [pic-a-yūn'], **Picayunish** [pic-a-yūn'-ish], *a.* De poco valor, mezquino. *Picayunish business*, Negocio de chucherías.

Piccalilli [pic-a-lil'-i], *s.* Legumbres de varias especies conservadas en vinagre con especias.

Piccaninny [pic'-a-nin-i], *s.* Niñito, particularmente el de raza negra.

Piccolo [pic'-o-lō], *s.* (Mús.) Flautín.

Pick [pic], *va.* 1. Escoger, elegir. 2. Coger, recoger. 3. Mondar, limpiar. *To pick one's teeth*, Mondarse o limpiarse los dientes. *To pick a bone*, Roer un hueso. *To pick a fowl*, Descañonar un ave. 4. Picar, agujerear o penetrar en alguna cosa con un instrumento punzante. 5. Picotear. 6. Robar, birlar o soplar con ligereza alguna cosa. 7. Forzar o abrir por fuerza alguna cerradura con una herramienta.—*vn.* 1. Picar, comer alguna porción pequeña de comida. 2. Hacer alguna cosa con exagerada nimiedad o delicadeza. *To pick off*, (1) Arrancar, quitar. (2) Tirar con arma de fuego apuntando cuidadosamente a un blanco determinado. *To pick out*, Escoger o elegir una cosa entre otras ; coger o atrapar algo con cuidado ; separar, quitar o arrancar con violencia. *To pick up*, Coger, recoger o alzar lo que estaba caído ; juntar lo esparcido ; sacar de un apuro ; recobrar la salud. *To pick a hole in one's coat*, Sacar a relucir una falta de otra persona ; buscar camorra. *I have a bone to pick with him*, Tengo que ajustar cuentas con él, o tengo con él una cuenta pendiente. *To pick a quarrel*, Buscar pendencia sin provocación.

Pick, *s.* 1. Herramienta de escultor y de cantero ; pico, instrumento de hierro puntiagudo para excavar en tierras duras, caminos, etc. 2. Escogimiento, derecho de elección. 3. Cantidad de ciertas mieses que se recogen con las manos. 4. En el arte de tejer, el golpe que empuja la lanzadera del telar. 5. Hilo ; el número de los hilos en una pulgada determina el valor relativo de la tela de algodón. 6. (Impr.) Mancha en un pliego impreso. *A pick of hops*, Cosecha de lúpulo u hombrecillo. *Pick and pick*, (Tejido) Variedad simétrica de matices producida por la alternación de hilos de diferentes colores. *Ear-pick*, Limpiaoídos o escarbaoídos.

Pickaback, Pickapack [pic'-a-pac], *adv.* (Fam.) Sobre los hombros ; a modo de fardo o del mismo modo que si fuera un fardo.

Pickax, Pickaxe [pic'-ax], *s.* Pico, especie de azadón.

Picked [pik'-ed], *a.* 1. Espinoso, que tiene espinas o púas. 2. Puntiagudo.

Picked [pict], *pp.* y *a.* Escogido con cuidado o para un fin especial ; de la mejor calidad. *Picked fruit*, Frutas de la mejor calidad. *Picked men*, Hombres o soldados escogidos.

Picker [pik'-er], *s.* 1. Escogedor. 2. El que con facilidad toma parte en algún negocio. 3. Escardador. 4. (En los telares) Recibidor. *A picker of quarrels*, Camorrista, pendenciero.

Pickerel [pik'-er-el], *s.* 1. Lucio pequeño, pez de agua dulce. Esox. 2. Sollo pequeño.

Pickerel-weed [pic'-er-el-wīd], *s.* Hierba acuática perenne, tipo de una familia de plantas acuáticas. Pondeteria.

Picket [pik'-et], *s.* 1. Estaca puntiaguda, piquete. 2. (Mil.) Piquete.

Picket, *va.* 1. Cercar con estacas o piquetes. 2. Poner o colocar de guardia. 3. Atar un caballo a la estaca. 4. Castigar a los soldados con el servicio de piquete.

Picket-guard, *s.* (Mil.) Piquete, centinelas avanzados.

Picking [pik'-ing], *s.* La acción y el efecto del verbo *pick* en todas sus acepciones ; por ejemplo, recolección, cosecha (de frutos, etc.) ; quite, arrancamiento ; picadura, roedura ; limpia, monda ; elección, escogimiento ; hurto, robo. En plural, desperdicios, resíduos, desechos ; también hurtos, arrebañaduras, raterías.

Pickle [pik'-l], *s.* 1. Salmuera, escabeche, adobo. 2. Cualquier cosa puesta en escabeche o adobo. 3. Fruta o legumbre conservada en vinagre. 4. (Fam.) Estado, condición, situación ; úsase en este último sentido para expresar desprecio. *Mixed pickles*, (1) Varias legumbres, como pepinos, cebollas y coliflor, adobados en vinagre. (2) Mezcla, cosas o personas incongruas. *To have a rod in pickle*, Tenérsela guardada a uno.

Pickle, *va.* Escabechar, adobar, conservar en vinagre, adobo, salmuera o escabeche. *Pickled cucumbers*, Pepinillos encurtidos. *Pickled herrings*, Arenques salados. *Pickled fish*, Pescado en escabeche. *Pickled salmon*, Salmón escabechado.

Picklock [pic'-loc], *s.* 1. Ganzúa, alambre fuerte y encorvado para abrir una cerradura; llave falsa. 2. Ladrón nocturno. 3. La lana más fina, escogida.

Pickpocket [pic'-pok-et], **Pickpurse** [pic'-pūrs], *s.* Ratero, raterillo, el que hurta de las faltriqueras o bolsillos de otros.

Pickthank [pic'-thanc], *s.* Entremetido.

Pick-up (of an auto) [pic'-up], *s* 1. Aceleración, desarrollo de velocidad (de un automóvil). 2. Pequeño camión de carga. 3. Fonocaptor.

Picnic [pic'-nic], *s.* 1. Partida de campo, merienda al aire libre en la que cada cual contribuye parte de las provisiones. 2. (Ger. E. U.) Ocupación o deber fácil y agradable.—*vn.* Tener una partida de campo, merienda o romería, o concurrir a ella.

Picotee [pic-o-tí'], *s.* Variedad de clavel doble.

Picrate [pic'-rêt], *s.* Picrato, sal formada con ácido pícrico o trinitrofénico.

Picric [pic'-ric], *a.* Excesivamente amargo. *Picric acid*, Ácido pícrico o trinitrofénico ($C_6H_3N_3O_7$) compuesto amarillo cristalizable; se emplea para teñir y como ingrediente de ciertos compuestos explosivos.

Pict [pict], *s.* Picto, individuo de un antiguo pueblo que habitaba la Caledonia (A. D. 296–844)

Pictography [pic-tog'-ra-fi], *s.* Pictografía, escritura ideográfica.

Pictorial, *a.* 1. Pictórico, que pertenece a la pintura. 2. Gráfico.

Picturable [pic'-chur-a-bl], *a.* Que puede dibujarse o pintarse.

Picture [pic'-tiūr], *s.* 1. Pintura, retrato, cuadro, fotografía. 2. Descripción, delineación verbal. 3. Imagen, retrato, semejanza; lo que se asemeja a alguna cosa o la sugiere; escena.

Picture, *va.* 1. Pintar, dibujar; hacer un cuadro. 2. Figurar, describir. 3. Imaginar, formar una imagen en la mente.

Picture gallery [pic'-tiūr gal'-ẹr-i], *s* Museo de pinturas.

Picture-like [pic'-tiūr-laic], *a* Semejante a una pintura.

Picturesque [pic-tiūr-esc'], *a.* Pintoresco.

Picturesqueness [pic-tiūr-esc'-nes], *s.* Calidad de pintoresco.

Picture tube [pic'-tiūr tiūb], *s.* Teletubo.

Picture window, *s.* Ventana al exterior que enmarca una vista agradable.

Piddle [pid'-l], *vn.* 1. Pellizcar la comida, comer muy poco á poco y como con desgana. 2. Emplearse en bagatelas. 3. Orinar: voz que usan los niños.

Piddler [pid'-lẹr], *s* El que come sin ganas.

Pidgin-English [pij-in-in'-glish], *s.* Inglés chapurrado, mezcla de inglés con vocablos chinos, portugueses y malayos; sirve en ciertas ciudades de China y del Oriente para entenderse los indígenas y los extranjeros. (< *business* y *English.*)

Pie [pai], *s.* 1. Pastel, empanada. *Veal pie*, Empanada de ternera. *Mince pie*, Pastel de picadillo ó de carne. *He intends to have his finger in the pie*, Él se propone meter también cuchara. 2. (Orn.) Marica. 3. (Impr.) *V.* PI.

Piebald [pai'-bōld], *a.* Manchado de varios colores.

Piece [pīs], *s.* 1. Remiendo, fragmento, pedazo, pieza. 2. Pintura, retrato. 3. Pieza, un cañón de artillería. 4. Pieza, cualquier especie de moneda. 5. Fusil. 6. Composición, obra, escrito; cualquier artefacto. 7. Pieza, la porción de un tejido que se fabrica de una vez en el telar. 8. Trozo, pedazo de una pieza mayor cortada y rota; retal, retazo. *A piece of wit*, Una gracia, una agudeza. *Of a piece (with)*, De la misma clase ó calidad; enterizo; de una sola pieza, de un solo pedazo. *To give one a piece of one's mind*, Soltarle a uno cuatro frescas, decirle las verdades del barquero, ponerlo como un trapo o como nuevo. *A piece of news*, Una noticia, un informe. *A piece of advice*, Un consejo. *A piece of folly*, Un acto de locura. *A piece of furniture*, Un mueble. *A piece of ground*, Un solar, una porción de tierra. *A piece of paper*, *of wood*, Un pedazo de papel, de madera. *To come to pieces*, Desarmarse, deshacerse, separarse las piezas o fragmentos de una cosa. *To cut to pieces* o *in pieces*, Cortar en pedazos; destrozar (un ejército). *To tear to* o *in pieces*, Romper en pedazos, rasgar, desgarrar en tiras. *To pull to pieces*, Despedazar, desgarrar, hacer trizas. *A fowling-piece*, Una escopeta. *A (broken) piece of a bottle*, Un tiesto o casco de botella.

Piece, *va.* 1. Aumentar alguna cosa añadiéndole una pieza o pedazo de lo mismo. 2. Juntar, unir. 3. Remendar.—*vn.* Juntarse, unirse una cosa con otra. *To piece out*, Alargar, aumentar o engrandecer añadiendo retazos; (fig.) aumentar, prolongar *To piece up*, Remendar, reparar.

Pieceless [pīs'-les], *a.* Que es todo de una pieza o que no está dividido en pedazos.

Piecemeal [pīs-mīl], *adv.* En pedazos.—*a.* Dividido.—*s.* Fragmento, pedazo. *By piecemeal*, A pedacitos, a bocaditos.

Piecer [pīs'-ẹr], *s* El que añade o remienda.

Pied [paid], *a.* De varios colores, manchado, abigarrado

Piedness [paid'-nes], *s.* Variedad o diversidad de colores

Pie-plant [pai'-plant], *s.* Ruipóntico, rapóntico, planta de huerta, cuyos pecíolos ácidos se emplean en pastelería. Rheum rhaponticum.

Pier [pīr], *s.* 1. Estribo de puente. 2. Pilar, pilón, estribo, sostén de obra de albañilería, de madera o de hierro. 3. Entrepaño de pared. 4. Muelle, malecón, desembarcadero; muelle, escollera, espolón. *Pier-glass*, Tremó, espejo largo colocado en el entrepaño de una sala. *Pier-table*, Consola, mueble que se coloca entre dos ventanas.

Pierage [pīr'-ẹj], *s.* Muellaje, derecho que se paga por el uso de un muelle.

Pierce [pīrs], *va.* 1. Penetrar, agujerear, taladrar, introducir algún cuerpo en otro. 2. Excitar o mover las pasiones, traspasar el corazón, conmover. 3. Abrir camino por medio de la fuerza.—*vn.* 1. Penetrar, llegar a lo interior de un cuerpo rompiendo o dividiendo su unión física. 2. Ser afectuoso, patético, atractivo o persuasivo. 3. Alcanzar o comprender alguna cosa dificultosa. 4. Llegar lo agudo del dolor o sentimiento a lo interior del alma. *Pierced with sorrow*, Traspasado de dolor. *Pierced with holes*, Acribillado, hecho una criba.

Piercer [pīrs'-ẹr], *s.* Taladro; aguijón.

Piercingly [pīrs'-ing-li], *adv.* Agudamente.

Pierian [pai-í'-ri-an], *a.* Pierio, referente a las musas, y a la Pieria, región de la antigua Macedonia.

Pietism [pai'-et-izm], *s.* 1. Pietismo, doctrina de los pietistas, secta luterana que prefirió el recogimiento al culto público. 2. Piedad, más particularmente mojigatería, mística afectada.

Pietist [pai'-et-ist], *s.* 1. Pietista, partidario del pietismo luterano. 2. Misticón, beato.

Piety [pai'-e-ti], *s.* 1. Piedad, devoción, reverencia hacia Dios; religiosidad (en general). 2. (Ant.) Piedad, atención, respeto y reverencia que se debe a los padres, a los mayores o a la patria.

Piezometer [pai-ez-om'-e-tẹr], *s.* Piezómetro, instrumento destinado a medir la compresibilidad de los líquidos. (< Gr.)

Pig [pig], *s.* 1. Cochino, cerdo, marrano, puerco, particularmente cuando es gorrino o pequeño; cochinillo, lechón. *Sucking-pig*, Lechoncillo. *Pig-sty*, Zahurda, la pocilga en que se encierran los puercos. 2. Masa oblonga de metal después de fundida en un molde basto, como de arena; tejo, lingote, pigote, galápago o barra; v. g. *Pig-lead*, Un lingote de plomo. *To buy a pig in a poke*, Cerrar un trato a ciegas sin saber bien lo que se hace. *Pig-iron*, Hierro en lingotes; goa, barra, masa de hierro colado. *Pig-pen*, Pocilga.

Pig, *vn.* 1. Parir la puerca. 2. Conducirse o vivir como cochinos.

Pigeon [pij'-un], *s.* Pichón, palomo, paloma. *Pigeon-hearted*, Tímido, cobarde. *Pigeonhole*, (1) División que hay en los escritorios para guardar cartas y papeles. (2) *pl.* Un juego antiguo. *Pigeon-house*, *pigeon-loft*, Palomar. *Pigeon-pie*, Pastel de pichones. *Pigeon-toed*, (1) Que tiene los pies parecidos a los de un pichón; peristerópodo. (2) Que tiene los dedos del pie dirigidos hacia dentro.

Pigeon-breast [pij'-un-brest], *s* Deformidad causada por la raquitis, que deprime la caja del pecho por ambos lados y hace sobresalir el esternón. *Pigeon-breasted*, Que padece dicha deformidad.

Pigeonfoot [pij'-un-fut], *s* (Bot.) Pie de milano.

Pigeon-livered [pij'-un-liv-ẹrd], *a* Apacible, quieto; medroso.

Pigeonry [pij'-un-ri], *s.* Palomar, paraje donde se recogen y crían las palomas.

Piggery [pig'-ẹr-i], *s.* Zahurda, lugar para criar cochinos.

Piggin [pig'-in], *s.* 1. Cubeta, vasija pequeña de madera, con reborde saliente para servir como mango; también, cucharón con mango largo y vasija poco profunda. 2. Cántaro, cacharro, vasija de barro.

Piggish [pig'-ish], *a.* Que se porta como un cochino; voraz, puerco, sucio.

Piggishness [pig'-ish-nes], *s.* Voracidad; porquería, suciedad.

Piggyback [pig'-i-bac], *s.* (F.C.) Servicio de remolques en plataformas de ferrocarril. —*a.* Sobre los hombros.

Pig-headed [pig-hed'-ed], *a.* Terco, obstinado, perverso.

Pigmean, *a.* *V.* PYGMEAN.

Pigment [pig'-mẹnt], *s.* Colores, los materiales de varios colores preparados para pintar; afeite; pigmento, cualquier substancia que da color a los tejidos animales o vegetales. 2. Vino ricamente aromatizado con especias y endulzado con miel.

Pigmy [pig'-mi], *s.* Pigmeo. *V.* PYGMY.

Pignoration [pig-no-ré'-shun], *s.* Empeño, pignoración.

Pig-nut [pig'-nut], *s.* (Bot.) 1. (E. U.) Nuez de un nogal de América y el árbol que la produce. Carya porcina o glabra. 2. (Bot.) Bulbocástano, una planta oficinal.

Pike [paic], *s.* 1. Lucio, pez de agua dulce. Esox lucius. 2. Pica, especie de lanza larga. 3. *V.* SPIKE.

Pike, *s.* 1. Camino de barrera; camino real, calzada. 2. Barrera de portazgo. (Abrev. de TURNPIKE.)

Piked [paict o pik'-ed], *a.* Puntiagudo.

Pikeman [paic'-man], *s.* Piquero, el soldado armado con pica.

Pikestaff [paic'-staf], *s.* Asta de pica.

Pilaster [pi-las'-tẹr], *s* Pilastra, columna cuadrada.

Pilau [pi-lō'], *s.* Pilau.

Pilchard [pilch'-ard], **Pilcher** [pilch'-ẹr], *s.* Arenque menor, sardina arenque.

Pile [pail], *s.* 1. Pila, montón, rimero. 2. Pira, hoguera, montón de combustibles. 3. Estaca, pilote, madero fuerte que se hinca en el suelo para afianzar un cimiento. *V.* SPILE. 4. Edificio grande y macizo. 5. Pelo de los animales. 6. (Art.) Montón de balas. 7. Pelillo en las telas de lana; pelo, pelusilla, parte fina y aterciopelada del paño y varias telas. 8. Pila galvánica. *Piles,* Almorranas. *Pile-drawer,* Aparato para sacar o arrancar pilotes. *Pile-driver,* Martinete, máquina para clavar pilotes. *Pile-hoop,* Vilorta, loriga, anillo de hierro que se pone alrededor de la cabeza de un pilote para impedir que se hienda. *Pile-shoe,* Zueco, guarda de metal puesta al extremo de un pilote. *He has made his pile,* (Ger.) Ha hecho su agosto, se ha enriquecido.

Pile, *va.* 1. Amontonar, apilar. 2. Clavar, empujar pilotes. 3. Poner pelo o pelusa a una tela.

Piler [pail'-ẹr], *s.* Amontonador.

Pilework [pail'-wŭrk], *s.* Pilotaje, estructura de pilotes.

Pilfer [pil'-fẹr], *va.* y *vn.* Ratear, hurtar cosas de poco valor con destreza y sutileza.

Pilferer [pil'-fẹr-ẹr], *s.* Ratero.

Pilfering [pil'-fẹr-ing], *s.* Ratería.

Pilferingly [pil'-fẹr-ing-li], *adv.* Con ratería, rateramente.

Pilfery [pil'-fẹr-i], *s.* (Poco us.) Ratería, el hurto de cosas de poco valor.

Pilgarlic [pil-gār'-lic], *s.* (Bajo) Miserable, pobrete; la persona que ha perdido los cabellos a consecuencia de una enfermedad asquerosa.

Pilgrim [pil'-grim], *s.* Peregrino, romero.

Pilgrim, *vn.* Peregrinar.

Pilgrimage [pil'-grim-ej], *s.* Peregrinación.

Piliferous, Piligerous [pi-lif'-ẹr-us, pi-lij'-ẹr-us], *a.* (Zool.) Peludo, que tiene pelo, pelusa o borra.

Piling [pai'-ling], *s.* 1. Acto o procedimiento de preparar y de clavar pilotes. 2. Pilotes colectivamente; estructura de pilotes.

Pill [pil], *s.* 1. Píldora. 2. Cualquier cosa que produce náuseas o que no es fácil de evitar. 3. (Ger.) Pesadilla, persona muy fastidiosa.

Pillage [pil'-ej], *s.* Pillaje, botín, saqueo, latrocinio, rapiña.

Pillage, *va.* Pillar, hurtar, robar.

Pillager [pil'-aj-ẹr], *s.* Pillador, saqueador.

Pillar [pil'-ar], *s.* 1. Columna, pilar. 2. Masa columnar, v. g. de carbón en una mina. 3. (Biol.) Columela, columna. 4. (Fig.) Soporte, sostén. *He was a pillar of the church,* Era firme sostén de la iglesia.

Pillar-box [pil'-ar-box], *s.* (Gran Bretaña) Buzón.

Pillared [pil'-ard], *a.* Sostenido por columnas.

Pillbox [pil'-bex], *s.* 1. Pildorera, estuche para píldoras. 2. Sombrero chico de mujer, con copa redonda, sin ala. 3. (Mil.) Fortín con ametralladoras.

Pillion [pil'-yun], *s.* Albarda, sillón, la parte de la silla en que se sientan las mujeres a caballo detrás del jinete.

Pilloried [pil'-o-rid], *a.* Empicotado.

Pillory [pil'-o-ri], *s.* Picota, cepo, tabla con agujeros para las manos y cabeza, en donde se ponía a los malhechores a la vergüenza.

Pillory, *va.* Empicotar, poner a un malhechor a la vergüenza en una picota o argolla.

Pillow [pil'-ō], *s.* 1. Almohada. 2. *Pillow of the bowsprit,* (Mar.) Tragante o descanso del bauprés. *Pillows of the mast-heads,* (Mar.) Almohadas de las jarcias. *Pillow-case, pillow-slip,* Funda de almohada. *Pillow-sham,* Cubierta de adorno para almohada.

Pillow, *va.* Poner alguna cosa sobre la almohada.

Pilose [pai'-lōs], *a.* Peludo, velloso, con pelo o vello.

Pilosity [pi-les'-i-ti], *s.* Abundancia de pelo.

Pilot [pai'-lẹt], *va.* 1. Guiar, conducir. 2. Pilotar, pilotear.

Pilot, *s.* 1. Piloto. *Coast-pilot,* Piloto práctico de costa. *Sea-pilot,* Piloto de altura. 2. Carta de marear. 3. Instrumento para corregir la desviación de una brújula. 4. Guía, consejero. 5. La limpiavía de una locomotora, bastidor triangular, colocado cerca de los carriles para apartar los objetos que obstruyen la vía. *Pilot-bird,* Pájaro-piloto, ave que en el mar de las Antillas indica a los navegantes la proximidad de la tierra. *Pilot-boat,* Bote del piloto, embarcación en que salen los pilotos al encuentro de los buques para guiarlos al entrar en puerto; lleva un número en la vela mayor. *Pilot-bread,* Galleta. *Pilot fish,* Piloto, pez de mar, que se ve a menudo en latitudes cálidas en compañía de los tiburones. *Pilot-house,* Garita o mirador de timonel, en que se pone el piloto cuando está de guardia.

Pilotage [pai'-lẹt-ẹj], *s.* 1. Pilotaje. *Book of pilotage,* Derrotero. *Rates of pilotage,* Timonaje. 2. Pilotaje, el sueldo del piloto.

Pilot light [pai'-lẹt lait], *s.* Luz piloto.

Pilous, Pileous [pai'-lus, pai'-lẹ-us], *a.* Piloso, peludo.

Pimenta [pi-men'-ta] o **Pimento** [pi-men'-to], *s.* Pimienta de Jamaica.

Pimp [pimp], *s.* Alcahuete.

Pimp, *vn.* Alcahuetear.

Pimpernel [pim'-pẹr-nel], *s.* (Bot.) Anagálida, planta conocida con el nombre vulgar de *hierba pajarera.* Pertenece a la familia de las primuláceas. Por cerrarse sus flores al aproximarse el mal tiempo se llama *poor man's weather-glass.* Anagallis arvensis.

Pimpinel [pim'-pi-nel], *s.* (Bot.) Pimpinela. Pimpinella saxifraga.

Pimping [pimp'-ing], *a.* (Fam.) Pequeño, fútil, mezquino, miserable.

Pimple [pim'-pl], *s.* Grano, tumorcillo; botón, postilla, pupa, buba; barrillos.

Pimpled [pim'-pld], *a.* Engranujado, granujiento.

Pin [pin], *s.* 1. Alfiler. *Hair-pins,* Alfileres de gancho, horquillas para el cabello. 2. Bagatela, cosa de poco valor. *I don't care a pin,* No se me da un bledo, un pito, un ardite o tres pepinos. 3. Prendedor, broche. 4. Clavo, perno, chabeta; clavija, pasador. 5. Bolo, trozo de palo aguzado para que se tenga derecho en el suelo. *Pin of wood,* Clavija, cabilla, saetín, perno. *Linch-pin of a wheel,* Pezonera. *Larding-pin,* Aguja de mechar. *Rolling-pin,* Hataca, rodillo. *Block-pins,* (Mar.) Pernos de motones. *Belaying-pins,* (Mar.) Cabillas de probados y jarcias. *Pin-clover,* (Bot.) Alfilerilla. *Pin-feather,* Pluma que empieza a salir, pluma rudimentaria. *Pin-feathered,* Que no tiene todavía plumas. *Pin-head,* Cabeza de alfiler; objeto muy pequeño. *Pin-maker,* Afilerero, fabricante de alfileres. *Pin-point,* Punta de alfiler; minuciosidad, nimiedad.

Pin, *va.* 1. Prender con alfileres. 2. Asegurar alguna cosa; fijar o unir una cosa a otra; asir y tener firmemente de cualquier manera. 3. (Germ.) Coger, tomar furtivamente, hurtar. *To pin up a gown,* Arremangar, recoger o levantar un vestido asegurándolo con alfileres. *To pin one's reason to a woman's petticoat,* Ser esclavo de los caprichos de una mujer. *To pin one's faith to u on,* Confiar absolutamente en. *To pin one's opinion upon another's sleeve,* Adherirse al parecer de alguien, identificarse con su opinión.

Pin, *va.* Encerrar, enjaular. *V* PEN.

Pinafore [pin'-a-fōr], *s.* Delantal (sin mangas) para niño.

Pinang [pi-nang'], *s.* Areca, palmera de Filipinas, y su fruto, con el que se hace el buyo.

Pinaster [pi- (o pai-) nas'-tẹr], *s.* Pinastro, aznacho, variedad de pino de la región mediterránea.

Pincase [pin'-kês], *s.* Alfiletero, cajita para alfileres.

Pincers [pin'-sẹrz], *s. pl.* 1. Pinzas, tenacillas. 2. (Zool.) Pinza. 3. (Mil.) Movimiento de pinzas.

Pinch [pinch], *va.* 1. Pellizcar; comprimir o apretar una cosa entre un dedo y el pulgar o entre los cantos de dos cuerpos duros. 2. Apretar con pinzas o tenazas. 3. Apretar, oprimir, perseguir, estrechar a alguno persiguiéndole. 4. Limitar mucho los gastos. 5. Examinar una cosa desentrañándola.—*vn.* 1. Apretar, acosar, hacerse sentir mucho alguna cosa. 2. Ahorrar, ser frugal, excusar gastos. *To pinch off,* Arrebatar, agarrar, llevarse violentamente una cosa. *He who wears the shoe knows where it pinches,* Cada uno sabe dónde le aprieta el zapato. *To pinch one's self,* Privarse de lo necesario. *My shoe pinches,* Me aprieta el zapato.

Pinch, *s.* 1. Pellizco. 2. Polvo o pulgarada, la porción de cualquier cosa menuda que puede tomarse con las yemas de los dedos. 3. Dolor, tormento, pena, angustia; opresión, aprieto, apuro, extrema necesidad. *He is* o *he finds himself in a pinch,* Se halla en un apuro. *A pinch of snuff,* Un polvo de rapé. *Upon a pinch,* Cuando fuere menester, llegado el caso. *To be a pinch,* Estar en pena. 4. Esquina, pico. 5. Abolladura.

Pinchbeck [pinch'-bec], *s.* Similor o similoro.

Pincher [pinch'-ẹr], *s.* Pellizcador.—*pl.* Tenacillas.

Pinchfist [pinch'-fist], **Pinchpenny** [pinch'-pen-i], *s.* Hombre tacaño, ruin o miserable.

Pinch-hit [pinch-hit'], *vn.* 1. En el juego de beisbol, batear en lugar de otro. 2. Substituir a otro en una emergencia.

Pinching-tongs [pinch'-ing-tōngz], *s.* Tenazuelas que forman un molde en la fabricación del vidrio.

Pincushion [pin'-cush-un], *s.* Acerico, almohadilla pequeña en que clavan las mujeres sus alfileres.

Pine [pain], *s.* 1. (Bot.) Pino, cualquier árbol del género Pinus de la familia de las coníferas. 2. Madera de cualquier pino. 3. Piña, anana. *V.* PINEAPPLE. 4. (Des.) Miseria, padecimiento. *Cluster pine, V.* PINASTER. *Scotch pine,* Pino de Escocia, pino silvestre. *Pine-barren,* Terreno estéril y arenoso cubierto de pinos. *Pine-marten,* Marta cibelina. *Pine-needle,* Hoja acicular de pino. *Pine-tree,* Pino, árbol. *Pine-tree State,* El Estado norteamericano de Maine, llamado así por sus bosques de pinos.

Pine, *vn.* 1. Desfallecer, estar lánguido, descaecer perdiendo el vigor y las fuerzas. Se emplea a menudo con la prep. *away. She pined away after her husband's death,* Ella descaeció después de la muerte de su marido. 2. Desear con vehemencia (seguido por la prep. *for*). *To pine for a new world,* Anhelar, desear vivamente una nueva vida.—*va.* 1. Hacer debilitarse a alguno, causarle languidez, hacerle consumir a fuerza de sentimientos. 2. Lamentar en silencio, sentir interiormente algún mal. *To pine one's self to death,* Morirse de pena.

Pineal [pin'-ẹ-al o pai'-nẹ-al], *a.* Que tiene figura de piña. *Pineal gland* Glándula pineal en el cerebro.

Pine-apple [pain'-ap-l], *s.* Piña, anana. *The kernel of a pine-apple,* El corazón de la anana.

Pine-branch [pain'-branch], *s.* Rama de pino.

Pinery [pai'-nẹr-i], *s.* 1. Invernadero para criar ananas. 2. Pinar, bosque de pinos.

Piney [pai'-ni], *a. V.* PINY.

Ping [ping], *s.* El silbido de una bala al cruzar por el aire. (Imitativo.)

Ping-pong [ping'-pong], *s.* Ping pong, juego parecido al tenis.

Pinguid [pin'-gwid], *a.* Pingüe, craso, gordo, pingüedinoso.

Pinhead [pin'-hed], *s.* 1. Cabeza de un alfiler. 2. Algo pequeñísimo. 3. Persona de muy poca inteligencia.

Pinhole [pin'-hōl], *s.* 1. El agujero que hace el alfiler. 2. Punto diminuto transparente en una prueba negativa fotográfica.

Pining [pain'-ing], *a.* Lánguido. *Pining away, s.* Languidez.

Pinion [pin'-yun], *s.* 1. Piñón, el huesecillo último de las alas del ave. 2. Ala, y a veces también una pluma de la misma ala y el alón. 3. Piñón de reloj. 4. Esposas, prisiones para atar las manos.

Pinion, *va.* 1. Atar las alas. 2. Maniatar, atar y ligar las manos a uno.

Pinioned [pin'-yund], *a.* Alado, que tiene alas; maniatado.

Pink [pink], *s.* 1. (Bot.) Clavel, dianto, planta y su flor del género Dianthus. 2. Cualquier flor parecida al clavel. 3. Color de rosa, rojo muy claro. 4. Tipo de excelencia o de perfección, dechado, modelo. *The pink of politeness,* Dechado de cortesía. 5. Pez pequeño de color rojizo.—*a.* Rojizo claro, de color de clavel. *Pink eyes,* Ojos pequeños.

Pink, *va.* 1. Ojetear, hacer ojetes en la ropa. 2. Picar, adornar una tela con calados.

Pinker [piŋk'-ẹr], *s.* El que pica las telas de seda.

Pinkeye [piŋk'-ai], *s.* 1. Catarro epidémico, contagioso y febril de los caballos, acompañado de oftalmia. 2. (Med.) Oftalmia contagiosa de las personas, caracterizada por el enrojecimiento de los ojos.

Pink-eyed [piŋk'-aid], *a.* Ojialegre.

Pinking [piŋk'-ing], *s.* Picado, recortado; guiñadura. *Pinking-iron,* Instrumento de hierro para picar las telas en forma de festones.

Pinky [piŋk'-i], *a.* Rosado, de color rojizo claro.

Pin-money [pin'-mun-i], *s.* Alfileres, la cantidad de dinero que se señala a las señoras casadas para sus gastos particulares.

Pinna [pin'-a], *s.* 1. (Bot.) Una sola hojuela de una hoja pinada. 2. Oreja, pabellón externo del oído. 3. (Zool.) Ala, aleta, u órgeno semejante.

Pinnace [pin'-ẹs], *s.* (Mar.) Pinaza, embarcación pequeña de remo y vela.

Pinnacle [pin'-a-cl], *s.* Pináculo, chapitel, la parte superior y más alta de algún edificio: cima. cumbre.

Pinnacle, *va.* Edificar con pináculos o chapiteles.

Pinnate [pin'-êt], **Pinnated** [pin'-êt-ed], *a.* 1. (Bot.) Pinado, que tiene la figura de una pluma, hablando de las hojas compuestas de las plantas. 2. Que tiene partes o apéndices parecidos a alas.

Pinnatifid [pin-at'-i-fid], *a.* (Bot.) Pinatífido, que tiene las hojas divididas y dispuestas en forma de pluma, hablando de las plantas.

Pinner [pin'-ẹr], *s.* 1. El que asegura con alfileres, pernos, clavijas, etc. 2. *V.* PINAFORE. 3. Una especie de toca de mujer.

Pinnule [pin'-ūl], *s.* 1. (Zool.) Aleta pequeña. 2. (Bot.) Pínula, hojuela de una hoja pinada.

Pinochle [pi-nuc'-l], *s.* Pinocle, juego de naipes.

Pinpoint [pin'-point], *s.* Punta de alfiler.—*va.* Precisar, determinar con gran precisión.

Pint [paint], *s.* Pinta, medida de áridos y líquidos en Inglaterra y en los Estados Unidos que equivale a 47 centilitros.

Pintail [pin'-têl], *s.* 1. Especie de ánade de cola larga del hemisferio septentrional. Dafila acuta. 2. Gallo silvestre de cola puntiaguda de la América del Norte. Pediœcetes phasianellus.

Pintle [pin'-tl], *s.* (Art.) Clavija del cabezal y eje. *Pintles of the rudder,* (Mar.) Machos de timón.

Pinwheel [pin'-hwīl], *s.* 1. Fuego artificial construído de manera que cuando se enciende gira rápidamente alrededor de un eje, formando una rueda de fuego. 2. Rueda de espigas, que tiene espigas o cabillas en su periferia en lugar de dientes. 3. Molino de viento, hecho de papel; juguete de los niños.

Piny [pai'-ni], *a.* Pinoso, referente o relativo a los pinos y abetos; cubierto o coronado de pinos. *Piny tallow,* Sebo vegetal sacado del fruto de la Vateria indica.

Pioneer [pai-o-nīr'], *s.* 1. Explorador de un país; el que va delante apartando obstáculos y preparando el camino. 2. (Mil.) Gastador, zapador.—*va.* y *vn.* Explorar, ir delante preparando el camino; abrir un camino; guiar; ser explorador.

Piony [pai'-o-ni], *s.* (Dial.) Peonía.

Pious [pai'-us], *a.* 1. Pio, piadoso, devoto, religioso. 2. Que demuestra un espíritu reverente. 3. Practicado bajo pretexto de religión. 4 (Ant.) Que profesa a sus padres respeto y cariño. *A pious deed* Una obra piadosa. *A pious fraud* Un mojigato malvado.

Piously [pai'-us-li], *adv.* Religiosamente, piadosamente.

Pip [pip], *s.* 1. Pepita, enfermedad que padecen las aves en la lengua. 2. La semilla de una manzana, naranja, etc. 3. Punto de un naipe, dado o dominó.

Pip, *va.* Romper el cascarón; dícese de los polluelos.—*vn.* Piar ciertas aves. *V.* PEEP.

Pipe [paip], *s.* 1. Tubo, cañón, conducto, caño. 2. Pipa para fumar. 3. Caramillo, churumbela, instrumento músico; pito o silbo del contramaestre. *Pipes of an organ,* Cañones de órgano. *Bagpipe,* Gaita. *Clyster-pipe,* Cañoncito de jeringa. *Windpipe,* Gaznate, tráquea. 4. Silbo, silbido, nota o llamada aguda y penetrante. 5. Pipa, medida de líquidos. *Pipe-staves,* Duelas, las costillas de las pipas y cubas. *Elbow-pipe,* Tubo acodillado. *Gas-pipe,* Tubo, cañería de gas. *Water-pipe,* Cañería, conducto de agua. *Stopped pipe,* Cañón de órgano, que tiene su extremo superior cubierto; tubo tapado. *Suction pipe*, Tubo de aspiración, tubo aspirante de succión. *The bowl of a pipe*, El hogar o fogón de una pipa. *To smoke the pipe of peace*, Fumar la pipa de paz, uno tras otro; costumbre de los indios norteamericanos.

Pipe, *va.* 1. Tocar la flauta u otro instrumento semejante. 2. Articular, proferir en tono alto. 3. Llamar por medio del pito de contramaestre. 4. Proveer de caños o tubos; conducir por cañería. *To pipe water from a spring*, Conducir agua por cañería desde un manantial. 5. Entre las costureras, hacer en cordoncillo.—*vn.* 1. Tocar el caramillo o la gaita. 2. Silbar, producir un sonido penetrante.

Pipe-clay [paip'-clé], *s.* Tierra de pipa, especie de arcilla que se emplea para fabricar pipas y limpiar los equipos militares.—*va.* Blanquear con tierra de pipa.

Pipefish [paip'-fish], *s.* Pez de mar muy delgado, con el cuerpo cubierto de escamas óseas. Syngnathus.

Pipeline [paip'-lain], *s.* Cañería, conducto.

Pipe-office [paip'-ef-is], *s.* En tiempos pasados, una oficina del ramo de hacienda en Inglaterra.

Pipe organ [paip ōr'-gan], *s.* (Mús.) Órgano.

Piper [paip'-ẹr], *s.* Flautista, gaitero. *To pay the piper*, Sufrir las consecuencias de una mala acción; pagar los platos rotos.

Piperine [pip'-ẹr-in], *a.* Pimentoso. —*s.* Piperina, substancia incolora y cristalina que se halla en la pimienta.

Pipe-tree [paip'-trī], *s.* (Bot.) Lila.

Pipette [pi-pet'], *va.* Gotear, sacar o desviar un líquido por medio de un gotero.—*s.* Gotero, pipeta, tubo pequeño, a menudo graduado, que se emplea para trasladar pequeñas cantidades de líquido de una vasija a otra.

Piping [paip' ing], *a.* 1. Tocando el caramillo. 2. Hirviente, hirviente, muy caliente; silbador, que silba. 3. Propio de la música no marcial, o caracterizado por ella.

Pipit [pip'-it], *s.* Pajarito parecido a la alondra.

Pipkin [pip'-kin], *s.* Pucherito.

Pippin [pip'-in], *s.* (Bot.) Esperiega, una variedad de manzana.

Piquancy [pī'-can-si], *s.* Picante, acrimonia.

Piquant [pī'-cant], *a.* Punzante, picante; áspero, mordaz.

Piquantly [pī'-cant-li], *adv.* Agriamente; mordazmente.

Pique [pīc], *s.* 1. Pique, desazón, desabrimiento, desavenencia ligera. *I have no pique against him*, No le tengo ojeriza. 2. Pundonor, delicadeza, puntillo.

Pique, *va.* y *vn.* 1. Picar, enojar, provocar. 2. Ofender, irritar. 3. Picarse, preciarse de alguna cosa haciendo de ella punto de honor; jactarse. 4. Picarse, ofenderse, enojarse.

Piqué [pi-ké'], *s.* Piqué, tela de algodón cuyo tejido forma unos como granillos redondos o cuadrados. (Fr.)

Piquet [pi-ket'], *s.* 1. Juego de los cientos. *To play at piquet*, Jugar a los cientos. 2. (Mil.) Piquete, guardia avanzada.

Piracy [pai'-ra-si], *s.* Piratería.

Piragua [pi-rā'-gwa], *s.* Piragua.

Pirate [pai'-rẹt], *s.* 1. Pirata, forbante, el ladrón que roba por el mar. 2. Pirata, el que roba la propiedad de otro, y particularmente el impresor que sin derecho imprime obras ajenas.

Pirate, *vn.* Piratear.—*va.* 1. Apropiarse sin derecho una propiedad literaria. 2. Pillar, hurtar, robar.

Piratical [pai-rat'-i-cal], *a.* Pirático.

Pirn [pẹrn], *s.* (Esco.) 1. Huso o carrete pequeño. 2. Ovillo, hilo, en una lanzadera. 3. Carrete, bobina de torno para hilar. 4. Argadijo, devanadera de la caña de pescar.

Pirogue [pi-rōg'], *s.* 1. Piragua, canoa de una pieza; de aquí, cualquier bote pequeño. 2. Barco grande sin quilla, que tiene el fondo plano para navegar por ríos poco profundos.

Pirouette [pir-ū-et'], *s.* 1. Pirueta, vuelta que da el caballo sin mudar terreno. 2. Pirueta en el baile.

Piscary [pis'-ca-ri], *s.* Privilegio de pesca en aguas de la propiedad de otra persona.

Piscatory [pis'-ca-to-ri], *a.* Piscatorio, que pertenece a la pesca o pesquería.

Pisces [pis'-iz], *s. pl.* 1. Los peces, una clase de los vertebrados. 2. (Astr.) Piscis, duodécimo signo del zodíaco.

Pisciculture [pis-i-cul'-chur], *s.* Piscicultura, arte de repoblar de pesca los ríos y estanques.

Piscinal [pis'-i-nal], *a.* Lo que pertenece a la piscina.

Piscivorous [pis-siv'-o-rus], *a.* Ictiófago, que se mantiene de pescado.

Pish [pish], *inter.* ¡Bah! ¡Quita allá! Exclamación de desprecio.

Pismire [pis- ó piz'-mair], *s.* Hormiga.

Piss [pis], *vn.* (Vulg.) Orinar.—*s.* Orina.

Pistachio [pis-tē'-sho o pis-ta'-sho], *s.* (Bot.) Alfóncigo o pistacho, fruta de un árbol del mismo nombre.

Pistil [pis'-til], *s.* (Bot.) Pistilo, el órgano femenino de las flores.

Pistillary [pis'-til-ẹ-ri], *a.* Perteneciente al pistilo.

Pistillate [pis'-til-ēt], *a.* Pistilado, que tiene pistilo; particularmente, que tiene pistilos, y no estambres.

Pistol [pis'-tẹl], *s.* Pistola, arma de fuego pequeña y corta. *Pocket-pistol*, Pistolete, cachorro. *Pistol-shot*, Pistoletazo, tiro de pistola. *Case* o *brace of pistols*, Par de pistolas. *Two* o *three-barrelled pistol*, Pistola de dos o tres cañones o tiros.

Pistol, *va.* Tirar con pistola; matar a uno de un pistoletazo.

Pistole [pis-tōl'], *s.* Doblón.

Pistolet [pis-to-let'], *s.* Pistolete, cachorro o cachorrillo.

Piston [pis'-ten], *s.* (Mec.) Émbolo, macho. *Piston ring*, Aro o anillo de émbolo o de pistón. *Piston rod*, Vástago sujetador del émbolo.

Pit [pit], *s.* 1. Hoyo, el hueco o concavidad que queda después de sacada la tierra. 2. Abismo, profundidad sin término. 3. Hoyo, sepultura. 4. Area de un teatro ocupada por las lunetas o butacas. *The armpit*, El sobaco. *The pit of the stomach*, La boca del estómago. *Coal-pit*, Mina de carbón de piedra. *Sand-pit*, Mina de arena que se saca para hacer argamasa. *Gravel-pit*, Cascajal o cascajar. *Turf-pit*, Hornaguero. *To be at the pit's brink*, Estar al borde del precipicio, estar con un pie en la sepultura. *Pit-coal*, Hulla, carbón mineral. *Pit-head*, Pozo de mina. *Pit-saw*, Sierra larga para aserrar maderos sobre un hoyo o foso; sierra que se maneja entre dos.

Pit, *va.* 1. Poner alguna cosa en un agujero. 2. Comprimir una cosa haciendo que forme hoyos. 3. Formar agujeritos en alguna cosa. 4. Incitar a uno a reñir.

Pitapat [pit'-a-pat], *s.* Palpitación de corazón; paso ligero y apresurado. —*adv.* Con una rápida sucesión de golpecitos; (fam.) pit, pat; tictac.

Pitch [pich], *s.* 1. Punto, grado de elevación; punto extremo. 2. Grado de inclinación de una pendiente; declive, bajada; inclinación con respecto al horizonte. 3. Declive, de un tejado. 4. (Mec.) Trecho que adelanta una rosca a cada vuelta; también, paso de un diente de encaje. 5. (Mús.) Grado más o menos alto de un tono, diapasón; el diapasón con referencia a un tipo. 6. En los juegos, lanzamiento, el acto de lanzar, o la distancia a que llega el objeto lanzado. *Pitch-pipe*, Diapasón de voz, instrumento que sirve para entonar la voz o un instrumento músico. *He came to that pitch*, Llegó a ese extremo. *The highest pitch of glory*, La cumbre, el pináculo, el más alto punto de gloria.

Pitch [pich], *s.* 1. Pez, la resina del pino espesada por medio del fuego; brea, alquitrán. *Pitch-brush*, Escopero. *Pitch-kettle*, Caldero de brea. *Pitch-ladle*, Cucharón de embrear. *Pitch-pine*, Pino de tea. 2. Jugo resinoso que exudan los pinos.

Pitch, *va.* 1. Tirar, arrojar, lanzar al aire (moviendo el brazo como un péndulo); en el juego de *base-ball*, arrojar la pelota al jugador que tiene la maza o *bat*. 2. Empujar, meter algo en la tierra, v. g. estacas; de aquí, colocar, ordenar. *A pitched battle*, Batalla campal. 3. Fijar, plantar. *To pitch a tent*, Plantar una tienda de campaña. 4. Embrear, dar con brea, empegar. 5. (Mús.) Graduar el tono, dar el diapasón.—*vn.* 1. Arrojar por bajo mano; arrojar de una manera cualquiera. 2. Caerse alguna cosa hacia abajo. 3. Caer de cabeza. 4. Escoger. 5. Instalarse, fijarse, establecerse. 6. Arfar, cabecear el buque de popa a proa. *To pitch into*, (Fam.) Acometer, embestir. *To pitch in*, (Fam.) Empezar algo con decisión y energía.

Pitcher [pich'-ẹr], *s.* 1. Cántaro, bocal, vasija de barro para llevar o traer agua. 2. Piqueta, herramienta para abrir la tierra; una forma de pie de cabra. 3. Arrojador, el que arroja o lanza; en el juego de *base-ball*, el que tira la pelota al que tiene la maza. 4. (Bot.) Forma de hoja muy particular parecida a un cántaro.

Pitcher-plant [pich'-ẹr-plant], *s.* Cualquiera de las plantas que tienen hojas o pecíolos en forma de bocal o urna, como la nepenta, sarracenia, y darlingtonia.

Pitchfork [pich'-fōrk], *s.* 1. Horca o percha que usan los labradores. 2. Diapasón, instrumento de dos brazos paralelos para graduar el tono de un instrumento músico o de la voz.

Pitchiness [pich'-i-nes], *s.* Obscuridad; negrura, color de pez.

Pitching [pich'-ing], *a.* Inclinado, en declive.—*s.* 1. Arfada, cabezada de un buque. 2. Lanzamiento, la acción de lanzar ó arrojar. *Pitching-pence,* (Gr. Bret.) Contribución que se paga por poner en venta las mercancías en las ferias.

Pitchstone [pich'-stōn], *s.* Un vidrio volcánico que á menudo contiene cristales porfíricos y esferitas, y que presenta un lustre resinoso. Difiere de la obsidiana en que contiene mucha mayor cantidad de agua.

Pitch-tree [pich'-trī], *s.* Abeto píceo, abeto de Noruega, la Abies excelsa.

Pitchy [pich'-i], *a.* 1. Embreado, dado con brea ó pez; que tiene las propiedades de la pez. 2. Negro, obscuro, triste.

Piteous [pit'-ẹ-us], *a.* 1. Lastimoso, que mueve á compasión ó excita simpatía. 2. Compasivo, tierno.

Piteously [pit'-ẹ-us-li], *adv.* Lastimosamente.

Piteousness [pit'-ẹ-us-nes], *s.* Compasión, ternura.

Pitfall [pit'-fēl], *s.* Trampa, hoya ligeramente cubierta para ocultarla; añagaza, peligro latente.

Pith [pith], *s.* 1. Meollo de planta ó árbol. 2. Tuétano. 3. Fuerza, robustez. 4. Medula, energía, vigor de pensamiento y estilo. 5. Medula; la parte esencial de alguna cosa. *The pith of life,* Lo mejor de la vida.

Pith, *va.* 1. Matar, destruyendo la medula espinal. 2. Quitar el meollo á una planta.

Pithily [pith'-i-li], *adv.* Enérgicamente, fuertemente.

Pithiness [pith'-i-nes], *s.* Energía, eficacia.

Pithless [pith'-les], *a.* Falto de meollo; endeble, sin fuerza, sin energía, necio.

Pithy [pith'-i], *a.* 1. Enérgico, eficaz; meduloso. 2. Que contiene la parte esencial de un asunto; expresivo, lacónico, efectivo. *A pithy saying,* Un dicho enérgico y expresivo, de mucha miga.

Pitiable [pit'-i-a-bl], *a.* 1. Lastimoso, sensible, patético, digno de compasión. 2. Despreciable, desestimado.

Pitiful [pit'-i-ful], *a.* 1. Lastimoso, sensible. 2. Despreciable, detestable.

Pitifully [pit'-i-ful-i], *adv.* Lastimosamente; despreciablemente.

Pitifulness [pit'-i-ful-nes], *s.* 1. Ternura, compasión, piedad, misericordia. 2. Ruindad.

Pitiless [pit'-i-les], *a.* Desapiadado, cruel, inhumano, duro de corazón.

Pitilessly [pit'-i-les-li], *adv.* Cruelmente, inhumanamente.

Pitilessness [pit'-i-les-nes], *s.* Inhumanidad, dureza de corazón.

Pitman [pit'-mạn], *s.* (*pl.* PITMEN). 1. Aserrador de foso; y particularmente, pocero, el minero que tiene á su cargo la maquinaria subterránea. 2. (*pl.* PITMANS) (Mec.) Barra de conexión; vara que conecta una pieza giratoria con otra que tiene movimiento de vaivén.

Pittance [pit'-ans], *s.* 1. Pitanza ó ración, originalmente la porción de comida que se repartía á cada uno, v. g. en los conventos; pequeño donativo que se hace por caridad. 2. Porcioncilla, porción pequeña de alguna cosa.

Pitted [pit'-ed], *a.* Cavado, picado. *Pitted with the small-pox,* Picado de viruelas.

Pituitary [pi-tiū'-i-tẹ-ri o pit'-yu-i-tẹ-ri], *a.* Pituitario.

Pituitous [pi-tiū'-i-tus], *a.* Pituitoso.

Pity [pit'-i], *s.* 1. Piedad, misericordia, lástima, compasión. *I feel no pity for him,* No le tengo lástima. 2. Lástima, el objeto que excita la compasión: en este sentido tiene plural. *It is a pity that his book is lost,* Es lástima que se haya perdido su libro. *It is a thousand pities,* Es muchísima lástima. *For pity's sake, from pity,* Por piedad.

Pity, *va.* Compadecer, tener lástima.—*vn.* Lastimarse, apiadarse, tener piedad, enternecerse. *He is greatly to be pitied,* Es muy digno de lástima.

Pivot [piv'-ut], *s.* 1. Espigón, gorrón, quicio, pivote. 2. Eje, polo, alma. 3. *V. Pivot-man. Pivot-gun,* Cañón giratorio, colisa. *Pivot-hole o collar,* Rangua, buje o quicio de eje. *Pivot-man,* Guía, el soldado que se halla en el flanco sobre el cual se opera una conversión.

Pivot, *va.* Colocar sobre un eje; proveer de un gorrón o espigón.—*vn.* Girar sobre un eje o pivote.

Pivotal [piv'-ut-al], *a.* De la naturaleza de un gorrón o eje; se aplica al punto sobre el cual gira un asunto, una conversación, etc.

Pixy [pix'-i], *s.* (*pl.* PIXIES). Entre la gente del pueblo inglés, una especie de hada o duende.

Pizza [pit'-zah], *s.* Torta muy condimentada de la cocina italiana, hecha de harina con salsa de tomate y que generalmente contiene también anchoas, queso, etc.

Placability [plē-ca-bil'-i-ti], **Placableness** [plé'-ca-bl-nes], *s.* Placabilidad; dulzura, clemencia.

Placable [plé'-ca-bl], *a.* Placable, aplacable.

Placard [plac'-ard], *s.* 1. Cartel, anuncio; la proclama que se fija en las esquinas para noticia del público. 2. Herrete o plancha que lleva el nombre del dueño.

Placard [pla-cārd'], *va.* Publicar o hacer manifiesta alguna cosa; fijar en las esquinas algún cartel o noticia al público.

Placate [plé'-kēt], *va.* Aplacar, apaciguar, conciliar, sosegar.

Place [plēs], *s.* 1. Lugar, sitio, paraje, espacio en que está colocado un objeto. *In all places,* En todas partes. 2. (Mil.) Plaza, fortaleza, puesto militar. 3. Residencia, mansión. 4. Lugar, texto, pasaje de un escrito o de un libro. 5. Colocación, orden de prioridad, posición; punto, grado en orden de precedencia. 6. Empleo, dignidad, oficio público, plaza. 7. Lugar, camino; lugar, asiento; recepción, buena acogida. 8. Plaza en una ciudad, espacio abierto cuadrado; también callejón sin salida, o una calle corta y estrecha. *A place of refuge,* Asilo. *In the first place,* En primer lugar. *To give place,* Dar la preeminencia, ceder el paso. *In the next place,* Luego, después. *In place of,* En lugar de, en vez de. *In no place,* En ninguna parte. *A watering-place,* (1) Aguadero, abrevadero; (2) estación balnearia, punto de baños. *To take place,* Verificarse, tener efecto, sobrevenir, suceder, pasar, ocurrir un suceso.

Place, *va.* 1. Colocar, poner alguna cosa en un paraje determinado. 2. Fijar, establecer, plantar. 3. Prestar a interés, poner dinero á ganancia. *To place in order,* Arreglar, poner en orden. 4. Señalar, asignar, destinar a un deber. *I have placed (out) my son,* He colocado a mi hijo.

Placebo [pla-sī'-bo], *s.* (Med.) Placebo.

Placeman [plēs'-man], *s.* Empleado público, oficinista.

Placement [plēs'-mẹnt], *s.* Colocación, empleo.

Placenta [pla-sen'-ta], *s.* 1. (Bot.) Placenta, la parte del fruto a que están prendidas las semillas. 2. (Anat.) Placenta.

Placental [pla-sen'-tal], *a.* Perteneciente a la placenta, o enlazado con ella; provisto de placenta.

Placer [plas'-ẹr], *s.* Placer, lavadero de oro. (< Esp.)

Placer [plé'-sẹr], *s.* Colocador, el que coloca.

Placid [plas'-id], *a.* Plácido, quieto, sosegado, benigno, apacible.

Placidity [pla-sid'-i-ti], **Placidness** [plas'-id-nes], *s.* Apacibilidad, afabilidad, dulzura, suavidad.

Placidly [plas'-id-li], *adv.* Apaciblemente, suavemente, dulcemente.

Placit [plas'-it], *s.* Decreto, resolución, orden.

Placket [plak'-et], *s.* 1. Abertura en la parte superior de un zagalejo o una saya. 2. (Des.) Guardapiés.

Placoid [plac'-eid], *a.* Parecido a una plancha o placa; dícese de ciertas escamas de los tiburones y de las rayas. (< Gr. πλακώδης.)

Plagal [plé'-gal], *a.* (Mús.) Plagal, se dice de un modo musical en que la quinta es aguda y la cuarta grave.

Plagiarism [plé'-ji-a-rizm], *s.* Plagio, usurpación de los pensamientos u obras literarias de otro.

Plagiarist [plé'-ji-a-rist], *s.* Plagiario, el que roba los pensamientos o escritos ajenos y los vende por suyos.

Plagiarize, Plagiarise [plé-ji-a-raiz], *va.* En las obras literarias o artísticas, plagiar, apropiarse los pensamientos de otros y darlos por suyos.—*vn.* Cometer o hacer plagios.

Plague [plēg], *s.* 1. Peste, enfermedad contagiosa y muy destructiva. 2. Plaga, miseria, calamidad. 3. Peste, majadero, majadería, joroba, cualquier cosa muy enfadosa o molesta.

Plague, *va.* 1. Atormentar, afligir, molestar, inquietar, vejar, importunar. 2. Jorobar, infestar, apestar, plagar.

Plaguily [plēg'-i-li], *adv.* (Fam.) Molestamente.

Plaguy [plēg'-i], *a.* (Fam.) Enfadoso, molesto; apestado.

Plaice [plēs], *s.* Platija, pez de la familia de los pleuronéctidos. Pleuronectes platessa.

Plaid [plēd], *s.* 1. Capa suelta de sarga listada que usan los montañeses de Escocia. 2. [plad o plēd] Listados en cuadro, o a lo ancho y a lo largo.—*a.* [plad o plēd] 1. Que tiene un dibujo cuadriculado, de rayas que se cruzan en ángulos rectos. 2. En cuadros de varios colores.

Plain [plēn], *a.* 1. Lleno, raso, igual, sin tropiezo ni embarazo alguno. 2. Liso, que no tiene adorno; sencillo. 3. Ingenuo, llano, abierto; liso, sincero. 4. Puro, simple, común; simple, sencillo, modesto, que no tiene lujo ni riquezas. 5. Llano, claro, evidente, distinto. *In plain*

Spanish, En buen castellano. *Plain people*, (1) Gente sencilla. (2) Gente humilde, común, de origen obscuro. 6. Verdadero, puro; acabado, rematado. 7. Falto de belleza personal, ordinario, feo. *A very plain girl*, Una joven o muchacha más bien fea que bonita, sin belleza alguna. *Plain food*, Alimento simple, sencillo. *Plain-chant, plain-song*, Canto llano, canto plano, o de iglesia. *Plain work*, Costura sencilla, lisa, a diferencia de la que tiene algún adorno. *Plain truth*, La pura verdad o sin disfraz alguno. *Plain man*, (1) Hombre sincero. (Fam.) Hombre a la pata la llana. (2) El hombre que no es bien parecido. *In plain terms*, En términos claros. *To be plain with one*, Hablar claro a uno, decirle francamente lo que se siente.—*adv.* 1. Claramente, distintamente. 2. Llanamente, sinceramente, con lisura o tersura y verdad.—*s.* 1. Llano, el campo o terreno igual, llanada. 2. (Des.) Campo de batalla. *Plain-dealer*, Hombre de buena fe, hombre de bien, hombre sincero. *Plain-dealing*, Buena fe, sinceridad en el trato, honradez. *Plain-hearted*, Sencillo, sincero, bueno, sin doblez. *Plain-heartedness*, Sinceridad. *Plain-spoken*, Sencillo, claro y sincero en sus palabras.

Plain, *va.* Allanar, hacer llana alguna cosa.

Plain-clothes man [plên-clōdhz' man], *s.* 1. Detective. 2. Oficial de policía no uniformado.

Plaining [plên'-ing], *s.* (Poét.) Queja, lamento.

Plainly [plên'-li], *adv.* 1. Llanamente. 2. Llanamente, con ingenuidad. 3. De veras. *I tell you plainly I can not*, Le digo a Vd. de veras que no puedo. 4. Claramente, sencillamente, francamente.

Plainness [plên'-nes], *s.* 1. Llanura, igualdad. 2. Sencillez. 3. Sinceridad, franqueza. 4. Claridad.

Plainsman [plênz'-man], *s.* Llanero.

Plaint [plênt], *s.* Quejido, queja, lamento.

Plaintful [plênt'-ful], *a.* Quejoso; lloroso, doliente, dolorido.

Plaintiff [plên'-tif], *s.* Demandante, el actor litigante que demanda en juicio.

Plaintive [plên'-tiv], *a.* Lamentoso, lastimoso, dolorido.

Plaintively [plên'-tiv-li], *adv.* De un modo lastimoso.

Plaintiveness [plên'-tiv-nes], *s.* El estado o calidad que constituye a una cosa lamentosa o dolorida.

Plait [plêt], *s.* 1. Pliegue, el doblez que se hace en la ropa. 2. Trenza, cordoncillo. *V.* BRAID. *Plait of hair*, Trenza de cabellos.

Plait, *va.* 1. Plegar, hacer dobleces o pliegues. 2. Alechugar, rizar, encarrujar. 3. Tejer, trenzar.

Plaiter [plêt'-ẹr], *s.* Plegador.

Plaiting [plêt'-ing], *s.* Plegadura, pliegue.

Plan [plan], *s.* 1. Plan, designio, proyecto formulado para alcanzar algún resultado. 2. Plan o modelo de alguna cosa; plano. 3. Icnografía, delineación de la planta de un edificio o buque; plano, proyección. 4. Diseño, esbozo, bosquejo, de una obra literaria o artística. 5. Método, hábito, modo usual, costumbre.

Plan, *va.* 1. Trazar, delinear algún plan; proyectar. 2. Urdir, tramar, fraguar.

†**Planch** [planch], *va.* (Des.) Entarimar, entablar.

Plancher [planch'-ẹr], *s.* 1. Entarimado, suelo o techo entarimado de una habitación. 2. Tabla de madera. (Fr.)

Planchet [planch'-et], *s.* Tejuelo, pieza de metal preparada para estampar el cuño sobre ella.

Planchette [plan-shet'], *s.* 1. Grafómetro. *V.* CIRCUMFERENTOR. 2. Plancheta, tablita provista de un lápiz y dos ruedas; de este aparato se creía en otro tiempo que escribía independientemente de la voluntad de las personas que lo tocaban.

Plane [plên], *a.* Llano; (bot.) que tiene una superficie llana.—*s.* 1. Plano, superficie plana. 2. Cepillo, instrumento de carpintería. 3. *V.* PLANE-TREE. *Plane-table*, (1) Plancheta, instrumento topográfico de los agrimensores que sirve principalmente para levantar planos. (2) Tablilla inclinada para disponer los minerales. *Bench-plane*, Garlopa, cepillo de banco. *Jack-plane*, Garlopa de alisar. *Rabbet-plane*, Cepillo de ranurar. *Dovetail-plane*, Guillame de ensamblar.

Plane, *va.* 1. Allanar. 2. Acepillar, alisar.

Plane, *s.* Aeroplano, avión.

Plane geometry [plên jẹ-em'-e-tri], *s.* Geometría plana.

Planer [plên'-ẹr], *s.* 1. Acepillador. 2. Cepillo mecánico, acepilladora, máquina de acepillar para madera o para metal. 3. (Impr.) Tamborilete, aplanador, tablita cuadrada que se asienta y va golpeando la parte superior de la forma, para que las letras queden todas á igual altura.

Plane-tree [plên'-trî], *s.* (Bot.) Plátano, cualquiera de los varios árboles del género Platanus. El plátano americano se llama vulgarmente *sycamore* o *buttonwood*.

Planet [plan'-et], *s.* (Astr.) Planeta, astro opaco que gira con movimiento propio y periódico alrededor del sol.

Planetarium [plan-e-tê'-ri-um], *s.* Planetario, máquina que representa los movimientos de los planetas.

Planetary [plan'-et-ẹ-ri], *a.* Planetario, que pertenece a los planetas.

Planetoid [plan'-et-eid], *s.* Planeta menor.

Planet-struck [plan'-et-struc], *a.* Asombrado, atolondrado, atónito, confundido.

Planifolious [plan-i-fō'-li-us], *a.* (Bot.) Planifolio u hojiplano, compuesto de hojas llanas o lisas.

Planing [plên'-ing], *s.* Acepilladura, acción de acepillar. *Planing-machine*, Máquina de acepillar (para madera o metal), cepillo mecánico; acepilladora.

Planipetalous [plan-i-pet'-al-us], *a.* Planipétalo, que tiene los pétalos llanos o lisos.

Planish [plan'-ish], *va.* Alisar, allanar, pulir, aplanar.

Planisher [plan'-ish-ẹr], *s.* Planador.

Plank [planc], *s.* Tablón, tabla gruesa. *Planks of a ship*, (Mar.) Tablaje, tablazón.

Plank, *va.* Entablar, entarimar, cubrir con tablas alguna cosa. *To plank the deck*, (Mar.) Entablar la cubierta.

Planner [plan'-ẹr], *s.* Trazador, persona que forma un plan, un proyecto.

Plano-concave [plê'-no-cen'-kêv], *a* Planocóncavo: dícese de lo que es cóncavo por un lado y plano por otro.

Plano-conical [plê'-no-cen'-i-cal], *a.* Planocónico.

Plant [plant o plqnt], *s.* 1. Planta, nombre genérico de todo vegetal. 2. Planta, se llama así particularmente toda mata o hierba. 3. Planta, el asiento del pie. 4. Planta, plantel, instalación completa de maquinaria, herramientas, edificios, etc., necesarios para alguna empresa mecánica. *Plant-food*, Lo que sirve para fomentar el crecimiento de las plantas. *Plant-louse*, Pulgón, cualquier insecto áfido. *A perennial plant*, Una planta perenne, la que vive más de dos años.

Plant, *va.* 1. Plantar, meter en la tierra el vástago de un árbol o de otra planta para que vegete y crezca. 2. Colocar, poner, sentar una cosa fijamente. 3. Plantar, clavar en la tierra una cosa. 4. Plantar, fundar, establecer; engendrar. 5. Adornar un lugar poniendo plantas en él. *To plant a cannon*, Sentar, colocar un cañón.

Plantain [plan'-ten], *s.* (Bot.) 1. Plátano, planta cuya fruta se come, hierba tropical perenne. Musa paradisiaca. 2. Llantén, planta; tipo de la familia de las plantagíneas.

Plantar [plan'-tar], *a.* Plantar, perteneciente a la planta del pie.

Plantation [plan-tê'-shun], *s.* 1. Plantación, planta, el acto de plantar. 2. Plantío, el lugar o sitio plantado. 3. Colonia, un establecimiento de nuevos pobladores. 4. Ostral, ostrera, criadero de ostras. 5. Finca de cultivo mayor. *Sugar plantation*, (Amer.) Ingenio, trapiche, hacienda de azúcar. *Coffee plantation*, Cafetal. *Plantation hoes*, Azadones.

Planter [plan'-tẹr], *s.* 1. Plantador, cultivador. 2. Colono, el que cultiva la tierra en las colonias americanas.

Plantigrade [plan'-ti-grêd], *a.* Plantígrado, que anda apoyado en la planta de los pies, como el hombre, los osos, etc.—*s.* Animal plantígrado.

Planting [plant'-ing], *s.* Plantación, plantel.

Plantlet, Plantule [plqnt'-let, plant'-yūl], *s.* (Bot.) 1. Plantita, planta pequeña. 2. El embrión de la semilla cuando acaba de desplegarse en virtud de la germinación.

Plaque [plqc], *s.* 1. Plancha, chapa, o disco de metal, de porcelana u otro material embellecido artísticamente, v. g. para adornar las paredes. 2. Broche, o cosa semejante. 3. (Zool.) Disco o estructura parecido a un plato. (Fr.)

Plash [plash], *s.* 1. Charquillo, charco pequeño, aguazar, lagunajo. 2. La rama cortada y entretejida con otras.

Plash, *va.* 1. Enramar, entretejer ramas. 2. Hacer ruido moviendo o turbando el **agua**.

Plashing [plash'-ing], *s.* La entretejedura de ramas para hacer una empalizada o cerca.

Plashy [plash'-i], *a.* Pantanoso.

Plasm [plazm], *s.* 1. ¿Molde, matriz. 2. La forma de *plasma* en las voces compuestas, como *bioplasm*.

Plasma [plas'-ma o plaz'-ma], *s.* 1.

Plasma, la parte líquida de la sangre o de la linfa en circulación, en la que se encuentran las substancias nutritivas. 2. (Min.) Prasma (plasma), variedad verdusca de calcedonia.

Plasma physics [plas'-ma fiz'-ics], *s.* Física del plasma.

Plasmic [plas'-mic], *a.* Plasmal, que se refiere al plasma; protoplásmico, formativo.

Plaster [plas'-ter], *s.* 1. Yeso, sulfato de cal, para cubrir o lavar las paredes. *Plaster of Paris*, Yeso, sulfato calcinado de cal. 2. Argamasa, mezcla de arena y cal para obras de albañilería; estuco. 3. Emplasto, medicamento. *Blister-plaster*, Vejigatorio, cantárida. *Mustard plaster*, Sinapismo. *Healing plaster* o *salve*, Disecativo, ungüento.

Plaster, *va.* 1. Enyesar, enlucir, revocar o cubrir con yeso; sacar a plana. 2. Emplastar, poner emplastos sobre una parte enferma.

Plaster cast [plas'-ter cast], *s.* Yeso, enyesado, vendaje de yeso.

Plasterer [plas'-ter-er], *s.* 1. Enjalbegador, revocador. 2. Plasmante, el que hace figuras de yeso o barro.

Plastic [plas'-tic o plas'-tic], *a.* 1. Plástico, perteneciente a la plástica. 2. Que da forma a una cosa, formativo. 3. Plástico, que puede ser modelado en una forma cualquiera. 4. (Cir.) Eficaz para renovar las partes perdidas, o para modificar las mal formadas.

Plasticity [plas-tis'-i-ti], *s.* Plasticidad, calidad de plástico; capacidad de ser modelado; facultad o propiedad formativa.

Plastic surgery [plas'-tic sur'-jer-i], *s.* Cirugía plástica, autoplastia, anaplastia.

Plastography [plas-tog'-ra-fi], *s.* 1. Plastografía. 2. El acto o procedimiento de imitar la escritura o letra de otro; falsificación.

Plastron [plas'-tron], *s.* 1. Peto, pechera, porción de una prenda de vestir, de un escudo, etc., que cubre el pecho. 2. (Zool.) Concha inferior de las tortugas; parte semejante de los anfibios.

Plat [plat], *s.* 1. (Mar.) Baderna. 2. Pedazo de tierra señalado a un uso particular. *V.* PLOT. 3. Mapa o plano de un terreno medido o partido. 4. Especie de cintilla de paja o junco para hacer sombreros de mujer.

Plat, *va.* 1. Entretejer, trenzar. 2. Trazar, delinear un plano o un mapa; disponer un terreno para usos particulares.

Platane [plat'-en], *s.* *V.* PLANE-TREE.

Platband [plat'-band], *s.* 1. (Agr.) Acirate, espacio que se dispone algo elevado en los jardines para plantar flores. 2. Tablas, el espacio entre dos hileras de árboles. 3. (Arq.) Faja de la cornisa.

Plate [plêt], *s.* 1. Plancha o lámina de medal o vidrio. 2. Plata labrada. *Gold and silver plate*, Vajilla. 3. Plato, vasija baja y redonda con una concavidad en medio. 4. Plato, porción de comida servida a la mesa. 5. Palio, el premio que se señalaba en las corridas de caballos al que llegaba primero. 6. Plancha (de un grabado); estereotipo, clisé; electrotipo. 7. Placa o plancha, lámina de vidrio o de celuloide, sobre la cual se ha tomado una prueba negativa o se ha hecho alguna otra imagen o cuadro. 8. Vidrio cilindrado. 9. Pedazo de gutapercha, etc., en la cual se insertan uno o varios dientes artificiales. 10. *V. Plate armor*. *Plate-brass*, Latón en planchas. *Copper-plate engraver*, Grabador en dulce o de láminas. *Unsilvered plates*, Láminas de cristal sin azogue o desazogadas. *Dry plates*, Placas secas de fotografía. *Wet plates*, Placas húmedas de fotografía, que hoy sólo se emplean en ciertos casos especiales. *Plate armor*, Blindaje, planchas de armadura. *Plate-culture*, Cultivación de las bacterias en gelatina o en otros medios nutritivos extendidos en capas muy tenues, v. g. sobre láminas de vidrio. *Plate-holder*, Portaplaca fotográfico; bastidor ligero impenetrable a la luz que lleva una o más comúnmente dos placas fotográficas. Se llama también *dark slide*. *Plate-glass*, Vidrio cilindrado. *Plate-mark*, (1) Prueba, marca (de las monedas de plata u oro); (2) marca de contraste (en el borde de una estampa). *Plate-paper*, Papel de primera calidad para estampas. *Plate matter*, Material para periódicos fundido en clisés estereotípicos, para venderlo a varios periódicos que lo usan simultáneamente. *Plate-powder*, Polvos para pulir la vajilla. *Plate-rack*, (1) Vasar en el que se ponen los platos para que goteen; (2) bastidor para sostener las placas fotográficas mientras se secan. *Plate-warmer*, Estufa para calentar los platos. *Plates*, (Mar.) Chapas. *Back-stay-plates*, (Mar.) Cadenas de los brandales.

Plate, *va.* 1. Planchear, cubrir alguna cosa con planchas de metal; platear, dorar, niquelar, por medio de la galvanoplastia. 2. Batir hoja, labrar el oro u otro metal reduciéndolo a hojas o planchas.

Plateau [pla-tō'], *s.* (*pl.* PLATEAUX o PLATEAUS). 1. Altillanura, altiplanicie, mesa que se extiende sobre una altura. 2. ¿Fuente ancha para el centro de la mesa.

Plateful [plêt'-ful], *s.* La cantidad contenida en un plato.

Platen [plat'-en], *s.* 1. (Impr.) Platina, cuadro, en ciertas máquinas de imprimir y de escribir. 2. En maquinaria, platina, mesa que sostiene el material que se trabaja.

Platform [plat'-fōrm], *s.* 1. Plataforma, especie de tablado o andamio; terraplén. 2. Tribuna, lugar elevado desde donde se dirige la palabra a una asamblea. 3. Andén de ferrocarril. 4. Plataforma al extremo de un carro urbano, ómnibus, etc. 5. Programa, declaración formal de principios, hecha por un cuerpo político, religioso u otro.

Platina [pla-tí'-na o plat'-i-na], *s.* 1. Platino, metal blanquizco. *V.* PLATINUM. 2. Alambre torcido de plata.

Platinum [plat'-i-num], *s.* Platino, el más pesado de todos los metales.

Platitude [plat'-i-tiūd], *s.* 1. Perogrullada, verdad de Perogrullo; verdad trivial. 2. Calidad de trivial, vulgar.

Platonic [pla-ten'-ic], *a.* Platónico, que pertenece o se refiere a Platón.

Platonism [plê'-to-nizm], *s.* Platonismo, sistema filosófico de Platón, y su doctrina.

Platoon [pla-tūn'], *s.* Pelotón, un pequeño cuerpo de soldados.

Platter [plat'-er], *s.* Fuente, plato grande, por lo común de loza; antiguamente se hacía de peltre.

Platting [plat'-ing], *s.* Especie de cintillo de paja, junco o astilla para hacer sombreros de mujer.

Plaudit [plō'-dit], *s.* Aplauso, aclamación.

Plausibility [plōz-i-bil'-i-ti], **Plausibleness** [plōz'-i-bl-nes], *s.* Plausibilidad.

Plausible [plōz'-i-bl], *a.* Plausible, especioso, aparente.

Plausibly [plōz'-i-bli], *adv.* Plausiblemente, con plausibilidad.

Play [plê], *vn.* 1. Jugar, entretenerse, divertirse, recrearse. 2. Jugar, juguetear, travesear, enredar, retozar. 3. Jugar, burlarse unos con otros o unos de otros. 4. Jugar, competir con otro en algún juego. *To play at cards*, Jugar a los naipes. 5. Tocar, tañer, hablando de instrumentos músicos o de alguna orquesta. 6. Jugar, ponerse alguna cosa compuesta de varias piezas en movimiento y ejercicio; estar corriente o franco, hablando de los muelles, llaves o piezas que juegan en las máquinas. 7. Flotar, ondular, ondear. 8. Representar en público. —*va.* 1. Disparar, tirar. 2. Hacer andar una máquina o ponerla en movimiento. 3. Remedar, hacer el papel de. 4. Representar una comedia, un papel. 5. Tocar un instrumento músico, una pieza, etc. 6. Jugar una partida de cualquier juego. 7. Burlar o chasquear á alguno. *To play away one's money*, Jugar o perder al juego el dinero que se posee. *To play on a musical instrument*, Tocar o tañer un instrumento músico, como el violín, piano, etc. *To play upon one*, Burlarse de uno, hacer mofar de. *To play upon*, Hacer equívoco de vocablos. *To play a set* o *game*, Jugar un partido o una partida. *To play false*, Engañar. *To play one a trick*, Engañar a uno, hacerle una mala jugada, pegarle un petardo. *To play off*, Hacer alarde, desplegar; pretender, ostentar; hacer jugar; poner en oposición o contraposición. *To play the fool*, Hacerse el tonto. *To play the knave*, Engañar. *To play (the) truant*, Hacer novillos, no asistir a la escuela, al aula, etc.

Play, *s.* 1. Juego; divertimiento y ejercicio de recreación. 2. Representación de una pieza dramática y la misma pieza dramática. 3. Juego, la acción de jugar a un juego sujeto a reglas. 4. Juego, la disposición en que se hallan unidas algunas cosas entre sí, de modo que sin desunirse o separarse puedan ponerse en acción y movimiento, ya a la vez, ya de por sí. *To come in play*, Entrar en juego, hacer uno su parte en una cosa ejecutada entre muchos. 5. Juego. *V.* GAMBLING. 6. El modo de tocar un instrumento o de representar una pieza dramática. 7. Libertad para obrar; vuelo, remonte, hablando de las pasiones de la imaginación, etc. 8. Movimiento ligero y rápido; reflejo de colores o de luces. *A child full of play*, Un muchacho travieso o enredador. *To play fair play*, Jugar limpio, obrar con sinceridad, sin trastienda, de veras. *To play foul play*, Entrampar en el juego; engañar. *By fair play*, Sinceramente, con pureza. *In play*, En chanza, de burlas. *A play upon words*, Equívoco de vocablos. *Foul*

play, Mala jugada, perfidia. *Play-actor*, Actor, cómico.
Playback [plê'-bac], *s.* Reproducción en magnetófono.
Playbill [plê'-bil], *s.* Cartel de teatro, programa de una función teatral.
Playboy [plê'-bōi], *s.* Muchacho travieso, calavera, hombre de mundo.
Play-day [plê'-dê], *s.* Día de huelga, día de descanso.
Play-debt [plê'-det], *s.* Deuda contraída en el juego.
Player [plê'-ẹr], *s.* 1. Jugador. 2. Holgazán, haragán. 3. Comediante, cómico, actor. *Strolling player*, Cómico de la legua. 4. Tocador, músico, tañedor, instrumentista.
Player piano [plê'-ẹr pi-a'-no], *s.* Pianola, piano mecánico.
Playfellow [plê'-fel-o], *s.* Compañero de juego, así entre jugadores como entre niños.
Playful [plê'-ful], *a.* Juguetón, travieso.
Playgame [plê'-gêm], *s.* Juego de niños.
Playgoer [plê'-gō-ẹr], *s.* Persona que frecuenta los teatros.
Playground [plê'-graund], *s.* Patio de recreo, particularmente el que está inmediato a una escuela.
Playhouse [plê'-haus], *s.* 1. Teatro, casa de comedias; sala de espectáculos. 2. Casita de juguete para niños.
Playing-card [plê'-ing-cārd], *s.* Naipe, baraja, carta.
Playlet [plê'-let], *s.* Entremés teatral, comedia corta.
Playmate, *s.* *V.* PLAYFELLOW.
Playsome [plê'-sum], *a.* (Ant.) Juguetón, retozón.
Plaything [plê'-thing], *s.* Juguete.
Playwright [plê'-rait], *s.* Compositor de comedias, tragedias u óperas.
Plaza [plā'-za o plā'-tha], *s.* Plaza, lugar espacioso dentro de poblado, particularmente en una ciudad española o hispano-americana. (Esp.)
Plea [plī], *s.* 1. El acto o forma de abogar. 2. Alegación, alegato, defensa que hace un abogado ante un tribunal. 3. Apología, disculpa, excusa, pretexto. 4. Súplica, instancia. *A plausible plea*, Una excusa, disculpa plausible. *Plea in abatement*, Instancia de nulidad.
Pleach [plīch], *va.* Entretejer ramas.
Plead [plīd], *vn.* 1. Orar, argüir en un tribunal de justicia. 2. Raciocinar o argüir con otro alegando razones. 3. Abogar, defender en juicio la causa de un reo.—*va.* 1. Defender en juicio. 2. Alegar o exponer razones. 3. Disculpar, excusar, interceder. *To plead guilty*, Confesar que se ha cometido el delito de que se va a juzgar al reo. *To plead not guilty*, Negar la acusación. *To plead for*, Militar o argüir en favor de.
Pleadable [plīd'-a-bl], *a.* Que se puede alegar en un pleito, o en defensa de alguna cosa.
Pleader [plīd'-ẹr], *s.* 1. Abogado, el que aboga en un tribunal de justicia. 2. Abogado, defensor; todo el que sostiene el pro o contra de alguna opinión.
Pleading [plīd'-ing], *s.* Alegación, defensa.—*pl.* (For.) Debates, litigios; alegaciones.
Pleasant [plez'-ant], *a.* 1. Delicioso, agradable. 2. Placentero, alegre, vivo. 3. Divertido.
Pleasantly [plez'-ant-li], *adv.* Deliciosamente, alegremente, de una manera grata.
Pleasantness [plez'-ant-nes], *s.* Delicia, alegría, gusto, agrado, placer, satisfacción, recreo.
Pleasantry [plez'-ant-ri], *s.* 1. Gusto. 2. Agudeza, dicho agudo; chocarrería, chanza.
Please [plīz], *va.* 1. Deleitar, agradar, dar gusto. 2. Contentar, complacer.—*vn.* 1. Placer, agradar, gustar, gozar. 2. Querer, gustar, tener a bien, hallar por bueno. *To be pleased*, Complacerse, recrearse, deleitarse. *Do as you please*, Haga Vd. lo que guste. *Please God*, o *if God please*, o *if it please God*, ¡Dios lo quiera! ¡plegue á Dios! *Hard to please*, Difícil de contentar. *Ill-pleased*, Malcontento. *Please to come as soon as you can*, Sírvase Vd. venir lo más pronto que pueda. *Please to go in*, Sírvase Vd. entrar. *Please, sir*, *If you please*, Con permiso de Vd.
Pleaser [plīz'-ẹr], *s.* El hombre agradable que hace la corte a alguna persona para ganar su afecto o su favor.
Pleasing [plīz'-ing], *a.* Agradable, placentero, jovial, alegre.
Pleasingly [plīz'-ing-li], *adv.* Agradablemente.
Pleasingness [plīz'-ing-nes], *s.* La calidad que constituye a una cosa agradable o deleitosa.
Pleasurable [plezh'-ur-a-bl], *a.* Deleitante, divertido, festivo: dícese también de las personas que se entregan á los placeres.
Pleasurableness [plezh'-ur-a-bl-nes], *s.* Cualidad de lo que es agradable; agrado, atractivo, deleite.
Pleasure [plezh'-ur], *s.* 1. Gusto, placer, deleite, agrado, satisfacción, complacencia. *What is your pleasure, madam?* ¿Qué quiere Vd., señora? ¿qué es lo que Vd. desea? ¿en qué puedo complacer a Vd.? *It gives me great pleasure to see you*, Me alegro mucho de ver a Vd. *I shall do it with great pleasure*, Lo haré con mucho gusto. 2. Deleite sensual. *Woman of pleasure*, Cortesana. 3. Arbitrio, propia voluntad. *At his own pleasure*, Como él quiera, como le plazca.
§**Pleasure**, *va.* Complacer, dar gusto a otro; servir, favorecer, hacer favor a uno.
Pleasure-ground [plezh'-ur-graund], *s.* El jardín o praderas dispuestos con orden y hermosura; parque, jardín de recreo.
Pleat [plīt], *va.* (Fam.) Plegar, hacer dobleces o pliegues.—*s.* Pliegue, doblez, plegadura en la ropa. *V.* PLAIT.
Plebeian [plẹ-bī'-yan], *a.* y *s.* Plebeyo, pechero; vulgar, bajo, común.
Plebeianism [plẹ-bī'-yan-izm], *s.* 1. Condición de plebeyo, estado de la plebe. 2. Vulgaridad, la conducta de los plebeyos.
Plebiscite [pleb'-i-sit], *s.* 1. Plebiscito, resolución tomada por todo un pueblo a pluralidad de votos. 2. Plebiscito, ley romana votada por los plebeyos a propuesta del tribuno.
Plectrum [plec'-trum], *s.* Plectro, instrumento pequeño para tocar las cuerdas de la lira, cítara, etc.
Pledge [plej], *s.* 1. Prenda, la alhaja que se da en seguridad de una deuda o contrato. 2. Fianza; rehén. 3. Promesa.
Pledge, *va.* 1. Empeñar, dar o dejar alguna cosa en prenda, dar fianza. 2. Corresponder uno al brindis que se le hace. 3. Comprometerse.
Pledgee [plej-ī'], *s.* (For.) Depositario, la persona en quien se deposita alguna prenda.
Pledgeless [plej'-les], *a.* Desprovisto de fianza, de garantía.
Pledger [plej'-ẹr], *s.* 1. Depositante, depositador, el que deposita alguna cosa. 2. El que corresponde al brindis que se le dirige.
Pledget [plej'-et], *s.* Planchuela, plancha de hilas que se pone sobre una llaga o herida.
Pleiades [plī'-ya-dīz], *s.* (Astr.) Pléyadas o pléyades, grupo de estrellas en la constelación de Tauro, seis o siete de las cuales son perceptibles a la simple vista.
Pleiocene, *a.* *V.* PLIOCENE.
Pleistocene [plais'-to-sīn], *s.* El período cuaternario, la época más reciente de la historia geológica.
Plenarily [plī'-na-ri-li], *adv.* Plenariamente, llenamente.
Plenariness [plī'-na-ri-nes], *s.* Plenitud, calidad de pleno.
Plenary [plī'-na-ri], *a.* 1. Plenario, lleno, entero. 2. (For.) Plenario, que ha cumplido con todas las formalidades que previenen las leyes.
Plenipotential [plen-i-po-ten'-shal], *a.* Autorizado con poder pleno.
Plenipotentiary [plen-i-po-ten'-shi-ẹ-ri], *s.* y *a.* Plenipotenciario (representante diplomático), revestido de plenos poderes.
Plenish [plen'-ish], *va.* (Esco. o ant.) Llenar, rellenar.
Plenist [plī'-nist], *s.* El filósofo que niega que hay vacuo ó vacío en la naturaleza.
Plenitude [plen'-i-tiūd], *s.* Plenitud, abundancia.
Plenteous [plen'-tẹ-us], *a.* Copioso, fructífero, fértil, abundante.
Plenteously [plen'-tẹ-us-li], *adv.* Copiosamente, abundantemente.
Plenteousness [plen'-tẹ-us-nes], *s.* Abundancia, fertilidad.
Plentiful [plen'-ti-ful], *a.* Copioso, abundante, fértil.
Plentifully [plen'-ti-ful-i], *adv.* Abundantemente.
Plentifulness [plen'-ti-ful-nes], *s.* Copia, fertilidad.
Plenty [plen'-ti], *s.* 1. Copia, abundancia. 2. Profusión, demasía.
Plenum [plī'-num], *s.* Pleno, plenitud de la materia en el espacio; espacio, lo opuesto a vacuo.
Pleonasm [plī'-o-nazm], *s.* 1. Pleonasmo, figura de construcción que se comete cuando en la oración se acumulan palabras superfluas. 2. (Med.) Exceso en el volumen o número.
Pleonast [plī'-o-nast], *s.* El que acostumbra usar palabras superfluas.
Pleonastic, Pleonastical [plī-o-nas'-tic, al], *a.* Redundante, pleonástico.
Pleroma [plẹ-rō'-ma], *s.* 1. Condición de lleno o abundante, plenitud; lo que llena. 2. La naturaleza espiritual divina.
Plerophoria [plī-ro-fō'-ri-a], *s.* (Poco us.) Persuasión firme, certidumbre.
Plerotic [plẹ-ret'-ic], *a.* (Med.) Que tiene el poder o la facultad de criar carne.
Plesiosaurus [plī-si-o-sō'-rus], *s.* Plesiosauro, género de reptiles gigantescos del cual sólo se conocen algunos restos fósiles.
Plethora [pleth'-o-ra], **Plethory** [pleth'-o-ri], *s.* Plétora, repleción, superabundancia, exceso.

Plethoric, Plethorical [pleth'-o-ric o plẹ-ther'-ic, al], *a.* Pletórico, repleto.

Pleurisy [plū'-(o plū'-) ri-si], *s.* Pleuritis, pleuresía, inflamación de la pleura.

Pleuritic, Pleuritical [plu-rit'-ic, al], *a.* Pleurítico.

Pleuron [plū'-ron], *s.* (Zool.) Parte o prominencia de un lado.

Pleuropneumonia [plū'-ro-niu-mō'-ni-a], *s.* 1. Pleuroneumonía, enfermedad contagiosa del ganado mayor, inflamación simultánea de la pleura y del pulmón. Se llama también *cattle-plague* (peste del ganado). 2. Pleuroneumonía, inflamación simultánea de la pleura y del pulmón en el hombre.

Plexiform [plex'-i-fērm], *a.* 1. Plexiforme, en forma de redecilla; complicado. 2. (Anat.) Que tiene la forma de plexo.

Pleximeter [plex-im'-ẹ-tẹr], *s.* Plexímetro, chapa de marfil o de goma endurecida que sirve para practicar la percusión mediata.

Plexus [plec'-sus], *s.* 1. Enlace, entrelazamiento de partes en forma de redecilla. 2. (Anat.) Plexo, tejido de varios nervios.

Pliability [plai-a-bil'-i-ti], *s.* Flexibilidad, docilidad, cualidad de doblarse sin romperse.

Pliable [plai'-a-bl], *a.* 1. Flexible, que se puede doblar o torcer fácilmente. 2. Dócil, manejable, de disposición flexible, que cede fácilmente a un influjo moral.

Pliableness [plai'-a-bl-nes], **Pliancy** [plai'-an-si], *s.* Flexibilidad, blandura, docilidad.

Pliant [plai'-ant], *a.* 1. Flexible, dócil, blando, fácil de doblarse sin romperse. 2. Dócil, manejable, que cede fácilmente a un influjo moral, de disposición flexible.

Pliantness [plai'-ant-nes], *s.* Docilidad o flexibilidad de carácter.

Plica [plai'-ca], *s.* Pliegue. *Plica polonica*, Plica polónica, enfermedad de los cabellos que es endémica en Polonia.

Plicate [plai'-kêt], **Plicated** [plai'-kêt-ed], *a.* (Bot.) Plegado sobre sí mismo, como un abanico.

Plication [pli-kê'-shun], ‡**Plicature** [plic'-a-tiūr], *s.* Plegadura, pliegue.

Pliers [plai'-ẹrz], *s. pl.* Alicates, especie de tenazas. *Flat-pointed pliers*, Tenacillas de boca. *Sharp-pointed pliers*, Tenacillas de punta.

Plight [plait], *va.* 1. Empeñar, dar o dejar en prenda. *Plight* nunca se aplica a una propiedad, y en esto difiere de *pledge*. 2. Prometer en matrimonio, contraer esponsales.

Plight, *s.* 1. Promesa, empeño, compromiso solemne; esponsales, promesa de matrimonio. 2. Estado, condición; comúnmente, un estado apurado, embarazo, perplejidad. 3. (Des.) Pliegue. *V.* PLAIT. *A sorry* (o *woeful*) *plight*, Un estado lastimoso.

Plighter, *s.* Prometedor; el que empeña; la persona que contrae esponsales.

Plinth [plinth], *s.* Plinto, el cuadrado sobre que asienta el toro de la basa de la columna.

Pliocene [plai'-o-sīn], *a.* Plioceno; dícese de un terreno terciario (de Europa), en el que se encuentran los fósiles más recientes. (<Gr. pleiōn, más, y kainós, reciente.)

Plod [plod], *vn.* 1. Afanarse mucho; trajinar, andar de una parte a otra con trabajo. 2. Estudiar con aplicación y constancia; trabajar con perseverancia, trabajar de un tirón (expresión familiar).

Plodder [plod'-ẹr], *s.* El que se aplica mucho a un estudio, aunque sea sin utilidad.

Plodding [plod'-ing], *s.* El acto de estudiar con aplicación.

†**Plonket** [ploŋ'-ket], *s.* Especie de tela de lana gruesa.

Plot [plot], *s.* 1. Espacio pequeño de terreno destinado a un uso particular. *V.* PLAT. *Grass-plot*, Césped. *Garden-plot*, Jardincito, cuadro de flores. *Ground-plot*, Terreno, solar, de un edificio. 2. Plano, la delineación que se saca de un terreno, mapa. 3. Conspiración, conjuración, trama. 4. Enredo, nudo, intriga. (Fam.) Entruchada. 5. Plan, proyecto, idea. 6. Estratagema, astucia, fingimiento y enredo artificioso.

Plot, *va.* 1. Delinear, formar la planta de algún edificio o plaza. 2. Trazar, idear.—*vn.* 1. Conspirar. 2. Urdir, tramar.

Plotful [plot'-ful], *a.* Abundante en tramas, enredos o maquinaciones; lleno de intrigas.

Plotter [plot'-ẹr], *s.* Conspirador, conjurado; tramador.

Plotting [plot'-ing], *s.* 1. La delineación de algún terreno. 2. Conspiración, trama.

Plotting-scale [plot'-ing-skêl], *s.* Instrumento para levantar planos de terrenos.

Plough, Plow [plau], *s.* 1. Arado, instrumento para arar la tierra. 2. Lengüeta, instrumento con que el encuadernador recorta las hojas de los libros. 3. Instrumento para apartar o desviar obstáculos o para pasar a través de ellos, v. g. la máquina que se emplea para apartar la nieve. (*Plough* ha sido la forma usual, pero hoy día se ha restablecido la forma *plow*, más antigua.)

Plough, Plow, *vn.* Arar, labrar la tierra.—*va.* Arar. *To plough in*, Cubrir arando. *To plough up*, (1) Romper, partir, como con un arado. (2) Remover, arrancar del suelo, arándolo. *To plough with one's heifer*, (1) Arar con la novilla, es decir, tratar con la mujer para alcanzar alguna cosa del marido. (2) Usar los bienes de otro en provecho propio. *To put one's hand to the plough*, Empezar a hacer una cosa. *Gang-plough*, Arado de reja múltiple. *Snow-plough*, Quitanieves (para los ferrocarriles). *Plough-plane*, Guillame, acanalador, especie de cepillo.

Plough-alms [plau'-āmz], *s.* Contribución que cada arado pagaba antiguamente a la Iglesia.

Ploughboy [plau'-boi], *s.* Cualquier muchacho que está empleado en los oficios inferiores de la labranza, y por extensión cualquier muchacho patán e ignorante.

Plougher [plau'-ẹr], *s.* Arador, surcador.

Ploughing [plau'-ing], *s.* Aradura, labranza.

Ploughland [plau'-land], *s.* Tierra labrantía o de pan llevar.

Ploughman, Plowman [plau'-man], *s.* 1. Arador, el que ara y cultiva la tierra. 2. Patán, campesino, rústico. 3. El hombre de campo que es muy fuerte y trabajador.

Plough-Monday [plau'-mun-dê], *s.* El primer lunes después de la Epifanía.

Ploughshare, Plowsock [plau'-shār], *s.* Reja de arado. *Ploughstaff*, Arrejada.

Ploughwright [plau'-rait], *s.* El que hace arados.

Plover [pluv'-ẹr], *s.* 1. Avefría, ave de las costas del género Charadrias. 2. Algún ave semejante. *Bastard plover*, Frailecillo. *V.* LAPWING.

Plow [plau], *s.* *V.* PLOUGH.

Pluck [pluc], *va.* 1. Tirar o traer hacia sí alguna cosa con fuerza; arrancar, derribar, derrocar, echar por tierra: en estas significaciones este verbo lleva tras sí regularmente *off*, *on*, *away*, *up* o *into*. 2. Desplumar, pelar, quitar las plumas al ave. *To pluck up heart* o *spirit*, Hacer de tripas corazón.

Pluck, *s.* 1. Valor, ánimo, resolución ante el peligro. 2. Arranque, tirón. 3. Asadura; hígado, corazón y bofes (de un animal).

Plucker [pluk'-ẹr], *s.* Arrancador.

Plucky [pluk'-i], *a.* Animoso, valeroso, valiente.

Plug [plug], *s.* 1. Tapón, tarugo o llave de fuente, émbolo. *Fire-plug*, Llave o caño que abastece de agua en un incendio. 2. Porción de tabaco torcido. *Plug tobacco*, Tabaco curado o torcido. 3. (Fam.) Cualquier artículo gastado o que no sirve para nada; en especial, rocín, penco, caballo de poco valor. 4. (Ger.) Sombrero de copa.

Plug, *va.* 1. Atarugar, tapar con tapón o tarugo. *To plug melons* o *other fruits*, (Fam.) Calar melones, etc. 2. Orificar, rellenar la picadura de una muela o de un diente.

Plugger [plug'-ẹr], *s.* Orificador, instrumento que sirve para orificar.

Plum [plum], *s.* 1. Ciruela, fruto del ciruelo; ciruelo, el árbol mismo que da las ciruelas. 2. Pasas, la uva seca y puesta en cajas, particularmente las que se usan para guisar. 3. (Fam. Ingl.) La cantidad de cien mil libras esterlinas; riquezas, muchos bienes de fortuna. 4. La parte óptima de alguna cosa, lo mejor. *Dried plums*, Ciruelas pasas. *Green gage plum*, Ciruela claudia. *Plum-cake*, Bollo o bizcocho con pasas de Corinto y pasas comunes. *Plum-curculio*, Curculio, gorgojo, muy destructivo para las frutas del ciruelo, del melocotonero y del peral. *Plum-pudding*, Pudín, manjar inglés cocido en agua y compuesto de harina, tuétano de vaca, pasas comunes y de Corinto, especias y algún licor alcohólico. *Plum-pie*, Torta, pastel de ciruelas; también pastel que contiene pasas comunes y de Corinto. *Plum-tree*, Ciruelo.

Plumage [plū'-mẹj], *s.* Plumaje, conjunto de plumas del ave.

Plumb [plum], *s.* Plomada.—*adv.* A plomo, perpendicularmente.

Plumb, *va.* 1. Sondar, sondear. 2. Aplomar, examinar con la plomada. 3. Instalar (en un edificio) cañerías para gas, agua y albañales.

Plumbaginous [plum-baj'-i-nus], *a.* Plombaginoso, de plombagina o grafito; parecido a la dentelaria.

Plumbago [plum-bê'-gō], *s.* 1. Lápiz plomo, grafito, plombagina; se emplea para fabricar lápices y crisoles, y para lubricar. 2. (Bot.) Dentelaria, plumbago, género de plantas con flores color de plomo.

Plumbean [plum'-bẹ-an], **Plumbeous** [plum'-bẹ-us], *a.* Plúmbeo, plomizo, plomado.

Plumber [plum'-ęr], *s.* Plomero, el que trabaja en cañerías o plomo.
Plumbing [plum'-ing], *s.* 1. Arte u oficio del plomero; instalación de cañerías en un edificio. 2. Emplomadura, tubería, sistema de tubos para dichos usos.
Plumb-line [plum'-lain], *s.* Cuerda de plomada o sonda; nivel, instrumento para examinar si está igual un plano.
Plume [plūm o pliūm], *s.* 1. Pluma, plumaje, penacho de plumas. 2. Orgullo, altivez. 3. (Bot.) *V.* PLUMULE.
Plume, *va.* 1. Ajustar o componer las plumas. 2. Desplumar, pelar, quitar las plumas. 3. Adornar con plumas. *To plume one's self upon*, Vanagloriarse de alguna cosa. 4. Pelar, desollar, desplumar, sacar el dinero a alguno.—*vn.* Emplumar o emplumecer.
Plume-alum [plūm-al'-um], *s.* Alumbre de pluma.
Plumeless [plūm'-les], *a.* Implume.
Plumigerous [plū-mij'-ęr-us], *a.* Plumoso o plumado.
Plumiped [plū'-mi-ped], *s.* Ave calzada: dícese de la que tiene plumas en los pies.—*a.* Plumípedo, con patas cubiertas de plumas.
Plummet [plum'-et], *s.* Plomada (instrumento que usan los albañiles, carpinteros, etc.); sonda, sondaleza de los marineros.
Plumose [plū'-mōs], **Plumous** [plū'-mus], *a.* Plúmeo, plumoso.
Plump [plump], *a.* 1. Gordo, rollizo, regordete, gordiflón. *Plump man*, Hombre rechoncho. *Plump face*, Cara llena. 2. Brusco, claro, sin reserva.—*adv.* De golpe, á plomo, de repente.—*s.* Grupo apretado; bandada de aves, espesura de árboles.
Plump, *va.* Engordar, hinchar.—*vn.* Caer a plomo; hincharse, ponerse gordo y corpulento.
Plumpness [plump'-nes], *s.* Gordura, corpulencia.
Plumpy [plump'-i], *a.* Gordo, lleno, rollizo.
Plumula [plū'-miu-la], *s.* (Orn.) Plúmula, plumón, pluma muy delgada y sedosa.
Plumule [plū'-miul], *s.* 1. (Orn.) Plúmula, pluma blanda. 2. (Bot.) Plúmula, la parte del verdadero embrión de las simientes que sale fuera de la tierra.
Plumy [plū'-mi], *a.* Plumado, plumoso.
Plunder [plun'-dęr], *va.* 1. Pillar, tomar a viva fuerza lo que pertenece a un enemigo; despojar. 2. Saquear, pillar, hurtar, robar.
Plunder, *s.* 1. Pillaje, saqueo, despojo, lo que se toma por fuerza a un enemigo. 2. Pillaje, robo, botín, pecorea.
Plunderer [plun'-dęr-ęr], *s.* Saqueador, pillador, ladrón.
Plunge [plunj], *va.* 1. Zambullir, zampuzar, somorgujar, sumergir, chapuzar, meter en el agua, 2. Anegar, sumergir a uno en penas, en miseria, etc. 3. Precipitar, exponer a uno a alguna ruina. 4. Rempujar, meter alguna cosa a rempujones.—*vn.* 1. Sumergirse, meterse de repente debajo del agua. 2. Precipitarse, arrojarse inconsideradamente a ejecutar o decir alguna cosa. 3. Dar manotadas o coces como hacen los potros no domados.
Plunge, *s.* 1. Sumersión, zampuzo, zambullida. 2. Movimiento repentino y violento. 3. (Des.) Estrecho, aprieto, apuro. *Plunge-bath*, Baño suficientemente grande para zambullirse en él.
Plungeon [plun'-jun], *s.* (Orn.) Somorgujo, mergo.
Plunger [plunj'-ęr], *s.* 1. Buzo, somorgujador. 2. (Mec.) Émbolo de bomba.
Plunging [plunj'-ing], *s.* El acto de dar manotadas y brincos los caballos sin domar.
Pluperfect [plū-pęr'-fect], *a.* (Gram.) Pluscuamperfecto.—*s.* Pluscuamperfecto, tiempo que indica que una cosa estaba ya hecha, o podía estarlo, cuando se hizo otra.
Plural [plū'-ral], *a.* Plural, más de uno. *The plural number*, El número plural.—*s.* Plural, el número que designa la pluralidad. *In the plural*, En plural.
Pluralism [plū'-ral-izm], *s.* 1. Pluralidad, calidad de ser más de uno. 2. Pluralidad de los beneficios, posesión de más de un beneficio eclesiástico a la vez.
Plurality [plū-ral'-i-ti], *s.* 1. Pluralidad, multitud. 2. Pluralidad, mayoría, el mayor número.
Plurally [plū'-ral-i], *adv.* En sentido plural, en el número plural.
Plus [plus], *adv.* 1. Más: es voz latina. 2. Más de cero; positivo.
Plush [plush], *s.* Tripe, felpilla, tela felpada. *Silk plush*, Felpa de seda, especialmente para sombreros.
Plutarchy [plū'-tar-ki], *s.* Gobierno por los ricos, forma de la oligarquía. (< Gr.)
Plutocracy [plu-tec'-ra-si], *s.* Plutocracia, poder, reino del dinero.
Plutocrat [plū'-to-crat], *s.* Plutócrata, acaudalado político.
Plutocratic [plū-to-crat'-ic], *a.* Plutocrático.
Plutonian [plu-tō'-ni-an], *a.* Plutónico. *V.* PLUTONIC.—*s.* Plutonista, partidario del plutonismo. *V. Plutonic theory.*
Plutonic [plu-ten'-ic], *a.* 1. Plutomano, perteneciente a Plutón, dios de los infiernos entre los antiguos. 2. Plutónico, ígneo, debido a la acción del fuego. *Plutonic rocks*, Rocas plutónicas. *Plutonic theory*, Plutonismo, doctrina o teoría que atribuye la formación de las capas del globo a la acción del fuego interior.
Plutonist [plū'-to-nist], *s.* Plutonista, partidario del plutonismo, de la teoría plutónica.
Plutonium [plū-tō'-ni-um], *s.* Plutonio.
Pluvial [plū'-vi-al], *a.* Pluvial, que proviene de la lluvia o se refiere a ella; lluvioso.—*s.* Capa pluvial.
Pluviometer [plū-vi-em'-e-tęr], *s.* Pluvímetro, pluviómetro, instrumento para medir la lluvia que cae en lugar y tiempo dados.
Ply [plai], *va.* 1. Trabajar con ahinco, formar, disponer o ejecutar alguna cosa. 2. Ocupar, dar que hacer; usar con diligencia; manejar (la aguja, el remo). 3. Instar, solicitar con importunidad.—*vn.* 1. Ir y venir entre dos puntos; hacer viajecitos. *The ferry which plies between San Francisco and Tiburon*, El vapor de puerto que hace viajes entre San Francisco y Tiburón. 2. Afanarse por hacer algo con exactitud y presteza. 3. Ir de prisa. 4. Barloventear, voltejear a barlovento.
Ply, *s.* 1. Pliegue, doblez, hoja o capa de una tela, de una alfombra o manguera, etc. 2. Propensión, inclinación. *Three-ply*, De tres dobleces o capas.
Plying [plai'-ing], *s.* 1. Solicitación importuna. 2. (Mar.) Esfuerzo de vela contra el viento.
Plywood [plai'-wud], *s.* Madera terciada.
Pneumatics [niu-mat'-ics], *s.* Neumática (ciencia física).
Pneumatology [niu-ma-tel'-o-ji], *s.* Neumatología, tratado sobre las cosas espirituales.
Pneumonia [niu-mō'-ni-a], *s.* (Med.) Neumonía, inflamación del pulmón, que se llama perineumonía o pulmonía.
Pneumococcus [niu-mo-cec'-us], *s.* (Med.) Neumococo.
Poa [pō'-a], *s.* Poa, género de plantas de la familia de las gramíneas. La especie llamada *Kentucky blue-grass* es la más conocida. Poa pratensis.
Poach [pōch], *va.* 1. Cocer, dar un hervor ligero a alguna cosa. *To poach eggs*, Pasar huevos por agua rompiéndolos. 2. Pillar, robar, hurtar. 3. (Des.) Herir con un instrumento aguzado.—*vn.* Cazar furtivamente en tierras vedadas con el objeto de hurtar la caza.
Poacher [pōch'-ęr], *s.* El que caza en tierras vedadas para hurtar lo cazado.
Poachiness [pōch'-i-nes], *s.* Humedad.
Poaching [pōch'-ing], *s.* El acto de cazar sin licencia para hurtar la caza.
Poachy [pōch'-i], *a.* Dícese del terreno que forma hoyos al pisarlo el ganado; húmedo, pantanoso.
Pochard [pō'-chard], *s.* Pato de mar del género Aythya, con la cabeza y el cuello rojizos.
Pock [pec], *s.* Viruela, pústula, postilla. *Pock-marked*, Marcado de viruelas.
Pocket [pek'-et], *s.* 1. Bolsillo, faltriquera. 2. (Fig.) Bolsa; interés. 3. Bolsa, cavidad, receptáculo: en una mina, cavidad que contiene el mineral (pepitas de oro); nasa para pescados. *In pocket*, Que tiene ganancia pecuniaria. *Out of pocket*, De su bolsillo, habiendo perdido dinero. *Pocket-book*, (1) Portamonedas, bolsa. (2) Librito de memoria, cartera. (3) Dinero, recursos o medios pecuniarios. *Pocket-comb*, Peinecito de bolsillo. *Pocket-handkerchief*, Pañuelo de bolsillo. *Pocket-knife*, Navaja. *Pocket dictionary*, Diccionario manual, de bolsillo. *Pocket-flap*, Cartera del bolsillo. *Pocket-hole*, Boca de faltriquera. *Pocket-gopher*, *V.* GOPHER. *Pocket-money*, Alfileres, dinero para gastos particulares.
Pocket, *va.* Embolsar, meter alguna cosa en el bolsillo o faltriquera. *To pocket an affront*, Tragarse una injuria, o quedarse con ella en el cuerpo. *To pocket up*, Tomar alguna cosa clandestinamente.
Pocketed [pek'-et-ed], *a.* Lo que se toma furtivamente.
Pocketknife [pek'-et-naif], *s.* Cortaplumas, navajita de bolsillo.
Pockiness [pek'-i-nes], *s.* Calidad o condición de estar picado de viruelas.
Pocky [pek'-i], *a.* 1. Picado de viruelas. 2. Buboso, sifilítico.
Pod [ped], *s.* 1. Vaina, legumbre, la

corteza en que están encerradas algunas legumbres; cápsula de una planta. 2. Manada, rebaño, colección de animales, especialmente de focas, ballenas, o morsas. 3. La ranura o canal longitudinal que hay en ciertos taladros y barrenas.

Pod, *vn.* 1. Llenarse, hincharse. 2. Criar vainas. 3. Hacer que las focas y vacas marinas se reunan en grupos o rebaños para matarlas.

Podagric, Podagrical [po-dag'-ric, al], *a.* Gotoso.

Podder [ped'-er], *s.* El que recoge legumbres.

Podge [pej], *s.* (Prov. Ingl.) Charco, cenagal, lamedal.

Podium [pō'-di-um], *s.* (*pl.* PODIA) Podio.

Podometer [po-dem'-e-ter], *s.* Podómetro, instrumento para contar los pasos que uno da o las vueltas que da una rueda. *V.* PEDOMETER, que es más común.

Poem [pō'-em], *s.* 1. Poema, cualquiera obra en verso. 2. Obra en prosa cuyo estilo muestra imaginación y belleza poéticas.

Poesy [pō'-e-si], *s.* 1. Poesía, ciencia que enseña a componer y hacer versos. 2. Poesía, la misma obra o escrito compuesto en verso. 3. (Des.) Lema, mote, sentencia breve que se graba en una sortija o cosa semejante. *V.* POSY.

Poet [pō'-et], *s.* Poeta. *Poet-laureate,* Poeta laureado, archipoeta.

Poetaster [po-et-as'-ter], *s.* Poetastro, poeta despreciable.

Poetess [pō'-et-es], *sf.* Poetisa.

Poetic, Poetical [po-et'-ic, al], *a.* Poético.

Poetically [po-et'-ic-al-i], *adv.* Poéticamente.

Poetics [po-et'-ics], *s.* Poética, el tratado que contiene los preceptos del arte de componer obras de poesía.

Poetize [pō'-et-aiz], *vn.* Poetizar, versificar, hacer o componer versos.

Poetry [pō'-et-ri], *s.* 1. Poética; poesía. 2. Lo que es poético. 3. Versos, poema, obra poética.

Poh [pō], *inter.* ¡Puf! ¡bah! ¡quiá! interjección que expresa aversión o desprecio.

Poignancy [pei'-nan-si], *s.* 1. Punta, el sabor que va tirando á agrio. 2. Picante, la acerbidad o acrimonia con que algunas cosas irritan el paladar. 3. Picante, acrimonia, aspereza o mordacidad en el decir.

Poignant [pei'-nant], *a.* 1. Picante, acerbo. 2. Punzante. 3. Acre, mordaz, satírico, picante.

Poignantly [pei'-nant-li], *adv.* Picantemente, mordazmente, satíricamente.

Point [peint], *s.* 1. Punta, extremo muy agudo. 2. Herramienta o utensilio con un extremo puntiagudo; v. g. punta, especie de buril que usan los abridores y tallistas; en Inglaterra, aguja, carril móvil (término de ferrocarril); en plural, cambiavía. 3. Agujeta, cordón con herrete. 4. Punto, fin u objeto con que se hace una cosa. 5. Punta, promontorio. 6. Punto, pundonor, puntillo. 7. Agudeza, sal, chiste ingenioso. 8. Punto, la parte más pequeña que se considera indivisible. 9. Punto, instante, momento. 10. Punto, momento crítico, ocasión oportuna. 11. Punto, el estado actual de cualquier especie o negocio. 12. Rumbo, la división del plano en la rosa náutica. 13. Punto, paraje determinado a que se dirige alguna cosa. 14. Puntería. 15. Punta, toda especie de encaje. 16. Punto, parte o cuestión de alguna ciencia. 17. Punto musical. 18. (Gram.) Cualquier signo de puntuación, particularmente entre los impresores, punto final. *Points,* Puntos, las vocales en la lengua hebrea. 19. Punto tipográfico, unidad de medida para el tamaño de los tipos. 20. Punto, tanto, unidad de cuenta en los juegos. 21. Rabo, cola de un animal. *To speak to the point,* Ir al caso o a lo principal, dejarse de rodeos. *At the point of death,* En artículo de muerte. *At all points,* Enteramente, *Point-blank,* (1) Directamente, en línea recta. (2) Cara a cara, en facha, en términos formales. *To be at points,* Estar de punta, de cuernos o contrapuestos. (Mex.) Estar quebrados. *I was on the point of coming,* Estaba a punto (o a pique) de venir, iba a venir. *In point,* Al caso, a propósito. *In point of,* En cuanto, tocante a, con respecto a. *To come to the point,* Llegar al caso, al punto; encajar bien. *Knotty point,* Punto espinoso, cuestión difícil. *To carry one's point,* Salirse con la suya. *He has made five points,* Ha hecho cinco tantos.

Point, *va.* 1. Apuntar, aguzar, afilar, adelgazar. 2. Apuntar, señalar, indicar. 3. Puntuar. 4. Apuntar, dirigir, asestar el tiro de un arma. 5. Apuntar, señalar alguna palabra o frase con puntos en lo escrito. 6. (Albañ.) Juntar, llenar con argamasa los huecos o intersticios e igualarlos con la llana.—*vn.* 1. Apuntar, señalar con el dedo. 2. Parar, mostrar la caza como hacen los perros de muestra. 3. Señalar, enseñar, dar a conocer.

Point-blank [peint'-blanc], *a.* 1. Que tiene una dirección horizontal; a quema ropa. 2. Directo, positivo, formal.—*adv.* Directamente, en línea recta, diametralmente; en facha; positivamente, en términos formales.—*s.* Tiro a quema ropa, tiro asestado.

Pointed [peint'-ed], *a.* 1. Puntiagudo, puntuado, agudo. 2. Picante, epigramático, satírico. 3. Dirigido a una persona particular; acentuado. 4. (Arq.) Ojival.

Pointedly [peint'-ed-li], *adv.* Sutilmente, de un modo picante; con acento y fuerza; explícitamente, en términos formales.

Pointedness [peint'-ed-nes], *s.* Picantez; aspereza, acrimonia.

Pointer [peint'-er], *s.* 1. Indicador, índice, lo que indica; en particular, manecilla (de reloj), apuntador, puntero. 2. Perro de punta y vuelta, ventor, pachón, braco inglés. 3. *pl.* Las dos estrellas de la Osa mayor, en cuya dirección se halla la estrella polar.

Point Four [peint fōr], *s.* Punto Cuatro, programa de ayuda extranjera propuesto por el Presidente Truman de los Estados Unidos.

Pointing [peint'-ing], *s.* 1. Acto de afilar o apuntar; afiladura, aguzadura; acto de quitar las puntas. 2. Señalamiento, indicación, el acto de señalar o indicar; particularmente, puntuación; división de las palabras para cantar en la iglesia; acción de juntar o llenar los huecos o grietas con argamasa; puntería (de artillería). 3. Maduración de un absceso. 4. (Mar.) Rabo de rata.

Pointing-stock [peint'-ing-stec], *s.* Objeto de irrisión, hazmerreír.

Point lace [peint lēs], *s.* V. NEEDLEPOINT.

Pointless [peint'-les], *a.* Obtuso, sin punta.

Point of honor [peint ev en'-er], *s.* Pundonor.

Poise [peiz], *s.* Equilibrio, contrapeso; balanza; reposo.

Poise, *va.* 1. Equilibrar, balancear. 2. Igualar en peso, hacer equivaler una cosa a otra. 3. Cargar con algún peso. 4. Pesar, examinar con madurez alguna cosa. 5. Contrapesar, equiparar, cotejar una cosa con otra. 6. Abrumar, oprimir con algún peso grave.

Poison [pei'-zn], *s.* 1. Veneno. *Poison-nut,* Nuez vómica. 2. Veneno, ponzoña, cualquier cosa gravemente nociva a la salud. *Poison-oak, poison-ivy,* Especie de zumaque que causa en muchas personas una dermatitis o inflamación de la piel. Rhus toxicodendron, o en los estados norteamericanos del Pacífico. Rhus diversiloba. *Poison-sumac, poison-elder,* (1) Zumaque, árbol venenoso al tacto. (2) Mata, lo mismo que *poison-oak.*

Poison, *va.* 1. Envenenar, atosigar, emponzoñar. 2. Corromper, inficionar.

Poisoner [pei'-zn-er], *s.* Envenenador; corruptor, seductor.

Poisoning [pei'-zn-ing], *s.* Envenenamiento, emponzoñamiento; estado mórbido debido a una substancia venenosa.

Poisonous [pei'-zn-us], *a.* Venenoso, emponzoñado.

Poisonousness [pei'-zn-us-nes], *s* Venenosidad.

Poitrel [pei'-trel], *s.* Antepecho, la armadura que en tiempos pasados cubría el pecho del caballo de batalla.

Poke [pōk], *s.* 1. Empuje, empujón; picadura; la acción de empujar o de picar. 2. Collera con apéndice que sirve para impedir a las bestias que salgan de un cercado. 3. Perezoso, el que se mueve lentamente. 4. Gorra de mujer con ala anterior muy saliente.

Poke, *s.* 1. Barjuleta, bolsa; saquillo. 2. *V.* POKEWEED.

Poke, *va.* 1. Empujar, golpear con alguna cosa puntiaguda, picar. 2. Impeler por medio de un empujón o una picadura.—*vn.* 1. Andar perezosamente, gastar tiempo. 2. Andar a tientas, buscar alguna cosa a obscuras, particularmente cuando se busca á tientas con un palo u otro instrumento largo. *To poke the fire,* Hurgar la lumbre, atizar el fuego. *To poke fun at,* Burlarse, mofarse de alguno. *To poke the nose everywhere,* Meterse en todo.

Poker [pōk'-er], *s.* 1. Hurgón, atizador, hierro para menear y revolver la lumbre. 2. Juego de naipes, en el cual los jugadores apuestan sobre el valor de sus manos y la mano más alta gana todo lo apostado.

Pokerish [pō'-ker-ish], *a.* 1. Alarmante o que tiende a alarmar. 2. (Fam.) Tieso, rígido, inflexible.

Pokeweed [pōk'-wīd], *s.* (Bot.) Hierba carmín, fitolaca, hierba lisa y perenne común al borde de los caminos en los Estados Unidos y el Canadá. Es medicinal, y las bayas se emplean en Portugal para dar color al vino de Oporto. Phytolacca decandra.

Poky [pō'-ki], *a.* 1. Flojo, pesado, falto de espíritu ; lento. 2. (Ingl.) Desharrapado, mal vestido. 3. (Ingl.) Constreñido, apretado.

Polar [pō'-lar], *a.* Polar, que pertenece a los polos ; que pertenece a los polos magnéticos ; que proviene o se halla cerca de los polos. *Polar-stone,* (Con.) Especie de equino petrificado.

Polar bear [pō'-lar bār], *s.* Oso polar, oso blanco.

Polariscope [po-lar'-i-scōp], *s.* Polariscopio, instrumento para demostrar o medir la polarización de la luz, o para examinar substancias (como el azúcar) con luz polarizada.

Polarity [po-lar'-i-ti], *s.* 1. Polaridad, facultad de tener o de poder adquirir polos ; cualidad de tener polos opuestos. 2. *V.* POLARIZATION.

Polarization [pō''-lar-i-zé'-shun], *s.* 1. Calidad de tener o adquirir polaridad. 2. Polarización, modificación de la luz de modo que no pueda reflejarse en ciertas direcciones.

Polarize, Polarise [pō'-lar-aiz], *va.* Polarizar, comunicar polaridad o polarización a una cosa.

Pole [pōl], *s.* 1. Polo, cualquiera de los extremos del eje de la esfera.* 2. Pértiga, vara larga ; cualquier palo largo. 3. Una viga o un palo largo clavado en el suelo. *Pole-mast,* (Mar.) Palo y mastelero de una sola pieza. *Under bare poles,* (Mar.) A palo seco o a la bretona. *Pole of a coach,* Lanza de coche. 4. Percha, instrumento de diez pies geométricos de largo ; medida de diez y seis pies y medio. 5. Polaco, el natural de Polonia. *The South Pole,* El Polo Sur. *The poles of a magnet,* Los polos de un imán.

Pole, *va.* 1. Empujar o hacer andar con palos. 2. Llevar, sostener sobre palos. 3. Armar con palos. 4. Agitar con pértiga.—*vn.* Impeler un barco con pértiga.

Pole-axe [pōl'-ax], *s.* Hachuela de mano.

Polecat [pōl'-cat], *s.* 1. Veso. Putorius fœtidus. 2. Mofeta.

Polemic, Polemical [po-lem'-ic, al], *a.* Polémico.

Polemic, *s.* Controversista, el que escribe o trata sobre puntos dogmáticos.

Polestar [pōl'-stār], *s.* 1. Cinosura, estrella muy resplandeciente en la constelación de la Osa menor. 2. Norte, guía.

Pole vault [pōl vōlt], *s.* Salto con pértiga o garrocha.

Police [po-līs'], *s.* Policía. *Police headquarters,* Cuartel de policía.

Policed [po-līst'], *a.* Arreglado, bien administrado.

Police dog [po-līs' dog], *s.* Perro policía.

Policeman [po-līs'-man], *s.* Policía, gendarme.

Policewoman [po-līs'-wum-an], *s.* Mujer policía, agente femenino de policía.

Policy [pol'-i-si], *s.* 1. Arte, astucia ; prudencia, sagacidad en la dirección y manejo de los asuntos. 2. Curso o plan de acción ; particularmente, política, dirección de los negocios públicos. 3. Póliza de seguro.

Policyholder [pol'-i-si-hōld'-er], *s.* Asegurado, poseedor de una póliza de seguro.

Polio [pōl'-i-ō], *s.* Contracción de *Poliomyelitis,* poliomielitis, parálisis infantil.

Poliomyelitis [pol-i-o-mai-e-lai'-tis], *s.* Poliomielitis, parálisis infantil.

Polish [pol'-ish], *va.* 1. Pulir, pulimentar, alisar por medio de la frotación, dar lustre, bruñir. 2. Pulir, limar, civilizar a una persona rústica o tonta ; morigerar, hacer cortés, suavizar las costumbres, ilustrar el entendimiento.—*vn.* Recibir lustre o pulimento.

Polish, *s.* 1. Pulimento, bruñido, tersura, lustre. 2. Cortesía, urbanidad. 3. Barniz, substancia empleada para dar lustre.

Polish [pō'-lish], *a.* Polaco, que pertenece a Polonia.—*s.* Polaco, la lengua eslava que hablan los polacos.

Polisher [pol'-ish-er], *s.* Pulidor, bruñidor (operario o instrumento).

Polite [po-lait'], *a.* Pulido, cortés, urbano, bien criado ; que tiene finos modales.

Politely [po-lait'-li], *adv.* Urbanamente, cortésmente.

Politeness [po-lait'-nes], *s.* Cortesía, urbanidad, buena crianza.

Politic [pol'-i-tic], *a.* 1. Político, sagaz, diestro, astuto. 2. Bien concebido para alcanzar un fin ; especioso. 3. Que consta de ciudadanos ; adecuado al bien público, político. *Body politic,* Cuerpo político, de ciudadanos.

Political [po-lit'-i-cal], *a.* 1. Político, que pertenece al gobierno civil o a la administración general de un Estado ; que trata de la política o del gobierno. 2. Político, perteneciente a un partido. *Political economy,* Economía política. 3. (Des.) Sagaz, astuto.

Politically [po-lit'-i-cal-i], *adv.* Políticamente.

Politician [pol-i-tish'-an], *s.* 1. Político, estadista. 2. Hombre astuto y artificioso.

Politicize [po-lit'-i-saiz], *va.* Dar carácter político.

Politics [pol'-i-tics], *s. pl.* 1. Política, la ciencia o arte que trata de la administración y manejo de los negocios públicos. 2. Negocios públicos desde el punto de vista de un partido. 3. Opiniones políticas, preferencia de partido.

Polka [pōl'-ka], *s.* Polca, baile muy conocido, originario de Polonia ; y la música de ese baile.

Polka dots [pō'-ka dots], *s. pl.* Diseño de bolitas distribuidas en una tela.

Poll [pōl], *s.* 1. Cabeza de una persona ; y de aquí, la persona misma. 2. Matrícula o lista de los que votan en una elección y la votación en una elección.—*pl.* Paraje donde se vota. 3. Capitación, repartimiento de tributos o contribuciones por cabezas.

Poll, *va.* 1. Descabezar, descopar, desmochar, quitar la cima o copa a los árboles. 2. Descornar, quitar los cuernos a las reses. 3. Encabezar, formar una matrícula con los nombres de las personas que se deben incluir para el objeto con que se forma ; preguntar la opinión política de esas personas. 4. Encabezar, registrar o poner en matrícula a uno. 5. Votar en las elecciones. 6. Contar los votos.—*vn.* Dar voto en las elecciones.

Pollack, Pollock [pol'-ac, pol'-oc], *s.* Pescadilla, pez de mar del género gádido, parecido al bacalao. Pollachius.

Pollard [pol'-ard], *s.* 1. Árbol desmochado o descopado. 2. (Ict.) Coto. *V.* CHUB. 3. Salvado. 4. Ciervo u otro animal que ha perdido las astas.

Pollard, *va.* (Poco us.) Podar, descopar o desmochar.

Pollen [pol'-en], *s.* 1. (Bot.) Polen o polvillo fecundante del órgano masculino de las plantas. 2. Salvado fino.

Poller [pōl'-er], *s.* 1. Votante, el que tiene voto en una elección. 2. Registrador de votantes. 3. Desmochador, el que desmocha árboles. 4. (Poco us.) Barbero.

Pollex [pol'-ex], *s.* Pólice, el dedo primero o radial de un vertebrado ; pulgar.

Pollination [pol-i-nē'-shun], *s.* (Bot.) Polinización.

Polling [pōl'-ing], *s.* Votación, acción de votar ; escrutinio de los votos. *Polling-booth,* Local donde se vota. *Polling-place,* Paraje donde se hace el escrutinio de los votos.

Polliwig, Polliwog [pol'-i-wig, wog] *s.* (Fam.) Renacuajo. *V.* TADPOLE.

Pollutant [pol-lūt'-ant], *s.* Contaminante.

Pollute [pol-lūt' o pol-liūt'], *va.* Manchar, ensuciar. 2. Contaminar, corromper moralmente, viciar. 3. Desflorar, violar, deshonrar ; profanar. 4. Impurificar, mancillar, quitar la pureza ceremonial (entre los judíos).—*a.* (Poco us.) Mancillado, deshonrado, contaminado.

Pollutedness [pol-lūt'-ed-nes], *s.* Polución, contaminación ; desfloración, deshonor, violación.

Polluter [pol-lūt'-er], *s.* Corrompedor, corruptor, contaminador ; desflorador.

Pollution [pol-lū'-shun], *s.* Polución, contaminación, profanación.

Pollux [pol'-ux], *s.* Pólux, estrella fija de la constelación Géminis. *V* CASTOR.

Polly [pol'-i], *s.* (Fam.) Mariquita, nombre familiar usado en vez de *Mary ;* también, una cotorra.

Polo [pō'-lo], *s.* Polo, juego de pelota a caballo.

Polonaise [pō-lo-nēz'], *s.* 1. Polonesa, prenda de vestir de mujer a modo de gabán corto, ceñido a la cintura. 2. (Mús.) Polaca. 3. Polonesa, polaca, mujer de Polonia.

Poltroon [pol-trūn'], *s.* 1. Poltrón, collón, cobarde, pusilánime. 2. Poltrón, haragán, holgazán.

Poly [pō'-li], *s.* Polio, planta vivaz, especie de germandria. Teucrium polium.

Poly- [pol'-i]. Prefijo griego que significa muchos o varios.

Polyacoustic [pol-i-a-cūs'-tic o caus-tic], *a.* Poliacústico, que multiplica los sonidos.

Polyandry [pol-i-an'-dri], *s.* 1. Poliandria, estado de la mujer que tiene más de un marido. 2. Sistema social que incluye la pluralidad de maridos.

Polyanthus [pol-i-an'-thus], *s.* (Bot.) Poliantes, tuberosa, nardo, planta bulbosa con muchas flores fragantes y blancas.

Polybasic [pol''-i-bē'-sic], *a.* (Quím.)

Polibásico, que contiene dos átomos o más de hidrógeno, los cuales se pueden reemplazar por una base o por radicales básicos.
Polybasite [pol''-i-bê'-sait o po-lib'-a-sait], *s.* Polibasito, mineral de plata, negro como el hierro, y compuesto de plata, antimonio y azufre (Ag_9SbS_6).
Polycarpous [pel-i-cār'-pus], *a.* (Bot.) Policarpio, que tiene muchos frutos o pericarpios.
Polychromatic [pel''-i-cro-mat'-ic], *a.* Policromático, que presenta varios colores o cambios de color.
Polychrome [pel'-i-crōm], *a.* Policromo, hecho o impreso en varios o en muchos colores.—*s.* Cuadro o estatua ejecutados en varios colores.
Polyclinic [pel-i-clin'-ic], *s.* 1. Policlínica, institución en que se da instrucción clínica sobre toda clase de enfermedades. 2. Hospital general para el tratamiento de todas las enfermedades.
Polyester [pel-i-es'-tęr], *s.* Poliéster.
Poliethylene [pel-i-eth'-i-lin], *s.* Polietileno.
Polygamist [po-lig'-a-mist], *s.* Polígamo, polígama, el que practica la poligamia o sostiene su legalidad.
Polygamous [po-lig'-a-mus], *a.* 1. Polígamo, que se refiere a la poligamia. 2. (Zool.) Que se une o tiene cópula con más de uno del sexo opuesto. 3. (Bot.) Polígamo, que tiene sobre el mismo pedúnculo flores hembras y hermafroditas.
Polygamy [po-lig'-a-mi], *s.* Poligamia, el estado de un hombre casado con muchas mujeres, o de una mujer casada con muchos maridos a un tiempo.
Polyglot [pel'-i-glet], *a.* 1. Poligloto, escrito en varias lenguas. 2. Poligloto, que sabe muchas lenguas.
Polygon [pel'-i-gen], *s.* Polígono, figura de varios lados.
Polygonum [po-lig'-o-num], *s.* Polígono, género de plantas de la familia de las poligonáceas; contiene muchas especies, entre las que son muy conocidas el alforfón, la centinodia y la sanguinaria.
Polygraphy [po-lig'-ra-fi], *s.* Poligrafía, el arte de escribir usando muchas clases de cifras desconocidas y el arte de descifrarlas.
Polyhedral, Polyhedrous [pel-i-hi'-drus], **Polyhedrical** [pel-i-hi'-dric-al], *a.* Poliedro, que tiene muchas superficies.
Polyhedron [pel-i-hi'-drǫn], *s.* Poliedro, cuerpo sólido de muchas superficies planas.
Polymer [pel'-i-mer], *s.* Polímero.
Polymer chemistry [pel'-i-mer kem'-is-tri], *s.* Química de polímeros.
Polymeric [pel''-i-mer'-ic], *a.* (Quím.) Polímero, que contiene los mismos elementos y en la misma cantidad relativa, pero cuyo peso molecular es diferente.
Polymerism [po-lim'-ęr-izm], *s.* Calidad de polímero.
Polymerization [po-lim-er-i-zê'-shun], *s.* Polimerización.
Polymerize [pel'-i-mer-aiz], *va.* Polimerizar.
Polymorph [pel'-i-mērf], *s.* 1. (Quím.) Substancia que posee o presenta el polimorfismo. 2. Ser u organismo polimorfo.
Polymorphism [pel-i-mēr'-fizm], *s.* Polimorfismo, calidad del ser o del mineral que se presenta bajo varias formas sin cambiar de naturaleza.
Polymorphous, Polymorphic [pel-i-mēr'-fus, fic], *a.* Polimorfo.
Polynesian [pel'-i-nî-shan], *a.* Polinesiano o polinesio, perteneciente a la Polinesia.
Polynomial [pel-i-nō'-mi-al], *a.* De varios términos.—*s.* (*Syn.* POLYNOME) 1. Polinomio, cantidad algebraica que contiene varios términos. 2. Vocablo científico que consta de más de tres palabras.
Polyp [pel'-ip], *s.* Pólipo, animalillo gelatinoso, particularmente cuando es compuesto; zoófito.
Polypary [pel'-ip-ę-ri], *s.* Polipero, formación calcárea o córnea, hecha por varios zoófitos; zoófito compuesto.
Polypetalous [pel-i-pet'-al-us], *a.* Polipétalo, de muchas hojas o pétalos.
Polyphonic [pel-i-fen'-ic], *a.* Polifónico.
Polypody [po-lip'-o-di], *s.* (Bot.) Polipodio, planta.
Polypus [pel'-i-pus], *s.* 1. Pólipo, especie de zoófito. *V.* POLYP. 2. Pólipo, especie de tumor blando que se forma en las ventanas de la nariz u otra membrana mucosa.
Polysaccharide [pel-i-sac'-a-raid], *s.* Polisacárido.
Polyscope [pel'-i-scōp], *s.* Poliscopio, instrumento óptico que multiplica los objetos.
Polysyllabic, Polysyllabical [pel-i-si-lab'-ic, al], *a.* Polisílabo, polisilábico, que consta de más de tres sílabas.
Polysyllable [pel-i-sil'-a-bl], *s.* Polisílabo, la voz que consta de muchas sílabas, particularmente de más de tres.
Polysyndeton [pel-i-sin'-de-ten], *s.* (Ret.) Polisíndeton, figura que consiste en emplear repetidamente las conjunciones.
Polytechnic [pel''-i-tec'-nic], *a.* Politécnico, que abraza o practica muchas artes.—*s.* 1. Escuela politécnica, en que se enseñan las artes industriales. 2. Exhibición industrial.
Polytheism [pel'-i-thi-izm], *s.* Politeísmo, la doctrina que enseña que hay más de un Dios.
Polytheist [pōl'-i-thi-ist], *s.* Politeísta, el que admite muchos dioses.
Polytheistic, Polytheistical [pel-i-thi-is'-tic, al], *a.* Politeísta, perteneciente o relativo al politeísmo, o que lo profesa.
Polyvalent [pel-i-vê'-lent], *a.* Polivalente.
Polyvinyl [pel-i-vain'-l], *a.* Polivinílico.
Polyzoan [pel-i-zō'-an], *a.* Polizoico, relativo a los zoófitos compuestos. —*s.* Individuo de un cuerpo compuesto o colonia de pólipos polizoicos, o zoófitos parecidos a las plantas, particularmente los que tienen un tubo digestivo corto.
Pomace [pum'-es], *s.* El desecho de manzanas después de sacar la sidra.
Pomaceous [po-mê'-shus], *a.* 1. Pomáceo, relativo a las pomas o manzanas, o hecho de ellas. 2. (Bot.) Pomáceo, relativo a un pomo, o fruta de pipa, o a los árboles de las rosáceas que producen pomos.
Pomade [po-mêd'], *s.* Pomada, especie de ungüento hecho de varios ingredientes olorosos.
Pomander [po-man'-dęr], *s.* (Ant.) Bola o poma olorosa.
Pomatum [po-mê'-tum], *s.* Pomada para los cabellos.
Pome [pōm], *s.* Pomo, cualquier fruta de pipa; pericarpio carnoso de muchas celdillas en que se hallan las pepitas; como la manzana, el membrillo y la pera.
Pomegranate [pem'-gran-ẹt], *s.* 1 (Bot.) Granado, el árbol que produce la granada. 2. Granada, la fruta del granado.
Pomiferous [po-mif'-ęr-us], *a.* Pomífero, que produce pomas o manzanas.
Pommel [pum'-ęl], *s.* 1. Pomo del arzón de una silla; pomo de la empuñadura de una espada, o de la culata de un cañón. 2. (Arq.) Perilla, bolilla, bala redonda. *Pommel of a sword*, Pomo de una espada. *Pommel of a saddle*, Pomo del arzón de la silla.
Pommel, *va.* Cascar, dar a uno golpes hasta hacerle cardenales.
Pomological [po-mo-lej'-ic-al], *a.* Pomológico, que se refiere a la pomología.
Pomology [po-mel'-o-ji], *s.* Pomología, el arte de cultivar los árboles frutales; el conocimiento y estudio de la producción y conservación de las frutas.
Pomona [pō-mō'-na], *s.* Pomona, diosa de las frutas y huertas.
Pomp [pemp], *s.* Pompa, fausto, vanidad, grandeza, esplendor.
Pompadour [pem'-pa-dūr], *s.* 1. Forma de peinado en que se dispone el cabello cepillándolo directamente hacia arriba desde la frente. 2. Especie de corpiño de escote bajo y cuadrado.
Pompeian [pem-pi'-an o pem-pê'-ian], *a.* Pompeyano, relativo a la ciudad de Pompeya.
Pomposity [pem-pes'-i-ti], *s.* Fausto, pompa, ostentación; afectación en el lenguaje o los modales.
Pompous [pem'-pus], *a.* Pomposo, ostentoso.
Pompously [pem'-pus-li], *adv.* Pomposamente, magníficamente.
Pompousness [pem'-pus-nes], *s.* Esplendor artificioso, pompa.
Poncho [pen'-chō], *s.* Poncho, prenda de vestir.
Pond [pend], *s.* Estanque de agua, pantano, laguna pequeña. *Horse-pond*, Abrevadero. *Fish-pond*, Pecina, vivero, nansa. *Mill-pond*, Represa de molino. *Pond-snail*, Limnea, molusco gasterópodo.
Ponder [pen'-dęr], *va.* Ponderar, pesar, examinar con madurez. *To ponder on*, Considerar, reflexionar.
Ponderable [pen'-dęr-a-bl], *a.* Ponderable, que se puede pesar.
Ponderosity [pen-dęr-es'-i-ti], *s.* 1 Ponderosidad, peso, gravedad. 2. Pesadez, languidez, falta de animación, de viveza; verbosidad. 3. Cosa de peso o de importancia.
Ponderous [pen'-dęr-us], *a.* 1. Ponderoso, pesado. 2. Importante, lo que es de importancia. 3. Impulsivo, lo que impele a la ejecución de algo.
Ponderously [pen'-dęr-us-li], *adv.* Pesadamente.
Ponderousness [pen'-dęr-us-nes], *s.* Ponderosidad, pesadez, peso.
Pondweed [pend'-wid], *s.* (Bot.) Potamogeton.
Pongee [pen-ji'], *s.* Variedad de tela de seda cruda.
Poniard [pen'-yard], *s.* Puñal.
Poniard, *va.* Herir con puñal, dar puñaladas.
Pontage [pent'-ẹj], *s.* Pontazgo, pon-

taje, el derecho que se paga por pasar los puentes y que se destina a repararlos.

Pontee [pen-tī'], *s.* *V.* PONTIL.

Pontiff [pen'-tif], *s.* Pontífice, el Papa.

Pontific, Pontifical [pen-tif'-ic, al], *a.* 1. Pontifical, perteneciente al sumo pontífice y a los obispos y arzobispos; pontificio, perteneciente al pontífice. 2. Que toca y pertenece a los jefes del sacerdocio de cualquier religión. 3. (Des.) El que edifica puentes.

Pontifical, *s.* 1. Pontifical, el libro de ceremonias pontificias y de las funciones episcopales. 2. *pl.* Pontificales, el conjunto o agregado de los ornamentos que sirven al obispo para la celebración de los oficios divinos.

Pontifically [pen-tif'-ic-al-i], *adv.* Pontificalmente, según la práctica y estilo de los obispos o pontífices.

Pontificate [pen-tif'-i-kêt], *s.* Pontificado, papado, la dignidad de pontífice y el tiempo que el pontífice goza de esta dignidad.

Pontil [pen'-til], **Ponty** [pen'-ti], *s.* Pontil, varilla de hierro a propósito para fabricar sopletes de vidrio.

Pontoon, Ponton [pen-tūn'], *s.* 1. Pontón, barco chato y estrecho que sirve para pasar ríos y construir puentes. 2. (Mar.) Chata, barco chato provisto de pescantes, etc. *V.* LIGHTER. 3. Cajón o cilindro impermeable que se emplea para poner a flote una embarcación sumergida. *Pontoon bridge*, Puente de barcas, pontón flotante. 4. (Aer.) Flotador de hidroavión.

Pony [pō'-ni], *s.* 1. Haca, jaco, caballo que no llega a la marca. 2. Entre colegiales, traducción que se emplea en la preparación de las lecciones. 3. Vaso muy pequeño para licor.

Poodle [pū'-dl], *s.* Perro de lanas; perro que tiene el pelo largo y sedoso, negro o blanco por lo común, y que es a menudo muy inteligente.

Pooh [pū o pu], *inter.* ¡Bah! ¡ah! (interjección de desdén).

Pooh-pooh [pū'-pū], *va.* y *vn.* Rechazar con desprecio; burlar, mofar; hablar con desprecio.

Pool [pūl], *va.* Formar una polla, hucha, un fondo o capital común que ha de dividirse según lo convenido. *Pool your issues*, Reconciliar las diferencias de opinión, ponerse de acuerdo sobre asuntos controvertidos.—*vn.* Formar un charco.

Pool, *s.* 1. Charco. 2. Charca. 3. Hoya (de río). 4. Piscina. 5. Billar, trucos. 6. Yacimiento (de petróleo). *Pool reactor*, Reactor nuclear sumergido. *Pool table*, Billar, mesa de trucos.

Pool, *s.* 1. Polla, nombre que se da en algunos juegos de naipes al dinero que se juega. 2. Combinación para especular en fondos o valores públicos. 3. Combinación de sociedades, de compañías de ferrocarriles, etc., para fijar de acuerdo los precios o cotizaciones y para dividirse las ganancias proporcionalmente.

Poop [pūp], *s.* (Mar.) Popa o toldilla. *Poop-royal*, (Mar.) Chopeta.

Poop, *va.* Dar o embestir por la popa; dícese del mar o de otra embarcación.

Poor [pūr], *a.* 1. Pobre, necesitado, menesteroso, mendigo. 2. Pobre, escaso, que no es completo o carece de algo. 3. Pobre, humilde, abatido, de poco valor, de poco mérito. 4. Pobre, infeliz, desdichado, desgraciado. 5. Tacaño, miserable. 6. Pobre, inútil, lo que para nada sirve. 7. Estéril, seco. 8. Falto de vigor, indispuesto, malo, enfermizo. 9. (Fam.) Flaco, seco, enjuto de carnes. 10. Despreciativo, que desprecia; malo. *A poor horse*, Un penco, un caballo de poco valor, que para nada sirve. *A poor opinion of one*, Mala o despreciativa opinión de alguien. *A poor night*, Una mala o incómoda noche. *Poor thing*, Pobrecito, pobrecillo.—*s.* Los pobres. †*Poor-john*, Merluza salada.

Poor farm [pūr farm], *s.* Asilo campestre para los pobres.

Poorly [pūr'-li], *adv.* Pobremente, infelizmente, abatidamente.—*a.* (Fam.) Ligeramente enfermo. *I am poorly*, Estoy malo, no me siento bien. *He is very poorly*, Está bastante malo.

Poorness [pūr'-nes], *s.* 1. Pobreza, necesidad, estrechez, miseria; carestía. 2. Pobreza, escasez o cortedad de ánimo o de otras prendas del alma. 3. Pobreza, esterilidad, falta o escasez de alguna cosa.

Poor-rate [pūr'-rêt], *s.* Contribución, que se paga en Inglaterra para mantener a los pobres.

Poor-spirited [pūr-spir'-it-ed], *a.* Abatido, bajo, ruin, cobarde.

Poor-spiritedness [pūr-spir'-it-ed-nes], *s.* Poquedad, cobardía, bajeza, pusilanimidad.

Pop [pep], *s.* Chasquido, sonido ligero y repentino.

Pop, *va.* 1. Meter o empujar de repente; ofrecer inopinadamente. 2. Hacer producir un sonido repentino y explosivo.—*vn.* Entrar o salir de sopetón; llegar, presentarse de repente. *To pop out* u *off*, Huir precipitadamente, desaparecer repentinamente, evadir una dificultad. *To pop him off*, Dejarle con la palabra en la boca. *To pop the question*, (Fam.) Hacer una declaración de amor; pedir la mano de una mujer.

Popcorn [pep'-cōrn], *s.* 1. Palomitas, rosetas de maíz reventado. 2. Maíz con que se hace lo anterior.

Pope [pōp], *s.* 1. Papa, la cabeza suprema de la Iglesia católica romana. 2. Cualquier sacerdote de la Iglesia griega.

Popedom [pōp'-dum], *s.* Papado, la dignidad de Papa.

Popery [pop'-er-i], *s.* Papismo, nombre que dan los protestantes a la religión católica romana; término despectivo.

Pope's-eye [pōps'-ai], *s.* Nombre vulgar de una glándula situada en medio del muslo de un carnero o buey; estimada como buen bocado. *Pope's-head*, (Ingl.) Escobillón para limpiar bóvedas. *Pope's-nose*, Obispillo o rabadilla de ave.

Popgun [pep'-gun], *s.* Una escopetilla que arroja una bolita o un tapón de corcho con chasquido; (Amer.) cerbatana.

Popinjay [pep'-in-jê], *s.* 1. (Orn.) Loro, papagayo. 2. (Orn.) Picamaderos. 3. Pisaverde, el mozuelo que presume de galán.

Popish [pōp'-ish], *a.* Papal, papista, perteneciente al Papa o a la Iglesia católica romana.

Popishly [pōp'-ish-li], *adv.* A la manera de los papistas o católicos; papalmente, pontificalmente.

Poplar [pep'-lar], *s.* (Bot.) Álamo o chopo temblón, cualquier árbol del género Populus, particularmente el álamo blanco, y el de Italia. *White* o *silver poplar*, Pobo, álamo blanco. *Lombardy poplar*, Álamo de Italia.

Poplin [pep'-lin], *s.* Poplín, popelina, tela listada, lustrosa, que tiene la urdimbre de seda y la trama de estambre; se hacen también variedades inferiores sin seda alguna.

Popliteal [pep-li-tī' al o pep-lit'-e-al], *a.* Poplíteo, perteneciente a la corva. *Syn.* POPLITIC [pep-lit'-ic].

Popper [pep'-er], *s.* 1. Lo que produce chasquido; arma de fuego. 2. Tostador de maíz.

Poppet [pep'-et], *s.* 1. *V.* PUPPET. 2. Válvula de huso. 3. (Mar.) Columna de basada, puntal grueso que se apoya contra el fondo del buque que se va a echar al mar.

Poppy [pep'-i], *s.* (Bot.) 1. Adormidera, amapola, cualquier planta del género Papaver. 2. Una de las plantas de otros géneros de las paveráceas. *California poppy*, Amapola de California, que se llamaba familiarmente entre los mejicanos, "copa de oro" o "torosa;" su flor es de color anaranjado brillante. Eschscholtzia Californica.

Poppycock [pep'-i-cec], *s.* (Ger. E. U.) Tontería presumida, majadería.

Poppy-head [pep'-i-hed], *s.* Cabeza de adormidera.

Populace [pep'-yu-les], *s.* Populacho, la plebe, el cuerpo principal del pueblo; a menudo, en sentido despectivo, el pueblo bajo, gentuza.

Popular [pep'-yu-lar], *a.* 1. Popular, perteneciente al pueblo o a la plebe. 2. Popular, amado del pueblo. 3. Popular, lo que es común en el pueblo o entre el populacho. *Popular applause*, Aura popular.

Popularity [pep-yu-lar'-i-ti], *s.* Popularidad, la aceptación y aplauso que uno goza entre el pueblo.

Popularize [pep'-yu-lar-aiz], *va.* Popularizar, propagar entre el pueblo, acreditar a una persona o cosa en el concepto público.

Popularly [pep'-yu-lar-li], *adv.* Popularmente.

Populate [pep'-yu-lêt], *vn.* Poblar, multiplicar.

Population [pep-yu-lê'-shun], *s.* 1. Población, el número total de habitantes de un lugar o una extensión dada de territorio. 2. Población, acción de poblar, de proveer de habitantes, de multiplicarlos.

Populous [pep'-yu-lus], *a.* Populoso.

Populously [pep'-yu-lus-li], *adv.* Con mucha gente.

Populousness [pep'-yu-lus-nes], *s.* La abundancia de población; población, el estado de cualquier país en cuanto al número de sus habitantes.

Porcate [pōr'-kêt], *a.* Surcado; con surcos longitudinales.

Porcelain [pōr'-se-lên], *s.* Porcelana, china, loza fina y translúcida.

Porcelain-shell [pōr'-se-lên-shel], *s.* Porcelana, concha de Venus, un marisco.

Porcelane, Porcelaneous [pōr'-se-lên, pōr-se-lê'-ne-us], *a.* De porcelana, o parecido a ella.

Porch [pōrch], *s.* Pórtico, vestíbulo, entrada, portal.

Porcine [pōr'-sin], *a.* Porcuno, propio del puerco.
Porcupine [pōr'-kiu-pain], *s.* Puerco espín, erizo grande, animal roedor.
Pore [pōr], *s.* Poro.
Pore, *vn.* Ojear, mirar con atención, tener los ojos fijos en algo.
Poriness [pōr'-i-nes], *s.* Porosidad.
Pork [pōrc], *s.* 1. Carne de puerco. *Fresh pork*, Tocino fresco. *Salt pork*, Tocino salado. 2. (Ant.) Cochino, puerco, cerdo. *Pork-chop*, Chuleta, costilla de cerdo. *Corned pork*, Carne de puerco salada.
Pork-eater [pōrk'-īt-ẹr], *s.* Comedor de carne de puerco.
Porker [pōrk'-ẹr], *s.* Puerco, cochino, cerdo, marrano.
Pornographic [pēr-no-graf'-ic], *a.* Pornográfico, obsceno.
Pornography [pēr-neg'-ra-fi], *s.* Pornografía, obscenidad.
Porosity [po-res'-i-ti], **Porousness** [pō'-rus-nes], *s.* 1. Porosidad, la propiedad o calidad de poroso. 2. Poro.
Porous [pēr'-us o pō'-rus], *a.* Poroso.
Porphyritic, Porphyritical [per-fi-rit'-ic, al], *a.* Porfídico, que contiene pórfido o presenta la apariencia de tal; que contiene cristales relativamente grandes en una base vidriosa o finamente granulada.
Porphyry [per'-fi-ri], *s.* Pórfido, una roca ígnea cualquiera con base que encierra cristales de feldespato o de cuarzo.
Porpoise, Porpus [pēr'-pus], *s.* 1. Puerco marino o marsopa, cetáceo del género Phocæna; tiene unos cinco pies de longitud. 2. Marsuino, cetáceo pequeño, particularmente del género delfín.
Porraceous [per-rē'-shus], *a.* Verdoso.
Porrect [per-rect'], *a.* (Zool.) Extendido horizontalmente.
Porridge [per'-ij], *s.* 1. Gachas, puches, alimento hecho con harina cocida en agua o leche hasta que tome consistencia. 2. Potaje, caldo o guisado de legumbres. *Milk-porridge*, Sopa de leche. *Porridge-dish*, Sopera.
Porridge-pot [per'-ij-pet], *s.* Marmita, cazuela.
Porringer [per'-in-jẹr], *s.* Escudilla, vasija algo ligera que tiene los lados verticales y algunas veces, asas.
Port [pōrt], *s.* 1. Puerto; lugar de entrada y salida para las embarcaciones. *To touch at a port*, Hacer escala. *Free port*, Puerto franco o libre de derechos. *Bar-port*, Puerto con barra. *Close-port*, Puerto cerrado. 2. Porta, portañola, ventanilla; abertura en el costado de un buque, sea para un cañón ó para dar luz y aire. *V.* PORT-HOLE. *Ballast-ports*, Portas de alastrar. *Port-sill*, Batiporte, batiente. *Light-ports*, Ventanillas. *Port-tackle*, Aparejuelo de las portas. 3. Puerta. 4. (Mec.) Porta, orificio para el paso de un flúido motor. 5. (Mar.) Babor. *Hard a port*, A babor todo. *The ship heels to port*, El buque cae sobre babor. 6. Porte, presencia, continente, aire o garbo de una persona. 7. Vino de Oporto. 8. Porte, la capacidad de la nave para el transporte. *Port-fire*, Lanzafuego, botafuego.
Port, *va.* y *vn.* 1. Poner, o andar a babor. 2. (Mil.) Llevar un fusil diagonalmente con relación al cuerpo. *Port the helm*, A babor el timón.
Portable [pōrt'-a-bl], *a.* 1. Manual, portátil. *Portable typewriter*, Máquina de escribir portátil. 2. Sufrible, llevadero.
Portableness [pōrt-a-bl-nes], *s.* La propiedad de ser manual, portátil o llevadero.
Portage [pōrt'-ẹj], *s.* 1. Porte, lo que se paga por llevar alguna cosa de un lugar a otro. 2. Conducción, transporte, acarreo, porte de barquichuelos y víveres desde un cuerpo navegable de agua a otro. 3. Carga, cargazón, lo que se transporta o lleva.
Portal [pōr'-tal], *s.* (Arq.) 1. Portal, portada, particularmente si es grande e imponente. 2. Construcción arquitectónica que incluye las entradas y portadas de una gran iglesia, etc.
Port-caustic [pert-cōs'-tic], *s.* Portacauterio, cajita en que se lleva el cauterio o que sirve para aplicarlo.
Port-crayon [pōrt-crē'-ẹn], *s.* Lapicero, tubo metálico en que se pone el lápiz común o el de pastel.
Portcullis [port-cul'-is], *s.* (Fort.) Rastrillo formado por una reja fuerte y tupida, que se sube y baja.
Porte (The) [pōrt], *s.* La Puerta otomana; el gobierno del imperio turco.
Portemonnaie [pōrt'-mẹn-nē''], *s.* Portamonedas, pequeña bolsa o estuche con cierre, para llevar dinero. (Fr.)
Portend [pōr-tend'], *va.* Pronosticar, anunciar o indicar un acontecimiento que está para suceder; presagiar.
Portent [pōr-tent' o pōr'-tent], *s.* Portento, señal que indica lo que va a suceder, y particularmente prodigio que trae consigo señales de mal agüero.
Portentous [pōr-ten'-tus], *a.* 1. Portentoso, ominoso, azaroso, de mal agüero. 2. Prodigioso, portentoso, monstruoso, espantoso; que causa pasmo o terror.
Porter [pōr'-tẹr], *s.* 1. Portador, porteador, el que lleva o trae de una parte a otra; mozo de cordel, mandadero. 2. Portero. *Porter's lodge*, Portería. 3. Portador, cualquier cosa que se usa para llevar o soportar. 4. Una especie de cerveza fuerte de color pardo que posee propiedades tónicas.
Porterage [pōr'-tẹr-ẹj], *s.* 1. Empleo u oficio de un mozo de cordel. 2. Porte, porteo, precio de transporte que se paga a un mozo de cordel.
Porterhouse steak [pōr'-tẹr-haus stêk], *s.* Variedad de bistec de solomillo grueso.
Portfolio [pōrt-fō'-li-o], *s.* 1. Cartera, bolsa en que se guardan materiales de escribir, dibujos, grabados, etc. 2. (Fig.) Cartera, oficio de un ministro de Estado.
Port-hole [pōrt'-hōl], *s.* Ventanilla abierta en el costado de un buque para dar luz y aire; porta, portañola, tronera.
Portico [pōr'-ti-cō], *s.* Pórtico, especie de portal cubierto y fundado sobre columnas, que se construye a la entrada de un edificio; soportal, atrio.
Porticoed [pōr'-ti-cōd], *a.* Provisto de pórtico, o de pórticos.
Portière [pōr-tiār'], *s.* Cortina de puerta, cortinaje que sirve en vez de puerta o para adorno. (Fr.)
Portion [pōr'-shun], *s.* 1. Porción, parte. 2. Cuota, parte fija y determinada. 3. La parte de herencia que pertenece a cada uno de los hijos en los bienes que quedaron de sus padres. 4. Dote, la hacienda que lleva la mujer cuando se casa.
Portion, *va.* 1. Partir, dividir, repartir, distribuir, asignar una parte. 2. Dotar.
Portioner [pōr'-shun-ẹr], *s.* Repartidor.
Portionless [pōr'-shun-les], *a.* Sin porción, y particularmente, sin dote.
Portliness [pōrt'-li-nes], *s.* Porte majestuoso, aire de dignidad de una persona.
Portly [pōrt'-li], *a.* 1. Corpulento, rollizo, gordiflón, algo grueso. 2. Majestuoso, serio, grave.
Portman [pōrt'-man], *s.* Habitante de alguno de los cinco puertos del canal de Inglaterra.
Portmanteau [pōrt-man'-to], *s.* Portamanteo, maleta ligera.
Portrait [pōr'-trêt], *s.* Retrato, pintura, efigie o fotografía que representa la imagen de alguna persona; figuradamente, descripción exacta de una persona.
Portrait-painter [por'-trêt-pênt'-ẹr], *s.* Retratista.
Portraiture [pōr'-trê-tiūr o chur], *s.* 1. Retrato, pintura, bosquejo. 2. Representación de un objeto.
Portray [pōr-trê'], *va.* Retratar, formar la imagen de alguna cosa; representar natural y vivamente, ya dibujando, pintando, esculpiendo, o describiendo con palabras; pintar, hacer un retrato.
Portrayal [pōr-trê'-al], *s.* Representación, delineación, retrato.
Portreeve [pōrt'-rīv], *s.* Antiguamente en Inglaterra alcalde de una ciudad marítima.
Portress [pōr'-tres], *sf.* Portera.
Portuguese [pōr'-chu-gīz o por-chu-gīs'], *a.* Portugués, de Portugal.—*s.* 1. Portugués, portuguesa, habitante de Portugal. 2. Portugués, idioma de Portugal. *Portuguese man-of-war*, Fisalia, acalefo de los mares tropicales.
Portulaca [pōr-tiu-lê'-ca ó pōr-tiu-lak'-a], *s.* Género de plantas, tipo de la familia de las portulacáceas, que incluye la verdolaga; una planta cualquiera de este género.
Pose [pōz], *va.* 1. Tomar o hacer tomar una actitud; poner o colocar en cierta actitud o postura, como hace un pintor o escultor. 2. Proponer, afirmar una proposición.—*vn.* Ponerse o colocarse en actitud o postura dadas.
Pose [pōz], *va.* Parar, confundir, dejar a uno parado sin que sepa qué hacerse; acorralar a uno o dejarle sin salida o respuesta.
Pose [pōz], *s.* Postura, posición del cuerpo entero, o de una parte de él; particularmente, actitud o postura que ha de reproducirse en un retrato o estatua.
Poser [pōz'-ẹr], *s.* 1. Cuestión o problema difícil; argumento perentorio que reduce al silencio. 2. En algunas escuelas inglesas, examinador; el que confunde o acorrala.
Posit [pez'-it], *va.* 1. En lógica, afirmar, proponer como principio o hecho. 2. Disponer, colocar, poner con relación a otros cuerpos.
Position [po-zish'-un], *s.* 1. Posición, el modo en que está colocada alguna cosa; positura, postura, situación. 2. Postura, actitud, disposición de las partes del cuerpo. 3. Esfera o radio de influencia, trabajo, o deber; situación elevada. 4. El acto de afirmar un principio o proposi-

ción; proposición, aserto. 5. (Mat.) Procedimiento para hallar el valor de una cantidad no conocida asumiendo una o más hipótesis; regla de falsa posición.

Positional [po-zish'-un-al], *a.* Perteneciente a la posición, postura o situación de una cosa.

Positive [pez'-i-tiv], *a.* 1. Positivo, real, verdadero; que existe; opuesto a negativo. 2. Absoluto, que no tiene relación con otra cosa; inherente; opuesto a relativo. 3. Explícito, formal, preciso, enfático; opuesto a implicado. 4. Prescrito por autoridad competente; imperativo (opuesto a discrecional); expreso, escrito, dependiente de autoridad, convenido (opuesto a natural). 5. Cierto, seguro, asegurado. 6. Terco, porfiado. 7. Primario, principal (opuesto a negativo); que lleva el signo de más +, mayor que cero. 8. Positiva; dícese de la electricidad que tiene una potencia relativamente alta. 9. (Foto.) Positivo, que tiene las luces y las sombras en su relación natural en vez de invertidas. 10. (Gram.) Positivo, del grado positivo.—*s.* 1. Afirmación, lo que es cierto. 2. Lo positivo, lo que se puede conocer por los sentidos. 3. Ley absoluta, imperativa. 4. Prueba positiva, cuadro que presenta las luces y sombras como en la naturaleza. 5. (Gram.) Grado positivo de comparación. 6. (Elec.) Plancha, polo, etc., positivos.

Positively [pez'-i-tiv-li], *adv.* Positivamente, absolutamente; perentoriamente.

Positiveness [pez'-i-tiv-nes], **Positivity** [pez-i-tiv'-i-ti], *s.* 1. El estado de lo que es positivo o absoluto. 2. Porfía, terquedad, obstinación, contumacia.

Positivism [pez'-i-tiv-izm], *s.* 1. Positivismo, calidad de atenerse a lo positivo. 2. Positivismo, sistema de filosofía que sólo admite lo evidente o claramente demostrado. 3. Certeza, o la aserción de la certeza, en el conocimiento.

Positivist [pez'-i-tiv-ist], *s.* Positivista, partidario del sistema filosófico del positivismo.

Positron [pez'-i-tren], *s.* (Elec.) Positrón.

Posologic, Posological [po-so-lej'-ic, al], *a.* Posológico, perteneciente a la posología.

Posology [po-sel'-o-ji], *s.* 1. Posología, parte de la terapéutica que trata de las dosis en que deben administrarse los medicamentos. 2. (Mat.) Doctrina o ciencia de la cuantidad.

Posse [pes'-e], *s.* 1. Posibilidad. 2. *V.* Posse Comitatus. 3. (Vulg.) Gentío.

Posse Comitatus [pes'-e com-i-tê'-tus], *s.* El número de alguaciles u otras personas, que el alguacil mayor (*sheriff*) tiene autoridad de juntar para evitar desórdenes, tumultos, etc.

Possess [pez-zes' o pes-ses'], *va.* 1. Poseer, gozar, tener en su poder. 2. Tomar, apoderarse, hacerse dueño de algo. 3. Señorear, dominar. 4. Hacer adquirir o poner en posesión a uno de lo que no tiene. 5. Tener a uno poseído o poseso algún espíritu infernal.

Possessed [pez-zest'], *pp.* Poseso, poseído. *One possessed,* Energúmeno.

Possession [pez-zesh'-un], *s.* 1. Posesión, el acto de poseer y la misma cosa poseída. 2. Propiedad, riquezas, bienes. 3. Posesión, el estado del poseso o poseído, del que se halla bajo la influencia del demonio.

Possessive [pez-zes'-iv], *a.* Posesivo; poseyente, que denota posesión. *Possessive case,* Caso posesivo en la gramática inglesa, que corresponde al caso genitivo. Su signo es el apóstrofo (').

Possessor [pez-zes'-er], *s.* Poseedor, el que tiene la posesión de alguna cosa.

Posset [pes'-et], *s.* Leche cortada con vino o con un ácido, azucarada, mezclada con especias, y a menudo espesada con pan.

Possibility [pes-i-bil'-i-ti], *s.* Posibilidad, lo posible; cosa posible, contingencia.

Possible [pes'-i-bl], *a.* Posible.

Possibly [pes'-i-bli], *adv.* 1. Posiblemente. 2. Quizá, quizás, acaso, por ventura.

Possum [pes'-um], *s.* (Fam.) *V.* Opossum. *To play possum,* Desatenderse, no hacer caso; por alusión a la costumbre de la zorra mochilera de fingirse muerta cuando se alarma mucho o se ve cogida.

Post [pōst], *s.* 1. Posta, correo, estafeta, el sistema de transportar la correspondencia ordinaria. 2. Propio, mensajero que se envía con alguna carta de una parte a otra. 3. Puesto, paraje señalado para las operaciones militares. 4. Puesto, empleo. dignidad. 5. Poste, un pilar de piedra o madera. 6. Situación, asiento. 7. Especie, tamaño, del papel de escribir. *To travel by post,* Correr la posta o ir en posta. *Foot-post,* Propio, correo de a pie. *Penny post,* Cartero, el que reparte por las casas las cartas del correo. *To be tossed from pillar to post,* Andar de Herodes a Pilatos. *I took my post,* Tomé mi puesto, fuí a mi puesto. *By return of post,* A vuelta de correo.—*a.* †Sobornado, ganado para cometer una acción ruin. (Ant.) Pronto, rápido. *Postboy,* Postillón. *Post-chaise, post-coach,* Silla o coche de posta. *Post-horse,* Caballo de posta. *Post-house,* Casa de postas donde se tienen y cuidan los caballos de posta. *Post-card, V. Postal card. Post-note, V. Postal note. Post-road,* Camino de posta o correo. *Post-town,* El pueblo donde hay administración de correos.

Post, *adv.* Con rapidez, por la posta, de prisa.

Post, *vn.* Ir en posta o correr la posta.—*va.* 1. Apostar, situar, colocar en algún puesto o sitio; dar aviso en un lugar público; hacer saber; anunciar. 2. Cartelear, poner carteles infamatorios. 3. Echar al correo o a la estafeta. 4. (Com.) Pasar los asientos de un libro al libro mayor; hacer los asientos de las operaciones mercantiles. 5. (Fam.) Informar, dar a entender, proveer de informes.

Postage [pōst'-êj], *s.* Porte de correos, precio fijo para el transporte de correos. *Postage stamp,* Sello de correo, sello de franqueo. (Amer.) Estampilla. *Postage meter,* Medidor de franqueo.

Postal [pōs'-tal], *a.* Postal, perteneciente al correo o a las cartas. *Postal card,* Tarjeta postal. *Postal convention,* Convenio postal entre dos países. *Postal note,* Billete de correo, pagadero al portador, por una suma menor de cinco pesos. *Postal order,* (Gr. Bret.) Orden postal, billete semejante al anterior, pero cuyo importe está impreso en el mismo documento.

Post-communion [pōst-com-miūn'-yun], *s.* El oficio o rezo divino después de la comunión.

Post-date [pōst-dêt'], *va.* Posfechar, poner fecha posterior a la verdadera.

Post-date, *s.* Posfecha, fecha posterior a la verdadera.

Postdiluvial, Postdiluvian [pōst-di-lū'-vi-al, an], *s.* y *a.* Postdiluviano.

Poster [pōst'-er], *s.* 1. Cartel. 2. Colocador o fijador de carteles. 3. Correo; el que viaja en posta o de prisa.

Posterior [pes-tī'-ri-er], *a.* Posterior, trasero, que está detrás o viene después. *Posteriors,* Nalgas, partes posteriores.

Posteriority [pes-tī-ri-er'-i-ti], *s.* Posterioridad.

Posterity [pes-ter'-i-ti], *s.* Posteridad, la raza, prole que proviene del mismo ascendiente; descendientes, hijos; también, la descendencia o generación venidera.

Postern [pōs'-tern], *s.* 1. Puerta trasera, entrada particular; puerta pequeña, postigo. 2. (Fort.) Postigo, poterna.

Post-existence [pōst-eg-zis'-tens], *s.* Existencia venidera.

Postfix [pōst'-fix], *va.* Añadir un sufijo.—*s.* Sufijo; letra, sílaba o palabra añadida al fin de otra.

Postgraduate [pōst-grad'-yu-êt], *s.* y *a.* Posgraduado.

Post-haste [pōst-hêst'], *a.* Hecho a toda prisa, como la del correo.—*s.* Diligencia, presteza en ir y venir, como la del correo.—*adv.* A rienda suelta.

Posthumous [pes'-tiu-mus o chu-mus], *a.* 1. Póstumo, nacido después de la muerte del padre; algunas veces, extraído del cadáver de la madre. 2. Póstumo, publicado después de la muerte del autor.

Postil [pes'-til], *s.* Postila, apostilla, la glosa o nota breve puesta al margen de algún impreso o manuscrito, particularmente de la Sagrada Escritura.

Postilion [pōs-til'-yun], *s.* 1. Delantero, sota, hablando de cocheros. 2. (Des.) Postillón, el que guía una silla de posta y el mozo de posta.

Postliminium [pōst-li-min'-i-um, **Postliminy** [post-lim'-i-ni], *s.* Postliminio, ficción del derecho romano, por la cual los que en la guerra quedaban prisioneros de los enemigos, recobraban los derechos de ciudadanos al regresar a la ciudad.

Postlude [pōst'-lūd o liūd], *s.* Postludio, pieza para el órgano que se toca después del oficio divino.

Postman [pōst'-man], *s.* Cartero; correo.

Postmark [pōst'-mārk], *s.* Matasellos.

Postmaster [pōst'-mas-ter], *s.* Administrador de correos, director de correos.

Postmaster-general [pōst'-mas-ter-jen'-er-al], *s.* Director general de correos.

Post-meridian [pōst-me-rid'-i-an], *a.* Postmeridiano, de la tarde; comúnmente se abrevia en P.M.

Post mortem [pōst mōr'-tem], *adv.* (Lat.) Después de la muerte. ***Post-mortem,*** *s.* Necropsia, autopsia.

Post-nuptial [pōst-nup'-shal], *a.* Hecho o sucedido después del matrimonio.
Post office [pōst ef'-is], *s.* Casa de correos, correo. *Post-office box,* Apartado postal o casilla de correo. *Post-office branch,* Estafeta, sucursal de correos.
Post-paid [pōst'-pêd], *a.* Franco, franco de porte ; porte pagado.
Postpone [pōst-pōn'], *va.* 1. Diferir, suspender. 2. Posponer, colocar alguna cosa en lugar inferior, apreciarla menos que otra, estimar menos que, tener en menos.
Postprandial [pōst-pran'-di-al], *a.* Referente al tiempo que sigue a la comida principal ; que sucede después de comer.
Postscript [pōst'-script], *s.* 1. Posdata, la cláusula o capítulo que se añade a la carta ya escrita. 2. (En los papeles públicos) Alcance.
Postulant [pes'-chu-lant o tiu-lant], *s.* 1. Postulante, el que hace una petición. 2. Novicio, postulador que quiere hacerse sacerdote o religioso.
Postulate [pes'-tiu-lêt], *va.* 1. Postular, pedir para prelado de una iglesia a un sujeto que según derecho no puede ser elegido. 2. Admitir una cosa sin pruebas.
Postulate, *s.* 1. Postulado, principio tan claro que no necesita prueba ni demostración. 2. (Mat.) Admisión de un primer principio para establecer una demostración.
Postulation [pes-tiu-lê'-shun], *s.* 1. Postulación, el acto de postular. 2. †Petición, instancia, súplica. 3 Suposición que no necesita prueba, acción de suponer alguna cosa como verdadera, o un hecho.
Posture [pes'-chur], *s.* 1. Postura, modo de tener o poner el cuerpo. 2. Positura, pie, estado, disposición, la situación buena o mala en que uno se halla con respecto a sus negocios o fortuna.
Posture, *va.* Colocar, poner alguna cosa en un paraje y postura particular.
Posture-master [pes'-chur-mas'-tẹr], *s.* El maestro que enseña el modo de poner el cuerpo en ciertas posturas estudiadas.
Posy [pō'-zi], *s.* 1. Ramillete de flores. 2. Mote o cifra en un anillo o en otra cosa, particularmente en versos. (Abrev. de *poesy.*)
Pot [pet], *s.* 1. Marmita ; olla ; puchero ; vaso más profundo que ancho. 2. Pote, taza de metal para beber. 3. La cantidad contenida en una olla. 4. Apuesta, hucha, puesta, lo que se pone al juego. 5. Mucho dinero, una gran suma. *Flower-pot,* Tiesto, florero. *Melting-pot,* Crisol. *To go to pot,* Ir al crisol, estar arruinado, ir hacia la destrucción. *To keep the pot boiling,* (1) Mantenerse en actividad. (2) Procurar los medios de vivir. *Pot-companion,* Compañero de taberna. *Pot-hanger,* Llares. *Pot-herb,* Hortaliza. *Pot-lid,* Cobertera de olla, tapadera de pote o de marmita. *Pot-luck,* Comida ordinaria ; equivale en castellano a la frase "hacer penitencia ;" comer lo que haya en una casa donde no se esperaban convidados. *To take pot-luck,* Hacer penitencia. *Pot-valiant,* Valeroso a fuerza de beber licores fuertes : dícese del que es valiente sólo cuando está bebido.
Pot, *va.* 1. Cocer en una olla o marmita. 2. Poner en tiestos con tierra. 3. Cerrar, preservar o conservar en marmitas para purgar o limpiar. 4. (Ger.) Procurar, buscar, como se hace en la caza.—*vn.* 1. Tirar (contra una persona o cosa). 2. Beber, achisparse.
Potable [pō'-ta-bl], *a.* Potable, que se puede beber.
Potash [pet'-ash], *s.* 1. Potasa, álcali que se obtiene de las cenizas de los vegetales. 2. Potasio hidratado (KOH), cuerpo blanco, sólido, licuescente, muy alcalino y de propiedades cáusticas.
Potassium [po-tas'-i-um], *s.* Potasio, metal blanco descubierto por Humphry Davy en la potasa.
Potation [pō-tê'-shun], *s.* 1. Acción de beber ; bebida ; trago. 2. Desarreglo en el beber.
Potato [po-tê'-tō], *s.* Patata, papa, bulbo de la raíz que echa la planta del mismo nombre. Solanum tuberosum. *Sweet* o *Spanish potato,* Batata, o patata dulce o de Málaga. (Cuba) Boniato. (Mex.) Camote. *Potato-beetle, potato-bug,* Doríforo, insecto coleóptero de los crisomélidos, amarillento, con diez rayas sobre los élitros ; se alimenta de las hojas de la patata y es muy destructivo. Doryphora decemlineata. *Potato-blight, potato-rot,* Enfermedad de las patatas, a veces aniquiladora, como en 1845 en Irlanda.
Potbellied [pet'-bel-id], *a.* Panzudo, ventrudo, barrigudo.
Potbelly [pet'-bel-i], *s.* Barrigón, barriga grande.
Potboiler [pet'-beil'-ẹr], *s.* Libro, pintura, etc. hecho de prisa únicamente con propósitos pecuniarios.
Poteen [po-tīn'], *s.* Aguardiente de granos de Irlanda (whisky), que se hace ilegalmente. (Ir.)
Potency [pō'-ten-si], *s.* Potencia, fuerza ; poder, influjo, autoridad.
Potent [pō'-tent], *a.* 1. Potente, poderoso, fuerte ; que tiene fuerza física, vigor ; que tiene fuerza moral, convincente. 2. Poderoso, eficaz, influyente, que ejerce gran autoridad.
Potentate [pō'-ten-têt], *s.* Potentado.
Potential [pō-ten'-shal], *a.* 1. Potencial, posible, existente en potencia, pero no real. 2. Virtual, capaz de existir, pero no existente todavía. 3. (Fís.) Potencial, existente por razón de su posición, en contraposición al movimiento ; dícese de la energía. 4. (Gram.) Potencial, que indica la posibilidad o el poder. 5. Eficaz, potente, poderoso.—*s.* 1. Cosa posible o virtual. 2. (Gram.) El modo potencial. 3. Energía potencial, potencia motriz, fuerza capaz de poner en movimiento un cuerpo o una máquina. *Potential mode* (o *mood*), El modo como que se emplean los auxiliares *may, can, must, should, would,* con un infinitivo.
Potentiality [pō-ten-shi-al'-i-ti], *s.* Potencialidad, la mera capacidad de la potencia independiente del acto.
Potentially [pō-ten'-shal-i], *adv.* Potencialmente, virtualmente.
Potently [pō'-tent-li], *adv.* Potentemente, poderosamente.
Potentness [pō'-tent-nes], *s.* Potencia, poder.
Pother [pedh'-ẹr], *s.* Baraúnda, alboroto, bullicio.
Pother, *va.* y *vn.* Atormentar, fastidiar, molestar ; alborotar sin substancia ; poner en desorden.
Potholder [pet'-hōld'-ẹr], *s.* Portaollas.
Pothook [pet'-huc], *s.* 1. Llares, aparato para suspender encima del fuego los calderos y marmitas. 2. Garabato, las letras o escritos mal formados.
Potion [pō'-shun], *s.* Poción, brebaje, pócima, bebida medicinal.
Potpie [pet'-pai], *s.* Torta o pastel de carne y verduras.
Potpourri [pō-pū-rī'], *s.* Menjurje o menjunje ; olla podrida. (Fr.)
Potsherd [pet'-shẹrd], *s.* Tiesto, casco, pedazo de una vasija de barro rota.
Pot shot [pet' shet], *s.* Tiro o ataque a mansalva o que viola las reglas del deporte.
Pottage [pet'-êj], *s.* Potaje.
Potter [pet'-ẹr], *s.* Alfarero. *Potter's clay,* Arcilla, barro, tierra de alfareros. *Potter's ware,* Alfarería, vasijas de barro.
Pottern-ore [pet'-ẹrn-ōr], *s.* Vidriado, mineral que se vitrifica por medio del calor ; término anticuado.
Pottery [pet'-ẹr-i], *s.* 1. Alfarería o alfar, fábrica de vasijas de barro. 2. Alfarería, arte de construir vasijas de barro. 3. Efectos de alfarería, vajilla de barro.
Pottle [pet'-l], *s.* 1. Pote, jarro, vaso de beber. 2. Azumbre, medida líquida de cuatro cuartillos. 3. Cesta o cesto pequeño para frutas. *Pottle-bellied,* Panzudo, barrigudo, corpulento.
Pouch [pauch], *s.* 1. Saco pequeño, bolsillo, faltriquera. 2. (Zool.) Bolsa, órgano semejante a un saco para contener huevos o hijuelos. 3. (Bot.) Silícula ; cualquier bolsa o saquillo. *Mail-pouch,* Mala, valija del correo.
Pouch, *va.* 1. Embolsar, meter en el bolsillo. 2. Tragar o engullir.—*vn.* Hacer pucheritos. (Amer.) Jirimiquear. *V. To* POUT.
‖**Poulp** [pūlp], *s.* Pulpo, molusco octópodo. *V.* OCTOPUS.
Poulterer [pōl'-tẹr-ẹr], *s.* Pollero, gallinero.
Poultice [pōl'-tis], *s.* Cataplasma, emplasto.
Poultice, *va.* Poner una cataplasma.
Poultry [pōl'-tri], *s.* Aves caseras o de corral colectivamente, como gallinas, capones, pollos, pavos, etc. *Poultry-yard,* El corral donde se crían las aves caseras.
Pounce [pauns], *s.* 1. Acción de asir con las garras. 2. Garra del ave de rapiña. 3. Grasilla, goma sandáraca reducida a polvo. 4. Cisquero o muñequilla de carbón molido para estarcir algún dibujo ; hoy día se llama *stamping-powder.*
Pounce, *va.* 1. Horadar, agujerear. 2. Asir con las garras. 3. Polvorear con grasilla. 4. Alisar (un sombrero) frotándolo.
Pound [paund], *s.* 1. Libra, peso que consta de doce (*troy*) o diez y seis onzas. 2. Libra esterlina, la cantidad de veinte chelines de Inglaterra, o $4.86 en América o 25.20 pesetas. 3. Corral de concejo ; corral en que se encierra el ganado perdido o embargado. 4. Depósito. *Pound-foolish,* Gastador, derrochador. *Pound-breach,* Traslado ilegal del ganado encerrado en el corral de concejo.
Pound, *va.* 1. Golpear pesada y repetidamente ; machacar o moler. 2. Encerrar, poner en encierro o depósito. *V.* IMPOUND.

Poundage [paund'-éj], *s.* 1. Tanto por libra; derecho de tanto por libra de peso. 2. Costo de rescatar el ganado acorralado por otros. 3. Acto de acorralar el ganado perdido o embargado.

Poundcake [paund kêk], *s.* Pastel o torta hechos con una libra de cada ingrediente.

Pounder [paund'-ęr], *s.* 1. Golpeador. 2. Criada, pala de lavar la ropa. 3. Cualquiera cosa que toma su denominación del número de libras que tiene. *A thirty-six pounder*, Cañón de a treinta y seis. 4. Triturador, bocarte de un molino para minerales. 5. (Ingl.) El que paga un alquiler de cierto número determinado de libras.

Poundkeeper, Poundmaster [paund'-kīp'-ęr, mqs-tęrl, *s.* Empleado que tiene a su cargo un corral de concejo.

Pound-weight [paund'-wêt], *s.* El peso de una libra.

Pour [pōr], *va.* 1. Echar o vaciar líquidos de una parte a otra. 2. Emitir, arrojar, echar fuera alguna cosa continuadamente. 3. Desembolsar pródigamente; dejar caer, desparramar copiosamente.—*vn.* 1. Fluir, correr con rapidez. 2. Caer, descender, precipitarse profusamente; llover. 3. Salir en masa, venir en muchedumbres, llegar a montones. 4. Esparcirse grandemente. *The northern hordes poured over Italy*, Las hordas del norte cayeron sobre Italia. *The ants poured out of the hill*, Las hormigas salieron a montones del hormiguero. *To pour out of one vessel into another*, Trasegar líquidos; vaciar los líquidos de una parte a otra. *To pour down*, Llover a cántaros, diluviar.

Pourer [pōr'-ęr], *s.* Trasegador, vaciador.

Pout [paut], *s.* 1. Mueca que se hace contrayendo los labios, señal de ceño o mal humor. 2. Abadejo; mustela de río. Gadus luscus.

Pout, *vn.* Poner mal gesto, ponerse ceñudo, enfurruñarse, amohinarse. (Fam.) Estar de hocico. *Pouting fellow*, Hombre ceñudo; cara de vinagre.

Pouter [paut'-ęr], *s.* 1. Hombre ceñudo, que pone mala cara. 2. Guturosa, buchona; paloma de cuello grueso; paloma que tiene la costumbre de dilatar la parte anterior del cuello.

Poverty [pov'-ęr-ti], *s.* 1. Pobreza, necesidad, estrechez, indigencia, miseria. 2. Falta de substancia, de elementos o de propiedades. 3. Aridez, insuficiencia; tibieza (de sentimientos).

Powder [pau'-dęr], *s.* 1. Polvo, colección de partículas sueltas de una substancia seca. 2. Polvos de tocador. 3. Pólvora. *Powder-box*, Polvera. *Powder room*, 1. Salón-tocador para señoras. 2. Pañol de pólvora, Santabárbara.

Powder, *va.* 1. Pulverizar, polvificar, moler, desmenuzar y reducir a polvos alguna cosa. 2. Polvorear, esparcir polvo sobre alguna cosa. 3. Salar, rociar con sal.

Powdering [pau'-dęr-ing], *s.* Polvoreamiento, empolvamiento, el acto de pulverizar o el de polvorear; el polvo esparcido.

Powdering-tub [pau'-dęr-ing-tub], *s.* Saladero, la vasija en que se sala la carne.

Powdery [pau'-dęr-i], *a.* Polvoriento, lleno o cubierto de polvo; desmenuzable.

Power [pau'-ęr], *s.* 1. Facultad, poder, potencia, virtud de hacer alguna cosa. 2. Potencia motriz; fuerza realmente empleada; pujanza. 3. Poder, potestad, dominio, imperio, autoridad, jurisdicción; también, documento legal que confiere tal poder o autoridad. 4. Gran fuerza que produce su efecto. 5. Potencia, el producto que resulta de la multiplicación continua de un número por sí mismo. 6. Poder, las fuerzas militares de un Estado. 7. Potentado, potestad. 8. El estado o cuerpo político de una nación importante e influyente; potencia. 9. Potencia, fuerza mecánica, cualquier forma de energía capaz de hacer trabajo. 10. (Ópt.) Potencia, facultad de aumentar que tiene un lente. 11. Ente celeste, divinidad. 12. (Vulg.) Una gran cantidad, gran número, muchedumbre. *Power-house*, Edificio en que están los dínamos, las máquinas de vapor u otros motores primitivos, y de donde se transmite la fuerza mecánica a las varias partes de un ferrocarril eléctrico, de un sistema de talleres, etc. *As much as lies in his power*, En cuanto está en su poder, en cuanto de él depende. *Heating-power*, Potencia (fuerza) calorífica. *Propelling-power*, Fuerza motriz, propulsora. *Horse-power*, *V.* HORSE-POWER, en su lugar alfabético. *A power of attorney*, Un poder, una procuración. *Civil power*, Autoridad civil. *Refractive power, dispersive power*, Facultad de refracción, fuerza dispersiva.

Powerboat [pau'-ęr-bōt], *s.* Lancha de motor.

Power brake [pau'-ęr brêc], *s.* Servofreno.

Power dive [pau'-ęr daiv], *s.* Picada de un avión a todo motor.

Powerful [pau'-ęr-ful], *a.* 1. Poderoso, eficaz, fuerte. 2. Intenso, que tiene gran energía o actividad. 3. Que posee gran autoridad, o que muestra altas cualidades de cuerpo o de ánimo; potente. 4. Que produce gran efecto en el ánimo; convincente.

Powerfully [pau'-ęr-ful-i], *adv.* Poderosamente, eficazmente, con mucha fuerza.

Powerfulness [pau'-ęr-ful-nes], *s.* Poderío, fuerza, energía, eficacia.

Powerless [pau'-ęr-les], *a.* Impotente, ineficaz.

Power plant [pau'-ęr plant], *s.* Central eléctrica, central generadora de fuerza motriz.

Power shovel [pau'-ęr shuv'-l], *s.* Pala mecánica.

Powwow [pau'-wau], *vn.* 1. Tratar a los enfermos por medio de conjuros. 2. Reunirse un cuerpo deliberante. 3. (Fam. E. U.) Producirse una algarabía en una reunión o conferencia.—*s.* 1. Conjurador indio. 2. Conjuración para curar a los enfermos. 3. Baile, festín, holgorio que precede a una cacería. 4. Concilio.

Pox [pex], *s.* Una enfermedad cualquiera que produce erupciones pustolosas, particularmente la sífilis y las viruelas. *Small-pox*, Viruelas. *Pox* o *French pox*, (Vulg.) Mal venéreo o gálico. *Chicken-pox*, Viruela loca. *Cow-pox*, Vacuna.

Practicable [prac'-ti-ca-bl], *a.* Practicable, factible, hacedero; accesible.

Practicability, Practicableness [prac'-ti-ca-bl-nes], *s.* La posibilidad de hacer una cosa.

Practicably [prac'-ti-ca-bli], *adv.* Posiblemente; prácticamente.

Practical [prac'-ti-cal], *a.* 1. Práctico, factible. 2. Útil. *Practical joke*, Broma pesada. *Practical nurse*, Enfermera por la práctica, sin haberse graduado.

Practically [prac'-ti-cal-i], *adv.* Prácticamente.

Practicalness [prac'-ti-cal-nes], *s.* La propiedad o calidad de práctico.

Practice, Practise [prac'-tis], *s.* 1. Práctica, uso, costumbre. 2. Práctica, el ejercicio de alguna cosa en cuanto se distingue de la teoría. 3. Práctica, método, modo. 4. Una regla de aritmética. *Gun practice*, Ejercicio de cañón. *To be in good practice*, Tener buena parroquia, clientela. *To make it one's practice to*, Acostumbrarse a.

Practise, Practice, *va.* Practicar, ejercer, ejercitar alguna cosa.—*vn.* 1. Practicar, usar continuadamente alguna cosa. 2. Negociar secretamente. 3. Ejercer la medicina; ejercer cualquier arte u oficio. 4. Ensayarse. *To practise at a target*, Tirar al blanco. *To practise with the rifle*, Ejercitarse en la carabina. *To practise on the fears of*, Explotar los temores de.

Practiser [prac'-tis-ęr], *s.* 1. Practicante. 2. Práctico; se usa substantivamente esta palabra para designar a los profesores de medicina. 3. El que usa habitualmente estratagemas o malas artes.

Practitioner [prac-tish'-un-ęr], *s.* Práctico, el que ejerce su profesión; aplícase más comúnmente al médico.

Præ-. Prefijo latino. *V.* PRE-.

Prænomen [pri-nō'-men], *s.* Prenombre. *V.* PRENOMEN.

Præmunire, *s.* (For.) *V.* PREMUNIRE.

Pragmatic [prag-mat'-ic], *a.* 1. Práctico, perteneciente a la consumación del deber u oficio; relativo a los asuntos civiles de un Estado soberano. 2. Pragmático, filosófico, ocupado en la evolución científica de las causas y efectos; dícese de la historia, poesía, etc. *Pragmatic sanction*, Pragmática sanción, la pragmática; el edicto imperial que servía de ley fundamental.

Pragmatical [prag-mat'-ic-al], *a.* 1. Entremetido, impertinente, oficioso; que pretende dictar o gobernar a los demás. 2. Vulgar, trivial.

Pragmatically [prag-mat'-i-cal-i], *adv.* Impertinentemente; magistralmente.

Prairie [prê'-ri], *s.* Pradera, pradería, extensión de terrenos llanos sin árboles y cubiertos de hierba, particularmente en parte del oeste de los Estados Unidos. *Prairie-chicken*, Chocha, cerceta de las praderas: el Tympanuchus americanus o el Pedioecetes phasianellus. *Prairie-dog*, Marmota, roedor del género Cynomys, de las praderas de la América del Norte. Cynomys ludovicianus.

Praise [prêz], *s.* 1. Alabanza, elogio, encomio. 2. Celebridad, fama, renombre, reputación. 3. Loa, alabanza dirigida a Dios; homenaje por gracias o favores recibidos.

Praise, *va.* 1. Celebrar, aplaudir. 2.

Alabar, glorificar, loar, ensalzar. 3. Bendecir, expresar gratitud por favores recibidos. *The Lord be praised*, Alabado sea el Señor.

Praiser [prêz'-ęr], *s.* Loador, admirador, aprobador.

Praiseworthily [prêz'-wŏr-dhi-li], *adv.* Loablemente, de una manera que merece alabanzas.

Praiseworthiness [prêz'-wŏr-dhi-nes], *s.* Calidad de loable, de lo que es digno de alabanza; naturaleza loable.

Praiseworthy [prêz'-wŏr-dhi], *a.* Digno de alabanza, loable.

Praline [prā-lîn'], *s.* Variedad de dulce de almendra típico de Nueva Orleans, E.U.

Pram [pram], *s.* Barco chato usado en Holanda.

Prance [prqns], *vn.* Cabriolar, cabriolear, dar o hacer cabriolas.—*va.* Hacer cabriolar.

Prancer [prqn'-sęr], *s.* Caballo que cabriola.

Prancing [prqn'-sing], *s.* 1. Acción de ponerse de manos los caballos. 2. Aire altanero, modo de andar campante y garboso.

Prandial [pran'-di-al], *s.* Perteneciente a una comida. (< Lat. prandium, almuerzo.)

Prank [prank], *va.* Hermosear, adornar.—*vn.* Vestirse de una manera vistosa, exagerada, con pretensiones.

Prank, *s.* Travesura, chasco, locura, extravagancia.

Prankish [prank'-ish], *a.* Dispuesto o propenso a hacer travesuras.

Prase [prêz], *s.* (Min.) Prasio.

Prate [prêt], *va.* Charlar, hablar mucho sin substancia.

Prate, *s.* Charla, plática o conversación sin substancia.

Prater [prêt'-ęr], *s.* Charlante, charlador, charlatán.

Pratic [prat'-ic] ó **Pratique** [pra-tîc'], *s.* (Mar.) Práctica, el permiso que se da a la tripulación de una embarcación, para que entre en algún puerto y desembarque.

Prating [prêt'-ing], *s.* Charlatanería, el acto de charlar.

Pratingly [prêt'-ing-li], *adv.* Con charla vana, locuazmente.

Prattle [prat'-l], *vn.* Charlar, proferir como los niños.

Prattle, *s.* Parlería, habla de los niños; de aquí, charla, charlatanería.

Prattler [prat'-lęr], *s.* Charlador.

Pravity [prav'-i-ti], *s.* Pravedad, iniquidad, perversidad.

Prawn [prōn], *s.* Langostin, crustáceo comestible muy parecido al camarón pero mayor. Palæmon serratus. (< Lat. perna.)

Praxis [prac'-sis], *s.* 1. Práctica, ejercicio con un fin determinado. 2. Colección de ejemplos, modelos, etc., como los de la gramática.

Pray [prê], *vn.* 1. Orar, invocar, rezar a Dios. 2. Rogar, pedir, suplicar. *Pray what is your name?* Sírvase Vd. decirme su nombre, o tenga Vd. la bondad de decirme su gracia.—*va.* Suplicar, rogar, pedir con sumisión y humildad alguna cosa.

Prayer [prār o prā'-ęr], *s.* 1. Oración, súplica, rezo, deprecación o ruego que se hace a Dios. *The Lord's Prayer*, La oración dominical o el Padre nuestro. 2. Súplica, ruego, petición, plegaria. *The Book of Common Prayer*, El ritual de las Iglesias anglicana y americana episcopal. *Prayer-meeting*, Reunión para orar y alabar a Dios.

Prayer-book [prār'-buk], *s.* Libro de devociones, ejercicio cotidiano, devocionario: en especial, ritual que en las Iglesias anglicana y americana episcopal se llama *The Book of Common Prayer*.

Prayerful [prār'-ful], *a.* Piadoso, que reza mucho; entregado á la oración.

Prayerfulness [prār'-ful-nes], *s.* Piedad, devoción; inclinación a rezar.

Prayerless [prār'-les], *a.* Que descuida el rezo; que no reza, que no ora.

Prayerlessness [prār'-les-nes], *s.* Omisión, olvido o descuido del rezo, de la oración.

Pre- [prî]. Prefijo latino que significa ante, delante.

Preach [prîch], *va.* 1. Predicar, exponer la palabra divina. 2. Recomendar con instancia.—*vn.* Predicar, reprender públicamente los vicios y exhortar a la virtud.

Preacher [prîch'-ęr], *s.* Predicador.

Preaching [prîch'-ing], *s.* Predicación, acción de predicar; la doctrina predicada.

Preachment [prîch'-męnt], *s.* Prédica, plática o sermón; arenga.

Preacquaint [prî-ąc-cwênt'], *va.* Hacer saber o advertir de antemano.

Preacquaintance [prî-ac-cwênt'-ans], *s.* Conocimiento previo, anterior.

Preadamite [prî-ad'-am-ait], **Preadamitic** [prî-ad-am-it'-ic], *a.* Preadamita, anterior a Adán; que se supone ha existido antes que Adán.

Preamble [prî'-am-bl], *s.* Preámbulo; exordio, prefación.—*va.* Introducir como preliminar, hacer preceder de un preámbulo.

Prebend [preb'-end], *s.* 1. Prebenda, ciertos beneficios eclesiásticos en las catedrales. 2. Prebendado, canónigo.

Prebendary [preb'-en-dę-ri], *s.* 1. Prebendado, canónigo que recibe las rentas de una prebenda. 2. Dignidad u oficio de prebendado.

Precarious [prę-kê'-ri-us], *a.* 1. Precario, sujeto a continuo riesgo de pérdida; dependiente de la voluntad de otro, o de la casualidad; incierto. 2. Peligroso, arriesgado, que puede ocasionar daño. 3. Que no está firmemente establecido, que no es fijo; indigno de confianza. *Precarious conclusions*, Conclusiones indignas de confianza.

Precariously [prę-kê'-ri-us-li], *adv.* Inciertamente, precariamente.

Precariousness [prę-kê'-ri-us-nes], *s.* Condición precaria o peligrosa; incertidumbre, falta de certeza.

Precaution [prę-cō'-shun], *s.* 1. Precaución, reserva, cautela para impedir, obstáculos o daños posibles, o para asegurar o hacerse dueño de alguna propiedad. 2. Cuidado que se toma de antemano para precaver algún mal.

Precaution, *va.* Precaver, precautelar, prevenir algún riesgo.

Precautionary [prę-cō'-shun-ęr-i], *a.* Precaucionado, de precaución; destinado á precaver algún mal. *A precautionary signal*, Señal de precaución (del Departamento de Señales Meteorológicas).

Precautious [prę-cō'-shus], *a.* Precavido, cauto.

Precede [prę-sîd'], *va.* 1. Anteceder, preceder; de aquí, sobresalir, llevar la preferencia. 2. Colocar, poner alguna cosa delante de otra; proveer de un preludio.—*vn.* 1 Ir delante de otra persona; tener la primacía. 2. Acontecer primeramente.

Precedence [prę-sî'-dens], **Precedency** [prę-sî'-den-si], *s.* Prioridad, anterioridad; precedencia, superioridad.

Precedent [prę-sî'-dent], *a.* Precedente, antecedente.

Precedent [pres'-ę-dent], *s.* 1. Precedente, ejemplar, lo que se ha hecho en igual caso otras veces, antecedente, cosa que se puede invocar como ejemplo o razón. 2. Decisión judicial que se considera como regla y sirve para guiar decisiones subsiguientes.

Precedently [prę-sî'-dent-li], *adv.* Antecedentemente, anticipadamente.

Preceding [prę-sîd'-ing], *a.* Anterior, que precede.

Precentor [prę-sen'-tęr], *s.* Chantre, dignidad de alguna iglesia catedral o colegiata.

Precept [prî'-sept], *s.* 1. Precepto, mandato u orden que el superior intima. 2. (For.) Mandato, hecho por escrito.

Preceptive [prę-sep'-tiv], *a.* Preceptivo, didáctico, didascálico; que da preceptos para la conducta moral.

Preceptor [prę-sep'-tęr], *s.* Preceptor, maestro, el que enseña.

Precession [prę-sesh'-un], *s.* 1. Precedencia. 2. (Astr.) Precesión de los equinoccios.

Precinct [prî'-sinct], *s.* 1. Límite, lindero; lugar cerrado o cercado. 2. Distrito jurisdiccional, división menor territorial, sometida a una autoridad administrativa. 3. Inmediación de un palacio o de una corte. *Voting precinct*, Distrito electoral.

Precious [presh'-us], *a.* 1. Precioso, costoso, de gran valor, muy apreciado, muy estimado. 2. Caro, amado, que excita el amor. 3. (Irón.) Famoso, altivo; sin valor, sin mérito. 4 (Fam.) Bastante, considerable. *Precious stones*, Piedras preciosas. *A precious scoundrel*, Un gran belitre.

Preciously [presh'-us-li], *adv.* Preciosamente; a gran precio.

Preciousness [presh'-us-nes], *s.* Preciosidad, valor elevado, la calidad que da á una cosa cualquiera el carácter de preciosa.

Precipice [pres'-i-pis], *s.* 1. Precipicio, despeñadero. 2. Situación peligrosa; la ruina temporal o espiritual.

Precipitable [prę-sip'-i-ta-bl], *a.* Que puede precipitarse.

Precipitance [prę-sip'-i-tans], **Precipitancy** [prę-sip'-i-tan-si], *s.* Precipitación, inconsideración; prisa inconsiderada.

Precipitant [prę-sip'-i-tant], *a.* 1. Que se precipita, que se lanza hacia adelante con gran velocidad, o que cae de cabeza. 2. Precipitado, arrojado, arrebatado.—*s.* (Quím.) Precipitante, cualquiera de los agentes que producen la precipitación.

Precipitantly [prę-sip'-i-tant-li], *adv.* Precipitadamente, con mucho apresuramiento.

Precipitate [prę-sip'-i-têt], *va.* 1. Precipitar, despeñar, arrojar. 2. Precipitar, acelerar, apresurar demasiado una cosa. 3. Precipitar, exponer a uno a ruina temporal o espiritual. 4. (Quím.) Precipitar, separar el ingrediente disuelto y hacerlo caer en polvo al fondo del disolvente.—*vn.* 1. Precipitarse, despeñarse, caer al fondo. 2. Precipitarse, arrojarse a algún peligro ó meterse en él. 3. (Quím.) Caer bajo la forma de precipitado.

Precipitate [prẹ-sip'-i-têt], *a.* 1. Precipitado, que se precipita; que cae, corre o se hace lanzar de un lugar elevado. 2. Precipitado, que obra sin debida reflexión, inconsiderado, arrebatado. 3. Urgido o propuesto prematuramente.—*s.* Precipitado, cualquier cosa que se precipita al fondo de una vasija por medio de una operación química.

Precipitately [prẹ-sip'-i-têt-li], *adv.* Precipitadamente; apresuradamente.

Precipitation [prẹ-sip-i-té'-shun], *s.* 1. Precipitación, acción o procedimiento de precipitar; la acción química de precipitar; inconsideración, demasiada prisa para o en hacer alguna cosa. 2. Depósito de humedad (lluvia o nieve) desde la atmósfera sobre la superficie de la tierra.

Precipitous [prẹ-sip'-i-tus], *a.* 1. Precipitoso, pendiente, escarpado. 2. Precipitoso, arrojado.

Precise [prẹ-sais'], *a.* 1. Preciso, puntual, exacto, no equívoco; estricto, escrupuloso. 2. Formal; afectado. 3. Que no tiene error apreciable; no más que y no menos que. 4. Particular, singular, idéntico. *The precise spot,* El paraje idéntico. *Precise manners,* Maneras formales.

Precisely [prẹ-sais'-li], *adv.* 1. Precisamente, exactamente. 2. Formalmente.

Preciseness [prẹ-sais'-nes], *s.* Precisión, exactitud; afectación ó gravedad afectada; formalismo, ceremonia.

Precisian [prẹ-sizh'-an], *s.* El que contiene, limita o restringe; rigorista; el que es nimiamente escrupuloso; formulista.

Precision [prẹ-sizh'-un], *s.* 1. Precisión, limitación exacta, exactitud. 2. Precisión de estilo, la calidad que expresa exactamente lo que el escritor se propone.

Precisive [prẹ-sai'-siv], *a.* Precisivo, que prescinde; preciso, estricto.

Preclude [prẹ-clūd'], *va.* 1. Prevenir, impedir o estorbar alguna cosa anticipadamente. 2. Echar fuera, excluir. (< Lat. præcludo.) *The one does not preclude the other,* Lo uno no excluye lo otro. *To preclude the possibility of,* Hacer imposible.

Precocious [prẹ-cō'-shus], *a.* 1. Precoz, que tiene desarrolladas prematuramente las facultades mentales. 2. Precoz, maduro antes del tiempo natural, prematuro, adelantado.

Precociousness [prẹ-cō'-shus-nes], **Precocity** [prẹ-ces'-i-ti], *s.* Precocidad, madurez anticipada; desarrollo prematuro de las facultades mentales.

Precogitate [prẹ-cej'-i-têt], *va.* Premeditar.

Precogitation [prẹ-cej-i-té'-shun], *s.* Premeditación.

Precognition [prī-ceg-nish'-un], *s.* Precognición, conocimiento anticipado, conocimiento previo.

Precompose [prī''-cem-pōz'], *va.* Componer de antemano.

Preconceit [prī-cen-sīt'], *s.* Concepto anticipado.

Preconceive [prī-cen-sīv'], *va.* Concebir, opinar o imaginar anticipadamente.

Preconception [prī-cen-sep'-shun], *s.* Preocupación, concepto anticipado, concepción formada de antemano.

Preconcert [prī-cen-sẹrt'], *va.* Concertar de antemano.

Preconcert [prī-cen'-sẹrt], *s.* Acuerdo anticipado, lo convenido con anterioridad.

Preconization [prẹ-cen-i-zé'-shun], *s.* Preconización.

Preconsign [prī-cen-sain'], *va.* Consignar anteriormente.

Precontract [prī-cen-tract'], *va.* Contratar con anterioridad.

Precontract [prī-cen'-tract], *s.* Contrato anticipado o antecedente.

Precordial [prẹ-cēr'-di-al], *a.* Precordial, relativo al diafragma, o á las partes anteriores del corazón.

Precursive, Precursory [prẹ-cūr'-siv, so-ri], *a.* Precursor, que va delante; que advierte, informa o predice de antemano.

Precursor [prẹ-cūr'-sẹr], *s.* Precursor, el o lo que va delante, que precede a un hombre o un acontecimiento y anuncia su venida.

Predaceous [prẹ-dé'-shus], *s.* Que vive de las presas que hace: dícese comúnmente de los animales carniceros.

Predatory [pred'-a-to-ri], *a.* Perteneciente a hurto o rapiña; de presa, de botín; rapaz, voraz.

Predeceased [prī-dẹ-sīst'], *a.* Muerto antes que otro.

Predecessor [pred-ẹ-ses'-ẹr ó prī-dẹ-ses'-ẹr], *s.* Predecesor, antecesor; antepasado, abuelo; persona que ha precedido a alguien en el ejercicio de las mismas funciones.

Predestinarian [prẹ-des-ti-né'-ri-an], *a.* Perteneciente, relativo a la predestinación; que cree en esta doctrina. —*s.* El que cree y defiende la doctrina de la predestinación.

Predestinate [prẹ-des'-ti-nêt], *va.* Predestinar, destinar de antemano o desde el principio de las cosas.

Predestination [prẹ-des-ti-né'-shun], *s.* 1. Predestinación, destinación anterior de alguna cosa. 2. (Teol.) Predestinación, ordenación de la voluntad divina con que *ab æterno* tiene elegidos a los que por medio de su gracia han de lograr la gloria.

Predestinator [prẹ-des'-ti-nê-tẹr], *s.* 1. El que arregla y ordena de antemano. 2. El que cree en la predestinación.

Predestine [prẹ-des'-tin], *va.* Predestinar; ordenar de antemano.

Predeterminate [prī-dẹ-tẹr'-mi nêt], *a.* Predeterminado, determinado de antemano.

Predetermination [prī-dẹ-tẹr-mi-né'-shun], *s.* Predeterminación.

Predetermine [prī-dẹ-tẹr'-min], *va.* Predeterminar o determinar con anterioridad.

Predial [prī'-di-al], *a.* Predial, que toca o pertenece a los predios; que consta de bienes raíces.

Predicable [pred'-i-ca-bl], *a.* Predicable, que se puede afirmar o decir de un sujeto.—*s.* (Lóg.) Predicable, categorema.

Predicament [prẹ-dic'-a-mẹnt], *s.* Predicamento, clase, categoría; estado, condición; particularmente, trance apurado, embarazoso, situación difícil o divertida.

Predicamental [prẹ-dic-a-men'-tal], *a.* Predicamental.

Predicate [pred'-i-kêt], *va.* Predicar o más comúnmente predicarse, decir, afirmar o negar en la enunciación una cosa de otra.—*vn.* Afirmarse.

Predicate [pred'-i-ket], *s.* 1. (Gram.) Predicado, lo que se afirma ó niega en una proposición. 2. Calidad inherente á una cosa o que se afirma de ella; atributo.

Predication [pred-i-ké'-shun], *s.* Afirmación de alguna cosa.

Predict [prẹ-dict'], *va.* Predecir, decir de antemano lo que ha de acaecer; profetizar, pronosticar.

Prediction [prẹ-dic'-shun], *s.* Predicción, profecía.

Predictive [prẹ-dic'-tiv], *a.* Que predice, que anuncia de antemano.

Predictor [prẹ-dic'-tẹr], *s.* Adivino, pronosticador.

Predigestion [prī-di-jes'-chun], *s.* 1. La digestión artificial o peptonización del alimento, v. g. para las personas achacosas. 2. Masticación, insalivación, funciones preliminares de la digestión.

Predilection [prī-di-lec'-shun], *s.* Predilección, preferencia.

Predisponent [prī-dis-pō'-nent], *a.* Predisponente, que predispone, que causa una predisposición.

Predispose [prī-dis-pōz'], *va.* Predisponer, disponer con anticipación; preparar para recibir alguna impresión.

Predisposed [prī-dis-pōzd'], *a.* Predispuesto.

Predisposition [prī-dis-po-zish'-un], *s.* 1. Predisposición, disposición natural, propensión, predilección. 2. Predisposición, circunstancia que facilita el desarrollo de una enfermedad.

Predominance [prẹ-dem'-i-nans, **Predominancy** [prẹ-dem'-i-nan-si], *s.* Predominio, predominación; ascendiente, superioridad en fuerza, influencia o grado.

Predominant [prẹ-dem'-i-nant], *a.* Predominante.

Predominate [prẹ-dem'-i-nêt], *va.* Predominar, prevalecer, mandar o influir con predominio.

Pre-election [prī-ẹ-lec'-shun], *s.* Elección hecha por resolución anterior.

Pre-eminence [prī-em -i-nens], *s.* Preeminencia, excelencia especial; superioridad de posición, calidad o excelencia (algunas veces de maldad); supremacía.

Pre-eminent [prī-em'-i-nent], *a.* 1. Preeminente, de primer orden o mérito, supremo (rara vez en mala parte). 2. Extraordinario, extremo, superlativo.

Pre-empt [prī-empt'], *va.* (E. U.) Obtener el derecho de preferencia en la compra de terrenos públicos; establecer un título anterior.—*vn.* Apropiar un terreno público por el privilegio de compra anterior.

Pre-emptible [prī-emp'-ti-bl], *a.* Sujeto al derecho de compra de una persona determinada.

Pre-emption [prī-emp'-shun], *s.* 1. El derecho de comprar antes que otros. 2. (Ingl.) El privilegio que gozaba antiguamente el rey de comprar las provisiones para la casa real, con preferencia a todos sus súbditos.

Pre-emptor [prī-emp'-tẹr], *s.* El que goza el derecho de comprar un terreno con preferencia a todo otro comprador, por ser verdadero colono.

Preen [prīn], *va.* Limpiar, concertar y componer sus plumas las aves.

Pre-engage [prī-en-gêj'], *va.* Empeñar, obligar o comprometer a uno por medio de una promesa anticipada.

Pre-establish [prī-es-tab'-lish], *va.* Preestablecer, establecer de antemano o á prevención.

Pre-exist [prī-eg-zist'], *vn.* Preexistir, existir antes.

Pre-existence [prī-eg-zist'-ens], *s.* 1. Preexistencia, existencia anterior. 2. Existencia del alma antes de la vida humana, como la afirmaron Pitágoras, Platón y otros filósofos.

Pre-existent [prī-eg-zist'-ent], *a.* Preexistente.

Prefabricated [prī-fab'-ri-kêt-ed], *a.* Prefabricado, construído de antemano.

Preface [pref'-ĝs], *s.* 1. Prefación, prefacio, prólogo; discurso preliminar y corto de un libro; se diferencia de la introducción. 2. Cualquier prólogo, o acción preliminar.

Preface, *va.* Hacer o poner un prólogo a un libro; decir alguna cosa en forma de introducción al discurso que se va a hacer.—*vn.* Decir, o hacer, a manera de prólogo.

Prefatory [pref'-a-to-ri], *a.* Preliminar; de la naturaleza de un prólogo, que sirve de prólogo.

Prefect [prī'-fect], *s.* 1. Prefecto, una dignidad, un poder tutelar jefe entre los romanos. 2. En Francia y en el Perú, prefecto, gobernador de una provincia o departamento.

Prefectship [prī'-fect-ship], *s.* Prefectura, dignidad o territorio de un prefecto.

Prefecture [pref'-ec-tiūr], *s.* Prefectura; funciones o jurisdicción de un prefecto; también, el edificio oficial para su uso.

Prefer [prg-fęr'], *va.* 1. Preferir, anteponer. 2. Elevar, exaltar. 3. Proponer en público; ofrecer solemnemente; exhibir o manifestar alguna cosa; presentar. 4. Dar preferencia, como a un acreedor antes de otros. Se usa con la prep. *to,* algunas veces con *above,* y rara vez *before.*

Preferable [pref'-ęr-a-bl], *a.* Preferible, más deseable, digno de escogimiento.

Preferableness [pref'-ęr-a-bl-nes], *s.* El estado de lo que es preferible o digno de anteponerse a otra cosa.

Preferably [pref'-ęr-a-bli], *adv.* Preferiblemente; por preferencia, de preferencia.

Preference [pref'-ęr-ens], *s.* Preferencia, la acción de preferir, el estado de ser preferido, o la cosa preferida.

Preferential [pref-ęr-en'-shal], *a.* Que posee, constituye, implica, o procede de la preferencia.

Preferment [prg-fęr'-mgnt], *s.* 1. Promoción, elevación a alguna dignidad o empleo más eminente que el que uno tenía. 2. Puesto, empleo u oficio honorífico o lucrativo.

Preferred [prg-fęrd'], *a.* Preferente, preferido, predilecto. *Preferred stock,* Acciones preferentes (en finanzas).

Preferrer [prg-fęr'-ęr], *s.* El que prefiere.

Prefigurative [prg-fig'-yur-a-tiv], *a.* Que muestra por figuras, por tipos anteriores.

Prefigure [prg-fig'-yur], *va.* Prefigurar, representar anticipadamente la forma o figura de alguna cosa.

Prefix [prg-fix'], *va.* 1. Prefijar, determinar o señalar anticipadamente. 2. Fijar, establecer.

Prefix [prī'-fics], *s.* (Gram.) Prefijo, la partícula o sílaba puesta delante de una palabra o término que hace variar su significación.

Pregnancy [preg'-nan-si], *s.* 1. Preñez, preñado, el estado de la mujer en cinta o de la hembra preñada. 2. Fertilidad, fecundidad. 3. (Fig.) Importancia, gravedad.

Pregnant [preg'-nant], *a.* 1. Preñada, embarazada, encinta, dícese de la mujer; mientras que *gravid* se aplica comúnmente al órgano, y a las hembras de los animales que han concebido. 2. Fértil, abundante, copioso. 3. Fecundo en consecuencias, grave, que conduce a resultados importantes; seguido comúnmente de *with.* 4. Lleno, repleto; que importa mucho. 5. En retórica y en lógica, que implica más de lo que se expresa.

Pregnantly [preg'-nant-li], *adv.* Copiosamente, abundantemente, plenamente.

Prehensible [pre-hen'-si-bl], *a.* Capaz de ser aprehendido o asido.

Prehensile [prg-hen'-sil], *a.* Prensil; dícese en zoología de las colas de algunos animales cuando pueden enroscarlas alrededor de un cuerpo y suspenderse de ellas.

Prehension [prg-hen'-shun], *s.* Aprehensión, acción de aprehender física o mentalmente.

Prehistoric, Prehistorical [prī-his-tor'-ic, al], *a.* Prehistórico, perteneciente a la prehistoria, a los tiempos a que no alcanza la historia.

Prejudge [prī-juj'], †**Prejudicate** [prī-jū'-di-kêt], *va.* Prejuzgar, juzgar o formar juicio de alguna cosa antes del tiempo debido, y generalmente se usa por condenar antes de hacer un examen completo de lo que se condena.

Prejudgment [prī-juj'-mgnt], *s.* Prejuicio, juicio o condenación sin examen.

†**Prejudicate** [prī-jū'-di-kêt], *a.* Juzgado o condenado sin examen; preocupado, que tiene preocupaciones.

Prejudication [prī-jū-di-kê'-shun], *s.* El acto de juzgar de antemano sin previo examen.

Prejudice [prej'-u-dis], *s.* 1. Prevención, prejuicio, preocupación del ánimo o de la voluntad; prevención, juicio anticipado, opinión prematura a favor o en contra de una persona. 2. Perjuicio, daño, detrimento.

Prejudice, *va.* 1. Preocupar, prevenir, imbuir o impresionar el ánimo o la voluntad de alguno. 2. Perjudicar, hacer daño, causar pérdida a otro.

Prejudicial [prej-u-dish'-al], *a.* Perjudicial, dañoso, nocivo.

Prejudicially [prej-u-dish'-al-i], *adv.* Perjudicialmente, con perjuicio.

Prelacy [prel'-a-si], *s.* 1. Prelacía, dignidad u oficio de prelado. 2. Episcopado; el cuerpo de obispos.

Prelate [prel'-et], *s.* Prelado.

Prelateship [prel'-et-ship], *s.* Prelacía, prelatura.

Prelature, Prelatureship [prel'-a-tiūr], *s.* Prelatura, prelacía.

Prelect [prg-lect'], *va.* Leer, hacer una lectura ante alguna sociedad o corporación.

Prelection [prg-lec'-shun], *s.* Lección, lectura, discurso.

Prelector [prg-lec'-tęr], *s.* Lector, instructor en una universidad.

Prelibation [prī-lai-bê'-shun], *s.* Gusto anticipado.

Preliminarily [pre-lim'-i-ng-ri-li], *adv.* Preliminarmente, por vía de introducción, de una manera preparatoria.

Preliminary [prg-lim'-i-ng-ri], *a.* Preliminar, antecedente, preparativo, introductorio; que sirve de prefación.—*s.* Preliminar, paso iniciativo, acto preparativo para alguna cosa.

Prelude [prī'-liūd o prel'-yūd], *s.* 1. Preludio, lo que precede y sirve de entrada; prelusión, acción que indica lo que ha de ser la función principal. 2. (Mús.) Preludio, tiento, floreo, arpegio; también, una pieza corta de música que se toca antes de una ceremonia o representación. 3. Presagio, cosa precursora, lo que anuncia un acontecimiento venidero.

Prelude [prg-liūd'], *va.* (Mús.) Florear, hacer floreos.—*vn.* Servir de introducción.

Preludial [prg-lū'-di-al], *a.* Introductorio, de la naturaleza de un preludio; que sirve de prólogo.

Prelusive [prg-lū'-siv], *a.* Previo, introductorio, que presagia.

Premature [prī-ma-tiūr'], *a.* Prematuro, intempestivo, precoz, que está maduro o desarrollado antes de tiempo; que se ha hecho, dicho, o concluído antes del tiempo conveniente. *Premature fruit, premature judgment,* Fruto prematuro, juicio prematuro.

Prematurely [prī-ma-tūr'-li], *adv.* Prematuramente; antes del tiempo debido.

Prematureness [prī-ma-tiūr'-nes], **Prematurity** [prī-ma-tiū'-ri-ti], *s.* Madurez o sazón antes de tiempo.

Premaxillary [prī-max'-il-ę-ri], *a.* Premaxilar, colocado delante de la quijada superior.

Premedical [prī-med'-i-cal], *a.* Preparatorio para estudiar medicina.

Premeditate [prg-med'-i-têt], *va.* Premeditar, meditar de antemano; proyectar y resolver anticipadamente.—*vn.* Pensar de antemano.

Premeditation [prg-med-i-tê'-shun], *s.* Premeditación, acción de premeditar; designio que ha precedido a la ejecución de un crimen; meditación juiciosa sobre alguna cosa antes de ejecutarla.

Premier [prī'-mi-ęr], *s.* Primer ministro, el ministro principal del estado.—*a.* Primero, principal.

Premillennial [prī-mil-en'-i-al], *a.* Anterior al milenio.

Premise [prg-maiz'], *va.* Decir o exponer alguna cosa con anterioridad o anticipadamente a otra; sentar o establecer premisas.

Premise [prem'-is], *s.* 1. Premisa, cada una de las dos primeras proposiciones de un silogismo. 2. *pl.* (For.) (1) Asertos, aserciones anteriores, que van delante; hechos afirmados anteriormente. (2) Aquella parte de un instrumento auténtico que da a conocer la fecha, los nombres de los individuos, el terreno, predio u otra cosa transferida, y la razón o precio. 3. *pl.* Predio rústico o urbano, casa, tierra, posesiones. *In the premises,* Tocante al asunto de que se trata; en el particular, en esto, acerca de.

Premium [prī'-mi-um], *s.* 1. Premio, galardón, remuneración. 2. Prima o premio de un seguro, la cantidad que se paga al asegurador. 3. Prima, la cantidad prometida o dada por premio en ciertas especulaciones mercantiles; interés, beneficio, premio. *Bottomry premium*, Premio de un seguro marítimo, por el riesgo de mar. 4. Premio, prima, aumento de valor sobre el nominal o el de par que adquieren ciertas acciones, fondos, o dinero; aumento de valor en la moneda.

Premonish [prẹ-men'-ish], *va.* (Ant.) Prevenir, advertir antes.

Premonition [prî''-mo-nish'-un], *s.* Prevención, advertencia o aviso anticipado.

Premonitory [prẹ-men'-i-to-ri], *a.* Preventivo, que previene á otra cosa, que presagia, o amonesta.

Premonstrant, Premonstratensian [prẹ-men'-strant, stra-ten'-si-an], *s.* Orden premonstratense, fundada en Francia por San Norberto, con canónigos regulares.

Premunire [prî''-miū-nai'-ri], *s.* Usase esta palabra entre los jurisconsultos para expresar una ley penal, a la cual se da este nombre porque principia con dicha palabra; o el delito contra el que se ha dado aquella ley.

Premunition [prî''-miū-nish'-un], *s.* Acción de fortalecer contra el peligro o la objeción; estado de defensa.

Prenatal [prî-nê'-tal], *a.* Prenatal, antenatal.

Prenomen [prẹ-nō'-men], *s.* Prenombre, el nombre que entre los romanos precedía al de familia.

†**Prenominate** [prî''-nem'-i-nêt], *va.* Nombrar primero o con anterioridad.

Prenotion [prẹ-nō'-shun], *s.* Prenoción, noción anticipada o primer conocimiento de una cosa.

Prentice [pren'-tis], *s.* (Fam.) Aprendiz: voz común en otros tiempos. *V.* APPRENTICE.

Prenticeship [pren'-tis-ship], *s.* Aprendizaje.

Preoccupancy [prî-ec'-yu-pan-si], *s.* 1. El acto de tomar posesión antes que otro. 2. Preocupación, la anticipación o prevención en la adquisición de una cosa.

Preoccupant [prẹ-ec'-yu-pant], *s.* El que preocupa alguna cosa.

Preoccupation [prî'ec-yu-pê'-shun], *s.* 1. Preocupación, anticipación en la adquisición de una cosa; el acto o derecho de preocupar; estado de posesión anterior. 2. Preocupación del ánimo. 3. (Des.) Objeción anticipada.

Preoccupied [prẹ-ec'-yu-paid], *pp.* y *a.* 1. Absorto en las propias ideas o en los negocios. 2. Que ha sido ocupado anteriormente. 3. Ya en uso, v. g. un nombre científico.

Preoccupy [prẹ-ec'-yu-pai], *va.* 1. Preocupar, ocupar antes. 2. Preocupar, prevenir el ánimo.

Preordain [prî-ōr-dên'], *va.* (Teo.) Preordinar, determinar de antemano.

Preordination [prî-ōr-di-nê'-shun], *s.* (Teo.) Preordinación.

Prepaid [prî-pêd'], *a.* Franco de porte, con porte pagado.

Preparation [prep-a-rê'-shun], *s.* 1. Preparación, acción y efecto de preparar; disposición, adaptación. 2. Preliminar, precaución; hecho que sirve para poner por obra algún plan o designio. 3. El hecho o cualidad de estar o ser preparado, dispuesto, listo. 4. Cosa preparada, como un compuesto medicinal o químico, o una muestra para el estudio científico. 5. Preparación, el procedimiento de componer o de manipular. 6. Estudio preliminar, instrucción, v. g. para un colegio, o para los negocios. *Preparations for war*, Preparativos de guerra.

Preparative [prẹ-par'-a-tiv], *a.* Preparativo, preparatorio, que prepara y dispone.—*s.* Preparativo, la cosa dispuesta y preparada.

Preparatory [prẹ-par'-a-to-ri], *a.* Preparatorio, previo, antecedente; que sirve de introducción, preliminar.

Prepare [prẹ-pār'], *va.* 1. Preparar, prevenir, disponer, aparejar, poner en disposición propia para alcanzar el fin que se desea. 2. Proveer de lo necesario o lo conveniente. 3. Disponer el ánimo hacia un estado conveniente o deseable.—*vn.* Prepararse, disponerse, ponerse en disposición de hacer alguna cosa.

Preparedly [prẹ-pār'-ed-li], *adv.* Con las medidas oportunas tomadas de antemano.

Preparedness [prẹ-pār'-ed-nes], *s.* Estado de preparación.

Preparer [prẹ-pār'-ẹr], *s.* Preparador, el que prepara; preparativo.

Prepay [prî''-pê'], *va.* (*pret.* y *pp.* PREPAID). Pagar adelantado, pagar anticipadamente; franquear una carta.

Prepayment [prî-pê'-mẹnt], *s.* Pago adelantado; franqueo.

Prepense [prẹ-pens'], *a.* Premeditado, concebido o imaginado antes; por lo común en la locución legal "*with malice prepense*," maliciosa y premeditadamente.

Preponderance [prẹ-pen'-dẹr-ans], **Preponderancy** [prẹ-pen'-dẹr-an-si], *s.* Superioridad de peso, de influencia, de fuerza, de número; preponderancia.

Preponderant [prẹ-pen'-dẹr-ant], *a.* Preponderante, predominante.

Preponderate [prẹ-pen'-dẹr-êt], *va.* y *vn.* 1. Preponderar, pesar una cosa más que otra. 2. Preponderar o hacer más fuerza una opinión que otra. 3. Arrastrar, llevarse tras sí. 4. Tener más influencia, crédito o influjo.

Preposition [prep-o-zish'-un], *s.* Preposición, parte indeclinable de la oración que precede a la palabra regida; denota la relación que entre sí tienen las palabras.

Prepositional [prep-o-zi'-shun-al], *a.* Preposicional, que tiene la fuerza o naturaleza de una preposición.

Prepositive [prẹ-pez'-i-tiv], *a.* Prepositivo, antepuesto, prefijo; particularmente, prefijo delante de la palabra regida.—*s.* Palabra o partícula prepositiva.

Prepositor [prẹ-pez'-i-tẹr], *s.* (Ingl.) Decurión, el estudiante señalado por el maestro para tomar la lección a los demás y cuidar de ellos.

Prepossess [prẹ-pez-zes'], *va.* 1. Preocupar, llenar de preocupaciones; impresionar, imbuir en favor de (rara vez en sentido despectivo). 2. Tomar posesión de algo antes que otro; preocupar.

Prepossessing [prî-pez-zes'-ing], *a.* Que produce opinión favorable desde luego, atractivo; que predispone a favor de algo.

Prepossession [prẹ-pez-zesh'-un], *s.* 1. Preocupación, primera impresión que produce una cosa en el ánimo; prevención, opinión preconcebida a favor (raramente en disfavor) de alguna persona o cosa. 2. Preocupación, ocupación o posesión anterior.

Preposterous [prẹ-pes'-tẹr-us], *a.* 1. Prepóstero, absurdo, contrario a la naturaleza o a la razón; evidentemente impracticable. 2. (Des.) Por su origen, trastrocado, hecho al revés o fuera de tiempo. (Fam.) Descabellado, sin son ni ton.

Preposterously [prẹ-pes'-tẹr-us-li], *adv.* Absurdamente, sin razón, prepósteramente.

Preposterousness [prî-pes'-tẹr-us-nes], *s.* Preposteración, trabucación, trastorno o inversión de orden.

Prepotency [prẹ-pō'-ten-si], *s.* Prepotencia, predominio.

Prepuce [prî'-piūs], *s.* Prepucio, piel móvil que cubre el balano.

Prerequire [prî-rẹ-cwair'], *va.* Requerir antes, demandar de antemano.

Prerequisite [prî-rec'-wi-zit], *a.* Que se necesita de antemano.—*s.* Requisito necesitado con anticipación para la ejecución de una cosa.

Prerogative [prẹ-reg'-a-tiv], *s.* Prerogativa, privilegio exclusivo o especial.—*a.* Privilegiado.

Presage [pres'-êj], **Presagement** [prẹ-sêj'-mẹnt], *s.* Presagio, pronóstico.

Presage [prẹ-sêj'], *va.* Presagiar, pronosticar.

Presageful [pres'-ej-ful], *a.* Que contiene agüero o presagio; ominoso.

Presbyope [pres'-bi-ōp], *s.* Présbite, el que ve mucho mejor los objetos lejanos que los inmediatos a causa de la vejez.

Presbyopia, Presbyopy [pres-bi-ō'-pi-a, pi], *s.* Presbicia, presbitopia, presbiopia, defecto del présbite, estado del que ve mejor de lejos que de cerca debido a la rigidez del lente cristalino, como sucede en la vejez.

Presbyter [pres- o prez'-bi-tẹr], *s.* Presbitero, sacerdote.

Presbyterial [pres- o prez-bi-tî'-ri-al], *a.* Presbiteral.

Presbyterian [pres-bi-tî'-ri-an], *a.* Presbiteriano, perteneciente al gobierno de la iglesia por los ancianos (en contraposición a la independencia y a la prelacía).—*s.* Presbiteriano, miembro de la secta protestante que niega la inferioridad de los presbiteros respecto de los obispos.

Presbyterianism [pres-bi-tî'-ri-an-izm], *s.* Presbiterianismo, secta o doctrina de los presbiterianos; gobierno de la iglesia por los ancianos.

Presbytery [pres'- (o prez'-) bi-ter-i], *s.* 1. (Biblia) Presbiterio, consejo de ancianos en la Iglesia cristiana; cuerpo de ancianos, sean sacerdotes o legos. 2. Presbiterianismo, el sistema de gobierno de una iglesia por presbíteros o ancianos, en oposición a la prelacía y a la independencia. 3. La junta de sacerdotes presbiterianos dentro de un distrito determinado, con un anciano por cada iglesia; tribunal eclesiástico de los presbiterianos. 4. (Arq.) Presbiterio, coro. *V.* CHANCEL.

Prescience [prî'-shi-ens], *s.* Presciencia, conocimiento anticipado de las cosas futuras.

Prescient [prî'-shi-ent], *a.* Presciente, que sabe lo futuro, que sabe de antemano; también, dotado de vista penetrante.

Prescind [prę-sind'], *va.* y *vn.* 1. Prescindir; separar o apartar una cosa de otra. 2. Prescindir, separar mentalmente una cosa de otra á que está realmente unida.

Prescribe [prę-scraib'], *va.* 1. Prescribir, señalar, ordenar, determinar alguna cosa. 2. Recetar a un enfermo, dar instrucciones para el uso de un remedio.—*vn.* 1. Dar leyes o reglas; particularmente, prescribir un remedio que se ha de emplear, el régimen que ha de seguir un enfermo. 2. (For.) Prescribir, adquirir un derecho por una larga posesión o por prescripción; perderse, invalidarse por el transcurso del tiempo.

†**Prescript** [prí'-script], *s.* 1. Norma, regla. 2. Receta del médico.—*a.* Prescrito.

Prescriptible [prę-scrip'-ti-bl], *a.* 1. Prescriptible; que se puede prescribir. 2. (For.) Adquirible por la prescripción.

Prescription [prę-scrip'-shun], *s.* 1. Prescripción, acción de prescribir o de dirigir; dirección autoritativa. 2. Precepto, regla. 3. Receta medicinal; también, familiarmente, el medicamento así prescrito. 4. (For.) (1) Revindicación o reivindicación, modo de adquirir el dominio de una propiedad por la posesión larga y no interrumpida; también, el número determinado de años después de los cuales se puede reclamar la prescripción. (2) Modo de perder un derecho o título por no haberlo alegado dentro de un plazo señalado; el número de años después de los cuales no puede alegarse un título o derecho no reclamado; el plazo en que prescribe o se pierde el derecho de incoar un procedimiento criminal.

Prescriptive [prę-scrip'-tiv], *a.* 1. Sancionado, autorizado por la costumbre y por el uso prolongado. 2. (For.) Adquirido por usufructo o uso inmemorial.

Presence [prez'-ens], *s.* 1. Presencia, asistencia personal; el estado de una persona que se halla delante de otra, o en el mismo paraje que otra. 2. Presencia, el talle, figura o disposición del cuerpo, proximidad. 3. Presencia, viva memoria de alguna cosa; algo impalpable, pero cercano y perceptible á los sentidos, como una aparición. 4. Asistencia, corte, asamblea de personas, v. g. ante un gran personaje. 5. (Ant.) El salón del palacio donde el monarca recibe su corte. 6. Serenidad. *Presence of mind,* Presencia de ánimo.

Presence-chamber [prez'-ens-chêm'-bęr], **Presence-room** [prez'-ens-rūm], *s.* Sala de estrado, sala de recibimiento.

Present [prez'-ent], *a.* 1. Presente, que está delante o en presencia de otro, o concurre con él en el mismo lugar. 2. Presente, actual, hablando de cosas que existen en el tiempo en que uno vive. (Com.) Actual, corriente. *The present month,* El mes actual o corriente. 3. Presente, que está actualmente fijo en el ánimo. 4. (Ant.) Pronto, dispuesto, aparejado. 5. (Ant.) Atento, cuidadoso. *At present,* Al presente, ahora. *To be present,* Presenciar, asistir, concurrir.

Present, *s.* 1. Presente, el don, alhaja o regalo que una persona da a otra. 2. Carta de mandamiento.—*pl.* Las escrituras presentes. *Know all men by these presents,* Sepan todos por las presentes. *To all to whom these presents shall come, greeting,* A todos los que las presentes vieren, salud. 3. (Gram.) Tiempo presente. *Presents remove difficulties,* Dádivas quebrantan peñas.

Present [prę-zent'], *va.* 1. Presentar, introducir, dar a conocer; poner delante de alguien. 2. Presentar, dar graciosa y voluntariamente algún regalo, ofrecer, regalar. 3. Presentar, manifestar, mostrar. 4. Presentar un beneficio eclesiástico. 5. Representar, exponer. 6. Apuntar, asestar (un arma). 7. (For.) Denunciar, citar. *To present arms,* (Mil.) Presentar las armas. *To present one's self,* Presentarse, ofrecerse. *To present a person with a thing,* Regalar una cosa a alguien.

Presentable [prę-zent'-a-bl], *a.* Presentable, que puede presentarse, ofrecerse, mostrarse, exhibirse o representarse.

Presentation [prez-en-tê'-shun], *s.* 1. Presentación; acción de presentar, de ofrecer; introducción; particularmente, ofrecimiento formal de un regalo. 2. Exhibición, representación, manera de exhibir o de presentar algo a la mente. 3. Presentación, posición del feto al nacer. *On presentation.* (Com.) A presentación.

Presentative [prę-zent'-a-tiv], *a.* 1. Que tiene relación con la presentación mental. 2. Que tiene derecho de presentación.

Present-day [prez'-ent-dê'], *a.* De la actualidad, de hoy.

Presentee [prez-en-tí'], *s.* Presentado, el sujeto propuesto o nombrado para ocupar un beneficio eclesiástico.

Presenter [prę-zent'-ęr], *s.* Presentador, el que presenta o propone para un beneficio eclesiástico; el que hace un regalo.

Presential [prę-zen'-shal], *a.* Presencial, que implica la verdadera presencia; presente en realidad, manifiesto.

Presentiment [prę-sen'-ti-męnt], *s.* Presentimiento, cierto movimiento interior que hace presagiar lo que ha de acontecer; especialmente, idea de que amenaza una calamidad o desgracia.

Presently [prez'-ent-li], *adv.* 1. Presentemente, luego, de aquí a poco, dentro de poco. 2. (Ant.) Inmediatamente, incontinenti, al punto, sin dilación.

Presentment [prę-zent'-męnt], *s.* 1. Presentación, acción de presentar; manera o estado de ser presentado. 2. Representación, retrato; semejanza. 3. Parte, conducta, manifestación del carácter. 4. Denuncia o acusación ante un tribunal.

Preservable [prę-zęrv'-a-bl], *a.* Preservable, que se puede preservar.

Preservation [prez-ęr-vê'-shun], *s.* Preservación, conservación.

Preservative [prę-zęrv'-a-tiv], *a.* Preservativo, que tiene virtud o eficacia para preservar; conservador.—*s.* Preservativo, lo que sirve para preservar o que tiende a preservar; defensa, salvaguardia.

Preservatory [prę-zęrv'-a-to-ri], *a.* Preservativo, que tiene la facultad de preservar o proteger.

Preserve [prę-zęrv'], *va.* 1. Asegurar, poner o mantener en seguridad; proteger contra un daño o preservar, sacar de peligro, librar de la destrucción o de la muerte. 2. Preservar, guardar, conservar, mantener en buen estado. 3. Preservar, poner al abrigo de la corrupción; conservar, hacer almíbar, almibarar.—*vn.* Hacer conservas de frutas, confitarlas o almibararlas. *To preserve the health,* Conservar la salud. *To preserve appearances,* Guardar las apariencias.

Preserve, *s.* Conserva, confitura.

Preserver [prę-zęrv'-ęr], *s.* 1. Preservador, confitero. 2. Antiguamente conservero. 3. Conservador, el que protege o defiende contra la destrucción o el mal.

Preside [prę-zaid'], *vn.* 1. Presidir. 2. Gobernar, dirigir: (úsase con la prep. *over*).

Presidency [prez'-i-den-si], *s.* Presidencia; superintendencia; funciones de presidente; tiempo durante el cual ejerce sus funciones un presidente.

President [prez'-i-dent], *s.* Presidente, funcionario elegido o nombrado para presidir una corporación, sociedad o asamblea de personas y dirigir sus deliberaciones; particularmente, el jefe del poder ejecutivo en las repúblicas.

Presidental [prez-i-dent'-al], *a.* De, o perteneciente a un presidente; que preside.

Presidential [prez-i-den'-shal], *a.* Presidencial, perteneciente a una presidencia, o a un presidente; que preside.

Press [pres], *va.* 1. Aprensar, prensar, apretar, estrujar u oprimir en una prensa. 2. Aprensar, apretar; afligir, oprimir, angustiar; estrujar a una persona. 3. Compeler, obligar; impeler con violencia. 4. Apresurar, dar priesa. 5. Apretar, instar con eficacia. 6. Apretar, estrechar, acosar, perseguir de cerca. 7. Recalcar, ajustar o apretar mucho una cosa sobre otra. 8. Hacer levas, enganchar soldados. *V. To* IMPRESS. 9. Abrazar estrechamente, acariciar. 10. Acosar, incomodar, hostigar, fatigar; abrumar, causar pena. 11. Alisar o dar forma por medio de la presión, satinar.—*vn.* 1. Obrar por el peso o la fuerza; ejercer presión. 2. Avanzar sobre, adelantarse con ardor o enérgicamente, hacer esfuerzos para progresar; apresurarse. 3. Urgir, instar con vehemencia, apurar. 4. Agolparse la gente alrededor de una persona o cosa, apiñarse. 5. Acercarse demasiado por pura curiosidad; instar importunamente. 6. Hacer fuerza con algún argumento, razón, etc. *To hot-press,* Prensar con planchas calientes. *To press a benefit upon one,* Hacer a uno algún favor a su pesar. *To press down,* Apretar o estrujar a uno hasta hacerle caer o hasta dejarlo inmóvil. *He pressed him to his breast,* Le estrechó contra su pecho. *Pressed for money,* Necesitado; impulsado por la falta de dinero. *To press clothes,* Alisar, planchar la ropa. *To press on, to press forward,* Impeler hacia adelante, hacer adelantar; apresurarse, adelantarse con ardor. *The feet press the ground,* Los pies pisan el suelo.

Press, *s.* 1. Turba, muchedumbre de gente. 2. Acción de esforzarse hacia adelante o de apiñarse. 3.

Prisa, urgencia de asuntos; peso (de los negocios). *Press of business*, Presión, urgencia de los negocios. 4. Prensa, máquina que sirve para apretar o exprimir, para alisar y dar lustre a los tejidos, para imprimir y otros usos. *Wine-press*, Prensa de lagar. *Cloth-press*, Prensa de paños. 5. Prensa de impresor; imprenta en general y sus productos; también, el conjunto de los redactores, gacetilleros, repórters, etc., empleados en los diarios o periódicos. 6. Armario, cajón de madera en forma de alacena para poner ropa y otras cosas. 7. Leva, recluta, enganche. *V.* IMPRESSMENT. *To go to press, to send to press*, Poner en prensa. *To correct for the press*, Corregir pruebas de imprenta. *Liberty of the press*, Libertad de la prensa, de imprenta. *Press-proof*, (1) La última prueba tomada antes de imprimir. (2) Una prueba tomada con cuidado. *Hot press, cold press*, Prensa para satinar, en caliente o en frío.

Presser [pres'-ẹr], *s.* Aprensador.

Pressgang [pres'-gang], *s.* Ronda de matrícula, empleada para enganchar o hacer levas para la marina o el ejército.

Pressing [pres'-ing], *a.* 1. Urgente, que insta; importante. 2. Importuno, pesado en sus solicitaciones. —*s. V.* PRESSURE. *Pressing-boards*, Cartones lustrosos para prensar paño. *Pressing-iron*, Plancha.

Pressingly [pres'-ing-li], *adv.* Apretadamente, urgentemente.

Pressman [pres'-man], *s.* 1. Prensador, el que tiene a su cargo una prensa; prensista (tipográfico). 2. Obrero que prensa el paño. 3. Reclutador, el que engancha gente para la marina o el ejército. 4. El hombre, soldado o marinero alistado en el servicio público.

Press-money [pres'-mun-i], *s.* Enganche o enganchamiento, el dinero que se da a alguno en la Gran Bretaña para que siente plaza de soldado.

Press-room [pres'-rūm], *s.* Taller de imprenta, local donde están las prensas de imprimir.

Pressure [presh'-ur], *s.* 1. Presión, la acción de apretar, estrujar o comprimir; prensadura, acción de prensar; el estado de ser apretado, prensado o comprimido. 2. Fuerza mecánica, medida comúnmente en libras; fuerza mecánica de cualquier especie. 3. Fuerza moral determinante, impulso eficaz. 4. Urgencia, prisa, ímpetu, exigencia sobre el tiempo o la energía de alguien. 5. Ahogo, opresión, aprieto, congoja, vejación, apretura.

Pressure cooker [presh'-ur cuk'-ẹr], *s.* Olla a presión. (Mex.) Olla express.

Pressurize [presh'-ur-aiz], *va.* (Aer.) Sobrecomprimir. *Pressurized cabin*, Cabina a presión.

Presswork [pres'-wūrk], *s.* 1. (Impr.) Manejo y manipulación de la prensa tipográfica; también, tirada, el trabajo hecho por la prensa. 2. Ebanistería hecha con chapas colocadas al través, encoladas y prensadas mientras están calientes.

Prestation [pres-tê'-shun], *s.* Pago de dinero, v. g. por peaje; el hacer un servicio o deber; antiguamente, préstamo, cantidad que los clérigos anglicanos pagaban anualmente a los obispos.

Prester [pres'-tẹr], *s.* Preste; desusado, excepto en la locución *Prester John*, Preste Juan, soberano cristiano legendario que en la edad media se suponía reinaba en el Oriente (más tarde reconocido como la Abisinia).

Prestidigitation [pres"-ti-dij-i-tê'-shun], *s.* Prestidigitación, juegos de manos.

Prestidigitator [pres-ti-dij'-i-tê'-tər], *s.* Prestidigitador.

Prestige [pres'-tij], *s.* Prestigio, buena reputación, fama, influencia moral o autoridad basada en el poder o los triunfos pasados.

Prestimony [pres'-ti-mo-ni], *s.* Prestimonio, prestamera, prebenda eclesiástica de la Iglesia católica romana.

Presto [pres'-tō], *adv.* 1. En música, en compás vivo y animado. 2. Presto, luego, al instante.

Presumable [prẹ-ziū'-ma-bl], *a.* Presumible; razonable.

Presumably [prẹ-ziū'-ma-bli], *adv.* Sin examen; por presunción.

Presume [prẹ-ziūm'], *va.* 1. Presumir, suponer o creer alguna cosa sólo por indicios; afirmar sin prueba. 2. Presumir, estar muy satisfecho o pagado de sí. 3. Atreverse a hacer una cosa sin derecho o permiso para hacerla.—*vn.* Vanagloriarse, jactarse. *To presume on* o *upon*, Suponer; contar con; imaginarse; vanagloriarse de. *To presume upon*, Estar muy satisfecho o pagado de, contar con, tener demasiada confianza en algo.

Presumed [prẹ-ziūmd], *a.* Presunto.

Presumer [prẹ-ziūm'-ẹr], *s.* Un presumido; un hombre arrogante o presuntuoso.

Presumption [prẹ-zump'-shun], *s.* 1. Presunción, sospecha, conjetura. 2. Presunción, vanidad, confianza en sí mismo. 3. La confianza que se tiene en una cosa presupuesta. 4. Argumento muy fuerte. 5. Temeridad, acción de emprender alguna cosa contra las probabilidades ordinarias. *The presumption is that it will take place*, Puede presumirse, pensarse, que eso se realizará.

Presumptive [prẹ-zump'-tiv], *a.* 1. Presuntivo, supuesto, presupuesto, que da origen a una presunción, fundado sobre una presunción o un testimonio probable; que puede creerse razonablemente. 2. (Des.) Presuntuoso.

Presumptively [prẹ-zump'-tiv-li], *adv.* Según presunción, por vía de conjetura.

Presumptuous [prẹ-zump'-chu-us o tiu-us], *a.* 1. Presuntuoso, presumido, arrogante, vano, insolente, irreverente. 2. Atrevido, arrojado, que confía excesivamente.

Presumptuously [prẹ-zump'-chu-us-li], *adv.* Presuntuosamente.

Presumptuousness [prẹ-zump'-chu-us-nes], *s.* Presunción, calidad de presuntuoso o arrogante; orgullo, arrogancia, vana confianza; irreverencia.

Presuppose [prî-sup-pōz'], *va.* Presuponer; implicar como antecedente; suponer de antemano.

Presupposition [prî-sup-po-zish'-un], *s.* Presuposición, presupuesto.

Pretence [prẹ-tens'], *s.* Lo mismo que PRETENSE.

Pretend [prẹ-tend'], *va.* 1. Aparentar, mostrar o dar a entender lo que no es o lo que no hay, dar por pretexto, fingir; hacerse el, o que. 2. Pretender, intentar. 3. Pretender, procurar o solicitar alguna cosa. 4. Afirmar falsamente; alegar sin verdad.—*vn.* 1. Afectar; presumir o preciarse de; aspirar a lograr alguna cosa o creer tener derecho a ella. 2. Disfrazarse.

Pretender [prẹ-tend'-ẹr], *s.* Pretendiente, pretensor; en la historia de Inglaterra, el hijo y el nieto de Jaime II.

Pretendingly [prẹ-tend'-ing-li], *adv.* Arrogantemente, presuntuosamente.

Pretense [prẹ-tens'], *s.* 1. Pretexto, motivo simulado, causa aparente, supuesta razón aparente para ocultar un motivo; ficción, máscara, velo. 2. Pretensión, afectación, simulación. 3. Pretensión, el derecho bien o mal fundado que alguno juzga tener a una cosa. 4. Intención, designio, proyecto.

Pretenseless [prẹ-tens'-les], *a.* Falto de pretensiones.

Pretension [prẹ-ten'-shun], *s.* 1. Pretensión, el derecho bien o mal fundado que alguno juzga tener sobre una cosa; pretexto. 2. Ostentación de un carácter particular, sea simulada o mal entendida; afectación. 3. Afirmación atrevida o presuntuosa.

Pretentious [prẹ-ten'-shus], *a.* Con pretensiones, afectado, vanaglorioso, presumido; llamativo.

Preter- [prî'-tẹr], *s.* Prefijo latino que significa fuera de, más o más allá.

Preterit, Preterite [pret'-ẹr-it], *a.* (Gram.) Pasado, pretérito.—*s.* Tiempo pretérito o pasado del verbo. *V.* AORIST.

Preterition [pret-ẹ-rish'-un], *s.* 1. Preterición, pretermisión. 2. (Ret.) Preterición, figura que consiste en aparentar que se quiere omitir o pasar por alto aquello mismo que se dice expresamente.

Preterlapsed [prî-tẹr-lapst'], *a.* Pasado, ido.

Pretermission [prî-tẹr-mish'-un], *s* Pretermisión, omisión.

Preternatural [prî'-tẹr-nach-ur-al], *a* Preternatural, extraordinario, inexplicable; poco común; se diferencia de antinatural.

Preternaturally [prî'-tẹr-nach-ur-al-i], *adv.* Preternaturalmente.

Preternaturalness [prî'-tẹr-nach-ur-al-nes], *s.* El estado o calidad de preternatural.

Pretext [prî'-text o prẹ-text'], *s.* Pretexto, motivo fingido, razón ficticia; excusa, socolor.

Pretor [prî'-tər], *s.* Pretor, magistrado romano.

Pretorian, Pretorial [prẹ-tō'-ri-an, al], *a.* 1. Pretoriano, pretorial, tocante o perteneciente al pretor. 2. Pretoriano, se aplica a los soldados de la guardia de los emperadores romanos.

Prettily [prit'-i-li], *adv.* Lindamente, bonitamente; agradablemente.

Prettiness [prit'-i-nes], *s.* Lindeza; calidad de bonito; cierta belleza, elegancia o gentileza; gracia.

Pretty [prit'-i], *a.* 1. Lindo, bien parecido, bonito, moderadamente bello o hermoso. 2. Afectado; lindo, hablando irónicamente. 3. Mediano, ni muy pequeño ni muy grande, pasadero; suficiente, bastante. 4. Agradable, dulce, encantador, precioso. *A pretty while*, Un buen rato.—*adv.* Algo, algún tanto, un poco. *Pretty well*, Medianamente, tal cual, no mal, bastante bien. *Pretty near*, Bastante cerca, poco más o menos. a corta diferencia.

Pretzel [pret'-sęl], *s.* Galleta muy salada de origen alemán, por lo general en forma de nudo.

Prevail [prę-vêl'], *vn.* 1. Prevalecer, vencer, ser superior, poder o valer más; sobresalir, predominar. 2. Influir, tener influjo; obrar con eficacia. 3. Persuadir, inducir, lograr, conseguir, alcanzar de una persona que haga lo que se quiere. 4. Esparcirse o extenderse grandemente, estar en boga general; ser muy frecuente. *To prevail on, upon, over* o *against*, Ser superior, tener más fuerza, dominar, vencer; supeditar. *To prevail on, upon* o *with*, Persuadir, inducir, convencer. *He prevailed upon me to come*, Me persuadió a que viniese. *Mohammedanism prevails throughout northern Africa*, El mahometismo predomina en todo el norte de África. *It is a fashion which prevails*, Es una moda que está en boga.

Prevailing [prę-vêl'-ing], *a.* 1. Muy esparcido, extendido, general, común. 2. Predominante, poderoso, eficaz.

Prevalence [prev'-a-lens], **Prevalency** [prev'-a-len-si], *s.* 1. Predominio, superioridad, fuerza predominante, eficacia, preponderancia. 2. Uso o aceptación general, ocurrencia común, frecuencia.

Prevalent [prev'-a-lent], *a.* 1. Superior, sobresaliente, predominante, poderoso, dominante. 2. General, grandemente esparcido, de frecuente ocurrencia, común. 3. Victorioso, eficaz.

Prevalently [prev'-a-lent-li], *adv.* Eficazmente, poderosamente.

Prevaricate [prę-var'-i-kêt], *vn.* 1. Usar de lenguaje ambiguo o evasivo para engañar; representar falsamente. 2. (For.) Prevaricar, emprender un negocio de mala fe con objeto de que salga mal, o asumir la defensa de un cliente para hacerle traición.

Prevarication [prę-var-i-kê'-shun], *s.* 1. Afirmación que engaña, aserto equívoco, ambiguo: mentira. 2. Subterfugio; dolo, superchería. 3. (For.) Prevaricato, el crimen del abogado o procurador que hace traición a su parte, favoreciendo a la contraria.

Prevaricator [prę-var'-i-kê-tęr], *s.* Prevaricador, el que representa falsamente, el que engaña con lenguaje ambiguo: término menos ofensivo que *liar* (mentiroso).

Prevent [prę-vent'], *va.* 1. Prevenir, precaver, estorbar, impedir. 2. Prevenir, adelantarse o anticiparse a alguno. 3. (Ant.) Preceder, guiar, ir delante guiando y facilitando el camino.—*vn.* (Des.) Venir antes de tiempo.

Preventative [prę-vent'-a-tiv], *a.* y *s.* V. PREVENTIVE.

Preventer [prę-vent'-ęr], *s.* Estorbador, el que o lo que impide o precave; especialmente, (Mar.) soga, berlinga, cadena o perno auxiliar. *Preventer-brace*, Contrabraza. *Preventer-tacks*, Contraamuras. *Preventer-lifts*, Contraamantillos. *Preventer-shrouds*, Contraobenques. *Preventer-sheets*, Contraescotas. *Preventer-stay*, Estay folar. *Preventer-backstays*, Contrabrandales.

Prevention [prę-ven'-shun], *s.* 1. Estorbo, embarazo, la acción de estorbar o impedir; también, lo que impide o sirve de obstáculo. 2. (Des.) La acción de ir delante o de tomar la delantera; la acción de preceder. *Prevention is better than cure*, (prov.) Lo mejor es curarse en salud.

Preventive [prę-ven'-tiv], *a.* 1. Impeditivo; que sirve para proteger contra daño: preservativo, lo que tiene virtud de preservar. 2. (Des.) Preventivo, que previene a otra cosa. *Preventive service*, Resguardo militar, fuerza empleada en Inglaterra para impedir el contrabando.—*s.* Preservativo, profiláctico; medida preventiva o profiláctica.

Preventively [prę-ven'-tiv-li], *adv.* Prevenidamente, anticipadamente, de antemano.

Preview [pri'-viū], *s.* Exhibición previa, representación especial (de algún espectáculo) antes de verlo el público.

Previous [pri'-vi-us], *a.* Previo, anticipado, antecedente, anterior, de antemano. *Previous notice*, Aviso dado de antemano. *The previous question*, La cuestión previa. *Previous to*, Antecedente; antes de. V. PREVIOUSLY.

Previously [pri'-vi-us-li], *adv.* De antemano, anticipadamente, anteriormente. *Previously to July*, Antes de julio.

Previse [prę-vaiz'], *va.* 1. Prever; conocer de antemano. 2. Prevenir, avisar o amonestar de antemano.

Prevision [prę-vish'-un], *s.* Previsión, conocimiento o juicio de lo futuro.

Prewar [prę'-wēr], *a.* De la preguerra, de antes de la guerra.

Prey [prê], *s.* 1. Presa, cualquier animal asido por otro para su alimento; de aquí, botín, pillaje, despojo. 2. Víctima. 3. Rapiña, robo. *Beast of prey*, Animal de rapiña, animal carnicero. *Bird of prey*, Ave de rapiña. *To fall a prey to*, Ser presa de.

Prey, *vn.* (con *on* o *upon*). 1. Devorar sus presas los animales carniceros. 2. Rapiñar, hurtar, pillar, robar, hacer presa. 3. Irse consumiendo la salud, la vida, etc.; minar, arruinar gradualmente. 4. Pesar, hacer fuerza en el ánimo la razón de alguna cosa; oprimir, agobiar.

Price [prais], *s.* 1. Precio, el dinero que se paga por alguna cosa. 2. Precio, valor o estimación. 3. Premio, galardón. *Market price*, Precio de mercado, precio corriente. *Set price*, Precio fijo. *Trade price*, Precio con rebaja para los que hacen el mismo comercio. *Full* o *selling price*, Precio de venta al menudeo. *Opening price, closing price*. Primer curso, último curso (en la Bolsa). *At any price*, A todo precio; cueste lo que cueste, o lo que costare. *To set a price upon one's head*, Poner a precio la cabeza de alguno. *Price-list*, Lista de precios; cotización.

Price, *va.* 1. Valuar, estimar, apreciar, fijar el precio de alguna cosa. 2. (Fam.) Preguntar o pedir el precio de. *A priced catalogue*, Un catálogo con precios.

Price control [prais' con-trol], *s.* Control de precios.

Price-current [prais-cur'-ent], *s.* La lista de los precios corrientes por mayor, derechos, etc., de los géneros.

Priceless [prais'-les], *a.* 1. Inapreciable, demasiado precioso para admitir precio; sin precio. 2. (Des.) Bajo precio, sin valor ni mérito.

Prick [pric], *va.* 1. Punzar, picar, herir de punta. 2. Fijar por la punta algún instrumento. 3. Apuntar, señalar o marcar alguna cosa con la punta de un instrumento; de aquí, escoger: en otro tiempo, poner en música una canción. 4. Aguzar, avivar, picar, excitar, estimular; pinchar. 5. (Mar.) Compasear la carta de marear. 6. Enderezar o aguzar las orejas; prestar atención. 7. Perseguir una liebre por medio de pistas.—*vn.* 1. Tener o causar la sensación de una punzada o picadura; picarse. 2. Galopar; arrimar las espuelas o dar de espuelas. 3. Apuntar hacia arriba. 4. (Prov. Ingl.) Avinagrarse, ponerse ácido. *To prick on o forward*, Aguijonear, pisar, aguzar, avivar, estimular. *To prick up*, Enderezar, poner derecha una cosa. *To prick up one's ears*, Aguzar las orejas, aguzar los oídos, oír o escuchar muy atentamente; amusgar. *To prick off* o *out*, En jardinería, transplantar muy arrimadas las plantas tiernas, por vía de preparación para ponerlas en macetas o cuadros. *To prick the sails*, (Mar.) Recoser las velas.

Prick, *s.* 1. Punzón, aguijón, acicate; cualquier instrumento puntiagudo. 2. Puntura, herida con instrumento punzante; picadura, punzada. 3. Punzada, el sentimiento interior que causa alguna cosa que aflige el ánimo; espina, escrúpulo o remordimiento de conciencia. 4. Pista, rastro, huella de venado o liebre. 5. Punto, momento; el tiempo fijo en que se hace alguna cosa. 6. El blanco a que tiran los ballesteros. *To kick against the pricks*, Dar o tirar coces contra el aguijón; obstinarse en resistir a una fuerza superior.

Prick-eared [prik'-ird], *a.* Amusgado; despierto, vivo; impertinente.

Pricker [prik'-ęr], *s.* 1. Punzón, instrumento puntiagudo; alesna o lesna. 2. El que pica. 3. Jinete, el que espolea o da espuela al caballo.

Pricket [prik'-et], *s.* 1. Punta sobre que se puede asegurar una vela. 2 Siempreviva menor. 3. El gamo de un año cumplido.

Pricking [prik'-ing], *s.* 1. Picadura. 2. Punzada, dolor agudo que repite de cuando en cuando.

Prickle [pric'-l], *s.* Pincho, púa. espina. *Thorn prickle*, Abrojo.

Prickliness [pric'-li-nes], *s.* Calidad de espinoso; abundancia de púas, espinas o pinchos.

Prickly [pric'-li], *a.* Espinoso. *Prickly heat*, Salpullido o sarpullido.

Prickly-pear [pric'-li-pār''], *s.* Nopal, tunal, higuera de Indias; cualquier cacto del género Opuntia.

Pride [praid], *s.* 1. Orgullo, presunción, vanidad, engreimiento. 2. Insolencia, altivez. 3. Ostentación, jactancia o vanagloria. 4. Hermosura notable; belleza, amabilidad; ornamento; de aquí, majestuosidad, pompa, aparato. 5. Dignidad, elevación, esplendor, ostentación. 6. Amor propio. 7. Conocimiento interior de la juventud o del poder;

fuego, ardor; de aquí, (des.) propensión al coito que tienen las hembras de algunos animales cuando están salidas. *He takes pride in doing good*, Se precia o gloria en hacer bien.
Pride, *va.* Ensoberbecerse, picarse, preciarse o jactarse de alguna cosa regularmente buena. *To pride one's self*, Enorgullecerse, ensoberbecerse.
Prideful [praid'-ful], *a.* Orgulloso, altanero; también, vano.
Prier [prai'-ęr], *s.* Escudriñador.
Priest [prīst], *s.* Sacerdote, presbítero, cura; el que preside las ceremonias de un culto religioso.
Priestcraft [prīst'-crgft], *s.* Supercheria, artimaña, embuste o fraude de los ministros de la religión.
Priestess [prīst'-es], *sf.* Sacerdotisa.
Priesthood [prīst'-hud], *s.* Clero, clerecía; el estado eclesiástico; el sacerdocio.
Priestliness [prīst'-li-nes], *s.* Las maneras o modales de los sacerdotes.
Priestly [prīst'-li], *a.* Sacerdotal, perteneciente a un sacerdote o a un cura; que conviene a un cura.
Priestridden [prīst'-rid-n], *a.* Gobernado o dirigido completamente por sacerdotes.
Prig [prig], *vn.* (Prov. Ingl.) Regatear, bajar el precio.
Prig, *s.* Mozuelo presumido, pisaverde; pedante.
Priggish [prig'-ish], *a.* Algo presumido y afectado.
Priggishness, Priggism [prig'-ish-nes, prig'-izm], *s.* Maneras o modales de un pisaverde o un pedante.
Prill [pril], *s.* *V.* BRILL.
Prim [prim], *a.* Peripuesto, afectado, puesto de veinticinco alfileres.
Prim, *va.* Ataviar, poner a uno petimetre o muy majo; hacer carocas o carantoñas.
Primacy [prai'-ma-si], *s.* Primacía, la dignidad y jurisdicción del primado.
Prima facie [prai'-ma fé'-shi-ī o prī'-ma fg'-ki-ę], locución latina. Prima facie, a primera vista.
Primage [prai'-męj], *s.* (Mar.) Capa.
Primal [prai'-mal], *a.* Primero, que está al principio; original, principal, lo más importante.
Primarily [prai'-ma-ri-li], *adv.* Primariamente, originalmente; sobre todo, principalmente.
Primariness [prai'-ma-ri-nes], *s.* Primado, primacía, prioridad.
Primary [prai'-ma-ri], *a.* 1. Primario, primero; primitivo, original, radical. 2. Principal, de primer orden, fundamental. 3. Elemental, del primer grado, el más bajo. —*s.* 1. Primero, lo que ocupa el primer puesto en importancia. 2. (E. U.) Reunión de los electores de un partido antes de una elección, para nombrar los candidatos. 3. Pluma grande de las que sirven a las aves para volar.
Primary education [prai'-ma-ri ed-yu-kē'-shun], *s.* Educación primaria o elemental.
Primate [prai'-met], *s.* Primado, el primero y más preeminente de todos los arzobispos y obispos de un reino. *Primates*, Orden primero de la clase de los mamíferos.
Primateship [prai'-met-ship], *s.* Primado, dignidad del primado.
Prime [praim], *s.* 1. La primavera de la vida, el estado de mayor vigor o hermosura. 2. El principio de alguna cosa; la madrugada, el alba, el amanecer, el principio del día y a veces se toma por toda la mañana. 3. Apice, el último grado de perfección. 4. Flor, nata, lo mas escogido o selecto de alguna cosa. 5. Prima, una de las horas canónicas. 6. Señal o signo (') que se pone arriba y hacia la derecha de una letra o guarismo; la pulgada, o el minuto designado por este signo.—*a.* 1. Que está en su mayor verdor o en su estado más floreciente. 2. Primero, original, principal. *At prime cost*, Al precio de pie de fábrica; a coste y costas. 3. Primoroso, excelente. 4. Primo, número divisible solamente por sí mismo y por la unidad. 5. Marcado con el signo '. *Prime minister*, Primer ministro, el ministro principal del estado.
Prime, *va.* 1. Aparejar, preparar. 2. (Fam.) Advertir, avisar, noticiar; informar sobre lo que se ha de decir o hacer. 3. Cebar, poner pólvora en la cazoleta de un arma de fuego cargada. 4. Imprimar, cubrir con la primera capa de colores o de argamasa.—*vn.* 1. Servir de cebo; de aquí, poner una persona o cosa en estado de preparación para hacer algo. 2. Llevar agua con el vapor dentro del cilindro; dícese de una caldera de vapor.
Primely [praim'-li], *adv.* 1. En alto grado, muy bien, excelentemente. 2. (Des.) Primeramente, originalmente.
Primeness [praim'-nes], *s.* Primacía, primor, excelencia.
Primer [prim'-ęr], *s.* 1. Cartilla para los niños. 2. Originalmente, el devocionario de Nuestra Señora. 3. Dos grados de letra de imprenta; es decir *long primer*, entredós, filosofía, letra de diez puntos; y *great primer*, texto, letra de dieciocho puntos.
Primeval [prai-mī'-val], *a.* Primitivo, primero, original.
Primigenial [prai-mi-jī'-ni-al], *a.* Primigenio, primogénito; primígeno, original, primario; constitutivo, elemental.
Priming [prai'-ming], *s.* 1. El acto de prepararse o alistarse. 2. Cebo, la pólvora que se pone en las cazoletas de las armas de fuego. 3. Lo que es preliminar, o relativamente pequeño, en comparación con otra cosa. 4. Imprimación, la primera capa de colores u óleo que se da a una superficie. 5. En las máquinas de vapor, el primer chorro de mezcla de vapor y agua. *Priming-horn*, Polvorín, el frasco para el cebo.
Primitial [prai-mish'-al], *a.* (Poco us.) Perteneciente a las primicias.
Primitive [prim'-i-tiv], *a.* 1. Primitivo, original; antiguo, que pertenece al principio, al origen, o a los tiempos antiguos; radical, que no es derivado. 2. (Biol.) Rudimentario, original, que se halla en estado temprano de su desarrollo. 3. Primitivo, radical, de donde se derivan otras palabras.
Primitively [prim'-i-tiv-li], *adv.* Originalmente, primitivamente, al principio.
Primly [prim'-li], *adv.* De una manera peripuesta; puesto de veinticinco alfileres.
Primness [prim'-nes], *s.* Precisión, exactitud, formalidad o gravedad afectada; remilgo o dengue en las mujeres.
Primogenial [prai-mo-jī'-ni-al], *a.* *V.* PRIMIGENIAL.
Primogeniture [prai-mo-jen'-i-chur o tiūr], *s.* 1. Prioridad de nacimiento; derecho de nacimiento. 2. Primogenitura.
Primordial [prai-mōr'-di-al], *s.* Origen, primer principio.
Primordial, Primordiate [prai-mōr'-di-ęt], *a.* Primordial.
Primrose [prim'-rōz], *s.* 1. (Bot.) Prímula o primavera, una planta y su flor. 2. Color amarillo verdoso claro.—*a.* 1. Perteneciente a la prímula o de su color; amarillo verdoso claro. 2. Florido, gayo.
Primum-mobile [prai'-mum-meb'-i-li], *s.* (Astr.) Primer móvil.
Prince [prins], *s.* 1. Príncipe, soberano, monarca. 2. Príncipe, el hijo de un monarca; descendiente varón de una casa real; el que goza de este título de honor. 3. Príncipe, el primero y más excelente en su línea. *Petty prince*, Principillo, principote. *Prince Rupert's drops*, *V.* RUPERT'S DROPS. *Prince of the power of the air, prince of this world*, (Bíblico) Satanás. *Prince of Wales*, Príncipe de Gales, título del heredero del trono en Inglaterra.
Princedom [prins'-dum], *s.* Principado, soberanía.
Prince-like [prins'-laic], *a.* Correspondiente a un príncipe o semejante a él.
Princeliness [prins'-li-nes], *s.* Cualidad que conviene a un príncipe; munificencia, nobleza, magnificencia.
Princely [prins'-li], *a.* 1. Semejante a un príncipe o característico de él; digno de un príncipe, grande, noble, munífico. 2. Propio de un príncipe; real, magnífico, regio; faustoso, fastuoso, fastoso, augusto. —*adv.* Como un príncipe, digno de un príncipe.
Prince's-feather [prins'-ez-fedh'-ęr], *s.* (Bot.) 1. Polígono, planta herbácea anua, con espigas de flores color de rosa. Polygonum orientale. 2. Amaranto (de Méjico).
Princess [prin'-ses], *sf.* Princesa; hija de un monarca, o de una casa real; esposa de un príncipe; reina, o mujer soberana de un Estado..
Principal [prin'-si-pal], *a.* 1. Principal, que tiene el primer lugar y estimación. 2. Principal, el que está a la cabeza de algún negocio, y en este sentido se usa como substantivo en ambas lenguas.—*s.* 1. Principal, jefe, presidente, gobernador; director de una escuela u otro establecimiento de educación. 2. (For.) Causante, comitente, constituyente. 3. Principal, capital, la cantidad de dinero que se pone a censo, rédito o a ganancias y pérdidas.
Principality [prin-si-pal'-i-ti], *s.* 1. Principado, soberanía. 2. (Ant.) Superioridad, predominio. —*pl.* (Ant.) En el Nuevo Testamento, potestades celestiales o demoníacas.
Principally [prin'-si-pal-i], *adv.* Principalmente, primeramente, en primer lugar.
Principalness [prin'-si-pal-nes], *s.* La calidad de ser principal ó jefe.
Principia [prin-sip'-i-a], *s. pl.* Primeros principios; en especial, título de la gran obra de Sir Isaac Newton. (Lat.)
Principle [prin'-si-pl], *s.* 1. Principio constitutivo, causa primitiva o primera; fundamento, motivo, causa,

origen. 2. Carácter esencial; esencia. 3. Verdad general, axioma, postulado, proposición admitida como punto de partida. 4. Principio, máxima, regla de conducta. 5. (Quím.) Elemento de los cuerpos; constituyente esencial de un compuesto o de una substancia a la cual da su carácter.

Principle, *va.* Imbuir, infundir principios o máximas en el entendimiento; fijar en el ánimo. Se emplea principalmente en el participio pasado. *Men principled against bribery*, Hombres de principios opuestos al cohecho.

Prink [princ], *vn.* y *va.* 1. Ataviarse, adornarse; presumir; acicalarse para llamar la atención. 2. Tener ínfulas, asumir un aire altanero.

Print [print], *va.* 1. Estampar, imprimir, dejar señalada la figura de una cosa en otra. 2. Imprimir, hacer ejemplares de (una cosa) por medio de la prensa. 3. Imprimir, hacer estampar, dar a la prensa o publicar algún libro o escrito. 4. Imprimir, reproducir por medio de la acción de la luz, o de un procedimiento de transferencia. También, en sentido figurado, fijar en el ánimo.—*vn.* 1. Imprimir, ejercer el arte de la tipografía. 2. Sufrir la acción de la luz, cambiar de color; dícese del papel sensibilizado de fotografía. *Printed by*, Impreso por; imprenta de. *Printed for*, Impreso para.

Print, *s.* 1. Impresión, estampa, la calidad y forma de la letra de algún impreso u obra impresa. 2. Impresión; material impreso; caracteres impresos colectivamente. 3. Impreso, el escrito impreso en una o en pocas hojas; papel suelto o volante, diario, etc. 4. Impresión, la marca, señal o huella que una cosa deja en otra. 5. Lámina, plancha, estampa. 6. Indiana, tela impresa. 7. Molde, lo que sirve para dar una forma. 8. Ejemplar positivo sacado de una prueba negativa. *In print*, (1) Impreso; ya en venta, abastecido. (2) (Des.) Con exactitud, con formalidad. *Out of print*, Agotado, vendido. *Butter print*, Molde para mantequilla. *Prints* o *printed goods*, Zarazas. (Amer.) Quimones. *Print-shop*, Tienda en que se venden estampas o grabados. *Print-works*, Taller de estampar telas.

Printed goods [print'-ed gudz], *s. pl.* Tela estampada, tela con diseños.

Printed matter [print'-ed mat'-ẹr], *s.* Impresos.

Printer [print'-ẹr], *s.* Impresor. *Printer's ink*, Tinta de imprenta. *Printer's mark*, Pie de imprenta. *Printer's proof*, Prueba de imprenta, prueba tipográfica.

Printing [print'-ing], *s.* 1. Imprenta, tipografía; arte u oficio de imprimir letras, caracteres o figuras en papel, telas, etc. 2. Impresión, la acción y efecto de imprimir; lo que está impreso. *V.* PRESSWORK. *Printing-frame*, (Foto.) Marco de imprimir. *Printing-machine*, *printing-press*, Prensa, máquina para imprimir o para estampar telas. *Printing-office*, Imprenta. *Printing-types*, Caracteres de imprenta, letras de molde, tipo.

Printless [print'-les], *a.* Lo que no deja señal, impresión ni huella.

Prior [prai'-ẹr], *a.* Anterior, antecedente, precedente, prior.—*s.* Prior, prelado en algunas órdenes religiosas.

Priorate [prai'-er-ēt], *s.* Priorato, el oficio o dignidad de prior o priora; el tiempo que dura este oficio.

Prioress [prai'-er-es], *sf.* Priora.

Priority [prai-er'-i-ti], *s.* Prioridad, anterioridad, antelación. *Priority of debt*, Prelación de los acreedores.

Priorship [prai'-ẹr-ship], *s.* Priorazgo, priorato.

Priory [prai'-ẹr-i], *s.* Priorato, convento en que tiene jurisdicción un prior o una priora.

Prisage [praiz'-ẹj], *s.* El derecho del fisco a una parte de las presas.

Prism [prizm], *s.* 1. Prisma, sólido determinado por dos bases planas, paralelas e iguales, y por tantos paralelogramos cuantos lados tenga cada base; en óptica, pieza de cristal en forma de prisma triangular; sirve para descomponer la luz. 2. El espectro solar.

Prismatic, Prismatical [priz-mat'-ic, al], *a.* 1. Prismático, refractado o formado por un prisma; parecido al espectro solar. 2. Prismático, parecido a un prisma; perteneciente a un prisma.

Prismatically [priz-mat'-i-cal-i], *adv.* En forma de prisma.

Prismoid [priz'-meid], *s.* Sólido de forma parecida a la del prisma.

Prison [priz'-n], *s.* Prisión, cárcel, edificio público donde se encierra a los presos. *Prison-house*, Cárcel, prisión. *Prison-ship*, Buque prisión, embarcación destinada a guardar o conducir presos. *Prison-fever*, *jail-fever*, El tifo, de una forma maligna. *Keeper of a prison*, Alcaide, carcelero.

Prison, *va.* Encarcelar. *V. To* IMPRISON.

Prison-bars [priz'-n-bārz], **Prison-base** [priz'-n-bēs], *s.* *V. Prisoner's base.*

Prisoner [priz'-n-ẹr], *s.* Preso, prisionero. *The prisoner at the bar*, El acusado, el preso que está presente ante el tribunal. *Prisoner's base*, Rescate, juego de muchachos.

Prisonment [priz'-n-mẹnt], *s.* Encierro. *V.* IMPRISONMENT.

Pristine [pris'-tin], *a.* Prístino, primitivo, original, que pertenece a los tiempos primitivos.

Pritchel [prich'-el], *s.* (Vet.) Contrapunzón.

Prithee [pridh'-i]. (Corrupción de *I pray thee.*) Te ruego.

Prittle-prattle [prit'-l-prat'-l], *s.* (Fam.) Charla, habladuría.

Privacy [prai'-va-si], *s.* 1. Retiro, soledad, aislamiento. 2. Secreto, asunto que se conserva secreto, o en privado. 3. Retrete, paraje adonde se retira el que quiere estar solo: sitio de retiro.

Private [prai'-vet], *a.* 1. Secreto, oculto; solo, solitario, retirado. 2. Privado, que se ejecuta a vista de pocos, familiar y domésticamente; que no es público; propio, particular, peculiar o personal a cada uno; raso, sin graduación. 3. Reticente, poco dispuesto a comunicarse. *In private*, Particularmente; en secreto, en particular. *A private man*, Un particular. *Private staircase*, Escalera secreta o excusada.—*s.* 1. Soldado raso; antiguamente, simple particular. 2. *pl.* Partes pudendas. *A private hearing*, Una audiencia secreta, a puertas cerradas. *They wish to be private*, Quieren estar solos. *At one's private expense*, A costa propia. *Private theatricals*, Comedias caseras.

Private enterprise [prai'-vet en'-tẹr-praiz], Empresa particular.

Privateer [prai-va-tīr'], *s.* 1. Corsario, navío o embarcación armada en corso, tripulada por simples particulares y a su costa, con licencia de su gobierno para capturar embarcaciones extranjeras en tiempo de guerra. 2. Corsario, el tripulante de un buque corsario.

Privateer, *vn.* Armar en corso, cruzar contra el enemigo a bordo de un buque corsario. *To go privateering*, Ir o salir a corso.

Privateersman [prai-va-tīrs'-man], *s.* Corsario, el capitán de un barco armado en corso.

Privately [prai'-vet-li], *adv.* Secretamente, ocultamente.

Privateness [prai'-vet-nes], *s.* 1. El estado de la persona que vive como particular, o que vive en la obscuridad. 2. Secreto, silencio. 3. Retiro, recogimiento, apartamiento.

Privation [prai-vé'-shun], *s.* 1. Privación, carencia, falta de bienestar; cosa dura, penible. 2. *V.* DEPRIVATION. 3. Privación, exoneración, el acto de privar de un empleo u oficio.

Privative [priv'-a-tiv], *a.* 1. Privativo, que causa privación. 2. (Gram.) Privativo, que significa privación; que muda la significación al negativo.—*s.* 1. Negación, no existencia. 2. (Gram.) Prefijo que indica negación; también, adjetivo que indica la ausencia de lo que es ordinariamente inherente; como "ciego," falto de vista.

Privet [priv'-et], *s.* (Bot.) Alheña, ligustro, un arbusto. Ligustrum vulgare. *Mock privet*, Ladierna.

Privilege [priv'-i-lej], *s.* Privilegio, favor, beneficio; gracia, prerogativa, inmunidad, exención concedida a ciertas personas solamente, o bajo especiales condiciones. *Writ of privilege*, Auto de excarcelación.

Privilege, *va.* Privilegiar, exceptuar de un gravamen o carga; conceder una exención, prerrogativa, favor o beneficio.

Privily [priv'-i-li], *adv.* Secretamente, ocultamente.

Privity [priv'-i-ti], *s.* 1. Conocimiento particular, conocimiento en común con otro de un asunto privado; en derecho, relación mutua o sucesiva a los mismos derechos de propiedad. 2. Confianza; secreto.

Privy [priv'-i], *a.* 1. Consabidor, el que juntamente con otro sabe alguna cosa; confidente, cómplice; instruído, informado, enterado. 2. Privado, escondido, secreto, excusado, clandestino. 3. Particular, propio, destinado a usos particulares; personal. *Privy council*, El consejo privado.—*s.* 1. Parte interesada, partícipe con otro; cómplice. 2. Privada, secreta, letrina, lugar excusado.

Prize [praiz], *s.* 1. Premio, recompensa, galardón. *He drew a prize in the lottery*, Él se sacó un premio en la lotería. 2. Presa, el botín que se hace al enemigo en conformidad con las leyes de la guerra; buque apresado. *Prize-master*, Capitán o cabo de presa. 3. Ganancia, ventaja inesperada; buena suerte. *To carry the prize*, Llevar, conseguir o ganar el premio. *Prize-court*, Tribunal marítimo que juzga las presas. *Prize-fight*, Pugilato, lucha en público entre dos combatientes para ganar un premio. *Prize-money*, Parte de una presa que toca a cada uno de los oficiales y tripulantes que la han hecho. *Prize-ring*, Espacio de dieciseis a veinticuatro pies cuadrados, rodeado de una cuerda y en el cual se verifican los pugilatos. *The prize-ring*, Pugilismo como profesión.

Prize, *s.* (Prov. Ingl.) Alzaprima, punto de apoyo de una palanca.

Prize, *va.* 1. Apreciar, estimar, valuar, tasar. 2. (Prov. Ingl.) Alzaprimar, levantar con alzaprima.

Prize-fighter [praiz'-fait-ẹr], *s.* Púgil, pugilista; el que pelea públicamente por una recompensa.

Prize-office [praiz'-ef-is], *s.* La oficina en que se despachan todos los negocios relativos a las presas hechas en la guerra.

Prizer [praiz'-ẹr], *s.* Apreciador; tasador, valorador.

Pro [prō], *s.* Pro, es la afirmativa de una cuestión o su extremo favorable. *Neither pro nor con*, Ni en pro ni en contra.

Probabilism [preb'-a-bil-izm], *s.* Probabilismo, doctrina teológica que sostiene ser lícito seguir la opinión meramente probable, en contraposición a la más probable.

Probabilist [preb'-a-bil-ist], *s.* Probabilista, el que profesa el probabilismo.

Probability [preb-a-bil'-i-ti], *s.* 1. Probabilidad, verisimilitud, calidad de probable; evento o afirmación probable. 2. (E. U.) Predicción concerniente al tiempo, especialmente los boletines oficiales de la Oficina de Señales Meteorológicas. *In all probability*, Según toda probabilidad.

Probable [preb'-a-bl], *a.* Probable, verisímil.

Probably [preb'-a-bli], *adv.* Probablemente.

Probang [prō'-bang], *s.* Sonda esofágica, varilla delgada y flexible con una esponja en su extremidad.

Probate [prō'-bêt], *a.* Que se refiere a la comprobación de un testamento. *Probate court*, Tribunal encargado de la comprobación de los testamentos, y que tiene jurisdicción en las curadurías.—*s.* Prueba, justificación o verificación de los testamentos en el tribunal privativo y el certificado de esta verificación.

Probation [prō-bê'-shun], *s.* 1. Prueba, evidencia, testimonio. 2. Prueba, la acción y efecto de probar. 3. Prueba, experiencia, examen, ensayo o tentativa que se hace de alguna cosa. 4. Probación noviciado.

Probational [pro-bê'-shun-al], **Probationary** [pro-bê'-shun-ẹ-ri], *a.* Probatorio, que sirve de evidencia, de ensayo, o para comprobación.

Probationer [pro-bê'-shun-ẹr], *s.* 1. Novicio, el religioso que no ha profesado. 2. Novicio, el principiante en cualquier arte o facultad.

Probationership [pro-bê'-shun-ẹr-ship], *s.* Noviciado.

Probative [prō'-ba-tiv], *a.* Probatorio, que sirve de prueba.

Probator [pro-bê'-tẹr], *s.* 1. Examinador, aprobador. 2. (Der. ant. inglés) Acusador, el que intenta probar que una persona ha cometido algún delito.

Probatory prō'-ba-to-ri], *a.* Probatorio.

Probatum est [prō-bê'-tum est]. Está o queda probado. Es voz latina.

Probe [prōb], *s.* 1. (Cir.) Tienta. 2. Prueba, ensayo, lo que prueba o ensaya. *Probe-scissors*, Tijeras de cirujano, con puntas bulbosas.

Probe, *va.* 1. Tentar, reconocer con la tienta alguna herida. 2. Escudriñar, probar, registrar; indagar.

Probe rocket [prōb' rek-et], *s.* (Aer.) Proyectil de sondeo.

Probity [preb'-i-ti], *s.* Probidad, honradez, hombría de bien; veracidad, sinceridad.

Problem [preb'-lem], *s.* Problema.

Problematic, Problematical [preb-lem-at'-ic, al], *a.* Problemático, dudoso, incierto.

Problematically [preb-lem-at'-ic-al-i], *adv.* Problemáticamente.

Proboscis [pro-bes'-is], *s.* Probóscide, trompa o nariz del elefante; la trompa o trompetilla de los insectos dípteros, u órgano semejante en varios invertebrados. En sentido festivo se aplica a veces a la nariz humana; hocico largo.

Procacious [pro-kê'-shus], *a.* (Ant.) Procaz, desvergonzado, atrevido.

Procedure [pro-sî'-jur o pro-sîd'-yūr], *s.* 1. Proceder, procedimiento, conducta; un acto, o una serie de actos; manera de obrar. 2. Procedimientos judiciales, actuación, modo de proceder en justicia.

Proceed [pro-sîd'], *vn.* 1. Ir adelante, dirigirse al fin propuesto, adelantar, avanzar; andar; proseguir, continuar lo empezado. *Proceed*, Prosiga o continúe Vd. *After proceeding some distance*, Después de haber avanzado o andado algunos pasos. 2. Proceder, pasar de una cosa a otra. *To proceed to business*, Ir a lo que importa; poner manos a la obra. 3. Proceder, provenir, dimanar, seguirse, salir. *Water proceeds from the fountain*, El agua procede de la fuente. 4. Obrar, proceder, portarse, empezar a ejecutar una serie de acciones, especialmente proceder en justicia contra alguno. 5. Proceder, originarse, venir por generación. 6. Recurrir, acudir, echar mano de, valerse de. *To proceed to blows*, Llegar a las manos, acudir a los golpes. *To proceed to strong measures*, Recurrir a, echar mano de medidas rigurosas.

Proceeder [pro-sîd'-ẹr], *s.* Adelantador, el que adelanta; el que hace progresos en alguna cosa.

Proceeding [pro-sîd'-ing], *s.* 1. Procedimiento, conducta, porte, acto, proceder, transacción. *The day's proceedings*, Las transacciones del día. *A cautious proceeding*, Una medida de precaución; conducta cautelosa. 2. Forma u orden judicial, modo de actuar en justicia, procedimiento; proceso, autos. 3. *pl.* Acta de una asamblea o sociedad.

Proceeds [prō'-sîdz], *s. pl.* Resultados materiales de una acción o proceder; productos, réditos.

Procellarian [pro-sel-lê'-ri-an], *a.* Procelario, perteneciente o parecido a la procelaria (ave de San Pedro).

Process [pres'-es], *s.* 1. Procedimiento, serie sistemática de operaciones en la producción de alguna cosa (natural o artificial); manipulación, el modo y orden con que se trabaja en la química y en varias artes. 2. Progreso, continuación, adelantamiento; serie, sucesión; transcurso del tiempo. *Process of time*, El lapso o trascurso del tiempo. *In process of time*, Con el tiempo. 3. Proceso, el agregado de autos que se forman para alguna causa o pleito civil; forma, expediente, trámite judicial, o modo de actuar en las causas civiles o eclesiásticas. 4. (Anat. y Zool.) Eminencia, protuberancia, excrecencia. 5. (Bot.) Toda extensión de una uperficie o apéndice accesorio.

Process [prō-ses'], *va.* Someter (alguna materia) a un proceso especial. *Processed cheese*, Queso preparado con un método especial.

Procession [pro-sesh'-un], *s.* Procesión. *Funeral procession*, Acompañamiento fúnebre.

Procession, *vn.* (Poco us.) Andar en procesión.

Processional [pro-sesh'-un-al], *a.* Procesional, que se ordena en forma de procesión o que pertenece a ella.—*s.* 1. Procesionario, libro. 2. Himno que se canta durante una procesión religiosa.

Processionary [pro-sesh'-un-ẹ-ri], *a.* Procesional, perteneciente a una procesión. *Processionary moth*, Lepidóptero nocturno que marcha en filas formando cuña, y cuyas orugas se alimentan de las hojas del roble.

Procidence [pres'-i-dens], *s.* (Med.) Procidencia, prolapso.

Prociduous [pro-sid'-yū-us], *a.* Dícese del útero, etc., cuando se halla en estado de procidencia.

Proclaim [pro-clêm'], *va.* 1. Proclamar, promulgar; publicar, propalar. 2. Antiguamente, en Inglaterra, proscribir, poner fuera de la ley.

Proclaimer [pro-clêm'-ẹr], *s.* El que promulga o proclama.

Proclamation [prec-la-mê'-shun], *s.* 1. Proclamación, la publicación de algún decreto, edicto, bando o ley. 2. Decreto, edicto, bando, ley, pragmática.

Proclitic [pro-clit'-ic], *a.* (Gram.) Proclítico; dícese de la voz monosílaba que se une con la siguiente.

Proclivous [pro-clai'-vus], *a.* Inclinado hacia adelante; se dice de los dientes incisivos.

Proclivity [pro-cliv'-i-ti], *s.* Propensión, prontitud, proclividad; facilidad en ejecutar alguna cosa.

Proconsul [pro-cen'-sul], *s.* Procónsul, magistrado de la república romana.

Proconsular [pro-cen'-siu-lar], *a.* Proconsular, que se refiere a un procónsul.

Proconsulate, Proconsulship [pro-cen' siu-lêt, sul-ship], *s.* Proconsulado.

Procrastinate [pro-cras'-ti-nêt], *va.* y *vn.* Procrastinar, diferir, dilatar, dejar de un día para otro, retardar; ser moroso.

Procrastination [pro-cras-ti-nê'-shun], *s.* Dilación, demora, tardanza, detención.

Procrastinator [pro-cras'-ti-nê-tẹr], *s.* El que es moroso, tardo o poco diligente en lo que debe hacer; vulgarmente, pelmazo.

Procreant [prō'-crẹ-ant], *a.* Productivo, que procrea; conducente a la reproducción, reproductivo; relacionado con la generación.

Procreate [prō'-crẹ-êt], *va.* Procrear engendrar, producir.

Procreation [prō-crẹ-ê'-shun], *s.* Procreación, generación, producción.

Procreative [prō'-crẹ-ê-tiv], *a.* Generativo, productivo.

Procreativeness [prō'-crę-ê-tiv-nes], *s.* La facultad o potencia de procrear.
Procreator [prō'-crę-ê-tęr], *s.* Procreador; padre.
Procrustean [pro-crus'-tę-an], *a.* De Procusto, característico de él o de sus hechos.
Procrustes [pro-crus'-tīz], *s.* Procusto, nombre de un tirano muy cruel que se aplica a los que son intolerantes en sus dictámenes.
Proctor [prec'-tęr], *s.* 1. Procurador, el que en virtud de poder o facultad de otro ejecuta en su nombre alguna cosa. 2. Procurador de la curia eclesiástica. 3. Abogado en el tribunal del almirantazgo. 4. Censor de una universidad, funcionario encargado de vigilar a los alumnos y de hacer observar los reglamentos.
Proctorage [prec'-ter-ēj], *s.* Manejo de los negocios (por un procurador).
Proctorial [prec-tō'-ri-al], *a.* De procurador; que se refiere al censor académico.
Proctorship [prec'-tęr-ship], *s.* Procuración, procuraduría, oficio de procurador.
Procumbent [pro-cum'-bent], *a.* 1. Postrado, inclinado, doblado hacia el suelo. 2. (Bot.) Procumbente, tendido, yacente: dícese de las plantas.
Procurable [pro-kiūr'-a-bl], *a.* Asequible, que puede conseguirse, alcanzarse; proporcionable.
Procuracy [prec'-yu-ra-si], *s.* Procuración; gestión, manejo de negocios o intereses ajenos.
Procuration [prec-yu-rê'-shun], *s.* 1. Acción de procurar, de obtener; en especial, alcahuetería. 2. (For.) Procuración, poder o comisión que una persona da a otra para que en su nombre haga o ejecute alguna cosa; y el documento en que se da dicho poder. *Procuration-fee,* Derecho de comisión sobre un préstamo.
Procurator [prec'-yu-rê-tęr], *s.* Procurador.
Procuratorial [prec-yu-ra-tō'-ri-al], *a.* Hecho por procurador.
Procuratory [prec'-yu-ra-to-ri], *s.* (Poco us.) El poder o instrumento legal para obrar en nombre del que lo da.—*a.* Tocante o perteneciente a la procuración o agencia.
Procure [pro-kiūr'], *va.* 1. Lograr, obtener, conseguir; procurar, hacer las diligencias para conseguir lo que se desea. 2. Causar, ocasionar. 3. Alcahuetear.—*vn.* Alcahuetear, andar en tercerías.
Procurement [pro-kiūr'-męnt], *s.* 1. Obtención, logro, consecución. 2. El acto de causar, de poner por obra, de efectuar. *They think it done by her procurement,* Creen que se ha hecho por su causa, a solicitud suya o por haberlo ella procurado.
Procurer [pro-kiūr'-ęr], *s.* 1. El que logra, alcanza o consigue alguna cosa. 2. Alcahuete.
Procuress [pro-kiūr'-es], *sf.* Alcahueta, tercera.
Procyon [prō'-si-en], *s.* Proción, estrella en la constelación del Can Menor, muy notable por su movimiento variable.
Prod [pred], *va.* Punzar, pungir, empujar o golpear con un instrumento puntiagudo; picar.—*s.* 1. Cualquier instrumento puntiagudo; pincho, aguijón. 2. Picadura, pinchazo, pungimiento, empuje efectuado con un instrumento puntiaguido. (Prob. < islandés *broddr,* clavo.)
Prodigal [pred'-i-gal], *a.* 1. Pródigo, manirroto, derrochador. 2. Pródigo, muy generoso o liberal.—*s.* Gastador, disipador.
Prodigality [pred-i-gal'-i-ti], *s.* Prodigalidad, profusión.
Prodigally [pred'-i-gal-i], *adv.* Pródigamente.
Prodigious [pro-dij'-us], *a.* 1. Enorme, vasto, inmenso, excesivo, extraordinario. 2. (Des.) Prodigioso, portentoso.
Prodigiously [pro-dij'-us-li], *adv.* Enormemente, excesivamente, extraordinariamente, prodigiosamente.
Prodigiousness [pro-dij'-us-nes], *s.* Prodigiosidad, enormidad de extensión, estatura, cantidad o grado.
Prodigy [pred'-i-ji], *s.* 1. Maravilla, persona o cosa extraordinaria; lo que causa admiración. 2. Monstruo, monstruosidad. 3. (Ant.) Prodigio, portento.
Prodrome [prō'-drōm], **Prodromus** [pred'-ro-mus], *s.* 1. (Med.) Pródromo, malestar que precede a una enfermedad. 2. Curso o tratado preliminar; prolegómeno.
Produce [pro-diūs'], *va.* 1. Producir, criar, engendrar. 2. Sacar o dar a luz una cosa, exponerla a la vista. 3. Causar o ser causa de alguna cosa, efectuar; conducir a. 4. Producir, presentar o exhibir alguna cosa en juicio. 5. Manufacturar, fabricar; hacer. 6. (Geom.) Prolongar, alargar una línea.—*vn.* Producir, dar producto o resultado conveniente. *Vice produces misery,* El vicio engendra la miseria. *The inhabitants produced their hidden stores,* Los habitantes presentaron las provisiones que habían escondido.
Produce [pred'-iūs], *s.* Producto, producción, la cosa producida; particularmente los rendimientos de una hacienda de campo; provisiones.
Producer [pro-diū'-sęr], *s.* Productor, producente, productor.
Producible [pro-diū'-si-bl], *a.* Producible, lo que se puede producir, exhibir o mostrar.
Product [pred'-uct], *s.* 1. Producto, producción, la cosa producida; alguna cosa obtenida como resultado de una operación o trabajo. 2. Producción, obra del entendimiento o del arte. 3. Producto, el número que resulta de la multiplicación de otros dos o más números. 4. Producto, provento, renta.
Productile [pro-duc'-til], *a.* Dúctil, susceptible de alargarse sin romperse.
Production [pro-duc'-shun], *s.* 1. Producción, el acto o procedimiento de producir; en economía política, acto de producir para el consumo. 2. Producto. 3. Producción, composición, obra del ingenio.
Productive [pro-duc'-tiv], *a.* 1. Productivo, que tiene la virtud o la facultad de producir. 2. Fecundo, fértil, que da buenas cosechas.
Productiveness [pro-duc'-tiv-nes], *s.* Calidad de productivo; fertilidad, fecundidad.
Productivity [pro-duc-tiv'-i-ti], *s.* Productividad.
Proem [prō'-em], *s.* Proemio, prólogo, prefacio; exordio.
Proemial [pro-em'-i-al], *a.* Proemial, tocante o perteneciente al proemio.
Proethnic [pro-eth'-nic], *a.* Característico de una raza prehistórica antes de su subdivisión (v. g. una lengua materna).
Profanation [pref-a-nê'-shun], *s.* Profanación, profanamiento, profanidad, impiedad, irreligión.
Profane [pro-fên'], *a.* 1. Profano, irreligioso, impío; impuro. 2. Profano, secular, en contraposición a sagrado o religioso.
Profane, *va.* 1. Profanar, violar, aplicar alguna cosa sagrada a usos profanos, o tratarla con irreverencia. 2. Profanar, prostituir, hacer uso indecente de una cosa: desperdiciar, hacer mal uso de algo.
Profanely [pro-fên'-li], *adv.* Profanamente, impíamente.
Profaneness [pro-fên'-nes], *s.* Impiedad, profanación. *V.* PROFANITY.
Profaner [pro-fên'-ęr], *s.* Profanador, el que profana una cosa sagrada.—*a. comp.* Más profano.
Profanity [pro-fan'-i-ti], *s.* 1. Lenguaje o acto profano; impiedad, blasfemia. 2. La calidad de profano; irreverencia a las cosas sagradas.
Profess [pro-fes'], *va.* 1. Declarar, manifestar abiertamente su ánimo o intento. 2. Profesar, seguir alguna religión u opinión abierta y públicamente. 3. Profesar, ejercer o enseñar en público alguna facultad o arte.—*vn.* Profesar, declarar abiertamente. *Professed foe,* Enemigo declarado. *Professed friend,* Amigo decidido. *A professed monk* o *nun,* Un religioso profeso; o una religiosa profesa, una monja.
Professed, Profest [pro-fest'], *pp.* del verbo *To* PROFESS, Profeso.
Professedly [pro-fes'-ed-li], *adv.* Declaradamente, manifiestamente, abiertamente, públicamente.
Profession [pro-fesh'-un], *s.* 1. Profesión, destino, empleo, ejercicio, el modo de vida que requiere una educación liberal o el trabajo mental más bien que el manual. 2. Profesión, protestación, declaración pública de la creencia, opinión, doctrina, etc., de cada uno. 3. Oferta, ofrecimiento, palabra.
Professional [pro-fesh'-un-al], *a.* 1. Profesional, que se refiere a una profesión o la practica; apto para una profesión. 2. Profesional, que tiene relación con una profesión particular; opuesto a *amateur* (aficionado). *Professional duties,* Deberes profesionales.—*s.* 1. El que por profesión y por dinero compite en los juegos o diversiones. 2. Sujeto hábil en su profesión.
Professionally [pro-fesh'-un-al-i], *adv.* Por vía de profesión; de profesión; en su profesión.
Professor [pro-fes'-ęr], *s.* 1. Profesor, catedrático, el que enseña públicamente alguna facultad, arte, ciencia o doctrina. 2. Profesor, el que ejerce públicamente alguna facultad o ciencia. 3. Partidario, el que sigue alguna opinión o partido.
Professorial [pro''-fes-sō'-ri-al], *a.* De profesor; profesoral, relativo a un catedrático o profesor.
Professorship [pro-fes'-ęr-ship], *s.* 1. Oficio de profesor, dignidad de catedrático. 2. Cátedra.
Proffer [pref'-ęr], *va.* Proponer, ofrecer algo para su aceptación.
Proffer, *s.* Oferta, propuesta, ofrecimiento; la cosa ofrecida.
Proficience [pro-fish'-ens], **Proficiency** [pro-fish'-en-si], *s.* Estado o calidad

de adepto o proficiente; maña, habilidad; perfeccionamiento en un arte.
Proficient [pro-fish'-ent], *a.* Proficiente, adelantado, versado, instruído en una ciencia, un arte; hábil.
Profile [prō'-fil o prō'-fail], *s.* 1. Contorno, recorte; diseño en perfil o como en una sección vertical. 2. Perfil, el rostro humano representado de lado; el contorno del cuerpo visto de lado.
Profile, *va.* Retratar o pintar de perfil.
Profit [pref'-it], *s.* 1. Provecho, beneficio, ventaja, utilidad, producto. 2. Ganancia, utilidad o interés pecuniario; exceso de los ingresos o cantidades recibidas sobre los desembolsos o gastos. *Gross profit,* Ganancia total. *Net profit,* Ganancia neta, beneficio neto. *Profit and loss,* Ganancias y pérdidas. *To make profit of a thing,* Sacar ventaja de una cosa, hacer su agosto. *To yield profit,* Dar ganancia, o provecho.
Profit, *va.* Aprovechar a, servir, ser útil, ventajoso para; hacer bien; ayudar.—*vn.* 1. Sacar utilidad o provecho de alguna cosa, utilizarse; lucrar, ganar. 2. Mejorarse; servir, ser útil, traer beneficio. *To profit by experience,* Ganar, mejorarse, por la experiencia. *To be profited by,* Ganar en.
Profitability [pref-it-a-bil'-i-ti], *s.* 1. Rentabilidad. 2. Provecho, utilidad. 3. Ventaja.
Profitable [pref'-it-a-bl], *a.* 1. Rentable. 2. Util, provechoso, ventajoso.
Profitableness [pref'-it-a-bl-nes], *s.* Ganancia, lucro; ventaja, provecho.
Profitably [pref'-it-a-bli], *adv.* Provechosamente, útilmente, ventajosamente.
Profiteer [pref-i-tīr'], *s.* Explotador que se aprovecha de las circunstancias para ganar demasiado dinero.—*vn.* Obtener ganancias elevadas aprovechándose de alguna circunstancia, p. ej. la guerra.
Profitless [pref'-it-les], *a.* Sin ventaja, sin provecho; inútil.
Profit sharing [pref'-it shār'-ing], *s.* Distribución de ganancias entre los trabajadores.
Profligacy [pref'-li-ga-si], *s.* Estragamiento, libertinaje, desenfreno; disolución, abandono, corrupción desvergonzada.
Profligate [pref'-li-get], *a.* Abandonado, entregado a los vicios; libertino, libre, licencioso, desmandado, perdido.—*s.* Un hombre libertino, disipado, relajado, perdido, calavera, vicioso o de vida airada.
Pro forma [prō fēr'-ma]. Locución latina que se usa para significar o que una cosa se hace meramente por cumplir con alguna fórmula o que es fingida. *Pro forma accounts,* Cuentas simuladas. *Pro forma bills,* Letras simuladas o supuestas.
Profound [pro-faund'], *a.* 1. Profundo, hondo. 2. Profundo, recóndito, abstruso. 3. Profundo, grande, extremo en su clase. 4. Profundo, intenso o denso en su especie. 5. Profundo, humilde en sumo grado. —*s.* 1. Profundo, abismo. 2. Profundo, mar, océano.
Profoundly [pro-faund'-li], *adv.* Profundamente.
Profoundness [pro-faund'-nes], *s.* Profundidad, penetración.
Profoundness, Profundity [pro-fun'-di-ti], *s.* 1. Profundidad, hondura. 2. Profundidad, sublimidad o grandeza de ciencia o ingenio.
Profuse [pro-fiūs'], *a.* Profuso; pródigo.
Profusely [pro-fiūs'-li], *adv.* Profusamente; pródigamente.
Profuseness [pro-fiūs'-nes], **Profusion** [pro-fiū'-zhun], *s.* Profusión, prodigalidad; abundancia, copia, superabundancia; gastos extravagantes.
Prog [preg], *va.* (Esco.) *V. To* PROD. —*vn.* (E. U.) Buscar a la ventura, v. g. las almejas a lo largo de la playa.—*s.* 1. (Fam. o Ger.) Víveres o provisiones que se obtienen merodeando o mendigando; bucólica, comida o vianda de cualquier especie. 2. (Esco.) Pinchazo, picadura.
Progenitor [pro-jen'-i-tęr], *s.* Progenitor; ascendiente en línea directa.
Progeny [prej'-e-ni], *s.* Progenie, progenitura, casta, descendientes.
Prognathism [preg'-na-thizm], *s.* Prognatismo, calidad de prognato.
Prognathous [preg'-na-thus], *a.* Prognato, que tiene las quijadas prolongadas.
Prognosis [preg-nō'-sis], *s.* (Med.) 1. Conclusión o predicción respecto a la marcha futura y terminación de una enfermedad; también, el arte de pronosticar lo que debe suceder en las enfermedades por los síntomas que presentan. 2. Cualquier pronóstico o predicción; presciencia.
Prognosticable [preg-nes'-ti-ca-bl], *a.* Pronosticable.
Prognostic [preg-nes'-tic], *s.* Pronóstico, juicio conjetural que se hace de lo que ha de suceder: en medicina, síntoma indicativo de la terminación de una enfermedad.—*a.* Pronóstico, que sirve para indicar lo que ha de suceder.
Prognosticate [preg-nes'-ti-kēt], *va.* Pronosticar, indicar de antemano.
Prognostication [preg-nes-ti-kē'-shun], *s.* Pronosticación, acción de pronosticar; lo que pronostica, presagio, pronóstico.
Prognosticator [preg-nes'-ti-kē-tęr], *s.* Pronosticador.
Program, Programme [prō'-gram], *s.* 1. Anuncio o cartel en que se indican por su orden las partes que forman una función pública. 2. Curso de procedimientos dispuesto de antemano; cartel, enumeración o lista de las tareas y deberes ordinarios o cotidianos; prospecto. 3. Programa; prólogo, introducción.
Program [prō'-gram], *va.* Programar.
Program director [prō'-gram di-rect'-ęr], *s.* Programador.
Programmer [prō'-gram-er], *s.* Programador.
Programming [prō'-gram-ing], *s.* Programación.
Progress [preg'-res], *s.* 1. Progreso, aprovechamiento, adelantamiento; desarrollo, mejoramiento, adelanto. 2. Viaje, jornada, curso; carrera, p. ej. la del séquito de un monarca: corriente; paso, pasaje. *To make slow progress,* Adelantar lentamente. *Dinner was in progress,* Estaban comiendo.
Progress [pro-gres'], *vn.* Progresar, hacer progresos o adelantamientos en alguna cosa.
Progression [pro-gresh'-un], *s.* 1. Progresión, adelantamiento, la acción de ir o dirigirse hacia adelante. 2. (Mat.) Progresión, serie de números o cantidades en proporción continua.
Progressional [pro-gresh'-un-al], *a.* Progresivo.
Progressive [pro-gres'-iv], *a.* Progresivo, que va hacia adelante; que aspira al progreso o lo favorece; que va mejorando, perfeccionándose.
Progressive, *s.* Progresista.
Progressively [pro-gres'-iv-li], *adv.* Progresivamente.
Progressiveness [pro-gres'-iv-nes], *s.* Calidad de progresivo, estado de progreso; marcha progresiva, adelanto.
Prohibit [pro-hib'-it], *va.* 1. Prohibir, vedar. 2. Impedir, embarazar. *Prohibited goods,* Contrabando o géneros prohibidos.
Prohibiter [pro-hib'-it-ęr], *s.* El que prohibe alguna cosa; impedidor.
Prohibition [pro-hi-bish'-un], *s.* 1. Prohibición; auto prohibitorio. 2. (E. U.) Prohibición legal de la manufactura y venta de licores alcohólicos como bebida.
Prohibitionist [pro-hi-bish'-un-ist], *s.* Partidario de la prohibición; en especial, (E. U.) partidario de prohibir por la ley la fabricación y venta de licores alcohólicos para el consumo público como bebida.
Prohibitive [pro-hib'-it-iv], **Prohibitory** [pro-hib'-i-to-ri], *a.* Prohibitivo, prohibitorio; que implica prohibición.
Project [pro-ject'], *va.* 1. Echar, arrojar, despedir. 2. Delinear, trazar. 3. Proyectar, idear, trazar.—*vn.* Volar, salir fuera de la línea perpendicular, hacer o formar proyectura o vuelo; proyectar.
Project [prej'-ect], *s.* Proyecto, idea, pensamiento; dibujo, diseño, plan.
Projector [pro-ject'-ęr], *s.* 1. Proyectista. 2. Proyector, aparato de proyección de películas cinematográficas.
Projectile [pro-jec'-til], *a.* 1. Impelido o puesto en movimiento por alguna fuerza o potencia. 2. Arrojador, que arroja o lanza. 3. Arrojadizo, que se puede arrojar o se destina a ser arrojado.—*s.* Proyectil, cuerpo arrojadizo que se lanza para herir o matar.
Projection [pro-jec'-shun], *s.* 1. Lanzamiento, el acto de lanzar o arrojar. 2. Proyección, el acto de comunicar movimiento a algún cuerpo arrojadizo. 3. Plan, minuta o borrón de un proyecto, de un pensamiento, etc. 4. Delineación. 5. El punto crítico de una preparación culinaria o de otra clase.
Prolapsus [pro-lap'-sus], *s.* (Med.) Prolapso, procidencia, caída o descenso de una víscera u órgano movible.
Prolate [prō'-lēt], *a.* Alargado, en dirección a los polos.
Proleg [prō'-leg], *s.* Una de las patas carnosas abdominales de muchas larvas de insectos, como de las orugas; pie de apoyo, o falso.
Prolegomenon [pro-leg-em'-en-en], *s.* Prolegómeno, tratado que se pone al principio de una obra para establecer los principios que contiene.
Prolepsis [pro-lep'-sis], *s.* 1. Prolepsis, anticipación; figura retórica por la cual se anticipa una objeción, refutándola de antemano.
Proleptic, Proleptical [pro-lep'-tic, al], *a.* Previo, antecedente.
Proleptically [pro-lep'-ti-cal-i], *adv.* Anticipadamente, previamente.
Proles [prō'-līz], *s.* Prole, hijos; en derecho, descendencia, hijos legítimos.

Proletarian [prō-le̤-tē'-ri-an], *a.* Proletario; bajo, vulgar, despreciable. —*s.* 1. Proletario, persona de la clase última o más pobre. 2. Gañán, jornalero, peón.
Proletariat [pro-le̤'tē'-ri-at], *s.* Proletariado, la clase de los proletarios; en su empleo primitivo, populacho, gentuza; en el uso moderno y socialista, la clase obrera, como creadora de la riqueza; operarios, trabajadores.
Prolicide [prō'-li-said], *s.* Infanticidio, el crimen de matar a su propio hijo antes o después de su nacimiento.
Proliferate [pro-lif'-e̱r-ēt], *va.* Producir, dar.—*vn.* Reproducirse, particularmente con rapidez, como las celdillas en la formación de los tejidos.
Proliferous [pro-lif'-e̱r-us], *a.* 1. Prolífero, que produce prole o descendientes. 2. (Bot.) Que tiene un desarrollo excesivo de partes u órganos.
Prolific, Prolifical [pro-lif'-ic, al], *a.* 1. Prolífico, fértil, fecundo, muy productivo. 2. *V.* PROLIFEROUS.
Prolifically [pro-lif'-ic-al-i], *adv.* Fecundamente, abundantemente.
Prolification [pro-lif-i-kē'-shun], *s.* 1. Generación, el acto de engendrar. 2. (Bot.) Proliferación, la producción poco común o excesiva de partes accesorias o superfluas, sean de la misma naturaleza o diferentes.
Prolificness [pro-lif'-ic-nes], *s.* Fecundidad, fertilidad.
Prolix [prō'-lix o pro-lix'], *a.* Prolijo, demasiado largo, dilatado, difuso; fastidioso, enfadoso.
Prolixity [pro-lix'-i-ti], **Prolixness** [pro-lix'-nes], *s.* Prolijidad, estado o calidad de prolijo; verbosidad.
Prolixly [pro-lix'-li], *adv.* Prolijamente.
Prolocutor [pro-lec'-yu-te̱r o prel-o-kiū'-te̱r], *s.* 1. Intercesor, el que habla o gestiona en pro de otro. 2. Presidente de una asamblea o junta del clero.
Prolocutorship [prel-o-kiū'-te̱r-ship], *s.* El oficio o dignidad de presidente.
Prologue [prō'-leg], *s.* Prólogo, exordio, prefacio.
Prolong [pro-lēng'], *va.* 1. Prolongar, alargar, dilatar, extender. 2. (Des.) Diferir, retardar.
Prolongation [pre-lon̤-gē'-shun], *s.* Prolongación, dilatación, extensión.
Prolonge [pro-lenj'], *s.* (Mil.) Prolonga, la cuerda que une el avantrén con la cureña. (Fr.)
Prolusion [pro-lū'-zhun], *s.* Prolusión, preludio, introducción.
Promenade [prem-e̱-nād'], *vn.* Pasearse.—*s.* 1. Paseo, acción de pasearse; paseo ceremonioso. 2. Paseo, sitio o lugar público destinado a pasear. (Fr.)
Promethean [pro-mī'-the̱-an], *a.* De Prometeo, que pertenece o se refiere a Prometeo.
Prominence [prem'-i-nens], **Prominency** [prem'-i-nen-si], *s.* 1. Estado de lo que es prominente o eminente; eminencia, altura; distinción, importancia. 2. Prominencia, protuberancia; lo que hace salidizo; (Arq.) salidizo, resalto.
Prominent [prem'-i-nent], *a.* 1. Prominente, saliente, proyectante, que se eleva sobre lo que está a su inmediación, en relieve. 2. Conspicuo por su posición, carácter o importancia; eminente, sobresaliente, distinguido. *Prominent eyes,* Ojos saltones. *Prominent figures,* Figuras de alto relieve.
Promiscuous [pro-mis'-kiu-us], *a.* 1. Promiscuo, mezclado confusamente, compuesto de individuos o partes mezclados confusamente. 2. Ejercido o repartido sin distinción; común, no restringido, sin restricción.
Promiscuously [pro-mis'-kiu-us-li], *adv.* Promiscuamente, sin orden; en común.
Promiscuousness [pro-mis'-kiu-us-nes], *s.* Mezcla, confusión.
Promise [prem'-is], *s.* 1. Promesa, palabra dada, prometido. 2. Espectativa, esperanza. (Bíbl. y ant.) Promisión. 3. Prometido, alguna cosa prometida; la ejecución u obtención de lo prometido. *To break one's promise,* Faltar a su palabra, o promesa. *Land of promise,* Tierra de promisión.
Promise, *va.* 1. Prometer, ofrecer hacer o no hacer (una cosa); hacer promesa de dar alguna cosa. 2. Hacer concebir una esperanza. 3. (Ant. o fam.) Prometer, asegurar o aseverar.—*vn.* 1. Prometer, hacer promesas; empeñarse a hacer o no hacer alguna cosa. 2. Dar buenas esperanzas; anunciarse, hacer concebir esperanzas; prometerse, tener gran esperanza o confianza en que se logrará alguna cosa.
Promise-breaker [prem'-is-brē'-ke̱r], *s.* El que no cumple con sus promesas o falta a su palabra.
Promisee [prem-is-ī'], *s.* (For.) El o la que ha recibido una promesa.
Promiser [prem'-is-e̱r], *s.* Prometedor.
Promising [prem'-is-ing], *a.* Prometedor, que promete mucho, que es de gran esperanza.
Promisor [prem'-is-e̱r], *s.* Autor de una promesa; prometedor.
Promissorily [prem'-is-o-ri-li], *adv.* Por vía de promesa.
Promissory [prem'-is-o-ri], *a.* Promisorio, que encierra en sí promesa. *Promissory note,* Pagaré, vale, escrito por el cual se compromete el firmante a pagar una cantidad.
Promontory [prem'-en-to-ri], *s.* Promontorio, cabo o punta de tierra que entra en el mar.
Promote [pro-mōt'], *va.* 1. Promover, fomentar, hacer adelantar, favorecer, desarrollar, extender, establecer, aumentar; alentar, hacer florecer. 2. Promover, ascender, elevar a uno a otro empleo más preeminente que el que tenía. *To promote the arts and sciences,* Hacer florecer las artes y las ciencias.
Promoter [pro-mōt'-e̱r], *s.* 1. Promotor, promovedor, el que da el impulso principal. 2. Promovedor, el que ayuda (obteniendo un capital o de otra manera) a promover o establecer una empresa rentística o de comercio.
Promotion [pro-mō'-shun], *s.* Promoción, acción de promover o estado de ser promovido; elevación, ascenso de alguno a una dignidad, grado o empleo superior al que tenía.
Promotive [pro-mō'-tiv], *a.* Promovedor, que tiende a fomentar, promover, adelantar, alentar o favorecer.
Prompt [prempt], *a.* 1. Pronto, dispuesto, aparejado para la ejecución de alguna cosa; puntual, exacto en hacer las cosas a su tiempo sin dilatarlas. 2. Hecho o ejecutado de todo corazón o de buena voluntad; que sucede al tiempo debido o señalado. *Prompt payment,* Pago puntual (en la fecha señalada). *Prompt cash,* Pago al contado, inmediato.
Prompt, *va.* 1. Impulsar, excitar, hurgar, incitar, conmover. 2. Sugerir, insinuar, advertir o hacer a uno acordarse de alguna cosa. 3. Apuntar; dar ocasión, mover.
Prompter [prempt'-e̱r], *s.* 1. Admonitor, el que amonesta; la persona que incita a obrar. 2. Apuntador, el que apunta; apuntador de teatro.
Promptitude [prempt'-i-tiūd], **Promptness** [prempt'-nes], *s.* Prontitud, presteza, rapidez de decisión y de acción; facilidad, buena voluntad.
Promptly [prempt'-li], *adv.* Prontamente, a su tiempo, al momento.
Promulgate [pro-mul'-gēt], *va.* Promulgar, publicar alguna cosa solemnemente, proclamar.
Promulgation [pro-mul-gē'-shun], *s.* Promulgación.
Promulgator [pro-mul-gē'-te̱r], *s.* Promulgador.
Promulge [pro-mulj'], *va.* (Ant.) Promulgar. *V. To* PROMULGATE.
Promulger [pro-mul'-je̱r], *s.* Promulgador, publicador.
Pronate [prō'-nêt], *va.* Poner o echar boca abajo.
Pronation [pro-nē'-shun], *s.* Pronación, un movimiento por el cual el antebrazo y la palma de la mano se vuelven hacia abajo,
Pronator [pro-nē'-te̱r], *s.* Pronador, músculo del antebrazo que sirve para volver la palma de la mano hacia tierra.
Prone [prōn], *a.* 1. Inclinado hacia abajo. 2. Echado boca abajo. 3. Precipitoso, pendiente. 4. Prono, inclinado, dispuesto, propenso.
Proneness [prōn'-nes], *s.* 1. Inclinación hacia abajo; pendiente, cuesta. 2. Inclinación, propensión o disposición a alguna cosa mala.
Prong [preng], *s.* Cualquier instrumento puntiagudo; parte saliente como la púa, diente o punta de un tenedor o de una horca de labrador.
Prongbuck, *s.* *V.* PRONGHORN y SPRINGBOK.
Pronged [prengd], *a.* Dentellado, dentado, provisto de púas. *A four-pronged fork,* Un tenedor de cuatro dientes.
Pronghorn [preng'-hērn], *s.* Antílope de las Montañas Roqueñas. Antilocapra americana.
Pronominal [pro-nem'-i-nal], *a.* Pronominal, de la naturaleza del pronombre; concerniente al pronombre.
Pronoun [prō'-naun], *s.* Pronombre, parte de la oración.
Pronounce [pro-nauns'], *va.* 1. Pronunciar, proferir, articular las palabras; articular correctamente. 2. Pronunciar, decir, recitar una arenga, un discurso, etc. 3. Pronunciar, fallar, dar sentencia.—*vn.* Hablar magistralmente.
Pronounceable [pro-nauns'-a-bl], *a.* Pronunciable, que se puede pronunciar o articular.
Pronouncer [pro-nauns'-e̱r], *s.* Pronunciador.
Pronouncing [pro-naun'-sing], *pa.* del verbo PRONOUNCE.—*a.* De pronun-

ciación, que enseña la pronunciación. *A pronouncing dictionary*, Un diccionario de pronunciación.

Pronunciation [pro-nun-si- (o shi-) é'-shun], *s.* Pronunciación, el acto o la manera de pronunciar palabras; articulación; articulación solemne, v. g. para bendecir.

Proof [prūf], *s.* 1. Prueba, la razón, argumento, etc., con que se prueba algo; lo que demuestra la verdad o falsedad de alguna cosa. 2. Prueba, el ensayo o experiencia que se hace de alguna cosa. 3. Prueba, la consistencia y firmeza de alguna cosa; impenetrabilidad; también, armadura impenetrable. 4. Prueba, la primera plana que se tira para corregir las erratas de imprenta. 5. Grado regulador, que sirve de tipo para los licores alcohólicos. 6. Prueba, la primera impresión de un negativo. 7. (Mat.) Operación por la cual se comprueba la exactitud de un cálculo. *Proof-reader*, Corrector de pruebas. *Proof-sheet*, Pliego de prueba, prueba.—*a.* 1. Empleado en probar, cotejar o corregir. 2. Impenetrable, que está hecho a prueba o que es de prueba. *Proof brandy*, Aguardiente de prueba. *Bomb-proof*, A prueba de bomba. *Water-proof*, A prueba de agua, impermeable. *To be proof against*, Ser o estar á prueba de. *Proof against all temptations*, A prueba de toda tentación. *Proof spirit*, Licor que contiene alcohol por la mitad de su volumen. *The proof of the pudding is in the eating*, Al freir será el reir.

Proofless [prūf'-les], *a.* Falto de prueba, no probado; sin fundamento.

Proofread [prūf'-rīd], *va.* Corregir pruebas de imprenta.

Prop [prep], *va.* 1. Sostener, apoyar, impedir que caiga una cosa; apuntalar; poner un rodrigón, etc. 2. (Fig.) Sostener, apoyar, mantener firme, sustentar.

Prop, *s.* 1. Apoyo, puntal. 2. Apoyo, amparo, columna, báculo. 3. Sostén, cualquier cosa que sirve para sostener a otra; apeo, paral, sustentáculo; (Min.) entibo, ademe; (Agr.) rodrigón, tentemozo; machón, contrafuerte. *Props of the cut-water*, (Mar.) Escoras del tajamar.

Propagable [prep'-a-ga-bl], *a.* Que puede propagarse, que es capaz de propagación.

Propaganda [prep-a-gan'-da], *s.* 1. Propaganda, congregación pontificia fundada en Roma para propagar el catolicismo. 2. De aquí, propaganda, cualquier asociación para propagar doctrinas.

Propagandist [prep-a-gan'-dist], *s.* & *a.* Propagandista, propagador. *Propagandist doctrine*, Doctrina propagandista.

Propagate [prep'-a-gêt], *va.* 1. Propagar, multiplicar la especie, engendrar. 2. Propagar, dilatar, extender, aumentar. 3. Engendrar, causar, ocasionar, formar.

Propagation [prep-a-gé'-shun], *s.* 1. Propagación, la multiplicación de la especie. 2. Propagación, la dilatación o extensión de alguna cosa.

Propagator [prep'-a-gêt-er], *s.* Propagador.

Propel [pro-pel'], *va.* Impeler, mover alguna cosa hacia adelante; servir como un medio de propulsión o impulsión; lanzar (un proyectil).

Propellent [pro-pel'-ent], *a.* Motor, propulsor, que hace mover, o empuja hacia adelante.

Propeller [pro-pel'-er], *s.* 1. Impulsor, el o lo que impele. 2. Hélice, parte del mecanismo propulsor de un buque de vapor; propulsor en general. 3. Buque de hélice. *Screw propeller*, Propulsor de hélice.

Propense [pro-pens'], *a.* (Ant.) Propenso, inclinado, dispuesto.

Propension [pro-pen'-shun], **Propensity** [pro-pen'-si-ti], *s.* Propensión, tendencia, hacia lo bueno o (más frecuentemente) hacia lo malo.

Proper [prep'-er], *a.* 1. Propio, conveniente, idóneo, á propósito, apto para algún fin. 2. Propio, conforme al uso, conveniente, correspondiente, justo, correcto. 3. Propio, peculiar, particular. 4. Propio, natural, en contraposición a lo postizo o accidental. 5. Justo, exacto, literal, plano. 6. (Ant. o Prov.) Esbelto, bien dispuesto, de buena presencia, bien parecido; aseado. 7. (Ant.) Propio, mismo. *Proper sense*, Sentido propio, justo o literal. *Proper surroundings*, Alrededores, medio, atmósfera, circunstancias propias, convenientes.

Properly [prep'-er-li], *adv.* Propiamente, justamente, convenientemente; correctamente; oportunamente, con mucha razón, a propósito. *Properly speaking*, Hablando claro; hablando en términos precisos, etc.

Properness [prep'-er-nes], *s.* Propiedad, la calidad particular que conviene privativamente a alguna cosa.

Propertied [prep'-er-tid], *a.* Propietario, que posee bienes.

Property [prep'-er-ti], *s.* 1. Propiedad, calidad particular o privativa. 2. Propiedad, derecho de posesión, dominio; derecho o interés legal de valor; el derecho de ejercer una ocupación o empleo particular. 3. Propiedad, lo que puede ser poseído legalmente; hacienda, los bienes poseídos. *Personal property*, Bienes muebles, los que pueden acompañar a la persona del dueño. *Real property*, Bienes inmuebles, bienes raíces. *A man of large property*, Un gran hacendado, un rico propietario. 4. *Properties*, *s. pl.* Trajes, vestidos, armas, etc., propias y usadas en el tiempo y lugar en que se supone la acción de un drama.

Prophecy [pref'-e-si], *s.* 1. Profecía hecha por inspiración divina; predicción de las cosas futuras. 2. Plática o discurso hecho bajo inspiración divina.

Prophesier [pref'-e-sai-er], *s.* Profeta, el que predice.

Prophesy [pref'-e-sai], *va.* 1. Profetizar, predecir, especialmente bajo la inspiración divina; prefigurar. 2. Hablar o proferir en nombre de Dios; interpretar, declarar.—*vn.* 1. Hablar por influencia divina; comunicar entre Dios y el hombre. 2. Profetizar; predecir.

Prophet [pref'-et], *s.* 1. Profeta, el que transmite mensajes divinos o que interpreta la voluntad divina. 2. Profeta, el que predice lo venidero; especialmente el profeta inspirado. 3. Guía, superior religioso.

Prophetess [pref'-et-es], *sf.* Profetisa.

Prophetic, **Prophetical** [pro-fet'-ic, al], *a.* Profético: que predice.

Prophetically [pro-fet'-i-cal-i], *adv.* Proféticamente.

Propheticalness, **Propheticality** [pro-fet'-i-cal-nes], *s.* La calidad que constituye a una cosa profética.

Prophylactic [prō-fi-lac'-tic o pref-i-lac'-tic], *a.* Profiláctico, preservativo, preventivo.

Prophylaxis [prō-fi-lac'-sis], *s.* Profilaxis, higiene, tratamiento médico preventivo.

Propinquity [pro-pin'-cwi-ti], *s.* 1. Propincuidad, cercanía (de lugar). 2. Proximidad (de tiempo). 3. Propincuidad, parentesco.

Propitiable [pro-pish'-i-a-bl], *a.* Que se puede propiciar o volver propicio, favorable.

Propitiate [pro-pish'-i-êt], *vn.* Propiciar, ablandar. aplacar, conciliar.

Propitiation [pro-pish-i-é'-shun], *s.* 1. Propiciación, acción de volver propicio. 2. Propiciación, lo que hace propicio; sacrificio que se ofrece a Dios para aplacarle.

Propitiator [pro-pish'-i-ê-ter], *s.* Propiciador.

Propitiatory [pro-pish'-i-a-to-ri], *a.* Propiciatorio, que tiene virtud de mover y hacer propicio.—*s.* 1. Propiciación. 2. Propiciatorio, placa de oro que en la ley antigua se colocaba sobre el arca de la Alianza.

Propitious [pro-pish'-us], *a.* 1. Propicio, benéfico, benigno, inclinado a hacer bien. 2. De buen agüero, feliz, favorable.

Propitiously [pro-pish'-us-li], *adv.* Propiciamente, favorablemente.

Propitiousness [pro-pish'-us-nes], *s.* Calidad de propicio; beneficencia, naturaleza favorable, favor, benignidad.

Proplasm [prō'-plazm], *s.* (Poco us.) Matriz, molde.

Prop-leg [prep'-leg], *s.* (Ento.) *V.* PROLEG.

Propolis [prō'-po-lis o prep'-o-lis], *s.* Propóleos, tanca, betún de las abejas. Se llama también cera aleda. *V.* BEE-GLUE.

Proponent [pro-pō'-nent], *s.* Proponente, proponedor.

Proportion [pro-pōr'-shun], *s.* 1. Proporción, relación de las partes entre sí o con el todo; extensión, número o grado relativos. 2. Proporción debida, ajuste conveniente, simetría, forma, tamaño. 3. (Mat.) Proporción, la semejanza o igualdad de dos razones. *In proportion*, En proporción, en correspondencia, a medida que. *Out of proportion*, Desproporcionado.

Proportion, *va.* Proporcionar, disponer y ordenar una cosa en la debida proporción; formar con simetría.

Proportionable [pro-pōr'-shun-a-bl], *a.* Proporcionable, proporcionado.

Proportionably [pro-pōr'-shun-a-bli], *adv.* Proporcionablemente, proporcionadamente.

Proportional [pro-pōr'-shun-al], *a.* Proporcional, perteneciente a la proporción o que la incluye.—*s.* Proporcional, número o cantidad proporcional.

Proportionality [pro-pōr-shun'-al-i-ti], *s.* Proporcionalidad.

Proportionally, *adv.* Proporcionalmente, en proporción.

Proportionate [pro-pōr'-shun-et], *a.* Proporcionado, en debida proporción con algo; competente.

Proportionate [pro-pōr'-shun-ĕt], *va.* Proporcionar, ajustar en proporción.
Proportionateness [pro-pōr'-shun-et-nes], *s.* Proporcionalidad, proporción.
Proportionment [pro-pōr'-shun-mẹnt], *s.* Acción y efecto de proporcionar.
Proposal [pro-pō'-zal], *s.* Propuesta, proposición, ofrecimiento, oferta que ha de ser considerada o aceptada.
Propose [pro-pōz'], *va.* 1. Proponer, ofrecer algo para su consideración o aceptación; ofrecer, presentar. 2. Proponer, pensar, tener intención de, formar un designio.—*vn.* 1. Proponerse, hacer propósito, hacer resolución de. 2. Ofrecer, en especial hacer una oferta de matrimonio.
Proposer [pro-pōz'-ẹr], *s.* Proponente, proponedor.
Proposition [prep-o-zish'-un], *s.* 1. Proposición, una oración breve en que se afirma o niega alguna cosa. 2. Proposición, la acción de proponer; propuesta. 3. Expresión de un juicio por medio de palabras. 4. Lo que se propone como asunto del discurso; exposición de un tema; propósito. 5. (Mat.) Proposición, cualquier principio que se establece y ha de ser demostrado.
Propositional [prep-o-zish'-un-al], *a.* Considerado como una proposición.
Propound [pro-paund'], *va.* 1. Proponer. 2. Sentar o sostener una proposición. 3. Hacer preguntas a uno.
Propounder [pro-paund'-ẹr], *s.* Proponente, proponedor.
Propped [prept], *pret.* y *pp.* del verbo *To* PROP.
Propretor [pro-prī'-tẹr], *s.* Propretor, magistrado de la antigua Roma.
Proprietary [pro-prai'-ẹ-tẹ-ri], *a.* Propietario, que tiene derecho exclusivo a una cosa.—*s.* 1. Propietario, dueño. 2. Conjunto de propietarios. 3. Derecho exclusivo a la posesión: justa pretensión a la propiedad de una cosa.
Proprietor [pro-prai'-ẹ-tẹr], *s.* Propietario, la persona, o una de las personas, que tienen derecho a una cosa, o al título legal de la misma.
Proprietress [pro-prai'-ẹ-tres], *sf.* Propietaria.
Propriety [pro-prai'-ẹ-ti], *s.* 1. Concordancia con el uso establecido, conveniencia, conducta o acción conveniente, decencia en los modales. 2. Exactitud y uniformidad gramatical y retórica; propiedad, perfecta conveniencia de la palabra o estilo con el asunto que se expresa; sentido propio (de los vocablos). *To offend against propriety,* Faltar a las reglas de la buena crianza.
Propt, *pp. irr.* de *To* PROP.
Propulsion [pro-pul'-shun], *s.* Propulsión, propulsa; impulso, impulsión.
Propulsive [pro-pul'-siv], **Propulsory** [pro-pul'-so-ri], *a.* Propulsor, que hace adelantar, que propende a avanzar.
Propylæum [pro-pi-lī'-um], *s.* Propíleo, entrada o vestíbulo de un templo.
Propylene [prō'-pi-līn], *s.* (Quím.) Propileno, carburo de hidrógeno gaseoso, incoloro, de gusto algo dulce.
Pro rata [pro rē'-ta], *a.* (Com.) Prorrata, a proporción.
Prorate [prō-rēt'], *va.* Prorratear.
Prore, *s.* (Poét. y raro) Proa, prora.
Prorogation [pro-ro-gē'-shun], *s.* Prorogación, ampliación, prolongación, extensión, continuación o dilatación del tiempo señalado para una cosa. *The prorogation of the session of Parliament,* Suspensión de las sesiones del Parlamento hasta cierto día señalado.
Prorogue [pro-rōg'], *va.* 1. Prorogar, ampliar, extender, dilatar o continuar el tiempo señalado. 2. Diferir. *To prorogue Parliament,* Suspender las sesiones del Parlamento hasta un día señalado.
Prosaic [pro-zē'-ic], *a.* 1. Prosaico, tocante o parecido a la prosa; que está en prosa. 2. No imaginativo, falto de interés, común, trivial.
Prosaically [pro-zē'-ic-al-i], *adv.* Prosaicamente, de un modo prosaico.
Prosaicism, Prosaism [pro-zē'-i-sizm, prō'-za-izm], *s.* Estilo, carácter prosaico; frase, locución prosaica; prosaísmo.
Proscenium [pro-sī'-ni-um], *s.* Proscenio, el lugar entre la escena y la orquesta.
Proscribe [pro-scraib'], *va.* 1. Proscribir, declarar a uno reo de muerte; poner a uno fuera de la protección de las leyes; expulsar de la sociedad. 2. Condenar, reprobar, hablando de doctrinas, máximas, etc.; prohibir, vedar.
Proscriber [pro-scraib'-ẹr], *s.* El que proscribe, prohibe o veda.
Proscription [pro-scrip'-shun], *s.* Proscripción, acción de proscribir, de poner fuera de la ley, o de la sociedad.
Proscriptive [pro-scrip'-tiv], *a.* Proscriptivo, que proscribe o condena; perteneciente a, o de la naturaleza de la proscripción.
Prose [prōz], *s.* 1. Prosa, la forma corriente y suelta del lenguaje, sin aligación de pies y consonantes. 2. Habla común, trivial y tediosa.—*a.* Prosaico, de prosa, en prosa; insulso, fastidioso.
Prosect [pro-sect'], *va.* Preparar disecciones anatómicas para alguna demostración.
Prosecute [pres'-ẹ-kiūt], *va.* 1. Proseguir, seguir, continuar, llevar adelante. 2. Anhelar, buscar o seguir con empeño; pretender, solicitar. 3. Procesar, hacer causa a uno.—*vn.* Querellarse ante el juez; seguir un pleito; sostener una acusación criminal.
Prosecution [pres-ẹ-kiū'-shun], *s.* 1. Prosecución, la acción de proseguir una cosa. 2. Seguimiento de una causa criminal.
Prosecutor [pres'-ẹ-kiū-tẹr], *s.* El que prosigue o continúa alguna cosa; el actor o acusador en una causa criminal.
Prosecutrix [pres-ẹ-kiū'-trix], *sf.* Acusadora, demandante en una causa criminal.
Proselyte [pres'-ẹ-lait], *s.* Prosélito, persona convertida a una religión, a una secta, a un partido, o a alguna opinión.
Proselyte, Proselytize [pres'-ẹ-li-taiz], *va.* Convertir, hacer prosélitos.
Proselytism [pres'-e-li-tizm], *s.* Proselitismo, el acto de hacer prosélitos; estado de conversión.
Proser [prōz'-ẹr], *s.* Prosista, hablador sin substancia, escritor enojoso, insulso.
Prosily [prō'-zi-li], *adv.* Prosaicamente, de un modo prosaico.
Prosiness [prō'-zi-nes], *s.* Calidad de prosaico; insulsez.
Proslavery [pro-slē'-vẹr-i], *a.* Partidario de la esclavitud o de la política de no intervención en lo relativo a la esclavitud.
Prosing [prōz'-ing], *s.* Charla, plática o conversación sin substancia y fuera de propósito.
Prosodian [pres-ō'-di-an], *s.* El que conoce bien la prosodia.
Prosodic, Prosodiac, Prosodial [pres-ed'-ic, pres-ō'-di-ac, al], *a.* Prosódico, perteneciente a la prosodia; conforme a las reglas de la prosodia.
Prosody [pres'-o-di], *s.* Prosodia, la parte de la gramática que enseña la pronunciación y cantidad de las sílabas.
Prosopopœia [pres-o-po-pī'-ya], *s.* Prosopopeya, personificación, figura por la cual se hace hablar u obrar a una persona muerta o ausente, y también a los animales o cosas inanimadas.
Prospect [pres'-pect], *va.* y *vn.* 1. Catear, (Amer.) buscar, descubrir minerales o minas. 2. Dar buenas esperanzas, prometer.
Prospect, *s.* 1. Perspectiva, vista o aspecto de diversos objetos mirados de lejos. 2. Perspectiva, lo que se prevé o espera; indicación que justifica una expectativa o esperanza; aspecto, futura probabilidad fundada en las indicaciones presentes. 3. Situación con respecto a los puntos cardinales; la dirección en que se halla el frente de una cosa. 4. Indicación de la presencia de un mineral. 5. (Des.) Vistillas, lugar alto desde donde se ve y descubre mucho terreno. *These houses afford a fine prospect,* Estas casas tienen hermosas vistas. *There is no prospect of his coming,* No hay esperanzas de que venga; no tiene trazas de venir. *The house has a western prospect,* La casa da al poniente. *A prospect of gold,* Indicación (pepita o polvo) de oro.
Prospective [pro-spec'-tiv], *a.* 1. Anticipado, venidero, que está por venir, o en expectativa. 2. Previsor, prevenido, que mira hacia adelante o toma en cuenta lo futuro.—*s.* Vista, perspectiva.
Prospectively [pro-spec'-tiv-li], *adv.* Con relación a lo futuro; en perspectiva.
Prospectus [pro-spec'-tus], *s.* Prospecto, el anuncio que se hace de algún plan o proyecto, o de alguna obra antes de darse a luz.
Prosper [pres'-pẹr], *va.* Prosperar, acrecentar en bienes.—*vn.* 1. Prosperar, gozar de fortuna o prosperidad. 2. Medrar, mejorar de fortuna.
Prosperity [pres-per'-i-ti], *s.* Prosperidad, felicidad, fortuna.
Prosperous [pres'-pẹr-us], *a.* 1. Próspero, feliz, dichoso, afortunado, favorable. 2. Floreciente; propicio *Prosperous gales,* Vientos propicios.
Prosperously [pres'-pẹr-us-li], *adv.* Prósperamente.
Prosperousness [pres'-pẹr-us-nes], *s* Prosperidad.
Prostate [pres'-tēt], *s.* (Anat.) Próstata, glándula situada al principio de la uretra en el hombre y los mamíferos machos.
Prostatic [pres-tat'-ic], *a.* Prostático, perteneciente o relativo a la próstata.
Prosthenic [pres-then'-ic], *a.* Prosté-

nico, que tiene fuerza o preponderancia de fuerza en las partes delanteras. (< Gr.)
Prosthesis [pres'-thes-is], *s.* 1. Prótesis, adición de una o más letras a una palabra, especialmente al principio. 2. (Cir.) La operación de hacer partes artificiales y ajustarlas al cuerpo, como los dientes postizos, piernas de corcho, etc.
Prostitute [pres'-ti-tiūt], *va.* Prostituir, exponer á todo género de torpeza y sensualidad.
Prostitute, *s.* 1. Mercenario. 2. Prostituta, ramera.—*a.* 1. Prostituto, prostituido, venal. 2. Vil, entregado a los vicios, deshonrado, envilecido.
Prostitution [pres-ti-tiu'-shun], *s.* Prostitución.
Prostrate [pres'-trêt], *a.* 1. Postrado, humillado, prosternado. 2. Echado a la larga. 3. (Biol.) Procumbente, echado.
Prostrate, *va.* 1. Echar a tierra o por el suelo; tender a la larga. 2. Postrar, demoler, derribar; arruinar. 3. Postrarse, hincarse de rodillas. 4. (Med.) Postrar, enflaquecer, quitar el vigor a alguno.
Prostration [pres-trê'-shun], *s.* 1. Postración; acción y efecto de tender a la larga, etc. 2. Postración, abatimiento, depresión. 3. (Med.) Postración, abatimiento por la excitación o por el esfuerzo muy sostenido; se diferencia del agotamiento (*exhaustion*).
Prostyle [prō'-stail], *s.* (Arq.) Próstilo.
Protagonist [prōt-ag'-o-nist], *s.* Protagonista, personaje principal del drama griego; jefe.
Protasis [pret'-a-sis], *s.* 1. (Gram.) Prótasis, cláusula de un período condicional que contiene la condición o antecedente; primera parte de un período compuesto que se completa con la segunda, llamada apódosis. 2. Antiguamente, prótasis, exposición del drama.
Protean [prō'-te-an], *a.* 1. De Proteo, que se refiere a Proteo. 2. Que cambia fácilmente de forma.
Protect [pro-tect'], *va.* Proteger, amparar, defender, patrocinar, favorecer.
Protection [pro-tec'-shun], *s.* 1. Protección, amparo, patrocinio. 2. Protección, proteccionismo, sistema económico que, para proteger la industria y el comercio de un país, dificulta la importación de productos extranjeros, recargando los derechos de aduana. 3. Salvoconducto, pasaporte.
Protectionism [pro-tec'-shun-izm], *s.* Proteccionismo, sistema económico de los proteccionistas. *V.* PROTECTION, 2ª acep.
Protective [pro-tec'-tiv], *a.* 1. Protector, que sirve de abrigo. 2. Protector, que protege. *Protective coloring,* Coloración protectora, mimetismo. *Protective tariff,* Tarifa (o arancel) proteccionista.
Protective [pro-tect'-iv], *a.* Protector, protectorio, que protege, que sirve de abrigo.—*s.* 1. Alguna cosa que protege; amparo, abrigo. 2. Cubierta aséptica para una herida.
Protector [pro-tect'-er], *s.* Protector, patrono, patrocinador.
Protectorate [pro-tec'-ter-êt], **Protectorship** [pro-tec'-ter-ship], *s.* Protectorado, protectoría, el oficio, dignidad o jurisdicción de protector.
Protegé [pro'-tê-zhê'], *s.* Protegido, favorito.
Protegée [pro-tê-zhê'], *s.* Protegida, favorita.
Proteid [prō'-te-id], *s.* Compuesto muy complejo y amorfo por lo común, que contiene carbono, hidrógeno, nitrógeno y azufre; se halla en casi todos los sólidos y líquidos de los organismos animales y vegetales, en forma viscosa, o desleída.
Protein [prō'-te-in], *s.* Proteína, substancia sacada de dichos compuestos; se considera hoy como producto artificial.
Protest [pro-test'], *vn.* Protestar, declarar solemnemente su dictamen o parecer.—*va.* Protestar una letra de cambio, hacer o sacar protesto contra el que no la quiere aceptar o pagar después de haberla aceptado. *To protest for non-acceptance,* Protestar por falta de aceptación. *To protest for non-payment,* Protestar por falta de pago.
Protest [prō'-test], *s.* Protesta, protesto. *To accept a bill under protest,* Aceptar una letra bajo o so protesto. *Protest of a bill,* Protesto de una letra de cambio o libranza.
Protestant [pret'-es-tant], *a.* 1. Protestante, el que protesta. 2. Protestante, nombre que se da a las religiones anglicana, luterana y calvinista y a las sectas que se derivan de ellas.
Protestant, *s.* Protestante, nombre que se da a los que profesan cualquiera de las sectas protestantes.
Protestantism [pret'-es-tant-izm], *s.* Protestantismo, la creencia de los protestantes.
Protestation [pret-es-tê'-shun], *s.* Protestación; protesta, declaración solemne de una opinión, etc.
Protester [pro-test'-er], *s.* El que protesta.
Prothonotary [pro-then'-o-te-ri], *s.* Protonotario, el principal y primero de los notarios. *Prothonotary warbler,* Pájaro cantor del Sur de los Estados Unidos, de vivo color amarillo, con la espalda aceitunada y las alas y cola cenicientas. Protonotaria citrea.
Prothonotaryship [pro-then'-o-te-ri-ship], *s.* Protonotariato.
Proto- [prō'-to]. Prefijo derivado del griego que significa primero; en química significa el más bajo.
Protocol [prō'-to-cel], *s.* 1. Trazo, esbozo, v. g. de un tratado; declaración o memoria informal de un acuerdo entre dos países; acta de una conferencia. 2. Protocolo, registro.
Protology [pro-tel'-o-ji], *s.* *V.* PREFACE.
Proton [prō'-ten], *s.* (Fís. y Quím.) Protón.
Protoplasm [prō'-to-plazm], *s.* (Biol.) Protoplasma (m.), sarcodo, la substancia viscosa, contráctil, semilíquida, algo granulosa que constituye la porción principal de una célula animal o vegetal.
Protoplasmic, Protoplasmal [prō-to-plaz'-mic, mal], *a.* Protoplasmático, perteneciente o parecido al protoplasma, o formado por él.
Prototype [prō'-to-taip], *s.* Prototipo, el original de alguna copia.
Protoxid [prōt-ox'-id], *s.* Protóxido, el óxido que contiene un solo átomo de oxígeno.
Protozoa [prō-to-zō'-a], *s. pl.* Protozoarios, clase diversamente determinada del reino animal, que comprende los seres compuestos de una sola célula, o de un solo grupo de células que no se pueden separar en tejidos diferentes.
Protract [pro-tract'], *va.* 1. Alargar, prolongar, dilatar, diferir en tiempo. 2. Levantar un plano; trazar un mapa por medio del pitipié y del semicírculo (transferidor). 3. (Anat.) Extender, empujar o impulsar hacia adelante.
Protracter [pro-tract'-er], *s.* 1. Alargador. 2. *V.* PROTRACTOR.
Protractile [pro-tract'-il], *a.* Capaz de ser impulsado o extendido hacia adelante.
Protraction [pro-trac'-shun], *s.* Prolongación, dilatación.
Protractive [pro-trac'-tiv], *a.* Dilatorio.
Protractor [pro-tract'-er], *s.* 1. Transferidor, instrumento para medir o trazar ángulos. 2. (Anat.) Músculo que mueve un miembro hacia adelante. 3. *V.* PROTRACTER, 1ª acep.
Protrude [pro-trūd'], *va.* Empujar, impeler, llevar hacia adelante.—*vn.* Empujarse o moverse hacia adelante, salir al aire.
Protrusible, Protrusile [pro-trū'-si-bl, sil], *a.* Que puede ser extendido o impulsado hacia adelante.
Protrusive [pro-trū'-siv], *a.* Que impulsa hacia adelante, que hace salir o proyectar.
Protrusion [pro-trū'-zhun], *s.* El acto de empujar o llevar una cosa hacia adelante; rempujón, empujón.
Protuberance, Protuberancy [pro-tiū'-ber-ans], *s.* 1. Protuberancia, prominencia, de los huesos o de otras partes del cuerpo. 2. Prominencia, la elevación de una de las partes de cualquier cuerpo sobre las que están alrededor.
Protuberant [pro-tiū'-ber-ant], *a.* Prominente, saliente.
Protuberate [pro-tiū'-ber-êt], *vn.* Sobresalir, formar prominencia.
Proud [praud], *a.* 1. Soberbio, orgulloso, altivo, atrevido, envanecido, presumido, presuntuoso, fiero, ufano. 2. Alto, quisquilloso, engreído; grande, noble. 3. Arrogante, insolente, impaciente. 4. Soberbio, magnífico, pomposo, ostentoso, espléndido, grande. 5. (Med.) Fungoso. 6. (Des.) Salida: dícese de las hembras de los animales. *He is very proud of his birth,* Está muy pagado de su nacimiento. *A proud day for Athens,* Un gran día para Atenas. *Proud-stomached,* Altivo, arrogante. *Proud titles,* Títulos pomposos.
Proudly [praud'-li], *adv.* Soberbiamente, orgullosamente; pomposamente.
Provable [prūv'-a-bl], *a.* Probable, persuasible, que puede ser demostrado.
Prove [prūv], *va.* (*pret.* PROVED, *pp.* PROVED o PROVEN). 1. Probar, justificar, manifestar, hacer patente, mostrar. 2. Probar, examinar, experimentar. 3. Abrir y hacer público un testamento con las fórmulas prescritas por las leyes.—*vn.* 1. Resultar, venir a parar, salir bien o mal, según la prueba, hallarse. 2. (Ant.) Hacer prueba o experiencia de una cosa. *It will prove otherwise,* Saldrá de otro modo. *Prove all things,* Probadlo todo. *To prove incorrect,* Resultar inexacto. *To prove useful,* Ser o resultar útil. *If what*

you say prove true, Si lo que Vd. dice resulta verdadero. *To prove one's self*, Mostrarse, hacer prueba de, mostrar que uno es. *To prove the patience of*, Poner a prueba la paciencia de.

†**Proveditor** [pro-ved'-i-tẹr], *s.* *V.* PURVEYOR.

Proven [prūv'-n], *pp. irr.* de PROVE (limitado a los tribunales o a documentos judiciales). Probado, demostrado. *Not proven*, Veredicto admisible en el derecho escocés, que declara la acusación como no probada, aunque tampoco refutada.

Provender [prev'-en-dẹr], *s.* Provisión de heno y grano para el ganado.

Proverb [prev'-ẹrb], *s.* 1. Proverbio, adagio o refrán; apotegma. 2. Sentencia enigmática. 3. Alguna cosa proverbial; ejemplo típico o notorio.

Proverbial [pro-vẹr'-bi-al], *a.* 1. Proverbial. 2. Conocido, notorio.

Proverbialist [pro-vẹr'-bi-al-ist], *s.* Proverbiador; proverbista.

Proverbially [pro-vẹr'-bi-al-i], *adv.* Proverbialmente.

Provide [pro-vaid'], *va.* 1. Proveer, prevenir, proporcionar, tener prontas las cosas necesarias para algún fin. 2. Proveer, abastecer, surtir; dar, suministrar. 3. Atesorar. 4 Estipular, contratar mutuamente.—*vn.* 1. Proveer; proporcionar medios para el uso futuro; abastecer de víveres. 2. Precaverse, tener cuidado, encargarse de; tomar precauciones, prepararse. 3. Hacer una estipulación previa. *To provide against*, Precaver, prevenir anticipadamente algún riesgo, daño o peligro. *To provide for*, Proveer, cuidar de antemano; dar a uno lo que necesita; estar preparado para algún acontecimiento, negocio, etc.; tomar precauciones. *Provided that*, Con tal que; siempre que; como, bajo condición; bien entendido.

Providence [prev'-i-dens], *s.* 1. Providencia, previsión, prevención o disposición anticipada. 2. Providencia divina, o simplemente Providencia, la mira y cuidado que tiene Dios acerca de sus criaturas. 3. Prudencia, frugalidad, economía.

Provident [prev'-i-dent], *a.* Próvido, providente, prevenido; cuidadoso, cauto, circunspecto, prudente, avisado.

Providential [prev-i-den'-shal], *a.* Providencial, que resulta de o que evidencia la acción de la providencia divina.

Providentially [prev-i-den'-shal-i], *adv.* Providencialmente, por la sabia disposición de la Providencia.

Providently [prev'-i-dent-li], *adv.* Próvidamente, prudentemente.

Provider [pro-vaid'-ẹr], *s.* Proveedor, provisor.

Province [prev'-ins], *s.* 1. Provincia, una de las partes en que generalmente se dividen los reinos o estados. 2. El oficio, empleo, obligación o incumbencia particular de cada uno; competencia; departamento. *That is not my province*, Eso no me toca, no me pertenece o no es encargo mío, o eso no es de mi cargo. *It is the province of*, Pertenece o está al cargo de.

Provincial [pro-vin'-shal], *a.* 1. Provincial, perteneciente a una provincia (de un mismo estado). 2. Provincial, rudo, campesino, grosero.

Provincial, *s.* 1. Provincial, el natural o habitante de una provincia; que no es de la capital. 2. Provincial, el religioso que tiene el gobierno y superioridad sobre todas las casas y conventos de una provincia.

Provincialism [pro-vin'-shal-izm], *s.* Provincialismo, modo particular de hablar de los habitantes de una provincia.

Provincialist [pro-vin'-shal-ist], *s.* Provincial, el que usa de provincialismos; habitante de una provincia.

†**Provine** [pro-vain'], *s.* Provena, serpa, el mugrón de la vid o el sarmiento que se planta para que eche raíces.

Provine, *va.* Amugronar o ataquizar las vides.

Proving [prūv'-ing], *s.* Prueba, acción y efecto de probar. *Proving-ground*, Lugar para probar los cañones y otras armas de fuego y las municiones para las mismas.

Provision [pro-vizh'-un], *s.* 1. Provisión, prevención de comestibles o de otras cosas necesarias; víveres, bastimentos. 2. Provisión, los comestibles u otras cosas recogidas. 3. La acción de proveerse, prevenirse o disponerse; precaución o medidas de precaución. 4. Señalamiento, asignación de alimentos, asistencias, etc. 5. Ajuste, convenio, estipulación. 6. Requisito. *Till farther provision be made*, Hasta más proveer.

Provisional [pro-vizh'-un-al], *a.* Provisional; establecido, dispuesto, o mandado interinamente.

Provisionally [pro-vizh'-un-al-i], *adv.* Provisionalmente, interinamente.

Proviso [pro-vai'-zo], *s.* Caución, estipulación, condición provisional.

Provisor [pro-vai'-zẹr], *s.* Proveedor, un oficio en los colegios.

Provisory [pro-vai'-zo-ri], *a.* Provisorio, provisional, condicional; temporero.

Provocation [prev-o-kē'-shun], *s.* 1. Provocación, lo que provoca, causa ira o resentimiento. 2. Incitamento, estímulo para ejecutar una cosa.

Provocative [pro-vō'-ca-tiv o pro-vec'-a-tiv], *a.* Provocativo, estimulante. —*s.* Llamativo, lo que puede estimular o producir apetito.

Provocativeness [pro-vō'-ca-tiv-nes], *s.* La calidad o propiedad de excitar el apetito.

Provoke [pro-vōk'], *va.* 1. Provocar, irritar o estimular a uno para que se enoje. 2. Provocar, excitar, incitar, inducir. 3. Provocar, facilitar, ayudar, causar, promover. 4. (Des.) Desafiar.—*vn.* Causar enojo, excitar la cólera de alguno.

Provoker [pro-vōk'-ẹr], *s.* Provocador.

Provoking [pro-vōk'-ing], *a.* Provocativo, provocante.

Provokingly [pro-vōk'-ing-li], *adv.* Insolentemente, de un modo provocativo.

Provost [prev'-ust], *s.* 1. Preboste, el sujeto que es cabeza de una comunidad o la preside y gobierna. 2. (Mil.) [pro-vō'] Preboste de ejército.

Provost-marshal [pro-vō'-mār'-shal], *s.* Preboste o capitán preboste de un ejército.

Provostship [prev'-ust-ship], *s.* Prebostazgo, prebestad, prebestadgo.

Prow [prau], *s.* Proa, la parte delantera de una embarcación; tajamar.—*a.* (Des.) Valeroso.

Prowess [prau'-es], *s.* Proeza, hazaña, valentía.

Prowl [praul], *va.* 1. Recorrer. 2. Rapiñar, hurtar; estafar.—*vn.* Andar o vagar de una parte a otra en busca de presa o pillaje.

Prowler [praul'-ẹr], *s.* Vagamundo, andorrero; el que anda vagando; ladrón, estafador.

Proximal [prex'-i-mal], *a.* (Biol.) Próximo, relativamente más cercano al centro del cuerpo; lo opuesto a *distal*.

Proximate [prex'-i-mēt], *a.* Próximo, inmediato; que tiene conexión inmediata con otra cosa. *Proximate principle*, Principio inmediato.

Proximately [prex'-i-met-li], *adv.* Próximamente, inmediatamente.

Proximity [prex-im'-i-ti], *s.* Proximidad, cercanía, inmediación.

Proximo [prex'-i-mo], *adv.* En el mes o del mes que viene; en abreviatura, *prox.*

Proxy [prex'-i], *s.* 1. Procuración, comisión, poder. *To marry by proxy*, Casarse por poder. 2. Apoderado, poderhabiente, el que tiene poder de otro para ejecutar algo en su nombre. (Contracción de *Procuracy.*)

Prude [prūd], *sf.* Mojigata, remilgada, gazmoña que afecta honestidad, modestia o santidad.

Prudence [prū'-dens], *s.* Prudencia, cordura, discreción.

Prudent [prū'-dent], *a.* Prudente, cuerdo, discreto, circunspecto.

Prudential [prū-den'-shal], *a.* Prudencial, que toca a la prudencia; dictado por la prudencia.

Prudentiality [prū-den-shi-al'-i-ti], *s.* (Poco us.) El estado o calidad de lo que es prudente; prudencia.

Prudentially [prū-den'-shal-i], *adv.* Prudencialmente.

Prudentials [prū-den'-shalz], *s.* Máximas de prudencia.

Prudently [prū'-dent-li], *adv.* Prudentemente.

Prudery [prūd'-ẹr-i], *s.* Melindre, remilgo, la afectada y demasiada delicadeza en las acciones o en el modo de ejecutarlas; gazmoñería, mojigatez, la afectación de modestia, honestidad o prudencia.

Prudish [prūd'-ish], *a.* Gazmoño, mojigato, el que afecta modestia, honestidad o prudencia; serio o grave con afectación.

Pruinous [prū'-i-nus], *a.* Harinoso; parecido a la escarcha; polvoriento, como la pelusilla blanco-azulada sobre la hoja de la col.

Prune [prūn], *va.* y *vn.* 1. Podar, cortar o quitar las ramas superfluas de los árboles y plantas. 2. Escamondar los árboles. 3. Limpiar alguna cosa quitando lo superfluo. *To prune up*, Vestir, adornar. 4. Limpiar y componer sus plumas las aves. *V.* PREEN.

Prune, *s.* Ciruela pasa; ciruela.

Prunella, Prunello [pru-nel'-o], *s.* 1. Carro de oro, especie de tela de que antiguamente se hacían las togas que gastan los ministros de la Iglesia anglicana; y hoy sólo se usa para las palas del calzado. 2. Bruñola, especie de ciruela.

Pruner [prūn'-ẹr], *s.* Podador.

Pruniferous [pru-nif'-ẹr-us], *a.* Que produce o lleva ciruelas.

Pruning [prū'-ning], *s.* Acción de podar o mondar; poda, monda, remonda, limpia de los árboles. *Pruning-hook*, Podón, márcola, corvillo.

Pruning-knife, Cuchilla para podar. *Pruning-shears,* Podaderas, tijeras para podar.

Prurience [prū'-ri-ens], **Pruriency** [prū'-ri-en-si], *s.* Comezón, prurito; particularmente, curiosidad liviana; sensualidad.

Prurient [prū'-ri-ent], *a.* 1. Dispuesto a la lascivia o liviandad. 2. Que padece prurito o comezón; anheloso.

Pruriginous [pru-rij'-i-nus], *a.* (Med.) Pruriginoso, que pertenece a la comezón, picazón, prurito o prurigo.

Prurigo [prū-rai'-go], *s.* (Med.) Erupción papulosa de la piel acompañada de viva comezón.

Prussian [prush'-an o prū'-shan], *a.* y *s.* Prusiano, natural de Prusia o lo perteneciente a este reino. *Prussian blue,* Azul de Prusia.

Prussiate [prus'-i-ēt], *s.* (Quím.) Prusiato, sal formada de ácido prúsico con alguna base.

Prussic [prus'-ic o prū'-sic], *a.* (Quím.) Prúsico. *Prussic acid, V. Hydrocyanic acid.*

Pry [prai], *va.* y *vn.* 1. Espiar, acechar, atisbar, observar, reconocer. Se usa particularmente con *out. To pry out a secret,* Arrancar un secreto. *To pry into other people's concerns,* Meterse en asuntos ajenos, meterse uno en lo que no le toca; curiosear, entremeterse, sonsacar. 2. Alzaprimar, mover o levantar con una palanca.

Pry, *s.* 1. Mirada escrudiñadora y taimada. 2. Curioso, indiscreto. 3. (Fam.) Palanca, barra o palo para levantar un peso.

Psalm [sām], *s.* Salmo; cántico sagrado que contiene alabanzas; himno.

Psalmist [sām'-ist o sal'-mist], *s.* Salmista; por antonomasia, David.

Psalmody [sal'-mo-di o sām'-o-di], *s.* Salmodia.

Psalter [sēl'-tẹr], *s.* Salterio o libro de salmos; en especial las versiones de las Iglesias católica y anglicana.

Psaltery [sēl'-tẹr-i], *s.* 1. Salterio, instrumento músico de los antiguos hebreos, de forma no conocida. 2. Salterio, instrumento músico de la edad media, con trece cuerdas y una tabla harmónica.

Pseudo [siū'-dō], *a.* Seudo o falso: adjetivo griego que se pone delante de algunas voces.

Pseudography [siū-deg'-ra-fi], *s.* 1. Escritura u ortografía incorrecta. 2. Escritura falsa, falsificación.

Pseudomorph [siū'-do-mērf], *s.* 1. Seudomorfo, mineral que tiene la forma exterior cristalina de otro mineral. 2. Forma irregular o falsa.

Pseudomorphic, Pseudomorphous [siū-do-mēr'-fic, fus], *a.* Seudomorfo, que ha tomado la forma de cristales extraños a su especie.

Pseudonym [siū'-do-nim], *s.* 1. Seudónimo, nombre ficticio empleado por un autor para que se ignore el suyo propio. 2. (Biol.) El nombre vernáculo.

Pseudonymous [siū-den'-i-mus], *a.* Seudónimo, de nombre supuesto.

Pseudo-philosopher [siū-do-fi-les'-o-fẹr], *s.* Seudofilósofo, filosofastro.

Pseudo-philosophy [siū-do-fi-les'-o-fi], *s.* Seudofilosofía.

Pseudopod [siū'-do-ped], *s.* (Biol.) Seudópodo, una prolongación temporal del protoplasma de una célula o de un animal unicelular, que le sirve para tomar su alimento, para moverse, etc.

Pshaw [shō], *inter.* ¡Vaya! ¡fuera! ¡quita! ¡malhaya! ¡puf!

Psoriasis [so-rai'-a-sis], *s.* Soriasis, enfermedad crónica de la piel que presenta grupos de escamas.

Psyche [sai'-ki], *s.* Psique.

Psychedelic [sai-kẹ-del'-ic], *a.* Psicodélico o sicodélico.

Psychiatrist [sai-kai'-a-trist], *s.* (Med.) Psiquiatra o siquiatra.

Psychiatry [sai-kai'-a-tri], *s.* (Med.) Psiquiatría o siquiatría.

Psychic, Psychical [sai'-kic, al], *a.* 1. Psíquico, referente a las facultades del alma, desde el punto de vista intelectual y moral. 2. Natural, como opuesto a espiritual.

Psychoanalysis [sai-cō-a-nal'-i-sis], *s.* (Med.) Psicoanálisis o sicoanálisis.

Psychoanalyst [sai-cō-an'-a-list], *s.* Psicoanalista o sicoanalista.

Psychoanalytic [sai-cō-an-a-lit'-ic], *a.* Psicoanalítico o sicoanalítico.

Psychoanalyze [sai-cō-an'-a-laiz], *va.* Psicoanalizar o sicoanalizar, hacer psicoanálisis o sicoanálisis.

Psychological, Psychologic [sai-co-lej'-ic, al], *a.* Psicológico. *Psychological testing,* Psicotecnia.

Psychologist [sai-cel'-o-jist], *s.* Psicólogo, el que estudia o está versado en la psicología.

Psychology [sai-cel'-o-ji], *s.* Psicología, la ciencia que trata del alma humana, sus facultades y funciones; también, tratado sobre el alma.

Psychomancy [sai'-co-man-si], *s.* Sicomancia, arte supersticiosa de evocar o llamar los manes o las almas de los muertos.

Psychopathic [sai-co-path'-ic], *a.* (Med.) Psicopático o sicopático.

Psychopathology [sai-co-pa-thel'-o-ji], *s.* Psicopatología.

Psychopathy [sai-ce'-pa-thi], *s.* Psicopatía.

Psychophysics [sai-co-fiz'-ics], *s.* Psicofísica.

Psychosis [sai-cō'-sis], *s.* (Med.) Psicosis o sicosis.

Psychosomatic [saik-o-so-ma'-tic], *a.* Psicosomático.

Psychotechnological [sai-co-tec-no-lej'-ic-al], *a.* Psicotécnico.

Psychotherapy [sai-co-ther'-a-pi], *s.* (Med.) Psicoterapia o sicoterapia.

Psychrometer [sai-crem'-ẹ-tẹr], *s.* Psicrómetro.

Ptolemaic [tel-ẹ-mē'-ic], *a.* Tolemaico, lo que pertenece al sistema astronómico de Tolomeo.

Ptomain, Ptomaine [tō'-ma-in], *s.* Ptomaína, alcaloide ponzoñoso por lo común, que se deriva de materias animales en estado de descomposición. (< griego ptoma, cadáver.)

Ptyalism [tai'-a-lizm], *s.* Tialismo, salivación, babeo.

Puberty [piū'-bẹr-ti], *s.* 1. Pubertad, la edad en que adquieren las personas de ambos sexos aptitud para reproducirse. 2. (Bot.) El período en que una planta empieza a echar flores.

Pubescent [piu-bes'-ent], *a.* 1. Pubescente, cubierto de pelos, particularmente de pelos delgados, cortos y suaves, como las hojas de ciertas plantas; que tiene pelusa, velloso. 2. Púber: dícese de la persona que ha llegado a la edad de la pubertad.

Pubic [piū'-bic], *a.* Pubiano, púbico; que se refiere al pubis o a la región púbica.

Public [pub'-lic], *a.* 1. Público, común, que pertenece a todo el pueblo. 2. Público, notorio, patente, manifiesto. 3. General, universal. 4. Público: se aplica a la potestad, autoridad, espíritu, etc., cuando se tienen o poseen para el bien de todo el pueblo o cuando se emplean en él. *Public-house,* (1) Posada, taberna, hostería, fonda. (2) (Ingl.) Cervecería, establecimiento autorizado para vender bebidas embriagantes. *To make public,* Publicar o hacer pública alguna cosa.—*s.* Público, el común del pueblo. *In public,* En público, públicamente, a la vista de todos. *Public-hearted,* Animado del bien público, ansioso por el bien del pueblo. *Public-spirited,* Patriótico; el que prefiere el bien común o del público a su interés particular.

Publican [pub'-li-can], *s.* 1. Publicano, arrendador o cobrador de derechos públicos entre los romanos. 2. (Vulg.) Mesonero, posadero, tabernero.

Publication [pub-li-kē'-shun], *s.* 1. Publicación, el acto de publicar. 2. La acción de poner en venta alguna obra impresa, y la misma obra publicada.

Publicist [pub'-li-sist], *s.* 1. Publicista, el autor que escribe sobre el derecho público, o de los estados o naciones. 2. Escritor sobre asuntos de interés público.

Publicity [pub-lis'-i-ti], *s.* Publicidad, notoriedad.

Publicize [pUb'-li-saiz], *va.* Publicar, divulgar.

Publicly [pub'-lic-li], *adv.* Públicamente, a la vista de todos.

Public utility [pub'-lic yu-til'-i-ti], *s.* Empresa de servicios públicos.

Public works [pub'-lic wurks], *s. pl.* Obras públicas.

Publish [pub'-lish], *va.* 1. Publicar, hacer manifiesta al público alguna cosa. 2. Publicar un libro, anunciar que está de venta.

Publisher [pub'-lish-ẹr], *s.* Publicador, editor, el que publica un libro o escrito y lo pone en venta.

Publishing house [pUb'-lish-ing haus], *s.* (Casa) editorial, casa editora.

Puccoon [puc-cūn'], *s.* Orcaneta, onoquiles, planta norteamericana de la familia de las borragíneas. Lithospermum canescens. (Nombre indio.)

Puck [puc], *s.* Coco, fastasma, duende legendario de los ingleses, como el del "Sueño de una noche de verano" de Shakespeare.

Pucker [puk'-ẹr], *va.* Arrugar, hacer pliegues.—*s.* 1. Pliegue, arruga. 2. (Fam.) Agitación, perplejidad, embrollo.

Pudding [pud'-ing], *s.* 1. Pudín o pudingo, cierta masa sabrosa hecha por lo común de harina, azúcar, leche y huevos. 2. Manjar farináceo, que se come con carne, o como plato principal de una comida. 3. Salchicha, morcilla. *Black-pudding,* Morcilla. (Amer.) Morcón.

Pudding-dish [pud'-ing-dish], **Pudding-pan** [pud'-ing-pan], *s.* Cazuela o tartera para hacer el pudín.

Puddle [pud'-l], *s.* 1. Lodazal, cenagal. 2. *V.* PUDDLING.

Puddle, *va.* 1. Afinar, convertir en hierro batido, agitando sin cesar el hierro derretido y eliminando el carbono. 2. Cimentar, cubrir el fondo de un canal para que no filtre. 3. Enlodar; enturbiar el agua con lodo.

Puddler [pud'-lęr], *s.* 1. El que enloda o cimenta con lodo; refinador de hierro. 2. Utensilio para agitar el metal derretido. 3. Horno de afinar.

Puddling [pud'-ling], *s.* 1. Acto y efecto de cimentar o enlodar, o de batir el hierro, agitándolo en el horno de afinación. 2. Amasijo, masa de arcilla y tierra gredosa para cimentar.

Puddly [pud'-li], *a.* Lodoso, cenagoso.

Pudency [piū'-den-si], *s.* Modestia, pudor.

Pudgy [puj'-i], *a.* (Fam.) Corto y grueso, v. g. las manos; regordete, gordiflón.

Pudicity [piū-dis'-i-ti], *s.* Pudicicia, pudor, modestia, recato.

Puerile [piū'-ęr-il], *a.* Pueril, que es propio de muchachos.

Puerility [piū-ęr-il'-i-ti], *s.* Puerilidad, muchachada.

Puerperal [piū-ęr'-pęr-al], *a.* (Med.) Puerperal, perteneciente o que se refiere al parto; que resulta del parto.

‡**Puerperous** [piū-ęr'-pęr-us], *a.* Parturiente, de parto; que pare.

Puet [piū'-et], *s.* (Orn.) Gallineta.

Puff [puf], *s.* 1. Resoplido, bufido, soplo, bocanada de humo. 2. Borla para empolvar o echar polvos en el pelo. 3. Bollos, rizado, abanillo de las vueltas, tocados, etc., de los vestidos de mujer. 4. La exageración en alabar y recomendar alguna cosa para llamar la atención sobre ella. 5. *V.* PUFFBALL. *Puff of wind*, Ventarrón, ventolera. *Puff-paste*, Hojaldre, hojuela de pasta. *Spanish puff*, Buñuelo. *Puff-adder*, Víbora muy venenosa de África, con cuyo veneno emponzoñan los indígenas sus saetas. Clotho arietans.

Puffball [puf'-bōl], *s.* Bejín, pedo de lobo, hongo redondo del género Lycoperdon.

Puff, *va.* 1. Hinchar, inflar o llenar alguna cosa de aire. 2. Soplar, apartar algo de donde estaba por medio del viento. 3. Ensoberbecer, engreir, envanecer. 4. Alabar o ensalzar desmedidamente una persona o cosa con el objeto de llamar la atención hacia ella y de hacerla parecer mejor y más excelente de lo que en sí es. (Fam.) Cacarear.—*vn.* 1. Inflarse, hincharse con aire alguna cosa. 2. Inflarse, hincharse, engreirse, envanecerse. 3. Bufar, manifestar enojo o desprecio. 4. Resoplar, fumar, resollar con fuerza, jadear, hipar. 5. Mover alguna cosa muy agitadamente. *To puff at*, Bufar haciendo desprecio de alguna cosa; despreciar. *To puff away*, Disipar á soplos, disiparse una cosa por la acción del viento; arrojar a una persona o cosa de donde estaba, dando resoplidos o con enojo o desprecio. *To puff from*, Arrancar de repente alguna cosa del sitio que ocupaba por medio de una ráfaga de viento, una bocanada de aire o un soplo. *To puff with pride*, Llenar o henchir de viento o vanidad; ponerse inflado, soplado, hinchado o hueco de vanidad.

Puffer [puf'-ęr], *s.* El que resopla o sopla; el que es jactancioso, vanaglorioso o muy inflado de vanidad; el que pondera desmedidamente alguna cosa.

Puffin [puf'-in], *s.* 1. (Orn.) Alca de pico muy deprimido. Fratercula. 2. (Bot.) Bejín.

Puffiness [puf'-i-nes], *s.* 1. Hinchazón, regularmente de estilo. 2. (Med.) Hinchazón, intumescencia que cede a la presión.

Puffing [puf'-ing], *s.* 1. Hinchazón, el efecto de hincharse, envanecerse o engreirse. 2. La acción de soplar, inflar, hinchar o de apartar algo de su lugar por medio del viento. 3. Ponderación desmesurada del mérito o valor de algo. 4. Una especie de bollo.—*a.* Abofellado, fofo, hueco: dícese de las telas, cintas y otros géneros, y de los vestidos que no se doblan o apañan bien.

Puffingly [puf'-ing-li], *adv.* Hinchadamente; con afan.

Puffy [puf'-i], *a.* Flatulento; hinchado, inflado, entumecido. *A swelling, puffy style*, Un estilo pomposo o campanudo.

Pug [pug], *s.* 1. *V. Pug-dog.* 2. Nariz roma. 3. Nombre cariñoso que se da regularmente a los monos, a los perros pequeños y á veces a las personas. *Pug-dog*, Faldero, perrillo de pelo corto y nariz roma. *Pug-nose*, Nariz roma, respingada, cuya punta mira hacia arriba. *Pug-nosed*, Romo.

Pug, *va.* 1. Cimentar, embarrar, el fondo de un canal, enlodar con arcilla. 2. Llenar con argamasa para apagar el sonido.

Pugging [pug'-ing], *s.* 1. Amasijo, mezcla grosera de arcilla y aserrín que se pone entre los pisos para amortiguar el ruido. 2. Acción de forrar, de cimentar.

Pugh [pū o puh], *inter.* ¡Fuera! ¡puf! voz que indica desprecio, y particularmente que una cosa huele muy mal.

†**Pugil** [piū'-jil], *s.* Pulgarada.

Pugilism [piū'-jil-izm], *s.* Pugilismo o pugilato, la lid a puñadas.

Pugilist [piū'-jil-ist], *s.* Púgil.

Pugilistic [piū-jil-is'-tic], *a.* De pugilato, perteneciente al pugilato.

Pug-mill [pug'-mil], *a.* Artesa de ladrillería; amasadera, maquina en que se muele y mezcla la arcilla.

Pugnacious [pug-nē'-shus], *a.* Pugnaz, belicoso.

Pugnacity [pug-nas'-i-ti], *s.* Pugnacidad.

Puisne [piū'-nę], *a.* (For.) Reciente, nuevo; inferior; pequeño, poco considerable; el que es más joven que otro que se llama segundo o segundón con respecto al primero. Forma antigua de *Puny*.

Puissance [piū'-is-ans], *s.* Pujanza, fuerza, poder, potencia.

Puissant [piū'-is-ant], *a.* Pujante, poderoso, fuerte.

Puissantly [piū'-is-ant-li], *adv.* Poderosamente, fuertemente.

Puke [piūc], *s.* (Vulg.) Vomitivo.

Puke, *va.* y *vn.* (Vulg.) Vomitar.

Pulchritude [pul'-cri-tiud], *s.* Pulcritud, esmero en el adorno y aseo de la persona; hermosura, aseo, donaire.

Pule [piūl], *vn.* 1. Piar como un pollo. 2. Gemir, llorar.

Pulic [piū'-lic], *s.* (Bot.) Pulguera, zaragatona.

Pulicene, Pulicose [piū'-li-sīn, piū'-li-cōs], *a.* (Poco us.) Perteneciente a las pulgas; pulgoso, lleno de pulgas.

Puling [piū'-ling], *s.* 1. Pío, voz del pollo. 2. Gritería de niños; gemido.

Pulkha [pul'-ka], *s.* Trineo de Laponia, con el espaldar alto y cuadrado; tira de él un solo rengífero.

Pull [pul], *va.* 1. Tirar, atraer o traer hacia sí con violencia, estirar. *To pull ahead*, (Mar.) Tirar avante. 2. Coger, recoger; obtener asiendo y tirando. 3. Sacar. 4. Rasgar, desgarrar, hacer tiras. 5. Bogar, remar, conducir remando. 6. Sacar una prueba con la prensa de mano. —*vn.* Tirar con esfuerzo, tirar de una cuerda. *To pull asunder* o *away*, Arrancar, separar con violencia o quitar por fuerza una cosa de donde estaba. *To pull back*, Tirar, apartar o retirar hacia atrás, hacer recular o cejar. *To pull down*, Derribar, subvertir, demoler; degradar, privar, deponer; bajar, humillar, abatir. *To pull in*, Tirar, traer o atraer hacia adentro; cerrar. *To pull in pieces*, Hacer pedazos. *To pull off*, Tirar, quitar, sacar alguna cosa a viva fuerza, arrancar; deshacer o desbaratar; levantar, quitar una cosa que estaba encima de otra o la cubría, como un sello, un parche, una máscara, etc. *To pull out*, Tirar, quitar, sacar, arrancar. *To pull up*, Extirpar, arrancar de cuajo o de raíz, desarraigar; alzar, levantar. *To pull the wool over one's eyes*, Engañar a uno como un chino, jugársela a uno de codillo.

Pull, *s.* 1. Tirón, estirón, sacudimiento, sacudida. 2. Contienda, combate.

Pullback [pul'-bac], *s.* Estorbo, lo que tira hacia atrás o impide adelantar.

Puller [pul'-ęr], *s.* El que tira o arranca.

Pullet [pul'-et], *s.* Polla, la gallina medianamente crecida.

Pulley [pul'-i], *s.* Polea, garrucha. *Pulley-piece*, (Mar.) Armadura de barca.

Pullulate [pul'-yu-lēt], *vn.* 1. Pulular, germinar, ahijar o multiplicar mucho las plantas. 2. Pulular, se dice de los errores que se multiplican o crecen.

Pullman [pul'-man], *s.* Variedad de coche dormitorio o salón muy usada en los Estados Unidos de América. (Del nombre de su inventor.)

Pulmonary [pul'-mo-nę-ri], **Pulmonic** [pul-men'-ic], *a.* Pulmonar, pulmoníaco, que pertenece o se refiere a los pulmones. *Pulmonary artery*, Arteria pulmonar.

Pulmotor [pul-mō'-tęr], *s.* Pulmotor, aparato para respiración artificial.

Pulp [pulp], *s.* 1. Pulpa, la parte más carnosa del cuerpo animal. 2. Pulpa, arila, la carne o parte mollar de las frutas. 3. Pulpa, masa blanda y húmeda; pasta para hacer papel. 4. (Bot.) Arila, tegumento propio de ciertas semillas, como la del café.

Pulpiness [pulp'-i-nes], *s.* Estado pulposo, calidad de pulposo.

Pulpit [pul'-pit], *s.* Púlpito. *Pulpit-cloth*, Paño de púlpito.

Pulpous [pul'-pus], **Pulpy** [pul'-pi], *a.* Pulposo, mollar.

Pulpousness [pul'-pus-nes], *s.* La calidad de pulposo.

Pulque [pul'-kē], *s.* Pulque, bebida fermentada del maguey.

Pulsate [pul'-sēt], *vn.* Pulsar, latir una arteria, el corazón, etc.; latir con impulso rítmico.

Pulsatile [pul'-sa-til], *a.* 1. Pulsativo, de latido; dícese de la cosa que pulsa. 2. (Mús.) De percusión.

Pulsation [pul-sé'-shun], *s.* Pulsación, latido.
Pulsative [pul'-sa-tiv], *a.* Pulsativo, pulsador, que pulsa.
Pulsator [pul-sé'-tẹr], *s.* Golpeador, apaleador.
Pulsatory [pul'-sa-to-ri], *a.* Pulsador, que pulsa, que late, que produce pulsaciones; dícese del movimiento más bien que de la cosa.
Pulse [puls], *s.* 1. Pulso, el latido de la arterias que es perceptible al tacto. 2. Pulsación, vibración. *To feel one's pulse,* Tomar el pulso; tantear o sondear con arte la voluntad de una persona.
Pulse, *s.* Legumbres colectivamente (de las leguminosas), v. g. garbanzos, habas, lentejas, etc. (< Fr. ant. pouls < lat. puls, potaje.)
Pulse, *vn.* Pulsar, latir las arterias o el corazón.
Pulsion [pul'-shun], *s.* Impulso, virtud impulsa.
Pulsometer [pul-sem'-ẹ-tẹr], *s.* Pulsómetro, aparato de bomba que funciona por medio del vapor.
Pultaceous [pul-té'-shus], *a.* Pultáceo, que tiene la consistencia de la papilla.
§**Pulverable, Pulverizable** [pul'-vẹr-a-bl], *a.* Pulverizable, que se puede reducir fácilmente a polvo.
Pulverization [pul-vẹr-i-zé'-shun], *s.* Pulverización.
Pulverize [pul'-vẹr-aiz], *va.* Pulverizar, reducir á polvo.
Pulverizer [pul-vẹr-aiz'-ẹr], *s.* Lo que o el que pulveriza.
Pulverulence [pul-ver'-u-lens], *s.* Abundancia de polvo, polvareda.
Pulverulent [pul-ver'-u-lent], *a.* Polvoriento, lleno o cubierto de polvo.
Pulvillus [pul-vil'-us], *s.* Especie de cojinete que tienen las patas de muchos insectos, p. ej. la mosca.
Puma [piū'-ma], *s.* (Zool.) Puma, tigre americano, de unos cuatro pies de longitud. (Nombre peruano.) Felis concolor.
†**Pumicate** [piū'-m.i-két], *va.* *V.* PUMICE.
Pumice o **Pumice-stone** [pum'-is, stōn], *s.* Piedra pómez.
Pumice [pum'-is (o piū''-mis)], *va.* Apomazar, allanar o pulir con piedra pómez.
Pumiceous [piū-mish'-us], *a.* Perteneciente a la piedra pómez, o que la contiene.
Pump [pump], *s.* 1. Bomba, máquina para sacar agua o hacer circular un flúido, o para comprimirlo, llevándolo o impeliéndolo por aberturas o cañerías. *Suction-pump,* Bomba aspirante. *Lifting-pump,* Bomba elevadora. *Force-pump,* Bomba impelente. *Air-pump,* Máquina neumática; bomba de aire, en las máquinas de vapor. *Feed-pump, donkey-pump,* Bomba alimenticia. *Chain-pump,* Bomba de cadena. *Pump-dale,* (Mar.) Dala. *Pump-hook,* (Mar.) Sacanabo. *To fetch the pump,* (Mar.) Cargar la bomba. *To man the pump,* (Mar.) Armar la bomba. *To work a pump,* Hacer funcionar una bomba. 2. Zapato de hombre, fino y de suela delgada.
Pump, *va.* y *vn.* 1. Dar a la bomba, sacar agua de la bomba, bombear. 2. Sondear, tantear. 3. Sonsacar, examinar con astucia. 4. Bañar a chorro. *Pumping-shaft,* Pozo en que se hallan las bombas de una mina.
Pumper [pump'-ẹr], *s.* 1. Bombero, el que saca agua con una bomba. 2. Sonsacador, el que tantea, sondea o sonsaca.
Pumpernickel [pum'-pẹr-nic''-l], *s.* Especie de pan de cebada, de que usan principalmente los campesinos de Alemania.
Pumpkin [pump'-kin, fam. puṇ'-kin], †**Pumpion** [pump'-yun], *s.* Calabaza.
Pun [pun], *s.* Equívoco, chiste, juego de vocablos.
Pun, *vn.* 1. Jugar del vocablo, decir equívocos. 2. Burlarse de alguno con equívocos o retruécanos.
Punch [punch], *va.* 1. Punzar, horadar con punzón. 2. (Fam.) Dar puñetazos; empujar con el codo o con la mano; dar golpes con la mano.
Punch, *s.* 1. Punzón, instrumento de hierro que remata en punta y sirve para horadar; sacabocado o sacabocados. 2. Ponche, bebida compuesta de licores espirituosos, agua, limón y azúcar. 3. (Fam.) Golpe. 4. Arlequín o bufón de los volatines.—*a.* Fuerte, gordo. *Conductor's punch,* Sacabocados de conductor (en los ferrocarriles).
Punch-bowl [punch'-bōl], *s.* Ponchera, la taza para hacer ponche.
Puncheon, †**Punchin** [punch'-un], *s.* 1. Medida de líquidos que contiene veinte arrobas. 2. Punzón; cuño.
Puncheon, *s.* (Carp.) Pie derecho, poste grueso de madera que se pone en pie debajo del caballete de un edificio.
Puncher [punch'-ẹr], *s.* Punzador, el que punza u horada.
Punchinello [pun-chi-nel'-o], *s.* 1. Polichinela, bufón, gracioso. 2. Títere, en los juegos de saltimbanquis. 3. Hombre cachigordete.
Punching bag [punch'-ing bag], *s.* Balón para práctica de boxeo.
Punctate, Punctated [punc'-têt, ed], *a.* 1. (Bot. y Zool.) Puntuado, sembrado de puntos o de glándulas internas translúcidas. 2. Formado en punta, puntiagudo.
Punctilio [punc-til'-yo], *s.* Puntillo, punto de honra, delicadeza o pundonor.
Punctilious [punc-til'-yus], *a.* Puntilloso, nimiamente escrupuloso o pundonoroso; muy puntilloso, demasiado delicado en puntos de honor y trato, demasiado exacto o preciso.
Punctiliousness [punc'-til-yus-nes], *s.* Pundonor o escrupulosidad nimia; exactitud, atención minuciosa a los pormenores.
Puncto [punc'-tō], *s.* Punto de toque en la esgrima.
Punctual [puṇc'-tiu-al], *a.* 1. Puntual, diligente y exacto. 2. Puntual, indudable, cierto. 3. Preciso, fijo, cierto, determinado.
Punctuality [puṇc-tiu-al'-i-ti], **Punctualness** [puṇc'-tiu-al-nes], *s.* Puntualidad, exactitud.
Punctually [puṇc'-tiu-al-i], *adv.* Puntualmente, exactamente.
Punctuate [puṇc'-tiu-êt o puṇc'-chu-êt], *va.* Puntuar, señalar con puntos; colocar las notas o signos ortográficos.—*vn.* Usar signos de puntuación.
Punctuation [puṇc-tiu-é'-shun], *s.* Puntuación, el arte de puntuar, y el conjunto de puntos o signos ortográficos de un escrito.
Puncture [punc'-chur o puṇc'-tiur], *va.* Punzar, agujerear con un instrumento puntiagudo, picar.—*s.* 1. Puntura, agujero hecho con algún instrumento puntiagudo, punzadura, punzada, picadura, picada. 2. (Zool.) Concavidad menuda, hoyo.
Pundit [pun'-dit], *s.* Bracmán sabio, particularmente el versado en el conocimiento del idioma sanscrito, así como en las ciencias, leyes y religión de la India.
Pungency [pun'-jen-si], *s.* 1. Picante, naturaleza picante, poder de picar o punzar; la acerbidad o acrimonia que tienen algunas cosas que exacerban el sentido del gusto. 2. Punta, sabor, picante. 3. Picante, la acrimonia o mordacidad en el decir.
Pungent [pun'-jent], *a.* 1. Picante, que afecta los órganos de los sentidos, especialmente los del gusto y el olfato, con una sensación picante. 2. Acre, mordaz, acerbo, áspero. 3. (Zool.) Propio para picar. 4. (Bot.) Que termina en una punta dura.
Punic [piū'-nic], *a.* Púnico, perteneciente a los cartagineses; entre los romanos, falso, pérfido.—*s.* Lengua púnica, idioma de los cartagineses.
Puniceous [piū-nish'-us], *a.* Purpúreo; morado claro.
Puniness [piū'-ni-nes], *s.* Pequeñez; delicadeza de salud.
Punish [pun'-ish], *va.* 1. Castigar, mortificar, afligir con una restricción o pérdida, como pena, o con el propósito de corregir o reformar; penar. 2. Castigar, pegar, imponer una pena en expiación de una falta o un crimen.
Punishable [pun'-ish-a-bl], *a.* Punible, digno de castigo; sujeto a castigo por la ley.
Punishableness [pun'-ish-a-bl-nes], *s.* La propiedad que constituye a una persona o cosa digna de castigo.
Punisher [pun'-ish-ẹr], *s.* Castigador.
Punishment [pun'-ish-mẹnt], *s.* Castigo. (Fam.) Vapuleo, serie de golpes, p. ej. en un pugilato.
Punitive [piū'-ni-tiv], **Punitory** [piū'-ni-to-ri], *a.* Penal, punitivo.
Punk [punc], *s.* Yesca.—*a.* (fam.) 1. Muy malo, de ínfima calidad. 2. (fam.) Malo en cuanto a salud.
Punka [pun'-ka], *s.* Abanico; particularmente un abanico grande en el Indostán, que consiste en un marco o bastidor movible cubierto de tela y suspendido del techo. Lo mueve un sirviente y a veces un aparato mecánico. (< Indio, pankha.)
Punning [pun'-ing], *s.* Costumbre de hacer retruécanos o juegos de vocablos.
Punster [pun'-stẹr], *s.* Truhán; el que hace retruécanos; jugador de vocablos.
Punt [punt], *va.* 1. Impeler un barco, empujando con una vara contra el fondo. 2. Llevar, conducir, en un barquichuelo. 3. En el juego de la pelota de viento, impeler la pelota golpeándola con el pie; de aquí, dar, impeler.—*vn.* 1. Ir cazando o pescando en una lancha o barquichuelo; también, impeler un bote, empujándolo. 2. Impeler una pelota golpeándola con los pies.
Punt, *vn.* Apuntar, parar: úsase en ciertos juegos para indicar el acto de apuntar o poner dinero a las cartas.
Punt [punt], *s.* 1. Barquichuelo que tiene el fondo plano: se usa en aguas poco profundas y se impulsa con una vara. 2. (Mar.) Plancha de agua. 3. Golpe que se da con el pie a la pelota de viento después de soltarla y antes de que toque en el suelo.

Punter [punt'-ẹr], *s.* 1. El que impele la pelota de viento golpeándola con el pie. 2. El que apunta, o pone dinero a las cartas en ciertos juegos.
Puny [piū'-ni], *a.* Débil, enfermizo; tierno; chico, pequeño; inferior.
Pup [pup], *vn.* Parir la perra.
Pup, *s.* Cachorro, cachorrito.
Pupa [piū'-pa], *s.* Ninfa, crisálida o dormida; el tercer grado de un insecto que pasa por una metamorfosis completa.
Pupil [piū'-pil], *s.* 1. Pupila, la niña del ojo. 2. Discípulo, alumno, alumna. 3. Pupilo, el menor que está bajo la dirección de un tutor o ayo.
Pupilage [piū'-pil-ėj], *s.* Pupilaje, el estado del que se halla bajo la dirección de un ayo o tutor, o a pupilo.
Pupilary, Pupillary, Pupilar [piū-pil-ẹ-ri], *a.* Pupilar, perteneciente á un pupilo o á la niña del ojo. *Pupilary margin*, Borde de la pupila del ojo.
Pupipara [piu-pip'-a-ra], *s. pl.* (Ento.) Pupíparos, división de insectos dípteros, que conservan sus huevos en el abdomen hasta que se han transformado en ninfas; son parásitos de otros animales, v. g. las garrapatas de los murciélagos.
Puppet [pup'-et], *s.* 1. Títere, muñeco, figurilla que se mueve artificiosamente. 2. Títere, voz de desprecio empleada respecto a una persona que obra bajo la autoridad de otra. 3. Monuelo, voz de cariño. 4. (Mec.) Válvula de huso; se llama también, *puppet-valve*. *Puppet-man*, Titiritero. *Puppet-show*, Representación de títeres; comedia de muñecos.
Puppy [pup'-i], *s.* 1. Cachorro, perrillo. 2. Trasto, monicaco, nombre de desprecio que se da al enfadoso impertinente; pisaverde.
Puppy, *va.* y *vn.* *V. To* PUP.
Puppy-headed [pup'-i-hed'-ed], *a.* Lerdo, pesado.
Puppyish [pup'-i-ish], *a.* Parecido a un cachorro; á la manera de un pisaverde.
Puppyism [pup'-i-izm], *s.* Fatuidad; monerías.
Pur [pūr], *s.* y *v.* *V.* PURR.
Purblind [pūr'-blaind], *a.* Cegato, corto de vista, que sufre ofuscamiento de la vista.
Purchasable [pūr'-chas-a-bl], *a.* Comprable, que puede adquirirse por dinero.
Purchase [pūr'-chės], *va.* 1. Comprar, mercar, adquirir por dinero el dominio de una cosa. 2. Ganar, obtener, adquirir por medio de esfuerzo, o con peligro. *He purchased it dearly*, Le costó caro. *I have purchased it by great labour*, Buen trabajo me ha costado ganarlo. 3. (Des.) Expiar una falta pagando una multa.
Purchase, *s.* 1. Compra; adquisición, el acto de comprar; adquisición por medio de dinero u otro equivalente de cambio; o por esfuerzo o peligro. 2. Compra, adquisición, lo que se ha comprado. 3. Ventaja mecánica. *V.* LEVERAGE. 4. (Mec.) Fuerza; potencia; aparato.
Purchaser [pūr'-ches-ẹr], *s.* Comprador; adquiridor, adquirente.
Pure [piūr], *a.* 1. Puro, libre, sin mezcla, exento de toda substancia extraña, limpio, claro. 2. Puro, limpio, sin mancha ni mancilla, exento de imperfecciones, de toda mancha moral; inocente; tambien, que no está echado á perder, alterado ni corrompido; pulido, clásico (de dicción). 3. Puro, casto, inmaculado; santo, virtuoso. 4. Puro, simple, mero, sencillo.
Purée [piū-rê'], *s.* Puré (de papas, de manzana, etc.)
Purely [piūr'-li], *adv.* Puramente, meramente, simplemente, de una manera pura; sin mezcla, sin corrupción ni delito; inocentemente, castamente. *Purely accidental*, Meramente accidental, fortuito.
Pureness [piūr'-nes], *s.* 1. Pureza, limpieza, claridad. 2. Pureza, inocencia, integridad; castidad. 3. Pureza en las voces, frases y expresiones.
†**Purfile** [pūr'-fil], **Purfle** [pūr'-fl], *s.* Perfil, orla, orilla, borde ricamente adornado; (Her.) especie de galón de oro.
Purfle, *va.* Orlar o guarnecer los extremos de alguna ropa; bordar, recamar.
Purfling [pūr'-fling], *s.* Borde de adorno.
Purgation [pūr-gê'-shun], *s.* 1. Purgación, purificación, la acción de purgar o purificar; en particular, de exonerar el vientre por medio de un purgante. 2. (For.) Purgación, el acto de purgar o desvanecer los indicios o nota que resultan contra una persona delincuente.
Purgative [pūr'-ga-tiv], *a.* Purgativo, purgante.—*s.* Purgante, medicamento cuyo uso interno produce evacuaciones alvinas.
Purgatorial [pūr-ga-tō'-ri-al], *a.* Lo que pertenece al purgatorio.
Purgatory [pūr'-ga-to-ri], *s.* Purgatorio, el lugar donde las almas de los que mueren en gracia expían pecados veniales.
Purge [pūrj], *va.* 1. Purgar, purificar, limpiar, separando todo lo que es impuro, extraño o superfluo; acrisolar. 2. Purgar, desvanecer las sospechas, indicios o nota que existen contra alguno; justificar. 3. Purgar con purga medicinal. 4. Clarificar.—*vn.* Purificarse.
Purge, *s.* 1. Purga, purgante. 2. Purgación, acción u operación de purgar.
Purger [pūrj'-ẹr], *s.* Purificador, purgador; purga, purgante.
Purging [pūrj'-ing], *a.* Purgativo.—*s.* 1. Purgación, purificación, la acción y efecto de purgar. 2. Diarrea. 3. Purificación, expiación.
Purification [piū-ri-fi-kê'-shun], *s.* Purificación, en los mismos sentidos que en castellano.
Purificative [piu-rif'-i-ca-tiv], **Purificatory** [piu-rif'-i-ca-to-ri], *a.* Purificatorio.
Purificator [piū-ri-fi-kê'-tẹr], *s.* Purificador, un paño de lino con el cual el sacerdote enjuga el cáliz.
Purifier [piū'-ri-fai-ẹr], *s.* Purificador.
Puriform [piū'-ri-fōrm], *a.* Puriforme, que tiene la apariencia de pus.
Purify [piū'-ri-fai], *va.* 1. Purificar, hacer puro o claro, quitar o extraer de cualquier cosa todo aquello que le es extraño; limpiar, refinar, clarificar. 2. Librar del pecado o de su corrupción. 3. Purificar, limpiar según las ceremonias de una religión; librar de manchas. 4. Purificar o refinar un idioma, dejándolo castizo y libre de impropiedades.—*vn.* Purificarse.
Purifying [piū'-ri-fai-ing], *s.* Purificación, la acción u operación de purificar.
Purim [piū'-rim], *s.* Purim, fiesta de los judíos.
Purism [piūr'-izm], *s.* Purismo, calidad de purista; pureza afectada, particularmente en el empleo de las palabras.
Purist [piūr'-ist], *s.* Purista, el que afecta pureza en el lenguaje o la observa con nimia escrupulosidad.
Puritan [piū'-ri-tan], *s.* 1. Puritano, nombre dado en Inglaterra (1559) a una secta de protestantes que se preciaban de observar una religión más pura. Se oponían al ritualismo y a las tradiciones humanas, y sostenían la libertad de conciencia y los derechos populares. Al principio tuvo sentido despectivo. 2. Colono de la Nueva Inglaterra.
Puritanic, Puritanical [piū-ri-tan'-ic, al], *a.* Puritano, que pertenece á los puritanos; riguroso, severo, rígido.
Puritanism [piū'-ri-tan-izm], *s.* Puritanismo, la doctrina de los puritanos.
Purity [piū'-ri-ti], *s.* Pureza, integridad; castidad; limpieza; inocencia; exactitud en las voces, frases y expresiones; la calidad o el estado de lo puro en cualquier sentido.
Purl [pūrl], *vn.* 1. Murmurar o susurrar los arroyos. 2. Ondear o hacer ondas el agua; hacer ondas la luz; undular.—*s.* Suave murmullo. (< Sueco, porla.)
Purl, *va.* Perfilar, guarnecer con un bordado o fleco, orlar.—*s.* 1. Perfil, orla, guarnición de bordado; espiral de hilo de oro o plata. 2. Pliegue de vestido. 3. Variedad de punto o encaje del siglo XVI. (< Purfle.)
Purl [pūrl], *s.* Cerveza o vino de ajenjos; cerveza aromatizada. *Purlman*, El que vende dicha bebida.
Purlieu [pūr'-liū], *s.* Las tierras que confinan con algún monte o vedado; lindes, mojoneras de un campo o de una heredad; límites, confines, lindero.
Purlin [pūr'-lin], *s.* (Arq.) Viga que sostiene los cabrios.
Purling [pūrl'-ing], *s.* Murmullo suave de una pequeña corriente de agua.—*a.* y *pa.* Que susurra o murmura.
Purlingly [pūrl'-ing-li], *adv.* A la manera de un suave murmullo, suavemente.
Purloin [pūr-loin'], *va.* Hurtar, robar, ratear.
Purloiner [pūr-loin'-ẹr], *s.* Ladrón, ratero.
Purparty [pūr'-pār-ti], *s* (For.) Parte, división.
Purple [pūr'-pl], *a.* 1. Purpúreo, dícese del color que resulta de la mezcla del rojo y azul y que tira a violado; de aquí, imperial, regio. 2. (Poét.) Purpurino, purpúreo; teñido de sangre, sangriento.—*s.* 1. Púrpura, color purpúreo. 2. Vestido de color de púrpura propio de los reyes; de aquí, dignidad de los reyes y de los cardenales. *Purples*, Pintas; tabardillo pintado.
Purple, *va.* Purpurar, teñir de púrpura.
Purplish [pūr'-plish], *a.* Purpurino algo purpúreo.
Purport [pūr'-pōrt], *s.* 1. Significado, sentido, tenor de algún escrito; in-

tento, la cosa intentada. 2. Contenido, la substancia de algún escrito o instrumento, no expresada con las palabras exactas que deberían emplearse.

Purport [pūr-pōrt'], *va.* y *vn.* Significar, querer decir, implicar; dar a entender.

Purpose [pūr'-pus], *s.* 1. Mira, intención, designio, proyecto, efecto. 2. Ventaja práctica, efecto o resultado práctico, utilidad, resulta, consecuencia; uso, caso. 3. Resolución fija, determinación, constancia. 4. Intento; tenor, significación. 5. Propósito; proposición; cuestión, materia de discusión. *To the purpose,* A o al propósito. *To no purpose,* Inútilmente. *To small purpose,* Para bien poco. *To very little purpose,* Casi para nada. *On purpose,* Expresamente, de propósito, de intento, adrede. *To the purpose,* (Fam.) De perilla; como anillo al dedo. *To my purpose,* Según lo que deseo, según mi intención, según las miras que tengo. *As for the purpose,* En cuanto al objeto, a propósito. *To speak to the purpose,* Hablar (como hace) al caso, como se debe. *What they say is not to the purpose,* Lo que dicen no viene al caso, está fuera del caso. *For what purpose?* ¿Con qué fin, para qué? *Common purposes,* Usos ordinarios. *Public purposes,* Utilidades públicas, usos públicos. *To come to the purpose,* Ir al grano, o al caso. *What purpose would that answer?* ¿Para qué serviría eso?

Purpose, *va.* y *vn.* Proponer, determinar o hacer algún propósito; tener la intención de; proponer o proponerse, tener designio de, formar una resolución; contar con algo.

Purposely [pūr'-pus-li], *adv.* Adrede, de intento, de propósito, expresamente.

Purr [pūr], *s.* 1. El susurro que hace el gato cuando está satisfecho. 2. Marisco bivalvo comestible. Tapes decussata.

Purr, *vn.* Susurrar, hilar los gatos cuando están contentos; producir un sonido bajo, continuo y zumbante como el de un carrete.—*va.* Mostrar los gatos su aprobación por medio del susurro. (Imitativo.)

Purr, Purre, Pirr [pūr], *s.* (Prov. Ingl.) Charadrio, alcaraván, ave. Se llama también, *dunlin.*

Purse [pūrs], *s.* 1. Bolsa, bolso o bolsillo. 2. Recursos, posibles, efectivo. 3. Suma de dinero ofrecida como premio o regalo.

Purse, *va.* 1. Embolsar, echar, meter o guardar el dinero en la bolsa. 2. Cerrar una cosa formando pliegues como los de una bolsa.

Purseful [pūrs'-ful], *a.* Rico.—*s.* La cantidad que contiene una bolsa.

Purse-net, Purse-seine [pūrs'-net, sên], *s.* Bolsa de cordones.

Purse-proud [pūrs'-praud], *a.* Dícese del que tiene mucho orgullo por ser rico; plutocrático.

Purser [pūrs'-ẹr], *s.* (Mar.) Mayordomo, sobrecargo, contador de navío.

Pursiness [pūr'-si-nes], *s.* Dificultad en la respiración; de aquí, gordura

Purslane, Purslain [pūrs'-lẹn], *s.* (Bot.) Verdolaga, planta rastrera.

Pursuable [pūr-siū'-a-bl], *a.* Proseguible.

Pursuance [pūr-siū'-ans], *s.* Prosecución, continuación.

Pursuant [pūr-siū'-ant], *a.* Hecho en consecuencia o en conformidad con alguna cosa.

Pursue [pūr-siū'], *va.* y *vn.* 1. Perseguir, hacer padecer o sufrir a alguno. 2. Perseguir, seguir, acosar, ir tras del que huye o en su seguimiento. 3. Proseguir, continuar; seguir, adoptar. 4. Proceder contra alguno, procesarle. 5. Procurar, solicitar.

Pursuer [pūr-siū'-ẹr], *s.* 1. Perseguidor. 2. La persona que procura con empeño el logro de algún objeto.

Pursuit [pūr-siūt'], *s.* 1. Perseguimiento, acosamiento, seguimiento, la acción de ir tras uno o de acosarle. 2. Persecución, el acto de perseguir. 3. Conato, empeño, esfuerzo en la ejecución de alguna cosa. 4. Prosecución, continuación o seguimiento de alguna cosa; busca, solicitud. 5. Ocupación, pretensión. *Pursuits, s. pl.* Ocupaciones, estudios, investigaciones, tareas.

Pursuit plane [pūr-siūt' plên], *s.* Avión de combate.

Pursuivant [pūr'-swi-vant], *s.* Persevante o prosevante, oficial inferior al faraute, y este al heraldo o rey de armas en la antigua caballería.

Pursy [pūr'-si], *a.* Corto de aliento, asmático; que resuella con fatiga; de aquí, obeso.

Purtenance [pūr'-ten-ans], *s.* (Ant.) Pertenencia; en especial, la asadura de un animal.

Purulent [piū'-ru-lent], *a.* Purulento.

Purvey [pūr-vê'], *va.* y *vn.* 1. Proveer, surtir, procurar, suministrar. 2. Proveer, abastecer de lo necesario para hacer una cosa.

Purveyance [pūr-vê'-ans], *s.* Abastecimiento; abasto, provisión de los bastimentos necesarios.

Purveyor [pūr-vê'-ẹr], *s.* Abastecedor, surtidor, suministrador.

Purview [pūr'-viū], *s.* 1. Extensión, esfera, alcance de una cosa, p. ej. de la autoridad oficial, o de una historia. 2. Cuerpo o substancia de un estatuto; límite o alcance de una disposición legal.

Pus [pus], *s.* Pus, humor que se segrega en los tejidos inflamados, como en las úlceras, o en las heridas no cicatrizadas.

Push [push], *va.* 1. Empujar, impeler con fuerza hacia adelante. 2. Llevar adelante con energía, proseguir con empeño, promover. 3. Obligar, estrechar, apretar. 4. Importunar, molestar. 5. (Ant.) Herir de punta; embestir.—*vn.* 1. Ejercer presión regular al mover alguna cosa; dar impulso; lo opuesto a *draw,* tirar hacia sí. 2. Adelantarse, apresurarse, darse prisa; hacer todos los esfuerzos para lograr alguna cosa. 3. Acometer; dar una topetada los animales cornudos. *To push away,* Empujar a distancia, alejar, rechazar; apartar con la mano. *To push back,* Rechazar, hacer retroceder. *To push down,* Abatir, derribar, echar por tierra; forzar, empujar hacia abajo. *To push forward,* Adelantarse dando empujones. *To push one's self forward,* Entrar uno donde no se le llama; abrirse camino en el mundo. *To push further,* Seguir adelante. *To push in,* Hacer entrar, introducir empujando; entremeterse, meterse uno donde no le llaman. *To push off,* Apartar con la mano; alejarse del muelle, de la ribera u orilla: hacerse mar adentro. (Mar.) Desatracar. *To push on,* Echar adelante, incitar, aguijonear; empujar, hacer adelantarse, apresurar. *Push on!* ¡Adelante! *To push out,* Empujar hacia fuera, hacer salir; echar, expulsar; alejarse de la ribera, desatracar, hacerse mar adentro.

Push, *s.* 1. Impulso, impulsión, empujón, empuje, empujo. 2. Asalto, ataque. 3. Conato, esfuerzo; (fam.) energía, actividad resuelta. 4. Momento crítico, emergencia, apuro, aprieto, prueba. *He has been put to a push,* Se ha visto en un apuro. 5. (Mec.) Lo que se empuja para inducir acción, v. g. un botón de presión. *Push-button,* Botón o perilla que, bajo presión, establece o corta una corriente eléctrica; botón de presión. *Push-pin* (1) Juego de alfileres. (2) Pasador de la caja del reloj.

Pushball [push'-bol], *s.* 1. Pelota gigantesca para un juego especial. 2. Juego en que se emplea dicha pelota.

Pushing [push'-ing], *a.* Activo, diligente, eficaz; emprendedor; vigoroso, robusto, fuerte.

Pushover [push'-ō-vẹr], *s.* 1. Adversario débil. (Mex.) Pichón. 2. Problema de fácil solución.

Pusillanimous [piū-si-lan'-i-mus], *a.* Pusilánime, cobarde, falto de ánimo.

Puss [pus], *s.* 1. Miz, minino, voz de que ordinariamente se usa para llamar a los gatos; por extensión, una muchacha o joven. *A sly puss,* Una muchacha taimada. 2. Liebre. 3. *V.* PUSS-MOTH. *Puss-in-the-corner,* El juego de muchachos llamado "de las cuatro esquinas."

Pussy [pus'-i], *s.* Gatita (forma diminutiva). *Pussy-cat,* (1) Gata, gato. 2. (Bot.) El amento del sauce llamado *pussy-willow. Pussy-willow,* Sauce pequeño americano que tiene amentos sedosos al principiar la primavera. Salix discolor.

Pustular [pus'-tiu-lar], *a.* Pustoloso, relativo a las pústulas.

Pustulate [pus'-tiu-lêt], *vn.* Formar en pústulas, hacerse pústulas, cubrirse de ampollas.

Pustule [pus'-tiūl], *s.* Pústula, postilla pequeña. (Vulg.) Grano, nacido.

Pustulous [pus'-tiu-lus], *a.* Postilloso, pustuloso.

Put [put], *va.* (*pa.* PUTTING, *pret.* y *pp.* PUT). 1. Poner, colocar. 2. Poner, disponer o prevenir alguna cosa. 3. Poner, confiar, cometer, entregar. 4. Poner, dedicar a alguno o inclinarle a que tome algún empleo u oficio. 5. Poner, reducir o estrechar a una persona a que haga algo contra su voluntad. 6. Poner, exponer, proponer, presentar para ser discutido. hacer o dirigir (una pregunta). 7. Expresar en palabras, declarar, interpretar. 8. Arrojar, lanzar con un movimiento del brazo hacia arriba y adelante. 9. (Ant.) Poner, imponer, obligar a alguna cosa.—*vn.* 1. Dirigir su rumbo o curso, dirigirse. 2. (Ant.) Ir, moverse. 3. Brotar, germinar, arrojar el árbol sus hojas, flores, botones o renuevos. *To put about,* (1) (Mar.) Cambiar de rumbo. (2) Molestar, turbar, desconcertar. *To put asunder.* Apartar.

To put away, Apartar, quitar, poner a un lado; echar fuera, despedir; desterrar; repudiar. *To put back*, Apartar, retirar hacia atrás; retroceder, volver atrás; perder el terreno, atrasar, retardar. (Mar.) Arribar, volver de arribada. *To put back the clock*, Atrasar el reloj. *To put by*, Arrimar, arrinconar, desviar, apartar, poner a un lado; despachar, despedir, echar fuera; disuadir o desviar de un propósito; eludir, evitar; estorbar, distraer; rehusar; despreciar, no hacer caso; refutar. *To put down*, Deprimir, abatir, humillar; dar un tapaboca o un remoquete; hacer callar a uno; suprimir, abolir, hacer caer en desuso alguna cosa; impugnar, confutar; poner debajo. *To put down in writing*, Asentar, notar, poner por escrito. *To put forth*, Extender, alargar la mano u otra cosa; publicar, dar a luz; producir, brotar, germinar o arrojar las plantas; proponer; emplear el poder, la fuerza, etc., para el logro de una cosa. (Mar.) Dejar un puerto. *To put forward*, Llevar adelante; apresurarse, adelantarse. *To put one's self forward*, Presentarse; hacerse o darse a conocer. *To put in*, Insertar, ingerir, introducir una cosa entre otras; indicar para un empleo u oficio; volver a poner en su lugar, v. g. un miembro dislocado; hacer esfuerzos, hacer algo con vigor; entrar en un lugar para procurarse abrigo, provisiones o asistencia. (Mar.) Entrar en un puerto. *To put in a claim*, Alegar, hacer presente o reclamar un derecho; demandar, o poner una demanda. *To put in at*, Arribar a un sitio de abrigo. *To put in fear*, Amedrentar, intimidar. *To put in for*, Pretender, solicitar; hacer oposición a algún destino; salir a la palestra o ponerse entre los pretendientes a alguna dignidad, oficio, etc. *To put in mind*, Recordar. *To put in practice*, Poner en uso, usar, ejercitar. *To put in print*, Imprimir. *To put in writing*, Poner por escrito. *To put into*, Unir; meter dentro de, guardar en; hacer declarar, expresar. *To put into port*, (Mar.) Arribar, entrar de arribada en un puerto. *To put off*, Diferir, dilatar, dejar para otro tiempo; dejar o desistir de una obra, etc.; quitarse algo de encima del cuerpo, despojarse de alguna cosa que se llevaba puesta; poner a un lado, apartar; poner en voga, acreditar, recomendar; dar al público; entretener; desentenderse; embocar, encajar. Salir a la mar; echar el bote al agua. *Put off your clothes*, Desnúdese Vd. *To put on*, Ponerse alguna cosa; atribuir, hacer algún cargo, imputar, acusar; incitar, promover; imponer una pena; engañar o engañarse; empezar un nuevo género de vida; hacerse pasar uno por lo que no es. *Put on your hat*, Cúbrase Vd., póngase Vd. el sombrero. *To put on shore*, Echar a tierra, desembarcar. *To put out*, Brotar, arrojar o germinar las plantas; echar, sacar, expeler o arrojar a una persona o cosa del lugar que ocupaba; despedir, despachar, echar fuera; apagar o matar la lumbre, la luz o el fuego; cegar, dejar ciego; borrar lo escrito o impreso; poner dinero a interés, dar a logro; sacar o dar a luz; publicar, divulgar; olvidar las máximas o resoluciones que uno se había propuesto seguir; distraer. *To put out of all hope*, Quitar o hacer perder completamente la esperanza; hacer caer en la desesperación. *To put out of doors*, Poner en la calle. *To put out of heart*, Desalentar. *To put out of joint*, Dislocar o desencajar los huesos. *To put out of order*, Desordenar, descomponer, sacar las cosas de su quicio o de su puesto; desconcertar, echar a perder alguna cosa. *To put out the flag*, Enarbolar una bandera. *To put one out*, Aturdir, confundir; perturbar, cortar, sonrojar, avergonzar, dejar parado, confuso, chafado o despatarrado a alguno; turbar o desordenar. *To put over*, Enviar, remitir o dirigir a uno a otra persona para tomar informes; remitirse, referirse; diferir, dilatar, posponer. Conducir al otro lado; navegar por travesía, atravesar. *To put to*, Dejar, abandonar; exponer; sujetar a; consignar a; unir, como se hace con las caballerías; añadir, aumentar; ayudar; echar, juntar los animales machos con las hembras para la generación. *To put to bed*, Acostar, desvestir y poner en cama, como se hace con los niños; disponer a una mujer para el parto. *To put to flight*, Hacer huir. *To put to his oath*, Hacer prestar juramento en justicia. *To put to death*, Quitar la vida, hacer morir, matar. *To put to it*, Añadir, aumentar; perturbar, atormentar, incomodar; apretar, estrechar, acosar, perseguir de cerca; obligar, precisar, poner las peras a cuarto. *To be put to it*, Hallarse en un aprieto, verse entre la espada y la pared. *To put to sea*, Hacerse a la vela. *To put to the sword*, Pasar a cuchillo. *To put to the vote*, Recoger los votos; poner a votación. *To put to the venture*, Arriesgar, aventurar, poner en peligro. *To put together*, Acumular, juntar, acopiar, amontonar, hacinar, reunir. *To put to rights*, Poner en orden, arreglar debidamente. *To put up*, Poner a un lado o en su propio lugar; preservar, encajonar (las frutas); hacer conservas; guardar, esconder, ocultar; adelantarse o ir hacia alguno; pretender, solicitar, salir a la palestra, ponerse entre los pretendientes a algún empleo, oficio, etc.; dejar impune un delito; exponer al público; salir de repente; acumular, amontonar; hacer brotar o germinar una planta. *To put up a thing for sale*, Poner una cosa en venta. *To put up a prayer*, Rogar, pedir, suplicar; hacer una oración o deprecación. *To put up at*, Apearse en, alojarse en. *To put up to*, Incitar, urgir, instigar a alguno para que ejecute lo que se desea; empeñar en algún asunto; enseñar, dar instrucciones sobre algo. *To put up with*, Sufrir sin quejarse; aguantar, tolerar, sufrir; perdonar o disimular una falta; tener paciencia; conformarse con. *To put upon*, Poner o colocar sobre; imponer como obligación o deber; exponer a algún riesgo, hacer padecer; engañar. *To put a trick upon one*, Hacer una mala partida o pegar un petardo a alguno. *To put upon trial*, Poner a prueba o someter a juicio. *To put a stop*, Impedir, hacer alto, poner fin a. *To put an end*, Acabar. *To put one's hand to the plough*, Poner manos a la obra. *Put the case*, Suponga Vd., dé Vd. por sentado.

Put, *pret.* y *pp.* de *To* PUT.

Put [put], *s.* 1. Acción del verbo *put* en cualquiera de sus acepciones, particularmente golpe, tiro, lanzamiento. 2. Especie de juego de naipes. 3. (E. U.) Contrato por el cual una persona adquiere, mediante pago, el privilegio de vender o remitir a otra determinado artículo por un precio estipulado; lo opuesto a *call*.

Put [put], *s.* (Prov. Ingl.) Patán, palurdo.

Putamen [piu-tē'-mẹn], *s.* 1. (Bot.) Pepita. 2. (Anat.) Parte exterior del núcleo cerebral.

Putative [piū'-ta-tiv], *a.* Putativo, reputado, supuesto.

Puteal [piū'-tẹ-al], *s.* Brocal de un pozo.

Putlog [put'-leg], *s.* (Arq.) Almojaya, palo de andamio, cualquiera de los palos que entran en los mechinales para formar los andamios.

Putredinous [piu-tred'-i-nus], *a.* Podrido, corrompido, pútrido, que tiene su origen en la putrefacción; de olor fétido.

Putrefaction [piu-trẹ-fac'-shun], *s.* Putrefacción, corrupción, acto o procedimiento de pudrirse, corromperse; calidad de podrido.

Putrefactive [piu-trẹ-fac'-tiv], *a.* Putrefactivo, corruptivo; perteneciente a la putrefacción; expuesto a pudrirse; que puede causar putrefacción.

Putrefactiveness [piu-trẹ-fac'-tiv-nes], *s.* La tendencia a la putrefacción; corruptibilidad.

Putrefiable [piū'-trẹ-fai"-a-bl], *a.* Que puede pudrirse.

Putrefy [piū'-trẹ-fai], *va.* 1. Pudrir o podrir, corromper, podrecer, hacer descomponer con olor fétido, resolver en podre alguna cosa. 2. Hacer gangrenoso o carioso.—*vn.* Pudrirse, corromperse, podrecer, echarse a perder, hacerse fétido por la pudrición.

Putrescence [piu-tres'-ens], *s.* Pudrición, pudrimiento, putrefacción, corrupción.

Putrescent [piu-tres'-ent], *a.* Podrido, pútrido, que se halla en estado de putrefacción.

Putrilage [piū'-tri-lệj], *s.* (Med.) Materia pútrida, gangrenosa.

Putrid [piū'-trid], *a.* Podrido, pútrido, corrompido.

Putt [put], *s.* Tirada en el juego de golf enfocada hacia el agujero.

Puttee [put-i'], *s.* Polaina.

Putter [put'-ẹr], *s.* En el juego de golf, *putter*, bastón empleado para hacer caer la pelota en el agujero.

Putter [put'-ẹr], *vn.* (Fam.) Inquietarse por bagatelas, entretenerse en cosas que no valen la pena. *V.* POTTER.

Putty [put'-i], *s.* 1. Masilla (o potea), pasta de greda levigada mezclada con aceite de linaza que usan los vidrieros. 2. *V. Putty-powder.* *Putty-powder, jewelers' putty*, Óxido de estaño, a veces mezclado con óxido de plomo; polvos para pulir el vidrio, los metales, la joyería, etc.

Putty, *va.* Cubrir o llenar con masilla.

Puzzle [puz'-l], *s.* 1. Embarazo, embrollo; pena, inquietud; perplejidad. 2. Acertijo, adivinanza, enigma.

Puzzle, *va.* Embrollar, enredar, confundir, aturrullar: poner dificultades u obstáculos; inquietar, molestar.—*vn.* Enredarse, embrollarse, confundirse.

Puzzler [puz'-lẹr], *s.* Embrollador, enredador, inquietador, molestador, zumbón.

Pygmean [pig-mí'-an] o **Pygmy** [pig'-mi], *a.* Pigmeo.

Pygmy, *s.* Pigmeo, enano.

Pyloric [pi-ler'-ic], *a.* Pilórico, relativo al píloro.

Pylorus [pi-lō'-rus], *s.* (Anat.) Píloro, el orificio inferior del estómago.

Pyorrhea [pai-ẹ-rí'-a], *s.* (Med.) Piorrea.

Pyracanth [pir'-a-canth], *s.* (Bot.) Piracanta, especie de níspero, de fruto astringente; especie de espino siempre verde, que se halla en el mediodía de Europa. Cratægus pyrocantha.

Pyralis [pir'-a-lis], *s.* Pirausta, insecto al que se le atribuye la propiedad de poder vivir en el fuego; insecto lepidóptero nocivo.

Pyramid [pir'-a-mid], *s.* Pirámide. (1) Monumento grande en forma de pirámide cuadrilateral. (2) (Mat.) Sólido que tiene por base un polígono cualquiera y cuyas caras son triángulos que se unen en un vértice.

Pyramidal [pi-ram'-i-dal], **Pyramidical** [pir-a-mid'-i-cal], *a.* Piramidal.

Pyramidically [pir-a-mid'-i-cal-i], *adv.* Piramidalmente.

Pyramidicalness [pir-a-mid'-i-cal-nes], *s.* La forma piramidal.

Pyre [pair], *s.* Pira, hoguera.

Pyrargyrite [pir-ār'-ji-rait], *s.* (Min.) Argiritroso, mineral que se llama vulgarmente plata roja o plata antimonio-sulfurada (Ag_3SbS_3).

Pyrenean [pir-ẹ-ní'-an], *a.* Pirenaico, perteneciente o relativo a los montes Pirineos.

Pyretic [pai- (o pi-) ret'-ic], *a.* 1. Pirético, febril, con fiebre; que proviene de la fiebre. 2. Febrífugo, que quita la fiebre.—*s.* Medicamento febrífugo.

Pyrex [pai'-rex], *s.* Loza refractaria, resistente a la lumbre.

Pyrexia [pai-rec'-sia], *s.* Pirexia, fiebre, condición febril; también, paroxismo de fiebre.

Pyriform [pir'-i-fōrm], *a.* Piriforme, que tiene forma de pera.

Pyrite [pir'-ait], *s.* Marcasita, bisulfuro de hierro, opaco, de color amarillo claro (FeS_2).

Pyrites [pi-rai'-tīz], *s.* (Min.) Pirita, mineral compuesto de azufre con hierro u otro metal; marquesita. *Martial pyrites,* Sulfureto de hierro, pirita marcial.

Pyritic, Pyritous [pai-rit'-ic, pir'-i-tus], *a.* Piritoso, perteneciente o parecido a la pirita; que tiene las propiedades de ésta.

Pyro-, Pyr- [pai'-rō]. Prefijo griego que significa fuego.

Pyro [pai'-rō], *s.* (Fam.) Abreviatura de ácido pirogálico.

Pyroacetic [pai-rō-a-set'-ic], *a.* Piroacético. *Pyroacetic acid* o *spirit,* Ácido o espíritu piroacético.

Pyroacid [pai-rō-as'-id], *s.* Ácido pirogenado, el que se obtiene sometiendo otro ácido a la acción del calor.

Pyrogallic [pai-ro-gal'-ic], *a.* Pirogálico. *Pyrogallic acid* o *pyrogallol,* Ácido pirogálico; compuesto blanco cristalino que se obtiene sometiendo el ácido gálico a la acción del calor ($C_6H_3(OH)_3$). Se emplea mucho en fotografía.

Pyrogenous [pai-rej'-en-us], *a.* 1. Pirógeno, producido por la fusión, ígneo. 2. Febril, que excita la fiebre.

Pyrography [pai-rog'-ra-fi], *s.* Pirografía, el arte o procedimiento de producir un diseño sobre madera por medio de una punta hecha ascua o de una llama fina; también, el de estampar madera con planchas o cilindros calientes.

Pyroligneous, Pyrolignous [pai'-ro-lig'-nẹ-us, nus], *a.* Pirolignoso, producido por la destilación de la madera.

Pyrology [pai-rel'-o-ji], *s.* Pirología, análisis por medio del soplete.

Pyrolusite [pai-ro- (o pir-o-) lū'-sait], *s.* Pirolisita, binóxido de manganeso blando, metálico, negruzco o gris de acero.

Pyromagnetic [pai-ro-mag-net'-ic], *a.* Piromagnético, que se refiere a las variaciones en la intensidad magnética, producidas por el cambio de la temperatura.

Pyromancy [pai'-ro-man-si], *s.* Piromancia, adivinación por el fuego.

Pyrometer [pai- (o pi-) rem'-ẹ-tẹr], *s.* Pirómetro, instrumento para medir las temperaturas muy elevadas.

Pyromorphous [pai-ro-mōr'-fus], *a.* Piromorfo, que se cristaliza por el calor.

Pyrophorus [pi-ref'-o-rus], *s.* Piróforo, una composición que se inflama al contacto del aire.

Pyrophosphate [pai-ro-fes'-fêt], *s.* (Quím.) Pirofosfato, una sal del ácido pirofosfórico.

Pyrotechnic, Pyrotechnical [pir-o-tec'-nic, al], *a.* Pirotécnico, que pertenece a los fuegos artificiales o al arte de hacerlos.

Pyrotechnics [pai-ro-tec'-nics], *s.* Pirotécnica.

Pyrotechny [pir'-o-tec-ni], *s.* Pirotecnia, el arte de hacer la pólvora o cualquiera de las invenciones de fuego, ya sean éstas de artificio o de las usadas en la guerra. Algunos han dado este nombre a la química.

Pyroxene [pai'-rex-īn o pir'-ex-īn], *s.* Piróxeno, bisilicato de cal, magnesio o manganeso.

Pyroxylin [pi- (o pai-) rex'-i-lin], *s.* Piroxilina, piróxilo, algodón pólvora; producto explosivo que se obtiene sumergiendo el algodón u otra fibra vegetal en una mezcla de iguales pesos de ácido nítrico y ácido sulfúrico, lavándolo y secándolo después.

Pyrrhic [pir'-ic], *s.* Pirriquio, pie compuesto de dos sílabas breves.—*a.* Pírrico, perteneciente a un pirriquio, o a una antigua danza guerrera.

Pyrrhonean [pir-o-ní'-an], **Pyrrhonist** [pir'-o-nist], *a.* y *s.* Pirronista, que duda o afecta dudar de todo.

Pyrrhonism [pir'-o-nizm], *s.* Pirronismo, escepticismo, duda universal.

Pythagorean [pi-thag-o-rí'-an o pith-a-gō'-rẹ-an], *a.* Pitagórico, perteneciente a la doctrina de Pitágoras.

Pythian [pith'-i-an], *a.* Pitio, perteneciente a los juegos de Apolo en Delfos.

Python [pai'-then], *s.* 1. Pitón, serpiente grande y no venenosa que aplasta su presa entre sus pliegues; boa del Antiguo Mundo. 2. Pitón, serpiente enorme que acudía a las cuevas del Parnaso y fué muerta por Apolo.

Python, *s.* Adivino, adivina, espectro adivinador; también, ventrílccuo.

Pythoness [pith'-o-nes], *sf.* Pitonisa, especie de adivina o maga.

Pyx [pics], *s.* Copón, píxide, la cajita en que se guarda la hostia.

Q

Q [kiū]. Se pronuncia en inglés como en castellano la *c* fuerte. *Que, qui,* en principio o medio de dicción, se pronuncian *cue, cui;* y en las voces derivadas del francés como *c.* Ejemplos: banquet, *báncuet;* quiver, *cuiver.* En las voces derivadas del francés, cuando estas sílabas están al fin de dicción, en unas se pronuncia como *c,* y en otras como en castellano, v. g. antique, *antic;* etiquette, *étiquet.*

Quack [cwac], *vn.* 1. Graznar como un pato. 2. Charlatanear, charlar, chacharear, echar bocanadas o baladronadas; jactarse.—*s.* Graznido, grito del pato.

Quack, *s.* y *a.* 1. Charlatán, el que charla mucho jactándose y ponderando sus conocimientos en las ciencias o artes. 2. Curandero, matasanos, el que hace de médico sin serlo. 3. Empírico, matasanos, mal médico, medicastro.

Quackery [cwak'-ẹr-i], *s.* Charlatanería, habladuría, baladronada.

Quad [cwed], *s.* (Fam.) 1. (Impr.) Cuadrado, cuadratín. *V.* QUADRAT. 2. (Teleg.) *V.* QUADRUPLEX. 3. *V.* QUADRUPLET. 4. Cuadrángulo o patio, como el de un colegio o de una cárcel; de aquí, cárcel.

Quadra [cwed'-ra], *s.* (Arq.) 1. Bastidor, marco. 2. Plinto, el miembro más bajo de un podio.

Quadragesima [cwed''-ra-jes'-i-ma], *s.* Cuadragésima, cuaresma.

Quadragesimal [cwed-ra-jes'-i-mal], *a.* Cuadragesimal, que pertenece a la cuaresma.

Quadrangle [cwed'-raŋ-gl], *s.* 1. Cuadrángulo, figura que se compone de cuatro ángulos. 2. (Arq.) Patio cuadrado u oblongo, como el que suele haber dentro de un colegio u otro edificio grande.

Quadrangular [cwed-raŋ'-giu-lar], *a.* Cuadrangular, que tiene o forma cuatro ángulos.

Quadrant [cwed'-rant], *s.* 1. Cuadrante, la cuarta parte del círculo. 2. Cuadrante de altura, instrumento matemático, instrumento astronómico reemplazado hoy por el sextante u octante. 3. (Elec.) *V.* HENRY.

Quadrantal [cwed-ran'-tal], *a.* (Mat.) Cuadrantal.

Quadrat [cwed'-rat], *s.* Cuadrado, cuadratín, pieza cuadrada de metal más baja que las letras y que se pone entre éstas para formar los espacios.

Quadrate [cwed'-rêt], *a.* 1. Cuadro, cuadrado: dícese de todo lo que tiene cuatro lados iguales. 2. (Des.) Lo que contiene números cuadrados.—*s.* 1. (Anat.) Hueso o músculo cuadrado. 2. (Astr.) Aspecto de los astros en que distan de sí 90°; cuadrado. 3. (Mús.) Becuadro (♮).

Quadrate, *vn.* 1. Cuadrar, adaptarse, conformarse, ajustarse o venir bien una cosa con otra. 2. Equilibrar un cañón en la cureña.

Quadratic [cwed-rat'-ic], *a.* Cuadrático, perteneciente al cuadro o cuadrado. *Quadratic equation*, Ecuación cuadrática, cuadrática.—*s.* Cuadrática, ecuación que encierra el cuadrado de la raíz que se busca.

Quadrature [cwed'-ra-tiūr o chur], *s.* 1. Cuadratura, reducción de una figura curvilínea á un cuadrado. 2. Cuadratura, el aspecto cuadrado de la luna con el sol; posición relativa de dos cuerpos celestes que se hallan á una distancia de 90° uno del otro, al ser vistos desde el centro de un tercer cuerpo.

Quadrennial [cwed-ren'-i-al], *a.* 1. Cuadrienal, que comprende o dura cuatro años. 2. Que sucede una vez cada cuatro años.

Quadribasic [cwed-ri-bé'-sic], *a.* (Quím.) Cuadribásico, que tiene cuatro átomos de hidrógeno, reemplazables por radicales básicos.

Quadrifarious [cwed-ri-fé'-ri-us], *a.* (Biol.) Dispuesto en cuatro filas ó hileras.

Quadrifid [cwed'-ri-fid], *a.* Hendido en cuatro partes.

Quadriga [cwed-rai'-ga], *s.* Cuadriga, carro antiguo tirado por cuatro caballos de frente.

Quadrilateral [cwed-ri-lat'-ẹr-al], *a.* Cuadrilátero, que tiene cuatro lados.—*s.* Figura que tiene cuatro lados.

Quadrilateralness [cwed-ri-lat'-ẹr-al-nes], *s.* Calidad de cuadrilátero.

Quadrille [cwa-dril'], *s.* 1. Cuadrilla, conjunto de las cinco figuras de una contradanza bailadas sin interrupción; en ella cada grupo comprende cuatro parejas. 2. La música de este baile. 3. Cuatrillo, cascarela, un juego de naipes entre cuatro.—*vn.* Bailar el baile así llamado o tocar la música del mismo.

Quadrillion [cwed-ril'-yun], *s.* Cuadrillón, número cardinal; según el sistema americano y francés, la quinta potencia de mil, o la unidad seguida de quince ceros; por el sistema inglés, la cuarta potencia de un millón, la unidad seguida de veinticuatro ceros.

Quadrilocular [cwed-ri-lec'-yu-lar], *a.* (Bot.) Cuadrilocular, que está dividido en cuatro compartimientos.

Quadrinomial [cwed-ri-nō'-mi-al], *a.* Cuadrínomo, compuesto de cuatro términos.—*s.* Cuadrinomio, cantidad algebraica que consta de cuatro términos.

Quadripartite [cwed-rip'-ar-tait ó cwed-ri-pār'-tait], *a.* Cuádruple, que se compone de cuatro partes.

Quadripartitely [cwed-ri-pār'-tait-li], *adv.* De un modo cuádruple.

Quadriphyllous [cwed-ri-fil'-us], *a.* Cuadrifolio, que tiene cuatro hojas.

Quadrireme [cwed'-ri-rīm], *s.* Galera con cuatro bancos de remos.

Quadrisyllable [cwed-ri-sil'-a-bl], *s.* Cuadrisílabo.

Quadrivium [cwed-riv'-i-um], *s.* Cuadrivio, el lugar donde concurren cuatro sendas o caminos.

Quadroon [cwed-rūn'], *s.* Cuarteron, hijo de blanco y mulata o de mulato y mujer blanca.

Quadrumana [cwed-rū'-ma-na], *s. pl.* Cuadrumanos, orden de mamíferos que en las cuatro extremidades tienen el dedo pulgar separado de modo que puede tocar a los otros dedos.

Quadrumanous [cwed-rū'-ma-nus], *a.* Cuadrumano, que tiene cuatro manos.

Quadruped [cwed'-ru-ped], *s.* Cuadrúpedo, el animal de cuatro pies.

Quadrupedal [cwed-rū'-pẹ-dal], *a.* Cuadrupedal, de cuatro pies, o perteneciente a ellos.

Quadruple [cwed'-ru-pl], *a.* Cuádruple.—*s.* Pieza de ocho o de cuatro doblones.

Quadruplet [cwed'-ru-plet], *s.* Juego de cuatro cosas que funcionan como una sola; v. g. una bicicleta de cuatro asientos.

Quadruplex [cwed'-ru-plex], *a.* Cuádruple, cuádruplo; dícese de un sistema telegráfico en que se pueden enviar a la misma vez cuatro mensajes, dos en cada dirección.—*s.* Instrumento telegráfico cuádruple.

Quadruplicate [cwed-rū'-pli-kēt], *va.* Cuadruplicar, multiplicar por cuatro.

Quadruplication [cwed-ru-pli-ké'-shun], *s.* Cuadruplicación.

Quadruply [cwed'-ru-pli], *adv.* Al cuádruplo, cuatro veces tanto o cuatro tantos más.

Quære [cwī'-ri], *s.* Voz latina que significa busca; una nota en los autos para expresar que alguna cosa se ha de investigar o averiguar. *V.* QUERY.

Quaff [cwqf], *va.* Beber a grandes tragos; beber con gusto.—*vn.* Beber demasiado.

Quaffer [cwqf'-ẹr], *s.* Bebedor desmedido; borracho.

‡**Quag** [cwag], **Quagmire** [cwag'-mair], *s.* Tremedal, el sitio o paraje cenagoso que con poco movimiento retiembla.

Quagga [cwag'-a], *s.* (Zool.) Cuaga, mamífero del África meridional, parecido a la cebra. Equus quagga.

Quaggy [cwag'-i], *a.* Pantanoso; blando.

Quahaug, Quahog [cwō'-heg], *s.* Marisco redondo, común en la costa norteamericana del Atlántico y estimado como alimento. Venus mercenaria. *V.* CLAM.

Quail [cwēl], *s.* 1. (Orn.) Codorniz, ave gallinácea. 2. Colín, ave gallinácea de la América del Norte; ave semejante del género Callipepla. 3. Turnice, gallinácea.

Quail, *va.* 1. (Ant.) Intimidar. 2. (Ant.) *V. To* QUELL.—*vn.* Desanimarse, descorazonarse, perder el valor.

Quail-pipe [cwēl'-paip], *s.* Reclamo de codornices.

Quaint [cwēnt], *a.* 1. De apariencia anticuada y extraña, pero no desagradable; raro, a la vez que gracioso, gentil, o lindo. 2. Original, singular, fantástico. 3. (Ant.) Primorosamente labrado; que sirve de adorno. *She is so quaint*, Ella tiene un ingenio tan original.

Quaintly [cwēnt'-li], *adv.* Graciosamente, con gracia; lindamente; fantásticamente, de una manera singular, original, extraña.

Quaintness [cwēnt'-nes], *s.* Primor, singularidad, apariencia anticuada.

Quake [cwēc], *vn.* Temblar, tembloquear o tembletear, temblar con frecuencia; estar agitado por sacudimientos cortos y frecuentes; estremecerse, oscilar; ser movedizo.

Quake, *s.* Temblor, movimiento trémulo; tiritona.

Quaker [cwēk'-ẹr], *s.* Cuáquero, cuákero, temblador, nombre que se da a ciertos sectarios; ellos prefieren el nombre de "*Friends*," amigos. Se distinguen por la sencillez y severidad de sus costumbres.

Quakerism [cwēk'-ẹr-izm], *s.* La doctrina y maneras de los cuáqueros.

Quaking [cwēk'-ing], *pa.* de QUAKE. Que tiembla; movedizo. *Quaking-grass*, (1) Cualquiera de las plantas gramíneas del género Briza; en particular Briza media. (2) La planta gramínea que se llama comúnmente *rattlesnake-grass.* Glyceria Canadensis.

Qualifiable [cwel-i-fai'-a-bl], *a.* Calificable, que puede calificarse; susceptible de modificaciones.

Qualification [cwel-i-fi-ké'-shun], *s.* 1. Calificación, la acción y efecto de calificar á una persona o cosa. 2. Requisito, la circunstancia ó condición que se requiere para alguna cosa; calidad, cualidad natural o adquirida que hace a una persona o cosa propia para un puesto, objeto o destino; en especial, capacidad o poder legal; adaptación. 3. Modificación, restricción; negación parcial; atenuación, mitigación.

Qualificator [cwel-i-fi-kē'-tẹr], *s.* Calificador del santo oficio.

Qualified [cwel'-i-faid], *pp.* y *a.* 1. Idóneo, apto, competente, que posee las cualidades necesarias. 2. Limitado, restringido, modificado.

Qualify [cwel'-i-fai], *va.* 1. Hacer apto o idóneo para alguna colocación, empleo u ocupación. 2. Dotar, adornar la naturaleza de dotes y prerrogativas. 3. Habilitar, hacer hábil y capaz a alguno. 4. Calificar, dar por buena o mala una cosa según sus cualidades y circunstancias. 5. Modificar, limitar, restringir. 6. Templar, suavizar. *A person qualified to exercise an employment*, Una persona capaz de ejercer un empleo o con los requisitos necesarios para desempeñarlo. *A man well qualified*, Un hombre dotado de bellas prendas.—*vn.* 1. Prepararse, hacer lo necesario para poder desempeñar un cargo, o gozar determinadas ventajas. 2. (E. U.) Prestar juramento, antes de entrar en funciones. *A qualified voter*, Elector habilitado, que ha cumplido con la ley. *To qualify the sense of words*, Modificar el sentido de las palabras. *An adjective qualifies a noun*, El adjetivo califica al nombre. *To qualify liquors*, Saborear o diluir los licores.

Qualitative [cwel'-i-ta-tiv], *a.* Cualitativo, que denota cualidad; que se refiere únicamente a la cualidad. *Qualitative analysis*, Análisis cualitativo.

Quality [cwel'-i-ti], *s.* 1. Calidad o cualidad, la propiedad natural de cada cosa; lo que hace que una cosa sea lo que es; elemento característico. 2. Condición; grado; grado de excelencia; prenda, excelencia relativa. 3. Natural, genio, índole. 4. Propiedad, poder o virtud de producir efectos determinados. 5. Papel, parte especial, función. 6. (Prov. o des.) Posición social, el conjunto o cuerpo de los nobles o las personas de distinción. *Man of quality*, Hombre de buena cuna, de distinción.

Qualm [cwām], *s.* 1. Acceso de náusea. 2. Delicadeza de conciencia; escrúpulo moral; remordimiento.

Qualmish [cwām'-ish], *a.* 1. Con náuseas. 2. Escrupuloso.

Qualmishness [cwām'-ish-nes], *s.* El estado de la persona que tiene predisposición a náuseas.

Quandary [cwen'-da-ri], *s.* Incertidumbre, duda, suspensión; laberinto.

Quantitative [cwen'-ti-ta-tiv], *a.* Cuantitativo, que se refiere á la cantidad. *Quantitative analysis*, Análisis cuantitativo, el que se emplea para determinar la cantidad de cada elemento o ingrediente.

Quantity [cwen'-ti-ti], *s.* 1. Cantidad, cuantidad, propiedad de alguna cosa que se puede aumentar ó disminuir o que está sujeta a número, peso o medida. 2. Medida o peso indeterminado. 3. Cantidad, porción grande o pequeña de alguna cosa. 4. Cantidad, el tiempo que se emplea en pronunciar una sílaba; duración relativa de las notas musicales. 5. (Elec.) La fuerza de una corriente, en contraposición a la potencia o intensidad.

Quantum [cwen'-tum], *s.* Tanto, la cantidad a que llega alguna cosa.

Quarantine [cwer'-an-tīn], *s.* 1. Cuarentena, el espacio de tiempo que están en el lazareto o privados de comunicación los que se presume vienen de países inficionados o contagiados. 2. Lazareto, lugar destinado para hacer la cuarentena. 3. Cuarenta días. 4. (For.) El derecho que la ley de Inglaterra concedía a las viudas de continuar en posesión de la casa de su marido por cuarenta días después del fallecimiento de éste.

Quarrel [cwer'-el], *s.* 1. Quimera, pendencia, riña, contienda. *To pick a quarrel*, Armar pendencia. 2. Altercación, porfía, disputa. 3. Desavenencia, rompimiento de amistades. 4. Motivo o causa de disputa. 5. El diamante con que se corta el cristal. 6. Una especie de flecha usada antiguamente con extremidad cuadrada. 7. *V.* QUARRY, 5ª acep.

Quarrel, *vn.* 1. Reñir, pelear; disputar, contender. 2. Desamistarse, discordar, desavenirse mutuamente. 3. Tachar, poner en alguna cosa faltas o tachas. *To quarrel with one's bread and butter*, Quitarse el pan de la boca, perjudicarse a sí mismo.

Quarreller [cwer'-el-er], *s.* Quimerista.

Quarrelsome [cwer'-el-sum], *a.* Pendenciero, quimerista; irascible.

Quarrelsomely [cwer'-el-sum-li], *adv.* Alborotadamente, con gana de reñir.

Quarrier [cwer'-i-er], *s.* Cantero, picapedrero, obrero que trabaja en las canteras.

Quarry [cwer'-i], *s.* 1. Cantera, el sitio de donde se saca piedra para labrar; mina. (< Fr. ant. quarrière < Lat. quadratus.) 2. El ave en que hace presa el halcón; presa. 3. (Des.) Un montón de caza muerta. (< Fr. curée < cuir. *piel* < Lat. corium.) 4. Cuadrado, cuadro, rombo. 5. Cuadrado o rombo pequeño de vidrio, teja, etc. 6. *V.* QUARREL, 6ª acep. (< Fr. ant. quarre < Lat. quadratus.)

Quarry, *va.* 1. Sacar piedra o trabajar en una cantera. 2. (Des.) Devorar, hacer presa.

Quarryman [cwer'-i-man], *s.* Cavador de cantera, dueño de una cantera; cantero, picapedrero, obrero en una cantera.

Quart [cwōrt], *s.* 1. Cuarto de galón, medida líquida de Inglaterra que corresponde a la media azumbre de España. 2. Una vasija que sirve para medir líquidos. 3. (Mús.) Cuarta, intervalo de cuatro tonos.

Quart [cārt], *s.* 1. (Esgr.) *V.* CARTE. 2. Cuarta en el juego de los cientos. (Fr. quarte.)

Quartan [cwōr'-tan], *a.* Perteneciente a la cuarta en una serie; particularmente que sucede cada cuarto día.—*s.* Cuartana, calentura intermitente que se repite cada cuarto día.

Quartation [cwōr-tē'-shun], *s.* (Metal.) Liga de una parte de oro con tres de plata en el procedimiento de separar el oro de sus impurezas, disolviendo éstas con la plata en el ácido nítrico.

Quarter [cwōr'-ter], *s.* 1. Cuarto, cuarterón o cuarta parte de cualquiera cosa; cuarto de quintal, en otro tiempo 28 libras, hoy 25 libras; trimestre, cuarto del año; cuarto del dólar, moneda de 1.25 pesetas o cinco reales vellón. 2. Cuarta, la división de los medios vientos; de aquí, origen, el lugar de donde proviene cualquiera cosa. 3. Cuartel, barrio, paraje o sitio particular de alguna población. 4. Barriada, vecindad, parte de alguna comarca; distrito, región. *From all quarters*, De todas partes. 5. (Mil.) Cuartel, el sitio o paraje en que está alojado o acuartelado un cuerpo de soldados. *Winter quarters*, Cuarteles de invierno. 6. Estación, sitio, puesto señalado, como el de los oficiales y de la tripulación en un buque de guerra; ordinariamente en plural. 7. Morada, residencia temporal; cuartos alquilados; generalmente en plural. 8. Región que comprende la cuarta parte, poco más o menos, de un espacio; cada una de cuatro partes correlativas, como las de un zapato, del casco de una caballería, etc. 9. Cuarterón, entrepaño. 10. (Mar.) Cuadra de popa. *Wind on the quarter* o *quartering wind*, (Mar.) Viento a la cuadra. *Quarter-cask*, Cuarterola. *Quarter-cloths*, (Mar.) Empavesadas. *Quarter-day*, El día en que principia cada una de las cuatro estaciones del año; día en que se paga el alquiler. *Quarter-deck*, (Mar.) Alcázar. *Quarter-deck ladder*, Escalera de costado, o escalera real. *Quarter-gunners*, (Mar.) Artilleros de brigada de marina. *Quarter-netting*, (Mar.) Redes de combate. *Quarter-pieces*, (Mar.) Montantes. *Quarter-plates*, Tamaño de una placa fotográfica de 3¼ por 4¼ pulgadas; placa o cuadro de este tamaño. *Quarter-point*, (Mar.) Cuarto viento o rumbo de la brújula. *Quarter-rails*, (Mar.) Batayolas. *Quarter-section*, En los Estados Unidos y el Canadá, el cuarto de una milla cuadrada; pieza de terreno de media milla cuadrada o 160 acres. *Quarter-sessions*, Tribunal formado por tres magistrados inferiores o jueces de paz, que se reunen una vez cada trimestre en todos los condados de Inglaterra, para juzgar a los acusados de ciertos delitos leves. *Quarter wind*, (Mar.) Viento por anca. *All hands to quarters*, Todos a su puesto. *In quarters*, En cuartos; en cuarteles o en campamento; en cuartos alquilados. *They took up their quarters at*, Se alojaron en o en casa de. *From another quarter*, De otra parte. *The moon is then in its third quarter*, La luna está entonces en su tercer cuarto.—*a.* Cuarto, que tiene la cuarta parte de una cosa.

Quarter, *s.* Cuartel, gracia, acto de hacer gracia de la vida a un enemigo que no puede defenderse y rendido a discreción; de aquí, clemencia, indulgencia. *To ask for, to cry quarter*, Pedir gracia. *To give no quarter*, No dar cuartel.

Quarter, *va.* 1. Cuartear, partir o dividir en cuartas partes; descuartizar, hacer cuartos. 2. Partir, romper a la fuerza. 3. Dividir en cuarteles una población. 4. Acuartelar, repartir la tropa en cuarteles. 5. Dar de comer o mantener a uno con comida sea por dinero o sin él. 6. Alojar, hospedar. 7. (Her.) Cuartelar los escudos de armas.

Quarterage [cwōr'-ter-ēj], *s.* Sueldo o salario que se paga cada trimestre.

Quarterback [cwer'-ter-bac], *s.* En el futbol americano, uno de los cuatro jugadores colocados detrás de la línea.

Quartered [cwōr'-terd], *a.* 1. Partido o separado en cuatro partes. 2. Hecho de madera dividida o aserrada a lo largo en cuartos, para mostrar la veta. 3. Alojado, acuartelado. *Quartered oak*, Madera de roble aserrado a lo largo en cuartos para mostrar la veta.

Quarterly [cwer'-ter-li], *a.* Que contiene la cuarta parte; que se hace cada tres meses, trimestral. *Quarterly wages*, Salario de un trimestre. *The quarterly review*, La revista trimestral, un periódico que se publica cada tres meses.—*s.* Periódico que sale a luz cada tres meses.

Quarterly, *adv.* 1. Una vez cada trimestre. 2. En cuartos, por cuartos.

Quarterman [cwer'-ter-man], *s.* (Mar.) Sotomaestro.

Quarter-master [cwer'-ter-mas'-ter], *s.* (Mil.) Cuartelmaestre, comisario ordenador; (Mar.) cabo de brigadas, oficial inferior que ayuda al piloto y tiene a su cargo las brújulas, los aparatos de señales, etc. *Quartermaster-general*, Intendente de ejército.

Quartern [cwōr'-tern], *s.* (Ingl.) 1. La cuarta parte de ciertas medidas y pesos; como de un cuartillo. 2. *Quartern loaf*, Pan de cuatro libras.

Quartet, Quartette [cwōr-tet'], *s.* 1. Cuarteto, composición vocal o instrumental para cuatro voces. 2. Las cuatro personas que tocan ó cantan esta composición. 3. (Poét.) Cuarteto, estrofa de cuatro versos. 4. Cuatro cosas de una misma clase.

Quartile [cwōr'-til], *s.* Cuadrado o aspecto cuadrado en la astrología.

Quarto [cwōr'-tō], *a.* En cuarto: dícese del libro cuyo pliego doblado forma cuatro hojas u ocho páginas. —*s.* Un libro en cuarto.

Quartz [cwōrts], *s.* (Min.) Cuarzo, cristal de roca; llámase así el pedernal o sílice puro; óxido de silicio (SiO_2), el más duro de los minerales comunes; abunda en las rocas y es elemento esencial del granito.

Quartzose, Quartzous, Quartzy [cwōrts'-ōs, cwōrts'-us], *a.* Cuarzoso, que contiene cuarzo, o compuesto de cuarzo.

Quash [cwosh], *va.* 1. Someter, oprimir, suprimir por fuerza, domar. *To quash a rebellion,* Suprimir o sofocar una revolución. 2. (For.) Anular, invalidar, abrogar, derogar.—*vn.* Estremecerse al oir algún ruido.

Quasi- [cwē'-sai o cwā'-sī]. Prefijo latino que significa casi o "como si."

Quasi-contract [cwé'-sai-cen-tract], *s.* Cuasicontrato.

Quassia o **Quassia Wood** [cwash'-ia o cwosh'-i-a, wud], *s.* (Bot.) Leño o palo de cuasia (quasia) o simarruba; es muy amarga y tiene propiedades tónicas.

Quassin [cwas'-in o cwes'-in], *s.* El principio amargo de la cuasia, un compuesto blanco cristalizable.

Quater-cousin [ké'-tẹr-cuz-n], *s.* Primo en cuarto grado; amigo.

Quaternary [cwa-tẹr'-na-ri], *a.* 1. Cuaternario, compuesto de cuatro cosas; dispuesto de cuatro en cuatro. 2. Cuarto en orden. 3. Cuadrángulo. 4. De la época cuaternaria.—*s.* Época la más reciente de la historia geológica.

Quaternion [cwa-tẹr'-ni-un], *s.* 1. Cuaternidad. 2. Una fila de cuatro soldados; juego o sistema de cuatro.

Quatrain [cwōt'-rên], *s.* Cuarteto, combinación métrica de cuatro versos.

Quaver [cwẹ'-vẹr], *vn.* 1. Gorgoritear, gorjear, trinar, hacer quiebros con la voz en la garganta. 2. Temblar, moverse alguna cosa con un movimiento trémulo.

Quaver, *s.* 1. Gorjeo, trino; pasaje en la música; trino en los instrumentos. 2. (Mús.) Corchea, un signo de la música. *Quaver rest,* Aspiración de corchea.

Quavering [cwé'-vẹr-ing], *s.* Gorgorito, trinado, trino.

Quay [kī], *s.* Muelle, malecón; desembarcadero artificial donde pueden cargar y descargar las embarcaciones.

Queachy, Queechy [cwīch'-i], *a.* Movedizo, que tiembla bajo los pies, como el terreno húmedo o pantanoso.

Quean [cwīn], *s.* 1. Mujercilla, la mujer de mala vida. 2. Una joven o muchacha.

Queasiness [cwī'-zi-nes], *s.* Debilidad, flaqueza de estómago; hastío, desgana, inapetencia.

Queasy [cwī'-zi], *a.* 1. Nauseabundo: dícese del que es propenso al vómito. 2. Nauseabundo, nauseoso, nauseativo, que provoca al vómito o produce náuseas. 3. Fastidioso, que causa hastío. 4. Asqueroso, que da asco. 5. Delicado, nimio, escrupuloso. 6. Delicado, expuesto a contingencias; difícil de manejar o tratar.

Queen [cwīn], *sf.* 1. Reina, la esposa del rey. 2. Mujer soberana de un reino. 3. Mujer que brilla más que las otras en una fiesta o solemnidad. *Queen dowager,* Reina viuda. 4. El caballo en los naipes. 5. La dama en el juego de damas y la reina en el ajedrez. 6. Reina (de las abejas); la sola hembra completamente desarrollada en un enjambre de abejas u hormigas. *Queen consort,* Esposa del rey, que no tiene parte en el gobierno. *Queen regent,* Reina regente. *Queen regnant,* Reina reinante, la que ejerce el dominio por derecho propio. *Queen-of-the-meadows,* Espírea, ulmaria, "reina de los prados," género de plantas de la familia de las rosáceas. Spiræa ulmaria.

Queen-bee [cwīn'-bī], *s.* Reina de las abejas; abeja maesa.

Queenhood [cwīn'-hud], *s.* Realeza, estado o condición de una reina.

Queenly [cwīn'-li], *a.* Parecido a una reina; que tiene el carácter o el porte de una reina; de reina, regio; propio de una reina.

Queenship [cwīn'-ship], *s.* Dignidad, dominio o poder de una reina.

Queer [cwīr], *a.* 1. Raro, extraño, original, singular. 2. Cuestionable, desfavorable, no propicio, misterioso. 3. Estrafalario, estrambótico. —*s.* (Ger.) 1. Moneda falsa. 2. Maricón, marica.

Queerly [cwīr'-li], *adv.* Particularmente, singularmente, raramente, misteriosamente.

Queerness [cwīr'-nes], *s.* Rareza, particularidad, ridiculez.

Quell [cwel], *va.* 1. Hacer cesar, hacer ceder; subyugar, sojuzgar. *To quell tumults,* Apaciguar o sosegar tumultos. 2. Apaciguar, calmar, aquietar, mitigar (v. g. un dolor).—*vn.* ¿Minorarse, ir á menos, apaciguarse, calmarse.

Queller [cwel'-ẹr], *s.* Opresor, domador, sojuzgador.

Quench [cwench], *va.* 1. Apagar, matar la lumbre, la luz, el fuego y también se dice de la sed; ahogar, extinguir. 2. Apagar, sosegar, extinguir alguna pasión de ánimo. 3. Extinguir, acabar, borrar la memoria de alguna cosa. 4. Destruir.

Quenchable [cwench'-a-bl], *a.* Extinguible, apagable, destruible.

Quencher [cwench'-ẹr], *s.* Apagador.

Quenchless [cwench'-les], *a.* Inextinguible, que no se puede apagar; implacable, que no se puede calmar.

Quercine [cwẹr'-sin], *a.* De encinas o robles, perteneciente a estos árboles.

Quercitron [cwẹr-sit'-run], *s.* 1. Corteza del roble negro americano con que se tiñe de amarillo. 2. El roble negro americano. Quercus tinctoria.

Quercus [cwẹr'-cus], *s.* Género típico de las quercíneas, que comprende los robles y las encinas.

Querent [cwī'-rent], *s.* Querellante, el que se querella.

Querist [cwī'-rist], *s.* Inquiridor, preguntador; la persona curiosa o preguntona.

Querl, Quirl [cwẹrl] (E. U.), *va.* Dar vueltas, doblar en redondo.—*s.* Sinuosidad, doblez redondeada, enroscadura.

Quern [cwẹrn], *s.* Molino de mano antiguo (para granos).

Querulous [cwer'-u-lus], *a.* Querelloso, quejoso, dispuesto a quejarse; de índole inclinada a la murmuración.

Querulously [cwer'-u-lus-li], *adv.* Querellosamente, quejosamente, con sentimiento.

Querulousness [cwer'-u-lus-nes], *s.* La disposición a quejarse continuamente.

Query [cwī'-ri], *s.* 1. Cuestión, pregunta a que se debe responder; de aquí, una duda. 2. Signo de duda o interrogación; nota que se pone para que se investigue la exactitud de alguna cosa; se indica a menudo con el signo interrogativo (?).

Query, *va.* 1. Expresar una duda respecto á; marcar con un signo de interrogación. 2. Preguntar, inquirir, pesquisar.—*vn.* 1. Dudar de. 2. Preguntar, proponer cuestiones o hacer preguntas.

Quest [cwest], *s.* 1. Pesquisa, inquisición, averiguación. 2. Busca, buscada. 3. (Des.) El conjunto de los que van en busca de alguna cosa.

Question [cwes'-chun], *s.* 1. Cuestión, pregunta, interrogación. 2. Cuestión, proposición de que se trata, asunto; materia u objeto de discusión o de deliberación; problema. 3. Cuestión, disputa, debate, controversia. 4. Proposición que ha de resolverse o discutirse en una asamblea deliberante. 5. Objeción interpuesta o admitida; duda. 6. †Cuestión de tormento. 7. †Examinación jurídica. *The question is,* El caso es. *Leading question,* Pregunta hecha de modo que indica la respuesta que se ha de dar. *Out of the question,* Fuera de la cuestión, que no es digno de consideración, que no se debe pensar en ello. *Past question,* Fuera de duda, indudablemente, ciertamente. *To ask one a question,* Hacer a uno una pregunta. *To beg the question,* Suponer lo que está bajo discusión. *To call in question,* Poner en cuestión, en duda. *To be beside the question,* Salirse de la cuestión. *To put a question,* Hacer una pregunta, dirigir una interpelación. *The previous question was put and carried,* Pidieron y votaron la cuestión previa. *Not a fair question,* Pregunta no permitida, pregunta indiscreta. *What is the question?* ¿De qué se trata? *That is the question,* Hé ahí la cuestión, lo que se ha de examinar, decidir; hé ahí de lo que se trata. *There can be no question about it,* No cabe duda acerca de ello.

Question, *vn.* 1. Inquirir, preguntar, escudriñar. 2. Cuestionar, poner en cuestión o en duda; dudar que; también, hacer objeción a, tachar, recusar, controvertir.—*va.* 1. Preguntar, examinar a uno por preguntas. 2. Dudar, dificultar. 3. Desconfiar, no tener confianza. *He questions my prudence,* Desconfía de mi prudencia.

Questionable [cwes'-chun-a-bl], *a.* Cuestionable, que puede ponerse en cuestión; expuesto a sospecha o cuestión; dudoso, sospechoso.

Questionableness [cwes'-chun-a-bl-nes], *s.* Calidad o estado de lo cuestionable; naturaleza sospechosa, dudosa, controvertible.

Questioner [cwes'-chun-ẹr], *s.* Inquiridor, preguntador, preguntón.

Questionist [cwes'-chun-ist], *s.* 1. En la Universidad de Cambridge, aspirante a un grado. 2. (Des.) Escudriñador, inquiridor.

Questionless [cwes'-chun-les], *a.* Que no hace pregunta.—*adv.* (Des.) Ciertamente, sin duda.

Questionnaire [cwes'-chun-ār], *s.* Cuestionario, interrogatorio.

Questor [cwes'-tẹr], *s.* Cuestor, magistrado romano.

Questus [cwes'-tus], *s.* (For.) Bienes adquiridos y no heredados.

Quetzal [ket-sal'], *s.* 1. Quetzal, ave de Guatemala. 2. Quetzal, moneda guatemalteca.

Queue [kiū], *s.* 1. Cola, trenza de cabellos en forma de cuerda. 2. Fila, hilera de personas que esperan en el orden de su llegada. 3. Cola, como la de un violín. (Fr. < lat. cauda, cola.)

Quibble [cwib'-l], *vn.* 1. Sutilizar, buscar escapatorias; evadir el punto en cuestión o la verdad llana y lisa, por medio de argucias. 2. (Des.) Jugar del vocablo, decir equívocos.—*s.* Subterfugio, escapatorio, evasión de un punto o cuestión; argucia, sutileza.

Quibbler [cwib'-lẹr], *s.* Tramoyista.

Quibblingly [cwib'-ling-li], *adv.* De una manera evasiva; con argucias y sutilezas.

Quick [cwic], *a.* 1. Veloz, acelerado, ligero, pronto, hecho con celeridad; rápido, presto; que llega en poco tiempo. *Be quick*, Despáchese Vd., dése Vd. prisa. 2. Vivo, diligente, ágil, activo. 3. Ardiente, penetrante. 4. Vivo, viviente. *Quick work*, (Mar.) Obra viva. 5. Vivo de genio, despierto de inteligencia; que responde fácilmente a las impresiones. 6. Irritable, petulante. 7. Preñada, embarazada, en cinta; se dice más comúnmente, *quick with child.* 8. Que produce interés o provecho; disponible, efectivo. *A quick motion*, Un movimiento rápido, veloz. *A quick ear*, Un oído vivo, fino. *A quick wit*, Una inteligencia viva. *A quick fire*, Un fuego ardiente. *A quick pulse*, Pulso irritable; se distingue del pulso frecuente. *The quick and the dead*, Los vivos y los muertos. *To be quick about* o *at anything*, Hacer de prisa una cosa, ejecutarla prontamente.—*adv.* Con presteza, vivamente, velozmente, rápidamente. *Quick-eyed*, De ojos vivos, con vista penetrante. *Quick-grass*, *V.* COUCH-GRASS. *Quick-scented*, Que tiene el olfato fino. *Quick-sighted*, Que tiene vista aguda, penetrante. *Quick-sightedness*, Agudeza de vista, penetración. *Quick-tempered*, Fácil de encolerizarse, irascible, colérico. *Quick-witted*, De inteligencia viva, agudo, perspicaz. *Quick-hedge*, Seto vivo. *Quick-match*, Mecha de estopilla, cuerdamecha.

Quick, *s.* 1. Lo que tiene vida, particularmente la carne viva, lo vivo; (fig.) la sensibilidad. *To cut* o *sting to the quick*, Herir a uno en lo vivo. 2. (Bot.) Planta de seto. *V.* QUICKSET.

Quickbeam [cwic'-bīm], *s.* (Bot.) Fresno silvestre.

Quicken [cwic'-n], *va.* 1. Vivificar, dar vida, resucitar, devolver la vida. 2. Acelerar, urgir, avivar; apresurar. 3. Avivar, excitar, aguzar, animar.—*vn.* 1. Avivarse, vivificarse, recibir vida. 2. Moverse de prisa. 3. Sentir moverse la criatura: dícese de una madre.

Quickener [cwic'-n-ẹr], *s.* 1. Vivificador, el que vivifica. 2. Avivador, el que aviva.

Quickening [cwic'-n-ing], *s.* 1. Acción y efecto de vivificar, o de hallarse vivo. 2. En la jurisprudendia médica, la primera vez que la mujer preñada siente moverse el feto dentro de la matriz, por lo general en la semana décimaoctava de la preñez.

Quickfreeze [cwic-frīz'], *va.* Congelar rápidamente.

Quicklime [cwic'-laim], *s.* Cal viva.

Quickly [cwic'-li], *adv.* Prontamente, con presteza.

Quickness [cwic'-nes], *s.* Presteza, vivacidad, prontitud, celeridad, actividad; sagacidad, viveza, penetración.

Quicksand [cwic'-sand], *s.* Arena movediza.

Quickset [cwic'-set], *s.* 1. Arbusto o árbol con que se hace un seto, particularmente el espino blanco. 2. Seto vivo. *Quickset hedge*, Seto vivo.

Quickset, *va.* Cercar con un seto vivo; plantar con el espino majuelo.

Quicksilver [cwic'-sil-vẹr], *s.* Azogue, mercurio.

Quicksilvered [cwic'-sil-vẹrd], *a.* Azogado, dado de azogue o mercurio.

Quickstep [cwic'-step], *s.* 1. (Mús.) Marcha escrita en compás acelerado; pasacalle. 2. Paso acelerado.

Quid [cwid], *s.* Un pedacito de cualquier cosa que se está mascando, v. g. de tabaco; o la porción de heno medio mascado que cae de la boca de un caballo.

Quiddity [cwid'-i-ti], *s.* 1. Esencia. 2. Cavilación, argucia, distinción u objeción fútil, ligera.

Quiddle [cwid'-l], *vn.* Gastar el tiempo en pequeñeces, divertirse en bagatelas.

Quidnunc [cwid'-nuṇc], *s.* Curioso insaciable, persona que quiere saber todo lo que pasa; novelero, amigo de cuentos.

Quiesce [cwai-es'], *vn.* 1. Aquietarse, callarse. 2. Convertirse en muda una letra.

Quiescence [cwai-es'-ens], **Quiescency** [cwai-es'-en-si], *s.* Quietud, reposo, descanso.

Quiescent [cwai-es'-ent], *a.* 1. Quieto, descansado, falto de movimiento, en reposo. 2. No agitado, tranquilo, libre de ansiedad o emoción. 3. Mudo, que no se pronuncia.

Quiet [cwai'-et], *a.* 1. Quedo, quieto, falto de movimiento. 2. Pacífico, apacible, dulce de genio, sosegado, tranquilo.—*s.* Quietud, sosiego, reposo, descanso, tranquilidad, calma.

Quiet, *va.* Aquietar, apaciguar, sosegar, tranquilizar.

Quieter [cwai'-et-ẹr], *s.* Apaciguador.

Quietism [cwai'-et-izm], *s.* 1. Tranquilidad de ánimo. 2. Quietismo, molinismo.

Quietist [cwai'-et-ist], *s.* Quietista, molinista.

Quietly [cwai'-et-li], *adv.* Quietamente, pacíficamente, con sosiego.

Quietness [cwai'-et-nes], **Quietude** [cwai'-ẹ-tiūd], *s.* Quietud, sosiego, tranquilidad, paz, reposo.

Quietus [cwai-ī'-tus], *s.* Carta de pago, finiquito; descanso; muerte.

Quill [cwil], *s.* 1. Pluma grande de las alas o de la cola de las aves; cañón de pluma. 2. Cañón o pluma para escribir; también, un escritor y con el artículo significa la profesión literaria. 3. La púa del puerco espín. 4. Parte cilíndrica, parecida al cañón de una pluma; canilla, cañita de tejedor. *Quill-men*, Gente de pluma.

Quill, *s.* Estría, albardilla redondeada o pliegue cilíndrico.

Quilling [cwil'-ing], *s.* Faralá, vuelo de un material plegado; cada uno de los pliegues de ese material.

Quilt [cwilt], *s.* Colcha o cobertura acolchada para la cama; sobrecama colchada.

Quilt, *va.* Colchar, acolchar.

Quilter [cwilt'-ẹr], *s.* Colchonero.

Quilting [cwilt'-ing], *s.* 1. (Mar.) Cajera. 2. El acto de acolchar. 3. *Quiltings*, Cotines colchados.

Quinary [cwai'-na-ri], *a.* Quinario, que consta de cinco partes.

Quince [cwins], *s.* 1. (Bot.) Membrillo, fruto amarillento y ácido que produce el árbol del mismo nombre. 2. Membrillo o membrillero, árbol o arbusto que produce los membrillos. Cydonia vulgaris. *Japan* o *Japanese quince*, Membrillo japonés, arbusto de adorno, estimado por sus flores encarnadas o carmesíes.

Quincuncial [cwin-cuṇ'-shal], *a.* Que tiene la figura de quincunce o tresbolillo.

Quincunx [cwiṇ'-cuṇcs], *s.* 1. Quincunce, tresbolillo, plantío de árboles en cuadro, uno en cada esquina y otro en medio. 2. Quincunce, una medida y peso pequeño. 3. (Astr.) El aspecto de un astro distante de otro cinco signos.

Quindecagon [cwin-dec'-a-gon], *s.* Quindecágono, figura de quince lados y otros tantos ángulos.

Quinia, Quinin, Quinine [cwin'-ia, cwin'-in, cwai'-nain o ki-nīn'], *s.* Quinina, alcaloide activo, febrífugo, que se extrae de la quina.

Quinidin, Quinidine [cwin'-i-din], *s.* Quinidina, compuesto blanco cristalizable, isómero de la quinina, contenido en la quina.

Quinquagesima [cwin-cwa-jes'-i-ma], *s.* Período de cincuenta días. *Quinquagesima Sunday*, Domingo de quincuagésima, el que precede al primero de cuaresma.

Quinnat [cwin'-at], *s.* El salmón del río Columbia en las costas del Pacífico del Norte. Oncorhynchus chonicha.

Quinquangular [cwin-cwaṇ'-giu-lar], *a.* Que tiene cinco ángulos.

Quinquefoliate [cwin-cwe-fō'-li-êt], *a.* Quinquefoliado, quinquedigitado, de cinco hojas.

Quinquelobate [cwin-cwe-lō'-bêt], *a.* Que tiene cinco lóbulos.

Quinquennial [cwin-cwen'-i-al], *a.* Quinquenal, que dura un quinquenio o sucede una vez en cinco años.

Quinquina [cwin-cwai'-na], *s.* Quinaquina.

Quinsy [cwin'-zi], *s.* Angina, esquinancia, inflamación de las amígdalas, especialmente cuando es supurativa.

Quint [cwint], *s.* 1. Registro de órgano que suena una quinta más alta que los teclados que se tocan. 2. El conjunto de cinco. 3. La cuerda E del violín. 4. Quinta, cinco cartas de un palo seguidas en orden en algunos juegos.

Quintain [cwin'-ten] o **Quintin** [cwin'-tin], *s.* Poste o pilar que se ponía antiguamente en los picaderos.

Quintal [cwin'-tal], *s.* Quintal, el peso de cien libras o cuatro arrobas.

Quintessence [cwin-tes'-ens], *s.* Quinta esencia, lo más puro y acrisolado de cualquiera cosa.

Quintessential [cwin-te-sen'-shal], *a.* Perteneciente a la quinta esencia.

Quintet, Quintette [cwin-tet'], *s.* Quinteto, trozo de música compuesto para cinco voces o cinco instrumentos; también las cinco personas que lo ejecutan.

Quintillion [cwin-til'-yun], *s.* Número cardinal; entre los franceses y los americanos, la sexta potencia de

mil; el guarismo uno seguido de dieciocho ceros; en el sistema inglés, la quinta potencia de un millón.
Quintuple [cwin'-tiu-pl], *a.* Quíntuplo.
Quip, *s.* Pulla, chufleta, dicho picante; chanza pesada, sarcasmo.
Quire [cwair], *s.* 1. Mano de papel; cuaderno compuesto de 24 o 25 hojas. *Book in quires,* Libro en papel o sin coser. 2. Juego de todas las hojas necesarias para hacer un libro; de aquí, libro. 3. (Ant.) Coro. *V.* CHOIR.
Quire [cwair], *va.* Plegar el papel en manos.
Quire, *vn.* (Poco us.) Cantar en concierto, cantar a coro.
Quirk [cwẹrk], *s.* 1. Desvío repentino, vuelta corta, recodo. 2. Arranque de la imaginación, capricho; pulla, expresión aguda y picante. 3. Sutileza, delicadeza, distinción artificiosa; argucia, escapatoria, refugio, rodeo. 4. Aire de música muy corto. 5. Copada, caveto, muesca pequeña entre las molduras.
Quirk, *va.* Acanalar, estriar; hacer copadas o cavetos. *Quirking plane,* Cepillo de cavetos.
Quirky [cwẹr'-ki], *a.* 1. Lleno de argucias, artificioso, que emplea escapatorias. 2. Que consta de vueltas o recodos.
Quirt [cwẹrt], *s.* Látigo con mango corto de madera o cuero rígido y correa de cuero crudo retorcido. (< Esp. cuerda.)
Quisling [cwiz'-ling], *s.* Quisling, traidor de su patria.
Quit [cwit], *va.* (*pret.* y *pp.* QUIT o QUITTED). 1. Dejar, abandonar, parar, cesar de, desistir; renunciar, ceder, resignar; por extensión, salir, alejarse de. 2. (Ant.) Pagar; hacer pago de, o para. 3. (Fam. o des.) Absolver, dar por libre, descargar; de aquí, eximir, desembarazar, justificar. *V.* ACQUIT.—*vn.* Desistir de, o cesar de hacer una cosa. *To quit an employment,* Dejar, abandonar un empleo. *To give notice to quit,* Dar aviso o notificar para que se deje una casa, habitación, etc. *To quit work,* Cesar de trabajar. *Quit your nonsense,* Basta de tonterías. *He quit the place for good,* Salió del lugar para siempre. *To quit cost,* Pagar los gastos, reembolsar. *To quit scores,* Ajustar, arreglar cuentas con alguno, desquitarse con alguien.
Quit, *pp.* de *To* QUIT. Libertado, libre, descargado, absuelto.
Quitchgrass [cwich'-gras], *s.* (Bot.) Grama, planta gramínea que echa raíces profundas y muy difícil de extirpar. *V.* COUCH-GRASS. Triticum repens.
Quitclaim [cwit'-clêm], *va.* Renunciar o ceder un título o reclamación. —*s.* (For.) Renuncia, cesión definitiva sin reserva alguna que hace una persona a favor de otra, ya se trate de una demanda, reclamación, litigio judicial, o derecho de acción. *Quitclaim deed,* Documento que contiene la renuncia a la propiedad de un terreno.
Quite [cwait], *adv.* 1. Completamente, perfectamente, totalmente, enteramente, absolutamente. 2. En grado considerable, bastante, muy.
Quitrent [cwit'-rent], *s.* Censo feudal que pagaba antiguamente el dueño de una propiedad y por medio del cual se libraba del servicio feudal.
Quits [cwits], *inter.* En paz: expresión que se usa cuando se paga enteramente un alcance o deuda. *To be quits,* (Fam.) Estar o quedar en paz o corrientes; salir o ser pata o patas; quedar pagado.
Quittance [cwit'-ans], *s.* 1. Finiquito, descargo, desempeño, pago, satisfacción. 2. Recompensa, remuneración.
Quitter [cwit'-ẹr], *s.* El que abandona o renuncia una cosa.
Quiver [cwiv'-ẹr], *s.* Carcaj, aljaba.
Quiver, *vn.* Temblar, estremecerse.
Quivered [cwiv'-ẹrd], *s.* Armado con aljaba; metido como flecha en aljaba.
Quivering [cwiv'-ẹr-ing], *s.* Tremor, temblor.
Quixotic [cwix-ot'-ic], *a.* Quijotesco, relativo o parecido a Don Quijote: de aquí, romancesco o caballeresco hasta la extravagancia.
Quixotism [cwix'-ẹt-izm], *s.* Quijotismo, porte o modo de proceder ridículo.
Quiz [cwiz], *s.* 1. Cuestión o sugestión disparatada o poco seria; chanza, chulada, burla: acertijo, enigma. 2. Burlón, zumbón, chancero, candongo, chuleador. 3. (Fam.) El acto de preguntar a un discípulo o a una clase oralmente o por escrito.
Quiz, *va.* 1. Candonguear, chulear, chancear. 2. Mirar, con un lente, con un monóculo. 3. Examinar a un discípulo o clase haciéndoles preguntas. *Quizzing-glass,* Monóculo, lente para un ojo.
Quizzical [cwiz'-i-cal], *a.* 1. Burlón, dado a chulear o chasquear. 2. Raro, singular, extraño.
Quodlibet [cwed'-li-bet], *s.* 1. (Mús.) Fantasía, miscelánea, a veces poco armoniosa. 2. Sutileza, punto delicado y disputable.
Quodlibetic, Quodlibetical [cwed-li-bet'-ic, al], *a.* 1. No restringido a un asunto particular; discutido a voluntad por gusto o curiosidad. 2. Dado a sutilezas y argucias como ejercicio intelectual.
†**Quoif** [cweif], *s.* Cofia, escofieta. *V.* COIF.
Quoin [cwein o coin], *s.* 1. (Arq.) Adaraja, piedra saliente, diente, ángulo de una pared: esquina, ángulo exterior de un edificio; clave, piedra cuneiforme con que se cierra el arco o bóveda. 2. (Mec.) Cuña, o pieza cuneiforme de que se usa para algún fin; cuña de imprenta, para apretar la forma. *Stowing-quoins,* (Mar.) Cuñas de abarrotar, abarrotes.—*va.* Acuñar, meter cuñas.
Quoit [cweit], *s.* Tejo, disco de hierro con un agujero redondo en el centro, de que se usa en un juego parecido al de los tejos.—*pl.* Especie de juego de tejos.
Quoit, *vn.* Jugar al tejo.—*va.* (Poco us.) Tirar el tejo a la raya.
Quondam [cwen'-dam], *a.* De tiempos anteriores, de otro tiempo, que fué. *My quondam king,* Mi antiguo rey o el que fué mi rey en otro tiempo.
Quorum [cwō'-rum], *s.* 1. Junta o número suficiente de personas pertenecientes a un cuerpo deliberante o a una corporación para resolver o determinar algún asunto. 2. (Ingl.) Comisión especial de jueces de paz.
Quota [cwō'-ta], *s.* Cuota, parte o porción determinada que toca a cada uno; prorrata, contingente. *Quota of troops,* Contingente de tropas.
Quotable [cwō'-ta-bl], *a.* Citable, que puede citarse o es digno de ser citado.
Quotation [cwo-tê'-shun], *s.* 1. Citación, el acto de citar. 2. Cita, las palabras citadas; párrafo de un libro, citado por vía de aclaración o prueba en apoyo. 3. (Com.) Cotización, indicación del precio de las mercancías. 4. *Quotation-mark,* Virgulilla, signo tipográfico que se pone al principio y al fin de un pasaje citado (". . ."). En inglés se emplean comas invertidas al principio y apóstrofos al fin.
Quote [cwōt], *va.* 1. Citar, notar, repetir, reproducir un párrafo de un escrito o discurso, como aclaración, autoridad o prueba en apoyo. 2. (Com.) Cotizar, indicar el precio de un artículo.
Quoter [cwōt'-ẹr], *s.* Citador, el que cita.
Quoth [cwōth], *v. imp.* *Quoth I,* Dije yo, digo yo. *Quoth he,* Él dijo.
Quotha [cwō'-tha], *inter.* ¡De veras! ¡vaya! Expresa ordinariamente algún desprecio.
Quotidian [cwo-tid'-i-an], *a.* Cotidiano, diario, que sucede cada día.—*s.* Calentura cotidiana.
Quotient [cwō'-shent], *s.* Cociente. *Intelligence Quotient, I.Q.,* Cociente intelectual.
Quoting [cwōt'-ing], *s.* Citación, el acto de citar.
Quran [kū-rān'], *s.* Alcorán. *V.* KORAN.

R

R [ar]. Se pronuncia en general como en castellano. La *r* sola se pronuncia muchas veces como *rr,* y las dos *rr* como una sola *r.* A la sílaba *er,* cuando es final, se le da el sonido de *ar* o *or,* como si estuviera sola y separada de la dicción; v. g. desire (*desaiar*); digger (*digguer*). Como abreviatura, *R* quiere decir *rey* o *real,* o en las recetas de los médicos, *recipe,* esto es, *toma.*
Rabbet [rab'-et], *va.* (Carp.) Acepillar un pedazo de madera para que ajuste con otro; hacer con el inglete una ranura en la madera; rebajar con el guillame.
Rabbet, *s.* 1. Ranura, rebajo o ensambladura de dos pedazos de madera para que encajen uno en otro. *Rabbet-plane,* Guillame, cepillo angosto y largo. 2. (Mar.) Alefriz.
Rabbi [rab'-ai], **Rabbin** [rab'-in], *s.* Rabí, rabino, el doctor de la ley judaica.
Rabbinic, Rabbinical [rab-in'-ic, al] *a.* Rabínico.
Rabbinist [rab'-in-ist], *s.* Rabinista.
Rabbit [rab'-it], *s.* 1. Conejo, pequeño animal roedor del género Lepus. *Doe-rabbit,* Coneja. *Young rabbit,* Gazapillo, gazapo. *Rabbit nest* o *hole,* Conejera. *Welsh rabbit,* (Fam.) Quesadilla, tostada con queso; queso tostado, sazonado, y que se sirve generalmente con tostada. 2. (Mar.) Alefriz.
Rabbit-warren [rab'-it-wōr-en], *s.* Conejera, conejar; madriguera.
Rabble [rab'-l], *s.* 1. La gentuza, gentualla, canalluza, canalla, la ínfima plebe. 2. Gentío, muchedumbre.
Rabble, *s.* Hurgón o botador de

punta curva, como el que se usa en las fundiciones.

Rabid [rab'-id], *a.* 1. Rabioso, que padece el mal de rabia. 2. Que proviene de la rabia o pertenece a ella. 3. Rabioso, fanático, violento, furioso, feroz.

Rabies [rê'-bi-iz], *s.* Rabia, hidrofobia, enfermedad a menudo mortal que se desarrolla en los perros y se transmite al hombre por la mordedura del animal atacado.

Raccoon [rac-cūn'], *s.* Mapache, cuadrúpedo carnívoro nocturno de América, de la familia de los úrsidos.

Race [rês], *s.* 1. Raza, casta; serie continua de los descendientes que provienen de la misma estirpe; casta, especies de los animales domésticos; descendencia, prole, generación; familia, tribu, pueblo. 2. Linaje, generación, genealogía. 3. Clase, especie de seres o animales con caracteres que los unen o los separan de otros. 4. (Ant.) Sabor o gusto particular, como el del vino. (Fr.) *The human race*, El género humano.

Race, *s.* 1. Carrera, apuesta, lucha de velocidad, ya sea a pie o a caballo; en botes o yates, en trineos o coches, nadando o patinando; carreras para ganar un premio. 2. De aquí, una competencia cualquiera. 3. Progresión, y particularmente carrera, movimiento acelerado. 4. Duración de la vida; curso, carrera. 5. Corriente de agua violenta o rápida o el canal para ella; canal estrecho, caz, saetín. 6. Paso, carrera de la lanzadera. 7. Sendero circular para un caballo que pone en movimiento un motor. (< A.-S. raes.) *To run a race*, Luchar a la carrera, a correr. *The Derby races*, Las carreras de Derby. *Race-course*, (1) Lugar o campo para carreras. (2) Canal de molino, saetín. *Race-cup*, Premio de carrera. *Race-ground*, Campo de carreras; terreno dispuesto para las carreras de caballos. *Race-horse*, Caballo criado para las carreras.

Race, *va.* 1. Obligar a correr de prisa (como para ganar un premio). 2. Correr, disputar el premio de una carrera.—*vn.* 1. Correr con mucha ligereza, de prisa. 2. Moverse la maquinaria a un paso acelerado.

Racer [rê'-sẹr], *s.* 1. Corredor, el que disputa el premio de la carrera o corre por apuesta. 2. Caballo de carrera.

Race track [rês trac], *s.* Hipódromo.

Raceway [rês'-wê], *s.* Canal de agua artificial, canal de molino, caz, saetín.

Rachis [rê'-kis], *s.* (*pl.* RACHIDES o RACHISES). 1. Raquis, eje central de una inflorescencia. 2. Cañón de pluma. 3. Raquis, espinazo.

Rachitic [ra-kit'-ic], *a.* 1. Raquítico, que padece raquitis. 2. Perteneciente a un raquis.

Racial [rê'-shal], *a.* Racial. *Racial integration*, Integración racial. *Racial segregation*, Separación racial.

Racily [rê'-si-li], *adv.* De una manera picante.

Racism [rê'-sizm], *s.* Racismo, creencia en la superioridad racial de un grupo.

Racist [rê'-sist], *s.* Racista.

Rack [rac], *s.* 1. Instrumento para extender alguna cosa: tormento; potro o cuestión de tormento. *To put to the rack*, Dar tormento. 2. Dolor, pena, angustia. 3. Rueca, palo a que se afirma el lino para hilarlo. 4. Cremallera, barra dentada que se mueve por medio de una rueda dentada también. *Rack and pinion*, Engranaje de cremallera y piñón. 5. Morillos de asador. 6. Enrejado de madera dentro del cual se pone el heno para el ganado. 7. Nubarrón. 8. Astillero o percha en que se ponen astas, picas o lanzas. *Racks of a cart*, Adrales, laderas de carro. 9. Destrucción; desusado excepto en la locución *To go to rack and ruin*, Caer en ruinas y destrucción.

Rack, *va.* 1. Dar tormento. 2. Atormentar, afligir, molestar. 3. Apretar, oprimir con exacciones violentas. 4. Vagar o moverse apresuradamente de una parte a otra. 5. Trasegar, mudar el licor de una vasija a otra. *To rack wine*, Trasegar el vino. 6. Alargar, extender.

Racket [rak'-et], *s.* 1. Baraúnda, confusión. 2. Jerga, habla confusa. 3. Raqueta, paleta para jugar al volante.

Racking [rak'-ing], *s.* 1. Tortura. 2. Remordimiento de conciencia; tortura de ánimo. 3. Trasiego de vino u otros licores.

Rackrent [rac'-rent], *s.* Arriendo o arrendamiento exorbitante.

Racy [re'-si], *a.* 1. Picante, lleno de interés, vigoroso (estilo o lenguaje). 2. De aroma o sabor peculiar, agradable y característico. 3. Perteneciente a la raza, al tipo o al origen.

Radar [rê'-dār], *s.* (Radio) Radar.

Radial [rê'-di-al], *a.* 1. Que pertenece al radio, o al rayo; que parte del centro, que tiene radios. 2. (Zool.) Radial, perteneciente al hueso radio, o a una parte divergente del centro. 3. (Bot.) Perteneciente a la ligulada de la flor compuesta.

Radiance [rê'-di-ans], **Radiancy** [rê'-di-an-si], *s.* Brillo, resplandor, esplendor, brillantez, lucimiento.

Radiant [rê'-di-ant], *a.* Radiante, radioso, resplandeciente, brillante.—*s.* 1. (Geom.) Línea recta que procede de un punto dado, alrededor del cual se supone que gira. 2. Punto luminoso de donde emana la luz. 3. Lo que despide rayos.

Radiantly [rê'-di-ant-li], *adv.* Con brillo, con esplendor, con alegría.

Radiate [rê'-di-êt], *vn.* Radiar, despedir o arrojar rayos de luz, salir como los rayos de luz; echar rayos, centellear, relumbrar.—*va.* Dar luz, llenar de luz, iluminar, irradiar.

Radiate, Radiated [rê'-di-êt, ed], *a.* 1. Radiado, dispuesto en forma de radio, que parte de un centro común. 2. Partido o separado en rayos, o marcado con rayos. 3. (Zool.) Radiado, que tiene simetría de radios; perteneciente a la división de los animales radiados. 4. (Bot.) Que tiene florecillas liguladas.

Radiation [rê-di-ê'-shun], *s.* Radiación, irradiación. *Radiation sickness*, Enfermedad provocada por la radiación.

Radiator [rê'-di-ê-tẹr], *s.* Radiador.

Radical [rad'-i-cal], *a.* 1. Radical. 2. Extremo. 3. Extremista.—*s.* Radical.

Radicalism [rad'-i-cal-izm], *s.* Radicalismo.

Radicand [rad'-i-cand], *s.* Radicando.

Radicate [rad'-i-kêt], *va.* Arraigar.

Radicle [rad'-i-cl], *s.* Radícula.

Radio [rê'-di-ō], *s.* 1. Radio. 2. Radiocomunicación. *Radio amateur*, Radioaficionado. *Radio announcer*, Locutor de radio. *Radio astronomy*, Radioastronomía. *Radio beacon*, Radiobaliza, radiofaro. *Radio broadcasting*, Radiodifusión. *Radio communication*, Radiocomunicación, radiotelecomunicación. *Radio compass*, *Radio direction finder*, Radiocompás. *Radio frequency*, Radiofrecuencia. *Radio listener*, Radioescucha, radioyente. *Radio message*, Radiograma. *Radio navigation*, 1. Radionavegación. 2. (Aer.) Radioaviación. *Radio navigator*, Radionavegante. *Radio station*, Radiodifusora, estación. *Radio telescope*, Radiotelescopio. *Radio tube*, Lámpara de radio, válvula. *Radio wave meter*, Ondímetro.

Radioactive [rê-di-o-ac'-tiv], *a.* Radiactivo, radioactivo.

Radioactivity [rê-di-o-ac-tiv'-i-ti], *s.* Radiactividad, radioactividad.

Radiobiology [rê-di-o-bai-el'-o-ji], *s.* Radiobiología.

Radiobroadcast [rê-di-o-brōd'-cast], *va.* Radiodifundir.

Radiocarbon [rê-di-o-kar'-bun], *s.* Radiocarbono. *Radiocarbon dating*, Determinación de antigüedad con radiocarbono.

Radiochemistry [rê-di-o-kem'-is-tri], *s.* Radioquímica.

Radioelement [rê-di-o-el'-ẹ-mẹnt], *s.* Radioelemento.

Radiogram [rê'-di-o-gram], *s.* Radiograma.

Radiograph [rê'-di-o-graf], *s.* Radiografía.—*va.* Radiografiar.

Radiographer [rê-di-eg'-ra-fer], *s.* Radiógrafo.

Radiography [rê-di-eg'-ra-fi], *s.* Radiografía.

Radioisotope [rê-di-o-ai'-so-top], Radioisótopo.

Radiolocation [rê-di-o-lo-kê'-shun], *s.* Radiolocalización.

Radiologist [rê-di-el'-o-jist], *s.* Radiólogo.

Radiology [rê-di-el'-o-ji], *s.* Radiología.

Radioman [rê'-di-o-man], *s.* Radiotécnico.

Radiometer [rê-di-em'-ẹ-tẹr], *s.* Radiómetro.

Radiophone [rê'-di-o-fōn], *s.* 1. Radioteléfono. 2. (Fís.) Radiófono.

Radiophoto [rê-di-o-fō'-tō], *s.* Radiofotografía.

Radioscopy [rê-di-es'-co-pi], *s.* Radioscopia.

Radiosensitive [rê-di-o-sen'-si-tiv], *a.* Radiosensitivo.

Radiosonde [rê-di-o-send'], *s.* Radiosonda.

Radiotechnology [rê-di-o-tec-nel'-o-ji], *s.* Radiotécnica, radiotecnia.

Radiotelegram [rê-di-o-tel'-ẹ-gram], *s.* Radiograma.

Radiotelegraph [rê-di-o-tel'-ẹ-graf], *s.* Radiotelegrafía.

Radiotelephone [rê-di-o-tel'-e-fōn], *s.* 1. Radiotelefonía. 2. Radioteléfono.

Radiotherapy [rê-di-o-ther'-a-pi], *s.* Radioterapia.

Radish [rad'-ish], *s.* Rábano.

Radium [rê'-di-um], *s.* Radio.

Radius [rê'-di-us], *s.* Radio.

Radon [rê'-den], *s.* Radón.

Raffia [raf'-i-a], *s.* Rafia.

Raffish [rê'-fish], *a.* 1. Chillón,

vulgar. 2. Extravagante, adefesiero.

Raffle [raf'-l], *va.* y *vn.* Rifar, sortear. *To raffle off*, Rifar. —*s.* Rifa, sorteo, tómbola. *Charity raffle*, Tómbola (de beneficiencia).

Raft [raft], *s.* 1. Balsa, almadía; jangada. 2. (E. U.) Amontonamiento de troncos de árboles en un río. 3. (Ger.) Gran número, montón.

Raft, *va.* Llevar sobre una balsa o jangada.

Rafter [raft'-er], *s.* Cábrio, viga.

Raftport [raft'-pōrt], *s.* (Mar.) Porta de cañón, tronera.

Rag [rag], *s.* 1. Trapo, andrajo, harapo, jirón. 2. *pl.* Vestidos usados, rasgados. 3. Canto agudo o saliente de un trozo de metal o de una roca; risco.

Ragamuffin [rag'-a-muf-in], *s.* Andrajoso, hombre vil y despreciable; mendigo, pordiosero; trapiento, pelagatos, chispero.

Rage [rêj], *s.* 1. Rabia, ira, enojo, furor, arrebato de cólera. 2. Furor, furia, violencia, vehemencia, intensidad extrema (de las cosas). 3. Ardor, anhelo. 4. (Fam.) Antojo, cosa que todos o muchos desean con vehemencia; boga, moda.

Rage, *vn.* Rabiar, enojarse, enfurecerse, encolerizarse.

Ragged [rag'-ed], *a.* 1. Roto, andrajoso, trapiento. 2. Desigual, escabroso, áspero.

Ragingly [rêj'-ing-li], *adv.* Rabiosamente, airadamente.

Raglan [rag'-lan], *s.* Raglán, gabán holgado de hombre. *Raglan sleeves*, mangas raglán (muy holgadas, típicas de dicho gabán).

Ragman [rag'-man], *s.* Trapero.

Ragout [ra-gū'], *s* Guisado, estofado. (Fr.)

Ragstone [rag'-stōn], *s* Especie de piedra de amolar.

Ragtime [rag'-taim], *s.* Música popular sincopada.

Ragweed [rag'-wīd], *s.* (Bot.) Ambrosía.

Raid [rêd], *va.* 1. Invadir súbitamente, como para hacer la guerra o pillar. 2. (Fam.) Entrar o apoderarse por fuerza legal.—*vn.* Merodear, hacer una invasión, pillar.—*s.* Correría, irrupción, incursión hostil; invasión repentina, prendimiento.

Rail [rêl], *s.* 1. Barra, baranda, barandilla, antepecho, barrera. 2. Riel, carril, cada una de las barras de hierro o acero que, colocadas paralelamente, forman el carril sobre que ruedan las locomotoras y los coches de ferrocarriles y tranvías. 3. (Mar.) Batayola, cairel, galón. *Head-rails*, (Mar.) Perchas. *Roughtree-rails*, (Mar.) Barandas. *Waist-rails*, (Mar.) Varengas. 4. Carril, considerado como medio de transporte. *By rail*, Por ferrocarril. *To run off the rails*, Descarrilar.

Rail, *s.* Ave zancuda, género típico de la familia de los rálidos; tiene las alas y la cola cortas, las patas, los dedos y el pico largos.

Rail, *va.* 1. Cercar con balaustradas, barandillas o barreras. 2. Poner rieles o carriles.—*vn.* Injuriar de palabra, emplear un lenguaje insolente y ultrajante; decir mal; se emplea con *at* o *against*.

Railer [rêl'-er], *s.* Maldiciente, murmurador.

Railing [rêl'-ing], *s.* 1. Serie de barras; barandilla, balaustrada, cerca, estacada, verja, enverjado. 2. Carriles, material para una vía férrea. 3. Lenguaje injurioso.

Raillery [rêl'-er-i o ral'-er-i], *s.* Chocarrería, bufonada satírica; burla.

Railroad [rêl'-rōd], *va.* (E. U.) Apresurar, hacer algo rápidamente, como con la rapidez de un tren.

Railroad, Railway [rêl'-rōd, rêl'-wê], *s.* (En la Gran Bretaña se usa más la palabra *railway;* en los Estados Unidos, *railroad.*) 1. Ferrocarril, vía férrea, camino de hierro sobre el que van los coches o material rodante. 2. Sistema de carriles, estaciones, material rodante, etc., empleado en el transporte por ferrocarril. 3. Corporación o personas que poseen o explotan una línea férrea. *Railroad car*, Carro, coche de ferrocarril. *Railroad crossing*, Encrucijada, crucero; cruce de vía; también, lugar en que el camino ordinario corta la vía férrea. *Railroad gauge*, Entrevía, anchura entre los carriles de una vía férrea. *Railroad siding*, Desviadero, vía suplementaria; en Cuba, chucho. *Street railroad* o *railway*, Ferrocarril urbano, tranvía; sea eléctrico o de sangre. *Narrow-gauge railway*, Ferrocarril de vía estrecha o angosta.

Raiment [rê'-ment], *s.* Ropa, traje, prendas de vestir.

Rain [rên], *vn.* Llover. *It rains*, Llueve. *To rain pitchforks*, Llover chuzos. *To rain bucketsful*, Llover a cántaros. *Rain or shine*, Que llueva o no; con buen o mal tiempo.—*va.* Hacer llover, hacer caer alguna cosa en mucha abundancia.

Rain, *s.* 1. Lluvia. 2. Caída de lluvia; caída de alguna cosa a manera de lluvia. *Heavy rain*, Aguacero.

Rainbow [rên'-bō], *s.* Arco iris.

Raincoat [rên'-cōt], *s.* Impermeable, abrigo impermeable.

Rainfall [rên'-fōl], *s.* 1. Aguacero, caída de lluvia. 2. Cantidad de lluvia y de nieve derretida y medida como lluvia, que cae en un período de tiempo determinado.

Rain forest [rên' fer-est], *s.* Bosque húmedo, bosque tropical, bosque de zona de gran precipitación pluvial.

Rain-ga(u)ge [rên'-gêj], *s.* Pluviómetro, udómetro, pluvímetro, instrumento para medir la lluvia que cae en lugar y tiempo dados.

Rainproof [rên'-prūf], *a.* Impermeable, a prueba de lluvia.

Rain-water [rên'-wō-ter], *s.* Agua llovediza.

Rainy [rên'-i], *a.* Lluvioso.

Raise [rêz], *va.* 1. Levantar, alzar, poner en pie, poner derecho. 2. Levantar, construir, fabricar, edificar. 3. Levantar, aumentar, subir, dar mayor incremento, mayor valor o un precio más alto a alguna cosa. 4. Levantar, engrandecer, enhiestar, elevar, ensalzar, exaltar, promover. 5. Animar, excitar, incitar, poner en movimiento. 6. Causar, ocasionar, producir, hacer nacer, hacer crecer, criar; cultivar; hacer concebir, inspirar, dar lugar a, hacer surgir, hacer brotar. 7. Resucitar, vivificar, dar vida, revivir, poner en estado de actividad o vigor. 8. Levantar, reclutar, alistar. 9. Sacar contribuciones; recoger o juntar dinero sacándoselo a otros por cualquier medio. 10. Levantar, quitar lo impuesto, poner fin a, abandonar. *To raise a siege*, Levantar un sitio. *To raise an outcry*, Exclamar; armar un alboroto. *To raise the country*, Sublevar, alborotar, revolucionar un país. *To raise the nap of the cloth*, Perchar los paños, sacarles el pelo con el palmar. *To raise the dust*, Hacer o levantar polvo. *To raise pride in one*, Inspirar orgullo. *To raise the curtain* (en el teatro), Correr o levantar el telón.

Raiser [rêz'-er], *s.* 1. Levantador, el que alza o levanta; el que engrandece, exalta o ensalza. 2. Causador, productor, autor. 3. Fundador. 4. El que saca contribuciones; el que levanta ejércitos.

Raisin [rê'-zn], *s.* Pasa, la uva seca *Bloom raisins*, Pasas gorronas.

Raising [rêz'-ing], *s.* 1. Crianza. 2. Levantamiento. 3. Izamiento (de una bandera, etc.).

Raj [rāj], *s.* Soberanía, señorío (Indio.)

Raja, Rajah [ra'-ja], *s.* Rajá, soberano de la India.

Rake [rêk], *s.* 1. Rastro, mielga, rastrillo, instrumento de los labradores y hortelanos. 2. (Mar.) Lanzamiento, la caída para afuera de la roda o codaste. 3. Calavera, tunante, libertino o perdido (contracción de *Rakehell*). *Coal rake* u *oven rake*, Hurgón.

Rake, *va.* 1. Recoger con rastrillo, rastrillar; raer. 2. Rebuscar, escudriñar, buscar, mirar o examinar con atención. 3. Pasar por encima con el movimiento de un rastrillo; raspar ligeramente. 4. Cubrir, arrastrando tierra u otra cosa. 5. (Mil.) Enfilar, tirar a lo largo de; (Mar.) barrer de popa a proa.—*vn.* 1. Usar del rastro o de la mielga. 2. Buscar a tientas, buscar minuciosamente, escudriñar; ahorrar, acumular con cuidado. 3. Pasar con rapidez o violencia. 4. Tunar, vaguear, andar vagando, vivir como un libertino.

Rake, *vn.* Inclinarse, estar fuera de la perpendicular.

Raker [rêk'-er], *s.* 1. Raedera, raspadera. 2. Rastrillador, raedor; el que recoge alguna cosa con rastro o rastrillo.

Rakish [rêk'-ish], *a.* 1. Libertino, licencioso, perdido, disoluto. 2. (Mar.) Que tiene los mástiles inclinados hacia atrás de una manera insólita.

Rally [ral'-i], *va.* 1. (Mil.) Reunir y reanimar, rehacer, replegar, volver a juntar las tropas fugitivas o dispersas y ponerlas de nuevo en orden. 2. Ridiculizar; dar chanza o zumba.—*vn.* 1. (Mil.) Reunirse, reanimarse; recobrar las fuerzas, el vigor. 2. Burlarse o reírse de alguno, chancearse, zumbarse. *A rallying-word*, Grito o voz de batalla o de guerra: voz para animar las tropas o la gente.

Rally, *s.* 1. Unión o reunión pronta para un fin común, v. gr. de tropas dispersas. 2. Recuperación, acto de recobrar la condición normal después de un período de agotamiento o depresión; acción rápida y vigorosa de cualquier especie.

Ram [ram], *s.* 1. Morueco, carnero padre. 2. Instrumento para dar o aplastar con golpes fuertes; pisón. 3. Espolón, remate de la proa de los buques acorazados; también, ariete, buque blindado con espolón. 4. Ariete, máquina militar para batir las murallas. 5. Aries, signo del zodíaco.

Ram, *va.* 1. Apisonar, dar, golpear con un pisón, espolón o ariete. 2. Impeler con violencia, hacer entrar por fuerza; apretar; atacar un arma. 3. Atestar, henchir; atracar. *To ram down a paving*, Apisonar o pisonar el empedrado.

Ramadan [ram-a-dan'], *s.* Ramadán, la cuaresma de los mahometanos, noveno mes del año musulmán.

Ramble [ram'-bl], *vn.* 1. Vagar, corretear, ir a la ventura, andar vagando sin dirección fija. 2. Hacer algo o hablar sin objeto determinado. 3. Dar vueltas, serpentear. 4. Mostrar falta o carencia de plan o sistema: dícese de las cosas.

Ramble, *s.* 1. Correría, acción de ir de una parte a otra sin dirección, sin objeto fijo. 2. Sendero que serpentea, que tiene muchas vueltas y revueltas.

Rambler [ram'-bler], *s.* Vagabundo, vagamundo, tunante, callejero.

Ramie [ram'-i], *s.* 1. Ramio, planta perenne de la familia de las urticáceas propia de las Indias Orientales, con muchos tallos y hojas acorazonadas; la Bœhmeria nivea. 2. Fibra fina sacada de esta planta, y que empieza a usarse en sustitución del algodón; ramina.

Ramification [ram-i-fi-kê'-shun], *s.* Ramificación.

Ramify [ram'-i-fai], *vn.* Ramificarse, dividirse en ramas.—*va.* Dividir una cosa en ramificaciones.

Ramjet engine [ram'-jet en'-jin], *s.* (Aer.) Motor de retropropulsión a base de aire comprimido y combustible.

Rammer [ram'-er], *s.* 1. Maza. *Paving rammer*, Pisón, empedrador. 2. Atacador. 3. La baqueta de fusil o escopeta.

Rammish [ram'-ish], *a.* Que huele a chotuno; también, libidinoso.

Ramose [ra-mōs'], **Ramous** [rê'-mus], *a.* Ramoso.

Ramp [ramp], *s.* 1. Rampa, declive. 2. (Des.) Salto, brinco, pernada, zancada.

Ramp, *vn.* 1. Saltar, brincar; bailar, enredar o divertirse dando saltos o brincos. 2. Trepar como planta.—*va.* Sesgar.

Rampage [ram'-pêj], *s.* (Fam.) Alboroto, agitación turbulenta; brinco dado con cólera o violencia.

Rampancy [ram'-pan-si], *s.* Exuberancia, superabundancia, extravagancia en acciones o sentimientos.

Rampant [ram'-pant], *a.* 1. Exuberante, excesivo, desenfrenado, no restringido; lozano, que crece con abundancia. 2. (Her.) Rampante, en ademán de agarrar o asir. 3. (Arq.) Que tiene un estribo o contrafuerte más alto que otro.

Rampart [ram'-pārt], *s.* 1. Plataforma, terraplén; muralla, el terraplén con su parapeto. 2. Baluarte, amparo, defensa.

Rampion [ram'-pi-un], *s.* (Bot.) Rapónchigo, planta perenne de Europa, de raíz comestible; también una de varias otras plantas.

Ramrod [ram'-red], *s.* Baqueta de fusil; atacador de cañón.

Ramshackle [ram'-shac-l], *a.* Próximo a caerse en pedazos; viejo y descuidado; poco sólido.

Ramulose, **Ramulous** [ram'-yu-lōs, lus], *a.* (Biol.) Ramoso, que tiene muchas ramitas o ramas pequeñas.

Ran [ran], *pret.* de *To* RUN.

Rana [rê'-na], *s.* 1. Rana. 2. Príncipe; título del jefe reinante en varias partes de la India.

Ranch [ranch], *s.* (E. U. del Oeste) 1. Rancho, granja donde se cría ganado en grande escala. 2. Granja.

Rancher [ranch'-er], *s.* Hacendado, dueño de un rancho.

Rancid [ran'-sid], *a.* Rancio, de olor o gusto fuerte, el de substancias oleosas que empiezan a echarse a perder; acedo; rancioso.

Rancidness [ran'-sid-nes], **Rancidity** [ran'-sid-i-ti], *s.* Rancidez, ranciadura, lo rancio; olor rancioso, como el del aceite añejo.

Rancor [ran'-cer], *s.* Rencor, enemistad antigua, encono, inquina, malicia, odio profundo.

Rancorous [ran'-cer-us], *a.* Rencoroso: vengativo, malévolo.

Rancour, *s.* *V.* RANCOR.

Rand, *s.* Calzo del zapato.

Random [ran'-dum], *s.* 1. Falta de propósito o intención definidos; ventura, acaso; se emplea hoy sólo en la locución, *At random*, A la ventura, por acaso; a diestro y siniestro, al tuntún, a trochemoche. 2. Desatino, desacierto; cosa hecha o escogida sin método.—*a.* Fortuito, impensado, casual; desatinado. *Random shot*, (Art.) Tiro por elevación.

Randy, **Randie** [ran'-di], *a.* (Esco.) Desordenado, tumultuoso, alborotado.

Rang, *pret.* de *To* RING.

Range [rênj], *va.* 1. Recorrer, pasar, repasar, particularmente buscando alguna cosa; andar vagando; navegar, pasar cerca de la costa. 2. Colocar, ordenar, poner en hileras, en filas; arreglar. 3. Arreglar, clasificar, disponer en clases, divisiones sistemáticas o partidos; colocar en orden.—*vn.* 1. Vagar. 2. Colocarse; proseguir un rumbo. 3. Extenderse, estar situado en la misma dirección o en una línea paralela a otra; de aquí, tomar el mismo partido. 4. Variar, pasar de un punto a otro. *The thermometer may range forty degrees in one day*, El termómetro puede variar cuarenta grados (Fah.) en un día. 5. Tener lugar igual o correspondiente. 6. Ir, caminar: dícese de los proyectiles con referencia a su alcance y dirección.

Range, *s.* 1. Extensión o espacio en que cabe alguna cosa o al través del cual se mueve; período de tiempo que separa las reapariciones periódicas de una cosa; duración. 2. Vasta extensión de terrenos de pasto. 3. Alcance, v. g. el de un arma de fuego; extensión en que se hace sentir una influencia; duración. 4. Fila, hilera, ringlera, línea. 5. Clase, orden. 6. Línea de un tiro de artillería; sitio para tirar al blanco. *Range of a cable*, (Mar.) Aduja de cable. 7. Reja de cocina; fogón de rejas. 8. *Ranges*, *pl.* (Mar.) Cornamusas, piezas para amarrar varios cabos de labor. *Range of mountains*, Cordillera de montañas.

Range finder [rênj' faind-er], *s.* (Mil.) Telémetro.

Ranger [rênj'er], *s.* 1. Guardamayor de bosque. 2. Tunante, tuno, bribón, ladrón. 3. Perro ventor.

Ranine [rê'-nin], *a.* Perteneciente o parecido a la rana.

Rank [rank], *a.* 1. Lozano, exuberante, fértil; espeso, cerrado. 2. Rancio; que tiene olor fuerte y desabrido; fétido. 3. Insigne, acabado, rematado. 4. Grosero, áspero, basto.—*s.* 1. Fila, la serie de hombres puestos en línea; hilera, ringlera. 2. Clase, orden, grado de dignidad. 3. Calidad, dignidad o empleo honorífico. *A man of rank*, Hombre de condición o de distinción.

Rank, *va* Poner en fila, colocar, ordenar, disponer.—*vn.* Colocarse, alinearse.

Rankish [rank'-ish], *a.* Algo rancio.

Rankle [ran'-cl], *vn.* Enconarse, inflamarse, irritarse.

Rankly [ranc'-li], *adv.* 1. Toscamente, groseramente. 2. Pomposamente. 3. Ranciamente.

Rankness [ranc'-nes], *s.* 1. Exuberancia, fertilidad, fecundidad, abundancia. 2. Olor muy fuerte. 3. Carácter excesivo.

Ransack [ran'-sac], *va.* 1. Escudriñar, rebuscar, explorar o registrar todas las partes de. 2. (Des.) Saquear, pillar, robar.

Ransacking [ran'-sak-ing], *s.* Rebusco.

Ransom [ran'-sum], *s.* 1. Rescate, la cantidad que se paga para obtener la libertad de un preso o de un esclavo, o de mercancías capturadas o retenidas; también, en otros tiempos, multa considerable. 2. Rescate, obtención de la libertad mediante el pago de una suma.

Ransom, *va.* Rescatar, redimir, librar del cautiverio, de presidio, etc., pagando un rescate o una indemnización.

Ransomless [ran'-sum-les], *a.* Irrescatable, irredimible, que no se pue de rescatar o redimir.

Rant [rant], *vn.* Declamar con extravagancia, delirar, disparatar; vocear.

Rant, *s.* Lenguaje altisonante, campanudo, retumbante.

Ranter [rant'-er], *s.* Declamador, orador que emplea vehemencia inútil, energúmeno.

Ranunculaceous [ra-nun"-kiu-lê'-shus], *a.* Ranunculáceo, que se refiere a la familia de las ranunculáceas.

Ranunculus [ra-nun'-kiu-lus], *s.* (Bot.) Ranúnculo, botón de oro; género de plantas y su flor, típico de las ranunculáceas.

Rap [rap], *va.* y *vn.* 1. Golpear o dar un golpe vivo y repentino. *To rap at the door*, Tocar o llamar a la puerta. 2. Proferir de una manera seca y violenta.

Rap, *va.* (*pret.* y *pp.* RAPT o RAPPED). 1. Arrebatar; generalmente en el participio pasado *rapt*. 2. Quitar, tomar alguna cosa con violencia; tomar ávidamente para llevárselo.

Rap, *s.* 1. Golpe, ligero y vivo o el sonido de él; sopapo. *A rap on the knuckles*, Golpecito dado sobre los artejos. 2. Medio penique falso o contrahecho; de aquí fruslería, cosa sin valor. *I don't care a rap*, No se me da (importa) un bledo. 3. Madeja, cadejo de 120 yardas de hilo. *Rap on the nose*, Papirote.

Rapacious [ra-pê'-shus], *a.* 1. Rapaz, que tiene inclinación o está dado al hurto, robo o rapiña. 2. Voraz, acostumbrado a tomar por fuerza el alimento.

Rapaciously [ra-pê'-shus-li], *adv.* Con rapacidad.

Rapaciousness [ra-pê'-shus-nes], **Rapacity** [ra-pas'-i-ti], *s.* Rapacidad.

Rape [rêp], *s.* 1. Rapto, fuerza, la violencia que se hace a una mujer para gozarla; estupro. *To commit a rape*, Forzar a una mujer; cometer un rapto. 2. Rapiña, robo; acción de coger y llevarse algo. 3. Escobajo, el racimo separado de las uvas. 4. (Bot.) Nabo silvestre, colza, planta de cuya semilla se saca aceite. *Rape-seed*, Nabina o simiente de colza o nabo silvestre. 5. Filtro para hacer vinagre.

Raphe [rê'-fi o ra'-fê], *s.* Rafe, rugosidad o línea saliente a modo de costura, como las de la lengua, el periné y el escroto.

Rapid [rap'-id], *a.* Rápido, veloz; raudo; que se mueve con celeridad; que está hecho o acabado en poco tiempo; que va prontamente al término.—*s.* Recial, raudal, corriente impetuosa de los ríos; caída desde menor altura que la de una catarata; se usa generalmente en plural.

Rapidity [ra-pid'-i-ti], **Rapidness** [rap'-id-nes], *s.* Rapidez, velocidad, celeridad.

Rapidly [rap'-id-li], *adv.* Rápidamente, velozmente.

Rapier [rê'-pi-er], *s.* Espadín; florete, espetón, estoque; arma blanca con la que sólo se puede herir de punta.

Rapine [rap'-in], *s.* Rapiña, robo; violencia, fuerza.

Rapparee [rap-a-rî'], *s.* Nombre dado antiguamente en Irlanda a cierta clase de ladrones.

Rappee [rap-pî'], *s.* Rapé o tabaco rapé.

Rapper [rap'-er], *s.* 1. Golpeador; medio espiritista. 2. Llamador o aldabón de puerta. 3. (Vulg.) Un juramento.

Rapping [rap'-ing], *s.* Llamada.

Rapport [rap-pōrt' o ra-pōr'], *s.* Armonía, concordancia de relación, relación simpática. (Fr.)

Rapscallion [rap-scal'-yun], *s.* Vagabundo, canalla.

Rapt [rapt], *a.* Transportado, encantado, en éxtasis.

Raptorial [rap-tō'-ri-al], *a.* 1. De presa, rapaz. 2. Propio para asir y retener una presa.

Rapture [rap'-chur], *s.* 1. Rapto, enajenamiento, pasmo, éxtasis, arrebatamiento, arrobamiento, transporte. 2. Acto o expresión de arrobamiento, del mayor placer.

Raptured [rap'-churd], *a.* (Poco us.) Absorto, arrobado, arrebatado, transportado, fuera de sí.

Rapturous [rap'-chur-us], *a.* Maravilloso, pasmoso, hechicero.

Rapturously [rap'-chur-us-li], *adv.* Con éxtasis, con transportes, con el mayor placer.

Rare [rār], *a.* 1. Raro, que sucede pocas veces; que no se halla frecuentemente, poco común. 2. Muy apreciado por causa de rareza, de gran valor; sobresaliente, excelente; precioso. 3. Asado imperfectamente, que conserva el color de la carne cruda y sus jugos; medio crudo: dícese de la carne. *V.* UNDERDONE. 4. Raro, ralo (de la atmósfera). 5. Muy esparcido en el espacio; lejanos entre sí.

Rarebit [rār'-bit], *s.* Tostada con queso. *V.* RABBIT.

Raree-show [rār'-i-shō], *s.* Tutilimundi, mundinovi.

Rarefaction [rar-e-fac'-shun], *s.* Rarefacción.

Rarefiable [rar'-e-fai-a-bl], *a.* Capaz de rarefacción.

Rarefy [rar'-e-fai], *va.* Rarificar, rarefacer, enrarecer; dilatar un cuerpo por la dispersión de sus partículas en un espacio mayor.—*vn.* Rarefacerse, extenderse, dilatarse.

Rarely [rār'-li], *adv.* Raramente, por maravilla, rara vez.

Rareness [rār'-nes], *s.* 1. Rareza, calidad de lo poco común; singularidad; superioridad, excelencia. 2. Tenuidad. *V.* RARITY, 3ª acep.

Rareripe [rār'-raip], *a.* Precoz, que madura temprano.—*s.* Fruta precoz, particularmente ciertas variedades del melocotón.

Rarity [rar'-i-ti], *s.* 1. Raridad, rareza. 2. Cosa a que se atribuye gran precio a causa de su rareza. 3. Raridad, tenuidad, calidad de raro o ralo; lo opuesto a densidad.

Rascal [ras'-cal], *s.* Pícaro, bribón, bellaco, pillo, un hombre bajo, vil, ruin o indigno; belitre.

Rascality [ras-cal'-i-ti], *s.* Bellaquería, ruindad, carácter pícaro; acción vil o ruin; pillada.

Rascallion [ras-cal'-yun], *s.* Un villano, uno de la gentualla o de la ínfima plebe; un canalla.

Rascally [ras'-cal-i], *a.* Vil, bajo, ruin, indigno, infame.

Rase [rêz], *va.* 1. Arrasar, destruir, echar por tierra. 2. (Ant.) Rasar, pasar rozando. 3. (Des.) *V.* ERASE.

Rash [rash], *a.* Temerario, inconsiderado, atolondrado, irreflexivo, precipitado.—*s.* Roncha; sarpullido, erupción del cutis.

Rasher [rash'-er], *s.* Lonja, torrezno.

Rashly [rash'-li], *adv.* Temerariamente, imprudentemente, con precipitación.

Rashness [rash'-nes], *s.* 1. Temeridad, audacia, arrojo, irreflexión, precipitación. 2. Acción temeraria o inconsiderada.

Rasorial [ra-sō'-ri-al], *a.* Que cava la tierra con las uñas en busca de alimento, como la gallina; perteneciente a las gallináceas.

Rasp [rasp], *s.* 1. Escofina, raspa, raspador, rascador. 2. La acción o el sonido de escofinar.

Rasp, *va.* Raspar; escofinar.

Raspatory [ras'-pa-to-ri], *s.* Raspador, instrumento quirúrgico para igualar un hueso cariado.

Raspberry [raz'-ber-i], *s.* 1. (Bot.) Frambuesa. 2. Frambueso, planta que produce las frambuesas.

Raspberry-bush [raz'-ber-i-bush], *s.* (Bot.) Frambueso.

Rasping [rasp'-ing], *a.* Raedor, raspante; ronco, áspero; de aquí, irritante, que irrita o veja, atormentador.—*s.* Raspadura, raedura.

‡**Rasure** [rê'-zhur], *s.* Raspadura, raedura, borradura, testadura.

Rat [rat], *s.* 1. Rata, pequeño cuadrúpedo roedor que infesta las casas, los graneros, las embarcaciones, etc. 2. Como término de desprecio, el obrero que pide o acepta un jornal menor que el acordado, o el que se niega a tomar parte en una huelga o que toma el lugar de un huelgista; en la Gran Bretaña, desertor, tránsfuga de un partido; renegado. 3. (E. U.) Postizo para el pelo. *To smell a rat*, Oler el poste. *Rat-trap*, Ratonera. *Rat-catcher*, Cazador de ratas o ratones. *Rat-poison*, Cualquier veneno para matar ratas. *Rat-tail file*, Lima de cola de rata.

Rat, *va.* y *vn.* 1. (Fam.) Reemplazar los operarios que pertenecen a un gremio por otros no agremiados. 2. (Fam.) Trabajar por menor jornal que el fijado por los gremios de oficio; no tomar parte en una huelga. 3. Cazar ratas.

Ratable [rêt'-a-bl], *a.* 1. Sometida a contribucion por la ley. 2. Valuado, tasado, proporcionalmente. 3. Valuable, que puede valuarse.

Ratably [rêt'-a-bli], *adv.* A prorrata o según prorrata.

Ratafia [rat-a-fî'-a], *s.* Ratafía, especie de rosoli hecho con aguardiente y almendras de albaricoque.

Ratan [ra-tan'], *s.* Rota, caña de Indias; roten, junco o bastón hecho del tallo de la rota. *V.* RATTAN.

Ratany, Ratanhy [rat'-a-ni], *s.* Ratania, arbusto del Perú, de raíz muy astringente. Krameria triandra.

Ratch [rach], *s.* Una rueda de reloj que tiene doce dientes.

Ratchet [rach'-et], *s.* 1. Rueda, dentada con fiador; fiador, (Amer.) trinquete. 2. Diente del caracol en la relojería.

Rate [rêt], *s.* 1. Tasa, razón, proporción, medida de alguna cosa; cantidad o grado relativo o comparativo. *At the rate of*, A razón de. 2. Precio o valor fijo; (Com.) curso, tasa, tipo. 3. Clase, grado, orden, clase de un navío o de una embarcación (buque mercante). 4. Variación diaria del reloj. 5. Modo, manera. *At any rate*, De todos modos, de cualquier modo; sea como se fuere. *An extravagant rate*, Precio exorbitante. 6. (Gran Bret.) Derecho parroquial; contribución impuesta para usos locales en contraposición a las del gobierno general. *Book of rates*, Arancel de los derechos de aduana. *First-rate*, De primera clase, lo mejor. *Market rate*, Tipo del mercado. *A first-rate author*, Un escritor de primer orden. *A first-rate singer*, Un cantante de primera fuerza. *Poor-rate*, Tasa o contribución para socorrer á los pobres. *A second-rate ship*, Un buque de segunda clase. *At that rate*, De ese modo; si es así. *At the rate you are going on*, Al paso que va Vd. *At a furious rate*, A todo correr.

Rate, *va.* 1. Tasar, valuar, apreciar, arreglar y fijar el valor relativo de alguna cosa. 2. Imponer, repartir una tasa o derecho (sobre). 3. Tomar la medida de; calcular la variación diaria de un reloj o cronómetro, comparándolo con un regulador de hora exacta.—*vn.* Ser estimado o valuado; tener valor.

Rate, *va.* y *vn.* Regañar, reñir a uno; poner a alguno como nuevo. *V.* BERATE.

Rateable [rêt'-a-bl], *a.* *V.* RATABLE.

Rateen, *s.* *V.* RATTEEN.

Rather [radh'-er o radh'-er], *adv.* 1. De mejor gana; más bien, antes; puede ser; tal vez, quizá; algo, un poco. 2. Antes, con preferencia a otra cosa. 3. Antes bien, más presto. 4. Por mejor decir; al contrario. 5. (Fam.) Muy; en sentido irónico. *I would rather go than stay*, Más quisiera irme que quedarme. *I had rather*, (o mejor) *I would rather*, Me gustaría más, preferiría. *This work is rather expensive*, No deja de ser cara esta obra. *He was rather* *noisy*, No dejaba de meter bastante bulla. *I would rather not*, Expresión muy común entre los ingleses para denotar que ciertamente no quiere una persona la cosa que le ofrecen, y corresponde a de veras no la quiero, o ciertamente no me gusta; más bien no. *Men loved darkness rather than light*, Los hombres prefirieron las tinieblas á la luz. *The rather as, the rather for*, Tanto más que; tanto mejor que. *She is rather pretty*, Es bastante bonita. *The yellow, or rather the buff, tint*, El matiz amarillo, o por mejor decir, el de ante.

Ratification [rat-i-fi-kē'-shun], *s.* Ratificación, confirmación, aprobación.

Ratifier [rat'-i-fai-ẹr], *s.* Ratificador.

Ratify [rat'-i-fai], *va.* Ratificar, aprobar o confirmar.

Rating [rēt'-ing], *s.* Determinación de una tasa, precio o grado.

Ratio [rē'-shi-o], *s.* 1. Razón, relación de grado, número, etc.; cantidad relativa, proporción. 2. (Mat.) Razón, relación entre dos números o dos cantidades de la misma naturaleza. 3. (Ant.) Razón, causa, argumento. *In the inverse ratio*, En razón inversa.

Ratiocinate [rash-i-os'-i-nēt], *vn.* Raciocinar.

Ration [rē'-shun o rash'-un], *s.* (Mil.) Ración, la porción de pan, carne, forraje, etc., que se da para cada día en el ejército o en la marina.

Ration [rē'-shun], *va.* Racionar, distribuir artículos de primera importancia cuando hay escasez.

Rational [rash'-un-al], *a.* 1. Racional; fundado en la razón. 2. Razonable, según razón; motivado. 3. Juicioso, de juicio. 4. Racional, que sólo se concibe por la razón.

Rational, *s.* Un ser racional.

Rationale [rash-o-nē'-li], *s.* Explicación de las razones en que se funda alguna cosa.

Rationalism [rash'-un-al-izm], *s.* 1. Racionalismo, sistema de opiniones deducidas de la razón sola; lo opuesto a *supernaturalism*. 2. La doctrina de que la razón proporciona ciertos elementos que son base de la experiencia y sin los cuales la experiencia es imposible; lo contrario de *empiricism*, empirismo.

Rationalist [rash'-un-al-ist], *s.* El que procede, obra o explica alguna cosa solamente por las reglas de la razón.

Rationalistic, Rationalistical [rash-un-al-is'-tic, al], *a.* Racionalista, perteneciente al racionalismo; conforme con los principios del racionalismo.

Rationality [rash-un-al'-i-ti], **Rationalness** [rash'-un-al-nes], *s.* Racionalidad, la conveniencia o conformidad de las cosas con la razón.

Rationalization [rash-un-al-i-zē'-shun], *s.* Racionalización.

Rationalize [rash'-un-al-aiz], *va.* 1. Explicar racionalmente. 2. Reorganizar racionalmente.

Rationally [rash'-un-al-i], *adv.* Racionalmente.

Rationing [rē'-shun-ing], *s.* Racionamiento, distribución de artículos de primera importancia en época de escasez.

Ratlin [rat'-lin] o **Ratling** [rat'-ling], *s.* Mar.) Rebenque, flechaste.

Ratoon [ra-tūn'], *s.* 1. Vástago, renuevo que brota de la raíz de una planta desbrozada, como de la caña de azúcar. 2. Una de las hojas de en medio en la planta del tabaco.

Ratsbane [rats'-bēn], *s.* Arsénico, un veneno mineral.

Rattan, Ratan [rat-tan'], *s.* 1. Roten, rota (rotino); (Amer.) bejuco; planta de los géneros Calamus o Rhapis, de la familia de las palmeras; su tallo largo y flexible. 2. Bastón o varilla de roten.

Ratteen [ra-tīn'], *s.* Ratina, tela de lana que tiene granillo.

Rattle [rat'-l], *vn.* 1. Zumbar, zurrir, hacer un ruido bronco y confuso; rechinar, hacer ruido con golpes repetidos ludiendo entre sí cuerpos poco sonoros. 2. Hablar rápida y tontamente, parlotear. 3. Moverse o funcionar con ruido desapacible. —*va.* 1. Sonar o tocar alguna cosa de modo que haga ruido; hacer producir una serie de sonidos breves y agudos en rápida sucesión; sacudir con ruido. 2. Atolondrar o aturdir con ruido. 3. Proferir, articular, o producir de una manera ruidosa. 4. (Mar.) Atar los rebenques a. *The wind rattled the shutters*, El viento sacudió los postigos de la ventana. *To rattle away*, Parlotear; rodar a distancia, haciendo ruido. *To rattle in the throat*, Tener un moribundo el hipo o sarrillo; familiarmente, hervirle el pecho. (Mex.) Tener el estertor.

Rattle, *s.* 1. Sonido o ruido repetido vivamente; rechino, zumbido, zurrido. 2. Sonajero o sonajillas de niños; matraca; también la serie de anillos sueltos y córneos en la cola de la culebra de cascabel. 3. Parla, charla; habla rápida y ruidosa. *The rattles*, (1) Estertor del moribundo. (2) *V.* CROUP.

Rattleheaded [rat'-l-hed-ed], *a.* Ligero de cascos, casquivano.

Rattlepate [rat'l-pēt], **Rattleskull** [rat'-l-scul], *s.* Hablantín, hablanchín.

Rattlesnake [rat'-l-snēc], *s.* Culebra de cascabel, crótalo. *Rattlesnake-root*, Lechera; hierba perenne del género Prenanthes, con raíz gruesa y amarga.

Rattling [rat'-ling], *s.* El hipo o sarrillo de los moribundos; estertor; ruido; rechino; zollipo o sollozo con hipo.—*a.* (Ger.) Vivo, sorprendente, alegre.

Raucous [rō'-cus], *a.* Ronco, de sonido áspero, bronco.

Ravage [rav'-ẹj], *va.* Saquear, pillar; asolar, talar, destruir.

Ravage, *s.* Asolamiento, ruina, destrozo, destrucción; saqueo.

Ravager [rav'-ẹj-ẹr], *s.* Pillador, saqueador; asolador.

Rave [rēv], *vn.* 1. Delirar, desvariar; disparatar, decir extravagancias; encolerizarse, enfurecerse, ponerse fuera de sí o salirse de sus casillas. 2. Obrar, moverse o arrojarse de una manera tumultuosa y ruidosa; correr con ímpetu como un torrente. También se usa este verbo en sentido activo. *To rave after*, Querer a toda costa, despepitarse por algo. *He raved about his painting*, Disparataba con motivo de su cuadro.

Ravel [rav'-l], *va.* 1. Deshilar, deshilachar, destejer, deshacer un tejido; desenlazar; a menudo con *out*. 2. (Ant.) Enredar, enmarañar (acepción original).—*vn.* 1. Deshilarse, destorcerse; deshacerse; se usa a menudo con *out*. 2. (Ant.) Enredarse, confundirse. *To ravel out*, Deshilarse un tejido.

Ravelin [rav'-lin], *s.* (Fort.) Rebellín, obra exterior separada de la fortificación.

Raveling, Ravelling [rav'-l-ing], *s.* 1. Hilacha. 2. Acto de deshilachar o deshilacharse.

Raven [rē'-vn], *s.* (Orn.) Cuervo, ave omnívora de gran tamaño, con las plumas de la garganta largas y lanceoladas. Corvus corax.—*a.* Negro y luciente como el plumaje del cuervo.

Raven [rav'-n], *va.* y *vn.* 1. Apresar, proporcionarse algo con violencia; prender por fuerza. 2. Devorar, tragar con voracidad; echarse sobre la presa, hacer presa de.—*s.* Presa, botín; alimento obtenido a viva fuerza; despojo, rapiña.

Ravening [rav'-n-ing], *s.* Rapiña, voracidad.—*pa.* de *To* RAVEN.

Ravenous [rav'-n-us], *a.* Voraz, hambriento, tragón, golosazo; rapaz.

Ravenously [rav'-n-us-li], *adv.* Vorazmente.

Ravin [rav'-in], *s.* Presa, rapiña.

Ravine [ra-vīn'], *s.* Barranca, quebrada, hondonada.

Raving [rēv'-ing], *s.* Desvarío, delirio.—*pa.* de *To* RAVE.

Ravingly [rēv'-ing-li], *adv.* Disparatadamente, locamente.

Ravish [rav'-ish], *va.* 1. Arrebatar, llevar tras sí, atraer, encantar. 2. Estuprar, forzar a una mujer. 3. (Ant.) Arrebatar, quitar, tomar por fuerza.

Ravisher [rav'-ish-ẹr], *s.* Estuprador, forzador; arrebatador.

Ravishing [rav'-ish-ing], *pa.* Encantador, pasmoso, embriagador.

Ravishingly [rav'-ish-ing-li], *adv.* De una manera encantadora.

Ravishment [rav'-ish-mẹnt], *s.* 1. Rapto, transporte, éxtasis, arrobamiento. 2. Fuerza, estupro, violación de una mujer.

Raw [rō], *a.* 1. Crudo, que no está cocido, asado o frito; no aderezado ni guisado. 2. Raído, desollado vivo, que no está cubierto con pellejo o piel, o que está lastimado: dícese también de los huesos que no tienen carne encima. 3. Crudo, frío y húmedo. 4. Sin preparar, crudo, en estado natural; verde; no suavizado o sin tono, v. g. los colores; bruto, sin refinar, sin purificar. 5. Nuevo, nuevamente hecho o fabricado. 6. Novato, falto de experiencia, poco versado, ignorante, indisciplinado. *Raw weather*, Tiempo crudo o frío y húmedo. *Raw silk*, Seda cruda o en rama. *Raw spirits*, Licores puros o sin mezcla. *A raw apple*, Una manzana cruda. *Cucumbers are generally eaten raw*, Los pepinos se comen generalmente crudos. *Raw flesh*, Carne desollada, viva. *Raw soldiers, troops*, Soldados bisoños, tropas bisoñas, mal aguerridas. *Raw hand*, Tirón, novato, novicio. *Raw material*, Materia bruta, materia prima. *Raw sugar*, Azúcar bruto, sin refinar.

Rawboned [rō'-bōnd], *a.* Huesudo, membrudo; magro, enjuto.

Raw deal [rō dīl'], *s.* Mala pasada.

Rawhead [rō'-hed], *s.* Espectro, fantasma, espantajo. *Rawhead and bloody bones*, Coco, espantajo de niños.

Rawhide [rō'-haid], *a.* Hecho de cuero crudo.—*s.* 1. Cuero crudo, sin curtir. 2. Látigo hecho de este cuero.

Rawish [rō'-ish], *a.* Algo crudo; un poco frío u húmedo.

Rawness [rō'-nes], *s.* Crudeza, falta de experiencia.

Ray [rê], *s.* 1. La línea a lo largo de la cual se propaga una forma cualquiera de energía radiante; rayo de luz. 2. Rayo, una de las varias líneas que salen de un objeto. 3. Rayo, línea recta por donde se considera que va o se dirige una cosa. 4. Línea, raya; fila derecha. 5. (Zool.) Parte o prominencia parecida a un rayo; como la espina de la aleta de los peces, el brazo de una estrella de mar, etc. 6. (Bot.) Lígula, florecilla ligulada de las sinantéreas. 7. Raya, pez cartilaginoso, que tiene el cuerpo muy ancho y aplanado por delante.

Ray, *va.* 1. Rayar, hacer rayas; proveer de rayas. 2. Emitir.

Ray-cloth [rê'-clōth], *s.* Paño que no está teñido.

Ray-grass [rê'-grqs], *s.* (Bot.) Joyo, cominillo.

Rayon [rê'-qn], *s.* Rayón, fibra de celulosa modificada.

Raze [rêz], *va.* 1. Arrasar, demoler, echar por tierra, destruir enteramente. 2. *V.* Razel. 3. (Ant.) Extirpar; tachar, borrar.

Razee [ra-zí'], *va.* 1. Rebajar, v. g. reducir a menor grado un buque de guerra. 2. Reducir, minorar, cercenar, abreviar.—*s.* Un buque rebajado, o reducido a menor porte.

Razor [rê'-zqr], *s.* Navaja de barbero o de afeitar, verduguillo. *To set a razor,* Amolar una navaja de afeitar; vaciarla. *Razor-grinder,* Vaciador de navajas de afeitar. *Razor-strop,* Suavizador, asentador de navajas. *Razor-sheath* o *razor-shell,* Navaja, una especie de marisco.

Razor-bill [rê'-zqr-bil], *s.* (Orn.) Alca, ave palmeada.

Razor blade [rê'-zqr blêd], *s.* Hoja de afeitar.

Re [rí]. Partícula inseparable que denota repetición o acción retrógrada.

Re [rê], *s.* Re, segunda nota de la escala musical.

Reabsorb [rí-ab-sērb'], *va.* Reabsorber; absorber o embeber de nuevo lo que se había derramado, extravasado.

Reabsorption [rí-ab-sērp'-shun], *s.* Reabsorción, acción de absorber de nuevo.

Reaccess [rí-ac'-ses], *s.* Visita repetida; (Med.) recidiva, vuelta.

Reach [rích], *va.* 1. Alargar, extender, tender. 2. Alcanzar. 3. Llegar o alcanzar a alguna cosa distante; conseguir; penetrar. 4. Alcanzar o llegar hasta algún término. 5. Coger o tomar alguna cosa de un paraje distante y darla. *Reach me my hat,* Alcánceme Vd. el sombrero; entrégueme Vd. mi sombrero. 6. Lograr, obtener, conseguir (con esfuerzo).—*vn.* 1. Extenderse, llegar. 2. Alcanzar, penetrar; esforzarse. 3. Coger alguna cosa con la mano. 4. (Mar.) Ceñir el viento, navegar de bolina. *He reached out his plate,* Alargó su plato. *To reach home,* Llegar a casa. *The letter reached me,* La carta llegó a mis manos. *To reach the heart,* Llegar al corazón, tocar al corazón. *As far as the eye could reach,* Tan lejos como alcanzaba la vista. *To reach into,* Penetrar en. *To reach after,* Procurar, hacer esfuerzos para alcanzar u obtener. *To reach back,* Remontar, alcanzar. *To reach down,* Bajar, descender. *In an overcoat which reached below his knees,* En un sobretodo que le llegaba más abajo de las rodillas.

Reach, *s.* 1. Alcance, extensión. *Reach of thought,* Capacidad. 2. Alcance, poder, facultad; capacidad. *It is not within my reach,* No puedo alcanzarlo; no está a mi alcance, o no puedo entenderlo bien; capacidad de llegar, de tocar con la mano o con algo que se tiene en la mano; de aquí, alcance, extensión de la inteligencia, de la influencia mental. 3. Punto, posición, o resultado ganados o asequibles. 4. Extensión no interrumpida de una corriente de agua; vista. 5. Lanza o barra que une el eje posterior de un vehículo con la parte delantera. 6. (Mar.) El acto de navegar, o la distancia navegada en una sola bordada. *Out of reach,* Fuera de alcance. *One boundless reach of sky,* Una extensión ilimitada de cielo.

React [rí-act'], *va.* 1. Reaccionar, producir una acción como en respuesta o resistencia a otra. 2. Rechazar, resistir a la acción de un cuerpo por una fuerza contraria. 3. Obrar recíprocamente dos o más agentes químicos o físicos.

Reactance [rg-act'-ans], *s.* Reactancia, reacción de autoinducción.

Reaction [rí-ac'-shun], *s.* 1. Reacción, acción opuesta o contraria; la tendencia hacia un estado precedente u opuesto; la fuerza que opone el cuerpo impelido a la del impulsor. 2. Acción mutua o recíproca de agentes químicos. 3. Cualquier acción debida a un estímulo.

Reactionary [rg-ac'-shun-g-ri], *a.* Reaccionario.—*s.* y *a.* Derechista, reaccionario (en sus tendencias políticas).

Reactionist [rg-ac'-shun-ist], *s.* Reaccionario, partidario conservador, contrario a la revolución.

Reactive [rg-act'-iv], *a.* Reactivo, que causa, produce u opera reacción; que tiende a operar una reacción, o que tiene la fuerza de obrar en sentido contrario.

Reactor [rí-ac'-tgr], *s.* (Elec.) Reactor.

Read [ríd], *va.* (*pret.* y *pp.* Read [red]). 1. Leer; pasar la vista por lo escrito, pronunciando o no las palabras. 2. Leer alto, proferir los sonidos que de ordinario se dan a las palabras. 3. Comprender, leer, ver, percibir, reconocer; descubrir o comprender por caracteres, signos o rasgos. 4. Interpretar, explicar; imputar, v. g. una significación oculta. 5. Leer, observar o anunciar las indicaciones de un instrumento. 6. Saber por medio de libros. 7. Estudiar, aprender. 8. (Mús.) Leer, seguir de un modo inteligente, tocar o cantar las notas de una composición. 9. Producir un resultado cualquiera por medio de la lectura. *To read one to sleep,* Adormecer (a uno) leyendo. 10. Enseñar, como con un libro; amonestar, aconsejar, avisar.—*vn.* 1. Leer, notar o comprender los caracteres o el contenido de un libro o manuscrito. 2. Leer, saber; se usa a menudo con *of* o *about.* 3. Leer en alta voz el contenido de un libro o manuscrito. 4. Aprender leyendo, estudiar; entregarse al estudio, practicar mucho la lectura. Se usa a menudo con *up.* 5. Leerse, aparecer en la lectura. 6. Comprender o expresar la música escrita. 7. Dar una conferencia pública o una serie de ellas. *The deed having been read,* Dada lectura del instrumento auténtico. *To read offhand,* Leer de corrida. *To read between the lines,* Leer entre líneas, es decir, inferir lo que no está expresado claramente. *To read by sound,* Recibir un despacho telegráfico, oyendo los sonidos del instrumento receptor. *To read out,* Expulsar a un miembro de una asociación. *The passage reads thus,* El pasaje dice así o lee así: (presenta esta variante). *To read law,* Leer, estudiar derecho. *To read about,* Leer acerca de algo, hacer un curso de, aprender leyendo. *To read again, to read over again,* Volver a leer, leer otra vez. *To read on,* Proseguir o continuar leyendo. *To read over,* Leerlo todo, recorrer un escrito. *To read aloud,* Leer en alta voz.

Read [red], *pp.* del verbo *To* Read. Leído; que se instruye leyendo; instruído, erudito. *Well-read man* Hombre leído o erudito.

Readable [ríd'-a-bl], *a.* Leíble, legible, que se puede leer; de lectura fácil y agradable.

Readability, Readableness [ríd-a-bil'-i-ti, ríd'-a-bl-nes], *s.* Calidad de legible; de aquello cuya lectura causa placer.

Reader [ríd'-gr], *s.* 1. Lector, el que lee. 2. Libro de lectura. *Lay-reader,* Lego autorizado para leer las oraciones en una iglesia.

Readily [red'-i-li], *adv.* Prontamente, luego; con placer, de buena gana.

Readiness [red'-i-nes], *s.* 1. Calidad de dispuesto, preparado a o listo para; en condición conveniente. 2. Prontitud, facilidad, aptitud, desembarazo. *Readiness of wit,* Viveza o vivacidad de talento o de ingenio. 3. Voluntad, gana, buena voluntad, disposición favorable. *Readiness of speech,* Facilidad de palabra. *Readiness in doing anything,* Prontitud para hacer alguna cosa. *We had got all in readiness,* Todo lo habíamos preparado.

Reading [ríd'-ing], *s.* 1. Lección, lectura, acción de leer, en cualquiera de las acepciones de este verbo; relación pública; lectura de un proyecto de ley. 2. Estudio de los libros; investigación literaria, educación literaria. 3. Lectura, lo que se lee, o que se señala para su lectura. 4. La indicación de un instrumento graduado. 5. Lección, variante, texto; la forma en que aparece algún pasaje, palabra o cosa en un manuscrito o libro determinado. 6. Glosa, interpretación, de una adivinanza, etc.; delineación. —*a.* Que lee mucho; que le gusta mucho leer. *Reading-room,* Gabinete de lectura; sala donde hay libros, o diarios y publicaciones periódicas para leer. *Reading matter,* Material de lectura; la parte literaria o de noticias en algún periódico, en oposición a los anuncios.

Readjust [rí-ad-just'], *va.* 1. Ajustar de nuevo; poner en su primer estado. 2. Ajustar de una manera diferente; poner en relación diferente.

Readmission [rî-ad-mish'-un], *s.* Readmisión.
Readmit [rî-ad-mit'], *va.* Readmitir, volver a admitir, admitir de nuevo.
Readorn [rî-a-dōrn'], *va.* Readornar, adornar de nuevo.
Ready [red'-i], *a.* 1. Preparado, dispuesto, aparejado para alguna cosa, aprestado; provisto de todo lo que es necesario; en condición para usar u obrar. *Ready to burst,* A pique de reventar. *To make ready,* Preparar. 2. Inclinado, propenso, dispuesto. 3. Que está para; no lejos de; en el momento de. 4. Listo, pronto; contante, de contado; que no se difiere. *Ready money,* Dinero contante. *Ready payment,* Paga pronta. 5. Fácil, lo que no cuesta trabajo. 6. A la mano, al alcance; socorrido, útil, disponible sin dilación. 7. Pronto, ligero. *All things are ready,* Todo está listo, todo se halla dispuesto. *Ready for departure,* Preparado para salir o irse, listo para la marcha. *A ready retort,* Una réplica pronta. *Ready to find fault,* Inclinado a poner faltas. *A ready method,* Un método fácil. *He was ready to die,* Estaba para morir, en vísperas de morir. *Ready-made,* Ya hecho; confeccionado. *Ready-witted,* De ingenio vivo, pronto.—*adv.* (Poco us.) Prontamente, presto.
Reaffirmance [rî-af-fẹr'-mans], *s.* Segunda confirmación o afirmación; aseveración.
Reagent [rî-ê'-jent], *s.* (Quím.) Reactivo, cualquier agente químico que se usa para descubrir los cuerpos simples que entran en la composición de los compuestos.
Real [rî'-al], *a.* 1. Real, verdadero, que existe de hecho; no imaginario ni teórico. 2. Efectivo, genuino; no artificial, no falso ni contrahecho; sincero. 3. (For.) Perteneciente o referente a las tierras o bienes raíces; que se refiere a las cosas en contraposición a las personas. *Real sherry wine,* Vino de Jerez legítimo. *Real property,* Propiedad inmueble, bienes raíces. *Real estate,* Bienes raíces.—*s.* Real, una moneda de España. *A real vellon,* Un real de vellón, la vigésima parte de un peso o duro, igual a *a half dime* o cinco centavos de los Estados Unidos.
Realgar [rî-al'-gar], *s.* Rejalgar, sulfuro rojo de arsénico.
Realism [rî'-al-izm], *s.* 1. Realismo, la negación del ideal; copia de la naturaleza sin ninguna idealidad, en la literatura y en las artes. 2. Doctrina filosófica de los realistas.
Realist [rî'-al-ist], *s.* Realista, el que mira las ideas abstractas como seres reales; el que sostiene la doctrina de que el hombre puede ver y ve verdaderos objetos externos.
Realistic [rî-al-is'-tic], *a.* 1. Realista, conforme a los principios y métodos del realismo. 2. Que parece estar vivo (a veces, en sentido despectivo).
Reality [rî-al'-i-ti], *s.* 1. Realidad, entidad. 2. Carácter o cosa real. 3. (Raro. For.) *V.* REALTY. *In reality,* En realidad, en verdad.
Realizable [rî'-al-aiz''-a-bl], *a.* Realizable, que se puede realizar.
Realization [rî''-al-i-zê'-shun], *s.* Realización.
Realize [rî'-al-aiz], *va.* 1. Percibir como realidad; comprender la verdadera naturaleza de algo; sentir, apreciar completa y vivamente; considerar, admitir como real. 2. Realizar, hacer real; poner en existencia verdadera. 3. Hacer parecer como verdadero: presentar al ánimo como existente. 4. Ganar, obtener como ganancia o provecho. 5. (Com.) Realizar, vender géneros, convertir su propiedad en dinero contante. *His hopes could never be realized,* Sus esperanzas no pudieron realizarse jamás. *To realize much profit from,* Obtener grandes ganancias de algo.
Really [rî'-al-i], *adv.* Realmente, efectivamente, verdaderamente.
Realm [relm], *s.* 1. Reino. *The peers of the realm,* Los pares o grandes del reino; los próceres. 2. Dominio, jurisdicción o alcance de un poder o influencia cualquiera. 3. División del globo con respecto a su fauna.
Realty [rî'-al-ti], *s.* (For.) Bienes raíces; fincas, bienes heredados, patrimonio en tierras.
Ream [rîm], *s.* Resma, el mazo de veinte manos de papel.
Ream [rîm], *va.* Ensanchar o aumentar gradualmente un agujero.
Reamer [rîm'-ẹr], *s.* Escariador.
Reanimate [rî-an'-i-mêt], *va.* Reanimar, hacer revivir, dar nuevas fuerzas o vigor; resucitar.
Reannex [rî-an-ecs'], *va.* Reunir, unir de nuevo, volver a unir.
Reap [rîp], *va.* 1. Segar, cortar y recoger las mieses; cosechar los frutos de un campo. 2. Obtener o sacar fruto de alguna cosa. *What benefit shall you reap by it?* ¿Qué provecho sacará Vd. de ello?—*vn.* 1. Hacer el agosto, hacer la siega, hacer la cosecha por medio de una segadora o de otro modo. 2. Recibir como recompensa, o como fruto de su trabajo.
Reaper [rîp'-ẹr], *s.* 1. Segador, el que siega. 2. Segadora, máquina para segar las mieses. Contiene a menudo una agavilladora o mecanismo para atar los haces. *V.* HARVESTER.
Reaping [rîp'-ing], *s.* Siega, cosecha; acción de segar, de hacer el agosto. *Reaping-hook,* Hoz, segadera, instrumento para segar las mieses. *Reaping-machine,* Segadora; máquina con que se cortan y agavillan las mieses. *Reaping-time,* Siega, el tiempo de segar las mieses.
Reappear [rî-ap-pîr'], *vn.* Reaparecer.
Reappearance [rî-ap-pîr'-ans], *s.* 1. Reaparición, nueva aparición. 2. Segunda entrada en escena de un actor.
Reappoint [rî-ap-peint'], *va.* Designar o fijar de nuevo; dar una nueva cita, y particularmente nombrar de nuevo para un empleo.
Reapportion [rî-ap-pōr'-shun], *va.* Proporcionar otra vez, repartir de nuevo.
Rear [rîr], *a.* Postrero, trasero, que está, se queda o viene detrás; último, posterior. *Rear wall,* Pared trasera o posterior.—*s.* 1. Fondo, la parte posterior. 2. Lugar o posición a espaldas o detrás de alguna persona o cosa. 3. (Mil.) Retaguardia; la última clase. *Rear-guard,* Retaguardia. *Rear rank,* Ultima fila. *To be in the rear,* Estar a la cola. *To bring up the rear,* Cerrar la marcha, hacer o formar la cola.
Rear, *va.* 1. Levantar, alzar, ensalzar, elevar. 2. Erigir, construir. 3. Criar, cuidar de alguna persona desde su niñez hasta la edad madura; educar, instruir. 4. Levantar desde una condición caída; reanimar, ensalzar, exaltar.—*vn.* Encabritarse (el caballo). *To rear a family,* Criar una familia. *To rear a building,* Erigir, construir un edificio. *The horse reared,* El caballo se encabritó.
Rear-admiral [rîr-ad'-mi-ral], *s.* Contraalmirante.
Rearm [rî-arm'], *va.* Rearmar.
Rearmament [rî-ār'-ma-mẹnt], *s.* Rearme.
Rearrange [rî-a-rênj'], *va.* Volver a arreglar.
Rear-view mirror [rîr'-viū mir'-ẹr], *s.* Espejo de retrovisión.
Rearward [rîr'-ward], *a.* Postrero, que viene último ó á la cola.—*adv.* Detrás, hacia ó en la parte posterior.—*s.* (Ant.) Retaguardia; la última clase.
Reason [rî'-zn], *s.* 1. Razón, la facultad de discurrir; la potencia intelectual; racionalidad. 2. Fundamento, motivo, causa. 3. Razón, justicia, derecho. 4. Razón, argumento, prueba. 5. (Lóg.) Principio o motivo lógico para pensar, antecedente; premisa, particularmente la premisa menor. 6. Intuición, conocimiento infuso. 7. Moderación. *To yield to reason,* Ceder a la razón. *In reason,* Con derecho, en buena justicia. *We will give him anything in reason,* Le daremos lo que sea justo. *By reason of,* A causa de. *It stands to reason,* Así lo quiere, lo pide la razón. *There is reason to suspect that fellow,* Hay motivos para tener sospechas de ese individuo.
Reason, *vn.* Razonar, raciocinar; debatir, disputar.—*va.* Investigar, escudriñar, examinar; discutir.
Reasonable [rî'-zn-a-bl], *a.* 1. Racional, razonable; conforme o según la razón; dirigido por la razón, que piensa u obra según los consejos de la razón; justo, equitativo. 2. Arreglado, mediano, mediocre.
Reasonableness [rî'-zn-a-bl-nes], *s.* Racionalidad; naturaleza razonable, conformidad con la razón; moderación; justicia, equidad.
Reasonably [rî'-zn-a-bli], *adv.* Razonablemente.
Reasoner [rî'-zn-ẹr], *s.* Razonador, el que razona o discute.
Reasoning [rî'-zn-ing], *s.* Raciocinio, argumento, discurso.
Reasonless [rî'-zn-les], *a.* Sin razón, desrazonable.
Reassemble [rî-as-sem'-bl], *va.* Juntar de nuevo, reunir, recoger.
Reassert [rî-as-sẹrt'], *va.* Asegurar, afirmar de nuevo.
Reassign [rî-as-sain'], *va.* Asignar, destinar o repartir de nuevo; retroceder.
Reassume [rî-as-siūm'], *va.* Reasumir, volver a tomar.
Reassumption [rî-as-sump'-shun], *s.* Reasunción.
Reassurance [rî-as-shūr'-ans], *s.* 1. Confianza establecida; afirmación repetida, certeza restablecida. 2. (Com.) Segundo seguro, el acto de volver a asegurar las mercancías o géneros por haber quebrado, o temerse que quiebren los primeros aseguradores.
Reassure [rî-as-shūr'], *va.* Alentar; volver a asegurar.
Reattachment [rî-at-tach'-mẹnt], *s.* (For.) El reembargo de alguna cosa.

Rebate [rẹ-bêt'], *va.* y *vn.* 1. Rebajar, deducir, disminuir de una cuenta, de una factura; hacer una rebaja. 2. Embotar.
Rebate, Rebatement [rī-bêt'-mẹnt], *s.* Rebaja, descuento, deducción; diminución.
Rebec [rī'-bec], *s.* Rabel, la forma primitiva del violín, con una, dos, o tres cuerdas.
Rebel [reb'-el], *a.* y *s.* Rebelde.
Rebel [rẹ-bel'], *vn.* Rebelarse, levantarse, sublevarse, alzarse.
Rebellion [rẹ-bel'-yun], *s.* Rebelión, levantamiento, revuelta, sublevación.
Rebellious [rẹ-bel'-yus], *a.* Rebelde, amotinado, sedicioso, sublevado.
Rebelliously [rẹ-bel'-yus-li], *adv.* Con rebeldía.
Rebelliousness [rẹ-bel'-yus-nes], *s.* Rebeldía, falta de obediencia o subordinación.
Rebirth [rī-bẹrth'], *s.* Renacimiento.
Reblossom [rī-blos'-um], *vn.* Volver a florecer; florecer de nuevo.
Rebound [rẹ-baund'], *vn.* 1. Repercutir; botar, saltar la pelota. 2. Volverse contra. 3. (Des.) Resonar. *The jest rebounded on him,* La burla se volvió contra él; la espada se le volvió garabato.—*va.* Rechazar.
Rebound, *s.* Resalto, repercusión, rebote.
Rebounding [rẹ-baund'-ing], *s.* Rebote.
Rebroadcast [rī-brōd'-cạst], *s.* Retransmisión radiodifusora.
Rebuff [rẹ-buf'], *s.* 1. Desaire, mala acogida. 2. Repulsa, denegación. 3. Resistencia, repentina y viva; jaque, vencimiento.
Rebuff, *va.* 1. Rechazar, rebatir co violencia. 2. Desairar, denegar, acoger mal.
Rebuild [rī-bild'], *va.* (*pret.* y *pp.* REBUILT). Reedificar, construir de nuevo.
Rebuke [rẹ-biūk'], *va.* 1. Reprender, censurar; dar una reprimenda; regañar, reñir. 2. (Ant.) Hacer callar, refrenar por medio de un mandato o una orden.
Rebuke, *s.* 1. Reprensión, reprimenda, amonestación, censura. 2. Bofetada.
Rebuker [rẹ-biūk'-ẹr], *s.* Reprensor, censor.
Rebury [rī-ber'-i], *va.* Enterrar, sepultar por segunda vez o de nuevo; volver a enterrar.
Rebus [rī'-bus], *s.* Un jeroglífico acertijo; quisicosa; manera peculiar de expresar palabras o frases por la representación de objetos cuyos nombres tienen semejanza a las palabras o las sílabas de que se componen.
Rebut [rẹ-but'], *va.* (For.) Refutar, contradecir por prueba en contrario.—*vn.* Replicar, responder á la dúplica del demandante.
Rebuttal [rẹ-but'-al], *s.* Refutación, acción de refutar; la presentación de pruebas para refutar una deposición ya hecha.
Rebutter [rẹ-but'-ẹr], *s.* (For.) 1. Respuesta a una contrarréplica. 2. El que refuta, o que presenta testimonio en contrario.
Recalcitrant [rī-cal'-si-trant], *a.* Recalcitrante; rehacio, obstinado en la resistencia.
Recalcitrate [rī-cal'-si-trêt], *vn.* Recalcitrar, resistir con tenacidad a quien se debe obedecer.
Recall [rẹ-cōl'], *va.* 1. Revocar, anular, hacer volver, mandar volver. 2. Traer a la memoria, recordar. 3. Quitar el cargo o empleo. *To recall an ambassador,* Retirar a un embajador de su misión, mandarle volver a su país. *I can not recall the circumstances,* No puedo recordar las circunstancias.
Recall, *s.* 1. Revocación. 2. El acto de volver a llamar.
Recant [rẹ-cant'], *va.* y *vn.* Retractarse, desdecirse. *He was obliged to recant,* Le obligaron a cantar la palinodia.
Recantation [rī-can-tê'-shun], *s.* Retractación, recantación, palinodia.
Recanter [rẹ-cant'-ẹr], *s.* El que se desdice.
Recap [rī'-cap], *s.* Capa de caucho que se superpone a neumáticos gastados.—[rī-cap'], *va.* 1. Recubrir neumáticos gastados. 2. Recapitular, resumir.
Recapacitate [rī-ca-pas'-i-têt], *va.* Recapacitar.
Recapitulate [rī-ca-pit'-yu-lêt], *va.* Recapitular, resumir.
Recapitulation [rī-ca-pit-yu-lê'-shun], *s.* Recapitulación, resumen; resunción.
Recaption [rī-cap'-shun], *s.* (For.) Nuevo embargo, secuestro o prisión.
Recapture [rī-cap'-chur], *va.* Volver a tomar; represar.
Recapture, *s.* Represa de una embarcación; acción de prender o capturar de nuevo.
Recast [rī-cạst'], *va.* (*pret.* y *pp.* RECAST). 1. Fundir otra vez, volver a fundir. 2. Formar, amoldar, de nuevo, cambiando la forma, disposición, etc., v. g. de un discurso u obra dramática. 3. Calcular de nuevo. 4. Arrojar otra vez.
Recede [rẹ-sīd'], *vn.* 1. Cejar, retroceder, recular; retirarse, alejarse. 2. Desistir, volverse atrás; desdecirse. 3. Inclinarse o tenderse a distancia, formar declive, apartarse. *He receded from his demand,* Desistió de su demanda.
Receipt [rẹ-sīt'], *s.* 1. Recibimiento, cobranza. 2. Lo que se recibe; ingresos, sumas o cantidades recibidas. 3. Recibo, el escrito en que se declara haber recibido dinero u otra cosa. 4. Receta, memoria de aquello de que se debe componer alguna cosa. *V.* RECIPE. 5. (Ant.) Receptoría. *Receipt and outgo,* Entrada y salida. *On receipt of,* Al recibo de. *Receipt-book,* Registro de recetas; (Com.) libro de ingresos o recibos. *Receipt in full* (*of all demands*), Recibo por saldo de cuenta
Receipt, *va.* Dar recibo de algo, extender el recibo de un pago.
Receipted, *pp.* Que lleva un recibo.
Receivable [rẹ-sīv'-a-bl], *a.* Recibidero, admisible. *Bills receivable,* Valores a recibir, o por cobrar.
Receive [rẹ-sīv'], *va.* 1. Recibir, tomar lo que se da o presenta. 2. Recibir, aceptar, aprobar, admitir. 3. Recibir, admitir, hospedar, acoger. 4. Recibir, percibir, cobrar. 5. Concebir. 6. Recibir, comulgar. *To receive rents,* Cobrar rentas. *To receive one graciously,* Hacer buena acogida a alguno.
Receivedness [rẹ-sīv'-ed-nes], *s.* Aceptación, aprobación.
Receiver [rẹ-sīv'-ẹr], *s.* 1. Recibidor, depositario. 2. Encubridor de hurtos. 3. (Elec.) Receptor. *Telephone receiver,* Audífono.
Receivership [rẹ-sīv'-ẹr-ship], *s* Sindicatura.
Receiving set [rẹ-sīv'-ing set], *s.* Radiorreceptor.
Recension [rẹ-sen'-shun], *s.* 1. Revisión crítica de un texto, y el mismo texto revisado. 2. Crítica, examen crítico.
Recent [rī'-sent], *a.* Reciente, moderno, nuevo, fresco, flamante, acaecido no ha mucho tiempo.
Recently [rī'-sent-li], *adv.* Recientemente, nuevamente, hace poco.
Recentness [rī'-sent-nes], *s.* Novedad; fecha, origen reciente.
Receptacle [rẹ-sep'-ta-cl], *s.* 1. Receptáculo, cualquiera cosa que sirve para contener otras. 2. (Bot.) Receptáculo, extremo del pedúnculo, casi siempre grueso y carnoso, donde se asientan las hojas ó verticilos de la flor.
Receptacular [rẹ-sep-tac'-yu-lar], *a.* Perteneciente o relativo a un receptáculo.
Reception [rẹ-sep'-shun], *s.* Recepción, el acto de recibir, y el estado de ser recibido; acogimiento, acogida; readmisión; afección o pasión del ánimo; dictamen u opinión generalmente aceptada o admitida.
Receptionist [rẹ-sep'-shUn-ist], *s.* Recepcionista, recibidor.
Receptive [rẹ-sep'-tiv], *a.* Capaz de recibir; que tiene la facultad de recibir; dispuesto a recibir.
Recess [rẹ-ses'], *s.* 1. Nicho, alcoba; la parte entrante en la pared de un cuarto. 2. Suspensión de cualquiera empresa, acción o trabajo; vacaciones, interrupción de trabajos; prórroga. 3. Retiro, el lugar apartado y distante del concurso y bullicio de la gente; soledad, escondrijo. *The most secret recesses of the human heart,* Lo más escondido o lo más oculto del corazón humano.
Recession [rẹ-sesh'-un], *s.* 1. Retirada, retiro, la acción de retirarse. 2. Restitución, desistimiento; concesión. 3. (Com.) Recesión.
Recessional [rẹ-sesh'-un-al], *s.* Himno que se canta cuando el sacerdote o el coro dejan el presbiterio después del servicio divino.
Rechange [rī'-chênj], *va.* Recambiar.
Recharge [rī-chārj'], *va.* 1. Acusarse mutuamente; acusar al acusador. 2. Recargar, cargar o acometer de nuevo.
Recharge, *s.* Recarga.
†**Recheat** [rī-chīt'], *s.* Toque de trompa por el montero cuando los perros han perdido de vista la caza.
Recidivation [rẹ-sid-i-vê'-shun], *s.* Reincidencia, la recaída en alguna culpa o pecado.
Recipe [res'-i-pẹ], *s.* 1. Récipe o receta de médico. 2. Instrucciones para hacer un guiso o preparar un plato.
‡**Recipience,** ‡**Recipiency** [rẹ-sip'-i-ens, en-si], *s.* Acción de recibir; facultad de recibir.
Recipient [rẹ-sip'-i-ent], *s.* Recipiente, el que o lo que recibe.—*a.* Recipiente.
Reciprocal [rẹ-sip'-ro-cal], *a.* Recíproco, mutuo; alternativo, que obra por movimiento de vaivén.—*s.* 1. El cuociente obtenido dividiendo la unidad por un número. 2. Una cosa que alterna con otra.
Reciprocally [rẹ-sip'-ro-cal-i], *adv.* Recíprocamente, mutuamente.
Reciprocalness [rẹ-sip'-ro-cal-nes], *s.* Reciprocidad, mutua correspondencia.

Reciprocate [rę-sip'-ro-kêt], *va.* Producir un movimiento de vaivén; hacer pasar adelante y atrás; dar y recibir mutuamente.—*vn.* Reciprocar, obrar recíprocamente. *Reciprocating motion*, Movimiento alternativo o de vaivén.

Reciprocation [rę-sip-ro-kê'-shun], *s.* Reciprocación, reciprocidad; acto de dar y recibir mutuamente; alternación, alternativa; movimiento alternativo.

Reciprocity [res-i-pres'-i-ti], *s.* Reciprocidad, calidad de recíproco; derecho u obligación recíproca; particularmente, derechos o ventajas iguales y mutuos entre los ciudadanos de dos países respecto á los privilegios comerciales que han de gozar ambos.

Recision [rę-sizh'-un], *s.* Cortadura, resección.

Recital [rę-sai'-tal], *s.* 1. Relación, narración; repetición. 2. Recitación en público de algo que se ha confiado a la memoria. 3. (Mús.) El acto de tocar una composición una sola persona. 4. Explicación, repetición.

Recitation [res-i-tê'-shun], *s.* Recitación.

Recitative [res-i-ta-tîv'], *s.* Recitativo o recitado, estilo músico en que se canta recitando.—*a.* Recitativo.

Recite [rę-sait'], *va.* 1. Recitar, referir, narrar, relatar, contar hechos o detalles; entrar en los pormenores. 2. Decir o pronunciar de memoria; recitar, recitar una lección. 3. Citar.

Reciter [rę-sai'-tęr], *s.* Recitador.

Reck [rec], *va.* y *vn.* (Poét. o ant.) Tener cuidado o inquietarse de. *He recked not of danger*, No le inquietó el peligro.

Reckless [rec'-les], *a.* Descuidado, atrevido, temerario precipitado; indiferente, sin miramiento, con desvergüenza; atolondrado respecto al peligro.

Recklessness [rec'-les-nes], *s.* 1. Descuido, atrevimiento, falta de atención, abandono a los vicios; ociosidad, indiferencia, inconsideración. 2. Indiferencia, apatía.

Reckon [rec'-n], *va.* 1. Contar, numerar. 2. Estimar, considerar. *I shall reckon it a favour*, Lo miraré como un favor. 3. Poner en el número de, en el grado de.—*vn.* 1. Contar, computar, calcular; formalizar una cuenta. 2. Pagar una multa. 3. Contar, fiar, tener confianza; con *on* o *upon*, contar con. *I reckon on your friendship*, Cuento con la amistad de Vd. 4. (Prov. o ant.) Suponer, creer.

Reckoner [rec'-n-ęr], *s.* 1. Contador, calculador. 2. Libro u otro expediente para facilitar una computación. *Ready-reckoner*, Libro de cuentas ya hechas.

Reckoning [rec'-n-ing], *s.* 1. Cuenta; cuenta de cargo y data; cuenta de huésped. 2. Cuenta, suposición; cálculo. 3. Ajuste de demandas o cuentas. 4. Escote. 5. (Mar.) Estima. *Dead reckoning*, (Mar.) Rumbo estimado, estima, cálculo aproximado de la distancia recorrida por un buque, según la guíndola. *To be out in one's reckoning*, Estar lejos de la cuenta, engañarse en el cálculo. *Reckoning-book*, Libro en que se sienta lo que se recibe y gasta o de cuenta y razón. *Every one must pay his reckoning*, Cada uno debe pagar su escote.

Reclaim [rę-clêm'], *va.* 1. Reformar, corregir; amansar, domesticar. 2. Reducir alguna cosa al estado que se requiere; volver al estado de cultivo las tierras incultas, desiertas o inundadas. 3. Reclamar, oponerse; pedir en contra.

Reclaimable [rę-clêm'-a-bl], *a.* Reclamable, que puede ser reclamado, corregido o cultivado.

Reclaimant [rę-clêm'-ant], *s.* (Poco us.) Disidente, el que se opone a alguna determinación o reclama contra ella.

Reclamation [rec-la-mê'-shun], *s.* Reclamación, restauración.

Reclinate [rec'-li-nêt], **Reclined** [reclaind'], *a.* Que se inclina hacia abajo.

Reclination [rec-li-nê'-shun], *s.* 1. Reclinación; acción de inclinarse. 2. Ángulo que forma el plano de un reloj de sol con un plano vertical que lo entrecorta en una línea horizontal.

Recline [rę-clain'], *va.* Reclinar, inclinar.—*vn.* Recostarse, descansar, reposar.

Recline, *a.* (Poco us.) Reclinado, inclinado.

Reclose [rî-clōz'], *va.* Volver á cerrar.

Reclothe [rî-clōdh'], *va.* Volver a vestir, vestir de nuevo.

Recluse [rę-clūs'], *a.* Recluso, encerrado, retirado del mundo o de la vista pública.—*s.* Una persona retirada del mundo, persona que vive en el retiro, en el aislamiento.

Reclusely [rę-clūs'-li], *adv.* Retiradamente.

Recluseness [rę-clūs'-nes], *s.* Retiro, recogimiento, estado de la persona que vive encerrada; soledad, aislamiento.

Reclusion [rę-clū'-zhun], *s.* Reclusión, retirada del mundo.

Reclusive [rę-clū'-siv], *a.* Que proporciona retiro, que vive en el aislamiento o el retiro.

Recognition [rec-og-nish'-un], *s.* 1. Reconocimiento, el acto de reconocer; examen. 2. Recuerdo, memoria. 3. Agradecimiento; saludo amistoso.

Recognizable [rec-og-nai'-za-bl], *a.* Que puede ser reconocido.

Recognizance [rę-cog'-ni-zans], *s.* Reconocimiento; obligación, sumisión con condición de hacer un acto determinado, v. gr. comparecer ante un tribunal.

Recognize [rec'-og-naiz], *va.* 1. Reconocer. 2. Declarar que se tiene conocimiento de una cosa; reconocer, admitir formalmente. 3. Confesar, admitir, conceder.—*vn.* Subscribir una obligación auténtica.

Recognize [rî-cog'-naiz], *va.* Volver a conocer, a percibir.

Recognizee [rę-cog-ni-zî'], *s.* (For.) La persona a cuyo favor se da algún vale.

Recognizor [rec'-og-nai-zęr], *s.* (For.) El que da algún vale a favor de otro.

Recoil [rę-coil'], *s.* 1. Reculada; coz, retroceso, rebufo de un arma de fuego. 2. Repugnancia, temor. *Recoil-spring*, Resorte para disminuir el rebufo.

Recoil, *vn.* 1. Recular de horror o repugnancia, quedarse helado; retirarse. 2. Cejar, retroceder. 3. Volver atrás. 4. Rebufar (un arma de fuego). *The blood recoils with horror at the sight*, La sangre se hiela en las venas ante tal cuadro.

Recoin [rî-coin'], *va.* Acuñar de nuevo.

Recoinage [rî-coin'-ęj], *s.* Refundición de la moneda; moneda nueva.

Recollect [rec-ol-lect'], *va.* 1. Acordarse, traer a la memoria, recordar. 2. Recobrarse, volver en sí.

Recollect [rî-col-lect'], *va.* Recoger, juntar de nuevo; reunir.

Recollect, Recollet [rec'-o-lęct], *s.* Recoleto, miembro de una orden reformada de franciscanos.

Recollection [rec-ol-lec'-shun], *s.* 1. Memoria, recuerdo, recordación, reminiscencia. 2. Recuerdo, memoria, la cosa traída a la memoria.

Recommence [rî-com-ens'], *va.* Empezar de nuevo.

Recommencement [rî-com-ens'-męnt], *s.* La acción de comenzar de nuevo alguna cosa.

Recommend [rec-ęm-mend'], *va.* 1. Recomendar, alabar, empeñarse por alguno elogiándole; encomendar, poner al cuidado de uno. 2. Aconsejar, avisar por lo que toca a un curso de acción.

Recommendable [rec-ęm-mend'-a-bl], *a.* Recomendable; digno de alabanza.

Recommendation [rec-om-men-dê'-shun], *s.* 1. Recomendación. 2. Recomendación, la alabanza o elogio que se hace de alguno con el fin de recomendarle á otro.

Recommendatory [rec-om-men'-da-to-ri], *a.* Recomendatorio.

Recommender [rec-om-mend'-ęr], *s.* El que recomienda.

Recommit [rî-com-mit'], *va.* 1. Someter de nuevo a una comisión (de un cuerpo deliberante). 2. Volver a mandar prender a alguno que había sido puesto en libertad bajo fianza.

Recommitment [rî-com-mit'-męnt], **Recommittal** [rî-com-mit'-al], *s.* El acto de remitir a una comisión, o de volver a prender al que había sido puesto en libertad bajo fianza.

Recompact [rî-com-pact'], *va.* Reunir, volver a unir, volver a pegar.

Recompense [rec'-om-pens], *va.* 1. Recompensar, compensar, satisfacer, dar el equivalente; reintegrar. 2. Indemnizar; resarcir de un daño.

Recompense, *s.* Recompensa, equivalente devuelto; compensación, indemnización.

Recompilement [rî-com-pail'-męnt], *s.* Nueva compilación.

Recompose [rî-com-pōz'], *va.* 1. Volver a componer; tranquilizar de nuevo. 2. Recomponer, rehacer; componer de nuevo (la luz blanca); lo contrario de *decompose*, descomponer.

Recomposition [rî-com-po-zish'-un], *s.* 1. Nueva composición. 2. (Quím.) Recomposición.

Reconcilable [rec-on-sail'-a-bl], *a.* Reconciliable, componible; conciliable, que puede concordar con algo; compatible.

Reconcilableness [rec-on-sail'-a-bl-nes], *s.* La disposición a reconciliarse; posibilidad de reconciliación, calidad de conciliable.

Reconcilably [rec-on-sai'-la-bli], *adv.* De una manera compatible.

Reconcile [rec'-on-sail], *va.* 1. Reconciliar, componer o ajustar diferencias; restablecer la amistad entre personas enojadas. 2. Conciliar, componer, concordar, arreglar (una querella), poner de acuerdo; adaptar. 3. Restablecer. *I can not reconcile myself to his way of thinking,* No puedo adaptarme a su modo de pensar. *To reconcile one's self to,* Resolverse o determinarse a. *If you can reconcile it to your conscience,* Si Vd. puede conciliarlo con su conciencia.

Reconcilement [rec'-en-sail-mẹnt], *s.* Reconciliación, la acción de reconciliar, o el estado de hallarse reconciliado.

Reconciler [rec-en-sail'-ẹr], *s.* Reconciliador; conciliador, pacificador.

Reconciliation [rec-en-sil-i-é'-shun], *s.* Reconciliación; conciliación, ajuste, acomodamiento; renovación de la amistad; acuerdo entre cosas que parecen opuestas, diferentes o incompatibles.

Reconciliatory [rec-en-sil'-i-a-to-ri], *a.* Reconciliador, que reconcilia o tiende a reconciliar.

Recondense [rî-cen-dens'], *va.* Volver a condensar.

Recondite [rec'-en-dait], *a.* 1. Recóndito, secreto, oculto, impenetrable. 2. Profundo; que trata, que se ocupa en asuntos abstrusos.

Recondition [rî-cen-dish'-un], *va.* Reacondicionar, reparar, restaurar.

Reconduct [rî-cen-duct'], *va.* Conducir de nuevo, volver a conducir.

Reconnoisance [rî-cen'-i-sans], *s.* Reconocimiento; examen de una región, v. g. para operaciones militares.

Reconnoitre [rec-o-nei'-tẹr], *va.* Reconocer, examinar el estado de las cosas para dar parte de él; examinar con la vista; inspeccionar, v. g. los militares, ingenieros o geólogos.

Reconquer [rî-coṇ'-kẹr], *va.* Reconquistar.

Reconsecrate [rî-cen'-sî-crêt], *va.* Volver a consagrar.

Reconsider [rî-cen-sid'-ẹr], *va.* Considerar de nuevo, volver a considerar; someter a nuevo examen una cuestión ya debatida.

Reconsideration [rî-cen-sid-ẹr-é'-shun], *s.* El acto de considerar de nuevo; el acto de someter a nueva discusión una propuesta rechazada anteriormente.

Reconstruct [rî''-cen-struct'], *va.* Reedificar, construir de nuevo; en los Estados Unidos, reorganizar y reintegrar en la Unión un Estado separado de ella.

Reconvene [rî-cen-vîn'], *va.* Convocar, juntar o reunir de nuevo.

Reconvention [rî-cen-ven'-shun], *s.* (For.) Reconvención.

Reconversion [rî-cen-vẹr'-shun], *s.* Reconversión.

Reconvey [rî-cen-vé'], *va.* 1. Volver a llevar o enviar; volver a poner una cosa en su antiguo sitio. 2. Retroceder; transferir a un poseedor anterior.

Record [rẹ-cōrd'], *va.* 1. Registrar, notar o poner alguna cosa en los libros de registro; inscribir una relación auténtica u oficial de algo; protocolar; archivar. 2. Celebrar la memoria de alguna cosa, fijar en el ánimo, imprimir en la memoria. 3. Indicar, registrar. 4. (Ant.) Referir, relatar. *Where the barometer recorded but 28.5 inches,* Donde el barómetro indicó no más que 28.5 pulgadas (726 milímetros).

Record [rec'-ẹrd], *s.* 1. Registro, copia auténtica de un documento; protocolo, historia; recuerdo. 2. Relación de suceso consignados en un libro para conservarlos. 3. Disco que reproduce sonidos musicales o de otra clase en un gramofono. 4. Registro de actos, en especial de los atletas; también el más notable de esos actos. 5. Atestación, testimonio. *Records,* Archivo; papeles archivados; fastos; memorias. *Old records,* Archivos. *Keeper of the records,* Archivero. *On* o *upon record,* Registrado; (fig.) inscrito en los anales de la historia. *There is no record of it in history,* No hay nota de ello, no se hace mención de ello en la historia. *To make a record,* Tomar razón, registrar, archivar; también, igualar o superar al más notable ejercicio atlético que se recuerda.

Recorder [rẹ-cōrd'-ẹr], *s.* 1. Registrador, archivero. 2. Juez recopilador, magistrado o ministro superior que recopila y examina la evidencia o resultado de las deposiciones de los testigos para que el jurado (*jury*) decida; y que dicta la sentencia (*verdict*) según la decisión del jurado. 3. Indicador, contador, aparato para indicar.

Recordership [rẹ-cōrd'-ẹr-ship], *s.* Cargo o función de registrador o archivero, y el tiempo de su duración.

Recount [rẹ-caunt'], *va.* Recontar; referir, relatar; recitar, detallar, mencionar con pormenores.

Recount [rî-caunt'], *va.* Contar de nuevo.

Recount [rî'-caunt], *s.* Repetición de una cuenta; cuenta hecha de nuevo.

Recoup [rẹ-cūp'], *va.* 1. Retener (alguna cosa debida) para indemnizarse. 2. Obtener compensación por una pérdida. 3. Reparar (una pérdida), indemnizar, resarcir.

Recourse [rẹ-cōrs'], *s.* 1. Recurso, remedio, auxilio, refugio. 2. (For.) Recurso, derecho de acción contra una persona o una propiedad para obtener garantías. 3. Acceso, entrada al trato o comunicación.

Recover [rẹ-cuv'-ẹr], *va.* 1. Recobrar, volver a cobrar lo que antes se tenía. 2. Reparar, remediar, resarcir. *To recover a loss,* Resarcir un daño. 3. (For.) Obtener fallo judicial contra alguien. 4. (Ant.) Rescatar, restablecer, reparar a alguno de la enfermedad o mal que ha padecido. 5. Alcanzar, lograr. —*vn.* 1. Restablecerse de una enfermedad, ir recobrando la salud perdida; volver a un estado o condición anterior. 2. (For.) Ganar un pleito. *To recover one's health,* Restablecerse, recobrar la salud. *To recover one's self,* Volver en sí; tomar valor.

Recover [rî-cuv'-ẹr], *va.* Volver a cubrir o tapar.

Recoverable [rẹ-cuv'-ẹr-a-bl], *a.* Curable; recuperable; exigible, que se puede lograr por medio de un pleito. *The debt was recoverable,* Era exigible la deuda. *No damages are recoverable,* No se deben daños y perjuicios.

Recoverableness [rẹ-cuv'-ẹr-a-bl-nes], *s.* El estado o la calidad de recuperable.

Recovery [rẹ-cuv'-ẹr-i], *s.* 1. Recobro, recuperación; acto de recobrar, de volver a entrar en posesión de una propiedad, de volver a ganar. 2. Mejoría, convalecencia, restablecimiento de la salud. 3. El acto de hacer libres los bienes vinculados. 4. Fallo, decisión judicial en favor de alguien. 5. Remedio. *It is a thing past recovery,* No tiene remedio. *Past recovery,* Desahuciado, sin remedio; en estado crítico.

Recreancy [rec'-re-an-si], *s.* Deslealtad, apostasía; pusilanimidad.

Recreant [rec'-rẹ-ant], *a.* 1. Falso, desleal; apóstata. 2. Cobarde, apocado, pulsilánime.

Recreate [rec'-rẹ-êt], *va.* Recrear, deleitar, divertir; aliviar.

Recreate [rî''-crẹ-êt'] *va.* Crear o criar de nuevo.

Recreation [rec-rẹ-é'-shun], *s.* Recreación, recreo, entretenimiento, diversión, pasatiempo; descanso.

Re-creation [rî''-crẹ-é'-shun], *s.* Nueva creación, formacion de nuevo.

Recreative [rec'-rẹ-a-tiv], *a.* Recreativo, agradable; entretenido.

Recreativeness [rec'-rẹ-a-tiv-nes], *s.* La calidad de lo que divierte o agrada.

Recrement [rec'-rẹ-mẹnt], *s.* 1. (Med.) Recremento, cualquier flúido devuelto a la sangre después de separado de ella. 2. (Ant.) Recremento; hez, escoria.

Recriminate [rẹ-crim'-i-nêt], *va.* y *vn.* Recriminar, acusar al acusador, acusarse mutuamente.

Recrimination [rẹ-crim-i-né'-shun], *s.* Recriminación, acto de recriminar.

Recriminative, Recriminatory [rẹ-crim'-i-na-tiv, to-ri], *a.* Recriminador, recriminativo, perteneciente a la recriminación o que la contiene.

Recriminator [rẹ-crim'-i-né''-tẹr], *s.* (For.) Recriminador.

Recross [rî-cres'], *va.* Volver a pasar.

Recrudesce [rî-cru-des'], *vn.* Recrudecer, recrudecerse, tomar nuevo incremento un mal físico o moral; encrudecerse.

Recrudescence [rî-cru-des'-ens], *s.* Encrudecimiento, recrudescencia, acción y efecto de recrudecer; aumento o actividad mayor de los fenómenos morbosos después de una mejoría sensible.

Recrudescent [rî-cru-des'-ent], *a.* Recrudescente, que recrudece.

Recruit [rẹ-crūt'], *va.* 1. Abastecerse, proveerse uno de lo que necesita; de aquí, restablecer, reparar, rehacer; reemplazar. 2. Reclutar tropas. *To recruit one's self,* Reparar las fuerzas, restablecerse.—*vn.* Restablecerse, reponerse, rehacerse; reanimarse, recobrar la salud o la fuerza.

Recruit, *s.* 1. (Mil.) Recluta, soldado bisoño; marinero novicio. 2. El reemplazo de cualquiera cosa que hace falta.

Recruiting [rẹ-crūt'-ing], *s.* Recluta, el acto de reclutar o reemplazar.

Recrystallize [rî-cris'-tal-aiz], *va.* y *vn.* Volver o volverse a cristalizar; cristalizar o cristalizarse de nuevo.

Rectal [rec'-tal], *a.* Relativo o perteneciente al recto.

Rectangle [rec'-taṇ-gl], *s.* Rectángulo, paralelogramo de ángulos rectos.

Rectangled [rec-taṇ'-gld], **Rectangular** [rec-taṇ'-giu-lar], *a.* Rectangular, que tiene ángulos rectos.

Rectangularity [rec-taṇ-giu-lar'-i-ti], **Rectangularness** [rec-taṇ'-giu-lar-nes], *s.* El estado o calidad de lo que es rectangular.

Rectangularly [rec-taṇ'-giu-lar-li], *adv.* Con ángulos rectos.

Rectifiable [rec'-ti-fai-a-bl], *a.* Rectificable; que se puede rectificar, capaz de ser corregido.

Rectification [rec-ti-fi-ké'-shun], *s.* Rectificación, acción de rectificar: (1) enmendación; (2) el procedimiento de refinar o purificar (un líquido) por destilaciones repetidas; (3) (Mat.) determinación de una línea recta cuya longitud es igual al arco de una curva.

Rectifier [rec'-ti-fai-ęr], *s.* Rectificador, el que o lo que rectifica; particularmente un refinador de licores espirituosos.

Rectify [rec'-ti-fai], *va.* (*pret.* y *pp.* RECTIFIED). 1. Rectificar, corregir, enmendar, reformar. 2. Rectificar los licores y darles mayor perfección o purificar por cristalizaciones repetidas.

Rectilineal [rec-ti-lin'-ę-al], **Rectilinear** [rec-ti-lin'-ę-ar], *a.* Rectilíneo, que se compone de líneas rectas.

Rectitude [rec'-ti-tiud], *s.* 1. Rectitud, derechura. 2. Rectitud en las acciones, equidad.

Rector [rec'-tər], *s.* 1. Rector, párroco, cura propio. 2. Jefe, superior, principal de ciertos colegios u otros establecimientos de educación.

Rectoral [rec'-to-ral], **Rectorial** [rec-tō'-ri-al], *a.* Rectoral, relativo o perteneciente a un rector.

Rectorate [rec'-tęr-êt], *s.* Rectorado. el oficio y cargo de rector y el tiempo que dura; rectoría.

Rectorship [rec'-tər-ship], *s.* *V.* RECTORATE.

Rectory [rec'-tər-i], *s.* 1. Habitación de un rector, casa de un cura, particularmente cuando forma parte de la propiedad de una iglesia. 2. (Ingl.) Rectoría, feligresía de un cura con sus edificios, tierras y rentas.

Rectum [rec'-tum], *s.* (Anat.) Recto, la tercera y última porción del intestino grueso.

Recumbency, Recumbence [rę-cum'-ben-si], *s.* 1. Estado o postura del que está reclinado. 2. (Des.) Reposo, descanso. 3. (Des.) La acción de esperar con confianza.

Recumbent [rę-cum'-bent], *a.* Recostado, reclinado.

Recuperate [rę-kiū'-pęr-êt], *va.* 1. Recuperar, recobrar, volver a ganar. 2. ¿*V.* RECOUP.—*vn.* (E. U.) Restablecerse, recobrar la salud o las fuerzas.

Recuperation [rę-kiū-pęr-é'-shun], *s.* Recuperación.

Recuperative [rę-kiū'-pęr-a-tiv], **Recuperatory** [rę-kiū'-pęr-a-to-ri], *a.* Recuperativo, que tiende o pertenece a la recuperación.

Recur [rę-cūr'], *vn.* 1. Acaecer, suceder, otra vez o repetidas veces, particularmente a intervalos regulares; volver, presentarse de nuevo. *A recurring paroxysm,* Un paroxismo que se repite. 2. Ofrecerse a la imaginación o a la memoria. 3. (Des.) Recurrir, acudir.

Recurrence [rę-cur'-ens], **Recurrency** [rę-cur'-en-si], *s.* 1. Repetición, reaparición. 2. Recurso.

Recurrent [re-cur'-ent], *a.* 1. Que vuelve de vez en cuando; periódico. 2. (Anat.) Recurrente, que corre hacia atrás, como una arteria, o un nervio.

Recurve, Recurvate [re-cūrv', êt], *va.* Encorvar, torcer hacia atrás o abajo.

Recurved [re-cūrvd'], **Recurvous** [re-cūr'-vus], *a.* Encorvado.

Recusancy [rec'-yu-zan-si], *s.* La acción de recusar y la calidad de recusante.

Recusant [rec'-yu-zant], *s.* y *a.* Recusante, no conformista, el que rehusa en Inglaterra reconocer la supremacía del rey en materias de religión.

Recusation [rec-yu-zé'-shun], *s.* (For.) Recusación, acto de recusar a un juez por motivo de parentesco, predisposición contra una de las partes, etc.

Recycle [rę-sai'-cl], *va.* Recircular.

Red [red], *a.* 1. Colorado, rojo, encarnado; rubio. 2. Revolucionario, anárquico.—*s.* 1. Rojez, el color rojo, el encarnado, el color encarnado; color parecido al de la sangre. 2. Uno de muchos colores rojos. 3. Republicano rojo; ultraradical en sus opiniones. *Adrianople* o *Turkey red,* Carmesí. *The Red Sea,* El Mar Rojo. *Cherry red,* Rojo cereza. *A deep red,* Un rojo subido. *Light red,* Rojo claro. *To turn red,* Ponerse colorado, sonrojarse. *Red ant,* (1) Hormiga leonada, la hormiga común de las casas; Monomoriun pharaonis. (2) Hormiga que esclaviza a otras. *Red cedar,* Cedro colorado; junípero; tuya de la costa del Pacífico. *Red chalk,* Creta roja, creta colorada con el peróxido de hierro. *Red deer,* Ciervo común (Cervus elaphus); ciervo de Virginia. *Red-haired,* De pelo rojo o de un rubio ardiente. *Red herring,* Arenque seco y ahumado. *Red man,* Indio de América. *Red liquor, red mordant,* Disolución de acetato de alúmina, empleado como mordiente en el tinte. *Red scale,* Insecto rojizo de los cóccidos, perjudicial a los naranjos. *Red snow,* Nieve colorada por el alga Protococcus nivalis, que se halla en gran abundancia en las regiones árticas. *Red silver,* Plata roja, mineral de plata rojizo; pirargirita; proustita. *Red spider,* Ácaro rojo, cresa roja. *Red thrush,* Tordo rojo. *Red ocher,* Ocre rojo. *Red-tapist,* Formalista, covachuelista, empleado del Gobierno. *Red tape,* (1) Balduque, cinta estrecha (rojiza) para atar legajos; (2) (fig.) formalismo, apego a la rutina, exclusivismo de escuela.

Redan [rę-dan'], *s.* (Fort.) Estrella, fortificación con ángulos entrantes y salientes.

Red-baiting [red-bêt'-ing], *s.* Acosamiento de los comunistas.

Redbird [red'-bərd], *s.* (Orn.) 1. Cardenal. 2. Tángara, (fam.) tángara escarlata. 3. Pinzón real.

Red-blooded [red-blud'-ed], *a.* 1. Valiente, intrépido. 2. Viril.

Red-book [red'-buc], *s.* El registro de las personas que tienen tierras, pensiones o empleos por el rey; guía de la corte.

Redbreast [red'-brest], *s.* (Orn.) Pitirrojo, petirrojo, pechicolorado.

Redbud [red'-bud], *s.* (Bot.) Botón encarnado, árbol de Judas, algarrobo loco.

Redcap [red'-cap], *s.* 1. Cardelina, jilguero europeo. 2. Cargador (en las estaciones de ferrocarril).

Redcoat [red'-cōt], *s.* Casaca colorada: voz con que designan en Inglaterra a los soldados.

Red-coral [red-cer'-al], *s.* Coral rojo, especie de zoófito.

Red Cross, *s.* 1. Cruz de San Jorge, emblema de los ingleses. 2. Cruz griega, roja sobre fondo blanco. *Red Cross Society,* Sociedad de la Cruz Roja, formada para socorrer a los enfermos y heridos en la guerra. *Red-cross knight,* Templario; caballero de la orden de San Jorge.

Redden [red'-n], *va.* Teñir de color rojo o encarnado.—*vn.* Ponerse colorado; ruborizarse.

Reddish [red'-ish], *a.* Bermejizo, rojizo; que tira a rojo.

Reddishness [red'-ish-nes], *s.* Bermejura, el color bermejo.

Redditive [red'-i-tiv], *a.* (Poco us.) Dícese en gramática de la partícula que responde a una pregunta.

Reddle [red'-l], *s.* Almazarrón, almagre.

Redeem [rę-dīm'], *va.* 1. Recomprar, adquirir de nuevo; volver a tomar posesión de una cosa enajenada, reembolsando su valor al que la posee. 2. Redimir, rescatar, libertar; sacar del cautiverio. 3. Redimir del pecado y sus consecuencias: se dice de Jesucristo. 4. Cumplir una promesa, una palabra dada. 5. Resarcir, recompensar, reintegrar, reparar. *To redeem out of pawn,* Desempeñar.

Redeemable [rę-dīm'-a-bl], *a.* Redimible, rescatable.

Redeemer [rę-dīm'-ęr], *s.* Redentor, el Salvador del mundo.

Redeeming [rę-dīm'-ing], *a.* Que rescata, redime o libra; que recompensa, que reembolsa.—*s.* Redención, rescate; recompensa, reintegro.

Redemption [rę-demp'-shun], *s.* 1. Redención, rescate; la acción de rescatar o redimir, o la calidad de rescatado. (1) Liberación de una propiedad gravada con hipoteca, desempeño de bienes muebles. (2) Pago de una deuda u obligación. 2. Redención del pecado por la expiación de Jesucristo.

Redemptional [rę-demp'-shun-al], **Redemptory** [rę-demp'-to-ri], *a.* Perteneciente a la redención o rescate.

Redemptioner [rę-demp'-shun-ęr], *s.* Dábase antiguamente este nombre a los europeos que se comprometían a servir por un espacio determinado de tiempo, en pago de su traslación a los Estados Unidos de América.

Redemptive [rę-demp'-tiv], *a.* De rescate, que sirve para rescatar o redimir; relacionado con la redención.

Red-gum [red'-gum], *s.* 1. Especie de árbol australiano del género Eucalyptus. 2. Añublo, tizón de las mieses. 3. Granos que salen en la cara a los niños recién nacidos.

Red-handed [red-hand'-ed], *a.* Que tiene las manos ensangrentadas, como las de un asesino; en flagrante, en el acto.

Redhead [red'-hed], *s.* y *a.* Pelirrojo.

Redhibition [red-hi-bish'-un], *s.* Redhibición, rescisión de venta por ocultación de vicio en la cosa vendida.

Redhibitory [red-hib'-i-to-ri], *a.* Redhibitorio, perteneciente a la redhibición.

Red-hot [red'-hot], *a.* 1. Candente, ardiente, enrojecido al fuego. 2. (Fig.) Demasiado entusiasta; extremo. *A red-hot partizan,* Un partidario extremo. *Red-hot poker,* (Bot.) Trítomo, planta del sur de África que lleva una espiga de flores rojo anaranjadas.

Redintegrate [red-in'-tę-grêt], *va.* Reintegrar, restablecer en estado perfecto.

Redintegrate, *a.* Reintegrado, restablecido; renovado.
Redintegration [red-in-te-grê'-shun], *s.* Reintegración, reintegro; restauración, renovación, restablecimiento.
Redirect [rî-di-rect'], *a.* (For.) Dícese del examen de un testigo, después de las repreguntas, por la parte que primero lo examinó.
Red-lead [red-led'], *s.* Minio, bermellón, azarcón, rúbrica sinópica.
Red-letter [red-let'-er], *a.* Indicado por una o más letras rojas. *Red-letter day,* Día de fiesta o feriado; de aquí, día favorable, propicio.
Redly [red'-li], *adv.* Con color rojo, rojizamente.
Redness [red'-nes], *s.* Encarnado, rojo; rojez, rojura, bermejura.
Redolence [red'-o-lens], **Redolency** [red'-o-len-si], *s.* Fragancia o fragrancia, perfume.
Redolent [red'-o-lent], *a.* Fragante, fragrante, oloroso.
Redouble [re-dub'-l], *va.* Reduplicar, redoblar, aumentar; repetir frecuentemente.—*vn.* Redoblarse, aumentarse dos veces tanto.
Redoubt [re-daut'], *s.* (Fort.) *V.* REDOUT.
Redoubtable [re-daut'-a-bl], *a.* Formidable, terrible.
Redound [re-daund'], *vn.* 1. Operar por su turno; de aquí, contribuir, redundar, venir a parar una cosa en perjuicio o daño de otro, provenir, resultar. 2. (Des.) Recudir, resaltar, recaer. *Undertakings which will redound to the honour of their country,* Empresas que contribuirán a la gloria de su país.
Redout, Redoubt [re-daut'], *s.* Reducto, fuerte de varios lados, sin baluarte; fortificación de tierra para uso provisional.
Redowa [red'-o-a], *s.* Baile parecido a la polka y al vals, y la música del mismo.
Redraft [rî-draft'], *s.* 1. Nuevo dibujo, copia, o borrón. 2. Resaca, letra de cambio contra el endosante de otra protestada, para reembolsarse.
Redraw [rî-drō'], *va.* Hacer un segundo dibujo o borrón, una segunda copia.—*vn.* (Com.) Resacar, girar una letra de resaca.
Redress [re-dres'], *va.* 1. Enderezar; corregir, enmendar, reformar, rectificar; hacer justicia. 2. Aliviar o aligerar el peso, carga, etc. 3. Aliviar, consolar. *To redress grievances,* Deshacer agravios.
Redress, *s.* Reforma, corrección, enmienda, enderezamiento; desagravio; alivio, consuelo. *To seek redress,* Buscar justicia, buscar la reparación de algún agravio.
Redresser [re-dres'-er], *s.* Reformador, enderezador de tuertos.
Redressible [re-dres'-i-bl], *a.* Reformable, corregible; capaz de ser aliviado.
Redressive [re-dres'-iv], *a.* (Poco us.) Consolatorio; correctivo, reformatorio.
Redsear [red-sîr'], *vn.* Abrirse el hierro cuando se le martilla estando muy caliente; partirse, quebrarse.
Redshank [red'-shanc], *s.* (Orn.) Especie de maubecha del género Totanus.
Redskin [red'-skin], *s.* Piel roja, indio de América.
Redstreak [red'-stric], *s.* Manzana de rosa.
Red tape [red têp], *s.* 1. Cinta roja 2. Papeleo, expedienteo.
Redtop [red'-top], *s.* Especie de agrostis o agróstida, planta gramínea de cultivo.
Reduce [re-diūs'], *va.* 1. Reducir, dar una forma o condición determinadas. 2. Reducir, convertir, reformar, enmendar. 3. Reducir, disminuir, minorar. 4. Reducir, sujetar, someter, sojuzgar; poner en orden. 5. Degradar, envilecer. 6. (Arit. y Álg.) Cambiar la denominación de los números. 7. (Cir.) Reducir, volver a su lugar partes dislocadas; volver alguna cosa al lugar donde antes estaba o al estado que antes tenía. 8. (Quím.) Desoxidar un mineral; separar de una tierra, de un óxido, el metal que contienen. *To reduce to the ranks,* Volver a las filas; convertir a un oficial en simple soldado. *Reducing-scale,* Escala de reducción; escala de partes iguales para reducir las dimensiones de un plano.
Reducer [re-diūs'-er], *s.* Reductor, reducidor; (Art. y Of.) empate en disminución.
Reducible [re-diūs'-i-bl], *a.* Reducible, que se puede reducir.
Reduction [re-duc'-shun], *s.* Reducción, reducimiento, acción y efecto de reducir o disminuir; disminución; conquista; desoxidación. *Reduction-works,* Establecimiento metalúrgico para la extracción del metal de los minerales; fundición.
Reductive [re-duc'-tiv], *a.* Reductivo, perteneciente a la reducción.
Reductively [re-duc'-tiv-li], *adv.* Por consecuencia.
Redundance [re-dun'-dans], **Redundancy** [re-dun'-dan-si], *s.* Redundancia, exceso, superabundancia. *Redundance of words,* Pleonasmo.
Redundant [re-dun'-dant], *a.* 1. Redundante, superabundante, superfluo, excesivo. 2. Redundante, recargado en el estilo, verboso, tautológico.
Redundantly [re-dun'-dant-li], *adv.* Superfluamente.
Reduplicate [re-diū'-pli-kêt], *va.* Reduplicar, redoblar, reiterar, multiplicar.
Reduplicate, *s.* Reduplicado, duplicado, reiterado.
Reduplication [re-diū-pli-kê'-shun], *s.* Reduplicación.
Reduplicative [re-diū'-pli-ca-tiv], *a.* Reduplicativo, reduplicado.
Redwing [red'-wing], *s.* 1. Tordo rojo del antiguo continente. 2. Mirlo americano con manchas rojas sobre las alas. Algelæus.
Redwood [red'-wud], *s.* 1. Árbol inmenso de California de las coníferas, o su madera; la Sequoia sempervirens. 2. Algún otro árbol de madera rojiza, como el sándalo rojo, el sibucao, etc.
Re-echo [rî-ec'-o], *vn.* Responder o resonar el eco.
Reed [rîd], *s.* 1. (Bot.) Caña, planta hueca y nudosa que se cría en lugares húmedos; especialmente planta de los géneros Phragmitis y Arundo. La caña común es Phragmitis communis. También el tallo de esta planta. *Reed-cane,* Caña. 2. (Mús.) Caña, lengüeta; laminilla delgada, elástica, de caña, madera, o metal, que casi tapa una abertura, produciendo los tonos musicales de los órganos, etc. 3. Churumbela, un instrumento semejante a la chirimía; de aquí, poesía pastoral. 4. Tubo que contiene pólvora y la conduce al agujero de explosión en una mina. 5. (Arq.) Baqueta, junquillo, moldura semicilíndrica. 6. Peine (cárcel), una parte de los telares donde se juntan los hilos. 7. (Poét.) Flecha, saeta. 8. Abomaso, el cuarto o verdadero estómago de los rumiantes. *Reed-bird, V.* BOBOLINK (Dolichonyx). *Reed-bunting,* Emberizo, verderol; verderón de los cañaverales. Emberiza schœniclus. *Reed-mace,* Enea, planta del género Typha. *Reed-organ,* Armonio, órgano pequeño provisto de lengüetas (de latón) y de teclado. *Reed-work,* Lengüetería del órgano.
Reedy [rîd'-i], *a.* 1. Lleno de cañas, cañado, cañoso. 2. Parecido a una caña o a una lengüeta. 3. De tono delgado y agudo, como el producido por una lengüeta.
Reef [rîf], *s.* 1. Arrecife, escollo o banco de políperos situado casi á flor de agua. 2. Bajío, banco de arena en el mar. 3. (Australia) Filón, vena metálica. 4. (Mar.) Rizo. *To take in a reef,* Tomar un rizo. *To let out a reef,* Largar un rizo. *Reef-band,* Faja de rizos. *Reef-cringle,* Anillo de vela. *Reef-knot,* Nudo de rizos. *Reef-line,* Cabo de tomar rizos. *Reef-tackles,* Aparejuelos o palanquines de rizos.
Reef, *va.* (Mar.) Tomar rizos á las velas, acortarlas cuando hay mucho viento; disminuir la extensión de las velas plegando una parte y amarrándola a la verga. *To be close-reefed,* (Mar.) Estar con todos los rizos tomados.
Reek [rîk], *s.* (Esco.) 1. Humo, vaho, vapor. 2. Aventura, hazaña (en sentido burlesco), calaverada.
Reek, *va.* y *vn.* Ahumar, exponer al humo; humear, vahear, vahar. Hoy implica un olor desagradable. *To reek with sweat,* Humear de sudor. *To reek with filth,* Estar excesivamente sucio.
Reeky [rîk'-i], *a.* Ahumado, ennegrecido. *V.* AULD REEKIE.
Reel [rîl], *s.* 1. Aspa, devanadera, argadijo, carrete; utensilio giratorio que sirve para aspar o devanar madejas, etc. 2. Un baile como una contradanza, vivo y animado, y la música del mismo. *Reel of a log,* (Mar.) Carretel. *Fishing-reel,* Carrete, para cuerda de pescar. *Hose-reel,* Carretel para manguera. *Reel-click,* Retén, fiador, para regularizar el movimiento de la cuerda de pescar.
Reel, *va.* Aspar, recoger el hilo en el aspa haciéndolo madeja.—*vn.* Hacer eses, dar vueltas y giros como un borracho; vacilar al andar; bambolear.
Re-elect [rî-e-lect'], *va.* Reelegir, elegir de nuevo.
Re-election [rî-e-lec'-shun], *s.* Reelección, elección repetida.
Re-embark [rî-em-bārk'], *va.* y *vn.* Reembarcar; reembarcarse, embarcarse otra vez.
Re-embarkation [rî-em-bar-kê'-shun], *s.* Reembarco, embarco, embarcación.
Re-emergence [rî-e-mer'-gens], *s.* Reaparición; nueva aparición.
Re-enact [rî-en-act'], *va.* Establecer u ordenar de nuevo.
Re-enactment [rî'-en-act-ment], *s.* Restablecimiento, revalidación (de una ley).
Re-enforce [rî-en-fōrs'], *va.* Reforzar,

añadir nuevas fuerzas a, fortalecer; proveer de tropas adicionales.—*s.* Lo que da más fuerza o fortalece; parte de un cañón cerca de la culata, más gruesa que el resto; refuerzo de tela, etc.

Re-enforcement [rî-en-fōrs'-mẹnt], *s.* Refuerzo, nuevo socorro; tropas o embarcaciones adicionales en auxilio de otras.

Re-engage [rî-en-gêj'], *va.* Empeñar, alquilar, apalabrar, comprometer, enganchar, o acometer de nuevo.

Re-engagement [rî-en-gêj'-mẹnt], *s.* Empeño o combate renovado; nuevo empeño o ataque; acción de estipular o apalabrar segunda vez.

Re-enlist [rî-en-list'], *va.* y *vn.* Alistar o alistarse de nuevo; enganchar o engancharse de nuevo.

Re-enter [rî-en'-tẹr], *va.* 1 Volver a entrar; entrar de nuevo. 2. Repasar con el buril.

Re-entering [rî-en'-tẹr-ing], *a.* *V.* RE-ENTRANT.

Re-enthrone [rî-en-thrōn'], *va.* Volver a entronizar; reentronizarse.

Re-entrance [rî-en'-trans] o **Re-entry** [rî-en'-tri], *s.* 1. Segunda entrada, entrada repetida. 2. *Re-entry,* (For.) La acción de volver a entrar en posesión de tierras, habitaciones, rentas, etc.

Re-entrant [rî-en'-trant], *a.* Reentrante, dícese de un ángulo.

Re-establish [rî-es-tab'-lish], *va.* Restablecer.

Re-establishment [rî-es-tab'-lish-mẹnt], *s.* Restablecimiento, restauración.

Reeve [rîv], *va.* (Mar.) Pasar, guarnir, introducir un cabo en el motón.

Reeve, *s.* Mayordomo. Esta palabra sólo existe ya en algunos compuestos, como *port-reeve,* sheriff (= shire-reeve), etc.

Re-examine [rî-eg-zam'-in], *va.* Reexaminar.

Re-examination [rî-eg-zam-i-nê'-shun], *s.* Reexaminación.

Re-export [rî-ex-pōrt'], *va.* Reexportar, volver a exportar; exportar lo que había sido importado.

Refashion [rî-fash'-un], *va.* Rehacer, modelar, de nuevo.

Refasten [rî-fas'-n], *va.* Atar, amarrar, asegurar, unir de nuevo; volver a atar.

Refection [rẹ-fec'-shun], *s.* Refección, refacción, refocilación, alimento moderado.

Refective [rẹ-fec'-tiv], *a.* Refocilador, que refocila o repara.—*s.* Restaurador.

Refectory [rẹ-fec'-to-ri], *s.* Refectorio; el comedor, la sala destinada para comer.

Refer [rẹ-fẹr'], *va.* 1. Referir, remitir, enviar; dirigir, encaminar u ordenar alguna cosa para algún fin, dirigir para informes. 2. Someter al examen o consideración (de otra persona); someter a la decisión de un árbitro. 3. Asignar, atribuir. —*vn.* 1. Referirse, hacer relación una cosa á otra, aludir. 2. Referir á otra persona, a un banco, etc., para que dé recomendaciones o informes. 3. Dirigirse a, recurrir a, acudir. 4. Apuntar, dar a conocer por medio de una cruz, asterisco u otro signo de imprenta. *He refers to the Bank of T——,* Refiere (para informes) al Banco de T——.

Referee [ref-ẹ-rî'], *s.* Árbitro, arbitrador, el sujeto a cuya decisión queda alguna cosa.

Reference [ref'-ẹ-rens], *s.* 1. Referencia, remisión; alusión, mención. 2. Nota, señal u otra indicación en un libro o escrito que refiere al lector a otro pasaje o libro. 3. La persona a quien se puede acudir (para informes o recomendación); fiador; la misma recomendación; referencia, aviso del crédito de que puede gozar una persona, casa de comercio, etc. 4. Arbitramento o arbitramiento. *On reference to,* Dirigiéndose a. *With reference to,* Con referencia, con relación a; en cuanto a, respecto.

Referendum [ref-ẹr-en'-dum], *s.* 1. Acción de someter algo un diplomático a su gobierno, v. gr. una proposición no contenida en sus instrucciones. 2. Referendum, especie de plebiscito sobre ciertas cuestiones políticas o económicas.

Referential [ref-ẹr-en'-shal], *a.* Que contiene un informe; que se refiere a algo.

Referment [rẹ-fẹr-mẹnt'], *va.* Fermentar de nuevo, volver a fermentar.

Referrible, *a.* *V.* REFERABLE.

Refill [rẹ'-fil], *s.* Repuesto (de un envase comercial).—[rẹ-fil'], *va.* Volver a llenar.

Refine [rẹ-fain'], *va.* Refinar, purificar, pulir, perfeccionar alguna cosa; hacer o hacerse cortés y cultivado, elegante.—*vn.* 1. Sutilizar, discurrir con demasiada sutileza, astucia, malicia, etc. 2. Purificarse o hacerse algo más puro. 3. Pulirse, hacerse demasiado delicado o afectado. *To be refined,* Ser muy prendado, distinguirse por su cortesía, urbanidad o cultura.

Refinedly [rẹ-fain'-ed-li], *adv.* Afectadamente.

Refinedness, *s.* *V.* REFINEMENT.

Refinement [rẹ-fain'-mẹnt], *s.* 1. Refinación, la acción de refinar. 2. Refinadura, la acción de refinar metales o licores. 3. La demasiada delicadeza, sutileza o esmero en lo que se discurre, inventa o hace. 4. Adelantamiento, en elegancia o pureza. 5. Astucia refinada. 6. Afectación de elegancia o elegancia afectada. 7. Prendas, dotes, elegancia, gracias, adorno.

Refiner [rẹ-fain'-ẹr], *s.* Refinador, persona o cosa que refina.

Refinery [re-fai'-nẹr-i], *s.* Refinería, lugar donde se purifica alguna materia cruda, v. gr. el azúcar o el petróleo.

Refining [rî-fain'-ing], *s.* Refinadura de metales o licores, etc.

Refit [rẹ-fit'], *va.* 1. Reparar, componer, aderezar, rehabilitar. 2. (Mar.) Embonar o reparar el casco de una embarcación.

Reflect [rẹ-flect'], *va.* y *vn.* 1. Reflejar, reflectar, reverberar, devolver, hablando de la luz, el calor, el sonido o algún cuerpo elástico. 2. Reflejar, rechazar, repercutir. 3. Reflejar, devolver una imagen. 4. Repensar, volver a pensar, discurrir o reflexionar. 5. Reflexionar, considerar, pensar con atención. 6. Improperar, dar en rostro a alguno con una mala acción, echar en cara a, reprobar, hacer observaciones injuriosas. 7. Desdorar, deslustrar, deslucir, manchar. 8. Recaer o refluir en; ser responsable de. *Errors of wives reflect on husbands,* Los maridos pagan las faltas de las mujeres.

Reflecter [rẹ-flect'-ẹr], *s.* Reverbero, el cuerpo que refleja.

Reflection [rẹ-flec'-shun], *s.* 1. Reflexión de los rayos de la luz, etc., reverberación; imagen producida por reflexión. 2. Reflexión, consideración, meditación. 3. Censura, nota, tacha, baldón. 4. (Anat.) Doblez, el efecto de doblar una cosa sobre sí misma. *On, upon, reflection,* Pensando en ello. *They will not bear any reflections upon their nephew,* No sufren que se diga mal de su sobrino.

Reflective [rẹ-flect'-iv], *a.* 1. Reflexivo, que refleja o reflecta. 2. Reflexivo, que reflexiona; meditativo, meditabundo.

Reflector [rẹ-flect'-ẹr], *s.* 1. (Ópt.) Reflector, lo que refleja, como un espejo de metal pulimentado; telescopio de reflexión. 2. (Des.) El que reflexiona, medita o considera atentamente.

Reflex [rî'-flex], *a.* 1. Reflejo, dirigido hacia atrás. 2. (Fís.) Perteneciente a una acción reflexiva o producido por ella. *Reflex action* (*motion* o *movement*), Acción refleja, la producida por la transmisión de un impulso aferente a un centro nervioso, y su reflexión de allí como impulso eferente, independientemente de la volición; v. g. el pestañeo involuntario cuando se amenaza al ojo.—*s.* 1. Imagen producida por la reflexión; una simple copia. 2. Reflejo, reverberación, resalto de la luz o del color de un cuerpo en otro.

Reflex [rẹ-flex'], *va.* Reflejar, dirigir, inclinar o volver hacia atrás.

Reflexion [rẹ-flec'-shun], *s.* (Ant.) Reflexión: úsase siempre en sentido físico y no moral. *V.* REFLECTION.

Reflexive [rẹ-flex'-iv], *a.* (Gram.) Reflexivo, aquello cuya acción recae sobre el mismo que la ejecuta. *Reflexive pronoun, reflexive verb,* Pronombre, verbo reflexivo.

Reflexively [rẹ-flex'-iv-li], *adv.* Reflexivamente.

Reflorescence [rî-flo-res'-ens], *s.* El acto de reflorecer.

Reflourish [rî-flur'-ish], *vn.* Reflorecer.

Reflow [rî-flō'], *vn.* Refluir, volver hacia atrás o hacer retroceso un líquido.

Refluence, Refluency [ref'-lu-ens, en-si], *s.* Reflujo, el estado o calidad de refluente; acción de refluir.

Refluent [ref'-lu-ent], *a.* Refluente, que refluye, que vuelve hacia atrás.

Reflux [rî'-flux], *s.* Reflujo, movimiento hacia atrás, o en dirección opuesta; menguante, decadencia.

Reforest [rî-fer'-est], *va.* Restablecer bosques.

Reforestation [rî-fer-es-tê'-shun], *s.* Reforestación, restablecimiento de bosques.

Reform [rî-fōrm'], *va.* 1. Volver a formar. 2. Reformar, restituir una cosa a su antigua forma. 3. [rẹ-fōrm'] Reformar, corregir, enmendar, cambiar de malo á mejor, o persuadir a otros a que se enmienden; hacer mejor moralmente, librar de malas costumbres. 4. (Mil.) Reformar, licenciar parte de las tropas de un ejército, cuerpo, etc.—*vn.* Reformarse, corregirse, enmendarse.

Reform, *s.* Reforma, arreglo, cambio favorable y progresivo, especialmente en la administración. *Civil-service reform*, (E. U.) Reforma en el servicio civil, nacional, o de un Estado particular.

Reformation [ref-er-mé'-shun], *s.* 1. Reforma, el acto de reformar o enmendar, y la calidad de reformado; enmienda en el método de vida o en las maneras. 2. Reforma, la gran revolución religiosa del siglo XVI, que terminó con el establecimiento del protestantismo. 3. [rí"-fer-mé'-shun] Nueva formación, acción y efecto de formar de nuevo.

Reformative [rę-fōrm'-a-tiv], *a.* Reformador, que forma de nuevo.

Reformatory [rę-fōrm'-a-to-ri], *a.* Reformatorio, que tiene autoridad o tendencia para producir reforma o enmienda.—*s.* Casa de corrección, establecimiento destinado á corregir individuos culpables de delitos; cuando es para jóvenes se llama *reform school.*

Reformer [rę-fōrm'-ęr], *s.* 1. Reformador, reformista. 2. Uno de los que emprendieron la Reforma protestante.

Reformist [rę-fōrm'-ist], *s.* Religioso reformado.

Refract [rę-fract'], *va.* Refringir, refractar, hacer cambiar de dirección al rayo que pasa de un medio á otro de diferente densidad.

Refracted [rę-fract'-ed], *a.* Refracto.

Refraction [rę-frac'-shun], *s.* Refracción, la desviación del rayo de luz que pasa de un medio a otro de diferente densidad.

Refractive [rę-fract'-iv], *a.* Refringente, que refringe; refractor, que causa refracción.

Refractor [rę-fract'-ęr], *s.* Telescopio de refracción; refractor.

Refractorily [rę-frac'-to-ri-li], *adv.* Tercamente, obstinadamente, de un modo incorregible.

Refractoriness [rę-frac'-to-ri-nes], *s.* Contumacia, obstinación, terquedad, porfía.

Refractory [rę-frac'-to-ri], *a.* 1. Refractario, contumaz, terco, díscolo, obstinado, indócil, rebelde, incorregible. 2. (Quím.) Infundible, que resiste a los medios ordinarios de reducción.

Refragable [ref'-ra-ga-bl], *a.* Capaz de impugnación, lo que se puede refutar.

Refrain [rę-frên'], *va.* Refrenar, contener, reprimir, moderar, detener. —*vn.* Refrenarse, abstenerse de obrar o intervenir, dejar de hacer, contenerse, guardarse de hacer una cosa.

Refrain, *s.* Estrambote, estribillo, verso o copla que se repite a intervalos en una canción o estancia.

Refrangibility [rę-fran-ji-bil'-i-ti], **Refrangibleness** [rę-fran'-ji-bl-nes], *s.* Capacidad de ser refractado, como la de los rayos de luz.

Refrangible [rę-fran'-ji-bl], *a.* Capaz de refracción.

Refresh [rę-fresh'], *va.* 1. Refrescar, poner fresco, renovar, volver á dar vigor, vivificar. 2. Refrescar, templar el calor, enfriar. 3. Refrigerar, aliviar, descansar, tomar algún descanso, alivio o recreo.—*vn.* Refrescarse, recobrar nuevas fuerzas, rehacerse.

Refresher [rę-fresh'-ęr], *s.* Refrescador, refrigerador, el o lo que refresca.

Refreshing [rę-fresh'-ing], *a.* Refrescante, refrigerante; que alivia; a menudo en sentido sarcástico, como *refreshing impudence*, descaro, frescura.—*s.* Refrescadura.

Refreshment [rę-fresh'-męnt], *s.* 1. Refresco, refrigerio, alivio, lo que da nueva fuerza o vigor. 2. Refresco, alimento moderado que se toma para reparar las fuerzas; agasajo de refrescos, dulces, etc., que se hace en las visitas o reuniones. En este sentido se usa en pluràl, por regla general.

Refrigerant [rę-frij'-ęr-ant], *a.* Refrigerante, refrigerativo, que disminuye el calor, que enfría.—*s.* Refrigerante, medicamento o remedio que disminuye el calor.

Refrigerate [rę-frij'-ęr-ét], *va.* Refrigerar, refrescar, hacer que se ponga fría alguna cosa, enfriar.

Refrigerating [rę-frij'-ęr-ét-ing], *s.* Refrigeración.

Refrigeration [rę-frij-ęr-é'-shun], *s.* Refrigeración, enfriamiento, acción y efecto de enfriar.

Refrigerative [rę-frij'-ęr-a-tiv], *a.* Refrigerante.—*s.* Refrigerante.

Refrigerator [rę-frij'-ęr-é"-tęr], *s.* 1. Lo que enfría; refrigerador, caja o cuarto para conservar algo frío por medio de hielo; garapiñera. 2. Refrigerante, vaso que rodea el capitel de un alambique o su serpentín, para enfriar pronto. *Refrigerator car*, (F.C.) Carro de refrigeración; furgón provisto de una cámara de hielo para el transporte de artículos maleantes.

Refrigeratory [rę-frij'-ęr-a-to-ri], *s.* (Quím.) Refrigeratorio, vaso con agua para templar el calor en la destilación.—*a.* Refrigerativo, refrigerante.

Refuel [rí-fiū'-el], *vn.* Repostar combustible.

Refuge [ref'-yūj], *s.* 1. Refugio, acogida, amparo, protección contra un peligro o una calamidad. 2. Abrigo, asilo, lo que abriga o protege; plaza fuerte, guarida. 3. Recurso, expediente, subterfugio.

Refugee [ref-yū-jí'], *s.* Refugiado; el que huye hacia un asilo para ponerse un seguridad, especialmente el que en tiempos de persecución o de conmociones políticas huye a un país o ciudad extranjeros.

Refulgence [rę-ful'-jens], **Refulgency** [rę-ful'-jen-si], *s.* Refulgencia, resplandor, claridad, esplendor, brillantez.

Refulgent [rę-ful'-jent], *a.* Refulgente, brillante, resplandeciente, esplendente.

Refund [rę-fund'], *va.* 1. Restituir; volver a pagar, reembolsar. 2. [rí-fund'] Consolidar una deuda; reemplazar por un empréstito recién consolidado.

Refundable [rę-fund'-a-bl], *a.* Que se puede restituir o volver a pagar.

Refusable [rę-fiūz'-a-bl], *a.* Recusable, que se puede recusar.

Refusal [rę-fiūz'-al], *s.* 1. Negativa, repulsa, denegación; desaire. 2. Elección, opción, el privilegio de aceptar o recusar, o rehusar; la preferencia para hacer una cosa.

Refuse [rę-fiūz'], *va.* y *vn.* 1. Recusar, negar, no conceder lo que se pide, no consentir, no permitir, no convenir. 2. Rehusar, desechar, no aceptar, repulsar, denegar. 3. Desairar.

Refuse [ref'-yus], *s.* Desecho, zupia, desperdicio; sobra, residuo.—*a.* Rechazado, desechado, como sin valor.

Refuser [rę-fiū'-zęr], *s.* El que recusa o rehusa.

Refutable [rę-fiū'-ta-bl], *a.* Refutable, que puede ser refutado.

Refutation [ref-yu-té'-shun], **Refutal** [rę-fiū'-tal], *s.* Refutación.

Refutatory [rę-fiū'-ta-to-ri], *a.* Refutatorio, que tiende a refutar o sirve para ello.

Refute [rę-fiūt'], *va.* Refutar, contradecir.

Regain [rę-gên'], *va.* Recobrar, recuperar; volver a ganar lo perdido; ganar de nuevo; conseguir, acercarse otra vez.

Regal [rí'-gal], *a.* Real, regio, perteneciente a un rey; propio de un rey.—*s.* Organillo portátil y muy pequeño del siglo XVI.

Regale [rę-gél'], *va.* Regalar, agasajar, festejar; recrear, deleitar.

†**Regale** [rę-gé'-lę], *s.* (*sing.* de REGALIA). 1. Patronato regio, prerrogativa real. 2. (Ant.) Banquete, festín suntuoso, holgorio; regalo; complacencia.

Regalement [rę-gél'-męnt], *s.* Regalo, presente, dádiva.

Regalia [rę-gé'-li-a], *s. pl.* 1. Insignias reales. 2. Insignias, distintivos, adornos propios de algunos cuerpos.

Regality [rę-gal'-i-ti], *s.* Realeza, soberanía, poder soberano.

Regally [rí'-gal-i], *adv.* Soberanamente, como rey, de un modo regio.

Regard [rę-gārd'], *va.* 1. Observar o mirar de cerca, reparar, atender, poner atención. 2. Considerar desde cierto punto de vista, reputar, juzgar, estimar. 3. Estimar, hacer aprecio y estimación de alguno, hacer caso de alguna cosa, apreciar; hacer alto; respetar, venerar. 4. Tocar, pertenecer, tener relación a, concernir, mirar a. *As regards*, Tocante a, en cuanto a, por lo que toca a. *As regards that I can not agree with you*, En cuanto a eso, no puedo convenir con Vd.

Regard, *s.* 1. Miramiento, atención, circunspección, consideración. 2. Respeto, veneración, acatamiento. *I profess a great regard for him*, Le estimo mucho. *With regard to what you say*, En cuanto a lo que Vd. dice. 3. Reputación, fama común. 4. Respecto, relación; con *with* o *in*, y seguido de *to* u *of*. *With regard to, in regard to* u *of*, Con relación a, en cuanto a, relativamente a. 5. Consideración, afectos, amistades; fórmula de urbanidad. 6. Mirada. *With the kindest regards*, Con la mayor consideración. *My kindest regards*, Mil afectos de mi parte. *To have a great regard for*, Tener mucha consideración por, hacer gran caso de. *Without any regard to*, Sin miramientos. *Regard being had* (*to*), Atendido que, en vista de.

Regardant [rę-gārd'-ant], *a.* (Her.) Mirante.

Regarder [rę-gārd'-ęr], *s.* Espectador, mirón, mirador; un inspector de los montes vedados del rey.

Regardful [rę-gārd'-ful], *a.* Atento, circunspecto; cuidadoso.

Regardfully [rę-gārd'-ful-i], *adv.* Atentamente, respetuosamente.

Regarding [re-gārd'-ing], *prep.* Con relación a, relativamente á, en cuanto a. *Anxious regarding his plans.* Ansioso en cuanto a sus planes.

Regardless [rę-gārd'-les], *a.* Descuidado, negligente; desacatado, indiferente.

Regardlessly [rẹ-gārd'-les-li], *adv.* Descuidadamente, desatentamente.
Regardlessness [rẹ-gārd'-les-nes], *s.* Descuido, negligencia; desacatamiento.
Regatta [rẹ-gat'-a], *s.* Regata, contienda entre botes u otras embarcaciones menores, para ganar una apuesta.
Regency [rí'-jen-si], *s.* 1. Regencia, el gobierno de un reino cuando el príncipe no puede gobernar por cualquiera causa. 2. Regencia, el gobierno de un regente; también el conjunto de regentes.
Regeneracy [rẹ-jen'-ẹr-a-si], *s.* Regeneración, acción y efecto de regenerar.
Regenerate [rẹ-jen'-ẹr-êt], *va.* 1. Regenerar, reproducir. 2. Reengendrar. 3. (Teol.) Renovar espiritualmente; infundir buenos principios.
Regenerate, *a.* Regenerado, reengendrado; nacido a una nueva vida, renovado espiritualmente.
Regenerateness [rí-jen'-ẹr-ẹt-nes], **Regeneration** [rí-jen-ẹr-ê'-shun], *s.* Regeneración; renacimiento.
Regenerative [rẹ-jen'-ẹr-a-tiv], *a.* Regenerador, que regenera.
Regeneratory [rẹ-jen'-ẹr-a-to-ri], *a.* Regeneratorio, que tiene la propiedad de regenerar o renovar.
Regent [rí'-jent], *a.* 1. Regente, que ejerce autoridad en lugar de otro. 2. Regente, reinante; que rige o gobierna.—*s.* 1. Regente, regenta, el o la que rige un reino en nombre y lugar del rey. 2. Gobernador, gobernante. 3. Regente, miembro de una universidad encargado de ciertas funciones especiales de administración.
Regentship [rí'-jent-ship], *s.* Regencia, empleo de regente.
Regerminate [rí-jẹr'-mi-nêt], *vn.* Retoñar, germinar o brotar de nuevo.
Regermination [rí-jẹr-mi-nê'-shun], *s.* La acción de brotar de nuevo.
Regicidal [rej-i-sai'-dal], *a.* Regicida, que mata a un rey o reina; perteneciente al regicidio.
Regicide [rej'-i-said], *s.* 1. Regicidio, asesinato de un rey o reina. 2. Regicida, el que mata a un rey o soberano.
Régime [rê-zhím'], *s.* Régimen, manera o sistema de gobernar: administración particular; sistema social. (Fr.)
Regimen [rej'-i-men], *s.* 1. Régimen, dieta, observancia metódica de las prescripciones higiénicas en cuanto á los alimentos, vestidos, ejercicio, etc. 2. Gobierno metódico, sujeción, freno. 3. (Gram.) Régimen, dependencia mutua que tienen las partes de la oración, expresada con o sin preposiciones, según los casos.
Regiment [rej'-i-mẹnt], *s.* 1. Regimiento, cierto número de compañías de soldados de que es jefe un coronel. 2. (Des.) Regimiento, gobierno.
Regimental [rej-i-ment'-al], *a.* Regimental, perteneciente a un regimiento. *Regimentals,* Uniforme militar.
Region [rí'-jun], *s.* 1. Región, extensión indefinida aunque considerable; área: dícese hablando de la tierra, del aire o del cuerpo humano. 2. Región, país, distrito, comarca; lugar, espacio. 3. (Anat. y Zool.) Región, porción del cuerpo.
Regional [rí'-jun-al], *a.* Regional, perteneciente a una región; local, topográfico.
Register [rej'-is-tẹr], *s.* 1. Registro, asiento o apuntamiento de alguna cosa; relación formal u oficial, y el libro que la contiene; rol, lista, archivo, protocolo; libro de parroquia. 2. Registrador; escribano de hipotecas. *V.* REGISTRAR. *Register of a ship,* Matrícula de navío. *Register-ships,* (Mar.) Navíos de registro, los que tenían permiso del rey de España para traficar en los puertos de América. 3. Lo que registra; aparato mecánico para registrar ciertos hechos, como la velocidad, la presión, etc.; o para contar el valor de los billetes de pasaje, el dinero cobrado en las tiendas, etc. 4. (Quím.) Registro, celosía, placa o plancha de los hornos que sirve para abrirlos o cerrarlos y regular el calor. 5. (Mús.) (1) Compás de la voz o de un instrumento; (2) registro, listón de madera que puesto o retirado cambia las voces del órgano. 6. (Com.) Certificado de nacionalidad; documento de aduana que contiene la descripción de un buque, su nombre, cabida, nacionalidad, dueños, etc. 7. (Impr.) Registro, la correspondencia igual de las dos páginas de una misma hoja.
Register, *va.* 1. Registrar, inscribir en un registro o en una lista. 2. Notar según una escala.—*vn.* 1. Inscribir uno su nombre en un registro. 2. (Impr.) Estar en un registro. *To register a letter,* Certificar una carta.
Registrar [rej'-is-trar], **Registrary** [rej'-is-tra-ri], *s.* Registrador, el empleado a cuyo cargo está algún registro.
Registration [rej-is-trê'-shun], *s.* Asiento, registro; empadronamiento, encabezamiento.
Registry [rej'-is-tri], *s.* 1. Asiento. 2. Archivo, el lugar o paraje en que se guardan papeles o instrumentos. 3. Protocolo, registro.
Reglet [reg'-let], *s.* 1. (Arq.) Filete, moldura pequeña. 2. (Impr.) Corondel, regleta.
Regnant [reg'-nant], *a.* Reinante, predominante.
Regorge [rí-gōrj'], *va.* 1. Vomitar. 2. Tragar muy aprisa, zampar. 3. Volver a tragar.
Regraft [rí-grqft'], *va.* Ingerir o ingertar de nuevo.
Regrant [rí-grqnt'], *va.* Volver a conceder.
Regrate [rẹ-grêt'], *va.* 1. Antiguamente, monopolizar, hacer monopolio, revender provisiones en el mismo lugar de su primera venta a un precio mayor. 2. Raspar, quitar la superficie exterior de una piedra para darle mejor apariencia.
Regress [rí'-gres], *s.* Regreso, retorno, vuelta.
Regress [rẹ-gres'], *vn.* 1. Regresar, volver, retornar. 2. (Astr.) Retrogradar, moverse en dirección opuesta a la del movimiento general de los astros.
Regression [rẹ-gresh'-un], *s.* Regresión, retrocesión o el acto de volver atrás.
Regressive [rẹ-gres'-iv], *a.* Retrógrado, que vuelve o retorna; retroactivo.
Regret [rẹ-gret'], *s.* 1. Pesadumbre, cuidado, sentimiento; dolor al recordar algún acontecimiento pasado; pesar. 2. Compunción, dolor de conciencia, tristeza llena de remordimientos. 3. *pl.* (Fam.) Pésame, recusación; excusa cortés que se da como respuesta a una invitación.
Regret, *vn.* Sentir, tener pena, dolor o pesadumbre; echar de menos.
Regrettable [rẹ-gret'-a-bl], *a.* Que ha de ser sentido; propio para causar pesadumbre.
Regular [reg'-yu-lar], *a.* 1. Regular, regulado, que es o está ajustado, y conforme a una regla, que está en regla. 2. Arreglado, que guarda regla y orden, gobernado por una regla o reglas, metódico; que vuelve o se repite sin omisión. 3. Regular, conforme a ley o costumbre; autorizado debidamente, permanente. 4. (Mil.) Regular, perteneciente a un ejército permanente. *A regular doctor,* Un médico titulado o examinado; el médico llamado por otros alópata.—*s.* 1. Soldado que pertenece a un ejército permanente. 2. El que está empleado regularmente. 3. Regular, el que vive bajo una regla en un instituto religioso. *As regular as clockwork,* Tan bien ordenado como un reloj. *He is a regular attendant at church on Sundays,* Asiste regularmente a la iglesia los domingos.
Regularity [reg-yu-lar'-i-ti], *s.* Regularidad, conformidad, simetría, método, buen orden.
Regularly [reg'-yu-lar-li], *adv.* Regularmente.
Regulate [reg'-yu-lêt], *va.* 1. Regular, regularizar, arreglar, ordenar, poner y mantener en orden. 2. Medir, ajustar, dirigir, disciplinar, ajustar según regla y método.
Regulation [reg-yu-lê'-shun], *s.* Regulación, arreglo, método; reglamento, orden, regla de conducta o de gobierno; mandato. *Regulation size, length,* Tamaño, longitud de reglamento.
Regulative [reg'-yu-la-tiv], *a.* Reglamentario, regulador, que tiende o sirve para regular.
Regulator [reg'-yu-lê-tẹr], *s.* 1. Regulador; el que regula, arregla u ordena alguna cosa. 2. Regulador, reloj que sirve de norma para el arreglo de los demás relojes. 3. Regulador, mecanismo que en las máquinas, particularmente en las de vapor, sirve para regular el movimiento; índice que acelera o atrasa la marcha de un reloj.
Regulus [reg'-yu-lus], *s.* 1. (Quím.) Régulo, la parte más pura de los minerales, que en estado de fusión cae al fondo del crisol. 2. (Astr.) Régulo, estrella blanca de primera magnitud en la constelación León.
Regurgitate [rí-gūr'-ji-têt], *va.* Volver a echar, echar otra vez, volver a verter o a trasegar.—*vn.* (Med.) Regurgitar, salirse algún líquido o humor de la parte que le contiene por la mucha abundancia.
Regurgitation [rí-gūr-ji-tê'-shun], *s.* Regurgitación.
Rehabilitate [rí-ha-bil'-i-têt], *va.* Rehabilitar, restablecer, reintegrar en su primer estado o capacidad, en sus anteriores derechos, títulos o privilegios.
Rehabilitation [rí-ha-bil-i-tê'-shun], *s.* Rehabilitación.
Rehash [rí-hash'], *va.* Volver a picar, esto es, dar nueva forma a una cosa (se emplea despreciativamen-

te).—*s.* Algo rehecho con materiales usados antes; fárrago.
Rehearsal [rẹ-hẹrs'-al], *s.* 1. Repetición, la acción de repetir; recitación, relación. 2. Ensayo, la prueba de una pieza de teatro o de música, por lo común en privado.
Rehearse [rẹ-hẹrs'], *va.* 1. Repetir, recitar, referir. 2. Repasar; ensayar una pieza de teatro o de música, para poder corregirla antes de la representación pública.
Reign [rên], *vn.* 1. Reinar, poseer y ejercer el poder soberano. 2. Reinar, dominar, predominar. 3. Reinar, prevalecer, estar en boga, estar muy valida alguna cosa.
Reign, *s.* 1. Soberanía, reino, poder soberano. 2. Predominio, dominio, influencia predominante. 3. Reinado, espacio de tiempo en que gobierna un rey o reina.
Reigning [rên'-ing], *a.* Reinante, predominante, prevaleciente.
Reimburse [rî-im-būrs'], *va.* 1. Reembolsar, devolver el dinero desembolsado. 2. Indemnizar.
Reimburser [rî-im-būr'-sẹr], *s.* El que reembolsa o indemniza.
Reimbursement [rî-im-būrs'-mẹnt], *s.* Reembolso.
Reimpregnate [rî-im preg'-nêt], *va.* Impregnar de nuevo.
Reimpregnation [rî-im-preg-nê'-shun], *s.* (Quím.) Nueva impregnación.
Reimpression [rî-im-presh'-un], *s.* Reimpresión, impresión repetida; nueva edición. *V.* REPRINT.
Rein [rên], *s.* Rienda, tanto en el sentido físico como en el moral; correa de las bridas; (fig.) gobierno, dirección. *To give rein to,* Aflojar las riendas, dar licencia para obrar como se quiera. *To take the reins,* Tomar las riendas, tomar la dirección del gobierno.
Rein, *va.* 1. Gobernar; dirigir por medio de riendas. 2. Refrenar, tener en freno, contener.
Reincarnation [rî''-in-car-nê'-shun], *s.* Reencarnación, reincorporación en la carne, una de las series en la transmigración de las almas.
Reincorporate [rî-in-cōr'-po-rêt], *va.* Reincorporar, volver á incorporar.
Reincorporation [rî-in-cōr-po-rê'-shun], *s.* Reincorporación.
Reindeer [rên'-dîr], *s.* Reno, rangífero, rengífero, un cuadrúpedo de los países más septentrionales, parecido al ciervo. (Rangifer tarandus.)
Reinfect [rî-in-fect'], *va.* Infectar o inficionar de nuevo, volver a inficionar.
Reinforce [rî-in-fōrs'], *va.* *V.* RE-ENFORCE.
Reinforcement, *s.* *V.* RE-ENFORCEMENT.
Reingratiate [rî-in-grê'-shi-êt], *va.* Volver a hacer entrar en gracia.
Reins [rênz], *s.* 1. Riñones, o la región de los riñones. 2. Las partes interiores; de aquí, los afectos y las pasiones.
Reinsert [rî-in-sẹrt'], *va.* Insertar o ingerir de nuevo una cosa en otra.
Reinstate [rî-in-stêt'], *va.* 1. Reinstalar, reintegrar, volver a poner en el estado precedente, restablecer; volver á revestir de autoridad. 2. En los seguros contra incendios, reparar o reponer, en lugar de pagar el valor de la propiedad dañada.
Reinsurance [rî-in-shūr-ans], *s.* Seguro de una propiedad ya asegurada; reparto de un seguro cuantioso entre varias compañías.
Reinsure [rî-in-shūr'], *va.* Asegurar por segunda vez, volver a asegurar.
Reinvest [rî-in-vest'], *va.* Dar nueva autoridad o renovar la que se dió.
Reinvigorate [rî-in-vig'-er-êt], *va.* Vigorizar o fortificar de nuevo.
Reinvigoration [rî-in-vig-er-ê'-shun], *s.* El acto de reforzar o vigorizar de nuevo.
Reissue [rî-ish'-ū], *va.* 1. Reimprimir (un libro, publicación, etc.). 2. Emitir por segunda vez (como una película cinematográfica).—*s.* Reimpresión, reaparición.
Reiterate [rî-it'-ẹr-êt], *va.* Reiterar, repetir, decir o ejecutar algo repetidas veces.
Reiteratedly [rî-it'-ẹr-ê''-ted-li], *adv.* Reiteradamente, repetidas veces.
Reiteration [rî-it-ẹr-ê'-shun], *s.* Reiteración, repetición.
Reject [rẹ-ject'], *va.* 1. Rechazar, rebatir, repulsar. 2. Desechar, no admitir, rehusar, repugnar; despreciar, desestimar.
Rejectable [rẹ-ject'-a-bl], *a.* Recusable, inadmisible.
Rejecter, Rejector [rẹ-ject'-ẹr, ẹr], *s.* El que rechaza, rebate o repugna.
Rejection [rẹ-jec'-shun], *s.* Rechazamiento, desecho, la acción de desechar, rechazar, etc.
Rejective [rẹ-jec'-tiv], *a.* Rechazador, que tiende a rechazar o rehusar.
Rejectment [rẹ-ject'-mẹnt], *s.* Desecho, cosa que no sirve; también, rechazamiento.
Rejoice [rẹ-jois'], *vn.* Regocijarse, recrearse, sentir júbilo, alegría.—*va.* Regocijar, alegrar, dar o causar alegría.
Rejoicing [rẹ-jois'-ing], *s.* Alegría, fiesta, regocijo, júbilo.—*a.* Gustoso, agradable, divertido, alegre.
Rejoin [rẹ-join'], *va.* Reunirse, volver a juntarse, volver a la compañía de; reunirse después de una separación (activo en inglés).—*vn.* 1. Replicar, responder a una respuesta. 2. (For.) Contrarreplicar, contestar contradiciendo la réplica del demandador.
Rejoinder [rẹ-join'-dẹr], *s.* Respuesta, réplica; contrarréplica.
Rejoint [rî-joint'], *va.* 1. (Alb.) Llenar las degolladuras con mortero. 2. Reponer, reunir las junturas o articulaciones de algo.
Rejudge [rî-juj'], *va.* Rever, volver a ver, revistar, examinar o juzgar de nuevo.
Rejuvenate [rẹ-jū'-vẹ-nêt], *va.* Rejuvenecer, remozar.
Rejuvenation [rẹ-jū-ve-nê'-shun], *s.* Remozamiento, el acto de remozar, de renovar.
Rejuvenescence [rî-jū-vẹ-nes'-ens], **Rejuvenescency** [rî-jū-vẹ-nes'-en-si], *s.* Renovación de la juventud; acción y efecto de rejuvenecerse.
Rekindle [rî-kin'-dl], *va.* Volver a encender; inflamar, despertar o excitar de nuevo.
Relapse [rẹ-laps'], *vn.* 1. Recaer, volver alguno a adolecer de la enfermedad de que padeció; sufrir una recaída o recidiva. 2. Recaer, volver a caer en algún error, delito, etc.; reincidir; renegar, pasarse de un culto a otro.
Relapse, *s.* Recaída; reincidencia, repetición de una falta; recidiva de una enfermedad.
Relate [rẹ-lêt'], *va.* 1. Relatar, referir, contar, narrar. 2. Emparentar, contraer parentesco.—*vn.* Estar en relación o asociación de pensamiento o de hecho; tocar, pertenecer, ser concerniente a, referirse.
Related [rẹ-lê'-ted], *pp.* y *a.* Conexo, que está en relación o enlace (con); emparentado, consanguíneo; del mismo género, de la misma familia.
Relater [rẹ-lêt'-ẹr], *s.* Relator, el que narra o relata.
Relation [rẹ-lê'-shun], *s.* 1. Relación, respecto; consonancia, conexión, concernencia, interdependencia. 2. Referencia, alusión. 3. Relación, comunicación o correspondencia de una persona o cosa con otra. 4. Parentesco. 5. Pariente, parienta. *All his relations,* Toda su parentela. *Near relation,* Pariente cercano. 6. Relación, narración. *In relation to,* Con relación a, respecto a.
Relationship [rẹ-lê'-shun-ship], *s.* Parentesco, conexión por consanguinidad o afinidad; estado o calidad de ser emparentado.
Relative [rel'-a-tiv], *a.* 1. Relativo, que tiene relación con, que se refiere a; pertinente. 2. Relativo, inteligible sólo en relación con otra cosa, que no existe por sí mismo. 3. Relativo, que representa un antecedente. *Relative greatness,* Grandeza relativa.—*s.* 1. Pariente, deudo. 2. Pronombre relativo. 3. Cualquier cosa que tiene relación con otra.
Relatively [rel'-a-tiv-li], *adv.* Relativamente, por comparación.
Relativeness [rel'-a-tiv-nes], *s.* El estado de lo que tiene relación con otra cosa.
Relativism [rel'-a-tiv-izm], *s.* Relativismo.
Relativist [rel'-a-tiv-ist], *s.* Relativista.
Relativistic [rel-a-tiv-is'-tic], *a.* Relativista.
Relativity [rel-a-tiv'-i-ti], *s.* Relatividad. *Theory of relativity,* Teoría de la relatividad.
Relax [rẹ-lax'], *va.* 1. Relajar, aflojar, laxar; ablandar. 2. Aflojar, soltar lo que estaba tirante. 3. Relajar, anular o relevar de alguna obligación. 4. Relajar, esparcirse o divertir el ánimo, solazar. 5. Relajar, disminuir la pena o castigo. 6. Abrir; desatar. 7. Aliviar el estreñimiento. 8. Hacer lánguido, languidecer.—*vn.* Aflojar, ceder o perder algo de su rigor o severidad.
Relaxation [rî-lax- o rel-ax-ê'-shun], *s.* 1. Aflojamiento, flojedad de lo que estaba tirante. 2. Relajación, descanso o intermisión en algún trabajo o tarea; descanso, reposo, recreo, distracción, mitigación, lenidad. 3. Relajamiento de nervios, músculos, etc.
Relay [rî'-lê], *s.* 1. Relevo. 2. Remuda. 3. Carrera de relevos. 4. Tramo (de carrera). 5. Posta. 6. (Elec.) Relevador, relé.—*va.* Reexpedir. *Relay race,* Carrera de relevos.
Release [re-lîs'], *va.* 1. Soltar, dar libertad a un preso. 2. Libertar, poner en libertad. 3. Libertar, eximir de alguna obligación; ceder, condonar, remitir; relajar, aflojar, relevar, apartarse, renunciar; eximir, exonerar. 4. Aliviar los dolores, los pesares.
Release, *s.* 1. Libertad, soltura. 2. Remisión de una pena; alivio en los sufrimientos, en los pesares;

aligeramiento final de algo opresivo. 3. Descargo, exoneración de una obligación; el recibo de una deuda firmado por el acreedor; finiquito. 4. Un modo de traspasar la posesión de cualquier heredad. 5. Cesión (de un derecho); abandono de una pretensión. *Deed of release*, Acta de cesión.

Releasee [rg-lîs-î'], *s.* (For.) La persona a cuyo favor se otorga una escritura de cesión o finiquito.

Releasement [rg-lîs'-mgnt], *s.* (Poco us.) El acto de descargar o libertar.

Releasor [rg-lîs'-gr], *s.* (For.) El que otorga un finiquito o acta de cesión.

Relegate [rel'-g-gêt], *va.* Desterrar, relegar; colocar en posición inferior u obscura; apartar.

Relegation [rel-g-gê'-shun], *s.* Relegación, como a obscuridad, destierro.

Relent [rg-lent'], *vn.* 1. Apiadarse, compadecerse, enternecerse, ceder, aplacarse, desenojarse. 2. (Des.) Relentecer, ponerse tierna y blanda alguna cosa, ablandarse, templarse. *His heart relents*, Su corazón se enternece.

Relenting [rg-lent'-ing], *a.* Enternecido, dispuesto a enternecerse o a ceder.—*s.* Enternecimiento, desenojo; sentimiento de compasión.

Relentless [rg-lent'-les], *a.* Desapiadado, empedernido, implacable, inexorable.

Relessee, Relessor, *s.* *V.* RELEASEE, RELEASOR. (Formas irregulares.)

Relevancy, Relevance [rel'-g-van-si, vans], *s.* Cualidad de pertinente o aplicable; aplicabilidad.

Relevant [rel'-g-vant], *a.* 1. Pertinente, a propósito, aplicable, apropiado. 2. (Poco us.) Que alivia o auxilia.

Reliability, Reliableness [re-lai-a-bil'-i-ti, re-lai'-a-bl-nes], *s.* Calidad del que o de lo que es digno de confianza.

Reliable [rg-lai'-a-bl], *a.* Seguro, digno de confianza, confiable; discreto, prudente, de sano juicio.

Reliance [rg-lai'-ans], *s.* Confianza, seguridad.

Reliant [rg-lai'-ant], *a.* Confiado, particularmente el que tiene confianza en sí mismo.

Relic [rel'-ic], *s.* 1. Reliquia, residuo o resto de lo que ha desaparecido o está destruido. 2. Reliquia, cosa apreciada en memoria de alguien fallecido, como un santo o mártir; memento.

Relict [rel'-ict], *s.* Viuda.

Relief [rg-lîf'], *s.* 1. Alivio, alejamiento completo o parcial de un mal que aflige el cuerpo o el ánimo; aligeramiento. 2. Consuelo, socorro, ayuda caritativa; lo que alivia el pesar; refuerzo. 3. (Mil.) Relevo, mudanza de centinela. 4. Desagravio, satisfacción o compensación de la injuria u ofensa recibida; reparación. 5. Relieve, realce, en obras de escultura o arquitectura; labor o figura que resalta en una superficie plana. 6. Parte que aparentemente se destaca en una pintura. 7. Elevación de una persona; hecho u objeto que descuella. *High relief, low relief*, Alto relieve, bajo relieve. *To stand in bold relief*, Resaltar vigorosamente. *Indoor relief*, Socorro dado a los indigentes en una casa de caridad. *Outdoor relief*, Socorro a domicilio.

Relievable [rg-lîv'-a-bl], *a.* Consolable, capaz de alivio.

Relieve [rg-lîv'], *va.* 1. Relevar, remediar, socorrer, librar completa o parcialmente de algo doloroso u opresivo, o de sus efectos. 2. Aliviar, consolar. 3. (Mil.) Relevar, mudar la centinela. 4. Desagraviar, hacer justicia. 5. Mitigar, suavizar, vivificar el estilo o lenguaje. 6. Poner en relieve, hacer resaltar una labor o figura.

Reliever [rg-lîv'-gr], *s.* El que socorre o releva.

Relieving-tackle [rg-lîv'-ing-tac'-l], *s.* (Mar.) Pluma, un aparejo que se hace firme al palo de la chata cuando la nave cae de quilla y se está carenando.

Relievo [rg-lîv'-o], *s.* Relieve. *V.* RILIEVO.

Relight [rî-lait'], *va.* Volver a encender o encender de nuevo.—*vn.* Volver a desmontarse de un caballo; volver a bajarse de un carruaje.

Religion [rg-lij'-un], *s.* Religión, culto que se tributa a Dios y el conjunto de creencias religiosas de un individuo o de un país.

Religionary [rg-lij'-un-g-ri], *a.* Religioso, perteneciente a la religión.

Religionary, Religionist [rg-lij'-un-ist], *s.* Religionario, religionista.

Religionism [rg-lij'-un-izm], *s.* Religiosidad, ejercicio o práctica de una religión; es voz despectiva.

Religious [rg-lij'-us], *a.* 1. Religioso, pío, devoto. 2. Perteneciente o que se refiere a una religión. 3. Verdaderamente fiel, concienzudo. 4. Religioso, perteneciente a una orden monástica.

Religiously [rg-lij'-us-li], *adv.* Religiosamente; exactamente, puntualmente.

Religiousness [rg-lij'-us-nes], *s.* Religiosidad, piedad, moralidad religiosa.

Relinquish [rg-lin'-cwish], *va.* 1. Abandonar, dejar, ceder. 2. Dejar de demandar o pretender; resignar, renunciar (a).

Relinquishment [rg-lin'-cwish-mgnt], *s.* Abandono, dejación, cesión.

Reliquary [rel'-i-cwg-ri], *s.* 1. Relicario, la caja o lugar en que se guardan las reliquias de los santos. 2. (For.) El que después de haber presentado sus cuentas resulta deudor de cierta suma; el que paga poco a poco.

Relish [rel'-ish], *s.* 1. Gusto, apetencia, sabor. 2. Gusto agradable de los alimentos o bebidas; (fig.) cualidad que hace a una cosa agradable. 3. Sainete, sabor. 4. Cata, la porción pequeña de alguna cosa que se da para catar o probar. *A relish for good literature*, Un gusto por la buena literatura. *He has no relish for studying*, No le agrada estudiar.

Relish, *va.* 1. Saborear, dar sabor, gusto o sainete a las cosas. 2. Gustar de, tener afición a alguna cosa. —*vn.* 1. Saber bien, tener buen gusto; ser sabroso. 2. Gustar, agradar.

Relishable [rel'-ish-a-bl], *a.* Gustoso, sabroso, apetitoso.

Relishableness [rel'-ish-a-bl-nes], *s.* La calidad que hace agradable, gustosa o sabrosa alguna cosa.

Relive [rî-liv'], *vn.* Revivir, vivir de nuevo.

Relocate [rî'-lō-kêt], *va.* Establecer de nuevo, colocar en un nuevo lugar.

Relocation [rî-lō-kê'-shun], *s.* Nueva colocación.

Reluctance [rg-luc'-tans], **Reluctancy** [rg-luc'-tan-si], *s.* Repugnancia; desgana, disgusto, mala gana. *With reluctance*, De mala gana.

Reluctant [rg-luc-tant], *a.* Repugnante, que no quiere, que no tiene ganas; no dispuesto a ceder; que obra con repugnancia.

Relume [rg-lūm'], †**Relumine** [rg-lū'-min], *va.* Volver a encender. *V.* REKINDLE.

Rely [rg-lai'], *vn.* Confiar en, tener confianza en, contar con; asegurarse de, fiarse en o de; se usa con *on* o *upon*. *Do not rely upon them*, No se fíe Vd. de ellos, no cuente Vd. con ellos. (< Lat. religo.)

Remain [rg-mên'], *vn.* 1. Quedar, restar, faltar; quedarse atrás después del alejamiento o de la destrucción de otras personas o cosas; quedarse solo. 2. Remanecer, permanecer, persistir, continuar en un estado determinado. *They remained a fortnight in Caracas*, Se quedaron quince días en Caracas. *She still remains a maiden*, Aun permanece soltera o aun no se ha casado. *It only remains to tell you*, Sólo resta decirle a Vd. o sólo tengo ya que decir a Vd.

Remainder [rg-mên'-dgr], *s.* Resto, residuo, resta, alcance.—*a.* Restante, que queda de una cantidad, de una cuenta, etc.

Remains [rg-mênz'], *s. pl.* 1. Cadáver, el cuerpo muerto del hombre. 2. Sobras, restos, reliquias. 3. Las obras póstumas de un autor. 4. Esqueletos humanos; ruinas.

Remake [rî-mêk'], *va.* Rehacer, volver a hacer, hacer de nuevo.

Remand [rg-mand'], *va.* 1. Volver a llamar; traer o enviar a alguno al paraje donde había estado antes. 2. (For.) Volver a enviar a la prisión; enviar a otro tribunal.

Remand, Remandment [rg-mand', mgnt], *s.* Nuevo envío a la prisión; mandato judicial para el traslado a otro tribunal.

Remark [rg-mārk'], *s.* Observación, advertencia, nota, reparo.

Remark, *va.* 1. Expresar con palabras o por escrito; hacer observaciones; señalar, distinguir. 2. Notar, observar; reparar.

Remarkable [rg-mārk'-a-bl], *a.* Reparable, notable, interesante, considerable o digno de consideración, o atención; extraordinario, poco común, que puede excitar admiración.

Remarkableness [rg-mārk'-a-bl-nes], *s.* Singularidad; la calidad que hace a una cosa notable o digna de atención particular.

Remarkably [rg-mārk'-a-bli], *adv.* Notablemente, extraordinariamente.

Remarker [rg-mārk'-gr], *s.* Observador; anotador.

Remarriage [rî-mar'-ij], *s.* Segundas nupcias.

Remarry [rî-mar'-i], *va.* y *vn.* Casar o casarse de nuevo; volver a casar o casarse.

Remediable [rg-mî'-di-a-bl], *a.* Remediable; curable.

Remedial [re-mî'-di-al], *a.* Reparador; de la naturaleza de un remedio.

Remediless [rem'-g-di-les], *a.* Irremediable, sin recurso; incurable; irreparable.

Remedy [rem'-g-di], *s.* 1. Remedio, medicamento. *It is past remedy*, No tiene remedio; es incurable. 2. Remedio, el medio que se toma para reparar algún daño; recurso.

Remedy, *va.* Curar, sanar, remediar, reparar.
Remember [rẹ-mem'-bẹr], *va.* 1. Acordarse, tener presente o retener en la memoria, rememorar. 2. Acordarse, hacer memoria. 3. Mentar, hacer mención de alguna cosa; recordar, traer a la memoria.—*vn.* Acordarse. *Remember me to her,* Déle Vd. expresiones mías.
Rememberer [rẹ-mem'-bẹr-ẹr], *s.* Recordante.
Remembrance [rẹ-mem'-brans], *s.* 1. Memoria, retentiva. *To call to remembrance,* Traer a la memoria; acordarse de alguna cosa. 2. Relación o apuntamiento de. 3. Recuerdo, aviso. 4. Memoria, recuerdo, señal.
Remembrancer [rẹ-mem'-brans-ẹr], *s.* 1. Recordador, el que recuerda alguna cosa; recuerdo, lo que trae a la memoria. 2. Un empleado en la tesorería general de Inglaterra.
Remind [rẹ-maind'], *va.* Acordar, recordar, avisar, excitar y mover a otro a que tenga presente alguna cosa, poner en la memoria; reavivar la memoria.
Reminder [rẹ-maind'-ẹr], *s.* Recuerdo, lo que trae algo a la memoria; advertencia.
Remindful [rẹ-maind'-ful], *a.* 1. Rememorativo, que sirve para hacer recordar; que sirve de aviso. 2. Atento, cuidadoso, vigilante.
Reminisce [rem-i-nis'], *vn.* Tener reminiscencias, narrar recuerdos.
Reminiscence [rem-i-nis'-ens], **Reminiscency** [rem-i-nis'-en-si], *s.* Reminiscencia.
Reminiscent [rem-i-nis'-ent], *a.* Que recuerda lo pasado.
Reminiscential [rem-i-nis-en'-shal], *a.* Perteneciente a la reminiscencia.
Remiped [rem'-i-ped], *a.* Remípedo, que tiene las patas en forma de remos.—*s.* Animal remípedo.
Remiss [rẹ-mis'], *a.* Remiso, flojo, lento, perezoso, negligente; falto de energía. *Remiss in duty,* Lento, negligente en cumplir con su deber. *To grow remiss,* Entibiarse, aflojar.
Remissibility [rẹ-mis-i-bil'-i-ti], *s.* Calidad de remisible o perdonable.
Remissible [rẹ-mis'-i-bl], *a.* Remisible, perdonable.
Remission [rẹ-mish'-un], *s.* 1. Remisión, la acción de remitir; particularmente, remisión, perdón, absolución de culpa o delito. 2. Remisión, disminución o mengua de actividad o fuerza. 3. (Med.) Remisión, disminución temporal del rigor de una enfermedad. 4. Rebaja, minoración, v. g. de una multa. 5. Descanso en el trabajo o estudio. 6. Remesa. *V.* REMITTANCE.
Remissly [rẹ-mis'-li], *adv.* Flojamente, negligentemente.
Remissness [rẹ-mis'-nes], *s.* Remisión, flojedad, negligencia y poca solicitud en la ejecución de alguna cosa.
Remissory [rẹ-mis'-o-ri], *a.* Remisorio, que tiene virtud o facultad para remitir o perdonar.
Remit [rẹ-mit'], *va.* 1. Remitir, enviar dinero de una parte a otra; transmitir. 2. Remitir, perdonar culpas, hacer gracia. 3. Exonerar, eximir de una multa u otra pena; dejar de exigir. 4. Relajar, aflojar. 5. Referir, someter, a la consideración de otro.—*vn.* 1. Enviar dinero; hacer remesas. 2. Disminuir; debilitarse, hacerse más llevadera alguna cosa; bajar, templarse, suavizarse. *The fever begins to remit,* La calentura empieza a bajar.
Remitment [rẹ-mit'-mẹnt], *s.* Remisión, acción y efecto de remitir; gracia, perdón, exoneración; remesa.
Remittal [rẹ-mit'-al], *s.* 1. Cesión, renuncia, abandono. 2. Remesa. *V.* REMITTANCE.
Remittance [rẹ-mit'-ans], *s.* Remesa, la remisión de dinero o valores que se hace de una parte a otra; letra de cambio; también los valores enviados.
Remittent [rẹ-mit'-ẹnt], *a.* Remitente, que tiene aumentos y disminuciones alternativas sin cesación completa, v. g. una fiebre.—*s.* Fiebre o calentura remitente.
Remitter [rẹ-mit'-ẹr], *s.* 1. Remitente, el que hace una remesa; el que compra una libranza postal. 2. (For.) Restitución, v. g. a un derecho o título anterior.
Remnant [rem'-nant], *s.* 1. Remanente, resto, residuo; retal, retazo de alguna tela. 2. Los verdaderos siervos de Jehová; de aquí, en el uso literario reciente, los pocos espíritus escogidos, en cuanto al cultivo, la inteligencia, etc.
Remodel [rî-med'-el], *va.* Modelar de nuevo; reconstruir.
Remonetize [rî-mun'-ẹ-taiz], *va.* Remonetizar, restablecer como moneda legal.
Remonstrance [rẹ-men'-strans], *s.* 1. Representación, súplica motivada, el acto de hacer reconvenciones. 2. Reprensión, amonestación, reconvención. 3. La custodia o viril en que se pone la hostia en las iglesias católicas. *V.* MONSTRANCE.
Remonstrant [rẹ-men'-strant], *a.* Motivado, que contiene motivos o razones eficaces.—*s.* El que representa a lo vivo; protestante.
Remonstrate [rẹ-men'-strêt], *vn.* Representar a lo vivo; objetar, reconvenir, oponer, presentar razones contra.
Remora [rem'-o-ra], *s.* 1. Rémora, un pez notable por tener en la cabeza una placa oval cuyos bordes membranosos le sirven para adherirse a cuerpos submarinos, formando con ella el vacío. 2. Un instrumento de cirugía usado antiguamente.
Remorse [rẹ-mōrs'], *s.* 1. Remordimiento, compunción, dolor que se siente por haber cometido una mala acción. 2. (For.) Compasión, piedad.
Remorseful [re-mōrs'-ful], *a.* Lleno de remordimientos; tierno, compasivo.
Remorseless [rẹ-mōrs'-les], *a.* Cruel, insensible a los remordimientos.
Remorselessly [rẹ-mōrs'-les-li], *adv.* Sin remordimiento, sin piedad.
Remorselessness [rẹ-mōrs'-les-nes], *s.* Crueldad, apatía ante la desgracia.
Remote [rẹ-mōt'], *a.* 1. Remoto. 2. Lejano. 3. Ajeno. 4. Leve, mínimo. 5. Inabordable. *Remote control,* Telemando, teledirección. *To operate by remote control,* Teledirigir, teleguiar.
Remote-control [re-mōt-cẹn-trōl'], *a.* Teledirigido, teleguiado.
Remotely [rẹ-mōt'-li], *adv.* Remotamente, lejos, a lo lejos.
Remoteness [rẹ-mōt'-nes], *s.* Alejamiento, distancia.
Remount [rî-maunt'], *va.* 1. Remontar, volver a montar, subir de nuevo. 2. (Mil.) Remontar, hacer la remonta, dar nuevos caballos a los soldados.—*vn.* Volver a subir.
Removability [rẹ-mūv-a-bil'-i-ti], *s.* 1. Movilidad, facultad de moverse. 2. Amovilidad, calidad de amovible (un funcionario o sus funciones).
Removable [rẹ-mūv'-a-bl], *a.* 1. Removible, que se puede remover o alejar; transportable. 2. Amovible (de personas).
Removal [rẹ-mūv'-al], *s.* 1. Remoción, acto y efecto de remover; removimiento; alejamiento, apartamiento; traslado de un lugar a otro. 2. Cambio de lugar; cambio de morada. 3. Deposición. 4. Alivio, curación, quite. 5. Acto de poner fin o término a alguna cosa; (a veces, asesinato). *From our removal from Havana,* Desde nuestra salida de la Habana.
Remove [rẹ-mūv'], *va.* 1. Remover, alejar, desviar, mudar una cosa de un lugar a otro; alzar o levantar la casa. 2. Remover, deponer del empleo o destino. 3. Alejar, apartar; quitar. 4. Destruir, poner fin, hacer desaparecer.—*vn.* Mudarse, trasladarse de un paraje a otro, alejarse, apartarse, cambiar de sitio, cambiar de habitación. *Remove that chair,* Quite Vd. esa silla. *We must remove him from his post,* Es menester destituirle de su puesto. *They will remove on the first of May* Cambiarán de casa el primero de mayo.
Remove, *s.* 1. Cambio de puesto o paraje, mudanza, mudada. 2. Partida, el acto de partir de un lugar para ir a otro. 3. Escalón, el grado que se sube en dignidad. 4. Grado de parentesco; grado, paso, intervalo. 5. Plato o entrada de una comida.
Remover [rẹ-mūv'-ẹr], *s.* El que remueve.
Remunerability [rẹ-miū-nẹr-a-bil'-i-ti], *s.* La capacidad de ser remunerado.
Remunerable [rẹ-miū'-nẹr-a-bl], *a.* Remunerable, capaz o digno de recompensa.
Remunerate [rẹ-miū'-nẹr-êt], *va.* Remunerar, recompensar, premiar.
Remuneration [rẹ-miū-nẹr-ê'-shun], *s.* Remuneración, recompensa, retribución.
Remunerative [rẹ-miū'-nẹr-a-tiv], *a.* Remuneratorio; ganancioso, provechoso, lucrativo.
Remunerator [rẹ-miū'-nẹr-ê-tẹr], *s.* Remunerador.
Renaissance [rẹ-nê-sūns'], *s.* 1. Renacimiento, vuelta a la vida. 2. Renacimiento, dícese en especial del restablecimiento de las artes y literatura que comenzó a mediados del siglo XV; fué como la aurora de los tiempos modernos. (Fr.)
Renal [rî'-nal], *a.* Renal, que pertenece a los riñones.
Renard [ren'-ard], *s.* Zorro. *V.* REYNARD.
Renascence, Renascency [rẹ-nas'-ens, en-si], *s.* 1. Renacimiento. 2. *V.* RENAISSANCE, 2ª acep.
Renascent [rẹ-nas'-ent], *a.* Renaciente.
Rencounter [ren-cau -tẹr], *s.* 1. Reencuentro, choque, combate, refriega. 2. Quimera, pendencia, riña casual, colisión hostil repentina.
Rencounter, *va.* y *vn.* 1. Encontrar, hallar impensadamente. 2. Encontrarse al enemigo de repente, embestirse, acometerse, atacarse.

Rend [rend], *va.* y *vn.* 1. Lacerar, hacer pedazos, desgarrar, rasgar, hender. 2. Separar, desunir. 3. Remover a viva fuerza; arrancar.
Rend, *s.* (Mar.) Costura de los tablones.
Render [rend'-ẹr], *s.* 1. Desgarrador. 2. Pago de un arriendo o alquiler.
Render, *va.* 1. Hacer, cambiar dando un carácter determinado. 2. Dar, suministrar, prestar, rendir. 3. Interpretar, v. g. una composición musical. 4. Traducir. 5. Volver, devolver, restituir. 6. Derretir y clarificar. 7. Aplicar algo a una pared, v. g. la primera capa de yeso. *To render thanks to God*, Dar gracias á Dios. *To render assistance to*, Prestar auxilio a. *To render justice*, Hacer justicia. *To render smooth*, Alisar. *To render tallow*, Derretir el sebo. *To render into Spanish*, Traducir al castellano.
Rendering [ren'-dẹr-ing], *s.* 1. Acción de dar, devolver o asignar. 2. Traducción, versión. 3. Interpretación artística. 4. Acto de derretir y clarificar. *Rendering-pan*, Caldera para extraer la manteca.
Rendezvous [ren'-dẹ-vū ó rāñ'-de-vū], *s.* 1. Cita para concurrir en un día u hora convenida á un lugar ó sitio previamente señalado. 2. Lugar señalado para juntarse o reunirse. (Fr.)
Rendezvous, *vn.* Acudir, juntarse, reunirse en paraje y hora señalados. (Fr.)
Rendible [rend'-i-bl], *a.* Que puede ser desgarrado o lacerado.
Rending [rend'-ing], *s.* Quebranto, dolor o pesar agudo.
Rendition [ren-dish'-un], *s.* 1. Versión, traducción. 2. Interpretación artística. 3. Rendición, acción de rendirse. 4. La cantidad producida o redituada, rédito.
Renegade [ren'-ẹ-gêd], **Renegado** [ren-ẹ-gé'-do], *s.* 1. Renegado, apóstata de su fe religiosa. 2. Desertor. 3. Vagamundo, perdido.
Renege, Renig [rẹ-nīg' o rẹ-nīj'; rẹ-nig'], *vn.* En los naipes, no jugar carta del palo que ha jugado otro, teniéndola.
Renew [rẹ-niū'], *va.* y *vn.* 1. Renovar, renovarse, hacer o hacerse nuevo. 2. Hacer, comenzar de nuevo; hacer revivir. 3. (Teol.) Regenerar espiritualmente.
Renewable [rẹ-niū'-a-bl], *a.* Renovable.
Renewal [rẹ-niū'-al], *s.* Renovación.
Reniform [ren'-i-fẹrm], *a.* Reniforme, que se parece a un riñón ó tiene su figura.
Renitency [rẹ-nai'-ten-si], *s.* Renitencia, repugnancia a hacer o admitir una cosa.
Rennet [ren'-et], *s.* 1. Cuajo. 2. Cuajaleche, cardo lechero. 3. Quimosina.
Rennin [ren'-in], *s.* Quimosina, fermento del cuajo.
Renominate [rī-nom'-i-nêt], *va.* Nombrar de nuevo, particularmente para un segundo período del mismo cargo o empleo.
Renounce [rẹ-nauns'], *va.* 1. Renunciar. 2. Rechazar, negar, renegar, abandonar, abjurar. 3. En los naipes, no jugar carta de un palo, teniéndola.
Renouncement [rẹ-nauns'-mẹnt], *s.* Renuncia.
Renovate [ren'-o-vêt], *va.* 1. Renovar. 2. Limpiar enteramente, purificar.
Renovation [ren-o-vê'-shun], *s.* Renovación, acción y efecto de renovar; limpiadura: en teología, regeneración.
Renovator [ren'-o-vê"-tẹr], *s.* Renovador, el ó lo que renueva.
Renown [rẹ-naun'], *s.* Renombre, fama, gloria, reputación, celebridad. *A man of renown*, Un hombre célebre.
Rent [rent], *s.* 1. Renta; arrendamiento; alquiler, arriendo; también, el derecho de recibir esa compensación. 2. Desgarrón, rasgón, desgarro; rotura, rompimiento, cuarteadura; cisma. *Rent-free, adv.* Sin pagar alquiler. *Rent-day*, Día de pagar el alquiler o arrendamiento.
Rent, *va.* 1. Arrendar, tomar en arrendamiento alguna renta o posesión. 2. Arrendar, dar en arriendo, alquilar.
Rentable [rent'-a-bl], *a.* Arrendable.
Rental [rent'-al], **Rent-roll** [rent'-rōl], *s.* 1. Renta, arriendo; producto total de una propiedad alquilada. 2. Lista de rentas.
Renter [rent'-ẹr], *s.* Rentero, arrendador, aquilador.
Renunciation [rẹ-nun-shi-é'-shun], *s.* Renuncia, renunciación.
Reopen [rī-ō'-pn], *va.* Volver á abrir.
Reorder [rī-ōr'-dẹr], *va.* 1. Volver a pedir o encargar. 2. Arreglar, ordenar.
Reorganization [rī-ōr-gan-i-zê'-shun], *s.* Reorganización.
Reorganize [rī-ōr'-gan-aiz], *va.* Reorganizar.
Rep [rep], *s.* Cierto tejido de superficie cordelada.
Repair [rẹ-pār'], *va.* 1. Reparar, componer, aderezar, recorrer. *To repair a house*, Reparar, recorrer una casa. 2. Resarcir, recompensar. 3. Suplir, cumplir lo que falta; acudir, aplicar, embonar, restaurar, renovar; (Mar.) carenar.
Repair, *vn.* 1. Ir a alguna parte, encaminarse a, irse; retirarse, refugiarse. 2. Volver; dirigirse a, recurrir a.
Repair, *s.* 1. Reparo, reparación, restauración, compostura. 2. Recorrida, embonada o reparo del casco de una embarcación. 3. (Ant.) Morada, asilo, guarida. *Out of repair*, Descompuesto. *Repair-shop*, Taller de reparaciones, particularmente de las máquinas.
Repairer [rẹ-pār'-ẹr], *s.* Reparador.
Reparable [rep'-a-ra-bl], **Repairable** [rẹ-pār'-a-bl], *a.* Reparable.
Reparation [rep-a-ré'-shun], *s.* 1. Reparación, renovación. 2. Recompensa; satisfacción, compensación.
Reparative [rẹ-par'-a-tiv], *a.* Reparativo, restaurativo, que tiene virtud de reparar o restaurar.
Repartee [rep-ar-tī'], *s.* Respuesta o réplica aguda o picante; agudeza, chiste, donaire; gracia.
Repartition [rī-par-tish'-un], *s.* Repartimiento, repartición.
Repass [rẹ-pas'], *va.* Repasar, volver a pasar; pasar en dirección opuesta.
Repassage [rẹ-pas'-ẹj], *s.* Libertad o permiso de pasar.
Repast [rẹ-past'], *s.* Refrigerio, comida, alimento. *Light repast*, Colación. *To make a light repast*, Tomar un refrigerio; hacer colación, tomar un pisto.
Repatriate [rī-pé'-tri-êt], *va.* Repatriar, enviar o conducir a su patria al que está fuera de ella.
Repay [rẹ-pé'], *va.* Volver a pagar, recompensar, retornar, restituir; reconocer un beneficio recibido, dar un equivalente; pagar en la misma moneda.—*vn.* Hacer un pago, dar satisfacción o desquite.
Repayment [rī-pé'-mẹnt], *s.* Pago, devolución de lo comprado o gastado.
Repeal [rẹ-pīl'], *va.* Abrogar, anular, revocar, abolir, como una ley.
Repeal, *s.* Revocación, abrogación, anulación.
Repealable [rẹ-pīl'-a-bl], *a.* Revocable, anulable, abrogable, capaz de ser abrogado.
Repealer [rẹ-pīl'-ẹr], *s.* Revocador, anulador.
Repeat [rẹ-pīt'], *s.* (Mús.) Repetición, línea de puntos que se pone en la pauta para indicar que un trozo de música debe ejecutarse dos veces.
Repeat, *va.* 1. Repetir, volver a hacer o decir; reiterar. 2. Recitar de memoria, repasar, ensayar.
Repeatedly [rẹ-pīt'-ed-li], *adv.* Repetidamente, repetidas veces.
Repeater [rẹ-pīt'-ẹr], *s.* 1. Repetidor. 2. Reloj de repetición. 3. Arma (de fuego) de repetición. 4. Repetidor, instrumento para transmitir de nuevo señales telegráficas. 5. (E. U.) El que vota o procura votar más de una vez en la misma elección.
Repel [rẹ-pel'], *va.* 1. Repeler, rechazar, hacer retroceder por fuerza; refutar. 2. Repeler, alejar; lo contrario de atraer. 3. (Med.) Repercutir los humores.—*vn.* Rechazar, resistir; tener una cualidad o tendencia repulsiva.
Repellent [rẹ-pel'-ent], *a.* 1. Repelente, que repele o rechaza. 2. A prueba de agua, impermeable.—*s.* 1. Impermeable, tela. 2. (Med.) Remedio repercusivo.
Repent [rī'-pẹnt], *a.* (Zool.) Rastrero, que se arrastra; (Bot.) que echa raíces desde un tallo horizontal. (< Lat. repens.)
Repent [rẹ-pent'], *va.* y *vn.* Arrepentirse (de), tener pesar de haber hecho alguna cosa ofensiva o de haber pecado. *You will repent it*, Le pesará a Vd.
Repentance [rẹ-pent'-ans], *s.* Arrepentimiento, penitencia, contrición.
Repentant [rẹ-pent'-ant], *a.* Arrepentido, que se arrepiente, contrito.
Repentant, Repenter [rẹ-pent'-ẹr], *s.* Penitente, arrepentido.
Repenting [rẹ-pent'-ing], *s.* Arrepentimiento.
Repentingly [rẹ-pent'-ing-li], *adv.* Con pesar o arrepentimiento.
Repeople [rī-pī'-pl], *va.* Repoblar, volver a poblar.
Repercuss [rī-pẹr-cus'], *va.* Repercutir, reverberar, rechazar.
Repercussion [rī-pẹr-cush'-un], *s.* Repercusión, reverberación, rechazo; frecuente reiteración del mismo tono, nota o acorde.
Repercussive [rī-pẹr-cus'-iv], *a.* Repercusivo.
Repertoire [rep-ẹr-twār'], *s.* *V.* REPERTORY, 2ª acep. (Fr.)
Repertory [rep'-ẹr-to-ri], *s.* 1. Depósito (ant. repositorio), lugar donde se recogen las cosas; colección. 2. Repertorio, reportorio, lista de obras dramáticas o musicales que están por representar. 3. Tabla en que las cosas están dispuestas de tal modo que se pueden hallar fácilmente; lista, índice.

Repetition [rep-ẹ-tí'-shun], *s.* Repetición, reiteración; repaso; acción de repetir y lo que se repite.

Repine [rẹ-pain'], *vn.* Afligirse, apurarse, quejarse, murmurar, ser muy dado a hallar o poner faltas.

Repiner [rẹ-pain'-ẹr], *s.* Murmurador, sentidor, triste, melancólico.

Repining [rẹ-pain'-ing], *s.* Pesar; murmuración, queja, descontento quejoso.

Replace [rẹ-plês'], *va.* 1. Reemplazar. 2. Reponer, colocar. 3. Poner un substituto en lugar de otra persona. 4. Devolver, reembolsar; restituir. 5. Colocar en otro lugar.

Replaceable [rẹ-plês'-a-bl], *a.* Reemplazable, que se puede reemplazar o reponer.

Replacement [rẹ-plês'-mẹnt], *s.* 1. Remplazo, reposición, reintegración. 2. Colocación en su lugar. 3. Pieza de repuesto. 4. Substitución.

Replait [rî-plêt'], *va.* Plegar repetidas veces.

Replant [rẹ-plant'], *va.* Replantar, plantar de nuevo.

Replantation [rẹ-plan-tê'-shun], *s.* La acción de volver a plantar.

Replenish [rẹ-plen'-ish], *va.* Rellenar, llenar, surtir generosamente; proveer con abundancia.

Replenishment [rẹ-plen'-ish-mẹnt], *s.* Acción y efecto de llenar, proveer, o surtir.

Replete [rẹ-plît'], *a.* Relleno, repleto, lleno. *Replete with,* Lleno de.

Repletion [rẹ-plî'-shun], **Repleteness** [rẹ-plît'-nes], *s.* Repleción, plenitud.

Repleviable [rẹ-plev'-i-a-bl], *a.* Que se puede desembargar.

Replevin [rẹ-plev'-in], *s.* (For.) 1. Procedimiento para recobrar la posesión de una propiedad ilegalmente retenida. 2. Auto de desembargo.

Replevin, Replevy [rẹ-plev'-i], *va.* Desembargar, alzar el embargo o secuestro; recobrar, recuperar.

Replica [rep'-li-ca], *s.* 1. (Bellas artes) Duplicado ejecutado por el artista mismo y que se considera como original. 2. (Mús.) Pasaje que se ha de ejecutar segunda vez. (Ital.)

Replicant [rep'-li-cant], *s.* Replicador, replicante, el que responde.

Replicate [rep'-li-kẹt], *a.* Replegado, plegado hacia atrás, como el ala de un insecto, o la parte superior de una hoja sobre la inferior.

Replication [rep-li-ké'-shun], *s.* 1. Réplica, respuesta. 2. (For.) Réplica del actor contradiciendo la respuesta del demandado. 3. Una repetición o copia. 4. Pliegue sistemático de una superficie.

Reply [rẹ-plai'], *s.* Réplica, respuesta, contestación.

Reply, *va.* 1. Contestar, responder a lo que se habla o escribe. 2. Replicar, instar, argüir con otro.

Report [rẹ-pōrt'], *va.* 1. Esparcir, divulgar; referir, contar; informar, hacer relación, dar parte, noticia, o hacer exposición; manifestar. 2. Relatar, dar cuenta por razón de observación o indagación personal. 3. Certificar formal u oficialmente (un resultado, una condición).—*vn.* 1. Hacer relación, dar parte. 2. Servir como repórter o noticiero. 3. (E. U.) Comparecer en un paraje señalado, o ante alguien y anunciarse. *It is reported,* Corre la voz, se dice. *To be reported* o *reported of,* Ser objeto de informes favorables o desfavorables. *To report progress,* Exponer el estado de la cuestión.

Report, *s.* 1. Relación, parte, noticia, manifiesto, anuncio, informe. 2. Voz, rumor, opinión. *Flying report,* Noticia volandera, suelta. *There was a report of his arrival,* Corrió la voz de su llegada. *By report,* Según se dice. 3. Fama, reputación pública. 4. Relación de pleitos o causas. 5. *Report of fire-arms,* Estallido, tiro, trueno, traquido. *Report of a gun,* Un cañonazo. *Report of a musket,* Un escopetazo. *Report of a pistol,* Un pistoletazo, un trabucazo. 6. Declaración de efectos hecha en la aduana.

Report card [re-pōrt' card], *s.* Calificación escolar periódica.

Reporter [rẹ-pōrt'-ẹr], *s.* 1. Taquígrafo, repórter, el que busca y recoge noticias para los periódicos. 2. Relator, redactor de las causas o pleitos importantes en los tribunales. *Reporter's gallery,* Tribuna de los taquígrafos o de los periodistas (en una asamblea legislativa).

Repose [rẹ-pōz'], *va.* 1. Extender en una postura de descanso; reponer por medio del descanso. 2. Fijar, fiar, confiar, poner su confianza o esperanza en.—*vn.* 1. Reposar, dormir, descansar. 2. Estar seguro, tener seguridad; fiarse de. 3. Tenderse a la larga, reclinarse, recostarse.

Repose, *s.* 1. Reposo, descanso, tranquilidad, sueño. 2. Calma, quietud; moderación en los modales.

Reposite [rẹ-poz'-it], *va.* Depositar, reponer.

Reposition [rî-po-zish'-un], *s.* Reposición, restablecimiento.

Repositor [rẹ-poz'-i-tẹr], *s.* Reponedor, el o lo que repone; en particular, repositor, instrumento que se usa en casos de prolapso.

Repository [rẹ-poz'-i-to-ri], *s.* Repositorio, depósito, despensa, lugar en que se pueden guardar géneros; también, lugar de exhibición y venta, almacén, tienda.

Repossess [rî'-poz-zes'], *va.* Recobrar, recuperar. *To repossess one's self of,* Volver a tomar posesión de algo.

Repossession [rî-poz-zesh'-un], *s.* Reposesión, recuperación de una posesión.

Repoussé [rẹ-pū-sé'], *a.* Trabajado en relieve al martillo, abollonado. *Repoussé work,* Trabajo al martillo en relieve, abollonadura. (Fr.)

Reprehend [rep-rẹ-hend'], *va.* Reprender, reñir, censurar, tachar.

Reprehender [rep-rẹ-hend'-ẹr], *s.* Reprensor.

Reprehensible [rep-rẹ-hen'-si-bl], *a.* Reprensible, censurable.

Reprehensibleness [rep-rẹ-hen'-si-bl-nes], *s.* La calidad que constituye a una cosa reprensible o digna de reprensión.

Reprehension [rep-rẹ-hen'-shun], *s.* Reprensión, amonestación, censura; paulina, fraterna.

Reprehensive [rep-rẹ-hen'-siv], *a.* Reprensor, que indica o contiene una reprensión; propenso a reprender, a reconvenir.

Represent [rep-rẹ-zent'], *va.* 1. Representar, manifestar, describir, por medio de palabras, cuadros o personificaciones; hacer el papel de; recitar en público. 2. Presentar de nuevo a la mente. 3. Estar en lugar de otro, hacer las veces de, ser apoderado de alguien.

Re-present [rî"-prẹ-zent'], *va.* Presentar de nuevo, en particular de un modo diferente.

Representable [rep-rẹ-zent'-a-bl], *a.* Representable, que se puede representar; digno de representación.

Representation [rep-rẹ-zen-tê'-shun], *s.* 1. Representación, acción y efecto de representar. 2. Lo que representa o exhibe algo por medio de semejanza, como un modelo, una figura, un cuadro, una descripción o ejecución de una obra dramática. 3. Derecho de hacer las veces de otro; también el derecho de ser representado en una asamblea legislativa. 4. Asamblea de representantes. 5. Representación, manifestación, aserto, afirmación.

Re-presentation [rî-prez-en-tê'-shun], *s.* Presentación segunda o nueva.

Representative [rep-rẹ-zen'-ta-tiv], *a.* 1. Representativo, apto o autorizado para representar; que sirve para representar; típico. 2. Representante, que hace las veces de otro, que hace el papel de delegado o agente.—*s.* 1. Representante, el que representa a una persona ausente; delegado nombrado por elección para un cuerpo legislativo; en los Estados Unidos, miembro de la cámara popular del Congreso o de la Legislatura de un estado. 2. Símbolo, tipo, ejemplo típico.

Representatively, *adv.* Por delegación o poder, como representante.

Representer [rep-rẹ-zent'-ẹr], *s.* Representante.

Repress [rẹ-pres'], *va.* Sojuzgar, sujetar, reprimir, domar.

Repression [rẹ-presh'-un], *s.* Represión, la acción y efecto de represar o de reprimir.

Repressive [rẹ-pres'-iv], *a.* Represivo, que sirve para reprimir o refrenar.

Reprieve [rẹ-prîv'], *va.* 1. Suspender la ejecución de una sentencia de muerte. 2. Aliviar, o libertar temporalmente de peligro, pena o dolor.

Reprieve, *s.* 1. La dilación o la suspensión temporal en la imposición de un castigo. 2. Suspensión temporal del dolor.

Reprimand [rep-ri-mqnd'], *va.* Reprender, corregir; reñir, y especialmente censurar, reconvenir en público.

Reprimand [rep'-ri-mand], *s.* Reprensión, corrección; reprimenda, sofrenada, pública o privada.

Reprint [rẹ-print'], *va.* Reimprimir, imprimir de nuevo.

Reprint [rî'-print], *s.* Reimpresión, nueva edición de una obra; copia hecha en otro país.

Reprisal [rẹ-praiz'-al], *s.* Represalia.

Reprise [rẹ-praiz'], *s.* 1. Represalia. 2. Estribillo de copla.

Reproach [rẹ-prōch'], *va.* Improperar, baldonar, reprochar, vituperar, increpar, reconvenir, dar en rostro a alguno con algún mal hecho, echar en cara; vituperar, afear, censurar. *They were reproached as devoid of courage,* Se les increpó por su falta de valor. *What have they to reproach him with?* ¿Qué tienen que echarle en cara?

Reproach, *s.* Improperio, baldón, reproche, oprobio; tacha, nota, infamia, causa de reproche o culpa; vituperación, reconvención, increpación. *Free from reproach,* Exento de tacha o faltas.

Reproachable [rẹ-prōch'-a-bl], *a.* Censurable, reprensible, digno de reproche o increpación.

Reproachableness [rẹ-prōch'-a-bl-nes], *s.* La calidad que constituye a una cosa digna de censura o reprensible.

Reproachful [rẹ-prōch'-ful], *a.* Que contiene o expresa reproche, improperio, tacha o reconvención; increpador, injurioso; ceñudo; infame. *A reproachful look,* Una mirada reprochadora, ceñuda. *Reproachful words,* Palabras injuriosas. *Reproachful life,* Vida infame o licenciosa.

Reproachfully [rẹ-prōch'-ful-i], *adv.* De una manera increpadora, por vía de improperio u oprobio; con ceño.

Reproachfulness [rẹ-prōch'-ful-nes], *s.* Calidad de lo que es digno de improperio, tacha o reproche; reconvención; ceño; oprobio, disposición a improperar o vituperar.

Reprobate [rep'-ro-bēt], *a.* 1. Malvado, vicioso, abandonado a los vicios; privado de todo sentimiento del deber, réprobo. 2. (Ant.) Falso, de mala ley; bajo, inferior.

Reprobate, *va.* Reprobar, condenar; desaprobar, no aprobar.

Reprobation [rep-ro-bé'-shun], *s.* Reprobación, desaprobación, condenación.

Reprobative, Reprobatory [rep'-ro-bé''-tiv, rep''-ro-bé'-to-ri], *a.* Reprobador, reprobatorio, que reprueba.

Reproduce [ri-pro-diūs'], *va.* Reproducir, volver a producir o producir de nuevo.

Reproduction [ri-pro-duc'-shun], *s.* 1. Reproducción, el acto o poder de reproducir: (1) en biología, reproducción, generación de animales o plantas; (2) reminiscencia, el procedimiento de la memoria que presenta de nuevo al conocimiento interior objetos conocidos anteriormente. 2. Reproducción, la cosa reproducida; renacimiento del drama; copia, traslado del original, en las bellas artes.

Reproductive, Reproductory [ri-pro-duc'-tiv], *a.* Reproductivo, reproductor, perteneciente a la reproducción; empleado en la reproducción física o mental.

Reproof [rẹ-prūf'], *s.* Improperio, reprensión, censura, tacha echada en cara a uno, peluca.

Reprovable [rẹ-prūv'-a-bl], *a.* Censurable, tachable, reprensible.

Reprove [rẹ-prūv'], *va.* 1. Culpar, censurar autoritativa, directa y abiertamente. 2. Acusar, expresar desaprobación (de un acto o hecho); reprender, condenar. 3. (Ant.) Convencer.

Reprover [rẹ-prūv'-ẹr], *s.* Reprensor, censor.

Reptant [rep'-tant], *a.* Rastrero, que se arrastra.

Reptile [rep'-til], *a.* 1. Reptil, que camina rozando la tierra con el vientre. 2. Bajo, taimado, vil; venenoso.—*s.* 1. Reptil. 2. Persona vil y baja.

Reptilian [rep-til'-i-an], *a.* De reptil, perteneciente a los reptiles.

Reptilious [rep-til'-i-us], *a.* Semejante a un reptil.

Republic [rẹ-pub'-lic], *s.* 1. República. 2. Comunidad de personas.

Republican [rẹ-pub'-lic-an], *a.* y *s.* Republicano.

Republicanism [rẹ-pub'-lic-an-izm], *s.* 1. Republicanismo, sistema republicano de gobierno. 2. Predilección por los principios republicanos. 3. Política del partido republicano de los Estados Unidos.

Republication [ri-pub-li-ké'-shun], *s.* 1. Segunda o nueva publicación; copia hecha en otro país. 2. Renovación de un testamento.

Republish [ri-pub'-lish], *va.* Publicar de nuevo.

Repudiable [rẹ-piū'-di-a-bl], *a.* Repudiable.

Repudiate [rẹ-piū'-di-ēt], *va.* 1. Repudiar; renunciar, echar o lanzar de sí. 2. Repeler a la mujer propia.

Repudiation [rẹ-piū-di-é'-shun], *s.* Repudiación, repudio.

Repugnance [rẹ-pug'-nans], **Repugnancy** [rẹ-pug'-nan-si], *s.* Repugnancia, desgana, aversión.

Repugnant [rẹ-pug'-nant], *a.* Repugnante, contrario, incompatible, opuesto; inconsistente.

Repugnantly [rẹ-pug'-nant-li], *adv.* Con repugnancia, de muy mala gana.

Repulse [rẹ-puls'], *s.* Repulsa, rechazo, rehuso; sofión.

Repulse, *va.* Repulsar, desechar, repeler.

Repulsion [rẹ-pul'-shun], *s.* 1. (Fís.) Repulsión. 2. Estado de ser repulsado; aversión, repugnancia, mala acogida.

Repulsive [rẹ-pul'-siv], *a.* Repulsivo, repugnante, chocante, que rechaza, que causa aversión.

Repulsiveness [re-pul'-siv-nes], *s.* Carácter repugnante, chocante; lo que rechaza toda familiaridad.

Reputable [rep'-yu-ta-bl], *a.* 1. Honroso, decoroso, honorífico, estimable, digno de estimación. 2. Lícito, exento de tacha. *Reputable conduct,* Conducta decorosa, exenta de tacha.

Reputably [rep'-yu-ta-bli], *adv.* Honrosamente, con decoro.

Reputation [rep-yu-té'-shun], *s.* Reputación buena o mala; estimación, fama, crédito, nombre, renombre, nombradía. *To ruin anybody's reputation,* Dar mala reputación a alguien. *Of no reputation,* Sin reputación.

Repute [rẹ-piūt'], *va.* Reputar, estimar, juzgar, tener por. *To be reputed,* Pasar por, estar reputado por, ser juzgado como. *Reputed father,* Padre putativo.

Repute, *s.* Fama, crédito, reputación, estimación; opinión común. *In good repute,* De buena reputación. *In evil repute,* De mala fama.

Reputedly [rẹ-piūt'-ed-li], *adv.* Según la opinión común.

Request [rẹ-cwest'], *s.* 1. Petición, pedimento, ruego, súplica, encargo, instancia, solicitud. 2. Crédito, estimación, boga. *At the request of,* A petición, a solicitud de. *In request,* En boga, en crédito; en lenguaje comercial, pedido, buscado.

Request, *va.* Rogar, pedir, suplicar, encargar, solicitar. *To request an answer,* Pedir una contestación, una respuesta.

Requicken [ri-cwic'-n], *va.* Reanimar, hacer revivir.

Requiem [ri'-cwi-em], *s.* 1. Misa de requiem o de difuntos. 2. Descanso, paz, quietud.

Requirable [rẹ-cwair'-a-bl], *a.* Que se puede requerir o solicitar.

Require [rẹ-cwair'], *va.* 1. Requerir, demandar, solicitar, pedir alguna cosa como de derecho. 2. Requerir, necesitar, exigir; haber menester o hallar indispensable. *To require one to report,* Requerir de alguno que dé informes sobre algo. *The work will require money and men,* La obra exigirá dinero y hombres.

Requirement [rẹ-cwair'-mẹnt], *s.* Demanda, requerimiento, el acto de pedir con autoridad; requisito, lo que se requiere para alguna cosa, necesidad. *The requirements of health,* Los cuidados que exige la salud.

Requirer [rẹ-cwair'-ẹr], *s.* Requeridor, solicitador.

Requisite [rec'-wi-zit], *a.* Necesario, preciso, indispensable.—*s.* Requisito.

Requisiteness [rec'-wi-zit-nes], *s.* Necesidad, precisión.

Requisition [rec-wi-zish'-un], *s.* 1. Pedimento, petición, demanda formal, requisición. 2. Necesidad, requisito, menester. 3. Cualidad de ser solicitado, boga. *In requisition,* En boga; pedido, buscado. 4. (For.) Requisitoria, requerimiento, pedido.

Requisitory [rẹ-cwiz'-i-to-ri], *a.* 1. Que implica una petición, demanda o súplica. 2. (Poco us.) Demandado, pedido, solicitado.

Requital [rẹ-cwai'-tal], *s.* 1. Retorno, paga, satisfacción, compensación por lo bueno o lo malo; desquite, pena del talión. *In requital of,* En pago, en compensación de. 2. Premio, galardón, recompensa.

Requite [rẹ-cwait'], *va.* 1. Retornar, pagar en la misma moneda, volver satisfaciendo o recompensando; desquitar, vengar una injuria. 2. Reconocer, pagar, recompensar. *He requited me evil for good,* Me ha devuelto mal por bien.

Reredos [rir'-des], *s.* 1. Retablo, adorno arquitectónico, que se coloca detrás de un altar. 2. Placa de hierro que se pone en el fondo de un hogar o chimenea.

Reroute [ri-rūt'], *va.* Reenrumbar, reencaminar.

Rerun [ri'-run], *s.* Repetición, por ejemplo de una película.

Rescind [rẹ-sind'], *va.* Rescindir, anular, abrogar.

Rescission [rẹ-sizh'-un], *s.* Rescisión, anulación, abrogación.

Rescissory [rẹ-sis'-o-ri], *a.* (For.) Rescisorio, que tiene el poder de rescindir.

Rescribe [rẹ-scraib'], *va.* (Des.) 1. Rescribir, contestar. 2. Volver a escribir la misma cosa.

Rescript [ri'-script], *s.* Rescripto, edicto.

Rescuable [res'-kiu-a-bl], *a.* Que puede ser rescatado o librado de algún peligro o riesgo.

Rescue [res'-kiu], *va.* Librar, libertar; recobrar, rescatar; preservar, sacar de algún peligro o riesgo. (Fam.) Quitar o sacar de las manos.

Rescue, *s.* Libramiento, recobro; la acción de libertar con violencia a un preso; socorro, preservación de un peligro o de un enemigo.

Rescuer [res'-kiu-ẹr], *s.* Librador, libertador.

Research [rẹ-sẹrch'], *s.* Escudriñamiento, averiguación o examen diligente de una cosa; investigación sistemática y científica.

Research [ri-sẹrch'], *va.* y *vn.* Buscar o escudriñar de nuevo.

Researcher [ri-sẹrch'-ẹr], *s.* Científico investigador, rebuscador.

Reseat [ri-sīt'], *va.* 1. Sentar o asentar de nuevo. 2. Poner un fondo o asiento nuevo. *To reseat a chair*, Poner asiento nuevo a una silla.

Resect [rẹ-sect'], *va.* Acortar, cercenar, cortar una porción de (un hueso o nervio).

Resection [rẹ-sec'-shun], *s.* Acortamiento, resección, operación de cortar una porción de un hueso o nervio.

Reseize [rî-sîz'], *va.* Volver a tomar; coger o apresar de nuevo.

Reseizure [rî-zîzh'-yur], *s.* Segunda toma o presa de alguna cosa.

Resemblance [rẹ-zem'-blans], *s.* Semejanza, similitud, conformidad; lo que se asemeja, imagen exterior, retrato fiel.

Resemble [rẹ-zem'-bl], *va.* 1. Asemejarse, parecerse. *He resembles his father*, Se parece a su padre. 2. (Des.) Asemejar; comparar, poner en paralelo.

Resent [rẹ-zent'], *va.* Resentirse, dar muestras de sentimiento o pesar; encolerizarse, tomar una cosa como injuria o afrenta, indignarse.

Resenter [rẹ-zent'-ẹr], *s.* El que se resiente de un agravio.

Resentful [rẹ-zent'-ful], *a.* Enfadadizo, vidrioso, el que se enfada con facilidad; resentido.

Resentment [rẹ-zent'-mẹnt], *s.* Resentimiento, enojo y mala voluntad en vista del mal verdadero o supuesto hecho contra sí mismo o los amigos de uno; disgusto profundo y persistente, desazón, pesar.

Reservation [rez-ẹr-vê'-shun], *s.* 1. Reservación, acción y efecto de reservar, y la cosa reservada. 2. Restricción mental, segunda intención, pensamiento secreto, lo que sobreentiende cautelosamente el que habla. 3. Reserva, reservación; término forense. 4. Separación o destino de una porción designada de territorio, bajo las leyes territoriales de los Estados Unidos, para un uso particular, v. g. para residencia de una tribu de indios; también, el territorio así reservado.

Reserve [rẹ-zẹrv'], *va.* 1. Reservar, guardar para en adelante, guardar alguna cosa para otra ocasión. 2. Tener por suyo, retener, conservar. 3. Exceptuar, excluir de alguna cosa concedida o estipulada.

Reserve, *s.* 1. Reserva, reservación, guarda o custodia de una cosa para otro tiempo o uso; reservación de tierras. 2. Reserva, circunspección, cautela, silencio en lo que a uno se refiere; reticencia; recato, modestia. 3. Reservación, excepción. 4. (Mil.) Reserva, retén. *Without reserve*, Sin reserva, sin excepción, enteramente.

Reserved [rẹ-zẹrvd'], *a.* 1. Reservado, modesto, cauteloso, circunspecto, discreto, distante. 2. Retenido, guardado, preservado.

Reservedly [rẹ-zẹrv'-ed-li], *adv.* Reservadamente, bajo sigilo; con reserva, con cautela.

Reservedness [rẹ-zẹrv'-ed-nes], *s.* Reserva, cautela, circunspección, recato.

Reserver [rẹ-zẹrv'-ẹr], *s.* El que reserva.

Reservist [rẹ-zẹrv'-ist], *s.* Soldado de reserva.

Reservoir [rez'-ẹr-vwōr], *s.* Depósito, regularmente de agua, que puede ser charca, estanque, arca o algibe: por extensión se da también este nombre al depósito de cualquier otra cosa.

Reset [rî-set'], *va.* Poner, colocar, o fijar de nuevo.—*s.* Acción de poner o fijar otra vez; o lo que está fijado o puesto de nuevo.

Reset [rẹ-set'], *va.* (Der. esco.) Recibir objetos hurtados.

Resetter [rẹ-set'-ẹr], *s.* (Der. esco.) El receptador o recibidor de objetos hurtados.

Resettle [rî-set'-l], *va.* Restablecer, repoblar, poblar de nuevo.—*vn.* Restablecerse, poblarse, fijarse de nuevo. *To resettle in the same parish*, Fijarse de nuevo en la misma parroquia.

Resettlement [rî-set'-l-mẹnt], *s.* Restablecimiento.

Reship [rî-ship'], *va.* y *vn.* Reembarcar o reembarcarse; transportar en retorno o de vuelta.

Reshipment [rî-ship'-mẹnt], *s.* 1. Reembarco, reembarque, acción de transportar segunda vez. 2. La cosa reembarcada o transportada por segunda vez.

Reside [rẹ-zaid'], *vn.* 1. Residir, morar en algún lugar. 2. Residir, estar o formar parte de, ser inherente.

Residence [rez'-i-dens], *s.* 1. Residencia, morada, domicilio, habitación o lugar donde se vive. 2. El acto de residir, o la calidad de residente; vecindad. *Certificate of residence*, Carta de vecindad; certificación de residencia.

Residency [rez'-i-den-si], *s.* 1. *V.* RESIDENCE. 2. En la India inglesa la habitación oficial del representante del gobernador-general, v. g. en la corte de un príncipe indígena.

Resident [rez'-i-dent], *a.* 1. Residente, que reside o mora en un lugar. 2. Permanente, no migratorio: dícese de las aves. 3. Inherente.—*s.* 1. El que o lo que reside, en cualquier sentido; particularmente, vecino, el que tiene casa y hogar en un pueblo, habitante. 2. Residente: llámase así el ministro que reside en alguna corte extranjera, sin el carácter de embajador.

Residentiary [rez-i-den'-shi-ẹ-ri], *a.* y *s.* Residente.

Resider [rẹ-zaid'-ẹr], *s.* Residente, morador, habitante.

Residual [rẹ-zid'-yu-al], **Residuary** [rẹ-zid'-yu-ẹ-ri], *a.* 1. Restante, perteneciente a un residuo, de la naturaleza de un residuo; lo que queda cuando han desaparecido todas las cosas de un mismo género, o todas las causas conocidas. *Residual magnetism*, Magnetismo restante, el que queda después de suprimida la fuerza imanante. 2. *Residuary*, (For.) Que está en relación con el resto de una herencia o que se refiere a él. *Residuary legatee*, Legatario universal.

Residue [rez'-i-diū], *s.* Residuo, resto, resta, sobrante.

Residuum [rî-zid'-yu-um], *s.* Residuo, lo que queda de una substancia con la que se ha hecho alguna operación; resta, lo que queda después de cualquier procedimiento de sustracción.

Resign [rẹ-zain'], *va.* 1. Dimitir, resignar, renunciar, ceder, hacer dejación. 2. Resignarse, rendirse, entregarse o humillarse a la voluntad de otro.

Resign [rî-sain'], *va.* Firmar de nuevo, firmar otra vez.

Resignation [rez-ig-nê'-shun], ¿**Resignment** [rẹ-zain'-mẹnt], *s.* Resignación, conformidad con la voluntad de Dios.

Resignee [rez-i-nî' o re-zain-î'], *s.* Resignatario, el eclesiástico en cuyo favor ha resignado otro un beneficio.

Resigner [rẹ-zain'-ẹr], *s.* Resignante, el que resigna un beneficio.

Resilience [rẹ-zil'-i-ens], **Resiliency** [rẹ-sil-i-en-si], ¿**Resilition** [rez-i-lish'-un], *s.* Resalto, elasticidad, el poder, acto o efecto, de volver a una posición anterior.

Resilient [rẹ-zil'-i-ent], *a.* Resaltante, elástico.

Resin [rez'-in], *s.* Resina, substancia amorfa e inflamable que fluye de algunos árboles, naturalmente o por incisión.

Resinaceous [rez-in-ê'-shus], *a.* *V.* RESINOUS, 1ª acepción.

Resiniferous [rez-i-nif'-ẹr-us], *a.* Resinífero, que produce resina.

Resinoid [rez'-in-eid], *a.* Parecido a una resina.—*s.* Substancia que se parece a una resina.

Resinous [rez'-in-us], *a.* 1. Resinoso, de la naturaleza de las resinas, o que contiene resina. 2. Obtenido de la resina, como la electricidad.

Resinousness [rez'-in-us-nes], *s.* La calidad de lo que es resinoso.

Resist [rẹ-zist'], *va.* y *vn.* Resistir, rechazar, repeler; oponerse; impedir, detener por la inercia; esforzarse en poner obstáculos, en contrariar, en hacer frustrar un proyecto, etc.; negarse a. *To resist the evidence of one's senses*, Negarse a admitir el testimonio de los sentidos.

Resistance, Resistence [rẹ-zist'-ans], *s.* 1. Resistencia, oposición, defensa. 2. Fuerza que impide un movimiento; impedimento, obstáculo. 3. (Elec.) Resistencia, la cualidad de un cuerpo que limita la fuerza de una corriente eléctrica. *Resistance-box*, Caja del carrete de resistencia. *V.* RHEOSTAT. *Resistance-coil*, Rosca, carrete, de alambre aislado de resistencia eléctrica conocida, del que se usa para medir las resistencias no conocidas.

Resistant, Resistent [rẹ-zist'-ant, ent], *a.* Resistente, que resiste.

Resistibility [rẹ-zist-i-bil'-i-ti], *s.* La calidad de resistible.

Resistible [rẹ-zist'-i-bl], *a.* Resistible.

Resistless [rẹ-zist'-les], *a.* 1. Irresistible, que, o a quien, no se puede resistir. 2. Que no ofrece resistencia, indefenso.

Resistor [rî-zis'-ter], *s.* Resistencia.

Resoluble [rez'-o-lu-bl], *a.* 1. Soluble, que se puede disolver, desatar, o desleir. 2. Resoluble.

Resolute [rez'-o-lūt], *a.* Resuelto, determinado; firme, constante.

Resolutely [rez'-o-lūt-li], *adv.* Resueltamente.

Resoluteness [rez'-o-lūt-nes], *s.* Resolución, determinación, firmeza, ánimo, constancia.

Resolution [rez-o-lū'- (o liū'-) shun], *s.* 1. Resolución, determinación, ánimo, valor, arresto; firmeza, constancia. 2. Resolución, determinación de algún asunto; el propósito, línea de conducta o acuerdo tomado. 3. Resolución, solución de alguna duda o dificultad, de un problema o de una ecuación. 4. Análisis, la solución de las partes de algún compuesto; resolución, disolución de un todo; análisis químico, mecánico o mental; descomposición. 5. Resolución, la propuesta formal que se ofrece á la aceptación, o que se acepta por un cuerpo legislativo o deliberante. 6. Resolución de un tumor, de una inflamación, etc. *Man of resolution*, Hombre de tesón; hombre determinado o decidido.

Resolutive [rez'-o-lū-tiv], *a.* (Poco us.) Resolutivo.

Resolvable [rẹ-zelv'-a-bl], *a.* Resoluble, lo que se puede resolver, analizar, o aclarar.

Resolve [rẹ-zelv'], *va.* y *vn.* 1. Resolver o resolverse, determinar, decidir, decidirse, declarar, declararse; tratar de, estar dispuesto á. 2. Expresar o declarar como opinión o intención; tomar un acuerdo; aprobar por medio de votos. 3. Resolver, analizar. 4. Resolver, convertir, reducir un todo á partes menudas deshaciéndolo; descomponer en sus partes constituyentes. 5. Enterar, explicar alguna cosa. 6. Resolver, desatar, dar solución a una dificultad ó a una duda. 7. Resolver, disipar, desvanecer humores, tumores, etc. 8. (Fig.) Transformarse en o reducirse una cosa a otra mejor. 9. ¿Fijarse en una opinión. 10. (Ant.) Derretir, desleír. —*vr.* Resolverse, cambiar un cuerpo deliberante de una forma de organización o proceder a otra.—*vn.* Resolverse, tomar una resolución; decidirse a, determinarse. *I have resolved upon it*, Me he decidido, he determinado. *The House resolved to take up the bill*, La Cámara resolvió aprobar el proyecto de ley.

Resolve, *s.* Resolución, determinación, propósito.

Resolvedly [rẹ-zelv'-ed-li], *adv.* Resueltamente, valerosamente.

Resolvedness [rẹ-zelv'-ed-nes], *s.* Resolución determinada.

Resolvent [rẹ-zelv'-ent], *a.* Resolvente, que tiene la facultad de resolver o descomponer una cosa en sus elementos o partes constituyentes.—*s.* Solutivo, el medicamento que tiene la virtud de disipar los humores o tumores; todo lo que tiene el poder de resolver, en cualquier sentido.

Resolver [rẹ-zelv'-ẹr], *s.* El que resuelve, determina o disuelve.

Resonance [rez'-o-nans], *s.* Resonancia, retumbo, la calidad de sonoro; resonación.

Resonant [rez'-o-nant], *a.* 1. Resonante, retumbante, reverberante, repercusivo, hablando de un paraje que refleja bien o demasiado el sonido. 2. Sonoro, sonoroso, hablando de voces o instrumentos.

Resonator [rez'-o-nê''-tẹr], *s.* Resonador, lo que resuena; la faringe con las fosas nasales, y el nombre de ciertos aparatos.

Resorcinol, Resorcin [rez-ēr'-sin-ōl], *s.* Resorcina, compuesto cristalizable ($C_6H_6O_2$) de los derivados del ácido fénico, que se emplea en medicina, y como base de ciertos colores purpurinos rojos.

Resorption [rẹ-sērp'-shun], *s.* Reabsorción, resorción.

Resorptive [rẹ-sērp'-tiv], *a.* Reabsorbedor, relativo a la reabsorción, o causado por ella.

Resort [rẹ-zērt'], *vn.* 1. Acudir, recurrir, frecuentar, concurrir. 2. Ir o ponerse en camino para alguna parte; venir, llegar o concurrir en abundancia personas o cosas a algún lugar. 3. (For.) Faltar a lo prometido o pactado.

Resort, *s.* 1. Concurso, concurrencia; visita, el acto de visitar o frecuentar un lugar; también, el lugar o sitio frecuentado, punto de reunión. 2. Recurso, acción de recurrir a alguno; el medio que se emplea en un caso urgente; refugio. 3. (Ant.) Gran copia de gente junta en un mismo lugar.

Resorter [rẹ-zērt'-ẹr], *s.* El que concurre a algún sitio o le frecuenta o visita.

Resound [rẹ-zaund'], *va.* 1. Publicar, repetir, repercutir el sonido. 2. Cantar, celebrar. *The echo resounded his lamentations*, El ecó repitió sus lamentos.—*vn.* 1. Resonar, retumbar, hacer gran ruido o estruendo. 2. Devolver o reforzar un sonido; formar eco; llenarse de sonido. 3. Mostrar resonancia. 4. Tener fama, ser célebre o celebrado.

Resound [rī-saund'], *va.* Volver a sonar, sonar repetidas veces.

Resource [rẹ-sōrs'], *s.* 1. Recurso, arbitrio, medio, expediente. 2. Facultad de hallar, procurar o aplicar los medios convenientes, el poder de ejecución (*sing.* o *pl.*) 3. *pl.* Recursos, posibles, medios pecuniarios; ventajas naturales de un país.

Resourceful [rẹ-sōrs'-ful], *a.* Fértil en recursos o expedientes; lleno de medios o ventajas.

Resourceless [rẹ-sōrs'-les], *a.* Desprovisto de recursos, o de ventajas naturales.

Resow [rī-sō'], *va.* Resembrar.

Respect [rẹ-spect'], *va.* 1. Respetar, venerar, tener respeto a una persona, acatar, estimar; tener como sagrado o inviolable. 2. Mirar, apreciar, hacer caso de alguna cosa. 3. Tocar, tener relación una cosa a otra, concernir, referir. *It respects you directly*, Le toca a Vd. en derechura. *To respect persons*, Dejarse influir demasiado por el estado social; ceder a las circunstancias exteriores de la persona con perjuicio del derecho y la equidad.

Respect, *s.* 1. Respecto, la razón, relación o proporción de una cosa con otra. 2. Miramiento, respeto, veneración, acatamiento, atención, consideración a las personas beneméritas o a lo que es justo. *To show respect*, Tener respeto a alguno. 3. Carácter respetable. 4. Consideración, motivo. *With respect to what you say*, Tocante a lo que Vd. dice. *In some respect*, De algún modo. *In other respects*, Por otra parte. 5. Porte que indica deferencia; en plural, *respects*, memorias, expresiones, recuerdos, cumplimientos que se hacen o envían por cortesía unas personas a otras. *Out of respect for you*, Por consideración a Vd., por Vd. *In respect to* (rara vez *of*), Con respecto a; en comparación de. 6. Acepción, tendencia, disposición indebida, en detrimento de la justicia.

Respectability, Respectableness [rẹ-spect-a-bil'-i-ti, rẹ-spect'-a-bl-nes], *s.* Respetabilidad, calidad de respetable; crédito, carácter o posición honoríficos. *Of no respectability*, Sin consideración, en situación dudosa u obscura.

Respectable [rẹ-spect'-a-bl], *a.* 1. Respetable, estimable, honroso, de buen nombre, en buena reputación. 2. Pasable, tal cual, bastante bueno, considerable; mediano. *A respectable man*, Hombre de mucho respeto, de crédito sentado; hombre formal. *Respectable talents*, Talentos bastante notables, de consideración.

Respectably [rẹ-spect'-a-bli], *adv.* 1. Respetablemente, con respeto. 2. Pasablemente, bastante bien, medianamente.

Respected [rẹ-spect'-ed], *a.* Considerado, respetado, estimado.

Respecter [rẹ-spect'-ẹr], *s.* El que respeta. *To be a respecter of persons*, Hacer acepción de personas.

Respectful [rẹ-spect'-ful], *a.* Respetuoso, respetoso, lleno de respeto.

Respectfully [rẹ-spect'-ful-i], *adv.* Respetuosamente, respetosamente.

Respectfulness [rẹ-spect'-ful-nes], *s.* Conducta respetuosa.

Respecting [rẹ-spect'-ing], *prep.* Con respecto a, en cuanto a, relativamente a, por lo que toca a.

Respective [rẹ-spect'-iv], *a.* Respectivo, relativo o referente a una cosa particular; cada uno, particular; que se contrae particularmente a alguno; sendo.

Respectively [rẹ-spect'-iv-li], *adv.* Respectivamente, relativamente.

Respirable [rẹ-spair'-a-bl o res'-pi-ra-bl], *a.* Respirable, que se puede respirar, propio para la respiración.

Respiration [res-pi-ré'-shun], *s.* 1. Respiración, acción de aspirar y de respirar el aire. 2. (Bot.) Respiración, acción de tomar las plantas el oxígeno, y después de su oxigenación expeler los productos de ésta. 3. El sonido que se oye en la auscultación.

Respirator [res'-pi-rê-tẹr], *s.* Respirador, aparato de alambre fino, o de gasa, que se pone sobre la boca o la nariz como protección contra el frío, el polvo, el humo, etc.

Respiratory [rẹ-spair'-a-to-ri o res'-pi-ra-to-ri], *a.* Respiratorio, que sirve para la respiración o que pertenece a ella; causado por la respiración.

Respire [rẹ-spair'], *vn.* 1. Resollar, respirar; tener vida, vivir. 2. †Descansar, aliviarse del trabajo, tomar aliento.—*va.* 1. Respirar, inspirar y arrojar el aire o gas. 2. Exhalar, echar vaho.

Respite [res'-pit], *s.* 1. Suspensión de la ejecución de la pena capital. 2. Pausa; plazo, respiro, tregua.

Respite, *va.* Dar treguas, suspender o diferir una cosa; conceder plazo o espera.

Resplendence [rẹ-splen'-dens], **Resplendency** [rī-splen'-den-si], *s.* Resplandor, brillo, lustre.

Resplendent [rẹ-splen'-dent], *a.* Resplandeciente, brillante.

Resplendently [rẹ-splen'-dent-li], *adv.* Lustrosamente, brillantemente.

Respond [rẹ-spend'], *vn.* 1. Responder, contestar a lo que se habla o escribe. 2. Responder; corresponder; venir bien, ajustarse una cosa a otra.

Respondent [rẹ-spend'-ent], *s.* Respondedor; demandado.

Responsal [rẹ-spen'-sal], *s.* Respuesta litúrgica.

Response [rẹ-spens'], *s.* 1. Respuesta, contestación a una pregunta o carta. 2. En el oficio divino la respuesta que da la congregación a lo que dice el oficiante. 3. Réplica a una objeción en los argumentos.

Responsibility [rẹ-spen-si-bil'-i-ti], *s.* 1. Responsabilidad. 2. Deber, obligación, fideicomiso o depósito; aquello de que es uno responsable. 3. Solvencia; también la capacidad de ejecutar un contrato

Responsible [rę-spen'-si-bl], *a.* 1. Responsable, obligado a satisfacer algún cargo, deber, deuda u otro servicio. 2. Que tiene capacidad, mental y moral, para distinguir entre lo bueno y lo malo, y para ser legalmente responsable por su conducta: perteneciente a dicha capacidad o condición. 3. Solvente. 4. Abonado; que envuelve o implica responsabilidad u obligación. *A responsible post,* Un puesto de responsabilidad.

Responsibleness [rę-spen'-si-bl-nes], *s.* Responsabilidad.

Responsive [rę-spen'-siv], *a.* 1. Respondiente; correspondiente, que concuerda con, idóneo, conforme. 2. Respondedor, que responde, que constituye una respuesta. 3. (For.) Que contiene respuesta pertinente.

Responsiveness [rę-spen'-siv-nes], *s.* Calidad de lo que corresponde a otra cosa o concuerda con ella; simpatía, conformidad.

Responsory [rę-spen'-so-ri], *a.* Que responde, que contiene respuesta.—*s.* (Poco us.) Responsorio, ciertas preces y versículos que se dicen en el rezo divino.

Rest [rest], *s.* 1. Descanso, tregua, interrupción o cesación de la ocupación o trabajo, o de una acción o movimiento cualquiera; sueño, reposo. 2. Reposo de los muertos, el descanso final o último. 3. Quietud, paz, tranquilidad. 4. Sustentáculo, apoyo, arrimo, estribo; esperanza final. 5. Resto, residuo, sobra. 6. Los demás, los otros. 7. Descansadero, el lugar donde se descansa. 8. Cuja, ristre. 9. Pausa en la música y el signo que la indica. 10. Cesura en la poesía. *To disturb a person's rest,* Turbar el reposo de alguien. *To have a good night's rest,* Pasar una buena noche, dormir bien. *To take rest,* Tomar descanso. *Give me the rest,* Déme Vd. lo restante, lo demás. *Minim rest,* (Mús.) Media pausa.

Rest, *vn.* 1. Descansar, dormir, reposar; apoyar, afianzar. 2. Morir, tener descanso en el sepulcro. 3. Parar, estar quedo o sin movimiento. 4. Estar en paz, tener el ánimo sosegado. 5. Estar sostenido por; estar tendido, establecido o fundado sobre; apoyarse en, reposar, yacer. 6. Fiarse en, atenerse a, poner su confianza en; contar con alguien. 7. (For.) Dar una parte por terminada la vista de un pleito. 8. Allanarse a algún convenio. 9. Quedar, permanecer. *Rest assured,* Esté Vd. seguro. 10. Restar, quedar.—*va.* Poner a descansar, hacer cesar un trabajo o esfuerzo; y (*vr.*) ponerse a descansar; poner, apoyar o asentar una cosa sobre otra para que esté cómoda o quieta. *Rest from your task,* Descanse Vd. de su tarea. *To rest against,* u *on, a tree,* Apoyarse en o contra un árbol. *To rest on one's word,* Fiar en la palabra de alguno. *To retire to rest,* Retirarse a descansar, acostarse o dormir.

Restaurant [res'-to- (o tō-) rant], *s.* Restaurante, fonda, lugar donde se sirve de comer. (Fr.)

Restful [rest'-ful], *a.* 1. Lleno de reposo, que da descanso. 2. Quieto, sosegado, tranquilo. *A restful scene,* Una escena tranquila, reposada.

Restfully [rest'-ful-i], *adv.* Tranquilamente, reposadamente.

Rest-harrow [rest-har'-o], *s.* (Bot.) Rémora de arado o detienebuey.

Restiff [res'-tif], *a.* (Ant.) *V.* RESTIVE.

Resting [rest'-ing], *s.* Reposo, descanso. *Resting-place,* (1) Lugar de descanso; (fig.) el sepulcro. (2) Meseta de escalera.

Restitution [res-ti-tiū'-shun], *s.* 1. Restitución, restablecimiento, recobro. 2. Reparación, acción de dar un equivalente, como por un daño o por una pérdida; indemnización. 3. Recuperación de una posición o condición anterior. 4. (Fís.) Propiedad de elasticidad.

Restive [rest'-iv], *a.* Repropio: dícese de los caballos y mulos tercos y reacios y también de las personas; pertinaz, obstinado.

Restiveness [rest'-iv-nes], *s.* Terquedad, obstinación, rebeldía.

Restless [rest'-les], *a.* 1. Inconstante, mudable. 2. Inquieto, impaciente. 3. Insomne, desvelado, falto de sueño. 4. Desasosegado.

Restlessness [rest'-les-nes], *s.* Insomnio, vigilia, desvelo; desasosiego; agitación continua; inquietud, impaciencia.

Restock [ri-stec'], *va.* Renovar, surtir nuevamente.

Restorable [rę-stōr'-a-bl], *a.* Restituíble.

Restoration [res-to-rē'-shun], *s.* 1. Restauración, el acto de restaurar, reparar, o reponer alguna cosa en el estado o estimación que tenía; rehabilitación, restablecimiento, renovación. 2. La cosa restablecida o restaurada a su estado original, v. gr. una obra de arte. 3. Restauración, el restablecimiento de los Estuardos en Inglaterra, de los Judíos en Palestina después de la cautividad babilónica, etc. 4. (Teol.) Redención final del pecado, salvación universal.

Restorative [rę-stōr'-a-tiv], *a.* y *s.* Restaurativo, restaurante, que tiene el poder de restaurar; medicamento que restaura las fuerzas.

Restore [rę-stōr'], *va.* 1. Restituir, restablecer una cosa en el estado que antes tenía; reparar, reconstruir. 2. Reproducir, reedificar, representar como antes existía, con la ayuda de materiales o restos existentes. 3. Recuperar, recobrar, restaurar, restablecer después de una interrupción; devolver la salud. 4. Restituir, devolver lo que ha sido perdido, tomado o quitado; compensar, resarcir, dar un equivalente. 5. Reponer, reintegrar, colocar a uno en el empleo o estado de que fué privado. *To restore one to liberty,* Darle a uno su libertad, ponerle en libertad.

Restore [rī-stōr'], *va.* Depositar o almacenar de nuevo.

Restorer [rę-stōr'-ęr], *s.* Restaurador.

Restoring [rę-stōr'-ing], *s.* Restauración; restitución.

Restrain [rę-strēn'], *va.* 1. Restringir, restriñir, detener, apretar; reprimir, contener, refrenar. 2. Impedir. 3. Restriñir, constreñir, limitar, coartar. 4. (For.) Prohibir, vedar la comisión de un acto ilegal.

Restrainable [rę-strēn'-a-bl], *a.* Restringible.

Restrainedly [rę-strēn'-ed-li], *adv.* Con restricción.

Restrainer [rę-strēn'-ęr], *s.* Restringente, lo que restringe; especialmente en fotografía, un agente químico que retarda la acción del revelador.

Restraint [rę-strēnt'], *s.* Sujeción, limitación, refrenamiento, freno, constreñimiento; oposición; prohibición.

Restrict [rę-strict'], *va.* Restringir, limitar, ceñir o coartar.

Restriction [rę-stric'-shun], *s.* Restricción, limitación o modificación.

Restrictive [rę-stric'-tiv], *a.* Restrictivo, que restringe, ciñe o limita; que sirve para limitar o restringir.

Restrictively [rę-stric'-tiv-li], *adv.* Limitadamente.

Rest room [rest rūm], *s.* 1. Sala de descanso. 2. Retrete. excusado.

Resubjection [rī-sub-jec'-shun], *s.* Nueva sujeción o el acto de volver a caer bajo el yugo de alguno después de haberlo sacudido una vez.

Result [rę-zult'], *vn.* 1. Seguirse, inferirse, como consecuencia o resultado; ser efecto físico o lógico. 2. Resultar, venir a parar, acabar, terminar en; tener un resultado: (seguido de *in*). *This will result in good (or evil),* Esto acabará en bien (o en mal).

Result, *s.* 1. Resulta, resultado; ilación, consecuencia; efecto, conclusión. 2. Resulta, lo que últimamente se resuelve en alguna conferencia o deliberación; decisión aprobada por una asamblea deliberante.

Resultance [rę-zul'-tans], *s.* Resultado, resultancia.

Resultant [rę-zult'-ant], *a.* Resultante.—*s.* 1. Resultante, fuerza o velocidad que resulta de la concurrencia de otras en un mismo punto, o la que produce el mismo efecto que las demás juntas. 2. Lo que se sigue como consecuencia, resultado.

Resulting [rę-zult'-ing], *pa.* 1. Resultante, que dimana como consecuencia, efecto o conclusión. 2. (For.) Que vuelve a ser o recaer. *Resulting use,* Usufructo que vuelve a recaer en quien lo ha instituído.

Resumable [rę-ziū'-ma-bl], *a.* Que se puede reasumir.

Resume [rę-ziūm'], *va.* 1. Empezar de nuevo, continuar después de una interrupción. 2. Reasumir; recobrar la posesión de algo, reocupar, recuperar lo perdido o tomado; volver a tomar.—*vn.* Tomar el hilo, reanudar. *To resume a journey,* Volver a ponerse en viaje, en camino. *To resume a business,* Reanudar un negocio. *To resume a discourse,* Tomar el hilo de un discurso.

Resumption [rę-zump'-shun], *s.* Reasunción; recobro.

Resumptive [rę-zump'-tiv], *a.* Que vuelve a tomar o a resumir.

Resurface [rī-sūr'-fēs], *va.* Revestir, poner nueva superficie.

Resurrect [rez''-ur-rect'], *va.* (Fam.) 1. Volver a la vida, o al uso y aceptación. 2. Desenterrar, exhumar. *To resurrect a doctrine,* Volver a poner una doctrina en aceptación corriente.

Resurrection [rez-ur-rec'-shun], *s.* 1. Resurrección. 2. Renovación, restablecimiento. *Resurrection-men,* Los que desentierran los muertos para venderlos a los disectores.

Resurvey [rî-sūr-vê'], *va.* 1. Apear, deslindar, medir de nuevo un terreno. 2. Rever, volver a ver.—*s.* [rî-sūr'-vê] Nuevo apeo, deslinde, o medición de terreno.
Resuscitate [rî-sus'-i-têt], *va.* Resucitar, hacer revivir; renovar.—*vn.* Resucitar, volver a la vida.
Resuscitation [rî-sus-i-tê'-shun], *s.* Resurrección, renacimiento, renovación.
Resuscitative [rî-sus'-i-ta-tiv], *a.* Resucitador, que tiende a resucitar o puede hacer revivir o resucitar.
Ret [ret], *va.* Enriar, embalsar el cáñamo o el lino.
Retail [rî-têl'], *va.* 1. Vender por menor, revender, regatonear. 2. Decir o relatar una cosa detalladamente.
Retail [rî'-têl], *s.* Venta por menor; reventa. *To sell by retail,* Vender al por menor o al menudeo.
Retailer [rî-têl'-ẹr], *s.* Lonjista, tendero, comerciante por menor, revendedor.
Retain [rẹ-tên'], *va.* 1. Retener, guardar, conservar. 2. Tomar a sueldo o ajustar a un mozo, sirviente, etc.; especialmente, contratar un abogado, pagarle honorarios anticipados. —*vn.* Pertenecer, ser dependiente o criado. (Arq.) Servir de sostén. *To retain youthful vigour,* Conservar el vigor de la juventud. *Retaining-fee, V.* RETAINER, 4ª acep. *Retaining-wall,* Pared maestra, muro de apoyo.
Retainable [rẹ-tên'-a-bl], *a.* Que se puede retener.
Retainer [rẹ-tên'-ẹr], *s.* 1. Adherente, partidario. 2. Dependiente, criado, acompañante de otro en un campamento. 3. Retenedor. 4. El honorario o estipendio que se paga anticipadamente a un abogado para que defienda un a causa o pleito.
Retainer fee [rẹ-tên'-ẹr fî], *s.* Iguala.
Retake [rî-têc'], *va.* Volver a tomar.
Retaliate [rẹ-tal'-i-êt], *va.* Talionar, castigar con la pena del talión; pagar en la misma moneda; desquitarse, vengarse
Retaliation [rẹ-tal-i-ê'-shun], *s.* Desquite, despique; desagravio, satisfacción; pago, retorno; defensa. *By way of retaliation,* Por vía de represalias. *Law of retaliation,* Ley del talión.
Retaliative [rẹ-tal'-i-a-tiv], *a.* Vengativo; que se desquita.
Retaliatory [rẹ-tal'-i-a-to-ri], *a.* Que usa de represalias, se desquita o paga en la misma moneda.
Retard [rẹ-tārd'], *va.* 1. Disminuir la velocidad, retardar, atrasar. 2. Retardar, detener, diferir, dilatar. —*vn.* (Des.) Atrasarse.
Retardation [ret-ar-dê'-shun], *s.* Retardación, retardo, atraso; acción de retardar el movimiento; dilación.
Retarder [rẹ-tārd'-ẹr], *s.* El o lo que retarda o impide.
Retardment [rẹ-tārd'-mẹnt], *s.* (Poco us.) Retardo.
Retch [rech], *vn.* Esforzarse para vomitar, arquear.
Rete [rî'-tî], *s.* Redecilla, disposición parecida a la de los vasos y nervios. (Lat. = red.)
Retent [rẹ-tent'], *s.* Lo retenido, guardado, o conservado.
Retention [rẹ-ten'-shun], *s.* 1. Retención, la acción y efecto de retener; acto de guardar una cosa en poder o posesión de uno; conservación de una costumbre u opinión. 2. La facultad de retener o conservar. 3. Retentiva, memoria.
Retentive [rẹ-ten'-tiv], *a.* 1. Retentivo, que tiene virtud de retener. 2. (Med.) Retentriz, potencia o poder de retener.
Retentiveness [rẹ-ten'-tiv-nes], *s.* Retentiva, facultad, poder de retener; tenacidad (de la memoria).
Reticence [ret'-i-sens], **Reticency** [ret'-i-sen-si], *s.* 1. Reticencia, la calidad, la costumbre o el acto de guardar silencio, o de ser reservado, sobre lo que debiera decirse. 2. (Ret.) Reticencia.
Reticent [ret'-i-sent], *a.* Reticente.
Reticle [ret'-i-cl], *s.* (Astr.) Retículo, redecilla de alambres, que sirve de micrómetro y para otros usos en los telescopios, etc.
Reticular [rẹ-tic'-yu-lar], *a.* Reticular, en forma de red; perteneciente a un retículo.
Reticulate [rẹ-tic'-yu-lêt], *va.* Formar un tejido en forma de red.
Reticulate, Reticulated [rẹ-tic'-yu-lêt-ed], *a.* Reticulado, retífero, trenzado, formado en redecilla, enrejado o trenza.
Reticulation [rẹ-tic-yu-lê'-shun], *s.* Disposición en forma de red.
Reticule [ret'-i-kiūl], *s.* 1. Ridículo, bolsa de señora para llevar el pañuelo, el bordado de aguja, artículos pequeños, etc. 2. *V.* RETICLE.
Reticulum [rẹ-tic'-yu-lum], *s.* 1. Retículo, tejido en forma de red. 2. Redecilla, segunda de las cuatro cavidades en que se divide el estómago de los rumiantes.
Retiform [ret'-i-fērm o rî'-ti-fērm], *a.* Con líneas que se cruzan a manera de red.
Retina [ret'-i-na], *s.* Retina, membrana del fondo del ojo que contiene el aparato nervioso esencial para la visión.
Retinitis [ret-i-nai'-tis o nî'-tis], *s.* Retinitis, inflamación de la retina.
Retinoid [ret'-i-neid], *a.* Resiniforme, parecido a una resina. (< Gr. rhetine, resina.)
Retinue [ret'-i-niū], *s.* 1. Tren, comitiva, acompañamiento de criados. 2. Serie de resultados.
Retire [rẹ-tair'], *vn.* 1. Retirarse; retroceder, volver atrás. 2. Retirarse, refugiarse, ponerse en salvo. 3. Dejar algún empleo público. 4. Recogerse, apartarse, separarse. *A retired life,* Vida privada. *To retire from business,* Retirarse de los negocios.—*va.* 1. Pagar completamente y retirar de la circulación comercial. *To retire the bonds of a city,* Retirar los bonos de una ciudad. 2. Jubilar, retirar, un oficial del ejército o de la marina. 3. (Ant.) Remover, apartar, separar.
Retired [rẹ-taird'], *pa.* 1. Retirado; secreto, apartado, aislado, solitario. 2. Retirado, jubilado. *To live a retired life,* Llevar una vida retirada, solitaria; vivir lejos del mundo. *Retired officer,* Oficial retirado. *To put on the retired list,* Poner en retiro, conceder la jubilación.
Retiredly [rẹ-taird'-li], *adv.* Solitariamente, privadamente.
Retiredness [rẹ-taird'-nes], *s.* Retiro, recogimiento, soledad.
Retirement [rẹ-tair'-mẹnt], *s.* 1. Retiro, retiramiento. 2. Retiro, lugar apartado; la morada o asilo a donde uno se retira a pasar una vida sosegada. 3. Retiro, el estado del que se ha separado del mundo, de los negocios, etc.; jubilación.
Retiring [rẹ-tair'-ing], *pa.* 1. Recatado; modesto, discreto. 2. Perteneciente a un empleado jubilado o militar en situación de retiro.
Retorsion [rẹ-tēr'-shun], *s.* Ley del talión, ojo por ojo, y diente por diente.
Retort [rẹ-tērt'], *va.* 1. Redargüir; pagar una palabra descortés o picante con otra igual o más fuerte. (Fam.) Retrucar. 2. Encorvar, doblar, torcer. 3. Replicar. 4. (Des.) Rechazar, repeler.
Retort, *s.* 1. Redargución; réplica aguda, picante o mordaz; acción de redargüir. 2. Retorta, vasija de forma especial que sirve para las operaciones químicas.
Retorter [rẹ-tērt'-ẹr], *s.* El que replica o redarguye.
Retortion [rẹ-tēr'-shun], *s.* Retorcimiento; retorsión.
Retouch [rî-tuch'], *va.* Retocar, volver a tocar, modificar, dar la última mano. *To retouch an essay, a painting,* Retocar un ensayo, un cuadro.—*s.* Retoque, última mano.
Retoucher [rî-tuch'-ẹr], *s.* El que retoca, particularmente las impresiones fotográficas para perfeccionarlas.
Retrace [rẹ-três'], *va.* 1. Volver a seguir las huellas o pisadas de alguno; traer o representar a la memoria o a la imaginación la idea de una cosa pasada. 2. Repasar, narrar, recitar. 3. Retrazar, volver a trazar.
Retract [rẹ-tract'], *va.* 1. Retractar, desdecir una declaración, palabras, etc.; denegar, retirar. 2. Retraer, encoger, como las uñas de un gato. —*vn.* 1. Retractarse, desdecirse, cantar la palinodia. 2. Encogerse, retirarse, retraerse.
Retractable, Retractible [rẹ-tract'-a-(i-)bl], *a.* Retractable, que se puede retractar, o encoger.
Retractation [rẹ-trac-tê'-shun], *s.* Retractación.
Retractile [rẹ-tract'-il], *a.* Retráctil, se dice de las uñas de los animales que se hallan ocultas en el estado de reposo.
Retraction [rẹ-trac'-shun], *s.* Retracción; contracción; retractación; renuncia.
Retractive [rẹ-tract'-iv], *a.* Que retira o retracta.
Retractor [rẹ-tract'-ẹr], *s.* El o lo que retrae; en particular, un músculo retractor; también, un instrumento o aparato destinado a levantar las carnes después de cortadas, en una amputación.
Retread [rẹ-tred'], *va.* 1. Volver a andar, volver a pisar. 2. Recubrir. *To retread a tire,* Recubrir una llanta o neumático.
Retreat [rẹ-trît'], *s.* 1. Retiro, soledad. 2. Retirada, en lugar que sirve de acogida segura; refugio, asilo. 3. (Mil.) Retirada. *To sound the retreat,* Tocar retirada. 4. (Arq.) Releje. 5. Receso.
Retreat, *vn.* Retirarse, refugiarse.
Retrench [rẹ-trench'], *va.* 1. Cercenar, cortar, acortar, disminuir. 2. (Mil.) Atrincherar.—*vn.* Reducirse o ceñirse a sus medios, vivir con economía, cercenar los gastos.
Retrenchment [rẹ-trench'-mẹnt], *s.* 1. Cercenadura, cercenamiento, rebaja, diminución. 2. Atrincheramiento, trinchera.

Retribution [ret-ri-biū'-shʊn], *s.* Retribución, recompensa; especialmente, imposición de una pena.

Retributive [rẹ-trib'-yu-tiv], **Retributory** [rẹ-trib'-yu-to-ri], *a.* 1. Retribuyente, que retribuye, que tiende a remunerar o a castigar. 2. Distributivo. *Retributive justice*, Justicia distributiva.

Retrievable [rẹ-trīv'-ɑ-bl], *a.* Recuperable; reparable.

Retrievableness [rẹ-trīv'-ɑ-bl-nes], *s.* El estado o la condición de lo que puede repararse.

Retrieval [rẹ-trīv'-ɑl], *s.* El acto o procedimiento de recuperar, restaurar, etc.; reintegración de una pérdida o quiebra.

Retrieve [rẹ-trīv'], *va.* 1. Recuperar, mejorar de condición o estado, recobrar, restablecer, restaurar. 2. Reparar, componer, remediar las malas consecuencias de algo, expiar. 3. Buscar y traer a la mano; se dice de los perros.—*vn.* Hallar y traer algo los perros, como la caza muerta o herida.

Retriever [rẹ-trīv'-ẹr], *s.* 1. El o lo que recobra o restaura. 2. Perro adiestrado para buscar y traer la caza, sabueso.

Retro- [rī'-tro o ret'-ro]. Prefijo que significa atrás o hacia atrás, y que a veces implica oposición.

Retroact [rī''-tro-act'], *va.* Obrar en oposición o hacia atrás; tener fuerza retroactiva.

Retroaction [rī-tro-ac'-shʊn], *s.* (For.) Retroacción, ficción legal que supone a una cosa anterior al tiempo en que sucedió.

Retroactive [rī-tro-ac'-tiv], *a.* Retroactivo, que obra o tiene fuerza sobre el tiempo anterior.

Retrocede [rī'-tro-sīd o ret'-ro-sīd], *va.* Retroceder, ceder a uno el derecho o cosa que él había cedido antes.—*vn.* Retroceder, volver hacia atrás.

Retrocession [rī-tro-sesh'-ʊn], *s.* Retrocesión, retroceso; movimiento retrógrado; inclinación hacia atrás.

Retrofiring [ret'-ro-fair-ing], *s.* Retrodisparo.

Retroflex [ret'-ro-flex], *a.* Que muda bruscamente de dirección doblándose hacia atrás.

Retroflexion [ret-ro-flec'-shʊn], *s.* Retroflexión, inflexión hacia atrás; se dice particularmente del fondo del útero.

Retrogradation [ret-ro-grɑ-dē'-shʊn], *s.* Retrogradación.

Retrograde [ret'-ro-grēd], *a.* Retrógrado; contrario, opuesto.

Retrograde, *vn.* Retrogradar, retroceder.

Retrogression [rī-tro- (o ret-ro-) gresh'-ʊn], *s.* Retrogradación.

Retrogressive [rī-tro-gres'-iv], *a.* Retrógrado, que va o vuelve hacia atrás; que se inclina hacia abajo.

Retro-rocket [re'-tro rɒk-et], *s.* (Aer.) Retrocohete.

Retrospect [ret'-ro-spect], *s.* Reflexión o consideración de las cosas pasadas.

Retrospection [ret-ro-spec'-shʊn], *s.* El acto y la facultad de considerar las cosas pasadas.

Retrospective [ret-ro-spec'-tiv], *a.* Retrospectivo, que se refiere al tiempo pasado.

Retroversion [ret-ro-vẹr'-shʊn], *s.* Retroversión, inclinación hacia un lado o hacia atrás; dícese particularmente de la matriz.

Return [rẹ-tūrn'], *vn.* 1. Volver, ir otra vez al paraje donde uno ha estado ya; regresar (al lugar de donde se salió); retornar. 2. Volverse, irse de nuevo, aparecer o presentarse de nuevo. 3. Volver, repetir, reiterar o empezar de nuevo lo mismo que se había hecho antes. 4. Restituirse o volver al estado anterior. 5. Responder, reponer, replicar. 6. Volver a la posesión de alguien.—*va.* 1. Devolver, transmitir, remitir; volver a enviar. 2. Volver, corresponder, pagar, retribuir. 3. Volver, restituir lo que se ha recibido o tomado. 4. Dar cuenta o hacer relación, especialmente de una manera oficial a los superiores de uno, o a determinada autoridad. 5. Dar en cambio, recompensar, agradecer o reconocer (un favor, etc.); corresponder. 6. Dar como aumento, interés o provecho; ser origen o manantial de; redituar, producir (utilidad). 7. Elegir, anunciar como elegido para un cuerpo legislativo. *To return to the same kind of life*, Volver a las andadas. *To return answer*, Dar respuesta. *To return a kindness*, Corresponder a un beneficio. *To return good for evil*, Devolver bien por mal. *To return thanks*, Dar las gracias. *To return a verdict*, Dar, pronunciar un jurado su fallo. *To return home*, Regresar a casa. *They were about to return*, Estaban a punto de volver. *She has not yet returned*, Ella no está de vuelta todavía.

Return, *s.* 1. Retorno, regreso. 2. Ganancia, utilidad, provecho, rédito. 3. Retorno, reconocimiento de un beneficio, pago, paga, satisfacción, recompensa, retribución. 4. Retorno, cambio o trueque de unas mercaderías por otras. 5. Vicisitud, revolución. 6. Vuelta, repetición de alguna cosa. 7. Remesa, remisión de alguna cosa de una parte a otra. 8. Relación, cuenta que se da de alguna cosa. 9. Restitución, la acción de restituir. 10. Recaída. 11. (Arq.) Continuación de las molduras hasta alguna esquina. 12. Relación, parte oficial; (*pl.*) lista, nómina, padrón o censo; (Mil.) lista de muertos y heridos. 13. Respuesta, réplica, redargüición. 14. Reaparición, retorno. 15. (Ingl.) Elección, nombramiento para el Parlamento. *To make a return*, (1) Hacer una relación oficial; (2) redituar, producir utilidad o ganancia; (3) devolver, corresponder, hacer restitución; (4) pagar en la misma moneda, desquitarse, no quedar a deber nada; responder, sacudirse. *Goods of a quick return*, Mercancías de pronto despacho. *On my return from*, A mi regreso de. *In return*, En cambio, en recíproca correspondencia. *Return-ticket*, Billete de ida y vuelta. *Return-request*, (E. U.) Solicitud impresa o escrita en un sobre para que se devuelva la carta a ciertas señas, si no se entrega en un plazo determinado. *Election returns*, Colección de datos e informes sobre el resultado de una elección. *By return of post*, A vuelta de correo.

Returnable [rẹ-tūrn'-ɑ-bl], *a.* 1. Que se puede retornar o volver. 2. (For.) Devolutorio, debido y exigido en tiempo y lugar determinados; v. gr. una citación judicial.

Returner [rẹ-tūrn'-ẹr], *s.* Persona que devuelve, restituye, o vuelve a enviar; el que remite dinero.

Retuse [rẹ-tiūs'], *a.* Muy obtuso, terminado en una extremidad redondeada con el centro deprimido; se dice de hojas y conchas.

Reunion [rī-yūn'-yʊn], *s.* 1. Reunión; reconciliación; nueva unión, cohesión o concordia. 2. Reunión, conjunto de personas reunidas.

Reunite [rī-yu-nait'], *va.* Reunir, juntar; reconciliar.—*vn.* Reunirse, volver a unirse, reconciliarse.

Revaluation [rī-val-yu-ē'-shʊn], *s.* Revaluación.

Revamp [rī-vamp'], *va.* Poner nueva pala a un zapato; de aquí, remendar, rehacer.

Reveal [rẹ-vīl'], *va.* 1. Revelar, manifestar o descubrir algún secreto. 2. Revelar, manifestar Dios lo futuro o lo que está oculto.

Revealer [rẹ-vīl'-ẹr], *s.* Revelador, el que revela.

Reveille [rẹ-vēl'-yẹ o rev-el-ī'], *s.* (Mil.) Diana, el toque militar al romper el día.

Revel [rev'-el], *vn.* Jaranear, andar en borracheras; divertirse con gran ruido o algazara.

Revel, *s.* Algazara, regocijos ruidosos; jarana, borrachera, banquete con gran algazara.

Revelation [rev-e-lē'-shʊn], *s.* 1. Revelación, acción y efecto de revelar, y también la cosa revelada, especialmente la revelación divina. 2. (Fil.) Conocimiento inmediato de lo verdadero. 3. Apocalipsis, el último de los libros del Nuevo Testamento.

Reveller [rev'-el-ẹr], *s.* Jaranero, la persona que gusta de andar en fiestas estrepitosas; hombre disoluto.

Revelry [rev'-el-ri], *s.* Jarana, borrachera, banquete estrepitoso, regocijos ruidosos.

Revenge [rẹ-venj'], *va.* Vengar, tomar satisfacción del agravio o injuria recibida; vengarse de; aplicar una pena en cambio de otro mal sufrido. *To revenge an affront*, Vengarse de una afrenta.

Revenge, *s.* 1. Desquite, despique, desagravio, ley del talión. 2. Venganza.

Revengeful [rẹ-venj'-ful], *a.* 1. Vengativo. 2. Vengador.

Revengefully [rẹ-venj'-ful-i], *adv.* Con venganza.

Revengefulness [rẹ-venj'-ful-nes], *s.* Venganza, ansia de vengarse.

Revengingly [rẹ-venj'-ing-li], *adv.* Con venganza.

Revenue [rev'-e-niū], *s.* 1. Rentas públicas, ingresos del Estado, el producto total de las contribuciones, tasas, impuestos, derechos de aduanas, etc. 2. Renta, rédito, entrada (de los bienes de un particular). *Revenue officer*, Empleado de aduana. *Revenue stamp*, Timbre del impuesto.

Reverberant [rẹ-vẹr'-bẹr-ɑnt], *a.* Repercusivo; retumbante, resonante.

Reverberate [rẹ-vẹr'-bẹr-ēt], *va.* y *vn.* 1. Resonar, retumbar, repetir el sonido; hacer eco. 2. Reverberar, reflejar la luz; rechazar.

Reverberation [rẹ-vẹr-bẹr-ē'-shʊn], *s.* Retumbo, eco o repercusión del sonido; rechazo; reverberación o reflexión de la luz y el calor.

Reverberator [rẹ-vẹr'-bẹr-ē''-tẹr], *s.* Reverberador, lo que reverbera o refleja el sonido, la luz, el calor; reverbero.

Reverberatory [re-ver'-ber-a-to-ri], *s.* Horno de reverbero.—*a.* De reverbero, que reverbera o refleja, destinado a producir reverberación. *Reverberatory furnace,* Horno de reverbero.
Revere [rê-vír'], *va.* Reverenciar, respetar, venerar, honrar.
Reverence [rev'-e-rens], *s.* 1. Reverencia, respeto, veneración. 2. Reverencia, inclinación del cuerpo o de parte de él en señal de respeto. 3. Reverencia, el título honorífico que se da a las personas religiosas. *To do, to pay reverence,* Rendir homenaje; inclinarse, hacer reverencia. *Saving your reverence,* Salvo vuestro respeto.
Reverence, *va.* Reverenciar, respetar, venerar.
Reverend [rev'-er-end], *a.* 1. Reverendo, venerable. 2. Reverendo, el tratamiento que se da a las dignidades eclesiásticas. *Right reverend* (tratamiento que se da a un obispo), Muy reverendo, o *Most reverend* (a un arzobispo), Reverendísimo.
Reverent [rev'-er-ent], *a.* Reverente; sumiso, humilde, lleno de respeto.
Reverential [rev-er-en'-shal], *a.* Reverencial, respetuoso.
Reverentially [rev-er-en'-shal-i], **Reverently** [rev'-er-ent-li], *adv.* Reverencialmente, respetuosamente.
Reverie, Revery [rev'-er-i], *s.* Estado del ánimo preocupado por ideas vagas; ensueño; arrebato, rapto, arrobamiento, distracción.
Reversal [re-ver'-sal], *s.* 1. Trastrocamiento, trastrueco; (For.) revocación de un fallo o una sentencia. 2. En el espectro solar, el cambio de una línea obscura en una brillante y viceversa.
Reverse [re-vers'], *va.* 1. Trastrocar, volver al revés, volver lo de arriba abajo, volver patas arriba; invertir, poner lo de dentro afuera. 2. Volcar, voltear, trastornar. 3. (For.) Revocar, anular, abolir. 4. Poner o mudar una cosa en lugar de otra. 5. (Mec.) Comunicar un movimiento o efecto opuesto; dar contravapor. *He quickly reversed the engine,* A toda prisa dió contravapor a la locomotora.—*vn.* Cambiarse en lo contrario o volver a un estado anterior. *Reversing lever, gear,* Palanca de retroceso o inversión, aparato que invierte el movimiento de una máquina de vapor.
Reverse, *s.* 1. Lo contrario, lo opuesto. *Quite the reverse,* Todo lo contrario. 2. Respaldo, el lado extremo o superficie de atrás, inferior o secundario; en especial, reverso o revés de una moneda o medalla. 3. Cambio a una posición, dirección o estado opuestos. 4. Vicisitud, mudanza, contratiempo, descalabro.
Reversedly [re-vers'-ed-li], *adv.* Con lo de arriba abajo; al revés.
Reverseless [re-vers'-les], *a.* Que no se puede trastrocar o mudar de arriba abajo.
Reversible [re-vers'-i-bl], *a.* 1. Capaz de ser volteado o trastrocado; que admite posición o dirección opuesta; de dos caras. 2. Revocable por la ley, anulable.
Reversion [re-ver'-shun], *s.* 1. Futura, la sucesión de empleo o renta a que uno tiene derecho después de la muerte de otro. 2. Reversión, vuelta de una heredad a su precedente poseedor o sus herederos; derecho de reversión.
Reversionary [re-ver'-shun-e-ri], *a.* Que toca a uno por derecho de reversión.
Reversioner [re-ver'-shun-er], *s.* El que tiene derecho de reversión o sucesión.
Revert [re-vert'], *va.* (Ant.) Trastrocar, volver al revés; volver atrás. —*vn.* 1. Retroceder, volverse atrás, mirar atrás, volver a una posición, condición o estado anteriores. 2. Tomar el hilo, referirse a alguna cosa anteriormente conocida o mencionada. 3. (Biol.) Volver hacia una forma hereditaria, anterior o primitiva, o mostrar algunos de sus rasgos característicos. 4. Volver o tocar a uno por derecho de reversión.
Revert, *s.* (Mús.) Vuelta.
Revertible [re-vert'-i-bl], *a.* Reversible, que ha de volver al poseedor precedente.
Revery, *s.* *V.* REVERIE.
Revest [rî-vest'], *va.* 1. Volver a vestir. 2. Restablecer en la posesión de algún empleo.
†**Revestiary** [re-vest'-i-a-ri], *s.* Guardarropa. *Revestiary of a church,* Sacristía.
Revet [re-vet'], *va.* Revestir la pared con cal, piedra u otros materiales.
Revetment [re-vet'-ment], *s.* (Fort.) Revestimiento de una muralla o pared; pared fuerte destinada a sostener las tierras.
Revictual [rî-vit'-l], *va.* Volver a proveer de víveres.
Review [re-viū'], *va.* 1. Rever, ver de nuevo; examinar, considerar, repasar. 2. Volver a ver, ver otra vez. 3. (Mil.) Revistar, pasar revista a la tropa. 4. Criticar, dar cuenta de; analizar una obra.—*vn.* Escribir o hacer una revista.
Review, *s.* 1. Revista, la segunda vista o examen de una cosa hecho con cuidado y diligencia; recordación, repaso. 2. Revista, nombre dado a algunas obras periódicas en que se analizan y examinan críticamente las producciones literarias. 3. (Mil.) Revista o reseña de la tropa. 4. Escrutinio. *Quarterly review,* Revista trimestral.
Reviewer [re-viū'-er], *s.* 1. El que escribe en los periódicos llamados revistas; crítico, el que da cuenta de las publicaciones nuevas en una revista; revistero. 2. Revisor, el que revé o pasa revista; examinador, inspector.
Revile [re-vail'], *va.* Ultrajar, despreciar, injuriar, disfamar.
Revilement [re-vail'-ment], *s.* Contumelia, oprobio, injuria, ultraje.
Reviler [re-vail'-er], *s.* Injuriador.
Reviling [re-vail'-ing], *s.* Oprobio, injuria, ultraje.
Revilingly [re-vail'-ing-li], *adv.* Injuriosamente, afrentosamente, con oprobio.
Revisal [re-vai'-zal], *s.* Revista, revisión, para corregir y perfeccionar; segundo examen.
Revise [re-vaiz'], *va.* 1. Rever, volver a examinar detenidamente alguna cosa. 2. Revisar, modificar, corregir por una autoridad; mejorar, reformar. *Revised, pp.* Revisado, examinado de nuevo, corregido. *Revised Version,* La traducción corregida de la Biblia en inglés, hecha por un grupo de literatos ingleses y uno de americanos, en los años 1870 a 1884. *V Authorized Version.*
Revise, *s.* 1. Revista. 2. (Impr.) La segunda prueba de un pliego. *Second revise,* La tercera prueba del pliego que se está imprimiendo.
Reviser, Revisor [re-vaiz'-er], *s.* Revisor, censor, el que revé o corrige, particularmente pruebas de imprenta.
Revision [re-vizh'-un], *s.* 1. Revisión, el acto de rever. 2. Versión o edición revisada o corregida.
Revisit [rî-viz'-it], *va.* Volver a visitar, visitar de nuevo.
Revisory [re-vai'-zo-ri], *a.* Revisor, que revisa o revé. *A revisory commission,* Una comisión revisora.
Revival [re-vai'-val], *s.* 1. Restauración, restablecimiento. 2. Renovación de interés por la religión; despertamiento religioso.
Revivalist [re-vai'-val-ist], *s.* El que contribuye al despertamiento del sentimiento religioso.
Revive [re-vaiv'], *vn.* 1. Revivir, volver a vivir, tener nueva vida. 2. Revivir, restablecerse, renovarse o reanimarse después de un estado de descaimiento; cobrar nuevo vigor; volver en sí, recobrar los sentidos. 3. Renacer, florecer de nuevo.—*va.* 1. Resucitar, dar nueva vida a un muerto. 2. Restablecer, renovar, restaurar. 3. Avigorar, dar nuevo vigor; despertar, avivar; animar, excitar. 4. Restablecer, volver a poner en vigor (una ley, costumbre, etc.). 5. Hacer recordar, despertar la memoria. *Trade begins to revive,* El comercio empieza a revivir. *To revive the memory of great men,* Hacer revivir la memoria de los grandes hombres.
Reviver [re-vaiv'-er], *s.* Vivificador.
Revivification [rî-viv-i-fi-kê'-shun], *s.* Vivificación, revivificación.
Revivify [rî-viv'-i-fai], *va.* y *vn.* Revivificar, hacer revivir; dar nueva vida, nuevo vigor; restablecerse, revivir.
Reviviscency [rev-i-vis'-en-si], *s.* Renovación de vida.
Revocable [rev'-o-ca-bl], *a.* Revocable, que se puede revocar.
Revocableness [rev'-o-ca-bl-nes], *s.* Calidad de revocable.
Revocation [rev-o-kê'-shun], *s.* 1. Revocación, acción y efecto de revocar. 2. (For.) Anulación de un instrumento, acto o promesa por parte de quien los hizo.
Revoke [re-vōk'], *va.* Revocar, anular, invalidar, declarar nulo lo que se ha hecho (una ley, un testamento, etc.).—*vn.* Renunciar, no jugar la carta del palo que se pide.
Revolt [re-vōlt' o re-volt'], *vn.* 1. Rebelarse, levantarse, sublevarse, amotinarse. 2. Desertar, cambiar de casaca.—*va.* 1. Rebelar, revolucionar, sublevar. 2. Chocar excesivamente, indignar, irritar.
Revolt, *s.* 1. Revuelta, sublevación, levantamiento. 2. Rebelión, rebeldía. 3. Deserción.
Revolter [re-volt'-er], *s.* Rebelde, sublevado, amotinado.
Revolting [re-vōlt'-ing o re-volt'-ing], *a.* Que causa horror o repugnancia.
Revoltingly [re-vōlt'-ing-li], *adv.* De un modo repugnante en alto grado.
Revolute [rev'-o-lūt (o liūt)], *a.* (Bot.) Enrollado hacia atrás, doblados los márgenes sobre la superficie inferior.
Revolution [rev-o-lū'- (o liū'-) shun], *s.* 1. Revolución, rotación, vuelta al mismo punto: dícese de los plane-

tas, del tiempo, de las estaciones y de los siglos; cada uno de los giros completos de un astro en su órbita. 2. Revolución, cualquier giro, vuelta, o sinuosidad sobre un eje, v. g. una espiral. 3. Repetición de cambios o acontecimientos sucesivos; ciclo; espacio de tiempo que transcurre entre esas repeticiones. 4. Revolución, mudanza violenta en los negocios de un Estado o en la forma de su gobierno.

Revolutionary [rev-o-lū'-shun-ẹ-ri], *a.* Revolucionario, perteneciente á una revolución en el Estado; que tiende á producir una revolución. —*s.* Revolucionario, partidario de una revolución política.

Revolutioner [rev-o-lū'- (o liū'-) shun-ẹr], **Revolutionist** [rev-o-lū'- (o liū'-) shun-ist], *s.* Revolucionario, el partidario de una revolución política.

Revolutionize [rev-o-lū'-shun-aiz], *va.* Revolucionar, conmover, sublevar, trastornar.

Revolvable [rẹ-volv'-a-bl], *a.* Que puede girar, capaz de dar vueltas.

Revolve [rẹ-volv'], *vn.* 1. Revolverse, moverse en línea curva de modo que vuelva periódicamente al punto de partida. 2. Girar, moverse alrededor o circularmente, rodar. 3. Moverse en ciclos, suceder periódicamente. 4. Ser considerado bajo todos los aspectos.—*va.* 1. Arrollar, revolver, hacer girar o mover en una órbita o círculo. 2. Hacer rodar, dar vueltas sobre un eje. 3. Revolver, discurrir, meditar, contemplar.

Revolver [rẹ-volv'-ẹr], *s.* El o lo que gira o rueda; en especial, revólver, pistola que contiene varias recámaras en un cilindro giratorio: invención americana (de Colt).

Revolving credit [rẹ-volv'-ing cred'-it], *s.* Crédito rotativo.

Revolving door [rẹ-volv'-ing dōr], *s.* Puerta giratoria.

Revue [rẹ-viū'], *s.* Revista teatral.

Revulsion [rẹ-vul'-shun], *s.* 1. Cambio repentino, v. g. en las ideas; reacción fuerte de cualquiera especie. (Med.) Revulsión, reacción. 2. Apartamiento, retroceso; separación violenta, reculada.

Revulsive [rẹ-vul'-siv], *a.* (Med.) Revulsivo, revulsorio, que causa una fuerte reacción.

Reward [rẹ-wōrd'], *va.* Premiar, remunerar, recompensar, gratificar.

Reward, *s.* 1. Premio, recompensa, remuneración; gratificación, hallazgo, salario. 2. Merecido, el castigo o pena.

Rewardable [rẹ-wōrd'-a-bl], *a.* Digno o capaz de premio.

Rewarder [rẹ-wōrd'-ẹr], *s.* Premiador, remunerador.

Reword [rī-wūrd'], *va.* 1. Repetir en otras palabras, expresar de otra manera. 2. Repetir las mismas palabras.

Reynard [rē'-nard o ren'-ard], *s.* Zorro, maese zorro.

Rhapontic [ra-pen'-tic], *s.* Rapóntico, planta. *V.* RHUBARB.

Rhapsodist [rap'-so-dist], *s.* 1. Rapsodista, el que hace o compone rapsodias. 2. El que se expresa con exagerado sentimiento.

Rhapsodize [rap'-so-daiz], *va.* y *vn.* Cantar o recitar centones o rapsodias.

Rhapsody [rap'-so-di], *s.* Rapsodia, centón, obra compuesta de diferentes trozos debidos a varios autores.

Rhea [rī'-a], *s.* 1. Rea, hija de Urano y madre de los dioses. 2. Ave parecida al avestruz que habita en las llanuras de la América del Sur.

Rhenish [ren'-ish], *a.* Perteneciente o relativo al río Rin ó a sus riberas. —*s.* Vino del Rin.

Rheostat [rī'-o-stat], *s.* Reóstato, aparato que sirve para medir la resistencia eléctrica de los conductores.

†**Rheotome** [rī'-o-tōm], *s.* Reótomo. interruptor eléctrico.

Rhetoric [ret'-o-ric], *s.* 1. Retórica, el arte de hablar con propiedad y elegancia. 2. Libro de texto sobre el discurso o la retórica. 3. Retóricas, sofisterías ó razones que no son del caso.

Rhetorical [rẹ-ter'-i-cal], *a.* Retórico, que pertenece a la retórica.

Rhetorically [rẹ-ter'-i-cal-i], *adv.* Retóricamente.

Rhetorician [ret-o-rish'-an], *s.* Retórico, persona versada en los principios y reglas de la retórica, o que la enseña.

Rheum [rūm], *s.* Reuma, destilación, fluxión; romadizo.

Rheumatic [rū-mat'-ic], *a.* Reumático, perteneciente al reumatismo o que lo padece.

Rheumatism [rū'-ma-tizm], *s.* Reumatismo, enfermedad que se manifiesta por dolores mudables más o menos vivos en los músculos o las articulaciones.

Rheumy [rū'-mi], *a.* Lleno de humedad o de humor acre.

Rh factor [ar eich fac'-tẹr], *s.* (Med.) Factor Rh.

Rhinoceros [rai-nes'-e-res], *s.* Rinoceronte, un animal cuadrúpedo paquidermo, con uno o dos cuernos cortos y encorvados sobre la nariz, y con el labio superior movedizo y prensil. (Lat. < Gr.)

Rhinoplastic [rai''-no-plas'-tic], *a.* (Cir.) Rinoplástico, que forma una nariz; concerniente a la rinoplastia.

Rhinoplasty [rai'-no-plas''-ti], *s.* (Med.) Rinoplastia, operación quirúrgica que consiste en rehacer una nariz cortada, extirpada o deshecha por cualquier causa.

Rhizome, Rhizoma [rai'-zōm, rai-zō'-ma], *s.* (Bot.) Rizoma, tallo horizontal y subterráneo: se llama también *rootstock.*

Rhizopod [rai'-zo-ped], *s.* Animal rizópodo, ejemplar de una división de los protozoarios.

Rhodian [rō'-di-an], *a.* Rodio, perteneciente a la isla de Rodas o a sus habitantes.

Rhodium [rō'-di-um], *s.* (Min.) Rodio, un metal que se halla mezclado con platina.

Rhododendron [rō-do-den'-dren], *s.* (Bot.) Rododendro, género de plantas de la familia de las ericáceas; arbusto de este género.

Rhomb [remb], **Rhombus** [rem'-bus], *s.* Rombo, paralelogramo que consta de cuatro lados iguales y tiene dos ángulos mayores que los otros dos.

Rhombic [rem'-bic], *a.* Que tiene figura de rombo.

Rhomboid [rem'-beid], *s.* (Geom.) Romboide, paralelogramo cuyos lados contiguos son desiguales y dos de sus ángulos mayores que los otros dos.

Rhomboidal [rem-bei'-dal], *a.* Romboidal, parecido á la figura del romboide o romboide.

Rhombus, *s.* *V.* RHOMB.

Rhumb [rumb], *s.* 1. (Mar.) Rumbo, cada una de las direcciones del viento o divisiones de la brújula, igual a 11° 15'. 2. *Rhumb* o *rhumb-line,* Línea loxodrómica.

Rhubarb [rū'-barb], *s.* 1. Ruibarbo, raíz medicinal purgante. 2. Ruipóntico, rapóntigo, planta que se cultiva en los huertos por sus tallos mollares y ácidos.

Rhumba, rumba [rum'-ba], *s.* Rumba.

Rhyme, Rime [raim], *s.* Rima, consonancia; poesía o poema. *Without rhyme or reason,* Sin ton ni son. (< A.-S. *rīman,* contar, < *rīm,* número.)

Rhyme, Rime, *vn.* Versificar, hacer versos; rimar. *V.* RIME.

Rhymer, Rimer [raim'-ẹr], **Rhymester** [raim'-stẹr], *s.* Versista, el que hace versos.

Rhythmic, Rhythmical [rith'-mic, al o ridh'-mic, al], *a.* Rítmico; armónico.

Rhythm [rithm], **Rhythmus** [rith'-mus], *s.* 1. Ritmo, proporción entre el tiempo de un movimiento y el de otro diferente; combinación métrica. 2. Cadencia, medida; armonía. 3. (Med.) Periodicidad, ocurrencia en paroxismos.

Rib [rib], *va.* Marcar con rayas, listones o filetes; hacer una tela con listones salientes; proveer de costillas; encerrar como dentro de un costillar.

Rib [rib], *s.* 1. Costilla, el hueso largo y encorvado que nace del espinazo y viene hacia el pecho. 2. Cualquier pedazo de madera u otro material que fortalece el costado de alguna cosa: faja, listón largo y estrecho parecido a una costilla, como una moldura saliente de un tejado; cabrio, viga de tejado; cuaderna; varilla o ballena (de paraguas); tirante, varenga de hierro; vivo (en las telas o medias). 3. (Bot.) Costilla, nervadura gruesa de las hojas. 4. Costilla, la mujer propia; en alusión a la frase del Génesis. *Ribs of a ship,* Ligazones de navío. *Ribs of a parrel,* (Mar.) Liebres de racamento.

Ribald [rib'-ald], *s.* Hombre bajo e impúdico.—*a.* Obsceno, lascivo, groseramente abusivo, toscamente chistoso, insultante.

Ribaldry [rib'-ald-ri], *s.* Lenguaje bajo, vulgar, obsceno o deshonesto.

Riband [rib'-and], *s.* (Ant.) *V.* RIBBON.

Rib-bands [rib'-bandz], *s.* (Mar.) Bagaras, piezas de madera clavadas contra las cuadernas.

Ribbed [ribd], *a.* Provisto de costillas.

Ribbon [rib'-ẹn], *s.* 1. Colonia, cinta o listón de seda. 2. Cinta, listón, faja; parecido a una cinta, como el muelle de un reloj o una lista pintada sobre el costado de una embarcación. 3. *pl.* (Fam.) Riendas. *Satin ribbons,* Cintas o listones de raso. *Velvet ribbons,* Cintas de terciopelo. *Silk plush ribbon,* Cinta rizada de felpa. *Hat-band ribbon,* Cinta para sombreros. *Hat-bindery ribbon,* Rivecillo para sombreros. *Waist ribbon,* Cinta para cinturones. *Ribbon-grass,* Alpiste (Phalaris arundinacea), género de gramíneas, de hojas anchas con listas blancas longitudinales.

Ribbon, *va.* Encintar, adornar o engalanar con cintas.

Ribbon, *a.* Hecho de cinta, o semejante a una cinta.

Ribbon-weaver [rib'-ẹn-wīv'-ẹr], *s.* Cintero, tejedor de cintas.

Riboflavin [ri-bo-flê'-vin], *s.* Riboflavina.

Rib-roast [rib'-rōst], *s.* Costillas para asar.—*va.* (Des.) Zurrar, moler a palos.

Ribwort [rib'-wūrt], *s.* (Bot.) Llantén lanceolado.

Rice [rais], *s.* (Bot.) Arroz, planta gramínea y su fruto. Oryza sativa. *Rice-field*, Arrozal, campo sembrado de arroz. *Rice-bird*, *V.* BOBOLINK. Se llama así en los Estados Unidos del Sur, porque se alimenta de arroz en el otoño. Dolichonyx oryzivorus. *Rice-paper*, (1) Papel de paja de arroz. (2) Papel de China; papel vegetal muy delicado que emplean los chinos para pintar flores, insectos, etc., de varios colores y para hacer flores artificiales. Proviene de una planta vivaz, Fatsia papyrifera, cuya medula se corta en rollos delgados.

Rich [rich], *a.* 1. Rico, opulento, acaudalado, hacendado. 2. Precioso, costoso, de precio, compuesto de materiales raros o preciosos; de valor, suntuoso. 3. Abundante, copioso, generoso; fértil, pingüe. *Rich soil*, Tierra pingüe. *Rich wine*, Vino generoso. 4. Rico, sabroso, muy grato al paladar; dulzarrón; a menudo implica exceso perjudicial de manteca o grasas; muy sazonado. 5. Rico, excelente, muy bueno en su clase; abundante en cualidades recomendables. 6. (Fam.) Muy jocoso; divertido o ridículo. *A rich soil*, Un suelo rico, fértil, fecundo. *Rich jewels*, Joyas costosas, de mucho valor. *Rich hues*, Matices ricos, vivos. *Rich gravy*, Pringue, salsa demasiado grasa. *A rich joke*, Un chiste muy divertido.

Riches [rich'-ez], *s. pl.* 1. Riqueza, opulencia, abundancia de bienes y cosas preciosas. 2. Esplendor, pompa, magnificencia.

Richly [rich'-li], *adv.* 1. Ricamente, opulentamente, magníficamente. 2. Copiosamente, abundantemente.

Richness [rich'-nes], *s.* 1. Riqueza, opulencia; primor, suntuosidad, magnificencia. 2. Fertilidad. 3. Abundancia, copia. 4. Pinguosidad, crasitud; calidad de lo rico en general o de lo que da buenas ganancias.

Rick [ric], *s.* Niara, rima o rimero de haces de grano o heno.

Rickets [rik'-ets], *s.* Raquitis, raquitismo, enfermedad de la temprana niñez, caracterizada por el reblandecimiento de los huesos y consecuente deformidad.

Rickety [rik'-et-i], *a.* 1. Desvencijado, cayéndose, que está para caerse por falta de solidez. 2. Raquítico, que padece de raquitis.

Rickshaw [rik'-shē], *s.* Vehículo japonés tirado por un hombre.

Ricochet [ric-o-shê'], *va.* Hacer fuego de rebote.—*vn.* Rebotar sobre una superficie una o varias veces, como hace una bala de cañón cuando se dispara casi horizontalmente, —*s.* (Art.) Fuego de rebote.

Rid [rid], *va.* 1. Desembarazar, desocupar. 2. (Ant.) Librar, libertar, redimir. 3. (Ant.) Desechar, expeler. *To rid one's self of a troublesome business*, Zafarse de algún asunto escabroso, de una carga o de la que ofende; librar. *To rid one's self of*, Desembarazarse de. *To be o to get rid of*, Estar exento; desembarazarse o librarse de; deshacerse de.

Rid, 1. *pret.* y *pp.* de *To* RID. 2. (Ant.) *pret.* de *To* RIDE.

Riddance [rid'-ans], *s.* 1. Libramiento o preservación de un mal o peligro. 2. Zafada, la acción de zafarse de alguna cosa que molesta. *To make a clear riddance*, Desembarazar alguna parte de las personas o cosas que estorban.

Ridden [rid'-n], *pp.* de *To* RIDE.

Riddle [rid'-l], *s.* 1. Enigma, adivinanza, pregunta intrincada. 2. Cualquier cosa difícil de atinar o comprender.—*va.* Resolver enigmas.—*vn.* Hablar enigmáticamente. (<A.-S. *raedels*, consejo.)

Riddle, *va.* y *vn.* 1. Acribillar, agujerear en muchas partes con balas de fusil, etc. 2. Cribar, acribar, pasar al través de una criba.—*s.* Criba, cribo, cedazo grueso, especialmente el empleado en una fundición o para lavar el oro. (< A.-S. *hridder*, criba.)

Ride [raid], *vn.* (*pret.* RODE, *pp.* RIDDEN). 1. Cabalgar, andar, ir o pasear a caballo; manejar, enseñar o adiestrar un caballo. 2. Ruar, andar en coche o carruaje. 3. Moverse o caminar una cosa puesta encima de otra. 4. Flotar, sostenerse en un flúido; estar fondeado; andar por el mar o estar en él. *To ride at anchor*, Surgir, estar fondeado.—*va.* 1. Sentarse y ser llevado sobre algo; correr. 2. Flotar sobre las olas, henderlas, dominarlas. 3. Montar, guiar un caballo; atravesar a caballo; andar por, o viajar, cualquiera que sea el medio empleado. *Can you ride?* ¿Sabe Vd. montar a caballo? *To ride down*, Echar a tierra y pisar paseando a caballo; de aquí, pisotear, tratar insolente y arrogantemente. *To ride out*, (Mar.) Luchar felizmente contra una tempestad. *To ride shanks' mare*, (Fam.) Andar a pie. *To ride easy*, (Mar.) Mantenerse bien al ancla.

Ride, *s.* 1. Paseo a caballo o en coche. 2. El espacio de terreno destinado para paseo.

Rideau [ri-dō'], *s.* (Fort.) Elevación de tierra para proteger un campamento. (Fr.)

Rider [raid'-ẹr], *s.* 1. Caballero, cabalgador; jinete; picador; biciclista. 2. Ruante, el que va en coche o carruaje. 3. El cochero u otra persona que maneja los caballos de un carruaje, y también los que corren caballos. 4. Cosa que va a horcajadas sobre otra, ya sea real o figuradamente; nombre que se da algunas veces a una hoja añadida a un instrumento ya concluido, y a las cláusulas añadidas a las leyes aprobadas en el Parlamento.

Riders [raid'-ẹrz], *s. pl.* (Mar.) Sobreplanes, especie de cuadernas o costillas interiores. *Floor-riders*, Sobreplanes del fondo. *After-floor-riders*, Sobreplanes popeses del fondo. *Lower futtock-riders*, Genoles de sobreplanes. *Second futtock-riders*, Ligazones de sobreplanes.

Ridge [rij], *va.* Alomar, formar lomos o camellones; cubrir con listones salientes o arrugas.—*vn.* Estar marcado con arrugas o listones salientes.

Ridge, *s.* 1. Cualquier protuberancia que se levanta desigualmente y que es larga en proporción a su anchura y altura; listón saliente, arruga, elevación prolongada, serie de colinas, serranía, serrijón; cerro. 2. Cumbre, cima o pico de montaña. 3. Escollo, arrecife, banco de piedra que sale del mar. 4. Caballón, el lomo que se levanta en el campo arado entre surco y surco; camellón. 5. Caballete, el lomo que se levanta en medio del tejado. *A ridge of hills*, Una cadena de colinas, cerro. *Ridge-ropes of the head-nettings*, (Mar.) Nervios de las redes de proa. *Ridges of a horse's mouth*, Las arrugas que tienen los caballos en el paladar. *Ridge-pole*, *ridge-plate*, Cima, madero que termina la armazón del alero.

Ridgy [rij'-i], *a.* Desigual, que se levanta con desigualdad, cerril; que tiene listones salientes.

Ridicule [rid'-i-kiūl], *s.* 1. Ridiculez, extravagancia. 2. Ridículo, el dicho que ridiculiza a alguno.

Ridicule, *va.* Ridiculizar, escarnecer, tornar en ridículo, hacer mofa de alguien.

Ridiculous [ri-dic'-yu-lus], *a.* 1. Ridículo, risible. 2. Ridículo, extravagante, nimio.

Ridiculously [ri-dic'-yu-lus-li], *adv.* Ridículamente.

Ridiculousness [ri-dic'-yu-lus-nes], *s.* Calidad de ridículo.

Riding [raid'-ing], *s.* 1. La acción de andar a caballo o en coche; paseo a caballo o en coche; excursión, cabalgata. 2. Distrito o porción en que se dividen algunos condados en Inglaterra.—*a.* Lo que se emplea para caminar a caballo o en coche. (Mar.) Fondeado. *Riding easy*, (Mar.) Descansado al ancla. *Riding hard*, (Mar.) Tormentoso al ancla. *Riding-cloak*, *riding-coat*, Redingote. *Riding-habit*, Traje de montar. *Riding-hood*, Capirote, gabán, capilla, capucho. *Riding-school*, Picadero, escuela de equitación. *Riding-whip*, *riding-rod*, Látigo de montar.

†**Rie** [rai], *s.* (Bot.) Centeno. *V.* RYE.

Rife [raif], *a.* 1. Abundante en número o cantidad; muy esparcido, corriente, común. 2. Lleno, seguido de *with*. *Rumours of war were rife*, Los rumores de guerra eran cosa corriente. *The small-pox has been very rife this year*, Este año ha habido epidemia de viruelas ó han sido muy comunes las viruelas.

Rifely [raif'-li], *adv.* Abundantemente, comúnmente.

Rifeness [raif'-nes], *s.* Abundancia, frecuencia.

Riffraff [rif'-raf], *s.* Gentuza, canalla, desperdicio: dícese de la gente más baja.

Rifle [rai'-fl], *va.* 1. Robar, pillar. (< F. ant. rifler.) 2. Rayar un arma de fuego.—*vn.* Proveer a un arma de fuego de raya o muesca espiral.

Rifle, *s.* Carabina, escopeta con cañón estriado por dentro, rifle. *Rifle range*, 1. Alcance de un tiro del rifle. 2. Lugar en que se puede tirar al blanco.

Rifleman [rai'-fl-man], *s.* Escopetero, carabinero, riflero, el hombre armado con rifle o que es hábil en su manejo.

Rifler [rai'-flẹr], *s.* Pillador, robador.

Rift [rift], *s.* 1. Hendedura, rendija, grieta, reventón; cuarteadura.

2. Desemboque, vado, sitio poco profundo en un arroyo. 3. Espuma que forman las olas al romperse en la playa.

Rift, *va.* Hender, dividir.—*vn.* Reventar; regoldar.

Rig [rig], *va.* 1. Ataviar, asear, adornar; con *out.* 2. Aparejar, equipar; con *out* o *up.* *To rig out a boom,* (Mar.) Botar afuera.

Rig, *s.* 1. Aparejo, disposición especial de los mástiles, jarcias, velas, etc., en el casco de un buque. 2. (Fam.) Modo de vestir, traje; tren de carruaje y caballos para pasear en coche; apresto, aparejo, equipo; aparato de pesca. 3. (Prov.) Burla, mala partida.

Rigadoon [rig-a-dūn'], *s.* Rigodón, baile, especie de contradanza provenzal.

Rigger [rig'-ẹr], *s.* (Mar.) Aparejador.

Rigging [rig'-ing], *s.* 1. (Mar.) Aparejo, el conjunto de velas, jarcia y motonería de un buque. 2. (Ger.) Vestido.

Right [rait], *a.* 1. Recto, justo, equitativo, sincero, razonable, honesto. 2. Derecho, recto, justo, conforme a la ley moral o a la voluntad de Dios. 3. Idóneo, propio, conveniente; fundado. 4. Verdadero, cierto, real, que ni es falso ni erróneo; legal, legítimo. 5. Derecho, igual, no torcido ni inclinado a uno u otro lado, directo, que está en línea recta. 6. Bien arreglado, convenientemente dispuesto, ajustado, en buen orden. 7. Derecho (lo contrario de izquierdo). 8. Sano, en buen estado de cuerpo o de ánimo. 9. Derecho; dícese del lado mejor acabado en las telas. *The right way,* El camino recto o directo. *Right angle,* Ángulo recto. *The right side,* El lado derecho (de una tela). *To be right,* Tener razón. *Right sailing,* (Mar.) Navegación recta o por alguno de los cuatro puntos cardinales. *Right-angled,* De ángulos rectos, rectangular. *Right-minded,* Recto, honrado. —*inter.* ¡Bien! ¡bueno!—*adv.* 1. Rectamente, justamente, exactamente, perfectamente, precisamente. 2. Derechamente, en derechura. 3. Muy. 4. Inmediatamente, al instante. 5. Ahora mismo. *It is right,* Está bien; está justo. *You are right* o *you are in the right,* Tiene Vd. razón. *Right or wrong,* A tuertas o a derechas, con razón o sin ella. *You say right,* Dice Vd. bien, tiene Vd. razón. *Right reverend,* Reverendísimo. *Right honourable,* Muy honorable, o respetable.—*s.* 1. Derecho, la ley moral; justicia, equidad, rectitud. 2. Razón, lo que está conforme con los hechos o con la verdad, que no contiene maldad ni error. 3. Derecho; título justo y equitativo; propiedad, dominio. 4. Poder, autoridad. 5. Privilegio, prerrogativa. 6. La derecha, lo opuesto a la izquierda. *To rights,* Derechamente, derecho, sin torcer. *To the right,* A la derecha. *On his right,* A su derecha. *To maintain one's right,* Sostener su derecho. *To set to rights,* Poner en orden; componer; reconciliar. *Right of way,* Derecho de vía.

Right, *va.* 1. Hacer justicia, proceder con justicia. *To right one's self,* Tomarse justicia por su mano. 2. (Mar.) Adrizar o levantar una embarcación que estaba ladeada.

Rightabout [rait'-a-baut], *s.* 1. Media vuelta. 2. Vuelta hacia la derecha.

Right away [rait a-wê'], *adv.* Inmediatamente, en seguida.

Righteous [rai'-chus], *a.* Justo, recto, equitativo; honrado.

Righteously [rai'-chus-li], *adv.* Justamente, rectamente, honradamente.

Righteousness [rai'-chus-nes], *s.* Rectitud, justicia, equidad; honradez.

Righter [rai'-tẹr], *s.* El que hace justicia; enderezador de tuertos o agravios.

Rightful [rait'-ful], *a.* Legítimo, justo, recto.

Rightfully [rait-ful-i], *adv.* Legalmente, rectamente, justamente.

Rightfulness [rait'-ful-nes], *s.* Derechura; justicia, rectitud, equidad.

Right-hand [rait'-hand], *a.* 1. Situado o perteneciente a mano derecha. 2. Se dice de la persona con quien más se cuenta o en quien se confía principalmente. *Right-hand man,* (Fam.) El brazo derecho, el colaborador principal; el auxiliar en quien se confía sobre todo.

Right-handed [rait-hand'-ed], *a.* 1. Que se sirve ordinariamente de la mano derecha; de aquí, mañoso, hábil. 2. Que rueda o gira de izquierda a derecha, como las manecillas de un reloj. 3. Hecho o dado con la mano derecha. *Right-handed screw,* Tornillo (de rosca) a la derecha.

Rightist [rait'-ist], *s.* Derechista, conservador.

Rightly [rait'-li], *adv.* Rectamente, justamente, bien, como se debe; exactamente; directamente.

Rightness [rait'-nes], *s.* Rectitud, justicia; derechura.

Right off [rait ef], *adv.* En seguida.

Rigid [rij'-id], *a.* Tieso; rígido, inflexible; austero, severo; rigoroso; estricto, exacto, como el razonamiento.

Rigidity [ri-jid'-i-ti], *s.* 1. Rigidez, rigor, austeridad; tesura. 2. Tosquedad, falta de garbo, gracia o aire; terquedad.

Rigidly [rij'-id-li], *adv.* Tiesamente; inflexiblemente; con rigidez.

Rigidness [rij'-id-nes], *s.* Rigidez inflexibilidad.

Riglet [rig'-let], *s.* *V.* Reglet.

Rigmarole [rig'-ma-rōl], *s.* Jerigonza, galimatías, desatino; un conjunto de palabras vacías de sentido.

Rigor, Rigour [rig'-ẹr], *s.* 1. Rigor, la tesura preternatural de los nervios que los hace inflexibles. 2. Rigor de calentura. 3. Rigor, severidad, dureza, austeridad; tesón, terquedad. 4. Rigor, exactitud en lo que es justo y recto. 5. Tesura, dureza, inflexibilidad de las cosas.

Rigorous [rig'-ẹr-us], *a.* Rigoroso, severo, cruel.

Rigorously [rig'-ẹr-us-li], *adv.* Rigorosamente.

Rigorousness [rig'-ẹr-us-nes], *s.* Severidad, rigor.

Rigour (es la manera usual de escribir esta palabra en Inglaterra). *V.* Rigor.

Rile [rail], *va.* (Prov. o fam.) Sulfurar, encolerizar. *V.* Roil.

Rill [ril], *s.* Riachuelo, arroyuelo.

Rillet [ril'-et], *s.* Arroyuelo. *V.* Rivulet.

Rim [rim], *s.* 1. Canto, borde, margen, orilla. 2. Cerco, arco. *The rim of the belly,* El peritoneo.

Rime [raim], *s.* 1. Escarcha. 2. Resquicio, hendedura, rendija, agujero, abertura.

Rime, Rhyme [raim], *va.* y *vn.* (Rhyme es forma etimológicamente incorrecta, aunque muy usada.) 1. Rimar, versificar; componer en rima. 2. Rimar, ser una voz consonante de otra; corresponder, convenir, armonizarse; se dice de las cosas.

Rimer, Rhymer [rai'-mẹr], *s.* Rimador, versista; también, poetastro.

Rimose [rai'-mōs o rai-mōs'], **Rimous** [rai'-mus], *a.* Hendido, rajado, que tiene grietas.

Rimy [raim'-i], *a.* Escarchado, blanco con escarcha; frío.

Rind [raind], *s.* Corteza, hollejo.

Rind, *va.* Descortezar, quitar el hollejo.

Rinderpest [rin'-der-pest], *s.* Morriña, enfermedad epidémica de los ganados que causa gran mortandad. (Al. < *rind, pl. rinder* (ganado) y *pest,* peste.) *V.* Murrain.

Ring [ring], *s.* 1. Círculo, cerco, cualquier objeto circular que tiene una abertura casi igual a su diámetro; anillo, aro, arillo, cintillo; virola; argolla. 2. Sortija, anillo; aro de oro u otro metal que se lleva, principalmente para adorno, en los dedos de la mano. *Staple-ring,* Argolla con espiga. 3. Circo, arena, como para una carrera, lucha o espectáculo. 4. Corro o corrillo de gente. 5. Combinación de varias o muchas personas, frecuentemente para fines ilícitos o censurables, v. g. en los negocios o en la política. 6. Ojera, círculo amoratado alrededor de los ojos. *A wedding ring,* Un anillo de boda. *A seal ring,* Una sortija que sirve de sello. *Ear-ring,* Zarcillo. *Ring-bolt,* (Mar.) Cáncamo, argolla. *Ring-bone,* (Vet.) Sobrehueso de caballo. *Ring-dial,* Reloj de sol en un anillo. *Ring-ropes,* (Mar.) Bozas rabizadas. *Ring-streaked,* Rayado en círculo. *Ring-shaped,* Anular.

Ring, *s.* 1. Campaneo o repique de campanas; el juego de campanas de una torre. 2. (Mar.) Arganeo, virola con chaveta. 3. Sonido, ruido, rumor, susurro; estruendo.

Ring [ring], *va.* 1. Rodear, formar corro alrededor de; circundar. 2. Poner un anillo; anillar, ensortijar; adornar con anillos, sortijas o argollas. 3. (Hort.) Quitar una tira circular de corteza.—*vn.* 1. Moverse en círculo o en espiral. 2. Formar círculo.

Ring, *va.* (*pret.* Rang, a veces Rung; *pp.* Rung). 1. Sonar, tocar, tañer. 2. Repicar o tañer campanas. 3. Anunciar, proclamar, celebrar, v. g. con un repique de campanas. 4. Repetir a menudo o con énfasis; reiterar. 5. Llamar, convocar, por medio de una campana. —*vn.* 1. Sonar, dar de sí un sonido sonoro como una campana. 2. Sonar mucho, clara o fuertemente; retiñir, retumbar, resonar. 3. Zumbar los oídos. 4. Estar lleno del ruido, fama o nombre de una cosa.

Ring-dove [ring'-duv], *s.* Paloma torcaz, zurita o zorita

Ringent [rin'-jẹnt], *a.* (Bot.) Bostezante; dícese de la corola gamopétala bilabiada, que tiene los labios muy apartados.

Ringer [ring'-er], *s.* Campanero, tocador de campanas.
Ringing [ring'-ing], *pa.* Resonante, retumbante; que repica, que toca las campanas. *A ringing cheer,* Viva resonante.—*s.* 1. Acción de sonar o hacer tocar las campanas; campaneo, repique de campana; retintín (del sonido de una campana). 2. (Hort.) Acción de quitar una tira circular de la corteza.
Ringleader [ring'-lîd-er], *s.* Cabeza de partido o bando; cabecilla, abanderizador.
Ringlet [ring'-let], *s.* 1. Anillejo, círculo. 2. Sortija, bucle en el cabello, rizo. (Cuba) Crespo.
Ringtail [ring'-têl], *s.* (Orn.) Especie de milano.
Ringworm [ring'-wūrm], *s.* Tiña, enfermedad del cutis: aparece en manchas circulares y la causa un parásito fungoso.
Rinse [rins], *va.* 1. Lavar, limpiar, inundando o sumergiendo en un líquido. 2. Enjuagar, aclarar.
Rinser [rins'-er], *s.* Lavandero, el que limpia.
Rinsing [rins'-ing], *s.* Enjuagadura, acción de enjuagar, y el líquido con que se enjuaga; lo que se quita enjuagando.
Riot [rai'-et], *s.* 1. Tumulto, sedición, alboroto, motín, asonada. 2. Desenfreno, desorden, exceso; borrachera.
Riot, *vn.* 1. Andar en borracheras, vivir desenfrenadamente, entregarse a los vicios. 2. Causar alborotos, sediciones, tumultos o motines.
Rioter [rai'-et-er], *s.* Hombre disoluto, bullicioso o sedicioso; alborotador, amotinador, abanderizador. (Fam.) Bullanguero, jaranero, libertino.
Riotous [rai'-et-us], *a.* 1. Sedicioso, faccioso, amotinado. 2. Desenfrenado, desarreglado, libertino, disoluto.
Riotously [rai'-et-us-li], *adv.* Desenfrenadamente, disolutamente; bulliciosamente.
Riotousness [rai'-et-us-nes], *s.* Disolución, desenfreno, desorden; el estado de la persona o personas que están alborotadas o fuera de orden.
Rip [rip], *va.* 1. Rasgar, lacerar, romper, dividir (una tela) a lo largo de una línea de resistencia mínima; comúnmente con *up, open,* u *off:* hender. 2. Descoser, soltar. *To rip up,* Rajar. *To rip off a plank,* (Mar.) Descoser un tablón. 3. Penetrar al fondo de, sondear; poner a descubierto; descubrir un secreto; se usa con *up.* 4. Aserrar la madera en la dirección general de la veta; (carp.) hilar, linear.—*vn.* Henderse, romperse. *To rip off,* Rajar, abrir de golpe, quitar, arrancar. *To rip open,* Abrir, volver a abrir. *To rip out,* Soltar, dejar escapar, hablar con vehemencia. *To rip out an oath,* Jurar con violencia, jurar a la ligera, blasfemar. *Ripsaw,* Sierra de hender o máquina para aserrar tablas.
Rip, *s.* 1. Laceración, rasgadura, rasgón, paraje rasgado o roto. 2. Sierra de hender. *V. Rip-saw.*
Riparian [rai-pê'-ri-an], *a.* Ribereño, que pertenece a la ribera de un río.
Riparious [rai-pê'-ri-us], *a.* (Bot. y Zool.) Ribereño, que vive o se cría a lo largo de las riberas de un río.
Ripe [raip], *a.* 1. Maduro, sazonado, en sazón. 2. Acabado, consumado, que se acerca a la perfección. 3. Pronto, preparado, a propósito. 4. Rosado, colorado; parecido a la madurez del fruto.
Ripen [raip'-n], *vn.* Madurar, llegar a madurez.—*va.* Madurar, poner alguna cosa en estado de madurar.
Ripely [raip'-li], *adv.* Maduramente; a propósito.
Ripeness [raip'-nes], *s.* Madurez.
Ripper [rip'-er], *s.* El que rasga o descose.
Ripping [rip'-ing], *s.* 1. Rompimiento, la acción de romper. 2. Laceración, la acción de lacerar. 3. Descubrimiento.
Ripple [rip'-l], *va.* Formar pequeñas ondas, rizar la superficie del agua.—*vn.* 1. Agitarse, rizarse la superficie del agua. 2. Sonar como el agua que corre sobre un lecho áspero o pedregoso; murmurar.
Ripple, *va.* Desgargolar, sacudir el cáñamo para que despida el cañamón.
Ripple, *s.* 1. Oleadita, escarceo del agua, pequeña onda producida por una brisa suave, o al correr del agua sobre un lecho pedregoso. 2. Cualquier sonido semejante al murmullo de las aguas. 3. Ondulación, rizo, algo parecido a una oleadita.
Ripple, *s.* Un peine que sirve para desgargolar.
Rippling [rip'-ling], *s.* 1. La acción de desgargolar el cáñamo. 2. El escarceo del agua cuando lo produce una brisa suave o el lecho pedregoso de un arroyo.
Riprap [rip-rap'], *va.* Reforzar por medio de piedras partidas o deshechas.—*s.* 1. Piedras trituradas para hacer cimientos o muros, particularmente para formar una base o cimiento en agua profunda. 2. Cimiento hecho de piedras echadas en montón. (< Dina. *rips-raps,* desperdicios.)
Rise [raiz], *vn.* (*pret.* ROSE, *pp.* RISEN). 1. Ascender, subir una cosa hacia arriba; elevarse, levantarse. 2. Levantarse, ponerse en pie (después de arrodillarse, sentarse o acostarse); de aquí, suspender sus tareas una asamblea deliberante, cerrar una sesión. 3. Levantarse, salir de la cama. 4. Nacer, asomar por el horizonte; salir el sol. 5. Nacer, salir: dícese de las plantas cuando empiezan a despuntar. 6. Saltar, salir, brotar alguna cosa de la tierra. *That stream rises from a spring,* Aquel arroyo nace de un manantial. 7. Levantarse, sublevarse, rebelarse. 8. Levantarse, suscitarse una disputa, una competencia, etc. 9. Ascender, subir o adelantar en empleo o dignidad; aumentar en fortuna, hacerse más rico. 10. Hincharse hacia arriba. *A river rises after rain,* Un río sube, se hincha o aumenta después de la lluvia. 11. Encarecerse, subir o aumentarse el precio de una cosa. 12. Elevarse en el estilo; elevarse o ensalzarse en honores, fama o fortuna. 13. Resucitar. *The Lord is risen indeed,* El Señor ha resucitado en verdad. *To rise up against any one,* Acometer a alguno. 14. Provenir, motivar, nacer, originarse. *To rise to one's feet,* Ponerse en pie, levantarse. *That rises (o arises) from your negligence,* Eso proviene de la negligencia de Vd. Sinónimo, ARISE.
Rise [rais o raiz], *s.* 1. Levantamiento, erección, la acción y efecto de levantar o levantarse. 2. Elevación, altura, eminencia. 3. Subida, la acción y efecto de subir; ascensión. 4. Subida, el sitio o lugar en declive, que va subiendo. 5. Subida, la mejoría o elevación de las cosas con respecto a su estado o precio. 6. Crecida, creciente (de un río, etc.); alza en los fondos públicos. *Rise and fall in the public stocks,* Alza y baja en los fondos públicos. 7. Salida del sol. 8. Fuente, principio, origen, manantial, causa. 9. Elevación, ascenso en grado, honores, riquezas, reputación, etc.; elevación de la voz. *A rise of ground,* Una elevación del terreno. *The rise of a hill,* La pendiente de una colina. *The rise of mercury in the thermometer,* La subida del mercurio en el termómetro.
Risen, *pp.* de *To* RISE.
Riser [raiz'-er], *s.* 1. El que se levanta. *An early riser,* Madrugador, el que madruga. *Late riser,* Persona que se levanta tarde. 2. Contrahuella, la cara vertical de un peldaño de escalera.
Risibility [riz-i-bil'-i-ti], *s.* Risibilidad, la facultad de reir.
Risible [riz'-i-bl], *a.* 1. Risible, lo que causa risa. 2. Risible, ridículo, digno de risa o burla.
Rising [raiz'-ing], *a.* Naciente, nuevo, saliente.—*s.* 1. Levantamiento, renacimiento, vuelta a la vida; sublevación, insurrección, motín; acto de asomar en el horizonte; término de una sesión. 2. (Prov. Ingl. y E. U.) Levadura, fermento; también la cantidad de masa que se prepara de una vez. 3. Prominencia, protuberancia; en especial, lobanillo, lupia.
Risk [risk], *s.* Riesgo, contingencia, peligro. *To run a risk,* Correr peligro.
Risk, *va.* Arriesgar, poner en riesgo, aventurar, exponer.
Risker [risk'-er], *s.* El que arriesga.
Risky [risk'-i], *a.* 1. Peligroso, arriesgado, expuesto a riesgos. 2. Imprudente, arriesgado, temerario.
Risorial [rai-sō'-ri-al], *a.* Reidor, reidero, perteneciente a la risa; que causa risa.
Rite [rait], *s.* Rito, la ceremonia solemne o religiosa; acto u observancia ceremonial. *Funeral rites,* Ritos fúnebres o exequias.
Ritual [rit'-yu-al], *a.* Ritual, ceremonial.—*s.* 1. Formalidad o método prescrito para una ceremonia religiosa o ceremonial; sistema o conjunto de ritos. 2. Ritual, libro que enseña el orden de las sagradas ceremonias.
Ritualism [rit'-yu-al-izm], *s.* Ritualismo, el estudio de los ritos o el exagerado apego a ellos; ritualidad, observancia de las formalidades prescritas para hacer una cosa.
Ritualist [rit'-yu-al-ist], *s.* Ritualista, rubriquista.
Ritualistic [rit-yu-al ist'-ic], *a.* Ritualista, apegado al ritualismo, que aprecia mucho los ritos, particularmente los de la Iglesia antes de la Reforma.
Ritually [rit'-yu-al-i], *adv.* Según el ritual o los ritos; conforme a los ritos.
Rival [rai'-val], *a.* Émulo, contrario, opuesto.—*s.* Rival, competidor.
Rival, *va.* 1. Competir, emular, entrar en competencia con alguno; rivalizar con; ser el igual de otro.

2. (Ant.) Ser rival o competidor de alguien; esforzarse en alcanzar el mismo fin a que otro aspira.—*vn.* Rivalizar.

Rivalry [rai'-val-ri], *s.* Rivalidad, competición, emulación; lucha o esfuerzo para obtener un fin que otro se propone alcanzar al mismo tiempo; esfuerzo para igualar o exceder a otro en mérito o perfección.

Rive [raiv], *va.* (*pret.* RIVED, *pp.* RIVED o RIVEN). Rajar, hender. —*vn.* Henderse.

River [riv'-er], *s.* 1. Río. 2. (Fig.) Río, copia, flujo copioso, torrente. *River-basin,* Cuenca de río, el área que desagua. *River-bed,* Lecho, álveo, madre, de un río. *Up (the) river,* Río arriba. *Down (the) river,* Río abajo. *River-dragon,* Cocodrilo, caimán. *River-god,* Dios tutelar de río. *River-horse,* Hipopótamo.

Riverside [riv'-er-said], *s.* y *a.* Orilla de un río; ribera, el espacio a lo largo de un río.

Rivet [riv'-et], *s.* Remache, la vuelta de la punta de un clavo remachado; roblón.

Rivet, *va.* 1. Remachar, asegurar un clavo después de introducido doblándole la punta. 2. Roblar, doblar o remachar una pieza de hierro para asegurarla. 3. Remachar, asegurar o afianzar fuertemente alguna cosa.

Rivulet [riv'-yu-let], *s.* Riachuelo, río pequeño.

RNA, ribonucleic acid [ār-en-ê', rai-bō-niū-clî'-ic as'-id], *s.* Acido ribonucleico.

Roach [rōch], *s.* Escarcho, pez europeo ciprinoide con aletas rojizas. (Leuciscus rutilus.)

Roach, *s.* Cucaracha.

Road [rōd], *s.* 1. Camino, camino real; vía abierta al paso del público, particularmente desde una población a otra; vía, carretera. 2. Camino, el viaje que se hace de una parte a otra. *The high road,* El camino real. 3. (Mar.) Rada, bahía o ensenada en la que pueden anclar los buques. *By-road,* Atajo, trocha, camino privado o poco frecuentado. *Cross-road,* Encrucijada; camino de atajo. *Turnpike road,* Camino con portazgo, calzada; y familiarmente, camino real. *Road-bed,* Fundación de un camino; construcción sobre la que se asientan los rieles de un ferrocarril. *Road-roller,* Pisón, rodillo para allanar caminos. *Road-runner,* Pájaro, cuclillo de tierra, de cola larga, de los Estados Unidos del Sudoeste; habita en las llanuras y corre con gran velocidad.

Roadbed [rōd'-bed], *s.* 1. Infraestructura. 2. Calzada (de carretera).

Roadblock [rōd'-blec], *s.* 1. (Mil.) Barricada. 2. Obstáculo colocado en caminos, particularmente por representantes de la autoridad.

Roadhouse [rōd'-haus], *s.* Posada o restaurante cerca de una carretera.

Roadster [rōd'-ster], *s.* 1. Caballo que anda bien; también, bicicleta para los caminos ordinarios. 2. (Mar.) Un buque al ancla.

Roadway [rōd'-wê], *s.* Carretera, calzada, parte del camino reservada para los carruajes.

Roam [rōm], *vn.* Vagar, vaguear, andar vagando sin dirección fija, correr acá y acullá.—*va.* Correr, corretear.

Roamer [rōm'-er], *s.* Vagamundo; el que vaguea.

Roan [rōn], *a.* Roano, ruano; se aplica al caballo cuyo pelo está mezclado de gris, de bayo y blanco; dase también en inglés el nombre de *roan* al color del caballo que en castellano se llama rodado, que es el blanco con manchas negras.—*s.* 1. Caballo ruano; color ruano. 2. Badana curtida de color ruano, o que imita el marroquín.

Roar [rōr], *vn.* 1. Rugir, bramar como el león u otra bestia feroz. 2. Aullar, dar aullidos. 3. Bramar: dícese del mar y de los vientos. 4. Mugir el toro.

Roar, *s.* 1. Rugido, el bramido del león. 2. Grito, gritería, vocerío. 3. Bramido, estruendo, ruido grande. 4. Mugido, el bramido del toro.

Roary [rōr'-i], *a.* (Poco us.) Rociado.

Roast [rōst], *va.* 1. Asar; cocer la carne o un manjar en el asador o en el horno. 2. Tostar o calentar mucho; calentar hasta un grado extremo, calcinar. 3. (Fam.) Burlarse, mofarse; chiflar, rechiflar (con ironía).

Roast, *a.* Asado, tostado (abrev. de *roasted*). *Roast meat,* Asado o carne asada. *Roast beef,* Carne de vaca asada, rosbif.—*s.* Carne asada, o una pieza a propósito o que está para asar; asado. *To rule the roast,* (Vulg.) Mandar, tener vara alta, gobernar.

Roaster [rōst'-er], *s.* Cocinero que asa; asador, tostador, persona que asa o tuesta; tostador, aparato para tostar o calcinar; animal u objeto a propósito para ser asado.

Roasting [rōst'-ing], *ger.* de *To* ROAST. —*s.* 1. Acción de asar, de tostar; tostadura. 2. En metalurgia es el acto de quemar el mineral para disipar su materia volátil; torrefacción, calcinación, beneficio por medio del fuego. 3. Burla pesada, rechifla; zurra.

Rob, *va.* Robar, coger y llevarse una propiedad con violencia y sin derecho; pillar; saquear; quitar, hurtar; privar. *To rob on the highway,* Saltear. *To rob a stage-coach,* Robar una diligencia. *To rob Peter to pay Paul,* Robar a Pedro para pagar a Pablo.

Robber [rob'-er], *s.* Robador, ladrón, salteador de caminos, saqueador, despojador del bien ajeno.

Robbery [rob'-er-i], *s.* Robo, la acción de robar; robo a mano armada; salteamiento, pillaje, saqueo.

Robe [rōb], *s.* 1. Manto, toga, traje talar o ropa larga que se lleva por encima de otros vestidos, particularmente como señal de oficio ó dignidad; traje de ceremonia. 2. Túnico; alguna cosa que cubre, como un manto. 3. Manta de coche, de pieles u otro material, cubierta de abrigo. *A counsellor's robe,* Garnacha. *Robe of state,* Traje de gala. *Master of the robes,* Jefe de la guardarropa.

Robe, *va.* Vestir de gala o de ceremonia; vestir, ataviar.—*vn.* Vestirse, ponerse trajes; cubrirse. *Fields robed with green,* Campos cubiertos de verdura. *Robing-room,* Guardarropa, sitio para ponerse y quitarse los trajes de ceremonia; vestuario de las iglesias.

Robin, Robin-redbreast [rob'-in, red'-brest], *s.* 1. (Orn.) Pechicolorado, petirrojo, pájaro europeo de unas cinco pulgadas de largo. (Erythacus rubecola.) 2. Petirrojo, tordo norteamericano, algo parecido al pechicolorado, pero mayor, pues mide diez pulgadas de largo.

Robot [rō'-bet], *s.* 1. Robot, autómata mecánico. 2. Piloto automático de aviones.

Robustness [ro-bust'-nes], *s.* Robustez, fuerza, vigor.

Rock [rec], *s.* 1. Roca, peñasco; escollo, laja. 2. Fundamento sólido o inmutable; solidez, defensa, protección, amparo. 3. Arrecife, laja, algo sobre lo cual se puede naufragar; causa de ruina o daño. 4. (Prov. o des.) Rueca. *Chalk rock,* Roca cretácea. *Trap rock,* Roca dolerita. *V.* TRAP. *Rock alum* (*roche alum*), Alumbre de roca, alumbre en estado nativo. *Rock-bound,* Rodeado de peñascos. *Rock-candy,* Azúcar candi. *Rock-crusher,* Máquina para triturar rocas o minerales.

Rock, *va.* 1. Mecer. 2. Arrullar; calmar, sosegar.—*vn.* Bambolear, oscilar.

Rock bottom [rec bet'-um], *s.* Lo más profundo, el fondo.

Rock-crystal [rec'-cris-tal], *s.* (Min.) Cristal de roca, cuarzo.

Rocker [rek'-er], *s.* 1. Columpio de una cuna; una de las piezas curvas sobre que se mece una cuna o silla mecedora; (E. U.) silla mecedora. 2. Cunera.

Rocket [rek'-et], *s.* 1. Cohete, volador. 2. Jaramago de los jardines; una de varias plantas de la familia de las crucíferas del género Hesperis; hespéride. *Base rocket,* Reseda. *Sky-rocket,* Cohete.

Rocket launcher [rek'-et lānch'-er], *s.* Lanzacohetes.

Rocket missile [rek'-et mis'-il], *s.* Proyectil-cohete.

Rocket plane (rek'-et plên], *s.* Avión cohete.

Rocketry [rek'-et-ri], *s.* Cohetería.

Rocket ship [rek'-et ship], *s.* Navecohete, barco para lanzar proyectiles-cohete.

Rock garden [rec gār'-dn], *s.* Jardín rocoso.

Rockiness [rek'-i-nes], *s.* 1. Gran número de rocas o montañas. 2. El estado de lo que se halla lleno de peñascos; naturaleza roqueña.

Rocking [rek'-ing], *pa.* Mecedor; vacilante, oscilatorio. *Rocking-chair,* Mecedora, (Cuba) columpio. *Rocking-horse,* Caballo mecedor, caballito de madera, cuyos pies descansan sobre dos arcos que permiten al jinete mecerse en él.

Rocking, *s.* Balanceo.

Rock-oil [rek'-eil], *s.* Petróleo.

Rock-ribbed [rec'-ribd], *a.* Inflexible, fuerte, firme.

Rock-salt [rec'-sōlt], *s.* Sal de piedra, sal gema.

Rock-water [rec'-wō-ter], *s.* Agua cristalina de las rocas.

Rockwork [rec'-wūrc], *s.* Grutesco, roca artificial, conjunto de piedras aseguradas con argamasa y dispuestas de modo que imitan una roca natural.

Rocky [rek'-i], *a.* Peñascoso, roqueño, roquero, formado de rocas, lleno de rocas; duro, endurecido. *The Rocky Mountains,* Las Montañas Roqueñas.

Rococo [ro-cō'-cō], *a.* y *s.* Churrigueresco; estilo arquitectónico en que abundan los adornos con profusión excesiva y de mal gusto.

Rod [rod], *s.* 1. Varilla, vara, caña, rama pequeña de una planta leñosa; bastón (de mando, varita de mago, etc.); de aquí, disciplina, corrección; dominación, poder. *Angling-rod*, Caña de pescar. *Curtain-rod*, Varilla de cortina. 2. Vara de medir; pértica, medida de dieciseis pies y medio o poco más de cinco metros; vara de alguacil o de otro cargo análogo. 3. (Mec.) Vástago, barra, varilla, vara que forma parte de una máquina. 4. Varillas, manojo de mimbres para azotar a los niños. 5. Uno de los cuerpos microscópicos parecidos a varillas que se hallan en la retina. 6. Línea particular de alcurnia o linaje; raza, tribu. *Black-rod*, Nombre que se da al ujier de la cámara de los pares de Inglaterra. *Connecting rod*, Biela. *To rule with a rod of iron*, Gobernar con el palo, con mano de hierro. *To give the rod*, Dar azotes, azotar.

Rode [rōd], *pret.* de *To* RIDE.

Rodent [rō'-dent], *a.* Roedor, que roe; perteneciente al orden zoológico de los roedores.—*s.* Roedor, animal del orden de los roedores.

Rodeo [ro-dé'-o], *s.* Rodeo, jaripeo.

Roe [rō], *s.* 1. Corzo. 2. Hueva, huevecillos de los pescados.

Roebuck [rō'-buc], **Roe-deer** [rō'-dīr], *s.* Corzo, un animal pequeño rumiante, muy veloz y tímido. (Capreolus caprea.)

Roentgen rays [rŭnt'-gen rês], *s. pl.* Rayos de Roentgen, una forma de energía radiante, desarrollada por medio del llamado tubo de Crookes; fueron descubiertos en 1895, en Würzburg, Alemania, por el profesor W. C. Roentgen. Se parecen a la luz porque se dirigen en línea recta y afectan las películas sensitivas fotográficas. Se diferencian de la luz porque todavía no han sido refractados ni polarizados; pasan fácilmente al través de varias substancias opacas, como la madera y la carne. Por medio de estos rayos se pueden ver y fotografiar las sombras de los huesos, de balas, cálculos, etc., en las partes carnosas del cuerpo, por ser estos objetos más opacos que la carne.

Rogation [rō-gé'-shun], *s.* 1. Rogaciones, letanías en las procesiones de las cuatro témporas. 2. Proyecto de ley presentado al pueblo romano. 3. Ruego, súplica. *Rogation-week*, Semana de rogaciones.

Rogue [rōg], *s.* 1. Bribón, pícaro, villano, ruin, vagamundo. 2. Perillán: voz familiar y cariñosa; tunante, astuto, travieso. *A cunning rogue*, Un pícaro taimado. *To be a great rogue*, (Fam.) Ser caña. *A thorough rogue*, Pícaro de cuatro suelas. *Rogues' yarn*, (Mar.) Hilo de ladrones. 3. (Der. inglés) Pordiosero, mendigo holgazán y robusto; vagabundo. 4. Elefante feroz y peligroso, separado del resto de la manada.

Roguery [rōg'-er-i], *s.* Picardía, ruindad; travesura, retozo.

Rogues' gallery [rōgz gal'-e-ri], *s.* Galería de retratos de delincuentes buscados por la policía.

Roguish [rōg'-ish], *a.* 1. Pícaro, ruin, travieso, picaresco. 2. Juguetón, chistoso, decidor. *Roguish eyes*, Ojos picarescos, burlones, ojitos traviesos.

Roguishly [rōg'-ish-li], *adv.* Pícaramente.

Roguishness [rōg'-ish-nes], *s.* Picardía; ladronera, tunantada, bribonada; mala partida, partida de tuno. *The roguishness of his look*, Lo picaresco, lo travieso de su mirada.

Roil [rell], *va.* 1. Enturbiar o espesar algo agitándolo; enlodar. 2. Vejar, irritar. (Á veces se dice familiarmente, *rile*.)

Roister [reist'-er], *vn.* Bravear, fanfarronear, echar bravatas.—*s.* Fanfarrón, baladrón.

Role [rōl], *s.* Papel de un actor; funciones ó carácter asumidos. (Fr.)

Roll [rōl], *va.* 1. Rodar, hacer rodar. 2. Volver, girar, voltear, dar vuelta o vueltas a alguna cosa. 3. Arrollar, fajar. 4. Rollar, arrollar papel, cinta, tela, etc. 5. Laminar, pasar por el laminador; cilindrar, extender en rodillos. 6. Alisar, allanar por medio de un rodillo (de pastelero) o de un alisador. 7. Envolver (con o sin rotación del objeto envuelto). 8. Empujar o llevar hacia adelante sobre rodillos. 9. Dar de sí los sonidos musicales de una manera llena y creciente.—*vn.* 1. Rodar, dar vueltas sobre el suelo o cualquier plano. 2. Volver, girar, rodar, andar o moverse alrededor o en torno, correr o moverse sobre ruedas; girar sobre un eje. 3. Revolver, revolverse; agitarse las olas. 4. Menear los ojos o moverlos de uno a otro lado. 5. Voltear o caer dando vueltas. 6. Ondear, ondular, moverse como las olas; moverse tumultuosamente, fluctuar, flotar sobre un mar agitado. 7. Retumbar, producir un sonido profundo y resonante, como el trueno. 8. Bambolearse, moverse de un lado a otro. 9. Arrollarse en forma de cilindro u ovillo: ser allanado, alisado o extendido con un rodillo. 10. Vivir con lujo; manar, tener abundancia de algo. 11. Dar un redoble de tambores. *To roll about*, Rodar, divagar, andar de acá para allá. *To roll down*, Bajar rodando una cuesta, una escalera, etc. *To roll in money*, Nadar en dinero. *To roll up*, Rollar, arrollar; hacer un ovillo. *To roll a walk with a roller*, Allanar la tierra con un rodillo.

Roll, *s.* 1. Rodadura, la acción de rodar. 2. Rodador, lo que rueda o cae rodando. 3. Rollo de papel, de cinta, de tabaco, etc.; rodillo, cilindro de madera o metal; tela rollada en forma de cilindro. *V.* ROLLER. 4. Rollo o volumen: dícese de los libros de los antiguos por la figura que les daban. 5. Rol, lista, nómina, catálogo, matrícula. 6. Documentos públicos que han sido archivados, y a veces también se toma por los archivos donde se guardan. 7. Redoble (de tambores); retumbo del trueno. 8. Bamboleo. 9. Superficie ondeante, ondulante, como la del mar. 10. (Arq.) Roleo, voluta. 11. Bollo, mollete. *Master of the rolls*, La segunda dignidad judicial en Inglaterra. *French roll*, Pan francés, panecillo. *Silver-smith's roll*, Cilindro de escarchar.

Roll call [rōl cōl], *s.* Lista, pase de lista.

Roller [rōl'-er], *s.* 1. Rodillo, cilindro que rueda para disminuir la fricción: cilindro muy pesado para allanar la tierra. 2. Venda, faja. 3. Rodillo, alisador, palo redondo que usan algunos menestrales para alisar, pulir o estirar. 4. (Mar.) Polines, rolletes, roldana. 5. Ola larga y creciente.

Roller bearing [rōl'-er bār'-ing], *s.* Cojinete de rodillos.

Roller coaster [rōl'-er cōst'-er], *s.* Montaña rusa.

Roller skate [rōl'-er skêt], *s.* Patín de ruedas.

Roller towel [rōl'-er tau'-el], *s.* Toalla sin fin.

Rollick [rel'-ic], *vn.* Travesear, moverse con aire retozón; portarse indolente y jovialmente.

Rollicking, *ger.* y *a.* Que se mueve de una manera negligente o fanfarrona; jovial; juguetón, travieso.

Rolling [rōl'-ing], *a.* y *ger.* de *To* ROLL. 1. Rodadero, rodadizo; que rueda, que da vueltas. 2. Undulado, entrecortado por colinas y valles. 3. Vuelto hacia atrás o hacia abajo como lo que está bajo un rodillo.—*s.* Rodadura, movimiento de lo que rueda; acto de rodar o de la persona que emplea una herramienta de laminar. *Rolling prairies*, Praderadas entrecortadas, ondulantes. *Rolling-mill*, (1) Establecimiento para hacer láminas, barras, rieles o varillas de metal, trabajándolo entre pares de cilindros. (2) Laminador, máquina para laminar los metales. *Rolling-plant*, (1) *V. Rolling-mill*, 1ª acep. (2) *V. Rolling-stock*. *Rolling-pin*, Rodillo de pastelero. *Rolling-stock*, Material rodante, el conjunto de locomotoras, coches, vagones, carros, etc., de un ferrocarril. *Rolling stone*, Rodillo de piedra para allanar la tierra. *Rolling-tackle*, (Mar.) Aparejo de rolin.

Roll-top desk [rōl'-tep desk], *s.* Escritorio con tapa corrediza.

Roly-poly [rō'-li-pō''-li], *a.* Rechoncho, gordiflón.—*s.* 1. Pudín en forma de rollo, cocido o sometido a la acción del vapor. 2. (Fam.) Persona gordiflona.

Romaic [ro-mê'-ic], *a.* Romaico, perteneciente al idioma o al pueblo griego moderno, o característico de ellos.

Roman [rō'-man], *a.* 1. Romano, relativo a Roma o á los romanos. 2. Semejante a un romano por su carácter; noble, valeroso; también, austero, severo. 3. Católico romano, papal. *Roman letter*, *Roman type*, Letra romana, tipo romano, forma ordinaria de caracteres de imprenta. *Roman candle*, Candela romana, pieza de fuegos artificiales.

Romance, Romanic [ro-mans', ro-man-ic], *a.* Romance; aplícase á cada una de las lenguas modernas derivadas del latín popular, entre las cuales se distinguen el español, el italiano y el francés.

Romance [ro-mans'], *s.* Romance; ficción, cuento, fábula.

Romance, *vn.* Mentir; fingir fábulas.

Romancer [ro-mans'-er], *s.* 1. Romancero, el que compone romances. 2. Mentiroso, chismeador, chismoso.

Romancist [ro-man'-sist], *s.* Romancero, escritor de romances.

Romanesque [ro''-man-esc'], *a.* 1. Romanesco, románico; dícese de cierto estilo de arquitectura caracterizado por el arco redondo y por su general solidez. 2. Romance; dícese en particular del provenzal o la lengua de *oc*.

Romanist [rō'-man-ist], *s.* y *a.* Un católico romano.

Romantic, Romantical [ro-man'-tic, al], *a.* 1. Quijotesco: dícese del modo, porte ridículo o empeños extravagantes de alguno. 2. Romántico, novelesco, que pertenece a los romances y novelas; extravagante, improbable, ridículo. 3. Encantado: dícese de los sitios amenos y deliciosos. 4. Fabuloso, fingido, de novela, de cuento.

Romantically [ro-man'-tic-al-i], *adv.* Extravagantemente, ridículamente.

Romanticism [ro-man'-ti-sizm], *s.* Romanticismo.

Romish [rōm'-ish], *a.* 1. Romano, que pertenece a los romanos. 2. Romano, que pertenece al Papa o a la Iglesia católica.

Romp [remp], *s.* 1. La muchacha retozona que es amiga de juguetear con descompostura. 2. El retozo descompuesto y poco modesto.

Romp, *vn.* Retozar, brincar o juguetear descompuestamente.

Rompers [rēmp'-ẹrz], *s. pl.* Mameluco, trajecito de niño de una sola pieza en forma de pantalón.

Rompish [remp'-ish], *a.* Inclinado a retozos o juegos poco modestos.

Rondeau [ren'-dō], *s.* 1. Redondilla. 2. (Mús.) Rondó.

Rondo [ren'-do], *s.* 1. (Mús.) Rondó, cierta composición musical. 2. Redondilla.

Rood [rūd], *s.* 1. La santa cruz o el crucifijo. 2. Un cuarto de acre cuadrado. 3. Pértica. *V.* Rod. *Rood-screen*, Gloria, mampara del presbiterio. *Roodloft*, Crucero.

Roof [rūf], *s.* 1. Tejado, techado, techo de bóveda; (poét.) bóveda, cielo. 2. Paladar, la parte interior y superior de la boca. 3. Imperial de un coche o diligencia. 4. Casa, hogar, habitación. *Rooftree*, Cumbrera, maderamen de techo; el techo mismo. *Flat roof*, Azotea; techo casi horizontal. *Gambrel roof*, Techo a la holandesa. *Mansard roof*, Techo aboardillado, a la francesa. *Slate roof*, Techo de pizarras. *Tile roof*, Tejado, techo cubierto de tejas.

Roof, *va.* 1. Techar, cubrir con techo. 2. Encerrar en una casa; abrigar, alojar.

Roof garden [rūf gar'-dn], *s.* Azotea con jardín.

Rooftile [rūf'-tail], *s.* Teja, cobija.

Roofed [rūft], **Roofy** [rūf'-i], *a.* Techado.

Rook [ruc], *s.* (Orn.) 1. Corneja de pico blanco. 2. Roque, torre, pieza del juego de ajedrez. 3. (Des.) Trampista, tramposo, fullero.

Rookery [ruk'-ẹr-i], *s.* 1. Los árboles donde hacen sus nidos muchas cornejas. 2. Nido de las aves marinas; lugar donde anualmente se reunen las focas para procrear. 3. Alojamiento viejo y en mal estado; también, vecindario bajo, vil.

Rooky [ruk'-i], *a.* Habitado por cornejas.

Room [rūm], *vn.* (Fam.) Habitar ciertas piezas, alojarse.—*s.* 1. Lugar, paraje, sitio. 2. Lugar, el espacio que ocupa cualquier cuerpo; puesto. 3. Lugar, causa, motivo, razón para hacer o no hacer una cosa. 4. Lugar, tiempo, ocasión, oportunidad. 5. Cuarto, aposento, cámara, pieza de una casa. *The next room*, La pieza inmediata. *A front room*, Aposento o cuarto a la calle. *A back room*, Cuarto o pieza interior. *State-rooms*, (Mar.) Camarotes principales; pañol. *There is no room for your horse*, No hay cabida para el caballo de Vd. *There is room for one*, Hay puesto para una persona. *To give room*, Hacer lugar retirarse, dar puesto. *To make room*, Abrir paso, hacer lugar, despejar la vía. *There is no room for doubt*, No hay duda posible. *Dining-room*, Comedor. *Drawing-room*, Salón. *Room-mate*, Compañero de cuarto; la persona que habita un cuarto con otra u otras.

Roomer [rūm'-ẹr], *s.* Inquilino en un cuarto.

Roomy [rūm'-i], *a.* Espacioso, dilatado, capaz.

Roost [rūst], *s.* 1. Pértiga de gallinero; de aquí, cualquier lugar provisional de descanso. *Henroost*, Gallinero. 2. Sueño, descanso, reposo, hablando de las aves domésticas. 3. (E. U.) Perchada, reunión de aves perchadas en un mismo sitio. *To rule the roost*, Dominar, mandar, como el gallo de pelea sobre los otros.

Roost, *vn.* 1. Dormir o descansar las aves en una pértiga. 2. (Fest.) Estar alojado en alguna parte. *To come home to roost*, No hay deuda que no se pague.

Rooster [rūst'-ẹr], *s.* Gallo, el macho de las aves domésticas o de corral.

Root [rūt], *s.* 1. Raíz de los árboles y plantas. 2. Raíz, la parte inferior o el pie de cualquiera cosa. 3. Raíz, origen, principio de donde procede una cosa; estirpe, tronco, el fundador de una familia. 4. (Gram.) Raíz, voz primitiva o lo que queda de ella, después de quitarle los prefijos y subfijos. 5. Raíz: metafísicamente hablando se dice de las pasiones o afectos que están profundamente fijos en el alma. 6. (Arit.) Raíz, número que multiplicado por sí mismo produce la potencia. *Roots*, Raíces: dase este nombre genérico más particularmente a las plantas de las cuales se come la parte que está bajo tierra. 7. (Mús.) Base, nota fundamental. 8. Raigón (de diente). *Root-stock*, Rizoma. *Cube root*, Raíz cúbica. *To take root* o *strike root*, Echar raíces, arraigarse. *The root of all evil*, La raíz, el origen de todos los males.

Root, *vn.* y *va.* 1. Arraigar, echar o criar raíces. 2. Hozar, levantar la tierra con el hocico. 3. Arraigarse o afianzarse alguna planta en la tierra. 4. Arraigarse, inveterarse los males, vicios, etc. 5. Arraigarse, echar raíces en el alma o hacer en ella una impresión profunda alguna pasión o afecto; imprimir, grabar profundamente. 6. Estar establecido, fijo en alguna parte. *To root up* o *out*, Arrancar de raíz, desarraigar; extinguir, extirpar; desterrar.

Root beer [rūt bīr], *s.* Cerveza de baja graduación alcohólica hecha de raíces.

Rooted [rūt'-ed], *a.* Radical; arraigado.

Rootedly [rūt'-ed-li], *adv.* Radicalmente; fijamente.

Rootlet [rūt'-let], *s. dim.* Raicilla, radícula.

Rooter [rūt'-ẹr], *s.* 1. El o lo que desarraiga, u hoza como un puerco o jabalí; el que arranca de raíz. 2. (Ger.) El que anima por medio de aplausos; aplaudidor.

Rooty [rūt'-i], *a.* 1. Lleno de raíces. 2. Parecido á raíces.

Rope [rōp], *s.* 1. Soga, cuerda, cordel, maroma. 2. Sarta, ristra, trenza; hilera, fila. *Rope of onions*, Ristra de cebollas. *Ropes of a ship*, (Mar.) Jarcia, cordaje. *Rope's end*, Chicote de cabo. *Entering-rope*, Guardamancebo del portalón. *Bolt-rope*, Relinga. *Buoy-rope*, Orinque. *Guest-rope*, Guía de falsa amarra. *Rope-yard*, Cordelería. *To be at the end of one's rope*, Quedarse en la calle, estar sin recursos. *Rope-bands, pl.* (Mar.) Envergues. *Rope-dancer*, Volatín, bailarín de cuerda. *Rope-ladder*, Escala de cuerdas. *Rope-maker*, Cordelero, soguero. *Rope's-end*, Castigar, golpeando con un cabo de cuerda. *Rope-work*, Obra, trabajo hecho de cuerdas. *To know the ropes*, Saber cuántas son cinco; entender bien un asunto.

Rope, *va.* 1. Atar, amarrar o unir por medio de una cuerda. 2. Rodear con soga (como un circo ó arena). 3. (E. U.) Coger con un lazo. —*vn.* Hacer hebras o madeja. *To rope in*, (Ger. E. U.) Atraer a una empresa, engañar con arte y maña.

Rope-trick [rōp'-tric], *s.* 1. Cualquier juego de manos que se ejecuta con cuerdas. 2. (Des.) Picardía o villanía que merece la horca.

Ropewalk [rōp'-wēc], *s.* Cordelería, soguería, paraje largo cubierto donde se fabricaban cordeles o sogas; hoy lo ha sustituído la maquinaria perfeccionada. *Rope-walker*, Volatinero, persona que con habilidad y arte anda y voltea por el aire sobre una maroma.

Ropeyarn [rōp'-yārn], *s.* (Mar.) Filástica.

Ropiness [rōp'-i-nes], *s.* Viscosidad; tenacidad.

Ropish [rōp'-ish], **Ropy** [rōp'-i], *a.* Viscoso, pegajoso, glutinoso.

Roquet [ro-kē'], *va.* En el juego de *croquet*, dar la bola de un jugador contra otra.—*s.* Acción de chocar la bola de un jugador contra la de otro.

Rosaceous [ro-zē'-shus], *a.* Róseo, rosáceo, perteneciente a la familia de plantas cuyo tipo es el rosal.

Rosary [rō'-za-ri], *s.* 1. Rosario. 2. Rosario, rezo de este nombre. 3. Guirnalda o corona de rosas; de aquí, colección de piezas literarias escogidas. 4. Cuadro de rosas; jardín de rosales.

Rose [rōz], *pret.* de *To* Rise.

Rose [rōz], *s.* 1. Rosal, planta que produce las rosas; género, tipo de las rosáceas. 2. Rosa, flor del rosal. 3. Color de rosa. 4. Lo que tiene alguna semejanza a una rosa; rosa, roseta, lazo de cintas para adorno; (Arq.) rosetón; el remate circular y lleno de orificios del caño de una regadera. *Honey of roses*, Miel rosada. *Rose-bush*, (Bot.) Rosal. *Every rose has its thorn*, (prov.) A cada gusto su susto; o no hay rosa sin espinas. *Dog-rose*, Agavanzo, escaramujo, rosal silvestre. Se llama también *wild brier*. *Bengal* o *monthly rose*, Rosa de China; rosa de todo el año. *Tea-rose, tea-scented rose*, Cualquiera de las numerosas variedades de rosas con fragancia semejante a la de la rosa de te. *Under the rose*, Bajo cuerda, secretamente. *Rose-beetle, rose-bug, rose-chafer*, Varios escarabajos o insectos coleópteros dañinos a los rosales. *Rose-window*, Ventana con florón o rosetón.

Roseate [ro'-zg-êt], *a.* Rosado; róseo.

Rosebud [rōz'-bud], *s.* 1. Capullo de rosa. 2. Una joven en la flor de su juventud.

Rosegall [rōz'-gōl], *a.* Zarzarrosa, la flor del escaramujo.

Rosemary [rōz'-mê-ri], *s.* (Bot.) Romero, rosmarino, arbusto aromático de la familia de las labiadas, con flores azules.

Roseola [ro-zî'-o-la], *s.* Sarpullido, erupción de manchas rosadas.

Roset [rō'-zet], *s.* Rosicler, el color encendido parecido al de la rosa encarnada.

Rosette [ro-zet'], *s.* 1. Rosa, roseta, lazo de cintas que sirve de adorno o de distintivo; rosetón, adorno de arquitectura. 2. Cosa semejante a una rosa.

Rosewater [rōz'-wō-tęr], *s.* Agua rosada, agua de rosas.

Rosewood [rōz'-wud], *s.* Palo de rosa; árbol del género Dalbergia.

Rosied [rō'-zid], *a.* Rosado, adornado con rosas.

Rosin [rez'-in], *s.* 1. Trementina, resina que despide el pino. 2. *V.* RESIN.

Rosin, *va.* Dar con resina.

Rossoli [res'-o-li], *s.* Rosoli, licor.

Roster [res'-tęr], *s.* 1. Escalafón, registro de personal. 2. Lista, nómina, matrícula. 3. (Mil.) Lista de deberes, orden de prestar servicio.

Rostral [res'-tral], *a.* Rostral, perteneciente a un pico o rostro de ave, o a un espolón; (Zool.) que tiene rostro.

Rostrate [res'-trêt], *a.* Adornado con espolones de galeras u otros buques.

Rostriform [res'-tri-fōrm], *a.* En forma de rostro.

Rostrum [res'-trum], *s.* 1. Tribuna, plataforma desde donde habla un orador, o el que preside; los oradores colectivamente. 2. La tribuna en que arengaban los oradores romanos. 3. Rostro, el pico del ave; hocico; parte sobresaliente. 4. (Mar.) Rostro, la punta de la proa o del espolón que sobresale. 5. Cañón de alambique.

Rosy [rō'-zi], *a.* 1. Róseo, rosado, de rosa; sonrojado, que se sonroja. 2. (Fig.) Glorioso, agradable, lisonjero; optimista. 3. Rosado, que está compuesto de rosas. *Rosy-fingered*, Con dedos de rosa; epíteto homérico de la aurora. *Rosy-hued*, Rosado, color de rosa; con tez rosada.

Rot [ret], *vn.* 1. Pudrirse o podrirse; corromperse, echarse a perder, malearse. 2. Padecer de morriña las ovejas. 3. Corromperse moralmente. 4. Irse consumiendo poco a poco; estar estancado; ir a menos.—*va.* 1. Pudrir, resolver en podre. 2. Enriar. *V.* RET.

Rot, *s.* 1. Putrefacción, podre, podredumbre. 2. Enfermedad que agota, como las de los pulmones; morriña, una enfermedad que da a las ovejas. 3. (Bot.) Una de varias formas de descaecimiento en las plantas, causado por los hongos y las bacterias. 4. (Ger.) Borricada, dicho tonto, opinión necia.

Rota [rō'-ta], *s.* 1. Rol, nómina, lista de nombres que indica el orden y clase de sus deberes. *V.* ROSTER. 2. Orden de los deberes u obligaciones de uno, rutina. 3. Una asociación política que hubo en Inglaterra en el tiempo de las guerras civiles.

Rotary [ro'-ta-ri], *a.* Giratorio, rotante, que rueda o da vueltas como una rueda. *Rotary club*, Club rotario. *Rotary press*, Máquina rotativa.

Rotate [rō'-têt], *va.* y *vn.* 1. Girar, dar vueltas, o hacer rodar sobre un eje. 2. Alternar, cambiar, como las cosechas, los funcionarios, etc.; desamelgar un terreno.—*a.* 1. (Bot.) Rotante en forma de rueda, como la corola de ciertas flores. 2. (Ento.) Que forma círculo alrededor de una parte.

Rotating [rō-têt'-ing], *a.* Rotativo, giratorio.

Rotation [ro-tê'-shun], *s.* Rotación, turno, alternativa, vicisitud. *In rotation* o *by rotation*, Por turno, alternativamente. *Rotation of crops*, Desamelgamiento, rotación de las cosechas.

Rotative [rō'-ta-tiv], **Rotatory** [rō'-ta-to-ri], *a.* 1. Rotante, rotatorio, que está en rotación o que la causa. 2. (*Rotatory*) Alternativo, sucesivo.

Rotator [ro-tê'-tęr], *s.* Lo que causa rotación; músculo rotador.

Rote [rōt], *s.* Las palabras aprendidas sólo por rutina. *To learn by rote*, Aprender de memoria, como el papagayo.

Rotiform [rō'-ti-fōrm], *a.* Rotiforme, en forma de rueda.

Rotogravure [rō-to-gra-viūr'], *s.* Rotograbado.

Rotor [rō'-tęr], *s.* Rotor, indicador giratorio. *Rotor hub*, Cubo de rotor.

Rotten [ret'-n], *a.* Podrido, corrompido; endeble. *Rotten egg*, Huevo empollado. *Rotten trick*, Acción de pícaro.

Rottenness [ret'-n-nes], *s.* Podredumbre, putrefacción.

Rotten-stone [ret'-n-stōn], *s.* Trípol o trípoli (tierra podrida), substancia usada para pulir.

Rotund [ro-tund'], *a.* Rotundo, redondo, circular, esférico; orbicular.

Rotunda [ro-tun'-da], *s.* Rotonda, rotunda, salón o edificio circular que generalmente tiene cúpula.

Rotundity [ro-tun'-di-ti], *s.* 1. Rotundidad, redondez. 2. Objeto o protuberancia redondos.

Rouble [rū'-bl], *s.* *V.* RUBLE.

Rouge [rūzh], *s.* 1. El encarnado, el color encarnado. 2. Arrebol, colorete, afeite que se ponen en el rostro las mujeres. 3. Azafrán de Marte, rojo de joyero para pulir. *V.* CROCUS.—*a.* Colorado, encarnado.

Rouge, *va.* y *vn.* Arrebolarse, afeitarse, darse la cara con arrebol o colorete, o tenerla compuesta con este afeite; pulir con azafrán de Marte.

Rough [ruf], *a.* 1. Áspero, tosco, escabroso: dícese de lo que no está llano, liso o igual en la superficie; erizado; peludo, encrespado; desgreñado, mal peinado. 2. Tosco o áspero al tacto. 3. Áspero, acerbo o agrio al gusto. 4. Bronco, ingrato al oído. 5. Áspero, escabroso, hablando de caminos. 6. Duro, cruel, severo, áspero de genio, desapacible, rígido. 7. Bruto, tosco, inculto, grosero, brusco, insolente, arrogante. 8. Tempestuoso, borrascoso. 9. Formado o ejecutado de prisa, no acabado; aproximativo, general. *Rough diamond*, Diamante en bruto. *Rough wine*, Vino áspero. *Rough sea*, Mar alborotado. *Rough wind*, Viento borrascoso. *Rough words*, Palabras duras y chocantes. *A rough sketch*, Boceto, bosquejo. *A rough guess*, Una valuación aproximada. *Rough with prickles*, Erizado de púas. *A dog with rough hair*, Un perro de pelo encrespado. —*s.* 1. Estado tosco, en bruto, no pulido o mal acabado. 2. Vista general, aproximada. 3. Pillo, alborotador. *V.* RUFFIAN. *Rough-draft, draught*, Bosquejo, boceto.

Rough, *va.* 1. Hacer, poner áspero, tosco, escabroso. 2. Labrar imperfectamente. *To rough-draw*, Bosquejar, trazar rudamente. *To rough-hew*, Formar el modelo tosco de alguna cosa; desbastar, cortar toscamente sin allanar. *To rough it*, Pasar trabajos, vivir en duras condiciones. *To rough-dry*, Secar, enjugar (de prisa y corriendo) sin planchar. *Rough-rider*, (1) Jinete que cabalga de una manera descuidada. (2) Escudero instructor, el que adiestra los caballos. *Rough-shod*, Herrado con herraduras para el hielo (es decir, con clavos); se halla a menudo en la locución, *to ride rough-shod*, ir en derechura al grano, conducirse de una manera imperiosa.

Roughage [ruf'-êj], *s.* Forraje o alimento áspero de difícil digestión.

Rough-and-ready [ruf-and-red'-i], *a.* Tosco de maneras pero de eficaz acción.

Rough-and-tumble [ruf-and-tum'-bl], *a.* Rudo y desordenado pero resistente.

Roughcast [ruf'-cgst], *va.* Hacer alguna cosa toscamente; bosquejar una figura o cuadro.

Roughcast, *s.* Modelo en bruto.

Roughen [ruf'-n], *va.* Poner áspero. —*vn.* Volverse rudo.

Rough-hewn [ruf'-hiūn], *a.* Desbastado, mal acabado; a menudo en sentido figurado; rudo, tosco, de modales groseros.

Roughly [ruf'-li], *adv.* Ásperamente, rudamente, tempestuosamente, desapaciblemente, desagradablemente.

Roughness [ruf'-nes], *s.* 1. Aspereza, rudeza, tosquedad, desigualdad (de la superficie). 2. Severidad, dureza (en la disciplina). 3. Grosería de modales o de conducta; rudeza de genio, calidad de brusco. 4. Calidad de lo que está mal acabado o no trabajado. 5. Tempestad, tormenta.

Rouleau [rū-lō'], *s.* Paquetito de dinero, rollo, cucurucho, alcartaz.

Roulette [rū-let'], *s.* 1. Ruleta, cierto juego de azar. 2. Roleta, disco de acero templado de que usan los grabadores. (Fr.)

Round [raund], *a.* 1. Redondo, circular, orbicular, cilíndrico, esférico. 2. Que tiene superficie curva; no angular ni plano; convexo o cóncavo. 3. Lleno, hablando de los períodos; fácil, cuando se trata del estilo. 4. Redondo, cabal, sin picos ni quebrados, hablando de cuentas o de números. 5. Grande, cuantioso; liberal, amplio. 6. Franco, claro, sincero, liso, llano, ingenuo. 7. Cómodo en el andar, vivo, veloz, acelerado. 8. De cadencia llena, de tono sonoro. 9. Franco, justo, honrado. 10. Semicircular, ó caracterizado por el arco semicircular. *A round assertion*, Una afirmación rotunda, clara y positiva. *To make round*, Redondear, dar figura redonda. *A round fee*, Gajes u honorarios amplios, generosos. *To bring up with a round turn*, Obligar a hacer una parada repentina.—*s.* 1. Círculo, orbe, esfera, redondez. 2. Vuelta, giro, rotación, revolución. 3. Paso, escalón, peldaño, uno de los palos atravesados en una escalera portátil. 4. (Mil.) Ronda. 5. Andanada de cañones; salva, descarga de muchas armas de fuego a un tiempo; tiro, descarga, una sola carga de municiones de guerra. 6. Ruta, camino, circuito. 7. Rutina, serie de movimientos repetidos. 8. Un baile. 9. Redondilla, canción corta, compuesta de modo que produce un efecto armónico al cantarla varias voces que empiezan a intervalos sucesivos. 10. Tajada redonda de carne de buey. *In the whole round of our life*, En todo el curso de nuestra vida. *To go the rounds*, Ir de ronda. *Every one fired five rounds*, Cada uno hizo cinco disparos.—*adv.* Circularmente, redondamente, en circunferencia; por todas partes, por todos lados.—*prep.* Alrededor de; en contorno. *Round the world*, Por todo el mundo. *My head turns round*, Se me va la cabeza. *To take a round*, Dar una vuelta. *To go round*, Andar alrededor. *All the year round*, Todo el año.

Round, *va.* 1. Cercar, rodear, ceñir, abrazar todo alrededor, dar vuelta una cosa alrededor de otra. 2. Redondear. 3. Moverse alrededor. 4. Relevar, fabricar alguna cosa en relieve o resalte. *To round in*, (Mar.) Halar en redondo. *To round up the beams*, Volver para arriba los baos.—*vn.* 1. Redondearse, hacerse redondo. 2. Susurrar, hablar al oído, hablar quedo. 3. Rondar.

Roundabout [raund'-a-baut], *a.* Indirecto, vago, que hace rodeos; desviado.—*s.* 1. Chaqueta, chaleco. 2. Tío vivo. *V. Merry-go-round.* 3. Danza a la redonda.

Roundel [raun'-del], **Roundelay** [raun'-dl-lê], *s.* 1. Una melodía sencilla. 2. Redondilla. 3. Baile en círculo. *Roundel*, La figura redonda.

Round-hand [raund'-hand], *s.* Carácter de letra que suprime los ángulos, haciendo todos los trazos redondeados.

Roundhead [raund'-hed], *s.* Cabeza redonda: apodo que se daba antiguamente a los puritanos en Inglaterra.

Round-house [raund'-haus], *s.* 1. (Mar.) Toldilla, la cubierta superior de un navío en la parte de popa o la que cubre la cámara alta. 2. (E. U.) Rotunda, casa de máquinas, edificio semicircular para las locomotoras con una plataforma giratoria en su centro.

Roundish [raund'-ish], *a.* Algo o casi redondo.

Roundly [raund'-li], *adv.* Redondamente; claramente, sin cumplimientos, abiertamente; francamente; absolutamente; ligeramente.

Roundness [raund'-nes], *s.* Redondez; claridad, sinceridad, buena fe.

Round number [raund num'-bęr], *s.* Número redondo.

Round-shouldered [raund shōl'-dęrd], *a.* Algo jorobado, cargado de espaldas.

Round steak [raund stêk], *s.* Bistec de mediana calidad.

Round table [raund' tê'-bl], *s.* Mesa redonda. *Round-table discussion*, Discusión de mesa redonda.

Round trip [raund trip], *s.* Viaje redondo, viaje de ida y vuelta.

Round-up [raund'-up], *va.* Rodear, recoger los hatos en un rodeo.—*s.* Rodeo de hatos para marcarlos con hierro candente o para reunirlos.

Round robin [reb'-in], *s.* Petición, memorial en que las firmas están dispuestas en círculo para que no se sepa quién ha firmado primero.

Rouse [rauz], *va.* 1. Despertar, cortar el sueño al que está durmiendo. 2. Despertar, hacer que uno vuelva sobre sí o recapacite; excitar, animar, poner en acción. 3. Levantar la caza, hacerla salir de su nido o cama. 4. (Mar.) Halar o arronzar un calabrote o cable.—*vn.* 1. Despertar, dejar de dormir. 2. Despertar, hacerse más advertido o avisado.

†**Rouse**, *s.* Tragazo, trago demasiado grande de licor.

Rouser [rauz'-ęr], *s.* 1. Despertador, excitador. 2. (Fam.) Bola, mentira, embuste.

Roust [raust], *va.* (Fam.) Despertar y hacer huir o cazar.—*vn.* Ser activo, moverse con energía.

Roustabout [raust'-a-baut''], *s.* (E.U. y Aus.) Peón, trabajador de cubierta en los vapores de río; también, gañán.

Rout [raut], *s.* 1. Rota, derrota de un ejército, huída en confusión. 2. Jabardo, jabardillo, garulla, chusma, junta o reunión de gente baja. 3. (Ant.) Tertulia, reunión de gente decente.

Rout, *va.* 1. Derrotar, vencer y poner en confusión, hacer huir, destruir. 2. Arrojar, sacar o hacer salir con violencia, como de un retiro; con *out*, por lo común.

Route [rūt], *s.* 1. Ruta, itinerario, derrota. 2. Camino, carretera. 3. Rumbo. 4. Trazado.—*va.* 1. Enrumbar, encaminar. 2. Predisponer.

Routine [rū-tīn'], *a.* 1. Rutinario. 2. Rutinero. 3. Soso, insulso. 4. Mediano, regular.

Routine [rū-tīn'], *s.* Rutina, serie de actos prescritos o habituales; costumbre, estilo o hábito adquiridos por mera práctica.

Rove [rōv], *va.* Corretear.—*vn.* 1. Vagar, vaguear, errar, correr acá y acullá. 2. Disparar una especie de flecha que los ingleses llaman *rover*. *To rove about the seas*, Piratear.

Rove, *va.* (Art. y Of.) 1. Unir y alargar las madejas, torcer el hilo antes de encanillarlo, pasándolo entre pares de cilindros arrolladores. 2. Enhebrar, pasar por un ojo o agujero; pasar una cuerda por una polea.

Rove [rōv], *s.* 1. Madeja de lana tirada. 2. Anillo de metal que se usa como remache de clavo en la construcción de barcos. 3. Correría, acto de correr acá y acullá.

Rover [rōv'-ęr], *s.* 1. Errante, andorrero, tunante, vago, vagamundo. 2. Veleta, la persona inconstante y mudable. 3. Ladrón, pirata. 4. Una especie de flecha.

Roving [rōv'-ing], *s.* Primera torsión que se da a un hilo de algodón, lana, etc.—*a.* Errante.

Row [rō], *s.* 1. Hilera, fila, línea. 2. Paseo en lancha o bote.

Row [rō], *vn.* (Mar.) Remar, trabajar con el remo.—*va.* Bogar, conducir remando: pasear por agua. *Rowboat*, Bote, lancha, barca de remos. *Row-lock*, Chumacera, escalamera.

Row [rau], *vn.* Pelearse, armar un zipizape, tomar parte en un alboroto.—*s.* Camorra, zipizape; zambra, quimera, alboroto. (< rouse.)

Rowdy [rau'-di], *s.* y *a.* Pillo, pelafustán, quimerista, alborotador. (Méx.) Lépero, pelagatos, canalla.

Rowdyism [rau'-di-izm], *s.* Pillería, pelagatería; alboroto.

Rowel [rau'-el], *s.* Rodajuela o estrella de espuela. 2. (Vet.) Sedal.

Rowel, *va.* Poner un sedal.

Rowen [rau'-en], *s.* 1. Segunda cosecha en el mismo campo. 2. (Prov.) *pl.* Campo que queda en rastrojo para dar pastos en el otoño.

Rower [rō'-ęr], *s.* Remero, bogador.

Royal [rei'-al], *a.* 1. Real, que pertenece a un rey o monarca. 2. Regio, majestuoso, magnífico, noble, magnánimo, ilustre. 3. De calidad o tamaño superior. 4. Eminentemente agradable o primoroso. *We had a royal time*, Nos divertimos en grande.—*s.* 1. Un tamaño de papel; es de 19 por 24 pulgadas para escribir y de 20 por 25 para imprenta. 2. (Mar.) Juanete, la vela más alta. 3. Mogote de ciervo.

Royalist [rei'-al-ist], *s.* Realista, partidario de los reyes.

Royally [rei'-al-i], *adv.* Regiamente, a lo regio, a manera de rey; magníficamente, noblemente.

Royalty [rei'-al-ti], *s.* 1. Realeza, soberanía, dignidad real; majestad real. 2. Los emblemas de la soberanía, que se expresan metafóricamente por las palabras corona y cetro. 3. Regalía, parte de las utilidades que paga el editor, fabricante, etc., al autor, inventor o propietario que se han reservado ciertos privilegios. 4. Derechos, regalías, prerrogativas reales.

Rub [rub], *va.* 1. Estregar, fregar, limpiar, frotar, rascando o estregando una cosa con otra. 2. Rozar, tocar ligeramente dos cosas entre sí. 3. Rascar, frotar con las uñas u otra cosa la piel. 4. Raspar, raer un papel, una lámina, etc. 5. Inquietar, incomodar, fastidiar.—*vn.* 1. Estregarse o frotarse dos cosas entre sí. 2. Desenredarse, salir o librarse de algún peligro o enredo, adelantarse con dificultad. 3. Producir un efecto mental, particularmente un efecto duro o penoso; hastiar, molestar. *To rub away*, Continuar frotando o estregando; quitar frotando. *To rub along* u *on*, Ir viviendo con trabajo; salir de apuros. *To rub down a horse*, Limpiar un caballo. *To rub in*, Hacer penetrar por los poros frotando o refregando; (fam.) reiterar, insistir demasiado. *To rub off*, Quitar; limpiar una cosa estregándola con otra. *To rub out*, Borrar. *To rub the wrong way*, Frotar a contrapelo; de aquí causar irritación, contradecir, incomodar. *To rub up*, Aguijonear, excitar, animar; retocar, repasar, pulir, pulimentar.

Rub, *s.* 1. Frotamiento, ludimiento, colisión de dos cuerpos uno con otro. 2. Estregamiento, estregadura. 3. Tropiezo, embarazo, obstáculo, dificultad. 4. Sarcasmo, denuesto; algo que ofende el amor propio.

Rubbish [rub'-ish], *s.* Escombro, ripio, rudera, broza, ruinas; morralla, desecho, zupia, desperdicio; andrajos.

Rubber [rub'-ęr], *a.* Hecho de caucho o goma elástica. *Rubber cloth,* Tela revestida de caucho. *Rubber dam,* Hoja de caucho de que se sirven los dentistas para mantener seca la cavidad de un diente.—*s.* 1. Caucho, hule, goma elástica (en Perú, jebe); llámase también, *India-rubber. Hard rubber,* Vulcanita, caucho químicamente compuesto con azufre y expuesto a la acción del calor; substancia que tiene muchas aplicaciones. 2. El que estrega alguna cosa. 3. Rodilla, estropajo, aljofifa para estregar o limpiar; estregadera; escofina; cualquiera cosa con que se estrega, limpia, frota o raspa. 4. Partida en el juego llamado *whist.*

Rubber band [rub'-ęr band], *s.* Bandita de goma elástica o de caucho.

Rubber heel [rub'-ęr hîl], *s.* Tacón de goma o de caucho.

Rubberize [rub'-ęr-aiz], *va.* Engomar, encauchar, impregnar con goma o caucho, p. ej. la seda.

Rubber plant [rub'-ęr plant], *s.* Cauchera, planta del hule.

Rubbers [rub'-ęrz], *s. pl.* Zapatos de goma o de caucho.

Rubber-sheathed [rub'-ęr-shîdhd], *a.* Encauchado.

Rubber stamp [rub'-ęr stamp], *s.* Sello de goma.—*va.* 1. Sellar con sello de goma. 2. (vul.) Aprobar rutinariamente.

Rubble [rub'-l], *s.* 1. Ripios, cascote, morrillo, piedras, de forma irregular; se llama también *rubble-stone.* 2. Enripiado, mampostería; por otro nombre, *rubble-work.*

Rub down [rub daun], *s.* Fricción, masaje.—*va.* Friccionar, dar masaje.

Rubefacient [rū-be-fé'-shient], *a.* Rubefaciente, que causa rubefacción. —*s.* Tópico para producir rubefacción de la piel.

Rubescent [rū-bes'-ent], *a.* Que empieza a rubificar, a ponerse colorado.

Rubicund [rū'-bi-cund], *a.* Rubicundo.

Rubied [rū'-bid], *a.* Encendido como rubí o de color de rubí.

Rubiform [rū'-bi-fōrm], *a.* Rojo, rubio.

Rubify [rū'-bi-fai], *va.* Rubificar, poner colorada alguna cosa.

Rubiginous [rū-bij'-i-nus], *a.* 1. Que tiene color herrumbroso o mohoso; pardo-rojo. 2. Atacado por el añublo o tizón.

Ruble [rū'-bl], *s.* Rublo, moneda rusa de plata que vale unas cuatro pesetas; papel moneda que valía 51 centavos o sea 2.67 pesetas.

Rubric [rū'-bric], *a.* Rubro, rojo, rojizo.—*s.* 1. Rúbrica, regla que enseña la práctica de las ceremonias y ritos de la Iglesia (porque solían estamparse con letras encarnadas). 2. Rúbrica, rasgo o señal que ponen algunos despues de su firma.

Rubstone [rub'-stōn], *s.* Piedra de amolar o afilar.

Ruby [rū'-bi], *s.* 1. Rubí, piedra preciosa de color rojo o de carmín transparente. 2. Carmín, color encarnado vivo. 3. Piedra preciosa en la máquina de un reloj.—*a.* Rubicundo, de rojo vivo; semejante a un rubí.—*va.* Rubificar, enrojecer; hacer parecer a un rubí. *Ruby-throat,* Colibrí norteamericano del género Trochilus; el macho tiene la garganta de un rojo vivo metálico.

Ruche [rūsh], *s.* Rizado de muselina o cinta para los vestidos (o mangas) de mujer. (Fr.)

Rudd [rud], *s.* Leucisco, pez europeo de agua dulce. (Leuciscus.)

Rudder [rud'-ęr], *s.* Timón, la pieza de madera que sirve para gobernar el buque; gobernalle. *Rudder-pintles,* (Mar.) Machos del timón.

Ruddiness [rud'-i-nes], *s.* 1. Color de rubí; rubicundez. 2. Hermosura y encendimiento del color del rostro; tez lustrosa y encendida.

Ruddy [rud'-i], *a.* Colorado, rubio. *A ruddy face,* El rostro con colores muy vivos, cara de tomate.

Rude [rūd], *a.* 1. Rudo, brutal, rústico, grosero, impolítico, descortés. *Rude language,* Lenguaje brutal. 2. Violento, turbulento; severo, inflexible. 3. Tosco, basto, ignorante, sin crianza, sin educación. 4. Informe, imperfecto, mal hecho. 5. Desigual, escabroso. *To be rude,* Ser descortés o grosero, portarse con poca modestia o con poca crianza.

Rudely [rūd'-li], *adv.* Rudamente, ásperamente, groseramente, brutalmente; con poca delicadeza.

Rudeness [rūd'-nes], *s.* Grosería, descortesía; rudeza, dureza, aspereza; brutalidad, insolencia; ignorancia.

Rudiment [rū'-di-ment], *s.* Rudimento, cualquiera de los primeros principios de un arte, ciencia o profesión; principio. 2. Lo que es rudimentario; parte, órgano, estructura rudimentarios, germen.

Rudimental [rū-di-ment'-al], *a.* Rudimental, perteneciente o relativo a los rudimentos.

Rudimentary [rū-di-men'-ta-ri], *a.* 1. Rudimental, rudimentario, de la naturaleza de un rudimento; en estado de rudimento; germinal, elemental. 2. Que queda imperfectamente desarrollado; abortivo.

Rue [rū], *va.* Llorar, lamentar, sentir, ponderar un infortunio.—*vn.* Compadecerse, sentir, arrepentirse, estar pesaroso. *You will rue the day of your birth,* Lamentará Vd. el día en que nació. *You shall rue it,* Te ha de pesar.

Rue, *s.* 1. (Bot.) Ruda, planta, tipo de las rutáceas. 2. Infusión o decocción hecha de esta planta; trago amargo o ácido.

Rueful [rū'-ful], *a.* Lamentable, lastimoso, triste, deplorable; terrible.

Ruefully [rū'-ful-i], *adv.* Tristemente.

Ruff [ruf], *s.* 1. Lechuguilla, el cuello o cabezón que se usaba antiguamente. 2. Aspereza, la calidad de áspero que tienen las cosas. 3. Apéndice natural, como un collar de plumas salientes o de pelo alrededor del cuello de un ave o de un mamífero. 4. Paloma moñuda. 5. Pavo marino.

Ruffian [ruf'-i-an o ruf'-yan], *s.* Malhechor, ladrón, bandolero.—*a.* Brutal, inhumano, semejante a un bandolero o merodeador. *Ruffianish, a.* Propio de un malvado; tunantón.

Ruffianly, Ruffian-like [ruf'-i-an-li, laic], *a.* Forajido, no sujeto a la ley; parecido a un bandido.

Ruffle [ruf'-l], *va.* 1. Desordenar, confundir; desazonar, enfadar. 2. Rizar, hacer dobleces en la ropa y otras cosas; adornar con puños o manguitos. 3. Incomodar, irritar; vejar.—*vn.* 1. Rizarse, tomar en dobleces; de aquí, moverse alguna cosa tremolando en el aire. 2. Fastidiarse, incomodarse, aburrirse. 3. (Ant.) Alborotarse, exasperarse.

Ruffle, *va.* Tocar marcha (los tambores).

Ruffle, *s.* 1. Vuelta o puño de camisola. 2. Vuelo de las mangas de mujer. 3. Enojo, irritación, conmoción temporal; también, escarceo del agua. 4. Un toque de tambor en la milicia. *Laced ruffles,* Vueltas de encaje.

Rug [rug], *s.* 1. Paño burdo. 2. Frazada, manta peluda muy basta. 3. Perro de lanas o de aguas. 4. Ruedo, tapete; felpudo.

Rugate [rū'-gęt], *a.* *V.* RUGOSE.

Rugged [rug'-ed], *a.* 1. Áspero, desigual, tosco, escabroso. 2. Basto, inculto, desapacible. 3. Descomedido, desvergonzado, severo; arrugado, ceñudo, regañón. *That rugged teacher, adversity,* Aquel maestro severo, la adversidad. 4. Peludo. 5. Bronco, ingrato al oído. 6. (Fam. E. U.) Robusto, vigoroso. 7. Tempestuoso, borrascoso. *A rugged beard,* Unas barbas incultas.

Ruggedly [rug'-ed-li], *adv.* Rudamente, ásperamente.

Ruggedness [rug'-ed-nes], *s.* Rudeza, aspereza.

Rugose, Rugous [rū'-gōs, rū'-gus], *a.* Rugoso, lleno de arrugas; arrugado, rizado.

Ruin [rū'-in], *s.* 1. Ruina, caída, decadencia; bancarrota; pérdida de reputación u honra, corrupción, vicio. 2. Estado de ruina, desolación o degradación; perdición. 3. Ruina, causa de destrucción. *To bring one to ruin,* Perder a uno. *Ruins,* Escombros, ruinas o despojos de fábricas o edificios arruinados; residuos.

Ruin, *va.* Arruinar, derribar, demoler, destruir; empobrecer; seducir.—*vn.* 1. Caer en ruinas, arruinarse; decaer. 2. Producir o causar ruina.

Ruination [rū-in-é'-shun], *s.* Arruinamiento, ruina, perdición.

Ruinous [rū'-in-us], *a.* Ruinoso; pernicioso, fatal, funesto.

Ruinously [rū'-in-us-li], *adv.* Perniciosamente, ruinosamente.

Rulable [rū'-la-bl], *a.* 1. Que se puede gobernar, mandar o dirigir; sujeto a reglas. 2. Permisible según regla; lícito, permitido.

Rule [rūl], *s.* 1. Mando, poder, autoridad, señorío. 2. Regla, modelo o ejemplo que debe servir de medida para ajustar las acciones y pensamientos; método o principio de acción. 3. Regla, el listón que sirve para echar o trazar las líneas derechas; cartabón. 4. Regularidad, buen orden. 5. Auto, fallo de un tribunal; también, regla, estatuto. 6. Raya, filete, regla de imprenta. 7. Raya, línea rayada o reglada. 8. Reglamento. *To be the rule,* Ser de regla, de reglamento. *To bear rule,* Mandar. *To make it a rule to,* Hacerse una regla, una ley, de. *Two-foot rule,* Regla de dos pies de largo.

Rule, *va.* 1. Gobernar, mandar; reprimir, subyugar, contener, moderar. 2. Establecer una regla, un reglamento; dirigir, disciplinar, decidir según reglas. 3. Arreglar, conducir. 4. Rayar, marcar con rayas o líneas; marcar o trazar con una regla, reglar. *To rule paper*, Reglar papel. *To rule out*, (For.) No admitir, no recibir, desechar.—*vn.* 1. Señorear, dominar, tener mando o autoridad; regir. 2. Poner, sentar, establecer, una regla que debe observarse; formular una decisión. 3. Tener influencia predominante, prevalecer. 4. (Com.) Quedar, permanecer en determinado nivel o estado. *To rule over*, Regir, gobernar, dominar. *He is ruled by his wife*, Su mujer le manda.

Ruler [rūl'-ẹr], *s.* 1. Gobernador, el que tiene el supremo mando. 2. Regla para trazar las líneas derechas. *Parallel ruler*, Regla para trazar paralelas.

Ruling [rūl'-ing], *s.* 1. Decisión, fallo u orden de un tribunal, un juez o una persona que preside. 2. Rayadura, acción de rayar o trazar líneas. *Ruling-machine*, Máquina para rayar. *Ruling-pen*, Tiralíneas.

Rum [rum], *s.* 1. Ron, aguardiente de caña dulce. (Méx.) Chinguirito. 2. (Fam.) Cualquier licor embriagante.—*a.* (Fam. Ingl.) 1. Extraño, singular. 2. Que da placer.

Rumble [rum'-bl], *va.* y *vn.* 1. Producir un sonido sordo y continuo o de redoble, como el trueno; retumbar, rugir. 2. Moverse, avanzar haciendo ese sonido. 3. Alborotar, hacer tumulto; estar en tumulto o alboroto.

Rumble, *s.* 1. Ruido, rumor, sonido sordo y prolongado; estruendo producido por un carruaje o tren. 2. Asiento elevado detrás de un coche.

Rumble seat [rum'-bl sīt], *s.* Asiento elevado detrás de un automóvil.

Rumen [rū'-men], *s.* Omaso, panza o primer estómago de los rumiantes.

Ruminant [rū'-mi-nant], *a.* y *s.* 1. Rumiador, rumiante. 2. Meditativo.

Ruminate [rū'-mi-nêt], *va.* 1. Rumiar, masticar segunda vez lo que han comido los animales rumiantes. 2. Rumiar, considerar despacio y pensar con reflexión y madurez alguna cosa.

Rumination [rū-mi-né'-shun], *s.* Rumia, rumiadura; meditación, consideración.

Rummage [rum'-ẹj], *va.* y *vn.* 1. Revolver, explorar, de una manera desordenada; escudriñar, andar revolviendo todo lo que se encuentra. 2. Agitar bien (un líquido o el contenido de un barril, etc.). 3. (Con *out* o *up*) Hallar, algo que se ha buscado sin orden ni método.—*vn.* Ir buscando y rebuscando por todas partes, trastornándolo todo.—*s.* Revuelta, trastorno, desorden; acto de rebuscar desordenadamente, de prisa y revolviendo.

Rummager [rum'-ẹj-ẹr], *s.* Saqueador, explorador.

Rummy [rum'-i], *s.* Variedad de juego de naipes.

Rumor, Rumour [rū'-mẹr], *s.* Rumor, voz no confirmada que corre entre el público.

Rumor, *va.* Esparcir o divulgar alguna noticia; hacer correr un rumor. *It is rumoured*, Se dice.

Rumorer [rū'-mẹr-ẹr], *s.* El que esparce noticias.

Rump [rump], *s.* Rabadilla u obispillo de ave; anca; nalga de animal y a veces también de hombre en desprecio; solomo de vaca. *Rump Parliament*, Nombre que se da en la historia inglesa a ciertos períodos del parlamento en el tiempo de Cromwell. (Voz de desprecio.)

Rumple [rum'-pl], *va.* Arrugar, hacer pliegues o protuberancias irregulares.

Rumple, *s.* Arruga, doblez o pliegue irregulares.

Rumrunner [rum-run'-ẹr], *s.* Contrabandista en bebidas alcohólicas.

Run [run], *va.* (*pret.* RAN, *pp.* RUN, *ger.* RUNNING). 1. Hacer correr, (en cualquiera de sus acepciones intransitivas), recorrer. 2. Introducir con precipitación una cosa en otra, hacer entrar, herir de punta; picar. 3. Arrojar con violencia. 4. Efectuar corriendo, ejecutar, hacer. 5. Cazar (correr). 6. Descargar, verter, echar de sí, manar. 7. Hacer derretirse o liquidarse. 8. Coser en una línea continua. 9. Aventurar, arriesgar. 10. Derretir, fundir. 11. Manejar, dirigir (una máquina, institución, empresa). 12. Conducir, llevar o dirigir el juicio o la imaginación.—*vn.* 1. Correr, ir corriendo, seguir corriendo, pasar o caminar con velocidad; pasar como un meteoro; volar, hender el aire; moverse rápidamente de un punto a otro; viajar; apresurarse, huir. 2. Correr el tiempo; correr peligro. 3. Cambiarse o pasar rápidamente de un estado a otro; resbalarse, deslizarse. 4. Correr, ir tras uno, seguir o buscar a alguno. 5. Competir, lidiar, ser competidor. *To run for Congress*, Ser competidor de otros para un puesto en el Congreso. 6. Correr, estar admitido o recibido; estar en fuerza una costumbre, opinión, etc., estilarse, acostumbrarse; estar en actividad; hallarse en operación, como una máquina. 7. Correr, decirse o saberse públicamente una cosa. 8. Desarrollarse por medio de acrecimiento o transición; frecuentemente con *in, into, to* o *up*. *To run to seed*, Granar. 9. Ocupar el entendimiento o imaginación en la contemplación de un asunto; con *on* o *upon*. 10. Proceder, continuar o proseguir en la ejecución de una cosa con orden fijo y determinado; repetirse en sucesión. 11. Correr, fluir, manar, gotear un líquido; derretirse o liquidarse un cuerpo. 12. Correr, perseguir, acosar; acometer o arremeter impetuosamente. 13. Correr, pasar, tener curso; extenderse a lo largo, ya sea distancia o dirección. 14. Correr a porfía. 15. Ser el estilo de un escrito fácil y flúido. 16. Ocurrir o suceder algo; ser, existir con las naturales variaciones de tamaño, calidad, etc. 17. Tender, ir hacia, inclinarse, tener predisposición hacia algo. 18. En música, tocar una serie de notas en sucesión rápida. 19. Presentarse gran número de personas a retirar dinero de un banco. 20. Rezumarse, derramarse. 21. Hacer contrabando. *To run about*, Andar de una parte a otra o correr de acá para allá sin objeto determinado. *To run across*, Atravesar corriendo; hallar (casualmente), encontrar; extenderse en. *A friend whom I ran across in London*, Un amigo con quien me encontré en Londres. *To run after*, Anhelar por, aspirar a; buscar con ansia alguna cosa. *To run against*, Chocar, topar, encontrarse, darse encontrones; oponerse; ser una cosa contraria u opuesta a otra. *To run aground*, Zozobrar, encallar. *To run ahead*, Correr delante; llevar ventaja. *To run along*, Correr un flúido o líquido, la voz, un sonido, etc., por todo un espacio. *To run away*, Huir, escapar, tomar soleta, zafarse. *To run away with*, Arrebatar, precipitar. *To run back*, Retroceder, volver pies atrás; volver el pensamiento o la imaginación a la contemplación de una cosa pasada. *To run behind*, Correr detrás; quedarse atrás; no hacer frente a sus gastos. *To run by*, Ser conocido por; pasar por, por vía de. *To run counter*, Oponerse; correr en una dirección opuesta. *To run down*, Agobiar, oprimir, envilecer; cansar o quebrantar a una persona o a un animal haciéndole correr demasiado; fluir, destilar, gotear, chorrear. *To run foul of*, (Mar.) Chocar, abordar. *To run in*, Coincidir; convenir; ocupar enteramente. *To run into*, Ocuparse, emplearse; pasar. *To run in the blood* o *in the family*, Seguir o extenderse por generaciones sucesivas; estar en la sangre. *To run into the ground*, (Fam. E. U.) (1) Llevar al exceso; (2) tener mal éxito, manejar mal y fracasar. *To run off*, Pasar rápidamente de una cosa a otra; imprimir; decir sin estudio, ensartar, repetir. *To run on*, Mencionar de paso; continuar. *To run out* Salir, o salirse corriendo; esparcirse, escurrirse, correrse o fluir una cosa; atrasarse o gastar más de lo que se tiene de renta; acabarse o concluirse; extenderse o dilatarse; consumir. *To run over*, Rebosar, derramarse, salirse un líquido del vaso u otra cosa que lo contiene; decir, contar o referir una cosa con todos sus pormenores; repasar, volver a pasar o contar; recorrer, registrar o mirar con cuidado. *To run through*, Atravesar, pasar de parte a parte; traspasar, atravesar, pasar de una parte a otra. *To run to*, Acudir, correr o ir con diligencia al socorro de alguno. *To run under*, Navegar a la altura de algún lugar. *To run up*, Recorrer con la imaginación alguna cosa anterior a otra; levantar, dar más altura; coser de una manera provisional; contar o sumar rápidamente; incurrir, contraer por medio de repetidas adiciones; crecerse, aumentarse; construir de prisa; alzar, levantar en alto (bandera, etc.); estrecharse, encogerse un tejido mojado; (E. U. del Oeste) ahorcar. *To run up and down*, Correr de una parte a otra. *To run upon*, Acometer, encontrarse, chocarse. *To run races*, Efectuar carreras; apostar carreras, apostar a correr. *To run the hazard* o *the danger*, Correr peligro. *To run to seed*, Granar, desarrollar las simientes con exceso. *To run the gantlet*, Pasar por baquetas. *The title runs thus*, El título dice así. *To run aground*, Varar. *To run out a warp*, (Mar.) Tender una espía. *To run close-hauled*, (Mar.) Correr a bolina halada. *To run in for the land*, Andar con la proa a tierra. *The sled runs over the snow*, El trineo se desliza sobre la nieve. *The watch has run down*, El reloj se ha parado. *To* *run to leaves*, Desarrollar las hojas con exceso. *A sore which runs*, Una úlcera que supura. *The note has yet twenty days to run*, El pagaré vence dentro de veinte días. *The memory of man runs not to the contrary*, No hay memoria de un ejemplo en contrario.

Run, *s.* 1. Corrida, carrera, curso. 2. Vuelta, viajecito, excursión ; también, adelantamiento regular o continuo. 3. Curso o período de operación ; también, lo que se produce o ejecuta en ese período (v. g. en una fábrica). 4. Curso, movimiento de un líquido ; lo que fluye : especialmente un arroyuelo. 5. Curso, serie, continuación. 6. Voluntad, gusto, libre uso, libertad de ir y venir á voluntad. 7. Aceptación, aprobación. 8. Carrera, hilera. 9. La acción de acudir muchas personas a sacar sus depósitos de un banco. 10. Sitio frecuentado, especialmente por los animales ; terreno de pasto. 11. Migración, v. g. de los peces al lugar del desove, ribazón. 12. Caída, dirección relativa. 13. (Mús.) Sucesión rápida de notas. 14. Aptitud para correr. 15. (Mar.) Racel, cada uno de los delgados que la nave lleva a popa y a proa. *Good* o *ill run at play*, Buena o mala suerte en el juego. *A day's run*, (Mar.) Singladura, el camino que hace una embarcación en veinte y cuatro horas. *In the long run*, Al fin, al cabo ; a la corta o a la larga ; tarde o temprano.

Runabout [run'-a-baut], *s.* 1. Persona callejera. 2. Automóvil pequeño. 3. Lancha pequeña de motor.

Runagate [run'-a-gêt], *s.* Renegado, apóstata ; vagamundo.

Runaway [run'-a-wê], *a.* y *s.* 1. Fugitivo, desertor ; que huye. 2. Efectuado o causado por medio de la fuga. *Runaway match*, Casamiento que sigue a un rapto o una fuga.

Runcinate [run'-si-nêt], *a.* (Bot.) Dentado, con los dientes inclinados hacia atrás.

Rundlet [rund'-let], *s.* Barrilejo, barril pequeño.

Rune [rūn], *s.* 1. Runa, cada uno de los caracteres que empleaban en la escritura los antiguos escandinavos. 2. Cualquier verso, poema, sentencia o dicho obscuros ; misterio.

Rung, *pret.* y *part.* de *To* Ring.

Rung [rung], *s.* 1. Paso, escalón, cualquiera de los peldaños de una escalera de mano. 2. (Mar.) Varengas, planes.

Runic [rū'-nic], *a.* Rúnico, runo ; perteneciente o relativo a las runas o al idioma de los godos y dinamarqueses.—*s.* Una forma de caracteres modernos de imprenta, v. g. runic.

Runlet, Runnel [run'-el], *s.* Arroyuelo. *V.* Rivulet.

Runner [run'-ẹr], *s.* 1. Corredor ; correo, mensajero. 2. Vástago, renuevo ; (Prov. Ingl.) tallo delgado, echado a la larga, que se arraiga por nudos y extremos. 3. La parte sobre que un objeto corre o se desliza ; corredera. 4. Corredera, la muela superior del molino. 5. Anillo movible ; pasador corredizo. 6. Operador de una máquina o locomotora. *Runner of a tackle*, (Mar.) Amante de aparejo. *Runner of a crowfoot*, (Mar.) Perigallo de araña.

Runner-up [run'-ẹr-up], *s.* Concursante que queda en segundo lugar.

Runnet [run'-et], *s.* *V.* Rennet.

Running [run'-ing], *s.* Carrera, corrida, curso.—*a.* 1. Corredor. 2. Que fluye, que contiene pus. 3. Corriente, que corre. *Running board*, Estribo de un automóvil. *Running gear*, Tren de rodaje, ejes y ruedas de un vehículo. *Running horse*, Caballo corredor. *Running sore*, Una herida con pus. *Running water*, Agua corriente.

Runnion [run'-yun], *s.* Pelafustán, pandorgo, persona despreciable.

Run-off [run'-ōf], *s.* 1. Agua de desagüe. 2. Carrera o competencia final para determinar el vencedor.

Runt [runt], *s.* 1. Redrojo, el animal más pequeño y débil de una lechigada o hato ; animal detenido en su crecimiento. 2. Enano.

Runway [run'-wê], *s.* 1. Vía o sendero por el que corre algo. 2. Lecho de un arroyo. 3. Senda por la que pasan animales. 4. Pista de aterrizaje para aviones.

Rupee [rū-pī'], *s.* Rupía, una moneda del Indostán ; vale dos chelines, 48 centavos, o unas 2.36 pesetas. *A lac* o *lakh of rupees*, Cien mil rupías.

Rupture [rup'-chur], *s.* 1. Rompimiento, rotura. 2. Rompimiento, riña, desavenencia, hostilidad. 3. Potra, hernia, quebradura.

Rupture, *va.* Reventar, romper o hacer pedazos una cosa, quebrar, separar con violencia.—*vn.* Abrirse, henderse, sin extrema violencia.

Rupturewort [rup'-chur-wūrt], *s.* (Bot.) Milengrana, herniaria.

Rural [rū'-ral], *a.* Rural, campesino, campestre, rústico.

Rurality [rū-ral'-i-ti], **Ruralness** [rū'-ral-nes], *s.* La calidad de lo que es rural o propio del campo.

Rurally [rū'-ral-i], *adv.* Ruralmente.

Ruse [rūz], *s.* Astucia, engaño, estafa ; acción con que se pretende engañar.

Rush [rush], *s.* 1. Junco, junquillo, enea. 2. Friolera, bagatela, cosa de poco valor. 3. *V.* Rushlight. *It is not worth a rush*, No vale un bledo o un ardite. *Rush-bottomed*, Con fondo de junco. *Rushlight*, Una especie de vela o lamparilla de noche con pábilo de junco. *Rush-mat*, Estera de junco.

Rush, *s.* 1. Ímpetu, movimiento furioso ; método o procedimiento enérgico. 2. Prisa grande, presión, demanda extraordinaria ; gran cantidad de algo que causa ímpetu o prisa. 3. Concurso, gentío, agolpamiento de gente, apretura. 4. (E. U.) Lucha, contienda violenta entre dos grupos de personas, cada uno de los cuales procura rechazar al otro. 5. Carrera precipitada.

Rush, *vn.* Arrojarse, abalanzarse, tirarse, dispararse : dícese de una persona o de un animal que da una embestida o salto impetuoso.—*va.* Empujar o arrojar con violencia, ejecutar con precipitación. *To rush forward*, Abalanzarse, arrojarse con ímpetu. *To rush in*, Entrar de rondón. *To rush in upon*, Sorprender. *To rush out*, Salir precipitadamente. *To rush through*, Ejecutar con precipitación o de prisa ; exponerse atrevidamente.

Rush hour [rush aur], *s.* Hora de mayor tránsito.

Rush order [rush ōr-dẹr], *s*: Pedido urgente.

Rust-proof [rust'-prūf], *a.* Inoxidable.

Rushy [rush'-i], *a.* Juncoso, lleno de juncos.

Rusk [rusc], *s.* Galleta, rosca.

Russet [rus'-et], *a.* 1. Bermejizo ; color mezcla de anaranjado y purpúreo ; vulgarmente, moreno rojizo o amarillento. 2. Burdo, tosco, grosero. 3. Acabado, pero no teñido de negro ; aplícase al calzado.—*s.* 1. Color producido por la mezcla de anaranjado y purpúreo. 2. Vestido de labrador o de un hombre del campo. 3. Variedad de manzana de color verdusco con manchas pardas.

Russeting [rus'-et-ing], *s.* Manzana de rosa, pera de rosa.

Russia [rush'-a o rū'-sha], *s.* 1. Rusia. *V.* Apéndice. 2. Piel de Rusia ; vaqueta de Moscovia.

Russian [rush'-an o rū'-shan], *a.* Ruso, de Rusia.—*s.* Ruso, natural o habitante de Rusia.

Rust [rust], *s.* 1. Orín, herrumbre, robín, el moho u óxido que cría el hierro o cualquier otro metal ; el óxido rojizo de hierro. 2. (Bot.) Añublo, tizón, enfermedad que ataca los trigos y se debe a un honguillo parásito ; el hongo que produce esa enfermedad. 3. Orín, mancha, defecto. *Rust of corn*, Tizón. *To gather rust*, Enmohecerse, criar moho u orín.

Rust, *vn.* 1. Enmohecerse, ponerse mohoso, cubrirse de moho o de orín. 2. Enmohecerse, embotarse : dícese del entendimiento o valor cuando se entorpecen por la falta de ejercicio.—*va.* 1. Enmohecer, poner mohoso, cubrir de orín una cosa de metal. 2. Entorpecer el entendimiento, el valor o el ingenio por no ponerlo en ejercicio.

Rustic [rus'-tic], *a.* 1. Rústico, agreste, villano, campesino ; sencillo, sin artificio ; inculto, grosero. 2. Que nota o pertenece a algún estilo irregular de trabajo o adorno propio del campo.—*s.* Patán, villano, rústico, hombre del campo.

Rustical [rus'-tic-al], *a.* (Ant.) Rústico, áspero.

Rustically [rus'-tic-al-i], *adv.* Rústicamente.

Rusticity [rus-tis'-i-ti], *s.* Rusticidad, simplicidad ; grosería, rudeza.

Rustily [rust'-i-li], *adv.* Con herrumbre, enmohecimiento o falta de uso.

Rustiness [rust'-i-nes], *s.* El estado de lo que se halla cubierto de orín o moho ; falta de uso.

Rustle [rus'-l], *va.* y *vn.* 1. Susurrar, hacer, o hacer producir una serie de sonidos rápidos y suaves (como los de las hojas, de las sedas, etc.) ; producir un sonido de rozamiento. 2. (Ger. E. U.) Conducirse con energía y actividad.—*s.* Rozamiento, ruido que hacen las hojas, las sedas, cuando se las frota o agita ; susurro.

Rustler [rus'-lẹr], *s.* 1. El o lo que susurra o produce ruido parecido al roce. 2. (Ger. E. U.) Hombre activo o emprendedor.

Rusty [rust'-i], *a.* 1. Oriniento, mohoso, herrumbroso, tomado de herrumbre o producido por ella. 2. Parecido a orín o herrumbre en el color ; rojizo o amarillento. 3. Entorpecido, debilitado por falta de uso ; que ha perdido su habilidad por falta de práctica. 4. Ronco, rudo, bronco (de tonos o sonidos). *Rusty bacon*, Tocino rancio.

Rut [rut], *va.* Hacer carriles, rodadas o surcos en el camino o suelo; (fig.) arrugar.—*s.* 1. Carril, rodada, la impresión o señal que deja la rueda en la tierra por donde pasa. 2. Costumbre, hábito arraigados; sendero trillado, pisado. (< route.)

Rut, *vn.* Bramar los venados, ciervos y otros animales cuando están en celo; estar en celo.—*s.* 1. Brama, unión del macho con la hembra, celo, excitación sexual en varios animales, v. g. los venados. 2. Mugido, bramido; ruido, batahola, alboroto. (Fr. < Lat. *rugitus*, rugido.) *Rutting-time*, Tiempo de brama, estación del celo.

Rutabaga [rū-ta-bê'-ga], *s.* Rutabaga, nabo sueco, variedad de nabo.

Ruth [rūth], *s.* (Ant.) Compasión, conmiseración; desgracia, miseria.

Ruthless [rūth'-les], *a.* Cruel, endurecido, insensible, falto de piedad.

Ruthlessly [rūth'-les-li], *adv.* Cruelmente, inhumanamente.

Ruthlessness [rūth'-les-nes], *s.* Crueldad, falta de piedad, de compasión; apatía por las desgracias ajenas.

Ruttish [rut'-ish], *a.* 1. Que tiende a hacer o correr en las rodadas. 2. Lascivo, libidinoso; salido.

Rutty [rut'-i], *a.* Lleno de carriles.

Rye [rai], *s.* 1. (Bot.) Centeno, especie de grano; planta gramínea y sus simientes. 2. (Fam. E. U.) Whisky destilado de centeno. *Rye-worm*, Gusano, larva de una mosca europea (Oscinis pumilionis), nociva a los tallos del centeno. *Spurred rye*, Centeno atizonado; cornezuelo. *V.* Ergot.

Rye bread [rai bred], *s.* Pan de centeno.

Rye-grass [rai'-gras], *s.* (Bot.) Grama de centeno.

Ryot [rai'-ot], *s.* En el Indostán, el que tiene tierras en arriendo perpetuo; labrador, villano. (Angloindio.)

S

El sonido de la *s* varía mucho en la lengua inglesa: en muchas voces tiene un sonido agudo, como en *soon, yes, muffs;* y en otras suave, como en *praise, ribs, churches.* Cuando precede a la *h*, tiene un sonido especial que conserva también en la mayor parte de las voces en que está seguida de *u* o *ion*, como en *pleasure, evasion.* En algunas voces es muda, como en *island, viscount.* *'s* es signo del posesivo o genitivo; también, contracción de *is*, es. *It's good*, Es bueno.—Como abreviatura significa la *S, sociedad, sud* o *sur;* como F. R. S., Miembro de la Sociedad Real. S. E., Sudeste; S. S. E., Sudsudeste, etc.

Sabal [sê'-bal o sa'-bal], *s.* Sabal, género de palmeras de los trópicos, que tienen hojas grandes en forma de abanico.

Sabaoth [sab'-ê-oth o sa-bā'-ōth], *s. pl.* Los ejércitos; es palabra hebrea. (< Heb. tsebāōth.)

Sabbatarian [sab-a-tê'-ri-an], *a.* y *s.* Nombre de unos sectarios que guardaban con el mayor rigor la fiesta del domingo; y por extensión se llama así a los que observan muy estrictamente la abstinencia de todo trabajo en este día.

Sabbath [sab'-ath], *s* Sábado, el día séptimo de la semana destinado entre los judíos al descanso, y por extensión se da este nombre a toda cesación de trabajo, pena o dolor, al tiempo de descanso, y al domingo, por ser el día dedicado entre los cristianos al reposo y al ejercicio de los deberes de la religión. *The Christian Sabbath*, Domingo, el primer día de la semana. *Sabbath-breaker*, Infractor o quebrantador del domingo. *Sabbath-day*, El día dedicado a obras de piedad y al reposo.

Sabbatical, Sabbatic [sab-bat'-i-cal], *a.* Sabático, perteneciente al sábado entre los judíos.

Sabbatism [sab'-a-tizm], *s.* La observancia supersticiosa y rígida del sábado.

Sabæan, Sabean [sê-bî'-an], *a.* *V.* Sabian.

Saber, Sabre [sê'-ber], *s.* Sable, arma blanca; espada de un solo filo. (< Fr. sabre.)—*va.* Acuchillar, herir a sablazos.

Sabian [sê'-bi-an], *a.* Sabeo, perteneciente a los sabeos o a su culto.—*s.* Sabeo, adorador del sol, entre los persas y caldeos; secta que reconoció la unidad de Dios.

Sabianism, *s.* Sabeísmo.

Sabine [sab'-in], *s.* (Bot.) Sabina. *V.* Savin.

Sable [sê'-bl], *s.* Cebellina, especie de comadreja o marta y también la piel de dicho animal.—*a.* (Her.) Sable, negro.

Sabot [sa-bō'], *s.* 1. Zueco, almadreña. 2. Disco adherido a un proyectil para hacerle mantener determinada posición dentro del cañón de un arma de fuego. 3. Pieza de empalme para acortar una cuerda del arpa. (Fr.)

Sabotage [sab-o-tāzh'], *s.* Sabotaje. —*va.* Sabotear.

Saboteur [sab-o-ter'], *s.* Saboteador.

Sabre [sê'-ber], *s* *V.* Saber.

Sac [sac], *s.* (Biol.) Saco, bolsa membranosa; cavidad o receptáculo.

Saccate [sak'-et o êt], *a.* En forma de bolsa o saco.

Sacchariferous [sac-a-rif'-er-us], *a.* Sacarífero, que da o produce azúcar.

Saccharimeter, Saccharometer [sac-a-rim- (o rom'-) e-ter], *s.* Sacarímetro, sacarómetro, instrumento que sirve para determinar la cantidad de azúcar contenida en un líquido.

Saccharin [sac'-a-rin], *s.* 1. Sacarina, compuesto azucarado que se obtiene del alquitrán de hulla. 2. Otro compuesto de un sabor amargo.

Saccharine [sac'-a-rin o rain], *a.* Sacarino, azucarado.

Saccharose [sac'-a-rōs], *s.* Azúcar (de caña, de remolacha) que desvía la luz polarizada hacia la derecha.

Sacerdotal [sas-er-dō'-tal], *a.* Sacerdotal.

Sacerdotalism [sas-er-dō'-tal-izm], *s.* Carácter y métodos sacerdotales; celo por las cosas sacerdotales; también, artimaña de un ministro de la religión.

Sachem [sê'-chem], *s.* Jefe hereditario de una tribu de indios norteamericanos; cacique.

Sachet [sa-shê'], *s.* Saquito para polvos perfumados. (Fr.)

Sack [sac], *s.* 1. Saco, saca, costal, talega. 2. Medida de tres fanegas. 3. Saco, el saqueo de una plaza. 4. Chaqueta, casaca suelta con mangas que usaron las personas de uno y otro sexo en los siglos XVII y XVIII; bata de mujer. 5. (Des.) Vino dulce de Canarias.

Sack, *va.* 1. Meter en sacos. 2. Saquear. *To sack up*, Ensacar.

Sackbut [sac'-but], *s.* 1. Sacabuche, un instrumento músico primitivo parecido al trombón. 2. En la Biblia, un instrumento de cuerda.

Sackcloth [sac'-clōth], *s.* 1. Arpillera, brea. 2. Cilicio.

Sack coat [sac cōt], *s.* Saco holgado de hombre.

Sacker [sak'-er], *s.* Saqueador, el que saquea.

Sackful [sac'-ful], *s.* Costal o saco lleno; lo bastante para llenar un saco.

Sacrament [sac'-ra-ment], *s.* 1. El juramento o ceremonia solemne que impone una obligación. 2. Sacramento. 3. El sacramento de la eucaristía. *To receive the sacrament*, Comulgar.

Sacramental [sac-ra-ment'-al], *a.* Sacramental.

Sacramentarian [sac-ra-men-tê'-ri-an], *a.* Sacramental, perteneciente a los sacramentos o a los sacramentarios. —*s.* Sacramentario, el que rechaza la doctrina luterana de la eucaristía.

Sacramentary [sac-ra-men'-ta-ri], *a.* Sacramental, concerniente a los sacramentos.—*s.* Sacramentario, antiguo libro que contenía todas las ceremonias y oraciones usadas en la celebración de los sacramentos.

Sacred [sê'-cred], *a.* Sagrado, sacro, consagrado; santo, concerniente a la religión; en relación con seres divinos o sobrenaturales; digno de reverencia; inviolable. *His sacred majesty*, La persona sagrada del rey.

Sacredly [sê'-cred-li], *adv.* Sagradamente, inviolablemente, religiosamente, santamente.

Sacredness [sê'-cred-nes], *s.* Santidad, carácter sagrado; consagración a Dios o a su culto; inviolabilidad.

Sacrific [sa-crif'-ic], *a.* Empleado en un sacrificio, de sacrificio.

Sacrifice [sac'-ri-faiz o fais], *va.* 1. Sacrificar, inmolar. 2. Sacrificar, abandonar, renunciar o perder una cosa por conservar otra. 3. Destruir, matar.—*vn.* Sacrificar, ofrecer sacrificios.

Sacrifice [sac'r-i-fais o faiz], *s.* 1. Sacrificio, el acto de sacrificar u ofrecer a la deidad alguna cosa y la misma cosa sacrificada u ofrecida; víctima. 2. Sacrificio, renunciación de alguna cosa apreciable hecha con repugnancia por amor, respeto o reconocimiento. 3. Pérdida sufrida sin compensación; destrucción, v. g. de una o más vidas. 4. (Com.) Sacrificio, rebaja en los precios que anula la ganancia o implica pérdida.

Sacrificer [sac'-ri-faiz-er], *s.* Sacrificador.

Sacrificial [sac-ri-fish'-al], *a.* Sacrificador, que pertenece a los sacrificios; empleado en los sacrificios; de la naturaleza de un sacrificio; ofrecido como expiación del pecado.

Sacrilege [sac'-ri-lej], *s.* Sacrilegio, lesión o violación de alguna cosa sagrada.

Sacrilegious [sac-ri-lî'-jus], *a.* Sacrílego.

Sacrilegiously [sac-ri-lî'-jus-li], *adv.* Sacrílegamente.

Sacring [sê'-cring], *s.* (Ant.) Consagración, el acto de consagrar. *Sacring-bell*, *V. Sanctus bell.*

Sacrist [sê'-crist], *s.* 1. *V.* Sacristan. 2. Copista de música y encargado de los libros de coro de una iglesia.

Sacristan [sac'-ris-tan], *s.* Sacristán, el empleado que cuida de los ornamentos y del aseo de la iglesia y sacristía.
Sacristy [sac'-ris-ti], *s.* Sacristía (de una iglesia).
Sacrum [sê'-crum], *s.* Sacro, hueso del espinazo, formado por cinco vértebras entre la región lumbar y el cóccix.
Sad [sad], *a.* 1. Triste, lúgubre, pensativo, melancólico. 2. Infausto, lastimoso, calamitoso. 3. Malo, perverso, cruel, funesto. 4. (Ant.) Obscuro, sombrío o triste en el color. 5. (Fam.) Travieso, malicioso, dispuesto a hacer diabluras. 6. (Prov.) Pesado, indigesto; se dice del pan. *Sad news,* Noticias infaustas o funestas. *To grow sad,* Entristecerse. *To make sad,* Entristecer, afligir. *A sad fellow,* Diablillo, hombre malicioso; un pícaro.
Sadden [sad'-n], *va.* y *vn.* 1. Entristecer, contristar, causar o dar tristeza, poner triste. 2. Hacer más obscuro un color. 3. Entristecerse, melancolizarse, ponerse triste.
Saddle [sad'-l], *s.* 1. Silla de montar (a caballo o en bicicleta). (S. Amer.) Galápago, silla de caballo. 2. Cojinete relleno de material blando (pelote, etc.) para el lomo de un caballo. 3. Entre carniceros, cuarto trasero de una res. 4. Lo que tiene la forma o posición de una silla. *Saddleback,* Cuesta o montaña con dos cumbres separadas por una ligera depresión. *Saddle of mutton,* Lomos de carnero. *Saddle-bow,* Arzón. *Saddle-cloth,* Mantilla de silla. *Saddle-tree,* Fuste de silla. *Pack-saddle,* Basto, albarda. *Saddle-backed,* Ancho de espaldas; encorvado. *Saddle-bag,* Alforja. (Mex.) Cojinillo. *Saddle-horse,* Caballo de silla. *Saddle-maker, V.* SADDLER. *Saddle-shaped,* En forma de silla de montar; (Geol.) en arco, encorvado y sin fractura en la cima.
Saddle, *va.* 1. Ensillar, poner o echar la silla al caballo u otro animal cuadrúpedo. 2. Cargar, poner a cuestas.
Saddle-galled [sad'-l-gōld], *a.* Lastimado por la silla. (Mex.) Desollado, en el sentido de despellejado.
Saddler [sad'-lẹr], *s.* Sillero, el que hace sillas de montar.
Saddlerock [sad'-l-rec], *s.* (E. U.) Ostra grande de primera calidad oriunda de Long Island, Estado de Nueva York.
Saddlery [sad'-lẹr-i], *s.* Herraje de talabartero o sillero.
Sadducee [sad'-yu-sî], *s.* Saduceo, miembro de una secta judía que negaba la inmortalidad del alma.
Sadism [sād'-izm], *s.* Sadismo.
Sadist [sād'-ist], *s.* Sadista.
Sadly [sad'-li], *adv.* Tristemente, miserablemente, mal. *Sadly hurt,* Herido de peligro. *To be sadly off,* Tener uno sus asuntos en mal estado.
Sadness [sad'-nes], *s.* Tristeza, pesadumbre, melancolía, abatimiento; aspecto tétrico, serio.
Sae [sê], *adv.* (Esco.) Así. *V.* So.
Saengerfest, Sängerfest [seng'-ẹr-fest], *s.* Fiesta musical en la que compiten dos o más sociedades corales. (Alemán.)
Safe [sêf], *a.* 1. Seguro, salvo, ileso, libre y exento de todo peligro, daño o riesgo. 2. Intacto, sin lesión. 3. Seguro, que ofrece toda clase de seguridades; hablando de personas, leal, digno de confianza. 4. Cierto, exento de duda o error. 5. Incapacitado para dañar u ofender, p. ej. por estar encarcelado, o haber muerto. *It is not safe for us to stay here,* No estamos seguros aquí. *Safe conscience,* Conciencia pura o tranquila. *I wish you safe home,* Deseo que llegue Vd. con felicidad. *Safe and sound,* Sano y salvo.
Safe, *s.* Lugar seguro para guardar objetos; en especial, caja de seguridad, arca o cofre fuerte a prueba de fuego o de ladrones; también, alacena para conservar carnes o manjares, despensa. *Safe-keeping,* Depósito, guardia o custodia segura; acto y efecto de poner una cosa en seguridad.
Safe-conduct [sêf-cen'-duct], *s.* Convoy, salvoconducto.
Safe-deposit box, safe-deposit vault [sêf-de-pez'-it bex,vōlt], *s.* Caja de seguridad (en un banco, etc.)
Safeguard [sêf'-gārd], *s.* Salvaguardia, defensa; carta de seguridad; escolta; defensa, abrigo.
Safeguard, *va.* Guardar, proteger.
Safely [sêf'-li], *adv.* Seguramente, sin peligro, á salvo, felizmente.
Safeness [sêf'-nes], *s.* Estado o condición de hallarse en seguridad.
Safety [sêf'-ti], *s.* Seguridad, resguardo, salvamento; exención de todo mal, daño o perjuicio. *Safety-belt,* Cinto de seguridad, salvavidas. *Safety-lamp,* Lámpara de seguridad, o de Davy, para los mineros: lámpara envuelta en tela metálica. *Safety-match,* Fósforo que se enciende solamente sobre una superficie especialmente preparada. *Safety-pin,* Imperdible, alfiler de seguridad. *Safety-valve,* Válvula de seguridad (en las máquinas de vapor).
Safety island [sêf'-ti ai'-land], *s.* Plataforma de seguridad (en las calles de mucho tránsito.)
Safety razor [sêf'-ti rê'-zer], *s.* Navaja de afeitar de seguridad.
Saffron [saf'-run], *s.* (Bot.) Azafrán (planta [Crocus sativus], las hebras o los estigmas de las flores, y el color).—*a.* Azafranado, de color de azafrán.
Sag [sag], *va.* Hacer ceder o doblegar por el medio.—*vn.* 1. Ceder a su propio peso, doblegarse, hundirse, particularmente en el medio; doblegarse, colgar toscamente. 2. Aflojar, flaquear, como bajo un infortunio. 3. (Mar.) Irse a la ronza. 4. Tardar, ser lento de movimiento.—*s.* Hundimiento. (< sueco, sacka.)
Saga [sê'-ga o sā'-ga], *s.* Saga, leyenda de los escandinavos.
Sagacious [sa-gê'-shus], *a.* Sagaz, vivo, sutil, penetrante.
Sagaciously [sa-gê'-shus-li], *adv.* Sagazmente, astutamente.
Sagaciousness [sa-gê'-shus-nes], **Sagacity** [sa-gas'-i-ti], *s.* Sagacidad, astucia; penetración, sutileza. *Sagacity* es voz más usada.
Sagapenum [sag-a-pî'-num], *s.* Sagapeno, serapino, una gomorresina de Egipto y Persia, algo transparente, amarga y con olor de ajo.
Sage [sêj], *s.* 1. (Bot.) Salvia, planta de la familia de las labiadas. *Sage-brush,* Artemisia, una especie parecida, arbusto. *Sage-cheese,* Queso aromatizado con hojas de salvia. 2. Sabio, filósofo.—*a.* Sabio; prudente; grave, sagaz; cuerdo.
Sagely [sêj'-li], *adv.* Sabiamente; cuerdamente, prudentemente.
Sageness [sêj'-nes], *s.* Sabiduría; gravedad; prudencia, cordura.
Sagittal [saj'-i-tal], *a.* Sagital.
Sagittary [saj-i-tê'-ri], **Sagittarius** [saj-i-tê'-ri-us], *s.* (Astr.) Sagitario.
Sago [sê'-go], *s.* (Bot.) Sagú, meollo de varias especies de palma de la India oriental, muy alimenticio.
Sahib [sā'-ib], *s.* Señor; tratamiento empleado en Persia y en el Indostán.
Said [sed], *pp.* de SAY. (For.) Citado, antedicho, ya nombrado.
Sail [sêl], *s.* (Mar.) 1. Vela, el paño de lona extendido sobre un palo y verga a fin de recibir el viento e impeler la nave. *Main-sail,* Vela mayor. *Main-top-sail,* Gavia. *Main-top-gallant-sail,* Juanete mayor. *Main-top-gallant-royal,* Sobrejuanete mayor. *Fore-sail,* Trinquete. *Fore-top-sail,* Velacho. *Fore-top-gallant-sail,* Juanete de proa. *Mizzen-sail,* Mesana. *Mizzen-top-sail,* Sobremesana. *Mizzen-top-gallant-sail,* Juanete de mesana. *Stay-sail,* Vela de estay. *Fore-stay-sail,* Trinquetilla. *Studding-sail,* Rastrera, ala. *Sprit-sail,* Cebadera. *To set sail,* Hacerse a la vela. *To strike sail,* Arriar una vela. 2. Vela, la misma embarcación. (En este sentido el plural no lleva *s*, y tiene la misma forma que el singular.) 3. Velas, número de embarcaciones. *Fleet of seventeen sail of the line,* Escuadra de diez y siete navíos de línea. 4. Excursión, paseo en barco de vela. *Sail-boat,* Barco de vela; barca, yate. *Sail-cloth,* Lona, lienzo para velas y toldos. *Sail-loft,* Tinglado, almacén de velas o lona; taller donde se hacen velas. *Sail-maker,* Fabricante de velas.
Sail, *vn.* 1. Darse a la vela, hacerse a la vela, dar las velas al viento, navegar. 2. Viajar por mar, río o lago; ir en una embarcación. 3. Volar sin aletear; flotar, ir por el aire (una nube). 4. (Fam.) Pasar sobre, moverse majestuosamente.—*va.* 1. Navegar, manejar o guiar una embarcación. 2. Navegar por, viajar en, cruzar en una embarcación. *To sail back,* Tomar puerto, entrar a descansar en algún puerto. *To sail along the coast,* Costear. *To sail before the wind,* (Mar.) Navegar a dos puños. *To sail with the wind on the beam,* (Mar.) Navegar con el viento a través. *To sail with a scant wind,* (Mar.) Navegar de bolina. *To sail close-hauled,* (Mar.) Navegar ciñendo el viento.
Sailable [sêl'-a-bl], *a.* Navegable (a la vela).
Sailer [sêl'-ẹr], *s.* Navío, buque, embarcación que sirve para navegar. *Good* o *fine sailer,* Navío velero.
Sailfish [sêl'-fish], *s.* Variedad de pez espada.
Sailing [sêl'-ing], *s.* 1. Acto de darse a la vela. 2. Navegación, arte de navegar. *Plain sailing,* (1) Avance, adelantamiento sin dificultades, literal o figuradamente; coser y cantar. (2) *V. Plane sailing. Plane sailing,* Acción de navegar sobre la carta de marear. *Great-circle sailing,* Navegación circular. *Sailing orders* o *instructions,* (1) Orden de salida o marcha dada a un buque de guerra. (2) Instrucciones que da el oficial naval de un convoy a los capitanes de los buques mercantes para que comprendan sus

señales y respondan a ellas, y para indicarles un punto de reunión en caso de ser dispersados por una tempestad.

Sailor [sêl'-ṣr], *s.* Marinero, hombre de mar. *Sailor's wages*, Mesadas, soldadas, sueldo de los marineros o de la tripulación.

Sailyard [sêl'-yard], *s.* Verga.

Saint [sênt], *s.* 1. Santo, la persona de virtud y piedad eminentes; (en el Nuevo Testamento, cualquier cristiano fiel); en especial, santo, santa, persona canonizada por la Iglesia. 2. Un ángel.—*a.* Santo; como título se escribe con mayúscula, y por lo común en abreviatura, St. *St. Andrew's cross*, Cruz de San Andrés; también, nombre de una planta de la familia de las hipericíneas. *St. John's wort*, Hierba de San Juan, hipérico, corazoncillo. *St. Vitus's dance*, Corea (baile de San Vito), enfermedad caracterizada por movimientos convulsivos. *St. Bernard*, Perro grande y sagaz, oriundo del hospicio de San Bernardo en los Alpes. *St. John's-bread*, Algarrobo, árbol. *V.* CAROB.

Saint, *va.* Canonizar.—*vn.* Fingir santidad.

Sainted [sênt'-ed], *a.* Santo; piadoso, virtuoso; sagrado.

Saint-like [sênt'-laic], *a.* Propio de un santo o de los santos.

Saintliness [sênt'-li-nes], *s.* Santidad, santificación.

Saintly [sênt'-li], *adv.* Santamente; piadosamente, virtuosamente.

Saintship, Sainthood [sênt'-ship], *s.* Santidad, carácter de santo.

Saith [seth]. (Ant.) Dice; 3ª *pers. pres. indic.* del verbo *To* SAY, decir. *What saith it?* ¿Qué dice?

Sake [sêc], *s.* Causa, motivo, fin, objeto, razón; amor, respeto, consideración. *For God's sake*, Por amor de Dios. *For brevity's sake*, En obsequio de la brevedad. *Do it for my sake*, Hágalo Vd. por mí. *For your sake*, Por Vd., por respeto a o de Vd., en obsequio o gracia de Vd. (Vulg.) Por mor de Vd. *For politeness' sake*, Por política.

Sal [sal], *s.* Sal; término de química o farmacia. *Sal ammoniac*, Sal amoniaco, cloruro de amoniaco. *Sal soda*, Sosa, carbonato de sodio para lavar.

Salaam, Salam [sa-lām'], *va.* y *vn.* Saludar a la oriental.—*s.* Reverencia oriental profunda, que se hace con la palma de la mano derecha sobre la frente.

Salable [sêl'-a-bl], *a.* Vendible, que puede ser vendido; de fácil venta.

Salableness [sêl'-a-bl-nes], *s.* La calidad que constituye a una cosa vendible o de despacho.

Salacious [sa-lé'-shus], *a.* Salaz, lascivo, lujurioso.

Salaciousness [sa-lé'-shus-nes], **Salacity** [sa-las'-i-ti], *s.* Salacidad, lascivia, lujuria.

Salad [sal'-ad], *s.* Ensalada. *Salad-bowl*, Ensaladera. *Salad dish*, Plato para la ensalada. *Salad dressing*, Salsa para la ensalada. *Salad greens*, Verduras para ensalada (tales como lechuga, espinaca, etc.). *Salad oil*, Aceite para ensalada (generalmente de oliva).

Salamander [sal'-a-man-dṣr], *s.* Salamandra, salamanquesa.

Salamander's-hair o **wool** [sal'-a-man-dṣrz-hār o wul], *s.* (Min.) Asbesto; amianto.

Salary [sal'-a-ri], *va.* ‡Asalariar, dar jornal, salario o sueldo.—*s.* Salario; sueldo, paga, jornal. *Salaried*, *pp.* Asalariado, que recibe un salario.

Sale [sêl], *s.* 1. Venta, acción y efecto de vender. 2. Almoneda, venta a pública subasta. 3: Oportunidad de vender; demanda por parte de los compradores; voga, mercado. *Sale by auction*, Almoneda, subasta. *For sale* u *on sale*, De venta; ofrecido o pronto para la venta. *On sale or return*, Contrato o pacto de retroventa.

Saleable, Saleableness. *V.* SALABLE, SALABLENESS.

Salep [sé'-lep], *s.* Salep, raíz seca del satirión.

Sale price [sêl' prais], *s.* 1. Precio de venta. 2. Precio en barata o realización.

Saleratus [sal-ṣr-é'-tus], *s.* Bicarbonato de sosa o potasa para usos culinarios.

Sales agent [sêlz ê'-jent], *s.* Agente vendedor.

Salesclerk [sêlz'-clṣrk], *s.* Dependiente, vendedor (en una tienda).

Salesgirl [sêlz'-gṣrl], *s.* Dependienta, vendedora (en una tienda).

Saleslady [sêlz-lê'-di], *s.* Dependienta (en una tienda).

Salesman [sêlz'-man], *m.* Vendedor, el que vende géneros en una tienda.

Salesmanship [sêlz'-man-ship], *s.* Arte de vender.

Salesperson [sêlz'-pṣr-sn], *s.* Dependiente, vendedor (en una tienda).

Sales quota [sêlz cwō'-ta], *s.* Cuota de ventas fijada a cada vendedor.

Sales resistance [sêlz re-zist'-ans], *s.* Resistencia a los argumentos de los vendedores.

Salesroom [sêlz'-rūm], *s.* Sala de ventas, sala de exhibición de mercancías.

Sales tax [sêlz tax], *s.* Impuesto sobre las ventas.

Saleswoman [sêlz'-wum-an], *sf.* Vendedora, la que vende géneros en una tienda; vulgarmente, *saleslady*.

Salic [sal'-ic], *a.* Sálico. *Salic law*, Ley sálica, en virtud de la cual sólo podían reinar en Francia los príncipes varones.

Salicin, Salicine [sal'-i-sin], *s.* Salicina, compuesto blanco, amargo y febrífugo ($C_{13}H_{18}O_7$) que se saca de la corteza de ciertos sauces y álamos; se emplea contra el reumatismo.

Salicylate [sal'-is-il-êt], *s.* Salicilato, sal formada con ácido salicílico y una base.

Salicylic [sal-is-il'-ic], *a.* Salicílico, perteneciente a ciertos sauces o derivado de ellos. *Salicylic acid*, Ácido salicílico, compuesto blanco y cristalizable ($C_7H_6O_3$), contenido en varias plantas y también se hace sintéticamente del ácido fénico. Es antiséptico y se emplea en medicina.

Salience [sé'-li-ens], *s.* Condición de saliente o salido; proyección, salidizo.

Salient [sé'-li-ent], *a.* Saltante, saliente, salido.

Saliferous [sa-lif'-ṣr-us], *a.* (Geol.) Salífero, que contiene sal.

Salify [sal'-i-fai], *va.* (Quím.) Salificar, formar una sal.

Saline [sé'-lain o sa-lain'], **Salinous** [sa-lai'-nus], *a.* Salino, que consiste en sal; que contiene sal; que tiene propiedades de sal.—*s.* Una sal de magnesio o de uno de los álcalis.

Salineness [sa-lain'-nes], *s.* La calidad o propiedad de salino.

Saliva [sa-lai'-va], *s.* Saliva.

Salival [sa-lai'-val], **Salivary** [sal'-i-vṣ-ri], *a.* Salival; salivoso.

Salivate [sal'-i-vêt], *va.* (Med.) Excitar la secreción excesiva y continua de saliva.

Salivation [sal-i-vé'-shun], *s.* Babeo, salivación, la excreción abundante de saliva, producida ordinariamente por algún remedio.

Salk vaccine [sok vac sin'], *s.* Vacuna Salk, vacuna contra la poliomielitis.

Sallet [sal'-et], *a.* Celada, especie de yelmo del siglo XV. (Fr. salade < Ital. celata.)

Sallow [sal'-o], *a.* Cetrino, descolorido, amarillo, pálido, lívido; se dice principalmente de la piel humana.—*s.* (Bot.) Sarga, una especie de sauce.

Sally [sal'-i], *s.* 1. (Mil.) Salida, surtida. 2. Paseo, excursión. 3. Ímpetu, arranque, pronto de alguna pasión o del genio; arrancada. 4. Despropósito; desahogo; un repente o una viveza nacida de irreflexión; humorada, extravagancia. 5. (Arq.) Salidizo, saliente, vuelo. *Sallies of wit*, Agudezas, rasgos, dichos prontos y vivos; ocurrencias graciosas o saladas. *To make sallies into the country*, Recorrer un terreno, dar frecuentes paseos por el campo.

Sally, *vn.* Salir, hacer una salida repentinamente; salir, avanzar con ánimo resuelto.

Sallyport [sal'-i-pōrt], *s.* (Fort.) Surtida, la puerta por donde los sitiados hacen sus salidas.

Salmon [sam'-un], *s.* 1. Salmón, pez de mar de carne rosada. 2. Color de la carne de salmón, anaranjado rosado. *Salmon louse*, Lombriz que se halla en las agallas del salmón.

Salmon-trout [sam'-un-traut], *s.* Trucha salmonada.

Saloon [sa-lūn'], *s.* 1. En E.U., una cantina o taberna donde se venden licores. 2. Sala de asamblea. 3. Sala grande de un vapor. 4. Vagón-salón en un ferrocarril.

Sal soda [sal sō'-da], *s.* Carbonato de sodio.

Salt [sōlt], *s.* 1. Sal, cloruro de sodio, substancia cristalina de sabor propio bien señalado y muy soluble en el agua. 2. (Quím.) Sal, cuerpo compuesto de un ácido y una base. 3. *pl.* Sales medicinales; cuando no se especifica, sal de higuera, sulfato de magnesia. 4. Sabor, gusto. 5. Sal, agudeza, gracia o viveza en lo que se dice.—*a.* 1. Salado, impregnado de sales; salobre, que tiene sabor de sal; salino. 2. Curado o conservado con sal. 3. Que contiene agua salada o que crece en ella. *Salt-box*, Caja para guardar la sal en la cocina, salero de cocina. *Saltcellar*, Salero de mesa. *Salt-bush*, Cualquiera de ciertas hierbas de Australia, principalmente del género Atriplex, especie de ceñiglo de la familia de las quenopodeas. Abundan en los saladares del interior y dan buen pasto. *Salt-junk*, Carne de buey dura, seca y salada para rancho de marinero. *Salt-lick*, Lamedero, lugar adonde acuden los animales para lamer la sal de depósitos superficiales. *Glauber's salt*, Sal de Glauber, sulfato de sodio. *Rochelle salt*, Tartrato de potasio y sodio. *Rock salt*, Sal gema. *Not (to be) worth one's salt*, No valer uno el pan que come. *To be sent* o *to go up Salt River*, (Ger. E. U.) Ser vencido; dícese de candidatos políticos, y es alusión a un pequeño río del Kentucky. *Salt-mines*, Minas de sal, salinas. *Salt-maker*, Salinero, el que trabaja en las minas de sal o en las salinas. *Salt meat*, *s.* Carne salada; cecina. *Salt-pan*, (1) Caldera o vasija en que se hace la sal evaporando el agua salada; (2) saladar, *V. Salt-pit*. *Salt-pit*, Saladar, lagunajo, el sitio donde se cría o obtiene la sal por evaporación natural; salina. *Salt-spring*, Fuente de agua salada. *Salt-tub*, Saladero. *Salt-works*, Salina, lugar donde se hace, beneficia o cuaja la sal.

Salt, *va.* 1. Salar, sazonar con sal, curar con sal; salpimentar. 2. (Fig.) Sazonar; purificar. 3. (Ger.) Depositar fraudulentamente mineral rico en una mina sin valor.

Saltant [sal'-tant], *a.* Saltante.

Saltation [sal-tê'-shun], *s.* Saltación; palpitación.

Saltatorial [sal-ta-tō'-ri-al], **Saltatory** [sal'-ta-to-ri], *a.* Saltón.

Salter [sōlt'-ẹr], *s.* 1. Salador, el que sala. 2. Salinero, el que vende sal.

Saltern [sōlt'-ẹrn], *s.* Salina, el lugar donde se beneficia la sal.

Saltier [sal'-tīr], *s.* (Her.) Sotuer, cruz o aspa de San Andrés.

Saltigrade [sal'-ti-grêd], *a.* Saltígrado, que anda a saltos; aplícase en particular a una clase de arañas.

Saltine [selt-īn'], *s.* Galleta de soda.

Salting [sōlt'-ing], *s.* Salazón, acción de salar. *Salting-tub*, Saladero.

Saltish [sōlt'-ish], *a.* Sabroso, algo salado.

Saltless [sōlt'-les], *a.* Soso, desabrido, insulso, insípido.

Salt marsh [sōlt' mārsh], *s.* Saladar o marisma.

Saltness [sōlt'-nes], *s.* Sabor de sal; saladura.

Saltpeter, **Saltpetre** [solt-pī'-tẹr], *s.* Nitro, salitre. *Saltpetre-house*, Salitrería. *Saltpetre-maker*, Salitrero.

Salt-rheum [sōlt-rūm'], *s.* Enfermedad del cutis, eczema o herpes.

Saltwort [selt'-wūrt], *s.* Barrilla, sosa, nombre de diferentes plantas de los géneros Salsola y Salicornia.

Salty [sōlt'-i], *a.* Sabroso, un poco salado; salobre, salobreño.

Salubrious [sa-lū'-bri-us], *a.* Salubre, saludable.

Salubrity [sa-lū'-bri-ti], **Salubriousness** [sa-lū-bri-us-nes], *s.* Salubridad.

Salutary [sal'-yu-tẹ-ri], *a.* Saludable, salubre, sano, salutífero.

Salutation [sal-yu-tê'-shun], *s.* Salutación, saludo; bienvenida, enhorabuena, parabién.

Salutatory [sa-lū'-ta-to-ri], *a.* Saludador.—*s.* La oración con que principian los ejercicios el día de recepción de grados en los colegios y universidades americanos; discurso de bienvenida.

Salute [sa-lūt'], *va.* 1. Saludar, mostrar a otro benevolencia, respeto o deferencia. 2. Honrar con una salva de artillería o fusilería, o porte de armas; enarbolar el pabellón, etc., saludar. 3. (Ant.) Besar.—*vn.* Ofrecer un saludo.

Salute, *s.* 1. Salutación; saludo, acción o actitud de saludar. 2. Salva, descarga de armas en honor de alguien; saludo hecho portando el arma; honras militares, navales, u otras de carácter oficial. 3. Beso, abrazo.

Salvability [sal-va-bil'-i-ti], **Salvableness** [sal'-va-bl-nes], *s.* La posibilidad de ser redimido, de salvarse o ir a la gloria.

Salvable [sal'-va-bl], *a.* Que puede salvarse.

Salvage [sal'-vẹj], *s.* 1. Salvamento. 2. Derecho de salvamento que se cobra de las cosas salvadas de un naufragio. 3. Lo recuperado en un incendio o un naufragio.—*va.* Salvar (en un naufragio, incendio, etc.).

Salvage-money [sal'-vẹj-mun'-i], *s.* Derecho de salvamento.

Salvation [sal-vê'-shun], *s.* Salvación, estado del que se halla libre de peligro; salvación, consecución de la bienaventuranza eterna. *Salvation Army*, Ejército de Salvación, una organización religiosa fundada por Guillermo Booth en 1865 con el nombre de "Misión cristiana," y que tomó el presente nombre en 1878.

Salve [sāv], *s.* Emplasto, ungüento; auxilio, socorro, remedio. *Lip-salve*, Pomada para los labios.

Salve, *va.* 1. Curar una herida o úlcera aplicando ungüentos o emplastos. 2. Salvar, socorrer, remediar, auxiliar. 3. Salvar, evitar algún inconveniente, impedimento, dificultad o riesgo.

Salver [sal'-vẹr], *s.* Salvilla, bandeja.

Salvia [sal'-vi-a], *s.* (Bot.) Salvia.

Salvo [sal'-vo], *s.* 1. Reservación, excusa, escapatoria, subterfugio; restricción mental; excepción. 2. Salva de artillería, saludo militar o naval.

Samara [sa-mê'-ra o sam'-a-ra], *s.* (Bot.) Nombre de un fruto indehiscente, o semilla alada, como las del olmo, el fresno y el arce.

Samaritan [sa-mar'-i-tan], *a.* Samaritano, samarita, de Samaria.—*s.* 1. Samarita, samaritano. 2. Persona benévola; en alusión a la parábola de San Lucas.

Samba [sam'-ba], *s.* Samba, baile y canto populares del Brasil.

Sambo [sam'-bo], *s.* 1. Un negro; apodo muy común. 2. Zambo.

Same [sêm], *a.* Mismo, idéntico; igual. *The same*, Lo mismo, la misma cosa, otro tanto; todo uno. *It is all the same to me*, Para mí es todo uno; no me importa; lo mismo me da. *Much the same as*, Casi como. *If it is the same to you*, Si le es a Vd. lo mismo, o igual.

Sameness [sêm'-nes], *s.* 1. Identidad. 2. Semejanza fiel.

Samlet [sam'-let], *s.* Salmón pequeño, salmonete. (En vez de *Salmonet.*)

Samovar [sā'-mo-vār], *s.* Urna rusa de cobre destinada a contener agua hirviendo, v. g. para hacer te.

Samp [samp], *s.* (E. U.) Maíz descortezado sin moler o gachas hechas con él.

Samphire [sam'-fair], *s.* (Bot.) Hinojo marino.

Sample [sam'-pl], *s.* 1. Muestra, prueba. 2. Ejemplo, dechado, patrón.

Sample, *va.* Sacar una muestra de algo; probar o examinar por medio de una porción o muestra.

Sample book [sam'-pl buk], *s.* Muestrario, libro de muestras.

Sampler [sam'-plẹr], *s.* 1. El que prueba o examina por medio de muestras; el que prepara o exhibe muestras de artículos de comercio. 2. Dechado, labor de las niñas.

Sanative [san'-a-tiv], *a.* Curativo, sanativo, que sana.

Sanatorium [san-a-tō'-ri-um], *s.* 1. Lugar adonde acuden las gentes para conservar la salud, v. g. una estación balnearia o un punto de veraneo en los climas tropicales. 2. Casa de salud, sanatorio, establecimiento adonde los enfermos van voluntariamente á someterse a un régimen especial, bajo la dirección de un médico especialista.

Sanctification [saṇc-ti-fi-kê'-shun], *s.* Santificación; consagración.

Sanctifier [saṇc'-ti-fai-ẹr], *s.* Santificador.

Sanctify [saṇc'-ti-fai], *va.* Santificar.

Sanctimonious [saṇc-ti-mō'-ni-us], *a.* Beato, mojigato, parecido o semejante á santo.

Sanctimoniously [saṇc-ti-mō'-ni-us-li], *adv.* Con santimonia o apariencia de santidad.

Sanctimoniousness [saṇc'-ti-mō'-ni-us-nes], *s.* Apariencia de santidad, aire falso de santidad, mojigatería.

Sanctimony [saṇc'-ti-mo-ni], *s.* 1. Santimonia, santidad. 2. Apariencia de santidad; beatería.

Sanction [saṇc'-shun], *s.* 1. Sanción, el acto solemne por el que se ratifica, autoriza o confirma una ley o estatuto. 2. Sanción, establecimiento o ley; mandato, decreto. 3. Ratificación, confirmación; justificación. —*va.* Sancionar, dar fuerza de ley; autorizar, ratificar, validar; venir en apoyo de, confirmar.

Sanctitude [saṇc'-ti-tiūd], *s.* (Ant.) Carácter sagrado, santidad.

Sanctity [sanc'-ti-ti], *s.* 1. Santidad, el estado o la naturaleza de sagrado o santo; pureza espiritual. 2. Calidad de sagrado, solemnemente obligatorio, o inviolable; inviolabilidad.

Sanctuary [saṇct'-yu-ẹ-ri], *s.* 1. Santuario, lugar santo o sagrado; templo, altar de santo. Entre los israelitas, la parte más retirada del tabernáculo o templo. 2. Asilo, refugio sagrado. *To take sanctuary*, Acogerse a sagrado.

Sanctum [sanc'-tum], *s.* Paraje sagrado; familiarmente, una pieza reservada, una oficina particular. *Sanctum sanctorum*, Sanctasanctórum.

Sanctus [saṇc'-tus], *s.* Sanctus, parte de la misa antes del canon, en que se repite esta palabra tres veces. *Sanctus bell*, Campanilla que sirve para anunciar la elevación de la sagrada hostia en la misa.

Sand [sand], *s.* 1. Arena, partículas o granos pequeños de piedra sueltos o separados. 2. Arenal, tierra estéril cubierta de arena. 3. *pl.* (1) Arenales, playa de arena; regiones donde no se halla más que arena. (2) Partículas o granos arenosos semejantes a los del reloj de arena; de aquí, momentos de tiempo o de vida. 4. (Ger. E. U.) (1) Fuerza de carácter, sufrimiento; valor. (2) Dinero contante, caudales. *Sand-bank*, Banco de arena. *Small sand*, Arenilla. (Mex.) Marmajita o margajita. *Sand-bag*, Saco de arena, saco para arena; se emplea para construir fortificaciones, para lastre, etc., y también como arma ofensiva. *Sand-bar*, Barra, banco de arena en la embocadura de un río, o a lo largo de playas, etc. *Sand-blast*, Aparato para impeler un chorro de arena a fin de desgastar o grabar modelos en el vidrio, mármol, etc. *Sand-fly*, Mosca de los arenales, insecto pequeño muy incómodo del género Simulium. *Sand-glass*, Reloj de arena. *Sand-wasp*, Avispa de arena, toda avispa que cava en la tierra. *Sand-bath*, (Quím.) Baño de arena. *Sand-blind*, Corto de vista. *Sand-box*, (1) Salvadera (para echar arenilla sobre lo que se escribe). (2) Depósito de arena que se pone en una locomotora y sirve para echar arena delante de las ruedas e impedir que resbalen.

Sand, *va.* Enarenar, cubrir o mezclar con arena.

Sandal [san'-dal], *s.* Sandalia, especie de calzado suelto hecho de una suela que se asegura al tobillo con correas.

Sandalwood [san'-dal-wud], *s.* Sándalo, árbol de la India, y su madera olorosa. *Red sandalwood* o *sanderswood*, Madera de sándalo rojo (el Pterocarpus santalinus).

Sandarac, Sandarach [san'-da-rac], *s.* 1. Sandáraca, la resina del enebro; grasilla. 2. *V.* REALGAR.

Sandbag [sand'-bag], *s.* Saco de arena.

Sandblast [sand'-blast], *s.* Chorro de arena.—*va.* Limpiar (paredes, etc.) mediante un chorro de arena.

Sandbox-tree [sand'-box-trí], *s.* (Bot.) Hura, especie de nogal de América.

Sand dune [sand diūn], *s.* Duna.

Sanded [sand'-ed], *a.* 1. Arenoso, arenisco, lleno o cubierto de arena. 2. Color de arena; marcado con puntos menudos, pecoso.

Sanders [san'-derz], *s.* (Bot.) Sándalo. *V.* SANDALWOOD.

Sandiness [sand'-i-nes], *s.* 1. Naturaleza arenosa. 2. Rubio ardiente de la tez o cabellera.

Sandiver [sand'-i-ver], *s.* Anatrón, la sal y espuma del vidrio que se saca en las fábricas.

Sandpaper [sand'-pê-per], *s.* Papel de lija.

Sandpiper [sand'-pai-per], *s.* Actitis o tringa, ave zancuda semejante a la agachadiza, que por lo común frecuenta las orillas del mar en bandadas.

Sandpit [sand'-pit], *s.* Arenal.

Sandstone [sand'-stōn], *s.* Piedra arenisca, roca que consta de granos de cuarzo.

Sandstorm [sand'-stōrm], *s.* Tormenta de arena.

Sandwich [sand'-wich], *s.* Sandwich, emparedado. *Sandwich man*, Individuo metido entre dos carteles anunciadores que ambula por las calles.—*va.* Colocar entre dos capas, intercalar.

Sandy [sand'-i], *a.* 1. Arenoso, arenisco; abundante en arena; que consta o está cubierto de arena; de arena, o que la contiene. 2. Rufo, del color de la arena, rubio ardiente.

Sane [sên], *a.* Sano de mente; que está en posesión de todas sus facultades mentales; que proviene de una mente sana.

Saneness [sên'-nes], *s.* Sanidad del ánimo.

Sang [sang], *pret.* de *To* SING.

Sang, Sheng, *s.* Instrumento chino de viento que contiene trece tubos.

Sangaree [san-ga-rí'], *s.* Sangría, bebida que se compone de vino tinto, agua, azúcar, una raja de limón, etc. (< Esp. sangría.)

Sanguiferous [san-gwif'-er-us], *a.* Sanguífero; sanguificativo.

Sanguifier [san'-gwi-fai-er], *s.* La cosa que se puede convertir en sangre por medio de la digestión y sanguificación.

Sanguify [san'-gwi-fai], *vn.* Sanguificar, criar sangre.

Sanguinariness [san'-gwi-ne-ri-nes], *s.* Calidad de sanguinario.

Sanguinary [san'-gwi-ne-ri], *a.* Sanguinario, cruel, bárbaro, inhumano.

Sanguine [san'-gwin], *a.* 1. Sanguíneo, sanguino, de color de sangre. 2. Sanguíneo: dícese de uno de los temperamentos o complexiones. 3. Ardiente, violento, vehemente; atrevido, temerario, impetuoso; confiado, lleno de esperanza.—*s.* Color de sangre.

Sanguinely [san'-gwin-li], *adv.* Ardientemente; confiadamente, con esperanzas de buen éxito.

Sanguineness [san'-gwin-nes], *s.* 1. Estado o calidad del que está lleno de esperanza, confianza, ardor o arrojo; originalmente, temperamento sanguíneo. 2. Plenitud de sangre, plétora; color de sangre en la piel.

Sanguineous [san-gwin'-e-us], *a.* 1. Sanguino, que abunda en sangre o la aumenta y cría. 2. Sanguíneo, sanguino, que pertenece a la sangre, que constituye la sangre. 3. Encarnado, de color de sangre.

Sanhedrin, Sanhedrim [san'-he-drin, drim], *s.* 1. Sanedrín, sanhedrín o sinedrio, el consejo supremo de los judíos, compuesto de 71 personas. 2. (Fig.) Todo consejo o asamblea.

Sanies [sê'-ni-iz], *s.* (Med.) Sanies, sanie, podre, pus icoroso, materia corrompida, verdosa y fétida, que sale de las úlceras.

Sanious [sê'-ni-us], *a.* Purulento, sanioso, icoroso.

Sanitarian [san-i-tê'-ri-an], *a.* Sanitario, perteneciente a la salud pública o a las reglas de la higiene.—*s.* Promovedor de una reforma sanitaria.

Sanitarium [san-i-tê'-ri-um], *s.* *V.* SANATORIUM (2ª acep.).

Sanitary [san'-i-te-ri], *a.* Sanitario, higiénico, relativo a la salud. *Sanitary napkin*, Servilleta sanitaria, almohadilla higiénica.

Sanitation [san-i-tê'-shun], *s.* Saneamiento, higiene.

Sanity [san'-i-ti], *s.* Juicio sano, sentido común; sanidad, estado sano de la inteligencia, del espíritu y de la voluntad.

Sanskrit, Sanscrit [san'-skrit], *s.* y *a.* Sánscrito, lengua sagrada del Indostán, que tiene gran afinidad con las principales de Europa.

Santon [san'-ten], *s.* Santón, monje o fraile turco. (Esp.)

Santonin, Santonine [san'-to-nin], *s.* Santonina, cuerpo cristalizable y ponzoñoso que se extrae del semencontra (Santonica), una variedad de artemisa. Se emplea como vermífugo.

Sap [sap], *s.* 1. Savia, el jugo o suco nutricio de los árboles y plantas. 2. (Mil.) Zapa, una especie de mina. 3. *V.* *Sap-wood.* *Sap-green*, Verde del jugo del ramno. *Sap-wood*, Albura, alburno, la madera nueva próxima a la corteza de un árbol.

Sapajou [sap'-a-jū], *s.* Sapajú, cierta especie de mono (del género Cebus) llamado también llorón.

Sap, *va.* 1. Zapar, minar una muralla o fortificación. 2. Minar, abrir camino por debajo de tierra. 3. Minar, procurar cautelosamente la ruina o destrucción de una cosa.—*vn.* Caminar por mina o debajo de tierra; obrar ocultamente o por bajo mano; introducirse furtiva y cautelosamente en alguna parte.

Sapan-wood [sa-pan'-wud], *s.* Sapán, madera de tinte de la India.

Sapful [sap'-ful], *a.* Lleno de savia.

Saphenous [sa-fí'-nus], *a.* (Anat.) Superficial, manifiesto; dícese de ciertas venas y nervios de la pierna.

Sapid [sap'-id], *a.* Sabroso, gustoso, deleitable al paladar.

Sapidity, Sapidness [sa-pid'-i-ti, sap'-id-nes], *s.* Sabor, gusto, de los alimentos.

Sapience [sê'-pi-ens], *s.* Sabiduría, (ant.) sapiencia.

Sapient [sê'-pi-ent], *a.* Sabio.

Sapiential [sê-pi-en'-shal], *a.* (Poco us.) Sapiencial; perteneciente a la sabiduría; instructivo.

Sapling [sap'-ling], *s.* Renuevo, árbol joven; de aquí, un joven, y en particular, cachorro de lebrel.

Saponaceous [sap-o-nê'-shus], *a.* Jabonoso, saponáceo, que tiene la naturaleza o las propiedades del jabón.

Saponifiable [sa-pon-i-fai'-a-bl], *a.* Saponificable.

Saponification [sa-pon"-i-fi-kê'-shun], *s.* Saponificación, el procedimiento o resultado de hacer jabón o saponificar.

Saponify [sa-pon'-i-fai], *va.* Saponificar, convertir en jabón.

Saporific [sap-o-rif'-ic], *a.* Saporífero, que causa sabor.

Sapper [sap'-er], *s.* (Mil.) Zapador, el que zapa.

Sapphic [saf'-ic], *a.* Sáfico, que se refiere a la poetisa griega Safo.—*s.* Sáfico, especie de verso.

Sapphire [saf'-air], *s.* 1. Zafir o zafiro, piedra preciosa de color cerúleo, variedad dura y transparente del corindón. 2. Color azul obscuro, cerúleo.

Sappiness [sap'-i-nes], *s.* 1. El estado o la calidad de lo que abunda en savia, jugosidad. 2. Mentecatería, conducta pueril.

Sappy [sap'-i], *a.* 1. Que abunda en savia. 2. Jugoso, que abunda en jugos. 3. Inmaturo; mentecato, débilmente sentimental, propenso a puerilidades.

Saraband [sar'-a-band], *s.* Zarabanda, tañido y danza española de carácter majestuoso, en tres tiempos. Es de origen morisco. (< Per. serbend, canto.)

Saracen [sar'-a-sen], *s.* Sarraceno; enemigo muslímico de los cristianos de la edad media.

Saracenic [sar-a-sen'-ic], *a.* Sarracénico, perteneciente á los sarracenos; moro. (Gr. < Ar.)

Sarasin, Sarasine, *s.* *V.* SARRASIN.

Sarbacand [sār'-ba-cand], *s.* Cerbatana. (F. ant. sarbacane.)

Sarcasm [sār'-cazm], *s.* Sarcasmo, ironía acerba, burla o sátira picante.

Sarcastic, Sarcastical [sar-cas'-tic, al], *a.* Sarcástico, mordaz, picante, irónico.

Sarcastically [sār-cas'-tic-al-i], *adv.* Mordazmente, sarcásticamente.

Sarcel [sār'-sel], *s.* Una de las plumas del alón de cualquier ave, y particularmente del halcón.

Sarcenet [sārs'-net], *s.* *V.* SARSENET.

Sarco-, Sarc-. Formas de combinación del griego *sarx*, carne.

Sarcocarp [sãr'-co-carp], *s.* (Bot.) Sarcocarpio, la parte carnosa de un fruto drupáceo entre la piel y el hueso o endocarpio; v. g. en un pérsico.
Sarcocele [sãr'-co-sîl], *s.* Sarcocele, tumor duro y sólido del testículo; enfermedad cística del testículo.
Sarcocolla [sãr-co-col'-a], *s.* Sarcócola, goma de un árbol de Persia.
Sarcologic, Sarcological [sar-co-loj'-ic, al], *a.* Sarcológico, referente a la sarcología.
Sarcology [sãr-col'-o-ji], *s.* Sarcología, la parte de la anatomía que trata de las partes blandas.
Sarcoma [sãr-cō'-ma], *s.* Sarcoma, tumor o excrecencia que se cría en alguna parte del cuerpo sin cambio de color; frecuentemente es maligno.
Sarcomatous [sar-cem'-a-tus o sar-cō'-ma-tus], *a.* Sarcomatoso, referente al sarcoma; de la naturaleza del sarcoma.
Sarcophagous [sãr-cef'-a-gus], *a.* Carnívoro: dícese del animal que se mantiene de carne.
Sarcophagus [sãr-cef'-a-gus], *s.* 1. Sarcófago, ataúd de piedra o tumba en forma de cofre. 2. Sarcófagos, variedad de piedra caliza empleada por los griegos para sepulcros; se suponía consumir las carnes de los cadáveres depositados en ella.
Sarcophagy [sãr-cef'-a-ji], *s.* La costumbre de comer carne.
Sarcotic [sãr-cet'-ic], *a.* (Cir.) Sarcótico, que produce o regenera la carne.—*s.* Medicamento sarcótico.
Sard, Sardel, Sardine [sãrd, sãr'-del, sãr'-din], *s.* Sardio, especie de cornerina; se considera y emplea como piedra preciosa.
Sardel [sãr'-del], *s.* Sardina; también otro pececillo clupeido.
Sardine [sar-dîn'], *s.* Sardina, arenque menor; uno de los varios pececillos que se conservan en aceite.
Sardinian [sar-din'-i-an], *a.* Sardo, de Cerdeña.
Sardonic [sar-den'-ic] o **Sardonian** [sar-dō'-ni-an], *s.* 1. Sardónico, insincero y burlón; burlador. 2. Antiguamente, forzado, no natural (risa). *Sardonic laughter,* Risa sardónica.
Sardonyx [sãr'-do-nics], *s.* Sardónice, piedra preciosa, sardonio, sardónique o sardónix, variedad de ónice que consta de capas de calcedonia de colores claros, alternadas con capas rojizas de cornerina.
Sargasso [sar-gas'-o], *s.* Sargazo, alga marina con vejiguillas entallecidas y llenas de aire.
Sark [sãrk], *s.* (Prov. Ingl.) Camisa (de hombre o mujer); de aquí, mortaja.
Sarmentum [sãr-men'-tum], **Sarment** [sar'-ment], *s.* Sarmiento, tallo o vástago rastrero. *V.* RUNNER.
Sarmentose [sãr-men'-tōs], *a.* Sarmentoso, parecido al sarmiento, que produce tallos rastreros.
Sarrasin [sar'-a-sin], *s.* Rastrillo de defensa. *V.* PORTCULLIS.
Sarsaparilla [sar-sa-pa-ril'-a], **Sarsa** [sar'-sa], *s.* (Bot.) Zarzaparrilla.
Sarsenet, Sarsnet [sãrs'-net], *s.* Tafetán de Florencia, especie de tela delgada de seda que se emplea para forros.
Sartorial [sar-tō'-ri-al], *a.* Sartorio, de sastre; perteneciente a un sastre.
Sash [sash], *va.* Poner una banda, cíngulo o ceñidor a una persona.
Sash, *s.* 1. Banda o faja de seda que usan los oficiales militares, ya terciada, ya ceñida; cíngulo, cinturón, ceñidor, cinto. 2. Bastidor o marco de ventana, o vidriera; vidriera corrediza, la que se sube y baja con poleas y cuerdas. 3. Chal largo y muy angosto.
Sassafras [sas'-a-fras], *s.* (Bot.) Sasafrás, árbol americano de las lauráceas; también la corteza de las raíces, cuya infusión es un estimulante aromático.
Sat, *pret.* y *pp.* del verbo *To* SIT.
Satan [sê'-tan], *s.* Satanás, el diablo, el jefe de los ángeles caídos.
Satanic, Satanical [sa-tan'-ic, al], *a.* Satánico, diabólico, infernal.
Satanically [sa-tan'-ic-al-i], *adv.* Diabólicamente, satánicamente.
Satchel [sach'-el], *s.* Burjaca o bursaca; mochila, bolsa, maletilla, saco de mano.
Sate [sêt], *va.* Hartar, saciar a uno de comida. *V.* SATIATE.
Sateen [sa-tîn'], *s.* Rasete. cierta tela lustrosa de algodón y a veces de estambre.
Satellite [sat'-el-ait], *s.* 1. (Astr.) Satélite. *Man-made satellite,* Satélite artificial. 2. Satélite, subalterno obsequioso, persona que asiste o acompaña a otra que se halla en el poder.
Satiable [sê'-shi-a-bl], *a.* Saciable, que puede saciarse.
Satiate [sê'-shi-êt], *va.* 1. Saciar, hartar, llenar; satisfacer completamente los deseos o pasiones. 2. Saturar, colmar, sobrecargar, sobrellenar.—*vn.* Hartarse, saciarse.
Satiate, *a.* Harto, saciado, satisfecho; saturado.
Satiation [sê-shi-ê'-shun], *s.* Hartazgo, el acto y efecto de hartarse o saciarse; saciedad.
Satiety [sa-tai'-e-ti], *s.* Saciedad, hartura, plenitud que sobrepasa los deseos; repleción.
Satin [sat'-in], *s.* Raso, tela de seda lustrosa, tupida y suave. *Satin-bird,* Pájaro muy vistoso de Australia, (Ptinolorynchus holosericeus). *Satin-damask,* Raso con rico dibujo de flores o arabescos, lisos o en relieve. *Satin-flower,* Lunaria, planta y su flor.
Satinet [sat'-in-et], *s.* 1. Satinete, cotonía arrasada, especie de tela fuerte de lana y algodón. 2. Rasete, especie de raso delgado.
Satinwood [sat'-in-wud], *s.* Palo águila, madera dura y lustrosa, una de varias maderas de las Indias orientales y occidentales que se emplean en la ebanistería.
Satiny [sat'-in-i], *a.* Arrasado, parecido al raso o propio de él.
Satire [sat'-air], *s.* Sátira, obra en que se motejan las costumbres, vicios, etc, 2. Sátira, cualquier dicho agudo, picante y mordaz.
Satiric, Satirical [sa-tir'-ic, al], *a.* Satírico, que contiene una sátira; de la naturaleza de la sátira.
Satirically [sa-tir'-ic-al-i], *adv.* Satíricamente.
Satirist [sat'-ir-ist], *s.* Escritor de sátiras, autor satírico.
Satirize [sat'-ir-aiz], *va.* Satirizar, motejar con sátiras, escribir sátiras.
Satisfaction [sat-is-fac'-shun], *s.* 1. Satisfacción, contento, cumplimiento del deseo o gusto. 2. Satisfacción, recompensa o reparación por algún delito, agravio o injuria. 3. Lo que satisface o recompensa; razón, reparación, compensación; pago (de una deuda o cuenta). *In full satisfaction of a debt, of a demand,* En pago final de una deuda, en saldo de una cuenta.
Satisfactorily [sat-is-fac'-to-ri-li], *adv.* Satisfactoriamente, suficientemente; de una manera satisfactoria o convincente.
Satisfactoriness [sat-is-fac'-to-ri-nes], *s.* Calidad de satisfactorio.
Satisfactory [sat-is-fac'-to-ri], *a.* Satisfactorio, que da o produce satisfacción o contento; expiatorio; suficiente.
Satisfy [sat'-is-fai], *va.* 1. Satisfacer, saciar un gusto o una pasión, contentar. 2. Satisfacer, aquietar y sosegar las pasiones de ánimo. 3. Satisfacer, recompensar, resarcir, pagar. 4. Satisfacer, dar solución a alguna duda o dificultad.—*vn.* Satisfacer, dar satisfacción a.
Satrap [sê'-trap o sat'-rap], *s.* Sátrapa, gobernador de una provincia en la antigua Persia.
Satrapy [sê'-tra-pi], *s.* Satrapía, territorio gobernado por un sátrapa.
Saturable [sat'-yu-ra-bl], *a.* Saturable, capaz de saturación.
Saturate [sat'-yu-rêt], *va.* 1. (Quím.) Saturar, echar en un líquido toda la cantidad de un sólido que puede disolverse en él. 2. Empapar, mojar; imbuir, inculcar completamente; llenar al extremo.
Saturation [sat-yu-rê'-shun], *s.* Saturación.
Saturday [sat'-ūr-dê], *s.* Sábado, séptimo y último día de la semana.
Saturant [sat'-yu-rant], *a.* Saturador, que posee la virtud de saturar.—*s.* Substancia que neutraliza la acidez o la alcalinidad de otra.
Saturn [sat'-ūrn], *s.* 1. Saturno, uno de los planetas, el sexto en orden de la distancia desde el sol (♄). 2. Saturno, una de las divinidades latinas.
Saturnalia [sat''-ūr-nê'-li-a], *s.* 1. Saturnales, fiestas en honor del dios Saturno. 2. Época o escenas de licencia y desorden.
Saturnalian [sat-ūr-nê'-li-an], *a.* Saturnal, de las saturnales; licencioso.
Saturnian [sa-tūr'-ni-an], *a.* 1. Saturnal, feliz, dichoso; perteneciente a la edad dorada. 2. Saturnal, perteneciente al planeta Saturno.
Saturnine [sat'-ūr-nin], *a.* 1. Saturnino, bajo la influencia del planeta Saturno; melancólico, triste, silencioso, poco sociable. 2. (Ant. Quím.) Plomizo, perteneciente al plomo. *Saturnine poisoning,* Envenenamiento por el plomo.
Satyr [sat'-er o sê'-ter], *s.* 1. Sátiro, divinidad mitológica de los bosques, con orejas semejantes a las de la cabra. 2. Persona muy lasciva.
Sauce [sōs], *s.* 1. Salsa, mezcla de varias cosas desleídas para condimentar los guisados. 2. Plato hecho con pulpa de frutas cocida ligeramente con azúcar. 3. (Fam.) Lenguaje impertinente o impudente. *Sauce-boat, sauce-dish,* Salsera.
Sauce, *va.* 1. Condimentar, sazonar. 2. (Fam.) Ser impertinente; decir desvergüenzas, insolencias.
Saucebox [sōs'-box], *s.* El muchacho o persona desvergonzada y atrevida.
Saucepan [sōs'-pan], *s.* Cacerola, cazo pequeño con un mango largo para hacer salsas y otros guisos.

Saucer [sō'-sęr], *s.* 1. Platillo que se pone debajo de las tazas o jícaras. 2. Platillo usado para servir las confituras, frutas, etc.; salsera. 3. (Mar.) Parte que recibe el espigón del cabrestante.

Saucily [sō'-si-li], *adv.* Descaradamente, desvergonzadamente, con impudencia o insolencia.

Sauciness [sō'-si-nes], *s.* Descaro, insolencia, impudencia, desvergüenza.

Saucisse [sō-sīs'], *s.* (Art.) Salchicha, saco embetunado y lleno de pólvora para dar fuego a una min (Fr.)

Saucy [sō'-si], *a.* Descarado, atrevido, desvergonzado, insolente, impudente.

Sauerkraut [saur'-kraut], *s.* Col ácida, preparación alemana de col desmenuzada, sazonada con sal y fermentada bajo presión.

Saunter [sān'-tęr o sōn'-tęr], *vn.* Vagar, andar ocioso, despacio y sin objeto; de aquí, haraganear.

Sauntering [sān'-tęr-ing], *s.* Vagancia, acción de vagar ocioso.

Saurian [sō'-ri-an], *a.* Saurio, parecido a un lagarto.—*s. pl.* Saurios, los reptiles conocidos con el nombre de lagartos.

Sausage [sō'-sęj], *s.* Salchicha, chorizo, longaniza. *Large sausage,* Salchichón. (Prov.) Butifarra.

Savable, Saveable [sēv'-a-bl], *a.* Conservable, salvable, que se puede salvar o conservar.

Savage [sav'-ęj], *a.* 1. Salvaje, que no está domesticado, silvestre; feroz; bárbaro, inculto. 2. Salvaje, no civilizado, que vive de una manera ruda o primitiva. 3. Feroz, cruel, enfurecido. 4. (Poco us.) Inculto, inhabitado, alejado de las habitaciones humanas.—*s.* Salvaje, el hombre bárbaro o inculto.

Savagely [sav'-ęj-li], *adv.* Bárbaramente, cruelmente, inhumanamente.

Savageness [sav'-ęj-nes], **Savagery** [sav'-ęj-ri], *s.* Salvajez; barbarie, ferocidad, crueldad.

Savanna [sa-van'-a], *s.* Sabana, campo grande cubierto de hierbas, y por extensión cualquier pradera muy extensa sin árboles.

Savant [sę-vān'], *s.* Sabio, persona erudita.

Save [sēv], *va.* 1. Salvar, librar de algún riesgo o peligro, poner en seguro; guardar, conservar. 2. Ahorrar, excusar algo del gasto; economizar, conservar las cosas no gastándolas con profusión. 3. Salvar, dar la bienaventuranza eterna. 4. Salvar, evitar algún inconveniente, obstáculo o riesgo. 5. Aprovecharse de, tomar o emplear a propósito, en tiempo oportuno. 6. Ahorrar, evitar, excusar penas, trabajos, molestias, etc. 7. Reservar, proteger, eximir. *To save quarrels,* Impedir o prevenir las contiendas. *To save harmless,* Sanear, indemnizar. *God save the king!* ¡Dios salve al rey! ¡Viva el rey!

Save, *prep.* Salvo, excepto.—*conj.* Sino, a menos que, si no es más que.

Saveall [sēv'-ōl], *s.* Cualquier objeto que sirve para recoger fragmentos ó desechos; p. ej. baloncita, arandela o cazoleta que se pone en el candelero para consumir los cabitos de las velas.

Saver [sēv'-ęr], *s.* Libertador; el que guarda, ahorra o economiza.

Savin [sav'-in], *s.* (Bot.) 1. Sabina, junípero, árbol conífero (Juniperus Sabina). 2. Cedro rojo. (Juniperus virginiana.)

Saving [sēv'-ing], *a.* 1. Ahorrativo, frugal, económico; que no hace gastos inútiles, que no es pródigo. 2. Salvador, que salva. 3. Sin pérdida, ni ganancia. 4. Calificativo, que hace excepción o reserva. *A saving clause,* Cláusula que contiene una salvedad o reserva.—*s.* 1. Economía, ahorro, el acto de ahorrar o lo que se ahorra. 2. Excepción en favor de una cosa. 3. *pl.* Ahorros. *Savings account,* Cuenta de ahorros. *Savings bank,* Banco de ahorros, caja de ahorros.—*prep.* Con excepción de, fuera de, excepto.

Savingly [sēv'-ing-li], *adv.* Económicamente, parcamente.

Savingness [sēv'-ing-nes], *s.* Ahorro, economía; frugalidad.

Savior, Saviour [sē'-vięr], *s.* Salvador, el Redentor del género humano.

Savoir-faire [sę-vwer-fār'], *s.* Don de gentes.

Savor, Savour [sē'-vęr], *s.* 1. Sabor, gusto; olor, perfume, u olor y sabor combinados. 2. Sabor, calidad aproximada o carácter determinado.

Savor, Savour, *va.* 1. Saborear, dar sabor y gusto. 2. (Ant.) Tener gusto a.—*vn.* 1. Saber, tener sabor perceptible al gusto. 2. Oler, exhalar algún olor. 3. Tener sabor u olor a alguna cosa (con *of*); manifestar una calidad determinada. En este último sentido se usa casi siempre moralmente hablando. *Words savouring of pride,* Palabras de orgulloso dejo.

Savorily [sē'-ver-i-li], *adv.* Con gusto, sabrosamente.

Savoriness [sē'-ver-i-nes], *s.* Paladar; fragancia.

Savory [sē'-ver-i], *s.* (Bot.) Ajedrea, hierba anual olorosa que se usa como condimento.

Savory, Savoury, *a.* Sabroso, fragante, aperitivo, agradable.

Savour, *s.* y *v.* *V.* SAVOR. Forma usual en Inglaterra.

Savoy [sa-vei'], *s.* (Bot.) Variedad de col o berza con hojas arrugadas.

Savoyard [sa-vei'-ard], *a.* y *s.* Saboyano, de Saboya; natural de Saboya.

Saw [sō], *s.* 1. Sierra; serrucho, instrumento para aserrar. *Hand-saw,* Sierra o serrucho de mano. *Pit-saw* o *whip-saw,* Serrucho, sierra grande con dos asideros. *Tenon-saw,* Sierra de ingletes. 2. Refrán, proverbio, sentencia. *Band saw,* Sierra continua (de hoja sin fin). *Cross-cut saw,* Sierra de trozar. *Fret saw,* Sierra de calar. *Compass* o *keyhole saw,* Sierra de rodear, de punta, para abrir bocallaves. *Jig saw,* Sierra de vaivén. *Sawbuck,* (E. U.) Caballete de aserrador con extremos en forma de X. *Saw-blade,* Hoja de sierra. *Saw-fly,* Mosca de sierra, tentredo, insecto himenóptero, cuya hembra con su largo ovipositor penetra las plantas y la madera blanda y deposita sus huevos en la incisión. *Saw-set,* Trabador, triscador, instrumento para triscar los dientes de una sierra.

Saw, *pret.* del verbo *To* SEE.

Saw, *va.* (*pp.* SAWED y SAWN). Serrar, aserrar.—*vn.* 1. Ser cortado o capaz de ser cortado con una sierra. 2. Usar una sierra; ejecutar movimientos como los del que maneja una sierra.

Sawdust [sō'-dust], *s.* Aserraduras, serrín.

Sawer [sō'-ęr], *s.* Aserrador. *V.* SAWYER, 1ª acep.

Sawfish [sō'-fish], *s.* Priste, pez marino del orden de los selacios, cuya mandíbula superior, a modo de espolón o espada, tiene espinas laterales, triangulares y muy fuertes.

Sawmill [sō'-mil], *s.* Molino de aserrar.

Sawn [sōn], *pp. irr.* de SAW. Aserrado.

Sawpit [sō'-pit], *s.* Aserradero.

Saw-wort [sō'-wūrt], *s.* (Bot.) Serrátula.

Saw-wrest [sō'-rest], *s.* Triscador. *V. Saw-set,* en SAW.

Sawyer [sō'-yęr], *s.* 1. Aserrador, serrador o más bien chiquichaque, el aserrador de piezas grandes. 2. (E. U.) Árbol que ha caído en un río. *V.* SNAG. *Sawhorse* o *trestle,* Caballete de aserrador.

Sax [sacs], *s.* Hachuela de pizarrero.

Saxicolous [sax-ic'-o-lus], *a.* Saxátil, que se cría entre peñas.

Saxhorn [sax'-hērn], *s.* (Mús.) Bombardino.

Saxifrage [sac'-si-frēj], *s.* (Bot.) Saxífraga, género de plantas.

Saxon [sax'-un], *a.* Sajón, de Sajonia, perteneciente a los sajones o a su lengua.—*s.* 1. Sajón, sajona, habitante de Sajonia. 2. Lengua sajona. 3. Anglosajón, aquel cuya lengua materna es el inglés; de aquí, inglés puro y castizo, en oposición al que usa palabras o construcciones latinas.

Saxophone [sax'-o-fōn], *s.* Saxofono, instrumento con embocadura semejante a la del clarinete y unas 20 llaves.

Say [sē], *s.* 1. Habla, la locución o palabras que se hablan, discurso, afirmación; lo que uno ha dicho o tiene que decir. 2. Derecho o turno de hablar o elegir.

Say, *va.* (*pret.* y *pp.* SAID). 1. Decir, hablar, pronunciar alguna cosa; recitar, repetir. 2. Decir, alegar, afirmar. 3. Suponer, presumir como probable o verdadero o como hipótesis provisional. *To say over again,* Volver a decir, repetir o decir segunda vez. *That is to say,* Esto es decir o quiere decir. *I have something to say to you,* Tengo que hablar con Vd. *Say you so?* ¿Lo dice Vd. de veras? *No sooner said than done,* Dicho y hecho. *To say a lesson,* Recitar una lección. *My watch says quarter past twelve,* Mi reloj señala las doce y cuarto. *It is said, they say,* Se dice, dicen.—*vn.* Decir, hacer una aserción. *To say on,* Continuar hablando. *I say!* ¡Hola! ¡escucha, oye! *All he could say for himself,* Todo lo que pudo decir o alegar en su favor.

Saying [sē'-ing], *s.* Dicho, lo que se dice; aserto, relato; adagio, sentencia, proverbio. *An old saying,* Refrán antiguo. *As the saying is,* Como se dice, como dijo el otro.

Scab [scab], *s.* 1. Costra de una herida o úlcera. 2. Roña, especie de sarna que padecen las bestias. 3. Sarnoso, roñoso; apodo que se da al hombre ruin; de aquí (reciente), despreciativamente, obrero que no pertenece a un gremio, o que no quiere hacer causa común con él.

Scab, *vn.* Criar costra sobre una llaga o herida.
Scabbard [scab'-ard], *s.* 1. Vaina de espada. 2. Funda de botón; toda cobertura.
Scabbed [scabd], **Scabby** [scab'-i], *a.* 1. Cubierto de costras, costroso. 2. Sarnoso, roñoso. 3. Vil, despreciable, ruin.
Scabbiness [scab'-i-nes], *s.* La calidad de ser costroso, roñoso o sarnoso y el estado del que padece costras o roña.
Scabies [ské'-bi-íz o scg'-bi-es], *s.* Sarna. *V.* ITCH.
Scabious [ské'-bi-us], *a.* Sarnoso.—*s.* (Bot.) Escabiosa, planta del género Scabiosa, de la familia de las dipsáceas.
Scabrous [skê'-brus], *a.* Escabroso, desigual, áspero a causa de puntos pequeños o irregularidades diminutas; se usa particularmente en botánica y zoología.
Scabrousness [skê'-brus-nes], *s.* Escabrosidad.
Scabwort [scab'-wūrt], *s.* (Bot.) Énula campana. *V.* ELECAMPANE.
Scad [scad], *s.* 1. Escombro, pez. *V.* HORSE-MACKEREL. 2. Alosa, sábalo.
Scaffold [scaf'-old], *s.* 1. Andamio para sostener a los obreros o los materiales, v. g. en la construcción de un edificio. 2. Cadalso para ejecutar a un reo; patíbulo. 3. Tablado, andamio para un espectáculo o fiesta.
Scaffold, *va.* 1. Construir tablados, instalar o poner andamios. 2. Entablar, tender los cadáveres sobre una especie de andamio, como hacen ciertas tribus indias.
Scaffolding [scaf'-old-ing], *s.* 1. Construcción temporal de tablados o andamios; material para andamios. 2. Armazón, bastidor de apoyo, sostén, particularmente en embriología.
Scaglia [scgl'-ya], *s.* Piedra caliza italiana que corresponde a la greda de Inglaterra.
Scalable [skê'-la-bl], *a.* Que se puede escalar.
Scalariform [scg-lar'-i-fērm], *a.* Escaleriforme, que tiene forma de escalera; dícese en biología de células las o vasos que presentan esa apariencia.
Scalawag, **Scallawag** [scal'-a-wag], *s.* (Ger. E. U.) Tuno, bribón; animal inferior o sin valor.
Scald [scōld], *va.* 1. Escaldar, quemar con algún líquido hirviendo o caliente. 2. Coger ligeramente en un líquido muy caliente. 3. Limpiar con agua muy caliente.
Scald,[1] *s.* 1. Quemadura, escaldadura, lesión de la piel y de la carne causada por un líquido hirviente. 2. Quema, acción de escaldar.
Scald[2] [scāld o scōld], *s.* Escalda, poeta de los antiguos escandinavos.
Scald,[3] *s.* *V.* SCALL.
Scald, *a.* Tiñoso; vil, ruin, miserable.
Scaldhead [scōld'-hed], *s.* Tiña, especie de lepra.
Scale [skêl], *s.* 1. Platillo de balanza, y también la balanza misma. 2. Libra, un signo del zodíaco. 3. Escama (de peces y de reptiles). 4. Escama, costrita de la piel; formación parecida a una escama, p. ej. en las alas de las mariposas. 5. Costra, costrita. 6. (Bot.) Escama, hoja abortada o rudimentaria, cuyo color varía mucho. 7. Incrustación en las calderas; chispa, revestimiento de óxido que se forma sobre el hierro calentado. 8. Lámina pequeña de algún metal; laminita o plancha, hoja o capa muy pequeña de alguna cosa. 9. Escala, escalera portátil; escalón. 10. Escalada. 11. (Mat.) Escala o pitipié, línea dividida en partes iguales; escala, instrumento o medida matemática; escala de un mapa. 12. (Mús.) Gama. 13. Graduación regular, división de una cosa en grados. *Pair of scales*, Peso de cruz. *Money-scales*, Pesillo para pesar el oro y la plata. *Scale-beam*, Ástil o brazo de balanza. *Scales of iron*, Las chispas que salen del hierro blando cuando se le martilla. *Scale-insect*, Cualquiera de los insectos cóccidos, o pulgón de la corteza. Las hembras adultas carecen de alas y secretan una escama escutiforme bajo la cual se abrigan. Muchas especies son muy perjudiciales a los árboles frutales. *Scale-pan*, Platillo de balanza. *On a large scale*, En gran escala, en grande. *On a small scale*, En pequeña escala, en pequeño.
Scale,[1] *va.* 1. Escamar, quitar las escamas; descortezar. 2. Quitar el cardenillo a los metales. 3. Cercenar, escatimar. 4. Cubrir con escamas. 5. Incrustar.—*vn.* Descostrarse; separarse en hojas o láminas delgadas; incrustarse.
Scale,[2] *va.* 1. Escalar, subir, encaramarse. 2. Medir por escala, hacer un dibujo por escala. 3. Reducir (sueldos, jornales o salarios) según una escala. 4. Balancear, averiguar el peso por medio de balanzas; comparar, pesar, igualar.—*vn.* Servir como escalera.
Scaled [scêld], *pa.* 1. Escamado, que tiene quitadas las escamas. 2. Escamoso, que tiene escamas. 3. Subido, escalado.
Scalene, **Scalenous** [sca-lín', us], *s.* (Geom.) Triángulo escaleno.
Scaliness [skê'-li-nes], *s.* Escamosidad, calidad de escamoso.
Scaling [skêl'-ing], *s.* 1. Escamadura, la acción de escamar. 2. Escalada, la acción de escalar una fortaleza. *Scaling-ladders*, Escalas de sitio.—*pa.* de *To* SCALE.
Scall [scel], *s.* Tiña, erupción cutánea pustulosa, a menudo epidémica entre los niños; erupción costrosa o escamosa.
Scalled [scōld], *a.* Tiñoso, que padece tiña; costroso.
Scallion [scal'-yun], *s.* (Bot.) Ascalonia, cebolleta.
Scallop [scel'-up], *s.* 1. Peine, molusco bivalvo, pechina. 2. Venera, concha que llevaban como señal los romeros. 3. Recortadura, festón semicircular, recorte, onda. 4. Vasija en que se cuecen o se sirven ostras; originalmente fué una concha grande o venera.
Scallop, *va.* 1. Festonear, hacer cortaduras en forma de dientes o festones. 2. Asar ostras, cocerlas en su concha.
Scalp [scalp], *s.* Cuero cabelludo, la piel y los cabellos que cubren el cráneo, particularmente como trofeo de guerra entre los salvajes.
Scalp, *va.* 1. Levantar los tegumentos que cubren el cráneo; levantar el pellejo que cubre el cráneo, llevándose el cabello pendiente de él. 2. (Fam.) Comprar y vender a precios reducidos (v. g. billetes de ferrocarril).
Scalpel [scal'-pel], *s.* Escalpelo; bisturí, instrumento de hoja fina y aguda empleado en cirugía y en las disecciones.
Scalping [scalp'-ing], *s.* Acción de arrancar la piel del cráneo, como hacen los salvajes con los enemigos vencidos. *Scalping-knife*, Cuchillo que se usa para levantar los tegumentos del cráneo dejándoles pendientes los cabellos.
Scaly [skêl'-i], *a.* 1. Escamoso, escamudo; que está cubierto de escamas; de la naturaleza de una escama. 2. Incrustado (caldera). 3. (Fam.) Vil, ruin, deshonrado.
Scammony [scam'-o-ni], *s.* (Bot.) Escamonea, planta trepadora de Levante con raíces tuberosas; y la resina seca de sus raíces, que es un purgante muy activo.
Scamp [scamp], *s.* Bribón, tuno, pícaro; originalmente, vagabundo, fugitivo.
Scamper [scam'-pgr], *vn.* Escaparse de prisa, huir, poner pies en polvorosa.—*s.* Fuga, huída precipitada.
Scan [scan], *va.* 1. Escudriñar, examinar cuidadosamente. 2. Escandir, medir las sílabas o los pies que tiene un verso; leer versos marcando los pies que tienen.
Scandal [scan'-dal], *s.* 1. Escándalo; difamación, maledicencia. 2. Oprobio, ignominia, mancha, infamia, causada por conducta deshonrosa o vergonzosa; baldón, caída. *Scandal-bearer*, *scandal-monger*, Murmurador, detractor, el que va de una a otra parte diciendo mal de los demás.
Scandalize [scan'-dal-aiz], *va.* 1. Difamar; acusar falsamente. 2. Escandalizar, causar escándalo.
Scandalous [scan'-dal-us], *a.* Escandaloso; vergonzoso, infame; chocante, ofensivo, calumnioso, difamatorio.
Scandalously [scan'-dal-us-li], *adv.* Ignominiosamente; escandalosamente; de una manera difamante.
Scandalousness [scan'-dal-us-nes], *s.* Calidad de escandaloso u ofensivo, carácter escandaloso.
Scandent [scan'-dent], *a.* Trepador; que trepa, o que sirve para trepar.
Scandinavian [scan-di-né'-vi-an], *a.* y *s.* Escandinavo, lo perteneciente a la Escandinavia; el natural de este país, o su lengua.
Scanning [scan'-ing], *s.* Acción de escandir versos.
Scansion [scan'-shun], *s.* La medida de los versos por sus pies, escansión.
Scansorial [scan-sō'-ri-al], *a.* Trepador, que trepa; apto para trepar, que tiene la costumbre de trepar. A veces se escribe también *Scansorious.*
Scant [scant], *va.* Escasear, cercenar, limitar la provisión de algo; de aquí, dar de mala gana o insuficientemente, estrechar, dar escasa ración, acortar los gajes o los alimentos.—*vn.* (Mar.) Bajar en fuerza, caer, disminuirse; también, cambiar a una dirección menos favorable.
Scant, *a.* Escaso, parco, apenas suficiente; corto, limitado; angosto, estrecho; insuficientemente provisto de alguna cosa.
Scantily [scant'-i-li], **Scantly** [scant'-

li], *adv.* Escasamente, parcamente, estrechamente, a duras penas; insuficientemente.
Scantiness [scant'-i-nes], *s.* Estrechez, angostura y corta capacidad; escasez, rareza de una cosa; falta de espacio, de extensión; proporciones estrechas, restringidas, exigüidad, insuficiencia.
Scantle [scan'-tl], *va.* (Ant.) Dividir en pequeñas porciones.
Scantling [scant'-ling], *s.* 1. Cuartón, todo madero de cinco pulgadas o menos en cuadro, de que se usa para pies derechos, etc.; colección de cuartones. 2. Modelo y tamaño prescritos para una parte cualquiera del casco de una embarcación. *The scantlings,* (Mar.) Las grúas de tablas.
Scantly, *adv.* (Ant.) *V.* SCANTILY.
Scantness [scant'-nes], *s.* *V.* SCANTINESS.
Scanty [scant'-i], *a.* 1. Corto, estrecho, pequeño, falto de extensión. 2. Limitado en número o cantidad, escaso. 3. Económico, parsimonioso, que ahorra.
cape [skêp], *s.* 1. (Bot.) Bohordo, tallo herbáceo radical que no tiene hojas y que sirve para sostener las flores y el fruto de algunas plantas, como el narciso. 2. (Ento.) Parte semejante a un tallo cerca de la base, p. ej. de una antena. 3. (Orn.) Cañón entero de una pluma. 4. Fuste de una columna. 5. El grito de una agachadiza asustada.
Scape-goat [skêp'-gōt], *s.* 1. El chivo que los judíos acostumbraban poner en libertad en la fiesta de la expiación. 2. Persona obligada a sufrir por las culpas de otras.
Scapegrace [skêp'-grês], *s.* Persona incorregible; pícaro, travieso, bribón.
Scapement [skêp'-ment], *s.* En relojería, escape. *V.* ESCAPEMENT.
Scaphoid [scaf'-eid], *a.* En forma de nave, navicular; escafoideo, parecido a un esquife.—*s.* Navicular o escafoides, hueso del carpo.
Scapula [scap'-yu-la], *s.* Escápula, omoplato, hueso de la espaldilla.
Scapular [scap'-yu-lar], **Scapulary** [scap'-yu-le-ri], *a.* Escapular, que pertenece a la escápula.—*s.* 1. Escapulario, tira de tela que cuelga sobre el pecho y la espalda y sirve de distintivo a varias órdenes religiosas; también, escapulario pequeño que usan por devoción los católicos seglares. 2. (Cir.) Vendaje para el omoplato.
Scar [scār], *s.* 1. Cicatriz, chirlo, señal que queda después de curada una herida o llaga. 2. Toda marca o señal que resulta de una lesión. 3. (Ict.) Escaro.
Scar, *va.* Hacer alguna herida o cicatriz en el cuerpo.
Scar (Ingl.), **Scaur** (Esco.), *s.* Roca, pelada y solitaria; peñasco.
Scarab [scar'-ab], **Scarabee,** *s.* Escarabajo sagrado, ateuco, insecto coleóptero al que daban culto los antiguos egipcios. (Ateuchus sacer.)
Scarabæid [scar-a-bī'-id], *a.* y *s.* Escarabídeo, perteneciente o parecido al escarabajo; género numeroso de insectos coleópteros.
Scaramouch [scar'-a-mauch], *s.* Botarga, bufón.
Scarce [scārs], *a.* 1. Raro, que no es abundante. 2. Escaso, que se encuentra o halla pocas veces; que no sucede a menudo; que escasea con relación a la demanda. *Money is scarce,* El dinero anda escaso.
Scarce, Scarcely [scārs'-li], *adv.* Apenas, con dificultad, no bien, luego que.
Scarceness [scārs'-nes], **Scarcity** [scārs'-i-ti], *s.* Carestía, penuria, escasez; rareza, raridad.
Scare [scār], *va.* Espantar, causar miedo o espanto; amedrentar, intimidar. *To scare away,* Espantar o ahuyentar la caza, los pájaros, etc.
Scarecrow [scār'-crō], *s.* 1. Espantajo, maniquí para espantar los cuervos y otras aves. 2. Lo que da miedo. 3. Espantajo, esperpento, persona estrafalaria o desgalichada.
Scarf [scārf], *s.* 1. Banda, cuando pasa del hombro al costado; faja, cuando ciñe la cintura. 2. Corbata, corbata ya preparada y colgante. 3. *Scarf* o *scarf-joint,* (Carp.) Ensamblaje, ensambladura, de dos piezas de madera; uno de los maderos cortados para ensamblarlo.
Scarf, *va.* 1. Ensamblar, unir varias piezas de madera entre sí para formar una obra. 2. Adornar con una banda; terciar, poner en banda.
Scarfing [scārf'-ing], *s.* Acción de ensamblar; ensambladura, encabezadura, empalme.
Scarf pin [scārf pin], *s.* Alfiler de corbata.
Scarfskin [scārf'-skin], *s.* Cutícula, epidermis.
Scarification [scar-i-fi-kê'-shun], *s.* Escarificación, sajadura, el acto de escarificar y las ligeras incisiones que produce esa operación.
Scarificator [scar'-i-fi-kê''-tor], *s.* Escarificador, instrumento con varias puntas aceradas o lancetas, que se usa para escarificar.
Scarifier [scar'-i-fai-er], *s.* 1. Sajador, escarificador, el que escarifica. 2. *V.* SCARIFICATOR. 3. Especie de cultivadora.
Scarify [scar'-i-fai], *va.* 1. Escarificar, hacer incisiones en la piel, sirviéndose del escarificador, de una lanceta o de un bisturí; sajar. 2. Revolver la superficie del terreno. 3. (Fig.) Criticar severamente; satirizar de una manera mordaz.
Scarious, Scariose [skê'-ri-us, ōs], *a.* (Bot.) Escarioso; seco, delgado, membranáceo y no verde.
Scarlatina [scār-la-tī'-na], *s.* *V.* SCARLET-FEVER.
Scarlet [scār'-let], *s.* Escarlata, grana, color fino encarnado vivo que tiende a anaranjado, y el paño teñido del mismo color. *Scarlet-oak,* (Bot.) Coscoja.—*a.* Bermejo, de color escarlata.
Scarlet-fever [scār'-let-fī'-ver], *s.* Escarlatina, escarlata, fiebre contagiosa, caracterizada por un sarpullido escarlata sobre la piel y en la garganta, y al que sigue la exfoliación de la epidermis.
Scarp [scārp], *va.* Hacer escarpa, cortar en declive.—*s.* (Fort.) Escarpa; declive, pendiente.
Scarry [scār'-i], *a.* Que tiene cicatrices.
Scary [scār'-i], *a.* (Fam.) Predispuesto a asustarse, pusilánime.
Scat [scat], *inter.* ¡Zape! voz que se usa para espantar al gato y otros animales pequeños.
Scathe [skêdh], **Scath** [scath], *va.* Desbaratar, dañar severamente, hacer gran daño.
Scathe, *s.* Desbarate, desbarato, el acto y efecto de desbaratar o dañar.
Scatheless [skêdh'-les], *a.* Libre de daño o perjuicio; sano y salvo.
Scatter [scat'-er], *va.* 1. Esparcir, disipar, alejar cosas una de otra; malgastar, disipar. 2. Dispersar, hacer huir, vencer.—*vn.* Dispersarse, esparcirse; disiparse, partir en muchas direcciones diferentes. *Scatter-brain,* Persona atolondrada, casquivana. *Scatter-brained,* Atolondrado, voluble, inconstante.
Scattered [scat'-erd], *a. part.* 1. Disperso, disipado; esparcido. 2. (Bot.) Apartado, irregular, sin apariencia alguna de orden regular. *Scattered flock,* Rebaño disperso.
Scatteringly [scat'-er-ing-li], *adv.* Esparcidamente.
Scavenge [scav'-enj], *va.* Limpiar o retirar la basura, particularmente de las calles.
Scavenger [scav'-en-jer], *s.* 1. Basurero, el que se lleva o saca la basura de las calles y letrinas. 2. Animal que se alimenta de carroña. *Scavenger-beetle,* Escarabajo que se alimenta de carroña, especialmente un clavicornio.
Scend [send], *vn.* Arfar, cabecear el buque levantando alternativamente la popa y la proa.
Scenario [se-nā'-ri-o], *s.* Guión (de una película u obra teatral).
Scene [sīn], *s.* 1. Escena, perspectiva, vista, paisaje; una localidad y todo lo que con ella se relaciona. 2. Escena, sitio o tablado del teatro en que se representa una obra dramática u otro espectáculo; teatro, lugar donde sucede un acontecimiento, real o fingido. 3. Escena, división de un acto; la acción ó asunto de la pieza que se representa. 4. Escena, escenario, las decoraciones del teatro. 5. Acción notable, extraordinaria, sea o no intencional; especialmente un arrebato, un impulso apasionado, un escándalo. *To bring on the scene,* Poner en escena. *The scene of war,* El teatro de la guerra. *The scene is at Granada,* La escena pasa en Granada. *Scene-painter,* Pintor escénico, o de decoraciones.
Sceneful [sīn'-ful], *a.* Abundante en escenas o imágenes.
Scenery [sīn'-er-i], *s.* 1. Perspectiva, vista, paisaje. 2. Decoraciones teatrales; escenario.
Scenic [sen'-ic ó sī'-nic], *a.* Escénico, tocante o perteneciente a la escena; artístico; pintoresco.
Scenographical [sen-o-graf'-i-cal], *a.* Escenográfico.
Scenographically [sen-o-graf'-i-cal-i], *adv.* Escenográficamente.
Scenography [se-neg'-ra-fi], *s.* Escenografía, la perfecta delineación y representación de un objeto en perspectiva.
Scent [sent], *s.* 1. Olfato, el sentido con que se percibe el olor. 2. Olor, perfume, la fragancia o el mal olor que exhala alguna cosa. 3. Rastro, la senda o camino que lleva la caza y se descubre por el olor; pista.
Scent, *va.* 1. Oler, percibir con el olfato. 2. Perfumar. 3. Concebir una sospecha de algo.—*vn.* Seguir la pista, rastrear.
Scentless [sent'-les], *a.* 1. Desprovisto del sentido del olfato; que no halla la pista. 2. Inodoro, sin olor; que no tiene olor.
Sceptic [skep'-tic], *a.* Escéptico. *V.* SKEPTIC.

Scepticism [skep' ti-sizm], *s.* Escepticismo. *V.* SKEPTICISM.
Scepter, Sceptre [sep'-tęr], *s.* Cetro, insignia de los emperadores y reyes.
Sceptred [sep'-tęrd], *a.* 1. Que lleva o tiene cetro. 2. Real, regio.
Schedule [sked'-yul], *va.* Incluir en una lista, catálogo o inventario; inventariar, hacer una lista de.—*s.* 1. (For.) Añadidura, aditamento. 2. Lista, catálogo. 3. Plan, programa. 4. Horario (de los trenes). 5. Temario.
Schematic [skę-mat'-ic], *a.* Esquemático; de la naturaleza de un plan, diseño o representación generales; de una constitución general, típico.
Scheme [skīm], *s.* 1. Plan, proyecto, designio. 2. Planta, esquema, modelo; diseño, bosquejo en perfil, diagrama, construcción gráfica. 3. Sistema, arreglo, disposición. 4. Treta, artificio sutil.
Scheme, *va.* y *vn.* Formar un plan, proyectar; trazarse un plan; formar proyectos.
Schemer [skīm'-ęr], *s.* Proyectista, invencionero.
Schism [sizm'], *s.* 1. Cisma, escisión o separación en una Iglesia. 2. Cisma, cuerpo eclesiástico separado de un cuerpo mayor o más antiguo. 3. División, desavenencia.
Schismatic [siz-mat'-ic], *s.* Cismático, el fundador o partidario de un cisma.
Schismatic, Schismatical [siz-mat'-ic-al], *a.* Cismático, perteneciente al cisma; que implica cisma.
Schismatically [siz-mat'-ic-al-i], *adv.* Cismáticamente.
Schismatize [siz'-ma-taiz], *vn.* Tomar parte en un cisma.
Schist [shist], *s.* Esquisto, toda roca que fácilmente se divide en hojas.
Schistose, Schistous, Schistic [shist'-ōs, us, ic], *a.* Esquistoso; de la naturaleza del esquisto o parecido a él.
Schizophrenia [skit-so-frī'-ni-a], *s.* Esquizofrenia.
Schizophrenic [skit-so-fren'-ic], *a.* Esquizofrénico.
Schnaps [shnaps], *s.* Ginebra de Holanda; cualquier licor alcohólico destilado. (Alemán.)
Scholar [scol'-ar], *s.* 1. Escolar, estudiante; discípulo. 2. Hombre erudito, docto o literato; letrado, sabio o sabia. 3. El que adquiere conocimientos de cualquier especie. 4. El estudiante que en las universidades de Inglaterra goza una beca pensionada en algún colegio. *Day scholar,* Externo, discípulo externo. *Fellow-scholar,* Condiscípulo, camarada de colegio o escuela, de estudios. *A classical scholar,* Humanista, helenista, latinista. *To be no scholar,* Haber recibido poca instrucción; no saber leer ni escribir.
Scholarly, Scholar-like [scol'-ar-li, laik], *a.* De estudiante, de escolar, que conviene a un estudiante.—*adv.* Como sabio, como hombre letrado.
Scholarship [scol'-ar-ship], *s.* 1. Saber, el conocimiento de las ciencias o de las letras; erudición, ciencia. 2. Educación literaria. 3. Beca, plaza o prebenda en algún colegio, fundada para la manutención de un estudiante.
Scholastic [sco-las'-tic], *a.* 1. Escolástico; estudiantino, estudiantil; perteneciente a las escuelas o a la educación. 2. Escolástico, que se refiere a la teología de la edad media; pedantesco.
Scholastical [sco-las'-tic-al], *a.* Escolástico, escolar, estudiantino, estudiantil.
Scholastically [sco-las'-tic-al-i], *adv.* Escolásticamente.
Scholasticism [scol-las'-ti-sizm], *s.* Escolasticismo; el método o las sutilezas de las escuelas.
Scholiast [scō'-li-ast], *s.* Escoliador, el que hace anotaciones, glosas y escolios.
Scholium [scō'-li-um], *s.* Escolio, nota breve gramatical o crítica que se pone a un texto para explicarlo; observación matemática que se refiere a una demostración precedente.
School [scūl], *s.* 1. Escuela, la casa o paraje donde se enseña; una institución para la enseñanza. 2. El cuerpo de alumnos de una escuela. 3. Cualquier clase o ejercicio de una escuela. 4. Todos los discípulos de un maestro (filósofo o doctor célebre, artista, etc.) o sistema; el sistema mismo. 5. Esfera o medios de enseñanza o de disciplina. 6. Método de vida. *Common school,* Escuela libre y pública de los Estados Unidos. *Boarding-school,* Pupilaje, la casa donde se admiten pupilos para vivir en ella y recibir educación. *Fencing-school,* Sala o escuela de esgrima. *Dancing-school,* Sala o escuela de baile. *Charity-school,* Escuela gratuita. *Law school,* Escuela de derecho. *In school,* En clase. *To go to school,* Entrar en clase. *School book,* Un libro usado en las escuelas. *Schoolboy,* Muchacho de escuela. *Schoolfellow,* Condiscípulo. *Schoolgirl,* Niña que va a la escuela. *Schoolhouse,* La escuela, casa de escuela. *Private school,* Escuela particular, a diferencia de la pública. *Public school,* Escuela pública, la establecida y mantenida por la autoridad civil. *School-teacher,* Maestro o maestra de escuela.
School,[1] *va.* 1. Instruir, enseñar. 2. Amaestrar, adiestrar. 3. Reprender enseñando su obligación al que faltó a ella, disciplinar.
School,[2] *vn.* Ir o moverse juntos, como los peces; moverse en masa.—*s.* Ribazón, manjúa, majal, la multitud de peces que nadan juntos, como en tropa.
School board [scūl' bōrd], *s.* Junta de educación.
Schooling [scūl'-ing], *s.* 1. Instrucción dada o adquirida en una escuela; enseñanza preparatoria. 2. Precio de la escuela, remuneración pagada a un maestro de escuela.
Schoolman [scūl'-man], *s.* 1. Un erudito muy versado en las disputas y controversias de las escuelas. 2. Escritor sobre teología escolástica.
Schoolmaster [scūl'-mas-tęr], *s.* Maestro de escuela; maestro, el o lo que forma, instruye y guía.
Schoolmate [scūl'-mēt], *s.* Compañero de colegio, de escuela, de clase.
Schoolmistress [scūl'-mis-tres], *sf.* Maestra de niños o niñas.
Schooner [scūn'-ęr], *s.* (Mar.) 1. Goleta, embarcación con dos palos (hoy con tres y aun cuatro) y velas cangrejas. 2. (E. U.) Furgón con toldo que usan los emigrantes en las llanuras del Oeste de los Estados Unidos. 3. (Fam. E. U.) Vaso alto y grande para cerveza.
Schorl, Shorl [shōrl], *s.* (Miner.) Chorlo; turmalina, en particular la variedad negra.
Sciagraph [sai'-a-graf], *s.* Sección vertical arquitectónica que representa el interior de un edificio; esciagrafía.
Sciagraphic, Sciagraphical [sai-a-graf'-ic, al], *a.* Relativo a la esciagrafía.
Sciagraphy [sai-ag'-ra-fi], *s.* Esciagrafía, averiguación de la hora por la sombra que proyectan los astros; también el arte de sombrear (dibujos).
Sciatheric, Sciatherical [sai-a-ther'-ic, al], *a.* Esciatérico, perteneciente a los relojes de sol.
Sciatica [sai-at'-i-ca], *s.* Ciática, neuralgia de la cadera y del muslo, es decir, del nervio ciático.
Sciatic, Sciatical [sai-at'-ic, al], *a.* Ciático, isquiático, que se refiere a la cadera. *The sciatic nerve,* El nervio ciático.
Science [sai'-ens], *s.* 1. Ciencia, conocimiento, sabiduría. 2. Certidumbre, destreza, habilidad de ejecución que resulta del conocimiento que se tiene de algo. 3. Conjunto, sistema de conocimientos sobre un asunto.
Science fiction [sai'-ens fic'-shun], *s.* Ciencia y fantasía.
Sciential [sai-en'-shal], *a.* Que produce el saber, o que conduce a la ciencia; inteligente, hábil, instruído.
Scientific, Scientifical [sai-en-tif'-ic, al], *a.* 1. Científico. 2. De acuerdo con las reglas, principios o procedimientos de la ciencia; sistemático, exacto. 3. Versado en la ciencia o en una ciencia; sabio, muy hábil.
Scientifically [sai-en-tif'-i-cal-i], *adv.* Científicamente.
Scientist [sai'-en-tist], *s.* Científico, sabio.
Scimeter, Scimitar [sim'-i-tęr], *s.* Cimitarra. *V.* SIMITAR.
Scintilla [sin-til'-a], *s.* Centella, chispa; de aquí, partícula, traza, tilde, jota.
Scintillant [sin'-til-ant], *a.* Centelleante, que echa chispas.
Scintillate [sin'-ti-lēt], *vn.* Chispear, centellear.
Scintillation [sin-ti-lē'-shun], *s.* Chispazo.
Sciolist [sai'-o-list], *s.* Erudito a la violeta, semisabio.
Scion [sai'-ǫn], *s.* 1. Verduguillo, rama destinada a ser injertada o plantada; también, esqueje. 2. Vástago, renuevo, tallo tierno de un árbol o planta. 3. Hijo, hija o descendiente.
Scioptic [sai-op'-tic], *a.* Escióptico, perteneciente a la cámara obscura.
Scirrhous [sir'-us o skir'-us], *a.* Escirroso, endurecido; canceroso.
Scirrhus [skir'-us], *s.* Escirro, tumor endurecido; tumor duro canceroso.
Scissel [sis'-ęl], *s.* Desperdicios, desechos de metal, escoria.
Scission [sish'-un], *s.* 1. Escisión, fisión. 2. Corte, separación.
Scissor [siz'-ęr], *va.* y *vn.* Cortar o cortarse con tijeras.
Scissors [siz'-ęrz], *s. pl.* Tijeras.
Scissure [sish'-ur], *s.* Cisura, hendedura, cortadura longitudinal.
Sclerosis [sclę-rō'-sis], *s.* Esclerosis, toda especie de endurecimiento morboso de los tejidos.
Sclerotic [sclę-ret'-ic], *a.* 1. Esclero-

so, denso, endurecido, dícese particularmente de la esclerótica o córnea opaca del ojo. 2. Que padece esclerosis.

Scobs [scebs], *s.* 1. Escobina, aserraduras, rasuras, limaduras. 2. Escoria. 3. Un álcali.

Scoff [scef], *vn.* Mofarse, burlarse o hacer burla (úsase con *at*).

Scoff, *s.* Mofa, escarnio, burla

Scoffer [scef'-ẹr], *s.* Mofador.

Scoffingly [scef'-ing-li], *adv.* Con mofa y escarnio.

Scold [scōld], *va.* y *vn.* Regañar, reñir, rezongar, refunfuñar. *A scolding-match,* (Fam.) Una pelotera.

Scolding [scōld'-ing], *a.* Regañón, regañador.

Scollop [scel'-up], *s.* y *v.* *V.* SCALLOP.

Scolopendra [scel-o-pen'-dra], *s.* (Ent.) Escolopendra, ciempiés.

Scomber [scem'-bẹr], *s.* Escombro, caballa, género típico de los escombéridos.

Sconce [scens], *s.* 1. Baluarte, defensa. 2. (Fam.) Cabeza; el contenido del cráneo; seso, juicio, sentido. 3. Yelmo. 4. Anaquel fijo. 5. Multa.

Sconce, *s.* Candelabro de pared; linterna provista de una pantalla exterior. (Mex.) Pantalla.

Sconce, *va.* 1. Fortificar con un baluarte o defensa. 2. Multar, imponer una pena pecuniaria.

Scoop [scūp], *s.* 1. Cuchara o cucharón; paleta, pala cóncava (de mano); utensilio que sirve para traspalar la hulla, para rastrear las ostras, para tomar porciones de harina, azúcar, etc. 2. Acto de cavar o ahuecar. 3. Paletada, la cantidad cavada o sacada de una vez. 4. Cavidad en forma de taza; hueco. 5. (Mar.) Vertedor, achicador.

Scoop, *va.* 1. Sacar con cucharón o achicador, vaciar. 2. Cavar, socavar.

Scooper [scūp'-ẹr], *s.* El que achica o socava; cavador.

Scoot [scūt], *vn.* 1. (Fam. E. U.) Irse de prisa; tomar las de Villadiego. 2. Pasar, volar, ligeramente por encima de una cosa, como un ave.

Scooter [scūt'-ẹr], *s.* 1. Patineta, patinete. (Mex.) Patín del diablo. 2. Velero de fondo plano para el agua o hielo.

Scope [scōp], *s.* 1. Alcance de vista o acción; punto de mira; lugar, espacio en que ejercer las facultades. 2. Objeto, fin, intento, designio, intención. *To have free scope,* Tener carta blanca para hacer lo que se quiera, no tener freno ni sujeción, obrar libremente. *To give full scope to the imagination,* Dar rienda suelta a la imaginación.

-scope. Sufijo que significa indicador; se emplea principalmente en los nombres de los instrumentos de observación; v. g. *telescope,* telescopio.

Scorbutic, Scorbutical [scēr-biū'-tic, al], *a.* Escorbútico.

Scorbutically [scēr-biū'-tic-al-i], *adv.* Con escorbuto, con propensión al escorbuto o como si lo padeciera.

Scorch [scērch], *va.* 1. Chamuscar, quemar por encima o por afuera; tostar. 2. Agostar, abrasar (el sol) con calor extremo.—*vn.* 1. Quemarse, secarse. 2. Agostarse, abrasarse (las plantas). 3. (Ger.) Moverse o ser impelido a gran velocidad.

Scorcher [scērch'-ẹr], *s.* 1. Lo que chamusca o abrasa. 2. Persona o cosa que se mueve o puede moverse a gran velocidad, como un caballo, un ciclista, etc.

Scorching [scērch'-ing], *a.* Ardiente, abrasador, caliente.

Scordium [scēr'-di-um], *s.* (Bot.) Escordio, germandria acuática.

Score [scōr], *s.* 1. Muesca, canalita, incisión, entalladura; señal, marca, línea, raya. 2. Cuenta, escote; deuda. 3. De aquí, mala voluntad, diferencia, controversia; también, razón, motivo, cuenta, consideración. 4. Talla, el número de tantos en los juegos. 5. (Mús.) Partitura, conjunto de las partes de una composición musical; los pliegos o el libro que las contienen. 6. Veintena, veinte. *To pay one's score,* Pagar sus deudas, su escote. *Put that to my score,* Póngame Vd. eso en cuenta. *On the score of,* En consideración a, con motivo de. *Upon what score?* ¿Con qué motivo? ¿por qué razón? *An opera in score,* Una ópera puesta en partitura. *Threescore,* Sesenta. *Fourscore,* Ochenta. *Sixscore,* Ciento veinte.

Score, *va.* 1. Rayar, marcar con líneas, muescas o cortaduras; escoplear. 2. Marcar con latigazos, azotar; de aquí, censurar severamente. 3. Borrar, tachar, testar. 4. Apuntar, sentar, poner en cuenta; llevar a una cuenta. 5. Ganar tantos en un juego. 6. (Mús.) Escribir la parte correspondiente a instrumento de orquesta.—*vn.* 1. Marcar la tarja, sentarse en cuenta; marcar los tantos en un juego. 2. Ganar tantos en un juego; obtener una ventaja. 3. Hacer muescas, rayas o señales.

Scorer [scōr'-ẹr], *s.* 1. Marcador, el que marca; el que lleva cuenta de las jugadas o de los tantos ganados por los que toman parte en un juego cualquiera. 2. Martillo, instrumento que emplean los leñadores para marcar los árboles.

Scoria [scō'-ri-a], *s.* 1. Escorias volcánicas, fragmentos de lava. 2. Escoria, la hez de los metales.

Scoriaceous [scō-ri-é'-shus], *a.* Escoriáceo, que se asemeja a la escoria o participa d , ella.

Scorification [scō-ri-fi-kē'-shun], *s.* Escorificación, el acto y efecto de escorificar.

Scoriform [scō'-ri-fērm], *a.* Escoriforme, que tiene el aspecto de escoria.

Scorify [scō'-ri-fai], *va.* 1. Escorificar, separar el oro o la plata de un mineral, fundiéndolo con plomo. 2. Reducir a escoria o hez.

Scorn [scērn], *va.* y *vn.* 1. Despreciar, desdeñar; rechazar desdeñosamente, profesar desprecio por. 2. Mofar, escarnecer, hacer escarnio. 3. Burlarse de uno, ponerle en ridículo. *My friends would scorn me if,* Mis amigos me despreciarían si.

Scorn, *s.* 1. Desdén, desprecio; sentimiento o tratamiento desdeñoso debido a la mala opinión que se tiene de una persona o de un objeto. 2. Irrisión, escarnio, expresión de desdén, mofa. 3. Objeto de desdén, de desprecio. *He is the scorn of all the town,* Es objeto del desprecio de toda la ciudad.

Scorner [scērn'-ẹr], *s.* Desdeñador, escarnecedor.

Scornful [scērn'-ful], *a.* Desdeñoso, insolente, lleno de desprecio.

Scornfully [scērn'-ful-i], *adv.* Desdeñosamente, despreciablemente, con desdén.

Scornfulness [scērn'-ful-nes], *s.* Calidad de desdeñoso. *The scornfulness of his look,* Lo desdeñoso de su mirada.

Scorpio [scēr'-pi-ō], *s.* (Astr.) Escorpión, una constelación del Zodíaco, y su signo.

Scorpion [scēr'-pi-ọn], *s.* 1. Escorpión, alacrán. 2. Escorpión, constelación del zodíaco. 3. Especie de látigo o azote. *Scorpion-fly,* Panorpo, escorpión mosca, insecto neuróptero cuya cola se parece á la del escorpión. *Scorpion-grass,* Una especie cualquiera de miosotis, v. g. la "Nomeolvides."

Scorpion-wort [scēr'-pi-ọn-wūrt], *s.* (Bot.) Hierba del alacrán.

Scot [scet], *s.* (Ant.) Escote; tasa, contribución. *Scot and lot* Derechos parroquiales. *Scot-free,* Libre de escote; impune.

Scot, *s.* Escocés, escocesa, persona natural de Escocia.

Scotch [scech], *va.* 1. Escoplear, hacer muescas, hacer cortes o cortaduras pequeñas en alguna cosa. 2. Herir ligeramente. 3. Allanar la piedra con un pico. 4. Poner una galga o amarra a un vehículo. *We have scotched the snake, not killed it,* Hemos herido pero no matado esta serpiente.

Scotch, *s.* 1. Cortadura, corte, incisión. 2. Línea trazada en el suelo, p. ej. para jugar al infernáculo. *V.* HOP-SCOTCH. 3. Calzo, cuña, galga, amarra de un carruaje.

Scotch, Scottish [scet'-ish], *a.* Escocés, lo perteneciente a Escocia. *Scotch thistle,* Cardo borriquero; cardo, emblema nacional de Escocia. *Scotch-collops, s. pl.* Ternera cortada en tajadas o picada. *Scotch-fiddle,* (Vulg.) Sarna.

Scotcher [scech'-ẹr], *s.* Travesaño.

Scotchman, Scotsman [scech'-man, scets'-man], *s.* Escocés, el natural de Escocia.

Scotism [scō'-tizm], *s.* Escotismo, doctrina escolástica de Escoto (Duns Scot) fundador del realismo y adversario de los tomistas.

Scotograph [scet'-o-graf], *s.* 1. Instrumento que ayuda a los ciegos a escribir, y sirve también para escribir en la obscuridad.

Scotomy [scet'-o-mi], *s.* Escotomía, vértigo.

Scoundrel [scaun'-drel], *s.* Belitre, bergante, un pícaro, un bribón, un hombre vil y ruin.

Scoundrelism [scaun'-drel-izm], *s.* Picardía, bajeza.

Scoundrelly [scaun'-drel-i], *adv.* De pícaro, de bribón, bajo, vilmente.

Scour [scaur], *va.* 1. Fregar, estregar. 2. Limpiar, ahuyentar de una parte a los que son perjudiciales en ella. 3. Limpiar, quitar la suciedad de una cosa estregándola; lavar; recorrer, componer; blanquear. *To scour cloth,* Escurar el paño o sacarle el aceite con greda y jabón. 4. Purgar con violencia. 5. Formar, v. gr. el cauce de un arroyo, disminuyendo por el roce. 6. Pasar atravesando con cuidado, recorrer, explorar. 7. Correr, pasar rápidamente cerca de algo. 8. Ahuyentar, expeler.—*vn.* 1. Limpiar, estregar, los utensilios de una casa. 2. Corretear, correr de una parte a otra. 3. Soltársele a uno el vientre. *To scour about,* Vagar, ser un vagamundo. *To scour away,* Huirse.

Scourer [scaur'-ẹr], *s.* 1. Limpiador, sacamanchas. 2. Purga.
Scourge [scūrj], *s.* Azote, correa, látigo, instrumento de corrección; lo que agota o mata; castigo severo; calamidad.
Scourge, *va.* 1. Azotar, dar con un látigo, flagelar, dar golpes con unas disciplinas. 2. Castigar (por delitos o faltas con intención de corregir); mortificar, hostigar, acosar.
Scourger [scūrj'-ẹr], *s.* Azotador, castigador, mortificador.
Scouring [scaur'-ing], *s.* 1. Fregado, fregadura, estregadura, acción de fregar o estregar; acción de escurar o desengrasar. 2. Diarrea.
Scout [scaut], *s.* (Mil.) Descubridor, explorador, batidor del campo; centinela avanzada; espía.
Scout, *vn.* (Mil.) Reconocer secretamente los movimientos del enemigo, ir como explorador.
Scout, *va.* 1. Rechazar con desdén. 2. (Con *at*) Burlarse, reirse de algo o de alguien.
Scoutmaster [scaut-mqs'-tẹr], *s.* Jefe de niños exploradores.
Scovel [scuv'-l], *s.* (Prov.) Escobón, el deshollinador para limpiar un horno.
Scow [scau], *s.* Chalana.
Scowl [scaul], *vn.* Mirar con ceño poner mala cara, ponerse ceñudo, poner mal gesto, enfurruñarse.—*va.* Rechazar, repeler.
Scowl, *s.* Ceño, sobrecejo, semblante ceñudo, enfadado, disgustado o emperrado.
Scowling [scaul'-ing], *s.* El acto de mirar de sobrecejo, mal gesto o ceño.
Scowlingly [scaul'-ing-li], *adv.* Con ceño.
Scrabble [scrab'-l], *va.* 1. Escarabajear, garabatear. 2. Recoger, amontonar de prisa.—*vn.* 1. Emborronar, trazar caracteres irregulares o informes. 2. (Fam.) *V.* SCRAMBLE. —*s.* Acción de escarabajear, de emborronar.
Scrag [scrag], *s.* 1. Cualquier cosa flaca o macilenta y basta o aspera; pedazo de carne magra, particularmente del cuello; el cuello. 2. *V.* REMNANT.
Scragged, Scraggly [scrag'-ed, li], *a.* 1. Áspero, desigual, escabroso. 2. Flaco, descarnado.
Scraggedness [scrag'-ed-nes], **Scragginess** [scrag'-i-nes], *s.* Flaqueza, extenuación; aspereza, desigualdad.
Scraggy [scrag'-i], *a.* Áspero, desigual; flaco, macilento, descarnado.
Scramble [scram'-bl], *va.* 1. Preparar, arreglar, de prisa o confusamente. 2. Preparar huevos revolviéndolos mientras se fríen.—*vn.* 1. Trepar, andar con ayuda de pies y manos, o subir gateando a una altura; trepar, las plantas. 2. Hacer esfuerzos para alcanzar; contender o disputar ansiosamente acerca de quién ha de coger una cosa. *To scramble for,* Esforzarse por coger o alcanzar. *To scramble over,* Pasar gateando. *To scramble up,* Trepar, subir. *Scrambled eggs,* Huevos revueltos.
Scramble, *s.* 1. Trepa, la acción de trepar o subir gateando a una altura. 2. Lucha, esfuerzo para obtener algo, contienda o pelea entre dos o más personas por agarrar o posesionarse de una cosa; arrebatiña, hecho desordenado. 3. (Aer.) Despegue de emergencia.
Scrambler [scram'-blẹr], *s.* 1. El que disputa con otro u otros por agarrar algo. 2. Trepador, el que trepa o sube gateando a una altura.
Scrap [scrap], *s.* 1. Migaja, mendrugo, sobras. 2. Pedacito, fragmento. *Scrap book,* Libro de recortes. *Scrap heap,* Montón de desechos o desperdicios. *Scrap iron, scrap metal,* Hierro viejo, despojos de metal o de hierro. *Scrap of paper,* Pedazo de papel.
Scrape [scrêp], *va.* y *vn.* 1. Raer, raspar la superficie de alguna cosa para quitar o borrar algo de ella. 2. Arañar, recoger con afán de varias partes y en pequeñas porciones lo necesario para algún fin; amontonar poco a poco. 3. Hacer un ruido desagradable tocando en la superficie de una cosa; rascar o tocar mal un instrumento. 4. Hacer cortesías o reverencias con muy poca gracia. *To scrape out,* Borrar o quitar algo de la superficie de una cosa raspándola. *To scrape off,* Quitar raspando. *To scrape together,* Amontonar a fuerza de industria y ahorro. *To scrape acquaintance with,* Insinuarse, entrar en las buenas gracias de alguien.
Scrape, *s.* 1. Raspadura, acción y efecto de raspar; ruido de raspar, roce de los pies en el suelo. 2. Enredo, maraña; embarazo, dificultad, berenjenal, empeño, lance apretado. 3. Cortesía tosca o con poca gracia. *I am out of the scrape,* Zafé el cuerpo, salí de enredos.
Scraper [scrêp'-ẹr], *s.* 1. Rascador, raspador, instrumento para raspar o rascar. 2. Arañador de dinero. 3. Aprendiz o persona que toca mal el violín. 4. (Mar.) Rasquetas. 5. Estregadera, raedera; garatura (del pelambrero).
Scraping [scrêp'-ing], *s.* 1. Raedura, raspadura, acción de raspar, de raer. 2. Raspaduras, lo que se saca raspando. 3. *pl.* Ahorros, cosas amontonadas.
Scratch [scrach], *va.* y *vn.* 1. Rascar, raspar; raer, arañar; garrapatear. 2. Rasguñar o hacer un rasguño o araño. 3. Rayar (el vidrio). 4. Escribir mal, garrapatear. 5. Cavar, excavar raspando. 6. Cancelar, borrar, testar. *To scratch out one's eyes,* Sacar a uno los ojos con las uñas.
Scratch, *s.* 1. Rasguño, araño, arañazo, rascadura; marca o incisión hecha en una superficie; raya ligera, arañazo. 2. La línea desde la cual parten los que se disputan el premio en una carrera. 3. *pl.* Galápago, espundia, enfermedad en el casco del caballo. 4. Peluca para una parte de la cabeza. 5. (E. U.) En el juego de billar, bambarria, chiripa, acierto o logro casual. *Scratches,* Grietas en los pies de los caballos. *V.* la 3ª acep.
Scratcher [scrach'-ẹr], *s.* Arañador, el que araña o rasguña.
Scratchingly [scrach'-ing-li], *adv.* Arañando, rascando.
Scratch pad [scrach pad], *s.* Cuaderno de apuntes, cuaderno para borrador.
Scratchwork [scrach'-wūrk], *s.* Pintura al fresco.
Scrawl [scrēl], *va.* Garrapatear, garabatear, escribir mal, hacer garabatos.
Scrawl, *s.* Escrito desigual o cosa escrita de prisa y mal; lo que está escrito o dibujado sin habilidad; garabatos, garrapatos.
Scrawler [scrēl'-ẹr], *s.* Garabateador, el que escribe garabatos.
Scrawny [scrē'-ni], *a.* Flaco, enjuto y huesoso, falto de carnes.
Scrawniness [scrē'-ni-nes], *s.* Flaqueza, flacura, falta de carnes.
Scream [scrîm], *va.* Gritar, proferir en voz alta y penetrante; dar alaridos; vociferar, vocear.—*vn.* Chillar, gritar, dar gritos agudos o penetrantes.
Scream, *s.* Grito, alarido que comúnmente denota miedo o dolor; grito agudo o penetrante, chillido.
Screamer [scrîm'-ẹr], *s.* El que o lo que grita o vocea; ave gritadora, como el camique de la América meridional; las hay de varias especies.
Screaming [scrîm'-ing], *s.* Gritería, acción de dar un grito; vocería, alarida.
Screech [scrîch], *vn.* Dar alaridos o chillidos.
Screech, *s.* Chillido, grito, alarido.
Screechowl [scrîch'-aul], *s.* (Orn.) Zumaya o zumacaya, alucón; toda lechuza que da chillidos en vez de graznar.
Screechy [scrîch'-i], *a.* Chillante, que se asemeja a un chillido; agudo, penetrante y discorde.
Screed [scrîd], *s.* 1. Tirada crítica; invectiva, arenga. 2. Plantilla, gálibo; listón, tira de madera o capa de mortero que se pone a intervalos en una pared para igualar la superficie. 3. Jirón, tira larga, retazo.
Screen [scrîn], *s.* 1. Biombo, mampara, algo que separa o intercepta; cancel, pantalla, antipara, persiana; tabique, reja; albitana, cerca para resguardar las plantas de la acción del viento; de aquí, abrigo, defensa. 2. Pantalla de chimenea. 3. Criba, harnero, zaranda.
Screen, *va.* 1. Abrigar, ocultar, esconder; proteger, defender; sustraer (a un castigo). 2. Cribar, cerner. *Screenings, s. pl.* Desperdicios, restos de alguna cosa pasada por una criba o harnero.
Screenplay [scrîn'-plê'], *s.* Argumento de película cinematográfica.
Screw [scrū], *s.* 1. Tornillo, cilindro de metal, madera, etc., ahuecado en espiral por su superficie exterior; también, tuerca, rosca, cilindro hueco rayado en espiral en su superficie interior. 2. Tornillo, clavo cilíndrico con filete en espiral; lo que se parece a un tornillo; hélice; vapor de hélice; concha de hélice. 3. Vuelta de tornillo. 4. (Ger.) Cicatero, tacaño; también, presión, fuerza. *Set-screw, thumb-screw, binding-screw,* Tornillo montado o de presión. *Right-handed screw,* Tornillo de filete a la derecha. *Left-handed screw,* Tornillo zurdo o reverso. *Round-head screw,* Tornillo de cabeza redonda (de gota de sebo). *Screw steamer,* Vapor de hélice. *Screw eyes,* Armellas. *Screw nails,* Clavos de rosca. *Female screw,* Tuerca. *Screw-tap,* Matriz o molde para hacer tornillos. *Cork-screw,* Tirabuzón, sacacorchos. *Screw-plate,* Taraja. *Screw-taps for the screw-plate,* Mochuelos de taraja. *Screw-wrench,* Atornillador. *Screw-driver,* Desatornillador.
Screw, *va.* 1. Atornillar, torcer o afianzar con tornillo. 2. Retorcer; afear alguna cosa retorciéndola. 3. Forzar, apretar, comprimir, oprimir, estrechar. 4. Torcer, defor-

mar; hacer gestos con la boca o cara.—*vn.* 1. Retorcerse o dar vueltas una cosa en forma de rosca o espiral. 2. Ejercer extorsión u opresión. *To screw down,* Atornillar, cerrar, fijar, con tornillo. *To screw in,* Hacer entrar una cosa en otra dándole vueltas o revolviéndola como se hace a un tornillo; insinuar, introducir alguna palabra o discurso con maña en una conversación. *To screw out,* Hacer salir a viva fuerza alguna cosa de donde estaba metida; echar a perder algo al sacarlo de donde estaba. *To screw out of one,* Sonsacar con astucia y maña. *To screw one's wits,* Darse de las astas, calentarse los sesos.

Scribble [scrib'-l], *va.* 1. Escribir de prisa y sin cuidado (letra o estilo). 2. Escarabajear, borrajear, garrapatear.

Scribble, *s.* Escrito de poco mérito o mal formado.

Scribbler [scrib'-lẹr], *s.* Escritor o autor de poca nota.

Scribe [scraib], *s.* 1. Escritor; escribiente. 2. Notario público. 3. Escriba, doctor de la ley entre los hebreos.

Scribe, *va.* 1. Marcar, rayar, con un instrumento puntiagudo. 2. Ensamblar, ajustar, corrocar, esgarabotar.

Scrimmage [scrim'-ẹj], *s.* Contienda, jaleo, lucha cuerpo a cuerpo, escaramuza.

Scrimp [scrimp], *va.* y *vn.* Estrechar, reducir, acortar; ser parsimonioso, portarse con tacañería o sordidez. —*a.* Estrecho, reducido, corto.—*s.* Mísero, un avaro.

Scrimpingly [scrimp'-ing-li], *adv.* De una manera mezquina, parsimoniosa o sórdida.

Scrimpy [scrimp'-i], *a.* (Fam.) Demasiado estrecho, escaso, desmasiado corto; reducido, muy pequeño.

Scrip [scrip], *s.* 1. Cédula, esquela. 2. Certificado o certificación de un banco o compañía atestando que el accionista tiene interés en uno u otra. 3. Bolsa, morral, zurrón, taleguilla. (En vez de *Script.*) *Scripholder,* Tenedor de vales o certificados provisionales.

Script [script], *s.* 1. Escritura, mano, carácter ordinario de letra. 2. (Impr.) Plumilla inglesa, tipo que imita la forma de la letra escrita. 3. (For.) Escritura, v. g. un testamento o codicilo. (< Lat.)

Scriptural [scrip'-chur-al], *a.* Bíblico, contenido en la Sagrada Escritura, o autorizado por ella.

Scripturally [scrip'-chur-al-i], *adv.* De una manera bíblica; conforme a la Sagrada Escritura.

Scripture [scrip'-chur o tiụr], *s.* Escritura, la Escritura sagrada de cualquier pueblo; en especial, la Biblia.

Scrivener [scriv'-nẹr], *s.* (Ingl. ó ant.) 1. Escribano, notario público. 2. Antiguamente, el que tenía por oficio prestar dinero a interés.

Scrobiculate [scro-bic'-yu-lêt], *a.* (Bot. y Zool.) Que tiene gran número de hoyuelos.

Scrofula [scref'-yu-la], *s.* Lamparón, escrófula, estado orgánico que predispone a la consunción mesentérica o pulmonar.

Scrofulous [scref'-yu-lus], *a.* Escrofuloso, que tiene lamparones, que padece de escrófula.

Scroll [scrōl], *s.* 1. El rollo de papel o pergamino que contiene un escrito o se destina a escribir en él. 2. Rasgo, traza o diseño en lugar de un sello. 3. Adorno en espiral; encaracolado, voluto, roleo. *Scroll-saw,* Sierra de contornear.

Scrotal [scrō'-tal], *a.* Escrotal, relativo al escroto.

Scrotocele [scrō'-to-sīl], *s.* Escrotocele, hernia completa que desciende al escroto.

Scrotum [scrō'-tum], *s.* Escroto, bolsa que contiene los testículos.

Scrub [scrub], *va.* Fregar, estregar; limpiar fregando o rascando; restregar (con la mano o con un estropajo).

Scrub, *a.* 1. Achaparrado, desmirriado; inferior, mezquino. 2. En que participan luchadores novicios o poco hábiles. (Se dice de carreras, etc.)—*s.* 1. Belitre, un hombre vil. 2. Estropajo; escoba vieja; una cosa inútil y despreciable.

Scrubby [scrub'-i], **Scrubbed** [scrubd], *a.* Estropajoso; vil, despreciable, bajo; achaparrado.

Scruff [scruf], *s.* Nuca, parte alta de la cerviz, unión de la cabeza y el espinazo.

Scruple [scrū'-pl], *s.* 1. Escrúpulo, duda. 2. Escrúpulo, la tercera parte de una dracma, peso de veinte granos; se indica con el signo ℈. 3. Cualquiera cantidad muy pequeña.

Scruple, *vn.* Escrupulizar, tener duda; vacilar por razones de conciencia.

Scrupulous [scrū'-piu-lus], *a.* 1. Escrupuloso, delicado, riguroso, concienzudo; dudoso, temeroso; cuidadoso, cauto. 2. Exacto, preciso, estricto, exigente.

Scrupulously [scrū'-piu-lus-li], *adv.* Escrupulosamente.

Scrupulousness [scrū'-piu-lus-nes], *s.* Escrupulosidad, delicadeza de conciencia; calidad de escrupuloso o concienzudo; exactitud, nimiedad en el examen y averiguación de las cosas.

†**Scrutable** [scrū'-ta-bl], *a.* Escudriñable.

Scrutineer [scrū-ti-nīr'], *s.* Escudriñador; oficial inglés que examina los votos en una elección.

Scrutinize [scrū'-ti-naiz], *va.* Escudriñar, examinar en sus detalles o a fondo, averiguar, inquirir, sondear.

Scrutinous [scrū'-ti-nus], *a.* Curioso.

Scrutiny [scrū'-ti-ni], *s.* Escrutinio, averiguación, examen.

Scrutoire [scrū-twōr'], *s.* Escritorio, papelera. (Fr.)

Scuba [scū'-ba], *s.* Escafandra autónoma. *Scuba gear,* Equipo para buceo, escafandra autónoma.

Scud [scud], *vn.* Correr, volar o moverse rápidamente; atravesar de prisa; correr como una embarcación en una borrasca, con pocas velas puestas, o sin ellas. *To scud before the wind,* Correr viento en popa. *To scud before the sea,* (Mar.) Correr con mar en popa. *To scud under bare poles,* (Mar.) Correr a palo seco. *To scud with both sheets aft,* (Mar.) Correr a dos puños.—*s.* 1. Carrera precipitada, el acto de correr o moverse rápidamente. 2. Nubes ligeras, impulsadas por el viento; celaje; la variedad de nubes próximas a la tierra; también, espuma del mar.

Scuddle [scud'-l], *vn.* (Des.) Huir, apretar a correr.

Scuff [scuf], *va.* y *vn.* (Fam.) 1. Ponerse áspera una superficie con el uso o desgaste. 2. Arrastrar los pies al andar.

Scuffle [scuf'-l], *s.* Quimera a puñetazos, pendencia, contienda, riña, altercación, reyerta a fuerza de agarrar, de tirar o de empujar. (Fam.) Retozo, jugueteo.

Scuffle, *vn.* Reñir, pelear, altercar. (Fam.) Retozar, juguetear.

Sculk [sculk], *vn.* *V.* SKULK.

Sculker [sculk'-ẹr], *s.* *V.* SKULKER.

Scull [scul], *s.* 1. Remo de espadilla, remo largo colocado a popa de una barquilla y que puede bogarlo un hombre solo. 2. Remo ligero y corto de espadilla. 3. Botecito, barquilla para remar con espadilla.

Scull, *va.* y *vn.* Cinglar, impeler un bote con un solo remo colocado a popa, y moviéndolo alternativamente a uno y otro lado.

Scullboat [scul'-bōt], *s.* Barquillo, botecito; (Mar.) serení.

Sculler [scul'-ẹr], *s.* Bote de un remero; remero de bote; cinglador, el que cingla.

Scullery [scul'-ẹr-i], *s.* Espetera; fregadero.

Scullion [scul'-yun], *s.* 1. Marmitón, pinche, galopín de cocina. *Scullion wench,* Fregona. 2. Sollastre, ente vil, despreciable.

Sculper [scul'-pẹr], *s.* Buril, cincel. Se escribe también, SCORPER.

Sculpin [scul'-pin], *s.* 1. Coto espinoso, pez inferior que tiene la cabeza grande y espinosa. 2. (Nueva Ingl.) Perjudicador; persona despreciable.

Sculptor [sculp'-tẹr], *s.* Escultor, el que modela efigies en barro o las esculpe en piedra, bronce, etc.; cincelador (en metales).

Sculptress [sculp'-tres], *f.* Escultora, la mujer que esculpe o entalla.

Sculptural [sculp'-chur-al], *a.* Escultural, relativo a la escultura, como arte, o propio de ella.

Sculpture [sculp'-chur], *s.* Escultura, el arte de esculpir y entallar.

Sculpture, *va.* 1. Esculpir, labrar o formar una efigie o imagen en madera, mármol o piedra. 2. Entallar, cincelar.

Sculpturesque [sculp-chur-esc'], *a.* Característico de la escultura o parecido a ella; fría o serenamente bello; majestuoso.

Scum [scum], *s.* 1. Nata, espuma, la materia impura o inútil que sobrenada en algunos licores cuando están en ebullición o fermentación; conjunto de plantas diminutas sobre el agua estancada; espuma, burbujas. 2. Hez, escoria; (fig.) desecho. *Scum of metals,* La escoria o deshecho de los metales. *Scum of the people,* La hez del pueblo, la canalla.

Scum, *va.* Espumar, quitar la espuma, la nata o la escoria que arrojan de sí los líquidos a su superficie.

Scumble [scum'-bl], *va.* Templar los colores de una pintura o dibujo frotándolos con un color relativamente seco, dar glacis. *Scumbling,* Glacis, unión de colores.

Scummy [scum'-i], *a.* Espumoso, cubierto de escoria, o de la naturaleza de ésta.

Scup [scup], *s.* Pez comestible común en la costa oriental de los Estados Unidos. Stenotomus chrysops.

Scupper [scup'-ẹr], *s.* Imbornal o embornal, uno de los agujeros que hay sobre la cubierta para vaciar el agua. *Scupper-nails*, Estoperoles.

Scurf [scūrf], *s.* 1. Caspa, descscamación harinosa de la cutícula, epidermis exfoliada en escamas; tiña de los árboles. 2. Cualquier partícula de cosa sucia o substancia escamosa adherida a una superficie.

Scurfiness [scūrf'-i-nes], *s.* El estado de lo que tiene caspa o epidermis exfoliada en escamas.

Scurfy [scūrf'-i], *a.* Casposo, costroso.

Scurrility [scur-ril'-i-ti], *s.* Baldón, improperio; lenguaje grosero; broma baja, soez; bufonería, bufonada.

Scurrilous [scur'-il-us], *a.* Vil, grosero, bajo; chocante; injurioso; difamatorio, oprobioso.

Scurrilously [scur'-il-us-li], *adv.* Injuriosamente, groseramente.

Scurry [scur'-i], *va.* y *vn.* Moverse o hacer mover precipitadamente; escaparse de prisa; apretar a correr. —*s.* 1. Movimiento precipitado. 2. Prisa, vuelta, remolino. (< Scour, 6 y 7 acep.

S-curve [es'-cūrv], *s.* Curva en S (en los caminos).

Scurvied [scūr'-vid], *a.* Escorbútico, atacado de escorbuto.

Scurvily [scūr'-vi-li], *adv.* Vilmente; groseramente; mezquinamente, ignominiosamente.

Scurviness [scūr'-vi-nes], *s.* Ruindad; malignidad, indignidad; torpeza, vileza.

Scurvy [scūr'-vi], *s.* Escorbuto, enfermedad caracterizada por manchas lívidas bajo la piel, inflamación y sanguinolencia de las encías y agotamiento general; la causa el uso prolongado a bordo de carnes saladas sin legumbres frescas. —*a.* 1. Vil, ruin, despreciable, bajo. 2. (Des.) Escorbútico.

Scurvy-grass [scūr'-vi-gras], *s.* (Bot.) Coclearia.

Scut [scut], *s.* (Prov. Ingl.) Colita, rabito, rabo o cola pequeña.

Scutate [skiū'-têt], *a.* 1. (Zool.) Escutiforme, cubierto de placas en forma de escamas. 2. (Bot.) Escuteliforme, que tiene forma de escudo.

Scutch [scuch], *va.* Agramar, espadillar, macerar a golpes el lino, cáñamo, etc.

Scutcheon [scuch'-un], *s.* 1. Escudo de armas. 2. Escudete de metal; plancha con el nombre de una persona.

Scutcher [scuch'-ẹr], *s.* Agramadera, útil para agramar.

Scutellate, Scutellated [skiū'-tel-ét, ed], *a.* Escuteloide, que tiene forma de escudo o de fuente.

Scutiform [skiū'-ti-fōrm], *a.* Escutiforme, en forma de escudo.

Scuttle [scut'-l], *s.* 1. Escotillón, puerta o tapa cerradiza en el suelo de la embarcación. *Cabin-scuttles*, (Mar.) Luces o lumbreras de camarote. *Scuttles of the mast*, (Mar.) Fogonaduras. 2. Cualquier agujero. 3. Cubo metálico para carbón; se llama también *coal-scuttle* o *coal-hod*. 4. Carrera corta; paso acelerado.

Scuttle, *va.* Hacer aberturas en el fondo, en los lados o en la cubierta de un buque; echar a pique.—*vn.* Apretar a correr. *V.* SCURRY. *To scuttle a vessel*, Barrenar un barco, para echarlo a pique.

Scythe [saidh], *s.* Guadaña, dalle (para segar o cortar la hierba).

Scythian [sith'-i-an], *a.* Escita, escítico, relativo o perteneciente a la Escitia o a sus naturales.—*s.* Escita.

'sdeath [sdeth], *inter.* que denota ira, impaciencia o énfasis.

Sea [sī], *s.* 1. Mar, toda el agua salada que rodea la tierra; océano. 2. Mar, considerable extensión del océano rodeada en parte de tierra; menos frecuentemente, lago grande. 3. Olaje, oleada, oleaje; ola grande, el curso de las ondas. 4. Mar, la abundancia excesiva o vasta extensión de una cosa. 5. Cualquier cosa muy tempestuosa. *At sea*, (1) En el mar. (2) No saber qué hacer, estar perplejo. *Beyond sea*, Allende el mar, ultramarino. *The main sea*, Alta mar, mar ancha. *Narrow sea*, Estrecho de mar. *Heavy sea*, Oleada, ola fuerte. *High-swelling sea*, Mar de leva. *The sea runs very high*, La mar está muy crecida. *To put to sea*, Salir a la mar, hacerse a la vela. *Half-seas-over*, Medio borracho. *A high sea*, Una mar gruesa. *Sea-bank*, (1) Muralla de mar, especie de dique opuesto a las aguas del mar. (2) Orilla del mar. *Sea-beat, sea-beaten*, Batido o golpeado por las olas de la mar. *Sea-biscuit*, Galleta de marinero. *Sea-boat*, Embarcación marinera. *A good sea-boat*, Embarcación velera. *Sea-born*, Nacido en la mar, marino. *Sea-breach*, Irrupción de mar que rompe un dique. *Sea-bream*, Besugo, pez de los espáridos. *Sea-breeze*, Brisa, viento de mar, que sopla del mar hacia tierra. *Sea-brief*, (Mar.) Carta de mar o marítima. *Sea-built*, Construido para la mar o para navegar. *Sea-cabbage, sea-colewort, sea-kale*, (Bot.) Berza marina. *Sea-calf*, Foca o becerro marino. *Sea-cap*, Gorra de marinero. *Sea-captain*, Capitán de navío o de otra embarcación. *Sea-card*, (Mar.) Rosa náutica. *Sea-chart*, (Mar.) Carta de marear. *Sea-coal*, Carbón de piedra (el transportado por mar). *Sea-cob*, Gaviota. *Sea-compass*, Brújula o aguja de marear. *Sea-cucumber*, Cohombro de mar, holoturia que recibe este nombre a causa de su figura. *Sea-dragon*, Araña o dragón marino, un pez. *Sea-eagle*, Halieto, águila pescadora, ave marítima rapaz, de plumaje leonado y cola blanca. Haliætus. *Sea-ear*, Oreja de mar, aulone, molusco gasterópodo. *Sea-egg*, *V. Sea-urchin*. *Sea-fennel*, (Bot.) Hinojo marino. *Sea-fight*, Batalla o combate naval. *Sea-fish*, Pez o pescado de mar. *Sea-fowl*, Ave marítima o ave de mar; conjunto de aves marinas. *Sea-gate*, (1) Oleada larga. (2) Punto de salida al mar. (3) Compuerta de marea. *Sea-girt*, Rodeado o cercado por el mar. *Sea-green*, (*a.*) Verdemar. (*s.*) Color verde azulado obscuro, como el del mar. *Sea-gull*, Gaviota, ave de los láridos. *Sea-hedgehog*, Equino. *Sea-hog*, Marsopa, marsopla o cachalote. *Sea-holly*, (Bot.) Cardo corredor. *Sea-holm*, Isleta no habitada. *Sea-horse*, Caballo marino, hipocampo; hipopótamo. *Sea-king*, Rey de piratas de los pueblos del norte. *Sea-legs*, Pie marino, facultad de andar por la cubierta de un buque sin caerse ni dar tumbos. *Sea-letter*, Patente de mar, documento que lleva un buque neutral y que indica su nacionalidad, matrícula, clase de cargamento, etc. *Sea-lettuce*, Lechuga de mar, alga marina verde que se usa a menudo como alimento. Ulva lactuca. *Sea-level*, Nivel del mar. *Sea-lion*, León marino, foca de largas orejas. *Sea-lungs*, Pólipo coelentorado (ctenophora). *Sea-mark*, Valiza, boya, señal que se pone con palo, mástil, tonel o cualquier otra cosa en los parajes donde la navegación es peligrosa. *Sea-mew*, Gaviota, particularmente la europea. *Sea-monster*, Monstruo marino. *Sea-moss*, (1) Carolina, ova, alga marina comestible, especialmente la rosada. (2) Polípero marino parecido al musgo. *Sea-nettle*, Ortiga de mar, acalefo que causa picazón en la piel. *Sea-nymph*, Ninfa marina. *Sea-onion*, Cebolla albarrana, escila marítima. *Sea-ooze*, Cieno de mar. *Sea-otter*, Nutria marina. *Sea-pen*, Pluma de mar, pólipo en forma de pluma rizada. *Sea-piece*, Pintura marítima o naval, pintura que representa cualquiera cosa perteneciente al mar o a la navegación. *Sea-pool*, Marisma; lago o laguna de agua salada. *Sea-porcupine*, Cierto pez espinoso de mar. *Sea-raven*, (1) *V.* SCULPIN. (2) Cormorán, ave afín al pelícano. *Sea-risk*, Riesgo o peligro de mar. *Sea-rocket*, (Bot.) Alga marina. *Sea-room*, Alta mar, espacio suficiente para maniobrar una embarcación. *Sea-rover*, Pirata; corsario. *Sea-serpent*, Serpiente acuática o de mar; animal marino enorme, parecido a la serpiente, que algunos pretenden haber visto. *Sea-service*, El servicio de marina o de mar. *Sea-shark*, Tiburón. *Sea-shell*, Concha marina. *Sea-star*, *V.* STARFISH. *Sea-term*, Término naval, voz náutica. *Sea-tossed*, Batido por el mar. *Sea-unicorn*, Unicornio de mar, nombre vulgar del narval. *Sea-urchin*, Equino, erizo de mar; equinodermo. Echinus. *Sea-voyage*, Viaje por mar. *Sea-wall*, Muralla de mar, especie de dique para romper el ímpetu de las olas; banco de arena, piedras, etc., arrojadas por el mar. *Sea-walled*, Rodeado o protegido por el mar, como por una pared. *Sea-water*, Agua del mar, agua salada. *Sea-wave*, Ola. *Sea-wolf*, Lobo marino.

Sea-anemone [sī-a-nem'-o-nẹ], *s.* Anémone de mar, especie de actinia, pólipo que se parece a la flor del mismo nombre.

Sea-bass [sī'-bas], *s.* Serrano, pez de mar muy estimado, abundante desde la Florida hasta el Cabo Cod, en Massachusetts; se llama también *bluefish* y *blackfish* o *rock-bass*. Centropristis striatus.

Seaboard [sī'-bōrd], *a.* Vecino al mar, o cerca de él.—*s.* Orilla, borde del mar.

Sea-coast [sī'-cōst], *s.* Costa marítima, orilla, borde del mar.

Sea-cow [sī'-cau], *s.* Manato, manatí, vaca marina.

Sea-dog [sī'-dog], *s.* 1. Foca común. 2. León marino, foca grande de California. 3. Tiburón espinoso, perro de mar. 4. Marinero viejo o persona aficionada al mar; también, pirata, filibustero; (fam.) lobo marino.

Seafarer [sī'-fār-ẹr], *s.* Marinero, navegante.

Seafaring [sī'-fār-ing], *a.* Marino, marinero, navegante.

Seafood [sī'-fūd], *s.* Mariscos.

Seagoing [sī'-go-ing], *a.* 1. Propio

para la navegación de altura. 2. Navegante, experto en la navegación por alta mar.

Seal [sîl], *s.* 1. Sello para cerrar las cartas y la impresión que hace en la oblea o lacre. 2. Selladura, la acción de sellar. 3. El lacre que tiene la señal formada por el sello; señal o marca característica. 4. El acto de sellar, concluir o poner fin a una cosa. 5. Sello; firma; autenticación, fianza; sacramento. *Great seal*, Gran sello. *Privy seal*, Sello privado (o pequeño). *To affix one's seal*, Poner uno su sello. *Under the hand and seal of*, Firmado y sellado por. *Keeper of the seals*, Guardasellos. (< Fr. ant. *seel*, < Lat. *sigillum*, sello.)

Seal, *va.* 1. Sellar, poner el sello sobre una cosa. 2. Sellar, estampar una cosa en otra. 3. Sellar, concluir, poner fin. 4. Sellar, afirmar, afianzar, confirmar. 5. Cerrar una carta, un paquete, con lacre u otra substancia. 6. Santiguar; bautizar, confirmar. 7. Guardar secreto. *To seal up*, Cerrar. 8. Poner una chapeleta para impedir el retroceso de gas o aire.

Seal, *vn.* Cazar focas.—*s.* Foca, becerro marino, mamífero acuático y carnívoro que vive principalmente en las latitudes árticas. (< A.-S. seol.)

Sealer [sîl'-ẹr], *s.* 1. Sellador. 2. Cazador de focas.

Sealing-wax [sîl'-ing-wax], *s.* Lacre.

Seal-ring [sîl'-ring], *s.* Sortija con sello.

Sealskin [sîl'-skin], *s.* Piel de foca o una prenda de vestir hecha de ella.

Seam [sîm], *s.* 1. Costura, línea visible de unión entre dos partes o piezas. 2. Grieta, hendedura, rendija, raja. 3. Listón saliente o reborde que se forma al juntar dos cosas, o que queda en una pieza de fundición al salir del molde. 4. Costurón, cicatriz; arruga. 5. (Geol.) Filón, vena, capa delgada, yacimiento de mineral o roca. 6. Sutura. (Mar.) Costura de los tablones. *To pay the seams*, (Mar.) Embrear las costuras.

Seam, *va.* 1. Hacer costuras, coser. 2. Señalar con cicatrices.

Seamaid [sî'-mêd], *sf.* Sirena.

Seaman [sî'-man], *s.* 1. Marinero, hombre de mar; marino experimentado. 2. Tritón, el macho de la sirena. *Seaman's wages*, Sueldos o mesadas de los marineros.

Seamanship [sî'-man-ship], *s.* La habilidad o pericia en la navegación o en el arte de hacer maniobrar una embarcación.

Seamless [sîm'-les], *a.* Sin costura. *Seamless hose*, Medias sin costura.

Seamster [sîm'-stẹr], *sm.* (Ant.) Costurero.

Seamstress [sîm'-stres], *sf.* Costurera, la mujer que tiene por oficio coser ropa blanca. Se escribe también **Sempstress**.

Seamy [sîm'-i], *a.* Que tiene o muestra costuras; (fig.) lo peor. *The seamy side*, El lado peor, el aspecto menos favorable.

Seance [sé'-ãns], *s.* Sesión; en especial, reunión de espiritistas. (Fr.)

Seaplane [sî'-plên], *s.* Hidroavión.

Seaport [sî'-pōrt], *s.* Puerto de mar.

Sear [sîr], *a.* Seco, marchito, ajado; dícese ordinariamente de las plantas que se han sacado.

Sear, *va.* 1. Disecar, marchitar, tostar, chamuscar. 2. Cauterizar, quemar la superficie de una cosa. 3. Hacer calloso o insensible.

Sear, *s.* Linguete o fiador en la llave de un arma de fuego que mantiene el gatillo en seguro o montado. *Sear-spring*, Muelle real.

Searce [sẹrs], *va.* Cerner harina.

Search [sẹrch], *va.* y *vn.* 1. Explorar, escudriñar, buscar, registrar, hallar buscando. *To search a house*, Registrar una casa. 2. Inquirir, indagar. 3. Tentar, reconocer con la tienta la cavidad de una herida; probar, poner a prueba. 4. Investigar, indagar, hacer pesquisas o averiguaciones, informarse de. *To search after*, Preguntar por alguno; indagar, inquirir. *To search into*, Examinar, investigar. *To search for*, Buscar, tratar de descubrir; inquirir o procurar; hallar alguna cosa. *To search out*, Hallar o encontrar alguna cosa buscándola.

Search, *s.* 1. Registro, el acto de registrar. *The right of search*, El derecho de registrar o visitar un barco. 2. Pesquisa, averiguación. 3. Busca, buscada, el acto de buscar. *Search-light*, Holofote, luz eléctrica con reflector que proyecta un rayo luminoso de gran intensidad; se usa mucho en la navegación por la costa y en los buques de guerra.

Searchable [sẹrch'-a-bl], *a.* Que puede de buscarse, escudriñarse, explorarse.

Searcher [sẹrch'-ẹr], *s.* 1. Buscador, escudriñador, pesquisidor, indagador, inquiridor; vista, inspector, empleado de aduana encargado de registrar el equipaje de los viajeros. 2. Todo instrumento o aparato empleado para examinar o investigar; gato, instrumento con garfios que sirve para escudriñar el interior de un cañón; sonda para las piedras de la vejiga; buscador, ocular de microscopio.

Searching [sẹrch'-ing], *a.* Penetrante, escrutador; completo, cabal.

Search-warrant [sẹrch'-wer''-ant], *s.* Mandato judicial disponiendo el registro de una casa, lugar u objeto.

†**Sear-cloth** [sîr'-clōth], *s. V.* CERECLOTH.

Seashore [sî'-shōr], **Seaside** [sî'-said], *s.* Ribera, costa u orilla del mar.

Seasick [sî'-sic], *a.* Mareado, que se marea.

Seasickness [sî'-sic-nes], *s.* Mareamiento, mareo, náuseas causadas por el balanceo de un buque; indisposición muy molesta.

Season [sî'-zn], *s.* 1. Estación, una de las cuatro partes en que se divide el año. 2. Sazón, tiempo determinado, tiempo oportuno o conveniente; temporada; período de tiempo. 3. Época, momento; tiempo fijo. *Dull season*, (Com.) Estación muerta. *In season, in due season*, En tiempo oportuno. *To be in season*, Ser de la estación, del tiempo. *In season*, En sazón, a su tiempo.

Season, *va.* 1. Sazonar, dar sazón al manjar; condimentar. 2. Imbuir, persuadir, infundir. 3. Sazonar, poner las cosas en el punto y madurez que deben tener. 4. Templar, moderar, hacer más agradable, o menos riguroso y severo. 5. Aclimatar, acostumbrar, habituar. —*vn.* 1. Secarse, endurecerse, v. g. el maderaje. 2. Sazonarse, madurarse, hacerse propio para el uso; aclimatarse (una persona).

Seasonable [sî'-zn-a-bl], *a.* Oportuno, conveniente, favorable, a propósito, de estación.

Seasonably [sî'-zn-a-bli], *adv.* En sazón, oportunamente.

Seasoned [sî'-znd], *a.* 1. Sazonado. 2. Picante, curado. 3. Aclimatado, habituado. *Seasoned traveler*, Viajero consumado.

Seasoner [sî'-zn-ẹr], *s.* Sazonador.

Seasoning [sî'-zn-ing], *s.* 1. Sazón, condimento que se da a los manjares. 2. Salsa o sal de un cuento o de un escrito; sainete de un dicho, etc.; lo que se añade para aumentar el placer del goce. 3. El procedimiento de secarse y endurecerse (la madera). 4. Aclimatación.

Seat [sît], *s.* 1. Asiento, cualquiera cosa que sirve para sentarse, silla, banco. 2. Asiento, fondo, parte de la silla en que uno se coloca. 3. Fondillos de los calzones; nalga. 4. Sitio, posición, paraje o lugar en que se halla situada alguna cosa. 5. Residencia, morada, domicilio. *Country-seat*, Sitio, casa de campo. 6. Privilegio, derecho o manera de sentarse.

Seat, *va.* 1. Sentar, asentar, colocar en asientos. 2. Tener asientos para (personas). 3. Colocar o acomodar a alguno en un empleo elevado. 4. Asentar, poner alguna cosa de manera que esté firme. 5. Poner un asiento a una silla; echar fondillos (a un pantalón). *The hall will seat eight hundred*, La sala tiene asientos para ochocientas personas.

Seating [sît'-ing], *s.* 1. Acción de sentar o de sentarse. 2. Material para entapizar las sillas o sofás. 3. (Mec.) Lecho, base.

Seating capacity [sît'-ing ca-pas'-i-ti], *s.* Cupo, cabida.

Seaward [sî'-ward], *adv.* Hacia el mar.—*a.* Dirigido hacia el mar.

Seaway [sî'-wê], *s.* 1. Ruta oceánica. 2. Vía fluvial que permite la navegación de embarcaciones marítimas. 3. Mar gruesa o alborotada.

Seaweed [sî'-wîd], *s.* 1. Alga marina (y aun la que vive en el agua dulce); ova. 2. Toda planta que crece en el mar.

Seaworthy [sî'-wūr-dhi], *a.* Dícese de la embarcación que es a propósito para navegar.

Sebaceous [sẹ-bé'-shius], *a.* Sebáceo, seboso, perteneciente o parecido al sebo, que contiene materia pingüe.

Sebacic [sẹ-bas'-ic], *a.* Sebácico, que proviene de la grasa, del cebo. *Sebacic acid*, Ácido sebácico.

Sebate [sî'-bêt], *s.* Sebato, sal formada de ácido sebácico con alguna base.

Secant [sî'-cant], *a.* Cortante, que divide en dos partes.—*s.* Secante, línea que corta una superficie, o plano que corta un cuerpo; secante, el radio prolongado hasta encontrarse con la tangente.

Secede [sẹ-sîd'], *vn.* Apartarse, separarse de un cuerpo político o religioso.

Seceder [sẹ-sîd'-ẹr], *s.* Separatista, el que se aparta.

Secession [sẹ-sesh'-un], *s.* Apartamiento, separación, antiguamente secesión.

Secessionist [se-sesh'-un-ist], *s.* Partidario de la separación; secesionista, el que en la guerra civil de los Estados Unidos mantenía el derecho de los Estados del Sur a la separación política.

Seclude [se-clūd], *va.* Apartar, excluir, alejar á alguien de una compañía o sociedad; alejarse de otros; encerrar, confinar en estado de aislamiento. *Secluded,pp.* Alejado, apartado, desviado; retirado en el aislamiento, en la soledad.

Seclusion [se-clū'-zhun], *s.* 1. Separación; exclusión, aislamiento, soledad. 2. Lugar apartado.

Second [sec'-und], *a.* 1. Segundo, lo que sigue inmediatamente al primero. *Second son,* Segundón. 2. Secundario, subordinado; inferior. 3. Segundo, otro, idéntico a otro. *Second-class,* De segunda clase, de grado inferior. *Second-hand,* De segunda mano, de lance, que ha sido poseído o usado por otro; por intermedio de otro. *Second-rate,* De segunda clase o categoría. *The twenty-second,* El vigésimo segundo. *To be second to none,* No ser inferior a nadie.—*s.* 1. Segundo, brazo derecho; el que ayuda a otro en una empresa, en un negocio; apoyo, auxilio; defensor, sostenedor. 2. Padrino, el que apadrina a otro en un desafío. 3. Segundo, una de las sesenta partes en que se divide el minuto de hora o de grado. 4. Segunda, intervalo músico entre dos sonidos sucesivos. *The second best,* El mejor después del primero. En los certámenes, el accésit. *To come off second best,* Llevar lo peor, o la peor parte en una contienda.

Second, *va.* 1. Apoyar, sostener, apadrinar, ayudar, auxiliar, favorecer; apoyar un proyecto de ley en los cuerpos deliberantes, como preliminar a su discusión o aceptación. 2. Segundar, asegundar, ser segundo o seguirse al primero.

Secondarily [sec'-und-e-ri-li-], *adv.* Secundariamente, en segundo lugar.

Secondary [sec'-und-e-ri], *a.* 1. Secundario, de segunda clase, influencia o grado; subordinado, subalterno; subsecuente; resultante; accesorio; que depende de otro; que gira alrededor de un planeta principal. 2. De, o perteneciente a una corriente eléctrica inducida o a su circuito.—*s.* 1. Lugarteniente, delegado, diputado. 2. Algo de tamaño o importancia secundarios. 3. (Astr.) Círculo secundario; planeta secundario, satélite. 4. Una de las plumas grandes que crecen en la segunda articulación del ala de un ave. 5. Ala posterior de las mariposas y otros insectos.

Seconder [sec'-und-er], *s.* El que apoya, secunda o sostiene la proposición que ha hecho algún otro.

Second-hand [sec'-und-hand], *s.* 1. Segunda mano, la posesión que se recibe del primer poseedor. 2. Manecilla de reloj que indica los segundos. *At second-hand,* Por imitación; secundariamente; de segunda mano, de lance.

Second lieutenant [sec'-und liu-ten'-ant], *s.* Subteniente.

Secondly [sec'-und-li], *adv.* En segundo lugar.

Second nature [sec'-und nê'-chur], *s.* Hábito, costumbre, arraigo.

Second-sight [sec'-und-sait], *s.* Conocimiento de lo futuro.

Secrecy [sî'-cre-si], *s.* 1. Secreto, silencio cuidadoso, sigilo. 2. Soledad, retiro. 3. Fidelidad en guardar sigilo o secreto.

Secret [sî'-cret], *a.* 1. Secreto, oculto. 2. Secreto, retirado, escondido. 3. Secreto, callado, reservado, que no se sabe generalmente. 4. Callado, reservado, silencioso, que guarda un secreto. 5. Obsceno, vergonzoso, que no debe salir á luz.—*s.* 1. Secreto, el silencio cuidadoso de no revelar lo que se quiere tener oculto, y la misma cosa que se quiere guardar callada. 2. Secreto, una cosa no conocida o sabida sólo por una o muy pocas personas. 3. Razón oculta; lo que cuando es conocido, explica; llave. 4. *pl.* Partes pudendas o genitales. *In secret,* Secretamente, en secreto. Secreto; cuidado o disimulación silenciosa; la cosa que se oculta o no se descubre.

Secretary [sec'-re-te-ri], *s.* 1. Secretario, el que cuida de la correspondencia de otros y escribe sus cartas, despachos y documentos públicos o privados. 2. Secretario, ministro, funcionario cuyo empleo es presidir y dirigir un ministerio. 3. Escritorio, papelera, mueble. *Secretary of State,* Ministro de Estado. *Secretary of War,* Ministro de la guerra. *Secretary-bird,* Secretario (Serpentarius), ave de rapiña de África.

Secretaryship [sec'-re-te-ri-ship], *s.* Secretaría, el cargo o empleo de secretario.

Secrete [se-crît'], *va.* 1. Desviar, esconder, tener secreto, ocultar, encubrir. 2. (Med.) Secretar, separar, elaborar algo de la sangre o de la savia por el procedimiento de la secreción.

Secretion [se-crî'-shun], *s.* 1. Secreción, el procedimiento por el cual se separan de la sangre o de la savia ciertos elementos para convertirse en nuevas substancias. 2. Secreción, la substancia secretada. 3. Ocultación, escondimiento, el acto de esconder.

Secretive [se-crî'-tiv], *a.* 1. Secreto, callado, silencioso, reservado, dispuesto a ocultar. 2. Secretivo, secretorio, que promueve la secreción.

Secretiveness [se-crî'-tiv-nes], *s.* Inclinación a ocultar o esconder.

Secretly [sî'-cret-li], *adv.* Secretamente, ocultamente.

Secretness [sî'-cret-nes], *s.* 1. Secreto, sigilo. 2. La calidad que constituye a uno propio para guardar un secreto.

Secretory [se-crî'-to-ri], *a.* Secretorio, perteneciente á la secreción; que secreta o que sirve para la secreción.

Secret service [sî'-cret ser'-vis] *s.* Policía secreta.

Sect [sect], *s.* 1. Secta, la comunidad de hombres que siguen la doctrina y opinión particular de algún maestro célebre, especialmente en materias religiosas; denominación, una comunión que no está de acuerdo con una iglesia establecida. 2. Partido, pandilla, orden.

Sectarian [sec-tê'-ri-an], *a.* y *s.* Sectario, que profesa o sigue alguna secta con tesón; fanático.—*s.* Sectario, miembro (fanático) de una secta.

Sectarianism [sec-tê'-ri-an-izm], *s.* Carácter o tendencia de secta; adhesión excesiva a una secta.

Sectary [sec'-ta-ri], *s.* Sectario, secuaz; discípulo.

Sectile [sec'-til], *a.* Sectil, que se puede cortar, dividir o separar en secciones.

Section [sec'-shun], *s.* 1. Sección, cortadura, división; parte, porción distinta, subdivisión de un capítulo o de una ley; en los Estados Unidos, área de terreno público, una milla en cuadro que contiene 640 acres y constituye la trigésimasexta parte de una municipalidad o *township.* 2. Sección, corte, representación de un edificio, de una máquina, de una formación geológica, etc., de manera que muestre el interior. 3. Corte muy delgado de alguna cosa, especialmente para su examen con el microscopio. 4. (Impr.) El signo §, que indica una subdivisión. *Section-cutter,* Instrumento para cortar secciones muy delgadas para el examen microscópico.

Sectional [sec'-shun-al], *a.* 1. Seccionario, perteneciente a una parte; local. 2. Hecho de secciones, como un vapor.

Sectionalism [sec'-shun-al-izm], *s.* Regionalismo, prejuicios regionales.

Sector [sec'-ter], *s.* 1. (Geom.) Sector, parte del círculo comprendida entre dos radios y el arco comprendido entre ellos. 2. Un instrumento matemático o astronómico en forma de sector geométrico; compás de proporción.

Secular [sec'-yu-lar], *a.* 1. Secular, seglar, mundano, temporal. 2. Secular: dícese del clero no sujeto a las reglas monásticas. 3. Secular, lo que sucede una vez en un siglo. 4. Efectuado en el curso de un siglo o siglos.—*s.* Seglar, lego, por oposición a eclesiástico, sea secular o regular.

Secularity [sec-yu-lar'-i-ti], **Secularness** [sec'-yu-lar-nes], *s.* El apego a las cosas mundanas.

Secularly [sec'-yu-lar-li], *adv.* A lo seglar o como seglar; como un hombre apegado al mundo.

Secularization [sec-yu-lar-i-zê'-shun], *s.* Secularización, acción y efecto de secularizar.

Secularize [sec'-yu-lar-aiz], *va.* Secularizar, hacer secular o mundano; transferir la jurisdicción civil de un distrito o de un país de manos de eclesiásticos a las de seglares.

Secundine [sec'-un-dain], *s.* Secundina, túnica o membrana que cubre el feto.

Secure [se-kiūr'], *a.* 1. Seguro, tranquilo, sin temor o inquietud. 2. Descuidado, negligente, que no hace caso, lleno de confianza. 3. Seguro, libre y exento de peligro, daño o riesgo. 4. Seguro, cierto, indudable. 5. Confiado en sí mismo.

Secure, *va.* 1. Asegurar, resguardar, poner en seguridad o al abrigo; salvar, proteger, poner en salvo. 2. Asegurar, dar firmeza y seguridad a una cosa, afianzar; dar garantías. 3. Encerrar, aprisionar, poner bajo llave, impedir que algo se escape o pierda. 4. Lograr, obtener, adquirir, hacerse dueño de. *To secure one,* Asegurar o poner en lugar seguro a una persona; prender. *I have secured my place,* He obtenido ya un asiento.

Securely [se-kiūr'-li], *adv.* Seguramente, con seguridad, sin riesgo; tranquilamente.

Secureness [se-kiūr'-nes], *s.* Seguridad, calidad de seguro; falta de cuidado.

Security [se-kiū'-ri-ti], *s.* 1. Seguridad, el estado de las cosas que las hace firmes, seguras y libres de todo riesgo y peligro; protección, defensa. 2. Seguridad, tranquilidad, confianza; también exceso de confianza, falta de cautela, descuido. 3. Seguridad. fianza, obligación de indemnidad a favor de alguno.—*pl.* Vales, valores, garantías de pago. *To stand security*, Salir fiador por otro. *Security risk*, Persona de dudosas antecedentes y peligrosa para la seguridad nacional.

Sedan [sẹ-dan'], *s.* 1. Sedán, automóvil sedán. 2. Silla de manos.

Sedate [sẹ-dêt'], *a.* Sereno, apacible, sosegado, formal, serio, juicioso.

Sedately [sẹ-dêt'-li], *adv.* Tranquilamente, formalmente.

Sedateness [sẹ-dêt'-nes], *s.* Serenidad, tranquilidad, calma, quietud.

Sedative [sed'-a-tiv], *a.* Sedativo, calmante.—*s.* Sedativo, medicamento calmante.

Sedentariness [sed'-en-tẹ-ri-nes], *s.* Pereza, poltronería, falta de actividad.

Sedentary [sed'-en-tẹ-ri], *a.* 1. Sedentario: aplícase á la vida o ejercicio de poca acción y movimiento. 2. Poltrón, flojo, perezoso. 3. (Zool.) Sedentario, que queda fijado o unido a un objeto.

Sedge [sej], *s.* (Bot.) Juncia, cárice, esparganio, cualquiera planta de la familia de las ciperáceas; vulgarmente, junco, enea. *Sedge-warbler, sedge-bird*, Curruca, pajarillo cantor de Europa.

Sedgy [sej'-i], *a.* Cubierto de juncias o cárices.

Sediment [sed'-i-mẹnt], *s.* 1. Sedimento, hez, poso, zurrapas. 2. (Geol.) Detritus transportado o depositado por el agua.

Sedimental [sed-i-men'-tal], *a.* Sedimental, perteneciente a los sedimentos.

Sedimentary [sed-i-men'-ta-ri], *a.* Sedimentario, sedimentoso, que participa de la naturaleza del sedimento o está formado por él. *Sedimentary rocks*, Rocas sedimentarias.

Sedimentation [sed-i-men-té'-shun], *s.* Sedimentación.

Sedition [sẹ-dish'-un], *s.* Sedición, tumulto, levantamiento popular contra la autoridad; motín, revuelta, sublevación.

Seditious [sẹ-dish'-us], *a.* 1. Sedicioso. 2. Culpable de sedición, faccioso, tumultuoso; amotinado.

Seditiously [sẹ-dish'-us-li], *adv.* Sediciosamente.

Seditiousness [sẹ-dish'-us-nes], *s.* Calidad de sedicioso; excitación a la sedición.

Seduce [sẹ-diūs'], *va.* 1. Seducir, desviar del deber, de la rectitud o de la verdad, instigar a alguna cosa mala. 2. En especial, seducir á una mujer.

Seducement [sẹ-diūs'-mẹnt], *s.* Seducción, acción de seducir o los medios empleados para ello.

Seducer [sẹ-diūs'-ẹr], *s.* Seductor, seductora; el o la que seduce.

Seducible, Seduceable [sẹ-diūs'-i-bl], *a.* Capaz de ser seducido o de dejarse seducir.

Seduction [sẹ-duc'-shun], *s.* Seducción.

Seductive [sẹ-duc'-tiv], *a.* Seductivo, atractivo, halagüeño; persuasivo.

Seductress [sẹ-duc'-tres], *sf.* Seductora, la que seduce o corrompe.

Sedulity [sẹ-diū'-li-ti], *s.* Diligencia, aplicación, ahinco, cuidado.

Sedulous [sed'-yu-lus], *a.* Diligente, aplicado, cuidadoso, asiduo.

Sedulousness [sed'-yu-lus-nes], *s.* Ahinco, cuidado celoso, diligencia, asiduidad, aplicación.

Sedum [sí'-dum], *s.* (Bot.) Extenso género de plantas de la familia de las crasuláceas; comprende la faba crasa, la siempreviva, etc. *V.* STONECROP.

See [sí], *s.* Silla pontifical o episcopal; sede, diócesis o episcopado.

See, *va.* (*pret.* SAW, *pp.* SEEN, *ger.* SEEING). 1. Ver, percibir con los ojos; mirar, observar. 2. Ver, percibir con la mente: concebir, comprender, conocer. 3. Ver, distinguir, descubrir, reparar; notar, inquirir, indagar, informarse; también conocer, sufrir. *See whether I am right*, Averigüe Vd. si tengo razón. *I have seen better days*, He conocido mejores tiempos. 4. Ver, visitar a un sujeto o estar con él con un objeto cualquiera, tener relaciones con alguien; hacer o recibir visitas. 5. Acompañar, escoltar. 6. Tener como cargo o cuidado (seguido de cláusula que empiece con *that*). *See that the work be done*, Cuide Vd. de que se haga el trabajo.—*vn.* 1. Ver, percibir con la vista. 2. Discernir, penetrar, comprender. 3. Preguntar, informarse, considerar, advertir; reflexionar; pensar en algo. *To see afar off*, Ver de lejos, ver a lo lejos. *To see for*, Buscar, inquirir. *To see into*, Ver y examinar una cosa a fondo, ver el interior de una cosa o penetrar en ella. *To see one another*, Visitarse, verse. *I'll see about it*, Yo lo veré, yo lo pensaré. *Let me see*, Déjeme Vd. ver, pensar o examinar (la cosa de que se trata). *To see a person home*, Acompañar a una persona a su casa. *Let's see, let us see*, Veamos; a ver. *I see*, Ya veo, ya comprendo. *To see out*, Ver u oir hasta el fin; ver partir; eclipsar, dejar deslucido a otro. *To see through*, Comprender, reconocer; llevar a cabo; ayudar a uno en la ejecución de algo. *To see to*, Tener cuidado, pensar, poner atención en algo. *See to it*, Tenga Vd. cuidado de ello, piense Vd. en ello.

See, *inter.* ¡Mira!

Seed [síd], *s.* 1. Semilla, simiente; grano de los vegetales. *Seed of a fruit*, Pepita, cuesco. *Animal seed*, Esperma, semen. 2. Origen, causa primitiva, principio productivo. 3. Progenie, casta, generación. *Seed-basket*, Sembradera, cesto para grano. *Seed-bud*, Botón, el germen o rudimento del fruto. *Seed-corn*, Trigo o maíz para sembrar. *Seed-drill*, Sembradora, máquina de sembrar. *Seed-lac*, Laca seca en granos. *Seed-vessel*, Pericarpio, la parte de una planta en que están contenidas las semillas. *To run to seed*, Producir semillas, convertirse todo en semillas; agotarse. *Seed-cake*, Bollo o torta hecha con semillas aromáticas (anisado). *Seedlip, seedlop*, Sementero. *Seed-plot*, Semillero, plantel.

Seed, *va.* 1. Sembrar, esparcir las semillas. 2. Adornar con figuras parecidas a semillas. 3. Despepitar.—*vn.* 1. Sembrar semillas. 2. Granar, desgargolar, llegar a la madurez, y producir la semilla.

Seeder [síd'-ẹr], *s.* Sembradora, máquina de sembrar.

Seediness [síd'-i-nes], *s.* La condición o calidad de lo que está lleno de simiente.

Seed-pearl [síd'-pẹrl], *s.* Aljófar, rostrillo, granillos de perlas.

Seed-time [síd'-taim], *s.* Sementera, siembra.

Seedling [síd'-ling], *s.* Planta de semillero.

Seedsman [sídz'-man], *s.* 1. Sembrador, el que siembra granos. 2. Tratante en semillas o simientes.

Seedy [síd'-i], *a.* 1. Granado, lleno de granos, abundante en semillas. 2. Desharrapado, pobre y andrajoso, descamisado.

Seeing [sí'-ing], *s.* Vista, visión, el acto de ver.—*conj. Seeing* o *seeing that*, Visto que, siendo así que, puesto que.

Seek [sík], *va.* (*pret.* y *pp.* SOUGHT). 1. Buscar, ir en busca de, procurar hallar alguna cosa. 2. Inquirir; solicitar, pretender. 3. Intentar, procurar. 4. Preguntar, interrogar, suplicar. 5. Acudir, dirigirse, recurrir.—*vn.* Buscar, hacer preguntas o diligencias para hallar. *To seek after*, Buscar, inquirir; solicitar, pretender; perseguir; pesquisar. *To seek for*, Andar buscando, inquiriendo o preguntando por una cosa; procurar conseguir un objeto. *To seek of*, Solicitar. *To seek out*, Buscar por todos lados; pesquisar, hacer pesquisas o investigaciones; solicitar, hacer esfuerzos por conseguir un fin; seguir los perros la caza por el olfato. *To seek to*, Acudir. *To seek one's life*, Querer matar o asesinar a uno.

Seeker [sík'-ẹr], *s.* Buscador, inquiridor, investigador.

Seel [síl], *va.* 1. Tapar o coser los ojos a los halcones. 2. Cerrar los ojos; cegar. 3. *vn.* Tumbarse sobre una banda. *V. To* HEEL.

Seem [sím], *vn.* 1. Parecer, tener apariencia o señales de, darse un aire a alguno. 2. Parecerle a uno alguna cosa. *It seems*, Parece, según parece.

Seemer [sím'-ẹr], *s.* El que parece.

Seeming [sím'-ing], *s.* Apariencia, parecer, exterior; particularmente, apariencia falsa.—*a.* Aparente, especioso, parecido; que tiene apariencia de algo.

Seemingly [sím'-ing-li], *adv* Al parecer, aparentemente.

Seemingness [sím'-ing-nes], *s.* Exterioridad, apariencia; plausibilidad.

Seemliness [sím'-li-nes], *s.* Gracia, gallardía; decoro, decencia, bien parecer; propiedad, la conformidad y correspondencia que deben guardar las cosas y personas entre sí.

Seemly [sím'-li], *a.* Decente, propio, correspondiente, decoroso, que conviene. *It is not seemly to*, No conviene que.—*adv.* Decentemente, de una manera conveniente.

Seen [sín], *pp.* de *To* SEE.

Seep [síp], *va.* y *vn.* (E. U. y Esco.) 1. Colar, pasar. 2. Colarse, rezumarse, pasar al través de los poros o intersticios. 3. Perder un líquido por haberse derramado o rezumado.

Seepage [síp'-ẹj], *s.* Coladura de un líquido; cantidad de un flúido que pasa por los poros de algo y se pierde.

Seer [sír], *s.* 1. Profeta, adivinador, el que prevé los acontecimientos futuros. 2. [sí'-ẹr] Veedor, el que ve o mira.

Seersucker [sír'-suk-ẹr], *s.* (Com.) Sirsaca, carranclán fino y rayado de la India.

Seesaw [sí'-sō], *s.* 1. Vaivén, movimiento alternativo. 2. Juego de muchachos, y la tabla de que se sirven para este juego.—*a.* De vaivén, que vacila.

Seesaw, *vn.* Balancear, dar o hacer balances.

Seethe [sídh], *va.* (*pp.* SEETHED, y antiguamente SODDEN o SOD). Hacer cocer, hacer hervir.—*vn.* Hervir, bullir, ponerse en movimiento algún licor por la acción del calor. *To seethe over,* Derramarse el líquido o salirse de su continente por estar hirviendo.

Seether [sídh'-ẹr], *s.* Caldera, marmita.

Seething [sídh'-ing], *a.* Hirviente, efervescente.

Segment [seg'-mẹnt], *s.* 1. Segmento, parte cortada o dividida; sección. 2. Segmento de un círculo.

Segmentation [seg-men-té'-shun], *s.* Acción y efecto de dividir en segmentos.

Segregate [seg'-rẹ-gêt], *va.* y *vn.* Segregar, separar o apartar una cosa de otra; segregarse.—*a.* Segregado, apartado, separado; selecto.

Segregation [seg-rẹ-gé'-shun], *s.* Segregación, separación, apartamiento.

Seidlitz [sed'-lits], *a.* De Seidlitz, en Bohemia. *Seidlitz powders,* Polvos de Seidlitz, que poseen propiedades alcalinas y constan de dos partes, un bicarbonato alcalino y uno ácido con ácido tartárico.

Seignior [sín'-yẹr], *s.* Señor.

Seignorage [sín'-yer-ệj], *s.* 1. Tasa que recibe un gobierno por acuñar monedas de oro y plata. 2. Ganancia de un gobierno obtenida en la acuñación de monedas. 3. *V.* ROYALTY, 3ª acep.

Seine [sên], *va.* y *vn.* Pescar con buitrago o red barredera.—*s.* Buitrago, red barredera.

Seismic, Seismical [sais'-mic, al], *a.* Seísmico, perteneciente a los terremotos o producido por ellos. (< Gr. *seismos,* temblor.)

Seismograph, Seismometer [sais'-mo-grạf, sais-mem'-e-tẹr], *s.* Seismógrafo, seismómetro, instrumento que señala automáticamente los fenómenos de un terremoto, mide su dirección, su intensidad, etc.

Seismology [sais-mel'-o-ji], *s.* Seismología, ciencia que trata de los terremotos.

Seizable [síz'-a-bl], *a.* Capaz de o expuesto a ser asido o embargado.

Seize [síz], *va.* y *vn.* 1. Asir, agarrar, coger. 2. Embargar, secuestrar bienes o efectos. 3. Apoderarse una pasión de ánimo de alguna persona. 4. (For.) Tomar bajo la custodia de la ley; poner en posesión. 5. (Mar.) Amarrar, dar una ligadura. *To seize on,* Apoderarse, agarrar con firmeza una cosa. *To seize upon,* Coger, agarrar o asir una cosa echándose sobre ella; embargar. *To seize again,* Volver a agarrar o asir lo que se había soltado; volver a embargar lo que se había desembargado. *To be seized with fear,* Sobrecogerse de miedo. *To be seized* (o *seised*) *of,* (For.) Estar en posesión de, poseer.

Seizer [síz'-ẹr], *s.* Agarrador, secuestrador; el que ase, embarga, o se apodera de algo. Como término forense se escribe también SEIZOR y SEISOR.

Seizin, Seisin [síz'-in], *s.* (For.) Posesión, el acto de poseer, y la cosa poseída; el acto de apoderarse o de tomar posesión; apoderamiento.

Seizing [síz'-ing], *s.* 1. El acto de asir o tomar posesión de una cosa y la misma cosa de que se toma posesión. 2. La cuerda con que se amarra; acción de atar las jarcias con una cuerda.

Seizure [sí'-zhur], *s.* 1. El acto de asir. 2. La cosa asida o agarrada. 3. Captura, la acción de apoderarse de alguna cosa por fuerza; embargo, secuestro.

Sejant, Sejeant [sí'-jant], *a.* (Her.) Sentado, que se representa sentado.

Sel [sel], *s.* (Esco.) *V.* SELF.

Seldom [sel'-dum], *adv.* Raramente, rara vez.

Select [sẹ-lect'], *va.* Escoger, entresacar; tomar con preferencia a otro o entre muchos; elegir.

Select, *a.* 1. Selecto, escogido, tomado con preferencia a otros. 2. (Fam.) Exclusivo. *Select society,* Sociedad selecta, escogida. *Selectman,* Consejero municipal en la Nueva Inglaterra; por lo común, uno de tres.

Selected [sẹ-lect'-ed], *a.* Escogido, seleccionado.

Selection [sẹ-lec'-shun], *s.* 1. Selección, elección, escogimiento. 2. Lo elegido o escogido; colección hecha con cuidado.

Selective [se-lect'-iv], *a.* Perteneciente o relativo a la selección; que escoge.

Selectman [sẹ-lect'-man], *s.* Funcionario municipal en los estados de Nueva Inglaterra, E.U.

Selectness [sẹ-lect'-nes], *s.* La calidad o propiedad de ser selecto.

Selector [sẹ-lect'-ẹr], *s.* El que elige o escoge.

Selenite [sel'-ẹ-nait], *s.* 1. Selenites, selenita, espejuelo, variedad vítrea y nacarada, por lo general transparente, del sulfato de cal. 2. Sal del ácido selenioso. 3. Selenita, habitante posible o imaginario de la luna.

Selenium [se-lí'-ni-um], *s.* (Quím.) Selenio, metaloide que se reduce con facilidad a polvo; notable por las variaciones de su resistencia eléctrica bajo la influencia de la luz y del calor.

Self [self], *a.* (*pl.* SELVES). 1. Mismo, idéntico, propio; desusado excepto en el compuesto *selfsame.* 2. Puro, no mezclado (colores).—*s.* 1. Persona, personalidad, individuo. 2. Se, sí mismo; yo mismo. *Self* se une a los pronombres personales, a algunos adjetivos posesivos y al pronombre *one* para formar pronombres reflexivos o para dar más fuerza a la expresión. *The selfsame thing,* La misma cosa. *Myself,* Yo mismo, me. *Himself, herself, itself,* Se. *Ourselves, yourselves, themselves,* Nos, os, se. *One's self* o *oneself,* Sí mismo, se. *Thy gracious self,* Tu graciosa persona. *My other self,* Mi otro yo. *To lay a thing by itself,* Poner una cosa aparte. *To live like one's self,* Vivir según su calidad. Esta palabra se usa muy frecuentemente en composición. La mayor parte de estas voces tienen el sentido que claramente les da su segundo componente; algunas que requieren explicación se hallarán aquí. *Self-abased,* Humillado por la conciencia de su propia falta o vergüenza. *Self-binder,* Máquina de segar, con atador automático. *Self-centered,* Concentrado en sí mismo. *Self-command,* Dominio sobre sí mismo. *Self-complacency,* Complacencia en sí mismo. *Self-conceit,* Egotismo, vanidad, arrogancia. *Self-conceited,* Presumido, arrogante, presuntuoso. *Self-confidence,* Confianza en sí mismo. *Self-conscious,* (1) Consciente de sí mismo con exageración. (2) Esciente, conocedor de la propia existencia. *Self-contradiction,* Contradicción consigo mismo. *Self-control,* Imperio sobre sí mismo. *Self-convicted,* Convicto por confesión propia; que se condena a sí mismo. *Self-deception,* La acción de engañarse a sí mismo o de formarse ilusiones vanas. *Self-defense,* Defensa propia, personal. *Self-delusion, V. Self-deception. Self-denial,* Abnegación de sí mismo. *Self-denying,* Que hace abnegación de sí mismo. *Self-devotion,* Dedicación de una persona, de sus deseos e intereses al servicio de una causa o de otra persona. *Self-esteem,* Estimación, buena opinión de sí mismo; a veces, demasiado buen concepto de sí mismo. *Self-evident,* Patente, evidente por sí mismo; que lleva la convicción al ánimo con sólo enunciarlo. *Self-examination,* Examen de sí mismo, examen de conciencia. *Self-existence,* Existencia por sí mismo, independiente de todo otro ser; uno de los atributos de Dios. *Self-existent, self-existing,* Existente por sí mismo, en virtud de su propia esencia o naturaleza. *Self-government,* (1) Dominio, imperio, sobre sí mismo; (2) gobierno de un pueblo por sí mismo. *Self-importance,* Altivez; concepto extravagante de la importancia propia. *Self-instructor,* El maestro de sí mismo. *Self-interest,* El propio interés. *Self-love,* Amor propio, amor de sí mismo. *Self-luminous,* Luminoso por su propia naturaleza, que emite luz. *Self-moving,* Automotor, que se mueve por sí mismo. *Self-murder,* Suicidio. *Self-murderer,* Suicida. *Self-possession,* Sangre fría, tranquilidad de ánimo, calma. *Self-preservation,* Preservación de sí mismo. *Self-regulating,* Regulador automático. *Self-reliance,* Confianza en sí mismo, en el propio juicio, en los propios recursos. *Self-reliant,* Confiado en sí mismo. *Self-righteous,* Que es justo en la propia estimación. *Self-righteousness,* Estado o calidad de justo en la propia estimación. *Self-sacrifice,* Sacrificio o subordinación de sí mismo o de los propios deseos al deber o al bien de otros. *Self-sufficience, self-sufficiency,* Presunción, confianza desmedida en sí mismo. *Self-sufficient,* (1) Que tiene entera confianza en sí mismo, en su fuerza; de aquí, orgulloso, arrogante. (2) Que se basta a sí mismo. *Self-will,* Obstinación, terquedad, porfía. *Self-willed,* Obstinado, terco.

Self-address [self-ạ-dres'], *va.* Rotular.

Self-assurance [self-a-shūr'-ans], *s.* Confianza en sí mismo.

Self-contained [self con-tênd'], *a.* Reservado, independiente.

Self-controlled [self-cọn-trōld'], *a.* Dueño de sí mismo.

Self-expression [self-ex-presh'-un], *s.* Expresión de la personalidad.

Self-heal [self'-hīl], *s.* (Bot.) Sanícula, planta.

Selfial [self'-i-al], *a.* Relativo o perteneciente a sí mismo; personal, particular.

Self-improvement [self-im-prūv'-ment], *s.* Mejoramiento de sí mismo.

Self-induction [self-in-dʊc'-shʊn], *s.* (Elec.) Autoinducción.

Self-indulgence [self-in-dʊl'-jens], *s.* Satisfacción de los propios deseos.

Selfish [self'-ish], *a.* 1. Interesado, ensimismado, egoísta. 2. Que cree o enseña que el amor propio es causa principal de los actos humanos.

Selfishly [self'-ish-li], *adv.* Interesadamente; con mucho amor propio, por egoísmo.

Selfishness [self'-ish-nes], *s.* Egoísmo, amor propio, egotismo.

Self-made [self-mêd'], *a.* Formado por esfuerzo propio.

Self-propulsion [self-pro-pʊl'-shʊn], *s.* Autopropulsión.

Self-same [self'-sêm], *a.* Idéntico.

Self-satisfied [self-sat'-is-faid], *a.* Ensimismado.

Self-service [self-sẹr'-vis], *s.* Autoservicio.

Self-starter [self-stārt'-ẹr], *s.* Arranque automático.

Self-sufficiency [self-sʊ-fish'-en-si], *s.* Autosuficiencia.

Self-winding [self-waind'-ing], *a.* De cuerda automática.

Sell [sel], *va.* (*pret.* y *pp.* SOLD). 1. Vender, traspasar a otro la propiedad de la cosa que uno posee, por un precio convenido. 2. Vender: se dice respecto de las cosas inmateriales cuando se las sacrifica al interés. 3. Vender, entregar por dinero; hacer traición.—*vn.* 1. Vender, hacer el comercio, traficar. 2. Venderse, ser vendido, hallar compradores; tener buen despacho una cosa o venderse bien. *To sell for ready money,* Vender al contado. *To sell on credit,* Vender al fiado o a plazos. *To sell underhand,* Vender bajo mano. *To sell off,* Vender el todo de muchas cosas juntas. *To sell by auction,* Almonedear. *To sell at retail, wholesale,* Vender al por menor, al por mayor.

Sellender [sel'-en-dẹr], *s.* Úlcera carnosa en el corvejón del caballo.

Seller [sel'-ẹr], *s.* Vendedor.

Selters, Seltzer [sel'-ters, seltz'-ẹr], *s.* Agua de Seltz, agua mineral que contiene mucho ácido carbónico.

Selvage [sel'-vẹj], *s.* 1. Orilla de paño. 2. Borde, orilla, particularmente cuando es diferente del resto. *Selvages,* (Mar.) Estrobos para los obenques y brandales.

Semantics [sem-an'-tics], *s. pl.* Semántica.

Semaphore [sem'-a-fōr], *s.* Semáforo, aparato para hacer señales, especialmente con brazos, discos, pabellones o linternas movibles; telégrafo de señales (en los ferrocarriles).

Semblance [sem'-blans], *s.* Semejanza, exterior, apariencia; ademán, máscara, velo, ficción; imagen; forma visible o imaginaria.

Semen [sí'-men o sé'-men], *s.* 1. Semen, substancia que para la generación tienen los animales del sexo masculino. 2. (Bot.) Simiente, semilla.

Semester [sẹ-mes'-tẹr], *s.* Semestre.

Semi- [sem'-i]. Semi: prefijo que usado en composición significa medio, la mitad de cualquiera cosa. *Semiannual,* Semianual, semestral; que se verifica cada seis meses.

Semiannual [sem-i-an'-yu-al], *a.* Semestral.

Semiannular [sem-i-an'-yu-lar], *a.* Semianular; que tiene la figura de un medio anillo.

Semibreve [sem'-i-brīv], **Semibrief** [sem'-i-brīf], *s.* (Mús.) Semibreve, redonda, la figura o nota fundamental de la música, que vale un compás menor. *Semibreve rest,* Aspiración de semibreve.

Semicircle [sem'-i-sẹr-cl], *s.* Semicírculo, medio círculo.

Semicircular [sem-i-sẹr'-kiu-lar], **Semicircled** [sem'-i-sẹr-cld], *a.* Semicircular.

Semicolon [sem-i-cō'-lẹn], *s.* Punto y coma (;), signo ortográfico.

Semidiameter [sem-i-dai-am'-ẹ-tẹr], *s.* Semidiámetro.

Semidiapason [sem-i-dai-a-pé'-sẹn], *s.* (Mús.) Semidiapasón.

Semidiaphanous [sem-i-dai-af'-a-nus], *a.* Semidiáfano.

Semidouble [sem'-i-dub-l], *a.* (Bot.) Semidoble, que tiene los estambres exteriores convertidos en pétalos y los interiores perfectos.—*s.* Semidoble, el oficio o fiesta de la Iglesia romana que se celebra con menor solemnidad que los oficios y fiestas dobles.

Semifinals [sem-i-fai'-nals], *s. pl.* Semifinales.

Semifloret [sem'-i-flō-ret], *s.* (Bot.) Semiflósculo, florecita terminada en figura de lengüeta que forma parte de una flor compuesta.

Semifluid [sem-i-flū'-id], *a.* Semiflúido, que no es del todo flúido.

Semiglobular [sem-i-glob'-yu-lar], *a.* Semiesférico.

Semilunar, Semilunary [sem-i-lū'-nar, i], *a.* Semilunar, que tiene figura de media luna.

Semimetal [sem-i-met'-al], *s.* Semimetal, metal imperfecto.

Semimonthly [sem-i-mʊnth'-li], *a.* Quincenal.

Seminal [sem'-i-nal], *a.* 1. Seminal, lo perteneciente al semen o lo que lo contiene. 2. (Bot.) Seminal, lo que pertenece a las semillas de las plantas.

Seminar [sem'-i-nār], *s.* Seminario, reunión del profesor con estudiantes para realizar trabajos de investigación.

Seminary [sem'-i-nẹ-ri], *s.* 1. Seminario, la casa o lugar destinado para educación de niños y jóvenes. 2. Seminario, el principio o raíz de que nacen o se propagan algunas cosas. 3. Semillero, sitio en que se crían las plantas hasta la época en que han de transplantarse: (sentido original). *Theological seminary,* Seminario eclesiástico.—*a.* 1. Seminal. 2. Perteneciente a un seminario.

Semination [sem-i-né'-shʊn], *s.* (Ant.) 1. Sembradura, la acción de sembrar; diseminación. 2. (Bot.) El esparcimiento natural de las semillas.

Seminific, Seminifical [sem-i-nif'-ic, al], *a.* Seminal, que produce simiente o semen.

Semiopaque [sem-i-o-pêc'], *a.* Medio obscuro, casi opaco.

Semipedal [sem'-i-ped-al], *a.* Lo que mide o contiene medio pie.

Semiquadrate [sem-i-cwed'-rêt], **Semiquartile** [sem-i-quōr'-til], *s.* (Astr.) Semicuadrado, el aspecto de dos planetas cuando distan entre sí cuarenta y cinco grados.

Semiquaver [sem'-i-cwê-vẹr], *s.* (Mús.) Semicorchea.

Semisextile [sem-i-sex'-til], *s.* (Astr.) Semisextil, el aspecto de dos astros que distan entre sí treinta grados.

Semispheroidal [sem-i-sfẹ-reid'-al], *a.* Que tiene figura de media esferoide.

Semite [sem'-ait], *a.* Semítico, perteneciente a los semitas.—*s.* **Semita,** persona de la raza semítica.

Semitic [sẹ-mit'-ic], *a.* Semítico, concerniente a Sem, o a los pueblos clasificados entre sus descendientes. —*s.* Conjunto de las lenguas semíticas.

Semitertian [sem-i-tẹr'-shan], *s.* Semiterciana, terciana que participa de sencilla y doble.

Semitone [sem'-i-tōn], *s.* (Mús.) Semitono, intervalo equivalente a la mitad de un tono.

Semitonic [sem-i-ten'-ic], *a.* Relativo a un semitono; de medio tono.

Semivowel [sem'-i-vau-el], *s.* Semivocal.

Semiweekly [sem-i-wīc'-li], *a.* Bisemanal.—*adv.* Bisemanalmente. —*s.* Publicación bisemanal.

Semiyearly [sem-i-yīr'-li], *a.* Semestral, semianual.—*adv.* Semestralmente, semianualmente.

Sempiternal [sem-pi-tẹr'-nal], *a.* Sempiterno, que tiene principio pero no tiene fin.

Senary [sen'-a-ri], *a.* Senario, compuesto de seis unidades; que contiene seis.

Senate [sen'-ẹt], *s.* 1. Senado, junta de los senadores; el más alto de los dos cuerpos legislativos de los países constitucionales (v. g. los Estados Unidos, España, Francia, e Italia). 2. La junta directiva de ciertas universidades. 3. Consejo, un cuerpo legislativo. 4. Cualquier junta o concurrencia de personas graves, respetables y circunspectas. *Senate-house,* Senado, el lugar donde se juntan los senadores; casa de ayuntamiento.

Senator [sen'-a-tẹr], *s.* Senador, miembro de un senado; consejero.

Senatorial [sen-a-tō'-ri-al], *a.* 1. Senatorio, perteneciente o relativo al senado o al senador. 2. (E. U.) Que tiene derecho de elegir un senador, v. g. un distrito senatorio.

Senatorship [sen'-a-ter-ship], *s.* El empleo o dignidad de senador.

Send [send], *v.* (*pret.* y *pp.* SENT), *va.* 1. Enviar, despachar, mandar una persona a alguna parte. 2. Enviar, remitir cosas de una parte a otra. 3. Emitir, arrojar, producir. 4. Difundir, extender, propagar. 5. Enviar, conceder, dar; hacer venir, sobrevenir o acontecer; infligir. 6. Hacer mirar hacia algo o alguien.—*vn.* Enviar, despachar, un agente, mensaje o mensajero. *To send away,* Despedir a un criado; enviar a escardar o despedir a alguno ásperamente. *To send back,* Mandar volver, enviar de vuelta, enviar otra vez, hacer volver. *To send down,* Enviar abajo, hacer bajar. *To send for,* Enviar a buscar, enviar a llamar, enviar por uno o a decirle que venga; enviar o despachar a una persona para que traiga consigo a otra o alguna cosa. *To send in,* Hacer entrar, mandar entrar, venir o servir; anunciar, decir su nombre; introducir. *To send word,* Mandar o pasar aviso, participar una noticia por escrito o por un propio, enviar un mensaje o recado por medio de una persona. *To send forth,* Enviar adelante, hacer marchar; producir, dar a luz; publicar, promulgar; empujar; emitir, exhalar. *To send forward,* Enviar hacia adelante. *To send off,* Expedir, hacer partir. *To send up,* (1) Enviar arriba, mandar subir. (2) (Fam. E. U.) Enviar a la cárcel.

Send, *vn.* (Mar.) Cabecear la embarcación de proa a popa. *V.* SCEND.

Sender [send'-er], *s.* El que envía. (Com.) Expedicionario.

Senega [sen'-e-ga], **Seneca, Seneka,** *s.* (Bot.) Serpentaria.

Senescence [se-nes'-ens], *s.* Senectud, vejez.

Senescent [se-nes'-ent], *a.* Que envejece; característico de la vejez.

Seneschal [sen'-e-shal], *s.* Senescal o mayordomo mayor.

Senile [sí'-nil o nail], *a.* Senil, que pertenece a los viejos y a la vejez.

Senior [sí'-nior], *a.* 1. Mayor, de mayor edad. 2. Más antiguo o anciano por su cargo o título; superior en grado o dignidad. 3. Perteneciente al último año del curso de estudios en un colegio americano. —*s.* Antiguo, anciano. *Senior of a college,* Antiguo de colegio, que en algunas partes se llama también senior.

Senior high school [sí'-nior hai scūl], *s.* Los dos últimos años de una escuela secundaria.

Seniority [sí-nior'-i-ti], *s.* 1. Antigüedad. 2. Precedencia. *Seniority scale,* Escalafón.

Senna [sen'-a], *s.* (Bot.) Sen o sena.

Se'nnight [sen'-nait], *s.* (Prov. o ant.) El espacio de siete días con sus noches; semana. *This day se'nnight,* Hoy hace ocho días; de hoy en ocho días.

Senocular [sen-oc'-yu-lar], *a.* Que tiene seis ojos (como ciertas arañas).

Sensation [sen-sé'-shun], *s.* 1. Sensación, la impresión de los objetos en los órganos de los sentidos percibida por el cerebro. 2. Lo que produce sentimientos de interés o excitación; estado de excitación.

Sensational [sen-sé'-shun-al], *a.* 1. De sensación; que produce excitación o que se destina a producirla. 2. Que se refiere a la sensación, a la percepción por los sentidos.

Sense [sens], *s.* 1. Sentido, la potencia o facultad que tienen los seres animados de percibir las impresiones de los objetos externos. 2. Sentido, entendimiento, razón, seso (a menudo en plural). *A man of sense,* Hombre de juicio. 3. Sentido, el modo particular de entender una cosa o el juicio que se forma de ella; el juicio del mayor número. 4. Sensación, percepción por los sentidos; sentimiento, percepción moral. 5. Sentido, significado, interpretación, significación. *To gratify one's senses,* Satisfacer los sentidos. *Common sense,* Sentido común.

Senseless [sens'-les], *a.* 1. Insensible, falto de sentimiento; privado de sentido, que no puede sentir, que no tiene conciencia de sí mismo. 2. Insensato, estólido, necio, absurdo, falto de razón. *Senseless of,* Insensible a.

Senselessly [sens'-les-li], *adv.* Insensatamente, de un modo insensato.

Senselessness [sens'-les-nes], *s.* Tontería, insensatez, necedad, absurdo.

Sensibility [sen-si-bil'-i-ti], *s.* 1. Sensibilidad, la facultad de percibir las impresiones que recibimos de los objetos externos. 2. Sensibilidad, la predisposición o propensión de los sentidos a recibir de una manera viva o fuerte las impresiones exteriores. 3. Precisión, hablando de instrumentos.

Sensible [sen'-si-bl], *a.* 1. Sensible, capaz de sentir; capaz de producir impresiones en los sentidos; perceptible por los sentidos; sensitivo, perceptible o percibido por la inteligencia. 2. Sensitivo, capaz de emociones. 3. Convencido, persuadido. 4. Cuerdo, razonable, juicioso, sensato. 5. (Poco us.) Sensitivo, afectado por los cambios más ligeros. *To be sensible,* Tener tacto, buen juicio; conocer, estar persuadido; ver, concebir. *To be sensible of,* Hacerse cargo de. *I am sensible (that) I have done amiss,* Estoy persuadido de que he hecho mal.

Sensibleness [sen'-si-bl-nes], *s.* 1. La posibilidad de que una impresión sea percibida por los sentidos. 2. Sensación, sensibilidad. 3. Impresión, sentimiento producido en el ánimo por alguna cosa que lo aflige. 4. Cordura, sensatez.

Sensibly [sen'-si-bli], *adv.* 1. Perceptiblemente, sensiblemente. 2. Exteriormente. 3. Juiciosamente, con prudencia y cordura.

Sensitive [sen'-si-tiv], *a.* 1. Sensitivo, sensible, impresionable, de viva sensibilidad; que afecta a los sentidos; en fotografía, sensibilizado, hecho sensible a la acción de la luz. 2. Sensitivo, perteneciente a los sentidos. *Sensitive-plant,* Sensitiva, planta que al tocarla se contrae como si tuviera sensación: (Mimosa pudica) planta de la familia de las leguminosas.

Sensitively [sen'-si-tiv-li], *adv.* Sensiblemente, con pesar, con sentimiento.

Sensitiveness [sen'-si-tiv-nes], *s.* Sensibilidad, calidad de sensitivo o sensible, así física como mentalmente.

Sensitize [sen'-si-taiz], *va.* Sensibilizar, hacer sensible, particularmente a la acción de la luz (v. g. la placa fotográfica). *Sensitized paper,* Papel sensibilizado (para fotografía).

Sensorial [sen-sō'-ri-al], *a.* Sensorio, perteneciente al sensorio o a la sensación.

Sensorium [sen-sō'-ri-um], **Sensory** [sen'-so-ri], *s.* Sensorio, cualquiera de los órganos de los sentidos.

Sensory [sen'-so-ri], *a.* Sensorio, perteneciente a la facultad de sentir; que produce la sensación.

Sensual [sen'-shu-al], *a.* 1. Sensual, que pertenece a los sentidos o al apetito carnal; carnal, lo contrario de espiritual. 2. Sensual, lascivo, lujurioso, voluptuoso.

Sensualist [sen'-shu-al-ist], *s.* Persona sensual o dada a la sensualidad, a la satisfacción de los sentidos. 2. (Filos.) Sensualista, partidario del sensualismo.

Sensuality [sen-shu-al'-i-ti], *s.* Sensualidad, lascivia, voluptuosidad; el estado o calidad de sensual; entregado o los placeres sensuales.

Sensualize [sen'-shu-al-aiz], *va.* Hacer sensual, voluptuoso o lascivo.

Sensually [sen'-shu-al-i], *adv.* Sensualmente, con sensualidad, voluptuosamente.

Sensuous [sen'-shu-us], *a.* Afectivo, patético; que afecta los sentidos; que se deriva de los sentidos o se refiere a ellos; tierno, apasionado. Se diferencia de *sensual.*

Sensuousness [sen'-shu-us-nes], *s.* Afición a lo bello y a los objetos o adornos de lujo; calidad de los sentidos, de ser susceptibles a las influencias externas.

Sent, *pret.* y *pp.* de *To* SEND.

Sentence [sen'-tens], *s.* 1. Sentencia, dictamen, juicio o parecer que da uno acerca de la cosa sobre que se le consulta. 2. Sentencia, declaración de juicio o resolución de un juez, vistos los méritos de una causa. 3. Sentencia, dicho grave y sucinto. 4. (Gram.) Sentencia, período, frase, párrafo breve que contiene sentido completo.

Sentence, *va.* Sentenciar, condenar.

Sentential [sen-ten'-shal], *a.* (Gram.) De frase, perteneciente a un período completo.

Sententious [sen-ten'-shus], *a.* 1. Sentencioso, abundante en sentencias, en máximas. 2. Lacónico, breve; enérgico, expresivo en su lenguaje.

Sententiously [sen-ten'-shus-li], *adv.* Sentenciosamente.

Sententiousness [sen-ten'-shus-nes], *s.* Laconismo, brevedad con energía.

Sentience [sen'-shi-ens], *s.* Conciencia, sensibilidad.

Sentient [sen'-shi-ent], *a.* Senciente, que siente o tiene sensación, dotado de la facultad de percibir por los sentidos; lo contrario de inanimado y vegetal.—*s.* Senciente, el que siente.

Sentiment [sen'-ti-ment], *s.* 1. Sentimiento, afecto, impresión que se siente en el ánimo, sea de alegría, de tristeza, etc.; sentimiento noble, tierno o artístico y su expresión; también la cualidad de afectar o de ser afectado por una emoción delicada, intelectual o afectuosa. 2. Sentimiento de simpatía o afecto personal hacia una persona del sexo opuesto, a diferencia del amor o la pasión. 3. Sentimiento, dictamen, opinión o juicio interior que se forma de las cosas. 4. Sentido, pensamiento (expresados en palabras); brindis. *A man of honourable sentiments,* Hombre de nobles sentimientos.

Sentimental [sen-ti-men'-tal], *a.* Sentimental, que pertenece a los sentimientos o afectos; propenso a sentimientos tiernos; que los excita; muy sensible.

Sentimentalist [sen-ti-men'-tal-ist], *s.* Persona sentimental, propensa al sentimiento más bien que a la razón, o que afecta gran sensibilidad.

Sentimentality [sen-ti-men-tal'-i-ti], *s.* Afectación de exquisita sensibilidad o de afectos muy tiernos.

Sentimentalize [sen-ti-men' tal-aiz], *va.* y *vn.* Afectar gran sensibilidad

Sentinel [sen'-ti-nel], **Sentry** [sen'-tri], *s.* 1. Centinela, el soldado que está de guardia; el acto de hacer guardia. *To stand sentry,* Estar de centinela o estar de facción. 2. Lo que sirve de guarda o protección. *Sentry-box,* Garita de centinela.

Sepal [sep'-al], *s.* (Bot.) Sépalo, cada una de las hojuelas del cáliz.

Separable [sep'-a-ra-bl], *a.* Separable, capaz de separarse.

Separably [sep'-a-ra-bli], *adv.* De manera que se pueda separar.

Separate [sep'-a-rêt], *va.* 1. Separar,

dividir, desunir, apartar cosas que están juntas o unidas; desviar. 2. Ocupar una posición entre dos cosas; poner a parte. 3. Considerar separadamente; estimar como cosas diferentes.—*vn.* Apartarse, desunirse, separarse.

Separate [sep'-a-ret], *a.* Separado, desunido, segregado, sin lazo, distinto, diferente; separado del cuerpo.

Separately [sep'-a-ret-li], *adv.* Separadamente, a parte, sin conexión, distintamente; uno a uno.

Separateness [sep'-a-ret-nes], *s.* Estado de separación.

Separation [sep-a-ré'-shun], *s.* 1. Separación, desunión; acción de separar; estado de separación. 2. Análisis químico, descomposición de un mixto en sus elementos constitutivos. 3. Separación, divorcio.

Separatist [sep'-a-re-tist], *s.* Cismático, el que se ha separado de la religión dominante en su país.

Separative [sep'-a-re-tiv], *a.* Separativo, que separa o tiende á la separación; distintivo.

Separator [sep'-a-ré"-ter], *s.* 1. Separador, cualquier útil o aparato para separar las cosas, como el zurrón del grano. 2. Separador, el o lo que separa.

Separatory [sep'-a-re-to-ri], *a.* Separatorio, vasija que usan los químicos para separar los licores.

Sepia [sí'-pi-a o sé'-pi-a], *s.* 1. Sepia, materia colorante que se saca de la jibia, tratándola con álcalis; color de sepia; dibujo hecho con sepia. 2. Sepia, jibia. *V.* CUTTLEFISH. 3. Jibión, hueso de la jibia.—*a.* Perteneciente á la sepia, hecho en sepia.

Sepoy [sí'-pei], *s.* Cipayo, el soldado natural de la India oriental que sirve en los regimientos indígenas que mantienen allí los ingleses.

Sepsis [sep'-sis], *s.* 1. Sepsis, putrefacción venenosa. 2. Infección procedente de un virus pútrido que contiene organismos microscópicos.

Sept [sept], *s.* Raza, casta, generación, linaje.

Septal [sep'-tal], *a.* 1. De septo, perteneciente a un septo o que lo forma. 2. Perteneciente á un linaje.

Septangle [sept'an-gl], *s.* Heptágono, figura de siete ángulos y siete lados.

Septangular [sept-an'-giu-lar], *a.* Heptagonal, heptágono, con siete ángulos.

September [sep-tem'-ber], *s.* Septiembre, el noveno mes del año.

Septemia, Septæmia [sept-í'-mi-a], *s.* Septicemia, estado morboso de la sangre que resulta de materias pútridas o sépticas.

Septenary [sep'-te-ne-ri], *a.* Septenario, lo que se compone de siete.—*s.* El número siete.

Septennial [sep-ten'-i-al], *a.* Sieteñal, que dura un septenio, que sucede una vez en siete años.

Septentrion, Septentrional [sep-ten'-tri-en-al], *a.* Septentrional, del norte.

Septet [sep-tet'], *s.* Grupo de siete personas, cosas o partes; compañía de siete cantores o tañedores; composición musical en siete partes.

Septic [sep'-tic], *a.* Séptico, putrefactivo, que causa putrefacción, pútrido. *Septic tank,* Fosa séptica.

Septicæmia, Septicemia [sep-ti-sí'-mi-a], *s.* Septicemia, envenenamiento de la sangre. *V.* SEPTEMIA.

Septicemic [sep-tis-í'-mic], *a.* Séptico, perteneciente al emponzoñamiento de la sangre.

Septifarious [sep-ti-fé'-ri-us], *a.* Que tiene siete especies o caminos diferentes.

Septifluous [sep-tif'-lu-us], *a.* Que fluye por siete corrientes o conductos.

Septilateral [sep-ti-lat'-er-al], *a.* Que tiene siete lados.

Septillion [sep-til'-yun], *s.* Septillón, un número cardinal; según la numeración francesa y americana, la octava potencia de mil; según la numeración inglesa, la séptima potencia de un millón.

Septuagenary [sep-tiu-aj'-e-ne-ri], *a.* Septuagenario, que consiste o se compone de setenta.

Septuagesima [sep-tiu-a-jes'-i-ma], *s.* Septuagésima, el tercer domingo anterior a la primera semana de cuaresma.

Septuagesimal [sep-tiu-a-jes'-i-mal], *a.* Septuagésimo.

Septuagint [sep'-tiu-a-jint], *s.* Los setenta, la versión griega del Antiguo Testamento, llamada así por ser, según se suponía, obra de setenta intérpretes.

Septum [sep'-tum], *s.* (Anat.) Septo, la cosa que divide o separa a otras entre sí.

Septuple [sep'-tiu-pl], *a.* Séptuplo.

Sepulchral [se-pul'-cral], *a.* Sepulcral, fúnebre.

Sepulcher, Sepulchre [sep'-ul-ker], *s.* Sepulcro, sepultura.

Sepulcher, Sepulchre [sep'-ul-ker], *va.* Sepultar, enterrar, poner en un sepulcro.

Sepulture [sep'-ul-chur o tiūr], *s.* Sepultura, entierro.

Sequacious [se-cwé'-shus], *a.* 1. Siguiente, que sigue; que va detrás de otra cosa; secuaz. 2. Logicamente consecutivo o consistente.

Sequaciousness, Sequacity [se-cwé'-shus-nes, se-cwas'-i-ti], *s.* La acción de seguir a otro.

Sequel [sí'-cwel], *s.* 1. Secuela, lo que sigue como porción final; párrafo o capítulo final. 2. Resultado, consecuencia, éxito de una cosa. *In the sequel,* En seguida, después.

Sequence [sí'-cwens], *s.* 1. Serie, continuación ordenada y sucesiva de cosas. 2. Orden de sucesión; arreglo. 3. Efecto, consecuencia. 4. (Mús.) Sucesión regular de frases melodiosas y semejantes en diferentes diapasones. *Sequence of a suit of cards,* Runfla de un palo, en los naipes.

Sequent [sí'-cwent], *a.* Siguiente, en orden de tiempo; (?)consiguiente.

Sequester [se-cwes'-ter], *va.* 1. Separar, apartar, retirar. 2. Secuestrar, poner en secuestro. 3. Privar a uno de lo que poseía hasta que se decida una controversia o se satisfaga una demanda.—*vn.* Renunciar; v. g. la renuncia que hace una viuda a toda intervención en la liquidación de la herencia de su marido.

Sequestrable [se-cwes'-tra-bl], *a.* Que se puede secuestrar y separar; capaz de división.

Sequestrate [se-cwes'-trêt], *va.* 1. Secuestrar, apropiar o confiscar para uso del gobierno; tomar posesión provisional de algo a consecuencia de un acuerdo equitativo entre acreedores. 2. (Ant.) Retirar, apartar, separar.

Sequestration [sec-wes-tré'-shun], *s.* 1. Secuestración de bienes. 2. Separación, retiro. 3. Privación del uso y de las utilidades de alguna cosa.

Sequestrator [sec-wes-tré'-ter], *s.* Secuestrador, el que secuestra.

Sequin [sí'-cwin], *s.* Cequí o cequín, moneda de oro de Venecia y Levante.

Sequoia [se-cwei'-a], *s.* Nombre de un árbol y de un género de árboles gigantescos de California, pertenecientes a las coníferas. Sequoia sempervirens (*redwood*), palo rojo, y Sequoia gigantea (*big tree*), árbol grande.

Seraglio [se-ral'-yō o se-rāl'-yō], *s.* 1. Serrallo, el antiguo palacio de los sultanes en Constantinopla. 2. Harem; de aquí, burdel, lupanar.

Serai [se-rā'-i], *s.* 1. En Oriente, posada, hostal. 2. Serrallo, palacio.

Serape [se-rā'-pê], *s.* Sarape, manta mejicana.

Seraph [ser'-af], *s.* Serafín, ángel o espíritu del primer coro celestial.

Seraphic, Seraphical [se-raf'-ic, al], *a.* Seráfico.

Seraphine [ser'-a-fīn], *s.* Organo de salón o pórtatil, el de lengüetas. Voz casi anticuada.

Seraskier [ser-as-kīr'], *s.* Serasquier, general de ejército o generalísimo entre los turcos.

Sere [sīr], *a.* Seco, marchito.

Serenade [ser-e-nêd'], *s.* Serenata, música que se toca durante la noche para festejar a alguien.

Serenade, *va.* Dar una serenata.

Serene [se-rīn'], *a.* 1. Sereno, claro, despejado de nubes y nieblas. 2. Sereno, apacible, sosegado, tranquilo. 3. De exaltada posición; aplícase a ciertos príncipes y personajes elevados en Alemania y Francia. *Most serene,* Serenísimo.

Serenely [se-rīn'-li], *adv.* 1. Serenamente, con serenidad y despejo. 2. Con sosiego y apacibilidad de ánimo.

Sereneness [se-rīn'-nes], *s.* Serenidad de ánimo, tranquilidad, calma.

Serenity [se-ren'-i-ti], *s.* 1. Serenidad, claridad, despejo de nubes en el cielo. 2. Serenidad, sosiego, apacibilidad. 3. Tranquilidad, calma, paz, quietud. 4. Serenidad, título de honor que se da a algunos príncipes.

Serf [serf], *s.* Siervo, criado o esclavo ocupado en la labranza y anejo al suelo, al terruño, con el cual se transmite; (fig.) esclavo.

Serfdom [serf'-dum], *s.* Servidumbre, estado o condición de los siervos o esclavos.

Serge [serj], *s.* Sarga, tela fuerte de seda o más comúnmente de estambre que forma cordoncillo. *Silk serge,* Sarga de seda. *Woollen serge,* Anascote. *Serge-maker,* Fabricante de sarga.

Sergeancy [sār'-jen-si], *s.* *V.* SERGEANTSHIP.

Sergeant [sār'-jent], *s.* 1. Sargento, oficial subalterno en la milicia inmediatamente superior al cabo. 2. Alguacil, ministro inferior de justicia. 3. (Ingl.) Abogado de primera clase. *Sergeant at arms,* Macero del rey; oficial de las asambleas legislativas que ejecuta los mandatos del presidente y mantiene el orden.

Sergeantship [sār'-jent-ship], *s.* Sargentía, el empleo y oficio de sargento; grado de sargento.

Serial [sí'-ri-al], *a.* 1. Consecutivo, perteneciente a una serie; a manera de serie. 2. Publicado por series, por entregas, y a intervalos regulares. 3. Sucesivo, dispuesto en hileras o filas.—*s.* Obra que se publica por entregas, por series.

Serially [sí'-ri-al-i], *adv.* En serie; por serie.

Sericate [ser'-i-kêt], *a.* Sedoso; velludo.

Sericeous [se-rish'-ius], *a.* Sérico, que contiene seda o que es de la naturaleza de ésta; lustroso como seda; en botánica, cubierto de pelusa muy suave y tupida.

Sericulture [sí-ri-cul'-chur], *s.* Sericicultura, industria que tiene por objeto la producción de la seda.

Series [sí'-ri-iz], *s.* Serie, continuación ordenada y sucesiva de las cosas; enlace, encadenamiento, unión.

Serin [ser'-in], *s.* Verderón, pinzoncillo verdoso parecido al canario; se cría a menudo en pajarera. Serinus hortulinus.

Serio-comic [sí''-ri-o-com'-ic], *a.* Seriocómico.

Serious [sí'-ri-us], *a.* 1. Serio, sensato, reflexivo, grave, severo. 2. Serio, formal; verdadero, sincero. 3. Serio, grave, importante, de consecuencia. 4. Solemne, particularmente en lo relativo a la religión. *Are you serious?* ¿Habla Vd. de veras? ¿habla Vd. formalmente? *A serious business,* Asunto de gravedad.

Seriously [sí'-ri-us-li], *adv.* Seriamente, de veras, fuera de chanza, formalmente, con formalidad.

Seriousness [sí'-ri-us-nes], *s.* Seriedad, gravedad.

Serjeant, *s. V.* SERGEANT.

Sermocination [ser-mes-i-né'-shun], *s.* (Ret.) Una forma de prosopopeya en que uno responde a la pregunta que él mismo ha hecho.

Sermon [ser'-mun], *s.* 1. Sermón, discurso cristiano hecho para el púlpito, oración evangélica. 2. Cualquier discurso de carácter grave y formal; exhortación, amonestación, reprensión particular. *Funeral sermon,* Oración fúnebre. *Collection of sermons,* Sermonario.

Sermonize [ser'-mun-aiz], *va.* 1. Predicar la palabra de Dios. 2. Predicar, sermonear, reprender o echar sermones.

Seron, Seroon [se-rūn'], *s.* Serón, zurrón, sera grande en que se llevan higos, dátiles, pasas, etc. *A seroon of indigo,* Un zurrón de añil. *A seroon of cinnamon,* Churla de canela. *A seroon of cocoa,* Sobornal de cacao.

Serosity [se-res'-i-ti], *s.* Serosidad, la parte más acuosa de un humor animal.

Serotine [ser'-o-tin], *s.* Especie de murciélago.

Serotinous [se-ret'-i-nus], *a.* (Bot.) Serondo, serotino; aplícase a los frutos tardíos, que maduran ya avanzada la estación.

Serous [sí'-rus], *a.* Seroso, que produce serosidad o suero, o es semejante a estos líquidos.

Serpent [ser'-pent], *s.* 1. Serpiente, sierpe, animal que se arrastra por la tierra. 2. Buscapiés, una especie de cohete sin varilla que corre muy arrimado a la tierra. 3. Serpentón, instrumento músico de viento, especie de bajón. 4. Persona traidora, llena de malicia. 5. Satanás.

Serpentigenous [ser-pen-tij'-e-nus], *a.* Nacido de serpiente.

Serpentine [ser'-pen-tin o tain], *a.* 1. Serpentino, que se asemeja o pertenece a la serpiente o sierpe. 2. Serpentino, caracoleado, que se mueve caracoleando como la serpiente. *Serpentine marble,* Serpentina, especie de mármol manchado como piel de serpiente.—*s.* 1. Serpentina, piedra de color verde, rojizo o amarillo, a veces transparente y otras opaca; un silicato de magnesio. 2. (Des.) Serpentín, variedad de alambique.

Serpentine, Serpentize [ser'-pen-taiz], *vn.* Serpentear, andar haciendo vueltas o tornos, como la serpiente.

Serpiginous [ser-pij'-i-nus], *a.* Serpiginoso: dícese del que tiene serpigo o de lo que toca a este mal.

Serpigo [ser-pí'-go], *s.* Serpigo, erupción cutánea a modo de tiña seca.

Serrate, Serrated [ser'-ēt, ed], *a.* Dentellado; (Bot.) serrado, cuyos dientes se dirigen hacia adelante.

Serration [ser-ré'-shun], *s.* Endentadura, recortadura semejante a la de los dientes de una sierra.

Serrature [ser'-a-chur o tiūr], *s.* (Biol.) Estructura serrada, endentadura.

Serried [ser'-id], *part. a.* Apretado, compacto en filas o hileras, como los soldados.

Serum [sí'-rum], *s.* Suero, la parte más acuosa de la sangre o de la leche.

Servable [serv'-a-bl], *a.* Servible, que puede ser servido.

Servant [serv'-ant], *s.* 1. Criado, sirviente, persona que sirve a otra por un salario. *Woman-servant, servant-girl, servant-maid,* Criada. *Servant-man,* Criado. 2. Siervo, esclavo. 3. Servidor, el que por cortesía se pone a la disposición de otro.

Serve [serv], *va.* 1. Servir, estar al servicio de otro, trabajar para otro. 2. Servir, estar sujeto a otro o estar a sus órdenes. 3. Servir, aprovechar, valer alguna cosa o ser de alguna utilidad; ayudar, ser útil. 4. Servir de tal o cual cosa, hacer las veces de otro, auxiliar a otro; prestar servicios. 5. Servir, asistir a la mesa llevando a ella los manjares. 6. Servir, ejercer algún empleo o cargo en propiedad o como substituto de otro. 7. Maniobrar, mantener en acción, hacer funcionar (v. g. un cañón). 8. Servir, tener las cosas el efecto o uso para que se destinan o ser a propósito para el objeto que se intenta conseguir con ellas; bastar, ser suficiente, satisfacer, contentar. 9. Servir, obsequiar, divertir. 10. Abastecer, surtir, v. g. con aprovisionamiento regular o hecho en períodos fijos. 11. (For.) Entregar una citación o requerimiento. 12. Servir, prestar culto o adoración a Dios. 13. (Mar.) Aforrar. 14. Portarse para con alguien, recompensar, tratar. 15. En la crianza de ganado, cubrir el macho a la hembra.—*vn.* 1. Servir, ser criado, estar al servicio de otro, emplearse en interés de otro. 2. Estar en sujeción. 3 Cumplir los deberes de un empleo, servir a su país, como en el ejército o en la marina. 4. Bastar, ser suficiente y eficaz; de aquí, ser favorable, conveniente o apto para algún propósito. 5. Sacar o dar saque, tirar, arrojar la pelota en el juego de este nombre. *To serve for,* Servir de. *To serve himself of,* Servirse de o hacer uso de. *To serve an office,* Servir un empleo, desempeñar algún puesto público. *To serve one a trick,* Jugar a uno una mala partida, pegarle un chasco. *To serve one's ends,* Servir o ser útil para que otro consiga lo que intenta. *To serve one's turn,* Bastar, ser suficiente. *To serve out one's time,* Acabar el tiempo de servicio. *To serve the time,* Andar con el tiempo, contemporizar. *I'll serve him in his kind,* Le pagaré en la misma moneda. *When occasion shall serve,* Cuando la ocasión sea favorable. *To serve a warrant,* Intimar o ejecutar un auto de prisión.

Server [serv'-er], *s.* 1. Servidor, el que sirve. 2. Lo que se emplea para servir, como una bandeja o una vajilla.

Service [ser'-vis], *s.* 1. Servicio, el acto y tiempo de servir como criado, dependiente, empleado, soldado o marinero; la condición o el trabajo de un criado. 2. Servidumbre, el acto de servir en la casa real y en las de los grandes. 3. Servicio, el uso útil que se hace de una cosa; utilidad, ventaja. 4. Culto divino, los divinos oficios; la celebración de los oficios. 5. Servicio, favor, asistencia, ayuda, el obsequio que se hace en beneficio de un igual o de un amigo. 6. Servicio; tomado absolutamente es el militar o el naval. 7. Servicio, cubierto, entrada, el número de platos que se ponen y mudan juntos en la mesa. 8. Acomodo, conveniencia de una persona para servir en una casa. 9. (For.) (1) Deber, obligación que tiene un criado o un arrendatario. (2) Entrega legal de una citación a la persona designada. 10. (Mar.) Forro de cable. 11. (Bot.) *V.* SERVICE-TREE. *I am at your service,* Estoy a la disposición de Vd. *It is of no service,* No vale nada, de nada sirve. *Out of service,* Desacomodado, sin acomodo, sin conveniencia. *To see service,* Servir, prestar servicio. *To be of service to,* Ser útil a, servir.

Serviceable [ser'-vis-a-bl], *a.* 1. Servible, que puede servir. 2. Capaz de prestar largo servicio; duradero. 3. (Ant.) Servicial, diligente en servir; oficioso.

Serviceableness [ser'-vis-a-bl-nes], *s.* Calidad de servicial o duradero.

Serviceably [ser'-vis-a-bli], *adv.* Útilmente, duraderamente.

Service station [ser'-vis sté'-shun], *s.* Taller de reparaciones de automóviles.

Service-tree [serv'-is-trí], *s.* Serbal, árbol de la familia de las rosáceas. (Pyrus domestica o Sorbus); su fruta se llama sorba y serba.

Servient [ser'-vi-ent], *a.* (For.) Subordinado; contrapuesto a *dominant.*

Servile [ser'-vil], *a.* 1. Servil, bajo, abyecto; abatido, humilde. 2. Perteneciente a esclavos o propio de ellos; digno de un esclavo. 3. Adulador, lisonjero. 4. (Gram.) Servil, que no pertenece a la raíz de la palabra.—*s.* 1. Esclavo, o individuo de espíritu servil. 2. Letra o sílaba servil, que no es de la forma de su radical.

Servilely [ser'-vil-li], *adv.* Servilmente, de una manera servil; con bajeza.

Servileness [ser'-vil-nes], **Servility** [ser-vil'-i-ti], *s.* 1. Servidumbre, esclavitud, estado de siervo. 2. Servidumbre, la sujeción de las pasiones o afectos que dominan la voluntad. 3. Bajeza, vileza de ánimo.

Serving [sęrv'-ing], *a.* Sirviente, que sirve, que está al servicio de otro.—*s.* Acción de servir. *Serving-maid,* Criada, sirvienta. *Serving-mallet,* (Mar.) Maceta de forrar. *Serving-man,* Sirviente, criado.

Servitor [sęr'-vi-tęr], *s.* 1. Partidario; compañero en una expedición o conquista con respecto al jefe que la manda. 2. Servidor, el que se ofrece á la disposición de otro. 3. Un fámulo de colegio en la universidad de Oxford.

Servitorship [sęr'-vi-tęr-ship], *s.* Famulato, el empleo de fámulo de un colegio.

Servitude [sęr'-vi-tiūd], *s.* 1. Servidumbre, esclavitud; estado de sujeción; domesticidad, condición de criado o sirviente; dependencia de otro. 2. (Angloindio) Servicio militar o naval. 3. (For.) Bienestar, alivio. *V.* EASEMENT.

Servomotor [serv'-o-mō-ter], *s.* Servomotor.

Sesame [ses'-a-mę], *s.* Ajonjolí, sésamo, planta herbácea anual de la India, de cuyo fruto se extrae aceite.

Sesamoid [ses'-a-meid], *a.* Sesamoide, que se parece al sésamo.—*s.* Término aplicado a los huesecillos o cartílagos que se desarrollan en el espesor de las articulaciones.

Sesqui-. Prefijo que significa uno y medio.

Sesquialter, Sesquialteral [ses-cwi-al'-tęr, al], *a.* Sesquiáltero: se aplica a la proporción o cantidad que contiene una mitad más, como nueve respecto de seis.

Sesquioxide [ses-cwi-ex'-id], *s.* Sesquióxido, óxido que contiene la mitad más de oxígeno que el protóxido.

Sesquipedal [ses-cwip'-ę-dal], **Sesquipedalian** [ses-cwi-pę-dé'-li-an], *a.* Sesquipedal, que tiene pie y medio de largo.

Sesquitertian [ses-cwi-tęr'-shan], *a.* Sesquitercio: se dice del número que contiene en sí otro y además una tercera parte de él, como ocho respecto de seis.

Sessile [ses'-il], *a.* (Biol.) Sesil, fijado inmediatamente en la base; que carece de sostén o tallo particular.

Session [sesh'-un], *s.* 1. Sesión, junta de una corporación organizada, de una compañía, de magistrados ó senadores; reunión, asamblea de los miembros de una corporación. 2. Todo el tiempo que duran las sesiones de una junta, un congreso, etc. 3. El tribunal inferior y el cuerpo gobernante de la Iglesia presbiteriana. 4. Llámanse en Inglaterra *sessions* ciertas juntas de los magistrados de los condados en las que, constituyendo un tribunal, juzgan varios delitos.

Sessional [sesh'-un-al], *a.* Relativo a una sesión.

Set [set], *va.* (*pret.* y *pp.* SET). 1. Asentar, sentar, poner derecho o en pie. 2. Poner, colocar, fijar, disponer una cosa en el sitio, grado u orden que debe tener; montar; plantar (en la tierra). 3. Poner, fijar, poner fijo, inmóvil; de aquí, embarazar, detener, impedir; desarrollar en forma rudimentaria, como el fruto o simiente. 4. Establecer, determinar, ordenar, señalar, destinar. 5. Arreglar, poner en orden para el uso; preparar, alistar, poner o parar en el juego; reducir a regla. 6. Estimar, considerar, reputar (con *at*); valuar, fijar un precio (con *by* u *on*). 7. Engastar, encajar y embutir una cosa en otra. 8. Trabar, triscar los dientes de la sierra alternando a uno y otro lado. 9. Poner en movimiento en una dirección dada. 10. Embarazar, inquietar, perturbar la mente. 11. (Impr.) Parar tipo, componer: a menudo con *up.* 12. Poner algunos versos en música; también, dar, fijar el tono (de un himno, etc.). 13. (Cir.) Reducir una dislocación. 14. Hacer empollar (las gallinas). 15. Tender, poner lazos; (Mar.) tender, desplegar.—*vn.* 1. Ponerse el sol o los astros u ocultarse bajo el horizonte. 2. Cuajarse un líquido o convertirse en sólido. 3. Pararse, quedarse parada ó fija alguna persona o cosa; fijarse, detenerse. 4. Componer, poner alguna letra en música. 5. (Fam.) Empollar (la gallina). 6. Moverse o fluir (una corriente) en una dirección dada; tender, inclinarse. 7. Aplicarse a alguna cosa o dedicarse a ella con esmero. 8. Empezar a desarrollarse un fruto rudimentario; transformarse las flores en semillas o frutos. 9. (Fam.) Sentar, caer bien una prenda de vestir. *To set at liberty,* Poner en libertad. *To set to work,* Poner a la obra. *To set a house on fire,* Pegar fuego a una casa. *To set great store by,* Dar mucha importancia a una cosa. *To set right,* Colocar bien; corregir, rectificar. *To set a bone,* Poner un hueso en su lugar. *To set fast,* Sujetar, consolidar; adelantar un reloj. *To set thinking,* Hacer pensar. *To set a task,* Imponer una tarea. *To set about,* Emprender una cosa o ponerse a hacerla, dedicarse a algún empleo, ocupación o destino. *To set abroad,* Divulgar, publicar o hacer pública alguna cosa. *To set afloat,* Poner a flote; esparcir, hacer circular. *To set again,* Reponer, volver a poner, colocar otra vez. *To set against,* Indisponer o poner mal a uno con otro, incitar o irritar a alguno en contra de otro; oponer u oponerse. *To set agoing,* Hacer ir; poner en juego o movimiento; dar impulso. *To set aground,* Arrendar un terreno. *To set a razor,* Afilar una navaja de afeitar. *To set a page,* Componer una página. *To set apart,* Poner a parte, dejar para otra vez; arrinconar o abandonar por algún tiempo. *To set aside,* Dejar alguna cosa o suspender su ejecución para hacerla después, poner a un lado o a parte; despreciar, no hacer caso; rechazar; abrogar, anular. (Fam.) Arrinconar. *To set at defiance,* Provocar, desafiar, apostárselas con otro. *To set at naught,* Despreciar, tener en nada. *To set at rest,* Poner en reposo; dejar una cosa. *To set away,* Quitar, separar, echar a un lado. *To set back,* Recular, hacerse atrás; llevar hacia atrás. *To set before,* Presentar, poner a la vista; dar a escoger una cosa poniéndola a la vista. *To set by,* Estimar, hacer aprecio, hacer caso, considerar, reputar; abandonar por un poco de tiempo la ejecución de una cosa. *To set down,* Poner en tierra ó por tierra; desembarcar (un viajero); depositar; poner por escrito, hacer algún apunte; resolver una cosa definitivamente; considerar como verdad establecida; atribuir, acusar, imputar; censurar ó humillar; poner más bajo. *To set forth,* Manifestar; exponer, representar; promulgar; exponer, dar a conocer, enunciar; hacer valer (razones); ensalzar, alabar; avanzar, adelantarse, irse, marcharse, ponerse en camino; levantar, poner más alta alguna cosa; arreglar o poner en orden; enviar una expedición. *To set forward,* Adelantar, ganar la delantera; promover; empujar, impeler, llevar hacia delante; acercar; animar, dar aliento; ponerse en camino, irse. *To set from,* Salir de una parte, emprender la marcha. *To set in,* Subir, fluir con constancia hacia tierra; dícese de la marea, y por extensión de cualquier influencia general; comenzar, ponerse a; encajar, embutir; y (des.) poner a una persona en estado de que principie a hacer algo. *To set off,* Poner a parte; reservar, separar del resto por medio de una línea o linde; comparar, contraponer; poner en relieve, realzar, adornar, hermosear, embellecer, poner bonito o hermoso, componer o adornar un gabinete, casa, etc.; salir de alguna parte, partir; salir los caballos de las barreras para principiar la corrida en las carreras de caballos. *To set on,* Determinar, resolver; fijar la atención en alguna cosa; acometer, arremeter, atacar, asaltar; emplear a alguno para que haga una cosa determinada; animar, incitar, azuzar; echar a andar, marcharse; emprender un asunto, negocio u ocupación. *He set on the mob,* Incitó al populacho. *To set one's mind on,* Aplicarse a. *To set on edge,* Dar dentera. *To set on shore,* Desembarcar. *To set one's hand to,* Poner su firma, firmar (un convenio); (fig.) aceptar, aprobar. *To set one's house in order,* Arreglar sus negocios y particularmente prepararse para la muerte. *To set out,* Echar a andar, irse, marcharse, ponerse en camino, partir, emprender un viaje; mostrar, hacer ver, dar a conocer; proveer de equipos o pertrechos; publicar, manifestar, hacer patente; dar a luz; dar principio a alguna cosa, principiar a ejercer algún oficio, empleo u ocupación; asignar, señalar; adornar, hermosear; trazar los contornos de una figura; fluir hacia afuera, como la marea o una corriente; plantar (un árbol, legumbres, etc.). *To set to,* Aplicarse con vigor; ponerse a trabajar. *To set to rights,* Rectificar; poner una cosa en orden. *To set one to work,* Poner a alguno a trabajar, darle trabajo o hacer que trabaje. *To set pen to paper,* Escribir, poner la pluma sobre el papel. *To set together,* Poner en orden; juntar, poner junto. *To set up,* Ensalzar, exaltar, elevar; erigir, fundar, instituir o levantar; enderezar o poner derecha o empinada una cosa; adelantarse o ponerse delante; hacer una proposición; establecer y establecerse; empezar alguno a traficar por sí o por su cuenta; principiar un sistema nuevo de vida; hacer profesión pública de una opinión, de una virtud, etc., preciarse de; poner a la vista; (Impr.) componer; dar un grito; hacer ruido; meter bulla. *To set up a coach,* Echar coche. *To set up a shop,* Poner tienda. *To set up a tent,* Levantar una tienda. *To* *set up for*, Darse uno por lo que no es; darse por lo que es; erigirse en medianero, dictador, etc.; preciarse de; concurrir. *To set up for one's self*, Obrar por sí; trabajar por su cuenta. *To set up to sale*, Poner en venta. *To set upon*, Echar a andar; echarse sobre uno, acometer, asaltar; fijar la atención; determinar resueltamente. *To be set upon by footpads*, Ser atacado por salteadores. *To set a price*, Fijar un precio. *To set a stone*, Engastar una piedra preciosa. *To set a time*, Señalar un tiempo o plazo determinado. *To set free*, Libertar, poner en libertad. *To set nets*, Poner lazos. *To set one over a thing*, Dar a uno el encargo de hacer o de inspeccionar la ejecución de una cosa. *To set one's hand to*, Firmar. *To set one's mind against*, Concebir odio o tirria contra alguno. *To set sail*, Hacerse a la vela.

Set, *a.* 1. De opinión fija; obstinado, terco, resuelto. 2. Señalado, establecido por autoridad; prescrito. 3. Regular, arreglado, ajustado, formal, estudiado; reflexionado. 4. Puesto, sentado, colocado; fijo, inmóvil. 5. Hecho, construido, fabricado, fijo, montado, engastado.

Set,[1] *s.* 1. Juego, un determinado número de cosas que tienen cierta proporción y conexión entre sí; colección, serie, grupo, clase; compañía, cuadrilla, banda, hablando de personas. *A set of books*, Una colección de libros. *Set of buckles*, Juego de hebillas. *Set of diamonds*, Aderezo de diamantes. (Mex.) Terno de diamantes. *Set of horses*, Tiro de caballos para arrastrar un coche o carruaje; yunta de caballos para arar. *Set of bed-curtains*, Colgadura de cama. *A set of oars, of chairs*, Un juego de remos, de sillas. 2. Conjunto o agregado de muchas cosas. *Set of china*, Servicio de porcelana. *Set of teeth*, Carrera de dientes, dentadura. *Set form*, Formulario. 3. Juego, la disposición en que están unidas ciertas cosas, siempre más de dos, de suerte que sin separarse puedan ejecutar algún movimiento. 4. Acción y efecto de dar dirección, posición o forma fija; curso, movimiento, tendencia; encorvadura; porte; triscamiento de los dientes de ciertas sierras. 5. Ocaso o puesta del sol. 6. Planta o pie de árbol, plantel, tallo listo para plantarlo. 7. Un fruto en su estado rudimentario.

Set,[2] *s.* Ajuste o caída de una prenda de vestir. *V.* FIT.

Setaceous [sẹ-té'-shus], *a.* Cerdoso, cerdudo.

Setback [set'-bac], *s.* 1. Obstáculo, impedimento al paso, embarazo; vuelta forzosa a un punto por donde se pasó antes. 2. Contracorriente.

Set-bolt [set'-bōlt], *s.* (Mar.) Botador, perno de trabante.

Set-down [set'-daun], *s.* Reprimenda; (fam.) peluca.

Set-off [set'-ef], *s.* (For.) 1. Compensación; cualquier contrapeso, tanto en el sentido recto como en el figurado. 2. Adorno; brillo, relieve, lo que realza. 3. Parte saliente de una pared. *V.* OFFSET. 4. La acción de reconocer un deudor la justicia de la petición de su acreedor, presentando al propio tiempo alguna demanda contra él que iguale la deuda o parte de ella.

Seton [sí'-tn], *s.* (Cir. y Vet.) Sedal.

Setose, Setous [sí'-tōs, sí'-tus], *a.* Cerdoso.

Setscrew [set'-scrū], *s.* Tornillo de sujeción o de presión.

Settee [set-í'], *s.* 1. Canapé. 2. (Mar.) Bajel de dos palos que se emplea en el mar Mediterráneo.

Setter [set'-ẹr], *s.* 1. El o lo que pone, coloca o fija. 2. Perro de ajeo; perro adiestrado para indicar la caza por medio de una postura fija. 3. Espión, espía. 4. Corchete, alguacil. 5. El que compone música para adaptarla a versos o letra.

Setting [set'-ing], *s.* 1. Ocultación aparente del sol y de los astros debajo del horizonte. 2. Acción y efecto de colocar, fijar, engastar, embutir, etc. 3. Alguna cosa engastada, embutida, etc., la cosa insertada. 4. Engaste, engastadura, montadura, el marco en que está puesta una cosa; de aquí, cercado, alrededor. 5. (Fam.) Nidada, un número de huevos juntos para ser empollados. *Setting of the wind* o *current*, (Mar.) Dirección del viento o la corriente.

Setting, *a.* Poniente. *Setting sun*, Sol poniente.

Settle [set'-l], *s.* Escaño.

Settle, *va.* 1. Colocar, dar colocación a una persona. 2. Fijar, asegurar, afirmar, arreglar. 3. Establecer, estatuir leyes, reglamentos, etc.: poner en el comercio, dar una profesión, estado; casar. 4. Hacer a una cosa más unida o compacta. 5. Colonizar, poblar, establecer en un país. 6. Clarificar, quitar la hez. 7. Sosegar, calmar, serenar. 8. Aclarar un pasaje, quitarle toda ambigüedad; determinar el sentido de un texto; resolver, decidir. 9. Decidir, determinar, poner fin a, fijar la opinión; acabar. 10. Arreglar, poner en orden. 11. Liquidar una cuenta, pagar una deuda. 12. Hacer firme y transitable un camino.—*vn.* 1. Reposarse, asentarse, hacer sedimento, caer al fondo de algún líquido una parte de lo que está disuelto o suspenso en él. 2. Establecerse o fijar su residencia en algún paraje. 3. Disponer un método de vida; tomar estado; casarse; instalarse. 4. Fijarse una cosa o permanecer quieta por mucho tiempo en un paraje. 5. Sosegarse, calmar, serenarse. 6. Contraerse. 7. Dar en dote, señalar o asignar una cantidad de dinero como arras a la esposa. 8. Decidirse, determinarse, elegir; ponerse resueltamente a hacer alguna cosa. 9. Hacer arreglos con acreedores; saldar una cuenta. 10. Posarse; reposar. 11. Dejarse caer gradualmente, ir al fondo. *To settle to the bottom*, Ir al fondo. *To be settled*, Estar domiciliado. *The Puritans settled New England*, Los puritanos colonizaron la Nueva Inglaterra. *This last blow settled him*, Este último golpe acabó con él. *To settle the succession to the throne*, Regularizar la sucesión al trono. *To settle down*, Ponerse a; fijarse, detenerse. *Let the wine settle*, Deje Vd. reposar el vino. *To settle an estate upon one*, Instituir o nombrar a uno irrevocablemente heredero de alguna propiedad. *To settle upon*, Constituir la dote o señalar la propiedad que tiene la mujer al tiempo de su casamiento, para que no pueda entrar en la posesión del marido; decidirse a. *I have settled upon him a good annuity*, Le he constituído una buena renta vitalicia. *To settle disputes*, Componer las disputas o pendencias; zanjar las dificultades; convenirse, arreglar, hacer las paces entre los que están reñidos. *To settle accounts*, Ajustar cuentas.

Settledness [set'-ld-nes], *s.* Estabilidad, permanencia; el estado fijo de alguna cosa.

Settlement [set'-l-mẹnt], *s.* 1. La acción de establecer. 2. Establecimiento, la colocación o suerte estable de alguna persona; instalación de un cura párroco, etc. 3. Colonia, el sitio o lugar donde se establecen colonos. 4. (Ingl.) Asiento, domicilio. 5. El acto de posesionar legalmente. 6. Dote que se da en arras a una mujer, y la acción de constituir o señalar la dote que una mujer lleva al matrimonio. 7. Acomodo, empleo, destino. 8. Ajuste, finiquito, convenio; (Com.) liquidación. *Act of settlement*, Ley que ha fijado la sucesión al trono de Inglaterra en la casa de Hanover.

Settler [set'-lẹr], *s.* 1. El que compone, arregla y fija alguna cosa. *Settler of averages*, El medidor de averías o el que fija el importe de las averías. 2. El colono que se establece por primera vez en una colonia. 3. Poblador, establecedor, fundador.

Settling [set'-ling], *s.* 1. Establecimiento, colonización, arreglo; la acción del verbo *settle* en todas sus acepciones. 2. *pl.* Heces, zurrapas; sedimento, poso.

Set-to [set-tū'], *s.* Lucha, combate, disputa, debate.

Setup [set'-up], *s.* Arreglo, disposición, organización.

Setwall [set'-wōl], *s.* Valeriana común de Europa.

Seven [sev'-n], *a.* y *s.* Siete, número cardinal y su signo. *The seven wonders of the world*, Las siete maravillas del mundo.

Sevenfold [sev'-n-fōld], *a.* Séptuplo, siete veces una cantidad.—*adv.* Siete veces.

Sevenscore [sev'-n-scōr], *a.* Ciento cuarenta, siete veces veinte.

Seventeen [sev'-n-tīn], *a.* y *s.* Diez y siete.

Seventeenth [sev'-n-tīnth], *a.* Décimo séptimo, el ordinal de diez y siete.

Seventh [sev'-nth], *s.* y *a.* Séptimo. *Seventh heaven*, Séptimo cielo, éxtasis.—*s.* (Mús.) Séptima.

Seventieth [sev'-n-ti-eth], *a.* Septuagésimo, número ordinal de setenta.

Seventy [sev'-n-ti], *a.* y *s.* Setenta, siete veces diez.

Sever [sev'-ẹr], *va.* 1. Separar, apartar, cortar, desunir, hacer una división o separación entre dos cosas que están unidas o que deben estarlo. 2. Arrancar, sacar, quitar o separar con violencia alguna cosa. 3. Partir, romper, deshacer.—*vn.* Separarse, desunirse, entreabrirse; partirse.

Several [sev'-ẹr-al], *a.* 1. Diversos, varios, algunos; más de uno o de dos, sin ser numerosos. 2. Diverso, distinto, solo, considerado como individuo, separado. 3. Particular, singular. 4. (For.) Distinto, relacionado individual y separadamente; respectivo.—*s.* Cada persona o cosa tomada por sí; varios, cada uno en particular. *Our several claims,* Nuestras reclamaciones respectivas.

Severally [sev'-ẹr-al-i], *adv.* Separadamente, distintamente, individualmente; a parte, cada uno de por sí. *Jointly and severally,* Solidariamente.

Severalty [sev'-ẹr-al-ti], *s.* (For.) Posesión privativa de un terreno.

Severance [sev'-ẹr-ans], *s.* Separación, partición. *Severance pay,* Salario al que se despide de un empleo.

Severe [sẹ-vīr'], *a.* 1. Severo, doloroso, acre, riguroso. 2. Severo, riguroso, áspero, duro, cruel, inexorable. 3. Severo, exacto, rígido, conforme a reglas rígidas, que rechaza todo ornato de estilo; austero. 4. Severo, grave, serio, mesurado. *A severe test,* Una prueba dura, severa. *A severe blow,* Un rudo golpe. *A severe climate,* Un clima riguroso. *A severe cold,* Un fuerte resfriado.

Severely [sẹ-vīr'-li], *adv.* Severamente, cruelmente; con rigor, con severidad; estrictamente, rigurosamente.

Severity, Severeness [sẹ-ver'-i-ti, sẹ-vīr'-nes], *s.* 1. Severidad, rigor, aspereza, crueldad. 2. Severidad, observancia rígida, exactitud, puridad y austeridad de estilo; austeridad. 3. Severidad, seriedad, gravedad. *Severity of life,* Austeridad de vida. *The severity of a test,* El rigor de una prueba.

Sew [sō], *va.* Coser, juntar con aguja o lesna e hilo.—*vn.* Coser, ocuparse cosiendo. *To sew again,* Recoser. *To sew up,* Encerrar, coser en.

Sew [siū], *va.* (Prov. Ingl.) Desaguar un estanque, vaciar.

Sewage [siū'-ẹj], *s.* Drenaje. V. SEWERAGE.

Sewer [sō'-ẹr], *s.* Cosedor, el que cose.

Sewer [siū'-ẹr], *s.* 1. Albañal, el canal o conducto para expeler las inmundicias; alcantarilla, desaguadero. 2. (Des.) Maestresala.

Sewerage [siū'-ẹr-ẹj], *s.* 1. Desagüe sistemático por medio de albañales o cloacas; la conducción de las inmundicias desde los edificios. 2. Sistema de albañales o alcantarillas. *Sewerage system,* Alcantarillado.

Sewing [sō'-ing], *s.* Costura, el acto de coser; lo que se ha cosido a la aguja. *Sewing-machine,* Máquina de coser. *Sewing-needle,* Aguja de coser. *Sewing-thread,* Hilo de coser o para coser; hilo de número.

Sex [sex], *s.* 1. Sexo, condición orgánica que distingue al macho de la hembra en los animales y en las plantas. 2. Sexo, absolutamente hablando se entiende en inglés del femenino o de las mujeres en general.

Sexagenarian [sex-a-je-né'-ri-an], *s.* Sexagenario, persona de edad entre los sesenta y los setenta años.

Sexagesima [sex-a-jes'-i-ma], *s.* Sexagésima, domínica segunda de las tres que se cuentan antes de la primera de cuaresma.

Sexagesimal [sex-a-jes'-i-mal], *a.* Sexagesimal, basado en el número sesenta; que procede por potencias de sesenta.

Sexangled [sex'-aṇ-gld], **Sexangular** [sex-aṇ'-giu-lar], *a.* Sexangular.

Sexangularly [sex-aṇ'-giu-lar-li], *adv.* Sexangularmente.

Sexennial [sex-en'-i-al], *a.* Que dura seis años, acontece cada seis años o pertenece al sexenio.

Sexless [sex'-les], *a.* Neutro, que no tiene sexo.

Sexology [sex-ol'-o-ji], *s.* Sexología.

Sextain [sex'-tẹn], *s.* Sextilla, composición métrica que consta de seis versos.

Sextant [sex'-tant], *s.* 1. La sexta parte de un círculo. 2. Sextante, un instrumento astrónomico, usado principalmente por los marinos para determinar la latitud de un lugar. 3. Constelación pequeña.

Sextile [sex'-til], *s.* (Astr.) Sextil, el aspecto de dos astros que distan entre sí sesenta grados.

Sextillion [sex-til'-yun], *s.* Sextillón, un número cardinal; según la numeración americana y francesa la séptima potencia de mil; según la numeración inglesa, la sexta potencia de un millón.

Sextodecimo [sex-to-des'-i-mō], *a.* y *s.* Dieciseisavo.

Sexton [sex'-tẹn], *s.* Sacristán de una iglesia que cuida del edificio, de los entierros, etc.; en lo antiguo, sepulturero, el que por oficio abría las sepulturas.

Sextuple [sex'-tiu-pl], *a.* Séxtuplo.

Sexual [sex'-yu-al], *a.* Sexual, que concierne al sexo; que tiene sexo o se caracteriza por él; generativo, genital.

Sexuality [sex-yu-al'-i-ti], *s.* Sexualidad, condición de lo que tiene sexo o está caracterizado por él.

Sexually [sex'-yu-al-i], *adv.* De una manera sexual; respecto al sexo.

Shabbily [shab'-i-li], *adv.* Vilmente, ruinmente, mezquinamente; con vestidos usados, rapados.

Shabbiness [shab'-i-nes], *s.* Vileza, bajeza, miseria, roñería; estado andrajoso, desharrapado.

Shabby [shab'-i], *a.* 1. Usado, rapado, andrajoso, en mal estado, ensuciado por el largo uso. 2. Desharrapado, descamisado; mísero, ruin, tacaño. 3. Vil, bajo, despreciable, indigno de un hombre honrado.

Shack [shac], *s.* 1. (E. U. y Canadá) Choza, cabaña tosca o de troncos. 2. (E. U. y prov. Ingl.) Pasto de bellotas; pasto para el invierno.

Shackle [shac'-l], *va.* 1. Encadenar, atar, ligar con cadenas; poner obstáculos o trabas, estorbar. 2. (Elec.) Poner un aislador entre los extremos (cortados) de algo, v. g. de un alambre.

Shackle [shac'-l], *s.* 1. Anillo o argolla de metal (para atar a un preso), grillo, esposa. 2. Grillo, traba, impedimento. 3. Cadena, grillete; eslabón o gancho para unir los coches de ferrocarril. *Shackle-bolt,* Cáncano de grillete; perno de horquilla.

Shad [shad], *s.* Alosa, sábalo, saboga; pez del género Alosa.

Shaddock [shad'-oc], *s.* Pamplemusa, árbol de las Antillas parecido al naranjo, y su fruta. Citrus decumana.

Shade [shēd], *s.* 1. Sombra, la obscuridad causada por la interceptación de los rayos de la luz. 2. Sombra, el color obscuro y bajo que se pone entre los demás colores que sobresalen en una pintura. 3. Matiz, graduación de un color. 4. Matiz, diferencia ligera; poco, cantidad pequeña. 5. Cortina para minorar la luz; pantalla, lo que sirve para interceptar la luz o proteger contra los rayos de luz, el polvo, etc.; pantalla, sombrerillo de lámpara; visera de gorra; toldo. 6. Sombra, espectro, fantasma. 7. Sombra, la representación o semejanza imperfecta de alguna cosa. 8. Un sitio obscuro o cubierto de sombras; sombra, la que hacen los árboles, que también se llama umbría. 9. Exterior, ligera apariencia; ficción, máscara, imagen. *Window-shades,* Cortinas de encerado para ventanas. *Glass shade,* Guarda brisa, brisero.

Shade, *va.* 1. Obscurecer, privar de la luz y claridad. 2. Asombrar, cubrir con la sombra; ocultar una cosa de modo que no le dé la luz. 3. Entoldar, cubrir algún sitio con toldos para resguardarse del sol o del calor. 4. Abrigar, esconder, amparar, proteger, poner al abrigo de o dar abrigo. 5. Sombrear, poner sombras en la pintura o dibujo; matizar, juntar, casar acertadamente diversos colores. 6. Rasguear las letras, hacer ciertos trazos más gruesos que otros al escribir.

Shader [shē'-dẹr], *s.* El que obscurece.

Shadeless [shēd'-les], *a.* Privado de sombra.

Shadily [shē'-di-li], *adv.* Con sombra, en la sombra; de una manera sospechosa.

Shadiness [shē'-di-nes], *s.* La calidad y estado de lo que se halla cubierto de sombra o bajo la sombra.

Shadoof [sha-dūf'], *s.* Útil para sacar agua, especie de palanca usada en Oriente y en el Nilo. (<árabe.)

Shadow [shad'-o], *s.* 1. Sombra, obscuridad que produce en un cuerpo otro que se interpone entre él y la luz; sombrajo, sombraje. 2. Sombras, obscuridad, tinieblas: dícese poéticamente. 3. Sombra, el fondo obscuro o partes sombreadas de una pintura. 4. Cualquier sitio obscuro o cubierto de sombras. 5. Sombra, espectro, fantasma. 6. Compañero inseparable o lo que sigue a otra cosa como si fuese su sombra. 7. Tipo, representación mística de alguna cosa. 8. Traza o apariencia ligera; el más leve grado, poco. 9. Sombra, refugio, amparo, protección.

Shadow, *va.* 1. Anublar, obscurecer, dar sombra, poner a la sombra. 2. Representar imperfectamente o de un modo misterioso; representar por medio de un símbolo, simbolizar. 3. Seguir, acompañar de cerca como una sombra; espiar, cazar, como hace un perro. 4. Matizar. —*vn.* 1. Anublarse, obscurecerse. 2. Casarse o confundirse los colores.

Shadowboxing [shad'-o-bex'-ing], *s.* Boxeo con un contendiente imaginario a manera de entrenamiento.

Shadowy [shad'-o-i], *a.* 1. Umbroso, umbrío; obscuro, sombreado, tenebroso. 2. Obscuro, sin realidad, vago; indefinido; que tiene relación con un espectro. 3. Típico, simbólico.

Shady [shēd'-i], *a.* 1. Opaco, obscuro, sombrío, lleno de sombra; que hace sombra. 2. Al abrigo de los rayos y del calor del sol; refrescado por la sombra. 3. Impropio de la luz o que la evita; moralmente sospechoso.

Shaft [shaft], *s.* 1. Flecha, dardo.

saeta, arma arrojadiza; también mango de un arma. 2. Chapitel de una torre; caña o fuste de columna: (Mec.) eje, árbol, astil; barra larga y cilíndrica, particularmente si gira; limón o limonera de carro; lanza de coche; varas de las sillas de manos. 3. Cañón o tubo de pluma. *Shafts of a carriage*, Varas y juego de un coche. (< A.-S. sceaft.)

Shaft, *s.* 1. Socavón, tiro o pozo de mina, para la ventilación o para extraer materiales. 2. Túnel de un horno de fundición. (< Ale. schacht.)

Shag [shag], *s.* 1. Pelo áspero y lanudo. 2. Felpa, tejido que tiene pelo por el haz; (Amer.) tripe; jergón. 3. Cormorán, cuervo marino. *Shag-bag*, Guitón, pícaro; pordiosero.

Shag, *va.* y *vn.* (*pret.* y *pp.* SHAGGED). Hacer peludo, velludo; hacer escabroso, desigual; colgar o yacer en forma de mechón pesado.

Shagbark [shag'-bārk], *s.* Caria (blanca). *V.* HICKORY.

Shagged [shag'-ed], *a.* Velludo; acharrado.

Shagginess [shag'-i-nes], *s.* Calidad de peloso o afelpado.

Shaggy [shag'-i], *a.* 1. Peludo, velludo, hirsuto; afelpado, lanudo; de aquí, escabroso, áspero, desigual. 2. Cubierto de pelo, lana, etc., desigual y enredado.

Shagreen [sha-grīn'], *s.* 1. Piel de zapa, lija que se emplea para alisar maderas, etc. 2. Especie de cuero granilloso, teñido de verde por regla general y que proviene del Oriente.

Shah [shā], *s.* 1. Chah, soberano de Persia. 2. Título de honor común en los países mahometanos, como adición al nombre.

Shake [shêk], *va.* (*pret.* SHOOK (†SHAKED), *pp.* SHAKEN). 1. Sacudir, menear con fuerza, agitar o mover rápida o violentamente alguna cosa, hacer bambolear o bambonear. 2. Arrojar, lanzar, despedir con ímpetu. 3. Debilitar; poner a una cosa en riesgo o peligro; (y fig.) desalentar, amilanar. 4. Despertar repentinamente, excitar, agitar; estorbar o dañar a causa de un choque: (a veces con *up*). 5. Estrechar la mano. 6. (Mús.) *V.* TRILL. 7. (Fam. E. U.) Desembarazarse, librarse de algo, echar de sí, despedir.—*vn.* 1. Bambonear o bambolear; vacilar, titubear. 2. Temblar, moverse con movimiento inquieto y perturbado. 3. Temblar, tener mucho miedo. *To shake one's head*, Mover la cabeza. *The wind shakes the house*, El viento hace temblar la casa. *To shake hands*, Darse un apretón de manos. *To shake hands with*, Darse la mano, despedirse; dar la mano a otro, ponerse de acuerdo. *To shake for fear*, Temblar de miedo. *To shake from*, Echar de sí, poner a un lado. *To shake in*, Introducir una cosa sacudiéndola o meneándola violentamente. *To shake off*, Sacudir una cosa para que se mueva; hacer caer una cosa a fuerza de sacudirla; zafarse de, echar de sí, libertarse de algo que incomoda. *To shake to pieces*, Sacudir o menear violentamente alguna cosa hasta que caiga en pedazos. *To shake out*, Sacudir, hacer salir, hacer caer. *To shake out of*, Arrancar. *To shake up*, Sacudir, remover; agitar, poner en debida forma sacudiendo. *To shake with laughter*, Morirse de risa, o perecer de risa.

Shake, *s.* 1. Concusión, sacudimiento, sacudida, impulso dado a una cosa. 2. Vibración; movimiento de undulación causado por un impulso dado al cuerpo que se mueve. 3. La acción de darse o apretarse las manos. 4. Tabla de ripia desigual y no raspada que se usa para cubrir chozas, etc. 5. *pl.* Escalofrío de la fiebre intermitente. 6. (Ger.) Periquete; instante. 7. (Mús.) Trino. *V.* TRILL. 8. Duela. *V.* SHOOK. 9. Grieta, hendedura en un tronco.

Shakedown [shêk'-daun], *s.* 1. Cama improvisada. 2. (fam.) Variedad de baile ruidoso y rápido. 3. (fam.) Extorsión, exigencia de dinero por compulsión o persuasión.

Shaken [shê'-kn], *pp.* del verbo SHAKE. Sacudido; agitado; rajado, hendido (madero).

Shake-up [shêk'-up], *s.* 1. Sacudimiento. 2. Reorganización con cambio de personal.

Shaking [shêk'-ing], *s.* Sacudimiento; temblor.

Shaker [shêk'-ęr], *s.* 1. Temblador, temblante; sacudidor. 2. Miembro de una secta religiosa de personas célibes y comunistas de los Estados Unidos.

Shakespearian [shêk-spīr'-i-an], *a.* Perteneciente o relativo a Shakespeare, o en el estilo de este autor.

Shako, Shacko [shak'-ō], *s.* Chacó, morrión militar.

Shaky [shê'-ki], *a.* 1. Habitualmente trémulo; vacilante, débil, poco firme. 2. (Com.) Falta de crédito o solvencia; indigno de confianza. 3. Agrietado, hendido.

Shale [shêl], *s.* Arcilla esquistosa que se hiende fácilmente en láminas frágiles y desiguales.

Shall [shal], *v. defec.* (*pret.* SHOULD. *V.* la SINOPSIS). Úsase como auxiliar para denotar el tiempo futuro del verbo en el modo indicativo. Deber, haber de. En las oraciones afirmativas *shall* se usa en la primera persona para anunciar simplemente un acontecimiento venidero, y en las segundas y terceras para expresar mandato, amenaza o promesa. *I shall do it*, Lo haré o tengo intención de hacerlo. *You shall do it*, Lo hará Vd., yo mando que Vd. lo haga o yo aseguro que le obligaré a Vd. a hacerlo; Vd. ha de hacerlo. *He shall go*, Él irá, yo le haré ir, yo haré que vaya o yo prometo hacerle ir. En las oraciones interrogativas *shall* sirve en la primera persona para expresar simplemente la interrogación, en la segunda para averiguar la intención de la persona a quien se pregunta, y en la tercera para indagar la voluntad de la persona con quien hablamos, respecto al supuesto de la oración. *Shall I go to town?* ¿Voy a la ciudad? ¿debo ir a la ciudad? ¿iré a la ciudad? ¿quiere Vd. que vaya a la ciudad? *Thou shalt not kill*, No matarás. *Shall you go to town?* ¿Irá Vd. a la ciudad? ¿piensa Vd. ir a la ciudad? ¿tiene Vd. intención de ir a la ciudad? *How shall we spend the evening?* ¿Cómo pasaremos la velada? Después de otro verbo *shall* en la segunda y tercera persona sirve simplemente para anunciar. *He says that he shall set out to-morrow*, Dice que partirá mañana.

Shallop [shal'-up], *s.* Chalupa, barco prolongado mayor que el esquife o bote; bote abierto, de cualquier tamaño.

Shallot [shal-lot'], *s.* Chalote ascalonia, planta afín al ajo.

Shallow [shal'-ō], *a.* 1. Somero, inmediato a la superficie, que tiene poco fondo, poco profundo. 2. Superficial, trivial, insípido; necio, bobo. *A shallow stream*, Una corriente poco profunda.—*s.* (Mar.) Bajío, banco de arena. *Shallow-brained, shallow-pated*, Aturdido, ligero de cascos, necio.

Shallowness [shal'-o-nes], *s.* 1. Falta de hondura; poca profundidad. 2. Ligereza, necedad, falta de reflexión, bobada.

Shaly [shê'-li], *a.* De, o perteneciente a la arcilla esquistosa.

Sham [sham], *va.* y *vn.* Engañar, chasquear, hacer una burla, dar un chasco; fingir, hacer creer una cosa falsa; usar de ficción. *To sham Abraham*, (Mar.) Fingir una enfermedad.

Sham, *s.* Socolor, pretexto, apariencia falsa; fingimiento, ilusión, impostura.—*a.* Fingido, disimulado, no genuino, supuesto; postizo. *Sham-fight*, Batalla figurada, combate fingido. *A sham quarrel*, Una contienda simulada.

Shamble [sham'-bl], *vn.* Andar bamboleándose o con paso poco seguro. —*s.* Modo de andar bamboleándose; paso poco seguro. (< scamble.†)

Shambles [sham'-blz], *s. pl.* 1. Matadero, el lugar o sitio donde se matan las reses; lugar donde ha ocurrido una matanza. 2. Carnicería, el sitio donde se vende la carne para el abasto público. (< A.-S. *scamel* < lat. *scamellum*, banquillo.)

Shambling [sham'-bling], *a.* Que se mueve inseguramente, renqueando. —*pa.* de SHAMBLE.

Shame [shêm], *s.* 1. Vergüenza, rubor, bochorno, empacho. 2. Pundonor. 3. Vergüenza, ignominia, oprobio, deshonra, afrenta. *For shame! shame on you!* ¡Qué vergüenza! ¡qué asco! ¡bah!

Shame, *va.* 1. Avergonzar, causar vergüenza; afrentar, deshonrar. 2. Impeler, incitar, por un sentimiento de vergüenza: con *into* o *out of*. *To shame one out of his negligence*, Echar en cara a uno su negligencia, hacerle sonrojar por su descuido.

Shamefaced [shêm'-fêst], *a.* Tímido, vergonzoso, modesto, pudoroso.

Shamefacedly [shêm'-fêst-li], *adv.* Vergonzosamente, con rubor o modestia.

Shamefacedness [shêm'-fêst-nes], *s.* Timidez, modestia, pudor, vergüenza, rubor, empacho.

Shameful [shêm'-ful], *a.* 1. Vergonzoso, ignominioso, bochornoso, oprobioso, deshonroso, afrentoso. 2. Deshonesto, indecente.

Shamefully [shêm'-ful-i], *adv.* Vergonzosamente, ignominiosamente; indignamente, indecentemente.

Shameless [shêm'-les], *a.* 1. Desvergonzado, sin vergüenza, descarado, desollado. 2. Hecho sin la menor vergüenza; falto de decoro, de pudor.

Shamelessly [shêm'-les-li], *adv.* Desvergonzadamente, atrevidamente, descaradamente, sin empacho, desahogadamente.

Shamelessness [shêm'-les-nes], *s.* Desvergüenza, descaro, desuello, avilantez, impudencia.

Shammy, Shamois [sham'-i], *s.* Gamuza, especie de cabra montés. *Shamois-leather,* Gamuza: escríbese a veces *Shammy-leather.* *V.* CHAMOIS.

Shampoo [sham-pū'], *va.* 1. Lavar y limpiar la cabeza, frotándola con espuma de jabón y agua. 2. Frotar con fuerza el cuerpo de una persona que sale de un baño caliente.—*s.* El acto de frotar el cuerpo, o de limpiar la cabeza; líquido que sirve para este objeto. (< Indostánico *chāmpnā,* apretar.)

Shamrock [sham'-rec], *s.* (Bot.) Trébol, como emblema nacional de Irlanda; también, una de otras varias plantas trifolioladas, p. ej. la acedera.

Shank [shanc], *s.* 1. Pierna, la parte del cuerpo del animal que está entre la rodilla y el pie. 2. Zanca, pierna larga de las aves. 3. Asta o ástil, el mango o parte más larga de algún instrumento; tallo, soporte comparado a una pierna; cuerpo del tipo; fuste de una columna; enfranque de un zapato; rabo o cola de botón. 4. (Bot.) *V.* PEDICEL o FOOTSTALK. 5. (Ger. E. U.) Resto o última parte. *The shank of the evening,* La última parte de la anochecida. *Shank of an anchor,* Asta de ancla. *Spindle shank,* Pierna de un huso. *Shank-painter,* (Mar.) Boza de la uña del ancla.

Shanked [shanct], *a.* Enastado, que tiene asta o mango; de piernas, de tallo. *Long-shanked,* Zancudo, con zancas largas.

Sha'n't [shant]. (Fam.) Abreviación de *shall not* (no deberá).

Shanty [shan'-ti], *s.* (*pl.* SHANTIES). Cabaña, choza; abrigo desvencijado o provisional.

Shape [shêp], *va.* y *vn.* (*pp.* SHAPED, rara vez SHAPEN; y antiguamente SHOPEN). 1. Formar, dar figura o forma, modelar, tallar. 2. Proporcionar, ajustar a un fin particular, modificar; disponer, ordenar un rumbo o marcha determinados. 3. Imaginar, concebir, figurarse alguna cosa. *To shape a course,* (Mar.) Ponerse en rumbo.

Shape, *s.* 1. Hechura, forma, figura; contorno de los objetos. 2. Talle, la disposición o proporción del cuerpo humano. 3. Expresión desarrollada o fórmula definida de algo; aplicación. *To put an idea into shape,* Hacer aplicación de una idea. 4. Exterior, apariencia, aspecto. 5. Modelo, ejemplar, norma. 6. (Fam.) Manera, modo de hacer.

Shapeless [shêp'-les], *a.* Informe, disforme, desproporcionado, imperfecto.

Shapelessness [shêp'-les-nes], *s.* Irregularidad o deformidad en la forma o figura de una cosa.

Shapeliness [shêp'-li-nes], *s.* Simetría, belleza, proporción.

Shapely [shêp'-li], *a.* Simétrico, que tiene simetría; que está bien hecho o bien proporcionado.

Shaper [shê'-pęr], *s.* Persona o instrumento que da forma; máquina de tallar o estampar.

Shard [shārd], *s.* 1. (Ant.) Tiesto, casco, el pedazo quebrado de alguna vasija de barro. 2. Élitro (v. g. de un coleóptero).

Share [shār], *va.* 1. Distribuir, repartir entre muchos; con *between* o *among.* 2. Participar, recibir de otro alguna cosa como parte que toca a uno; tener parte en algo; gozar o soportar con otros. 3. Dividir, compartir, partir; con *with.* 4. Cortar, separar.—*vn.* Participar, tener parte en alguna cosa o tocar algo de ella. *To share alike,* Repartir igualmente, tener una parte igual.

Share, *s.* 1. Parte, porción de una cosa dividida o repartida entre varios. 2. Cuota, parte que toca a cada persona que participa en un negocio; (y Com.) acción, parte o porción del fondo de una compañía de comercio, y el papel o vale que representa cada parte. 3. Interés, participación, porción asignada. *To hold a share,* Tener interés en alguna cosa, tener o poseer una acción de alguna compañía. 4. Reja del arado. *To each his share,* A cada uno su parte. *Share and share alike,* Por igual, por partes iguales. *On shares,* Con condición de tener una parte. *Railway share,* Acción de ferrocarril. *Paid-up share,* Acción liberada. *To fall to the share of,* Tocar, caer en parte.

Sharebone [shār'-bōn], *s.* Hueso del empeine, del pubis.

Sharecropper [shār-crep-ęr], *s.* Mediero, inquilino.

Shares [shār'-ęr], *s.* Repartidor; partícipe.

Shareholder [shār'-hōld-ęr], *s.* (Com.) Accionista, el dueño de una o más acciones.

Sharer [shār'-ęr], *s.* Repartidor; partícipe.

Shark [shārk], *s.* 1. Tiburón, pez marino voracísimo de carne humana. 2. Gato, el ladrón ratero que hurta con astucia y engaño. 3. (Des.) Gatada.

Shark, *va.* Gatear, petardear, hurtar.—*vn.* Ratear, hurtar cosas pequeñas con destreza y sutileza.

Sharker [shārk'-ęr], *s.* Petardista. *V.* SHARPER.

Sharp [shārp], *a.* 1. Agudo, lo que tiene la punta, filo o corte delgado y sutil, puntiagudo, aguzado, cortante. 2. Que forma un ángulo agudo, abrupto, angular. 3. Agudo, perspicaz, de vivo ingenio, astuto, mañoso. 4. De aguada vista, de buen oído. 5. Agudo, penetrante. 6. Acre, mordaz, picante, agrio; sarcástico. 7. Severo, rígido; vivo, violento. 8. Ansioso, ardiente; vehemente, penetrante, áspero (v. g. la arena); pronto; impetuoso, fogoso, vivo (combate, debate); vigilante, atento; mordaz, excesivamente frío (viento, escarcha); listo, avisado. 9. Distinto, claramente delineado o definido. 10. (Mús.) Elevado más alto que su propio tono; precedido de un sostenido.—*s.* 1. (Mús.) Sostenido, (♯) signo musical que indica elevación de un semitono; el mismo tono así indicado. 2. Aguja de coser de la forma más larga y más delgada. 3. Estafador. 4 (Fest. E. U.) De aquí, maestro en un arte, sujeto hábil, experto.—*adv.* 1. De una manera severa, sarcástica. 2. (Fam.) Al instante, exactamente, puntualmente. *We shall go at four o'clock sharp,* Iremos a las cuatro en punto. *Look sharp,* Está o estad alerta. *A sharp knife,* Un cuchillo cortante. *A sharp needle, roof,* Una aguja puntiaguda, un techo puntiagudo, o en punta. *Sharp sight,* Vista penetrante. *Sharp features,* Facciones enjutas. *Sharp criticism,* Una crítica acerba. *Sharp-edged,* Afilado, agudo, aguzado. *Sharp-eyed,* De vista penetrante. *Sharp-pointed,* Puntiagudo, de punta aguda, acerada.

Sharp, *va.* 1. Afilar, aguzar. 2. Elevar medio tono; marcar con un sostenido.—*vn.* 1. (Mús.) Cantar o tocar más alto que el tono debido. 2. Ratear; engañar, trampear, petardear.

Sharp bend [shārp bend], *s.* Curva cerrada (en una carretera).

Sharpen [shār'-pn], *va.* 1. Afilar, aguzar, adelgazar; amolar. 2. Aguzar o sutilizar el ingenio. 3. Hacer más severo, intenso, acre, fogoso o ansioso.—*vn.* Aguzarse, hacerse más agudo, más vivo o picante; afilarse.

Sharpener [shār'-pn-ęr], *s.* Amolador, afilador. *Pencil-sharpener,* Cortalápiz.

Sharper [shārp'-ęr], *s.* 1. Fullero. 2. Caballero de industria.

Sharpie [shār'-pi], *s.* (Fam.) Púa.

Sharply [shārp'-li], *adv.* 1. Con filo, corte o punta. 2. Severamente, rigorosamente. 3. Agudamente, vivamente. 4. Agudamente, sutilmente, ingeniosamente.

Sharpness [shārp'-nes], *s.* 1. Agudeza, sutileza o delicadeza en los filos, cortes o puntas. 2. Agudeza, sutileza, perspicacia, viveza de ingenio. 3. Acrimonia, aspereza, mordacidad. 4. Acritud, agrura, acrimonia. 5. Violencia, rigor. 6. Destemple, inclemencia del tiempo.

Shatterproof [shat'-ęr-prūf], *a.* Inastillable.

Sharpshooter [shārp'-shūt-ęr], *s.* Tirador experto.

Sharp-sighted [shārp'-sait-ed], *a.* Perspicaz, el que tiene vista de lince o muy penetrante.

Sharp-visaged [shārp'-viz-ejd], *a.* Cariaguileño.

Sharp-witted [shārp'-wit-ed], *a.* Agudo de ingenio.

Shatter [shat'-ęr], *va.* 1. Destrozar, hacer pedazos o astillas, hacer añicos alguna cosa; estrellar, romper alguna cosa de un golpe haciéndola pedazos. 2. Arruinar la salud, distraer, perturbar.—*vn.* 1. Hacerse pedazos, quebrarse, romperse. 2. Tener un sonido como el de las cosas al romperse; dar un estallido.

Shatter-brained [shat'-ęr-brênd], **Shatter-pated** [shat'-ęr-pêt-ed], *a.* Atronado.

Shattery [shat'-ęr-i], *a.* Desmenuzable, quebradizo, que se puede reducir fácilmente a pedazos.

Shave [shêv], *va.* 1. Rasurar, quitar o cortar la barba o el cabello, rapar. 2. Afeitar, hacer o cortar la barba. 3. Raspar, raer alguna cosa quitando una parte de su superficie. 4. Rozar, tocar o tropezar ligeramente. 5. Cortar alguna cosa reduciéndola a partes muy menudas.—*vn.* 1. Afeitarse, hacerse la barba. 2. Llevarse la mejor parte en un trato o negocio.

Shave, *s.* Afeitada, rasurada.

Shaveling [shêv'-ling], *s.* Hombre rapado; monje o fraile.

Shaver [shêv'-ęr], *s.* 1. Barbero, el que afeita. 2. Desollador, el que hace su negocio, el que no mira más que su interés. 3. Robador, ladrón. 4. (Fam.) Muchacho, jovencito. *He is a keen shaver,* Es trujamán experto.

Shaving [shêv'-ing], *s.* 1. Raedura, la parte menuda que se rae de alguna cosa. 2. Raspadura, rasura, lo que se quita de la superficie raspando. *Shaving-brush*, Brocha de afeitar. *Shaving-dish*, Bacía. *Shaving-knife*, Navaja de afeitar. *Cloth-shaving*, Paño de afeitar. *Shaving-soap*, Jabón para afeitarse. *Shavings* (*of wood*), Acepilladuras, virutas, alisaduras. *Shavings of hartshorn*, Raeduras de cuerno de ciervo.

Shaw [shō], *s.* (Prov. brit.) Bosquecillo, bosque pequeño, soto.

Shawl [shōl], *s.* Chal, pañolón, pañuelo grande o manteleta. (Amer.) Manta, pañuelos para rebozo.

Shawm [shōm], *s.* (Ant.) Oboe, instrumento músico.

She [shī], *pron. fem.* 1. Ella, aquella; (delante de un pronombre relativo) la que, aquella que. *She who speaks*, La que habla. 2. La hembra. *She-ass*, Borrica, burra. *She-goat*, Cabra.

Sheaf [shīf], *s.* (en *pl.* SHEAVES). 1. Gavilla, haz, garba, un manojo de cañas de trigo, centeno o cebada atadas. 2. Paquete, lío. 3. *V.* SHEAVE. *Sheaf of arrows*, Haz de flechas.

Sheaf, *va.* Agavillar.

Shear [shīr], *va.* (*pret.* SHEARED o SHORE, *pp.* SHEARED o SHORN). 1. Atusar, recortar o igualar el pelo con tijera; trasquilar. 2. Tundir, cortar el pelo de los paños e igualarlo con la tijera. 3. Esquilar, quitar con la tijera el pelo, vellón o lana de los ganados. 4. Cortar cualquier cosa mediante el roce o presión de otras dos, como cortar hierba con los dientes, etc. *Shearing-time*, Esquileo, el tiempo en que se esquilla. *Shearing-machine*, Esquiladora mecánica.

Shearer [shīr'-ẹr], *s.* Esquilador, trasquilador, el que esquila.

Shears [shīrz], *s. pl.* 1. Tijeras grandes; cizallas, tijeras para cortar los metales. 2. Las correderas de un torno o de una máquina para taladrar. 3. Cualquier cosa que tiene la figura de tijeras. 4. *V.* SHEERS.

Shearman [shīr'-man], *s.* Esquilador; tundidor.

Shearwater [shīr'-wō-tẹr], *s.* Pico-tijera, ave marina del género Puffinus.

Sheath [shīth], *s.* 1. Vaina, caja, funda, estuche. 2. Cubierta, lo que cubre una parte o un órgano, v. g. la parte inferior de las hojas en las plantas gramíneas.

Sheathe [shīdh], *va.* 1. Envainar, meter en la vaina. 2. Poner vaina a una espada o puñal. 3. Defender alguna cosa poniéndole un forro o cubierta, aforrar. 4. Embotar la acritud o acrimonia de las partículas acres de los cuerpos. *To sheathe a ship's bottom*, (Mar.) Aforrar el fondo de un navío.

Sheathing [shīdh'-ing], *s.* 1. Forro exterior, lo que forma una funda o cubierta. 2. El acto de envainar o forrar. 3. Forro exterior de navío. *Copper-sheathing*, (Mar.) Forro de cobre. *Pump-sheathing*, (Mar.) Forro de bomba de agua. *Sheathing-nails*, Clavos de entablar.

Sheathless [shīth'-les], *a.* Sin vaina, sin estuche; desenvainado.

Sheath-winged [shīth-wingd], *a.* Armado de estuches para cubrir las alas.

Sheave [shīv], *s.* 1. Roldana, rueda de una polea, garrucha. 2. Rueda excéntrica o su disco. *Lignumvitæ sheaves*, (Mar.) Roldanas de palo santo. *Sheave-holes of the sheets*, (Mar.) Escorteras.

Sheaves [shīvz], *pl.* de SHEAF.

Shed [shed], *va.* (*pret.* y *pp.* SHED). 1. Arrojar, quitarse, desprenderse de algo, como una culebra de su piel o un ave de sus plumas; mudar. 2. Verter, derramar, hacer correr. 3. Esparcir, dejar caer. 4. Exhalar, emitir. *To shed feathers*, Pelechar.—*vn.* Caer, desunirse, separarse; mudar los cuernos algunos animales.

Shed [shed], *s.* 1. Vertiente, superficie inclinada que vierte el agua. 2. En composición significa efusión o derramamiento. 3. Separación, reparto. 4. El declive o la bajada de una colina. (<A.-S. *scāde*, separado.)

Shed, *s.* 1. Sotechado, soportal, cobertizo, tinglado. 2. Tejadillo o colgadizo que sale de una pared para servir de cobertizo a algún puesto de vender o a otra cosa; cabaña, barraca. (Var. de SHADE.)

Shedder [shed'-ẹr], *s.* Derramador, el que vierte o derrama.

Sheen, *s.* Resplandor, brillantez; particularmente un lustre o brillo débil, como el de la luz reflejada.

Sheeny [shīn'-i], *a.* Lustroso, luciente, brillante.

Sheep [shīp], *s.* (*sing.* y *pl.*). 1. Oveja, carnero, rumiante del género Ovis. 2. *pl.* Ovejas: llámase así en sentido místico a los feligreses o fieles con respecto a sus obispos o párrocos. 3. Papanatas, hombre simple. 4. Badana, piel de carnero preparada para la encuadernación. *Sheep-bot*, Mosca de carnero, o su larva, que infesta la nariz de los carneros. *Sheepcote*, *Sheepfold*, Redil, el cercado o corral para encerrar el ganado. *Sheep-dog*, Perro de pastor. *Sheep-dip*, (1) Decocción insecticida, v. g. de tabaco, en la cual se zabulle a los carneros para librarlos de parásitos. (2) Limpiadura de la lana antes de esquilar. *Sheep-dung*, Sirle, sirria. *Sheep-hook*, Cayado. *Sheep-master*, Ganadero, el dueño de ganado lanar. *Sheep-shearer*, Esquilador de carneros. *Sheep-shank*, (1) La pierna de un carnero. (2) (Mar.) Margarita en un cabo. *Sheepwalk*, (Gran Bret.) Dehesa, tierra destinada solamente para pasto del ganado lanar.

Sheepish [shīp'-ish], *a.* Vergonzoso, corto de genio; tímido, pusilánime.

Sheepishly [shīp'-ish-li], *adv.* Tímidamente, con pusilanimidad o falta de ánimo.

Sheepishness [shīp'-ish-nes], *s.* Empacho, timidez, cortedad de genio; pusilanimidad.

Sheep's-eye [shīps'-ai], *s.* Mirada al soslayo; ojeada modesta y amorosa.

Sheep-shearing [shīp'-shīr-ing], *s.* Esquileo, acción de esquilar y la época en que se esquila el ganado lanar.

Sheepskin [shīp'-skin], *s.* Piel de carnero, badana.

Sheer [shīr], *a.* 1. Puro, claro, sin mezcla, absoluto, consumado, cabal. 2. Muy fino y delgado, ligero (v. g. un tejido). 3. Escarpado, casi vertical, a pico.—*adv.* De un golpe, de una vez.—*s.* (Mar.) Arrufo, arrufadura, la corvadura que hacen las cubiertas y costados de los barcos. *A ship with a great sheer*, (Mar.) Bajel muy arrufado.

Sheer, *vn.* (Mar.) Alargarse, desviarse del rumbo o derrota. *To sheer off*, Huirse, largarse, escaparse.

Sheers, Sheer-legs [shīrz], *s.* Cabria de arbolar, aparato para levantar grandes pesos.

Sheet [shīt], *s.* 1. Pedazo ancho y muy delgado de cualquier objeto o substancia: v. gr. sábana, pieza de lienzo para cubrir la cama. 2. Pliego, hoja de papel, pedazo de papel de cierto tamaño; un diario; hoja, lámina delgada de metal, vidrio, madera, etc. 3. Cualquier cosa grande extendida; superficie grande y ancha, p. ej. la de una extensión de agua. 4. En plural, hojas, en la significación de un libro o escrito. 5. (Mar.) Escota, cuerda o maroma con que se templa la vela de la nave alargándola o acortándola. 6. Vela; uso literario. *Winding-sheet*, Mortaja, la sábana en que se envuelven los cadáveres. *Top-sail sheets*, (Mar.) Escotines. *To haul aft the sheets*, (Mar.) Cazar las escotas. *To haul home the top-sail sheets*, (Mar.) Cazar el escotín a besar. *To ease off the sheets*, (Mar.) Dar un salto a las escotas. *To let fly the sheets*, (Mar.) Arriar las escotas en banda. *To sail with flowing sheets*, (Mar.) Navegar a escota larga. *Sheet-anchor*, Esperanza, el ancla mayor de un buque; (fig.) áncora de salvación, apoyo seguro, último recurso. *Sheet-cable*, Cable mayor, cable de forma o esperanza. *Sheet-lightning*, Relámpago a manera de un resplandor muy extenso, y que es debido al reflejo de un relámpago lejano.

Sheet, *va.* 1. Ensabanar, cubrir o envolver en sábanas. 2. Proveer de o suministrar sábanas. 3. Envolver en alguna cosa grande; extender en láminas u hojas. *To sheet a bed*, Poner sábanas en una cama.

Sheeting [shīt'-ing], *s.* Tela para hacer sábanas. *Russia sheeting*, Brin de Rusia.

Sheet metal [shīt met'-al], *s.* Hoja metálica, metal laminado.

Sheik [shīk o shēk], *s.* Jeque, anciano o superior entre los árabes; jefe de familia o de tribu en los países mahometanos.

Shekel [shec'-l], *s.* 1. Siclo, moneda usada entre los hebreos. 2. Peso usado entre los asirios y los babilonios. 3. *pl.* (Ger.) Dinero.

Sheldrake [shel'-drēk], *s.* 1. Tadorna, ave acuática de Europa muy parecida al ánade, de cualquiera de los géneros Tadorna o Casarca. 2. Mergánsar. 3. *V.* CANVASBACK. Se escribe también *shelduck* y *skeldrake*.

Shelf [shelf], *s.* (*pl.* SHELVES). 1. Anaquel o estante de armario, de alacena o de vasares; entrepaño; tabla fija a la pared para sostener objetos. 2. Bajío, banco de arena.

Shell [shel], *s.* 1. Casco, la parte exterior de cualquiera cosa cuando es dura y consistente. 2. Cáscara de nuez, de huevo, de avellana, etc. 3. Vaina, vainilla, la corteza de algunas legumbres. 4. Silicua, la corteza de las semillas de las plantas silicuosas. 5. Concha, la cubierta exterior de los animales testáceos o crustáceos. 6. La parte exterior de una cosa. 7. Corteza, la exterioridad de alguna cosa inmaterial. 8. (Art.) Bomba, proyectil hueco metálico, lleno de una substancia explosiva; también, cápsula metálica para un arma de retrocarga. 9. (Poét.) La lira en su forma primitiva, una concha de tortuga con cuerdas. 10. (Mar.) Casco o caja de motón. *Shell-gold*, Oro de concha u oro molido para dorar. *Shell-proof*, A prueba de bomba. *Shell-silver*, Plata de concha. *Shell-work*, Obra de concha.

Shell, *va.* 1. Descascarar, descortezar, quitar las cáscaras, cortezas o vainas. 2. Encerrar en una cáscara, vaina o casco. 3. Bombardear, lanzar bombas. 4. (E. U.) Separar los granos de maíz de la mazorca.—*vn.* Descascararse; levantarse la cubierta de una cosa en costras.

Shellac [shel'-ac o shel-ac'], *s.* Goma laca en hojuelas.

Shellbark [shel'-bārk], *s.* Caria; cada una de las dos especies, Carya alba o sulcata, o sus frutos.

Sheller [shel'-ẹr], *s.* Descascarador.

Shellfire [shel'-fair], *s.* Cañoneo, fuego de metralla.

Shell-fish [shel'-fish], *s.* Marisco, animal acuático provisto de concha, v. g. un molusco o un crustáceo.

Shell shock [shel shoc], *s.* Condición psiconeurótica que sufren soldados expuestos a los peligros de la guerra moderna.

Shelly [shel'-i], *a.* Conchudo, cubierto de conchas.

Shelter [shel'-tẹr], *s.* 1. Guarida, amparo, abrigo, abrigaño; todo lo que protege contra un peligro o contra la intemperie; casa, vivienda, hogar. 2. Protector, defensor. 3. Protección, asilo, refugio.

Shelter, *va.* 1. Guarecer, abrigar, poner al abrigo o a cubierto, dar casa o habitación. 2. Refugiar, acoger, amparar, proteger, defender. 3. Encubrir, ocultar, tapar.—*vn.* Refugiarse, guarecerse, acogerse.

Shelterless [shel'-tẹr-les], *a.* Desamparado, sin asilo, sin refugio; desabrigado.

Shelve [shelv], *va.* 1. Poner sobre un anaquel; (fig.) poner a un lado, diferir indefinidamente, retirar. 2. Proveer de estantes o anaqueles.

Shelve, *vn.* Inclinarse gradualmente, estar en pendiente. (< islandés, *skelgja*, declive.)

Shelves, *pl.* de SHELF.

Shelving [shelv'-ing], *a.* Inclinado, lo que está en declive o pendiente. —*s.* 1. Conjunto de estantes ó anaqueles; material para construir anaqueles. 2. Lugar inclinado, en declive; tonga, tongada.

Sheol [shī'-ol], *s.* El mundo inferior, los infiernos, el lugar de los muertos. (Heb.)

Shepherd [shep'-ẹrd], *s.* 1. Pastor, el que guarda y guía ovejas y carneros. 2. Zagal. 3. Pastor, párroco, cura, el que tiene cura de almas. *Shepherd-dog*, Perro de pastor. *V.* COLLIE. *Shepherd's crook*, Cayado de pastor. *Shepherd's purse* o *pouch*, (Bot.) Bolsa de pastor. *Shepherd's watch*, Hierba pajarera, anagálida.

Shepherdess [shep'-ẹrd-es], *sf.* Pastora, zagala, doncella aldeana.

Sherbet [shẹr'-bet], *s.* Sorbete, refresco hecho del zumo de alguna fruta, con azúcar, agua, esencia, etc., y al que se da cierto grado de congelación.

Sherd [shẹrd], *s.* Tiesto, casco, pedazo quebrado de alguna vasija de barro.

Sherif [sher-īf' o sher'-if], *s.* 1. Jerife, descendiente de Mahoma por su hija Fátima. 2. Magistrado principal de la Meca. (< árabe, *sharif*, noble.)

Sheriff [sher'-if], *s.* Jerife, el magistrado a quien está encargada la ejecución de las leyes en cada condado de Inglaterra o de los Estados Unidos; es casi equivalente al cargo de Alguacil mayor. (< A.-S. scir-*gerēfa*; shire-reeve.)

Sherry [sher'-i], *s.* Vino de Jerez.

Shew, Shewed, Shown. (Ant.) *V.* SHOW.

Shibboleth [shib'-o-leth], *s.* Palabra que sirve de prueba o de santo y seña (término bíblico).

Shield [shīld], *s.* 1. Escudo, broquel. arma defensiva. 2. Escudo, egida, amparo, patrocinio. 3. Protector, defensor. 4. (Her.) Escudo de armas, el espacio en que se representan los blasones de una familia. 5. Una parte que protege; todo lo que sirve para cubrir o proteger alguna cosa. *Shield-bearer*, Escudero, el que lleva el escudo; también, falena (del género Aspidisca) cuya larva es nociva a los árboles frutales. *Shield-fern*, Cualquier helecho del género Aspidium; aspidia.

Shield, *va.* Escudar, amparar, resguardar, defender.

Shift [shift], *va.* 1. Cambiar, hacer mudar de lugar, sitio o puesto a una cosa; transportar, conducir, llevar de un paraje a otro; trasladar de un paraje o de un tiempo a otro. 2. Cambiar por otra u otras cosas de la misma clase; vestirse o quitarse algo del cuerpo.—*vn.* 1. Cambiarse, mudarse de un paraje a otro. 2. Ingeniarse, darse maña, buscar arbitrios, discurrir trazas y modos para conseguir o ejecutar una cosa. 3. Tergiversar, usar de frases equívocas. 4. (Des.) Mudarse el vestido, la camisa, etc., ponerse otra ropa blanca. *To shift about*, Cambiar completamente de dirección. *To shift for one's self*, Mirar por sí mismo; ingeniarse o buscar arbitrios y recursos para salir por sí mismo de algún mal paso. *To shift off*, Eludir la dificultad, salir o librarse de algún aprieto por medio de artificios: cuando se toma en buen sentido corresponde también a tomar un sesgo, un medio, un temperamento o un arbitrio en cualquier asunto, pero más generalmente es andar u obrar con ardides, con doblez o con segunda. *To shift a tackle*, (Mar.) Enmendar un aparejo. *To shift the helm*, Cambiar el timón. poner el timón a la contra. *To shift the royal*, Despasar el ayuste. *To shift a berth*, Mudar fondo. *To shift the cargo*, Volver la estiva. *The ballast shifts*, El lastre se corre.

Shift, *s.* 1. Cambio, el acto de cambiar de lugar, dirección o forma, o una cosa por otra. 2. Sustitución, la cosa sustituída por otra; recurso, expediente, el medio extraordinario para el logro de algún fin; y de aquí, artimaña, artificio, maña, astucia, subterfugio, fraude, evasión, efugio, excusa frívola y sólo por salir del paso. 3. Camisa de mujer. 4. Tanda de obreros; tarea, el tiempo que trabaja cada tanda de operarios. *To make shift*, Hallar el medio de, arreglarse para. *To make shift without*, Pasarse sin.

Shiftable [shift'-a-bl], *a.* Mudable.

Shifter [shift'-ẹr], *s.* 1. El que traslada o cambia algo, v. g. la escena de un teatro. 2. Tramoyista, el que usa de ficciones y engaños; invencionero.

Shiftless [shift'-les], *a.* Falto de recursos, perezoso, ineficiente.

Shillalah, Shillelah [shi-lé'-la], *s.* Palo, porra fuerte, generalmente de encina o de endrino. (Irlandés, de una baronía famosa por sus encinas.)

Shilling [shil'-ing], *s.* 1. Chelín, moneda británica que vale doce peniques, o sea 1.25 pesetas. 2. El real fuerte, moneda española de plata equivalente a 12½ centavos y que circuló por mucho tiempo en los Estados Unidos.

Shill-i-shall-i ó **Shilly-shally** [shil'-i-shal'-i], *vn., adv.* y *a.* Estar irresoluto, no saber qué hacer. Repetición de *shall I?* que se usa para expresar familiarmente duda o indecisión. (Fam.) Con que sí, y con que no.

Shimmer [shim'-ẹr], *vn.* Despedir luz o claridad trémula, lucir con intermitencias.—*s.* Luz incierta o trémula; débil resplandor.

Shimmy [shim'-i], *s.* 1. Baile en que se mueven mucho las caderas y los hombros. 2. Vibración anormal, como la de las ruedas delanteras de un automóvil.

Shin [shin], *s.* Espinilla, la parte anterior de la canilla de la pierna.

Shindy [shin'-di], *s.* Alboroto, pendencia ruidosa en la que se dan y reciben golpes.

Shine [shain], *vn.* 1. Lucir, relucir, brillar, resplandecer, relumbrar. 2. Relucir, sobresalir, resaltar alguna virtud. 3. Lucir, sobresalir, distinguirse una persona por sus prendas, ingenio, etc., sobresalir, exceder. 4. Favorecer, ser propicio.—*va.* Pulir, bruñir, dar lustre (v. g. a los zapatos).

Shine, *s.* 1. Resplandor, lustre, brillo. 2. Buen tiempo, claridad. *Sunshine*, Claridad del sol. 3. (Ger. E. U.) Inclinación, afecto, gusto.

Shiner [shai'-nẹr], *s.* 1. El que o lo que brilla o hace relucir. 2. (Fam.) Moneda lustrosa o de oro. 3. Pez plateado.

Shingle, *va.* 1. Cubrir con ripias o tajamaniles. 2. Cortar los cabellos por igual y muy cortos en toda la cabeza. 3. Batir el hierro, expeler las impurezas por medio de golpes o presión fuertes.

Shingle [shiṇ'-gl], *s.* 1. Ripia, tablita delgada para cubrir las casas. (Cuba) Tejamaní. (Mex.) Tajamanil. 2. (Fest. E. U.) Muestra pequeña con el nombre de una persona, como para oficina, bufete, etc.

Shingle, *s.* Cascajo, piedra redondeada y gastada por el agua, y mayor que el cascajo ordinario.

Shingles [shiṇ'-glz], *s.* Zoster, enfermedad cutánea, sintomática de un desorden nervioso, que se presenta en forma de erupción vesicular o pustulosa.

Shining [shain'-ing], *a.* Brillante, resplandeciente, luciente.—*s.* Lucimiento, esplendor, lustre; resplandor, brillo.

Shinto, Shintoism [shin'-tō, izm], *s.* Culto de los primitivos japoneses, especie de culto de los antepasados.

Shiny [shai'-ni], *a.* Lustroso, brillante, resplandeciente, luciente.

Ship [ship], *s.* Nave, bajel, navío,

buque, embarcación de cubierta y con velas. *Ship of the line*, (Mar.) Navío de alto bordo o de línea. *Ship of war*, Navío, buque de guerra. *Merchant ship*, Buque mercante. *Store-ship*, (Mar.) Navío almacén. *To ballast a ship*, (Mar.) Lastrar un buque. *Burden of a ship*, (Mar.) Porte, capacidad de carga de un buque. *Ship-biscuit*, Galleta. *V.* HARDTACK. *Ship-boy*, (1) Paje de escoba. (2) Grumete. *Ship-builder*, Constructor de buques, ingeniero naval. *Ship-chandler*, Proveedor de buques (lona, jarcia, etc.). *Ship-chandlery*, Cabullería, tienda de artículos de marina; jarcia, etc. *Ship-fever*, Tifus; así llamado porque era en otro tiempo común a bordo. *Ship-load*, Cargamento, cargazón. *Ship-money*, Antiguo derecho sobre buques.

Ship, *va.* 1. Embarcar, poner a bordo. 2. Transportar por mar; y en el comercio, transportar por ferrocarril o de cualquier otro modo. 3. Contratar y recibir a bordo la tripulación. 4. Recibir a bordo de cualquiera embarcación, p. ej. una ola. 5. Armar, montar los mástiles, el timón, los remos.—*vn.* 1. Ir a bordo, embarcarse. 2. Alistarse como marinero. *To ship the oars*, Armar los remos.

Shipboard [ship'-bōrd], *s.* (Mar.) Bordo; se usa solamente en las frases adverbiales *a-shipboard* u *on shipboard*, a bordo.

Shipmaster [ship'-mas-tẹr], *s.* (Mar.) Capitán de embarcación.

Shipmate [ship'-mêt], *s.* Camarada de a bordo.

Shipment [ship'-mẹnt], *s.* Embarque, envío, remesa, cargo, cargamento.

Shipper [ship'-ẹr], *s.* 1. Cargador, el que entrega a una compañía de transportes los objetos que desea expedir. 2. (Com.) Lo que se puede transportar sin deterioro en la calidad, aroma o sabor.

Shipping [ship'-ing], *s.* 1. Navíos o bajeles colectivamente. 2. Embarques, expedición de mercancías.—*a.* Naval, marítimo, relativo a embarques, relativo a expedición de mercancías. *Shipping clerk*, Dependiente encargado de remisiones. *Shipping charges*, Gastos de embarque o de expedición. *Shipping documents*, Documentos de embarque o de expedición. *Shipping room*, Departamento de embarques o de expedición de mercancías.

Shipshape [ship'-shêp], *a.* Bien orientado, en buen orden, bien arreglado, bien instalado, como a bordo de un buque.

Shipworm [ship'-wūrm], *s.* Broma, especie de carcoma que se introduce en la madera de los buques y la destruye. Teredo.

Shipwreck [ship'-rec], *s.* 1. Naufragio, pérdida o ruina de la embarcación en el mar. 2. Los restos de un naufragio. 3. Desastre, desgracia.

Shipwreck, *va.* Causar naufragio; echar a pique alguna embarcación. *To be shipwrecked*, Naufragar. *Shipwrecked*, Naufragado, que se ha ido a pique.

Shipwright [ship'-rait], *s.* Carpintero de ribera; constructor de buques.

Shipyard [ship'-yārd], *s.* Astillero (de construcción naval).

Shire [shīr ó shair], *s.* Condado, cada una de las divisiones territoriales de la Gran Bretaña.

Shirk [shẹrk], *s.* El que falta a su obligación o trabajo, que se empereza.

Shirk, *va.* y *vn.* 1. Evitar, esquivar, eludir la ejecución de algo, faltar, desatender la obligación o trabajo. 2. (Des.) Trampear, defraudar.

Shirr [shẹr], *va.* 1. Acordonar, fruncir en líneas paralelas. 2. Pasar huevos por crema o nata en vez de agua.—*s.* 1. Acordonamiento, pliegues que se hacen por medio de hilos de fruncir. 2. Hilo de caucho o goma, tejido en una tela para hacerla elástica.

Shirred [shẹrd], *pp.* y *a.* 1. Acordonado. 2. Provisto de hilos de goma elástica. 3. Pasado por crema (huevos).

Shirt [shẹrt], *s.* 1. Camisa de hombre. 2. Revestimiento o forro interior de un horno de fundición. *Shirt-bosom, shirt-front*, Pechera de camisa. *Shirt-sleeve*, Manga de camisa. *In one's shirt-sleeves*, En mangas de camisa. *Shirt-waist*, Corpiño de camisa, prenda de vestir que llega sólo a la cintura, llevada por las mujeres y los niños.

Shirting [shẹrt'-ing], *s.* Tela para hacer camisas.

Shittah-tree [shit'-a-trī], *s.* Arbol asiático, especie de acacia. *Shittim(-wood)*, Setim, la madera de este árbol, de la que se supone que se sirvió Moisés para construir el tabernáculo y el arca de la alianza.

Shiver [shiv'-ẹr], *s.* 1. Temblor, escalofrío. 2. Cacho o pedazo pequeño de una cosa. 3. Cachivache, trozo, pedazo, fragmento, casco; la parte o porción de cualquiera cosa que se rompe, revienta o salta en pedazos. 4. †(Mar.) Roldana. *V.* SHEAVE.

Shiver, *vn.* 1. Tiritar de frío, temblar de miedo, calofriarse. 2. Cascarse, hacerse pedazos, quebrantarse.—*va.* 1. Estrellar, romper alguna cosa de un golpe haciéndola pedazos, hacer astillas, añicos; vibrar, sacudir. 2. Disponer una vela de modo que bata al viento en lugar de recibirlo de lleno.

Shivering [shiv'-ẹr-ing], *s.* 1. Horripilación, calofrío, temblor, estremecimiento. 2. Quebranto, desmembramiento.

Shivery [shiv'-ẹr-i], *a.* 1. Trémulo, parecido a un escalofrío. 2. Predispuesto a calofriarse. 3. Friolento, friolero o frío. 4. Quebradizo.

Shoal [shōl], *s.* 1. Sitio en que el agua es poco profunda. 2. Bajío, banco de arena. *By shoals*, A cientos. 3. Concurrencia, multitud, muchedumbre; cardume, manjúa. *V.* SCHOOL. *Shoal of herrings*, Cardume de arenques.—*a.* Poco profundo, bajo. *Shoal water*, Agua poco profunda.

Shoal, *va.* y *vn.* 1. Disminuir en profundidad. 2. Atroparse, juntarse en tropas; reunirse una gran muchedumbre.

Shoaliness [shōl'-i-nes], *s.* Falta de profundidad, calidad de somero.

Shoaly [shōl'-i], *a.* Lleno de sitios poco profundos en el agua, o de bajíos o bancos de arena.

Shock [shec], *s.* 1. Choque, encuentro violento, colisión, concusión, sacudimiento; reencuentro, combate. 2. Agitación súbita del ánimo; emoción pasmosa. 3. (Med.) Agotamiento de las funciones corporales, v. g. a consecuencia de una lesión repentina. 4. Conmoción, sacudimiento del cuerpo producido por la electricidad. 5. Ofensa; desazón.

Shock, *s.* 1. Hacina, el montón donde se juntan y ordenan los haces de trigo u otro grano. 2. Mechón de cabellos toscos y enredados. 3. Perro lanudo. *Shock-dog*, Perro de lanas.—*a.* Afelpado, lanudo.

Shock, *va.* y *vn.* 1. Sacudir, mover violentamente. 2. Ofender, disgustar. 3. Chocar, encontrarse con violencia una cosa con otra. 4. Chocar, provocar, enojar a otros. 5. Chocar, disgustar, enfadar; horrorizar, herir. 6. Hacinar, hacer hacinas de grano.

Shock absorber, *s.* Amortiguador.

Shocking [shek'-ing], *a.* Espantoso, horrible, chocante, que disgusta, choca o hiere; ofensivo.

Shockproof [shec'-prūf], *a.* A prueba de choques.

Shock troops, *s. pl.* Tropas especialmente escogidas para la ofensiva en la guerra.

Shock wave [shec' wêv], *s.* Onda de choques.

Shoddy [shed'-i], *a.* 1. Hecho de lana artificial o que la contiene. 2. Falso, no legítimo.—*s.* 1. Lana artificial, imitada. 2. Tela que contiene imitación de lana. 3. (Fam.) Ostentación vulgar, impostura.

Shoe [shū], *s.* 1. Zapato, el calzado del pie. 2. Algo que se asemeja a un zapato por su posición o su uso; p. ej. la herradura de las caballerías; suela de trineo, zapata de ancla; galga de carruaje; (Mar.) calzo, soler; contera de bastón o de la vaina de un arma blanca; canal para conducir el trigo o el mineral a la tolva, etc. *Shoe-black*, Limpiabotas. *Horse-shoe*, Herradura de caballo. *Shoe of a wheel*, Llanta. *Wooden shoes*, Zuecos, chanclos. *Shoe-blacking*, Betún para zapatos. *Shoestring, shoe-lace, shoe-tie*, Cordón o lazo de zapato. *To cast a shoe*, Desherrarse un animal. *I would not stand in his shoes*, (Coll.) No quisiera hallarme en su pellejo, o no le arriendo la ganancia.

Shoe, *va.* (*pret.* SHOD, *pp.* SHOD o SHODDEN). Calzar; guarnecer la parte inferior de alguna cosa con otra más fuerte. *To shoe a horse*, Herrar un caballo.

Shoeing [shū'-ing], *s.* El acto de herrar.

Shoemaker [shū'-mê-kẹr], *s.* Zapatero.

Shoemaking [shū'-mêk-ing], *s.* Zapatería, fabricación o comercio de calzado.

Shoe polish [shū pel'-ish], *s.* Betún o grasa para calzado.

Shoer [shū'-ẹr], *s.* Persona que calza; y particularmente herrador, el que hierra las caballerías.

Shoe store [shū stōr], *s.* Zapatería, tienda de calzado.

Shoe tree [shū trī], *s.* Horma para zapato.

Shole [shōl], *s.* (Mar.) Solera, trozo de tablón sobre que se apoyan las escoras cuando el terreno es flojo.

Shone [shōn, y por algunos shen], *pret.* de *To* SHINE.

Shoo [shū], *va.* y *vn.* Ahuyentar (las aves domésticas) gritando "shoo"; vocear o gritar "shoo."—*inter.* ¡Fuera! se usa para ahuyentar las gallinas.

Shook [shuk], *pret.* de *To* SHAKE.

Shoot [shūt], *va.* (*pret.* y *pp.* SHOT). 1. Tirar, dar, herir o matar con arma de fuego; fusilar, pasar por las armas. 2. Arrojar, lanzar, disparar, despedir alguna cosa con impulso y violencia, tirar, como una saeta o dardo. 3. Tirar, descargar un arma de fuego. 4. Descargar, vaciar el contenido de algo. 5. Empujar, hacer salir. 6. Traspasar, atravesar rápidamente, pasar por encima ó por debajo de. 7. Volar, hacer saltar con pólvora. 8. Ajustar (a una línea) cepillando.—*vn.* 1. Tirar, disparar las armas. 2. Lanzarse, correr rápidamente, v. g. un proyectil; caer una estrella. 3. Brotar, espigar, germinar; crecer. 4. Latir, punzar, sentir algún dolor agudo y repentino. 5. Sobresalir. *To shoot an arrow*, Lanzar un flecha. *To shoot a bear*, Matar un oso. *To shoot a deserter*, Fusilar a un desertor. *To shoot a bolt*, Echar, correr un cerrojo. *To shoot rapids*, Pasar, salvar el recial de un río. *To shoot forth*, Lanzarse o abalanzarse. *To shoot off*, Tirar, descargar (un arma); llevarse. *To shoot through*, Atravesar. pasar de parte a parte.

Shoot, *s.* 1. Vástago, pimpollo, el renuevo o ramo tierno del árbol o planta. 2. Recial, lugar angosto de un río, por el cual se precipitan las aguas impetuosamente. 3. Artesa inclinada, *V.* CHUTE. 4. Tiro, la acción y efecto de tirar.

Shooter [shūt'-ẹr], *s.* Tirador.

Shooting [shūt'-ing], *s.* 1. Caza con escopeta. 2. Tiro. 3. Latido doloroso, punzada.

Shop [shep], *s.* 1. Tienda, paraje donde se venden géneros por menor; en los Estados Unidos se llama comúnmente *store*, almacén. *Baker's shop*, Panadería. 2. Taller u oficina donde se trabaja alguna manufactura. *Silversmith's shop*, Platería. *Jeweller's shop*, Joyería, platería. *Watch-maker's shop*, Relojería. *To shut up shop*, Cerrar la tienda, el almacén; desistir de una empresa. *To smell of the shop*, Oler a tienda, sugerir demasiado la propia ocupación. *To talk shop*, Hablar con exceso, sin necesidad o fuera de tiempo de la propia ocupación, oficio o negocios. *Shop-bill*, (Ingl.) Lista de mercancías que se pone en el escaparate de una tienda. *Shop-boy, shop-girl*, Mancebo, muchacha de almacén. *Shop-walker, floor-walker*, Vigilante (para impedir raterías en tienda o almacén).

Shop, *vn.* (Fam.) Andar de tienda en tienda comprando.

Shopkeeper [shep'-kīp-ẹr], *s.* Tendero, mercader al por menor.

Shoplifter [shep'-lift-ẹr], *s.* El ladrón que ratea algo en una tienda.

Shoplifting [shep'-lift-ing], *s.* Ratería hecha en una tienda durante las horas de venta.

Shopping [shep'-ing], *s.* Compra. *Shopping center*, Centro comercial. *To go shopping*, 1. Ir de compras. 2. Ir de tiendas.

Shop window [shep win'-dō], *s.* Vitrina, escaparate o vidriera de tienda.

Shopwoman [shep'-wum-an], *sf.* Tendera, la que despacha en una tienda.

Shore [shōr], *s.* 1. Costa, ribera, grao, playa; borde, orilla de un río o lago. *To go on shore*, (Mar.) Ir a tierra. 2. Puntal, costón; (Mar.) escora, botante; (Min.) entibo, ademe. *Shore of a pair of shears*, (Mar.) Puntal diagonal de cabria. *Along shore*, Cerca de tierra. *A bold shore*, Una costa escarpada. *Close inshore*, Arrimado a la tierra.

Shore, *va.* 1. Apuntalar, poner puntales. 2. (Mar.) Escorar. 3. Llevar a tierra, a la orilla. 4. Circundar, como lo hace una orilla o ribera.

Shore leave [shōr līv], *s.* (Mar.) Permiso para ir a tierra.

Shoreline [shōr'-lain'], *s.* 1. Costa o ribera. 2. Contorno de la playa.

Shorn, *pp.* de To SHEAR.

Short [shērt], *a.* 1. Corto, de poca extensión; de escasa estatura; corto, de poca duración. 2. Limitado, circunscrito; breve, sucinto, conciso, compendiado. 3. Brusco, seco, malhumorado, de áspero trato. 4. Que no alcanza, inadecuado, deficiente. 5. Próximo, cercano, que debe llegar u ocurrir en tiempo no lejano. 6. Corto de alcances. 7. Quebradizo, que se desmiga fácilmente (como una pasta). 8. (Com.) Algo que el vendedor no tiene en su posesión al venderlo, pero que se obliga a entregarlo en época determinada. 9. Breve, que se pronuncia rápidamente; que no lleva acento. *To fall short of one's expectations*, No salir con lo que se esperaba. *Within a short time*, Dentro de poco tiempo. *Short of money*, Escaso de dinero. *The translation falls short of the original*, La traducción no llega o es inferior al original. *In short*, En suma, en resumen. *A very short while*, Un ratito. *Short of this*, Fuera de esto, además de esto, amén de esto. *In a short time*, Luego, pronto. *To be short, to cut short* o *in short*, Para abreviar. *To be short of*, Estar lejos de; no responder a. *To be short of money*, Andar escaso de dinero. *To come short of*, Faltar, no alcanzar, no corresponder, estar lejos de. *To cut short*, Cortar la palabra, interrumpir bruscamente; destruir, hacer cesar; abreviar. *To fall short*, Estar corto; escasear, faltar. *To grow short*, Hacerse corto, comenzar a ser corto. *To run short*, Faltar. *To take short*, Tomar o coger de improviso. *Short-handed*, Que carece de un número suficiente de operarios, marineros, etc. *Short-bodied*, Que tiene el cuerpo pequeño. *Short-breathed*, Que respira con dificultad. *Short-nosed*, Romo, chato, de nariz aplastada. *Short ribs*, Costillas falsas. *Short-winded*, Asmático, corto de respiración. *Short-waisted*, Corto de talle.

Short, *s.* 1. Sumario, resumen, compendio. 2. Sílaba o vocal breve. 3. *pl.* Salvado mezclado con harina gruesa. 4. *pl.* En la fabricación de cuerdas, el cáñamo de calidad inferior. 5. *pl.* Calzón corto. *The short and the long of it*, En resumidas cuentas.—*adv.* Brevemente, breve.

Shortage [shērt'-ēj], *s.* 1. Escasez, falta. 2. Desfalco, déficit.

Shortcake [shērt'-kēk], *s.* Torta de frutas.

Short-change [shērt'-chēnj'], *va.* Defraudar al dar el vuelto, engañar.

Short circuit [shērt sẹr'-kit], *s.* Corto circuito.—*va.* Causar un corto circuito.

Shortcoming [shērt'-cum-ing], *s.* 1. Defecto, falta de completa ejecución; negligencia del deber, omisión. 2. Falta de los productos usuales, de las cosechas acostumbradas.

Shorten [shērt'-n], *va.* 1. Acortar, recortar, hacer más corto. 2. Abreviar, compendiar, resumir. 3. Recortar, cercenar lo que sobra en alguna cosa. 4. Impedir, limitar, restringir. 5. Hacer quebradiza la pastelería.—*vn.* Acortarse, abreviarse, disminuirse.

Shortening [shērt'-n-ing], *s.* 1. Acción de acortar, de abreviar. 2. Lo que hace quebradiza una cosa, v. gr. la manteca o mantequilla usada para hacer quebradizas las pastas, los hojaldres, etc.

Shorthand [shērt'-hand], *s.* Taquigrafía, estenografía.

Shorthorn [shērt'-hērn], *s.* Ganado vacuno de cuernos cortos.

Short-lived [shērt'-laivd], *a.* Corto de vida; pasajero, que dura poco.

Shortly [shērt'-li], *adv.* 1. Presto, luego, al instante. 2. Brevemente, en pocas palabras.

Short-necked [shērt'-nect], *a.* Cuellicorto, el que tiene el cuello o pescuezo corto.

Shortness [shērt'-nes], *s.* 1. Cortedad; pequeñez. 2. Brevedad de palabras. 3. Flaqueza de memoria. 4. Defecto, imperfección. *Shortness of breath*, Respiración dificultosa, asma.

Shorts [shērts], *s. pl.* 1. Calzoncillos. 2. Calzones cortos de hombre o de mujer. *Bathing shorts*, Calzones de baño.

Short sale [shērt sēl], *s.* Venta de valores u otra propiedad que no se poseen al momento pero que se espera adquirir más tarde en condiciones más favorables.

Short-sighted [shērt'-sait-ed], *a.* Cegato, el que es miope o corto de vista, y el que es rudo o de cortos alcances. *Short-sightedness*, (1) Miopía, cortedad de vista. (2) Cortedad de alcances.

Short-tempered [shērt-tem'-pẹrd], *a.* De mal carácter.

Short-term [shērt'-tẹrm], *a.* De período breve.

Short wave [shērt wēv], *s.* (Radio) Onda corta.

Shot, *s.* 1. Munición, postas o municiones; perdigones, la munición menuda que sirve para cargar las escopetas. 2. Bala, proyectil sólido. *Grape-shot*, Metralla. *Shot between wind and water*, Balazo a flor del agua. 3. Tiro, la acción de tirar o disparar; el acto de lanzar un arma arrojadiza, y particularmente de descargar un arma de fuego. 4. Tiro, alcance, la distancia a que llega lo que se arroja o dispara. *Within pistol-shot*, A tiro de pistola. 5. Tirador, el que se ejercita en tirar. 6. Tirada, jugada, v. g. en el billar. 7. *V.* BLAST. 8. Escote, la parte que a prorrata cabe a cada uno de los que se han divertido o comido en compañía. *V.* SCOT. *Bird shot, fowling shot*, Munición menuda. *Buck shot, deer shot*, Munición de balines, postas. *Cannon shot*, Cañonazo. *A good shot*, Un buen tirador. *Shot gauge*, Vitola para calibrar proyectiles. *Shot-tower*, Torre para hacer municiones. *Not by a long shot*, (Ger.) Ni por asomo, ni con mucho.

Shot-put [shet'-put], *s.* Lanzamiento del peso, en el deporte.

Shotgun [shet'-gun], *s.* Escopeta, arma de fuego ligera para cazar.

Shotten [shet'-n], *a.* (Prov. o des.) 1. Dislocado. 2. Desovado: dícese de los peces cuando han soltado sus huevos o huevas. 3. Cuajado (leche).

Should [shud], *pret.* de SHALL. Indica un tiempo condicional y en general se usa en los mismos casos en que se emplea *shall* en el futuro de indicativo, aunque el uso de *should* no es tan fijo como el de *shall*. *Should* se usa muy frecuentemente como verbo defectivo con la significación de deber o haber de. *I should go*, Yo iría o yo debería ir. *If I should go*, Si yo fuese. *If you should go*, Si Vd. fuera o fuese. *You should go*, Vd. debería ir. *I should love him*, Yo le amaría. *I should be very sorry*, Sentiría mucho. *Should I do that?* . . . ¿Si yo hiciera eso? . . . *Should* se encuentra también solo en la oración para evitar la repetición del verbo que se ha usado inmediatamente antes. *Should be*, Expresión muy común que se usa casi siempre irónicamente para expresar que una persona o cosa no es lo que debería ser. *For fear he should fall*, Por temor de que él se cayese. *I should have seen you earlier*, Yo hubiera debido verle á Vd. más temprano. *Should he not come in a day or two*, Si no viniese dentro de uno o dos días.

Shoulder [shōl'-der], *s.* 1. Hombro, la parte alta de la espalda del hombre de donde nacen los brazos. 2. Brazuelo; cuarto delantero, la parte más alta de las patas delanteras de los cuadrúpedos. 3. (Fig.) Lo que sostiene o apoya; sostén, soporte, parte saliente: contera de bastón, virola de cuchillo, rodete mecánico; (Mec.) espaldón de espiga; regatón de lanza, etc. *Shoulder bone* o *blade*, Espaldilla, omoplato, escápula. *Shoulder of pork*, Pernil. *To give one the cold shoulder*, Recibir a uno con indiferencia o fríamente; no hacerle caso. *Shoulder-of-mutton sail*, Vela triangular, guaira. *Shoulder to shoulder*, Hombro a hombro, cooperando y apoyándose mutuamente, como una fila de soldados. *Shoulder-belt*, Tahalí. *Shoulder-knot*, Charretera mocha, capona. *Shoulder-strap*, (1) Correón (de los silleteros, aguadores, etc.). (2) Charretera, divisa militar de oro, plata o seda que se asegura al hombro; dragona.

Shoulder, *va.* 1. Empujar con insolencia. 2. Echar, cargar al hombro. *Shoulder arms*, (Mil.) Armas al hombro. *Broad-shouldered*, Ancho de espaldas.

Shout [shaut], *va.* 1. Vocear, exclamar. 2. Afectar voceando; repeler, animar con gritos.—*vn.* Exclamar, dar gritos y voces en señal de triunfo o para incitar o mover los ánimos; vitorear, dar vivas, aclamar. *To shout at*, Silbar a alguno; reprobar con voces, gritos o silbidos lo que alguno hace o dice.

Shout, *s.* Exclamación, aclamación, gritería. *Shout of applause*, Viva.

Shouter [shaut'-er], *s.* Gritador, el que grita y exclama.

Shouting [shaut'-ing], *s.* Vocerío, gritería; aclamación.—*a.* Que vocea, o mueve los ánimos dando gritos.

Shove [shuv], *va.* y *vn.* 1. Empujar, hacer fuerza para mover o separar alguna cosa; impeler, llevar adelante. 2. Llevar un barco con sogas por encima del agua. 3. Moverse hacia adelante con velocidad. *To shove along* o *forward*, Empujar o llevar hacia adelante; hacer avanzar o adelantarse. *To shove away*, Rechazar, alejar. *To shove back*, Hacer retroceder. *To shove off*, Alejarse de, dejar. *To shove from*, Empujar, rechazar a empujones. *To shove out*, Empujar hacia afuera, hacer salir.

Shove, *s.* Empellón, empujón.

Shovel [shuv'-l], *s.* Pala. *A shovel hat*, Sombrero de canal que usan los clérigos en Inglaterra. *Fire shovel*, Badila.

Shovel, *va.* Traspalar, mover o pasar con la pala alguna cosa de un lado o otro.

Shovel-board [shuv'-l-bōrd], *s.* Tabla para jugar al tejo; y el mismo tejo (juego).

Shovelful [shuv'-l-ful], *s.* Palada.

Show [shō], *va.* (*pret.* SHOWED, *pp.* SHOWN ó SHOWED). 1. Mostrar, exponer a la vista o en público, enseñar; hacer ver. 2. Señalar, mostrar, descubrir, manifestar. 3. Probar, demostrar. 4. Publicar, dar á conocer una cosa. 5. Enseñar, explicar. 6. Conducir.—*vn.* Parecer, tener apariencia o señales de; dar señal. *To show forth*, Exponer, mostrar; publicar, manifestar. *To show in* o *into*, Introducir o meter a alguno en alguna parte. *Show her in*, Hágala Vd. entrar. *To show off*, Hacer ver, descubrir; dejar ver. *To show (one's self) off*, Darse importancia. *To show up*, Hacer subir; exponer, descubrir un fraude, descorrer un velo; presentarse á la hora o en el día señalados.

Show, *s.* 1. Espectáculo público; exhibición o la cosa exhibida; muestra, lo que esta expuesto á la vista; títeres. 2. Ostentación, boato, prosopopeya, pompa. 3. Manifestación, lo que manifiesta; seña, indicación, promesa. 4. Apariencia con o sin realidad; pretexto, máscara, velo. 5. (Fam. E. U.) Oportunidad, lance, suerte. *To make show of anger*, Aparentar enfado. *In open show*, Públicamente. *To make a fine show*, Hacer gran papel. *To make a show of riches*, Hacer gala de sus riquezas. *Show-bill*, Cartel, cartelón. Muestrario de tienda, caja de muestras. *Show-window*, Ventana o escaparate de tienda. *Cattle-show*, Exposición de ganado. *A vote by show of hands*, Votación que se efectúa alzando las manos. *With a show of friendship*, Con apariencia de amistad; bajo pretexto de amistad.

Showbread [shō'-bred], *s.* Panes de proposición, los que se ofrecían todos los sábados en la ley antigua y se ponían en el tabernáculo.

Showcase [shō-kēs], *s.* Muestrario, vitrina, mostrador.

Shower [shau'-er], *s.* 1. Lluvia, nubada de corta duración, aguacero. *A heavy shower*, Chaparrón, turbión. 2. Lluvia, copia, abundancia. *Shower-bath*, Baño de ducha, chorro de agua que se aplica al cuerpo humano.

Shower [shō'-er], *s.* Mostrador, el que muestra.

Shower, *va.* 1. Mojar o anegar con lluvia. 2. Derramar. 3. Distribuir con liberalidad.—*vn.* 1. Llover, caer agua de las nubes. 2. Llover, venir o caer sobre uno alguna cosa con abundancia.

Showeriness [shau'-er-i-nes], *s.* Tiempo lluvioso.

Showerless [shau'-er-les], *a.* Sin lluvia, que no tiene nubadas.

Showery [shau'-er-i], *a.* Lluvioso, abundante en aguaceros.

Showily [shō'-i-li], *adv.* Vistosamente, ostentosamente, magníficamente.

Showiness [shō'-i-nes], *s.* Ostentación, vista, esplendor, magnificencia.

Showman [shōw'-man], *s.* 1. Hábil empresario de espectáculos. 2. Dueño o director de algún circo u otro espectáculo.

Showmanship [shō'-man-ship], *s.* Habilidad para la presentación de espectáculos teatrales.

Shown, *pp.* de *To* SHOW.

Show room [shō rūm], *s.* Sala de exhibiciones (de mercancía, etc.)

Showy [shō'-i], *a.* Ostentoso, magnífico, suntuoso, vistoso.

Shrank, *pret.* de *To* SHRINK.

Shrapnel [shrap'-nel], *s.* Granada de metralla, bomba llena de balas y con carga de pólvora, para hacerla volar en un momento dado. (< del nombre de un general inglés.)

Shred [shred], *va.* Picar, hacer pedazos muy pequeños alguna cosa, desmenuzar.

Shred, *s.* 1. Cacho, tira, pedazo pequeño; retazo, harapo. 2. Fragmento, partícula; punto, átomo, nada, jota, tilde.

Shrew [shrū], *s.* 1. Sierpe, víbora, mujer de mal genio, maligna y turbulenta. 2. Musgaño, musaraña, mamífero carnicero muy pequeño. Sorex vulgaris.

Shrewd [shrūd], *a.* 1. Astuto, perspicaz, de vivo ingenio, sagaz, sutil. 2. (Ant.) Artificioso, solapado. 3. (Ant.) Agudo, cortante. 4. (Des.) Enfadoso, enojoso; maligno. *A man of shrewd discernment*, Un hombre de sutil discernimiento. *A shrewd question*, Una pregunta astuta.

Shrewdly [shrūd'-li], *adv.* 1. Astutamente, con astucia, sagazmente, sutilmente. 2. (Ant.) Con artificio, con cautela, solapadamente.

Shrewdness [shrūd'-nes], *s.* 1. Sagacidad, travesura, astucia, sutileza de genio. 2. (Ant.) Malignidad, maldad; agudeza, mordacidad.

Shrewish [shrū'-ish], *a.* Regañón, regañador, quimerista, pendenciero; diabólico.

Shrewishness [shrū'-ish-nes], *s.* Perversidad, maldad; travesura; mal genio.

Shrewmouse [shrū'-maus], *s.* Musgaño, musaraña.

Shriek [shrīk], *vn.* Chillar, dar chillidos; gritar, dar gritos.

Shriek, *s.* Chillido; grito de espanto o dolor. *To utter a shriek*, Dar un chillido.

Shrift [shrift], *s.* Confesión auricular ó sacramental del penitente, y la acción de oir el confesor al penitente; absolución.

Shrike [shraik], *s.* Pega reborda, avé notable por su rapacidad. (Lanius borealis ó excubitor.)

Shrill [shril], *a.* Agudo, penetrante, sutil: se aplica al sonido.

Shrill, *va.* y *vn.* Chillar, producir un sonido agudo, sutil y penetrante.

Shrillness [shril'-nes], *s.* La aspereza del sonido y de la voz.

Shrilly [shril'-li], *adv.* Ásperamente, agudamente, con un ruido penetrante.

Shrimp [shrimp], *s.* 1. Camarón, crustáceo marino comestible. Crangon vulgaris. 2. Enano, hombre pequeño, de muy poca estatura.
Shrine [shrain], *s.* 1. Relicario, caja o urna para guardar reliquias. 2. Altar, o sepulcro de santo; capilla; paraje o cosa consagrados por razones históricas, religiosas, u otras.—*va.* *V.* ENSHRINE.
Shrink [shrink], *vn.* (*pret.* SHRANK, SHRUNK, *pp.* SHRUNK, SHRUNKEN, y antiguamente SHRINKED). 1. Encogerse, contraerse alguna cosa ocupando menos lugar, estrecharse, angostarse, acortarse; disminuir. 2. Evitar un peligro o huir y apartarse de él; retroceder; temblar, estremecerse; retirarse. 3. Encogerse, apocarse el ánimo.—*va.* Encoger, contraer. *To shrink from danger,* Retirarse del peligro. *To shrink for fear,* Temblar de miedo. *To shrink back,* Retirarse a la vista de algún peligro o de alguna cosa desagradable; detenerse en la ejecución de alguna cosa por temor a las consecuencias. *To shrink away,* Acortarse, angostarse; desaparecer por grados; sustraerse, huir. *To shrink up,* Estrechar, estrecharse; encogerse, arrugarse por efecto de la sequedad; temblar, estremecerse. *To shrink on,* Asegurar firmemente en su lugar, v. g. la llanta de una rueda.
Shrink, *s.* Encogimiento, acortamiento, contracción de nervios causada por miedo u horror.
Shrinkage [shrink'-ẹj], *s.* Merma, disminución de volumen de los metales, de la madera u otras materias; el peso o volumen perdidos a consecuencia de esa disminución.
Shrinkingly [shrink'-ing-li], *adv.* Encogiéndose, retrocediendo, con vacilación.
Shrive [shraiv], *va.* (*pret.* SHROVE o SHRIVED, *pp.* SHRIVEN o SHRIVED). Confesar, oír el confesor al penitente.—*vn.* 1. Oír en confesión, imponer la penitencia y dar la absolución. 2. Confesar los pecados y recibir la absolución.
Shrivel [shriv'-l], *vn.* Arrugarse, encogerse; acorcharse las frutas; encarrujarse, ensortijarse (hilo, pelo, hojas, etc.); a menudo con la prep. *up.*—*va.* 1. Arrugar, doblar, encoger. 2. Estrechar; disminuir el alcance, vigor o actividad de algo.
Shriven [shriv'-n], *pp.* de *To* SHRIVE.
Shroud [shraud], *s.* 1. Mortaja, la vestidura que ponen, o la sábana en que envuelven al cadáver para sepultarlo. 2. Cubierta, carpeta, vestidura.
Shrouds, *s. pl.* 1. (Mar.) Obenques, cabos gruesos que encapillan en la cabeza del palo y bajan a las mesas de guarnición, fijándose en las bigotas de las cadenas. 2. Retenidas, cadenas que sirven para asegurar la chimenea de un vapor. *Bowsprit-shrouds,* Mostachos del bauprés. *Main-shrouds,* Obenques mayores. *Preventer-shrouds,* Obenques volantes. *Main-top-gallant-shrouds,* Obenquitos del juanete mayor. *Bumkin-shrouds,* Pie de servioleta. *Futtock-shrouds,* Arraigadas.
Shroud, *va.* 1. Amortajar, poner la mortaja a un difunto. 2. Cubrir, ocultar, guarecer, abrigar.—*vn.* Guarecerse, refugiarse, encogerse.
Shrove [shrōv], *s.* *V.* SHRIFT; se usa solamente en voces compuestas, v. g.
Shrovetide [shrōv'-taid], **Shrove Tuesday** [shrōv' tiūz-dê], *s.* Martes de carnestolendas o de carnaval, el día que precede al miércoles de ceniza.
Shrub [shrub], *s.* 1. (Bot.) Arbusto; mata. (< A.-S. scrob.) 2. Especie de bebida que se hace de aguardiente de caña, limón y azúcar. (< árabe, sharab.)
Shrubbery [shrub'-ẹr-i], *s.* Plantío de arbustos o arbolitos; repajo, matorral, maleza.
Shrubby [shrub'-i], *a.* Parecido a un arbusto; lleno de arbustos. *Shrubby place,* Maleza, matorral.
Shrug [shrug], *vn.* Encogerse de hombros en señal de emoción (descontento, asombro, indiferencia).—*va.* Encoger, contraer.
Shrug, *s.* Encogimiento de hombros.
Shrunk, *pret.* y *pp.* de *To* SHRINK.
Shrunken, *pp.* de *To* SHRINK.
Shuck [shuc], *va.* Descascarar, descortezar; en los Estados Unidos, quitar el hollejo al maíz, o la concha a una ostra.—*s.* (Prov.) 1. Cáscara, vaina, hollejo. 2. (E. U.) Concha de ostra o almeja.
Shudder [shud'-ẹr], *vn.* Estremecerse, temblar de miedo o de horror.
Shudder, Shuddering [shud'-ẹr-ing], *s.* Temblor, estremecimiento producido por horror o miedo.
Shuffle [shuf'-l], *va.* y *vn.* 1. Barajar, mezclar y revolver unas personas o cosas con otras; empujar, hacer pasar de un lado a otro. 2. Barajar los naipes o mezclarlos entre sí antes de repartirlos. 3. Poner en confusión, desordenar. 4. Reunir o echar muchas cosas juntas, con fraude o prisa; poner a un lado descuidadamente; se usa con las preposiciones *up, out, off, in,* etc. 5. Eludir o evitar una dificultad saliendo de ella con algún artificio. 6. Trampear, entrampar, usar de algún artificio o fraude. 7. Tergiversar, ir buscando efugios con rodeos o trampas. 8. Hacer esfuerzos, proceder con dificultad. 9. Arrastrar los pies, andar de un modo irregular; taconear al bailar. *To shuffle along,* Arrastrar los pies; hacer esfuerzos para salir de un mal paso. *To shuffle into,* Introducir a alguno con artificio o cautela. *To shuffle off,* Evadirse, huir de una dificultad; hacer esfuerzos por salir de un mal paso; echar fuera, despedir. *To shuffle up,* Formar algo tumultuosa o fraudulentamente. Hacer las cosas a la carrera, o de cochite hervite.
Shuffle, *s.* 1. Barajadura, el acto de barajar o confundir el orden de las cosas. 2. Treta, fraude, artificio, evasión, efugio fraudulento para salir de una dificultad. 3. Mezcla, confusión, desorden; movimiento desordenado. *Shuffleboard,* *V.* SHOVELBOARD.
Shuffler [shuf'-lẹr], *s.* Tramoyista, el que usa de ficciones y engaños; petardista, enredador, embrollón, chismoso, maula.
Shuffling [shuf'-ling], *s.* 1. Confusión, desorden. 2. Tramoya, enredo, chisme, embrollo. 3. Tropezón, tropiezo.
Shun [shun], *va.* y *vn.* Huir, evitar; escaparse, recatarse de.
Shunt [shunt], *va.* 1. Desviar: en Inglaterra, apartar un tren, hacerlo pasar a otra vía. *V.* SWITCH. 2. Establecer una vía adicional para la corriente eléctrica; distribuir por medio de conductores. 3. Evadir, eludir; echar el cascabel a uno.—*vn.* Desviarse, usar de una cambiavía (de ferrocarril o eléctrica); de aquí, mudar de curso o de opinión. (A.-S. *scyndan,* apresurarse, huir, afín a *shun.*)
Shut [shut], *va.* (*pret.* y *pp.* SHUT). 1. Cerrar, encerrar. 2. Cerrar, prohibir, impedir; se usa con las preposiciones *against* o *to.* 3. Cerrar, negar a uno la entrada. 4. Concluir o acabar alguna cosa. 5. Encoger. 6. Cerrar, ajustar.—*vn.* Cerrarse, apretarse, estrecharse o apiñarse. *To shut against,* Cerrar a. *To shut from,* Excluir de, ocultar a. *To shut off,* Impedir la entrada (al vapor, etc.), impedir que algo fluya, interceptar. *To shut out,* Impedir que uno entre cerrándole la puerta; evitar que el ánimo se ocupe en una cosa. *To shut out rain,* Impedir que entre la lluvia. *To shut close,* Cerrarse bien. *To shut down on,* (Fam.) Hacer cesar, suprimir, reprimir. *To shut up,* Cerrar completamente; callarse, dejar de hablar; concluir, acabar, terminar; tapar; condenar (una puerta, ventana, etc.); aprisionar. *To shut up shop,* *V.* SHOP.
Shut, *s.* Cerradura; postigo.—*a.* 1. Cerrado. 2. Sordo, poco sonoro. 3. (Gram.) Sordo, cerrado; dícese de ciertas consonantes como t, p, k, b. 4. (Prov.) Libre, exento. *Are you shut of him?* ¿Se descartó Vd. de él?
Shut-down [shʊt'-daun], *s.* Cesación de trabajo (en una fábrica, planta, etc.)
Shut-in [shʊt'-in], *s.* Inválido recluído en un hospital o en su casa.
Shut-out [shʊt'-aut], *s.* 1. Encerramiento para impedir la entrada. 2. En los deportes, triunfo en que el lado contrario no logra ningún punto.
Shutter [shut'-ẹr], *s.* 1. Cerrador, el que cierra. 2. Cerradura, todo lo que cierra; obturador de una cámara fotográfica. 3. Contraventana, postigo de ventana.
Shuttle [shut'-l], *s.* Lanzadera, un instrumento de los tejedores.
Shuttlecock [shut'-l-coc], *s.* Volante, rehilete.
Shy [shai], *a.* 1. Tímido, miedoso, fácil de asustar. 2. Reservado, cauteloso, esquivo, vergonzoso, contenido. 3. Prudente, circunspecto, precavido. 4. Evasivo, que huye o escapa. 5. Huraño, intratable.
Shy, *va.* 1. Hacer desviar; se usa con *off* o *away.* 2. Echar con un movimiento lateral.—*vn.* Desviarse repentinamente, como con espanto: se dice de un caballo.—*s.* *V.* FLING.
Shyly [shai'-li], *adv.* Con esquivez, reserva o cautela; tímidamente, con sospecha; con circunspección.
Shyness [shai'-nes], *s.* Esquivez, desapego; reserva excesiva.
Shyster [shai'-stẹr], *s.* (Fam. E. U.) Abogado de mala reputación, trapisondista.
Si [sī], *s.* Si, séptima nota de la escala música.
Siamese [sai-a-mīs'], *a.* Siamés, perteneciente o relativo al reino de Siam.—*s.* Siamés, el natural o habitante de Siam.
Siberian [sai-bī'-ri-an], *a.* Siberiano, de Siberia.

Sibilation [sib-i-lé'-shun], *s.* Silbido.
Sibyl [sib'-il], *s.* Sibila, profetisa, adivina.
Siccative, Siccant [sic'-a-tiv, sic'-ant], *s.* y *a.* Secante, desecativo, que hace secar prontamente; término de arte.
Sicilian [si-sil'-ian], *a.* y *s.* Siciliano, de Sicilia.
Sick [sic], *a.* 1. Malo, enfermo, doliente. 2. Ahitado, ahito con náusea (sentido corriente en Inglaterra). 3. Disgustado, fastidiado. 4. Corrompido. *I am sick of him,* Estoy harto de él o me tiene muy disgustado o cansado. *The sick,* Los enfermos. *Sick to death,* Enfermo de peligro, de muerte. *To be sick at the stomach,* Tener náuseas. *To be sick at heart,* Llevar la muerte en el alma. *Sick-bed,* Lecho de enfermo.
Sick, *va.* Buscar; en imperativo para incitar a un perro a morder o atacar; de aquí, animar, excitar al ataque.
Sicken [sic'-n], *va.* 1. Enfermar, causar enfermedad, poner enfermo; dar asco, dar ganas de vomitar. 2. Debilitar, extenuar.—*vn.* 1. Enfermar, caer enfermo. 2. Hartarse, fastidiarse, cansarse. 3. Tener hastío o asco de alguna cosa. 4. Debilitarse, extenuarse. *Our heart sickens at the sight of him,* Nuestro corazón se despedaza o desgarra a su vista.
Sickening [sic'-n-ing], *a.* Nauseabundo, asqueroso, repugnante.
Sickish [sik'-ish], *a.* 1. Enfermizo, algo malo. 2. Nauseabundo, que da asco.
Sickishly [sik'-ish-li], *adv.* De un modo nauseabundo, asquerosamente.
Sickle [sic'-l], *s.* Hoz, segadera, instrumento para segar las mieses y hierbas.
Sickle cell [sic'-l sel], *s.* Célula falciforme.
Sickliness [sic'-li-nes], *s.* Achaque, indisposición habitual; estado enfermizo; insalubridad.
Sickly [sic'-li], *a.* 1. Enfermizo, achacoso, malsano, valetudinario. 2. Lánguido, endeble, débil.
Sickness [sic'-nes], *s.* 1. Enfermedad, indisposición, mal, falta de salud. 2. Basca, náusea. *Falling sickness,* Epilepsia. *Sickness rate,* Morbilidad.
Side [said], *s.* 1. Lado, costado, cada una de las partes del cuerpo del animal desde el nacimiento del brazo hasta el hueso de la cadera. 2. Lado, lo que está a la derecha o a la izquierda de un todo. 3. Orilla, margen; falda, ladera. 4. Lado, facción, partido, bando, parte. 5. Lado, cara, una de dos o más superficies o partes contrapuestas. 6. Lazo de parentesco. 7. (Mar.) Bordo, costado, banda. *Starboard side,* (Mar.) Banda de estribor. *Side of the waist,* (Mar.) Amurada del combés. *Lee-side,* (Mar.) Costado de sotavento. *Weather-side,* (Mar.) Costado de barlovento. *Right* o *wrong side of a stuff,* La cara o revés de una tela. *He is of my side,* Está por mí, es de mi partido o sigue mi opinión. *This and the other side,* Por acá y por allá. *The right or left side,* El lado derecho o izquierdo. *By the side of,* Al lado de, por el lado de. *On this side,* A, de, o por este lado. *On that side,* De o por aquel lado. *On the other side,* Del o al otro lado; más allá; a la otra parte. *On all sides,* Por todas partes. *Relations by the mother's side,* Parientes por parte de madre. *Side-arms,* Armas blancas.—*a.* Lateral, de lado; oblicuo. *Side-wheel, a.* Que tiene ruedas a los costados (vapor).—*s.* Rueda lateral; una de las dos ruedas de paleta de un vapor.
Side, *va.* y *vn.* 1. Tomar parte por alguno o declararse por él. 2. Declararse por un partido, facción o bando. 3. Unirse con alguno. 4. Igualar. *To side with one,* Ser del mismo partido u opinión.
Sideboard [said'-bōrd], *s.* 1. Aparador. 2. Adral (de camión).
Sideburns [said'-burnz], *s. pl.* Patillas.
Side dish [said' dish], *s.* Entremés, platillo.
Sideface [said'-fés], *s.* Cabeza de perfil.
Side light [said lait], *s.* 1. Luz lateral. 2. Información que se obtiene incidentalmente.
Side line [said' lain], *s.* Negocio u ocupación accesorios.
Sidelong [said'-lōng], *a.* Lateral, de lado.—*adv.* Lateralmente, de lado.
Sideral, *a.* *V.* SIDEREAL.
Sideration [sid-ẹr-é'-shun], *s.* (Poco us.) Nombre dado a la parálisis, apoplejía y gangrena, por suponerse que estos males eran causados por la influencia de los astros.
Sidereal [sai-dí'-re-al], **Sideral** [sid'-ẹr-al], *a.* Sidéreo, perteneciente a las estrellas.
Sidesaddle [said'-sad-l], *s.* La silla que usan las mujeres para montar a caballo.
Sideshow [said'-shō], *s.* Diversión secundaria (en un circo, etc.).
Sidestep [said'-step], *va.* 1. Hacerse a un lado. 2. Evadir (alguna situación, un problema, etc.).
Sideswipe [said'-swaip], *va.* (fam.) Rozar oblícuamente a manera de golpe.
Side-taking [said'-ték-ing], *s.* El empeño que se toma por una facción o partido.
Side-track [said'-trac], *va.* (E. U.) Desviar, apartar un carro o vagón de ferrocarril, para desembarazar la vía principal; (fig.) desviar, alejar de la dirección o del asunto principal; reducir a la inacción.—*vn.* Ir sobre un apartadero.—*s.* Apartadero, desviadero. *V.* SIDING, 1ª acepción.
Sidewalk [said'-wōc], *s.* Acera. (Mex.) Banqueta.
Sideways [said'-wéz], **Sidewise** [said'-waiz], *adv.* De lado, oblicuamente, al través.
Siding [said'-ing], *s.* 1. Apartadero, desviadero (de ferrocarril), ramal inmediato a la vía principal, por el que se desvían los coches de un tren. 2. Costaneras, el entablado de los costados. 3. La acción de empeñarse en un partido o facción.
Sidle [sai'-dl], *vn.* 1. Ir de lado por algún paso estrecho. 2. Estar echado de lado.
Siege [sīj], *s.* Sitio, asedio, cerco. *To lay siege to a fortress,* Poner sitio a una fortaleza.
Sienna [si-en'-a], *s.* Tierra de Siena; color moreno anaranjado que usan los pintores.
Sierra [si-er'-a], *s.* Sierra, cadena de montañas.
Sieve [siv], *s.* 1. Cedazo, tamiz; zaranda, criba, cribo. 2. Persona gárrula que repite cuanto se le dice. 3. Canasto que contiene dos tercios de fanega. *Sievemaker,* Cedacero, fabricante de tamices.
Sift [sift], *va.* 1. Cerner, separar con el cedazo la harina del salvado; pasar o cerner por tamiz; cribar, zarandear, pasar por la criba o la zaranda. 2. Examinar, escudriñar. 3. Dividir, separar una cosa de otra.—*vn.* Caer o pasar al través de un tamiz o cedazo. *To sift out,* Inquirir, investigar. *To sift a question to the bottom,* Examinar una cuestión a fondo.
Sifter [sift'-ẹr], *s.* Cernedor, persona o cosa que cierne; escudriñador; cedazo, zaranda, criba.
Sigh [sai], *vn.* 1. Suspirar, dar suspiros; lamentar, llorar. 2. Suspirar, desear ardientemente, anhelar; a menudo con la prep. *for.*—*va.* (Poét.) Decir suspirando; lamentar; algunas veces con la prep. *out. To sigh away,* Consumir (el tiempo) en suspiros.
Sigh, *s.* Suspiro.
Sighingly [sai'-ing-li], *adv.* Suspirando, con suspiros.
Sight [sait], *s.* 1. Vista, la facultad o potencia de ver. 2. Vista, el objeto de la visión. 3. Vista, los ojos o cada uno de ellos separadamente. 4. Vista, la acción y efecto de ver, y el modo con que se mira; alcance de la visión, y de lo que con ella se descubre. 5. Conocimiento claro de alguna cosa; oportunidad para investigar o estudiar; opinión, parecer. 6. Espectáculo, objeto que causa admiración u horror. 7. Visera de morrión. 8. Mira o punto del cañón de escopeta. 9. Puntería, acto de apuntar con un arma de fuego; observación hecha con un instrumento. 10. Agujero, abertura para mirar. *At sight,* A primera vista, a libro abierto. (Com.) A la vista. *To come in sight,* Asomarse, empezar a aparecer. *To pay at sight,* Pagar a la vista. *Ten days after sight,* A diez días vista.
Sight, *va.* 1. Avistar, alcanzar con la vista; ver con un instrumento. 2. Poner miras a un arma. 3. Apuntar a un blanco.
Sighted [sait'-ed], *a.* Que tiene vista; se emplea en composición. *V. Far-sighted, short-sighted, sharp-sighted.*
Sightless [sait'-les], *a.* 1. Ciego, falto de vista. 2. Que está fuera de vista.
Sightly [sait'-li], *a.* Vistoso, hermoso, deleitable o agradable á la vista.
Sightseeing [sait'-si-ing], *s.* Acto de visitar objetos o puntos de interés.
Sightseer [sait'-si-ẹr], *s.* Persona que visita puntos u objetos de interés.
Sign [sain], *s.* 1. Signo, señal, nota, indicio. 2. Portento, milagro. 3. Tablilla, muestra o señal que se pone encima de alguna puerta para dar a entender un lugar de negocio o de recreo. 4. Signo, constelación del zodíaco. 5. Firma, rúbrica. 6. Seña, la señal con que se da a entender una cosa sin hablar. 7. Señal, huella, vestigio. *To make the sign of the cross,* Hacer la señal de la cruz. *Sign manual,* Firma del soberano (en Inglaterra); firma o rúbrica de una persona. *Signboard,* Muestra de establecimiento.
Sign, *va.* 1. Señalar, poner señal en alguna cosa. 2. Firmar, rubricar.

3. Representar, significar. 4. Hacer señas.
Signal [sig'-nal], *a.* Insigne, señalado, notable, memorable.—*s.* 1. Señal, aviso. 2. Signo, indicio. *A signal exploit,* Una hazaña señalada, memorable. *A signal failure,* Fracaso completo. *Sailing-signals,* Señales de hacerse á la vela. *Signal-code,* Código o sistema de señales, especialmente en el mar. *Signal-light,* Fanal. *Signalman,* Guardavía, el que hace señales.
Signalize [sig'-nal-aiz], *va.* Señalar, distinguir; singularizar, particularizar; hacer notable.
Signally [sig'-nal-li], *adv.* Insignemente, grandemente; señaladamente.
Signatory [sig'-na-to-ri], *s.* y *a.* Signatario, firmante.
Signature [sig'-na-chur o tiūr], *s.* 1. Subscripción, la firma en una carta o en cualquier otra cosa. 2. Signatura, señal de imprenta en los pliegos para su coordinación. 3. (Mús.) Signatura, signo o signos que se ponen a la derecha de la llave en el pentagrama, para indicar la entonación de las notas (signos de bemol o sostenido). 4. (Ant.) Señal, marca.
Signer [sain'-ęr], *s.* Firmante, el que firma o ha firmado.
Signet [sig'-net], *s.* 1. Sello; el sello privado del rey. 2. Signáculo, la impresión de un sello sobre el papel.
Significance [sig-nif'-i-cans], **Significancy** [sig-nif'-i-can-si], *s.* 1. Significación, calidad de expresivo o significante. 2. Energía, eficacia, énfasis. 3. Importancia, momento, consecuencia, peso.
Significant [sig-nif'-i-cant], *a.* 1. Significante, expresivo, significativo; enfático, enérgico. 2. Importante, que es de algún momento o consecuencia. 3. Que figura, que tiene un significado oculto o encubierto.
Significantly [sig-nif'-i-cant-li], *adv.* Expresivamente, con energía y fuerza.
Significantness [sig-nif'-i-cant-nes], *s.* La calidad que constituye a una cosa significativa o importante.
Signification [sig-nif-i-ké'-shun], *s.* Significación, significado, sentido de alguna frase o palabra; la acción de significar o demostrar.
Significative [sig-nif'-i-ca-tiv], *a.* Significativo, expresivo, enérgico; que tiene una significación, particularmente una significación oculta.
Significatory [sig-nif'-i-ca-to-ri], *a.* (Poco us.) Significativo.—*s.* (Des.) Señal, indicio.
Signify [sig'-ni-fai], *va.* 1. Significar, notificar, declarar, manifestar, hacer saber; dar a entender. 2. Significar, representar una cosa a otra distinta de sí misma; ser signo o indicio de algo, denotar. 3. Importar, ser de alguna consecuencia.—*vn.* Tener sentido; importar, ser de alguna consecuencia. *What does it signify?* ¿Qué importa? ¿qué significa eso?
Signor, Signior [sín'-yęr], *s.* Señor. Es voz italiana. *The grand signior,* El gran señor o el sultán.
Signiory [sín'-yęr-i], *s.* Señorío, dominio; ancianidad.
Signpost [sain'-pōst], *s.* Poste o pilar de alguna muestra o señal.
Silage [sai'-lēj], *s.* Ensilaje.
Silence [sai'-lens], *s.* 1. Silencio, taciturnidad; privación voluntaria de hablar, quietud. 2. Silencio, secreto. *Death-like silence,* Silencio sepulcral. *To put to silence,* Reducir al silencio. *Silence gives consent,* Quien calla otorga.—*inter.* ¡Silencio! ¡punto en boca! voz con la cual se manda callar.
Silence, *va.* 1. Imponer silencio, mandar o hacer callar. 2. Parar, detener el movimiento de algo, aquietar.
Silencer [sai'-lens-ęr], *s.* Silenciador, apagador.
Silent [sai'-lent], *a.* 1. Silencioso, mudo, que no produce sonido; taciturno, callado. 2. Que no hace mención o alusión. 3. Quieto, tranquilo, sosegado, calmoso. 4. (Com.) Comanditario, perteneciente a la comandita. *Silent partner,* Socio comanditario. *To remain silent,* Callar, guardar silencio, no chistar. *Be silent,* Calle Vd.
Silently [sai'-lent-li], *adv.* Silenciosamente, sin ruido; sin hacer mención de una cosa o pasándola por alto.
Silentness [sai'-lent-nes], *s.* Silencio.
Silex [sai'-lex], *s.* *V.* SILICA.
Silhouette [sil-u-et'], *va.* Hacer aparecer en silueta.—*s.* Silueta, imagen de perfil, tomada por el contorno de la sombra.
Silica [sil'-i-ca], *s.* Sílice, binóxido de silicio, ácido silícico, substancia que constituye la mayor parte del cuarzo, arena, pedernal, y piedras semejantes.
Silicate [sil'-i-két], *s.* Silicato, sal compuesta de ácido silícico y una base.
Silicic [si-lis'-ic], *a.* Silícico, perteneciente a la sílice. *Silicic acid,* Ácido silícico, sílice.
Silicious [si-lish'-us], *a.* Silícico, silíceo, que consta de sílice o cuarzo. *Silicious earth,* Tierra primitiva o sencilla de sílice o pedernal.
Silicon [sil'-i-cęn], *s.* (Quím.) Silicio, elemento no metálico, el más abundante después del oxígeno.
Siliqua [sil'-i-cwa], *s.* 1. Silicua, un antiguo peso romano. 2. *V.* SILIQUE.
Silique [si-líc'], *s.* (Bot.) Silicua, la vaina producida solamente por las plantas crucíferas.
Siliquous [sil'-i-cwus], **Siliquose** [sil'-i-cwōs], *a.* Silicuoso, que tiene silicua o vaina.
Silk [silk], *a.* Hecho de seda, sedoso, sedeño. *A silk hat,* Un sombrero de copa.—*s.* 1. Seda. 2. Tejido de seda. *Raw silk,* Seda cruda o en rama. *Sewing-silk,* Seda para coser. *Black corded silk,* Paño de seda. *Figured silk,* Seda labrada. *Floss silk,* Seda floja; escarzo, atanquía, filadiz. *Shot silk,* Seda tornasolada. *Twilled silk,* Tela cruzada de seda. *Watered silk,* Seda ondeada, muaré. *Silk-cotton,* Seda vegetal, borrilla de las simientes del bómbice, que se emplea para rellenar almohadones, etc. *Silk-cotton-tree,* Bómbice, ceiba. *Silk goods,* Géneros de seda. *Silk-throwing,* Torcedura de la seda. *Waste silk,* Borra de seda. *Silk-dyer,* Tintorero de sedas. *Silk-thrower, silk-throwster,* Devanador o torcedor de seda. *Silk-weaver,* Tejedor de seda.
Silken [silk'-n], *a.* 1. Sedoso, hecho de seda; sedeño; blando, suave. 2. Vestido de seda.
Silkiness [silk'-i-nes], *s.* Blandura, molicie, suavidad; lisonja; sonsaca.
Silk-screen process [silk'-scrín pres'-es], *s.* Serigrafía.
Silkweed [silk'-wíd], *s.* 1. Asclepias, planta americana del género Asclepias (o Gomphrena), cuyas semillas tienen una pelusilla sedosa. 2. Alga del género Conferva.
Silk-worm [silk'-wūrm], *s.* Gusano de seda, larva de una mariposa nocturna de los bombícidos.
Silky [silk'-i], *a.* 1. Hecho de seda. 2. Sedoso, sedeño, que tiene las propiedades de la seda; suave como la seda; lustroso.
Sill [sil], *s.* Umbral de puerta; (carp.) solera, viga de carrera, antepecho de ventana; nabo; madero horizontal para sostener otras piezas. *Cap-sill,* (Min.) Cabezal, cumbrera. *Ground-sill,* Solera, viga de carrera. *Window-sill,* Antepecho, poyo de ventana.
Sillily [sil'-i-li], *adv.* Simplemente, tontamente, neciamente.
Silliness [sil'-i-nes], *s.* Simpleza, bobería, tontería, necedad.
Silly [sil'-i], *a.* 1. Necio, tonto, mentecato, imbécil; inocente, cándido, fácil de engañar. 2. Sencillo, ingenuo, sin artificio. 3. (Fam.) Bobo, baboso, babieca, papamoscas.
Silo [sai'-lō], *s.* 1. Silo. 2. (Mil.) Plataforma subterránea de lanzamiento.
Silt [silt], *s.* Cieno, fango, aluvión; sedimento térreo arrastrado y depositado por las aguas.—*va.* y *vn.* Obstruir o obstruirse con aluvión; también, colar, pasar al través.
Silurian [si-lū'-ri-an], *s.* y *a.* Edad siluriana, paleozoica; (*a.*) paleozoico (y fig.), estorbador, el que pone obstáculos en asuntos públicos o legislativos.
Silver [sil'-vęr], *s.* 1. Plata, metal precioso.—*a.* De plata, hecho de plata; plateado. *A silver voice,* Voz argentina o sonora como la plata. *Silver leaf,* Hoja de plata. *Crude mass of silver,* Plata bruta, o en bruto. (Prov.) Plata virgen. 2. Monedas de plata consideradas como dinero. 3. Vajilla o servicio de mesa de plata. *Silver alloy,* Aleación de plata. *Silver foil,* Hoja de plata. *Silver plate,* Artículos plateados, mercadería plateada. *Silver-plated,* Plateado. *Silver thimble,* Dedal de plata. *Silver-beater,* Batihoja, batidor de plata. *Silver-fir,* (Bot.) Abeto. *Silver-lace,* Encaje o galón de plata. *Silver-mine,* Mina de plata. *Silver-ore,* Mineral de plata. *Silver-thistle,* (Bot.) Acanto o branca ursina. *Silver-weed,* (Bot.) Agrimonia.
Silver fox [sil'-vęr fox], *s.* Zorro plateado.
Silver, *va.* 1. Platear, dar la blancura o el brillo de la plata.
Silvering [sil'-vęr-ing], *s.* 1. Capa de plata aplicada sobre alguna cosa. 2. Plateadura, arte o procedimiento de platear; azogamiento. 3. (Foto.) Acto de sensibilizar el papel con una sal de plata.
Silver-plate [sil'-vęr plēt], *va.* Enchapar, platear.
Silver-plated [sil'-vęr plēt'-ed], *a.* Enchapado, plateado.
Silver screen [sil'-vęr scrín], *s.* Pantalla cinematográfica.
Silversmith [sil'-vęr-smith], *s.* Platero, el artífice que labra la plata; fabricante de efectos de plata.

Silverware [sil'-vẹr-wār], *s.* Plata labrada; vajilla de plata; artículos de plata.
Silver wedding [sil'-vẹr wed'-ing], *s.* Bodas de plata.
Silvery [sil'-vẹr-i], *a.* 1. Plateado, dado de plata. 2. Argentino, que se asemeja a la plata en lustre, color o sonido.
Simian [sim'-i-an], *s.* Simio o mono. —*a.* Perteneciente o parecido a un mono.
Similar [sim'-i-lar], *a.* 1. Similar, homogéneo. 2. Semejante, similitudinario, que se parece o tiene semejanza con otra cosa.
Similarity [sim-i-lar'-i-ti], *s.* Semejanza, conformidad, homogeneidad.
Similarly [sim'-i-lar-li], *adv.* Semejantemente.
Simile [sim'-i-lī o le], *s.* Símil, ejemplo, parábola; similitud, comparación.
Similitude [si-mil'-i-tiūd], *s.* 1. Similitud, semejanza. 2. Ejemplo, comparación.
Simioid, Simious [sim'-i-eid, sim'-i-us], *a.* De mono o simio; parecido al mono.
Simitar [sim'-i-tar], *s.* Cimitarra, arma de acero que tiene el corte afilado, la figura corva y remata en punta.
Simlin, *s.* (E. U. del Sur y del Oeste) Variedad de calabaza.
Simmer [sim'-ẹr], *vn.* Hervir a fuego lento.
Simon-pure [sai'-mẹn-piūr], *a.* Auténtico, genuino, puro.
Simoom, Simoon [si-mūm', mūn'], *s.* Simún, viento abrasador que reina en el Sahara y en la Arabia. (< árabe = envenenado.)
Simous [sai'-mus], *a.* Que tiene nariz chata y vuelta hacia arriba.
Simper [sim'-pẹr], *vn.* Sonreirse, comúnmente sonreirse bobamente o con afectación. (< noruego, *semper.*)
Simper, *s.* Sonrisa, por lo común sonrisa tonta o afectada.
Simple [sim'-pl], *a.* 1. Simple, manso, apacible, sencillo, llano, ingenuo. 2. Simple, puro, sencillo, que no tiene mezcla ni composición; mero, no complicado. *Simple substance*, Substancia sencilla o elemento de alguna cosa. 3. Simple, fácil de engañar; mentecato, necio, bobo. 4. Poco importante, insignificante, ordinario.—*s.* Simple, planta, hierba o mineral que sirve por sí sola para medicina. *Simple manners*, Modales sencillos. *Simple-hearted*, Sencillo, franco, sincero. *Simple-minded*, Sencillo, cándido, ingenuo. *Simple-mindedness*, Sencillez, candor.
Simpleton [sim'-pl-tẹn], *s.* Simplón, simplonazo.
Simplicity [sim-plis'-i-ti], *s.* 1. Sencillez, ingenuidad, llaneza, candor. 2. Simplicidad, el estado de lo que no es compuesto. 3. Simpleza, bobería, necedad, imbecilidad.
Simplification [sim-pli-fi-ké'-shun], *s.* Simplificación, acción o procedimiento de simplificar.
Simplify [sim'-pli-fai], *va.* Simplificar, hacer una cosa más sencilla o menos complicada.
Simply [sim'-pli], *adv.* 1. Sencillamente, sin arte. 2. Simplemente, sin añadidura ni composición. 3. Meramente, solamente. 4. Simplemente, tontamente.
Simulant [sim'-yu-lant], *a.* Que simula, imita o finge; que tiene la forma o apariencia (de una cosa dada); se emplea especialmente en biología.
Simulate [sim'-yu-lêt], *va.* Simular, fingir.
Simulation [sim-yu-lé'-shun], *s.* Simulación, doblez de ánimo, hipocresía.
Simultaneity, Simultaneousness [sim-ul-ta-nī'-i-ti, sim-ul-té'-nẹ-us-nes], *s.* Simultaneidad, calidad de simultáneo.
Simultaneous [sim-ul- (o sai-mul-) té'-nẹ-us], *a.* Simultáneo, que existe, se hace o sucede a un mismo tiempo.
Simultaneously [sim-ul-té'-nẹ-us-li], *adv.* Simultáneamente, a un tiempo, de conformidad.
Sin [sin], *s.* 1. Pecado, transgresión de la ley de Dios o de sus preceptos; maldad. 2. Transgresión, falta, ofensa.
Sin, *vn.* Pecar, faltar a la ley de Dios o a sus preceptos.
Sinapism [sin'-a-pizm], *s.* Sinapismo, cataplasma de mostaza.
Since [sins], *adv.* 1. Desde que, desde, desde entonces. *Ever since*, Desde entonces. 2. Antes de ahora. *Some months since*, Algunos meses ha. *Long since*, Hace mucho tiempo. *Not long since*, Hace poco, de poco acá. *It is half an hour since the train left*, Hace media hora que partió el tren.—*conj.* Ya que, puesto que, en vista de; pues, pues que. *Since 'tis so*, Siendo esto así o puesto que es así.—*prep.* Desde, después.
Sincere [sin-sīr'], *a.* 1. Sincero, real, verdadero, genuino. 2. Sincero, sin doblez, franco, abierto.
Sincerely [sin-sīr'-li], *adv.* Sinceramente, verdaderamente; francamente, con franqueza y buena fe.
Sincereness [sin-sīr'-nes], **Sincerity** [sin-ser'-i-ti], *s.* Sinceridad, integridad, franqueza.
Sinciput [sin'-si-put], *s.* Sincipucio, coronilla, el vértice de la cabeza. *V.* OCCIPUT.
Sine [sain], *s.* (Mat.) Seno, perpendicular tirada desde el extremo de un arco de círculo al radio que pasa por el otro extremo. *Coversed sine*, Cosenoverso. *Versed sine*, Senoverso.
Sine [sai'-nī], *prep.* (Lat.) Sin. *Sine die*, Indefinidamente, sin día señalado para reunirse de nuevo; hasta nueva orden. *Sine qua non*, Cosa o condición esencial.
Sinecure [sai'-nẹ-kiūr o sin'-ẹ-kiūr], *s.* Renta o sueldo sin empleo, beneficio simple. (Vul.) Una olla boba.
Sinew [sin'-yū], *va.* Fortalecer o juntar como con tendones; proveer de tendones, dar fuerza.—*s.* 1. Tendón, cuerda fibrosa. 2. Nervio, fortaleza, la parte más firme y poderosa de alguna cosa.
Sinewed [sin'-yūd], **Sinewy** [sin'-yū-i], *a.* Nervoso, nervioso; fuerte, robusto.
Sinful [sin'-ful], *a.* Pecaminoso, malvado, mal inclinado, corrompido, perverso, perdido. *A sinful man*, Pecador. *A sinful woman*, Pecadora.
Sinfully [sin'-ful-i], *adv.* Malvadamente, con maldad, de un modo criminal.
Sinfulness [sin'-ful-nes], *s.* Maldad, corrupción, perversidad, mala conducta.
Sing [sing], *vn.* y *va.* (*pret.* SANG o SUNG, *pp.* SUNG). 1. Cantar, hacer con la voz modulaciones armoniosas y agradables. 2. Murmurar el arroyuelo. 3. Gorjear los pájaros. 4. Gorjearse o hacer gorgoritos los niños cuando principian a hablar. 5. Rechinar; zumbar (los oídos). 6. (Poét.) Cantar, celebrar. 7. *To sing out*, Gritar, dar voces; avisar. *To sing out of tune* (o *false*), Cantar falso. *To sing a child to sleep*, Dormir a un niño cantando.
Singe [sinj], *va.* 1. Chamuscar, quemar alguna cosa ligeramente por la parte exterior; socarrar, sollamar, aperdigar un ave, purificar algo pasándolo por las llamas. 2. Dañar, perjudicar. *Her reputation was singed*, Su reputación quedó perjudicada.
Singer [sing'-ẹr], *s.* Cantor, cantora.
Singer [sin'-jẹr], *s.* El o lo que chamusca o sollama.
Singing [sing'-ing], *s.* Canto, música vocal, concierto, armonía. *Singing bird*, Pájaro cantor. *Singing book*, Cuaderno de solfa, de canto. *Singing-master*. Maestro de canto, el que enseña a cantar.
Single [sin'-gl], *a.* 1. Único, simple, solo, no doble. *Single block*, (Mar.) Motón sencillo. *Not a single word*, Ni una sola palabra. 2. Particular, individual. 3. Solo, sin compañía. 4. Soltero, soltera. 5. Puro, incorrupto. *To live single*, Vivir en el estado de celibato. *A single sole*, Una suela sencilla. *A single man or woman*, Un soltero, una soltera. *Single-handed*, (1) Solo, sin ayuda; (2) manco, que tiene una sola mano; (3) que se puede usar con una sola mano. *Single-loader*, Arma de fuego de retrocarga que recibe un solo cartucho de una vez; contrapuesto a *repeater*. *Single-minded*, Ingenuo, sincero, sin doblez. *Single combat*, Combate singular. *Single-hearted*, Sencillo de corazón, cándido, ingenuo. *Single life*, Celibato.
Single, *va.* 1. Singularizar, particularizar. 2. Separar, retirar. 3. Tomar por sí solo.
Single-breasted [sin'-gl-brest'-ed], *a.* De una sola hilera de botones. (Aplícase a sacos de hombre.)
Single file [sin'-gl fail], *adv.* En hilera, uno tras otro.
Singleness [sin'-gl-nes], *s.* Sencillez, llaneza, sinceridad, ingenuidad.
Single-track [sin'-gl-trac], *a.* De una sola vía. *Single-track mind*, Mente estrecha, de interés muy limitado.
Singly [sin'-gli], *adv.* Individualmente, sencillamente; de uno en uno, uno a uno, separadamente; francamente, abiertamente.
Singsong [sing'-sēng], *s.* 1. Cadencia uniforme. 2. Sonsonete, verso malo; gorigori. *V.* DOGGEREL.
Singular [siṇ'-giu-lar], *a.* 1. Sencillo, singular; aislado, que está aparte, peculiar. 2. Singular, extraño, extraordinario, raro, excelente. 3. (Ant.) Único, sin ejemplo. *Singular conduct*, Conducta singular, extraña. *The singular number*, El número singular.
Singularity [siṇ-giu-lar'-i-ti], **Singularness**, *s.* 1. Particularidad, distinción. 2. Singularidad, cosa extraordinaria, rara o excelente.
Singularize [siṇ'-giu-lar-aiz], *va.* Singularizar, particularizar.
Singularly [siṇ'-giu-lar-li], *adv.* Singularmente, separadamente, particularmente.
Sinic [sin'-ic], *s.* Chinesco, chino.

Sinical [sin'-ic-al], *a.* Relativo al seno de un arco.
Sinister [sin'-is-tęr], *a.* 1. Siniestro, izquierdo. 2. Siniestro, viciado, avieso, mal intencionado. 3. Siniestro, infeliz, funesto, aciago.
Sinistrad [sin'-is-trad], *adv.* Hacia el lado izquierdo del cuerpo.
Sinistral [sin'-is-tral], **Sinistrorse** [sin'-is-trōrs], *a.* Siniestro, izquierdo, vuelto hacia la izquierda.
Sinistrous [sin'-is-trus], *a.* Siniestro, malvado, depravado.
Sinistrously [sin'-is-trus-li], *adv.* 1. Siniestramente, depravadamente. 2. Hacia la izquierda.
Sink [siŋk], *vn.* (*pret.* SANK o SUNK, *pp.* SUNK o SUNKEN). 1. Hundirse, sumirse, irse abajo. 2. Hundirse, sumergirse, irse a pique una nave. 3. Hundirse, bajarse, sentarse o apretarse una obra, un monte, etc. 4. Pasar o penetrar una cosa por medio o hasta el interior de otra; dejarse penetrar, calar; imprimirse o fijarse una cosa, v. g. en la memoria. 5. Bajarse, descender, desaparecer. 6. Bajar, disminuir menguar; debilitarse, sucumbir, perecer. 7. Dejarse caer, ceder a su propio peso. 8. Abatirse, acoquinarse, amilanarse. 9. (Ant.) Arruinarse, decaer, declinar, empeorar, ir a menos.—*va.* 1. Hundir, sumergir, echar a lo hondo. *To sink a ship,* (Mar.) Echar a pique un buque. 2. Cavar, penetrar. 3. Deprimir, abatir, humillar. 4. Destruir, exterminar, extinguir. 5. Disminuir, bajar, rebajar. 6. Abatir, derribar, hacer caer. 7. Disipar (bienes, fortuna, etc.). 8. Suprimir, ocultar, hacer desaparecer. 9. Decorar por medio de líneas o calados; inscribir o hacer una incisión en algo, p. ej. en un cuño. *To sink away,* Pasar la vida indolentemente o sin utilidad alguna. *To sink down,* Caer por grados; penetrar profundamente. *To sink under,* Atribularse en o con, anonadarse. *Sinking-fund,* Fondo de amortización. *Sinking spirit,* Abatimiento de ánimo. *The water sinks,* El agua baja, disminuye. *The moon was sinking,* La luna iba desapareciendo. *The stone sank into his forehead,* La piedra penetró en su frente. *To sink on one's knees,* Caer de rodillas.
Sink, *s.* 1. Alcantarilla, albañal. 2. Sentina, cualquier lugar lleno de inmundicia.
Sinker [siŋk'-ęr], *s.* Hundidor, el que o lo que hunde; plomo para la cuerda de pescar. *Die-sinker* o *punch-sinker,* Tallador, abridor o grabador en hueco.
Sinless [sin'-les], *a.* Impecable, exento de pecado, puro.
Sinlessness [sin'-les-nes], *s.* Impecabilidad.
Sinner, *s.* Pecador, pecadora.
Sin-offering [sin'-ef-ęr-ing], *s.* El sacrificio propiciatorio ofrecido por los pecados.
Sinople [sin'-o-pl], *s.* 1. (Her.) Sinople, verde. 2. Un cuarzo ferruginoso de Hungría.
Sinter [sin'-tęr], *s.* Toba, materia calcárea o silícea depositada en manantiales.
Sinuate [sin'-yu-ēt], *va.* Formar oblicuidades, sinuosidades o senos.—*a.* Sinuoso, ondulado.
Sinuation [sin-yu-é'-shun], *s.* Tortuosidad, corvadura.
Sinuosity [sin-yu-es'-i-ti], *s.* Sinuosidad.
Sinuous [sin'-yu-us], *a.* Sinuoso.
Sinus [sai'-nus], *s.* 1. Seno, ensenada, bahía, la parte del mar que se interna entre dos puntas de tierra. 2. Seno, cavidad, abertura, hueco, concavidad.
Sip [sip], *va.* Beborrotear, echar sorbitos, traguitos o copitas; absorber lentamente; chupar, extraer.
Sip, *s.* Sorbo, trago pequeño. *A little sip,* Sorbito.
Siphon [sai'-fen], *s.* Sifón, cañón o tubo corvo que sirve para sacar licores y para otros varios usos.
Sipper [sip'-ęr], *s.* Sorbedor, el que sorbe.
Sippet [sip'-et], *s.* Sopita, sopilla, sopa, pedazo de pan empapado en algún licor.
Sir [sęr], *s.* 1. Señor, término de cortesía. 2. Título que se da en Inglaterra, puesto siempre delante del nombre de bautismo, a los barones y a los caballeros de las órdenes militares. 3. A veces se toma por hombre. *Sir knight,* Señor caballero.
Sire [sair], *s.* 1. Padre. 2. Se usa hablando de los animales irracionales: v. g. *This horse had a good sire,* Este caballo tuvo buen padre. 3. Algunas veces se usa en composición, como *grand-sire,* abuelo; *great grand-sire,* bisabuelo. 4. Señor, tratamiento del soberano.
Sire, *va.* Engendrar, producir, hablando de animales y particularmente de caballos.
Siren [sai'-ren], *s.* 1. Sirena, ninfa legendaria del mar, mitad mujer y mitad ave, que por la dulzura de su canto arrastraba a los navegantes hacia los escollos; de aquí una mujer peligrosa y hechicera. 2. Cantadora melodiosa. 3. Aparato para producir un silbido fuerte por medio del vapor. *V.* FOGHORN.—*a.* Encantador.
Sirius [sir'-i-us], *s.* (Astr.) Sirio, canícula, la estrella más brillante del firmamento.
Sirloin [sęr'-lein], *s.* Lomo de buey o vaca; la parte que queda encima del riñón.
Sirocco [si-rec'-o], *s.* Siroco o jaloque, el viento que viene de la parte intermedia entre levante y mediodía. *V.* SIMOOM.
Sirrah [sir'-a], *s.* Malandrín, pícaro: es voz de baldón y desprecio.
Sirup [sir'-up], *s.* Jarabe, el zumo de vegetales cocido con azúcar.
Siruped [sir'-upt], *a.* Dulce como jarabe.
Sirupy [sir'-up-i], *a.* Semejante a jarabe.
Siskin [sis'-kin], *s.* Verderón, pájaro del género Spinus.
Sissy [sis'-i], *s.* 1. Marica, Maricón. 2. Bragazas.
Sister [sis'-tęr], *sf.* 1. Hermana, la que tiene los mismos padres que otra persona o el padre o madre solamente. 2. Hermana, la mujer de la misma creencia, del mismo ser o naturaleza, de la misma especie o de la misma profesión que otra. *The sister kingdom,* Denominación con que los ingleses designan a Irlanda y los irlandeses a Inglaterra. *Foster sister,* Hermana de leche. *The Three* o *Fatal Sisters,* Las Parcas.
Sister-blocks [sis'-tęr-blecs], *s.* (Mar. Motones herrados.
Sister-in-law [sis'-tęr-in-lē], *sf.* Cuñada, hermana política.
Sisterhood [sis'-tęr-hud], *s.* 1. Hermandad, el oficio u obligación de hermana. 2. Conjunto de hermanas. 3. Hermandad, congregación de mujeres bajo ciertas reglas o votos.
Sisterly [sis'-tęr-li], *a.* Con hermandad, como corresponde a hermanas; perteneciente a las hermanas.
Sistrum [sis'-trum], *s.* Sistro, instrumento músico a manera de matraca que usaban los antiguos egipcios en las ceremonias del culto de Isis.
Sit [sit], *vn.* (*pret.* SAT (y ant. SATE), *pp.* SAT). 1. Sentarse, asentarse, estar sentado. 2. Sentarse, poner el cuerpo en alguna disposición o de algún modo particular; posarse, permanecer inmóvil y en pie (como las aves). 3. Estar situada o colocada una cosa. 4. Fijarse algo profundamente en el ánimo, en el corazón, etc. 5. Sentar, venir o ajustar bien o mal un vestido, un adorno, etc. 6. Sentar bien o mal una cosa, agradar o ser conforme y conveniente al gusto. 7. Hallarse reunida alguna junta, consejo, asamblea, etc. 8. Estar en sesión los individuos de una junta, tribunal, etc. 9. Sostenerse en el puesto que se ocupa estando sentado; mantenerse a caballo. 10. Descansar, apoyarse sobre alguna cosa. 11. Empollar. 12. Servir de modelo a un pintor o fotógrafo; tomar una posición determinada para un fin especial.—*va.* Asentar, sentar, poner a uno en un asiento. *To sit by,* Sentarse junto a uno o arrimado a una persona. *To sit close,* Juntarse, acercarse. *Sit by me,* Siéntese Vd. a mi lado. *He sits a horse well,* Se tiene o se mantiene bien a caballo, monta bien. *To sit down,* Sentarse, estar sentado; residir, morar; quedar satisfecho. *To sit down before a fortress,* Bloquear una fortaleza o principiar a ponerle sitio. *To sit for one's picture,* Sentarse delante de un retratista para que haga el retrato. *To sit out,* Estar desocupado o sin puesto ni empleo, estar holgando; perseverar. *To sit up,* Sentarse el que estaba echado; velar. *To sit upon,* Juzgar, cuando se habla de jueces; estar reunidos en sesión los individuos de una junta, asamblea, etc. *Sit still,* Esté Vd. quieto, no se levante Vd. *To sit well,* Venir bien una cosa con otra.
Sitar [sit'-ar], *s.* Guitarra oriental que tiene dos cuerdas de alambre del mismo tono, y una de acero, un cuarto de tono más alta que aquellas.
Sit-down strike [sit'-daun straic], *s.* Huelga de brazos caídos.
Site [sait], *s.* Sitio, situación, solar.
Sited [sait'-ed], *a.* Puesto, colocado, situado.
Sith [sith], *adv., prep.* y *conj.* (Des. o poét.) *V.* SINCE.
Sitter [sit'-ęr], *s.* 1. El que se sienta o está sentado; en particular, la persona que se hace retratar o fotografiar. 2. El ave que está empollando huevos.
Sitting [sit'-ing], *s.* 1. La acción de sentarse y la postura que uno tiene cuando está sentado. 2. El tiempo que está uno delante del pintor para que le retrate. 3. Sesión, junta. 4. Sentada, asentada. 5. Empolladura, la acción de empollar huevos;

también, nidada o cría de pajarillos.—*a.* 1. Sentado, de persona sentada; ave que empolla. 2. (Bot.) Sesil, sin pedimento. *V.* SESSILE.
Sitting room [sit'-ing rūm], *s.* Sala de recibo.
Situate [sit'-yu-ēt o sich'-u-ēt], *a.* Situado, colocado.
Situation [sit-yu-ē'-shun o sich-u-ē'-shun], *s.* 1. Situación, estado, vecindad, cercanía, localidad. 2. Acomodo, plaza, empleo, ocupación. 3. Combinación de circunstancias, complicación; situación, punto en el desarrollo de una obra literaria que excita vivamente el interés. *In a situation,* Con empleo, empleado. *Out of a situation,* Sin empleo, cesante.
Six [six], *a.* y *s.* Seis. *Six and seven,* Confusión, desorden. *At sixes and sevens,* A la buena ventura, en estado de descuido, desorden, confusión o contrariedad.
Sixpence [six'-pens], *s.* Seis peniques o medio chelín, moneda de plata en Inglaterra; vale 63 céntimos.
Sixpenny [six'-pen-i], *a.* Que vale o se vende por seis peniques; de aquí, mezquino, miserable.
Sixscore [six'-scōr], *a.* Ciento veinte, seis veces veinte.
Sixshooter [six-shūt'-ęr], *s.* Revólver con cilindro de seis cartuchos.
Sixteen [six'-tīn], *a.* y *s.* Diez y seis.
Sixteenth [six'-tīnth], *a.* Décimosexto. *The sixteenth century,* El siglo décimosexto o diez y seis.
Sixth [sixth], *a.* y *s.* Sexto. *Sixth sense,* Sexto sentido, profunda intuición.
Sixth, *s.* 1. La sexta parte de cualquiera cosa. 2. (Mús.) Sexta, una de las concordancias originales. *The sixth of June,* El seis de junio. *Edward the Sixth,* Eduardo Sexto.
Sixthly [sixth'-li], *adv.* En sexto lugar.
Sixtieth [six'-ti-eth], *a.* Sexagésimo. —*s.* Una de las sesenta partes iguales de una cosa.
Sixty [six'-ti], *a.* y *s.* Sesenta.
Sizable, Sizeable [saiz'a-bl], *a.* Que tiene tamaño proporcionado; algo grande.
Sizar [sai'-zar], *s.* Estudiante que goza de una beca en la universidad de Cambridge y en el colegio de la Trinidad (*Trinity*) de Dublín; en otro tiempo, "fámulo," estudiante sirviente.
Size [saiz], *s.* 1. Tamaño, talle; calibre, dimensión; corpulencia, estatura, grandor. 2. Marco de zapatero. 3. Tipo de medida; cantidad especificada. (<Fr. *assise,* medida.) *Size of ropes,* (Mar.) Mena, el grueso de cabos y cuerdas.
Size, *s.* 1. Substancia viscosa y pegajosa; engrudo; disolución de materia gelatinosa, como la cola, el almidón o la resina, que se emplea para encolar el papel. 2. Cola de retazo, sisa empleada para dorar. (<Ital. ant. sisa.)
Size, *va.* 1. Ajustar, arreglar, igualar, hacer venir una cosa a la medida de otra. 2. Fijar, arreglar: dícese comúnmente de los pesos y medidas; distribuir o clasificar según tamaño. 3. Evaluar, apreciar, tasar.
Size, *va.* 1. Engrudar, encolar, pegar una cosa a otra con cualquier materia glutinosa. 2. Lavar una pared para blanquearla.
Sized [saizd], *a.* Que pertenece al tamaño, magnitud o grandor de las cosas. *Large-sized ropes,* (Mar.) Cabos de mena mayor.
Sizer [saiz'-ęr], *s.* 1. Instrumento para medir el tamaño de las perlas. 2. *V.* SIZAR.
Siziness [sai'-zi-nes], *s.* Viscosidad.
Sizing [saiz'-ing], *s.* 1. Encoladura, acción de encolar. 2. Cola; capa de cola.
Sizy [sai'-zi], *a.* Viscoso, pegajoso.
Sizz [siz], *vn.* Chisporrotear, silbar.
Sizzle [siz'-l], *va.* y *vn.* (Prov.) Quemar, chamuscar, quemarse o chamuscarse produciendo un silbido, como sucede bajo la acción violenta del calor.—*s.* (Fam.) Sonido como de silbido; chisporroteo; temperatura excesivamente alta.
Skate [skēt], *va.* Patinar, deslizarse sobre el hielo u otra superficie lisa, sirviéndose al efecto de patines.—*s.* 1. Patín, especie de calzado armado de hierro para correr sobre el hielo. 2. Lija. *Roller-skate,* Patín de ruedas.
Skater [skē'-tęr], *s.* Patinador.
Skean [skīn], *s.* Daga, puñal irlandés antiguo.
Skedaddle [skę-dad'-l], *vn.* (Ger.) Tomar las de Villadiego; poner pies en polvorosa.
Skee [skī], *s.* Especie de patín noruego para deslizarse sobre el hielo y la nieve; consiste en una plancha de madera larga y estrecha, a la cual se asegura la parte anterior del pie.
Skeet [skīt], *s.* (Mar.) Bañadera, especie de cucharones para bañar las velas, cubiertas o costados de la embarcación.
Skein [skēn], *s.* Madeja, mazo, cadejo. *To wind off a skein,* Devanar una madeja.
Skeletal [skel'-et-al], *a.* De esqueleto, perteneciente al esqueleto; que forma esqueleto.
Skeleton [skel'-ę-ton], *a.* Que consiste meramente en un esqueleto o armazón; extenuado.—*s.* 1. Esqueleto, armazón descarnada y completa del cuerpo animal. 2. Armazón o armadura; esbozo o plan de una cosa, particularmente de una obra literaria. *Skeleton key,* Llave maestra.
Skep [skep], *s.* (Prov. brit.) Especie de cesto para llevar trigo; colmena, casa de abejas.
Skeptic, Sceptic [skep'-tic], *s.* Escéptico, el que duda de todo y particularmente de la religión cristiana.
Skeptical [skep'-ti-cal], *a.* Escéptico.
Skeptically [skep'-ti-cal-i], *adv.* Escépticamente.
Skepticism [skep'-ti-sizm], *s.* Escepticismo.
Sketch [skech], *s.* 1. Diseño, esbozo, bosquejo, la primera mano que se da a una pintura u otra obra material. 2. Esquicio, boceto, traza, rasguño, borrón, el primer diseño de una obra de pintura o escultura. 3. Bosquejo, borrón, el plan de cualquier obra intelectual.
Sketch, *va.* 1. Esquiciar, trazar, delinear, rasguñar una figura, un cuadro, etc. 2. Bosquejar una pintura o cualquier obra material. 3. Bosquejar, presentar o hacer el bosquejo o borrón de una obra intelectual.
Sketchily [skech'-i-li], *adv.* A manera de esbozo, bosquejo o boceto.
Sketchiness [skech'-i-nes], *s.* Calidad o condición de esbozo, bosquejo o borrón.
Sketchy [skech'-i], *a.* Bosquejado, esquiciado; no acabado.
Skew [skiū], *a.* Oblicuo, torcido, atravesado, al sesgo, de través.—*s.* 1. Movimiento, curso o posición oblicuos. 2. Mirada al sesgo, oblicua.
Skew, *va.* Poner al sesgo; dar forma o poner oblicua o torcidamente; echar de través.—*vn.* 1. Andar o moverse oblicuamente. 2. Mirar al sesgo.
Skewer [skiū'-ęr], *s.* Aguja de lardear; espetón.
Skewer, *va.* 1. Espetar. 2. Afianzar con espetones.
Ski [skī], *s.* Esquí.—*vn.* Esquiar. *Ski lift,* Telesquí, teleférico.
Skid [skid], *va.* Proveer de baraderos; poner, arrastrar o tirar sobre baraderos o carenotes.—*s.* 1. Carenote, baradero. 2. Calzo, rastra (de rueda).
Skid row [skid rō], *s.* Hampa, barrio de holgazanes y degenerados.
Skiff [skif], *s.* Esquife, bote o barco pequeño.
Skilful [skil'-ful], *a.* Práctico, experimentado, diestro, hábil, experto.
Skilfully [skil'-ful-i], *adv.* Diestramente, sagazmente, mañosamente.
Skilfulness [skil'-ful-nes], *s.* Habilidad, destreza, capacidad o arte para hacer una cosa.
Skill [skil], *s.* Conocimiento práctico; habilidad, destreza, saber; maña o gracia en hacer o para hacer una cosa; arte, artificio.
Skilled [skild], *a.* Práctico, instruído; diestro, hábil.
Skilless [skil'-les], *a.* Inexperto; falto de conocimiento o destreza.
Skillet [skil'-et], *s.* Marmita pequeña; cacerola o cazuela pequeña.
Skim [skim], *va.* 1. Desnatar, quitar la nata a la leche u otros líquidos. 2. Espumar, quitar la espuma. 3. Pasar ligeramente por encima de una cosa tocando su superficie. 4. Tratar superficialmente acerca de alguna cosa.—*vn.* Deslizarse o moverse una cosa con rapidez por encima de otra, tocando suavemente su superficie. *To skim the ocean,* (Mar.) Peinar las olas. *To skim along,* Rozar, resbalar. *To skim over,* Resbalar, rozar; recorrer un libro; tocar ligeramente una cuestión.
Skim, *s.* Acción de desnatar o espumar; espuma, desecho.
Skimble-scamble [skim'-bl-scam'-bl], *a.* (Fam.) Desordenado, extravagante.
Skimmer [skim'-ęr], *s.* Espumadera.
Skim-milk [skim'-milk], *s.* Leche desnatada; voz que se usa a menudo para indicar inferioridad.
Skimp [skimp], *va.* (Fam.) 1. *V.* STINT. 2. Ejecutar con descuido.—*vn.* 1. Ser mezquino o tacaño. 2. Hacer un trabajo con poco cuidado.
Skimpy [skim'-pi], *a.* 1. Corto, escaso. 2. Tacaño, que escatima.
Skin [skin], *s.* 1. Cutis, pellejo sutil que cubre exteriormente el cuerpo humano; piel de un animal, tegumento. *He is nothing but skin and bone,* Está en los huesos. *I would not be in his skin,* No quisiera hallarme en su pellejo. 2. Cuero, piel del animal que sirve para hacer pergamino, cordobán, suela y otras cosas. 3. Odre; pellejo o cuero que sirve para contener líquidos. 4. Pellejo, tegumento o capa exterior que cubre ciertos frutos. *Sheepskin dressed with wool,* Zalea. *Foreskin,* Prepucio. *Scarf skin,* Epider-

mis, cutícula. *Skin deep*, Superficial, no más profundo que el cutis. *Calf skin*, Piel de becerro. *Sheep skin*, Badana, zalea. *Dressed skin*, Piel adobada o curtida.

Skin, *va.* 1. Desollar, quitar el pellejo o la piel. 2. Cubrir con la piel o pellejo. 3. Cubrir superficialmente.—*vn.* Cubrirse de pellejo o tegumento; cicatrizarse. *To skin over*, Curarse o cicatrizarse una llaga o herida; cuajarse superficialmente; hacerse costras.

Skin diving [skin daiv'-ing], *s.* Buceo sin escafandra pero con un dispositivo que permite la respiración en el agua.

Skinflint [skin-flint], *s.* Avaro, cicatero, miserable.

Skin graft [skin' graft], *s.* Piel para injertos.

Skinless [skin'-les], *a.* Desprovisto de pellejo, sin piel o que tiene una película muy delgada, como ciertas frutas y granos.

Skinner [skin'-ęr], *s.* 1. Pellejero, el que tiene por oficio vender y adobar los pellejos. 2. Peletero, el que trabaja o vende pieles finas.

Skinned [skind], *a.* Que tiene pellejo; hecho de cuero; correoso.

Skinniness [skin'-i-nes], *s.* Flaqueza, falta de carnes; extenuación.

Skinny [skin'-i], *a.* Flaco, falto de carnes.

Skin test [skin' test], *s.* Cutirreacción.

Skin-tight [skin'-tait], *a.* Ceñido al cuerpo.

Skip [skip], *va.* 1. Pasar por alto, omitir. 2. Saltar ligeramente por encima de algo. 3. Hacer saltar sucesivamente, como salta una piedra plana sobre el agua.—*vn.* 1. Saltar ligeramente, brincar, cabriolar, triscar, dar o hacer cabriolas. 2. Dar saltos o pernadas, brincar hacia alguna cosa o desde ella. 3. Pasar por alto sin hacer caso de (lo escrito o impreso).

Skip, *s.* 1. Cabriola, salto, brinco. 2. Omisión, acción de pasar por alto sin hacer caso.

Skipjack [skip'-jac], *s.* Hombre de fortuna, elevado desde el arroyo, o desde el lodo.

Skipper [skip'-ęr], *s.* 1. Persona o cosa que brinca o salta. 2. Un bailarín o bailarina. 3. Escombresocio, pez. 4. Especie de mariposa; debe su nombre a la manera como vuela. 5. Gusanillo de queso.

Skipper, *s.* Maestro o patrón de una pequeña embarcación; paje de escoba. *Skipper's daughter*, Cabrilla de mar.

Skipping [skip'-ing], *s.* Acción de saltar. *Skipping-rope*, Comba, cuerda para el juego de niños llamado también comba.

Skippingly [skip'-ing-li], *adv.* A saltos, a brincos.

Skirmish [skęr'-mish], *s.* Escaramuza, pelea ligera; contienda, pendencia.

Skirmish, *vn.* Escaramuzar.

Skirmisher [skęr'-mish-ęr], *s.* Escaramuzador.

Skirret [skir'-et], *s.* (Bot.) Chirivía, planta de las umbelíferas.

Skirt [skęrt], *s.* 1. Falda, saya, faldilla, la parte del vestido desde la cintura abajo; también, enagua. 2. Faldón, falda suelta al aire o la parte inferior de una colgadura, etc.; orla, filete. 3. Orilla, margen, borde.

Skirt, *va.* 1. Orillar, guarnecer la orilla de una tela o ropa. 2. Poblar, adornar o formar la orilla o el margen de un río, monte, país, etc.

Skit [skit], *s.* 1. Pasquín, sátira breve. 2. Burla, capricho.

Skittish [skit'-ish], *a.* 1. Espantadizo, que fácilmente se asusta, tímido. 2. Retozón, inclinado a retozar. 3. Repropio, terco, reacio. 4. Caprichoso, quisquilloso, suspicaz. 5. Voluble, inconstante.

Skittishly [skit'-ish-li], *adv.* Caprichosamente.

Skittishness [skit'-ish-nes], *s.* Desenvoltura; volubilidad, inconstancia.

Skittle [skit'-l], *s.* Bolo, juego de bolos; por lo común en plural.

Skive [skaiv], *va.* 1. Raspar, adelgazar, p. ej. el cuero. 2. Moler y pulir, v. g. la superficie de una joya. —*s.* Disco de joyero para pulir el diamante.

Skiver [skai'-vęr], *s.* 1. Cuero hendido con cuchillo; cuero para pastas. 2. Cuchillo o máquina para raspar o adelgazar.

Skulk [sculc], *vn.* Andar a sombra de tejado; ocultarse, substraerse a la vista.

Skull [scul], *s.* 1. Cráneo; calavera, casco de la cabeza de un animal vertebrado. 2. Remo para cinglar. *V.* SCULL.

Skullcap [scul'-cap], *s.* 1. Casquete, gorra muy ajustada a la cabeza. 2. Sincipucio. *V.* SINCIPUT. 3. Escutelaria, planta de la familia de las labiadas, hierba anual de los lugares pantanosos.

Skunk [skunk], *s.* 1. Zorrillo. 2. Canalla.

Sky [skai], *s.* 1. Región etérea, cielo, firmamento, el orbe diáfano que rodea la tierra. *Cloudy sky*, Cielo turbio o encapotado. 2. Atmósfera. 3. Tiempo, la constitución o temperamento del aire. 4. Una nube. 5. Una sombra. *Sky-blue*, Azul celeste. *Sky-born*, Nacido en el cielo. *Sky-clad*, (Fam.) Desnudo. *Sky-high*, Tan alto como el cielo.

Skyey [skai'-i], *a.* Etéreo.

Sky-colour [skai'-cul-ęr], *s.* Color azul o celeste.

Sky-coloured [skai'-cul-ęrd], **Sky-dyed** [skai'-daid], *a.* Azul celeste, el color semejante al que muestra el cielo cuando está claro: hablando poéticamente, color cerúleo.

Skylark [skai'-lārc], *s.* (Orn.) Alondra, calandria. Alauda arvensis. —*vn.* (Fam.) Chacotear, estar de chacota, triscar, jaranear. *Skylarking*, Chacota, jarana.

Skylight [skai'-lait], *s.* Claraboya, lumbrera, montera; ventanilla que mira al cielo.

Skyline [skai'-lain], *s.* 1. Línea del horizonte. 2. Perspectiva de una ciudad con rascacielos.

Skyrocket [skai'-rek-et], *s.* Cohete.

Skysail [skai'-sēl], *s.* (Mar.) Sosobre, vela ligera colocada encima del sobrejuanete.

Skyscraper [skai'-scrēp-ęr], *s.* Rascacielos.

Skyward, Skywards [skai'-ward, wardz], *adv.* Hacia el cielo.

Slab [slab], *s.* 1. Costero, el madero que se saca de la parte más exterior del árbol. 2. Losa, piedra alisada; plancha o pedazo plano y grueso de metal, piedra u otro material.

Slabber [slab'-ęr], *vn.* Babear, expeler o echar de sí la baba o saliva; dejar caer el alimento líquido al comer; ensuciar, hacer un lodazal.

Slabberer [slab'-ęr-ęr], *s.* 1. Baboso, la persona que echa babas. 2. Ensuciador, el que ensucia.

Slabbering [slab'-ęr-ing], *s.* 1. Babeo, el acto de babear. 2. El acto de derramar, ensuciar o mojar.

Slabby [slab'-i], *a.* 1. Espeso, viscoso. 2. Mojado, lleno de humedad.

Slac [slac], *a.* 1. Flojo, poco apretado o poco tirante. 2. Flojo, perezoso, negligente, descuidado, tardo. 3. Lento, tardo, sosegado, espacioso. 4. Que fluye lentamente. *Slack water*, Estado del mar entre flujo y reflujo. *Trade is slack*, El comercio no marcha bien, decae. *Slack ropes*, (Mar.) Cabos sueltos o en banda.—*s.* 1. Cabo de cuerda colgante; parte de una cuerda que no está bastante tirante. 2. Cisco, carbón menudo.

Slack, Slacken [slac'-n], *va.* y *vn.* 1. Aflojar, poner floja una cosa que estaba tirante. 2. Ablandar, poner blanda una cosa que estaba endurecida. 3. Apagar, v. g. la cal. 4. Aflojar, amainar, amortiguar. 5. Remitir; diferir, tardar, descuidar. 6. Despegar o despegarse. 7. Aflojar, entibiarse, perder el vigor, aplicación, etc. 8. Decaer, desfallecer. 9. Relajar, laxar o ablandar. 10. Relajar, aliviar. *The fever slackens*, Cede la calentura. *The wind slackens*, El viento amaina. *To slack up*, Retardar, detener la rapidez de algo: aflojar, amainar.

Slacker [slak'-ęr], *s.* Cobarde, el que elude pelear en la guerra.

Slackly [slac'-li], *adv.* Flojamente, lentamente.

Slackness [slac'-nes], *s.* 1. Flojedad, remisión, descuido. 2. Debilidad.

Slacks [slacs], *s. pl.* Pantalones holgados (de hombre o de mujer).

Slag [slag], *s.* 1. Escoria, la hez de los metales. 2. Escoria volcánica.

Slain [slēn], *pp.* del verbo *To* SLAY.

Slake [slēk], *va.* 1. Apagar, extinguir. 2. Remojar; desleír. 3. Moderar. 4. Aflojar, ceder, bajar o disminuirse la fuerza o vigor de una cosa.—*vn.* Apagarse, llegar a ser hidratado; dícese de la cal. *To slake lime*, Apagar la cal. *To slake one's thirst*, Apagar uno la sed.

Slalom [sla'-lem], *vn.* Esquiar zigzagueando.

Slam [slam], *va.* 1. Arrojar, tirar o empujar con violencia y estrépito. *To slam the door*, Cerrar de golpe, o dar un golpe a la puerta. 2. Dar capote, hacer uno de los jugadores en alguna mano todas las bazas.—*vn.* Cerrarse o dar de golpe y con estrépito.

Slam, *s.* 1. Empuje o cierre con estrépito y violencia. 2. Capote en el juego.

Slander [slan'-dęr], *va.* Calumniar, denigrar, infamar, hablar mal.

Slander, *s.* 1. Calumnia, acusación falsa, denigración, mancha o borrón en la fama de alguno, impostura. 2. Infamia, descrédito, deshonra.

Slanderer [slan'-dęr-ęr], *s.* Calumniador, impostor, maldiciente.

Slandering [slan'-dęr-ing], *s.* Murmuración, maledicencia.—*a.* Maldiciente, calumnioso.

Slanderous [slan'-dęr-us], *a.* Infamatorio, calumnioso.

Slanderously [slan'-dęr-us-li], *adv.* Calumniosamente.

Slang, *s.* 1. Jerga, jerigonza (germanía), lenguaje popular inelegante y no autorizado; o empleo de expresiones correctas, pero dándoles un sentido impropio o grotesco. 2. Jacarandina, caló, lenguaje propio de ladrones, gitanos y gentuza. (< sling.)

NOTA.—La abreviatura (Ger.) usada en esta Parte II se refiere por lo general a la primera acepción y rara vez a la segunda.

Slangy [slang'-i], *a.* 1. De la naturaleza de la jerga, que le pertenece o la contiene. 2. Dado al uso de la jerga.

Slank [slank], *pret.* del verbo SLINK.

Slant [slant], *va.* y *vn.* Dar una dirección oblicua; inclinarse, sesgarse.

Slant [slant], **Slanting** [slant'-ing], *a.* Sesgado, oblícuo; inclinado, en declive.—*s.* 1. Dirección oblicua; plano inclinado, declive. 2. Pulla, chufleta, dicho sarcástico.

Slantingly [slant'-ing-li], **Slantwise** [slant'-waiz], *adv.* Sesgadamente, de través o al través.

Slap [slap], *va.* Golpear, dar un golpe: regularmente se usa para denotar un golpe con la mano abierta o una manotada. *To slap one over the face*, Dar una bofetada o bofetón; dar un sopapo.

Slap, *s.* Manotada, el golpe dado con la mano, y por extensión cualquier golpe dado con una cosa ancha. *Slap on the face*, Bofetada, bofetón.—*adv.* De golpe y porrazo, de sopetón.

Slapdash [slap'-dash], *a.* y *adv.* (Fam.) De una vez, de un golpe.

Slapstick [slap'-stic], *s.* Comedia grotesca en que abundan los porrazos.

Slash [slash], *va.* Acuchillar, dar cuchilladas.—*vn.* Tirar tajos y reveses con una espada, a trochemoche.

Slash, *s.* Cuchillada, corte en carne viva; chirlo, jabeque; latigazo, azote; en especial, corte, cortadura en una tela.

Slat [slat], *va.* y *vn.* Arrojar con violencia o con un empellón; lanzar con descuido; sacudirse, hacer ruido.

Slat [slat], *s.* Tablilla, pedazo delgado y estrecho de madera y algunas veces de metal o piedra. *Blind-slat*, Tablilla de persiana.

Slatch [slach], *s.* (Mar.) 1. El medio de un cabo suelto. 2. Intervalo de buen tiempo.

Slate [slêt], *s.* 1. Pizarra, especie de piedra que se divide en hojas delgadas para cubrir los tejados. 2. Pizarra para escribir. 3. (E. U.) Lista de candidatos preparada de antemano; programa redactado con anticipación. *Slate-coloured*, De color de pizarra. *Slate-pencil*, Pizarrín, pizarrete. *Slate-quarry*, Pizarral, cantera de pizarra.

Slate, *va.* Empizarrar, cubrir con pizarra.

Slater [slêt'-er], *s.* Pizarrero, el que cubre los tejados con pizarra; herramienta con canto de pizarra para quitar el pelo de las pieles.

Slattern [slat'-ern], *a.* Puerco, desaliñado.—*s.* Mujer desaliñada.

Slatternly [slat'-ern-li], *adv.* Desaliñadamente.—*a.* Puerco, desaliñado.

Slaty [slé'-ti], *a.* Pizarreño, que participa de la naturaleza de la pizarra; que consiste de pizarra o se parece a ella.

Slaughter [slō'-ter], *s.* Carnicería, matanza, mortandad de gente, estrago que se hace en la guerra.

Slaughter, *va.* 1. Matar atrozmente, hacer una carnicería; hacer pedazos. 2. Matar animales en la carnicería.

Slaughter-house [slō'-ter-haus], *s.* Matadero.

Slaughterman [slō'-ter-man], *s.* Matador, asesino.

Slaughterous [slō'-ter-us], *a.* Mortífero, destructivo.

Slav [slav], *a.* Eslavo. *V.* SLAVONIC.—*s.* Persona de la raza eslava.

Slave [slêv], *s* 1. Esclavo, esclava, persona sin libertad, bajo el dominio de otra. 2. Esclavo, el que se somete a sus pasiones. *Slave-driver*, Capataz de esclavos. *Slave-born*, Nacido en la esclavitud. *Slave-holder*, Amo, propietario de esclavos. *Slave-holding*, Poseedor de esclavos. *Slave-coffle*, Cuadrilla de esclavos para venderlos.

Slave, *vn.* Trabajar como esclavo.—*va.* (Poét. o ant.) Esclavizar.

Slaver [slê'-ver], *s.* Negrero, persona o buque que hace el tráfico de negros para venderlos como esclavos.

Slaver [slav'-er], *s.* Baba.

Slaver, *vn.* Babosear.

Slaverbit [slav'-er-bit], *s.* La cadena de las saliveras del freno del caballo.

Slaverer [slav'-er-er], *s.* Baboso, el que babosea.

Slavery [slê'-ver-i], *s.* 1. Esclavitud, servidumbre, el estado de esclavo. 2. Esclavitud, servidumbre, yugo, el estado de sujeción injusta y forzada en que un superior tiene a su inferior o el fuerte al débil.

Slavic [slav'-ic], *a.* *V.* SLAVONIC.

Slavish [slêv'-ish], *a.* Servil, bajo, humilde.

Slavishly [slêv'-ish-li], *adv.* Servilmente.

Slavishness [slêv'-ish-nes], *s.* 1. Bajeza, vileza. 2. Servidumbre, esclavitud.

Slavism [slav'-izm], *s.* Eslavismo, conjunto de rasgos característicos de los eslavos.

Slavonian [sla-vō'-ni-an], *a.* 1. Esclavón, relativo a la Esclavonia, parte del imperio austro-húngaro. 2. *V.* SLAVONIC.

Slavonic [sla-ven'-ic], *a.* 1. Eslavo, esclavón, relativo a los pueblos o a las lenguas de origen eslavo. *V.* SLAV. 2. *V.* SLAVONIAN.

Slaw [slō], *s.* Col cortada en rebanadas y servida cruda o cocida como ensalada.

Slay [slê], *va.* (*pret.* SLEW, *pp.* SLAIN). Matar, dar muerte violenta, quitar la vida.

Slay, **Sley** [slê], *s.* Peine, instrumento que guía los hilos de un telar.

Slayer [slê'-er], *s.* Matador; asesino. *Man-slayer*, Homicida.

Sleave [slīv], *s.* Seda o hilo destorcido.

Sleazy [slé'-zi o slī'-zi], *a.* Falto de firmeza en su textura, flojo, ligero. *Sleazy cloth*, Paño de soplillo.

Sled [sled], *va.* y *vn.* Llevar o pasearse sobre una narria; usar una narria.—*s.* Narria, rastra, vehículo sin ruedas para ir por la nieve o el hielo.

Sledge [slej], *va.* y *vn.* Transportar o viajar en una rastra o narria.—*s.* 1. Rastra, narria, carretón sin ruedas destinado por lo común a ser arrastrado sobre el hielo o la nieve por caballerías. 2. Macho, el mazo grande que tienen en las herrerías para forjar el hierro.

Sleek [slīc], *a.* 1. Liso, bruñido, alisado. 2. Suave, blando; zalamero, insinuante, de palabras melífluas: en los Estados Unidos, generalmente, *slick*. *V.* SLICK.

Sleek, *va.* 1. Peinar o componer el pelo o la lana. 2. Alisar, pulir, poner lisa o lustrosa alguna cosa. 3. Hacer menos desagradable u ofensivo; aquietar, pacificar.

Sleekly [slīk'-li], *adv.* Con lisura, igualdad o lustre.

Sleekness [slīk'-nes], *s.* Lisura, igualdad y lustre de una superficie.

Sleeky [slīk'-i], *a.* 1. *V.* SLEEK. 2. (Esco.) Zalamero, socarrón, taimado.

Sleep [slīp], *va.* y *vn.* (*pret.* y *pp.* SLEPT). 1. Dormir, descansar o reposar en el sueño. 2. Dormir o dormirse, descuidarse u obrar en algún negocio con poca actividad o solicitud. 3. Reposar, descansar; también, yacer muerto. 4. Dormir una cosa o no hablarse de ella. 5. Entumecerse un miembro por hallarse interrumpida la circulación de la sangre. 6. Girar sin movimiento perceptible: dícese de un trompo o peonza. *To sleep away*, Disipar o malgastar el tiempo durmiendo. *To sleep like a top*, Dormir como un lirón. *To sleep on*, Seguir durmiendo. *To sleep one's liquor away*, Dormir la mona, desollar el lobo, o la zorra. *To sleep over*, Consultar con la almohada, posponer una decisión hasta pasada la noche; considerar maduramente; vivir locamente, pasar el tiempo sin provecho. *To sleep upon*, No hacer caso de una cosa; descuidarse en el cumplimiento de su obligación. *To sleep in Jesus*, Estar muerto, dormir en el Señor, estar gozando de Dios. *To sleep soundly*, Dormir a pierna suelta; dormir profundamente, con sueño profundo.

Sleep, *s.* 1. Sueño, el acto de dormir; descanso, reposo. 2. Estado de inacción, de inercia o reposo; muerte, el reposo del sepulcro. 3. (Bot.) Posición que toman durante la noche las hojas de las plantas. *To go to sleep*, Dormirse. *To put to sleep*, Adormecer. *Sleep-walker*, Somnámbulo. *Sleep-walking*, Somnambulismo.

Sleeper [slīp'-er], *s.* 1. El que duerme. 2. (E. U.) Coche dormitorio. *V.* *Sleeping-car*. 3. Animal adormecido durante el invierno.

Sleeper, *s.* Durmiente, carrera, travesaño, vigueta; (Mar.) curva de yugo que se sitúa por la parte interior, aplicando sus brazos contra los yugos inferiores o contra el forro. (< noruego, sleip.)

Sleepily [slīp'-i-li], *adv.* Con somnolencia, pesadez o torpeza.

Sleepiness [slīp'-i-nes], *s.* Somnolencia, adormecimiento; letargo.

Sleeping [slīp'-ing], *s.* Sueño, reposo, descanso.—*pa.* Durmiente; calmante, adormecedor. *Sleeping-car*, Coche dormitorio de ferrocarril. En Inglaterra se llama más comúnmente *sleeping-carriage* o *coach*. *Sleeping-draft* o *potion*, Bebida calmante, narcótico. *Sleeping-partner*, Comanditario.

Sleeping sickness, *s.* (Med.) Encefalitis letárgica.

Sleepless [slīp'-les], *a.* Desvelado, falto de sueño. *Sleepless night*, Noche que se pasa en vela.

Sleeplessness [slīp'-les-nes], *s.* Insomnio, desvelo.

Sleepy [slīp'-i], *a.* 1. Soñoliento, adormecido. 2. Soporífero, soporoso; letárgico.

Sleepyhead [slīp'-i-hed], *s.* Dormilón.

Sleet [slīt], *s.* Agua nieve, nieve o granizo mezclado con lluvia.

Sleet, *vn.* Caer agua nieve, nevar y llover al mismo tiempo; caer granizo menudo.

Sleety [slīt'-i], *a.* Lo que contiene agua nieve.

Sleeve [slīv], *s.* 1. Manga, la parte de la vestidura que cubre los brazos hasta la muñeca. 2. (Mec.) Dedal largo, tubo o cilindro hueco que rodea un árbol o vara. 3. Junta de manguito o manguito de tuerca. *To laugh in the sleeve at,* Reirse con disimulo de alguna persona o cosa. *To say in one's sleeve,* Decir para su capote o para su sayo. *To hang on one's sleeve,* Estar una persona sujeta o dependiente de la voluntad de otra. *To wear one's heart on one's sleeve,* Llevar el corazón en la mano. *Hanging sleeves,* Mangas perdidas. *Sleeve-band,* Cinta con que se aprieta la manga. *Sleeve-button,* Botón de manga. *Sleeve-coupling,* Junta de manguito. *Sleeve-links,* Gemelos de mangas. *Sleeve-nut,* Manguito de tuerca; tuerca larga con filete a la derecha en un extremo y filete a la izquierda al otro, para juntar y acercar dos barras o tubos.

Sleeved [slīvd], *a.* Que tiene mangas, antiguamente mangado. *A sleeved waistcoat.* Chupa con mangas

Sleeveless [slīv'-les], *a.* 1. Sin mangas, que no tiene mangas. 2. (Ant.) Falto de razón o fundamento, fuera de camino. *Sleeveless tale,* Fábula absurda o ridícula.

Sleigh [slê], *s.* Trineo, vehículo ligero y sin ruedas para caminar sobre la nieve y el hielo.

Sleighing [slê'-ing], *s.* 1. Acción de ir en trineo. 2. La condición de los caminos que permite el uso de un trineo.

Sleight [slait], *s.* Ardid, artificio, estratagema, astucia, maña. *Sleight of hand,* Juego de manos.

Slender [slen'-dęr], *a.* 1. Delgado, sutil, tenue, de poco diámetro o circunferencia en proporción al largo o altura. 2. Flaco, débil, enclenque, falto de vigor, delicado. 3. Escaso, de poca base o fundamento. 4. Pequeño, corto, insuficiente; mediano. 5. Delgado en sonido o calidad; falto de volumen. *Slender estate,* Hacienda corta, pocos haberes. *Slender income,* Renta corta. *A slender pittance,* Una escasa pitanza. *Slender waist,* Cintura o talle delgado. *Slender wit,* Entendimiento limitado; ingenio o saber superficial; corto mérito. *Slender dinner,* Comida escasa.

Slenderness [slen'-dęr-nes], *s.* 1. Delgadez, sutileza, delicadeza. 2. Tenuidad, debilidad. 3. Escasez, falta de abundancia. 4. Pequeñez. 5. Debilidad, falta de vigor, falta de solidez.

Slept, *pp.* y *pret.* del verbo *To* SLEEP.

Sleuth [sliūth], *s.* 1. Pista, rastro de un hombre o animal. 2. (fam.) Detective. *Sleuth-hound,* Sabueso ventor. —*va.* Hacer el papel de detective.

Slew, *pret.* del verbo *To* SLAY

Sley [slê], *va.* Dividir o torcer en hilos; poner la urdimbre en el telar.—*s.* Peine de tejedor. *V.* SLAY.

Slice [slais], *va.* 1. Rebanar, hacer rebanadas; cortar haciendo tiras o tajadas; a menudo con *up.* 2. Tajar, cortar, partir, dividir; se usa frecuentemente con *off.*

Slice, *s.* 1. Rebanada, tajada, lonja. 2. Una de las varias herramientas que se emplean para rebanar o partir; pala; espátula.

Slicer [slai'-sęr], *s.* 1. Rebanador, el o lo que rebana. 2. Sierra circular o aparato de hender de los joyeros.

Slick [slik], *va.* Alisar, hacer lindo, lustroso u oleoso.—*a.* 1. Liso, resbaladizo, de tersura grasienta. 2. De palabras melifluas, adulador, rendido. 3. (Fam.) Diestro; mañosamente hecho.—*s.* Punto liso sobre la superficie del agua o en el pelo de un animal. (< sleek.)

Slicker [slik'-ęr], *s.* 1. Impermeable. 2. (vul.) Pillo, trampista.

Slid, *pret.* y *pp.* del verbo *To* SLIDE.

Slidden, *pp.* del verbo *To* SLIDE.

Slide [slaid], *vn.* 1. Resbalar, deslizarse, irse los pies por encima de una superficie lisa. 2. Escabullirse, escurrirse o deslizarse una cosa. 3. Correr o resbalar por encima del hielo. 4. Salirse, huirse o escurrirse de entre las manos. 5. Correr, pasar, deslizarse o irse una cosa fácilmente. 6. Irse introduciendo, ir entrando, penetrar una cosa en otra poco a poco, y también se dice de las opiniones, modas, etc. 7. Errar, pecar. 8. No hacer caso de; con *let. Let the matter slide,* No haga Vd. caso del asunto.—*va.* Hacer colar, introducir o hacer recibir por medio de algún artificio una opinión, argumento, etc. *To slide away,* Colarse, pasar sin ser observado; deslizarse o escurrirse una cosa de entre las manos. *To slide in,* Introducirse en una parte sin ser sentido; introducir una cosa con maña y artificio. *To slide into,* Pasar imperceptiblemente de un estado a otro, y regularmente se usa para expresar el pase de lo bueno a lo malo. *To slide over,* Pasar ligeramente; recorrer ligera o superficialmente una cosa.

Slide, *s.* 1. Tapa corrediza; tapa o pantalla fotográfica; portaobjetos para el microscopio o para la linterna óptica; cajón que se abre deslizándose. 2. Resbalón, acción de resbalar. 3. Sitio donde resbalan las personas o cosas; resbaladero, para deslizarse sobre la nieve; plano inclinado; paso llano y fácil; muesca, encaje (de un bastidor.) 4. Falla, dislocación de una veta; desmoronamiento, caída de una masa de tierra. 5. Diapositiva, transparencia. 6. (Mús.) Ligado. *Slide-bolt,* Pestillo corredizo, cerrojo de seguridad. *Slide-rest,* (Mec.) Soporte de corredera, carrillo portaherramientas (de un torno). *Slide-valve,* Válvula de corredera.

Slide projector [slaid' pro-ject'-ęr], *s.* Linterna de proyección.

Slider [slaid'-ęr], *s.* El que resbala.

Slide rule [slaid' rūl], *s.* Regla de cálculo.

Sliding [slaid'-ing], *s.* Deslizamiento, la acción y efecto de deslizar. *Sliding knot,* Nudo escurridizo.

Slight [slait], *a.* 1. Ligero, leve, de poca importancia, de poco momento. 2. Pequeño, corto, breve, limitado. 3. Negligente, descuidado. 4. Necio, imprudente. 5. Fútil, débil, sin fuerza. 6. Flojo, delgado.—*s.* Desaire, descuido, indiferencia, una acción u omisión que implica falta de cortesía, o desprecio; menosprecio. *To make slight of,* Despreciar, menospreciar, hacer poco caso de alguien o algo.

Slight, *va.* 1. Menospreciar, despreciar, desdeñar, desestimar, no hacer caso, desairar, ver mal, sonrojar. 2. Hacer o ejecutar algo con poco cuidado. *V.* SHIRK. *To slight,* Hacer una cosa con descuido o poco cuidado; tratar a una persona con poco aprecio o menospreciarla.

Slighter [slait'-ęr], *s.* Menospreciador, desairador, indiferente; el que descuida.

Slightingly [slait'-ing-li], *adv.* Con desprecio.

Slightly [slait'-li], *adv.* 1. Sin fuerza, ligeramente. *Slightly wounded,* Ligeramente herido. 2. Negligentemente, descuidadamente.

Slightness [slait'-nes], *s.* 1. Debilidad, falta de vigor. 2. Descuido, negligencia.

Slim [slim], *a.* 1. Delgado, sutil, tenue. 2. Poco lógico, débil. 3. Insubstancial, construído ligeramente, poco sólido. 4. Falto de vigor, enclenque. 5. Insuficiente, escaso, magro, flaco.

Slime [slaim], *s.* 1. Cualquiera substancia viscosa o mucilaginosa, particularmente la sucia y adhesiva; lama, légamo, barro pegajoso; fango; exudación mucosa de ciertos animales y plantas. 2. Lodo mineral. 3. Cualquiera cualidad o cosa repugnante.—*va.* y *vn.* 1. Ensuciar, cubrir o cubrirse de lama, légamo o exudación mucosa. 2. Deslamar, quitar el légamo o substancia viscosa.

Slimy [slai'-mi], *a.* Viscoso, pegajoso, legamoso; mucoso.

Sling [sling], *s.* 1. Honda, instrumento hecho de cuero o cuerda para arrojar piedras con violencia. 2. Hondazo. 3. El vendaje en que descansa un brazo roto, dislocado o herido; barbiquejo, cabestrillo. 4. (Mar.) Eslinga. *Slings of the yard,* Cruz de la verga; estribos de las vergas. *Slings of the buoy,* Guarnición de la boya.

Sling, *s.* (E. U.) Bebida compuesta de aguardiente, whisky o ginebra con azúcar y nuez moscada. (< alem. *schlingen,* tragar.)

Sling, *va.* 1. Tirar con honda; tirar, arrojar. 2. Colgar, suspender como en un cabestrillo; izar, columpiar o subir en alto, eslingar con una cuerda o polea.—*vn.* 1. Oscilar repentinamente; ir girando. 2. Moverse con paso suelto y fácil.

Slinger [sling'-ęr], *s.* Hondero.

Slingshot [sling'-shot], *s.* Tirador.

Slink [slink], *vn.* (*pret.* y *pp.* SLUNK o SLANK.) Escabullirse, escaparse, escurrirse furtivamente.

Slink, *va.* y *vn.* (reg.) Abortar, malparir; dícese de las bestias.

Slip [slip], *va.* (*pret.* y *pp.* SLIPPED o SLIPT). 1. Tirar, echar a un lado o arrojar una cosa que oprime o sujeta; hacer mover suave y fácilmente. 2. Meter o introducir secretamente. 3. Soltar, desatar; separar o arrancar una cosa de otra. 4. Dejar. 5. Perder alguna cosa por descuido o negligencia. 6. (Mar.) Largar (soltar), un cable o cabo. 7. Malparir (la bestia). 8. Dislocarse un hueso. 9. (Ant.) Recorrer, mirar o considerar alguna cosa superficialmente.—*vn.* 1. Resbalar, deslizarse, irse los pies. 2. Salirse alguna cosa de su lugar. 3. Resbalar, caer en alguna falta o error. 4. Escapar, huirse, dejar un lugar o sitio repentinamente. 5. Pasar rápidamente sin ser visto ni sentido. 6. Deslizarse, decir o hacer una cosa con descuido o inadvertencia. 7. Borrarse algo de la memoria u olvidarlo. *To slip away,* Desaparecerse, marcharse o huirse precipitadamente. *To slip down,* Dejarse caer. *To slip into,* Introducirse alguno donde no le llaman; insinuarse en el ánimo de una persona con maña. *To slip off,* Quitarse alguna cosa de encima del cuerpo. *To slip out,* Salir de alguna parte sin ser observado o con disimulo; dislocarse un hueso. *To slip out a word,* Escaparse alguna palabra. *To slip one's clothes on,* Vestirse de prisa. *To slip the cable,* (Mar.) Alargar el cable por el ojo o por el chicote.

Slip, *s.* 1. Resbalón, el acto de resbalar. 2. Desliz, falta, tropiezo. 3. Esqueje, estaca; vástago desgajado. 4. Escapada, huída. 5. Tira, pedazo largo y angosto. 6. Pasaje o espacio largo en proporción a su anchura: en los Estados Unidos, espacio entre dos muelles, dique, embarcadero, como un *ferry-slip.* 7. Equivocación, error, engaño. 8. Falta, ligera dislocación de los estratos. 9. (Impr.) Galerada, molde que aun no está en páginas. 10. Lo que se pone o quita fácilmente, como una funda de almohada o una prenda de vestir holgada; guardapiés, zagalejo; traílla, la cuerda o correa con que se lleva al perro atado. *Slip of paper,* Tira de papel. *Slip of the tongue,* Lapsus linguæ, yerro de lengua. *Glass slip,* Portaobjetos para el microscopio; con el objeto montado en su lugar se llama *slide.*

Slipboard [slip'-bōrd], *s.* Corredera.

Slipknot [slip'-net], *s.* Lazo corredizo.

Slip-on [slip'-en], *s.* Prenda de vestir que entra por la cabeza. *Slip-on sweater,* Suéter o chaqueta tejida que no tiene botonadura.

Slipper [slip'-ẹr], *s.* Chinela, pantuflo, zapato ligero y bajo, zapatilla.

Slipperiness [slip'-ẹr-i-nes], *s.* 1. La calidad que constituye a una cosa resbaladiza. 2. La facilidad en deslizarse o resbalarse. 3. El estado de lo que es muy movedizo o poco firme.

Slippery [slip'-ẹr-i], *a.* 1. Resbaladizo, escurridizo, deslizadizo. 2. Movedizo, poco firme, poco sólido: dícese regularmente del terreno. 3. Que se escapa de entre las manos; engañador, indigno de confianza. *A slippery witness,* Un testigo engañador, indigno de confianza.

Slipshod [slip'-shed], *a.* En chancletas. *To go slipshod,* (Fam.) Andar o ir en chancleta, o chancletas.

Slit [slit], *va.* (*pret.* y *pp.* SLIT o SLITTED). 1. Hacer una larga incisión (en algo). 2. Tajar, cortar a lo largo en tiras o jirones.

Slit, *s.* Raja, hendedura; corte relativamente largo; abertura larga y estrecha.

Slitting [slit'-ing], *s.* y *pa.* de SLIT. Acción de dar un corte largo, o de cortar largas tiras. *Slitting-mill,* (1) Taller donde se cortan planchas de metal en tiras para hacer clavos. (2) Sierra de disco empleada por los joyeros para labrar las piedras preciosas. (3) Sierra múltiple para aserrar tablillas, etc.

Sliver [sliv'-ẹr], *va.* y *vn.* 1. Cortar, romper o romperse en trozos largos, a lo largo. 2. Desgajar, desgajarse, romperse.

Sliver, *s.* 1. Brizna, astilla. *V.* SPLINTER. 2. Torzal, mecha de fibras textiles.

Sloats [slōts], *s. pl.* Teleras de carro.

Slobber, *s.* Baba. *V.* SLAVER.

Slobber [sleb'-ẹr], *va.* Babosear.

Sloe [slō], *s.* Endrina, la fruta del endrino; también, el mismo endrino.

Slogan [slō'-gan], *s.* Grito de combate o de llamada, originalmente de los montañeses de Escocia.

Sloop [slūp], *s.* (Mar.) Balandra, embarcación pequeña. *Sloop-of-war,* (Mar.) Corbeta, embarcación de guerra.

Slop [slep], *va.* 1. Verter, derramar. 2. Verter agua u otro líquido sobre algo; mojar, ensuciar, enlodar.—*vn.* Verterse, derramarse.

Slop, *s.* 1. La mancha que se hace dejando caer algún líquido; lugar mojado. 2. *pl.* Agua sucia; desechos líquidos. 3. *pl.* Atole, u otro alimento líquido (por desprecio): zupia, purrela, aguachirle. *Slop-basin, slop-bowl,* Barreño o receptáculo para aguas sucias. *Slop-jar,* Jarro o tinaja para aguas sucias, particularmente pieza de un juego de tocador. *Slop-pail, slop-bucket,* Cubo o tina para agua sucia.

Slope [slōp], *s.* 1. Sesgo, la oblicuidad o torcimiento de alguna cosa hacia un lado; escotadura. 2. Declive, declivio, descenso, bajada, loma. 3. Escarpa.—*a.* Sesgo, torcido, inclinado, en pendiente.—*adv.* Al sesgo, oblicuamente.

Slope, *va.* 1. Sesgar, cortar o partir en sesgo; formar en declive. 2. Escotar una tela.—*vn.* 1. Inclinarse al horizonte, estar en declive. 2. Ir oblicuamente, moverse en un carril o plano inclinado.

Sloping [slōp'-ing], *a.* Inclinado, en declive.

Slopingly [slōp'-ing-li], *adv.* Sesgadamente, al sesgo.

Sloppiness [slep'-i-nes], *s.* Calidad de mojado y sucio; estado cenagoso.

Slops [sleps], *s. pl.* Equipaje de los marineros. *Slop-room,* Pieza en una embarcación inglesa donde se guardan, despachan y venden ropas y otros efectos. *Slop-work,* Efectos de pacotilla; cualquier trabajo barato.

Sloppy [slep'-i], *a.* 1. Mojado y sucio; lodoso, cenagoso, lleno de lodo o cieno. 2. Hecho de una manera descuidada.

Slosh [slesh], *va.* y *vn.* *V.* SPLASH. —*s.* *V.* SLUSH.

Slot [slet], *s.* 1. (Mec.) Muesca, ranura, canal o hendedura larga y estrecha. (< A.-S. slāt.) 2. Pista, huella de venado. (< islandés.)

Slot, *va.* 1. Ajustar en una ranura. 2. Acanalar, cortar una ranura o muesca.

Sloth [slōth], *s.* 1. Pereza, negligencia, dejadez, flojedad, inercia. 2. Perezoso, un animal arbóreo de la América tropical.

Slothful [slōth'-ful], *a.* Perezoso, tardo, lento; dejado, negligente.

Slothfully [slōth'-ful-i], *adv.* Perezosamente, flojamente, con dejadez.

Slothfulness [slōth'-ful-nes], *s.* Pereza, tardanza, pesadez, haraganería.

Slot-machine [slet-ma-shīn'], *s.* Máquina con ranuras para monedas en que se juega dinero.

Slouch [slauch], *s.* 1. Mirada cabizbaja; inclinación del cuerpo. 2. Patán, rústico, villano.

Slouch, *va.* y *vn.* 1. Estar cabizbajo como un patán o rústico. 2. Poner una cosa más baja o caída y suelta de lo que estaba. *Slouch-hat,* Sombrero gacho o con las alas caídas.

Slough [slau], *s.* Lodazal, el sitio pantanoso y lleno de lodo; (fig.) abismo. *The slough of despond,* El abismo de la desesperación.

Slough [slū], *s.* (E. U.) 1. Pantano; canal de agua, abra llena de cañas. 2. Lodazal.

Slough [sluf], *va.* y *vn.* Echar o ser echado, como el tejido muerto: echar de sí una costra.—*s.* 1. El pellejo suelto o fuera del cuerpo de ciertos animales que lo mudan: en la culebra y en la serpiente se llama camisa y en algunos insectos tela: por extensión se dice también a veces del pellejo humano. 2. Escara de una herida ó úlcera; el tejido muerto separado y desechado de las partes vivas.

Sloughy [slau'-i], *a.* Lodoso, pantanoso.

Sloughy [sluf'-i], *a.* Que tiene tejidos muertos y desechados, o que es propio de ellos.

Sloven [sluv'-n], *s.* Persona desaliñada y desaseada.

Slovenliness [sluv'-n-li-nes], *s.* 1. Desaliño, desaseo en el vestir. 2. Asquerosidad, porquería. 3. Negligencia, descuido, dejadez.

Slovenly [sluv'-n-li], *a.* 1. Desaliñado, desaseado, puerco, sucio. 2. Dejado, descuidado.—*adv.* Desaliñadamente, con desaseo, con dejadez.

Slow [slō], *va.* y *vn.* Retardar, aflojar el paso, diferir; ir más despacio; a menudo con las preposiciones *up* o *down.*—*s.* 1. Tardío, lento, pausado, detenido, tardo en obrar, en moverse o en cualquiera otra cosa. 2. Tardío, tardo, que sucede después de tiempo oportuno. 3. Tardo, lento, torpe, pesado. 4. Tarto, torpe, poco expedito en comprender las cosas o en explicarse. *Slow coach,* Indolente, perezoso, negligente, dejado. *Slow-paced,* Pesado en el andar. *Slow-witted,* Torpe, estúpido. *My watch goes too slow,* Mi reloj atrasa.

Slowly [slō'-li], *adv.* Lentamente, pausadamente, con lentitud.

Slow motion [slō mō'-shun], *s.* Movimiento lento, tardío. *Slow motion camera,* Cámara lenta.

Slowness [slō'-nes], *s.* 1. Lentitud, tardanza, detención. 2. Pesadez o torpeza de entendimiento, negadez. 3. Dilación, retardación, retardo. 4. Deliberación.

Slowworm [slō'-wūrm], *s.* Cecilia, serpiente pequeña.

Slub [slub], *va.* Torcer un poco (torzales de lana) antes de encanillar; ovillar.—*s.* Hilo muy poco retorcido, mechón. (Términos técnicos.)

†**Slubber** [slub'-ẹr], *va.* 1. Hacer alguna cosa de mala gana o con prisa intempestiva, chafallar. 2. Manchar, ensuciar.—*vn.* Estar muy de prisa,

hacer algo muy de prisa y aturdidamente.
Slubber, *s.* Canillero, el que hace canillas o mechones de hilo; ovillador de lana.
Sludge [sluj], *s.* Lodo, cieno.
Slue [slū], *va.* (*pa.* SLUING, *pp.* SLUED). 1. Revirar, mover a un lado como sobre un eje. 2. Volver, girar.—*s.* Giro, vuelta.
Slug [slug], *s.* 1. Haragán, holgazán, zángano. 2. Babosa, caracol que se cría sin concha; también, la larva de un tentredo (mosca de sierra) u otro insecto parecido a la babosa. 3. El pedazo de metal que se mete en algún arma de fuego en lugar de bala. 4. (Impr.) Lingote, tira de metal más gruesa que un renglón.
Slug, *va.* Cargar (un arma de fuego) con trozos de metal en lugar de balas.
Slug, *va.* y *vn.* (Ger.) Dar fuertes puñadas.
Sluggard [slug'-ard], *s.* Haragán, holgazán.
Sluggish [slug'-ish], *a.* Perezoso, flojo, dejado, descuidado, indolente.
Sluggishly [slug'-ish-li], *adv.* Perezosamente, lentamente, con flojedad.
Sluggishness [slug'-ish-nes], *s.* Pereza, flojedad, negligencia, dejadez.
Sluice [slūs], *s.* 1. Canal, acequia, acueducto; azud; compuerta, especie de puerta pequeña en los canales o en las presas de ríos. 2. (Fig.) Salida, la cosa al través de la cual sale o fluye algo.
Sluice, *va.* 1. Mojar. regar, por medio de acequias; lavar la tierra que contiene el mineral en una acequia. 2. Soltar la presa o quitar la compuerta de un canal, acequia, etc.
Sluicy [slūs'-i], *a.* Que fluye en torrente, como el agua luego que se suelta una presa.
Slum [slum], *s.* Barrio bajo y sucio de una población; garito.—*vn.* Visitar los barrios bajos, particularmente cuando se hace por mera curiosidad.
Slumber [slum'-bęr], *vn.* 1. Dormitar, estar medio dormido; (poét.) dormir. 2. Dormirse o descuidarse uno en las obligaciones de su empleo u oficio o en lo que tiene que hacer.
Slumber, *s.* Sueño ligero y tranquilo.
Slumberous [slum'-bęr-us], *a.* Soñoliento, soporífero.
Slump [slump], *vn.* Romper una costra y hundirse en una materia blanda cualquiera, como la nieve; (fam.) salir mal, faltar, hacer bancarrota —*s.* Rompimiento y hundimiento; desplome; mal éxito, quiebra.
Slung, *pret.* y *pp.* del verbo *To* SLING.
Slung-shot [slung'-shot], *s.* Rompecabezas, arma ofensiva de los malhechores.
Slunk, *pret.* y *pp.* del verbo *To* SLINK.
Slur [slūr], *va.* 1. Menospreciar, rebajar, desdorar a alguno. 2. Pasar ligeramente, ocultar. 3. Hacer algo o hablar de una manera descuidada o confusa; juntar palabras o sílabas. 4. (Mús.) Ligar las notas. 5. Manchar, ensuciar.
Slur, *s.* 1. Reparo, observación en desdoro; estigma; borrón o mancha ligera en la reputación. 2. (Mús.) Ligadura, línea, curva (⌢ o ⌣) que indica que las notas han de encadenarse. 3. (Impr.) Porción manchada de una impresión.
Slush [slush], *va.* 1. Ensebar, engrasar con una substancia lubricante. 2. (Alb.) Llenar de argamasa; generalmente con la preposición *up*. 3. Lavar, echando agua sobre un puente o cubierta.—*s.* 1. Materia blanda y mojada, como la nieve que se derrite, o el fango: cieno, lodo blando. 2. Grasa lubricante; pintura para evitar el enmohecimiento.
Slushy [slush'-i], *a.* Cubierto de nieve a medio derretir o de cieno; parecido a estas substancias.
Slut [slut], *sf.* 1. Perra, la hembra del perro. 2. Una mujer sucia o asquerosa; en otro tiempo se aplicaba también a los hombres.
Sluttish [slut'-ish], *a.* Asqueroso, puerco, sucio, desaliñado, despreciable.
Sluttishness [slut'-ish-nes], *s.* Asquerosidad, porquería, suciedad.
Sluttishly [slut'-ish-li], *adv.* Asquerosamente.
Sly [slai], *a.* Astuto, taimado, pícaro, socarrón, disimulado, artificioso, falso, martagón, marrajo. *Sly blade*, Encallecido en astucias, camastrón, gran perillán.
Slyboots [slai'-būts], *s.* (Fam.) Mañuelas, martagón, mátalas-callando, sueco, socarrón; la persona astuta y cauta que sabe manejar diestramente sus negocios.
Slyly [slai'-li], *adv.* Astutamente, disimuladamente, con artificio, con maña, con segunda; a hurtadillas, callandito, bonitamente.
Slyness [slai'-nes], *s.* Mañuela, socarronería, la maña con astucia y bellaquería; disimulo; con segunda o con segunda intención.
Smack [smac], *vn.* 1. Saber, tener algún sabor particular. 2. Oler o tener sabor u olor: dícese de las opiniones, doctrinas, etc. *His language smacks of atheism*, Su lenguaje huele a ateismo o tiene sabor u olor de ateísmo. 3. Saborearse, hacer ruido desuniendo los labios, como después de catar o probar alguna cosa. 4. Besarse mutuamente estrechando los labios.—*va.* Besar, dar un beso.
Smack, *s.* 1. Sabor, gusto. 2. Tintura, conocimiento ligero ó superficial. 3. Gusto, semejanza, resabio, tintura; el residuo que queda de alguna cosa que ha estado unida á otra, después de separarse. 4. Un poco o una cantidad corta de cualquier cosa. 5. La acción de separar los labios haciendo ruido con ellos. 6. Beso fuerte y ruidoso, o que se oye. 7. Manotada. 8. Chasquido de látigo. 9. (Mar.) Esmaque, embarcación pequeña.
Smacker [smak'-ęr], *s.* Beso o golpe con ruido.
Small [smōl], *a.* 1. Pequeño, menudo, chico; corto. 2. Poco; de poco momento, peso o importancia. 3. Falto de amplitud moral ó mental; corto, despreciable, mezquino. 4. Que funciona o que comercia de una manera limitada. 5. Débil, flojo. 6. Tierno, blando; fino, delgado, de poco bulto o volumen. 7. Obscuro, bajo, vulgar, plebeyo. *To cut small*, Hacer pedazos menudos alguna cosa. *Small print*, Carácter de letra muy menuda. *To make small*, Achicar.—*s.* 1. La parte estrecha de cualquiera cosa y en particular del lomo, canto o filo. 2. Cosa o cantidad pequeña.—*adv.* En tono bajo o suave. *Small arms*, Armas blancas. *Small-beer*, Cerveza débil o floja. *Small-clothes*, Calzones cortos. *Small coal*, Carbón menudo, cisco. *Small fry*, Los peces pequeños en general; de aquí, gente menuda o cosas pequeñas. *Small talk*, Conversación sin importancia, vulgaridades. *The small hours*, Las primeras horas de la mañana, la una, las dos, etc. *Small craft*, Conjunto de embarcaciones menores; (fig.) cosas o personas pequeñas en general. *Small pica*, V. PICA. *A small voice*, Una vocecita, una voz delgada (ó suave). *Small wares*, Mercería.
Smallage [smōl'-ęj], *s.* Apio particularmente en estado silvestre.
Smallish [smōl'-ish], *a.* Algo pequeño, corto, menudo.
Smallness [smōl'-nes], *s.* Pequeñez; debilidad.
Small potatoes [smōl po-tē'-tōz], *s. pl.* Algo o alguien de mínima importancia.
Smallpox [smōl'-pex], *s.* Viruelas.
Smalt [smōlt], *s.* Esmalte, un vidrio azul obscuro, teñido por el óxido de cobalto; esmaltín que sirve para pintar.
Smart [smārt], *s.* 1. Escozor, dolor vivo y punzante. 2. Dolor, aflicción. 3. (Vulg.) Bullebulle, el que afecta viveza y actividad; muchacho muy despierto.—*a.* 1. Punzante, agudo, acerbo, agrio, picante. 2. Vivo, eficaz, activo, vivaracho; (E. U.) inteligente, despierto, hábil, de talento, avisado, despejado, ingenioso, despavilado. 3. Agudo, ingenioso, sutil. 4. Mordicante, mordaz, picante. 5. (Ingl.) Elegante, petimetre, a la moda; estimable, gallardo.
Smart, *vn.* 1. Escocer, percibir una sensación muy desagradable parecida á la de una quemadura. 2. Escocer, sentir en el ánimo una impresión desagradable, dolerse. *I will make you smart for it*, Le haré a Vd. arrepentirse.
Smarten [smārt'-n], *va.* Hermosear, embellecer; hacer a uno gallardo, donoso.
Smartly [smārt'-li], *adv.* 1. Agudamente, vivamente, sensiblemente. 2. Agudamente, con agudeza de ingenio, con finura, con delicadeza.
Smartness [smārt'-nes], *s.* 1. Agudeza, vigor. 2. Viveza, vivacidad, perspicacia de ingenio, agudeza, sutileza.
Smash [smash], *va.* y *vn.* 1. Hacer pedazos o añicos; hacer astillas, romper o romperse de golpe; (fam.) hacer bancarrota. 2. Machacar, allanar, aplastar.—*s.* 1. Machacamiento, acto de machacar o romper; se usa a menudo con la prep. *up*; ruina, quiebra. 2. Bebida de licores espirituosos. (< sueco, *smaska*.) *To go to smash*, Arruinarse, quebrar.
Smashup [smash'-up], *s.* 1. Choque o colisión desastrosos. 2. Quiebra total.
Smatter [smat'-ęr], *vn.* 1. Saber una cosa superficialmente y muy por encima. 2. Hablar superficialmente y sin conocimiento.
Smatterer [smat'-ęr-ęr], *s.* El que sabe una cosa superficialmente o a medias.
Smattering [smat'-ęr-ing], *s.* Tintura, conocimiento superficial de una cosa o de varias.

Smear [smīr], *va.* 1. Salpicar, untar, cubrir de una substancia viscosa, emporcar, ensuciar. 2. Calumniar, difamar.—*s.* 1. Mancha, embarradura. 2. Calumnia, difamación.

Smeary [smīr'-ɪ], *a.* Graso; pegajoso.

Smegma [smeg'-ma], *s.* 1. (Med.) Esmegma, secreción sebácea, particularmente de las partes genitales. 2. Jabón y cualquiera cosa que limpia como el jabón.

Smegmatic [smeg-mat'-ic], *a.* (Poco us.) Jabonoso, saponáceo.

Smell [smel], *va.* (*pret.* y *pp.* SMELLED o SMELT.) 1. Oler, percibir con el olfato. 2. Oler, percibir, descubrir, conocer; olfatear, oliscar. *To smell a rat,* Oler el poste. *I will smell him out,* Yo le descubriré.—*vn.* 1. Oler, despedir o echar de sí fragancia o hedor. *It smells good,* Huele bien. 2. Oler, parecerse o tener señas y visos de alguna cosa ordinariamente mala. *To smell of,* Oler a. *To smell strong,* Despedir un olor fuerte.

Smell, *s.* 1. Olfato, sentido del olfato. 2. Olor; perfume. 3. Fragancia o hediondez. 4. Olor, traza, vestigio. *To be offensive to the smell,* Herir, ofender el olfato.

Smeller [smel'-ẹr], *s.* Oledor, el que huele.

Smellfeast [smel'-fīst], *s.* Parásito, gorrista, mogollón.

Smelling [smel'-ing], *s.* El acto de oler. *Smelling-bottle,* Vasito o redomilla para olores. *Smelling salts,* Sales aromáticas. *Sweet-smelling, a.* Oloroso, odorífero. *Foul-smelling, a.* Hediondo, que huele mal.

Smelt, *pret.* y *pp.* del verbo *To* SMELL.

Smelt [smelt], *s.* Esperlán, pez plateado comestible del género Osmerus (o de otro género afín). Osmerus eperlanus o mordax.

Smelt, *va.* Fundir, derretir minerales para extraer el metal.

Smelter [smelt'-ẹr], *s.* Fundidor.

Smew [smiū], *s.* Harla, mergo pequeño del antiguo mundo.

Smift [smift], *s.* (Min.) Mecha de minero.

Smilax [smaɪ'-lax], *s.* 1. Esmílaco o esmílax, planta liliácea y trepadora, oriunda del sur de África; se cultiva mucho para hacer guirnaldas y festones. Myrsophyllum asparagoides. 2. Cualquier planta del género Smilax.

Smile [smaɪl], *vn.* 1. Sonreirse, reirse un poco o levemente. 2. Manifestar alegría o lozanía. *The meadows smile,* Ríen los prados. 3. Favorecer, ser propicio. *Fortune smiles on him,* La fortuna le favorece. 4. Despreciar o no hacer caso de alguna cosa sonriéndose.—*va.* Expresar o efectuar por medio de una sonrisa. *To smile one's thanks,* Dar las gracias con una sonrisa. *To smile at, on* o *upon,* Sonreir a uno, favorecer. *To smile assent,* Consentir con una sonrisa.

Smile, *s.* 1. Sonrisa. 2. Aspecto agradable o risueño. 3. Disposición favorable o propicia; favor, bendición.

Smiling [smaɪl'-ing], *a.* Risueño, sonriente.

Smilingly [smaɪl'-ing-lɪ], *adv.* Con cara risueña, con sonrisa, sonriendo.

Smirch [smẹrch], *va.* 1. Ensuciar, tiznar, mancillar, deslucir. 2. (Fig.) Desdorar, denigrar, difamar, deshonrar.

Smirk [smẹrk], *vn.* Sonreirse con desenvoltura; sonreirse agradablemente, tener cara de risa. *To smirk upon,* Mirar risueño. *Smirking look,* Cara risueña.

Smirker [smẹrk'-ẹr], *s.* El que muestra risa en el semblante.

Smit, *pp.* o *pret.* del verbo *To* SMITE.

Smitch [smich], *s.* (Fam.) Pedacito, partícula.

Smite [smaɪt], *va.* (*pret.* SMOTE o SMIT, *pp.* SMITTEN o SMIT). 1. Herir, golpear. 2. Afligir, castigar. 3. Herir o tocar al alma, mover o excitar algún afecto, ganar el corazón. *She has smitten you,* Te ha encantado o te ha robado el corazón o el alma. *It smites my heart,* Me llega al alma. 4. Quemar o abochornar el calor las tierras o frutos. 5. Arruinar, destruir, asolar. 6. Cortar, partir o romper por medio de un golpe. 7. (Ant.) Matar, quitar la vida.—*vn.* Venir con fuerza repentina; chocar.

Smiter [smaɪt'-ẹr], *s.* El que hiere o aflige; golpeador.

Smith [smith], *s.* Forjador de metales. *Blacksmith,* Herrero. *Smith and farrier,* Herrador, albéitar. *Locksmith,* Cerrajero. *Goldsmith,* Orífice. *Silversmith,* Platero.

Smithereens [smidh-ẹr-īnz'], *s. pl.* (Fam.) Añicos, fragmentos producidos por golpes.

Smithery [smith'-ẹr-ɪ], *s.* 1. Herrería, el arte u oficio del herrero. 2. Herrería, taller en que se funde el hierro o en que se hacen obras de hierro en grueso.

Smitten, *pp.* de *To* SMITE.

Smithy [smith'-ɪ], *s.* Forja, hornaza de herrero o cerrajero.

Smock [smoc], *s.* Camisa de mujer. *Smock-frock,* Blusa de obrero o labriego. *Smock-faced,* De cara afeminada.—*a.* (Des.) Afeminado, parecido a una mujer.

Smog [smog], *s.* Mezcla de niebla y humo propia de algunas grandes ciudades.

Smoke [smōk], *s.* Humo, vapor espeso que exhala lo que se está quemando. *To end in smoke,* Volverse humo, o agua de cerrajas. *Smoke-consumer,* Aparato o útil fumívoro que sirve para consumir más completamente los gases de la combustión. *Smoke-consuming,* Fumívoro. *Smoke-house,* Cuarto cerrado para ahumar o acecinar carnes, pieles, etc. *Smoke-jack,* Torno de asador que se mueve por medio del humo. *Smoke-stack,* Chimenea, cañón por donde pasa el humo (de un vapor, locomotora, etc.). *Smoke-tree,* Arbusto o árbol de adorno (Rhus cotinus) con largos tallos parecidos a plumas; zumaque veneciano.

Smoke, *vn.* 1. Humear, echar de sí humo. 2. Arder, estar encendido. 3. Moverse con velocidad levantando polvo. 4. Oler, descubrir. 5. Fumar, consumir tabaco en cigarro o pipa.—*va.* 1. Ahumar, poner al humo alguna cosa para que se cure; sahumar. 2. Fumar, quemar tabaco en hoja; aspirar el humo del tabaco. 3. Ahumar, ahogar con humo; echar, hacer salir por medio del humo; se usa frecuentemente con la prep. *out.* 4. (Ant.) Oler, descubrir, indagar. *To smoke out,* Expeler a uno con intención de que no vuelva.

Smoke-dry [smōk'-draɪ], *va.* Ahumar, secar al humo.

Smokeless [smōc'-les], *a.* Desahumado; sin humo, que no da humo. *Smokeless powder,* Pólvora sin humo.

Smoker [smōk'-ẹr], *s.* 1. Sahumador; fumador. 2. Caja o aparato con que se echa humo sobre las abejas para aquietarlas. 3. (E. U.) Coche de fumar. 4. (Fam.) Tertulia en que se permite fumar.

Smoke screen [smōk scrīn], *s.* Cortina de humo.

Smoking [smōk'-ing], *s.* Acción de ahumar o de fumar. *Smoking-car* (*smoking-carriage* en Inglaterra), Coche de fumar. *No smoking* (*allowed*), Se prohibe fumar.

Smoking jacket [smōk'-ing jak'-et], *s.* Batín, saco holgado de casa.

Smoky [smōk'-ɪ], *a.* Humeante; humoso.

Smolder, Smoulder [smōl'-dẹr], *vn.* 1. Arder sin llama y humear. 2. Existir en estado latente.

Smooth [smūdh], *a.* 1. Liso, pulido, bruñido, alisado. 2. Llano, igual; uniforme, sin variación; fácil, libre de impedimentos ú obstáculos. 3. Suave, mansa, hablando de la corriente; suave, dulce, delicado, tierno. 4. Lisonjero, halagüeño, adulador, carantoñero. 5. Cortés, afable. 6. (Gram. griega) No aspirado; contrapuesto a *rough.* 7. Que no tiene un sabor acídulo ni astringente; se dice de los licores. *A smooth surface,* Una superficie lisa, igual. *Smooth water,* Agua mansa. *Smoothbore,* Anima lisa. *Smooth-faced,* (1) Barbilampiño, sin barba; (2) alisado; (3) de semblante apacible y sereno. *Smooth-grained,* Que tiene vetas lisas. *Smooth-sliding,* Que se desliza con suavidad e igualdad. *Smooth-paced,* Lo que anda con paso igual. *Smooth-shaven,* Que está rasurado por igual. *Smooth-spoken, smooth-tongued,* De palabras melifluas, lisonjeras.

Smooth, *va.* 1. Allanar, poner llana o igual la superficie de alguna cosa. 2. Alisar, poner lisa alguna cosa. 3. Allanar, facilitar. 4. Pacificar, aquietar; calmar, ablandar, lisonjear. *Smoothing-iron,* Hierro para alisar. *Smoothing-plane,* Cepillo corto.

Smoothly [smūdh'-lɪ], *adv.* 1. Igualmente, con igualdad, sin desigualdad. 2. Lisamente, llanamente. 3. Fácilmente, libremente. 4. Blandamente, inocentemente. 5. Halagüeñamente, con halagos, con blandura, afablemente.

Smoothness [smūdh'-nes], *s.* 1. Lisura, igualdad y lustre de la superficie, llanura. 2. Bruñido, tersura. 3. Suavidad, dulzura o dulzor de las cosas al gusto. 4. Blandura, suavidad o dulzura en el estilo, en el discurso, etc.

Smote [smōt], *pret.* de *To* SMITE.

Smother [smudh'-ẹr], *va.* 1. Ahogar, sofocar, impedir la respiración; también, hacer morir por falta de aire. 2. Ahogar, apagar (fuego, llama). 3. Suprimir, ocultar, disfrazar. 4. Embadurnar, embarrar. 5. Hablando de cocina, encerrar y cocer algo dentro de una masa apretada.—*vn.* 1. Ahogarse, asfixiarse, carecer de respiración. 2. Estar oculto por falta de aire, v. g. un fuego. 3. (Fig.) Hallarse oculto, suprimido.

Smother, *s.* 1. Supresión, el efecto

de suprimir; ahoguío, sofocación. 2. Humareda, polvareda.

Smotheringly [smudh'-ęr-ing-li], *adv.* De un modo que ahoga o capaz de sofocar, ahogando.

Smoulder, *v.* *V.* SMOLDER.

Smouldering [smōl'-dęr-ing], *a.* Lleno de humo sin salida, sofocante.

Smudge [smuj], *va.* 1. Tiznar, manchar con tizne u hollín; ensuciar. 2. (E. U.) Fumigar, ahumar, v. g. para ahuyentar los mosquitos o evitar la escarcha.—*s.* 1. Tizne, hollín; ensuciamiento con una materia seca u hollín. 2. Fuego humoso para ahuyentar los insectos, impedir la escarcha, o acecinar la carne. 3. Raspas de pintura y barniz, que sirven para cubrir los techos de los coches y carros antes de ponerles una cubierta de lona. (Var. de *smutch.*)

Smudgy [smuj'-i], *a.* 1. Tiznado, holliniento, ensuciado. 2. Humeante, v.g. un fumigador, llamado *smudge,* 2ª acep.

Smug [smug], *a.* Atildado, pulido con afectación, nimiamente compuesto y satisfecho de sí mismo.

Smuggle [smug'-l], *va.* 1. Hacer o ejercer el contrabando, matutear, entrar o sacar géneros por alto. 2. Pasar o introducir algo clandestinamente, a escondidas.—*vn.* Hacer contrabando.

Smuggler [smug'-lęr], *s.* Contrabandista, metedor, matutero.

Smuggling [smug'-ling], *s.* Comercio de contrabando, metedurĺa.

Smugly [smug'-li], *adv.* Pulidamente, afectadamente.

Smugness [smug'-nes], *s.* Afectación y nimiedad en el vestir.

Smut [smut], *s.* 1. Tiznón, la mancha que se hace en alguna cosa untándola con tizne; suciedad. 2. Tizón, tizoncillo, enfermedad de las plantas producida por un hongo parásito. 3. Obscenidad, impureza, palabras sucias u obscenas.

Smut, *va.* 1. Tiznar, manchar o señalar con tizne; ensuciar. 2. Atizonar, añublar. 3. Destizonar, quitar el tizón de los granos. 4. (Fig.) Mancillar la reputación, echar un baldón, infamar.—*vn.* Añublarse, atizonarse los trigos.

Smutch [smuch], *va.* Tiznar, manchar con tizne, hollín u otro unto semejante. (< sueco, *smutsa.*)

Smuttily [smut'-i-li], *adv.* 1. Con humo o tizne, suciamente. 2. Impúdicamente, deshonestamente, obscenamente.

Smuttiness [smut'-i-nes], *s.* 1. Tizne, el humo que se pega a las cosas; tiznón, la mancha que deja el tizne. 2. Obscenidad, impureza.

Smutty [smut'-i], *a.* 1. Tiznado, manchado con tizne, hollín o carbón. 2. Humoso: se dice del lugar que contiene humo o donde se esparce. 3. Añublado, atizonado: se dice de los granos que tienen la enfermedad llamada tizón o añublo. 4. Obsceno, impuro.

Snack [snac], *s.* 1. Parte, porción. *To go snacks,* Ir a medias, compartir. 2. Tentempie, refrigerio, una comida ligera.

Snaffle [snaf'-l], *s.* Brida con muserola; bridón, bocado de freno sin camas; se llama también *snaffle-bit.*

Snaffle, *va.* 1. Refrenar, sujetar y reducir al caballo con el freno. 2. Refrenar, contener, reprimir. 3. Ganguear, hablar por la nariz.

Snag [snag], *s.* 1. Nudo en la madera, ramo desgajado, protuberancia. 2. Sobrediente, diente que sale sobre otro. 3. Pitón, punta de las astas del ciervo. 4. (E. U.) En los ríos del Oeste, tronco de un árbol fijo al fondo por un extremo y casi a flor de agua por el otro; de aquí, cualquier obstáculo oculto e ignorado. *To strike a snag,* Chocar contra un tronco sumergido; encontrar un obstáculo no sospechado. *Snag-boat,* Buque de vapor para arrancar árboles fijos en el fondo de un río.

Snagged [snag'-ed], *a.* Lleno de sobredientes; nudoso.

Snaggy [snag'-i], *a.* 1. Lleno de troncos de árbol, v. g. un río. 2. Nudoso, lleno de nudos o tocones (árbol. pantano). 3. Parecido a una rama desgajada, á un nudo o un pitón.

Snail [snêl], *s.* 1. Caracol, molusco gasterópodo. 2. Babosa, caracol gasterópodo sin concha (principalmente en los E. U.). 3. Posma, persona roncera, lerda y pesada. *Snail-clover,* Alfalfa, mielga. *Snail-pace,* Paso de tortuga, de caracol.

Snake [snêk], *s.* 1. Culebra, serpiente; también en sentido figurado. 2. Lagarto, lagartija u otro animal anfibio de forma semejante. *Snake-killer,* (1) Secretario, un ave. (2) *V. Road-runner.*

Snake, *va.* 1. (Fam. E. U.) Tirar de algo por un extremo arrastrándolo por el suelo. 2. Efectuar algo por medio de movimientos parecidos á los de las culebras.—*vn.* Culebrear; embutir, entrañar.

Snakeroot [snêk'-rūt], *s.* (Bot.) Serpentaria. *Virginian snakeroot,* Serpentaria de Virginia, díctamo de Virginia. *Indian snakeroot,* Raíz de serpiente.

Snake's-head [snêcs'-hed], **Snakeweed** [snêc'-wīd], *s.* (Bot.) Bistorta, dragontea, dracúnculo.

Snakewood [snêk'-wud], *s.* Madera medicinal de las Indias Orientales.

Snaky [snêk'-i], *a.* 1. Que pertenece o se asemeja a la culebra; culebrino, serpentino; serpenteando, culebreando, tortuoso, formando eses. 2. Astuto, solapado; insinuante, traidor. 3. (E. U.) Lleno de culebras.

Snap [snap], *va.* 1. Hacer estallar una cosa; dar, apretar, cerrar con golpe o estallido. 2. Romper, destrozar, hacer pedazos o astillas una cosa con ruido y violencia. 3. Agarrar a alguno, echar la mano o la garra, asir de repente y con precipitación; a menudo con la prep. *up.* 4. Interrumpir a uno con petulancia, cortarle la palabra. 5. (Fam.) Fotografiar instantáneamente, y a menudo fotografiar a uno sin que él lo sepa. 6. (E. U.) Lanzar por el aire.—*vn.* 1. Chasquear, dar un chasquido. 2. Estallar una cosa, romperse o quebrarse dando un estallido. 3. Lanzarse rápidamente, como cuando la tensión cesa de repente. 4. Coger de golpe, procurar coger; tirar a morder; por lo común con la prep. *at.* 5. Emitir, o parecer emitir luz; dícese de los ojos. 6. Hablar severa y abruptamente. 7. Fallar, no salir un tiro. *To snap in two,* Quebrar, romper en dos pedazos. *To snap at,* Tirar una mordiscada, tirar a morder o procurar morder. *To snap one's fingers,* Castañetear; burlarse de.

Snap, *s.* 1. Chasquido, sonido rápido y agudo; castañeteo (con los dedos). 2. Estallido, el sonido que hace una cosa al henderse o abrirse de golpe. 3. Corchete, cerrajita, garra que se cierra con chasquido. 4. Mordiscón, mordedura; cierre repentino, como el de las garras de una trampa. 5. Galletica. *V. Ginger-snap.* 6. (Fam.) Vigor de carácter o de estilo; energía. 7. Período corto (de frío).—*a.* Hecho o ejecutado repentinamente, sin consideración o sin demora. *Snap-shot,* (1) Disparo hecho rápidamente, sin apuntar. (2) Fotografía tomada instantáneamente, sin preparación.

Snapdragon [snap'-drag-un], *s.* 1. Hierba becerra, cualquier especie del antirrino. Antirrhinum. 2. Tenazas de vidriero. 3. Juego que consiste en coger con los dedos pasas, etc., que se ponen en aguardiente ardiendo.

Snapper [snap'-ęr], *s.* 1. Mordedor. 2. Pez comestible de gran tamaño del género Lutjanus (u otro afín) que se halla en el Golfo de México. 3. *V. Snapping turtle.* *Snappers,* Castañuelas, castañetas.

Snapping [snap'-ing], *s.* Acción del verbo *snap* en cualquiera de sus acepciones. *Snapping turtle,* Gran tortuga voraz, particularmente la Chelydra serpentina, común en la América del Norte.

Snappish [snap'-ish], *a.* 1. Mordaz; regañón, agrio, mohino, pendenciero. 2. Arisco; pronto o dispuesto a morder, como un perro.

Snappishly [snap'-ish-li], *adv.* Mordazmente; agriamente, con aspereza.

Snappishness [snap'-ish-nes], *s.* Aspereza, sequedad o despego en el trato.

Snare [snār], *s.* 1. Cepo, lazo, buitrón, trampa para coger la caza y los animales monteses. 2. Lazo, garlito, celada, asechanza para ofuscar y engañar a una persona. 3. Trampa, petardo, la apariencia engañosa con que se deslumbra o se burla a alguno. 4. Tirante para templar un tambor. *Snare-drum,* Tambor con tirantes de cuerda.

Snare, *va.* Enmarañar, enredar, tender trampas o lazos.—*vn.* Usar de trampas o cepos.

Snarl [snārl], *vn.* Regañar, dar muestras de enfado, gruñir entre dientes.—*s.* Regaño; gruñido entre dientes; (fam.) contienda, riña.

Snarl, *va.* y *vn.* 1. Enredar, enmarañar; enredarse, enmarañarse; confundir. 2. Embutir, estampar (artículos huecos de metal).—*s.* 1. Nudo, hilo enredado; cabellos desgreñados; complicación, enredo. 2. (Fam.) Riña, escaramuza. 3. Nudo en la madera.

Snarler [snārl'-ęr], *s.* Regañón, el que tiene costumbre de regañar.

Snarly [snārl'-i], *a.* Enredoso, insidioso.

Snatch [snach], *va.* 1. Arrebatar, coger o tomar alguna cosa con precipitación. 2. Agarrar, echar la mano o la garra, asir de repente. 3. Arrebatar, quitar o tomar con violencia. 4. Transportar o llevar de una parte a otra con precipitación.—*vn.* 1. Procurar agarrar o arrebatar. 2. Tirar á morder, tirar un mordisco.

Snatch, *s.* 1. El acto de echar la garra o agarrar. 2. Arrebatamiento, la acción de arrebatar. 3. Arrebatiña, el acto de arrojarse muchos en confusión a coger algo. 4. Una pequeña porción de cualquier cosa; un bocado, hablando de comida; un pequeño espacio o intervalo, hablando de tiempo. 5. Respuesta evasiva.

Snatcher [snach'-ẹr], *s.* Arrebatador.

Snatchingly [snach'-ing-li], *adv.* Arrebatadamente, precipitadamente.

Sneak [snīk], *vn.* 1. Venir o irse a la sordina, a cencerros tapados o secretamente. 2. Arrastrar o andar arrastrando por la tierra. 3. Obrar con bajeza o ruindad. 4. Ratear. *To sneak along,* Andar cabizbajo.

Sneaker [snīk'-ẹr], *s.* 1. El que obra con bajeza. 2. (Prov. Ingl.) Tacita de ponche u otra bebida.

Sneaking [snīk'-ing], *a.* 1. Furtivo, a hurtadillas, ratero; servil, bajo, vil. 2. Mantenido o concebido secretamente. *A sneaking fondness,* Afición que se guarda secreta.

Sneakingly [snīk'-ing-li], *adv.* Servilmente, con bajeza; rateramente.

Sneakingness [snīk'-ing-nes], *s.* Bajeza, lisonja baja; vileza, ruindad.

Sneak thief [snīk thīf], *s.* Ratero, ladrón de poca monta.

Sneck, Snecket [snec, snek'-et], *s.* Colanilla, pasadorcillo, aldaba de puerta. *Sneck-drawer,* Ladrón; persona dolosa.

Sneer [snīr], *vn.* 1. Mirar o hablar con desprecio. 2. Fisgarse o burlarse sonriéndose.

Sneer, *s.* 1. Mirada de desprecio. 2. Fisga, risa falsa o burlona, mofa, escarnio.

Sneerer [snīr'-ẹr], *s.* Mofador, fisgón, escarnecedor.

Sneering [snīr'-ing], *a.* Burlón, mofador, escarnecedor.—*s.* Escarnio, rechifla.

Sneeringly [snīr'-ing-li], *adv.* Con desprecio; escarneciendo; con aire desdeñoso.

Sneeze [snīz], *vn.* Estornudar, dar un estornudo.

Sneeze, *s.* Estornudo.

Sneezing [snīz'-ing], *s.* Estornudo, acción de estornudar. *Sneezing-powder,* Cebadilla.

Snick [snic], *va.* (Esco.) Cortar (como con tijeras).—*s.* (Prov. Ingl.) Corte pequeño, tijeretada. *Snick and snee, snick or snee,* (Ant.) Riña a navajazos o cuchilladas; también, jocosamente, un cuchillo.

Snicker [snik'-ẹr], **Snigger** [snig'-ẹr], *vn.* Reirse tontamente o con desprecio; dar risotadas.

Snide [snaid], *a.* (Ger.) Fraudulento, engañoso, socarrón, bellaco.

Sniff [snif], *va.* 1. Atraer alguna cosa con el aliento por medio de inhalaciones rápidas y cortas. 2. Dar un respingo, como expresión de desprecio o desdén.—*vn.* Resollar con fuerza hacia adentro; oler; sorberse los mocos; algunas veces como expresión de sospecha, desprecio o resentimiento.—*s.* 1. Acción de respirar, o aspirar prontamente; olfateo rápido. 2. Lo que se aspira oliendo o respirando prontamente.

Sniffle [snif'-l], *s.* Lloriqueo, moqueo.—*vn.* Lloriquear, moquear.

Sniggle [snig'-l], *vn.* (Ingl.) Pescar anguilas en presa; entrampar, enmarañar.

Snip [snip], *va.* Tijeretear, dar tijeretadas; cortar con tijeras. *To snip off,* Cortar de un golpe con tijeras.

Snip, *s.* 1. Tijeretada. 2. Pedazo pequeño; cosa o persona pequeña. *A snip of a girl,* Una muchachita. 3. Parte, porción.

Snipe [snaip], *s.* 1. Agachadiza, ave zancuda del género Gallinago; gallina de agua. 2. (Poco us.) Zote, zopenco.

Sniper [snaip'-ẹr], *s.* Tirador o cazador emboscado.

Snipper [snip'-ẹr], *s.* El que tijeretea o corta con tijeras.

Snippet [snip'-et], *s.* 1. Parte o porción pequeña; pitanza. 2. Gallineta pequeña; (lo usan los ingleses en la India y África).

Snivel [sniv'-l], *s.* Moquita, el moco líquido que destila de la nariz.

Snivel, *vn.* 1. Moquear, echar mocos. 2. Llorar como una criatura. 3. Jeremiquear, hacer pucheros. (Mex.) Jirimiquear.

Sniveller [sniv'-l-ẹr], *s.* 1. Lloraduelos, el que es muy llorón. 2. El que es mocoso o echa muchos mocos.

Snivelly [sniv'-l-i], *a.* Que tiene moco; llorón, que hace pucheros.

Snob [snob], *s.* Esnob o snob, persona ignorante y jactanciosa.

Snobbery [snob'-ẹr-i], *s.* Esnobismo.

Snobbish [snob'-ish], *a.* Esnob, ignorante y jactancioso.

Snobbishness [snob'-ish-ness], *s.* Esnobismo, ignorancia jactanciosa.

Snood [snūd], *s.* 1. (Esco.) Cintillo, cinta para la cabellera de que usaron las jóvenes solteras escocesas; (emblema de la virginidad). 2. (Dial.) Sedal (Prov. sotileza), trozo de crin o hilo de tripa para asegurar un anzuelo. *V.* Snell.

Snooze [snūz], *vn.* (Fam.) Dormitar, dormir la siesta; estar amodorrado, soñoliento.—*s.* (Fam.) Sueño ligero.

Snore [snōr], *va.* Pasar (el tiempo) roncando.—*vn.* Roncar, hacer ruido con el resuello cuando se duerme.

Snore, *s.* Ronquido.

Snorer [snōr'-ẹr], *s.* Roncador, el que ronca.

Snoring [snōr'-ing], *s.* Ronquido.

Snorkel [snōr'-kl], *s.* Doble tubo de respiración para submarinos. *Snorkel pen,* Pluma fuente que se llena de tinta mediante un tubo aspirante.

Snort [snōrt], *va.* y *vn.* Resoplar, bufar como un caballo fogoso.

Snot [snot], *s.* (Bajo) Moco que sale de la nariz.

Snotty [snot'-i], *a.* (Bajo) Mocoso, lleno de mocos; sucio.

Snout [snaut], *va.* Proveer de hocico, boquerel o embocadura.—*s.* 1. Hocico, el morro de los animales, y en estilo burlesco se aplica también a las personas. 2. Jeta u hocico de puerco. 3. Trompa de elefante. 4. Cañón de un fuelle, tobera; boquerel de manguera, embocadura de un cañón. *Snout-beetle,* Gorgojo. *Snout-ring,* Narigón para puercos.

Snow [snō], *s.* 1. Nieve, vapor condensado por el frío y resuelto en copos blancos. 2. Algo que se parece a la nieve. 3. Nieves, nevada, nevasca. *Snowbird,* (1) Pinzón de las nieves, pájaro americano que vuela en bandadas durante el invierno. Junco hyemalis. (2) *V. Snow-bunting. Snow-blind,* Cegado por la reverberación de la luz sobre la nieve. *Snow-blindness,* Ceguera causada por la reverberación de la luz sobre la nieve. *Snow-broth,* Agua de nieve o de cualquier líquido muy frío. *Snow-bunting,* Verderón de las nieves, pájaro de los fringílidos; el macho en la estación de la cría es blanco de nieve con manchas negras. Plectrophenax nivalis. *Snow-capped* [capt], Coronado de nieve, con la cima cubierta de nieve. *Snow-drift,* Montón, masa de nieve acumulada por el viento. *Snow-plough,* Limpianieves (de ferrocarril). *Snow-shed,* Guardaaludes, estructura de maderos construída sobre la vía férrea para protegerla contra los derrumbamientos de masas de nieve desde las alturas vecinas. *Snow-shoe,* Zueco, calzado para andar sobre la nieve. *V.* Skee. *Snowslide, snowslip,* Alud, avalancha de nieve. *Snow-storm,* Nevasca, nevada, nevisca; borrasca de nieve.

Snow, *vn.* Nevar, caer nieve.—*va.* 1. Cubrir, obstruir, detener o aprisionar con nieve; se usa con *in, over, under,* o *up.* 2. Dejar caer como nieve; nevar.

Snowball [snō'-bōl], *va.* Lanzar bolas de nieve.—*s.* Pella o pelota de nieve.

Snowbound [snō'-baund], *a.* Bloqueado o incomunicado por la nieve.

Snowdrop [snō'-drop], *s.* (Bot.) Campanilla blanca; flor de la leche, planta de las amarilídeas. Galanthus nivalis. *Snowdrop-tree,* Árbol pequeño del género Halesia.

Snowfall [snō'-fōl], *s.* Nevada.

Snowflake [snō-flêk], *s.* 1. Copo de nieve. 2. Verderol de las nieves. 3. (Bot.) Campanilla.

Snowshoe [snō'-shū], *s.* Raqueta de nieve.

Snowsuit [snō'-siūt], *s.* Traje-pantalón (generalmente infantil) que protege contra la nieve y el frío.

Snow-white [snō'-hwait], *a.* Nevado, blanco como la nieve.

Snowy [snō'-i], *a.* 1. Nevoso, que frecuentemente tiene nieve. 2. De nieves, cargado de nieve, dispuesto á nevar. 3. Nevado, blanco como la nieve. 4. Puro, sin mancha.

Snub [snub], *va.* 1. Desairar, acoger mal, tratar con aspereza. 2. Reprender, reñir, regañar. 3. Parar de repente.

Snub, *s.* 1. Represión, repulsa, desaire. 2. Nariz chata.—*a.* Chato; corto y ancho; dícese de la nariz. *Snub-nosed,* El que tiene la nariz roma y ancha.

Snuff [snuf], *s.* 1. Moco o pavesa de candela y la misma candela cuando está casi toda concluída. 2. El olor que despide de sí una cosa. 3. Tabaco en polvo, polvo, polvillo; rapé. 4. (Vulg.) Refunfuñadura. *Snuff-taker,* Tomador de rapé.

Snuff, *va.* 1. Atraer o introducir una cosa en la nariz con el aliento. *To snuff up,* Tomar por la nariz. 2. Oler, percibir el olor de alguna cosa. 3. Despabilar, limpiar o quitar la pavesa o pábilo a la vela.—*vn.* Resoplar hacia adentro, (vulg.) sorberse los mocos. *V. To* Sniff.

Snuffbox [snuf'-box], *s.* Caja de tabaco en polvo o de rapé; tabaquera.

Snuffer [snuf'-ẹr], *s.* 1. Despabilador, el que despabila. 2. *pl.* Despabiladeras, las tijeras con que se despabila o quita el pábilo a la luz.

Snuffiness [snuf'-i-nes], *s.* Condición de lo que está cubierto de tabaco o rapé.

Snuffle [snuf'-l], *vn.* Ganguear, hablar gangoso, hablar por las narices.—*s.* 1. Gangueo, acción de ganguear. 2. *pl.* Romadizo, catarro nasal.

Snuffy [snuf'-i], *a.* Cubierto de tabaco; que huele a rapé.

Snug [snug], *a.* 1. Abrigado estrecha y cómodamente; bien puesto, lindo, bonito. 2. Estrecho o compacto; ajustado, con lugar suficiente pero no demasiado; conveniente, cómodo, acomodado.—*s.* (Mec.) Tope, reborde.

Snuggery [snug'-ẹr-i], *s.* (Fam.) Pieza o habitación cómoda y bien arreglada; en las fondas inglesas, pieza inmediata al mostrador de licores.

Snuggle [snug'-l], *vn.* Dormir abrigado.

So [sō], *adv.* 1. Así, del mismo modo que, así como, por lo mismo; por tanto, por consiguiente; a causa de, así pues; lo mismo que. 2. Tal, tan o tanto, tan . . . como, tanto como; correlativo de *as.* 3. De modo o de manera que. 4. Por tanto, por lo cual, por cuya razón. 5. Con tal que, con esta condición o bajo la condición de. 6. A este punto, a este tiempo; entonces; a tal punto, de modo que, tan bien como. 7. Casi, poco más o menos. 8. Lo, ello, eso; (se emplea para evitar la repetición de una voz o de una frase). 9. Sea, así sea; bien, bueno. 10. (Fam.) ¿Verdad, de veras? (por elipsis en vez de *is it so?*).—*conj.* Bien, supuesto que. *So as to,* De manera que. *So much,* Tanto. *So much as,* Siquiera, a lo menos. *So, then,* Con que, de modo que. *So that,* De suerte que, de modo que, de tal manera que. *So be it,* Amen, así sea, quiéralo Dios. *And so forth,* Y así de lo demás, y todo lo demás. *If it be so that,* Si fuese así, si fuese verdad que. *So much as,* Por mucho que. *So so,* Así, así, tal cual, medianamente; bien bien o bueno bueno, como exclamación para expresar que se ha concluído una cosa o que se sabe algo. *Do you so?* ¿Hace Vd. eso? *They are not so,* No lo son, no son así. *If so,* Si así es, o de ese modo. *I hope so; I think so,* Así lo espero; lo creo. *How so?* ¿Cómo es eso? *Why so?* ¿Por qué así? *So-called,* Llamado así; seudo (delante de un nombre), supuesto. *So much for,* Hé aquí lo que es; hé ahí. *So far,* Hasta aquí, hasta ahí; tan lejos. (*Mr.*) *So and so,* Señor Fulano, fulano de tal. *Be he never so powerful,* Por poderoso que sea. *If ever so little,* Por poco que.—*inter.* ¡So! (para que se paren las caballerías ó vacas).

Soak [sōk], *va.* 1. Empapar, remojar, poner en remojo alguna cosa para que se empape. 2. Empapar, mojar, humedecer del todo, regar. 3. Chupar o embeber en sí por los poros; absorber. 4. Beber con exceso.—*vn.* 1. Remojarse, estar puesto en remojo. 2. Calarse, introducirse algún líquido en un cuerpo poroso: con *in, into* o *through.* 3. Beborrotear, empinar el codo.

Soak, *s.* 1. Procedimiento o acto de empapar, remojo. 2. El líquido en que se empapa alguna cosa. 3. (Fam.) Bebedor, borrachón, zampacuartillos; orgía en que se bebe mucho.

Soakage [sōk'-ẹj], *s.* Remojo, acción de remojar o remojarse; merma, cantidad de líquido que se rezuma y se pierde.

Soaker [sōk'-ẹr], *s.* 1. El o lo que empapa o remoja. 2. (Fam.) Borrachón de vicio.

Soap [sōp], *s.* Jabón, pasta o masa que sirve para lavar y blanquear la ropa y otras cosas; un compuesto cualquiera de un ácido grasiento y una base. *Soap-ashes,* Las cenizas que quedan después de hacer jabón. *Soap-ball,* Jaboncillo, bola de jabón. *Soap-boiler,* Jabonero; caldera para jabón. *Soap-bubble,* Ampolla de jabón. *Soap-earth,* V. STEATITE. *Soap-house,* Jabonería. *Soap-maker,* Jabonero. *Soap-suds,* Jabonaduras.

Soap, *va.* Jabonar, o enjabonar, lavar con jabón.

Soap opera [sōp ōp'-ẹr-a], *s.* Comedia sentimental transmitida periódicamente por radio o televisión en capítulos sucesivos, dedicada a las amas de casa.

Soapstone [sōp'-stōn], *s.* Esteatita, galaxía; jaboncillo, jabón de sastre.

Soapwort [sōp'-wūrt], *s.* (Bot.) Saponaria.

Soapy [sōp'-i], *a.* Jabonoso, saponáceo, que tiene las cualidades del jabón.

Soar [sōr], *vn.* 1. Remontarse, elevarse en el aire. 2. Remontarse, encumbrarse, elevarse, sublimarse; aspirar, anhelar. *Soaring style,* Estilo muy elevado o sublime.—*s.* Vuelo o remonte de las aves hacia lo alto.

Sob [sob], *s.* Sollozo, suspiro.

Sob, *vn.* Sollozar, suspirar.

Sober [sō'-bẹr], *a.* 1. Cuerdo, sano en su juicio, sensato; sereno, con el ánimo tranquilo; de sangre fría. 2. Grave, serio, sabio, modesto. 3. Sobrio, templado, moderado, arreglado, especialmente en el beber. 4. Sobrio, no embriagado. 5. Obscuro, sombrío, de color apagado. *To get* o *grow sober,* Recobrar la sobriedad; volverse sensato y formal; no beber más. *In sober earnest,* De veras, con seriedad, formalmente. *The sober plumage of a wren,* El plumaje sombrío de un troglodita.

Sober, *va.* Desemborrachar, sacar a uno del estado de borracho; de aquí, poner grave, serio, o pensativo.—*vn.* Volverse sobrio, cuerdo, moderado, sensato. *To sober down,* Serenar o serenarse; hacer volver o volverse cuerdo; sosegar, sosegarse.

Soberly [sō'-bẹr-li], *adv.* Sobriamente, con moderación o templanza; juiciosamente.

Soberness [sō'-bẹr-nes], **Sobriety** [so-brai'-e-ti], *s.* 1. Sobriedad, templanza; moderación, cordura. 2. Seriedad, gravedad. 3. Calma, sangre fría.

Socage [soc'-ẹj], *s.* (Der. feudal) La tenencia, ocupación o posesión de alguna tierra en censo, foro o por un cánon, o cualquier otro servicio determinado.

Soccer [sok'-ẹr], *s.* Fútbol, balompié.

Sociable [sō'-shi-a-bl], *a.* Sociable, amigable, familiar, comunicativo.

Sociability [sō-shi-a-bil'-i-ti], **Sociableness** [sō'-shi-a-bl-nes], *s.* Sociabilidad, franqueza.

Sociably [sō'-shi-a-bli], *adv.* Sociablemente, francamente, amigablemente.

Social [sō'-shal], *a.* 1. Social, sociable, afable, franco. 2. Social, perteneciente a la sociedad. 3. Organizado para vivir en sociedad, como una raza o pueblo. 4. (Zool.) Social, que vive en comunidad; p. ej. las abejas, hormigas o avispas: agregado, compuesto, colonial.

Socialism [sō'-shal-izm], *s.* Socialismo, sistema que se propone reconstruir la sociedad sobre nuevas bases, sustituyendo la asociación a la competencia, y a la lucha de los intereses; se diferencia del comunismo.

Socialist [sō'-shal-ist], *a.* y *s.* Socialista, partidario del socialismo.

Socialistic [sō-shal-ist'-ic], *a.* Socialista, perteneciente al socialismo.

Socialization [sō-shal-i-zê'-shun], *s.* Socialización.

Socialize [sō'-shal-aiz], *s.* Socializar.

Socialized medicine [sō'-shal-aizd med'-i-sin], *s.* Medicina estatal.

Social science [sō'-shal sai'-ens], *s.* Ciencia social.

Social security [sō'-shal sẹ-kiū'-ri-ti], *s.* Seguro social.

Social service [sō'-shal ser'-vis], **social work** [sō'-shal wūrk], *s.* Servicio social, servicio de beneficencia.

Social worker [sō'-shal wūrk'-ẹr], *s.* Asistente social.

Society [so-sai'-e-ti], *s.* 1. Sociedad, la unión de los hombres entre sí formada por la naturaleza o por las leyes. 2. Sociedad, academia, junta o reunión para cultivar o promover las ciencias o las artes. 3. Compañía, sea para objetos de comercio o para otra cosa. 4. Compañía, trato amistoso o civil; visita o tertulia en las casas. *Fashionable society,* La buena, la alta sociedad.

Sociological [so-shi-o-loj'-ic-al], *a.* Sociológico.

Sociologist [so-shi-ol'-o-jist], *s.* Sociólogo.

Sociology [so-shi-ol'-o-ji], *s.* Sociología, ciencia que estudia las leyes de la evolución y organización de la sociedad.

Sock [soc], *s.* 1. Calcetín, escarpín, media calceta. 2. Zueco, especie de calzado que usaban los cómicos antiguos. 3. Reja de arado, particularmente de quita y pon.

Socket [sek'-et], *s.* Cualquier hueco en que encaja alguna cosa; cuenca, encaje, contera; el cañón de candelero donde se mete la vela, y la arandela o cazoleta del mismo cañón. *Socket of the eye,* Cuenca del ojo. *Socket of a tooth,* Alvéolo de un diente. *Socket of the capstan,* (Mar.) Concha de cabrestante.

Socratic, Socratical [so-crat'-ic, al], *a.* Socrático, lo perteneciente o relativo a Sócrates.

Sod [sod], *va.* (*pret.* SODDED, *ger.* SODDING). Cubrir de césped un terreno.—*s.* Césped, turba, terrón.

Soda [sō'-da], *s.* Sosa, soda; carbonato u óxido de sodio; sal soda. *Soda-fountain,* Fuente de agua de soda. *Soda-water,* Agua de soda, la cargada de gas ácido carbónico y de un poquito de sosa.

Soda cracker [sō'-da crak'-ẹr], *s.* Galleta de soda.

Sodality [so-dal'-i-ti], *s.* Cofradía, hermandad.

Sodden [sed'-n], *va.* Mojar, empapar con agua, saturar.—*vn.* Empaparse, mojarse; ponerse blanda o corrompida una cosa.

Sodden, *pp.* del verbo *To* SEETHE. 1. Mojado, empapado en agua. 2. Que parece cocido o medio cocido.

Sodden-witted [sed'-n-wit-ed], *a.* Débil, bobo, tonto.
Sodic [sō'-dic], *a.* (Quím.) Perteneciente al sodio; término poco usado.
Sodium [sō'-di-um], *s.* Sodio, elemento metálico color de plata y alcalino.
Sodomy [sed'-ǫm-i], *s.* Sodomía, delito contrario á las leyes de la naturaleza.
Soever [so-ev'-ęr], *adv.* Que sea; quiera, por o por más. Esta voz hace siempre relación á un pronombre o adverbio que está en la misma frase. *What great thing soever,* Cualquier acción señalada que. *Whosoever,* Quienquiera. *Wheresoever,* Donde quiera. *Howsoever,* Como quiera, de cualquier modo que sea. *Which way soever,* Por donde quiera, de cualquier modo que sea.
Sofa [sō'-fa], *s.* Sofá, canapé ancho y cómodo.
Soft [sōft], *a.* 1. Blando, suave al tacto, mole, suavecito; dúctil, maleable, flexible, que cede fácilmente. 2. Liso, dulce y suave al tacto. 3. Melodioso, de sonido débil y grato al oído; no fuerte ni áspero. 4. Benigno, tierno, blando; delicado, sensible a la impresión del aire. 5. Pastoso, jugoso, cuando se habla de la suavidad y blandura de una cosa. 6. Atento, cortés, obsequioso; apacible; fácil, dócil. 7. De matices delicados, templado; no reluciente ni demasiado vivo. 8. Afeminado. 9. Dulce, sin sales minerales, que puede disolver el jabón: aplícase al agua. 10. (Gram.) Sibilante; sonante, vocal ó fuerte. 11. Bituminoso: dícese de la hulla en contraposición al carbón de piedra. *A soft skin,* Un cutis suave. *Soft iron,* Hierro dulce ó maleable. *A soft voice,* Una voz dulce, suave, baja. *A soft answer turneth away wrath,* Una respuesta dulce disipa la ira. *Soft water,* Agua dulce.—*inter.* ¡Poco a poco! ¡quedo, quedito! ¡despacio!—*adv.* (Des.) Blandamente, suavemente, flexiblemente.
Soft-boiled [sōft-beild'], *a.* Pasado por agua. *Soft-boiled eggs,* Huevos tibios, huevos pasados por agua.
Soft coal [sōft cōl], *s.* Carbón bituminoso.
Soften [sōf'-n], *va.* 1. Ablandar, reblandecer, poner blanda ó suave una cosa dura ó tiesa. 2. Mitigar, templar, amansar, suavizar. 3. Enternecer o mover a compasión; aplacar al que está enojado. 4. Enervar, afeminar.—*vn.* 1. Ablandarse, reblandecerse. 2. Templarse, amansarse, enternecerse.
Softener [sōf'-n-ęr], **Softner** [sōf'-nęr], *s.* 1. El ó lo que ablanda. 2. El que templa, amansa o aplaca a uno. 3. Brocha ancha para casar ó amortiguar los colores.
Softening [sōf'-n-ing], *pa.* del verbo SOFTEN.—*s.* Reblandecimiento; blandura; enternecimiento; suavidad.
Softish [sōft'-ish], *a.* Blandito, blandujo.
Softly [sōft'-li], *adv.* Blandamente, callandito, boniticamente, suavemente, tranquilamente, sin ruido; lentamente, con lentitud, paso a paso. *Speak softly,* Hable Vd. bajo.
Softness [sōft'-nes], *s.* 1. Blandura, la calidad de las cosas blandas. 2. Blandura, dulzura, afabilidad en el trato. 3. Complacencia, deferencia, atención para con los deseos de los demás. 4. Afeminación, pusilanimidad.
Soft-pedal [sōft-ped'-al], *va.* (vul.) Reprimir, suavizar.
Soft-soap [soft-sōp'], *va.* (vul.) Dar coba, halagar con fines mezquinos.
Softwood [sōft'-wud], *s.* 1. Madera blanda. 2. Madera de árbol conífero.
Soggy [seg'-i], *a.* Empapado en agua; húmedo y pesado; mojado.
Soil [seil], *va.* 1. Ensuciar, emporcar, manchar. 2. Abonar, estercolar, engrasar las tierras.
Soil, *va.* Alimentar con verde en un corral o cercado; purgar con alimento verde. (< Fr. *souler,* llenar.)
Soil, *s.* 1. Terreno, la tierra considerada repecto de sus cualidades vegetativas. 2. Región. *Native soil,* El país natal. *Soil good for wheat,* Terreno a propósito para trigo. 3. Suciedad, mancha, porquería. 4. Mancha, borrón en la fama de alguno. 5. Abono, estiércol.
Soiling [seil'-ing], *s.* 1. Ensuciamento. 2. Alimento verde, alcacer para las bestias.
Soirée [swa-rē'], *s.* Tertulia. (Fr.)
Sojourn [sō'-jūrn o so-jūrn'], *vn.* Residir o morar en un paraje o lugar por algún tiempo.
Sojourn, *s.* Morada o residencia casual o por algún tiempo.
Sojourner [sō'-jūrn-ęr], *s.* Morador, residente temporal, transeunte.
Soke [sōc], *s.* 1. Un privilegio de exención de ciertos servicios concedido a algunos arrendatarios. 2. El derecho de jurisdicción que algunos señores tenían para castigar los delitos cometidos en sus posesiones.
Sol [sel o sōl], *s.* 1. Sueldo, moneda de cobre de Francia; sol, moneda de plata del Perú. 2. [sōl] Sol, nota de música. 3. [sel] El sol, dios del sol.
Solace [sel'-ęs], *va.* Solazar, divertir; consolar; recrear, alegrar.—*vr.* *To solace one's self,* Consolarse, solazarse, recrearse, divertirse.
Solace, *s.* Consuelo, alivio, recreo, complacencia.
Solanaceous [sel-a-nē'-shus], *a.* Solanáceo, perteneciente a la familia de plantas que incluye el tomate, la patata, el tabaco, etc.
Solar [sō'-lar], *a.* Solar, relativo al sol. *Solar system,* Sistema solar. *Solar year,* Año solar.
Solar battery [sō'-lar bat'-ęr-i], *s.* Batería solar.
Solarium [so-lē'-ri-um], *s.* Solana, pieza para tomar el sol.
Solar plexus [sō'-lar plec'-sus], *s.* (Anat.) Plexo solar.
Sold [sōld], *pret.* y *pp.* del verbo TO SELL. *Sold out,* Agotado, vendido en su totalidad.
Soldan [sel'-dan], *s.* (Ant.) Sultán, gran señor, el emperador de los turcos.
Solder [sed'-ęr o sel'-dęr], *va.* Soldar, pegar y unir con metal.
Solder, *s.* Soldadura, el metal a propósito para soldar.
Solderer [sed'-ęr-ęr], *s.* Soldador, el que tiene el oficio de soldar.
Soldering [sed'-ęr-ing], *s.* Soldadura, acción de soldar. *Soldering-iron,* Soldador, el instrumento con que se suelda.
Soldier [sōl'-jęr], *s.* 1. Soldado, soldado raso. 2. Militar, el que profesa la milicia; también guerrero experto, valiente, o esforzado. *A foot-soldier,* Soldado de a pie o de infantería.
Soldier-like [sōl'-jęr-laic], **Soldierly** [sōl'-jęr-li], *a.* Soldadesco, marcial, militar, perteneciente a los soldados.
Soldiership [sōl'-jęr-ship], *s.* 1. Soldadesca, el ejercicio y la profesión de soldado. 2. La conducta de los soldados. 3. Talentos militares.
Soldiery [sōl'-jęr-i], *s.* Soldadesca, el conjunto de los soldados.
Sole [sōl], *va.* Solar, echar suelas a los zapatos. *To half-sole,* Poner o echar medias suelas.
Sole, *s.* 1. Planta del pie; suela del zapato. 2. Lenguado, pez del género Solea de la familia de los pleuronéctidos. 3. Suelo, la superficie inferior de cualquiera cosa que toca la tierra. *Sole of a gun-carriage,* Solera de cureña. *Sole of the rudder,* Zapata del timón.—*a.* 1. Unico, solo. 2. (For.) Soltero, soltera. *A sole proprietor,* Unico propietario. *The sole support of a numerous family,* El unico sostén de una numerosa familia.
Solecism [sel'-ę-sizm], *s.* 1. (Gram.) Solecismo, error en la construcción o sintaxis. 2. Una falta cualquiera, incongruencia.
Solecistic, Solecistical [sel-e-sis'-tic, al], *a.* Incongruo, incongruente, que falta a las reglas de la sintaxis.
Solecize [sel'-e-saiz], *vn.* Cometer solecismos.
Sole-leather [sōl'-ledh-ęr], *s.* Suela, cuero de suela.
Solely [sōl'-li], *adv.* Unicamente, solamente.
Solemn [sel'-em], *a.* 1. Solemne, grave. 2. Augusto, majestuoso, grave, serio, circunspecto.
Solemness [sel'-em-nes], *s.* Seriedad, gravedad, carácter o tono solemne.
Solemnity [so-lem'-ni-ti], *s.* 1. Solemnidad, pompa. 2. Solemnidad, rito, ceremonia, fiesta. 3. Gravedad, seriedad.
Solemnization [sel-em-ni-zē'-shun], *s.* Solemnización, celebración, celebridad.
Solemnize [sel'-em-naiz], *va.* Solemnizar, celebrar solemnemente. *To solemnize a marriage,* Celebrar un matrimonio.
Solemnly [sel'-em-li], *adv.* Solemnemente, majestuosamente; con todas las formalidades.
Soleness [sōl'-nes], *s.* (Poco us.) Independencia, el estado de hallarse solo y sin dependencia de otro.
Solenoid [sō'-len-eid], *s.* Solenoide, hilo eléctrico, la forma más sencilla de un imán.
Sol-fa [sōl-fā'], *va.* y *vn.* Solfear, cantar marcando el compás y pronunciando los nombres de las notas.
Solicit [so-lis'-it], *va.* 1. Solicitar, pretender o buscar alguna cosa con diligencia y cuidado; pedir con instancia; importunar, rogar. 2. Pedir, implorar. 3. Solicitar, inducir, incitar a hacer alguna cosa; excitar el deseo; en especial incitar a cometer una acción ilícita.—*vn.* Pedir, hacer una petición o solicitud.
Solicitation [so-lis-i-tē'-shun], *s.* Solicitación.
Solicitor [so-lis'-i-ter], *s.* 1. Procurador, agente, solicitador o diligenciero, el que solicita en nombre de otro. 2. Solicitador, persona que

pide o ruega. *Solicitor in Chancery*, Procurador o abogado en el tribunal de la chancillería.

Solicitous [so-lis'-i-tus], *a.* Solícito, deseoso (con *about* o *for*); que siente solicitud o se interesa por algo, atento a o por; inquieto, cuidadoso, ansioso por algo.

Solicitously [so-lis'-i-tus-li], *adv.* Solícitamente, diligentemente, ansiosamente.

Solicitude [so-lis'-i-tiūd], *s.* Solicitud, cuidado, afán, instancia cuidadosa.

Solid [sel'-id], *a.* 1. Sólido, consistente. 2. Sólido, compacto, macizo. 3. Sólido, firme, fuerte, denso; sano. 4. Sólido, verdadero. 5. Sólido, real, efectivo, duradero; grave, sesudo.—*s.* 1. Sólido, la parte del cuerpo animal que contiene los flúidos. 2. (Geom.) Sólido, cuerpo que tiene extensión, anchura y altura o profundidad.

Solidarity [sel-i-dar'-i-ti], *s.* 1. Solidaridad. 2. Mancomunidad.

Solid-fueled [sel-id-fiū'-ld], *a.* De combustible sólido.

Solid geometry [sel'-id je-em'-e-tri], *s.* Geometría del espacio.

Solidification [so-lid-i-fi-kē'-shun], *s.* Solidificación; consolidación.

Solidify [so-lid'-i-fai], *va.* Solidificar, hacer sólido, volver sólido un cuerpo líquido o gaseoso.—*vn.* Volverse sólido.

Solidity [so-lid'-i-ti], *s.* 1. Solidez, firmeza, dureza, densidad. 2. Solidez, verdad, certeza; integridad.

Solidly [sel'-id-li], *adv.* Sólidamente, firmemente.

Solid state physics [sel'id stêt fiz'-ics], *s.* Física del estado sólido.

Solidungulate, Solidungulous [sel-id-uŋ'-giu-lêt, lus], *a.* Solípedo, que tiene la pezuña entera.

Solifidian [sel-i-fid'-i-an], *s.* y *a.* El que cree que basta la fe sin las buenas obras para salvarse.

Soliloquize, Soliloquise [so-lil'-o-cwaiz], *vn.* Hacer un soliloquio, un monólogo; soliloquiar, hablar a solas.

Soliloquy [so-lil'-o-cwi], *s.* Soliloquio, habla o discurso de una persona a solas, o consigo misma.

Soliped [sel'-i-ped], *s.* Solípedo, el animal cuyos pies no están hendidos, como los del caballo.

Solitaire [sel'-i-tār], *s.* 1. Solitario, diamante u otra joya que se engasta separadamente. 2. Solitario, uno de los varios juegos en que toma parte una sola persona.

Solitarily [sel'-i-te-ri-li], *adv.* Solitariamente, en soledad, sin compañía.

Solitariness [sel'-i-te-ri-nes], *s.* Soledad, retiro.

Solitary [sel'-i-te-ri], *a.* 1. Solitario, que vive en la soledad. 2. Solitario, retirado, poco frecuentado, desierto, desamparado, hablando de sitios o parajes. 3. Solo, único; hecho, ejecutado o sucedido aisladamente. 4. (Zool.) Solitario, que vive solo o en parejas; simple, no compuesto. 5. Incomunicado, dícese de una clase de prisión.—*s.* Solitario, ermitaño.

Solitude [sel'-i-tiūd], *s.* 1. Soledad, vida solitaria, la falta de compañía. 2. Soledad, desierto, paraje solitario.

Sollar [sel'-ar], *s.* 1. Descanso, plataforma en una mina. 2. Cámara elevada en una iglesia.

Solo [sō'-lo], *s.* (Mús.) Solo, la composición que uno canta solo o que se toca con un solo instrumento.

Solomon's-seal [sel'-o-munz-sīl], *s.* (Bot.) Sello de Salomón, planta liliácea con flores verdosas. Polygonatum.

Solstice [sel'-stis], *s.* (Astr.) Solsticio, época en que el sol está más distante del ecuador. *Summer solstice*, Solsticio de verano o estival. *Winter solstice*, Solsticio hiemal o de invierno.

Solstitial [sel-stish'-al], *a.* Solsticial, relativo a los solsticios.

Solubility [sel-yu-bil'-i-ti], **Solubleness** [sel'-yu-bl-nes], *s.* Solubilidad.

Soluble [sel'-yu-bl], *a.* Soluble.

Solute [so-lūt'], *a.* (Bot.) Completamente separado, libre; contrapuesto a adnato.

Solution [so-lū'-shun], *s.* 1. Solución, desleimiento de una cosa sólida y el compuesto que resulta de este desleimiento. 2. Solución, desenlace de una dificultad o de un argumento. 3. Resolución de una duda, de un problema o ecuación. 4. Separación, desunión.

Solutive [sel'-yu-tiv], *a.* Solutivo; laxativo, laxante.

Solvability, Solvableness [sel-va-bil'-i-ti, sel'-va-bl-nes], *s.* Solubilidad, calidad de soluble.

Solvable [selv'-a-bl], *a.* Disoluble, soluble, que se puede resolver o disolver: dícese de un argumento o de un problema.

Solve [selv], *va.* 1. Desenredar, desenlazar, librar de perplejidades; aclarar. 2. Resolver, solver, disolver, explicar.

Solvency [sel'-ven-si], *s.* Solvencia, posibilidad de pagar uno sus deudas.

Solvent [selv'-ent], *a.* 1. Solvente o resolvente, que puede desleir o desatar. 2. Solvente, abonado, que puede pagar sus deudas.—*s.* 1. Disolvente, menstruo, líquido que puede disolver una substancia. 2. (Med.) Medicamento que se emplea para disolver las concreciones u obstrucciones mórbidas de un órgano.

Solvible [selv'-i-bl], *a.* Soluble. *V.* Solvable.

Somatic, Somatical [so-mat'-ic, al], *a.* 1. Corporal, corpóreo, físico. 2. Perteneciente a la cavidad del cuerpo o a sus paredes.

Somatology [so-ma-tel'-o-ji], *s.* 1. Somatología, la ciencia de los cuerpos orgánicos, especialmente del cuerpo humano, que comprende la anatomía y la fisiología. 2. La parte de la física que trata de la materia y de sus propiedades.

Somber, Sombre [sem'-ber], *a.* 1. Sombrío, obscuro, nebuloso. 2. Triste, tétrico, severo, lúgubre, melancólico.

Sombrous [sem'-brus], *a.* (Poét.) *V.* Somber.

Some [sum], *a.* 1. Algo de, un poco, expresando una cantidad indeterminada. 2. Algún, alguno, alguna, unos pocos, ciertos, expresando un número indeterminado. 3. Algunos, algunas personas, ciertas personas. 4. Uno, alguno, cualquier o cualquiera. 5. Unos, unas, poco más o menos; cerca de. *Give me some bread*, Deme Vd. pan o un poco de pan. *Some time since*, Hace algún tiempo. *Some two thousand*, Unos dos mil. *Some persons say*, Algunos, o ciertas personas dicen. *Some shoes*, Zapatos, unos zapatos. *Some difficulty*, Cierta dificultad.—*pron.* Algunos, algunas; unos y otros; parte, una parte, una porción. *Some are rich and some poor*, Unos son ricos y otros pobres. *Are there any matches? There are some.* ¿Hay fósforos? Sí, los hay. *Give me some*, Deme Vd. unos cuantos.

-some, *sufijo*: desinencia, que se emplea en la formación de ciertos adjetivos que indican una cantidad regular o suficiente de la cualidad expresada; v. gr. blithe*some*, alegre, lleno de alegría; quarrel*some*, pendenciero, irascible.

Somebody [sum'-bed-i], *s.* 1. Alguien, alguna persona; persona no conocida o no especificada. 2. Una persona de suposición, un personaje. *Somebody else*, Algún otro.

Somehow [sum'-hau], *adv.* De algún modo o manera.

Somersault [sum'-er-sēlt], **Somerset** [sum'-er-set], *s.* Salto mortal, el que dan los volatines en el aire.

Something [sum'-thing], *s.* 1. Alguna cosa, algo; una cosa no especificada. 2. Cosa que tiene existencia real. 3. Cosa de importancia y suposición. *Something strange*, Algo de extraño. *Something else*, Otra cosa. *I have something to do*, Tengo que hacer.—*adv.* Algo, algún tanto. *This is something like*, Esto sí que me gusta.

Sometime [sum'-taim], *adv.* En algún tiempo, en otro tiempo, antiguamente.

Sometimes [sum'-taims], *adv.* Algunas veces, a veces, de cuando en cuando.

Somewhat [sum'-hwet], *s.* 1. Alguna cosa, algo; un poquito, poco más o menos, por poco que sea. 2. Sujeto o cosa de consecuencia.—*adv.* Algo, algún tanto, un poco. *Somewhat busy*, Algo ocupado.

Somewhere [sum'-hwār], *adv.* En alguna parte. *Somewhere else*, En alguna otra parte.

Somite [sō'-mait], *s.* Segmento en la serie de los que teóricamente forman un cuerpo (particularmente de los articulados). Se llama también *somatome*. (< Gr. *soma*, cuerpo.)

Somnambulist [sem-nam'-biu-list], *s.* Somnámbulo, el que estando dormido se levanta de la cama y anda como si estuviera despierto.

Somnambulism [sem-nam'-biu-lizm], *s.* Somnambulismo, estado del somnámbulo.

Somniferous [sem-nif'-er-us], *a.* Somnífero, soporífero.

Somnific [sem-nif'-ic], *a.* Narcótico, soporífero.

Somniloquism, Somniloquence [sem-nil'-o-cwizm, cwens], *s.* Somnilocuencia, el acto o la costumbre de hablar durante el sueño.

Somnolence [sem'-no-lens], **Somnolency** [sem'-no-len-si], *s.* Somnolencia, inclinación a dormir, gana de dormir.

Somnolent [sem'-no-lent], *a.* 1. Soñoliento, poseído de sueño, o muy inclinado a él. 2. Soñoliento, adormecedor que tiende a causar sueño.

Son [sun], *s.* 1. Hijo: dícese del hijo varón con relación al padre o a la madre. 2. Hijo, descendiente; como *The sons of Adam*, Los hijos de Adán. 3. Hijo de confesión, hijo espiritual. 4. Hijo, expresión de cariño. 5. Hijo o natural de un

país o pueblo. 6. Hijo: se usa para expresar una cosa producida por otra con respecto a la cosa que la produjo. 7. Hijo, la segunda persona de la Santísima Trinidad. *Godson*, Ahijado. *Grandson*, Nieto.
Son-in-law [sun'-in-lō], *s.* Yerno.
Sonant [sō'-nant], *a.* 1. Sonante; dícese de las vocales, y de ciertas consonantes, como la *n*, *g*, *th*, *b*, en contraposición a *surd*, *voiceless*, mudas. 2. Sonante, sonoro, que resuena.
Sonar [sō'-nār], *s.* Contracción de la expresión inglesa *SOnic NAvigation RAnging*, dispositivo para conocer la presencia y situación de submarinos y otros objetos sumergidos.
Sonata [so-nā'-ta], *s.* (Mús.) Sonata, composición instrumental para piano en tres o cuatro movimientos; contrapuesto a *cantata*.
Song [seng o sēng], *s.* 1. Canción, cantar, cantinela, copla, canto; balada, poema lírico. 2. Poesía, verso. 3. Bagatela, nimiedad, poca cosa. *To sell for a mere song*, Vender por un pedazo de pan. *To sing the same song*, Cantar la misma cantinela, repetir la misma cosa. *An old song*, Bagatela. *To sing a song*, Cantar una canción. *Drinking song*, Canción báquica. *Love song*, Canción de amor. *The Song of Songs, the Song of Solomon*, El Cantar de los Cantares. *Song-book*, Cancionero, libro de canciones.
Songful [sēng'-ful], *a.* Melodioso, lleno de canto.
Songless [seng'-les], *a.* Que no canta; sin canto.
Song sparrow [sēng spar'-o], *s.* Gorrión canoro.
Songster [sēng'-stęr], *s.* Cantor, el que sabe cantar; pájaro cantor.
Songstress [sēng'-stres], *sf.* Cantora, cantarina, cantatriz.
Song writer [sēng rait'-ęr], *s.* Compositor de canciones.
Sonic [sen'-ic], *a.* Sónico. *Sonic barrier*, Barrera sónica.
Soniferous [so-nif'-ęr-us], **Sonorific** [sen-o-rif'-ic], *a.* Sonante, sonoro.
Sonnet [sen'-et], *va.* y *vn.* Celebrar con sonetos; componer sonetos.—*s.* Soneto, composición métrica de catorce versos.
Sonometer [sen-e'-me-tęr], *s.* Sonómetro.
Sonorous [so-nō'-rus], *a.* Sonoro, de buen sonido, sonoroso; retumbante, resonante.
Sonorously [so-nō'-rus-li], *adv.* Sonoramente, armónicamente.
Sonship [sun'-ship], *s.* Filiación, calidad de hijo; relación del hijo para con sus padres.
Soon [sūn], *adv.* Presto, pronto, prontamente; temprano; de buena gana. *As soon as*, Luego que, tan pronto como. *As soon as I saw him*, Luego que le ví. *Too soon*, Demasiado temprano o demasiado pronto. *How soon shall you be back?* ¿Cuánto tardará Vd. en volver? *Soon after*, Luego después, inmediatamente después. *Sooner*, Antes. *I would sooner die*, Antes la muerte; preferiría morir. *Soon after sunrise*, Poco después de salir el sol. *Sooner or later*, Tarde o temprano.
Soonest [sūn'-est], *adv.* Superlativo de SOON. Lo más pronto posible. *At the soonest*, Cuanto antes.
Soot [sut o sūt], *va.* Cubrir de hollín o ensuciar con él.—*s.* Hollín.
Sooted [sut'-ed], *a.* Holliniento.
Sooth [sūth], *a.* (Esco. o ant.) Agradable, delicioso; verdadero, real.—*s.* (Des.) Verdad, realidad.
Soothe [sūdh], *a.* 1. Calmar, ablandar, apaciguar, suavizar. 2. Agradar, complacer, lisonjear. 3. Paliar, excusar.
Soother [sūdh'-er], *s.* 1. Apaciguador, el que calma, ablanda o suaviza. 2. (Des.) Lisonjero, adulador.
Soothing [sūdh'-ing], *a.* Calmante, dulcificante, consolador; tierno, dulce.—*s.* Acción de calmar, apaciguar, suavizar o paliar.
Soothingly [sūdh'-ing-li], *adv.* Con dulzura, con tono acariciador; tiernamente.
†**Soothsay** [sūth'-sê], *vn.* Adivinar, decir lo que está por venir: decir la buena ventura.
Soothsayer [sūth'-sê-ęr], *s.* 1. Adivino. 2. *V.* MANTIS.
Sootiness [sut'-i-nes], *s.* La calidad de estar una cosa llena de hollín; fuliginosidad.
Sooty [sut'-i], *a.* 1. Holliniento, que tiene hollín. 2. Fuliginoso, denegrido, obscurecido, tiznado.
Sop [sep], *s.* 1. Sopa, pedazo de pan o de otra cosa empapado en cualquier líquido para comerlo. 2. Dádiva, regalo, lo que se da para apaciguar o aplacar a alguien. 3. Cualquier masa húmeda o empapada.
Sop, *va.* 1. Ensopar, empapar. 2. Hacer embeber o absorber.
Sophi [sō'-fi], *s.* *V.* SUFI.
Sophism [sef'-izm], *s.* 1. Sofisma, argumento falaz. 2. Doctrina de los antiguos sofistas.
Sophist [sef'-ist], *s.* 1. Sofista, nombre antiguo de los profesores de filosofía y retórica. 2. Sofista, el que se vale de sofismas para engañar.
Sophistic, Sophistical [so-fis'-tic, al], *a.* Sofístico, fingido, de la naturaleza del sofisma.
Sophistically [so-fis'-tic-al-i], *adv.* Sofísticamente.
Sophisticalness [so-fis'-tic-al-nes], *s.* Sofistería, aparente y fingida sutileza de los argumentos y razones.
Sophisticate [so-fis'-ti-kêt], *va.* 1. Sofisticar, hacer sofismas. 2. Sofisticar, falsificar, alterar o adulterar alguna cosa.
Sophisticated [so-fis'-ti-kêt-ed], *a.* 1. Complejo, complicado. 2. Refinado, astuto.
Sophistication [so-fis-ti-kê'-shun], *s.* 1. Complejidad. 2. Refinamiento, esmero.
Sophistry [sef'-is-tri], *s.* Sofistería, argumento falaz.
Sophomore [sef'-o-mōr], *s.* En los colegios, estudiante de segundo año (en un curso completo de cuatro años).
Soporiferous [so-per-if'-ęr-us], *a.* Soporífero, narcótico, que causa sueño.
Soporiferousness [so-per-if'-ęr-us-nes], *s.* La virtud o calidad soporífera.
Soporific [so-po-rif'-ic o sep-o-rif'-ic], *a.* Soporífero, soporoso, que causa, motiva o inclina al sueño.—*s.* Medicamento soporífero, que hace dormir.
Sopping [sep'-ing], *a.* Mojado. *Sopping wet*. Empapado.
Soppy [sep'-i], *a.* Mojado, saturado de humedad; blando y muy húmedo.
Soprano [so-prā'-no], *a.* De tiple o soprano.—*s.* 1. Tiple, soprano, la más aguda de las voces humanas. 2. Las notas o la música propias de esa voz. 3. Tiple, persona que tiene este tono de voz. (Ital.)
Sorb [sērb], *s.* Sorba o serba, el fruto del serbo o serbal y el mismo serbal o serbo.
Sorcerer [sēr'-sęr-ęr], *s.* Hechicero.
Sorceress [sēr'-sęr-es], *sf.* Hechicera.
Sorcery [sēr'-sęr-i], *s.* Hechizo, encantación, encanto; hechicería.
Sordes [sēr'-dîz], *s. pl.* Sarro, substancia feculenta que se adhiere a los dientes (como en algunas clases de fiebre); el pus o materia de las llagas.
Sordet [sēr'-det], *s.* *V.* SORDINE.
Sordid [sēr'-did], *a.* 1. Avariento, tacaño, codicioso. 2. Sórdido, impuro, indecente, escandaloso; vil, bajo. 3. (Ant.) Sórdido, sucio; (sentido antiguo).
Sordidly [sēr'-did-li], *adv.* Codiciosamente, con codicia y bajeza.
Sordidness [sēr'-did-nes], *s.* 1. Sordidez, mezquindad, miseria. 2. Bajeza, vileza. 3. Sordidez, suciedad, porquería o fealdad de alguna cosa.
Sordine [sēr'-dîn], *s.* Sordina, lo que se pone a un instrumento músico para apagar su tono.
Sore [sōr], *s.* 1. La parte del cuerpo que está dolorida; una parte escoriada; una llaga o úlcera; lastimadura, matadura (del ganado). 2. Mal, dolor; pena, memoria dolorosa; controversia.—*a.* 1. Delicado, tierno, dolorido, malo. 2. Escrupuloso, resentido. 3. Doloroso, penoso, violento, vehemente. *Sore ears*, Mal de oídos. *Sore eyes*, Mal de ojos, ojos enfermos. *The sore place*, La parte enferma. *A sore sight*, Un espectáculo doloroso.—*adv.* (Ant.) Muy penosamente.
†**Sorel** [ser'-el], *a.* y *s.* *V.* SORREL.
Sorely [sōr'-li], *adv.* Penosamente.
Soreness [sōr'-nes], *s.* 1. Dolencia, mal. 2. El estado de una llaga o úlcera muy dolorida. 3. Amargura o intensidad de una pena.
Sore throat [sōr thrōt], *s.* Dolor de garganta.
Sorghum [sēr'-gum], *s.* 1. Sorgo, zahina, planta gramínea que se cultiva por su jugo sacarino. Andropogon sorghum. 2. (E. U.) Melaza que se hace con el jugo del sorgo.
Sorites [so-rai'-tîz], *s.* Sorites, argumento lógico compuesto de muchas proposiciones encadenadas.
Sororiation [so-ro-ri-ê'-shun], *s.* (Med.) Desarrollo progresivo de los pechos de una joven; el período de ese desarrollo.
Sororicide [so-rer'-i-said], *s.* El asesinato de una hermana.
Sorority [so-rer'-i-ti], *s.* Hermandad de mujeres con fines sociales.
Sorosis [so-ro'-sis], *s.* 1. (Bot.) Un fruto compuesto y mollar, como la piña o anana. 2. (E. U.) Hermandad, sociedad de mujeres.
Sorrel [sęr'-el], *a.* Alazán rojo: se aplica al caballo que es de color alazán.—*s.* 1. Color alazán o rojizo. 2. Caballo u otro animal alazán. 3. Gamo en su tercer año. 4. (Bot.) Acedera, hierba del género Rumex. *Field-* o *sheep-sorrel*, Acedera pequeña. Rumex acetosella. *Wood-sorrel*, Acederilla, oxálide blanca. Oxalis acetosella.
Sorrily [ser'-i-li], *adv.* Mal, malamente, pésimamente, lastimosamente.
Sorriness [ser'-i-nes], *s.* Ruindad, vileza, bajeza; mediocridad.
Sorrow [ser'-o], *s.* 1. Pesar, dolor, sentimiento. *Full of sorrow*, Lleno de pesar. 2. Tristeza, pesadumbre, pena, sinsabor, desabrimiento. *To*

my sorrow, Con gran sentimiento mío. *Sorrow-stricken*, Agobiado de dolor.

Sorrow, *vn.* Entristecerse, ponerse triste y melancólico.

Sorrowful [ser'-o-ful], *a.* Pesaroso, afligido, angustiado, lleno de sentimiento o pena; triste, melancólico, que expresa pesar; doloroso, lastimoso.

Sorrowfully [ser'-o-ful-i], *adv.* Con angustia, con pena, con aflicción, con sentimiento.

Sorrowfulness [ser'-o-ful-nes], *s.* Angustia, pesar, tristeza, aflicción.

Sorrowing [ser'-o-ing], *s.* Aflicción, tristeza; lamentación.

Sorrowless [ser'-o-les], *a.* Sin pena, sin dolor, sin aflicción.

Sorry [ser'-i], *a.* 1. Apesadumbrado, pesaroso, triste, afligido, desconsolado. 2. Triste, melancólico, funesto. 3. Despreciable, ruin, vil, pícaro, malvado. 4. Pobre, escaso, miserable, pobrete. *I am sorry for it*, Lo siento. *I am sorry for you*, Lo siento por Vd. *A sorry sight*, Un triste espectáculo.

Sort [sōrt], *s.* 1. Suerte, género, especie, clase, calaña. *Three sorts of wine*, Tres clases de vino o vino de tres clases. 2. Suerte, calidad, condición. 3. Clase u orden de personas; conjunto de personas. 4. Manera, modo, forma. *In like sort*, De la misma suerte. *All sorts of people*, Toda clase de gentes. *Out of sorts*, (1) Indispuesto; (2) malhumorado, triste, apesumbrado; (3) (Impr.) falto de una clase o fundición especial de letra o guarismos.

Sort, *va.* 1. Separar o dividir en distintas clases; se usa a menudo con *over*. 2. Colocar, ordenar, arreglar; a menudo con *out*. 3. ¿Proporcionar, conformar, adaptar.—*vn.* (Como *vn.* es desusado) 1. Hermanarse, unirse con otros de la misma especie. 2. Ajustarse, acomodarse una cosa con otra. 3. Salir o suceder alguna cosa bien o mal.

Sortable [sōrt'-a-bl], *a.* Acomodado, conveniente, apto, oportuno.

Sortie [sōr'-tī], *s.* Salida que hace un número de tropas de la plaza sitiada. (Fr.)

Sortilege [sōr'-ti-lej], *s.* 1. Sortilegio. 2. Sorteo, la acción de sortear.

So-so [sō'-sō], *a.* Pasadero, pasable. —*adv.* Así, así, en forma regular.

Sot [set], *s.* 1. Zaque, el hombre borracho. 2. Zote, hombre ignorante y torpe.

Sot, *va.* Atontar, aturdir, atolondrar.—*vn.* Beborretear hasta embriagarse.

Sottish [set'-ish], *a.* 1. Torpe, rudo, tardo. 2. Embotado, entorpecido por los excesos.

Sou [sū], *s.* Sueldo, moneda que ha tenido distinto valor según los tiempos; hoy, moneda de cobre de cinco céntimos.

Souchong [sū-shong'], *s.* Nombre de una variedad de té negro.

Sough [suf o sau], *va.* y *vn.* Producir un sonido como de suspiro, v. g. el del viento entre las ramas de los pinos; susurrar, murmurar.—*s.* 1. Susurro, suspiro profundo, murmullo. 2. (Prov. Ingl.) Desaguadero subterráneo.

Sought [sōt], *pret.* y *pp.* del verbo *To* SEEK.

Soul [sōl], *s.* 1. Alma, el espíritu inmortal del hombre. 2. Alma, lo que es principio de la vida en todos los seres vivientes. 3. Alma, esencia, virtud principal. 4. Alma, individuo, persona, criatura racional. *There was not a soul in the house;* No había nadie en casa. 5. Alma, viveza, espíritu, gallardía. 6. Fuerza o fervor individual; cordialidad, corazón; ardor, móvil; nobleza, generosidad. 7. Espíritu separado del cuerpo. *With all my soul*, Con el mayor gusto, con toda mi alma, con mis cinco sentidos. *Upon my soul*, En mi ánima o en mi conciencia.

Souled [sōld], *a.* Animado, el que tiene alma racional; se usa en composición.

Soulful [sōl'-ful], *a.* Lleno de lo que apela al alma o a los sentimientos y los satisface; conmovedor, espiritual. A este adjetivo corresponden el adverbio *soulfully* y el substantivo *soulfulness.*

Soulless [sel'-les], *a.* Desalmado, vil, bajo, ruin, despreciable; sin conciencia.

Soulscot [sōl'-scet], †**Soulshot** [sōl'-shet], *s.* La limosna que se da por la misa de difuntos.

Sound [saund], *a.* 1. Sano, sin lesión o enfermedad alguna. 2. Sano, perfecto, entero. 3. Puro, seguro, ortodoxo: cuando se habla de doctrinas. 4. Seguro, cierto, indudable. 5. Recto, justo, firme. 6. Profundo; completo, cabal. 7. Solvente, que puede cumplir sus obligaciones. *Sound sleep*, Sueño profundo.—*adv.* Sanamente, vigorosamente.—*s.* 1. Mar poco profundo. 2. Sonda, cualquier paraje en la mar donde la sondaleza alcanza al fondo. 3. El estrecho del Sund, a la entrada del Mar Báltico. 4. Tienta, sonda, instrumento de cirugía. 5. Son, sonido; vibración de un cuerpo sonante. 6. Alcance del oído. 7. Ruido; apariencia grande en las cosas. 8. Vejiga natatoria (del pez). *Sound-post*, El alma del violín. *Sound reasoning*, Raciocinio sólido, seguro. *Sound-board*, V *Sounding-board*. *Of sound and disposing mind and memory*, (For.) De mente y memoria sanas; capaz de hacer testamento.

Sound, *va.* 1. Sonar, tocar, tañer, hacer que alguna cosa emita un sonido. *To sound the alarm*, Tocar al arma. 2. Celebrar, publicar. 3. Dar aviso, mandar, prescribir u ordenar por medio de un sonido. 4. Probar por el sonido; auscultar o percutir; examinar por medio de los sonidos.—*vn.* 1. Sonar, hacer o causar ruido. 2. Sonar, hacer una cosa alusión a otra. 3. Ser llevado por el sonido; esparcirse, divulgarse. 4. Dar una señal por medio de un toque o sonido.

Sound, *va.* 1. (Mar.) Sondar o sondear, echar la plomada para cerciorarse de la profundidad del agua. 2. Sondar o sondear, inquirir o rastrear cautelosamente alguna cosa; sondar o tantear. 3. (Med.) Sondar, tentar, reconocer con la tienta.

Sounder [saund'-er], *s.* 1. Resonador, el o lo que da un sonido; resonador telegráfico que transmite un mensaje por medio del sonido. 2. Sondeador, aparato para sondear, p. ej. en el mar. 3. Tienta.

Sounding [saund'-ing], *a.* Sonante, sonoro; retumbante. *High-sounding*, Sonoro, retumbante, campanudo. *Sounding-board*, Tabla de armonía (de un piano); secreto, cajón de los órganos; tornavoz, sombrero de púlpito.—*s.* 1. Acción de sonar, resonar, sondar, o tentar. 2. (Mar.) Braceaje, medida por brazas; sonda. 3. *pl.* Sondas, cantidad de brazas. 4. Muestras, v. g. de conchas sacadas del agua por el sondeador. *Sounding-lead*, (Mar.) Escandallo. *Lead-sounding*, Sonda de escandallo. *Sounding-line*, Sondaleza. *Off* o *out of soundings*, Fuera de sondas.

Soundless [saund'-les], *a.* 1. Mudo, sin sonido. 2. Insondable.

Soundly [saund'-li], *adv.* Sanamente, con salud; vigorosamente; firmemente; verdaderamente, seguramente, con rectitud y justicia. *To sleep soundly*, Dormir profundamente.

Soundness [saund'-nes], *s.* 1. Sanidad, salud; vigor, firmeza. 2. Verdad, rectitud, pureza. 3. Fuerza, solidez. 4. Rectitud, justicia. 5. Pureza de la fe, ortodoxia.

Soundproof [saund'-prūf], *a.* Insonoro, a prueba de ruidos.

Sound track [saund' trac], *s.* Banda o huella de sonido de una película cinematográfica.

Sound wave [saund wêv], *s.* Onda sonora.

Soup [sūp], *s.* Sopa, caldo de carne o legumbres; se diferencia de *broth*, que es caldo solo, colado. *Pease-soup* o *pea-soup*, Sopa de guisantes. *Milk-soup*, Sopa de leche. *Soup-ladle*, Cucharón. *Soup-plate*, Plato hondo o sopero. *Soup-tureen*, Sopera. *Mock turtle soup*, Imitación de la sopa de tortuga. *In the soup*, (Fest. E. U.) En apuros, en aprieto.

Sour [saur], *s.* Agrio, zumo ácido o substancia agria.—*a.* 1. Agrio, ácido, acerbo al gusto. 2. Agrio, acre, áspero, desabrido. 3. Penoso, doloroso. *Sour apple*, Manzana agria o verde. *Sour dock*, Acedera. *Sour-krout*, *sourcrout*, Berza ácida. *V.* SAUERKRAUT. *To taste sour*, Tener gusto agrio. *To turn sour*, Volverse agrio. *A sour countenance*, Un aspecto avinagrado. *Sour-gourd*, Pan de mico, árbol de la familia de las malváceas. Adansonia. *Sour grass*, Acedera pequeña.

Sour, *va.* 1. Agriar, acedar, poner agria o aceda alguna cosa. 2. Agriar, desabrir, exasperar, irritar, indisponer los ánimos o las voluntades. 3. Descontentar, desagradar. 4. Macerar; hacer fermentar (la cal).—*vn.* 1. Agriarse, ponerse agria alguna cosa; revenirse, fermentar. 2. Mostrar un genio acre; irritarse, enojarse. 3. Corromperse, echarse a perder. 4. Volverse áspera, viscosa y perjudicial a las mieses; se dice de la tierra.

Source [sōrs], *s.* 1. Creador, originador; origen. 2. Lugar donde se halla algo, o de donde se saca; principio. 3. Manantial, el origen del agua u otra cosa. *To have from a good source*, Saber de buena tinta.

Sour grapes [saur grêps], *s. pl.* (fig.) Uvas verdes.

Sourish [saur'-ish], *a.* Agrillo, algo agrio. *This wine has a sourish taste*, Este vino tiene punta de agrio.

Sourly [saur'-li], *adv.* Agriamente, ásperamente.

Sourness [saur'-nes], *s.* 1. Acedía, el sabor acedo y agrio; agrio, agrura. 2. Acrimonia, la aspereza o desabrimiento en el genio o en las palabras.

Souse [saus], *s.* 1. Salmuera, adobo;

escabeche; la cabeza, patas u orejas de cerdo adobadas. 2. (E. U. y Prov. Ingl.) Zambullida (en el agua). 3. Ataque repentino, lanzamiento de un halcón sobre su presa. —*adv.* Zas, con violencia.

Souse, *va.* 1. Zabullir, chapuzar, meter en el agua. 2. Arrojar, derramar, verter un líquido. 3. Escabechar, poner en escabeche; adobar. 4. Arrojarse, dar un golpe con violencia, como hace el ave de rapiña a la presa.—*vn.* Lanzarse, arrojarse como el ave de rapiña se arroja sobre la presa.

South [sauth], *s.* 1. Mediodía, sud o sur, la parte meridional de la esfera, punto cardinal opuesto al norte. 2. Comarca o región situada en dirección al sur. 3. (E. U.) Los estados que se separaron de la Unión en 1861. 4. (Des.) Viento del sur. —*a.* Meridional, austral, del sur, del mediodía. *South wind,* Viento del sur. *The South Pole,* El Polo Sur. *To be south,* Dar a mediodía. *South Sea,* Mar Pacífico o del sur.—*adv.* 1. Hacia el mediodía, por la parte del sur. 2. Desde el sur.

Southeast [sauth-îst'], *s.* Sudeste, el punto que media entre el este y el sud.—*a.* Sudeste, del sudeste, al sudeste.

Southeaster [sauth-îst'-ęr], *s.* Temporal o viento de sudeste.

Southeasterly [sauth-îst'-ęr-li], *a.* y *adv.* Hacia el sudeste, al sudeste; que sopla del sudeste. *Southeastern,* Del sudeste, perteneciente o situado al sudeste.

Souther [saudh'-ęr], *s.* Viento o borrasca del sur.

Southerly [sudh'-ęr-li], *a.* Casi meridional, hacia el sur o mediodía; del sur, que proviene del sur.

Southern [sudh'-ęrn], *a.* Meridional, austral; del sur; situado al sur. *The Southern Cross,* La Cruz del Sur; constelación del hemisferio austral. *Southernmost,* Lo más al sur, lo más al mediodía.

Southerner [sudh'-ęrn-ęr], *s.* Persona nativa del sur de E.U.A.

Southernwood [sudh'-ęrn-wud], *s.* (Bot.) Abrótano, lombriguera.

Southing [saudh'-ing], *a.* Que camina hacia el sur.—*s.* 1. Diferencia de latitud medida hacia el sur. 2. Posición extrema de un astro hacia el sud en su movimiento diurno.

Southmost [sauth'-mōst], *a.* El más cercano al mediodía.

Southron [sudh'-ron], *s.* Habitante del sur, especialmente un inglés; término que en otro tiempo emplearon despreciativamente los escoceses.

Southward [sauth'-ward], *s.* Las regiones del sur o mediodía.

Southward, Southwardly [sauth-ward-li], *adv.* Hacia el mediodía. *Southward of the line,* Al sur de la línea (ecuador).

Southwest [sauth-west'], *s.* Sudoeste, punto entre el sud y el oeste.—*a.* Sudoeste, del sudoeste, al sudoeste.

Southwester [sauth-west'-ęr], *s.* 1. Viento, borrasca o tempestad del sudoeste. 2. Chapona, sueste, sombrero de lona encerada, con el ala estrecha por delante y muy ancha por detrás. *Southwesterly, a.* y *adv.* Del sudoeste, hacia el sudoeste; que sopla del sudoeste. *Southwestern,* Del sudoeste, perteneciente o situado al sudoeste. *Southwestward,* Hacia el sudoeste.

Souvenir [sū-ve-nír'], *s.* Memoria, prenda de recuerdo, lo que sirve para traer lo pasado a la memoria.

Sovereign [suv'-ęr-en o sev'-ęr-ęn], *s.* 1. Soberano, monarca, el que tiene la autoridad suprema. 2. Moneda inglesa de oro del valor de veinte chelines.—*a.* 1. Soberano, supremo, independiente, superior a todo en su género o clase. 2. Soberano, singular, preeminente; de eficacia segura; lo más influyente o poderoso.

Sovereignly [sev- o suv'-ęr-en-li], *adv.* Soberanamente, perfectamente, excelentemente.

Sovereignty [sev- o suv'-ęr-en-ti], *s.* Soberanía.

Soviet [sō-vi-et'], *s.* y *a.* Soviet, soviético.

Sow [sau], *s.* 1. Puerca, marrana, la hembra del puerco. *V.* Pig. 2. Un pedazo de plomo según sale de la fundición. 3. Goa, el pedazo de hierro según sale de la hornaza donde se funde la mina. 4. *Sow* o *sowbug,* Cochinilla de tierra, insecto isópodo (Oniscus) que se cría en parajes húmedos. *Sow-pig,* Lechona. *Wild-sow,* Jabalina o puerca montés, la hembra del jabalí. *Sowthistle,* Cerraja, cardo ajonjero, planta semejante a la achicoria. Sonchus.

Sow [sō], *va.* y *vn.* (*pret.* Sowed, *pp.* Sown o Sowed). 1. Sembrar, arrojar y esparcir, como las semillas por la tierra; empanar, sembrar grano. 2. Sembrar, desparramar, esparcir, propagar.—*vn.* Sembrar, hacer la sementera; literal y figuradamente. *To sow one's wild oats,* (Fig. fam.) Correr sus mocedades, hacer travesuras juveniles.

Sowbread [sau'-bred], *s.* (Bot.) Pamporcino o pan porcino, una planta.

Sowens, Sowans [sau'-enz], *s. sing.* y *pl.* (Esco.) Puches o gachas preparadas con los desechos de la harina de avena.

Sower [sō'-ęr], *s.* 1. Sembrador, el que siembra; desparramador, el que desparrama; sembradera, máquina para sembrar. 2. Propagador, el que propaga.

Sowing [sō'-ing], *s.* Sementera, siembra, acción de sembrar los granos; sembradura. *Sowing-machine,* Sembradera, instrumento o máquina para sembrar. *Sowing-time,* Sementera, tiempo a propósito para sembrar.

Sown [sōn], *pp.* del verbo *To* Sow.

Soy bean [sei bīn], *s.* (Bot.) Soya.

Spa [spā], *s.* 1. Paraje frecuentado por razón de sus aguas minerales. 2. Manantial de aguas minerales.

Space [spēs], *va.* Espaciar; (Impr.) poner espacios entre las palabras o las líneas.—*s.* 1. Espacio; extensión (limitada o ilimitada), trecho; distancia; área. 2. Espacio, el intervalo de tiempo; de aquí, un poco de tiempo. 3. Tiempo, sazón, oportunidad. 4. Intersticio. 5. (Impr.) Espacio, pieza de metal más baja que la letra y más delgada que un cuadratín de ene, para dividir una dicción de otra. 6. (Mús.) Espacio, intervalo que hay entre raya y raya del pentagrama. *Space between,* El espacio intermedio. *A space,* Algún tiempo, un poco de tiempo, durante algún tiempo, por algún tiempo.

Space capsule [spēs cap'-siūl], *s.* Cápsula espacial.

Spacecraft [spēs'-craft], *s.* Nave espacial.

Space fiction [spēs' fic-shun], *s.* Ficción científica, novelas de aventuras interplanetarias.

Space flight [spēs' flait], *s.* Vuelo espacial.

Spaceman [spēs'-man], *s.* Astronauta, piloto espacial, cosmonauta.

Spacemanship [spēs'-man-ship], *s.* Destreza o maestría aeronáutica o de los aeronautas.

Space medicine [spēs' me-di-sin], *s.* Medicina espacial.

Space platform [spēs plat'-fērm], *s.* Platforma espacial.

Space probe [spēs' prōb], *s.* Misión exploradora espacial.

Space rocket [spēs' rek'-et], *s.* Proyectil-cohete.

Spaceship [spēs'-ship], *s.* Astronave.

Space station, *s.* Estación astral.

Space suit [spēs' sūt], *s.* Traje para vuelos espaciales.

Space travel [spēs' trav'-el], *s.* Astronáutica, viajes astronáuticos o interestelares.

Spacious [spé'-shus], *a.* Espacioso, vasto, amplio, extenso, de mucho espacio; capaz, ancho.

Spaciously [spé'-shus-li], *adv.* Espaciosamente, con gran extensión.

Spaciousness [spé'-shus-nes], *s.* Espaciosidad, capacidad, extensión, amplitud.

Spade [spēd], *s.* 1. Azadón (en figura de pala), legón (laya), con que se labra la tierra; (su hoja es más angosta y plana que la de la pala). 2. Un ciervo o gamo de tres años. 3. Espadas, uno de los cuatro palos de que se compone la baraja de naipes. 4. Animal castrado.

Spade, *va.* Azadonar, cavar con azadón.

Spadeful [spēd'-ful], *s.* Azadonada, cantidad que puede contener o remover un azadón.

Spadix [spé'-dix], *s.* (Bot.) Espádice, (m.) receptáculo común de varias flores, encerrado en la espata.

Spaghetti [spa-get'-i], *s.* Macarrón a la italiana.

Spain [spēn], *s.* España.

Spake [spēk], *pret. ant.* del verbo *To* Speak.

Span [span], *s.* 1. Palmo, la distancia que hay desde la punta del dedo pulgar de la mano abierta y extendida hasta el extremo del dedo meñique, y que se estima en nueve pulgadas. 2. Instante, momento, rato breve, espacio pequeño de tiempo. 3. (Arq.) Tramo, luz de puente; ojo, apertura de arco o bóveda. 4. Tronco, pareja; (E. U. pareja de caballos; África del sur, de bueyes). 5. Lo que mide o limita; traba; (Mar.) eslinga; amante. *Span-rope,* (Mar.) Nervio. *Spanshackle,* (Mar.) Suncho, abrazadera o cepo del pescante del ancla. *Span-new,* (Ant. o dial.) Flamante, enteramente nuevo. *Spanworm,* Oruga o larva de los geometrinos.

Span, *va.* 1. Medir a palmos; medir con la mano. 2. Alcanzar, llegar de un lado a otro; echar sobre, extenderse sobre. 3. Amarrar, ligar, atar.—*vn.* Proceder por etapas o jornadas regulares.

Span, *pret. ant.* del verbo *To* Spin.

Spandrel (o **Spandril**) [span'-drel], *s.* (Arq.) Enjuta, embecadura; tímpano, espacio triangular entre dos arcos.

Spangle [span'-gl], *s.* 1. Lentejuela,

planchita de metal plana y reluciente. 2. Cualquier cuerpo luminoso o cualquiera cosa que relumbra.

Spangle, *va.* Adornar alguna cosa con lentejuelas. *Spangled skies*, El cielo estrellado.

Spaniard [span'-yard], *s.* 1. Español; natural o habitante de España. 2. Arbusto espinoso de la Nueva Zelandia.

Spaniel [span'-yel], *s.* Perro de aguas, de tamaño pequeño o mediano, con orejas grandes y colgantes y pelo largo y sedoso. (< Fr. espagneul < español.)

Spanish [span'-ish], *a.* Español, de España; que se refiere o pertenece a aquel país.—*s.* Español, el lenguaje castellano. *Spanish bayonet*, Cualquier especie de yuca, particularmente Yucca aloifolia. *Spanish broom*, Retama de España, atocha. *Spanish chalk*, Esteatita, jaboncillo. *Spanish-black*, Negro de España; corcho quemado. *Spanish-flies, s. pl.* Cantáridas. *Spanish-leather*, Cordobán cuero de Córdoba. *Spanish mackere*, Escombro de ambas costas del Atlántico. *Spanish main*, La parte del Mar de las Antillas inmediata a la América del Sur, con inclusión del camino que solían seguir los buques mercantes españoles en sus viajes entre Europa y América. *Spanish moss*, Musgo negro o de Florida, planta epifítica de la familia de las bromeliáceas. Los tallos secos se emplean en tapicería. *Spanish soap*, Jabón de Castilla.

Spanish America [span'-ish a-mer'-i-ca], *s.* América Hispana, Hispanoamérica.

Spanish-American [span'-ish-a-mer'-i-can], *a.* y *s.* Hispanoamericano.

Spank [spank], *va.* Golpear con la mano abierta o con un objeto sobre las nalgas; dar nalgadas.—*vn.* Correr, ir de prisa.

Spanker [spank'-er], *s.* 1. El o lo que da nalgadas. 2. Maricangalla, vela del palo de mesana. 3. (Fam.) Alguna cosa extraordinariamente grande y hermosa. 4. (Fam.) El o lo que va rápidamente, a grandes pasos.

Spanking [spank'-ing], *a.* 1. Que se mueve rápidamente, pronto, veloz. 2. (Fam.) Extraordinariamente grande o hermoso.

Spanner [span'-er], *s.* 1. El o lo que mide o alcanza; en especial una entre varias clases de herramientas; llave de pasador. 2. *V. Spanworm*, al fin del título SPAN.

Spar [spār], *s.* 1. Espato, especie de fósil reluciente. 2. Un palo delgado y corto. 3. (Mar.) Berlinga, percha, bordón, mástil. 4. Asna, cabrio, cabrial, madero redondo que forma parte de una grúa o cabria de enarbolar. 5. Lucha a puñadas. *Iceland spar*, Espato de Islandia. *Spar-deck*, Cubierta de guindaste.

Spar, *vn.* Fingir un combate a puñadas, como hacen los púgiles para ejercitarse.—*va.* 1. Proveer de berlingas o mástiles; mover o alzar por medio de mástiles y poleas. 2. (Des.) Atrancar o cerrar; cerrar con una tranca.

Spare [spār], *va.* 1. Ahorrar, economizar, excusar gastos o moderarlos; economizar o conservar las cosas para que no se gasten o consuman, guardar o reservar una cosa; pasar o pasarse sin alguna cosa. 2. Perdonar, dejar libre a alguno de la pena que merecía; ahorrar, abstenerse de injuriar o molestar; hacer gracia de; permitir vivir. 3. Dispensar de, dar, conceder, conferir, disponer de.—*vn.* 1. Hacer gracia, usar de clemencia; de aquí, abstenerse, detenerse, refrenarse, desistir. 2. Ser frugal, ahorrativo; vivir con frugalidad y economía. *Not to spare one's self*, No economizar su trabajo, sus esfuerzos. *To spare the life of a prisoner*, Perdonar la vida a un prisionero, permitirle vivir. *To have to spare*, Tener de sobra. *Can you spare this book?* ¿Puede Vd. privarse de este libro?

Spare, *a.* 1. Disponible a voluntad. 2. Sobrante, de sobra, que está de repuesto para un caso de necesidad o reserva; suplementario, adicional. 3. Descarnado, delicado, débil, amaricado en la complexión y figura. 4. Escaso, sobrio, no abundante; apenas suficiente. *Spare time*, Tiempo desocupado. (Fam.) Ratos perdidos; horas de descanso. *Spare hours*, Horas de recreo o perdidas para el trabajo. *Spare money*, Dinero de repuesto o de reserva, dinero ahorrado para una necesidad. *Spare of speech*, Escaso de palabras, que habla poco. *Spare bed*, Cama de repuesto o de sobra. *To spare at the spigot and let out at the bunghole*, (prov.) Economizar una gota y desperdiciar una bota. *Spare stores*, (Mar.) Pertrechos de respeto. *Spare rigging*, (Mar.) Cordaje de respeto. *Spare deck*, (Mar.) Crujía; postizas.

Spareness [spār'-nes], *s.* Magrura; escasez; ahorro; frugalidad.

Sparer [spār'-er], *s.* Ahorrador, la persona que ahorra.

Sparerib [spār'-rib], *s.* Costilla de puerco casi descarnada.

Spare tire [spār tair], *s.* Llanta o neumático de refacción.

Sparing [spār'-ing], *a.* 1. Escaso, corto, limitado, poco; de abastecimiento limitado. 2. Frugal, económico, ahorrativo, sobrio. *Sparing in commendations*, Sobrio de elogios. *Sparing efforts*, Esfuerzos limitados.

Sparingly [spār'-ing-li], *adv.* 1. Escasamente, parcamente, frugalmente, económicamente. 2. Rara vez, con poca frecuencia. 3. Cautamente, con precaución, con prudencia. *To live sparingly*, Vivir parcamente.

Sparingness [spār'-ing-nes], *s.* 1. Ahorro, escasez, ahorramiento. 2. Precaución, cautela.

Spark [spārk], *s.* 1. Chispa, partícula encendida de fuego. 2. (Poét.) Centella, la chispa que se desprende del pedernal herido. 3. Resplandor pasajero, emanación brillante, chispa eléctrica; centella, punto reluciente. 4. Vislumbre. 5. Chispa, diamante muy pequeño. 6. Petimetre, pisaverde, el joven que cuida demasiadamente de su compostura. 7. Amante, galán. *A spark of reason*, Una vislumbre de razón, un destello de buen sentido. *A spark of life*, Un átomo de vida. *Spark-arrester, spark-catcher*, Chispero, sombrerete (de locomotora).

Spark, *vn.* 1. Chispear, echar chispas, centellear. 2. Formar chispas eléctricas o pequeños arcos, v. g. en el conmutador: dícese de los dínamos.—*va.* (Fam.) Galantear, pretender en matrimonio.

†**Sparkish** [spārk'-ish], *a.* Alegre, vivo; galán, vestido de gala.

Sparkle [spārk'-l], *s.* Centella, chispa, vislumbre.

Sparkle, *vn.* 1. Chispear, despedir chispas o resplandores; centellear. 2. Chispear, relucir, o brillar mucho. 3. Chispear, producir burbujas, como ciertos vinos.

Sparkler [spārk'-ler], *s.* La persona que tiene los ojos muy vivos o como suele decirse, que echan chispas.

Sparkling [spārk'-ling], *pa.* Centelleante, brillante; chispeante, espumoso. *Sparkling eyes*, Ojos brillantes, chispeantes. *Sparkling wine*, Vino que chispea.

Sparklingly [spārk'-ling-li], *adv.* Con brillantez o brillo; con esplendor.

Sparklingness [spārk'-ling-nes], *s.* Brillantez, brillo, lustre, esplendor.

Spark plug [spark plug], *s.* Bujía.

Sparrow [spar'-o], *s.* 1. Gorrión, pardal; pájaro de color obscuro, particularmente del género Passer. 2. Otro pájaro cantor parecido al gorrión.

Sparrowgrass [spar'-o-gras], *s.* (Fam.) Espárrago. (Corrupción de *asparagus.*)

Sparrowhawk [spar'-o-hēc], *s.* Gavilán, ave de rapiña. (Accipiter.)

Sparse [spārs], *a.* Esparcido, desparramado, difundido en pequeño número, no denso.

Sparsely [spārs'-li], *adv.* Aquí y allá, a grandes trechos, no densamente.

Sparsity [spār'-si-ti], *s.* Calidad de disperso o esparcido.

Spartan [spār'-tan], *a.* Espartano, de Esparta.—*s.* Espartano, habitante o natural de Esparta.

Spasm [spazm], *s.* Espasmo, contracción violenta e involuntaria de los músculos.

Spasmodic [spaz-med'-ic], *a.* Espasmódico, convulsivo.

Spasmodically [spaz-med'-ic-al-i], *adv.* Espasmódicamente; por saltos, a ratos.

Spastic [spas'-tic], *a.* Espástico. *V* SPASMODIC.

Spat [spat], *pret.* y *pp.* del verbo *To* SPIT.

Spat, *va.* y *vn.* Desovar los mariscos o moluscos.—*s.* Huevas de los mariscos o moluscos, particularmente de la ostra; ostras pequeñas hasta que se fijan en un lugar. (< *spat*, pret. de *spit.*)

Spat, *va.* y *vn.* (E. U.) 1. Dar un golpe ligero con la mano; dar palmadas; también, reñir ligeramente. 2. Azotar (la lluvia). *V.* PATTER.—*s.* 1. Manotada, manotón con la mano abierta; sopapo, bofetada. 2. Gota grande de lluvia; salpicadura, salpicón. 3. (E. U.) Riña, disputa. *V.* PAT.

Spathe [spēdh], *s.* (Bot.) Espata, bolsa membranácea que envuelve muchas flores; en especial, espádice.

Spathic [spath'-ic], *a.* (Min.) Espático, parecido al espato.

Spatial, Spacial [spē'-shal], *a.* Del espacio, perteneciente a él, o de su naturaleza.

Spats [spats], *s. pl.* Polainas.

Spatter [spat'-er], *va.* y *vn.* 1. Salpicar, manchar con agua sucia. 2. Rociar, esparcir en gotas. 3. Difamar, quitar la fama o la reputación.

Spatter, *s.* 1. Salpicadura; rociamiento, rociada; acción y efecto de salpicar, de rociar. 2. Salpicadura, la substancia con que se salpica o rocía. 3. Ruido como de la lluvia que cae.

Spatterdashes [spat'-ęr-dash-ez], *s. pl.* Polainas.

Spatterdock [spat'-ęr-dec], *s.* Núfar, lirio amarillo acuático. (Nuphar o Nymphea advena.)

Spattle [spat'-l], *va.* (Cerám.) Motear la vajilla de loza. *Spattling-machine,* Máquina para motear los objetos de cerámica.

Spatula [spat'-yu-la], *s.* Espátula, paleta de acero de que usan los boticarios, los esmaltadores, los escultores, etc.

Spatulate [spat'-yu-lêt], *a.* Espatulado, en forma de espátula; estrecho en la base y redondeado por el extremo, forma de muchas hojas.

Spavin [spav'-in], *s.* Esparaván, enfermedad que padecen las caballerías en la articulación del corvejón.

Spawn [spēn], *s.* 1. Freza, huevas de los peces, anfibios, moluscos o crustáceos. 2. Producto o fruto de una cosa. En este sentido sólo se usa en desprecio. 3. Ostras pequeñas antes de fijarse; también pececillos. *V.* SPAT. 4. (Bot.) Micelio de un honguillo (como el de la seta).

Spawn, *va.* y *vn.* 1. Desovar, poner sus huevos o huevas los peces, anfibios o moluscos. 2. Producir o soltar de sí alguna cosa, como desovan los peces. 3. Engendrar, procrear; proceder, dimanar. En este último sentido es voz de desprecio. *Spawn of the devil,* (Vulg.) Hijo del diablo o demonio.

Spawner [spēn'-ęr], *sf.* Pez hembra.

Spawning [spēn'-ing], *s.* Freza, desove, el acto de desovar los peces. *Spawning-time,* Desove, el tiempo en que desovan los peces.

Spay [spê], *va.* Castrar las hembras de los animales.

Speak [spīk], *va.* y *vn.* (*pret.* SPOKE y ant. SPAKE; *pp.* SPOKEN, ant. SPOKE). 1. Hablar, articular, pronunciar, proferir palabras o voces; expresarse en un idioma; decir. 2. Perorar, arengar, hacer alguna arenga o razonamiento. 3. Razonar, conversar, disputar. 4. Hablar, rogar, abogar o interceder por una persona. 5. Hablar, revelar, hacer mención, dar aviso; explicarse. 6. Sonar. 7. Proclamar, celebrar. 8. Hablar a otro, dirigirse a uno, llamar un buque a otro con bocina. *To speak about,* Hablar de, tratar de. *To speak fair,* Hablar bien de algo o de alguien. *To speak for,* (1) Hablar a favor, o en nombre de otro. (2) Ser prueba, evidencia de algo. *To speak for itself,* Hablar por sí mismo, ser manifiesto. *To speak one's mind,* Decir lo que se piensa, hablar en plata. *To speak out,* Hablar claro, o en romance; hablar atrevidamente. *To speak to,* Hablar a; (fam.) poner de oro y azul, reprender. *To speak up,* Hablar en voz alta, elevar la voz; osar hablar; decir claridades. *To speak thick,* Hablar con media lengua, hablar tartajoso. *To speak through the nose,* Ganguear, hablar gangoso. *So to speak,* Por decirlo así. *Not to be on speaking terms,* (1) No conocer a uno sino de vista; no tener trato con alguien. (2) No hallarse en buenos términos con otra persona.

Speakable [spīk'-a-bl], *a.* 1. Decible, capaz de decirse o hablarse. 2. ¿Capaz de hablar.

Speaker [spīk'-ęr], *s.* 1. El que habla, vocero. 2. Orador, el que arenga o habla en público. 3. Presidente de un cuerpo legislativo. *The Speaker of the House,* El presidente de la cámara de los diputados. *An easy* o *ready speaker,* Un orador de fácil palabra.

Speakership [spī'-ker-ship], *s.* Oficio o cargo del presidente de una asamblea legislativa.

Speaking [spīk'-ing], *a.* Parlante, que habla. *A speaking likeness,* Un retrato viviente, que está hablando.—*s.* Habla, discurso; declamación. *Speaking-tube,* Tubo acústico (para hablar entre dos piezas algo distantes una de otra) o desde la calle a uno de los pisos. *Speaking-trumpet,* Bocina, especie de trompeta que sirve para hablar de lejos; portavoz.

Spear [spīr], *s.* 1. Lanza, azagaya, venablo. 2. Arpón de pesca. 3. (Poét.) Lancero. 4. Brizna, tallo delgado de hierba. *Pump-spear,* (Mar.) Asta de bomba. *Spear-box,* (Mar.) Guarnición de bomba. *Spear-grass,* Hierba de los prados. Poa pratensis. *Spear-head,* Punta de lanza. *Spear-wort,* Un ranúnculo, francesilla llama.

Spear, *va.* Alancear, atravesar o prender con lanza o con arpón.—*vn.* Brotar.

Spear fishing [spīr' fish-ing], *s.* Pesca con arpón.

Spearmint [spīr'-mint], *s.* (Bot.) Hierbabuena puntiaguda, menta verde.

Special [spesh'-al], *a.* 1. Especial, extraordinario, singular, que se diferencia de lo común, ordinario o general. 2. Especial, particular, privativo, peculiar; destinado para una cosa determinada. 3. Específico, que caracteriza y distingue una especie de otra; de especie, diferencial.

Special delivery [spesh'-al de-liv'-ęr-i], *s.* Entrega inmediata. (Aplícase a correspondencia.) *Special-delivery stamp,* Timbre de entrega inmediata.

Specialist [spesh'-al-ist], *s.* Especialista, persona que se dedica a una ciencia o arte, o que descuella en ellas.

Specialization [spesh-al-i-zê'-shun], *s.* Especialización.

Specially [spesh'-al-i], *adv.* Especialmente, singularmente, particularmente, sobre todo.

Speciality [spesh-i-al'-i-ti], *s.* Especialidad, calidad de especial.

Specialize [spesh'-al-aiz], *vn.* Especializar, especializarse.

Specialty [spesh'-al-ti], *s.* 1. Especialidad, empleo o estudio limitado a una clase determinada de trabajo; las tareas de un especialista. 2. Artículo fabricado para uso especial; artículo que se vende principal o exclusivamente. 3. (For.) Cualquiera obligación hecha y firmada formalmente.

Specie [spī'-shę], *s.* Dinero contante en oro o plata; numerario.

Species [spī'-shīz], *s.* (*sing.* y *pl.*) 1. (Biol.) Especie, grupo de animales o plantas subordinado al género (genus) y capaz de multiplicarse entre sí ilimitadamente. 2. Especie, razón general o concepto que comprende a muchos individuos de la misma naturaleza. 3. De aquí, en el lenguaje popular, clase, género, suerte, variedad; forma. 4. (Ant.) Especie, imagen o idea de algún objeto que se representa en el alma. 5. (Farm.) Polvos compuestos.

Specific, Specifical [spę-sif'-ic, al], *a.* 1. Específico, que caracteriza y distingue una cosa de otra. 2. Específico: dícese del medicamento que se supone capaz de curar una enfermedad determinada. 3. Expreso, formal, preciso; especificado, determinado, distinto. 4. Peculiar. *Specific name,* Nombre específico, el de la especie; sigue siempre al del género y principia generalmente con letra minúscula.

Specific, *s.* Específico o medicamento específico.

Specifically [spę-sif'-i-cal-i], *adv.* 1. Específicamente, de un modo específico. 2. En cuanto a su naturaleza o diferencia específica. 3. En un sentido o caso particular.

Specification [spes-i-fi-kê'-shun], *s.* Especificación; la mención individual o particular de una cosa.

Specific gravity [spę-sif'-ic grav'-i-ti], *s.* Gravedad específica.

Specify [spes'-i-fai], *va.* Especificar, declarar con individualidad, mencionar específicamente.

Specimen [spes'-i-men], *s.* Muestra, ejemplar.

Specious [spī'-shus], *a.* 1. Especioso, plausible, recto y verdadero en apariencia; por lo común sólo en apariencia. 2. (Ant.) Especioso, hermoso, vistoso.

Speciousness [spī'-shus-nes], *s.* Calidad de especioso.

Speck [spec], **Speckle** [spec'-l], *s.* 1. Manchita, mácula, punto descolorido en alguna cosa; nube en un ojo; lunar, señal. 2. Punto, cosa muy pequeña; partícula, átomo.

Speck, Speckle, *va.* Abigarrar, manchar, señalar con manchitas; espolvorear, motear.

Spectacle [spec'-ta-cl], *s.* 1. Espectáculo, lo que se expone a la vista pública; ostentación. 2. Espectáculo, suceso lastimoso, exhibición deplorable. 3. *pl.* Anteojos, lunetas de vidrio o cristal que sirven para corregir algún defecto de la visión o para proteger los ojos de la luz demasiado viva; gafas. 4. *pl.* (Zool.) Marcas o señales a manera de gafas.

Spectacled [spec'-ta-cld], *a.* El que lleva o usa anteojos.

Spectacular [spec-tac'-yu-lar], *a.* Espectacular, caracterizado por fausto y magnificencia.—*s.* Programa espectacular de televisión, de carácter extraordinario.

Spectator [spec-tê'-tęr], *s.* Espectador, el que mira con atención.

Spectatress [spec-tê'-tres], *sf.* Espectadora.

Specter, Spectre [spec'-tęr], *s.* Espectro, visión, fantasma.

Spectral [spec'-tral], *a.* 1. Espectral, perteneciente a un espectro o fantasma. 2. (Ópt.) Espectral, relativo a los espectros solares o causado por ellos.

Spectrology [spec-trel'-o-ji], *s.* Espectrología, el ramo de la ciencia que trata del análisis espectral.

Spectrometer [spec-trem'-e-tęr], *s.* Espectrómetro, aparato para el análisis espectral.

Spectroscope [spec'-tro-scōp], *s.* Espectroscopio, instrumento óptico que sirve para estudiar el espectro luminoso.

Spectroscopic, Spectroscopical [spec-tro-scep'-ic, al], *a.* Espectroscópico, que se refiere al espectroscopio o se ve con él.

Spectrum [spec'-trum], *s.* 1. Espectro, imagen con los colores del arco iris, producida por la descomposición de la luz. 2. Imagen de un objeto reluciente que se ve después de apartar de él la vista. *Solar spectrum*, Espectro solar.
Specula [spec'-yu-la], *s. pl.* Espejos. *V.* SPECULUM.
Specular [spec'-yu-lar], *a.* 1. Especular, terso, limpio, que tiene las cualidades de un espejo. 2. (Des.) Auxiliar de la vista.
Speculate [spec'-yu-lêt], *va.* y *vn.* 1. Especular, meditar, contemplar, considerar, reflexionar. 2. Especular, hacer una compra o inversión que puede ofrecer pérdida, pero con la esperanza de obtener una ganancia.
Speculation [spec-yu-lé'-shun], *s.* 1. Especulación, la acción y efecto de especular. 2. Un proyecto o pensamiento que se ha discurrido o meditado, pero que no se ha puesto en práctica. 3. Especulativa, teórica; en oposición a la práctica en las artes y ciencias. 4. Meditación, contemplación o consideración detenida de alguna cosa. 5. (Com.) Especulación, acción de comprar, vender, etc., para obtener una ganancia.
Speculative [spec'-yu-la-tiv], *a.* 1. Especulativo, contemplativo. muy pensativo, dado a la especulación o contemplación. 2. Especulativo, teórico, que termina sólo en la especulación de las cosas. 3. Especulador (en sentido comercial).
Speculatively [spec'-yu-la-tiv-li], *adv.* Especulativamente, teóricamente; por vía de especulación (intelectual o comercial).
Speculativeness [spec'-yu-la-tiv-nes], *s.* Carácter especulativo.
Speculator [spec'-yu-lê-tgr], *s.* 1. Especulador, la persona que especula comercialmente. 2. (Des.) Un observador, un contemplador.
Speculum [spec'-yu-lum], *s.* 1. Espejo. 2. (Cir.) Espéculum: nombre dado a varios instrumentos de cirugía que sirven para tener dilatadas las cavidades mientras se las examina.
Sped, *pret.* y *pp.* de *To* SPEED.
Speech [spîch], *s.* 1. Habla, lenguaje, palabra o facultad de hablar. 2. Habla, conversación; el acto de hablar; dicho, expresión hecha por palabras. *To lose one's speech*, Perder el habla. 3. Discurso (manuscrito o impreso); oración, arenga. 4. Idioma o lengua particular; dialecto; (fig.) cualquier modo de expresar el pensamiento por sonidos o señales.
Speechless [spîch'-les], *a.* 1. Mudo, privado de la facultad de hablar. 2. Cortado, sobrecogido, callado, turbado, desconcertado, sin habla.
Speechlessness [spîch'-les-nes], *s.* Mudez, la falta de habla.
Speechmaker [spîch'-mê-kgr], *s.* El que hace arengas.
Speed [spîd], *va.* (*pret.* y *pp.* SPED o SPEEDED). 1. Ayudar, dar ayuda o auxilio; favorecer; hacer salir bien o que tenga buen éxito alguna cosa. 2. Despachar, expedir, resolver y determinar algún negocio; acelerar el paso o movimiento. 3. Enviar a uno de prisa; apresurar, dar prisa, acelerar. *May Heaven speed this undertaking!* ¡El cielo favorezca esta empresa!—*vn.* 1. Ir, moverse o hacer alguna cosa con presteza y prontitud, despacharse, darse prisa. 2. Salir bien, tener buen éxito, tener acierto en lo que se emprende. 3. Hallarse en cualquiera situación buena o mala.
Speed, *s.* 1. Rapidez; el acto y estado de progresar rápidamente; presteza, velocidad, prisa, apresuramiento, diligencia. 2. Carrera, medida o razón del movimiento; velocidad relativa; (Mec.) andar. 3. Éxito, suceso, salida, fin, despacho bueno o malo de una cosa. *High speed*, Galope o carrera tendida. *With all speed*, A toda prisa, con toda la celeridad posible. *At full speed*, A toda velocidad; (hablando de personas) a carrera tendida, velozmente; (hablando de caballos) a escape, a rienda suelta, a escape tendido; (de carruajes) a la carrera, a todo correr. *To make speed*, Hacer diligencia, acelerarse, apresurarse.
Speedboat [spîd'-bōt], *s.* Lancha rápida.
Speeder [spîd'-gr], *s.* Corredor, el que corre a velocidades excesivas.
Speedily [spîd'-i-li], *adv.* Rápidamente, velozmente; de prisa, pronto, con toda diligencia, con apresuramiento.
Speediness [spîd'-i-nes], *s.* Celeridad, velocidad, rapidez; prontitud, diligencia, prisa.
Speed limit [spîd lim'-it], *s.* Límite de velocidad.
Speedometer [spî-dem'-e-tgr], *s.* Velocímetro, celerímetro.
Speed-up [spîd'-up], *s.* Aceleramiento.
Speedway [spîd'-wê], *s.* Autopista, supercarretera.
Speedwell [spîd'-wel], *s.* (Bot.) Verónica, planta de las escrofulariáceas.
Speedy [spîd'-i], *a.* 1. Ligero, veloz, rápido, que se mueve con velocidad. 2. Pronto, diligente, acelerado, vivo, que emplea poco tiempo en hacer una cosa. *A speedy answer*, Una contestación pronta.
Speer, Speir [spîr], *va.* y *vn.* (Esco.) Buscar para descubrir; indagar, preguntar, inquirir. *To speer at*, Informarse, preguntar.
Speiss [spais], *s.* Compuesto que consta de los arseniuros y sulfuros de ciertos metales (como el cobre, el hierro y el níquel), que se concentran en la fundición de algunos minerales.
Spell [spel], *s.* 1. Hechizo, encanto. 2. Turno, orden y alternativa entre varios sujetos para el trabajo; tanda. 3. Tanda, tarea que se señala para un tiempo determinado. 4. (Fam.) Poco tiempo. *By spells*, Por turnos, a su vez. *A spell of eight hours*, Tanda (o tiempo) de ocho horas. *Spellbound*, Encantado, bajo el poder del encanto.
Spell, *va.* (*pret.* y *pp.* SPELLED o SPELT). 1. Deletrear, pronunciar o escribir cada letra separada y de por sí. 2. Descifrar, p. ej. una inscripción; aprender calentándose los sesos, estudiar; se usa a veces con *over* o *out*. 3. Hechizar, encantar.—*vn.* 1. Formar palabras con las letras; particularmente, escribir correctamente o con buena ortografía. 2. (Poét. y poco us.) Contemplar, meditar.
Spell, *va.* (Fam. o Prov.) Relevar, reemplazar, tomar el puesto de otro en alguna ocupación. *To spell the pump*, Rendir los marineros a la bomba. *To spell the watch*, Llamar a la guardia.
Speller [spel'-gr], *s.* El que deletrea.
Spelling [spel'-ing], *s.* 1. Deletreo, acción de deletrear; arte de deletrear correctamente; ortografía. 2. Manera como se deletrea una palabra y la misma palabra deletreada.
Spelt [spelt], *s.* (Bot.) Espelta.
Spelt, *pret.* y *pp.* del verbo SPELL.
Spelter [spel'-tgr], *s.* Cinc (término del comercio).
Spelt-wheat [spelt'-hwît], *s.* Escanda, espelta, una especie de trigo.
Spencer [spen'-sgr], *s.*, Especie de sobretodo, que se llevaba al principio del siglo XIX.
Spend [spend], *va.* (*pret.* y *pp.* SPENT). 1. Gastar, expender, emplear el dinero en alguna cosa. 2. Malgastar, disipar. 3. Gastar, consumir, destruir, extinguir. 4. Gastar, echar a perder. 5. Gastar, ocupar, emplear. *I shall spend the winter with my sister*, Pasaré el invierno con mi hermana. 6. Cansar, fatigar.—*vn.* 1. Hacer gastos. 2. Gastarse, perderse, consumirse. *To spend a mast*, (Mar.) Perder un palo.
Spender [spend'-gr], *s.* 1. El que gasta. 2. Gastador, el que gasta mucho, pródigo, manirroto.
Spending [spend'-ing], *s.* Gasto.
Spendthrift [spend'-thrift], *s.* Pródigo, gastador, manirroto, derrochador, malgastador.
Spent, *pret.* y *pp.* del verbo *To* SPEND.
Sperm [spgrm], *s.* Esperma, semen.
Spermaceti [spgr-ma-sî'-ti o set'-i], *s.* Espermaceti o esperma de ballena, substancia grasienta que se saca del aceite contenido en la cabeza de los cachalotes. *Sperm-oil, spermaceti-oil*, Aceite de esperma, de cachalote.
Spermatic, Spermatical [spgr-mat'-ic, al], *a.* Espermático, perteneciente a la esperma, que conduce o contiene semen.
Spermatize [spgr'-ma-taiz], *vn.* Arrojar esperma.
Spermatology, Spermology [spgr-ma-tel'-o-ji, spgr-mel'-o-ji], *s.* Espermatología, la parte de la biología que trata de la esperma, o de las semillas en general.
Spermatozoon [spgr-ma-to-zō'-gn], *s.* (*pl.* -ZO'-A). Espermatozoide, espermátulo o espermatozoario; cuerpo filamentoso y viviente que se halla en el semen de los animales y que da a éste su facultad fecundante.
Sperm-whale [spgrm'-hwêl"], *s.* Cachalote, un gran cetáceo. Physeter macrocephalus.
Spew [spiū], *va.* y *vn.* Vomitar, echar algo del estómago; arrojar, echar con aborrecimiento.
Spewing [spiū'-ing], *s.* Vómito.
Sphalerite [sfal'-gr-ait], *s.* Mineral, un sulfuro de cinc, amarillo, pardo o negro, translúcido o diáfano.
Sphenoid [sfî'-neid], *a.* Esfenoidal, encajado a modo de cuña.—*s.* Esfenoides, hueso impar, en medio de los de la base del cráneo.
Spheral [sfîr'-al], *a.* 1. Esférico, redondeado, simétrico. 2. Referente a las esferas celestes; armonioso.
Sphere [sfîr], *s.* 1. Esfera, cuerpo esférico. 2. Globo, sea celeste o terrestre. 3. Esfera, el círculo o extensión de los conocimientos científicos, y la clase, estado o condición de las personas; círculo de acción, extensión de poder o influencia.

Sphere, *va.* Colocar en una esfera; redondear, poner redonda alguna cosa.
Spheric [sfer'-ic], *a.* 1. Celestial, perteneciente á un astro, o a las esferas en que los antiguos suponían colocados a los astros; exaltado. 2. *V.* SPHERICAL.
Spherical [sfer'-ic-al], *a.* 1. Esférico, de forma de esfera o globo. 2. Planetario, perteneciente á los planetas.
Spherically [sfer'-ic-al-i], *adv.* En forma esférica.
Sphericalness [sfer'-ic-al-nes], **Sphericity** [sfe-ris'-i-ti], *s.* Esfericidad, redondez; forma esférica.
Spheroid [sfí'-reid], *s.* Esferoide. cuerpo cuya figura se aproxima a la de la esfera.
Spheroidal [sfí-reid'-al], *a.* Esferoidal, que tiene forma o figura de esferoide.
Spherule [sfer'-yūl o ūl], *s.* Esfera menuda, glóbulo, esférula.
Sphincter [sfinc'-ter], *s.* (Anat.) Esfínter, un músculo que rodea una abertura o tubo y sirve para cerrarlo.
Sphinx [sfincs], *s.* 1. Esfinge (*f.*); monstruo fabuloso, con cabeza de mujer y cuerpo de león, que proponía enigmas y devoraba a los que no podían explicarlos. La esfinge egipcia no tenía alas, la griega sí. 2. Persona misteriosa o enigmática. 3. Esfinge (*m.*), género de insectos lepidópteros. *V.* HAWK-MOTH.
Sphygmic [sfig'-mic], *a.* Esfígmico, relativo al pulso; pulsátil, que pulsa. (Gr.)
Sphygmograph [sfig'-mo-graf], *s.* Esfigmógrafo o esfigmómetro, instrumento que sirve para medir el pulso.
Spicate, Spical, Spicated [spai'-kêt, ed, spai'-cal], *a.* 1. (Bot.) Espigado, dispuesto en espigas; se dice de las flores. 2. (Orn.) Espolonado, que tiene espuela.
Spice [spais], *s.* 1. Especia, cualquiera de las drogas con que se sazonan las viandas. 2. Saborete, lo que da sabor, gusto o interés; grano, dosis. 3. (Poét.) Olor aromático, perfume agradable. *Spice-bush*, Benjuí, arbusto americano aromático (Lindera benzoin) de las lauráceas. *Spices*, Especiería, especias. *The spice*, (Fig.) La nata, la flor de.
Spice, *va.* Especiar, echar especias, sazonar o condimentar con especias; (fig.) dar gusto o picante a una cosa, dicho o escrito.
Spicer [spais'-er], *s.* 1. El que sazona con especias. 2. (Des.) Especiero, el que vende especias o trata en ellas.
Spicery [spais'-er-i], *s.* 1. Especiería, droguería. 2. Dispensa o lugar donde se guardan las especias. 3. Propiedad o carácter aromático.
Spicily [spai'-si-li], *adv.* De una manera picante.
Spick-and-span [spic-and-span], *a.* Nuevo, flamante, fresco.
Spicknel [spic'-nel], *s.* (Bot.) Pinillo oloroso, hierba perenne de Europa. Meum athamanticum.
‡**Spicosity** [spai-ces'-i-ti], *s.* La calidad de tener espigas o aristas.
Spicula [spic'-yu-la], *s.* 1. (Bot.) Espiguita, espiga menuda. 2. *V.* SPICULE.
Spicular [spic'-yu-lar], *a.* 1. Parecido a un dardo o a una aguja; puntiagudo; que tiene puntas o púas. 2. Picante, mordaz. *A spicular epigram*, Un epigrama mordaz.
Spicule [spic'-yūl], *s.* Cuerpo pequeño y puntiagudo, púa. 1. (Zool.) Púa que se halla en los invertebrados, como la esponja. 2. (Bot.) Espiguita, espiguilla. 3. *pl.* Agujas de la escarcha o hielo, la única forma en que puede existir la humedad a grandes alturas de la atmósfera.
Spicy [spai'-si], *a.* 1. Que produce especias o abunda en ellas. 2. Aromático, que tiene fragancia, especiado. 3. (Fig.) Sabroso, picante.
Spider [spai'-der], *s.* 1. Araña, insecto arácnido. 2. Arácnido, lo que es semejante a la araña. 3. *Spider* o *spider-crab*, Araña de mar, cangrejo de patas largas y delgadas. (Maia o Macrocheira.) 4. Sartén con mango largo; originalmente cazo con pies. *Spider-like*, Parecido a una araña. *Spiderflower*, Una especie cualquiera del género Cleome. *Spider-line*, Hilo de tela de araña para micrómetros. *Spider's web*, Telaraña.
Spiderwort [spai'-der-wūrt], *s.* (Bot.) Pasajera, una especie cualquiera del género Tradescantia; hierba perenne con flores azules obscuras de tres pétalos.
Spigot [spig'-et], *s.* Llave de fuente, tapón para cerrar la espita.
Spike [spaic], *s.* 1. Espiga de grano; inflorescencia con flores sesiles dispuestas juntamente a lo largo de un eje común. 2. Espigón, clavo largo, perno. 3. Punta o punta larga. 4. (Bot.) Alhucema, espliego. *Oil of spike*, Aceite de espliego.
Spike, *va.* 1. Afianzar, sujetar o clavar con espigones. 2. Aguzar, adelgazar por la punta. 3. Clavar, tapar o inutilizar el oído de un cañón. *To spike a cannon*, (Mil.) Clavar un cañón.
Spikelet [spaik'-let], *s. dim.* Espiguita, espiguilla; espiga secundaria (en las gramíneas).
Spikenard [spaic'-nard], *s.* 1. Nardo, confección aromática hecha de las hojas del nardo y sus espigas. 2. (Bot.) Espicanardo, espique o nardo. (Nardostachys Jatamansi.) 3. Hierba americana (Aralia racemosa) que se parece a la zarzaparilla silvestre. 4. Uno de los varios aceites vegetales.
Spiky [spai'-ki], *a.* Parecido a un clavo, puntiagudo; armado de púas.
Spile [spail], *va.* 1. Horadar un barril y ponerle espita, tapón o espiche. 2. Clavar estacas o pilotes.—*s.* 1. Pilote (estaca). *V.* PILE. 2. Clavija de madera que sirve de tapón; espiche; también, agujero en un barril o tonel que permite la entrada del aire o la salida de los gases de fermentación. 3. (E. U.) Llave de sangrar el arce azucarero.
Spiling [spai'-ling], *s.* Pilotaje, conjunto u obra de pilotes.
Spill [spil], *s.* (Prov.) 1. Astilla de madera. 2. Clavillo; fósforo de cartón.
Spill, *va.* (*pret.* y *pp.* SPILLED o SPILT). 1. Derramar, verter, dejar caer; perder: dícese de las substancias líquidas y polvorientas o de objetos pequeños y sueltos. 2. Arrojar, volcar. 3. Destruir, desperdiciar, malbaratar, disipar. 4. (Mar.) Apagar, descargar el viento del seno de una vela para aferrarla. —*vn.* Derramarse, verterse, volcarse; rebosar; perderse o destruirse.
Spiller [spil'-er], *s.* Sedal de caña de pescar.
Spilling-lines [spil'-ing-lainz], *s.* (Mar.) Trapas de las velas.
Spillway [spil'-wê], *s.* Canal de desagüe.
Spin [spin], *va.* (*pret.* SPUN, ant. SPAN, *pp.* SPUN). 1. Hilar, reducir el algodón, lino, cáñamo, lana, seda, a hilo, etc. 2. Alargar, prolongar; decir, contar, parlotear; a menudo con *out*. *To spin out long discourses*, Hacer largos discursos. 3. Hacer girar (como gira una peonza). 4. Hacer durar, procurar que pase el tiempo.—*vn.* 1. Hilar, ejercer el arte de hilar. 2. Correr hilo a hilo; hilar, echar filamentos viscosos las arañas o los gusanos de seda y formar con ellos telarañas o capullos. 3. Girar; moverse en derredor como un huso. 4. *V.* SPURT.
Spinach, Spinage [spin'-ej], *s.* (Bot.) Espinaca.
Spinal [spai'-nal], *a.* Espinal. *Spinal column*, Espina dorsal, espinazo.
Spindle [spin'-dl], *s.* 1. Huso, instrumento de madera con que se hila; instrumento de hierro que se introduce en un cañón para devanar seda; broca. 2. Gorrón, eje, carretel, árbol sobre el cual gira una cosa. 3. Cosa muy delgada que se supone parecida a un huso. *Spindle of the vane*, (Mar.) Huso, eje o fierro de la grímpola. *Spindle of the capstan*, (Mar.) Pínola del cabrestante. *Spindle of the steering-wheel*, (Mar.) Maza de la rueda del timón. *Spindle-legged*, *-shanked*, Zanquivano, el que tiene las piernas largas y delgadas. *Spindle-shaped*, Fusiforme, en figura de huso.
Spindle, *vn.* Crecer los tallos de las plantas muy altos y delgados.
Spindle-tree [spin'-dl-trí], *s.* (Bot.) Bonetero, arbusto de Europa. Euonymus.
Spine [spain], *s.* 1. Espinazo o espina; columna vertebral. 2. Espina, púa delgada o puntiaguda.
Spinel [spi-nel'], *s.* Espinel, especie de rubí.
Spinet [spin'-et], *s.* Espineta, clavicordio pequeño.
Spinnaker [spin'-a-ker], *s.* Una vela grande en forma de foque para regatas, y que se pone al lado opuesto de la vela mayor.
Spinner [spin'-er], *s.* 1. Hilador, hilandera, hilandero. 2. Araña de jardín. 3. *V.* SPINNERET.
Spinneret [spin'-er-et], *s.* Fileras, órgano propio de la araña o del gusano de seda, que les sirve para tejer la telaraña o la seda.
Spinning [spin'-ing], *s.* Hila, acción o arte de hilar, filatura. *Spinning-jenny*, Telar o aparato para hilar más de un hilo a la vez. *Spinning-mule*, Telar para hilar algodón. *V.* MULE. *Spinning-wheel*, Torno de hilar.
Spinose [spai'-nōs], *a.* Espinoso, lleno de espinas.
Spinosity [spai-nes'-i-ti], *s.* Dificultad, cosa espinosa, difícil o intrincada, perplejidad, enredo.
Spinous [spai'-nus], *a.* Espinoso.
Spinster [spin'-ster], *sf.* 1. (Des.) Hilandera, la mujer que hila. 2. Soltera, la mujer que no se ha casado nunca, especialmente si es ya de alguna edad.
Spiny [spai'-ni], *a.* 1. Espinoso, pro-

visto de espinas. 2. Penoso, difícil, inquietante.

Spiracle [spir'-a-cl], *s.* 1. Respiradero, abertura u orificio para dar paso al aire o al agua al respirar; estigma, orificio de las tráqueas de los insectos; estoma, poro microscópico que se halla en la epidermis de las plantas; respiradero de los cetáceos. 2. Cono muy pequeño formado en la lava líquida por los gases que de ella se escapan.

Spiral spai'-ral], *a.* Espiral; dispuesto en espiral o en hélice.—*s.* 1. Espira, curva espiral que partiendo de un punto y aumentando progresivamente su radio, da vueltas en torno de sí misma a manera de caracol. 2. Hélice.

Spirally [spai'-ral-i], *adv.* Espiralmente, en figura o a modo de espiral.

Spire [spair], *s.* 1. Espira, línea curva que sin cerrar el círculo va dando vueltas en forma de caracol. 2. Obelisco, pirámide; torre. 3. La aguja o chapitel de un campanario o torre. 4. Tallo delgado, brizna de hierba. 5. Cúspide, cima, de alguna cosa.

Spire, *va.* Edificar con chapitel.—*vn.* 1. Rematar en punta. 2. Germinar, como la cebada al hacer cerveza.

Spirit [spir'-it], *s.* 1. Espíritu, substancia incorpórea o inmaterial. 2. Espíritu, alma racional. 3. Espíritu, ánimo, valor, energía, brío, esfuerzo, denuedo. 4. Viveza, agudeza, fuego, ardor, fogosidad. 5. Espectro, fantasma, visión. 6. Hombre de corazón, espíritu emprendedor. 7. Elación, fortaleza, grandeza de alma. 8. Espíritu, genio o inclinación para una cosa. 9. Ingenio, talento. 10. Genio, condición, carácter especial; motivo, principio de acción. 11. Espíritu, el verdadero sentido o intento; opuesto a letra. 12. Espíritu, el vigor o la energía natural que alienta y fortifica el cuerpo. 13. Extracto o quinta esencia de una cosa. 14. El licor espirituoso que ha sido sacado por destilación, particularmente el alcohol. *Spirits, s. pl.* (1) Espíritus, los vapores sutilísimos que se exhalan de un licor o cuerpo cualquiera. (2) Espíritus, las partes más sutiles y puras de los cuerpos. (3) Humor o buen humor, la buena disposición en que uno se halla para ejecutar una cosa; alegría, vivacidad, viveza. *To be in good* o *high spirits*, Estar alegre, de buen humor o contento. *To have a high spirit*, Tener el alma grande; ser altivo. *Spirits* o *spirit of wine*, Espíritu de vino, alcohol común. *Spirits of turpentine*, Aceite de trementina, aguarrás. *Low spirits*, Abatimiento. *High spirits*, Alegría, buen humor. *To keep up one's spirits*, Mantener el valor. *Spirit-stirring*, Animador, que estimula el valor. *To show spirit*, Mostrar buen ánimo. *Pyroxylic spirit, wood spirit*, Éter piroleñoso, alcohol metílico. *Ardent spirits*, Licores espirituosos. *Spirit-lamp*, Lámpara de alcohol. *Spirit-level*, Nivel de aire (en el éter y el alcohol). *The Spirit*, El Espíritu Santo.

Spirit, *va.* 1. Llevar, conducir secreta y misteriosamente como por medio de un espíritu; arrebatar, llevarse; se usa con *away* u otro adverbio. 2. (Ant.) Incitar, animar, dar espíritu.

Spirited [spir'-it-ed], *a.* Vivo, fogoso, brioso; lleno de vida, de fuerza, de vigor; arrebatado. *A spirited horse*, Un caballo fogoso, impetuoso. *High-spirited*, Que posee grandeza de alma. *Low-spirited*, Que es cobarde o se amilana con facilidad. *Mean-spirited*, De ánimo mezquino, estrecho; miserable.

Spiritedly [spir'-it-ed-li], *adv.* Animosamente, con espíritu, vigor o energía.

Spiritedness [spir'-it-ed-nes], *s.* Arrebato, calor, energía; ardor; corazón, valor; vigor, ánimo, fuerza.

Spiritism [spir'-it-izm], *s.* Espiritismo; voz de uso no bien determinado. *V.* SPIRITUALISM.

Spiritless [spir'-it-les], *a.* 1. Abatido, amilanado, sin espíritu o vigor; sin carácter, gastado; sin imaginación. 2. Sin espíritu, sin alma, muerto.

Spiritlessly [spir'-it-les-li], *adv.* Sin vigor, sin espíritu, sin energía.

Spiritlessness [spir'-it-les-nes], *s.* Abatimiento, amilanamiento, falta de vigor o energía.

†Spiritous [spir'-it-us], *a.* 1. Espiritoso o espirituoso, refino o refinado. *Spiritous liquors*, Licores espirituosos. 2. Vivo, activo.

Spiritual [spir'-it-yu-al], *a.* 1. Espiritual, incorpóreo, que consta de espíritu; mental, intelectual, inmaterial. 2. Espiritual, que pertenece al espíritu; santo, puro; que no es carnal, sensual ni corporal; que proviene del Espíritu Santo. 3. Espiritual, eclesiástico, en oposición a temporal o civil; piadoso, religioso. 4. *V.* SPIRITUALISTIC.

Spiritualism [spir'-it-yu-al-izm], *s.* 1. Espiritismo, doctrina de los que creen en la comunicación con los espíritus mediante una persona que se llama médium. 2. Espiritualismo, sistema filosófico opuesto al materialismo, que acepta la existencia de seres espirituales y en particular la inmortalidad del alma. 3. Espiritualidad.

Spiritualist [spir'-it-yu-al-ist], *s.* 1. Espiritista, partidario del espiritismo. 2. Espiritualista, partidario del espiritualismo.

Spiritualistic [spir''-it-yu-al-is'-tic], *a.* Espiritista, perteneciente al espiritismo moderno.

Spirituality [spir-it-yu-al'-i-ti], *s.* 1. Espiritualidad, inmaterialidad; calidad de espiritual, de santo y puro; carácter o naturaleza espiritual; vida interior. 2. Los bienes espirituales o eclesiásticos.

Spiritualization [spir-it-yu-al-i-zé'-shun], *s.* 1. El acto de espiritualizar. 2. (Quím. ant.) Espiritualización, la acción de extraer las partes espirituosas de los cuerpos.

Spiritualize [spir'-it-yu-al-aiz], *va.* 1. Espiritualizar, dar carácter espiritual; tratar, considerar como si tuviese sentido espiritual. 2. Animar, vivificar.

Spiritually [spir'-it-yu-al-i], *adv.* Espiritualmente; con el carácter de espíritu, en espíritu.

Spirituous [spir'-it-yu-us], *a.* 1. Espiritoso o espirituoso, destilado; que contiene alcohol; embriagante, ardiente. 2. (Des.) Espiritoso, vivo, animoso, que tiene mucho espíritu. *Spirituous liquors*, Licores espirituosos o ardientes.

Spirituousness [spir'-it-yu-us-nes], *s.* La calidad de ser un licor espirituoso.

Spirometer [spai-rom'-e-ter], *s.* Espirómetro, instrumento para medir la capacidad de los pulmones.

Spirt [spert], *va.* y *s.* *V.* SPURT.

Spiry [spai'-ri], *a.* (Poét. o des.) Piramidal, espiral; con numerosos campanarios.

†Spissated [spis'-é-ted], *a.* Espesado.

Spit [spit], *s.* 1. Asador, varilla puntiaguda de hierro que se introduce en la carne para asarla. 2. Lengua de tierra o banco de arena largo y estrecho que se extiende mar adentro desde la orilla. 3. (Prov. Ingl.) Azadonada. *Turnspit*, Asador, máquina para asar.

Spit, *s.* 1. Escupidura, escupitajo, esputo, escupido; saliva. 2. Escupidura, el acto de escupir. 3. Espuma o huevos de varios insectos. *Spitbox*, Escupidera.

Spit, *va.* (*pret.* y *pp.* SPIT, SPAT). 1. Escupir. 2. Arrojar, impulsar o echar en ráfagas o gotas.—*vn.* 1. Escupir, salivar, echar saliva o esputos, gargajear. 2. Producir sonido semejante al que se hace escupiendo. 3. Caer en gotas o copos dispersos.

Spit, *va.* (*pret.* y *pp.* SPITTED). 1. Espetar, clavar en el asador; atravesar de parte a parte. 2. Ensartar en una varilla.

Spitchcock [spich'-coc], *va.* Dividir un ave o pescado a lo largo y asarlos.

Spitchcock, *s.* Anguila tajada y asada.

Spite [spait], *s.* 1. Rencor, despecho, malevolencia, odio, mala voluntad. 2. Acción de malquerencia; lo que se hace por rencor; vejación. *Spite of* o *in spite of*, A pesar de, a despecho, contra la voluntad o gusto de alguno. *In spite of all my endeavours*, A pesar de todos mis esfuerzos.

Spite, *va.* Dar pesar, causar indignación; picar, impacientar; mostrar resentimiento, vejar maliciosamente.

Spitfire [spit'-fair], *s.* Persona colérica, dada a decir palabras duras o maliciosas.

Spiteful [spait'-ful], *a.* Rencoroso, enconoso; malicioso, maligno, malévolo.

Spitefully [spait'-ful-i], *adv.* Malignamente, con rencor, con tirria; por despecho; con el deseo de hacer daño.

Spitefulness [spait'-ful-nes], *s.* Malignidad, malevolencia, malicia, rencor, encono; deseo de perjudicar que proviene de irritación y mala voluntad.

Spitter [spit'-er], *s.* 1. El que espeta. 2. Escupidor. 3. Gamezno, el gamo pequeño y nuevo.

Spittle [spit'-l], *s.* Saliva, humor acuoso que se forma en la boca; escupido, esputo, gargajo.

Spittoon [spit-tūn'], *s.* Escupidera, recipiente para escupir.

Spitvenom [spit'-ven-um], *s.* Veneno arrojado por la boca.

Spitz [spits], *s.* Perro pequeño de hocico puntiagudo y pelo largo y tupido; perro de Pomerania. (Alemán < *spitze*, punto.)

Splanchnic [splanc'-nic], *a.* Esplánico, perteneciente o relativo a las vísceras.—*s.* Un nervio esplánico.

Splanchnology [splanc-nol'-o-ji], *s.* Esplanología, parte de la anatomía que trata de las vísceras.

Splash [splash], *va.* 1. Chapotear,

hacer saltar, golpear el agua. 2. Salpicar, humedecer con un líquido (como agua sucia); enlodar.—*vn.* Chapotear, golpear el agua con los pies o las manos.—*s.* 1. Salpicadura, acto de salpicar, o chapotear; ruido, choque del agua. 2. Salpicadura, mancha de agua sucia que ha salpicado.

Splashboard [splash'-bōrd], *s.* Guardafango (de un vehículo).

Splashy [splash'-i], *a.* Cenagoso, lodoso, sucio; húmedo.

Splatter [splat'-ẹr], *va.* y *vn.* Hacer un ruido ligero como de chapoteo; también, hablar entre dientes, hablar en vascuence.

Splay [splê], *va.* 1. Achaflanar, hacer en chaflán. 2. Exponer a la vista, mostrar; cortar un ave, un pez, etc. 3. Despaldar o despaldillar a un caballo.—*a.* Extendido, desplegado, ancho; pesado.—*s.* Alféizar, derrame que hace la pared en el corte de una ventana o puerta.

Splayfoot, Splayfooted [splê'-fut, ed], *a.* Que tiene los pies aplastados o vueltos hacia afuera.

Splaymouth [splê'-mauth], *a.* Boquiancho.

Spleen [splīn], *s.* 1. Bazo, órgano esponjoso que está en el hipocondrio izquierdo; antiguamente se consideraba como el asiento de varios afectos. (De aquí los sentidos figurados.) 2. Ira, rencor, odio, animosidad, mal humor. 3. Hipocondría, vapores hipocondríacos. 4. Esplín, melancolía. *To vent one's spleen,* Descargar uno la bilis o el rencor.

Spleened [splīnd], *a.* Privado del bazo.

Spleenful [splīn'-ful], *a.* Bilioso, colérico, enfadoso, regañón, triste, melancólico.

Spleenish [splīn'-ish], *a.* (Poco us.) Algo caprichudo o regañón; algo bilioso o melancólico.

Spleenless [splīn'-les], *a.* Blando, suave, apacible.

Spleenwort [splīn'-wūrt], *s.* (Bot.) Escolopendra, culantrillo, doradillo, cualquier helecho del género Asplenium. (Llamado así porque varias especies se empleaban en otro tiempo para curar las enfermedades del bazo.)

Spleeny [splīn'-i], *a.* Triste, melancólico, bilioso; irritable, enfadadizo.

Splendent [splen'-dent], *a.* Esplendente; resplandeciente.

Splendid [splen'-did], *a.* 1. Esplendente, brillante, resplandeciente. 2. Espléndido, magnífico. 3. Ilustre, glorioso, heroico.

Splendidly [splen'-did-li], *adv.* Espléndidamente.

Splendor, Splendour [splen'-dẹr], *s.* Esplendor, pompa, magnificencia; brillantez, gran resplandor.

Splenetic [sple-net'-ic o splen'-ẹ-tic], *a.* Atrabiliario, atrabilioso, bilioso, melancólico; caprichudo, regañón, de mal humor.

Splenic [splen'-ic], *a.* Esplénico, perteneciente o relativo al bazo. *Splenic artery,* Arteria esplénica.

Splenotomy [sple-not'-o-mi], *s.* Esplenotomía, operación para extirpar el bazo.

Splice [splais], *va.* 1. Ayustar, entrelazar las puntas de dos cabos; empalmar. 2. Unir, juntar, empalmar, maderos. 3. (Fest.) Unir en matrimonio. *To splice the main brace,* (Ger.) Tomar un trago de licor espirituoso.

Splice, *s.* (Mar.) Ayuste, empalme, de cabo. *To bend with a splice,* (Mar.) Ajustar con costura. *Eye-splice,* (Mar.) Costura de ojo. *Long-splice,* (Mar.) Costura larga o española, ayuste largo. *Short-splice,* (Mar.) Costura corta o flamenca; empalmadura.

Splicing [splais'-ing], *s.* Ayuste, empalme. *Splicing-fid,* (Mar.) Pasador, para abrir los cabos y ayustar.

Splint [splint], *va.* Entablillar, asegurar con tablillas un miembro fracturado o lastimado.—*s.* 1. Tira plana y delgada, particularmente la que sirve para hacer cuévanos, asientos de sillas, etc.; astilla. 2. Tablilla para entablillar los miembros rotos o descoyuntados. 3. *V. Splint-bone. Splint-bone,* Sobrehueso, uno de los pequeños huesos rudimentarios laterales, en las patas del caballo y otros animales afines.

Splinter [splin'-tẹr], *va.* 1. Astillar, hacer astillas, hender en fragmentos. 2. Entablillar o entabletar un miembro fracturado.—*vn.* Hacerse pedazos, romperse en astillas.

Splinter, *s.* 1. Cacho, astilla, esquirla, brizna, de un cuerpo sólido; por lo general, es agudo y angular más bien que plano. 2. Rancajo, punta o astilla de madera clavada en la carne. 3. Astillazo que salta de una piedra cuando se está labrando.

Split [split], *va.* (*pret.* y *pp.* SPLIT o SPLITTED). 1. Hender, dividir, partir, rajar; estrellar. *Let us split the difference,* Partamos la diferencia. 2. Dividir, hender o separar a lo largo. *V.* RIVE. 3. Dividir en dos o más capas, como se hace con el cuero. 4. Dividir, desunir los ánimos introduciendo discordias.—*vn.* 1. Henderse, estrellarse, rajarse, romperse; estallar. 2. Dividirse en dos o más partidos opuestos. 3. Henderse, rajarse a lo largo. *To split upon a rock,* Estrellarse contra una roca. *To split with laughing,* Reventar de risa.—*s.* 1. Hendedura, hendidura, grieta, abertura longitudinal. 2. División, cisma, rompimiento. 3. Raja, pedazo separado. —*a.* 1. Hendido (longitudinalmente). 2. Limpiado y acecinado (el pescado).

Split-level [split-lev'-el], *a.* De piso escalonado.

Splitter [split'-ẹr], *s.* Hendedor, el que hiende o raja.

Splotch [splech], *va.* Manchar o ensuciar con manchitas de diferente color.—*s.* Manchita de color distinto de las que la rodean; borrón.

Splurge [splūrj], *vn.* Hacer gran papel; hacer alarde vanidoso.—*s.* Ostentación vana de sí mismo. (Voz imitativa.)

Splutter [splut'-ẹr], *va.* y *vn.* Farfullar, hablar indistinta y atropelladamente.—*s.* Chisporroteo; sonido como el que se produce al farfullar. Baraúnda, batahola, confusión. (Variación de *Sputter.*)

Spoil [spoil], *va.* 1. Inutilizar, echar a perder; deteriorar, destruir la utilidad o belleza de una cosa; estropear. 2. Corromper, pervertir, arruinar. 3. Pillar, robar; despojar, saquear, robar. 4. Mimar demasiado. —*vn.* 1. Inutilizarse, corromperse, dañarse, echarse a perder alguna cosa. 2. Hacer pillaje o robo. *Spoiled child,* Niño mimado, gachón, consentido.

Spoil, *s.* 1. Despojo, botín; lo que se coge al enemigo. 2. *pl.* (E. U.) Los gajes o beneficios de un cargo público; recompensa por servicios políticos. 3. Pillaje, robo. 4. ¿Camisa o despojo de serpiente o culebra, la piel de que se desnuda.

Spoiler [spoil'-ẹr], *s.* 1. Despojador, desposeedor; robador, ladrón. 2. Corruptor, pervertidor, el que echa a perder a otro corrompiéndole o contemplándole.

Spoilsman [spoilz'-man], *s.* (E. U.) El que trabaja por un partido político por los gajes del oficio; partidario del reparto de los despojos entre los que mandan.

Spoke [spōk], *s.* 1. Radio de rueda, rayo de rueda. 2. Barra que se introduce en la rueda para impedir que gire. 3. Escalón de escalera. 4. (Mar.) Cabilla del timón.—*va.* Poner rayos a una rueda. *Spoke-shave,* Rebajador de rayos.

Spoke, *pret.* del verbo *To* SPEAK.

Spoken, *pp.* del verbo *To* SPEAK. Hablado.

Spokesman [spōcs'-man], *s.* Interlocutor, el que habla en nombre de otro, o lleva la voz o la palabra en nombre de otros.

Spoliation [spo-li-ê'-shun], *s.* 1. Despojo. 2. (For.) Espoliación de bienes.

Spondaic [spen-dê'-ic], *a.* Espondaico, lo perteneciente o que se compone de pies espondeos.

Spondee [spen'-dī], *s.* (Poét.) Espondeo, pie que consta de dos sílabas largas.

Spondyl [spen'-dil], *s.* 1. Espondil o vértebra. 2. Ensambladura.

Sponge [spunj], *s.* 1. Esponja, animal fijo y marino por regla general, sin tentáculos y con poros en la pared del cuerpo. 2. Esponja, producción marina, masa flexible y porosa habitada por pólipos, que con mucha facilidad absorbe cualquier líquido y lo suelta comprimiéndola. 3. Todo utensilio parecido a una esponja que sirve como absorbente; lanada o escobillón; masa para hacer pan; masa de metales finamente divididos. 4. Mogollón, gorrista, parásito humano. *Sponge-cake,* Bizcocho, bizcochuelo, bollo ligero y esponjoso.

Sponge, *va.* 1. Borrar o limpiar alguna cosa con esponja. 2. Atraer y chupar la substancia o bienes de otros. 3. Comer de gorra; chasquear; meterse de mogollón. 4. Escobillonar.—*vn.* 1. Embeberse como una esponja. 2. Pescar o recoger esponjas. 2. Vivir de gorra, comer de gorra.

Spongelet [spunj'-let], *s.* 1. (Bot.) *V.* SPONGIOLE. 2. Esponjita, esponja pequeña.

Sponger [spunj'-ẹr], *s.* Esponja, pegote, mogollón, gorrista, gorrón.

Sponginess [spun'-ji-nes], *s.* La calidad que constituye a una cosa esponjosa.

Sponging [spunj'-ing], *s.* 1. Socaliña, estafa, pillería. 2. Limpiamiento o limpiadura. *Sponging-house,* (Ingl.) La casa de un alguacil donde quedaban detenidos provisionalmente los presos por deudas.

Spongiole [spun'-ji-ōl], *s.* (Bot.) Espongiola, la extremidad esponjosa de las raíces tiernas.

Spongy [spun'-ji], *a.* 1. Esponjoso, esponjado, lleno de poros, que es de la calidad de la esponja. 2. Embebido, empapado, lleno como una esponja.

Sponsion [spen'-shun], *s.* Fianza u obligación que uno contrae de responder por otro.

Sponson [spen'-sen], *s.* Barbeta lateral saliente de los buques de guerra, para que los cañones de borda puedan disparar en dirección a proa y popa.

Sponsor [spen'-ser], *s.* 1. Fiador, fianza, el que abona a otro. 2. Padrino o madrina de bautismo.

Sponsor, *va.* Auspiciar, fomentar, apadrinar.

Spontaneity [spen-ta-ní'-i-ti], *s.* Espontaneidad, voluntariedad, cualidad de espontáneo.

Spontaneous [spen-tê'-ne-us], *a.* 1. Espontáneo, que tiene su principio en sí mismo; que se hace o se produce por sí mismo y no por una causa exterior. 2. Que se produce o se cría sin trabajo humano; indígena, silvestre; esporádico. *Spontaneous generation*, Generación espontánea. *V.* ABIOGENESIS.

Spontaneously [spen-tê'-ne-us-li], *adv.* Espontáneamente, voluntariamente.

Spontaneousness [spen-tê'-ne-us-nes], *s.* Espontaneidad, voluntariedad.

Spontoon [spen-tūn'], *s.* Media pica con garfio de que se usaba para prender a los malhechores.

Spook [spūk], *s.* (Fam. y fest.) Fantasma, aparición, coco.

Spool [spūl], *s.* 1. Canilla en que los tejedores devanan el hilo o la seda; carrete o carrillo pequeño. 2. La cantidad de hilo que contiene la canilla.

Spool, *va.* Encañar, encanillar, devanar en canilla o en carrete. *Spooling-wheel*, El torno para devanar la seda.

Spoom [spūm], *vn.* (Ant.) Pasar con velocidad; (Mar.) navegar, viento en popa.

Spoon [spūn], *s.* Cuchara. *Table spoon*, Cuchara (para sopa). *Dessert spoon*, Cucharilla de postre. *Teaspoon*, Cucharilla de café. *Knife, fork, and spoon*, Cubierto.

Spoon, *va.* y *vn.* Usar una cuchara; alzar con cuchara; pescar con garfio de cuchara.

Spoon, *vn.* (Fam.) Hacer cocos; enamorarse de una manera sentimental.

Spoonbill [spūn'-bil], *s.* (Orn.) 1. Ave de cuchara, espátula, ave zancuda. 2. Pez notable por el achatamiento y prolongación de las mandíbulas.

Spoondrift [spūn'-drift], *s.* (Mar.) Rocío del mar.

Spoonful [spūn'-ful], *s.* Cucharada.

Spoonmeat [spūn'-mít], *s.* El manjar que se come con cuchara.

Spoonwort [spūn'-wūrt], *s.* (Bot.) Coclearia.

Spoor [spūr], *s.* (África holandesa del Sur) Pista, huella de un animal salvaje.

Sporadic [spo-rad'-ic], *a.* (Med.) Esporádico: solo, aislado; caso de una enfermedad que no es epidémico ni endémico, sino aislado.

Spore ([spōr], *s.* 1. (Bot.) Espora (o esporo), corpúsculo reproductor de las plantas criptógamas, análogo a las semillas. 2. (Biol.) Espora (o esporo), cuerpo redondo u ovoide, menudo, orgánico, que se desarrolla en un nuevo individuo, como en los protozoarios y las bacterias. 3. Organismo diminuto, germen.

Sport [spōrt], *s.* 1. Juego, retozo; burla, chanza. 2. Juguete, diversión, divertimiento, entretenimiento, recreo, pasatiempo. 3. Juguete, objeto de risa y broma. 4. Cacería a caballo o a pie, partida de pesca, natación. 5. (Biol.) Animal o planta que exhibe variación espontánea del tipo normal. *Field-sports*, Diversiones del campo, como la caza, etc. *To make sport of*, Burlarse de.

Sport, *va.* 1. Divertirse, alegrarse, regocijarse. 2. Ostentarse, vanagloriarse.—*vn.* 1. Chancear, juguetear, estar de burla, de juego o de chunga; andarse con chanzas o con burlas; estrenar, lucir. 2. (Biol.) Variar de repente o espontáneamente del tipo normal.

Sportful [spōrt'-ful], *a.* Festivo, alegre, chistoso, placentero, agradable.

Sportfulness [spōrt'-ful-nes], *s.* Juguete, diversión; humor alegre, divertido.

Sporting [spōrt'-ing], *a.* Deportivo.

Sportive [spōrt'-iv], *a.* Festivo, alegre, juguetón, retozón; aficionado a bromear.

Sportively [spōrt'-iv-li], *adv.* De un modo retozón o festivo.

Sportiveness [spōrt'-iv-nes], *s.* Alegría, juego, festividad, holganza, chanza, retozo.

Sportless [spōrt'-les], *a.* Triste, sin gana de juego, sin diversión.

Sportsman [spōrts'-man], *s.* Cazador, el que caza por diversión; pescador; aficionado a las diversiones campestres.

Sportsman-like [spōrts'-man-laik], *a.* Aficionado a los ejercicios atléticos, a la caza, pesca, natación, etc.; conforme a las reglas de estas diversiones.

Sportsmanship [spōrts'-man-ship], *s.* Espíritu deportivo. *Good sportsmanship*, Caballerosidad deportiva, honradez deportiva. (Aplícase también a otras actividades fuera del deporte.)

Sportswoman [spōrts'-wum-an], *f.* Mujer aficionada a los ejercicios de destreza y fuerza y a las diversiones al aire libre

Spot [spot], *s.* 1. Sitio, lugar o paraje particular. *Upon the spot*, En el sitio mismo, en el acto, al punto, inmediatamente; también, alerta, despierto. *He was on the spot*, Estaba alerta, en el sitio mismo. *He died upon the spot*, Murió en el acto. *In spots*, (Fam.) En algunos respectos; aquí y allí. 2. Un espacio pequeño de terreno, trozo de tierra. 3. Mancha, la impresión que hace en algún cuerpo la cosa que cayendo sobre él muda su color; borrón. 4. Mancha, la deshonra que se hereda o se contrae; mácula, borrón, deshonra, ignominia, desgracia. 5. Lunar, mancha natural en cualquier parte del cuerpo. 6. Tacha, el defecto en las calidades morales.

Spot, *va.* 1. Abigarrar, motear, poner a una cosa varios colores sin orden ni unión. 2. Manchar, ensuciar haciendo perder el color. 3. Manchar, deslustrar la fama o la reputación. 4. Corromper, alterar o mudar 5. Tachonar, sembrar de.

Spot cash [spot cash], *s.* Dinero contante y sonante.

Spotless [spot'-les], *a.* Limpio, inmaculado, sin mancha.

Spotlessness [spot'-les-nes], *s.* Inocencia, el estado del que no tiene tacha, mancha o defecto.

Spotlight [spot'-lait], *s.* (Teat.) 1. Reflector. 2. Farol de luz concentrada. *To be on the spotlight*, Hacerse conspicuo.

Spotted [spot'-ed], *a.* y *pp.* 1. Manchado, ensuciado con manchas. 2. Moteado, con manchas; apulgarado, v. g. la ropa blanca; esquizado, como el mármol. *Spotted fever*, Tabardillo pintado, la fiebre del tabardillo.

Spotter [spot'-er], *s.* 1. La persona que mancha o ensucia; el que mancha o deshonra. 2. (Fam.) Persona empleada en los tranvías para anotar disimuladamente el número de pasajes que cobra el conductor.

Spottiness [spot'-i-nes], *s.* Estado o calidad de lo que tiene manchas.

Spotty [spot'-i], *a.* Lleno de manchas, puerco, sucio.

Spousal [spau'-zal], *s.* (Ant.) Nupcias, casamiento, desposorios (generalmente en plural).—*a.* (Poét.) Matrimonial, nupcial, conyugal.

Spouse [spauz], *s.* Esposo, esposa.

Spouseless [spauz'-les], *a.* Soltero o viudo; sin esposo, sin esposa.

Spout [spaut], *s.* 1. Caño o cañón por donde sale el agua a chorro; tubo de desagüe; canilla de tonel, espita; gárgola o figurón que arroja el agua por la boca en las canales de los tejados. 2. Cuello de vasija; pico de cafetera, de tetera. *Water-spout*, Surtidor de agua que salta, tromba o manga marina, remolino; chaparrón, turbión. *Rain-spout*, Lluvia muy abundante.

Spout, *va.* y *vn.* 1. Arrojar o echar agua u otro líquido con mucho ímpetu. 2. Salir, saltar o hacer salir o saltar cualquier líquido con mucho ímpetu. 3. Borbotar, salir a borbotones o con mucha fuerza el agua u otro líquido. 4. Chorrear, correr a chorro. 5. (Fam.) Decir de una manera declamatoria; recitar, declamar. *To spout down*, Llover a chaparrones. *To spout up*, Resaltar, salir o saltar el agua hacia arriba.

Sprain [sprên], *va.* Torcer violentamente los ligamentos que rodean alguna articulación sin dislocar el hueso. *He has sprained his ankle*, Se ha torcido el tobillo.

Sprain, *s.* Torcedura o tensión violenta de los tendones o ligamentos sin dislocación.

Sprang, *pret.* del verbo *To* SPRING.

Sprat [sprat], *s.* Clupeo; pez parecido el arenque (Clupea sprattus); anchoa californica; arenque pequeño.

Sprawl [sprōl], *va.* y *vn.* 1. Tenderse a la larga; tender o mover, tenderse o moverse con los miembros en posición poco graciosa. 2. Tener una posición extendida y falta de gracia (p. ej. las viñas).—*s.* El acto de tenderse sin gracia, o esa posición misma.

Spray [sprê], *va.* 1. Rociar, pulverizar un líquido, esparcirlo en partículas menudas. 2. Rociar, aplicar el líquido pulverizado, como se hace con el rociador.—*vn.* Rociar, esparcir un líquido en menudas gotas.—*s.* 1. Rociada, rocío, agua u otro líquido que se esparce en gotas menudas; espuma del mar. 2. Rociador. *V.* ATOMIZER.

Spray, *s.* 1. Ramita de árbol o

planta que lleva otras ramitas o flores; ramaje menudo. 2. Dibujo o adorno parecido a una colección de ramillas o flores. (< danés, sprag.)

Spraying [sprē'-ing], *s.* 1. Rociadura. 2. Pulverización.

Spread [spred], *va.* (*pret.* y *pp.* SPREAD). 1. Tender, extender, alargar, desplegar, engrandecer la superficie de algo; desenvolver. 2. Esparcir, divulgar, difundir o extender noticias, doctrinas, etc.; publicar, diseminar, propagar. 3. Esparcir o difundir luz, olor, etc. 4. Envolver, cubrir de una capa delgada. 5. Desplegar a la vista; exhibir. 6. Pertrechar, equipar a propósito con cosas arregladas en orden. 7. Tender, alejar, forzar más a parte, a mayor distancia una cosa de otra.—*vn.* 1. Extenderse, alargarse, desplegarse. 2. Esparcirse, difundirse. 3. Desarrollarse, propagarse; exhalarse. 4. Alejarse por fuerza. *To spread abroad,* Esparcir, divulgar, hacer una cosa pública, y también susurrarse, correr o saberse una cosa que estaba secreta. *To spread over,* Cubrir una cosa con otra extendiéndola por toda su superficie. *To spread the cloth,* Poner la mesa.

Spread, *s.* 1. Extensión, dilatación, amplitud. 2. Expansión, dilatación. 3. Ámbito. 4. Desarrollo; propagación. 5. Colcha de cama; tapete de mesa, mantel. 6. (Fam.) Festín, banquete.

Spreader [spred'-ẹr], *s.* Divulgador; el o lo que esparce.

Spreading [spred'-ing], *a.* 1. Extenso, ancho; que se extiende: (Bot.) divergente; frondoso. 2. Que se esparce, que se propaga. *Under a spreading chestnut-tree,* Debajo de un castaño frondoso.—*s.* Acción y efecto del verbo *spread;* extensión, propagación, etc.

Spree [sprī], *vn.* Beber mucho, emborracharse.—*s.* Borrachera, jarana, juerga. V. CAROUSAL.

Sprig [sprig], *s.* 1. Ramita, rama pequeña, renuevo, pimpollo. 2. Tachuela sin cabeza.

Sprig, *va.* Adornar con ramitas; bordar ramos o flores.

Spriggy [sprig'-i], *a.* Ramoso.

Sprightliness [sprait'-li-nes], *s.* Viveza, despejo, alegría, vivacidad.

Sprightly [sprait'-li], *a.* Alegre, despejado, despierto, vivo, vivaracho.

Spring [spring], *va.* (*pret.* SPRANG o SPRUNG, *pp.* SPRUNG). 1. Soltar el resorte o muelle (de una trampa, una cerradura, etc.). 2. Presentar a la vista, producir o ejecutar de repente o inesperadamente. 3. Hacer volar o saltar una mina. 4. Combar, encorvar por fuerza una cosa, esforzar demasiado; rendir un palo o verga. 5. (Arq.) Arrancar o vaciar un arco o bóveda; principiarlos de un punto dado. 6. Insertar una cosa en un lugar donde cabe muy apretadamente, encorvándola o forzándola. 7. Saltar por encima; pasar por arriba de algo saltando. 8. Ojear la caza, espantarla o ahuyentarla con voces para que se levante.—*vn.* 1. Saltar, brincar. 2. Salir o saltar un líquido. 3. Salir con mucha fuerza; aparecerse de repente. 4. Moverse súbitamente, como con una fuerza elástica o por medio de un resorte. 5. Alabearse, combarse, desviarse de un plano o línea normal. 6. Brotar, arrojar, apuntar los árboles y plantas; echar o arrojar hierba o cualquier otra cosa la tierra. 7. Nacer, proceder, provenir, tomar su origen, derivar de; venir, dimanar, originarse, traer su origen. 8. Levantarse, elevarse más arriba que los objetos circunvecinos. 9. Comenzar, nacer, empezar a levantarse un arco o bóveda. *To spring again,* Renacer, brotar de nuevo, volver a saltar. *To spring at,* Lanzarse sobre; procurar llegar de un salto. *To spring away,* Saltar a un lado, lanzarse de un salto. *To spring back,* Saltar hacia atrás; retroceder, recular. *To spring forth,* Brotar, crecer; salir; lanzarse, precipitarse. *To spring forward,* Abalanzarse, arrojarse, tirarse, dispararse. *To spring up,* Nacer, brotar, crecer, desarrollarse; salir a luz, presentarse a la vista; subir, engrandecerse. *To spring upon,* Abalanzarse a. *To spring aleak,* (Mar.) Descubrir una vía de agua, hacer agua el buque. *The chamois sprang from rock to rock,* La gamuza saltaba de roca en roca. *To spring a charge of perjury,* Hacer inesperadamente una acusación de perjurio.

Spring, *s.* 1. Resorte, elasticidad, fuerza elástica; muelle, resorte; cualquier cuerpo elástico que vuelve a su forma normal cuando cesa de estar comprimido. *Spring-lock,* Cerradura de golpe. 2. Salto, brinco, corcovo; reculada, movimiento súbito con fuerza. 3. Energía o potencia, causa de acción. 4. Primavera, estación del año en la cual comienzan las plantas a brotar y crecer. 5. Manantial, el nacimiento del agua o fuente; surtidor. *Spring-water,* Agua de fuente. 6. Manantial, origen, principio. 7. Entrada de agua; tangidera; barloa. 8. Combadura, o la cosa combada. (Esta voz forma muchos compuestos, en su mayor parte de significación evidente.) *Spring-back,* Lomo plegado (de un libro de contabilidad, de registros). *Spring-board,* Trampolín. *Spring mattress,* Colchón de muelles.

Spring beauty [spring biū'-ti], *s.* (Bot.) Claitonia.

Springbok [spring'-bok], *s.* Gacela del Sur de África con una faja blanca a lo largo del cuello. (Gazella euchore.)

Springer [spring'-ẹr], *s.* 1. Saltador, brincador. 2. (Arq.) Imposta; sotabanco, cojinete, sillar de arranque. 3. Perro de España, hábil en ojear la caza.

Spring-halt [spring'-hōlt], *s.* Cojera de caballo.

Springiness [spring'-i-nes], *s.* Elasticidad, resorte, fuerza elástica.

Springlike [spring'-laik], *a.* Primaveral.

Springtide [spring'-taid], *s.* Estación de primavera. *Spring-tide,* Marea fuerte en las épocas del novilunio y plenilunio.

Springy [spring'-i], *a.* 1. Elástico. 2. Lleno de fuentes o manantiales.

Sprinkle [sprin'-cl], *va.* 1. Asperjar, rociar, esparcir; regar o desparramar en gotas. 2. Polvorear, empolvar (con azúcar, sal, especias, etc). 3. Distribuir aquí y allá, sembrar; arrojar o esparcir cosas de modo que caigan separadas. 4. Bautizar rociando.—*vn.* 1. (Impers.) Lloviznar, llover un poco, como al principio de un aguacero. *It sprinkles,* Está lloviznando. 2. Caer en gotas o en partículas.

Sprinkle, *s.* La cantidad pequeña de cualquier cosa que se esparce o derrama rociando algo; caída en gotas o partículas o lo que cae de esta manera; de aquí, pequeña cantidad, una pizca, un poco.

Sprinkler [sprin'-klẹr], *s.* El o lo que asperja o derrama; (1) regadera; (2) aspersorio, instrumento con que se rocía; hisopo para esparcir agua bendita.

Sprinkling [sprin'-kling], *s.* 1. Lo que se esparce; pequeña cantidad, una pizca, un poco. 2. Aspersión, rociadura, esparcimiento de gotas de un líquido. 3. Diversidad de colores. *A sprinkling of rain,* Una lluvia fina, una llovizna. *A sprinkling of knowledge,* Una pizca de conocimiento.

Sprint [sprint], *vn.* Correr como en las carreras de apuesta.—*s.* Corrida, carrera corta y rápida.

Sprit, *s.* (Mar.) Botavara, verga de abanico.

Sprite [sprait], *s.* 1. Espíritu aéreo, duende, trasgo; hada. 2. (Ant.) Fantasma, espectro.

Spritsail [sprit'-sêl], *s.* (Mar.) Cebadera. *Spritsail braces,* Brazos de cebadera. *Spritsail-top-sail,* (Mar.) Sobrecebadera.

Sprocket [sprok'-ẹt], *s.* 1. Diente de rueda, cabilla para el engranaje de rueda y cadena. 2. Erizo, rueda de cabillas; rueda para engranarse en una cadena; se llama también *sprocket-wheel. Sprocket-gear,* Engranaje de rueda y cadena (como en una bicicleta).

Sprout [spraut], *va.* 1. Hacer germinar o brotar. 2. Quitar los botones o vástagos.—*vn.* 1. Germinar, brotar el germen; arrojar hojas, flores o renuevos; echar botones. 2. Crecer. 3. Extenderse en ramificaciones.

Sprout, *s.* Vástago, renuevo, retoño. *Sprouts, s. pl.* Bretones, los renuevos o tallos del bretón.

Spruce [sprūs], *a.* Lindo, pulido, gentil.—*s.* (Bot.) Pruche, pinabete, especie de abeto del género Picea. *Essence of spruce,* Esencia o jugo de pruche. *Norway spruce,* Pinabete, pícea de Noruega. Picea excelsa. *Hemlock spruce,* Abeto del Canadá. *Douglas spruce, V.* PINE. *Black spruce,* Abeto negro.

Spruce, *vn.* Vestirse con esmero.

Sprucely [sprūs'-li], *adv.* Lindamente, bellamente, vivamente.

Spruceness [sprūs'-nes], *s.* Lindeza, hermosura, belleza, gentileza.

Sprue [sprū], *s.* 1. (Fundición) Bebedero de molde; escoria del orificio de colada. 2. (Local, E. U.) Aftas. *V.* THRUSH.

Sprung [sprung], *pret.* y *pp.* del verbo *To* SPRING. *A sprung mast,* (Mar.) Palo rendido.

Spry [sprai], *a.* Vivo, listo, ágil, activo en sus movimientos. (< Sueco.)

Spryness [sprai'-nes], *s.* Agilidad, presteza, calidad de listo.

Spud [spud], *s.* 1. Uno de los diversos utensilios parecidos á un azadón o a un escoplo; escarda; limpiaojos (de cirujano); navaja corta. 2. (Prov.) (1) Mano de criatura; (2) patata.

Spume [spiūm], *s.* Espuma o nata que sobrenada en los líquidos en estado de ebullición o fermentación.

Spume, *vn.* Espumar, echar o hacer espuma.

Spumescent [spiu-mes'-ent], *a.* Lo que arroja de sí mucha espuma cuando se pone á hervir.

Spumous [spiū'-mus], **Spumy** [spiū'-mi], *a.* Espumoso, espumajoso, espumante.

Spun [spun], *pret.* y *pp.* del verbo *To* SPIN.

Spunge [spunj], *s.* 1. Esponja. 2. (Art.) Lanada.—*s.* y *v.* *V.* SPONGE. (Forma antigua, pero recomendada recientemente por la Sociedad Filológica.)

Spunging-house [spunj'-ing-haus], *s.* La casa adonde llevaban a los deudores antes de ponerlos en la cárcel. *V. Sponging-house.*

Spun glass [spun glas], *s.* Vidrio hilado.

Spungy [spun'-ji], *a.* 1. Esponjoso. 2. Húmedo.

Spunk [spuŋk], *s.* 1. Yesca. 2. (Fam.) Corazón, genio (violento), coraje, valor; también, enojo.

Spunky [spuŋk'-i], *a.* (Fam.) Vivo, valeroso, valiente; también, enfadadizo, enojadizo.

Spunyarn [spun'-yārn], *s.* (Mar.) Meollar. *Three-yarn spunyarn,* (Mar.) Meollar de tres filásticas.

Spur [spūr], *s.* 1. Espuela para picar un jinete a la caballería en que va montado. 2. Espuela, aguijón, estímulo; excitación. 3. Espolón del gallo; uña puntiaguda; pincho; acicate. *Artificial cock-spurs,* Navajas de gallo. 4. Estribación, estribo, risco, saliente brusco de una colina o montaña. 5. (Bot.) Prolongación en forma de cucurucho detrás de ciertas flores. *On the spur of the moment,* Incontinenti, de prisa, bajo el impulso del momento. *Spur-gear,* Rueda dentada. *Spur-gearing,* Engranaje de ruedas dentadas. *Spur-wheel,* Rueda de engranaje recto. *To win one's spurs,* Ganar la dignidad de caballero; ejecutar una hazaña o acción notable que da fama y renombre. *Spurs of the beams,* (Mar.) Pernadas de los baos. *Spurs of the bitts,* (Mar.) Curvas de las bitas.

Spur, *va.* y *vn.* 1. Espolear, picar con la espuela. 2. Espolear, poner espuelas, avivar, incitar, estimular. 3. Hacer andar o mover a viva fuerza. 4. Calzar o ponerse las espuelas en el pie, en una bota, etc. 5. Andar muy de prisa, apretar el paso. 6. Viajar con toda diligencia. *To spur on,* Espolear, aguijar, avivar o estimular mucho; adelantarse o avanzar con osadía e intrepidez.

Spurgall [spūr'-gōl], *va.* Espolear, herir o picar haciendo herida con la espuela.

Spurgall, *s.* Espoleadura, la picadura o llaga que hace la espuela.

Spurge [spūrj], *s.* (Bot.) Lechetrezna, titímalo, euforbio; cualquier planta del género Euphorbia.

Spurge-laurel [spūrj'-lō-rel], *s.* (Bot.) Mecereón, lauréola. Daphne laureola.

Spurious [spiū'-ri-us], *a.* 1. Espurio, adulterado, contrahecho, degenerado, no genuino. 2. Espurio, bastardo. 3. (Biol.) Falso. 4. (Bot.) Aparente, pero no real y verdadero.

Spuriously [spiū'-ri-us-li], *adv.* Falsamente, de un modo espurio.

Spuriousness [spiū'-ri-us-nes], *s.* 1. Falsedad, falsificación. 2. La calidad o estado de ser espuria, adulterada o contrahecha alguna cosa. 3. Bastardía, la calidad del que es bastardo o hijo espurio.

Spurn [spūrn], *va.* 1. Desdeñar, despreciar, menospreciar; tratar o mirar con desprecio, rechazar con desdén. 2. Rechazar a puntapiés; cocear o acocear.—*vn.* Oponerse con insolencia o desprecio; desechar con desdén, rechazar desdeñosamente. *To spurn away,* Echar fuera a puntapiés.

Spurn, *s.* Coz; maltrato, ajamiento.

Spurning [spūrn'-ing], *s.* Desdén, menosprecio; tratamiento insolente y lleno de desprecio.

Spurred [spūrd], *a.* 1. Con espuelas; con espolones. 2. (Biol.) Que tiene espuela o espolón; atizonado (como ciertos granos). *Spurred rye,* Centeno atizonado. *V.* ERGOT.

Spurrer [spūr'-ęr], *s.* El que espolea.

Spurrey, *s.* *V.* SPURRY.

Spurry [spur'-i], *s.* (Bot.) Espérgula, esparcilla.

Spurt [spūrt], *va.* y *vn.* Arrojar (un líquido) en chorro o a chorros; hacer salir o salir en chorro; brotar, salir impetuosamente.—*s.* 1. Chorro, derrame repentino de un líquido. 2. Explosión de ira. (< A.-S.)

Spurt, *vn.* Hacer un esfuerzo repentino y extremo; esforzarse por breve tiempo con toda energía o rapidez.—*s.* 1. Aumento de energía o rapidez por poco tiempo; esfuerzo extraordinario de poca duración. 2. Período breve. (< islandés.)

Sputter [sput'-ęr], *va.* y *vn.* 1. Escupir con ruido; chisporrotear; silbar (quemándose). 2. Farfullar, barbotar, hablar entre dientes confusamente; hablar con volubilidad e irritación.

Sputnik [s-put-nik], *s.* Sputnik, satélite ruso.

Sputter, *s.* 1. Chisporroteo, el acto de chisporrotear; acción de farfullar. 2. Saliva que se arroja farfullando; saliva.

Sputterer [sput'-ęr-ęr], *s.* 1. Escupidor, gargajiento, gargajoso, el que escupe mucho. 2. Faramallero, faramallón.

Sputum [spiū'-tum], *s.* Esputo, lo que se arroja en cada expectoración; expectoración característica de tal o cual enfermedad.

Spy [spai], *s.* Espía, persona enviada al campo enemigo para informarse de sus planes; emisario secreto; el que vigila las acciones de otro.

Spy, *vn.* 1. Columbrar, ver desde lejos. 2. Espiar, observar con aplicación intensa. 3. Explorar, reconocer un país; examinar o descubrir por medio de procedimientos ocultos; con *out.* *To spy out,* Atisbar, divisar, columbrar. *Spyboat,* Barca exploradora. *Spyglass,* Anteojo de larga vista, catalejo.

Squab [scwōb], *a.* 1. Acabado de salir de la cáscara; implume. 2. Rechoncho, cachigordo, regordete: dícese del que es gordo y muy pequeño.—*s.* 1. Pichón, pichoncillo. 2. Persona rechoncha, regordeta. 3. Cojín muy relleno; canapé lleno de crin o pluma.—*adv.* Zas, voz con que se expresa el sonido de un golpe repentino o el mismo golpe.

Squabble [scwob'-l], *vn.* Reñir, andar en pendencias o en contestaciones, armar querellas o disputas disputar.

Squabble, *s.* Pendencia, riña, querella, disputa, contienda, sarracina o tremolina.

Squabbler [scwob'-lęr], *s.* Pendenciero, amigo de armar riñas o pendencias.

Squab-pie [scwob'-pai], *s.* (Ingl.) Pastel hecho con carne de carnero, cebolla y lonjas de manzanas en capas alternadas.

Squad [scwed], *s.* (Mil.) Escuadra de soldados o de la policía; pelotón; pequeño grupo de personas. *Squad drill,* Ejercicio de pelotón.

Squadron [scwed'-run], *s.* 1. (Mar.) Escuadra de naves de guerra; división de una armada. 2. Escuadrón, una de las porciones en que se divide un regimiento de caballería; consta de dos *troops* o pelotones. 3. Cuadro, la formación de un cuerpo de tropas en figura cuadrada; un conjunto o número de soldados en formación.

Squadroned [scwed'-rund], *a.* (Mil.) Escuadronado, formado en escuadrones.

Squalid [scwel'-id], *a.* De apariencia mezquina y pobre, desaliñado, sucio.

Squalidness, **Squalidity** [scwel'-id-nes, scwe-lid'-i-ti], *s.* Mezquindad, pobreza, suciedad.

Squall [scwōl], *va.* y *vn.* Chillar, dar chillidos; vocear como un niño encolerizado.—*v. impers.* Estar borrascoso; soplar en ráfagas.

Squall, *s.* 1. Chillido, sonido de la voz agudo y desapacible. 2. (Mar.) Racha, golpe repentino de viento, pero que dura poco; chubasco. *Southerly squall,* (Mar.) Racha, solana. *Violent squall,* (Mar.) Ráfaga, movimiento violento del aire. *Squall of wind and rain,* (Mar.) Chubasco.

Squaller [scwōl'-ęr], *s.* Chillador, chillón, el que chilla mucho.

Squally [scwōl'-i], *a.* Chubascoso, borrascoso.

Squalor [scwōl'-ęr o scwé'-lōr], *s.* Suciedad, inmundicia, mugre.

Squamoid [scwé'-meid], *a.* Parecido a una escama, escamoso.

Squamose [scwé'-mōs], **Squamous** [scwé'-mus], *a.* Escamoso, cubierto o provisto de escamas; en forma de escamas, lamelar.

Squander [scwen'-dęr], *va.* 1. Malgastar, gastar pródigamente, disipar, desperdiciar, malbaratar. 2. (Ant.) Dispersar.

Squanderer [scwen'-dęr-ęr], *s.* Malbaratador, gastador, disipador, pródigo.

Square [scwār], *a.* 1. Cuadrangular, cuadrado, cuadrángulo. *Twelve inches square,* Doce pulgadas en cuadro. 2. Paralelo, exactamente correspondiente; en ángulos rectos, rectangular. 3. Cuadrado, perfecto, exacto, justo, cabal, sin defecto ni imperfección; honrado, equitativo, justo. 4. Ancho, con líneas comparativamente rectas. 5. (Fam.) Abundante, que satisface; p. ej. *A square meal,* Una comida completa. 6. Horizontal, y en ángulos rectos con la quilla; se dice de las vergas. 7. (Mat.) Elevado a la segunda potencia. *A square man,* Un hombre bien formado o bien proporcionado. *Square dealing,* Buena fe, honradez en los tratos. *To be square,* (Fam.) Estar a mano, o corrientes, o pagados. *Square measure,* Medida cuadrada o de superficie. *The account is square,* La cuenta está justa.

Square root, (Mat.) Raíz cuadrada. *Square-rigged*, (Mar.) Aparejo de cruzamen. *Square-sail*, (Mar.) Vela redonda. *Square-yard*, (Mar.) Verga redonda. *Square-timbers*, (Mar.) Maderos escuadrados.—*s.* 1. (Geom.) Cuadro, cuadrado, figura de cuatro lados iguales y cuatro ángulos rectos. 2. Cuadrado, el producto de un número multiplicado por sí mismo; la segunda potencia. 3. Objeto cuadrado o casi cuadrado; v. gr. cristal de ventana; casilla de tablero de damas. 4. Plaza, lugar ancho y cuadrado cercado de casas. 5. (Amer.) Manzana de casas en una población. 6. Escuadra, instrumento compuesto comúnmente de dos reglas que forman un ángulo recto; cartabón. 7. Nivel, la proporción debida, orden; exactitud, proceder honrado, equidad. 8. Cuadro formado por las tropas. *Out of square*, Que no está en ángulo recto o a escuadra.

Square, *va.* 1. Cuadrar, formar en cuadro. 2. Escuadrar, formar en ángulos rectos. 3. (Mat.) Cuadrar, reducir a un cuadrado o a su valor; multiplicar un número por sí mismo. 4. Medir, reducir á una misma medida. 5. (Carp.) Cuadrar, trabajar los maderos en cuadro. 6. Ajustar, arreglar, acomodar; hacer el balance de una cuenta. 7. Conformar o ajustar; (Mar.) bracear en cuadro; colocar las vergas paralelas a la cubierta y en ángulos rectos con la quilla.—*vn.* 1. Cuadrar, estar en ángulos rectos, conformarse o ajustarse una cosa con otra. 2. Convenir, concordarse, estar en exacta conformidad; corresponder a un aserto. 3. Tomar una actitud pugilística; se usa con *off*, por regla general. *To square the circle*, Cuadrar el círculo, construir geométricamente un cuadrado equivalente al área de un círculo dado. *To square the yards*, (Mar.) Poner las vergas en cruz.

Square dance [scwār dans], *s.* Contradanza, especie de lanceros.

Squarely [scwār'-li], *adv.* En cuadro, cuadradamente; convenientemente, justamente, honradamente.

Squareness [scwār'-nes], *s.* Cuadratura, la calidad o condición de cuadrado.

Squash [scwosh], *s.* 1. Cualquier cosa blanda o inmatura. 2. Aplastamiento; masa u objeto aplastado o magullado. 3. La colisión de los cuerpos blandos entre sí; caída de un cuerpo blando y pesado.

Squash, *s.* Cidracayote (calabaza), fruto mollar y comestible de varias hierbas anuales rastreras y americanas, de las cucurbitáceas; también la planta misma. *Summer squash*, Cidracayote de verano; se come verde cocida y sin quitarle las semillas. *Squash-vine*, Cucúrbita, cidracayote, planta. *Squash-beetle*, Coleóptero crisomélido (Diabrotica vittata), con rayas amarillas y negras, que se alimenta del cidracayote, del melón, y plantas semejantes. (< Ind. amer. *asquash*, pl. de *asq*, verde, poco maduro.)

Squash, *va.* Aplastar, deshacer la figura que tenía alguna cosa haciéndola una plasta; magullar.

Squat [scwot], *vn.* 1. Agacharse, agazaparse, acurrucarse, ponerse en cuclillas. 2. Establecerse en u ocupar un terreno público o ajeno sin justo título.

Squat, *a.* 1. Agachado, puesto en cuclillas. 2. Rechoncho, grueso y corto.—*s.* Porrazo, caída repentina.

Squatter [scwot'-ęr], *s.* Advenedizo, entremetido, injusto ocupante, colono usurpador. (Mex. fam.) Paracaidista.

Squaw [scwō], *s.* Mujer o muchacha india (de la América del Norte).

Squawk [scwōc], *vn.* 1. Graznar. 2. (fig.) Delatar, denunciar.

Squeak [scwīc], *vn.* 1. Chillar, dar un chillido; producir un sonido agudo y discordante (una rueda, etc.). 2. Romper el silencio por miedo de algún daño.

Squeak, *s.* Grito, quejido lastimoso.

Squeal [scwīl], *vn.* 1. Gritar, dar alaridos; lanzar gritos agudos de mayor duración que los del *squeak*. 2. (Ger.) Hacer delaciones.—*s.* Grito penetrante como el de un cerdo. (< sueco.)

Squeamish [scwīm'-ish], *a.* 1. Fastidioso, enfadoso; nimio, demasiado delicado o escrupuloso. 2. Fastidiado, disgustado; con náuseas. *Squeamish stomach*, Estómago delicado.

Squeamishly [scwīm'-ish-li], *adv.* Fastidiosamente, enfadosamente; con náuseas.

Squeamishness [scwīm'-ish-nes], *s.* Fastidio, disgusto, delicadeza excesiva.

Squeegee [scwī'-jī], *va.* Alisar, allanar una estampa fotográfica con un cilindro alisador.—*s.* Alisador de goma que se usa en la fotografía.

Squeeze [scwīz], *va.* 1. Apretar, comprimir; estrechar; estrujar, exprimir el jugo. 2. Exprimir, estrujar; tupir. 3. Poner en cierta posición o lugar por medio de fuerza o presión; apretar fuertemente. 4. Arrancar el tributo, las contribuciones, etc.; acosar, agobiar; disminuir los jornales hasta el más bajo tipo. 5. Hacer un molde o impresión en papel húmedo por medio de la presión. *To squeeze in*, Hacer entrar apretando. *To squeeze out*, Hacer salir, exprimir. *To squeeze through*, Pasar o hacer pasar al través (por fuerza). *To squeeze to death*, (Fam.) Matar a apachurrones.—*vn.* Escaparse o salirse alguna cosa que estaba oprimida.

Squeeze, *s.* 1. Apretadura, presión, compresión, apretón. 2. Facsímile de una moneda o inscripción, que se obtiene oprimiendo sobre ella una substancia blanda.

Squeezer [scwīz'-ęr], *s.* Exprimidor (de frutas, etc.)

†**Squelch** [scwelch], *s.* Caída fuerte, porrazo.

Squelch [scwelch], *va.* 1. Hacer callar a uno, dar un tapaboca, humillándole; desconcertar. 2. Poner fin; derrotar, vencer, sojuzgar; se usa a menudo con *out*.—*vn.* Ser vencido, desconcertado.

Squib [scwib], *s.* 1. Cohete, cañuto de papel lleno de pólvora u otra materia combustible; buscapié. 2. Sátira, chiste, chanza.

Squib, *va.* y *vn.* Usar de sátiras o pullas; atacar con ellas.

Squid [scwid], *s.* 1. Calamar, molusco con diez tentáculos, de que se usa mucho para cebo. 2. Cebo artificial, que tiene a menudo la forma de un pez.

Squint [scwint], *a.* 1. Ojizaino, que mira atravesado y con malos ojos. 2. Bizco, bisojo: dícese de la persona que por vicio o defecto de los ojos tuerce la vista.

Squint, *s.* 1. Estrabismo, enfermedad o vicio de los ojos bizcos. 2. Mirada bizca; mirada furtiva; también, vista parcial. 3. Tendencia indirecta. *To have a squint*, Bizquear, mirar bisojo. *To give a squint at*, Mirar de soslayo.

Squint, *va.* y *vn.* 1. Bizquear, mirar bizco o atravesado. 2. Ladear o torcer la vista o los ojos.

Squint-eyed [scwint'-aid], *a.* 1. Ojizaino, bizco, bisojo. 2. Atravesado, torcido y de mala intención; ambiguo, obscuro.

Squinting [scwint'-ing], *s.* (Med.) Estrabismo, estrambosidad, la enfermedad o vicio de los bizcos o bisojos.

Squintingly [scwint'-ing-li], *adv.* Con un modo de mirar atravesado, como un bizco.

Squire [scwair], *s.* 1. Escudero, el paje o sirviente que llevaba el escudo al caballero en la antigua caballería. 2. Escudero, título de hidalguía en Inglaterra; propietario de antigua heredad; (local, E. U.) alcalde, juez de paz. *Squire Brown*, Señor Brown. *V.* ESQUIRE.

Squire, *va.* Acompañar a una persona por cortesía y como caballero.

Squirm [scwęrm], *vn.* 1. Torcerse, encorvar el cuerpo como a consecuencia de un dolor o sufrimiento. 2. Mostrar señales de dolor o pena. 3. (Con *out*) Escaparse con trabajo, con poca destreza.—*s.* Torcimiento; movimiento causado por el dolor.

Squirrel [scwęr'-el o scwir'-el], *s.* Ardilla, arda, mamífero roedor del género Sciurus; se halla en todo el mundo, excepto en Australia.

Squirt [scwęrt], *va.* y *vn.* Arrojar algún líquido con fuerza y violencia; hacer salir o salir a chorros; jeringar. *Squirting cucumber* Cohombro de asno. Ecballium elaterium. *V.* ELATERIUM.

Squirt, *s.* 1. Chorro, golpe de alguna cosa líquida que sale con fuerza. 2. Jeringazo, el acto de jeringar. 3. Jeringa, instrumento con el cual se arroja con violencia alguna cosa líquida.

Squirter [scwęrt'-ęr], *s.* El que jeringa o arroja un líquido con una jeringa.

St., *s.* Abreviatura de *Saint*, San o Santo.

Stab [stab], *va.* y *vn.* 1. Herir o matar a puñaladas, dar de puñaladas; atravesar con un arma puntiaguda. 2. Atravesar el corazón, dar una puñalada.

Stab, *s.* 1. Puñalada, la herida que se da con el puñal; estocada. 2. Golpe mortal.

Stabber [stab'-ęr], *s.* Asesino, el que mata alevosamente.

Stability [sta-bil'-i-ti], *s.* 1. Estabilidad, calidad de estable; permanencia, duración, solidez, consistencia. 2. Constancia, firmeza, fijeza en las resoluciones.

Stabilization [stē-bl-i-zē'-shun], *s.* Estabilización.

Stabilize [stē'-bl-aiz], *va.* Estabilizar, fijar.

Stable [stē'-bl], *a.* Estable, establecido firmemente; durable, permanente; firme, fijo, constante, decidido, de principios o conducta fijos y sin cambio; sólido.—*s.* 1. Establo, caballeriza; cuadra para albergar las caballerías o el ganado vacuno. 2. Conjunto de caballos de carrera.

Stable, *va.* Meter los caballos en la cuadra o el ganado en el establo.—*vn.* Vivir en establo como las bestias.

Stable-boy [stê'-bl-bɵi], **Stable-man** [stê'-bl-man], *s.* Establero, mozo de caballos.

Stableness [stê'-bl-nes], *s.* Estabilidad. *V.* STABILITY.

Stabling [stê'-bling], *s.* 1. Acción de meter los caballos en la cuadra o el ganado en el establo. 2. Lugar o comodidad en una cuadra o establo.

Staccato [sta-cā'-tō], *a.* (Mús.) Staccato, voz italiana que significa destacado.

Stack [stac], *s.* 1. Niara, rima o rimero (de haces de grano o heno). 2. Pila o hacina de leña o de heno, cónica por lo común, montón; pabellón de fusiles. 3. Ringlera o fila de fogones o cañones de chimenea. 4. (Fam.) Copia, abundancia.

Stack, *va.* Hacinar, el heno o leña; apilar, amontonar; poner las armas en pabellones.

Stacte [stac'-te], *s.* Estacte, licor oloroso sacado de la mirra fresca molida y lavada en agua.

Stadia [stê'-di-a], *s.* 1. Estación provisional de los agrimensores. 2. Estadia, instrumento topográfico para medir distancias.

Stadium [stê'-di-um], *s.* 1. Estadio, lugar público en la Grecia antigua para las carreras a pie. 2. Estadio, medida griega de longitud de 185 metros o 600 pies ingleses. 3. Grado de progreso o adelantamiento.

Stadtholder [stat'-hōl-der], *s.* Estatúder, el jefe de la antigua república de Holanda.

Staff [staf], *s.*(*pl.* STAVES o STAFFS). 1. Báculo, palo, cayado. 2. Apoyo, sostén, alivio, arrimo. 3. Palo o bastón que se usa como arma ofensiva y defensiva; garrote. 4. Vara, insignia de jurisdicción y empleo. 5. Vara de agrimensor; jalón de mira; alidade. 6. (Mil.) Estado mayor de un ejército; plana mayor de un regimiento. 7. Conjunto de personas asociadas para llevar a cabo alguna empresa particular; p. ej. *The editorial staff*, El conjunto de redactores, la redacción. 8. (Mús.) Pentagrama, las cinco líneas paralelas que se usan para notar las notas de la música. 9. Asta (de lanza, pica, bandera, etc.). 10. Sonda acanalada que sirve de guía al litótomo. *Ensign-staff*, (Mar.) Asta de bandera de popa. *Jack-staff*, (Mar.) Asta de bandera de proa. *Flag-staff*, Asta de bandera. *Staff-officer*, Oficial de estado mayor. *Medical staff*, Cuerpo de sanidad militar.

Staff, *s.* Compuesto plástico, que consta principalmente de yeso mezclado con un poco de cemento, glicerina y dextrina en agua; se usa para edificar provisionalmente o para adorno de edificios. (prob. < *stuff*.)

Staff-tree [staf'-trî], *s.* (Bot.) Aladierno.

Staffwood [staf'-wud], *s.* Duelas, botada, la madera para toneles.

Stag [stag], *s.* 1. Ciervo, mamífero rumiante, particularmente cuando tiene cinco o más años de edad y puntas terminales en las astas. 2. El macho de otros venados o animales cervales. 3. (Fam.) Varón, en contraposición a la mujer. (< islandés, *steggr*, animal macho.)

Stag-beetle [stag'-bî-tl], *s.* Ciervo volante, escarabajo cornudo de los lucánidos; el macho tiene las quijadas enormemente desarrolladas y parecidas a las astas del ciervo. Lucanus.

Stage [stêj], *s.* 1. Tablado, andamio que se levanta para algún espectáculo o fiesta. 2. Escenario, tablas, escena, parte del teatro o de la sala concierto, en que se verifica la representación; teatro. 3. De aquí, la profesión de actor. 4. Teatro, escena de acción. 5. Parada, descansadero; etapa, jornada, distancia recorrida sin detención; distancia que separa dos puntos en que descansan los viajeros. 6. Grado, estado; progreso, período de una enfermedad. 7. Disco, portaobjetos (de microscopio). 8. (E. U.) Diligencia. *V. Stage-coach.* 9. (Arq.) Escalón, paso de escalera. *Hanging-stage*, Plancha de viento; andamio para los pintores. *To bring upon the stage*, Poner en escena. *To come* o *to go upon the stage*, Entrar en escena. *To go off, to quit the stage*, Abandonar la escena; retirarse del teatro. *By short stages*, A pequeñas etapas, a cortas jornadas. *Stage of growth*, Grado de crecimiento. *Stage-micrometer*, Micrómetro del portaobjetos. *Mechanical stage*, Disco de microscopio que puede moverse en dos direcciones en ángulos rectos. *Stage-coach*, Diligencia o coche de diligencia, coche público para los viajeros. *Stage-driver*, Mayoral, cochero de diligencia. *Stage-horse*, Caballo de parada; caballo de diligencia.

Stage, *va.* Representar, exhibir en público; arreglar para el escenario.—*vn.* Viajar en diligencia.

Stagecraft [stêj'-craft], *s.* Habilidad para las producciones teatrales

Stagefright [stêj'-frait], *s.* Terror que inspira el público.

Stage lights [stêj laits], *s. pl.* Candilejas, luces en el proscenio de un teatro.

Stager [stêj'-er], *s.* 1. Caballo de diligencia. 2. (Fest.) Hombre experimentado y que conoce el mundo.

Staggard [stag'-ard], *s.* Ciervo de cuatro años.

Stagger [stag'-er], *vn.* 1. Hacer eses, dar vueltas o giros como un borracho; bambolear. 2. Desmayarse, perder el sentido. 3. Vacilar, titubear, dudar, estar incierto, no estar resuelto.—*va.* 1. Causar vértigos o vahidos. 2. Asustar, dar o causar susto. 3. Hacer vacilar, dudar o titubear. 4. Hacer bambolear, temblar o tambalear.

Staggers [stag'-erz], *s.* 1. Vértigo, especie de apoplejía que padecen los caballos, y el ganado lanar. 2. Vértigo, vahido.

Staghound [stag'-haund], *s.* Sabueso o perro para cazar ciervos.

Staging [stê'-jing], *s.* 1. Andamiaje, plataforma provisional. 2. Tráfico y conducción por medio de diligencias y ómnibus.

Stagnant [stag'-nant], *a.* Estancado, detenido, encharcado, estantío; que cesa de circular.

Stagnate [stag'-nêt], *vn.* 1. Estancarse, detenerse; estar estancado, llegar a ponerse cenagoso, encharcándose. 2. Estar embotado, embotarse; volverse inactivo o inerte.

Stagnation [stag-nê'-shun], *s.* Estagnación, estancación, estancamiento, sea en sentido literal o figurado; paralización de los negocios.

Stag party [stag par'-ti], *s.* Fiesta de hombres solos.

Staid [stêd], *a.* Grave, serio, sosegado.

Staid [stêd], *pret.* y *pp.* de *To* STAY.

Staidness [stêd'-nes], *s.* Gravedad, sosiego, carácter serio.

Stain [stên], *va.* 1. Manchar, ensuciar; chafarrinar. 2. Manchar, ajar, desdorar, empañar la fama, la reputación, etc. 3. Colorar, teñir, como el vidrio o la madera; pintar cristales. 4. Teñir, impregnar de color un tejido para hacer más visible su estructura microscópica.—*vn.* Recibir o comunicar un tinte o color, teñirse. *A bacillus which stains readily with anilin colours*, Un bacilo que se tiñe fácilmente con los colores de anilina. *Stained glass*, *s.* Vidrio de color.

Stain, *s.* 1. Mancha, mácula, borrón. 2. Tinte, color con que se tiñe. 3. Deslustre, deshonra, desdoro.

Stainer [stên'-er], *s.* El que mancha o ensucia; el que tiñe; el que desdora o deslustra. *Glass-stainer*, Colorador de vidrios, fabricante de vidrios de color.

Stainless [stên'-les], *a.* Limpio, libre de manchas, inmaculado. *Stainless steel*, Acero inoxidable.

Stair [stār], *s.* 1. Escalón, peldaño. 2. *pl.* Escalera, una serie de escalones. *One pair of stairs*, El primer alto o el primer piso. *Spiral* o *corkscrew stairs*, Escalera de caracol. *Flight of stairs*, Tramo de escalera. *Stair-carpet*, Alfombra de escalera. *Stair-rod*, Varilla para sujetar la alfombra de escalera. *Up-stairs*, Arriba, en el piso superior. *Down-stairs*, Abajo, en el piso inferior. *To go* o *come up-stairs*, Subir la escalera. *To go* o *come down-stairs*, Bajar la escalera.

Staircase [stār'-kês], *s.* Escalera; caja de escalera.

Stairway [stār'-wê], *s.* Escalera. *V.* STAIRCASE.

Stake [stêc], *s.* 1. Estaca, poste; jalón, estaquilla; rodrigón, palo que se pone para apoyar las vides y árboles tiernos. 2. Pira, poste al que se ata a una persona para quemarla viva. 3. Tas, yunque pequeño. *Stake-boat*, Bote anclado para marcar la dirección y distancias en las regatas.

Stake, *s.* 1. Apuesta; posta en los juegos de envite; tosta o polla. 2. Riesgo, peligro, contingencia. 3. Premio (de contienda). 4. Interés en una empresa; ganancia o pérdida contingente.

Stake, *va.* 1. Estacar; fijar o poner palos, estacas, etc., para que sostengan o apoyen algo. 2. Poner, apostar. 3. Poner en el juego. 4. Arriesgar, exponer. *To stake all*, Envidar el resto, echar el resto, aventurarlo todo.

Stalactite [sta-lac'-tait], *s.* Estalactita, una especie de concreción pétrea que se forma en las bóvedas de las cavernas.

Stalactitic [stal-ac-tit'-ic], *a.* Estalactítico.

Stalagmite [sta-lag'-mait], *s.* Estalagmita, concreción pétrea en el piso de una caverna; parte opuesta a la estalactita, y que a menudo se une con ésta.

Stalder [stōl'-dẹr], *s.* Cerco de madera para sostener los toneles.
Stale [stêl], *a.* Añejo, viejo, rancio, añejado; alterado, deteriorado. *To grow stale,* Añejarse, enranciarse.—*s.* 1. Cerveza que ha principiado á volverse agria. 2. Mate en el juego de ajedrez; tablas. 3. Orines (del ganado).
Stale, *va.* Añejar, hacer viejo.—*vn.* Mear, orinar (los caballos y el ganado).
Stalely [stêl'-li], *adv.* De mucho tiempo.
Stalemate [stêl'-mêt], *s.* Tablas, empate, en el juego de ajedrez.—*va.* Hacer tablas en el juego de ajedrez.
Staleness [stêl'-nes], *s.* Vejez, antigüedad; rancidez.
Stalk [stōk], *va.* 1. Cazar a la espera; acercarse a hurtadillas para matar. 2. Pasar sobre algo con porte majestuoso.—*vn.* 1. Andar con paso majestuoso afectando señorío. 2. Andar a hurtadillas, avanzar a paso de lobo.
Stalk, *s.* 1. Paso levantado y orgulloso. 2. Tallo, pie, tronco; eje de las plantas, particularmente las herbáceas. 3. Pedúnculo, rabo de flor, de fruta; pecíolo, rabo de hoja; troncho de ciertas hortalizas, raspa de las uvas. *Partial flower-stalk,* Pedunculillo o pedúnculo parcial. 4. (Zool.) Tallo, parte que sostiene. 5. Cualquier pie o sostén, como el de una copa.
Stalking-horse [stōk'-ing-hōrs], *s.* 1. El caballo verdadero ó figurado que sirve a los cazadores para ocultarse y cazar. 2. Máscara, disfraz.
Stalky [stōk'-i], *a.* Duro como el tallo.
Stall [stōl], *s.* 1. Pesebre, compartimiento de una cuadra o establo donde se encierra y se da de comer a un caballo o una vaca. 2. Puesto, tienda portátil, puestecillo de cosas para vender; tabla de carnicería; tabanco, puesto público de cosas de comer para la gente pobre. 3. Silla o asiento de un prebendado en el coro. 4. Asiento de luneta o butaca de teatro. 5. Compartimiento de explotación en una mina de carbón. *Butcher's stall,* Tabla de carnicero. *Cobbler's stall,* Zapatería de viejo.
Stall, *va.* 1. Encerrar, meter ó tener encerrada o atada al pesebre una res en el establo, especialmente para cebarla. 2. Instalar, investir, poner en posesión de una cosa. 3. Atascar, atollar, meter en el barro; parar o detener con obstáculos.—*vn.* Estar atascado, atollado; hundirse en el cieno, en la nieve, etc. *The train was stalled in a snowstorm,* El tren quedó detenido por una nevada.
Stall-fed [stōl'-fed], *a.* Cebado a estaca, mantenido en establo.
Stallion [stal'-yun], *s.* Caballo padre, garañón, el destinado para la cría.
Stalwart [stōl'-wart ó stal'-wart], **Stalwarth** [stel'-wūrth], *a.* (Ant.) 1. Fuerte, duro, firme, bravo. 2. Digno de guardarse ó mantenerse. 3. (E. U.) Constante; fiel a su partido político.
Stamen [stê'-men], *s.* (*pl.* STAMENS, rara vez STAMINA). Estambre, órgano masculino de la flor, que contiene el polen.
Stamina [stam'-i-na], *s.* 1. Fuerza vital, vigor. 2. Sostén, la parte firme de un cuerpo, la que sirve de apoyo. (Este vocablo, hoy singular, fué en su origen el plural de STAMEN.)
Staminal [stam'-i-nal], *a.* 1. Estaminal, concerniente a los estambres. 2. Relativo a la fuerza vital, esencial.
Staminate [stam'-i-nêt], *a.* 1. Estaminífero, provisto de estambres, pero sin pistilos. 2. Estamíneo, que tiene estambres.
Stamineous [sta-min'-ẹ-us], *a.* Estamíneo, estaminoso, relativo o perteneciente a los estambres.
Stammer [stam'-ẹr], *va.* y *vn.* Tartamudear; balbucear o balbucir.—*s.* Tartamudeo; balbucencia o balbuceo.
Stammerer [stam'-ẹr-ẹr], *s.* Tartamudo.
Stamp [stamp], *vn.* Patear, patalear, dar patadas o golpes con los pies en el suelo.—*va.* 1. Estampar, señalar o imprimir una cosa en otra. 2. Sellar; timbrar (papel, cartas); fijar el sello de correo; estampillar, marcar con una estampilla. 3. Acuñar. 4. Machacar, moler, majar. 5. Patear, golpear con los pies. 6. Atribuir una cualidad distintiva; marcar, infamar, estigmatizar. 7. Marcar, imprimir, fijar en la mente.
Stamp, *s.* 1. Impresión, marca o señal que deja una cosa que se estampa en otra y la misma cosa que hace la señal. 2. Imagen grabada en madera o metal. 3. Cuño, troquel para sellar la moneda; cuño, sello, la señal o marca que queda impresa en la moneda. 4. Estampador, mano de mortero; instrumento o útil para estampar. 5. Sello o marca, la señal que se pone en las cosas que pagan derechos; timbre, sello legal; sello de correos, estampilla. 6. (Min.) Bocarte, máquina para quebrantar y machacar el mineral antes de fundirlo. *Stamps,* Papel sellado. *Stamp-duties,* Derechos de papel sellado o de sello. 7. Temple, calidad de la índole, humor o genio; suerte, clase; laya, calaña. *Stamp act,* Ley del timbre. *Stamp-office,* Oficina del timbre. *Postage stamp,* Sello de correos o de franqueo. *To bear the stamp of,* Llevar el timbre, la estampilla de; llevar la señal, marca o sello de algo. *Men of the same stamp,* Hombres de la misma calaña.
Stampede [stam-pīd'], *va.* y *vn.* 1. Ahuyentar, con estampido; hacer huir con terror pánico (dícese de un rebaño, una turba, etc.). 2. Obrar por común impulso, tomar de repente un acuerdo, v. gr. en una reunión política.—*s.* 1. Estampida, huída con terror pánico. 2. Movimiento repentino e impulsivo de un gran número de personas o animales. (< esp. amer. estampida.)
Stamper [stamp'-ẹr], *s.* 1. Estampador; impresor. 2. Herramienta o máquina para estampar o machacar; pilón, punzón de forja, bocarte; triturador que se emplea en la fabricación de la pólvora.
Stamping [stamp'-ing], *s.* 1. Timbrado, timbre, acción de estampar, de estampillar, de timbrar; pataleo, pateo. 2. Machaqueo, trituración. *Stamping-machine,* Estampador mecánico; máquina de perforar. *Stamping-mill,* Bocarte, molino triturador de minerales.
Stanch [stanch], *va.* 1. Restañar la sangre. 2. Estancar o detener el curso de alguna cosa líquida.—*vn.* ¿Estancarse, detenerse.
Stanch, *a.* 1. Firme, seguro, celoso, verdadero, constante, fiel, adicto. 2. Sano, bien acondicionado, en buen estado; que no está roto. *A stanch friend,* Un amigo fiel, adicto. *A stanch ship,* Un buque fuerte, sólido. *A stanch hound,* Un sabueso seguro, que no pierde la pista.
Stanchion [stan'-shun], *s.* Puntal, el madero que se pone hincado en la tierra firme para sostener las paredes u otras cosas. *Stanchions of a ship,* (Mar.) Puntales. *Quarter stanchions,* (Mar.) Candeleros o grampones. *Awning-stanchions,* (Mar.) Candeleros del toldo.
Stanchless [stanch'-les], *a.* Lo que no se puede restañar o detener.
Stanchness [stanch'-nes], *s.* Firmeza, resolución, determinación, celo.
Stand [stand], *vn.* (*pret.* y *pp.* STOOD). 1. Estar en pie o derecho, estar de pie o levantado, estar en posición vertical; mantenerse derecho. 2. Sostenerse, tenerse tieso o firme, resistir. 3. Permanecer, quedarse o subsistir en algún paraje. 4. Pararse, detenerse, hacer alto, hacer mansión en algún sitio. 5. Cesar, pararse, quedar suspenso, parado o sin movimiento, suspenderse. 6. Mantenerse firme, resistir; durar. 7. Subsistir en un estado fijo. 8. Tenerse, ponerse, estar en cierta postura. 9. Enderezarse o ponerse de punta. 10. Poseer rectitud moral. 11. Estar situado, estar colocado, hallarse. 12. Tener un puesto determinado con respecto a la clase o al orden. 13. Persistir, perseverar. 14. Ser consistente, acordar, convenir; quedar de acuerdo, quedar corrientes. 15. Estar, hallarse, tener, ser. 16. Estar mal satisfecho, poner tachas u objeciones; ser exigente o difícil. *One must not stand upon trifles,* No hay que pararse en fruslerías. 17. Valer, tener fuerza o valor. 18. Consistir, estribar una cosa en otra; depender lógicamente; se usa con *on, upon,* o *by.* 19. Presentarse como candidato u opositor. 20. Erizarse el pelo. 21. Tomar una dirección, hacer correr, dirigirse. *To stand on the same tack,* Correr la misma bordada, correr bajo las mismas amuras.—*va.* 1. Poner derecho, colocar, hacer tener derecho. 2. Aguantar, sufrir, tolerar, llevar con paciencia. 3. Someterse, soportar. 4. Importar, ser útil, ser de provecho. 5. (Fam.) Pagar el coste de algo. *To stand treat,* Pagar una comida, una convidada. 6. Sostener, defender, resistir. *To stand about,* Rodear, cercar. *To stand against,* Oponerse, resistir; mantenerse firme contra alguno. *To stand alone,* Estar, mantenerse solo; ser el único de su especie. *To stand aloof* (*from*), Mantenerse separado de algo, lejos; no participar en algo. *To stand aside,* Apartarse, mantenerse alejado. *To stand back,* Retroceder; mantenerse detrás. *To stand by,* Sostener, favorecer, ayudar, auxiliar; atenerse a una cosa, contar con; hallarse presente sin tomar parte en lo que se hace; estar cerca, quedarse allí; sostenerse o apoyarse. (Mar.) Velar, estar listo, mantenerse listo. *To stand by* o *to*

an award, Sujetarse al juicio de árbitros. *To stand by itself*, Estar solo o apartado. *To stand by the halliards*, (Mar.) Velar la driza. *I stood by at the operation*, Yo asistí á la operación; me hallaba presente. *Stand by me*, Esté Vd. a mi lado; ayúdeme usted. *To stand far off*, Mantenerse o estar lejos. *To stand for*, Estar por, estar en lugar de, representar; significar, querer decir; solicitar, pretender, presentarse como candidato u opositor; sostener, defender, ser del partido, opinión, etc., de otro, mantener o sostener una opinión; dirigirse a o hacia, llevar rumbo hacia. *A mark which stood for the highest grade*, Una señal que indicaba el grado más alto. *Who stood for the child?* ¿Quiénes sacaron de pila al niño? *To stand fire*, Aguantar el fuego (del enemigo). *To stand forth*, Adelantarse, ponerse o mantenerse delante; avanzar; presentarse. *To stand from under*, Alejarse de alguna cosa que está por caer. (Imper.) ¡Agua va! *To stand in*, Costar, montar, importar tanto; hablando de cantidades. *To stand in a person's light*, Quitar la luz a alguno, hacer sombra, tanto en el sentido recto como en el figurado; causar daño o perjuicio a alguno. *To stand in awe of*, Sentir temor de alguien o algo. *To stand in hand*, Importar, ser ventajoso o importante. *To stand in need*, Tener necesidad o necesitar. *To stand in good stead*, Servir, ser útil. *To stand inshore*, (Mar.) Correr hacia la tierra. *To stand in the way*, Cerrar el paso; hallarse en el camino, impedir, ser un obstáculo. *To stand off*, Mantenerse a cierta distancia, estar separado; negar, no conceder lo que se desea; no convenir en una cosa; no ser amigos, tener las voluntades desunidas; evitar el encontrarse o el verse; hacerse o volverse atrás; salir hacia fuera. *Stand off*, Hágase usted allá, sepárase Vd., no se acerque o no se arrime Vd. *To stand off and on*, (Mar.) Bordear, barloventear, vuelta al mar, vuelta a la tierra. *To stand on end* o *to stand upon an end*, Erizarse, mantenerse derecho, quedar vertical. *To stand on tiptoe*, Ponerse de puntillas. *To stand out*, Mantenerse firme, sostenerse con resolución y firmeza, resistir, hacer frente, oponerse abiertamente; separarse, apartarse; no convenir, negar o no conceder una cosa; salir mucho una cosa de la superficie, resaltar, destacarse, estar en relieve, formar eminencias o protuberancias. *To stand out to sea*, Llevar la proa al mar. *Stand out of the way!* ¡Quítese Vd. de en medio! ¡Fuera! *It stands to reason*, Es conforme a razón, es razonable. *To stand together*, Mantenerse juntos, concertarse y adherirse. *To stand to it*, Mantenerse firme en una contienda. *To stand towards*, Acercarse. *To stand under*, Sufrir, sostener; estar bajo, estar colocado debajo de. *To stand up*, Levantarse, alzarse, ponerse en pie; hacer o formar un partido o reunión para defender algo. *To stand up for*, (1) Defender, mantener, sostener, apoyar. (2) Personarse por, sacar la cara por. *To stand upon*, Estar colocado sobre, estar en; adherirse a; interesar, concernir, tocar, pertenecer; estimar, valuar, hacer mucho caso de una cosa; picarse de, tener su orgullo en; insistir. *Do not stand upon ceremony*, Sin cumplimientos, no gaste Vd. cumplimientos. *To stand with*, Acordarse, convenirse; estar conforme con; disputar, andar en contestaciones. *To stand still*, Estarse quieto; estancarse el agua. *Stand still!* ¡Esté Vd. quieto! ¡no se mueva Vd.! *To stand sentry*, Estar de facción o de centinela. *As the case stands*, En el estado en que se hallan las cosas.

Stand, *s.* 1. El puesto o sitio donde está uno esperando. 2. Posición, situación, estación, el punto o paraje señalado para que alguno se ponga en él; lugar en que uno se dedica ordinariamente a sus asuntos o negocios. 3. Construcción sobre la cual pueden ponerse personas o cosas; plataforma, tribuna; mostrador (de comerciante); puesto en un mercado; velador para poner la luz, consola; salvilla para servir la bebida; estante, vasar; mesita; atril (de música); estante, pie, sostén, soporte. 4. Parada, pausa o alto, la acción de pararse o detenerse. 5. Parada, el término de la acción de una cosa; estado de lo inactivo. 6. Oposición, resistencia. 7. El estado fijo de una cosa que ni puede adelantar ni retroceder. 8. Armamento, equipo completo de armas y munición para un solo soldado. 9. Vegetación sobre el campo, v. g. de las hierbas. *Cruet-stand*, Taller, angarillas, pie de las ampolletas de aceite y vinagre que se usan en las mesas. *To keep a stand*, Quedarse siempre en el mismo estado. *Flower-stand*, Estante para flores, jardinera, portaramillete; tenducho de flores. *Music-stand*, Pupitre para papeles de música, estrado para orquesta.

Standard [stand'-ard], *s.* 1. Marco o patrón para servir de norma; ley, medida de extensión, de cantidad, de valor o de precio que se establece por la ley o de común asenso. 2. Patrón, modelo, dechado, norma, regla fija. 3. Ley; grados de fino del oro o la plata.

Standard, *s.* 1. Árbol o palo que se queda en pie derecho. 2. (Mar.) Curva capuchina. 3. Mueble fijo o pesado. 4. Estandarte, insignia de la milicia; estandarte, pétalo superior (o posterior) de la corola papilionácea.—*a.* Regulador; que sirve de tipo de modelo o de marco; de ley; clásica (una obra). *Standard authors*, Autores clásicos. *Standard gauge*, (1) Medida o marco que sirve de norma. (2) Entrevía común de ferrocarril, la de 56½ pulgadas. *Standard work*, Obra maestra o clásica.

Standard-bearer [stand'-ard-bār-ęr], *s.* Portaestandarte, portaguión.

Standardization [stand'-ard-i-zé'-shun], *s.* Estandardización.

Standard of living [stand'-ard ef liv'-ing], *s.* Standard o nivel de vida.

Standard time [stand'-ard taim], *s.* Hora astronómica.

Standby [stand'-bai], *s.* Adherente fiel; persona o cosa digna de confianza.

Stander [stand'-ęr], *s.* 1. El que está en pie. 2. (Des.) Árbol que está en pie mucho tiempo; resalvo.

Standing [stand'-ing], *a.* 1. Derecho o en pie, levantado, de pie; erecto, con pedestal, con pie. 2. Permanente, fijado, establecido; fijo o establecido permanentemente. 3. Duradero, estable, constante. 4. Estancado, encharcado, sin vertiente o sin salida. 5. Fijo, que no puede moverse con facilidad. *Standing army*, Ejército permanente. *Standing-place, standing-room*, Sitio en que se está de pie, o en que se puede estar de pie. *Standing-room only*, Espacio sólo para estar en pie (donde los asientos están todos tomados). *Standing water*, Agua muerta, remansada, encharcada o estancada, el agua que no corre. *Standing trees*, Los árboles que quedan en pie en los montes después de una corta. 6. (Mar.) Muerto, arraigado. *Standing rigging*, (Mar.) Jarcia muerta, aparejo fijo.

Standing, *s.* 1. Posición, carácter o calidad de las personas o familias en la estimación de otras; posición relativa. 2. Posición, puesto, sitio o paraje destinado para colocarse; sitio o paraje que tiene bastante firmeza y solidez para poder mantenerse de pie en él. 3. La duración de alguna cosa; fecha. 4. Antigüedad, la calidad de ser antiguo. 5. Parada; acción de quedarse en pie. *Of four years' standing*, Que tiene cuatro años de fecha; establecido desde hace cuatro años. *Friends of old standing*, Amigos antiguos, amigos de mucho tiempo. *We are of the same standing*, Somos contemporáneos, o somos iguales. *A person of high standing*, Persona o sujeto de consecuencia, posición o carácter. (Fam.) Sujeto de alto copete.

Standish [stand'-ish], *s.* Escribanía de mesa.

Stand-pipe [stand'-paip], *s.* Columna, tubo de alimentación de agua, en un depósito.

Standpoint [stand'-peint], *s.* Puesto, posición con relación a la que se consideran las cosas; punto de vista. (Análogo al *standpunkt* alemán.)

Standstill [stand'-stil], *s.* Parada, alto; pausa completa; descanso. *To be at a standstill*, Quedar parado, no andar.

Stanhope [stan'-hōp], *s.* Cabriolé ligero y descubierto de un solo asiento.

Stank [stank], *pret.* de *To* STINK.

Stannic [stan'-ic], *a.* Estánnico, perteneciente al estaño, particularmente en sus compuestos más altos.

Stanza [stan'-za], *s.* (Poét.) Estancia, estrofa, grupo de cuatro o más líneas en rima; cada uno de esos grupos o divisiones de un poema.

Stapes [sté'-piz], *s.* (Anat.) Estribo, el huesecillo más interior del oído. (Lat.)

Staple [sté'-pl], *s.* 1. Género, producción principal de un país (o de una comarca). 2. Elemento o material principal. 3. Hebra o filamento de algodón o de lana (para determinar su grado o calidad). 4. Materia prima, materia bruta. 5. Emporio de comercio, mercado.—*a.* 1. Principal, producido y vendido regular y constantemente. 2. Ajustado o establecido según las leyes del comercio, conforme a los usos o leyes del comercio. 3. Vendible, de buena calidad. (< Fr. ant. estaple.) *Staple commodities*, Las principales manufacturas o géneros de algún emporio o escala de comercio.

Staple, *s.* Cerradero, la chapa de hierro en que entra y se asegura el pestillo o cerrojo; picolete, grapa o chapa en forma de U con extremos puntiagudos. (< A.-S. stapel.)

Staple, *va.* Clasificar las hebras (de lana) según su longitud. *Short-stapled, long-stapled,* De hebra corta, de hebra larga.

Stapler [stê'-plęr], *s.* 1. Engrapador. 2. Comerciante en productos de consumo principal.

Star [stār], *s.* 1. Estrella, uno de los cuerpos luminosos que aparecen en el cielo de noche. *Shooting stars,* Estrellas errantes o voladoras. 2. Estrella, hado, suerte, destino. 3. Cruz, placa, la insignia honorífica que llevan los caballeros de varias órdenes. 4. Asterisco, marca de referencia o cita en los libros. 5. Actor, actriz que hace el papel principal; el que sobresale en su profesión. *Binary* o *double star,* Estrella doble, par de estrellas que giran alrededor de su centro común de gravedad. *North star, pole-star,* Estrella polar. *Star of Bethlehem,* (Bot.) Leche de gallina. *Star-paved,* Sembrado o lleno de estrellas, estrellado. *Star-proof,* Que no puede ser atravesado por la luz de las estrellas. *Star-shaped,* Esteliforme, en forma de estrella. *Star-spangled,* Sembrado de estrellas; dícese en especial del pabellón de los Estados Unidos. *Star-stone,* Piedra de estrella, especie de fósil.

Star-apple [stār'-ap-l], *s.* (Bot.) Crisofillo.

Starboard [stār'-bord], *s.* (Mar.) Estribor, el costado derecho de una embarcación.

Starch [stārch], *s.* 1. Almidón, fécula, substancia blanca, pulverulenta, insípida e inodora $(C_6H_{10}O_5)n$, insoluble en el agua fría y en alcohol, que se extrae de todos los vegetales excepto los hongos. 2. Engrudo de almidón. 3. (Fig.) Modales rígidos; coraje, brío.

Starch, *va.* Almidonar, atiesar, la ropa blanca con almidón.

Star-chamber [stār'-chêm-bęr], *s.* Un tribunal criminal que hubo antiguamente en Inglaterra, llamado por algunos antiguos escritores españoles cámara estrellada.

Starched [stārcht], *a.* 1. Almidonado. 2. Tieso, nimiamente grave y circunspecto.

Starcher [stārch'-ęr], *s.* Almidonador o almidonadora.

Starchly [stārch'-li], *adv.* Tiesamente, fuertemente; con afectación.

Starchmaker [stārch'-mê-ker], *s.* Almidonero, el que hace almidón.

Starchness [stārch'-nes], **Starchedness** [stārch'-ed-nes], *s.* Tesura, gravedad excesiva y con afectación.

Starchy [stārch'-i], *a.* 1. Almidonado, engrudado; (fig.) tieso, de modales rígidos. 2. De almidón, combinado con almidón; (med.) feculoso.

Stare [stār], *va.* Clavar o fijar la vista, encararse con alguno; hacer que uno haga o deje de hacer algo por medio de miradas fijas y penetrantes; mirar de fijo.—*vn.* 1. Abrir grandes ojos; mirar con asombro, con insolencia. 2. Saltar a la vista; salir una cosa en la superficie de otra. 3. Enderezarse, levantarse los cabellos. *To stare in the face.* Dar en cara o en los ojos, saltar a los ojos, venirse á los ojos, ser tan claro como la luz del día, ser una cosa tan clara que no se puede negar.

Stare, *s.* Mirada fija, mirada con los ojos dilatados; mirada atontada o de asombro.

Starer [stār'-ęr], *s.* El que clava la vista en algún objeto.

Starfish [stār'-fish], *s.* Estrella de mar, asteria, animal marino equinodermo de brazos radiados.

Star-gazer [stār'-gêz-ęr], *s.* Astrónomo, astrólogo.

Star-gazing [stār'-gêz-ing], *s.* El acto de mirar a las estrellas.

Staring [stār'-ing], *pa.* 1. Abierto, grande, fijo; que mira fijamente. 2. Que salta a la vista; llamativo. *Staring colours,* Colores llamativos, muy vivos.

Stark [stārc], *a.* 1. Tieso, rígido, como en la muerte; de aquí, muerto. 2. (Fig.) Tieso, inflexible, severo. 3. Completo, cabal; puro. 4. (Ant.) Fuerte, vigoroso, poderoso. *Stark madness,* Locura completa. *Stark nonsense,* Pura tontería. *Stark and stiff,* Rígido, muerto.—*adv.* Completamente, enteramente. *He is stark mad,* Está rematadamente loco o es un loco rematado. *Stark naked,* Completamente desnudo, en cueros.

Starkly [stārc'-li], *adv.* Tiesamente, totalmente, del todo.

Starless [stār'-les], *a.* Sin estrellas; sin la luz de las estrellas.

Starlight [stār'-lait], *s.* Luz de las estrellas.—*a.* Estrellado. *Starlight night,* Noche estrellada o muy clara.

Starlike [stār'-laik], *a.* Estrellado, lustroso, brillante, radiante como una estrella o como las estrellas.

Starling [stār'-ling], *s.* 1. (Orn.) Estornino; pájaro del antiguo continente (Sturnus); también, pájaro americano del género Sturnella. 2. El ángulo o esquina del estribo de un puente.

Starred [stārd], *a.* Estrellado, lleno de estrellas; adornado con estrellas; afortunado.

Starry [stār'-i], *a.* 1. Estrellado, sembrado de estrellas o de puntos brillantes. 2. Alumbrado por las estrellas. 3. Centelleante, radiante como las estrellas. 4. Esteliforme, que tiene la forma de una estrella. 5. Estelar, perteneciente o relativo a las estrellas.

Starwort [stār'-wūrt], *s.* (Bot.) Estrellada.

Start [stārt], *va.* 1. Suscitar, mover por primera vez; (1) sobrecoger, asustar; ojear o espantar la caza; hacer levantar (un animal o ave), desemboscar, hacer salir un animal montés de su guarida; (2) poner en movimiento, hacer funcionar o marchar (una cosa inanimada); dar la señal de partida; (3) aflojar, dislocar. 2. Principiar, dar nueva dirección; originar, empezar. 3. Proponer de una manera inesperada, poner sobre el tapete; suscitar objeciones. 4. Trasegar, sacar el contenido de (un tonel, etc.); desfondar; alabear, despegar, (madera). 5. (Ant.) Descubrir, inventar.—*vn.* 1. Sobrecogerse, sobresaltarse, asustarse, estremecerse, conmoverse súbitamente por alguna pasión. 2. Saltar, dar un salto, levantarse de repente. 3. Partir, ponerse en camino; principar la carrera; emprender cualquier negocio; coger o tomar la delantera; estrenarse, comenzar. 4. Salir, proceder, ir adelante; proceder, derivar. 5. Aflojarse de su lugar; descoyuntarse; alabearse, combarse (como la madera). 6. (Ant.) Desviarse, apartarse. *To start aside,* Echarse a un lado, ladearse. *To start after,* Salir, empezar a perseguir o buscar; partir después (de otra cosa). *To start back,* Saltar hacia atrás; partir a la vuelta. *To start for,* Partir, ponerse en camino hacia; presentarse como candidato. *To start from,* Salir, partir de un lugar; tomar su origen; comenzar. *To start off,* Salir; partir, ponerse en camino; principiar a moverse. *To start out,* Principiar a hacer una cosa, irse, marcharse. *To start out of one's sleep,* Despertarse sobresaltado. *To start up,* Levantarse precipitadamente, ponerse derecho; elevarse; salir a luz alguna cosa de repente; ponerse en movimiento, empezar a funcionar (una máquina). *To start a car,* Dar la señal para que un coche del tranvía se ponga en camino. *To start a subject,* Poner un asunto sobre el tapete. *To start wine,* Trasegar el vino.

Start, *s.* 1. Estremecimiento, agitación repentina; sobresalto, susto repentino o de una impresión imprevista. 2. Partida; primer paso, primer movimiento, comienzo, principio. 3. Salto, bote, la acción de apartarse de pronto para evitar un encuentro imprevisto. 4. Ímpetu, arranque, pronto de alguna pasión o del genio; estampida. 5. Arranque, la acción de partir de carrera para proseguir corriendo. 6. Delantera, distancia en que uno se adelanta a otro; ventaja. 7. Grieta, raja, aflojamiento. *To get the start,* Coger la delantera. *By starts,* A saltos, por botes. *By fits and starts,* A saltos y corcovos. *To give a start,* Asustar, dar un susto. *Upon the start,* Al primer paso, al principio, en el momento de partir.

Starter [stārt'-ęr], *s.* 1. El que da la señal de partida (de un automóvil o en una carrera). 2. Palanca de marcha en las máquinas. 3. El perro que levanta la caza. 4. Arranque o marcha de un automóvil. *Self-starter,* Marcha automática (de un auto). *Elevator starter,* Jefe de ascensoristas.

Starting [stārt'-ing], *s.* 1. Sobresalto, estremecimiento. 2. Partida. 3. Impulso, movimiento repentino. 4. (Mec.) Salida, arrancada, acto de poner en movimiento (una máquina). 5. Comienzo. *Starting-point,* Punto de partida. *Starting-place* o *starting-post,* La barrera de donde se arranca a correr.

Startle [stār'-tl], *va.* Espantar, asustar, dar miedo: sobrecoger, alarmar, hacer estremecer.—*vn.* (Ant.) Sobresaltarse, sobrecogerse, temblar de miedo.

Starvation [stār-vê'-shun], *a.* Que causa o que tiende a causar inanición o indigencia.—*s.* Inanición, debilidad grande por falta de alimento; el acto de morir de hambre o el estado de padecer hambre; la muerte procedente de la falta de alimento; por extensión, indigencia, carencia de cualquier cosa esencial a la vida.

Starve [stārv], *vn.* 1. Morir de hambre, morirse de hambre. 2. Perecer, morir por falta de alimento. 3. Sufrir mentalmente, o hallarse sumido en la miseria. 4. (Ingl.) Morir de frío.—*va.* 1. Matar de hambre, hacer morir por falta de alimento. 2. Hambrear, sujetar a una persona por hambre; reducir a un estado de extrema hambre. 3. (Ingl.) Hacer morir de frío; helar. 4. Amilanar, privar de fuerza o vigor. *To starve one's self*, Dejarse morir de hambre.

Starveling [stārv'-ling], *s.* El animal extenuado por falta de alimento o muerto de hambre.—*a.* Hambriento, muerto de hambre, famélico, hambrón.

Stasis [stê'-sis], *s.* (Med.) Estancación de la sangre, particularmente en los vasos capilares.

State [stêt], *s.* 1. Estado, modo de existencia, relación a las circunstancias, condición, ser actual o disposición en que se halla o considera una persona o cosa. 2. Estado, el cuerpo político de una nación; en especial, uno de los Estados Unidos de América. 3. Estado, el país o dominio de algún príncipe. 4. Fausto, pompa, aparato, gran ceremonia; dignidad, grandeza. 5. Trono, dosel, el asiento real usado en los actos de ceremonia majestuosa. 6. El gobierno civil, en contraposición al eclesiástico. *State affairs*, Negocios públicos, negocios o asuntos de estado. *In a state of*, o *to*, En estado de. *Married state*, Matrimonio. *Single state*, Celibato. *In state*, Con gran pompa, de gran ceremonia. *To lie in state*, Estar expuesto en cama de respeto. *Secretary of State*, Ministro de Estado, de Relaciones Exteriores.

State, *a.* 1. De estado; político, público. 2. De lujo; usado en grandes ceremonias; propio para ocasiones de pompa. 3. De un estado de los Estados Unidos. *State paper*, Documento del Estado; pliego, documento o tratado político. *State-house*, (E. U.) Edificio del Estado, en que se reune la legislatura de un estado. *State's evidence*, (1) Testimonio aducido en una causa criminal; (2) el cómplice que por librarse del castigo declara sobre un delito en perjuicio de otros. *State prison*, *V.* PENITENTIARY.

State, *va.* 1. Exponer, enunciar, declarar formal o particularmente, hablando o por escrito; relatar, decir, contar. 2. (For.) Declarar como cosa positiva. 3. (Álg.) Proponer, plantear (un problema).

Statecraft [stêt'-crąft], *s.* Política, el arte de gobernar, de dirigir los asuntos públicos.

Stated [stê'-ted], *a. part.* Establecido, que sucede en épocas señaladas o fijas; regular, fijo, perteneciente a los cuerpos en equilibrio; opuesto a dinámico.

Stateliness [stêt'-li-nes], *s.* 1. Grandeza, majestad, aparato majestuoso, dignidad. 2. Fausto o pompa afectada; altivez.

Stately [stêt'-li], *a.* Augusto, sublime, majestuoso, imponente, soberbio; con apariencia de grandeza y magnificencia; lleno de dignidad, grande, excelso, noble, elevado. *A stately edifice*, Un soberbio edificio. *Stately manners*, Modales nobles, llenos de dignidad.—*adv.* (Poco us.) Majestuosamente, suntuosamente.

Statement [stêt'-męnt], *s.* 1. Declaración, exposición, acción de declarar o exponer; resumen, narración, relación, cuenta. 2. Relato, informe. 3. Cuenta y razón.

Stateroom [stêt'-rum], *s.* 1. Camarote, cuarto particular para dormir, como en un vapor o coche dormitorio; contiene generalmente dos camas. 2. Gran salón, o pieza principal de un palacio.

Statesman [stêts'-man], *s.* Estadista, político; hombre de Estado notable por su talento.

Statesmanlike [stêts'-man-laik], *a.* De una manera propia de un hombre de Estado, o estadista.

Statesmanship [stêts'-man-ship], *s.* Calidad de estadista. *V.* STATECRAFT.

Stateswoman [stêts'-wum-an], *sf.* La mujer que se mezcla en los asuntos de estado.

Static, Statical [stat'-ic, al], *a.* Estático.

Static, *s.* Parásitos. *Static suppressor*, Antiparásito, antiparasitario.

Statics [stat'-ics], *s.* Estática, la ciencia que trata del equilibrio de los cuerpos.

Station [stê'-shun], *s.* 1. El puesto donde se coloca alguno; lugar señalado. 2. Paradero, estación de ferrocarril o de la policía. 3. Condición o posición social. 4. En agrimensura, punto desde el cual o alrededor del cual se hacen las medidas de ángulos o distancias; también, la distancia que sirve de medida normal. 5. Puesto militar, parada, descansadero. *Station-house*, Edificio donde están de guardia los ministros de la policía; estación de ferrocarril para viajeros; habitación de los individuos de una estación de salvamento.

Station, *va.* Apostar, disponer, colocar.

Stationary [stê'-shun-ę-ri], *a.* 1. Estacionario, estacional. 2. Fijo, sin movimiento. 3. Que continúa en el mismo estado, sin hacer progreso alguno. *Stationary engine*, Máquina fija.

Stationer [stê'-shun-ęr], *s.* Papelero, el que vende papel, tinta, lacre y demás efectos necesarios para escribir.

Stationery [stê'-shun-er-i], *s.* Papel y avíos necesarios para escribir. *Stationery store*, Papelería.

Station wagon [stê'-shun wag'-un], *s.* Camioneta.

Statist [stê'-tist], *s.* Estadístico, el versado en la estadística.

Statistical, Statistic [sta-tis'-tic-al], *a.* Estadístico, perteneciente a la estadística; que contiene tablas estadísticas; que trata de la estadística, o dado a ella.

Statistician [stat-is-tish'-an], *s.* Estadístico, persona versada en trabajos estadísticos.

Statistics [sta-tis'-tics], *s.* 1. Estadística, conjunto de datos relativos al estado social. 2. †Estadística, ciencia.

Statoscope [stat'-o-scōp], *s.* (Fís.) Estatoscopio.

Statuary [stat'-yu-ę-ri], *s.* 1. Estatuas consideradas colectivamente. 2. Estatuaria; estatuario, escultor.

Statue [stat'-yu], *s.* Estatua.

Statuesque [stat-yu-esk'], *a.* Parecido a una estatua.

Statuette [stat-yu-et'], *s.* Estatua pequeña. (Fr.)

Stature [stat'-yur], *s.* Estatura, altura, talla, tamaño.

Status [stê'-tus], *s.* 1. Manera de ser; condición o relación legal. 2. Posición relativa.

Statute [stat'-yūt], *s.* Estatuto, ley, pragmática, decreto, reglamento.

Statutory [stat'-yu-to-ri], *a.* Perteneciente o relativo a un estatuto, establecido por la ley.

Staunch [stąnch], *a.* Sano de quilla y costados. *V.* STANCH.

Stave [stêv], *va.* (*pret.* STAVED o STOVE). 1. Romper las duelas; quebrar una cosa, abriendo un agujero; quebrantar, destrozar. 2. Agujerear una cosa destrozándola, o rompiéndola, desfondar. 3. Cubrir de duelas, poner duelas. 4. Rechazar, desviar como con un bastón; retardar, diferir; se usa con *off*, por lo general. 5. Descabezar algún barril o tonel para desocuparlo. *To stave and tail*, Separar a los perros cuando riñen dándoles de palos y tirándoles de la cola.

Stave [stêv], *s.* 1. Duela de barril, tabla de tonel. *Staves and heading*, Duelas y fondos. 2. Tabla recta que forma parte del brocal de un pozo. 3. (Mús.) Pentagrama. 4. Estrofa, estancia.

Staves, *s.* 1. [stêvs] *pl.* regular de STAVE. 2. [stāvz] *pl.* irregular de STAFF.

Stay [stê], *s.* 1. Morada, mansión, el acto o tiempo de quedarse en un paraje; parada, detención, estancia. 2. (For.) Cesación temporal de un procedimiento judicial. 3. Embarazo, impedimento, obstáculo. 4. Lo que reprime o apoya; puntal; apoyo, sostén; sustentáculo, atesador, fiador; (Arq.) arbotante, apeo, estribo; tentemozo. 5. Varilla de ballena en un corsé; en plural, una forma antigua de corsé. 6. Estabilidad, fijeza, perseverancia, persistencia. (< Fr. ant. estaye.) *Make no stay*, No se detenga Vd. *I shall make some stay in London*, Me detendré algo en Londres.

Stay, *s.* (Mar.) Estay, cabo grueso que sirve para sostener un palo o mastelero por la parte delantera. (< A.-S. stæg.) *Main-stay*, Estay mayor. *The ship missed stays*, El buque falló la virada. *Stay-sails*, Velas de estay. *Fore-stay*, Estay de trinquete. *Foretop-stay*, Estay del velacho.

Stay, *vn.* (*pret.* y *pp.* STAYED o STAID). 1. Quedarse, permanecer, estarse, continuar en el mismo sitio, en el mismo estado o en la misma situación. 2. Parar o pararse, cesar en el movimiento o en la acción, no pasar adelante. 3. Tardar, detenerse. 4. (Des.) Aguardarse, esperarse.—*va.* 1. Parar, detener o impedir el movimiento o acción de otro. 2. Contener, poner freno, reprimir. 3. Sostener, apoyar. *To stay away*, Quedar alejado, ausentarse, no parecer. *To stay for*, Aguardar o esperar a uno. *To stay from*, Impedir la acción o efecto de una cosa; separar; torcer o hacer torcer el camino. *To stay in*, Quedarse en su casa, no salir. *To stay on*, Quedar sobre, descansar sobre; permanecer, continuar en el mismo estado. *To stay out*, Quedarse fuera, no entrar. *To stay up*, Velar, no acostarse. *Stay-at-home*, Casero, persona que rara vez sale de su casa. *Stay-a-while*, Mata espinosa que se adhiere a cuantos la rozan. *To*

stay the stomach, Tomar una ligera refacción, tomar las once.
Stayer [stê'-ẹr], *s.* El que permanece, se queda ó está quieto en una parte; el que para ó detiene; el que apoya ó favorece.
Stays [stêz], *s. pl.* *V.* STAY,[1] 5ª acep.
Stead [sted], *s.* 1. Lugar, sitio; las veces de; (precedido de *in*). 2. Auxilio, ayuda. 3. (Des.) Armazón de cama. *V.* BEDSTEAD. *In his stead*, En su sitio, en su lugar; en vez de él. *In stead of*, En lugar de, en vez de. *V.* INSTEAD. *To stand in stead*, Ser útil, servir una cosa para lo que se quiere destinarla.
Steadfast, Stedfast [sted'-fast], *a.* 1. Fijo, firme, estable, permanente. 2. Constante, inmutable. 3. Resuelto, determinado.
Steadfastly [sted'-fast-li], *adv.* Firmemente, con constancia, con resolución. *He fixed his eyes steadfastly on her*, Él estuvo con los ojos clavados en ella.
Steadfastness [sted'-fast-nes], *s.* 1. Inmutabilidad, estabilidad. 2. Firmeza, constancia, resolución, persistencia.
Steadily [sted'-i-li], *adv.* Firmemente; invariablemente.
Steadiness [sted'-i-nes], *s.* 1. Firmeza, la seguridad en que se halla una cosa que no falsea ni se mueve; estabilidad. 2. Firmeza, entereza, constancia. 3. Regularidad, conducta arreglada, morigerada.
Steady [sted'-i], *a.* 1. Firme, fijo, seguro, asegurado. 2. Juicioso, formal, asentado, prudente. 3. Firme, constante, no variable; que se mueve o funciona con regularidad. 4. Libre de excesos; de vida arreglada.
Steady, *va.* Hacer firme, sostener, fijar alguna cosa.
Steak [stêk], *s.* Tajada de carne para asar. *Beef-steak*, Tajada de vaca, bistec.
Steal [stîl], *va.* y *vn.* (*pret.* STOLE, *pp.* STOLEN). 1. Robar, hurtar, pillar, estafar con tretas y engaños. 2. Pretender o arrogarse algo sin derecho, v. g. la calidad de autor; cometer plagio. 3. Introducirse clandestinamente o sin ser observado; pasar furtivamente, a hurtadillas. 4. Colarse, escabullirse, escapar sin ser visto. 5. Robar o atraer con eficacia y como violentamente el afecto o ánimo. *To steal away from*, Quitar del medio, hacer desaparecer, ocultar, esconder. *Thou shalt not steal*, No hurtarás. *To steal along*, Pasar en silencio, deslizarse sin ruido, avanzar a paso de lobo. *To steal away, to steal off*, Marcharse a hurtadillas; escabullirse. *To steal down*, Descender furtivamente. *To steal forth*, Salir clandestinamente. *To steal in, into*, Penetrar furtivamente, introducirse a hurtadillas. *To steal over*, Ganar insensiblemente, apoderarse suavemente de algo; deslizarse a escondidas. *To steal up*, Subir a ocultas, clandestinamente. *To steal upon*, Aproximarse sin ruido, sorprender; apoderarse de algo; deslizarse, penetrar calladamente.—*s.* (Fam.) Hurto, el acto de hurtar; robo.
Stealer [stîl'-ẹr], *s.* Ladrón, el que roba o hurta.
Stealing [stîl'-ing], *s.* Hurto, robo; la acción de hurtar, y la cosa robada.
Stealth [stelth], *s.* La calidad o costumbre de obrar a hurtadillas ó en secreto. *By stealth*, A hurtadillas, a escondidas, de oculto, a escondite, en secreto.
Stealthy [stelth'-i], *a.* Furtivo, hecho de oculto o a escondidas.
Steam [stîm], *s.* 1. Agua en el estado gaseoso; vapor, o vaho que exhala todo cuerpo húmedo que se calienta; en especial el flúido elástico producido por la ebullición del agua. 2. Niebla, vaho visible. *Steam-engine*, Máquina de vapor. *To cut off, to expand, to shut off steam*, Cortar, disminuir, interrumpir, el vapor. *To get up* o *generate steam*, Producir o generar vapor. *With all steam on*, A todo vapor. *Steam is on*, Hay presión. *Superheated, surcharged steam*, Exceso de vapor. *High-pressure steam*, Vapor a alta presión. *Steam-chest*, Caja o cámara de vapor. *Steam-gauge*, Manómetro de vapor. *Steam-hammer*, Martinete de vapor. *Steam-pipe*, Cañería o conducto de vapor.
Steam, *va.* 1. Saturar con vapor; someter a la acción del vapor. 2. Secar, quitar la humedad a una cosa, v. g. los adobes.—*vn.* 1. Vahear, emitir o echar de sí vaho o vapor. 2. Moverse por medio del vapor. 3. Evaporarse o reducirse a vapor.
Steamboat [stîm'-bōt], *s.* Barco de vapor, vapor de río.
Steamer [stîm'-ẹr], *s.* 1. Barco, vapor. 2. Vaporizador. *Steamer rug*, Manta de viaje. *Steamer trunk*, Baúl de camarote.
Steamfitter [stîm-fit'-ẹr], *s.* Montador de calderas de vapor.
Steamheat [stîm-hît'], *s.* Calefacción mediante vapor.
Steamroller [stîm-rōl'-ẹr], *s.* 1. Apisonadora. 2. (Fig.) Actividad arrolladora, fuerza abrumadora. —*va.* Abrumar.
Steamship [stîm'-ship], *s.* Vapor, buque de vapor. *Steamship line*, Línea marítima, línea de vapores.
Steam shovel [stîm' shuv-l], *s.* Pala mecánica.
Stearic [stî-ar'-ic], *a.* Esteárico, de estearina o relativo a ella. *Stearic acid*, Ácido esteárico, contenido en las grasas sólidas de los animales, y también en algunos de los aceites vegetales.
Stearin [stî'-ar-in], *s.* Estearina, compuesto blanco y cristalizable ($C_3H_5(C_{18}H_{35}O_2)_3$) contenido en las grasas.
Steatite [stî'-a-tait], *s.* Esteatita.
Steed [stîd], *s.* Caballo de regalo, corcel.
Steel [stîl], *s.* 1. Acero. 2. Arma o instrumento hecho de acero, p. ej. espada, cuchillo, etc. 3. (fig.) Dureza, firmeza. *Alloy steel*, Aleación de acero. *Ball-bearing steel*, Acero para cojinetes. *Bessemer steel*, Acero Bessemer. *Chrome steel*, Acero cromado o al cromo. *Damask steel*, Acero damasquinado. *Stainless steel*, Acero inoxidable. *Steel wool*, Lana de acero (para limpieza).
Steel, *va.* 1. Acerar, poner acero, cubrir o armar de acero. 2. Fortalecer, endurecer, hacer más firme, acorazar. 3. Dar apariencia de acero a una cosa.—*a.* Hecho ó compuesto de acero o parecido a él; de aquí, endurecido, inflexible, duro, sin piedad. *Steel-blue*, Azulado como ciertos aceros. *Steel-clad*, Cubierto o armado de acero. *Steel-engraving*, Grabado en acero. *Steel-pen*, Pluma de acero. *Tincture of steel*, (Ingl.) Tintura de cloruro de hierro. *Steel-works*, Talleres en que se fabrica el acero. *Tool-steel*, Acero de superior calidad y de gran temple que se usa para hacer herramientas cortantes.
Steeliness [stîl'-i-nes], *s.* Dureza, insensibilidad.
Steel mill [stîl' mil], *s.* Acería.
Steelworker [stîl'-wurk'-ẹr], *s.* Obrero en una fundición de acero.
Steely [stîl'-i], *a.* 1. Acerado, con acero o de acero. 2. (Poét.) Acerino, de acero o perteneciente a este metal. 3. Fuerte, inflexible, firme, duro.
Steep [stîp], *a.* Escarpado, derecho, pino, rápido.—*s.* Precipicio, despeñadero, altura o cuesta muy difícil de subir.
Steep, *va.* 1. Empapar, penetrar con algún líquido, macerar. 2. Mojar completamente, impregnar, remojar; poner en infusión. 3. Embalsar, enriar (el cáñamo o el lino). —*vn.* Mezclarse gradualmente en una infusión. *To steep tea*, Poner el té en infusión. *Steeping-tub*, (Mar.) Tina de desalar. *Steeping-trough*, El sitio donde los cerveceros echan la cebada para entallecer.—*adj.* (Fam.) Excesivo, exorbitante.
Steeping [stîp'-ing], *s.* Mojadura, maceración; acción de empapar, de remojar, o de enriar.
Steeple [stî'-pl], *s.* 1. Campanario, torre elevada de una iglesia. 2. Iglesia (el edificio); nombre dado por los primeros cuáqueros.
Steeplechase [stî'-pl-chês''], *s.* Corrida a caballo por el campo, con tapias, zanjas u otros obstáculos.
Steepled [stî'-pld], *a.* Con torre o campanario.
Steeplejack [stî'-pl-jac], *s.* Reparador de espiras, chimeneas, torres, etc.
Steepness [stîp'-nes], *s.* Calidad de escarpado o pendiente.
Steer [stîr], *s.* 1. Novillo, novillejo, utrero. 2. (E. U.) Buey de cualquier edad que sea.
Steer [stîr], *va.* 1. Gobernar, guiar o dirigir el rumbo o la embarcación. 2. Guiar o manejar la rueda o el volante de un vehículo.—*vn.* 1. Navegar, andar bien o mal una nave. 2. Gobernarse, conducirse. 3. Estar sujeto a la acción del timón o de cualquier direcciön. *To steer clear of*, Evitar chocar con algo, mantenerse alejado de.
Steerage [stîr'-ẹj], *s.* 1. Antecámara de un bajel, proa, rancho de la gente, que ocupan principalmente los inmigrantes. 2. Alojamiento de los marineros, oficiales más jóvenes, sirvientes, etc. (en un buque de guerra). 3. Gobierno, dirección; la acción de gobernar o dirigir. *To have steerage-way*, (Mar.) Tener salida para gobernar. *Steerage passenger*, Pasajero de proa, de bodega, o de combés. *Steerage-way*, Estela, surco del buque; movimiento de una embarcación suficiente para poder gobernarla por el timón.
Steering wheel [stîr'-ing hwîl], *s.* 1. Volante (de un automóvil). 2. (Mar.) Rueda del timón.
Steersman [stîrz'-man], *s.* (Mar.) Piloto, timonel, timonero.

Stellar [stel'-ar], *a.* Astral, estrellar, relativo o perteneciente á las estrellas.
Stellate [stel'-ēt], *a.* Estrellado, de forma estrellada, parecido a las estrellas.
Stelliform [stel'-i-fōrm], *a.* Esteliforme, en forma de estrella.
Stellular [stel'-yu-lar], *a.* Estrellado, sembrado de pequeñas estrellas.
Stellionate [stel'-yun-ēt], *s.* (For.) Estelionato, el delito que comete el que vende una finca como libre no siéndolo.
Stem [stem], *s.* 1. Tallo, tronco, cuerpo principal de un árbol, arbusto o planta, el eje que sube. 2. Vástago, pedúnculo de una flor, fruta u hoja; pecíolo. 3. Una parte delgada cualquiera que se asemeja más o menos al tallo del árbol, al pedúnculo de la flor, etc.; pie (de copa); cañón de pluma; barra, rasgo perpendicular que se añade al cuerpo de una nota. 4. (Mar.) Roda, roa, tajamar, un trozo derecho de madera en el cual se unen los costados del bajel por la parte delantera. *A woody stem,* Un tallo leñoso. *Herbaceous stems,* Tallos herbáceos. *From stem to stern,* De proa a popa. *Stem-winder,* Reloj de bolsillo al que se da cuerda por medio de un muñón al extremo del eje. *Stem-winding,* Remontoir; aplícase al reloj de bolsillo sin llave.
Stem, *va.* 1. Navegar contra la corriente, ir contra viento o marea. 2. Oponerse a la corriente o a las opiniones más aceptadas; resistir. 3. Hacer impermeable una unión o encaje, tapándola o cubriéndola. 4. Quitar los pedúnculos; desgranar (p. ej. las uvas, las pasas). 5. Poner patas o pies a una cosa. *To stem the torrent,* Detener el torrente. *To stem the tide,* Rendir la marea.
Stemless [stem'-les], *a.* Sin pie o sostén; sin pedúnculo; en botánica, acaule, sin tallo.
Stempel, Stemple [stem'-pl], *s.* 1. Estemple, montante, asnado, madero grueso con que se aseguran de trecho en trecho los costados de la mina. 2. Travesaño de madera.
Stemson [stem'-sun], *s.* (Mar.) Contrarroda, sobrerroda, trabazón de palos fuertes que asegura la roda del navío.
Stench [stench], *s.* Hedor, hediondez; también en sentido figurado.
Stencil [sten'-sil], *va.* 1. Estarcir, hacer letras o dibujos calados con un patrón. 2. Pintar con un modelo calado.—*s.* 1. Patrón, modelo calado para estarcir. 2. Adorno hecho con planchas de estarcir.
Stenciler [sten'-sil-ẹr], *s.* El que estarce letras o dibujos, particularmente para adornar los techos de las habitaciones.
Stenograph [sten'-o-graf], *s.* 1. Carácter o escritura en la estenografía. 2. Máquina parecida a la de escribir para hacer caracteres fonéticos.
Stenographer [sten-og'-ra-fẹr], *s.* Estenógrafo, taquígrafo, persona que ejerce la estenografía.
Stenographic [sten-o-graf'-ic], *a.* Estenográfico, perteneciente a la estenografía.
Stenography [stẹn-og'-ra-fi], *s.* Taquigrafía o estenografía. *V.* SHORTHAND.
Stenotyping [sten'-o-taip'-ing], *s.* Estenomecanografía.
Stentor [sten'-tẹr], *s.* 1. En la Ilíada, Estentor, heraldo famoso a causa de su voz formidable; de aquí, cualquier persona de voz notablemente fuerte. 2. Infusorio del género Stentor.
Stentorian [sten-tō'-ri-an], *a.* Estentóreo, muy fuerte y grueso; dícese de la voz.
Step [step], *va.* (*pret.* y *pp.* STEPPED o STEPT). 1. Colocar, poner o mover el pie, como al andar. 2. Ejecutar, llevar a cabo dando los pasos necesarios; atravesar o medir dando pasos; se usa a menudo con *off.* 3. Plantar un mástil.—*vn.* 1. Dar un paso, mover el pie o los pies como al andar, correr o bailar; avanzar, retroceder o mudar de posición con un movimiento del pie. 2. Andar una corta distancia, pasear, dar una vuelta. 3. Andar paso a paso, gravemente o con dignidad y resolución. *To step after,* Seguir o ir detrás. *To step aside,* Desviarse, apartarse, ponerse a un lado. *To step back,* Retroceder, volver atrás; volver o tornar el pensamiento hacia lo pasado. *To step down,* Bajar, descender. *To step forth,* Presentarse resueltamente; ir andando con pasos mesurados o muy poco a poco. *To step in,* Entrar en un carruaje o subir a él; entrar, venir de repente, ocurrirse a la imaginación. *To step on,* Poner el pie sobre algo, pisar; andar sobre. *To step out,* Salir, dar un paso fuera; bajar, v. g. de un carruaje. *To step over,* Atravesar, pasar de una parte a otra. *To step short,* (Mil.) Dar pasos de quince pulgadas cada uno, acortando el paso. *To step up,* Subir.
Step, *s.* 1. Paso, la acción de andar el espacio o distancia que naturalmente se adelanta de un pie á otro, y el mismo espacio. 2. Paso, este mismo espacio tomado como medida. 3. Paso o escalón, el peldaño de escalera; umbral de puerta. 4. Paso, un espacio muy corto. 5. Escalón, el grado a que se asciende en la consecución de una cosa o el paso y modo con que alguno adelanta en lo que desea. 6. Paso, el adelantamiento que se hace en cualquiera cosa. 7. Pisada, paso, la huella que queda impresa al andar. 8. Paso, el modo de andar. 9. Paso, el modo de vida de alguno o su conducta. 10. (Mús.) Intervalo equivalente a un grado de la escala o del pentagrama. 11. Pedestal de máquina, quicio de eje vertical; (Mar.) carlinga, madero fijo sobre la quilla en el que entra la mecha del palo. *Steps, pl.* Pasos, diligencias para la prosecución de algún negocio. *Step of a mast,* Carlinga. *By such steps,* Por tales medios. *To retrace one's steps,* Volver sobre sus pasos. *To take a step,* Dar un paso; tomar alguna medida. *In step,* De acorde, en unión (como en la marcha).
Step-. Prefijo que en composición tiene la significación de parentesco de afinidad, como *Step-father,* Padrastro. *Step-mother,* Madrastra. *Step-son,* Hijastro. *Step-daughter,* Hijastra. *Step-brother,* Medio hermano. *Step-sister,* Media hermana.
Stepladder [step'-lad-ẹr], *s.* Escalera de mano.
Steppe [step], *s.* Estepa.
Stepping-stone [step'-ing-stōn], 1. Pasadera, estriberón. 2. (Fig.) Escalón. 3. (Fig.) Trampolín.
Stercoraceous [ster-co-rē'-shus], *a.* Estercoráceo, perteneciente al estiércol.
Stere [stīr o stār], *s.* Estéreo, medida métrica para áridos; un metro cúbico.
Stereographic, Stereographical [ster-ẹ-o-graf'-ic, al], *a.* Estereográfico, perteneciente á la estereografía.
Stereography [ster-ẹ-eg'-ra-fi], *s.* Estereografía, el arte de representar los sólidos sobre un plano.
Stereometer [ster-ẹ-em'-ẹ-tẹr], *s.* Estereómetro, instrumento para medir el volumen de un cuerpo.
Stereometry [ster-ẹ-em'-ẹ-tri], *s.* Estereometría, el arte de medir los sólidos.
Stereophonic [ster-ẹ-o-fe'-nic], *a.* Estereofónico.
Stereopticon [ster-ẹ-op'-ti-con], *s.* Estereóptico, linterna mágica doble de que se usa para reflejar alternativamente las imágenes sobre una mampara.
Stereoscope [ster'-ẹ-o-scōp], *s.* Estereoscopio, instrumento óptico con dos lentes prismáticos, en que se ven como de relieve las figuras de un dibujo o fotografía doble.
Stereoscopic [ster-ẹ-o-scep'-ic], *a.* Estereoscópico, perteneciente al estereoscopio o propio para usarlo en él. *Stereoscopic pictures,* Cuadros estereoscópicos, *Stereoscopic camera,* Cámara estereoscópica.
Stereotype [ster'-ẹ-o-taip], *va.* 1. Estereotipar, clisar; convertir las formas de caracteres movibles en planchas permanentes. 2. Estereotipar, imprimir con planchas firmes y estables en lugar de las comunes hechas con letras sueltas; imprimir de una manera indeleble.—*s.* Estereotipo, clisé; plancha de metal de estereotipar, que se saca de una matriz; letra o viñeta clisada. *Stereotype plate,* Plancha estereotípica, clisé.
Stereotyped [ster'-ẹ-o-taipd], *a.* 1. Estereotipado. 2. Sin originalidad.
Stereotyping [ster'-ẹ-o-taip'-ing], *s.* Estereotipia.
Sterile [ster'-il], *a.* 1. Estéril, infructífero, que no engendra; que no contiene polen o no produce un pistilo. 2. Que no produce, sin ventaja, sin resultado.
Sterility [stẹ-ril'-i-ti], *s.* Esterilidad, condición ó calidad de estéril.
Sterilization [ster-il-i-zē'-shun], *s.* Esterilización.
Sterilize [ster'-il-aiz], *va.* 1. Esterilizar, hacer infecundo. 2. Destruir las bacterias u otros organismos microscópicos. *To sterilize milk,* Hervir la leche para destruir las bacterias.
Sterilizer [ster'-il-aiz-ẹr], *s.* Esterilizador; aparato para destruir las bacterias.
Sterling [stẹr'-ling], *a.* 1. Esterlina, epíteto por el cual se distingue la moneda legítima de Inglaterra. 2. Genuino, hecho a ley, puro, verdadero. *A pound sterling,* Una libra esterlina.
Stern [stẹrn], *a.* 1. Austero, duro rígido; severo, inflexible, cruel. 2. Áspero, agrio de genio; que infunde miedo, que repele.—*s.* 1. (Mar.) Popa, el remate posterior de un bajel. *Stern-fast,* Codera. *Square-stern,* Popa llana. *Pink-stern,* Popa de pinque. *Stern-frame,* Cuaderna de popa o del cuerpo popés. *Stern-port,* (Mar.) Porta de guardatimón.

2. La parte o extremidad posterior de cualquiera cosa, cola. *Stern-chase*, Caza en que la nave que persigue va siguiendo en la estela de la otra. *Stern-chaser*, Pieza de retirada. *Stern-post*, Codaste, estambor, guardatimón, pieza fijada en la quilla y que sostiene el timón. *Stern-sheets*, El espacio que queda a popa de los bancos de un bote. *Sternway*, Reculada, cía, movimiento de retroceso. *Stern-wheeler*, (E. U.) Bote de vapor, de poco calado, que tiene a popa una sola rueda grande de paleta.

Sternly [stẹrn'-li], *adv.* Austeramente, severamente, rigurosamente.

Sternness [stẹrn'-nes], *s.* Austeridad, severidad, rigor, dureza, aspereza de genio.

Sternum [stẹr'-num], *s.* (Anat.) Esternón, hueso situado en la parte anterior y media del tórax.

Sternutative [stẹr-nū'-ta-tiv], *a.* (Poco us.) Estornutatorio, que hace estornudar.

Sternutatory [stẹr-nū'-ta-to-ri], *s.* Estornutatorio, el medicamento que hace estornudar.

Steroid [ster'-oid], *s.* Esteroide.

Stertor [stẹr'-ter], *s.* Estertor, respiración ronca y anhelosa.

Stertorous [ster'-tōr-us], *a.* Esterto roso, caracterizado por el estertor.

Stet [stet]. (Impr.) Reténgase.

Stethoscope [steth'-o-scōp], *s.* Estetoscopio, instrumento acústico para explorar el estado del pecho.

Stethoscopic [steth-o-scop'-ic], *a.* Estetoscópico, relativo al estetoscopio.

Stevedore [stī'-vẹ-dōr], *s.* Estibador, cuyo oficio es estibar o descargar la carga de los buques. (< Esp.)

Stew [stiū], *va.* y *vn.* Estofar, cocer a fuego lento.—*s.* 1. Estofado, guisado; carne o pescado estofados. 2. (Fam.) Estado de excitación nerviosa y ansiedad; agitación mental. 3. (Ant.) Estufa, aposento recogido y abrigado al que se da calor artificialmente. 4. *pl.* (Ant.) Burdel, lupanar. *Stew-pan*, La cazuela o cacerola donde se estofa la carne.

Steward [stiū'-ard], *s.* 1. Administrador; el que administra o maneja una propiedad o los asuntos de otro. 2. Mayordomo de mesa o de colegio; a bordo, despensero, el que tiene a su cargo la despensa y los camarotes de los viajeros: senescal. *Steward of a farm*, (Cuba) Mayoral. *Steward of a dinner*, etc., Comisionado, encargado de un convite, función, etc. *Steward's room*, Despensa.

Stewardess [stiū'-ar-des], *sf.* 1. (Mar.) Camarera de a bordo. 2. (Aer.) Azafata, aeromoza.

Stewardship [stiū'-ard-ship], *s.* Mayordomía.

Sthenic [sthen'-ic], *a.* 1. Que manifiesta energía o actividad, como una parte o un órgano. 2. Que tiene el poder de inspirar o animar.

Stich [stic], *s.* 1. Un versículo de la Biblia. 2. Verso, línea de poesía; se usa frecuentemente en composición; v. gr. *hemistich*, hemistiquio. 3. Hilera de árboles.

Stick [stic], *s.* 1. Palo, palillo, pedazo de madera largo y delgado; vara, raja de leña. 2. Pieza de madera de construcción. 3. Bastón, vara que se lleva en la mano. 4. Ristra, serie de cosas dispuestas en sarta. 5. Estique, instrumento de madera que usan los escultores para modelar en barro. 6. Arco (para instrumento de cuerda). *Sticks*, *pl.* Támaras o rozo, leña menuda de palitos, astillas, etc., para quemar; chabasca, ramitas delgadas. *Broomstick*, Palo de escoba. *Composing-stick*, Componedor, el instrumento en que componen y forman las líneas los cajistas. *Round stick*, Taco en el juego de billar. *Shooting-stick*, (Impr.) Atacador de imprenta. *Stick of sealing-wax*, Barra de lacre. *Drum-sticks*, Palillos de tambor o bolillos. *Chop-sticks*, Paletillas para comer. *Fan-sticks*, Varillas de abanico. *To pick up sticks*, Recoger la leña menuda o támaras. *Blow with a stick*, Bastonazo, garrotazo.

Stick, *s* Herida o golpe penetrante con arma o instrumento punzante; estocada.

Stick, *s.* 1. Estado de hallarse pegadas unas cosas a otras. 2. Acción de parar, parada; demora, dilación; vacilación, escrúpulo.

Stick, *va.* (*pret.* y *pp.* STUCK). 1. Hacer penetrar, hacer entrar un instrumento de punta; hundir, pasar o atravesar con puñal u otro instrumento puntiagudo. 2. Hincar, introducir o clavar una cosa en otra; fijar alguna cosa con un instrumento puntiagudo; sujetar, fijar con alfileres, tachuelas, etc 3. Matar o herir de una puñalada o cuchillada. 4. Picar, punzar; llenar de puntas; cubrir de algo que penetra. *A paper stuck with pins*, Un papel cubierto o bien provisto de alfileres.—*vn.* 1. Cogerse, ser mantenido o apoyado para no hundirse. 2. Hacer comba hacia fuera, hacer barriga, sobresalir; se usa con *out*, *through* y *from*. (< A.-S. stecan.) *To stick in*, Clavar, picar, punzar, encajar; hundirse. *To stick out*, Salir, sobresalir, hacer barriga; mantenerse firme, no ceder, resistir. *His bones stick out*, Se le ven los huesos, está descarnado.

Stick, *va.* (*pret.* y *pp.* STUCK). 1. Pegar, juntar, unir con una substancia adhesiva. 2. (Ger.) Confundir, aturrullar. 3. (Ger.) Engañar. 4. Componer tipo. 5. (Agr.) Plantar jalones.—*vn.* 1. Pegarse, adherirse o unirse una cosa con otra tenazmente. 2. Pegarse, estar siempre con uno a su pesar o introducirse en una parte sin ser llamado. 3. Pegarse, insinuarse alguna cosa en el ánimo. 4. Pararse, detenerse; dudar, tener escrúpulo, fluctuar, vacilar. 5. Perseverar, ser constante en alguna cosa. 6. Atollarse, meterse en algún empeño o embarazo del que no se puede salir fácilmente. *To stick at it*, (Fam.) Persistir. *To stick at*, Detenerse, sentir escrúpulo de; acusar la conciencia o tener cargo de conciencia. *He sticks at everything*, (Fam.) Se ahoga en poca agua. *He sticks at nothing*, (Fam.) Nada le detiene o contiene, de nada tiene escrúpulo. *To stick fast*, Pegarse, adherirse fuertemente. *To stick close*, Mantenerse juntos; unirse fuertemente. *To stick in the mire*, Hundirse en el cieno. *To stick by*, Sostener, apoyar; pegarse a alguno. *To stick to*, Pegarse o adherirse tenazmente: obstinarse, preocuparse fuertemente, aferrarse a una idea, opinión; atenerse a.

Sticker [stik'-ẹr], *s.* Etiqueta engomada.

Stickiness [stik'-i-nes], *s.* 1. Tenacidad, la dificultad en desasirse o despegarse una cosa de otra. 2. Viscosidad, glutinosidad.

Sticking-plaster [stik'-ing-plas-tẹr], *s.* Emplasto adhesivo, tafetán inglés o de Inglaterra.

Stickle [stic'-l], *vn.* Altercar, disputar o porfiar acerca de menudencias; insistir o vacilar por razones de poca importancia.

Stickleback [stic'-l-bac], *s.* Espino, pez pequeño de aguas dulces o saladas.

Stickler [stic'-lẹr], *s.* Un disputador porfiado o cansado; el que es partidario ardiente o defiende con ardor a su partido.

Stickpin [stic'-pin], *s.* Alfiler de corbata. (Mex.) Fistol.

Sticky [stik'-i], *a.* Pegajoso, viscoso, tenaz.

Stiff [stif], *a.* 1. Tieso; duro, firme y sólido, que con dificultad se dobla o rompe. 2. Envarado, entorpecido, torpe, embotado, que funciona con dificultad o fricción. 3. Rígido, duro, inflexible; tenso, tendido. 4. Espeso, viscoso, consistente. 5. Obstinado, terco. 6. Afectado, poco natural, que carece de gracia. 7. Duro; hablando del estilo. 8. Fuerte, que tiene movimiento fuerte y regular. 9. Difícil, severo. 10. (Com.) Firme en los precios. 11. (Mar.) Que aguanta bien el viento; que se inclina poco cuando lleva mucho velamen. *To grow stiff*, Estirarse, endurecerse. *Stiff breeze*, Brisa fuerte. *A stiff paste*, Una pasta espesa. *Stiff gale*, Viento fuerte. *Stiff news*, Noticias fundadas o dignas de creerse. *Stiff neck*, (1) Afección reumática de los músculos del cuello. (2) Torticoli. *V. Wry neck.*

Stiffen [stif'-n], *va.* 1. Atiesar, poner tieso o tirante; endurecer, dar firmeza; espesar. 2. Envarar o entorpecer los miembros. 3. Arrecir de frío.—*vn.* 1. Atiesarse o ponerse tiesa una cosa, endurecerse; enderezarse; espesarse. 2. Envararse o entorpecerse los miembros. 3. Obstinarse.

Stiffener [stif'-n-ẹr], *s.* Abultador, colchoncillo, cojinillo; atiesador; contrafuerte de zapato.

Stiff-hearted [stif'-hārt-ed], *a.* Obstinado, terco.

Stiff-necked [stif'-nect], *a.* Obstinado, terco, pertinaz, testarudo, cabezudo.

Stiffly [stif'-li], *adv.* Tiesamente, obstinadamente, inflexiblemente.

Stiffness [stif'-nes], *s.* 1. Tesura, inflexibilidad; rigidez de lo que no se puede doblar; imposibilidad de moverse. 2. (Med.) Rigor, tensión preternatural que impide el movimiento. 3. Inflexibilidad, terquedad, obstinación; modales severos, altaneros. 4. Dureza de estilo. 5. Espesura, consistencia de una masa. *Stiffness of limbs*, Envaramiento o entorpecimiento de los miembros.

Stifle [staī'-fl], *va.* 1. Sufocar, ahogar. 2. Apagar, extinguir, acabar, terminar, poner fin. 3. Suprimir, callar, ocultar.—*vn.* Ahogarse, morir por falta de respiración.

Stigma [stig'-ma], *s.* 1. Borrón, mancha, nota de infamia; antiguamente, marca, señal que se hacía con un hierro candente. 2. Estigma, extremo superior del pistilo destinado a recibir el polen. 3. (Anat. y Zool.) Marco o poro; orificio de la tráquea en los insectos. 4. Estigma, llaga milagrosa (correspondiente a las cinco heridas de Jesucristo).

Stigmatic [stig-mat'-ic], *a.* 1. Señalado con una marca; (ant. de infamia); ignominioso; de aquí, deformado, desfigurado. 2. (Bot.) Estigmático, referente al estigma de una flor.

Stigmatize [stig'-ma-taiz], *va.* 1. Estigmatizar, señalar con una nota de infamia. 2. Marcar con estigmas, como los puntos que presenta la piel en el sarampión.

Stile [stail], *s.* 1. Un portillo con escalones para pasar de un cercado a otro. 2. Gnomon, el estilo de hierro con que se señalan las horas en los relojes de sol. 3. Estilo. *V.* STYLE. *Turn-stile,* Un torno en forma de cruz que se pone en algunos sitios o cercados para pasar fácilmente.

Stiletto [sti-let'-o], *s.* 1. Verduguillo, un puñal o estoque pequeño con tres cortes. 2. Punzón, instrumento puntiagudo para agujerear.

Still [stil], *va.* 1. Acallar, aplacar o sosegar el llanto; hacer callar, hacer cesar un ruido cualquiera. 2. Acallar, aquietar, aplacar, apaciguar. 3. Parar o detener el movimiento de alguna cosa. 4. (Des.) Destilar, alambicar.

Still, *a.* 1. Inmóvil, que no puede moverse; fijo, que está sin movimiento; tranquilo, quedo. 2. Silencioso, quieto, que guarda silencio, que no hace ruido; de aquí, suavizado, de sonido débil; apacible, sosegado, 3. Sin efervescencia; dícese de los vinos. 4. Muerto, inanimado. *Still water,* Agua encharcada o tranquila. *Still wine,* Vino no espumoso. *Still as the grave,* Silencioso como la tumba. *The air is still,* La atmósfera está tranquila. *To stand still,* Detenerse, permanecer quedo, no moverse. *Still life,* Naturaleza muerta (en una pintura). *Still-born,* Aborto, que ha nacido muerto.—*s.* 1. Silencio, calma, tranquilidad, quietud, sosiego. 2. Alambique, vaso que sirve para destilar.—*adv.* 1. Todavía, aun, sin cesar, siempre, hasta ahora. 2. No obstante, sin embargo, a pesar de eso. 3. Más, además. *Still more,* Todavía más, aun más.

Still-burn [stil'-būrn], *va.* Quemar por la destilación.

Stiller [stil'-ẹr], *s.* 1. Persona que apacigua, que calma. 2. (Prov. Ingl.) Disco que se coloca sobre un cubo lleno para impedir que el líquido salpique.

Stilling [stil'-ing], *s.* Poino, el codal que sustenta y sirve de apoyo a las cubas en la bodega.

Stilly [stil'-li], *a.* (Poét.) Tranquilo, silencioso; suave, de sonido débil. —*adv.* Silenciosamente, quietamente.

Stillness [stil'-nes], *s.* Silencio, sosiego, calma, quietud, tranquilidad.

Stilt [stilt], *s.* 1. Zanco, palo con horquilla o estribo en que se afirma el pie para andar. 2. Prisma o trípode de barro para sostener un artículo de alfarería en el horno. 3. (Esco.) Esteva del arado. 4. Zanco de manto, ave del orden de las zancudas, género Himantopus.

Stilted [stilt'-ed], *a.* Subido en zancos, hinchado, pomposo, engreído.

Stimulant [stim'-yu-lant], *a.* Estimulante, que estimula, que excita o es propio para excitar.—*s.* 1. Estimulante, lo que excita, lo que aguijonea. 2. Remedio estimulante, substancia que excita la acción orgánica del sistema humano; en plural, licores embriagantes.

Stimulate [stim'-yu-lêt], *va.* 1. Estimular, aguijonear, punzar, avivar. 2. (Med.) Estimular, avivar o acelerar la acción orgánica de las partes del cuerpo.—*vn.* 1. Servir como estímulo o aguijón. 2. Tomar estimulantes o licores embriagantes.

Stimulation [stim-yu-lê'-shun], *s.* 1. Estímulo, aguijón, incitamiento para obrar. 2. Estimulación, la acción y efecto de estimular.

Stimulative [stim'-yu-la-tiv], *a.* Estimulante.—*s.* Estímulo; excitación.

Stimulus [stim'-yu-lus], *s.* 1. Estímulo, aguijón; motivo, incentivo. 2. Estimulante, lo que determina una excitación en un nervio o músculo. 3. (Bot.) Dardo, aguijón.

Sting [sting], *va.* y *vn.* (*pret.* y *pp.* STUNG). 1. Picar, pinchar, hacer una picadura, usar de un aguijón. 2. Causar o producir tormento la memoria de una cosa. 3. Atormentar, carcomer, remorder la conciencia.

Sting, *s.* 1. Aguijón, la púa o punta aguda con que pican algunos insectos. 2. Punzada, picadura, picada. 3. Cualquier cosa que produce un dolor vivo o que punza; (Bot.) púa, filamento hueco y tieso que secreta un flúido picante, como el de las ortigas. 4. Remordimiento de conciencia. 5. Aguijón, estímulo.

Stingily [stin'-ji-li], *adv.* Avaramente, miserablemente, tacañamente.

Stinginess [stin'-ji-nes], *s.* Tacañería, avaricia, miseria, ruindad.

Stinging [sting'-ing], *s.* Picadura, punzada, punzadura.

Stingless [sting'-les], *s.* Que no tiene aguijón; sin púa.

Stingo [stiṇ'-go], *s.* (Vulg.) Cerveza añeja.

Stingy [stin'-ji], *a.* 1. Mezquino, tacaño, ruin, avaro, miserable. 2. Escaso, poco, limitado.

Stink [stiṇk], *vn.* (*pret.* STANK o STUNK, *pp.* STUNK). Heder, oler mal, apestar.

Stink, *s.* Hedor, hediondez.

Stinkard [stink'-ard], *s.* La persona hedionda o muy puerca.

Stinker [stink'-ẹr], *s.* Cualquier cosa hedionda o que arroja de sí muy mal olor.

Stinking [stiṇk'-ing], *a.* Hediondo.

Stinkingly [stiṇk'-ing-li], *adv.* Hediondamente, con hediondez; vilmente, cobardemente.

Stinkingness [stink'-ing-nes], *s.* Hediondez.

Stinkpot [stiṇk'-pot], *s.* Olla llena de materiales hediondos; bomba asfixiante.

Stint [stint], *va.* 1. Limitar, restringir dentro de límites fijos; proporcionar o servir escasamente. 2. Señalar, repartir una tarea determinada.—*vn.* Ceñirse, ser económico o parsimonioso.

Stint, *s.* 1. Cuota, porción fija o determinada, v. g. tarea de trabajo. 2. Límite, restricción. 3. Maubecha pequeña, tríngido, ave de las escolopácidas. Tringa.

Stipe [staip], *s.* (Bot.) 1. Estipo, el tallo de las palmas y de las plantas que llevan fronde. 2. Estipo, el sustentáculo de cualquier órgano de las plantas y particularmente del sombrerete en los hongos.

Stipend [stai'-pend], *s.* Estipendio, sueldo o salario pagado en épocas fijas como compensación de servicios prestados; en Escocia, sueldo de un clérigo.

Stipendiary [stai-pen'-di-ẹ-ri], *a.* Estipendiario.—*s.* Estipendiario, el que hace algún servicio por estipendio señalado.

Stipitate [stip'-i-têt], *a.* (Bot.) Estiposo, que tiene estipo, que está mantenido por un sustentáculo.

Stipple [stip'-l], *va.* Picar, puntear, hacer puntitos, dibujando, pintando o grabando.—*s.* Picado, punteado. (< Holan. stippelen.)

Stippling [stip'-ling], *s.* Picado, acto o procedimiento de dibujar, de grabar picando.

Stiptic, Stiptical [stip'-tic, al], *a.* Estíptico, que tiene virtud de apretar, constreñir o astringir.

Stipulate [stip'-yu-lêt], *va.* 1. Estipular, especificar las cláusulas o palabras de un convenio. 2. Mencionar expresamente; especificar, particularizar.—*vn.* Estipular, contratar mutuamente.

Stipulate, *a.* Estipulífero, provisto de estípulas.

Stipulation [stip-yu-lê'-shun], *s.* 1. Estipulación, acción de estipular, calidad de estipulado. 2. Estipulación, cláusula, condición, convenio enunciado en un contrato; convenio, contrato mutuo; pacto.

Stipule [stip'-yūl], *s.* 1. (Bot.) Estípula, apéndice foliáceo en la base del pecíolo de ciertas hojas. 2. (Orn.) Pluma reciente.

Stir [stẹr], *va.* 1. Cambiar de lugar las partes componentes de un todo, mover o menear una cosa, particularmente con un movimiento circular, como con una cuchara. 2. Agitar, alterar, revolver, enturbiar, inquietar, irritar. 3. Suscitar, animar, incitar; conmover, excitar los afectos y sentimientos. 4. Agitar, ventilar o controvertir una cuestión o materia de negocios o de ciencias. *To stir the fire,* Atizar o avivar la lumbre.—*vn.* 1. Moverse o menearse, ponerse en movimiento. 2. Mudar de posición, moverse, cambiar de lugar. 3. Levantarse temprano. 4. (Ant.) Agitarse, bullir o no estarse quieto. *To stir up,* Conmover, excitar, animar, aguijonear; poner en movimiento; despertar.

Stir, *s.* 1. Movimiento, conmoción, actividad en alguna cosa. 2. Interés, público o general, excitación, conmoción. 3. Estruendo, alboroto.

Stirrer [stẹr'-ẹr], *s.* 1. Promovedor, movedor, promotor, motor; instigador, incitador. 2. Madrugador, el que madruga.

Stirring [stẹr'-ing], *s.* 1. Movimiento. 2. El acto de levantarse por la mañana.—*a.* 1. Activo, acostumbrado a una vida activa. 2. Alentador, animador.

Stirrup [stir'-up o stẹr'-up], *s.* 1. Estribo, pieza en que apoya el pie el jinete. 2. (Mar.) Estribo. *Stirrups of the yards or of the horses,* (Mar.) Estribos de guardamancebos de las vergas. *Stirrups of the yard-arms,* (Mar.) Estribos de los pelones de las vergas. *Stirrups of the chain-plates,* (Mar.) Estribos de las cadenas.

Stirrup-bearer, Tirante de estribo. *Stirrup-leather*, Ación, la correa de que cuelga el estribo.

Stitch [stich], *va.* 1. Coser, unir con aguja, seda, hilo, etc., dos pedazos de cualquiera cosa. 2. Coser, unir, juntar.—*vn.* Coser o hacer bordados; coser, tener el oficio de sastre o costurera. *To stitch up*, Remendar; recoser lo que estaba descosido. *To stitch down*, Ribetear.

Stitch, *s.* 1. Puntada, punto, el paso de la aguja por la tela que se va cosiendo. 2. Punto, cada una de las lazadas o nuditos de las medias, calcetas, etc. 3. Punzada, dolor punzante. 4. Caballón o surco que traza el arado. 5. Distancia, jornada, división o porción de un viaje. (< A.-S. stice, < radical de *stick*,[1] verbo.) *Back-stitch*, Punto atrás, pespunte. *Cross-stitch*, Punto cruzado, punto de escarpín. *Chain-stitch*, Punto de cadena. *Lock-stitch*, Punto de cadeneta. *Lock-stitch* o *chain-stitch sewing-machines*, Máquinas de coser punto de cadeneta o de cadena.

Stitcher [stich'-ẹr], *s.* 1. Cosedor, cosedora; ribeteadora, persona que cose. 2. En la encuadernación, máquina para coser los libros.

Stitching [stich'-ing], *s.* 1. Pespunte, hilera de puntos en una tela. 2. Punto atrás.

Stithy [stith'-i], *s.* 1. Fragua. *V.* SMITHY. 2. Yunque o ayunque, bigornia.

Stiver [staī'-vẹr], *s.* Moneda holandesa; un ochavo; una blanca.

Stoat [stōt], *s.* El armiño, particularmente en su pelaje de verano, que es moreno rojizo por encima y amarillo por debajo.

Stock [stec], *s.* 1. Tronco, la parte de los árboles y plantas desde el suelo hasta donde se divide en ramas; también, ingerto, el árbol ingerido. 2. Tronco, estirpe o cepa de una familia o linaje; estirpe, familia, linaje. 3. (For.) Línea directa de una familia. 4. Ganado en general; se llama comúnmente *live stock*. 5. (Com.) Capital comercial; valores, acciones; en plural, surtido de mercancías; mercancías almacenadas. 6. Acopio, provisión cuantiosa; fondo; abundancia, cantidad de primeras materias; enseres; muebles; efectos existentes. 7. Mango, manija; berbiquí de barrena; caja de fusil; aquella parte de un mecanismo que sirve para apoyar o mantener las piezas vivas. *Stock of a gun*, Caja de escopeta. 8. (Mar.) Grada de construcción, astillero. *A ship on the stocks*, (Mar.) Navío en las gradas o en el astillero. *Stock-blocks*, (Mar.) Polines de la grada. *Stock of an anchor*, (Mar.) Cepo de ancla. 9. Corbatín, especie de corbata. 10. Baceta o monte, los naipes que quedan después de haber dado. 11. Alelí. *V.* GILLYFLOWER. 12. Leño, el trozo del árbol después de cortado; de aquí, tronco, zoquete, estólido, un hombre tonto o insensible. 13. *Stocks*, Cepo, prisión, antiguo instrumento de castigo en el cual se sujetaban los pies o brazos del delincuente. 14. Colonia de abejas, abejar. *To lay in a stock*, Hacer provisión, surtir sus almacenes; proveerse. *Stock in trade*, Mercancías disponibles en almacén. *To take (account of) stock*, Hacer inventario. *Live stock*, Ganados. *Stock farmer*, Ganadero. *Joint-stock company*, Sociedad por acciones, sociedad anónima. *Railroad stocks*, Acciones de ferrocarril. *Stock-yard*, Corral para ganados; corral grande en que se encierra el ganado destinado al matadero o al transporte. *Stock-broker*, Corredor de valores públicos; corredor de vales; agiotista. *Stock-dove*, (Orn.) Paloma torcaz. *Stock-fish*, Bacalao seco, pejepalo, una especie de merluza seca. *Stock-gillyflower*, (Bot.) Alelí doble. *Stock-jobber*, Agiotista, el que negocia en los efectos o valores públicos, a menudo de un modo irregular. *Stock-jobbing*, Agiotaje de valores públicos.

Stock, *va.* 1. Proveer, abastecer, surtir, llenar. 2. Acumular, juntar, acopiar. 3. Encepar, poner en un cepo.

Stockade [stek-ēd'], *va.* Empalizar, rodear de empalizadas.—*s.* 1. Empalizada, estacada, fila de estacas clavadas en tierra. 2. Construcción de pilotaje para proteger un muelle.

Stock company [stec cum'-pa-ni], *s.* (Com.) 1. Sociedad anónima. 2. (Teat.) Compañía teatral de repertorio.

Stockholder [stec'-hōld-ẹr], *s.* Accionista.

Stockinet [stek"-i-net'], *s.* Elástica, tejido elástico propio para ropa interior.

Stocking [stek'-ing], *va.* Proveer de medias; poner las medias a uno.—*s.* Media, la vestidura de la pierna y del pie. *Silk stockings*, Medias de seda. *Worsted stockings*, Medias de lana o de estambre. *Thread stockings*, Medias de hilo. *Knit stockings*, Medias de punto. *Wove stockings*, Medias de telar.

Stocking-frame [stek'-ing-frēm], *s.* Telar de medias.

Stocking-weaver [stek'-ing-wīv-ẹr], *s.* Tejedor de medias.

Stockish [stek'-ish], *a.* Estúpido, insensible, como un tronco, duro.

Stock market [stec mār'-ket], *s.* Bolsa de valores.

Stockpile [stec'-pail], *s.* Acumulación de materias primas y otros productos para hacer frente a escaseces.

Stockpile, *va.* Acumular materias primas para hacer frente a escaseces.

Stockroom [stec' rūm], *s.* Depósito de mercancías (en un almacén, oficina, etc.).

Stocks [stecs], *s. pl.* 1. Cepo, especie de prisión. 2. Valores públicos, acciones. 3. Gradas de construir buques. *V.* STOCK.

Stock-still [stec'-stil], *a.* Inmoble, inmóvil (como un poste).

Stocky [stek'-i], *a.* Rechoncho.

Stodgy [stej'-i], *a.* Regordete.

Stoic [stō'-ic], *s.* Estoico, el filósofo que seguía la escuela de Zenón; de aquí, persona indiferente al placer o al dolor; también, ascético severo.

Stoical [stō'-ic-al], **Stoic**, *a.* 1. Estoico, perteneciente a la secta o filosofía estoica. 2. Estoico, severo, firme, inflexible e imperturbable como un estoico.

Stoically [stō'-i-cal-i], *adv.* Estoicamente, de un modo inflexible e imperturbable.

Stoicism [stō'-i-sizm], *s.* Estoicismo, la doctrina o secta de los estoicos.

Stoke [stōk], *va.* y *vn.* Atizar, mantener vivo el fuego en las máquinas de vapor.

Stoker [stō'-kẹr], *s.* Fogonero, el que cuida del fuego.

Stole [stōl], *s.* 1. Estola, vestidura para la celebración de oficios sagrados. 2. Estola, chal. *Fur stole*, Estola de piel.

Stole, **Stolen**, *pret.* y *pp.* del verbo *To* STEAL.

Stolid [stel'-id], *a.* Estólido; impasible, estúpido.

Stolon [stō'-len], *s.* 1. (Bot.) Estolón, rama horizontal o nueva planta que nace del nudo de otra. 2. (Zool.) Prolongacion del cuerpo de varios animales, como los corales.

Stomach [stum'-ac], *s.* 1. Estómago, la parte del cuerpo en que se hace la primera digestión de los alimentos. 2. Barriga, abdomen; uso común, pero inexacto. 3. Apetito, gana de comer; afición, inclinación.

Stomach, *va.* Aceptar sin oposición; sufrir, aguantar.

Stomachal [stum'-ac-al], *a.* Estomacal, perteneciente al estómago o que aprovecha al estómago; cordial.

Stomacher [stum'-ak-ẹr], *s.* Peto, prenda de vestir que se pone en el pecho.

Stomaching [stum'-ak-ing], *s.* Resentimiento.

Stomachless [stum'-ac-les], *a.* Sin estómago; desganado, sin gana o sin apetito.

Stomatitis [stō"-ma-taī'-tis], *s.* Estomatitis, inflamación de la boca.

Stone [stōn], *s.* 1. Piedra, un cuerpo natural, sólido y duro. 2. Roca, como material. 3. Trozo de piedra con forma propia para un uso especial; v. gr. piedra de molino, de amolar; piedra sepulcral. 4. Piedra preciosa. 5. Piedra, cálculo, la materia dura que se engendra en el cuerpo humano, particularmente en los riñones y en la vejiga. 6. Hueso, cuesco, pepita de las frutas. 7. (Ingl.) Un peso de catorce libras en general y de ocho para la carne. 8. (Bajo) Testículo. *Mill-stone*, Muela o piedra de molino. *Flint-stone*, Piedra de escopeta, de lumbre o de pedernal. *Imposing-stone*, (Impr.) Piedra de imponer. *To leave no stone unturned*, No dejar piedra por mover, no economizar ningún esfuerzo, hacer todo lo posible. *Stone-breaker*, *V.* *Stone-crusher*. *Stone-coal*, Carbón de piedra; carbón muy duro o antracita. *Stone-cold*, Frío como la piedra, como el mármol. *Stone-colour*, Color de la piedra expuesta al aire; gris azulado. *Stone-crusher*, Triturador o bocarte de piedra. *Stone-cutting*, Labra de las piedras. *Stone-dead*, Muerto como una piedra. *Stone-mason*, Albañil. *Stone-parsley*, Amomo, perejil perenne. *Stone-pine*, Pino dulce del Mediterráneo. *Stone's cast*, *stone's throw*, Tiro de piedra, distancia a que alcanza una piedra lanzada con la mano. *Stone-blind*, Enteramente ciego, física o mentalmente. *Stone-cutter*, Picapedrero, cantero, el que labra las piedras. *Stone-fruit*, Fruta de hueso. *Stone-hawk*, (Orn.) Halcón apedreado. *Stone-pit*, *stone-quarry*, Cantera.—*a.* De piedra, hecho de piedra.

Stone, *va.* 1. Apedrear; asaltar o matar a pedradas. 2. Quitar los cuescos o huesos a las frutas. 3. Revestir de piedras, trabajar en albañilería.

Stonebreak [stōn'-brēk], *s.* (Bot.) Quebranta-piedras, saxífraga (traducción del nombre botánico saxífraga).

Stone-deaf [stōn'-def'], *a.* Sordo como una tapia.

Stoner [stō'-nẹr], *s.* Apedreador: despepitador de frutas.

Stoneware [stōn'-wār], *s.* Cacharro de barro.

Stonework [stōn'-wūrc], *s.* Obra hecha de piedra o cantería.

Stony [stō'-ni], *a.* 1. Pedregoso, lleno de piedras. 2. (Ant. o poét.) De piedra, hecho de piedra; pétreo. 3. Duro, inflexible, inexorable. 4 Petrificante, que transforma en piedra.

Stood [stud], *pret.* y *pp.* del verbo STAND.

Stooge [stūj], *s.* 1. (Teat.) El que ayuda subrepticiamente a un actor. (Mex.) Palero. 2. El que ejecuta tareas serviles para otra persona.

Stool [stūl], *s.* 1. Banquillo sin respaldo; taburete, escabel. 2. Tarimilla, banqueta. *V.* FOOTSTOOL. 3. Sillico, silleta; y de aquí, cámara, excremento, evacuación de vientre: (comúnmente en plural). 4. Planta madre; vástago acodado. 5. Señuelo o añagaza (para atraer las aves). *Stool of repentance,* Banquillo de arrepentimiento (derivado de una antigua costumbre escocesa). *Stool-pigeon,* (1) Cimbel, cimillo. (2) Persona empleada para embaucar a otras. *Close-stool, night-stool,* Sillico para excrementos. *To go to stool,* Hacer del cuerpo, ir a la secreta. *Foot-stool,* Escabel, tarimilla para poner los pies.

Stoop [stūp], *vn.* 1. Encorvarse, combarse, inclinarse hacia adelante. 2. Encorvarse o bajarse hasta el suelo. 3. Bajarse, someterse, sujetarse. 4. Bajarse, humillarse, abatirse; emplearse en cosas menos honoríficas que las pertenecientes a alguno por su clase o estado. 5. Ceder, rendirse. 6. Condescender, acomodarse al gusto y voluntad de otro. 7. Lanzarse, arrojarse como el halcón se arroja sobre la presa.—*va.* Someter o sujetar; hacer bajar; bajar la cabeza.

Stoop,[1] *s.* 1. Inclinación hacia adelante y abajo; también, inclinación habitual de los hombros hacia adelante. 2. Descenso, caída de alguna dignidad o estado a otro inferior. 3. Caimiento, declinación, abatimiento. 4. Caída del halcón sobre la presa.

Stoop,[2] *s.* (E. U.) Gradería, pórtico exterior, meseta descubierta a la entrada de una casa.

Stoop,[3] **Stoup** [stūp], *s.* 1. Copa o frasco para beber. 2. Pila de agua bendita.

Stoopingly [stūp'-ing-li], *adv.* Hacia abajo, con inclinación hacia abajo.

Stop [stọp], *va.* 1. Detener, parar, impedir que una cosa siga el movimiento que lleva; cortar, interceptar. 2. Detener, suspender, diferir, dilatar la ejecución de una cosa; reprimir, refrenar de antemano. 3. Tapar, cerrar o cubrir algún agujero o abertura. 4. Retener, v. g. los salarios o jornales. *To stop a leak,* Tapar, cegar una vía de agua. *To stop the progress of vice,* Detener los progresos del vicio. *To stop the way,* Obstruir el camino, cerrar el paso.—*vn.* 1. Parar o pararse, cesar el movimiento o la acción, detenerse, hacer alto. 2. Llegar al fin, cesar. 3. (Fam.) Quedarse algún tiempo, alojarse o morar en algún paraje o casa. 4. (Mús.) Cambiar el tono o diapasón por medio de un agujero o un traste. *To stop up,* Tapar, cerrar. *To stop one's career,* Cortarle a uno los pasos. *To stop one's mouth,* Tapar la boca, no dejar hablar. *Stop a moment,* Deténgase Vd. un instante. *My watch has stopped,* Mi reloj se ha parado. *To stop short,* Quedarse cortado. *To stop payment,* (Com.) Suspender los pagos; dar punto a los negocios. *Not to stop at,* No pararse en, no contentarse con, no mirar en.

Stop, *s.* 1. Parada, la acción de parar o detenerse; pausa, alto. 2. Interrupción; suspensión, detención. 3. Dilación, retardación, retardo. 4. Oposición, obstáculo, impedimento, embarazo. 5. Cesación; represión. 6. (Mús.) Palanca, tecla o mango para cambiar el diapasón de un instrumento de música; traste de guitarra; registro de órgano. 7. Punto, signo de puntuación. *Full stop,* Punto final. 8. (Mec.) Retén, fiador, seguro. *To put a stop to,* Suspender, poner término a, hacer cesar. *To make a stop,* Hacer alto, detenerse; hacer una pausa. *To come to a dead stop,* Cortarse, pararse repentinamente. *Stop-gap,* Lo que cierra un agujero; (Mar.) abarrote. Se usa también como adjetivo.

Stopcock [stọp'-coc], *s.* 1. Llave de fuente. 2. Canilla de tonel; espita.

Stop light [stọp' lait], *s.* Señal luminosa de parada.

Stopover [stọp'-ō'-vẹr], *s.* Escala, parada intermediaria en el camino.

Stoppage [stọp'-ēj], *s.* 1. Obstrucción, cesación de movimiento, detención, embarazo, impedimento. 2. Retención (sobre los sueldos). *Stoppage in transit,* (For.) Embargo hecho por el vendedor de las mercancías durante su transporte a manos del comprador, en caso de insolvencia de éste.

Stopper [stọp'-ẹr], *va.* Entapouar, tapar con un tapón; (Mar.) bozar, amarrar con bozas.—*s.* 1. Persona o cosa que tapa, que cierra; tarugo, tapón; (Mar.) bozas, pedazos cortos de cabo grueso que sirven para suspender cualquier cuerpo pesado o para tener un cable. 2. Persona o cosa que detiene. *Anchor-stopper,* (Mar.) Capón. *Stopper-bolts,* (Mar.) Argollas de boza.

Stopple [stọp'-l], *va.* Entaponar, atarugar, o cerrar con tapón.—*s.* Tapón.

Stop signal [stọp sig'-nal], *s.* Señal de parada.

Stop watch [stọp' wọch], *s.* Cronómetro, reloj cuya marcha se inicia y detiene a voluntad. Se utiliza en deportes.

Storage [stōr'-ēj], *s.* 1. Almacenaje, acción y efecto de almacenar, de guardar en almacén. 2. Espacio para almacenar las mercancías. 3. Almacenaje, lo que se paga por guardar en un almacén.

Storage battery [stōr-ēj bat'-ẹr-i], *s.* Acumulador, batería de acumuladores.

Store [stōr], *s.* 1. Copia, abundancia, gran cantidad, acopio, provisión. 2. *pl.* Pertrechos, equipos; víveres, provisiones; municiones, bastimentos. 3. Almacén, depósito. 4. En los Estados Unidos y en algunas colonias inglesas, tienda, almacén. *V.* SHOP. *Store of victuals,* Provisiones de boca. *Stores for an army,* Municiones, pertrechos o provisiones de guerra.—*a.* Almacenado, guardado en almacén.

Store, *va.* 1. Surtir, proveer, abastecer; municionar, pertrechar. *To store a ship,* (Mar.) Abastecer un buque. 2. Atesorar, guardar, acumular, acopiar; tener en reserva. 3. Almacenar, poner o guardar en almacén.

Storer [stōr'-ẹr], *s.* El que atesora, acumula, acopia o guarda.

Storehouse [stōr'-haus], *s.* Almacén.

Storekeeper [stōr'-kīp-ẹr], *s.* 1. Guardaalmacén; jefe de déposito; tendero, comerciante. 2. (Mar.) Pañolero, magacenero.

Storeroom [stōr'-rūm], *s.* (Mar.) Despensa; pañol. *Boatswain's storeroom,* (Mar.) Pañol de proa.

Storied [stō'-rid], *a.* 1. Historiado, que tiene una historia notable. 2. Historiado, adornado con cuadros históricos. 3. Referido por la historia. 4. Que tiene pisos.

Stork [stōrc], *s.* (Orn.) Cigüeña.

Storm [stōrm], *s.* 1. Tempestad, tormenta, borrasca; vendaval; conmoción de la atmósfera, por lo regular con lluvia, etc. *A thunder-storm,* Tronada. *A rain and wind storm,* Turbonada. *Snow-storm,* Tormenta de nieve, nevasca. 2. Tormenta, adversidad, calamidad, desgracia o infelicidad en el estado de una persona. 3. Asalto, el ataque para apoderarse a viva fuerza de una plaza o puesto. 4. Conmoción, tumulto, alboroto. 5. Acometimiento tumultuoso, lluvia (particularmente de proyectiles). *To raise, to stir up a storm,* Levantar una tempestad, promover desórdenes. *To take by storm,* Tomar por asalto. *Storm-beaten, storm-beat, storm-tossed,* Azotado, combatido por la tempestad. *Storm-petrel* o *stormy petrel, V.* PETREL. *Storm-sail,* Tallavientos, vela pequeña de trinquete que se usa en las borrascas.

Storm, *va.* Asaltar, tomar por asalto, atacar a viva fuerza.—*vn.* 1. (Impersonal) Tempestar, haber tempestad, haber tormenta. *It stormed yesterday,* Ayer hubo tempestad. 2. Levantarse una borrasca o tempestad. 3. Reventar o estallar de cólera, prorrumpir en injurias, denuestos o invectivas.

Stormbird [stōrm'-bẹrd], *s.* Procelaria, ave que anuncia borrasca en el mar.

Storm door [stōrm dōr], *s.* Contrapuerta, doble puerta (para proteger contra el viento y el frío).

Storminess [stōrm'-i-nes], *s.* Estado borrascoso, tempestuoso.

Stormy [stōrm'-i], *a.* 1. Tempestuoso, borrascoso. 2. Violento, turbulento.

Storm window [stōrm win'-dō], *s.* Contraventana, doble ventana (para proteger contra el viento y el frío).

Story [stō'-ri], *s.* 1. Historia, relación de las cosas pasadas. 2. Cuento, fábula, conseja; historieta, noveleta. (Fam.) Cuento de viejas, hablilla. 3. Enredo, trama de una obra literaria o dramática. 4. (Fam.) Mentira, fábula; eufemismo usado generalmente por los niños o para con los niños. 5. Anécdota. 6. Alto, cada uno de los pisos o suelos de una casa. *A house three stories* *high,* Casa de tres altos o de tres pisos. *As the story goes,* Según se dice, según cuenta la historia. *A true story,* Una historia o anécdota verdadera. *Fairy story,* Cuento de hadas.

Story, *va.* 1. Historiar, narrar. 2. Colocar las cosas poniéndolas ordenadamente unas debajo de otras.

Story-teller [stō'-ri-tel-ęr], *s.* Cuentista, chismeador, chismoso; embustero, el que dice con frecuencia mentiras.

Stout [staut], *a.* 1. Fornido, robusto, corpulento; fuerte, vigoroso, firme. 2. Resuelto, intrépido, animoso. 3. Terco, inflexible.—*s.* Cerveza fuerte.

Stoutly [staut'-li], *adv.* Vigorosamente, valientemente; con resolución.

Stoutness [staut'-nes], *s.* 1. Valor, ánimo, fuerza. 2. Intrepidez, arrojo. 3. Terquedad, obstinación; aspereza.

Stove [stōv], *s.* 1. Estufa (para caldear una habitación); estufa de cocina; hornillo para poner fuego. 2. Estufa, pieza para secar. 3. (Ingl.) Estufa para plantas. 4. Horno cerámico. (< Hol. stoof.) *Foot-stove,* Rejuela.

Stove, *pret.* y *pp.* de *To* STAVE.

Stow [stō], *va.* 1. Ordenar, colocar con orden; llenar de una manera compacta o metódica; hacinar. 2. (Mar.) Estibar, arrumar. 3. Ocultar; también, alojarse. *To stow in bulk,* (Mar.) Arrumar a bulto.

Stowage [stō'-ej], *s.* 1. Arreglo, colocación en su sitio; el estado de la cosa que se halla almacenada o guardada. 2. Sitio, espacio donde se guardan o almacenan cosas. 3. El dinero que se paga por el almacenaje. 4. (Mar.) Estiba; arrumaje. *To shift the stowage,* (Mar.) Mudar la estiba.

Stowaway [stō'-a-wē''], *s.* Polizón, el que se oculta en un buque o tren de ferrocarril para obtener pasaje gratis.

Stower [stō'-ęr], *s.* Estibador.

Strabismus [stra-biz'-mus], *s.* (Med.) Estrabismo, defecto visual de los bizcos.

Straddle [strad'-l], *vn.* Estar en pie o andar esparrancado o muy abierto de piernas; ponerse a horcajadas.—*s.* 1. Acción de ponerse a horcajadas. 2. El espacio que separa las piernas del que se pone a horcajadas.

Straggle [strag'-l], *vn.* 1. Extraviarse, descaminarse o andar descaminado del cuerpo principal o de sus compañeros. 2. Rodar, andorrear, corretear, ir de una parte a otra. 3. Extenderse más de lo ordinario las ramas de algún árbol o arbusto. 4. Estar disperso, hallarse a intervalos irregulares. *Straggling soldier,* Soldado rezagado. *Straggling branches,* Ramas dispersas, apartadas.

Straggler [strag'-lęr], *s.* 1. Rezagado, el que se queda atrás. 2. Vagamundo, tunante. 3. La rama que sale más que las otras. 4. Objeto aislado o desviado.

Straight [strēt], *a.* 1. Derecho, recto; que no es rizado ni pasudo; sin inclinación ni torcedura. 2. Justo, equitativo; correcto, exacto. 3. Directo, recto, sin rodeos, libre de estorbos. *Straight timbers,* Palos derechos.—*adv.* 1. Directamente, en derechura, en línea recta. 2. Luego, al punto, inmediatamente. *To make straight,* Enderezar o poner derecha una cosa. *To make straight again,* Volver a enderezar lo que se había torcido. *Straight line,* Línea recta.

Straight (poker), *s.* Escalerilla (en el juego de poker).

Straightaway [strēt'-a-wē], *adv.* Adelante, en línea recta.—*s.* Curso directo.

Straightedge [strēt'-ej], *s.* Regla o barra de metal o madera para trazar líneas rectas.

Straighten [strē'-tn], *va.* 1. Enderezar, poner derecho. 2. Sacar del desorden, arreglar; se usa a menudo con *up.*

Straightener [strē'-tn-ęr], *s.* El que pone una cosa en el estado que debe tener.

Straightforward [strēt-fōr'-ward], *a.* Que no desvía, que anda derecho; de aquí, honrado, de corazón recto, sincero.—*adv.* Directamente adelante. Se escribe también *straightforwards.*

Straightly [strēt'-li], *adv.* 1. En línea recta, directamente. 2. Con mucha tensión.

Straightness [strēt'-nes], *s.* Rectitud, derechura; tensión.

Strain [strēn], *va.* 1. Extender con esfuerzo; estirar, ensanchar o alargar una cosa con violencia o más de lo que es debido. 2. Llevar al extremo o más allá de lo que es debido y razonable. 3. (Mec.) Forzar, desformar permanentemente; obligar demasiado; torcer, retorcer. 4. Constreñir, incomodar, molestar, inquietar. 5. Apretar a uno contra sí abrazándole. 6. Colar, pasar por manga, cedazo, etc., algún líquido; se usa frecuentemente con *out.*—*vn.* 1. Esforzarse, hacer grandes esfuerzos. 2. Filtrarse, colarse. *To strain the voice,* Forzar la voz o levantarla más de lo que se debe. *To strain close,* Comprimir. *Do not strain yourself,* No se canse Vd., no se violente Vd. *To strain a point,* Hacer un esfuerzo. *To strain milk,* Colar la leche. *The ship is strained,* (Mar.) Se han levantado o largado las costuras.

Strain, *s.* 1. Tensión; estiramiento, estirón; esfuerzo. 2. Lesión o daño que se sufre a consecuencia de un esfuerzo excesivo; contorsión, retorcimiento, torcedura, esguince. *V.* SPRAIN. 3. Estilo, tono, modo de hablar o de pensar. 4. (Mús.) Aire, melodía; acorde, acentos. 5. Parte distintiva de un poema, canto; composición en verso. 6. Estirpe, descendencia, raza, linaje; clase. 7. Genio o disposición heredada. *Strain of madness,* Vena de locura. *Melodious strains,* Acordes melodiosos. *Too high a strain,* Un tono demasiado alto. *A strain of buff-coloured pansies,* Una clase de pensamientos color de ante.

Strainer [strēn'-ęr], *s.* Colador, coladera, coladero, pasador.

Strait [strēt], *a.* 1. Estrecho, angosto. 2. Estrecho o íntimo, hablando de la amistad o del parentesco. 3. Estrecho, rígido, austero, exacto. 4. Estrecho, escaso, apretado, miserable. 5. (Des.) Recto, derecho. —*s.* 1. Estrecho, el brazo angosto de mar. 2. Garganta de una montaña; desfiladero, angostura o paso estrecho. 3. Estrecho, aprieto, peligro, riesgo. *Strait-jacket, strait-waistcoat,* Camisa de fuerza.

Straiten [strē'-tn], *va.* 1. Acortar, ceñir, limitar; angostar, cercenar. 2. Estrechar, reducir a menos espacio; disminuir. 3. Estrechar, apretar, reducir a estrechez o aprieto: incomodar.

Strait-laced [strēt'-lēst], *a.* 1. Metido en prensa, apretado, muy comprimido. 2. Estricto, estrecho, demasiado riguroso. 3. Santurrón.

Straitly [strēt'-li], *adv.* 1. Estrechamente; estrictamente, rigorosamente. 2. Íntimamente, con intimidad.

Straitness [strēt'-nes], *s.* 1. Estrechez, angostura, corta extensión de lugar o tiempo. 2. Estrechez, aprieto, lance apretado. 3. Estrechez, escasez notable, penuria, falta de lo necesario. 4. Rigor, severidad, austeridad.

Strake [strēc], *s.* (Mar.) Traca o hilada, costura de tablas de popa a proa. *To heel a strake,* (Mar.) Tumbarse de una traca; hablando de la embarcación.

Stramonium [stra-mō'-ni-um], *s.* 1. Estramonio, planta de las solanáceas. 2. Droga obtenida de esa planta, que usan los asmáticos.

Strand [strand], *va.* y *vn.* Encallar; echarse sobre la costa; en sentido figurado, quedarse desamparado.—*s.* Costa, marina, playa del mar; rara vez, ribera de un río; arenal a la orilla de un río. (< A.-S. strand.)

Strand, *va.* 1. Romper uno de los cabos de una cuerda. 2. Torcer, retorcer los cabos de un cordel.—*s.* 1. Cabo, una de los hilos de que se compone una cuerda. 2. Hebra, fibra, filamento. (< Holandés. *streen,* madeja.) *Heart-strand,* Corazón de un cabo.

Strange [strēnj], *a.* 1. Extraño, singular, raro, sorprendente, extraordinario; singularmente bueno o malo. 2. Extraño, que no es de la misma casa o familia, que pertenece a otra parte; de una clase o carácter diferente; desconocido. 3. Forastero, el que no es del lugar donde está. 4. Extranjero, el que es o viene de país extraño. 5. De modales huraños, reservado, poco tratable. *A strange face,* Cara desconocida.—*inter.* ¡Cosa rara! ¡cáspita! *To make strange, to make one's self strange,* (1) Mostrar o afectar asombro, sorpresa o ignorancia: con *of.* (2) Pretender ser extranjero. *Strange woman,* En la Biblia, ramera.

Strangely [strēnj'-li], *adv.* 1. Extrañamente, singularmente, extraordinariamente. 2. Como los extranjeros; con relación a extranjeros.

Strangeness [strēnj'-nes], *s.* 1. Extranjería, la condición o calidad de ser uno extranjero o de otro dominio o país. 2. Extrañeza, reserva, alejamiento, esquivez. 3. Maravilla. 4. Extravagancia o desarreglo en el porte o conducta.

Stranger [strēn'-jęr], *s.* 1. Extranjero, el extraño o el que no pertenece a la casa, familia, corporación, etc., de que se trata, desconocido. 2. Extranjero, el que es de otra nación. 3. El que no conoce o no sabe alguna cosa especificada; con *to.* *A child who is still a stranger to the world,* Un hijo que todavía no conoce el mundo. *He is a stranger to me,* Me es desconocido. *You are a great stranger here,* Se vende Vd. muy caro, no se le ve a Vd.

Strangle [stran'-gl], *va.* 1. Estrangular; dar garrote. 2. Ahogar, sofocar. 3. Reprimir, suprimir.—*vn.* Padecer estrangulación, morir estrangulado, estrangularse.

Strangle hold [stran'-gl hōld], *s.* 1. (Lucha) Llave con que se semiasfixia al adversario. 2. Lo que priva de libertad de movimiento o expresión.

Strangler [straŋ'-glẹr], *s.* 1. El que ahoga o da garrote. 2. El que extingue o sofoca alguna cosa.

Strangles [straŋ'-glz], *s.* Estrangol, hinchazón que padecen las caballerías en la garganta.

Strangulate [stran'-giu-lêt], *va.* Estrangular.

Strangulated [stran'-giu-lê''-ted], *a. part.* 1. (Med.) Estrangulado, estrechado de tal manera que se halla suspendida la circulación. 2. (Bot. y Zool.) Estrechado a intervalos, como por medio de vendas o cuerdas.

Strangulation [straŋ-giu-lé'-shun], *s.* 1. Estrangulación, acción y efecto de estrangular; ahogamiento, la acción y efecto de ahogar o de dar garrote. 2. (Med.) Estrangulación, toda constricción ejercida sobre una parte de manera que suspenda la circulación.

Strap [strap], *s.* 1. Correa, tira de cuero larga, estrecha y flexible; una tira de paño. 2. Cuero, asentador de navajas. *V.* STROP. 3. Capona, charretera mocha; tirante o trabilla de pantalón. 4. (Mar.) Gaza, cabo con que se guarnecen los motones por la parte exterior de su circunferencia. 5. Oreja de zapato; tirante de bota. 6. Correones, sopandas de coche; precinta, trabilla.

Strappado [stra-pā'-dō o pé'-dō], *s.* 1. Estrapada, antiguo suplicio militar. 2. En sentido lato, paliza, zurra de palos.

Strapping [strap'-ing], *a.* (Fam.) Abultado. *Strapping woman,* Mujerona.

Strata [strê' ta], *s. pl.* de STRATUM.

Stratagem [strat'-a-jem], *s.* 1. Estratagema, ardid de guerra. 2. Estratagema, astucia, fingimiento o engaño artificioso.

Strategic, Strategetic, Strategetical [stra-tej'-ic o tí'-jic; strat-ẹ-jet'-ic, al], *a.* Estratégico.

Strategic Air Command [stra-tí-jic ār' co-mand], *s.* Mando Aéreo Estratégico.

Strategist [strat'-ẹ-jist], *s.* Estratégico, persona versada en el arte de la estrategia.

Strategy [strat'-e-ji], *s.* 1. Estrategia, el arte de dirigir las operaciones militares para conseguir la victoria. 2. El empleo de astucia y estratagemas en los negocios, la política, etc. (<Gr. strategía.)

Stratify [strat'-i-fai], *va.* Estratificar, colocar por capas o lechos.

Stratosphere [stra'-to-sfir], *s.* Estratosfera.

Stratum [stré'-tum], *s.* Estrato, lecho o capa de cualquiera cosa que está tendida naturalmente sobre otra. (1) Estrato, capa de roca; (2) (Anat. y Zool.) capa de tejido.

Stratus [stré'-tus], *s.* Nube que se presenta en forma de faja, a poca altura sobre el horizonte.

Straw [strō], *s.* 1. Paja. 2. Un comino, un bledo, una nonada o fruslería. *I don't care a straw,* No me importa un pito. *Stack of straw,* Pajar. *To break a straw,* Reñir.—*a.* 1. Hecho o relleno de paja. 2. De ningún valor, falso, ficticio. *Straw bail,* Caución o fianza simuladas. *Straw bond,* Bono o caución ficticios. *Straw colour,* Color de paja, amarillo claro. *Straw-bed,* Jergón de paja. *Straw-built,* Pajizo, hecho de paja. *Straw-coloured,* Pajizo claro, de color de paja; pajado. *Straw-hat,* Sombrero de paja. *Straw-worm,* Gorgojo.

Strawberry [strō'-ber-i], *s.* 1. (Bot.) Fresa, la mata que produce la fresa. 2. Fresa, la fruta producida por la planta de este nombre.

Strawberry-tree [strō'-ber-i-trí], *s.* (Bot.) Madroño, árbol de las ericáceas.

Straw vote [strō vōt], *s.* Escrutinio exploratorio.

Stray [strê], *vn.* 1. Descarriarse, extraviarse, andar descarriado; perder el camino, andar vagando sin saber el camino. 2. Errar, faltar a la justicia y equidad; desviarse del deber.

Stray, *s.* 1. Descarriamiento, descarrío, la acción de descarriar o descarriarse. 2. Una persona o animal descarriado o perdido.

Streak [strík], *s.* 1. Raya, lista, línea de color distinto del que tiene el fondo de una cosa; reguero; rayo de luz. 2. Vena, rasgo de ingenio; traza, pizca; también, antojo, capricho. 3. Raspadura, color del polvo fino de un mineral cuando está limado. 4. (Mar.) Costura de tablas, traca, hilada. *V.* STRAKE. (<A.-S. *strica,* < *strican,* andar.)

Streak, *va.* Rayar, hacer líneas de varios colores; barajar o entreverar colores.

Streaky [strík'-i], *a.* Rayado, alistado, veteado, abigarrado; bordado.

Stream [strím], *s.* 1. La corriente, flujo o curso del agua u otro líquido que corre. 2. Arroyo, río, torrente. 3. Flujo, movimiento de lo que sale o entra sin intermisión, v. g. de la gente; chorro (de líquido, gas, luz, etc.). 4. Corriente, el curso que llevan algunas cosas. (Fig.) Fuente. *Stream of words,* Flujo de palabras. *Stream-anchor,* Anclote, ancla de espía. *A small stream,* Arroyuelo. *In the stream,* En franquicia. *Down stream, up stream,* Agua abajo, agua arriba. *Against the stream,* Contra la corriente. *Stream tin,* Estaño de aluvión, en grano.

Stream, *va.* y *vn.* 1. Correr, manar o fluir los líquidos. 2. Manar, brotar; salir en abundancia y a modo de un torrente. 3. Arrojar o derramar alguna cosa con abundancia y sin interrupción. 4. Lavar, v. g. los minerales, en agua corriente. 5. Hacer ondear; flotar, extenderse ondeando, como una bandera. 6. Moverse llevando tras sí un rastro de luz, como un meteoro. *To stream the buoy,* (Mar.) Echar la boya al agua.

Streamer [strím'-ẹr], *s.* Flámula, gallardete, banderola; faja de luz en una aurora boreal; bandera o cinta pendiente.

Streamlet [strím'-let], *s.* Arroyuelo, arroyo pequeño; hilo de agua.

Streamline [strím'-lain], *va.* Dar líneas aerodinámicas, dar formas que permitan flujo continuo.

Streamlined [strím'-laind], *a.* 1. Aerodinámico, modernizado. 2. Adelgazado.

Streamy [strím'-i], *a.* 1. Que abunda en agua corriente, surcado de arroyos; que mana a chorros. 2. Parecido a rayos de luz o que los echa.

Street [strít], *s.* Calle, camino público en una población, y el espacio que queda entre las dos aceras formadas por las casas. *By-street,* Calle apartada, callejuela. *Cross street,* Calle traviesa. *Main street,* Calle mayor, principal. *Street car,* Carro urbano, coche de tranvía. *Street railway,* Tranvía, ferrocarril urbano. *Street-walker,* Mujer pública o prostituta.

Strength [strength], *s.* 1. Fuerza, vigor, robustez. 2. Fuerza, virtud, eficacia; potencia motriz; potencia intelectual o moral; poder en general; facultad de obrar o sufrir; validez, fuerza legal; fuerza, vigor, nervio del estilo o de las palabras; fuerza o fuerzas, la gente de guerra y demás aprestos militares. 3. Fortaleza, consistencia, firmeza, tenacidad, solidez de una cosa material. 4. Fortaleza o vigor de ánimo. 5. Grado de intensidad, de vehemencia; grado de potencia o de concentración; seguridad, confianza (que nace del sentimiento de la propia fuerza). 6. (Ant.) Fuerza, una plaza murada y guarnecida para defenderse. *By strength of,* A fuerza de. *The strength of public opinion,* La fuerza de la opinión pública.

Strengthen [streng'-thn], *va.* 1. Fortalecer, fortificar, dar fuerza y vigor. 2. Confirmar, corroborar, reforzar. 3. Animar, alentar, infundir brío.—*vn.* Fortalecerse, coger o cobrar fuerzas; hacerse fuerte o más fuerte, reforzarse.

Strengthener [streng'-thn-ẹr], *s.* Corroborante.

Strenuous [stren'-yu-us], *a.* 1. Estrenuo, fuerte, persistente, enérgico; acérrimo, tenaz. 2. Que necesita gran esfuerzo. *To be strenuous,* Tener entereza, no doblegarse o no condescender con facilidad; ser activo en sumo grado.

Strenuously [stren'-yu-us-li], *adv.* Acérrimamente, con mucha fuerza y vigor; vigorosamente, enérgicamente.

Strenuousness [stren'-yu-us-nes], *s* Ánimo, esfuerzo, vigor, fortaleza, ardor, celo.

Streptococcus [strep-to-coc'-us], *s.* Estreptococo.

Streptomycin [strep-to-mai'-sin], *s.* (Med.) Estreptomicina.

Stress [stres], *s.* 1. Fuerza, peso, importancia, entidad, consideración, valor; punto esencial. 2. Violencia, tensión, fuerza que se hace o se padece. 3. Influencia ejercida por la fuerza, compulsión, coacción. 4. Acento tónico, fuerza, énfasis. *By stress of weather,* (Mar.) Á causa de un temporal. *Stress of the war,* Lo recio de la guerra. *Stress of the voice,* El esfuerzo que se hace con la voz en las sílabas en que está el acento. *To lay great stress upon,* Dar mucha importancia a; insistir, apoyar fuertemente sobre, algo, hacer hincapié.

Stress, *va.* Sujetar a tensión o peso, como se hace con un madero; dar importancia o énfasis a; meter en dificultades, acongojar.

Stretch [strech], *va.* y *vn.* 1. Extender, alargar, tender; poner muy tensa o estirada alguna cosa. 2. Estirar, extender o alargar alguna cosa más de lo que se debe; dilatar. 3. Violentar o dar una interpretación o sentido siniestro a un texto, ley, etc. 4. Hacer un gran esfuerzo, forzar; hacer violencia; exagerar, llevar al extremo. 5. (Mar.) Hacer toda fuerza de vela. *To stretch out to sea*, (Mar.) Tirar a la mar. 6. Alargarse, extenderse, dar de sí, dilatarse, estirarse; ocupar cierto espacio; (fig.) esforzarse, exagerar. 7. Desplegarse. *To stretch as far as*, Extenderse, llegar hasta. *To stretch the wings*, Extender las alas. *To stretch forth*, Alargar, extender. *To stretch out*, Extender, estirar, alargar; extenderse, desplegarse, yacer desplegado; prolongar o prolongarse. *Stretched in bed*, Tendido en la cama o tendido a la larga. *To stretch one's self*, Esperezarse o desperezarse.

Stretch, *s.* 1. Extensión, dilatación. 2. Estirón, esfuerzo. 3. Violencia o interpretación forzada del sentido de un texto, ley, etc. 4. (Fam.) El punto a donde puede llegar la acción o esfuerzo de una cosa. 5. (Mar.) Bordada, el camino que hace una embarcación entre dos viradas. *The stretch of its wings was three feet*, La extensión de sus alas era de tres pies. *The utmost stretch of imagination*, El mayor esfuerzo de la imaginación.

Stretcher [strech'-ẹr], *s.* 1. El o lo que alarga o estira. 2. Camilla, cama portátil para conducir los heridos; andas, féretro con varas. 3. En albañilería, un ladrillo o piedra que yace a lo largo de la hilera. 4. Viga, madero largo, tirante que se emplea en la construcción; (Mar.) codaste, codal. 5. Pedestal, el madero contra el cual pone los pies el remero para bogar. *Carpet-stretcher*, Atiesador para alfombras. *Glove-stretcher*, Ensanchador de guantes. *Wire-stretcher*, Estirador de alambre.

Stretching [strech'-ing], *s.* La acción y el efecto del verbo *stretch*, en cualquiera de sus acepciones; tendedura, alargamiento, estiramiento; dilatación; esperezo (después de dormir).

Strew [strū], *va.* (*pp.* STREWED y STREWN). Esparcir, derramar, desparramar; sembrar, salpicar. *To strew with flour* o *with sugar*, Espolvorear o polvorear con harina o con azúcar. *To strew with salt*, Polvorear con sal.

Stria [straı'-a], *s.* (*pl.* STRIÆ [straı'-ī]). (Arq.) 1. Estría, la media caña que tienen a lo largo las columnas y pilastras. 2. Las rayas o surcos de ciertas conchas.

Striate [straı'-ēt], *va.* Estriar, marcar con estrías.

Striate, Striated [straı'-ēt, ed], *a.* Estriado, formado en estrías.

Striation, Striature [straı-ē'-shun, straı'-a-tiūr], *s.* Estriación, disposición en estrías; estriatura.

Stricken [stric'-n], *pp.* del verbo *To* STRIKE. 1. Herido (particularmente por un proyectil). 2. Afligido, agobiado. 3. Entrado en años.

Strickle [stric'-l], *s.* (Prov. Ingl.) Rasero, instrumento que sirve para rasar o igualar las medidas de áridos.

Strict [strict], *a.* 1. Estricto, rígido, estrecho, ajustado, puro. 2. Exacto, riguroso, escrupuloso. 3. Severo, áspero. 4. (Zool.) Limitado, ceñido, estrecho. 5. Ajustado, apretado. 6. Estirado, tirante.

Strictly [strict'-li], *adv.* Exactamente, rigurosamente, con rigor, con severidad, estrictamente; puntualmente.

Strictness [strict'-nes], *s.* 1. Exactitud, puntualidad, regularidad. 2. Severidad, rigor, austeridad; escrupulosidad. 3. Tirantez.

Stricture [stric'-chur], *s.* 1. Sello, marca o impresión hecha en una cosa. 2. Observación o reflexión ligera hecha sobre un discurso, un escrito, etc. 3. Contracción o estrechez de un canal o conducto en un cuerpo; constricción.

Stride [straıd], *s.* Tranco, trancada o zancada, un paso largo.

Stride, *va.* (*pret.* STRODE, *pp.* STRIDDEN, antiguamente STRID; *pa.* STRIDING). 1. Pasar a zancadas, cruzar a grandes trancos. 2. Cabalgar, montar a horcajadas.—*vn.* Atrancar, dar trancos, zancadas o pasos largos.

Strident [straı'-dent], *a.* Estridente; aplícase al sonido agudo, desapacible y chirriante.

Stridor [straı'-dor], *s.* Estridor, sonido agudo, desapacible y chirriante. (Lat.)

Stridulate [strid'-yu-lêt], *vn.* Estridular, producir un ruido ligeramente agudo y penetrante; chirriar ciertos insectos.

Stridulation [strid-yu-lê'-shun], *s.* Estridulación, acción o efecto de estridular.

Strife [straıf], *s.* Contienda, disputa, refriega, pleito, debate; antipatía.

Strigil [strij'-il], *s.* Estrigila, especie de raedera de bronce, hueso o marfil que usaban los antiguos en el baño para raer la piel.

Strike [straıc], *va.* (*pret.* STRUCK, *pp.* STRUCK o STRICKEN, y ant. STROOK). 1. Golpear, sacudir o dar golpes; pegar; atravesar de un golpe, herir; hacer impresión sobre algo; sacar fuego por medio de un golpe; cortar, separar, quitar; (en este sentido se usa con *off*). 2. Arrojar con violencia una cosa contra otra. 3. Acuñar o sellar moneda. 4. Contratar; convenir, concertar; hacer un balance. 5. Imprimir o fijar fuertemente en la memoria, en el ánimo, etc. 6. Herir o tocar haciendo impresión, como en la vista, en la imaginación, etc. 7. Mover o conmover repentinamente el ánimo. 8. Chocar, encontrar y ver repentinamente; de aquí, descubrir, divisar. 9. Borrar, tachar, rayar; se usa con *out*, *off*, *from* o alguna cláusula adverbial. 10. Arriar, calar; bajar una vela; levantar el campo. *To strike the colours or the flag*, Arriar la bandera. *To strike on a rock*, (Mar.) Escollar. *To strike soundings*, (Mar.) Sondear, tocar el fondo (sondeando). 11. Tocar, tañer o dar el martillo en la campana del reloj; dar la hora; batir un tambor; hacer resonar. *The clock strikes twelve*, El reloj da las doce. 12. Dejar de trabajar para obtener por ese medio una concesión. 13. Dar golpe, hacer eco, hacer impresión o llamar la atención alguna cosa; sorprender, sorprenderse, causar admiración, amedrentar. —*vn.* 1. Golpear, dar golpes; tropezar, dar; aporrear, batir. 2. Sonar, dar o hacer sonido. 3. (Mar.) Varar, encallar la embarcación; amainar las velas. 4. Suceder casualmente; encontrarse, tropezar con; se usa con *upon*. 5. Entrar atrevida o repentinamente en un sendero o camino; ir adelante, avanzar; también, brotar, estallar, manifestar. 6. Declararse en huelga, para obtener aumento de jornales, disminución de horas de trabajo o corrección de abusos. 7. Arriar el pabellón, rendirse. 8. Echar raíces; fijarse en las conchas, como lo hacen las ostras pequeñas. 9. Tomar cierta dirección, como los estratos geológicos. 10. Esparcirse, acabarse poco a poco, o cambiarse, p. ej. los colores de una tela. 11. Penetrar; saturarse de sal, como el pescado salado. *To strike against* o *upon*, Chocar o encontrarse un cuerpo con otro; estrellarse. *To strike a lead* [līd], Encontrar una veta o vena de mineral; de aquí (fam.), hallar el medio de obtener una ganancia o conseguir buen éxito. *To strike back*, Dar golpe por golpe. *To strike at*, Atacar, acometer, atacarse; alcanzar el tiro de una arma arrojadiza o de una de fuego. *To strike down*, Echar abajo de uno o muchos golpes; derribar, hacer caer; aterrar, echar por tierra. *To strike for*, (Fam.) Dirigirse hacia; acometer, atacar en favor o defensa de. *To strike home*, Alcanzar el punto deseado, dar en el hito o en el clavo. *To strike in*, Meterse, desaparecer de la superficie; juntarse, unirse a otros después que éstos han empezado; interrumpir; conformarse con, adaptarse a; entrar repentinamente. *To strike into*, Comenzar repentinamente; entrar, penetrar, hundirse en. *To strike in with*, Conformarse, convenir, condescender. *To strike off*, Borrar, cancelar, rayar; cortar o separar alguna parte de un todo, quitar; (fam.) imprimir, hacer una tirada. *To strike off one's head*, Cortar la cabeza a uno. *To strike on*, Dar contra, tropezar, encontrar, descubrir. *To strike out*, Borrar, cancelar, testar; producir algún efecto por medio de la colisión de dos cuerpos; formar o producir algún designio, resolución, plan, etc., por un esfuerzo repentino del ánimo; arrojarse, lanzarse, hacer un esfuerzo nadando o patinando. *To strike through*, Mostrarse repentinamente una cosa por medio de otra diversa; traspasar, atravesar, pasar de parte a parte; calar. *To strike up*, Producir un sonido cualquiera por medio de golpes; tocar, tañer. *To strike with admiration*, Llenar de admiración o chocar. *To strike fire*, Sacar fuego del pedernal con el eslabón. *To strike work*, Hallar trabajo, y (rara vez) declararse en huelga. *A thought strikes me*, Me ocurre un pensamiento, tengo una idea. *As it strikes me*, Según me parece, a mi juicio, en mi opinión. *To strike blind*, Cegar o poner ciego de repente.

Strike, *s.* 1. Golpe, acción de dar, pegar o golpear. 2. Huelga, cesación del trabajo por cierto número de trabajadores. 3. (Fam.) Descubrimiento de un filón o del mineral que se buscaba; buen éxito completo o inesperado. 4. Rasero; medida. *V.* STRICKLE.

Strikeblock [straıc'-bloc], *s.* (Carp.) Cepillo bocel.

Strikebreaker [straıc'-brêk'-ẹr], *s.* Esquirol, rompehuelgas.

Striker [straık'-er], *s.* 1. Golpeador, el que golpea. 2. Huelguista, trabajador que deja el trabajo y se declara en huelga.

Striking [straik'-ing], *a.* 1. Que sorprende y admira; fuerte, obvio, parecido, semejante; de bulto, patente, evidente, seguro. *Striking news,* Noticias extraordinarias o muy inesperadas. 2. Que hace huelga.

String [string], *s.* 1. Cordón, cuerdecita por lo común redonda de hilo, etc., para colgar o atar algo; bramante. 2. Cualquier hilo en que se ha ensartado alguna cosa y las cosas ensartadas; ristra. 3. Cinta, presilla, cordel. 4. La cuerda de un arco. 5. Hilera, un número de cosas colocadas en orden sucesivo. 6. Cuerda de cualquier instrumento músico. 7. Fibra, nervio, tendón. 8. Cadena, encadenamiento. 9. Cuelga, ristra. *A string of onions,* Ristra de cebollas. *A string of carriages, of lies,* Una hilera de carruajes, una sarta de mentiras. 10. (Mar.) Durmiente del alcázar y castillo.

String, *va.* 1. Encordar, poner cuerdas a los instrumentos de música o a otra cosa cualquiera. 2. Templar algún instrumento músico de cuerdas. 3. Ensartar, enhilar; encordelar; enhebrar; atar con bramante. 4. Estirar, poner tensa o estirada una cosa. 5. Quitar las fibras, las briznas. *To string up,* (Fam.) Ahorcar. *To string out,* Extender como un cordón.—*vn.* 1. Extenderse (la gente) en línea larga e irregular. 2. Presentar la apariencia de hebras o briznas.

String bean [string bīn], *s.* Habichuela verde, judía. (Mex.) Ejote.

Stringed [stringd], *a.* Encordado, encordelado; ensartado. *Stringed instrument,* Instrumento de cuerda.

Stringency [strin'-jen-si], *s.* Calidad de riguroso, estricto o severo; severidad, estrechez

Stringent [strin'-jent], *a.* 1. Estricto, riguroso, severo. 2. Impedido por obstáculos. 3. Que aprieta, que comprime; (Com.) estancado.

Stringer [string'-er], *s.* 1. Durmiente, madero pesado que sirve de apoyo. 2. El que encuerda, enhiebra, ensarta, etc.

Stringless [string'-les], *a.* Que no tiene cuerdas.

Stringy [string'-i], *a.* Fibroso, filamentoso; tenaz, duro, correoso.

Strip [strip], *va.* (*pret.* y *pp.* STRIPPED ó STRIPT). 1. Desnudar, despojar, quitar a uno el vestido o lo que tiene encima. 2. Despojar o privar a uno de lo que goza o tiene. 3. Robar. 4. Descortezar, quitar la corteza. 5. Ordeñar hasta agotar. 6. Desgarrar o cortar en tiras o jirones. 7. Desnudar, quitar lo que cubre o se halla encima, como se hace en varias operaciones mecánicas. *To strip a mast,* (Mar.) Desaparejar un palo. *To strip off,* Desnudar.

Strip, *s.* Tira, faja, pedazo angosto y comparativamente largo (de madera, de tela); jirón. *V.* STRIPE. *Narrow strip,* Tirita, tirilla. *Weather-strip,* Gualdrín.

Stripe [straip], *va.* Rayar, hacer rayas. *Striped and plaid,* Rayado y listado.

Stripe, *s.* 1. Raya, lista, banda o línea de color diferente de la superficie contigua. 2. Banda, trozo largo de tela. 3. Cardenal, la señal amoratada que queda en el cuerpo de resultas de un golpe. 4. Carácter distintivo: calaña, clase; género.

Striped [straipt], *a.* Listado, rayado, con franjas.

Stripling [strip'-ling], *s.* Mozalbete, mozuelo.

Striptease [strip-tīz'], *s.* (Teat.) Espectáculo en que una actriz se desnuda poco a poco.

Strive [straiv], *vn.* (*pret.* STROVE, *pp.* STRIVEN). 1. Esforzarse, procurar, hacer lo posible para conseguir alguna cosa. 2. Empeñarse en adquirir o conseguir algo, familiarmente pernear o trabajar mucho en la consecución de una cosa. 3. Debatir, disputar, contender; oponerse, estar en oposición una cosa con otra. 4. Competir una cosa con otra. *To strive for mastery,* Disputarse la supremacía.

Striver [straiv'-er], *s.* Competidor.

Strobile [streb'-il], *s.* (Bot.) Estróbilo, nombre dado a los frutos de las coníferas; reunión de frutos cubiertos o velados. (Lat. < Gr. στρόβιλος < *strepho.* torcer.)

Stroboscope [streb'-os-cōp], *s.* Estroboscopio.

Strode [strōd], *pret.* de *To* STRIDE.

Stroke [strōk], *s.* 1. Golpe, el choque de un cuerpo contra otro; acción de golpear; golpe o tiro que alcanza o hiere á alguno. 2. Cada uno de los movimientos repetidos de una serie, como los de un émbolo o remo; remada, curso o carrera del émbolo o pistón; dirección o extensión de dicho movimiento. 3. Toque en la pintura; pincelada, plumada. 4. Fractura, cardenal o herida causada por un golpe; cualquier daño causado como por un golpe; golpe, infortunio o desgracia repentina. 5. Golpe en las obras de ingenio, la parte que tiene más gracia y oportunidad en ellas. *I know his stroke,* Conozco su modo de obrar. 6. Campanada de reloj. *It is on the stroke of eight,* Están al dar las ocho. 7. Acción eficaz, hazaña; suceso, éxito. 8. Ligero movimiento acariciador. 9. (Med.) Ataque. *Stroke of a pen* o *pencil,* Plumada, pincelada. *Stroke of wit,* Chiste, gracia, humorada, dicho gracioso, especie salada.

Stroke, *va.* 1. Pasar la mano por la espalda, halagar, acariciar. 2. Frotar suavemente. 3. Ranurar la piedra con cincel (en líneas iguales y paralelas). 4. Alisar los pliegues con la aguja.

Stroll [strōl], *vn.* Tunar, vagar, vaguear, andar vagando; callejear, pasearse.—*s.* Paseo voluntario; vagancia, callejeo. *To take, to go for, a stroll,* Dar un paseo, pasearse.

Stroller [strōl'-er], *s.* 1. El que se pasea o anda lentamente o sin objeto fijo; tunante, vagamundo o vagabundo. 2. Cómico ambulante, de la legua.

Strolling [strōl'-ing], *a. part.* Vagamundo, que vaga; que se pasea ociosamente; ambulante.

Strong [strōng], *a.* 1. Fuerte, forzudo, vigoroso, robusto, muscular, que tiene grandes fuerzas. 2. Fuerte, que tiene mucha resistencia; que produce impresión notable sobre los sentidos. que posee una cualidad en alto grado; sólido, firme, concentrado; espirituoso, de cuerpo, que contiene mucho alcohol. 3. Capaz, hábil. 4. Violento, impetuoso; de aquí, vivo, brillante, picante. 5. Fuerte, sano. 6. Ardiente, activo, eficaz, enérgico; celoso, caluroso. 7. Resuelto, determinado. 8. (Com.) Que manifiesta tendencia al alza, como el mercado o los precios. *Strong meat,* Carne difícil de digerir. *His army is ten thousand strong,* Tiene un ejército de diez mil hombres. *A strong partizan,* Un celoso partidario. *A strong argument,* Un argumento poderoso. *Strong box,* Cofre fuerte, caja de hierro para guardar valores. *Strong-minded,* De carácter, de inteligencia vigorosa; despreocupado, descreído. *Strong-backed,* Ancho de caderas, robusto. *Strong-bodied,* Corpulento, robusto. *Strong-bodied wine,* Vino de mucho cuerpo. *Strong-fisted, strong-handed,* Fuerte de manos y puños. *Strong-hand,* Fuerza, violencia.

Strongly [strōng'-li], *adv.* Fuertemente, rigorosamente, vehementemente; con violencia.

Stronghold [strōng'-hōld], *s.* Plaza fuerte; lugar hecho fácilmente defendible por la naturaleza o por el arte.

Strongroom [strōng'-rūm], *s.* Cuarto acondicionado para guardar cosas de valor.

Strontium [stren'-shi-um], *s.* (Quím.) Estroncio, elemento amarillento; se emplean sus sales en la pirotecnia para producir llamas rojas.

Strontium 90 [stren'-shi-um nain'-ti], *s.* Estroncio 90.

Strop [strep], *va.* Asentar navajas, suavizar la navaja con el cuero.—*s.* 1. Suavizador o asentador de navajas; tira de cuero o lona que sirve para afilar las navajas de afeitar. 2. (Mar.) Estrovo, cordaje de las poleas.

Strophe [strō'-fī], *s.* Estrofa; estancia, cualquiera de las partes simétricamente iguales de que consta una oda, canción, etc.

Strove [strōv], *pret.* del verbo *To* STRIVE.

Struck, *pret.* y *pp.* del verbo *To* STRIKE.

Structural [struc'-chur-al], *a.* Perteneciente a la estructura, caracterizado por la estructura o que la tiene.

Structuralize [struc'-chur-al-aiz], *va.* Estructurar, disponer.

Structure [struc'-chur], *s.* 1. Construcción, el efecto de construir; lo que se construye; combinación de partes relacionadas, p. ej. una máquina, un edificio, etc. 2. Estructura, hechura, distribución y unión orgánica de las partes u órganos en un cuerpo u objeto. 3. (Ant.) Edificación. *The microscopic structure of malachite,* La estructura microscópica de la malaquita.

Struggle [strug'-l], *vn.* 1. Bregar, forcejar, resistirse para desasirse, soltarse o librarse de algo. 2. Esforzarse o hacer esfuerzos para conseguir algo. 3. Luchar, contender, agitarse.

Struggle, *s.* Esfuerzo, contienda, lucha, disputa; resistencia.

Strum [strum], *va.* y *vn.* Arañar, tañer un instrumento de cuerda de una manera descuidada, ruidosa y sin expresión.

Strumpet [strum'pet], *s.* Ramera, puta, mujer abandonada.

Strung, *pret.* y *pp.* del verbo STRING.

Strut [strut], *vn.* 1. Contonearse, pavonearse. 2. Inflarse, ensoberbecerse.

Strut, Strutting [strut'-ing], *s.* Contoneo, la acción de contonearse; paso arrogante, altanero.

Strut, *s.* 1. Riostra, jabalcón, tornapunta de caballete. 2. Instrumento de hueso o madera que se usa ajustando los pliegues de una lechuguilla.

Strychnin, Strychnine, o **Strychnia** [stric'-nin, stric'-ni-a], *s.* Estricnina, alcaloide sumamente venenoso que se extrae de las habas de varias especies de Strychnos, particularmente de la nuez vómica. Es un compuesto blanco y cristalizable ($C_2H_{22}N_2O_2$) muy usado en medicina.

Stub [stub], *s.* 1. Tocón, cepa, de un árbol pequeño, arbusto o mata; lo que queda de un tronco o tallo después de cortada la parte principal. 2. Zoquete; parte o pieza corta que sobresale de una superficie; fragmento, resto. 3. (E. U.) En un libro de cheques, talón, matriz. *Stub-book*, Libro talonario. *Stub-iron*, Hierro hecho de clavos viejos de herradura. *Stub pen*, Pluma de escribir con punta muy roma. *Stub-twist*, Hierro de varios colores hecho con clavos de herradura usados; sirve para hacer cañones de fusil.

Stub, *va.* 1. (E. U.) Dar o tropezar contra una cosa situada casi al nivel del suelo. 2. Extirpar, arrancar sacando las raíces. 3. Quitar los tocones o cepas. 4. Reducir a un tocón; hacer cachigordete.

Stubbed [stubd], *a.* 1. Cortado o extirpado por el tronco. 2. Grueso y corto. 3. Fuerte, vigoroso, como un tronco. 4. Grosero, áspero de trato o modales.

Stubbiness [stub'-i-nes], *s.* El estado de lo que es corto y grueso.

Stubble [stub'-l], *s.* Rastrojo, el residuo de la mies después de segada. (< Fr. prob. < Lat. stipula.)

Stubborn [stub'-ərn], *a.* 1. Cabezudo, obstinado, contumaz, terco, testarudo, porfiado, tenaz. 2. Inflexible, inquebrantable, intratable. *Stubborn facts*, Hechos innegables.

Stubbornly [stub'-ərn-li], *adv.* Obstinadamente, inflexiblemente, tercamente.

Stubbornness [stub'-ərn-nes], *s.* Obstinación, aferramiento, terquedad, pertinacia; porfía.

Stubby [stub'-i], *a.* Cachigordete; gordo, corto y tieso.

Stub-nail [stub'-nêl], *s.* Puntilla, hita.

Stucco [stuc'-o], *va.* y *vn.* Revestir, cubrir de estuco; formar adornos de estuco.—*s.* 1. Estuco, yeso fino para encostrar las paredes. 2. Trabajo de estuco; cualquier cemento o argamasa para el exterior de los edificios.

Stuck [stuc], *pret.* y *pp.* del verbo STICK.

Stud[1] [stud], *s.* 1. Poste de tabique, pie derecho, poste intermedio y corto. 2. Tachón, tachuela grande, clavo de adorno; botón de camisa. 3. Refuerzo de eslabón. (< A.-S. studu.)

Stud,[2] *s.* Yeguada, caballada, manada de yeguas y caballos padres. (< A.-S. stod.) *Stud-book*, Registro genealógico de caballos. *Stud-horse*, Caballo padre.

Stud, *va.* Tachonar, adornar con tachones.

Studding-sails [stud'-ing-sêlz], *s. pl.* (Mar.) Velas ligeras que se extienden más afuera que las mayores en los peñoles de las vergas. *Lower studding-sails*, Rastreras. *Upper studding-sails*, Alas.

Student [stiū'-dent], *s.* 1. Estudiante, discípulo, persona que estudia. 2. Sabio, letrado. *Law or medical student*, Pasante de abogado o médico.

Studied [stud'-id], *a.* 1. Estudiado, hecho con cuidado, premeditado. 2. (Des.) Docto, versado o instruído.

Studier [stud'-i-ər], *s.* El que ha cultivado o cultiva con esmero alguna ciencia.

Studio [stiū'-di-ō], *s.* Estudio, taller de un artista.

Studio couch [stiū'-di-ō cauch], *s.* Sofá cama.

Studious [stiū'-di-us], *a.* 1. Estudioso, aplicado al estudio. 2. Cuidadoso, solícito, diligente. 3. Estudiado, hecho con deliberación.

Studiously [stiū'-di-us-li], *adv.* Estudiosamente, diligentemente, con aplicación.

Studiousness [stiū'-di-us-nes], *s.* Estudiosidad, aplicación al estudio.

Study [stud'-i], *s.* 1. Estudio, la aplicación a saber y comprender alguna ciencia o arte. 2. Estudio, aplicación, cuidado o diligencia para hacer alguna cosa. 3. Meditación profunda. 4. Embarazo, perplejidad. 5. Estudio, instrucción, conocimientos adquiridos. 6. Estudio, la pieza donde una persona tiene su biblioteca y estudia. *To be in a brown study*, Estar absorto en una idea; estar pensando en las avutardas; mirar las telarañas.

Study, *va.* 1. Estudiar, aplicarse á aprender alguna facultad o ciencia. 2. Estudiar, observar o examinar con cuidado. 3. Aprender a fuerza de aplicación. 4. Considerar, meditar; idear, proyectar, discurrir medios, aplicarse a; se usa a menudo con *out* o *up*. *To study up a scheme*, Estudiar un plan o proyecto. —*vn.* 1. Estudiar, estar pensando o discurriendo de intento en alguna cosa. 2. Procurar, hacer las diligencias para conseguir lo que se desea.

Stuff [stuf], *s.* 1. Material, la materia que se requiere para hacer alguna cosa; materia prima. 2. Esencia, parte elemental, elemento fundamental, sea material o espiritual. 3. Bienes en general; mobiliario, mueblaje, los muebles de una casa. 4. Cosa de poco o ningún valor y estimación; droga; desechos, desperdicios; ideas o sentimientos sin valor; fruslería; se usa muchas veces con interjección. 5. Tejido o tela de cualquier especie; particularmente, todo tejido de lana que es más delgado y ligero que el paño; estofa. *Silk and cotton stuff*, Filoseda. 6. Jarope, cualquier droga o medicamento. 7. Betún, compuesto de sebo, trementina, etc., para preservar el maderamen de una embarcación. 8. Tablas, tablillas. *Thick stuff*, (Mar.) Tablones.—*inter.* ¡ Bagatela ! ¡ niñería ! ¡ fruslería ! (< Fr. ant. étoffe, < Lat. *estupa*, estopa.)

Stuff [stuf], *va.* 1. Henchir, llenar; colmar, rellenar. 2. Rehenchir, llenar de borra, lana o crin; en taxidermia, rehenchir, rellenar la piel de un animal. 3. Atestar; apretar. 4. Mechar; introducir especias o hierbas aromáticas en la carne. *To stuff a turkey*, Rellenar un pavo. 5. Tapar, atascar (las narices o boca).—*vn.* Atracarse, engullir, llenarse de comida; tragar.

Stuffing [stuf'-ing], *s.* 1. El material con que se atesta o rellena una cosa; atestadura, (mec.) empaquetado; relleno culinario; borra, pelote de telas de lana. 2. Relleno, la acción y efecto de rellenar. *Stuffing-box*, (Mec.) Caja de empaquetado, prensa-estopas.

Stuffy [stuf'-i], *a.* 1. Mal ventilado; que causa sensación de malestar. 2. Que impide la respiración.

Stultify [stul'-ti-fai], *va.* 1. Embrutecer, atontar, hacer parecer absurdo, inconsistente o contradictorio; se emplea frecuentemente como verbo reflexivo. 2. (For.) Alegar locura o estupidez.

Stum [stum], *s.* Mosto, el zumo exprimido de la uva antes de fermentar y hacerse vino; vino fermentado en parte. *V.* MUST.

Stum, *va.* Hacer cesar la fermentación (del mosto), añadiendo mostaza u otros ingredientes. (< Holan. *stom*, silencioso.)

Stumble [stum'-bl], *vn.* 1. Tropezar, dar con los pies en un estorbo; dar un traspié, un paso en falso; moverse de una manera incierta o desatinada. 2. Hallar casualmente alguna persona o cosa o dar por casualidad con ella; con *on* o *upon*.—*va.* 1. Hacer tropezar a uno; hacer á uno dar un traspié o deslizarse. 2. Ofender.

Stumble, *s.* Traspié, tropiezo, resbalón; desliz, paso en falso (en sentido recto y figurado); desatino.

Stumbler [stum'-blər], *s.* Tropezador el que tropieza.

Stumbling-block [stum'-bling-bloc], **Stumbling-stone** [stum'-bling-stōn], *s.* Tropezadero, tropiezo; piedra de escándalo.

Stump [stump], *s.* 1. Tocón, cepa, el resto del tronco de un árbol que sobresale de la tierra después de cortado. 2. En general, la parte de un cuerpo sólido que queda después de haber separado o cortado una porción considerable de su substancia. *Stump of a finger*, Tocón o zoquete de un dedo. *Stump of a leg*, Muñón de una pierna. *Stump of a tooth*, Raigón de un diente. *Cabbage-stump*, Troncho de berza. *Up a stump*, (Fam. E. U.) Estar en un brete, verse perplejo. 3. *pl.* Las piernas; generalmente en la locución. *to stir one's stumps*, (fam. E. U.) mover las piernas, es decir, ponerse en movimiento, zarandearse. 4. Tribuna o estrado desde donde se pronuncia un discurso político; de aquí, arenga política en tiempo de elecciones. 5. (Fam.) Desafío, invitación a una controversia. 6. Esfumino, rollito de piel suave o de papel cortado en punta para esfumar.—*a.* 1. Parecido a un tocón. 2. Perteneciente a una arenga política. *Stump-speaker*, Orador político.

Stump, *va.* 1. Pronunciar un discurso electoral. 2. (Fam.) Desafiar, provocar; hacer parar por razón de obstáculos verdaderos o imaginarios; tropezar, dar contra un obstáculo, v. g. con el pie.—*vn.* 1. Andar renqueando, renquear; andar sobre los muñones de piernas amputadas. 2. (Fam.) Pronunciar discursos políticos.

Stumpy [stump'-i], *a.* 1. Lleno de tocones o trozos. 2. Parecido a un tocón; cachigordete, rechoncho.

Stun [stun], *va.* 1. Aturdir con un golpe; privar del sentido por medio de una conmoción cerebral. 2. Atolondrar, ensordecer, por algún tiempo, v. g. por medio de un ruido explosivo. 3. Aturrullar, dejar pasmado.—*s.* Choque, golpe o sacudimiento que aturde o deja estupefacto; aturdimiento, el efecto de aturdir.

Stung [stung], *pret.* y *pp.* del verbo STING.

Stunner [stun'-ẹr], *s.* 1. El o lo que aturde, atolondra o aturrulla. 2. (Ger.) Cosa extraordinaria, de apariencia o efecto sorprendente.

Stunt[1] [stunt], *va.* Impedir crecer o no dejar medrar; detener en el crecimiento; hacer achaparrado. *To grow stunted,* Achaparrarse o no crecer los árboles.—*s.* 1. Detenimiento, en el progreso o desarrollo; cesación del crecimiento. 2. Animal o cosa achaparrados.

Stunt,[2] (fam. E. U.) *va.* Hacer ejercicios corporales de fuerza y destreza.—*s.* Suerte o ejercicio corporal que requiere pericia y destreza.

Stupe [stiūp], *s.* (Med.) Fomentación, compresa; el paño empapado en un cocimiento para fomentar alguna llaga.

Stupe, *va.* Fomentar, aplicar paños empapados en un cocimiento a una parte enferma.

Stupefacient [stiū-pẹ-fê'-shent], *a.* Estupefaciente, que causa estupor, falta de sensación o pasmo.—*s.* Un medicamento narcótico.

Stupefaction [stiū-pẹ-fac'-shun], *s.* Estupefacción, pasmo o estupor; atolondramiento, aturdimiento, asombro.

Stupefier [stiū'-pẹ-fai-ẹr], *s.* Lo que causa estupidez o insensibilidad.

Stupefy [stiū'-pẹ-fai], *va.* 1. Embrutecer, entorpecer los sentidos o las facultades; dejar estupefacto. 2. Atontar, atolondrar; asombrar, causar gran sorpresa, dejar turulato.

Stupendous [stiu-pen'-dus], *a.* Estupendo; inmenso, vasto; de tamaño, volumen o grado maravilloso.

Stupendously [stiu-pen'-dus-li], *adv.* Estupendamente, de un modo asombroso.

Stupid [stiū'-pid], *a.* 1. Estúpido, insensato, notablemente torpe en comprender o en raciocinar. 2. Tosco, grosero. *A stupid thing,* Una patochada, tontada o brutalidad.

Stupidity [stiu-pid'-i-ti], **Stupidness** [stiū'-pid-nes], *s.* Estupidez, tontería, embrutecimiento.

Stupidly [stiū'-pid-li], *adv.* Torpemente, estúpidamente, con insensatez.

Stupor [stiū'-pẹr], *s.* 1. Estupor, entorpecimiento de los sentidos o de las facultades intelectuales. 2. Atontamiento, torpeza notable para comprender, estupidez densa.

Sturdily [stūr'-di-li], *adv.* Robustamente, resueltamente; firmemente, porfiadamente, vigorosamente.

Sturdiness [stūr'-di-nes], *s.* 1. Fuerza, fortaleza. 2. Terquedad, obstinación.

Sturdy [stūr'-di], *a.* 1. Fuerte, robusto, de buena y cabal salud; endurecido, vigoroso. 2. Bronco, terco, firme e inflexible, resuelto. *Sturdy beggars,* Mendigos robustos o que pueden trabajar.

Sturgeon [stūr'-jun], *s.* Esturión, pez de gran tamaño de los mares septentrionales; se le llama también sollo, aunque inexactamente. Acipenser.

Stutter [stut'-ẹr], *vn.* Tartamudear, hablar con dificultad, entrecortadamente y repitiendo las sílabas; tartalear en la pronunciación.—*s.* Tartamudeo, la acción o el vicio de tartamudear o tartalear.

Stutterer [stut'-ẹr-ẹr], *s.* Tartamudo, el que tartamudea; farfulla, el que habla balbuciente y de prisa.

Sty [stai], *s.* (*pl.* STIES). 1. Zahurda, pocilga o cochiquera. 2. Zaquizamí, habitación sucia; lupanar, burdel. 3. Orzuelo del ojo, tumor inflamatorio del borde libre de un párpado.

Stygian [stij'-i-an], *a.* Estigio, infernal, lo que pertenece á la laguna Estigia.

Style[1] [stail], *s.* 1. Estilo, el modo y forma de escribir o hablar particular a cada uno; manera de expresar el pensamiento; dicción distintiva y característica. 2. Estilo, el uso y moda que hay y se guarda comúnmente; manera de obrar; manera, moda, tono, género. *Style of address,* Tratamiento; encabezamiento. *Old style,* Año conforme al cómputo de Julio César. *New style,* Cómputo del año conforme a la corrección de Gregorio XIII en 1582. El primero es 13 días más tarde que el segundo. 3. Estilo o modo peculiar de pintar o de componer en la música; carácter de la composición y ejecución; carácter general de las obras de un artista. 4. Estilo, un punzón de hierro con el cual escribían los antiguous sobre tablillas preparadas con una capa de cera. 5. Útil para grabar; estilete de cirugía. 6. (Zool.) Punzón, prolongación o parte puntiaguda. 7. Título, apellido, renombre o epíteto. (Fr. < Lat. *stilus,* estaca.)

Style,[2] *s.* 1. Estilo o gnomon del reloj de sol. 2. (Bot.) Estilo, la parte del pistilo que está entre el estigma y el embrión. (< Lat. romance, *stylus* < Gr. *stylos,* pilar.)

Style, *va.* Intitular, nombrar, dar o poner un nombre, título o renombre.

Stylet [stai'-let], *s.* 1. Estilete, cualquier instrumento delgado y puntiagudo; punzón pequeño. 2. (Zool.) Prolongación puntiaguda.

Stylish [stai'-lish], *a.* Elegante, a la moda, de buena forma y estilo.

Stylist [stail'-ist], *s.* Estilista. Consultor respecto a estilos de ropa, peinados, etc.

Stylograph [stai'-lo-grạf], **Stylographic pen** [stai-lo-grạf'-ic pen], *s.* Pluma estilográfica, pluma fuente. V. FOUNTAIN PEN.

Styloid [stai'-loid], *a.* Estilóideo, parecido a un estilo o punzón.

Stylus [stai'-lus], *s.* 1. Estilo, punzón. 2. Aguja de fonógrafo.

Styptic [stip'-tic], *a.* y *s.* (Med.) Estíptico, que tiene virtud de astringir y de contener la hemorragia.

Stypticity [stip-tis'-i-ti], *s.* Estipticidad.

Styrax [stai'-rax], *s.* (Bot.) Estoraque, el género típico de las plantas estiráceas.

Styx [stix], *s.* Estigia, laguna del infierno mitológico.

Suable [siū'-a-bl], *a.* Que puede ser perseguido en justicia.

Suasion [swê'-zhun], *s.* Persuasión; anticuado, excepto en la locución, *moral suasion.*

Suasive [swê'-siv], (ant.) †**Suasory** [swê'-so-ri], *a.* Persuasivo, suasorio; persuasivo, que persuade con facilidad.

Suave [swêv o swāv], *a.* Suave, tratable, de modales corteses, afable.

Suavity [swav'-i-ti], *s.* Suavidad, dulzura, blandura, delicia.

Sub- [sub]. Prefijo que unido con otras voces significa el grado inferior de alguna cosa.

Subacetate [sub-as'-ẹ-têt], *s.* (Quím.) Subacetato.

Subacid [sub-as'-id], *a.* 1. Agrillo. 2. (Med.) Subácido.

Subacrid [sub-ac'-rid], *a.* Asperillo.

Subaerial [sub-ê-i'-ri-al], *a.* Subaéreo, formado en la superficie de la tierra, al raso.

Subalmoner [sub-al'-mun-ẹr], *s.* Teniente de limosnero.

Subaltern [sub-ōl'-tẹrn o sub'-al-tẹrn], *a.* Subalterno, inferior, subordinado, dependiente.—*s.* 1. Oficial subalterno; alférez, teniente, oficial inferior al capitán. 2. (Lógica) Clase o naturaleza especificada como comprendida en otra general.

Subalternant [sub-al-tẹr'-nant], *a.* En lógica, universal, en contraposición a particular.—*s.* Proposición universal.

Subalternate [sub-al-tẹr'-nêt], *a.* 1. Sucesivo; que alterna o sigue por turno. 2. Subordinado.

Subaqueous [sub-ê'-cwẹ-us], *a.* Subacuático, que está, vive o se mueve debajo del agua.

Subastringent [sub-as-trin'-jent], *a.* Algo astringente.

Subbase [sub'-bês], *s.* (Arq.) El miembro más bajo de una base.

Subbass, Subbase [sub'-bês], *s.* Registro grave del pedal de un órgano.

Subcarbonate [sub-car'-bo-nêt], *s.* (Quím.) Subcarbonato, sal en que el ácido carbónico se encuentra con exceso de base.

Subchanter [sub-chạnt'-ẹr], *s.* Sochantre, una dignidad eclesiástica.

Subclavian [sub-clé'-vi-an], *a.* (Anat.) Subclavio.

Subcommittee [sub-com-mit'-i], *s.* Una comisión parcial nombrada de entre los individuos de otra para un objeto particular.

Subconscious [sub-con'-shus], *a.* Subconsciente.

Subcontract [sub-con'-tract], *s.* Subcontrato, contrato que hace a su vez el contratista de una obra o trabajo.

Subcontractor [sub-con-trac'-tẹr], *s.* Subcontratista, el que toma en subarriendo o subcontrato.

Subcontrary [sub-con'-tra-ri], *a.* (Lóg.) Subcontraria, una proposición.

Subcordate [sub-cōr'-dét], *a.* Subcordiforme, de forma muy aproximada a la de un corazón.

Subcostal [sub-cos'-tal], *a.* Lo que está debajo de las costillas.

Subcutaneous [sub-kiu-tê'-nẹ-us], *a.* Subcutáneo, que está debajo del cutis. *V.* HYPODERMIC.

Subdeacon [sub-dī'-cn], *s.* Subdiácono.

Subdeaconship [sub-dī'-cn-ship], *s.* Subdiaconato.

Subdean [sub-dīn'], *s.* Subdecano o vice-decano.

Subdecuple [sub-dec'-yu-pl], *a.* Subdécuplo, que contiene una parte de diez.

Subdivide [sub-di-vaid'], *va.* Subdividir.

Subdivision [sub-di-vizh'-un], *s.* Subdivisión; en botánica y zoología, división o grupo subordinado.

Subdominant [sub-dom'-i-nant], *s.*

(Mús.) Subdominante, la cuarta nota de un escala.

Subduce [sub-diūs'], **Subduct** [sub'duct'], *va.* Substraer, quitar, sacar.

Subduction [sub-duc'-shun], *s.* 1. El acto de quitar alguna cosa de donde estaba. 2. Substracción.

Subdue [sub-diū'], *va.* 1. Sojuzgar, subyugar, sujetar, dominar, mandar con violencia. 2. Domar; enternecer, suavizar. 3. Sojuzgar, conquistar, vencer con habilidad o industria; mejorar las tierras; extirpar las malas hierbas. *In a subdued tone,* En tono sumiso; bajando la voz. *To subdue one's flesh,* Mortificar el cuerpo o reprimir los impulsos y apetitos de la carne.

Subduer [sub-diū'-er], *s.* Sojuzgador, conquistador.

Subduement [sub-diū'-ment], *s.* Conquista; sujeción.

Subduple [sub'-diu-pl], **Subduplicate** [sub-diū'-pli-kêt], *a.* Subduplo.

Suberic [siu-ber'-ic], *a.* Subérico, extraído del corcho.

Subfamily [sub-fam'-i-li], *s.* (Biol.) División primaria de una familia; tribu, subfamilia.

Subfusk [sub-fusc'], *a.* (Ant.) Algo moreno u obscuro.

Subgenus [sub-jī'-nus], *s.* (Biol.) Subgénero, subdivisión primaria de un género.

Subindicative [sub-in-dic'-a-tiv], *a.* Que indica de una manera indirecta.

Subjacent [sub-jê'-sent], *a.* Subyacente, situado debajo de otra cosa o más bajo que ella.

Subject [sub-ject'], *va.* 1. Sujetar, someter, sojuzgar, dejar sujeto a. 2. Exponer, arriesgar. 3. Presentar, colocar una cosa delante para que se la considere y juzgue y se disponga de ella. 4. Sujetar, poner en estado de dependencia, subordinar. 5. (Ant.) Someter, poner debajo.

Subject [sub'-ject], *a.* 1. Sujeto, expuesto o propenso a alguna tendencia o agencia. 2. Sujeto, sometido a otro, avasallado, que está bajo la dependencia de otro. 3. Situado debajo o a los pies de otra cosa.—*s.* 1. Súbdito, súbdita; vasallo. 2. Sujeto, materia, aquello de que se trata actualmente, asunto, argumento, tema: (Gram.) sujeto, término de una proposición de la cual se afirma o niega alguna cosa, y particularmente el caso nominativo. 3. Sujeto, lo mismo que persona cuando se trata de sus buenas o malas cualidades. 4. La materia u objeto de alguna ciencia o arte; idea o plan general de una obra artística; asunto. 5. Cadáver destinado a la disección para explicar o enseñar la anatomía; persona expuesta a una enfermedad o que la padece. *Subject-matter,* Asunto, materia de que se trata.

Subjection [sub-jec'-shun], *s.* 1. Sujeción, yugo, dependencia, servidumbre. 2. Sujeción, el acto de sujetar o sujetarse.

Subjective [sub-jec'-tiv], *a.* 1. Subjetivo, que se refiere al sujeto pensante; en contraposición a objetivo. 2. Subjetivo, que tiene relación con el sujeto de que se trata.

Subjectively [sub-jec'-tiv-li], *adv.* Subjetivamente, de una manera subjetiva.

Subjectiveness, Subjectivity [sub-jec'-tiv-nes, sub-jec-tiv'-i-ti], *s.* Subjetividad, calidad de subjetivo.

Subjoin [sub-join'], *va.* Añadir al fin, sobreañadir, juntar a.

Subjugate [sub'-ju-gêt], *va.* Subyugar, conquistar, someter, sujetar.

Subjugation [sub-ju-gê'-shun], *s.* Sujeción, servidumbre, yugo.

Subjunction [sub-junc'-shun], *s.* La acción de añadir al fin; sobreañadidura.

Subjunctive [sub-junc'-tiv], *a.* Subjuntivo, del modo subjuntivo, perteneciente al modo del verbo que denota la suposición, la duda, la condición o dependencia.—*s.* (Gram.) Subjuntivo, modo subjuntivo.

Subkingdom [sub'-king"-dum], *s.* Subreino, división primaria del reino animal o vegetal.

Sublapsary [sub-lap'-sa-ri], *a.* (Poco us.) Lo sucedido después de la caída del primer hombre.

Sublease, [sub-līs'], *va.* Subarrendar. V. SUBLET.

Sublet [sub-let'], *va.* Subarrendar, arrendar a otro una parte o todo el trabajo que uno mismo se ha obligado a hacer por contrata; arrendar a otro lo que se tenía arrendado.

Sublevation [sub-le-vê'-shun], *s.* 1. Alza, elevación. 2. Sublevación.

Sublimate [sub'-li-mêt], *s.* (Quím.) Sublimado, la parte más sutil y volátil de los mixtos, extraída de las partes crasas por medio del fuego. *Corrosive sublimate,* Solimán, sublimado corrosivo, cloruro sobreoxigenado de mercurio.

Sublimate, *va.* 1. (Quím.) Sublimar, elevar por medio del fuego las partes volátiles de los cuerpos, y volver a solidificarlas. 2. Sublimar, separar de la escoria; (fig.) refinar, purificar.

Sublimation [sub-li-mê'-shun], *s.* 1. Sublimación. 2. Refinamiento, perfección, quinta esencia.

Sublime [sub-laim'], *a.* 1. Sublime, excelso, elevado, exaltado. 2. Majestuoso, imponente, solemne. 3. Del grado más alto, supremo, extremo, el más grande. 4. (Poét.) Altivo, orgulloso, arrebatado, transportado.—*s.* El estilo sublime o elevado.

Sublime, va. y vn. 1. Sublimar, exaltar, engrandecer, ensalzar o poner a gran altura. 2. (Quím.) Sublimar o sublimarse.

Sublimely [sub-laim' li], *adv.* **Sublimemente, elevadamente, de un modo sublime.**

Sublimeness [sub-laim'-nes], **Sublimity** [sub-lim'-i-ti], *s.* **Sublimidad, grandeza, exaltación, elevación o altura de alguna cosa.**

Sublingual [sub-lin'-gwal], *a.* (Anat.) Sublingual, situado debajo de la lengua.

Sublunar [sub-lū'-nar], **Sublunary** [sub'-lu-na-ri], *a.* Sublunar, que está debajo de la luna; terreno, terrestre, terráqueo.

Submachine gun [sub-ma-shīn' gun], *s.* Metralleta.

Submarine [sub-ma-rīn'], *a.* Submarino, que está debajo de la superficie del mar.

Submaxillary [sub-mac'-sil-e-ri], *a.* Submaxilar, situado debajo de la mandíbula inferior.

Submediant [sub-mī'-di-ant], *s.* (Mús.) Sexta nota de la escala.

Submerge [sub-merj'], ‡**Submerse** [sub-mers'], *va.* 1. Sumergir, zambullir, meter alguna cosa debajo del agua; de aquí, ahogar. 2. Sumergir, anegar, inundar.—*vn.* Zambullirse, sumergirse, yacer debajo del agua; estar escondido o enterrado, oculto a la vista.

Submergence, Submersion [sub-mer'-jens, shun], *s.* Sumersión, acción y efecto de sumergir.

Subministration [sub-min-is-trê'-shun], *s.* Suministración.

Submission [sub-mish'-un], *s.* 1. Sumisión, sometimiento, la acción y efecto de someterse; obediencia. 2. Sumisión, rendimiento, deferencia, obsequio, respeto; resignación. 3. (Ant.) El reconocimiento de una falta, la confesión de un error. 4. (For.) Acción de referir o someter, o el acuerdo de someter el punto controvertido al arbitraje.

Submissive [sub-mis'-iv], *a.* Sumiso, obediente, rendido, sometido, obsequioso.

Submissively [sub-mis'-iv-li], *adv.* Humildemente, respetuosamente, con sumisión, rendimiento o respeto.

Submissiveness [sub-mis'-iv-nes], *s.* Obsequio, sumisión, rendimiento.

Submit [sub-mit'], *va.* 1. Someter, sujetar (en este sentido es generalmente verbo reflexivo). 2. Someter, referir o dejar una resolución o determinación al juicio, fallo, discreción o arbitrio de otro. 3. Presentar como el propio parecer o versión.—*vn.* 1. Someterse, sujetarse, rendirse, conformarse, consentir en una cosa, ceder. 2. Estar sometido. *We must all submit,* No hay más remedio que someternos, o tenemos que consentir o conformarnos.

Subnormal [sub-nōr'-mal], *a.* Anormal, inferior al grado normal. *Subnormal temperature,* Temperatura bajo la normal.—*s.* (Mat.) Subnormal, parte del eje de una curva comprendida entre la ordenada y la normal.

Suboctave [sub-oc'-têv], **Suboctuple** [sub-oc'-tiu-pl], *a.* Subóctuplo.

Suborbital [sub-ōr'-bit-al], *a.* Suborbital, situado debajo de la órbita del ojo.

Suborder [sub'-ōr"-der], *s.* 1. (Bot. y Zool.) Suborden, división primaria de un orden. 2. (Arq.) Orden subordinado, empleado principalmente para adorno.

Subordinacy [sub-ōr'-di-na-si], *s.* Subordinación, sujeción.

Subordinate [sub-ōr'-di-net], *a.* Subordinado, inferior, dependiente o bajo las órdenes de otro.

Subordinate, *va.* 1. Subordinar, poner o colocar en un orden o categoría inferior; de aquí, tener o considerar como de menor importancia. 2. Someter, sujetar.

Subordinately [sub-ōr'-di-net-li], *adv.* Subordinadamente, como dependiente, como inferior a otro.

Subordination [sub-ōr-di-nê'-shun], *s.* Subordinación.

Suborn [sub-ōrn'], *va.* Sobornar, corromper, cohechar.

Subornation [sub-ōr-nê'-shun], *s.* Soborno, la acción de sobornar, cohecho.

Suborner [sub-ōrn'-er], *s.* Sobornador, cohechador, el que soborna.

Subperitoneal [sub-per-i-to-nī'-al], *a.* Subperitoneal, situado debajo de la superficie adherente del peritoneo.

Subpœna [sub-pī'-na], *s.* Comparendo, la citación que un superior o un juez hace a una persona, mandándola comparecer bajo alguna pena.—*va.* Notificar por medio de una citación de comparendo; emplazar.

Subpolar [sub-pō'-lar], *a.* Subpolar, situado debajo del polo o inmediato a él.

Subrector [sub-rec'-tẹr], *s.* Vicerector, subrector; subregente (de colegio).

Subreption [sub-rep'-shun], *s.* Subrepción, la acción oculta y á escondidas, y la ocultación de algún hecho o de alguna circunstancia importante en un hecho.

Subrogation [sub-ro-gê'-shun], *s.* Subrogación.

Subscribe [sub-scraib'], *va.* y *vn.* 1. Subscribir, suscribir, dar el consentimiento firmando al pie o al fin de algún escrito. 2. Certificar uno con su firma; firmar, rubricar. 3. Subscribir, convenir con el dictamen de otro; aprobar, consentir, dar el consentimiento. 4. Subscribirse a una obra. 5. Subscribirse para la ejecución de cualquier empresa, anticipando una suma determinada para tener derecho a las ganancias.

Subscriber [sub-scraib'-ẹr], *s.* 1. Subscriptor, suscriptor, el que subscribe o firma. 2. Subscriptor, el que subscribe o contribuye a alguna obra o a cualquiera otra empresa u objeto.

Subscript [sub-script], *a.* y *s.* Cualquier cosa escrita debajo de otra.

Subscription [sub-scrip'-shun], *s.* 1. Subscripción, la acción y efecto de subscribir. 2. Subscripción, la firma de una carta o documento. 3. Subscripción, la acción de contribuir a cualquiera empresa. 4. La suma o número individual o total que se subscribe para cualquier objeto. 5. Pacto, convenio en cuanto está demostrado por la firma del que lo hace.

Subsection [sub-sec'-shun], *s.* Subdivisión, clase menor.

Subsecutive [sub-sec'-yu-tiv], *a.* Subsiguiente, subsecuente.

Subsequence [sub'-se-cwens], *s.* Subsecuencia.

Subsequent [sub'-se-cwent], *a.* Subsiguiente.

Subsequently [sub'-se-cwent-li], *adv.* Posteriormente, subsiguientemen-

Subserve [sub-sẹrv'], *va.* Servir, estar subordinado, servir como instrumento o de instrumento; favorecer.—*vn.* Servir como subordinado.

Subservience [sub-sẹr'-vi-ens], **Subserviency** [sub-sẹr'-vi-en-si], *s.* Servicio, utilidad, socorro; la acción de servir de instrumento en la ejecución de una cosa y la aptitud para ello.

Subservient [sub-sẹr'-vi-ent], *a.* Subalterno, subordinado, inferior; obsequioso; útil, apto o a propósito para servir de instrumento.

Subserviently [sub-sẹr'-vi-ent-li], *adv.* Subordinadamente, de un modo secundario pero útil; útilmente.

Subside [sub-said'], *vn.* 1. Apaciguarse, calmarse, cesar una tempestad, agitación, o pasión turbulenta; minorar, cesar. 2. Bajar, rebajar, ir a un nivel más bajo (un flúido); desplomarse, dejarse caer. 3. Sumergirse, irse a fondo (como las heces).

Subsidence [sub-sai'-dens], **Subsidency** [sub-sai'-den-si], *s.* 1. Apaciguamiento, calma. 2. Desplome, desmoronamiento. 3. Sumersión, acción de sumergir o de irse a fondo.

Subsidiary [sub-sid'-i-e-ri], *a.* 1. Subsidiario. 2. Auxiliar, que ayuda.

Subsidize [sub'-si-daiz], *va.* Subvencionar, dar un subsidio; suministrar fondos á una empresa (p. ej. a una línea de vapores).

Subsidy [sub'-si-di], *s.* Subsidio, ayuda, socorro en dinero que da el Estado a una empresa individual o comercial considerada como de interés público; subvención. 2. Subsidio, dinero que da un Estado a una potencia aliada.

Subsign [sub-sain'], *va.* Subscribir, firmar.

Subsist [sub-sist'], *vn.* 1. Subsistir, permanecer, durar alguna cosa o conservarse. 2. Subsistir, existir, vivir, estar por sí en su propia naturaleza y ser. 3. Sustentarse, tener con que vivir y mantenerse de un modo correspondiente a su estado o calidad.—*va.* Alimentar o mantener a uno.

Subsistence [sub-sist'-ens], *s.* 1. Existencia. 2. Subsistencia, sustento. 3. Calidad de subsistente; también, una cualidad inherente. *Subsistence money,* La cantidad de dinero que se necesita o se emplea en mantenerse o en el sustento diario.

Subsistent [sub-sist'-ent], *a.* 1. Subsistente, que subsiste. 2. Inherente.

Subsoil [sub'-soil], *va.* Arar, voltear la tierra con un arado de subsuelo. —*s.* Subsuelo, capa de tierra situada inmediatamente debajo del terreno superficial.

Substance [sub'-stans], *s.* 1. Substancia, la entidad o esencia que subsiste o existe por sí. 2. Substancia, ser, esencia, naturaleza de las cosas. 3. Substancia, la parte más esencial de una cosa. 4. Realidad, la existencia física y real de una cosa. 5. Substancia, lo mismo que cuerpo o materia. 6. Substancia, la hacienda, caudal o bienes.

Substantial [sub-stan'-shal], *a.* 1. Substancial, que pertenece a la substancia, es propio de ella o la incluye. 2. Real, existente, verdadero. 3. Corpóreo, material. 4. Substancial, substancioso. 5. Fuerte, vigoroso, sólido. 6. Acomodado, el que tiene medios de subsistir o es moderadamente rico.—*s.* Lo que tiene substancia; realidad, cosa real. *Substantials,* Las partes esenciales o más importantes.

Substantiality [sub-stan-shi-al'-i-ti], *s.* 1. Realidad, la existencia física y real. 2. Corporeidad, la calidad de corpóreo.

Substantialize [sub-stan'-shal-aiz], *va.* (Poco us.) Hacer real y efectiva alguna cosa.

Substantially [sub-stan'-shal-i], *adv.* Substancialmente; realmente; sólidamente.

Substantialness [sub-stan'-shal-nes], *s.* Firmeza, fuerza, duración.

Substantiate [sub-stan'-shi-êt], *va.* 1. Verificar, establecer, comprobar, justificar. 2. (Ant.) Dar cuerpo. *V.* EMBODY.

Substantival [sub'-stan-tiv-al], *a.* 1. (Gram.) Substantivo, perteneciente a un nombre o substantivo. 2. Existente por sí mismo.

Substantive [sub'-stan-tiv], *a.* 1. (Gram.) Substantivo, que puede usarse como nombre substantivo; que denota existencia. 2. Que tiene substancia o realidad; de aquí, duradero. 3. Esencial. 4. Expresado explícitamente. 5. Que tiene individualidad distinta; que posee medios o recursos independientes, v. g. un país.—*s.* 1. Nombre, substantivo; cualquier cosa que se emplea como substantivo, p. ej. una forma del verbo, una locución o cláusula. 2. El o lo que es independiente.

Substantively [sub'-stan-tiv-li], *adv.* 1. Substancialmente, en substancia, esencialmente. 2. Substantivamente, como substantivo.

Substitute [sub'-sti-tiut], *va.* Substituir, poner una persona o cosa en lugar de otra.

Substitute, *s.* Substituto, la persona o cosa que substituye a otra.

Substitution [sub-sti-tiū'-shun], *s.* Substitución; reemplazo: acción y efecto de substituir.

Substratum [sub-strê'-tum], *s.* Lecho, capa o cama debajo de otras.

Substructure [sub-struc'-chur], *s.* (Arq.) Infraestructura, soporte, las partes de un edificio que están debajo de todas las otras. Se contrapone a *superstructure,* superestructura.

Substylar [sub-stai'-lar], *a.* Substilar: dase este nombre a una línea en la gnomónica.

Subsultus [sub-sul'-tus], *s.* (Med.) Sacudimiento de los músculos; síntoma grave de ciertas fiebres.

Subtangent [sub-tan'-jent], *s.* (Geom.) Subtangente.

Subtend [sub-tend'], *va.* 1. (Geom.) Subtender, estar opuesto a. 2. (Bot.) Encerrar o abrazar en la axila.

Subtense [sub-tens'], *s.* (Geom.) Subtensa, cuerda.

Subter- [sub'-tẹr]. Prefijo que en composición significa debajo; opuesto a *super,* sobre.

Subterfluent [sub-tẹr'-flu-ent], **Subterfluous** [sub-tẹr'-flu-us], *a.* (Poco us.) Lo que fluye o corre por debajo de otra cosa.

Subterfuge [sub'-tẹr-fiūj], *s.* Subterfugio, efugio, evasión, salida, excusa falsa.

Subterranean [sub-tẹr-rê'-ne-an], **Subterraneous** [sub-tẹr-rê'-ne-us], *a.* Subterráneo, que está debajo de tierra.

Subterraneousness [sub-tẹr-rê'-ne-us-nes], *s.* El estado de lo que es subterráneo o se halla debajo de tierra.

Subtile [sub-til], *a.* 1. Sutil, delicado, tenue, etéreo; refinado; penetrante. *A subtile spider's web,* Una telaraña sutil. *A subtile perfume,* Un perfume penetrante. 2. Sutil, perspicaz, ingenioso, penetrante, agudo. 3. Artero, artificioso, astuto. *V.* SUBTLE. (La tendencia actual es a emplear *subtile* como atributo de las cosas y *subtle,* como característico del ánimo.

Subtilely [sub'-til-li], *adv.* Sutilmente, con sutileza, astutamente.

Subtileness [sub'-til-nes], *s.* Sutileza, sutilidad, finura, astucia.

Subtilize [sub'-til-aiz], *va.* y *vn.* 1. Sutilizar, adelgazar una cosa. 2. Sutilizar, limar o pulir una cosa.—*vn.* Sutilizar, discurrir ingeniosamente: por lo regular se toma en mala parte.

Subtilty [sub'-til-ti], *s.* 1. Sutileza, sutilidad, delgadeza o tenuidad. 2. La demasiada sutileza, delicadeza ó esmero. 3. Astucia, artificio, artería.

Subtle [sut'-l], *a.* 1. Sutil, astuto, artificioso, mañoso, artero. 2. Perspicaz, penetrante, agudo; demasiado refinado. 3. Apto, hábil, mañoso. 4. Ejecutado con arte primoroso, ingeniosamente ideado. 5. *V.*

SUBTILE, en cualquiera de sus acepciones.

Subtleness [sut'-l-nes], **Subtlety** [sut'-l-ti], *s.* Sutileza, astucia, artificio.

Subtly [sut'-li], *adv.* Sutilmente, delicadamente, artificiosamente.

Subtract [sub-tract'], *va.* 1. Substraer, apartar, separar. 2. (Arit.) Restar, substraer un número menor de otro mayor.

Subtraction [sub-trac'-shun], *s.* 1. Substracción, la acción y efecto de substraer. 2. (Arit.) Resta o substracción.

Subtrahend [sub'-tra-hend], *s.* Substraendo, sustraendo.

Subtreasury [sub-trezh'-u-ri], *s.* Subtesorería, sucursal de la tesorería de los Estados Unidos para el recibo y desembolso de los ingresos y pagos del gobierno.

Subtreasurer [sub-trezh'-ur-er], *s.* Subtesorero.

Subtropic, Subtropical [sub-trop'-ic, al], *a.* 1. Subtropical, de cualidades intermedias entre las de las zonas templadas y las tropicales. 2. Perteneciente a la región cercana a los círculos tropicales.

Subulate [siū'-biu-lēt], *a.* (Biol.) Subulado, alesnado.

Suburb [sub'-ūrb], *s.* Suburbio, arrabal o aldea cerca de la ciudad.

Suburban [sub-ūrb'-an], *a.* Suburbano.—*s.* Residente en un suburbio.

Suburbanite [sub-urb'-an-ait], *s.* El que vive en un suburbio.

Suburbia [su-būr'-bi-a], *s.* 1. Suburbios, alrededores, extramuros barrios residenciales o ciudades que rodean una metrópolis. 2. Tipo de vida que los caracteriza.

Subvene [sub-vīn'], *vn.* Suceder, acontecer (de modo que ayude o socorra); subvenir; intervenir, interponerse.

Subvention [sub-ven'-shun], *s.* Subvención, la acción y efecto de subvenir o amparar; ayuda. *V.* SUBSIDY.

Subversion [sub-ver'-shun], *s.* Subversión, ruina, estrago, trastorno o destrucción.

Subversive [sub-ver'-siv], *a.* Subversivo.

Subvert [sub-vert'], *va.* Subvertir, destruir, trastornar, arruinar.

Subverter [sub-vert'-er], *s.* Subversor, destructor.

Subvertible [sub-vert'-i-bl], *a.* Subvertible, que se puede subvertir; trastornable, destruible.

Subway [sub'-wē], *s.* Subterráneo, ferrocarril subterráneo, metro, metropolitano.

Subworker [sub-wūrk'-er], *s.* Ayuda, ayudante.

Sucaryl [suc'-ar-il], *s.* Nombre comercial de un compuesto azucarado parecido a la sacarina.

Succeed [suc-sīd'], *vn.* y *va.* 1. Suceder, entrar en lugar de otro o seguirse a él. 2. Suceder, llenar una persona o cosa el hueco de otra u ocupar su lugar. 3. Salir bien de alguna empresa o empeño; conseguir, lograr, acertar. 4. Hacer salir bien una empresa o empeño; hacer prosperar. *To succeed in doing a thing,* Acertar, lograr hacer una cosa. *Nothing succeeds with them,* Nada les sale bien. *Maria Theresa succeeded to the throne,* María Teresa sucedió en el trono. *To succeed each other* o *one another,* Sucederse (los unos a los otros).

Succeeder [suc-sīd'-er], *s.* Sucesor, el que sucede a otro o entra en su lugar.

Succeeding [suc-sīd'-ing], *a.* Subsiguiente, que sigue inmediatamente a otra cosa; futuro.

Success [suc-ses'], *s.* 1. Suceso, salida, resultado o fin bueno, buen éxito, fortuna, ventaja o triunfo. 2. (Ant. o fam.) Mal resultado. 3. Persona o asunto afortunados.

Successful [suc-ses'-ful], *a.* Próspero, dichoso, afortunado, exitoso, feliz, que ha salido bien.

Successfully [suc-ses'-ful-i], *adv.* Felizmente, prósperamente, con felicidad o buen éxito.

Successfulness [suc-ses'-ful-nes], *s.* Feliz éxito, buen suceso, dicha.

Succession [suc-sesh'-un], *s.* 1. Sucesión, la acción de suceder. 2. Linaje, descendencia. 3. Sucesión o herencia; derecho de sucesión; advenimiento al trono.

Successive [suc-ses'-iv], *a.* Sucesivo, que sigue o va después de otra cosa.

Successively [suc-ses'-iv-li], *adv.* Sucesivamente, consiguientemente.

Successiveness [suc-ses'-iv-nes], *s.* (Poco us.) Sucesión.

Successless [suc-ses'-les], *a.* Desafortunado, desgraciado, infeliz.

Successor [suc-ses'-er], *s.* 1. Sucesor, el que sucede a otro. 2. Heredero.

Succinate [suc'-si-nēt], *s.* (Quím.) Succinato, sal del ácido succínico.

Succinct [suc-sinct'], *a.* 1. Sucinto, breve, compendioso. 2. (Ento.) Enfaldado, sostenido por un hilo de seda, como la ninfa de una mariposa.

Succinctly [suc-sinct'-li], *adv.* Sucintamente, compendiosamente, con brevedad, con precisión, en pocas palabras.

Succinctness [suc-sinct'-nes], *s.* Brevedad, concisión.

Succinic [suc-sin'-ic], *a.* 1. Succínico, que se deriva del succino o ámbar. 2. Que se halla en el ámbar (v. g. un insecto).

Succor, Succour [suc'-er], *va.* Socorrer, ayudar, auxiliar, dar socorro.

Succor, Succour, *s.* Socorro, ayuda, auxilio, favor, asistencia. *To fly, to run for succor,* Volar, correr en busca de socorro.

Succorer [suc'-er-er], *s.* Socorredor, el que socorre, auxiliador.

Succorless [suc'-er-les], *a.* Desamparado, sin protección, sin ayuda.

Succory [suc'-o-ri], *s.* (Bot.) Achicoria. *V.* CHICORY.

Succotash [suc'-o-tash], *s.* (E. U.) Guiso de maíz tierno y frijoles o habas tiernas. (< nombre indígena, sickquatash.)

Succour, *v.* y *s.* *V.* SUCCOR. (Forma preferida en Inglaterra.)

Succulency [suc'-yu-len-si], *s.* Jugosidad.

Succulent [suc'-yu-lent], *a.* Suculento, jugoso.

Succumb [suc-cum'], *vn.* 1. No poder llevar o aguantar un trabajo o una carga; quedar rendido o vencido debajo de otro. 2. Morir. *He succumbed to his wounds,* Murió de sus heridas.

Succussion [suc-cush'-un], *s.* Sacudimiento, la acción de sacudir.

Such [such], *a.* 1. Tal, igual, semejante; cierto. 2. Enfáticamente, cosa extremada, intolerable. *We are come to such a pass,* Hemos llegado a situación tan extrema. *Such a place,* Cierto lugar.—*pron.* Tal, un tal; el que, la que, los que, las que; aquel, aquella, aquello. *There is no such thing,* No hay tal cosa. *At such a time,* En tal tiempo. *Mr. such a one,* Don fulano, o el señor fulano de tal. *Such as,* El que, los que, lo que, cualquiera que.

Suck [suc], *va.* y *vn.* 1. Chupar, sacar o atraer con los labios un jugo o substancia. 2. Mamar, atraer y sacar la leche de los pechos. 3. Extraer o sacar alguna cosa formando un vacío o casi vacío por medio de la rarefacción o extracción del aire, como el agua que se extrae con las bombas. 4. Chupar o ir sustrayendo la hacienda de otro con pretextos y engaños. *To suck in,* Embeber, chupar. *To suck out* o *up,* Extraer o sacar algo chupando o por medio de una bomba; dar a la bomba; vaciar una cosa sacando lo que contenía a fuerza de chupar; sacar una cosa de otra.

Suck, *s.* 1. (Med.) Succión, la acción de chupar o de extraer algo chupando. 2. La acción de mamar. 3. Leche, lo que dan las madres o amas a sus criaturas. *To give suck,* Amamantar, dar de mamar.

Sucker [suk'-er], *s.* 1. Chupador, el que chupa. 2. Chupadero, lo que chupa. 3. Chupón. 4. Émbolo y el sopapo de bomba. 5. Tubo aspirador. 6. Caramelo, paleta de dulce. 7. (vul.) Bobo, persona cándida y crédula.

†**Sucket** [suk'-et], *s.* Dulce que se chupa, como el caramelo.

Sucking [suk'-ing], *s.* Chupadura, la acción de chupar; la acción de mamar. *Sucking-fish,* Rémora: (Echeneis remora). *Sucking pig,* Lechoncillo.

Suckle [suc'-l], *va.* 1. Amamantar, dar la teta, dar de mamar. 2. Criar, nutrir a un niño con la leche de los pechos.

Suckling [suc'-ling], *s.* Mamantón, la cría o la criatura que está aún mamando.

Sucrose [siū'-crōs], *s.* El compuesto blanco y cristalizable que se conoce bajos los nombres de azúcar de caña, de remolacha, de arce, según su origen, pero idéntico químicamente $(C_{12}H_{22}O_{11})n$.

Suction [suc'-shun], *s.* Succión, el acto de chupar; la producción de un vacío parcial en un espacio inmediato a un flúido sujeto a presión, con lo cual el líquido fluye en un receptáculo. *Suction-hose,* Manguera de alimentación. *Suction-pump,* Bomba aspirante.

Suctorial [suc-tō'-ri-al], *a.* 1. Chupador, chupadero, apto o propio para chupar o para adherir. 2. Que vive o se alimenta chupando.

Sudanese, Soudanese [sū''-da-nīs' o nīz'], *a.* Sudanés, del Sudán o perteneciente a él.—*s.* Sudanés, habitante o negro de esta región de África.

Sudation [siu-dē'-shun], *s.* Sudor excesivo.

Sudatory [siū'-da-to-ri], *a.* 1. Sudorífero, que promueve el sudor. 2. Que transpira o suda.—*s.* 1. Sudorífico, agente que produce sudor. 2. Sudadero, el lugar en el baño destinado para sudar.

Sudden [sud'-en o sud'-n], *a.* 1. Repentino, pronto, no prevenido, imprevisto, súbito. 1. Apresurado, ideado, usado o hecho de prisa; precipitado.—*s.* (Des.) Repentón, suceso o lance que sobreviene sin pensar.

On a sudden, De repente, sin esperarse, súbitamente.

Suddenly [sud'-en-li], *adv.* Repentinamente, de repente, súbitamente.

Suddenness [sud'-en-nes], *s.* Precipitación, calidad de repentino.

Sudoriferous [siu-der-if'-er-us], *a.* Sudorífero, que causa o produce sudor.

Sudorific [siu-der-if'-ic], *a.* Sudorífico, que promueve el sudor.—*s.* Sudorífico, medicamento que hace sudar.

Suds [sudz], *s. pl.* 1. Jabonaduras, el agua que queda mezclada con el jabón y su espuma. 2. Espuma. *To be in the suds*, (Vulg.) Verse apurado.

Sue [siū], *va.* y *vn.* 1. Poner por justicia; perseguir o demandar a alguno en justicia. 2. Seguir un pleito; procesar o hacer causa a alguno. 3. Ganar un pleito o una demanda. 4. Ejecutar u obligar a uno por justicia a pagar lo que debe. 5. Rogar, pedir, suplicar.—*vn.* Pretender en matrimonio, galantear. *To sue for*, Pedir o demandar judicialmente. *To sue for damages*, Demandar por daños y perjuicios. *To sue out*, Conseguir u obtener una cosa a fuerza de ruegos.

Suede [swêd], *s.* Piel de ante. *Suede cloth*, Tela parecida a la piel de ante.

Suet [siū-et], *s.* Sebo, grasa dura y sólida de la región de los riñones (de los bueyes, corderos, etc.).

Suety [siū'-et-i], *a.* Seboso.

Suffer [suf'-er], *va.* y *vn.* 1. Sufrir, padecer algún dolor, pesar, etc. 2 Sufrir, tolerar, aguantar, llevar algún mal con paciencia, sufrimiento y tolerancia. 3. Sufrir, permitir; admitir. 4. Sufrir alguna pena o castigo. 5. Causar daño o detrimento. *To suffer for*, Sufrir, padecer por, llevar la pena de algo. *To be suffered*, Tolerable, soportable. *Not to be suffered*, Intolerable, insoportable.

Sufferable [suf'-er-a-bl], *a.* Sufrible, sufridero, soportable, tolerable.

Sufferableness [suf'-er-a-bl-nes], *s.* El estado de lo que puede tolerarse.

Sufferably [suf'-er-a-bli], *adv.* De un modo soportable.

Sufferance [suf'-er-ans], *s.* 1. Tolerancia, permisión, consentimiento tácito. 2. (Ant.) Sufrimiento, paciencia, conformidad, resignación, tolerancia, aguante. 3. (Ant.) Pena, dolor, trabajo, tormento. 4. En las aduanas, permiso para expedir ciertas clases de efectos.

Sufferer [suf'-er-er], *s.* 1. Sufridor, el que sufre dolor físico o moral; doliente. 2. Perdidoso. 3. El que tolera tácitamente. *Fellow-sufferer*, Compañero de infortunio. *A sufferer in* o *by*, Víctima de.

Suffering [suf'-er-ing], *s.* Pena, dolor (físico o moral), el padecimiento o la pérdida sufrida, tormento.—*pa.* Paciente, doliente.

Suffice [suf-fais'], *vn.* Bastar, ser suficiente.—*va.* Satisfacer, ser bastante o suficiente. *Suffice it to say*, Baste decir.

Sufficiency [suf-fish'-en-si], *s.* 1. Suficiencia, capacidad o idoneidad para algún fin u objeto. 2. Lo suficiente, lo bastante o lo que basta, lo que es menester. 3. Cualidad, eficacia. 4. Presunción, exagerada confianza en sí mismo, alto concepto del propio valor. *Self-sufficiency*, Presunción en las fuerzas propias.

Sufficient [suf-fish'-ent], *a.* 1. Suficiente, bastante, lo que es menester. 2. Suficiente, bastante o capaz para alguna cosa; apto, idóneo. *Sufficient witness*, Testigo sin tacha.

Sufficiently [suf-fish'-ent-li], *adv.* Suficientemente, bastantemente, bastante: bastante bien.

Suffix [suf-fix'], *va.* Añadir, anexar, como sufijo o afijo.

Suffix [suf'-ix], *s.* 1. Sufijo, afijo, sílaba o letra que se añade al final de una palabra para modificar la significación de ésta. 2. Cualquier título o designación añadidos.

Suffocate [suf'-o-kêt], *va.* 1. Sofocar, sufocar, ahogar, impedir el aliento o la respiración. 2. Matar sofocando. 3. Apagar, extinguir, ahogar, v. g. un fuego.—*vn.* Sofocarse, ahogarse, perder la respiración.

Suffocating [suf'-o-kêt-ing], *a.* Sofocante, sofocador, que ahoga.

Suffocation [suf-o-kê'-shun], *s.* Sofocación, ahogo, impedimento de la respiración.

Suffocative [suf'-o-ca-tiv], *a.* Sofocante, sofocador.

Suffragan [suf'-ra-gan], *a.* Auxiliar. —*s.* 1. Sufragáneo: dícese de un obispo con respecto a su metropolitano. 2. Obispo auxiliar.

Suffrage [suf'-rêj], *s.* 1. Sufragio, voto en favor de alguna medida u opinión: de aquí, aprobación, consentimiento. 2. El derecho o privilegio de votar.

Suffragette [suf-ra-jet'], *s.* Sufragista, partidaria del voto femenino.

Suffragist [suf'-ra-jist], *s.* Sufragista, partidario del sufragio femenino.

Suffuse [suf-fiūz'], *va.* Difundir, extender; derramar, verter, cubrir con un color o tinte. *Cheeks suffused with blushes*, Mejillas cubiertas de rubor.

Suffusion [suf-fiū'-zhun], *s.* 1. (Med.) Sufusión o efusión de humores debajo del cutis. 2. Sufusión, congestión ligera difundida. 3. Mezcla de colores en el plumaje.

Sugar [shug'-ar], *s.* 1. Azúcar, compuesto dulce cristalizable ($C_{12}H_{22}O_{11}$) que se saca principalmente del jugo de la caña dulce y de la remolacha. 2. Cualquier cosa muy dulce. *Beet-sugar*, Azúcar de remolacha. *Grape-sugar*, Azúcar de uvas, glucosa. *Maple-sugar*, Azúcar de arce. *Sugar-beet*, Remolacha. *Sugar-bowl*, Azucarero. *Sugar-cane*, Caña dulce o de azúcar. *Loaf-sugar*, Azúcar de pilón. *Brown* o *clayed sugar*, Azúcar moreno o terciado, cogucho; (Amer.) chancaca, panoche, panela. *White* o *refined sugar*, Azúcar refinado. *Sugar-candy*, Azúcar piedra o cande. *Sugar-coated*, Garapiñado, cubierto de azúcar. *Sugar-plum*, Confite, dulce. *Sugar of lead*, Azúcar de plomo o sal de saturno. *Sugar-house*, Ingenio o trapiche donde se fabrica el azúcar; refino u oficina donde se refina. *To sweeten with sugar*, Azucarar, confitar.

Sugar, *va.* 1. Azucarar, endulzar o suavizar el mal sabor de una cosa con azúcar; también en sentido figurado. 2. (E. U. y Canadá) Hacer el azúcar de arce.

Sugar mill [shug'-ar mil], *s.* Trapiche, molino de azúcar.

Sugary [shug'-ar-i], *a.* 1. Azucarado, sacarino, compuesto de azúcar, dulce. 2. Goloso, aficionado al azúcar y a los dulces. 3. (Fig.) Meloso, seductivo, halagüeño.

Suggest [su-jest' o sug-jest'], *va.* 1. Sugerir, echar una indirecta, insinuar, informar indirecta y discretamente. 2. Sugerir, advertir o acordar alguna especie. 3. Sugerir, instigar una acción, influir para que se ejecute.

Suggestion [su-jes'-chun o sug-jes'-chun], *s.* Sugestión, la acción de sugerir y la cosa sugerida; instigación.

Suggestive [su o sug-jes'-tiv], *a.* Sugerente, que sugiere; que inspira el ánimo o estimula la reflexión.

Suicidal [siu-i-sai'-dal], *a.* 1. Que pertenece o que tiende al suicidio. 2. Destructor de sí mismo, ruinoso a sus propios intereses.

Suicide [siū'-i-said], *s.* 1. Suicidio, el acto de quitarse la vida. 2. Suicida. 3. (Fig.) Ruina política, social, o comercial que uno mismo se atrae o causa.—*vn.* (Vulg.) Suicidarse.

Suing [siū'-ing], *s.* 1. Solicitación o diligencia para conseguir alguna cosa. 2. Galanteo, pretensión en matrimonio. *V.* SUIT, 2ª acep.

Suit [siūt], *s.* 1. Petición, súplica, solicitación. 2. Galanteo, obsequio o cortejo hecho a una mujer. 3. Pleito o litigio judicial. 4. Juego, un número determinado de cosas que tienen cierta conexión o correspondencia entre sí; colección completa de cosas semejantes, reunión, surtido. 5. Vestido, el conjunto de prendas que componen el abrigo del cuerpo. *I have bought four suits of clothes*, He comprado cuatro vestidos completos. 6. Palo en la baraja. 7. *V.* SUITE, 2ª acep. *Suit of hangings*, Colgaduras. *A suit of armor*, Una armadura completa. *Suit in chancery*, Procedimiento ante la cancillería. *To bring (a) suit*, Entablar un pleito, incoar una demanda judicial. *To follow suit*, (1) Jugar el mismo palo; (2) seguir el ejemplo, imitar lo que otro hace.

Suit, *va.* y *vn.* 1. Adecuar, proporcionar, acomodar, ajustar o casar dos o más cosas para que digan bien entre sí o para que hagan buen juego. 2. Adaptar, acomodar o hacer venir bien una cosa con otra. 3. Venir, ajustarse, acomodarse o conformarse una cosa a otra o una cosa con otra. 4. Convenir, concordar. 5. Sentar, caer o venir bien un vestido o adorno; ser aparente o bueno. *This coat does not suit me*, No me sienta esta levita. *That suits you very well*, Eso le conviene a Vd. perfectamente; eso le va o cae a Vd. muy bien. *He is well suited with his place*, Está muy contento con su empleo.

Suitable [siūt'-a-bl], *a.* Conforme, proporcionado, conveniente.

Suitableness [siūt'-a-bl-nes], *s.* Conformidad, igualdad, conveniencia.

Suitably [siūt'-a-bli], *adv.* De una manera conveniente, conforme.

Suitcase [siūt'-kês], *s.* Maleta.

Suite [swit], *s* 1. Serie, continuación ordenada y sucesiva de cosas. 2. Séquito de un alto personaje; tren, acompañamiento, comitiva. *Suite of apartments*, Vivienda o habitación con varias piezas o aposentos; vivienda.

Suitor [siū'-ter], *s.* 1. Pretendiente. suplicante, el que pretende o suplica; aspirante; postulante. 2. Aman-

te, pretendiente, cortejo, el que galantea o hace la corte a una mujer. 3. Pleiteante, el que pleitea.
Sulcate, Sulcated [sʊl'-kêt, ed], *a.* Surcado, que tiene surcos largos y angostos; acanalado.
Sulfa drugs [sʊl'-fa drʊgs], *s. pl.* V. SULPHA DRUGS.
Sulfanilamide [sʊl-fa-ni'-la-maid], *s.* (Med.) Sulfanilamida.
Sulfapyridine [sʊl-fa-pi'-ri-dain], *s.* (Med.) Sulfapiridina.
Sulfate, Sulfid, Sulfur, Sulfuric, etc. *V.* SULPHATE, SULPHUR, etc.
Sulfathiazole [sʊl-fa-thai'-a-zōl], *s.* (Med.) Sulfatiazol.
Sulfonamide [sul-fen'-g-maid], *s.* Sulfonamida.
Sulk [sulk], *vn.* Estar malcontento o de mal humor; ser terco u obstinado.
Sulkiness [sʊl'-ki-nes], *s.* Mal humor, ceño; estado de la persona que refunfuña.
Sulky [sʊl'-ki], *a.* 1. Malcontento, caprichudo, regañón, áspero de genio, vinagre. 2. Obstinado, terco.
Sulky, *s.* (*pl.* SULKIES). Calesín de un solo asiento. solitario.
Sullen [sʊl'-en], *a.* 1. Malcontento; malévolo. 2. Intratable, duro de genio, berrinchudo. 3. Remolón, taciturno, cazurro.
Sullenly [sʊl'-en-li], *adv.* Ásperamente, con ceño, de mal humor; tercamente.
Sullenness [sʊl'-en-nes], *s.* 1. Ceño, enojo, berrín o berrinche, demostración de enfado; mal humor o mal genio, tristeza sombría. 2. Obstinación, terquedad, pertinacia.
Sully [sʊl'-i], *va.* Manchar, ensuciar, tachar, mancillar, ennegrecer.—*s.* Mancha.
Sulpha drugs [sʊl'-fa drʊgz], *s. pl.* Sulfonamidas.
Sulphate [sʊl'-fêt], *s.* (Quím.) Sulfato, sal de ácido sulfúrico con una base.
Sulphid, Sulphide [sʊl'-fid], *s.* Sulfuro, compuesto de azufre con un elemento o radical.
Sulphite [sʊl'-fait], *s.* Sal de ácido sulfuroso.
Sulphur [sʊl'-fur], *s.* Azufre, elemento amarillo claro, no metálico, que se halla en muchas partes en estado nativo.
Sulphurate, Sulfurate [sʊl'-fiu-rêt], *va.* 1. Blanquear, v. g. los sombreros de paja, con vapores de azufre. 2. Azufrar.
Sulphureous [sʊl-fiū'-re-us], **Sulphurous** [sʊl'-fur-us], *a.* Sulfúreo, azufroso, azufrado. que tiene azufre.
Sulphuric [sʊl-fiū'-ric], *a.* Sulfúrico, perteneciente al azufre, o procedente de él. *Sulphuric acid,* Ácido sulfúrico, líquido muy corrosivo (H_2SO_4) que se usa en las artes; aceite de vitriolo.
Sulphurwort [sʊl'-fur-wūrt], *s.* (Bot.) Servato. Debe su nombre al jugo amarillo de las raíces y en otro tiempo se consideraba como medicinal.
Sultan [sʊl'-tan], *s.* Sultán, nombre que dan los turcos a su emperador.
Sultana [sʊl-tā'-na], **Sultaness** [sʊl'-tan-es], *sf.* Sultana, la primera de las mujeres del sultán.
Sultriness [sʊl'-tri-nes], *s.* Bochorno.
Sultry [sʊl'-tri], *a.* Abochornado, caluroso, bochornoso, sin ventilación, sofocante.
Sum [sum], *s.* 1. Suma, el agregado de muchas cosas; particularmente se toma por el de dinero, y en este caso corresponde muy frecuentemente a cantidad. 2. Suma, sumario, resumen, compendio, o recopilación de alguna cosa. 3. Suma, la conclusión o substancia de alguna cosa y también su resultado. 4. Cima, lo sumo, lo último. *For a certain sum agreed upon,* Por cierta cantidad alzada.
Sum, *va.* 1. Sumar, juntar dos o más números o cantidades. 2. Sumar, recopilar, compendiar, abreviar alguna materia difusa o extensa. *To sum up,* Recapitular, resumir.
Sumac, Sumach [sū'-mac, shū'-mac], *s.* 1. (Bot.) Zumaque, cualquier arbusto o árbol del género Rhus. 2. Polvos de las hojas secas de ciertas especies de zumaque, que se emplean para curtir y teñir.
Summarily [sum'-a-ri-li], *adv.* Sumariamente, en compendio, en pocas palabras.
Summarize [sʊm'-ar-aiz], *va.* Epitomar, resumir, reducir.
Summary [sum'-a-ri], *a.* Sumario, breve, compendioso, sucinto, corto. —*s.* Sumario, resumen, compendio o suma.
Summer [sum'-er], *a.* Estival o estivo, de verano.—*s.* 1. Verano, estío. *Indian summer,* El Veranillo de San Martín, de 15 de octubre a 15 de noviembre. *Summer-house,* Cenador, glorieta de jardín. *Summer solstice,* Solsticio de verano. *Summer-time, -tide,* Estío, estación de verano. *Summer-boarder,* Veraneante. *Summer-fallow, va.* Arar en el verano y dejar en barbecho. 2. (Poét.) Año de vida, particularmente de vida alegre; período próspero.
Summer, *s.* 1. Viga solera, viga maestra. 2. Sotabanco, piedra grande sobre una columna para sostener una o más bóvedas. *Summer-tree,* Los traveseros en que descansan las vigas maestras.
Summer, *vn.* Veranear, pasar el verano.—*va.* Calentar; preservar del frío.
Summer resort, *s.* Centro de veraneo.
Summersault [sum'-er-sōlt], **Summerset** [sum'-er-set], *s.* Salto mortal.
Summit [sum'-it], *s.* Ápice, el extremo superior de una cosa, cima, punta; cima, cumbre, de un edificio, montaña, etc.
Summit conference [sum'-it cen'-fer-ens], *s.* Reunión en la cima.
Summon [sum'-un], *va.* 1. Citar, ordenar a alguno que se presente en fecha y lugar señalados. 2. Citar, notificar, requerir por auto de juez; requerir o pedir la inmediata presencia de alguien o algo, dar o servir como señal para presentarse; convocar; mandar. 3. Excitar, animar. 4. Intimar la rendición. *To summon away,* Llamar aparte, mandar alejarse. *To summon back,* Llamar, volver a llamar.
Summoner [sum'-un-er], *s.* El que cita o notifica.
Summons [sum'-unz], *s.* Citación, notificación, requerimiento; intimación; aviso o amonestación hecha con autoridad.
Summum bonum [sum'-um bō'-num], *s.* El sumo bien.
Sump [sump], *s.* 1. Sumidero, pozo perdido, pozanco, (en las minas), estanque en una salina. 2. Hoyo de albañilería cubierto de arcilla para recibir los metales fundidos. (<Holan. *somp,* pantano.)
Sumpter [sump'-ter], *s.* Caballo o mulo de carga, acémila.
Sumption [sump'-shun], *s.* Premisa mayor de un silogismo.
Sumptuary [sump'-chu-e-ri], *a.* 1. Suntario, que pertenece al arreglo, suspensión o moderación de los gastos o del lujo en las comidas y vestidos. 2. (Poco us.) Que hace las veces de una acémila.
Sumptuous [sump'-chu-us], *a.* Suntuoso, magnífico, espléndido, pomposo.
Sumptuously [sump'-chu-us-li], *adv.* Suntuosamente, con esplendor, con pompa.
Sumptuousness [sump'-chu-us-nes], *s.* Suntuosidad, magnificencia, pompa.
Sun [sun], *s.* 1. Sol, el astro que nos alumbra de día. 2. Sol, cualquier astro que es centro de un sistema planetario. 3. Sol, cualquiera cosa sumamente espléndida ó que da luz física ó moral. 4. Solana, el sitio donde el sol da de lleno. *Under the sun,* Debajo del sol, en este mundo. *The sun rises, sets,* El sol sale, se pone. *The sun is up, is down,* El sol ha salido ya, se ha puesto. *Sunbath,* Exposición del cuerpo á los rayos directos del sol; algunas veces con un fin terapéutico. *Sunproof,* Á prueba de sol. *Sun-spot,* Mácula, mancha obscura, irregular, en la cara del sol, dentro de los 35° de su ecuador.
Sun, *va.* Asolear, poner al sol, secar al sol. *To sun one's self,* Tomar el sol.
Sunbeam [sun'-bīm], *s.* Rayo de sol.
Sunbeat [sun'-bīt], *a.* Asoleado, calentado por el sol; iluminado por el sol.
Sunbird [sun'-berd], *s.* Suimanga. ave de las Indias orientales.
Sunbonnet [sun'-ben-et], *s.* Gorra ó cofia de mujer para andar al sol, especie de papalina.
Sunbright [sun'-brait], *a.* Resplandeciente como el sol.
Sunburning [sun'-būrn-ing], *s.* Quemadura del sol.
Sunburnt [sun'-būrnt], *a.* Tostado por el sol, asoleado; atezado.
§**Sunclad** [sun'-clad], *a.* Brillante, lustroso.
Sundae [sun'-dê], *s.* Helado con salsa de frutas y nueces.
Sunday [sun'-dê], *s.* Domingo, el primer día de la semana. el día del Señor. *Sunday-letter,* Letra dominical. *Sunday-school,* Escuela dominical; conjunto de los discípulos y maestros de dicha escuela.
Sunder [sun'-der], *s.* Dos, dos partes.
Sunder [sun'-der], *va.* y *vn.* Separar, apartar, dividir; romper ó romperse; separarse.
Sundew [sun'-diū], *s.* (Bot.) Rocío del sol, cualquier planta del género Drosera; notables por ser insectívoras.
Sundial [sun'-dai-al], *s.* Reloj de sol, cuadrante.
Sundown [sun'-daun], *s.* 1. Puesta del sol. *V.* SUNSET. 2. (E. U.) Sombrero de ala ancha para las mujeres.
Sundries [sun'-driz], *s. pl.* (Com.) Géneros diversos.
Sundry [sun'-dri], *a.* Varios, muchos, diversos.
Sunfast [sun'-fast], *a.* De color firme, a prueba de sol.
Sunfish [sun'-fish], *s.* 1. Ojón, pez de mar del género Mola, de cuerpo muy corto (como cortado por detrás) y forma redondeada. 2. Pez

norteamericano de agua dulce, semejante a la perca; pertenece al género Lepomis.
Sunflower [sun'-flau-gr], *s.* (Bot.) Girasol, helianto.
Sung, *pret.* y *pp.* del verbo *To* SING.
Sunglasses [sun'-glas'-ez], *s. pl.* Anteojos para el sol.
Sunhemp [sun'-hemp], *s.* (Bot.) Cáñamo de sol; especie de cáñamo de las Indias orientales.
Sunk, *pret.* y *pp.* del verbo *To* SINK
Sunlamp [sun'-lamp], *s.* Lámpara de rayos ultravioleta usada en terapéutica.
Sunless [sun'-les], *a.* Sin calor o sin sol; sombrío; sin luz, obscuro.
Sunlight [sun'-lait], *s.* La luz del sol.
Sunlike [sun'-laik], *a.* Semejante o parecido al sol; resplandeciente.
Sunny [sun'-i], *a.* 1. Resplandeciente, semejante al sol. 2. Asoleado, expuesto al sol; tostado por el sol, atezado. 3. Brillante como el sol. *Sunny day*, Día claro. 4. (Fig.) Alegre, risueño. *A sunny smile*, Una sonrisa alegre.
Sunparlor, sunporch [sun'-pār'-lər, sun'-pōrch], *s.* Solana.
Sunrise [sun'-raiz], **Sunrising** [sun'raiz-ing], *s.* 1. Salida o nacimiento del sol. *Before sunrise*, Antes de salir el sol o antes de amanecer. 2. Oriente.
Sunset [sun'-set], *s.* La puesta o el ocaso del sol. *Until sunset*, Hasta que el sol se ponga.
Sunshade [sun'-shêd], *s.* Quitasol o sombrero de anchas alas.
Sunshine [sun'-shain], *s.* 1. Solana, el sitio o paraje donde el sol da de lleno. 2. El influjo del sol; la claridad del sol. *In the sunshine*, Al sol.
Sunshiny [sun'-shain-i], *a.* Claro o resplandeciente como el sol.
Sunstroke [sun'-strōk], *s.* Insolación, congestión repentina del cerebro, a menudo con síntomas semejantes a los de la apoplejía, y causada por el calor excesivo.
Sunward [sun'-ward], *adv.* Hacia el sol.
Sunwise [sun'-waiz], *adv.* Con el sol (en su movimiento diurno).
Sup [sup], *va.* Sorber, beber a sorbos.—*vn.* Cenar.
Sup, *s.* Sorbo, bocanada de cualquiera cosa líquida.
Super- [siū' pgr]. Prefijo que en composición significa *sobre*.
Superable [siū' pgr-a-bl], *a.* Superable, que se puede vencer.
Superabound [siu-pgr-a-baund'], *vn.* Superabundar, abundar con exceso.
Superabundance [siu-pgr-a-bun'-dans], *s.* Superabundancia, lo superfluo.
Superabundant [siu-pgr-a-bun'-dant], *a.* Superabundante, superfluo.
Superabundantly [siu-pgr-a-bun'-dant-li], *adv.* Superabundantemente.
Superadd [siu-pgr-ad'], *va.* Sobreañadir, añadir con exceso.
Superaddition [siū-pgr-a-dish'-un], *s.* 1. Sobreañadidura, añadidura o adición excesiva. 2. Lo que se añade o adiciona en demasía.
Superannuate [siu-pgr-an'-yu-êt], *va.* Inhabilitar o declarar a uno inhábil para ejercer u obtener algún cargo a causa de su mucha edad; jubilar, dar retiro a una persona de mucha edad por estar imposibilitada de ejercer su cargo. *Superannuated*, *pp.* Imposibilitado, viejo, fuera de servicio; anticuado, añejo; jubilado.
Superb [siu-pgrb'], *a.* Soberbio, grande, magnífico, espléndido.
Superbly [siu-pgrb'-li], *adv.* Soberbiamente.
Supercargo [siu-pgr-cār'-go], *s.* Sobrecargo, encomendero: dícese del que se embarca en un buque de comercio como comisionado para la venta del cargamento o parte de él, por cuenta del dueño.
Supercharge [siu'-pgr-chārj], *va.* Sobrecargar, sobrealimentar.
Supercharger [siu'-pgr-charj'-gr], *s.* Compresor, sobrecargador, sobrealimentador.
Superciliary [siu-pgr-sil'-i-g-ri], *a.* Perteneciente a la ceja; situado en la sobreceja.
Supercilious [siu-pgr-sil'-i-us], *a.* Arrogante, altanero, altivo, fiero; imperioso.
Superciliousness [siu-pgr-sil'-i-us-nes], *s.* Arrogancia, altanería, altivez, orgullo, presunción.
Superconductivity [siu-pgr-con-duc-tiv'-i-ti], *s.* Superconductividad.
Superdominant [siu-pgr-dom'-i-nant], *s.* (Mús.) La nota inmediata a la dominante y más alta que ella, la sexta de la escala.
Superdreadnought [siu-pgr-dred'-nōt], *s.* Acorazado.
Supereminence [siu-pgr-em'-i-nens], **Supereminency** [siu-pgr-em'-i-nen-si], *s.* Supereminencia, la elevación o exaltación en que una persona o cosa, montaña, colina, etc., se halla respecto de otra.
Supereminent [siu-pgr-em'-i-nent], *a.* Supereminente, eminentísimo, muy elevado.
Supererogate [siu-pgr-er'-o-gêt], *vn.* Hacer más de lo que uno tiene obligación de hacer o ejecutar.
Supererogation [siu-pgr-er-o-gê'-shun], *s.* Supererogación, cosa ejecutada sobre o además de los términos de la obligación.
Superessential [siu-pgr-es-sen'-shal], *a.* Sobreesencial, que es más que esencial.
Superexcellent [siu-pgr-ec'-sel-ent], *a.* Sobreexcelente, muy excelente.
Superfetate [siu-pgr-fi'-têt], *vn.* Concebir la hembra estando preñada.
Superfetation [siu-pgr-fg-tê'-shun], *s.* Superfetación, la segunda preñez en la hembra durando la primera.
Superficial [siu-pgr-fish'-al], *a.* 1. Superficial, que toca o pertenece a la superficie, está o se queda en ella. 2. Superficial, aparente, sin solidez ni substancia, insubstancial.
Superficiality [siu-pgr-fish-i-al'-i-ti], **Superficialness** [siu-pgr-fish'-al-nes], *s.* Superficialidad, calidad de superficial.
Superficially [siu-pgr-fish'-al-i], *adv.* Superficialmente, ligeramente, por encima.
Superficiary [siu-pgr-fish'-i-g-ri], *s.* El que edifica una casa sobre terreno de otro y paga el censo, que en estilo forense se llama superficionario.
Superficies [siu-pgr-fish'-i-iz], *s.* Superficie, la parte externa o exterior de los cuerpos o su área. (Lat.)
Superfine [siū'-pgr-fain], *a.* Superfino.—*s.* El paño superfino o más fino.
Superfineness [siu-pgr-fain'-nes], *s.* La calidad de superfino.
Superfluous [siu-pgr' flu-us], *a.* Superfluo, que está demás, sobrante.
Superfluousness [siu-pgr'-flu-us-nes], **Superfluity** [siu-pgr-flū'-i-ti], *s.* 1. Superfluidad, demasía. 2. Superfluidad, lo superfluo o lo que está demás.
Superflux [siu'-pgr-flux], *s.* Superfluidad, lo superfluo.
Superheat [siu-pgr-hit'], *va.* Recalentar.
Superheterodyne [siu-pgr-het'-gr-o-dain], *s.* y *a.* (Radio) Superheterodino.
Superhighway [siu'-pgr-hai'-wê], *s.* Autopista.
Superhuman [siu-pgr-hiū'-man], *a.* Sobrehumano.
Superimpose [siu-pgr-im-pōz'], *va.* Sobreponer, poner encima de otra cosa.
Superimposition [siu-pgr-im-po-zish'-un], *s.* Superposición, colocación de una cosa encima de otra.
Superincumbent [siu-pgr-in-cum'-bent], *a.* Que está colocado en la superficie; que yace encima de otra cosa.
Superinduce [siu-pgr-in-diūs'], *va.* Sobreañadir, añadir con exceso o sobre lo que se había añadido antes; producir o ser causa de algo como adición a otra cosa que existía anteriormente.
Superinduction [siu-pgr-in-duc'-shun], *s.* El acto de sobreañadir.
Superinjection [siu-pgr-in-jec'-shun], *s.* Inyección repetida o que se hace inmediatamente después de otra.
Superintend [siu-pgr-in-tend'], *va.* Vigilar, celar, cuidar solícitamente; dirigir.
Superintendence [siu-pgr-in-tend'-ens], **Superintendency** [siu-pgr-in-ten'-den-si], *s.* Superintendencia.
Superintendent [siu-pgr-in-tend'-ent], *s.* Superintendente, la persona a cuyo cargo está la dirección y cuidado de alguna cosa.
Superior [siu-pi'-ri-gr], *a.* 1. Superior, que está más alto o en lugar más prominente con respecto a otra cosa. 2. Superior, que es más excelente o digno que otra cosa. 3. Superior, que excede a otra cosa en vigor, virtud, etc.—*s.* Superior, la persona que manda, gobierna o dirige a otras.
Superiority [siu-pi-ri-or'-i-ti], *s.* 1. Superioridad, preeminencia, excelencia. 2. Superioridad, autoridad, dominio.
Superlative [siu-pgr'-la-tiv], *a.* Superlativo, lo más grande o excelente en su clase.
Superlatively [siu-pgr'-la-tiv-li], *adv.* Superlativamente, en grado superlativo, extremadamente, en sumo grado.
Superlunar [siu-pgr-lū'-nar], *a.* (Poco us.) Que está encima de la luna o más arriba que ella.
Superman [siu'-pgr-man], *s.* Superhombre.
Supermarket [siu'-pgr-mār'-ket], *s.* Supermercado.
Supernatural [siu-pgr-nach'-u-ral o nat'-yu-ral], *a.* Sobrenatural, que excede o pasa los términos de la naturaleza.
Supernaturally [siu-pgr-nach'-u-ral-i], *adv.* Sobrenaturalmente.
Supernaturalness [siu-pgr-nach'-u-ral-nes], *s.* Calidad de sobrenatural.
Supernumerary [siu-pgr-niū' mgr-g-ri], *a.* Supernumerario, que está sobre el número señalado; suplementario, superfluo.—*s.* Supernumerario; figurante, comparsa (de teatro); cosa suplementaria.
Superpose [siu-pgr-pōz'], *va.* Sobreponer, superponer, colocar sobre otra

cosa; en geometría, suponer que una figura está sobrepuesta a otra.
Superposition [siu-pęr-po-zish'-un], *s.* Superposición, acción de sobreponer; calidad de sobrepuesto.
Superpower [siu'-pęr-pau-ęr], *s.* Superpotencia.
Superreflection [siu-pęr-rę-flec'-shun], *s.* Reflexión o inflexión de un rayo de luz o de una imagen que ya ha sido reflejada.
Superroyal [siu-pęr-rei'-al], *s.* Forma de papel de 20 por 28 pulgadas para escribir y de 22 por 28 para imprenta; en Inglaterra de 19½ por 27½.
Supersaliency [siu-pęr-sé'-li-en-si], *s.* El acto de saltar encima de alguna cosa.
Supersaturate [siu-pęr-sat'-yu-ręt], *va.* Supersaturar.
Superscribe [siu-pęr-scraib'], *va.* Sobreescribir, escribir o poner un letrero en alguna cosa; poner sobreescrito a una carta.
Superscript [siu'-pęr-script], *s.* Carácter sobrescrito.
Superscription [siu-pęr-scrip'-shun], *s.* 1. La acción de sobreescribir. 2. Sobreescrito.
Supersede [siu-pęr-sid'], *va.* Sobreseer, hacer diferir o suspender; invalidar, hacer inútil o vana alguna cosa; impedir.
Supersedeas [siu-pęr-sí'-de-as], *s.* (For.) El auto jurídico en que se manda sobreseer o desistir de algún proceso legal.
Superserviceable [siu-pęr-sęr'-vis-a-bl], *a.* Demasiado servicial, excesivamente oficioso.
Supersession [siu-pęr-sesh'-un], *s.* Sobreseimiento; anulación.
Supersonic [siu-pęr-son'-ic], *a.* Supersónico.
Superstition [siu-pęr-stish'-un], *s.* 1. Superstición, modo excesivo, indiscreto o vano en las prácticas de piedad o del culto religioso. 2. Superstición, culto que se da a quien no se debe o que se da de un modo indebido. 3. Superstición, nimia exactitud o esmero vano en el cumplimiento y observancia de algunas cosas, sobre todo en la moral.
Superstitious [siu-pęr-stish'-us], *a.* Supersticioso; nimiamente escrupuloso.
Superstitiously [siu-pęr-stish'-us-li], *adv.* Supersticiosamente.
Superstitiousness [siu-pęr-stish'-us-nes], *s.* Superstición, calidad de supersticioso.
Superstructure [siu-pęr-struc'-chur], *s.* Superestructura.
Supervene [siu-pęr-vín'], *vn.* Sobrevenir, supervenir, acaecer o suceder; seguir inmediatamente a otra cosa.
Supervenient [siu-pęr-ví'-ni-ent], *a.* Superveniente, añadido, adicional.
Supervention [siu-pęr-ven'-shun], *s.* Supervención.
Supervise [siu-pęr-vaiz'], *va.* Inspeccionar, revistar, vigilar o celar por incumbencia u oficio la ejecución de una cosa.
Supervision [siu-pęr-vizh'-un], *s.* Superintendencia.
Supervisor [siu-pęr-vai'-zęr], *s.* 1. Sobrestante, superintendente, inspector. 2. (E. U.) Funcionario de una municipalidad que tiene parte en la gestión administrativa de la misma. *Board of Supervisors,* La junta administrativa de una ciudad o de un condado.
Supination [siu-pi-né'-shun], *s.* 1. La situación o posición del que está echado boca arriba. 2. Supinación, el movimiento de volver la palma de la mano hacia arriba.
Supine [siu-pain'], *a.* 1. Supino, que está echado boca arriba. 2. Supina: aplícase a la ignorancia que procede de negligencia o descuido en aprender lo que se puede y debe saber. 3. Negligente, indolente, descuidado.
Supine [siú'-pain], *s.* (Gram.) Supino, una de las partes de la conjugación del verbo latino.
Supinely [siu-pain'-li], *adv.* Boca arriba; descuidadamente, con negligencia.
Supineness [siu-pain'-nes], †**Supinity** [siu-pin'-i-ti], *s.* 1. La situación o postura del que está echado boca arriba. 2. Descuido, negligencia, dejadez.
Supper [sup'-ęr], *s.* Cena, el alimento que se toma por la noche; también, banquete. *The Lord's Supper,* La última cena o la institución de la Eucaristía.
Supperless [sup'-ęr-les], *a.* Sin cenar.
Supper-time [sup'-ęr-taim], *s.* La hora de cenar.
Supping [sup'-ing], *s.* El acto de sorber; el acto de cenar.
Supplant [sup-plant'], *va.* 1. Suplantar, derribar a uno de su empleo, fortuna, favor o valimiento para ponerse en su lugar y alzarse con lo que el otro goza o para instalar a otro en su lugar. 2. Desbancar a uno de un puesto. 3. Dar una zancadilla.
Supplanter [sup-plant'-ęr], *s.* Suplantador, el que suplanta a otro.
Supplanting [sup-plant'-ing], *s.* Suplantación, la acción y efecto de suplantar.
Supple [sup'-l], *a.* 1. Flexible, manejable, que se deja doblar fácilmente. 2. Flexible, blando, dócil, obediente, deferente. 3. Adulatorio, lisonjero.
Supple, *va.* y *vn.* 1. Hacer flexible y manejable alguna cosa. 2. Hacer dócil u obediente a una persona. 3. Ablandarse, hacerse flexible.
Supplement [sup'-lę-męnt], *s.* 1. Suplemento. *Supplement of a newspaper,* Alcance, suplemento. 2. El ángulo que se añade a otro para formar dos ángulos rectos.
Supplemental [sup-lę-ment'-al], **Supplementary** [sup-lę-ment'-a-ri], *a.* 1. Suplementario, suplemental; que suple o puede suplir a otra cosa; adicional. 2. Suplementario, dícese del ángulo que sumado con otro completa 180 grados.
Suppleness [sup'-l-nes], *s.* Flexibilidad, blandura; docilidad, condescendencia.
Suppliant [sup'-li-ant], *a.* Deprecatorio; humilde, rendido, postrado. —*s.* Suplicante, el que suplica.
Suppliant, Supplicant [sup'-li-cant], *s.* Suplicante, en un pedimento o memorial.
Supplicate [sup'-li-kêt], *va.* Suplicar, rogar, pedir.
Supplication [sup-li-ké'-shun], *s.* Súplica, suplicación, petición, ruego.
Supplicatory [sup'-li-ca-to-ri], *a.* Que expresa súplica o ruego.
Supply [sup-plai'], *va.* 1. Suplir, completar, acabalar, integrar o llenar lo que falta en alguna cosa. 2. Surtir, abastecer, proveer; suministrar, proporcionar, dar. 3. Suplir, poner o ponerse una persona o una cosa en el lugar que otra ocupaba o había de ocupar.
Supply, *s.* 1. Provisión, abastecimiento, surtido; conjunto de cosas necesarias para un objeto. 2. Cantidad suficiente para un uso dado; acopio de provisiones. 3. Substituto, beneficiado temporal. 4. *pl.* Pertrechos, materiales, víveres, enseres. *To be in want of supplies,* Carecer de provisiones. *Demand and supply,* Demanda y oferta o existencia (en economía política).
Support [sup-pōrt'], *va.* 1. Sostener, mantener, impedir la caída de algo, servir de apoyo; apoyar (el peso de). 2. Proveer, suministrar fondos. 3. Sostener, v.g. un trato o diálogo. 4. Soportar, sufrir, tolerar. 5. Asistir, amparar, ayudar. 6. Defender, atestiguar, probar, demostrar. 7. (Teatro) Hacer un papel subordinado a otro; hacer un papel. *To support a family,* Mantener a una familia. *To support one's self,* Mantenerse, ganarse la vida.
Support, *s.* 1. Sostén, el acto de sostener y aquello con que se sostiene. 2. Apoyo, protección. 3. Sustento, lo necesario para vivir. *In support of,* En favor de, en apoyo de; para sostener, apoyar, etc. *Point of support,* Punto de apoyo.
Supportable [sup-pōrt'-a-bl], *a.* Soportable, tolerable, llevadero; sostenible.
Supportableness [sup-pōrt'-a-bl-nes], *s.* La propiedad o calidad que hace soportable o llevadera alguna cosa.
Supportably [sup-pōrt'-a-bli], *adv.* De una manera tolerable, soportable.
Supporter [sup-pōrt'-ęr], *s.* 1. Sostenimiento, sustentáculo. 2. Apoyo, amparo, columna. 3. Sosteniente, sostenedor. 4. Defensor, protector. 5. (Her.) Soporte, cada una de las figuras de animales que sostienen el escudo de armas; se usa casi siempre en plural. 6. (Arq.) Atlante o telamón.
Supposable [sup-pōz'-a-bl], *a.* Que se puede suponer o que es de suponer; no inconcebible.
Supposal [sup-pōz'-al], *s.* Suposición.
Supposableness [sup-pōz'-a-bl-nes], *s.* La capacidad de poderse suponer una cosa; probabilidad.
Suppose [sup-pōz'], *va.* 1. Suponer, dar por sentada alguna cosa sin prueba ni autoridad. 2. Suponer, fingir o presuponer alguna cosa. 3. Imaginar algo; creer sin examen. *It is to be supposed,* Es de creer o se puede suponer. *Supposing it to be true,* Suponiendo que sea esto verdad. *Supposing that,* Dado caso que.
Supposer [sup-pōz'-ęr], *s.* Suponedor.
Supposition [sup-o-zish'-un], *s.* Suposición, hipótesis.
Suppositional [sup-o-zish'-un-al], *a.* Hipotético, supositivo, que se funda en suposición o hipótesis.
Supposititious [sup-pez-i-tish'-us], *a.* 1. Supuesto, falso, ilegítimo, fingido. 2. Supuesto, imaginado.
Supposititiousness [sup-pez-i-tish'-us-nes], *s.* Suposición, falsedad; substitución de una cosa por otra.
Suppositive [sup-pez'-i-tiv], *a.* Supuesto.
Suppositively [sup-pez'-i-tiv-li], *adv.* En suposición.
Suppository [sup-pez'-i-to-ri], *s.* Supositorio, cala; preparación sólida y medicinal para ser introducida en algún conducto, cavidad u órgano interno.

Suppress [sup-pres'], *va.* 1. Suprimir, detener, estorbar o impedir el curso de alguna cosa. 2. Suprimir, ocultar, no explicar lo que se debe en alguna materia, omitir o callar de propósito. 3. Destruir.

Suppression [sup-presh'-un], *s.* 1. Supresión; represión, acción de reprimir. 2. (Med.) Suspensión de una secreción; falta de secreción, a diferencia de retención.

Suppressive [sup-pres'-iv], *a.* Represivo, que tiende a reprimir o que puede reprimir; que suprime o ahoga.

Suppressor [sup-pres'-ẹr], *s.* Supresor, el que suprime.

Suppurate [sup'-yu-rêt], *va.* Supurar, criar pus o materia alguna herida o llaga.—*vn.* Supurar, echar pus o materia.

Suppuration [sup-yu-rê'-shun], *s.* Supuración, la acción y efecto de supurar.

Suppurative [sup'-yu-ra-tiv], *a.* Supurativo, que hace supurar.

Supralapsarian [siu-pra-lap-sê'-ri-an], *a.* (Poco us.) Lo sucedido antes de la caída del hombre.

Supramaxillary [siu-pra-max'-il-ẹ-ri], *a.* y *s.* Supramaxilar, relativo a la maxila o quijada superior.

Supramundane [siu-pra-mun'-dên], *a.* Sobrenatural, superior a las cosas terrenales.

Supranational [siu-pra-nash'-un-al], *a.* Supranacional.

Suprarenal [siu-pra-rí'-nal], *a.* Suprarenal, que está colocado encima de los riñones.

Supremacy [siu-prem'-a-si], *s.* Supremacía, autoridad suprema, estado de supremo.

Supreme [siu-prîm'], *a.* Supremo, lo más elevado, lo más grande.

Supremely [siu-prîm'-li], *adv.* Supremamente, en el más alto grado.

Sura [sū'-ra], *s.* Sura, capítulo del Corán.

Surah [sū'-ra o siū'-ra], *s.* Tela fina y cruzada de seda de la India.

Sural [siū'-ral], *a.* Sural, que pertenece a la pantorrilla.

Surbase [sūr'-bês], *s.* 1. Cornisa, moldura sobre un pedestal. 2. Moldura o borde por encima de una base.

Surcease [sūr-sís'], *vn.* Cesar, suspenderse; acabarse enteramente.

Surcease, *s.* (Ant.) Cesación.

Surcharge [sūr-chārj'], *s.* 1. Sobrecarga, sobrepeso, más carga. 2. Sobrecarga, recargo, nuevo gravamen.

Surcharge, *va.* Sobrecargar, recargar, cargar con exceso.

Surd [sūrd], *a.* y *s.* 1. Sordo, no vocal ni sonante; producido por los órganos vocales sin voz ni tono; por ejemplo las consonantes *p*, *t*, *s*, o *k*. opuesto a sonante. 2. (Mat.) Irracional, que no puede ser expresado en números racionales; v. g. la raíz cuadrada de dos.

Sure [shūr], *a.* 1. Seguro, cierto, indudable, hablando de noticias o hechos. 2. Seguro, infalible, efectivo, hablando de medios, recursos, remedios, etc. 3. Seguro, firme, sentado, hablando del paso, de la mano, del pulso, etc. 4. Seguro, firme, constante, estable, que no está en peligro de faltar o de caerse. *To be sure,* Seguramente, sin duda; ya se ve. *To be sure of foot,* Tener el pie o paso seguro. *To be sure to,* No faltar, no carecer. *To make sure,* Asegurar, cerciorar. *To make sure of,* Asegurarse de, apoderarse de; contar con o sobre alguien.—*adv.* (Fam. o des.) Ciertamente, indudablemente, sin duda alguna. *Sure enough,* A buen seguro, con certeza.

Sure-footed [shūr'-fut-ed], *a.* Dícese del animal que no tropieza y de los afectos de ánimo que obran sin interrupción.

Surely [shūr'-li], *adv.* Ciertamente, seguramente, sin duda. Úsase generalmente de un modo expletivo para afirmar más.

Sureness [shūr'-nes], *s.* Certeza, seguridad. *V.* SURETY.

Surety [shūr'-ti], *s.* 1. Seguridad, exención de riesgo o el estado de las cosas que las hace firmes, seguras y libres de todo riesgo o peligro. 2. Seguridad, certeza que se tiene de que una cosa no faltará o no engañará. 3. Seguridad, fianza, responsabilidad de daños u obligación a favor de alguno, regularmente en materia de intereses. 4. Seguridad o caución que se da o se toma. 5. Fiador, obligado, el que se obliga por otro. *Of a surety,* De seguro, como cosa cierta. *To be surety for,* Ser fiador, salir garante; responder de alguien o algo.

Suretyship [shūr'-ti-ship], *s.* Seguridad, fianza u obligación de indemnidad en favor de alguno.

Surf [sūrf], *s.* Marejada; olaje, embate del mar al romper sobre la playa. (Variación de *sough.*)

Surface [sūr'-fês], *va.* Poner o hacer una superficie sobre algo; allanar, alisar, igualar.—*s.* Superficie, sobrefaz, la parte externa o exterior de alguna cosa. *To skim the surface of,* Rozar la superficie; correr de prisa y superficialmente.

Surfacer [sūr'-fa-sẹr], *s.* 1. Cepillo mecánico para igualar superficies. 2. El que iguala o allana una superficie, como con un cepillo mecánico.

Surfboard [sūrf'-bōrd], *s.* Tabla para flotar sobre la rompiente.

Surfboat [sūrf'-bōt], *s.* Lancha para una marejada fuerte.

Surfeit [sūr'-fit], *va.* y *vn.* 1. Ahitar, hartar, saciar; atracar, sobrecargar de alimentos. 2. Saciar o satisfacer el ánimo. 3. Ahitarse, saciarse, hartarse de comida o bebida.

Surfeit, *s.* Ahito, empacho, exceso en comer y beber; indigestión, embarazo gástrico o del estómago.

Surfeiter [sūr'-fit-ẹr], *s.* Glotón, el que come o bebe con exceso.

Surge [sūrj], *s.* Olaje, oleada; prolongadas ondulaciones del mar: el acto de levantarse y moverse las olas.

Surge, *vn.* Agitarse o embravecerse el mar; levantarse e hincharse, y moverse hacia adelante las olas.—*va.* Hacer mover hacia adelante con movimiento de expansión, v. g. las olas, las ondas sonoras, etc. *To surge the capstan,* Lascar el cabrestante.

Surgeon [sūr'-jun], *s.* 1. Cirujano. 2. Médico del ejército o la armada. *Surgeon-dentist,* Cirujano dentista. *Surgeon-general,* En los E. U., médico mayor, jefe de sanidad militar o naval, con grado equivalente al de general de ejército.

Surgery [sūr'-jẹr-i], *s.* Cirugía.

Surgical [sūr'-ji-cal], *a.* Quirúrgico, que pertenece a la cirugía.

Surgy [sūr'-ji], *a.* Agitado o embravecido como el mar.

Surliness [sūr'-li-nes], *s.* Grosería, mal genio, mal humor; entono.

Surloin [sūr'-loin], *s.* Solomillo. *V.* SIRLOIN. (Etimológicamente *surloin* debería ser la forma preferible, como más exacta.)

Surly [sūr-li], *a.* 1. Arisco, insolente; áspero de genio; impertinente. 2. Grosero, tosco, rudo, v. g. una respuesta. 3. Furioso, tempestuoso, p. ej. el tiempo. *A surly dog,* Un perro arisco.

Surmise [sūr-maiz'], *va.* Conjeturar, suponer, imaginar alguna cosa sin fundamento o razón suficiente.

Surmise, *s.* 1. Conjetura, imaginación; aprensión falsa, juicio o discurso sin fundamento; noción imperfecta. 2. Indirectas, rumores.

Surmount [sūr-maunt'], *va.* 1. Vencer, superar, a fuerza de voluntad. 2. Sobrepujar, pasar por encima de una cosa; levantarse o elevarse sobre ella. 3. Pasar, sobrepujar.

Surmountable [sūr-maunt'-a-bl], *a.* Vencible, superable.

Surmullet [sūr-mul'-et], *s.* Barbo marino, pez del género Mullus (Mullus surmerletus).

Surname [sūr'-nêm], *s.* 1. Apellido, el nombre o sobrenombre de la familia. 2. Renombre o epíteto que se añade al nombre de una persona.

Surname [sūr-nêm'], *va.* Apellidar, nombrar, denominar, llamar con algún renombre o título a una persona.

Surpass [sūr-pɑs'], *va.* Sobresalir, sobrepujar, superar, exceder.

Surpassing [sūr-pɑs'-ing], *a.* Sobresaliente, superior, que sobrepuja a los demás; excelente.

Surplice [sūr'-plis], *s.* Sobrepelliz, vestidura de lienzo que usa el clero en las funciones de su ministerio.

Surpliced [sūr'-plist], *a.* Con sobrepelliz, que lleva sobrepelliz.

Surplus, Surplusage [sūr'-plus, ẹj], *s.* Sobrante, demasía, sobras, lo que sobra de alguna cosa.

Surplus value [sūr'-plus val'-yu], *s.* Plusvalía.

Surprise [sūr-praiz'], **Surprisal** [sūr-prai'-zal], *s.* 1. Sorpresa, la acción por la cual se sorprende. 2. Estado de sorpresa; admiración, asombro, emoción producida por algo que sucede súbitamente; ataque repentino.

Surprise, *va.* 1. Sorprender, sobrecoger, coger descuidado o de improviso. 2. Sorprender, dejar admirado o maravillado.

Surprising [sūr-praiz'-ing], *a.* Maravilloso, asombroso, admirable, que causa sorpresa.

Surprisingly [sūr-praiz'-ing-li], *adv.* Pasmosamente, maravillosamente, de un modo admirable.

Surrealism [sẹr-rí'-al-izm], *s.* Surrealismo.

Surrebut [sūr-rẹ-but'], *vn.* (For.) Triplicar; replicar por tercera vez.

Surrebutter [sūr-rẹ-būt'-ẹr], *s.* (For.) Tríplica; la respuesta del demandante a la contrarréplica del demandado.

Surrejoinder [sur-rẹ-join'-dẹr], *s.* (For.) La respuesta que se da a la réplica del contrario.

Surrender [sur-ren'-dẹr], *va.* 1. Rendir, entregar a otro, y particularmente poner en manos del enemigo. 2. Ceder, traspasar, renunciar a, abandonar, entregar. 3. Renunciar a favor de otro.—*vn.* Ceder, rendirse, entregarse.

Surrender, *s.* 1. Rendición, entrega. 2. Renuncia o dejación voluntaria; abandono, sumisión. 3. (For.) Cesión de bienes. *The surrender of a right*, La renuncia de un derecho.
Surreptitious [sur-rep-tish'-us], *a.* Subrepticio, hecho oculta o fraudulentamente.
Surreptitiously [sur-rep-tish'-us-li], *adv.* Subrepticiamente, fraudulentamente.
Surrey [sur'-e̱], *s.* (E. U.) Vehículo ligero para paseo; tiene comúnmente dos asientos y algunas veces capota.
Surrogate [sur'-o-gêt], *va.* Subrogar, substituir o poner una persona o cosa en lugar de otra.
Surrogate, *s.* 1. Subrogado, delegado de un juez eclesiástico. 2. (Local, E. U.) (For.) Juez de testamentarías, o de bienes de difuntos o intestados.
Surround [sur-raund'], *va.* 1. Circundar, cercar, rodear. 2. Rodear, circundar, constituir una cerca o borde alrededor de algo; ceñir. 3. Asediar, v. g. una plaza o fortaleza.
Surrounding [sur-raund'-ing], *s.* 1. *pl.* Alrededores, contornos o cualquiera parte de ellos. 2. El acto del que rodea o ciñe.
Surtax [sūr'-tax], *s.* Impuesto adicional.
Surtout [sūr-tūt'], *s.* Sobretodo ajustado al cuerpo. (Fr.)
Surveillance [sūr-vêl'-yans], *s.* Vigilancia, acción de vigilar; estado del que se halla vigilado. (Fr.)
Survey [sūr-vê'], *va.* 1. Apear, acotar, medir o deslindar las tierras y heredades. 2. Mirar, inspeccionar o reconocer desde lo alto. 3. Inspeccionar, examinar, vigilar o celar por incumbencia u oficio los edificios, etc., y tasarlos. 4. Mirar una cosa examinándola. *To survey a coast*, (Mar.) Reconocer una costa y levantar el plano de ella.
Survey [sūr'-vê], *s.* 1. Apeo o deslinde de tierras o heredades; también, un departamento o cuerpo para practicar la agrimensura; medición. 2. Perspectiva, vista o aspecto de muchos objetos juntos mirados de lejos. 3. Reconocimiento, inspección, examen, vista.
Surveying [sūr-vê'-ing], *s.* Agrimensura, arte de medir terrenos y levantar planos.
Surveyor [sūr-vê'-e̱r], *s.* 1. Agrimensor, apeador, medidor de tierras. 2. Sobrestante, superintendente. 3. Perito. *Surveyor of the navy*, (Mar.) Inspector de marina. *Surveyor of the custom-house*, Vista de la aduana.
Surveyorship [sūr-vê'-er-ship], *s.* El empleo de agrimensor, inspector o visitador.
Survival [sūr-vai'-val], *s.* 1. Supervivencia, la acción de sobrevivir. 2. Persona o cosa que sobrevive; costumbre que ha durado mucho más tiempo que las condiciones que la originaron. *Survival of the fittest*, (Biol.) La supervivencia de los más idóneos; la conservación y propagación de ciertas formas favorecidas en la lucha por la existencia (teoría de la evolución).
Survive [sūr-vaiv'], *vn.* 1. Sobrevivir, vivir después de muerto otro. 2. Vivir o durar una cosa más que otra.
Survivor o **Surviver** [sūr-vai'-ve̱r], *s.* El que sobrevive á otro ó vive después de su muerte.
Survivorship [sūr-vai'-ve̱r-ship], *s.* Supervivencia, la acción y efecto de sobrevivir.
Susceptibility [sus-sep-ti-bil'-i-ti], *s.* Susceptibilidad, la disposición a recibir las impresiones.
Susceptible [sus-sep'-ti-bl], *a.* 1. Susceptible, capaz de recibir o dispuesto a admitir en sí. 2. Sensible, que recibe fácilmente las impresiones morales; que se conmueve fácilmente, impresionable. *He is very susceptible*, (Fam.) Es muy enamorado.
Susceptibly [sus-sep'-ti-bli], *adv.* De una manera susceptible.
Susceptive [sus-sep'-tiv], *a.* Susceptivo, susceptible.
Suspect [sus-pect'], *va.* y *vn.* 1. Imaginar la existencia de algo; conjeturar, suponer, tener una opinión sin certidumbre. 2. Recelar; desconfiar de; inferir la culpa posible de una persona sin pruebas, sin razón suficiente. 3. Sospechar, formar o tener sospecha; tener por sospechoso.
Suspect, *s.* Persona sospechada de un delito; persona vigilada como sospechosa.
Suspectedly [sus-pect'-ed-li], *adv.* De una manera sospechosa; de manera que excita las sospechas.
Suspend [sus-pend'], *va.* 1. Suspender, colgar, poner pendiente una cosa en el aire. 2. Suspender, interrumpir, cesar, aplazar; detener o parar por algún tiempo la ejecución de una cosa. 3. Suspender, privar temporalmente a uno del ejercicio de su empleo o ministerio. 4. Hacer depender.—*vn.* (Com.) Suspender pagos.
Suspender [sus-pend'-e̱r], *s.* El o lo que suspende; cada uno de los tirantes del pantalón.
Suspense [sus-pens'], *s.* 1. Suspensión, duda o detención en algún movimiento del ánimo, incertidumbre. 2. Suspensión, detención, parada o interrupción.—*a.* (Poco us.) 1. Suspenso, parado, detenido. 2. Suspenso, irresuelto, irresoluto.
Suspension [sus-pen'-shun], *s.* Suspensión, acción de suspender; estado de lo que se halla suspendido; (Quím.) estado de una substancia que permanece en un líquido sin precipitarse; detención; cesación temporal; duda. *Suspension bridge*, Puente colgante o de suspensión. *Suspension of hostilities*, Suspensión de hostilidades, armisticio.
Suspensory [sus-pen'-so-ri], *a.* Suspensorio, que sirve para suspender. —*s.* Suspensorio, vendaje para sostener el escroto.
Suspicion [sus-pish'-un], *s.* 1. Sospecha, recelo, desconfianza; conjetura. 2. (Fam.) Pizca, grano, brizna.
Suspicious [sus-pish'-us], *a.* Suspicaz, desconfiado, receloso; sospechoso.
Suspiciously [sus-pish'-us-li], *adv.* Sospechosamente, con sospecha, de un modo sospechoso.
Suspiciousness [sus-pish'-us-nes], *s.* Recelo, suspicacia, desconfianza, inclinación a sospechar.
Suspiration [sus-pi-ré'-shun], *s.* (Des. o poét.) Suspiro.
Suspire [sus-pair'], *vn.* (Poét. o des.) 1. Suspirar, dar suspiros. 2. Respirar.
Sustain [sus-tên'], *va.* 1. Sostener, sustentar o mantener alguna cosa, llevar, soportar; (Mús.) prolongar con la misma fuerza. 2. Sostener, apoyar, afianzar. 3. Sostener, mantener o defender; establecer, probar. 4. Sostener, sustentar o dar lo necesario para mantenerse. 5. Sostener, ayudar, patrocinar. 6. Sostener, sufrir, tolerar, aguantar. *To sustain a loss*, Perder algo, sufrir una pérdida.
Sustainable [sus-tên'-a-bl], *a.* Sostenible, que se puede sostener; defendible, que se puede defender.
Sustainer [sus-tên'-e̱r], *s.* 1. Sostenedor, defensor, protector. 2. El que sufre.
Sustenance [sus'-ti-nans], *s.* Sostenimiento, sustento, mantenimiento; alimentos, víveres, manutención, subsistencia.
Sustentation [sus-ten-tê'-shun], *s.* 1. Sostenimiento, sustentación, sustentamiento. 2. Mantenimiento, sustento, y el acto de mantenerse o sustentarse.
Susurration [siu-sur-ê'-shun], *s.* Susurro.
Sutler [sut'-le̱r], *s.* Vivandero, vivandera (o cantinera); el o la que sigue a las tropas y les vende provisiones y licores.
Suttee [sut'-ti], *s.* Antigua costumbre que obligaba a la viuda india a sacrificarse en la misma hoguera que consumía el cadáver de su marido.
Suttle [sut'-l], *a.* y *s.* Neto; peso limpio.
Sutural [siū'-chur-al], *a.* Sutural, perteneciente a una sutura o colocado en ella.
Suture [siū'-chur], *s.* 1. Sutura, costura; unión de los huesos del cráneo; (Bot.) línea poco saliente, rafe, que a menudo indica la línea de dehiscencia de una flor o un pericarpio. 2. Sutura, acción de coser los labios de una herida para que se unan; también el hilo u otro material que se emplea en esta operación.
Suzerain [siū'-ze̱-rên], *s.* Persona revestida de suprema autoridad. (Fr.)
Svelte [sfelt], *a.* 1. Esbelto. 2. Airoso, elegante. 3. Aliñado.
Swab [sweb], *s.* Instrumento que consta de una substancia blanda y absorbente al extremo de un mango; se emplea para limpiar la boca de un paciente, el alma de un cañón, etc. (Mar.) Lampazo, estropajo grande hecho de filáciga.
Swab, *va.* Fregar, limpiar; (Mar.) lampacear, limpiar con lampazo.
Swabber [sweb'-e̱r], *s.* Paje de escoba, galopín.
Swaddle [swed'-l], *va.* Fajar, rodear, ceñir o envolver con fajas; generalmente significa envolver o fajar una criatura en pañales.
Swaddle, *s.* Faja.
Swaddling-band [swed'-ling-band], **Swaddling-cloth** [swed'-ling-clōth], *s.* Mantilla, pañal, envoltura de niños.
Swag [swag], *vn.* 1. Colgar, inclinarse alguna cosa hacia abajo por su propio peso. 2. Fachendear, echar plantas, echarla de bravo, de majo, de grande, de ingenio.
Swage [swêj], *va.* Estampar, dar figura al metal con una matriz.—*s.* Herramienta para hacer molduras en las fajas de hierro. *Swage-block*, Dicha herramienta; variedad de yunque.
Swagger [swag'-e̱r], *vn.* Baladronear, hacer o decir baladronadas; echarlas de valiente.

Swaggerer [swag'-ęr-ęr], *s.* Jaquetón, jaque, valentón, fanfarrón, baladrón.
Swaggy [swag'-i], *a.* Colgante, pendiente, que cuelga o está suspenso.
Swain [swên], *s.* Zagal, joven aldeano, pastorcillo; amante, enamorado.
†**Swale** [swêl], *vn.* *V.* SWEAL.
Swale, *s.* 1. Terreno bajo y pantanoso en ciertas estaciones. 2. (Prov. Ingl.) Sitio al abrigo del sol.
Swallow [swel'-ō], *s.* 1. (Orn.) Golondrino, golondrina, pájaro de la familia de los hirundínidos. 2. Vencejo, avión. *Swallow-tail*, Algo que por su forma se parece a la cola de la golondrina; cola de milano, especie de espiga de ensambladura. *Swallow-tailed coat*, Frac.
Swallow, *va.* 1. Tragar, deglutir, engullir, hacer pasar alguna cosa por el tragadero. 2. Recibir o hacer desaparecer; tragar; se usa comúnmente con *up*. 3. Tragar, recibir o creer alguna cosa de ligero y sin examinarla. 4. Soportar con paciencia y sumisión. 5. Retractar, retirar, desdecir. *To swallow up*, Tragar; absorber; sumir, precipitar como en un abismo; apropiar o hacer propia alguna cosa. *To swallow an insult*, Tolerar un ultraje.—*s.* 1. Bocado, trago, lo que se traga de una vez. 2. El acto de tragar, deglución. 3. Tragadero esófago. 4. Abismo, sima; agujero de un sumidero.
Swam [swam], *pret.* del verbo *To* SWIM.
Swamp [swemp], *s.* Pantano, terreno encharcado; sitio bajo y húmedo.
Swamp, *va.* 1. Sumergir, cubrir de agua; echar a pique un barco; hacer zozobrar. 2. Meter en terreno pantanoso; encharcar; de aquí, sumergir en dificultades, confundir en un tropel; arruinar, hundir.—*vn.* Caer en grandes dificultades, empantanarse, irse a pique; zozobrar.
Swampy [swemp'-i], *a.* Pantanoso.
Swan [swen], *s.* Cisne, ave palmípeda de cuello largo y flexible y plumaje blanco. *Swan-like*, Semejante al cisne. *Swandown, swan's down*, (1) Plumón de cisne. (2) Moletón, una tela muy suave. *V. Canton flannel.* (3) Paño de vicuña, tela de lana muy suave y gruesa. *Swanskin*, (1) Piel de cisne; (2) lanilla, bayeta superfina.
Swan song [swen sēng], *s.* Canto del cisne.
Swap [swep], *adv.* (Prov. Ingl.) De prisa, con presteza; vivamente.
Swap, *va.* Cambiar, cambalachear.—*vn.* Hacer cambalaches o trueques.—*s.* (Fam.) Cambalache, trueque, cambio.
Sward [swērd], *va.* Sembrar, cubrir de césped.—*vn.* Volverse verde, herboso, cubrirse de hierbas.—*s.* La haz o superficie de la tierra cubierta de hierbas, césped.
Sware, *pret.* (ant.) de *To* SWEAR.
Swarm [swērm], *s.* 1. Enjambre, copia grande de abejas o de seres vivientes y pequeños de cualquiera clase. 2. Enjambre, gentío, multitud de gente reunida. 3. Hormiguero.
Swarm, *va.* Ocupar en enjambres, producir en enjambres.—*vn.* 1. Enjambrar, jabardear, hacer mucha cría las abejas, y también salir en enjambres de la colmena. 2. Enjambrar, multiplicar o producir en abundancia. 3. Hervir, bullir, hormiguear de gente, de soldados, etc., para ponderar la muchedumbre. 4. Abundar o haber grande abundancia de alguna cosa; manar en abundancia.
Swarm, *va.* y *vn.* (Fam.) Trepar, subir, ayudándose con pies y manos.
Swart [swērt], *a.* 1. Prieto, moreno, atezado; negro. 2. Triste; contrario.
Swarthiness [swērth'-i-nes], *s.* Color moreno, atezamiento, tez morena.
Swarthy [swērth'-i], *a.* Atezado, tezado, tostado por el sol; moreno, negruzco, curtido.
Swash [swesh], *s.* 1. El impulso del agua cuando surte o fluye con violencia. 2. Canal angosto por el cual fluyen las mareas. *Swash-buckler*, Matasiete, espadachín, fanfarrón.
Swash], *va.* Verter, derramar o salpicar agua en bastante cantidad.—*vn.* 1. Hacer ruido como salpicando con agua. 2. Salpicar, hacer saltar el agua. 3. Baladronear; meter bulla o hacer mucho ruido.
Swasher [swesh'-ęr], *s.* Jaquetón, baladrón, fanfarrón.
Swashing [swesh'-ing], *pa.* 1. El acto de fanfarronear, de echarlas de valiente. 2. Violento, abrumador. *A swashing blow*, Un golpe violento.
Swashy [swesh'-i], *a.* Batiente, a la manera del mar.
Swastika [swas'-ti-ca], *s.* Svástika.
Swatch [swēch], *s.* Muestra pequeña de alguna tela o tejido.
Swath [swēth], *s.* 1. Faja de hierba que el guadañero deja tras sí; ringlera de heno o mies acabada de segar. 2. Guadañada, el espacio cortado de una vez por una máquina o útil; se emplea en sentido figurado en ambos casos.
Swathe [swêdh], *va.* Fajar, liar, rodear; envolver (una criatura).
Swathe, *s.* Faja, venda, atadura; pañal de niño.
Sway [swê], *va.* 1. Hacer que se incline o ladee alguna persona; de aquí, preocupar el ánimo o la voluntad de alguno. 2. Blandir o vibrar alguna cosa en el aire; mover con la mano, v. g. un cetro. 3. Mandar, dominar, gobernar; dirigir, ejercer influencia o autoridad sobre alguno; regir. 4. (Mar.) Izar, guindar.—*vn.* 1. Ladearse, inclinarse o torcerse una cosa por su propio peso hacia un lado. 2. Inclinarse o ladearse el ánimo hacia una cosa o persona. 3. Tener influjo, mando o dominio. *To sway up*, Guindar.
Sway, *s.* 1. Poder, imperio, dominación, mando, influjo. *To bear sway*, Llevar el cetro. *To hold sway*, Gobernar, regir, estar en el poder. 2. Vibración, la acción de vibrar o blandir un arma. 3. Sacudimiento, estremecimiento, bamboleo.
Sway-backed [swê'-bact], *a.* (fam.) Pando.
Sweal [swīl], *vn.* 1. Derretirse y correrse como el sebo de una vela. 2. Consumirse, quemarse despacio.
Swear [swār], *va.* y *vn.* (*pret.* SWORE, y *ant.* SWARE; *pp.* SWORN). 1. Jurar, afirmar o negar una cosa bajo juramento. 2. Jurar, declarar, ratificar, confirmar o prometer alguna cosa con juramento. 3. Jurar, echar votos o juramentos; blasfemar. 4. Jurar, resolverse u ofrecerse con juramento a hacer una cosa; prestar juramento 5. Hacer jurar o prometer a uno bajo juramento. 6. Juramentar, tomar juramento a alguno. *To swear by*, (Fam.) Poner confianza implícita en. *To swear in*, Hacer prestar juramento a. *The witness has been sworn*, El testigo ha prestado juramento.
Swearer [swār'-ęr], *s.* Jurador, votador, el que tiene el vicio de jurar.
Swearing [swār'-ing], *s.* Jura, juramento.
Sweat [swet], *s.* 1. Sudor, la serosidad que sale del cuerpo del animal por los poros en forma de gotas; secreción cutánea, transpiración. 2. Sudor, trabajo, fatiga. 3. Evaporación de humedad. *To be in a sweat*, Estar sudaudo, estar nadando en sudor. *By the sweat of his brow*. Con el sudor de su frente. *Sweat-shop*, Taller donde se trabaja un número excesivo de horas por jornal insuficiente.
Sweat, *va.* y *vn.* (*pret.* y *pp.* SWEAT o SWEATED). 1. Sudar, exhalar o expeler el sudor. 2. Sudar, trabajar con fatiga y desvelo, física o moralmente. 3. Exhalar o echar de sí humedad en forma de vapor; dejar salir por los poros; p. ej. una planta o un jarro; resudar. 4. Hacer sudar. 5. Echar de sí alguna cosa a modo de sudor. *To sweat out a distemper*, Curarse de una enfermedad por medio del sudor. 6. Sujetar las pieles a un procedimiento de fermentación para despojarlas del pelo. 7. Recortar o cercenar las monedas, especialmente de una manera ilegal. 8. Tomarse mucho trabajo, extenuarse, fatigarse.
Sweater [suet'-ęr], *s.* Chaqueta o blusa tejida. (Amer.) Suéter.
Sweatiness [swet'-i-nes], *s.* El estado de lo que se halla lleno de sudor; calor; humedad.
Sweating [swet'-ing], *s.* Transpiración, acción de sudar. *Sweating-room*, Sudadero, lugar del baño destinado para sudar. *Sweating-sickness*, Cierta fiebre epidémica que prevaleció en Inglaterra en los siglos catorce y quince.
Sweaty [swet'-i], *s.* Sudado, sudoso, en transpiración; trabajoso, laborioso; lo que hace sudar.
Swede [swīd], *s.* 1. Natural o habitante de Suecia. 2. Nabo sueco. *V.* RUTABAGA.
Swedish [swīd'-ish], *a.* Sueco, perteneciente a Suecia.—*s.* Idioma sueco.
Sweep [swīp], *va.* y *vn.* (*pret.* y *pp.* SWEPT). 1. Barrer, limpiar con la escoba. 2. Barrer, no dejar nada de lo que había en alguna parte. 3. Arrebatar, llevar con celeridad y violencia; arrastrar por; mover o hacer moverse una cosa a la fuerza y como barriéndola, en sentido literal o figurado; abrazar con la mirada. 4. Marchar pomposamente, llevar una cosa con pompa u orgullo. 5. Pasar o moverse con celeridad llevándose tras sí cuanto se encuentra. 6. Deshollinar o limpiar chimeneas. *To sweep away*, Robar o llevarse cuanto se halla; arrebatar, arrastrar. *To sweep the bottom*, (Mar.) Rastrear. *To sweep along*, Arrastrar con fuerza o majestuosamente; ostentar, desplegar; rozar.

To sweep down, Descender (barriendo); precipitarse en; descender. *To sweep*, Barrer; llevar, arrebatar. *To sweep up*, Barrer en montón; limpiar.

Sweep, *s.* 1. Barredura, barrido, el acto de barrer. 2. Destrucción violenta y general. 3. La figura o línea que describe en su movimiento una cosa agitada violentamente; vuelta, giro. 4. Alcance, extensión o área alcanzada; alcance de la vista; dirección o extensión de un movimiento no hecho en línea recta; curva, encorvadura. 5. El o lo que barre; deshollinador; pieza de una máquina a lo largo de la cual se efectúa un rozamiento; remo largo y pesado; cigoñal de pozo; aspa de molino. 6. Calzada o camino en forma curva delante de un edificio. 7. *pl.* Barreduras.

Sweeper [swîp'-ẹr], *s.* Barrendero, el que barre. *Carpet-sweeper*, Escoba mecánica para barrer alfombras. *Chimney-sweeper*, Deshollinador, limpiachimeneas.

Sweeper-bar [swîp'-ẹr-bār], *s.* (Art.) Travesaño de la amoladera.

Sweepings [swîp'-ingz], *s. pl.* Barreduras, la inmundicia que se junta con la escoba cuando se barre.

Sweep-net [swîp'-net], *s.* Esparavel, red redonda de pescar.

Sweepstakes [swîp'-stêcs], *sing.* y *pl.* 1. El que gana todo cuanto se apuesta o se juega. 2. Palio, el premio que se señalaba en la carrera al que llegaba primero.

Sweet [swît], *a.* 1. Dulce, grato, gustoso, agradable a los sentidos: dulce al gusto o al paladar; que no es ni ácido ni amargo, azucarado: que no está salado; suave, blando o grato al tacto; oloroso, fragante al olfato; melodioso, dulce y agradable al oído. 2. Hermoso, lindo, agradable o bello a la vista. 3. Benigno, suave, dulce, apacible, amable, cuando se habla del genio, del trato, etc.; encantador, agradable, que impresiona agradablemente el ánimo, la imaginación. 4. Fresco, que no está corrompido o no es añejo.—*s.* 1. Dulzura, deleite. 2. Cosa dulce; más usado en plural, dulces, golosinas. 3. Dulzura, placer, satisfacción. 4. Persona querida; querido, querida: es voz de cariño. *Sweet music*, Música suave, melodiosa. *A sweet face*, Una cara linda. *Sweet pinks*, Claveles olorosos, fragantes. *A sweet girl*, Una muchacha encantadora. *Sweet-apple, sweet-sop*, Anona, chirimoya. *Sweet cicely*, Perifollo. *V.* CICELY. *Sweet corn*, Variedad de maíz, preferida como comestible. *Sweet-fern*, Planta de la familia de las miricáceas. *Sweet-gum*, Liquidámbar de América y la goma que de él se obtiene. *Sweet herbs*, Hierbas olorosas que se usan como condimento. *Sweet-oil*, Aceite de oliva. *Sweet-pea*, Guisante de olor, arveja olorosa. *Sweet potato*, Camote; patata dulce; (Amer.) camote; (Cuba) boniato. *Sweet-tempered*, De carácter dulce, complaciente. *Sweet-tongued*, Melifluo, pico de oro. *Sweet-scented*, Perfumado. *Sweet-smelling*, Odorífero, fragante. *Sweet-spoken*, Melifluo. *Sweet-toothed*, Goloso. *Sweet-William*, (Bot.) Dianto, clavel barbado. *Sweet-willow, sweet-gale*, Mirto holandés, pimienta de Brabante, arbusto de las miricáceas. (Myrica Gale.)

Sweetbread [swît'-bred], *s.* Pancreas, glándula abdominal; o timo, glándula del cuello, cuando se emplean como alimento; lechecillas o mollejas de ternera.

Sweetbrier [swît'-brai-ẹr], *s.* (Bot.) Escaramujo oloroso, agavanzo.

Sweeten [swî'-tn], *va.* 1. Dulzurar, dulcificar, endulzar, poner dulce lo que no lo era; azucarar, edulcorar. 2. Suavizar, mitigar, moderar, aplacar; aumentar el placer de; dar encanto a. 3. Embalsamar; purificar, quitar los malos olores; hacer salubre.—*vn.* Endulzarse.

Sweetener [swî'-tn-ẹr], *s.* 1. Dulcificante, lo que dulcifica. 2. El que mitiga, calma o suaviza; el que palia.

Sweetflag [swît'-flag], *s.* (Bot.) Cálamo aromático.

Sweetheart [swît'-hārt], *s.* Enamorada, dulce amiga; querida, amante; la mujer a quien se corteja o galantea; se usa también a veces para significar galán, galanteador, cortejo, el amante de una mujer.

Sweeting [swît'-ing], *s.* 1. Camuesa, especie de manzana; variedad particular de manzana dulce. 2. (Ant.) Querido: voz de cariño.

Sweetish [swît'-ish], *a.* Algo dulce.

Sweetly [swît'-li], *adv.* Dulcemente, con dulzura, suavemente.

Sweetmeat [swît'-mît], *s.* Dulce, cualquiera especie de confitura en seco; dulces secos.

Sweetness [swît'-nes], *s.* Dulzura, calidad de dulce, melodioso, oloroso, o benigno; suavidad, blandura, apacibilidad, bondad.

Sweetrush [swît'-rush], *s.* (Bot.) Cálamo aromático. *V.* SWEETFLAG.

Swell [swel], *vn.* (*pp.* SWELLED o SWOLLEN). 1. Hincharse, engrosarse, llenarse y entumecerse alguna cosa por cualquiera causa que sea. 2. Hincharse, elevarse alguna parte del cuerpo; abotagarse. 3. Hincharse, envanecerse, engreirse, ensoberbecerse. 4. Escribir o hablar usando un estilo hinchado. 5. (Mar.) Embravecerse o agitarse el mar, hervir las olas.—*va.* 1. Hinchar, engrosar, inflar, entumecer; abultar. 2. Aumentar, agravar. 3. Hinchar, engreir, envanecer. 4. Cantar o tocar usando el crescendo y diminuendo combinados. *To swell to a great amount*, Elevarse a una gruesa suma. *Rains swell the rivers*, Las lluvias engrosan los ríos. *The sails swelled*, Se hincharon las velas. *Swollen with pride*, Inflado, hinchado de orgullo. *To swell out*, Arrojar el árbol sus hojas; espetarse, ampollarse, bufar.

Swell, *a.* 1. (Ger.) De petimetres, de mal gusto o de moda extremada. 2. Perteneciente a una hinchazón o torcedura.—*s.* 1. Entumecencia, hinchazón, bulto; cualquier aumento de volumen. 2. Oleada, ola larga y continua, oleaje, marejada; de aquí, ondulación del terreno. 3. Prominencia, protuberancia. 4. (Mús.) (1) La unión de crescendo y diminuendo, y los signos (< >) que la indican. (2) Aparato por el cual se puede aumentar o disminuir la fuerza del sonido. 5. (Ger.) Persona que sigue las modas con exageración. *Swell-organ*, Parte del órgano cuyos cañones están encerrados en una caja; órgano de expresión. *Swell-pedal*, Pedal de expresión.

Swelling [swel'-ing], *s.* 1. Hinchazón, el efecto de hincharse. 2. Tumor, abotagamiento de las carnes, bulto. 3. Cualquier prominencia, salida, chichón, bollo. 4. Acceso, transporte.—*pa.* de SWELL. Que se hincha, que infla o que se infla, etc. *Swelling sails*, Velas que se hinchan. *Swelling sea*, Mar agitada, de oleaje. *Swelling breast*, Seno agitado; pecho que se desarrolla.

Swelter [swel'-tẹr], *va.* y *vn.* 1. Abrumar de calor. 2. Ahogarse o estar abrumado de calor.

Swept, *pret.* y *pp.* del verbo SWEEP.

Swerve [swẹrv], *va.* Desviar, apartar de una dirección.—*vn.* Desviarse, apartarse, separarse, extraviarse.

Swift [swift], *va.* (Mar.) Tortorar, dar tortores. *To swift a boat*, (Mar.) Dar tortores a un bote.

Swift, *a.* 1. Veloz, acelerado, pronto, ligero, rápido. 2. Capaz de moverse con velocidad. 3. Pronto, repentino; que viene o sucede sin previo aviso. 4. Pronto, que obra sin tardar; vivo, diligente, activo.—*s.* 1. (Orn.) Vencejo, avión, pájaro semejante a la golondrina, notable por la rapidez de su vuelo. 2. Un ejemplar de varias clases de lagartos pequeños. 3. Carrete, devanadera con eje de quita y pon. 4. ¿Corriente o curso rápido de un río; torrente o avenida impetuosa. *A swift stream*, Una corriente rápida. *Swift-footed, swift of foot*, De paso rápido, ligero para correr. *Swift destruction*, Ruina repentina.

Swifter [swift'-ẹr], *s.* (Mar.) Tortor, andaribel; falso obenque.

Swiftly [swift'-li], *adv.* Velozmente, rápidamente, ligeramente.

Swiftness [swift'-nes], *s.* Velocidad, ligereza, rapidez, celeridad, prontitud en el movimiento.

Swig [swig], *va.* y *vn.* Beber a grandes tragos.

Swig, *va.* (Mar.) Aballestar, estirar una cuerda fija por un extremo, y atada por el otro a un objeto movible.—*s.* Acción de halar un cable o cabo que está amarrado por ambos extremos.

Swill [swil], *va.* 1. Beber con exceso. 2. Emborrachar, embriagar. 3. Lavar, enjuagar.

Swill, *s.* 1. Bazofia, alimento líquido para los puercos hecho con los restos de la cocina. 2. Tragantada, trago grande de algún licor.

Swiller [swil'-ẹr], *s.* Bebedor insaciable.

Swim [swim], *vn.* (*pret.* SWAM o SWUM, *pp.* SWUM). 1. Nadar, mantenerse el hombre u otro animal sobre el agua o ir sobre ella. 2. Nadar, ir una cosa por encima del agua sin hundirse. 3. Nadar, abundar en alguna cosa. 4. Llevarse o ir con la corriente; conformar uno su conducta a la moda o la opinión general. 5. Padecer vaguidos ó vahidos. *His head swims*, Se le va la cabeza. 6. Pasar alguna cosa por delante de la vista con un movimiento trémulo.—*va.* 1. Pasar á nado. 2. Hacer flotar. 3. Empapar, calar, mojar en el agua para que floten las partes más ligeras. *To swim away*, Salvarse a nado. *To swim over a river*, Atravesar un río a nado. *To swim with the tide*, Seguir la corriente o ir con la corriente.

Swim, *s.* 1. La acción o diversión de nadar. 2. Movimiento de deslizarse o bambolearse. *Swim bladder*, Vejiga natatoria. *Swim fin*, Aleta. *Swim trunks*, Taparrabo. *To be in the swim*, 1. Estar en auge. 2. Estar al corriente.

Swimmable [swim'-a-bl], *a.* Que se puede atravesar a nado.

Swimmer [swim'-ęr], *s.* Nadador.

Swimming [swim'-ing], *s.* 1. Natación. 2. Mareo, vahido, vértigo. —*a.* 1. Natatorio. 2. Nadador, natátil. 3. Lloroso. *Swimming hole*, Nadadero. *Swimming pool*, Piscina, alberca. *Swimming stroke*, Brazada. *To be fond of swimming*, Ser aficionado a nadar.

Swimmingly [swim'-ing-li], *adv.* A las mil maravillas, sin tropiezo.

Swindle [swin'-dl], *va.* Petardear, estafar, sonsacar, trampear, sacar dinero u otra cosa con pretextos falsos, pillar alguna cosa con tretas y engaños.

Swindler [swin'-dlęr], *s.* Estafador, petardista, trampista, tramposo.

Swine [swain], *s.* Marrano, puerco, cerdo, cochino. *Wild swine*, Jabalí. *Sea-swine*, Marsopa, marsopla o cachalote, un cetáceo. *Swine-plague*, Peste de los puercos, enfermedad infecciosa causada por un microbio, que ataca los pulmones y el aparato digestivo de los cerdos. *Swine-pox*, Variedad de viruelas locas. *Swine-thistle*, *V. Sow-thistle.*

Swine-bread [swain'-bred], *s.* 1. (Bot.) Trufa, criadilla de tierra. 2. Pan de puerco, planta. *V.* CYCLAMEN.

Swine-herd [swain'-hęrd], *s.* Porquero, porquerizo, el que guarda los puercos.

Swing [swing], *va.* (*pret.* SWUNG o ‡SWANG, *pp.* SWUNG). 1. Vibrar, hacer oscilar; balancear, bambolear, dar un movimiento trémulo a alguna cosa. 2. Mover, voltear o hacer dar vueltas en el aire; blandir (un arma). 3. Hacer girar sobre un punto o eje. 4. Hacer subir, engoznar, colocar sobre goznes. —*vn.* 1. Vibrar, oscilar, moverse libremente a uno y otro lado un cuerpo suspenso en el aire. 2. Columpiarse, moverse en el columpio. 3. Balancearse, dar o hacer balances. 4. Volverse, dar vueltas en alguna dirección fija, como sobre un eje. 5. (Mar.) Bornear, hacer cabeza, dar vuelta sobre las anclas. *To swing about*, Rodear o dar vueltas alrededor de alguna cosa. *Swing-back*, Respaldo de articulación de una cámara fotográfica. *Swing-bar*, *V.* SWINGLETREE. *Swing-plough*, Arado de reja reversible. *To swing around the circle*, Pasar por la serie completa. *To swing clear*, Evitar un choque.

Swing, *s.* 1. Vibración, oscilación, el movimiento libre e igual a un lado y a otro de un cuerpo suspenso en el aire. 2. Balanceo, bamboleo, balance. 3. Columpio, soga fija por sus extremos para columpiarse. 4. Inclinación o propensión irresistible. 5. Ímpetu de algún cuerpo puesto en movimiento; alcance. 6. Libre carrera o libertad desenfrenada. 7. Respaldo de articulación (de una cámara fotográfica). *Swing-tree of a gun carriage*, (Art.) Balancín de cureña. *In full swing*, En plena operación. *To give a swing*, Balancear.

Swing, *s.* Música de *jazz*, variedad de música popular de E.U.

Swinge [swinj], *va.* (SWINGED, *pa.* SWINGEING). Azotar, castigar, dar una felpa o una zurribanda.

Swinger [swing'-ęr], *s.* El que se columpia, voltea o da vueltas en el aire.

Swinging [swing'-ing], *s.* 1. Oscilación, vibración. 2. Balanceo. 3. Borneo.—*pa.* del verbo SWING.

Swingle [swiṇ'-gl], *va.* Espadillar, sacudir el lino o cáñamo con la espadilla.—*s.* 1. Espadilla, instrumento para espadillar lino o cáñamo. Se llama también *swinglestaff* y *swing-knife*. 2. La barra corta del mayal con que se golpea el trigo al trillarlo. 3. *V.* SWINGLETREE.

Swingletree [swiṇ'-gl-tri], *s.* Bolea, balancín de tiro, afianzado en la punta de la lanza de un coche o arado. Se escribe también *singletree*.

Swinish [swain'-ish], *a.* Porcuno, que es propio del puerco o perteneciente a él; cochino, grosero, sucio.

Swink [swiṇc], *vn.* (Esco. y ant.) Trabajar con exceso.

Swipe [swaip], *va.* 1. (Fam.) Dar un golpe fuerte. 2. (Ger.) Hurtar. —*s.* 1. (Fam.) Golpe fuerte. 2. Cigueñal o cigoñal, una pértiga que se usa para sacar agua.

Swirl [swęrl], *va.* y *vn.* Hacer girar o girar, como en torbellino; girar en remolino la nieve, el viento, el polvo o el agua.—*s.* 1. Remolino, torbellino; movimiento de lanzarse, como el de un pez. 2. Torcedura, forma espiral. (< noruego, *svirla.*)

Swish [swish], *va.* y *vn.* Mover o moverse con movimiento como de barrer y produciendo un sonido silbante.—*s.* Sonido silbante, como el de un látigo al cortar el aire; el movimiento que produce dicho sonido. (Voz imitativa.)

Swiss [swis], *a.* Suizo, de Suiza.—*s.* Suizo, suiza; habitante de Suiza.

Switch [swich], *s.* 1. Varilla, vara pequeña; (Amer.) cuje. 2. Moño de cabello natural o postizo en el peinado de las mujeres. 3. Aguja, (Amer.) cambiavía, carril movible o artificio para pasar un tren de uno a otro lado. 4. (Elec.) Conmutador, pieza de los aparatos eléctricos que sirve para cambiar de conductor una corriente. 5. Acción o operación de desviar un tren por medio de una aguja.

Switch, *va.* 1. Varear, dar golpes o sacudir con una vara; sacudir a uno el polvo, medirle las costillas. 2. Precintar, asegurar con cujes o flejes. 3. Desviar, hacer pasar a otra vía un coche o un tren de ferrocarril. 4. (Elec.) Mudar de un circuito a otro.

Switchback [swich'-bac], *s.* Vía de ferrocarril en zigzag.

Switchblade [swich'-blẽd], *s.* Puñal, cuchillo o navaja de hoja automática.

Switchboard [swich'-bōrd], *s.* Conmutador telefónico.

Switch box [swich'box], *s.* (Elec.) Caja de interruptores.

Switchman [swich'-man], *s.* Guarda-agujas, empleado encargado de manejar las agujas de ferrocarril.

Switchyard [swich'-yard], *s.* (F. C.) Patio de maniobras.

Swivel [swiv'-l], *va.* y *vn.* Girar sobre un eje.—*s.* 1. Alacrán, eslabón de vueltas o giratorio. 2. Pedrero, colisa, cañoncito que gira sobre un eje. 3. La lanzadera de un telar de cintas.

Swivel chair [swiv'-l chār], *s.* Silla giratoria.

Swivel-gun [swiv'-l-gun], *s.* Pedrero.

Swob. *s.* *V.* SWAB.

Swollen, Swoln [swōl'-n], *pp.* del verbo *To* SWELL.—*a.* Hinchado.

Swoon [swūn] *vn.* Desmayarse, desfallecer, perder el sentido.

Swoon, *s.* Desmayo, deliquio, desfallecimiento, pasmo, síncope.

Swoop [swūp], *va.* 1. Descender y agarrar la presa al vuelo o hallándose en movimiento; se usa a menudo con *up*. 2. Coger, agarrar.—*vn.* Caer, precipitarse sobre algo, como el ave sobre su presa.

Swoop, *s.* El acto de echarse un ave de rapiña sobre su presa.

Sword [sōrd], *s.* 1. Espada, arma blanca; sable. 2. (Fig.) Poder de la espada; dominio; derecho de vida y muerte; el poder militar en contraposición al civil. *Broadsword*, Espada ancha, sable. *Cut and thrust sword*, Espada-sable. *To put to the sword*, Pasar a filo de espada, pasar a cuchillo. *To fire and sword*, A fuego y sangre. *Sword-arm*, Brazo derecho. *Sword-belt*, Cinturón. *Sword-cane*, Bastón de estoque. *Sword-guard*, *sword-hilt*, Empuñadura, puño, guarda de la espada. *Sword-knot*, Borla de espada o espadín. *Sword-play*, Asalto y defensa con la espada. *Sword-shaped*, Ensiforme, que tiene la forma de una espada. *Sword-law*, La ley del más fuerte. *Sword-player*, Esgrimidor.

Swordfish [sōrd'-fish], *s.* Pez espada, pez del alta mar (Xiphias gladius).

Swordsman [sōrdz'-man], *s.* (*pl.* SWORDSMEN). 1. Tirador, hombre hábil en el manejo de la espada. 2. Soldado, hombre de espada.

Swore, *pret.* del verbo *To* SWEAR.

Sworn, *pp.* del verbo *To* SWEAR.

Swum, *pret.* y *pp.* del verbo *To* SWIM.

Swung, *pret.* y *pp.* del verbo *To* SWING.

Sybarite [sib'-a-rait], *s.* Sibarita, habitante de la antigua ciudad griega de Sibaris, famosa por su lujo.

Sybaritic, Sybaritical [sib-a-rit'-ic, al] *a.* Sibarítico; dícese del que es dado a la molicie y a los deleites; y de las fiestas, diversiones, etc., muy extravagantes y continuadas.

Sycamore [sic'-a-mōr], *s.* 1. (Bot.) Sicomoro, higuera sicomoro, árbol de Siria y Egipto. 2. (E. U.) Plátano de América, falso plátano, árbol afín al arce. *V.* BUTTONWOOD.

Sycophancy [sic'-o-fan-si], *s.* 1. La calidad, carácter o práctica de sicofante. 2. Adulación.

Sycophant [sic'-o-fant], *s.* Adulador, parásito, sicofante; gorrista, mogollón.

Syenite [sai'-en-ait], *s.* (Min.) Sienita, roca plutónica parecida al granito, pero que contiene muy poco o ningún cuarzo.

Syllabary [sil'-a-bę-ri], *s.* Silabario, lista o catálogo de caracteres que representan signos y sirve como alfabeto para escribir, p. ej. en el idioma japonés.

Syllabic, Syllabical [si-lab'-ic, al], *a.* Silábico.

Syllabically [si-lab'-ic-al-i], *adv.* Por sílabas.

Syllabicate [si-lab'-i-kēt], *va.* Silabear, dividir en sílabas.

Syllabication [si-lab-i-kē'-shun], *s.* Silabeo, el acto de formar sílabas.

Syllable [sil'-a-bl], *s.* 1. Sílaba. 2. Cualquiera cosa concisa o breve.
Syllable, *va.* (Poét. o des.) Proferir, articular, pronunciar.
Syllabub [sil'-a-bub], *s.* Bebida hecha con leche, vino y azúcar. *V.* SILLIBUB.
Syllabus [sil'-a-bus], *s.* Extracto, compendio, resumen de los principales puntos de un discurso.
Syllepsis [sil-lep'-sis], *s.* (Gram. y Ret.) Silepsis, la figura de construcción por la cual se forma una frase expresando lo que uno se propone decir, más bien que ateniéndose a las reglas gramaticales.
Syllogism [sil'-o-jizm], *s.* 1. Silogismo, argumento que consta de tres proposiciones, la última de las cuales se deduce de las otras dos. 2. Razonamiento deductivo en contraposición al inductivo.
Syllogistic, Syllogistical [sil-o-jis'-tic, al], *a.* Silogístico.
Syllogize [sil'-o-jaiz], *vn.* Silogizar, hacer silogismos o argüir en forma silogística.
Sylph [silf], *s.* 1. Silfo, sílfide (*f.*), nombre que los cabalistas daban a los duendes; una joven delgada y primorosa. 2. Colibrí sudamericano del género Cyanolesbia, con cola larga horcada y de colores brillantes.
Sylva [sil'-va], *s.* Conjunto de los árboles de las selvas.
Sylvan [sil'-van], *a.* Selvático, silvático, silvestre; de aquí, rústico, rural.—*s.* Silvano, dios de las selvas.
Symbiosis [sim-bai-ō'-sis], *s.* Simbiosis.
Symbol [sim'-bel], *s.* 1. Símbolo, figura emblemática o nota significativa, emblema, signo, tipo. 2. Signo, carácter, marca o abreviatura que representa algo, como una operación o cantidad en las matemáticas, una substancia en química, un planeta en astronomía, etc. 3. Símbolo, el credo o sumario de los artículos de la fe. *♃ is the symbol of Jupiter.* El signo ♃ es el símbolo de Jupiter. *The symbol of sulphuric acid is H_2SO_4.* El símbolo del ácido sulfúrico es H_2SO_4.
Symbolic, Symbolical [sim-bel'-ic, al], *a.* Simbólico.
Symbolically [sim-bel'-ic-al-i], *adv.* Simbólicamente.
Symbolic logic [sim-bel'-ic lej'-ic], *s.* Lógica simbólica.
Symbolism [sim'-bel-izm], *s.* Simbolismo, representación por medio de símbolos; sistema de símbolos.
Symbolization [sim-bel-i-zé'-shun], *s.* Simbolización.
Symbolize [sim'-bel-aiz], *va.* y *vn.* Simbolizar, parecerse una cosa a otra o representarla con semejanza; guardar mucha semejanza una cosa con otra.
Symbology [sim-bel'-o-ji], *s.* El arte de simbolizar, de representar por medio de símbolos.
Symmetrical [si-met'-ri-cal], **Symmetral** [sim'-e-tral], *a.* Simétrico, proporcionado, que tiene simetría.
Symmetrist [sim'-e-trist], *s.* La persona que tiene mucho esmero en guardar simetría en lo que hace.
Symmetrize [sim'-et-raiz], *va.* Hacer o poner simétrico.
Symmetry [sim'-e-tri], *s.* Simetría, la proporción y correspondencia de unas partes con otras y de estas con el todo.
Sympathetic, Sympathetical [sim-pa-thet'-ic, al], *a.* Simpático; que causa o experimenta simpatía; que obra por simpatía, que depende de ella; de acuerdo.
Sympathetically [sim-pa-thet'-i-cal-i], *adv.* Simpáticamente, con simpatía.
Sympathize [sim'-pa-thaiz], *vn.* 1. Compadecerse, simpatizar, acompañar a otro en el mismo sentimiento o dolor; aliviar las penas de alguno mostrando sentimiento por ellas. 2. Padecer una parte u órgano en simpatía con otra. 3. Convenir, armonizarse, ajustarse.
Sympathy [sim'-pa-thi], *s.* 1. Simpatía, la correspondencia natural o imaginada que tienen ciertos cuerpos entre sí. 2. Simpatía, la conformidad de genios e inclinaciones entre dos personas. 3. (Med.) Simpatía, la relación o correspondencia que existe entre la acción de dos órganos separados uno de otro.
Symphonic [sim-fen'-ic], *a.* 1. Sinfónico, perteneciente o relativo a la sinfonía. 2. Homónimo; dícese de los vocablos del mismo sonido.
Symphonious [sim-fō'-ni-us], *a.* Armonioso.
Symphonist [sim'-fo-nist], *s.* Sinfonista, el que compone sinfonías.
Symphony [sim'-fo-ni], *s.* Sinfonía, concierto de diferentes voces o instrumentos de música.
Symposium [sim-pō'-zi-um], *s.* 1. Festín o banquete amenizado con la conversación de los comensales. 2. De aquí, una colección de comentarios, opiniones o sueltos cortos que se publican juntos, v. g. en un periódico.
Symptom [simp'-tom o tum], *s.* 1. (Med.) Síntoma, cualquier fenómeno morboso o mudanza sensible en la apariencia o en el modo de funcionar los órganos. 2. Síntoma o señal que indica la existencia de alguna otra cosa.
Symptomatic, Symptomatical [simp-to-mat'-ic, al], *a.* Sintomático, perteneciente al síntoma, de la naturaleza de un síntoma o indicio; según los síntomas.
Symptomatically [simp-to-mat'-ic-al-i], *adv.* Sintomáticamente.
Symptomatology [simp-to-ma-tel'-o-ji], *s.* Sintomatología, la parte de la patología que trata de la observación y clasificación de los síntomas.
Synæresis [sin-er'-e-sis], *s.* *V.* SYNERESIS.
Synagogue [sin'-a-geg], *s.* 1. Sinagoga, el lugar o edificio en que se reunen los judíos a orar y a oir la doctrina de su religión. 2. Sinagoga, congregación o junta religiosa de los judíos.
Synalepha [sin-a-li'-fa], *s.* (Gram.) Sinalefa, reunión de dos sílabas en una sola por la elisión de una vocal.
Synchronic, Synchronical [sin-cren'-ic, al], *a.* Sincrónico, lo que sucede al mismo tiempo que otra cosa.
Synchronism [siṇ'-cro-nizm], *s.* Sincronismo, contemporaneidad, concurrencia de sucesos o eventos acaecidos a un mismo tiempo.
Synchronization [sin-cron-i-zé'-shun], *s.* Sincronización.
Synchronize [sin'-cron-aiz], *va.* Sincronizar.
Synchronous [siṇ'-cro-nus], *a.* Sincrónico, coetáneo, concurrente, simultáneo, que se hace al mismo tiempo.
Synchrotron [sin'-cro-tren], *s.* Sincrotrón.
Synclinal [sin-clai'-nal o sin'-cli-nal], *a.* Que se inclina hacia abajo por cada lado.
Syncopate [siṇ'-co-pêt], *va.* 1. Sincopar. 2. (Mús.) Hacer una síncopa.
Syncopation [sin-co-pê'-shun], *s.* 1. Síncopa, supresión de una letra o sílaba en medio de una palabra. 2. Síncopa musical.
Syncope [sin'-co-pe], *s.* 1. Síncope, la pérdida completa y repentina del sentido y movimiento. 2. (Gram.) Síncopa, la supresión de una letra o sílaba en medio de la dicción. 3. (Mús.) Síncopa, nota que se toca al fin de un tiempo y al principio de otro.
Syncretic [sin-cret'-ic], *a.* Sincrético.
Syncretism [sin'-cre-tizm], *s.* Sincretismo.
Syndic [sin'-dic], *s.* Síndico.
Syndicalism [sin'-di-cal-izm], *s.* Sindicalismo.
Syndicate [sin'-di-kêt], *va.* y *vn.* Combinar en una asociación comercial o manejar por medio de ella.—*s.* 1. Asociación de personas para la prosecución de una empresa que exige grandes caudales. 2. Sindicado, junta de síndicos.
Syne [sain], *adv.* (Esco.) Hace tiempo. *V.* SINCE o AGO.
Synecdoche [si-nec'-do-kê], *s.* Sinécdoque, figura retórica.
Syneresis [sin-er'-ê-sis], *s.* (Gram.) Sinéresis, figura por la cual se unen dos sílabas en una.
Synesis [sin'-es-is], *s.* (Gram. y Ret.) Construcción de acuerdo con el sentido más que con la sintaxis.
Synod [sin'-ed], *s.* Sínodo, el concilio que celebra el obispo con los eclesiásticos de su diócesis.
Synodal [sin'-o-dal], **Synodic, Synodical** [si-ned'-ic, al], *a.* Sinódico.
Synonym [sin'-o-nim], *s.* 1. Sinónimo, voz o palabra que tiene el mismo o casi el mismo sentido que otra: opuesto a *antonym.* 2. Equivalente de un vocablo en otra lengua.
Synonymize [sin-en'-i-maiz], *va.* Expresar una misma cosa con palabras diferentes o en otros términos.
Synonymous [sin-en'-i-mus], *a.* Sinónimo, que expresa la misma cosa con diferentes voces; dícese de una cosa respecto de otra con la cual tiene estrecha relación.
Synonymy [sin-en'-i-mi], *s.* Sinonimia, la calidad de expresar la misma cosa con diferentes voces.
Synopsis [sin-ep'-sis], *s.* Sinopsis, suma, sumario.
Synoptic, Synoptical [sin-ep'-tic, al], *a.* Sinóptico; perceptible o comprensible a primera vista.
Synovia [sin-ō'-vi-a], *s.* Sinovia, humor viscoso que lubrica las articulaciones del animal.
Synovial [sin-o'-vi-al], *a.* Sinovial, perteneciente a la sinovia o que la produce.
Syntactic, Syntactical [sin-tac'-tic, al], *a.* Sintáctico, perteneciente o relativo a la sintaxis.
Syntax [sin'-tacs], *s.* Sintaxis, la parte de la gramática que enseña el uso de las partes de la oración.
Synthesis [sin'-the-sis], *s.* 1. Síntesis, composición, lo contrario de *análisis;* reunión de substancias separadas, o de partes subordinadas en una nueva forma. 2. Combinación de los elementos radicales de una palabra en la formación de un idioma. 3.

(Lóg.) Razonamiento que procede del todo a una parte o de lo general a lo particular. 4. (Cir.) Reunión de partes divididas.

Synthesize [sin'-the-saiz], *va.* Sintetizar.

Synthetic, Synthetical [sin-thet'-ic, -al], *a.* 1. Sintético, relativo a la síntesis, lo contrario de analítico. 2. Sintético, fabricado químicamente. *Synthetic rubber,* Caucho sintético, caucho artificial.

Syphilis [sif'-i-lis], *s.* Sífilis, mal gálico, enfermedad específica, venérea, e infecciosa.

Syphilitic [sif-i-lit'-ic], *a.* Sifilítico, perteneciente a la sífilis, o que la padece.

Syphon [sai'-fen], *s.* Sifón. *V.* SIPHON.

Syren [sai'-ren], *s.* *V.* SIREN.

Syrian [sir'-i-an], *a.* y *s.* Sirio, de la Siria; habitante de la Siria moderna o antigua.

Syringa [si-rin'-ga], *s.* (Bot.) 1. Jeringuilla (Philadelfus), arbusto de adorno de la familia de las saxífragas. 2. Lila, género pequeño de arbustos de las oleáceas.

Syringe [sir'-inj], *s.* Jeringa, un instrumento para echar ayudas y hacer inyecciones.

Syringe, *va.* Jeringar, echar ayudas con una jeringa; lavar haciendo inyecciones.

Syrup [sir'-up], *s.* Jarabe. *V.* SIRUP.

System [sis'-tem], *s.* 1. Sistema, el orden y situación natural de muchas cosas que obran simultáneamente. 2. Sistema, el conjunto y enlace de principios o verdades relativas a una materia; clasificación metódica. 3. Un todo compuesto de partes constituyentes; p. ej. un sistema de ferrocarril. 4. (Biol.) Conjunto de estructuras orgánicas que obran en combinación; el sistema nervioso, digestivo, etc.

Systematic [sis-tem-at'-ic], *s.* y *a.* Sistemático.

Systematical [sis-tem-at'-i-cal], *a.* Sistemático, metódico, puesto con orden.

Systematically [sis-tem-at'-i-cal-i], *adv.* Sistemáticamente.

Systematize [sis'-tem-a-taiz], *va.* Reducir a sistema.

Systematizer [sis'-tem-a-taiz-er], *s.* El que sigue un sistema.

Systemic [sis-tem'-ic], *a.* 1. Sistemático. 2. Perteneciente al cuerpo como un todo.

Systole [sis'-to-le], *s.* Sístole, el movimiento del corazón y de las arterias cuando se contraen; opuesto al llamado *diástole.*

Systolic [sis-tol'-ic], *a.* Sistólico, relativo a la sístole.

Systyle [sis'-tail], *s.* (Arq.) Sistilo.

Syzygy [siz'-i-ji], *s.* (Astr.) Sizigia: término usado para denotar la conjunción o la oposición de algún planeta con el sol.

T

T [ti]. **Esta letra tiene en general el mismo sonido que en español, aunque un poco más fuerte. Cuando precede a una *i* seguida de vocal, se pronuncia como *sh*; v. g. en las palabras *nation* y *patient*: en muchas voces acabadas en *une, ure, ue,* etc., tiene el sonido de *ch,* como en *nature, virtue,* etc.: también es** algunas veces muda, p. ej. en *to listen, often, to soften,* etc.—La *th* tiene tres sonidos: uno suave, entre la *d* y la *z* castellana, como en *thus, that,* etc.; otro agudo, parecido al de la *z* española, como en *thin, thought,* etc.; y el último como el de la *t* simple, v. g. en *Thames, Thomas,* etc.

T, *s.* Algo que tiene la forma de la letra T, o la sección vertical semejante a una T. *T rail,* Riel o carril de hongo, en forma de T.

Tab [tab], *s.* 1. Jirón, lengüeta, proyección, apéndice o parte saliente de una cosa. 2. Cuenta. *To keep tab,* (Fam.) Llevar cuenta, poner en cuenta.

Tabard [tab'-ard], *s.* Tabardo, prenda de abrigo ancha y larga con las mangas bobas, que se usó en tiempos pasados.

Tabarder [tab'-ard-er], *s.* El que llevaba tabardo.

Tabasco [ta-bas'-cō], *s.* Salsa de pimienta de Tabasco.

Tabby [tab'-i], *s.* 1. Tabí, especie de tela de seda ondeada y prensada. 2. Gato moteado; y particularmente una gata.—*a.* 1. Ondeado, que tiene la apariencia de hacer ondas: dícese de las telas. 2. Abigarrado, salpicado de varios colores.

Tabby, *va.* Ondear y prensar las telas de seda formando en ellas aguas u ondas.

Tabefaction [tab-e-fac'-shun], *s.* Marasmo; enflaquecimiento, consunción.

Tabefy [tab'-e-fai], *vn* Extenuarse, debilitarse, enflaquecer.

Tabernacle [tab'-er-na-cl], *s.* 1. Tabernáculo, tienda: entre los judíos el lugar donde estaba el arca del testamento. 2. Tabernáculo, templo, santuario; cualquier habitación o vivienda en el lenguaje de la Sagrada Escritura.

Tabes [tē'-biz], *s.* (Med.) *V.* CONSUMPTION.

Tabetic [ta-bet' ic], *a.* Tábido, extenuado por una enfermedad.

Tabid [tab'-id], *a.* (Med.) Tábido, extenuado; macilento, debilitado.

Tabidness [tab'-id-nes], *s.* (Med.) Marasmo, consunción.

Tablature [tab'-la-tiūr], *s.* 1. (Anat.) Una de las láminas de tejido óseo que forman las paredes del cráneo. 2. Pintura mural.

Table [tē'-bl], *s.* 1. Mesa, un mueble para el servicio doméstico o para adorno. 2. Mesa, tomado absolutamente es la mesa para comer, y también la comida o manjares que se ponen o sirven en ella. *To keep a good table,* Tener buena mesa. 3. El conjunto de personas que están comiendo a un tiempo en la mesa. 4. Tabla, el índice de los libros o cualquier lista o catálogo dispuesto en orden sucesivo; clasificación o serie de números o signos dispuestos para facilitar su examen. 5. Tabla, pintura hecha en tabla o piedra. 6. Tabla, plancha, superficie plana o lisa de cualquier metal o piedra para grabar, esculpir o pintar en ella. 7. Palma de la mano. *Tables,* Tablas o tablas reales, un juego muy semejante al del chaquete. *To turn the tables,* Volverse la tortilla; hacer cambiar la suerte. *To turn the tables upon one,* Devolver la pelota a alguno. *Side-table.* Bufete, aparador. *Table-cloth,* Mantel (generalmente en plural, manteles); tela para manteles; alemanisco. *Table-covers,* Sobremesas: (Amer.) Cubremesas. *Table-land,* Mesa, meseta, terreno elevado y llano. *Table-linen,* Adamascado. *Table-set* o *service,* Vajilla, juego de artículos necesarios para poner completamente una mesa. *Table-boarder,* Pupilo, pensionista, el que come a la mesa, pero se aloja en otra parte. *Table-talk,* Propósitos de sobremesa; conversación familiar. *Table-beer,* Cerveza floja, cerveza de pasto. *Table-book,* Libro vistoso que se tiene por lo regular sobre una mesa; y (des.) una especie de librito de memoria para escribir con lápiz.

Table, *va.* y *vn.* 1. Dar carpetazo a un proyecto de ley; posponer la discusión o consideración de un acuerdo. 2. Poner sobre la mesa, v. g. un naipe. 3. Hacer el índice de algún escrito; hacer un catálogo en orden sucesivo. 4. (Carp.) Ensamblar, acoplar.

Table-spoon [tē'-bl-spūn], *s.* Cuchara de mesa o de sopa.

Table-spoonful [tē'-bl-spūn-ful], *s.* Cucharada.

Tablet [tab'-let], *s.* 1. Tableta, tablilla; hoja de marfil, etc., sobre la cual se puede escribir; juego o conjunto de hojas de papel unidas, o una sola de esas hojas. *V.* PAD. 2. Mesa pequeña o cualquier superficie plana pequeña; particularmente, plancha para una inscripción. 3. Tableta, medicamento en forma de pastilla cuadrada. *Votive tablet,* Tablilla, plancha grabada conmemorativa de un voto.

Tableware [tē'-bl-wār], *s.* Servicio de mesa.

Tabloid [tab'-loid], *s.* Pequeño periódico con noticias condensadas y muchas ilustraciones.—*a.* Comprimido o condensado, como una crítica, un drama, etc.

Taboo, Tabu [ta-bū'], *va.* Declarar tabú; (fig.) prohibir, excluir, desterrar.—*s.* Tabú, especie de prohibición religiosa de los habitantes de la Polinesia, por la que se consideran como sagrados ciertos objetos, lugares, días, personas, etc.; de aquí, preocupación, ostracismo.

Tabor, Tabour [tē'-ber], *s.* Tamboril, tambor pequeño; pandero.

Taborer [tē'-ber-er], *s.* Tamborilero.

Tabouret [tab-u-ret], **Taboret, Tabret** [tab'-ret], *s.* 1. Tambor pequeño o tamboril. 2. Taburete. 3. Bastidor de bordar.

Tabourine [tab-ur-īn'], *s.* Tamboril.

Tabular [tab'-yu-lar], *a.* 1. Perteneciente a una tabla; dispuesto en forma de lista o catálogo. 2. Tabular, en forma de placa o plancha; llano; laminado. 3. Cuadrado, formado en cuadros. 4. Computado con una tabla matemática.

Tabulate [tab'-yu-lēt], *va.* 1. Disponer en forma de tabla o lista; disponer en cuadros sinópticos. 2. Formar con una superficie plana.

Tabulated [tab'-yu-lēt-ed], *a.* Liso, plano, igual.

Tabulation [tab-yu-lē'-shun], *s.* Colocación, distribución en cuadros o listas.

Tachygraphic [tak-i-graf'-ic], *a.* Taquigráfico. *V.* STENOGRAPHIC.

Tachygraphy [ta-kig'-ra-fi], *s.* Taquigrafía, el arte de escribir con celeridad por medio de signos. *V.* STENOGRAPHY.

Tacit [tas'-it], *a.* Tácito, que sin expresarse se supone o infiere.
Tacitly [tas'-it-li], *adv.* Tácitamente, de un modo tácito.
Taciturn [tas'-i-türn], *a.* Taciturno, callado, que por costumbre gasta pocas palabras.
Tack [tac], *va.* 1. Atar, afianzar como con tachuelas; clavar ligeramente. 2. Pegar, coser o unir una cosa a otra; añadir como suplementario, anexar. *V.* APPEND.—*vn.* Virar, dar vuelta la nave para tomar otro rumbo; virar por avante, cambiar de bordada.
Tack, *s.* 1. Tachuela, clavito con cabeza; puntilla. 2. Lo que asegura; hilván. 3. (Mar.) (1) Amura, jarcia para fijar el ángulo de ciertas velas; (2) bordada, virada, el giro que hacen las embarcaciones a un lado y a otro alternativamente para ganar el viento. 4. De aquí, un cambio de política; nuevo plan de acción. *On the port tack*, Amurado a babor. *On the starboard tack*, Amurado a estribor. *To stand on the other tack*, Cambiar de amura.
Tackle [tac'-l], *va.* 1. Agarrar, asir, forcejear. 2. En el juego de *foot-ball*, salir al encuentro de un adversario y procurar impedir que corra.—*s.* 1. Aparejo, artificio para levantar o mover algo, combinación de cuerdas, poleas, ganchos, etc.; jarcia. 2. Todo género de instrumentos, aparejos, aperos, o avíos. *Fishing-tackle*, Enseres, avíos de pescar. 3. Acción de agarrar, o de impedir que otro corra. *Main-tackle*, Aparejo real. *Fore-tackle*, Aparejo del trinquete. *Stay-tackle*, Candeletón, estrinque. *Tack-tackle*, Aparejo de amurar. *Tackle-fall*, Tira de aparejo. *Tackle-hooks*, Ganchos de aparejos.
Tackling [tac'-ling], *s.* 1. Aparejo, palanquín. 2. Instrumentos, aperos, herramientas.
Tact [tact], *s.* 1. Tacto, discernimiento, buen sentido; finura, tino. 2. Tacto, sentido del tacto.
Tactical, Tactic [tac'-tic-al, tac'-tic], *a.* Táctico, perteneciente o relativo a la táctica.
Tactician [tac-tish'-an], *s.* Táctico, el instruido en la táctica militar o naval.
Tactics [tac'-tics], *s. pl.* 1. Táctica, el arte de los movimientos, formaciones o evoluciones militares o navales. 2. Manejo hábil; ardides.
Tactile [tac'-til], *a.* Tangible, referente al tacto; tocable, que se puede tocar.
Tactless [tact'-les], *a.* Falto de tacto, finura o tino; desatinado.
Tactual [tac'-chiū-al], *a.* Táctil.
Tadpole [tad'-pōl], *s.* Renacuajo, cría acuática de un animal anfibio, particularmente de la rana o el sapo, que respira por medio de agallas exteriores.
Ta'en [tên], *pp.* de *To* TAKE. (Esco.)
Taenia, Tenia [tí'-ni-a], *s.* 1. Banda, faja o cinta. 2. Tenia, solitaria, lombriz intestinal muy larga y en forma de cinta.
Taffeta [taf'-e-ta], **Taffety** [taf'-e-ti], *s.* Tafetán sencillo o liso.
Taffy [taf'-i], *s.* 1. Melcocha, arropía. 2. (Ger. E. U.) Zalamería.
Tag [tag], *s.* 1. Herrete; marbete, rótulo, cédula atada por un extremo; lo que está atado o cuelga. 2. Pingajo, arrapiezo. 3. Vedija desigual de lana en el cuello de un carnero.
Tag, *s.* Juego de muchachos, en el cual uno persigue a los demás hasta coger o tocar a uno de ellos.
Tag, *va.* 1. Herretear, echar herretes a alguna cosa; marcar con un marbete o rótulo. 2. Atar, afianzar. *Tagged lace*, Agujeta. 3. Seguir de cerca, marchar sobre los talones de alguno.
Tag, *va.* Alcanzar y tocar.
Tag day [tag dê], *s.* Día de colectas para beneficencia pública. Al contribuyente se le coloca en la solapa una etiqueta.
Tagrag [tag'-rag], *s.* Persona baja, vil y despreciable.
Tail [têl], *s.* 1. Cola, la extremidad que en la parte posterior tienen los animales, aves y peces. 2. Cola, la punta prolongada de algunas ropas talares. 3. Cola, la parte posterior o inferior de alguna cosa; la parte opuesta a la cabeza: apéndice terminal; rastro luminoso de un cometa; rasgo que se pone a una nota música y que la hace subir o bajar. 4. Acompañamiento, escolta. *To turn tail*, Volver la espalda, mostrar los talones, fugarse. *Bob tail*, Cola cortada. 5. (For.) Limitación de propiedad.
Tail, *va.* Tirar de la cola.
Tailblock [têl'-bloc], *s.* (Mar.) Motón de rabiza.
Tailed [têld], *a.* Rabudo, que tiene cola o rabo.
Tailing [têl'-ing], *s.* 1. *pl.* Restos, partes inferiores, particularmente de los minerales. 2. Extremo interior de un ladrillo o piedra dentro de una pared.
Tail light [têl' lait], *s.* Luz o farol de cola.
Tailor [tê'-lur], *s.* Sastre, el que tiene por oficio hacer vestidos. *Tailor-bird*, Pájaro oriental que cose o ensarta hojas con algodón para formar su nido. Sutoria sutoria.
Tailoress [tê'-lur-es], *sf.* Sastra, mujer que tiene por oficio hacer vestidos.
Tailor-made [tê'-lur-mêd], *a.* Hecho a la medida.
Tail-piece [têl'-pis], *s.* Florón o cualquier otro adorno grabado al fin de un libro o de un capítulo; (Tip.) culo de lámpara; cola de violín o guitarra.
Tail spin [têl' spin], *s.* (Aer.) Barrena.
Tailtackle [têl'-tac-l], *s.* (Mar.) Aparejo o palanquín de rabiza.
Tail wheel [têl' hwil], *s.* (Aer.) Rueda de cola.
Tail wind [têl' wind], *s.* Viento de cola o trasero, viento de popa.
Taint [tênt], *va.* 1. Manchar, ensuciar, inficionar. 2. Corromper, viciar, echar a perder; envenenar.—*vn.* Inficionarse.
Taint, *s.* Mácula, mancha, tanto en el sentido físico como en el moral: tacha, lunar; infección, corrupción.
Taintless [tênt'-les], *a.* Incorrupto, no contaminado, puro, sin mancha.
Take [têk], *va.* (*pret.* TOOK, *pp.* TAKEN). 1. Tomar, coger, asir o agarrar una cosa con la mano. 2. Tomar, recibir o aceptar de cualquier modo que sea. 3. Tomar, ocupar o adquirir por medio de la fuerza o por medio de artificios; apoderarse de. 4. Tomar, percibir o cobrar. 5. Tomar, quitar, hurtar o pillar; arrebatar, llevar; restar, deducir, substraer. 6. Tomar o hacer a uno prisionero; prender. 7. Escoger; de aquí, usar, emplear, adoptar. 8. Tomar, entender o interpretar alguna cosa en un sentido determinado. 9. Cautivar, embargar las potencias del alma; deleitar, causar deleite, gusto o placer. 10. Tomar, aprender o concebir alguna cosa. 11. Ejecutar cualquiera acción expresada generalmente por el substantivo que va unido con el verbo. 12. Contraer una enfermedad; resfriarse (con *cold*). 13. Informarse midiendo, pesando o computando. 14. Pasar por encima de, cruzar. *A horse takes a hedge*, El caballo salta por encima del seto. 15. Copiar, sacar una copia. 16. Tomar, tragar alguna cosa como medicina. 17. Suponer o dar por sentada alguna cosa. 18. Dar en alguna parte determinada. 19. Incluir en un curso, visitar.—*vn.* 1. Tomar, lograr; salir bien, tener buen éxito; causar gusto o agrado. 2. Quitar, abstraer o deducir alguna cosa; detraer, detractar, derogar. 3. Efectuarse una cosa, seguir el curso, orden o efecto natural. 4. Agarrarse, arraigarse, prender las plantas. 5. Encaminarse, dirigirse, ir o moverse hacia. 6. Prender el fuego. 7. Aplicarse, tener afición a, inclinarse naturalmente; se usa por lo común con *to*. 8. Hacer un cuadro, imagen o fotografía. *That takes a great deal of time*, Eso toma mucho tiempo. *Take my word for it*, Créame Vd. bajo mi palabra. *To take after*, Imitar, tomar por ejemplo; parecerse. *To take again*, Volver a tomar o tomar segunda vez. *To take asunder*, Separar, desunir, despegar. *To take away*, Quitar, sacar; llevarse; alzar o levantar la mesa; apartar o separar alguna cosa. *To take back*, (Fam.) Retractar, desdecirse. *To take down*, Bajar o poner más baja una cosa; bajar o conducir de alto abajo; abatir, humillar; tragar. *To take for granted*, Dar por sentado. *To take from*, Despojar, privar de, minorar, substraer. *To take in*, Cercar, rodear o ceñir; contener, comprender o incluir en sí; entender, comprender; admitir, recibir, tomar; acoger, recoger, dar asilo; contraer, disminuir el volumen de algo; encoger; ganar por conquista; (fam.) estafar, engañar. *To take in hand*, Emprender, tomar por su cuenta, tomar en mano. *To take into one's head*, Ponérsele a uno en la cabeza, metérsele en la mollera. *To take off*, Separar, quitar de delante o del medio, arrebatar; levantar o apartar, v. g. una máscara; destruir; invalidar o hacer nula y de ningún valor una cosa; tragar de un golpe; comprar; remedar, ridiculizar; copiar; sacar un retrato; despegar o separar dos cosas que estaban unidas entre sí. *To take off an arm*, Cortar, amputar un brazo. *To take off the edge of a knife*, Embotar un cuchillo; quitar el filo. *To take off from*, Debilitar, disminuir; apartar de, desviar de. *To take on*, Quejarse, lamentarse, melancolizarse, estar triste. *V.* también *To take upon*. *To take out*, Llevar o sacar afuera; hacer salir o echar a alguno de un paraje; sacar, quitar, arrebatar; arrancar, extraer. *To take the creases out of cloth*, Quitar los dobleces del paño o alisarlo.

To take out a patent, Obtener un privilegio de invención. *To take out of*, Extraer. *To take over*, (1) (Ingl.) Apoderarse, adquirir. tomar posesión de algo; (2) derivar. *To take to*, Aplicarse al estudio; tomar afición a alguna cosa; recurrir. *To take to heart*, Tomar a pechos. *To take to pieces*, Hacer pedazos; desarmar una cosa que tiene varias piezas; de aquí, confutar un argumento punto por punto. *To take up*, Tomar al fiado, tomar prestado; atacar; comenzar o dar principio a alguna cosa; ocupar la atención; recurrir en último resultado; prender, arrestar; ligar un vaso en las operaciones quirúrgicas; admitir una cosa sin examen; reprender, amonestar; principiar una cosa en el punto donde otro la dejó; alzar o levantar alguna cosa del suelo; ocupar o llenar un sitio cualquiera; comprender o incluir en sí; adoptar una opinión, doctrina, etc.; saldar, pagar (una letra de cambio, un pagaré, etc.); cobrar o recoger, hablando de contribuciones; aprovechar en el estudio o en cualquier otra materia; detenerse o contenerse; reformar uno su vida o sus costumbres. *To take up a quarrel*, Entremeterse en alguna disputa o pendencia. *To take up a space*, Ocupar o llenar completamente un sitio o espacio. *To take one up sharply*, Reprender a alguno agriamente. *To take up short*, Quedarse cortado. *To take up with*, Contentarse; vivir o habitar con; ocupar. *To take upon*, Tomar sobre sí algún cargo, obligación, responsabilidad, etc.; entremeterse, mezclarse o meterse en una cosa; afectar señorío, hacerse el personaje, el caballero; arrogarse, atribuirse. *To take upon trust*, Tomar a crédito; saber algo por haberlo oído decir; creer alguna cosa bajo la fe o crédito de otro. *To take upon one's self*, Tomar a su cargo o encargarse de la ejecución de una cosa. *To take with*, Agradar, satisfacer, contentar, gustar. *To take a journey*, Hacer un viaje. *To take a leap*, Dar un salto o brinco. *To take a liking to*, Aficionarse a. *To take a turn o a walk*, Dar una vuelta, un paseo. *To take a thing kindly*, Tomar una cosa en buen sentido, no tomarlo por donde quema; y también quedar contento de alguna cosa que otro ha hecho. *To take advice*, Aconsejarse o tomar consejo. *To take an oath*, Jurar o hacer juramento. *To take breath*, Tomar aliento, reposarse después de algún esfuerzo. *To take home*, Llevar, traer a casa. *To take care*, Cuidar, tener cuidado; ser cuidadoso, tener solicitud por algo. *To take the chair*, Tomar, ocupar el sillón presidencial, presidir. *To take the field*, Entrar en campaña, comenzar las hostilidades. *To take fire*, Encenderse; atufarse, tomar fuego. *To take fright at*, Atemorizarse de o por, sobresaltarse. *To take heed*, Estar alerta, tener cuidado, atender. *To take hold*, Coger, apoderarse. *To take landscapes*, Fotografiar o pintar paisajes. *To take leave of*, Despedirse de. *To take no trouble to gain an end*, No dar pie ni patada. *To take offence at*, Agraviarse de, picarse. *To take pains*, Esmerarse, darse la pena. *To take pity on*, Apiadarse o compadecerse de. *To take place*, Suceder, efectuarse, verificarse, tener efecto alguna cosa. *To take notice*, Poner atención. *Not to take notice*, No hacer caso, no poner cuidado. *Take notice*, (For.) Aviso, aviso o noticia al público; advertencia. *To take refuge*, Acogerse a. *To take sanctuary*, Acogerse a sagrado o tomar sagrado. *To take shelter*, Guarecerse. *To take ship*, Embarcarse. *To take the law*, Poner pleito. *To be taken ill*, Enfermar. *The enemy took to flight*, El enemigo huyó. *To take to business*, Ser aficionado a los negocios o consagrarse a ellos. *A book which will not take*, Un libro que no tendrá buen éxito, que no se venderá. *The daughter takes after her father*, La hija se parece o sale a su padre.

Take, *s.* 1. Toma, tomadura, acción de tomar, y la porción que se toma de una vez. 2. (Impr.) Tomada, la porción que toma el cajista de una vez. *Take-off*, (1) Imitación burlesca, caricatura. (2) El punto donde los pies dejan el suelo al saltar. *Take-up*, Atesador, pieza que estira el hilo en las máquinas de coser al levantarse la aguja.

Take-home pay [têk-hōm pê], *s.* Salario neto (después de haberse descontado los impuestos y otras sumas por diversos conceptos).

Taken, *pp.* de *To* TAKE.

Take-off [têk'-ōf], *s.* 1. Despegue (de un avión). 2. Partida o salida (en viaje). 3. (fam.) Imitación en son de caricatura.—*vn.* 1. Despegar (un avión). 2. Salir, partir (en un viaje).

Taker [tê'-kẹr], *s.* Tomador.

Taking [têk'-ing], *a.* 1. Encantador, seductor, atractivo, halagüeño. 2. (Fam.) Contagioso.—*s.* 1. Acción del que toma o embarga; secuestro, embargo. 2. Afición a alguna cosa; inclinación, afecto; se usa con *for*. 3. *pl.* Recibos. 4. (Fam.) Captura; de aquí, situación difícil, trance apurado.

Talc [talc], *s.* (Min.) Talco, esteatita, un silicato de magnesia blando y untuoso, fibroso o compacto.

Talcum powder [tal'-cum pau'-dẹr], *s.* Talco, polvo de talco.

Tale [têl], *s.* 1. Cuento, cuentecillo o narración de alguna aventura, incidente, etc. 2. Relación, relato. 3. Fábula, conseja. 4. Cuenta, operación aritmética.

Tale-bearer [têl'-bār-ẹr], *s.* Soplón, chismoso, cuentero.

Tale-bearing [têl'-bār-ing], *s.* Soplo, cuento o chisme.

Talent [tal'-ent], *s.* 1. Talento, dotes de la naturaleza. 2. Talento, aptitud notable, capacidad, habilidad natural, ingenio. 3. Talento, moneda o suma de monedas que usaron los antiguos.

Talented [tal'-ent-ed], *a.* Talentoso, que tiene talento.

Talent scout [tal'-ent scaut], *s.* Persona encargada de descubrir posibles futuros actores, cantantes, etc.

Tale-teller [têl' tel-ẹr], *s.* Chismeador, chismoso, correvedile.

Talisman [tal'-is- (o iz-) man], *s.* Talismán; carácter, figura o imagen adivinatoria y supersticiosa.

Talk [tōk], *va.* 1. Decir, hablar de; conversar sobre algo. 2. Hablar (un idioma).—*vn.* 1. Hablar, conversar. 2. Charlar, hablar mucho y fuera de propósito. 3. Contar, referir. 4. Razonar, conferenciar. *To talk away, to talk on*, Continuar hablando, hablar siempre; pasar el tiempo en hablar, en conversar. *To talk into*, Convencer a fuerza de hablar, persuadir, hacer ejecutar. *To talk out of*, Disuadir; sonsacar. *To talk over*, Discutir, persuadir, convencer. *To talk to the purpose*, Hablar al alma. *To talk up*, Pronunciarse, explicarse claramente; (fam.) discutir con intención de promover; alabar, engrandecer.

Talk, *s.* 1. Plática, conversación de una persona con otra. 2. Habla, la locución o palabras que se hablan. 3. Charla, cháchara, parloteo. 4. Voz común, fama, rumor. 5. El asunto de una conversación. *Small talk*, Palique, charla. (Vulg.) Dichitos.

Talkative [tōk'-a-tiv], *a.* Gárrulo, locuaz, charlante, amigo de charlar.

Talkativeness [tōk'-a-tiv-nes], *s.* Locuacidad, charlatanería, garrulidad, flujo de palabras.

Talker [tōk'-ẹr], *s.* 1. El que habla o conversa con otro. 2. Hablador, el que habla mucho, parlador, charlador. 3. Fanfarrón, el que hecha fanfarronadas.

Talking machine [tek'-ing ma-shīn'], *s.* Fonógrafo, tocadiscos.

Talking picture [tek'-ing pic'-tiūr], *s.* Película sonora, película hablada.

Talky, Talcky [talk'-i], *a.* *V.* TALCOSE.

Tall [tōl], *a.* 1. Alto, de alta talla o estatura. 2. Alto, elevado. 3. (Ant.) Excelente, admirable, renombrado.

Tallage [tal'-ẹj], *s.* Alcabala; impuesto.

Tallness [tōl'-nes], *s.* Altura, estatura, talla.

Tallow [tal'-o], *va.* Ensebar, untar con sebo.—*s.* Sebo. *Raw tallow*, Sebo puro o en rama. *Melted tallow*, Sebo colado. *Tallow-chandler*, Velero, el que hace velas de sebo. *Tallow-chandler's shop*, Velería. *Tallow-tree*. (Bot.) Árbol del sebo. *Tallow dip*, Vela de sebo.

Tallowy [tal'-o-i], *a.* Seboso, grasoso; del color o de la apariencia de sebo.

Tally [tal'-i], *s.* 1. Tarja, palo partido por el medio para ir marcando lo que se saca o compra fiado o da adelantado, haciendo muescas en él. 2. Cualquiera cosa hecha de modo que ajuste con otra.

Tally, *va.* 1. Ajustar, acomodar, hacer alguna cosa a medida de otra o de modo que venga bien con ella. 2. Tarjar, llevar la cuenta de alguna cosa señalando las partidas por rayas o muescas en una tarja o caña. *To tally the sheets*, (Mar.) Cazar y atracar las escotas.—*vn.* Cuadrar, conformarse o ajustarse una cosa con otra.

Tallyho, *inter.* Grito del cazador a los sabuesos.—*s.* Coche de cuatro caballos.

Tallyman [tal'-i-man], *s.* El tendero que da al fiado a los jornaleros lo que necesitan, bajo la condición de cobrar algo cada semana, cuando reciben su jornal.

Tally sheet [tal'-i shīt], *s.* Hoja para apuntar los tantos (en una elección, un juego, etc.).

Talmud [tal'-mud], *s.* Talmud, libro de los judíos que contiene su tradición, doctrina y ceremonias.

Talon [tal'-un], *s.* 1. Garra, el pie del ave de rapiña. 2. Talón de hoja de espada.
Talus [tê'-lus], *s.* 1. (Anat.) Astrágalo, hueso del tobillo; tobillo. 2. (Arq.) Pendiente, inclinación, talud. 3. (Geol.) Masa pendiente de fragmentos debajo de un peñasco. (Lat.)
Tamable [têm'-a-bl], *a.* Domable, domesticable, capaz de ser amansado, domado o domesticado.
Tamarind [tam'-a-rind], *s.* Tamarindo, árbol tropical oriundo de la India, y su fruto.
Tamarisk [tam'-a-risc], *s.* (Bot.) Tamarisco, tamariz.
Tambour [tam'-būr], *s.* 1. Tambor. 2. Tambor, para bordar y la obra hecha a tambor. 3. Tamboril. 4. Cancel de una iglesia; (arq.) tambor, el casco de una cúpula que estriba en los arcos torales.
Tambour, *va.* Bordar a tambor.
Tambourine [tam-bū-rīn'], *s.* Pandereta con cascabeles o con rodajas metálicas.
Tame [têm], *a.* 1. Amansado, domado, domesticado, manso. 2. Dócil, sometido, tratable. 3. Abatido, humilde, sumiso. 4. Pálido, falto de animación o efecto, sin color. *A tame narrative,* Un relato pálido, sin color.
Tame, *va.* 1. Domar, domesticar, amansar, hablando de fieras o animales. 2. Avasallar, abatir; suavizar, domeñar, poner dócil o tratable.
Tamely [têm'-li], *adv.* Humildemente, abatidamente, bajamente.
Tameness [têm'-nes], *s.* 1. Calidad de amansado o domesticado; domesticidad de los animales; mansedumbre. 2. Sumisión, timidez, cobardía, genio o carácter apocado.
Tamer [têm'-ẹr], *s.* 1. Domador, vencedor. 2. El que domestica animales.
Tamis [tam'-is], *s.* Tamiz, cedazo hecho de tela.
Tam-o'-shanter [tam'-o'-shan'-tẹr], *s.* (Esco.) Gorra de lana a manera de boina grande.
Tamkin [tam'-kin], *s.* (Art.) Tapaboca.
Tamp [tamp], *va.* Cebar el barreno de una cantera para volar la roca.
Tamper [tam'-pẹr], *vn.* Procurar alterar oficiosamente; entremeterse, meterse en camisa de once varas; se usa generalmente con *with.*
Tampon [tam'-pon], *s.* (Med.) Tapón.
Tam-tam [tam'-tam], *s.* Timbal, especie de tambor de la India y del oeste de África.
Tan [tan], *va.* 1. Curtir, zurrar, adobar o aderezar pieles. 2. Curtir, tostar, quemar, poner marchito o moreno, hablando del sol o del aire.
Tan, *s.* 1. Casca, la corteza del roble molida para curtir las pieles. 2. Moreno amarillento que tira a rojo. 3. Tez morena como requemada por el sol y el aire. *Tan-bark,* Casca para curtir. *Tan-pit* o *vat,* El tanque o pozo donde se adoban las pieles en las tenerías. *Tan-yard,* Tenería.
Tanager [tan'-a-jẹr], *s.* Tángara, pájaro de los tanágridos de vivos colores.
Tanbark [tan'-bārk], *s.* Casca, corteza de ciertos árboles para curtir las pieles.
Tandem [tan'-dem], *a.* Que tiene los caballos colocados en fila, uno tras otro.—*s.* 1. Dos o más caballos enganchados y guiados uno tras otro; el vehículo con los caballos así enganchados. 2. Bicicleta o biciclo de doble silla, para dos ciclistas.—*adv.* Uno delante de otro.
Tang [tang], *s.* 1. Resabio, el sabor que deja alguna cosa en la boca. 2. (Vulg.) Sainete, sabor, gusto. 3. Sonido, tañido, tono. 4. Cola, espiga, rabera de una herramienta; parte saliente.
Tang, *vn.* Retumbar, hacer ruido.
Tangency [tan'-jen-si], *s.* Tangencia, calidad de tangente.
Tangent [tan'-jent], *a.* y *s.* (Geom.) Tangente.
Tangential [tan-jen'-shal], *a.* De una línea tangente; que se mueve en tangente.
Tangerine [tan'-jẹ-rīn], *a.* y *s.* 1. Tangerino, tangerina, natural de Tánger o perteneciente a esta ciudad. 2. Naranja tangerina, variedad pequeña y aromática de corteza roja.
Tangibility [tan-ji-bil'-i-ti], *s.* La calidad que hace a una cosa capaz de ser percibida por el tacto.
Tangible [tan'-ji-bl], *a.* Tangible.
Tangle [taṇ'-gl], *va.* 1. Enredar, enmarañar, embrollar, embarazar. 2. Confundir.—*vn.* Enmarañarse, enredarse; confundirse.
Tangle, *s.* 1. Enredo o enlace desordenado de una cosa con otra; trenza de pelo. 2. Estado de confusión.
Tangle, *s.* Cada una de las dos especies de laminaria, alga marina.
Tangly [taṇ'-gli], *a.* 1. Enredado o desordenado. 2. Abundante en hierbas marinas.
Tango [tan'-go], *s.* Tango.
Tank [taṇk], *s.* Cisterna de madera o metal, aljibe, arca de aguas; (Amer.) tanque. *Tank-car,* Carro tanque, vagón de ferrocarril que lleva un tanque de hierro, por lo común de forma cilíndrica; sirve para transportar petróleo, etc. *Tank-engine,* Locomotora con tanque de agua encima de la caldera, pero sin ténder.
Tankage [taṇk'-ẹj], *s.* 1. Acto de poner en tanques. 2. Precio que se paga por guardar algo en tanques. 3. Cabida o capacidad de un tanque o tanques. 4. Residuo de las grasas.
Tankard [taṇk'-ard], *s.* Cántaro o jarro grande, a veces con tapa.
Tanker [tank'-ẹr], *s.* Barco petrolero.
Tannate [tan'-êt], *s.* (Quím.) Tanato, sal formada con ácido tánico.
Tanner [tan'-ẹr], *s.* Curtidor, zurrador, el que curte o adoba pieles.
Tannery [tan'-ẹr-i], *s.* Tenería o curtiduría.
Tannic [tan'-ic], *a.* (Quím.) Tánico, perteneciente a la casca, o que se saca de ella. *Tannic acid,* Ácido tánico, o tanino, compuesto astringente ($C_{14}H_{10}O_9$) que forma escamas brillantes cuando se saca de las nueces de agalla. Sirve para curtir y para hacer tinta.
Tannin [tan'-in], *s.* Tanino, principio curtiente. *V. Tannic acid.*
Tanning [tan'-ing], *s.* Curtimiento, zurra, procedimiento para adobar o aderezar las pieles.
Tansy [tan'-zi], *s.* (Bot.) Tanaceto. *Wild tansy,* Argentina.
Tantalize [tan'-ta-laiz], *va.* Atormentar a alguno mostrándole objetos o placeres que no puede alcanzar.
Tantalum [tan'-ta-lum], *s.* (Min.) Tántalo, cuerpo simple metálico.
Tantamount [tan'-ta-maunt], *a.* Equivalente, que equivale.
Tantivy [tan-tiv'-i], *adv.* De priesa, a rienda suelta.
Tantrum [tan'-trum], *s.* Acceso de cólera o petulancia.
Tap [tap], *va.* 1. Sacar un líquido; decentar un barril; horadar para poner la canilla a un tonel. 2. Extraer el jugo de un árbol por incisión.—*s.* 1. Canilla, espita, tubo o caño que se pone en la cuba para sacar el vino. 2. (Mec.) Taladro, herramienta en forma de tornillo para hacer el filete o rosca interior. 3. Licor especial o calidad particular de licor. 4. (Fam.) Mostrador de taberna. *On tap,* Contenido en un barril; que se saca de un barril, cubo o tonel. (A.-S. tæppan.)
Tap, *va.* y *vn.* 1. Golpear o tocar ligeramente. 2. Remontar (el calzado). 3. Dar golpecitos.—*s.* 1. Palmada suave, golpecito con una cosa pequeña. 2. Remiendo echado al talón de un zapato. 3. *pl.* Toque militar de corneta o tambor para apagar las luces. (<Fr. *taper,* < alemán *tappen.*) *To tap at the door,* Llamar dando golpecitos a la puerta.
Tape [têp], *s.* Cinta, cintilla, tejido de hilo o algodón; tira plana de metal delgado; (Amér.) melindre. *Tape line, tape measure,* Cinta para medir. *Linen tape,* Cinta de hiladillo. *Red tape,* (1) Balduque, cinta estrecha para atar legajos. (2, fig.) Expedienteo, formalismo, método rutinario (en el despacho de los asuntos públicos).
Tap dance [tap dans], *s.* Baile zapateado de los E. U.
Taper [tê'-pẹr], *s.* 1. Bujía, cerilla, vela pequeña; cirio (de iglesia); hacha, blandón. 2. Diminución gradual de tamaño en un objeto de forma prolongada.
Taper, *vn.* Ahusarse.—*va.* Ahusar, adelgazar.
Tape recorder [têp rẹ-cord'-ẹr], *s.* Magnetófono, grabadora de cinta.
Tape-recording [têp'-rẹ-cord-ing], *a.* Magnetofónico.
Taproom [tap'-rūm], *s.* Cantina, taberna.
Tapeworm [têp'-wūrm], *s.* Tenia, lombriz solitaria.
Tapestry [tap'-es-tri], *va.* Entapizar, adornar con colgaduras o tapices.—*s.* Tapiz; tapicería, colgadura.
Tapioca [tap-i-ō'-ca], *s.* Tapioca, fécula de la yuca brava o mandioca.
Tapir [tê'-pẹr], *s.* Tapir, mamífero paquidermo de los países intertropicales.
Tapis [tê'-pis], *s.* Tapete; se emplea sólo en la locución *on the tapis,* sobre el tapete (objeto de discusión).
Tapping [tap'-ing], *s.* La operación quirúrgica de la paracentesis o la extracción del agua del vientre de los hidrópicos.
Taproot [tap'-rūt], *s.* Tallo de la raíz; raíz principal.
Taps [taps], *s. pl.* (Mil.) Toque de queda.
Tapster [tap'-stẹr], *s.* Mozo de cervecería.
Tar [tār], *s.* 1. Alquitrán, brea, pez líquida. 2. En estilo vulgar significa marinero u hombre de mar, como apodo. (Abrev. de TARPAULIN, 3ª acep.) *Coal-tar,* Alquitrán de hulla. *Mineral tar,* Betún, al-

quitrán mineral. *Tar-box*, Caja que contiene ungüento de brea para los carneros. *Tar-water*, Agua de alquitrán.

Tar, *va.* 1. Alquitranar, embrear. 2. Brear, dar brega a alguno, molestarle o chasquearle. *To tar and feather*, Embrear y emplumar: antigua forma de castigo que todavía emplean las turbas en algunos casos.

Tarantella [tar-an-tel'-a], *s.* Tarantela, baile napolitano de movimiento muy vivo.

Tarantula [ta-ran'-tiu-la], *s.* Tarántula, una especie de araña de gran tamaño.

Tarbrush [tār'-brush], *s.* (Mar.) Escopero, pincel.

Tardigrade, Tardigradous [tār'-di-grêd, tār-dig'-ra-dus], *a.* Tardo, tardígrado, lento, pesado en su movimiento: dícese de los animales.

Tardily [tār'-di-li], *adv.* 1. Lentamente. 2. Tardíamente; pasado el tiempo oportuno; fuera de tiempo.

Tardiness [tār'-di-nes], *s.* Lentitud, tardanza.

Tardy [tār'-di], *a.* 1. Tardío, que sucede después del tiempo oportuno. 2. Tardo, lento; negligente, que obra de mala gana.

Tare [tār], *s.* 1. (Bot.) Cizaña. 2. (Bot.) Lenteja; algarroba común, o una de otras varias especies de plantas. 3. (Com.) Tara, la parte del peso que se rebaja en los géneros o mercancías por razón de la caja, saca u otro envase en que vienen incluidos; merma.

Tare, *va.* Destarar, restar la tara al pesar una cosa.

Tarentella, *s.* *V.* TARANTELLA.

Target [tār'-get], *s.* 1. Blanco a que se tira. 2. Tarja, especie de escudo o rodela. 3. (Fig.) Objeto de ataque, centro de observación *Target-practise*, Tiro al blanco.

Targum [tār'-gum], *s.* Targum, versión o traducción libre de partes del Antiguo Testamento en arameo o caldeo.

Tariff [tar'-if], *s.* Tarifa, arancel, tabla o catálogo de los derechos que deben pagar los géneros.

Tarlatan, Tarletan [tār'-la-tan], *s.* Tarlatana, muselina fina y algo transparente.

Tarn [tārn], *s.* (Ingl. y Esco.) Lago pequeño entre las montañas.

Tarnish [tār'-nish], *va.* 1. Deslustrar, empañar, deslucir, quitar el lustre. 2. Mancillar, deshonrar; disminuir la pureza de.—*vn.* Deslustrarse, deslucirse, perder el lustre; enmohecerse, tomarse de orín (hablando de los metales).—*s.* 1. Falta de lustre, deslustre; de aquí, mancha. 2. La película delgada y de color que se forma en la superficie del mineral expuesta al aire.

Taro [tā'-rō], *s.* Taro, planta alimenticia de varias islas del Océano Pacífico, particularmente la Colocasia esculenta; hay varias especies.

Tarpaulin [tar-pē'-lin] o **Tarpawling** [tār-pōl'-ing], *s.* 1. El cáñamo embreado; alquitranado o lienzo de alquitrán; encerado. *Tarpawling-nails*, (Mar.) Estoperoles. 2. Sombrero de cuero encerado. 3. (Fam.) Marinero, en son de burla.

Tarpeian [tār-pī'-an], *a.* De Tarpeya.

Tarpon [tār'-pen], *s.* Sábalo (pez).

Tarragon [tar'-a-gen], *s.* (Bot.) Tarragona.

Tarras [tar-ras'], *s.* *V.* TRASS.

Tarred [tārd], *a.* Embreado, alquitranado. *Tarred canvas coats of the masts*, (Mar.) Capas de fogonaduras.

Tarrier [tar'-i-ęr], *s.* 1. Tardador, el que tarda o se tarda. 2. (Dial.) *V.* TERRIER.

Tarry [tar'-i], *vn.* 1. Tardar, detenerse, pararse, quedarse atrás; aplazar la partida o la llegada. 2. Morar, habitar o estar de asiento en algún lugar.

Tarry [tār'-i], *s.* Cubierto de brea o de alquitrán; semejante al alquitrán o a la brea.

Tarsal [tār'-sal], *a.* Tarsal, que tiene relación con el tarso.

Tarsus [tār'-sus], *s.* 1. (Anat.) Tarso, empeine del pie. 2. Lámina de tejido conexivo en el párpado. 3. Tarso, la tercera articulación del pie de las aves. 4. (Zool.) Segmento terminal de las patas de los artrópodos.

Tart [tārt], *a.* 1. Acedo, agridulce, que tiene punta de agrio. 2. Acre, desapacible, picante, mordaz.

Tart, *s.* Tarta, pastelillo de fruta.

Tartan [tār'-tan], *s.* 1. Tartán, tela de lana con cuadros o listas cruzadas de diferentes colores. 2. El cuadro o dibujo de dicha tela. 3. Vestido de tartán. 4. (Mar.) Tartana, especie de embarcación con un solo mástil y una vela latina.

Tartar [tār'-tar], *s.* 1. Tártaro, sal que se forma dentro de las cubas de vino. *V.* ARGOL. 2. Sarro, incrustación que se forma sobre los dientes, principalmente el fosfato de cal. *Cream of tartar*, Crémor tártaro. *Tartar emetic*, Tártaro emético.

Tartar, *s.* Tártaro, habitante de la Tartaria. *To catch a Tartar*, Hallar uno la horma de su zapato; do cazar pensamos, cazados quedamos.

Tartarean [tār-tē'-rę-an], *a.* Tartáreo, infernal.

Tartareous [tar-tē'-rę-us], *a.* 1. Tartáreo, compuesto de tártaro o hecho de tártaro. 2. Infernal, tartáreo.

Tartaric [tar-tar'-ic], *a.* Tártrico, perteneciente al tártaro, o que se deriva de él; ácido tártrico.

Tartarize [tār'-tar-aiz], *va.* Tartarizar, impregnar o tratar con tártaro.

Tartarous [tār'-tar-us], *a.* Tartáreo, hecho de tártaro, compuesto de tártaro o que tiene las propiedades de tártaro.

Tartly [tārt'-li], *adv.* Agriamente, austeramente.

Tartness [tārt'-nes], *s.* 1. Agrura, acedía, sabor acedo o agrio. 2. Acrimonia, aspereza o desabrimiento en el genio o en las expresiones.

Tartrate [tār'-trêt], *s.* Tartrato, sal del ácido tártrico.

Task [tąsk], *s.* 1. Tarea, la obra o trabajo que se debe concluir en tiempo determinado y que reparten los maestros o los amos; deber, tarea (de un discípulo), lección que hay que aprender. 2. Trabajo molesto, labor, faena. *To take to task*, Reprender, regañar, censurar.

Task, *va.* Atarear, poner o señalar tarea.

Tasker [tąsk'-ęr], **Task-master** [tąsk' mąs-tęr], *s.* El que da, pone o señala tareas.

Tassel [tas'-el], *s.* 1. Borla o borlita de seda, oro o plata en figura de bellota, con muchos hilos. 2. Borla, especie de botón de seda, oro o plata de que salen muchos hilos, en figura de campanillas. 3. Inflorescencia de ciertas flores, v. g. las del maíz o del sauce.

Tasselled [tas'-eld], *a.* Adornado con borlas o campanillas.

Tasset [tas'-et], *s.* Escarcela.

Tastable [têst'-a-bl], *a.* Sabroso, que tiene sabor, que se puede gustar.

Taste [têst], *va.* y *vn.* 1. Gustar, sentir, percibir y distinguir con el paladar el gusto o sabor de las cosas. 2. Gustar, probar, catar, gustar de, tomar algo de. 3. Gustar, experimentar, ensayar. 4. Gustar, querer alguna cosa, tener complacencia en ella; agradar, parecer bien. 5. Saber o tener un sabor que puede percibir el sentido del gusto.

Taste, *s.* 1. Gusto, sensación de los sabores; sabor, gustadura; paladeo, saboreo. 2. Gusto, sentido por el cual se distinguen los sabores. 3. Cata, sorbo, trago, la porción pequeña de alguna cosa que se da para catar o probarla; (fig.) ligera cantidad, un poco, muy poco; muestra, ejemplar; ensayo, prueba, experimento. 4. Gusto, discernimiento; la facultad estética; facultad de sentir y discernir lo bello o lo excelencia artística. 5. Inclinación y aptitud especiales para una ocupación. 6. Manera con que se hace una obra o labor, en lo referente al buen gusto, a la gracia y elegancia de la misma. *A man of taste*, Hombre de gusto. *A matter of taste*, Cuestión de gusto. *To have a taste for*, Gustarle a uno una cosa, o tener gusto para hacerla.

Tastebud [têst'-bud], *s.* Papila del gusto.

Tasted [têst'-ed], *a.* Que tiene sabor o gusto particular.

Tasteful [têst'-ful], *a.* Conforme al buen gusto, que tiene buen gusto, hecho con gusto. 2. (Ant.) Sabroso.

Tastefully [têst'-ful-i], *adv.* Según el buen gusto, con gusto.

Tastefulness [têst'-ful-nes], *s.* Gusto, discernimiento, gracia, elegancia.

Tasteless [têst'-les], *a.* 1. Insípido, desabrido, soso o que no tiene sabor ni sazón. 2. Falto o privado del sentido del gusto. 3. Insípido, que no tiene espíritu o que no tiene gracia ni sal.

Tastelessly [têst'-les-li], *adv.* Insípidamente, sin gusto, sin sal, sin gracia.

Tastelessness [têst'-les-nes], *s.* Insipidez, falta de gusto o falta de viveza o gracia.

Taster [têst'-ęr], *s.* 1. Catador, el que cata o prueba la vianda o bebida. 2. Copita para catar o probar licores.

Tasty [têst'-ti], *a.* 1. Sabroso. 2. (Fam.) Hecho o expresado con gusto, con gracia o con sal; forma poco castiza. *Tasty food*, Alimentos sabrosos.

Tat [tat], *va.* y *vn.* Hacer encaje de hilo a mano, con lanzadera y por medio de lazos y nudos.

Tatar, Tartar [tā'-tār, tār'-tar], *s.* 1. Tártaro, natural de Tartaria; familia humana que comprende los turcos, los cosacos, etc. 2. Uno de los mogoles que en el siglo trece asolaron la Europa y el Asia. 3. Descendiente de dichos mogoles de la edad media, que habita al presente en Asia o Europa. (< Per. tātār.)

Tatter [tat'-ęr], *va.* Hacer andrajos, jirones o harapos; se usa casi exclusivamente en el participio pasado, *tattered*, harapiento.

Tatter, *s.* Andrajo, pingajo, arrapiezo, harapo. *To be all in tatters*, Estar hecho un andrajo o estar hecho jirones.

Tatting [tat'-ing], *s.* Encaje o guarnición de hilo, hecho a mano con lanzadera ; y el procedimiento empleado para hacerlo. *V.* TAT.

Tattle [tat'-l], *va.* Charlar, parlar, chacharear. *V.* BLAB.—*vn.* Chismear, traer y llevar chismes.

Tattle, *s.* Charla, cháchara, charlatanería ; chisme ; parlería, como la de los niños.

Tattler [tat'-lęr], *s.* 1. Charlador, parlador, hablador, chacharero. 2. (Orn.) Agachadiza del género Totamus, de pico recio y agudo.

Tattoo [tat-tū'], *s.* 1. (Mil.) Retreta, el toque del tambor que avisa a los soldados que se retiren al cuartel. 2. Figura dibujada en el cutis con tinta indeleble.

Tattoo, *va.* Pintar o pintarse el cutis con figuras, o rayarlo con colores.

Tattooing [tat-tū'-ing], *s.* La acción y efecto de pintarse figuras en el cutis; la figura así dibujada.

Taught [tōt], *pret.* y *pp.* del verbo TEACH.—*a.* (Des.) *V.* TAUT.

Taunt [tānt o tōnt], *va.* Mofar, hacer burla o zumba de alguna persona, dar chanza ; echar en cara, vituperar.

Taunt, *s.* Mofa, burla, escarnio, chanza, zumba.

Taunter [tānt'-ęr], *s.* Mofador, burlón, zumbón.

Tauntingly [tānt'-ing-li], *adv.* Con mofa, con vituperio ; en tono de sarcasmo ; en tono insultante.

Taunt-masted [tānt-mąst'-ed], *a.* (Mar.) De mucha guinda, demasiado alto.

Taupe [tōp], *s.* Gris pardo.

Taurine [tō'-rin o tō'-rain], *a.* 1. Taurino, de toro, semejante o relativo al toro. 2. (Astr.) Relativo al signo Tauro del zodíaco.

Taut [tōt], *a.* 1. (Mar.) Tieso, tendido. 2. Listo, preparado, en forma debida.

Tautology [tō-tel'-o-ji], *s.* Tautología, repetición de una misma idea en otros términos.

Tavern [tav'-ęrn], *s.* Taberna ; fonda, posada, establecimiento público donde por dinero se hospeda la gente ; figón. *Tavern-haunter*, El que frecuenta figones o tabernas. *Tavern-keeper*, Tabernero ; posadero.

Taw [tō], *va.* Curtir pieles blancas con alumbre, a diferencia de curtir corambres con zumaque.

Taw, *s.* Bolita de mármol con que juegan los niños; línea desde la cual los jugadores lanzan las bolas.

Tawdrily [tō'-dri-li], *adv.* De una manera chillona ; vistosamente y sin elegancia.

Tawdriness [tō'-dri-nes], *s.* Oropel, apariencia, brillo falso de oropel ; calidad de chillón (colores).

Tawdry [tō'-dri], *a.* Vistoso sin elegancia ; adornado con exceso ; de colores chillones ; dícese sólo de lo que relumbra mucho y vale poco.

Tawer [tō'-ęr], *s.* El curtidor que zurra o adoba las pieles con alumbre.

Tawny [tō'-ni], *a.* Curtido, moreno ; leonado, que tira a pardo y amarillo.

Tax [tax], *s.* 1. Impuesto, tributo, contribución, gabela que se paga al Estado ; estos nombres se usan comúnmente en plural. 2. Gabela, carga, servidumbre pesada. *Tax-collector*, *tax-gatherer*, Recaudador de contribuciones. *Tax-payer*, Contribuyente. *Tax-list*, Cédula, lista de bienes raíces sobre los cuales se han pagado las contribuciones.

Tax, *va.* 1. Imponer tributos o contribuciones. 2. (For.) Tasar costas, tasar las costas. 3. Cargar, abrumar ; exigir demasiado. 4. (Biblia) Registrar para la imposición de tributos. 5. (Fam.) Pedir como precio. 6. Acusar, hacer cargos ; se usa con *of* o *with*. *To tax with insincerity*, Tachar, acusar a alguien de doblez.

Taxable [tax'-a-bl], *a.* 1. Lo que se puede cargar o está sujeto a impuestos. 2. Pechero.

Taxation [tax-ē'-shun], *s.* 1. La imposición o repartimiento de derechos, contribuciones o impuestos. 2. (Des.) Imputación, la atribución de alguna culpa, falta o delito.

Taxer [tax'-ęr], *s.* 1. El que impone tributos. 2. Acusador, el que acusa.

Tax exempt, *a.* Exento de impuestos.

Tax-gatherer [tax'-gadh-ęr-ęr], *s.* Recaudador de tributos, impuestos o contribuciones.

Taxi [tax'-i], *vn.* 1. Ir en un taxi. 2. (Aer.) Deslizarse un avión sobre la superficie al despegar o al aterrizar.

Taxi, taxicab [tax'-i, tax'-i-cab], *s.* Taxi, automóvil de plaza.

Taxidermal, Taxidermic [tax-i-dęr'-mal, mic], *a.* Taxidérmico, relativo a la taxidermia.

Taxidermist [tax-i-dęr'-mist], *s.* Taxidermista, el que practica la taxidermia.

Taxidermy [tax-i-dęr'-mi], *s.* Taxidermia, arte de disecar los animales muertos para conservarlos con apariencia de vivos.

Taxonomy [tax-en'-o-mi], *s.* Taxonomía, la ciencia de clasificar, como parte de la biología.

T-bolt [tī'-bōlt], *s.* Perno en T.

Tea [tī], *s.* 1. Té : dase este nombre a un arbusto, a las hojas de este arbusto y a la infusión que se hace con ellas ; cha en Nueva España. 2. Cualquier infusión o decocción que sirve como bebida o medicamento. 3. Refección ligera de la tarde o prima noche ; también, reunión en la cual se sirve té. *Tea-board*, Batea, bandeja o azafate para servir el té. *Tea-canister*, Caja para te. *Tea-pot*, Tetera, vasija en que se hierve y se sirve el té. *Tea-kettle*, Marmita en que se tiene hirviendo el agua para hacer el té.

Tea ball [tī bel], *s.* Bolsita para hacer té.

Teacart [tī'-cārt], *s.* Mesita de ruedas para servir el té.

Teach [tīch], *va.* 1. Enseñar, dar lecciones. 2. Enseñar, doctrinar, dar documentos. 3. Instruir, informar, hacer saber.—*vn.* Tener por oficio la enseñanza pública o particular.

Teachable [tīch'-a-bl], *a.* Dócil ; susceptible de enseñanza.

Teachableness [tīch'-a-bl-nes], *s.* Docilidad ; capacidad para aprender, ansia de aprender o de instruirse.

Teacher [tīch'-ęr], *s.* 1. Maestro, preceptor, enseñador. 2. Predicador. *Assistant teacher*, Pasante, ayo, segundo maestro, sotamaestro.

Teaching [tīch'-ing], *s.* 1. Enseñanza, acción, arte u ocupación de enseñar. 2. Instrucción, doctrina, la cosa enseñada.

Teacup [tī'-cup], *s.* Taza para té ; cabida de dicha taza. *Teacupful*, Cabida de una taza para té ; unos 125 gramos.

Teak [tīk], *s.* Teca, árbol y madera más dura que el roble que se da en las Indias orientales. Tectona grandis.

Teal [tīl], *s.* (Orn.) Cerceta, zarceta, especie de ánade silvestre.

Team [tīm], *s.* 1. Equipo, bando. 2. Yunta (de bueyes, etc.).

Team, *va.* 1. Conducir con un tronco o una yunta. 2. Uncir, enganchar, poner el tiro a un vehículo.—*vn.* Guiar, por oficio, un tiro de caballos.

Teamster [tīm'-stęr], *s.* Conductor de tiro de caballos o bueyes.

Teamwork [tīm'-wūrk], *s.* Trabajo de cooperación, espíritu de solidaridad de un equipo.

Teapoy [tī'-pei], *s.* Mesita de adorno para servicio de té. (< Ind. tapai < Per. sāpāi.)

Tear [tīr], *s.* 1. Lágrima de los ojos ; lloro, llanto. 2. Gota, porción parecida a una gota.

Tear [tār], *s.* 1. Raja, rasgón, desgarradura. 2. (Ger.) Borrachera, jarana. *Wear and tear*, Desmejoramiento.

Tear, *va.* (*pret.* TORE, ant. TARE, *pp.* TORN). 1. Desgarrar, romper, despedazar, rasgar, hacer pedazos, lacerar. 2. Rasguñar, arañar. 3. Arrancar, separar una persona o cosa de otra con violencia. 4. Atormentar.—*vn.* 1. Separarse, dividirse algo cuando se tira de ello. 2. Menearse, moverse o correr con velocidad, precipitadamente. *To tear to tatters*, Hacer jirones. *To tear one's hair*, Arrancarse los cabellos. *To tear asunder*, Separar con violencia. *To tear away*, Arrancar, arrebatar ; desmembrar, separar. *To tear one's self away*, (Fam.) Arrancarse de un lugar, partir uno contra su voluntad. *To tear down*, Despedazar, destruir, echar por tierra. *To tear off*, Arrancar o separar con violencia ; arrojarse, ir precipitadamente. *To tear up*, Arrancar las plantas. *To tear along*, Correr a rienda suelta.

Tear bomb [tīr bem], *s.* Bomba lacrimógena.

Tearful [tīr'-ful], *a.* Lloroso, lagrimoso, lleno de lágrimas.

Tear gas [tīr' gas], *s.* Gas lacrimógeno.

Tea room [tī rūm], *s.* Salón o sala de té.

Tease [tīz], *va.* 1. Jorobar, molestar, atormentar, importunar, hacer rabiar. 2. Cardar, rastrillar, lana o lino. 3. Sacar el pelo al paño con la capota del cardón. 4. Despedazar, separar por medio de instrumentos, como los tejidos al examinarlos.—*s.* 1. El o lo que atormenta. 2. Acción o efecto de molestar o atormentar.

Teasel [tī'-zl], *s.* *V.* TEAZEL.

Teaser [tīz'-ęr], *s.* La persona o cosa importuna, molesta o enfadosa.

Teaspoon [tī'-spūn], *s.* Cucharita. *Teaspoonful*, Cucharadita.

Teat [tīt], *s.* 1. Pezón del pecho, tetilla. 2. Ubre, la teta del animal.

Teazel [tī'-zl], *s.* 1. Cardencha, cualquier planta de las dipsáceas; también, capota, la cabeza de la cardencha para levantar pelo en el paño. 2. Aparato mecánico que hoy usan los pelaires, en vez de la cabeza o capota de la cardencha, para sacar el pelo al paño.

Techily [tech'-i-li], *adv.* De mal humor, con aspereza o dureza de genio.

Technical [tec'-ni-cal], *a.* 1. Técnico. 2. Legalista. *Technical term,* Tecnicismo, voz técnica.

Technicality [tec-ni-cal'-i-ti], *s.* 1. Tecnicidad. 2. Tecnicismo. 3. Argucia.

Technically [tec'-ni-cal-i], *adv.* Técnicamente.

Technician [tec-nish'-un], *s.* Técnico.

Technicolor [tec'-ni-cul'-er], *s.* Tecnicolor.

Technics [tec'-nics], *s.* 1. Conjunto de principios de las artes en general. 2. Tecnicismo, conjunto de reglas, términos y métodos técnicos.

Technique [tec-nik'], *s.* Técnica, manera de ejecutar algo artísticamente, y en particular de tocar un instrumento de música según las reglas del arte. (Fr.)

Technocracy [tec-noc'-ra-si], *s.* Tecnocracia.

Technological [tec-no-loj'-ic-al], *a.* Tecnológico, perteneciente o relativo a la tecnología.

Technology [tec-nol'-o-ji], *s.* 1. Tecnología, conjunto de los conocimientos propios de los oficios mecánicos y de las artes industriales. 2. Aplicación de la ciencia a las artes.

Te Deum [tí di'-um], *s.* Te Deum, cántico cristiano.

Ted [ted], *va.* Extender o esparcir el heno o hierba recién segada para que se seque.

Tedder [ted'-er], *s.* 1. Traba, o trabas; impedimento, restricción. 2. El o lo que esparce el heno o la hierba para que se seque.

Tedious [tí'-di-us], *a.* Tedioso, fastidioso, enfadoso, molesto, pesado.

Tediously [tí'-di-us-li], *adv.* Fastidiosamente.

Tediousness [tí'-di-us-nes], *s.* 1. Tedio, fastidio, aburrimiento. 2. Pesadez.

Teem [tím], *va.* (Ant.) Parir, dar a luz la hembra; producir o causar una cosa a otra.—*vn.* 1. Estar llena alguna cosa, estar rebosando de, abundar en; hervir; hervir en o de. *A lake which teems with fishes,* Un lago lleno de peces, abundante en peces. 2. Parir, salir a luz o al público una cosa que no se sabía. 3. Verter el acero derretido.

Teemer [tím'-er], *s.* La hembra que pare.

Teeming [tím'-ing], *a. part.* 1. Prolífico, fecundo. 2. Lleno; que rebosa; producido en gran cantidad.

Teen-age [tín-éj'], *a.* Adolescente, de trece a diez y nueve años.

Teen-ager [tín-éj'-er], *s.* Adolescente, joven de trece a diez y nueve años.

Teens [tíns], *s. pl.* Los números cuyos nombres terminan en *-teen;* en especial de edad de trece a diez y nueve años. *She is not yet out of her teens,* Aun no llega a los veinte.

Teeter [tí'-ter], *vn.* Balancearse, columpiarse.—*s.* Movimiento oscilante; vaivén.

Teeth, *s. pl.* de TOOTH. *Wisdom-teeth,* Muelas del juicio.

Teeth, Teethe [tídh], *vn.* Endentecer. echar los dientes.

Teething [tídh'-ing], *s.* Dentición, formación y salida de los dientes; época o tiempo de la dentición.

Teetotal [tí-tō'-tal], *a.* 1. Entero, completo, total. 2. Relativo a la abstinencia completa de bebidas alcohólicas.

Teetotaler [tí-tō'-tal-er], *s.* El que se abstiene absolutamente del uso de bebidas alcohólicas.

Teetotalism [tí-tō'-tal-izm], *s.* Abstinencia completa de bebidas alcohólicas.

Tegmen [teg'-men], *s.* Cubierta: (Anat.) placa de hueso situada sobre el oído medio; (Ento.) élitro.

Tegument [teg'-yu-ment], *s.* Tegumento, cubierta exterior.

Te-hee [te-hí'], *vn.* Reir entre dientes.—*s.* Risa ahogada.

Telecommunication [tel-e-ce-miū-ni-ké'-shun], *s.* Telecomunicación.

Telegram [tel'-e-gram], *s.* Telegrama, despacho telegráfico, mensaje enviado por el telégrafo.

Telegraph [tel'-e-graf], *s.* Telégrafo, aparato para transmitir noticias con brevedad y a largas distancias.

Telegraph, *va.* y *vn.* Telegrafiar, enviar por el telégrafo; dictar despachos o entregarlos para su transmisión.

Telegrapher, Telegraphist [tel'-e-graf-er, ist, o tel-eg'-ra-fer, fist], *s.* Telegrafista, empleado de una oficina telegráfica o persona versada en telegrafía.

Telegraphic [tel-e-graf'-ic], *a.* Telegráfico, perteneciente o relativo al telégrafo.

Telegraphy [tel-eg'-ra-fi o tel'-e-graf-i], *s.* Telegrafía, el arte de construir y manejar los telégrafos.

Telemechanics [tel-e-me-can'-ics], *s.* Telemecánica.

Telemeter [tel-em'-e-ter], *s.* Telémetro.

Telemetering [tel-e-mít'-er-ing], *s.* Telemedición.

Telemetric [tel-e-met'-ric], *a.* Telemétrico.

Telemetry [tel-em'-e-tri], *s.* Telemetría.

Teleologic, Teleological [tel-e-o-loj'-ic, al], *a.* Teleológico, perteneciente a la teleología.

Teleology [tel-e-ol'-o-ji o tí-le-ol'-o-ji], *s.* Teleología, doctrina de las causas finales.

Telepathy [tel-ep'-a-thi o tel'-e-path-i], *s.* Telepatía, comunicación del pensamiento de una persona o otra por medios no generalmente reconocidos.

Telephone [tel'-e-fōn], *s.* Teléfono.—*va.* y *vn.* Telefonear. *Telephone book,* Guía telefónica. *Telephone booth,* Cabina telefónica. *Telephone office,* Central telefónica. *Telephone operator,* Telefonista.

Telephonic [tel-e-fon'-ic], *a.* Telefónico.

Telephony [te-lef'-o-ni], *s.* Telefonía.

Telephoto [tel-e-fō'-tō], *s.* (Trademark) Telefoto.—*a.* Telefotográfico. *Telephoto lens,* Teleobjetivo.

Telephotography [tel-e-fo-teg'-ra-fi], *s.* Telefotografía.

Teleplay [tel'-e-plé], *s.* Teleteatro.

Teleprinter [tel-e-print'-er], *s.* Teleimpresor.

Teleprompter [tel-e-prempt'er], *s.* (Trademark) Apuntador electrónico.

Teleran [tel-e-ran'], *s.* Telerán.

Telescope [tel'-e-scōp], *s.* Telescopio.

Telescope, *va.* y *vn.* Impeler o moverse dos cosas en dirección contraria y chocar de modo que una encaje en la otra, como las secciones de un telescopio o anteojo de larga vista.

Telescopic, Telescopical [tel'-e-scop ic, al], *a.* 1. Telescópico, perteneciente al telescopio; hecho con auxilio del telescopio. 2. Telescópico, que no se puede ver sino con el telescopio. 3. Que ve de lejos. 4. (Mec.) Con secciones que encajan una dentro de otra.

Teletype [tel'-e-taip], *s.* Teletipo.

Televiewer [tel-e-viū'-er], *s.* Televidente, telespectador.

Televise [tel'-e-vaiz], *va.* Televisar.

Television [tel-e-vizh'-un], *s.* Televisión. *Television camera,* Tomavistas. *Television set,* Televisor, telerreceptor. *Television studio,* Telestudio.

Tell [tel], *va.* y *vn.* (*pret.* y *pp.* TOLD). 1. Decir, principalmente cuando significa contar, mandar o adivinar. *Before I tell my fatal story,* Antes que yo diga o cuente mi lamentable historia. *Nobody can tell what will happen to-morrow,* Nadie puede decir o adivinar lo que sucederá mañana. *He told me to call again,* Me dijo o me mandó que volviera o que volviese. 2. Decir, informar, hacer saber. 3. Descubrir, revelar o decir algún secreto. *It will tell in his favour or against him,* Eso irá o será a su favor o en su contra. 4. Dar una orden o mandato a otro; disponer, ordenar. 5. Contar, numerar. 6. *vn.* Producir efecto. *He was told to do it,* Se le mandó hacerlo. *Every blow told,* Cada golpe produjo efecto.

Teller [tel'-er], *s.* 1. Relator de noticias o cuentos. 2. Computista. *Teller,* en la tesorería pública, o en los bancos, empleado, bajo las denominaciones de *Receiving teller,* Recibidor. *Paying teller,* Pagador. *Entering teller,* Contador. 3. Escrutador, el que recibe y cuenta los votos.

Telling [tel'-ing], *pa.* Que hace o produce efecto. *A telling speech,* Un discurso eficaz.

Telltale [tel'-tél], *s.* 1. Soplón, chismoso, chismeador, correvedile. 2. Indicador, aparato, generalmente automático, que da informes o noticias; axiómetro, instrumento que indica los movimientos del timón.

Telluric [tel-lū'-ric], *a.* Telúrico, de o perteneciente a la tierra o al telurio.

Tellurium [te-lū'-ri-um], *s.* (Min.) Telurio, un elemento no metálico y raro, de color entre plata y estaño.

Telpherage [tel'-fer-ēj], *s.* Transporte automático aéreo por medio de la electricidad, particularmente con un cable conductor provisto de motores independientes.

Temerarious [tem-er-ār'-i-us], *a.* Temerario, imprudente.

Temerity [te-mer'-i-ti], *s.* Temeridad, arrojo u osadía imprudente.

Temper [tem'-per], *va.* 1. Templar, moderar, entibiar o suavizar la fuerza de alguna cosa; atemperar. 2. Mezclar varios ingredientes entre sí para componer o formar un compuesto. 3. Atemperar, acomodar; temperar, ablandar. 4. Templar, dar a los metales aquel punto de dureza que requieren para su perfección.

Temper, *s.* 1. Condición, carácter, genio, disposición del ánimo. 2.

Temple, la calidad o el estado del genio y natural apacible o áspero; disposición, carácter. 3. Irritación, cólera, ira. 4. Moderación, calma, sangre fría. 5. Temple, el punto de dureza que se da a los metales. 6. Grado de densidad debida a una mezcla, v. g. en la argamasa. 7. Cal de defecación (para el azúcar). 8. (Ant.) Temperamento, la complexión, constitución o disposición del cuerpo.

Temperament [tem'-pęr-a-męnt], *s.* 1. Temperamento, la constitución o complexión propia de cada individuo. 2. (Mús.) Sistema de templar los instrumentos que practica una ligera alteración en los espacios muy breves, para evitar la disonancia o confusión de los sonidos. 3. Disposición mental.

Temperamental [tem-pęr-a-ment'-al], *a.* Propio y peculiar del temperamento físico o del temple moral de cada uno.

Temperance [tem'-pęr-ans], *s.* 1. Templanza, temperancia, moderación, sobriedad. 2. Paciencia, calma. 3. En especial el principio y la práctica de la abstinencia total de bebidas alcohólicas.

Temperate [tem'-pęr-et], *a.* 1. Templado, moderado, contenido, sobrio. 2. Abstemio, que no bebe vino ni licores alcohólicos. 3. Templado, ni frío ni caliente.

Temperately [tem'-pęr-et-li], *adv.* Moderadamente, templadamente.

Temperateness [tem'-pęr-et-nes], *s.* Templanza, moderación; serenidad de ánimo.

Temperature [tem'-pęr-a-tiūr], *s.* 1. Temperatura, el grado de calor de los cuerpos; temperie, la constitución y disposición del aire o ambiente. 2. (Des.) Constitución, temperamento; templanza, moderación.

Tempered [tem'-pęrd], *a.* 1. Templado, acondicionado. 2. Dispuesto, inclinado. *Ill-tempered,* Áspero, agrio de genio, mal condicionado. (Fam.) De la cáscara amarga. *Even-tempered,* De humor igual. *Good-tempered,* De buen temple o carácter.

Tempest [tem'pest], *s.* 1. Tempestad, tormenta, temporal. 2. Conmoción o perturbación de ánimo: tempestad o violencia de genio o natural. *Tempest-beaten,* Batido por la tempestad. *Tempest-tossed,* Sacudido por la tormenta.

Tempestuous [tem-pes'-chu-us], *a.* Tempestuoso, proceloso; borrascoso; impetuoso, turbulento.

Tempestuousness [tem-pes'-chu-us-nes], *s.* Tiempo proceloso, tempestad.

Templar [tem'-plar], *s.* 1. Templario, miembro de cierta orden de caballería, fundada en 1123 para proteger los caminos que debían de seguir los que iban a visitar los Santos Lugares; fué suprimida en 1312. 2. Fracmasón de la orden llamada Knights Templar, Caballeros del Temple, o Templarios. 3. (Ingl.) Estudiante de leyes, que habita en el Temple de Londres.

Template [tem'-plēt], *s.* *V.* TEMPLET.

Temple [tem'-pl], *s.* 1. Templo, edificio dedicado al culto de Dios o de una divinidad; por excelencia, el templo de Jerusalén que se destinaba al culto de Jehová: en Francia, templo protestante, en contraposición a iglesia católica romana. 2. Cada uno de los dos colegios de legistas que hay en Londres y en Paris, y que en otro tiempo estuvieron habitados por los templarios. 3. Sien, la parte de la cabeza que está al extremo de las cejas. 4. Vara o regla en los telares con púas en sus extremidades para mantener igual y extendida la tela: úsase por lo común en plural.

Templet [tem'-plet], *s.* 1. Patrón, modelo, gálibo, pieza plana de madera o metal que sirve para dar forma a alguna cosa. 2. Solera, cuña, piedra o madero corto y grueso para igualar el peso o empuje.

Tempo [tem'-pō], *s.* (Mús.) Ritmo, compás, grado relativo de movimiento; también, cadencia, modo o estilo particular del compás. (Ital.) *A tempo,* En debido compás. *Tempo rubato,* En compás irregular ("compás robado").

Temporal [tem'-po-ral], *a.* 1. Temporal, transitorio, pasajero. 2. Temporal, secular, en oposición a eclesiástico. 3. Temporal, perteneciente a las sienes.

Temporality [tem-po-ral'-i-ti], **Temporals** [tem'-po-ralz], *s.* Temporalidades, bienes seculares.

Temporally [tem'-po-ral-i], *adv.* Temporalmente, transitoriamente; con respecto a la vida presente.

Temporalty [tem'-po-ral-ti], *s.* 1. Seglares, los que no son eclesiásticos. 2. Bienes seculares.

Temporariness [tem'-po-rę-ri-nes], *s.* Duración temporal o pasajera, como opuesta a la eternidad.

Temporary [tem'-po-rę-ri], *a.* Temporario, temporal, que dura por limitado tiempo.

Temporize [tem'-po-raiz], *vn.* 1. Temporizar, diferir, ganar tiempo. 2. Temporizar, contemporizar; atenerse, someterse a las circunstancias.

Temporizer [tem'-po-raiz-ęr], *s.* Temporizador, entretenedor, el que gana tiempo dilatándolo.

Tempt [tempt], *va.* 1. Tentar, poner a prueba, solicitar al mal, al pecado; instigar, inducir, estimular. 2. Poner a prueba la paciencia de uno, provocar, excitar.

Temptable [tempt'-a-bl], *a.* El que es capaz de dejarse tentar, instigar o seducir a la comisión de una acción mala.

Temptation [temp-tē'-shun], *s.* 1. Tentación, la acción de tentar. 2. Tentación, movimiento interior que induce a lo malo. 3. Tentación, movimiento interior que provoca el deseo hacia alguna cosa.

Tempter [tempt'-ęr], *s.* 1. Tentador, el que tienta o induce al mal. 2. Tentador, el demonio o espíritu maligno.

Temptingly [tempt'-ing-li], *adv.* Con tentación.

Temptress [tempt'-res], *f.* Tentadora, mujer que fascina y atrae.

Ten [ten], *a.* y *s.* Diez.

Tenable [ten'-a-bl], *a.* Defensible, capaz de ser defendido o sostenido.

Tenacious [tę-nē'-shus], *a.* 1. Tenaz, que es difícil de despegarse, de partes muy unidas unas a otras; tieso, no flexible. 2. Tenaz, pegajoso, adhesivo. 3. Tenaz, que retiene fuertemente; terco, porfiado, firme en su intento o propósito.

Tenacity [tę-nas'-i-ti], *s.* 1. Tenacidad, calidad de adhesivo o pegajoso. 2. Tenacidad, terquedad, porfía.

Tenaciously [tę-nē'-shus-li], *adv.* Tenazmente, con tenacidad, con obstinación.

Tenaciousness [tę-nē'-shus-nes], *s.* Tenacidad, pertinacia, obstinación.

Tenail, Tenaille [tę-nēl'], *s.* (Fort.) Tenaza doble, obra exterior baja que se compone de dos flancos paralelos y una cara. (Fr.)

Tenaculum [tę-nac'-yu-lum], *s.* Tenáculo, instrumento quirúrgico en forma de gancho que se emplea para coger y sostener las arterias que deben ligarse.

Tenancy [ten'-an-si], *s.* Tenencia, posesión temporal de lo que pertenece a otro; estado o período de inquilinato o arrendatamiento; título legal.

Tenant [ten'-ant], *s.* 1. Arrendatario, arrendador, inquilino, rentero, el que tiene posesión temporal de alguna cosa que pertenece a otro. 2. Residente, morador, el que reside o mora en algún lugar. *Tenant for life,* Residente, usufructuario o inquilino vitalicio.

Tenant, *va.* Arrendar, tener en arriendo o en posesión temporal alguna cosa que pertenece a otro.

Tenantable [ten'-ant-a-bl], *a.* Habitable, a propósito para ser alquilado y ocupado.

Tenantless [ten'-ant-les], *a.* Desarrendado, sin inquilinos; deshabitado.

Tenantry [ten'-ant-ri], *s.* 1. Arriendo. 2. El conjunto de los arrendatarios de un hacendado o propietario.

Tench [tench], *s.* Tenca, pez europeo de agua dulce de los ciprínidos. (Tinca.)

Tend, *vn.* 1. Propender, tener tendencia, tender; tener por resultado, ejercer influencia en cierta dirección; contribuir. 2. Ir hacia, moverse, encaminarse o dirigirse en cierta dirección. (< Fr. tendre, < Lat. tendo, tender.) *Education tends to refinement,* La educación tiende al refinamiento. *His path tended upward,* Su sendero se dirigía hacia arriba.

Tend [tend], *va.* 1. Guardar, vigilar, velar, cuidar o tener cuidado de alguna cosa. 2. Atender, estar con cuidado y atención a lo que se hace. 3. (Des.) Asistir, acompañar. 4. (Mar.) Vigilar en un buque al ancla, para evitar que cuando cambie la marea se enreden el ancla y las cadenas.—*vn.* 1. Asistir, servir como criado o dependiente; con *on* o *upon.* 2. Estar atento a; ocuparse en; pensar en. (Abrev. de ATTEND.) *To tend a child,* Tener cuidado de un niño. *To tend a flock of sheep,* Vigilar un rebaño de carneros. *To tend upon a master,* Servir a un amo.

Tendance [ten'-dans], *s.* 1. (Ant.) Cuidado, atención. 2. (Des.) Corte; tren. *V.* ATTENDANCE.

Tendency [ten'-den-si], *s.* 1. Tendencia, propensión; dirección o inclinación hacia algún designio, fin o resultado. 2. Lo que tiende a causar un efecto.

Tender [ten'-dęr], *a.* 1. Tierno, blando, delicado, flexible; que cede a cualquier impresión extraña. 2. Tierno, delicado, compasivo, sensible, que se afecta fácilmente. 3. Capaz de afectos o sentimientos tiernos. 4. Delicado, afeminado. 5. Tierno, amoroso, afectuoso, cariñoso. 6. Indulgente, benigno. 7. Delicado, arduo, arriesgado. 8. Delicado, escrupuloso. 9. Tierno, se aplica al tiempo o a la edad de la niñez. *Tender of* u *over*, Cuidadoso de, solícito de los sentimientos de otros. *Tender-hearted*, Tierno de corazón, compasivo.

Tender, *s.* 1. Oferta, ofrecimiento, propuesta que se hace sobre cualquier asunto. 2. (For.) Oferta formal de pago; moneda que se ofrece en pago; también, sumisión, oferta formal de hacer cierto trabajo por una suma especificada.

Tender, *s.* 1. Escampavía, patache, bajel pequeño que ordinariamente sigue a otro mayor. 2. Ténder, (Amer.) alijo, carro que lleva el combustible y el agua para la locomotora. 3. Guarda, persona que cuida a alguno: servidor. (< Tend.[2])

Tender, *va.* 1. Ofrecer, presentar, proponer. 2. (For.) Ofrecer en pago sin condiciones.—*vn.* Hacer una oferta o propuesta.

Tender, *va.* 1. Enternecer, ablandar, poner tierno. 2. (Ant.) Estimar a uno, hacer caso de algo, querer.

Tenderfoot [ten'-dẹr-fut], *s.* (Ger. E. U. y Australia) El recién llegado que no está acostumbrado todavía a la vida en los bosques o en los campos de mineros, etc.; cualquier persona inexperta.

Tenderling [ten'-dẹr-ling], *s.* 1. Uno de los pitones de venado o ciervo. 2. (Poco us.) Favorito, persona mimada.

Tenderloin [ten'-dẹr-lein], *s.* Filete, la parte más jugosa y tierna del solomillo.

Tenderly [ten'-dẹr-li], *adv.* Tiernamente, con ternura y cariño.

Tenderness [ten'-dẹr-nes], *s.* 1. Terneza, ternura, delicadeza, suavidad: calidad de tierno. 2. Facilidad de enternecerse, dulzura, benevolencia. 3. Delicadeza, miramiento, escrupulosidad, nimiedad. 4. Afecto, cariño.

Tendinous [ten'-di-nus], *a.* Tendinoso, que tiene tendones o se compone de ellos.

Tendon [ten'-dọn], *s.* 1. Tendón, cuerda o cordón que une los extremos de los músculos a los huesos y sirve para el movimiento. 2. La ternilla del casco de caballo.

Tendril [ten'-dril], *s.* Zarcillo: en algunas plantas un cordoncillo o hilo que está enroscado a ellas y que en las vides se llama también tijeretas.

Tendriled [ten'-drild], *a.* Provisto de zarcillos; se usa para formar palabras compuestas.

Tenebrous [ten'-ẹ-brus], *a.* (Poét. o ant.) Tenebroso, obscuro.

Tenement [ten'-ẹ-mẹnt], *s.* 1. Habitación, vivienda, alojamiento, parte de una casa en que se aloja una familia; por lo común en una clase inferior de habitaciones. 2. (For.) Cualquier cosa de carácter permanente que puede poseerse en propiedad, como tierras, rentas, franquicias, etc. 3. Fábrica, edificio, y particularmente casa habitación.

Tenesmus [tẹ-nes'-mus], *s.* (Med.) Tenesmo, pujos.

Tenet [ten'-et], *s.* Dogma; aserción, aserto, proposición que se sienta como verdadera.

Tenfold [ten'-fōld], *a.* Décuplo, que contiene un número diez veces exactamente.—*adv.* De manera décupla.

Tennis [ten'-is], *s.* Tenis. *Tennis ball*, Pelota de tenis. *Tennis court*, Cancha de tenis. *Tennis tournament*, Torneo de tenis.

Tenon [ten'-ọn], *va.* 1. Espigar, formar espiga en un madero. 2. Juntar a espiga y mortaja.—*s.* 1. (Carp.) Espiga, almilla, la punta de algún madero o palo que entra en una mortaja. 2. Pieza que se pone a una estatua para reforzarla. *Tenon-saw*, Sierra de ingletes.

Tenor [ten'-ẹr], *s.* 1. Tenor, curso, constitución u orden firme y estable de alguna cosa. 2. Tenor, contenido, substancia y efecto de un escrito o instrumento; contenido literal de un escrito. 3. Carácter y tendencia generales. 4. (Mús.) Tenor, voz media entre las de contralto y barítono; persona que tiene esta voz. 5. Viola u otro instrumento de sonido intermedio entre el alto y el bajo.—*a.* De tenor, perteneciente a la voz o instrumento de tenor. *The even tenor of one's way*, Su método regular de vida.

Tenpenny [ten'-pen-i], *a.* De diez peniques, que vale diez peniques; también, clavo de cierto tamaño.

Tenpins [ten'-pinz], *s.* (E. U.) Juego con diez bolos de madera.

Tense [tens], *a.* Tieso, estirado, tenso, tirante.—*s.* (Gram.) Tiempo del verbo.

Tenseness [tens'-nes], *s.* Contracción, tensión, tirantez; el estado de lo que se halla tirante.

Tensibility [ten-si-bil'-i-ti], *s.* El estado y la disposición de lo que se puede estirar o poner tenso.

Tensible [ten'-si-bl], **Tensile** [ten'-sil], *a.* Capaz de tensión, que puede estirarse.

Tensile [ten'-sil], *a.* Tensor. *Tensile strength*, Resistencia a la tensión.

Tension [ten'-shun], *s.* 1. Tensión, extensión o dilatación de alguna cosa, tirantez. 2. Gran aplicación del espíritu. 3. (Mec.) Tensión; regulador del hilo en una máquina de coser. 4. Estado de tirantez en las relaciones entre dos gobiernos.

Tensive [ten'-siv], *a.* Tirante, estirado; causado por tensión o que la causa.

Tensor [ten'-sẹr], *s.* Tensor, músculo extensor.

Ten-strike [ten'-straik], *s.* Jugada en que se derriban los diez bolos con una sola bocha; de aquí, *To make a ten-strike*, Poner una pica en Flandes.

Tent [tent], *s.* 1. (Mil.) Tienda de campaña; pabellón. 2. Cualquiera habitación provisional. 3. Lechino, porción de hilas que unidas en figura de clavo se emplean en cirugía para varios usos. 4. (Zool.) Tela sedosa que cubre a ciertas orugas. 5. Tintillo, especie de vino de color rojo vivo. *Tent-bed*, Catre de tijera. *Tent-cloth*, Terliz. *To pitch tents*, Armar las tiendas de campaña; acamparse. *To strike the tents*, Plegar tiendas, levantar el campo. *Tent-pole*, Mástil, montante de tienda. *Tent-wine*, Vino de Alicante. *Dark-tent*, Tienda portátil con cámara obscura para usarla al aire libre. *Tent-caterpillar*, Oruga norteamericana gregaria que hila una tela grande y sedosa y es muy nociva. Clisiocampa americana.

Tent, *vn.* Alojarse en tienda o pabellón.—*va.* Tentar, reconocer con la tienta la cavidad de una herida.

Tentacle [ten'-ta-cl], *s.* 1. (Zool.) Tentáculo, apéndice móvil y blando (comúnmente de la cabeza) que tienen muchos moluscos y zoófitos y que les sirve para tocar y hacer presa. 2. (Bot.) Tentáculo, filamento glandular sensible.

Tentacular [ten-tac'-yu-lar], *a.* De la naturaleza de un tentáculo o perteneciente a él.

Tentative [ten'-ta-tiv], *a.* Que toca o pertenece a la tentativa, prueba o ensayo.—*s.* Tentativa, ensayo.

Tented [tent'-ed], *a.* Entoldado, cubierto con toldos, pabellones o tiendas.

Tenter [tent'-ẹr], *s.* Rama, especie de bastidor que se usa en las fábricas de paño para estirarlo en todas direcciones. *Tenter-hooks*, Clavijas de rama, escarpias o alcayatas. *To be on the tenters*, Hallarse entre la espada y la pared.

Tenter, *va.* Estirar con ganchos.—*vn.* Estirarse, alargarse, dilatarse.

Tenth [tenth], *a.* Décimo, deceno, el ordinal de diez. *Alphonso Tenth*, Alfonso Décimo. *The tenth of October*, El diez de octubre.—*s.* 1. La décima parte. 2. El diezmo.

Tenthly [tenth'-li], *adv.* En décimo lugar.

Tentwort [tent'-wūrt], *s.* (Bot.) Culantrillo.

Tenuirostral [ten''-yu-i-res'-tral], *a.* Tenuirrostro, que tiene pico delgado.

Tenuity [tẹ-niū'-i-ti], *s.* Tenuidad, raridad, sutileza, delgadez; rarefacción del aire o de un flúido.

Tenuous [ten'-yu-us], *a.* Tenue, delgado, delicado.

Tenure [ten'-yur], *s.* Tenencia, dependencia o enfiteusis en distrito de un señor directo, y también el modo como se tiene algo en arriendo.

Teocalli [ti-o-cal'-i], *s.* Teocalí, pirámide que servía de templo a los antiguos mejicanos.

Tepefaction [tep-ẹ-fac'-shun], *s.* El acto de entibiar, templadura.

Tepee [tī'-pi], *s.* Cabaña de los indios de E. U.

Tepefy [tep'-e-fai], *va.* y *vn.* Entibiar, hacer tibio; ponerse tibio.

Tepid [tep'-id], *a.* Tibio, templado, entre caliente y frío.

Tepidity [tẹ-pid'-i-ti], *s.* Tibieza.

Tepor [tī'-pẹr], *s.* Calor moderado.

Teratology [ter-a-tel'-o-ji], *s.* Teratología, parte de la biología que trata de las monstruosidades orgánicas.

Terce [tẹrs], *s.* Tercerola, una especie de tonel que contiene la tercera parte de un pipa. *V.* TIERCE.

Tercentenary [tẹr-sen'-tẹ-nẹ-ri], *a.* De tres siglos, de trescientos años.—*s.* Aniversario tricentésimo.

Terebinth [ter'-ẹ-binth], *s.* Alfóncigo, terebinto; arbolillo cuya madera exuda la trementina.

Terebinthinate [ter-e-bin'-thi-nēt], **Terebinthine** [ter-e-bin'-thin], *a.* Compuesto de trementina o mezclado con ella.

‡**Terebrate** [ter'-ẹ-brēt], *va.* Taladrar, barrenar con taladro, agujerear.

Terebration [ter-ẹ-brē'-shun], *s.* (Poco us.) La acción de taladrar o barrenar.

Teredo [tẹ-rī'-dō], *s.* Broma, un gusano que roe la madera y se halla frecuentemente en los lados y quilla de los bajeles.

Terete [ter-īt'], *a.* Cilíndrico o algo cónico; redondo en sección vertical.

Tergeminate, Tergeminous [tẹr-jem'-i-nêt, nus], *a.* (Bot.) Que tiene un par de hojuelas sobre cada uno de tres pecíolos secundarios.

Tergiversation [tẹr-ji-vẹr-sé'-shun], *s.* 1. Tergiversación, efugio, evasión. 2. Instabilidad, falta de constancia y firmeza.

Tergiversate [tẹr'-ji-vẹr-sêt], *vn.* (Poco us.) Tergiversar, ir buscando efugios con rodeos y trampas.

Term [tẹrm], *s.* 1. Término, dicción, vocablo, la voz o palabra con la cual se explica alguna cosa: particularmente, una voz técnica. 2. *pl.* Palabras significativas, discurso, oración. 3. (Lóg.) Palabras que pueden ser sujeto o atributo de la proposición; uno de los tres elementos de un silogismo. 4. Término, espacio de tiempo, plazo de tiempo determinado y prescrito: en este sentido llaman los ingleses término al tiempo en que los tribunales superiores de justicia están abiertos. 5. *pl.* Condiciones, estipulaciones propuestas, sean o no aceptadas: de aquí, relato, pie, base de un acuerdo, relaciones mutuas. *Upon what terms?* ¿En que términos? 6. Término, límite, confín, hablando de la extensión de lugar. 7. (Mat.) Lo que limita una línea, superficie o volumen: parte de una expresión algebraica unida a otra por el signo de adición o substracción. *The term of four years,* El plazo de cuatro años. *In set terms,* En términos escogidos. *To be on good terms with,* Estar sobre buen pie con, estar bien con. *Not on any terms,* Por ningún concepto, a ningún precio, de ninguna manera. *To bring to terms,* Traer a un arreglo, imponer condiciones. *To come to terms,* Decidirse a un arreglo, ceder, someterse. *To make terms,* Efectuar un acuerdo o arreglo, estar acordes. *Michaelmas term,* Época (de tribunal) de la festividad de San Miguel, del 24 de octubre al 21 de diciembre. *Hilary term,* Sesiones de los tribunales desde el 11 de enero al miércoles anterior a la Pascua de Resurrección.

Term, *va.* Nombrar, llamar.

Termagancy [tẹr'-ma-gan-si], *s.* Carácter pendenciero.

Termagant [tẹr'-ma-gant], *a.* Turbulento; pendenciero.—*s.* Sierpe, fiera, áspid: aplícase a la mujer de mal genio y que siempre está gruñendo o armando pendencias.

Termer [tẹrm'-ẹr], *s.* El abogado, procurador, agente, etc., que en Inglaterra sigue a los jueces a los diferentes puntos donde establecen su tribunal.

Terminable [tẹr'-mi-na-bl], *a.* Limitable.

Terminal [tẹr'-mi-nal], *a.* 1. Terminal, último y que pone término a una cosa. 2. (Zool.) Terminal, que forma la extremidad de una parte; (Bot.) que crece en la punta de una rama o tallo.—*s.* Punto o parte que termina; estación o figura terminal.

Terminate [tẹr'-mi-nêt], *va.* y *vn.* 1. Terminar, acabar, ser fin o término de una cosa. 2. Terminar, limitar, poner término, límite o fin. 3. Terminar, componer una desavenencia o disputa.

Termination [tẹr-mi-né'-shun], *s.* 1. Terminación, la acción y efecto de acabarse, terminarse o resolverse una cosa; fin, conclusión. 2. Limitación, la acción de limitar. 3. Límite, lindero, cabo, extremidad; en especial, el cabo de un conductor eléctrico. 4. Terminación, desinencia, la última sílaba de una voz según la variedad de sus significados.

Terminative [tẹr'-mi-nẹ-tiv], *a.* Terminativo.

Terminology [tẹr-mi-nel'-o-ji], *s.* 1. Terminología, el arte o ciencia del uso debido de los términos. 2. Conjunto de los términos técnicos o nomenclatura de una persona, clase o ciencia particulares.

Terminus [tẹr'-mi-nus], *s.* 1. Término final, fin; particularmente la estación terminal de un ferrocarril y la ciudad en que está situada dicha estación. 2. Término, límite, mojón. 3. Término arquitectónico.

Termite [tẹr'-mait], *s.* Termito, comején, hormiga blanca.

Terminer [tẹr'-mi-nẹr], *s.* (For.) La comisión que se da a los jueces ingleses para que oigan y determinen las causas en sus respectivos distritos.

Termless [tẹrm'-les], *a.* Ilimitado, que no tiene límites ni términos.

Termly [tẹrm'-li], *adv.* (Poco us.) (For.) En cada término.

Tern [tẹrn], *s.* Golondrina de mar, ave palmípeda semejante a la gaviota, pero menor. Sterna.—*a. V.* TERNATE.

Ternary [tẹr'-na-ri], *a.* Ternario, compuesto de tres.—*s.* Terna; ternario.

Ternate [tẹr'-nêt], *a.* Clasificado (arreglado de tres en tres.

Terpsichorean [tẹrp''-sic-o-rí'-an], *a.* De Terpsícore, del baile.

Terra [ter'-a], *s.* Tierra. (Lat.) *Terra alba,* Tierra de pipa. *Terra-cotta,* Tierra cocida (terracota). *Terra firma,* Tierra firme. *Terra incognita,* Tierra desconocida.

Terrace [ter'-ẹs], *va.* Terraplenar, hacer un terraplén o formar en terraplenes sucesivos.—*s.* 1. Terraplén, terrapleno, bancal, espacio elevado y llano que tiene uno o más lados inclinados. 2. Terraplén que sostiene una hilera de casas o las mismas casas así colocadas. 3. Terrado, azotea. 4. Balcón, galería abierta.

Terramycin [ter-a-mai'-sin], *s.* (Med.) Terramicina.

Terrane, Terrain [ter'-ên], *s.* (Geol.) Cualquier roca o serie de rocas relacionadas sin intermisión.

Terrapin [ter'-a-pin], *s.* Emido, tortuga de carne deliciosa, de la costa atlántica de los Estados Unidos. (Especialmente la Malaclemmys palustris.)

Terraqueous [ter-ê'-cwẹ-us], *a.* Terráqueo, compuesto de tierra y agua.

Terrene [ter-ín'], *a.* 1. Terreno, terrenal, que pertenece a la tierra. 2. Terrestre, mundano.

Terreplein [tār-plên'], *s.* (Fort.) Terraplén.

Terrestrial [ter-es'-tri-al], *a.* Terrestre, terreno.

Terrestrialness [ter-es'-tri-al-nes], *s.* La naturaleza y calidad de la tierra.

Terret [ter'-et], *s.* Portarriendas, uno de los dos anillos por donde pasan las riendas. (< Fr. *touret* < Lat. *tornus* < Gr. *tornos,* torno.)

Terrible [ter'-i-bl], *a.* 1. Terrible, pavoroso, espantoso, horroroso. 2. Tremendo, grande, desmedido, desmesurado.

Terribleness [ter'-i-bl-nes], *s.* Terribilidad.

Terribly [ter'-i-bli], *adv.* Terriblemente, espantosamente, horriblemente.

Terrier [ter'-i-ẹr], *s.* 1. Zorrero, perro zorrero o raposero, notable por su valor en la persecución de los animales nocivos. 2. (Ingl.) Nutria macho solitaria. 3. (For. ant. Ingl.) Descripción o catálogo de posesiones, heredades o bienes raíces.

Terrific [ter-rif'-ic], *a.* 1. Espantoso, terrífico, que amedrenta, que causa terror. 2. (fam.) Extraordinario, maravilloso.

Terrify [ter'-i-fai], *va.* Aterrar, causar terror, espantar, amedrentar.

Territorial [ter-i-tō'-ri-al], *a.* Territorial; en especial, perteneciente a uno o a todos los Territorios de los Estados Unidos.

Territory [ter'-i-to-ri], *s.* 1. Territorio, extensión de tierra sobre la cual ejerce su jurisdicción un estado soberano. 2. Extensión de tierra, región, distrito. 3. Comarca de los Estados Unidos no elevada todavía á la categoría de Estado y sometida a un régimen provisional.

Terror [ter'-ẹr], *s.* Espanto, terror, pavor, gran miedo; objeto de miedo, de espanto. (Fam.) Persona fastidiosa.

Terror-stricken [ter'-ẹr-strik''-n], *a.* Horrorizado, aterrado.

Terrorist [ter'-er-ist], *s.* Terrorista.

Terse [tẹrs], *a.* 1. Sucinto; breve y comprensivo; conciso, compendioso; limado y elegante sin afectación. 2. (Des.) Terso, liso, pulido.

Tersely [tẹrs'-li], *adv.* Concisa y elegantemente.

Terseness [tẹrs'-nes], *s.* Calidad de conciso y sucinto (en el estilo).

Tertian [tẹr'-shan], *a.* Terciano, que vuelve u ocurre cada tercer día.—*s.* Terciana, calentura intermitente que repite cada tercer día.

Tertiary [tẹr'-shi-ẹ-ri], *a.* 1. Terciario, tercero en orden o grado. 2. (Geol.) Terciario, de la época terciaria.—*s.* 1. Época geológica posterior a la cretácea. 2. (Orn.) Pluma terciaria de un ave.

Tessellate [tes'-el-êt], *va.* Taracear, hacer mosaicos.

Tessellate, Tessellated [tes'-e-lêt-ed], *a.* Taraceado, cuadriculado. *Tessellated pavement,* Pavimento mosaico.

Tessellation [tes-el-ê'-shun], *s.* 1. Mosaico, obra taraceada. 2. Arte o acto de hacer mosaicos.

Test [test], *s.* 1. Prueba, toque, examen que se hace de una persona o cosa. 2. Juicio o distinción que se hace entre dos cosas. 3. Piedra de toque, criterio, norma de juicio. 4. Juramento u otra prueba testimonial de los principios de la fe. 5. Reacción química, por medio de la cual se puede establecer la identidad de un compuesto o de uno de sus constituyentes; reactivo. *Test Act,* Una ley de Inglaterra por la cual se exigía que todo empleado hiciese juramento rechazando la transubstanciación y que recibiese la comunión según las ceremonias de la Iglesia anglicana. *To put to the test,* Experimentar, probar, poner á prueba. *To stand the test,* Ser de prueba, soportar la prueba. *Test-tube,* Probeta que se usa en los laboratorios. *Test-paper,* Papel reactivo.

Test, *s.* 1. Cubierta exterior rígida;

concha. 2. (Bot.) Tegumento exterior de una semilla.

Test, *va.* 1. Experimentar ensayar, hacer la prueba, el ensayo de algo. 2. Sujetar a condiciones que demuestran el verdadero carácter de una cosa.

Testable [tes'-ta-bl], *a.* Capaz de ser testigo o de servir de testigo.

Testacean [tes-tê'-şe-an], *a.* y *s.* Testáceo, que tiene concha; invertebrado provisto de concha.

Testaceous [tes-tê'-shus], *a.* Testáceo: que tiene concha dura.

Testament [tes'-ta-ment], *s.* 1. Testamento, declaración de la última voluntad que hace una persona disponiendo de sus bienes y hacienda. 2. El Viejo y Nuevo Testamento, los libros de la Sagrada Escritura.

Testamentary [tes-ta-men'-ta-ri], *a.* Testamentario.

Testate [tes'-têt], *a.* Que ha hecho testamento, que ha testado.

Testator [tes-tê'-ter], *s.* Testador, el que hace testamento.

Testatrix [tes-tê'-trics], *sf.* Testadora, la mujer que hace testamento.

Tested [test'-ed], *a.* Ensayado, probado, experimentado; examinado.

Tester [test'-er], *s.* 1. Probador, el que prueba o hace examen. 2. Cielo de cama. 3. (Ger. Ingl.) Medio chelín.

Testicle [tes'-ti-cl], *a.* Testículo, cada una de las glándulas seminales.

Testiculate [tes-tic'-yu-lêt], *a.* 1. En forma de testículo. 2. Que tiene testículos u organos parecidos a ellos. 3. (Bot.) Sólido y aovado como las raíces de ciertas plantas orquídeas.

Testificate [tes-tif'-i-kêt], *s.* (Der. esco.) Aserto solemne por escrito.

Testification [tes-ti-fi-kê'-shun], *s.* Testificación, el acto de testificar.

Testifier [tes'-ti-fai-er], *s.* Testigo, testificante.

Testify [tes'-ti-fai], *va.* 1. Testificar, atestiguar, afirmar. 2. Atestar, declarar bajo juramento o ante el juez. 3. Servir de prueba.—*vn.* 1. Dar testimonio, servir de testigo. 2. Servir de evidencia o indicación. 3. Aseverar.

Testily [tes'-ti-li], *adv.* Impertinentemente, con petulancia; con morosidad.

Testimonial [tes-ti-mō'-ni-al], *a.* Testimonial, que da testimonio, que hace fe.—*s.* 1. Prenda o prueba formal de amistad, recuerdo que se da a menudo en público. 2. Certificación o certificado en que se asegura la verdad de algún hecho.

Testimony [tes'-ti-mo-ni], *s.* 1. Testimonio, atestación, testificación, declaración. 2. Testimonio, prueba, justificación o comprobación de la certeza y verdad de alguna cosa. 3. (Bibl.) Tablas de la Ley, el decálogo; Libro de la Ley, el Antiguo Testamento. *I must bear testimony,* Debo hacer la justicia. *In testimony whereof,* En testimonio de lo cual.

Testiness [tes'-ti-nes], *s.* Enfado, enojo, mal humor, aspereza de genio.

Testudinate, Testudinated [tes-tiū'-di-nêt, ed], *a.* (Poco us.) Arqueado, formado en bóveda.

Testudo [tes tiū'-do], *s.* 1. Testudo, cubierta protectora que formaban los antiguos romanos con sus escudos al acercarse a la muralla de una plaza sitiada. 2. Tortuga, animal anfibio (nombre científico).

Testy [tes'-ti], *a.* Enojadizo, tétrico, descontentadizo.

Tetanic [te-tan'-ic], *a.* Tetánico, relativo al tétanos, o que lo produce.

Tetanoid [tet'-a-noid], *a.* Parecido al tétano, o que produce síntomas del tétanos.

Tetanus [tet'-a-nus], *s.* Tétanos, tétano, enfermedad nerviosa caracterizada por rigidez y tensión de los músculos sometidos al imperio de la voluntad.

Tête-a-tête [têt'-a-têt], *s.* Cara a cara, silla a silla, a solas. (Fr.)

Tether [tedh'-er], *s.* Traba, cuerda que se echa a los pies de un animal que se pone a pastar; maniota, lazo, brida.

Tether, *va.* Trabar, atar, restriñir.

Tetra-. Prefijo griego que significa cuatro.

Tetrachord [tet'-ra-cērd], *s.* (Mús.) Tetracordio, media octava.

Tetragon [tet'-ra-gon], *s.* (Geom.) Tetrágono, cuadrilátero.

Tetragonal [te-trag'-o-nal], *a.* Tetrágono, cuadrangular, que tiene cuatro ángulos.

Tetrahedral [tet-ra-hī'-dral], *a.* Tetraedral, tetraédrico, relativo al tetraedro.

Tetrahedron [tet-ra-hī'-dren], *s.* Tetraedro, sólido terminado por cuatro planos ó caras.

Tetrameter [tet-ram'-e-ter], *s.* Tetrámetro, verso de cuatro bases o medidas.

Tetrapetalous [tet-ra-pet'-a-lus], *a.* (Bot.) Tetrapétalo, compuesto de cuatro pétalos.

Tetrarch [tī'-trārc], *s.* Tetrarca, el señor de la cuarta parte de un reino o provincia.

Tetrarchate [tī-trārk'-êt], **Tetrarchy** [tet'-rar-ci], *s.* Tetrarquía, la dignidad del tetrarca.

Tetrastich [tet'-ra-stic], *s.* Toda composición poética de cuatro versos.

Tetter [tet'-er], *s.* Sarpullido, empeine, enfermedad vesicular del cutis.

Teuton [tiū'-ton], *s.* 1. Teutón, teutona, individuo de la raza germánica. 2. Los arios del noroeste de Europa con inclusión de los alemanes y los escandinavos.

Teutonic [tiu-ten'-ic], *a.* Teutónico, germánico.—*s.* Tudesco, idioma o idiomas de los teutones.

Tew [tiū], *va.* (Prov. o Com.) Cascar, trabajar; agramar. *To tew hemp,* Espadar o espadillar cáñamo.

Texan [tex'-an], *s.* y *a.* Tejano.

Text [text], *s.* 1. Texto, las palabras propias de un autor a distinción de las notas o comentarios que se hacen de ellas. 2. Verso o pasaje breve de la Sagrada Escritura. 3. De aquí, tema, tesis o asunto de un discurso. 4. Grado de letra o tipo; p. ej. *German text,* Tipo alemán. *Text-book,* Libro de texto; manual, libro de escuela; libro con espacios en blanco para notas o comentarios; libreto de ópera.

Text-hand [text'-hand], *s.* Escritura o carácter de letra muy grueso.

Textile [tex'-til], *a.* Textil, hilable, capaz de hilarse o de reducirse a hilos y ser tejido.

Textual [text'-yu-al], *a.* Textual, que conviene con el texto y es propio de él; versado en el texto.

Textualist [text'-yu-al-ist], *s.* Textualista, el que usa con frecuencia del texto de una obra, y también el que es dado a citar textos.

Texture [tex'-chur], *s.* 1. Textura, tejido, disposición y orden en los hilos de una tela, y por extensión se dice también de la disposición y orden de las fibras que componen las partes del cuerpo del animal. 2. Tela, tejido, obra tejida. 3. Textura, la colocación y orden de una cosa que se sigue o ata con otra.

Thallic [thal'-ic], *a.* Tálico, perteneciente o relativo al talio.

Thallium [thal'-i-um], *s.* Talio, elemento metálico poco común, de que se usa para formar aleaciones y en la fabricación del vidrio. Su espectro contiene una línea verde característica, de la cual recibe su nombre.

Than [dhan], *conj.* 1. Que: partícula comparativa. *Your house is larger than mine,* La casa de Vd. es mayor que la mía. *He has more money than I,* Tiene más dinero que yo. 2. De: se usa en lugar de que cuando va delante de los números, en sentido afirmativo. *Fewer than twenty,* Menos de veinte. *More than a thousand,* Más de mil. *More than once,* Más de una vez.

Thane [thên], *s.* Título antiguo de honor equivalente quizás a barón; caballero compañero de un rey; hacendado dueño de cierta extensión de terreno.

Thank [thank], *va.* Agradecer, expresar gratitud a uno, dar gracias a. *I shall thank you for that favour,* Le agradeceré a Vd. o le estimaré a Vd. que me haga ese favor. *Thank you,* Gracias. *Thank God,* A Dios gracias.—*s. pl.* Gracias, agradecimiento, acción de agradecer, expresión de gratitud. *Thanks to you,* Gracias a usted. *To return thanks,* Hacer presentes sus agradecimientos.

Thankful [thank'-ful], *a.* Grato, agradecido. *I am very thankful to him,* Le estoy muy reconocido.

Thankfully [thank'-ful-i], *adv.* Con gratitud o reconocimiento.

Thankfulness [thank'-ful-nes], *s.* Agradecimiento, gratitud, reconocimiento.

Thankless [thank'-les], *a.* 1. Desagradecido, ingrato, el que no reconoce los favores recibidos. 2. Lo que no merece gracias.

Thanklessness [thank'-les-nes], *s.* Desagradecimiento, ingratitud.

Thank-offering [thank'-ef-er-ing], *s.* Ofrecimiento en acción de gracias.

Thanksgiving [thancs'-giv-ing], *s.* 1. Acción de gracias; particularmente, reconocimiento por las mercedes recibidas de Dios. 2. Celebración pública en reconocimiento del favor de Dios; día señalado para esa celebración. *Thanksgiving Day,* Día de acción de gracias en reconocimiento de la protección y merced divinas; en los Estados Unidos es el último jueves de noviembre.

Thankworthy [thanc'-wūr-dhi], *a.* Digno de reconocimiento; meritorio.

That [dhat], *a.* Ese, esa, eso; el, la, aquello especialmente designado; este, cuando se refiere a frase o bien a una persona o cosa que no está presente, en cuyo caso se debe traducir por ese. *That boy,* Ese o este muchacho. *That book is better than this,* Ese (aquel) libro es mejor que éste.—*pron.* 1. Aquel, aquello, aquella, como pronombre demostrativo. 2. Que, quien, el cual, la cual, lo cual, como pronombre relativo, y puede hacer relación a personas o cosas. *That of,* El de, la de. *That which,* El que, la que, lo que. *What of that,* ¿Qué importa eso? ¿qué quiere Vd. decir con eso? ¿qué resulta de eso? *That* se usa frecuentemente para evitar la repetición de una palabra. *That way,* Por aquel camino, por allí. *That is,* Es decir o eso es. *That may be,* Eso puede ser, es posible. *See that,* Vea Vd. eso. *What street is that,* ¿Qué calle es esa? *Upon that,* Sobre esto, en cuanto á eso; luego. *All that is just,* Todo lo que es justo. *And all that,* Y todo eso; y otras hierbas. *To put this and that together,* Deducir conclusiones. *It was I, not he, that wrote it,* Fuí yo, y no él, quien lo escribió.—*conj.* 1. Porque. 2. Para que. 3. Que, de modo que. *So that, insomuch that,* Por cuanto; de modo que, de suerte que. *Not but that,* No es decir que. *Save that,* Salvo que. *Supposing that,* Supuesto que, dado caso que.

Thatch [thach], *s.* Cubierta de cañas, bálago, paja u hojas de palmera, que sirve de techado.

Thatch, *va.* Techar con bálago o cañas, o poner un techo de paja.

Thatcher [thach'-ẹr], *s.* Trastejador de cañas o bálago.

Thaumaturgic, Thaumaturgical [thō-mat-ūr'-jic, al], *a.* Taumaturgo, que hace prodigios.

Thaumaturgy [thō-mat-ūr'-ji], *s.* Taumaturgia, el arte de hacer milagros; mágico.

Thaw [thō], *vn.* 1. Deshelarse, derretirse, liquidarse lo que está helado. 2. Deshacerse los hielos.—*va.* Deshelar, liquidar lo que está helado. *It thaws,* Deshiela, se derrite la nieve o el hielo.

Thaw, *s.* 1. Deshielo, blandura del tiempo que deshace las nieves o el hielo. 2. El derretimiento o disolución de lo que está helado.

The [dhī o dhẹ sin énfasis y delante de una consonante], *art.* El, la; lo: *the* se usa delante de un substantivo tomado en sentido determinado (véase la Sinopsis de la Gramática inglesa). Delante de un comparativo no se traduce en español. *All the region,* Toda la región. *The poor,* Los pobres. *The more—the,* Cuanto más—tanto.

Theater, Theatre [thī'-a-tẹr], *s.* 1. Teatro, el edificio o paraje en que se junta el público a ver algún espectáculo o función. 2. Literatura y representaciones dramáticas, en general, en conjunto. 3. Anfiteatro, lugar provisto de gradas. 4. Cualquier paraje o región que es escena de los acontecimientos.

Theatric, Theatrical [thẹ-at'-ric, al], *a.* 1. Teatral, que pertenece o toca al teatro. 2. Fingido, como por un actor; hecho para producir efecto.

Theatrically [thẹ-at'-ric-al-i], *adv.* De un modo teatral.

Thee [dhī], *pron.* Te, a tí: el caso objetivo de la segunda persona del singular del pronombre personal; se emplea en la oración, en poesía y en prosa elevada.

Theft [theft], *s.* Hurto, la acción de hurtar y la misma cosa hurtada.

Thein, Theine [thī'-in], *s.* Teína, alcaloide contenido en el te.

Their [dhār], *pron. pos.* Su, suyo, suya, de ellos, de ellas. *Theirs,* El suyo, la suya, los suyos, las suyas, de ellos o de ellas.

Theism [thī'-izm], *s.* Teísmo; deísmo.

Theist [thī'-ist], *s.* Teísta, deísta.

Theistic, Theistical [thī-is'-tic, al], *a.* Teísta, del teísmo, de los teístas.

Them [dhem], *pron.* El caso objetivo de *They.* Los, las, les, ellos, ellas, á aquellos, á aquellas. *I love them,* Los o las amo.

Theme [thīm], *s.* 1. Tema, el asunto o materia de un discurso. 2. Tesis, disertación, particularmente en las escuelas y colegios. 3. (Mús.) Tema, motivo, sobre el cual se hacen variaciones.

Themselves [dhem-selvz'], *pron. pl.* Ellos mismos, ellas mismas; sí mismos: caso oblicuo del pronombre personal recíproco y a veces también se usa como nominativo.

Then [dhen], *adv.* 1. Entonces, en aquel tiempo, a la sazón. 2. Luego, después, en seguida. 3. En otro tiempo.—*conj.* 1. En tal caso, por consiguiente, pues. 2. Luego, por esta razón. *Now and then,* De cuando en cuando; de vez en cuando. *Now . . . then . . . ,* Ya . . . ya . . . *Now then,* Ahora pues, pues, por consiguiente. *And then,* Con esto; y además de esto; y entonces; y en seguida. *And what then?* ¿Y qué más? ¿y qué se seguirá de eso? —*a.* De entonces, de aquel tiempo; (uso cuestionable).

Thenar [then'-ar o thī'-nar], *a.* De la palma de la mano, o del juanete del pie.

Thence [dhens], *adv.* 1. Desde allí, de allí, hablando de lugar. 2. Desde entonces, desde ese tiempo, después de aquel tiempo. 3. De ahí, por eso, por esa razón, por ese motivo.

Thenceforth [dhens'-fōrth], *adv.* Desde entonces, de allí en adelante.

Thenceforward [dhens-fōr'-ward], *adv.* Desde entonces; en adelante.

Theocracy [thẹ-oc'-ra-si], *s.* Teocracia, el gobierno cuyos jefes son mirados como ministros o delegados de Dios.

Theocratic, Theocratical [thẹ-o-crat'-ic-al], *a.* Teocrático.

Theodolite [thẹ-od'-o-lait], *s.* Teodolito, instrumento geodésico que se usa para medir ángulos, distancias y alturas.

Theogony [thẹ-og'-o-ni], *s.* Teogonía, generación de los dioses del paganismo.

Theologian [thī"-o-lō'-ji-an], *s.* Teólogo, persona versada en la teología: profesor de teología.

Theological [thẹ-o-loj'-ic-al], *a.* Teologal, teológico.

Theologically [thẹ-o-loj'-ic-al-i], *adv.* Teológicamente.

Theologize [thẹ-ol'-o-jaiz], *va.* Hacer o convertir en teológico.—*vn.* Teologizar, discurrir sobre principios o razones teológicas.

Theologue [thẹ'-o-log], *s.* (Fam.) Estudiante de teología.

Theology [thẹ-ol'-o-ji], *s.* Teología, ciencia que trata de Dios y sus atributos.

Theorbo [thẹ-ōr'-bo], *s.* Tiorba, un instrumento músico del siglo XVII en forma de laúd.

Theorem [thī'-o-rem], *s.* 1. Teorema, proposición de una verdad especulativa que se puede demostrar. 2. (Geom.) Proposición en que se va a averiguar la verdad de una cosa.

Theoretic, Theoretical [thī-o-ret'-ic, al], **Theoric** [thī-er'-ic], *a.* Teórico, especulativo, que pertenece á la teoría; que comprende y entiende especulativamente la esencia de las cosas sin prueba práctica.

Theoretically [thī-o-ret'-i-cal-i], *adv.* Teóricamente, especulativamente.

Theoric [thẹ-er'-ic], *s.* Teórica, especulativa.—*a.* Teórico.

Theorist [thī'-o-rist], *s.* Teórico, el que no conoce más que la teoría de un arte o ciencia.

Theorize [thī'-o-raiz], *vn.* Exponer o formar teorías.

Theory [thī'-o-ri], *s.* 1. Teoría, teórica, especulativa, conocimiento teórico. 2. Teoría, serie de leyes que sirven para relacionar determinado orden de fenómenos. 3. La ciencia en contraposición al arte. 4. Explicación filosófica de los fenómenos.

Theosophic, Theosophical [thī-o-sef'-ic, al], *a.* Teosófico, perteneciente á la teosofía.

Theosophist [thẹ-es'-o-fist], *s.* Teósofo, el que profesa la teosofía.

Theosophy [thẹ-es'-o-fi], *s.* Teosofía, doctrina de varias sectas que pretenden admitir la verdad esencial existente como base de toda religión, filosofía y ciencia; la religión universal. (< Gr. theosophia.)

Therapeutic, Therapeutical [ther-a-piū'-tic, al], *a.* Terapéutico, curativo.

Therapeutics [ther-a-piū'-tics], *s.* Terapéutica, la parte de la medicina que trata del modo de obrar los medicamentos y de su aplicación.

Therapeutist [ther-a-piū'-tist], *s.* Persona versada en la terapéutica.

There [dhār], *adv.* 1. Allí, allá, ahí. 2. Allá, hacia aquel lugar, en aquella dirección. *There she is,* Héla ahí. *There is,* Allí está, helo ahí o allí, este o ese es, míralo allí. *There* forma con el verbo *to be* el impersonal *there be* que corresponde al verbo castellano *haber* usado como impersonal, con la diferencia que en inglés el verbo está en el mismo número que el nombre a que se refiere. *There can not be,* No puede haber. *There is a place,* Hay un lugar o un sitio. *There are many things,* Hay muchas cosas. *There was a king,* Hubo un rey. *There were many soldiers,* Había muchos soldados. *There* precede también a otros verbos para dar énfasis a la oración. *There came a man,* Vino un hombre. *Here and there,* De aquí para allí, acá y acullá.—*inter.* (Fam.) *There!* ¡Toma! y bien; ¡vaya!

Thereabout [dhār'-a-baut], **Thereabouts** [dhār'-a-bauts], *adv.* 1. Por ahí, por allá, por allí, cerca, en los contornos; acerca de; hablando de algún lugar o paraje, o del número, cantidad o estado de alguna cosa. 2. Tocante a eso.

Thereafter [dhār-ạf'-tẹr], *adv.* 1. Después de eso, en seguida. 2. Según, conforme, en conformidad.

Thereat [dhār-at'], *adv.* 1. Por eso; de eso. 2. Allá, en aquel paraje o lugar. 3. A aquel.

Thereby [dhār-bai'], *adv.* Con eso, por medio de eso; con ello, con aquello; de este modo.

Therefor [dhār-fōr'], *adv.* Para eso, por eso o por esto.

Therefore [dhār'-fōr ó dhẹr'-fōr], *adv.* y *conj.* 1. Por esto, por eso, por aquello, por esta razón, por tanto o por lo tanto, de consiguiente o a consecuencia de eso. 2. En recompensa de esto o de aquello.

Therefrom [dhār-frem'], *adv.* De allí, de allá; de eso, de aquello.
Therein [dhār-in'], *adv.* En esto, en aquello, en eso.
Thereinto [dhār-in-tū'], *adv.* En aquello, en eso; dentro de aquello o de esto.
Thereof [dhār-ef'], *adv.* De esto, de aquello, de ello.
Thereon [dhār-en'], *adv.* En eso, sobre eso.
Thereout [dhār-aut'], *adv.* De allí; fuera de allí; fuera de eso o de aquello.
Thereto [dhār-tū'], (ant.) **Thereunto** [dhār-un-tū'], *adv.* A eso, a ello.
Thereunder [dhār-un'-dẹr], *adv.* Debajo de eso.
Thereupon [dhār-up-en'], *adv.* En consecuencia de eso; sobre eso; al instante.
Therewith [dhār-widh'], *adv.* Con eso o con aquello; luego, inmediatamente.
Therewithal [dhār-widh ōl'], *adv.* A más, además; al mismo tiempo.
Theriac [thī'-ri-ac], **Theriacal** [thẹ-rai'-a-cal], *a.* Teriacal, triacal, de triaca o que contiene alguna de sus propiedades.
Thermal [thẹr'-mal], *a.* Termal, perteneciente al calor, caliente. *Thermal alarm,* Alarma automática que suena cuando la temperatura alcanza a cierto grado. *Thermal waters,* Aguas termales.
Thermic [thẹr'-mic], *a.* Termal, perteneciente o debido al calor.
Thermodynamics [thẹr''-mo-dai-nam'-ics], *s.* Termodinámica, parte de la física que trata de la fuerza mecánica del calor.
Thermoelectric [thẹr''-mo-ẹ-lec'-tric], *a.* Termoeléctrico, relativo a la termoelectricidad.
Thermoelectricity [thẹr''-mo-ī-lec-tris'-i-ti], *s.* Termoelectricidad, electricidad desarrollada por diferencias de temperatura.
Thermometer [thẹr-mem'-e-tẹr], *s.* Termómetro, instrumento que sirve para medir los grados del calor y del frío.
Thermonuclear [thẹr-mo-niū'-clir], *a.* Termonuclear.
Thermos bottle [thẹr'-mẹs bet'-l], *s.* Termos.
Thermoscope [thẹr'-mo-scōp], *s.* Termoscopio, una especie de termómetro.
Thermostat [thẹr'-mo-stat], *s.* Termostato, aparato para regular automáticamente la temperatura por medio de la expansión diferencial de ciertas substancias.
Thesaurus [thẹ-sē'-rus], *s.* 1. Antiguo almacén griego. 2. Almacén de palabras o de conocimientos; léxico o enciclopedia.
These [dhīz], *pron. pl.* de THIS. Estos, estas.
Thesis [thī'-sis], *s.* 1. Tesis, conclusión, la proposición que se sienta y que se intenta defender. 2. Cuestión, proposición. 3. Tesis, parte no acentuada del pie de verso; disminución del tono de la voz al pronunciar la tesis. *V.* ARSIS.
Thespian [thes'-pi-an], *a.* Trágico, dramático; relativo a Tespis, considerado como el padre de la tragedia griega.
Theurgy [thī'-ūr-ji], *s.* Teurgia, el poder de hacer cosas sobrenaturales por medios legítimos, como invocando a Dios.
Thew [thiū], *s.* Tendón, músculo particularmente en plural, fuerzas corporales.
They [dhē], *pron. pl.* de HE, SHE o IT. Ellos, ellas.
Thick [thic], *a.* 1. Espeso, denso, condensado. 2. Cenagoso, turbio, feculento. 3. Grueso, corpulento, macizo. 4. Continuado, repetido, frecuente. 5. Espeso, que está muy junto y apretado; abundante en. 6. Basto, grosero, tosco. 7. Sobrecargado de vapor, nebuloso, brumoso, sombrío. 8. Embotado, obtuso, de inteligencia torpe. 9. (Fam.) Íntimo, excesivamente familiar. *Thick-lipped,* Bezudo. *To speak thick,* Hablar con media lengua. *Thick of hearing,* Teniente de oído, duro de oído, que oye con dificultad.—*s.* 1. Grueso, espesor. 2. Lo más denso, nutrido, tupido o recio. *The thick of the fight,* Lo más fuerte del combate. *To go through thick and thin,* Atropellar por todo.—*adv.* Frecuentemente, continuadamente; de una manera fuerte. *Thick-headed,* Espeso, pesado, que tiene la cabeza dura; torpe de inteligencia. *Thick-set,* (1) Rechoncho, grueso, abultado de carnes. (2) Plantado muy espeso o dejando poco espacio entre las plantas o árboles. *Thick-skinned,* (1) De pellejo espeso; (2) paquidermo. *Thick stuff,* (Mar.) Tablones, palmejares. *Scarf thick stuff,* Palmejares de los escarpes.
Thicken [thic'-n], *va.* y *vn.* 1. Espesar, condensar lo líquido o lo flúido. 2. Espesar. 3. Dar fuerza, dar más valor, confirmar. 4. Engrosar, aumentar. 5. Crecer. 6. Condensarse, enturbiarse, cerrarse. *It thickens,* (Fam. fig.) ¡ Ya escampa !
Thickening [thik'-n-ing], *s.* 1. Espesura, acción y efecto de espesar. 2. Lo que sirve para condensar un líquido. 3. Lo que está engrosado o espesado.
Thicket [thik'-et], *s.* Bosquecito o monte espeso o muy frondoso; soto, espesura o frondosidad; matorral.
Thickish [thik'-ish], *a.* Algo espeso o denso; un poco turbio.
Thickly [thic'-li], *adv.* 1. Profundamente. 2. Con frecuencia, continuadamente. *Thickly settled,* Muy poblado.
Thickness [thic'-nes], *s.* 1. Espesor, espesura, densidad. 2. Espesor, la tercera dimensión de un cuerpo, en oposición al largo y al ancho. 3. Consistencia, el estado de las cosas líquidas cuando se coagulan y toman cuerpo. Grosor de un montón de papel, de las capas de alguna substancia, etc. *Thickness of hearing,* Dureza de oído.
Thick-skulled [thic'-skuld], *a.* Tardo, torpe, rudo, de cabeza dura.
Thief [thīf], *s.* 1. Ladrón, el que roba; estafador. 2. El o lo que causa una pérdida, v. g. de tiempo, de la reputación, etc. 3. (Prov.) Seta, pavesa o moco de una luz.
Thieve [thīv], *vn.* Hurtar, robar.
Thievery [thīv'-ẹr-i], *s.* 1. Latrocinio, hurto, robo, la acción y costumbre de hurtar o robar. 2. Hurto, robo, la cosa hurtada á robada.
Thievish [thīv'-ish], *a.* Inclinado a hurtar, dado al vicio del hurto.
Thievishness [thīv'-ish-nes], *s.* Latrocinio.
Thigh [thai], *s.* Muslo, la parte del cuerpo del animal desde la juntura de la cadera hasta la rodilla.
Thill [thil], *s.* Lanza, cada una de las varas de un carruaje cualquiera.
Thimble [thim'-bl], *s.* 1. Dedal. 2. (Mar.) Guardacabo. *Thimbleberry,* La frambuesa negra; y también, el frambueso de flor blanca; ambos del Canadá y los Estados Unidos.
Thin [thin], *a.* 1. Delgado, delicado, sutil. 2. Flaco, falto de carnes. 3. Ralo, claro, que no tiene densidad o solidez. 4. Poco, corto, ligero, escaso; delgado; tenue, pequeño. 5. Claro, poco trabado, que no está turbio o espeso. 6. Raro, diseminado, no espeso ni abundante; poco numeroso. 7. Escaso, pequeño, falto de ingredientes o cualidades características. *A thin plate of metal,* Una placa delgada de metal. *A thin crop,* Una cosecha escasa. *A thin disguise,* Un disfraz ligero. *Thin blood,* Sangre clara. *Thin air,* Aire enrarecido. *A thin suspicion,* Una sospecha sin fundamento. *To make thin,* Descarnar; hacer enflaquecer. *To grow thin,* Enflaquecer. *To make thinner,* Adelgazar.
Thin, *va.* 1. Enrarecer, atenuar, poner ralo. 2. Adelgazar. 3. Aclarar, clarificar los licores. 4. Aclarar, entresacar un bosque, una arboleda, etc. 5. Dejar claro, disminuir el número.
Thine [dhain], *pron.* Tuyo.—*a.* Tu, tus: se emplea en vez de *thy* delante de una vocal. *Thine eyes,* Tus ojos. *The glory is thine,* La gloria es tuya.
Thing [thing], *s.* 1. Cosa, en contraposición a persona; objeto, substancia. 2. Asunto, objeto o existencia no conocida o no caracterizada por un nombre definido; asunto, hecho. 3. Evento, circunstancia, acontecimiento. *Above all things,* Sobre todas las cosas o sobre todo. 4. *pl.* Cosas, efectos personales; hábitos, vestidos. 5. Se usa algunas veces por desprecio o como diminutivo hablando de personas. *I pity the poor little thing,* Tengo lástima del pobrecito o de la pobrecita. *Anything,* Algo, cualquier cosa que sea. *Anything but,* Otra cosa que, nada menos que. *No such thing,* No hay tal cosa; nada. *The thing,* Lo conveniente, lo que está de moda, lo necesario o lo que se desea. *To make a good thing of,* (Fam.) Sacar gran provecho de una cosa. *As things stand,* En el punto en que están las cosas.
Think [thiṇk], *va.* y *vn.* 1. Pensar, imaginar, meditar, discurrir, considerar, idear. 2. Pensar, reflexionar, examinar con cuidado. 3. Pensar, intentar hacer una cosa o hacer ánimo de ejecutarla. 4. Pensar, creer, juzgar, formar concepto. 5. Proponerse, formar designio, tener intención de. 6. (*vn.*) Traer a la memoria, pensar en; se usa con *on* o *upon.* *To think of, on* o *upon,* Pensar en, reflexionar acerca de, meditar, considerar; tener la mira en. *To think well* o *ill of one,* Pensar bien o mal de uno, tener buena o mala opinión de él. *As you think fit,* Como Vd. guste, como Vd. quiera. *To think scorn,* Desdeñarse. *Methinks, methought,* Me parece a mí, creía yo.
Thinker [thiṇk'-ẹr], *s.* Pensador.
Thinking [thiṇk'-ing], *s.* 1. Pensamiento, la acción y efecto de pensar; meditación, reflexión. 2. Juicio, parecer, opinión. *Way of thinking,* Modo de pensar, opinión, pare-

cer. *To my thinking,* A mi parecer, en mi opinión.

Thinly [thin'-li], *adv.* 1. Delgadamente, delicadamente. 2. Poco, en corto número. *Thinly sown,* Claro: dícese del sembrado.

Thinness [thin'-nes], *s.* 1. Tenuidad, delgadez, sutileza. 2. Escasez. 3. Raleza, lo contrario de espesura. 4. Fineza, ligereza. 5. Falta de viscosidad, poca consistencia.

Third [therd], *a.* Tercer, tercero, ordinal de *three,* tres. *Third rate,* De tercer orden, de tercera clase. *George the Third,* Jorge Tercero.—*s.* Tercio, la tercera parte. *Two-thirds,* Dos terceras partes.

Thirdborough [therd'-bur-o], *s.* Ministril, corchete.

Thirdly [therd'-li], *adv.* En tercer lugar.

Thirst [therst], *s.* 1. Sed, deseo o apetito de beber. *To quench the thirst,* Apagar la sed. 2. Sed, deseo vehemente o anhelo y gana ardiente de alguna cosa. *Thirst of riches,* Ansia o sed de riquezas.

Thirst, *va.* y *vn.* 1. Tener o padecer sed. 2. Desear con anhelo y ansia. 3. Desear beber. *To thirst after* o *for,* Ansiar, anhelar, desear con ansia o vehemencia.

Thirstiness [thers'-ti-nes], *s.* 1. Sed, deseo de beber. 2. Sed, el deseo o ansia ardiente por alguna cosa.

Thirsty [thers'-ti], *a.* 1. Sediento, que padece o tiene sed. 2. Sediento, que desea con ansia alguna cosa. *Bloodthirsty,* Sanguinario.

Thirteen [ther'-tîn], *a.* y *s.* Trece. *She is thirteen,* Ella tiene trece años.

Thirteenth [ther-tînth'], *a.* Décimotercio, ordinal de trece. *On the thirteenth of January,* El trece de enero.

Thirtieth [ther'-ti-eth], *a.* Trigésimo, ordinal de treinta.

Thirty [ther'-ti], *a.* y *s.* Treinta.

This [dhis], *a.* y *pron.* Este, esta, esto, que está presente; se refiere a lo que está presente o más cerca que otra cosa. *This plant,* Esta planta. *This or that,* Esto o aquello, el uno o el otro. *These three years I come seeking fruit,* Hace tres años que vengo a buscar fruta. *By this time,* Ahora, al presente, a este tiempo. *This is the way,* Este es el camino.

Thistle [this'-l], *s.* (Bot.) Cardo; una de varias plantas espinosas de la familia de las compuestas. *Canada thistle, cursed thistle,* Cardo silvestre. Cnicus arvensis. *Carline thistle,* Ajonjera, carlina común. *Fuller's thistle,* Cardón, cardencha, cardo de batanero. *Milk thistle, Our Lady's thistle,* Cardo lechoso, cardo de Nuestra Señora. *Thistledown,* Vello, borrilla de cardo. *Scotch thistle,* Cardo que se considera como emblema nacional de Escocia. *Thistle-finch, thistle-bird,* Jilguero. *V.* GOLDFINCH.

Thistly [this'-li], *adv.* Lleno de cardos.

Thither [dhidh'-er], *adv.* 1. Allá, hacia aquel lugar, en aquella dirección. 2. A ese fin, punto o resultado. *Hither and thither,* Acá y allá.

Tho' [dhō], *conj.* Contracción de THOUGH.

Thole [thōl], *s.* 1. Tolete, escálamo, gavilán donde se apoya el remo al tiempo de remar. *Thole-pin,* Tolete. 2. Uno de los dos asideros por donde se coge el mango de la guadaña.

Thong [thong], *s.* Correa o correhüela, tira larga de cuero.

Thor [thōr], *s.* El dios escandinavo de la guerra y de la agricultura, bienhechor de la humanidad.

Thoracic [tho-ras'-ic], *a.* Torácico, que pertenece al tórax.

Thoral [thō'-ral], *a.* Perteneciente á la cama.

Thorax [thō'-rax], *s.* 1. Tórax, cavidad del pecho de los animales vertebrados. 2. Región media del cuerpo de un insecto entre la cabeza y el abdomen.

Thorium [thor'-ium], *s.* (Quím.) Torio.

Thorn [thōrn], *va.* 1. Penetrar o traspasar con una espina o púa. 2. Asegurar con una espina. 3. Proveer de espinas para cualquier objeto.—*s.* 1. (Bot.) Espina, púa que nace del tejido leñoso o vascular de ciertas plantas. 2. Espino, arbusto del género Cratægus; majuelo. *V.* HAWTHORN. 3. Espina, pesadumbre, zozobra, cualquier cosa que molesta. *To be upon thorns,* Estar en ascuas.

Thorn-apple, *s.* (Bot.) Estramonio.

Thornback [thōrn'-bac], **Thornbut** [thōrn'-but], *s.* (Ict.) Raya espinosa o lija raya.

Thornless [thōrn'-les], *a.* Falto de espinas o púas.

Thorny [thōr'-ni], *a.* 1. Espinoso, lleno de espinas. 2. Espinoso, arduo, penoso.

Thorny-woodcock [thōr-ni-wud'-coc], *s.* Especie de limazo con cáscara.

Thorough [thur'-ō], *a.* Entero, cabal, completo, perfecto, acabado; consumado, perfecto: (en mala parte) loco rematado, pícaro consumado.—*prep.* (Des.) *V.* THROUGH.

Thoroughbred [thur'-o-bred], *a.* De sangre pura; osado, valeroso; de forma elegante.

Thoroughfare [thur'-o-fār], *s.* Paso, tránsito o camino libre por donde se puede pasar. *No thoroughfare,* No se pasa; calle cerrada; el público no entra.

Thorough-going [thur'-o-gō''-ing], *a.* Completo, muy eficaz, entero; que va hasta el fin.

Thoroughly [thur'-o-li], *adv.* Enteramente, cabalmente, a fondo.

Thorough-paced [thur'-ō-pêst], *a.* Cabal, completo, perfecto.

Thorough-wax [thur'-o-wax], *s.* Oreja de liebre. *V.* HARE'S-EAR.

Thoroughwort [thur'-o-wūrt], *s.* Eupatorio, hierba fuerte. *V.* BONESET.

Thorp [thōrp], *s.* Lugar, aldea.

Those [dhōz], *pron. pl.* de THAT. Aquellos, aquellas; esos, esas. *Those who* o *those which,* Los que o las que. *Those of,* Los de o las de.

Thou [dhau]. Tú, segunda persona del pronombre personal. *Thou* no se usa en inglés en el lenguaje familiar, a no ser por los cuáqueros; pero se usa frecuentemente en la poesía y en el estilo sublime. *Thou and thee,* Trato demasiado familiar.

Thou, *va.* Tutear; hablar o tratar con demasiada familiaridad; hablar a uno en tono de desprecio. *To thee and thou,* Tutear.

Though [dhō], *conj.* Aunque, bien que, no obstante, sin embargo, aun cuando. *What though,* Aun que, qué, importa que. *Though he were dead, yet shall he live,* Aun cuando él muera, vivirá. *As though,* Como si; como que; con todo.

Thought [thēt], *pret.* y *pp.* del verbo THINK.—*s.* 1. Pensamiento, el acto y efecto de pensar; la especie concebida o formada; meditación seria, reflexión. 2. Pensamiento, juicio, dictamen, opinión. 3. Designio, proyecto, intención. 4. Memoria, recordación. 5. Cuidado, solicitud, atención. 6. (Fam.) Poquito, una migaja. *To entertain ill thoughts of one,* Tener mala opinión de alguna persona. *The thought strikes me,* Me ocurre la idea. *To take thought,* Sentir inquietud. *To have some thoughts of,* Tener el proyecto o la idea de; pensar en.

Thoughtful [thēt'-ful], *a.* Pensativo, meditabundo; atento, cuidadoso, que piensa en.

Thoughtfully [thēt'-ful-i], *adv.* Cuidadosamente, solícitamente; de un modo muy pensativo o meditabundo; con reflexión, con inquietud.

Thoughtfulness [thēt'-ful-nes], *s.* Meditación profunda, reflexión; cuidado, afán, inquietud; previsión.

Thoughtless [thēt'-les], *a.* Atolondrado, descuidado, irreflexivo, inconsiderado, incauto; insensato, disipado, impróvido.

Thoughtlessly [thēt'-les-li], *adv.* Descuidadamente, negligentemente, sin consideración, sin reflexión, sin cuidado.

Thoughtlessness [thēt'-les-nes], *s.* 1. Descuido, omisión, inadvertencia. 2. Ligereza, indiscreción, atolondramiento.

Thousand [thau'-zand], *a.* 1. Mil, diez veces ciento. 2. También se usa indefinidamente para denotar un número o cantidad muy grande. *He will find a thousand occasions for doing it,* Hallará mil ocasiones de hacerlo.—*s.* 1. Mil. 2. Millar; guarismo que significa mil. *By thousands,* Por millares, a millares.

Thousandth [thau'-zandth], *a.* Milésimo, el ordinal de mil.—*s.* Milésima parte de un todo.

Thracian [thrê'-shan], *a.* Tracio, de la Tracia.—*s.* Tracio, habitante de la Tracia.

Thrall [thrēl], *s.* Esclavo, esclava; esclavitud, servidumbre.

Thrall, *va.* (Poét. o des.) Esclavizar, avasallar.

Thraldom [thrēl'-dum], *s.* Esclavitud, servidumbre.

Thrash [thrash], *va.* 1. Trillar o apalear grano; desgranar; batir; sacudir; apalear; azotar. 2. Golpear o dar de palos a alguno, zurrar. (Vulg.) Sobar.—*vn.* 1. Trillar el grano. 2. Arrojarse, agitarse, moverse violentamente. 3. Trabajar, ocuparse en cosas serviles.

Thrasher [thrash'-er], *s.* 1. Trillador, apaleador de granos. 2. Máquina para trillar. 3. Malviz, especie de tordo americano del género Harporynchus. 4. *V.* THRESHER.

Thrashing-floor [thrash'-ing-flōr], *s.* Era.

Thrasonical [thra-son'-i-cal], *a.* Jactancioso.

Thrave [thrêv], *s.* 1. (Prov. Ingl.) Veinticuatro gavillas de trigo. 2. (Des.) Dos docenas.

Thraw [thrē], *va.* (Esco.) 1. Torcer. 2. Frustrar, contrariar.

Thread [thred], *s.* 1. Hilo, torzal delgado. 2. Filete (de tornillo, de rosca). 3. Filamento, hilito. 4. Hilo, continuación de alguna cosa que se está haciendo. *Skein of thread,* Madeja de hilo. *Threadlike,* Semejante a hilo, como hilo, filiforme. *Thread and thrum,* Hilo e hilaza, mezcla de bueno y malo.

Thread, *va.* 1. Enhebrar. 2. Ensartar, colar, atravesar á lo largo, pasar por. 3. Coser.

Threadbare [thred'-bār], *a.* Raído, muy usado, gastado hasta verse los hilos.

Threadworm [thred'-wūrm], *s.* Lombricilla filiforme, ascáride; se llama también *pinworm*.

Threat [thret], *s.* Amenaza.

Threat, Threaten [thret'-n], *va.* 1. Amenazar, hacer amenazas á, aterrar. 2. Amenazar o amagar; hablando de cosas, es pronosticar algún mal.

Threatener [thret'-n-ẹr], *s.* Amenazador.

Threatening [thret'-n-ing], *s.* Amenaza, acción de amenazar.—*a.* Amenazador, terrible, amenazante.

Threateningly [thret'-n-ing-li], *adv.* Con amenazas.

¿**Threatful** [thret'-ful], *a.* Lleno de amenazas.

Three [thrī], *a.* Tres, número cardinal.—*s.* Tres, la suma de tres unidades; el guarismo que representa este número. *Three-celled*, Trilocular, que tiene tres células. *Three-cleft*, (Bot.) Trífido, que está dividido en tres. *Three-cornered*, Triangular; de tres cuernos, de tres esquinas o ángulos. *Three-decker*, Navío de tres puentes. *Three deep*, En tres hileras o filas. *Three-leaved*, Trifoliado, de tres hojas. *Three-parted*, (Bot.) Tripartido. *Three-ply*, Triple, de tres pliegues. *Three-legged*, De tres pies. *Three-lobed*, Trilobulado, dividido en tres lóbulos. *Three-quarter*, De las tres cuartas partes. *Three-stringed*, De tres cuerdas. *Three-valved*, De tres válvulas, de tres conchas.

Threefold [thrī'-fōld], *a.* Tríplice, triplo.

Threepence [thrī'-pens o fam. thrip'-ens], *s.* Tres peniques, moneda pequeña de plata que tenía este valor.

Threepenny [thrī'-pen-i o fam. thrip'-en-i], *a.* Vil, bajo, de poco valor.

Threepile [thrī'-pail], *s.* Terciopelo

Threescore [thrī'-scōr], *a.* y *s.* Sesenta; tres veces una veintena. *Threescore years and ten*, Setenta años.

Threnody [thren'-o-di], *s.* Treno, lamentación fúnebre por alguna calamidad.

Thresh, *va.* *V. To* THRASH.

Thresher [thresh'-ẹr], *s.* 1. Zorra marina, especie de tiburón. 2. Para otras acepciones, véase THRASHER.

Threshold [thresh'-hōld], *s.* 1. Umbral, quicio, piedra o madero colocado al pie de la abertura de una puerta; entrada. 2. Punto de partida de entrada.

Threw, *pret.* del verbo *To* THROW.

Thrice [thrais], *adv.* Tres veces; de una manera o grado triple; de aquí, completamente.

Thrid [thrid], *vn.* Colar, pasar por un paraje estrecho.

Thrift [thrift], *s.* 1. Economía, frugalidad, cuidado y prudencia en el manejo de sus negocios. 2. Ganancia, utilidad, ahorro. 3. Crecimiento rápido, desarrollo, como el de una planta. 4. (Bot.) Planta llamada también *sea-pink*, una de las varias especies del género Armeria.

Thriftily [thrif'-ti-li], *adv.* Frugalmente, económicamente.

Thriftiness [thrif'-ti-nes], *s.* Frugalidad, parsimonia, economía.

Thriftless [thrift'-les], *a.* Manirroto, pródigo; extravagante.

Thrifty [thrif'-ti], *a.* 1. Frugal, económico; de gastos moderados. 2. Próspero, feliz en los negocios. 3. Floreciente, que crece o se desarrolla con rapidez.

Thrill [thril], *va.* 1. Penetrar, hacer experimentar una emoción viva. 2. Hacer estremecerse.—*vn.* 1. Estremecerse o conmoverse por alguna pasión violenta; experimentar una emoción viva. 2. Penetrar, herir el oído con sonidos o gritos violentos y agudos. 3. Temblar, moverse temblando. *To thrill with pleasure*, Temblar de gusto. *To thrill the blood*, Hervir la sangre.

Thrilling [thril'-ing], *pa.* Que pasma, que conmueve; vivo.

Thrive [thraiv], *vn.* 1. Medrar, prosperar, adelantar, tener éxito, enriquecerse. 2. Crecer con vigor, desarrollarse.

Thriver [thraiv'-ẹr], *s.* El que medra o prospera.

Thrivingly [thraiv'-ing-li], *adv.* Prósperamente.

Thro' [thrū], *adv.* y *prep.* abrev. de THROUGH.

Throat [thrōt], *s.* 1. Garganta, la parte interior del cuello; también, gaznate. *I have a sore throat*, Me duele la garganta. *To cut the throat*, Degollar. 2. El camino principal de alguna parte. 3. Pasaje u orificio; (Bot.) entrada del tubo de la corola; garganta, parte estrecha. 4. (Mar.) Cangreja. *Throat-halliard*, (Mar.) Driza de cangreja. *Throat-pipe*, Traquiarteria. *Throat-seizing*, Garganteadura.

Throb [throb], *vn.* 1. Latir, palpitar. 2. Vibrar, de cualquier modo que sea. *V.* THRILL.

Throb, *s.* Latido, pulsación, palpitación.

Throe [thrō], *s.* Angustia, gran dolor; dolor de parto; agonía de la muerte.

Thrombosis [throm-bō'-sis], *s.* (Med.) Trombosis.

Throne [thrōn], *s.* 1. Trono, asiento regio; la sede de un obispo en una catedral. 2. Poder soberano; el que tiene el poder soberano. *Thrones*, *pl.* Tronos, hablando de los espíritus angélicos.

Throng [throng], *s.* Tropel de gente, multitud amontonada, muchedumbre.

Throng, *va.* 1. Apretar, rellenar cierto espacio. 2. Apretar o estrujar a uno la concurrencia muy numerosa y apiñada de gente.—*vn.* Venir en tropel, amontonarse la gente, acudir en gran número. *The audience thronged the hall*, El auditorio llenó la sala de bote en bote.

Throstle, *s.* 1. (Ingl.) *V.* THRUSH. 2. Máquina para torcer y devanar hilos; telar continuo. Hace un hilo más liso y más duro que la *spinning-mule*.

Throttle [thret'-l], *s.* 1. Gaznate, garguero; traquiarteria. 2. Válvula de cuello o de paso en las máquinas de vapor; también se llama *throttle-valve*.

Throttle, *va.* Ahogar, sofocar.—*vn.* Sofocarse, ahogarse, respirar con dificultad.

Through [thrū], *a.* Que va desde el principio hasta el fin con pocas paradas o sin ninguna. *A through train*, Tren terminal.—*adv.* 1. De un lado a otro. *I am wet through*, Estoy calado hasta los huesos, enteramente. 2. Desde el principio hasta el fin; todo el camino. 3. Hasta el fin; de parte a parte. 4. (Fam.) A buen fin.—*prep.* 1. Al través de, de un extremo a otro de; de parte a parte, de medio a medio. 2. Por medio de, por entre, de o al través; enteramente, del todo. *Through your influence*, Mediante el influjo de Vd.; por mediación de Vd. 3. En, en medio de; por. 4. Con motivo de, por efecto de, por causa de. *Fish swim through the water*, Los peces nadan por o en medio del agua. *Through all Spain*, Por toda España. *To carry through*, Llevar a buen fin. *To fall through*, Salir mal, fracasar. *This train runs through*, Este tren va hasta el término.

Throughout [thrū-aut'], *prep.* Por todo, en todo, a lo largo de; durante todo.—*adv.* En todas partes.

Throve [thrōv], *pret.* del verbo *To* THRIVE.

Throw [thrō], *va.* y *vn.* (*pret.* THREW, *pp.* THROWN). 1. Echar, arrojar, tirar, disparar, lanzar. 2. Echar, tirar, tender, derribar al suelo. 3. Echarse, arrojarse. 4. Tirar los dados. 5. Impeler, empujar con violencia; estrellar. 6. Desmontar, desarzonar, echar al suelo. 7. Echar, tirar algo apresurada ó negligentemente. 8. Despojarse de; desechar o mudar, v. g. como lo hace una serpiente con su piel. 9. Torcer la seda, convertir los filamentos en hilo. 10. Parir (la coneja y otros animales). 11. Perder con premeditación (una carrera, un juego). 12. Dar forma a los objetos de alfarería. *To throw away*, Arrojar, rechazar, desperdiciar, malgastar; desechar, echar a un lado; arrinconar. *To throw about*, Echar alrededor de; arrojar por uno y otro lado. *To throw aside*, Arrojar, poner de lado. *To throw back*, Rechazar hacia atrás; volver. *To throw by*, Poner en olvido, arrinconar, echar a un lado; despreciar. *To throw down*, Derribar, destruir, echar por tierra; subvertir, trastornar. *To throw in*, Echar dentro, arrojar en; intercalar, insertar; añadir; dar de más; dar además de lo convenido. *To throw off*, Echar o arrojar de sí o de alguna parte; expeler, hacer salir; dejar o renunciar una cosa. *To throw out*, Proferir, hacer creer; echar afuera, expeler; excluir; esparcir, exhalar; emitir, v. g. una opinión; hacer observaciones, insinuar. *To throw out of*, Arrojar por. *To throw up*, Arrojar por alto o en alto; echar al aire; elevar, levantar; renunciar a, abandonar, deshacerse de un cargo; vomitar. *To throw silk*, Torcer seda. *To throw overboard*, (Mar.) Echar en la mar o tirar a la mar. *To throw open*, Abrir de par en par.

Throw, *s.* 1. Tiro, el movimiento de una cosa arrojada o lanzada con violencia, y también el espacio que recorre la cosa así arrojada. 2. Un rato, un corto espacio de tiempo. 3. Golpe; esfuerzo. 4. *Within a stone's throw*, A tiro de piedra.

Throwback [thrō'-bac], *s.* Atavismo, retroceso.

Thrum [thrum], *s.* Cadillos; hilo basto; hilo destorcido.

Thrum, *va.* Rascar las cuerdas de un instrumento, tocarlas mal; golpear ligeramente con los dedos, tamborilear.—*s.* Sonido que se hace golpeando ligeramente.

Thrush [thrush], *s.* 1. (Orn.) Tordo, ave de los géneros Turdus o Merula; zorzal, malvís. 2. Afta, úlcera que se forma en la superficie interior de la boca. 3. (Vet.) Higo, enfermedad que ataca el talón del caballo.

Thrust [thrust], *va.* y *vn.* (*pret.* y *pp.* THRUST). 1. Introducir con violencia. 2. Empujar, impeler. 3. Apretar, estrechar, cerrar. 4. Entremeterse, meterse, mezclarse en lo que a uno no le toca. 5. Introducirse en alguna parte sin ser llamado. 6. Acometer con ímpetu y violencia, embestir con uno. 7. Obligar a hacer algo por fuerza. *To thrust aside*, Rechazar, empujar a un lado. *To thrust away*, Rechazar, apartar, arrojar, alejar. *To thrust back*, Rechazar. *To thrust down*, Echar abajo; introducir, hacer entrar. *To thrust forward*, Empujar hacia adelante, echar adelante. *To thrust in*, Meter o introducir por fuerza o con violencia. *To thrust out*, Echar ó arrojar afuera. *To thrust together*, Apretar o estrujar unas cosas con otras. *To thrust through*, Dar de puñaladas, atravesar de parte a parte con algún instrumento punzante. *To thrust upon*, Imponer a, hacer aceptar a; hacer creer cosas falsas á otro.

Thrust, *s.* 1. Empuje repentino; empuje a lo largo; empujón; estocada; lanzada; cualquier bote o golpe que se tira con un arma ó instrumento punzante. 2. Arremetida, ataque. 3. (Mec.) Empuje mutuo entre dos cuerpos en contacto; presión horizontal hacia el exterior: tracción; impulso del tornillo, empuje de la hélice. (Fís.) Empuje, potencia o capacidad de empuje.

Thud [thud], *vn.* Hacer un ruido sordo.—*s.* Sonido sordo y pesado, como el de un cuerpo duro que da contra otro comparativamente blando; el golpe que produce dicho sonido.

Thug [thug], *s.* 1. Miembro de una secta de asesinos fanáticos de la India. 2. De aquí, asesino.

Thumb [thum], *s.* Pulgar, el dedo primero y más grueso de los de la mano. *Thumb-nut*, Tuerca con orejetas. *Thumb-screw*, Tuerca con orejetas, tornillo de presión; antiguo instrumento de tortura.

Thumb, *va.* Manosear con poca destreza; emporcar alguna cosa con los dedos al manosearla.

Thumbnail [thum'-nêl], *s.* Uña del pulgar. *Thumbnail sketch*, Esbozo en miniatura.

Thumb notch [thum' noch], *s.* Recorte en diccionarios, índices, etc. para facilitar su consulta.

Thumbtack [thum'-tac], *s.* Chinche, tachuela.

Thump [thump], *s.* Porrazo, golpe que causa un sonido sordo; puñada.

Thump, *va.* y *vn.* 1. Aporrear, cascar, apuñear, acachetear. 2. Dar un porrazo o un golpe; golpear pesadamente.

Thunder [thun'-dẹr], *s.* 1. Trueno, el ruido que acompaña al rayo. 2. Cualquier estruendo ó ruido violento. 3. (Fig.) Rayo; denunciación fulminante, excomunión. *Thunder-storm*, Tormenta acompañada de truenos.

Thunder, *va.* y *vn.* 1. Tronar, oirse el ruido del trueno. 2. Tronar, dar estampidos o estallidos como los de las armas de fuego. 3. Tempestar, atronar, aturdir a voces o a gritos. 4. Fulminar o arrojar rayos. 5. Fulminar penas, excomuniones, etc. *It thunders*, Truena.

Thunderbolt [thun'-dẹr-bōlt], *s.* 1. Rayo o centella despedida de las nubes. 2. Fulminación, censura, excomunión eclesiástica.

Thunderclap [thun'-dẹr-clap], *s.* Trueno, rayo; tronada o tempestad con truenos.

Thunderer [thun'-dẹr-ẹr], *s.* Tonante o tronador.

Thunderous [thun'-dẹr-us], *a.* Tronador, que produce truenos.

Thunder-shower [thun'-dẹr-shau-ẹr], *s.* Tronada o tempestad con truenos, nubarrada o nubada acompañada de truenos.

Thunderstrike [thun'-dẹr-straic], *va.* Fulminar, herir con rayo o centella; aturdir o espantar con alguna cosa muy extraordinaria y sorprendente. Este verbo se usa poco a no ser en el participio pasado, *thunderstruck*, anonadado, estupefacto, turulato. *To be thunderstruck*, (Fam.) Quedarse helado o de una pieza.

Thurible [thiū'-ri-bl], *s.* Turíbulo, incensario, braserillo que sirve para incensar.

Thuriferous [thiu-rif'-ẹr-us], *a.* Turífero, que produce o lleva incienso.

Thurification [thiu-ri-fi-kê'-shun], *s.* Incensación, el acto y efecto de incensar.

Thursday [thūrz'-dê], *s.* Jueves, el quinto día de la semana.

Thus [dhus], *adv.* 1. Así, de este modo, de esta suerte, en estos términos. 2. Sí, tanto; a ese grado. 3. Siendo así, en estas condiciones. (*Thus* se limita hoy al estilo literario y formal, y lo reemplaza *so* en el uso ordinario.) *Thus it is*, Así es que, así es como. *Thus far*, Hasta aquí. *Thus much*, Basta no más, baste esto. *Thus it comes to pass*, Así es como viene a ser, a acontecer.

Thus [thus o thūs], *s.* Incienso, resina aromática.

Thwack [thwac], *va.* Aporrear, pegar, zurrar; golpear con alguna cosa plana o redondeada. *V.* WHACK.—*s.* Zurra, tunda, golpe dado con alguna cosa plana. (Var. de WHACK.)

Thwart [thwōrt], *a.* 1. Travesero, transversal, travieso. 2. (Ant.) Atravesado, perverso.—*s.* Banco de remeros, banco de bogar.

Thwart, *va.* 1. Impedir, contradecir, contrariar, suscitar obstáculos, contrarrestar. 2. (Ant.) Mover obstáculos, poner estorbos.—*vn.* (Poco us.) Ir en contra; estar en oposición con o a.

Thwartingly [thwōrt'-ing-li], *adv.* Opuestamente.

Thy [dhai]. Adjetivo posesivo correspondiente a *Thou*, Tu, tus.

Thyme [taim], *s.* (Bot.) Tomillo, cualquiera hierba olorosa del género Thymus.

Thymus [thai'-mus], *s.* Timo, glándula sin conducto eferente que se halla en el cuello de muchos vertebrados.

Thyroid [thai'-reid], *a.* Tiroideo. —*s.* Tiroides (glándula).

Thyrse, Thyrsus [thẹrs, thẹr'-sus], *s.* (Bot.) Tirso, Panoja de forma aovada; como las de la vid y la lila.

Thyself [dhai-self'], *pron. recip.* Tú mismo, tí mismo. *Love thy neighbour as thyself*, Ama a tu prójimo como a tí mismo.

Tiara [tai-ē'-ra o ti-ạ'-ra], *s.* Tiara, ornamento de la cabeza; diadema.

Tibia [tib'-i-a], *s.* 1. Tibia, el hueso más grueso (interior) de la pierna; un hueso semejante del ave. 2. Cuarta articulación de la pata de un insecto. 3. Flauta primitiva.

Tibial [tib'-i-al], *a.* Tibial, que pertenece al hueso tibia.

Tick [tic], *s.* 1. El golpe del reloj o cosa semejante; tic tac, ruido ligero producido por un movimiento acompasado. 2. Marca indicadora que se usa al confrontar una cosa. 3. Garrapata, rezno, un insecto que se agarra fuertemente a los animales. 4. Funda de almohada. 5. (Fam.) Crédito, préstamo de dinero o géneros sin más seguridad que la confianza que se tiene en el que lo recibe. *To buy upon tick*, Comprar al fiado. *Bed-tick*, Cotí o terliz con que se hacen almohadas y colchones.

Tick, *va.* 1. Sonar produciendo tic tac; indicar la hora con ruido ligero; se usa a menudo con *off*. 2. Confrontar, haciendo una marca indicadora.—*vn.* Hacer sonido de tic tac, batir.

Ticker [tik'-ẹr], *s.* El o lo que produce un sonido de tic tac; en especial, (1) (fam. E. U.) instrumento telegráfico receptor, particularmente un indicador de valores; (2) (Ger.) reloj de bolsillo.

Ticker tape [tik'-ẹr têp], *s.* Cinta de teletipo.

Tick, Ticken, [tik'-en], **Ticking** [tik'-ing], *s.* Terliz, cotí o cotín para colchones.

Ticket [tik'-et], *s.* 1. Billete, boleta, (Mex.) boleto; tarjeta de entrada; billete, cédula de transporte por ferrocarril. 2. Rótulo, marbete; marca que se pone a alguna cosa para reconocerla. 3. (E. U.) Balota; de aquí, lista de candidatos en una elección. *Excursion ticket, round-trip ticket*, Billete de ida y vuelta (F. C.). *Play-house ticket*, Boletín o boleta de teatro. *Lottery-ticket*, Cédula o billete de lotería.

Ticket, *va.* Fijar, pegar un rótulo o marbete a; rotular, marcar.

Tickle [tic'-l], *va.* 1. Hacer cosquillas. 2. Halagar, lisonjear, regalar los oídos, la vanidad, las pasiones, etc.—*vn.* Tener cosquillas.

Tickler [tic'-lẹr], *s.* El que hace cosquillas.

Tickling [tic'-ling], *s.* Cosquillas.

Ticklish [tic'-lish], *a.* 1. Cosquilloso, que siente mucho las cosquillas. 2. Instable, incierto. 3. Arduo, delicado, difícil.

Ticklishness [tic'-lish-nes], *s.* La propiedad de ser cosquilloso.

Tickseed [tic'-sīd], *s.* Cualquier planta del género Cercopsis, cuyas semillas parecen garrapatas.

Tick-tack, Tick-tock [tic'-tac], *s.* 1. Tic tac, sonido recurrente o reiterado como el producido por un reloj. 2. Chaquete, una especie de juego muy conocido.

Tid [tid], *a.* (Des.) Delicado, gustoso. *Tid-bit*, Golosina.

Tidal [tai'-dal], *a.* 1. De marea, determinado por las mareas; que crece y mengua periódicamente. 2. Periódico; regularizado o medido en cuanto al tiempo por el flujo y reflujo de la marea. *Tidal basin*, Dique de marea, en el cual la marea mengua y crece. *Tidal harbour*, Puerto en que se notan las mareas. *Tidal wave*, (1) Marejada, oleada de vasta extensión pero de pocos pies de altura, que sigue al sol y a la luna de este a oeste y causa las mareas. (2) Impropiamente, avenida o desbordamiento de la marea.

Tiddlywinks [tid'-li-winks], *s.* Juego en que se emplean pequeños discos de colores en una taza.

Tide [taid], *s.* 1. Marea, el flujo y reflujo de las aguas del mar. 2. Corriente; curso, marcha; flujo. 3. Tiempo, estación. *Time and tide*, El tiempo y la hora. *Springtide*, Estación de primavera. 4. Período de tiempo de seis horas y doce minutos, el intervalo que media entre pleamar y bajamar en el océano. *Whitsuntide*, Pentecostés. *The tide ebbs*, La marea mengua. *The tide flows*, La marea crece. *Flood tide*, Creciente, flujo, marea alta. *High* o *full tide*, Plenamar, pleamar. *Ebb tide, low tide*, Bajamar. *Tide-way*, Canal de marea. *Neap-tides*, Aguas chifles o muertas. *Spring-tide*, Agua viva, marea mayor. *To go with the tide*, Seguir la corriente.

Tide, *va.* 1. Llevar (la marea) hacia algún paraje. 2. Superar una dificultad; aguardar tiempo u ocasión más favorable; se usa con *over*. 3. Arrastrar, llevar por la marea. *To tide it up*, (Mar.) Montar con la marea.

Tideless [taid'-les], *a.* Que no tiene marea; sin marea.

Tidesman [taidz'-man], *s.* 1. *V.* TIDEWAITER. 2. Empleado cuyo oficio depende del estado de la marea.

Tidewaiter [taid'-wêt-er], *s.* El empleado de las aduanas a cuyo cargo está el cuidado de que los géneros que se desembarcan de los buques vayan a la aduana.

Tidewater [taid'-wō'-ter], *s.* Marejada.—*a.* Costanero.

Tidily [tai'-di-li], *adv.* Aseadamente; mañosamente, en buen orden.

Tidiness [tai'-di-nes], *s.* Aseo, buen arreglo, maña.

Tidings [tai'-dingz], *s. pl.* Nuevas, relato, noticias. (<A.-S. *tidan*, suceder.)

Tidy [tai'-di], *a.* 1. Airoso, bien dispuesto, limpio, aseado. 2. De disposición o hábitos metódicos. 3. (Des. o fam.) Considerable, bastante.—*s.* Funda para muebles.

Tidy, *va.* y *vn.* (Fam.) Asear, componer; poner en orden.

Tie [tai], *va.* (*pret.* y *pp.* TIED, *pa.* TYING). 1. Anudar, atar, ligar o enlazar dos o más cosas haciendo nudos; juntar con un lazo. 2. Unir o enlazar íntimamente; atar, encadenar. 3. Restringir dentro de límites, limitar, confinar. 4. Sentar el mismo número en la cuenta; traer a igualdad en la suma. 5. Unir las notas con un rasgo. *To tie up*, Arremangar, recoger, levantar; impedir, obstruir; poner fuera del gobierno o poder de alguien; envolver algo (en una cubierta).

Tie, *s.* 1. Lazo, atadura, ligadura, lo que sirve para atar o ligar. 2. Lazo, vínculo del matrimonio, de la amistad, etc.; apego, adhesión, unión. 3. Una trenza de pelo. 4. Par, igualdad cabal de número en pro y en contra. 5. Lo que sirve para atar; maroma, cordaje, ostaga. 6. (Mús.) Ligadura, línea curva que junta dos notas en el mismo grado del pentagrama. 7. Tirante, ligazón. 8. Traviesa de ferrocarril. 9. (E. U.) *pl.* Zapatos bajos atados con cordones. *Tie-beam*, Tirante; solera de puente.

Tier [tai'-er], *s.* Atador, lo que ata; lo que se ata; en especial, delantal de niño.

Tier [tîr], *s.* Fila, ringlera. *Tier of guns*, (Mar.) Andanada de cañones. *Cable-tier*, Pozo de cable. *Tier of a cable*, Andana.

Tierce [tîrs], *s.* 1. Tercerola, el tonel que contiene la tercera parte de una pipa. 2. (Mús.) Tercera, la consonancia que comprende el intervalo de dos tonos y medio. 3. Tercera, término del juego de los cientos. 4. Tercia, hora canónica. 5. En la esgrima, posición del puño vuelto hacia dentro.

Tiercet [tîr'-set], *s.* (Poét.) Tercerilla, terceto, composición métrica que consta de tres versos.

Tie-up [tai'-up], *s.* 1. Interrupción de trabajo por huelga, descompostura de maquinaria, etc. 2. Paralización momentánea del tráfico.

Tiff [tif], *s.* 1. Pique, disgusto; arranque, palabra picante. 2. Bebida, cualquier licor simple o compuesto.

Tiff, *va.* Merendar. (Angloindio.) —*vn.* Picarse, atufarse, reñir.

Tiffany [tif'-a-ni], *s.* Tafetán sencillo.

Tiger [tai'-ger], *s.* 1. Tigre, mamífero carnicero y feroz de la raza felina. 2. Jaguar. 3. Volante (criado). *Tiger-beetle*, Cicindela, insecto coleóptero. *Tiger-lily*, Lirio de tigre. (Lilium tigrinum.)

Tigerish [tai'-ger-ish], *a.* De tigre, parecido al tigre.

Tight [tait], *a.* 1. Bien cerrado, construido sólida y fuertemente; impermeable, impenetrable a los flúidos; (mar.) estanco. 2. Tirante, fuertemente apretado, tieso, tenso. 3. Premioso, estrecho, muy ajustado. *A tight shoe*, Un zapato demasiado estrecho. 4. (Com.) Escaso, difícil de obtener; dícese del dinero. 5. (Fam.) Compacto, acomodado. 6. (Fam. E. U.) Mezquino, miserable. 7. Difícil de pasar o de salir de. 8. (Fam.) Embriagado, borracho. *Tight fit*, Empalme muy ajustado. *Tight-fitting*, Muy ajustado. *Water-tight*, Estanco, impermeable. *Tight lacing*, Trabas; corsé demasiado ajustado. *To tie tight*, Apretar. *A tight ship*, (Mar.) Navío estanco.

Tighten [tai'-tn], *va.* y *vn.* Estirar, atiesar; apretar; atiesarse, ponerse más tenso.

Tight-lipped [tait'-lipt'], *a.* Reservado, callado, poco comunicativo.

Tightly [tait'-li], *adv.* Con firmeza, bien apretado; de una manera apretada, estirada, tiesa; con estrechez.

Tightness [tait'-nes], *s.* 1. Tensión, tirantez; 2. Estrechez. 3. Condición de lo que se halla bien cerrado; impermeabilidad. 4. Parsimonia, tacañería.

Tightrope [tait'-rōp], *s.* Cuerda tirante de volatinero.

Tights [taits], *s. pl.* Calzón ajustado para facilitar los movimientos y mostrar las formas.

Tight squeeze [tait scwiz], *s.* Aprieto, apuro, conflicto.

Tigress [tai'-gres], *sf.* La hembra del tigre.

Tike [taic], *s.* (Prov.) 1. Patán, rústico. 2. Perro degenerado.

Tilbury [til'-bur-i], *s.* Tílburi, birlocho anticuado para dos personas.

Tile [tail], *s.* 1. Teja, baldosa, pieza de barro cocido de varias figuras para cubrir los techos, suelos, etc. 2. Placa de porcelana, mármol u otro material que se usa para adornar las paredes, etc. *Ridge-tile*, Teja acanalada. *Dutch tiles*, Azulejos. *Tile-maker*, Tejero. *Tile-kiln*, Tejar, el lugar donde se fabrican las tejas.

Tile, *va.* 1. Tejar, cubrir de tejas. 2. Desaguar por medio de tejas. 3. Asegurar contra una intrusión.

Tiling [tail'-ing], *s.* 1. El acto o procedimiento de cubrir con tejas. 2. Tejas en general; tejado, el techo cubierto de telas.

Till [til], *s.* Cajón o gaveta para guardar dinero.—*prep.* Hasta, hasta donde.—*conj.* Hasta que.

Till, *va.* Cultivar, labrar, dar a la tierra las labores necesarias.

Tillable [til'-a-bl], *a.* Labrantío, capaz de cultivo. *Tillable land*, Tierra cultivable, labrantía o de pan llevar.

Tillage [til'-ĝj], *s.* Labranza, el trabajo de cultivar la tierra, cultivo de la tierra, la agricultura.

Tiller [til'-er], *s.* 1. Agricultor, labrador. 2. Mango, palanca; en especial, barra o caña del timón; de aquí, medio de guiar. 3. Retoño, renuevo, resalvo de un árbol. *Tiller-rope*, (Mar.) Guardín de la caña. *Tiller-hole*, (Mar.) Limera. *Tiller-transom*, (Mar.) Descanso de la caña del timón. *To ship the tiller*, (Mar.) Montar la caña del timón.

Tiller, *vn.* Echar retoños de la raíz.

Tilling [til'-ing], *s.* Labranza.

Tilt [tilt], *s.* 1. Inclinación desde la vertical o la horizontal; declive. 2. Justa o torneo, un ejercicio y fiesta militar de los antiguos caballeros. 3. Lanzada. 4. Tienda, cubierta, toldo, tendal. *Tilt-boat*, (Mar.) Carroza. *Tilt-hammer*, Martinete de báscula.

Tilt, *va.* 1. Empinar, inclinar, levantar en alto alguna cosa de modo que se salga lo que hay en ella. 2. Martillar, forjar con el martinete. 3. Apuntar la lanza. 4. Entoldar, cubrir con toldos.—*vn.* 1. Inclinarse hacia un lado, ladearse. 2. Justar, combatir en una justa.

Tilth [tilth], *s.* 1. Labranza, cultivo. 2. Profundidad a que alcanza el cultivo de un terreno.

Timbal, Tymbal [tim'-bal], *s.* Timbal, atabal.

Timber [tim'-ber], *s.* 1. Madera de construcción; maderamen, maderaje. 2. Árboles de monte; tronco de árbol; el mismo monte, los árboles no cortados. 3. Viga maestra, el madero principal de una fábrica. 4. Cuaderna, miembro; pieza de construcción que se levanta de dos lados de la quilla. *Filling-timbers*, (Mar.) Cuadernas de henchimiento. *Floor-timbers*, Varengas. *Stern-timbers*, Gambotas de popa. *Head-timbers*, Gambotas de proa. *Cant-timbers*, Cuadernas que no están perpendicularmente sobre la quilla. *Ship-timber*, Madera para construcciones navales. *Top-timbers*, Reveses. *Round timber*, Madera en troncos, tronco entero. *Squared timber*, Madera escuadrada. *Old timber*, Madera de demolición. *Standing timber,* Árboles en pie. *Timber-merchant,* Maderero, el que trata en madera. *Timber-sow,* Carcoma, gusano que roe la madera. *Timber-work,* Maderaje, maderamen, el conjunto de maderas para edificios, etc. *Timber-yard,* Astillero.

Timber, *va.* Enmaderar, proveer de madera de construcción.

Timbered [tim'-bẹrd], *adj. part.* 1. Cubierto de árboles crecientes o de monte alto. 2. Edificado, construido, provisto de madera.

Timberland [tim'-bẹr-land], *s.* Terrenos madereros.

Timber line [tim'-bẹr lain], *s.* Límite de la vegetación arbórea.

Timber wolf [tim'-bẹr wulf], *s.* Lobo gris.

Timbre [tim'-bẹr], *s.* 1. Timbre, calidad de una voz, de un instrumento músico. 2. (Her.) Timbre, la insignia que se coloca sobre el escudo de armas para distinguir los grados de nobleza.

Time [taim], *s.* 1. Tiempo, la medida de la duración de las cosas. 2. Tiempo, un término limitado; plazo. 3. Tiempo, sazón, oportunidad, la ocasión y coyuntura de hacer algo. 4. Tiempo, tomado por un largo espacio de él; edad, época; como *To take time,* Tomarse tiempo o dejar la ejecución de una cosa por un largo espacio de tiempo. 5. (Mús.) Compás, medida de los sonidos con respecto a su duración: grado del movimiento. *V.* TEMPO. 6. Vez (indicando la repetición). *At a time,* A la vez. *At times,* A veces. *Every time,* Cada vez, todas las veces. *Many times,* Muchas veces, a menudo. *Many and many a time,* Muchísimas veces. 7. Intervalo, el espacio de un tiempo a otro; hora, división del día indicada por el reloj. *What time is it?* ¿Qué hora es? *Tell me the time,* Dígame Vd. la hora. 8. El término de la preñez. 9. La hora del parto o de la muerte. 10. Relación temporal o inflexión que toma el verbo. *In time,* A tiempo, con el tiempo. *In our times,* En nuestros días. *From time to time,* De cuando en cuando. *The time to come,* Lo futuro, lo venidero. *Time out of mind,* Tiempo inmemorial. *In old times, in times of yore,* Antiguamente, en otros tiempos, en tiempos antiguos. *From this time forth,* Desde ahora, desde hoy en adelante, en lo venidero. *At any time,* Cuando Vd. guste o cuando Vd. quiera. *At no time,* Jamás. *At this time,* Al presente, ahora. *At that time,* En aquella ocasión, en aquel tiempo, entonces. *This time a twelvemonth,* De aquí a un año. *At all times,* En todos los tiempos, en todas las edades. *In a day's time,* En el espacio de un día. *In an hour's time,* En una hora. *In the day-time,* De día o por el día. *In the night-time,* De noche o por la noche. *To pass the time away,* Pasar el tiempo; recrearse, divertirse, darse una pavonada. *By that time,* Para entonces o entonces. *A woman near her time,* Una mujer en días de parir. *To take time by the forelock,* (prov.) Tomar o asir la ocasión por los cabellos. *From time to time,* De vez en cuando, de cuando en cuando. *A long time since,* Hace largo tiempo. *In no time,* En un instante, al momento, *Time enough,* Hay tiempo; es bastante pronto. *Behind time,* Atrasado, retardado. *There is no time to spare,* No hay tiempo que perder. *To lose time,* Perder el tiempo; retardar (el reloj). *At some time or other,* Un día u otro. *To keep time,* Guardar compás. *To beat time,* Marcar el compás. *To be on time,* (E. U.) Ser puntual. *Out of time,* Fuera de compás. *For the time being,* Por ahora, por o para entonces; de ahora, actual, en este tiempo. *Time-pleaser, time-server,* El que contemporiza o se acomoda con demasiada facilidad al gusto ajeno. *Time-serving,* Complaciente, contemplativo, lisonjero, que adora el sol que nace. *Time-table,* Cartel, cédula o lista de las horas en que suceden o se hacen ciertas cosas; p. ej. las horas de llegada y salida de trenes, barcos, etc. *Time-worn,* Usado, gastado por el tiempo.

Time, *va.* 1. Adaptar al tiempo, hacer alguna cosa a tiempo oportuno. 2. Concertar, arreglar el tiempo. 3. (Mús.) Llevar el compás.

Time card [taim' cārd], *s.* Tarjeta en que se marca la hora de entrada y salida de empleados o trabajadores.

Time-clock [taim'-clec], *s.* Reloj para marcar la hora de entrada y salida de empleados o trabajadores.

Time exposure [taim ex-pō'-zhur], *s.* Exposición de tiempo (en fotografía).

Timekeeper [taim'-kīp-ẹr], *s.* 1. Reloj; reloj astronómico. 2. Marcador de tiempo.

Timeless [taim'-les], *a.* 1. Independiente o superior a todas las limitaciones del tiempo; que no tiene fin. 2. Intempestivo, que se hace fuera de tiempo o de ocasión oportuna.

Time limit [taim' lim'-it], *s.* Plazo.

Timeliness [taim'-li-nes], *s.* Tiempo conveniente, oportunidad; calidad de oportuno.

Timely [taim'-li], *adv.* Temprano, con tiempo; bien pronto, a tiempo oportuno, a propósito.—*a.* Oportuno, en tiempo.

Timepiece [taim'-pīs], *s.* Cualquier reloj o instrumento que marca las horas.

Timer [taim'-ẹr], *s.* 1. Marcador de tiempo (persona o instrumento). 2. El que sirve o trabaja por determinado lapso.

Timid [tim'-id], *a.* Tímido, temeroso, que evita la publicidad; pusilánime, medroso.

Timidity [ti-mid'-i-ti], **Timidness** [tim'id-nes], *s.* Timidez, temor, miedo, pusilanimidad.

Timidly [tim'-id-li], *a.* Tímidamente, con temor, con miedo, con pusilanimidad.

Timorous [tim'-o-rus], *a.* Temeroso, medroso; asombradizo, espantadizo.

Tin [tin], *s.* 1. Estaño, metal maleable y blanco. 2. Hoja de lata, hojalata, lámina cubierta de estaño. 3. Objeto de hojalatería. 4. (Ger.) Dinero, moneda. *Tin-foil,* Hoja de estaño, alinde. *Tin-man,* Hojalatero, estañero. *Tin-plate,* Hoja de lata. *Tin-pot,* Jarro o vasija de hoja de lata. *Tintype,* (E. U.) Fotografía hecha sobre una plancha de hojalata. *V.* FERROTYPE. *Tinware,* Hojalatería, efectos de hojalata.

Tin, *va.* 1. Estañar, cubrir o bañar con estaño. 2. Cubrir, v. g. un tejado, con hoja de lata. 3. Meter en una caja o bote de hojalata. *To tin over,* Estañar completamente una cosa o cubrirla toda con estaño.

Tin can [tin can], *s.* Lata, bote.

Tincture [tiṇc'-chur], *s.* 1. Tintura, tinte, el color que queda en la cosa teñida. 2. Tintura, en farmacia es la solución de una substancia simple o compuesta en alcohol o espíritu de vino. 3. Tintura, el conocimiento superficial de alguna ciencia o arte; gusto, gustillo.

Tincture, *va.* 1. Teñir, colorar, tinturar. 2. Dar un sabor o un gusto particular a las cosas. 3. Tinturar, instruir o informar a grandes rasgos de alguna cosa.

Tinder [tin'-dẹr], *s.* Yesca, toda materia muy seca y dispuesta de suerte que cualquier chispa de fuego prenda en ella; mecha.

Tinderbox [tin'-dẹr-box], *s.* Yesquero.

Tine [tain], *s.* 1. Púa de rastrillo; diente de tenedor. 2. Angustia, aflicción de ánimo.

Tinea [tin'-ẹ-a], *s.* 1. Tínea, género típico de los tinéidos; polilla. 2. Tiña. *V.* RINGWORM.

Ting [ting], *va.* y *vn.* Dar o producir un solo sonido metálico y agudo.—*s.* Un sonido metálico solo y agudo, como el de una campana; retintín. (Imitativo.)

Tinge [tinj], *va.* 1. Colorar, teñir, dar un tinte ligero; colorear. 2. Dar ligero gusto a una cosa; modificar mezclando con algo.—*s.* 1. Tinte, color ligero, matiz. 2. Gusto, gustillo, cualidad comunicada por una substancia extraña.

Tingle [tiṇ'-gl], *vn.* 1. Picar, punzar, hormiguear, experimentar una picazón, como la que se siente en la piel cuando se expone al frío. 2. Producir picazón u hormigueo. *My ears tingle,* Me hormiguean las orejas.—*s.* 1. Picazón, hormigueo, comezón. 2. Retintín. *V.* JINGLE.

Tingling [tiṇ'-gling], *s.* Punzada de dolor, picazón, comezón.

Tinker [tiṇk'-ẹr], *va.* Remendar como lo hace un calderero; a veces, chafallar, remendar chapuceramente.—*vn.* 1. Trabajar como calderero o latonero. 2. Chafallar, remendar de un modo chapucero.—*s.* Latonero; calderero remendón; desabollador.

Tinkle [tiṇ'-kl], *va.* y *vn.* 1. Cencerrear, retiñir, hacer retintines; sonar o dejar oir ligeros sonidos metálicos repetidos. 2. Zumbar los oídos.

Tinkling [tiṇ-kling], *s.* Retintín, retín, sucesión de sonidos agudos, ligeros y sonoros.

Tinner [tin'-ẹr], *s.* 1. Minero de estaño. 2. Estañero, hojalatero.

Tinny [tin'-i], *a.* De estaño, perteneciente o parecido al estaño.

Tinsel [tin'-sel], *s.* 1. Oropel, laminitas de latón reluciente, lentejuelas; (fig.) falso brillo. 2. Brocadillo, restaño; tejido al que se pegan o cosen lentejuelas u oropel.—*a.* De oropel; que tiene brillo falso. —*va.* Adornar con oropel.

Tint [tint], *va.* Teñir, colorar, dar un color, matizar.—*s.* 1. Tinte, color con que se tiñe; matiz, grado de fuerza que se da a los colores. 2. Matiz, efecto de luz, sombra, etc., producido en el grabado cruzando las líneas, etc. *Neutral tint,* Matiz neutro.

Tinwork [tin'-wūrc], *s.* Fábrica o mina de estaño.

Tiny [tai'-ni], *a.* Muy pequeño, menudo.

Tip [tip], *s.* 1. Punta, extremidad, cabo. 2. Casquillo, regatón; virola que se pone al extremo de una cosa.

Tip, *s.* 1. Propina. 2. Aviso amistoso y útil, fundado en informes confidenciales. 3. Toque ligero, golpecito.

Tip, *va.* 1. Guarnecer o cubrir la extremidad o punta de una cosa con un metal cualquiera. 2. Golpear ligeramente o dar golpecitos suaves. 3. Ladear, inclinar, levantando un extremo o lado de. 4. (Fam.) Dar una propina. 5. (Ger.) Dar informes secretos respecto de algún suceso, particularmente cuando median apuestas.—*vn.* 1. Ladearse, inclinarse a un lado. 2. Hacer un regalo en dinero; dar propina. *To tip the wink*, Guiñar, dar guiñadas. *To tip at nine-pins*, Birlar, en el juego de bolos. *Tipped with silver*, Montado en plata.

Tippet [tip'-et], *s.* Palatina, adorno que usan las mujeres al cuello.

Tipple [tip'-l], *va.* y *vn.* 1. Beber con exceso, beborrotear, pero no hasta el extremo de embriagarse. 2. Achisparse, empinar el codo.

Tippler [tip'-lęr], *s.* Bebedor, el que bebe mucho o es aficionado a los licores. (Fam.) Tomista.

Tipsily [tip'-si-li], *adv.* Como borracho.

Tipstaff [tip'-stqf], *s.* 1. Alguacil de vara. 2. Vara de justicia.

Tipsy [tip'-si], *a.* 1. Borracho, embriagado, achispado. 2. Oscilante.

Tiptoe [tip'-tō], *s.* Punta del pie. *To walk on tiptoe* o *on one's tiptoes*, Andar de puntillas. *To be on tiptoe, to stand a-tiptoe*, Tenerse, ponerse de puntillas; estar aguardando, alerta.

Tip-top [tip'-tęp'], *a.* (Fam.) Lo mejor en su clase.—*s.* Cumbre, cima, el más alto punto.

Tirade [ti-rēd'], *s.* Tirada crítica: invectiva.

Tire [tair], *s.* Llanta, neumático. *Tire blowout*, Reventón de llanta o neumático. *Tire cover*, Cubrellantas. *Tire gauge*, Medidor de presión de las llantas o neumáticos.

Tire, *va.* Cansar, fatigar; aburrir, fastidiar, enfadar.—*vn.* 1. Cansarse, padecer cansancio o fatiga; aburrirse, fastidiarse. 2. Hacer presa en. *To tire out*, Cansar mucho, reventar de cansancio o fatiga.

Tired [taird], *a.* Cansado, fatigado, fastidiado.

Tiredness [taird'-nes], *s.* Cansancio, lasitud, demasiada fatiga.

Tireless [tair'-les], *a.* 1. Infatigable, incansable. 2. Falto de llanta (rueda).

Tiresome [tair'-sum], *a.* Tedioso, fastidioso, molesto, pesado, enfadoso.

Tiresomeness [tair'-sum-nes], *s.* Tedio, fastidio, aburrimiento, displicencia.

T-iron [tī-ai'-urn], *s.* Hierro en T.

Tirra-lirra [tir'-a-lir''-a], *s.* Nota melodiosa, como la de un pájaro o de una corneta.

'Tis [tiz]. Abreviatura poética de IT IS. *'Tis ill done*, Es o está mal hecho.

Tisane [ti-zqn'], *s.* Tisana, bebida medicinal. *V.* PTISAN.

Tisic [tiz'-ic], *s.* Tisis, tísica. *V.* PHTHISIC.

Tissue [tish'-ū], *s.* 1. (Biol.) Tejido, cada una de las agregaciones de elementos anatómicos, entrelazados o simplemente adheridos entre sí, que forman las partes sólidas de los cuerpos orgánicos. 2. Tejido ligero parecido a la gasa; originalmente, tisú, tela de oro o plata. 3. Serie conexa, encadenamiento; ficción. 4. Papel de seda. *Woody tissue*, Tejido leñoso. *The whole story is a tissue of fabrications*, Todo ello no es más que un tejido de mentiras. *Tissue-paper*, Papel de seda.

Tissue, *va.* Entretejer, mezclar en el tejido diferentes materias.

Tit [tit], *s.* 1. Paro. *V.* TOMTIT y TITLARK. 2. Haca, caballo pequeño. 3. Golpecito; en la locución *Tit for tat*, Taz a taz o taz por taz; tal para cual; esto por eso. *To give tit for tat*, No quedar a deber nada; estar a mano. (Vulg.) Estar pata, o patas.

Titanic [tai-tan'-ic], *a.* 1. Titánico, titanio, perteneciente o parecido a los Titanes; de aquí, vasto, gigantesco. 2. Titánico, perteneciente al titanio, particularmente en su más alto grado de combinación.

Titanium [ti-tē'-ni-um], *s.* (Min.) Titanio, metal gris.

Titbit [tit'-bit], *s.* Bocado regalado, trozo escogido.

Tithable [taidh'-a-bl], *a.* Diezmable, sujeto a pagar diezmo.

Tithe [taidh], *s.* 1. Diezmo. 2. La décima parte de una cosa; de aquí, una porción pequeña. *Collector of tithes*, Diezmero. *Tithe-free*, Libre o exento de diezmo.

Tithe, *vn.* Diezmar, pagar el diezmo; percibir y cobrar el diezmo.—*va.* Imponer tributo.

Tither [taidh'-ęr], *s.* Dezmero o diezmero, el que recauda el diezmo.

Tithing [taidh'-ing], *s.* 1. Diezmo, acción de levantar el diezmo. 2. Decena, el agregado de diez familias que se unían antiguamente para formar una subdivisión política en algunas provincias de Inglaterra.

Tithingman [taidh'-ing-man], *s.* El jefe de la subdivisión política llamada *tithing* en Inglaterra.

Tithymal [tith'-i-mal], *s.* (Bot.) Titímalo, lechetrezna.

Titillate [tit'-i-lēt], *va.* Titilar, causar titilación o una especie de cosquilleo agradable.

Titillation [tit-i-lē'-shun], *s.* Titilación, picazón suave que produce gusto o placer.

Titlark [tit'-lārc], *s.* Pipí de matorral, farlusa, pajarito parecido a la alondra. (Anthus pratensis.) *V.* PIPIT.

Title [tai'-tl], *s.* 1. Título, de un libro, de un capítulo, etc.; inscripción, rótulo o rotulata. 2. Título, nombre de dignidad o de una calidad honorífica. 3. Título, renombre o distintivo con que se conoce a alguna persona. 4. Título, la demostración auténtica del derecho que se tiene a alguna cosa; acta, título, documento que establece el derecho a una propiedad. 5. La portada o frontispicio de un libro.

Title, *va.* 1. Titular; intitular; conferir un título; dar el nombre de. 2. Titular, estampar el nombre en la cubierta o el lomo de un libro.

Title bout [tait'-l baut], *s.* En el boxeo, pelea de campeonato.

Titleless [tai'-tl-les], *a.* Lo que no tiene título ni nombre.

Title-page [tai'-tl-pēj], *s.* La portada o frontispicio de un libro; (Amer.) carátula.

Titling [tit'-ling], *s.* Farlusa o gorrión silvestre. *V.* TITLARK.

Titmouse [tit'-maus], *s.* (Orn.) Paro, pájaro pequeño que tiene el pico corto y cubierto de plumas.

Titrate [tit'-rēt], *va.* (Quím.) Graduar, determinar la fuerza de una disolución por medio de disoluciones típicas o análisis volumétrico.

Titration [ti-trē'-shun], *s.* El procedimiento del análisis volumétrico.

Titter [tit'-ęr], *vn.* Sonreirse, reir entre dientes, reir con disimulo.

Titter, Tittering [tit'-ęr-ing], *s.* Risa entre dientes, sonrisa.

Titterer [tit'-ęr-ęr], *s.* El o la que ríe entre dientes o sofocando la risa.

Tittle [tit'-l], *s.* 1. Tilde, vírgula, virgulilla. 2. Tilde, ápice, cosa mínima.

Tittle-tattle [tit'-l-tat-l], *s.* Charla, plática sin substancia.

Tittle-tattle, *vn.* Charlar; susurrar.

Titular [tit'-yu-lar], *a.* 1. Titular, nominal, que tiene solamente el nombre o título. 2. Titular, perteneciente a un título, revestido de un título.—*s.* Titular, el que tiene el título de un cargo.

Titularly [tit'-yu-lar-li], *adv.* Con sólo el título.

T-joint [tī'-joint], *s.* (F. C.) Unión en T.

Tmesis [tmī'-sis], *s.* División de las partes de una palabra compuesta por una palabra intercalada; v. gr. *to us ward*, para con nosotros; *from what* source *soever*, de cualquier origen que sea. (Gr. τμῆσις.)

TNT [tī-en-tī'], *s.* (Quím.) Abreviatura de *trinitrotoluene*, TNT, potente explosivo.

To [tū], *adv.* y *prep.* Hasta, hacia; a, en dirección hacia; también es el signo del infinitivo inglés. 1. Es *a* o *al*, cuando es signo del objeto indirecto o dativo, si éste no es un pronombre personal, y en general siempre que precede al nombre después de los verbos que significan movimiento, dirección, unión, pertenencia, preferencia o atención; como, *Give it to him*, Dáselo a él. *I'll go to London*, Iré a Londres. *I spoke to you*, Hablé a Vd. *I am going to speak to him*, Voy a hablarle. *It belongs to Peter*, Pertenece a Pedro. *I prefer this book to mine*, Prefiero este libro al mío. *I have no enmity to him*, No le tengo mala voluntad. *That is nothing to me*, Nada me importa eso. 2. Cuando denota la intención u objeto con que se ejecuta alguna cosa, corresponde a *para*, *por* o *a* en castellano. *She went there only to see me*, Fué allá sólo por verme, a verme, para verme o con sólo el objeto o la intención de verme. *I come to speak to him*, Vengo a hablarle, para hablarle o con el objeto de hablarle. 3. Después de un participio pasivo o de un adjetivo denotando su objeto, equivale a *para*. *Born to die*, Nacido para morir. *Ready to go out*, Dispuesto para salir. *That is lost to me*, Eso se perdió para mí. 4. Es también *que* en castellano, particularmente cuando expresa una acción futura o venidera. *We are still to see*, Tenemos todavía que ver. *To have to, to be obliged to,* Tener que, deber. *Why are we to go?* ¿Por qué tenemos que ir nosotros? 5. Hasta; tan lejos como. *To this day,* Hasta hoy o hasta el día de hoy. *To the number of,* Hasta el número de. *Even to,* Hasta. *I see to the bottom,* Veo hasta el fondo. 6. Hacia, a. *To the east was an open country,* Hacia el este se extendía un terreno llano. 7. En, cuando indica una relación de movimiento hacia algo. *From door to door,* De puerta en puerta. 8. Menos (marcando la hora). *It is ten minutes to nine,* Son las nueve menos diez minutos. 9. De o del. *He is a friend to the poor,* Es amigo de los pobres. *Philip the Second was son to Charles the Fifth,* o *was successor to Charles the Fifth,* Felipe Segundo fué hijo de Carlos Quinto o fué sucesor de Carlos Quinto. *Surgeon to the king,* Cirujano del rey. *The road to Madrid,* El camino de Madrid. *Woe to the man,* ¡ Ay del hombre, o infeliz del hombre! 10. En la mayor parte de los casos *to* no se traduce, cuando es signo de infinitivo. *He loves to travel,* Le gusta viajar. En otros casos se traduce por *a, de, para, a fin de,* según el sentido. *She has the desire to learn,* Ella tiene deseo de aprender. *Bound to succeed,* Resuelto a triunfar. *To arrive at the truth,* A fin de averiguar la verdad. *To* como signo del infinitivo se omite: (1) después de los verbos auxiliares *do, can, may, must, shall, will;* (2) después de *dare,* osar, atreverse, *help,* ayudar, *need,* necesitar, *please,* servirse, *go,* ir; (3) después del objeto de los verbos *bid,* mandar, *feel,* sentir, *have,* haber, *hear,* oir, *let,* dejar, *make,* hacer, y a veces, *find,* hallar y *know,* saber; (4) después de ciertas locuciones. *According to,* Según. *As to,* En cuanto a, por lo que toca á. *So as to,* De manera que, a fin de. *To and fro,* De acá para acullá; de aquí para allí. *To-and-fro motion,* Vaivén. *Twenty to one,* Veinte á uno. *Sharp to the taste,* Punzante al paladar. *Not to my knowledge,* No que yo sepa. *To my knowledge,* Me consta que. *To drink to excess,* Beber con exceso. *As to that,* Por lo que toca a eso, en cuanto a eso, respecto a eso. *For the time to come,* En lo venidero. *To the end that,* Á fin que. *I am glad to see you,* Me alegro de ver a Vd. *To speak to the purpose,* Hablar al caso. *To go to and again,* Ir y volver. *To and again,* De un lado y otro. *Face to face,* Cara a cara.

Toad [tōd], *s.* 1. Sapo, escuerzo, anfibio terrestre sin cola. 2. Cualquier persona como objeto de desprecio. *Toad-eater,* Pegote, parásito, sicofante.

Toadfish [tōd'-fish], *s.* Sapo marino.

Toadflax [tōd'-flax], *s.* (Bot.) Linaria, lino bastardo; planta de las escrofulariáceas; se llama también *butter-and-eggs,* mantequilla y huevos.

Toadstone [tōd'-stōn], *s.* (Min.) Piedra del sapo, batraquita: nombre vulgar de una especie de piedra llena de agujeritos y muy friable.

Toadstool [tōd'-stūl], *s.* (Bot.) Hongo bejín, hongo bastardo, cualquier seta venenosa.

Toady [tōd'-i], *va.* y *vn.* Adular servilmente; hacer zalamerías, ser zalamero.—*a.* Adulador, zalamero.

Toast [tōst], *va.* 1. Tostar, hacer asar, secar ó calentar a la lumbre. 2. (Fam.) Calentar o calentarse al fuego. 3. Brindar, echar un brindis a, beber a la salud de alguno.

Toast, *s.* 1. Tostada, rebanada de pan tostado. 2. Brindis, la acción de brindar a la salud de una persona.

Toaster [tōst'-ẹr], *s.* 1. El que brinda. 2. El o lo que tuesta, tostador; parrillas.

Tobacco [to-bac'-o], *s.* 1. Tabaco, las hojas curadas y preparadas del tabaco que se fuman, mastican o se toman por la nariz reducidas a polvo. 2. Tabaco, planta solanácea, originaria de la América tropical. Nicotiana tabacum. *Tobacco-heart,* Estado morboso del corazón debido al uso excesivo del tabaco. *Tobacco-pipe,* Pipa de tabaco. *Tobacco-pipe clay,* Tierra de pipa. *Tobacco-box,* Tabaquera. *Tobacco-pouch,* Bolsa para tabaco. *Tobacco-worm,* Oruga muy perjudicial al tabaco en los E. U. Protoparce carolina.

Tobacconist [to-bac'-o-nist], *s.* 1. Fabricante de tabaco. 2. Tabaquero, vendedor de tabaco, que en España se llama comúnmente estanquero.

Tobacco-stopper [to-bac'-o-step-ẹr], *s.* Tapador de pipa de tabaco.

Toboggan [to-beg'-an], *s.* Tobogán. —*vn.* Deslizarse en un tobogán. (fig.) Disminuir repentinamente en valor.

Tocsin [tec'-sin], *s.* Campana y campanada de alarma; toque, señal dada con una campana.

Tod [ted], *s.* (Ingl.) Zorro.

To-day [tū-dē'], *s.* El día presente; también, la época o siglo presente. —*adv.* Hoy.

Toddle [ted'-l], *vn.* Bambolear, marchar con paso incierto, como el de un niño.

Toddler [ted'-lẹr], *s.* Niño chiquito de dos a tres años de edad. *Toddler clothes,* Ropa de niño de esa edad.

To-do [tu-dū'], *s.* (Fam.) Confusión, trapisonda.

Toddy [ted'-i], *s.* 1. Ponche, bebida de licor espirituoso, agua caliente y azúcar; licor alcohólico en general. 2. Vino de palmera, jugo que exuda por las incisiones hechas en varias palmas.

Tody [tō'-di], *s.* Todi, pájaro verde de Jamaica, de la familia de los alciónidos.

Toe [tō], *s.* 1. Dedo del pie. 2. Uña, pezuña, parte delantera del casco del caballo y otros animales. 3. Extremo (de media, del calzado); el extremo inferior o pie de alguna cosa. *The great toe,* El dedo gordo del pie. *From top to toe,* De pies a cabeza.

Toe, *va.* 1. Tocar con los dedos del pie. 2. Asegurar con clavos un puntal. *Three-toed,* Con tres dedos.

Toenails [tō'-nēls], *s. pl.* Uñas de los dedos del pie.

Toga [tō'-ga], *s.* Toga, vestidura exterior de un ciudadano romano.

Togaed [tō'-gad], *a.* Togado, vestido de toga.

Together [tu-gedh'-ẹr], *adv.* 1. Juntamente, en compañía de otro. *Let us go together,* Vamos juntos. 2. A un tiempo o al mismo tiempo. 3. De seguida, sin interrupción. *Together with,* A una con, juntos. *Six weeks together,* Seis semanas seguidas. *Together,* (Mar.) A una.

Toggle [teg'-l], *s.* 1. Cazonete de aparejo. 2. Palanca acodillada. *Toggle-joint,* Junta de codillo.

Toggle switch [teg'-l swich], *s.* Interruptor de palanca acodillada, interruptor de presión.

Toil [teil], *vn.* 1. Trabajar, aplicarse con desvelo a la ejecución de alguna cosa; fatigarse, molestarse, trabajar mucho. 2. Adelantarse a paso lento. *To toil through,* Abrirse penosamente camino de parte a parte. *To toil up,* Subir con pena.

Toil, *s.* 1. Faena, trabajo, pena, fatiga, afán. 2. Red para pescar, cazar o para cualquiera otra cosa; generalmente en sentido figurado. *Toil of a spider,* Telaraña o red de araña.

Toilet [tei'-let], *s.* 1. Acto de vestirse. 2. Modo de vestir de una persona. 3. Tocador. 4. Retrete, excusado, lavatorio. *Toilet articles,* Artículos de tocador. *Toilet paper,* Papel de excusado. *Toilet water,* Agua de tocador.

Toilful [teil'-ful], *a.* Trabajoso, repleto de trabajos.

Toilsome [teil'-sum], *a.* Laborioso, trabajoso; penoso, fatigoso.

Toilsomely [teil'-sum-li], *adv.* Laboriosamente; fatigosamente.

Toilsomeness [teil'-sum-nes], *s.* Trabajo, afán; fatiga, penalidad que causa el trabajo prolijo o muy continuado.

Tokay [to-kē'], *s.* Uva de Hungría que se cultiva en California, y el vino que se hace de ella.

Token [tō'-cn], *s.* 1. Señal, muestra, marca, seña, nota. 2. Prenda, recuerdo, prueba de amistad. 3. Medalla, tanto, ficha de metal semejante a una moneda, que a veces ponen en circulación los comerciantes, dándoles un valor monetario determinado. *As a token of,* En señal de.

Token, *va.* Mostrar, denotar.

Tokology, Tocology [to-cel'-o-ji], *s.* Tocología, obstetricia. (< Gr.)

Told [tōld], *pret.* y *pp.* del verbo *To* TELL.

Toledan [to-lī'-dan], *a.* Toledano, de Toledo.

Tolerable [tel'-ẹr-a-bl], *a.* 1. Tolerable, sufrible; pasadero, llevadero. 2. Pasadero, medianamente bueno, mediocre.

Tolerableness [tel'-ẹr-a-bl-nes], *s.* La calidad de lo que es tolerable, pasadero o medianamente bueno.

Tolerably [tel'-ẹr-a-bli], *adv.* Tolerablemente, medianamente, así así.

Tolerance [tel'-ẹr-ans], *s.* 1. Tolerancia, indulgencia. 2. Paciencia.

Tolerant [tel'-ẹr-ant], *a.* Tolerante.

Tolerate [tel'-ẹr-ēt], *va.* Tolerar, permitir, disimular, llevar con paciencia.

Toleration [tel-ẹr-ē'-shun], *s.* Tolerancia; tolerancia civil.

Toll [tōl], *s.* 1. Peaje, portazgo o pontazgo, el derecho o impuesto pagado por los que viajan; derecho de molienda. *To pay toll,* Estar sujeto a peaje, pagar portazgo. *To take toll,* Cobrar una tasa, un peaje. *Toll-bridge,* Puente de peaje. *Toll-gate,* Barrera de peaje. *Toll-house,* Oficina de portazgos, domicilio del portazguero junto a la barrera. *Toll-man,* Peajero, portazguero. 2. El sonido de las campanas. *Miller's toll,* Maquila de molinero.

Toll, *va.* y *vn.* 1. Pagar o cobrar el derecho de portazgo. 2. Repicar; tañer, o tocar una campana, lentamente, con toques aislados repetidos a intervalos iguales. 3. Tocar á muerto (una campana). 4. Llamar o convocar con campana. *To toll the hour*, Dar la hora.

Tollbooth, *va.* Encarcelar, poner preso.

Toll call [tōl cōl], *s.* Llamada telefónica de larga distancia.

Toller [tōl'-ẹr], *s.* El que toca las campanas.

Toll-free [tōl'-frī], *a.* Exento de peaje.

Toll-gatherer [tōl'-gadh-ẹr-ẹr], *s.* Portazguero, el que cobra el derecho de portazgo.

Tomahawk [tem'-a-hēc], *va.* Golpear o matar con el hacha india llamada *tomahawk*.—*s.* Hacha de armas de los indios americanos.

Tomato [to-mā'-to], *s.* (Bot.) Tomate, planta de la familia de las solanáceas, y su fruto. Lycopersicum esculentum.

Tomb [tūm], *s.* Tumba, sepulcro.

Tombac [tem'-bac], *s.* Tumbaga, aleación de cobre y zinc.

Tomboy [tem'-bei], *s.* Marimacho, doncella pizpireta y respingona.

Tombstone [tūm'-stōn], *s.* Lápida o piedra sepulcral.

Tomcat [tem'-cat], *s.* Gato no castrado.

Tomcod [tem'-ced], *s.* Pez comestible de los gádidos (Microgadus), común en las costas norteamericanas. (< un nombre indígena.)

Tome [tōm], *s.* Tomo, libro grueso.

-tome, desinencia que significa corte o cortador.

Tomentose, Tomentous [tō'-men-tōs, to-men'-tus], *a.* (Bot.) Tomentoso, borroso, que tiene borra o tiene pelos muy tupidos.

Tomfool [tem'-fūl], *s.* Tonto, necio; también, persona divertida, chancera.

Tomfoolery [tem-fūl'-ẹr-i], *s.* Proceder o conducta necia.

To-morrow [tu-mer'-ō], *s.* El día de mañana, el día inmediato, que sigue al presente.—*adv.* Mañana.

Tomtit [tem'-tit], *s.* (Orn.) Paro. *V.* TIT.

Tampion [tem'-pi-ọn], *s.* (Art.) Tapaboca de un cañón.

Tomtom [tem'-tem], *s.* 1. Tamtam, especie de tambor indio. 2. Gongo. *V.* GONG.

Ton [tun], *s.* 1. Tonelada, medida de capacidad y el peso de dos mil libras o veinte quintales; este peso se llama *short ton*, en contraposición al *long ton* de 2,240 libras. 2. (Des.) Medida de dos toneles. *V.* TUN.

Tonal [tō'-nal], *a.* (Mús.) Tonal, relativo á los tonos o a la tonalidad.

Tonality [to-nal'-i-ti], *s.* 1. Tonalidad, sistema de sonidos que sirve de fundamento a una composición musical. 2. Conjunto de tonos que tiene un cuadro.

Tone [tōn], *s.* 1. Tono de la voz o del habla, y a veces también se toma por la misma voz o habla. 2. Tono o timbre en la música, intervalo de un segundo mayor. 3. Tonillo, modo particular de hablar o de leer. 4. Tono en medicina es el estado de tensión, elasticidad o firmeza propio y peculiar de cada órgano para ejercer su función respectiva. 5. Estilo o tendencia característica; tono. 6. Tono, efecto general de un cuadro, su armonía con relación el colorido y claroscuro; matiz de color.

Tone, *va.* 1. Dar el tono a; modificar el tono; entonar (cuadros, fotografías). 2. Templar. *V.* TUNE. 3. *V.* INTONE.—*vn.* 1. Corresponder en tono o matiz. 2. Tomarse un matiz dado. *To tone down*, (1) (Pint.) Suavizar el tono, pintar con colores menos vivos. (2) Moderar la calidad y volumen del sonido. (3) Modificar en cuanto á la expresión o al efecto. *To tone up*, (1) Aumentar la calidad o fuerza. (2) Elevar el tono músico. (3) Dar o adquirir mayor fuerza o vigor corporal.

Toneless [tōn'-les], *a.* Que está fuera de tono, sin estilo característico.

Tongs [tengz], *s. pl.* Tenazas, instrumento para prender, asir o agarrar alguna cosa; alicates. *Coal-tongs*, Tenazas de chimenea, para coger las brasas. *Oyster-tongs*, Gafas para pescar ostras. *Sugar-tongs*, Tenacillas para azúcar. *Hammer and tongs*, (Fam.) Con violencia, con todas sus fuerzas.

Tongue [tung], *s.* 1. Lengua, el órgano del gusto y de la palabra. 2. Lengua, idioma o modo de hablar de una nación. 3. Lengua, habla, lenguaje, lo que se habla. 4. Lengüeta, lo que tiene la forma de una pequeña lengua; espiga, saliente pequeño de una tabla; clavo de hebilla; lengua de tierra; badajo de campana. *Foul tongue*, Lengua maldiciente; (Med.) lengua cargada. *To hold the tongue*, Callar. *Tongue of a buckle*, Clavo de hebilla. *Tongue-tie*, *va.* Atar la lengua a uno, hacer callar.—*s.* Frenillo, defecto físico que impide a los niños mamar y hablar con facilidad. *Tongue-tied*, Con frenillo; con la lengua atada, mudo.

Tongue, *va.* 1. Modificar el sonido de (la flauta, corneta, etc.) por medio de la lengua. 2. Poner lengüetas para machihembrar. —*vn.* Usar de la lengua hablando o tocando un instrumento de viento; picotear.

Tongued [tungd], *a.* El o lo que tiene lengua. *A fine-tongued fellow*, Un zalamero, uno que usa palabras muy melosas.

Tongueless [tung'-les], *a.* 1. Mudo, sin habla. 2. Deslenguado, sin lengua. 3. Confuso, turbado. 4. Aquello de que nadie habla.

Tonic [ten'-ic], *a.* 1. Tónico, nombre dado a todo medicamento que excita la acción vital. 2. Tónico, perteneciente al tono o a los tonos; en música, perteneciente a la nota tónica o dominante. 3. Tenso, perteneciente a la tensión, (Med.) rígido, tieso.—*s.* 1. Tónico, medicamento fortificante. 2. (Mús.) Tónica (dominante) primera nota de la escala del tono en que está escrita una pieza de música.

Tonicity [to-nis'-i-ti], *s.* Tonicidad, calidad de tónico; salud y vigor en general.

To-night [tu-nait'], *s.* La noche inmediata, la que sigue al día de hoy; esta noche.—*adv.* Esta noche.

Toning [tōn'-ing], *s.* Entonación, el acto o procedimiento de entonar; en fotografía, el arte o acto de tratar una impresión plateada con una disolución de cloruro de oro para cambiarle el color y aumentar su permanencia.

Tonite [te-nait'], *s.* Tonita (explosivo).

Tonnage [tun'-ẹj], *s.* 1. Tonelaje o porte de un buque manifestado en toneladas; arqueo: también, arqueo o cabida del conjunto de los buques de un país. 2. Alcabala o derecho de aduana que se cobra a tanto por tonelada.

Tonsil [ten'-sil], *s.* Tonsila, amígdala, cuerpo glanduloso situado a uno y otro lado de la faringe.

Tonsilitis, Tonsillitis [ten-sil-ai'-tis], *s.* Amigdalitis, inflamación de las tonsilas.

Tonsillectomy [ten-sil-ec'-te-mi], *s.* (Med.) Amigdalotomía, extirpación de las amígdalas.

Tonsorial [tẹn-sō'-ri-al], *a.* Barberil, perteneciente a los barberos.

Tonsure [ten'-shur], *s.* 1. Tonsura, la acción de cortar el pelo. 2. Tonsura, grado preparatorio para recibir las órdenes menores, que confiere el prelado con la ceremonia de cortar al aspirante un poco de cabello. 3. Lugar de la cabeza en que se cortan esos cabellos.

Tontine [ten'-tīn], *s.* Tontina, una especie de fondo vitalicio en el que a proporción que mueren los capitalistas, se aumenta el situado de los que sobreviven.

Too [tū], *adv.* 1. Demasiadamente, demasiado. 2. Además, igualmente, también, así mismo, aun.

Took [tuk], *pret.* del verbo TAKE.

Tool [tūl], *va.* y *vn.* Marcar o adornar con una herramienta.—*s.* 1. Herramienta, apero, utensilio, trebejo, el instrumento que sirve para cualquier trabajo manual. 2. Por extensión, máquina como torno que se emplea para hacer máquinas. 3. La persona que sirve de instrumento a otra para hacer alguna cosa mala. *Edge-tool*, Instrumento cortante.

Toot [tūt], *va.* y *vn.* Tocar el cuerno de caza, una bocina o un silbato.

Tooth [tūth], *s.* (*pl.* TEETH). 1. Diente, hueso pequeño engastado en la quijada que sirve para mascar los manjares. *Back-tooth*, Muela. *Eye-tooth*, Colmillo. *Tooth-brushes*, Cepillos para dientes. 2. Diente de sierra, de rueda o de otro cualquier instrumento. 3. (Bot. y Zool.) Diente, dentecillo. 4. Gusto, paladar. 5. *pl.* (Fig.) Fuerza que hace oposición. *In the teeth of the wind*, Contra la fuerza del viento. *To have a sweet tooth*, Tener el paladar delicado, gustar de dulces y golosinas. *To show one's teeth*, Enseñar los dientes, amenazar. *To cast in the teeth*, Echar en cara, mostrar los dientes. *Tooth and nail*, Con todo tesón, con todo empeño, con todas sus fuerzas. *In spite of one's teeth*, A despecho, a pesar de uno.

Tooth, *va.* 1. Dentar, proveer de dientes. 2. Encajar unos dientes en otros. 3. (Mar.) Endentar.

Toothache [tūth'-ēk], *s.* Dolor de muelas.

Toothbrush [tūth'-brush], *s.* Cepillo de dientes.

Toothed [tūtht], *a.* Dentado, que tiene dientes. *Toothed wheel*, Rueda dentada.

Toothless [tūth'-les], *a.* Desdentado, que no tiene o ha perdido los dientes.

Toothpaste [tūth'-pēst], *s.* Dentífrico, pasta de dientes, pasta dentífrica.

Toothpick [tūth'-pic], *s.* Mondadientes, palillo, escarbadientes. *Tooth-pick case*, Palillero.

Toothshell [tūth'-shel], *s.* Dental, una especie de concha parecida á un diente.
Toothsome [tūth'-sum], *a.* Sabroso, gustoso, grato al paladar o al gusto.
Toothwort [tūth'-wūrt], *s.* (Bot.) Dentaria.
Tooting [tūt'-ing], *s.* El acto de tocar la trompa o la corneta; sonido de trompa.
Top [tep], *s.* 1. Cima, cumbre, cabeza, remate, coronilla, coronamiento (de pared), copa, punta, cielo, el extremo, lo más alto y elevado de cualquier cosa; y según esta sea se le aplican dichas voces. 2. Cumbre o ápice del favor, de la fortuna, de la gloria, etc. 3. Superficie. 4. El último grado; el puesto más elevado; la persona superior en alguna calidad moral a todas las demás. 5. Corona de la cabeza. 6. Tupé, el pelo que se trae en la parte anterior de la cabeza. 7. La cabeza o punta de una planta. *Tops of boots,* Campanas, vueltas de o para las botas. 8. Trompo, peón, con que juegan los muchachos haciéndole dar vueltas. *Whipping-top,* Peonza. *From top to bottom,* De arriba abajo. *From top to toe,* De pies á cabeza, de alto á bajo. 9. (Mar.) Cofa, tablero colocado horizontalmente en el cuello de un palo para afirmar la obencadura. *Main-top,* Cofa mayor. *Fore-top,* Cofa de trinquete. *Mizzen-top,* Cofa de mesana, *Top-mast,* Mastelero. *Top-block,* Motón de virador. *Top-lantern,* Farol de la cofa. *Top-rails,* Batayolas de las cofas. *Top-rope,* Amante del virador. *Top-sails,* Gavias. *Top-sail-sheets,* Escotines. *Top-tackle,* Aparejo del virador. *Top-armor, or armings,* Empavesadas de las cofas.—*a.* Lo más elevado en lugar, grado o posición; primero, principal.
Top, *va.* y *vn.* 1. Elevarse o levantarse por encima de otra cosa. 2. Sobrepujar. 3. Aventajar, exceder. 4. Predominar, exceder mucho en altura una cosa respecto de otra. 5. Predominar, prevalecer o tener más fuerza. 6. Cubrir el mango, el cabo, la punta o la extremidad de cualquier cosa con otra diversa. 7. Esforzarse, esmerarse. 8. Descabezar o desmochar los árboles. 9. Encumbrarse, llegar a la cumbre de alguna cosa. 10. (Fam.) Ejecutar alguna cosa a la perfección. *To top a yard,* (Mar.) Amantillar o embicar las vergas. *Topping lifts,* (Mar.) Amantillos.
Toparch [tō'-pārc], *s.* Toparca, (*m.*) persona principal en un lugar o en un territorio reducido. (< Gr.)
Topaz [tō'-paz], *s.* 1. Topacio, piedra preciosa amarilla compuesta de sílice, alúmina y fluor. 2. Topacio, colibrí del género Topaza, de vivos colores y de tamaño relativamente grande.
Topcoat [tep'-cōt], *s.* Abrigo o sobretodo liviano, gabán.
Tope [tōp], *vn.* Soplar, beber mucho.
Tope, *s.* Altar, bóveda o torre budista, construída para guardar reliquias. (< Hind. tōp.)
Toper [tō'-pẹr], *s.* Borrachón, bebedor. (Fam.) Tomista.
Topful [tep'-ful], *a.* Lleno hasta arriba.
Top-gallant [tep'-gal-ant], *s.* 1. (Mar.) Juanete, la vela que va encima de la gavia. 2. Cumbre, cima; cual quiera cosa muy elevada.
Tophaceous [to-fē'-shus], *a.* Tobáceo, calcáreo, arenisco.
Top-heavy [tep'-hev-i], *a.* Más pesado por arriba que por abajo.
Tophet [tō'-fet], *s.* 1. Lugar cercano á Jerusalén predilecto de los idólatras; y más tarde un lugar donde se quemaban las barreduras e inmundicias de la ciudad. 2. De aquí, el infierno.
Tophus [to'-fus], *s.* (Min.) Tofo, sarro, materia calcárea que se forma en torno de las articulaciones de los gotosos; sarro de los dientes.
Topiary [tō'-pi-a-ri], *a.* Que pertenece al arte de entretejer ramos.
Topic [tep'-ic], *s.* 1. Asunto, objeto de un discurso; tema. 2. *pl.* (Ret.) Lugares comunes, tópicos. 3. El remedio tópico o que se aplica directamente a la parte enferma.
Topical [tep'-ic-al], *a.* 1. Tópico, perteneciente a algún principio o punto general o a algún lugar determinado. 2. Local, limitado; que se emplea exteriormente.
Top-knot [tep'-net], *s.* Fontanche, un moño alto sobre la frente adornado con cintas.
Topless [tep'-les], *a.* Que no tiene cima o ápice.
Topman [tep'-man], *s.* Aserrador de arriba.
Topmost [tep'-mōst], *a.* Lo más alto.
Topnotch [tep'-nech], *a.* (fam.) De primera, excelente, insuperable.
Topographer [to-peg'-ra-fẹr], *s.* Topógrafo, el que describe o delinea algún terreno.
Topographic, Topographical [to-po-graf'-ic, al], *a.* Topográfico.
Topographist [to-peg'-ra-fist], *s. V.* TOPOGRAPHER.
Topography [to-peg'-ra-fi], *s.* 1. Topografía, descripción detallada o delineación de un terreno o región. 2. Conjunto de caracteres físicos de una región.
Topping [tep'-ing], *a.* 1. Eminente, distinguido. 2. De grandes pretensiones, empenachado, arrogante.—*s.* Cubierta, mango, punta, la extremidad o cabo que se pone a una cosa.
Toppingly [tep'-ing-li], *adv.* Aventajadamente, con todo primor.
Topple [tep'-l], *va.* Hacer caer, volcar.—*vn.* Volcarse o caer hacia adelante una cosa.
Top-sail [tep'-sēl], *s.* (Mar.) Gavia, vela de gavia. *To have the top-sails set,* (Mar.) Tener las gavias largas. *To back the top-sails,* (Mar.) Poner las gavias en facha.
Top-secret [tep sī'-cret], *a.* Estrictamente confidencial, absolutamente secreto.
Topsy-turvy [tep'-si-tūr'-vi], *adv.* Al revés, con lo de abajo arriba.
Toque [tōc], **Toquet** [to-ket'], *s.* 1. Cofia, toca, especie de gorra de mujer. 2. Toca, la alta cofia cónica de los antiguos Dux de Venecia.
Tor [tōr], *s.* 1. (Local) Peñasco, altura. 2. (Poco us.) Torre, torrecilla.
Torch [tōrch], *s.* Antorcha, hacha.
Torch-bearer [tōrch'-bār-ẹr], **Torcher** [tōrch'-ẹr], *s.* Hachero, el que alumbra con hacha.
Torch-light [tōrch'-lait], *s.* Luz de antorcha, en contraposición a la luz del sol.
Torch-thistle [tōrch'-this-l], *s.* (Bot.) Céreo, cirio.
Tore [tōr], *pret.* del verbo *To* TEAR.—*s.* 1. (Arq.) Tondino; toro; bocel. 2. (Prov. Ingl.) La hierba inútil que queda en los campos en invierno.
Toreumatography [to-rū-ma-teg'-ra-fi], *s.* La descripción de las escultúras y bajo relieves antiguos.
Torment [tēr-mẹnt'], *va.* Atormentar, afligir, causar molestia o enfado.
Torment [tēr'-mẹnt], *s.* Tormento, pena, dolor violento, angustia, tortura.
Tormenter, Tormentor [tēr-ment'-ẹr], *s.* Atormentador.
Tormentil [tēr'-men-til], *s.* (Bot.) Tormentila.
Torn, *pp.* del verbo *To* TEAR.
Tornado [tēr-nē'-do], *s.* Tornado, huracán que ocurre por lo general en el borde o límite sudeste de un ciclón.
Torpedo [tēr-pī'-dō], *s.* (*pl.* TORPEDOES). 1. Torpedo, aparato o máquina de guerra que sirve para volar barcos. 2. Torpedo, tremielga, tembladera, pez eléctrico o raya eléctrica. 3. Juguete que consiste en un fulminato y granos de arena gruesa, envueltos en papel de seda. *Torpedo-boat,* Torpedero, buque veloz para lanzar torpedos.
Torpid [tēr'-pid], †**Torpent** [tēr'-pent], **Torpescent** [ter-pes'-ent], *a.* Adormecido, entorpecido, privado de movimiento.
Torpor [tēr'-pẹr], **Torpidness** [tēr'-pid-nes], †**Torpitude** [tēr'-pi-tiud], *s.* 1. Entorpecimiento, pasmo o adormecimiento de algún miembro. 2. Letargo, apatía, estupor o embotamiento de los sentidos o del ánimo.
Torque [tērc], *s.* 1. Collar. 2. (Mec.) Esfuerzo de torsión.
Torrefaction [ter-ẹ-fac-shun], *s.* (Farm.) Torrefacción, el acto de torrar o tostar.
Torrefy [ter'-ẹ-fai], *va.* Torrar, tostar, secar a fuego.
Torrent [ter'-ent], *s.* 1. Torrente, corriente o avenida impetuosa de aguas. 2. Torrente, abundancia o muchedumbre de cosas que vienen a un mismo tiempo.
Torrential [ter-ren'-shal], *a.* Torrencial, que todo lo arrastra tras de sí en su carrera como un torrente.
Torrid [ter'-id], *a.* Tórrido, muy ardiente; tostado. *The torrid zone,* Zona tórrida, la que está entre los trópicos.
Torridness [ter'-id-nes], **Torridity** [ter-id'-i-ti], *s.* El estado o la calidad de lo que es muy ardiente.
Torsel [tēr'-sel], *s.* Torzal.
Torsion [tēr'-shun], *s.* Torcedura, torsión, acción y efecto de torcer. *Torsion balance,* Balanza de torsión.
Torso [tēr'-so], *s.* Torso, tronco de una estatua sin cabeza y sin miembros.
Tort [tērt], *s.* (For.) Tuerto, agravio, sinrazón.
Tortile [tēr'-til], *a.* Torcido, doblado.
Tortoise [tēr'-tus o tēr'-tis], *s.* Tortuga. *Tortoise-shell* o *turtle-shell,* Carey, concha de tortuga. *Sea tortoise* o *turtle,* Tortuga de mar. *Land tortoise,* Tortuga de tierra, galápago.
Tortuosity [tēr-tiu-es'-i-ti], *s.* 1. Tortuosidad. 2. Estragamiento de costumbres.
Tortuous [tēr'-tiu-us], *a.* Tortuoso, torcido, sinuoso.
Tortuousness [tēr'-tiu-us-nes], *s.* Tortuosidad.
Torturable [tēr'-chur-a-bl], *a.* Que puede ser atormentado.

Torture [tōr'-chur], *s.* 1. Tortura, cuestión de tormento. 2. Tormento, dolor.
Torture, *va.* 1. Atormentar, someter al tormento, hacer sufrir la tortura. 2. Atormentar o afligir la memoria de una cosa. 3. Torcer en una forma anormal; alterar el sentido, p. ej. de un texto.
Tortured [tōr'-churd], *a.* Atormentado. *Tortured to death*, Muerto en el tormento.
Torturer [tōr'-chur-ęr], *s.* Atormentador.
Tory [tō'-ri], *s.* Tory, nombre dado á uno de los dos grandes partidos políticos de Inglaterra, al que pertenecen los que se oponen a las reformas en la actual constitución del estado; conservador, opuesto a reformador. En la historia de la Revolución de los Estados Unidos significa *Realista*, o que sostenía al gobierno inglés.
Toryism [tō'-ri-izm], *s.* Las opiniones del partido tory en Inglaterra.
Toss [tes], *va.* 1. Tirar, arrojar o echar alguna cosa con la mano. 2. Tirar, lanzar, arrojar o disparar con violencia; lanzar al aire. 3. Agitar, mover bruscamente, en especial hacia arriba, v. gr. la cabeza; sacudir. *To toss in a blanket*, Mantear. 4. Agitar, discutir, repetir lo dicho.—*vn.* 1. Estar en continua agitación, no estarse quieto. 2. Corcovear, dar corcovos en el aire. *To toss one about* o *to and fro*, Traer a alguno al retortero o al pelotero, traerle engañado con falsas promesas. *To toss aside*, Arrojar a un lado; dejar de usar, no hacer caso de alguien o algo. *To toss off*, Tragar de golpe, beber sin tomar aliento; también, echar a un lado, disponer de. *To toss up*, Tirar o lanzar en alto; levantar o alzar algo; jugar a cara o cruz.
Toss, *s.* 1. Sacudimiento, sacudida. 2. Un modo de mover la cabeza con afectación hacia arriba.
Tosser [tes'-ęr], *s.* 1. Sacudidor, manteador. 2. Cualquiera persona o cosa que agita a otra.
Tossing [tes'-ing], *s.* 1. Sacudimiento, sacudida. 2. Agitación. 3. Manteamiento.
Tossingly [tes'-ing-li], *adv.* Con sacudidas o sacudimientos.
Tosspot [tes'-pet], *s.* (Ant.) Borrachón; glotón.
Tot [tet], *s.* Niño, niña que marcha con paso incierto. (< Islandés *tottr*, enano.)
Total [tō'-tal], *a.* Total, completo, entero, todo.—*s.* Total, el todo.
Totalitarian [to-tal-i-tār'-i-an], *a.* Totalitario, dictatorial.
Totality [to-tal'-i-ti], *s.* Totalidad.
Totalizator [tō'-tal-i-zē''-tęr], *s.* Máquina para registrar apuestas en las carreras de caballos.
Totally [tō'-tal-i], *adv.* Totalmente.
Tote [tōt], *va.* (Fam. E. U. del Sud) 1. Llevar carga sobre los hombros, cargar. 2. Entre los cortadores de árboles, acarrear provisiones y pertrechos desde el depósito o almacén a los bosques donde trabajan.
Totem, Totem pole [tō'-tem pōl], *s.* Totem, poste totémico.
T'other [tudh'-ęr]. Abreviatura vulgar de THE OTHER. El otro.
Totter [tet'-ęr], *vn.* 1. Bambolear, tambalear, temblar, estar para caer o estar cayéndose; desmoronarse, amenazar ruina, bambonearse. 2. Vacilar, titubear.
Tottering [tet'-ęr-ing], *a.* Vacilante; que bambonea o bambolea, que amenaza ruina.—*s.* 1. Bamboleo o bamboneo. 2. Vacilación.
Totteringly [tet'-ęr-ing-li], *adv.* De un modo vacilante.
Tottery [tet'-ęr-i], *a.* Vacilante, instable.
Toucan [tū-cān'], *s.* (Orn.) Tucán, ave trepadora de América del género Rhamphastos, notable por su enorme pico.
Touch [tuch], *va.* 1. Tocar, ponerse en contacto, particularmente con una parte del cuerpo; rozar ligeramente. 2. Tocar, poner la mano en una cosa sin cogerla; palpar. 3. Tocar, llegar, juntar una cosa a otra sin que quede espacio en medio. 4. Llegar a alguna parte. 5. Tocar o examinar los metales en la piedra de toque para saber su calidad y quilates. 6. Hacer relación a una persona o cosa. 7. Tocar o comunicar a uno un contagio físico o moral. 8. Mover, enternecer, imprimir en el corazón afectos de amor, piedad, etc., conmover; irritar, excitar la ira, aguijonear; herir, afligir. 9. Tocar, tratar de una cosa ligeramente. 10. Esquiciar, trazar. 11. Tocar, hacer son en algún instrumento hiriendo sus cuerdas. 12. Influir, tocar a; concernir, importar.—*vn.* 1. Tocar, estar cercano o contiguo, estar en contacto; tocarse. 2. Imponer las manos sobre una persona para curarla de una enfermedad, v. gr. los lamparones. *To touch at*, Llegar á algún paraje sin detenerse. *To touch at a port*, Hacer escala en algún puerto. *To touch off*, Descargar (un cañón); hacer o acabar de prisa, bosquejar. *To touch on*, Tocar, tratar de alguna materia ligeramente. *To touch on* o *upon*, Tocar en algún lugar o estar muy poco tiempo en él o de paso. *To touch up*, Retocar, corregir. *To touch upon a thing*, Tocar, hablar de una cosa por incidencia. *To touch one*, Tocar a uno, concernirle. *That touches him to the quick*, Le toca a lo vivo. *To touch and go*, (Mar.) Tocar y aparejar; tratar de un asunto ligeramente.
Touch, *s.* 1. Toque, el acto de tocar una cosa tentándola o palpándola o llegándose inmediatamente a ella; tocamiento, palpamiento, la acción y efecto de tocar. 2. Contacto, el acto de tocarse dos cuerpos. 3. Tacto, uno de los sentidos corporales, y el acto de tocar. 4. Toque, golpe; manera o método característico; ejecución, la última mano. 5. Toque en la pintura y escultura, pincelada, rasgo. 6. Cantidad pequeña de alguna cosa mezclada con otra; dolorcito, latido, dolor corto; un poco, una sospecha. 7. Indirecta. 8. Tiento, ensayo ligero. 9. La acción y la manera de tañer algún instrumento de música; también, la resistencia que opone el teclado a los dedos del que toca; tañimiento. 10. Buena inteligencia, armonía, simpatía, correspondencia. 11. Toque en el oro o plata con la piedra de toque. 12. Toque, la prueba, examen o experiencia que se hace de algún sujeto. 13. Movimiento interior del alma. *I wil have a touch at it*, Le daré un tiento. *Touch-and-go*, *a.* (1) Dispuesto á dispararse al más leve toque. (2) (Mar.) Que roza el fondo sin perder velocidad; que escapa a duras penas. (3) Ligero y alegre. U. t. c. s. *Touch-back*, *s.* (Término del juego de pelota llamado *foot-ball*) El acto de tocar el suelo con la pelota detrás de la meta del propio jugador, después de haberla lanzado con el pie uno de los jugadores del bando opuesto. *Touch-down*, (Término de *foot-ball*) El acto o la jugada consistente en tocar el suelo con la pelota detrás de la meta del campo enemigo.
Touchable [tuch'-a-bl], *a.* Tangible, que se puede tocar.
Touch-and-go [tuch'-and-gō'], *s.* Situación sumamente incierta o precaria.—*a.* Incierto, casual, inestable.
Touch-hole [tuch'-hōl], *s.* Fogón, oído del cañón.
Touchiness [tuch'-i-nes], *s.* 1. La disposición a picarse o resentirse fácilmente. 2. Iracundia, la propensión a la ira.
Touching [tuch'-ing], *prep.* Tocante, en orden a lo cual, por lo que toca á, concerniente a, en cuanto a, en orden a, acerca de.—*a.* Patético, lastimero, tierno, afectuoso.—*s.* Toque, acto de tocar; contacto.
Touchingly [tuch'-ing-li], *adv.* Patéticamente, tiernamente, de un modo afectuoso.
Touch-me-not [tuch'-mi-net], *s.* (Bot.) 1. Balsamina silvestre, planta del género Impatiens. 2. Nolimetángere, enfermedad del cutis. *V.* LUPUS.
Touchstone [tuch'-stōn], *s.* Piedra de toque; examen, prueba; criterio.
Touchy [tuch'-i], *a.* Vidrioso, enojadizo, quisquilloso, cosquilloso. *Touchy subject*, Tecla.
Tough [tuf], *a.* 1. Correoso, tenaz, flexible, que se extiende y se doblega fácilmente sin romperse. 2. Tieso, que no puede doblarse con facilidad. 3. Fuerte, duro, que no puede romperse sin esfuerzo; vigoroso, de gran fortaleza para el sufrimiento. 4. Viscoso, glutinoso. 5. (Fam.) Difícil, penoso.
Toughen [tuf'-n], *va.* y *vn.* Hacer o hacerse correoso; endurecer, hacer duro, llegar a ser duro.
Toughly [tuf'-li], *adv.* Fuertemente.
Toughness [tuf'-nes], *s.* 1. Flexibilidad. 2. Tenacidad; viscosidad. 3. Tesura, rigidez de lo que no se puede doblar.
Toupet [tū-pē'], **Toupee** [tū-pī'], *s.* Tupé, mechón de cabello.
Tour [tūr], *s.* 1. Viaje, peregrinación. *To take* o *make a tour*, Viajar. 2. Vuelta, paseo o viaje corto, excursión; circuito. 3. Vuelta, giro, revolución de los planetas. 4. Jornada, servicio; término militar de otros tiempos.
Tourism [tūr'-ism], *s.* Turismo.
Tourist [tūr'-ist], *s.* Turista, viajero, excursionista. *Tourist court*, Campo de turistas, especie de hotel para turistas.
Tourmaline [tęr'-ma-lin], *s.* Turmalina.
Tournament [tūr'-na-męnt], **Tourney** [tūr'-nę], *s.* Torneo, justa.
Tourney, *vn.* Tornear, combatir o pelear en el torneo.
Tourniquet [tūr'-ni-ket], *s.* Torniquete, instrumento quirúrgico para impedir la hemorragia en operaciones y heridas de las extremidades.

Tousle [tau'-zl], *va.* Desordenar, alborotar (el cabello); comúnmente en el participio pasado.

Tousled [tau'-zld], *a.* Desgreñado, despeinado (el cabello).

Touter [taut-ẹr], *s.* (Ingl. o fam.) Comisionista o mandadero de fonda; reclutador.

Tow [tō], *s.* Estopa, la borra del lino y del cáñamo. *Tow-head,* Persona que tiene los cabellos de color rubio subido o alborotados. *Tow-headed,* Que tiene los cabellos muy rubios.

Tow, *s.* 1. Lo que va o está remolcado o espiado; bajeles, barcos, etc. 2. Atoaje o espía, la maniobra de espiar un barco. *Tow-boat,* Barco remolcador. *Tow-line, tow-rope,* Cabo de remolque, sirga, remolque. *Tow-path,* Camino de sirga.

Tow, *va.* Remolcar, atoar, espiar, halar, tirar o llevar á remolque por medio de un cabo que se tiende por la proa, amarrado a un anclote o al muelle. *To take in tow,* (Mar.) Tomar a remolque.

Towage [tō'-ẹ̄j], *s.* 1. Derechos de sirga. 2. Atoaje o espía, la maniobra de atoar o espiar un barco.

Toward, Towards [tō'-ard, ardz], *prep.* Hacia, con dirección a; con, para con; cerca, cerca de, cosa de, alrededor de; con respecto a, tocante a. *Toward* o *towards evening,* Hacia o cerca del anochecer. *Toward God,* Para con Dios.

Toward, Towardly [tō'-ard-li], *a.* Dócil, complaciente, deferente.

Towardliness [tō'-ard-li-nes], **Towardness** [tō'-ard-nes], *s.* Docilidad, complacencia, deferencia.

Towel [tau'-el], *s.* Toalla, paño de manos, tela de lino o lienzo para enjugar una cosa frotándola. *Roller towel,* Toalla continua, giratoria.

Tower [tau'-ẹr], *s.* 1. Torre de iglesia, campanario, etc. 2. Torre, torreón; ciudadela, fortaleza. 3. Vuelo alto, elevación. 4. Un peinado muy elevado que se usaba antiguamente. *The Tower of London,* La Torre de Londres.

Tower, *vn.* 1. Elevarse una cosa a una altura desmesurada. 2. Remontarse o tomar viento libre las aves cuando vuelan muy alto.

Towered [tau'-ẹrd], **Towery** [tau'-ẹr-i], *a.* Torreado, guarnecido de torres.

Towhee [tō-hwī'], *s.* Pájaro americano de los fringílidos, parecido a un pinzón. Pipilo erythrophthalmus. (Nombre imitativo de su canto.) *V.* CHEWINK.

Towing-path [tō'-ing-pạth], *s.* (Mar.) Sirguería.

Town [taun], *s.* 1. Ciudad; villa, pueblo grande: dícese no sólo de la población material sino también del vecindario de ella; cualquiera población un poco considerable, y en Inglaterra se da el nombre de *town* a toda población que goza del privilegio de tener mercado, cualquiera que sea el número de sus habitantes, y que no es la sede de un obispado. 2. (E. U.) Municipalidad; subdivisión de un condado. 3. (Ingl.) Plaza, cualquiera porción o número de casas rodeadas de muros. *A fortified town,* Plaza de armas. *A trading town,* Ciudad mercantil. *Seaport town,* Ciudad marítima, puerto de mar. *In town,* En la ciudad; en la metrópoli. *On the town,* (E. U.) (1) Indigente, que no tiene para vivir más que los socorros de la ciudad. (2) Que vive de la prostitución. *Man about town,* Hombre acaudalado que vive en la ociosidad y cómodamente, y frecuenta los clubs y lugares públicos. *Women of the town,* Damas cortesanas, rameras. *Town clerk,* Secretario de ayuntamiento. *Town crier,* Pregonero. *Town hall,* Casa de ayuntamiento o casa consistorial. *Town house,* (1) Casa consistorial, casa de ayuntamiento o ayuntamiento, casa de consejo, y en algunas partes de España consistorio. (2) La casa que uno tiene en la ciudad, cuando se habla de una persona que tiene otra fuera de ella: los ingleses regularmente entienden por *town house* la casa que se tiene en Londres.

Township [taun'-ship], *s.* 1. (E. U.) Territorio de una ciudad; cuerpo municipal; subdivisión de un condado. 2. Extensión de terrenos públicos de los Estados Unidos, de seis millas cuadradas. 3. (Ingl.) Límites o territorio de una ciudad.

Townsman [taunz'-man], *s.* 1. Vecino de alguna villa o pueblo. 2. Conciudadano, paisano, el que es de la misma ciudad o pueblo que otro.

Towntalk [taun'-tēc], *s.* La cosa o suceso que es pasto de la conversación en un pueblo.

Towzer [tau'-zẹr], *s.* 1. Hombre travieso o revoltoso. 2. Nombre propio de un perro.

Toxemia [tex-ī'-mi-a], *s.* Toxemia, envenenamiento de la sangre.

Toxic, Toxical [tex'-ic, al], *a.* 1. Venenoso, ponzoñoso, tóxico. 2. Causado por ponzoña o veneno.

Toxicological [tex-i-co-lej'-ic-al], *a.* Toxicológico, perteneciente o relativo a la toxicología.

Toxicology [tex-i-cel'-o-ji], *s.* Toxicología, parte de la medicina que trata de los venenos.

Toxin [tex'-in], *s.* Toxina.

Toy [tei], *s.* 1. Chuchería, miriñaque, o juguete de niños. 2. Objeto menudo que imita a otro mayor y que sirve de entretenimiento y diversión. 3. Retozo, retozadura. 4. (Ant.) Humorada, capricho, cuento.

Toy, *va.* y *vn.* 1. Jugar, enredar, retozar, divertirse. 2. Loquear, juguetear, estar de chacota. 3. Regodearse o deleitarse haciendo caricias y halagos.

Toyish [tei'-ish], *a.* Juguetón; menudo y caprichoso; semejante a un miriñaque.

Toyshop [tei'-shop], *s.* La tienda donde se venden chucherías, miriñaques o juguetes de niños.

Trabecular, Trabeculate [tra-bec'-yu-lar, lēt], *a.* (Biol.) Perteneciente a una faja que sirve de apoyo, particularmente al parenquima o a las fibras del tejido celular de un órgano, v. gr. del bazo.

Trace [trēs], *s.* 1. Rastro, huella, pisada. 2. Vestigio, rastro, señal o apariencia de lo que fué. 3. Pizca; cantidad o calidad apenas perceptible. 4. Tirante o tiradera que se pone a las mulas o caballos.

Trace, *va.* 1. Trazar, delinear, hacer las líneas de un dibujo. 2. Calcar, copiar en una placa transparente. 3. Rastrear, seguir la huella o la pista. 4. Trazar, señalar el camino, la conducta, etc., que se debe seguir. 5. Formar idea de una cosa por algún vestigio o resto de ella o de otra. 6. Imitar o seguir el ejemplo, el estilo, etc. 7. Investigar, descubrir, escudriñar; rastrear. *Tracing-line,* (Mar.) Perigallo. 8. Recorrer, seguir su camino por, o a lo largo de.

Traceable [trēs'-a-bl], *a.* Que se puede trazar o rastrear; aquello cuyo rastro se puede seguir.

Tracer [trē'-sẹr], *s.* 1. Trazador; investigador, escudriñador; imitador. 2. Tiralíneas, instrumento de dibujante. 3. Cédula o fórmula de investigación, que se envía de un punto a otro para averiguar el paradero de cartas extraviadas en el correo.

Tracery [trē'-sẹr-i], *s.* 1. (Arq.) Recortaduras, adornos góticos en piedra. 2. Randa. 3. Arte de trazar o de hacer recortaduras.

Trachea [trē'-kẹ-a], *s.* 1. Tráquea, traquearteria, conducto cartilaginoso por el cual pasa el aire desde la laringe a los bronquios y pulmones. 2. Tráquea, conducto del aire en ciertos artrópodos, como los insectos. 3. (Bot.) Ducto, vasos en espiral.

Tracheal [trē'-kẹ-al], *a.* Traqueal, perteneciente o relativo a la tráquea.

Tracheotomy [trē-kẹ-et'-o-mi], *s.* Traqueotomía, operación quirúrgica, incisión en la tráquea para extraer un cuerpo extraño o para impedir la sofocación del paciente en ciertas enfermedades.

Trachyte [trac'-ait], *s.* (Min.) Traquita, roca volcánica, áspera al tacto.

Trachytic [tra-kit'-ic], *a.* Traquítico, perteneciente a la traquita o parecido a ella.

Tracing [trē'-sing], *s.* 1. Acción de trazar. 2. Calco, copia hecha en papel transparente.

Track [trac], *s.* 1. Vestigio, rastro, huella, pisada. 2. Rodada, carril, el surco que dejan en los caminos las ruedas de los carros o carruajes. 3. (Mar.) Estela, la señal que el navío deja en el agua cuando va navegando. 4. Rumbo, ruta; curso. 5. Camino trillado, senda o vereda muy pasajera. 6. Vía, los carriles de una vía férrea; carril sobre el que puede moverse alguna cosa. 7. Campo de carreras. *Double track,* (F. C.) Vía doble. *Side-track,* Desviadero. *V.* SIDE. *Track-walker,* Guardavía, empleado que tiene a su cargo la vigilancia constante de un trozo de la vía férrea.

Track, *va.* 1. Rastrear, seguir el rastro, buscar alguna cosa por él o seguir á alguno por las pisadas. 2. (Mar.) Sirgar. *Tracking-path,* Sirguería. *Tracking-rope,* Sirga.

Trackage [trak'-ẹ̄j], *s.* 1. Tirada, remolque. 2. Carril, el conjunto de rieles de un ferrocarril. *A trackage of eight hundred miles,* Extensión de rieles de ochocientas millas.

Tracker [trak'-ẹr], *s.* (Mar.) Sirguero.

Trackless [trac'-les], *a.* Que no presenta rastro o vestigio de que hayan andado por encima.

Track meet [trac'mīt], *s.* Competencia de pista y campo.

Tract [tract], *s.* 1. Trecho, espacio o extensión de lugar. 2. Región, comarca, un espacio grande de territorio. 3. Curso, serie, continuación. 4. Folleto, discurso, especialmente sobre un tema de religión o de moral; opúsculo. *A tract of land,* Un terreno erial o sin cultivo.

Tractable [trac'-ta-bl], *a.* 1. Tratable, manejable, complaciente, dócil. 2. Fácil de manejar o trabajar.
Tractably [trac'-ta-bli], *adv.* Afablemente, dócilmente, con dulzura en el trato.
Tractate [trac'-têt], *s.* Tratado breve, opúsculo, folleto.
†**Tractile** [trac'-til], *a.* Dúctil.
Traction [trac'-shun], *s.* 1. Tracción, acción y efecto de traer, particularmente de arrastrar los coches o carros sobre una vía o superficie, v. g. del ferrocarril. 2. Contracción, tensión de un músculo. 3. Tracción o fricción de las ruedas sobre una vía.
Traction engine [trac'-shun en'-jin], *s.* Tractor, máquina de tracción.
Tractive [tract'-iv], *a.* Traedor, que trae.
Tractor [trac'-ter], *s.* Tractor.
Trade [trêd], *s.* 1. Comercio, tráfico; negocio, trato. 2. Ocupación, oficio, ejercicio: generalmente se entiende del comercio o artes mecánicas en contraposición a la profesión de las ciencias o artes liberales. 3. Conjunto de artesanos del mismo oficio. 4. Volumen del tráfico y cambio (de dinero) hecho en cualquier lugar determinado. 5. (E. U.) En la política, convenio de mala ley. *Trade-mark,* Marca de fábrica. *Trade-union* o *trades-union,* Gremio de oficios, sociedad de obreros formada para favorecer sus intereses comunes. *What trade does he follow?* ¿Qué oficio tiene?
Trade, *va.* y *vn.* 1. Negociar, comerciar, tratar. 2. Traficar, vender, cambiar.
Traded [trêd'-ed], *a.* Versado, práctico.
Trade-in [trêd'-in], *s.* Trueque, objeto dado como pago parcial para la compra de otro similar. Úsase también como verbo activo.
Trade publication [trêd pub-li-kê'-shun], *s.* Publicación de determinada rama de la industria o del comercio.
Trader [trêd'-ẹr], *s.* 1. Negociante, comerciante, traficante, negociador. 2. Factor.
Trade school [trêd scūl] *s.* Escuela vocacional, escuela de artes y oficios.
Trades-folk [trêdz'-fōc], **Trades-people** [trêdz'-pī-pl], *s.* La gente menestral o artesana.
Tradesman [trêdz'-man], *s.* 1. Tendero, mercader, el que tiene tienda. 2. Artesano, menestral.
Trade-winds [trêd'-windz], *s. pl.* Vientos alisios, vientos generales, monzones en el Océano Índico.
Trading [trêd'-ing], *s.* Comercio, trato.—*a.* Mercantil, comercial. *Trading post,* Factoría. *Trading stamps,* Sellos de premio.
Tradition [tra-dish'-un], *s.* 1. Tradición, noticia de alguna cosa antigua que viene de padres a hijos y se comunica por relación sucesiva de unos a otros. 2. Costumbre antigua que casi tiene fuerza de ley. 3.
Traditional [tra-dish'-un-al], *a.* Tradicional, comunicado por tradición.
Traditionally [tra-dish'-un-al-i], *adv.* Por tradición.
Traditive [trad'-i-tiv], *a.* (Ant.) Transmitido o transmisible, que se transmite o se puede transmitir de edad en edad por medio de la tradición.
Traduce [tra-diūs'], *va.* Detractar, disfamar, decir mal de uno, murmurar de él, vituperar o afear su conducta; calumniar, denigrar.
Traducer [tra-diūs'-ẹr], *s.* Calumniador, detractor, difamador, murmurador.
Traducible [tra-diūs'-i-bl], *a.* Que puede ser difamado o calumniado.
Traduction [tra-duc'-shun], *s.* (Poco us.) 1. Calumnia, denigración. 2. (Des.) Propagación; derivación.
Traffic [traf'-ic], *s.* 1. Tráfico, comercio. 2. Tránsito, transporte. 3. Mercadería, géneros. *Traffic lane,* Vía para el tránsito. *Traffic light,* Semáforo, farol o luz de tránsito. *Traffic sign,* Señal de tránsito.
Traffic, *va.* Negociar, trocar efectos, vender.—*vn.* 1. Traficar, comerciar o negociar en géneros o mercaderías. 2. Hacer alguna cosa vil o infame por interés.
Trafficker [traf'-ik-ẹr], *s.* Traficante, comerciante.
Tragacanth [trag'-a-canth], *s.* Tragacanto, adraganto, goma blanquecina que se obtiene de varias especies de Astragalus.
Tragedian [tra-jī'-di-an], *s.* 1. El escritor de tragedias. 2. El actor que representa tragedias.
Tragedy [traj'-e-di], *s.* 1. Tragedia, obra dramática en que se representan sucesos de gran trascendencia o muy conmovedores, por personajes ilustres y con desenlace generalmente funesto. 2. Tragedia, cualquier suceso fatal, funesto, desgraciado o infausto.
Tragic, Tragical [traj'-ic, al], *a.* 1. Trágico, que pertenece a la tragedia. 2. Trágico, fatal, funesto, desgraciado.
Tragically [traj'-ic-al-i], *adv.* Trágicamente, fatalmente, infaustamente.
Tragicalness [traj'-ic-al-nes], *s.* Tristeza, horror, calamidad, infortunio.
Tragicomedy [traj-i-com'-e-di], *s.* Tragicomedia, uno de los géneros en que se han dividido las piezas dramáticas.
Tragicomical [traj-i-com'-i-cal], *a.* Tragicómico, jocoserio, cosa entre lastimosa y risible.
Trail [trêl], *va.* y *vn.* 1. Rastrear, seguir a algún animal por el rastro; cazar siguiendo la pista. 2. Arrastrar o llevar arrastrando una cosa por el suelo. 3. Llevar colgando alguna cosa larga. 4. Arrastrar o llevar tras sí. *Trailing arbutus, V.* ARBUTUS y MAYFLOWER.
Trail, *s.* 1. Rastro, pisada, huella, pista. 2. Cola, la punta prolongada del vestido o de otra cosa que se lleva arrastrando; cola (de meteoro). 3. Sendero, vereda, v. g. la senda que cruza un yermo. 4. Circunstancia o circunstancias que sugieren y guían las pesquisas en dirección o sentido determinados. *Trail of light,* Rastro luminoso. *A false trail,* Una pista falsa. *Trailboard,* (Mar.) Moldura entre las curvas bandas.
Trailer [trêl'-ẹr], *s.* 1. Carro de remolque. 2. Remolque-habitación. *Trailer court,* Estacionamiento para dichas habitaciones.
Train [trên], *va.* 1. Disciplinar, ejercitar o hacer que uno aprenda alguna cosa mediante el ejercicio y práctica de ella. 2. Amaestrar, enseñar, criar, adiestrar: en esta significación va casi siempre con la partícula *up.* 3. Preparar, poner en cierta condición física prescrita, por medio de la dieta y el ejercicio. 4. Poner en espaldera, hacer trepar o dirigir en una dirección particular (una planta). 5. Apuntar un cañón.—*vn.* 1. Criar, dar enseñanza, someter a un régimen. 2. Seguir un curso metódico de ejercicios gimnásticos, o de otra clase. *To train a horse,* Amaestrar o adiestrar un caballo. *To train soldiers,* Disciplinar tropa.
Train, *s.* 1. Procesión; fila de vehículos; tren de ferrocarril. 2. Reguero de pólvora. 3. Séquito, tren, comitiva; recua. 4. Serie, continuación ordenada. 5. La cola de las aves; cola de vestido. 6. (Mec.) Tren, serie de piezas que obran juntas para transmitir el movimiento. 7. Lazo, celada; trampa. *Train-tackle,* Palanquines de retenida de cañón. *Down train,* Tren descendente, tren de ida. *Up train,* Tren ascendente, tren de regreso. *Excursion train,* Tren de ida y vuelta, de recreo. *Freight train,* (E. U.) *goods train,* (Ingl.) Tren de mercancías, tren de carga. *Through train,* Tren directo o terminal.
Trainbands [trên'-bandz], *s. pl.* Milicias, cuerpos militares formados por los vecinos de algún país o ciudad.
Trainbearer [trên'-bār-ẹr], *s.* Caudatario.
Trainer [trên'-ẹr], *s.* Maestro, director, el que enseña o dirige.
Training [trên'-ing], *s.* La acción de enseñar alguna cosa por medio de la práctica; educación, instrucción. *Training-school,* (E. U.) Escuela de instrucción práctica y ejercicio (v. gr. para preparar e instruir a las enfermeras).
Trainload [trên'-lōd], *s.* Carga completa de un tren.
Train-oil [trên'-eil], *s.* Aceite de ballena.
Traipse [trêps], *vn.* (Prov.) *V.* TRAPES.
Trait [trêt], *s.* Golpe, toque; rasgo, acción; forma, figura, facción.
Traitor [trê'-tẹr], *s.* Traidor.
Traitorous [trê'-tẹr-us], *a.* Pérfido, aleve, alevoso, traidor.
Traitorously [trê'-tẹr-us-li], *adv.* Traidoramente, alevosamente, con perfidia.
Traitress [trê'-tres], *sf.* Traidora.
‡**Traject** [tra-ject'], *va.* Tirar, arrojar; traspasar. *V. To* THROW.
Trajection [tra-jec'-shun], *s.* Pasaje, el acto de pasar de una parte a otra.
Trajectory [tra-jec'-to-ri], *s.* Trayectoria, curva que describe el proyectil de un arma de fuego.
†**Tralatitious** [tral-a-tish'-us], *a.* Traslaticio, metafórico.
Tram [tram], *s.* 1. (Ingl.) Tranvía; coche de tranvía. 2. Riel plano; carril de tranvía. 3. Carreta de carbón. *Tram-car,* (Ingl.) Coche de tranvía. *Tramway, tramroad,* (1) Tranvía, ferrocarril urbano; (2) camino provisto de rieles planos, para vehículos de ruedas.
Trammel [tram'-el], *s.* 1. Impedimento, obstáculo, estorbo. 2. Trabas que ponen a los caballos para que sienten el paso. 3. Llares, garabato pendiente de una chimenea. 4. Compás de vara; compás de elipse.
Trammel, *va.* Trabar, poner trabas; estorbar, embarazar con limitaciones, impedir.

Tramontane [tra-mon'-tên], *a.* Tramontano, ultramontano, situado más allá de los montes; que viene del otro lado de los montes.—*s.* Extranjero, bárbaro; originalmente, el que vive o es natural de alguna parte situada del otro lado de los montes, con respecto al sitio donde o de que se habla.

Tramp [tramp], *va.* 1. Andar con paso pesado; pisar con fuerza. 2. Andar o viajar a pie.—*vn.* 1. Pisar pesadamente; ir, andar, marchar a pie. 2. Corretear, vagabundear.

Tramp, *s.* 1. Marcha pesada y continua, como de una muchedumbre. 2. Ruido producido por una marcha pesada y continua. 3. Viaje o paseo largo a pie. 4. (E. U.) Vago, peón, el que camina o viaja a pie; en especial, vagabundo, correntón. 5. Vapor que va de puerto en puerto, tomando carga donde la haya.

Trample [tram'-pl], *va.* 1. Hollar, pisotear o pisar repetidamente alguna cosa. 2. Pisar, poner bajo los pies; hollar, menospreciar, ajar o tratar con desprecio: por lo común con *on.* —*vn.* Marchar pesadamente, torpemente (en sentido literal y figurado); pisar muy fuerte.

Trampler [tram'-plęr], *s.* Pisador, el que pisa.

Trampoline [tram-po-lîn'], *s.* Trampolín.

Trance [trąns], *s.* 1. Rapto, éxtasis, arrobamiento del ánimo, enajenamiento. 2. Estado de insensibilidad: (1) síncope prolongado; (2) catalepsia, condición hipnótica.

Tranced [trąnst], *a.* Arrobado, elevado, arrebatado, enajenado.

Tranquil [traņ'-cwil], *a.* Tranquilo, sosegado, pacífico, apacible.

Tranquilize, tranquillize [tran'-cwil-aiz], *va.* Tranquilizar, sosegar, calmar, aquietar.

Tranquilizer [tran-cwil-aiz'-ęr], *s.* Tranquilizante, calmante.

Tranquilizing [tran-cwil-aiz'-ing], Calmante, tranquilizador.

Tranquillity [traņ-cwil'-i-ti], *s.* Tranquilidad, sosiego, reposo, calma, quietud.

Tranquilly [traņ'-cwil-li], *adv.* Tranquilamente, con quietud, con sosiego.

Trans-, tran-. Prefijo que significa al través de, más allá, por entre.

Transact [trans-act'], *va.* Llevar a cabo, hacer, ejecutar, conducir, despachar o dar curso a un negocio.

Transaction [trans-ac'-shun], *s.* 1. Manejo, conducta de cualquier asunto; transacción. 2. Negociación, negocio, asunto, lo que está hecho. 3. *pl.* Trabajos de una sociedad docta; memorias. *Let me know all the transactions,* Dígame Vd. todo lo que pasa o todo lo que pase. *During these transactions,* Mientras pasaba o sucedía esto.

Transactor [trans-act'-ęr], *s.* Negociador, el que negocia.

Transalpine [trans-al'-pin], *a.* Transalpino, situado al otro lado de los Alpes, particularmente al norte, es decir, el lado más lejano de Roma.

Transatlantic [trans-at-lan'-tic], *a.* Trasatlántico. *Transatlantic airship,* Aeronave trasatlántica. *Transatlantic liner,* Barco trasatlántico, trasatlántico.

Transcend [tran-send'], *va.* 1. Sobrepujar, elevarse sobre alguien o algo en excelencia o grado; sobresalir. 2. Exceder, propasar, pasar de los límites.—*vn.* Ser trascendente, transcendental o sobresaliente.

Transcendence [tran-sen'-dens], **Transcendency** [tran-sen'-den-si], *s.* 1. Trascendencia, excelencia, superioridad marcada; mérito trascendente. 2. (Teol.) Existencia superior y más allá de la de otros seres; existencia de Dios, aparte del universo y no limitada por el tiempo ni el espacio.

Transcendent [tran-sen'-dent], *a.* 1. Sobresaliente, excelente en sumo grado. 2. Trascendente, superior al universo material; espiritual.

Transcendental [tran-sen-den'-tal], *a.* 1. Trascendental, no comprendido en las categorías; que traspasa los límites de la ciencia experimental. 2. Eminente o excelente en sumo grado, sobresaliente. 3. Superior o fuera del sentido común o contrario a él.

Transcendently [tran-sen'-dent-li], *adv.* Excelentemente, primorosamente.

Transcontinental [trans-con-ti-nent'-al], *a.* Transcontinental.

Transcribe [tran-scraib'], *va.* Transcribir, copiar, trasladar un escrito o impreso.

Transcriber [tran-scraib'-ęr], *s.* Copiante, amanuense. (Amer.) Escribiente.

Transcript [tran'-script], *s.* Trasunto, copia o traslado de un original.

Transcription [tran-scrip'-shun], *s.* 1. Transcripción. 2. Trasunto, traslado, copia. 3. Radiodifusión a base de discos fonográficos. 4. Disco empleado con este fin.

Transcriptive [tran-scrip'-tiv], *a.* Perteneciente a la copia o al traslado.

Transcriptively [tran-scrip'-tiv-li], *adv.* Por medio de copia.

Transe, *s.* (Poco us.) *V.* TRANCE.

Transept [tran'-sept], *s.* El crucero de una iglesia; el espacio entre el altar y el coro.

Transfer [trans-fęr'], *va.* 1. Transferir, transportar, pasar ó llevar una cosa desde un lugar a otro. 2. Transferir, ceder o renunciar a otro el derecho o la posesión de una cosa; en este sentido va acompañado por lo común de *to* y algunas veces de *upon.*

Transfer [trans'-fęr], *s.* 1. Traspaso, acción y efecto de traspasar; transferencia, acción y efecto de transferir; traslación, transporte. 2. La cosa transferida o traspasada. 3. Lugar, método o medio de transferir. 4. Traspaso, acta de cesión de una propiedad.

Transferable [trans-fęr'-a-bl], *a.* Transferible, que puede ser transferido o traspasado; que se puede trasladar.

Transferee [trans-fęr-î'], *s.* Cesionario, persona á cuyo favor se hace la cesión de bienes.

Transference [trans-fęr'-ens], *s.* Transferencia, acción y efecto de transferir.

Transfiguration [trans-fig-yu-ré'-shun], *s.* Transfiguración, mudanza de una figura en otra.

Transfigure [trans-fig'-yur], *va.* Transformar, transmutar, mudar de figura.

Transfix [trans-fix'], *va.* Traspasar o atravesar con una cosa puntiaguda.

Transfixion [trans-fic'-shun], *s.* Transfixión, la acción de herir pasando de una parte a otra.

Transform [trans-fōrm'], *va.* 1. Transformar, cambiar la forma de algo, metamorfosear, transmutar. 2. Convertir, cambiar el carácter o la naturaleza de. 3. (Mat.) Cambiar una expresión en otra equivalente.—*vn.* Transfigurarse, transformarse.

Transformable [trans-fōrm'-a-bl], *a.* Transformable, convertible, que se puede transformar.

Transformation [trans-fōr-mé'-shun], *s.* Transformación, la mudanza de una forma o figura en otra; cambio, conversión; metamorfosis; en la alquimia, transmutación.

Transformative [trans-fōrm'-a-tiv], *a.* Transformativo, que tiene virtud de transformar.

Transformer [trans-fōrm'-ęr], *s.* Transformador, el o lo que transforma; en especial, aparato eléctrico para convertir una corriente en otra de cantidad y potencial diferentes (más bajas o más altas).

Transfuse [trans-fiūz'], *va.* 1. Transfundir, transvasar, echar un licor poco a poco de un vaso en otro. 2. Transfundir, hacer pasar cierta cantidad de sangre de las venas de una persona o un animal a las de otro. 3. Restablecer (las fuerzas).

Transfusion [trans-fiū'-zhun], *s.* Transfusión, la acción de transfundir.

Transgress [trans-gres'], *va.* 1. Traspasar, transgredir, violar o quebrantar alguna ley, estatuto o precepto. 2. Propasar, exceder, ir más allá de los límites.—*vn.* 1. Transgredir una ley; pecar. 2. En geología, tapar.

Transgression [trans-gresh'-un], *s.* Transgresión, quebrantamiento de alguna ley.

Transgressor [trans-gres'-ęr], *s.* Transgresor.

Transient [tran'-shent], *a.* Pasajero, transitorio, transeunte.

Transiently [tran'-shent-li], *adv.* Ligeramente, de paso, de un modo transitorio.

Transistor [tran-sis'-ter], *s.* Transistor, aparato eléctrico que remplaza al tubo al vacío.

Transit [tran'-sit], *s.* 1. Tránsito, paso o acto de pasar. 2. Pasaje o vía determinada, particular. 3. (Astr.) Tránsito, el paso de un astro sobre el disco de otro; paso de un astro por el meridiano de un lugar dado.

Transition [trans-ish'-un], *s.* 1. Tránsito, el paso o la acción de pasar de un lugar, condición o estado a otro; mudanza. 2. Transición, artificio oratorio con que se pasa de un discurso a otro. 3. (Mús.) Transición. *V.* MODULATION.

Transitional, Transitionary [trans-ish'-un-al], *a.* Perteneciente a la transición o al tránsito.

Transitive [trans'-i-tiv], *a.* Transitivo; se aplica al verbo cuya acción recae directamente sobre el complemento.

Transitively [trans'-i-tiv-li], *adv.* De un modo transitivo.

Transitorily [tran'-si-to-ri-li], *adv.* Transitoriamente.

Transitory [tran'-si-to-ri], *a.* Transitorio, caduco, perecedero, de corta duración.

Translatable [trans-lét'-a-bl], *a.* Traducible, que se puede traducir.

Translate [trans-lét'], *va.* 1. Traducir, verter de un idioma a otro; explicar, interpretar. 2. Trasladar a un obispo de una silla episcopal a otra. 3. Transformar, cambiar. 4. Dar a conocer, explicar, aclarar. 5. (Ant.)

Arrebatar al cielo. *To translate into English*, Traducir al inglés.

Translation [trans-lé'-shun], *s.* 1. Translación, la acción de transportar, transferir, trasladar o mudar de un paraje a otro; traslación de un obispo, la acción de mudarle de un obispado a otro. 2. Traducción, versión, traslación, la acción de traducir de un idioma a otro. 3. (Ret.) Traslación.

Translator [trans-lé'-tər], *s.* 1. Traductor, el que traduce de una lengua a otra. 2. Repetidor telegráfico.

Transliterate [trans-lit'-ər-êt], *va.* Representar las letras de una lengua, o su sonido, por las letras de otra.

Translocation [trans-lo-ké'-shun], *s.* Mudanza recíproca de unas cosas al lugar de otras.

Translucency [trans-lū'-sen-si], *s.* Translucidez, calidad de translúcido.

Translucent [trans-lū'-sent], **Translucid** [trans-lū'-sid], *a.* 1. Translúcido, que deja pasar la luz sin permitir distinguir los objetos; semitransparente. 2. Transparente (inexactamente).

Transmarine [trans-ma-rīn'], *a.* Ultramarino, que está al otro lado del mar.

Transmigrate [trans'-mi-grêt], *vn.* Transmigrar, mudar de habitación de un país a otro.

Transmigration [trans-mi-gré'-shun], *s.* 1. Transmigración, la mudanza de habitación de un país a otro hecha por una familia o una nación entera. 2. La transmigración de las almas o la transmigración pitagórica.

Transmigratory [trans-mai'-gra-to-ri], *a.* Que pasa de una condición o estado a otro.

Transmissibility [trans-mis-i-bil'-i-ti], *s.* Calidad de transmisible.

Transmissible [trans-mis'-i-bl], *a.* Transmisible, susceptible de transmisión.

Transmission [trans-mish'-ʊn], *s.* 1. Transmisión. 2. Emisión. 3. (Mec.) Caja de cambios.

Transmissive [trans-mis'-iv], *a.* Transmisible; que se debe a la transmisión, transmitido.

Transmit [trans-mit'], *va.* 1. Transmitir, ceder o traspasar lo que se posee al dominio de otro. 2. Conducir, transferir, trasladar.

Transmittable, **Transmittible** [trans-mit'-a-bl], *a.* Transmisible, que se puede transmitir o conducir.

Transmittal [trans-mit'-al], *s.* Transmisión, la acción de transmitir.

Transmitter [trans-mit'-ər], *s.* 1. Transmisor, lo que transmite. 2. Transmisor (telegráfico o telefónico).

Transmutable [trans-miū'-ta-bl], *a.* Transmutable.

Transmutably [trans-miū'-ta-bli], *adv.* De un modo transmutable.

Transmutation [trans-miu-té'-shun], *s.* 1. Transmutación, conversión, mudanza. 2. Cambio de estado, mudanza sucesiva, alternación; cambio de un metal vil en precioso.

Transmute [trans-miūt'], *va.* Transmutar, convertir o mudar una cosa en otra; cambiar la naturaleza, substancia o forma.

Transmuter [trans-miūt'-ər], *s.* El o lo que transmuta.

Transnatation [trans-na-té'-shun], *s.* El acto de nadar de un lado a otro.

Transom [tran'-sum], *s.* 1. Travesaño, el madero que atraviesa una abertura; de aquí, ventana pequeña encima de una puerta, que sirve para dar ventilación. 2. (Art.) Telera, una de las piezas de madera que juntan las gualderas de las cureñas. 3. (Mar.) Yugo o peto de popa. *Wing transoms*, Yugos principales o de la cruz o popa. *Deck-transoms*, Yugos de la cubierta. *Helm-port-transoms*, Contra-yugos. *Hilling-transoms*, Yugos de henchimiento.

Transparency [trans-pār'-en-si], *s.* 1. Transparencia, diafanidad, calidad de transparente. 2. Transparente, letrero o cuadro sobre tela, vidrio u otra substancia transparente, detrás del cual se ponen una o más luces. 3. Diapositiva, transparencia.

Transparent [trans-pār'-ent], *a.* 1. Transparente, diáfano. 2. (Fig.) Fácil de entender o discernir; también, franco, sincero.

Transpicuous [tran-spic'-yu-us], *a.* (Poco us.) Transparente, claro a la vista.

Transpierce [trans-pīrs'], *va.* Traspasar, penetrar, atravesar de una parte a otra.

Transpiration [tran-spi-ré'-shun], *s.* Transpiración, expulsión insensible de algún humor o líquido por los poros.

Transpire [tran-spair'], *va.* Transpirar, echar de sí por medio de la transpiración.—*vn.* 1. Transpirar, evaporarse insensiblemente; rezumarse. 2. Translucirse, empezarse a saber lo que estaba oculto. 3. (Neol. y erróneo) Acontecer, suceder.

Transplant [trans-plant'], *va.* Transplantar, mudar las plantas de un paraje á otro para que prevalezcan.

Transplantation [trans-plan-té'-shun], *s.* Transplantación, trasplante.

Transport [trans-pōrt'], *va.* 1. Transportar, llevar de un paraje a otro; particularmente, deportar, desterrar, extrañar, enviar de un estado a otro país; llevar a presidio. 2. Arrebatar, llevar tras sí; conmover, transportar.

Transport [trans'-pōrt], *s.* 1. Transportamiento, arrobamiento, rapto, efecto de una viva pasión; acceso. 2. Transporte, el acto de transportar. 3. Transporte, la embarcación para llevar o conducir soldados, las municiones de guerra, etc.; dícese también, *Transport ship* o *Transport vessel*. 4. El criminal que ha sido condenado a la pena de extrañamiento o deportación.

Transportable [trans-pōrt'-a-bl], *a.* Capaz de ser transportado.

Transportation [trans-pōr-té'-shun], *s.* 1. Transportación. 2. Extrañamiento, deportación o destierro a otro país. 3. (E. U.) Vehículos que se usan para el transporte; también, el coste del transporte.

Transporter [trans-pōrt'-ər], *s.* El que transporta.

Transposal [trans-pōz'-al], *s.* Transposición.

Transpose [trans-pōz'], *va.* 1. Transponer, mudar de un lugar a otro alguna cosa. 2. Quitar o mudar de su lugar o puesto. 3. (Mús.) Escribir o tocar en un tono lo que está escrito en otro.

Transposition [trans-po-zish'-un], *s.* Transposición, la acción de transponer.

Transship [trans-ship'], *va.* Transbordar.

Transshipment [trans-ship'-mənt], *s.* Transbordo, el traslado de la carga de un buque o carro a otro, para que continúe sin interrupción el transporte de dicha carga.

Transubstantiate [tran-sub-stan'-shi-êt], *va.* Transubstanciar, convertir totalmente de una substancia en otra.

Transubstantiation [tran-sub-stan-shi-é'-shun], *s.* Transubstanciación, conversión total de una substancia en otra; en especial, del pan y el vino en el cuerpo y sangre de Nuestro Señor Jesucristo, en la Eucaristía.

Transudation [tran-siu-dé'-shun], *s.* Trasudor, sudor tenue y leve; transpiración.

Transumption [tran-sump'-shun], *s.* (Ant.) El acto de tomar o coger alguna cosa de una parte para llevarla a otra.

Transvection [trans-vec'-shun], *s.* El acto de conducir sobre alguna cosa.

Transversal [trans-vər'-sal], *a.* Transversal, que atraviesa de un lado a otro.—*s.* Transversal, línea transversal.

Transversally [trans-vər'-sal-i], *adv.* (Poco us.) Transversalmente.

Transverse [trans-vərs'], *a.* Transversal, transverso, que está al través.

Transversely [trans-vərs'-li], *adv.* Transversalmente, oblicuamente.

Transversion [trans-vər'-shun], *s.* El acto de volver transversalmente.

Trap [trap], *s.* 1. Trampa, cepo, armadijo para coger ladrones o animales dañinos. *Mouse-trap*, Ratonera. 2. Garlito, red, lazo. *To be caught in the trap*, Caer en el garlito, o en la trampa. (Méx.) Caer en la ratonera. 3. Entre tiradores, aparato que en un momento dado deja salir un animal u objeto destinado a servir de blanco, v. gr. un pichón vivo o una bola de vidrio. 4. Válvula de sumidero, construcción que sirve para retener en un punto fijo una cantidad de líquido que sólo permite el paso a las inmundicias. 5. *V.* TRAP-DOOR. 6. (Fam.) Un carruaje. 7. *pl.* Efectos personales. 8. Juego del palo corvo.

Trap, **Trap-rock** [trap'-rec], *s.* Roca parduzca e ígnea, como el basalto, de estructura columnar.

Trap, *va.* 1. Hacer caer en el lazo, en la trampa o en el garlito; armar lazos o asechanzas. 2. Enjaezar, adornar.

Trap-door [trap'-dōr], *s.* Una especie de puerta disimulada que se abre por medio de algunos resortes ocultos. *Trap-door spider*, Araña de gran tamaño que habita en hoyos cilíndricos hechos en la tierra y protegidos por una puertecilla con gozne, de una substancia sedosa. Cteniza Californica.

Trape, *vn.* (Fam. o des.) *V.* TRAPES

Trapes, **Traipse** [trêps], *vn.* Mangonear; andar vagando o tunando.

Trapes [trêps], *s.* (Vulg.) Mujer ociosa y desaliñada.

Trapeze [tra-pīz'], *s.* Trapecio, palo corto suspendido por sus extremos con cuerdas y que sirve para hacer ejercicios gimnásticos.

Trapezium [tra-pī'-zi-um], *s.* 1. (Geom.) Trapezoide, cuadrilátero irregular que no tiene ningún lado paralelo a otro. 2. (Anat.) Trapecio, hueso radial del carpo.

Trapezoid [trap-ẹ-zoid'], *s.* (Geom.) Trapecio, cuadrilátero irregular que tiene paralelos solamente dos de sus lados.

Trapezoidal [trap-e-zoid'-al], *a.* Trapezoidal, de figura de trapecio.

Trapper [trap'-ẹr], *s.* El que pone trampas o lazos para coger animales de piel vendible.

Trappings [trap'-ingz], *s. pl.* Jaeces; adornos, galas.

Trapshooting [trap'-shūt'-ing], *s.* Tiro de pichón, tiro al vuelo.

Trapstick [trap'-stic], *s.* Pala o palo corvo.

Trash [trash], *s.* 1. Heces, porquería, desecho, zupia o cualquiera otra cosa de ninguna entidad ni valor. 2. Una persona vil o indigna. 3. La tierra, greda o cualquiera otra cosa del mismo género que comen las jóvenes que están opiladas.

Trash, *va.* Podar; deshojar, quitar las hojas.

Trashy [trash'-i], *a.* Vil, despreciable, inútil, de ningún valor.

Trauma [trē'-ma o trau'-ma], *s.* Cualquier lesión del cuerpo causada por violencia; herida. (Gr.)

Traumatic [trē-mat'-ic], *a.* Traumático, relativo a las heridas o al traumatismo. *Traumatics, s.* Los medicamentos vulnerarios.

Travail [trav'-ẹl], *vn.* 1. Trabajar, afanarse, hacer esfuerzos. 2. Estar de parto, padecer los dolores de parto.—*va.* (Des.) Cansar, fatigar, atoratormentar, mortificar, aquejar.

Travail, *s.* 1. Afán, fatiga, trabajo. 2. Dolores de parto.

Travel [trav'-el], *va.* y *vn.* 1. Viajar, hacer viajes, andar viajando; caminar; particularmente, visitar países extranjeros. 2. Volar o pasar con celeridad el tiempo, las noticias, etc. 3. Trabajar, afanarse.

Travel, *s.* 1. Viaje, la jornada o camino que se hace de una parte a otra. 2. Afán, fatiga. 3. (Mec.) Movimiento de un mecanismo; carrera del émbolo o pistón. 4. *pl. Travels,* Viajes, relación de las cosas que algún viajero ha observado en sus viajes. *Travel-stained, travel-soiled,* Manchado por el polvo del camino. *Travel-worn,* Fatigado por el viaje.

Traveler, Traveller [trav'-el-ẹr], *s.* 1. Viajante, viajero. 2. (Mar.) Arraca de las vergas de juanete.

Traveler's check [trav'-el-ẹrz chek], *s.* Cheque de viajeros.

Traveling [trav'-el-ing], *a.* Viajero. *Traveling companion,* Compañero de viaje. *Traveling salesman,* Agente viajero.

Travelogue [trav'-el-og], *s.* Conferencia sobre un viaje, generalmente con ilustraciones.

Traversable [trav'-ẹrs-a-bl], *a.* Atravesable, que se puede atravesar; negable, contestable.

Traverse [trav'-ẹrs], *a.* Travieso, que está atravesado o puesto al través. *Traverse-course,* (Mar.) Rumbo compuesto. *Traverse-board,* Tabla que lleva dibujada la rosa marina de los vientos; de uso antiguo. *Traverse-table,* Libro del diario; tabla de las diferencias de latitud, etc.—*s.* 1. Cualquier cosa que está colocada de modo que cruza a otra; travesaño; travesero; cerco travesero. 2. (Fort.) Través, trinchera con parapeto pequeño. 3. (Geom.) Línea transversal. 4. El acto de recorrer o viajar; viaje, pasaje. 5. Negación, acto de negar; objeción legal. 6. (Mar.) Bordada en dirección oblicua. 7. En agrimensura, línea corta que parte de una línea principal y sirve para determinar la posición de un punto lateral. *Traverses of fortune,* Reveses de fortuna. *Traverse-jury, V. Petit-jury.*

Traverse, *va.* 1. Atravesar, cruzar. 2. Recorrer o atravesar todo un espacio determinado. 3. Examinar o escudriñar con cuidado. 4. (For.) Negar, oponerse o hacer oposición á alguna sentencia o resolución judicial por los medios legales. 5. Estorbar, impedir, contrariar, poner obstáculos o impedimentos.—*vn.* 1. Atravesarse, hacer vaivén, moverse de un lado a otro. 2. Dar vueltas, girar como sobre un eje.

Travesty, *va.* Disfrazar; trovar, imitar burlescamente, presentar o tomar las cosas bajo una forma ridícula.—*s.* Imitación grotesca o burlesca; el acto de disfrazar; tratamiento burlesco de un tema elevado o noble.

Trawl [trōl], *va.* Arrastrar el albareque. *V.* TROLL.—*vn.* Pescar con albareque.—*s. V. Trawl-line* y *Trawl-net. Trawl-line,* Cuerda gruesa y muy larga, provista de boyas y de la cual cuelgan a cortos trechos sedales con anzuelos cebados: se usa en la pesca del bacalao. *Trawl-net,* Red de gran tamaño en forma de saco, remolcada por un bote.

Tray [trê], *s.* 1. Bandeja, salvilla; (Amer.) azafate (de plata, metal o charol). 2. Encaje, cajoncito; caja ligera, poco profunda y sin tapa, que se usa en los baúles, en las colecciones científicas, etc. (< A.-S. *treg.*) *Tea-tray,* Bandeja, batea. *Chopping-tray,* Artesilla de cocina.

Treacherous [trech'-ẹr-us], *a.* Aleve, pérfido, falso, engañador; indigno de confianza. *Treacherous memory,* Memoria infiel o que olvida fácilmente las cosas. *A treacherous smile,* Risa falsa o risa de traidor.

Treacherously [trech'-ẹr-us-li], *adv.* Traidoramente, a traición, pérfidamente.

Treacherousness [trech'-ẹr-us-nes], *s.* La calidad de traidor, pérfido o falso.

Treachery [trech'-ẹr-i], *s.* Perfidia, deslealtad, traición, falsedad.

Treacle [trî'-cl], *s.* 1. Melote, miel de cañas, miel de prima, jarabe de azúcar. 2. Triaca, composición de varios medicamentos simples.

Tread [tred], *va.* y *vn.* (*pret.* TROD, *pp.* TRODDEN). 1. Pisar, hollar, poner el pie sobre alguna cosa. 2. Andar por encima de alguna cosa; sentir algo bajo los pies; apretar con el pie. 3. Pisotear. 4. Patalear, dar patadas en el suelo violentamente. 5. Hollar, ajar, abatir, pisar o despreciar. 6. Caminar con majestad o dándose importancia. 7. Pisar, (en las aves); gallear, cubrir el gallo a las gallinas. *To tread inward* o *outward,* Andar metiendo los pies hacia dentro o volviéndolos hacia fuera. *To tread back,* Desandar, volver atrás. *To tread in the footsteps of one,* Seguir las pisadas de alguno o imitarle. *Trodden path,* Camino trillado.

Tread, *s.* 1. Pisa, la acción de pisar. 2. Pisada, la huella o señal que deja estampada el pie en la tierra. 3. Pisada o pisadura, la parte sobre la cual se apoya algo al moverse o que sirve para pisar; escalón de escalera; cara de rueda, de corredera o de riel; centro del torno. 4. Galladura.

Treader [tred'-ẹr], *s.* Pisador.

Treadle [tred'-l], *s.* 1. Cárcola, el listón de madera o metal en que ponen el pie los torneros y tejedores. 2. Galladura (del huevo), chalaza.

Treadmill [tred'-mil], *s.* 1. Molino de rueda de escalones, mecanismo que servía antiguamente como medio de castigo. 2. (Fig.) Uniformidad fatigosa del trabajo o esfuerzo.

Treason [trî'-zn], *s.* 1. Traición, falta de lealtad debida al Estado 2. Perfidia, falsedad. *High treason,* Alta traición o delito de lesa majestad. *Petit* o *petty treason,* Llamábase en Inglaterra traición pequeña o baja al delito de asesinato cuando un criado mataba a su amo, una mujer a su marido o un fiel a su prelado.

Treasonable [trî'-zn-a-bl], *a.* Pérfido, desleal, traidor, de traición.

Treasonableness [trî'-zn-a-bl-nes], *s.* El estado o la calidad que constituye a uno traidor; traición.

Treasure [trezh'-ur], *s.* Tesoro, abundancia de caudal y dinero guardado y conservado; riquezas acumuladas; lo que es precioso o muy estimado. *Treasure-house,* Tesorería. *Treasure-trove,* Tesoro hallado, tesoro de oro, plata, etc., que alguien halla y no tiene dueño conocido.

Treasure, *va.* Atesorar, recoger tesoros y riquezas; guardar con cuidado.

Treasurer [trezh'-ur-ẹr], *s.* Tesorero. *Treasurer of the navy,* Tesorero general de marina.

Treasury [trezh'-ur-i], *s.* Tesorería, la oficina o despacho del tesorero. *King's treasury,* El real erario, la tesorería general.

Treat [trît], *va.* 1. Tratar, portarse (de cierta manera) para con alguno. 2. Tratar, manejar una cosa materialmente, aplicar un procedimiento particular a una cosa. 3. Tratar, escribir, discurrir o disputar sobre alguna materia; expresar por medio del arte. 4. Agasajar, regalar, pagar el coste de alguna comida o más particularmente de alguna bebida; pagar una convidada. —*vn.* 1. Tratar de, tratar, negociar, ajustar, conferir y hablar sobre algún negocio para conformar y avenir a los interesados en él. 2. Negociar, arreglar un tratado. 3. (Fam.) Regalar, pagar el coste de la comida o bebida de otro.

Treat, *s.* 1. Trato, convite, banquete, festín. 2. Complacencia, regalo, gran placer. *A high treat,* Un gusto grande, un gran placer. *To stand treat,* (Fam.) Convidar a alguno, esto es, hacer o pagar el gasto; obsequiar.

Treatise [trî'-tis], *s.* Tratado; escrito, discurso que comprende las especies concernientes a una materia particular.

Treatment [trît'-mẹnt], *s.* 1. Trato, modo de tratar o tratarse. 2. Tratamiento, modo de tratar una persona o cosa; método que se emplea para la curación de una enfermedad; procedimiento metalúrgico.

Treaty [trî'-ti], *s.* 1. Tratado, ajuste, convenio concluido entre dos o más gobiernos. 2. Negociación para llegar a un acuerdo.

Treble [treb'-l], *a.* 1. Tríplice, triplo, triple. 2. (Mús.) Atiplado, tiplisonante. *A treble block,* (Mar.) Cuadernal de tres ojos.

Treble, *va.* Triplicar, multiplicar por tres.—*vn.* Triplicarse, multiplicarse tres veces.

Treble, *s.* (Mús.) Tiple, la voz más alta en la consonancia música.

Trebly [treb'-li], *adv.* Triplicadamente, tres veces tanto.

Tree [trī], *s.* 1. Árbol, el mayor de los vegetales; vegetal leñoso cuya altura no baja de 20 pies. 2. Dibujo, cuadro en forma de árbol. 3. Madero, trozo pesado de madera. 4. Horca; cruz. *Tree of life* o *lignum vitæ,* Árbol de la vida, guayaco, palo santo. *Fruit-tree,* Árbol frutal. *Genealogical tree,* Árbol genealógico. *Tree-fern,* Helecho arborescente, helecho de árbol. *Tree-frog, tree-toad,* Rana arbórea del género Hyla o de otro afín. *Tree mallow,* Lavatera de árbol, planta malvácea. *Tree of heaven,* Árbol del cielo, ailanto, árbol originario de las Molucas. *Tyburn tree,* La horca. *Up a tree,* (Fam.) (1) Puesto entre la espada y la pared; (2) desinteresado, neutral.

Treenail [trī'-nêl, fam. trun'-el], *s.* (Mar.) Cabilla, clavija de palo larga y redonda que se usa en la construcción de los buques.

Trefoil [trī'-feil], *s.* 1. Trébol. *V.* CLOVER. 2. Adorno en forma de hoja de trébol. *Marsh trefoil,* Trébol palustre. *Shrub trefoil,* Citiso, ervellada, corona de rey.

Trek [trek], *vn.* (*pret.* y *pp.* TREKKED). (África del sur) 1. Viajar de un lugar a otro en carromatos. 2. Emigrar. 3. Tirar de una carga.

Trellis [trel'-is], *s.* Enrejado; espalera o espaldar de los jardines.

Tremble [trem'-bl], *vn.* 1. Temblar, tembloquear o tembletear. 2. Temblar, tener mucho miedo, estremecerse. 3. Tiritar de frío. 4. Temblar, amenazar ruina. 5. Trinar, hacer trinos con la voz o con un instrumento.

Trembling [trem'-bling], *s.* Temor. —*a.* Que tiembla, temblante, tembloso, trémulo. *Trembling poplar, trembling-tree,* Temblón, álamo temblón, particularmente el americano.

Tremblingly [trem'-bling-li], *adv.* Trémulamente, con temblor o temblando.

Tremendous [trẹ-men'-dus], *a.* Tremendo, formidable, digno de ser temido; que causa pasmo por su magnitud, fuerza o consecuencias.

Tremendously [trẹ-men' dus-li], *adv.* De un modo tremendo.

Tremendousness [trẹ-men'-dus-nes], *s.* Terribilidad; susto; espanto, miedo.

Tremor [trem'-ẹr], *s.* Tremor, temblor; vibración.

Tremulous [trem'-yu-lus], *a.* Trémulo, tremulento, que tiembla.

Tremulously [trem'-yu-lus-li], *adv.* Trémulamente.

Tremulousness [trem'-yu-lus-nes], *s.* Temblor, calidad de trémulo.

Trench [trench], *va.* y *vn.* 1. Surcar, hacer surcos; hacer zanjas, fosos o cauces. 2. Atrincherar, cerrar o ceñir con trincheras: en este sentido lleva tras sí por lo común la preposición *about.* 3. Usurpar o apropiarse lo ajeno. *V.* ENCROACH. *To trench upon the liberty of the citizens,* Atacar la libertad de los ciudadanos. *To trench the ballast,* (Mar.) Separar el lastre con mamparos.

Trench, *s.* 1. Foso, zanja, caz, cauce. 2. (Mil.) Trinchera.

Trenchant [trench'-ant], *a.* 1. Afilado, cortante. 2. Desabrido, mordaz, picante como la sátira.

Trench coat [trench cōt], *s.* Trinchera, abrigo impermeable.

Trencher [trench'-ẹr], *s.* 1. Trinchero, un plato de madera para trinchar; bandeja. 2. Las viandas, la comida; los placeres de la mesa; de aquí, la mesa. ‡*Trencher-friend, trencher-fly*(†), Parásito, gorrón, gorrista, pegote. *Trencherman,* Comedor; compañero de mesa. *Trenchermate,* Compañero de mesa.

Trench fever [trench fīv'-ẹr], *s.* Tipo de fiebre que les da a los soldados en las trincheras.

Trench mouth [trench mauth], *s.* Inflamación en las encías, especie de piorrea.

Trend [trend], *vn.* Tomar rumbo o dirección, dirigirse, tender, inclinarse.—*s.* Dirección o rumbo en general; inclinación hacia un punto particular, tendencia.

Trendle [tren'-dl], *s.* (Prov. o des.) *V.* TRUNDLE.

Trental [tren'-tal], *s.* Treintenario de misas.

Trepan, *va.* 1. (Cir.) Trepanar, hacer la operación del trépano. 2. (Esco.) Coger en el garlito.

Trepanner [trẹ-pan'-ẹr], *s.* 1. El cirujano que hace la operación del trépano. 2. Engañador.

Trephine [tre-fain' o tref'-in], *va.* Trepanar.—*s.* Trefino, especie de trépano pequeño.

‡**Trepid** [trep'-id], *a.* Trépido, trémulo; opuesto a *intrepid.*

Trepidation [trep-i-dé'-shun], ‡**Trepidity** [tre-pid'-i-ti], *s.* Trepidación, miedo, terror.

Trespass [tres'-pas], *va.* 1. Quebrantar, traspasar o violar alguna ley, precepto o estatuto, antiguamente transgredir; pecar, faltar. 2. Infringir, violar, ofender; se usa con *against.* *To trespass on one's patience,* Abusar de la paciencia de alguno. 3. Ocupar ilegítimamente la propiedad de otro.

Trespass, *s.* 1. Transgresión, traspaso, el quebrantamiento o violación de alguna ley, precepto, etc.; ofensa, culpa, pecado. 2. Ocupación ilegítima e injusta de la propiedad ajena.

Trespasser [tres'-pas-ẹr], *s.* Transgresor, violador de una ley; pecador.

Tress [tres], *s.* Trenza; rizo de cabellos; en plural, cabellos abundantes.

Tressed [trest], *a.* Trenzado.

Trestle [tres'-l], *s.* 1. Caballete, madero que descansa sobre cuatro pies divergentes; caballete de aserrador. 2. Obra de celosía y caballete para sostener los durmientes de un puente de ferrocarril, etc. *Trestle-trees, pl.* (Mar.) Baos de los palos. *Cross and trestle-trees,* (Mar.) Baos y crucetas. *Trestle-work,* Obra (puente) de caballete.

Trevet [trev'-et], *s.* *V.* TRIVET.

Trevis [trev'-is], *s.* (Esco.) 1. Viga o barra; travesaño. 2. Tabique entre dos compartimientos de un establo.

Trey [trê], *s.* Naipe o dado señalado con tres puntos; el tres.

Tri- [trai]. Prefijo que significa tres, tres veces.

Triable [trai'-a-bl], *a.* 1. Que se puede experimentar. 2. Averiguable en juicio.

Triad [trai'-ad], *s.* Triada, reunión de tres personas ó cosas.—*a.* (Quím.) Que vale tres en combinación.

Trial [trai'-al], *s.* 1. Esfuerzo, ensayo, probadura, tentativa. 2. Conocimiento adquirido por experiencia; prueba; desgracia, aflicción. 3. Ensayo, muestra o experiencia. 4. Juicio. (For.) El día de la vista de una causa o proceso; el examen judicial de una causa criminal para pronunciar sentencia. *To bring a prisoner to trial,* Poner en juicio o en tela de juicio a una persona acusada de algún delito. *Trial by jury,* Juicio por jurado. *The trial lasted six weeks,* El pleito (o el proceso) duró seis semanas. *On trial,* A prueba. *Trial trip,* Viaje de prueba.

Trial and error [trai'-al and er'-ẹr], *s.* Procedimiento experimental.

Trial order [trai'-al er'-dẹr], *s.* Pedido de prueba.

Trial run [trai'-al run], *s.* Representación teatral por cierto tiempo a manera de prueba.

Triangle [trai'-aṇ-gl], *s.* 1. Triángulo. 2. (Mús.) Triángulo, instrumento de percusión que consiste en una varilla de metal plegada en forma de triángulo, la cual se hace sonar golpeándola con otra varilla metálica. *Isosceles triangle,* Triángulo isósceles. *Spherical triangle,* Triángulo esférico.

Triangular [trai-aṇ'-giu-lar], *a.* Triangular.

Triangulate [trai-aṇ'-giu-lêt], *va.* Dividir o disponer en triángulos; en particular, ligar por medio de triángulos los puntos notables de una comarca para levantar su plano.

Triassic [trai-as'-ic], *a.* y *s.* (Geol.) Triásico, la división más baja de la época mesozoica.

Tribal [trai'-bal], *a.* De una tribu, perteneciente a una tribu.

Tribe [traib], *s.* 1. Tribu, una de las partes en que se dividía el pueblo entre los antiguos. 2. Raza, casta. 3. (Biol.) Grupo de plantas o de animales de un orden o grado no determinado.

Triblet [trib'-let], *s.* Un instrumento que usan los plateros para hacer anillos.

Tribulation [trib-yu-lé'-shun], *s.* Tribulación, congoja, pena, aflicción.

Tribunal [trai-biū'-nal], *s.* Tribunal, el lugar destinado para la administración de justicia; juzgado.

Tribune [trib'-yūn], *s.* 1. Tribuno, magistrado civil y también un jefe militar entre los romanos; cualquier campeón de la plebe. 2. Tribuna, lugar elevado desde donde se dirige la palabra a una asamblea.

Tribuneship [trib'-yūn-ship], *s.* Tribunado, la dignidad del tribuno civil.

Tributary [trib'-yu-tẹ-ri], *a.* 1. Tributario, que está obligado a pagar tributo en reconocimiento de dominio u obsequio. 2. Sujeto, subordinado.—*s.* Tributario.

Tribute [trib'-yut], *s.* Tributo. *To pay the tribute of nature,* Morir, pagar tributo a la muerte.

Trice [trais], *s.* Momento, instante, tris; se usa sólo en la locución *in a trice,* en un abrir y cerrar de ojos.

Trice, *va.* (Mar.) Izar, hacer subir por medio de una jarcia; también, amarrar, ligar.

Tricennial [trai-sen'-i-al], *a.* Tricenal, de treinta años.
Triceps [trai'-seps], *s.* Tríceps, músculo que tiene tres cabezas.
Trichina [tri-cai'-na], *s.* Triquina, helminto pequeño que vive en lo interior de los músculos de los animales vertebrados y se transmite de unos a otros por la vía digestiva.
Trichinosis [trik-i-nō'-sis], *s.* Triquinosis, enfermedad ocasionada por la presencia de triquinas en el cuerpo.
Trichotomy [trai-cot'-o-mi], *s.* La división en tres partes.
Trick [tric], *s.* 1. Treta fraudulenta, engaño, fraude, superchería, embuste, artería, astucia, socaliña. *A knavish trick,* Acción ruin. *He played me a trick,* Me jugó una pieza. *To play tricks,* Hacer suertes. (Fam.) Hacer travesuras. 2. Chasco, burla; travesura, parchazo. 3. Costumbre, hábito adquirido, maña. 4. Baza, en el juego de naipes.
Trick, *va.* 1. Engañar, defraudar, jugar una pieza, pegar un parchazo. 2. Ataviar, componer, asear; por lo común, con *out.*—*vn.* Trampear, vivir de trampas.
Tricking [trik'-ing], *s.* Atavío, adorno.
Trickish [trik'-ish], *a.* Astuto, artificioso, aleve, mañoso, embustero, trapacero.
Trickle [tric'-l], *vn.* Gotear, correr a gotas, caer gota á gota; escurrir.
Trickster [tric'-stęr], *s.* Engañador, embaucador; maula, gato.
Tricksy [tric'-si], *a.* 1. Juguetón, retozón, travieso. 2. Artificioso, aleve, embustero.
Tricky [trik'-i], *a.* 1. Falso, artificioso, trapacero. 2. Vicioso (el animal).
Tricolor, Tricolour [trai'-cul-er], *a.* Tricolor, de tres colores.—*s.* Bandera nacional de los franceses.
Tricorporal [trai-cōr'-po-ral], *a.* Que tiene tres cuerpos.
Tricuspid [trai-cus'-pid], *a.* Tricúspide, que tiene tres puntas o tres eminencias.
Tricycle [trai'-si-cl], *s.* Triciclo, velocípedo de tres ruedas.
Tride [traid], *a.* Trido, menudo y vivo: dícese del paso del caballo.
Trident [trai'-dent], *s.* Tridente, el cetro de tres puntas de Neptuno.
Tridentiferous [trai-den-tif'-ęr-us], *a.* Tridentífero, que lleva tridente.
Triduan [trid'-yu-an], *a.* Triduano, de tres días.
Triennial [trai-en'-i-al], *a.* Trienal, que dura tres años o sucede cada tercer año.
Trier [trai'-ęr], *s.* 1. Experimentador, ensayador. 2. Juez, censor, examinador. 3. Toque, ensayo, prueba.
Trifallow [trai'-fal-o], *va.* Terciar, dar la tercera reja a las tierras antes de sembrarlas.
Trifid [trai'-fid], *a.* Trífido, hendido o abierto por tres partes.
Trifle [trai'-fl], *s.* 1. Bagatela, paparrucha, fruslería, friolera, cualquier cosa de poca substancia y valor; nada, poca cosa. 2. Crema aromatizada, confección ligera. *To stop at trifles,* Reparar en pelillos.
Trifle, *va.* Emplear en bagatelas, malgastar (el tiempo).—*vn.* 1. Obrar ligeramente, no hacer caso de una cosa; ser ligero, hablar con ligereza. 2. Chancear, juguetear, emplear o gastar el tiempo en cosas vanas e inútiles; se usa por lo general con *with.* 3. Manosear, palpar, juguetear, jugar con algo ligeramente y sin objeto, v. gr. un abanico; se usa con *with.* *V.* DALLY y TOY. *To trifle with one,* Burlarse de uno; gastar chanzas con una persona; entretener á alguno, jugar con él. *To trifle away time,* Malgastar el tiempo o emplearlo en bagatelas.
Trifler [trai'-flęr], *s.* Persona frívola, casquivana.
Trifling [trai'-fling], *a.* Frívolo, vano, inútil; inconsiderable, de ninguna consecuencia. *Trifling story,* Un cuento insípido o que hace dormir.
Triflingly [trai'-fling-li], *adv.* Frívolamente, inútilmente, sin consecuencia.
Triflingness [trai'-fling-nes], *s.* Frivolidad, ligereza; insignificancia, poca importancia.
Trifoliate, Trifoliated [trai-fō'-li-êt-ed], *a.* Trifoliáceo, que tiene tres hojas.
Trifoliolate [trai-fō'-li-o-lêt], *a.* Trifoliado, de tres hojuelas.
Triform [trai'-fōrm], *a.* Triforme.
Trifurcate, Trifurcated [trai-fūr'-kêted], *a.* Trifurcado, que tiene tres ramales; tricótomo.
Trig [trig], *va.* Atar o trabar las ruedas de un carruaje, impedir que una rueda dé vueltas.—*s.* Calzo de rueda o de barril; galga.
Trig, *a.* 1. Bien puesto, bien acicalado. 2. Sano, en buen estado, firme. (<Islandés *tryggr,* verdadero.)
Trigamy [trig'-a-mi], *s.* El estado del que ha sido tres veces casado o del que ha contraído terceras nupcias; el estado del que se halla casado con tres mujeres a un tiempo.
Trigger [trig'-ęr], *s.* 1. Gatillo, disparador (de un arma de fuego). 2. Pararruedas, calzo que detiene una rueda al bajar por algún terreno pendiente.
Triglyph [trai'-glif], *s.* (Arq.) Triglifo, un miembro del friso dórico.
Trigon [trai'-gon], *s.* 1. Triángulo, trígono. 2. Trígono. *V.* TRINE.
Trigonal [trig'-o-nal], *a.* Triangular; de tres ángulos.
Trigonometric, Trigonometrical [trig-o-no-met'-ric, al], *a.* Trigonométrico.
Trigonometry [trig-o-nom'-e-tri], *s.* Trigonometría, el arte que enseña la resolución analítica de los triángulos, tanto planos como esféricos.
Trilateral [trai-lat'-ęr-al], *a.* Trilátero, trilateral.
Trilateralness [trai-lat'-ęr-al-nes], *s.* La calidad de lo que es trilátero.
Trilingual [trai-lin'-gwal], *a.* Trilingüe, que está en tres lenguas, o que las emplea.
Triliteral [trai-lit'-ęr-al], *a.* Trilítero, de tres letras. *Triliteral languages,* Idiomas trilíteros, la familia semítica de lenguas.
Trill [tril], *s.* Trino, trinado, quiebro de la voz.
Trill, *va.* Trinar, hacer trinos, quiebros o trinados.—*vn.* Gotear, correr gota a gota.
Trillion [tril'-yun], *s.* Trillón, un millón de millones según la numeración francesa y americana; según la inglesa, la tercera potencia de un millón.
Trillium [tril'-i-um], *s.* (Bot.) Trilio.
Trilobate [trai-lō'-bêt], *a.* Trilobado, que tiene tres lóbulos.
Trilobite [trai'-lo-bait o tril'-o-bait], *s.* Trilobites, especie de artrópodo fósil.
Trilogy [tril'-o-ji], *s.* Trilogía, conjunto de tres obras dramáticas que continúan el mismo tema general.
Trim [trim], *a.* Bien puesto, en buen estado, ajustado con precisión; bien cuidado; ataviado, acicalado.
Trim, *va.* 1. Dar forma a, restablecer la figura, ajustar, adaptar; en carpintería, alisar, desbastar. 2. Desbastar, poner en orden quitando cantos y esquinas; podar, mondar (plantas); cortar (los cabellos, la barba). 3. Despabilar una lámpara o vela; por extensión, quitar los carbonos de una lámpara eléctrica de arco y reemplazarlos con otros nuevos. 4. Componer, adornar; guarnecer (un vestido), franjear, orillar. 5. Balancear, igualar o equilibrar los pesos de dos cosas.—*vn.* 1. Vacilar, titubear entre dos partidos; nadar entre dos aguas. 2. Estar o mantenerse en equilibrio (una embarcación). *To trim off,* Afeitar, recortar e igualar los bojes, espalderas u otras plantas. *To trim up,* Adornar, hermosear, componer. *To trim a discourse,* Pulir un discurso. *To trim a lamp* o *a light,* Despabilar una lámpara o vela. *To trim a ship,* (Mar.) Orientar un buque. *To trim the sails,* Orientar las velas. *To trim the hold,* Abarrotar.
Trim, *s.* 1. Atavío, adorno, aderezo. *She was in her nicest trim,* Estaba de veinte y cinco alfileres o estaba muy compuesta. 2. Traje, vestido; estilo (adorno o aspecto). 3. La disposición en que se arreglan las diversas partes de un buque para que navegue bien; también, el grado comparativo de inmersión de la proa y popa. *Trim of the hold,* Disposición de la estiva. *Trim of the sails,* Disposición de las velas. *Out of sailing trim,* Mal dispuesto para navegar, pesado.
Trimeter [trim'-e-tęr], *s.* Trímetro (verso), que consta de tres medidas o seis pies.
Trimly [trim'-li], *adv.* Primorosamente, con buen arreglo, bien.
Trimmed [trimd], *a.* Ataviado, adornado. *Sharp trimmed,* (Mar.) A la trinca.
Trimmer [trim'-ęr], *s.* 1. El que ajusta, desbasta, poda, etc. 2. Veleta, hombre de todos partidos. 3. Herramienta o máquina para igualar y desbastar.
Trimming [trim'-ing], *s.* 1. Guarnición de vestido, franja, orla. 2. Desbaste; ajuste; arreglo; poda. 3. *pl.* Accesorios, pertenencias, como los enmaderamientos de adorno o la ferretería de una casa. *He will give him a good trimming,* (Fam.) Él le ajustará la golilla, él le dará una buena felpa.
Trinal [trai'-nal], *a.* Triple, compuesto de tres o que consta de tres.
Trine [train], *s.* (Astr.) El aspecto trino de los planetas, cuando distan entre sí ciento veinte grados.
Trinitarian [trin-i-tę'-ri-an], *s.* y *a.* Trinitario.
Trinitrotoluene [trai-nai-trō-tōl-iū'-in], *s.* (Quím.) Trinitrotolueno, explosivo muy potente. Úsase más en la forma abreviada de TNT.
Trinity [trin'-i-ti], *s.* 1. Trinidad, la unión de tres personas en un solo Dios. 2. *V.* TRIAD y TRIO. *Trin-*

ity House, La casa del gremio de marineros y pilotos en Inglaterra.
Trinket [trin'-ket], *s.* Joya, dije, adorno pequeño, bujería, chuchería, cosa de poco valor para componerse.
Trinomial [trai-nō'-mi-al], *a.* 1. (Biol.) Que tiene tres nombres ó términos, el genérico, el específico y el subespecífico. 2. (Álg.) Que consta de tres términos.—*s.* Trinomio, cantidad algebraica compuesta de tres términos.
Trio [trī'-o ó trai'-o], *s.* 1. Triada, reunión de tres. 2. (Mús.) Trío, composición para tres voces o para tres instrumentos.
Trip [trip], *va.* 1. Hacer caer a uno echándole la zancadilla. 2. Armar un lazo o zancadilla, usar de alguna treta o artificio. 3. Coger a uno en falta o cogerle un renuncio. 4. Bailar ligera o ágilmente; mover los pies ligeramente y con ritmo. 5. (Mec.) Soltar, disparar; desatar. 6. Zarpar, levar anclas.—*vn.* 1. Tropezar, trompicar, resbalar, deslizarse los pies. 2. Deslizarse, decir o hacer una cosa con descuido e indeliberadamente, equivocarse, engañarse, tener un desliz o un descuido. 3. (Mar.) Zarpar. 4. Correr, andar con pasos ligeros, andar muy aprisa. 5. Dar una vuelta; hacer un viaje corto. *To trip the anchor*, (Mar.) Hacer que el ancla largue el fondo; levar el ancla. *Trip-hammer*, Martinete de fragua. *V. Tilt-hammer.*
Trip, *s.* 1. Vuelta, un viaje corto, excursión. 2. Resbalón, el acto de resbalar; caída, desliz, paso falso. 3. Paso o movimiento ágil. 4. (Mar.) Bordada de una embarcación que barloventea. 5. Zancadilla, la acción de atravesar o echar el luchador el pie por detrás del de su contrario para derribarlo.
Tripartite [trip'-ar-tait o trai-pārt'-ait], *a.* Tripartido, tripartito.
Tripe [traip], *s.* Tripas, cuajar, estómago de un animal rumiante preparado como alimento. *Tripe-woman*, Tripicallera, la mujer que vende tripas y callos.
Tripedal [trip'-e-dal], *a.* Lo que tiene tres pies.
Tripetalous [trai-pet'-a-lus], *a.* (Bot.) Tripétalo, que tiene tres pétalos.
Triphthong [trif'-thong], *s.* (Gram.) Triptongo, tres vocales combinadas en una sola emisión de la voz.
Triple [trip'-l], *a.* Tríplice, triplo.—*va.* Triplicar. *Triple-expansion*, De triple expansión, con tres cilindros de tamaños graduados en los que el vapor se dilata sucesivamente, v. gr. en una máquina de vapor para buques.
Triplet [trip'-let], *s.* 1. Terno, número de tres de una misma especie. 2. Cada uno de tres hermanos nacidos de un parto. 3. Tercerilla, una composición poética.
Triplex [trai'-plex], *a.* Tríplice, de tres partes.
Triplicate [trip'-li-kēt], *a.* Triplicado, triplo, tres tanto, tres veces más.—*s.* Triplicado, tercera copia de algo.
Triplication [trip-li-kē'-shun], *s.* La acción de triplicar.
Triplicity [trai-plis'-i-ti], *s.* Triplicidad.
Triply [trip'-li], *adv.* Triplemente, de una manera triple, por triplicado.
Tripmadam [trip'-mad-am], *s.* (Bot.) Hierba puntera.
Tripod [trai'-pod], *s.* El o la trípode; aparato de tres pies para sostener instrumentos geodésicos, fotográficos, etc.
Tripoli [trip'-o-li], *s.* Trípoli, un género de greda silícea con que se pule y da lustre a los cristales, metales, etc. *V. Rotten-stone.*
Tripper [trip'-er], *s.* Andarín ágil, el que se mueve con ligereza; el que da una zancadilla; el o lo que suelta, disparador.
Tripping [trip'-ing], *a.* Veloz, ligero, ágil.—*s.* 1. Baile ligero y a saltos. 2. Tropiezo, tropezón, traspié, paso falso.
Trippingly [trip'-ing-li], *adv.* Velozmente, con agilidad y ligereza.
Triptote [trip'-tōt], *s.* Triptoto, nombre que tiene solamente tres terminaciones.
Trireme [trai'-rīm], *s.* (Ant.) Trirreme, galera de tres órdenes de bancos de remeros por banda.
Trisagion [tris-ē'-gi-on], *s.* Trisagio, himno en honor de la Santísima Trinidad.
Trisect [trai-sect'], *va.* Trisecar, tripartir, dividir en tres partes.
Trisection [trai-sec'-shun], *s.* Trisección, la acción de trisecar o dividir una cosa en tres partes.
Tristful [trist'-ful], *a.* (Ant.) Triste, melancólico.
Trisyllabic, Trisyllabical [trai-si-lab'ic, al], *a.* Trisílabo: dícese de la dicción o palabra de tres sílabas.
Trisyllable [trai-sil'-a-bl o tris-sil'-a-bl], *s.* Palabra o dicción trisílaba, la que consta de tres sílabas.
Trite [trait], *a.* Usado, repetido, envejecido, trillado; trivial, vulgar.
Tritely [trait'-li], *adv.* Vulgarmente.
Triteness [trait'-nes], *s.* Vulgaridad, trivialidad, cosa muy usada o muy común.
Tritheism [trai'-the-izm], *s.* Triteísmo, una herejía.
Triton [trai'-ton], *s.* 1. Tritón, deidad marina. 2. Gasterópodo del género Tritón. 3. Salamandra pequeña, batracio acuático.
Tritone [trai'-tōn], *s.* (Mús.) Trítono, intervalo de tres tonos.
Triturable [trit'-yu-ra-bl], *a.* Triturable, que se puede triturar.
Triturate [trit'-yu-rēt], *va.* Triturar, reducir a polvo.
Trituration [trit-yu-rē'-shun], *s.* Trituración, la acción de triturar.
Triumph [trai'-umf], *s.* 1. Triunfo, vencimiento, victoria. 2. Triunfo, la solemnidad y aplauso con que se celebra una victoria; la entrada solemne y pomposa en Roma con que se honraba en la antigüedad a los generales vencedores. 3. Alegría grande; brillo semejante a una pompa triunfal.
Triumph, *vn.* 1. Triunfar, entrar en triunfo. 2. Triunfar, vencer en la guerra o en una disputa. 3. Gloriarse de haber vencido; hacer alarde de alguna ventaja o vencimiento.
Triumphal [trai-um'-fal], *a.* Triunfal.—*s.* Triunfo.
Triumphant [trai-um'-fant], *a.* 1. Triunfante, victorioso. 2. Triunfante, glorioso, exaltado.
Triumphantly [trai-um'-fant-li], *adv.* Triunfantemente, en triunfo, victoriosamente; con alegría insolente.
Triumpher [trai'-umf-er], *s.* Triunfador.
Triumvir [trai-um'-vir], *s.* Triunviro, uno de los tres magistrados romanos que formaban el triunvirato.
Triumvirate [trai-um'-vi-rēt], *s.* Triunvirato.
Trivet [triv'-et], *s.* Trébedes (de cocina), trípode.
Trivia [triv'-i-a], *s. pl.* Trivialidades.
Trivial [triv'-i-al], *a.* Trivial, vulgar, ordinario, bajo; frívolo.
Trivially [triv'-i-al-i], *adv.* Trivialmente; comúnmente; frívolamente.
Trivialness [triv'-i-al-nes], *s.* Trivialidad; vulgaridad; frivolidad, poca importancia.
Triweekly [trai-wīk'-li], *a.* 1. Que sucede o se hace tres veces por semana. 2. Que se hace o sucede cada tercera semana.
Troat [trōt], *vn.* Bramar, hacer oir su voz el venado cuando está en celo.
Trocar [trō'-cār], *s.* Trocar, instrumento quirúrgico que sirve para dar salida a un flúido, v. g. en la hidropesía.
Trochaic, Trochaical [trō-kē'-ic, al], *a.* Trocaico, lo que consta de troqueos.
Trochanter [tro-can'-ter], *s.* 1. (Anat.) Trocánter, nombre de dos apófisis de la parte superior del fémur. 2. (Ento.) Segunda articulación de la pata de un insecto. (Gr.)
Troche [trō'-kī], *s.* Tablilla, trocisco, que contiene un medicamento pulverizado mezclado con azúcar y goma.
Trochee [trō'-kī], *s.* (Poét.) Troqueo, pie que consta de una sílaba larga y otra breve.
Trochlea [troc'-le-a], *s.* (Anat. y Zool.) Trocla, superficie parecida á una polea, en ciertas articulaciones, como entre el húmero y el cúbito. Su adjetivo es *trochlear.*
Trochoid [trō'-coid], *a.* Que gira sobre su propio eje.—*s.* Trocoide, curva generada por la revolución de un círculo sobre otro.
Trod, Trodden, *pret.* y *pp.* del verbo *To* Tread.
†**Trode** [trōd], *pret.* del verbo Tread.
Troglodyte [trog'-lo-dait], *s.* 1. Troglodita, habitante de las cavernas; aplícase a una raza prehistórica. 2. (Fig.) Ermitaño, solitario. 3. Mono semejante al hombre. 4. Reyezuelo, troglodita. *V.* Wren.
Trogon [trō'-gon], *s.* Trogón, género de pájaros tropicales de brillante plumaje.
Trojan [trō'-jan], *a.* y *s.* Troyano, de Troya.
Troll [trōl], *va.* 1. Cantar en sucesión (las partes de una canción), cantar de una manera alegre. 2. Pescar con caña por la popa de un bote o barco. 3. Voltear, dar vueltas a alguna cosa.—*vn.* 1. Cantar o cantarse alegremente. 2. Pescar con caña. 3. Girar, moverse circularmente. 4. Rodar, andorrear, corretear.
Troll, *s.* 1. Cantar que se entona en partes sucesivas. 2. Rodadura, movimiento de rodar o girar. 3. Carrete de la caña de pescar. 4. (Mit.) Gnomo, enano.
Trolley [trol'-e], *s.* Trole, rueda pequeña con muesca para que gire en contacto con un conductor eléctrico y comunique la corriente al coche de tranvía. *Trolley bus*, Trolebús.
Trolling [trōl'-ing], *s.* El procedimiento o acto de pescar tirando el anzuelo y cordel por la popa de una embarcación y casi á flor de agua.
Trollop [trol'-op], *s* Gorrona, mujer desaliñada y poco recatada.

Trombone [trem'-bōn], *s.* Trombón, sacabuche, instrumento músico de metal.

Troop [trūp], *s.* 1. Tropa, junta de mucha gente unida y acuadrillada entre sí para algún fin; cuadrilla, turba. 2. Tropa, el cuerpo de soldados o gente de guerra. 3. Tropa, conjunto de gente de guerra a caballo. *Troops,* Tropas, ejército.

Troop, *vn.* 1. Atroparse, juntarse la gente en cuadrillas. 2. Juntarse, tumultuarse, agavillarse la gente. 3. Marchar en cuerpo o en orden militar. 4. Marchar en compañía de otros muchos. *To troop away* o *off,* Retirarse en cuerpo o en cuadrillas.

Trooper [trūp'-ęr], *s.* Soldado de a caballo.

Trope [trōp], *s.* Tropo, uso de una expresión en sentido figurado; lenguaje figurado.

Trophic [tref'-ic], *a.* Trófico, perteneciente a la nutrición y a sus procedimientos.

Trophied [trō'-fīd], *a.* Adornado de trofeos.

Trophy [trō'-fī], *s.* 1. Trofeo, despojo del enemigo vencido. 2. Trofeo, monumento público en memoria del vencimiento. 3. (Poét.) Trofeo, triunfo.

Tropic [trep'-ic], *s.* Trópico: dase este nombre a dos círculos menores de la esfera que se consideran paralelos al ecuador.

Tropical [trep'-i-cal], *a.* 1. (Astr.) Tropical, que pertenece al trópico o círculo menor de la esfera. 2. (Ret.) Trópico: dícese del estilo en que se usan mucho los tropos.

Tropological [trep-o-lej'-i-cal], *a.* Tropológico, trópico, figurado.

Tropology [tro-pel'-o-ji], *s.* Tropología, el empleo de lenguaje figurado.

Troposphere [tre'-pos-fīr], *s.* Troposfera.

Trot [tret], *va.* 1. Hacer trotar. 2. Pasar al trote por encima de algo. —*vn.* 1. Trotar, ir o caminar al trote. 2. Trotar, andar de prisa o con celeridad.

Trot, *s.* 1. Trote, modo de andar del caballo más levantado y vivo que el paso regular. 2. Andar o movimiento constante. 3. Niño, niña. *V.* TOT.

Troth [treth o trōth], *s.* 1. Verdad, fe, fidelidad. *In troth,* En verdad. 2. Esponsales.

Trotter [tret'-ęr], *s.* Caballo trotón. *Trotters* o *sheep's trotters,* Manos o pies de carnero.

Troubadour [trū'-ba-dūr], *s.* Trovador, poeta provenzal de la Edad Media.

Trouble [trub'-l], *va.* 1. Disturbar, perturbar, causar disturbio. 2. Desazonar, afligir, inquietar, molestar, enfadar, aguar el gusto a uno; atribular. 3. Incomodar, dar que hacer; importunar. *Do not trouble yourself,* No se moleste Vd. 4. Revolver, enturbiar, poner turbio. 5. Pedir, rogar, suplicar (fórmula de cortesía). *May I trouble you to hand me the book?* ¿Tiene Vd. la bondad de darme el libro? *What need you trouble yourself?* ¿Por qué se incomoda o se apura Vd.? *Do not trouble my head with it,* No me quiebre Vd. la cabeza con eso.

Trouble, *s.* 1. Turbación, confusión, disturbio, desorden. 2. Molestia, inquietud, incomodidad. 3. Aflicción, calamidad, pena, congoja. *Can you do it without trouble?* ¿Puede Vd. hacerlo sin molestarse? 4. Enfado, impertinencia, engorro. *To be in trouble,* Estar inquieto, estar agitado, estar afligido; hallarse en un apuro, sufrir alguna calamidad. *To be at the trouble to,* Tomarse la pena de. *To give trouble, to put to trouble,* Dar que hacer. *It is not worth the trouble,* No vale la pena.

Troubled [trub'-ld], *pp.* del verbo TROUBLE. *I am troubled with the gout,* Padezco mal de gota. *To fish in troubled water,* Pescar en agua turbia, o en río revuelto.

Troubler [trub'-lęr], *s.* Alborotador, perturbador, inquietador.

Trouble shooter [trub'-l shūt'-ęr], *s.* (fam.) El encargado de descubrir y allanar o corregir fallas.

Troublesome [trub'-l-sum], *a.* 1. Penoso, molesto, oneroso, fatigoso, pesado, gravoso. 2. Importuno, molesto, enfadoso, impertinente, incómodo, fastidioso.

Troublesomeness [trub'-l-sum-nes], *s.* 1. Penalidad, molestia, incomodidad. 2. Incomodidad, impertinencia.

Troublous [trub'-lus], *a.* 1. Turbulento, confuso, tumultuoso. 2. Inquieto, impaciente.

Trough [trēf], *s.* 1. Artesa, gamella, gamellón; dornajo, cubeta. (Am.) Batea. *Stone trough,* Pilón. 2. Depresión larga y estrecha, como entre dos colinas o el intermedio o espacio entre dos olas.

Trounce [trauns], *va.* (Fam.) Zurrar, dar palos, castigar severamente.

Troupe [trūp], *s.* Compañía de cómicos, acróbatas, etc. (Fr.)

Trouper [trūp'-ęr], *s.* Comediante de la legua, actor que viaja. *A good trouper,* Persona que sabe viajar sin importarle incomodidades.

Trousers [trau'-zęrz], *s. pl.* Pantalones; calzones largos o de marinero.

Trousseau [trū'-sō], *s.* Ajuar de novia.

Trout [traut], *s.* Trucha, pez delicado que se coge en los ríos y arroyos. *Trout flies,* Moscas artificiales para la pesca de truchas.

Trout-hook [traut'-huk], *s.* Anzuelo de trucha.

Trover [trō'-vęr], *s.* (For.) El derecho de repetir contra quien ha hallado o posee por cualquier título los bienes ajenos y no los quiere entregar a su dueño.

Trowel [trau'-el], *s.* Trulla, llana, palustre, instrumento que usan los albañiles.

Troy [trei], **Troy-weight** [trei'-wēt], *s.* Peso de troy, peso para el oro, la plata y las drogas medicinales, que es de doce onzas cada libra.

Truancy [trū'-an-si], *s.* Novillos, ausencia de la escuela sin permiso; haraganería.

Truant [trū'-ant], *s.* y *a.* Holgazán, haragán, ocioso, tunante. *To play the truant,* Hacer novillos, ausentarse de la escuela sin licencia.

Truce [trūs], *s.* 1. Tregua, cesación temporal de hostilidades, suspensión de armas. 2. Descanso, interrupción, intermisión, intervalo.

Truck [truc], *va.* y *vn.* Trocar, permutar, cambiar, hacer un cambio o trueque; traficar, vender.—*s.* 1. Efectos para vender o trocar, particularmente los de fácil manejo. 2. (E. U.) Hortalizas para el mercado. 3. (Fam.) Artículos sin valor; desechos, desperdicios, zupias. 4. (Fam.) Cambio, permuta, trueque.

Truck *va.* y *vn.* Acarrear, transportar por medio de camiones. —*s.* 1. Camión, carretón fuerte para transportar mercancías pesadas. 2. Carretilla de mano para barriles, cajas, baúles, etc. *Truck frame,* Bastidor para camión. *Dumping truck,* Volquete.

Truckage [truk'-ēj], *s.* Carreteo, y el precio que se paga por llevar efectos en carretones.

Truckle [truc'-l], *vn.* Someterse, ceder, sujetarse, besar la correa; estar en un estado de sujeción e inferioridad.

Truckle-bed [truc'-l-bed], *s.* Carriola, cama con ruedas que puede rodarse debajo de otra cama más alta.

Truckman [truc'-man], *s.* 1. Carretero. 2. Trocador, el que hace trueques.

Truculence [trū'-kiu-lens], *s.* Fiereza, crueldad.

Truculent [trū'-kiu-lent], *a.* Truculento, cruel.

Trudge [truj], *vn.* Andar o ir a pie; caminar con afán, fatiga y trabajo.

True [trū], *a.* 1. Verdadero, cierto, seguro, efectivo. 2. Verdadero, real, sin engaño, doblez o tergiversación, ingenuo, sincero; verídico. 3. Genuino, puro, propio y natural. 4. Fiel, constante, leal; exacto. *A true translation,* Traducción que concuerda con su original. *True-blue,* Leal, fiel. *True-born,* Legítimo, verdadero; de nacimiento legítimo. *True-bred,* De casta legítima. *True-hearted,* Leal, sincero, fiel, franco, de buena fe. *True-heartedness,* Fidelidad, sinceridad, franqueza, buena fe.

True bill [trū bil], *s.* Acusación de parte de un gran jurado.

True-love [trū'-luv], *a.* (Bot.) Pariseta de cuatro hojas, hierba París o uva de oso.

True-lover's knot [trū'-luv-ęrs net], *s.* Lazo de amor.

Trueness [trū'-nes], *s.* Fidelidad, sinceridad, candidez, franqueza.

Truepenny [trū'-pen-i], *s.* (Fam.) Hombre de bien, mozo honrado.

Truffle [truf'-l], *s.* (Bot.) Criadilla de tierra, trufa, hongo subterráneo.

Truism [trū'-izm], *s.* 1. Verdad indudable y que no puede negarse. 2. (Fam.) Verdad evidente, pero no importante; perogrullada.

Truly [trū'-li], *adv.* Verdaderamente, en verdad; realmente, en realidad; exactamente, con precisión; sinceramente, de buena fe. *Yours truly, yours very truly,* Su afectísimo, su seguro servidor.

Trump [trump], *s.* 1. (Poét. o ant.) Trompeta, clarín. 2. Triunfo, en el juego de naipes. *Diamonds are trumps,* Oros son triunfos. *To put to one's trumps,* Apretarle a uno las clavijas, estrecharle en un discurso o argumento. 3. (Fam.) Persona muy agradable; un real mozo. 4. (Esco.) Birimbao.

Trump, *va.* 1. Fallar, jugar triunfo. 2. Engañar. *To trump up,* Forjar; idear, suponer o inventar; tomado siempre en mala parte.

Trumpery [trump'-ęr-i], *s.* 1. Hojarasca, oropel, cualquier cosa de poco valor o utilidad; bujería, baratija. 2. Palabras vanas, inútiles o de poca substancia, piropo, relumbrón. 3. Engaño, fraude, falsedad.

Trumpet [trump'-et], *s.* Trompeta, clarín; trompa, instrumento músico militar. *Speaking-trumpet,* Bocina. *Hearing-trumpet, ear-trumpet,* Trompetilla acústica. *Trumpet-creeper, trumpet-vine,* Jazmín trompeta, planta trepadora con flores escarlata en forma de trompeta. (Tecoma radicans.) *Trumpet-honeysuckle,* Madreselva. (Lonicera sempervirens.) *Trumpet-tongued,* Vocinglero, con lengua de trompeta. *Trumpet-shell,* Trompa o bocina marina.

Trumpet, *va.* 1. Pregonar a son de trompeta, trompetear. 2. Modelar en forma de boca de trompeta.—*vn.* Dar de sí un sonido como de trompeta.

Trumpeter [trump'-et-ęr], *s.* 1. Trompetero, trompeta. 2. Pregonero, el que publica y hace patente alguna cosa. 3. Agamí, ave sudamericana de las zancudas. (Psophia crepitans.) 4. Trompa marina, pez cetáceo.

Truncate [trun'-kêt], *va.* Truncar o troncar, cortar la cima o la extremidad de algo.

Truncate, Truncated, *a.* Truncado, cortado; terminado bruscamente en su extremidad.

Trundle [trun'-dl], *s.* 1. Rodaja, rueda pequeña. 2. *V. Trundle-bed.* 3. Rodadura, la acción de rodar. 4. ¿Rueda baja; carreta de ruedas bajas. *Trundle-bed,* Carriola, cama baja ó tárima con ruedas. *Trundle-shot,* (Mar.) Palanquetas. *Trundle-tail,* Cola redonda.

Trundle, *va.* y *vn.* Rodar, moverse por la tierra dando vueltas.

Trunk [truṇc'], *a.* De, o perteneciente a un cuerpo principal. *Trunk line,* Línea principal de un sistema de transportes, p. ej. un ferrocarril o un canal.—*s.* 1. Tronco, la parte inferior de los árboles desde el suelo hasta donde se divide en ramas. 2. Tronco, el cuerpo humano o de algún otro animal sin la cabeza, piernas o brazos. 3. Tronco, la parte principal de una cosa dividida en ramales, como las arterias, venas, etc. 4. Fuste de columna. 5. Baúl o cofre. *Nests of trunks,* Juegos de cuatro cofres o baúles. 6. Trompa, la nariz del elefante. 7. Cañón o conducto cuadrangular de madera, v. g. en un órgano. *Trunk-hose,* Calzones largos de los siglos XVI y XVII. *Trunk-maker,* Cofrero.

Trunks [truṇks], *s. pl.* Calzones cortos de hombre.

Trunnion [trun'-yun], *s.* 1. (Art.) Muñón, cada una de las dos piezas cilíndricas que sostienen a un cañón sobre la cureña. *Trunnion plates,* Chapos de testera, contramuñoneras. 2. Tuerca de cilindro oscilante.

Truss [trus], *s.* 1. Braguero para las quebraduras, suspensorio. 2. Armadura, armazón, conjunto de piezas principales de un puente ú otra construcción. 3. Mazorca, conjunto de flores terminales. 4. Haz, atado, lío, paquete, brazado. En Inglaterra, 36 libras de paja y 60 de heno hacen un *truss.* *Truss-maker,* El que hace bragueros ó suspensorios.

Truss, *va.* 1. Atirantar, apuntalar, sostener con una armazón. 2. Espetar; afianzar el ave antes de guisarla. 3. (Ant.) Empaquetar, enfardelar, hacer un lío o fardo. *To truss up,* Empaquetar, liar; ahorcar como criminal.

Trust [trust], *s.* 1. Confianza, seguridad o esperanza firme en otra persona, confidencia. 2. (For.) Fideicomiso, cargo, depósito, cualquier cosa confiada a la honradez o fidelidad de otra persona. 3. Crédito por el cual se presta a uno alguna cosa sin más seguridad que la confianza que en él se tiene. 4. Crédito por el cual se admite y cree algo; crédito en sentido comercial. 5. El estado de la persona en quien se ha hecho confianza. 6. Esperanza, expectación, creencia. 7. (Com.) Combinación, asociación de compañías industriales para fijar la producción, precio, etc., de una mercadería, o para asumir la dirección y las ganancias de un negocio. *A place of great trust,* Un puesto de mucha importancia. *To give upon trust,* Dar fiado. *In trust,* En confianza, en depósito. *Trust deed of sale,* (For.) Escritura de venta condicionada.

Trust, *va.* y *vn.* 1. Confiar, tener confianza en o hacer confianza de, contar con. 2. Confiar, esperar con firmeza y seguridad. 3. Confiar, encargar y fiar. 4. Confiarse, fiarse, poner su confianza en. 5. Creer, dar crédito. 6. Vender al fiado. 7. Creer en, dar fe, aceptar como verdadero. 8. Esperar con confianza; estimar algo como verdadero, deseando a la vez que lo sea.

Trustee [trus-tī'], *s.* Tenedor de bienes; encomendero, el que tiene a su cargo la propiedad de otro, depositario; fidei-comisario.

Truster [trust' ęr], *s.* Fiador, el que fía.

Trusteeship [trus-tī'-ship], *s.* Oficio o funciones de administrador o depositario.

Trustily [trust'-i-li], *adv.* Fielmente; lealmente, honradamente.

Trustiness [trust'-i-nes], *s.* Fidelidad, probidad, integridad y honradez en las acciones.

Trustless [trust'-les], *a.* Pérfido, inconstante, sin fe, sin que merezca confianza o crédito.

Trusthworthiness [trust'-wūr-dhi-nes], *s.* Integridad, honradez.

Trustworthy [trust'-wūr-dhi], *a.* Digno de confianza, seguro.

Trusty [trust'-i], *a.* 1. Fiel, leal, constante, íntegro, que merece confianza o crédito. 2. Fuerte, seguro, que no cede fácilmente.

Truth [trūth], *s.* 1. Verdad, la total correspondencia de lo que se dice o expresa con lo que interiormente se juzga. 2. Verdad, axioma. 3. Fidelidad, constancia. 4. Realidad. 5. Exactitud. 6. Honradez. *Of a truth* o *in truth,* A la verdad o en verdad; en realidad, seriamente.

Truthful [trūth'-ful], *a.* Verídico; verdadero, conforme a la verdad.

Truthless [trūth'-les], *a.* 1. Falso, contrario a la verdad. 2. Sin fe, desleal.

Try [trai], *va.* (*pret.* y *pp.* TRIED). 1. Examinar, ensayar, probar, hacer prueba. 2. Experimentar, probar y examinar prácticamente las virtudes o propiedades de una cosa. 3. Tentar, probar, tantear. 4. Tentar, intentar, poner los medios para lograr algo. 5. Procesar; juzgar o examinar algún pleito o causa criminal; formar causa a uno. 6. Procurar, emprender, intentar. 7. Decidir o terminar una diferencia. 8. Purificar, refinar por medio de la calefacción; afinar los metales. 9. Imponer una carga a, fatigar (v. g. la vista).—*vn.* 1. Esforzarse, ensayar, procurar, hacer lo posible. 2. †(Mar.) Capear. *We shall try it out,* Veremos en qué para.—*s.* Prueba, ensayo, esfuerzo.

Trying [trai'-ing], *a. part.* Penoso, difícil de soportar; fatigoso; contrariador.

Tryout [trai'-aut], *s.* Prueba, examen, ensayo.

Try-sail [trai'-sêl], *s.* (Mar.) La vela mayor de un paquete. *Try-sail-mast,* Pie de amigo de la mayor.

Try-square [trai'-scwār], *s.* Escuadra de precisión.

Tryst [trist o traist], *s.* Cita o lugar de cita. *To bide tryst,* Acudir a una cita, ser exacto a la cita.

Tsetse [tset'-sę], *s.* Tsetsé, mosca chupadora de sangre del interior del continente africano. Su picadura no causa daño al hombre, pero es mortal para el ganado mayor y los caballos. Glossina morsitans.

T-shirt [tī'-shęrt], *s.* Camiseta de mangas muy cortas que suele usarse exteriormente.

Tub [tub], *va.* 1. Encubar, poner en una cuba. 2. Bañar (a uno) en bañera.—*vn.* Bañarse en bañera.—*s.* 1. Cuba, recipiente de madera redondo formado de varias duelas; tina de madera. 2. Cantidad que puede contener una cuba. 3. Lo que se parece a una cuba; bote pesado. 4. Cubeta, tonel pequeño. 5. Baño tomado en una bañera. *Bath-tub,* Bañera, baño. *Mash-tub,* Cuba de tracear la cerveza. *Wash-tub,* Cuba, tina de lavar.

Tuba [tiū'-ba], *s.* Tuba (instrumento musical).

Tube [tiūb], *va.* Proveer de un tubo o tubos.—*s.* 1. Tubo, cañón, cañuto, fístola o cualquier otro conducto largo y muy delgado; sifón. 2. (Anat.) Conducto, órgano tubular, particularmente el que conduce aire.

Tuber [tiū'-bęr], *s.* 1. (Bot.) Tubérculo, porción corta y engrosada de un tallo subterráneo, como la patata. 2. (Anat.) Hinchazón, prominencia.

Tubercle [tiū'-bęr-cl], *s.* 1. Eminencia natural, poco notable, particularmente de un hueso. 2. (Med.) Tubérculo, tumorcillo granular, producto morboso dentro de un órgano; en los pulmones causa la consunción pulmonar. 3. (Bot.) Excrecencia pequeña.

Tubercular [tiu-bęr'-kiu-lar], *a.* 1. Tuberculoso; en forma de nudo o excrecencia. 2. (Med.) Tuberculoso, relativo o perteneciente al tubérculo; de la naturaleza de los tubérculos.

Tuberculin [tiu-bęr'-kiu-lin], *s.* Tuberculina, preparación para el diagnóstico de la tuberculosis.

Tuberculosis [tiu-bęr-kiu-lō'-sis], *s.* Tuberculosis, tuberculización, enfermedad diatésica que consiste en el desarrollo de tubérculos en uno o varios órganos, especialmente en los pulmones.

Tuberculous, Tuberculose [tiu-ber'-kiu-lus], *a.* Tuberculoso, tuberculífero, que padece tuberculosis, que tiene tubérculos.

Tuberose [tiū'-bę-rōs], *s.* (Bot.) Tuberosa, jacinto oriental.

Tuberous [tiū'-bęr-us], *a.* 1. Tuberoso, que presenta tuberosidades, nudos o excrecencias. 2. Tuberoso.

Tubing [tiūb'-ing], *s.* Tubería, tubo en secciones; sistema de tubos.
Tubipore. [tiū'-bi-pōr], *s.* Género de zoófitos.
Tubular [tiū'-biu-lar], *a.* Tubular, largo y hueco como tubo o cañón.
Tubulated [tiū'-biu-lêt-ed], **Tubulous** [tiū'-biū-lus], *a.* Con tubos, que tiene tubos.
Tubule [tiū'-biul], *s.* Tubo pequeño.
Tuck [tuc], *s.* 1. Alforza o pliegue para disminuir el largo de una bata, vestido, falda, etc. 2. Cartera, prolongación de una de las cubiertas de un libro, cuya extremidad se inserta en un corte o en una presilla de la otra cubierta. 3. (Mar.) Falda, arca de popa. 4. (Des.) Estoque, espada angosta y larga.
Tuck, *va.* 1. Arremangar, recoger o encoger lo que cuelga. 2. Meter entre la ropa; arropar, tapar y cubrir bien a uno con ropa. *To tuck up one's clothes*, Arremangarse.
Tucker [tuk'-ęr], *s.* 1. El o lo que hace alforzas; alforzador de máquinas de coser. 2. Escote, especie de adorno que cubre el pecho de las mujeres.
Tucker, *va.* (Fam. E. U.) Cansar, fatigar; por lo común con *out*. *To be tuckered out*, Estar muy cansado.
Tuesday [tiūz'-de], *s.* Martes, el tercer día de la semana. *Shrove Tuesday*, Martes de carnestolendas.
Tuff [tuf], *s.* Tufo, piedra esponjosa volcánica compuesta de fragmentos.
Tuft [tuft], *s.* 1. Copete, conjunto de cosas pequeñas y flexibles que están atadas por la base; v. gr. borla, lazo, penacho; mazorca de hierbas, de flores, etc.; ramillete; mechón de cabellos en lo alto de la frente; melena de crines, de lana. 2. Reunión de pequeños vasos sanguíneos en un punto, a manera de nudo. *Tuft of hair*, Moño. *Tuft-hunter*, Zalamero, adulador de los poderosos.
Tuft, *va.* 1. Adornar con borlas, lazos o penachos. 2. Separar en grupos, en mazorcas o en ramilletes. 3. En tapicería, fijar a intervalos regulares con copetes o botones.
Tufty [tuft'-i], *a.* 1. Afelpado, felpudo, velludo. 2. Encopetado. 3. Lleno de lazos, borlas, etc.
Tug [tug], *va.* Tirar con fuerza, hacer fuerza hacia sí, arrastrar con esfuerzo; halar, remolcar.—*vn.* Luchar, esforzarse.
Tug, *s.* 1. Tirada con esfuerzo o la acción de tirar de una cosa con toda violencia. 2. Esfuerzo grande hecho para arrancar o tirar de alguna cosa. 3. Remolcador de vapor. *Tug-boat*, Remolcador. *V.* 3ª acep.
Tugger [tug'-er], *s.* El que tira o arranca con mucha fuerza.
Tug-of-war [tug-ev-wōr'], *s.* 1. Competencia en que dos grupos tiran de una cuerda. 2. Lucha por la supremacía.
Tuition [tiu-ish'-un], *s.* 1. Tutoría, instrucción; enseñanza. 2. Precio de la enseñanza o instrucción.
Tulip [tiū'-lip], *s.* (Bot.) Tulipán, planta y flor.
Tulip-tree [tiū'-lip-trī], *s.* (Bot.) Tulípero, árbol grande de la familia de las magnoliáceas, con flores parecidas a las del tulipán. Liriodendron tulipifera.
Tulle [tūl], *s.* Tul.
Tumble [tum'-bl], *vn.* 1. Caer, dar en tierra. 2. Hundirse, desplomarse, venir abajo o al suelo, venir a tierra. 3. Rodar abajo, bajar rodando. 4. Voltear, dar alguna cosa vueltas por sí misma o dar vueltas o saltos como los volteadores; saltar, dar saltos o brincos; revolcarse. 5. (Ger.) Comprender, entender.—*va.* 1. Arrojar con descuido y con bastante fuerza. 2. Desordenar, desarreglar, trastornar, derribar; volcar. 3. Ajar o arrugar los vestidos. *To tumble down*, Hundirse, caer. *To tumble into bed*, Echarse en la cama. *To tumble out*, Echar fuera de, arrojar con violencia. *To tumble over*, Trastornar, volcar, poner lo de arriba abajo. *Tumble-down*, Que amenaza ruina, destrozado.
Tumble, *s.* Caída, vuelco, voltereta.
Tumblebug [tum'-bl-bug], *s.* Escarabajo pelotero, que hace una bola de estiércol para depositar en ella sus huevos.
Tumbler [tum'-blęr], *s.* 1. Volteador, el que da vueltas, saltabanco, titiritero. 2. Vaso sin pie para beber, a diferencia de la copa. 3. Pichón volteador. *The tumbler of a lock*, Rodete fiador, de cerradura.
Tumbrel [tum'-brel], *s.* 1. (Art.) Carro de artillería. 2. Chirrión, carro de basura.
Tumefaction [tiu-mę-fac'-shun], *s.* (Med.) Tumefacción, la hinchazón o elevación de alguna parte del cuerpo.
Tumefy [tiū'-mę-fai], *va.* Hacer entumecerse o hincharse.
Tumescence [tiū-mes'-ęns], *s.* Tumescencia, principio de un tumor.
Tumescent [tiū-me'-sent], *a.* Tumefacto, tumescente.
Tumid [tiū'-mid], *a.* 1. Túmido, hinchado; prominente. 2. Túmido, inflado, hablando del estilo.
Tumidity, Tumidness [tiu-mid'-i-ti], *s.* Hinchazón; turgencia.
Tumor, Tumour [tiū'-męr], *s.* Tumor, hinchazón, y bulto que se forma en alguna parte del cuerpo.
Tumular [tiū'-miu-lar], *a.* Tumulario, en forma de montecillo.
Tumulose [tiū'-miu-lōs], *a.* Montañoso, lleno de montecillos.
Tumult [tiū'-mult], *s.* 1. Tumulto, alboroto, motín, desorden; concurso grande de gente que causa desorden. 2. Agitación de ánimo.
Tumultuarily [tiu-mult'-yu-a-ri-li], *adv.* Tumultuariamente, desordenadamente.
Tumultuariness [tiu-mult'-yu-a-ri-nes], *s.* Turbulencia, disposición a levantar tumultos.
Tumultuous [tiu-mult'-yu-us], *a.* 1. Tumultuario, tumultuoso, que causa o levanta tumultos o que está sin orden ni concierto. 2. Turbulento, confuso, alborotado y desordenado.
Tumultuously [tiu-mult'-yu-us-li], *adv.* Tumultuariamente, en tumulto; sin orden ni concierto.
Tumultuousness [tiu-mult'-yu-us-nes], *s.* Turbulencia, tumulto.
Tumulus [tiū'-miu-lus], *s.* Túmulo, montón de tierra, que por lo general cubría una sepultura.
Tun [tun], *s.* 1. Tonel, cubeta o barril grande. 2. Cuba o tanque de cervecero para la fermentación; contiene a menudo unos 3,000 litros o más. 3. Cantidad de cerveza fermentada de una vez. 4. Tonelada, medida indeterminada y bastante grande; v. g. de dos pipas de vino (252 galones). *V.* Ton.
Tun, *va.* Entonelar, envasar, embarrilar vino u otros licores.
Tuna (o **tunny**) **fish** [tiū'-na, tun'-i fish], *s.* Atún.
Tunable [tiūn'-a-bl], *a.* 1. Que se puede templar. 2. (Des.) Armonioso, musical.
Tunableness [tiūn'-a-bl-nes], *s.* Melodía, armonía.
Tunably [tiūn'-a-bli], *adv.* Armoniosamente, con armonía o melodía.
Tunbellied [tun'-bel-id], *a.* Barrigudo, panzudo.
Tundra, Toondra [tun'-dra], *s.* Tundra, llanura undulada de Rusia y Siberia, cubierta de musgo y a veces húmeda o pantanosa. (< Ruso.)
Tune [tiūn], *s.* 1. Tono, la canción métrica para la música compuesta de varias coplas; tonada. 2. Tono, el sonido que hace la voz cuando se habla o canta y el que hace un instrumento cuando se toca. 3. Concordancia o armonía, tanto hablando de la música como hablando metafóricamente de costumbres, actos morales, etc. 4. Tono, el estado particular del ánimo y a veces también del cuerpo para ejecutar, aprender, etc. *The fiddle is in tune* o *out of tune*, El violín está templado o destemplado.
Tune, *va.* 1. Templar un instrumento músico. 2. Cantar armoniosamente. 3. Poner acordes dos o más cosas o ajustarlas perfectamente entre sí.—*vn.* 1. Modular, cantar con armonía y variedad de la voz. 2. Ajustarse o concertar dos o más voces o instrumentos.
Tuneful [tiūn'-ful], *a.* Armonioso, acorde, melodioso.
Tuneless [tiūn'-les], *a.* Desentonado, disonante, discordante, fuera de tono.
Tuner [tiūn'-ęr], *s.* Afinador de instrumentos musicales.
Tungstate [tung'-stêt], *s.* Tungstato, sal formada con ácido túngstico.
Tungsten [tung'-sten], *s.* (Quím.) Tungsteno, metal polvoriento, de color plomizo, duro y pesado.
Tungstic [tung'-stic], *a.* (Quím.) Túngstico, de tungsteno o derivado de él, particularmente en sus más altas combinaciones.
Tunic [tiū'-nic], *s.* 1. Túnica, vestidura interior, con o sin mangas, que usaban los antiguos. 2. Vestidura exterior moderna fruncida al talle, o ceñida con un cinturón, v. g. una blusa o un ropaje exterior. 3. Túnica, telilla o película que cubre algunos órganos de las plantas. 4. (Anat.) Túnica, membrana sutil que cubre algunas partes del cuerpo.
Tunicata [tiū-ni-kê'-ta], *s. pl.* Tunicados, división de animales invertebrados y marinos que tienen forma de saco.
Tunicated [tiū'-ni-kêt-ed], *a.* (Bot.) Membranoso, formado de túnicas o membranas.
Tunicle [tiū'-ni-cl], *s.* 1. Túnica, tegumento o envoltura. 2. Túnica fina, ligera o delicada. 3. Tunicela, vestidura eclesiástica.
Tuning [tiūn'-ing], *s.* Temple, acción y efecto de templar. *Tuning-fork*, Diapasón. *Tuning-hammer*, *tuning-key*, Templador, llave de afinador.
Tunnage [tun'-ęj], *s.* El derecho de tonelada que se cobraba en las aduanas. *V.* Tonnage.

Tunnel [tʊn'-el], *s.* 1. Túnel, socavón, o paso subterráneo, abierto artificialmente para el paso de trenes, para conducir aguas, o establecer otra comunicación. 2. Embudo. *V.* FUNNEL. 3. Cañón de chimenea, de ladrillera, etc. *Tunnel-net,* Red profunda ancha por la boca y de forma cónica.

Tunnel, *va.* 1. Hacer, construir un socavón o túnel a través de una colina o por debajo de un río. 2. Disponer en forma de túnel o socavón.

Tunny (o **tuna**) **fish** [tʊn'-i, tiūn'-a fish], *s.* Atún.

Tup [tʊp], *s.* Morueco, carnero padre.

Tup, *vn.* (Prov. Ingl.) Topetar como los carneros.

Tupelo [tiū'-pel-o], *s.* Cualquiera de varios árboles americanos del género Nyssa; nisa. (Nombre indígena.)

Turban [tūr'-ban], *s.* 1. Turbante, tocado con que los orientales se cubren la cabeza. 2. Tocado de mujer. 3. Sombrero moderno para mujeres y niños, con ala muy estrecha o sin ella. 4. Espira de molusco univalvo.

Turbaned [tūr'-band], *a.* Que tiene o lleva turbante.

Turbary [tūr'-ba-ri], *s.* El derecho de cavar turbas o céspedes de tierra, y el sitio donde se cavan.

Turbid [tūr'-bid], *a.* 1. Turbio, túrbido, espeso; cenagoso. 2. Turbulento, confuso, turulato, en estado de confusión.

Turbidity, Turbidness [tūr-bid'-i-ti, tūr'-bid-nes], *s.* Turbiedad, calidad de turbio; turbia.

Turbinate, Turbinated [tūr'-bi-nēt, ed], *a.* 1. Lo que tiene figura espiral, y el movimiento que se hace formando esta figura. 2. (Bot.) En forma de peonza.

Turbine [tūr'-bin], *s.* Turbina, rueda hidráulica que gira sobre un eje vertical y que aprovecha la mayor parte posible de la fuerza motriz.

Turbojet, *s.* Turborreactor; avión de turborreacción.

Turboprop [tʊr'-bo-prɵp], *s.* Avión de turbohélice.

Turbot [tūr'-bɵt], *s.* Rodaballo, rombo.

Turbulence [tūr'-biu-lens], **Turbulency** [tūr'-biu-len-si], *s.* Turbulencia, alboroto, tumulto, confusión.

Turbulent [tūr'-biu-lent], *a.* 1. Turbulento, agitado, tumultuoso, violento. 2. Predispuesto a la sublevación o insubordinación. 3. Que tiende a disturbar o poner en confusión. *A turbulent sea,* (Mar.) Mar bravo. *Turbulent weather,* (Mar.) Tiempo tormentoso. *Turbulent temper,* Genio turbulento o inquieto.

Turbulently [tūr'-biu-lent-li], *adv.* Turbulentamente, agitadamente, con confusión.

Turcism [tūrk'-izm o tūr'-sizm], *s.* Religión, sistema político o rasgo característico de los turcos.

Turcois [tūr'-coiz], *s.* *V.* TURQUOISE.

Turcoman, *s.* *V.* TURKOMAN.

Turdoid [tūr'-deid], *a.* Parecido o perteneciente a los tordos o túrdidos.

Tureen [tiu-rīn'], *s.* Sopera, vasija honda en que se sirve la sopa.

Turf [tūrf], *s.* 1. Césped, trozo de tierra cubierto de hierba menuda. 2. Turba. *V.* PEAT. 3. Alfombra de hierba. 4. Circo. terreno donde se efectúan las carreras de caballos: ocupación de hacer correr caballos: en la locución *the turf.*

Turf, *va.* Encespedar, cubrir con céspedes.

Turfiness [tūrf'-i-nes], *s.* La abundancia de césped o de turba.

Turfy [tūrf'-i], *a.* 1. Cubierto de céspedes; parecido al césped. 2. Perteneciente á las carreras de caballos. *Turfy ground,* Cespedera.

Turgescence [tūr-jes'-ens], **Turgescency** [tūr-jes'-en-si], *s.* 1. Turgencia, hinchazón. 2. (Fig.) Engreimiento, envanecimiento.

Turgescent [tūr-jes'-ent], *a.* Turgente, que se hincha o abulta.

Turgid [tūr'-jid], *a.* 1. Túmido, inflado, hinchado. 2. (Fig.) Ampuloso, engreído, pomposo; se dice del estilo.

Turgidity [tūr-jid'-i-ti], **Turgidness** [tūr'-jid-nes], *s.* El estado de turgencia o hinchazón.

Turk [tūrk], *s.* 1. Turco, turca; otomano, natural de Turquía. 2. *V.* TATAR. 3. Musulmán.

Turkey [tūr'-ke], *s.* (Orn.) Pavo, pava: (Mex.) Guajalote: (Cuba) Guanajo. *Turkey corn,* (Bot.) Maíz. *Turkey millet,* (Bot.) Alcandía. *Turkey-gobbler,* Pavo o guanajo. *Turkey-buzzard,* Aura, (Mex.) zopilote, buitre americano. Cathartes aura.

Turkish [turk'-ish], *a.* Turco. *Turkish bath,* Baño turco. *Turkish towel,* Toalla gruesa y afelpada propia para el baño.—*s.* Idioma turco.

Turkois [tūr'-coiz], *s.* *V.* TURQUOISE.

Turkoman [tūr'-ko-man], *s.* 1. Turcomano, pueblo del Turquestán de origen turco. 2. Persona natural del Turquestán.

Turkscap [tūrcs'-cap], *s.* 1. (Bot.) Martagón, especie de lirio. 2. Melocacto común.

Turmeric [tūr'-mer-ic], *s.* Cúrcuma, planta de la India parecida al jengibre; y su raíz, de que se saca color amarillo.

Turmoil [tūr'-meil], *s.* Disturbio, inquietud, baraúnda, alboroto.

Turmoil, *vn.* Inquietarse, estar en agitación.

Turn [tūrn], *va.* 1. Volver, dar vuelta o vueltas a alguna cosa. 2. Volver, mudar, cambiar, de un estado a otro. 3. Volver, poner a alguna persona o cosa en el estado que antes tenía. 4. Volver, torcer o inclinar una cosa de un lado a otro; volver o tornar lo de arriba abajo. 5. Volver, cambiar, convertir o transformar una cosa en otra. 6. Volver, hacer mudar a fuerza de persuasión o razones la opinión que se tenía; convertir; pervertir. 7. Volver, verter, traducir o trasladar de una lengua a otra. 8. Volver, dirigir, encaminar o enderezar una cosa a otra material o inmaterialmente. 9. Volver, rechazar. 10. Alterar, variar, cambiar. 11. Tornear, trabajar al torno. 12. Aplicar o destinar una cosa a un uso diferente del que antes tenía. 13. Adaptar una cosa a otra. 14. Discurrir, reflexionar. 15. Embotar. 16. Hacer circular dinero, géneros, etc. 17. Transferir. 18. Hacer vertiginoso; dar asco o náuseas.—*vn.* 1. Volver, girar, rodar, andar o moverse alrededor o en torno. 2. Voltear, dar alguna cosa vueltas por sí misma. 3. Dar vueltas, andar rodando, andar de acá para allá. 4. Volver, torcer o dejar el camino o línea recta. 5. Volverse a, inclinar el cuerpo o el rostro hacia alguna persona o cosa determinada. 6. Mudarse, transformarse, mudar de posición, de situación, de estado, de opinión, etc. 7. Hacerse o llegar uno a ser lo que antes no era. 8. Mudarse, desdecirse, cambiar de casaca. 9. Volverse o avinagrarse el vino, acedarse la leche. 10. Estribar, fundarse; depender de. 11. Trastornársele o írsele a uno la cabeza. *To turn about,* Volverse hacia otra parte; rodar o andar dando vueltas alrededor. *To turn against,* Hacer frente; defenderse. *To turn aside,* Descaminar, alejar; alejarse, ponerse a un lado. *To turn away,* Despedir o despachar, hacer que se vuelvan las personas o cosas que ya no se necesitan; despedir o echar a una persona; desviar o desviarse, volver o volverse al otro lado: apartar o separar; echar, sacar o arrojar con violencia; deshacerse de. *To turn back,* Volver atrás o volver otra vez, volverse; volver o devolver una cosa a la persona de quien se recibió, restituir; retroceder, desandar lo andado. *To turn down,* Plegar, doblar. *To turn from,* Desviar de; apartarse de. *To turn in,* Replegar, plegar muchas veces, hacer pliegues; doblar hacia dentro. *To turn in and out,* Serpear o serpentear. *To turn into,* Mudar, cambiar, transformar, convertir; transformarse, mudar de forma o de figura. *She is turned of forty,* Ella tiene cuarenta años cumplidos. *To turn off,* Cerrar una llave o canilla; despachar, arrojar o echar a una persona con desprecio, echar a cajas destempladas, despedir o echar enhoramala; renunciar, hacer dejación de alguna cosa; apartar, separar o divertir el pensamiento, la atención, etc.; mudar de camino o tomar otro camino; llevar a cabo, ejecutar. *To turn off a day's work,* Llevar a cabo el trabajo del día. *To turn out,* (1) Echar fuera, expeler, arrojar, lanzar, echar con violencia; volver lo de dentro afuera, llegar a ser; resultar. (2) (Mar.) Levantarse; (3) echar al campo los animales. *So it turned out,* Así resultó, sucedió que. *To turn over,* Transferir, pasar a otro; diferir, dilatar; enviar; volver la hoja de un libro. *To turn over a new leaf,* Enmendarse, empezar vida nueva. *To turn to,* Recurrir o acudir a uno; transformar o transformarse; volverse hacia una persona o cosa; dirigirse hacia. *To turn to advantage* o *to account,* Sacar ventaja o utilidad de una cosa; hacer que redunde en beneficio. *To turn to good account,* Sacar provecho de una cosa. *To turn to and fro,* Volver de un lado a otro. *To turn to windward,* (Mar.) Barloventear, abarloar. *To turn up,* Arregazar, arremangar; volver el triunfo en los juegos de naipes; acontecer, suceder; venir a mano, reaparecer. *To turn up the ground,* Cavar la tierra, disponer la tierra para el cultivo. *To turn upon,* Estribar, fundarse, apoyarse; producir un suceso, desgracia, etc., cualquier efecto en alguna persona o lugar; recaer sobre; revolver sobre. *To turn upside down,* Trastornar, volver lo de arriba abajo; zozobrar un navío. *To turn home,* Retirarse, volverse o irse a casa. *To turn one home,* Enviar a alguno a casa. *To turn physician*, Hacerse médico o recibirse de médico. *To turn short*, Dar media vuelta; volverse bruscamente. *To turn tail*, Andar u obrar con doblez o con segunda; buscar rodeos. *To turn the brain*, Volver loco. *To turn the head*, Trastornar la cabeza o el juicio; volverse loco. *To turn the scale*, Hacer inclinarse la balanza; volver la tortilla. *To turn the stomach*, Causar asco o hastío; causar náuseas. *My head turns*, Se me va la cabeza, me da vueltas la cabeza. *Turn over* o *please turn over*, (p. t. o.), A la vuelta.

Turn, *s.* 1. Vuelta, giro, movimiento circular. 2. Rodeo, revuelta. 3. Vuelta, paseo corto, viaje a sitio poco distante. 4. Turno, vez, tanda; alternación, orden sucesivo o alternado de las cosas. 5. Ocasión, oportunidad. 6. Mudanza, cambio; fase, faz. 7. Proceder, procedimiento, modo de obrar, portarse o comportarse las personas. 8. Genio, inclinacion, propensión. 9. Acción, pasada buena o mala que se hace a alguno; chasco, pieza; servicio, favor, asistencia. 10. Provecho, utilidad. 11. Forma, figura, hechura. 12. Modo de decir las cosas; colocación de las voces de una sentencia. *To take a turn*, Dar una vuelta, un paseo. *To take another turn*, Cambiar de faz. *Things have taken a different turn*, Las cosas han tomado otro aspecto. *By turns*, Por turno, alternativamente. *He has a turn for agriculture*, Es aficionado a la agricultura o tiene inclinación a la agricultura. *It is your turn*, A Vd. le toca. *At every turn*, A cada instante, a cada momento. *A friendly turn*, Un favor. *An ill-natured turn*, Un chasco pesado, una pieza.

Turnbuckle [tūrn'-buc''-l], *s.* Torniquete o eslabón giratorio para apretar estáys.

Turncoat [tūrn'-cōt], *s.* El que muda de partido o de opiniones, el que cambiar de casaca; desertor, renegado, apóstata.

Turn down [tūrn daun'], *va.* 1. Rechazar, reclinar, rehusar. 2. Voltear hacia abajo. *To turn down the bedspread*, Doblar hacia abajo la sobrecama. *To turn down one's coat collar*, Doblar hacia abajo el cuello del abrigo.

Turner [tūrn'-ẹr], *s.* 1. Torneador, tornero. *Turner's lathe*, Torno. 2. Gimnasta, miembro de un club atlético.

Turning [tūrn'-ing], *s.* 1. Vuelta, rodeo; las vueltas y revueltas que hace una cosa tortuosa. 2. Recodo, ángulo, rodeo (de una calle, río, etc.). 3. *pl.* Virutas que se hacen torneando. *Turning-point*, (1) Punto decisivo, crisis. (2) Punto donde se trueca la dirección de un movimiento.

Turnip [tūr'-nip], *s.* Nabo, planta hortense y su raíz comestible.

Turnkey [tūrn'-kī], *s.* Bastonero o ayudante del alcaide de una cárcel; demandadero de una cárcel.

Turnout [tūrn'-aut], *s.* 1. Tren, séquito, conjunto de personas que concurren a una reunión o diversión pública. 2. Vía doble o lateral en un camino angosto; desviadero corto en un ferrocarril. 3. Equipaje, carruaje de lujo. 4. Producto de una fábrica en un tiempo dado. 5. Salida de personas; en especial, huelga de obreros.

Turnover [tūrn'-ō-vẹr], *a.* Doblado hacia abajo, p. ej un cuello de camisa.—*s.* 1. Vuelco; vuelta. 2. Variedad de pastelillo. 3. Utensilio para dar vuelta a los guisos. 4. Cambio de partido, opinión, etc. 5. Ciclo en el movimiento de mercancías. 6. Proporción en el cambio de personal de una empresa.

Turnpike [tūrn'-paik], *s.* 1. Camino en que hay barreras de portazgo; camino público. 2. Barrera, los maderos que se ponen en algún camino público para el cobro del portazgo o de los derechos que se pagan para componer los caminos; portazgo. 3. *V.* TURNSTILE.

Turn signals [tūrn' sig'-nalz], *s. pl.* Luces intermitentes, luces direccionales.

Turnsole [tūrn'-sōl], *s.* (Bot.) Tornasol, girasol.

Turnspit [tūrn'-spit], *s.* El galopín de cocina que da vueltas al asador de mano.

Turnstile [tūrn'-stail], *s.* Torniquete.

Turnstone [tūrn'-stōn], *s.* (Orn.) Revuelvepiedras.

Turntable [tūrn'-tê-bl], *s.* 1. (F.C.) Plataforma giratoria, placa giratoria. 2. Plato tocadiscos. 3. Giratoria.

Turpentine [tūr'-pen-tain], *s.* Trementina, la goma que destilan el pino, abeto, enebro y otros árboles de la misma especie. *Turpentine-tree*, Terebinto, especie de alfóncigo.

Turpeth [tūr'-peth], *s.* 1. Turbit, raíz del albohol turbit, planta parecida a la jalapa. 2. *Turpeth mineral*, Turbit mineral, sulfato mercurial de propiedades eméticas.

Turpitude [tūr'-pi-tiūd], *s.* Torpeza, vileza, infamia; deshonestidad.

Turquoise [tūr-cois'], *s.* Turquesa, piedra preciosa azul.

Turret [tur'-et], *s.* Torrecilla, torre pequeña.

Turreted [tur'-et-ed], *a.* Hecho en figura de torre o que se eleva como una torre.

Turtle [tūr'-tl], *s.* 1. Tortuga de mar. 2. (Impr.) Bastidor grueso en forma de segmento de cilindro, que se usa para sostener el tipo en una prensa giratoria. 3. *V. Turtle-dove. Turtle-dove*, Tórtola. *Small land turtle*, (Amer.) Tortuga de tierra, galápago, jicotea. *Turtle-shell*, Carey. *To turn turtle*, Zozobrar, volverse hacia arriba el casco de una embarcación.

Tuscan [tus'-can], *a.* Toscano, de Toscana.—*s.* 1. Toscano, natural de Toscana. 2. Toscano, el más puro de los dialectos italianos.

Tush [tush], *inter.* (Ant.) ¡Tararira! ¡bah! interjección para expresar impaciencia o desprecio.

Tusk [tusk], *s.* 1. Colmillo, diente agudo de algunas fieras. 2. Punta parecida a un diente.

Tusked [tuskt], **Tusky** [tusk'-ī], *a.* Colmilludo.

Tussle [tus'-l], *va.* y *vn.* (Fam.) Luchar con; tener una agarrada, una sarracina.—*s.* Sarracina, refriega con desorden, pendencia.

Tussock [tus'-ec], *s.* 1. Montecillo de hierbas crecientes o de cárices. 2. Penacho de pelo o de plumas. *Tussock-moth*, Mariposa nocturna del género Orygia, cuya oruga tiene penachos peludos.

Tut, *inter.* ¡Tate! ¡Basta! ¡Quita allá! Se usa para expresar ligera reprensión o impaciencia.

Tutelage [tiū'-tel-ẹj], *s.* Tutela, tutoría, el cargo de tutor.

Tutelar [tiū'-te-lar], **Tutelary** [tiū'-te-le-ri], *a.* Tutelar. *A tutelar angel*, Ángel de la guardia. *A tutelar saint*, Santo tutelar o patrón.

Tutor [tiū'-tẹr], *s.* Tutor, ayo, preceptor.

Tutor, *va.* 1. Enseñar, instruir. 2. Señorear, mandar imperiosamente.

Tutorage [tiū'-tẹr-ẹj], *s.* Tutoría o tutela.

Tutoress [tiū'-tẹr-es], *sf.* Tutriz, aya.

Tutty [tut'-ī], *s.* Tutía, atutía, óxido de cinc impuro que se obtiene en los hornos de fundición y sirve como polvo para pulir.

Tuwhit, **Tuwhoo** [tu-hwit', tu-hwū'], *vn.* Gritar el buho.—*s.* Grito del buho.

Tuxedo [tux-ī'-do], *s.* Smoking.

Twaddle [twed'-l], *va.* y *vn.* Charlar, parlotear, chacharear con aire de persona docta.—*s.* Habladuría, charla; palique; tonterías, disparates.

Twain [twên], *a.* (Ant.) Dos.

Twang [twang], *va.* y *vn.* 1. Producir un sonido agudo y penetrante. 2. Restallar, chasquear o estallar alguna cosa como la honda o el látigo. 3. Tañer, hiriendo las cuerdas de un instrumento músico.

Twang, *s.* 1. Retintín, el modo y tonillo afectado de hablar; acento muy fuerte al pronunciar. 2. Cualquier sonido agudo y penetrante, como el de una cuerda música de la cual se tira.

Twangling [twang'-ling], *s.* Ruido desapacible.

'Twas [twez]. Contracción de IT WAS. Fué.

Tweak [twīc], *va.* Pellizcar y torcer, apretar entre los dedos.—*s.* Pellizco, sacudida.

Tweed [twīd], *a.* Hecho del paño cruzado de este nombre.—*s.* Paño cruzado escocés de lana, por lo general de dos colores.

Tweedle [twī'-dl], *va.* Manosear, tentar y tocar ligeramente con las manos.

Tweedledee [twī'-dl-dī], **Tweedledum** [twī-dl-dum'], *s.* Sonido semejante al del violín; dos cosas entre las cuales hay la menor diferencia posible.

'Tween [twīn], *prep.* Entre; contracción de BETWEEN.

Tweeter [twī'-ter], *s.* Altavoz para sonidos gudos.

Tweezers [twīz'-ẹrz], *s. pl.* Tenacillas, pinzas pequeñas para objetos diminutos.

Twelfth [twelfth], *a.* Duodécimo, número ordinal de doce.—*s.* 1. Una de doce partes iguales. 2. (Mús.) Duodécima, intervalo de una octava más una quinta. *Twelfth Night*, Víspera del día de Reyes, de la Epifanía.

Twelfth-tide [twelfth'-taid], *s.* El día de los Reyes o la Epifanía.

Twelve [twelv], *a.* y *s.* Doce. *Twelvemonth*, Un año o doce meses. *Twelvepenny*, De a doce peniques. *Twelvescore*, Doce veces veinte, doscientos cuarenta.

Twentieth [twen'-tī-eth], *a.* Vigésimo, ordinal de veinte.

Twenty [twen'-tī], *a.* y *s.* Veinte. *Twenty-one*, Veintiuno. *Twenty-nine*, Veintinueve.

'Twere [twẹr]. Fuese o fuere; contracción de IT WERE.

Twibil [twai'-bil], *s.* Una especie de hacha de dos filos.

Twice [twais], *adv.* 1. Dos veces. 2. Al doble, duplicadamente. *Twice-born,* Renacido.

Twiddle [twid'-l], *va.* (Fam. o dial.) Tocar ligeramente; hacer dar vueltas.

Twig [twig], *s.* 1. Ramita, rama pequeña (de árbol). 2. Rama pequeña de una arteria u otro vaso.

Twilight [twai'-lait], *s.* 1. Crepúsculo. 2. Cualquier luz débil. 3. Aprehensión o percepción indistinta. *By twilight,* Entre dos luces.—*a.* Obscuro, sombrío, crepuscular.

Twilight sleep [twai'-lait slip], *s.* Anestesia parcial para partos.

Twill [twil], *va.* Tejer con líneas diagonales; cruzar un tejido.—*s.* Tela cruzada; cruzado.

Twin [twin], *s.* 1. Gemelo, mellizo: (Mex.) Cuate: (Cuba) Jimagua: (Amer.) Morocho. 2. (Astr.) Géminis, signo boreal, el tercero de los del zodíaco.—*a.* 1. Gemelo, gemela. 2. Doble; gemíneo, en parejas.

Twin, *vn.* 1. Nacer mellizo. 2. Parir dos o más hijos de un parto. 3. Hermanearse, parearse.

Twin-born [twin'-bērn], *a.* Mellizo, gemelo.

Twine [twain], *va.* 1. Torcer, formar de muchos hilos una cuerda; enroscar, enredar o liar alrededor o dando vueltas. 2. Unir o combinar una cosa con otra de modo que formen un cuerpo entre sí.—*vn.* 1. Enroscarse, ensortijarse. 2. Caracolear, hacer tornos, dar vueltas. *To twine about,* Abrazar.

Twine, *s.* 1. Hilo de acarreto o bramante. (Amer.) Hilo mestizo, guita. (Mex.) Mecate. *Fine twine,* Mecatito. *Sail-twine,* (Mar.) Hilo de vela. 2. Enroscadura, el efecto de enroscarse. 3. Abrazo.

Twinge [twinj], *va.* y *vn.* Causar un dolor agudo o una pena a otro, hacer mal a alguien, atormentar; padecer un dolor local agudo y repentino.

Twinge, *s.* Dolor agudo o punzante, y el tormento que causa; tirón de orejas: dolor de costado; pena del ánimo, remordimiento.

Twinkle [twiṇ'-kl], *vn.* 1. Centellear, chispear, despedir rayos de luz de una manera trémula. 2. Parpadear, mover los párpados; abrir y cerrar los ojos; pestañear guiñando.

Twinkle, Twinkling [twin'-kling], *s.* 1. Vislumbre, resplandor tenue de la luz. 2. La acción de parpadear; pestañeo, guiñada. 3. Momento, instante. *In the twinkling of an eye,* En un abrir y cerrar de ojos. 4. Vibración trémula.

Twinling [twin'-ling], *s.* Cordero mellizo.

Twin-screw [twin'-scrū], *a.* En arquitectura marítima, de doble hélice.

Twirl [twērl], *va.* Voltear, dar vueltas á una cosa como con los dedos.—*vn.* Volver, dar vueltas.

Twirl, *s.* Rotación, movimiento rápido alrededor de algo, vuelta dada en círculo, giro.

Twirler [twērl'-ēr], *s.* El o lo que da vueltas a una cosa; (fam. E. U.) tormenta giratoria, ciclón.

Twist [twist], *va.* 1. Torcer, dar vueltas a alguna cosa alrededor apretándola; retorcer, torcer mucho. 2. Entrelazar o entretejer una cosa con otra. 3. Tejer. 4. Trenzar o hacer trenzas. 5. Ceñir, rodear.—*vn.* 1. Insinuarse ó introducirse una cosa en otra muy íntimamente; enroscarse, envolverse 2. Torcerse; hacerse una rosca. 3. Retortijarse, ensortijarse. *Twisted bread,* Rosca, pan retorcido.

Twist, *s.* 1. Trenza, cualquiera cosa hecha de varias otras torcidas, tejidas, entretejidas o entrelazadas entre sí: cordoncillo, hilo de seda. 2. Torcedura, la acción y efecto de torcer. 3. Torzal, la unión de varias cosas que hacen como hebras torcidas y dobladas unas con otras. 4. Cada hilo o hebra de un cordón o cuerda y el mismo cordón. 5. Rollo de tabaco. *To give one's arm a twist,* Torcerse el brazo.

Twister [twist'-ēr], *s.* 1. Torcedor; cordelero, soguero, cabestrero. 2. Torcedor, instrumento que sirve para torcer o retorcer. 3. Entre marinos, torbellino, viento giratorio; en los Estados Unidos del Oeste, ciclón, gran tormenta. *V.* TORNADO. 4. Pelota arrojada con cierta torcedura peculiar o con movimiento giratorio sobre su eje.

Twit [twit], *va.* Molestar, recordando algo desagradable; reprender, dar en rostro con, echar algo en cara.

Twitch [twich], *va.* Tirar bruscamente.—*vn.* Moverse con una contracción espasmódica, encogerse.

Twitch, *s.* 1. Tensión o tirantez dolorosa de las fibras; retortijón. 2. Acción de tirar bruscamente; tirón repentino. 3. Acial.

Twitter [twit'-ēr], *vn.* Gorjear los pájaros.

Twitter, *s.* 1. Gorjeo (de los pájaros). 2. (Fam.) Estado de agitación del ánimo.

'Twixt [twicst]. Contracción de BETWIXT.

Two [tū], *a.* y *s.* Dos. *Two and two,* Dos a dos. *To kill two birds with one stone,* Matar dos pájaros de un tiro. *Two-legged animal,* Animal bípedo o de dos pies. *Two-cleft,* Bífido, hendido en dos. *Two-faced,* De dos caras; doble, no sincero, disimulado. *Two-horse,* De dos caballos, tirado por dos caballos; de la fuerza de dos caballos. *Two-edged,* Que tiene dos filos o cortes.

Two-fisted [tū-fist'-ed], *a.* (fam.) Viril, vigoroso.

Twofold [tū'-fōld], *a.* Doble, duplicado.—*adv.* Duplicadamente, al doble.

Two-handed [tū'-hand-ed], *a.* 1. De dos manos, que exige el uso de ambas manos a la vez. 2. Construido para usarlo dos personas. 3. Ambidextro. *Two-handed sword,* Espadón.

Twopenny [tū'-pen-i; fam. tup'-en-i], *a.* De dos peniques, del valor de dos peniques; de aquí, vil, de ningún valor.

Two-ply [tū-plai'], *a.* De dos capas, de dos tramas.

Two-seater [tū-sīt'-ēr], *s.* Vehículo de dos asientos.

Two-tongued [tū'-tungd], *a.* Falso, doble.

Two-way [tū-wē'], *a.* De dos direcciones; de tránsito en ambas direcciones.

Tycoon [tai-cūn'], *s.* Magnate industrial o político.

Tymbal [tim'-bal], *s.* Timbal, atabal.

Tympan [tim'-pan], *s.* 1. (Impr.) Tímpano, una hoja o más comúnmente varias hojas de papel colocadas en una prensa para mejorar la calidad de la tirada. 2. Tímpano, membrana u hoja delgada que se pone tensa. *V.* TYMPANUM, 3ª acep.

Tympanum [tim'-pa-num], *s.* 1. (Anat.) Tímpano, membrana extendida y tensa como la de un tambor, que separa el conducto auditivo externo del oído medio; el oído medio. 2. (Bot.) Timpanillo, membrana que tapa el orificio de la cápsula de ciertos musgos. 3. (Arq.) Tímpano, vacío que hay entre el cerramiento del frontis y su cornisa; timpanillo o tímpano, adorno en el arranque de un arco.

Tympany [tim'-pa-ni], *s.* (Ant.) Timpanitis. *V.* TYMPANITES.

Type [taip], *s.* 1. Tipo, símbolo, signo, figura. 2. Emblema, figura simbólica. 3. Tipo, ejemplar distintivo de un grupo o de una clase. 4. Tipo, letra de imprenta, y cada una de sus clases o variedades. 5. (Biol.) Plan, tipo, modelo de estructura; representación ideal de una especie. *Type-bar,* Línea de letras que se funde en una sola pieza. *Type-founder,* Fundidor de letras de imprenta. *Type-foundry,* Fundición de tipos. *Type-setter,* Cajista mecánico; máquina para componer tipos. *Type-setting,* Que compone tipos; composición de letras de imprenta. *Type-wheel,* Rueda tipográfica.

Typewrite [taip'-rait], *va.* y *vn.* (*pp.* TYPEWRITTEN). Escribir a máquina, poner algo por escrito con una máquina de escribir. *A type-written letter,* Una carta escrita a máquina. (Neol.)

Typewriter [taip'-rai''-tēr], *s.* 1. Persona que hace funcionar una máquina de escribir. 2. Máquina de escribir, la que produce letras impresas en vez de escritas.

Typewriting [taip'-rai''-ting], *s.* 1. El acto, arte, u operación de usar una máquina de escribir. 2. Trabajo hecho con dicha máquina.

Typhoid [tai'-feid], *a.* Tifoideo, parecido al tifus o a la fiebre tifoidea.—*s.* Fiebre tifoidea, caracterizada por gran postración e irritación de los intestinos, con diarrea.

Typhoon [tai-fūn'], *s.* Tifón, huracán del mar de la China.

Typhous [tai'-fus], *s.* Tífico, perteneciente o relativo al tifo.

Typhus [tai'-fus], *s.* (Med.) Tifo, tifus, fiebre aguda, continua, caracterizada por perturbación profunda del sistema nervioso y sanguíneo y por irritación del cerebro, a la que sigue el estupor. *Typhus abdominalis,* Fiebre tifoidea.

Typical [tip'-ic-al], *a.* Típico, figurativo, lo que sirve para representar otra cosa; simbólico, alegórico.

Typically [tip'-ic-al-i], *adv.* Figurativamente.

Typify [tip'-i-fai], *va.* Representar, simbolizar.

Typing [taip'-ing], *s.* Mecanografía, dactilografía, escritura en máquina.

Typist [taip'-ist], *s.* Mecanógrafo.

Typographer [tai-pog'-ra-fēr], *s.* Tipógrafo, impresor.

Typographical [tai-po-graf'-ic-al], *a.* 1. Tipográfico, lo que pertenece al arte de imprimir o a la imprenta. 2. Emblemático.

Typographically [tai-po-graf'-ic-al-i], *adv.* Tipográficamente.
Typography [tai-pog'-ra-fi], *s.* 1. Representación emblemática o figurativa. 2. Tipografía, imprenta, el arte de imprimir.
Tyrannic, Tyrannical [tai-ran'-ic, al], **Tyrannous** [tir'-an-us], *a.* Tiránico, cruel, despótico.
Tyrannically [tai-ran'-ic-al-i], **Tyrannously** [tir'-an-us-li], *adv.* Tiránicamente.
Tyrannicalness [tai-ran'-ic-al-nes], *s.* Calidad de tirano.
Tyrannicide [tai-ran'-i-said], *s.* Tiranicidio, la acción de quitar la vida a un tirano.
Tyrannize [tir'-an-aiz], *va.* y *vn.* 1. Tiranizar. 2. Obrar o proceder con tiranía, severidad, rigor o inclemencia.
Tyrant [tai'-rant], *s.* Tirano, déspota, señor absoluto y severo.
Tyranny [tir'-an-i], *s.* 1. Tiranía; gobierno absoluto; gobierno despótico. 2. Opresión, rigor, crueldad, severidad.
Tyre [tair], *s.* (Angloindio) Leche cuajada.
Tyrian [tir'-i-an], *a.* 1. Tirio, de Tiro, antigua ciudad fenicia. 2. Purpurino, de color tirio.—*s.* Tirio, natural de Tiro.
Tyro [tai'-rō], *s.* Tirón, bisoño, principiante, novicio, nuevo en algún arte o disciplina.
Tyrolese, Tyrolian [tir-o-lis', ti-rō'-li-an], *a.* y *s.* Tirolés, del Tirol; natural del Tirol.
Tythe, *s.* y *va.* *V.* TITHE.
Tzar, Tzarina, *s.* *V.* CZAR, CZARINA.
Tzetze, *s.* *V.* TSETSE.

U

U [yū], vigésima primera letra del alfabeto inglés, tiene tres diferentes sonidos: el uno es semejante al del diptongo castellano *iu*, como en *muse, tube, cure* (mius, tiub, quiur); se pronuncia también como en español en las voces *full, truth*, etc.; y por último tiene un sonido entre la *a* y la *o* españolas en *but, cut, tub*, etc. Véase la Introducción.
Ubiety [yu-bai'-e-ti], *s.* (Poco us.) La relación que una cosa tiene con el lugar donde se halla: es término escolástico.
Ubiquitarian [yu-bic-wi-tê'-ri-an], *a.* *V.* UBIQUITOUS.—*s.* El que cree en la ubicuidad de nuestro Redentor y por consiguiente admite su presencia corporal en la Eucaristía.
Ubiquitous, Ubiquitary [yu-bic'-wi-tus, te-ri], *a.* Ubicuo, omnipresente, que está o se halla en todas partes.—*s.* Ubiquitario. *V.* UBIQUITARIAN.
Ubiquity [yu-bic'-wi-ti], *s.* 1. Ubicuidad, existencia en todas partes al mismo tiempo; omnipresencia. 2. Existencia perenne, sin principio ni fin.
Udder [ud'-er], *s.* Ubre, teta de las hembras de los cuadrúpedos.
Udometer [yu-dom'-e-ter], *s.* Udómetro, instrumento para apreciar la cantidad de lluvia que cae en un paraje dado.
Ugh [u], *inter.* ¡Puf! ¡uf! Denota repugnancia o disgusto.
Uglily [ug'-li-li], *adv.* Feamente, deformemente, vilmente.
Ugliness [ug'-li-nes], *s.* 1. Fealdad, deformidad, disformidad. 2. Fealdad, torpeza, corrupción de costumbres.
Ugly [ug'-li], *a.* 1. Feo, disforme, deforme, malparecido; asqueroso. 2. Repugnante, contrario a la moral; que causa aversión. 3. Malo por su carácter o sus consecuencias. 4. (Fam. E. U.) Obstinado.
Uhlan [ū'-lan], *s.* Ulano, soldado de caballería armado con lanza, de los ejércitos austriaco y alemán.
Ukase [yū-kês'], *s.* Ucase, decreto del zar.
Ukulele [yū-ku-lê'-le], *s.* Guitarrita de cuatro cuerdas, originaria de Hawaii.
Ulcer [ul'-ser], *s.* Ulcera.
Ulcerate [ul'-ser-êt], *va.* Ulcerar.
Ulceration [ul-ser-ê'-shun], *s.* Ulceración.
Ulcered [ul'-serd], *a.* Ulcerado.
Ulcerous [ul'-ser-us], *a.* Ulceroso.
Ullage [ul'-ej], *s.* El hueco o vacío de un tonel, la parte que está sin llenar.
Ulmaceous [ul-mê'-shus], *a.* (Bot.) Ulmáceo, relativo a la familia cuyo tipo es el olmo.
Ulna [ul'-na], *s.* Cúbito, el hueso interior y más grueso de los dos que forman el antebrazo.
Ulnar [ul'-nar], *a.* Cubital, relativo al cúbito.
Ulster [ul'-ster], *s.* Levitón o sobretodo largo para uno y otro sexo.
Ulterior [ul-tī'-ri-er], *a.* Ulterior, que está de la parte de allá; oculto, no revelado; que viene después, posterior; secundario.
Ultima [ul'-ti-ma], *s.* Sílaba última o final de una palabra.
Ultimate [ul'-ti-met], *a.* 1. Último, final. 2. Fundamental, esencial; primario.
Ultimately [ul'-ti-met-li], *adv.* Últimamente; esencialmente.
Ultimatum [ul-ti-mê'-tum], *s.* 1. Ultimátum, en lenguaje diplomático, resolución terminante y definitiva, comunicada por escrito. 2. Cualquiera cosa última o fundamental.
Ultra- [ul'-tra]. Prefijo latino que significa más allá o además.—*a.* Exagerado, extremo.
Ultramarine [ul-tra-ma-rīn'], *s.* Ultramar, ultramarino, el color azul formado del lapislázuli.—*a.* Ultramarino, que está o se considera de la otra parte del mar.
Ultramodern [ul-tra-me'-dern], *a.* Ultramoderno.
Ultramontane [ul-tra-men'-ten], *a.* 1. Ultramontano, que está más allá o de la otra parte de los montes; al sur de los Alpes. 2. Ultramontano, ultracatólico, que se refiere al ultramontanismo.
Ultramontanism [ul-tra-men'-ta-nizm], *s.* Ultramontanismo, doctrina de los católicos intransigentes, que abogan sin reserva por la supremacía del Papa sobre el Estado.
Ultramundane [ul-tra-mun'-dên], *a.* Ultramundano.
Ultrasonic [ul-tra-sen'-ic], *a.* Ultrasónico. *Ultrasonic wave*, Ultrasonido.—*s.* Ultrasonido.
Ultrasound [ul-tra-saund'], *s.* Ultrasonido.
Ultraviolet [ul-tra-vai'-o-let], *a.* Ultravioleta. *Ultraviolet ray*, Rayo ultravioleta.
Ululate [ul'-yu-lêt o ū'-lu-lêt], *vn.* Ulular, gritar como un buho.
Ululation [ū-lu-lê'-shun], *s.* Ululato, clamor, grito como el del buho.
Umbel [um'-bel], *s.* (Bot.) Umbela, inflorescencia cuyos pedúnculos nacen en el mismo punto y se elevan a igual o casi igual altura, a modo de quitasol.
Umbellate, Umbellated [um'-bel-êt, ed], **Umbelliferous** [um-bel-if'-er-us], *a.* (Bot.) Umbelífero, aparasolado, dispuesto en figura de parasol o umbela.
Umber [um'-ber], *s.* 1. Tierra de sombra usada por los pintores; tierra parda que consta de un óxido hidratado de hierro mezclado con óxido manganésico y arcilla. 2. (Ict.) Umbla, umbra.
Umber, *va.* Sombrear, hacer obscuro, como con tierra de sombra.
Umbilical [um-bil'-ic-al], *a.* Umbilical, que pertenece o se refiere al ombligo; central.
Umbilicus [um-bi-lai'-cus], *s.* 1. Ombligo. 2. Depresión o concavidad semejante a un ombligo, v. g. en una planta o concha.
Umbo [um'-bō], *s.* Cazoleta de broquel.
Umbrage [um'-brêj], *s.* 1. Pique, resentimiento; sentimiento que causa el verse aventajado u obscurecido por otro; sentimiento producido por una injuria. 2. Sombra, la que hacen los árboles; umbría; sombrajo.
Umbrageous [um-brê'-jus], *a.* Sombrío, umbroso.
Umbrella [um-brel'-a], *s.* Paraguas; quitasol, sombrilla.
Umpirage [um'-pi-rêj], *s.* Arbitramento.
Umpire [um'-pair], *s.* 1. Árbitro, arbitrador, el componedor amigable de alguna disputa o contienda. 2. Árbitro dirimente, el que decide en caso de desavenencia o empate entre los árbitros.—*va.* y *vn.* Arbitrar, decidir o juzgar como árbitro.
Un- [un]. Prefijo que significa no; se usa para expresar negación o estado incompleto, y corresponde muchas veces a des- o in-.
Unabased [un-a-bêst'], *a.* No abatido; no envilecido.
Unabashed [un-a-basht'], *a.* Descocado, falto de rubor o de vergüenza.
Unabated [un-a-bêt'-ed], *a.* No disminuido; completo, cabal.
Unabbreviated [un-ab-bri'-vi-êt-ed], **Unabridged** [un-a-brijd'], *a.* No abreviado; que no está compendiado; no reducido.
Unable [un-ê'-bl], *a.* Inhábil, incapaz, impotente; imposibilitado.
Unabsolved [un-ab-selvd'], *a.* No absuelto; que no está perdonado; que no ha recibido la absolución.
Unaccented [un-ac'-sent-ed], *a.* No acentuado, falto de acento.
Unacceptable [un-ac-sept'-a-bl], *a.* Inaceptable; poco conveniente, desagradable.
Unacceptableness [un-ac-sept'-a-bl-nes], *s.* Calidad de inaceptable.
Unaccessible [un-ac-ses'-i-bl], *a.* Inaccesible.
Unaccommodated [un-ac-cem'-o-dêt-ed], *a.* Desacomodado, falto de los medios convenientes para mantener su estado.
Unaccompanied [un-ac-cum'-pa-nid], *a.* Desacompañado, solo, sin compañía; sin acompañamiento.
Unaccomplished [un-ac-cem'-plisht], *a.* 1. Incompleto, imperfecto, no acabado. 2. Falto de prendas o gracias.
Unaccountable [un-ac-caunt'-a-bl], *a.*

Inexplicable, extraño, extraordinario; que no se puede explicar; que no se puede concebir.

Unaccountably [un-ac-caunt'-a-bli], *adv.* Extrañamente; de un modo extraordinario, raro; de un modo que no puede explicarse.

Unaccustomed [un-ac-cus'-tumd], *a.* Desacostumbrado, fuera del uso y costumbre común; insólito, no habitual.

Unacknowledged [un-ac-nel'-ejd], *a.* No reconocido; negado; inconfeso, no declarado; por contestar, v. gr. una carta de la cual no se ha acusado recibo.

Unacquainted [un-ac-cwênt'-ed], *a.* Desconocido, ignorado, que no conoce, que no sabe. *I am entirely unacquainted with it,* Me es del todo desconocido. *To be unacquainted,* No conocer; ignorar.

Unadjusted [un-ad-just'-ed], *a.* No ajustado, no arreglado.

Unadmired [un-ad-maird'], *a.* Despreciado, no apreciado; olvidado.

Unadmonished [un-ad-men'-isht], *a.* No amonestado, no aconsejado.

Unadored [un-a-dōrd'], *a.* No adorado.

Unadorned [un-a-dōrnd'], *a.* Desadornado, sin adorno.

Unadulterated [un-a-dul'-tẹr-ēt-ed], *a.* Genuino, puro; natural, sin mezcla, no falsificado.

Unadventurous [un-ad-ven'-chur-us], *a.* Prudente, circunspecto, no atrevido; que no se arriesga.

Unadvisable [un-ad-vaiz'-a-bl], *a.* Poco cuerdo, que no es prudente o conveniente.

Unadvised [un-ad-vaizd'], *a.* Imprudente, indiscreto; inconsiderado; hecho sin reflexión.

Unadvisedly [un-ad-vaiz'-ed-li], *adv.* Imprudentemente, temerariamente.

Unadvisedness [un-ad-vaiz'-ed-nes], *s.* Imprudencia, indiscreción, temeridad.

Unaffected [un-af-fect'-ed], *a.* 1. Real, verdadero, ingenuo, natural, sincero, sin artificio. 2. Natural, sencillo, franco, sin afectación. 3. Que no se conmueve, que se mantiene impasible o inalterable.

Unaffectedly [un-af-fect'-ed-li], *adv.* Sencillamente, naturalmente, sin afectación.

Unaffectedness [un-af-fect'-ed-nes], *s.* Sencillez, lisura, ingenuidad, naturalidad.

Unaffecting [un-af-fect'-ing], *a.* Que no mueve los afectos del ánimo; frío, insípido.

Unaided [un-ēd'-ed], *a.* Sin ayuda, sin socorro.

Unalarmed [un-a-lārmd'], *a.* Quieto, tranquilo, en reposo, no turbado.

Unalienable [un-ēl'-yen-a-bl], *a.* Inajenable, inalienable.

Unalienably [un-ēl'-yen-a-bli], *adv.* De un modo inalienable.

Unalleviated [un-al-lī'-vi-ēt-ed], *a.* No aliviado.

Unallied [un-al-laid'], *a.* 1. Falto de parientes o allegados; no afín. 2. Diverso, sin relación alguna.

Unallowable [un-al-lau'-a-bl], *a.* Inadmisible.

Unallowed [un-al-laud'], *a.* Ilícito, no permitido.

Unalloyed [un-al-leid'], *a.* Que no tiene liga o no está mezclado; cabal, completo, absoluto.

Unalterable [un-ōl'-tẹr-a-bl], *a.* Inalterable; invariable, inmutable.

Unalterableness [un-ōl'-tẹr-a-bl-nes], *s.* Inalterabilidad.

Unalterably [un-ōl'-tẹr-a-bli], *adv.* Inalterablemente.

Unambiguous [un-am-big'-yu-us], *a.* Claro, indudable, que no admite duda.

Unambitious [un-am-bish'-us], *a.* No ambicioso, sin ambición.

Un-American [un-a-mer'-i-can], *a.* No americano; que carece de los rasgos característicos de los Estados Unidos, ya se trate de sus habitantes, costumbres, política, etc.

Unamiable [un-ē'-mi-a-bl], *a.* Que no es amable; nada amable.

Unamiableness [un-ē'-mi-a-bl-nes], *s.* Falta de amabilidad.

Unanalyzed [un-an'-a-laizd], *a.* No analizado.

Unanimity [yu-na-nim'-i-ti], *s.* Unanimidad, conformidad de sentimientos, unión de voluntades.

Unanimous [yu-nan'-i-mus], *a.* Unánime, que está de común acuerdo.

Unanimously [yu-nan'-i-mus-li], *adv.* Unánimemente, de común acuerdo.

Unanimousness [yu-nan'-i-mus-nes], *s.* Unanimidad.

Unannealed [un-ạn-nīld'], *a.* No recocido, no templado.

Unanointed [un-a-neint'-ed], *a.* Que no ha sido ungido; que no ha recibido la extremaunción.

Unanswerable [un-an'-sẹr-a-bl], *a.* Incontrovertible, incontestable, indisputable, que no admite duda o disputa; tan convincente que no admite respuesta.

Unanswerableness [un-an'-sẹr-a-bl-nes], *s.* Calidad de incontrovertible o indisputable.

Unanswerably [un-an'-sẹr-a-bli], *adv.* Indisputablemente.

Unanswered [un-an'-sẹrd], *a.* 1. Por contestar, no contestado. 2. No respondido; no impugnado. 3. Que no es recompensado como se debe; no reconocido.

Unappalled [un-ạp-pōld'], *a.* Intrépido, arrojado.

Unapparelled [un-ạp-par'-eld], *a.* Desnudo, sin vestido.

Unapparent [un-ạp-pār'-ent], *a.* Invisible, que no aparece a la vista.

Unapparently [un-ạp-pār'-ent-li], *adv.* Sin apariencia; invisiblemente.

Unappealable [un-ạp-pīl'-a-ble], *a.* Que no admite apelación a un tribunal superior; de última instancia, conclusivo, final.

Unappeasable [un-ạp-pīz'-a-bl], *a.* Implacable.

Unappeasableness [un-ạp-pīz'-a-bl-nes], *s.* Implacabilidad.

Unapplied [un-ạp-plaid'], *a.* Que no se aplica o destina a una cosa determinada.

Unapportioned [un-ạp-pōr'-shund], *a.* Que no es proporcionado.

Unapprehended [un-ap-rẹ-hend'-ed], *a.* No entendido.

Unapprehensive [un-ap-rẹ-hen'-siv], *a.* Lerdo, tardo de ingenio, falto de comprensión; incauto, sencillo.

Unapproachable [un-ạp-prōch'-a-bl], *a.* Inaccesible.

Unapproachableness [un-ạp-prōch'-a-bl-nes], *s.* Inaccesibilidad.

Unappropriated [un-ạp-prō'-pri-ē-ted], *a.* No concedido, destinado ni reservado para un uso especial; impropio, no adecuado a una persona o conjunto de personas en particular.

Unapproved [un-ạp-prūvd'], *a.* Desaprobado.

Unapt [un-apt'], *a.* 1. Poco inclinado, poco propenso; inverosímil. 2. Inepto, incapaz; nada a propósito; inhábil; lerdo.

Unaptly [un-apt'-li], *adv.* Ineptamente, mal, sin maña, sin habilidad.

Unaptness [un-apt'-nes], *s.* Ineptitud, inaptitud, falta de inclinación; torpeza de ingenio.

Unarmed [un-ārmd'], *a.* 1. Desarmado, sin armas; sin defensa. 2. (Zool. y Bot.) Inerme, desprovisto de púas, espinas, placas, etc.

Unarticulated [un-ar-tic'-yu-lē-ted], *a.* Inarticulado, no pronunciado.

Unascertainable [un-as-ẹr-tēn'-a-bl], *a.* Inaveriguable, que no se puede descubrir o determinar.

Unashamed [un''-a-shēmd'], *a.* Que no tiene vergüenza.

Unasked [un-ạskt'], *a.* No solicitado, no llamado, no convidado.

Unaspirated [un-as'-pi-rēt-ed], *a.* Dícese de las letras que no se aspiran al pronunciarlas.

Unaspiring [un-as-pair'-ing], *a.* Modesto; exento de ambición.

Unassailable [un-as-sēl'-a-bl], *a.* Incapaz de ser asaltado, atacado o combatido.

Unassailed [un-as-sēld'], *a.* No acometido.

Unassayed [un-as-sēd'], *a.* No ensayado; no intentado.

Unassignable [un-as-sain'-a-bl], *a.* No cesible, no transferible.

Unassimilated [un-as-sim'-i-lēt-ed], *a.* No asimilado.

Unassisted [un-as-sist'-ed], *a.* Sin socorro, sin auxilio, sin ayuda.

Unassociated [un-as-sō'-shi-ēt-ed], *a.* Solo, no asociado; que no forma parte de una compañía o sociedad.

Unassuaged [un-as-swējd'], *a.* No mitigado; no ablandado.

Unassuming [un-as-siūm'-ing], *a.* Modesto, nada atrevido, nada presuntuoso.

Unassured [un-as-shūrd'], *a.* 1. Que no está asegurado; poco seguro. 2. Que no merece confianza.

Unattached [un-ạt-tacht'], *a.* 1. Suelto, que no está pegado o unido a otra cosa. 2. En especial, (1) no embargado por motivo de una deuda; (2) (Mil.) de reemplazo, no destinado a un cuerpo o regimiento.

Unattackable [un-at-tac'-a-bl], *a.* Inatacable, que no se puede atacar.

Unattainable [un-ạt-tēn'-a-bl], *a.* Inasequible, que no se puede alcanzar o lograr.

Unattainableness [un-ạt-tēn'-a-bl-nes], *s.* Imposibilidad de lograr, obtener o alcanzar una cosa.

Unattainted [un-ạt-tēnt'-ed], *a.* Incorrupto.

Unattempted [un-ạt-tempt'-ed], *a.* No experimentado, no ensayado, no intentado.

Unattended [un-ạt-tend'-ed], *a.* Solo, sin comitiva, sin séquito, sin acompañamiento. *Unattended to,* Descuidado, negligente.

Unattenuated [un-ạt-ten'-yu-ēt-ed], *a.* Que no está atenuado.

Unattested [un-ạt-test'-ed], *a.* No atestiguado, falto de atestación.

Unattired [un-ạt-taird'], *a.* No ataviado o adornado.

Unattractive [un-ạt-trac'-tiv], *a.* Falto de atracción, poco atractivo.

Unattributed [un-ạt-trib'-yu-ted], *a.* Que no se atribuye.

Unattuned [un-ạt-tiūnd'], *a.* Desentonado.

Unau [yū'-nō], *s.* El perezoso común del Brasil, mamífero desdentado, con dos dedos en cada pie. (Cholopus didactylus.)

Unauthentic, Unauthentical [un-ē-then'-tic, al], *a.* Falto de autenticidad, que no es auténtico; (For.) no legalizado; apócrifo, inventado.

Unauthorized, Unauthorised [un-ē'-ther-aizd], *a.* Desautorizado, sin autorización.

Unavailable [un-a-vêl'-a-bl], *a.* Infructuoso, inútil; no disponible, no utilizable, no aprovechable.

Unavailableness [un-a-vêl'-a-bl-nes], *s.* Ineficacia, inutilidad, condición de lo no disponible.

Unavailing [un-a-vêl'-ing], *a.* Inútil, vano, infructuoso, ineficaz.

Unavenged [un-a-venjd'], *a.* Inulto, que queda sin venganza.

Unavian [un-ē'-vi-an], *a.* No semejante o un ave.

Unavoidable [un-a-veid'-a-bl], *a.* Inevitable, ineluctable.

Unavoidableness [un-a-veid'-a-bl-nes], *s.* La calidad de lo que no se puede evitar.

Unavoidably [un-a-veid'-a-bli], *adv.* Inevitablemente.

Unavowed [un-a-vaud'], *a.* No declarado abiertamente; inconfeso.

Unawarded [un-a-wōrd'-ed], *a.* No determinado o juzgado.

Unaware [un"-a-wār'], *a.* 1. Que ignora una cosa determinada; que no presta atención a. 2. (Ant.) Descuidado, negligente. *To be not unaware,* No ignorar, estar impuesto de.

Unawares [un-a-wārz'], **Unaware** [un-a-wār'] (poét.), *adv.* Inopinadamente, repentinamente, de improviso; sin pensar, inadvertidamente; sin premeditación.

Unawed [un-ōd'], *a.* Falto de pavor, falto de temor respetuoso.

Unbacked [un-bact'], *a.* 1. Sin ayuda, sin apoyo (rentístico). 2. Que carece de respaldo, como un taburete.

Unbailable [un-bêl'-a-bl], *a.* Que no admite fianza.

Unbalanced [un-bal'-anst], *a.* 1. Que no está en equilibrio, no balanceado. 2. (Com.) No ajustado para su balance; dícese de las cuentas. 3. Falto de equilibrio mental, lunático, destornillado.

Unbankable [un-bank'-a-bl], *a.* Que no puede depositarse ni cobrarse en un banco.

Unbaptized [un-bap-taized'], *a.* No bautizado; de aquí, no cristiano, impío, profano.

Unbar [un-bār'], *va.* Desatrancar, quitar la tranca o los barrotes.

Unbarrel [un-bar'-el], *va.* Sacar de un tonel o barril lo que contiene.

Unbated [un-bē'-ted], *a.* (Ant.) 1. Que no tiene embotada la punta (espada). 2. No disminuido. *V.* UNABATED.

Unbearable [un-bār'-a-bl], *a.* Intolerable, insufrible, que no se puede sufrir o llevar con paciencia.

Unbearably [un-bār'-a-bli], *adv.* Insoportablemente.

Unbearded [un-bīr'-ded], *a.* 1. Imberbe. 2. Falto de aristas, no barbado.

Unbeaten [un-bī'-tn], *a.* 1. No pisado, no frecuentado. 2. No batido; no apaleado; no golpeado. 3. Invicto, no derrotado.

Unbecoming [un-bg-cum'-ing], *a.* Indecente, indecoroso; impropio, mal parecido, que sienta o cae mal, que no conviene al lugar, a las circunstancias; que no sienta bien al que lo lleva (vestido o adorno).

Unbecomingly [un-bg-cum'-ing-li], *adv.* Indecorosamente, de una manera impropia, inconveniente.

Unbecomingness [un-bg-cum'-ing-nes], *s.* Indecencia, falta de decencia o de decoro.

Unbedded [un-bed'-ed], *a.* 1. No dispuesto en lechos o capas; que no está plantado en los cuadros de un jardín. 2. (Des.) Levantado de la cama; estorbado.

Unbefriended [un-bg-frend'-ed], *a.* Sin amigos.

Unbefitting [un-bg-fit'-ing], *a.* Inconveniente, que no conviene.

Unbegotten [un-bg-get'-n], *a.* 1. Ingénito, no engendrado. 2. Increado, que existe por sí mismo.

Unbeheld [un-bg-held'], *a.* Que todavía no ha sido mirado.

Unbeknown [un-bg-nōn'], *a.* (Prov.) Desconocido; que ejecuta una acción desconocido, sin conocimiento de otro.

Unbelief [un-bg-līf'], *s.* 1. Incredulidad, dificultad o repugnancia en creer. 2. Incredulidad, irreligión, falta de fe.

Unbeliever [un-bg-līv'-er], *s.* Incrédulo, falto de fe religiosa, infiel.

Unbelieving [un-bg-līv'-ing], *a.* Incrédulo, infiel.

Unbeloved [un-bg-luvd'], *a.* Que no es amado.

Unbend [un-bend'], *va.* (*pret.* y *pp.* UNBENT o UNBENDED). 1. Enderezar lo que estaba doblado o torcido; aflojar, soltar lo que estaba tirante. 2. Dar descanso o aliviar de la fatiga; esparcir, distraer el ánimo, solazarse. 3. (Mar.) Desenvergar, desentalingar. *To unbend the sails,* Desenvergar las velas. *To unbend the anchor,* Desentalingar el ancla. *To unbend a cable,* Desentalingar un cable.

Unbending [un-bend'-ing], *a.* Inflexible, que no se encorva; que no se dobla, que no cede; resuelto o determinado firmemente.

Unbending, *a.* Laxante, destinado a diversión, de descanso.—*s.* Laxación, descanso.

Unbenign [un-bg-nain'], *a.* Maligno, malévolo; duro, nada cariñoso.

Unbent [un-bent'], *a.* Aflojado, flojo, suelto; destorcido.

Unbeseeming [un-bg-sīm'-ing], *a.* Mal visto, mal parecido, indecente.

Unbiased, Unbiassed [un-bai'-ast], *a.* Exento de prevención, de preocupación; imparcial.

Unbid [un-bid'], **Unbidden** [un-bid'-n], *a.* 1. Que no ha sido invitado. 2. Espontáneo, de propio movimiento; producido naturalmente.

Unbind [un-baind'], *va.* (*pret.* y *pp.* UNBOUND). Desatar; desvendar.

Unblamable [un-blêm'-a-bl], *a.* Inculpable, irreprensible, incensurable, inocente.

Unblamableness [un-blêm'-a-bl-nes], *s.* Inocencia.

Unblamed [un-blêmd'], *a.* Que no tiene tacha; inocente.

Unbleached [un-blīcht'], *a.* Crudo, no blanqueado: dícese de las telas.

Unblemished [un-blem'-isht], *a.* Irreprensible; sin mancha, sin tacha.

Unblest [un-blest'], *a.* Maldito; desdichado, infeliz, desgraciado.

Unblown [un-blōn'], *a.* 1. Que aun no se ha abierto; que aún está por florecer. 2. Mudo, que no se hace sonar (trompeta). 3. Que no está hinchado ni movido por el viento; no inflado.

Unblunted [un-blunt'-ed], *a.* Que no está embotado, desembotado.

Unblushing [un-blush'-ing], *a.* Que no se avergüenza, desvergonzado.

Unblushingly [un-blush'-ing-li], *adv.* Sin avergonzarse, descaradamente.

Unboastful [un-bōst'-ful], *a.* Modesto, contenido.

Unbodied [un-bed'-id], *a.* Incorpóreo, inmaterial; separado del cuerpo.

Unbolt [un-bōlt'], *va.* Desatrancar, tirar el cerrojo de.

Unbolted [un-bōlt'-ed], *a.* 1. Que no está cernido, no pasado por tamiz. 2. No asegurado con cerrojos, que se le ha quitado o corrido el cerrojo.

Unbonneted [un-ben'-et-ed], *a.* Desbonetado, sin bonete o sombrero.

Unbooted [un-būt'-ed], *a.* Descalzo, sin botas.

Unborn [un-bōrn'], *a.* Innato, que no ha nacido aún.

Unbosom [un-būz'-um], *va.* Abrir su pecho a uno; revelar un secreto, confiar o decir en confianza un secreto.

Unbottomed [un-bet'-umd], *a.* Insondable; infundado; sin fondo.

Unbought [un-bēt'], *a.* 1. Que no ha sido comprado, que se ha adquirido de balde. 2. Que no se ha vendido, hablando de mercancías.

Unbound [un-baund'], *a.* 1. No encuadernado. 2. Suelto, desatado. 3. *Pret.* y *pp.* de *To* UNBIND.

Unbounded [un-baund'-ed], *a.* Infinito, que no tiene fin, límite o término; ilimitado; libre, no empeñado.

Unbrace [un-brês'], *va.* Aflojar, soltar, desabrochar; destapar.

Unbraid [un-brêd'], *va.* Destejer, destrenzar; desenredar.

Unbreakable [un-brêk'-a-bl], *a.* Irrompible.

Unbreathed [un-brīdhd'], *a.* 1. No respirado, no comunicado a otro. 2. (Des.) No ejercitado.

Unbreathing [un-brīdh'-ing], *a.* Inanimado, inánime, que no respira.

Unbred [un-bred'], *a.* Descortés, malcriado, falto de educación; no acostumbrado a, no educado para.

Unbreeched [un-bricht'], *a.* Desbragado, sin bragas.

Unbribed [un-braibd'], *a.* Desinteresado; incorrupto, íntegro.

Unbridle [un-brai'-dl], *va.* Desenfrenar, desembridar.

Unbridled [un-brai'-dld], *a.* Desenfrenado, licencioso, que no tiene freno o sujeción en sus acciones.

Unbroached [un-brōcht'], *a.* Que no ha sido barrenado o decentado.

Unbroke [un-brōk'] (ant.), **Unbroken** [un-brō'-kn], *a.* 1. Intacto, que no está roto, entero. 2. Inviolado. 3. No interrumpido, regular; llano. 4. No debilitado, firme, fuerte. 5. No adiestrado (caballería).

Unbrotherly [un-brudh'-er-li], *a.* Indigno de un hermano.

Unbuckle [un-buc'-l], *va.* Deshebillar, soltar las hebillas.

Unburden [un-bōr'-dn], *va.* Descargar, quitar o aliviar la carga.

Unburied [un-ber'-id], *a.* Insepulto, no enterrado.

Unburned [un-bōrnd'], **Unburnt** [un-bōrnt'], *a.* No quemado.

Unburnished [un-bōr'-nisht], *a.* No bruñido.

Unburning [un-bōrn'-ing], *a.* Que no quema ni consume con su calor.

Unburthen [un-bōr'-dhen], *va.* *V.* UNBURDEN.

Unbusinesslike [un-biz'-nes-laik], *a.* Poco hábil, o que no conviene, para los negocios; poco práctico, poco serio.

Unbutton [un-but'-n], *va.* Desabotonar.

Uncage [un-kéj'], *va.* Sacar o hacer salir de una jaula, libertar.

Uncalled [un-cǫld'], *a.* No llamado, no citado, no pedido. *Uncalled for*, No merecido por las circunstancias; poco necesario, gratuito.

Uncancelled [un-can'-seld], *a.* No abolido, no anulado, no abrogado; no borrado.

Uncandid [un-can'-did], *a.* Falso, doble, falto de candor; desleal, poco sincero.

Uncanny [un-can'-i], *a.* (Esco.) 1. Misterioso, pavoroso. 2. Inhábil, incauto. 3. Poco seguro, peligroso. 4. Severo.

Uncanonical [un-ca-nen'-i-cal], *a.* Contrario u opuesto a los cánones.

Uncanvassed [un-can'-vast], *a.* No examinado; no solicitado.

Uncap [un-cap'], *va.* 1. Destapar, quitar la tapa o cubierta (como de una lente); quitar el casquillo de un fusil. 2. Quitar la superficie del panal (de miel).—*vn.* Saludar, quitándose la gorra o casquete.

Uncared [un-cãrd'], *a.* Desamparado, descuidado, abandonado (seguido de *for*).

Uncase [un-kés'], *va.* 1. Desenvainar, sacar de la caja o vaina; (Mil.) desplegar (la bandera); de aquí, revelar. 2. Desnudar.

Uncaught [un-cōt'], *a.* Aun no cogido.

Uncaused [un-cōzd'], *a.* Sin motivo, sin causa, lo que se hace sin razón.

Uncautious [un-cō'-shus], *a.* Incauto, impróvido. *V.* INCAUTIOUS.

Unceasing [un-sīs'-ing], *a.* Incesante, que no cesa; continuo.

Unceasingly [un-sīs'-ing-li], *adv.* Sin cesar, incesantemente, continuamente.

Unceremonious [un-ser-e-mō'-ni-us], *a.* Que no es ceremonioso, informal; descortés.

Uncertain [un-sẹr'-tẹn], *a.* 1. Incierto, dudoso. 2. Incierto, inconstante; precario. 3. Irresoluto, indeciso; que no sabe, que no está seguro de. 4. Variable, poco seguro; no fijado, no determinado. 5. Sin significación exacta.

Uncertainly [un-sẹr'-tẹn-li], *adv.* Inciertamente.

Uncertainty [un-sẹr'-tẹn-ti], *s.* Incertidumbre, duda, ambigüedad, irresolución; instabilidad, contingencia.

Unchain [un-chên'], *va.* Desencadenar, quitar las cadenas.

Unchangeable [un-chenj'-a-bl], *a.* Impermutable, inmutable.

Unchangeableness [un-chênj'-a-bl-nes], *s.* Inmutabilidad, estabilidad; constancia, firmeza de propósito.

Unchangeably [un-chênj'-a-bli], *adv.* Inmutablemente.

Unchanged [un-chênjd'], *a.* Invariado, no alterado.

Unchanging [un-chênj'-ing], *a.* Inalterable, inmutable.

Uncharitable [un-char'-i-ta-bl], *a.* Nada caritativo, duro.

Uncharitableness [un-char'-i-ta-bl-nes], *s.* Falta de caridad, dureza.

Uncharitably [un-char'-i-ta-bli], *adv.* Sin caridad.

Unchaste [un-chêst'], *a.* Impúdico, deshonesto, lascivo, incontinente.

Unchastity [un-chas'-ti-ti], *s.* Incontinencia, lascivia, impureza, impudicicia.

Unchecked [un-checkt'], *a.* 1. Desenfrenado, que no es reprimido, detenido, contenido. 2. Que no está confrontado, verificado.

Uncheerful [un-chīr'-ful], *a.* Triste, sombrío, melancólico, lúgubre.

Unchristian [un-cris'-chan], *a.* Anticristiano, opuesto o contrario a las leyes o máximas cristianas; indigno de un cristiano.

Unchronicled [un-cren'-i-cld], *a.* Que no ha sido escrito o de lo que no se ha hablado en ninguna crónica o historia.

Unchurch [un-chūrch'], *va.* 1. Excomulgar, expulsar de la iglesia. 2. Negar la validez de los sacramentos y órdenes de una iglesia: dícese p. ej. de una secta.

Uncial [un'-shal], *a.* Uncial: dícese de una clase de letra muy abultada que se halla en algunos manuscritos antiguos, entre los siglos IV y VIII.

Unciform [un'-si-fērm], *a.* Unciforme, en forma de gancho o corchete.

Uncircumcised [un-sẹr'-cum-saizd], *a.* Incircunciso.

Uncircumcision [un-sẹr-cum-sizh'-un], *s.* La falta de circuncisión.

Uncircumscribed [un-sẹr'-cum-scraibd], *a.* Incircunscripto.

Uncircumspect [un-sẹr'-cum-spect], *a.* Imprudente, inconsiderado.

Uncivil [un-siv'-il], *a.* Incivil, descortés, desatento, impolítico.

Uncivilly [un-siv'-il-i], *adv.* Groseramente.

Uncivilized [un-siv'-i-laizd], *a.* Bárbaro, tosco, salvaje, que no está civilizado.

Unclad [un-clad'], *pret.* y *pp.* del verbo UNCLOTHE. No vestido.

Unclarified [un-clar'-i-faid], *a.* Que no está purificado o clarificado.

Unclasp [un-clasp'], *va.* 1. Desabrochar; abrir el broche de un libro. 2. Librar de un abrazo.

Uncle [uŋ'-cl], *s.* 1. Tío, el hermano del padre o de la madre; el marido de la tía. 2. Hombre viejo; particularmente, negro viejo en los Estados Unidos del Sur. 3. (Ger.) *V.* PAWNBROKER. *Uncle Sam*, El gobierno o un representante típico de los Estados Unidos; explicación festiva de las iniciales U. S.

Unclean [un-clīn'], *a.* Inmundo, puerco, sucio, impuro; obsceno.

Uncleanliness [un-clen'-li-nes], *s.* Suciedad, inmundicia, falta de limpieza.

Uncleanly [un-clen'-li], *a.* Inmundo, puerco, impuro; indecente.

Uncleanness [un-clīn'-nes], *s.* Suciedad, asquerosidad; impureza, obscenidad.

Unclog [un-cleg'], *va.* Desembarazar, exonerar, descargar.

Uncloister [un-cleis'-tẹr], *va.* Exclaustrar; poner en libertad; sacar a una persona o cosa de donde estaba encerrada.

Unclose [un-clōz'], *va.* Abrir; descubrir, revelar.

Unclosed [un-clōzd'], *a.* Abierto; descercado.

Unclothe [un-clōdh'], *va.* (*pret.* y *pp.* regular y también UNCLAD). Desnudar, quitar la ropa, poner desnudo.

Unclouded [un-claud'-ed], **Uncloudy** [un-claud'-i], *a.* Claro, despejado, libre de nubes, sereno.

Unco [un'-cō], *a.* (Esco.) Singular, extravagante, poco familiar.—*adv.* Extraordinariamente bien, muy bien. (Abrev. de UNCOUTH.)

Uncoil [un-ceil'], *va.* Desarrollar, desenrollar, extender lo que estaba arrollado.

Uncoined [un-ceind'], *a.* No acuñado.

Uncollectable, Uncollectible [un-cel-ect'-a-bl], *a.* Que no se puede cobrar o recaudar; irrecuperable.

Uncollected [un-cel-ect'-ed], *a.* Disperso, no recogido.

Uncolored, Uncoloured [un-cul'-ẹrd], *a.* Descolorado, que no está teñido; incoloro, que carece de color; exento de preocupación.

Uncombed [un-cōmd'], *a.* Despeinado, no peinado; desgreñado.

Uncomeliness [un-cum'-li-nes], *s.* Fealdad; indecencia; falta de hermosura en las cosas; falta de gracia en las personas.

Uncomely [un-cum'-li], *a.* Indecente; feo; desagradable; grosero.

Uncomfortable [un-cum'-fẹrt-a-bl], *a.* Desconsolado, triste; que no se encuentra bien; penoso, desagradable, molesto, enfadoso, pesado, incómodo, que no es confortante.

Uncomfortableness [un-cum'-fẹrt-a-bl-nes], *s.* Incomodidad, penalidad, desconsuelo, malestar, molestia; desagrado.

Uncomfortably [un-cum'-fẹrt-a-bli], *adv.* Desconsoladamente; penosamente, trabajosamente, incómodamente; tristemente.

Uncommon [un-cem'-un], *a.* Poco frecuente, raro, extraño, extraordinario, nada común; de aquí, digno de observación.

Uncommonly [un-cem'-un-li], *adv.* Extraordinariamente; raramente, infrecuentemente, con poca frecuencia.

Uncommonness [un-cem'-un-nes], *s.* Rareza, singularidad, extrañeza.

Uncommunicated [un-cem-miū'-ni-kêt-ed], *a.* No comunicado.

Uncommunicative [un-cem-miū'-ni-kẹ-tiv], *a.* Poco comunicativo, reservado.

Uncompanionable [un-cem-pan'-yun-a-bl], *a.* Huraño, insociable.

Uncompelled [un-cem-peld'], *a.* Espontáneo, libre, voluntario, no compelido.

Uncompleted [un-cem-plīt'-ed], *a.* Inacabado, no completado, imperfecto.

Uncomplimentary [un-cem-pli-men'-ta-ri], *a.* Poco halagüeño.

Uncompounded [un-cem-paund'-ed], *a.* Simple, sencillo, que no tiene mezcla, que no está compuesto.

Uncompressed [un-cem-prest'], *a.* Que no está comprimido.

Uncompromising [un-cem'-pro-maiz-ing], *a.* Que no admite compromisos; inflexible, intratable, firme.

Unconceived [un-cen-sīvd'], *a.* Impensado; no concebido.

Unconcern [un-cen-sẹrn'], **Unconcernedness** [un-cen-sẹrn'-ed-nes], *s.* Indiferencia, descuido.

Unconcerned [un-cen-sẹrnd'], *a.* Indiferente, descuidado, negligente.

Unconcernedly [un-cen-sẹrn'-ed-li], *adv.* Indiferentemente, sin tomar interés.

Uncondemned [un-cen-demd'], *a.* Que no está condenado; tolerado, admitido; que no está prohibido, que no se desaprueba.

Unconditional [un-cen-dish'-un-al], *a.* Absoluto, sin condiciones, incondicional.

Unconditioned [un-cen-dish'-und], *a.* 1. Exento de condiciones, no limitado ni restringido. 2. (Fil.) In-

condicional, no limitado por condiciones de tiempo ó espacio; exento de relaciones, absoluto.
Unconfined [un-con-faind'], *a.* Libre, ilimitado, sin trabas, sin obstáculos.
Unconfirmed [un-con-fẹrmd'], *a.* Que no está confirmado, apoyado, establecido; que no ha recibido el rito de la confirmación.
Unconformability [un-con-fōrm-a-bil'-i-ti], *s.* Falta de conformidad; en geología, desacuerdo en el orden de sucesión entre una capa anterior y otra más reciente.
Unconformable [un-con-fōrm'-a-bl], *a.* Contrario, incompatible, que no se puede concordar con otra cosa, falto de conformidad; que presenta desacuerdo geológico.
Unconformity [un-con-fōrm'-i-ti], *s.* Desconformidad, desemejanza, falta de conformidad, desacuerdo; falta de paralelismo entre los estratos contiguos.
Unconfused [un-con-fiūzd'], *a.* Distinto, sin confusión; sin turbación, sin embarazo.
Uncongealable [un-con-jīl'-a-bl], *a.* Incongelable, que no puede ser congelado.
Uncongealed [un-con-jīld'], *a.* Incongelado, que no está helado.
Uncongenial [un-con-jī'-nial], *a.* 1. Poco simpático, antipático, sin afinidad. 2. Que no conviene a la naturaleza o al carácter de; desagradable.
Unconnected [un-con-nect'-ed], *a.* Inconexo, que no tiene conexión o relación con otra cosa.
Unconnectedly [un-con-nect'-ed-li], *adv.* De un modo inconexo.
Unconquerable [un-con'-kẹr-a-bl], *a.* Invencible, insuperable.
Unconscionable [un-con'-shun-a-bl], *a.* 1. Desrazonable, injusto, excesivo. 2. No sensato, falto de razón. 3. Falto de conciencia, que obra contra los dictados de ésta. *An unconscionable liar*, Un embustero de tomo y lomo.
Unconscionably [un-con'-shun-a-bli], *adv.* Sin razón, sin conciencia.
Unconscious [un-con'-shus], *a.* 1. Inconsciente, privado temporalmente de la conciencia de sí mismo. 2. No sabedor, que no sabe, que ignora. 3. De existencia ignorada o no conocida.
Unconsciously [un-con'-shus-li], *adv.* Sin tener conciencia de ello; sin saberlo, involuntariamente.
Unconsciousness [un-con'-shus-nes], *s.* 1. Inconsciencia. 2. Insensibilidad.
Unconsecrated [un-con'-sẹ-crêt-ed], *a.* No consagrado.
Unconstitutional [un-con-sti-tū'-shun-al], *a.* Inconstitucional, no conforme a la constitución del estado.
Unconstitutionality [un-con-sti-tū''-shun-al'-i-ti], *s.* Calidad de inconstitucional.
Unconstitutionally [un-con-sti-tū'-shun-al-i], *adv.* Inconstitucionalmente.
Unconstrainable [un-con-strên'-a-bl], *a.* Incapaz de ser constreñido; libre.
Unconstrained [un-con-strênd'], *a.* Libre, voluntario, espontáneo, hecho libremente.
Uncontrollable [un-con-trōl'-a-bl], *a.* Ingobernable; incontrastable, irresistible.
Uncontrollably [un-con-trōl'-a-bli], *adv.* Irresistiblemente, de un modo incontrastable.
Uncontrolled [un-con-trōld'], *a.* Sin freno, libre.
Unconventional [un-con-ven'-shun-al], *a.* Que no se ajusta a las reglas convenidas; informal, libre.
Unconverted [un-con-vẹrt'-ed], *a.* Infiel, no convertido.
Uncord [un-cōrd'], *va.* Desatar, deshacer la cuerda.
Uncork [un-cōrk'], *va.* Sacar el corcho o tapón de, destapar.
Uncorrected [un-cor-rect'-ed], *a.* Incorrecto, no corregido.
Uncorrupt [un-cor-rupt'], *a.* Incorrupto, no pervertido; honrado, íntegro. *V.* INCORRUPT.
Uncorrupted [un-cor-rupt'-ed], *a.* Incorrupto, no viciado o pervertido.
Uncostly [un-cest'-li], *a.* Que no es costoso, no dispendioso.
Uncountable [un-caunt'-a-bl], *a.* Innumerable, que no puede contarse.
Uncouple [un-cup'-l], *va.* Desatrahillar, quitar la trahilla; soltar; separar. *Uncoupled*, Soltado, suelto; de aquí, soltero, no casado.
Uncourtliness [un-cōrt'-li-nes], *s.* Falta de elegancia, grosería, maneras bruscas.
Uncourtly [un-cōrt'-li], *a.* Inelegante, que no tiene maneras cortesanas; incivil.
Uncouth [un-cūth'], *a.* 1. Tosco, grosero, sin gracia, imbécil; rústico. 2. Extraño, singular, extraordinario.
Uncouthly [un-cūth'-li], *adv.* Groseramente, toscamente, singularmente.
Uncouthness [un-cūth'-nes], *s.* Extrañeza, rareza, singularidad.
Uncover [un-cuv'-ẹr], *va.* 1. Destapar, descubrir, quitar lo que cubre. 2. Revelar, poner al descubierto, hacer saber abiertamente.—*vn.* Descubrirse, quitarse el sombrero o gorra.
Uncowl [un-caul'], *va.* Quitar la capucha de.
Uncreate [un-crẹ-êt'], *va.* (Poco us.) Aniquilar, privar de la existencia.
Uncreated [un-crẹ-êt'-ed], *a.* Increado; que no está creado todavía; por crear.
Uncropped [un-crept'], *a.* No recogido, no segado, no pacido o no roído.
Uncrossed [un-crōst'], *a.* No anulado; no frustrado.
Uncrowded [un-craud'-ed], *a.* Holgado, desahogado.
Uncrown [un-craun'], *va.* Destronar, privar de la corona.
Uncristallizable [un-cris-tal-aiz'-a-bl], *a.* Incristalizable.
Unction [uṇc'-shun], *s.* 1. Unción, la acción de ungir. 2. Unción, untura, untadura; también, ungüento. 3. La extremaunción. 4. Unción: dícese de lo que enternece y de lo que mueve el corazón a la piedad y amor de Dios.
Unctuosity [uṇc-chu-es'-i-ti], **Unctuousness** [uṇc'-chu-us-nes], *s.* Untuosidad.
Unctuous [uṇc'-chu-us], *a.* Untuoso, craso.
Unculled [un-culd'], *a.* No cogido; no escogido.
Uncultivable [un-cul'-ti-va-bl], *a.* Incultivable, que no se puede cultivar.
Uncultivated [un-cul'-ti-vêt-ed], *a.* 1. Inculto; que no tiene cultivo ni labor. 2. Inculto, rústico, grosero, que no tiene cultura.
Uncumbered [un-cum'-bẹrd], *a.* Desembarazado, libre.
Uncurbed [un-cūrbd'], *a.* Desenfrenado.
Uncurl [un-cūrl'], *va.* y *vn.* 1. Desenrizar el pelo, deshacer o descomponer los rizos. 2. Extender una cosa que estaba doblada, haciendo vueltas o circunvoluciones.
Uncurrent [un-cur'-ent], *a.* Que no tiene curso; que no es legal; no admitido.
Uncurtain [un-cūr'-ten], *va.* Quitar las cortinas de.
Uncustomary [un-cus'-tem-ẹ-ri], *a.* No habitual, no conforme a la práctica admitida, poco usual.
Uncut [un-cut'], *a.* Que no está cortado, que está entero o completo.
Undamaged [un-dam'-ejd], *a.* Ileso, libre de daño.
Undate [un-dêt'], *a.* Ondeado, que presenta undulaciones.
Undated [un-dê'-ted], *a.* 1. Sin fecha. 2. *V.* UNDATE.
Undaunted [un-dānt'-ed], *a.* Impávido, denodado; arrojado, ardiente, impertérrito, intrépido.
Undauntedly [un-dānt'-ed-li], *adv.* Intrépidamente, con osadía, con arrojo.
Undauntedness [un-dānt'-ed-nes], *s.* Intrepidez, arrojo, impavidez.
Undazzled [un-daz'-ld], *a.* No ofuscado.
Undecagon [un-dec'-a-gen], *s.* (Geom.) Endecágono, undecágono, figura de once lados y once ángulos.
Undecayed [un-dẹ-kêd'], **Undecaying** [un-dẹ-kê'-ing], *a.* Inmarcesible, incapaz de marchitarse; inalterable, duradero.
Undeceive [un-dẹ-sīv'], *va.* Desengañar, hacer conocer el engaño, advertir el error, hablar sin rebozo.
Undeceived [un-dẹ-sīvd'], *a.* Desengañado.
Undecided [un-dẹ-said'-ed], *a.* Indeciso, indeterminado, que no se ha decidido o determinado.
Undecipherable [un-dẹ-sai'-fẹr-a-bl], *a.* Indescifrable.
¿**Undecisive**, *a.* *V.* INDECISIVE.
Undeclinable [un-dẹ-clain'-a-bl], *a.* Indeclinable.
Undeclined [un-dẹ-claind'], *a.* Recto, derecho.
Undefaced [un-dẹ-fêst'], *a.* Entero, sano, no desfigurado.
Undefied [un-dẹ-faid'], *a.* No desafiado.
Undefiled [un-dẹ-faild'], *a.* Impoluto, puro, limpio, libre de mancha.
Undefinable [un-dẹ-fain'-a-bl], *a.* Indefinible.
Undefined [un-dẹ-faind'], *a.* Indefinido.
Undeformed [un-dẹ-fōrmd'], *a.* No desfigurado.
Undemonstrable [un-dẹ-men'-stra-bl], *a.* Indemostrable, que no se puede demostrar.
Undeniable [un-dẹ-nai'-a-bl], *a.* Innegable, incontestable, irrefragable.
Undeniably [un-dẹ-nai'-a-bli], *adv.* Irrefragablemente, de un modo incontestable o innegable.
Under [un'-dẹr], *a.* 1. Inferior, situado más abajo. 2. Subalterno, subordinado. 3. Bajo (de tono).—*prep.* y *adv.* 1. Debajo, denota dependencia o subordinación. 2. Debajo, más abajo, denota que una cosa está cubierta con otra. 3. Debajo, en un puesto inferior respecto al superior. 4. Bajo de, inferior a. 5. So: en español úsase sólo delante de las palabras *capa, color* y *pena*. 6. Soto: úsase sólo en composición. 7. Menos, menos que, por menos, en menos. 8. En; por; mediante, por el medio de; con relación a; que es

asunto u objeto de. *Under discussion,* En discusión. 9. En tiempo de, en la época de. 10. En virtud de; autorizado o atestiguado por. *Under my hand and seal,* Sellado y firmado por mí. 11. Conforme á, según. *Under contract,* Conforme al contrato. 12. Plantado o sembrado con. *A hectare under corn,* Una hectárea sembrada de maíz. *To be under restraint,* Estar sujeto. *To be under age,* Ser menor o no haber salido de la minoridad. *Under the care of,* Al cuidado de. *I am under an obligation to him,* Le debo favores. *Under sail, under canvas,* (Mar.) A la vela. *Under pain of death,* So pena de muerte. *Under arms,* Bajo las armas. *Under cover,* Al abrigo, a cubierto; dentro de un sobre. *To be under a cloud,* Hallarse en apuros, sufrir en su reputación. *To bring under,* Someter, sujetar. *To keep under,* Reprimir, subyugar, dominar. *Under steam,* Impelido por el vapor. *Under an assumed name,* Bajo un nombre supuesto. *The son is under tutors,* El hijo está sometido a sus tutores. *Under consideration,* En consideración. *Under* se usa muy frecuentemente en la formación de palabras compuestas.

Underage [un-dẹr-êj'] *a.* Menor de edad.

Underarmed [ʊn-dẹr-armd'], *a.* Sin suficientes armas.

Underbid [un-dẹr-bid'], *va.* Ofrecer menos que otro, particularmente por trabajo o materiales.

Underbind [un-dẹr-baind'], *va.* Atar por debajo.

Underbrush [un'-dẹr-brush], *s.* Maleza, los arbustos y arbolillos que crecen debajo de los grandes árboles.

Undercarriage [un-dẹr-car'-ij], *s.* 1. Bastidor de automóvil. 2. (Aer.) Tren de aterrizaje.

Undercharge [ʊn-dẹr-chārj'], *va.* 1. Cobrar menos que lo acostumbrado. 2. Cobrarle (a alguien) muy poco. 3. Cargar una arma con muy poco explosivo.

Underclerk [ʊn'-dẹr-clẹrk], *s.* Subsecretario o segundo secretario; escribiente.

Underclothes, Underclothing [ʊn'dẹr-clōdhs, clō'-dhing], *s.* Prendas de vestir interiores, ropa interior.

Under cover [ʊn'-dẹr cʊv'-ẹr], *adv.* En secreto, subrepticiamente.

Undercurrent [ʊn'-dẹr-cur''-ẹnt], *s.* Corriente inferior, debajo de la superficie; (fig.) tendencia obscura u oculta.

Undercut [ʊn-dẹr-cʊt'], *va.* 1. Socavar, cavar debajo de (v.g. una masa de hulla) para facilitar su extracción. 2. En tenis, cortar la pelota con golpe por debajo. 3. Vender a precios más bajos (que el competidor). 4. Trabajar por menos salario (que otros).—*s.* 1. Socava. 2. En tenis, golpe que se da por debajo a la pelota.

Underdeveloped [ʊn-der-dẹ-vel'-ẹpt], *a.* Subdesarrollado.

Underdevelopment [ʊn-der-dẹ-vel'-ẹp-mẹnt], *s.* Subdesarrollo.

Underdog [ʊn'-dẹr-deg], *s.* 1. Perdidoso. 2. Víctima. 3. El de abajo.

Underestimate [ʊn-dẹr-es'-ti-mêt], *va.* Subestimar.

Underexposure [un-dẹr-ex-pō'-zhur], *s.* Poca exposición (en una fotografía)

Underfeed [ʊn'-dẹr-fīd], *va.* 1. Desnutrir, alimentar muy poco. 2. Alimentar (una caldera) por debajo.

Underfilling [un-dẹr-fil'-ing], *s.* Cimiento de un edificio.

Underframe [ʊn'-dẹr-frêm], *s.* Infraestructura.

Underfurnish [un-dẹr-fūr'-nish], *va.* Escasear; proveer con menos de lo que se necesita.

Undergird [un-dẹr-gẹrd'], *va.* Ceñir por debajo.

Undergo [un-dẹr-gō'], *va.* (*pret.* UNDERWENT, *pp.* UNDERGONE). 1. Sufrir, padecer, aguantar, sostener, experimentar. 2. Pasar por; arrostrar, exponerse a, correr peligro o riesgo. 3. Estar sometido a, existir bajo.

Undergraduate [ʊn-dẹr-grad'-yu-êt], *s.* Alumno no graduado.

Underground [ʊn'-der-graund], *s.* 1. Subterráneo. 2. Metropolitano. 3. Resistencia.—*a.* Subterráneo. *Underground garage,* Aparcamiento subterráneo.

Undergrown [ʊn'-dẹr-grōn], *a.* Achaparrado, de talla menor que la mediana.

Undergrowth [ʊn'-dẹr-grōth], *s.* 1. Maleza, chamarasca, lo que nace debajo de los árboles grandes en los bosques y florestas. 2. Calidad de achaparrado o pequeño.

Underhand [un-dẹr-hand'], *adv.* Bajo mano, por bajo cuerda, clandestinamente.—*a.* Secreto, clandestino, socarrón, disimulado.

Underhanded [un-dẹr-hand'-ed], *a.* Disimulado, proseguido clandestinamente, con segunda intención.

Underlay [un-dẹr-lê'], *va.* Reforzar o fortalecer con alguna cosa puesta por debajo.—*vn.* Inclinarse un filón fuera de la perpendicular.—*s.* 1. (Impr.) Pedazo de papel, etc., que se pone debajo de ciertas partes de una forma para alzarlas al debido nivel. 2. (Min.) Inclinación de un filón.

Underlie [un-dẹr-lai'], *vn.* (*pret.* UNDERLAY, *pp.* UNDERLAIN). 1. Estar debajo. 2. *va.* Ser la razón fundamental o sostén de. *The principle that underlay his plan,* El principio que sirvió de fundamento a su plan. 3. ¿Estar sujeto a.

Underline [un-dẹr-lain'], *va.* Subrayar, notar las palabras con rayas puestas debajo de ellas.

Underling [ʊn'-dẹr-ling], *s.* 1. Un agente inferior. 2. Un hombre vil y despreciable; mequetrefe.

Underlying [un-dẹr-lai'-ing], *a.* Subyacente; fundamental.

Undermine [un-dẹr-main'], *va.* 1. Minar, cavar o abrir camino por debajo de la tierra. 2. Zapar, minar, abrir minas. 3. Minar los cimientos o los fundamentos de una cosa. 4. Dañar o injuriar por medios ocultos.

Undermost [ʊn'-dẹr-mōst], *a.* Infimo, el más bajo.—*adv.* Debajo de todo.

Underneath [un-dẹr-nīth'], *adv.* Debajo, en la parte inferior o en un paraje inferior.

Undernourished [ʊn-dẹr-nʊr'-ishd], *a.* Desnutrido, mal alimentado.

Underpaid [ʊn'-dẹr-pêd], *pp,* y *a.* Mal pagado, insuficientemente retribuído.

Underpart [ʊn'-dẹr-pārt], *s.* Parte inferior o no esencial.

Underpass [ʊn'-dẹr-pas], *s.* Paso bajo, paso inferior (en un camino, calle, etc.).

Underpay [un-dẹr-pê'], *va.* Pagar insuficientemente.—*s.* Retribución insuficiente.

Underpin [ʊn''-dẹr-pin'], *va.* Apuntalar, sostener desde abajo, cuando se quita un puntal anterior.

Underpinning [ʊn'-dẹr-pin'-ing], *s.* 1. Apuntalamiento (de un edificio). 2.(fam.) Las piernas de una persona.

Underpraise [un-dẹr-prêz'], *va.* Alabar una cosa menos de lo que merece.

Underprivileged [ʊn-dẹr-priv'-i-lejd], *s.* y *a.* Necesitado, desamparado, desvalido.

Underprize [un-dẹr-praiz'], *va.* Despreciar, desestimar, rebajar la estimación o valor de una cosa.

Underproduction [ʊn-dẹr-pro-dʊc'-shʊn], *s.* Producción insuficiente (para satisfacer la demanda).

Underprop [un-dẹr-prep'], *va.* Apuntalar.

Underrate [un-dẹr-rêt'], *va.* Despreciar, no dar a una cosa todo el valor o la estimación que se merece.

Underrun [un-dẹr-run'], *va.* 1. Correr por debajo. 2. (Mar.) Recorrer; poner un cable debajo de un barco y tirar de él. *To underrun the cables,* (Mar.) Recorrer los cables.

Underscore [un-dẹr-scōr'], *va.* Subrayar, poner una línea bajo una letra o palabra.

Under-secretary [un-dẹr-sec'-rẹ-tẹ-ri], *s.* Subsecretario.

Undersell [un-dẹr-sel'], *va.* Vender por menos o más barato que otro.

Underservant [un-dẹr-sẹr'-vant], *s.* Criado de escalera abajo.

Underset [un-dẹr-set'], *va.* Poner debajo.

Undershirt [un'-dẹr-shẹrt], *s.* Elástica, camiseta.

Undershot [un'-dẹr-shet], *a.* Impelido por agua que corre debajo; se dice de una rueda hidráulica.

Undersign [un-dẹr-sain'], *va.* Subscribir, firmar al pie de un escrito; se usa principalmente en el participio pasado, *undersigned,* infrascrito, el abajo firmado.

Undersized [un'-dẹr-saizd], *a.* De talla menor que mediana.

Underskirt [ʊn'-dẹr-skẹrt], *s.* 1. Fondo, refajo, enagua. 2. Falda principal de un vestido adornado con sobrefalda.

Underslung [ʊn'-dẹr-slʊng], *a.* Colgante, suspendido debajo del bastidor o del eje (de un vehículo).

Undersold [un-dẹr-sōld'], *pret.* y *pp.* del verbo UNDERSELL.

Understand [un-dẹr-stand'], *va.* y *vn.* (*pret.* y *pp.* UNDERSTOOD). 1. Entender, percibir, alcanzar, comprender. 2. Entender, saber, ser sabedor, tener claro conocimiento de. 3. Entender, conocer, penetrar. *I understand that,* Tengo entendido que. 4. Sobrentender, entender una cosa no expresa, pero que debe suponerse en vista de lo que antecede. *The preposition is understood,* La preposición está sobreentendida. *I gave him to understand,* Le dí a entender, le hice comprender. *That is understood,* Está entendido; por supuesto. *It being understood,* Bien entendido. *Be it understood,* Entiéndase.

Understanding [ʊn''-dẹr-stand'-ing], *s.* 1. Entendimiento, una de las tres potencias que se atribuyen al alma; comprensión. 2. Inteligencia, capacidad, conocimiento. 3. El espíritu en tanto que concibe. 4. Inteligencia, correspondencia, armonía, amistad recíproca. *A secret understanding*, Inteligencia, concierto o acuerdo secreto. *A good understanding*, Buena armonía. *To come to an understanding*, Convenirse; quedar o ponerse de acuerdo.—*a.* Inteligente, perito.

Understandingly [un''-dęr-stand'-ing-li], *adv.* De una manera inteligente.

Understate [un'-dęr-stêt], *va.* 1. Declarar con menos fuerza que la verdad merece. 2. Declarar como menos que lo verdadero.

Understatement [un'-dęr-stêt-ment], *s.* Expresión exageradamente moderada.

Understood, *pret.* y *pp.* del verbo *To* UNDERSTAND.

Understrapper [un'-dęr-strap-ęr], *s.* Substituto, agente inferior; el hombre que sirve de instrumento o apoyo de maldades.

Understudy [un'-dęr-stud-i], *s.* Actor listo para remplazar a otro en determinado momento.

Undertake [un''-dęr-têk'], *va.* y *vn.* 1. Emprender, comenzar alguna cosa que se supone difícil o peligrosa. 2. Emprender, tomar a su cargo, tomar por su cuenta, entrar en una empresa. 3. Emprender, determinarse a hacer o tratar alguna cosa. 4. Oponerse. 5. Responder, salir fiador. 6. Aventurar, arriesgar.

Undertaker [un'-dęr-tek-ęr], *s.* 1. Emprendedor; empresario; particularmente, el que prepara y dirige los entierros; (Amer.) zacateca. 2. El que toma a su cargo una empresa o le da comienzo; contratista.

Undertaking [un-dęr-tek'-ing], *s.* 1. Empresa, empeño; lo que se ha emprendido. 2. Oficio de preparar y dirigir entierros. 3. (For.) Empeño o garantía.

Undertone [un'-dęr-tōn], *s.* 1. Tono bajo de la voz. 2. Matiz suavizado de un color. 3. Sentido o indicación que se implica pero no se expresa.

Undertook, *pret.* del verbo *To* UNDERTAKE.

Undertow [un'-dęr-tō], *s.* Resaca, el movimiento de la ola al retirarse de la playa; también, contracorriente hacia el fondo del mar.

Undervaluation [un''-dęr-val-yu-é'-shun], *s.* Estimación muy baja, apreciación de algo en menos de lo que vale.

Undervalue [un''-dęr-val'-yū], *va.* Despreciar, dar menos valor a alguna cosa de lo que se debe; apreciar en menos.

Undervalue, *s.* Menosprecio, poco valor, escasa estimación.

Underwear [un'-dęr-wār], *s.* Ropa interior.

Underwent, *pret.* del verbo *To* UNDERGO.

Underwood [un'-dęr-wud], *s.* Monte bajo, los arbustos o árboles enanos que nacen entre los grandes. *V.* UNDERBRUSH.

Underwork [un-dęr-wūrk'], *va.* Competir con, trabajando por menos jornal.—*vn.* Trabajar menos de lo que se debe; dejar imperfecta alguna cosa por falta de trabajo.—*s.* Trabajo subordinado o de rutina.

Underworkman [un-dęr-wūrk'-man], *s.* El oficial u obrero que hace un trabajo manual bajo la dirección del maestro o de otro oficial superior a él.

Underworld [un'-dęr-wūrld], *s.* 1. Infierno. 2. Hampa, mundo del vicio, bajos fondos sociales.

Underwrit, Underwritten, *pp.* de *To* UNDERWRITE.

Underwrite [un-dęr-rait'], *va.* 1. Subscribir, firmar al pie de un escrito. 2. Asegurar, particularmente contra los riesgos del mar. 3. Obligarse o comprometerse a comprar todas las acciones de una nueva empresa o compañía, a las cuales no se subscribe el público.

Underwriter [un-dęr-rait'-ęr], *s.* Asegurador, corporación o persona que asegura mercancías u otras cosas.

Underwrote, *pret.* del verbo *To* UNDERWRITE.

Underwrought, *pret.* y *pp. ant.* del verbo *To* UNDERWORK.

Undescribed [un-dę-scraibd'], *a.* No descrito.

Undescried [un-dę-scraid'], *a.* No visto, no descubierto.

Undeserved [un-dę-zęrvd'], *a.* No merecido, inmerecido.

Undeservedly [un-dę-zęrv'-ed-li], *adv.* Sin mérito, sin merecerlo o sin haberlo merecido; injustamente.

Undeserving [un-dę-zęrv'-ing], *a.* Indigno de gozar o conseguir una cosa; no benemérito.

Undesigned [un-dę-zaind'], *a.* Involuntario, indeliberado, hecho sin intención.

Undesigning [un-dę-zain'-ing], *a.* Sincero, sencillo; el que obra sin malicia; el que hace una cosa sin objeto o designio determinado.

Undesirable [un-dę-zair'-a-bl], *a.* Que no es deseable, poco deseable.

Undesired [un-dę-zaird'], *a.* No deseado, no solicitado.

Undesiring [un-dę-zair'-ing], *a.* Negligente, tibio; no deseoso, indiferente.

Undesirous [un-dę-zair'-us], *a.* Que no desea, no deseoso.

Undestroyed [un-dę-streid'], *a.* No destruído.

Undetected [un-de-tec'-ted], *a.* Sin ser descubierto.

Undetermined [un-dę-tęr'-mind], *a.* Indeterminado, sin fijar, sin decidir; indeciso, incierto.

Undeterred [un-dę-tęrd'], *a.* Que no está asustado; no impedido, no estorbado.

Undeviating [un-dī'-vi-ét-ing], *a.* Regular, directo; que sigue su curso natural; sin rodeo, siempre el mismo.

Undevoted [un-dę-vōt'-ed], *a.* Opuesto; no dedicado a.

Undevout [un-de-vaut'], *a.* Indevoto, irreligioso, incrédulo.

Undid [un-did'], *pret.* de *To* UNDO.

Undigested [un-di-jest'-ed], *a.* Indigesto, no digerido; mal ordenado.

Undiminished [un-di-min'-isht], *a.* Entero, no disminuido.

Undine [un-dīn'], *s.* (Mit.) Ondina, ninfa de las aguas. (< Lat. *unda.*)

Undirected [un-di-rect'-ed], *a.* Que no está dirigido o no lleva dirección alguna; que no tiene gobierno; entregado a sí mismo; (carta) sin señas.

Undiscerned [un-di-zęrnd'], *a.* No descubierto.

Undiscernedly [un-di-zęrn'-ed-li], *adv.* Ocultamente.

Undiscernible [un-di-zęrn'-i-bl], *a.* Invisible, imperceptible.

Undiscernibly [un-di-zęrn'-i-bli], *adv.* Invisiblemente, imperceptiblemente.

Undiscerning [un-di-zęrn'-ing], *a.* Falto de discernimiento, falto de gusto.

Undisciplined [un-dis'-i-plind], *a.* Indisciplinado, falto de enseñanza; falto de corrección.

Undiscoverable [un-dis-cuv'-ęr-a-bl], *a.* Que no se puede descubrir; imposible de encontrar.

Undiscovered [un-dis-cuv'-ęrd], *a.* No descubierto o visto, escondido.

Undisguised [un-dis-gaizd'], *a.* Sin disfraz, cándido, franco, abierto, sencillo.

Undishonoured [un-dis-en'-ęrd], *a.* No deshonrado.

Undismayed [un-dis-mêd'], *a.* Que no ha perdido el ánimo o valor; que está o se mantiene firme.

Undisposed [un''-dis-pōzd'], *a.* No dispuesto. *Undisposed of*, Disponible, no vendido, no decidido de otra manera.

Undisputed [un-dis-piūt'-ed], *a.* Evidente, incontestable, incontrovertible.

Undissembled [un-di-sem'-bld], *a.* No disimulado, no disfrazado; franco, abierto, ingenuo.

Undissolving [un-diz-elv'-ing], *a.* Que no se derrite.

Undistempered [un-dis-tem'-pęrd], *a.* 1. Sano, bueno, que no padece enfermedad. 2. Tranquilo, sosegado, que nada tiene que lo inquiete.

Undistinctive [un-dis-tinc'-tiv], *a.* Indistintivo, que no hace distinción.

Undistinguishable [un-dis-tiṇ'-gwish-a-bl], *a.* Indistinguible, que no se puede distinguir.

Undistinguished [un-dis-tiṇ'-gwisht], *a.* 1. Indistinto, que no se distingue o no se diferencia. 2. Indistinto, que no se percibe clara y distintamente.

Undistinguishing [un-dis-tiṇ'-gwish-ing], *a.* Que no distingue o no hace diferencia alguna entre las cosas; que carece de discernimiento.

Undisturbed [un-dis-tūrbd'], *a.* Que no está turbado, inquietado; sin alteración ni desarreglo; quieto, tranquilo, no agitado; impasible, que por nada se turba.

Undivided [un-di-vaid'-ed], *a.* Indiviso, entero. *An undivided estate*, Una propiedad indivisa.

Undivulged [un-di-vuljd'], *a.* Secreto.

Undo [un-dū'], *va.* (*pret.* UNDID, *pp.* UNDONE). 1. Deshacer, anular el efecto de; reponer en el estado anterior. 2. Arruinar, perder: causar pesadumbre a. 3. Desatar, desliar; desarmar, desmontar. 4. No hacer, dejar sin hacer. *He intends to undo me*, Me quiere perder. *To come undone*, Deshacerse, desatarse. *To leave undone*, No hacer, dejar de hacer. *To remain undone*, Quedar por hacer. *I am undone*, Estoy perdido, estoy arruinado.

Undock [un-dec'], *va.* Sacar un buque del dique.

Undoing [un-dū'-ing], *s.* 1. Acción de deshacer. 2. Ruina, pérdida.

Undone [un-dun'], *pp.* del verbo UNDO.

Undoubted [un-daut'-ed], *a.* No dudado, evidente, fuera de duda, cierto.

Undoubtedly [un-daut'-ed-li], *adv.* Indudablemente.

Undrawn, *pp.* No sacado; no atraído, no arrastrado; que no ha sido sorteado (billete de lotería, etc.).

Undreamed [un-drīmd'], *a.* Impensado, inesperado. *Undreamed of*, Inopinado.

Undress [un-dres'], *va.* 1. Desnudar,

quitar la ropa. 2. Desvendar, quitar el vendaje de (una herida), etc.). —*vn.* Desnudarse.
Undress [un'-dres] *s.* Paños menores, ropa de levantarse; ropa de casa. *To be in an undress,* (Fam.) Estar de trapillo. *Undress,* (Mil.) Uniforme diario, traje de cuartel.—*a.* Perteneciente al traje diario; de aquí, informal.
Undried [un-draid'], *a.* Que aun no está seco o no secado; verde (frutos, etc.).
Undriven [un-driv'-n], *a.* Quieto, fijo; no impelido hacia ningún lado.
Undue [un-diū'], *a.* 1. Indebido, más que suficiente, excesivo, desmedido. 2. Irregular; ilícito, injusto, contra razón, ley o costumbre. 3. Que no es debido, no vencido.
Undulant fever [un'-diu-lant fī'-vęr], *s.* Fiebre mediterránea, fiebre de Malta.
Undulate [un'-diu-lēt], *vn.* Undular, ondear o hacer ondas, presentar la apariencia de una undulación.—*va.* Hacer ondear.
Undulation [un-diu-lé'-shun], *s.* Undulación, movimiento a modo del de las ondas.
Undulatory [un'-diu-la-to-ri], *a.* Undulatorio: dícese del movimiento semejante al de las ondas.
Unduly [un-diū'-li], *adv.* Indebidamente; ilícitamente.
Undutiful [un-diū'-ti-ful], *a.* Inobediente, desobediente, que falta a sus deberes. *An undutiful son,* Un mal hijo, un hijo desobediente.
Undutifully [un-diū'-ti-ful-i], *adv.* Inobedientemente, con inobediencia; sin respeto; contra su obligación.
Undying [un-dai'-ing], *a.* Imperecedero, que no muere; inmortal.
Unearth [un-ęrth'], *va.* Sacar de la tierra, desarraigar; revelar, descubrir.
Unearthly [un-ęrth'-li], *a.* Que no es terrenal, sobrenatural; aterrador, que infunde miedo, espantoso.
Uneasily [un-ī'z'-i-li], *adv.* Inquietamente, incómodamente, con mucho trabajo; penosamente.
Uneasiness [un-ī'z'-i-nes], *s.* Inquietud, desasosiego, incomodidad, disgusto, malestar; pena, pesadumbre.
Uneasy [un-ī'-zi], *a.* 1. Inquieto, cuidadoso, ansioso, desasosegado. 2. Impertinente, molesto, enfadoso, incómodo. 3. Embarazado, incomodado, que carece de gracia, desazonado. 4. Difícil de efectuar, dificultoso.
Uneaten [un-ī'-tn], *a.* No comido, no devorado.
Unedifying [un-ed'-i-fai-ing], *a.* Que no edifica con su ejemplo.
Uneducated [un-ed'-yu-kēt-ed], *a.* Falto de educación, sin instrucción; ignorante.
Uneffaced [un-ef-fēst'], *a.* Que no está borrado o cancelado.
Unelucidated [un-ę-lū'-si-dēt-ed], *a.* No elucidado, no aclarado.
Unemployed [un-em-ploid'], *a.* 1. Desocupado, sin ocupación, sin empleo; ocioso. 2. No empleado, no invertido, que no produce.
Unencumbered [un-en-cum'-bęrd], *a.* Sin trabas; exento de cargas de cualquiera clase.
Unending [un-end'-ing], *a.* Sin fin, perpetuo, eterno.
Unendowed [un-en-daud'], *a.* Indotado.
Unendurable [un-en-diūr'-a-bl], *a.* Inaguantable, insoportable.
Unenduring [un-en-diūr'-ing], *a.* Poco duradero, de corta duración.
Unengaged [un-en-gējd'], *a.* Desocupado, libre, no comprometido.
Unenjoyed [un-en-joid'], *a.* Que no se goza o no se ha gozado.
Unenjoying [un-en-joi'-ing], *a.* Que no goza.
Unenlarged [un-en-lārjd'], *a.* Estrecho; limitado.
Unenlightened [un-en-lai'-tnd], *a.* No iluminado.
Unenterprising [un-en'-tęr-praiz-ing], *a.* Que no es emprendedor.
Unentertaining [un-en-tęr-tên'-ing], *a.* Que no divierte o entretiene, insípido.
Unenumerated [un-ę-niū'-męr-ēt-ed], *a.* No numerado.
Unenviable [un-en'-vi-a-bl], *a.* Poco envidiable.
Unenvied [un-en'-vid], *a.* No envidiado, que no causa envidia.
Unequable [un-ī'-cwa-bl], *a.* Desigual, variable, irregular.
Unequal [un-ī'-cwal], *a.* 1. Desigual, que no es igual en extensión, duración o propiedades. 2. Ineficaz, insuficiente, inferior. 3. Desproporcionado; de aquí, no equitativo, injusto, parcial. 4. Falto de uniformidad. 5. (Bot.) Poco simétrico.
Unequalled [un-ī'-cwald], *a.* Sin igual, sin semejante, sin par, incomparable.
Unequally [un-ī'-cwal-i], *adv.* Desigualmente; fuera de proporción, insuficientemente.
Unequipped [un-ę-cwipt'], *a.* Que no está provisto de lo que necesita para un viaje, empresa, etc.
Unequivocal [un-ę-cwiv'-o-cal], *a.* Inequívoco, que no admite duda o equivocación.
Unerring [un-er'-ing], *a.* Infalible, sumamente cierto y seguro; inerrable.
Unerringly [un-er'-ing-li], *adv.* Infaliblemente, con toda seguridad y certidumbre.
Unespoused [un-es-pauzd'], *a.* Que no tiene defensor.
Unessayed [un-es-sēd'], *a.* No ensayado; no intentado.
Unesteemed [un-es-tīmd'], *a.* No estimado o apreciado.
Uneven [un-ī'-vn], *a.* 1. Desigual, que no es llano, escabroso, barrancoso, quebrado. 2. Desigual, que no corresponde o conviene con otra cosa; que no es regular o uniforme. 3. Impar, no divisible por dos.
Unevenly [un-ī'-vn-li], *adv.* Desigualmente.
Unevenness [un-ī'-vn-nes], *s.* 1. Desigualdad, escabrosidad o aspereza ocasionada por no estar llana una cosa; falta de regularidad. 2. Desigualdad, inconstancia, poca firmeza o estabilidad.
Uneventful [un-ę-vent'-ful], *a.* Exento de acontecimientos notables; tranquilo.
Uneventfully [un-ę-vent'-ful-i], *adv.* Tranquilamente, sin suceso notable, monótonamente.
Unexacted [un-eg-zact'-ed], *a.* Que no es exigido; que ha sido producido naturalmente y sin auxilio del arte.
Unexamined [un-eg-zam'-ind], *a.* No examinado.
Unexampled [un-eg-zam'-pld], *a.* Que no tiene igual, sin ejemplo, único en su línea.
Unexceptionable [un-ec-sep'-shun-a-bl], *a.* Libre de toda objeción o reparo; irreprensible; irrecusable.
Unexceptional [un-ec-sep'-shun-al], *a.* Que no hace excepción; ordinario, usual y corriente.
Unexcised [un-ec-saizd'], *a.* 1. No cortado. 2. Que no está sujeto al derecho de sisa.
Unexecuted [un-ec'-sę-kiut-ed], *a.* No ejecutado.
Unexemplified [un-eg-zem'-pli-faid], *a.* Que sucede por la primera vez; que no tiene ejemplar o igual.
Unexempt [un-eg-zempt'], *a.* No exento, sujeto.
Unexercised [un-ec'-sęr-saizd], *a.* Inexperto; no ejercitado, falto de ejercicio.
Unexhausted [un-eg-zēst'-ed], *a.* Inexhausto, no agotado.
Unexpanded [un-ex-pand'-ed], *a.* Encogido, no extendido.
Unexpected [un-ex-pect'-ed], *a.* Inesperado, impensado, no prevenido, inopinado; repentino, que no se esperaba.
Unexpectedly [un-ex-pect'-ed-li], *adv.* De repente, impensadamente, inesperadamente, inopinadamente, sin pensarlo; de improviso.
Unexpectedness [un-ex-pect'-ed-nes], *s.* Repentón, lance inesperado o imprevisto.
Unexpert [un-ex-pęrt'], *a.* Inhábil; inexperto, falto de experiencia.
Unexpired [un-ex-paird'], *a.* No acabado, no concluído.
Unexplored [un-ex-plōrd'], *a.* Inexplorado, no conocido, no descubierto.
Unexported [un-ex-pōrt'-ed], *a.* No extraído o llevado fuera del país.
Unexposed [un-ex-pōzd'], *a.* No expuesto (a la luz, etc.).
Unextended [un-ex-tend'-ed], *a.* No extendido, no abierto; sin extensión, sin dimensión.
Unexterminable [un-ex-tęr'-min-a-bl], *a.* Que no puede ser exterminado.
Unextinguishable [un-ex-tiŋ'-gwish-a-bl], *a.* Inextinguible.
Unfaded [un-fēd'-ed], *a.* No marchito, no ajado; que conserva sus colores o su frescura.
Unfading [un-fēd'-ing], *a.* Inmarcesible, que no pasa; imperecedero, imperdible.
Unfailing [un-fēl'-ing], *a.* 1. Inagotable, que produce siempre. 2. Seguro, cierto, que no puede faltar, infalible.
Unfair [un-fār'], *a.* Doble, falso; injusto; que no es honrado en sus tratos, que obra de mala fe.
Unfairly [un-fār'-li], *adv.* De mala fe; injustamente, con doblez.
Unfairness [un-fār'-nes], *s.* Falta de equidad; deslealtad, mala fe.
Unfaithful [un-fēth'-ful], *a.* Infiel, falto de fe; pérfido, desleal, traidor. *The unfaithful,* Los incrédulos, los infieles.
Unfaithfully [un-fēth'-ful-i], *adv.* Infielmente, deslealmente, pérfidamente.
Unfaithfulness [un-fēth'-ful-nes], *s.* Infidelidad, perfidia, alevosía, deslealtad.
Unfallen [un-fōl'-en], *a.* Que no ha caído, que está en pie.
Unfalsified [un-fōl'-si-faid], *a.* Verdadero.
Unfalteringly [un-fōl'-tęr-ing-li], *adv.* Sin vacilar.
Unfamiliar [un-fa-mil'-yar], *a.* Poco familiar, poco común; no conocido familiarmente.
Unfashionable [un-fash'-un-a-bl], *a.* Que no es de moda, que no sigue la

moda; opuesto a la moda, raro, singular.
Unfashionableness [un-fash'-un-a-bl-nes], *s.* La condición de no seguir los caprichos de la moda; llaneza en el vestir; el vestir a la antigua.
Unfashionably [un-fash'-un-a-bli], *adv.* Contra la moda.
Unfashioned [un-fash'-und], *a.* Informe, tosco, basto, que está sin limar o sin pulir.
Unfasten [un-fqs'-n], *va.* Desatar, soltar, aflojar.
Unfathered [un-fā'-dhẹrd], *a.* Huérfano de padre; que carece de autor.
Unfatherly [un-fā'-dhẹr-li], *a.* Indigno de un padre, desemejante a un padre.
Unfathomable [un-fadh'-um-a-bl], *a.* Insondable, impenetrable; que no tiene fondo.
Unfathomably [un-fadh'-um-a-bli], *adv.* De un modo insondable.
Unfavorable, Unfavourable [un-fé'-ver-a-bl], *a.* Contrario, adverso, no favorable, no propicio.
Unfavorably, Unfavourably [un-fé'-ver-a-bli], *adv.* Contrariamente, de una manera poco favorable.
Unfearing [un-fīr'-ing], *a.* Intrépido, animoso, sin temor.
Unfeasible [un-fīz'-a-bl], *a.* No hacedero, no factible, impracticable.
Unfeathered [un-fedh'-ẹrd], *a.* Implume, que no tiene plumas.
Unfeatured [un-fī'-churd], *a.* Disforme.
Unfed [un-fed'], *a.* Falto de alimento; no nutrido.
Unfeeling [un-fīl'-ing], *a.* Insensible, apático; duro de corazón, cruel.
Unfeelingly [un-fīl'-ing-li], *adv.* Cruelmente; insensiblemente.
Unfeigned [un-fênd'], *a.* Que no es fingido; real, verdadero, genuino; ingenuo.
Unfeignedly [un-fên'-ed-li], *adv.* Ingenuamente, sinceramente; verdaderamente.
Unfelt [un-felt'], *a.* No percibido, no sentido.
Unfenced [un-fenst'], *a.* Abierto, no cercado; que no tiene defensa.
Unfermented [un-fẹr-ment'-ed], *a.* No fermentado.
Unfertile [un-fẹr'-til], *a.* Infecundo, estéril.
Unfetter [un-fet'-ẹr], *va.* Desencadenar, quitar los grillos a, poner en libertad.
Unfigured [un-fig'-yurd], *a.* Lo que no representa forma o figura animal.
Unfilled [un-fild'], *a.* Vacío, no lleno; vacante.
Unfilial [un-fil'-yal], *a.* Que no conviene o no es propio de un hijo.
Unfinished [un-fin'-isht], *a.* Incompleto, imperfecto, no acabado, no concluído.
Unfit [un-fit'], *a.* Desconveniente, nada apto, poco propio para; poco hecho para; inepto, incapaz. (Se usa a menudo con *for* o *to.*)
Unfit, *va.* Inhabilitar, hacer incapaz o inhábil para alguna cosa.
Unfitly [un-fit'-li], *adv.* Impropiamente, incongruentemente; sin aptitud.
Unfitness [un-fit'-nes], *s.* Ineptitud, insuficiencia, falta de aptitud o de disposición; impropiedad.
Unfitting [un-fit'-ing], *a.* Impropio, poco o nada a propósito, desconvenible.
Unfix [un-fics'], *va.* 1. Soltar, aflojar. 2. Liquidar, deshelar.
Unfixed [un-ficst'], *a.* Errante, vacilante; irresoluto, voluble.
Unflagging [un-flag'-ing], *a.* Persistente, que no se cansa.
Unfledged [un-flejd'], *a.* Implume, que no tiene todavía plumas; inmaturo, inexperimentado.
Unfleshed [un-flesht'], *a.* No encarnizado; incruento, que no ha probado aún la sangre.
Unflinching [un-flinch'-ing], *a.* Que no retrocede; resuelto, no vencido.
Unfold [un-fōld'], *va.* 1. Desplegar, desdoblar, descoger, desarrollar, abrir una cosa plegada. 2. Revelar, descubrir, poner en claro, manifestar lo que está oculto, secreto o escondido; desencerrar.—*vn.* Abrirse, descubrirse, desarrollarse.
Unforbearing [un-fer-bār'-ing], *a.* Intolerante, poco indulgente, impaciente.
Unforbid [un-fẹr-bid'], **Unforbidden** [un-fẹr-bid'-n], *a.* Permitido, no prohibido.
Unforced [un-fōrst'], *a.* Sin estar obligado, libre; espontáneo, voluntario; natural, no fingido.
Unfordable [un-fōrd'-a-bl], *a.* Invadeable.
Unforeseen [un-fōr-sīn'], **Unforeknown** [un-fōr-nōn'], *a.* Imprevisto, inopinado, no previsto.
Unforfeited [un-fẹr'-fit-ed], *a.* No perdido.
Unforgetful [un-fẹr-get'-ful], *a.* No olvidadizo; que no olvida.
Unforgettable [un-fẹr-get'-a-bl], *a.* Inolvidable, imperecedero.
Unforgiving [un-fẹr-giv'-ing], *a.* Duro, inexorable, implacable.
Unforgotten [un-fẹr-get'-n], *a.* No olvidado, presente, fijo en la memoria.
Unformed [un-fẹrmd'], *a.* 1. Informe, sin forma regular, falto de estructura. 2. Crudo, de un carácter no completamente desarrollado. 3. (Biol.) No organizado, sin estructura. *Unformed stars,* Estrellas que se hallan fuera de una constelación.
Unfortified [un-fẹr'-ti-faid], *a.* 1. No fortificado, que no tiene murallas o fortificaciones. 2. Débil, endeble.
Unfortunate [un-fẹr'-chu-net], *a.* Desafortunado, infortunado, desgraciado, infeliz.
Unfortunately [un-fer'-chu-net-li], *adv.* Por desgracia, infelizmente.
Unfortunateness [un-fer'-chu-net-nes], *s.* Infortunio, desgracia, desventura.
Unfought [un-fōt'], *a.* Sin pelear o sin haber peleado. *Unfought for,* No disputado, sin lucha.
Unfound [un-faund'], *a.* No hallado; imposible de hallarse.
Unfounded [un-faund'-ed], *a.* 1. Infundado, sin fundamento. 2. No fundado ni establecido.
Unframed [un-frêmd'], *a.* Sin forma o figura.
Unfraught [un-frōt'], *a.* No cargado, exento de carga.
Unfreezable [un-frīz'-a-bl], *a.* Incongelable.
Unfrequent [un-frī'-cwent]. Poco o nada frecuente. *V.* INFREQUENT.
Unfrequented [un-frẹ-cwent'-ed], *a.* Solitario, poco o nada frecuentado.
Unfrequently [un-frī'-cwent-li], *adv.* Rara vez, raramente, por maravilla.
Unfriended [un-frend'-ed], *a.* Desamparado, sin protección, sin amigos.
Unfriendliness [un-frend'-li-nes], *s.* Falta de amistad, falta de benevolencia.
Unfriendly [un-frend'-li], *a.* 1. Aspero, poco amistoso, poco atento, seco, nada afable; enemigo. 2. Poco favorable, poco propicio, perjudicial.
Unfrock [un-frec'], *va.* Exclaustrar, privar del carácter eclesiástico.
Unfrozen [un-frō'-zn], *a.* No helado o convertido en hielo; deshelado.
Unfruitful [un-frūt'-ful], *a.* 1. Estéril, infructífero, que no da o no produce fruto. 2. Lo que no produce el fruto que se esperaba de ello; infructuoso.
Unfruitfulness [un-frūt'-ful-nes], *s.* Esterilidad, infecundidad; infructuosidad.
Unfulfilled [un-ful-fild'], *a.* No cumplido; no observado.
Unfunded [un-fund'-ed], *a.* No consolidado; sin fondos para el pago de los intereses.
Unfurl [un-fẹrl'], *va.* Desplegar, desdoblar, extender. *To unfurl the sails,* (Mar.) Desaferrar las velas.
Unfurnish [un-fẹr'-nish], *va.* 1. Desamueblar, quitar los muebles. 2. Despojar, desnudar.
Unfurnished [un-fẹr'-nisht], *pp.* y *a.* No amueblado, sin muebles; desprovisto.
Ungainliness [un-gên'-li-nes], *s.* Falta de gracia, torpeza.
Ungainly [un-gên'-li], *a.* Desmañado, falto de gracia, torpe, poco diestro, pesado.
Ungalled [un-gōld'], *a.* Que no está despellejado; libre de daño, no herido.
Ungartered [un-gār'-tẹrd], *a.* Sin ligas.
Ungathered [un-gadh'-ẹrd], *a.* No cogido; no recogido.
Ungear [un-gīr'], *va.* Desengranar, desconectar, desembragar.
Ungenerous [un-jen'-ẹr-us], *a.* Falto de generosidad; indigno, innoble, bajo.
Ungenerously [un-jen'-ẹr-us-li], *adv.* Sin generosidad; indignamente, bajamente.
Ungenial [un-jīn'-yal], *a.* Malsano, hablando de lo que hace daño a la salud; muy riguroso, hablando del clima; poco favorable a la naturaleza, a la constitución, a los hábitos adquiridos, etc.; áspero, rudo, brusco.
Ungenialness [un-jīn'-yal-nes], *s.* La falta de conformidad en las cosas con la salud, constitución, hábitos adquiridos, etc.
Ungenteel [un-jen-tīl'], *a.* Rudo, descortés, bajo, tosco, grosero, de mal tono, de mal gusto.
Ungentle [un-jen'-tl], *a.* Áspero, riguroso, severo, intratable, duro de genio.
Ungentlemanlike [un-jen'-tl-man-laic], **Ungentlemanly** [un-jen'-tl-man-li], *a.* Indigno de un hombre bien criado; que no conviene a un caballero.
Ungentleness [un-jen' tl-nes], *s.* Dureza de genio, rudeza, aspereza, severidad, falta de amabilidad en el trato.
Ungently [un-jent'-li], *adv.* Ásperamente, rudamente, con severidad.
Ungifted [un-gift'-ed], *a.* Que no está dotado de talento.
Ungird [un-gẹrd'], *va.* Desceñir; descinchar.
Ungirt [un-gẹrt'], *a.* Desceñido; suelto o sin atar.
Ungiving [un-giv'-ing], *a.* Que no da nada.
Unglazed [un-glêzd'], *a.* 1. Que no tiene vidrieras o sin vidrieras: dí-

cese de las ventanas. 2. No encharolado; no barnizado; no satinado (papel); que está sin vidriar: dícese de las vasijas de barro.

Unglorified [un-glō'-ri-faid], *a.* No glorificado, no honrado.

Unglove [un-gluv'], *va.* y *vn.* Quitar o quitarse los guantes.

Ungloved [un-gluvd'], *a.* Sin guantes.

Ungodliness [un-ged'-li-nes], *s.* Impiedad, irreligión, falta de piedad y religión.

Ungodly [un-ged'-li], *a.* Impío, malvado, irreligioso, profano.

Ungored [un-gōrd'], *a.* Ileso, que no está herido de cornada.

Ungorged [un-gōrjd'], *a.* Insaciable; no saciado.

Ungovernable [un-guv'-ęrn-a-bl], *a.* Indomable, ingobernable, indisciplinable, incapaz de gobierno, de dirección o de disciplina.

Ungovernableness [un-guv'-ęrn-a-bl-nes], *s.* Indocilidad.

Ungoverned [un-guv'-ęrnd], *a.* Desgobernado, desarreglado, desenfrenado, descomedido, desaforado; que no guarda regla ni orden.

Ungraceful [un-grês'-ful], *a.* Tosco, desairado, desgraciado, falto de gracia o de gentileza.

Ungracefulness [un-grês'-ful-nes], *s.* Tosquedad, falta de gracia o de gentileza.

Ungracious [un-grê'-shus], *a.* Desagradable, repugnante, ofensivo, chocante; falto de cortesía.

Ungraciously [un-grê'-shus-li], *adv.* Malvadamente, groseramente, sin gracia.

Ungraciousness [un-grê'-shus-nes], *s.* Descortesía, bellaquería, grosería.

Ungrammatical [un-gram-mat'-i-cal], *a.* Incorrecto, contrario a las reglas de la gramática.

Ungranted [un-grqnt'-ed], *a.* No concedido, no dado, no otorgado.

Ungranulated [un-gran'-yu-lêt-ed], *a.* Que no es granoso o no está hecho o formado de granos.

Ungrateful [un-grêt'-ful], *a.* 1. Desagradecido, ingrato, que olvida o desprecia los beneficios recibidos. 2. Desagradable, no agradable. 3. Ingrato: dícese del terreno poco fecundo.

Ungratefully [un-grêt'-ful-i], *adv.* 1. Ingratamente, desagradecidamente. 2. Desagradablemente, de mala gana, sin gusto.

Ungratefulness [un-grêt'-ful-nes], *s.* Ingratitud, desagradecimiento; desagrado.

Ungratified [un-grat'-i-faid], *a.* No satisfecho, no contentado.

Ungrounded [un-graund'-ed], *a.* Infundado, que no tiene razón ni fundamento.

Ungrudgingly [un-gruj'-ing-li], *adv.* De buena gana, con gusto, voluntariamente.

Ungual [uŋ'-gwal], *a.* 1. Perteneciente, o parecido a una uña o garra. 2. Que tiene uña, pesuña o garra. *Ungual bone,* Ungüis.

Unguarded [un-gārd'-ed], *a.* 1. Desguarnecido, sin guarda o sin defensa. 2. Descuidado, negligente; incauto, indiscreto.

Unguent [un'-gwent], *s.* Ungüento.

Unguicular [uŋ-gwic'-yu-lar], *a.* Unguiculado, que tiene los dedos terminados por uñas.

Unguided [un-gaid'-ed], *a.* No dirigido, no gobernado, sin guía.

Unguis [uŋ'-gwis], *s.* Uña, pesuña, garra o zarpa.

Ungulate [uŋ'-giu-lêt], *a.* y *s.* Ungulado (animal) que tiene casco o pesuña.

Unhabituated [un-ha-bit'-yu-ê-ted], *a.* Poco acostumbrado, no habituado.

Unhair [un-hār'], *va.* Apelambrar (las pieles).

Unhallowed [un-hal'-ōd], *a.* Profano, impío; profanado.

Unhammered [un-ham'-ęrd], *a.* No martillado.

Unhand [un-hand'], *va.* Soltar las manos.

Unhandily [un-han'-di-li], *adv.* Poco diestramente, desmañadamente.

Unhandsome [un-han'-sum], *a.* 1. Feo, desaliñado, falto de gracia o hermosura. 2. Innoble, bajo; doble, falso.

Unhandsomely [un-han'-sum-li], *adv.* 1. Groseramente, sin gracia; feamente, con fealdad, mal. 2. Con doblez; groseramente.

Unhandsomeness [un-han'-sum-nes], *s.* 1. Fealdad, falta de belleza. 2. Tosquedad, falta de gentileza. 3. Doblez; grosería.

Unhandy [un-han'-di], *a.* Desmañado, torpe, poco hábil, poco diestro.

Unhang [un'-hang], *va.* Descolgar, quitar las colgaduras; desprender (tapicerías). *To unhang the tiller,* Desmontar la caña del timón.

Unhappily [un-hap'-i-li], *adv.* Infelizmente, miserablemente, mal, por desgracia.

Unhappiness [un-hap'-i-nes], *s.* Infelicidad, desgracia, infortunio, mala ventura; miseria, desdicha, calamidad.

Unhappy [un-hap'-i], *a.* 1. Infeliz, desgraciado, desdichado: se aplica a personas y a cosas. 2. Desafortunado, desventurado: se aplica sólo a personas.

Unharbored [un-hār'-berd], *a.* Que no tiene puerto ni abrigo; desemboscado, salido del monte (dícese de la caza mayor).

Unharmed [un-hārmd'], *a.* Ileso, sano y salvo, que no ha recibido ningún daño.

Unharmful [un-hārm'-ful], *a.* Inocente, que no es nocivo o no hace daño.

Unharmonious [un-hār-mō'-ni-us], *a.* Desproporcionado, informe; discorde, disonante, discordante, falto de armonía.

Unharness [un-hār'-nes], *va.* 1. Desenjaezar, quitar los jaeces a los caballos. 2. Quitar las guarniciones a las bestias de carga. 3. Desarmar, quitar la armadura.

Unhasp [un-hqsp'], *va.* Soltar el pestillo.

Unhatched [un-hacht'], *a.* 1. No salido del cascarón. 2. No traslúcido, no descubierto, que no ha salido a luz.

Unhaunted [un-hānt'-ed], *a.* Poco concurrido, no frecuentado, solitario.

Unhead [un-hed'], *va.* Quitar el fondo de un barril.

Unhealed [un-hīld'], *a.* No curado.

Unhealthful [un-helth'-ful], *a.* Malsano, insalubre, que no es provechoso para la salud o es perjudicial a ella.

Unhealthiness [un-hel'-thi-nes], *s.* Insalubridad, calidad de malsano o contrario a la salud; la falta de salud.

Unhealthy [un-hel'-thi], *a.* 1. Enfermizo, achacoso, valetudinario, falto de salud. 2. Insalubre, malsano. *V.* UNHEALTHFUL.

Unheard [un-hęrd'], *a.* 1. Que no se oye o no se ha oído. 2. Desconocido, obscuro, sin fama. *Unheard of,* Inaudito, extraño, singular, nunca oído; sin ejemplo.

Unheated [un-hīt'-ed], *a.* No calentado, frío.

Unheeded [un-hīd'-ed], *a.* No atendido, despreciado: aplícase a aquello de que se hace poco caso.

Unheeding [un-hīd'-ing], *a.* Negligente, descuidado, distraído.

Unhelped [un-helpt'], *a.* Desamparado, no ayudado, no socorrido, sin auxilio.

Unhelpful [un-help'-ful], *a.* Inútil, que no da ayuda o auxilio.

Unhesitating [un-hes'-i-tê-ting], *a.* Que no vacila; pronto, listo.

Unhesitatingly [un-hes'-i-tê-ting-li], *adv.* Sin vacilar; prontamente.

Unhewn [un-hiūn'], *a.* Tosco, basto, bruto o en bruto; no pulido.

Unhindered [un-hin'-dęrd], *a.* Libre, sin trabas; no opuesto, no impedido.

Unhinge [un-hinj'], *va.* Desgoznar, desgonzar, desquiciar, sacar de quicio; desordenar, poner en confusión.

Unhitch [un-hich'], *va.* Descolgar, desatar, desenganchar.

Unholiness [un-hō'-li-nes], *s.* Impiedad, profanidad; maldad, perversidad.

Unholy [un-hō'-li], *adv.* Profano, impío, malvado, perverso.

Unhonored, Unhonoured [un-en'-ęrd], *a.* Despreciado, no venerado.

Unhood [un-hud'], *va.* Descapirotar, quitar el capirote a las aves.

Unhook [un-huk'], *va.* Desganchar, desenganchar, desaferrar; descolgar.

Unhoop [un-hup'], *va.* 1. Quitar los aros, arcos o cercos de los barriles o toneles. 2. Quitar el tontillo a las señoras.

Unhoped [un-hōpt'], *a.* Inesperado.

Unhopeful [un-hōp'-ful], *a.* Que no ofrece buenas esperanzas; falto de grandes esperanzas.

Unhorse [un-hōrs'], *va.* Botar o sacar de la silla al jinete, hacerle perder los estribos.

Unhospitable [un-hes'-pit-a-bl], *a.* *V.* INHOSPITABLE.

Unhouse [un-hauz'], *va.* Desalojar, echar a uno de la casa o alojamiento.

Unhuman [un-hiū'-man], *a.* Inhumano. *V.* INHUMAN.

Unhumbled [un-hum'-bld], *a.* No humillado; altanero, sin pudor, sin vergüenza.

Unhurt [un-hūrt'], *a.* Ileso, sano y salvo, que no ha recibido ningún daño.

Unhurtful [un-hūrt'-ful], *a.* Inocente.

Unhurtfully [un-hūrt'-ful-i], *adv.* Inocentemente.

Unhusbanded [un-huz'-band-ed], *a.* 1. No ahorrado, no economizado. 2. No labrado, inculto, sin cultivo.

Unhygienic [ūn-hai-jin'-ic], *a.* Antihigiénico.

Uniaxial, Uniaxal [yū-ni-ac'-si-al], *a.* De un solo eje.

Unicameral [yū-ni-cam'-ę-ral], *a.* Que consiste de una sola cámara; v. g. un cuerpo legislativo.

Unicorn [yū'-ni-cērn], *s.* Unicornio, animal fabuloso de un solo cuerno.

Unification [yū-ni-fi-kê'-shun], *s.* Unificación.

Unify [yū'-ni-fai], *va.* Unificar, unir.

Uniflorous [yū-ni-flō'-rus], *a.* Unifloro, de una sola flor.

Uniform [yū'-ni-fōrm], *a.* 1. Uniforme, que tiene la misma forma, invariable; semejante. 2. Acorde, armonioso, que conviene con otra cosa; consistente, constante.—*s.* Uniforme, traje reglamentario que usan los militares y otros empleados. *In full uniform,* De gran uniforme, de gala.

Uniformity [yū"-ni-fōrm'-i-ti], **Uniformness** [yū-ni-fōrm-nes], *s.* Uniformidad, conformidad o igualdad, semejanza de una cosa consigo misma o con otras.

Uniformly [yū'-ni-fōrm-li], *adv.* Uniformemente, correspondientemente, igual o concordemente, sin variación alguna.

Unilocular [yū"-ni-loc'-yu-lar], *a.* Que sólo tiene una célula o cámara.

Unimaginable [un-i-maj'-i-na-bl], *a.* Inimaginable, lo que no se puede imaginar.

Unimaginably [un-i-maj'-i-na-bli], *adv.* De un modo no imaginable.

Unimpaired [un-im-pārd'], *a.* 1. Intacto, ileso, inalterado. 2. No disminuído, no gastado, no usado.

Unimpeachable [un-im-pīch'-a-bl], *a.* Incensurable, intachable; irreprensible; digno de confianza.

Unimportant [un-im-pōrt'-ant], *a.* 1. Nada importante, que nada significa, insignificante. 2. Natural, sin afectación.

Unimpressionable [un-im-presh'-un-a-bl], *a.* Poco impresionable, poco conmovido, que no cede fácilmente a una impresión física o moral.

Unimpressive [un-im-pres'-iv], *a.* Que no impresiona, mueve o afecta.

Unimprovable [un-im-prūv'-a-bl], *a.* Incapaz de mejora, adelantamiento o reforma.

Unimprovableness [un-im-prūv'-a-bl-nes], *s.* Incapacidad de mejora o reforma.

Unimproved [un-im-prūvd'], *a.* No adelantado, no mejorado; inculto.

Unindustrious [un-in-dus'-tri-us], *a.* Desidioso, descuidado, dejado.

Uninflammable [un-in-flam'-a-bl], *a.* Incombustible.

Uninfluenced [un-in'-flu-enst], *a.* 1. No influído, libre de toda influencia. 2. Exento de preocupaciones.

Uninformed [un-in-fōrmd'], *a.* 1. Inculto, sin cultura, ignorante. 2. Inanimado.

Uninhabitable [un-in-hab'-it-a-bl], *a.* Inhabitable, que no se puede habitar.

Uninhabitableness [un-in-hab'-it-a-bl-nes], *s.* El estado de lo que no se puede habitar.

Uninhabited [un-in-hab'-it-ed], *a.* Inhabitado, desierto.

Uninjured [un-in'-jerd], *a.* Ileso, no dañado, que no ha recibido ningún daño; no perjudicado, intacto.

Uninscribed [un-in-scraibd'], *a.* Falto de inscripción.

Uninspired [un-in-spaird'], *a.* Que no ha recibido ninguna inspiración sobrenatural.

Uninstructed [un-in-struct'-ed], *a.* Rudo, ignorante, sin educación, sin instrucción.

Uninstructive [un-in-struc'-tiv], *a.* No instructivo.

Uninsured [un"-in-shūrd'], *a.* Que no está asegurado.

Unintelligent [un-in-tel'-i-jent], *a.* Falto de inteligencia, ignorante, estúpido.

Unintelligibility [un-in-tel-i-ji-bil'-i-ti], **Unintelligibleness** [un-in-tel'-i-ji-bl-nes], *s.* La incapacidad de ser entendido; obscuridad impenetrable; calidad de ininteligible.

Unintelligible [un-in-tel'-i-ji-bl], *a.* Ininteligible.

Unintelligibly [un-in-tel'-i-ji-bli], *adv.* De un modo o manera ininteligible.

Unintentional [un-in-ten'-shun-al], *a.* Hecho sin intención, objeto, plan o designio.

Unintentionally [un-in-ten'-shun-al-i], *adv.* Sin intención, sin quererlo, involuntariamente.

Uninterested [un-in'-ter-est-ed], *a.* Desinteresado.

Unintermitted [un-in-ter-mit'-ed], *a.* Continuo, continuado, sin intermisión.

Uninterrupted [un-in-ter-rupt'-ed], *a.* Continuo, no interrumpido, sin interrupción.

Uninterruptedly [un-in-ter-rupt'-ed-li], *adv.* Sin interrupción, continuamente.

Unintimidated [un-in-tim'-i-dêt-ed], *a.* No intimidado, no amedrentado.

Unintrenched [un-in-trencht'], *a.* No atrincherado.

Unintroduced [un-in-tro-diūst'], *a.* Entrometido, intruso, no presentado de un modo regular.

Uninvited [un-in-vait'-ed], *a.* No convidado, no rogado.

Union [yūn'-yun], *s.* 1. Unión, el acto de unir una cosa con otra; junta, reunión, coalición. 2. Unión, conformidad, concordia de los ánimos o dictámenes; confederación, liga o asociación; gremio de oficios. 3. Estado matrimonial. 4. Proporción, simetría, armonía. 5. Emblema de unión representado en un pabellón. 6. Unión, conexión para cañones o varillas. *Union Jack,* Pabellón de la Gran Bretaña e Irlanda reunidas.

Unionism [yūn'-yun-izm], *s.* 1. Unionismo. 2. Sindicalismo.

Uniparous [yu-nip'-a-rus], *a.* 1. (Bot.) Que tiene un solo eje o tallo. 2. Unípara: se dice de la hembra que pare uno a la vez.

Unipersonal [yū-ni-per'-so-nal], *a.* 1. Que existe en una sola persona. 2. (Gram.) *V.* IMPERSONAL.

Unique [yu-nîc'], *a.* Solo, sin igual, único en su género o especie; de aquí, singular, raro.

Unisexual [yu-ni-sex'-yu-al], *a.* 1. (Bot.) Unisexual, de un solo sexo. 2. (Ento.) Que consta de hembras solamente.

Unison [yū'-ni-sun], *s.* 1. Unisonancia, la concurrencia de dos o más voces, cuerdas o instrumentos en un mismo tono de música. 2. Unisón, concento músico por un mismo tono.—*a.* Unísono.

Unisonal [yū-ni-sō'-nal], *a.* Unísono, en unisonancia.

Unisonous [yū-ni-sō'-nus o yu-nis'-o-nus], *a.* 1. *V.* UNISONAL. 2. Que suena por sí mismo.

Unit [yū'-nit], *s.* 1. Unidad, una sola persona o cosa; lo que forma un todo. 2. Unidad, lo que constituye el número uno como indivisible y absoluto.

Unitarian [yū-ni-tê'-ri-an], *s.* Unitario, sectario que niega la doctrina de la Trinidad, que no reconoce en Dios más que una sola persona.

Unitarianism [yū-ni-tê'-ri-an-izm], *s.* Unitarismo, doctrina de los unitarios.

Unite [yu-nait'], *va.* 1. Unir, juntar dos o más cosas haciendo de ellas un todo. 2. Unir, concordar o conformar las voluntades, ánimos o pareceres.—*vn.* Unirse, juntarse, convenirse, concertarse.

United [yu-nait'-ed], *a.* Unido, juntado.

Unitedly [yu-nait'-ed-li], *adv.* Unidamente, juntamente, con unión; de acuerdo; de una vez.

Uniter [yu-nait'-er], *s.* La persona o cosa que une.

Unity [yū'-ni-ti], *s.* 1. Unidad, el estado de lo que es uno. 2. Unión, concordia, conformidad, armonía. 3. (Mat.) El número uno; la razón de dos cantidades iguales. 4. En literatura y en las artes, combinación en un conjunto homogéneo y artístico.

Univalve [yū'-ni-valv], *a.* Univalvo: dícese de los mariscos y conchas de una pieza.—*s.* Molusco univalvo, gasterópodo; concha de una pieza.

Universal [yū-ni-ver'-sal], *a.* 1. Universal, común, general, total, que se extiende a todo o lo comprende todo. 2. Que existe o que se considera como un todo. 3. (Art. y Of.) Universal, propio para una gran variedad de usos o aplicaciones.

Universalism [yū-ni-ver'-sal-izm], *s.* Universalismo, doctrina de la salvación final de todas las almas y de que lo bueno triunfará al fin universalmente.

Universalist [yū-ni-ver'-sal-ist], *s.* Universalista, partidario del universalismo.

Universality [yū-ni-ver-sal'-i-ti], *a.* Universalidad, generalidad, estado ó calidad de lo universal.

Universal joint [yū-ni-ver'-sal joint], *s.* (Mec.) Unión, junta o articulación universal o de Cardán.

Universally [yū-ni-ver'-sal-i], *adv.* Universalmente, generalmente.

Universe [yū'-ni-vers], *s.* Universo, el conjunto de todas las cosas creadas; mundo.

University [yū-ni-ver'-si-ti], *s.* 1. Universidad, establecimiento de instrucción superior donde se enseñan las ciencias y artes liberales. 2. Todos los estudiantes de ese establecimiento.

Univocal [yu-niv'-o-cal], *a.* 1. Unívoco, que tiene un solo sentido; no equívoco. 2. ¿Cierto, regular.

Univocally [yu-niv'-o-cal-i], *adv.* En un mismo, solo o único sentido.

Unjoin [un-join'], *va.* Separar, dividir, desunir.

Unjoint [un-joint'], *va.* Dislocar, desencajar, descoyuntar.

Unjointed [un-joint'-ed], *a.* Desunido; falto de articulaciones.

Unjoyful, Unjoyous [un-joi'-ful, un-joi'-us], *a.* Triste, melancólico, lúgubre, de mal humor.

Unjudged [un-jujd'], *a.* No juzgado, no decidido; pendiente, en litigio.

Unjust [un-just'], *a.* Injusto, inicuo, desrazonable, contrario a la justicia.

Unjustifiable [un-jus-ti-fai'-a-bl], *a.* Injustificable, inexcusable, sin disculpa, sin excusa.

Unjustifiableness [un-jus-ti-fai'-a-bl-nes], *s.* Falta de disculpa o excusa.

Unjustifiably [un-jus-ti-fai'-a-bli], *adv.* Inexcusablemente, de una manera injustificable.

Unjustly [un-just'-li], *adv.* Injustamente, inicuamente.

Unkempt [un-kempt'], *a.* 1. Despeinado, desgreñado, desmelenado. 2. (Fig.) Sin pulimento, sin arte, inculto, tosco.

Unkennel [un-ken'-el], *va.* 1. Desalojar o echar a un animal de su cama, madriguera, huronera, etc. 2. Poner al descubierto una cosa que estaba secreta.
Unkept [un-kept'], *a.* No retenido, no guardado.
Unkind [un-kaind'], *a.* Adusto, no benévolo, duro, poco amable; áspero, seco.
Unkindliness [un-kaind'-li-nes], *a.* Aspereza, dureza, severidad, rigor.
Unkindly [un-kaind'-li], *adv.* Duramente, ásperamente, con rigor o severidad, con desafecto, con poco cariño. *To treat one unkindly,* Maltratar a uno, no mostrarle afabilidad.
Unkindness [un-kaind'-nes], *s.* 1. Desafecto, desamor, falta de cariño o de afabilidad. 2. Malignidad, propensión o gusto en hacer o decir mal.
Unkink [un-kink'], *va.* Quitar las torceduras o los nudos.
Unknightly [un-nait'-li], *a.* Indigno de un caballero.
Unknit [un-nit'], *va.* Destejer, deshacer un tejido; desliar, deshacer.
Unknowable [un-nō'-a-bl], *a.* Incognoscible.
Unknowing [un-nō'-ing], *a.* Ignorante.
Unknowingly [un-nō'-ing-li], *adv.* Ignorantemente, sin saberlo.
Unknown [un-nōn'], *a.* 1. Oculto, desconocido, ignorado, no conocido antes, ignoto. 2. Mayor de lo que se cree o se imagina; superior a todo cómputo. 3. Incógnito, sin que se sepa, sin noticia de. *Unknown to me,* Sin mi noticia, sin saberlo yo, sin mi concurrencia o participación.
Unlabored, Unlaboured [un-lé'-bord], *a.* 1. No restringido, cómodo, natural, libre. 2. Natural, no producido por el trabajo; no cultivado. 3. Espontáneo, voluntario.
Unlaborious [un-la-bō'-ri-us], *a.* Fácil, que no cuesta trabajo, poco penoso.
Unlace [un-lēs'], *va.* Desabrochar; desenlazar; desatar.
Unlade [un-lēd'], *va.* 1. Descargar, quitar o aliviar la carga. 2. Desembarcar, sacar y poner en tierra lo que estaba embarcado.
Unladylike [un-lē'-di-laik], *a.* Impropio de una señora o dama; poco afeminado.
Unlaid [un-lēd'], *a.* y *pp.* de *To* UNLAY. 1. Que no está colocado ni puesto; en especial que no tiene líneas paralelas de filigrana (papel). 2. No apaciguado ni aquietado. 3. Destorcido (como los cabos de una cuerda).
Unlamented [un-la-ment'-ed], *a.* No lamentado, no llorado.
Unlatch [un-lach'], *va.* Abrir levantando el picaporte.
Unlawful [un-lō'-ful], *a.* Ilegal, ilícito, contrario u opuesto a las leyes; ilegítimo. *Unlawful interest,* Usura.
Unlawfully [un-lō'-ful-i], *adv.* Ilegalmente, ilegítimamente, ilícitamente, contra las leyes o en violación de las leyes. *Unlawfully born,* Ilegítimo, bastardo.
Unlawfulness [un-lō'-ful-nes], *s.* 1. Ilegalidad, calidad de ilegal. 2. Ilegitimidad.
Unlearn [un-lern'], *va.* Desaprender, olvidar lo que se ha aprendido.
Unlearned [un-lernd'], *pp.* y *a.* [un-lern'-ed]. Indocto, ignorante; ignorado, no aprendido; mal hecho.
Unleavened [un-lev'-nd], *a.* Ázimo, que no tiene levadura o fermento.
Unless [un-les'], *conj.* 1. A menos que, no sea que (seguido de verbo en subjuntivo): a menos de que, a menos de (seguido de verbo en infinitivo). 2. Excepto, si no, si no es (delante de un pronombre, etc.).
Unlessoned [un-les'-nd], *a.* No enseñado.
Unlettered [un-let'-erd], *a.* Indocto, iliterato.
Unlicensed [un-lai'-senst], *a.* No autorizado, sin privilegio, sin patente; sin permiso o licencia.
Unlicked [un-lict'], *a.* Mal formado, irregular.
Unlighted [un-lait'-ed], *a.* No iluminado, obscuro; no encendido.
Unlike [un-laic'], *a.* 1. Desemejante, diferente, disímil, distinto, nada parecido. 2. Inverosímil o inverisímil, improbable. *Not unlike,* Parecido, semejante.
Unlikelihood [un-laic'-li-hud], **Unlikeliness** [un-laic'-li-nes], *s.* Improbabilidad, inverisimilitud.
Unlikely [un-laic'-li], *a.* Inverosímil o inverisímil, improbable. —*adv.* Improbablemente, sin verosimilitud.
Unlikeness [un-laic'-nes], *s.* Disimilitud, desemejanza.
Unlimber [un-lim'-ber], *va.* y *vn.* Apartar el avantrén de un cañón, para estar pronto a disparar.
Unlimited [un-lim'-it-ed], *a.* 1. Ilimitado, sin límites ni término; indefinido. 2. Franco, absoluto.
Unlimitedly [un-lim'-it-ed-li], *adv.* Ilimitadamente, sin límites, sin medida.
Unlink [un-link'], *va.* Deseslabonar, desenlabonar, soltar los eslabones; separar, deshacer.
Unliquefied [un-lic'-wi-faid], *a.* No derretido; cuajado.
Unliquidated [un-lic'-wi-dē-ted], *a.* Indeterminado respecto a suma o cantidad; no pagado, no saldado.
Unload [un-lōd'], *va.* 1. Descargar, quitar o aliviar la carga; desahogar, aligerar. 2. (Fam. E. U.) Vender, particularmente en grandes cantidades; dícese de las mercancías averiables o difíciles de conservar en buen estado.—*vn.* Descargar la carga.
Unlock [un-loc'], *va.* 1. Abrir una cerradura (cerrada con llave). 2. (Impr.) Desapretar (las formas). 3. Dar libre acceso; hacer disponible. 4. Revelar (secreto).
Unlooked-for [un-luct'-fōr], *a.* Inesperado, inopinado.
Unloose [un-lūs'], *va.* Desatar.—*vn.* Hacerse pedazos.
Unloved [un-luvd'], *a.* Desamado, no amado.
Unloveliness [un-luv'-li-nes], *s.* Aspereza de genio, falta de amabilidad.
Unlovely [un-luv'-li], *a.* Desamable, desagradable, fastidioso.
Unloving [un-luv'-ing], *a.* Poco amante, poco afectuoso, que no ama.
Unluckily [un-luk'-i-li], *adv.* Desgraciadamente, desafortunadamente, por desgracia.
Unluckiness [un-luk'-i-nes], *s.* Desastre, desgracia, infortunio, mala suerte.
Unlucky [un-luk'-i], *a.* 1. Desgraciado, desafortunado, desdichado. 2. Funesto, infausto, azaroso, aciago, siniestro, de mal agüero.
Unlute [un-lūt'], *va.* Destapar, quitar el luten de las vasijas que están cubiertas o tapadas con él.
Unmade [un-mēd'], *a.* Increado; deshecho; que no se ha hecho aún o que se ha olvidado hacerlo.
Unmaidenly [un-mē'-dn-li], *a.* Impropio de una doncella.
Unmaimed [un-mēmd'], *a.* No mutilado, íntegro.
Unmake [un-mēk'], *va.* 1. Deshacer, destruir, aniquilar. 2. Deponer (autoridad).
Unman [un-man'], *va.* 1. Privar de fuerza viril o de firmeza; afeminar, acobardar, desanimar. 2. Desguarnecer, quitar la guarnición (de una plaza, una fortaleza). 3. Castrar, capar. 4. (Raro) Privar del juicio o de la razón.
Unmanageable [un-man'-ej-a-bl], *a.* Inmanejable, indómito, intratable.
Unmanaged [un-man'-ejd], *a.* No manejado, no domado; indisciplinado.
Unmanlike [un-man'-laic], **Unmanly** [un-man'-li], *a.* 1. Indigno de un hombre o contrario a los sentimientos que deben dirigir la conducta de los hombres. 2. Afeminado, enervado, muelle.
Unmanned [un-mand'], *a.* Que no está dirigido o gobernado por hombres.
Unmannered [un-man'-erd], *a.* Rudo, brutal, grosero; mal criado, soez.
Unmannerliness [un-man'-er-li-nes], *s.* Rudeza, brutalidad, mala crianza, descortesía, impolítica.
Unmannerly [un-man'-er-li], *a.* Impolítico, malcriado, mal educado, falto de crianza, descortés, grosero. —*adv.* Descortésmente, groseramente, sin política, sin crianza.
Unmarked [un-mārct'], *a.* No mirado, no observado, no señalado.
Unmarketable [un-mār'-ket-a-bl], *a.* Invendible, que no se halla en buen estado para el mercado; echado a perder, no pedido.
Unmarriageable [un-mar'-ij-a-bl], *a.* Incasable, no casadero; que no está en edad o condición de casarse.
Unmarried [un-mar'-id], *a.* Célibe, no casado; soltero, soltera.
Unmask [un-mask'], *va.* Desenmascarar, quitar la máscara a una persona; descubrir, descorrer o quitar el velo.
Unmasked [un-maskt'], *a.* Patente, manifiesto.
Unmastered [un-mas'-terd], *a.* No domado, no vencido; que no está todavía aprendido o adquirido.
Unmatchable [un-mach'-a-bl], *a.* Que no tiene par; único, incomparable.
Unmatched [un-macht'], *a.* Único, sin igual, sin par, sin nada que se le asemeje.
Unmeaning [un-mīn'-ing], *a.* Sin significación, vacío de sentido, que no significa nada. *Unmeaning words,* Palabras vanas o vacías de sentido; vulgarmente, greguería o jerga.
Unmeasurable [un-mezh'-ur-a-bl], *a.* Ilimitado, inmensurable, inmenso.
Unmeasured [un-mezh'-urd], *a.* Inmenso, infinito, ilimitado.
Unmeditated [un-med'-i-tēt-ed], *a.* Impensado, no meditado.
Unmeet [un-mīt'], *a.* Impropio, indigno, ajeno, extraño, poco conveniente.
Unmellowed [un-mel'-ōd], *a.* Inmaturo, no maduro o en sazón.
Unmelted [un-melt'-ed], *a.* No derretido.
Unmentionable [un-men'-shun-a-bl], *a.* Impropio, que no debe mencionar-

se,—*s. pl.* (Fest.) Calzones, pantalones.

Unmentioned [un-men'-shund], *a.* Que no está mencionado, designado, nombrado ; de que no se habla.

Unmerchantable [un-mẹr'-chant-a-bl], *a.* Invendible, no corriente.

Unmerciful [un-mẹr'-si-ful], *a.* 1. Inclemente, riguroso, cruel, desapiadado. 2. (Fam.) Excesivo, exorbitante, fuera de razón.

Unmercifully [un-mẹr'-si-ful-i], *adv.* Cruelmente, rigurosamente, desapiadadamente, inhumanamente, sin misericordia.

Unmercifulness [un-mẹr'-si-ful-nes], *s.* Inclemencia, crueldad, inhumanidad.

Unmerited [un-mer'-it-ed], *a.* Desmerecido, inmerecido.

Unmethodical [un-me-thod'-ic-al], *a.* Que no es metódico ; desarreglado, irregular, falto de método.

Unmindful [un-maind'-ful], *a.* Olvidadizo, que con facilidad se olvida de las cosas ; descuidado, dejado, negligente, que no hace caso, que no presta atención.

Unmindfulness [un-maind'-ful-nes], *s.* Descuido, dejadez, negligencia, falta de atención.

Unmingled [un-min'-gld], *a.* Puro, sin haberse mezclado.

Unmistakable [un-mis-têk'-a-bl], *a.* Inequívoco, que no puede tomarse por otra cosa ; evidente.

Unmitigated [un-mit'-i-gêt-ed], *a.* Duro, no mitigado, no suavizado ; desmesurado ; de aquí, tan malo como es posible serlo. *V.* UNCONSCIONABLE.

Unmixed, Unmixt [un-micst'], *a.* Puro, sin composición, sin mezcla ; simple, sencillo.

Unmolested [un-mo-lest'-ed], *a.* Quieto, tranquilo, no molestado.

Unmoor [un-mūr'], *va.* (Mar.) Desamarrar, quitar las amarras y levantar las anclas, desaferrar.

Unmortgaged [un-mōr'-gejd], *a.* No hipotecado, no dado en hipoteca.

Unmourned [un-mōrnd'], *a.* No llorado, no lamentado.

Unmoved [un-mūvd'], *a.* 1. Inmoto, que no se mueve. 2. Inmoble, inmovible, constante, firme e invariable. 3. Inalterable, impasible, no conmovido, no enternecido.

Unmoving [un-mūv'-ing], *a.* 1. Falto de movimiento. 2. Seco, árido, que no mueve los afectos del ánimo.

Unmuffle [un-muf'-l], *va.* 1. Destapar la cara, desembozarse. 2. Destapar o quitar la mufla de.

Unmusical [un-miū'-zi-cal], *a.* Disonante, discordante, discorde, poco musical.

Unmuzzle [un-muz'-l], *va.* Quitar el bozal a, desbozalar.

Unnamed [un-nêmd'], *a.* Innominado, no nombrado, anónimo, sin nombre.

Unnatural [un-nach'-ur-al], *a.* 1. Innatural, no natural, contrario a las leyes o a los sentimientos de la naturaleza ; cruel, monstruoso, inhumano. 2. Desnaturalizado, falto de los afectos o sentimientos naturales. 3. Forzado, artificial, fuera de lo natural. *An unnatural parent,* Un padre desnaturalizado.

Unnaturally [un-nach'-ur-al-i], *adv.* Contra la naturaleza o contra las leyes de la naturaleza.

Unnaturalness [un-nach'-ur-al-nes], *s.* La calidad que constituye a una cosa contraria a lo que es natural o común.

Unnavigable [un-nav'-i-ga-bl], *a.* Innavegable. *V.* INNAVIGABLE.

Unnecessarily [un-nes'-e-sẹ-ri-li], *adv.* Sin necesidad ; inútilmente ; fuera de propósito.

Unnecessariness [un-nes'-e-sẹ''-ri-nes], *s.* Superfluidad ; inutilidad ; falta de necesidad.

Unnecessary [un-nes'-e-sẹ-ri], *a.* Innecesario, excusado, superfluo, inútil.

Unneedful [un-nīd'-ful], *a.* Inútil, innecesario.

Unneighbourly [un-nê'-bor-li], *a.* Áspero, adusto ; nada cortés, poco atento con sus vecinos.

Unnerve [un-nẹrv'], *va.* Enervar, quitar las fuerzas, enflaquecer.

Unnerved [un-nẹrvd'], *a.* y *pp.* Enervado, debilitado, sin fuerzas.

Unnoted [un-nōt'-ed], *a.* Desapercibido, sin ser notado ; obscuro, sin reputación, poco conocido.

Unnoticed [un-nō'-tist], *a.* No observado, pasado por alto, dejado a parte.

Unnumbered [un-num'-bẹrd], *a.* Innumerable, sin número.

Unobjected [un-ob-ject'-ed], *a.* No imputado ; no objetado.

Unobjectionable [un-ob-jec'-shun-a-bl], *a.* Irreprensible, irrecusable ; exento de objeciones.

Unobsequious [un-ob-sī'-cwi-us], *a.* Que no es sumiso, no complaciente ; nada obsequioso.

Unobservable [un-ob-zẹrv'-a-bl], *a.* Imperceptible, inapreciable, que no se puede observar.

Unobservant [un-ob-zẹrv'-ant], **Unobserving** [un-ob-zẹrv'-ing], *a.* Inobservante, que no observa ; que no presta atención, que no hace caso.

Unobserved [un-ob-zẹrvd'], *a.* Desapercibido, no notado, que pasa o sucede sin observarse, sin llamar la atención o sin que se haga caso de ello.

Unobstructed [un-ob-struct'-ed], *a.* Libre, no obstruído, no impedido.

Unobstructive [un-ob-struc'-tiv], *a.* Que no impide o embaraza.

Unobtrusive [un-ob-trū'-siv], *a.* No intruso, no entremetido ; discreto, modesto.

Unobvious [un-ob'-vi-us], *a.* Que no es obvio o muy claro ; obscuro.

Unoccupied [un-oc'-yu-paid], *a.* Desocupado, vacante, libre ; sin ocupación. *Unoccupied land,* Baldío, erial.

Unoffending [un-of-fend'-ing], *a.* Sencillo, inocente ; que no puede hacer daño.

Unoffered [un-of'-ẹrd], *a.* No ofrecido.

Unofficial [un-of-fish'-al], *a.* Extraoficial, no oficial.

Unopened [un-ō'-pnd], *a.* Cerrado, que aun no se ha abierto.

Unoperative, *a.* *V.* INOPERATIVE.

Unopposed [un-op-pōzd'], *a.* Sin oposición o que no encuentra oposición.

Unorganized [un-ōr'-gan-aizd], *a.* Inorganizado, no organizado ; inorgánico, falto de estructura.

Unoriginal, Unoriginated, *a.* No original.

Unorthodox [un-ōr'-tho-dox], *a.* Heterodoxo.

Unostentatious [un-os-ten-tê'-shus], *a.* Libre de ostentación, de fausto ; no presumido, modesto, simple.

Unostentatiously [un-os-ten-tê'-shus-li], *adv.* Sin ostentación, simplemente.

Unowned [un-ōnd'], *a.* 1. Sin dueño. 2. Desconocido, no reconocido. 3. Mostrenco : se aplica a los objetos o bienes que no tienen dueño conocido.

Unoxidizable, Unoxidisable [un-oc-si-daiz'-a-bl], *a.* Inoxidable, que no se puede oxidar.

Unpacifiable [un-pas-i-fai'-a-bl], *a.* Que no admite pacificación ; turbulento, salvaje, amotinado.

Unpack [un-pak'], *va.* Desempaquetar, desempapelar, desenvolver, desembalar, desenfardar.

Unpaid [un-pêd'], *a.* No pagado, que no se ha pagado ; el que no recibe lo que se le debe ; el que trabaja sin recibir pago alguno.

Unpained [un-pênd'], *a.* Sin dolor, lo que no duele.

Unpainful [un-pên'-ful], *a.* Que no causa o produce dolor.

Unpainted [un-pênt'-ed], *a.* Que no está pintado ; sin afeites.

Unpaired [un-pārd'], *a.* Desapareado, no apareado ; no reunido.

Unpalatable [un-pal'-a-ta-bl], *a.* Desabrido, desagradable al paladar.

Unparalleled [un-par'-a-leld], *a.* Único, sin igual, sin par ; sin paralelo.

Unpardonable [un-pār'-dun-a-bl], *a.* Irremisible, que no merece perdón.

Unpardonably [un-pār'-dun-a-bli], *adv.* Irremisiblemente, sin remisión, sin perdón.

Unpardoned [un-pār'-dund], *a.* Que no está perdonado.

Unpardoning [un-pār'-dn-ing], *a.* Inexorable, implacable, que no perdona.

Unparliamentary [un-pār-li-ment'-a-ri], *a.* Contrario a las reglas del parlamento o a las que gobiernan a un cuerpo deliberante.

Unparted [un-pārt'-ed], *a.* Indiviso.

Unpartizan, Unpartisan [un-pār'-ti-zan], *a.* Exento de adhesión a un partido, no partidario.

Unpassionate [un-pash'-un-et], *a.* Desapasionado, imparcial.

Unpatented [un-pat'-en-ted], *a.* No privilegiado, sin patente.

Unpatronized [un-pat'-ron-aizd], *a.* Dícese del que no tiene quien le proteja o favorezca.

Unpaved, Unpaven [un-pêvd', un-pê'-vn], *a.* No empedrado.

Unpawned [un-pēnd'], *a.* Desempeñado, libre de empeño.

Unpayable [un-pê'-a-bl] *a.* Impagable, que no se puede pagar.

Unpeaceable [un-pīs'-a-bl], *a.* Revoltoso, amigo de riñas o querellas, alborotador.

Unpeaceful [un-pīs'-ful], *a.* Agitado, no apacible, desordenado.

Unpeg [un-peg'], *va.* Desenclavijar, abrir una cosa que está cerrada con clavijas.

Unpen [un-pen'], *va.* Soltar el ganado del redil ; librar de una prisión.

Unpensioned [un-pen'-shund], *a.* Sin pensión, no pensionado ; no jubilado, sin pensión de retiro.

Unpeople [un-pī'-pl], *va.* Despoblar.

Unperceivable [un-pẹr-sīv'-a-bl], *a.* Imperceptible ; ininteligible.

Unperceived [un-pẹr-sīvd'], *a.* No percibido, no descubierto.

Unperformed [un-pẹr-fōrmd'], *a.* No ejecutado, no hecho, no cumplido, por cumplir.

Unperjured [un-pẹr'-jẹrd], *a.* Libre de perjurio.

Unperplexed [un-pẹr-plecst'], *a.* Desenredado, desenmarañado.

Unpersuadable [un-pẹr-swêd'-a-bl], *a.* Impersuasible, terco.

Unperused [un-pẹ-rūzd'], *a.* No leído.

Unphilosophic, Unphilosophical [un-fil-o-sof'-ic, al], *a.* Antifilosófico, opuesto a la filosofía, poco filosófico

Unphilosophically [un-fil-o-sof'-ic-al-i], *adv.* Contra las reglas o máximas de la filosofía; contra el dictado de la razón.

Unpierced [un-pirst'], *a.* No penetrado, no traspasado.

Unpillared [un-pil'-ard], *a.* Sin columnas, sin pilares.

Unpillowed [un-pil'-ōd], *a.* Sin almohada.

Unpiloted [un-pai'-lot-ed], *a.* Que no es conducido por un piloto; sin guía, sin conductor.

Unpin [un-pin'], *va.* Desprender lo que está prendido con alfileres.

Unpinioned [un-pin'-yund], *a.* El que tiene las manos sueltas o sin trabas.

Unpitied [un-pit'-id], *a.* No compadecido, sin excitar compasión o lástima.

Unpitying [un-pit'-i-ing], *a.* Incompasivo, desapiadado, inclemente.

Unplaced [un-plêst'], *a.* Desacomodado, no colocado.

Unplagued [un-plêgd'], *a.* Libre de alguna cosa que cause dolor; no atormentado.

Unplanted [un-plant'-ed], *a.* Espontáneo, que no ha sido plantado; que crece espontáneamente.

Unplastered [un-plas'-terd], *a.* Que no está enyesado; que no está dado de estuco.

Unpleasant [un-plez'-ant], *a.* Desagradable, enfadoso, molesto, displicente.

Unpleasantly [un-plez'-ant-li], *adv.* Desagradablemente, enfadosamente, desabridamente.

Unpleasantness [un-plez'-ant-nes], *s.* Desagrado, disgusto, desazón, enfado.

Unpleased [un-plîzd'], *a.* Descontento, disgustado, enfadado, enojado.

Unpleasing [un-plîz'-ing], *a.* Desagradable, ofensivo, enfadoso, molesto.

Unpleasingly [un-plîz'-ing-li], *a.* Desagradablemente; ofensivamente.

Unploughed, Unplowed [un-plaud'], *a.* Inculto, no arado.

Unpoetic, Unpoetical [un-po-et'-ic, al], *a.* Que no es poético, que no está conforme con las reglas de la poesía.

Unpolished [un-pol'-isht], *a.* 1. Áspero, tosco, que no está liso, que no está pulido. 2. Basto, rudo, grosero, impolítico. *An unpolished diamond,* Diamante en bruto. *Unpolished ore,* Mineral sin bruñir.

Unpolite [un-po-lait'], *a.* Grosero, descortés, impolítico. *V.* IMPOLITE.

Unpolled [un-pōld'], *a.* No inscrito en la lista electoral; no incluido en el escrutinio; que no ha votado.

Unpolluted [un-pol-lūt'-ed], *a.* Impoluto, inmaculado, limpio, sin mancha.

Unpopular [un-pop'-yu-lar], *a.* Impopular, que es contrario a las opiniones dominantes, que no agrada al pueblo.

Unportable [un-pōrt'-a-bl], *a.* Que no se puede portear o llevar.

Unpossessed [un-pez-est'], *a.* No gozado, no poseído.

Unpossessing [un-pez-es'-ing], *a.* El que no posee o el que no tiene derecho a la posesión de alguna cosa.

Unpracticable [un-prac'-ti-ca-bl], *a. V.* IMPRACTICABLE.

Unpractised, Unpractical [un-prac'-tist], *a.* Inexperto, no versado, no enseñado.

Unpraised [un-prêzd'], *a.* No celebrado, que no es alabado.

Unprecedented [un-pres'-e-dent-ed], *a.* Inaudito, sin precedente o sin ejemplar.

Unpredictable [un-pre-dict'-a-bl], *a.* Que no se puede pronosticar.

Unpreferred [un-pre-ferd'], *a.* No antepuesto, no preferido; no elevado a alguna dignidad.

Unprejudiced [un-prej'-u-dist], *a.* No preocupado, libre o exento de preocupaciones; imparcial.

Unpremeditated [un-pre-med'-i-têt-ed], *a.* Inopinado; no premeditado, no pensado con anterioridad.

Unprepared [un-pre-pārd'], *a.* Desprevenido, desproveído, desprovisto, no preparado.

Unpreparedness [un-pre-pārd'-nes], *s.* Desprevención, falta de prevención.

Unprepossessed [un-prî-poz-est'], *a.* Libre de preocupaciones. *V.* UNPREJUDICED.

Unprepossessing [un-prî-poz-es'-ing], *a.* Poco atractivo, poco insinuante, que no inspira opinión favorable al principio, o a primera vista.

Unpressed [un-prest'], *a.* No prensado; no obligado, no forzado.

Unpretending [un-pre-tend'-ing], *a.* Modesto, moderado, falto de pretensión.

Unprevailing [un-pre-vêl'-ing], *a.* Nulo, írrito; no corriente; ineficaz.

Unprevented [un-pre-vent'-ed], *a.* No impedido a tiempo; sin obstáculo.

Unprincely [un-prins'-li], *a.* Indigno de un príncipe.

Unprincipled [un-prin'-si-pld], *a.* El que no tiene principios u opiniones fijas en la moral o en la religión; malvado.

Unprinted [un-print'-ed], *a.* 1. Manuscrito, no impreso. 2. Liso (se dice de tejidos).

Unprisoned [un-priz'-nd], *a.* Suelto, que no está preso.

Unprized [un-praizd'], *a.* No apreciado.

Unproclaimed [un-pro-clêmd'], *a.* No publicado, no proclamado.

Unproductive [un-pro-duc'-tiv], *a.* Improductivo, que no produce; estéril.

Unprofaned [un-pro-fênd'], *a.* Inviolado, no profanado.

Unprofessional [un-pro-fesh'-un-al], *a.* Que no pertenece a una profesión (liberal); extraño a una profesión; no profesional, contrario a las reglas de una profesión.

Unprofitable [un-pref'-it-a-bl], *a.* Poco ventajoso, no lucrativo, que no produce nada; inútil, vano, que para nada sirve.

Unprofitableness [un-pref'-it-a-bl-nes], *s.* Inutilidad.

Unprofitably [un-pref'-it-a-bli], *adv.* Inútilmente, sin provecho, sin beneficio.

Unprofited [un-pref'-it-ed], *a.* Inútil, sin provecho.

Unprohibited [un-pro-hib'-it-ed], *a.* No prohibido, permitido.

Unprolific [un-pro-lif'-ic], *a.* Poco prolífico; estéril, infecundo.

Unpromising [un-prem'-is-ing], *a.* De poca apariencia, que no promete mucho, que no da grandes esperanzas.

Unpronounceable [un-pro-nauns'-a-bl], *a.* Que no se puede pronunciar.

Unpronounced [un-pro-naunst'], *a.* Inarticulado, no pronunciado.

Unpropitious [un-pro-pish'-us], *a.* Infausto, no favorable, poco propicio.

Unproportionable [un-pro-pōr'-shun-a-bl], *a. V.* DISPROPORTIONABLE.

Unproportioned [un-pro-pōr'-shund], *a.* Desproporcionado, no adaptado.

Unpropped [un-prept'], *a.* Desapuntalado, sin apoyo.

Unprosperous [un-pres'-per-us], *a.* Desafortunado, desgraciado, infeliz.

Unprosperously [un-pres'-per-us-li], *adv.* Infelizmente, desgraciadamente.

Unprotected [un-pro-tect'-ed], *a.* Desvalido, sin protección; falto de impuestos protectores.

Unproved, Unproven [un-prūvd'], *a.* No probado, no demostrado.

Unprovided [un-pro-vaid'-ed], *a.* Desproveído, desprovisto, falto, cogido desprevenido. *Unprovided for,* No preparado a, no previsto. *Unprovided with,* Desprovisto de, que carece de.

Unprovoked [un-pro-vōct'], *a.* No provocado; sin motivo, sin provocación.

Unpruned [un-prūnd'], *a.* No podado.

Unpublished [un-pub'-lisht], *a.* Secreto, oculto, no publicado; inédito.

Unpunctual [un-punc'-chu-al], *a.* Inexacto, que no es puntual.

Unpunishable [un-pun'-ish-a-bl], *a.* Que no es punible, que no admite castigo.

Unpunished [un-pun'-isht], *a.* Impune, no castigado.

Unpurchased [un-pūr'-chest], *a.* No comprado.

Unpurged [un-pūrjd'], *a.* No purgado.

Unpurified [un-piū'-ri-faid], *a.* No purificado, no refinado.

Unpursued [un-pūr-siūd'], *a.* Quieto, no perseguido.

Unquailing [un-cwêl'-ing], *a.* Resuelto, no abatido, que no se desanima.

Unqualified [un-cwel'-i-faid], *a.* 1. Inhábil, inepto, incapaz, que no tiene las cualidades necesarias o no es a propósito para alguna cosa. 2. Que no tiene la autorización necesaria o legal. 3. Dado o hecho sin restricción; completo, entero. *They have his unqualified approbation,* Ellos tienen la entera aprobación de él.

Unqualify [un-cwel'-i-fai], *va.* Inhabilitar. *V.* DISQUALIFY.

Unquelled [un-cweld'], *a.* No sujeto, no abatido.

Unquenchable [un-cwench'-a-bl], *a.* Inextinguible, insaciable.

Unquenchableness [un-cwench'-a-bl-nes], *s.* La propiedad de lo insaciable o inextinguible.

Unquenched [un-cwencht'], *a.* No extinguido, no apagado.

Unquestionable [un-cwes'-chun-a-bl], *a.* Indudable, indiscutible, que no admite disputa.

Unquestionably [un-cwes'-chun-a-bli], *adv.* Indudablemente, sin duda, sin disputa.

Unquestioned [un-cwes'-chund], *a.* 1. Incontestable, indisputable. 2. Tenido por cierto, no dudado. 3. No examinado, no preguntado.

Unquickened [un-cwic'-nd], *a.* Inanimado.

Unquiet [un-cwai'-et], *a.* Inquieto, desasosegado; agitado, turbado.

Unquietly [un-cwai'-et-li], *adv.* Inquietamente, con desasosiego o inquietud.

Unquietness [un-cwai'-et-nes], *s.* Inquietud, desasosiego.

Unracked [un-ract'], *a.* No trasegado, no clarificado. *Unracked wine,* Vino por trasegar.

Unraked [un-rêct'], *a.* No rastrillado; no amontonado; no atizado, no limpiado.

Unravel [un-rav'-l], *va.* 1. Desenredar, deshacer el enredo; deshilar, sacar los hilos de un tejido. 2. Desembrollar, aclarar, explicar. 3. Desatar ó desenredar, dar salida á un lance, enredo ó trama en las piezas dramáticas.—*vn.* Desenredarse: desenlazarse.
Unravelment [un-rav'-el-mgnt], *s.* Desenlace (de una pieza).
Unreached [un-richt'], *a.* No alcanzado, no conseguido.
Unread [un-red'], *a.* No leído, sin leer; iliterato, indocto, ignorante.
Unreadiness [un-red'-i-nes], *s.* Pesadez; desprevención, falta de prevención o de preparación; lentitud; carencia de facilidad.
Unready [un-red'-i], *a.* 1. Lento; que no es pronto en ver o apreciar. 2. Desprevenido, que no está prevenido o preparado; que no está pronto o dispuesto.
Unreal [un-rí'-al], *a.* 1. No real, imaginario, vano, sin realidad. 2. Inmaterial, incorporal. 3. Insincero, falto de sinceridad.
Unreason [un-rí'-zn], *s.* Sinrazón, necedad, disparate.
Unreasonable [un-rí'-zn-a-bl], *a.* Inmoderado, excesivo, exorbitante, desrazonable.
Unreasonableness [un-rí'-zn-a-bl-nes], *s.* 1. Sinrazón, despropósito, falta de razón. 2. Exorbitancia.
Unreasonably [un-rí'-zn-a-bli], *adv.* Irracionalmente, exorbitantemente, excesivamente.
Unreclaimed [un-re-clêmd'], *a.* Incorregible, incapaz de corrección.
Unrecognizable [un-rec-eg-naiz'-a-bl], *a.* Irreconocible.
Unreconcilable [un-rec-en-sail'-a-bl], *a.* Implacable; incompatible; irreconciliable.
Unreconciled [un-rec'-en-saild], *a.* Enemistado; no reconciliado.
Unrecorded [un-re-cōrd'-ed], *a.* Sepultado en el olvido, no recordado en monumentos públicos; no archivado.
Unrecounted [un-re-caunt'-d], *a.* No referido.
Unrecoverable [un-re-cuv'-er-a-bl], *a.* Irrecuperable, que no se puede recobrar; irreparable, sin remedio, incurable.
Unrecovered [un-re-cuv'-erd], *a.* No recobrado.
Unrectified [un-rec'-ti-faid], *a.* No rectificado.
Unrecurring [un-re-cur'-ing], *a.* Que no se presenta de tiempo en tiempo; poco frecuente.
Unreduced [un-re-diūst'], *a.* No reducido, no sujetado.
Unreducible [un-re-diū'-si-bl], *a.* *V.* IRREDUCIBLE.
Unreeve [un-rív'], *va.* (Mar.) Despasar, desguarnir.
Unrefined [un-re-faind'], *a.* 1. No refinado, no purificado, en bruto. 2. Inculto, rudo, de estilo o modales poco cultos o refinados.
Unreformed [un-re-fōrmd'], *a.* 1. No reformado, no corregido. 2. Impenitente, obstinado en la culpa.
Unrefracted [un-re-fract'-ed], *a.* No refracto.
Unrefreshed [un-re-fresht'], *a.* No refrescado, no aliviado; cansado; no reanimado.
Unregarded [un-re-gārd'-ed], *a.* Desatendido, descuidado, desdeñado, despreciado.
Unregardful [un-re-gārd'-ful], *a.* Negligente, descuidado.
Unregenerate [un-re-jen'-er-êt], *a.* No regenerado.
Unregistered [un-rej'-is-terd], *a.* No archivado; no registrado, inscrito o apuntado.
Unreined [un-rênd'], *a.* Desenfrenado, libre.
Unrelated [un-re-lêt'-ed], *a.* 1. Que no tiene parentesco con otra persona. 2. Que no tiene relación o conexión con otra cosa, no afín.
Unrelenting [un-re-lent'-ing], *a.* Incompasivo, duro de corazón, inflexible.
Unreliable [un-re-lai'-a-bl], *a.* Indigno de confianza; que no merece creencia o fe (persona o cosa).
Unrelievable [un-re-lív'-a-bl], *a.* Incapaz de socorro.
Unrelieved [un-re-lívd'], *a.* No socorrido, no aliviado.
Unremediable [un-re-mí'-di-a-bl], *a.* *V.* IRREMEDIABLE.
Unremembered [un-re-mem'-berd], *a.* Olvidado, no recordado, sin decir o mencionar.
Unremembering [un-re-mem'-ber-ing], *a.* Que no se acuerda, trascordado, falto de memoria.
Unremembrance [un-re-mem'-brans], *s.* Olvido, falta de memoria.
Unremitted [un-re-mit'-ed], *a.* Continuo; no perdonado.
Unremitting [un-re-mit'-ing], *a.* Perseverante, constante, incansable.
Unremovable [un-re-mūv'-a-bl], *a.* *V.* IRREMOVABLE.
Unremoved [un-re-mūvd'], *a.* No removido; inmoble, incapaz de ser removido; no alejado, no desviado.
Unremunerative [un-re-miū'-ner-a-tiv], *a.* Que no es remunerador.
Unrepealed [un-re-píld'], *a.* No abrogado.
Unrepentant [un-re-pent'-ant], **Unrepented** [un-re-pent'-ed], **Unrepenting** [un-re-pent'-ing], *a.* Impenitente, obstinado en la culpa.
Unrepining [un-re-pain'-ing], *a.* Resignado, que no se queja.
Unrepiningly [un-re-pain'-ing-li], *adv.* Con resignación, con paciencia.
Unreplenished [un-re-plen'-isht], *a.* No lleno, no surtido o provisto.
Unrepresented [un-rep-re-zent'-ed], *a.* No representado, que no tiene representante.
Unreprievable [un-re-prív'-a-bl], *a.* Sentenciado a pena de muerte sin esperanza de perdón o de que se suspenda la ejecución de dicha pena.
Unreprieved [un-re-prívd'], *a.* Sentenciado a muerte sin orden para que se suspenda la ejecución de la sentencia.
Unreproved [un-re-prūvd'], *a.* Que no es reprendido, amonestado; irreprensible, que no se puede tachar o motejar.
Unrequested [un-re-cwest'-ed], *a.* Espontáneo, que no se ha pedido, rogado o demandado.
Unresented [un-re-zent'-ed], *a.* Que no excita la cólera o el resentimiento.
Unreserve [un-re-zerv'], *s.* Franqueza, ingenuidad, candor.
Unreserved [un-re-zervd'], *a.* 1. Que no es reservado, retenido; ilimitado, sin restricción. 2. Franco, abierto; libre.
Unreservedly [un-re-zerv'-ed-li], *adv.* Sin reserva; sin reticencia, francamente, abiertamente.
Unreservedness [un-re-zerv'-ed-nes], *s.* Candor, franqueza, ingenuidad.
Unresisted [un-re-zist'-ed], *a.* Sin resistencia; irresistible.
Unresistible [un-re-zist'-i-bl], *a.* *V.* IRRESISTIBLE.
Unresisting [un-re-zist'-ing], *a.* Que no resiste, que no ofrece resistencia, sin resistencia.
Unresolvable [un-re-zolv'-a-bl], *a.* Indisoluble, insoluble.
Unresolved [un-re-zolvd'], *a.* 1. Irresoluto, indeterminado, indeciso. 2. No desatado, no aclarado, que no está resuelto.
Unrespited [un-res'-pit-ed], *a.* 1. Que no tiene tregua; sin suspensión de una sentencia. 2. (Des.) Sin intermisión.
Unrest [un-rest'], *s.* Inquietud, desasosiego.
Unresting [un-rest'-ing], *a.* Que no descansa jamás; que no toma reposo.
Unrestored [un-re-stōrd'], *a.* No restituido, no recobrado; no devuelto; no restablecido.
Unrestrained [un-re-strênd'], *a.* 1. Desenfrenado, libre, licencioso, insubordinado; suelto. 2. Ilimitado, sin límites.
Unretracted [un-re-tract'-ed], *a.* Que no se ha retractado, que no se ha desdicho; no encogido ni retraído.
Unrevealed [un-re-víld'], *a.* Oculto, no revelado, que se guarda secreto.
Unrevenged [un-re-venjd'], *a.* Inulto, que queda sin vengar.
Unrevengeful [un-re-venj'-ful], *a.* Que no es vengativo.
Unreversed [un-re-verst'], **Unrevoked** [un-re-vōct'], *a.* No revocado.
Unrewarded [un-re-wērd'-ed], *a.* No premiado, no recompensado.
Unrhymed [un-raimd'], *a.* No rimado, falto de rima.
Unriddle [un-rid'-l], *va.* 1. Desatar o adivinar un enigma, explicar un problema. 2. Desenmarañar.
Unrifled [un-rai'-fld], *a.* 1. No rayado, de ánima lisa; aplícase a las armas de fuego. 2. No pillado ni saqueado; no escudriñado ni examinado.
Unrig [un-rig'], *va.* (Mar.) Desaparejar.
Unrighteous [un-rai'-chus], *a.* Inicuo, malo, perverso; injusto.
Unrighteously [un-rai'-chus-li], *adv.* Inicuamente, perversamente.
Unrighteousness [un-rai'-chus-nes], *s.* Iniquidad, perversidad, maldad; injusticia.
Unrightful [un-rait'-ful], *a.* Injusto, contrario a derecho; no legítimo.
Unrimed [un-raimd'], *a.* *V.* UNRHYMED.
Unripe [un-raip'], **Unripened** [un-rai'pnd], *a.* Verde, inmaturo, que no ha llegado a la madurez, que no está maduro.
Unripeness [un-raip'-nes], *s.* Falta de madurez.
Unrisen [un-riz'-n], *a.* Que no se ha levantado; que no ha salido todavía (astro).
Unrivalled [un-rai'-vald], *a.* Sin rival, sin igual o paralelo.
Unrivet [un-riv'-et], *va.* Quitar el roblón o el remache de los clavos.
Unrobe [un-rōb'], *va.* Quitar a uno el traje de ceremonia; desnudar.—*vn.* Desnudarse. *V.* DISROBE.
Unroll [un-rōl'], *va.* 1. Desarrollar, extender lo que estaba arrollado. 2. Desplegar a la vista.—*vn.* Abrirse desarrollándose; desarrollarse.
Unroof [un-rūf'], *va.* Destechar, quitar el techo.
Unroost [un-rūst'], *va.* Arrojar o echar de la percha de un gallinero:

y por extensión, echar á una persona de su puesto, empleo, etc.
Unroot [un-rūt'], *va.* Desarraigar, extirpar, arrancar de raíz.
Unrounded [un-raund'-ed], *a.* Que no está redondeado.
Unruffled [un-ruf'-ld], *a.* Calmado, tranquilo, sereno.
Unruled [un-rūld'], *a.* 1. No rayado, no reglado (papel). 2. Absoluto, independiente; lo que no tiene quien lo dirija o gobierne.
Unruliness [un-rū'-li-nes], *s.* Turbulencia, inquietud; desenfreno, desenfrenamiento.
Unruly [un-rū'-li], *a.* Indómito, desenfrenado, indomable, indomeñable; revoltoso, levantisco; terco, intratable; desarreglado.
Unrumple [un-rum'-pl], *va.* Quitar, deshacer los pliegues de; poner liso, llano.
Unsaddle [un-sad'-l], *va.* Desensillar, quitar la silla a las caballerías.
Unsafe [un-sêf'], *a.* Peligroso, no seguro, que tiene riesgo o peligro.
Unsafely [un-sêf'-li], *adv.* Peligrosamente.
Unsaid [un-sed'], *a.* No proferido, no mencionado, que no se ha dicho.
Unsalable [un-sêl'-a-bl], *a.* Invendible, que no se puede vender, lo que no tiene salida.
Unsalted [un-sōlt'-ed], *a.* Desalado; no salado.
Unsanctified [un-sanc'-ti-faid], *a.* Profano, no consagrado.
Unsanitary [un-san'-i-te-ri], *a.* Antihigiénico.
Unsaponifiable [un-sa-pen''-i-fai'-a-bl], *a.* Insaponificable, que no puede ser convertido en jabón.
Unsatiable [un-sé'-shi-a-bl], *a.* *V.* INSATIABLE.
Unsatisfactory [un-sat-is-fac'-to-ri], *a.* Poco satisfactorio, que no satisface ó no convence.
Unsatisfied [un-sat'-is-faid], *a.* No satisfecho, descontento; no harto; no convencido, no persuadido; no saldado.
Unsatisfying [un-sat'-is-fai-ing], *a.* Que no satisface, que no sacia.
Unsaturated [un-sat'-yu-rê-ted], *a.* No saturado; no combinado en el máximo grado (en química).
Unsavorily [un-sé'-vo-ri-li], *adv.* Desagradablemente, con sabor soso.
Unsavoriness [un-sé'-vo-ri-nes], *s.* 1. Insipidez; mal sabor. 2. Hediondez, mal olor.
Unsavory, Unsavoury [un-sé'-vo-ri], *a.* 1. Insípido, soso, desabrido; empalagoso. 2. Hediondo, fétido. 3. Desagradable, displicente; de mala conducta ó relacionado con alguna cosa moralmente mala. *To make unsavory,* Desazonar ó desabrir una cosa, ponerla sosa, insulsa ó insípida.
Unsay [un-sé'], *va.* Retractar lo que se ha dicho ó desdecirse de ello.
Unscanned [un-scand'], *a.* No medido con la vista, no escudriñado; no escandido (verso).
Unscared [un-scārd'], *a.* No espantado, no asustado.
Unscarred [un-scūrd'], *a.* Libre de cicatrices.
Unscholarly [un-scol'-ar-li], *a.* Impropio ó indigno de una persona instruida; iliterato, no erudito.
Unschooled [un-scūld'], *a.* Indocto, ignorante, falto de enseñanza.
Unscientific [un-sai-en-tif'-ic], *a.* No científico, poco científico.
Unscientifically [un-sai-en-tif'-ic-al-i], *adv.* De una manera poco científica.
Unscorched [un-scōrcht'], *a.* No chamuscado, no tostado, no quemado.
Unscratched [un-scracht'], *a.* Que no ha recibido ningún araño ó arañazo.
Unscreened [un-scrīnd'], *a.* 1. Descubierto; no protegido, sin defensa. 2. No pasado por la criba o harnero.
Unscrew [un-scrū'], *va.* Desatornillar, destornillar; (fig.) desenganchar, apartar, separar.
Unscriptural [un-scrip'-chur-al], *a.* No conforme con la Sagrada Escritura; no contenido en la Biblia.
Unscrupulous [un-scrū'-piu-lus], *a.* Poco escrupuloso, inmoral, falto de principios morales.
Unscrupulously [un-scrū'-piu-lus-li], *adv.* Sin moralidad, sin conciencia.
Unseal [un-sīl'], *va.* Desellar, romper o quitar el sello, abrir lo que está sellado.
Unsealed [un-sīld'], *a.* Desellado, sin sello, abierto, no sellado.
Unsearchable [un-serch'-a-bl], *a.* Inescrutable, inescudriñable; escondido, misterioso.
Unsearchableness [un-serch'-a-bl-nes], *s.* Inescrutabilidad.
Unseasonable [un-sī'-zn-a-bl], *a.* Intempestivo, fuera de sazón, fuera de propósito, inoportuno; indebido, poco conveniente. *At unseasonable hours,* A deshora o a deshoras.
Unseasonableness [un-sī'-zn-a-bl-nes], *s.* Despropósito.
Unseasonably [un-sī'-zn-a-bli], *adv.* Intempestivamente, fuera de propósito, fuera de tiempo o sazón, en mala ocasión.
Unseasoned [un-sī'-znd], *a.* 1. No sazonado, soso; no aclimatado. 2. No acostumbrado, no habituado; no aguerrido, no endurecido. 3. Verde, no seca (madera).
Unseat [un-sīt'], *va.* Quitar de un asiento o posición fija: (1) desarzonar, echar al suelo (de un caballo); (2) privar del derecho de tomar asiento como legislador; echar abajo (a un ministerio).
Unseaworthy [un-sī'-wūr-dhi], *a.* En mal estado para hacerse a la mar; incapaz de navegar.
Unseconded [un-sec'-ond-ed], *a.* No favorecido; no apoyado, no sostenido.
Unsectarian [un-sec-tê'-ri-an], *a.* No sectario, no propio de una secta; (escuela) abierta a todos.
Unsecure [un-se-kiūr'], *a.* Inseguro, en peligro. *V.* INSECURE.
Unseeing [un-sī'-ing], *a.* Ciego, falto de vista.
Unseemliness [un-sīm'-li-nes], *s.* Indecencia, indecoro.
Unseemly [un-sīm'-li], *a.* Indecente; indecoroso; malparecido, impropio.
Unseen [un-sīn'], *a.* 1. Invisible, que no se ve; no evidente. 2. Inapercibido, que no se ha visto; que no se ha visto más de una vez.
Unselfish [un-self'-ish], *a.* Desinteresado, no egoísta.
Unselfishly [un-self'-ish-li], *adv.* Desinteresadamente, sin egoísmo.
Unsensitized [un-sen'-si-taizd], *a.* No sensibilizado (película, papel, placa).
Unsent [un-sent'], *a.* No enviado. *Unsent-for,* No llamado, no enviado a llamar, no convidado.
Unseparated [un-sep'-a-rêt-ed], *a.* Indiviso.
Unserviceable [un-ser'-vis-a-bl], *a.* Inútil, sin utilidad ni ventaja, que no es bueno para nada.
Unserviceableness [un-ser'-vis-a-bl-nes], *s.* Inutilidad, calidad de inservible, carencia de idoneidad.
Unserviceably [un-ser'-vis-a-bli], *adv.* Inútilmente, sin provecho o ventaja.
Unset [un-set'] *a.* No plantado; no puesto.
Unsettle [un-set'-l], *va.* 1. Inquietar, alterar, perturbar. 2. Hacer incierta o poco segura alguna cosa, poner en desorden; desarreglar; trastornar (el espíritu, la razón). 3. Dislocar, remover, trastornar; conmover.
Unsettled [un-set'-ld], *a.* 1. Instable, poco estable, no fijado. 2. Que no tiene domicilio o residencia fija; vago. 3. Inconstante, irresuelto, indeterminado, incierto. 4. Pendiente, no acabado. 5. Desarreglado, descompuesto, turbado; turbio, que no ha hecho poso. 6. (Com.) No arreglado, no liquidado. 7. No habitado, no poblado, sin habitantes.
Unsevered [un-sev'-erd], *a.* Indiviso.
Unsex [un-sex'], *va.* Quitar las propiedades, hábitos, etc., que corresponden a su sexo; particularmente, hacer o hacer parecer poco femenino (a una mujer).
Unsexual [un-sex'-yu-al], *a.* Asexual, no característico o peculiar de uno de los sexos.
Unshackle [un-shac'-l], *va.* Destrabar, desencadenar, quitar las trabas a; libertar.
Unshaded [un-shêd'-ed], *a.* Que no está sombreado; que no tiene sombra.
Unshadowed [un-shad'-ōd], *a.* Claro, sereno, exento de sombra.
Unshakable [un-shêk'-a-bl], *a.* Inmutable, impasible.
Unshaken [un-shê'-kn], *a.* Firme, estable, seguro, inmoble, inmovible.
Unshamed [un-shêmd'], *a.* Descarado, desollado, desvergonzado, impudente.
Unshaped [un-shêpt'], **Unshapen** [un-shê'-pn], *a.* Disforme, informe, sin forma.
Unshapely [un-shêp'-li], *a.* Desproporcionado, que no tiene o guarda simetría.
Unshared [un-shārd'], *a.* Que no ha sido dividido; que no ha cabido a alguno en partición.
Unshaven [un-shêv'-n], *a.* No afeitado, sin estar afeitado.
Unsheathe [un-shīdh'], *va.* Desenvainar, sacar de la vaina.
Unshed [un-shed'], *a.* No derramado, no esparcido.
Unsheltered [un-shel'-terd], *a.* Desvalido, falto de abrigo o protección.
Unship [un-ship'], *va.* Desembarcar, sacar a tierra lo que está embarcado. *To unship the rudder,* (Mar.) Desmontar el timón. *To unship the oars,* (Mar.) Desarmar los remos.
Unshocked [un-shoct'], *a.* No ofendido, no disgustado.
Unshod [un-shod'], *a.* y *pp.* Descalzo; desherrado.
Unshoe [un-shū'], *va.* (*pret.* y *pp.* UNSHOD). Desherrar.
Unshorn [un-shōrn'], *a.* Que no ha sido esquilado. *Unshorn sheep,* Ovejas por esquilar.
Unshot [un-shot'], *a.* 1. Que no se ha descargado, no disparado. 2. No herido.
Unshriven [un-shriv'-en], *a.* No confesado, sin confesión sacerdotal.

Unshut [un-shut'], *a.* Abierto, no cerrado.
Unsifted [un-sift'-ed], *a.* No cernido, no cribado; que no se ha examinado cuidadosamente.
Unsightliness [un-sait'-li-nes], *s.* Fealdad, deformidad.
Unsightly [un-sait'-li], *a.* Feo, disforme, desagradable a la vista.
Unsilvered [un-sil'-vẹrd], *a.* No plateado, desplateado; no azogado.
Unsinful [un-sin'-ful], *a.* Impecable, que no peca; exento de pecado.
Unsisterly [un-sis'-tẹr-li], *a.* Indigno de una hermana.
Unsized [un-saizd'], *a.* No encolado, sin cola (papel).
Unskilful [un-skil'-ful], **Unskilled** [un-skild'], *a.* No diestro, desmañado, inhábil, inexperimentado; ignorante.
Unskilfully [un-skil'-ful-i], *adv.* Sin arte, sin conocimiento, mal, torpemente, con poca maña.
Unskilfulness [un-skil'-ful-nes], *s.* Desmaña, falta de habilidad o maña; inhabilidad.
Unslaked [un-slêct'], *a.* No apagado. *Unslaked lime,* Cal viva.
Unslaughtered [un-slō'-tẹrd], *a.* Que no ha sido muerto.
Unsleeping [un-slīp'-ing], *a.* En vela, siempre despierto.
Unsling [un-sling'], *va.* (Mar.) Quitar las relingas de; deslingar.
Unsmirched [un-smẹrcht'], *a.* Impoluto, limpio, sin mancha.
Unsmoked [un-smōct'], *a.* No ahumado; no fumado; (pipa nueva) en la cual no se ha fumado.
Unsociable [un-sō'-shi-a-bl], *a.* Insociable, intratable, huraño.
Unsociableness [un-sō'-shi-a-bl-nes], *s.* Insociabilidad.
Unsociably [un-sō'-shi-a-bli], *adv.* Insociablemente.
Unsocial [un-sō'-shal], *a.* Insocial, intratable, huraño.
Unsoiled [un-soild'], *a.* Impoluto, libre de mancha.
Unsold [un-sōld'], *a.* No vendido, no despachado; que no ha tenido salida.
Unsolder [un-sed'-ẹr], *va.* Quitar la soldadura.
Unsoldierlike [un-sōl'-jẹr-laic], **Unsoldierly** [un-sōl'-jẹr-li], *a.* Indigno de un soldado, contrario u opuesto a la disciplina militar.
Unsolicited [un-so-lis'-it-ed], *a.* No solicitado, no buscado.
Unsolicitous [un-so-lis'-it-us], *a.* Poco solícito, deseoso, o celoso de; poco cuidadoso de.
Unsolved [un-selvd'], *a.* Sin resolver, sin explicar, sin desatar; obscuro, confuso.
Unsophisticated [un-so-fis'-ti-kêt-ed], *a.* Puro, que no ha sido falsificado o adulterado; sencillo, no artificial; inexperimentado, falto de experiencia.
Unsorted [un-sērt'-ed], *a.* 1. No apartado, no separado. 2. Fuera de tiempo o de propósito.
Unsought [un-sēt'], *a.* Hallado o encontrado sin buscarlo.
Unsound [un-saund'], *a.* 1. Enfermizo, de poca salud; achacoso. 2. Defectuoso, que no es sano; falto de vigor, de fuerza, de solidez; poco firme; falto de salud, enfermo. 3. Sentido, hendido: dícese de la vasija que no está sana. 4. Erróneo, falso; heterodoxo, no ortodoxo. 5. Demasiado fofo o blando. 6. Podrido, corrompido.
Unsounded [un-saund'-ed], *a.* Que no ha sido sondeado o examinado con la sonda; que no se ha sondeado o sabido a fondo.
Unsoundness [un-saund'-nes], *s.* 1. Heterodoxia, oposición a las doctrinas ortodoxas. 2. Falta de solidez o de fuerza. 3. Corrupción.
Unsowed, Unsown [un-sōd', un-sōn'], *a.* No sembrado.
Unspared [un-spārd'], *a.* No ahorrado.
Unsparing [un-spār'-ing], *a.* 1. Liberal, generoso, pródigo, no económico. 2. Inhumano, falto de piedad, cruel.
Unsparingly [un-spār'-ing-li], *adv.* 1. Liberalmente, pródigamente, con profusión. 2. Sin piedad, inhumanamente.
Unspeakable [un-spīk'-a-bl], *a.* 1. Inefable, indecible, inexplicable. 2. (Fam.) Extremamente malo; execrable. *The unspeakable Turk,* El execrable turco.
Unspeakably [un-spīk'-a-bli], *adv.* Inefablemente, indeciblemente.
Unspecialized [un-spesh'-al-aizd], *a.* No específico; particularmente en biología no puesto aparte para un objeto determinado; general.
Unspecified [un-spes'-i-faid], *a.* No especificado, no mencionado.
Unspeculative [un-spec'-yu-la-tiv], *a.* No especulativo; no teórico.
Unsped [un-sped'], *a.* No despachado o expedido.
Unspent [un-spent'], *a.* Que no está agotado; no gastado, no debilitado.
Unsphere [un-sfīr'], *va.* Sacar de su esfera o lugar.
Unspiritual [un-spir'-it-yu-al], *a.* No espiritual, material, corporal; sensual.
Unspoiled [un-spoild'], *a.* No saqueado; ileso, libre de daño; intacto.
Unspotted [un-spot'-ed], *a.* Inmaculado, limpio, sin mancha.
Unsquared [un-scwārd'], *a.* No cuadrado.
Unstable [un-stê'-bl], *a.* Instable, poco estable; inconstante, variable, mudable, vacilante; irresoluto, indeciso.
Unstaid [un-stêd'], *a.* Voluble, mudable, ligero, atolondrado, inconstante.
Unstaidness [un-stêd'-nes], *s.* Indiscreción, imprudencia; inconstancia.
Unstained [un-stênd'], *a.* Inmaculado, libre de mancha; no teñido; sin color (vidrio).
Unstanched o **Unstaunched** [un-stāncht'], *a.* No restañado.
Unstatutable [un-stat'-yu-ta-bl], *a.* Ilegal, contrario o no conforme a los estatutos.
Unsteadfast [un-sted'-fast], *a.* Instable, inconstante, no fijo, irresoluto.
Unsteadfastness [un-sted'-fast-nes], *s.* Instabilidad, inconstancia.
Unsteadily [un-sted'-i-li], *adv.* Ligeramente, inconstantemente, de un modo inconsecuente; indiscretamente.
Unsteadiness [un-sted'-i-nes], *s.* Instabilidad, inconstancia.
Unsteady [un-sted'-i], *a.* Voluble, inconstante, veleidoso, inconsiguiente o inconsecuente, que no tiene firmeza o resolución; poco asegurado, poco fijo; poco firme, inseguro.
Unsteeped [un-stīpt'], *a.* No empapado.
Unstemmed [un-stemd'], *a.* No detenido, no restañado.
Unstep [un-step'], *va.* (Mar.) Desmontar, quitar un mástil de su hueco o encaje.
Unstimulated [un-stim'-yu-lêt-ed], *a.* No estimulado o incitado.
Unstinted [un-stint'-ed], *a.* No limitado; liberal.
Unstirred [un-stẹrd'], *a.* No movido, no meneado, no agitado.
Unstock [un-stec'], *va.* 1. Consumir el acopio de provisiones o de otra cosa; gastar el surtido de un almacén. 2. Desarmar o desmontar. 3. Quitar el mango.
Unstooping [un-stūp'-ing], *a.* Firme, invariable, que no cede o se doblega.
Unstop [un-step'], *va.* Abrir camino, dar paso libre; destapar.
Unstopped [un-stept'], *a.* Que no encuentra resistencia o que no halla nada que se le oponga.
Unstoried [un-stō'-rid], *a.* De que no habla la historia.
Unstormed [un-stōrmd'], *a.* Que no ha sido tomado por asalto.
Unstrained [un-strênd'], *a.* Natural, no violento.
Unstraitened [un-strê'-tnd], *a.* Ilimitado; cómodo.
Unstratified [un-strat'-i-faid], *a.* No dispuesto en capas o estratos.
Unstrengthened [un-strength'-end], *a.* Falto de apoyo.
Unstring [un-string'], *va.* 1. Desencordar, quitar las cuerdas a un instrumento de música. 2. Desliar, desatar, aflojar.
Unstruck [un-struc'], *a.* No conmovido, no asustado, impávido.
Unstrung, *pret.* y *pp.* del verbo *To* UNSTRING.
Unstudied [un-stud'-id], *a.* 1. Que no ha sido estudiado; que no ha sido premeditado, no preparado, natural. 2. No dado al estudio.
Unstuffed [un-stuft'], *a.* No llenado, no rellenado, no atiborrado.
Unsubdued [un-sub-diūd'], *a.* Indomado, no sujetado, no subyugado; indómito, invicto.
Unsubmissive [un-sub-mis'-iv], *a.* Insumiso, no sometido, rebelde.
Unsubstantial [un-sub-stan'-shal], *a.* Insubstancial, de poca o ninguna substancia; poco sólido; de poco valor; no real, imaginario; no duradero; inmaterial, no esencial.
Unsubsidized [un-sub'-si-daizd], *a.* Lo que no ha recibido subsidio, auxilio o socorro extraordinario.
Unsuccessful [un-suc-ses'-ful], *a.* Que no ha conseguido lo que esperaba, que ha salido mal; infructuoso, sin éxito, desgraciado, desafortunado, adverso.
Unsuccessfully [un-suc-ses'-ful-i], *adv.* Infelizmente, desafortunadamente.
Unsuccessfulness [un-suc-ses'-ful-nes], *s.* Infortunio, desgracia, desdicha.
Unsugared [un-shug'-ard], *a.* No azucarado.
Unsuggestive [un-sug-jes'-tiv], *a.* Que no sugiere.
Unsuitable [un-siūt'-a-bl], *a.* No adaptado, no apropiado; que no conviene, poco adecuado; desproporcionado, desigual, incongruente.
Unsuitableness [un-siūt'-a-bl-nes], *s.* Incongruencia, desconveniencia; incompatibilidad.
Unsuited [un-siūt'-ed], *a.* No a propósito, incongruo, impropio, incongruente.
Unsullied [un-sul'-id], *a.* Inmaculado, no ensuciado, puro, libre de mancha.
Unsung [un-sung'], *a.* No cantado, no celebrado en verso.
Unsunned [un-sund'], *a.* No expuesto al sol.

Unsupplied [un-sup-plaid'], *a.* Desprovisto, no abastecido, falto de lo necesario.
Unsupportable [un-sup-pōrt'-a-bl], *a.* V. INSUPPORTABLE.
Unsupported [un-sup-pōrt'-ed], *a.* Que no tiene apoyo o sostén; que no tiene quien lo defienda o apoye; no favorecido; no sostenido; no provisto.
Unsure [un-shūr'], *a.* Incierto, no seguro.
Unsurmountable [un-sūr-maunt'-a-bl], *a.* Insuperable. V. INSURMOUNTABLE.
Unsurpassable [un-sūr-pɑs'-a-bl], *a.* 1. Impasable. 2. Insuperable.
Unsurrendered [un-sur-ren'-dẹrd], *a.* No rendido, no entregado.
Unsurrounded [un-sur-raund'-ed], *a.* No rodeado o circundado.
Unsusceptible [un-sus-sep'-ti-bl], *a.* V. INSUSCEPTIBLE.
Unsuspected [un-sus-pect'-ed], *a.* No sospechado.
Unsuspecting [un-sus-pect'-ing], **Unsuspicious** [un-sus-pish'-us], *a.* Sencillo, que no es suspicaz; confiado, no inclinado a sospechar, no sospechoso, no receloso.
Unsustained [un-sus-tênd'], *a.* No apoyado, no sostenido, sin apoyo.
Unswathe [un-swêdh'], *va.* Desempañar, desvendar.
Unswayable [un-swê'-a-bl], *a.* Inflexible; que no se deja dirigir o influir; resuelto.
Unswear [un-swār'], *va.* y *vn.* (*pret.* UNSWORE, *pp.* UNSWORN). Abjurar; retractarse de un juramento.
Unsweetened [un-swî'-tnd], *a.* No dulcificado, sin endulzar.
Unswerving [un-swerv'-ing], *a.* Inmutable, firme. *Unswerving faith,* Fe inquebrantable.
Unsworn [un-swōrn'], *pp.* y *a.* No juramentado, que no ha prestado juramento.
Unsymmetrical [un-sim-met'-ric-al], *a.* Que carece de simetría, poco simétrico, asimétrico.
Unsympathetic [un-sim-pa-thet'-ic], *a.* Falto de simpatía, poco simpático, poco benévolo, que no simpatiza.
Unsystematic, Unsystematical [un-sis-tem-at'-ic, al], *a.* Que no es sistemático, falto de sistema.
Untack [un-tak'], *va.* Quitar las tachuelas; descoser, deshacer lo que está ligado.
Untainted [un-tênt'-ed], *a.* Inmaculado; que no está corrompido, no echado a perder; que no está viciado, infestado o apestado.
Untaken [un-tê'-cn], *a.* No tomado, no cogido. *Untaken up,* No ocupado, no llenado.
Untalked-of [un-tēct'-ev], *a.* De que no se habla, ni se hace mención.
Untamable [un-têm'-a-bl], *a.* Indomable; indomesticable.
Untamed [un-têmd'], *a.* Indómito, indomado, no domado, no suavizado, no domesticado; feroz: insumiso, rebelde.
Untangible [un-tan'-ji-bl], *a.* (Ant.) V. INTANGIBLE.
Untangle [un-taṇ'-gl], *va.* Desenredar, desenmarañar, desembarazar.
Untarnished [un-tār'-nisht], *a.* No mancillado, no deslucido, no deslustrado (en sentido literal y figurado); sin mancha.
Untasted [un-tést'-ed], *a.* Que no se ha gustado, probado o catado.
Untaught [un-tōt'], *a.* 1. Rudo, ignorante, mal criado. 2. Inexperto, novato, falto de experiencia.

Untaxed [un-taxt'], *a.* Exento de tasa, de contribución; no acusado.
Unteach [un-tîch'], *va.* (ant.) (*pret.* y *pp.* UNTAUGHT). Desenseñar, hacer olvidar lo que antes se había enseñado.
Unteachable [un-tîch'-a-bl], *a.* Incapaz de ser enseñado. *Unteachable man,* Hombre indócil.
Untempered [un-tem'-pẹrd], *a.* No templado, sin temple; no atemperado, no suavizado.
Untempted [un-tempt'-ed], *a.* No tentado, libre o exento de tentaciones.
Untenable [un-ten'-a-bl], *a.* 1. Lo que no se puede poseer. 2. Incapaz de defensa, insostenible.
Untenanted [un-ten'-ant-ed], *a.* Desarrendado, sin arrendatario; vacío, desocupado.
Untended, *a.* V. UNATTENDED.
Untender [un-ten'-dẹr], *a.* Duro, áspero, falto de ternura, insensible.
Untendered [un-ten'-dẹrd], *a.* No ofrecido.
Untented [un-tent'-ed], *a.* Que no tiene tiendas de campaña.
Unterrified [un-ter'-i-faid], *a.* Intrépido, no amedrentado, sin miedo.
Unthanked [un-thanct'], *a.* (Poco us.) Desagradecido o no agradecido, desestimado, que no se ha recibido con el debido reconocimiento.
Unthankful [un-thaṇc'-ful], *a.* Ingrato, desagradecido, desconocido.
Unthankfully [un-thaṇc'-ful-i], *adv.* Ingratamente, desagradecidamente.
Unthawed [un-thēd'], *a.* No deshelado.
Unthinking [un-thiṇk'-ing], *a.* Descuidado, desatento, indiscreto; irreflexivo.
Unthought-of [un-thēt'-ev], *a.* Impensado, descuidado; dado al olvido o echado en el olvido.
Unthread [un-thred'], *va.* Desenhebrar, deshilachar, sacar los hilos de algún tejido.
Unthrift [un-thrift'], *s.* 1. Carencia de ahorro, de economía; prodigalidad. 2. (Des.) Gastador, pródigo, el que gasta mucho.
Unthriftily [un-thrif'-ti-li], *adv.* Pródigamente.
Unthriftiness [un-thrif'-ti-nes], *s.* Prodigalidad.
Unthrifty [un-thrif'-ti], *a.* Pródigo, manirroto.
Unthriving [un-thraiv'-ing], *a.* El que no medra o no prospera.
Unthrone [un-thrōn'], *va.* Destronar, desposeer del trono.
Untidily [un-tai'-di-li], *adv.* Sin aseo, sin orden, sin arreglo ni limpieza.
Untidiness [un-tai'-di-nes], *s.* Descompostura, desaliño, falta de aseo y orden.
Untidy [un-tai'-di], *a.* Desaliñado, descompuesto, falto de orden y aseo, desaseado; sucio.
Untie [un-tai'], *va.* 1. Desatar, desprender, desenlazar o soltar lo atado, deshacer (un nudo). 2. Aflojar o soltar lo apretado. 3. (Des.) Aclarar, explicar, resolver una dificultad.
Until [un-til'], *prep.* Hasta.—*conj.* Hasta el punto en que; hasta el lugar o grado que, hasta que. *Until the hour comes,* Hasta que venga o llegue la hora.
Untile [un-tail'], *va.* Destejar, quitar las tejas de los tejados.
Untillable [un-til'-a-bl], *a.* No laborable, no arable.
Untilled [un-tild'], *a.* Inculto, no cultivado.

Untimbered [un-tim'-bẹrd], *a.* Falto de árboles crecientes, que carece de maderas de construcción; que no está guarnecido con maderaje.
Untimeliness [un-taim'-li-nes], *s.* Calidad de lo intempestivo, lo prematuro.
Untimely [un-taim'-li], *a.* Intempestivo, precoz, prematuro, adelantado, que no está en sazón, que es antes de tiempo.—*adv.* Intempestivamente, antes de tiempo, sin sazón, abortivamente.
Untinged [un-tinjd'], *a.* 1. No tinturado, no teñido; incoloro. 2. Libre de algún defecto o tacha.
Untirable [un-tair'-a-bl], *a.* Incansable, infatigable.
Untitled [un-tai'-tld], *a.* Que no tiene título, sin título.
Unto [un'-tū], *prep.* A, en, dentro; hacia. Forma poética o arcaica equivalente a *to*, excepto como signo del infinitivo.
Untold [un-tōld'], *a.* 1. Que no se ha referido, que no se ha dicho, no narrado. 2. No computable; desmedido, sumamente grande. *To leave untold,* No decir, no relatar, dejar en el tintero.
Untoothsome [un-tūth'-sum], *a.* Desagradable, no sabroso.
Untouched [un-tucht'], *a.* 1. Intacto, que no ha sido tocado; ileso. 2. Insensible, no conmovido, no afectado, que no se conmueve por nada.
Untoward [un-tō'-ard], *a.* 1. Displicente, enfadoso, incómodo, vejador; desfavorable, siniestro, adverso. 2. Indócil, que no cede fácilmente, testarudo, refractario.
Untowardly [un-tō'-ard-li], *adv.* Tercamente, indócilmente, perversamente; adversamente, infelizmente, siniestramente.
Untowardness [un-tō'-ard-nes], *s.* Perversidad, terquedad.
Untraceable [un-três'-a-bl], *a.* Que no se puede rastrear, inquirir o averiguar.
Untraced [un-trêst'], *a.* No hollado, no pisado, sin senda, sin huella; (dibujo) no calcado.
Untractable [un-tract'-a-bl], *a.* V. INTRACTABLE.
Untrading [un-trêd'-ing], *a.* Que no está dedicado al comercio.
Untrained [un-trênd'], *a.* Indisciplinado, indócil; no ejercitado, inexperimentado; que no está adiestrado.
Untrammelled [un-tram'-eld], *a.* Sin trabas; no limitado, libre.
Untransferable [un-trans-fẹr'-a-bl], *a.* No enajenable, que no se puede transferir o enajenar.
Untranslatable [un-trans-lê'-ta-bl], *a.* Intraducible, que no se puede traducir de un idioma a otro.
Untransparent [un-trans-par'-ent], *a.* Opaco, no transparente.
Untransportable [un-trans-pōrt'-a-bl], *a.* Intransportable, que no se puede transportar.
Untravelled [un-trav'-eld], *a.* No frecuentado por viajeros o pasajeros; dícese también del que no ha viajado por países extranjeros.
Untreasured [un-trezh'-urd], *a.* No atesorado.
Untried [un-traid'], *a.* Que no se ha experimentado, ensayado o probado; que no ha sido juzgado.
Untrimmed [un-trimd'], *a.* No guarnecido; no ajustado; (hort.) no escamondado; largo, no cortado, no

afeitado, descuidado (cabellos ó barbas).

Untrod, Untrodden [un-tred', n], *a.* Que no ha sido pisado ni hollado ó señalado con los pies; de aquí, no frecuentado.

Untroubled [un-trub'-ld], *a.* 1. Quieto, tranquilo, sosegado, apacible. 2. Claro, transparente.

Untrue [un-trū'], *a.* 1. Falso, que no es verdadero; incierto, contrario á la verdad, falto de realidad. 2. Falso, engañoso, pérfido, infidente.

Untruly [un-trū'-li], *adv.* Falsamente.

Untruss [un-trus'], *va.* Desatar.

Untrustiness [un-trust'-i-nes], *s.* Infidelidad, perfidia, falsedad, doblez.

Untrustworthiness [un-trust'-wūr"-dhi-nes], *s.* Calidad de lo que es indigno de confianza.

Untrustworthy [un-trust'-wūr"-dhi], *a.* Indigno de confianza.

Untrusty [un-trus'-ti], *a.* Infiel, pérfido, que no merece confianza.

Untruth [un-trūth'], *s.* 1. Falsedad, mentira. 2. Infidelidad, traición.

Untuck [un-tuc'], *va.* Deshacer un pliegue á; desguarnecer una cama.

Untunable [un-tiūn'-a-bl], *a.* Desentonado, discorde, disonante.

Untunableness [un-tiūn'-a-bl-nes], *s.* Falta de armonía.

Untune [un-tiūn'], *va.* 1. Hacer desentonar ó salir de tono; desacordar ó destemplar un instrumento. 2. Trastornar, sacar las cosas de su quicio.

Unturned [un-tūrnd'], *a.* No torneado; no movido. *To leave no stone unturned,* No dejar piedra por mover.

Untutored [un-tiū'-tərd], *a.* Malcriado, mal educado; que no ha sido instruído, enseñado ó disciplinado.

Untwine [un-twain'], *va.* 1. Desenrollar, desarrollar, desencoger lo que está arrollado. 2. Separar una cosa que está enroscada con otra.

Untwist [un-twist'], *va.* Destorcer, deshacer lo torcido.

Unurged [un-ūrjd'], *a.* No precisado, no obligado.

Unurned [un-ūrnd'], *a.* No colocado en una urna; de aquí, no enterrado.

Unused [un-yūzd'], *a.* Inusitado, no usado; insólito.

Unuseful [un-yūs'-ful], *a.* Inútil.

Unusual [un-yū'-zhu-al], *a.* Raro, extraordinario, extraño; inusitado; desacostumbrado.

Unusually [un-yū'-zhu-al-i], *adv.* Inusitadamente, raramente, rara vez.

Unusualness [un-yū'-zhu-al-nes], *s.* Rareza, raridad.

Unutterable [un-ut'-ər-a-bl], *a.* Inefable, inenarrable, inexplicable, indecible.

Unvalued [un-val'-yiūd], *a.* Desestimado, menospreciado. 2. Inestimable, que no tiene valor fijo.

Unvanquished [un-van'-cwisht], *a.* Invicto, no vencido.

Unvariable [un-vé'-ri-a-bl], *a.* *V.* INVARIABLE.

Unvaried [un-vé'-rid], *a.* Invariado, no mudado, no cambiado; uniforme, que es siempre lo mismo.

Unvariegated [un-vé'-ri-e-gêt-ed], *a.* Que no es de diversos colores.

Unvarnished [un-vār'-nisht], *a.* No barnizado, falto de barniz; sin adorno.

Unvarying [un-vé'-ri-ing], *a.* Que no varía, constante, uniforme.

Unvascular [un-vas'-kiu-lar], *a.* (Anat.) No vascular, falto de vasos.

Unveil [un-vêl'], *va.* Quitar el velo, descubrir lo que está cubierto, mostrar á la vista.

Unveiledly [un-vêl'-ed-li], *adv.* Á cara descubierta.

Unventilated [un-ven'-ti-lêt-ed], *a.* No ventilado.

Unveracious [un-ve-ré'-shus], *a.* Inverídico, que no dice la verdad.

Unversed [un-vərst'], *a.* Inexperto, falto de experiencia ó conocimiento, no versado, no práctico.

Unvexed [un-vecst'], *a.* No atormentado, quieto, tranquilo, sosegado.

Unviolated [un vai'-o-lêt-ed], *a.* Inviolado, que no ha sido infringido, contravenido; ileso, intacto.

Unvirtuous [un-vər'-chu-us], *a.* Vicioso, falto de virtud.

Unvisited [un-viz'-it-ed], *a.* No visitado.

Unvitiated [un-vish'-i-êt-ed], *a.* No viciado, no corrompido; puro.

Unvocal [un-vō'-cal], *a.* Que no tiene voz; no vocal, no pronunciado fuertemente; no melodioso, falto de canto.

Unvocalized, Unvowelled [un-vō'-cal-aizd, un-vau'-eld], *a.* Sin vocales.

Unwakened [un-wê'-cnd], *a.* No despierto.

Unwalled [un-wēld'], *a.* Sin murallas, sin muros; abierto; sin paredes.

Unwarily [un-wê'-ri-li], *adv.* Incautamente, inadvertidamente, imprudentemente, sin previsión, sin precaución.

Unwariness [un-wê'-ri-nes], *s.* Imprevisión, falta de precaución, falta de cuidado, de cautela.

Unwarlike [un-wēr'-laik], *a.* Que no es belicoso, pacífico.

Unwarned [un-wērnd'], *a.* No avisado, no prevenido, no advertido.

Unwarrantable [un-wer'-ant-a-bl], *a.* 1. Inexcusable, indisculpable, sin excusa ni disculpa. 2. Insostenible, que no se puede defender.

Unwarrantably [un-wer'-ant-a-bli], *adv.* Injustamente; de un modo inexcusable; de un modo que no puede admitir ninguna defensa.

Unwarranted [un-wer'-ant-ed], *a.* Incierto, que no es seguro ni fijo.

Unwary [un-wê'-ri], *a.* 1. Incauto, imprudente, inconsiderado, irreflexivo, que no pone cuidado en el peligro. 2. (Des.) Inopinado.

Unwashed [un-wēsht'], *a.* Puerco, sucio, que no se ha lavado. *The great unwashed,* (Fest.) El populacho, la canalla.

Unwasted [un-wêst'-ed], *a.* Entero, ileso, no consumido.

Unwasting [un-wêst'-ing], *a.* Que no se disminuye ó se consume, inagotable.

Unwatered [un-wē'-tərd], *a.* No regado.

Unwavering [un-wê'-vər-ing], *a.* Que no vacila; determinado, resuelto, constante.

Unweakened [un-wī'-cnd], *a.* No debilitado.

Unwearable [un-wār'-a-bl], *a.* Poco propio para ser llevado, que ya no puede usarse ó llevarse.

Unwearied [un-wī'-rid], *a.* 1. No cansado, no fatigado. 2. Infatigable, incansable.

Unweariedly [un-wī'-rid-li], *adv.* Sin cansarse, de una manera infatigable.

Unweave [un-wīv'], *va.* Destejer, deshacer el tejido; deshilar.

Unwed, Unwedded [un-wed', ed], *a.* Soltero, no casado.

Unweeded [un-wīd'-ed], *a.* No escardado.

Unweighed [un-wêd'], *a.* No pesado, sin ser pesado; que no ha sido escudriñado, examinado.

Unweighing [un-wê'-ing], *a.* Negligente, inconsiderado.

Unwelcome [un-wel'-cum], *a.* Que no es bienvenido, que no se ve con placer; mal recibido, mal acogido; desagradable, incómodo, importuno, que viene fuera de tiempo.

Unwell [un-wel'], *a.* 1. Indispuesto, que no está bien; enfermizo, malo. 2. Menstruante, la que está con el menstruo.

Unwept [un-wept'], *a.* No llorado, no lamentado; no vertido (lágrimas).

Unwet [un-wet'], *a.* Enjuto, que no está mojado; seco, sin humedad.

Unwhetted [un-hwet'-ed], *a.* Que no está afilado.

Unwhipped [un-hwipt'], *a.* No azotado.

Unwholesome [un-hōl'-sum], *a.* Malsano, insalubre, perjudicial á la salud; nocivo, malo.

Unwholesomeness [un-hōl'-sum-nes], *s.* Insalubridad, la calidad que hace á una cosa dañosa á la salud y el estado de lo que es insalubre.

Unwieldily [un-wīld'-i-li], *adv.* Pesadamente, de un modo dificultoso de manejar.

Unwieldiness [un-wīld'-i-nes], *s.* Pesadez, dificultad de manejarse ó moverse.

Unwieldy [un-wīld'-i], *a.* Pesado, ponderoso, abultado, que se mueve con dificultad.

Unwilling [un-wil'-ing], *a.* Desinclinado, que no quiere ó que no tiene deseo ó gana de hacer alguna cosa; mal dispuesto, de mala voluntad. *To be unwilling,* Tener repugnancia. *Willing or unwilling,* Que quiera que no quiera, á buenas ó á malas.

Unwillingly [un-wil'-ing-li], *adv.* De mala gana, con repugnancia, por fuerza, á duras penas.

Unwillingness [un-wil'-ing-nes], *s.* Mala gana, repugnancia.

Unwind [un-waind'], *va.* (*pret. y pp.* UNWOUND). Devanar (hilo); desenredar, desenmarañar, desembarazar.—*vn.* Devanarse, desarrollarse.

Unwise [un-waiz'], *a.* Imprudente, indiscreto; ignorante, tonto.

Unwisely [un-waiz'-li], *adv.* Neciamente; imprudentemente, indiscretamente.

Unwished [un-wisht'], *a.* No buscado, no deseado.

Unwithdrawing [un-widh-drē'-ing], *a.* Continuo; que no cede.

Unwitherable [un-widh'-ər-a-bl], *a.* Inmarcesible.

Unwithstood [un-widh-stud'], *a.* Sin oposición ni contradicción.

Unwitnessed [un-wit'-nest], *a.* Sin testigos; falto de evidencia.

Unwittily [un-wit'-i-li], *adv.* Sin gracia, tontamente, fastidiosamente.

Unwitting [un-wit'-ing], *a.* Que no tiene saber ni conocimiento de lo que se trata; que no sabe.

Unwittingly [un-wit'-ing-li], *adv.* Sin saberlo.

Unwomanly [un-wum'-an-li], *a.* Indigno de una mujer; que no conviene á una mujer.

Unwonted [un-wunt'-ed], *a.* 1. No acostumbrado, poco común, poco habitual, extraordinario. 2. (Des.) Insólito, desacostumbrado (se decía de personas).

Unwontedness [un-wunt'-ed-nes], *s.* Rareza, raridad, la calidad de ser rara alguna cosa.

Unwooded [un-wud'-ed], *a.* No poblado de árboles, sin bosque.

Unworking [un-wŭrk'-ing], *a.* Perezoso, holgazán; que no trabaja.

Unworkmanlike [un-wŭrk'-man-laic], *a.* Desmañado, sin maña, sin habilidad.

Unworshipped [un-wŭr'-shipt], *a.* No adorado.

Unworthily [un-wŭr'-dhi-li], *adv.* Indignamente.

Unworthiness [un-wŭr'-dhi-nes], *s.* Indignidad, falta de mérito; bajeza.

Unworthy [un-wŭr'-dhi], *a.* Indigno, falto de mérito, que no merece; vil, bajo.

Unwound [un-waund'], *a.* Sin cuerda (un reloj, etc.).

Unwounded [un-wūnd'-ed], *a.* No herido, ileso, libre de daño.

Unwove, Unwoven, *pret.* y *pp.* del verbo *To* UNWEAVE.

Unwrap [un-rap'], *va.* Desenvolver, descoger.

Unwreathe [un-rīdh'], *va.* Desenvolver, quitar la guirnalda; destrenzar, deshacer lo entretejido.

Unwrinkle [un-rin'-cl], *va.* Desarrugar.

Unwritten [un-rit'-n], *a.* Verbal, no escrito; tradicional, comunicado por tradición.

Unwrought [un-rōt'], *a.* No trabajado, no fabricado; en bruto; crudo; grosero. *Unwrought wax*, Cera virgen.

Unwrung [un-rung'], *a.* Destorcido, deshilado; no apretado, no exprimido; no arrancado, no violentado.

Unyielded [un-yīld'-ed], *a.* No cedido.

Unyielding [un-yīld'-ing], *a.* Inflexible, reacio, terco, que no cede.

Unyoke [un-yōk'], *va.* Desuncir, quitar el yugo; de aquí, separar, desunir.—*vn.* Ser libertado de un yugo; suspender el trabajo, cesar.

Up [up], *a.* Que se mueve o se inclina hacia arriba; levantado, sobre el horizonte; ascendiendo. *Up train*, Tren ascendente. *Up grade*, Terraplén, cuesta ascendente.—*s.* Lo alto, lo elevado, tierra elevada; estado de prosperidad: se usa principalmente en la locución *ups and downs*, altibajos.—*adv.* 1. Arriba, en lo alto, hacia arriba; lo contrario de *down*, abajo. 2. En pie o derecho; de pie o levantado. 3. Hasta, de manera que esté al mismo grado, nivel, etc. *Up to date*, Hasta la fecha, moderno, al día. 4. (Fam.) Informado en, en estado igual a, formando una partida igual. *Up to his tricks*, Tan pillo como él. *Up in geology*, Impuesto en geología. 5. Excitado, animado; en pie, sublevado, insurrecto; en progreso o ejecución. *To be up in arms*, Sublevarse, tomar las armas, insurreccionarse. *What's up?* ¿Qué pasa? ¿qué se trama? 6. En prominencia, bajo consideración. 7. Guardado en un lugar. *To lay up money*, Acumular dinero. *To put up preserves*, Preparar conservas de frutas. 8. Al término, llegado, acabado. *The hour is up*, Ha llegado la hora. *It is all up now*, Todo se acabó. 9. Completamente, en todo. *Twenty houses were burned up*, Veinte casas se quemaron completamente. *To go up*, Subir. *Hard up*, (Fam.) En apuros, a la cuarta pregunta. *Up hill*, Cuesta arriba. *Up-stairs*, Arriba, en lo alto de la escalera.—*prep.* Hacia arriba, a lo largo, subiendo; en lo alto de; en el interior de. *Up to*, Hasta; a la altura de; al corriente de; dispuesto a.—*inter.* ¡Arriba! *The sun is up*, El sol ha salido. *To be up*, Estar levantado, haberse levantado o salido de la cama; haberse levantado, amotinado o revolucionado; estar en una posición o situación elevada. *Now up, now down*, Tan pronto arriba como abajo. *Up there!* ¡Alto ahí! *Up, up!* ¡Arriba, levántese Vd.! *Drink it up*, Bébalo Vd. todo. *Up and down*, Acá y allá, por todas partes; arriba y abajo; por detrás y por delante, por todos lados; de un lado a otro.

Upas [yū'-pas], *s.* 1. Antiaro, árbol alto de Java, cuya resina es venenosa. 2. Algo moralmente mortal.

Upbear [up-bār'], *va.* (*pret.* UPBORE, *pp.* UPBORNE). Sostener en alto; levantar en alto.

Upbraid [up-brēd'], *va.* Echar en cara, vituperar, afear; reconvenir.

Upbraiding [up-brēd'-ing], *s.* Reconvención.

Upcast [up'-cast], *a.* Tirado o arrojado a lo alto.—*s.* 1. Tiro por alto en el juego de bolos. 2. Pozo de ventilación ascendente en una mina.

Upgrowth [up'-grōth], *s.* 1. Crecimiento, el procedimiento de crecer. 2. Lo que crece o ha crecido; lo que ha madurado.

Upheaval [up-hīv'-al], *s.* 1. Solevación, solevantamiento. 2. (Geol.) Levantamiento de la corteza terrestre. 3. Trastorno del orden establecido.

Upheave [up-hīv'], *va.* Solevantar, levantar con esfuerzo.—*vn.* Levantarse, alzarse.

Upheld [up-held'], *pret.* y *pp.* de *To* UPHOLD.

Up-hill [up'-hil], *a.* Difícil, penoso, fatigoso. (Fam.) Cuesta arriba.—*adv.* Bajo dificultades, con obstáculos.

Uphold [up-hōld'], *vn.* 1. Levantar en alto. 2. Sostener, apoyar, proteger, mantener.

Upholster [up-hōl'-stęr], *va.* 1. Guarnecer almohadones, sillas, sofás, etc.; proveerlos de relleno, resortes, cubiertas, etc. 2. Entapizar, adornar con tapices, colgaduras, etc. 3. Proveer de una cubierta de cualquier clase.

Upholsterer [up-hōl'-stęr-ęr], *s.* Tapicero; guarnecedor de sofás, etc.; el que tiene por oficio poner alfombras, cortinas, etc. *Upholsterer-bee*, *V.* LEAF-CUTTER.

Upholstery [up-hōl'-stęr-i], *s.* 1. Géneros de que se usa para guarnecer sillas, almohadones, etc. 2. Tapicería, conjunto de tapices de una pieza o un edificio. 3. Tapicería, arte y oficio de tapicero.

Upkeep [up'-kīp], *s.* 1. Sostenimiento, mantenimiento. 2. Costo de reparación.

Upland [up'-land], *s.* Terreno elevado, país montañoso.—*a.* Alto, elevado. *Upland cotton, uplands*, Algodón superfino.

Uplift [up-lift'], *va.* Levantar en alto o en vilo.

Upon [up-en'], *prep.* 1. Sobre, encima, en, con, cerca de, a, por. Corresponde a *on*, por lo general. *V.* ON. 2. De. *Cattle live upon grass*, Los ganados se alimentan de hierba. *To depend upon one*, Depender de alguien. 3. A. *Upon the right hand*, A mano derecha. *Upon the first opportunity*, A la primera ocasión. 4. *Upon*, seguido de un nombre de día o de una fecha, no se traduce, y lo mismo sucede con el gerundio. *Upon the fifth of May*, El cinco de mayo. *Upon seeing this*, Viendo esto. *Upon one's guard*, Prevenido. *Upon his coming*, Cuando venga. *To be upon duty*, Estar de facción. *I was upon a journey*. Yo estaba viajando. *Upon the whole matter*, Por lo demás, fuera de esto. *Upon my honour*, A fe mía. *Upon your arrival*, A la llegada de Vd. *He has nothing to live upon*, No tiene con qué vivir. *Upon Sunday*, El domingo. *Upon pain of death*, So pena de muerte, bajo pena de muerte. *Upon* corresponde en castellano a preposiciones muy diversas, tanto con respecto al lugar, como al tiempo y al modo: también se usa muy a menudo unida a los verbos para variar o modificar su significación.

Upper [up'-ęr], *a.* (comparativo de UP). 1. Superior, más alto o en lugar preeminente a otra cosa. 2. Superior, más elevado, más excelente o más eminente. *The upper regions*, Las altas regiones, las regiones superiores. *The upper House*, La cámara alta. *Upper case*, (Impr.) Caja alta, la que contiene las mayúsculas y versalitas. *Upper-hand*, Superioridad, ventaja. *Upper deck*, (Mar.) Cubierta alta. *Upper-works*, (Mar.) Obras muertas. *Upper-leather*, Pala de zapato.—*s.* 1. Pala del zapato. 2. Borceguíes que se llevan sobre el calzado.

Upper berth [up'-ęr bęrth], *s.* Cama o litera alta (en un tren, etc.).

Upper class [up'-ęr clas], *s.* Clase aristócrata.—*a.* 1. De la aristocracia. 2. De las clases superiores (de un colegio).

Uppercut [up'-ęr-cut], *s.* En el boxeo, golpe en corte de abajo arriba.

Uppermost [up'-ęr-mōst], *a.* Lo más alto, supremo, lo más elevado, lo más preeminente, excelente o eminente. *To be uppermost*, Predominar; estar encima.

Uppish [up'-ish], *a.* (Fam.) Engreído, altivo, soberbio.

Uppishness [up'-ish-nes], *s.* Altivez.

Upraise [up-rēz'], *va.* Exaltar; alzar, elevar.

Uprear [up-rīr'], *va.* Elevar, exaltar.

Upright [up'-rait], *a.* 1. Derecho, vertical, a plomo, recto; puesto en pie. 2. Recto, justo, equitativo. *Bolt upright*, Derecho como un huso, tieso como una barra de hierro. *To sit upright*, Estar derecho; incorporarse (en la cama).—*s.* (Arq.) El plan de un frontispicio; el alzado o diseño que muestra la obra en su frente; montante, pieza vertical.

Uprightly [up'-rait-li], *adv.* 1. Perpendicularmente, sin torcerse. 2. Derechamente, rectamente, con rectitud, sinceramente.

Uprightness [up'-rait-nes], *s.* 1. Elevación perpendicular. 2. Rectitud, probidad, integridad.

Uprise [up-raiz'], *vn.* Levantarse, elevarse.

Uprising [up-raiz'-ing], *s.* 1. La acción de levantarse de la cama; acción de salir por el horizonte o desde cualquier lugar más bajo. 2. Salida del sol. 3. Agitación grande entre mucha gente. 4. Motín, insurrección, sublevación. 5. Subida, cuesta.

Uproar [up'-rōr], *s.* Tumulto, batahola, alboroto, conmoción.

Uproarious [up-rōr'-i-us], *a.* Ruidoso, tumultuoso, particularmente con fiesta y algazara.
Uproot [up-rūt'], *va.* Desarraigar, arrancar de raíz.
Uprouse [up-rauz'], *va.* Despertar, excitar, mover.
Upset [up'-set], *va.* 1. Trastornar, poner lo de arriba abajo; volcar, hacer volcar (un carruaje). 2. De aquí, turbar mucho. 3. Desordenar, desarreglar. (Mar.) Zozobrar.
Upshot [up'-shet], *s.* Remate, fin, conclusión; suma total.
Upside [up'-said], *s.* La parte superior, lo de arriba. *Upside down,* Lo de arriba abajo, al revés; (fam.) patas arriba; en confusión.
Upstairs [up-stārz'], *adv.* Arriba, en el piso de arriba.
Upstart [up'-stārt], *s.* Hombre de fortuna, el villano o el hombre humilde que de repente se eleva a los honores, riquezas o poder.
Upstay [up-stē'], *va.* Sostener, apoyar.
Upstream [up'-strīm], *adv.* Aguas arriba.
Uptake [up-tēk'], *va.* Tomar o coger una cosa en las manos.
Upthrow [up'-thrō], *s.* *V.* UPHEAVAL, 1ª y 2ª aceps.
Up-town [up'-taun''], *a.* (Fam. E. U.) Perteneciente a la parte superior de una ciudad o residente en ella.—*adv.* En o hacia lo alto de la ciudad.
Upturn [up-tūrn'], *va.* Volver hacia arriba; volver patas arriba; de aquí, poner en confusión.
Upward [up'-ward], *a.* Lo que mira o se dirige hacia arriba.
Upward, Upwards [up'-wardz], *adv.* 1. Hacia arriba. 2. Más. *Ten pounds and upwards,* Diez libras o más. *Upwards and downwards,* Por arriba y por abajo.
Uræus [yu-rī'-us], *s.* Emblema de serpiente en el tocado de las divinidades y los reyes egipcios.
Uranic [yu-ran'-ic], *a.* 1. Uranio, relativo al espacio celeste; celeste, astronómico. 2. Uránico, relativo al segundo óxido de uranio.
Uranium [yu-rē'-ni-um], *s.* (Min.) Uranio. *Oxidulated uranium,* Uranio oxidulado, blanda pícea.
Uranus [yū'-ra-nus], *s.* Urano, planeta más distante del sol que Saturno.
Urate [yū'-rēt], *s.* Urato, sal del ácido úrico.
Urban [ūr'-ban], *a.* Urbano, situado en una ciudad o habitante de ella; parecido á una ciudad.
Urbane [ūr-bēn'], *a.* Cortesano, urbano, de buenas maneras.
Urbanity [ur-ban'-i-ti], *s.* Urbanidad, cortesanía, buen modo o buenos modales.
Urchin [ūr'-chin], *s.* 1. Niño travieso o malo; corresponde en general a bribonzuelo. 2. Erizo, animal rodeado de púas como espinas. 3. Erizo de mar.
Urea [yū'-re-a], *s.* Urea, principio inmediato de la orina (COH_4N_2), incoloro, soluble y cristalizable.
Uremia [yur-ī'-mi-a], *s.* Uremia, estado morboso ocasionado por la acumulación de urea en la sangre.
Uremic [yur-ī'-mic], *a.* Urémico, relativo á la uremia.
Ureter [yu-rī'-ter o yū'-re-ter], *s.* Uréter, el canal por donde desciende la orina de los riñones a la vejiga.
Urethra [yu-rī'-thra], *s.* Uretra, el canal excretor de la orina.
Urethral [yu-rī'-thral], *a.* Urético, uretral.
Urge [ūrj], *va.* 1. Impeler, empujar, apretar con fuerza en una dirección cualquiera, esforzar. 2. Incitar, excitar, estimular, hurgar. 3. Apresurar, acelerar. 4. Apretar, acosar, seguir de cerca. 5. Solicitar, importunar. 6. Urgir, instar, aguijonear, precisar.—*vn.* 1. Presentar, avanzar, sostener argumentos o pretensiones. 2. Estimular, animar, insistir sobre.
Urgency [ūr'-jen-si], *s.* Urgencia, aprieto o necesidad urgente.
Urgent [ūr'-jent], *a.* Urgente, importuno; insistente, imperativo.
Urgently [ūr'-jent-li], *adv.* Instantemente, con instancia.
Urger [ūrj'-er], *s.* El que compele, obliga o insta; solicitador, abrumador.
Uric [yū'-ric], *a.* Úrico, perteneciente a la orina o derivado de ella.
Urim [yū'-rim], *s. pl.* Objetos de adorno en el pectoral del gran sacerdote de los judíos.
Urinal [yū'-ri-nal], *s.* 1. Orinal, el vaso en que se recoge la orina. 2. Urinario, meadero cómodo y decente.
Urinalysis [yū-ri-nal'-i-sis], *s.* Urinálisis, análisis de la orina.
Urinary [yū'-ri-ne-ri], *a.* Urinario.
Urinate [yū'-ri-nēt], *vn.* Orinar, mear.
Urination [yū''-ri-nē'-shun], *s.* Acción de orinar.
Urinator [yū-ri-nē'-ter], *s.* Buzo, somormujador.
Urine [yū'-rin], *s.* Orina, orín.
Uriniferous [yu-rin-if'-er-us], *a.* Urinífero, que sirve para conducir la orina.
Urinous [yū'-ri-nus], *a.* Urinario, perteneciente a la orina o que participa de sus calidades. *A urinous odour,* Un olor como de orina.
Urn [ūrn], *s.* 1. Urna, vaso en forma de cofrecito para varios usos entre los antiguos: v. g. para guardar dinero, las cenizas de los muertos, etc. 2. Urna, vaso que tiene la boca más estrecha que el centro. 3. Recipiente para café o té.
Uroscopy [yu-ros'-co-pi], *s.* Uroscopia, inspección de la orina.
Urticaria [ur-ti-kē'-ri-a], *s.* (Med.) Urticaria.
Urtication [ūr-ti-kē'shun], *s.* Acción de picar con ortigas, particularmente flagelación practicada con ortigas frescas como tratamiento contra la parálisis.
Us [us], *pron.* Nos o nosotros, el caso objetivo o dativo de WE. *Give us this day our daily bread,* El pan nuestro de cada día dánosle hoy.
Usable, Useable [yūz'-a-bl], *a.* Que se puede usar, a propósito para el uso.
Usage [yū'-zej], *s.* 1. Trato, tratamiento, el modo de tratar a una persona o cosa. 2. Uso, costumbre, hábito, práctica corriente. 3. Empleo de formas o palabras, sancionado o no.
Usance [yū'-zans], *s.* 1. (Com.) Usanza, cierto término a que se libran las letras de cambio, el cual varía según los países. 2. (Ant.) Uso, aprovechamiento, empleo de alguna cosa. *To draw a bill at usance,* Librar una letra a uso o a estilo.
Use [yūs], *s.* 1. Uso, la acción y efecto de usar alguna cosa. 2. Uso, el servicio y aprovechamiento actual de una cosa; utilidad, provecho, ventaja: goce, manejo. 3. Necesidad, ocasión de emplear. 4. Uso, costumbre, hábito, práctica. *Uses of the sea,* (Mar.) Usos de la mar. 5. (For.) Uso, goce, derecho de usar de una cosa ajena con ciertas limitaciones. *Of use,* Útil, que sirve, que es a propósito para algún fin. *Of no use,* Inútil, que de nada sirve; que no viene al caso. *Out of use,* Sin uso, inusitado, olvidado; que no es de moda. *To be in use,* Estar en uso, servir, ser usado. *To be of no use,* No servir para nada, no ser de ninguna utilidad, ser inútil. *For the use of,* Para el uso de. *I have no further use for it,* No lo necesito ya; no me sirvo más de ello. *To make use of,* Hacer uso de, servirse de, usar de; utilizar. *To put to use,* Poner en uso.
Use [yūz], *va.* 1. Usar, emplear, gastar, hacer uso de, servirse o valerse de; usar de. 2. Practicar; poner en práctica; hacer práctica de. 3. Tratar, dar a alguno buen o mal trato, portarse bien ó mal con él. 4. Acostumbrar, habituar.—*vn.* Tener costumbre, hacer uno por costumbre; soler, acostumbrar; enseñarse o hacerse a sufrir trabajos, dolores, etc.; hoy siempre en imperfecto. *I used to go there,* Solía ir allá. *To use ill,* Maltratar o tratar mal. *They use the typewriter,* Ellos se sirven de la máquina de escribir. *To use one's self,* Acostumbrarse, habituarse. *To use up,* Usar completamente, gastar, consumir; agotar, fatigar con exceso.
Used [yūzd], *a.* 1. Usado, gastado. *Used car,* Automóvil de segunda mano. 2. Acostumbrado, habituado. *He is used to that,* Está acostumbrado a eso.
Useful [yūs'-ful], *a.* Util; provechoso, beneficioso.
Usefully [yūs'-ful-i], *adv.* Útilmente; con provecho.
Usefulness [yūs'-ful-nes], *s.* Utilidad.
Useless [yūs'-les], *a.* Inútil.
Uselessly [yūs'-les-li], *a.* Inútilmente.
Uselessness [yūs'-les-nes], *s.* Inutilidad.
User [yūz'-er], *s.* El que usa, se sirve o se vale de alguna cosa.
Usher [ush'-er], *s.* 1. Ujier, portero de cámara, conserje, aposentador: persona cuyo oficio es conducir a los asientos, como en una iglesia o en un teatro. 2. (Ingl.) Sotamaestro.
Usher, *va.* 1. Introducir; acompañar o ir delante, como aposentador. 2. Anunciar, dar la primera noticia.
Ustion [ust'-yun], *s.* Ustión, la acción de quemar; cauterización.
Usual [yū'-zhu-al], *a.* Usual, acostumbrado, ordinario, común, usado, habitual.
Usually [yū'-zhu-al-i], *adv.* Usualmente, comúnmente, ordinariamente, frecuentemente, regularmente, por lo regular, por lo común.
Usualness [yū'-zhu-al-nes], *s.* Costumbre, práctica muy usada y corriente; frecuencia.
Usufruct [yū'-ziu-fruct], *s.* Usufructo, el goce o disfrute de los frutos o rentas de una cosa sin tener la propiedad.
Usurer [yū'-zhiu-rer], *s.* Usurero, logrero, el que presta dinero con usura o a un interés exorbitante.
Usurious [yu-zhū'-ri-us], *a.* Usurario; que presta dinero a usura; en que hay usura.
Usuriousness [yu-zhū'-ri-us-nes], *s.* La

calidad que constituye á un contrato usurario.
Usurp [yu-zŭrp'], *va.* 1. Usurpar, tomar por fuerza y tener en posesión de uno sin derecho ni autoridad legal. 2. Usurpar, arrogarse como si se tuviera derecho a ello.
Usurpation [yū-zŭr-pê'-shun], *s.* Usurpación.
Usurper [yu-zŭrp'-ẹr], *s.* Usurpador.
Usury [yū'-zhu-ri], *s.* Usura, el interés exorbitante que se paga por el dinero prestado; originalmente, el préstamo de dinero a interés.
Utensil [yu-ten'-sil], *s.* Utensilio, lo que sirve para el uso y comodidad de la vida; herramienta o útil para el uso doméstico o agrícola. *Kitchen utensils,* Utensilios de cocina. *Farming utensils,* Aperos de labranza.
Uterine [yū'-tẹr-in], *a.* 1. Uterino, que pertenece al útero. 2. Uterino, se aplica a los hermanos de madre solamente.
Uterus [yū'-tẹ-rus], *s.* Útero, madre, matriz.
Utilitarian [yu-til-i-tê'-ri-an], *a* Utilitario, relativo a la utilidad; que sólo propende a conseguir lo útil; que antepone á todo la utilidad.—*s.* Utilitario, el que antepone a todo la utilidad.
Utilitarianism [yu-til-i-tê'-ri-an-izm], *s.* 1. Utilitarismo, sistema de los utilitarios, doctrina que hace la utilidad el fin y criterio de acción y la base de la moralidad. 2. Devoción a los intereses meramente materiales.
Utility [yu-til'-i-ti], *s.* Utilidad, ventaja.
Utilize, Utilise [yū'-til-aiz], *va.* Utilizar, emplear útilmente, aprovecharse de, hacer útil.
Utmost [ut'-mōst], *a.* Extremo, sumo; mayor, más grande; más posible; más distante; último, postrero.—*s.* Lo sumo, lo mayor, lo más sobresaliente a preeminente. *Do your utmost,* Haga Vd. cuanto pueda o todo lo que pueda.
Utopia [yu-tō'-pi-a], *s.* 1. Utopía, isla imaginaria que tenía un perfecto sistema social y político; descrita por Sir Thomas More. 2. Lugar, reino o condición idealmente perfectos.
Utopian [yu-tō'-pi-an], *a.* Imaginario, utópico, ideal.
Utricle [yū'-tri-cl], *s.* 1. (Biol.) Célula de un animal ó planta. 2. (Anat.) Cavidad pequeña parecida a una bolsita, que se halla en el laberinto del oído interno. 3. (Bot.) Utrículo, pequeño fruto que tiene un pericarpio abultado y membranáceo; vejiga o celdilla de aire en ciertas plantas acuáticas.
Utricular [yu-tric'-yu-lar], *a.* Utricular, parecido a un utrículo o a una célula de aire.
Utter [ut'-ẹr], *a.* 1. Total, todo, entero, cabal. 2. Extremo, excesivo, sumo. 3. Perentorio, terminante. 4. (Ant.) Exterior, de fuera, que está situado a la parte de afuera.
Utter, *va.* 1. Proferir, pronunciar ó articular las palabras. 2. Expresar, manifestar o representar con palabras lo que se siente. 3. Descubrir, publicar, revelar. 4. Dar circulación, emitir.
Utterable [ut'-ẹr-a-bl], *a.* Que se puede proferir o pronunciar.
Utterance [ut'-ẹr-ans], *s.* 1. Prolación, el acto de proferir o pronunciar; habla, lenguaje, expresión, estilo o modo de hablar. 2. La cosa proferída o expresada. 3. (Des.) Extremidad o extremo, el último punto.
Utterer [ut'-ẹr-ẹr], *s.* El que pronuncia o profiere; divulgador.
Utterly [ut'-ẹr-li], *adv.* Totalmente, enteramente, del todo; de lleno.
Uttermost [ut'-ẹr-mōst], *a.* Extremo, sumo.—*s.* Lo sumo. *V.* UTMOST.
U-turn [ū'-tūrn], *s.* Vuelta en U, vuelta completa.
Uvea [yū'-vẹ-a], *s.* Uvea, túnica del ojo, porción obscura del iris y de la coroides.
Uveous [yū'-vẹ-us], *a.* 1. Lo que pertenece a la úvea. 2. Parecido á una uva o á un racimo de uvas.
Uvula [yū'-viu-la], *s.* Úvula, campanilla, gallillo.
Uxoricide [ux-ŏr'-i-said], *s.* 1. Asesinato de la mujer propia. 2. El que asesina a su mujer.
Uxorious [ux-ō'-ri-us], *a.* Gurrumino: dícese del marido que contempla con exceso a su mujer.
Uxoriously [ux-ō'-ri-us-li], *adv.* Con gurrumina.
Uxoriousness [ux-ō'-ri-us-nes], *s.* Gurrumina, condescendencia y contemplación excesiva con la mujer propia.

V

V [vī] consonante se pronuncia en inglés como en español. En general los españoles confunden algo el sonido de esta letra con el de la *b*, aunque deben pronunciarse de muy diverso modo: para la *b* se han de juntar los labios por la parte exterior de la boca, y para la *v* los dientes superiores con el labio inferior.
V, *s.* 1. Pieza o dos piezas en forma de V; v. g. en maderas de construcción. 2. Guarismo romano que representa cinco. 3. (Fam. E. U.) Papel moneda del valor de cinco pesos.
Vacancy [vê'-can-si], *s.* 1. Vacuidad, calidad de vacío. 2. Vacío, espacio vacío, hueco; laguna, interrupción del pensamiento, 3. Vacante, puesto, destino o lugar que está por proveer, sin beneficiado. 4. Vacante, vacación, el tiempo de huelga o descanso.
Vacant [vê'-cant], *a.* 1. Vacío, desocupado, hueco; descargado. 2 Libre, desembarazado. 3. Vacante, lo que vaca. 4. Ocioso; lerdo, negligente; fútil.
Vacate [vê'-kêt], *va.* 1. Vaciar, dejar vacío; dejar vacante; dejar o renunciar la posesión de un empleo, dignidad, etc. 2. Anular, invalidar. *To vacate the sale,* Rescindir la venta.—*vn.* Dejar, salir, irse, marcharse; vacar.
Vacation [va-kê'-shun], *s.* 1. Vacación, días feriados, suspensión de los tribunales de justicia. 2. Vacación, suspensión de estudios, negocios o trabajo por algún tiempo, y el lugar o espacio de tiempo libre o desocupado. 3. Vacación, acción de vacar; anulación.
Vaccinate [vac'-si-nêt], *va.* Vacunar, inocular el flúido vacuno (u otro virus) como preservativo de la misma enfermedad que lo origina.
Vaccination [vac-si-nê'-shun], *s.* Vacunación, operación de vacunar.
Vaccine [vac'-sin], *a.* 1. Vacuno, perteneciente o relativo á las vacas. 2. Perteneciente á la vacuna.—*s.* Vacuna, virus de ciertos granos preparado para la vacunación o introducido por ella.
Vaccinia [vac-sin'-i-a], *s.* Vacuna, grano o viruela que sale a las vacas en las ubres y particularmente la vacuna inoculada.
Vacillate [vas'-i-lêt], *vn.* Vacilar; titubear, estar incierto, irresoluto; no estar firme.
Vacillation [vas-i-lê'-shun], *s.* Vaivén.
Vacuist [vac'-yu-ist], *s.* Vacuista, el filósofo que sostiene que existe el vacío.
Vacuity [va-kiū'-i-ti], *s.* 1. Vacuidad, estado de lo vacío, vacuo. 2. Espacio vacío, vacío. 3. Ociosidad, exención de esfuerzo mental. 4. Falta de inteligencia, estupidez. 5. Inanidad, falta de realidad, nada.
Vacuous [vac'-yu-us], *a.* 1. Vacío, desocupado. 2. Falto de inteligencia, mentecato.
Vacuum [vac'-yu-um], *s.* y *a.* Vacío, vacuo. *Vacuum bottle,* Termos. *Vacuum cleaner,* Aspiradora eléctrica o al vacío. *Vacuum pump,* Bomba al vacío. *Vacuum tube,* Tubo o válvula de vacío.
Vade-mecum [vê'-di-mi'-cum], *s.* Vademécum o vade.
Vagabond [vag'-a-bend], *a.* 1. Vagabundo, vagamundo, sin domicilio fijo. 2. Errante, que vaga acá y allá. 3. Fluctuante, al acaso.—*s.* Un vagamundo, un hombre sin casa ni hogar. *To play the vagabond,* Vagamundear.
Vagabondage [vag'-a-bend-ẹj], *s.* Estado o condición de vagabundo.
Vagary [va-gê'-ri], *s.* Capricho, extravagancia, humorada, antojo.
Vagina [va-jai'-na], *s.* 1. Vaina o cubierta parecida a una vaina. 2. Vagina, conducto sexual, que se extiende desde la vulva hasta la matriz. 3. (Bot.) Parte tubular que envuelve a otra.
Vaginal [vaj'-i-nal o va-jai'-nal], *a.* Vaginal, perteneciente a una vaina o a la vagina.
Vaginate [vaj'-i-nêt], *a.* 1. Envainado, contenido en una vaina, que tiene vaina. 2. Vaginado, tubular.
Vaginopennate [vaj-i-no-pen'-êt], *a.* Que tiene las alas cubiertas de una substancia callosa; coleóptero.
Vagrancy [vê'-gran-si], *s.* Tuna, la vida holgazana, libre y vagamunda.
Vagrant [vê'-grant], *a.* 1. Vagabundo, vagamundo, errante. 2. Que tiene curso o movimiento errante.—*s.* Un vago, un vagabundo.
Vague [vêg], *a.* 1. Vago, indeterminado, que carece de precisión; indistinto. 2. De origen incierto; no autenticado. 3. (Ant.) Vago, vagante, que anda ocioso sin oficio ni beneficio.
Vail [vêl], *s.* 1. Velo. *V.* VEIL. 2. (Local, Ingl.) Propina, gratificación que se da a los criados.
Vail, *va.* 1. Velar. *V.* VEIL. 2. (Des.) Bajar. *To vail one's bonnet,* Quitarse el sombrero.—*vn.* (Des.) Ceder, rendirse.
Vain [vên], *a.* 1. Vano, inútil, sin efecto, sin realidad, substancia o entidad. 2. Vano, vanidoso, presuntuoso, desvanecido. 3. Ostentoso, suntuoso, llamativo; se dice de las cosas. 4. Vano, insubsistente, poco durable o estable. 5. Vano, sin fundamento, razón o prueba. *In vain,* En vano, inútilmente. *To labour in vain,* Trabajar en balde.

Vainglorious [vên-glō'-ri-us], *a.* Vanaglorioso, vano, jactancioso, ufano.
Vaingloriously [vên-glō'-ri-us-li], *adv.* Vanagloriosamente, con jactancia.
Vaingloriousness [vên-glō'-ri-us-nes], *s.* Vanagloria.
Vainglory [vên-glō'-ri], *s.* Vanagloria, jactancia.
Vainly [vên'-li], *adv.* Vanamente, arrogantemente; inútilmente.
Vainness [vên'-nes], *s.* Vanidad, satisfacción de sí mismo, envanecimiento.
Vair [vār], *s.* 1. (Her.) Vero, piel de ardilla blanca y azul. 2. Especie de forro de pieles, blanco y azul, usado en los trajes de la nobleza (siglo XIV).
Valance [val'-ans], *s.* 1. Cenefa, doselera de cama colgada; gotera del dosel de una cama o de cortinas de ventana, orladura. 2. Damasco de seda, o de seda y lana, que sirve de cubierta a los muebles. Este tejido se llama también *valencia.*
Vale [vêl], *s.* 1. (Poét.) Valle, una llanura situada entre montañas o alturas. 2. Canal pequeño: reguera.
Vale [vê'-li o vg'-lê], *inter.* ¡Agur! ¡adiós!
Valediction [val-ẹ-dic'-shun], *s.* Vale, despedida; último vale.
Valedictory [val-ẹ-dic'-to-ri], *a.* De despedida o que pertenece a la despedida.—*s.* Discurso de despedida en los colegios, a fin de curso.
Valence [vê'-lens], *s.* (Quím.) Valencia, la propiedad poseída por los elementos o radicales de combinarse con otros elementos o de remplazarlos en una proporción definida y constante. También el grado de esta propiedad, según está representado por el hidrógeno, con el cual el átomo puede combinarse.
Valenciennes [va-lān-si-enz'], *s.* Encaje fabricado en Valenciennes, Francia.
Valentine [val'-en-tain], *s.* 1. La carta anónima y llena de requiebros o de sátiras que el día de San Valentín acostumbran escribir los jóvenes ingleses a sus conocidos. 2. El amante o cortejo que se elige el día de San Valentín (el 14 de febrero).
Valerian [va-lī'-ri-an], *s.* 1. (Bot.) Valeriana, hierba benedicta. 2. Medicamento preparado con la raíz de esta planta; se usa como antiespasmódico.
Valet [val'-et], *s.* 1. Criado. *Valet-de-chambre,* Ayuda de cámara. 2. Palo herrado y puntiagudo de que se usa para adiestrar los caballos.
Valetudinarian [val-e-tiu-di-nē'-ri-an], *a.* Valetudinario, enfermizo, delicado de salud.—*s.* La persona valetudinaria, enfermiza o delicada.
Valetudinary [val-e-tiū'-di-nẹ-ri], *a.* Valetudinario, débil o delicado de salud; de poca salud.
Valhalla [val-hal'-a], *s.* Valhala, sala de los muertos; palacio de la inmortalidad en la mitología escandinava.
Valiant [val'-yant], *a.* Valiente, esforzado, animoso, valeroso.
Valiantly [val'-yant-li], *adv.* Valientemente, con brío, con ánimo, esforzadamente.
Valiantness [val'-yant-nes], *s.* Valentía, valor, esfuerzo, aliento, ánimo.
Valid [val'-id], *a.* 1. Válido, apreciado o estimado generalmente, basado o sostenido en los hechos, justo; valedero. 2. (Ant.) Válido, fuerte, esforzado.
Validity [va-lid'-i-ti], **Validness** [val'-id-nes], *s.* Validez, calidad de válido.
Valise [va-līs'], *s.* Maleta, saco de viaje o de mano; valija.
Valkyr [val'-kir], **Valkyrie** (*pl.* VALKYRIES [val-kir'-i-iz]), *s.* Valquiria, una de las doncellas que sirven en los banquetes de Valhala, de donde son enviadas por Odín para elegir los que han de morir en el campo de batalla y para llevar sus almas al palacio de la inmortalidad.
Valley [val'-ẹ], *s.* 1. Valle, llanura de tierra entre dos alturas. 2. (Arq.) Gotera formada por el encuentro de dos declives de un techado.
Valor [val'-ẹr], *s.* Valor, brío, fortaleza, intrepidez en presencia del peligro.
Valorous [val'-ẹr-us], *a.* Valeroso, valiente, animoso, intrépido.
Valorously [val'-ẹr-us-li], *adv.* Valerosamente, con intrepidez, con arrojo.
Valour, *s. V.* VALOR. Forma preferida en Inglaterra.
Valuable [val'-yu-a-bl], *a.* 1. Precioso, estimable, apreciable. 2. Digno de atención o consideración, importante, que vale mucho.
Valuableness [val'-yu-a-bl-nes], *s.* 1. Preciosidad, estimabilidad. 2. Importancia de una cosa; valor.
Valuation [val-yu-ê'-shun], *s.* Tasa, valuación; avalúo.
Valuator [val-yu-ê'-tẹr], *s.* Tasador, avaluador.
Value [val'-yu], *s.* 1. Valor, utilidad o deseabilidad de una cosa; valor intrínseco. 2. Valor, precio del mercado. 3. Valor, aprecio, estimación. 4. Valor, significación exacta, sentido; importancia. 5. (Mús.) Valor, duración relativa de una nota. 6. (Biol.) Grado o lugar en una clasificación. *To set a great value on a thing,* Hacer mucho aprecio de una cosa.
Value, *va.* 1. Valuar, valorar, señalar el valor o la estimación de; tasar. 2. Estimar, apreciar, hacer mucho aprecio o estimación de una cosa. 3. Llevar cuenta de; hacer caso de; considerar, tomar en consideración.
Valueless [val'-yu-les], *a.* Indigno, despreciable, que no vale nada.
Valuer [val'-yu-ẹr], *s.* Tasador, apreciador, estimador.
Valvate [val'-vêt], *a.* 1. Valvulado, que sirve de válvula; parecido a una válvula; valvular. 2. Que tiene válvula o válvulas.
Valve [valv], *s.* 1. Válvula, cualquier artefacto que abre y cierra una abertura o pasaje a voluntad, para dejar escapar ó retener un flúido, gas, etc. 2. (Poco us.) Hoja de puerta. 3. (Anat.) Válvula, pliegue membranoso de los vasos del cuerpo, que abriéndose y cerrándose da o impide el paso a los humores. *Air valve,* Válvula atmosférica o de aire. *Ball valve,* Válvula esférica. *Cut-off valve,* Válvula de cortavapor. *Slide valve,* Válvula de corredera, de cajón. *Throttle valve,* Válvula de cuello o reguladora.
Valvular [valv'-yu-lar], *a.* Valvular, perteneciente a la válvula; de la naturaleza de una válvula. *Valvular heart-disease,* Enfermedad orgánica de las válvulas del corazón.
Valvule [valv'-yūl], *s.* Valvulilla, válvula pequeña.
Vamose [va-mōs' o vā'-mōs], *va.* y *vn.* (Ger. E. U.) Dejar prontamente; poner pies en polvorosa. (<vamos.)
Vamp [vamp], *s.* 1. Pala de zapato, empeine, capellada, la parte superior del calzado. 2. Algo que se añade a una cosa vieja para darle apariencia nueva. 3. (Fam.) Acompañamiento músico improvisado.
Vamp, *va.* 1. Echar capellada o empeine a. 2. Remendar una cosa vieja con otra nueva. 3. (Fam.) Improvisar un acompañamiento musical a. *To vamp a pair of shoes,* Echar capelladas a un par de zapatos.
Vampire [vam'-pair], *s.* 1. Vampiro, ente fabuloso o espectro que por las noches chupa la sangre de los vivos mientras duermen. 2. (Fig.) Vampiro, persona que se enriquece a expensas del pueblo; insaciable. 3. Vampiro, murciélago muy grande de la América tropical que chupa la sangre de los animales y del hombre, cuando los halla dormidos.
Van [van], *s.* 1. Vanguardia, la parte más avanzada de un ejército o armada. 2. Los jefes de una empresa. 3. (Ant.) Aventador; bieldo. (Abrev. de *Vanguard.*)
Van, *s.* 1. Carro grande o vehículo cubierto para el transporte de muebles. 2. (Ingl.) Furgón, coche de equipajes en los ferrocarriles; también, vehículo abierto o cubierto que usan los mercaderes para transportar mercancías ligeras. (Abrev. de *Caravan.*)
Vanadate [van'-a-dêt], *s.* (Quím.) Vanadato, sal de ácido vanádico.
Vanadic [va-nad'-ic], *a.* Vanádico, referente al vanadio.
Vanadium [va-nê'-di-um], *s.* (Quím.) Vanadio, metal blanco que se halla muy rara vez.
Van Allen radiation belt [van al'-en rê-di-ê'-shun belt], *s.* Zona de radiación Van Allen.
Vandal [van'-dal], *a.* Bárbaro, de vándalo.—*s.* Vándalo, hombre de una raza teutónica que en el siglo quinto saqueó a Roma; de aquí, el que con intención destruye o desfigura lo que es bello o artístico.
Vandalism [van'-dal-izm], *s.* Vandalismo, los hechos o el espíritu de los vándalos; espíritu de destrucción.
Vandyke, Vandyck [van-daik'], *a.* De o perteneciente a Antonio Van Dyck, pintor flamenco, o a su estilo, escuela, manera o traje.—*s.* 1. Un cuadro pintado por Van Dyck. 2. Cuello ancho o capa de lienzo y encaje, que cae sobre los hombros, parecido a los representados en retratos hechos por Van Dyck.
Vane [vên], *s.* 1. Veleta, banderilla de metal que se coloca en un sitio elevado para que señale la dirección en que viene el viento. 2. (Mar.) Grímpola. 3. Aspa de molino, paleta (de hélice). 4. Barba de pluma. 5. Pínula de instrumentos matemáticos. *Dog-vane,* Cataviento. *Vane-stock,* Armazón de la grímpola. *Vane-spindle,* Huso o hierro de la grímpola.
Vang [vang], *s.* (Mar.) Burra de mesana.
Vanguard [van'-gārd], *s.* Vanguardia.
Vanilla [va-nil'-a], *s.* 1. Vainilla, género de plantas orquídeas trepadoras y americanas, de flores olorosas.

2. Su fruto, que se suele mezclar con el chocolate.
Vanish [van'-ish], *vn.* Desvanecerse, desaparecer, ocultarse o quitarse de la vista con presteza.
Vanishing point [van'-ish-ing point], *s.* Punto de fuga (en la perspectiva).
Vanity [van'-i-ti], *s.* 1. Vanidad, falta de substancia, entidad o realidad; inutilidad. 2. Vanidad, fausto, ostentación, pompa vana, presunción. 3. Lo que es vano.
Vanity case [van'-i-ti kês], *s.* Polvera.
Vanman [van'-man], *s.* Conductor de vehículo transportador de muebles, etc.
Vanquish [van'-cwish], *va.* 1. Vencer, conquistar, rendir, sujetar (al enemigo o figuradamente). 2. Confutar o impugnar a uno.
Vanquishable [van'-cwish-a-bl], *a.* Vencible, que puede vencerse.
Vanquisher [van'-cwish-ęr], *s.* Vencedor.
Vantage [van'-tęj], *s.* Ventaja, superioridad sobre un competidor. *Vantage-ground*, La situación del que en una disputa o contienda posee alguna ventaja que no tiene su contrario.
Vapid [vap'-id], *a.* 1. Exhalado, evaporado; insípido (bebidas). 2. Pesado, falto de animación, de viveza.
Vapidity [va-pid'-i-ti], **Vapidness** [vap'-id-nes], *s.* Insipidez; el estado de lo que no tiene espíritu o fuerza por haberse evaporado.
Vapor, Vapour [vê'-pęr], *s.* 1. Vapor, vaho, exhalación; nube ligera, flúido visible en la atmósfera. 2. Vapor, flúido aeriforme, la forma gaseosa de una substancia que por lo general es sólida o líquida. 3. Lo transitorio e insubstancial. 4. Vanidad, presunción, soberbia, arrogancia. 5. *pl.* (Ant.) Vapores, melancolía, mal hipocondríaco o del bazo. *Vapor-bath*, Baño de vapor.
Vapor, *vn.* 1. Evaporarse, exhalarse. 2. Baladronear, hacer o decir baladronadas.—*va.* (Ant.) Evaporar, reducir una cosa a vapor; exhalar.
Vaporation [vap-o-rê'-shun], *s.* Vaporación, evaporación. *V.* EVAPORATION.
Vaporer [vê'-per-ęr], *s.* 1. Baladrón, fanfarrón; blasonador. 2. *V. Tussock-moth.*
Vaporish [vê'-per-ish], *a.* 1. Vaporoso, que echa de sí vapor. 2. Caprichoso.
Vaporizable [vê'-pęr-aiz"-a-bl], *a.* Que puede ser vaporizado.
Vaporization [vê"-pęr-i-zê'-shun], *s.* Vaporización.
Vaporize, Vaporise [vê'-pęr-aiz], *va.* Vaporizar, convertir en vapor; evaporar.—*vn.* Vaporizarse, disiparse en vapor.
Vaporizer [vê-pęr-aiz'-ęr], *s.* Vaporizador.
Vaporous [vê'-pęr-us], *a.* 1. Vaporoso, que tiene la naturaleza o carácter del vapor; nebuloso. 2. Cargado de vapores. 3. Hipocondríaco. 4. Vano, quimérico, caprichudo.
Vapory, Vapoury [vê'-pęr-i], *a.* 1. Vaporoso, que arroja de sí vapores; parecido al vapor. 2. Amilanado, hipocondríaco.
Vapour, Vapourish, etc. Formas usuales en Inglaterra.
Vara [vā'-ra], *adv.* (Esco.) Muy.
Variable [vê'-ri-a-bl], *a.* 1. Variable, alterable, mudable. 2. Inconstante, veleidoso. 3. (Mat.) Variable, que no tiene valor determinado.—*s.* 1. Lo que varía o está sujeto a mudanza. 2. (Mat.) Cantidad variable.
Variableness [vê'-ri-a-bl-nes], *s.* Instabilidad, inconstancia, ligereza.
Variably [vê'-ri-a-bli], *adv.* Variablemente.
Variance [vê'-ri-ans], *s.* 1. Variación, acción de variar, mudanza. 2. Discordia, desavenencia, oposición. *They are always at variance*, Siempre están riñendo, disputando, de cuernos, o de punta. (Mex.) Estar contrapunteados.
Variant [vê'-ri-ant], *a.* 1. Variante, que presenta variación, diverso. 2. Variable, inconstante, que tiende a variar; veleidoso. 3. Mudable, poco estable, indeciso.—*s.* Cosa que se diferencia de otra en la forma solamente; sinónimo estricto.
Variation [vê-ri-ê'-shun], *s.* 1. Variación, mudanza. 2. Grado en que varía una cosa. 3. (Gram.) Inflexión de nombres y verbos. 4. (Mús.) Floreos, variaciones de un tema musical. 5. (Astr.) Desigualdad del movimiento lunar; cambio en los elementos de una órbita. 6. (Biol.) Variación, desviación de la forma típica en estructura o funciones, como a consecuencia de las condiciones y circunstancias que rodean a la planta o animal descritos.
Varicella [var"-i-sel'-a], *s.* Viruelas locas. *V.* CHICKEN-POX.
Varicolored [vê'-ri-cul"-ęrd], *a.* Abigarrado, de varios colores.
Varicose [var'-i-cōs], *a.* Varicoso, que tiene o padece várices.
Varied [vê'-rid], *pp.* de VARY. Cambiado, variado, mezclado.
Variegate [vê'-ri-e-gêt], *va.* Jaspear, vetear, varetear, formar listas de diversos colores.
Variegation [vê-ri-e-gê'-shun], *s.* Jaspeadura; veteado, jaspeado.
Variety [va-rai'-e-ti], *s.* 1. Variedad, diversidad o diferencia de algunas cosas entre sí. 2. Colección de cosas diversas en un grupo. 3. Posesión de diferentes propiedades características por un solo individuo. 4. (Biol.) Variedad, subdivisión de una especie. 5. Clase limitada de cosas que se diferencian por ciertas propiedades comunes de una clase más extensa, a la cual pertenecen.
Variola [va-rai'-o-la], *s.* Viruela. (Lat.)
Variolous [va-rai'-o-lus], *a.* Varioloso, que pertenece a las viruelas.
Various [vê'-ri-us], *a.* 1. Vario, diverso, diferente. 2. Vario, inconstante, mudable. 3. Vario, que tiene variedad, siendo más de uno y fácil de distinguir; varios. 4. Desemejante, que tiene diversidad de aspecto o apariencia; veteado, abigarrado.
Variously [vê'-ri-us-li], *adv.* Variamente.
Varix [vê'-rics], *s.* Várice o variz, vena dilatada e hinchada.
Varlet [vār'-let], *s.* 1. Lacayo; camastrón. 2. (Ant.) Paje.
Varletry [vār'-let-ri], *s.* Chusma, el conjunto de gente soez, la canalla.
Varnish [vār'-nish], *s.* 1. Barniz, disolución de una o más substancias resinosas en alcohol, etc., y usada para dar lustre a los metales, maderas y otras cosas. 2. Barniz, la paliación, capa o color con que se disimula o encubre algo.
Varnish, *va.* 1. Barnizar, dar con barniz. 2. Paliar, disimular o encubrir los defectos de una cosa. 3. Cubrir una cosa con barniz o con cualquier otra substancia para adornarla.
Varnisher [vār'-nish-ęr], *s.* 1. Embarnizador, barnizador, charolista. 2. El que encubre o palia.
'Varsity [vār'-si-ti], *s.* y *a.* (Fam.) Universidad. (Corrupción de *university.*)
Varvel [vār'-vel], *s.* Uno de los anillos de metal que en tiempos pasados se fijaban a las patas del halcón y sobre el cual se grababa el nombre de su dueño.
Vary [vê'-ri], *va.* y *vn.* 1. Variar, diversificar. 2. Variar, cambiar, tener mudanzas o mutaciones. 3. Variar, mudar, hacer cambiar algo; mudarse, cambiarse, alterarse. 4. Discrepar, discordar, llegar a ser diferente; diferir en opiniones o sentimientos, estar en desacuerdo. 5. Desviarse a un lado; alejarse del norte o acercarse al norte la aguja imantada.
Vascular [vas'-kiu-lar], *a.* Vasculoso, vascular, perteneciente a los vasos de los seres orgánicos; que tiene vasos circulatorios y particularmente numerosos vasos sanguíneos.
Vascularity [vas-kiu-lar'-i-ti], *s.* Vascularidad, calidad de vascular, presencia de vasos circulatorios.
Vasculose [vas'-kiu-lōs], *a.* (Bot.) Vasculoso, vascular.
Vase [vês o vāz], *s.* Vaso, generalmente de adorno.
Vaseline [vas'-el-in (o īn)], *s.* Vaselina, substancia crasa que se saca de la brea del petróleo; variedad del *petrolatum* de la farmacopea americana. *V.* PETROLATUM.
Vasomotor [vas'-o-mō'-tęr], *a.* Que produce movimiento, ya de contracción, ya de dilatación, en las paredes de los vasos sanguíneos.
Vassal [vas'-al], *s.* 1. Vasallo, súbdito. 2. Esclavo, siervo.
Vast [vast], *a.* Vasto, extenso, extendido, dilatado; inmenso, muy numeroso, grande o crecido, enorme.—*s.* (Poét.) Inmensidad, espacio vasto.
Vastly [vast'-li], *adv.* En sumo grado, muy, mucho, excesivamente.
Vastness [vast'-nes], ‡**Vastitude** [vas'-ti-tiūd], *s.* Vastedad, calidad de vasto, número inmenso; grandeza, inmensidad.
Vasty [vast'-i], *a.* (Poét.) Vasto, enorme, inmenso.
Vat [vat], *s.* Tina, cuba grande. *A tanner's vat*, Noque, estanquillo o pozuelo en que ponen a curtir las pieles.
Vatican [vat'-i-can], *s.* 1. Vaticano, palacio pontificio en Roma. 2. Gobierno del Papa.
Vaticinate [va-tis'-i-nêt], *vn.* Vaticinar, adivinar.
Vaticination [va-tis-i-nê'-shun], *s.* Vaticinio, adivinación.
Vaudeville [vōd'-vil], *s.* 1. Zarzuela. 2. Jácara, romance, cantar del pueblo.
Vault [vōlt], *s.* 1. Bóveda, todo techo arqueado o artesonado. 2. Cueva, bodega, subterráneo como el en que se guarda el vino. 3. Cielo, firmamento. 4. Bóveda, lugar subterráneo en las iglesias para enterrar a los difuntos. 5. Privada, letrina. 6. Volteta, voltereta, salto.

Vault, *va.* Abovedar, hacer bóveda.—*vn.* Voltear, dar vueltas en el aire; saltar por encima, particularmente con ayuda de una percha o garrocha, o apoyando las manos sobre algo.

Vaulted [vōlt'-ed], *a.* Abovedado, arqueado, artesonado. *Vaulted sky,* La bóveda estrellada.

Vaulter [vōlt'-ẹr], *s.* Volteador, saltador, volatín.

Vaunt [vānt o vōnt], *va.* y *vn.* 1. Ostentar o manifestar orgullo o jactancia; hacer ostentación, gala o alarde de alguna calidad, acción, etc. 2. Jactarse, vanagloriarse, alabarse.

Vaunt, *s.* Jactancia, ostentación vana; gala, alarde.

Vaunter [vōnt'-ẹr], *s.* Baladrón, fanfarrón, blasonador.

Vauntingly [vōnt'-ing-li], *adv.* Con jactancia.

Veal [vīl], *s.* Ternera, la carne de ternero o ternera, y también se llama así a veces al mismo ternero vivo. *Veal-cutlet,* Tajada de ternera, chuleta. *Veal-pie,* Pastel de ternera.

Vectis [vec'-tis], *s.* Instrumento obstétrico de una sola hoja para facilitar el parto.

Vector [vec'-ter], *va.* Vectorizar, trazar vectores.

Vector, *s.* (Aer.) Vector.

Veda [vé'-da], *s.* Veda (literalmente ciencia); la ciencia divina de Brama, existente por sí misma; en plural, los cuatro libros sagrados de la India.

Vedette [vẹ-det'], *s.* Centinela o guardia avanzada de a caballo.

Veer [vīr], *vn.* (Mar.) Virar, cambiar de dirección, como el viento; (fig.) ser variable o veleidoso.—*va.* 1. Virar, dirigir el buque a otro rumbo. 2. Dejar arriar, aflojar, alargar. *To veer and haul,* Lascar y halar; largar y escasear. *The wind veers and hauls,* El viento se alarga y escasea. *To veer away the cable,* Arriar el cable.

Veery [vīr'-i], *s.* Tordo leonado y melodioso, común en todo el Este de la América del Norte. Turdus fuscescens.

Vegetable [vej'-ẹ-ta-bl], *s.* 1. Vegetal, vegetable, hortaliza, legumbre, verdura, la parte o el todo de una planta comestible. 2. En sentido científico, planta de cualquiera clase, vegetal.—*a.* 1. Vegetable, vegetal, lo que vegeta. 2. Perteneciente a las legumbres u hortalizas.

Vegetal [vej'-ẹt-al], *a.* 1. Vegetal, perteneciente o relativo a las plantas. 2. Que vegeta, común a las plantas y a los animales; p. ej. la nutrición, el crecimiento, etc.

Vegetarian [vej-ẹ-tê'-ri-an], *a.* y *s.* Fitófago, el que sólo se alimenta de vegetales.

Vegetarianism [vej-ẹ-tê'-ri-an-izm], *s.* Abstinencia de todo alimento animal; la teoría de que el alimento del hombre debería ser exclusivamente vegetal.

Vegetate [vej'-ẹ-têt], *vn.* 1. Vegetar, crecer. 2. Vegetar, vivir maquinalmente, con vida puramente orgánica.

Vegetation [vej-ẹ-tê'-shun], *s.* 1. Vegetación. 2. Vegetación, conjunto de las plantas en general.

Vegetative [vej'-ẹ-ta-tiv], *a.* 1. Vegetativo, vegetante, dotado de la calidad de vegetar; que hace vegetar; que concurre a las funciones de nutrición y reproducción. 2. Que tiene existencia meramente física.

Vegetativeness [vej'-ẹ-ta-tiv-nes], *s.* Potencia vegetativa.

Vehemence [vī'-hẹ-mens], **Vehemency** [vī'-hẹ-men-si], *s.* Vehemencia, impetuosidad, violencia.

Vehement [vī'-hẹ-mẹnt], *a.* Vehemente, impetuoso, violento; ansioso.

Vehemently [vī'-hẹ-mẹnt-li], *adv.* Vehementemente, patéticamente.

Vehicle [vī'-hi-cl], *s.* 1. Vehículo, cualquier carruaje u otro medio de transporte. 2. (Fís. y Med.) Vehículo, lo que sirve para hacer pasar una cosa más fácilmente, y con el mismo sentido se usa también en lo figurado. 3. (Fig.) Vehículo, lo que sirve para transmitir. 4. Excipiente.

Vehicular [vẹ-hic'-yu-lar], *a.* Perteneciente ó relativo al vehículo.

Veil [vêl], *va.* 1. Velar, cubrir con velo. 2. Encubrir, ocultar, disimular, disfrazar, tapar.

Veil, *s.* 1. Velo, prenda del traje femenino de calle, hecha de tul u otra tela ligera, con la cual suelen cubrirse las mujeres la cabeza o el rostro. 2. Velo, cortina o tela que cubre un objeto. 3. Velo, cubierta, disfraz, máscara, pretexto.

Vein [vên], *s.* 1. Vena, vaso sanguíneo que lleva la sangre al corazón. 2. Nervio del ala de un insecto. 3. (Bot.) Vena, nervio, hacecillo de hebras en las hojas de las plantas. 4. Vena, veta de metales en las minas; lo que llena una hendedura en la roca, particularmente cuando es depositado por soluciones acuosas; filón de mineral. 5. Vena; dase este nombre a las listas de varios colores que se hallan en algunas piedras y maderas. 6. Humor, genio. 7. La disposición favorable para hacer alguna cosa. 8. La inclinación del ingenio o talento. *A poetical vein,* Vena, numen poético.

Veined [vênd], **Veiny** [vên'-i], *a.* Venoso; veteado.

Vellicate [vel'-i-kêt], *va.* (Med.) Velicar, estimular.

Vellication [vel-i-kê'-shun], *s.* (Med.) Velicación.

Vellum [vel'-um], *s.* Vitela, piel de vaca o ternera adobada y muy pulida; cualquier pergamino.

Velocipede [vẹ-les'-i-pīd], *s.* Velocípedo, forma primitiva de la bicicleta; también, velocípedo de tres ruedas para niños.

Velocity [vẹ-les'-i-ti], *s.* Velocidad.

Velodrome [vel'-ō-drōm], *s.* Velódromo.

Velour o **Velure** [ve-lūr'], *s.* Variedad de terciopelo.

Velvet [vel'-vet], *s.* 1. Terciopelo, tela de seda velluda. 2. (Zool.) Vello, piel que cubre y nutre el cuerno de algunos animales cuando empieza a salir.—*a.* 1. Hecho de terciopelo. 2. Suave como el terciopelo, aterciopelado.

Velveteen [vel-vet-īn'], *s.* Pana, terciopelo de algodón.

Velvet-weaver [vel'-vet-wīv-ẹr], *s.* Terciopelero.

Velvety [vel'-vẹt-i], *a.* Aterciopelado, semejante al terciopelo, suave como él.

Venation [vẹ-nê'-shun], *s.* Venación, disposición de las venas, como en una hoja.

Venal [vī'-nal], *a.* 1. Venal, mercenario. 2. (Ant.) Venal, perteneciente a las venas. *V.* VENOUS.

Vend [vend], *va.* Vender; particularmente, llevar en un carretón y ofrecer a la venta.

Vendee [vend-ī'], *s.* Comprador.

Vender [vend'-ẹr], *s.* Vendedor, vendedora; vendedor ambulante, buhonero.

Vendetta [ven-det'-a], *s.* Vindicta, venganza personal, feudo de sangre entre dos personas o familias. (Ital.)

Vendible [ven'-di-bl], *a.* Vendible, venal, que está expuesto para venderse.—*s.* Cualquier cosa vendible; géneros de venta.

Vendibleness [ven'-di-bl-nes], *s.* La calidad y el estado que constituye a una cosa vendible.

Vendor [vend'-ẹr], *s.* Vendedor; forma más usada en documentos legales.

Vendue [ven-diū'], *s.* Venta en pública subasta. (Fr.)

Veneer [vẹ-nīr'], *va.* 1. Chapear, enchapar, cubrir (una superficie) con hojas delgadas, especialmente de maderas vistosas. 2. Revestir con chapas delgadas de otras substancias que la madera. 3. Tapar, ocultar lo desagradable, disfrazar.

Veneer, *s.* 1. Hoja para chapear, chapa de material para producir un efecto rico en una superficie. 2. Capa exterior y delgada que se da a una cosa para adorno. 3. Apariencia o elegancia meramente exterior.

Veneering [vẹ-nīr'-ing], *s.* 1. Chapeadura, el arte de chapear. 2. Material que sirve para hacer hojas de chapear.

Venenate [ven'-e-nêt], *va.* (Med.) Envenenado, emponzoñado.

Venenation [ven-e-nê'-shun], *s.* 1. Envenenamiento. 2. Veneno.

Venerable [ven'-ẹr-a-bl], *a.* 1. Venerable, digno de veneración; hoy implica generalmente vejez. 2. Venerable, que infunde reverencia; sagrado, consagrado.

Venerableness [ven'-ẹr-a-bl-nes], *s.* La calidad que constituye a una persona venerable o digna de veneración y respeto.

Venerably [ven'-ẹr-a-bli], *adv.* Venerablemente.

Venerate [ven'-ẹr-êt], *va.* Venerar, reverenciar, respetar, honrar (lo noble, lo viejo o lo sagrado).

Veneration [ven-ẹr-ê'-shun], *s.* Veneración, respeto.

Venerator [ven'-ẹr-ê-ter], *s.* Venerador.

Venereal [ve-nī'-rẹ-al], *a.* 1. Venéreo, que pertenece a la Venus o que procede del acto sexual. 2. Venéreo, transmitido por el coito con una persona que tiene el mal venéreo; perteneciente a las enfermedades así comunicadas. 3. Que excita el deseo sexual. 4. (Des.) De cobre.

Venereous [ve-nī'-re-us], *a.* Libidinoso, sensual, lascivo.

Venery [ven'-e-ri], *s.* 1. Venus, el acto venéreo, particularmente cuando es excesivo. 2. (Ant.) Montería o caza mayor, como de venados, jabalíes, etc.

Venesection [ven-ẹ-sec'-shun], *s.* Flebotomía, sangría.

Venetian [vẹ-nī'-shan], *a.* Veneciano, de Venecia.—*s.* Veneciano, natural de Venecia. *Venetian blinds,* Persianas, celosías. *Venetian chalk,* Talco gráfico. *Venetian window,* Ventana de tres aberturas o huecos separados.

Vengeance [ven'-jans], *s.* 1. Venganza, castigo retributivo, imposición de una pena merecida. 2. Despique, desquite, venganza rencorosa. *With a vengeance,* Con violencia, con fuerza, con toda su alma; extremamente.

Vengeful [venj'-ful], *a.* Vengativo.

Venial [vî'-ni-al], *a.* 1. Venial, remisible. 2. Permitido, lícito.

Venially [vî'-ni-al-i], *adv.* Venialmente, levemente, ligeramente.

Veniality, Venialness [vî-ni-al'-i-ti, vî'-ni-al-nes], *s.* Venialidad, calidad de venial.

Venire [ve-nai'-re], *s.* (For.) Orden de convocación del jurado; se llama así de la frase en ella contenida "venire facias."

Venison [ven'-zn o ven'-i-zn], *s.* Venado, carne de venado.

Venom [ven'-um], *s.* 1. Veneno, licor ponzoñoso que secretan ciertos animales, como las serpientes y los alacranes. 2. Ponzoña, lo que produce efecto ponzoñoso; maldad; rencor.

Venomous [ven'-um-us], *a.* 1. Venenoso, ponzoñoso. 2. Que comunica veneno; (fig.) dañoso, perjudicial. 3. Malo, rencoroso, maligno, propenso a obrar mal.

Venomously [ven'-um-us-li], *adv.* Venenosamente.

Venomousness [ven'-um-us-nes], *s.* Venenosidad; natural venenoso.

Venous [vî'-nus], *a.* 1. Venoso, perteneciente a las venas o contenido en ellas. 2. Veteado, marcado con venas o nervios; v. gr. el ala de un insecto. *Venous blood,* Sangre venosa; se diferencia de la arterial por su color más obscuro y por contener más ácido carbónico.

Vent [vent], *s.* 1. Respiradero, tronera, lumbrera, cualquier abertura por donde puede salir el aire y ventilarse una cueva, bodega, etc.; salida de cualquiera clase; ventosa, oído, fogón de un arma de fuego. 2. Ano. 3. Articulación, expresión, acción de pronunciar; úsase hoy por lo general en la locución *to give vent to,* dar expresión a, dar salida á. 4. Desahogo. *To give one's passion vent,* Desfogar o desahogar la cólera.

Vent, *va.* 1. Dar salida o abrir un respiradero, tronera, etc. 2. Descubrir o divulgar un proyecto, un secreto, etc.; expresar públicamente; articular. 3. Dejar escapar. 4. Dar libre carrera a; aliviar, dando salida a algo.

Ventail [ven'-têl], *s.* Ventalla (de casco).

Vental [ven'-tal], *a.* Del viento, perteneciente al viento.

Venter [vent'-er], *s.* 1. Cualquiera de las tres cavidades principales del cuerpo. 2. Vientre; de aquí, en derecho, madre.

Vent-hole [vent'-hōl], *s.* 1. (Art.) Fogón. 2. Venteadura de un barril o tonel. 3. Tronera o ventanillo de bodega. 4. Atabe de cañería.

Ventiduct [vent'-i-duct], *s.* Respiradero, conducto de aire, especialmente cuando es subterráneo.

Ventilate [ven'-ti-lêt], *va.* 1. Ventilar, producir circulación del aire en; renovar el aire de una habitación. 2. Ventilar, controvertir, disputar, discutir; examinar. 3. (Ant.) Aechar, aventar.

Ventilation [ven-ti-lê'-shun], *s.* 1. Ventilación, el movimiento del aire que pasa, corre o se transpira. 2. Ventilación, el acto de controvertir, disputar o contender sobre alguna cosa para examinarla.

Ventilator [ven'-ti-lê-ter], *s.* Ventilador, aparato o abertura para renovar el aire.

Ventose [ven'-tōs], *a.* Ventoso, flatulento; de aquí, hablador.

Ventral [ven'-tral], *a.* 1. Ventral, perteneciente al vientre. 2. (Bot.) Perteneciente a la superficie anterior de un organo. *Ventral fins,* Aletas abdominales.

Ventricle [ven'-tri-cl], *s.* (Anat.) Ventrículo: dase este nombre a dos cavidades del corazón y a cuatro del cerebro.

Ventricular [ven-tric'-yu-lar], *a.* Ventricular, relativo al ventrículo.

Ventriloquism, Ventriloquy [ven-tril'-o-cwizm, cwi], *s.* Ventriloquia, arte del ventrílocuo.

Ventriloquist [ven-tril'-o-cwist], *s.* Ventrílocuo, el que habla de tal modo que parece que la voz sale del vientre.

Venture [ven'-chur], *s.* 1. Riesgo, peligro. 2. Caso o empresa arriesgada; especulación en los negocios. 3. La cosa aventurada o arriesgada. *At a venture,* A ventura o a la ventura.

Venture, *vn.* 1. Osar, atreverse. 2. Aventurarse, arriesgarse. *To venture at, on* o *upon,* Probar ventura, pretender o emprender alguna cosa que se considera difícil de conseguir.—*va.* Aventurar, arriesgar. *To venture abroad, to venture out,* Atreverse a salir, arriesgarse fuera. *To venture in,* Aventurarse sobre; arriesgarse en. *To venture down,* Atreverse a descender. *To venture up,* Atreverse a subir; emprender la subida.

Venturer [ven'-chur-er], *s.* Aventurero.

Venturesome [ven'-chur-sum], *a.* 1. Atrevido, emprendedor, osado. 2. Aventurado, que envuelve riesgo o azar; dudoso.

Venturesomely [ven'-chur-sum-li], *adv.* Atrevidamente, arrojadamente.

Venturesomeness [ven'-chur-sum-nes], *s.* Arrojo, temeridad, carácter aventurero.

Venturous [ven'-chur-us], *a.* Osado, atrevido.

Venturously [ven'-chur-us-li], *adv.* Osadamente.

Venturousness [ven'-chur-us-nes], *s.* Arrojo, temeridad.

Venue [ven'-yū], *s.* (For.) Vecindad o paraje donde radica la causa del pleito. *A change of venue,* Cambio de tribunal en un pleito.

Venus [vî'-nus], *s.* 1. Venus, diosa romana del amor; originalmente la diosa latina de la primavera y de las vides. 2. (Astr.) Venus, el planeta más cercano a la tierra, y el astro más brillante en el firmamento después del sol y de la luna. *Venus's comb,* (Bot.) Peine de pastor. *Venus's looking-glass,* (Bot.) Campanilla, planta del género Specularia. *Venus's navelwort,* (Bot.) Ombligo de Venus, planta de las borrajíneas. *Venus's fan,* Especie de zoófito. *Venus's fly-trap,* Atrapa-moscas, planta sensitiva (Dionæa muscipula) con hojas que se cierran y aprisionan los insectos posados en ellas.

Veracity [ve-ras'-i-ti], *s.* Veracidad, la propiedad o hábito de decir siempre la verdad.

Veracious [ve-rê'-shus], *a.* 1. Veraz, verídico. 2. Verdadero.

Veranda [ve-ran'-da], *s.* Pórtico abierto o galería que se extiende a lo largo de uno o más lados de una casa.

Verb [verb], *s.* (Gram.) Verbo, una de las partes de la oración.

Verbal [ver'-bal], *a.* 1. Verbal, que se refiere a las palabras; que tiene relación con las palabras (más bien que con las ideas). 2. Verbal, de viva voz; proferido, no escrito. 3. Literal, palabra por palabra. 4. Verbal, derivado del verbo o que participa de su naturaleza. *A verbal contract,* Contrato verbal o de palabra.

Verbalism [ver'-bal-izm], *s.* Observación hecha de viva voz.

Verbally [ver'-bal-i], *adv.* Verbalmente; palabra por palabra.

Verbatim [ver-bê'-tim], *adv.* Al pie de la letra, palabra por palabra.

Verbena [ver-bî'-na], *s.* Verbena, planta herbácea anual que se cultiva en los jardines.

Verbiage [ver'-bi-ej], *s.* Verbosidad, el uso de palabras inútiles; superabundancia de palabras.

Verbose [ver-bōs'], *a.* Verboso, abundante en palabras inútiles, difuso, prolijo.

Verboseness, Verbosity [ver-bes'-i-ti], *s.* Verbosidad.

Verdancy [ver'-dan-si], *s.* Verdor, calidad de lo verde.

Verdant [ver'-dant], *a.* 1. Verde, que verdea; fresco. 2. Falto de experiencia, sencillo.

Verd-antique [verd"-an-tic'], *s.* 1. Verde antiguo, piedra de adorno que consta principalmente de serpentina. 2. Pátina verde que se forma en la superficie de los objetos antiguos de bronce.

Verderer [ver'-der-er], *s.* El guarda mayor del bosque real.

Verdict [ver'-dict], *s.* 1. Veredicto, el fallo del jurado; declaración o decisión sobre un hecho dictada por el jurado. *General verdict,* La decisión absoluta y sin reserva del jurado, tanto con respecto al hecho como á la ley. *Special verdict,* La decisión del jurado especificando simplemente el hecho y dejando al juez la aplicación de la ley. 2. Dictamen, parecer, voto.

Verdigris [ver'-di-grîs], *s.* 1. Verdete, acetato de cobre. 2. Cardenillo, verdín, la herrumbre u orín del cobre.

Verdin [ver'-din], *s.* Paro de Méjico, de cabeza amarilla. (Fr.)

Verditer [ver'-di-ter], *s.* Verdete, color azul o verde claro, hecho con el carbonato o acetato de cobre y que se emplea en pintura y tintorería.

Verdure [ver'-jur], *s.* Verde, verdura, verdor; vegetación.

Verdurous [ver'-jur-us], *a.* Verde; adornado de verde.

Verein [fer-ain'], *s.* Sociedad, asociación, unión. (Alem.)

Verge [verj], *s.* 1. Canto extremo, borde, margen, vera, veril. 2. Línea que deslinda o limita; círculo, anillo; de aquí, alcance, esfera, oportunidad. 3. Vara, insignia de jurisdicción y autoridad eclesiástica u otra. 4. Arbol de volante (en los escapes verticales de relojería). 5. (Arq.) Fuste de columna. 6. (Zool.) Verga, órgano de la generación en ciertos moluscos y crustáceos. 7. (Der. ingl.) El recinto de la jurisdicción del mayordomo de palacio.

On o upon the verge of, Al borde de; en vísperas de, a dos dedos de; á la extremidad de.
Verge, *vn.* Acercarse á, aproximarse á; tender.
Verger [vẹrj'-ẹr], *s.* 1. Alguacil de vara; macero de una universidad inglesa. 2. Aposentador, pertiguero de una catedral. *V.* USHER.
Verídical [vẹ-rid'-i-cal], *a.* Verídico.
Verifiable [ver-i-fai'-a-bl], *a.* Verificable, que se puede demostrar o comprobar.
Verification [ver-i-fi-kê'-shun], *s.* Verificación, comprobación, confirmación por argumento o evidencia.
Verify [ver'-i-fai], *va.* 1. Verificar, justificar, probar, comprobar, demostrar la exactitud de. 2. Cumplir, ejecutar (una promesa). 3. (For.) Afirmar bajo juramento.
Verily [ver'-i-li], *adv.* Verdaderamente, ciertamente, en verdad; sinceramente, en realidad.
Verisimilar [ver-i-sim'-i-lar], *a.* (Poco us.) Verosímil ó verisímil, que tiene apariencia de verdadero.
Verisimilitude [ver-i-si-mil'-i-tiūd], *s.* Verisimilitud, apariencia de verdad.
Veritable [ver'-i-ta-bl], *a.* Verdadero, cierto, real, genuino.
Verity [ver'-i-ti], *s.* Verdad, calidad de correcto, realidad; cosa realmente existente, hecho; máxima, axioma, principio.
Verjuice [vẹr'-jūs], *s.* 1. Agraz, zumo de la uva sin madurar. 2. Aspereza de modales o lenguaje; mordacidad.
Vermeil [vẹr'-mil], *s.* 1. Plata o bronce sobredorados. 2. Barniz transparente de agua. 3. Granate rojo anaranjado. 4. (Poét. o des.) Color bermellón.
Vermicelli [vẹr-mi-sel'-i o chel'-i], *s.* Fideos, especie de pasta o masa delgada, vermiforme.
Vermicide [vẹr'-mi-said], *s.* Vermífugo, medicamento que mata las lombrices intestinales.
Vermicular [vẹr-mic'-yu-lar], *a.* (Anat.) 1. Vermicular: dícese del movimiento de los intestinos. 2. Vermicular, que tiene figura de lombriz.
Vermiculate [vẹr-mic'-yu-lêt], *va.* Adornar con piezas en forma de ondulaciones.—*a.* Vermiforme, de figura de gusano; que tiene los movimientos de un gusano; insinuante.
Vermiculation [vẹr-mic-yu-lê'-shun], *s.* El movimiento vermicular o peristáltico de los intestinos, llamado así por parecerse al movimiento de las lombrices.
§**Vermicule** [vẹr'-mi-kiūl], *s.* Gusanillo, gusano pequeño, lombricilla.
Vermiform [vẹr'-mi-fōrm], *a.* Vermiforme, que tiene la forma o figura de lombriz o gusano; lombrizal. *Vermiform appendix*, Apéndice vermiforme del intestino ciego.
Vermifuge [vẹr'-mi-fiūj], *s.* Vermífugo, antihelmíntico, medicina contra las lombrices.
Vermilion [vẹr-mil'-yun], *s.* 1. Bermellón, cinabrio, sea natural o artificial. 2. Cualquier color sumamente rojo.
Vermilion, *va.* Enrojar, teñir de rojo.
Vermin [vẹr'-min], *s.* 1. Bicho, sabandija, cualquier animal dañino o nocivo, nombre colectivo para denotar los insectos parásitos, los ratones, gusanos, piojos, etc. 2. (Fig.) Gente despreciable y asquerosa.
Vermination [vẹr-mi-nê'-shun], *s.* La generación o producción de los parásitos, especialmente de las lombrices o de los piojos.
Verminous [vẹr'-mi-nus], *a.* (Med.) Verminoso, lleno de lombrices o con disposición a criarlas.
Vermivorous [vẹr-miv'-o-rus], *a.* Vermívoro, que come gusanos.
Vernacular [vẹr-nac'-yu-lar], *a.* 1. Indígena, vernáculo, del país natal. 2. Local, característico de una localidad ó país determinados. *Vernacular tongue*, La lengua nativa o el idioma vernáculo.
Vernal [vẹr'-nal], *a.* Vernal, que pertenece á la primavera, que sucede en la primavera; joven, de la juventud.
Vernier [vẹr'-ni-ẹr], *s.* Nonio, vernier, escala movible que forma parte de varios instrumentos para apreciar fracciones de las divisiones menores.
Veronese [ver-o-nīs'], *a.* y *s.* Veronés, veronense; natural de Verona.
Veronica [ve-ron'-i-ca], *s.* 1. Lienzo en que aparecen estampadas las facciones de Nuestro Señor Jesucristo. 2. (Bot.) Verónica, género de plantas de las escrofulariáceas.
Verrucose, Verrucous [ver'-u-cōs, cus], *a.* Verrugoso, cubierto de verrugas.
Versatile [vẹr'-sa-til], *a.* 1. Versátil, que tiene aptitud para tareas u ocupaciones nuevas y variadas. 2. Versátil, de genio o carácter inconstante o voluble. 3. Versátil, que se puede volver fácilmente (como sobre un quicio o eje).
Versatileness [vẹr'-sa-til-nes], **Versatility** [vẹr-sa-til'-i-ti], *s.* 1. Aptitud para muchas ocupaciones, posesión de variados talentos. 2. Veleidad, la calidad de lo que es versátil o de genio o carácter voluble e inconstante; mutabilidad, inconstancia.
Verse [vẹrs], *s.* 1. Verso, número determinado de sílabas que forman consonancia y cadencia. 2. Metro, copla, composición en verso. 3. Versículo, subdivisión pequeña de algún capítulo. *To make verses*, Versificar, hacer versos.
Versed [vẹrst], *a.* Versado, práctico o diestro en una materia o cosa. *Versed sine*, Seno verso, función trigonométrica.
Verseman [vẹrs'-man], *s.* Poeta, versista, el que hace versos.
Versicle [vẹr'-si-cl], *s.* Versículo; versículo, párrafo breve de un libro litúrgico.
Versification [vẹr-si-fi-kê'-shun], *s.* Versificación, acción, arte o práctica de hacer versos.
Versificator [vẹr'-si-fi-kê-tẹr], **Versifier** [vẹr'-si-fai-ẹr], *s.* Poeta, versista.
Versify [vẹr'-si-fai], *vn.* Versificar, hacer versos.—*va.* Recitar, decir o representar alguna composición en verso.
Version [vẹr'-shun], *s.* 1. Versión, traducción de una lengua a otra. 2. Versión, el modo que tiene cada uno de referir un mismo suceso. 3. Versión, operación obstétrica para cambiar la posición del feto cuando éste se presenta mal para el parto. *Authorized* o *King James's Version*, *Revised Version*, Dos versiones inglesas de la Biblia. *V.* AUTHORIZE y REVISE.
Verst [vẹrst], *s.* Medida longitudinal de Rusia, igual á 1.07 kilómetros.
Versus [vẹr'-sus], *prep.* En contra. Se abrevia **vs.** y se emplea en demandas y litigios, como por ej.: *The State vs. John Doe*, El Estado en contra de Fulano de Tal.
Vert [vẹrt], *s.* 1. (Der. inglés) Todo árbol, arbusto o cualquier otra planta que crece dentro de un bosque y puede ocultar á un ciervo. 2. (Her.) Sinople o sinoble.
Vertebra [vẹr'-tẹ-bra], *s.* Vértebra, cada uno de los huesos enlazados entre sí que forman el espinazo.
Vertebral [vẹr'-tẹ-bral], *a.* 1. Vertebral, perteneciente á las vértebras. 2. Vertebrado, provisto de vértebras.
Vertebrate [vẹr'-te-brẹt], *a.* Vertebrado, que tiene una columna vertebral.—*s.* Animal vertebrado.
Vertex [vẹr'-tecs], *s.* Vértice; cima, cumbre; extremidad superior de una pirámide, de un cono, etc.: cenit.
Vertical [vẹr'-ti-cal], *a.* Vertical, perpendicular al horizonte; que está directa y perpendicularmente sobre nuestro vértice o cabeza.
Verticality [vẹr-ti-cal'-i-ti], *s.* La situación o carácter vertical.
Vertically [vẹr'-ti-cal-i], *adv.* Verticalmente.
Verticillate [vẹr-tis'-i-let o ver-ti-sil'-et], *a.* (Bot.) Verticilado, dispuesto en verticilo.
Verticity [vẹr-tis'-i-ti], *s.* Verticidad, capacidad de moverse a varias partes o alrededor.
Vertiginous [vẹr-tij'-i-nus], *a.* 1. Vertiginoso, que padece vértigos. 2. Que tiende a causar vértigo. 3. Giratorio, que da vueltas.
Vertigo [vẹr'-ti-gō], *s.* Vértigo, vahído de cabeza.
Vervain [vẹr'-vên], *s.* (Bot.) Planta no cultivada del género Verbena.
Verve [vẹrv], *s.* 1. Energía, entusiasmo, fervor. 2. Inspiración artística.
Very [ver'-i], *a.* 1. Verdadero, real. 2. Grande, lo que tiene calidades comúnmente malas en grado eminente. *He is a very thief*, Es un ladrón consumado. 3. Idéntico, mismo. *At that very hour*, A aquella misma hora o precisamente a aquella hora. 4. Completo.—*adv.* Muy, mucho, sumamente. *Very much*, Mucho o muchísimo; muy (antes de un participio). *Very* se usa también de un modo expletivo para aumentar el énfasis de la oración.
Vesical [ves'-i-cal], *a.* Vesical, perteneciente o relativo a la vejiga.
Vesicant [ves'-i-cant], *a.* Vesicante.—*s.* Vejigatorio.
Vesicate [ves'-i-kêt], *va.* Aplicar cantáridas u otro estimulante capaz de levantar vesículas o ampollas en la piel o cutis, avejigar.
Vesication [ves-i-kê'-shun], *s.* La acción de levantar o producir vejigas o ampollas.
Vesicle [ves'-i-cl], *s.* Vesícula, vejigüela, vejiguilla; ampolla o quiste pequeño; protuberancia llena de aire que tienen ciertas plantas acuáticas.
Vesicular [vẹ-sic'-yu-lar], *a.* Vesicular, en forma de vesícula; vesiculoso.
Vesper [ves'-pẹr], *s.* 1. Véspero o héspero, la estrella vespertina. 2. Tarde, el anochecer. 3. Campana que llama a vísperas. 4. *pl.* Vísperas, una de las horas del oficio divino que se dice por la tarde.—*a.* Ves-

pertino, perteneciente a la tarde o a las vísperas.

Vespertine [ves'-pęr-tin], *a.* Vespertino.

Vessel [ves'-el], *s.* 1. Vasija, el vaso para echar o guardar licores u otras cosas. 2. Vaso, nombre dado por los anatómicos a los canales que contienen la sangre y la linfa en el cuerpo humano. 3. Buque, bajel, embarcación. 4. (Bot.) *V.* DUCT.

Vest [vest], *s.* 1. Chaleco. *V.* WAISTCOAT. 2. Chaqueta antigua de mujer; guarnición del vestido de mujer por el frente. 3. Elástica, camiseta interior. 4. Vestido, vestidura.

Vest, *va.* 1. Revestir (de autoridad), investir. 2. Investir, dar la investidura de alguna cosa; poner en posesión, dar a cargo. 3. Vestir, cubrir o adornar el cuerpo con el vestido. *To vest with*, Vestir de, revestir de. *To vest in*, Revestir de, investir de, poner en posesión de.

Vestal [ves'-tal], *s.* Vestal, entre los romanos la virgen consagrada a la diosa Vesta.—*a.* Virgíneo, virginal.

Vestiary [ves'-ti-ę-ri], *s.* (Ant.) Vestuario.

Vestibule [ves'-ti-biūl], *s.* Vestíbulo, atrio, pórtico, portal, zaguán.

Vestige [ves'-tij], *s.* 1. Vestigio, señal que queda de una cosa. 2. (Biol.) Parte u órgano, pequeño o atrofiado, aunque normalmente desarrollado en los antepasados.

Vestigial [ves-tij'-i-al], *a.* (Biol.) Que se ha atrofiado o degenerado.

Vesting [vest'-ing], *s.* Material para hacer chalecos.

Vestment [vest'-męnt], *s.* Prenda de vestir, vestido; vestidura de dignidad, de pompa; vestimenta que usan los sacerdotes; también, sabanilla (de altar).

Vest-pocket [vest-pek'-et], *a.* Para el bolsillo del chaleco. *Vest-pocket Dictionary*, Diccionario de bolsillo.

Vestry [ves'-tri], *s.* 1. Vestuario, habitación donde se guardan vestidos y se revisten los eclesiásticos y a veces los coristas. 2. Sacristía, una pieza contigua a la iglesia, donde se guardan las vestiduras, los ornamentos y otras cosas pertenecientes al culto divino. 3. En la Iglesia episcopal protestante, reunión de hombres que tiene a su cargo la administración de los asuntos de la parroquia. 4. En las iglesias no litúrgicas, capilla o cuarto para la escuela dominical contiguo a la iglesia. *Vestryman*, Miembro de la junta parroquial (*vestry*).

Vesture [ves'-chur], *s.* 1. Vestido, lo que viste o cubre, capa; traje, hábito. 2. En el antiguo derecho inglés, todo lo que cubre el terreno excepto los árboles.

Vetch [vech], *s.* (Bot.) Algarroba, alverjana o arverjona; cualquiera planta del género Vicia.

Vetchling [vech'-ling], *s.* Arveja, latiro, cualquiera planta del género Lathyrus.

Vetchy [vech'-i], *a.* Abundante en algarrobas.

Veteran [vet'-ęr-an], *s.* y *a.* 1. Veterano, militar viejo. 2. Veterano, hombre antiguo, práctico y experto en cualquier profesión o ejercicio.

Veterinarian [vet-ęr-i-nē'-ri-an], *s.* Albéitar, veterinario.

Veterinary [vet'-ęr-i-ne-ri], *a.* Veterinario, perteneciente a la veterinaria o a las enfermedades y lesiones de los animales domésticos y a su tratamiento. *Veterinary science*, Veterinaria.

Veto [vī'-tō], *va.* 1. Poner el veto a (v. g. a un proyecto de ley). 2. Vedar o prohibir con autoridad; rehusar la aprobación de.—*s.* 1. Veto, derecho que tiene el poder ejecutivo de negar la sanción de una ley votada por los cuerpos legislativos. 2. Acción de vedar, de poner el veto a; comunicación oficial en que se niega la sanción a un proyecto de ley. 3. Cualquier prohibición hecha con autoridad.

Vex [vecs], *va.* 1. Vejar, molestar; apesadumbrar, desazonar, hacer padecer a uno. 2. Enojar, irritar, enfadar, provocar, hacer salir a uno de sus casillas. (Vulg.) Moler, jorobar. 3. Turbar, perturbar. *To be vexed*, Incomodarse, enojarse, picarse.

Vexation [vecs-ē'-shun], *s.* Vejación, molestia, maltrato; provocación, enojo, enfado.

Vexatious [vecs-ē'-shus], *a.* Penoso, molesto, enfadoso; provocativo.

Vexatiousness [vecs-ē'-shus-nes], *s.* Molestia, vejación, inquietud.

Vexer [vecs'-ęr], *s.* El que inquieta, enfada, molesta o provoca.

Via [vai'-a o vī'-a], *prep.* Por la vía de, por. *Via Nicaragua*, Por Nicaragua.

Viability [vai-a-bil'-i-ti], *s.* Viabilidad, calidad de viable.

Viable [vai'-a-bl], *a.* Viable, capaz de vivir; que sale a luz con fuerza bastante para seguir viviendo.

Viaduct [vai'-a-duct], *s.* Viaducto, obra a manera de puente, para el paso de un camino sobre una hondonada.

Vial [vai'-al], *s.* Redoma, ampolleta; botella, vaso.

Viand [vai'-and], *s.* Vianda, la carne o comida que se sirve a la mesa.

Viatic [vai-at'-ic], *a.* De viaje, de viático.

Viaticum [vai-at'-i-cum], *s.* 1. Viático, prevención o provisión para algún viaje. 2. Viático, la comunión que se administra a los enfermos en peligro de muerte.

Vibrant [vai'-brant], *a.* Vibrante, que vibra.

Vibrate [vai'-brēt], *va.* 1. Vibrar, blandir, dar un movimiento trémulo a alguna cosa larga y delgada. 2. Vibrar, arrojar con ímpetu y violencia una cosa, especialmente hablando de las que en su movimiento hacen vibraciones.—*vn.* 1. Vibrar, moverse alguna cosa suspensa en el aire de un lado a otro, con movimiento igual. 2. Vibrar o moverse una cosa haciendo vibraciones.

Vibratile [vai'-bra-til], *a.* Vibrátil, a propósito para el movimiento vibratorio.

Vibration [vai-brē'-shun], *s.* Vibración: dícese del vaivén de un cuerpo libre suspenso en el aire, y del movimiento trémulo de las cuerdas tirantes, de los rayos de luz, etc.

Vibrative, Vibratory [vai'-bra-tiv, to-ri], *a.* Vibratorio, oscilatorio.

Viburnum [vai-būr'-num], *s.* Viburno, género de arbustos de las caprifoliáceas.

Vicar [vic'-ar], *s.* 1. Vicario, el que hace las veces de un superior en ciertas funciones, particularmente las eclesiásticas. 2. Teniente de cura de una parroquia; cura beneficiado.

Vicarage [vic'-ar-ēj], *s.* 1. Vicaría, vicariato, beneficio curado. 2. Vicaría, casa del vicario.

Vicarial [vai-kē'-ri-al], *a.* Vicarial, lo perteneciente al vicario y a su oficio.

Vicarious [vai-kē'-ri-us], *a.* 1. Vicario, hecho o ejecutado por vía de substitución; sufrido en vez de otro. 2. Diputado, delegado, substituto, que obra en virtud de poderes de otra persona o la substituye. 3. Vicarial, perteneciente al vicario.

Vicarship [vic'-ar-ship], *s.* Vicariato.

Vice [vais], *s.* 1. Vicio, maldad, habitual disposición al mal, malignidad; lo opuesto a virtud. 2. Vicio, defecto o imperfección del cuerpo o o del alma; falta, culpa, desliz. 3. El bufón de los volatines. 4. Vicio, resabio o mala costumbre del caballo. 5. *V.* VISE.

Vice [vai'-si], *prep.* En lugar de, en vez de. *Vice L——, retired*, En lugar de L——, jubilado. (< Lat. abl. de *vix*, vez.)

Vice- [vais]. Prefijo que sólo se usa en composición para significar que la persona de quien se habla tiene las veces o autoridad de aquella que denota la voz con que se forma la composición. *Vice-admiral*, (1) Vicealmirante, el jefe principal de una escuadra después del almirante. (2) Vicealmirante, uno de los grados de los oficiales generales de marina en Inglaterra. *Vice-admiralty*, Vicealmirantazgo. *Vice-agent*, Agente, la persona que hace algo en lugar de otro. *Vice-chancellor*, Vicecanciller, vicecancelario. *Vice-consul*, Vicecónsul, el que hace las veces de cónsul. *Vice-presidency*, Vicepresidencia, dignidad de vicepresidente y el tiempo que dura. *Vice-president*, Vicepresidente; en especial el Vicepresidente de los Estados Unidos de América.

Vicegerent [vais-ji'-rent], *s.* y *a.* Vicegerente, teniente, diputado, substituto.

Vicenary [vis'-e-na-ri], *a.* Vigésimo, que consta de veinte o que pertenece a veinte.

Viceregal [vais-rī'-gal], *a.* De virrey, perteneciente al virrey.

Viceroy [vais'-rei], *s.* Virrey, el que con este título gobierna en nombre y con autoridad del rey.

Viceroyalty [vais-rei'-al-ti], *s.* Virreinato.

Vice versa [vai'-sī vęr'-sa], *adv.* Viceversa.

Vicinage [vis'-i-nej], *s.* 1. Vecindad, cercanía o proximidad de unos parajes a otros. 2. Calidad de próximo o vecino.

Vicinal [vis'-i-nal], *a.* Vecino, cercano.

Vicinity [vi-sin'-i-ti], *s.* Vecindad, cercanía, proximidad.

Vicious [vish'-us], *a.* 1. Vicioso, entregado a los vicios, corrompido, depravado, entregado al mal. 2. Vicioso, defectuoso, imperfecto; (caballo) rehacio, asombradizo. 3. (Fam.) Maligno, rencoroso, enconado.

Vicious circle, *s.* Círculo vicioso.

Vicissitude [vi-sis'-i-tiūd], *s.* Vicisitud, orden o acontecimiento sucesivo o alternativo; alternativa, vuelta o retorno; mudanza; instabilidad.

Victim [vic'-tim], *s.* 1. Víctima, criatura viva ofrecida en sacrificio a una divinidad. 2. Persona sacrificada con un objeto cualquiera. 3. El que padece una condición enferma o un sentimiento mórbido. 4. El que ha sido embaucado, estafado.

Victimize [vic'-tim-aiz], *va.* (Fam.) Hacer víctima, estafar, embaucar.

Victor [vic'-tər], *s.* Vencedor, el que consigue una victoria.

Victoria [vic-tō'-ri-a], *s.* 1. (Bot.) Victoria, ninfea gigantea del Amazonas. 2. Carruaje bajo y ligero de cuatro ruedas, con cielo de quita y pon.

Victorian [vic-tō'-ri-an], *a.* Victoriano, relativo a Victoria, reina de la Gran Bretaña; v. gr. época victoriana.

Victorious [vic-tō'-ri-us], *a.* Victorioso.

Victoriously [vic-tō'-ri-us-li], *adv.* Victoriosamente.

Victoriousness [vic-tō'-ri-us-nes], *s.* Triunfo, victoria.

Victory [vic'-to-ri], *s.* Victoria, conquista; triunfo, vencimiento, vencida.

Victress [vic'-tres], *sf.* Vencedora.

Victual [vit'-l], *s.* Vitualla, el conjunto de cosas necesarias para la comida, víveres; úsase rara vez en singular en ambas lenguas.

Victual, *va.* Abastecer, proveer de bastimentos. *Victualling department,* (Ingl.) Administración naval, servicio de las subsistencias de la marina. *Victualling ship,* Buque que lleva los víveres para otro o para la flota.

Victualler [vit'-l-ẹr], *s.* 1. Abastecedor, proveedor, el que provee de bastimentos o vituallas. 2. Hostalero, bodegonero, el que tiene fonda, bodegón, etc., donde se da de comer. 3. El buque donde se llevan los bastimentos para una flota.

Vicugna, Vicuña [vi-cū'-nya], *s.* Vicuña, cuadrúpedo parecido al llama y originario del Perú, cuya lana es muy estimada.

Vide [vai'-di], *v.* Véase, véanse.

Videlicet [vi-del'-i-set], *adv.* A saber: comúnmente se escribe *viz.* *V.* Viz.

Video [vi'-deo], *s.* Televisión.

Viduity [vi-diū'-i-ti], *s.* (Poco us.) Viudedad.

Vie [vai], *va.* y *vn.* 1. Competir, contender dos o más personas entre sí, aspirar con empeño unos y otros a una misma cosa. 2. Disputar sobre una cosa; obrar o ejecutar algo en competencia; hacer una cosa por emulación.

Viennese [vi''-en-īs'], *a.* Vienés, vienesa, de Viena en Austria.—*s.* (*sing.* y *pl.*) Vienés, natural o habitantes de Viena.

View [viū], *va.* 1. Mirar; ver, percibir o examinar con la vista; mirar con atención, examinar, inspeccionar, reconocer. 2. Mirar mentalmente, considerar.

View, *s.* 1. Vista, la acción y efecto de ver. 2. Vista, el hecho mismo de ver y el modo con que se mira; vista intelectual; opinión, noción, parecer. 3. Vista, visión, la facultad o potencia de ver; el alcance a donde llega la vista. 4. Perspectiva, vista o aspecto de diversos objetos juntos mirados de lejos; cuadro, dibujo, lámina, particularmente lo que representa un paisaje; lo que se presenta a las miradas. 5. Vista, intento o propósito. 6. Examen, inspección o escrutinio de una cosa. 7. Apariencia. 8. (For.) Inspección hecha, v. g. por el jurado, de una propiedad o de un local o paraje. *With this view,* Con esta mira, con este intento. *At first view,* A primera vista. *At one view,* De una ojeada, de una mirada. *Field of view,* (Ópt.) Campo de la visión. *To take a nearer view of,* Ver, examinar de más cerca.

Viewer [viū'-ẹr], *s.* Veedor, el que ve, mira o registra con curiosidad; mirador, el que mira.

Viewfinder [viū-faind'-ẹr], *s.* En fotografía, visor o buscador.

Viewless [viū'-les], *a.* Invisible.

Viewpoint [viū'-point], *s.* Punto de vista.

Vigesimal [vai-jes'-i-mal], *a.* Vigésimo.

Vigil [vij'-il], *s.* 1. Vela, la acción de velar o la vigilia y el tiempo que se vela. 2. Vela, el ejercicio de devoción en las horas acostumbradas de descanso. 3. Vigilia, la víspera de alguna festividad en que se ayuna.

Vigilance [vij'-i-lans], **Vigilancy** [vij'-i-lan-si], *s.* 1. Desvelo, el estado del que no puede dormir. 2. Vigilancia, cuidado. *Vigilance committee,* Junta de vigilancia, para la administración de pronta justicia.

Vigilant [vij'-i-lant], *a.* Vigilante, cuidadoso, atento.

Vigilante [vij-i-lan'-tē], *s.* Vigilante. En E. U., miembro de un cuerpo especial de vigilancia privada.

Vigilantly [vij'-i-lant-li], *adv.* Con vigilancia y cuidado.

Vignette [vin-yet'], *va.* 1. Hacer una fotografía con fondo o borde cuya sombra va disipándose gradualmente. 2. Aviñetar, adornar con viñetas.—*s.* 1. Viñeta, un dibujo o estampita apaisada que se pone por adorno al principio o al fin de los libros o capítulos de una obra impresa. 2. Grabado, dibujo, fotografía, etc., la sombra de cuyo fondo va disipándose gradualmente hasta desaparecer.

Vigor, Vigour [vig'-ər], *s.* 1. Vigor, fuerza, actividad. 2. Energía, eficacia.

Vigorous [vig'-ər-us], *a.* Vigoroso.

Vigorously [vig'-ər-us-li], *adv.* Vigorosamente, con energía, con fuerza.

Vigorousness [vig'-ər-us-nes], *s.* Vigorosidad, robustez; actividad.

Vigour, *s.* *V.* Vigor; forma usual en Inglaterra.

Viking [vai'-king], *s.* Uno de los piratas del norte que infestaron las costas de Europa desde el siglo octavo hasta el undécimo.

Vile [vail], *a.* Vil, bajo, indigno, despreciable; malvado, perverso.

Vilely [vail'-li], *adv.* Vilmente, bajamente, servilmente.

Vileness [vail'-nes], *s.* Vileza, bajeza, infamia, abyección; acción o modo de pensar bajo y traidor.

Vilification [vil-i-fi-kē'-shun], *s.* Envilecimiento, acción de envilecer o vilipendiar; difamación.

Vilifier [vil'-i-fai-ẹr], *s.* Difamador, el que vilipendia.

Vilify [vil'-i-fai], *va.* 1. Envilecer, hacer despreciable una cosa. 2. Ajar, desacreditar, difamar, vilipendiar, calumniar.

Villa [vil'-a], *s.* Quinta, casa de campo.

Village [vil'-ẹj], *s.* Lugar, aldea, población pequeña y abierta.

Villager [vil'-a-jẹr], *s.* Lugareño, aldeano; villano.

Villain [vil'-ẹn], *s.* 1. Villano, bellaco, malvado. 2. Pechero, patán feudal.

Villainous, *a.* 1. Bellaco, vil, ruin; villano. 2. Malvado, capaz de grandes crímenes. 3. (Fam.) Muy malo, asqueroso, repugnante.

Villainously [vil'-a-nus-li], *adv.* Vilmente.

Villainousness [vil'-a-nus-nes], *s.* Maldad, perversidad, villanía.

Villainy, *s.* *V.* Villany.

Villanage [vil'-a-nẹj], *s.* *V.* Villenage.

Villanize [vil'-a-naiz], *va.* Avillanar, envilecer, hacer vil o despreciable.

Villanous [vil'-a-nus], *a.* *V.* Villainous.

Villany [vil'-a-ni], *s.* Villanía, vileza, bastardía, infamia.

Villatic [vil-at'-ic], *a.* (Ant.) Lugareño, de aldea.

Villose [vil'-ōs], **Villous** [vil'-us], *a.* Velludo; felpudo.

Villosity [vil-os'-i-ti], *s.* Vellosidad.

Villus [vil'-us], *s.* 1. (Anat.) Vello, cuerpo semejante a un pelo corto y suave que se halla en ciertas membranas, y especialmente en la mucosa del intestino delgado. 2. *pl.* Villi, (Bot.) Vellos, pelos largos y algo suaves.

Vim [vim], *s.* (Fam.) Fuerza o vigor; energía, espíritu. (Lat. acus. *vim,* de *vis,* fuerza.)

Viminal [vim'-i-nal], *a.* Mimbroso, hecho de mimbres.

Vinaceous [vai-nē'-shus], *a.* 1. Vinario, perteneciente al vino o a las uvas. 2. Vinoso, que tiene color rojo como el vino.

Vinaigrette [vin-ẹ-gret'], *s.* 1. Vasito o redomilla para contener una sal o esencia. 2. (Poco us.) Salpicón, salsa fría con vinagre.

Vincible [vin'-si-bl], *a.* Vencible, que puede ser vencido.

Vinculum [vin'-kiu-lum], *s.* Vínculo.

Vindicable [vin'-di-ca-bl], *a.* Sostenible, justificable, vindicable.

Vindicate [vin'-di-kēt], *va.* 1. Vindicar, defender, justificar. 2. (For.) Vindicar, recobrar justamente alguna persona aquello de que ha sido desposeída. 3. †Vengar.

Vindication [vin-di-kē'-shun], *s.* Vindicación, justificación, defensa.

Vindicative [vin'-di-kē''-tiv], *a.* Vindicativo, justificativo, vindicador.

Vindicator [vin'-di-kē''-tẹr], *s.* Defensor, protector, vindicador.

Vindicatory [vin'-di-ca-to-ri], *a.* Vindicativo, vindicatorio, justificativo; que contribuye a la vindicación.

Vindictive [vin-dic'-tiv], *a.* Vengativo, inclinado a tomar venganza de cualquier agravio.

Vindictively [vin-dic'-tiv-li], *adv.* Vengativamente, por venganza.

Vindictiveness [vin-dic'-tiv-nes], *s.* Ansia de venganza, carácter vengativo.

Vine [vain], *s.* 1. Parra, toda planta que tiene el tallo débil y rastrero o trepador; enredadera. 2. Vid, planta que produce las uvas; parra, una planta cualquiera del género Vitis. *Vine-clad,* Cubierto de enredaderas, de vides; por extensión, cubierto de viñas. *Vine-dresser,* (1) Viñador, deslechugador. (2) Oruga de una mariposa norteamericana que corta las hojas de la vid. *A vine-branch,* Un sarmiento. *Vine-knife,* Podadera. *Vine-fretter. vine-grub,* Pulgón de la vid. *Vine-leaf*, Hoja de vid o de sarmiento. *Vine-pest*, Filoxera; enfermedad de la vid. *Wild vine*, Vid silvestre. *Vine-stock*, Cepa, el tronco de la vid.

Vinegar [vin'-e-gar], *s.* 1. Vinagre, líquido ácido obtenido por la fermentación del vino, de la sidra, etc. 2. Vinagre, lo que es agrio metafóricamente; v. gr. una cara. *Vinegar aspect*, Cara de vinagre, cara áspera y desapacible.

Vinegar-cruet [vin'-e-gar-crū'-et], *s.* Vinagrera.

Vinery [vai'-ner-i], *s.* 1. Invernadero para las uvas. 2. Las vides en general.

Vineyard [vin'-yard], *s.* 1. Viña, viñedo, el terreno plantado de muchas vides. 2. (Fig.) Viña, lugar para cultura espiritual; la iglesia.

Vinous [vai'-nus], **Vinose** [vai'-nōs], *a.* 1. Vinoso, que tiene las calidades ó propiedades del vino. 2. (Zool.) De color de vino.

Vintage [vin'-tej], *s.* Vendimia; cosecha de uvas.

Vintager [vin'-tej-er], *s.* Vendimiador.

Vintner [vint'-ner], *s.* Vinatero, tabernero, tratante en vinos.

Viny [vai'-ni], *a.* Perteneciente á las vides o a las enredaderas: que produce vides o enredaderas.

Vinyl [vain'-l], *s.* (Quím.) Vinilo. —*a.* Vinílico.

Viol [vai'-ol], *s.* 1. Viola, instrumento músico de la edad media que tenía generalmente seis cuerdas; predecesor del violín. 2. Instrumento de cuerda parecido al violín. 3. (Mar.) Virador, calabrote afianzado con mojeles al cable y traído al cabrestante volante para mejor levar el ancla, cuando el cabrestante principal no basta.

Viola [vai'-o-la o vi-ō'-la], *s.* 1. Viola, instrumento de la misma figura que el violín, aunque algo mayor; alto. 2. *V.* VIOL, 2ª acep.

Violable [vai'-o-la-bl], *a.* Que puede ser violado.

Violaceous [vai-o-lē'-shus], *a.* Violáceo, de color de violeta; perteneciente a la violeta o a esta familia de plantas.

Violate [vai'-o-lēt], *va.* 1. Violar, quebrantar o traspasar la ley, preceptos, derechos, etc. 2. Violar, profanar las cosas sagradas. 3. Violar, forzar a una mujer, y si es doncella, se llama estuprar.

Violation [vai-o-lē'-shun], *s.* 1. Violación, la acción y efecto de violar o profanar. 2. Violación, la acción de forzar a una mujer. 3. Estupro, violación de una doncella.

Violator [vai'-o-lē-ter], *s.* 1. Violador. 2. Estuprador.

Violence [vai'-o-lens], *s.* 1. Violencia, fuerza o ímpetu en las acciones. 2. Violencia, vehemencia, impetuosidad. 3. Violencia, la fuerza con que se obliga á alguno a que haga lo que no quiere. 4. Violencia, la fuerza que se hace para sacar a una cosa de su estado u orden natural.

Violent [vai'-o-lent], *a.* 1. Violento, impetuoso, que obra con fuerza. 2. Violento, vehemente, arrebatado. 3. Fuerte, extremo. 4. Severo, duro, violento, que obra con fuerza indebida. 5. Que resulta de la fuerza externa o del daño.

Violently [vai'-o-lent-li], *adv.* Violentamente, con vehemencia, con impetuosidad.

Violet [vai'-o-let], *s.* 1. Violeta, una flor; toda planta del género Viola. 2. Color violado, el séptimo del espectro solar.—*a.* Violado, del color de la violeta.

Violet ray [vai'-o-let rê], *s.* Rayo violeta.

Violin [vai-o-lin'], *s.* 1. Violín, instrumento músico de cuatro cuerdas, que se toca con arco. 2. Violín, el que lo toca. *V.* VIOLINIST.

Violinist [vai-o-lin'-ist], *s.* Violín, violinista, el que toca el violín.

Violoncellist [vī''-o-len-chel'-ist o vai''-o-len-sel'-ist], *s.* Violoncelista, el que toca el violoncelo.

Violoncello [vī''-o-len-chel'-ō o vai''-o-len-sel'-ō], *s.* 1. Violoncelo, violonchelo, una especie de violón pequeño. 2. Violoncelo, registro pedal del órgano.

Viper [vai'-per], *s.* 1. Víbora, una especie de culebra venenosa. 2. Cualquiera persona o cosa dañina o dañosa.

Viperine [vai'-per-in], **Viperous** [vai'-per-us], *a.* Viperino, venenoso, nocivo; maléfico, pérfido.

Virago [vai-rē'-go], *s.* 1. Marimacho, Mari-Ramos, mujer regañona, colérica. 2. (Ant.) Marimacho, guerrera, amazona.

Virgilian [ver-jil'-i-an], *a.* Virgiliano, propio y característico del poeta Virgilio.

Virgin [ver'-jin], *s.* 1. Virgen, doncella, la mujer que no ha conocido varón. 2. Religiosa que ha hecho voto de virginidad. 3. Virgo, un signo del zodíaco. 4. (Zool.) Que produce huevos sin ser impregnada. —*a.* 1. Virginal, perteneciente á una virgen; modesto, casto. 2. Puro, incólume, inmaculado. 3. Virgen: se aplica a la tierra que no ha sido arada ni cultivada, a las cosas que están en su primera entereza, y a las producciones naturales que están en su ser primitivo, sin que las haya alterado el arte o el uso.

Virgin's-bower [ver'-jinz-bau-er], *s.* (Bot.) Clemátide.

Virginal [ver'-jin-al], *a.* Virginal, que pertenece a las vírgenes o es propio de ellas.

Virginal, Virginals [ver'-jin-alz], *s.* Espineta, clavicordio pequeño.

Virginity [ver-jin'-i-ti], *s.* Virginidad, el estado de la mujer que no ha conocido varón.

Virile [vai'-ril o vir'-il], *a.* 1. Viril, lo que es propio del varón; de aquí, procreativo. 2. Varonil, que tiene el vigor del varón, masculino.

Virility [vi-ril'-i-ti], *s.* Virilidad, carácter de lo viril; edad viril.

Virology [vai-rel'-o-ji], *s.* Virología.

Virtu [vir-tū'], *s.* 1. Calidad poco común, curiosa o hermosa; por lo común, en la locución *objects* o *articles of virtu*. 2. Gusto para objetos curiosos o raros. (Ital.)

Virtual [ver'-chu-al], *a.* Virtual.

Virtually [ver'-chu-al-i], *adv.* Virtualmente.

Virtue [ver'-chū], *s.* 1. Virtud: tiene las mismas acepciones en las dos lenguas, tanto en lo físico como en lo moral. 2. Castidad, particularmente de la mujer. *Virtues*, Virtudes, el quinto coro de los espíritus celestiales.

Virtuoso [ver-chū-ō'-sō], *s.* Persona aficionada a estudiar las antigüedades, las curiosidades de la naturaleza, las nobles artes o la música; particularmente, músico muy hábil. Es voz italiana.

Virtuous [ver'-chu-us], *a.* 1. Virtuoso, moralmente puro y bueno; digno de aprobación: dícese de las personas y de sus acciones, y cuando se habla de mujeres, regularmente se entiende casta. 2. (Ant.) Virtuoso, se aplicaba á las cosas que tienen la actividad y virtud natural que les corresponde; eficaz.

Virtuously [ver'-chu-us-li], *adv.* Virtuosamente.

Virtuousness [ver'-chu-us-nes], *s.* Virtuosidad, la calidad o propiedad que constituye a una persona o cosa virtuosa.

Virulence [vir'-yu-lens], *s.* 1. Virulencia, calidad de virulento, naturaleza sumamente ponzoñosa. 2. Malignidad, mordacidad.

Virulent [vir'-yu-lent], *a.* Virulento, venenoso, ponzoñoso; que tiene la naturaleza del virus; mordaz, maligno, cáustico.

Virulently [vir'-yu-lent-li], *adv.* Malignamente.

Virus [vai'-rus], *s.* Virus, el humor maligno de cualquier mal; principio morbífico que es el agente para la transmisión de varias enfermedades infecciosas; en sentido figurado, malignidad, infección moral, amargura mental, mordacidad.

Visage [viz'-ej], *s.* Rostro, cara, semblante; aspecto distintivo.

Visaged [viz'-ejd], *a.* De cara, de rostro, de semblante.

Viscera [vis'-se-ra], *s. pl.* de VISCUS.

Visceral [vis'-ser-al], *a.* 1. Visceral, perteneciente o relativo a las vísceras. 2. Ventral, abdominal.

Viscid [vis'-sid], *a.* 1. Viscoso, pegajoso, glutinoso. 2. (Fís.) Imperfectamente flúido; aplícase a una substancia, como el alquitrán, que cambia de forma bajo la influencia de una fuerza.

Viscidity [vis-sid'-i-ti], **Viscosity** [vis-cos'-i-ti], *s.* Viscosidad, calidad de viscoso.

Viscount [vai'-caunt], *s.* Vizconde, título de nobleza inmediato al de conde.

Viscountess [vai'-caunt-es], *sf.* Vizcondesa.

Viscous [vis'-cus], *a.* Viscoso, glutinoso, pegajoso.

Viscus [vis'-cus], *s.* (*pl.* VISCERA). Víscera, uno de los órganos contenidos en las grandes cavidades del cuerpo, el abdomen, el tórax y el cráneo; más común en plural, vísceras, entrañas.

Visa [vī'-za], *s.* Visa.

Viscose [vis'-cōs], *s.* (Quím.) Viscosa (para la fabricación de fibras textiles).

Vise [vais], *s.* Tornillo de banco, útil que sirve para asir y asegurar aquello en que se trabaja; torno.

Visé [vī-zé'], *va.* (*pret.* VISÉED [vi-zéd'], *pa.* VISÉING [vī-zé'-ing]). Visar una certificación poniendo en ella el visto bueno.—*s.* Visto bueno, certificación oficial que se pone en un pasaporte u otro documento. (Fr.)

Visibility [viz-i-bil'-i-ti], **Visibleness** [viz'-i-bl-nes], *s.* Visibilidad, calidad de visible.

Visible [viz'-i-bl], *a.* 1. Visible, que se puede ver, perceptible a la vista. 2. Visible, evidente, claro, manifiesto.—*s.* (Des.) La cosa visible.

Visibly [viz'-i-bli], *adv.* Visiblemente; evidentemente, manifiestamente.

Visigoth [viz'-i-geth], *s.* Visigodo, visigoda; godo del oeste.
Vision [vizh'-un], *s.* 1. Visión, vista, la facultad o el sentido de la vista; la acción de ver o el acto de la potencia visiva. 2. Visión, objeto de la vista. 3. Visión, fantasma, sueño; revelación inspirada y profética.
Visionary [vizh'-un-e-ri], *a.* 1. Imaginario, que carece de realidad; impracticable, infactible, que no se puede hacer. 2. Visionario, el que cree o se figura visiones o fantasmas.—*s.* Visionario, el hombre que se figura y cree con facilidad cosas quiméricas; hombre poco práctico.
Visit [viz'-it], *va.* 1. Visitar, ir a ver a alguno. 2. Visitar: dícese del reconocimiento o examen que hace una autoridad eclesiástica o civil de las personas o de los negocios que tienen relación con sus atribuciones. 3. (Teol.) Visitar, enviar Dios a los hombres algún consuelo, castigo o trabajo especial.—*vn.* Visitarse, irse a ver recíprocamente, hacer visitas, ir de visita.
Visit, *s.* 1. Visita, visitación, acto de cortesía. 2. Visita personal, de inspección y examen; v. gr. la ida del médico a la casa del enfermo; la visitación de un obispo, etc.
Visitable [viz'-it-a-bl], *a.* Visitable, lo que se puede visitar; lo que está sujeto a ser visitado o reconocido por alguna autoridad.
Visitant [viz'-it-ant], *s.* Visitador.
Visitation [viz-i-tê'-zhun], *s.* 1. Visitación, visita. 2. Inspección y examen oficiales, como de un establecimiento, colegio, etc.; visita de un obispo. 3. Disposición divina de gracia o de retribución; castigo del cielo. *Death by visitation of God,* Muerte natural.
Visitatorial [viz-i-ta-tō'-ri-al], *a.* Lo que pertenece a un visitador o a la autoridad que visita.
Visiting card [viz'-it-ing card], *s.* Tarjeta de visita.
Visitor, Visiter [viz'-it-er], *s.* Visitador.
Visor [viz'-er], *s.* *V.* VIZOR.
Visored [viz'-erd], *a.* *V.* VIZORED.
Vista [vis'-ta], *s.* Vista, perspectiva; perspectiva mental que comprende una serie de acontecimientos.
Visual [vizh'-yu-al], *a.* Visual.
Vital [vai'-tal], *a.* 1. Vital, perteneciente a la vida; que contribuye a la vida o le es necesario. 2. Esencial, indispensable; vital, de suma importancia. 3. Que afecta a la vida; fatal, mortal.
Vitality [vai-tal'-i-ti], *s.* Vitalidad, principio o fuerza vitales.
Vitalize [vai'-tal-aiz], *va.* Vivificar, hacer vital, dar vida; animar, reanimar.
Vitally [vai'-tal-i], *adv.* Vitalmente, de una manera vital; esencialmente.
Vitals [vai'-talz], *s. pl.* Las partes vitales de un ser viviente; (fig.) lo esencial, la vida.
Vitamin [vai'-ta-min], *s.* Vitamina.
Vitiate [vish'-i-êt], *va.* 1. Viciar, dañar, corromper, echar a perder. 2. Viciar, hacer nulo, invalidar.
Vitiation [vish-i-ê'-shun], *s.* Depravación, corrupción; estado de lo corrompido; invalidación (de un acto o contrato).
Viticulture [vit-i-cul'-chur o tiūr], *s.* Viticultura, cultivo de la vid; arte de cultivar las vides.
Viticulturist [vit-i-cul'-chur-ist], *s.* Viticultor, viticultora, persona perita en la viticultura.
Vitreous [vit'-re-us], *a.* 1. Vítreo, hecho de vidrio o que tiene sus propiedades. 2. Vítreo, parecido al vidrio en alguna propiedad; vidrioso. *Vitreous body* o *humor,* Humor vítreo del ojo.
Vitreousness [vit'-re-us-nes], *s.* Vidriosidad, la semejanza con el vidrio.
Vitrescent [vi-tres'-ent], *a.* Capaz de vitrificación.
Vitrifaction [vit-ri-fac'-shun], *s.* Vitrificación, acción o procedimiento de vitrificar; estado o calidad de lo vitrificado.
Vitriform [vit'-ri-fērm], *a.* Vítreo, que tiene la apariencia del vidrio.
Vitrify [vit'-ri-fai], *va.* Vitrificar.—*vn.* Vitrificarse, reducirse a vidrio.
Vitriol [vit'-ri-el], *s.* 1. Aceite de vitriolo, ácido sulfúrico. 2. Sulfato, vitriolo. *Blue* o *Roman vitriol,* Vitriolo azul, sulfato de cobre. *Green vitriol* o *copperas,* Vitriolo verde o marcial, caparrosa, sulfato de hierro. *White vitriol,* Vitriolo blanco, sulfato de cinc.
Vitriolic [vit-ri-el'-ic], †**Vitriolous** [vi-trai'-o-lus], *a.* 1. Vitriólico. 2. Cáustico, mordaz.
Vituperable [vi-tiū'-per-a-bl], *a.* Vituperable.
Vituperate [vi-tiū'-per-êt], *va.* Vituperar, censurar, decir mal.
Vituperation [vi-tiū-per-ê'-shun], *s.* Vituperación, el acto de vituperar ó censurar.
Vitus's Dance (St.) [vai'-tus-iz dans], *s.* Corea o baile de S. Vito, una enfermedad del sistema nervioso.
Viva voce [vai'-va vō'-sî], *adv.* De viva voz, de palabra.
Vivacious [vai-vê'-shus], *a.* 1. Vivo, animado, alegre, despejado. 2. (Poco us.) De larga vida. 3. (Bot.) Vivaz, perenne.
Vivaciousness [vai-vê'-shus-nes], **Vivacity** [vai-vas'-i-ti], *s.* 1. Vivacidad, viveza de genio, animación. 2. (Des.) Ancianidad, vida larga.
Vivarium [vai-vê'-ri-um], **Vivary** [vai'-va-ri o viv'-a-ri], *s.* Vivar, vivero.
Vives [vaivz], *s. pl.* 1. Glándula parótida del caballo. 2. Adivas, inflamación de las glándulas de los caballos.
Vivid [viv'-id], *a.* 1. Vivo, despejado, lleno de vida; intenso; brillante (color). 2. Vivo, de apariencia viviente; animado, enérgico. 3. Activo, que obra con vivo interés.
Vividly [viv'-id-li], *adv.* Vivamente, con vivacidad, con vigor.
Vividness [viv'-id-nes], *s.* Vivacidad, calidad de brillante; intensidad; fuerza, brillo.
Vivification [viv-i-fi-kê'-shun], *s.* Vivificación.
Vivify [viv'-i-fai], *va.* Vivificar, dar vida a; dar vigor, reanimar.
Viviparous [vai-vip'-a-rus], *a.* 1. (Zool.) Vivíparo: dícese del animal que pare los hijos vivos, a distinción de los que ponen huevos. 2. (Bot.) Que produce bulbos o simientes que germinan mientras están aún unidas a la planta.
Vivisect [viv'-i-sect], *va.* Disecar un animal vivo para hacer estudios fisiológicos.—*vn.* Practicar la vivisección.
Vivisection [viv-i-sec'-shun], *s.* Vivisección, disección de los animales vivos para fines científicos.
Vixen [vic'-sn], *s.* 1. Zorra o raposa, la hembra del zorro o raposo. 2. Mujer regañona, cólerica, displicente, quimerista.
Viz. *V.* VIDELICET. (Se lee generalmente *namely* o *to wit.*)
Vizard [viz'-ard], *s.* (Ant.) Visera, máscara, carátula.
Vizier, Vizir [vi-zîr' o viz'-yer], *s.* Visir o el gran visir, el primer ministro del imperio otomano.
Vizor [viz'-er], *s.* 1. Visera, ala pequeña que tienen en la parte anterior las gorras, etc., para resguardar la vista. 2. Visera, del yelmo.
Vizored [viz'-erd], *a.* Cubierto como con visera; con la visera baja o calada.
Vocable [vō'-ca-bl], *s.* Vocablo, palabra, sonido vocal.
Vocabulary [vo-cab'-yu-le-ri], *s.* 1. Vocabulario, lista de palabras, diccionario. 2. Nomenclatura, conjunto de palabras usadas por una persona o contenidas en una obra.
Vocal [vō'-cal], *a.* Vocal, oral. *Vocal cords,* Cuerdas vocales.
Vocalist [vō'-cal-ist], *s.* Cantor, cantora, particularmente los de voz cultivada; lo contrario de *instrumentalist.*
Vocality [vo-cal'-i-ti], **Vocalness** [vō'-cal-nes], *s.* La facultad de pronunciar las palabras.
Vocalization [vō''-cal-aiz-ê'-shun], *s.* Vocalización, acción y efecto de vocalizar.
Vocalize [vō'-cal-aiz], *va.* 1. Proferir o formar la voz, vocalizar. 2. Poner los puntos vocales, v. g. en fonografía, o en un idioma semítico.—*vn.* Vocalizar, solfear sin nombrar las notas.
Vocally [vo'-cal-i], *adv.* 1. Vocalmente, con la voz. 2. Verbalmente.
Vocation [vo-kê'-shun], *s.* 1. Vocación, oficio, carrera, profesión. 2. Llamamiento espiritual o que Dios hace al hombre para el servicio religioso.
Vocational [vo-kê'-shun-al], *a.* 1. Vocacional. 2. Profesional, práctico, relativo a un oficio o profesión. *Vocational guidance,* Orientación profesional. *Vocational school,* Escuela de artes y oficios, escuela profesional. *Vocational training,* Preparación o instrucción técnica o práctica. *Vocational tests,* Pruebas vocacionales de aptitud.
Vocative [vec'-a-tiv], *s.* Vocativo.
Vociferate [vo-sif'-er-êt], *vn.* Vociferar; clamorear.
Vociferation [vo-sif-er-ê'-shun], *s.* Vocería, grita, confusión de voces.
Vociferous [vo-sif'-er-us], *a.* Vocinglero, clamoroso.
Vogue [vōg], *s.* Crédito, estimación; moda. *To be in vogue,* Estar en boga, usarse mucho, ser de moda.
Voice [veis], *s.* 1. Voz, el sonido proferido con la boca por el hombre y algunos animales; calidad o carácter de ese sonido. 2. Facultad de hablar. 3. Opinión o elección expresados; sufragio, voz, voto. 4. Enseñanza, admonición, instrucción. 5. El que habla, particularmente en pro de otra persona. 6. (Gram.) Voz, del verbo.
Voice, *va.* 1. Poner en habla, expresar, proclamar, decir su parecer. 2. Dar el tono; acordar o templar un instrumento. 3. (Mús.) Escribir la parte vocal.

Voiced [voist], *a.* 1. (Gram.) Sonoro. 2. Expreso, expresado, formulado.
Voiceless [vois'-les], *a.* 1. Mudo. 2. (Gram.) Sordo.
Void [veid], *a.* 1. Vacío, desocupado, hueco; vacante. 2. (For.) Nulo, sin ningún efecto, sin valor ni fuerza. 3. Falto, privado, desprovisto. 4. Vano, falto de realidad.—*s.* Vacuo, vacío, el espacio enteramente desocupado.
Void, *va.* 1. Vaciar, desocupar, evacuar. 2. Dejar un lugar, desocuparlo o separarse de él. 3. Anular, invalidar, hacer nula alguna cosa. *To void out*, Echar fuera, arrojar.
Voidable [veid'-a-bl], *a.* 1. Anulable. 2. Que se puede evacuar o expeler.
Voidance [veid'-ans], *s.* Vaciamiento, la acción y efecto de vaciar.
Voider [veid'ęr], *s.* 1. El o lo que evacua, arroja, anula o vacía. 2. Cesta o canasta en que se llevaban antiguamente los residuos de la mesa o comida.
Voidness [veid'-nes], *s.* Vacuidad; nulidad.
Volant [vō'-lant], *a.* 1. Volante, que vuela; capaz de volar. 2. Ligero, ágil.
Volapük [vō''-la-pük'], *s.* Lengua internacional inventada en 1879 por el profesor suizo J. M. Schleyer.
Volar [vō'lar], *a.* Perteneciente a la palma de la mano o a la planta del pie.
Volatile [vel'-a-til], *a.* 1. Volátil, que tiene la propiedad de volatilizarse o exhalarse fácilmente a la temperatura ordinaria. 2. Voluble, ligero, inconstante. 3. Pasajero, transitorio.
Volatileness [vel'-a-til-nes], **Volatility** [vel-a-til'-i-ti], *s.* 1. Volatilidad, calidad de volátil, de transformarse en gas. 2. Voltariedad, volubilidad, instabilidad, ligereza.
Volatilization [vel-a-til-i-zé'-shun], *s.* Volatilización.
Volatilize [vel'-a-til-aiz], *va.* Volatilizar, sutilizar los cuerpos reduciéndolos a partes volátiles.—*vn.* Volatilizarse, transformarse en vapor o gas.
Volcanic [vel-can'-ic], *a.* Volcánico, perteneciente o relativo al volcán.
Volcano [vel-kê'-nō], *s.* Volcán, abertura en la tierra y más comúnmente en una montaña, por donde salen de tiempo en tiempo humo, llamas y materias encendidas o derretidas.
Vole [vōl], *s.* Arvícola, animal roedor de cola corta; ratón campestre.
Volition [vo-lish'-un], *s.* Voluntad, facultad de querer; volición, el acto en que la voluntad se determina por alguna cosa.
Volitional [vo-lish'-un-al], *a.* Volitivo, de la voluntad.
Volley [vel'-i], *s.* 1. Descarga de armas de fuego; andanada; salva. 2. Rociada de palabras picantes, de insultos, etc.
Volley, *va.* y *vn.* Lanzar una descarga de; ser descargado o sonar al mismo tiempo; estallar.
Volleyball [vel'-i-bol], *s.* Balonvolea, vólibol.
Volleyed [vel'-id], *a.* Tirado, descargado.
Volplane [vel-plên'], *vn.* Planear. (Aplícase a un avión.)
Volt [vōlt], *s.* Voltio, unidad práctica de la fuerza electromotriz; la fuerza que aplicada a un conductor de la resistencia de un ohmio produce una corriente de un amperio. (< Volta.) *Volt-ammeter, volt-meter*, Voltímetro, aparato que se emplea para medir potenciales eléctricas. *Volt-ampere*, *V.* WATT. *Volt-coulomb*, *V.* JOULE.
Volt [velt], *s.* La vuelta que se hace dar al caballo en el picadero.
Voltage [vōlt'-ęj], *s.* Voltaje, fuerza electromotriz expresada en voltios; conjunto de voltios que actúan en un sistema eléctrico.
Voltaic, *a.* 1. (Fís.) Voltaico, perteneciente a la electricidad que se desarrolla por medio de la acción química o del contacto; galvánico. 2. Perteneciente a Alejandro Volta, de Pavía.
Voltaism [vel'-ta-izm], *s.* Voltaísmo, galvanismo.
Volt-ampere [vōlt'-am-pīr], *s.* (Elec.) Voltamperio.
Volubility [vel-yu-bil'-i-ti], *s.* 1. Volubilidad, facilidad de expresión, verbosidad. 2. (Des.) Volubilidad, la facilidad de moverse alrededor de alguna cosa.
Voluble [vel'-yu-bl], *a.* 1. De fácil palabra. 2. Voluble, que gira fácilmente, dispuesto para dar vueltas. 3. (Bot.) Voluble, que sube en espiral.
Volume [vel'-yūm], *s.* 1. Volumen, un libro encuadernado. *A folio volume*, Un tomo en folio. 2. Un rollo formado por cualquier cosa arrollada; rollo de vitela sobre el cual escribían los antiguos. 3. Volumen, bulto; caudal de río. 4. Importe, suma, gran cantidad. 5. (Mat.) Volumen, espacio ocupado por un cuerpo. 6. Volumen, plenitud o cuantidad del sonido o del tono.
Volumetric [vel-yu-met'-ric], *a.* (Fís.) Volumétrico, perteneciente a la medida de los compuestos comparando los volúmenes.
Voluminous [vo-lū'-mi-nus], *a.* 1. Voluminoso, abultado, extenso. 2. Copioso, difuso. 3. Dícese del escritor que ha publicado muchas obras o de la obra que está escrita en muchos volúmenes.
Voluminously [vo-lū'-mi-nus-li], *adv.* En muchos tomos o volúmenes; copiosamente, abultadamente.
Voluminousness [vo-lū'-mi-nus-nes], *s.* El estado de lo que se halla contenido en muchos volúmenes o es voluminoso.
Voluntarily [vel'-un-tę-ri-li], *adv.* Voluntariamente, espontáneamente, de libre voluntad.
Voluntary [vel'-un-tę-ri], *a.* Voluntario, espontáneo, que nace de la voluntad libremente o que se hace de libre voluntad.—*s.* 1. Voluntario, el que se compromete a hacer o emprender una cosa voluntariamente. 2. Solo para órgano que se toca antes o después del oficio divino.
Volunteer [vel-un-tīr'], *s.* Voluntario, el que se ofrece para cualquier servicio por su propia voluntad; especialmente, el soldado que sirve sin haber sido reclutado.
Volunteer, *va.* y *vn.* Ofrecer o contribuir voluntariamente; servir como voluntario, sentar plaza; ofrecerse.
Voluptuary [vo-lup'-chu-ę-ri], *s.* Hombre voluptuoso o entregado a los placeres.
Voluptuous [vo-lup'-chu-us], *a.* 1. Voluptuoso, que proporciona o produce placer a los sentidos. 2. Voluptuoso, dado a los placeres del lujo o a los deleites sensuales. 3. De formas voluptuosas (mujer).
Voluptuously [vo-lup'-chu-us-li], *adv.* Voluptuosamente, lujuriosamente; con lujo.
Voluptuousness [vo-lup'-chu-us-nes], *s.* Sensualidad, deleite o placer sensual; voluptuosidad.
Volute [vo-liūt'], *s.* (Arq.) Voluta o roleo de columna (jónica o corintia).
Volvox [vel'vex], *s.* Vólvoce, género de algas de agua dulce, de forma esférica y dotadas de movimiento rotatorio.
Vomer [vō'-męr], *s.* Vómer, huesecillo impar de las fosas nasales.
Vomica [vem'i-ca], *s.* Vómica, una especie de bolsita membranosa llena de pus que suele formarse en el pulmón u otra víscera.
Vomic nut [vem'-ic nut], *s.* Nuez vómica. *V.* NUX-VOMICA.
Vomit [vem'-it], *va.* y *vn.* 1. Vomitar, arrojar violentamente lo que estaba en el estómago. 2. Vomitar, arrojar afuera con violencia; salir con violencia.
Vomit, *s.* 1. Vómito, lo que se vomita; acción de vomitar. 2. Vomitivo, el medicamento que hace vomitar.
Vomiting [vem'-it-ing], *s.* 1. Vómito, acción de vomitar. 2. Vómito, lo que se vomita.
Voodoo [vū'-dū], *s.* Conjunto de supersticiones aun existentes entre los negros y criollos de las Antillas y de los Estados Unidos del Sur, acerca de los hechizos, la magia, etc.
Voracious [vo-rê'-shus], *a.* Voraz, muy comedor, que devora; (apetito) devorador; rapaz.
Voraciously [vo-rê'-shus-li], *adv.* Vorazmente, con voracidad.
Voraciousness [vo-rê'-shus-nes], **Voracity** [vo-ras'-i-ti], *s.* Voracidad, calidad de voraz.
Vortex [vōr'-tecs], *s.* Remolino, torbellino, vórtice.
Vortical [vōr'-ti-cal], *a.* Vortiginoso, semejante al vórtice; que hace o forma torbellinos.
Votarist [vō'-ta-rist], *s.* (Poco us.) *V.* VOTARY.
Votary [vō'-ta-ri], *s.* El que se dedica o consagra a algún género particular de vida; el que está muy apasionado por alguna persona o cosa. *A votary of love*, Un amante, un enamorado. *A votary of learning*, Uno que se entrega al estudio.
Vote [vōt], *s.* 1. Voto, sufragio, parecer, dictamen; opinión expresada en una decisión o elección. 2. Medio por el cual se expresa un voto; por ejemplo, una palabra, una papeleta, o el acto de elevar la mano. 3. Votación, decisión. *To put to the vote*, Poner a votación, proceder a votar. *A casting vote*, Voto decisivo.
Vote, *va.* Votar, elegir o determinar por votos.—*vn.* Votar, dar uno su voto.
Voter [vōt'-ęr], *s.* Votante, voto, elector, la persona que vota o tiene derecho a votar.
Voting [vōt'-ing], *a.* Votante. *Voting machine*, Máquina electoral.
Votive [vō'-tiv], *a.* Votivo, dado u ofrecido por voto.
Vouch [vauch], *va.* 1. Poner o tomar a alguno por testigo. 2. Atestiguar, certificar, afirmar, atestar, testificar. 3. Apelar al testimonio de al.

guno.—*vn.* Dar testimonio de, salir fiador de; certificar.

Voucher [vauch'-ẹr], *s.* 1. Documento justificativo, particularmente el o lo que acusa recibo de dinero u objetos de valor. 2. Testigo, el que atestigua alguna cosa; fiador, responsable, garante.

Vouchsafe [vauch-sêf'], *va.* Conceder, permitir, otorgar.—*vn.* Condescender, dignarse.

Voussoir [vū-swār'], *s.* (Arq.) Dovela, clave de arco, piedra labrada con una cara convexa y otra cóncava. (Fr.)

Vow [vau], *s.* 1. Voto, promesa hecha de un modo solemne, particularmente a Dios, a la Virgen o a un santo. 2. Voto, cualquier promesa solemne de las que constituyen el estado religioso.

Vow, *va.* y *vn.* 1. Dedicar o consagrar a Dios. 2. Dedicar u ofrecer respetuosamente una obra, trabajo, etc., a alguna persona. 3. Votar, hacer voto. 4. Hacer solemnemente alguna promesa.

Vowel [vau'-el], *s.* Vocal, la letra que por sí forma sílaba; el sonido producido por la vibración de las cuerdas vocales.—*a.* Vocal.—*va.* Proveer de vocales, p. ej. un escrito árabe o hebreo.

Vox [vex], *s.* Voz (en la música). *Vox humana,* Registro de lengüeta para producir en el órgano tonos parecidos a la voz humana.

Voyage [vei'-ẹj], *s.* Viaje por mar, río o lago; navegación. *Voyage out and home,* Viaje redondo. *Twenty days' voyage,* Veinte días de viaje o de travesía.

Voyage, *vn.* Navegar, viajar por mar, río o lago, hacer un viaje por mar.—*va.* Transitar, pasar por.

Voyager [vei'-ẹj-ẹr], *s.* Viajero por mar; navegador.

Vulcan [vul'-can], *s.* 1. Vulcano, dios del fuego en la antigua Roma. 2. Planeta que se suponía existir entre el sol y Mercurio.

Vulcanite [vul'-can-ait], *s.* Vulcanita, variedad negruzca de caucho azufrado o vulcanizado.

Vulcanization [vul-can-aiz-ê'-shun], *s.* Vulcanización, el procedimiento de tratar el caucho con azufre a una temperatura elevada.

Vulcanize [vul'-can-aiz], *va.* Vulcanizar, combinar el caucho con azufre a una temperatura más o menos elevada; sujetar a la vulcanización.

Vulgar [vul'-gar], *a.* 1. Vulgar, lo que pertenece al vulgo. 2. Vulgar, común, ordinario. 3. Vulgar, vernáculo: dícese de las lenguas que se hablan, en contraposición a las lenguas muertas. 4. Público, generalmente sabido. 5. Vil, bajo, contrario al buen gusto.—*s.* Vulgo, plebe, populacho.

Vulgarism [vul'-gar-izm], *s.* Vulgaridad, expresión ofensiva al buen gusto; el modo de vivir correspondiente al vulgo.

Vulgarity [vul-gar'-i-ti], *s.* 1. Vulgaridad, la calidad o propiedad perteneciente al vulgo. 2. Vulgaridad, bajeza, dicho o hecho bajo; mal tono, modales vulgares.

Vulgarize, Vulgarise [vul'-gar-aiz], *va.* Vulgarizar, hacer vulgar.—*vn.* Conducirse de un modo vulgar, bajo.

Vulgarly [vul'-gar-li], *adv.* Vulgarmente, comúnmente; bajamente, como del vulgo.

Vulgate [vul'-gêt], *s.* y *a.* Vulgata, la versión latina de la Biblia aceptada por la Iglesia católica.

Vulnerability [vul-nẹr-a-bil'-i-ti], *s.* *V.* VULNERABLENESS.

Vulnerable [vul'-nẹr-a-bl], *a.* Vulnerable, que puede ser herido.

Vulnerableness [vul'-nẹr-a-bl-nes], *s.* La calidad de vulnerable.

Vulnerary [vul'-nẹr-ẹ-ri], *a.* Vulnerario, eficaz para curar llagas o heridas.—*s.* Medicamento vulnerario.

Vulpine [vul'-pin], *a.* 1. Zorruno, vulpino. 2. Astuto, ladino.

Vulture [vul'-chur], *s.* (Orn.) Buitre, ave de rapiña.

Vulturine, Vulturous [vul'-chur-in], *a.* Buitrero, perteneciente al buitre o que le es propio.

Vulva [vul'-va], *s.* Vulva, abertura exterior de la vagina.

Vulvar [vul'-var], *a.* De la vulva; perteneciente o relativo a la vulva.

Vyingly [vai'-ing-li], *adv.* De manera que emule o rivalice.

W

W [dub'-l-yū] es una letra ambigua en la lengua inglesa, siendo consonante al principio de dicción y vocal cuando forma diptongo en medio o al final de las palabras. Se pronuncia de un modo muy semejante a la *u* vocal castellana: es muda, cuando precede a la *r,* como en *wright, wrong;* cuando está delante de la *h* y *o,* como in *whole, who;* y en algunas otras voces, como *sword, answer,* etc.

Wabble [web'-l], *vn.* 1. (Fam.) Balancearse vacilando, como una peonza que gira lentamente. 2. Vacilar.—*s.* Movimiento irregular de cuerpos que están desigualmente equilibrados y en rotación.

Wabbly [web'-li], *a.* Que hace eses o se balancea vacilando.

Wacke [wak'-ẹ], *s.* Roca parda terrosa o arcillosa.

Wad [wed], *s.* 1. Manojo o atado de paja. 2. Borra o pelote para rehenchir cojines, sillas, etc. 3. (Art.) Taco, el bodoquillo que se pone sobre la carga en las piezas de artillería. 4. Mineral de manganeso y cobalto.

Wad, *va.* 1. Acolchar, emborrar, atacar. 2. Empaquetar con entreforro o algodón en rama para protección (v. gr. las mercancías preciosas); forrar con entretela.

Wad-hook [wed'-huc], *s.* (Art.) Sacatrapos.

Wadding [wed'-ing], *s.* Entretela, entreforro, lo que sirve para forrar, particularmente algodón en rama; conjunto de pelotes; taco.

Waddle [wed'-l], *vn.* Anadear, andar moviendo las caderas de un lado a otro, andar como el pato.

Wade [wêd], *va.* Atravesar a vado. —*vn.* 1. Vadear, pasar algún río sin echarse a nado; andar en el agua, en el barro, por entre las hierbas altas, en toda substancia que cede al pie. 2. Pasar o penetrar con dificultad.

Wader [wê'-dẹr], *s.* 1. El o lo que vadea. 2. *Wader* o *wading bird,* Zancudas, orden de aves.

Wadi [wed'-i], *s.* Valle que contiene el lecho de un torrente que generalmente se agota en la estación seca. (Árabe.)

Wae [wê], *a.* (Esco.) Triste, desgraciado.—*s.* *V.* WOE.

Wafer [wê'-fẹr], *va.* Poner una oblea; pegar o cerrar con oblea.—*s.* Oblea; hostia; barquillo. *Wafer-iron,* Barquillero, molde de hierro para hacer barquillos. *Wafer-man,* Oblcero, el que hace obleas; barquillero, el que hace y vende barquillos.

Waffle [wef'-l], *s.* Barquillo o suplicación; fruta de sartén.

Waft [waft], *va.* 1. Llevar por el aire o por encima del agua. 2. Hacer flotar, sobrenadar.

Waft, *s.* 1. Cuerpo flotante. 2. El movimiento de una bandera u otra cosa que se tremola para hacer alguna señal.

Waftage [waft'-ẹj], *s.* La conducción por el aire o por el agua.

Wafter [waft'-ẹr], *s.* Embarcación ligera; fragata; convoy, conserva.

Wafture [waft'-yur], *s.* Fluctuación, el acto y efecto de fluctuar o flotar.

Wag [wag], *va.* 1. Mover o menear ligeramente. *To wag the tail,* Colear. 2. Hacer gestos y movimientos ridículos.—*vn.* 1. Oscilar, inclinarse alternativamente en direcciones opuestas. 2. Proceder regularmente (vida). 3. Irse.

Wag, *s.* 1. Coleada, coleadura; movimiento alternativo de la cabeza. 2. Un chocarrero, retozón o juguetón; burlón; bufón; un tararira. *To play the wag,* Andarse en chanzas o con burlas, estar de chunga, gastar chanzas pesadas.

Wage, *s.* 1. Paga por algún servicio; comúnmente en plural. 2. †Prenda. *V.* WAGES. *Wage-earner, wage-worker,* Trabajador, jornalero, el que trabaja por un jornal.

Wage [wêj], *va.* 1. Hacer emprender con vigor, sostener. *To wage war,* Hacer guerra. 2. Preparar la alfarería, amasándola o trabajándola. *To wage one's law,* Llámase así en la jurisprudencia inglesa el derecho que tiene cualquiera persona ejecutada por deudas, de presentarse al tribunal para probar que no debe el todo o parte de lo que se le pide.

Wager [wê'-jẹr], *s.* 1. Apuesta, la acción de apostar, y también lo que se apuesta. 2. Prenda, cosa depositada. *To lay a wager,* Apostar, hacer una apuesta. *Wager of law,* La acción de ofrecer ante un tribunal la justificación o prueba de un hecho, etc.

Wager, *va.* Apostar.

Wagerer [wê'-jẹr-ẹr], *s.* Apostador, el que apuesta.

Wages [wê'-jez], *s. pl.* de WAGE. Salario, jornal, soldada, paga o recompensa por algún servicio. *Monthly wages,* Salario mensual; mesada.

Waggery [wag'-ẹr-i], *s.* Chocarrería, bufonada; travesura; bellaquería.

Waggish [wag'-ish], *a.* 1. Chocarrero, juguetón, retozón, bufón. 2. Dicho o hecho como gracia o bufonada.

Waggishness [wag'-ish-nes], *s.* Retozo, juguete, chocarrería; la propensión a gastar chanzas pesadas.

Waggle [wag'-l], *va.* Mover ligeramente de un lado a otro.—*vn.* Anadear; menearse; bullir.—*s.* Movimiento alternativo rápido, oscilación.

Wagnerian [wag-ni'-ri-an], *a.* Relativo a Ricardo Wagner, el compositor alemán de música, o a sus obras.

W X

Wagon, Waggon [wag'-un], *s.* 1. Galera, carro grande o carretón de cuatro ruedas para llevar géneros o equipajes; en general, cualquier vehículo de cuatro ruedas, coche. 2. (Ingl.) Vagón, furgón de ferrocarril para el transporte de géneros. *Wagon-load*, Galerada, carretada, la carga que cabe en una galera o carretón; unidad de medida. *Wagon-maker, waggon-maker, wagon-wright*, Carretero, el que hace carros.

Wagonage, Waggonage [wag'-un-ẹj], *s.* Porte, carretaje.

Wagontrain [wag'-un-trên], *s.* (Mil.) Tren de provisiones.

Wagtail [wag'-têl], *s.* (Orn.) Aguzanieve, nevatilla, motacila.

Waif [wêf], *s.* 1. Andorrero, (niño) errante, descuidado, sin hogar. 2. Algo llevado de aquí para allá, como por el viento o el agua; artículo desemparejado, perdido. 3. (For.) Cosa robada que el ladrón perseguido abandona en el camino; bienes mostrencos, los que no tienen dueño conocido.

Wail [wêl], *va.* y *vn.* 1. Deplorar o llorar los males, desdichas, etc. 2. Lamentar o lamentarse. 3. Gemir, dar gemidos y sollozos.

Wail, Wailing [wêl'-ing], *s.* Lamento, gemido, sollozo, clamor.

†**Wain** [wên], *s.* Carruaje. *Charles's Wain*, (Fam.) Osa Mayor.

Wainscot [wen'-scot], *s.* Enmaderamiento de ensambladura, el friso con que se cubren y adornan las paredes de una sala o gabinete.

Wainscot, *va.* Cubrir y adornar las paredes de una sala con piezas de ensambladura; entablar, guarnecer; poner friso de madera.

Wainscoting [wen'-scot-ing], *s.* Entablamento, entabladura; capa de mezcla que cubre la pared.

Waist [wêst], *s.* 1. Cintura, la parte inferior del talle. 2. (Hablando del vestido de las mujeres), justillo, corpiño, jubón, monillo, talle; ajustador. 3. (Mar.) Combés de una nave. *Waistboards*, (Mar.) Falcas, las tablas que se ponen en los cantos de las bordas para impedir la entrada de las olas. *Waistcloths*, (Mar.) Empavesadas.

Waistband [wêst'-band], *s.* Cintura de pantalón, de enagua.

Waistcoat [wêst'-cōt o wes'-cẹt], *s.* Chaleco, prenda de vestir sin mangas que llega hasta la cintura y que se lleva debajo de la levita o chaqueta. *Waistcoat button*, Botón de chaleco o chupa, botón pequeño.

Waistline [wêst'-lain], *s.* Cintura.

Wait [wêt], *va.* Esperar, aguardar; dilatar, diferir (la partida o un acto).—*vn.* 1. Estar aguardando o esperando, estar en expectativa. 2. Quedar dispuesto, listo a. 3. Servir; hacer servicios personales; ser criado, sirviente o mozo (de fonda). *To wait at table*, Servir a la mesa. *To wait for*, Esperar a; acechar. *To wait on* o *upon*, Ir a ver a alguno, visitar o hacer una visita; presentar sus respetos a; servir, seguir, servir a la mesa o como criado; seguirse, inferirse, ser una cosa consecuencia de otra; acompañar o ir acompañando, especialmente a los recién casados; poner cuidado en, velar sobre; volver a conducir a una persona al paraje de donde se salió con ella. *I shall have the honour to wait on you to-morrow*, Mañana tendré el gusto de ponerme a las órdenes de Vd.

Wait, *s.* 1. Espera, aguardamiento, acto de esperar; tardanza, detención, demora, el tiempo ocupado en aguardar. 2. *pl.* Unos músicos que tocan de noche por las calles en ciertas épocas del año y especialmente por Navidad. 3. (Des.) Asechanza, celada. *To lie in wait*, Asechar, poner asechanzas. *To lay wait*, Formar emboscada, preparar un paraje para un ataque.

Waiter [wêt'-ẹr], *s.* 1. Camarero, criado de fonda, mozo de café o taberna, sirviente, criado. 2. Azafate o bandeja para servir el café, el te, las bebidas, etc. *Dumb-waiter*, Ascensor doméstico (para elevar objetos de la cocina a los pisos altos): (en Ingl.) aparador giratorio.

Waiting [wêt'-ing], *s.* El acto de aguardar o esperar; servicio, el acto de servir. *Gentleman in waiting*, Gentilhombre de servicio. *Waiting-maid, waiting-woman, waiting-gentlewoman*, Doncella, camarera. *Waiting-room*, Sala para esperar; sala de descanso.

Waitress [wê'-tres], *s.* Criada, moza.

Waive [wêv], *va.* 1. Dejar pasar; renunciar temporalmente; ceder, resignar. 2. (Der. ant. Ingl.) Proscribir a una mujer.

Waiver [wêv'-ẹr], *s.* (For.) Renuncia voluntaria de un derecho, privilegio, o ventaja.

Waiving [wêv'-ing], *s.* (For. ant.) El acto de proscribir a una mujer; recusación de la protección de las leyes a una mujer.

Wake [wêk], *vn.* 1. Velar, estar sin dormir; velar, pasar la noche. 2. Despertar, despertarse, dejar el sueño, dejar de dormir. 3. Hacerse más vivo y advertido.—*va.* 1. Despertar, cortar o quitar el sueño. 2. Despertar, excitar, remover. 3. Resucitar. 4. Velar a los difuntos.

Wake, *s.* 1. Vela o vigilia de un muerto durante toda la noche; costumbre común entre los irlandeses. (Cuba y Méx.) Velorio. 2. (Gran Bret.) Vela, romería o fiesta de la dedicación de una iglesia, que antiguamente se guardaba velando toda la noche. 3. (Des.) Vela, vigilia, la acción de estar despierto. (< A.-S. wacu.) 4. (Mar.) Estela, la señal que la embarcación deja en el agua a su paso. (< Islandés *vök*, agujero.) *A ship in the wake of another*, (Mar.) Un bajel en la estela o las aguas de otro.

Wakeful [wêc'-ful], *a.* Vigilante, que vela o está despierto, que no tiene sueño o que no duerme.

Wakefully [wêc'-ful-i], *adv.* Vigilantemente.

Wakefulness [wêc'-ful-nes], *s.* Vigilia, desvelo, falta de sueño, insomnio; estado de una persona que no puede dormir.

Waken [wê'-cn], *vn.* Despertar, despertarse, dejar de dormir.—*va.* Despertar, avivar, hacer que uno vuelva en sí.

Wake-robin [wêc'-rob-in], *s.* (Bot.) 1. Aro o yaro, planta británica con hojas verdes obscuras y sagitadas. 2. (E. U.) Una especie cualquiera del género Trillium, hierba perenne de las liliáceas. Se llama también *birthroot.*

Waking [wê'-king], *s.* Vela, el tiempo que uno está en vela o despierto estado de vigilia.—*a.* 1. Que despierta. 2. Despierto, que no duerme. 3. De vela o vigilia; en que no se duerme. *Waking hours*, Horas de vela.

Wale [wêl], *va.* Hacer rayas sobre el cuerpo, azotar.—*s.* 1. Raya, señal hecha sobre la piel azotando. 2. Relieve, especie de labor o figura que se forma en el damasco y otras telas. 3. (Mar.) Cinta. *Main-wale*, Cinta principal o mayor. *Channel-wale*, Cinta de la segunda cubierta.

Wale-knot [wêl'-nẹt], **Wall-knot** [wōl'-nẹt], *s.* Nudo redondo y seguro.

Walk [wōk], *vn.* 1. Andar, ir al paso. 2. Pasear, pasearse; ir a pie; andar por gusto o por ejercicio. 3. Andar o caminar a paso corto, hablando de caballerías. 4. Obrar, conducirse, portarse; vivir. 5. Aparecer, hablando de fantasmas, espectros o duendes. 6. (Fam.) Irse obligado a ello, liar el petate, ser despedido.—*va.* 1. Pasear, sacar a pasear o hacer pasear; recorrer, andar en. 2. Atravesar, pasar de una parte a otra. 3. Conducir, dirigir; hacer ir al paso (un caballo). *To walk after*, Seguir a uno o ir tras él. *To walk away*, Irse, marcharse. *To walk back*, Volver, regresar. *To walk down*, Bajar, andar bajando. *To walk forth*, Salir. *To walk in*, Entrar, pasar adelante; pasearse en; (Bibl.) vivir en. *To walk out*, Salir, irse afuera. *To walk the hospitals*, Estudiar la clínica médica o quirúrgica en los hospitales. *To walk the streets*, Andar por las calles o pasear las calles. *To walk up*, Subir, andar subiendo: (con *to*) acercarse a. *To walk up and down*, Pasearse de arriba a abajo.

Walk, *s.* 1. Paseo, el acto de pasear o pasearse. 2. El modo de andar. 3. Paso, el movimiento seguido del caballo cuando no trota ni galopa. 4. Paseo, el lugar o sitio destinado para pasearse; senda; acera; alameda, camino cuyas orillas tienen árboles. *The street walk*, La calzada de la calle, el enlosado o entarimado. 5. Carrera, estado, empleo, vocación. 6. Método de vida, conducta, porte. *To go for a walk*, Ir a pasearse, ir a paseo. *The humble walks of life*, Las humildes sendas de la vida.

Walker [wōk'-ẹr], *s.* Paseador, andador; peatón, peón, el que anda a pie. *Night-walker*, Cantonera. *Street-walker*, Prostituta.

Walkie-talkie [wek'-i-te'-ki], *s.* Radioteléfono portátil.

Walking [wōk'-ing], *s.* Paseo, la acción de pasear o pasearse. *Walking-beam*, Balancín (de máquina vertical de vapor). *Walking-cane*, Bastón ligero. *Walking-staff*, Bordón, bastón. *Walking-stick*, (1) Bastón. (2) Insecto fasmídeo de cuerpo prolongado y parecido a las ramillas entre las cuales vive. *Walking-spirit*, Ánima en pena, duende, fantasma. *To give one his walking-ticket*, Despedirle, enviarle a pasear; darle calabazas.

Walkout [wōk'-aut], *s.* (Fam. E. U.) Huelga de obreros.

Walkover [wōk'-o"-vẹr], *s.* Triunfo fácil, o sin oposición apreciable.

Wall [wōl], *s.* 1. Pared. 2. Muralla, muro, obra de albañilería para cercar, separar, etc. 3. Muralla de un recinto fortificado; a menudo en plural. 4. Banco de roca natural; tapia. 5. Lado de cualquier cavidad, costado de vasija o receptáculo. *Partition-wall*, Tabique. *To take the wall*, Tomarse la acera, tomarse el mejor puesto sin querer cederlo a otro. *Main wall*, Pared maestra. *To be driven to the wall*, Verse entre la espada y la pared. *To go to the wall*, Verse obligado a rendirse, verse en apuros. *Wall-creeper*, (Orn.) Pico murario. *Wall-fruit*, Fruta de espalera o espaldera. *Wall-louse*, Chinche. *Wall-paper*, Papel de entapizar. *Wall-pepper*, (Bot.) Siempreviva, hierba puntera, fabacrasa británica. *Wall-piece*, Pieza o pedrero, cañón de muralla. *Wall-rue*, (Bot.) Ruda muraria. *Wall-tree*, Espaldera.

Wall, *va.* 1. Emparedar, tapiar. 2. Murar, cercar o guarnecer con muros o murallas; fortificar, murar, cerrar, tapiar.

Wallaby [wel'-a-bi], *s.* Especie menor de canguró.

Wallet [wel'-et], *s.* 1. Cartera. de bolsillo. 2. Alforjas, mochila.

Wall-eyed [wēl'-aid], *a.* 1. (Med.) Que tiene los ojos divergentes o muy abiertos; lo opuesto a bizco. 2. (Ant.) Zarco, el que tiene los ojos de un color azul muy claro.

Wall-flower [wēl'-flau-ẹr], *s.* 1. (Bot.) Alelí doble, planta crucífera. 2. Mujer a la que nadie saca a bailar, que se queda sin pareja en un baile.

Wallop [wel'-up], *vn.* Bullir, hervir. —*va.* (Ger.) Zurrar, tundir, castigar a golpes.—*s.* Linternazo, porrazo.

Wallow [wel'-ō], *vn.* 1. Moverse con pesadez o poca gracia. 2. Encenagarse, meterse o revolcarse en el cieno o porquería. 3. Sumergirse o estar encenagado en algún vicio. *To wallow in riches*, Manar en riquezas. *To wallow in pleasures*, Vivir en medio de los placeres.

Wallow, *s.* Revuelco, el acto de revolcarse.

Wallower [wel'-o-ẹr], *s.* El o la que se revolca en el fango o lodo.

Wallowing-place [wel'-o-ing-plēs], *s.* Cenagal; revolcadero.

Wallwort [wēl'-wūrt], *s.* (Bot.) 1. Yezgo, sauquillo europeo. 2. Oreja de monje, parietaria oficinal o berro de roca.

Walnut [wēl'-nut], *s.* (Bot.) 1. Nuez, el fruto del nogal o la madera de este árbol. 2. Nogal, árbol alto de la familia de las juglándeas y cuyo fruto es la nuez.

Walrus [wel'-rus], *s.* Morsa, mamífero de gran tamaño parecido a la foca. Vive en los mares árticos.

Waltron [wēl'-trun], *s.* Caballo marino.

Waltz [wēlts o vālts], *vn.* Valsar, bailar el vals.—*s.* Vals, baile de origen alemán, con movimiento giratorio; música de este baile. (< Al. walzer.)

Waltzer [wēlts'-ẹr], *s.* El o la que valsa; valsador, valsadora.

Waly [wē'-li], *inter.* (Prov. Ingl. ¡Ay!

Wamble [wem'-bl], *vn.* (Prov. o des.) Nausear, padecer bascas, ansias, náuseas o ganas de vomitar.

Wame [wēm], *s.* (Esco.) Vientre matriz.

Wampum [wem'-pum], *s.* Cuentas formadas de las partes interiores de conchas y enhebradas, que servían en lo antiguo como dinero y como adorno a los indios americanos.

Wan [wen], *a.* Pálido, descolorido. *To grow wan*, Palidecer, ponerse pálido.

Wand [wend], *s.* 1. Vara, ramo delgado. 2. Vara, insignia de autoridad ó jurisdicción. 3. Varita de virtudes, vara de adivinar. *Mercury's wand*, Caduceo.

Wander [wen'-dẹr], *va.* y *vn.* 1. Errar, andar vagando, vagar, vaguear. 2. Rodar, andorrear, corretear, andar de una parte a otra sin objeto fijo. 3. Discurrir, andar o caminar por diversas partes y lugares. 4. Delirar. 5. Extraviarse; desviarse del asunto, p. ej. durante una discusión.

Wanderer [wen'-dẹr-ẹr], *s.* Tunante, vagamundo, andorrero, vago; errante, extraviado. *Wanderer from*, Persona que se aleja o desvía de; transgresor.

Wandering [wen'-dẹr-ing], *s.* 1. Viajes o paseos de unas partes a otras sin objeto determinado. 2. Extravío, pérdida del camino. 3. Habla errante e incoherente, como la del que delira.—*a.* 1. Errante, que anda errante. 2. Descaminado, descarriado; delirante. 3. Vagamundo.

Wane [wēn], *vn.* Menguar, disminuir; decaer, ir en decadencia.

Wane, Waning [wēn'-ing], *s.* Decadencia, decremento, declinación, caimiento. *Wane of the moon*, Menguante de la luna.

Wangle [wan'-gl], *vn.* (fam.) Sacudirse, extricarse (de alguna dificultad, etc.)—*va.* Engatusar, persuadir con artificios o engaños. *To wangle an invitation*, Obtener una invitación con artimañas.

Wanness [wen'-nes], *s.* Palidez; descaecimiento, languidez, falta de fuerzas.

Want [wēnt], *va.* 1. Necesitar, haber menester, tener necesidad de alguna cosa; estar desprovisto de. 2. Hacer falta, sentir la necesidad de. 3. Querer, desear, tener o sentir deseo. *What do you want?* ¿Qué quiere Vd.? 4. Dispensarse de, pasarse sin.—*vn.* 1. Estar necesitado, indigente. 2. Carecer, tener falta de algo. 3. Faltar, no existir alguna prenda, calidad o circunstancia. *Who wants to enter into difficulties?* ¿Quién quiere meterse en dificultades? *I shall want your assistance*, Necesitaré su ayuda de Vd. *You are wanted*, Tienen necesidad de Vd., por Vd. preguntan. *Wanted*, (término de anuncios) Se necesita. *I want you to do it*, Quiero que Vd. lo haga.

Want, *s.* 1. Necesidad, la falta de las cosas necesarias para la conservación de la vida; pobreza, indigencia, miseria. 2. Falta, privación o carencia de una cosa necesaria o útil. *To be in want*, Estar pobre o necesitado. 3. La cosa que se necesita; falta de una cosa que se quiere tener. *For want of*, Por falta de. *To die of want*, Morir de miseria.

Wantage [wēnt'-ẹj], *s.* Lo que falta; déficit.

Wanting [wēnt'-ing], *a.* Falto, defectuoso, necesitado, escaso. *To be wanting*, Faltar.

Wanton [wen'-tẹn], *a.* 1. Juguetón, retozón, de buen humor, travieso. 2. Extravagante. 3. No atado, suelto (flotante). 4. Lascivo, inclinado a la lascivia; libre, licencioso, atrevido, disoluto. 5. Falto de razón inexcusable, imperdonable; sin provocación.—*s.* 1. Hombre o mujer lasciva. 2. Persona frívola.

Wanton, *vn.* 1. Retozar, juguetear, entretenerse jugueteando y retozando. 2. Hacer picardías, por maldad. 3. Pasar el tiempo en liviandades.

Wantonly [wen'-ten-li], *adv.* 1. Alegremente, con retozos; de picardía; de pura maldad; por hacer mal; sólo por juguete. 2. Lascivamente, inmodestamente.

Wantonness [wen'-ten-nes], *s.* 1. Lascivia, impudicicia, deshonestidad. 2. Licencia, libertad inmoderada, descompostura, desgarro. 3. Juguete, entretenimiento, chanza, chacota.

Wantwit [wēnt'-wit], *s.* Idiota, tonto.

Wapentake [wap'-en-tēk], *s.* Nombre antiguo de los distritos en que para ciertos fines se dividían los condados en Inglaterra.

Wapiti [wep'-i-ti], *s.* Gran ciervo de la América del Norte.

War [wēr], *s.* 1. Guerra, hostilidad armada entre naciones o partidos opuestos. 2. El arte militar, la profesión de las armas. 3. Las armas que se usan para hacer la guerra. 4. (Poét. o des.) Ejércitos. 5. Oposición, contrariedad. *War-dance*, Danza de los salvajes antes de ir a la guerra o en celebración de una victoria. *War to the knife*, Guerra a muerte. *Articles of war*, Código militar o naval. *Man-of-war*, Navío, buque de guerra. *War Department*, Ministerio de la guerra. *War-cry*, Grito de guerra (de nación o partido). *War-whoop*, Grito de guerra (de los indios americanos). *Warworn*, Usado o gastado por la guerra; abrumado por la guerra; se aplica particularmente a un veterano.

War, *vn.* Guerrear, estar en guerra.

Warble [wēr'-bl], *va.* Cantar con quiebros y trinos, como un pájaro; trinar, gorjear. *To warble her praises*, Cantar sus alabanzas (de una mujer).—*vn.* 1. Trinar, hacer quiebros y trinos con la voz; trinar, gorjear (los pájaros). 2. Murmurar (un arroyo).—*s.* Canto, gorjeo.

Warbler [wēr'-blẹr], *s.* 1. Cantor o músico que hace trinos. 2. Curruca, silvia, pájaro; nombre dado a varios pájaros de escaso canto.

Warbling [wēr'-bling], *a.* Melodioso; (arroyo) de suave murmullo.—*s.* Canto armonioso de una persona; canto, gorjeo, de las aves.

Ward [wērd], *va.* 1. Guardar, defender, proteger, preservar. 2. Parar o detener un golpe. *To ward off*, Evitar, desviar el golpe.—*vn.* Vigilar, velar.

Ward, *s.* 1. Pupilo o menor en tutela. 2. Barrio, cuartel o distrito de alguna ciudad. 3. Sala, división de hospital, de cárcel, etc. 4. Pupilaje, tutela, tutoría. 5. Guarda, el acto de guardar o custodiar. 6. Guardas de llave o cerradura. 7. Defensa, el arma con que uno se defiende; posición defensiva, en la que está uno a cubierto de la espada del adversario. 8. Guarda, guardián, conserje.

Warden [wēr'-dn], *s.* 1. Custodio, guardián, el que guarda o custodia alguna cosa. 2. Alcaide de una cárcel o carcelero. 3. Conserje, el que tiene a su cuidado ciertos establecimientos; en Inglaterra, director de ciertos colegios. 4. En la Iglesia anglicana, cada uno de los dos mayordomos que cuidan de los asuntos de una parroquia. *V.* CHURCH-WARDENS y VESTRY. *The wardens and vestry,* Los mayordomos y la junta parroquial. 5. Una especie de pera. *Warden of the Cinque Ports,* El gobernador de los Cinco Puertos, un empleo muy honorífico en Inglaterra. *The warden of a port,* Capitán de un puerto. *Wardens,* Maestros o jurados en algún oficio.

Wardenship [wēr'-dn-ship], *s.* El oficio de guarda o custodio; conserjería; bedelía; alcaidía.

Warder [wērd'-ęr], *s.* Guarda, guardia.

Wardmote [wērd'-mōt], *s.* Junta de barrio o cuartel para la dirección y gobierno de sus asuntos.

Wardrobe [werd'-rōb], *s.* 1. Guardarropa. 2. Conjunto de ropa que posee una persona.

Wardroom [wērd'-rūm], *s.* Cuartel de oficiales.

Wardship [wērd'-ship], *s.* Tutela, tutoría, pupilaje.

Ware [wār], *s.* 1. Mercadería, mercancía, artículos de la misma clase; se emplea por lo común en palabras compuestas; v. gr. *tableware,* vajilla de mesa; *earthenware,* loza, vajilla de barro. 2. *pl.* Géneros que se venden, mercancías, artículos de comercio. *Hardware,* Quinquillería. *China ware,* Porcelana, loza fina. *Hollow ware,* Ollas, marmitas, y otros artículos de hierro para cocinar. *Small wares,* Artículos menudos; mercería, pasamanería.—*a.* (Ant.) WARY y AWARE.

Warehouse [wār'-haus], *s.* Almacén, el edificio donde se guardan por junto los géneros; (1) lugar para guardar los efectos que todavía no están listos para el mercado; (2) almacén donde se cuidan géneros mediante pago. *Bonded warehouse,* Depósito, sitio donde se depositan las mercancías que aun no han pagado los derechos de aduana. *Warehouse-keeper, warehouseman,* Guardaalmacén; almacenero. *Warehouse-rent,* Almacenaje.

Warehouse [wār'-hauz], *va.* Almacenar, poner en almacén.

Wareroom [wār'-rum], *s.* Pieza para el almacenaje o para la venta de géneros o mercancías.

Warfare [wēr'-fār], *s.* 1. Guerra, el arte y profesión militar. 2. La vida del soldado, servicio militar. 3. Lucha, combate.

Warhead [wēr'-hed], *s.* Punta de combate.

Warhorse [wēr'-hērs], *s.* 1. Caballo de guerra o a propósito para la guerra. 2. (Fam.) El que ha tenido larga experiencia, especialmente en la guerra o en la política; veterano.

Warily [wār'-i-li], *adv.* Cautamente, cautelosamente, astutamente, con astucia.

Wariness [wār'-i-nes], *s.* Cautela, precaución, previsión prudente.

Warlike [wēr'-laik], *a.* Guerrero, belicoso, militar.

Warlock [wēr'-lec], *s.* (Ant.) Brujo; también, duende.

Warm [wērm], *a.* 1. Caloroso o caluroso, cálido, pero que no llega al estado de caliente (*hot*). 2. Cálido, que tiene cierto grado de calor; expuesto al calor; que no tiene invierno. 3. Ardiente, acalorado, vivo, activo, caliente, furioso, violento, celoso, conforme sea la cosa a que se aplica. 4. Conmovido, arrebatado, apasionado. 5. Muy unido, encariñado, afectuoso. 6. (Bellas artes) Que tiene matices predominantes de rojo o amarillo. 7. Recién hecho; fresco (la pista de la caza). 8. Cercano al objeto buscado; se dice en los juegos de niños. 9. (Fam.) Molesto, fastidioso, peligroso. *A warm climate,* Un clima cálido. *A warm friend,* Un amigo cariñoso, abnegado. *A warm heart,* Un corazón ardiente, generoso. *A warm temper,* Un carácter vivo, ardiente. *Warm work,* Tarea difícil, dura. *To be warm,* Tener calor, y familiarmente, estar sudando. *It is warm,* Hace calor. *To keep warm,* Conservar caliente. *To get warm,* Calentar, calentarse; comenzar a hacer calor; animarse. *To make warm,* Calentar. *Lukewarm,* Tibio. *Warm-blooded,* (1) De sangre caliente; dícese de los mamíferos y las aves; (2) entusiasmado, ardiente, apasionado. *Warm-hearted,* De corazón ardiente, afectuoso; simpático.

Warm, *va.* 1. Calentar, comunicar el calor. 2. Calentar, avivar, encender, enfervorizar. *To warm over,* Volver a calentar; calentar lo que estaba frío.

Warming-pan [wērm'-ing-pan], *s.* Calentador.

Warmly [wērm'-li], *adv.* Con calor, ardientemente, con ardor, con eficacia, con empeño.

Warmness [wērm'-nes], **Warmth** [wērmth], *s.* 1. Calor moderado. 2. Celo, ardor, fervor, ardimiento, viveza. 3. Fantasía, entusiasmo. *Warmth of colouring,* (Pint.) Color de fuego claro; color vivo.

Warn [wērn], *va.* 1. Precaver, avisar, caucionar. 2. Advertir, aconsejar. 3. Avisar anticipadamente, prevenir; notificar a.

Warning [wērn'-ing], *s.* 1. Amonestación, advertencia, aviso, caución; escarmiento; ejemplo terrorífico. 2. Notificación de dejar el servicio, o de salir de una casa o tienda alquilada. *To take warning,* Estar atento, precaverse. *To give warning,* Prevenir, advertir, avisar o hacer saber anticipadamente alguna cosa.

Warp [wērp], *s.* 1. Torcedura, alabeo, el estado de lo torcido, alabeado, retorcido o deformado; prevención del ánimo. 2. Urdiembre, urdimbre, el conjunto de hilos ya ordenados y dispuestos para el telar. 3. Espía, calabrote entalingado, jarcia que se usa para espiar una embarcación. 4. Capa o sedimento aluvial que el agua deposita sobre las tierras bajas. 5. Cierta medida longitudinal de soga o cordel. *Warp-beam,* Enjullo, plegador, cilindro sobre el cual el tejedor va arrollando la tela. *Warp and woof,* Trama y urdimbre.

Warp, *va.* 1. Torcer, desviar, deformar como por encogimiento o por el calor. 2. Dar a algo una tendencia falsa, prevenir el ánimo; retorcer. 3. Urdir, formar de la urdimbre una madeja en el urdidor para pasarla al telar. 4. (Mar.) Remolcar; hacer mudar de posición a la embarcación.—*vn.* 1. Torcerse; alabearse (madera). 2. Desviarse, alejarse, apartarse del camino recto. 3. (Hiland.) Urdir, estirar o preparar el hilo. 4. (Mar.) Ir a remolque, moverse a remolque, espiarse.

Warrant [wer'-ant], *va.* 1. Garantir, garantizar la calidad o suficiencia de; asegurar, salir o constituirse fiador o garante. 2. Responder, poner a cubierto, defender, preservar de; sanear. *I warrant you,* (Fam.) Yo se lo fío a Vd., yo se lo aseguro. 3. Autorizar, dar autoridad. 4. Justificar, ser fundamento o razón suficiente para (una creencia, conclusión, etc.). 5. Asegurar, afirmar, certificar. *I warrant it good,* Se lo garantizo a Vd. como bueno. *Reason warrants it,* La razón lo justifica.

Warrant, *s.* 1. (For.) Auto o decreto de prisión. 2. Cualquier cédula, oficio, escritura, etc., que confiere algún privilegio o gracia especial o reviste a una persona de algún poder o autoridad; autorización, poder, documento justificativo; (Com.) certificado de depósito. 3. Autoridad o apoyo de lo que se dice; testimonio; sanción. 4. Justificación, apología, razón. *Special warrant,* Llámase así en Inglaterra al auto dado por un magistrado mandando a los oficiales de justicia que conduzcan presa a su presencia a la persona nombrada en él. *General warrant,* Auto dado para prender a todas las personas implicadas en un delito: este auto es ilegal en Inglaterra si no se especifican en él las personas que deben ser presas. *Death-warrant,* La orden que se da al *sheriff* para que haga ajusticiar a un reo. *Warrant-officers,* Oficiales subalternos de mar. *Land-warrant,* Cédula emitida por el gobierno declarando que el poseedor tiene título a la cantidad de terrenos públicos en ella especificada.

Warrantable [wer'-ant-a-bl], *a.* Que se puede abonar, garantizar, justificar o defender.

Warrantableness [wer'-ant-a-bl-nes], *s.* Justificación; certeza, seguridad.

Warrantably [wer'-ant-a-bli], *adv.* Justificadamente.

Warrantee [wer-an-tī'], *s.* (For.) Afianzado, el que recibe alguna garantía.

Warranter [wer'-ant-ęr], *s.* El que autoriza; garante, fiador, fianza.

Warrantor [wer'-an-tęr], *s.* (Der.) Garante, fiador; correlativo de *warrantee.*

Warranty [wer'-ant-i], *s.* 1. (For.) Garantía, la acción de afianzar y asegurar lo estipulado en un contrato cualquiera; garantía del vendedor. *A warranty clause,* Cláusula de evicción y saneamiento. 2. Seguridad. 3. Autoridad para ejecutar alguna cosa.

Warren [wer'-en], *s.* 1. Conejera, conejar, vivar de conejos, soto de conejos o el sitio destinado para criar conejos. 2. Cercado para guardar la caza menuda; depósito para el pescado en los ríos.

Warrior [wēr'-yer ó wer'-i-ęr], *s.* Guerrero, soldado.

Warst [wārst], *a. super* (Escoc.) *V.* WORST.

Wart [wērt], *s.* 1. Verruga, excrecencia cutánea. 2. (Bot.) Verruga, excrecencia de la superficie de una planta. 3. Excrecencia en la cuartilla de los caballos.

Wartwort [wērt'-wērt], *s.* (Bot.) Verrucaria.

Warty [wōrt'-ĭ], *a.* Verrugoso, que tiene muchas verrugas; de la naturaleza de las verrugas.

Wary [wār'-ĭ], *a.* 1. Cauto, cauteloso, prudente, avisado, precavido contra engaños o peligros, circunspecto. 2. Astuto, artificioso, sagaz, sutil.

Was [wez], *pret.* del verbo *To* BE.

Wash [wesh], *va.* 1. Lavar, limpiar con agua u otro flúido; blanquear la ropa sucia. 2. Bañar, regar o tocar el agua alguna cosa; cubrir con agua; también llevarse algo el agua. 3. Lavar, purificar, quitar algún defecto o mancha. 4. Recubrir de una capa delgada de metal. 5. Dar una mano ligera de color sobre una superficie.—*vn.* 1. Lavarse. 2. Lavar ropa. 3. Gastarse por la acción del agua. 4. Moverse, como el agua, suavemente de aquí para allá. *To wash one's face or hands,* Lavarse la cara o las manos. *To wash away, off* o *out,* Lavar, borrar, hacer desaparecer; quitar lavando. *To wash down,* Separar una cosa de otra lavándolas; hacer bajar, tragar. *To wash over,* Sumergir, inundar; dar de otro color o dar una mano de otro color en la pintura. *To wash a picture,* Bañar una pintura o dar una mano de color transparente sobre otra.

Wash, *s.* 1. Lavadura, lavación, loción, ablución; lavatorio, la acción de lavar; de aquí, el conjunto de ropa lavada de una vez. 2. Preparación o mezcla que se usa para dar una capa, bañar o salpicar; agua de tocador, cosmético; loción, preparación líquida para uso externo. 3. El romper del agua sobre la orilla; el ruido que hace el agua moviéndose. 4. Superficie bañada por el mar o un río; pantano. 5. Aluvión, depósito, materias depositadas por el agua. 6. Bazofia, lavazas. 7. Un licor que se extrae de la cebada germinada y fermentada para destilar. *Wash-ball,* Bola de jabón, jaboncillo de olor. *Wash-board,* (1) Tablilla de lavandera (con superficie corrugada); (2) faja de madera en la parte baja de las paredes; (3) (Mar.) falca, batemar. *Wash-bowl* (*wash-hand-basin*), Jofaina, palangana. *Wash-house,* Lavadero. *Wash-leather,* Gamuza o imitación de ella. *Wash-off,* Fugitivo, que se destiñe. *Wash-pot,* Bacía; particularmente, vasija en que se da la última capa de estaño. *Wash-stand,* Palanganero, lavabo, aguamanil. *Wash-tub,* Cuba, artesón de lavar. *Wash of an oar,* (Mar.) Pala de remo.

Washer [wesh'-ẹr], *s.* 1. Lavador, lavandero, lavandera; el o la que lava; máquina para lavar. 2. Volandera, círculo de hierro plano puesto en los ejes de las ruedas; disco de cuero u otro material que sirve para empaquetadura en una manguera, etc.

Washer-woman [wesh'-ẹr-wum-an], *s.* Lavandera.

Washing [wesh'-ing], *s.* Lavadura, loción, lavatorio; blanqueadura. *Washing-machine,* Máquina para lavar. *Washing-soda,* Sosa para blanquear, carbonato de sodio.

Washout [wesh'-aut], *s.* 1. Deslave, derrubio. 2. (fam.) Fracaso, desilusión.

Washy [wesh'-ĭ], *a.* 1. Húmedo, mojado. 2. Débil, falto de solidez.

Wasp [wesp], *s.* Avispa, insecto himenóptero armado de un aguijón. Las avispas típicas sociales fabrican nidos de papel; las avispas solitarias construyen celdas de lodo o arena.

Waspish [wesp'-ish], *a.* 1. Enojadizo, caprichudo, de mal humor, áspero de genio, irascible. 2. Que tiene talle o cintura de avispa.

Waspishly [wesp'-ish-lĭ], *adv.* Enojadamente, ásperamente, con mal rumor.

Waspishness [wesp'-ish-nes], *s.* Mal genio, mal humor, aspereza de genio, naturaleza irascible.

Wassail [wes'-ẹl o was'-el], *s.* 1. Bebida hecha con manzanas, azúcar y cerveza, muy usada antiguamente en Inglaterra. 2. Borrachera, reunión alegre en que se cometen excesos en la bebida; orgía.

Wassail-bowl [wes'-ẹl-bōl], *s.* Taza, cubilete.

Wassailer [wes'-ẹl-ẹr], *s.* Borrachón, gran bebedor.

Wast [west]. Segunda persona del singular del *pret.* de *ind.* de *To* BE.

Waste [wēst], *va.* 1. Malgastar, disipar, destruir, echar a perder. 2. Gastar, ir consumiendo alguna cosa; agotar, quitar las fuerzas, hacer perder el vigor. 3. (Ant.) Desolar, arruinar, asolar, talar.—*vn.* Gastarse, irse consumiendo alguna cosa; usarse, alterarse, dañarse. *To waste away,* Descaecer, ir a menos, perder poco a poco la salud, vigor, etc.; menguar, disminuirse, irse consumiendo poco a poco; echar a perder.

Waste, *a.* 1. Desechado, inútil, sin importancia práctica, sin valor. 2. Desierto, inculto. 3. Desolado, arruinado. 4. Superfluo, sobrante.—*s.* 1. Despilfarro, gasto inútil, acción de malgastar. 2. Disminución de las fuerzas o vigor; decadencia. 3. Restos, despojos, desperdicios. 4. Baldío, terreno inculto, desierto; de aquí, extensión, inmensidad. 5. Artefacto o aparato de desagüe o para remover los desperdicios. 6. Desperdicio; destrozo, asolamiento, destrucción, daño. *Waste-basket,* Cesto para papeles y desechos. *Waste paper,* Papel de desecho. *Waste-pipe,* Tubo de desagüe, desaguadero.

Waste-book [wēst'-buk], *s.* Borrador, libro de memoria.

Wasteful [wēst'-ful], *a.* 1. Manirroto, gastador, pródigo, disipador. 2. Destructivo, dañoso, ruinoso.

Wastefully [wēst'-ful-ĭ], *adv.* Pródigamente.

Wastefulness [wēst'-ful-nes], *s.* Prodigalidad; gasto inútil.

Waster [wēst'-ẹr], *s.* Disipador, gastador.

Wasting [wēst'-ing], *a.* Que usa, agota o consume.—*s.* Consunción, agotamiento; acción del verbo *waste,* en cualquier sentido; lo que se agota o consume.

Wastrel [wēs'-trel], *s.* 1. Desperdicios. 2. Terreno no cultivado, pastos comunes.

Wasty [wēst'-ĭ], *a.* 1. Desierto, inculto. 2. Desechado, sobrante, sin importancia práctica.

Watch [wech], *s.* 1. Vela, la acción de velar; cuidado, vigilancia, observación vigilante. 2. Desvelo, vigilia, estado de vela, falta de sueño. 3. Centinela; guardia, sereno, vigilante. 4. Vela, velación, el período de tiempo durante el cual está de guardia un sereno; de aquí, cierta división de la noche. 5. (Mar.) Cuarto, servicio que hace cada una de las dos divisiones de la tripulación con sus oficiales, para velar por la seguridad de una nave; la duración de cada vela es de cuatro horas. *Watch and ward,* Patrulla, ronda. *Watch-glass,* (1) Cristal de reloj. (2) (Mar.) Ampolleta de media hora. *Larboard watch,* (Mar.) Guardia de babor. *Starboard watch,* (Mar.) Guardia de estribor. *Dog-watch,* (Mar.) Segunda guardia. *Morning-watch,* (Mar.) Guardia de la madrugada. *To set the watch,* (Mar.) Rendir la guardia. *To spell the watch,* (Mar.) Llamar a la guardia. 6. Muestra, reloj de faltriquera. *Repeating-watch,* Reloj de repetición. *Lever watch,* Reloj de escape. *Hunting-case watch,* Saboneta (de doble caja). *Open-faced watch,* Muestra (de una sola caja). *Stop watch,* Reloj de segundos muertos. *My watch is too fast, too slow,* Mi reloj adelanta, atrasa. *To wind a watch,* Dar cuerda a un reloj. *Watch-case,* Caja de reloj, relojera. *Watch-guard,* Cadena o cinta de reloj. *Watch-spring,* Muelle de reloj. *Watch-stand,* Porta-reloj. *Watch-tower,* Atalaya, torre de observación; garita. *Watch-work,* El mecanismo de un reloj de bolsillo. *To be upon the watch,* Estar alerta, estar a quién vive.

Watch, *va.* y *vn.* 1. Velar, estar sin dormir. 2. Velar, hacer centinela o guardia. 3. Velar, observar o cuidar atentamente alguna cosa. 4. Guardar, custodiar. 5. Espiar, observar.

Watcher [wech'-ẹr], *s.* Velador, observador, espía.

Watchful [wech'-ful], *a.* Vigilante, cuidadoso.

Watchfully [wech'-ful-ĭ], *adv.* Cuidadosamente.

Watchfulness [wech'-ful-nes], *s.* Vigilancia, cuidado; desvelo, falta de sueño.

Watch-house [wech'-haus], *s.* El cuerpo de guardia de la policía.

Watching [wech'-ing], *s.* Vigilancia; desvelo, falta de sueño; vela, el acto de vigilar, velar, guardar o espiar.

Watchmaker [wech'-mē-kẹr], *s.* Relojero.

Watchman [wech'-man], *s.* Sereno, guarda, la persona destinada para decir por la noche en voz alta la hora que es, y para rondar, prevenir los robos y avisar en caso de incendio.

Watchword [wech'-wurd], *s.* (Mil.) Contraseña, santo y seña, consigna que se da a un centinela.

Water [wō'-tẹr], *s.* 1. Agua (H_2O). *Rain-water,* Agua llovediza. *Fresh-water,* Agua dulce. *Spring-water,* Agua de fuente o de manantial. *Holy water,* Agua bendita. *Well-water* o *pump-water,* Agua de pozo. *Running water,* Agua viva o corriente. *Salt water,* Agua del mar, agua salada. 2. Cualquier extensión determinada de agua; v. gr. un lago, un río, un mar. *To go by water,* Ir por mar. *High water,* Marea alta. *Low water,* Marea baja. 3. Serosidad o humor de los animales; transpiración, lágrimas u orina. 4. Agua, preparación acuosa que tiene una substancia gaseosa o volátil en solución. *Ammonia water,* Agua amoniacal. *Chlorine water,* Agua de cloro. *Orange-flower water*, Agua de azahar. 5. Aguas, los visos que hacen las piedras preciosas. 6. Viso ondeante de los tejidos. 7. (Com.) Acciones que se emiten sin aumento del capital pagado para representarlas. *Smooth water*, Agua mansa, agua tranquila. *Still waters run deep*, (prov.) Del agua mansa líbreme Dios, que de la recia (*or* brava) me guardaré yo. *To swim under water*, Nadar entre dos aguas. *Water* se usa en inglés muy á menudo en composición para expresar lo que sirve para contener agua, y lo que está o crece en ella, etc. *Water-back*, Sistema de tubos en una estufa para la circulación de agua caliente. *Water-bath*, Baño de María. *Water-bird*, Ave acuática. *Water-boatman*, *water-bug*, Chinche de agua, insecto hemíptero que nada sobre su espaldar. *Water-borne*, Flotante, que flota o camina sobre el agua. *Water-brash*, Pirosis, sensación picante que va del estómago a la boca. *Water-butt*, *water-cask*, Vasija de agua, pipa. *Water-carriage*, (1) Transporte por agua. (2) Transporte del agua por medio de cañerías, etc. *Water-closet*, Letrina a la inglesa; retrete excusado. *Water-colours*, (Pint.) Aguadas, colores líquidos de que se usa en la pintura al temple; acuarela. *Painting in water-colours*, Pintura a la aguada o lo que se pinta con colores líquidos. *Water-course*, (1) Corriente de agua; río, arroyo. (2) Madre, lecho de un río o arroyo. (3) Derecho de aguas. *Water-cure*, (1) Hidroterapia, tratamiento de ciertas enfermedades por medio del agua. (2) Establecimiento de hidroterapia. *Water-dog*, (1) Perro de aguas. (2) (Fam.) Marinero viejo. *Water-engine*, Máquina hidráulica. *Water-gage*, *water-gauge*, Indicador de nivel de agua. *Water-gilding*, Loradura. *Water-gruel*, Una especie de polenta hecha con harina de avena mondada y cocida en agua. *Water-hammer*, Sacudimiento que hace el agua cuando se detiene su corriente de un modo repentino; también, martillo de agua (juguete). *Water-ice*, Sorbete; helado hecho con algún zumo de fruta sabrosa, azúcar y agua solamente. *Water-level*, Nivel de agua; instrumento para hacer las nivelaciones. *Water-lily*, (Bot.) Ninfea, nenúfar; cualquiera planta del género Castalia. *Yellow water-lily*, Nenúfar amarillo, lirio amarillo de agua. *Water-line*, (Mar.) Línea de agua, línea de flotación. *Load-water-line*, (Mar.) Línea de agua cargada. *Water-logged*, (Mar.) Anegado en agua. *Water-mark*, (1) La señal que se hace para saber a donde llega el agua. (2) Filigrana, marca translúcida hecha en el papel al tiempo de fabricarlo. *Water-mill*, Aceña, molino de agua. *Water-mint*, (Bot.) Hierbabuena acuática. *Water-mite*, Cresa de agua, pequeño insecto acuático de patas ciliadas que le permiten nadar. *Water-pail*, Cubo. *Water-pot*, Aguamanil; jarro para servir el agua; regadera. *Water-pitcher*, (1) Aguamanil, cántaro para agua. (2) (Bot.) Cualquier planta de la familia americana de las sarracenáceas. *Water-plantain*, Alisma. *Water-power*, (1) Fuerza motriz del agua aplicada a la maquinaria. (2) Caída o descenso en una corriente, de la cual puede obtenerse fuerza motriz. *Water-proof*, *a.* Impermeable, a prueba de agua.—*va.* Hacer impermeable.—*s.* Material impermeable; capote u otra prenda de vestir hecha de ese material. *Water-trough*, Abrevadero. *Water-tank*, Aljibe, cisterna, receptáculo para el agua. *Water-tower*, (1) Tubo de alimentación, el que sirve para la distribución del agua. (2) Armazón de acero semejante a una torre para sostener una manguera con la cual se hace llegar el agua a lo alto de los edificios. *Water-wheel*, Rueda hidráulica. *Water-ouzel* [ū'-zl], Cinclo de agua, pájaro. *Water-rail*, Rascón, ave zancuda. *Water-rate*, Costo del abono á las aguas de una ciudad. *Water-scorpion*, Escorpión de agua, nepa, insecto hemíptero. *Water-shed*, Vertiente de una montaña; línea divisoria de las aguas. *Water-side*, Borde u orilla de agua. *Water-soak*, *va.* Meter, empapar en agua. *Water-spaniel*, Perro fino de aguas. *Water-tight*, Impermeable, que no deja pasar el agua. *Water-rat*, Rata de agua. *Water-sail*, (Mar.) Vela de agua. *Water-sapphire*, Zafiro oriental. *Water-spring*, Manantial. *Water-way*, *s.* (1) Canal o corriente de agua como medio de comunicación. (2) *pl.* (Mar.) Trancaniles, canalones. *Water-worn*, Gastado, hecho liso por la acción del agua.

Water, *va.* Regar, humedecer, mojar, bañar. *To water cattle*, Abrevar, dar de beber al ganado. *To water ships*, (Mar.) Hacer aguada. *To water wine*, Aguar o bautizar el vino.—*vn.* Chorrear agua o humedad. *His mouth waters*, Le da dentera, se le hace agua la boca.

Water-cooled [wō'-tẹr-cūld], *a.* Enfriado por agua.

Water-cress [wō'-tẹr-cres'], *s.* (Bot.) Berro, planta crucífera comestible.

Waterfall [wō'-tẹr-fōl], *s.* Cascada, caída de agua.

Water-fowl [wō'-tẹr-faul], *s.* (Orn.) Ave acuática.

Water front [we'-tẹr frunt], *s.* Parte de la ciudad que da al mar, lago, etc.

Water glass [wō-tẹr glas], *s.* 1. Vaso para beber agua. 2. Nivel de agua. 3. Clepsidra.

Water heater [wō'-tẹr hīt'-er], *s.* Calentador de agua.

Watering [wō'-tẹr-ing], *s.* 1. Riego; acción del que riega, moja o abreva; irrigación. 2. (Mar.) Acción de hacer agua; aguada. 3. El hacer ondulaciones o visos ondeantes en algo, como adorno.

Watering-place [wō'-tẹr-ing-plês], *s.* 1. Aguadero o abrevadero. 2. El pueblo o paraje, ordinariamente a la orilla del mar, a donde concurre mucha gente a tomar baños y divertirse. 3. (Mar.) El lugar donde se hace aguada.

Watering-pot [wō'-tẹr-ing-pot], *s.* Regadera.

Watermelon [wō'-tẹr-mel'-un], *s.* (Bot.) Sandía, planta y su fruto. (S. Am.) Patilla.

Water meter [wō'-tẹr mī'-tẹr], *s.* Contador de agua.

Water ski [we-tẹr skī], *s.* Esquí acuático.

Water softener [wō'-tẹr sōf'-n-ẹr], *s.* Suavizador o adelgazador de agua.

Water-spout [wō'-tẹr-spaut], *s.* Manga, bomba marina, torbellino de agua.

Water tower [wō-tẹr tau'-er], *s.* Depósito elevado de agua.

Water wave [wō'-tẹr wêv], *s.* Ondulado al agua. Aplícase al cabello.

Water-work [wō'-tẹr-wūrk], *s.* 1. Cualquier máquina o artificio hidráulico, como cascadas, surtidores o chorros de agua que saltan, etc. 2. *pl.* Obras hidráulicas, sistema de máquinas, edificios y enseres para la distribución de las aguas.

Watery [wō'-tẹr-i], *a.* 1. Acuoso, ácueo, aguanoso; húmedo, lleno de agua. 2. Claro, ralo o líquido como agua. 3. Insípido, evaporado. 4. Lloroso.

Watt [wet], *s.* Vatio, cantidad de trabajo eléctrico equivalente a un julio por segundo; grado en que la fuerza electro-motriz es de un voltio, y la intensidad de la corriente un amperio.

Wattage [wet'-ej], *s.* Potencia en vatios.

Watt-hour [wet-aur], *s.* Vatio-hora.

Wattle [wet'-l], *s.* 1. Zarzo, el tejido de varas, cañas o mimbres. 2. Barbas de gallo, la excrecencia de carne roja que les cuelga a los gallos debajo del pico.

Wattle, *va.* Enzarzar, poner zarzas o cubrir algo con ellas; entretejer, entrelazar; asegurar con mimbres.

Wave [wêv], *s.* 1. Ola, onda. 2. Aguas, visos, vetas o desigualdades que forman algunas piedras, cristales, etc. *Beating of the waves*, Embate del agua o de las olas. *Shock of a wave*, Golpe de mar. 3. (Fís.) Onda, undulación, alteración del equilibrio de un cuerpo o de un medio, que se propaga de uno a otro punto con movimiento continuo. *Sound-wave*, *light-wave*, Onda del sonido, de la luz. 4. Undulación, movimiento semejante al de las ondas; movimiento de la mano, ademán. 5. Ola, lo que sobreviene a manera de oleaje, en gran volumen o con mucha fuerza; diluvio. 6. Apariencia ondulante en una tela. 7. Comba, curva que se halla en una superficie o canto ondulante. *Wave-offering*, Ofrenda de las primicias entre los judíos.

Wave, *va.* y *vn.* 1. Tremolar, batir, hablando de banderas, gallardetes, etc. 2. Agitar alguna cosa de modo que forme ondas. 3. Ondear, hacer ondas el agua. 4. Ondear, hacer que una cosa tenga la figura o el movimiento de las ondas. 5. Fluctuar o vacilar entre dos cosas o pareceres opuestos. 6. Blandir, mover alguna cosa con un movimiento trémulo. 7. Hacer señas.

Waved [wêvd], *a.* Ondeado.

Wavelength [wêv'-length], *s.* (Radio) Longitud de onda.

Waver [wê'-vẹr], *vn.* 1. Ondear, ondearse. 2. Fluctuar, vacilar, balancear, dudar, estar suspenso, estar perplejo o indeciso.

Wavering [wê'-vẹr-ing], *a.* Ligero, inconstante.—*s.* Irresolución, incertidumbre, vacilación.

Wavy [wê'-vi], *a.* Ondeado, undoso, que hace ondas o que se levanta a manera de ondas.

Wax [wacs], *s.* 1. Cera, substancia crasa que segregan las abejas. 2. Cera de los oídos. 3. Cera vegetal o mineral. 4. Lacre. *Wax-candle*, Vela de cera; cirio, bujía. *Wax-taper*, Blandón, hacha de cera. *Wax-tape*, Cerilla. (Amer.) Cerillo. *Wax in* *large cakes*, Cera en marquetas. *Wax-chandler*, Cerero. *Sealing-wax*, Lacre. *Ear-wax*, Cera de los oídos. *Shoemaker's wax*, Cerote de zapatero. *Maple-wax*, (E. U. y el Canadá) Substancia espesa que se obtiene cociendo la savia del arce sacarino. *Wax doll*, Muñeca de cera. *Wax-end*, Hilo encerado para coser calzado. Se escribe también *waxed end*. *Wax light*, Vela de cera; cerilla. *Wax-like*, Semejante a la cera. *Wax model(l)ing*, Modelado en cera.

Wax, *va.* Encerar, dar con cera alguna cosa.—*vn.* 1. Crecer, aumentarse. 2. Cundir; hacerse; ponerse, irse haciendo. *To wax warm*, Acalorarse, encenderse en cólera. *This opinion is waxing stronger every day*, Esta opinión se va haciendo más fuerte de día en día.

Waxen [wac'-sn], *a.* De cera; que consta totalmente o en parte de cera; semejante a la cera; plástico.

Wax paper [wacs pê'-pęr], *s.* Papel encerado.

Waxwing [wax'-wing], *s.* Pájaro con cresta y de plumaje pardo en su mayor parte, con los extremos de las plumas secundarias del ala guarnecidos de apéndices córneos parecidos a lacre encarnado o amarillo; picotera. Ampelis.

Waxwork [wax'-wũrk], *s.* Obra en cera; figura de cera.—*pl.* Colección de figuras de cera.

Waxy [wac'-si], *a.* 1. Semejante a cera; plástico, blando, que cede. 2. De color de cera. 3. Hecho de cera o abundante en ella; frotado o pulido con cera.

Way [wê], *s.* 1. Camino, vía, la tierra hollada por donde se transita; camino, senda, conducto, según sea la cosa de que se habla; pasaje, curso, canal; lugar para pasar; oportunidad para pasar, para ir o para venir. 2. Espacio recorrido; de aquí, espacio de terreno. 3. Curso o dirección; ruta, rota, derrota, camino de viaje. 4. Modo, medio o manera para hacer una cosa; expediente. 5. Uso, costumbre, hábito; máxima. 6. Conducta o modo de obrar; sistema, línea de conducta; manera de portarse. 7. Medio, medida, acto. 8. Modo, punto o relación. *He erred in two ways*, Erró de dos modos. 9. Paso de un lugar a otro; movimiento progresivo; adelantamiento. 10. *pl.* (Mec.) Maderos longitudinales de la basada para botar al agua un buque. 11. (Fam.) Estado o condición (de salud). 12. Estorbo, obstáculo. *Am I in your way?* ¿Estorbo a Vd.? ¿Sirvo a Vd. de estorbo? *Over the way* ó *Across the way*, A otro lado, en el otro lado, en frente. *Every way*, Por todas partes, de todos lados. *By the way*, De paso, de camino, de pasada, por incidencia. *Any way*, De cualquier modo, de cualquiera manera, como se quiera. *No way*, De ningún modo, de ninguna manera. *Crossway*, Travesía. *Pathway*, Senda, sendero. *Way in*, Entrada. *Way through*, Pasaje. *Way out*, Salida. *We are a great way off*, Estamos aún muy lejos o estamos muy distantes. *To go the same way*, Llevar el mismo camino. *To make way*, Atravesar, abrirse camino. *Make way!* ¡Fuera, fuera! apartarse, dejen Vds. pasar. *To go out of the way*, Extraviarse. *To keep out of the way*, Esconderse, ocultarse, evitar el encontrarse con alguno. *To have one's way*, (Fam.) Salirse con la suya. *Use your own way*, Hágalo Vd. como quiera o hágalo Vd. a su modo. *Go your ways*, Anda, vete. *Ways and means*, Medios y arbitrios. *To get under way*, (Mar.) Levar, comenzar a navegar, hacerse a la vela. *To fetch way*, (Mar.) Tener juego. *Ship's way*, (Mar.) Andar del bajel. *The ship has head-way*, (Mar.) El navío lleva vía. *To have stern-way*, (Mar.) Ir atrás. *Covered ó covert way*, (Fort.) Camino cubierto. *Cross way*, Encrucijada. *Milky way*, Vía láctea; camino de Santiago. *On the way*, En ruta, al pasar. *By way of*, Por la vía de, pasando por. *By the way*, De camino, al pasar por; sea dicho de paso. *On the way to*, En camino de, con rumbo a. *Out of the way*, Fuera del camino; escondido; poco ordinario, extraordinario, original. *To be out of the way*, Estar fuera del camino, desviarse. *You are out of the way*, Vd. no está en el buen camino. *To be in the way*, Estar en el camino o en la vía; incomodar, servir de estorbo. *To go the way of all things*, Ir donde todo va. *To go the way of all the earth*, Morir. *Right of way*, Derecho de paso por la propiedad de otro, servidumbre de paso.

Wayfarer [wê'-fãr-ęr], **Wayfaring-man** [wê'-fãr-ing-man], *s.* Pasajero, viajador, viajante, caminante.

Wayfaring [wê'-fãr-ing], *a.* Que camina, que va de viaje o de camino.

Waylay [wê-lê'], *va.* Insidiar, poner asechanzas o celadas, acechar o asechar.

Waylayer [wê-lê'-ęr], *s.* Acechador, espía.

Wayless [wê'-les], *a.* Sin sendero, vereda ni vestigio, sin camino.

Waymark [wê'-mārk], *s.* Mojón, poste para señalar el camino.

Way station [wê' stê'-shun], *s.* (F.C.) Estación intermedia.

Way train [wê' trên], *s.* (F.C.) Tren local.

Wayward [wê'-ward], *a.* 1. Díscolo, indócil, cabezudo, porfiado; que se aparta de la conducta debida. 2. Que no tiene curso definido, vacilante.

Waywardly [wê'-ward-li], *adv.* Porfiadamente, con indocilidad, con perversidad; malamente.

Waywardness [wê'-ward-nes], *s.* Indocilidad, perversidad; capricho, petulancia; malignidad, ruindad.

We [wî], *pron. prim. pers. pl.* de *I*. 1. Nosotros, nosotras. *We are all well*, Todos estamos buenos. *We are right*, Tenemos razón, hacemos bien en. 2. La gente en general, la especie humana; se expresa a menudo en español por el pronombre se. *We are told*, Se nos dice, nos dicen. 3. El escritor u orador.

Weak [wîc], *a.* 1. Débil, endeble, flojo, flaco, feble, tanto en lo físico como en lo moral. 2. Frágil, débil, sujeto a errar o pecar; falto de juicio o prudencia. 3. Deficiente en fuerza, estabilidad o eficacia (instrumento, estructura, parte); incapaz de sostener un ataque a viva fuerza; mal fortificado; sin recursos; no convincente; no apoyado en la razón, en la verdad; que no contiene bastantes principios activos, estimulantes, nutritivos; ligero. 4. Enfermizo, enclenque. 5. Imbécil. 6. Flojo de precio, cuyo precio va bajando. *The wheat market is weak*, El mercado de trigo está flojo, o en baja. 7. (Gram. ingl.) (Verbo) regular; que se conjuga añadiendo *ed*, *d*, o *t*, para formar el pretérito y el participio pasado; que forma el plural, añadiendo *s* o *es* al singular; (adjetivo) de comparación regular. *Weak-handed*, Que tiene escasos ayudantes; también, que tiene las manos débiles. *Weak-headed*, Débil o pobre de inteligencia. *Weak-kneed*, Que tiene las rodillas débiles; (fig.) falto de resolución, de energía. *Weak-minded*, Débil de espíritu, pobre de inteligencia; simple, mentecato. *Weak side*, El flaco, la flaqueza, la debilidad, fragilidad o falta principal por donde una persona claudica, y también la pasión que la domina; el lado débil.

Weaken [wî'-cn], *va.* 1. Debilitar, enflaquecer, quitar o disminuir las fuerzas. 2. Disminuir, atenuar.—*vn.* Enflaquecer, hacerse menos fuerte.

Weakfish [wîk'-fish], *s.* Pez americano, llamado así por lo delicado de su boca. Cynoscion.

Weakling [wîc'-ling], *s.* Alfeñique, persona delicada de cuerpo y complexión.

Weakly [wîc'-li], *adv.* Débilmente, sin vigor, sin fuerzas; fríamente.—*a.* Enfermizo, achacoso, enclenque.

Weakness [wîc'-nes], *s.* 1. Debilidad, falta de vigor y fuerzas, flaqueza, endeblez, flojedad. 2. Fragilidad, debilidad, considerada moralmente; el flaco o la parte flaca de una persona. 3. Imbecilidad, mentecatez.

Weal [wîl], *s.* 1. Felicidad, prosperidad, bien, bienestar. 2. Estado, república, interés público; hoy se usa sólo en ciertas locuciones.

Weald [wîld], *s.* Bosque. *V.* WOLD.

Wealth [welth], *s.* 1. Riqueza, abundancia de dinero, bienes o cosas preciosas; caudal. 2. Prosperidad; opulencia; gran abundancia.

Wealthily [welth'-i-li], *adv.* Ricamente, opulentamente.

Wealthy [welth'-i], *a.* Rico, opulento. *Wealthier*, Más rico.

Wean [wîn], *va.* 1. Destetar, apartar del pecho de la madre. 2. Apartar de algún vicio o costumbre anterior; enajenar el afecto de. *The child is being weaned*, Se está destetando al niño.

Weanling [wîn'-ling], *s.* Niño o animal recién destetado; desteto, hablando del ganado.

Weapon [wep'-n], *s.* 1. Arma; todo género de instrumento destinado para atacar y ofender. 2. *pl.* (Biol.) Púas, espinas; aguijones, garras, etc.; todos los medios de defensa de los vegetales y animales. *Deadly weapon*, Arma mortífera. *Cutting weapon*, Arma de corte, arma blanca.

Weaponed [wep'-nd], *a.* Armado, surtido de armas.

Weaponless [wep'-n-les], *a.* Desarmado, que no lleva armas.

Weaponry [we'-pen-ri], *s.* Armamentos, armas, arsenal.

Wear [wãr], *va.* (*pret.* WORE, *pp.* WORN). 1. Usar, llevar ó traer alguna cosa encima del cuerpo. 2. Mostrar, llevar usualmente, de una manera determinada. 3. Mostrar, tener aspecto o apariencia de, exhibir. 4. Gastar o consumir la cosa de que uno se sirve; consumir aniquilando o destruyendo lentamente, como lo hace el tiempo, el uso, etc.; disminuir por el roce. 5. Consumir gastando el tiempo. 6. Apurar, hacer perder la fuerza o paciencia; aburrir, enfadar.—*vn.* 1. Gastarse, consumirse o destruirse lentamente una cosa. 2. Pasarse, correr el tiempo. *To wear away*, Gastar o ir gastando, consumiendo o destruyendo; decaer; gastarse, consumirse. *To wear down*, Gastar, consumir, disminuir por el roce. *To wear off*, Usarse, gastarse; borrarse; pasarse, disiparse, desaparecer. *To wear on*, Pasarse lentamente. *To wear one's heart on one's sleeve*, Andar con la cara descubierta, llevar el corazón en la mano. *To wear out*, Gastar, romper o romperse a fuerza de uso; cansar, fastidiar. *To wear out one's patience*, Hacer perder la paciencia. *Worn to a thread, worn threadbare*, Gastado hasta dejar ver la trama; enteramente gastado. *To wear a youthful form*, Tener aspecto juvenil. *To wear a tall hat*, Llevar sombrero de copa, o de copa alta. *Worn-out clothes*, Vestidos usados. *To wear well*, Durar largo tiempo, ser duradero, estar bueno para usarse.

Wear, *va.* y *vn.* (Mar.) Virar; virar viento atrás. (Por VEER.)

Wear, *s.* 1. Uso, gasto, la acción y efecto de usar alguna cosa; acción de llevar, estado de lo llevado. 2. La cosa que se usa o gasta; moda, boga. *It is for my own wear*, Es para mi propio uso. *Very little the worse for wear*, Casi nuevo, casi sin usar. *Wear and tear*, Desgaste, deterioro. *Silk for summer wear*, Seda para verano.

Wear [wīr], *s.* *V.* WEIR.

Wearable [wār'-a-bl], *a.* Que se puede llevar, usar o gastar.

Wearer [wār'-er], *s.* El que lleva, gasta o usa alguna cosa.

Wearied [wī'-rid], *a.* Cansado, fatigado, enfadado, fastidiado.

Weariness [wī'-ri-nes], *s.* 1. Lasitud, cansancio, fatiga. 2. Enfado, fastidio.

Wearing [wār'-ing], *s.* 1. Acción o manera de llevar. 2. Desgaste, deterioro; pérdida (por el roce o por el tiempo). 3. Decaimiento, paso.—*a.* Que se lleva. *Wearing apparel*, Vestidos, ropaje, ropa exterior.

Wearisome [wī'-ri-sum], *a.* Tedioso, fastidioso, pesado, enfadoso; fatigante, cansado.

Weary [wī'-ri], *va.* Cansar, fatigar, aburrir, enfadar, molestar.—*vn.* Fatigarse, cansarse. *To weary out*, Moler, cansar la paciencia, fatigar.

Weary, *a.* 1. Cansado, abrumado, fatigado, rendido de cansancio. 2. Aburrido, enfadado, fastidiado. 3. Enfadoso, tedioso, fastidioso.

Weasel [wī'-zl], *s.* Comadreja, mamífero carnívoro del género Putorius.

Weather [wedh'-er], *s.* 1. Tiempo, estado atmosférico en una época dada, o en general. 2. (Fig.) Vicisitudes de la suerte. 3. Temporal, tempestad; el conjunto o uno cualquiera de los fenómenos meteorológicos ordinarios; frío, calor. *How is the weather to-day?* ¿Qué tiempo hace hoy? *It is bad weather, fine weather*, Hace mal tiempo, buen tiempo. *Weather Bureau*, Oficina de Señales Meteorológicas (en el Ministerio de Agricultura de Washington). *Weather-board*, (1) Tabla superpuesta; (2) lado del viento (de un buque). *Weather-boarding*, Solapadura de tablas; (Mar.) falcas, cubichete. *Weather-bound*, Detenido por el mal tiempo. *Weather-gauge*, Barlovento o lof; cualquier ventaja lograda. *Weather-proof*, A prueba del tiempo. *Weather-prophet*, Pronosticador de las mudanzas del tiempo. *Weather-signal*, Señal meteorológica (bandera, etc.), que se emplea para indicar las variaciones del tiempo. *Weather-tight*, A prueba de aire, impenetrable al aire. *Weather-side*, (Mar.) Costado de barlovento. *Weather-boards*, (Mar.) Falcas. *Weather-shore*, (Mar.) Costa de barlovento. *Weather-sheets*, (Mar.) Escotas de barlovento. *Hard a-weather*, Meter todo a barlovento. *Stress of weather*, Mal tiempo.—*a.* Al viento del lado del viento.

Weather, *va.* 1. Aguantar (el temporal), resistir a, sufrir, superar; sobrevivir á (la adversidad). 2. Orear, airear, poner alguna cosa á que le dé el aire; secar. 3. (Mar.) Montar o ganar barlovento; doblar, pasar más allá.—*vn.* 1. Sufrir cambios resultantes de la exposición al aire. 2. Resistir los efectos de los cambios atmosféricos. *To weather out*, Sufrir, superar. *The poor fellow weathers it out*, El pobre va tirando. *To weather a point*, Salirse con algo o conseguir una cosa venciendo algún obstáculo.

Weather-beaten [wedh'-er-bī-tn], *a.* Curtido, acostumbrado a las inclemencias del aire; gastado, extenuado, fatigado (por el mal tiempo). *A weather-beaten* o *weather-driven ship*, Bajel trabajado por la tormenta.

Weather-cock [wedh'-er-cec], *s.* 1. Gallo de campanario, la figura de gallo que sirve de remate a las veletas de las torres, o que forma por sí misma la veleta y señala la parte por donde viene el viento. 2. Veleta, persona inconstante, fácil o mudable. *Weather-eye*, Observación de las variaciones del tiempo; se usa principalmente en la locución *to keep one's weather-eye open*, estar alerta, ser circunspecto. *Weather-glass*, Una forma de barómetro. *Poor man's weather-glass*, (Bot.) Anagálida, hierba pajarera, cuyas flores no se abren en mal tiempo.

Weather forecast [wedh'-er fōr'-cast], *s.* Pronóstico del tiempo.

Weathering [wedh'-er-ing], *s.* (Geol.) Desgaste de las rocas por la acción atmosférica.

Weatherly [wedh'-er-li], *a.* (Mar.) Que va de bolina, de barlovento.

Weather report [wedh'-er re-pōrt'], *s.* Informe meteorológico.

Weather-strip [wedh'-er-strip], *s.* Burlete.—*va.* Acondicionar con burlete.

Weathertile [wedh'-er-tail], *va.* Poner tejas en la extremidad de una tapia o pared para resguardarla del tiempo.

Weather-vane [wedh'-er-vēn], *s.* Veleta de torre, de campanario, etc.

Weave [wīv], *va.* 1. Tejer; trenzar; cruzar una cosa con otra tejiéndolas. 2. Unir, reunir. 3. Entrelazar, interponer; construir con elaboración.—*vn.* Tejer, trabajar en telar.

Weaver [wīv'-er], *s.* 1. Tejedor, el artesano que teje telas, sean de seda o lana, etc. 2. *V. Weaver-bird.* 3. Araña tejedora. *Weaver-bird*, Tejedor, pájaro parecido a un pinzón, que construye nidos entrelazados. Vive en las regiones cálidas del Asia, Africa y Australia.

Weaving [wīv'-ing], *s.* Tejido, el arte y modo de tejer.

Weazen, Weazened [wī'-znd], *a.* *V.* WIZEN.

Web [web], *s.* 1. Tela, tejido, obra tejida. 2. Hoja o rollo de material, formados como una tela. 3. Trama, lazo; artificio engañoso, trampa. 4. Palmura, membrana que une los dedos de los palmípedos. 5. Tela de araña. 6. Barba o pelo de pluma. 7. Plancha (de metal) que une las partes de alguna cosa. *Cob-web*, Telaraña.

Webbed [webd], *a.* 1. Lo que está unido por medio de una telilla. 2. Palmípedo.

Webbing [web'-ing], *s.* 1. Cinta para cinchas. 2. Pretal.

Web-footed [web'-fut-ed], *a.* Palmeado, palmípedo.

Wed [wed], *va.* 1. Casar; tomar por marido o por mujer. 2. Dar en casamiento. 3. Unirse para siempre á, o emprender una cosa con intención de no dejarla nunca.—*vn.* Casarse, contraer matrimonio.

Wedded [wed'-ed], *pp.* Casado. *Wedded to his own opinion*, Testarudo, encasquetado, casado con su opinión.

Wedding [wed'-ing], *s.* 1. Boda, nupcias, casamiento, la celebración del matrimonio. 2. Aniversario de boda. *Silver wedding*, Las bodas de plata, el aniversario vigésimo quinto de la boda. *Golden wedding*, Bodas de oro, el aniversario quincuagésimo de la boda. *Wedding dress*, Traje nupcial, o de boda. *Wedding ring*, Anillo nupcial (de novio o novia).

Wedding cake [wed'-ing kēk], *s.* Pastel o torta de boda.

Wedge [wej], *s.* 1. Cuña para partir leña o abrir otros cuerpos duros, y cualquier otro cuerpo que tiene su figura. 2. (Geom.) Prisma triangular.

Wedge, *va.* 1. Acuñar, meter cuñas para rajar fácilmente alguna cosa. 2. Apretar, abrir o fijar con cuñas.

Wedlock [wed'-lec], *s.* Matrimonio, himeneo; poéticamente connubio.

Wednesday [wenz'-dê], *s.* Miércoles, el cuarto día de la semana. *Ash-Wednesday*, Miércoles de ceniza. *Wednesday morning*, El miércoles por la mañana.

Wee, *a.* (Fam. y esco.) Pequeño, chico.

Weed [wīd], *s.* 1. Hierbajo, mala hierba, cualquiera hierba nociva o inútil; también toda planta herbácea que se halla fuera de su propio lugar. 2. Lo que crece en abundancia dañosa o inútil. 3. (Fam.) Tabaco. 4. Prenda (de vestir) o ropa de luto. *Sea-weed*, Alga. *Widow's-weeds*, El vestido y los velos de luto de una viuda.

Weed, *va.* 1. Escardar, desarraigar ó arrancar las hierbas nocivas o inútiles. 2. Escardar, apartar lo malo de lo bueno. 3. Librar de alguna cosa ofensiva o dañosa.

Weed-ashes [wīd'-ash-ez], *s. pl.* Ceniza; potasa.

Weeder [wīd'-ẹr], *s.* 1. Escardador. 2. El que libra o separa de alguna cosa ofensiva o dañosa.

Weedhook [wīd'-huc], *s.* Escarda, azadilla con que se arrancan las hierbas nocivas.

Weedless [wīd'-les], *a.* Libre de malas hierbas o hierbajos.

Weedy [wīd'-i], *a.* Lleno de malas hierbas, por escardar.

Week [wīk], *s.* 1. Semana, el espacio de siete días; (fam.) ocho días. 2. Los seis días de trabajo. *So much a week,* Tanto por semana o a la semana. *The next week,* La semana que viene. *This day week,* De hoy en ocho días u ocho días ha.

Week-day [wīc'-dê], *s.* Feria, cualquiera de los días de la semana excepto el domingo; día de trabajo.

Week end [wīk'-end], *s.* Fin de semana.

Weekly [wīc'-li], *a.* Semanal, que sucede o se hace una vez a la semana; hebdomadario, de la semana. *Weekly paper,* Semanario.—*s.* Periódico semanal.—*adv.* Semanalmente, por semana, en todas las semanas o en cada una de ellas.

Weel [wīl], *a.* y *adv.* (Esco.) Bien. *V.* WELL.

Ween [wīn], *vn.* (Ant. o poét.) Imaginar, pensar, creer.

Weep [wīp], *va.* y *vn.* (*pret.* y *pp.* WEPT). 1. Llorar, verter lágrimas, hacer duelo o sentimiento por alguna cosa. 2. Llorar, verter o derramar lágrimas por algún pesar o placer. 3. Llorar, lamentar, condolerse de las calamidades o infortunios. 4. Llorar, destilar, caer el líquido gota a gota: dícese de algunas plantas. 5. Estar pendiente, inclinarse hacia el suelo. *To weep for,* Llorar de. *Weeping ash, weeping willow,* Fresno llorón, sauce llorón.

Weeper [wīp'-ẹr], *s.* 1. Llorador, el que llora. 2. Llorón, el que llora mucho. 3. Una tira de lienzo blanco muy fino que las mujeres inglesas acostumbraban ponerse en las vueltas del vestido negro en señal de luto riguroso.

Weeping [wīp'-ing], *s.* Lloro, lágrimas. *Weeping-grounds,* Tierras pantanosas o muy húmedas.

Weepingly [wīp'-ing-li], *adv.* Llorosamente, con lágrimas, con lloro.

†**Weet** [wīt], *vn.* Saber. *V.* WIT.

Weever [wī'-vẹr], *s.* Traquino, dragón marino; pez británico.

Weevil [wī'-vl], *s.* 1. Gorgojo, insecto coleóptero diminuto. 2. Cualquier insecto dañino para las mieses entrojadas. 3. Larva de una mosca perjudicial al trigo. (Diplosis tritici.)

Weft [weft], *s.* 1. Trama, hebra que pasa de un lado a otro de la urdimbre. *V.* WOOF. 2. (Des.) *V.* WAIF. *Weft of hair,* Trenza de cabello.

Weigelia [wai-jī'-li-a], *s.* (Bot.) Arbusto de adorno, oriundo de China y Japón, con flores rosadas. (Weigelia o Diervilla rosea.)

Weigh [wê], *va.* 1. Pesar, averiguar el peso de una cosa por medio de algún instrumento. 2. Pesar, examinar o considerar con relación al valor, a la importancia o a las ventajas de; poner en la misma balanza, apreciar. 3. Sobrecargar, agobiar, oprimir. 4. Levar anclas.—*vn.* 1. Pesar, tener o hacer tanto o cuanto, pesar una cosa. 2. Pesar, tener estimación y valor, ser digno de mucho aprecio, ser de importancia, ser estimado. 3. Pesar sobre, ser opresivo, estar a carga. 4. (Mar.) Levar anclas; hacerse a la vela. *To weigh down,* Pesar más una cosa que otra, exceder en peso; sobrepujar; hundirse una cosa por su propio peso; sobrecargar, oprimir. *To outweigh,* Sobrepesar. *To weigh out,* Pesar (en cantidades pequeñas). *To weigh anchor,* (Mar.) Levar el ancla. *This reason ought to weigh with you,* Esta razón debe ser de peso para Vd.

Weighable [wê'-a-bl], *a.* Capaz de ser pesado o vendido al peso.

Weighed [wêd], *a.* 1. Pesado. 2. Experimentado, de grande experiencia en alguna materia.

Weigher [wê'-ẹr], *s.* Pesador. *Public weigher,* Almotacén, juez de pesos y medidas.

Weighing [wê'-ing], *s.* 1. Peso, acción de pesar. 2. Pesada, cantidad pesada de una sola vez. *Weighing-machine,* Máquina para pesar.

Weight [wêt], *va.* Cargar un peso o con un peso; atar un peso a.—*s.* 1. Peso, pesantez, la fuerza natural con que los cuerpos se mueven hacia abajo, procedente de la pesadez o gravedad. 2. Pesadez, gravedad, la calidad de todo cuerpo grave. 3. Pesa, trozo de metal de un peso dado, que se emplea para pesar. 4. Peso, la gravedad determinada de una cosa, y también el instrumento que sirve para examinarla; masa, masa pesada. 5. Peso, carga, gravamen. 6. Peso, entidad, substancia, importancia. 7. Sistema graduado de pesas. *Overweight,* Sobrepeso. *Gross weight,* Peso bruto. *Net* o *neat weight,* Peso neto. *Defect in weight,* Desmedro. *Make-weight,* Añadidura. *Stamped weight,* Peso marcado, señalado o pasado por el contraste. *Hundred-weight,* Quintal. *By-weight,* Al peso. *To make weight,* Completar, hacer el peso. *It is worth its weight in gold,* Vale su peso en oro. *Standard weight,* Peso legal, peso normal o modelo.

Weightily [wêt'-i-li], *adv.* Pesadamente, con peso.

Weightiness [wêt'-i-nes], *s.* 1. Ponderosidad, pesadez, gravedad. 2. Solidez, firmeza, fuerza. 3. Importancia, momento.

Weightless [wêt'-les], *a.* Ingrávido.

Weightlessness [wêt'-les-nes], *s.* Ingravidez.

Weight lifting [wêt' lift'-ing], *s.* Halterofilia.

Weighty [wêt'-i], *a.* 1. Ponderoso, pesado. 2. Grave, serio, importante, de consecuencia.

Weir [wīr], *s.* 1. Paradera, compuerta del caz de una acequia, molino, etc.; esclusa de canales; presa o parada de ríos. 2. Nasa, cañal, cerco de cañas para pescar en las presas de los ríos. (<A.-S. wer.)

Weird [wīrd], *a.* Sobrenatural o que se refiere a ello; que despierta sentimientos supersticiosos; no terrestre. *The Weird Sisters,* Las Parcas.

Welcome [wel'-cum], *a.* 1. Bien venido, bien llegado, recibido con agrado. 2. Agradable, que se recibe con placer. 3. Admitido al goce de; que puede servirse de alguna cosa. *A welcome present,* Un regalo agradable. *You are welcome,* Sea Vd. bienvenido. *You are welcome to it,* Está al servicio de Vd.; a la disposición de Vd.; puede Vd. disponer de ello.—*inter.* ¡Bien venido! ¡bien llegado! modo de saludar a un recién llegado.—*s.* 1. Bienvenida, buena acogida; saludo de bienvenida; el parabién que se da a otro por haber llegado con felicidad; feliz llegada o arribo. 2. El gusto o agrado con que se recibe a alguno, y el agasajo con que se le obsequia.

Welcome, *va.* Dar la bienvenida a alguno.

Welcomer [wel'-cum-ẹr], *s.* El que acoge o da la bienvenida.

Weld [weld], *s.* (Bot.) Gualda, planta de que se sirven los tintoreros para teñir de amarillo. *V.* WOAD.

Weld, *va.* 1. Juntar o unir a golpe de martillo los pedazos de metal hechos ascua; soldar a martillo. 2. Unir en un todo homogéneo.—*s.* Soldadura a martillo en caliente.

Welding [weld'-ing], *s.* Soldadura.

Welfare [wel'-fār], *s.* Bienestar. *Welfare work,* Trabajo de beneficencia, obras caritativas.

Welkin [wel'-kin], *s.* (Poét.) Firmamento, cielo, el orbe diáfano que rodea la tierra.

Well [wel], *va.* Verter, derramar, como de manantial.—*vn.* Manar, salir como de manantial; correr, fluir.

Well, *s.* 1. Pozo para sacar agua, gas natural, o petróleo. 2. Fuente, manantial, nacimiento del agua. 3. Fuente, origen; lo que mana sin intermisión. 4. Cavidad, depresión o copa que se asemeja a un pozo; caja o pozo, el hueco que ocupa una escalera; vivar en una embarcación de pesca para conservar vivo el pescado; (Mar.) caja de bombas o sentina. *Well-borer, well-digger,* Pocero. *Well-curb,* Brocal (de pozo). *Well-hole,* Hueco o caja de escalera; boca de pozo. *Well-spring,* Manantial, fuente. *Well-sweep,* Cigüeñal o cigoñal, pértiga que se usa para sacar agua. *Well-water,* Agua de pozo. *Well-cleanser,* Pocero, el que limpia los pozos. *Well of a fishing-boat,* (Mar.) Pozo de barco pescador. *Well of a ship,* (Mar.) Arca de bomba.

Well, *a.* 1. Feliz, dichoso; bien hecho o arreglado, agradable. 2. Conveniente, ventajoso, que tiene cuenta. 3. Bueno, sano, sin lesión o enfermedad alguna. 4. Que está en buen estado, que se ha repuesto de alguna desgracia o infortunio. 5. (Ant.) Valido, favorecido.—*adv.* Bien, felizmente; favorablemente; suficientemente; convenientemente. *Well-nigh,* Casi; poco más o menos.—*conj.* Pues: sea. *As well,* Tan bien, lo mismo da. *As well as,* Así como, también como, tanto como, lo mismo que. *Well is he,* Dichoso aquel. *Well enough,* Bastante bien. *Well and good,* Enhorabuena, bien está. *Well, well!* ¡Bien! ¡bien! como Vd. quiera. *Well then,* Con que, pues bien. *Well* se usa muy frecuentemente en composición para expresar el buen estado de alguna cosa, o la calidad digna de alabanza en los nombres a que se junta. *It is well for you,* Afortunadamente para Vd. *All's well that ends well,* El fin corona la obra; hasta el fin nadie es dichoso. *All's well!* ¡Centinela alerta! *To be well off,* Tener medios de fortuna, hacer buenos negocios. *To be well to do,* Estar desahogado, tener el riñón bien cubierto. *To like well,*

Gustar bastante. *Full well*, Muy bien. *Well-accomplished*, Completo, consumado; lleno de perfecciones; muy bien educado. *Well-accustomed*, Muy hecho o muy acostumbrado, que tiene mucha experiencia en alguna cosa. *Well-acquainted*, Muy conocido o íntimamente conocido; bien enterado. *Well-adapted*, Bien adaptado o acomodado; muy a propósito para una cosa. *Well-advanced*, (1) Muy adelantado. (2) Lo que se propone con mucho fundamento. *Well-advised*, Bien aconsejado. *Well-affected*, Bien intencionado. *Well-appointed*, Bien equipado. *Well-balanced*, Bien equilibrado. *Well-behaved*, Cortés, urbano, bien criado, atento; que tiene buena conducta. *Well-born*, Bien nacido, que pertenece a buena familia. *Well-bred*, Bien criado, bien educado, cortés, político. *Well-disposed*, Caritativo, bien intencionado. *Well-doing*, Benéfico. (*s.*) Beneficencia, buenas acciones, buenas obras; prosperidad. *Well-favoured*, Hermoso, bien parecido, agradable a la vista. *Well-meaning*, Bien inclinado, honrado, sincero, ingenuo; a menudo tiene una significación algo despreciativa. *Well-meant*, Bien intencionado, hecho con buena intención. *Well-read*, Que ha leído mucho, instruído, erudito. *Well-spent*, Bien empleado, pasado honradamente. *Well-stricken*, Muy avanzado en años. *Well-spoken*, Que se expresa bien, bien dicho; urbano, de lenguaje y modales afables. *Well-stored*, Bien provisto; copioso. *Well-tasted*, Sabroso. *Well-timed*, Oportuno, hecho a propósito. *Well-to-do*, Que vive holgadamente, que tiene el riñón bien cubierto. *Well-turned*, (1) Simétrico o primoroso (como el trabajo hecho a torno); (2) construído o ejecutado con gracia o maña. *Well-wisher*, Amigo, partidario, la persona que tiene cariño o afecto a otra. *Well-worded*, Bien dicho, bien expresado. *Well-worn*, (1) Gastado, echado a perder por el uso; (2) llevado u ostentado decorosamente. *Well-wrought*, Bien trabajado.

Welladay [wel'-a-dê], *inter.* Hola; ay de mí.

Well-aimed [wel-êmd'], *a.* Certero.

Well-attended [wel-at-tend'-ed], *a.* Bien concurrido.

Well-being [wel'-bî''-ing], *s.* Felicidad, prosperidad, bienestar, comodidad.

Well done [wel' dun], *inter.* ¡Ánimo! ¡a las mil maravillas! ¡bien va!

Well-founded [wel-faund'-ed], *a.* Bien fundado, justo.

Well-grounded [wel-graund'-ed], *a.* Bien fundado.

Well-known [wel-nōn'], *a.* Bien conocido, famoso.

Well-off [wel-ōf'], *a.* Rico, adinerado, acomodado.

Well-spring [wel'-spring], *s.* Manantial, fuente.

Well-suited [wel-siūt'-ed], *a.* Adecuado. *Well-suited to each other*, Que congenian mutuamente.

Welsh [welsh], *a.* Galo, del país de Gales; perteneciente a Gales, al pueblo indígena de dicho país o a su lengua.—*s.* 1. Los galos, los naturales de Gales. 2. Idioma del país de Gales; dialecto de la lengua címrica. *Welsh girl*, Joven gala. *Welsh rabbit* (o *rarebit*), Tostada con queso; queso tostado o derretido que se sirve con pan tostado.

Welshman [welsh'-man], *s.* Galo, habitante o natural de Gales.

Welt [welt], *s.* 1. Ribete (de ropa); vira del zapato. 2. Costurón, señal que deja un latigazo. 3. (Fam.) El acto de azotar o de dar tundas.

Welt, *va.* 1. Ribetear, echar ribetes. 2. Azotar cruelmente de suerte que se formen costurones.

Welter [welt'-er], *vn.* 1. Introducirse en un flúido turbio. 2. Revolcarse en agua, cieno o lodo. 3. Hincharse o moverse las olas hacia adelante.—*s.* 1. Movimiento ondulante de las olas; de aquí, conmoción, agitación, tumulto. 2. Aquello en que algo o alguien se revuelca; cenagal, revolcadero.

Welterweight [welt'-er-wêt], *s.* En el boxeo, peso welter, peso mediano ligero.

Wen [wen], *s.* Lobanillo, lupia; excrecencia. *Wen on the throat*, Papera.

Wench [wench], *s.* 1. Moza, muchacha, una mujer joven de condición humilde; criada. 2. Mozuela: usado como término de desprecio. 3. (Fam. E. U.) Negra. 4. (Des.) Cantonera, andorra.

Wench, *vn.* Putañear.

Wend [wend], *va.* Dirigir (su curso), andar.—*vn.* Ir, continuar su camino; avanzar, pasar.

Went [went], *pret.* del verbo *To* Go: (pret. desusado de *wend*). *I went home*, Yo me fuí a casa.

Wentletrap [wen'-tl-trap], *s.* Escalaria, concha de escalera, molusco gasterópodo.

Wept, *pret.* y *pp.* del verbo *To* WEEP.

Were [wer], *pret. pl.* del verbo *To* BE, tanto subjuntivo como indicativo; en el subjuntivo es también singular. *You were*, Vd. era, estaba; Vd. fué, estuvo; Vds. eran, estaban, fueron, estuvieron; vosotros erais, estábais, etc. *If I were*, Si yo fuera o fuese, estuviera o estuviese. *As it were*, Por decirlo así; como si fuese. *If it were not so*, Si así no fuese. *Even though he were to see it, he would not believe it*, Aun cuando él lo viese no lo creería. *Were I asked my opinion*, Si me preguntasen mi opinión. *There were*, Había, hubo. *There were ten*, Había diez.

Wert [wert], 2ª *pers. sing.* indicativo y subjuntivo de WAS, pretérito del verbo to BE.

West [west], *s.* Oeste, poniente, occidente.—*a.* Occidental, del oeste.—*adv.* A poniente o hacia el poniente; hacia el occidente. *West End*, Barrio aristocrático de Londres, al oeste de Charing Cross. *West Indies*, Las Indias occidentales, las Antillas. *West-Indian*, De las Antillas, de las Indias occidentales.

Westerly [west'-er-li], *a.* Que se dirige a poniente; hacia el oeste. *In a westerly direction*, En dirección al oeste. *A westerly wind*, Viento del oeste.—*adv.* Hacia el oeste u occidente.

Western [west'-ern], *a.* Occidental, que está en el occidente o hacia el poniente; al oeste, que viene del oeste, o es característico del oeste; también, menguante.

Westernmost [west'-ern-mōst], *a.* Lo más el oeste, los más remoto hacia el oeste.

Westward, Westwardly [west'-ward, li], *adv.* A poniente, hacia occidente, hacia el oeste.

Westward, *a.* Que tiende al oeste, que está al oeste.

Wet [wet], *a.* Húmedo, mojado, humedecido, lluvioso. *Wet blanket*, Aguafiestas. *Wet paint*, Pintura fresca.—*s.* Humedad, agua, tiempo húmedo.

Wet, *va.* Mojar, humedecer.

Wether [wedh'-er], *s.* Carnero llano, el que está castrado.

Wetness [wet'-nes], *s.* Humedad.

Wet-nurse [wet'-nūrs], *s.* Ama de leche, ama de cría, nodriza.

Whack [hwak], *va.* (Fam.) Pegar, golpear, vapulear.—*vn.* 1. Golpear con ruido, dar una tunda, una zurra. 2. (Ger.) Ajustar cuentas; tener parte en, gozar con otros.—*s.* 1. Golpe ruidoso. 2. (Ger.) Parte, porción.

Whacking [hwak'-ing], *a.* (Fam.) Grueso, desmesurado, enorme.

Whale [hwêl], *va.* (Fam.) Azotar; vapulear, vapular, dar una tunda.

Whale, *vn.* Dedicarse a la pesca de la ballena.

Whale [hwêl], *s.* Ballena, mamífero cetáceo con figura de pez. *Whaleback*, Embarcación de cubierta cerrada y redondeada, que se usa en aguas peligrosas.

Whalebone [hwêl'-bōn], *s.* Ballena o barba de ballena, tira que se saca de la mandíbula superior de dicho cetáceo.

Whalefin [hwêl'-fin], *s.* Aleta de ballena.

Whale-oil [hwêl'-oil], *s.* Aceite o grasa de ballena.

Whaler [hwêl'-er], *s.* Ballenero, pescador de ballenas; buque ballenero, barco dedicado a la pesca de la ballena.

Whaling [hwêl'-ing], *s.* 1. El acto o la industria de pescar ballenas. 2. (Fam.) Tunda, zurra.

Whang [hwang], *va.* y *vn.* (Fam. o Prov.) Golpear (con resonancia); dar tundas.—*s.* Tunda.

Wharf [hwērf], *s.* (*pl.* WHARFS o WHARVES). Muelle, embarcadero o desembarcadero; construcción donde cargan y descargan los barcos cómodamente.

Wharfage [hwērf'-ēj], *s.* Muellaje, un derecho que se cobra por el uso de un muelle; derecho de muelle.

What [hwet], *pron.* 1. Que, qué cosa; cuál; el que, la que, lo que, aquello que. 2. Cuanto. *What time?* ¿Cuándo? *What time*, Cuando, al tiempo que, en el día que. *What a man!* ¡Qué hombre! *What man?* ¿Quién? *What though*, Sin embargo que, a pesar de que, aun cuando; ¿qué importa que? *What else?* ¿Y qué más? *What of that?* ¿Qué importa eso? *What is that?* ¿Qué es eso? *For what?* ¿Por qué? ¿para qué? *What if he should come?* ¿Y qué diría Vd. si viniese? *What more?* ¿Qué más? *What ho!* ¡Hola!—*adv.* En parte; tanto, sea. *What with hunger and what with weariness*, Parte por hambre y parte por cansancio. *To know what's what*, (Fam.) Comprender las cosas, estar en autos, estar al corriente. *What for*, (Fest) Qué clase de; (del alemán *was für*). *What for a dog have you?* ¿Qué clase de perro tiene Vd.?

Whatever [hwet-ev'-er], **Whatsoever** [hwet-so-ev'-er], *pron.* Cualquier o cualquiera cosa que, todo lo que, por cualquiera, sea lo o la que fuere, que sea.

What-not [hwet'-net], *s.* 1. Rinconera, estante, pequeño mueble con anaqueles. 2. (Fam.) Lo que Vd. guste, cualquiera cosa.

Wheal [hwîl], *s.* Raya amoratada en la piel causada por un latigazo o por las ortigas.

Wheat [hwît], *s.* (Bot.) Trigo.

Wheaten [hwî'-tn], *a.* Hecho de trigo.

Wheat-ear [hwît'-îr], *s.* (Orn.) Triguero, un pájaro pequeño.

Wheedle [hwî'-dl], *va.* Halagar, acariciar, persuadir con palabras halagüeñas, engaitar o engañar con lisonjas, popar o tratar con mucha blandura y regalo; sonsacar.

Wheel [hwîl], *s.* 1. Rueda, máquina circular que da vueltas sobre un eje; en sentido figurado, fuerza motriz. *Spinning-wheel*, Torno para hilar. *Wheel of the helm*, (Mar.) Rueda del timón. 2. Instrumento o aparato que se asemeja a una rueda o que tiene una rueda como elemento distintivo, v. g. una bicicleta, un fuego artificial giratorio, una polea, etc. 3. Rueda, máquina con que se daba suplicio en algunos países. *Balance-wheel*, Volante. 4. (Met.) Revolución, vuelta, rotación; acción de rodar, de dar vueltas. *To break upon the wheel*, Enrodar. *Wheel and axle*, Cabria, aparato para levantar pesos. *Cog-wheel*, Rueda dentada. *Driving-wheel*, Rueda motriz. *Fly-wheel*, Volante. *Paddle-wheel*, Rueda de paletas. *Potter's wheel*, Rueda de alfarero. *Breast wheel*, Rueda hidráulica de costado. *Catharine wheel*, (1) Rosa, ventana de rosetón; (2) sol, rueda de fuegos artificiales; (3) rueda catalina. *Wheel-animalcule*, Rotífero. *Wheel-barometer*, Barómetro de cuadrante. *Wheel-horse*, Caballo de varas (cuando va delante otro caballo). *Wheel-house*, Carroza o garita de timonel.

Wheel, *vn.* 1. Rodar, moverse por la tierra dando vueltas alrededor del eje o centro del cuerpo que se mueve. 2. Rodar, moverse alguna cosa con ruedas. 3. Rodar, divagar, andar de acá para allá o por muchas partes; girar, volar. 4. Rodar, suceder las cosas casualmente y como en el trascurso del tiempo. —*va.* 1. Rodar ó hacer rodar, transportar, llevar sobre ruedas. 2. Volver, girar, dar vuelta o vueltas a alguna cosa. 3. Proveer de una rueda. 4. Formar o trabajar con rueda. *To wheel about*, Rodar, divagar; dar vueltas, andar rodando o de acá para allá; no fijarse, cambiar muy fácilmente de opinión, de partido, etc.

Wheelbarrow [hwîl'-bar-ō], *s.* Carretón de una rueda; la carretilla o caja con una rueda en que llevan los albañiles los materiales.

Wheel base [hwîl' bês], *s.* Distancia entre ejes de vehículo.

Wheel chair [hwîl' chār], *s.* Silla de ruedas.

Wheeler [hwîl'-ẹr], *s.* 1. El que hace ruedas; el que rueda ó da vueltas. 2. Caballería uncida cerca de las ruedas. 3. Vapor de ruedas. *Stern-wheeler*, *V.* STERN. 4. Carretero.

Wheeling [hwîl'-ing], *s.* 1. Rodaje, transporte sobre ruedas; el acto o costumbre de usar una bicicleta. 2. Condición de los caminos en lo relativo al paso de vehículos de ruedas. 3. Movimiento de rotación.

Wheelman [hwîl'-man], *s.* 1. Timonero, timonel, el que gobierna una embarcación. 2. (Neol.) El que usa una bicicleta, biciclista, ciclista.

Wheelwright [hwîl'-rait], *s.* Carretero, el que hace carros, carretas o carruajes; el que hace juegos de ruedas para los carruajes.

Wheelwork [hwîl'-wūrk], *s.* El conjunto de ruedas de una máquina.

Wheeze [hwîz], *vn.* Jadear, respirar con dificultad y fatiga; respirar haciendo mucho ruido.

Whelk [hwelk], *s.* 1. Concha univalva espiral. 2. Tumorcillo, grano.

Whelp [hwelp], *s.* 1. Cachorro, el perro de poco tiempo, y también la cría de otros animales carnívoros. *Bear whelp*, Osezno. 2. Un muchacho u hombre muy joven: en este sentido se usa sólo por desprecio y para notar a un muchacho de atrevido y perverso.

Whelp, *vn.* Parir: por lo común se entiende de la perra ó la hembra de algunos otros animales carnívoros.

When [hwen], *adv.* Cuando, al tiempo que, o mientras que; desde que; que, en que. *When?* ¿Cuándo? ¿en qué tiempo? *Since when?* ¿Desde cuándo, de cuando acá? *Even when*, Aun cuando. *The moment when*, Al momento en que. *When I learned this*, Desde que oí o supe esto.

Whence [hwens], *adv.* De donde o desde donde, de que ó quien; de qué causa; por eso es que; por consiguiente. *Whence it may be seen*, De aquí se ve, o resulta. *From whence* es un pleonasmo poco usado.

Whencesoever [hwens-so-ev'-ẹr], *adv.* De donde quiera, de cualquier paraje que sea.

Whene'er [hwen-ār'], *adv.* y *conj.* *V.* WHENEVER.

Whenever [hwen-ev'-ẹr], **Whensoever** [hwen-so-ev'-ẹr], *adv.* Cuando quiera que, siempre que, en cualquier tiempo que sea, todas las veces que.

Where [hwār], *adv.* Donde, en que lugar, en donde, por donde, adonde. *Anywhere*, En cualquier parte, sitio o paraje, donde Vd. quiera. *Everywhere*, En todas partes, por todas partes.

Whereabout [hwār'-a-baut], *adv.* Hacia donde, hacia qué sitio, poco más o menos donde.

Whereabouts [hwār'-a-bauts], *s.* Lugar cercano a aquel en que se halla una persona o cosa; situación aproximada, paradero.

Whereas [hwār-az'], *conj.* Por cuanto, siendo así que, mientras que; cuando; por el contrario; pues que, ya que.

Whereat [hwār-at'], *adv.* A lo cual.

Whereby [hwār-bai'], *adv.* Por lo cual, con lo cual, por donde, de que; por medio del cual: ¿por qué? ¿cómo?

Wherefore [hwār'-fōr], *adv.* Por lo que, porque, por el cual motivo; por eso, por consiguiente.

Wherein [hwār-in'], *adv.* Donde, en donde, en lo cual, en que.

Whereinto [hwār-in-tū'], *adv.* En donde, dentro de lo que o dentro de lo cual, en lo cual, á lo que.

Whereof [hwār-ef'], *adv.* De lo cual, de que; ¿de qué?

Whereon [hwār-en'], *adv.* Sobre lo cual, sobre que.

Wheresoe'er [hwār-so-ār'], **Wheresoever** [hwār-sō-ev'-ẹr], *adv.* Donde quiera, en cualquiera parte que, en cualquier sitio que sea.

Whereto [hwār-tū'], **Whereunto** [hwār-un-tū'], *adv.* A lo que, a que.

Whereupon [hwār-up-en'], *adv.* Sobre que; entonces, así que sucedió esto.

Wherever [hwār-ev'-ẹr], *adv.* Donde quiera que, por donde quiera que, en donde quiera.

Wherewith [hwār-widh'], **Wherewithal** [hwār-widh-ōl'], *adv.* Con que, con lo cual; ¿con qué?—*s.* Los medios o recursos necesarios; dinero necesario.

Wherry [hwer'-i], *s.* 1. Esquife, barca, barco. 2. (Ingl.) Barca de pescador con cubierta y dos velas.

Wherry, *va.* Pasar en barco.

Wherryman [hwer'-i-man], *s.* Barquero.

Whet [hwet], *va.* 1. Afilar, amolar. 2. Agriar, exasperar: en este último sentido se usa casi siempre con la preposición *on.* 3. Excitar el apetito o dar apetito.

Whet, *s.* Afiladura, aguzadura; estímulo.

Whether [hwedh'-ẹr], *conj.* Si, sea, sea que, ora, ya.—*pron.* (Ant.) Cual, cual de los dos. *Whether you will or not*, Que quieras, que no quieras.

Whetstone [hwet'-stōn], *s.* Aguzadera, piedra de amolar o afilar.

Whetter [hwet'-ẹr], *s.* Amolador.

Whew [hwiū], *inter.* ¡Ah! ¡caramba! ¡cáspita! expresa asombro; ¡ay! expresa congoja.

Whey [hwê], *s.* Suero, la parte acuosa de la leche separada de la parte grumosa de ella.

Wheyey [hwê'-i], **Wheyish** [hwê'-ish], *a.* Seroso.

Which [hwich], *pron. rel.* 1. Que, el cual, la cual, los cuales, las cuales, cual, cuyo. *Which* se usa sólo para hacer relación a las cosas o a los animales, aunque antiguamente también se usaba para las personas; interrogativamente se dice de personas y cosas. 2. Lo que representa una cláusula o frase. *He says his copy is better printed, which is true*, Dice que su ejemplar está mejor impreso, lo que es cierto. *Which book do you prefer?* ¿Qué libro prefiere Vd.? *The canary which has a crest*, El canario que tiene cresta. *Both of which*, Ambos, los dos. *All of which, all which*, Todo esto. *In the progress of which*, En cuyo progreso. *Which will you have?* ¿Cuál quiere Vd.? *Which way?* ¿Por dónde? ¿por qué camino?

Whichever, **Whichsoever** [hwich-so-ev'-ẹr], *pron.* Cualquiera.

Whidah-bird [hwid'-a-bẹrd], *s.* (Zool.) Vidua, viuda, pájaro de Africa; las plumas de la cola del macho crecen extraordinariamente en la época del celo.

Whiff [hwif], *s.* Vaharada, el efecto de arrojar el vaho, aliento o respiración; bocanada de humo, soplo de viento.

Whiff, *va.* 1. Llevar por el aire, transportar con un soplo. 2. Echar bocanadas de humo o vaharadas. 3. Fumar (una pipa) echando bocanadas de humo.—*vn.* Lanzar o echar bocanadas.

Whiffle [hwif'-l], *va.* 1. Hacer bambolearse, hacer inclinar. 2. Hacer desparecer una cosa a soplos; poner a un lado o desechar alguna cosa con desprecio.—*vn.* Divertirse en bagatelas o cosas insignificantes; moverse o agitarse con mucha volubilidad; ser inconstante o voluble.

Whiffler [hwif'-lẹr], *s.* 1. Soplador,

el que sopla. 2. Veleta, hombre de poco más o menos. 3. (Ant.) Pífano; gaitero.

Whiffletree [hwif'-l-tri], *s.* V. SWINGLETREE.

Whig [hwig], *s.* Nombre de un partido político de Inglaterra que pide reformas liberales, liberal: de los Estados Unidos, (a) partidario de la revolución; (b) partido opuesto a *Democrat*, predecesor del actual partido republicano.

Whiggism [hwig'-izm], *s.* Las máximas, principios u opiniones políticas del partido llamado *Whig* en Inglaterra, que es el opuesto al *Tory*.

While [hwail], *s.* Rato, espacio corto de tiempo; vez. *A while ago*, Rato ha, hace algún tiempo. *A little while*, Un ratito. *A little while ago*, Hace poco, ahora mismo, poco tiempo ha, no hace mucho. *A while ago*, Rato ha. *All this while*, En todo este tiempo o durante todo este tiempo. *A while after*, Algo después o poco después. *For a while*, Durante algún tiempo o por algún tiempo. *In the mean while*, En el intervalo, entre tanto. *Between whiles*, De cuando en cuando, a intervalos. *'Tis not worth while*, No merece o no vale la pena.

While, †**Whiles** [hwailz], **Whilst** [hwailst], *adv.* Mientras, durante, entre tanto, en el ínterin. *While she sings, they converse*, Mientras ella canta, ellas conversan.

While, *va.* Pasar, hacer pasar (el tiempo). *To while away one's time*, Haraganear, pasar el tiempo; divertirse.

Whilom [hwail'-em], *a.* (Ant. o poét.) Anterior, del tiempo pasado.—*adv.* En otro tiempo; a veces.

Whim [hwim], **Whimsey** [hwim'-zi], *s.* 1. Antojo, capricho, fantasía, genialidad, extravagancia. *To be full of whims*, Ser lunático, tener rarezas, ser muy caprichoso o muy extravagante. 2. (Mec.) Cabria, trucha. *Whim-gin*, Cabria, trucha.

Whimper [hwim'-pęr], *vn.* Sollozar, llorar sin gritar, gemir, quejarse; lloriquear, fingir que se llora, como lo hacen los niños.—*s.* Quejido, lloriqueo. *V.* WHINE.

Whimsical [hwim'-zi-cal], *a.* 1. Caprichoso, caprichudo, fantástico, extravagante, ridículo. 2. Construído fantásticamente.

Whimsicality [hwim-zi-cal'-i-ti], *s.* La calidad de ser caprichoso o fantástico, extravagancia, ridiculez.

Whimsically [hwim'-zi-cal-i], *adv.* Caprichosamente, con extravagancia, de un modo raro.

Whimsicalness [hwim'-zi-cal-nes], *s.* Rareza, singularidad, extravagancia de genio, carácter raro; propensión a hacer las cosas de diverso modo que los demás.

Whimsy [hwim'-zi], *s.* *V.* WHIM, en ambas acepciones.

Whim-wham [hwim'-hwam], *s.* (Ant.) Bagatela; juguete.

Whine [hwain], *vn.* Llorar o lamentar sin ruido; quejarse, lamentarse; lloriquear (como hace un niño).

Whine, *s.* Quejido, lamento; lloriqueo.

Whining [hwain'-ing], *s.* Quejas.

Whinny [hwin'-i], *vn.* Relinchar (especialmente en voz baja).—*s.* Relincho, voz del caballo o la yegua.

Whinny, *a.* Abundante en hiniesta o tojo.

Whip [hwip], *va.* 1. Azotar, dar azotes; dar con vergas, flagelar. 2. Castigar á un niño, dándole azotes. 3. Efectuar con, o como con, golpes. 4. Asir, arrebatar, o coger con un movimiento rápido; úsase con preposición, v. gr. *away*, *in*, *off*, *on*, etc. 5. (Fam. E. U.) Exceder, sobresalir en una contienda; vencer. 6. Batir huevos, crema. 7. Hilvanar, filetear. 8. Dar varias vueltas con hilo a un pedazo de cuerda; envolver un cabo con cuerdecilla. 9. Izar con candeliza; levantar con precipitación. *To whip a horse*, Dar latigazos a un caballo. *It was whipped with black*, Estaba fileteado de negro.—*vn.* 1. Andar de prisa. 2. Echar repetidas veces el anzuelo en el agua. *To whip down*, Bajar corriendo o bajar volando. *To whip off a thing*, Despachar alguna cosa o negocio prontamente. *To whip out*, Zafarse, escaparse; llevarse alguna cosa con precipitación. *To whip up*, Agarrar, coger, tomar o asir algo de repente; subir corriendo o volando: (Mar.) izar con la candeliza; alzar levantar o subir con precipitación.

Whip, *s.* 1. Azote: látigo, zurriago; fusta, (Amer.) fuete. *Horse-whip*, Látigo. *Coachman's whip*, Manopla. *Whip-money*, Agujetas. 2. (Mar.) Palanquín de estay. *Whip and spur*, Con la mayor prisa, a todo correr. *Stroke of a whip*, Latigazo. *To crack a whip*, Hacer chasquear un látigo. *Whip-cord*, (1) Cordel de látigo. (Mex.) Pajuela. (2) Cordel de cuerda de tripa. *Whip-hand*, La mano que tiene el látigo; mano derecha; (fig.) ventaja. *To have the whip-hand of*, Tener la ventaja sobre, tener vara alta. *Whip-lash*, Punta de látigo.

Whip-graft [hwip'-graft], *va.* Ingertar a la inglesa. *Whip-grafting*, Ingerto inglés.

Whipped cream [hwipt crim], *s.* Crema batida.

Whipped potatoes [hwipt pō-tē'-tōs], *s. pl.* Puré de papas.

Whippet [hwip'-et], *s.* 1. Perro lebrero. 2. Cosa pequeña y veloz.

Whipping [hwip'-ing], *s.* Acción de azotar, flagelación. *To give a whipping*, Dar un latigazo, una mano de azotes. *Whipping-post*, La columna o poste a que atan a los reos para azotarlos.

Whippletree [hwip'-l-tri], *s.* V. SWINGLETREE.

Whippoorwill [hwip'-pur-wil''], *s.* Chotacabra americana, chotacabra chillona (Antrostornus vociferus). Nombre imitativo de su grito.

Whipsaw [hwip'-sē], *s.* Serrucho.

Whipstaff [hwip'-staf], *s.* (Mar.) Pinzote del timón.

Whipster [hwip'-stęr], *s.* Hombre ligero y ágil.

Whir, **Whirr** [hwęr], *va.* y *vn.* Girar, dar vueltas o llevarse con estruendo; zumbar; moverse o volar con ruido, rehilar.—*s.* Ruido que hacen las aves al remontar el vuelo: zumbido, sonido de un giro muy rápido.

Whirl [hwęrl], *va.* y *vn.* 1. Girar, dar vueltas alrededor o circularmente con mucha rapidez. 2. Hacer girar o dar vueltas en círculo. 3. Mover o moverse rápidamente.

Whirl, *s.* Giro, vuelta, rotación o movimiento circular muy rápido; cualquier cosa que se mueve circularmente con giros muy rápidos.

Whirlbat [hwęrl'-bat], *s.* Cualquier cosa que se mueve rápidamente para dar golpes; particularmente, cesto, especie de manopla guarnecida de hierro ó plomo de que usaban los púgiles antiguos en sus combates.

Whirlbone [hwęrl'-bōn], *s.* Rótula, choquezuela, el hueso de la rodilla.

Whirligig [hwęrl'-i-gig], *s.* 1. Perinola. 2. Tío vivo. *V. Merry-go-round.* 3. Cualquier cosa que se mueve circularmente con giros rápidos. 4. Girín, escarabajo de agua, insecto coleóptero de vivos colores metálicos.

Whirlpool [hwęrl'-pūl], *s.* Vórtice, remolino u olla de agua; agua que gira con violencia.

Whirlwind [hwęrl'-wind], *s.* Torbellino, remolino, viento violento que se mueve circularmente. (Fam.) *To raise a whirlwind*, Levantar una tremolina. *Sow the wind, and reap the whirlwind*, Quien siembra vientos recoge tempestades; o, haces mal, espera otro tal.

Whirr, *v.* y *s.* *V.* WHIR.

Whirring [hwęr'-ing], *s.* Zumbido de las alas o de ciertas máquinas.

Whish [hwish], *s.* (Fam.) Sonido agudo semejante al que hace una varita flexible cortando el aire. *V.* SWISH. (Voz imitativa.)

Whisk [hwisk], *s.* 1. Escobilla, cepillo. 2. Un movimiento pronto y violento. 3. Antiguamente una parte del vestido de mujer.

Whisk, *va.* 1. Cepillar, limpiar con escobilla, quitar el polvo. 2. Arrastrar o mover rápidamente.—*vn.* 1. Hopear, menear la cola los animales. 2. Moverse con velocidad alguna cosa. *To whisk away* u *off*, Quitar vivamente, hacer desaparecer; marcharse de prisa.

Whisker [hwisk'-ęr], *s.* Patilla, barbas á uno y otro lado de la cara; bigotes del gato.

Whiskey, **Whisky** [hwis'-ki], *s.* Aguardiente de grano; licor alcohólico que se obtiene destilando un compuesto amiláceo en estado de fermentación. *V.* USQUEBAUGH.

Whisper [hwis'-pęr], *va.* y *vn.* 1. Cuchichear o cuchuchear, hablar al oído; murmurar. 2. Susurrar, hablar quedo; hablar muy bajo o bajito. 3. Apuntar, soplar o sugerir á otro en voz baja lo que debe decir. 4. Secretear.

Whisper, *s.* Susurro, ruido sordo, cuchicheo, voz baja.

Whisperer [hwis'-pęr-ęr], *s.* 1. El que habla bajo. 2. Cuchicheador, el amigo de cuchichear o el que tiene el vicio de cuchichear. 3. Susurrador, el que susurra quedo.

Whispering [hwis'-pęr-ing], *s.* Cuchicheo; susurro; el acto de hablar quedo o bajito. *Whispering-gallery*, Una galería o corredor en forma de bóveda, construido de tal modo que en toda su extensión se puede oir el más pequeño ruido hecho en un punto cualquiera del mismo.

Whist [hwist], *a.* Silencioso, mudo, callado.—*inter.* ¡Chitón! ¡calla! ¡punto en boca!—*s.* Un juego de naipes parecido a la malilla, que se juega entre cuatro personas.

Whistle [hwis'-l], *va.* y *vn.* 1. Silbar, formar el silbo o silbido. 2. Chiflar, dar chiflidos. 3. Llamar a alguno dando silbidos. *To whistle down the wind*, Hablar por demás, gastar saliva en balde. *To whistle for*, Llamar dando silbidos; (fam.) buscar en vano lo que se desea.

Whistle, *s.* 1. Silbo, silbido. 2. Silbato, chiflato; pito. 3. El silbido del viento. 4. (Ger.) Pico, gaznate. *To pay (too) dear for one's whistle*, Pagar demasiado cara una chuchería, una bagatela. *To wet one's whistle*, (Ger.) Humedecerse el gaznate, beber. *Fog-whistle*, Pito de alarma en tiempo de niebla. *V. Fog-horn.*
Whistler [hwis'-lęr], *s.* Silbador.
Whistling [hwis'-ling], *s.* 1. Silbo, silbido, la acción de silbar. 2. Chiflido, la acción de chiflar. *Whistling-buoy*, Boya de pito de alarma.
Whit [hwit], *s.* Apice, jota, punto, la mínima parte de alguna cosa; algo, un poco. *Every whit*, De todo punto; enteramente. *Not a whit*, Nada de eso.
White [hwait], *a.* 1. Blanco; del color de la nieve; lo opuesto a negro. 2. Blanco, del color de la raza caucásica; rubio, blondo; también, pálido, descolorido. 3. Cano, hablando del pelo. 4. Puro, inmaculado, sin mancha; inocente. 5. Feliz, propicio. *Milk-white*, Blanco como la leche, de un blanco lechoso. *To get white*, Ponerse blanco. *To render white*, Blanquear. *White with age*, Encanecido por los años, por la edad. *White lie*, Mentirilla.—*s.* 1. Blancura, color blanco, reunión de todos los colores del espectro solar. 2. Blanco, una señal fija y determinada para apuntar cuando se tira. 3. La clara del huevo. 4. La parte blanca de los ojos, la esclerótica. 5. Persona blanca. *Spanish white*, Blanco de España, yeso mate. *Chinese white*, Blanco de la China, óxido de zinc. *White ant*, Hormiga blanca, termita. *V.* TERMITE. *White House*, La Casa Blanca, la residencia oficial del Presidente de los Estados Unidos. *White-lead*, Albayalde, cal de plomo. *White leather*, Baldés, piel curtida con alumbre. *White-livered*, Cobarde, doble, envidioso, maligno. *White meat*, Manjar blanco: lacticinio, manjar compuesto con leche. *White wine*, Vino blanco.
White, Whiten [hwai'-tn], *va.* Blanquear, poner blanca alguna cosa.—*vn.* Emblanquecerse.
White-collar [hwait-col'-ar], *a.* Oficinesco. *White-collar job*, Trabajo de oficina. *White-collar worker*, Oficinista.
White elephant [hwait el'-ę-fant], *s.* Elefante blanco, algo que cuesta mucho mantener y no presta utilidad alguna.
White feather [hwait fedh'-ęr], *s.* Pluma blanca, símbolo de cobardía.
Whitefish [hwait'-fish], *s.* 1. Pez de los lagos septentrionales, parecido al salmón. Coregonus. 2. Albur, cadoce; merlán; y *V.* MENHADEN. 3. La ballena blanca.
White gold [hwait gōld], *s.* Oro blanco.
White matter [hwait mat'-ęr], *s.* (Anat.) Materia blanca.
Whitener [hwai'-tn-ęr], *s.* Blanqueador.
Whiteness [hwait'-nes], *s.* 1. Blancura; palidez. 2. Pureza, candor.
Whitening [hwai'-tn-ing], *s.* Blanqueo, la acción y efecto de blanquear.
Whites [hwaits], *s.* 1. Flores blancas, leucorrea. 2. Flor de harina, la harina más blanca y más fina.
White sauce [hwait sōs], *s.* Salsa blanca.
White slavery [hwait slē'-vęr-i], *s.* Trata de blancas.
Whitethorn [hwait'-thōrn], *s.* (Bot.) Espino blanco.
Whitewash [hwait'-wesh], *s.* 1. Lechada, leche de cal, el blanqueo que se da a las paredes. 2. Blanquete, afeite con el cual se blanquea el rostro. 3. Informe en que se atribuye a uno virtudes que no tiene, o el acto de encubrir sus faltas.
Whitewash, *va.* 1. Blanquear, enlucir con yeso blanco una pared. 2. Encalar o blanquear con cal; enjalbegar. 3. Tapar ó encubrir las faltas o defectos. 4. (Fam. Ingl.) Poner a un deudor insolvente al abrigo de procedimientos ulteriores. 5. (Fam. E. U.) Vencer al partido opuesto en un juego, sin permitirle hacer tantos.
Whitewasher [hwait'-wesh-ęr], *s.* Encalador, blanqueador.
Whitewashing [hwait'-wesh-ing], *s.* 1. Blanqueo, encaladura, enjalbegadura, jalbegue. 2. *V.* WHITEWASH, 3ª acep.
Whither [hwidh'-ęr], *adv.* Adonde, a qué parte; ¿hasta dónde?; dondequiera.
Whithersoever [hwidh-ęr-so-ev'-ęr], *adv.* Adonde quiera.
Whiting [hwait'-ing], *s.* 1. Merlán, pez gádido; albur, cadoce. 2. Blino plateado. 3. Blanco de España, yeso mate, tiza, carbonato de cal que se usa para pulimentar.
Whitish [hwait'-ish], *a.* Blanquizco, blanquecino, que tira a blanco.
Whitishness [hwait'-ish-nes], *s.* Color blanquizco o color blanquecino.
Whitleather [hwit'-ledh-ęr], *s.* 1. Cuero adobado con alumbre, baldés, piel blanca. 2. Ligamento de la nuca.
Whitlow [hwit'-lō], *s.* Panadizo, panarizo.
Whit-Monday [hwit'-mun-dē], *s.* Lunes de Pentecostés.
Whitsuntide [hwit'-sun-taid], *s.* Pentecostés, fiesta del Espíritu Santo. *Whitsunday*, Día de Pentecostés.
Whittle [hwit'-l], *va.* 1. Cortar o formar con navaja. 2. Cercenar, ir disminuyendo poco a poco. 3. Aguzar, dar un corte agudo a.—*vn.* Cortar un pedazo de madera con una navaja.
Whittle, *s.* 1. Navajilla, navaja pequeña; cuchillito que se lleva a la cintura. 2. Una especie de manta lanuda usada antiguamente por las mujeres.
Whiz [hwiz], *vn.* Zumbar o silbar, producir un ruido agudo como el que hace una flecha o una bala que hiende el aire; moverse rápidamente con ese ruido.—*s.* Sonido entre zumbido y silbido. *Whizzing noise*, Zumbido.
Who [hū], *pron.* (interrogativo) ¿Quién? (relativo) Quien, que, la persona que. *Who is there?* ¿Quién está ahí? ¿quién va? Este pronombre se usa sólo hablando de personas. *As who should say*, Como si dijéramos, como quien dice.
Whoa [hwō], *inter.* ¡So! ¡cho o jo! (voz usada para hacer que se paren las bestias).
Whoever [hū-ev'-ęr], *pron.* Quienquiera que, cualquiera que.
Whole [hōl], *a.* 1. Todo, total, entero. 2. Sano, entero, libre de daño; en buena salud.—*s.* Total, el todo. *Upon the whole*, En el todo, en suma, en general.
Wholehearted [hōl-hārt'-ed], *a.* Cordial, de todo corazón, con entusiasmo.
Wholeness [hōl'-nes], *s.* Todo, integridad, totalidad.
Wholesale [hōl'-sēl], *a.* Al mayoreo, al por mayor.—*s.* Mayoreo, venta al por mayor.
Wholesaler [hōl-sēl'-ęr], *s.* Mayorista.
Wholesome [hōl'-sum], *a.* 1. Sano, saludable, que conduce a la salud. 2. Bienhechor, favorable a la virtud; moral.
Wholesomely [hōl'-sum-li], *adv.* Saludablemente.
Wholesomeness [hōl'-sum-nes], *s.* Salud, sanidad, salubridad; naturaleza sana.
Whole-wheat [hōl'-hwīt'], *a.* De trigo entero. *Whole-wheat bread*, Pan de trigo entero.
Wholly [hōl'-li], *adv.* Cabalmente, totalmente, enteramente.
Whom [hūm], *pron.* Acusativo de WHO. Quien, que, cual. *Whom have you seen?* ¿A quién ha visto Vd.? *He whom you revere*, Aquel a quien Vd. reverencia.
Whomsoever, *pron.* Acusativo de WHOSOEVER.
Whoop [hūp], *s.* 1. Algarada, gritería; grito de agitación o de estímulo. 2. Grito de señal. 3. Inspiración ruidosa y convulsiva después de un ataque de tos. 4. Grito de buho o lechuza.
Whoop, *vn.* 1. Huchear, chiflar, gritar, vocear. 2. Respirar ruidosa y convulsivamente, como después de un paroxismo de tos.—*va.* Insultar con gritos. *Whooping-cough*, Tos ferina o convulsiva.
Whop [hwēp], *va.* (Vulg.) Zurrar.
Whopper [hwēp'-ęr], *s.* (Fam.) 1. El que zurra. 2. Algo grande o notable, particularmente una gran mentira.
Whore, *vn.* 1. Putear. 2. En la Sagrada Escritura, dar culto a dioses falsos.—*va.* Putear, corromper por medio de la lascivia.
Whore [hōr], *s.* Puta, prostituta.
Whorish [hōr'-ish], *a.* Lascivo, putesco.
Whorl [hwērl o hwūrl], *s.* 1. Contrapeso de la rueca. 2. (Bot.) Verticilo, conjunto de hojas, flores u otros órganos en torno de un tallo. 3. (Zool.) Espiral de una concha univalva.
Whose [hūz]. Genitivo de WHO y WHICH. Cuyo, de quien.
Whoso [hū'-sō] (ant.), **Whosoever** [hū-sō-ev'-ęr], *pron.* Quienquiera, cualquiera.
Why [hwai], *adv.* y *conj.* Por qué. *Why so?* ¿Por qué así? *Why?* ¿Qué? *Why* se usa frecuentemente para dar énfasis al discurso, y en este caso deja de traducirse en castellano. *Why truly*, Pero verdaderamente.—*inter.* A veces se representa por si; p. ej.: *Why, I just saw it*, Si lo acabo de ver. *Why, he must be crazy*, Si debe estar loco; otras veces por ¡y bien! ¡pero! ¡cómo! *Why then!* ¡Pero, y qué! *Why, she is here!* ¡Y bien, aquí está ella! *Why, man alive!* ¡Cómo, hombre de Dios!
Wick[1] [wic], *s.* Torcida, mecha; pábilo.
Wick,[2] **wich**, *s.* Aldea o pueblo: se hallan en voces compuestas v. gr. *Berwick, Greenwich.*

Wicked [wik'-ed], *a.* 1. Malvado, perverso, inicuo. 2. Travieso, picaresco, juguetón.
Wickedly [wik'-ed-li], *adv.* Inicuamente, malamente, perversamente.
Wickedness [wik'-ed-nes], *s.* Maldad, iniquidad, perversidad, malignidad; vicio, pecado, impiedad, irreligión.
Wicker [wik'-ẹr], *a.* Mimbroso, tejido de mimbres.—*s.* 1. Mimbre, ramita flexible de sauce; mimbrera. 2. Cestería. *Wicker basket,* Cesto de mimbres. *Wickerwork,* Cestería, tejido o artículos hechos de mimbres.
Wicket [wik'-et], *s.* Portillo, postigo, portezuela.
Wide [waid], *a.* 1. Ancho, anchuroso, vasto, dilatado. 2. Extenso, amplio. 3. Del ancho de, de ancho. *Five inches wide,* Cinco pulgadas de ancho. 4. Remoto, apartado, lejano. 5. Que tiene amplitud intelectual; liberal; comprensivo. 6. Muy abierto, completamente desarrollado. *The wide world,* El ancho mundo.—*adv.* 1. Lejos, a gran distancia. 2. Anchamente. *Wide open,* Abierto del todo o de par en par. *Far and wide,* A lo ancho y a lo largo; por todas partes, por todos lados, completamente. *Wide-awake,* Bien despierto, sobre sí, vigilante. —*s.* Sombrero bajo con alas levantadas. *Wide-gauge, V. Broad-gauge. To cut a wide swath,* Hacer alarde, hacer ostentación de algo.
Wide-angle lens [waid-ang'-l lens], *s.* Lente gran angular.
Widely [waid'-li], *adv.* 1. Lejos, a gran distancia. 2. Extensamente, muy, mucho, anchamente.
Widen [wai'-dn], *va.* Ensanchar, extender, dilatar, aumentar en extensión.—*vn.* Ensancharse, dilatarse.
Wideness [waid'-nes], *s.* Anchura, anchor, extensión a lo ancho.
Widespread [waid'-spred], *a.* Diseminado, esparcido por todas partes.
Widgeon [wij'-un], *s.* Mareca, especie de pato.
Widow [wid'-ō], *s.* Viuda, la mujer a quien se le ha muerto el marido. *Widow-bird,* Viuda. *V.* WHIDAHBIRD. *Widow-wail,* Olivo enano, arbusto pequeño del género Cneorum. *Widow's weeds,* Prendas de luto de una viuda. *Mourning-widow,* Escabiosa, planta herbácea.
Widow, *va.* 1. Privar a una mujer de su marido. 2. Dotar con viudedad o dar una viudedad. 3. Privar de una cosa muy útil.
Widower [wid'-o-ẹr], *s.* Viudo, hombre cuya mujer ha muerto.
Widowhood [wid'-ō-hud], *s.* Viudez, viudedad.
Width [width], *s.* Anchura, anchor.
Wield [wīld], *va.* 1. Manejar, empuñar, usar con cabal efecto. 2. Ejercer autoridad sobre; mandar. *To wield the sword,* Manejar la espada, usarla con habilidad.
Wieldy [wīld'-i], *a.* Manejable.
Wienerwurst [wī'-nẹr-wurst], *s.* Variedad de salchicha.
Wife [waif], *s.* (*pl.* WIVES). 1. Esposa, mujer casada o simplemente mujer, cuando se habla con relación al marido. 2. Ama de casa. 3. Se usa también provincialmente para designar a una mujer empleada en algún oficio humilde.
Wifehood [waif'-hud], *s.* Estado de la mujer casada; carácter propio de una mujer casada; también, las esposas en general.
Wifeless [waif'-les], *a.* Que no tiene esposa, sin mujer.
Wifely [waif'-li], *adv.* Como mujer casada; que conviene a una esposa, propio de casadas.
Wig [wig], *s.* 1. Peluca o cabellera postiza. 2. Especie de torta. 3. (Fest. Ingl.) Juez. *Wig-maker,* Peluquero, fabricante de pelucas.
Wigged [wigd], *a.* Que lleva peluca.
Wiggle [wig'-l], *va.* y *vn.* (Fam.) Mover o moverse rápidamente de un lado a otro, torcerse, andar como un gusano.
Wight [wait], *s.* Persona, criatura racional.
Wigwag [wig'-wag], *va.* y *vn.* 1. Menear, moverse hacia adelante y hacia atrás. 2. Hacer señales con banderas.
Wigwam [wig'-wōm], *s.* 1. Choza o jacal de los Indios norteamericanos. 2. (Fam. E. U.) Gran edificio público que se usa para reuniones políticas, etc.
Wild [waild], *a.* 1. Silvestre, salvaje, que vive en los bosques, en los desiertos; no domesticado, bravo, feroz; que crece o se cría sin cultivo. *A wild boar,* Jabalí. 2. Desierto, inhabitado, solitario, despoblado. 3. Turbulento, alborotado, tosco; aturdido, disparatado; atronado, alocado, extraño, descabellado. 4. Desenfrenado, libre, desarreglado, desordenado; extravagante, loco, insensato. *Wild-eyed,* De ojos huraños. 5. Impetuoso, violento; de tempestad; borrascoso. 6. Fogoso, vivamente deseoso. 7. Lejano del curso debido, o del objeto propuesto o deseado.—*s.* Yermo, desierto, paraje despoblado. *Wild carrot,* Zanahoria silvestre. *Wildcat,* Atolondrado, irresponsable; úsase mucho hablando de especulaciones o empresas quiméricas. Gato silvestre. *To run wild,* (1) Volver (un jardín, etc.) al estado natural o primitivo; (2) desencadenarse. *To be wild in one's youth,* Tener una juventud borrascosa. *Wild conceits,* Disparates, desatinos, desvaríos.
Wilderness [wil'-dẹr-nes], *s.* 1. Desierto, yermo. 2. Tosquedad, selvatiquez, falta de cultura.
Wildfire [waild'-fair], *s.* 1. Cualquier composición de materias combustibles que se enciende con facilidad y es muy difícil de apagarse; fuego griego. 2. Erisipela, sarpullido.
Wild-goose [waild'-gūs], *s.* (Orn.) Ganso silvestre; ganso del Canadá.
Wild-goose-chase [waild'-gūs-chēs'], *s.* Caza de gansos silvestres; (fig.) empresa quimérica, insensata.
Wilding [waild'-ing], *s.* Manzana silvestre; planta que crece silvestre; árbol frutal con sus propias raíces que crece por entre frutales ingertos.
Wildly [waild'-li], *adv.* Sin cultivo; desatinadamente.
Wildness [waild'-nes], *s.* 1. La calidad de lo que está baldío o sin ningún cultivo. 2. Selvatiquez, tosquedad, rusticidad, falta de cultura, rudeza, brutalidad. 3. Estado salvaje, inculto; carácter salvaje; ferocidad, calidad de feroz. 4. Travesura o acción culpable por demasiada viveza. 5. Desvarío de la imaginación, locura.
Wild-oat [waild'-ōt], *s.* Avena loca o silvestre. *To sow one's wild-oats,* (Fam.) Hacer de las suyas; correrla; pasar sus mocedades.
Wild-stock [waild'-stoc], *s.* Árbol silvestre para ingerir o ingertar.
Wile [wail], *va.* 1. Desviar, atraer con astucia; corromper; vendar a uno los ojos. 2. Divertirse, pasar un rato: por lo común con *away.* *V.* WHILE.—*s.* Dolo, fraude, engaño; astucia.
Wilful [wil'-ful], *a.* 1. Porfiado, voluntarioso, temoso, testarudo, cabezudo; repropio, rehacio (se dice de las caballerías). 2. Voluntario, premeditado, lo que se ejecuta de intento ó lo que se hace con toda intención.
Wilfully [wil'-ful-i], *adv.* 1. Tercamente, obstinadamente. 2. Voluntariamente, con toda intención, de propósito o a propósito.
Wilfulness [wil'-ful-nes], *s.* Terquedad, obstinación; perversidad.
Wiliness [wai'-li-nes], *s.* Fraude, engaño; maña.
Will [wil], *s.* 1. Voluntad, facultad de querer; albedrío; discreción. 2. Acto de la voluntad, volición, elección o escogimiento. 3. Volición, decisión; entusiasmo práctico; energía de carácter. 4. Intención, resolución, designio. 5. Testamento, declaración de la última voluntad. 6. (Ant.) Gana, propensión, inclinación o deseo de alguna cosa. 7. (Ant.) Precepto, mandato. *At will,* A voluntad. *At one's will,* A su gusto. *Thy will be done,* Hagase tu voluntad. *To make one's will,* Hacer uno su testamento. *Ill-will,* Mala voluntad, malquerer, tirria, odio. *Good-will,* Cariño, buena voluntad, disposición o propensión favorable; buena intención. *Good-will of a house* o *shop,* La recomendación que da a sus parroquianos el que vende o traspasa una tienda o establecimiento, para que continúen favoreciendo al nuevo poseedor. *To have all things at will,* Tenerlo todo a medida de su deseo. *Will-o'-the-wisp,* Fuego fatuo, especie de meteoro.
Will, *va.* y *vn.* 1. Querer, desear. 2. Resolver, mandar. 3. Rogar, suplicar. 4. Testar o hacer testamento. *I will have him do it,* Quiero que él lo haga. *Do as you will,* Haga Vd. lo que quiera. *Will he, nill he,* Que quiera, que no quiera.—*Will,* signo verbal del futuro de indicativo inglés. (Véase la Introducción.) En las oraciones afirmativas sirve para expresar resolución, promesa o amenaza de parte de quien habla en la primera persona, y para anunciar o mandar en las segundas y terceras. *I will punish you,* Yo te castigaré, tengo voluntad de castigarte, estoy resuelto a castigarte o quiero castigarte. *You will receive the letter tomorrow,* Recibirá Vd. la carta mañana, anuncio a Vd. que recibirá la carta mañana, o creo que recibirá Vd. mañana la carta. En las oraciones interrogativas se usa *will* en las segundas personas, para indagar la voluntad del sujeto a quien se dirige la pregunta, y en la tercera persona, para averiguar la voluntad de esta tercera persona. *Will you go to London?* ¿Irá Vd. a Londres? ¿quiere Vd. ir a Londres? ¿tiene Vd. intención de ir a Londres? *Will your father give you leave?* ¿Le dará a Vd. licencia su padre? ¿sabe Vd. si le dará licencia su padre?

Willed [wild], *pret.* y *pp.* del verbo *To* WILL. *Ill-willed*, Maligno, el que tiene mala voluntad. *Self-willed*, Obstinado, terco.
Willing [wil'-ing], *a.* 1. Inclinado, pronto, deseoso. 2. Complaciente. 3. Ofrecido o hecho de buena gana; franco, voluntario. *God willing*, Mediante Dios, si Dios quiere. *To be willing*, Querer, no tener repugnancia. *To be willing to*, Querer, consentir en.
Willingly [wil'-ing-li], *adv.* Voluntariamente, de buena gana, con gusto.
Willingness [wil'-ing-nes], *s.* Buena voluntad, buena gana, gusto o buena disposición para hacer algo.
Willow [1] [wil'-ō], *s.* Sauce; cualquier árbol o arbusto del género Salix, de las salicíneas. *Weeping willow*, (Bot.) Sauce de Babilonia o de Judea, sauce llorón. *Willow-plot*, Saucedal, salceda. *Willow-herb*, Hierba perenne de la familia de las onagráceas. (Epilobium angustifolium.) Se llama también *Persian* o *French willow*, y crece en terrenos bajos. *Hairy willow-herb*, Especie británica de Epilobium. *Willow-warbler*, *willow-wren*, o *chiffchaff*, Curraquilla. Phylloscopus rufus. *Willow-oak*, Roble americano de gran tamaño, con hojas semejantes a las del sauce.
Willow,[2] *s.* Diablo, máquina para limpiar el algodón, la lana, el lino, etc.
Willowish [wil'-ō-ish], *a.* Que tiene color de sauce.
Willy-nilly [wil'-i-nil'-i], *a* y *adv.* Sin respeto a los deseos de otro, a fuerzas.
Wilt [1] [wilt], *va.* Marchitar, ajar, hacer decaer, volver mustio.—*vn.* 1. Marchitarse, secarse, perder su frescura una planta; (fig.) perder la energía o vitalidad. 2. (Ger.) Amansarse; ponerse en salvo repentinamente después de verse vencido.
Wilt, 2ª *pers. sing.* del presente de indicativo de WILL.
Wily [wai'-li], *a.* Astuto, falso, mañoso, cauteloso, insidioso.
Wimble [wim'-bl], *s.* Berbiquí, especie de barrena.
Wimple [wim'-pl], *s.* Toca; hoy griñón, toca de lienzo o seda que se ponen las monjas y beatas en la cabeza y les rodea el rostro.
Wimple, *va.* Tirar hacia abajo; cubrir con griñón.
Win [win], *va.* y *vn.* 1. Ganar, lograr o adquirir alguna cosa. 2. Ganar, conquistar. 3. Obtener, alcanzar. 4. Persuadir, atraer, arrastrar. 5. Llevarse, arrastrar tras sí. 6. Prevalecer, tener más poder o valor que otro.
Wince [wins], *vn.* Retroceder, recular como a consecuencia de un dolor o de un golpe; echar pie atrás; de aquí, cocear, tirar coces; mostrarse terco al ser reprendido.
Winch [winch], *s.* 1. Cigüeña de torno, manivela, manubrio en forma de codo que sirve para hacer girar el eje o árbol de una máquina. 2. Árgana, argüe, molinete, aparato para subir cosas de mucho peso; cabria.
Wind [wind, waind en poesía], *s.* 1. Viento, el aire en movimiento; una corriente de aire. 2. Viento, aire, el que se mueve por algún artificio. 3. Resuello, aliento, respiración. 4. Flatulencia, flato, ventosidad, pedo. 5. Cualquier cosa muy ligera y de poco momento. 6. Viento, husmo, el olor que viene de alguna cosa; un secreto dejado escapar o descubierto. *To get wind of a plot*, Husmear, descubrir una entruchada o intriga. 7. Viento, en náutica la dirección del viento o del aire movido en la atmósfera. *Wind-bound*, Detenido por falta de viento. *Westerly wind*, Viento de poniente. *Wind on the beam*, (Mar.) Viento derrotero. *Wind aft*, (Mar.) Viento en popa. *Wind on end or ahead*, (Mar.) Viento por la proa o a fil de roda. *Steady wind*, Viento hecho. *Land-winds*, Terrales. *Light winds*, (Mar.) Ventolinos. *Trade-winds*, Vientos alisios. *South-west winds*, Vendavales. *Quarter-wind*, (Mar.) Viento al anca o a la cuadra. *The wind is very high*, Hace mucho viento, o el viento es muy fuerte. *Between wind and water*, A flor del agua. *Puff of wind*, Soplo, ventolera. *Gale of wind*, Temporal, ventarrón. *Gust of wind*, Racha de viento, ráfaga, ventarrón. *In the wind's eye, in the teeth of the wind*, Directamente opuesto a la dirección del viento. *To keep the wind*, (Mar.) Navegar de bolina, mantenerse ciñendo el viento. *To sail against wind and tide*, Ir contra viento y marea. *Down the wind*, En decadencia, decayendo. *To take* o *to have* o *to get the wind*, Dominar a alguno; ganar la superioridad; ganar por la mano; anticiparse. *Something is in the wind*, Se trama algo.
Wind [1] [waind], *va.* (*pret.* y *pp.* WOUND o WINDED). 1. Serpear o serpentear; girar o moverse alrededor, hacer pasar espiralmente alrededor de un eje fijo. 2. Envolver, arrollar, abrazar. 3. Dar cuerda a, renovar la marcha de, arrollando una cuerda, un resorte, etc. 4. (Mar.) Virar; mudar o cambiar el rumbo de un buque; manejar, dirigir, gobernar, ganar influencia sobre. 5. Perseguir, seguir las vueltas o los rodeos de. 6. Devanar, hacer ovillos; tejer. 7. (Ingl.) Alzar con árgano o molinete.—*vn.* 1. Moverse o estar dispuesto de una manera circular o en espiral; serpentear. 2. Rodear, ir por rodeos o circunloquios; de aquí, insinuarse, lograr un fin con astucia. 3. Tener forma torcida. 4. Enroscarse, retortijarse, volverse, cambiarse. *To wind along*, Hacer eses, serpentear, seguir. *To wind about*, Enrollarse alrededor de; dar vuelta a. *To wind down*, Bajar dando vueltas, bajar serpenteando. *To wind off*, Devanar; desarrollar, desenredar. *To wind out*, Desenmarañar, desenredar lo que está enredado o enmarañado; desembarazarse, libertarse, salir de algún enredo o laberinto. *To wind up*, Concluir, acabar, finalizar. *To wind up a watch or clock*, Dar cuerda al reloj. *To wind up thread*, Devanar hilo, reducirlo a ovillos. *To wind a call*, (Mar.) Tocar el pito.
Wind [2] [wind], *va.* 1. Ventear, tomar el viento por el olfato. 2. Agotar, gastar el aliento o respiración de; también, recobrar la respiración. 3. Dar aire, exponer al viento, orear.
Wind [3] [wind o waind], *va.* y *vn.* 1. Soplar, echar viento por la boca. 2. Tocar un instrumento de viento.
Windage [wind'-ēj], *s.* (Art.) Viento de un cañón.
Wind-bound [wind'-baund], *a.* (Mar.) Detenido por vientos contrarios.
Winded [wind'-ed], *a.* *Short-winded*, Que respira dificultosamente. *Long-winded*, Largo; enfadoso, enmarañado.
Windegg [wind'-eg], *s.* Huevo huero.
Winder [waind'-ęr], *s.* 1. Argadillo, devanador, devanadera. 2. (Bot.) Planta enredadera. *V.* TWINER. 3. Escalón de abanico.
Windfall [wind'-fōl], *s.* 1. Fruta caída del árbol; fruta abatida por el viento. 2. Provecho, ganga, ventaja o ganancia inesperada.
Windflower [wind'-flau-ęr], *s.* (Bot.) Anémone, anémona.
Wind-gage, Wind-gauge [wind'-gēj], *s.* Anemómetro, instrumento que mide la fuerza y velocidad de los vientos.
Windgall [wind'-gōl], *s.* Aventadura, una enfermedad de los caballos.
Windgun [wind'-gun], *s.* Escopeta de viento.
Windiness [wind'-i-nes], *s.* 1. Tiempo ventoso; calidad de ventoso. 2. Ventosidad, flatulencia o flato. 3. Hinchazón, vanidad, presunción.
Winding [waind'-ing], *s.* 1. Vuelta, revuelta, giro, rodeo; recodo (de un camino). 2. El acto o la condición del que arrolla o envuelve. 3. Alabeo, comba, combadura. 4. (Elec.) Modo como se arrolla un alambre. *Windings and turnings*, Las vueltas y revueltas o los rincones y recovecos que hacen tortuosa a una cosa. *Winding of the voice*, La inflexión de la voz. *Winding-sheet*, Mortaja, la sábana en que se envuelve el cadáver. *Winding-stair*, Escalera de caracol u ojo. *Winding-tackle*, (Mar.) Aparejo de estrelleras o candelizas de combés. *Winding up*, (1) Acto de dar cuerda (v. g. a un reloj); (2) liquidación, conclusión; desenlace.—*a.* 1. Sinuoso, tortuoso, que serpea o serpentea, que se mueve haciendo vueltas o tornos como la serpiente. 2. Que se arrolla, que se enreda o envuelve.
Windlass [wind'-las], *s.* 1. Argüe, árgana o árgano, máquina para levantar cosas de gran peso. 2. (Mar.) Cabrestante pequeño o molinete, instrumento que se usa a bordo de las embarcaciones pequeñas para sacar las anclas del fondo y otros objetos. 3. En las minas de Méjico, malacate.
Windle [win'-dl], *s.* 1. (Prov.) Devanadera o cualquier cosa que se usa para para dar vueltas o envolver. 2. Medida desusada de 3.50 *bushels* o fanegas.
Windmill [wind'-mil], *s.* Molino de viento.
Window [win'-dō], *s.* Ventana; vidriera. *Glass window*, Vidriera. *Window-glass*, Vidrio de ventana o plano. *Window-shutter*, Postigo de ventana; contraventana. *Bay window, bow window*, Mirador, ventana saliente o cimbrada. *Dormer* o *garret window*, Lumbrera, tragaluz de bohardilla o desván. *Round* o *rose window*, Rosetón. *Show window*, Escaparate de una tienda. *Window-blind*, Contravidriera; también, celosía, transparente, persiana. *Window-frame*, Bastidor o marco de ventana. *Window-shade*, Persiana, transparente. *To look out of the window*, Mirar por la ventana.
Windpipe [wind'-paip], *s.* Tráquea, traquearteria.
Windrow [wind'-rō o win'-rō], *s.* Lí-

nea de hierba segada; montón de máiz o de turba.—*va.* Arrastrar el heno en una hilera o línea.

Windsails [wind'-seilz], *s. pl.* (Mar.) Mangueras de viento.

Windshield [wind'-shild], *s.* Guardabrisa, parabrisas. *Windshield wiper*, Limpiador de parabrisas.

Wind-up [waind'-up], *s.* Acción final; fin, término.

Windward [wind'-wɑrd], *a.* Al viento, expuesto al viento.—*s.* Barlovento, lado de donde sopla el viento.—*adv.* A barlovento. *The Windward Islands*, Las Islas de Barlovento. *A windward tide*, Marea contraria al viento. *To lie to windward*, Barloventear.

Windy [wind'-i], *a.* 1. Ventoso, tempestuoso, borrascoso. 2. Expuesto al viento, a barlovento. 3. Vano, dado al estilo hinchado o pomposo. 4. Flatulento. *It is windy*, Hace viento. *On the windy side*, Del lado del viento.

Wine [wain], *s.* 1. Vino, el zumo de las uvas exprimido y fermentado. 2. Vino, el zumo de otros vegetables que se cuece y fermenta al modo del de las uvas. *Sorry wine*, Zupia, purriela, vino malo. *Red wine*, Vino tinto. *Currant wine*, Vino de grosellas. *To season with wine*, Envinar. *Wine-cellar*, Bodega, cueva donde se guardan los vinos. *Wine-bibber*, Borracho, odre. *Wine-merchant*, Mercader de vino. *Wine-skin*, Odre, pellejo de vino. *Wine-taster*, Catador de vinos. *Wine-whey*, Suero con vino. *Wine-cooler*, Receptáculo para enfriar el vino. *Wine-fly*, Mosca pequeña del género Piophila que se cría en el vino, la sidra, etc. *Wine-glass*, Vaso para vino. *Wine-grower*, Viñadero, viticultor. *Wine-press*, Lagar. *Wine-measure*, Medida líquida, medida para vino. *Wine-palm*, Palmera de la cual se obtiene vino. *Wine-vault*, Candiotera, cueva para conservar el vino.

Wine (to), *va.* y *vn.* Convidar u obsequiar con vino; beber vino.

Winery [wai'-nɐr-i], *s.* Establecimiento para hacer vino; cuarto para afinar y conservar el vino, candiotera.

Wing [wing], *s.* 1. Ala, la parte del cuerpo de las aves o murciélagos, y de ciertos insectos, de que se sirven para volar. 2. Lo que proporciona o comunica movimiento veloz. *Upon the wings of the wind*, En alas del viento. 3. Vuelo, la acción de volar. *To take wing*, Volar. 4. (Mil.) Ala, la parte del ejército que cubre el centro. 5. Ala de un edificio, costado, flanco. 6. Cualquier lado, apéndice, parte, etc., semejante a un ala; apéndice foliáceo, uno de los dos pétalos de la corola papilionácea. *On the wing*, Al vuelo. *Wing-case, wing-cover, wing-sheath*, Élitro, estuche que cubre las alas de los insectos. *To be upon the wing*, Ir a salir, ir a marchar, estar para salir.

Wing, *va.* 1. Llevar, transportar sobre las alas; ejecutar por medio de las alas. 2. Pasar, atravesar, recorrer (volando). 3. Dar o prestar alas a, impeler. 4. Proveer de alas, dar o poner alas. 5. Flanquear, poner flancos. 6. Herir en el ala o en alguna parte análoga; dañar, incapacitar, inhabilitar.—*vn.* Alear, volar, mover las alas.

Wing chair [wing chãr], *s.* Sillón con respaldo en forma de alas.

Winged [wingd o wing'-ed], *a.* 1. Alado, que tiene alas; que vuela. 2. Que vuela como con alas; elevado, en éxtasis. 3. Lleno o poblado de seres alados. *Broken-winged*, Aliquebrado.

Wingless [wing'-les], *a.* Falto de alas, sin alas; áptero.

Wing spread [wing spred], *s.* Extensión de las alas de un avión o de un pájaro, etc.

Wingy [wing'-i], *a.* Alado.

Wink [wink], *vn.* 1. Cerrar los ojos y abrirlos rápidamente. 2. Guiñar; hacer señas guiñando; pestañear guiñando. 3. Pasar por alto, tolerar, disimular, dejar pasar una falta: en este sentido casi siempre lleva tras sí la partícula *at.* *A winking light*, Una luz poco clara.

Wink, *s.* 1. La acción de tener los ojos cerrados. 2. Pestañeo, el movimiento de cerrar y abrir los ojos guiñando. 3. Guiño, la acción de guiñar haciendo señas. 4. Ojeada, mirada pronta y ligera. *I did not sleep a wink all night*, No he cerrado los ojos en toda la noche, o no he podido pegar los ojos en toda la noche. *Without further winks or nods*, Sin más acá ni más allá. *To wink at a thing*, Hacerse el desentendido; no hacer alto en una cosa. *Forty winks*, (Fam.) Sueño de corta duración.

Winker [wink'-ɐr], *s.* 1. Guiñador, el que guiña; el que pestañea; el que tolera o disimula. 2. Anteojera (de caballo). 3. (Fam.) Pestaña. 4. El músculo con el cual se produce el pestañeo.

Winkingly [wink'-ing-li], *adv.* 1. Por medio de guiñadas o guiñando. 2. Con los ojos medio abiertos o entreabiertos. 3. Con tolerancia, con indulgencia. *Winking at*, Connivencia.

Winkle [win'-kl], *s.* Caracol marino, uno cualquiera de varios grandes gasterópodos, particularmente del género Fulgur.

Winner [win'-ɐr], *s.* Ganador, vencedor.

Winning [win'-ing], *s.* Ganancia, lucro.—*a.* 1. Atractivo, encantador, que lleva o arrastra tras sí; persuasivo, que gana la voluntad de otro. 2. Seguro del éxito. *Winning back*, Desquite, el acto de desquitarse. *Winning side*, El partido que triunfa, gana o lleva la ventaja.

Winnow [win'-ō], *va.* 1. Aventar, acchar, separar la paja del grano. 2. Examinar, escudriñar. 3. Agitar, batir el aire (como con alas). 4. Soplar; dispersar soplando.—*vn.* Abalear, acchar el grano. *Winnowing-machine*, Aventador, abalcador mecánico.

Winsome [win'-sum], *a.* Atractivo, que tiene apariencia o maneras atractivas o persuasivas, que gana el corazón.

Winter [win'-tɐr], *s.* 1. Invierno, la estación fría del año. *A hard winter*, Invierno crudo. *Winter clothes*, Ropa de invierno. *Winter season*, Invernada. *Winter's bark*, Corteza magelánica. *Winter-berry*, Apalachina, arbusto de la familia de las ilicíneas, con bayas escarlata. *Winter-bloom*, *V.* WICH-HAZEL. *Winter-solstice*, Solsticio hiemal. 2. Época triste o lúgubre. 3. (Poét.) Año.

Winter, *va.* 1. Hacer invernar. 2. Alimentar o conservar durante el invierno.—*vn.* Invernar, pasar el invierno. *Winter-kill*, (E. U.) Hacer perecer por la severidad del invierno.

Winter-beaten [win'-tɐr-bī-tn], *a.* Maltratado por el invierno.

Wintergreen [win'-tɐr-grin], *s.* (Bot.) 1. Pirola. 2. Gualteria, planta de la familia de las ericáceas.

Wintering [win'-tɐr-ing], *s.* 1. Acción de invernar o pasar el invierno. 2. Forraje y abrigo para el ganado durante el invierno.

Winterish [win'-tɐr-ish], *a.* Algo semejante al invierno.

Winterize [win'-ter-aiz], *va.* Acondicionar para uso invernal.

Winterless [win'-tɐr-les], *a.* Sin invierno frío; tropical.

Winterly [win'-tɐr-li] (ant.), **Wintry** [win'-tri], **Wintery**, *a.* Brumal, invernal o invernizo, lo perteneciente al invierno.

Wipe [waip], *va.* 1. Enjugar, frotar ligeramente; limpiar por medio de alguna cosa blanda y suave. 2. Quitar o separar frotando ligeramente; restregar, acepillar. 3. Aplicar la soldadura por medio de un pedazo de tela o cuero. *To wipe away*, Quitar sacudiendo, estregando o limpiando con suavidad. *To wipe off*, Borrar, cancelar; limpiar, lavar o quitar alguna cosa que ensuciaba o manchaba a otra. *To wipe out*, Borrar, cancelar, hacer nulo; destruir, hacer desaparecer. *To wipe out of*, Arrojar, defraudar.

Wipe, *s.* 1. Limpión, limpiadura ligera. 2. (Ger.) Golpe de lado, revés, manotón. *V.* SWIPE.

Wiper [waip'-ɐr], *s.* 1. Persona que enjuga o restriega. 2. Trapo, lienzo, útil, destinado a enjugar o usado para enjugar. 3. (Mec.) Leva, álabe, saliente fijado sobre un eje que tiene movimiento de desliz o frote.

Wire [wair], *va.* 1. Proveer de alambre; atar o liar con hilo metálico. 2. Coger (caza) con un lazo de alambre. 3. (Fam.) Transmitir por telégrafo.—*vn.* (Fam.) Enviar un telegrama; telegrafiar.—*s.* 1. Alambre, el hilo tirado de un metal dúctil. 2. El telégrafo eléctrico como medio de comunicación. 3. Cuerda de un instrumento músico. 4. Hilo fino metálico, o juego de líneas finamente rayadas en el foco de un telescopio. 5. Varilla de cortina. *Iron-wire*, Hilo o alambre de hierro. *Wires*, Arillos para aretes. *Wire-plate*, Hilera de tirar alambre. *Wire edge*, Filbán (de una navaja nueva, tijera, etc.). *Wire-gauge*, Calibrador de alambre. *Wire-gauze*, Gasa de alambre, tela metálica. *Wire-puller*, Titiritero; intrigante. *Wire-pulling*, Maquinaciones secretas, por bajo cuerda. *Wire-work*, Enrejado, alambrado. *Wire-worm*, Larva a modo de gusano de elátero.

Wireless [wair'-les], *s.* Abreviatura de *Wireless telegraph*, Telegrafía inalámbrica, *Wireless telephony*, Radiotelefonía, etc. (Ingl.) Radioemisora.—*va.* y *vn.* Comunicarse por radiograma. *Wireless transmission*, Transmisión por radio.

Wire tapping [wair tap'-ing], *s.* Conexión telefónica clandestina para interceptar mensajes.

Wiring [wair'-ing], *s.* 1. Alambrado. 2. Instalación de alambrado eléctico.

Wiry [wair'-i], *a.* 1. Hecho de alambre; reducido a alambre; semejante a un alambre; tieso, tenso. 2. De mucha resistencia; flaco pero fuerte y nervioso; dícese de las personas. 3. Débil: se dice del pulso.

Wis [wis], *vn.* (Des.) Pensar, creer.

Wisdom [wiz'-dum], *s.* 1. Sabiduría, cordura, prudencia, juicio, discreción; sentido común; buena conducta, buen modo de proceder. 2. Alto grado de conocimiento, erudición. 3. Dicho profundo. *Wisdom-tooth,* Muela cordal o del juicio. *A man of wisdom,* Hombre sabio, muy advertido, muy leído.

Wise [waiz], *a.* Sabio, docto, hábil; grave, cuerdo, juicioso, prudente, discreto, advertido, sentado, erudito, sabido. *A wise man,* Un sabio, un filósofo.—*s.* Modo, manera de ser, estar o hacer. Úsase en composición frecuentemente, como *otherwise,* de otro modo; *likewise,* también; *sidewise,* de lado; *in no wise,* de ningún modo, de ninguna manera, absolutamente.

Wiseacre [waiz'-ê-kẹr], *s.* Persona sabihonda, el que presume de sabio; de aquí, necio, tonto.

Wisecrack [waiz'-crac], *s.* Observación ingeniosamente chistosa.

Wisely [waiz'-li], *adv.* Sabiamente, con prudencia, con discreción, con cordura, juiciosamente; con mucha habilidad.

Wish [wish], *va.* 1. Desear, querer, apetecer lo que no se posee. 2. Pedir o suplicar para conseguir lo que se desea. 3. Anhelar, ansiar, desear con ansia o tener ansia o deseo vehemente de conseguir alguna cosa. 4. Estar inclinado o dispuesto a hacer algo. *I wish you joy,* Le doy a Vd. la enhorabuena o el parabién.—*inter. I wish!* ¡Ojalá! ¡Quiera el cielo!

Wish, *s.* 1. Anhelo, ansia, deseo; la cosa deseada. 2. Petición, demanda, expresión de un deseo. *Wish-bone,* Hueso de la pechuga en las aves; hueso delgado ahorquillado formado por la unión de las clavículas. Se le llama a veces *merry-thought.*

Wisher [wish'-ẹr], *s.* Deseador. *Well-wisher,* El que desea el bien de alguna persona.

Wishful [wish'-ful], *a.* Deseoso, ansioso, anheloso; ávido.

Wishfully [wish'-ful-i], *adv.* Ansiosamente, ardientemente, con anhelo.

Wishy-washy [wish'-i-wesh'-i], *a.* (Fam.) Débil, ligero, diluído (p. ej. una bebida); de aquí, flojo, falto de fuerza.

Wisp [wisp], *va.* 1. Acepillar, limpiar con escobilla. 2. *V.* CRUMPLE. —*s.* 1. Manojito de heno, paja larga u otra cosa; mechón, puñado de cabellos. 2. Escobilla pequeña. 3. Fuego fatuo. 4. Enfermedad que ataca los pies del ganado mayor.

Wist [wist], *pret.* del verbo *To* WIT. "*Moses wist not that his face shone,*" "Moisés no sabía que su rostro estaba resplandeciente."

Wistaria [wis-tê-rẹ-a], *s.* (Bot.) Wistaria, vistaria.

Wistful [wist'-ful], *a.* Pensativo, serio, atento.

Wistfully [wist'-ful-i], *adv.* Seriamente; atentamente; fijamente.

Wit [wit], *va.* y *vn.* (*pret.* WIST). (Ant.) Saber, recibir una noticia. *To wit,* A saber, es decir.

Wit, *s.* 1. Rasgo de ingenio, agudeza, dicho agudo, asociación de ideas que causa pasmo; sal. *V.* HUMOR. 2. Ingenio, el sujeto de mucha viveza de imaginación. 3. Entendimiento, ingenio; viveza de imaginación o fantasía; seso. 4. Juicio, discurso, prendas, conocimientos, luces. *Wits, pl.* Juicio, sentido, razón; industria. *The five wits,* Los cinco sentidos; también, las facultades intelectuales. *Ready wit,* Genio agudo. *Mother wit,* Sentido común, entendimiento natural. *To be at one's wit's end,* Estar, hallarse apurado, cortado; sin saber qué decir; perder la chaveta. *To be out of one's wits,* Estar fuera de juicio o fuera de sí; no saber uno lo que se hace. *To live by his wits,* Campar de golondro, vivir de gorra, o de expedientes, vivir y campar a costa ajena, ser un estafador o un petardista. *To be thought a wit,* Pasar por hombre de ingenio. *To have one's wits about one,* Conservar uno su presencia de ánimo.

Witch [wich], *s.* 1. Bruja, hechicera. 2. Vejarrona, mujer fea.

Witch, *va.* Encantar, maleficiar, hechizar, embrujar. *V. To* BEWITCH.

Witchcraft [wich'-crạft], **Witchery** [wich'-ẹr-i], *s.* 1. Brujería, hechicería, sortilegio, maleficio. 2. Encantamiento, poder mágico, fascinación.

Witch-elm [wich'-elm], *s.* (Bot.) *V.* WYCH-ELM.

Witch hazel [wich hê'-zl], *s.* (Bot.) 1. Hamamelis de Virginia. 2. Loción de Hamamelis de Virginia.

Witch-hunt [wich'-hunt], *s.* Persecución, campaña de desprestigio.

Witching [wich'-ing], *a.* Halagüeño, encantador, que fascina; mágico.

With [widh], *prep.* 1. Con, preposición que se usa para explicar el medio, modo o instrumento con que se hace una cosa; juntamente con, en compañía de. 2. De; toma muchas veces este sentido con los verbos y participios, y con ciertos adjetivos; por ejemplo: *To fill with water,* Llenar de agua. *Attended with,* Acompañado de. *Congenial with,* Que está en el carácter de. *Smitten with,* Enamorado de. *Taken with,* Encantado de. *With all my heart,* De todo corazón. 3. Por, contra, a, en, entre. *With all speed,* Con la mayor prisa, lo más pronto posible. *He does not find fault with it,* Nada tiene que decir. *I have nothing to do with you,* Nada tengo que ver con Vd. *With your leave,* Con permiso de Vd. *To struggle with adversity,* Luchar contra la adversidad. *Angry with,* Enfadado con. 4. En caso de, con respecto a, para con, concerniente. *Deal not harshly with me,* No sea Vd. duro para conmigo. *To go with,* (1) Convenir, sentar bien; (2) acompañar; (3) tomar el partido de. 5. Así que, luego que, inmediatamente, después de. *With that,* Así que dijo esto. *To have to do with,* Tener que habérselas con. *Away with him!* ¡Quítenlo de mi presencia! ¡fuera con él! ¡que muera! *It is so with the rich,* Así sucede entre los ricos. *I know not what course to take with them,* No sé qué partido tomar para con (o respecto a) ellos.

With-. Prefijo que indica oposición; contra, re. *To withdraw,* Retirar, remover. *To withhold,* Retener. *To withstand,* Oponerse a.

Withal [widh-ōl'], *adv.* 1. Además, a más de esto; también. 2. Por otra parte. 3. Al mismo tiempo. 4. (Ant.) Con.

Withdraw [widh-drō'], *va.* (*pret.* WITHDREW, *pp.* WITHDRAWN). 1. Quitar, privar; distraer; también alejar, descaminar, remover. 2. Retirar, apartar, separar. 3. Desdecir, retractar un aserto; retractarse.—*vn.* Retirarse, apartarse, separarse; irse, salir.

Withdrawal, ¿**Withdrawment** [widh-drō'-al, mẹnt], *s.* Retiro, retirada, el acto o hecho de retirar o de retirarse; acción de retirar un proyecto de ley presentado a un cuerpo legislativo.

Withdrew [widh-drū'], *pret.* del verbo WITHDRAW.

Withdrawing-room [widh-drō'-ing-rūm], *s.* 1. Retrete, cuarto pequeño destinado para retirarse. 2. *V.* DRAWING-ROOM.

Withe [with], *s.* 1. Mimbre. 2. Vencejo, atadero hecho de mimbres.

Wither [widh'-ẹr], *va.* 1. Marchitar, ajar, deslucir, poner mustias o secas las plantas. 2. Hacer perder las carnes o la fuerza muscular; agotar. 3. Hacer perecer o consumirse; también, avergonzar, sonrojar.—*vn.* Marchitarse, secarse, perder su frescura natural.

Wither-band [widh'-ẹr-band], *s.* La barra de hierro que sujeta los fustes de la silla de montar.

Witheredness [widh'-ẹrd-nes], *s.* 1. Ajamiento o marchitez de las flores, frutas, etc. 2. Sequedad.

Withers [widh'-ẹrz], *s. pl.* Cruz, la parte del cuerpo del caballo que está detrás del nacimiento del cuello.

Withhold [widh-hōld'], *va.* (*pret.* y *pp.* WITHHELD). 1. Detener, impedir, retener, apartar, contener. 2. Negar, rehusar.

Withholden [widh-hōld'-ẹn], *pp.* (Ant.) *V.* WITHHOLD.

Withholder [widh-hōld'-ẹr], *s.* Detentador; el que detiene, impide o rehusa.

Within [widh-in'], *prep.* 1. Dentro, adentro, en lo interior de. 2. Dentro de, en el espacio de, a la distancia de. 3. Al alcance de. *Within hearing,* Al alcance de la voz. 4, Debajo de. *Keep your expenses within your income,* Mantenga Vd. sus gastos dentro de los límites de sus ingresos. 5. Por poco; a, casi a, cerca de. *Within a short distance,* A poca distancia. *To reckon within an inch,* Calcular pulgada más o menos. *He was within a little of being killed,* Por poco lo matan. *From within,* De adentro. *Within four months,* Dentro de cuatro meses. *He is within,* Está dentro.—*adv.* 1. Interiormente, en la parte interior; de aquí, en el corazón o en la mente. 2. En casa, en su casa, en la habitación.

Without [widh-aut'], *prep.* 1. Sin, con falta de. 2. Fuera de, afuera. *Without my reach,* Fuera de mi alcance. 3. En lo exterior, por fuera. —*adv.* 1. Por afuera, por fuera, hacia fuera, de la parte de afuera. 2. Exteriormente, en lo exterior.—*conj.* Si no, sin que, a menos que, si no es que. *Without sin,* Sin pecado. *Without jesting,* Bromas aparte. *Without day,* Sin fecha. *To do* o *to go without,* Privarse de, pasarse sin. *Without being reminded,* Sin que alguien le llame la atención (a o hacia).

Withstand [widh-stand'], *va.* (*pret.* y *pp.* WITHSTOOD). Resistir, hacer resistencia u oposición, oponerse a; soportar.

Withstanding [widh-stand'-ing], *s.* Resistencia.

Witless [wit'-les], *a.* Necio, tonto, falto de ingenio o entendimiento.

Witling [wit'-ling], *s.* Truhán, chocarrero; el que afecta ingenio.

Witness [wit'-nes], *s.* 1. Testigo, espectador. 2. Testimonio, atestación de un hecho: el o lo que da fe, prueba; testigo (ante un tribunal). *To be a witness of,* Ser testigo de. *To bear witness to,* Dar testimonio, atestiguar. *In witness whereof,* En fe de lo cual. *Eye-witness,* Testigo de vista, testigo ocular. *Ear-witness,* Testigo de oídas, o auricular. *With a witness,* (Ant.) Efectivamente, con efecto.

Witness, *va.* 1. Ver o saber por experiencia personal; ser espectador de o concurrir a. 2. Atestiguar, testificar. 3. Firmar como testigo; establecer la autenticidad de un instrumento legal. 4. Exhibir alguna señal de; mostrar.—*vn.* Ser testigo de una cosa o presenciarla; servir de testigo.

Witted [wit'-ed], *a.* Ingenioso. *Quick-witted,* Perspicaz, vivo de ingenio.

Witticism [wit'-i-sizm], *s.* Dicho agudo, chiste, gracia, gracejo, chulada: frecuentemente se toma por chocarrería, bufonada o agudezas fuera de tiempo o poco delicadas.

Wittily [wit'-i-li], *adv.* Ingeniosamente, agudamente, con agudeza.

Wittiness [wit'-i-nes], *s.* Ingenio, sal, gracia, agudeza, chiste ingenioso y fino, concepto agudo; viveza de ingenio.

Wittingly [wit'-ing-li], *adv.* Conocidamente, adrede, de propósito.

Witty [wit'-i], *a.* 1. Ingenioso, lleno de ingenio, gracia o invención, agudo, chistoso, gracioso. 2. (Ant.) Satírico, mordaz, picante. *A witty saying,* Un chiste, una gracia o agudeza.

Witwall [wit'-wōl], *s.* (Prov. Ingl.) 1. Pico o picamaderos, un ave. 2. Oropéndola de Europa.

Wive [waiv], *vn.* Casarse, contraer matrimonio el hombre con la mujer. —*va.* 1. Casar, deposar, dar mujer. 2. (Poco us.) Tomar por mujer.

Wives [waivz], *s. pl.* de WIFE. Mujeres casadas, esposas.

Wizard [wiz'-ard], *a.* Hechicero, mago, que encanta.—*s.* 1. Brujo, hechicero, encantador, adivino. 2. Jugador de manos, titiritero.

Wizen [wiz'-n], *va.* y *vn.* Desecar, marchitar; desecarse, marchitarse; encogerse, estrecharse.—*a.* Encogido; marchito, ajado, mustio.

Wo o **Woe** [wō], *s.* Dolor, pena, angustia, pesar, aflicción; calamidad, infortunio, desastre, miseria. *Woe to you,* Pobre de tí, ay de tí.—*inter.* ¡Ay, infeliz! *Wo to the vanquished!* ¡Ay de los vencidos! *Woe is me!* ¡Desgraciado de mí! ¡pobre de mí! *Woe worth the day!* ¡Mal haya el día en que!

Woad [wōd], *s.* 1. Hierba pastel o glasto (en botánica, isátida): hierba de la familia de las crucíferas. 2. Tinte azul extraído de las hojas de esta planta. (Isatis tinctoria.)

Woaded [wōd'-ed], *a.* Teñido con glasto.

Wobble, *vn.* *V.* WABBLE.

Woden [wō'-den], *n. pr.* Lo mismo que *Odin;* forma anglosajona. El nombre sobrevive aún en la voz *Wednesday.*

Woebegone [wō'-be-gon], *a.* Abrumado de pesares o de desgracias, consumido por los infortunios, lleno de angustia.

Woful, Woeful [wō'-ful], *a.* 1. Triste, afligido, angustiado. 2. Lastimero, doloroso; calamitoso, funesto, desastroso. 3. Ruin, bajo, despreciable.

Wofully [wō'-ful-i], *adv.* Tristemente, ruinmente, miserablemente, funestamente, desastrosamente, dolorosamente.

Wold[1] [wōld], *s.* Campiña, espacio o comarca de tierras altas ligeramente inclinadas o con pequeñas eminencias. *V.* DOWN.

Wold,[2] *s.* Gualda. *V.* WELD.

Wolf [wulf], *s.* (*pl.* WOLVES). 1. Lobo. *She-wolf,* Loba. *Young wolf,* Lobezno, lobato, cachorro de lobo. 2. Mamífero semejante a un lobo. 3. Toda persona o cosa voraz, cruel o rapaz. 4. (Ento.) La larva destructiva de varios escarabajos y mariposas nocturnas. 5. Una especie de úlcera cancerosa. *V.* LUPUS. *To cry wolf,* Gritar "al lobo," dar falsa alarma (alusión a la fábula). *To have a wolf by the ears,* Ver las orejas al lobo, hallarse en gran peligro. *To have a wolf in the stomach,* Tener apetito voraz. *To keep the wolf from the door,* Cerrar la puerta al hambre, mantener alejada la pobreza o la necesidad.

Wolf-dog [wulf'-dog], *s.* 1. Mastín, perro grande para cazar lobos. 2. Perro-lobo. *Wolf-fish,* Lobo marino, pez grande con dientes sumamente fuertes.

Wolfish [wulf'-ish], *a.* Lobero, lo que es propio de lobos o pertenece a los lobos.

Wolfram [wul'-fram], *s.* Wolframio o tungsteno.

Wolf's-bane [wulfs'-bên], *s.* (Bot.) 1. Acónito. 2. Una especie europea de árnica.

Wolf's-milk [wulfs'-milk], *s.* (Bot.) Titímalo, lechetrezna.

Wolverine [wūl-ver-in], *s.* (Zool.) Especie de glotón norteamericano, carcayú. Gulo luscus.

Wolves [wulvz], *s. pl.* WOLF.

Woman [wum'-an], *s.* (*pl.* WOMEN [wim'-en]). 1. Mujer, criatura racional del sexo femenino. 2. La porción femenina de la raza humana; las mujeres colectivamente. 3. Carácter mujeril, el conjunto de las propiedades peculiares a las mujeres. 4. Mujer, criada, sirvienta. *Woman of the town,* Dama cortesana.

Woman-hater [wum'-an-hêt-er], *s.* Aborrecedor de las mujeres.

Womanhood [wum'-an-hud], *s.* El estado o la condición de mujer; el conjunto de las propiedades peculiares a las mujeres.

Womanish [wum'-an-ish], *a.* Mujeril, femenino, que pertenece a la mujer; afeminado, muelle, débil, pusilánime.

Womanize [wum'-an-aiz], *va.* (Poco us.) Afeminar.

Womankind [wum'-an-kaind], *s.* El sexo femenino considerado como el conjunto o agregado de todas las mujeres; mujeriego.

Womanliness [wum'-an-li-nes], *s.* Naturaleza o carácter adecuado a la mujer o propio de ella.

Womanly, Womanlike [wum'-an-li, laik], *a.* Mujeril, mujeriego, de mujer, propio o perteneciente a las mujeres; femenino, que conviene a la mujer; no masculino ni pueril. —*adv.* Mujerilmente, a manera de mujer, como una mujer.

Womb [wūm], *s.* 1. Útero, matriz, madre, víscera en que se concibe y alimenta el feto; de aquí, el sitio dondé una cosa es engendrada o dada a luz. 2. Cavidad que encierra algo; caverna, seno, entrañas.

Wombat [wem'-bat], *s.* Fascolomis, mamífero nocturno de los marsupiales de Australia.

Women [wim'-en], *s. pl.* de WOMAN.

Won [wun], *pret.* y *pp.* del verbo WIN.

Won, †**Wone** [wun], *vn.* (Esco. o des.) 1. Permanecer, residir, habitar. 2. Soler, tener costumbre.

Wonder [wun'-der], *va.* Querer saber, tener curiosidad por saber, preguntarse: (con una cláusula como complemento). *I wonder why he came,* Me pregunto por qué vino él. —*vn.* Admirarse, asombrarse, extrañar, mirar una cosa con admiración. *To wonder at,* Extrañar, maravillarse de, quedar admirado o espantado.

Wonder, *s.* 1. Admiración, el acto de admirar o admirarse. 2. Milagro, portento, pasmo, maravilla. *To do wonders,* Hacer maravillas. *Wonder-worker,* Fabricador de prodigios o milagros. *It is a wonder,* Es un prodigio. *No wonder,* No hay que extrañar, no es mucho o no es gracia.

Wonderer [wun'-der-er], *s.* Admirador, el o la que se maravilla.

Wonderful [wun'-der-ful], *a.* Admirable, maravilloso, portentoso, pasmoso.

Wonderfully [wun'-der-ful-i], *adv.* Admirablemente, maravillosamente, prodigiosamente, portentosamente; de una manera sorprendente, asombrosa o admirable. *Wonderfully well,* A maravilla, a las mil maravillas.

Wonderfulness [wun'-der-ful-nes], *s.* Naturaleza maravillosa o sorprendente; rareza.

Wondering [wun'-der-ing], *a. part.* y *pa.* Admirado, suspenso, que se maravilla de, que manifiesta sorpresa.

Wonderment [wun'-der-ment], *s.* 1. Sentimiento de admiración o sorpresa; embeleso. 2. Maravilla, cosa admirable, embeleso.

Wonder-struck [wun'-der-struc], *a.* Atónito, pasmado, espantado, asombrado.

Wondrous [wun'-drus], **Wonderous** [wun'-der-us], *a.* Extraño, maravilloso, admirable, portentoso, pasmoso, asombroso.

Wondrously [wun'-drus-li], *adv.* Pasmosamente, maravillosamente.

Wont [wunt], *a.* Acostumbrado, que usa o hace habitualmente. *To be wont, vn.* Soler, acostumbrar, tener costumbre de; estar ordinariamente en.

Wont [wunt], *s.* Uso, costumbre, hábito.

Won't [wōnt o wunt], abreviatura familiar de WILL NOT.

Wonted [wunt'-ed], *a.* Acostumbrado, usual, habitual, ordinario.

Wontedness [wunt'-ed-nes], *s.* (Poco us.) La costumbre o hábito de hacer alguna cosa, habituación.

Woo [wū], *va.* 1. Cortejar, galantear, enamorar, requerir de amores; pretender a una mujer. 2. (Ant.) Instar, invitar con instancia.—*vn.* 1. Enamoricarse; emplearse en cortejar o galantear. 2. Solicitar, rogar encarecidamente.

Wood [wud], *va.* 1. Proveer de madera. 2. Cubrir con bosques; convertir en selva.—*s.* 1. Bosque, selva, monte, cualquier paraje poblado de árboles; se usa a menudo en plural. 2. Madera, substancia dura y sólida de un árbol o arbusto; madero, palo, leña, leño, según los casos en que se hable. 3. Algo hecho de madera. *Coppice-wood*, Monte tallar. *Fire-wood*, Leña. *Split-wood*, Leña rajada o en astillas. *Cabinet-maker's wood*, Madera de ebanistería. *Cord-wood*, Leña hacinada de cuatro pies de largo que se vende por cuerdas. *V.* CORD. *Dye-wood*, Madera de tinte. *Drift-wood*, Madera de deriva o de flotación. *Sap-wood*, Albura; (Carp.) sámago. *Small wood*, Brusca, verdasca, leña menuda. *Warped wood*, Madera alabeada. *Wood-acid*; Ácido piroleñoso. *V. Wood-vinegar. Wood-anemone*, (Bot.) Anémona silvestre o de los bosques. *Wood-ant*, Hormiga leonada. *Wood-carving*, (1) El arte, método o procedimiento de esculpir en madera; (2) talla en madera. *Wood-chopper*, Leñador. *Wood-drink*, Cocimiento o infusión de maderas medicinales. *Wood-hole*, Leñera. *Wood-house*, Leñera, el paraje donde se encierra la leña. *Wood-lark*, (Orn.) Alondra, cogujada, calandria silvestre, un pájaro pequeño. *Wood-louse*, (Ent.) Cucaracha, crustáceo isópodo; también, carcoma. *Wood-note*, Música campestre. *Wood-nymphs*, *pl.* Dríades. *Wood-offering*, Leña para holocausto. *Wood-pease*, Guisante silvestre. *Wood-pigeon*, (Orn.) Paloma torcaz o paloma zura. *Wood-pile*, Pila de leña; hoguera. *Wood-screw*, Tornillo para madera. *Wood-shed*, Leñera, lugar destinado á guardar y hacinar la leña. *Wood-sorrel*, Cualquiera especie de oxálida; (Bot.) acedera silvestre. *Wood-stack*, Pila o montón de leña. *Wood-thrush*, Tordo pardo, notable por la dulzura de su canto, que se halla en el este de los Estados Unidos. Turdus mustelinus. *Wood-vinegar*, Vinagre de madera, ácido piroleñoso, un ácido acético impuro.

Wood alcohol [wud al'-co-hel], *s.* Alcohol metílico.

Woodbine [wud'-bain], *s.* (Bot.) 1. Madreselva de Europa (Lonicera periclymenum). 2. Trepadora virginiana. (Ampelopsis quinquefolia.)

Woodchuck [wud'-chuc], *s.* Marmota grande de América. Arctomys monex. (Corrupción del nombre indígena *wejack.*)

Woodcock [wud'-cec], *s.* Chocha, chochaperdiz o becada.

Woodcraft [wud'-crgft], *s.* Conocimiento y práctica en lo concerniente a la vida en los bosques.

Woodcut [wud'-cut], *s.* Grabado en madera.

Wood-cutter [wud'-cut-gr], *s.* 1. Leñador. 2. (Fam.) Grabador en madera.

Wooded [wud'-ed], *a.* Arbolado, plantado o cubierto de árboles; provisto de leña o de madera.

Wooden [wud'-n], *a.* 1. Hecho de palo o madera; grosero. 2. Semejante á un trozo de madera; rudo, torpe, sin espíritu, estúpido, mecánico. *Wooden bowl*, Artesilla de panaderos. *Wooden-head. wooden-headed*, Zote, zopenco, lerdo, estúpido, bolo. *Wooden shoes*, Zuecos. *Wooden spoon*, Cuchara de palo.

Woodiness [wud'-i-nes], *s.* Estado leñoso, calidad leñosa.

Woodland [wud'-land], *s.* Arbolado; la tierra plantada o cubierta de árboles.—*a.* Arbolado, cubierto de árboles; perteneciente a los árboles, a la leña o a la madera.

Woodless [wud'-les], *a.* Falto de madero o selvas, sin bosques.

Woodman [wud'-man], *s.* 1. Leñador. 2. Guardabosque; habitante de los bosques.

Woodpecker [wud'-pek-gr], *s.* Picamaderos, picaposte, pico, ave. *Ivory-billed woodpecker*, Carpintero real.

Woodruff [wud'-ruf], *s.* (Bot.) Aspérula, planta herbácea de la familia de las rubiáceas.

Woodsman [wudz'-man], *s.* El que vive o trabaja en el bosque; guardabosque, leñador.

Woodward [wud'-wērd], *s.* Guardabosque.

Woodwork [wud'-wūrk], *s.* Enmaderamiento, maderaje, maderamen, el conjunto de maderas para edificar o para otros usos.

Woody [wud'-i], *a.* 1. Leñoso; de la naturaleza de la madera. 2. Perteneciente o parecido a la madera. 3. Arbolado, abundante en madera; selvoso.

Wood-yard [wud'-yārd], *s.* Almacén de madera, el corral donde se apila la leña o madera.

Wooer [wū'-gr], *s.* Galanteador, pretendiente, el que obsequia; amante.

Woof [wūf], *s.* 1. Trama, la hebra que pasa de un lado a otro de la urdimbre; conjunto de hilos cruzados. *V.* WEFT. 2. Textura, la disposición y orden de los hilos en una tela.

Woofer [wū'-fer], *s.* Altavoz para sonidos graves.

Wooing [wū'-ing], *s.* Galanteo, cortejo.

Wooingly [wū'-ing-li], *adv.* Agradablemente, dulcemente.

Wool [wul], *s.* 1. Lana. 2. Pelo inferior de un animal cuya piel se utiliza en la peletería. 3. Cabello espeso y crespo, como el de un negro. 4. Algo que se parece a la lana; v. gr. la pelusa larga y blanda que cubre ciertas plantas e insectos. *All wool*, Todo de lana, de lana pura. *Coarse wool*, Lana burda o churla. *Fine carded wool*, Estambre. *Fleece wool*, Lana de vellón, toisón. *Cotton wool*, Algodón en rama, lana de algodón. *Long-staple wool*, Lana larga de cardar. *Short-staple wool*, Tundizno, lana corta. *Mineral wool*, Lana mineral, substancia de aspecto parecido al de la lana. *Natural wool*, Lana en bruto. *To dye in the wool*, Teñir la lana antes de hilarla; de aquí, confirmar, establecer firmemente una opinión. *Wool-ball*, Pelotón de lana, que a veces se encuentra en el estómago de un carnero. *Wool-bearing*, Lanar. *Wool-comber*, Cardador, cardadora de lana. *Wool-combing*, Cardadura de lana. *Wool-grower*, Criador de ganado lanar. *Woolpack*, (1) Saca o fardo de lana; (2) cúmulo (nube). *Wool-pated*, Que tiene los cabellos encrespados. *Woolsack*, El asiento del canciller y de los jueces en la cámara de los pares. *Wool-sorter*, Escogedor de lana. *Wool-sorter's disease*, Especie de envenenamiento de la sangre por medio de la lana infectada; probablemente ántrax. *Wool-stapler*, Comerciante en lanas. *Wool-winder*, Vellonero.

Wool-card [wul'-cārd], *s.* Carda, cardencha.

Woold [wūld], *va.* (Mar.) Trincar; pasar una soga o cadena en torno de una pieza jimelgada.

Wooled [wuld], *a.* Que tiene lana, con lana; forma a menudo palabras compuestas. *Fine-wooled*, Con lana fina.

Woolfell [wul'-fel], *s.* La piel a la cual no se ha quitado la lana.

Wool-gathering [wul'-gadh-gr-ing], *a.* Descarriado, divertido.—*s.* Ocupación trivial o sin objeto; distracción.

Woolen, Woollen [wul'-en], *a.* Hecho de lana; de lana (como mercadería).—*s.* Cualquier tela o tejido hecho de lana. *Woollens* o *woollen manufactures*, Manufactura de lana. *Woollen cloth*, Paño de lana. *Woollen-draper*, Pañero, comerciante en paños. *Woollen-dyer*, Tintorero de lana.

Woolly [wul'-i], *a.* 1. Lanudo, lanoso, que consta de lana; cubierto, vestido de lana o semejante a la lana; coposo; (cabello) crespo, pasudo. 2. (Bellas artes) Falto de detalles, vago y borroso. 3. (Meteo.) (Nube) que tiene la apariencia de la lana. 4. (Bot.) Lanoso, lanuginoso, que tiene una especie de lanilla o pelusa.

Woolman [wul'-man], *s.* Lanero.

Word [wūrd], *s.* 1. Palabra, vocablo, voz, sonido o conjunto de sonidos articulados que expresan una idea. 2. Palabra, representación gráfica de estos sonidos. 3. Palabra, habla, voz, la facultad de hablar. 4. Conversación corta o breve, pocas palabras; observación breve; de aquí, dicho, sentencia, apotegma. 5. Palabra, promesa, oferta. 6. Aviso, recado, mensaje. 7. Escritura, la palabra de Dios. 8. Palabra, Verbo, la segunda persona de la Santísima Trinidad. 9. Contraseña; señal, voz de mando, orden, mandato. 10. *pl.* Palabras mayores, disputa, contienda verbal. *To keep one's word*, Cumplir su palabra, tener palabra. *Take my word for it*, Créame Vd.; puede Vd. creerme bajo palabra. *Word-square*, Una disposición de vocablos en forma rectangular de modo que pueden ser leídos en líneas verticales u horizontales; por ejemplo:

F R E T
R E A R
E A S E
T R E E

Words of course, Cumplimientos. *Soft words*, Palabras dulces o melosas. *By word of mouth*, De boca, de viva voz. *By-word*, Proverbio. *High words*, Palabras mayores o dichos injuriosos. *Vain words*, Palabras al aire. *To write word, to send word*, Enviar a decir. *Big words*, Disputa; palabras mayores.

Word, *va.* 1. Expresar, explicar, enunciar. 2. Instar con palabras, afectar por medio de una palabra. *To word a letter*, Dictar bien una carta.

Word-book [wūrd'-buk], *s.* Vocabulario, léxico.

Word-catcher [wūrd'-cach-gr], *s.* Disputador.

Word-catching [wūrd'-cach-ing], *s* Disputa de palabras.

Wordiness [wŏrd'-i-nes], *s.* Verbosidad, prolijidad; expresión con abundancia de palabras.

Wording [wŏrd'-ing], *s.* Dicción, estilo, manera de expresarse en palabras; fraseología; palabras usadas, expresión, términos, redacción.

Wordless [wŏrd'-les], *a.* Falto de palabras, mudo.

Wordy [wŏrd -i], *a.* 1. Verbal, de la naturaleza de palabras o pertenecientes a ellas. 2. Verboso, difuso, abundante en palabras.

Wore [wōr], *pret.* del verbo *To* WEAR.

Work [wŏrk], *va.* 1. Trabajar, labrar, poner en obra; explotar (una mina, un privilegio, etc.); bordar; tallar (una piedra). 2. Fabricar, manufacturar; producir, hacer nacer (por medio del trabajo); trabajar en; preparar por medio de algún procedimiento. 3. Trabajar, formar o componer con arreglo y esmero las obras de ingenio. 4. Obrar sobre, influir, impeler, excitar, regir por medio de esfuerzo; a veces implica corrupción o soborno. 5. Investigar o resolver (un problema). 6. Hacer trabajar, obrar, mover, funcionar, ir o poner en movimiento; emplear, servirse, usar de (como instrumento); mover nerviosamento (los dedos); abrirse camino; hacer fermentar. 7. (Mar.) Maniobrar. 8. Causar, efectuar, poner por obra. —*vn.* 1. Trabajar, ocuparse en cualquier trabajo o ejercicio, estar empleado en algún negocio o tráfico. 2. Obrar, surtir efecto o hacer efecto alguna cosa. 3. Estar en movimiento o en acción; funcionar, ir, desempeñar. 4. Obrar u operar las medicinas. 5. Trabajar, darse pena para hacer algo, esforzarse para ejecutar alguna cosa. 6. Fermentar, ponerse un cuerpo en movimiento de fermentación. *To work one's self into favour,* Insinuarse en la amistad de alguno, ganar su favor. *To work one's self off,* Salir de un apuro a fuerza de trabajo o de fatigas, desembarazarse de un negocio complicado. *To work one's way,* Abrirse camino para la ejecución o el logro de alguna cosa. *To work against,* Trabajar contra; oponerse a. *To work at,* Trabajar en, ocuparse en o de. *To work down,* Hacer descender; descender, bajarse. *To work in,* Trabajar en; insinuarse en, entrar poco a poco. *To work into,* Entrar en, penetrar en. *To work out,* Acabar alguna cosa a fuerza de trabajo; borrar o expiar, cuando se habla de faltas, culpas, etc.; lograr o conseguir un objeto a fuerza de fatigas; ejecutar, efectuar; agotar (una mina). *To work round,* Volverse lentamente y con esfuerzo. *To work through,* Penetrar; atravesar a fuerza de trabajo, salir al otro lado. *To work up,* Labrar, dar forma a una cosa; servirse de; amasar; agotar, consumir; excitar, inflamar; elevarse, subir con esfuerzo; levantar. *To work upon,* Obrar sobre; trabajar en, estar ocupado en un trabajo manual; sublevar, excitar, mover a compasión. *To work to windward,* (Mar.) Barloventear, navegar de bolina, ceñir el viento.

Work, *s.* 1. Trabajo, ejercicio u obra de cualquier especie. 2. Fábrica, obra, tarea, lo que está por hacer, aquello en que se trabaja; costura, cosido; bordado, bordadura, dibujo hecho con la aguja. 3. Obra, trabajo, labor; producto del que trabaja manualmente o con la inteligencia; obra de un ingeniero; fortificación. 4. Fatiga. 5. Obra, toda suerte de acción moral. 6. Empleo u ocupación. 7. Fábrica, taller, establecimiento; en plural, por lo común. 8. *pl.* Rodaje, engranaje motor, movimiento, maquinaria. *Needle-work,* Labor de aguja. *Press-work,* Tirada. *Work-bag,* Saco de labor. *Work-box,* Caja de labor. *Work-days,* Días útiles o de trabajo. *To set to work,* Emplear, ocupar, dar empleo u ocupación. *To be at work,* Estar haciendo alguna cosa; estar ocupado en hacer algo; estar trabajando. *To be hard at work,* Estar muy afanado o muy ocupado en hacer algo. *Work-folk, work-folks, work-people,* Obreros, operarios. *Work-room,* Taller, pieza en que se trabaja.

Work, Working [wŏrk'-ing], *s.* 1. Maniobra de navío, faena. *Working aloft,* (Mar.) Maniobra alta. *Lubberly working,* Maniobra basta. 2. Trabajo, obra; operación; agitación.

Workable [wŏrk'-a-bl], *a.* 1. Que puede funcionar; que se puede hacer funcionar o trabajar (máquina). 2. Factible, practicable. 3. (Min.) Explotable. 4. Apto para el trabajo, capaz de trabajar. 5. Que puede ser influido o excitado.

Workaday [wurk'-a-dê], *a.* 1. Relativo a un día de trabajo. 2. Afanoso, laborioso, prosaico.

Workbook [wurk-buk], *s.* 1. Manual de trabajo. 2. Manual de estudios.

Work-day [wŏrk'-dê], **Working-day** [wŏrk'-ing-dê], *s.* Día de trabajo.

Worker [wŏrk'-ẹr], *s.* 1. Trabajador, obrero; operario. 2. Abeja u hormiga obrera (con los órganos sexuales no desarrollados) que trabaja en comunidad.

Work-fellow [wŏrk'-fel-ō], *s.* Compañero de trabajo, obrero.

Workhouse [wŏrk'-haus], *s.* 1. Hospicio, casa de misericordia, la destinada para albergar a los pobres. 2. Obrador, taller. 3. Casa de corrección en que recogen a los vagos y ociosos para que trabajen.

Working [wŏrk'-ing], *s.* 1. Que trabaja; que funciona, que se mueve. 2. De trabajo, adaptado al uso de un obrero o operario; obrero. 3. Usado o puesto aparte para conducir un negocio; activo, productivo. *Working capital,* Capital activo. *Working class,* La clase obrera, operaria. *Working beam,* Balancín. *Working-drawing,* (Arq.) Montea. *Working parts,* Piezas vivas, partes que funcionan. *Working-man,* Gañán, obrero u operario a jornal, jornalero.

Workman [wŏrk'-man], *m.* Artífice, labrador.

Workmanship [wŏrc'-man-ship], *s.* 1. Manufactura, artificio, trabajo de manos, hechura. 2. Habilidad o destreza del artífice. *A fine piece of workmanship,* Una obra perfectamente ejecutada, una obra maestra.

Works [wŏrks], *s. pl.* 1. Taller, fábrica. 2. Movimiento (de un reloj). 3. Engranaje de una máquina.

Workout [wŏrk'-aut], *s.* (vul.) Prueba, ensayo.

Work of art [wŏrk ev ārt], *s.* Obra de arte.

Workshop [wŏrc'-shop], *s.* Taller, obrador.

Work-woman [wŏrc'-wum-an], *f.* Costurera, obrera.

World [wŏrld], *s.* 1. Mundo, el con junto de todos los cuerpos que componen el universo. 2. Mundo, el modo de vida, trato y relaciones de los hombres. *For all the world,* Exactamente, cabalmente; rectamente. 3. Mundo, esfera o globo terrestre. 4. (Met.) Gente, gentío, muchedumbre o concurso de muchas personas, infinidad. 5. Mundo; en la mística se toma por los hombres corrompidos o profanos. *World without end,* Para siempre jamás; por los siglos de los siglos.

Worldliness [wŏrld'-li-nes], *s.* Carácter mundano; profanidad, vanidad mundana; apego ó afición desmedida á los halagos del mundo.

Worldly [wŏrld'-li], *a.* Mundano, terreno, que pertenece al mundo; humano, común.—*adv.* Profanamente, según el mundo.

World-wide [wŏrld'-waid], *a.* Mundial, del mundo entero.

Worm [wŏrm], *s.* 1. Gusano, animalillo invertebrado blando que se arrastra, como son las lombrices de tierra, las ascárides, etc.; lombriz que se cría en la tierra o se engendra en el cuerpo de los animales. 2. Larva rastrera de un insecto; oruga. 3. Polilla que se cría en la ropa; carcoma de la madera; coco, el gusanito que se cría en las legumbres y semillas; gorgojo, el que se cría en los granos; (fig.) gusano roedor, remordimiento, pesadumbre secreta. 4. Persona vil, despreciable; mortal débil comparable a un gusano. 5. (Mec.) Tornillo sin fin, rosca. 6. (Quím.) Serpentín. 7. Sacatrapos. *Still-worm,* Serpentín de alambique. *Worm in the conscience,* Gusano de la conciencia, el remordimiento. *Glow-worm,* Gusano de luz, luciérnaga. *Silk-worm,* Gusano de seda. *Vine-worm* o *vine-grub,* Pulgón de las viñas. *Worm fence,* Cercado en zigzag. *Worm-like,* Vermicular, semejante a un gusano. *Worm-tea,* Tisana vermífuga; infusión antihelmíntica. *Worm and wheel,* Engranaje de tornillo sin fin.

Worm, *vn.* Trabajar u obrar lentamente y por bajo mano.—*va.* 1. Insinuarse, entrar en, como un gusano; arrastrar; arrastrarse como un gusano. 2. Sacar, descargar por medio del sacatrapos; (fig.) echar o suplantar por medios secretos. 3. Quitar a los perros la lita que se dice tienen debajo de la lengua, para que no rabien. 4. *To worm a cable,* (Mar.) Embutir un cable.

Worm-eaten [wŏrm'-ī-tn], *a.* Carcomido, apolillado, roído, corroído o comido de gusanos; cocoso, dañado del coco.

Worm gear [wŏrm gīr], *s.* (Mec.) Rueda para tornillo sin fin.

Worm-holes [wŏrm'-hōlz], *s. pl.* Carcoma.

Wormwood [wŏrm'-wud], *s.* (Bot.) Ajenjo, planta amarga, perenne, del género artemisa. (Artemisia absinthium.)

Wormy [wŏrm'-i], *a.* Gusaniento, lleno de gusanos.

Worn [wōrn], *pp.* del verbo *To* WEAR. *Worn out,* Gastado, consumido por el uso; cansado, muy fatigado. *The sails are worn out,* Las velas son de media vida.

Worry [wur-i], *va.* 1. Acosar, perseguir, vejar, molestar, atormentar, jorobar. 2. Lacerar, desgarrar o matar mordiendo o sacudiendo.—*vn.* 1. Atormentarse, incomodarse, inquietarse. 2. Morder o lacerar, como los perros cuando riñen.

Worry, *s.* Cuidado, ansia, preocupación, tormento, molestia.

Worse [wŏrs], *a. comp.* de BAD, ILL o EVIL. 1. Peor, más malo, más imperfecto, inferior. 2. Más enfermo, peor, más malo. 3. Colocado en peor estación o situación. *You are worse than your word,* Vd. no cumple su palabra.—*adv.* Peor, de un modo más malo, más fuerte, más grandemente. *Worse and worse,* De mal en peor, peor que nunca; cada vez más malo (o peor); cada vez más fuerte. *To be worse,* Valer menos, ser más malo; estar peor. *To be worse off,* Estar menos bien, estar peor; ser menos feliz. *To become, to get, to grow worse,* Empeorarse; ponerse peor, ir peor. *To make, to render worse,* Empeorar. *So much the worse,* Tanto peor. *For the worse,* En mal. *Worse than ever,* Peor que nunca. *The cloak is but little the worse for use,* La capa está apenas usada.—*s.* Peoría, menoscabo, detrimento; lo peor. *He had the worse,* Llevó la peor parte.

Worsen [wŏrs'-n], *va.* y *vn.* (Poco us.) Hacer peor, empeorar; ponerse peor, empeorarse.

Worship [wŏr'-ship], *s.* 1. Culto, adoración. 2. Respeto, deferencia u honor que se tributa a la virtud, al poder, etc. 3. Dignidad, eminencia, excelencia. 4. Un tratamiento que se da en Inglaterra a los magistrados y a algunos empleados municipales, y corresponde unas veces a *merced* y otras a *señoría* en castellano. *Your worship,* Usía; vuestra merced.

Worship, *va.* Adorar, honrar, venerar o reverenciar con culto religioso; respetar.—*vn.* Dar culto.

Worshipful [wŏr'-ship-ful], *a.* Venerable, honorable, respetable, digno de honra, respeto o veneración. Es también palabra de tratamiento. *The worshipful president,* El respetable presidente. *Worshipful master* (entre los francmasones), El Venerable.

Worshipfully [wŏr'-ship-ful-i], *adv.* Respetablemente, honoríficamente, honrosamente, con adoración o veneración.

Worshipper [wŏr'-ship-ẹr], *s.* Adorador, el que da culto. *Worshipper of idols,* Idólatra.

Worshipping [wŏr'-ship-ing], *s.* Adoración, culto; accion de adorar.

Worst [wŏrst], *a. superl.* de BAD, ILL o EVIL. 1. Pésimo, malísimo, lo más malo, lo peor. 2. Lo más enfermo, lo más malo. 3. Lo más fuerte, lo más grande. *He is the worst of men,* Él es el más perverso de los hombres.—*adv.* Lo peor, lo más malo, lo más fuerte, lo menos.—*s.* Lo peor, lo más malo, el estado más desesperado o más calamitoso, la mayor miseria; inferioridad; mal andar. *I am at the worst,* Me hallo en el estado más triste, no puedo estar peor.

Worst, *va.* Vencer, rendir, sujetar, triunfar de.

Worsted [wŏrs'-ted], *pp.* del verbo WORST. Vencido.

Worsted [wurs'-ted o wust'-ed], *s.* 1. Estambre, la hebra de lana torcida. *Worsted stockings,* Medias de estambre. 2. Material que no es algodón ni seda y se emplea en la manufactura de fleco o galón.

Wort [wŏrt], *s.* 1. Planta, hierba; se usa en composición. 2. Legumbre del género de la col o berza; repollo. (<A.-S. *wyrt,* planta.) 3. La cerveza nueva que no ha fermentado y a veces también la que está fermentando. *Spleen-wort,* (Bot.) Hepática. (<A.-S. *wyrte* <*wyrt.*)

Worth [wŏrth], *vn.* (Ant.) Suceder, sobrevenir. *Woe worth the day,* véase bajo el título Wo.

Worth [wŏrth], *s.* 1. Mérito; consideración, importancia, entidad; de aquí, valor, precio. 2. Excelencia mental y moral.—*a.* 1. Digno, benemérito. 2. Que tiene mérito. 3. Que tiene dinero, rentas, etc. 4. Que vale; que tiene precio; de igual valor o precio que. *To be worth,* (1) Tener, poseer, cuando se habla de personas. (2) Valer, cuando se habla de cosas; valer la pena de; merecer, ser digno de. *He is worth a million,* Posee un millón. *A place worth keeping,* Una colocación o destino que vale la pena. *That is little worth,* Eso no vale gran cosa. *He is worth his weight in gold,* Él vale su peso en oro. *To be worth while,* Merecer o valer la pena de.

Worthily [wŏr'-dhi-li], *adv.* Dignamente, honorablemente; convenientemente, como corresponde; con justos motivos.

Worthiness [wŏr'-dhi-nes], *s.* Dignidad, mérito; excelencia, realce.

Worthless [wŏrth'-les], *a.* Indigno, falto de mérito; vil, bajo, de ningún valor.

Worthlessness [wŏrth'-les-nes], *s.* Indignidad, vileza; falta de mérito.

Worthy [wŏr'-dhi], *a.* Digno, benemérito, merecedor de recompensa u honor, acreedor a algún premio.—*s.* Héroe, varón ilustre y grande: en este sentido se usa comúnmente en plural.

†**Wot** [wot], *vn.* 1ª y 3ª *pers. sing. indic. pres.* de *To* WIT. Yo sé, él sabe.

Would [wud], *pret.* del verbo *To* WILL. Úsase también como verbo auxiliar en el subjuntivo y condicional; expresa también la inclinación, el deseo, la súplica o la costumbre, y la acción determinada o resuelta. *I would have her do it,* Yo querría que ella lo hiciese. *He would not do it,* No quiso hacerlo. *Do what he would,* Por más que él hacía. *I would learn the reason if I could,* Yo averiguaría la razón si pudiese. *I would do it,* Yo lo haría, lo hiciera o quisiera hacerlo. *Would to God!* ¡Ojalá! ¡plegue a Dios!

Would-be [wud'-bi], *a.* Titulado, presumido, supuesto o fingido. *A would-be poet,* Presumido de poeta.

Wound [wound], *pret.* y *pp.* del verbo *To* WIND. *He has wound up the clock,* Él ha dado cuerda al reloj.

Wound [wūnd o wound], *s.* 1. Herida, llaga, solución de continuidad en la piel y carne de un animal o en la corteza o substancia de un árbol o planta. 2. Ofensa, golpe, causa de pena o de pesar. *Incised wound,* Herida incisa, cortadura, incisión. *Lacerated wound,* Laceración. *Punctured wound,* Herida penetrante, picadura.

Wound [wūnd o wound], *va.* 1. Herir, hacer una herida, llagar. 2. Herir, ofender, dañar, agraviar, causar algún mal físico o moral.

Woundless [wūnd'-les], *a.* Sin herida, ileso.

Woundy [wūnd'-i], *a.* (Prov. o des.) Excesivo.

Woundwort [wūnd'-wŏrt], *s.* (Bot.) Vulneraria y varias especies de galiopsis; nombre dado a las plantas a las cuales se atribuye la virtud de curar las heridas.

Wove, Woven [wōv], *pret.* y *pp.* del verbo *To* WEAVE.

Wrack [rac], *s.* 1. Fuco, ova; vegetación y otros objetos que el agua arroja a la orilla. 2. Naufragio, ruina. 3. Despojos de naufragio. *To go to wrack,* Decaer, arruinarse, ir en decadencia; correr a su perdición.

Wrack, *s.* Montón de nubes: vapor flotante.

Wraith [rēth], *s.* Fantasma, espectro de una persona viva y que se suponía precursor de la muerte de dicha persona; aparecido, ánima en pena. (<Islandés *vörth,* guardián.)

Wrangle [raṇ'-gl], *vn.* Pelotear, reñir, disputar, contender.

Wrangle, *s.* Pelotera, pendencia, riña, contienda, disputa.

Wrangler [raṇ'-glẹr], *s.* 1. Pendenciero, disputador, amigo de disputas; originalmente, argumentador, defensor de una tesis. 2. En la Universidad de Cambridge, Inglaterra, el alumno que obtiene el primer grado en los exámenes de matemáticas.

Wrangling [raṇ'-gling], *s.* Disputa, quimera, zipizape, altercación.

Wrap [rap], *va.* (*pret.* y *pp.* WRAPPED o WRAPT). 1. Arrollar, rollar o revolver una cosa en sí misma. 2. Envolver, cubrir una cosa dando vueltas alrededor de ella con alguna otra. *To wrap up,* Rollar, arrollar; envolver; arrebatar, asombrar, llenar de admiración; contener; comprender. *He is wrapped up in his son,* (Fam.) El está encantado con su hijo. *She is wrapped up in herself,* Ella es muy presumida.

Wrap, *s.* Bata, abrigo, prenda de vestir holgada: en plural, todas las prendas exteriores que se llevan además de la ropa ordinaria, como capas, bandas, etc. *Wrap-rascal,* Abrigo ahuecado y por regla general de paño burdo; voz muy usada en el siglo dieciocho.

Wrapper [rap'-ẹr], *s.* 1. El que arrolla o rolla; el que envuelve; el que arrebata. 2. Envolvedero, envolvedor, cubierta, carpeta, papel. 3. Bata, peinador, ropaje holgado flotante. 4. (Fam.) Elástica, cualquier cosa que sirve para envolver. *Wrapper* (hablando del tabaco), Capa o envoltura.

Wrapping [rap'-ing], *s.* Envoltura, forro. *Wrapping paper,* Papel de envolver.

Wrath [rāth], *s.* Ira, furor, rabia, cólera, indignación.

Wrathful [rāth'-ful], *a.* Furioso, colérico, indignado, irritado.

Wrathfully [rāth'-ful-i], *adv.* Furiosamente, coléricamente, con indignación.

Wreak [ric], *va.* 1. Vengar, tomar satisfacción del agravio recibido. 2. Ejecutar alguna resolución violenta. *To wreak one's anger,* Descargar la cólera.

Wreath [rith], *s.* 1. Cualquiera cosa en figura de rosca o sortija. 2. Corona, guirnalda; festón, trenza. 3. Banda circular o espiral. *Bridal wreath*, Corona nupcial.

Wreathe [rídh], *va.* Ensortijar, enroscar, entrelazar, torcer; ceñir.

Wreck [rec], *s.* 1. Naufragio, pérdida de un buque; ruina, destrucción. 2. Buque naufragado, barco perdido. 3. Destrozos de bajel, objetos arrojados a la costa después de un naufragio. 4. Fuco, ova.

Wreck, *va.* y *vn.* 1. Naufragar, padecer naufragio; quebrarse o quebrantarse el buque, irse a pique. 2. Naufragar, perderse o salir mal de algún intento o negocio. 3. Hacer naufragar, causar naufragio. 4. Arruinar, perder a uno. *To go to wreck*, Ir a su ruina, a su pérdida; perderse. *To suffer wreck*, Naufragar. *Wrecking-car*, Coche, carro de auxilio (ferrocarril); surtido de herramientas para despejar de obstáculos una vía férrea.

Wreckage [rek'-ẹj], *s.* 1 Acción de naufragar o el estado de náufrago. 2. Despojos de naufragio.

Wrecker [rek'-ẹr], *s.* 1. Destructor. 2. Persona que roba los despojos de buques náufragos. 3. Persona o embarcación empleada para recobrar embarcaciones naufragadas o sus cargamentos. 4. Automóvil de auxilio.

Wren [ren], *s.* Reyezuelo, troglodita, abadejo; pajarillo de plumaje variado y vistoso.

Wrench [rench], *va.* 1. Arrancar, tirar o sacar con violencia; arrebatar torciendo. 2. Torcer, volver en sentido contrario y apretando; apartar una cosa del uso o destino propios. 3. Dislocar, desencajar, forzar, sacar de quicio. *To wrench one's foot*, Torcerse el pie.

Wrench, *s.* 1. Arranque; tirón violento; torcedura, arrancamiento. 2. Llave inglesa, llave para destornillar; palanca con ojo que sirve para dar vueltas a otras herramientas. *Monkey-wrench*, Llave inglesa.

Wrest [rest], *va.* 1. Arrancar, quitar a la fuerza o con violencia. 2. Apartar del sentido, carácter, destino o aplicación verdaderos; pervertir. *To wrest from*, Arrebatar.

Wrest, *s.* Violencia; contorsión, torcimiento; dislocación; fuerza; acción de arrancar retorciendo; aplicación falsa, mal uso, perversión; artificio, dolo; un instrumento que se usaba para templar los de música.

Wrestle [res'-l], *vn.* 1. Luchar, lidiar a brazo partido, esforzarse. 2. Disputar, altercar.

Wrestler [res'-lẹr], *s.* Atleta, luchador, el que lucha cuerpo á cuerpo.

Wrestling [res'-ling], *s.* Lucha. *Wrestling-place*, Palestra.

Wretch [rech], *s.* Un infeliz o un pobre infeliz, un hombre muy miserable o muy necesitado; un desventurado o un hombre que sufre mucho por cualquier causa o tiene poca fortuna; ente vil, despreciable; miserable.

Wretched [rech'-ed], *a.* 1. Infeliz, desdichado, miserable, desgraciado, desventurado. 2. Calamitoso, lastimero; lleno de aflicciones. 3. Vil, despreciable, perverso; mezquino. *To look wretched*, Tener aspecto lastimoso.

Wretchedly [rech'-ed-li], *adv.* Infelizmente, miserablemente, con muchos trabajos, con mucha miseria; ruinmente, vilmente.

Wretchedness [rech'-ed-nes], *s.* 1. Infelicidad, desdicha, miseria, desgracia, desventura. 2. Vileza, ruindad, bajeza. 3. Naturaleza miserable; pobreza; mala índole.

Wriggle [rig'-l], *vn.* 1. Bullir, menearse o agitarse con un movimiento continuado e irregular. 2. Insinuarse en el ánimo de alguno.—*va.* Mover o agitar alguna cosa con un movimiento irregular y continuo. *To wriggle away*, Escaparse alguna cosa a fuerza de moverse. *To wriggle into*, Insinuarse en. *To wriggle off*, Escaparse culebreando, retorciéndose. *To wriggle out of*, Salir de, escaparse, deslizarse fuera.

Wriggling [rig'-ling], *s.* Enroscadura, torcedura, movimiento análogo al de una lombriz de tierra; rosca, vuelta u onda, hablando del movimiento de las culebras.

Wright [rait], *s.* Artífice, artesano, obrero. *Wheelwright*, Tornero. *Cartwright*, Carretero. *Shipwright*, Carpintero de ribera o de buque, el que trabaja en los astilleros.

Wring [ring], *va.* (*pret.* y *pp.* WRUNG o WRINGED). 1. Torcer o dar vueltas a una cosa con violencia, comprimir torciendo. 2. Arrancar, quitar a la fuerza. 3. Estrujar, apretar con mucha fuerza. 4. Obligar a hacer o ejecutar alguna cosa por medios violentos o por fuerza. 5. Atormentar, aquejar. 6. Torcer, interpretar mal el sentido de algún escrito. 7. Forzar, encorvar, apartar de la posición normal (v. gr. un mástil).—*vn.* (Des.) Acongojarse, padecer angustias y tormentos. *To wring one's hands*, Retorcerse las manos. *Wrung from the poor*, Arrancado a los pobres. *To wring off*, Arrancar retorciendo. *To wring out*, Exprimir, hacer salir. *To wring water out of a garment*, Retorcer una prenda de vestir para exprimir el agua. *Wring-bolt*, Perno de atraca, clavija de apretar, argolla.

Wringer [ring'-ẹr], *s.* 1. Torcedor, torcedora, la persona que tuerce. 2. Exprimidor para la ropa.

Wrinkle [rin'-cl], *s.* 1. Arruga del rostro. 2. Arruga o doblez del paño. 3. Cualquiera aspereza o desigualdad.

Wrinkle, *va.* Arrugar, hacer arrugas; poner alguna cosa áspera o desigual. *To wrinkle one's brow*, Fruncir o arrugar las cejas. *To wrinkle up*, Arrugar, plegar.

Wrinkly [rin'-cli], *a.* Arrugado, lleno de arrugas.

Wrist [rist], *s.* Muñeca, articulación de la mano con el brazo.

Wristband [rist'-band], *s.* Puño de camisa.

Wristlet [rist'-let], *s.* Elástico (para retener un guante).

Wrist pin [rist pin], *s.* (Mec.) Eje de émbolo.

Wrist watch [rist woch], *s.* Reloj de pulsera.

Writ [rit], *s.* 1. Escrito; escritura; orden. 2. (For.) Auto, mandamiento o mandato jurídico, citación; auto o decreto de prisión. *Holy writ*, La Sagrada Escritura. *To issue a writ*, Dar una orden o un decreto.

Write [rait], *va.* (*pret.* WROTE, *pp.* WRITTEN). 1. Escribir, formar o figurar letras; inscribir. 2. Trazar, inscribir letras que representan sonidos o ideas. 3. Escribir, componer, producir como escritor o autor. 4. Imprimir o grabar una cosa fuertemente en el ánimo, en el corazón, etc.—*vn.* 1. Escribir, trazar o inscribir letras sobre una superficie. 2. Escribir, tener correspondencia por medio de cartas o esquelas. 3. Escribir, componer como escritor o autor. *To write after*, Copiar, escribir según un modelo. *To write back*, Contestar a la carta o esquela de otra persona. *To write down*, Poner por escrito, redactar. *To write out*, Escribir un relato completo de algo, escribir enteramente; copiar, trasladar, transcribir. *To write over again*, Volver a escribir, poner en limpio. *To write in a hurry*, Zurcir, hilvanar un discurso, un escrito, etc. *To write one's self*, Calificarse, tomar algún título, calidad, honor, etc. *To write down a person*, Publicar todo lo malo que se sabe de una persona; acabarla a escritos o publicaciones. *To write on*, Continuar escribiendo; escribir sobre. *To write a good hand*, Escribir bien, hacer buena letra, ser pendolista. *To write up*, (1) Ensalzar, encomendar al favor de alguien escribiendo; realzar, exaltar por medio de la pluma. (2) Describir completamente por escrito; poner al día o hasta la fecha (el libro mayor).

Writer [rait'-er], *s.* Escritor, autor; escribiente, amanuense.

Write off [rait ōf], *va.* 1. Cancelar (una cuenta, etc.). 2. Descontar por depreciación.

Writhe [raidh], *va.* Torcer, poner torcida alguna cosa.—*vn.* Acongojarse, padecer agonía o angustias, torcerse, dar vueltas con dolor.

Writing [rait'-ing], *s.* 1. Escritura, acción de escribir. 2. Escritura, mano, caracteres escritos. 3. Lo que está escrito o expresado en letras; escritura, escrito, manuscrito, obra o composición por escrito. *To commit to writing*, Poner por escrito. *In one's own writing*, De su puño y letra. *Writing-book*, Cuaderno de escritura. *Writing-machine*, Máquina para escribir. *Writing-desk*, Escritorio, bufete, escribanía. *Writing-master*, Maestro de escritura. *Writing-paper*, Papel para escribir.

Written, *pp.* del verbo *To* WRITE.

Wrong [reng o rōng], *s.* 1. Injuria, injusticia, agravio, perjuicio, detrimento conocido, mal, daño, perjuicio. 2. Culpa, sinrazón. 3. Error, extravío, falsedad. *You are in the wrong*, Vd. no tiene razón.—*a.* 1. Injusto, que viola el derecho o la justicia; malo, no derecho ni digno. 2. Erróneo, inexacto, incorrecto, falso; irregular, equivocado; que no conviene. *I took the wrong glove*, Cogí un guante en lugar de otro. *Wrong side*, Envés, el revés, el lado malo. *Wrong side out(ward)*, Al envés, al revés. *To be wrong*, Ser malo; no ser justo; no tener razón. *To be very wrong*, Tener mucha culpa. *That is wrong*, Eso no es justo, eso es malo, no es eso. *Wrong measures*, Medidas falsas, malas.—*adv.* Mal, sin razón, sin causa, injustamente; al revés. *Right or wrong*, A tuertas o a derechas, por fas o por nefas, a diestro o a siniestro; a trochemoche. *To be in the wrong*, No tener razón, estar equivocado. *To do wrong*, Obrar o hacer mal; hacer daño, causar perjuicio.

Wrong, *va.* 1. Hacer daño a, causar perjuicio, ofender. 2. Agraviar, injuriar, hacer alguna injusticia.
Wrong-doer [reng'-dū-ęr], *s.* El que es injusto con otro, el que injuria a otro; perverso.
Wrongful [reng'-ful], *a.* Injusto, inicuo, que hace u obra mal; supuesto, falso.
Wrongfully [reng'-ful-i], *adv.* Injustamente, sin razón, sin motivo o causa, falsamente.
Wrong-headed [reng'-hed-ed], *a.* Disparatado, el que tiene mala cabeza, desatinado, descabezado; terco, obstinado.
Wrong-headedness [reng'-hed-ed-nes], *s.* El estado o la disposición del que tiene sentimientos u opiniones extravagantes y las sostiene con tenacidad; terquedad, obstinación.
Wrongly [reng'-li], *adv.* Injustamente; mal; fuera de tiempo o de propósito.
Wrongness [rēng'-nes], *s.* Calidad de injusto; injusticia, maldad; falsedad, error, inexactitud.
Wrote [rōt], *pret.* del verbo *To* WRITE.
Wroth [rēth], *a.* (Ant.) Encolerizado, airado, enojado.
Wrought [rēt], *pret.* y *pp. irreg.* del verbo *To* WORK. (Hoy anticuado excepto en los sentidos de "forjado, labrado o efectuado.") *Wrought iron*, Hierro forjado o batido. *Wrought upon*, Influido. *Wrought up to*, Excitado, impelido a.
Wrung [rung], *pret.* y *pp.* del verbo *To* WRING. *A wrung mast*, (Mar.) Palo que hace comba.
Wry [rai], *a.* 1. Torcido, tuerto, no derecho, no recto; alejado, oblicuo. 2. Pervertido, alterado, mal interpretado. *Wry mouth, wry face*, Gesto, visajes. *Wry-neck*, Torticolis, mal o dolor que no deja poner derecha la cabeza.
Wryed [raid], *a.* Lo que está sesgado, torcido.
Wryly [rai'-li], *adv.* Sesgadamente, oblicuamente.
Wryneck [rai'-nec], *s.* 1. (Orn.) Torcecuello, pico del género Iynx (Iynx torquilla). 2. Torticoli, dolor reumático del cuello.
Wryness [rai'-nes], *s.* Condición de lo que es torcido u oblicuo.
Wych-elm [wich'-elm], *s.* Olmo escocés.
Wych-hazel, *s.* *V.* WICH-HAZEL.
Wye [wai], *s.* La letra Y, o algo en forma de y.

X

LA X [ecs], vigésima cuarta letra del alfabeto inglés, tiene dos sonidos, uno fuerte y otro suave. El primero equivale a *cs* en castellano; v. g. *excellence, execute, tax;* y el segundo a *gz*, pronunciando la *z* como en francés; v. g. *exalt, example, executor*. Ninguna palabra propiamente inglesa empieza con X; y en las derivadas del griego, que la tienen, como *Xenophon*, se les da el sonido de la *z* francesa. La X como número vale 10; y a causa de su forma en cruz, se usa como abreviatura de *Christ;* v. g. *Xmas*, por Christmas; *Xpher*, por Christopher. Lo mismo se hacía a veces en español.
Xanthein, Xantheine [zan'-the-in o ain], *s.* Xanteína, materia colorante amarilla y soluble, que existe en las flores.
Xanthic [zan'-thic], *a.* Xántico, amarillo o amarillento. *Xanthic acid*, Ácido xántico, compuesto pesado y líquido ($C_3H_6OS_2$).
Xanthin, Xanthine [zan'-thin, zan'-thain], *s.* 1. Xantina, compuesto blanco cristalizable contenido en la sangre, la orina y en otras secreciones animales. 2. Xantina, materia colorante amarilla e insoluble de ciertas flores.
Xanthous [zan'-thus], *a.* 1. Perteneciente al tipo amarillento o mogol de la raza humana. 2. Rubio, blondo, que tiene cabellos amarillentos.
Xanthoxylum [zan-thec'-si-lum], *s.* Xantóxilo, zantóxilo, género de árboles y arbustos de la familia de las rutáceas; las especies americanas se llaman fresno espinoso.
Xantippe [zan-tip'-ę], *s.* Jantipa, mujer de Sócrates; apodo que se da a una mujer pendenciera o regañona.
Xebec [zī'-bec], *s.* (Mar.) Jabeque, embarcación pequeña de tres palos que se usa en el Mediterráneo y en las costas de España, Portugal y Berbería.
Xenium [zī'-ni-um], *s.* (*pl.* XENIA). 1. Golosina, manjar delicado con que se obsequiaban mutuamente los antiguos en prenda de amistad. 2. Cuadro de caza, frutas o pescado, en una habitación destinada a huéspedes o amigos. 3. Presente o regalo que se da a un huésped o extranjero.
Xenodochium [zen''-o-do-cai'-um], *s.* Mesón, posada, hospicio.
Xenon [zen'-en], *s.* (Quím.) Xenón.
Xerocollyrium [zī-ro-co-lir'-i-um], *s.* Colirio seco, pomada, o ungüento para los ojos.
Xerophthalmia, Xerophthalmy [zę-ref-thal'-mi-a], *s.* Jeroftalmia, oftalmia seca o irritación de los ojos, con gran comezón.
Xerophyte [ser'-o-fait], *s.* Xerófila, planta de suelos secos.
Xerosis [zę-rō'-sis], *s.* Xerodermia, condición de sequedad anormal de la piel o de las membranas mucosas.
Xiphias [zif'-i-as], *s.* 1. Pez espada, xifia, jifia, pez de la familia de los escombéridos. 2. (Astr.) Jifia, dorada, una de las constelaciones del hemisferio austral.
Xiphoid [zif'-eid], *a.* Xifoideo.
Xoana [zō'-a-na], *s. pl.* Imágenes grabadas.
X rays [ecs rêz], *s. pl.* Rayos X, rayos Roentgen. *X-ray picture*, Radiografía. *X-ray specialist*, Radiógrafo.
Xylaloes [zai-lal'-ōz], *s.* Madera de áloe.
Xylobalsamum [zai-lo-bēl'-sa-mum], *s.* Jilobálsamo.
Xylocarpous [zai''-lo-cār'-pus], *a.* Que tiene un fruto duro y leñoso.
Xylocopa [zai-lo-cō'-pa], *s.* Jilocopo, xilocopo, insecto himenóptero.
Xylograph [zai'-lo-grąf], *s.* Grabado en madera, o estampa hecha de él.
Xylographer [zai-leg'-ra-fęr], *s.* Grabador en madera.
Xylography [zai-leg'-ra-fi], *s.* Xilografía, el arte de grabar o el grabado en madera.
Xylol, Xylene [zail'-ōl, zai'-lin], *s.* Xylole, hidrocarburo líquido, solvente de resinas.
Xylophagous [zai-lef'-a-gus], *a.* Xilófago, que come o roe la madera, como lo hacen varias larvas de insectos.
Xylophone [zai'-lo-fōn], *s.* Xilórgano, xilófono, armónica de madera.
Xyst [zist], *s.* 1. Xisto, sala o lugar cubierto destinado entre los antiguos a diversos ejercicios. 2. Paseo o terrado de jardín.
Xyster [zis'-tęr], *s.* Raspadera, instrumento quirúrgico para raer y raspar los huesos.

Y

Y [wai] se pronuncia como en castellano al principio de las voces, y en este caso se la considera en inglés como letra consonante. Cuando está al fin de las palabras se pronuncia como *i* castellana pronunciada rápidamente, y en este caso se la considera como vocal. También se halla la *y* en medio de algunas voces de derivación griega, como en *hydraulics*, la hidráulica; *hypothesis*, hipótesis, y entonces se pronuncia como el diptongo *ai* castellano.
Yacht [yet], *s.* (Mar.) Yate, embarcación de gala o de recreo; embarcación muy ligera, de vela o de vapor, destinada para recreo o regatas en ríos o lagos o en el mar.—*vn.* Viajar en yate; gobernar el yate.
Yachting [yet'-ing], *s.* Viaje en yate; el acto o la ocupación de dirigir un yate o de navegar en él.
Yachtsman, Yachter [yets'-man, yet'-ęr], *s.* Propietario o timonel de un yate.
Yak [yąk], *s.* Yak, rumiante bovino del Thibet, especie intermedia entre el búfalo y el toro. Lo domestican en el Asia central. Pœphigus grunniens.
Yam [yam], *s.* Ñame, raíz comestible de varias especies de Dioscorea.
Yank [yank], *va.* (Fam.) Tomar, quitar o dislocar por medio de un tirón repentino; dar un tirón.—*vn.* (Ingl.) 1. Moverse rápidamente. 2. Farfullar, regañar.—*s.* (Fam.) Tirón repentino, estirón.
Yankee [yan'-kę], *a.* Perteneciente a los yanquis o característico de ellos.—*s.* (Fam.) Yanqui, el natural o habitante de la Nueva Inglaterra; de aquí, ciudadano de los Estados del Norte y en general de todos los Estados Unidos, apodo que emplean principalmente los extranjeros. *Yankee doodle*, Canción popular de los norteamericanos.
Yap [yap], *vn.* (Prov.) Ladrar como un perrito.
Yard [yārd], *va.* Acorralar, apriscar.—*s.* 1. Corral, patio de una casa u otro edificio; cercado; por extensión, espacio descubierto situado delante o alrededor de una casa. 2. Parque, cercado de construcción. *Dock-yard*, Arsenal, taller de la marina, astillero. *Lumber-yard*, Leñera, depósito de maderas. 3. Yarda, una medida inglesa poco más larga que la vara castellana o de Burgos, equivalente a 0.914 metro. 4. (Mar.) Verga, nombre que se da a las piezas de madera que sirven para llevar las velas. *Yard-arms*, Penoles de las vergas. *Lateen-yards*, Vergas latinas. *Main-yard*, Verga mayor. *Main-topsail-yard*, Verga de gavia. *Sprit-sail-yard*, Verga de

cebadera. *Cross-jack-yard*, Verga seca o verga de gata. *Square yards*, Vergas redondas. *To brace the yards*, Bracear las vergas. *To top the yards*, Amantillar las vergas. *To top the yards a-port or a-starboard*, Amantillar a babor o estribor. *To square the yards*, Poner las vergas en cruz. 5. (Vulg.) Verga, miembro viril.

Yardland [yard'-land], *s.* Una medida de tierra que varía mucho según los diferentes condados en Inglaterra: en unos comprende sólo quince acres, en otros veinte, en otros cuarenta, etc.

Yardmaster [yārd-mas'-tẹr], *s.* Mayordomo, superintendente de un patio de ferrocarril.

Yardstick [yārd'-stic], *s.* Vara graduada que sirve para medir una yarda.

Yardwand [yārd'-wend], *s.* La medida de una yarda o de una vara inglesa.

Yare [yar], *a.* (Esco. o des.) 1. Manejable, pronto a responder al timón; se dice de un bajel. 2. Pronto, ligero, diestro o hábil para ejecutar algo.

Yarn [yārn], *s.* 1. Hilaza, hilo de lana; hilo de lino; popularmente, cualquier hilo; hilado. 2. (Fam.) Historia, cuento largo y extravagante. *To spin a yarn*, Hacer una hilaza; (fig.) referir una historia larga, hablar sobremanera. *Cotton yarn*, Hilo de torzal, hilaza de algodón. *Hemp yarn*, Hilaza o hilo de cáñamo. *Weaver's yarn*, Hilaza. *Rope-yarn*, (Mar.) Filástica. *Spun-yarn*, (Mar.) Meollar. *Tarred yarn*, Hilo negro, encerado ó alquitranado.

Yarrow [yar'-ō], *s.* Milenrama, mil hojas, aquilea; planta compuesta. Achillea millefolium.

Yaw [yē], *s.* 1. (Mar.) Guiñada. 2. *V.* YAWS.

Yaw, *va.* y *vn.* 1. (Mar.) Guiñar, mover la proa del buque apartándola hacia uno y otro lado, moviendo el timón. 2. Andar haciendo eses.

Yawing [ye'-ing], *s.* (Mar.) Guiñada.

Yawl [yēl], *s.* (Mar.) 1. Embarcación pequeña (Amer. yola), con aparejo de balandra y un mástil pequeño adicional en la popa. 2 Serení, especie de embarcación pequeña destinada al servicio de un navío. 3. Barca pescadora.

Yawn [yēn], *vn.* 1. Bostezar, abrir ancha o involuntariamente la boca. 2. Quedarse con la boca abierta; por extensión, suspirar por, anhelar. 3. Abrirse del todo, como pronto para engolfar o recibir alguna cosa.

Yawn, *s.* 1. Bostezo, la acción y efecto de bostezar. 2. Acción de abrirse del todo.

Yawner [yēn'-ẹr], *s.* Bostezador, el que bosteza mucho.

Yawning [yēn'-ing], *a.* Que bosteza, que está soñoliento, que se está cayendo de sueño.—*s.* Bostezo.

Yaws [yēz], *s.* Erupción cutánea y contagiosa de los trópicos, caracterizada por pequeños tubérculos rojizos; (*yaw, sing.* uno de los tubérculos).

Ye [yī], *nom. pl.* de THOU Vosotros, vos.

Yea [yē], *adv.* 1. Sí, ciertamente, verdaderamente. 2. Y aun, y además, no solamente . . . sino. *Yea or nay*, Sí ó no.—*s.* Sí, voto afirmativo. *The yeas and nays*, Los votos en pro y en contra; lista de los miembros de una asamblea o junta, con la indicación de sus votos. *V.* YES.

Yean [yīn], *vn.* Parir la oveja.

Yeanling [yīn'-ling], *s.* Cordero o cabrito mamantón.

Year [yīr], *s.* 1. Año, el espacio de doce meses, duración de una revolución de la tierra en su órbita alrededor del sol. 2. Año, el tiempo que emplea un planeta en recorrer su órbita; revolución. 3. *pl.* Años, edad, época de la vida; edad avanzada, vejez. *Once a year*, Una vez al año o cada año. *Every other year*, De dos en dos años o cada dos años. *New-year's day*, Día de año nuevo. *New-year's gift*, Aguinaldo. *Leap year*, Año bisiesto. *A man in years*, Un anciano, un hombre de edad o un hombre de mucha edad. *To grow in years*, Envejecer. *Last year*, El año último, el año pasado. *Next year*, El año próximo, el año que viene. *By the year*, Al año. *Of late years*, En estos últimos años. *Once a year*, Una vez al año. *One year with another*, Un año con otro. *To be in years*, Ser viejo. *To wish a happy New-year*, Desear feliz año nuevo.

Yearling [yīr'-ling], *s.* El animal que tiene un año. *Yearling bullock*, Becerro añal.

Yearly [yīr'-li], *a.* Anual, que sucede o se hace cada año; que dura por un año.—*adv.* Anualmente, todos los años, cada año o una vez al año.

Yearn [yẹrn], *vn.* Anhelar, desear vivamente, suspirar por; (con *for*); compadecerse, apiadarse, sentir interiormente un movimiento de piedad o compasión; (con *over*).

Yearning [yẹrn'-ing], *s.* Deseo ardiente acompañado de un sentimiento de ternura, de afecto; ternura, lástima, compasión.

Yeast [yīst], *s.* 1. Jiste, la espuma de la cerveza que fermenta y sirve para levadura; vegetación de un honguillo microscópico (Saccharomyces); fermento. 2. Espuma (de la mar agitada).

Yelk [yelk], *s.* (Dialecto) *V.* YOLK.

Yell [yel], *va.* y *vn.* Dar alaridos, gritar furiosamente, quejarse a gritos y con voces lastimeras. *To yell out*, Gritar, decir algunas palabras a gritos.

Yell, *s.* 1. Alarido, grito o quejido fuerte y lastimero. 2. Grito salvaje, grito feroz (como de guerra). 3. Grito formado con un conjunto de palabras acordadas de antemano; v. gr. el de los estudiantes de un colegio determinado.

Yellow [yel'-ō], *a.* 1. Amarillo, que es del color del oro, del limón, del latón, etc. 2. Rubio, dorado (hablando de los cabellos). *To grow yellow*, Amarillear.—*s.* Amarillo, color amarillo. *Chrome yellow*, Amarillo de cromo, cromato de plomo. *King's yellow*, Oropimento. *To become, to get, to grow* ó *to turn yellow*, Ponerse amarillo. *Yellow berries*, Bayas persas, semillas del cambrón de que se hace uso en el tinte; pizacantas. *Yellow-boy*, (Vulg.) Guinea u otra moneda de oro. *Yellow-bird*, (1) Acanta de América. Spinus tristis. (2) La silvia amarilla, "pájaro del estío." Dendroica estiva. (3) Chamariz u oropéndola (*golden oriole*). *Yellow bunting*, *V. Yellow-hammer*. *Yellow fever*, Fiebre amarilla, (fam. vómito negro). Se llama también *Yellow Jack*. *Yellow-hammer*, (1) Verderol, emberiza. (2) (E. U.) Colapto, pico grande del género Colaptes. *V.* FLICKER. *Yellow-jacket*, Avispa social del género Vespa, con rayas amarillas y cuya picadura es dolorosa. *Yellow spot*, (1) Mácula pequeña en el fondo del ojo, el sitio de la visión más aguda en todos los vertebrados; (2) mariposa americana con una mancha amarilla en las alas posteriores. *Yellow-throat*, Curruca de Marilandia, de pecho y cuello amarillos. Geothlypis trichas. *Yellow wood*, Fustete, cloreta, xantóxilo; maderas más ó menos amarillas de las que hay varias especies; en particular la Cladrastis tinctoria, árbol águila y la madera de satén de las Bahamas. *Yellow-lead*, Albayalde calcinado.

Yellowish [yel'-o-ish], *a.* Amarillento, que tira a amarillo o que amarillea.

Yellowishness [yel'-ō-ish-nes], *s.* El color amarillento o que tira a amarillo.

Yellowness [yel'-o-nes], *s.* Amarillez.

Yelp [yelp], *vn.* Latir, gañir, chillar el perro.—*s.* Gañido, chillido, grito agudo del perro lastimado o doliente.

Yen [yen], *s.* Unidad de la moneda japonesa, equivalente a cinco pesetas o un dólar. (< Chino *yuen*, redondo.)

Yelping [yelp'-ing], *s.* Gañido.

Yeoman [yō'-man], *s.* (*pl.* YEOMEN). 1. Hacendado, el que tiene hacienda en tierras; labrador acomodado. 2. Nombre de ciertos guardias del rey de Inglaterra. 3. (Mar.) Pañolero; en la marina de los E. U., guardaalmacén, almacenero, guardián. *Gunner's yeoman*, Pañolero de la Santa Bárbara. *Boatswain's yeoman*, Pañolero del pañol de proa.

Yeomanry [yō'-man-ri], *s.* 1. El conjunto o agregado de los hacendados de una provincia. 2. Uno de los cuerpos de guardias del rey de Inglaterra.

Yerk [yẹrk], *va.* (Prov. ó des.) *V. To* JERK.

Yes [yes], *adv.* Sí, partícula afirmativa; sí tal; bien está; verdaderamente.—Con el *yes* se contesta a la persona que nos llama, y corresponde a *¡ Señor !* o *¡ Señora ! ¿ qué manda, qué quiere Vd. ?* según la clase de superioridad o igualdad que tiene aquella respecto del que responde. Denotamos también con este adverbio quedar enterados de lo que otro nos dice, y entonces ha de traducirse por *Bien está; voy a hacerlo; ya voy*, con arreglo a los casos y antecedentes del discurso. —*Yes truly*, Verdaderamente, ciertamente.

Yes-man [yes'-man], *s.* Individuo servil, adulador que dice sí a todo.

Yester [yes'-tẹr], *a.* Pasado, último; que pertenece al día de ayer.

Yesterday [yes'-tẹr-dē], *s.* Ayer, el día de ayer.—*adv.* Ayer.

Yesternight [yes'-tẹr-nait], *s.* Anoche o la noche pasada.—*adv.* Ayer por la tarde.

Yet [yet], *conj.* Con todo, sin embargo; pero, empero.—*adv.* 1. Además, todavía, además de eso. 2.

Aún, hasta ahora, hasta aquí; á lo menos. *As yet*, Hasta ahora, hasta aquí. *Not yet*, Todavía no, aún no.

Yew [yū], *s.* 1. (Bot.) Tejo, árbol parecido al abeto; cualquier árbol o arbusto del género Taxus. 2. Madera de este árbol; arco hecho de esta madera. (<A.-S. īuv.)

Yield [yīld], *va.* 1. Producir utilidad o en retorno por el trabajo; redituar. *To yield six per cent.*, Producir, redituar seis por ciento. 2. Dar, dar de sí, ser origen natural de; ofrecer. 3. Ceder, admitir, conceder, deferir, condescender; devolver, restituir. 4. Acordar, admitir como verdadero, reconocer. 5. Permitir, sufrir; conceder, otorgar. *To yield consent*, Dar consentimiento, consentir.—*vn.* 1. Producir provecho por el trabajo, sacar utilidad. 2. Ceder; rendirse, sujetarse, someterse. 3. Asentir, convenir en lo que otro dice. *I yield to it*, Consiento en ello. 4. Flaquear, ceder, hacer lugar, como bajo presión. *To yield one's right*, Ceder su derecho. *To yield up*, Ceder, entregar; devolver; abandonar; entregar (el alma). *To yield to*, Ceder á, rendirse á; acceder á, consentir en; someterse á. *To yield to the temptation*, Ceder, sucumbir á la tentación.—*s.* 1. Rendición, acción de rendirse. 2. (For.) Rédito, rendimiento, renta, beneficio que rinde un capital.

Yielding [yīld'-ing], *a.* Fácil, complaciente; flojo; que cede o se somete con facilidad; condescendiente.

Yieldingly [yīld'-ing-li], *adv.* Libremente; flojamente.

Yieldingness [yīld'-ing nes], *s.* Facilidad en ceder o en condescender.

Yodel [yō'-dl], *va.* y *vn.* Cantar modulando la voz rápidamente desde el tono natural al falsete, y viceversa.—*s.* Acción de tararear una canción o un estribillo sin pronunciar las palabras. (<Alem. jodeln).

Yoke [yōk], *s.* 1. Yugo, el instrumento con que se une un par de bueyes. 2. Yugo, servidumbre, esclavitud. *To throw off the yoke*, Sacudir el yugo. 3. Barra de timón; balancín, pedazo de madera escotado que llevan los aguadores sobre los hombros. 4. *sing.* y *pl.* Yunta, cuando se habla de bueyes, y se usa también para expresar un par de otros animales, *Yoke of land*, Yugada.

Yoke, *va.* 1. Uncir, atar al yugo los bueyes. 2. Unir, juntar. 3. Sojuzgar, sujetar, reducir á la esclavitud; retener, reprimir.

Yoke-elm [yōk'-elm], *s.* (Bot.) Carpe, especie de olmo.

Yoke-fellow [yōk'-fel-ō], **Yokemate** [yōk'-mēt], *s.* Compañero en los trabajos.

Yolk [yōk o yōlk], *s.* 1. Yema de huevo, amarillo. 2. Una exudación jabonosa en la lana de las ovejas y carneros.

Yon [yen], †**Yond** [yend], **Yonder** [yen'-dẹr], *a.* y *adv.* Allí, allá: dícese de lo que está á la vista aunque algo distante. *Yonder he is*, Mírale allí.

Yore [yōr], *s.* (Ant. y poét.) Tiempos pasados, otro tiempo. *Of yore*, Tiempo hace o ha mucho tiempo; antaño, antiguamente, en otro tiempo.

You [yū]. Pronombre personal que se usa como caso oblicuo de la segunda persona y también como nominativo, correspondiendo en castellano á te, á vosotros, á Vd. o á Vds. en el primer caso, y á tú o Vd., vosotros o Vds. en el segundo. *You* también se usa en inglés indefinidamente, y en este caso se debe traducir en castellano por el pronombre indefinido. *As you come near it, you see nothing*, Al llegar cerca de ello, no se ve nada.

Young [yung], *a.* 1. Joven, mozo, en la edad de la juventud; que está en la primera parte de su desarrollo. 2. No avanzado, nuevo. 3. Lleno de vigor o frescura. 4. Nuevo, novicio, inexperimentado. 5. (Fam.) Más joven que otro u otra del mismo nombre, título o especie. *A young child*, Un niño. *A young man; a young girl, a young woman*, Un joven; una joven. *A young face*, Cara remozada. *A young plant*, Planta tierna.—*s.* Hijuelos, la cría de los animales. *Young one*, Hijuelo. *To grow young again*, Rejuvenecer. *To look young*, Tener la traza joven. *With young*, En cinta, preñada.

Younger [yuṇ'-gẹr], *a.* Más joven. *Younger brother*, Hermano menor. *To be the younger hand*, Ser pie o el último que echa la carta en el juego.

Youngish [yung'-ish], *a.* Mozuelo, jovencillo, tierno.

Youngling [yung'-ling], *s.* Pequeñuelo.

Youngster [yung'-stẹr], *s.* Jovencito, chico, mozalbete.

Younker [yuṇ'-kẹr], *s.* 1. Propietario campesino alemán. 2. (Ant.) Mozalbete, chico. 3. Señorito, joven.

Your [yūr], *pron.* Vuestro; de usted, de ustedes. *Your brothers, your sisters*, Vuestros hermanos, vuestras hermanas.

Yours [yūrz], *pron.* El vuestro, la vuestra, los vuestros, las vuestras; lo de usted que le pertenece. *You have my pen, and I have yours*, Vd. tiene mi pluma y yo tengo la de Vd. *This penknife is yours*, Este cortaplumas es de Vd. (el suyo). *I am yours*, Estoy á la disposición de Vd. *Yours truly*, Su seguro servidor (S. S. S.). *Yours very truly*, Su afectísimo.

Yourself [yūr-self'], *pron.* Tú mismo, Vd. mismo. *Yourselves, pl.* Vosotros o Vds. mismos.

Youth [yūth], *s.* 1. Juventud, mocedad, adolescencia, el período de la vida comprendida entre la niñez y la edad viril. 2. Un joven; juventud, el agregado o conjunto de jóvenes.

Youthful [yūth'-ful], *a.* Juvenil, joven, fresco, vigoroso, juguetón.

Youthfully [yūth'-ful-i], *adv.* De un modo juvenil, como muchacho.

Youthfulness [yūth'-ful-nes], *s.* Mocedad.

Yowl [yaul], *vn.* (Fam. o Prov.) Aullar, ladrar; dar alaridos, gritar.—*s.* Aullido, aúllo; grito fuerte (de aviso o advertencia); alarido. *V.* HOWL y YELL.

Yttria [it'-ri-a], *s.* Itria, substancia blanca, terrosa, insoluble, óxido de itrio. (Y_2O_3.)

Yttrium [it'-ri-um], *s.* (Quím.) Itrio, elemento metálico del grupo cerio; fué descubierto por medio de su espectro.

Yucca [yuc'-a], *s.* (Bot.) Yuca, género de plantas de la familia de las liliáceas; una planta de este género.

Yule [yūl], *s.* Navidad, tiempo de la Navidad o pascua.

Yunx [yuṇx], *s.* Género de pájaros cuyo tipo es el torcecuello. *V.* WRYNECK, 1ª acep.

Ywrought [i'-rōt], *pp.* ant. de *To* WORK. Trabajado, labrado. *V.* WROUGHT.

Z

Z [zī; se llama también zed en Inglaterra], vigésima sexta y última letra del alfabeto, cuya pronunciación inglesa se ve en *la clave corriente* y en las palabras siguientes.

Zabaism, *s.* *V.* SABAISM.

Zaffer, Zaffre [zaf'-ẹr], *s.* (Min.) Zafre, azul que se saca del cobalto; mineral de cobalto calentado con sílice.

Zambo [zam'-bō], *s.* *V.* SAMBO.

Zanana [za-nā'-na], *s.* *V.* ZENANA.

Zany [zē'-ni], *s.* El gracioso de las comedias italianas; un bufón, un truhán; simplonazo.

Zauschneria [zaush-nī'-ri-a], *s.* (Bot.) Planta califórnica de la familia de las onagráceas; se cultiva por sus flores carmesíes que se llaman familiarmente "trompeta de colibrí."

Zea [zī'-a ó zē'-a], *s.* (Bot.) Zea, género de altas plantas gramíneas. *Zea mays* es el maíz.

Zeal [zīl], *s.* Celo; fervor; ardor; amor ó afición desmedida, devoción entusiasta.

Zealot [zel'-ẹt], *s.* 1. Celador, entusiasta, el que es muy amante de la religión, de la patria, etc.; partidario inmoderado, fanático. 2. Miembro de un partido fanático judío (A. D. 6–70), en casi continua sublevación contra los romanos.

Zealotism [zel'-ẹt-izm], *s.* Celo ciego, fanatismo.

Zealotry [zel'-ẹt-ri], *s.* La conducta ó disposición de una persona celosa ó fanática.

Zealous [zel'-us], *a.* Celoso, el que cela, defiende ó toma mucho empeño en alguna causa.

Zealously [zel'-us-li], *adv.* Apasionadamente, con pasión y celo; con ardor.

Zealousness [zel'-us-nes], *s.* La propiedad de ser celoso; ardor, conato.

Zebec [zī'-bec], *s.* *V.* XEBEC.

Zebra [zī'-bra], *s.* Cebra, animal cuadrúpedo de África parecido al mulo, con listas transversales pardas o negras en toda la piel.

Zebu [zī'-biū], *s.* Zebú, cebú, buey de la India (Bos indicus) con giba en la cruz.

Zecchino [tsec-kī'-nō], **Zechin** [zek'-in], *s.* Cequí, moneda antigua de oro, del valor de unos dos pesos fuertes, acuñada en la república de Venecia.

Zed [zed], *s.* La letra z; zeda o zeta; casi siempre llamada *zi* en los Estados Unidos.

Zedoary [zed'-o-ẹ-ri], *s.* (Bot.) Cedoaria, raíz y planta aromática cuyas hojas se parecen á las del jengibre; se usa en medicina como tónico aromático y como perfume. Curcuma zedoaria.

Zeitgeist [tsait'-gaist], *s.* El espíritu de los tiempos; las tendencias intelectuales y morales que caracterizan cualquier siglo ó época. (Alem).

Zenana [zen-ä'-na], *s.* En la India, las habitaciones de las mujeres; el harén indio.

Zend [zend], *s.* Zendo, idioma de la familia indoeuropea usado antiguamente en las provincias septentrionales de Persia.

Zend-Avesta [zend"-a-ves'-ta], *s.* Zendavesta, colección de los libros sagrados de los persas, que contiene las doctrinas de Zoroastro.

Zenith [zí'-nith], *s.* 1. Cenit o zenit, el punto que en la esfera celeste está perpendicularmente sobre nuestra cabeza, opuesto al nadir. 2. Punto culminante de la prosperidad, cumbre; colmo de la grandeza.

Zephyr [zef'-ęr], *s.* 1. Céfiro, favonio, viento de la parte de poniente. 2. (Poét.) Céfiro, cualquier viento que sopla blanda y apaciblemente. 3. Hilaza floja de lana muy ligera de peso, para bordar.

Zephyrus [zef'-i-rus], *s.* Céfiro, Favonio.

Zeppelin [ze'-pe-lin], *s.* Zepelín.

Zero [zí'-rō], *s.* 1. Cero, el guarismo arábigo 0. 2. De aquí, la ausencia de cantidad, nada. 3. Punto en un pitipié o escala desde el cual se gradúa un termómetro, etc.; se mide generalmente en direcciones opuestas; de aquí, el punto más bajo.

Zest [zest], *va.* 1. Excitación agradable del ánimo que acompaña al ejercicio mental o físico. 2. Sainete, el sabor que se da a alguna cosa. 3. (Poco us.) Luquete, cortecita de naranja que se echa en el vino para darle gusto. 4. (Poco us.) Bizna, la membranita que hay entre los cachos de la nuez.

Zeta [zí'-ta o zé'-ta], *s.* Letra sexta del alfabeto griego.

Zetetic [zę-tet'-ic], *a.* Cetético, dado a resolver problemas o a pesquisas e investigaciones.

Zeus [ziūs], *s.* Nombre de la deidad suprema de los griegos, correspondiente al Júpiter de los romanos.

Zigote [sai'-gōt], *s.* (Biol.) Cigoto, huevo.

Zigzag [zig'-zag], *va.* y *vn.* Formar en zigzag; ir en zigzags, hacer zigzags.—*a.* Que está en una línea interrumpida con irregularidades a uno y otro lado.—*s.* Zisgás, zigzag, serie de líneas que forman ángulos entrantes y salientes.

Zinc [zinc], *s.* Cinc, zinc, metal blanco azulado y fácil de fundir. *Zinc chloride*, Cloruro de cinc. *Sulphate of zinc* o *white copperas*, Sulfato de cinc o caparrosa blanca. *Zinc blende*, Blenda, sulfuro de cinc nativo. *Zinc white*, Blanco de cinc, óxido de cinc.—*va.* Plaquear, dar una capa de cinc.

Zincite [zink'-ait], *s.* Oxido rojo de cinc.

Zincography [zin-cog'-ra-fi], *s.* El arte de grabar en zinc.

Zinnia [zin'-i-a], *s.* (Bot.) Zinnia.

Zion [zai'-ǫn], *s.* 1. Sión, colina de Jerusalén; de aquí, la antigua teocracia hebrea o la moderna Iglesia de Cristo. 2. Cielo.

Zip gun [zip' gun], *s.* Remachador de tipo de pistola; pistola o revolver de confección doméstica.

Zipper [zip'-ęr], *s.* Cremallera, cierre relámpago.

Zircon [zęr'-con], *s.* Circón, silicato adamantino de circonio de diversos colores. ($ZrSiO_4$.) Se usa como piedra fina.

Zirconium [zęr-cō'-ni-um], *s.* Circonio, metal muy raro cuyas sales tienen uso limitado.

Zither, Zithern [zith'-ęr, ęrn], *s.* Cítara, instrumento músico de cuerda algo parecido a la guitarra, que se toca con púa. (Alem.)

Zizyphus [ziz'-i-fus], *s.* (Bot.) Azufaifo, género de plantas de la familia de las rámneas.

Zocle [zō'-cl], *s.* *V.* SOCLE.

Zodiac [zō'-di-ac], *s.* 1. Zodíaco, faja o zona imaginaria que se extiende unos ocho grados a uno y otro lado de la eclíptica, y que contiene las doce constelaciones que el sol recorre aparentemente en los doce meses del año, así como los planetas mayores. 2. Circuito completo, círculo.

Zodiacal [zo-dai'-ac-al], *a.* Zodiacal, que pertenece al zodíaco.

Zoic [zō'-ic], *a.* 1. Zoico, concerniente al animal o a la vida animal. 2. En geología, que contiene fósiles; dícese de las rocas. (< Griego zōikos.)

Zoilism [zō'-il-izm], *s.* Crítica severa, censura inmotivada, como la de Zoilo, crítico griego.

Zollverein [tsōl'-fer-ain"], *s.* Unión aduanera alemana. (Alem.)

Zonal [zō'-nal], *a.* Perteneciente a una zona o banda; marcado con bandas o zonas.

Zone [zōn], *s.* 1. (Geog.) Zona, cualquiera de las cinco partes o bandas en que se considera dividida la superficie de la tierra de polo a polo. 2. Banda circular, faja; raya o línea de color diferente. 3. Originalmente, y hoy en poesía, cinturón o cíngulo.

Zoned [zōnd], *a.* 1. Zonado, marcado con fajas coloreadas y concéntricas. 2. Que lleva un cinto o cíngulo.

Zoneless [zōn'-les], *a.* Que no tiene cinto.

Zoo [zū], *s.* (Fam.) Jardín zoológico. (Abrev. de *zoological.*)

Zoochemistry [zō-o-kem'-is-tri], *s.* Zooquímica, química animal; es decir, química de los sólidos y líquidos contenidos en el cuerpo animal.

Zoogeny [zo-ej'-ę-ni], *s.* Zoogenia, la doctrina o el procedimiento del origen de los seres vivientes.

Zoogl͡œa [zō-o-glí'-a], *s.* Zoogloea, una colonia de bacterias que forma una masa gelatinosa. (< Gr. *zōon*, animal, y *gloios*, substancia pegajosa.)

Zoographer [zo-eg'-ra-fęr], *s.* Zoógrafo, el que escribe o compone un tratado de zoografía.

Zoographic, Zoographical [zō"-o-graf'-ic, al], *a.* Zoográfico, perteneciente o relativo a la zoografía.

Zoography [zo-eg'-ra-fi], *s.* Zoografía, descripción de la naturaleza y las propiedades de los animales.

Zoolatry [zo-el'-a-tri], *s.* Zoolatría, el culto y adoración de los animales.

Zoolite [zō'-o-lait], *s.* Zoolito, zoomorfito: los restos fósiles de un animal petrificado. Se escribe también Zoolith.

Zoological [zō-o-lej'-ic-al], *a.* Zoológico, perteneciente a la zoología.

Zoologist [zo-el'-o-jist], *s.* Zoólogo, el profesor de zoología.

Zoology [zo-el'-o-ji], *s.* 1. Zoología, la ciencia que trata de los animales. 2. El reino animal o ejemplares locales de él, considerados biológicamente. 3. Zoología, tratado científico sobre los animales.

Zoom [zūm], *vn.* (Aer.) Subir bruscamente en ángulo máximo.

Zoometry [zo-em'-e-tri], *s.* Zoometría, medición de los animales.

Zoonomy [zo-en'-o-mi], *s.* Zoonomía, las leyes de la vida animal.

Zoonosis [zō-o-nō'-sis], *s.* Zoonosis, enfermedad transmitible de animales a hombres.

Zoophagan [zō-ef'-a-gan], *s.* y *a.* Animal zoófago, carnívoro.

Zoophagous [zo-ef'-a-gus], *a.* Zoófago, que se alimenta de materias animales. (< Gr. ζωοφάγος.)

Zoophyte [zō'-o-fait], *s.* Zoófito, animal invertebrado que se asemeja algo a la planta en su forma y crecimiento: v. gr. el coral y la esponja.

Zoophytic, Zoophytical [zō"-o-fit'-ic, al], *a.* Zoofítico, de o perteneciente a los zoófitos.

Zoospore [zō'-o-spōr], *s.* (Bot) Zoósporo, esporo que puede moverse independientemente, como sucede con ciertas algas.

Zootic [zō-et'-ic], *a.* Zoótico; se dice de un terreno que contiene cuerpos organizados.

Zootomist [zo-et'-o-mist], *s.* Zootómico, el que hace la disección de los animales irracionales.

Zootomy [zo-et'-o-mi], *s.* Zootomía, disección de los cuerpos de los brutos o animales irracionales.

Zoroastrian [zō-ro-as'-tri-an], *a.* Zoroástrico, perteneciente a Zoroastro o a sus doctrinas.

Zoroastrianism [zō-ro-as'-tri-an-izm], *s.* Sistema religioso de Zoroastro, conocido como la religión de los magos.

Zouave [zū-āv'], *s.* Zuavo, soldado argelino de infantería al servicio de Francia, o el soldado francés o de otro país que lleva uniforme de zuavo.

Zounds [zaunds], *inter.* ¡Voto al chápiro! ¡por vida de sanes! ¡válgame Dios! (Corrupción de *God's wounds.*)

Zulu, Zooloo [zū'-lū], *a.* Zulú, perteneciente a los zulúes o a su idioma.—*s.* Zulú, individuo de ciertas tribus negras que habitan el África austral; su dialecto o idioma.

Zygoma [zig-ō'-ma], *s.* Cigoma, hueso del juanete; arco largo que une los huesos temporales y malares.

Zygomatic [zai-go-mat'-ic], *a.* (Anat.) Cigomático, perteneciente al cigoma o situado cerca de él.

Zygomorphous, Zygomorphic [zig"-o-mōr'-fus, fic], *a.* (Bot.) En forma de yugo; dícese de ciertas flores divisibles en mitades semejantes en un solo plano.

Zyme [zaim], *s.* 1. Un fermento. 2. Germen de enfermedad; lo que se considera causa específica de una enfermedad cimótica o infecciosa. (< Gr. zymê < *zeo*, cocer.)

Zymic [zim'-ic], *a.* Címico, concerniente a la fermentación o producido por ella.

Zymology [zai-mel'-o-ji], *s.* Zimología, tratado de la fermentación.

Zymosis [zai-mō'-sis], *s.* 1. Toda forma de fermentación; particularmente fermentacion morbífica. 2. Cualquiera enfermedad contagiosa o infecciosa producida por fermentación morbífica.

Zymotic [zai-met'-ic], *a.* Cimótico, relativo a la fermentación o producido por ella. *Zymotic disease*, Una enfermedad cualquiera epidémica, endémica o contagiosa.

Zythum [zai'-thum], *s.* Especie de cerveza usada en el antiguo Egipto.

Lista Alfabética de los Nombres De Países, Naciones, Provincias, Mares, Pueblos, Ríos, Montañas, Etc.

QUE NO SE ESCRIBEN DEL MISMO MODO

EN INGLÉS QUE EN ESPAÑOL.

CON el objeto de hacerla lo más corta posiole, no han sido comprendidos en ella los que tienen una misma ortografía en ambas lenguas, y los que pueden ser traducidos fácilmente con sólo mudar su terminación extranjera en la castellana; para lo cual se deberán observar las reglas siguientes.

Los acabados en *burg, burgh, bourg* y *borough* que no se hallen en la lista, se traducirán mudando solamente estas terminaciones en la castellana *burgo*, como *Augsburg*, Augsburgo; *Petersburg*, Petersburgo; *Hamburg*, Hamburgo; *Cobourg*, Coburgo; y *Peterborough*, Peterburgo, etc.

Hay muchos nombres geográficos universalmente conocidos que terminan en *e*, y se traducen con sólo mudar la *e* en *a*, como *Europe*, Europa; *Rome*, Roma, etc.

Los ingleses suelen designar algunos de los condados en que dividen la Gran Bretaña por medio de la terminación *shire* añadida al nombre del condado, distrito o provincia, como *Derbyshire*, que se traducirá El condado, distrito o provincia de Derby; *Yorkshire*, El condado de York, etc.

NOTA.—Los adjetivos derivados de los nombres propios se hallarán en sus respectivos lugares en el texto de este diccionario.

A

Aachen [ɑ'-ken] o **Aix-la-Chapelle** [êx-la-shɑ-pel'], Aquisgrán (Alemania).

Abyssinia [ab-i-sin'-i-ɑ], Abisinia. V. ETHIOPIA.

Achaea [ɑ-kî'-ɑ], Acaya (región de la antigua Grecia).

Addis Ababa [ad'-dis a'-bɑ-bɑ], Addis Abeba (Etiopía).

Admiralty Islands [ad'-mi-ral-ti ɑi'-lɑndz], Islas del Almirantazgo.

Adrianople [ad-ri-ɑ-nō'-pl] o **Edirne** [êd-îr'-nê], Adrianópolis o Andrinópolis (Turquía).

Adriatic Sea [ad-ri-at'-ic sî], Mar Adriático.

Aegean Sea [î-jî'-an sî], Mar Egeo.

Agincourt [a'-shin-our], Azincourt (Francia).

Aix-la-Chapelle. V. AACHEN.

Aleutian Islands [a-lū'-shɑn ɑi'-lɑndz], Islas Aleutianas.

Alexandria [al-ex-an'-dri-ɑ], Alejandría (Egipto).

Algeria [al-jî'-ri-ɑ], Argelia.

Algiers [al-jîrz'], Argel (ciudad de Argelia, África).

Alps [alps], Alpes (montañas del S. de la Europa central).

Alsace-Lorraine [ɑl-sɑ̄s' lō-rên'], Alsacia-Lorena.

Amazon River [am'-ɑ-zon], Río Amazonas.

Andalusia [an-dɑ-lū'-shi-ɑ], Andalucía (España).

Antarctic Ocean [an-tɑrc'-tic ō'-shan], Océano Antártico.

Antilles, Greater [grêt'-ęr an-tîl'-iz], Antillas Mayores.

Antilles, Lesser [les'-ęr an-tîl'-iz], Antillas Menores.

Antioch [an'-ti-oc], Antioquía (Turquía).

Antwerp [ant'-węrp], Amberes (Bélgica).

Apennines [ap'-ę-nɑinz], Apeninos (montañas de Italia).

Appalachian Mountains [ap-pęl-ê'-shan mɑun'-tenz], Montes Apalaches.

Arabian Sea [ɑ-rê'-bi-ɑn sî], Mar Arábigo.

Archipelago [ɑr-ki-pel'-ɑ-gō], El Archipiélago Griego o del Mar Egeo.

Arctic Ocean [ɑ̄rc'-tic ō'-shan), Océano Ártico.

Ardennes Mountains [ar-dênz' mɑun'-tenz], Sierra Ardenas.

Assisi [ɑ̄-sî'-sî], Asís (Italia).

Assyria [ɑ̄-sîr'-ia], Asiria.

Athens [ath'-ens), Atenas (Grecia).

Atlantic Ocean [at-lan'-tic ō'-ṣhan], Océano Atlántico.

Attica [at'-î-cɑ], Ática (Grecia).

Austria-Hungary [ōs'-tri-ɑ hʊn'-gɑ-ri], Austria-Hungría.

Avignon [ɑ̄-vî-nyen'], Aviñón (Francia).

B

Babylon [bab'-i-lęn], Babilonia.

Balearic Islands [ba-lear'-ic ɑi'-landz], Islas Baleares.

Balkans [bōl'-kɑns], Balcanes.

Baltic Sea [bōl'-tic sî], Mar Báltico.

Barbary Coast [bɑ̄r'-bɑ-ri cōst], Berbería (África).

Basle [bāl] o **Basel** [bā'-zel], Basilea (Suiza).

Bavaria [bɑ-vê'-ri-ɑ], Baviera (Alemania).

Bayonne [bɑ-yen'], Bayona (Francia).

Beirut o **Beyrouth** [bê-rut'], Beirut (Líbano).

Belgian Congo [bel'-ji-ɑn cen'-gō], Congo Belga.

Belgium [bel'-ji-ʊm], Bélgica.

Belgrade [bel-grêd'] o **Beograd** [bê'-o-grad], Belgrado (Yugoslavia).

Bengal [ben'-gel], Bengala.

Berne o **Bern** [bern], Berna (Suíza).

Bethlehem [beth′-le̩-hem], Belén (Jordania).
Beyrouth, V. BEIRUT.
Biscay [bis′-kê], Vizcaya (España).
Black Forest [blac fər′-est), Selva Negra.
Black Sea [blac sī], Mar Negro.
Blue Mountains [blū maun′-te̩nz], Montañas Azules.
Bologna [bō-lō′-nya], Bolonia (Italia).
Bordeaux [bōr-dō′], Burdeos (Francia).
Bosporus [bəs′-po-rʊs], Bósforo, Estrecho del.
Brazil [bra-zil′], Brasil.
Britain, Great [grêt brit′-an], Gran Bretaña.
British Columbia [brit′-ish co-lom′-bia], Colombia Británica.
British Guiana [brit′-ish gī-a′-na], Guayana Británica.
British Honduras [brit′-ish hon-dū-ras], Honduras Británica o Belice.
British Isles [brit′-ish ailz], Islas Británicas.
British Somaliland [brit′-ish sō-ma′-li-land], Somalia Británica.
Bruges [brūzh o brū′-jez], Brujas (Bélgica).
Brussels [brʊs′-elz], Bruselas (Bélgica).
Bucharest [bū′-ca-rest], Bucarest (Rumania).
Burgundy [bʊr′-gʊn-di], Borgoña.
Burma [bʊr′-ma], Birmania.
Byzantium [bi-zan′-shi-ʊm), Bizancio (nombre antiguo de Constantinopla). V. ISTANBUL.

C

Calcutta [cal-cʊt′-a], Calcuta (India).
Cambodia [cam-bō′-di-a], Camboja (Indochina).
Canal Zone. V. PANAMA CANAL ZONE.
Canary Islands [ca-nê′-ri ai′-landz], Islas Canarias.
Cantabrian Mountains [can-tê′-bri-an maun′-te̩nz], Cordillera Cantábrica.
Cape Breton Island [kêp bret′-en ai′-land], Isla Cabo Bretón (Nueva Escocia, Canadá).
Cape Horn [kêp hōrn], Cabo de Hornos.
Capetown [kêp′-taun], Ciudad del Cabo (Unión Sudafricana).
Cap Haitien [kêp hê′-shen], Cabo Haitiano.
Caribbean Sea [car-ī-bī′-an sī], Mar Caribe o de las Antillas.
Carpathian Mountains [car-pê′-thi-an maun′-tenz], Montes Cárpatos.
Carthage [car′-thêj], Cartago (antigua ciudad del África del Norte).
Cashmere o **Kashmir** [cash′-mīr], Cachemira (estado de la región del Himalaya).
Caspian Sea [cas′-pi-an sī], Mar Caspio.
Castile, New [niū cas-til′], Castilla la Nueva (España).
Castile, Old [ōld cas-til′], Castilla la Vieja (España).
Catalonia [cat-a-lō′-ni-a], Cataluña (España).
Caucasus [cō′-ca-sus], Cáucaso.
Cayenne [ca-yên′], Cayena (Guayana Francesa).
Central America [sen′-tral a-mer′-i-ca], Centro América o América Central.
Ceylon [se̩-lən′], Ceilán.
Champagne [shān-pañ′], Champaña (Francia).
Cologne [co-lōn′], Colonia (Alemania).
Constantinople [con-stan-ti-nō′-pl], Constantinopla (Turquía). V. ISTANBUL.
Copenhagen [cō-pen-hê′-gen], Copenhague (Dinamarca).
Corinth [cər′-inth], Corinto (Grecia).
Corsica [cər′-si-ca], Córcega (Isla del Mediterráneo).
Cracow o **Krakow** [crê′-cō], Cracovia (Polonia).
Crete o **Krete** [crīt], Creta (isla del Mediterráneo).
Cyprus [sai′-prus], Chipre (isla del Mediterráneo).
Czechoslovakia [chek-os-lo-va′-kia], Checoslovaquia.

D

Dalmatia [dal-mê′-shia], Dalmacia.
Damascus [da-mas′-cʊs], Damasco (Siria).
Danube [dan′-yūb], Danubio (río de Europa).
Dardanelles [dār-da-nelz′], Dardanelos (antiguamente Helesponto).
Dead Sea [ded sī], Mar Muerto.
Denmark [den′-mārk], Dinamarca.
Dordogne [dōr-dəñ′], Dordoña (río de Francia).
Douro [dū′-rō], o **Duero** [dwê′-ro], Duero (río de la península ibérica).
Dresden [dres′-den], Dresde (Alemania).
Dunkirk [dʊn′-ke̩rk], Dunquerque (Francia).
Dutch Guiana [dʊtch gī-a′-na] o **Surinam** [sū′-ri-nam], Guayana Holandesa o Surinam.

E

East Indies [īst in′-dīz], Indias Orientales.
Edinburgh [ed′-in-bʊrg], Edimburgo (Escocia).
Edirne, V. ADRIANOPLE.
Egypt [ī′-jipt], Egipto.
Elbe River [elb riv′-e̩r], Río Elba.
England [in′-gland], Inglaterra.
English Channel [in′-glish chan′-el], Canal de la Mancha.
Ephesus [ef′-e-sus], Efeso (antigua ciudad griega en Asia Menor).
Epirus [ī-pai′-rʊs], Epiro (Grecia).
Ethiopia [ī-thi-o′-pi-a], Etiopía (ant. Abisinia).
Euphrates [yū-frê′-tiz], Eufrates (río de Asia).

F

Falkland Islands [fək′-land ai′-landz], Islas Malvinas o Falkland.
Finland [fin′-land], Finlandia.
Flanders [flan′-derz], Flandes.
Florence [flər′-ens], Florencia (Italia).
France [frans], Francia.
French Equatorial Africa [french ī-cwa-tō′-ri-al af′ri-ca], África Ecuatorial Francesa.
French Guiana [french gī-a′-na], Guayana Francesa.
French Somaliland [french sō-ma′-li-land], Somalia Francesa.
Friendly Islands [frend′-ly ai′-landz], Islas de los Amigos o de la Amistad. V. TONGA.
Frisian Islands [frizh′-an ai′-landz], Islas Frisias.

G

Galilee [gal′-ī-lī], Galilea.
Garonne [ga-rən′], Garona (río de Francia).
Gascony [gas′-co-nī], Gascuña (Francia).
Gaul [gəl], Galia.
Geneva [je̩-nī′-va], Ginebra (Suiza)
Genoa [jen′-o-a], Génova (Italia).
Germany [jer′-man-i], Alemania.
Ghent [gent], Gante (Bélgica).
Gold Coast [gōld cōst], Costa de Oro (África Occidental).
Good Hope, Cape of [kêp ov gud hōp], Cabo de Buena Esperanza.
Great Britain [grêt brit′-an], Gran Bretaña.
Great Lakes [grêt lêks], Grandes Lagos.
Greece [grīs], Grecia.
Greenland [grīn′-land], Groenlandia.
Groningen [grən′-ing-en], Groninga (Holanda).

H

Hague, The [dhī hêg], La Haya (Holanda).
Haiti Island [hê′-ti ai′-land] o **Hispaniola** [is-pa-niō′-la], Haití o Santo Domingo o Isla Española.
Haiti, Republic of [re̩-pʊb′-lic əv hê′-ti], República de Haití.
Hangchow [hang′-chau], Hangcheú (puerto marítimo de China).
Hankow [han′-kau], Hankeú (ciudad de China).
Havana [ha-va′-na], Habana (Cuba).
Havre, Le [le̩ a′-vr], El Havre (puerto de Francia).
Hawaiian Islands [ha-wai′-yan ai′-landz], Islas Hawaii.
Hebrides [heb′-ri-dīz], Islas Hébridas.
Hellespont [hel′-es-pont], Helesponto. V. DARDANELLES.
Hispaniola [is-pa-niō′-la], Isla Española, Haití o Santo Domingo.
Holland [həl′-and], Holanda.
Holy Land [hō′-li land], Tierra Santa.
Horn, Cape [kêp hōrn], Cabo de Hornos.
Hungary [hʊn′-ga-ri], Hungría.

I

Iberian Peninsula [ai-bīr′-ian pen-in′-siu-la], Península Ibérica.
Iceland [ais′-land], Islandia.
Indian Ocean [in′-di-an ō′-shan], Océano Índico.
Indus [in′-dus], Indo (río de la India y Pakistán).
Ionian Sea [ai-ō′-ni-an sī], Mar Jónico.
Iraq [i-rak′], Irak.
Ireland [air′-land], Irlanda.
Istanbul [is-tan-bul′], Istambul (ant. Constantinopla).
Italian Somaliland [i-tal′-yan sō-ma′-li-land], Somalia Italiana.
Italy [it′-a-li], Italia.
Ivory Coast [ai′-vo-ri cōst], Costa de Marfil.

J

Japan [ja-pan′], Japón.
Jerusalem [je̩r-yus′-a-lem], Jerusalén.
Jordan [jōr′-dan], Jordania.
Jutland [jʊt′-land], Jutlandia.

K

Key West [kī west], Cayo Hueso (Florida, E.U.A.)
Korea [cō-rī'-a], Corea.
Kyoto [kī-ō'-tō], Kioto (Japón).

L

Lapland [lap'-land], Laponia.
Latin America [lat'-in a-mer'-i-ca], América Latina o América Ibera.
Lausanne [lō-zān'], Lausana (Suiza).
Lebanon [leb'-a-non], Líbano.
Leghorn [leg'-hōrn], Liorna (Italia).
Leningrad [len'-in-grad], Leningrado (ant. San Petersburgo y Petrogrado).
Libya [lī'-bia], Libia.
Liége [li-ezh'], Lieja (Bélgica).
Lille [līl], Lila (Francia).
Lisbon [liz'-bun], Lisboa (Portugal).
Lithuania [lith-yu-ê'-ni-a], Lituania.
London [lun'-dun], Londres (Inglaterra).
Lorraine [lō-rên'], Lorena. V. ALSACE-LORRAINE.
Louisiana [lu-i-zi-an'-a], Luisiana (E.U.A.).
Louvain [lū-vên' o lū-van'], Lovaina (Bélgica).
Lower California [lō'-er ca-li-for'-nia], Baja California (México).
Low Countries [lō cun'-tris], Países Bajos. V. NETHERLANDS.
Lucerne o **Luzern** [lū-sern'], Lucerna (Suiza).

M

Magellan, Strait of [strêt ov ma-jel'-an], Estrecho de Magallanes.
Mainz [maints], Maguncia (Alemania).
Majorca o **Mallorca** [ma-yer'-ca], Mallorca (isla del Mediterráneo).
Malay Peninsula [mê'-lê pen-in'-siū-la], Península de Malaca.
Maldive Islands [mal'-daiv ai'-landz], Islas Maldivas.
Marmora o **Marmara, Sea of** [sī ov mar'-ma-ra], Mar de Mármara.
Marseille o **Marseilles** [mar-sê], Marsella (Francia).
Martinique [mar-ti-nīc'], Martinica.
Mauritius [mō-rish'-i-us] o **Ile de France** [il de frans], Mauricio (isla británica en el Océano Índico).
Mediterranean Sea [med-i-ter-ê'-ne-an sī], Mar Mediterráneo.
Memphis [mem'-fis] Menfis (ant. capital de Egipto).
Meuse [mūz], Mosa (río de Francia y Bélgica).
Mexico [Mex'-i-co], Méjico o México.
Minorca o **Menorca** [min-er'-ca], Menorca (isla del Mediterráneo).
Mississippi River [mis-is-sip'-i riv'-er], Río Misisipi.
Missouri [mis-sū'-ri], Misuri (estado y río de E.U.A.).
Moluccas [mo-liū'-cas] o **Spice Islands** [spais ai'-landz], Islas Molucas o de las Especias.
Morocco [mo-rec'-o], Marruecos.
Moscow [mos'-cau], Moscú (U.R.S.S.)
Moselle [mō-zel'], Mosela (río de Francia y Alemania).

N

Naples [nê'-plz], Nápoles (Italia).
Near East [nīr īst], Cercano Oriente.
Netherlands [nedh'-er-landz], Países Bajos u Holanda.
Newfoundland [niū'-fund-land], Terranova.
New Orleans [niū ōr'-le-anz], Nueva Orleans (Luisiana, E.U.A.)
New South Wales [niū sauth wêlz], Nueva Gales del Sur.
New York [niū yōrk], Nueva York (E.U.A.).
New Zealand [niū zī'-land], Nueva Zelanda.
Niagara Falls [nai-ā'-ga-ra fōlz], Cataratas del Niágara.
Nice [nīs], Niza (Francia).
Nile [nail], Nilo (río de África).
Nineveh [nin'-e-ve], Nínive (ant. ciudad del imperio asirio).
Nippon [nip-en'], Nipón. V. JAPAN.
Normandy [nōr'-man-di], Normandía (Francia).
North America [north a-mer'-i-ca], Norte América o América del Norte.
North Pole [north pōl], Polo Norte.
Norway [nōr'-wê], Noruega.
Nova Scotia [nō'-va scō'-sha], Nueva Escocia.

O

Odessa [o-des'-a], Odesa (puerto de la U.R.S.S.).
Olympus, Mount [maunt o-lim'-pus], Monte Olimpo.
Ostend [es'-tend], Ostende (Bélgica).

P

Pacific Ocean [pa-sif'-ic ō'-shan], Océano Pacífico.
Palestine [pal'-es-tain], Palestina.
Panama Canal Zone [pa'-na-ma ca-nal' zōn], Zona del Canal de Panamá.
Papal States [pê'-pal stêts] o **States of the Church** [stêts ov dhi chūrch], Estados Pontificios.
Parnassus, Mount [maunt par-nas'-us], Parnaso (monte de Grecia).
Peloponnesus [pel-o-pen-nī'-sus], Peloponeso (Grecia).
Pennsylvania [pen-sil-vê'-nia], Pensilvania (E.U.A.).
Perugia [pe-rū'-ja], Perusa (Italia).
Petrograd [pe'-trō-grad], V. LENINGRAD.
Philadelphia [fil-a-del'-fi-a], Filadelfia (E.U.A.).
Philippines [fil'-ip-inz], Filipinas.
Phoenicia [fī-nish'-i-a], Fenicia.
Poland [pō'-land], Polonia.
Polish Corridor [pō'-lish cer'-i-dōr], Corredor Polaco.
Pompeii [pom-pê'], Pompeya (Italia).
Port-au-Prince [port-ō-prins'], Puerto Príncipe (Haití).
Port of Spain [port ov spên'], Puerto España (Trinidad).
Port Said [port sa-īd'], Puerto Said (Egipto).
Prague [prag], Praga (Checoslovaquia).
Pyrenees [pir'-i-nīz], Pirineos (cordillera entre España y Francia).

R

Rangoon [ran-gun'], Rangún (Birmania).
Red Sea [red sī], Mar Rojo.
Rhine [rain], Rhin o Rin (río de Europa).
Rhodes [rōdz], Rodas (isla del Mar Egeo).
Rhone [rōn], Ródano (río de Europa).
Rocky Mountains [rek'-i maun'-tenz], Montañas Rocosas.
Rouen [rū-an'], Ruan (Francia).
Russia [rush'-a], Rusia. V. UNION OF SOVIET SOCIALIST REPUBLICS (U.S.S.R.).

S

Salonika [sa-lo-nī'-ka] o **Thessalonike** [thes-a-lo-nī'-kê], Salónica (Grecia).
Sardinia [sar-dī'-ni-a] o **Sardegna** [sar-dê'-ña], Cerdeña (isla del Mediterráneo).
Saudi Arabia [sa-u'-di a-rê'-bi-a], Arabia Saudita.
Saxony [sac'-so-ni], Sajonia (ant. reino alemán).
Scandinavia [scan-di-nê'-vi-ā], Escandinavia.
Scheldt [shelt], Escalda (río de Bélgica).
Scotland [scot'-land], Escocia.
Seine [sên], Sena (río de Francia).
Siam [sai'-am], V. THAILAND.
Sicily [sis'-i-lī], Sicilia (isla del Mediterráneo).
Smyrna [smer'-na], Esmirna (Turquía).
Society Islands [so-sai'-e-tī ai'-landz], Islas de la Sociedad.
South America [sauth a-mer'-i-ca], Sud América o América del Sur.
South Pole [sauth pōl], Polo Sur.
Spain [spên], España.
Sparta [spar'-ta], Esparta (antigua ciudad de Grecia).
States of the Church [stêts ov dhi chūrch], V. PAPAL STATES.
Stockholm [stec'-hōlm], Estocolmo (Suecia).
St. Petersburg [sênt pīt'-ers-burg], V. LENINGRAD.
Stromboli [strom'-bō-li], Estrómboli (volcán al N. de Sicilia).
Surinam [su'-ri-nam], V. DUTCH GUIANA.
Sweden [swī'-den], Suecia.
Switzerland [swit'-ser-land], Suiza.
Syracuse [sir'-a-kiūs], Siracusa (Italia).
Syria [sir'-i-a], Siria.

T

Tagus [tê'-gus], **Tajo** [ta'-ho] or **Tejo** [tê'ho], Tajo (río de España y Portugal).
Tangier [tān-jīr'], Tánger (Marruecos).
Taurus Mountains [tō'-rus maun'-tenz], Montañas Tauro (Turquía).
Tehran o **Teheran** [tê-ran'], Teherán (Irán).
Texas [tec'-sas], Tejas (E.U.A.).
Thailand [tai'-land] o **Siam** [sai'-am], Thailandia o Siam.
Thames [temz], Támesis (río de Inglaterra).
Thebes [thībz], Tebas (antiguas ciudades de Grecia y de Egipto).
Thermopylae [ther-mep'-i-lī], Termópilas (desfiladero de Grecia).
Thessalonike [thes-a-lo-nī'-kê], V SALONIKA.
Thessaly [thes'-a-li], Tesalia (Grecia).
Thrace [thrês], Tracia.
Tokyo [tō'-ki-ō], Tokio (Japón).
Tonga [ton'-ga] o **Friendly Islands** [frênd'-li ai'-landz], Tonga o Islas de los Amigos o de la Amistad.

Toulon [tū-lōn'], Tolón (Francia).
Toulouse [tū-lūz'], Tolosa (Francia).
Trent [trent] o **Trento** [tren'-tō], Trento (Italia).
Troy [trəi], Troya.
Tunis [tū'-nis], Túnez.
Turkey [tʊr'-ki], Turquía.
Tuscany [tʊs'-ca-ni], Toscana (Italia).
Tyre [tair], Tiro (ant. puerto fenicio, actualmente puerto de Líbano).
Tyrrhenian Sea [tir-rī'-ni-an sī], Mar Tirreno.

U

Ukraine [ū'-krên], Ucrania.
Union of South Africa [yūn'-yʊn ov sauth a'-fri-ka], Unión Sudafricana.
Union of Soviet Socialist Republics (abbrv. **U.S.S.R.**), [yūn'-yʊn ov sō'-vi-et sō'-shal-ist rẹ-pʊb'-lics], Unión de Repúblicas Socialistas Soviéticas (abrev. URSS.).
United Kingdom [yu-nait'-ed king'-dʊm], Reino Unido (Gran Bretaña e Irlanda del N.).
United States of America [yu-nait'-ed stêts ov a-mer'-i-ca], Estados Unidos de América.
Ural Mountains [yū'-ral maun'-tẹnz], Montes Urales.

V

Vatican City [vat'-i-can sit'-i], Ciudad del Vaticano.
Venice [ven'-is], Venecia (Italia).
Versailles [ver-sêlz' o ver-sai'], Versalles (Francia).
Vesuvius [ve-siū'-vi-ʊs], Vesubio (monte y volcán de Italia).
Vienna [vi-en'-na], o **Wien** [vīn], Viena (Austria).
Virgin Islands [vẹr'-jin ai'-landz], Islas Vírgenes.

W

Wales [wêlz], Gales.
Warsaw [wōr'-sō], Varsovia (Polonia).
West Indies [west in'-diz], Indias Occidentales.
Windward Islands [wind'-ward ai'-landz], Islas de Barlovento.

Y

Yellow River [yel'-ō riv'-ẹr] o **Hwang Ho** [huang' hō], Río Amarillo o Hoang Ho.
Yellow Sea [yel'-ō sī] o **Hwang Hai** [huang hai'], Mar Amarillo.

Lista Alfabética de los Nombres Propios Más Comunes en la Lengua Inglesa,

INCLUSIVE BÍBLICOS E HISTÓRICOS, QUE SE ESCRIBEN DE MODO DIFERENTE EN ESPAÑOL

Abelard [a'-be-lārd], Abelardo.
Abraham [ê'-bra-ham], Abrahán.
Absalom [ab'-sa-lem], Absalón.
Achilles [a-kil'-īz], Aquiles.
Adalbert, Adelbert [ad'-al-bert, ad'-el-bert], Adalberto, Adelberto.
Adam [ad'-am], Adán.
Adelaide [ad'-e-lêd], Adelaida.
Adeline, Adela [ad'-e-lain, ad'-e-la], Adelina, Adela.
Adolphus [a-del'-fus], Adolfo.
Adrian [ê'-dri-an], Adrián o Adriano.
Æschylus [es'-ki-lus], Esquilo.
Æsop [ī'-sep], Esopo.
Agatha [ag'-a-tha], Águeda.
Agnes [ag'-nes], Inés.
Aileen [ai-līn'], V. HELEN.
Alan, Allen [al'-an, al'-en], Alano.
Alaric [al'-a-ric], Alarico.
Albert [al'-bert], Alberto.
Alexander [al-egz-an'-der], Alejandro.
Alexandra [al-egz-an'-dra], Alejandra.
Alexandrina, Alejandra o Alejandrina.
Alfred [al'-fred], Alfredo.
Alice [al'-is], Alicia.
Alphonso [al-fen'-zō], Alfonso, Alonso o Ildefonso.
Amadeus [am-a-dī'-us], Amadeo.
Ambrose, Ambrosius [am'-brōz], Ambrosio.
Amy [ê'-mi], Amata.
Anacreon [a-nac'-kri-on], Anacreón o Anacreonte.
Andrew [an'-drū], Andrés.
Ann, Anne, Anna [an], Ana.
Anselm [an'-selm], Anselmo.
Anthony, Antony [an'-to-ni], Antonio.
Antigonus [an-tī'-go-nus], Antígono.
Antiochus [an-tai'-ō-kus], Antioco.
Apuleius [a-pū-lī'-yus], Apuleyo.
Archibald [ārch'-i-bald], Archibaldo.
Archimedes [ar-ki-mī'-dīz], Arquímedes.
Aristophanes [ar-is-tē'-fa-nīz], Aristófanes.
Aristotle [ar-is-tē'-tl], Aristóteles.
Arnold [ār'-neld], Arnaldo.
Arthur [ār'-thur], Arturo.
Athanasius [ath-a-nê'-shius], Atanasio.
Attila [a'-ti-la], Atila.
Augustus [ē-gus'-tus], Augusto.
Augustin [ē'-gus-tin o (E. U.) ē-gus'-tin], **Austin** [ēs'-tin], Agustín.
Aurelius [ē-rī'-li-us], Aurelio, Aureliano.

Bacchus [ba'-kus], Baco.
Baldwin [beld'-win], Balduino.
Barnabas, Barnaby [bār'-na-bus, bi], Bernabé.
Bartholomew [bār-thel'-o-miū], Bartolomé.
Basil [bas'-il], Basilio.
Beatrice, Beatrix [bī'-a-tris, trix], Beatriz.
Belisarius [bel-is-a'-ri-us], Belisario.
Benedict [ben'-e-dict], Benedicto o Benito.
Benedicta, Benedicta o Benita.
Bernard [ber'-nārd], Bernardo.
Bertha [ber'-tha], Berta.
Bertram [ber'-tram], Beltrán.
Blaise [blês], Blas.
Bonaventura [bō-na-ven-tū'-ra], Buenaventura o Ventura.
Boniface [ben'-i-fês], Bonifacio.
Bridget [brij'-et], Brígida.

Cæsar [sī'-zer], César.
Camillus [ca-mil'-us], Camilo.
Caroline [car'-o-lain], Carolina.
Casimir [cas'-im-īr], Casimiro.
Caspar, Casper [cas'-par o per], Gaspar.
Cassandra [cas-san'-dra], Casandra.
Catharine [cath'-a-rin], **Catherine** [cath'-er-in], Catalina o Catarina.
Cato [kê'-to], Catón.
Cecil [ses'-il], Cecilio.
Cecile [ses-īl'], Cecilia.
Charles [chārlz], Carlos.
Charlotte [shār'-let], Carlota.
Charon [kê'-ron], Caronte.
Christ [craist], Cristo.
Christian [cris'-chan], Cristián.
Christine [cris-tīn'], Cristina.
Christopher [cris'-to-fer], Cristóbal.
Chrysostom [cris'-es-tem], Crisóstomo.
Cicero [sis'-e-rō], Cicerón.
Claude, Claudius [clēd, clē'-di-us], Claudio.
Clement [clem'-ent], Clemente.
Clotilda [clo-til'-da], Clotilde.
Clovis [clō'-vis], Clodoveo.
Conrad [cen'-rad], Conrado.
Constance [cen'-stens], Constanza.
Constantine [cen'-stan-tain o tin], Constantino.
Constantius [cen-stan'-shius], Constancio.
Cornelius [cēr-nīl'-yus], Cornelio.
Cyprian [sip'-ri-an], Cipriano.
Cyril, Cyrillus [sir'-il, si-ril'-us], Cirilo.
Cyrus [sai'-rus], Ciro.

Dagobert [dā'-go-bert], Dagoberto.
Daisy [dê'-si], Margarita.
Darius [da-rai'-us], Darío.
Dennis [den'-is], Dionisio.
Dominic [dem'-in-ic], Domingo.
Dorothy [der'-o-thi], Dorotea.

Edith [ī'-dith], Edita.
Edmund [ed'-mund], Edmundo.
Edward [ed'-ward], Eduardo.
Eleanor, Elinor [el'-e-a-ner, el'-a-nēr, el'-i-nēr], Leonor.
Elisha, Ellis [e-lai'sha], Eliseo.
Eliza [e-lai'-za], Elisa.
Elizabeth [e'liz'-a-beth], Isabel.
Ellen [el'-en], Elena.
Eloise [el-ō-īz'], Eloísa.
Emanuel, Emmanuel [em-man'-yu-el], Manuel.
Emil, Emile [ê'-mīl, e-mīl'], Emilio.
Emma, Ema o Manuela.
Emily [em'-i-li,] Emilia.
Erasmus [e-ras'-mus], Erasmo.
Ernest [er'-nest], Ernesto.
Esther [es'-ter], Ester.
Euclid [yū'-clid], Euclides.
Eugene [yu-jīn'], Eugenio.
Eugenie [yu-jīn'-i], Eugenia.
Euphemia [yu-fī'-mi-a], Eufemia.
Eusebius [yu-sī'-bi-us], Eusebio.
Eustace [yūs'-tês], Eustacio o Eustaquio.
Evangeline [i-van'-jel-īn], Evangelina.
Eve [īv], Eva.
Ezechias [e-zī'-ki-as], Ezequías. *V.* HEZEKIAH.
Ezekiel [e-zī'-ki-el], Ezequiel.

Felicia [fe-lish'-ia], Felisa.
Ferdinand [fer'-di-nand], Fernando.
Florence [fler'-ens], Florencia.

Frances [fran'-ses], Francisca.
Francis [fran'-sis], Francisco.
Frederica [fred-ẹ-rí'-ca], Federica.
Frederick, **Frederic** [fred'-ẹr-ic], Federico.

Gabrielle [ga-bri-êl'], Gabriela.
Gaius [gê'-yus], Gayo.
Genevieve [gen'-e-vív], Genoveva.
George [jōrj], Jorge.
Geraldine [jer'-al-din], Gerarda.
Gerard [je-rārd'], Gerardo.
Gertrude [gẹr'-trūd], Gertrudis.
Gervas [jer'-vas], Gervasio.
Gideon [gid'-ẹ-ẹn], Gedeón.
Gilbert [gil'-bẹrt], Gilberto.
Giles [jailz], Gil.
Godfrey [gəd'-fri], Godofredo.

Grace [grês], Engracia.
Gregory [greg'-o-ri], Gregorio.
Gustavus [gus-tê'-vus], Gustavo.
Guy [gai], Guido.

Hadrian [hê-dri-an], Adriano.
Hannah [han'-a], Ana.
Hannibal [han'-i-bal], Aníbal.
Harriet, **Henrietta** [har'-i-et], Enriqueta.
Helen [hel'-en], Elena.
Heloise [el-ō-íz'], Eloísa.
Henry [hen'-ri], Enrique.
Herbert [hẹr'-bẹrt], Herberto o Heriberto.
Herman [her'-man], Germán.
Hester [hes'-tẹr], Ester.
Hezekiah [hez-ẹ-kai'-a], Ezequías.
Hiero o **Hieron** [hai'-ẹ-ro o hai'-ẹ-ron], Herón.
Hieronymus [hai-ẹ-ron'-i-mus], Jerónimo. *V.* JEROME.
Hilary [hil'-a-ri], Hilario.
Hildebrand [hil'-de-brand], Hildebrando.
Hobart, **Hubert** [hiū'-bẹrt], Huberto.
Homer [hō'-mẹr], Homero.
Horace, **Horatio** [hor'-ẹs, ho-rê'-shi-ō], Horacio.
Hortense [hor-tens'], Hortensia.
Hosea [ho-zí'-a], Oseas.
Hugh [hiū], Hugo.
Humbert [həm'-bẹrt], Humberto.
Humphrey [hum'-fri], Hunfredo.

Ignatius [ig-nê'-shius], Ignacio.
Inez [ai-nês'], Inés.
Innocent [in'-ō-sent], Inocencio.
Ireneus [ai-rẹ-ní'-us], Ireneo.
Isabelle [iz-a-bel'-a], Isabel.
Isidore [is'-i-dōr], Isidro o Isidoro.

James [jêmz], Santiago, Jacobo, Jaime o Diego.
Jane [jên], Juana.
Jasper [jas'-pẹr], Gaspar.
Jeremiah [jer-ẹ-mai'-a], **Jeremy** [jer'-ẹ-mi], Jeremías.
Jerome [jẹ-rōm'], Jerónimo.
Jesus [jí'-sus], Jesús.
Jesus Christ [jí'-sus craist], Jesucristo.
Joachim [jō'-a-kim], Joaquín.
Joan [jō'-an o jōn], **Joanna** [jo-an'-a], Juana.
John [jon], Juan.
Jonah [jō'-na], Jonás.
Jonathan [jon'-a-than], Jonatán, Jonatás.
Joseph [jō'-zef], José.
Joshua [josh'-yu-a], Josué.
Josiah [jo-sai'-a], Josías.
Judith [jū'-dith], Judit.
Julian [jūl'-yan], Julián.
Juliet [jū'-li-et], Julia o Julieta.
Julius [jū'-li-us], Julio.
Justinian [jus-tin'-ian], Justiniano.

Katharine, **Katherine**, **Kathleen**, *V.* CATHERINE.

Ladislas [lê'-dis-las], Ladislao.
Lætitia, *V.* LETITIA, Leticia.
Lambert [lam'-bẹrt], Lamberto.
Lawrence, **Laurence** [lō'-rens], Lorenzo.
Lazarus [laz'-a-rus], Lázaro.
Leander [lẹ-an'-dẹr], Leandro.
Leo [lí'-ō], León.
Leonard [len'-ard], Leonardo.
Leonora, **Leonore** [li-ō-nor'-a, lí'-ō-nor], Leonor.
Leopold [lí'-o-pōld], Leopoldo.
Letitia, [le-tish'-ia], Leticia.
Lewis, **Louis** [lū'-is, lū'-i], Luis.
Livy [liv'-i], Livio.
Louisa [lu-í'-za], **Louise** [lu-íz'], Luisa.
Lucia [lū'-shi-a], Lucía.
Lucius [lū'-shi-us], Lucio.
Lucretia [lū-crí'-shi-a], Lucrecia.
Lucy [lū'-si], Lucía.
Luke [lūk], Lucas.
Luther [lū'-ther], Lutero.
Lycurgus [lai-cūr'-gus], Licurgo.
Lysander [lai-san'-dẹr], Lisandro.

Magdalen [mag'-da-len], Magdalena.
Mahomet [ma-ho'-met], Mahoma.
Malachi, **Malachy** [mal'-a-cai], Malaquías.
Marcel [mār''-sel'], Marcelo.
Margaret, **Margery** [mār'-ga-ret, mār'-jẹr-i], Margarita.
Maria [ma-rai'-a], María.
Marian, **Marion** [mar'-i-an], Mariana.
Mark [mārk], Marcos.
Martha [mār'-tha], Marta.
Martial [mār'-shal], Marcial.
Mary [mê'-ri], María.
Matilda, **Mathilda** [ma-til'-da], Matilde.,
Matthew [math'-iū], Mateo.
Matthias [mat-thai'-as], Matías.
Maurice, **Morice** [mō'-ris], Mauricio.
Maximilian [mac-si-mil'-i-an], Maximiliano.
Michael [mai'-kel], Miguel.
Miriam, **Marion** [mir'-i-am, mê'-ri-en], María (forma hebrea).
Mohammed [mō-ham'-med], Mahoma.
Moses [mō'-zez], Moisés.

Nathan [nê'-than], Natán.
Nathanael, **Nathaniel** [na-than'-(a)-i-el], Nataniel.
Nebuchadnezzar [nê-bu-kad-nes'-ar], Nabucodonosor.
Nehemiah [ní-hí-mai'-a], Nehemías.
Nero [ní'-ō], Nerón.
Nicholas [nic'-o-las], Nicolás.
Noah [nō'-a], Noé.

Octavius [oc-tê'-vi-us], Octavio.
Oliver [ol'-i-vẹr], Oliverio.
Osmond, **Osmund** [os'-mund], Osmundo.
Otho [ō'-thō], Otón.
Ovid [ov'-id], Ovidio.

Patrick [pat'-ric], Patricio.
Paul [pōl], Pablo.
Paulina, **Pauline** [pō-lai'-na, pō-lí'-na, lín], Paula o Paulina.
Pelaiah [pẹ-lê'-yā], Pelayo.
Peter [pí'-tẹr], Pedro.
Phædrus [fí'-drus], Fedro.
Philemon [fil-í'-mun], Filemón.
Phineas [fin'-ẹ-as], Fineas.
Philip [fil'-ip], Felipe.
Philippa [fi-lip'-a], Felipa.

Pius [pai'-us], Pío.
Plato [plê'-tō], Platón.
Pliny [plin'-i], Plinio.
Plutarch [plū'-tārc], Plutarco.
Pompey [pom'-pi], Pompeyo.
Prudence [prū'-dẹns], Prudencia.
Ptolemy [tol'-e-mi], Tolomeo.
Pyrrhus [pai'-rus], Pirro.

Quentin [cwen'-tin], Quintín.
Quintilian [cwin-til'-i-an], Quintiliano.

Rachael [rê'-chel], Raquel.
Rodolph [rō'-dolf], Rodolfo.
Randall, **Randolph** [ran'-dal, ran'-dolf], Randolfo.
Raphael [rê-fa-el'], Rafael.
Raymond [rê'-mond], Raimundo, Ramón.
Rebecca, **Rebekah** [rẹ-bec'-a], Rebeca.
Reginald [rej'-i-nald], Reinaldo, Reinaldos, Reginaldo.
Regulus [reg'-iū-lus], Régulo.
René [rẹ-nê'], René o Renato.
Reuben [rū'-ben], Rubén.

Reynold [rẹn'-old], Reinaldo. *V.* REGINALD.
Richard [rich'-ard], Ricardo.
Robert [rob'-ẹrt], Roberto.
Roderic, **Roderick** [rod'-er-ic], Rodrigo.
Rodolphus [ro-dol'-fus], **Rollo** [rol'-ō], Rodolfo.
Roger [roj'-ẹr], Rogerio o Roger.
Romulus [rom'-yu-lus], Rómulo.
Ronald [ron'-ald], Ronaldo.
Rosary [rō'-sar-i], Rosario.
Rose [rōz], Rosa.
Roland, **Rowland** [rō'-land], Rolando.
Rupert [rū'-pert], Ruperto.

Sallust [sal'-ust], Salustio.
Scipio [sip'-i-ō], Escipión.
Severus [se-ví'-rus], Severo.
Samson, **Sampson** [sam(p)'-sun], Sansón.
Sigismund [sij'-is-mund], Segismundo.
Silvanus, **Silvan** [sil-vê'-nus, sil'-van], Silvano.
Silvester, **Sylvester** [sil-ves'-tẹr], Silvestre.
Solomon [sol'-o-mẹn], Salomón.
Sophia [so-fai'-a], Sofía.
Stephen [stí'-ven], Esteban.
Strabo [strê-bō], Estrabón.
Susan, **Susanna** [sū'-zan, sū-zan'-a], Susana.

Terence [ter'-ens], Terencio.
Thaddeus [thad-dí'-us o thad'-ẹ-us], Tadeo.
Theobald, **Tybalt** [thí'-o-bald, tib'-alt], Teobaldo.
Theodore [thí'-o-dōr], Teodoro.
Theodoric [thí-od'-o-ric], Teodorico.
Theodosius [thí-o-dō'-shius], Teodosio.
Theophilus [thí-of'-i-lus], Teófilo.
Theresa [tẹ-rí'-sa o tê-rê'-sa], Teresa.
Thomas [tom'-as], Tomás.
Timothy [tim'-o-thi], Timoteo.
Titus [tai'-tus], Tito.
Toby [tō'-bi], Tobías.
Tristram [tris'-tram], Tristán.

Urban [ur'-ban], Urbano.
Uriah [yu-rai'-a], Urías.

Valentine [val'-en-tain], Valentín.
Veremond [ver'-e-mend o vê-rê-mēn'], Bermudo o Veremundo.
Vincent [vin'-sent], Vicente.
Virgil, Vergil, [vẹr'-jil], Virgilio.

Xavier [zav'-i-ẹr], Javier.
Xenophon [zen'-o-fẹn], Jenofonte

Xerxes [zẹrk'-sîz], Jerjes.

Walter [wel'-tẹr], Gualterio.
Wilhelmina, (al.) **Wilhelmine** [wil-hel-mî'-na, vil-hel-mî'-nẹ], Guillermina.

William [wil'-yam], Guillermo.

Yah-weh, Jehova [ja'-wê, je-hō'-va], Jehová.

Zachary [zac'-a-ri], Zacarías.
Zeno [zî'-nō], Zenón.
Zoroaster [zō''-ro-as'-tẹr], Zoroastro.

Lista Alfabética de los Nombres Propios de Personas

QUE SE USAN ABREVIADOS FAMILIARMENTE EN INGLES, CON SUS EQUIVALENTES EN CASTELLANO

De casi todos los equivalentes se pueden formar diminutivos o nombres familiares en castellano añadiéndoles una de estas terminaciones: *ito*, *ico*, *illo*. Dichos equivalentes pierden la letra final si es vocal, y mudan la *o* en *a* para los femeninos; y en los acabados en *co* o *ca* se convierten estas sílabas en *qu;* v. g. Francisco, *Francisquito;* Francisca, *Francisquita:* por esto sólo se insertan los que tienen un nombre irregular además del regular.

Alec [al'-ec] *por* **Alexander**, Alejandro.

Bab *por* **Barbara**, Bárbara, Barbarita.
Bart *por* **Bartholomew**, Bartolomé, Bartolo.
Bec, Becky [bek'-i] *por* **Rebecca**, Rebeca.
Bel, Belle [bel] *por* **Isabella**, Isabel.
Ben *por* **Benjamin**, Benjamín.
Bert, Bertie [bert; bẹr'-ti] *por* **Herbert** *o* **Albert**, Heberto o Alberto.
Bess, Beth, Betsy, Bessy, Betty, Lizzie *por* **Elizabeth**, Belita, Belica.
Biddy *por* **Bridget**, Brígida.
Bob, Rob *por* **Robert**, Roberto.
Bill, Billy *por* **William**, Guillermo.

Carrie *por* **Caroline**, Carolina.
Charley, Charlie *por* **Charles**, Carlos, Carlitos.
Cis *por* **Cecile**, Cecilia.
Clare [clār] *por* **Clara.**

Dan *por* **Daniel**, Daniel.
Davy *por* **David**, David.
Dick, Dicky *por* **Richard**, Ricardo.
Dol, Dolly *por* **Dorothy**, Dorotea.
Dorick [der'-ic] *por* **Theodoric**, Teodoro.
Di [dai] *por* **Diana**, Diana.

Eddy *por* **Edward** *o* **Edwin, Edgar** o **Edmund**, Eduardo, Edmundo.
Effie [ef'-i] *por* **Euphemia**, Eufemia.
Etta [et'-a] *por* **Henrietta**, Enriqueta.

Fan, Fanny *por* **Frances**, Francisca, Frasquita, Paquita, Panchita, Currita, Paca, Farruca.
Fred *por* **Frederick**, Federico.

Hal, Harry *por* **Henry**, Enrique.
Hatty, Hetty, Netty *por* **Henrietta**, Enriqueta.
Hodge [hej] *por* **Roger**, Rogerio.

Jack, Johnny *por* **John**, Juan.
Jeff *por* **Geoffrey** o **Jefferson.**
Jem, Jemmy *por* **James**, Santiago, Jaime, Jacobo.
Jerry *por* **Jeremiah, Jerome**, Jeremías, Jerónimo.
Jennie, Jenny *por* **Jane**, Juana.
Joe, Josy *por* **Joseph**, José, Pepe, Pepito, Pepillo.
Josie [jō'-zi] *por* **Josephine**, Pepa, Pepita, Pepilla.
Kate, Kitty, Kit *por* **Catharine**, Catalina, Catujita.
Kit *por* **Christopher**, Cristóbal, Tobalito.

Larry, Laurie, Lawrie *por* **Lawrence**, Lorenzo.
Len *por* **Leonard**, Leonardo.
Letty *por* **Letitia**, Leticia.
Libby, Lib, Lizzie, Liz *por* **Elizabeth**, Isabel.
Lulu [lū'-lū] *por* **Lucy** *y* **Louisa**, Lucía y Luisa, Luisita.

Madge, Meg *por* **Margery**, Margarita.
Mat *por* **Matthew**, Mateo.
Mat, Matty *por* **Martha**, Marta, *y* **Mathilda**, Matilde.
Maud [mēd] *por* **Mathilda.**
Mike [maik] *por* **Michael**, Miguel.
Mol, Molly *por* **Mary**, María, Mariquita, Maruca, Maruja.

Nan, Nancy *por* **Ann**, Ana.
Ned, Neddy, Teddy *por* **Edward** *o* **Edwin**, Eduardo.
Nel, Nelly *por* **Ellen** *y* **Eleanor**, Elena y Leonor.
Netty *por* **Henrietta**, Enriqueta.
Nick *por* **Nicholas**, Nicolás.

Pam *por* **Pamela**, Pamela.
Patty *por* **Pat, Patricia**, Patricia.
Peg, Peggy *por* **Margaret**, Margarita.
Pen *por* **Penelope**, Penélope.
Phil *por* **Philip**, Felipe.
Prue [prū] *por* **Prudence**, Prudencia.

Reta, Rita [rî'-ta] *por* **Margaret**, Margarita.

Sal, Sally *por* **Sarah**, Sara.
Sam *por* **Samuel**, Samuel.
Sil *por* **Silvester**, Silvestre.
Sim *por* **Simon**, Simón, Simoncito.

Ted, Teddy, Theo *por* **Theodore**, Teodoro.
Tilda *por* **Mathilda**, Matilde.
Tim *por* **Timothy**, Timoteo.
Tom, Tommy *por* **Thomas**, Tomás.
Tony *por* **Anthony**, Antonio, Toño, Antoñito.
Tracy *por* **Theresa**, Teresa.

Val *por* **Valentine**, Valentín.
Vin *por* **Vincent**, Vicente.

Walt *por* **Walter**, Gualterio.
Will *por* **William**, Guillermo.

Zach [zac] *por* **Zachary**, Zacarías.

Lista Alfabética de las Abreviaturas

MÁS USUALES EN INGLÉS

A. Academy, America.
a. accepted, acre, adjective, aged, answer, at.
aa. ana (de cada cosa). *Med.*
A. B. *Artium baccalaureus* (Bachelor of Arts).
abbr. abbreviated, abbreviation.
abt. about (poco más o menos).
A. C. *Ante Christum* (antes de Jesucristo).
A. C., AC, a. c. Alternating current.
acct., a/c. account.
ACTH. Adrenocorticotrophic hormone.
A. D. *Anno domini* (año de Cristo).
ad., adv. advertisement.
ad fin. *ad finem* (al fin).
adj. adjective, adjectival.
ad lib. *ad libitum* (a voluntad).
adv. adverb.
AFL, A. F. of L. American Federation of Labor.
Ala. Alabama.
A. M. *Anno mundi* (año del mundo); *artium magister* (maestro en artes); *ante meridiem* (antes del mediodía).
anon. anonymous.
AP, A. P. Associated Press.
arith. arithmetic.
Ark. Arkansas.
A.-S., AS. Anglo-Saxon.
at. wt. atomic weight.
athl. athletics.
Atty. Attorney.
Av., ave. Avenue.
av., avdp. avoirdupois.
avg. average.
AWOL, A. W. O. L., a. w. o. l. absent without leave (mil.)

b. born (nacido).
B. Bay, British.
B. A. Bachelor of Arts; Buenos Aires.
bal. balance (saldo).
Balt., Balto. Baltimore.
Bart., Bt. Baronet.
bbl. barrel.
B. C. Before Christ; British Columbia.
B. D. Bachelor of Divinity.
bds. boards (pasta).
bet. between.
B/L, b. l. bill of lading.
bldg. building.
bot. botany, botanical.
b. p. bills payable.—**bp.** bishop.
Br. Breton, British.
Bros. brothers.
bu., bus. bushel, bushels.

C. Cæsar, Caius, carbon, centigrade, Congress, conservative.
c. *caput*, cent, centime, centimeter, *centum*.
C. A. Central America.
Cal., Calif., California.
cap. capital (mayúscula); *caput* (capítulo).
Capt. captain.
carp. carpentry.
CC, c. c. carbon copy; cashier's cheque; chief clerk.
C. C. C. Civilian Conservation Corps (organismo oficial de E. U. A.).
C. E. civil engineer.
cf. *confer* (cotéjese); calf binding.
c. f. & i. cost, freight, and insurance.
C. G. Consul-general; Captain-general; Coast Guard.
cg. centigram(me).
ch. chapter; child, children.
chap. chapter.
Chas. Charles.
Ch. E. Chemical Engineer.
Chem. chemical, chemistry.
C. I. F., c. i. f. cost, insurance, and freight.
cir., circ. *circa* (hacia o alrededor).
civ. civil.
cl. cloth (pasta, de libros); centiliter.
c. l. carload.
cm. centimeter.—**cm.**^{2} square centimeter.—**cm.**^{3} cubic centimeter.
cml. commercial.
Co. Company, county, cobalt.
C. O. Commanding officer (mil.)
C. O. D. collect (o cash) on delivery.
Col. Colonel.
Col., Colo. Colorado.
coll., colloq. colloquial, colloquialism.
com., coml. commercial.
comp. comparative, compare; compiled; composer, compound.
con. conclusion, contra.
Cong. Congregational; Congressional; Congress.
conj. conjunction, conjugation.
Conn. (oficial) Connecticut.
constr. construction.
cont. containing; contents; continent; continued.
co-op. cooperative.
Cor. coroner.
cor. corpus, correction, correlative, correspondent; corner.
cp. compare (cotéjese, véase).
c. p. candlepower.
C. P. A., CPA Certified Public Accountant.
Cpl. Corporal.
C. R. Costa Rica.
Cr. credit; creditor.
cres. crescendo.
cs. cases (cajas).
C. S. Christian Science.
C S. T. Central Standard Time.
Ct. Connecticut, Court, Count.
cu., cub. cubic.
cur. currency; current.
c w. o. cash with order.
cwt. hundredweight(s).
C. Z. Canal Zone.

d. daughter, day, dead, denarius (penique), died, dime, dollar.
D. A. District Attorney.
Dan. Daniel; Danish.
D. A. R. Daughters of the American Revolution (organización de E. U. A.).
D. C. *Da capo;* District of Columbia; District Court.
D. D. Doctor of Divinity.
D. D. S. Doctor of Dental Surgery.
Dec. December.
def. definition, defined.
deg. degree.
Del. Delaware.
Dem. Democrat, Democratic.
Den. Denmark.
Dep., Dept. Department; deponent, deputy.
der., deriv. derivation, derived.
dft. defendant; draft.
D. G. *Dei gratia* (por la gracia de Dios).
dial. dialect, dialectical.
diam. diameter.
diff. difference, different, differs.
dig. digest.
dim. diminuendo, diminutive.
disc. discount; discovered.
dist. distance; district; distinguished.
div. divided; dividend; division; divorced.
D. L. O. Dead Letter Office.
DNA. Deoxyribosenucleic acid.
do. ditto (ídem, lo mismo).
dol., doll., $, dollar.
dom. domestic; dominion.
doz. dozen, dozens.
Dr. Debtor; doctor.
d. s. days after sight (giro bancario).
D. S. Doctor of Science.
DSC. Distinguished Service Cross.
D. S. T. Daylight Saving Time.
d. t. delirium tremens.
dup. duplicate.

E. East, eastern, earl, English.
ea. each.
eccl., eccles. ecclesiastic.
econ. economic; economy.
Ed. (Eds. *pl.***)** editor (redactor).
ed., edit. edited, edition.
e. g., ex. gr. *exempli gratia* (por ejemplo).
elec., elect. electrical, electricity.
elev. elevation.

enc., encl. enclosure.
E. N. E. East-northeast.
Eng. England, English.
eng. engin. engineering.
engr. engineer; engraved; engraving.
E. & O. E., e. & o. e. errors and omissions excepted.
Episc. Episcopal.
eq. equal, equivalent.
E. S. E. East-southeast.
esp. (espec.) especially.
Esq., Esqr. (*pl.* con **s**). Esquire.
est. established; estimate.
et al. *et alibi* (y en otra parte); *et alii* (y otros).
etc., &c. et cetera.
ethnol. ethnology.
et seq. *et sequentia* (y lo que sigue).
ex. example; export.
Ex., Exod. Exodus.
exam. examination.
Exc. Excellency.
exc. except; excellent.
Exch. Exchange; exchequer.
excl., exclam. exclamation, exclamatory.
Exec., Exr. Executor.
exec. executive; executor.
Execx., Exrx., Exx. Executrix.
ex lib. *ex libris* (from the books of).
exp. export, exported; express.
ext. extension; externally; extra; extract.

F. Felix, fellow, fluorin(e); France, French, Friday.
F., Fah., Fahr. Fahrenheit.
f. farthing, fathom, feminine, florin, folio, foot, franc, forte (música).
fac. facsimile.
F. A. M. Free and Accepted Masons.
fam. familiar, family.
F. B. I. Federal Bureau of Investigation.
FCC. Federal Communications Commission.
fcp., fcap. foolscap.
Feb. February.
fed. federal, federated, federation.
fem. feminine.
ff. folios, following, fortissimo.
FHA. Federal Housing Administration.
fig. figurative(ly), figure.
fin. financial.
Fin. Sec. Financial Secretary.
fl. florin; flourished.
Fla. Florida.
fl. oz. fluid ounce or ounces.
FM, F. M., f. m. frequency modulation (radio).
fm. fathom; from.
fo., fol. folio.
f. o. b. free on board.
fol., foll. following.
F. P. fire-plug.
Fr. France, Francis, French, Friday.
fr. fragments, franc, from.
fr., freq. frequent, frequentative.
Fri. Friday.
frt. freight.
Ft. Fort.—**ft.** feet, foot.
furn. furnished.
fut. future.
fwd. forward.

G., Ger., Germ. German, Germany.
g. genitive, gram(me), guide.
Ga. (Geo.) Georgia.
gal., gall. (*pl.* **gals.**) gallon.
G. A. R. Grand Army of the Republic.
G. B. Great Britain.
G. B. & I. Great Britain and Ireland.
g. c. m. greatest common measure.
gen. gender, general(ly), genus.
Gen. General, Genesis, Geneva.
gen., genit. genitive.
gent. gentleman.
geog. geographer, geographical, geography.
geol. geological, geologist.
geom. geometry, geometrical.
GHQ, G. H. Q. General Headquarters.
GI, G. I. General issue. (Aplícase al soldado de E. U. A. Véase el Vocab.)
gloss. glossary.
G. M. General Manager.
G. O. P. Grand Old Party (partido político republicano de E. U. A.).
Gov. Government, governor.
Gov. Ptg. Off. Government Printing Office.
Govt. Government.
G. P. O. General Post Office.
Gr. Greece, Greek.
gr. grain, gram(me), great.
grad. graduate, graduated.
gram. grammar, grammatical.
gro. gross.
GS, G. S. General Staff; Girl Scout
Gt. Br., Gt. Brit. Great Britain.
guar. guaranteed.

H. hydrogen.
h. Harbor, hardness, height, hour, hundred, husband.
h. c. l. high cost of living.
hd. head.
hdkf. handkerchief.
hdqrs. headquarters.
H. E. His Eminence, His Excellency; Hydraulic Engineer.
h. e. *hic est, hoc est* (esto es, eso es).
Heb., Hebr. Hebrews, Hebrew.
her. heraldic, heraldry.
hf. half.—**hf. cf.** half calf.
H. H. His (o Her) Highness; His Holiness (el Papa).
hhd. hogshead.
H. I. Hawaiian Islands.
H. I. H. His (o Her) Imperial Highness.
H. I. M. His (o Her) Imperial Majesty.
hist. historian, history, historical.
H. M. His (o Her) Majesty.
Hon. Honorable, honorary.
hort., hortic. horticulture.
hosp. hospital.
h. p. horse power; half pay.
HQ, H. Q., hq, h. q. headquarters.
hr. (*pl.* **hrs.**) hour.
H. R. H. His (o Her) Royal Highness.
H. S. H. His (o Her) Serene Highness.

ICBM. Intercontinental ballistic missile.
IRBM. Intermediate range ballistic missile.

mm. millimeter.—**m.²** square millimeter.—**m.³** cubic millimeter.
Mme. (Mmes. *pl.*) Madam.
Mo. Missouri; molybdenum; Monday.
M. O., m. o. money order.
mo. (*pl.* **mos.**), **mth.** month.
mod. moderato, modern.
Mon. Monday; Monsignor.
Mons. Monsieur.
Monsig. Monsignor.
Mont. Montana.
morn. morning.
M. P. Member of Parliament.
MP, M. P. military police.
M. P., m. p. melting point.
mph., m. p. h. miles per hour.
Mr. Mister, Master (Señor).
Mrs. Mistress (Señora).
MS. (*pl.* **MSS.**) manuscript.
m. s., M/S. months after sight (giro bancario).
m. s. l. mean sea level.
MST, M. S. T. Mountain Standard Time.
Mt. (**Mts.** *pl.*) Mount, mountain.
mus. music; museum.
myth. mythological, mythology.

N. North, Norse; nitrogen, Nero.
n. name, *natus* (nacido, da), neuter, nominative, noon, noun, number.
N. A. North America.
nat. national; native; natural.
NATO. North Atlantic Treaty Organization.
naut. nautical.
nav. naval, navigation.
N. B. New Brunswick, North Britain, North British; *nota bene* (nótese bien).
N. C. North Carolina; New Church.
n. d. no date (sin fecha).
N. Dak. North Dakota.
N. E. northeast, northeastern.
N. E., N. Eng. New England.
Neb., Nebr. (oficial). Nebraska.
Neth. Netherlands.
neut. neuter.
Nev. Nevada.
New Test. New Testament.
N. F. Newfoundland.
N. G. National Guard.
Ng. Norwegian.—**n. g.** no good.
N. H. New Hampshire.
N. J. New Jersey.
N. lat. North latitude.
N. M., N. Mex. New Mexico.
N. N. E. north-northeast.
N. N. W. north-northwest.
No. Number (**nos.** *pl.*); north.
N. O. New Orleans; natural order.
nom., nomin. nominative.
non seq. *non sequitur* (no sigue).
Norw. Norway, Norwegian.
Nos. numbers.
Nov. November.
N. P. Notary Public.
N. S. Nova Scotia; New School (teol.); New Style.
n. s. not specified.
N. S. W. New South Wales.
N. T. New Testament; new translation.
nt. wt. net weight.
n. u. name unknown.
Num., Numb. Numbers (Biblia).
N. W. Northwest.
N. Y. New York.
N. Z., N. Zeal. New Zealand.

O. Ohio; oxygen.
ob. *obit.* (murió), *obiter* (de paso).
obj. object, objection, objective.
obs. observation, observatory, obsolete.
Oct. October.
O. K. All correct (oll korrect, visto bueno).
Okla. Oklahoma.
Old Test., O. T. Old Testament.
Ont. Ontario.
O. P., OP, op, o. p. out of print.
op. opposite; opus (obra).
opt. optative, optical, optician, optics, optional.
Or. Oregon, Oriental.
orch. orchestra.
ord. ordained, order, ordinance.
Ore. (oficial), **Oreg.** Oregon.
org. organic, organized.
orig. original, originally.
oz. (**oz.** u **ozs.** *pl.*). ounce.

p. page, part, participle, past, piano (suave), pint, pipe, pole, population.

P. Phosphorus.
p. a. participial adjective.
Pa. Pennsylvania.
Pal. Palestine.—**pal.** paleontology.
P. and L. profit and loss.
par. paragraph, parallel, parish.
part. participle.
pass. passive.
pat. patent, patented.
path., pathol. pathology.
paym't, pay't. payment.
Pb. *Plumbum* (plomo).
P/C., p/c. petty cash; prices current.
pc. piece; price.
P. D., p. d. *per diem* (por día).
Pen., pen. peninsula.
Penn. Pennsylvania.
per an., per ann. *per annum* (por año).
per ct. per cent.
perf. perfect.
perh. perhaps.
pers. person, personal(ly)
pert. pertaining.
Peruv. Peruvian.
pf. perfect, preferred.
Pfc. Private, First Class. (Ejército de E. U. A.)
pfd. preferred.
Pg. Portugal, Portuguese.
Phar., Pharm. Pharmacy, pharmacopeia, pharmaceutical.
Ph. D. Doctor of Philosophy.
phil. philosophy.
Phil., Phila. (oficial). Philadelphia.
phon. phonetics.
phot., photog. Photographic, photography.
phys. physician, physics.
Phys. Sci. Physical Science.
P. I. Philippine Islands.
pkg. (**pkgs.** *pl.*) package.
pl. place, plate, plural.
plf., plff., pltff. plaintiff.
plup., plupf. pluperfect.
plur. plural, plurality.
p. m. *post meridiem* (tarde); post mortem.
P. M. Postmaster, *post meridiem* (tarde); paymaster.
pmkd. postmarked.
p. n., P/N. promissory note.
P. O. Post Office.
poet. poetic, poetical.
polit. political; politics.
polit. econ. political economy.
P. O. D. Post Office Department.
pop. popular(ly), population.
pos., posit. positive.
pos., poss. possession, possessive.
pot. potential.
pp. pages, pianissimo.
P. P., p. p. parcel post; past participle; postpaid.
ppd. postpaid, prepaid.
pr. pair, price, pronoun, proper, present.
P. R. Puerto Rico.
prec. preceding.
pref. preface, preference, prefix.
prep. preparation; preparatory; prepare; preposition.
Pres. President.
pret. preterit, past tense.
prin. principal(ly), principles.
print. printing.
priv. privative.
prob. probably; problem.
Prof. Professor.
pron. pronoun, pronunciation.
prop. properly, proposition.
Prot. Protestant.
pro tem. *pro tempore* (provisionalmente).
ht. height.
hyd. hydraulics, hydrostatics.

I. Idaho; Island.
i. intransitive; island.
Ia., Io. Iowa.
ib., ibid. *ibidem* (ibídem).
ich., ichth. Ichthyology.
id. *idem* (idem).
Ida. Idaho.
i. e. *id est* (esto es, es decir).
Ill. Illinois.
ill., illus. illustrated, illustration.
imp. imperial, imported, importer.
imp., imper. imperative.
imp., imperf., impf. imperfect (tense).
imp., impers. impersonal.
in. (*pl.* **ins.**) inch.
inc. inclosing; including; inclusive; income; incorporated; increase.
incog. incognito.
Ind. India, Indian, Indiana.
ind., indic. indicative.
indef. indefinite.
inf. infinitive; information.
init. initial.
in loc. cit. In the place cited.
insep. inseparable.
insp. inspector; inspected.
inst. instant, institute.
int. interest, interjection, international.
interj. interjection.
internat. international.
intr., intrans. intransitive.
inv. invented, inventor, invoice.
I. O. U. I owe you.
IQ, I. Q. intelligence quotient.
i. q. *idem quod* (lo mismo que).
irreg. irregular.
Is., Isl. Island, islands, isles.
It., Ital. Italian, Italic, Italy.

J. Judge, Julius, Jupiter.
Jan. January.
Jap. Japan, Japanese.
Jas. James.
J. C. Jesus Christ; Julius Cæsar; Justice Clerk.
Jno. John.
Jon., Jona. Jonathan.
Jos. Joseph.
Josh. Joshua.
J. P. Justice of the Peace.
jr., jun., junr. junior.
Judg. Judges.
Jul. Julian, Julius, July.
Jun. June, Junius.
Junc. Junction (empalme, f. c.).
juv. juvenile.

K. *Kalium*, potassium; King, Knight.
Kan., Kans., Kas. (oficial) Kansas.
K. C. Knight of Columbus.
Ken., Ky. (oficial) Kentucky.
K. G. Knight of the Garter.
kg. kilogram.
kilo., kilog. kilogram (me).
kilo., kilom., km. kilometer.
km. kilometer —**km.**^{2} square kilometer.
Knt., Kt. Knight.
kt. carat.
K. W. H., kw-h, kw-hr kilowatt-hour.
Ky. Kentucky.

L. Lucius, lady, lake, Latin, Liberal, *libra*, lithium, London, Lord.
l. latitude, league, length, line, liter o litre.
La. Lanthanum, Louisiana.
Lat. Latin —**lat.** latitude.
lb. (**lbs.** *pl.*) *libra*, pound.
l. c. lower case, left center, letter of credit.
L. C. L., l. c. l. less than carload lot.
l. c. m. least common multiple.
Leg., Legis. Legislature, legislative.
leg. legal; legislature.
Lev., Levit. Leviticus.
Lex. Lexicon.
L. G. Life Guards, Low German.
l. h. left hand.
Li. Lithium.
lib. *liber* (libro).
Lieut., Lt. Lieutenant.
lin. lineal, linear.
Linn. Linnæus, Linnean.
liq. liquid, liquor.
lith., lithog. lithograph, lithography.
log. logarithm.
lon., long. longitude.
loq. *loquitur* (habla).
L. S. *locus sigilli* (lugar del sello). —**l. s.** left side.
L. (o £) **s. d.** *Libræ, solidi, denarii*, Pounds, shillings, pence.
Lt. Lieutenant.
Ltd., ltd. limited.

M. Monday; Monsieur; thousand.
m. Married, masculine, meridiem (mediodía), meter, mile, minim, month, moon.—**m.**^{2} square meter.—**m.**^{3} cubic meter.
M. A. *Magister artium*, Master of Arts.
mach., machin. machinery, machinist.
mag. magazine; magnitude; magnetism.
Maj. Major.
man. manual (teclado).
Manit. Manitoba.
manuf. manufactured, manufacturer.
Mar., Mch. March.—**mar.** maritime.
marg. margin; marginal.
mas., masc. masculine.
Mass. Massachusetts.
math. mathematics.
Matt. Matthew.
max. maximum.
M. C. Master of Ceremonies; Medical Corps; Member of Congress (de E. U. A.)
mc, m. c. megacycle.
M. D. *Medicinæ doctor*, Doctor of Medicine.
Md. Maryland.
Mdlle. Mademoiselle.
mdse. merchandise.
M. E. Methodist Episcopal, Mining Engineer, Mechanical Engineer, Middle English.
Me. Maine.
meas. measure.
mech. mechanic, mechanical.
med. medical, medicine; medieval.
Medit. Mediterranean.
meg. megacycle.
Mem. memorandum.
mem. member; memorandum; memoir.
mer. meridian.
Messrs., MM. Messieurs.
met. metaphor; metaphysics; metropolitan.
metal., metall. metallurgy.
Meth. Methodist.
Mex. Mexican, Mexico.
mf. mezzo forte (algo fuerte).
mfd. manufactured.
mfg. manufacturing.
Mg. Magnesium.—**mg.** milligram.
Mgr. Manager; Monsignor.
mi. mile; mill.
Mich. Michigan, Michaelmas.
micros. microscopy.
mid. middle; midshipman.
mil., milit. military.
min., mineral. mineralogy.
min. minimum; mining; minor;

minute; mineralogy.
Minn. Minnesota.
misc. miscellaneous, miscellany.
Miss. Mississippi; mission, missionary.
ml. milliliter, millilitre.
Prov. Proverbs; Provençal, Provence, province, provincial.
prox. proximo (el mes que viene).
Prs. printers.—**prs.** pairs.
P. S. Postscript.
ps. pieces.
PST, P. S. T. Pacific Standard Time.
pt. part, payment, pint.
Pt. platinum, point, port.
P. T. A., PTA Parent-Teacher Association.
pta. peseta.
P. T. O. Please turn over.
pub. public, published, publisher.
Pub. Doc. Public Documents.
Pvt. Private (soldado raso de E. U. A.).
PW Prisoner of War.
pwt. pennyweight.
pxt. *pinxit* (lo pintó).

Q. Quebec, Queen, Quintus.
q. quasi, query, quintal.
Q., qu., ques. question.
q. e. *quod est* (lo cual es).
q. e. d. *quod erat demonstrandum* (lo que se trataba de demostrar).
q. e. f. *quod erat faciendum* (lo que se trataba de hacer).
q. l. *quantum libet* (tanto como se desee).—**ql.** quintal.
q. s. *quantum sufficit* (lo que baste); quarter-section.
qt. quantity, quart.—**qts.** quarts.
qu., qy. query.
Que. Quebec.
quot. quotation.
q. v. *quantum vis* (cuanto se quiera); *quod vide* (véase).

R. radical, railway, recipe, river; Republican.
r. rod, rood, rupee.
Rad. radical.—**rad.** radix (raíz).
R. A. F., RAF Royal Air Force (Inglaterra).
R. C. Roman Catholic, Red Cross.
rept., rec't., rect. receipt.
Rd. radium.
R. D. Rural Delivery.
rec'd., recd. received.
Rec. Sec. Recording Secretary.
ref. reference, referred, reformed, reformer.
reg. registry, regular.
Reg., Regt. Regent, regiment.
rel. relative(ly), religion, religious, relics.
rel. pron. relative pronoun.
rem. remark.
Rep. report, reporter, Representative.
Rep., Repub. Republic, Republican.
res. reserve; residence; resigned.
Rev. Revelation; revenue, Reverend (**Revs.** *pl.*), review.
Rev. Ver. Revised Version (de la Biblia).
R. F., r. f. radio frequency; rapid fire.
r. h. relative humidity.
Rh. Rhodium.—**r. h.** right hand.
R. H. Royal Highness.
rhet. rhetoric, rhetorical.
R. I. Rhode Island.
R. I. P. *requiescat in pace* (descanse en paz).
rit., ritard. *ritardando* (el compás).
riv. river.
R. N. Registered Nurse; Royal Navy.
Robt. Robert.
Rom. Cath. Roman Catholic.
rpm, r. p. m. revolutions per minute.
R. R. Railroad.
R. S. Recording Secretary; Revised Statutes.—**r. s.** right side.
R. S. V. P. *Répondez, s'il vous plaît.* (Sírvase Vd. contestar.)
Rt. Hon. Right Honorable.
Rt. Rev. Right Reverend.
R. W., Rw., Ry. Railway.

S. Saxon, Servius, Sextus; scribe, sign, society, south, sulphur, Sunday.
s. second, section (**ss.** *pl.*), series, shilling, singular, substantive.
S. A. Salvation Army; South America; South Africa.
S., Sab. Sabbath.
Sa., Sat. Saturday.
s. a. *secundum artem* (según arte); *sine anno* (sin fecha).
S. Am. South America.
San., Sans., Skr., Skt. Sanskrit.
Sax. Saxon, Saxony.
S. C. South Carolina; Supreme Court.
s. c., s. caps., sm. caps. small capitals (versalitas).
sc. scene; *scilicet* (a saber).
Scot. Scotch, Scotland; Scottish.
sculp., sculpt. *sculpsit* (lo esculpió); sculptor, sculptural, sculpture.
s. d. *sine die.*
S. Dak. South Dakota.
S. E. southeast, southeastern.
Sec. Secretary.—**sec.** second.
Sen. Senate, senator.
sep. separate.
Sep., Sept. September.
Serg., Sergt. Sergeant.
s. g. specific gravity.
sh. shilling.
So. South.
Soc. Society, Socrates.
sop. soprano.
Sp. Spain, Spanish; Spirit.
spec. special, specially.
sp. gr. specific gravity.
spt. seaport.
S. R. O. standing room only.
sq. square; *sequentes -tia* (siguiente(s)).
Sr. Senior, sir, strontium.
S. S. Sunday School, Sabbath School; Steamship.
s. s. steamship.
S. S. E. south-southeast.
S. S. W. south-southwest.
s. t. short ton.
St. Saint; strait, street.
st. stanza, stet, strophe.
ster., stg. sterling.
stge. storage.
stk. stock.
sts. streets.
sub. subject, substitute, suburb, suburban.
subj. subject, subjective, subjunctive.
suf., suff. suffix.
Sun., Sund. Sunday.
sup., super. superior, superfine.
Sup., Supp. Supplement.
Supt. Superintendent.
Surg., surg. Surgeon, surgery, surgical.
Surv. Surveying, surveyor.
S. W. southwest, southwestern.
Sw. Sweden, Swedish.
Swit., Switz. Switzerland.
syn. synonym, synonymous.
synop. synopsis.

T. Territory, Testament, Tuesday.
t. tenor, ton, town, transitive.
T. B., Tb, t. b. tuberculosis, tubercular.
tbs., tbsp. tablespoon.
tech. technical, technically.
tech., technol. technology.
tel., teleg. telegram, telegraph.
temp. temperature; temporary.
Tenn. Tennessee.
Ter., Terr. Territory.
Test. Testament (Biblia).
Tex. Texan, Texas.
Th., Thu., Thur., Thurs. Thursday.
theat. theatrical.
theol. theologian, theological, theology.
Tho., Thos. Thomas.
T. O. Turn over.
topog. topographical, topography.
tr. transpose, trill.
tr., trans. transitive, translation, translated, transaction, transportation.
transp. transportation.
trav. traveler, travels.
treas. treasurer, treasury.
trig., trigon. trigonometry
tsp. teaspoon.
TV television.
typ., typo., typog. typographer, typographic(al), typography.

U. Uranium.
u. c. upper case, (letra mayúscula).
U. H. F., u. h. f. ultra high frequency.
U. K. United Kingdom.
ult., ulto. ultimo (el mes pasado).
UN, U. N. United Nations.
UNESCO United Nations Educational, Scientific, Cultural Organization.
Univ. Universalist, university.
UNRRA United Nations Relief and Rehabilitation Administration.
U. P. United Press.
U. S. United States.
U. S. A. United States of America, United States Army.
U. S. M. United States Mail, United States Marines.
U. S. N. United States Navy.
U. S. S. United States Senate, United States Steamer.
U. S. S. R., USSR Union of Soviet Socialist Republics.
usu. usual, usually.

V. Vanadium, vector, venerable, vice, Victoria, violin, volunteers.
v. verse, versus (contra), village, vocative, volume.
v., vb. verb.
v., vid. *Vide* (Véase).
v. a. verb active, verbal adjective.
Va. Virginia.
val. value.
var. variant, variety.
Vat. Vatican.
Ven. Venerable.
Venez. Venezuela.
vet., veter. veterinary.
Vet. Surg. Veterinary surgeon.
v. i. verb intransitive.
Vice Pres. Vice-President.
v. imp. verb impersonal.
VIP, V. I. P. very important person (coll.).
v. irr. verb irregular.
viz. *videlicet* (a saber).
v. n. verb neuter.
voc. vocative.
vocab. vocabulary.
vol. volume (*pl.* **vols.**); volunteer.
vox pop. vox populi, voice of the people.
V. P. Vice-President.
V. S. Veterinary surgeon.
vs. *versus* (contra).
v. t. verb transitive.

vul., **vulg**. vulgar, vulgarly.
Vul., **Vulg**. Vulgate (Biblia).

w. week, wife.
W. Warden, Welsh, West, western, William, wolfram, Wednesday.
W., **w**. watt.
W. A. A. C. Women's Army Auxiliary Corps. (E. U. A.)
WAC Women's Army Corps (E. U. A.).
WAVES Women Accepted for Volunteer Emergency Service (Marina de E. U. A.)
We., **Wed**. Wednesday.
Wash. Washington (el estado).
w. c. water closet.
W. C. water closet; without charge.
WD, **W. D.** War Department (E. U. A.).
w. f., **wf**. wrong font (imprenta).
wh., **whr**. watt-hour.
Whf. wharf.
W. I. West Indies.
w. i. when issued (stocks).
Wis. (oficial), **Wisc**. Wisconsin.
Wk. week.
W. lon. West longitude.
Wm. William.
W. N. W. west-northwest.
Wp. Worship.
Wpful. Worshipful.
WRENS, **W. R. N. S.** Women's Royal Naval Service (Gran Bretaña).
W. S. W. west-southwest.
wt. weight.
W. Va. West Virginia.
Wyo. Wyoming.

Xmas. Christmas.

y. yard, year.
Y. B., **Yr. B.** Yearbook.
yd. (*pl.* **yds.**) Yard (medida).
Y. M. C. A. Young Men's Christian Association.
yr. (*pl.* **yrs.**) year, younger, your.
Y. W. C. A. Young Women's Christian Association.

Z. atomic number; zenith distance (astron.)
Z., **z**. zone.
Zn. Zinc.
Zool. Zoology, zoological.

Pesas y Medidas

(Weights and Measures)

PESAS
(Weights)

Ounce (avoirdupois)	28.35 grams.	Ton	2204.6 lbs.
Pound "	0.4536 kgs.	Kilogram	2.2046 lbs.
Long ton	1.0161 met. tons.	Gram	15.432 grains.
Short ton	0.9072 " "	Centigram	0.1543 "
Grain	0.0648 grams.		

LINEALES
(Linear)

Medidas de E.U.A. (U. S. Measures)		**Medidas Métricas** (Metric Measures)	
Mile	1.6093 kms.	Kilometer	0.62137 miles.
Naut. mile	1.853 "	Meter	39.37 inches.
Yard	0.9144 ms.	Decimeter	3.937 "
Foot	0.3048 ms.	Centimeter	0.3937 "
Inch	2.54 cms.	Millimeter	0.03937 "

SUPERFICIE
(Surface)

Acre	0.4453 hectares.	Sq. kilometer	247.104 acres.
Square mile	259 hectares.	Hectare	2.471 "
Square yard	0.8361 sq. meters.	Square meter	1550 sq. inches.
Square foot	929.03 sq. cms.	Square decimeter	15.50 " "
Square inch	6.4516 " "	Square centimeter	0.155 " "

VOLUMEN
(Cubic)

Cubic inch	16.387 cu. cm.	Cubic meter	1.308 cu. yards.
Cubic foot	0.0283 " ms.	Cubic decimeter	61.023 cu. inches.
Cubic yard	0.7646 " "	Cubic centimeter	0.0610 " "

CAPACIDAD
(Capacity)

Liquid quart	0.9463 liters.	Hectoliter	2.838 bushels
Dry quart	1.101 "		or 26.418 gallons.
Gallon	3.785 "	Liter	0.9081 dry qt.
Bushel	35.24 "		or 1.0567 liq. qts.

Monedas de América y de la Península Ibérica

(Monetary Units of America and the Iberian Peninsula)

Country	Monetary Unit
ARGENTINA	— Peso
BOLIVIA	— Boliviano
BRAZIL	— Cruzeiro
CANADA	— Dollar
CHILE	— Escudo
COLOMBIA	— Peso
COSTA RICA	— Colón
CUBA	— Peso
DOMINICAN REPUBLIC	— Peso
ECUADOR	— Sucre
EL SALVADOR	— Colón
GUATEMALA	— Quetzal
HAITI	— Gourde
HONDURAS	— Lempira
MEXICO	— Peso
NICARAGUA	— Córdoba
PANAMA	— Balboa
PARAGUAY	— Guaraní
PERU	— Sol
PORTUGAL	— Escudo
SPAIN	— Peseta
UNITED STATES OF AMERICA	— Dollar
URUGUAY	— Peso
VENEZUELA	— Bolívar

Spelling Reforms

OF THE ROYAL SPANISH ACADEMY

New definitive text in force as of 1 January, 1959

1. When *The Royal Academy Dictionary* authorizes two ways of accenting a given word, both forms will be given in the same entry, separated by the conjunction **o: quiromancia** o **quiromancía.**

2. The more common form will be entered first, but the alternate will be considered equally correct.

3. As concerns the alternate forms included for the first time in the 1956 edition of *The Royal Academy Dictionary*, the order of preference is reversed, to read as given, for the following entries:

pentagrama/pentágrama **reuma/reúma**

4. Dropping the initial consonant of words beginning with **ps-**, **mn-**, and **gn-** is now authorized: **sicología, nemotecnia, nomo.** Such traditional forms as **psicología, mnemotecnia,** and **gnomo** will be retained in the *Dictionary* and will continue to be the forms under which definitions will be provided.

5. The use of contracted forms such as **remplazo, remplazar,** and **rembolso, rembolsar** is now authorized. These forms are now entered in the *Dictionary* with a cross reference to the forms with double **e.**

6. A word used as the first element of a solid compound will be written without the accent mark it may have required as a separate word: **decimoséptimo, asimismo, rioplatense, piamadre.**

7. Adverbs ending in **-mente** are excepted from the foregoing rule, since they actually have two stresses: one on the adjective and the other on the noun **mente.** Pronouncing and spelling such adverbs as if they had one accent is incorrect. They will be pronounced and written with the same stress on the adjective as the latter would require as a separate word: **ágilmente, cortésmente, lícitamente.**

8. Compound nouns formed of verb, enclitic, and complement (such as **sabelotodo**) will be written without the accent mark that was formerly placed on the verb.

9. In hyphenated compounds formed of two or more adjectives, each element will retain its individual stress and written accent (if any): **hispano-belga, anglo-soviético, cántabro-astur, histórico-crítico- bibliográfico.**

10. Infinitives ending in **-uir** will continue to be written without an accent.

11. The verb **inmiscuir** may be conjugated either as a regular **-ir** verb or as all other verbs ending in **-uir** by the addition of **y** to the affected conjugated forms: **inmiscuyo.**

12. Any combination of an accented strong vowel and an unaccented weak vowel always constitutes a diphthong, and any required written accent on such a diphthong will be placed on the strong vowel. Any combination of an unaccented strong vowel and an accented weak vowel *does not* constitute a diphthong, and the respective weak vowel must always bear a written accent.

13. For writing purposes, the vowel cluster **ui** will always constitute a diphthong. Whenever the rules of accentuation require that this diphthong bear a written accent, it will be placed on the second of the weak vowels, that is on the **i: casuístico, benjuí.** It then follows that **ui** occurring in the penult will never bear a written accent: **casuista.**

14. Oxytones ending in **-ay, -ey, -oy** and **-uy** will never bear a written accent: **taray, virrey, convoy, maguey, Uruguay.**

15. The monosyllables **fue, fui, dio,** and **vio** will no longer bear a written accent.

16. The pronouns **éste, ése,** and **aquél,** as well as their respective feminine and plural forms, may be written without an accent whenever there is no risk of ambiguity.

17. The particle **aun** will bear a written accent (**aún**) and will be pronounced as a dissyllable when it can be replaced by **todavía** without changing the meaning of the sentence: **aún está enfermo; está enfermo aún.** In all other cases, that is when **aun** has the meaning of **hasta, también, inclusive** (or **siquiera** in negative sentences), it will be written without the accent: **aun los sordos han de oírme; no hizo nada por él ni aun lo intentó.**

18. When used as an adverb, the word **solo** may bear a written accent only in order to avoid confusion or ambiguity.

19. The accent will be dropped on **Feijoo, Campoo,** and all other oxytones ending in **-oo.**

20. As a general rule, foreign proper names should be written just as they appear in the original language, without any additional accent to make them conform to

Spanish. However, such foreign words may be accented as in Spanish when their original spelling and pronunciation permit. Geographical names that have already been incorporated into Spanish and adapted to its phonetic system should not be considered foreign words and should bear the written accent required by the rules of Spanish pronunciation.

21. The dieresis may only be used to show that the **u** in the combinations **gue** and **gui** should be pronounced. The dieresis may also be used when a special pronunciation is required for a special poetic effect.

22. Compounds of nationality should be written solid when there has been geographic and (or) political fusion: **hispanoamericano, checoslovaco.** When there has been no fusion, but rather opposition or contrast, the elements of the compound should be joined by a hyphen: **franco-prusiano, germano-soviético.**

23. Newly-formed compounds made up of two adjectives should be written with a hyphen and with only the second element inflected (that is, in agreement with the respective noun in gender and number): **tratado teórico-práctico, lección teórico-práctica, cuerpos técnico-administrativos.**

24. It will no longer be necessary to divide solid compounds so as to preserve their components intact. Such compounds may also be divided according to the general rules of syllabification: **no·sotros** or **nos·otros, de·samparo** or **des·amparo.** Words that contain a medial group consisting of a consonant plus **h** must be divided so as to begin the new line with the **h**: **al·haraca, in·humación, clor·hidrato, des·hidratar.**

25. Intervocalic **h** will no longer prevent vowels from diphthongizing: **de·sahu·cio, sahu·me·rio.** In order to avoid a diphthong with a preceding or following strong vowel, a written accent must be placed on the weak vowel when stressed: **vahído, búho, rehúso.**

The following are excerpts from the 1952 version of the spelling reforms of The Royal Spanish Academy. They were observed in the 1956 edition of *The Royal Academy Dictionary:*

16. Infinitives ending in **-aír, -eír,** and **-oír** will no longer bear a written accent. They will be written thus: **embair, sonreir, desoir.** The rules of pronunciation governing combinations of strong and weak vowels will be modified to exclude stressed **i** in infinitive endings.

18. Some verbs ending in **-iar** are radical-changing in that the **i** of the stem bears a written accent in the entire singular and the third person plural of the present indicative and the present subjunctive, as well as in the familiar command (as

envío, envías, envía, envían, envíe, envíes, envíe, envíen, envía from **enviar**). The following list shows those verbs in **-iar** that follow the aforesaid pattern of hiatus:

> **adiar, aliar, ampliar, arriar, ataviar, averiar, aviar, calofriar(se), cariar, contrariar, criar, cuantiar, chirriar, demasiar(se), desataviar, desaviar, descarriar, descriar(se), desliar, desvariar, desviar, enfriar, enlejiar, enriar, entrecriar, enviar, escalofriar(se), espiar, espurriar, estriar, expiar, extraviar, fiar** (and all its compounds), all verbs ending in **-grafiar, guiar, hastiar, istriar, liar, miar, piar, recriar, resfriar, rociar, triar, variar, vigiar.**

All verbs in **-iar** not in the preceding list are conjugated with a diphthong (**limpio, limpias, limpia,** etc.) with the exception of the following, which may be written either with a diphthong or hiatus:

> **afiliar, agriar, ansiar, auxiliar, conciliar, espaciar, expatriar, extasiarse, filiar, gloriar, historiar, inventariar, obviar, paliar, reconciliar, repatriar, vaciar, vanagloriarse, vidriar.**

19. The following rule is established for verbs ending in **-uar**: When the **u** is preceded by **c** or **g**, it will form a diphthong with the following vowel: **evacuar/eva·cuo, averiguar/averi·guo.** Otherwise hiatus and a written accent on the **u** will be the rule: **actuar/actúo, evaluar/evalúo.**

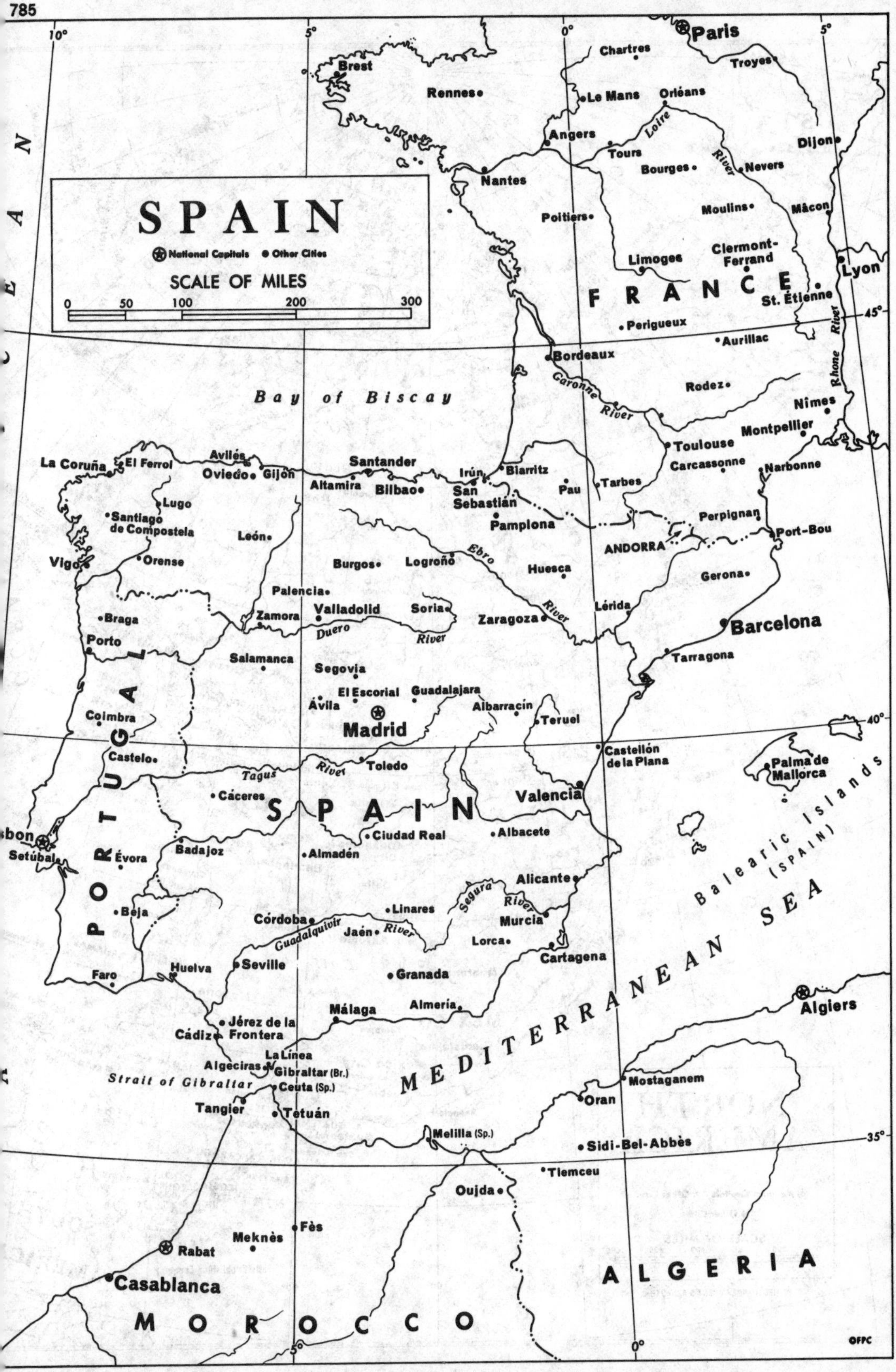

SPAIN

National Capitals · Other Cities

SCALE OF MILES

0 50 100 200 300

10° 5° 0° 5°

45° 40° 35°

Paris
Chartres
Brest
Troyes
Rennes
Le Mans
Orléans
Angers
Loire River
Dijon
Tours
Nantes
Bourges
Nevers
Moulins
Mâcon
Poitiers
Clermont-Ferrand
Limoges
Lyon
FRANCE
St. Étienne
Perigueux
Aurillac
Bordeaux
Rhone River
Garonne River
Rodez
Bay of Biscay
Nîmes
Montpellier
Toulouse
Carcassonne
Narbonne
Avilés
La Coruña
El Ferrol
Oviedo
Gijón
Santander
Irún
Biarritz
Altamira
Bilbao
San Sebastián
Pau
Tarbes
Lugo
Santiago de Compostela
Pamplona
Perpignan
León
Port-Bou
ANDORRA
Vigo
Orense
Burgos
Logroño
Ebro River
Huesca
Gerona
Palencia
Braga
Zamora
Valladolid
Soria
Zaragoza
Lérida
Duero River
Barcelona
Porto
Salamanca
Tarragona
Segovia
El Escorial
Guadalajara
Ávila
Albarracín
Teruel
Coimbra
Madrid
Castellón de la Plana
Castelo
Toledo
Palma de Mallorca
Tagus River
Cáceres
Valencia
PORTUGAL
SPAIN
Lisbon
Ciudad Real
Albacete
Setúbal
Évora
Badajoz
Almadén
Balearic Islands (SPAIN)
Alicante
Segura River
Beja
Linares
Córdoba
Murcia
Jaén
Guadalquivir River
Lorca
Seville
Cartagena
Faro
Huelva
Granada
MEDITERRANEAN SEA
Almería
Algiers
Málaga
Jérez de la Frontera
Cádiz
La Línea
Algeciras
Gibraltar (Br.)
Strait of Gibraltar
Ceuta (Sp.)
Mostaganem
Oran
Tangier
Tetuán
Melilla (Sp.)
Sidi-Bel-Abbès
Tlemceu
Oujda
Fès
Meknès
Rabat
ALGERIA
Casablanca
MOROCCO
OCEAN
OFPC

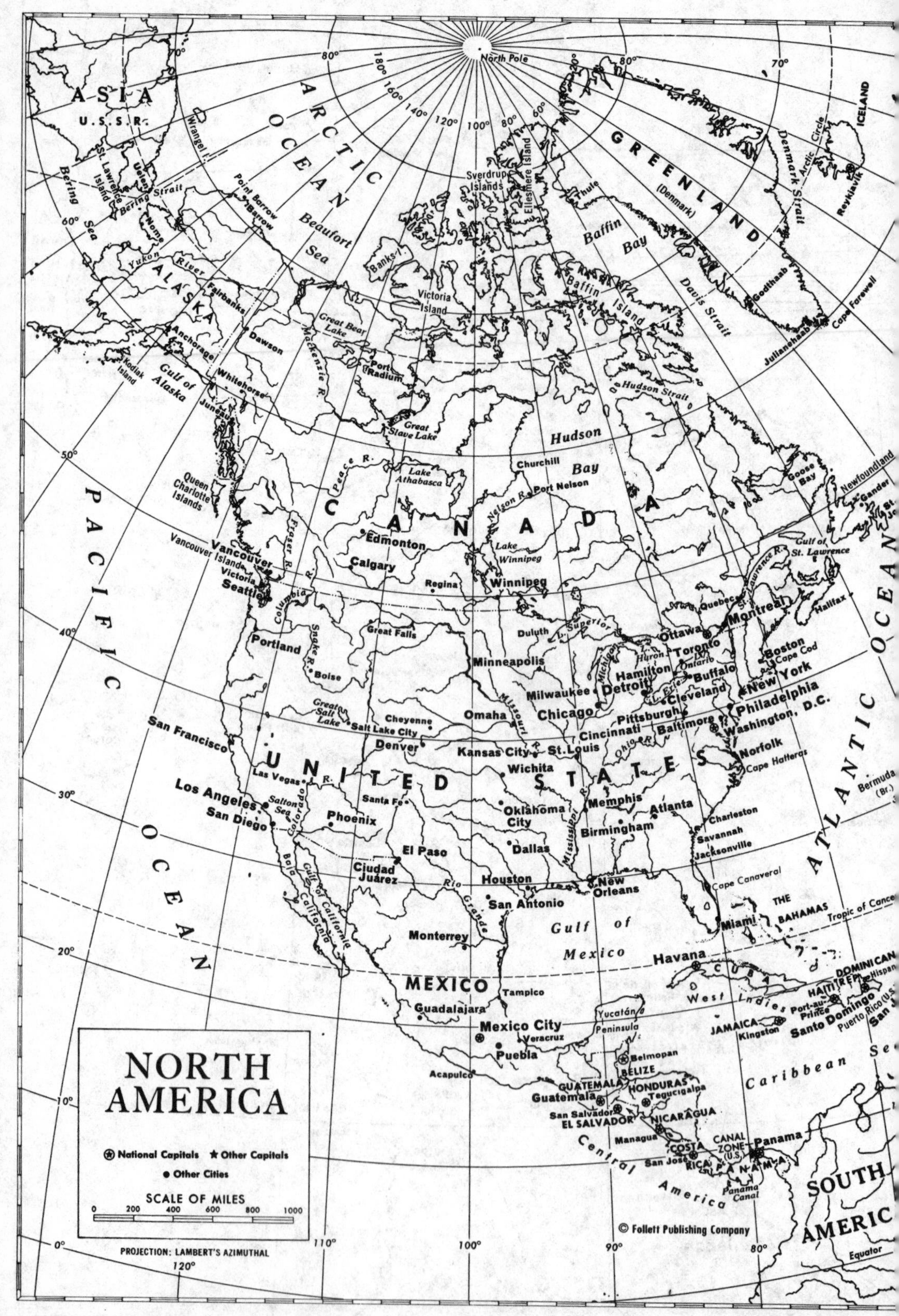
NORTH AMERICA
National Capitals
Other Capitals
Other Cities
SCALE OF MILES
0 200 400 600 800 1000
PROJECTION: LAMBERT'S AZIMUTHAL
© Follett Publishing Company
ARCTIC OCEAN
PACIFIC OCEAN
ATLANTIC OCEAN
CANADA
UNITED STATES
MEXICO
GREENLAND
(Denmark)
ALASKA
ASIA
U.S.S.R.
ICELAND
SOUTH AMERICA
Hudson Bay
Baffin Bay
Gulf of Mexico
Caribbean Sea
Central America
West Indies
Beaufort Sea
Bering Sea
Gulf of Alaska
North Pole
Tropic of Cancer
Arctic Circle
Equator

SOUTH AMERICA
ATLANTIC OCEAN
PACIFIC OCEAN
Caribbean Sea
Central America
Panama Canal
Lesser Antilles
Aruba (Neth.)
Curaçao (Neth.)
Bonaire (Neth.)
Port of Spain
TRINIDAD AND TOBAGO
Barranquilla
Cartagena
Maracaibo
L. Maracaibo
Barquisimeto
Valencia
La Guaira
Caracas
Ciudad Bolívar
VENEZUELA
Bucaramanga
Magdalena R.
Orinoco R.
Medellín
Manizales
Pereira
Bogotá
Cali
COLOMBIA
Pasto
Georgetown
GUYANA
Paramaribo
SURINAM
Cayenne
FR. GUIANA
Quito
ECUADOR
Guayaquil
Equator
Rio Negro
Amazon River
Manaus
Santarém
Belém
São Luís
Fortaleza
Teresina
Natal
João Pessoa
Recife
Maceió
Iquitos
Ucayali R.
Marañón R.
Madeira R.
Tapajós R.
Tocantins R.
Trujillo
PERU
BRAZIL
Cerro de Pasco
Lima
Callao
Machu Picchu (Ruins)
Cuzco
Puno
L. Titicaca
La Paz
BOLIVIA
Cochabamba
Oruro
L. Poopó
Sucre
Potosí
Arequipa
Arica
Iquique
Cuiabá
Brasília
São Francisco R.
Salvador
Belo Horizonte
Paraguay R.
PARAGUAY
Pilcomayo R.
Concepción
Asunción
Tropic of Capricorn
Antofagasta
Volta Redonda
Campinas
São Paulo
Niterói
Rio de Janeiro
Santos
Curitiba
Tucumán
Salado R.
Paraná R.
Uruguay R.
Pôrto Alegre
La Serena
Córdoba
Santa Fe
Paraná
San Juan
Mendoza
Viña del Mar
Valparaíso
Santiago
Rosario
URUGUAY
Rio Grande
Montevideo
Buenos Aires
Río de la Plata
La Plata
CHILE
ARGENTINA
Concepción
Mar del Plata
Colorado R.
Negro R.
Bahía Blanca
Puerto Montt
Falkland Islands (Br.)
Strait of Magellan
Tierra del Fuego
Punta Arenas
Cape Horn
South Georgia (Br.)
National Capitals
Other Capitals
Other Cities
SCALE OF MILES
0 200 400 600 800 1000
PROJECTION: SINUSOIDAL
10° 0° 10° 20° 30° 40° 50°
100° 90° 80° 70° 60° 50° 40° 30° 20° 10°

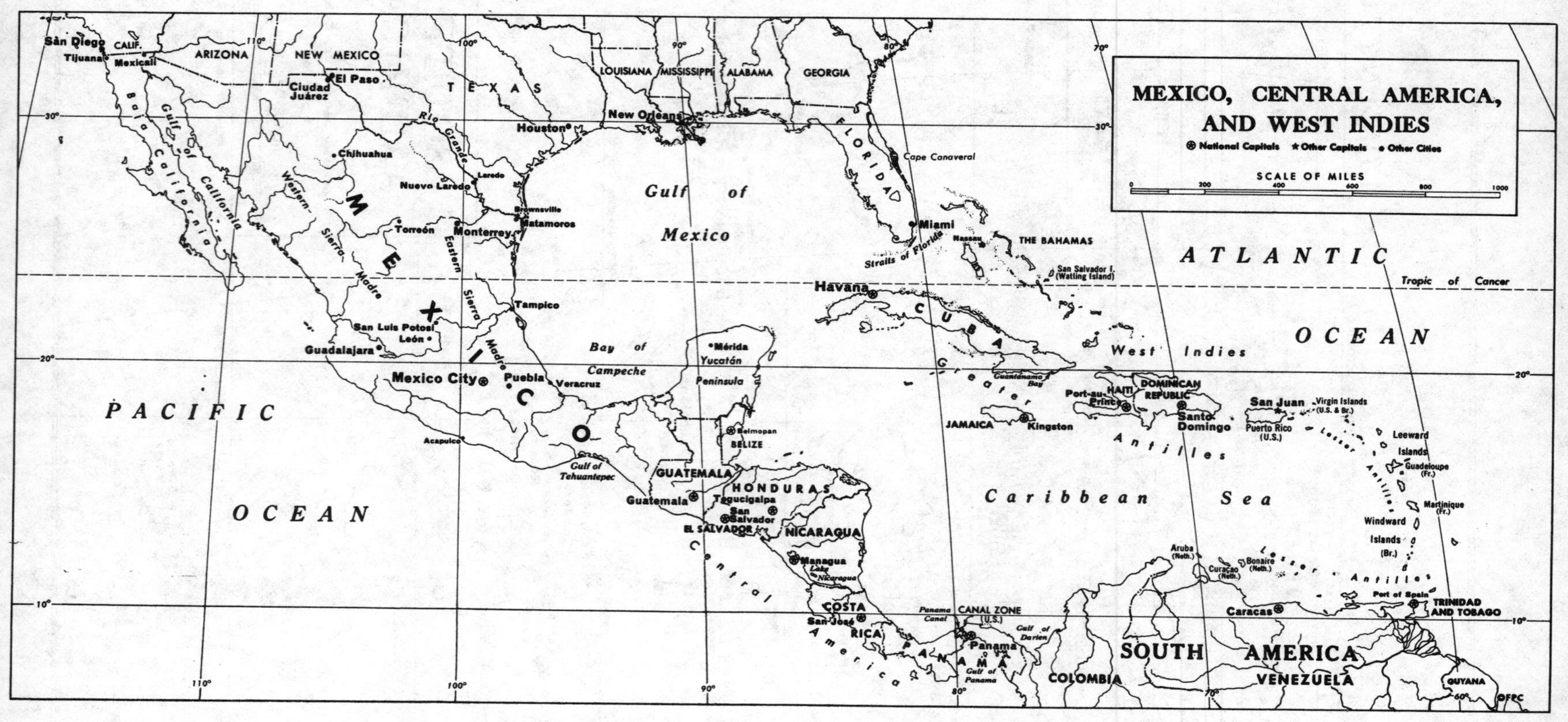

MEXICO, CENTRAL AMERICA, AND WEST INDIES
National Capitals
Other Capitals
Other Cities
SCALE OF MILES
0
200
400
600
800
1000
San Diego
CALIF.
Tijuana
Mexicali
ARIZONA
NEW MEXICO
El Paso
Ciudad Juárez
TEXAS
LOUISIANA
MISSISSIPPI
ALABAMA
GEORGIA
FLORIDA
New Orleans
Houston
Cape Canaveral
Miami
Nassau
THE BAHAMAS
San Salvador I. (Watling Island)
Straits of Florida
Gulf of Mexico
Baja California
Gulf of California
Chihuahua
Rio Grande
Laredo
Nuevo Laredo
Brownsville
Matamoros
Torreón
Monterrey
Western Sierra Madre
Eastern Sierra Madre
MEXICO
Tampico
San Luis Potosí
León
Guadalajara
Mexico City
Puebla
Veracruz
Bay of Campeche
Mérida
Yucatán Peninsula
Acapulco
Gulf of Tehuantepec
Belmopan
BELIZE
GUATEMALA
Guatemala
HONDURAS
Tegucigalpa
San Salvador
EL SALVADOR
NICARAGUA
Managua
Lake Nicaragua
COSTA RICA
San José
Central America
PANAMA
Panama
Panama Canal
CANAL ZONE (U.S.)
Gulf of Darien
Gulf of Panama
Havana
CUBA
Greater Antilles
Guantánamo Bay
JAMAICA
Kingston
Port-au-Prince
HAITI
DOMINICAN REPUBLIC
Santo Domingo
San Juan
Puerto Rico (U.S.)
Virgin Islands (U.S. & Br.)
West Indies
Leeward Islands
Guadeloupe (Fr.)
Martinique (Fr.)
Windward Islands (Br.)
Lesser Antilles
Caribbean Sea
Aruba (Neth.)
Curaçao (Neth.)
Bonaire (Neth.)
Caracas
Port of Spain
TRINIDAD AND TOBAGO
SOUTH AMERICA
COLOMBIA
VENEZUELA
GUYANA
ATLANTIC OCEAN
PACIFIC OCEAN
Tropic of Cancer
30°
20°
10°
110°
100°
90°
80°
70°
60°